Y0-AQW-144

3 1192 00325 7647

WITHDRAWN

47.50

REFERENCE
DOES NOT CIRCULATE

Who Was Who in America

Biographical Reference Works
Published by Marquis Who's Who, Inc.

Who's Who in America

Who's Who in America/Index by Professions

Who Was Who in America

   Historical Volume (1607-1896)

   Volume I (1897-1942)

   Volume II (1943-1950)

   Volume III (1951-1960)

   Volume IV (1961-1968)

   Volume V (1969-1973)

   Volume VI (1974-1976)

Who Was Who in American History — Arts and Letters

Who Was Who in American History — The Military

Who Was Who in American History — Science and Technology

Who's Who in the Midwest

Who's Who in the East

Who's Who in the South and Southwest

Who's Who in the West

Who's Who Biographical Record — Child Development Professionals

Who's Who Biographical Record — School District Officials

Who's Who of American Women

Who's Who in Government

Who's Who in Finance and Industry

Who's Who in Religion

Who's Who in the World

World Who's Who in Science

Directory of Medical Specialists

Directory of Osteopathic Specialists

International Scholars Directory

Marquis Who's Who Publications/

   Index to All Books

Who Was Who in America®

with World Notables

Volume-VI

1974-1976

With Index to All Who Was Who Volumes

R
920 07
W622
V.6

PS1276

EVANSTON PUBLIC LIBRARY,
1703 ORRINGTON AVENUE
EVANSTON, ILLINOIS 60201

MARQUIS
Who's Who

Marquis Who's Who, Inc.
200 East Ohio Street
Chicago, Illinois 60611 U.S.A.

Copyright 1976 by Marquis Who's Who, Inc. All rights reserved. No part of this publication may be reproduced, stored in a retrieval system or transmitted, in any form or by
any means, electronic, mechanical, photocopying, or otherwise, without the prior written
permission of the publisher, except in a magazine or newspaper article referring to a
specific listee.

Library of Congress Catalog Card Number 43-3789
International Standard Book Number 0-8379-0207-X
Product Code Number 030185

Distributed in the United Kingdom by
George Prior Associated Publishers
Rugby Chambers, 2 Rugby Street
London WC1N 3QU

Manufactured in the United States of America by
Kingsport Press, Inc., Kingsport, Tennessee 37662

Table of Contents

This index lists all names that appear in the seven Who
Was Who volumes, keying each name to the volume in
which the biographee is sketched.

Preface

The publication of Volume VI of WHO WAS WHO IN AMERICA is an important step forward in the growth of a series of biographical reference books that seek to reflect both American history and the genealogical heritage of this country. *Who's Who in America*, the distinguished major component of the series, has advanced the highest standards of biographical compilation throughout its three-quarters of a century of continuous publication. Its more recent companion volumes, the four books comprising the Marquis Regional Library, emanate from and extend the scope and coverage of *Who's Who in America*. As a consequence, and for the first time, a WHO WAS WHO IN AMERICA volume will contain the names of deceased Marquis biographees whose careers had been of an essentially regional significance and whose listings were in publications other than *Who's Who in America*. Thus, the magnitude of American career achievement, particularly that of a regional nature, persuaded us to broaden the standards for inclusion in Volume VI of WHO WAS WHO IN AMERICA.

In continuing improvements introduced with the immediate past volumes of WHO WAS WHO IN AMERICA, this new volume includes sketches of some Marquis biographees known to be 95 years of age or older. Lacking current information regarding these individuals, however, we make such inclusions in the hope that our apologies will be accepted should errors occur. Sketches of recently deceased world notables also are included, particularly of those international figures whose careers had a direct bearing on the course of recent American history.

Basically, however, the WAS books (to use the shortened form by which they are perhaps better known) inherited the unique characteristics that have made *Who's Who in America* both an internationally respected reference work and a household word here in the country of its origin.

Sketches, for example, have not only been prepared from information supplied by the biographees themselves, but have been approved personally — and frequently revised — before being printed in a Marquis publication during the subject's lifetime. As with all WAS volumes, many of these sketches have been scrutinized and revised by relatives or legal representatives of the deceased biographee. Except for the resulting changes and those occasional variations interjected by the compilers, the WAS biographies are printed precisely as they last appeared during the subject's lifetime. As a result, many contain personal data unavailable elsewhere. The preface to the first volume of *Who's Who in America* selected this fact as one of that volume's outstanding characteristics, and stated: "The book is autobiographical, the data having been obtained from first hand." It follows that WHO WAS WHO IN AMERICA is autobiographical to a distinctive degree. In that respect, it is unique among American biographical directories. And although condensed to the concise style that Marquis Who's Who, Inc. has made famous, the sketches contain all essential facts.

There results far more than a biographical directory of some 96,000 deceased American notables within the covers of these seven volumes. WHO WAS WHO IN AMERICA is a vital portion of American history from the early days of the colonies to mid-1976. It is authentic history. It is the autobiography of America.

Table of Abbreviations

The following abbreviations are frequently used in this book:

*Following a sketch signifies that the published biography could not be verified.

†Non-current sketches of WHO'S WHO IN AMERICA biographees who were born 95 or more years ago (see Preface for explanation).

A.A., Associate in Arts.
A.A.A., Agricultural Adjustment Administration; Anti-Aircraft Artillery.
A.A.A.S., American Association for the Advancement of Science.
AAC, Army Air Corps.
A. and M., Agricultural and Mechanical.
AAF, Army Air Force.
A.A.H.P.E.R., American Association for Health, Physical Education, and Recreation.
A.A.U.P., American Association of University Professors.
A.A.U.W., American Association of University Women.
AB, Alberta.
A.B., Bachelor of Arts.
ABC, American Broadcasting Company.
A.,B.&C.R.R., Atlanta, Birmingham & Coast R.R.
AC, Air Corps.
Acad., academy; academic.
ACAD, Arms Control and Disarmament Agency.
A.C.L.R.R., Atlantic Coast Line R.R.
A.C.L.U., American Civil Liberties Union.
A.C.P., American College of Physicians.
A.C.S., American College of Surgeons.
a.d.c., aide-de-camp.
adj., adjutant; adjunct.
adm., admiral.
adminstr., administrator.
adminstrn., administration.
Adminstrv., administrative.
adv., advocate; advisory.
advt., advertising.
A.E., Agricultural Engineer.
A.E. and P., Ambassador Extraordinary and Plenipotentiary.
AEC, Atomic Energy Commission.
AEF, American Expeditionary Forces.
aero., aeronautical; aeronautic.
AFB, Air Force Base.
A.F.D., Doctor of Fine Arts.
AFL (or A.F. of L) American Federation of Labor.
A.F.T.R.A., American Federation TV and Radio Artists.
agr., agriculture.
agrl., agricultural.
agt., agent.
agy., agency.
A.I.A., American Institute of Architects.
AID, Agency for International Development.
A.I.M., American Institute of Management.
AK, Alaska.
AL, Alabama.
Ala., Alabama.
A.L.A., American Library Association.
Amtrak, National R.R. Passenger Corporation.
Alta., Alberta.
Am., American, America.
A.M., Master of Arts.
A.M.A., American Medical Association.
A.M.E., African Methodist Episcopal.
Am. Inst. E.E., American Institute of Electrical Engineers.
Am. Soc. C.E., American Society of Civil Engineers.
Am. Soc. M.E., American Society of Mechanical Engineers.
A.N.A., Associate National Academician.

anat., anatomical.
ann., annual.
ANTA, American National Theatre and Academy.
anthrop., anthropological.
A.P., Associated Press.
apptd., appointed.
apt., apartment.
AR, Arkansas.
A.R.C., American Red Cross.
archeol., archaeological.
archtl., architectural.
Ariz., Arizona.
Ark., Arkansas.
ArtsD., Doctor of Arts.
arty., artillery.
AS, Air Service.
A.S.C.A.P., American Society of Composers, Authors and Publishers.
ASF, Air Service Force.
assn., association.
asso., associate; associated.
asst., assistant.
astron., astronomical.
astrophys., astrophysical.
ATSC, Air Technical Service Command.
A., T. & S. F. Ry., Atchison, Topeka & Santa Fe Ry.
atty., attorney.
AUS, Army of the United States.
Aux., Auxiliary.
Av., Avenue.
AZ, Arizona.

b., born.
B., Bachelor.
B.A., Bachelor of Arts.
B.Agr., Bachelor of Agriculture.
Balt., Baltimore.
Bapt., Baptist.
B. Arch., Bachelor of Architecture.
B. & A. R.R., Boston & Albany R.R.
B.A.S., Bachelor of Agricultural Science.
B.B.A., Bachelor of Business Administration.
BBC, British Broadcasting Corp.
BC, British Columbia.
B.C., British Columbia.
B.C.E., Bachelor of Civil Engineering.
B.Chir., Bachelor of Surgery.
B.C.L., Bachelor of Civil Law.
B.C.S., Bachelor of Commercial Science.
bd., Board.
B.D., Bachelor of Divinity.
B.Di., Bachelor of Didactics.
B.E., Bachelor of Education.
B.E.E., Bachelor of Electrical Engineering.
BEF, British Expeditionary Force.
B.F.A., Bachelor of Fine Arts.
bibl., biblical.
bibliog., bibliographical.
biog., biographical.
biol., biological.
B.J., Bachelor of Journalism.
Bklyn., Brooklyn.
B.L., Bachelor of Letters.
bldg., building.
B.L.S., Bachelor of Library Science.
Blvd., Boulevard.
B. & M. R.R., Boston & Maine R.R.
Bn., Battalion.
B.O., Bachelor of Oratory.
B. & O. R.R., Baltimore & Ohio R.R.
bot., Botanical.
B.P., Bachelor of Painting.

B.P.E., Bachelor of Physical Education.
B.Pd., Bachelor of Pedagogy.
B.Py., Bachelor of Pedagogy.
br., branch.
B.R.E., Bachelor of Religious Education.
brig. gen., brigadier general.
Brit., British; Britannica.
Bro., Brother.
B.S., Bachelor of Science.
B.S.A., Bachelor of Agricultural Science.
B.S.D., Bachelor of Didactic Science.
B.S.T., Bachelor of Sacred Theology.
B.Th., Bachelor of Theology.
bull., bulletin.
bur., bureau.
bus., business.
B.W.I., British West Indies.

CA, California.
Cal., California.
C.Am., Central America.
CAA, Civil Aeronautics Administration.
CAB, Civil Aeronautics Board.
CAC, Coast Artillery Corps.
Can., Canada.
CAP, Civil Air Patrol.
capt., captain.
CARE, Cooperative American Relief Everywhere.
Cath., Catholic.
cav., cavalry.
CBI, China, Burma, India Theatre of Operations.
C.B. & Q. R.R., Chicago, Burlington & Quincy R.R. Co.
CBS, Columbia Broadcasting System.
CCC, Commodity Credit Corporation.
C.,C.,C & St.L. Ry., Cleveland, Cincinnati, Chicago & St. Louis Ry.
CD, Civil Defense.
C.E., Civil Engineer, Corps of Engineers.
CENTO, Central Treaty Organization.
CERN, European Organization of Nuclear Research.
CEF, Canadian Expeditionary Force.
C. & E.I. R.R., Chicago & Eastern Illinois R.R.
C.G.W. R.R., Chicago Great Western Ry.
ch., church.
Ch.D., Doctor of Chemistry.
chem., chemical.
Chem.E., Chemical Engineer.
Chgo., Chicago.
Chirurg., Chirurgical.
chmm., Chairman.
chpt., Chapter.
Cie., (French) company.
Cia. (Spanish), Company.
CIA, Central Intelligence Agency.
CIC, Counter Intelligence Corps.
C.,I. & L. Ry., Chicago, Indianapolis & Louisville Ry.
Cin., Cincinnati.
CIO, Congress of Industrial Organizations.
Cleve., Cleveland.
climatol., Climatological.
clin., clinical.
clk., clerk.
C.L.U., Chartered Life Underwriter.
C.M., Master in Surgery.
C.M., St.P. & P. R.R., Chicago, Milwaukee, St. Paul & Pacific R.R. Co.
C. & N.-W. Ry., Chicago & Northwestern Ry.
CO, Colorado.
Co., Company.
C. of C., Chamber of Commerce.
C.O.F., Catholic Order of Foresters.
C. of Ga. Ry., Central of Georgia Ry.

col., colonel.
coll., college.
Colo., Colorado.
com., committee.
comd.., commanded.
comdg., commanding.
comdr., commander.
comdt., commandant.
commd., commissioned.
comml., commercial.
commn., commission.
commr., commissioner.
condr., conductor.
conf., conference.
Congl., Congregational; Congressional.
Conglist., Congregationalist.
Conn., Connecticut.
cons., consulting, consultant.
consol., consolidated.
constl., constitutional.
constn., constitution.
constrn., construction.
contbd., contributed.
contbg., contributing.
contbn., contribution.
contbr., contributor.
conv., convention.
coop. (or **co.op**), cooperative.
corp., corporation.
corr., correspondent; corresponding; correspondence.
C. & O. Ry., Chesapeake & Ohio Ry. Co.
C.P.A., Certified Public Accountant.
C.P.C.U., Chartered Property and Casualty Underwriter.
C.P.H., Certificate of Public Health.
cpl., corporal.
C.P. Ry., Canadian Pacific Ry. Co.
C.,R.I. & P. Ry., Chicago, Rock Island & Pacific Ry. Co.
C.R.R. of N.J., Central Railroad Co. of New Jersey.
C.S., Christian Science.
C.S.B., Bachelor of Christian Science.
CSC, Civil Service Commission.
C.S.D., Doctor of Christian Science.
C. & S. Ry. Co., Colorado & Southern Ry. Co.
C.,St.P.,M. & O. Ry., Chicago, St. Paul, Minneapolis & Omaha Ry. Co.
CT, Connecticut.
ct., court.
C.T., Candidate in Theology.
C.Vt. Ry., Central Vermont Ry.
C. & W.I. R.R., Chicago & Western Indiana R.R. Co.
CWS, Chemical Warfare Service.
cyclo., cyclopedia.
C.Z., Canal Zone.
CZ, Canal Zone.

d., daughter.
D., Doctor.
D.Agr., Doctor of Agriculture.
D.A.R., Daughters of the American Revolution.
dau., daughter.
D.A.V., Disabled American Veterans.
D.C., District of Columbia.
DC, District of Columbia.
D.C.L., Doctor of Civil Law.
D.C.S., Doctor of Commercial Science.
D.D., Doctor of Divinity.
D.D.S., Doctor of Dental Surgery.
DE, Delaware.
dec., deceased.
Def., Defense.

Del., Delaware.
del., delegate.
Dem., Democratic; Democrat.
D.Eng., Doctor of Engineering.
denom., denominational.
dep., deputy.
dept., department.
dermatol., dermatological.
desc., descendant.
devel., development.
D.F.A., Doctor of Fine Arts.
D.F.C., Distinguished Flying Cross.
D.H.L., Doctor of Hebrew Literature.
D. & H. R.R., Delaware & Hudson R.R. Co.
dir., director.
disch., discharged.
dist., district.
distbg., distributing.
distbn., distribution.
distbr., distributor.
div., division; divinity; divorce proceedings.
D.Litt., Doctor of Literature.
D., L. & W. R.R., Delaware, Lackawanna & Western R.R. Co.
D.M.D., Doctor of Dental Medicine.
D.M.S., Doctor of Medical Science.
D.O., Doctor of Osteopathy.
DPA, Defense Production Administration.
D.P.H., Diploma in Public Health.
Dr., Doctor, Drive.
D.R., Daughters of the Revolution.
D.R.E., Doctor of Religious Education.
D. & R.G.W. R.R. Co., Denver & Rio Grande Western R.R. Co.
Dr.P.H., Doctor of Public Health, Doctor of Public Hygiene.
D.Sc., Doctor of Science.
D.S.C., Distinguished Service Cross.
D.S.M., Distinguished Service Medal.
D.S.T., Doctor of Sacred Theology.
D.T.M., Doctor of Tropical Medicine.
D.V.M., Doctor of Veterinary Medicine.
D.V.S., Doctor of Veterinary Surgery.

E., East.
E. and P., Extraordinary and Plenipotentiary.
ECA, Economic Cooperation Administration.
eccles., ecclesiastical.
ecol., ecological.
econ., economic.
ECOSOC, Economic and Social Council (of the UN).
ed., educated.
E.D., Doctor of Engineering.
Ed.B., Bachelor of Education.
Ed.D., Doctor of Education.
edit., edition.
Ed.M., Master of Education.
edn., education.
ednl., educational.
EDP, electronic data processing.
E.E., Electrical Engineer.
EEC, European Economic Community.
EEG, electroencephalogram.
E.E. and M.P., Envoy Extraordinary and Minister Plenipotentiary.
EKG, electrocardiogram.
Egyptol., Egyptological.
elec., electrical.
electrochem., electrochemical.
electrophys., electrophysical.
E. M., Engineer of Mines.
ency., encyclopaedia.

Eng., England.
engr., engineer.
engring., engineering.
entomol., entomological.
environ., environmental.
EPA, Environmental Protection Agency.
epidemol., epidemiological.
ERDA, Energy Research and Development Administration.
ESSA, Elementary and Secondary School Act.
ESSA, Environmental Science Services Administration.
ethnol., ethnological.
ETO, European Theater of Operations.
Evang., Evangelical.
exam., examination; examining.
exec., executive.
exhbn., exhibition.
expdn., expedition.
expn., exposition.
expt., experiment.
exptl., experimental.

F.A., Field Artillery.
FAA, Federal Aviation Agency.
FAO, Food and Agriculture Organization (of the UN).
FBI, Federal Bureau of Investigation.
FCA, Farm Credit Administration.
FCC, Federal Communications Commission.
FCDA, Federal Civil Defense Administration.
FDA, Food and Drug Administration.
FDIA, Federal Deposit Insurance Administration.
FDIC, Federal Deposit Insurance Corporation.
F.E., Forest Engineer.
Fed., Federal.
Fedn., Federation.
Fgn., Foreign.
FHA, Federal Housing Administration.
FL, Florida.
Fla., Florida.
FMC, Federal Maritime Commission.
FOA, Foreign Operations Administration.
Found., Foundation.
frat., fraternity.
FSA, Federal Security Agency.
Ft., Fort.
FTC, Federal Trade Commission, Federal Tariff Commission.

G.-1 (or other number), Division of General Staff.
GA, Georgia.
Ga., Georgia.
GAO, General Accounting Office.
gastroent., gastroenterological.
GATT, General Agreement on Tariffs and Trade.
G.,C. & S.F. Ry., Gulf, Colorado & Santa Fe Ry. Co.
G.D., Graduate in Divinity.
gen., general.
geneal., genealogical.
geod., geodetic.
geog., geographical; geographic.
geol., geological.
geophys., geophysical.
gerontol., gerontological.
G.H.Q., General Headquarters.
GmbH., (German) company.
G.,M. & N. R.R., Gulf, Mobile & Northern R.R. Co.
G.,M. & O. R.R., Gulf, Mobile & Ohio R.R. Co.
G.N. Ry., Great Northern Ry. Co.
gov., Governor.
govt., government.
govtl., governmental.

GPO, Government Printing Office.
grad., graduated; graduate.
GSA, General Services Administration.
Gt., Great.
G.T. Ry., Grand Trunk Ry. System.
GU, Guam.
G.W. Ry. of Can., Great Western Ry. of Canada.
gynecol., genecological.

Hdqrs., Headquarters.
HEW, Department of Health, Education and Welfare.
H.H.D., Doctor of Humanities.
HHFA, Housing and Home Finance Agency.
HI, Hawaii.
H.I., Hawaiian Islands.
H.M., Master of Humanics.
hist., Historical.
HOLC, Home Owners Loan Corporation.
homeo., homeopathic.
hon., honorary; honorable.
Ho. of Dels., House of Delegates.
Ho. of Reps., House of Representatives.
Hort., Horticultural.
hosp., hospital.
HUD, Department of Housing and Urban Development.
H.T., Territory of Hawaii.
Hwy., Highway.
hydrog., hydrographic.

IA, Iowa.
Ia., Iowa.
IAEA, International Atomic Energy Agency.
IBM, International Business Machines Corp.
IBRD, International Bank for Reconstruction and Development.
ICA, International Cooperation Administration.
ICC, Interstate Commerce Commn.
I.C. R.R., Illinois Central R.R. System.
ID, Idaho.
Ida., Idaho.
I.E.E.E., Institute of Electrical and Electronics Engineers.
IFC, International Finance Corp.
I.G.N. R.R., International–Great Northern R.R.
IGY, International Geophysical Year.
IL, Illinois.
Ill., Illinois.
illus., illustrated.
ILO, International Labor Organization.
IMF, International Monetary Fund.
IN, Indiana.
Inc., Incorporated.
Ind., Indiana.
ind., independent.
Indpls., Indianapolis.
indsl., industrial.
inf., infantry.
info., information.
ins., insurance.
insp., inspector.
inst., institute.
instl., institutional.
instn., institution.
instr., instructor.
instrn., instruction.
internat., international.
intro., introduction.
I.R.E., Institute of Radio Engineers.
IRS, Internal Revenue Service.

JAG, Judge Advocate General.
J.B., Jurum Baccalaureus.
J.C.B., Juris Canonici Bachelor.

J.C.L., Juris Canonici Lector.
J.D., Doctor of Jurisprudence.
j.g., junior grade.
jour., journal.
jr., junior.
J.S.D., Doctor of Juristic Science.
jud., Judicial.
J.U.D., Juris Utriusque Doctor: Doctor of Both (Canon and Civil) Laws.

Kan., Kansas.
K.C., Knight of Columbus.
K.P., Knight of Pythias.
K.C.S. Ry., Kansas City Southern Ry.
KS, Kansas.
K.T., Knight Templar.
KY, Kentucky.
Ky., Kentucky.

LA, Louisiana.
lab., laboratory.
lang., language.
laryngol., laryngological.
LB, Labrador.
lectr., lecturer.
legis., legislation, legislative.
L.H.D., Doctor of Humane Letters.
L.I., Long Island.
L.I. R.R., Long Island R.R. Company.
lit., literary; literature.
Litt.B., Bachelor of Letters.
Litt.D., Doctor of Letters.
LL.B., Bachelor of Laws.
LL.D., Doctor of Laws.
LL.M., Master of Laws.
L. & N. R.R., Louisville & Nashville R.R.
L.R.C.P., Licentiate Royal Coll. Physicians.
L.R.C.S., Licentiate Royal Coll. Surgeons.
L.S., Library Science.
lt., lieutenant.
Ltd., Limited.
Luth., Lutheran.
L.V. R.R., Lehigh Valley R.R. Co.

m., marriage ceremony.
M., Master.
MA, Massachusetts.
M.A., Master of Arts.
mag., magazine.
M.Agr., Master of Agriculture.
maj., major.
Man., Manitoba.
M.Arch., Master in Architecture.
Mass., Massachusetts.
math., mathematical, mathematics.
MATS, Military Air Transport Service.
MB, Manitoba.
M.B., Bachelor of Medicine.
M.B.A., Master of Business Administration.
MBS, Mutual Broadcasting System.
M.C., Medical Corps.
M.C.E., Master of Civil Engineering.
M.C.S., Master of Commercial Science.
mcht., merchant.
M.C. R.R., Michigan Central R.R.
MD, Maryland.
Md., Maryland.
M.D., Doctor of Medicine.
M.Di., Master of Didactics.
M.Dip., Master in Diplomacy.
mdse., merchandise.
M.D.V., Doctor of Veterinary Medicine.
ME, Maine.

Me., Maine.
M.E., Mechanical Engineer.
mech., mechanical.
M.E. Ch., Methodist Episcopal Church.
M.Ed., Master of Education.
med., medical.
Med. O.R.C., Medical Officers' Reserve Corps.
Med. R.C., Medical Reserve Corps.
M.E.E., Master of Electrical Engineering.
mem., member.
Meml., Memorial.
merc., mercantile.
met., metropolitan.
metall., metallurgical.
Met.E., Metallurgical Engineer.
meteorol., meteorological.
Meth., Methodist.
metrol., metrological.
M.F., Master of Forestry.
M.F.A., Master of Fine Arts (carries title of Dr.).
mfg., manufacturing.
mfr., manufacturer.
mgmt., management.
mgr., manager.
M.H.A., Master of Hospital Administration.
MI, Michigan.
M.I., Military Intelligence.
Mich., Michigan.
micros., microscopical.
mil., military.
Milw., Milwaukee.
mineral., mineralogical.
Minn., Minnesota.
M.-K.-T. R.R., Missouri-Kansas-Texas R.R. Company.
M.L., Master of Laws.
M.L.D., Magister Legnum Diplomatic.
M.Litt., Master of Literature.
Minn., Minnesota.
Miss., Mississippi.
mktg., marketing.
Mlle., Mademoiselle.
M.L.S., Master of Library Science.
Mme., Madame.
M.M.E., Master of Mechanical Engineering.
MN, Minnesota.
mng., managing.
MO, Missouri.
Mo., Missouri.
Moblzn., Mobilization.
Mont., Montana.
M.P., Member of Parliament.
M.Pd., Master of Pedagogy.
M.P.E., Master of Physical Education.
M.P.H., Master of Public Health.
M.P.L., Master of Patent Law.
Mpls., Minneapolis.
M.P. R.R., Missour Pacific R.R.
M.R.E., Master of Religious Education.
MS, Mississippi.
M.S., Master of Science.
M.Sc., Master of Science.
M.S.F., Master of Science of Forestry.
M.S.T., Master of Sacred Theology.
M. & St. L. R.R., Minneapolis & St. Louis R.R. Company.
M.,St.P. & S.S.M. Ry., Minneapolis, St. Paul & Sault Ste. Marie Ry.
M.S.W., Master of Social Work.
MT, Montana.
Mt., Mount.
MTO, Mediterranean Theater of Operations.
mus., museum; musical.
Mus.B., Bachelor of Music.
Mus.D., Doctor of Music.

Mus. M., Master of Music.
Mut., Mutual.
mycol., mycological.

N., North.
N.A., National Academician; National Army.
N.A.A.C.P., National Association for the Advancement of Colored People.
NACA, National Advisory Committee for Aeronautics.
N.A.D., National Academy of Design.
N.Am., North America.
N.A.M., National Association of Manufacturers.
NARS, National Archives and Record Service.
NASA, National Aeronautics and Space Administration.
nat., national.
NATO, North Atlantic Treaty Organization.
NATOUSA, North African Theater of Operations, U.S. Army.
nav., navigation.
NB, New Brunswick.
N.B., New Brunswick.
NBC, National Broadcasting Company.
NC, North Carolina.
N.C., North Carolina.
N.,C. & St.L. Ry., Nashville, Chattanooga & St. Louis Ry.
ND, North Dakota.
N.D., North Dakota.
NDEA, National Defense Education Act.
NDRC, National Defense Research Committee.
NE, Nebraska.
N.E., Northeast.
N.E.A., National Education Association.
Neb., Nebraska.
neurol., neurological.
Nev., Nevada.
New Eng., New England.
NF, Newfoundland.
Nfld., Newfoundland.
N.G., National Guard.
NH, New Hampshire.
N.H., New Hampshire.
NIH, National Institutes of Health.
NIMH, National Institutes of Mental Health.
NJ, New Jersey.
N.J., New Jersey.
NLRB, National Labor Relations Bd.
NM, New Mexico.
N.M., New Mexico.
No., Northern.
NORAD, North American Air Defense.
N.O.W., National Organization for Women.
NPA, National Production Authority.
N.P. Ry., Northern Pacific Ry.
nr., near.
NRA, National Recovery Administration.
NRC, National Research Council.
NS, Nova Scotia.
N.S., Nova Scotia.
NSC, National Security Council.
NSF, National Science Foundation.
NSRB, National Security Resources Board.
NT, Northwest Territories.
N.T., New Testament.
numis., numismatic.
NV, Nevada.
NV or N/V, (Netherlands) company.
N.W., Northwest.
N. & W. Ry., Norfolk & Western Ry.
N.W.T., Northwest Territories.
NY, New York.
N.Y., New York.

N.Y.C., New York City.
N.Y.C. RR., New York Central R.R. Company.
N.Y.,C. & St.L. R.R., New York, Chicago & St. Louis R.R. Company.
N.Y.,N.H. & H. R.R., New York, New Haven & Hartford R.R. Company.
N.Y.,O. & W. Ry., New York, Ontario & Western Ry.

O., Ohio.
OAS, Organization of American States.
O.B., Bachelor of Oratory.
obs., observatory.
obstet., obstetrical.
O.D., Doctor of Optometry.
OCDM, Office of Civil and Defense Mobilization.
ODM, Office of Defense Mobilization.
OECD, Organization European Cooperation and Development.
OEEC, Organization European Economic Cooperation.
OEO, Office of Economic Opportunity.
ofcl., official.
OH, Ohio.
OK, Oklahoma.
Okla., Oklahoma.
ON, Ontario.
Ont., Ontario.
OPA, Office of Price Administration.
ophthal., ophthalmological.
ops., operations.
OPM, Office of Production Management.
OPS, Office of Price Stabilization.
O.Q.M.G., Office of Quartermaster General.
OR, Oregon.
O.R.C., Officers' Reserve Corps.
orch., orchestra.
Ore., Oregon.
orgn., organization.
ornithol., ornithological.
O.S.L. R.R., Oregon Short Line R.R.
OSRD, Office of Scientific Research and Development.
OSS, Office of Strategic Services.
osteo., osteopathic.
O.T., Old Testament.
O.T.C., Officers Training Camp.
otol., Otological.
otolaryn., otolaryngological.
O.T.S., Officers Training School.
O.U.A.M., Order United American Mechanics.
OWI, Office of War Information.
O.-W. R.R. & N. Co., Oregon-Washington R.R. & Navigation Company.

PA, Pennsylvania.
Pa., Pennsylvania.
paleontol., paleontological.
Pa. RR., Pennsylvania R.R.
path., pathological.
P.C., Professional Corporation.
Pd.B., Bachelor of Pedagogy.
Pd.D., Doctor of Pedagogy.
Pd.M., Master of Pedagogy.
PE, Prince Edward Island.
P.E., Protestant Episcopal.
Pe.B., Bachelor of Pediatrics.
P.E.I., Prince Edward Island.
P.E.N., Poets, Playwrights, Editors, Essayists and Novelists (Internat. Assn.).
P.E.O., women's organization.
penol., penological.
pfc., private first class.
PHA, Public Housing Administration.

pharm., pharmaceutical.
Pharm.D., Doctor of Pharmacy.
Pharm.M., Master of Pharmacy.
Ph.B., Bachelor of Philosophy.
Ph.C., Pharmaceutical Chemist.
Ph.D., Doctor of Philosophy.
Ph.G., Graduate in Pharmacy.
Phila., Philadelphia.
philol., philological.
philos., philosophical.
photog., photographic.
phys., physical.
Phys. and Surg., Physicians and Surgeons (College at Columbia U.).
physiol., physiological.
P.I., Philippine Islands.
Pitts., Pittsburgh.
Pkwy., Parkway.
Pl., Place.
P. & L.E. R.R., Pittsburgh & Lake Erie R.R.
P.M. R.R., Pere Marquette R.R. Co.
P.O., Post Office.
polit., political.
poly., polytechnic; polytechnical.
pomol., pomological.
PQ, Quebec (province).
PR, Puerto Rico.
P.R., Puerto Rico.
prep., preparatory.
pres., president.
Presbyn., Presbyterian.
presdl., presidential.
prin., principal.
proc., proceedings.
prod., produced (play production).
prodn., production.
prof., professor.
profl., professional.
prog., progressive.
propr., proprietor.
pros. atty., prosecuting attorney.
pro tem, pro tempore (for the time being).
psychiat., psychiatric.
psychol., psychological.
P.T.A., Parent-Teacher Association.
PTO, Pacific Theater of Operations.
pub., public; publisher; publishing; published.
publ., publication.
pvt., private.
PWA, Public Works Administration.

q.m., quartermaster.
Q.M.C., Quartermaster Corps.
Q.M.O.R.C., Quartermaster Officers' Reserve Corps.
quar., quarterly.
Que., Quebec (province).

radiol., Radiological.
RAF, Royal Air Force.
R.C., Roman Catholic.
RCA, Radio Corporation of America.
RCAF, Royal Canadian Air Force.
Rd., Road.
R.D., Rural Delivery.
R.E., Reformed Episcopal.
REA, Rural Electrification Administration.
rec., recording.
ref., reformed.
regt., regiment.
regtl., regimental.
rehab., rehabilitation.
Rep., Republican.
rep., representative.

Res., Reserve.
ret., retired.
rev., review, revised.
RFC, Reconstruction Finance Corporation.
R.F.D., Rural Free Delivery.
rhinol., rhinological.
RI, Rhode Island.
R.I., Rhode Island.
R.N., Registered Nurse.
roentgenol., roentgenological.
R.O.S.C., Reserve Officers' Sanitary Corps.
R.O.T.C., Reserve Officers' Training Corps.
R.P., Reformed Presbyterian.
R.R., Railroad.
R.T.C., Reserve Training Corps.
Ry., Railway.

s., son.
S., South.
S.A., (Spanish) Sociedad Anonima: (French) societe Anonyme.
SAC, Strategic Air Command.
SALT, Strategic Arms Limitation Talks.
S.A.L. Ry., Seaboard Air Line Ry.
S.Am., South America.
san., sanitary.
S.A.R., Sons of the Am. Revolution.
Sask., Saskatchewan.
S.A.T.C., Student's Army Training Corps.
Sat. Eve. Post, Saturday Evening Post.
savs., savings.
S.B., Bachelor of Science.
SBA, Small Business Administration.
SC, South Carolina.
S.C., South Carolina.
SCAP, Supreme Command Allies Pacific.
Sc.B., Bachelor of Science.
Sc.D., Doctor of Science.
S.C.D., Doctor of Commercial Science.
sch., school.
sci., science; scientific.
SCLC, Southern Christian Leadership Conference.
S.C.V., Sons of Confederate Veterans.
SD, South Dakota.
S.D., South Dakota.
S.E., Southeast.
SEATO, Southeast Asia Treaty Organization.
SEC, Securities and Exchange Commission.
sec., secretary.
sect., section.
seismol., seismological.
sem., seminary.
sgt., sergeant.
SHAEF, Supreme Headquarters, Allied Expeditionary Forces.
SHAPE, Supreme Headquarters Allied Powers in Europe.
S.I., Staten Island.
S.J., Society of Jesus (Jesuit).
SK, Saskatchewan.
S.J.D., Doctor Juristic Science.
S.M., Master of Science.
So., Southern.
soc., society.
sociol., sociological.
SOS, Service of Supply.
S.P. Co., Southern Pacific Co.
spl., special.
splty., specialty.
Sq., Square.
sr., senior.

S.R., Sons of the Revolution.
S.S., Steamship.
SSS, Selective Service System.
St., Saint; Street.
sta., station.
statis., statistical.
S.T.B., Bachelor of Sacred Theology.
Stbizn., Stabilization.
S.T.D., Doctor of Sacred Theology.
S.T.L., Licentiate in Sacred Theology; Lector of Sacred Theology.
St.L.-S.F. R.R., St. Louis-San Francisco Ry. Co.
supr., supervisor.
supt., superintendent.
surg., surgical.
S.W., Southwest.

T.A.P.P.I., Technical Association Pulp and Paper Industry.
Tb, Tuberculosis.
tchr., teacher.
tech., technical, technology.
technol., technological.
Tel. & Tel., Telephone and Telegraph.
temp., temporary.
Tenn., Tennessee.
Ter., Territory.
Tex., Texas.
T.H., Territory of Hawaii.
Th.D., Doctor of Theology.
Th.M., Master of Theology.
theol., theological.
TN, Tennessee.
tng., training.
topog., topographical.
T. & P. Ry., Texas & Pacific Ry. Co.
trans., transactions; transferred.
transl., transition.
transp., transportation.
treas., treasurer.
TV, Television.
TVA, Tennessee Valley Authority.
Twp., Township.
TX, Texas.
Ty., Territory.
typog., typographical.

U., University.
UAR, United Arab Republic.
U.A.W., International Union United Automobile, Aircraft, and Agricultural Implement Workers of American-AFL-CIO.
U.B., United Brethren in Christ.
U.D.C., United Daughters of the Confederacy.
U.K., United Kingdom.
UN. United Nations.
UNESCO, United Nations Educational, Scientific and Cultural Organization.
UNICEF, United Nations International Childrens Emergency Fund.
univ., university.
UNRRA, United Nations Relief and Rehabilitation Administration.
U.P., United Presbyterian.
U.P.I., United Press International.
U.P. R.R., Union Pacific R.R.
urol., urological.
U.S., United States.
U.S.A., United States of America.
USAAF, United States Army Air Force.
USAC, United States Air Corps.

USAF, United States Air Force.
USCG, United States Coast Guard.
USCGR, U.S. Coast Guard Reserve.
USES, United States Employment Service.
USIA, United States Information Agency.
USIS, United States Information Service.
USMC, United States Marine Corps.
USMCR, U.S. Marine Corps Reserve.
USMHS, United States Marine Hospital Service.
USN, United States Navy.
U.S.N.A., United States National Army.
U.S.N.G., United States National Guard.
USNR, United States Naval Reserve.
USNRF, United States Naval Reserve Force.
U.S.O., United Service Organizations.
USOM, United States Operations Mission.
USPHS, United States Public Health Service.
U.S.S., United States Ship.
USSR, Union of Soviet Socialist Republics.
U.S.V., United States Volunteers.
UT, Utah.

VA, Virginia.
Va., Virginia.
VA, Veterans Administration.
vet., Veteran; veterinary.
V.F.W., Veterans of Foreign Wars.
VI, Virgin Islands.
V.I., Virgin Islands.
vice pres., vice president.
vis., visiting.
VISTA, Volunteers in Service to America.
VITA, Volunteers in Technical Service.
vocat., vocational.
vol., volunteer; volume.
v.p., vice president.
vs., versus.
VT, Vermont.
Vt., Vermont.

W., West.
WA, Washington.
WAC, Women's Army Corps.
Wash., Washington (state).
WAVES, Womens Reserve, U.S. Naval Reserve.
W.C.T.U., Women's Christian Temperance Union.
WHO, World Health Organization (of the UN).
WI, Wisconsin.
W.I., West Indies.
Wis., Wisconsin.
W. & LE. Ry., Wheeling & Lake Erie Ry. Co.
WPA, Works Progress Administration.
WPB, War Production Board.
W.P.R.R. Co., Western Pacific R.R. Company.
WSB, Wage Stabilization Board.
WV, West Virginia.
W. Va., West Virginia.
WY, Wyoming.
Wyo., Wyoming.

YMCA, Young Men's Christian Assn.
YMHA, Young Men's Hebrew Assn.
YM and YWHA, Young Men's and Young Women's Hebrew Assn.
Y. & M.V. R.R., Yazoo & Mississippi Valley R.R.
YT, Yukon Territory.
Y.T., Yukon Territory.
YWCA, Young Women's Christian Assn.

zool., zoological.

ALPHABETICAL PRACTICES

Names are arranged alphabetically according to the surnames, and under identical surnames according to the first given name. If both surname and first given name are identical, names are arranged alphabetically according to the second given name. Where full names are identical, they are arranged in order of age—those of the elder being put first.

Surnames, beginning with De, Des, Du, etc., however capitalized or spaced, are recorded with the prefix preceding the surname and arranged alphabetically under the letter D.

Surnames beginning with Mac are arranged alphabetically under M. This likewise holds for names beginning with Mc; that is, all names beginning Mc will be found in alphabetical order after those beginning Mac.

Surnames beginning with Saint or St. all appear after names that would begin Sains, and such surnames are arranged according to the second part of the name, e.g., St. Clair would come before Saint Dennis.

Surnames beginning with prefix Van are arranged alphabetically under letter V.

Surnames containing the prefix Von or von are usually arranged alphabetically under letter V; any exceptions are noted by cross references (Von Kleinsmid, Rufus Bernhard; see Kleinsmid, Rufus Bernhard von).

Compound hyphenated surnames are arranged according to the first member of the compound.

Compound unhyphenated surnames common in Spanish are not rearranged but are treated as hyphenated names.

Since Chinese names have the family name first, they are so arranged, but without comma between family name and given name (as Lin Yutang).

Parentheses used in connection with a name indicate which part of the full name is usually deleted in common usage. Hence Abbott, W(illiam) Lewis indicates that the usual form of the given name is W. Lewis. In alphabetizing this type, the parentheses are not considered. However if the name is recorded Abbott, (William) Lewis, signifying that the entire name William is not commonly used, the alphabetizing would be arranged as though the name were Abbott, Lewis.

Who Was Who in America

AALDERS, CATHERINE ANN OLDING HEBB (MRS. LEWIS ELDON AALDERS), translator; b. Halifax, N.S., Can., Sept. 1, 1931; d. Peter Olding and Ann Joyce (Milne) Hebb; B.A., Dalhousie U., Halifax, 1953; m. Dr. Lewis Eldon Aalders, Sept. 8, 1954. Asst. to reference librarian N.S. Provincial Library, 1953-54; physics librarian Cornell U., Ithaca, N.Y., 1954-57; librarian Can. Agr. Research Sta., Kentville, N.S., 1959-60; Russian-English free-lance translator, Kentville, from 1960. Abstractor Russian bot. articles for Biol. Abstracts. Mem. A.L.A., Internat. Assn. Agr. Librarians and Documentalists, Am. Translators Assn., Assn. Profl. Translators, Inc., Internat. Platform Assn., Alpha Gamma Delta. Home: Kentville, N.S., Canada. Died Nov. 13, 1972; buried Mount Herman Cemetery, Dartmouth, N.S.

AARON, CHARLES DETTIE, physician; b. Lockport, N.Y., May 8, 1866; s. Abraham Higham and Hanna (Barnett) A.; M.D., U. of Buffalo, N.Y., 1891; Sc.D., Heidelberg U., 1910; m. Winifred Comstock, June 23, 1902; 1 dau., Josephine Comstock. Began practice of medicine at Detroit, 1891; city physician, 1893-95; became prof. gastroenterology and dietetics, Wayne U. Coll. of Medicine, 1905, now emeritus; cons. gastroenterologist to Harper, Receiving, Tuberculosis, Shurly and Alexander Blaine hosps. Fellow West London Medico-Chirurg. Soc. (Eng.), Am. Coll. Physicians, Am. Therapeutic Soc.; mem. A.M.A., Mich. State Med. Soc., Wayne County Med. Soc., Detroit Acad. Medicine (ex-pres.), Am. Gastroenterol. Assn. (founder and sec. 14 yrs.) Northern Tri-State Med. Soc. (ex-pres.), Mich. Authors' Assn., Mich. Acad. Science, Arts and Letters, Am. Med. Editors' and Authors' Assn., Assn. for the Study of Internal Secretions, Am. Congress Internal Medicine; hon. mem. Jackson Co. Med. Soc., Kalamazoo Acad. Medicine, Eugene Field Soc.; mem. Phi Rho Sigma, Alpha Omega Alpha. Republican. Mason. Author: Disease of the Stomach, 1911; Diseases of the Digestive Organs, 1915, 4th edit., 1927; also chapter on Dietetic Treatment of Disease (Oxford Index of Therapeutics), 1921, and many scientific papers in various foreign and American jours. Translator (from the German): Examination of the Feces by Means of the Test-Died, 1906 2d edit., 1909. Home: 748 Seminole Av. Office: 76 Adams Av., W., Detroit MI†

AARON, ELY MAYER, lawyer; b. Chgo., Apr. 29, 1896; s. Abraham B. and Fannie (Charness) A.; student U. Chgo., 1914-15; J.D., Northwestern U., 1918; m. Helen E. Strauss, Aug. 14, 1928; children Elizabeth (Mrs. Leonard Auerbach), William Henry. Admitted to Ill. bar, 1919, practiced in Chgo.; mem. Firm Aaron, Aaron, Schimberg Hess, and predecessor firms, 1970-75. Mem. Chgo. Mayor's Commn. on Human Relations, 1947-60, chmn., 1960-66; past chmn. Mayor's Com. New Residents; chmn. Chgo. chpt. Am. Jewish Com., 1946-52, later hon. chmn.; past nat. v.p., trustee Nat. Am. Jewish Com., later hon.; pres. Jewish Vocational Service and Employment Center, Chgo., 1941-46, life dir.; bd. dirs. Leadership Council Met. Chgo.; mem. exec. bd. Chgo. Com. on Urban Opportunity. Served with U.S. Army, World War 1. Fellow Am. Bar Found.; mem. Am., Ill. State, Chgo. bar assns. Clubs: City, Mid-Day, Standard (Chgo.); Lake Shore Country (Glencoe, Ill.); Harmonie (N.Y.). Home: Chicago Ill. Died Mar. 3, 1975.

AASGAARD, JOHAN ARND, clergyman; b. Albert Lea, Minn., Apr. 5, 1876; s. Anders Larsen and Maren Bergette (Hendrickson) A.; A.B., St. Olaf Coll., Northfield, Minn., 1898; candidate theology Luth. Theol. Sem., St. Anthony Park, Minn., 1901; B.D., Princeton Theol. Sem., 1906; studied U. of Wis., 1906-07; D.D., Wittenberg Coll., 1922; LL.D., Luther Coll., 1936; Th.D., Oslo U., 1938; L.H.D., Augustana College, 1940; S.T.D., St. Olaf College, 1944; m. Ragnhild Evangeline, daughter of Right Rev. G. Hoyme, Apr. 7, 1902; children—Gudrun Margaret, Valborg Ragnhild, Mary Elizabeth. Ordained Luth. ministry, 1901; pastor De Forest, Wis., 1901-11; mem. and sec. bd. of regents of ednl. insts. of United Luth. Ch., 1906-17; prof. ch. history, Luth. Sem., St. Anthony Park, Minn., 1906-07; 1st editor United Lutheran, 1908, 1909; editor Kirkebladet, 1910, 1911; pres. Concordia Coll., Moorhead Minn., 1911-25; pres. Evangelical Lutheran Church, 1925-54. Commissioner National Lutheran Council. 1925-56; Commander Grand Cross Royal Order of St. Olav (Norway). Mem. Norwegian-Am. Hist. Assn. (pres. 1954-57). Home: Cokato, Minn.†

ABARBANELL, LINA, actress, singer; b. Berlin, Germany, Jan. 3, 1880; d. Paul A. (musical dir.); studied for stage in Berlin, Vienna and New York; m. Edward Goldbeck, writer, Oct. 10, 1900. Made début in Neues Theatre, Berlin, 1895; appeared in grand opera at Posen, 1897, later at Royal Opera House, Berlin, in "Die Fledermaus"; toured Germany, Belgium, Denmark, Austria and Holland: came to U.S., 1905, and made first English-speaking début, in "The Student King," at Garden Theatre, New York, 1906; played in "The Merry Widow,", "The Love Cure," "Madame Sherry,", etc. Home: Evanston, Ill.†

ABBOTT, BUD, radio, stage and screen performer; b. Asbury Park, N.J., Oct. 2, 1898; s. Harry and Ray A.; ed. pub. sch., Coney Island, N.Y.; m. Jenny Mae Pratt, Sept. 17, 1918; children—William Bud, Victoria. Began as cashier in theatre, 1916; since then successively usher, asst. mgr., mgr. of theatre, actor, straightman, movie and radio star; movies include One Night in the Tropics, 1939 Buck Privates, In the Navy, Hold that Ghost, Keep 'em Flying, Pardon My Sarong, Abbott and Costello Meet Frankenstein. Sold 78 million dollars worth of War Bonds on a 31 day tour; entertained at 300 Army and Navy Camps. Mason (Shriner). Home: Encino, Cal. Died Apr. 24, 1974.

ABBOT, CHARLES GREELEY, astrophysicist; b. Wilton, N.H., May 31, 1872; s. Harris and Caroline Ann (Greeley) A.; S.B., Mass. Inst. Tech., 1894, S.M., 1895; D.Sc., Melbourne U., 1914, Case Sch. Applied Science, 1931, George Washington U., 1937; LL.D., U. Toronto, 1933; m. Lilliam E. Moore, Oct. 13, 1897; m. 2d, Virginia A. Johnston, June 9, 1954. Asst., Smithsonian Astrophys. Obs., 1895, aid, acting in 1896-1906, 1896, acting dir., 1907, dir., 1907-44; Asst. sec. Smithsonian Instn., 1918-28, sec., 1928-1944, research assoc., from 1944; home sec. Nat. Acad. Sciences, 1918-23. Draper medallist of Nat. Acad. Sciences; Rumford medallist Am. Acad. Arts and Scis. Fellow A.A.A.S.; mem. Astron. and Astrophys. Soc. Am., Philos. Soc. (Washington), Washington Acad. Sciences, Nat. Acad. Sciences, Soc. Astron. de France, Soc. Astron. Mexico, Acad. Modena, Deutsche Meteorol. Gesellschaft; hon. mem. Royal Meteorol. Soc.; asso. mem. Royal Astron. Soc. of Great Britain. Home: Hyattsville Md. Died Dec. 17, 1973.

ABBOTT, JANE DRAKE, author; b. Buffalo, N.Y., July 10, 1881; d. Marcus Motier and Mary Ann (Ludlow) Drake; student Cornell U.; m. Frank Addison Abbott, of Buffalo, Dec. 20, 1902; children—Frank Addison, Elizabeth Drake, Alice Ludlow. Chairman Erie Woman Suffrage Association, 1916; commissioner Girl Scouts of Buffalo and Erie County, 1919-24. Member Scribblers of Buffalo; member Alpha Phi. Democrat. Happy House, 1919; Highacres, 1920; Aprilly, 1921; Red Robin, 1922; Mingle Streams, 1923; Fideils, 1923; Laughing Last, 1924; Polly Put the Kettle On, 1925; Martha the Seventh, 1926; Juliet Is Twenty, 1927; (play) Stone, 1925; Black Flower, 1929; Heyday, 1929; Merridy Road, 1930; Kitty Frew, 1931; Bouquet Hill, 1931; Silver Fountain, 1932; Young Dalfreys, 1932; Miss Jolley's Family, 1933; Dicket, A Story of Friendships, 1933; Strangers in the House, 1935; Low Bridge, 1935; Row of Stars, 1937; Angels May Weep, 1938; also two plays for children, The Wonder Gate, and Light Heart. Home: Buffalo, N.Y.†

ABEGG, CARL JULIUS, food co. exec.; b. 1891. Dir., Nestle Alimentana, S.A., 1937-73, chmn., 1948-62, hon. chmn., 1962-73; hon. chmn. Zurich Ins. Co. Address: Vevey Vaud, Switzerland. Died August 1973.

ABERCROMBIE, THOMAS FRANKLIN, physician; b. Ga., June 5, 1879; s. Jesse and Elizabeth (Hatchett) A.; B.S., Douglasville Coll., 1898; M.D., Atlanta Coll. of Physicians and Surgeons (now Emory U.), 1903; D.P.H., Univ. of Ga., 1929; D.Sc., Emory U., 1936; m. Frances Clark Morris, Nov. 6, 1906; 1 dau., Frances Clark. In pvt. practice, 1903-11; mem. Rockefeller Sanitation Commn., 1911-13; commr. of health Brunswick and Glynn County, 1914-17; dir. Ga. State Dept. of Health 1917-47. Mem. com. of interchange of pub. health officers for League of Nations to study health conditions in Holland and England, 1924. Awarded L. G. Hardman Cup for distinguished service in public health, 1942. Mem. Med. Assn. of Ga., Southern Med. Assn. Democrat. Presbyn. Club: Men's Garden of Atlanta (pres. 1938-39). Home: Decatur, Ga.†

ABERNETHY, WILBUR MURRAH, dentist; b. Troy, Miss., June 28, 1910; s. Bobby Luster and Nelle Olive (Dunlap) A.; student Chickasaw Coll., Pontotoc, Miss., 1929; B.A., U. Miss., 1933, postgrad., 1958; D.D.S., U. Tenn., 1942; m. Jamie C. Hickman, July 24, 1941; children—Sylvia Nelle (Mrs. William Byron Harvey), Wilbur Nurrah II. Individual practice dentistry, Pontotoc, summer 1942, Oxford, Miss., 1946-75. Served to maj. AUS, 1942-46. Mem. LaFayette County Alumni Assn. U. Miss. (past pres.), Oxford Jr. C. of C., Plerre Fauchard Acad., Miss. Dental Soc., N.E. Miss. Dental Soc., Am. Dental Assn., Psi Omega, Pi Kappa Alpha. Baptist. Rotarian. Home: Oxford, Miss. Died Mar. 21, 1975; interred St. Peter's Cemetery, Oxford.

ABRAMS, CREIGHTON WILLIAMS, army officer; b. Springfield, Mass., Sept. 15, 1914; s. Creighton W. and Nellie (Randall) A.; B.S., U.S. Mil. Acad., 1936; grad. Command and Gen. Staff Coll., 1949, Army War Coll., 1953; m. Julia Harvey, Aug. 30, 1936; children—Noel (Mrs. William J. Bradley), Creighton Williams, John Nelson, Jeanne Rejane, Elizabeth Harvey, Robert Bruce. Commd. 2d lt. U.S. Army, 1936, advanced through grades to gen. 1964; troop officer 1st Cav. Div., 1936; assigned 1st Armored Div., 1940; successively regtl. adj., regtl. exec. officer, battalion comdr., combat command comdr. 4th Armored Div., 1941-45; assigned War Dept. Gen. 1945-46; dir. tactics Armored Sch., 1946-48; comdr. 63d Tank Battalion, Europe, 1949-53; chief staff I Corps, Korea, 1953, X Corps, Korea, 1954, IX Corps, Korea, 1954; chief staff Armored Center, 1955-56; dep. asst. chief staff res. components Dept. Army Gen. Staff, 1956-59; asst. div. comdr. 3d Armored Div., 1959-60; dep. chief staff operations Hdgrs. U.S. Army Europe, 1960; div. comdr. 3d Armored Div., 1960-62; asst. dep. chief staff mil. operations for civil affairs Dept. Army, 1962; dir. operations Office Dept. Chief Staff Mil. Operations, 1962; asst. dep. chief staff mil. operations and requirements and programs Dept. Army, 1962-63, dep. asst. chief staff force devel., 1963; comdg. gen. V Corps, 1963-64; vice chief staff, 1964-67, chief of staff, 1972-74; dep. comdr. U.S. Mil. Assistance Command, Vietnam, 1967-68; comdg. gen. U.S. forces Vietnam, 1968-72. Decorated D.S.C. with oak leaf cluster, Def. D.S.M., D.S.M. with 3 oak leaf clusters, Silver Star with Oak leaf; Legion of Merit with oak leaf, Bronze Star with V device, Joint Service Commendation Medal; Chevalier Legion Honor, Croix de Guerre (France); Distinguished Service Order (Great Britain); Ulchi Distinguished Service medal with gold star, Order Nat. Security Merit 2d class (Korea); knight grand cross 1st class Most Noble Order Crown Thailand; Nat. Order of Vietnam 1st Class, Republic of Vietnam Gallantry Cross with palm. Address: Washington, D.C. Died Sept. 4, 1974.

ABRAMS, DUFF ANDREW, cons. engr.; b. Grand Tower, Ill., Apr. 25, 1880; s. Hardin T. and Mary (Kuntz) A.; B.S. in C.E., U. of Ill., 1905, C.E., 1909; m. Leone Cronkhite, June 17, 1908; 1 dau., Edith Lenore; m. 2d, Eleanor R. Piercy. Assistant in engineering Experimental Station, University of Ill., 1905-08, asso. engr., research work on concrete and reinforced concrete, 1908-14; prof. in charge structural materials Research Lab., a joint project between Lewis Inst., Chicago and Portland Cement Assn., 1914-25; dir. of research Portland Cement Assn., Chicago, 1925-27, Internat. Cement Corp., New York, 1927-31; cons. engr., New York from 1931. Awarded Wason medal, Am. Concrete Inst., 1919; Turner gold medal, same, 1931; Brown medal, Franklin Inst., 1942. Fellow A.A.A.S.; Am. Soc. C.E. (com. on masonry dams), Am. Soc. for Testing Materials (com. on cement and concrete), Sigma Xi. Author of numerous papers on concrete and reinforced concrete. Home: New York City, N.Y.†

ABT, ARTHUR FREDERICK, pediatrician; b. Chgo., Sept. 7, 1898; s. Isaac A. and Lina A.; B.S., U. Chgo., 1918; M.D., Johns Hopkins, 1923; m. Alice Mitau, Mar. 25, 1928; children—Lina Abt Steele, Arthur. Resident house officer Johns Hopkins Hosp., 1923-24; resident physician Sarah Morris Hosp. for Children, Chgo., 1924-25; asso. prof. pediatrics Northwestern U. Med. Sch., 1926-53; attending pediatrician Chgo. Lying-In Hosp., 1925-31, Chgo. Maternity Center-Sarah Morris Hosp. for Children, 1930-53; pediatrician Northwestern U. Med. Sch. Polio Aid Team, and mem. Joint Maternal

Welfare Com., Cook County (Ill.), 1948-53; dir. radioisotope unit VA Hosp., Durham, N.C., also prof. pediatrics Duke U., 1953; past chief radioisotope service VA, Martinsburg, W.VA.; attending physician Gen. Med. Clinic, Johns Hopkins Hosp., Balt., 1969. Served as lt. comdr. USNR, 1940-45, naval liaison officer OSRD Com. on Med. Research; chem. warfare officer Hdqrs. 9th and 12th Naval Dists.; chem. warfare officer, 1943-44, overseas; on staff Adm. William Halsey, comdr. So. Pacific, 1944; med. officer on staff Adm. George Fort, comdr. Task Force 32, Pilau invasion; in charge evacuation of all (wounded) casualties; capt. Res. ret. Cons. in pediatrics U.S. Naval Hosp., Great Lakes, Ill., 1946-52. Recipient 50 year medal U. Chgo., 1968, Grad. medallion Johns Hopkins, 1973. Diplomate Am. Bd. Pediatrics. Fellow A.C.P.; mem. A.M.A., Soc. Pediatric Research, Am. Pediatric Soc., Am. Acad. Pediatrics, Soc. for Pediatric Research, Soc. for Exptl. Biology and Medicine, Chicago Pediatric Soc. (past pres.), Inst. of Medicine of Chgo., Am. Soc. Clin. Nutrition, Am. Inst. Nutrition, Pan Am. Med. Soc., Sigma Xi. Co-author: Year Book of Pediatrics, 1927-47. Author: Abt-Garrison History of Pediatrics, 1965. Contbr. chpts. pediatric subjects for De Lee's Obstetrics for Nurses, Collier's Ency., Brennemann's System of Pediatrics, A.M.A. Symposium Vitamins, Tb and Other Communicable Diseases (editor J. Arthur Myers), others; also articles on clin. and exptl. aspects pediatrics and nutrition. Home: Baltimore, Md. Died Mar. 25, 1974.

ACKER, GEORGE GERALD, educator; b. Venango, Pa., Oct. 4, 1914; s. George David and Mildred (Lilly) A.; A.B., Allegheny Coll., 1937; M.S., U. Okla., 1939; D.Sc., Central State U., 1966; m. Mary Margaret Sheppard, Feb. 4, 1942; children—Charles D., Frank W., Helen M. Instr. Bowling Green State U., 1946-48, asst. prof., 1949-59, asso. prof., 1960-69, prof., 1969-74, asst. chmn. biology dept., 1970, dir. biology field camp, 1960-74; dir. Ohio Jr. Acad. Sci., 1957-72, dir. emeritus, 1973-74, Ohio Jr. Sci. and Humanities Symposium, 1964-74; supt. Youth Sci. for The Ohio State Fair, 1962-74; adv. council Nat. Jr. Sci. and Humanities Symposium, 1969-71. Active Cub and Boy Scouts; mem. Gov.'s Com. on Traffic Safety, 1972-74. Served with AUS, 1941-46, ETO; Korean War, 1951-53. Decorated Bronze Star (2). Fellow Ohio Acad. Sci. (pres. 1972-73), A.A.A.S.; mem. Am. Inst. Biol. Sci., Am. Assn. Ichthyologists and Herpetologists, Internat. Soc. Theoretical and Applied Limnology, Ohio Council of Elementary Sch. Sci., A.A.U.P., Gt. Lakes Found., Internat. Assn. Gt. Lakes Research, Sigma Xi, Beta Beta Beta, Phi Sigma. Presbyn. (elder). Home: Bowling Green, Ohio. Died Sept. 3, 1974; interred Venango Cemetery, Venango, Pa.

ACKERMAN, WILLIAM COOPER, govt. ofcl.; b. Mt. Vernon, O., May 15, 1908; s. William Asa and Mildred (Cooper) A.; A.B. cum laude, Princeton, 1931; m. Margaret Green, June 3, 1933; children—Thomas Cooper, Constance Ackerman Hutchinson. Mem. editorial staff Cleve. Plain Dealer, 1932-36; mem. adminstr., staff Princeton, 1936-40; dir. reference dept. CBS, 1940-57, exec. dir. CBS Found., Inc., 1954-61, dir. spl. projects CBS News, 1957-61; spl. asst. Bur. Ednl. and Cultural Affairs, Dept. of State, 1961-62, 65-68, dep. pub. information and reports, 1962-65, dir. pub. information and reports, 1968-70, cons., 1970; staff Washington Internat. Center for spl. research projects, 1971; asst. coordinator of research Congl. Research Service, Library of Congress, from 1972. Exec. sec. Pres.'s Materials Policy Commn., Washington, 1951-52. Trustee, Merc. Library Assn., 1951-61, pres. 1959-60. Mem. Nat. Indsl. Conf. Bd. (council of execs. on co. contbns. 1955-61). Presbyn. (elder). Club: Saint Albans Tennis, Kenwood Golf and Country. Home: Washington, D.C. Died Oct. 26, 1974; interred Fredericktown, Ohio.

ACKLIN, ARTHUR ASHTON, business executive; born Carroll County, Ga., July 3, 1893; s. John Franklin and Izora (Johnson) A.; ed. pub. schs., Carrollton, Ga.; m. Edith Hunnicutt, Nov. 15, 1923. With The Coca-Cola Co., 1925-75, dir., 1938-75, former chmn. advisory com. The Coca-Cola Co. Served as pvt., U.S. Army, during World War I. Trustee Crawford W. Long Memorial Hospital, Atlanta. Baptist. Mason. Clubs: Capital City, Atlanta Athletic, Piedmont Driving (Atlanta). Home: Roswell, Ga. Died June 2, 1975.

ADAMS, BERTRAM MARTIN (BILL ADAMS), writer; b. of Am. parents in Eng., Feb. 24, 1879; s. Francis and Charlotte (Lee) A.; ed. pvtly. and at Weymouth Coll., Eng.; m. Dorothy V. Byrde, of Lausanne, Switzerland, Dec. 19, 1902; m Lucy Lockwood Hazard, June 11, 1936. Left college to go to sea; later worked as house painter, teamster, gardener, janitor, wood-chopper, milker, policeman, fruit tree specialist; in charge of casual camp "Y" at Camp Fremont, 1918, World War; began writing as contbr. to the Outlook, 1921, stories and verse appearing later in other mags. Author: Fenceless Meadows, 1923; Short Stories of Today and Yesterday, 1931; Wind in the Topsails (verse), 1931; Ships and Women, 1937. Home: Walnut Creek, Cal.†

ADAMS, CALVIN CHARLES, banker; b. Lubbock, Tex., May 12, 1925; s. Claude Edward and Nona Arabell (Griggs) A.; student Harvard, 1944-45; student exec. edn. program U. Cal. at Berkeley Grad. Sch. Bus., 1961; m. Phyllis Jeanne Wormley, July 3, 1946; children—Cynthia, Roger. With First Nat. Bank, Lubbock, 1939-42; with Bank Am., San Francisco, 1946, positions in domestic and internat. ops., 1948-62, overseas assignments include Bangkok, Thailand, Singapore, head loan adminstrn. No. Cal. brs., 1967-70, sr. v.p., adminstrv. officer finance in charge internat. loan, fgn. exchange and money ops., 1970-73. Mem. San Francisco Adv. Council Small Bus., 1969-70. Served with USNR, 1942-46. Mem. San Francisco C. of C. Club: Bankers (San Francisco). Home: Palo Alto, Calif. Died Aug. 23, 1973.

ADAMS, DONALD ALISON, b. Windsor, Wis., Sept. 7, 1881; g. Alison Dwight and Sarah (Lawson) A.; B.A., Carleton Coll., Northfield, Minn., 1903; LL.B., Yale, 1908; m. Edith Marion Nichols, of New Haven, Conn., May 19, 1910; children—Henry Sage, Eleanor, Asst. cashier Northfield Nat. Bank, 1903-05; practiced law, N.Y. City, 1908-10; instr. in business law, Yale, since 1915; gen. ins. business; dir. Broadway Bank & Trust Co. Elected pres. Rotary Internat., June 1925; sec. Civics Federation, New Haven, 4 yrs.; sec. Community Service, Inc., New Haven; mem. Bd. of Aldermen 2 terms. President of Chamber of Commerce of New Haven. Mem. Adelphic Soc. (Carleton Coll.), Phi Delta Phi. Republican. Conglist. Mem. Yale-Princeton Debate, 1906. Home: New Haven, Conn.†

ADAMS, FRANKLIN OLIVER, architect; b. La., July 5, 1881; s. Franklin Oliver and Susan (Drake) A.; B.S., Centenary Coll., La., 1901, student Univ. of Chicago, 1902, B.S., Mass. Inst. Tech., 1907; m. Caroline Kilbride, July 9, 1914; children—Franklin Oliver, III, Caroline. High sch. teacher and prin., 1901-04; in office of Newhall Blevins, architects, 1907; in office of Harry B. Wheelock, architect, 1909-14; opened own office in Tampa, Mar., 1914; asst. state architect of N.C., 1919-20; own office in Tampa from 1920. Assisted in organizing Tampa Builders Exchange, the Tampa Civic Art Commn.; mem. of Municipal Housing Com to study Negro housing conditions in Tampa; apptd. to Constructed Appeals Bd., under N.R.A. by Pres. Roosevelt; mem. Pres. Hoover's Building Congress. Fellow Am. Inst. Architects; mem. Fla. Assn. of Architects, Tampa Assn. of Architects, Kappa Alpha (Southern). Clubs: Tampa Executives' Club, Tampa Kiwanis (past pres.). Home: Tampa, Fla.†

ADAMS, HAROLD PLANK, govt. ofcl.; b. Wilmore, Ky., Dec. 18, 1912; s. Eleazer Tarrant and Evangeline (Plank) A.; B.S., U. Ky., 1934, Ed.D., 1949; M.A., Columbia, 1939; m. Sara Kinney, Aug. 8, 1956. Tchr., supr., adminstr. Fayette County (Ky.) Schs., 1934-41; tng. specialist U.S. War Dept. and Ford Motor Co., 1942-43; registration officer VA, 1946; asso. prof. edn. U. Ky., 1949-56; dep. chief edn. div. U.S. Operations Mission to Thailand, Dept. State, AID, 1956-60, chief edn. div. U.S. AID Mission to Paraguay, 1960-63, dep. chief edn. div. Bur. for Africa, Washington, 1963-66, chief edn. div. AID Mission to Uganda, 1966-70, dep. asst. dir. for edn. U.S. Operations Mission to Thailand, 1970-74. Chmn. gen. com. Nat. Study Secondary Sch. Evaluation, 1953-56; guest prof. Sch. Edn., U. N.C., 1955; cons. on tchr. edn. Govt. of Somalia, E. Africa, 1968. Served with AUS, World War II; MTO, ETO. Decorated Bronze Star medal with three oak leaf clusters. Mem. So. Assn. Colls. and Schs. (chmn. Ky. com. 1953-56), Assn. for Supervision and Curriculum Devel. (pres. Ky. chpt. 1955), Am. Assn. U. Profs., Am. Edn. Research Assn., N.E.A., Ky. Edn. Assn., Nat. Assn. Secondary Sch. Prins., Am. Assn. Sch. Adminstrs., Sigma Pi Sigma, Phi Delta Kappa, Kappa Delta Pi. Clubs: Kenwood Golf and Country (Washington); Westwood Country (Vienna, Va.); Royal Bangkok Sports; Asunción (Paraguay) Golf. Co-author: Basic Principles of Supervision, 1953; Basic Principles of Student Teaching, 1956. Editor and co-author Bull. of Bur. Sch. Service, U. Ky., 1949-54. Home: Bangkok, Thailand. Died Apr. 5, 1974.

ADAMS, JOHN DUNCAN, author; b. Toronto, Can., Dec. 16, 1879; s. George and Margaret (Cruikshank) A.; ed. Toronto Tech. Sch. and Parkdale Collegiate Inst., Toronto; unmarried. Came to U.S., 1895; connected with mech. dept. Parke, Davis & Co., Detroit, Mich., several yrs.; with Dept. of Interior, survey of public lands, from 1902. Became naturalized citizen of U.S., 1902. Author: Arts and Crafts Lamps, 1910; Metal Work and Etching, 1911; Lamps and Shades, 1912; When Mother Lets Us Carpenter, 1916; Carpentry for Beginners, 1917; Experiments with Alternating Current, 1919. Address: Phoneix, Ariz.†

ADAMS, KENNETH STANLEY, ret. oil co. exec.; b. Horton, Kan., Aug. 31, 1899; s. John Valentine and Louella (Stanley) A.; student U. Kan., 1917-20; LL.D., Drury Coll., 1955, Okla. Baptist U., 1959; m. 2d, Dorothy Glynn Stephens, Nov. 4, 1946; children—Mary Louise Hoy, Kenneth Stanley, Stepehn Stanley, Kenneth Glenn, Gary C., Stephanie, Lisa A. Warehouse clk. Phillips Petroleum Co. 1920-22, asst. operations mgr. prodn. dept., 1922-26, asst. to clk., accounting div., 1926, asst. sec. 1927, asst. sec., asst. treas., 1928-32, asst. to pres., 1932-35 dir. and mem. exec. com. 1935—, treas., asst. to pres., 1935-38, exec. v.p., 1938, pres. 1938-51, chmn. bd., 1951-68, chmn. emeritus, 1968—, also mem. finance com. Served in O.T.S., Camp Zachary Taylor Louisville, 1918; chmn. Dist. No. 2 Prodn. Com. under Petroleum Adminstrn. for War Mem. Am. Petroleum Inst., Mid-Continent Oil and Gas Assn., Independent Petroleum Assn., Sigma Chi. Presbyn. Mason (33 deg., K.T., Shriner, Jester). Clubs: Hillcrest Country (Bartlesville, Okla.); Cherokee (Afton, Okla). Home: Bartlesville, Okla. Died Mar. 30, 1975.

ADAMS, MILLER, restaurant exec.; b. Benton, Ill., Apr. 19, 1894; student Trinity Coll., Dublin, also Northwestern U.; m. Marion Phelan, Aug. 21, 1927 (dec.). Controller various mining firms, Chgo.; reorgn. accounting and adminstrv. division of Fred Harvey for Arthur Andersen & Co., 1928-30; asst. controller Fred Harvey, Chgo., 1930-31, controller, 1931-46, financial v.p., 1946-55, pres., 1955-59, dir., spl. cons., 1959-65; dir., spl. cons. Sky Chefs, Inc., 1959-69. Served with Motor Transport Corps, U.S. Army, World War I. Mem. Wine and Food Soc. Chgo. and Phoenix Nat., Chgo. restaurant assns., Am. Hotel Assn. Clubs: Edgewater Gold (Chgo.); Phoenix, Phoenix Country. Home: Phoenix, Ariz. Died Apr. 23, 1975.

ADAMS, PHILIP, b. of Am. parentage, Honolulu, T.H., June 26, 1881; s. Edward Payson and Ellen Germaine (Fisher), A.; A.B., Harvard, 1903; unmarried. Formerly instr. of English, U. of Wis., and was portrait and landscape painter; exhibited at San Francisco, Expn., 1915, and elsewhere. Editor of gen. and spl. orders, Bur. War Risk Ins., Aug. 1918-July 1920; chief of div. of passport control, Dept. of State, 1920-22; consul at Paris, France, 1922-24, at Valetta, Malta, 1924-26; sec. of Legation, Tirana, Albania, 1926. Unitarian. Clubs: University, Harvard (Washington); Twentieth Century (Boston); American (Paris).†

ADAMS, WESTON WOOLLARD, stock exchange exec.; b. Springfield, Mass., Aug. 9, 1904; s. Charles Francis and Lillias Mae (Woollard) A.; student Phillips Exeter Acad., 1921-23; B.A., Harvard, 1928; m. Mildred Culver Boyd, Jan. 8, 1933 (div. 1936); children—Abigail Mae (Mrs. Willys K. Silvers), John Weston; m. 2d, Nancy Evelyn Atkins, Sept. 26, 1936; children—Wendy Ann (Mrs. Shelby M. C. Davis), Weston Woollard. Mem. Boston Stock Exchange, from 1929, bd. govs., 1938-42, from 1964, v.p., 1953-62, pres., 1962-64; partner Weston W. Adams & Co., Boston, 1936-51, sr. partner, from 1951; pres. Boston Profl. Hockey Assn., Inc., 1936-51, 64-69, chmn., from 1964; chmn., pres. Boston Bruins; mem. N.Y. Stock Exchange, from 1946; chmn. bd. Boston Garden-Arena Corp., from 1951. Bd. govs. Nat. Hockey League. Served from lt. to comdr. USNR, 1942-46. Mem. Newcomen Soc. Clubs: Aleppo Temple, Tennis and Racquet, Harvard (Boston); Country (Brookline); Eastern Yacht (Marblehead Neck, Mass.); Caterpillar. Home: Brookline, Mass. Died Mar. 19, 1973.

ADAMS, WILLIAM ELIAS, surgeon; b. Nichols, Ia., May 1, 1902; s. Frank A. and Alvina W. (Mills) A.; B.S., M.D., U. Ia., 1926; m. Dr. Huberta Livingstone, June 9, 1928; 1 dau., Diana Isabella Livingstone Adams Morgan. Intern surgery U. Ia., 1926-27, instr. anatomy, 1927-28; Douglas Smith research fellow U. Chgo., 1928-29, asst. surgery, 1929-30, asst. resident, 1930-31, instr., resident surgery, 1931-33, instr., chief resident, 1933-35, asst. prof., 1936-40, asso. prof., 1940-47, prof., 1947-54, Raymond prof., 1954-67, Raymond prof. surgery emeritus, from 1967, chmn. dept. surgery, 1959-65; attending surgeon U. Chgo. Hosps., 1936-67, Billings Hosp., Chgo., 1936-67; asst. dir. A.C.S., 1967-73; sr. cons. surgeon Municipal Tb Sanitarium, Chgo., Great Lakes Naval Tng. Hosp., instr. surgery Washington U., St. Louis, 1933; guest asst. surgery U. Berlin, 1935-36; hon. prof. surgery U. Guadalajara (Mexico), 1955, U. Madrid (Spain), 1956; Fulbright guest prof. surgery U. Glasgow (Scotland), 1956. Treas. 1st Internat. Congress on Smoking, Health, 1963-66. Recipient Alexander B. Vishnevski medal Inst. Surgery, Moscow, Russia, 1966; certificate merit clin. and research surgery Vishnevski Inst., U. Moscow, 1966. Diplomate Am. Bd. Surgery, Am. Bd. Thoracic Surgery (founding mem., chmn., 1956-57). Fellow A.C.S. (sec. 1959-62), Am. Surg. Assn., Kansas City Acad. Medicine (hon.); hon. mem. Soc. Cancerol Mexico, Sociedad de Cirugia de Guadalajara; mem. Am. Assn. Thoracic Surgery (pres. 1959-60), Central Surg. Soc., A.M.A. (chmn. sect. diseases of chest 1965-66), Ill. (chmn. bd. trustees 1964-66, trustee 1958-67, 2d v.p. 1971-72), Chgo. (pres. 1970-71) med. socs., Chgo. Surg. Soc. (treas. 1948-52, pres. 1952-53), Chgo. Path. Soc. (pres. 1950), Chgo. Tb Soc. (pres. 1938), Soc. U. Surgeons (founding mem.), Internat. Soc. Surgery, Am. Coll. Chest Physicians (president Ill. chpt. 1960-61, nat. pres. 1967-68), U.S. and Mexico Med. Soc. (hon.), Soc. Clin. Surgery, Pan Am. Med. Assn. (N.Am. v.p. sect. gen. surgery), Am. Thoracic Soc., U. Chgo. Med. Alumni Assn. (pres. 1957-58), Sigma Xi, Alpha Kappa Kappa (grand internat. pres. 1965-71, grand primarius 1972-73), Alpha Omega Alpha (hon.). Presbyn. Mason. Clubs: Quadrangle, South Shore Country (Chgo.); Chikaming Country (Mich.). Contbr. articles to sci. jours., Ency. Brit., also chpts. surg. and physiology textbooks. Asso. editor Diseases of the Chest, 1958-72; editorial bd. Jour. Thoracic and Cardiovascular Surgery, from 1962; represented U.S.A. on internat. bd. editors Excerpta Medica, 1960-67. Home: Hopkinton, Ia. Died Nov. 25, 1973; buried Hopkinton (Ia.) Cemetery.

ADDERLEY, JULIAN EDWIN (CANNONBALL), Saxophonist; b. Tampa, Fla., Sept. 15, 1928; student U.S. Naval Sch. Music, Washington, 1952, Fla. Agrl. and Mech. Coll.; m. Olga James, June 1962. Dir. band Dillard High Sch., Ft. Lauderdale, Fla., 1948-56; debut Cafe Bohemia, N.Y.C., 1955; with brother, Nat Adderley, organizer ensemble for tour, 1955, on tour, 1955-57, 59; joined group Miles Davis, 1957, George Shearing's Band, 1959; rec. artist Em Arcy, 1955, Riverside, 1958-64, Capitol Records, 1964, others; appeared Newport Jazz Festival, Randalls Island, (N.Y.C.) Jazz Festival, Jazz at Philharmonic program, with various tours. Served with AUS, 1950-53; leader 36th Army Dance Band. Recipient citation (with Phil Woods), Ency. Jazz Yearbook, 1956; New Alto Star of Year award Down Beat mag., 1959; named on of Top Artists on Campus poll, 1968; Playboy mag. Poll winners award (readers) for 1st alto, 1962-71, All Stars award (musicians), 1962-71; Downbeat mag. winner Readers Poll, 1968-70. Recordings include: Black Messiah, Country Preacher, Fiddler on the Roof, In Person, Live Session, Mercy, Mercy, Price You got to Pay, Quintet, Walk TallIQuiet Nights, (with Nat Adderley) In New Orleans. Home: Corona, N.Y. Died Aug. 1975.

ADDICKS, LAWRENCE, consulting engr.; b. Phila., Mar. 3, 1878; s. Charles Henry and Mary Knox (Buzby) A.; special course U. of Pa.; B.S. in Mech. and Elec. Engring., Massachusetts Institute Technology, 1899; m. Mary Maulsby O'Brien, June 20, 1899. Supt. Chrome (N.J.) plant, U.S. Metals Refining Co., 1905-14; consulting engr. from 1914. Mem. Naval Consulting Bd. Fellow Am. Inst. Elec. Engrs.; mem. Am. Soc. Mech. Engrs., Am. Inst. Mining Engrs., Am. Soc. for Testing Materials, Electrochem. Soc. (past pres.), Mining and Metall. Soc. America, Instn. of Mining and Metallurgy (London). Episcopalian. Club: Chemists, Mining (New York). Author: Copper Refining, 1921. Editor: Silver in Industry, 1940. Home: Bel Air, Md.†

ADERHOLD, ARTHUR CHAIRRIER, prison warden; b. Carroll Co., Ga., June 2, 1881; s. James Baskin and Sarah Elizabeth (Boyd) A.; ed. rural consol. schs., Carroll Co., Ga.; m. Mittie Cash, Nov. 17, 1901; 1 son, Furman Houston. Asst. forman U.S. Penitentiary, Atlanta, Ga., 1906-08, custodial officer, 1908-18, record clk., 1918-27, dept. warden, 1927-29, warden, 1929-37; warden U.S. Penitentiary, Ft. Leavenworth, Kan., 1937-41. Mem. Warden's Assn. (pres. 1935), Am. Prison Congress. Methodist. Mason. Address: Atlanta, Ga.†

ADERS, ORAL MADISON, indsl. psychologist; b. nr. Tell City, Ind., Nov. 22, 1901; s. Abraham Peter and Emma (Lanman) A.; B.S., Ind. State U., 1929; postgrad. Ind. U., 1938, U. Cin., 1943; M.S., Purdue U., 1946; m. Frieda Marie Howell, June 4, 1924; children—Robert O., Lois Virginia (Mrs. Edmund D. Ludlow). Tchr. pub. schs., rural areas, Ind., 1920-42; indsl. psychologist Perfect Circle Corp., Hagerstown, Ind., 1942-62; pvt. practice indsl. psychology, 1947-74; propr. Aders Personnel Cons. Service; personnel cons., various cos.; dir. Richmond Supply Corp., Ind., 1954-74; guest instr. U. Wis., Miami U., Purdue U., Earlham Coll., 1950-62; past pres. Sales Edn. Center, Dayton, O. Bd. dirs. Wayne County Assn. Mental Health, 1949-61, pres., 1950-53; past pres. bd. Wayne County Child Guidance Clinic; past mem. corporate body United Ch. Bd. for World Ministries; b.d bd. dirs. Eastern Ind. Mental Health Services. Mem. Am. Soc. Tng. Dirs. (charter v.p.), Ind. Psychol. Assn., Ind. Tchrs. Assn., Ind. Indsl. Arts Assn., Iota Lambda Sigma. Mem. United Chs. of Christ. Mason, Rotarian. Contbr. articles to trade and profl. jours. Address: Hagerstown, Ind. Died Oct. 8, 1974; interred Brick Ch. Cemetery, Hagerstown.

ADLER, BETTY, librarian; b. Havana, Cuba, May 13, 1919; d. Pablo and Helene (Friedlein) Adler; B.A., Goucher Coll., 1937; M.L.S., Drexel U., 1938. Librarian, Enoch Pratt Free Library, Balt., 1938-41, from 1948; cons. to Office Coordinator Inter-Am. Affairs, Washington, 1941-48; editor, Menckeniana, from 1962. Recipient citations from gov. of Md. also mayor of Balt. Mem. Am., Md. library assns., Phi Beta Kappa. Indexer vols. 1-50 Md. Hist. Mag., 1961-71; translator, Basile 20th Century Mgmt., 1968. Home: Baltimore, Md. Died Mar. 10, 1973.

ADLER, JOEL B., physician; b. Bklyn., Mar. 27, 1934; s. Simon and Rose Adler; M.D., State U. N.Y. at Bklyn., 1959; m. Florra Feldman, June 23, 1957; children—Douglas, Alison. Intern, Kings County Hosp., Bklyn., 1959-60, resident in gen. surgery, 1960-62, fellow in trauma surgery, 1962; resident in orthopedic surgery Hosp. for Spl. Surgery, N.Y.C., 1962-65, staff orthopedic surgeon out-patient dept., 1965-67, 69-73; staff orthopedic surgeon Good Samaritan Hosp., Suffern, N.Y., 1965-73, dir. orthopedic surgery, 1971-73; staff orthopedic surgeon Meml. Hosp., Tuxedo, N.Y., 1965-73; dir. Regional Orthopedic Clinic of Rockland County (N.Y.); clin. instr. orthopedic surgery Cornell U. Sch. Medicine, N.Y.C., 1965-67, 69-73. Diplomate Am. Bd. Orthopaedic Surgery. Fellow N.Y. Acad. Medicine; mem. A.M.A., Am. Acad. Orthopaedic Surgeons, Physicians for Automotive Safety, Rockland County Med. Soc. Contbr. articles to med. jours. Home: Spring Valley, N.Y., Died Feb. 12, 1973; buried New Montefiore Cemetery, Pinelawn, L.I., N.Y.

ADLERBLUM, NIMA H., author; b. Jerusalem, Palestine, Aug. 4, 1886; d. Hayyim and Eva (Hakohen) Hirschensohn; brought to U.S., 1904; student Barnard Coll., also Paris, France; Ph.D., Columbia, 1926; m. Israel S. Adlerblum, Apr. 9, 1914; 1 dau., Ivria (Mrs. Alexander H. Sackton). Founder, mem. Am. Com. Translation and Dissemination John Dewey's and Am. philosophy in Latin Am.; also translation and dissemination Am. works in philosophy of edn.; founder Hadassah Nat. Cultural work, chmn. nat. com., mem. nat. bd. 1920-33; founder Exchange of Thought Movement, Am. and European scholars, 1920; research work throughout Europe, Near East, for studying problems of minority nationalities, Latin Am. for intercultural relationship and immigration of refugees. Life fellow Internat. Inst. Arts and Letters; mem. Am. Philos. Assn., InterAm. Congress Philosophy (elected editor of contemplated edit. of Contemporary Philos. Tendencies throughout the World), Internat. Congress of Philosophy, League for Indsl. Democracy, Hadassah, many other orgns. Author: A Study of Gersonides in his Proper Perspective, 1926; A Perscpective of Jewish Life through its Festivals, 1930 (transcribed into Braille); Memoirs of Childhood in Guardians of Our Heritage (Leo Jung editor), 1958; Sara Bayla and Her Times (Leo Jung editor) (translated into Hebrew); other biographies, chpts. in various publs. Contbr. articles to philos. jours. Home: Herzelia Israel. Died July 25, 1974.

AFFEL, HERMAN ANDREW, elec. engr.; b. Bklyn., Aug. 4, 1893; s. Herman and Catharine M.H. (Wittschen) A.; B.S., Mass. Inst. Tech., 1914; m. Bertha May Plummer, Apr. 20, 1918 (dec.); children—Herman Andrew, Priscilla (Mrs. Thomas G. Weilepp, Jr.); m. 2d, Dorothy Ruth Pape, Dec. 29, 1929. Research asst. Mass. Inst. Tech., 1914-16; engr. Am. Tel. & Tel. Co., 1916-31; engr. and exec. Bell Telephone Labs., Inc., 1931-58, ret. as asst. v.p., 1958, then cons.; cons. No. Electric. Co., Can. Former dir. YMCA and Community Fund, Ridgewood, N.J.; past pres. Ridgewood-Glen Rock council Boy Scouts Am. Mem. adv. coms. to mil. and other govt. agys. Recipient Modern Pioneers award Am. Mfrs. Assn., 1940; plaque Army Signal Corps, 1958. Registered profl. engr., Me., N.Y. Fellow I.E.E.E., A.A.A.S., Acoustical Soc. Am.; mem. Telephone Pioneers (life). Author numerous tech. articles on wire and radio communication. Inventions include coaxial cable for TV and other communication purposes; numerous patents in communications field. Home: Rome, Maine. Died Oct. 13, 1972; buried Lutheran Cemetery, Brooklyn, N.Y.

AGNEW, JANET MARGARET, ret. librarian; b. St. Paul, Nov. 1, 1903; d. Harry M. and Emmeline Marie (Brigham) A.; A.B., U. Man. (Can.), 1925, A.M., 1930; B.L.S., McGill U., 1933. Instr. library sch. McGill U., 1933-38; asst. prof. library sch. La. State U., 1939-42; librarian Sweet Briar Coll., 1942-47, Bryn Mawr Coll., 1947-69, formerly head librarian. Mem. A.L.A., Art Gallery Victoria, Victoria Nat. Hist. Soc. Club: Woman's University. Compiler: Southern Bibliography, 1939-42. Home: Victoria, B.C., Canada. Died Jan. 23, 1975.

AHERN, LEO JAMES, army officer; b. Miller, S.D., July 17, 1886; s. Matthew and Minnie (Corbett) A.; B.S., U.S. Military Academy, 1909. Commd. 2d lt., field arty., June 11, 1909; advanced through grades to col., June 1, 1938; temp. rank of brig. gen., Mar. 1943. Roman Catholic. Club: Army-Navy. Home: Washington, D.C. Died July 25, 1973.

AHLQUIST, MIRIAM SWEET (MRS. CARL GUSTAF AHLQUIST), home economist; b. Providence, Jan. 14, 1910; d. George Ernest and Jennie (Dillenbeck) Sweet; B.S., State Tchrs. Coll., Framingham, Mass., 1932; m. Carl Gustaf Ahlquist, Sept. 21, 1940; (dec. Apr. 1964); children—Robert Otto, Carl Erik. Owner, gen. mgr. Central Catering Service, Jamaica Plain, Mass., 1948-58; asst. dietitian John Hancock Mut. Life Ins. Co., Boston, 1958-61; food cons. United Fruit & Food Corp., Boston, 1962-63; food cons. West Roxbury, Mass., 1963-72; mgr., coordinator Mass. Gen. Hosp. Coffee Shop, Boston, 1965-67; mgr. coffee shop Glover Meml. Hosp., Needham, Mass., 1967-72. Head den mother Cub Scouts, 1949-52. Mem. Am., Mass. (chmn. comml. exhibits 1962, 63) home econs. assns., Home Economists in Bus. (sec. Boston 1960, 61, editor News Letter 1962, 63). Home: West Roxbury, Mass. Died Aug. 1, 1972.

AIELLO, GAETAN RUDOLPH, educator; b. Rome, Italy, Oct. 3, 1895; s. John and Ann-Christine (Luria) A.; came to U.S., 1903, naturalized, 1918; A.B. honoris causa, Amherst Coll., 1918, A.B., 1919; A.M., U. Ill., 1923; A.M. (Austin scholar), Harvard U., 1930, Ph.D., 1932; m. Josephine Malugani, Apr. 24, 1920 (dec. 1966); children—Vera-Viva (dec.), Lloyd Malugani, Cynthia (Mrs. Robert Allan Hurley); m. 2d, Frances M. Proteau, Feb. 3, 1967. Treas., Valtam Constrn. Co., Fordham U. Law Sch., 1919-20; supervising prin. Hebron (Ind.) High Sch., 1920-21; instr. Romance langs. U. Ill., 1921-23; asst. prof. Romance langs. and lit. Syracuse U., 1923-29; instr., tutor div. modern langs. Harvard, 1930-32; acting head, Spanish and Italian Dept., Amherst Coll., 1932-33; co-founder, co-dir. Cambridge (Mass.) Sch. Liberal Arts, jr. coll., 1934-36; founder, headmaster, headmaster emeritus Cambridge Acad., from 1936; cons., lectr. on edn. Mem. Cambridge City Republican Com. Mem. Nat. and Mass. Secondary Sch. Prin. Assn., Cambridge C. of C., Municipal Affairs Com., Harvard Sq. Bus. Men's Assn., Bishop Cheverus Gen. Assembly, Internat. Platform Assn. Elk, K.C. (4th deg), Rotarian. Author articles on indsl. subjects. Home: Duxbury, Mass. Died Sept. 1, 1973.

AIKEN, CONRAD POTTER, critic, poet; b. Savannah, Ga., Aug. 5, 1889; s. William Ford and Anna (Potter) A.; A.B., Harvard, 1911; m. Jessie McDonald, Aug. 25, 1912 (div. 1929); children—John Kempton, Jane Kempton, Joan Delano; m. 2d, Clarice Lorenz, 1930 (div. 1937); m. 3d, Mary Augusta Hoover, July 7, 1937. Consultant American letters Library of Congress. Author: (poems) Earth Triumphant and Other Tales, 1914; Turns and Movies, 1916; The Jig of Forslin, 1916; Nocturne of Remembered Spring, 1917; The Charnel Rose, 1918; The House of Dust, 1920; Punch, The Immortal Liar, 1921; Priapus and the Pool, 1922; Pilgrimage of Festus, 1923; Scepticisms—Notes on Contemporary Poetry, 1919; Priapus and the Pool, and Other Poems, 1925; Bring! Bring! and Other Stories, 1925; Blue Voyage (novel), 1927; Costumes by Eros (short stories), 1928; John Deth, and Other Poems, 1930; The Coming Forth by Day of Osiris Jones (poem), 1931; Preludes for Memnon (poems), 1931; Great Circle (novel), 1933; Among the Lost People (short stories), 1934; Landscape West of Eden (poems), 1934; King Coffin (novel), 1935; Time in the Rock (poems), 1936; A Heart for the Gods of Mexico (novel), 1939; The Conversation (novel), 1939; And in the Human Heart (poems), 1940; Brownstone Eclogues (poems), 1942; The Soldier, 1944; The Kid (poem) 1947; The Divine Pilgrim (poem), 1949; Skylight One (poems), 1949; Mr. Arcularis (play, with Diana Hamilton), 1949; The Short Stories of Conrad Aiken, 1950; Ushant: An Essay (an autobiography), 1952; Collected Poems, 1953; A Letter from Li Po (poems) 1956; Mr. Arcularis, 1957; Sheepfold Hill (poems), 1957; A Reviewer's ABC (criticism), 1958 (published as Collected Criticism 1968); The Collected Short Stories of Conrad Aiken, published 1960; Selected Poems, 1961; The Morning Song of Lord Zero (poems), 1963; The Collected Novels of Conrad Aiken, 1964; A Seizure of Limericks (poems), 1964; Cats and Bats and Things with Wings (poems), 1965; Tom, Sue, and the Clock (poem), 1966; Preludes (poems), 1966; Thee (poem), 1968; Collected Poems: 1916-1970, 1970; The Clerk's Journal, An Undergraduate Poem, 1971. Editor: Modern American Poets, 1922; Selected Poems Emily Dickinson, 1924; Am. Poetry (1671-1928), 1929; 20th Century American Poetry (anthology), 1963. Contbr. to Poets on Poetry, criticism, 1965. Compiler: Selected Poems, 1929. Contbg. editor, Dial, 1917-19. Awarded Pulitzer prize for best vol. of verse, 1929; Bryher Award, 1952, Nat. Book award for Collected Poems (1954). Apptd. to chair of poetry Library of Congress, 1950-52, fellow in Am. letters, 1947. Awarded Bollingen Prize, 1956; fellowship Am. Acad. Poets, 1957; gold medal for poetry Nat. Inst. Arts and Letters, 1958; Huntington Hartford Found. award in lit., 1961; St. Botolph award, 1964; Brandeis medal for poetry, 1967; National Medal for Lit., 1969. Mem. Am. Acad. Arts and Letters. Home: Savannah, Ga. Died Aug. 17, 1973.

AIKEN, PAUL C., lawyer, business executive; b. Macksville, July 24, 1910; son Robert Emmett and Florence Eva (Case) A.; A.B., U. of Kan., 1929; grad. work, Princeton, 1930-31; LL.B., George Washington U., 1934, LL.M., 1935; m. Camilla Lindsay, August 20, 1933; children—Carol Ann, Patricia, Paul. Asst. to secretary Western PowerLight and Telephone Co., Salina, Kan., 1929-30; econ. advisor, Consumers Adv. Bd., N.R.A., Washington, D.C., 1933-36; spl. counsel and asst. to chmn., Fed. Deposit Ins. Corp., Washington, D.C., 1937-40; law firm, Miller and Hornbeck, Cleveland, 1941-42; law practice Washington, Topeka, Kansas; assistant Postmaster General of the United States, 1947-50; pres. Gen. Truck Sales, Inc. Col. U.S. Army Res.; chief polit. activities sect. Office Mil. Govt., U.S. Zone (Germany), 1945-46; conducted first free elections in Germany after World War II, 1945-46; exec. Mil. Analysis Div., U.S. Strategic Bombing Survey, London, 1945; advisor on soldier voting, Office Sec. of War, Washington, D.C., 1944; exec. tactics div., Army Air Forces Board, Orlando, Fla., 1942-44. Mem. Officers Assn., Air Force Assn., Order of the Coif, Phi Beta Kappa, Sigma Phi Epsilon. Democrat (nominee for U.S. senator, Kan., 1950). Home: Washington, D.C. Died May 25, 1974.

AIKEN, WILLIAM HAMBLEN, paper co. exec.; b. Salado, Tex., May 24, 1916; s. Carl and Anna (Hamblen) A.; B.S. in Chem. Engring., Tex. A. and M. Coll., 1938; M.S. in Chemistry, Inst. Paper Chemistry, 1940, Ph.D., 1942; m. Rosemary Polk, Aug. 1, 1942; children—Rosemary, William Hamblen. Asst. mgr. chem. div. Goodyear Tire & Rubber Co., 1946-52; tech. dir. Gardner Board & Carton Co., 1952-59; v.p. research and devel. engring., dir. Personal Products Corp., 1959-61; v.p. research and devel. Union Bag-Camp Paper Corp. (now Union Camp Corp.), 1961-70, v.p. tech., 1970-74. Served to maj. AUS, 1942-46. Fellow A.A.A.S., T.A.P.P.I. (exec. com. 1961-64, pres. 1967-69, recipient award 1971), Internat. Acad. Wood Sci.;

mem. Am. Chem. Soc., N.Y. Acad. Sci., Am. Nat. Standards Inst. (dir. 1966-70), Sigma Xi. Home: Princeton, N.J. Died Oct. 17, 1974; buried Salado, Tex.

AILES, JOHN WILLIAM, III, naval officer; b. Donora, Pa., Sept. 9, 1907; s. Herbert and Margaret (Minford) A.; B.S., U.S. Naval Acad., 1930, postgrad., 1936-37; student Naval War Coll., 1942; m. Edith McIntire, June 10, 1930 (dec. 1961); children—John William IV, Robert H. (both USN), Anne; m. 2d, Margaret Sheehan Ailes. Commd. ensign USN, 1930, advanced through grades to rear adm., 1958; asst. gunnery officer U.S.S. Honolulu, Pearl Harbor, 1941; comdg. officer U.S.S. Cassin Young, 1944-45; chief staff to comdr. Crusier Div. 3, 1951-52, U.S.S. Tidewater, 1952-53; naval aide under sec. navy, 1953-55; comdg. officer U.S.S. Iowa, 1955-56; dir. Shore establishment devel. and maintenance div. Navy Dept., 1957-58; naval insp. gen., Washington, 1958-61; comdr. Cruiser-Destroyer Flotilla 6, 1961-63, comdr. service force U.S. Atlantic Fleet, 1963-65; ret., 1965; then staff NSF. Decorated Navy Cross, Silver Star medal, Legion of Merit, Bronze Star medal with gold star, Purple Heart, Navy unit commendation. Mem. Order of Carabao, Naval Order U.S., Naval Acad. Alumni Assn. Episcopalian. Club: Army-Navy (Washington). Home: Laurel, Md. Died July 30, 1974.

AKAR, JOHN J., diplomat, playwright, broadcaster; b. Rotifunk, Sierra Leone, May 20, 1927; s. Joseph Philip and Tikidankay (Mansaray) A.; student Otterbein Coll., 1946-49; B.A. in Polit. Sci., U. Cal. at Berkeley, 1950; student Lincoln's Inn, London, 1950-53, London Sch. Econs., 1950-52; Nuffield scholar U. Edinburgh (Scotland); m. Constance Eleanor Wright, Nov. 24, 1956; children—Jacqueline Jasmin, Pamela Juli, Melissa Dankay, Michelle Mayilla, Cynthia Collette, Emily Yama. Freelance broadcaster, 1950-55; with Voice of Am., 1955-56; dir. Sierra Leone Broadcasting System, 1957-67; sec. Sierra Leone Hotels and Tourist Bd., 1960-67; sec. Commonwealth Broadcasting Secretariat, London, 1967-69; ambassador to U.S. from Sierra Leona, 1969-75; high commr. to Can., 1970-75; an actor on stage and films; Danforth vis. lectr. to U.S., 1964-66. Mem. Sierra Leone Mus. Com.; chmn. Sierra Leone Nat. Mus., Monuments, and Relics Commn.; founder Nat. Dance Troupe of Sierra Leone. Chiefdom counsellor Bumpeh Chiefdom, Rotifunk, Sierra Leone. Hon. Trustee Baker U., Baldwin, Kan. Decorated Order Brit. Empire; chevalier Cedars of Lebanon, 1959; recipient Sierra Leone Independence medal, 1961; hon. doctorate Albright Coll., Reading Pa., Otterbein Coll., Westerville, O. Mem. A.F.T.R.A. Rotarian. Author (plays): Valley Without Echo, 1949; Cry Tamba, 1961; The Second Chance, 1954. Composer Sierra Leone nat. anthem. Home: Jamaica. Died June 23, 1975.

AKERS, LEWIS ROBESON, clergyman, author; b. Asheville, N.C., Aug. 25, 1881; s. William David and Mary Istalena (Robeson) A.; B.S., Asbury Coll., Wilmore, Ky., 1903, A.B., A.M., 1904, D.D., 1916; Harvard, summer 1909; European travel study, summers 1922, 31; B.D., Ashland (Ohio) Theol. Sem*, 1924; M.A. in Edn., U. of Ky., 1927; LL.D., Ohio Northern U., 1927; L.H.D., Southern Coll., 1929; Litt.D., McMurry Coll., 1929; m. Addie Avanelle Dyer, July 6, 1905; children—William Gerald, Lewis Robeson, Dorothy Dyer, Richard Lawrence. Ordained M.E. ministry, 1904; pastor Conesville, O., 1904-07, Nevada, O., 1907-11, Willard, 1911-15, Sebring, 1915-19, Ashland, 1919-24; prof. ethics, Ohio Wesleyan Sch. of Theology, 1917-23; v.p. Asbury Coll., 1924-25, pres., 1925-33; later minister La Belle View Meth Ch., Steubenville, O. Chaplain American Red Cross, World War. Del. Meth. Ecumenical Conf., Atlanta, 1931. Mem. Ohio Soc. S.R., Assn. Ky. Colls. and Univs. (pres. 1926-27), Assn. of Am. Conservative Colls. (pres. 1928-32), Pi Gamma Mu, Phi Delta Kappa. Ky. repr. of Nat. Council for Prevention of War. Rotarian. Lyceum lecturer. Author: The Red Road to Royalty, 1927; Tarry Ye, 1929; The Eighth Fear, 1945. Home: Steubenville, O.†

AKERS, SHELDON BUCKINGHAM, instn. ofcl.; b. Snowville, Va., Mar. 5, 1898; s. Montie Yost and Laura (Buckingham) A.; B.S., U. Va., 1922; A.M. in Econs., George Washington U., 1925; m. Ina Graham, Sept. 5, 1925; children—Sheldon B., Mary Elizabeth (Mrs. Thomas P. Graham). Staff mem. Inst. Econs., 1923-28; staff Brookings Instn., 1929-63, exec. mgr., controller, 1951-63. Mem. A.A.A.S. (chmn. investment and finance com.), Beta Gamma Sigma, Alpha Kappa Psi. The Fossils, Methodist. Author: The Government of Montgomery County, Maryland (with Lewis Meriam, others), 1941. Home: Bethesda, Md. Died Dec. 24, 1973; buried Rockville Union Cemetery, Rockville, Md.

AKIN, MARGARET CATHERINE ROUSE (MRS. AUSTIN FRANKLIN AKIN), physician; b. Boone, Ia., Apr. 18, 1913; d. Martin Francis and Margaret (Conry) Rouse; B.S. in Medicine, State U. Ia., 1936, M.D., 1936; m. Austin Franklin Akin, July 22, 1933. Children—Mary Patricia (Mrs. Charles Gordon Cloutier, Jr.), John Rouse. Intern Tri-State Hosp., Shreveport, La., 1936-37; practice medicine, Iowa, La., 1937-41, Shreveport, 1941-72; partner Family Clinic, Shreveport, 1964-72; mem. staff Physicians and Surgeons Hosp., Shreveport, staff pres., 1960; mem. staff Schumpert Hosp., Shreveport; mem. staff Willis Knighton Hosp., Shreveport, staff pres., 1958; clin. instr. medicine La. State U. Shreveport Sch. Medicine. Mem. La. State Bd. Practical Nurse Examiners. Chmn. Com. Health Care of Religious and Clergy of Diocese of Alexandria, 1962-72; bd. mem. Holidays for Humanity, 1964-72. Bd. dirs. Cath. Charities Dioceses of Alexandria. Mem. A.M.A., Am. Acad. Gen. Practice (dist. treas. 1966-68), La. State, Shreveport (rep. to internat. tb conf. 1965, v.p. 1954, dir.), Am. Assn. U. Women, Pan-Pacific Surg. Assn., League Women Voters (pres. Shreveport 1948), Cath. Physicians Guild, Alpha Omega Alpha, Theta Phi Alpha. Democrat. Roman Catholic. Club: Internat. Altrusa. Home: Shreveport, La. Died May 12, 1972.

AKIN, SPENCER BALL, army officer; b. Greenville, Miss., Feb. 13, 1889; s. Seddon Pleasants and Martha Giles (Chaffin) A.; B.S., Va. Mil. Inst., 1910; grad. Infantry Sch. (advanced course), 1926, Air Corps Tactical Sch., 1927, Command and Gen. Staff Sch., 1928, Army War Coll., 1936, General Staff Eligible List; m. Eleanor Holt Stone, June 8, 1910 (dec.); children—Eleanor (Mrs. Sheldon Smith), Martha Chaffin (widow of Capt. D. G. McMillin); commd. 2d lt. U.S. Army, 1910; promoted through grades to brig. gen., 1941, maj. gen. Nov. 3, 1943, chief signal officer on staff of Gen. Douglas MacArthur, chief signal officer Dept. of Army. Awarded D.S.C., D.S.M., D.S.M. with oak leaf cluster, Silver Star, Silver Star with oak leaf cluster, Air Medal, Legion of Merit, Distinguished Unit Badge with three clusters; Officer Legion of Honor (France); Hon. Comdr. Order of the British Empire (Gt. Britain): Grand Officer, Order of Nassau (Netherlands). Poor Richard Club citation for reorgn. of Army's system of mil. communication to needs of atomic warfare. Mem. Kappa Alpha (southern). Mason. Clubs: Army and Navy Country (Washington); Army and Navy (Manila); Rumson (N.J.). Home: Washington, D.C. Died Oct. 6, 1973.

ALBREN, EDWARD JOSEPH, govt. ofcl.; b. Manchester, N.H., Oct. 10, 1919; s. Frank and Anna (Wyderka) Albrewczenski; student St. Anselm's Coll., 1945-46; B.S., U. N.H., 1949; postgrad. U. Ala., 1948, George Washington U., 1950, Md. U., 1964; m. Mary Helen Stevenson, Sept. 24, 1959. Asst. head atomic energy and applied sci. br. Naval Facility Engring. Command, Washington, 1959-61, head nuclear, biol. and chem. def. br., from 1961. Served to capt. AUS, 1940-46. Decorated Purple Heart. Mem. Soc. Am. Mil. Engrs. Home: Silver Spring, Md. Died May 21, 1972; interred Arlington Nat. Cemetery, Arlington, Va.

ALBRIGHT, CHARLES CLINTON, univ. prof.; b. Brimfield, Ind., May 20, 1879; s. John Wallace and Sophia Emily (Bower) A.; B.S. in C.E., Purdue U., 1903, C.E., 1908; m. Adda Mabel Robinson, June 2, 1904; children—Mary Mildred (Mrs. Paul W. Jones), Helen Louise (Mrs. Robert R. Duff). With engring. corps, B.&O. R.R., 1903-04; asst. engr. to sr. asst. engr., gulf lines, A.T. & S.F. Ry. System, 1904-08; instr. civil engring., U. of Ill., 1908-09; successively asst. prof., asso. prof., prof. civil engring., Purdue U., 1909-24; staff officer, Pa. Dept. of Highways, Harrisburg, 1924-43; asst. coordinator, Army-Navy Coll. Training Program, Purdue U., 1943-46, prof. civil engring., 1946-49, retired; civil engineering consultant from 1949. Registered professional engineer Mem. city council, Lafayette, Ind., 1920-24. Mem. Ind. Nat. Guard, 1897-98; R.O.T.C., Ft. Sheridan-Ill., 1918. Life mem. Am. Ry. Engring. Assn.; mem. Purdue Alumni Assn., Chi Epsilon, Triangle. Republican. Methodist. Mason. Club: Purdue University. Home: Lafayette, Ind.†

ALBRIGHT, ROBERT CHOATE, newspaperman; b. Alexandria, Va., Sept. 1, 1903; s. Moore McCulloch and Harriet Estelle (Carden) A.; A.B., George Washington Univ., 1926; m. Irma Mary Smith, August 3, 1940; 1 daughter, Sara Louise. Reporter Washington Herald, 1926, Washington Post, 1926-28; financial writer, later Washington staff writer United Press Assn., 1928-30; nat. news writer, Washington Post, 1930-42; writer Time Mag. 1942-43; polit. writer Washington Post and Times-Herald, 1943-69. Mem. Standing Com. Correspondents (governing com. of Congressional press galleries), 1963-65. Mem. Nat. Press Club, Sigma Nu, Pi Delta Epsilon, Sigma Delta Chi. Episcopalian. Home: Bethesda, Md. Died Oct. 12, 1973; buried Cedar Hill Cemetery, Washington, D.C.

ALCORN, ROY ANVIL, ednl. adminstr.; b. Williamsville, Mo., Dec. 3, 1925; s. Scott and Delia Ann (Boxx) A.; B.S. in Edn., Southeast Mo. State Coll., 1955; M.A., George Peabody Coll. for Tchrs., 1958, Ed.D. in Edn., 1963; m. Virgie Lois Carter, Oct. 23, 1953; children—Martha Lynn, Daniel Sheridan, Joseph Dean, Elizabeth Ann, Walter Lee. Tchr. Mo. pub. schs., 1946-51; congl. aide to Mo. congressman, 1953-56; prin., high sch. Waynesville, Mo., 1956-58; supt. of schs., Eminence, Mo., 1958-61; asst. supt. schs., Wilmington, Del., 1963-65; supt. schs., Chesterfield County, Va., 1965-69, Roanoke City, 1969-72; chmn. edn. dept. George Peabody Coll. Tchrs., Nashville, 1972-73. Mem. exec. bd. Central Va. Ednl. TV, 1965-69. Trustee, Madison Coll., Harrisonburg, Va., 1972-73. Served with AUS, 1944-46, USAF, 1950-52. Recipient Freedoms Found. award, 1969. Mem. Am. Assn. Sch. Adminstrs., Va. Edn. Assn., N.E.A., Phi Delta Kappa, Kappa Delta Pi. Rotarian. Home: Antioch, Tenn. Died Apr. 10, 1973; interred Henson Cemetery, Ellsinore, Mo.

ALDERMAN, FRANK, banker; b. Batavia, N.Y., Sept. 9, 1879; s. Frank N. and Ida Julia (Starks) A.; LL.B., U. of Buffalo, 1900; m. Rossie L. Evans, Fort Myers, Mar. 15, 1905 (dec.); children—Dorothy Lois (dec.), Frank Cyrus, Jr.; m. 2d, Jennie S. Burgard, Sept. 29, 1937; admitted to Florida bar, 1901, since in practice at Fort Myers; officer and director First National Bank in Fort Myers from 1908, pres. from 1921; pres. First Nat. Co. of Fort Myers, Fort Myers Southern R.R. Co.; dir. Lee County Packing Co., Seminole Lumber & Mfg. Co., etc. Democrat. Mason, Elk. Home: Fort Myers, Fla.†

ALDERMAN, RHENAS HOFFARD, mortgage banker; b. Lithia, Fla., Dec. 9, 1881; s. Hiram and Sarah Jane (Gallagher) A.; Florida Conf. Coll., Leesburg, Fla., 1897-1901; A.B., Emery Coll., Oxford, Ga., 1904; student summers, Denver U., Columbia U.; m. Jane Katheryne Purnell, of Paris, Ky., May 22, 1906; 1 son, Rhenas Hoffard. Prin. high sch., Harrilson, Ga.; Prof. science, Southern Coll. (then at Sutherland, Fla.), 1905-07; pres. Russell Coll., Lebanon, Va., 1907-09; pres. Morris Harvey Coll., Barboursville, W.Va., 1909-14; pres. Southern Coll., 1914-25; later v.p. Session Loan and Trust Co., Marietta, Ga. Mem. Delta Tau Delta. Democrat. Mem. M.E. Ch., S. Rotarian. Home: Lakeland, Fla.†

ALDRICH, CHARLES SPAULDING, lawyer; b. Weathersfield, Vt., Apr. 1, 1871; s. Charles Frank and Abbie Louise (Spaulding) A.; prep. end., Vt. Acad., Saxton's River, Vt.; A.B., Brown University, 1894; A.M., Wesleyan University, Connecticut, 1896; LL.D. Keuka College, 1942; m. Helen Parker Drake, Sept. 9, 1897; 1 dau., Adeline. Admitted to N.Y. bar, 1898, and later practiced at Troy; mem. Murphy, Aldrich, Guy & Broderick (now Murphy, Aldrich, Guy, Broderick & Simon); director, atty. Pioneer Bldg. & Loan Assn., Troy, N.Y.; dir. Union Nat. Bank, Community Hotels Corporations, Ludlow Valve Manufacturing Company. Incorporated, W. & L. E. Gurley; president Hendrik Hudson Garage, Inc. Trustee Newton Theological Inst., Keuka Coll., Russell Sage College, Vt. Academy. Mem. Troy Citizens Corps, N.G.N.Y.; past pres. Troy Chamber of Commerce. Mem. N.Y. State Bar Assn., Rensselaer County Bar Assn. (ex-pres.), N.Y. State Hist. Soc., Delta Upsilon, Phi Beta Kappa. Republican. Club: Troy. Home: Troy, N.Y.†

ALDRICH, LOUISE BANISTER (MRS. TRUMAN ALDRICH), concert pianist; b. Harwood, Tex., Feb. 8, 1880; d. Robert Bolling and Corrilla (Nation) Banister; ed. pvt. sch., Huntsville, Ala., and St. Mary's Inst., Dallas, Tex., studied music under William H. Sherwood, Rafael Joseffy, Julia Rive King, Ernest Hutcheson and Irene Hale; m. Truman H. Aldrich, Jr., of Birmingham, Ala., Apr. 4, 1899. Professional début at Birmingham, Ala., Apr. 19, 1910; played with New York Symphony Orchestra, Theodore Thomas Orchestra, Russian Symphony Orchestra, Victor Herbert Orchestra, Atlanta Symphony Orchestra, Cincinnati Symphony Orchestra, Boston Symphony Orchestra; also recitals Chicago, Buffalo, Cincinnati, etc. Home: New York City, N.Y.†

ALDRICH, LYNN ELLIS, investor, consultant; born in the town of Bloomington, Illinois, May 17, 1890; s. Arthur E. and Jessie (Finch) A.; B.S., Beloit Coll., 1914; m. Marjorie M. Murdock, July 8, 1925 (dec. Oct. 1957); m. 2d, Elizabeth Moretz Williams, September 4, 1959. Clk. Washburn-Crosby Co., Mpls. and Milw. 1916-20; controller and asst. treas. Lowe Paper Co., Ridgefield, N.J., 1920-27; controller and asst. treas. The Chicago Daily News, and Chicago Daily News Prtg. Co., 1927-30, treas., 1931-44, vice pres., treas., 1944-45, dir., 1938-45; treas., dir. Daneco Corp., Chicago, 1931-45; pres. Great Lakes-Canadian-Inc., 1945-55; director North Am. Newspaper Alliance, Inc., 1931-45, Press Wireless, Inc., N.Y. City; director Boca Raton National Bank (Fla.), 1962-74. Commd. 1st lt. F.A. 2d O.T.C., Ft. Snelling, Minnesota, Nov. 27, 1917; artillery practice, Leon Springs, Tex., Dec. 1917-Jan. 1918; assigned 1st Corps Artillery Park, Jan. 1918; overseas, May 1918-Aug. 1919; participated in Marne, Aisne-Marne, Oise-Aisne, Meuse-Argonne offensives; with Army of Occupation and Am. forces in Germany; capt. F.A. Reserve, 1920-25. Trustee Beloit College, 1933-59, now life trustee. Mem. Beta Theta Pi. Republican. Presbyterian. Mason. Clubs: Boca Raton, Royal Palm Yacht and Country (commodore 1962-63) (Fla.). Home: Boca Raton, Fla. Died Sept. 21, 1974.

ALDRICH, WINTHROP WILLIAMS, former ambassador; b. Providence, Nov. 2, 1885; s. Nelson W. and Abby Pierce Chapman (Greene) A.; A.B., Harvard, 1907, J.D., 1910, LL.D., 1953; LL.D., Colgate U., 1937, Northeastern U., 1938, Washington and Jefferson Coll., 1939, Brown U., 1944, Lafayette Coll., 1945, Columbia, 1946, Bryant Coll., 1947, Georgetown U., 1952, Queen's U., Belfast, 1955, U. Liverpool (Eng.), 1956; D.S.C., N.Y. U., 1950; D.Sc., Stevens Inst. Tech., 1957, U. R.I., 1965, Tuskegee Inst., 1967; m. Harriet Alexander, Dec. 7, 1916; children—Winthrop Williams (dec.), Mary (Mrs. Robert Homans), Harriet (Mrs. Edgar A. Bering), Lucy (Mrs. George D. Aldrich),

Elizabeth Brewster (Mrs. J. Woodward Redmond), Alexander. Admitted to N.Y. bar, 1912; mem. firm Byrne, Cutcheon Taylor, 1916-17, Murray, Aldrich & Webb, 1919-29; pres. Equitable Trust Co., 1929; pres. Chase Nat. Bank, 1930-34, chmn. bd. dirs., 1934-53; ambassador to Ct. of St. James's, London, Eng., 1953-57. Mem. adv. com. Columbia Sch. Internat. Affairs; mem. vis. com. Harvard Center Internat. Affairs. Hon. trustee Presbyn. Hosp., N.Y.C., Riverside Ch., N.Y.C. Served as lt. USNR, 1917-18. Decorated Medal for Merit (U.S.); knight Grand Cross of Order Brit. Empire, asso. knight justice Order of St. John of Jerusalem, King's medal for Service in Cause of Freedom (Gt. Britain); comdr. Legion of Honor (France); comdr. Order of Leopold, grand officer Order of Crown (Belgium); grand officer Orange Nassau (Netherlands); grand officer Oak Crown (Luxembourgh); Knight comdr. Order of Pius IX (Vatican). Mem. Pilgrims U.S. (v.p., trustee). Clubs: White's (London); Royal Yacht Squadron (Cowes); Hope (R.I.); Racquet, Harvard, Knickerbocker, Brook, Century, Links, N.Y. Yacht (N.Y.C.). Home: New York City, N.Y. Died Feb. 25, 1974.

ALEXANDER, CHRISTINE, museum curator, archaeologist; b. Tokyo, Japan, Nov. 10, 1893 (parents U.S. citizens); d. Thomas Theron and Emma (Bicknell) Alexander; M.A., Cornell, 1915. Asst. dept. Greek and Roman art Met. Mus. Art, N.Y.C., 1923-26, asst. curator, 1926-30, asso. curator, 1930-48, curator 1948—59. Mem. Archaeol. Inst. Am., Soc. for Promotion Hellenic Studies (London, Eng.), Deutsches archaeologischen Institut. Club: Cosmopolitan (N.Y.C.). Author: Jewelry, The Art of the Goldsmith in Classical Times, 1927; Greek Jewelry, Arretine Relief Ware, 1943. Home: New York City, N.Y., Died Dec. 24, 1975.

ALEXANDER, CLYDE H., oil corp. exec.; b. Milbrook, Pa., Apr. 17, 1881; s. James H. and Alice May (Wilson) A.; student pub. schs.; m. Euna Mabel Tirk, December 24, 1908 (died November 9, 1959); children—Creston H., Glenn E., Helen Mae. Began career Pennsylvania oil fields, 1900-04; charge prodn. Douglas & Lacy Oil, 1905-07, Creston Oil Co., Bartlesville, Okla., 1907-10, Wolverine Oil Co., 1910-17; supt. prodn. Phillips Petroleum Co., 1923-34; chmn. Creslenn Oil Co.; dir. Transcontinental Gas Pipe Line. Mem. Independent Petroleum Assn. Am., Am. Petroleum Inst., Ind. Natural Gas Assn. Am. (dir.). Clubs: Petroleum, Athens Country (Athens), 25 Year Club of Petroleum Industry. Home: Trinidad, Tex.†

ALEXANDER, RAYMOND PACE, judge; b. Phila., Oct. 13, 1898; s. Hilliard Boone and Virginia Margaret (Pace) A.; B.S. in Econs. magna cum laude, U. Pa., 1920; postgrad. Columbia, summer 1921-22; LL.B., Harvard, 1923; LL.D., Shaw U., Va. State Coll., 1940; Litt.D., Western U., 1947, Campbell Coll., 1948; m. Sadie Tanner Mossell, Nov. 26, 1923; children—Mary Elizabeth (Mrs. Melvin Frank Brown), Rae Pace (Mrs. Thomas K. Minter). Admitted Pa. bar, 1923; mem. firm Raymond Pace Alexander, Phila., 1923-58; former gen. counsel Nat. Med. Assn., Nat. Bapt. Conv., Gen. Conf. A.M.E. Ch.; counsel Pa. Bapt. Conv., bd. bishops A.M.E. Ch.; counsel Pa., Phila. chpts. NAACP; counsellor Haitian embassy, Washington, 1946-49, hon. Haitian consul, Phila., 1948-56; specialist civil and criminal trial practice, state and fed. cts.; judge Common Pleas Ct. Phila., from 1959, sr. judge, from 1970. Mem. Phila. City Council, 1952-58, chmn. com. pub. property and pub. works. Vice chmn. Phila. County div. United Fund; past nat. dir. March of Dimes; nat. dir. Free Europe Com.; speaker Radio Free Europe to Iron Curtain Countries, 1954, 58; pres. Salute to Our Responsible Youth, from 1970; chmn. internat. legal edn. sect. World Peace Through Law Center, Washington and Geneva, Switzerland, from 1972; Am. specialist Dept. State to Scandanavia, 1965, Vietnam, S.E. Asia and India, 1966, to Middle East, Cyprus, Turkey, Lebanon, Iran, 1968; mem. adv. com. Bicentennial Com. Phila., 1973-74. Mem. past chmn. bd. mgrs. S.W. br. YMCA, Phila., 1948-58; vice chmn. capital fund dr. YMCA-YWCA Greater Phila.; founder, chmn. bd. trustees Dr. Virginia M. Alexander Scholarship Found.; bd. dirs. Phila. Grand Opera Co.; trustee Phila. Council Chs., Berean Coll., Phila.; nat. bd. dirs. Assn. Study Negro Life and History. Honored for outstanding achievement civil liberties Am. Jewish Congress, 1950; outstanding service to citizens of Phila., Barristers Club, 1951; other awards YMCA Phila., Phila. Assn. Pub. Sch. Tchrs.; C. Francis Stradford award Nat. Bar Assn., 1967; Carter G. Woodson award Assn. Study Negro Life and History, 1968; chancellor Phila. Cotillion Soc., 1958. Mem. Phila. Council Chs. (past dir.), Nat. (pres. 1929-30), Am., Pa., Phila. bar assns., Brandeis Law Soc., Phila. Crime Prevention Assn. (pres. 1967, dir. 1960, chmn. exec. com. 1970), Turkish-Am. Law Assn. (hon.), Am. Judicature Soc.; hon. mem. Bar Republic Haiti, Barrister's Library High Ct. India, Phi Beta Kappa, Beta Gamma Sigma. Baptist (past chmn. trustees). Co-founder, editor Nat. Bar Jour., 1940. Home: Philadelphia, Pa. Died Nov. 23, 1974.

ALEXANDERSON, ERNST FREDERIK WERNER, elec. engr., inventor; b. Upsala, Sweden, Jan. 25, 1878; s. Prof. A.M. and Amelie (von Heidenstam) A.; studied U. of Lund, 1896-97; grad. Royal Inst. Tech., Stockholm, 1900; post-grad. work, Koenigliche Technische Hochschule, Berlin; D.Sc., Union Coll., 1926; Ph.D., U. of Upsala, 1938; m. Edith B. Lewin, Feb. 1909 (died 1912); m. 2d, Gertrude Robart, Mar. 1914 (died 1948); married 3d Thyra Oxehufwud, June 1949. With General Electric Company from 1902, cons. engr. of same, to 1950; Was chief engr. RCA, 1920-24, cons., 1952-57. Inventor of Alexanderson high frequency alternator, multiple tuned antenna, vacuum tube radio telephone transmitter and tuned radio frequency receiver, which are generally used. Has done pioneer work in television, electric ship propulsion, railroad electrification and the amphidyne system of control. Has obtained more than 300 U.S. patents. Fellow Am. Inst. Elec. Engrs., Inst. Radio Engrs. (ex-pres.); mem. Royal Swedish Acad. Sciences, Sigma Xi. Decorated by King Gustav V, of Sweden, Knight Comdr. First Class Order North Star; Order of Polonia Restituta (Poland). Author of tech. papers. Awarded gold medal, Inst. Radio Engrs., John Ericsson medal, Edison and Cedegren medals, 1944; Valdemar Poulsen medal, 1946. Name inscribed on Wall of Fame at American Common, World's Fair, New York, 1940. Home: Schenectady, N.Y. Died May 1975.

ALFARO, VICTOR RICARDO, physician; b. Panama, Republic of Panama, Mar. 14 1907; s. Ricardo Joaquin and Amelia (Lyons) A.; came to U.S., 1922, naturalized, 1942; B.S. in Medicine, Georgetown U., 1927, M.D., 1929; postgrad. otolaryngology U. Pa., 1930-31, audiology and endaural surgery Northwestern U., 1951, laryngoscopy, laryngeal, surgery and bronchoesophagology Jackson Clinic, Temple U., 1943; m. Nancy Hamilton, June 24, 1929; children—Ricardo Joaquin II, Nancy Hamilton. Pvt. practice otolaryngology, Washington, from 1932; sr. attending otolaryngology Episcopal Eye, Ear and Throat Hosp., 1942-58; sr. attending otolaryngology Washington Hosp. Center, 1958-62; cons. otolaryngology Mt. Alto VA Hosp., 1949-55; cons. NIH, 1948-60, Washington Hosp. Center, from 1962; mem. faculty Sch. Medicine, Georgetown U., 1932-61, prof., head div. otolaryngology, 1949-61, prof. emeritus, from 1961. Bd. dirs. Deafness Research Found. Served to lt. col. M.C., AUS, 1942-46; ETO. Mem. Am. Soc. Otolaryngol. and Opthalmologic Allergy (past mem. council), A.M.A. (past chmn. sect. laryngol. otol. and rhinol.; past del. ho. dels.), Am. Laryngol., Rhinol. and Otol. Soc. (council, past sec., pres. from 1971), Med. Soc. D.C. (past pres.), Am. Acad. Ophthal. and Otolaryngol., Am. Laryngol. Assn., Am. Otol. Soc., Pan-Am. Soc. Otol., Laryngol. and Rhinol., Internat. Congress Otol. (chmn. com. local arrangements Washington 1957 del. for U.S. in Paris 1961, Tokyo 1965, Venice 1973), Washington Hearing Soc. (past mem. bd.). Home: Washington, D.C. Died Apr. 5, 1974; buried Mt. Olivet Cemetery, Washington, D.C.

ALI, ANWAR, govt. ofcl., economist; b. Gujranwala, West Pakistan, Feb. 16, 1913; s. Dost Mohamed and Raj Begum; B.A. with honors, Islamia Coll., Lahore, 1932, M.A. in Econs., 1934; m. Saeeda Kausar, Sept. 10, 1939; children—Saeed, Aisha. Asst. financial adviser to under-sec. Ministry Finance, Govt. India, 1943-47; dep. sec. Ministry Finance, Govt. Pakistan, 1947-52, joint sec., 1952-54; dir. Middle Eastern dept. IMF, Washington, from 1954; gov. Saudi Arabian Monetary Agy, Jedda, from 1958; dir. (rep. Govt. Pakistan) State Bank of Pakistan, 1952-54, Nat. Bank of Pakistan, 1949-53; rep. Pakistan various internat. meetings. Treas., Anglo Arabic Coll., New Delhi, 1945-47, Islamia, Coll., Karachi, 1950-51. Decorated Sitara-e-Quaid-Azam, 1961, Sitara-e-Pakistan, 1967. Fellow Internat. Banker Assn. Home: Jeddah, Saudi Arabia. Died Nov. 5, 1974.

ALLAN, DENISON MAURICE, educator; b. Hull, Eng., Sept. 15, 1897; s. Andrew and Mary Townsend (Mowbray) A.; student Brantford (Can.) Collegiate Inst.; A.B., A.M., Hampden-Sydney (Va.) Coll., 1916; postgrad. Columbia, 5 summers; A.M., Harvard, 1922, Ph.D., 1926; m. Sarah Evelyn Smith, Aug. 10, 1932; children—Denison Mowbray, David Blair. Came to U.S., 1910, naturalized, 1918. Prof. Modern langs. Hampden-Sydney Coll., 1920-21, prof. philosophy and psychology, 1923-69, coach debating, 1923-35, dir. Presbyn. Guidance Center, from 1970. Sprunt lectr. Union Theol. Sem., Richmond, 1944. Trustee Union Theol. Sem. in Va., Presbyn. Home, Lynchburg. Mem. adv. council on higher edn. Presbyn. Ch. U.S., mem. gen. assembly's com. on homes and orphanages; rep. Va. synod on State Council Chs. Served in C.W.S., U.S. Army, 1918. Mem. A.A.A.S., So. Soc. Philosophy Religion (pres. 1966-67), Am. Philos. Assn., So. Soc. Philosophy and Psychology, Va. Acad. Sci. (pres. 1938), Am. Psychol. Assn., Am. Personnel and Guidance Assn., Phi Beta Kappa, Sigma Upsilon, Tau Kappa Alpha, Chi Beta Phi, Sigma Chi, Omicron Delta Kappa. Democrat. Presbyn. Author: The Realm of Personality. Co-author: Church and Campus. Contbr. to psychol., philos. jours. Asso. editor Presbyn. Outlook. Home: Hampden-Sydney, Va. Died Sept. 11, 1974; interred Hampden-Sydney, Va.

ALLEN, CHARLES CLAFLIN, lawyer; b. St. Louis, Oct. 5, 1893; s. Charles Claflin and Carrie Louise (Richards) A.; A.B., Princeton, 1915; student Washington U. Law Sch., 1915-16, LL.B., St. Louis U., 1920; m. Mary Jane Thomson, Dec. 15, 1917; children—Mary Jane (Mrs. Erich G. Weissenberger), Charles Claflin. Admitted to Mo. bar, 1917; counsel Kauffman Smith & Co., St. Louis, 1920-29; counsel Boatmen's Nat. Bank, St. Louis, 1929-32, v.p., gen. counsel, 1933-35; gen. practice law, St. Louis, 1934-43; partner Lehmann & Allen, St. Louis, 1943-55, Allen & Allen, 1955-60, Lewis, Rice, Tucker, Allen & Chubb, 1960—. Chmn. St. Louis chpt. A.R.C., 1941-42, established St. Louis Blood Bank; mem. speaker's bur. United Fund of St. Louis. Mem. exec. com. Rehab. Center Greater St. Louis, 1931-43; bd. dirs. Episcopal Home for Children, 1945-49; trustee St. Luke's Hosp., St. Louis, 1944-56, Community Music Sch. of St. Louis. Served to capt. U.S. Army, 1917-18. Mem. Bar of St. Louis, Am., Mo., St. Louis bar assns., Am. Law Inst., Round Table, Phi Beta Kappa. Republican. Episcopalian (vestryman). Clubs: Princeton (pres. 1948-49), Noonday, St. Louis County (St. Louis). Home: St. Louis, Mo. Died Apr. 20, 1974.

ALLEN, EDWIN BROWN, ret. educator; b. Westerly, R.I., Nov. 3, 1898; s. John and Mary Frances (West) A.; E.E., Rensselaer Poly. Inst., 1920, M.S., 1930, Ph.D., 1934; A.M., Harvard, 1934; student Columbia, summer 1933, U. Chgo., summers 1935, 38, 41; m. Helen Cornelia Mackay, Sept. 3, 1927. Instr. math. Rensselaer Poly. Inst., 1920-27, asst. prof., 1927-34, prof. math. and astronomy, 1934-64, head dept. math., 1934-60, dean grad. sch., 1959-64, prof., dean emeritus, from 1964; dir. NSF Summer Inst., 1957-59. Dir. Gen. Electric Math. Fellowship Program, summers, 1952-59. Coordinator Naval Flight Prep. Sch., Rensselaer Poly. Inst., 1942-43, War Research, U.S. Arsenal, Watervliet, N.Y., 1943-45; cons. various pubs., industries. Mem. coms., N.Y. State Dept. Edn. Served with U.S. Army, 1918, Heavy Arty. O.T.S., 1918. Awarded U.S. Vol. Life Sav. medal and R.I. Boy Scout Life Sav. medal. Mem. Am. Math. Soc., Soc. for Symbolic Logic, Math. Assn. Am. (gov. 1949-52), Am. Oriental Soc., History of Sci. Soc., Am. Research Center Egypt (trustee 1951-63), Am. Schs. Oriental Research, Sigma Xi, Alpha Tau Omega, Eta Kappa Nu, Tau Beta Pi, Pi Mu Epsilon, Republican. Episcopalian. Mason (hon. 33; past dist. dept. grand master). Author: Vital Mathematics (with D. Maly and S. H. Starkey), 1944; Papers on Science in Orient; also numerous articles. Home: Troy, N.Y. Died Oct. 7, 1974.

ALLEN, FRANK WALLER, author; b. Milton, Trimble Co., Ky., Sept. 30, 1878; s. Frank Gibbs and Nancy (Maddux) A.; Summer Sch., U. of Chicago, Coll. of the Bible, Lexington, Ky.; A.B., Transylvania U., Ky., 1902; m. Anne Mary Meek, of Savannah, Ga., May 30, 1906. Newspaper work, Louisville, Ky., and Kansas City, Mo., 1897-1901; ordained Disciples of Christ ministry, 1904; pastor Odesa, Mo., 1904-08, Paris, Mo., 1908-14, 1st Ch., Springfield, Ill., 1914-17; prof. psychology and lecturer in lit., Springfield (Ill.) Coll. of Music and Allied Arts, 1917-1921. Mem. Sigma Upsilon, Kappa Sigma. Clubs: City, Midday. Author: My Ships Aground, 1900; Back to Arcady, 1905; The Maker of Joys, 1907; The Golden Road, 1910; The Lovers of Skye, 1913; Bread and Love, 1914; Brothers of Bagdad, 1916; Painted Windows, 1918; The Great Quest, 1918; My One Hundred Best Novels, 1919; Creative Living, 1926; Wings of Beauty, 1929. Contbr. on social conditions and lecturer before chautauquas and assemblies. Resigned from Disciples Ch., 1919. Home: Long Beach, Cal.†

ALLEN, FRED WILLIAM, JR., accountant; b. Houston, Oct. 30, 1901; s. Fred W. and Mattie (Cassagne) A.; student bus. coll., corr. schs.; m. Stella Matthews, July 19, 1927; 1 dau., Marjorie Nell (Mrs. C. Bryce Johnson). Pvt. practice pub. accounting, Houston, from 1924; sr. partner Allen & Inglish, C.P.A.'s. Mem. Am. Inst. C.P.A.'s, Tex. Soc. C.P.A.'s (past pres. Houston chpt.), Exec. Assn., C. of C. Methodist. Home: Houston, Tex. Died Dec. 2, 1973; buried Forest Park Lawndale, Houston, Tex.

ALLEN, FREDERICK MADISON, physician; b. Des Moines, Ia., Mar. 16, 1879; s. Madison Calvin and Harriet Amelia (McDaniel) A.; A.B., U. of Calif., 1902; student med. dept. U. of Chicago, 1 yr.; M.D., U. of Calif., 1907; m. Mary Belle Wishart, Oct. 22, 1921; children—Mary Belle, Dorothy Lewellyn; m. 2d, Anne Victorine Stacy, 1934. Research in diabetes, Harvard Med. Sch., 1909-12, Rockefeller Inst. for Med. Research, 1913-18; investigation and treatment of diabetes and other disorders of metabolism, as dir. of Physiatric Inst., Morristown, N.J., 1920-33; prof. staff N.Y. Polyclinic Hosp. and Med. Sch., New York Medical Coll. Introduced fasting or undernutrition treatment for diabetes, 1914. Capt. Med. Corps, U.S.A., 1 yr., 1918. Mem. A.M.A., Assn. Am. Physicians, Am. Soc. Exptl. Pathology, Am. Physiol. Soc., Pan-Am. Med. Assn., Harvey Soc., Acad. Medicine (New York), Alpha Delta Phi. Republican. Protestant. Author: Studies Concerning Glycosuria and Diabetes, 1913; Total Dietary Restriction in the Treatment of Diabetes (with Drs. E. Stillman and R. Fitz), 1919; Treatment of Kidney Diseases and High Blood Pressure, 1925; various articles on diabetes, hypertension, cancer, surgical refrigeration and shock treatment. Home: New York City, N.Y.†

ALLEN, GEORGE WALTON HOLKER, business exec.; b. St. Louis, Nov. 19, 1889; s. George W. and Lydia U. (McMillan) A.; ed. Bishops Coll. Sch., Lennoxville, P.Q., Can.; Ecole St. Ignace, Paris, France;

Morristown Sch., Morristown, N.J.; m. Gretchen Brooks Stevens, Apr. 18, 1911; children—Frederick Stevens, Elizabeth W. A. Lapey, Kathleen B.A. Forbes; m. 2d, Mrs. Elizabeth Lambert Barnes, Oct. 23, 1948. Vice president and director of the Enos & Sanderson Company, Buffalo; director, sec., treas. Owehgena Sanderson Co., Buffalo; dir., sec., treas. Owahgena Hosding Corp., Cazenovia; sec., dir. B. F. Gladding & Company, Inc., South Otelic. Vice chmn. home service div., Pasadena chapt., A.B.C. World War I; chmn. Cazenovia W.P.A. World War II. Mem. S.A.R., Mayflower Descendants, S.R., Newcomen Soc. of N.A. Republican. Episcopalian. Clubs: Saturn (Buffalo); Cazenovia (N.Y.); Vero Beach Country, Riomar (Vero Beach, Fla.). Home: Vero Beach, Fla. Died Oct. 29, 1973; buried Evergreen Cemetery, Cazenovia, N.Y.

ALLEN, GORDON FORREST, coll. ofcl.; b. Freedom, N.Y., Dec. 23, 1908; s. Earl and Louise (Owens) A.; A.B., Houghton Coll., 1930; M.S. in Edn., Cornell U., 1937; Ed.D., U. Buffalo, 1955; m. Faith Ellinwood, Apr. 11, 1936 (dec. July 19, 1967); children—Christopher G., Douglas F.; m. 2d, Elsa V. Benham, Oct. 9, 1968; stepchildren—Elsa Jane, Jeanne. Tchr. sci. and social studies, coach Groveland (N.Y.) High Sch., 1930-31; prin. Cuylerville (N.Y.) pub. schs., 1931-34; tchr. math., social studies Brighton High Sch., Rochester, N.Y., 1934-39, prin., 1939-47; prof. edn. State U. Coll. Edn., Brockport, N.Y., 1947-55, chmn. dept. edn., 1955-56, dean coll., 1956-64; acting pres. State U. N.Y. at Brockport, 1964-66, v.p. for acad. affairs, 1966-70, prof. emeritus, from 1970. Mem. N.E.A., N.Y. State Tchrs. Assn., Rochester Mus., Rochester Art Gallery, Phi Delta Kappa. Presbyn. Clubs: Torch, Rochester. Home: Brockport, N.Y. Died Sept. 19, 1973.

ALLEN, IDA BAILEY, home economist, dietitian, author; b. Danielson, Conn.; d. Frank Garvin and Ida Louise (Cogswell) Bailey; grad. Oread Inst. Domestic Sci., Worchester, Mass.; grad. dietitian, Met. Hosp., N.Y.C.; Dr. Oratorical Arts, Staley Coll., Mass.; m. Thomas Lewis Allen; children—Thomas Lewis (dec.), Ruth Elizabeth; m. 2d, William Brewster Chapman. Formerly dir. cooking schs., Worcester, Mass.; founder Mrs. Allen's School of Cookery, N.Y.C.; contbr. to Ladies Home Journal; diet editor Med. Rev. of Revs.; food editor Good Housekeeping Mag., Family Circle, Parade; lectr. bakers and cooks schs. Q.M. Dept. U.S. Army; contbr. to A.M.A. publ., Today's Health; cons. food and household industries. Recipient Medaillon de 'Arbalete Suisse (Switzerland), 1962. Author 56 books on cooking, homemaking and nutrition including: Youth After Forty, 1951 (translated into Japanese, French, Italian, Spanish); Solving the High Cost of Eating, 1952; Step-by-Step Picture Cook Book, 1953; Sandwich Book, 1955; Cook Book for Two, 1957; Gastronomique, A Cook Book for Gourmets, 1958, rev. edit., 1962; Best Loved Recipes of the American People, 1973. Daily column internat. syndicate, until 1968. Featured radio, TV, films. Address: Westport Conn. Died July 1973.

ALLEN, JEAN MALVEN (MRS. FREDERICK H. ALLEN), civic worker; b. College Point, N.Y., Mar. 23, 1901; d. Frank and Isadore (Wells) Malven; B.A. Vassar Coll., 1922; m. Frederick H. Allen, Jan. 1, 1927; children—Frederick H. III, Donald E., Nancy Jean (Mrs. John E. Rupke). Tchr. English, Langdon Meml. Mission Sch., Mt. Vernon, Ky., 1922-24; asst. publicity mgr. Gen. Assembly, U.P. Ch. U.S.A., Phila., 1925-26, mem. Bd. Nat. Missions, 1961-70. Trustee Coll. of Ozarks, 1963-69; mem. adv. council Boggs Acad., Keysville, Ga., 1961-70; mem. Nat. Presbyn. Health and Welfare Assn., 1961-70, sec., 1963-68. Home: Portland Me. Died Aug. 14, 1972.

ALLEN, JOHN ALPHEUS, chemist; b. Hebron, Me., Oct. 19, 1863; s. Prof. Oscar Dana and Fidelia Roberts (Totman) A.; grad. Sheffield Scientific School, Yale, 1883; unmarried. Asst. to curator metallurgy, U.S. Nat. Museum, 1884; chemist to Solid Steel Co., Alliance, O., 1887; asst. in herbarium Harvard Univ., 1892; made a published collection of mosses of the Cascade Mountains, 1898. Chemist to Nungesser Electric Battery Co., of Cleveland from 1903. Author: Tables for Iron Analysis, 1896 W9. Address: Cleveland, O†

ALLEN, LAURENCE EDMUND (LARRY), reporter; b. Mt. Savage, Md., Oct. 19, 1908; s. Laurence Bernard and Mary Caroline (Crowe) A.; student schs. several states, grad. high sch.; m. Helen Fazakerley Quisenberry. Began with Balt. News, 1926, later with Washington Herald and Huntington (W.Va.) Evening Herald; reporter, telegraph editor Charleston (W.Va.) Daily Mail, 1927-33; with Associated Press, 1933-60, as reporter and state editor Charleston bur., 1933-35, reporter Washington bur., 1935-37, fgn. cables desk, N.Y.C., 1937-38, European war corr., 1938-44, corr. Poland, 1945, 47, 49, chief of bur., Moscow, 1949, Tel Aviv, 1950, war corr., S.E. Asia, Singapore, 1951, French Union and Vietminh Indochina, 1951-55, Malaya, Thailand, Burma, 1956, Caribbean area, 1957-61; organized Am. Press Service specializing Latin Am., 1960—. Recipient Bronze Star for defending freedom press as prisoner of war, 1945; Croix de Guerre Fr. High Command, Indo China, frontline reporting, Nov. 1952. Received first award Nat. Headliners Club, 1941, for best news-reporting in covering Brit. Fleet operations; awarded Pulitzer prize for reporting on internat. affairs, May 5, 1942; Order of British Empire by King George VI, 1947. Republican. Contbr. many short stories to various publs., 1925-33. Home: Mexico City, Mexico Died May 1975.

ALLEN, ROBERT MCDOWELL, lawyer; b. Edinburg, Grundy Co., Mo., Oct. 29, 1878; s. Rev. Nelson McDowell and Carolina Josephine (Pelly) A.; A.B., Ky. State Coll., 1900; unmarried. Admitted to Ky. bar, 1901; head div. state food insp'n of Ky. State Expt. Sta., from 1900. Sec. Assn. of State and Nat. Food and Dairy Depts., 1902-07; sec. Internat. Pure Food Congress, La. Purchase Exp'n, St. Louis, 1904; sec. Permanent Comm'n on future Internat. Conf. concerning adulteration and misbranding of foods; mem. governing b'd Peoples Lobby. Mem. Phi Delta Theta. Has written various published addresses on Food Control Laws, Food Inspection, etc., and Govt. reports on food control work. Address: Lexington, Ky.†

ALLENDOERFER, CARL BARNETT, mathematician; b. Kansas City, Apr. 4, 1911; s. Carl William and Winifred (Barnett) A.; B.S., Haverford Coll., 1932; B.A. (Rhodes scholar), Oxford U., 1934; Ph.D., Princeton, 1937; mem. Inst. Advanced Study, 1948-49; m. Dorothy Holbrook, June 26, 1937; children—Robert Duff, James Holbrook, William Barnett. Prof. math. Haverford Coll., 1946-51; prof. math. U. Wash., Seattle, from 1951, exec. officer, 1951-62; Fulbright lectr. Cambridge (Eng.) U., 1957-58, Australia, 1963; mem. div. math. NRC, 1956-58, 62-65, commn. on math. Coll. Entrance Exam. Bd., 1955-59. Operations analyst U.S. Govt., World War II. Fellow A.A.A.S.; mem. Am. Math. Soc., Math. Assn. Am. (pres. 1959-60, chmn. com. on ednl. media 1963-66, Distinguished Service award 1972), Inst. Math. Statistics, Soc. for Indsl. and Applied Math., Nat. Council Tchrs. Math., Phi Beta Kappa, Sigma Xi. Club: Monday (Seattle). Author: Principles of Mathematics, 1955; Fundamentals of Freshman Mathematics, 1959; Mathematics for Parents, 1963; Fundamentals of College Algebra, 1967; Principles of Arithmetic and Geometry, 1971; Calculus of Several Variables and Differentiable Manifolds, 1974. Editor Am. Math. Monthly, 1952-56. Cons. editor in math. Macmillan Co., from 1958. Contbr. articles to profl. jours. Home: Seattle, Wash. Died Sept. 29, 1974; buried Mt. Moriah Cemetery, Kansas City, Mo.

ALLENSON, HAZEL SANDIFORD, artist, educator; b. Central Falls, R.I., Mar. 10, 1902; d. William and Emma (Oldham) Allenson; grad. tchr. tng. dept. (R.I. honor scholar) R.I. Sch. Design, 1924, B.S. in Art Edn., 1949; M.Ed., R.I. Coll., 1955; postgrad. Brown U. Extension courses, pvt. tchrs. art. Tchr. Gordon Sch., Providence, 1924; supr. art pub. schs., Avon, Randolph, Holbrook (all Mass.), 1925; tchr. Saturday classes R.I. Sch. Design, 1926-32; asst. to supr. art Providence Schs., 1926, writer art curriculum, 1947, 58, supr. art, 1964-69; made European tour of 10 countries with Am. Inst. Ednl. Travel, 1928; exhibited in group shows Providence Art Club, R.I. Sch. Design, Brown U., So. Printmaker's Rotary Exhbn., 1940-42, Grandfather's Barn Gallery, Lincoln, R.I., Old Slater Mill Blackstone Valley Show, Pawtucket, Province Art Club, 1970; poetry readings on Radio Sta. WJAR, Providence, 1943-46; critic tchr. for student tchrs. art R.I. Sch. Design, Brown U., 1949-64; represented in permanent collections, including Student Union Bldg., U. Fla. Organizer 2 first aid classes A.R.C., 1942; chmn. art Providence Book Fair, 1950; mem. R.I. Com. Nat. Scholastic Awards, from 1965. Recipient 1st award for Best of Show Grandfather's Barn Gallery, 1962-68, 1st awards Old Slater Mill All Blackstone Valley Show, 1962, 67, 3rd award, 1966. Mem. R.I. Edn. Assn., R.I. Art Tchrs. Assn., Providence Art Club, Nat. Art Edn. Assn., R.I. Assn. Supervision and Curriculum Devel., Providence Pub. Schs. Adminstrv. Staff Assn., R.I. Sch. Design Alumni Assn., R.I. Coll. Alumni Assn., Delta Kappa Gamma. Republican. Contbr. numerous articles to ednl. jours. Home: Central Falls R.I. Died Sept. 1973.

ALLERUP, PAUL RICHARD, editor; b. N.Y.C., June 11, 1912; s. Peter and Helga (Holm) A.; student Eastman Sch., N.Y.C., N.Y. U.; m. Ellen M. Hostrup, Apr. 8, 1938. With Internat. News Service, 1935-58, successively cub reporter, reporter bur. mgr. Cin., asst. bur. mgr. Columbus, O., asst. Pa. state mgr., asst. night editor Chgo., night editor, Chgo., N.Y.C., gen. news editor, asso. mng. editor, mng. editor, 1955-58; dir. spl. news projects and features editor U.P.I., N.Y.C., 1958-59, London news mgr., 1959-62, European gen. news mgr., U.P.I., 1962-66, editor Newsfeatures, from 1966. Served with AUS, 1944-46; ETO. Mem. Assn. Am. Corrs. (London). Clubs: Wig and Pen, Curzon (London). Address: New York City, N.Y. Died Dec. 1974.

ALLGOOD, MILES CLAYTON, congressman; b. Allgood, Ala., Feb. 22, 1878; s. William Barnett and Mary Matilda (Ingram) A.; State Normal Sch., Florence, Ala., 1898; m. Willie Randall Fox, of Montgomery, Ala., Feb. 1, 1917; children—Miles Clayton, Mary Fox, William David. Teacher pub. schs., 1898-1900; tax officer, Blount Co., Ala., 1900-09; also farmer; demonstration work, Blount Co.; later state auditor, Ala.; commr. of agr. and industry, Ala., 1918-22; mem. 68th to 72d Congresses (1923-33), 7th Ala. Dist., and 73d Congress (1933-35), 5th Alabama Dist. Del. at large to Dem. Nat. Conv., 1920. Democrat. Methodist. Mason, Odd Fellow, Woodman. Home: Gadsden, Ala.†

ALLIN, GEORGE R., army officer, supt. mil. acad.; b. Iowa City, Ia., Feb. 15, 1880; s. Thomas Banberry and Katherine (Detwiler) A.; Ph.B., U. of Ia., 1902; B.S., U.S. Mil. Acad., 1904; grad. Army War Coll., 1924; m. Jessie Pontius, Nov. 26, 1913; children—Elizabeth (Mrs. Edwin Richard Clarke), George R. Commd. 2d lt., U.S. Army, 1904, and advanced through grades to brig. gen., 1940; comd. 12th F.A. Brigade, World War I; comdt. Field Arty. Sch., Fort Sill, Okla., until retirement, 1942; later supt. Sewanee (Tenn.) Mil. Acad. Awarded Distinguished Service medal (World War I), Legion of Merit (World War II). Mem. Sigma Nu. Club: Army and Navy (Washington, D.C.). Home: Sewanee, Tenn.*†

ALLIS, JAMES ASHTON, banker; b. St. Paul, Jan. 5, 1881; s. Frederick and Lida (Ashton) A.; grad. Westminster Sch., Simsbury, Conn., 1898; m. Elizabeth Verrault, June 21, 1909; children—Frederick, Bayard. Bank examiner, 1910-20; v.p. State Bank, 1921-23; vice pres. Grace Nat. Bank, N.Y. City, 1924-51; dir. Fairchild Engine & Airplane Corp., 1942-58, chmn. bd., 1950-58. Fellow Am. Geog. Soc.; mem. Soc. Colonial Wars, S.R. (N.Y.), Vt. Hist. Soc., Appalachain Trail Conf., Torrey Bot., A.L.A., N.Y. Bot. Garden, New Eng. Bot. Club. St. James Ch. (vestryman 1946-52, warden 1955-57, treas. from 1950). Clubs: Explorers (dir. 1951-56, treas. 1951-57); Appalachian Mountain (v.p. 1925-26). Home: Upper Montclair, N.J.†

ALLISON, FRED, prof. physics; b. Glade Spring, Va., July 4, 1882; s. Robert Clark and Rebecca Jane (Clark) A.; A.B., Emory and Henry Coll., Emory, Va., 1904; post-grad. Johns Hopkins, 1907-08, 1910-11, U. of Chicago, summer, 1909; A.M., U. of Va., 1921, Ph.D., 1922; D.Sc., Ala. Poly. Inst., 1931; LL.D. from Emory and Henry Coll., 1933; m. Elizabeth Harriet Kelly, Aug. 24, 1915; children——Elizabeth Harriet (Mrs. R. T. Comer, Jr.), Fred. Prof. physics, Emory and Henry College, 1908-20, instructor and graduate student, University of Va., 1920-22; head prof. physics, Ala. Poly Inst., 1922-53, dean of graduate sch., 1949-53; director Auburn Research Foundation, Alabama Poly Institute, 1949-51; visiting prof. Emory and Henry Coll., 1953-55; vis. prof. physics U. Texas, summer 1955; sent as cons. in physics to Chulalongkorn U., Bangkok, Thailand, vis. prof. Huntingdon Coll., 1956-58. Cons. Operational Research Office, A.F. Missile Development Center, summer 1957, Holloman AFB, N.M. Awarded President and Visitors' Research Prize, U. of Va., 1925; Herty Research medal, 1933. Physics Bldg. Auburn U. named in his honor. Fellow Am. Phys. Soc. (chmn. S.E. sect. 1941), A.A.A.S. (George Pegram medal); mem. Ala. Acad. Sci. (pres. 1929), Phi Beta Kappa, Phi Kappa Phi, Sigma Xi; hon. mem. Ga. Acad. Science. Developed magneto-optic method of analysis, by means of which discovered with co-workers Element 87, 1930, Element 85, 1931. Author: College Physics Laboratory Instructions. Home: Auburn, Ala. Died Aug. 2, 1974.

ALLISON, ROBERT BURNS, newspaper editor; b. Mesa, Ariz., Aug. 23, 1916; s. George Lewis and Zelma (Babbitt) A.; student Ariz. State U., 1933-36; m. Ivon Hammock, Feb. 29, 1936 (dec. Feb. 2, 1969): 1 dau., Judith (Mrs. J.G.J. Samuels); m. 2d, Mary Oliver Wilson, July 19, 1969. Editor Flagstaff Jour. (Ariz.), 1936; reporter Phoenix Gazette, 1937-44, sports editor, from 1946. Served with AUS, 1944-46. Mem. Phoenix Press Club, Phoenix Press Box Assn., Football Writers Am. Assn., Golf Writers Assn. Am. (bd. dirs.), Sigma Delta Chi. Home: Phoenix Ariz. Died Apr. 5, 1974.

ALLTON, JAMES MILLER (TOM), businessman; b. Columbia, Mo., Mar. 3, 1895; s. James Miller and Mary Frances (Gans) A.; part time student U. Mo., 1914-24; m. Erma Euteneuer, Feb. 20, 1922; children—Mary Frances (Mrs. John M. Sneed), Barbara Louise (Mrs. John L. Knaus). Instr. indsl. arts dept. U. Mo., 1914-24; pres. Allton Automobile Co., Columbia, 1922-74, Automobile Dealers Insurors, Inc., 1946-56, Mid-Continent Casualty Co., 1952-56, Tipton Motor Co. (Mo.), 1951-59, Columbia Indsl. Devel. Corp., Columbia Improvement Corp., Mid-Mo. Devel. Council, Oak Wood Hills, Inc., until 1972, ABF Enterprises, Inc.; dir. Boone County Lumber Co. Mem. Columbia Indsl. Commn. Dir. Ford Dealers Advt. Fund, St. Louis br. Ford Motor Co. Campaign dir. United Fund, 1957, pres., 1967; mem. bd. Boone County Govtl. Study Group. Active United Community Funds Councils Am. Trustee Christian Coll., Columbia, U. Mo. Med. Sch. Found., Mo. Pub. Expenditure Survey. Trustee, sec. Mo. Cancer Research Center. Lab. Cancer Research Center named in his honor, 1975. Mem. Nat. Automobile Dealers Assn. (mil. com. for formation or Ordnance affiliated units 1942, dir., regional v.p.), Mo. Auto Dealers Assn. (1st pres. 1938; dir. since inception, treas), Columbia C. of C. (pres. 1937, 38, 39), Newcomen Soc. N. Am. Mason (32°, Shriner), Kiwanian (lt. gov. 1937, pres. Columbia 1936). Author: Blacksmithing (with R.W. Selvidge), 1924. Holder pvt. pilot license. Home: Columbia, Mo. Died June 16, 1974; cremated.

ALSOP, STEWART JOHONNOT OLIVER, mag. columnist; b. Avon, Conn., May 17, 1914; s. Joseph Wright and Corine Douglas (Robinson) A.; grad. Groton Sch., 1932; A.B., Yale, 1936, L.H.D., 1973; m. Patrica Hankey, June 1944; children—Joseph Wright, Ian Alexander Douglas, Elizabeth Winthrop, Stewart Johonnot Oliver, Richard Nicholas, Andrew Christian. Began as editor Doubleday Doran, N.Y.C.; after World War II, co-author (with brother Joseph) column Matter of Fact for N.Y. Herald Tribune Syndicate, 1945-58; nat. affairs contbg. editor Sat. Eve. Post, 1958-62, Washington editor, 1962-68; columnist Newsweek mag., from 1968. Enlisted in Kings Royal Rifle Corps, British Army, 1942; inf. platoon comdr. Italy, 1943; transferred to Am. Army as parachutist OSS, 1944; parachuted into France to join Maquis shortly after D-Day; resigned commn., 1945. Decorated Croix de Guerre with palm (France); mentioned in dispatches. Clubs: River (N.Y.C); Metropolitan (Washington). Author: (with Thomas Braden) Sub Rosa, 1945; (with Joseph Alsop) We Accuse, 1955; (with Joseph Alsop) The Reporter's Trade; Nixon and Rockefeller, 1960; The Center, 1968; Stay of Execution, 1973. Contbr. articles to Sat. Eve. Post, Life, Atlantic Monthly mags. Home: Washington, D.C. Died May 26, 1974.

ALSTON, ANGUS SORENSEN, telephone co. exec.; b. Salt Lake City, Dec. 22, 1914; s. Clinton A. and Martha Ellen (Sorensen) A.; student Colo. Coll., 1933-36; LL.D., So. Colo. State Coll., 1968; m. Fanny Christian, July 1, 1938 (dec. Sept. 1968); children—Clinton Angus, Joan Elizabeth (Mrs. R. R. Hare); m. 2d, Darlene Ullyot Norder, Sept. 27, 1969; stepchildren—Bonnie Sue Norder, Donna Lee Norder (Mrs. Walter Matthew Korchun). With Mountain Tel. & Tel. Co., 1936-61, v.p., Colo., 1954-58, v.p. co. personnel, 1958-61; v.p., gen. mgr. Bell Telephone Co. Pa., Pitts., 1962-64; exec. v.p. Am. Tel. & Tel. Co., 1967-70; pres. Southwestern Bell Telephone Co., 1970-73, chmn. bd., chief exec. officer, 1973-75; dir. Pepsico., Inc., Gen. Am. Life Ins. Co., Civic Center Redevel. Corp., Mississippi River Corp., First Nat. Bank, St. Louis, St. Louis Union Trust Co., First Union Inc., Alton Box Bd. Co. Mem. Commn. White House Fellows; mem. adv. bd. Radio Free Europe. Bd. dirs. St. Louis and St. Louis County YMCA, St. Louis Area council Boy Scouts Am., Civic Progress, Mo. Pub. Expenditure Survey, United Fund, Arts and Edn. Council, Cancer Research Center Devel. Council, U.S. Indsl. Payroll Savings Com., Municipal Opera, St. Louis Art Mus.; bd. dirs. Nat. Indsl. Pollution Council, also mem. utilities subcouncil; former chmn. Nat. Safety Council; charter trustee Colo. Coll.; trustee Washington U.; adv. trustee St. Louis Ednl. TV Commn. Mem. U.S., St. Louis chambers commerce, Phi Gamma Delta. Clubs: Old Warson Country, St. Louis Country, St. Louis, The Round Table; Bogey; Racquet, Noonday, Baltusrol. Home: Creve Coeur Mo. Died Jan. 12, 1975.

ALSTON, PHILIP HENRY, lawyer; b. Barbour County, Ala., Oct. 29, 1880; s. Augustus Holmes and Anna Maria (Ott) A.; A.B., Univ. Ala., 1900, LL.B., 1902; m. Mary Birnie Lewis, June 28, 1910; children—Philip Henry, Mary Birnie (Mrs. Fletcher Jordan, Jr.), James L., Anne Amanda (Mrs. John F. Glenn), Robert C. Admitted to Ala. bar, 1902, Georgia bar, 1903, later practiced in Atlanta; asso. with DuBignon & Alston, 1903-05. McDaniel, Alston & Black, 1905-10; mem. Robert C. and Philip H. Alston, 1911-21, Alston, Alston, Foster & Moise, 1921-38, Alston, Foster, Moise & Sibley, 1938-42, Alston, Foster, Sibley & Miller from 1942. Director Davison-Paxon Company (mem. exec. com.), Atlanta. Mem. adv. bd. Citizens & Southern Nat. Bank. Mem. Am., Ga. State and Atlanta (past pres.) bar assns. Maj., judge adv. gen. in World War. Mem. Atlanta Chamber of Commerce (past pres.). Mem. Sigma Nu. Democrat. Episcopalian. Clubs: Capital City, Piedmont Driving. Home: Atlanta, Ga.†

ALTER, WILBUR MCCLURE, justice; b. Allegheny, Pa., Dec. 17, 1879; s. D. G. and Ada V. (Lutz) A.; A.B., Denver U., 1903, LL.B., 1906; m. Florence E. Christy, Feb. 6, 1923; children—Wilbur McClure (dec.), Allen Grant, Lauren Lee. Admitted to Colo. bar, 1906, practicing at Cripple Creek; judge Dist. Ct., 4th Jud. District, Colo., 1923-28; justice Supreme Court, Colorado, 1928-33, 1944-55, chief justice Colorado Supreme Court, from 1955. Served as enlisted man, World War I. George W. Clayton Coll., Denver, and School of Mines, Golden, Colo. Comdr. American Legion, Dept. of Colo. Republican Mason; Justice Grand Forum, B.P.O.E. Home: Lakewood, Colo.†

ALTERMAN, ZIPORA STEPHANIA BALABAN, mathematician; b. Berlin, Germany, Aug. 6, 1925; d. Leon and Regina (Wischnitzer) Balaban; M.Sc., Hebrew U. Jerusalem, Israel, 1949, Ph.D., 1953; m. Israel Alterman, June 28, 1950; 1 son, Ilan M. Scientist, Israel Dept. Research and Devel., 1948-55; prof. applied math. Weizmann Inst., Rehovot, Israel, 1961-67; vis. research asso. U. Chgo., 1960-61; vis. prof. Hebrew U., 1961-65; vis. prof. Tel. Aviv (Israel) U., 1965-66, dir. Inst. Space and Planetary Sci., 1967-74, chmn. dept. environmental scis., 1968-74; vis. mem. Courant Inst. Math. Sci. N.Y. U., 1966-67. Mem. Israel Math. Union (past hon. sec.), Israel Soc. Geodesy and Geophysics (chmn. sect. seismology 1964, chmn. soc. 1967), Math. Union (past hon. sec.), Israel Soc. Geodesy and Geophysics (chmn. sect. seismology 1964—), Am. Math. Soc., Am. Geophys. Union, Seismol. Soc. Am., Israel Math. Union, Israel Union for Information Processing. Contbr. articles to tech. jours., chpts. in books. First to compute frequencies of free oscillations of earth, research in terrestrial spectoscopy, hydrodynamic stability; obtained complete theoretical seismograms for explosive and other point sources in a shpere; found propagation constants for sound and heat in rarefied gases. Office: Tel Aviv, Israel., Died Apr. 24, 1974.

ALTHER, JOSEPH G., research consultant; b. Chicago, Nov. 17, 1892; s. Nicholas and Magdalen (Schirmbeck) A.; ed. in pub. schs.; m. Elizabeth M. Kaebberich, Mar. 9, 1914; children—Marian E., Josephine. Began career with Universal Oil Products Co., research, development and licensing petroleum hydrocarbon, Chicago, 1915, sec., 1918-30, vice pres. of ops., 1928-44, acting pres., 1944-45; cons. research and develop., Evanston, Ill., after 1945; dir. Michigan Av. Nat. Bank, Chicago, 1945-48; chmn., dir. Benson & Assos., Inc., safety engring., Chicago, from 1946. Trustee Ill. Inst. Tech., Valmora (N.M.) Sanatorium. Republican. Mason (32, Shriner). Home: Evanston, Ill., Died Feb. 25, 1976.

ALTMAN, JULIAN ALLEN, mail order co. exec.; b. Wellsburg, W.Va., Nov. 2, 1911; s. Morris and Nellie (Solomon) A.; student Geneva Coll., 1927-28; A.B., Harvard, 1931, LL.B., 1934; M.B.A., U. Chgo., 1956; m. Katharine Goldschmidt, June 26, 1936; 1 son, Robert. Admitted to N.Y. Supreme Ct., 1936, Eastern Dist. and So. Dist. N.Y., 1936; practiced in N.Y.C., 1934-40; with Spiegel, Inc., Chgo., from 1946, controller, from 1956, treas., from 1967. Served with AUS, 1940-46. Decorated Bronze Star. Mem. Financial Execs. Inst., Chgo. Retail Controllers Assn. Club: Harvard of Chicago. Home: Chicago, Ill. Died Mar. 1, 1974.

ALTROCCHI, JULIA COOLEY (MRS. RUDOLPH ALTROCCHI), author, lectr.; b. Seymour, Conn., July 4, 1893; d. Harlan Ward and Nellie (Wooster) Cooley; A.B., Vassar Coll., 1914; spl. student U. Perugia, summer 1926; m. Rudolph Altrocchi, Aug. 26, 1920 (dec. May 1953); children—John Cooley, Paul Hemenway. Lectr. lit. and hist. subjects, univs., colls., socs. and clubs throughout U.S., from 1916. Recipient Poetry award Cal. Writers Guild of Los Angeles, 1937, 45; Stephen Vincent Benet award for hist. narrative poem, 1968. Mem. Internat. P.E.N., Nat. Poetry Soc. Am., Nat. League Am. Pen Women (past br. pres.), Cal. Writers Club (past pres.), Shakespearean Authorship Soc. London, Shakespeare Oxford Soc., Ina Coolbrith Circle San Francisco (hon.), Browning Soc. San Francisco (hon.; Dramatic Monologue award 1962), Poets of Pacific (hon.), Nat. Soc. Colonial Dames. Club: Town and Gown (Berkeley). Author: Poems of A Child, 1904; The Dance of Youth and Other Poems, 1917; Snow Covered Wagons; A Pioneer Epic (Silver medal, lit. award Commonwealth Club Cal.), 1936; Wolves Against the Moon, 1940; The Old California Trail, 1945; Spectacular San Franciscans, 1950; Girl With Ocelot and Other Poems (poetry award Commonwealth Club Cal. 1965), 1964, Contbr. articles on Cal., hist., lit. subjects, also poems to mags., bulls., jours., anthologies. Home: Berkeley Cal. Died Nov. 23, 1972.

ALWARD, HERBERT VAUGHAN, banker; b. New Brunswick, Can., Apr. 18, 1880; s. Freeman and Sarah (Keith) A.; student Provincial Normal Sch., Frederickton, N.B., 1896-97, Am. Inst. Banking, 1905-06, N.Y.U., 1906-08, 11-12; m. Kate Montelius, Sept. 8, 1910 (dec. Jan. 30, 1920); children—Kate (Mrs. George S. Campion), Herbert Vaughan; m. 2d Elizabeth Hailey, May 28, 1937. Came to U.S., 1901, naturalized, 1906. With Bank of Nova Scotia, Sussex, N.B., 1899-1901, First Nat. Bank, Missoula, Mont., 1901-06, Seaboard Nat. Bank, N.Y.C., 1906-08; cashier First Nat. Bank, Kalispell, Mont., 1908-15, Comml. Nat. Bank, Gt. Falls, Mont., 1915-16; v.p., cashier Fidelity Trust Co., Tacoma, Wash., 1916-19; asst. mgr. Bank of Cal., Tacoma, 1919-25, joint mgr., Seattle, 1925-27, mgr., Portland, 1927-36, v.p., cashier, sr. v.p., San Francisco, 1936-50, ret. 1950; dir. Edward Hines Lumber Co., Chgo. Adv. bd. R.F.C., Portland, Ore. Mem. C. of C. (dir. Portland, San Francisco), Cal. Bankers Assn. (pres. 1949-50). Episcopalian (treas. Diocese of Cal.). Home: Pebble Beach, Cal.†

ALWYNE, HORACE, educator; b. Lancashire, Eng., Oct. 13, 1891; s. Thalberg and Mary M. (Whittaker) A.; student Manchester (Eng.) Grammar Sch. and Royal Coll. of Music; m. Mildred Sewall Avery, Dec. 15, 1938. Came to U.S., 1913. Concert pianist from 1906; condr. orchestra and chorus, Manchester Grammar Sch., 1910-12; concert pianist and student, Berlin, Germany, 1912-13; head of piano dept., Skidmore Sch. of Arts (now Skidmore Coll.), Saratoga Springs, N.Y., 1914-21; asso. prof. music Bryn Mawr Coll., 1921-27, Alice Carter Dickerman prof. music and dir. dept. of music 1927-57, prof. emeritus music from 1957, vis. prof., 1958-65; John Hay Whitney Found. head piano dept. Bryn Mawr Conservatory of Music, from 1962; dir. music, Shipley Sch., Bryn Mawr, Pa., 1933-40; mem. faculty Surette Summer Sch. Music, Concord, Mass., 1922-26; lectr. in music, Curtis Inst. of Music, Philadelphia, Pa., 1926-28; Swarthmore Coll., summer 1943; vis. prof. Grinnell Coll., 1957-58; concert pianist recitals in Eng. Germany, Austria, Sicily and U.S.; soloist with Phila. Orchestra, New York Philharmonic, Detroit Symphony, Russian Symphony, Phila. String Sinfonietta, with BBC Orch. Hallé Orchestra and Bournemouth Symphony, also with well known quartets and chamber orgns. in U.S. Mem. bd. dirs. Settlement Music Sch. of Phila. Chamber String Sinfonietta, 1931-34. Hon. fellow Royal Coll. of Music (Manchester), 1924, gold medallist, 1912. Sir Charles Hallé Memorial Scholar, 1909-12; recipient Christian R. and Mary F. Lindback award for distinguished teaching ($1,000 grant), 1962. Pres. Soc. Contemporary Music, Phila., 1928-29; hon. dir. Tri-County Jr. Concerts Assn., Wayne, Pa. Home: Rosemont, Pa. Died Oct. 5, 1974.

AMELI, HOWARD WILMURT, lawyer; b. Brooklyn, N.Y., Oct. 12, 1881; s. Alonizo and Jessie Isabel (Robinson) A.; grad. Boys' High Sch., Brooklyn; A.B., Princeton, 1903; LL.B., New York Law Sch., 1905; m. Flora E. Maus, Aug. 10, 1918. Admitted to N.Y. bar, 1905, and began practice in Brooklyn; spl. asst. to atty. gen. of U.S., 1919-27; assistant in office of U.S. attorney, Eastern District of New York, 1927-29; became U.S. attorney, Eastern District of New York, 1929. Served as lieutenant senior grade, U.S. Navy, World War. Member Am. and Brooklyn bar assns. Am. Legion, Sons of Union Soldiers of Civil War (Lafayette Camp No. 140), Delta Chi. Republican. Mason. Clubs: Princeton, Invincible, Tiger Inn. Home: Brooklyn, N.Y.†

AMMAR, ABBAS MOUSTAFA, internat. civil servant; b. Shamma, Egypt, Dec. 10, 1907; s. Moustafa and Bahijah (Marzouk) A.; B.A. Cairo (Egypt) U., 1931, M.A., 1936; Ph.D., Manchester (Eng.) U., 1940; postdoctoral Cambridge (Eng.) U., 1941; m. Khadijah El-Shaarani, Nov. 12, 1942; 1 son, Moustafa. Lectr. socio-econs. Intermediate Coll. Commerce, Cairo, 1931-37; research work in social and cultural anthropology, Manchester and Cambridge Univs., 1937-42; lectr., asst. prof. social anthropology and socio-econs. Cairo U., 1942-47; head petitions div. trusteeship dept. UN, 1948-50, 51-52; dir.-gen. rural welfare dept. Egyptian Ministry Social Affairs, 1950-51, minister social affairs, 1952-54, minister edn., 1954; asst. dir.-gen. Internat. Labor Office, Geneva, 1954-64, dep. dir.-gen., 1964-74. Mem. higher com. Acad. Scis., Egypt. Trustee Internat. Council for Ednl. Devel. Author: Anthrogeographical Study of the Sinai Peninsula, 1936; Anthropological Study of the Arabs, 1946; Report on Adult Education and People's University for Workers, 1947; Report on Population Situation in Egypt, 1953; Reorganization of the Egyptian Village in a Decentralised Administration, 1954; The Peoples of Shargula: An Anthropo-Socio-Economic Study of the Eastern Province of the Nile Delta, 1946. Address: Geneva, Switzerland. Died Dec. 15, 1974.

AMMONS, EUGENE (GENE), tenor saxophonist; b. Chgo., Apr. 14, 1925; s. Albert Ammons; m; 2 children. Played with Billy Exstine and Woody Herman bands during 1940's; mem. two tenor combo with Sonny Stitt, later on own during 1950's; night club performances around Chgo., 1960-61; recording artist for Prestige, Argo, Verve records. Home: Chicago, Ill. Died Aug. 6, 1974.

AMSLER, HENRY MOORE, business exec., banker; b. Marienville, Pa., Mar. 20, 1896; s. Cornelius Washington and Ida (Moore) A.; student Wharton Sch., U. Pa., 1914; m. Jean Wilson, Sept. 27, 1918 (dec. 1964); children—Henry C., E. Wilson; m. 2d, Hannah Goheen, Aug. 1967. Supt., dir., pres. major owner Hamler Coal Co., Inc. and affiliated cos., Calrion, Pa., 1919-37; dir. First Seneca Bank & Trust Co., Oil City, Pa., 1932—, chmn. adv. bd. Clarion br. office; officer, pres., dir. Alta Co., Inc., Clarion; owner Amsler Co., Clarion; sr. partner Fishwell Co., Clarion, H & H Co., St. Petersburg, Fla. Mem. Clarion Town Council, 1930-42, pres., 1934-42. Trustee Polk State Sch., 1938-42, Clarion State Coll., 1946-58. Served as lt. comdr. USCGR World War II; sr. officer Gulf Coast Dist., USCG Aux., 1940-46. Mem. U.S., St. Petersburg (comdr. 1944-46), power squadrons, Delta Phi Delta, Phi Sigma Kappa. Presbyn. (trustee). Mason. Clubs: St. Petersburg (Fla.); Yacht; Oil City; Classic Car Club Am.; Packard International; Auburn Cord Duesenberg. Home: St. Petersburg, FLa. Died Jan. 26, 1975.

ANCERL, KAREL, conductor; b. Tucapy, Czechoslovakia, Apr. 11, 1908; s. Leopold and Ida (Ppreisz) A.; student master class composition and conducting, Conservatoire Music, Prague; m. Hana Glucklich, Oct. 5, 1946; children—George, Ivan. Condr., Liberated Theatre, Prague, 1930-33, Czechoslovakia Radio, 1933-39, Opera of 5th May, Prague, 1946-49; head condr. Czech Philharmonic Orch., 1950-68; chief condr. Toronto Symphony, from 1969; prof. conducting class Acad. Music, Prague, from 1949; guest condr., Europe, U.S., Asia, Australia. Recipient Laureate of State prize Czechoslovakia; 1958; Artist of Merit, 1965; Nat. Artist, 1967. Home: Toronto, Ont., Canada. Died July 3, 1973.

ANDERSEN, ANDREAS STORRS, educator, artist; b. Chgo., Oct. 6, 1908; s. Arthur Olaf and Mary (Storrs) A.; student Carnegie Inst. Tech., 1928-30, Acad. di Belli Arti, Rome, Italy, 1930-31. Art Inst. Chgo., 1931-34; diploma Brit. Acad. Fine Arts, Rome, 1931; m. Louise

Susan Spaulding, Oct. 6, 1934; children—Frances Stinson, Mary Ader. Mem. faculty U. Ariz., 1935-61, prof. art, head dept., 1940-61, dir. univ. art gallery, 1949-56; dir. Otis Art Inst. of Los Angeles County, 1961-74, pres., 1968-74; co-dir. Southwestern Indian Art Project, 1960-61; paintings exhibited Met. Mus. Art, Whitney Mus. Art, Cocoran Gallery Art, M.H. De Young Meml. Mus.; represented in permanent collections IBM Corp., U. Ariz., pvt. collections. Pres. emeritus Tucson Art Center. Fellow Royal Soc. Arts (London); mem. Nat. Assn. Schs. Art (dir. 1967-71), Am. Assn. U. Profs., Beta Theta Pi. Episcopalian. Art editor: Signs and Symbols in Christian Art, 1954. Home: Los Angeles, Cal. Died Oct. 28, 1974; buried Columbarium of St. Philips, Tucson, Ariz.

ANDERSON, ALAN ROSS, educator; b. Portland, Ore., Apr. 11, 1925; s. Ross E. and Selma (Wetteland) A.; B.A., Yale, 1950, Ph.D., 1955; M.Litt., Cambridge (Eng.) U., 1952; m. Carolyn Reed Willson, June 11, 1949; children—Nicholas George, Jeffrey Joseph, Elizabeth Grace, Timothy John. Faculty, Dartmouth Coll., 1954-55; faculty Yale, 1955-64, prof., 1962-64; Fulbright Lectr. U. Manchester, 1964-65; prof. U. Pitts., 1965-73, chmn. dept. philosophy, 1967-70. Dir. Basic Edn., Inc., 1958-64. Mem. selection com. Woodrow Wilson Fellowship Found., 1961-64, Am. Council Learned Socs., 1970-73. Served with Signal Corps, AUS, 1943-46. Mem. Kingsley Trust Assn., Am. Philos. Assn. (bd. officers 1970), Symbolic Logic, Mind Assn., Phi Beta Kappa, Chi Delta Theta. Author: Minds and Machines; Philosophical Problems; Entailment. Contbr. articles to profl. jours. Home: Pittsburgh, Pa. Died Dec. 5, 1973.

ANDERSON, ALVIN GEORGE, educator; b. Duluth, Minn., Apr. 21, 1911; s. August and Sigrid (Fogelberg) A.; B.C.E. with distinction, U. Minn., 1933, M.S., 1935, Ph.D., 1950; m. Dorothy Erickson, July 9, 1938 (dec. 1955); children—Shirley D. (Mrs. Donald H. Mills), Judith K. (Mrs. Ronald H. Spielbauer), Gail D. (Mrs. Craig J. Bagenstos); m. 2d, Geneva Nygren, Aug. 2, 1958. Asso. hydraulic engr. Dept. Agr., 1938-43; tech. aid OSRD, 1943-45; mem. faculty U. Minn., 1945—, prof. civil engring., 1959—, dir. St. Anthony Falls Hydraulic Lab., 1974-75; cons. in field, 1952-75. Fellow Am. Soc. C.E. (Norman medal 1961, Stevens award 1965); mem. Internat. Assn. Hydraulic Research, Am. Water Resources Assn., Soc. Engring. Edn., Sigma Xi, Tau Beta Pi. Lutheran. Author research papers on air entrainment, sediment transp., hydraulic structures. Home: Minneapolis, Minn. Died July 1, 1975; buried Lakewood Cemetery, Mpls.

ANDERSON, ANTON BENNETT, naval officer; b. Stanhope, N.J., Oct. 28, 1888; s. Martin and Louise (Benson) A.; B.S., U.S. Naval Acad., 1912; grad. Army Indsl. Coll., 1938; m. Miriam Thompson, Feb. 18, 1916; children—Frank C., Alister C., Ida L. (Mrs. J. M. Evans). Commd. ensign U.S. Navy, 1912, advanced through grades to rear adm., 1947; served aboard battleships and gunboat, 1912-17; flag lt., 1919; flag sec., 1922-24; instr. U.S. Naval Acad., 1924-26; comdr. U.S.S. Mervine, 1926-29; comdg. officer, Aviation Mechanics Sch., Great Lakes, Ill., 1929-31; gunnery officer, U.S.S. Lexington, 1931-33; Naval Acad., instr., 1933-36; comdr. destroyer div., Asiatic sta., 1936-38; with Office of Naval Operations, U.S. Navy Dept., 1938-42; chief of staff, amphibious force, South Pacific, 1943; comdr. transport div., 1943-44; pres., Bd. of Rev., Discharges and Dismissals, U.S. Navy Dept., 1945-46; ret. from active service, Jan. 1, 1947. Awarded spl. letter of commendation, Silver Star. Mem. U.S. Naval Inst. (sec.-treas., 1933-36), U.S. Naval Acad. Grads. Assn., Nat. Geog. Soc., Retired Officers Assn. Club: Army and Navy (Washington). Home: La Jolla Cal. Died Feb. 7, 1974.

ANDERSON, AXEL GORDON, ret. educator; b. Chgo., Dec. 24, 1904; s. Axel Walter and Wilma Adolphina (Oberg) A.; D.D.S., Loyola U., Chgo., 1927; m. Edith Catherine Hein, Nov. 28, 1928 (dec. 1959); children—Charles Peter, David John; m. 2d, Gladys A. Turley, Oct. 27, 1962; stepchildren—Ronald L. Turley, Thomas A. Turley, Jean C. Turley. Pvt. practice dentistry, Hinsdale, Ill., 1927-42; oral surgeon VA Hosp., Hines, Ill., 1946-57; lectr. clinician to med. and dental socs., 1946-57; prof. oral and maxillofacial surgery, head dept. U. Ill. Coll. Dentistry, 1957-73, clin. prof. surgery Coll. Medicine, 1957-73, dir. Hosp. Oral Surgery, 1957-73; cons. Hinsdale Hosp., West Side VA Hosp., Chgo., 1967-74. Served to lt. comdr. Dental Corps. USNR, World War II. Diplomate Am. Bd. Oral Surgery. Fellow Am. Coll. Dentists; mem. Am., Ill. dental assns., Chgo. Dental Soc., Chgo. Soc. Oral Surgeons, Omicron Kappa Upsilon, Delta Sigma Delta. Home: Hindsdale Ill. Died Mar. 12, 1974.

ANDERSON, CARL HAROLD, custom house broker; b. Boise, Ida., June 6, 1926; s. Carl Oscar Harold and Wanda Mae (Johnson) A.; B.A., Ida U., 1947; m. Hollis Patigian, Sept. 28, 1957; 1 dau., Stacie K. (Mrs. Robert H. Nelson). Pres., W.J. Byrnes & Co., Inc., air div. W.J. Byrnes, San Francisco, 1966-74. Mem. World Trade Club, Custon House Brokers Assn., San Francisco Press Club, San Francisco Comml. Club, Screen Actors Guild. Home: Sausalito, Cal. Died Apr. 10, 1974.

ANDERSON, CHARLES JOSEPH, educator; b. Thomson, Minn., Aug. 9, 1880; s. Carles and Caroline A.; grad. State Normal Sch., Superior, Wis., 1903; Ph.B., U. of Wis., 1913, Ph.M., 1927; post-grad. work, U. of Chicago; LL.D., Ripon Coll., 1939; m. Ada B. Maricle, June 24, 1908; 1 son, John Eugene. Prin. high sch., Galesville, Wis., 1912-15; supt. schs. Stoughton, Wis., 1915-21; asst. state supt. pub. instr., Wis., 1921-26; asso. prof. edn., U. of Wis., 1926-28, dir. Sch. of Edn., 1928-30, dean 1930-47, emeritus dean from 1947, U. of Wis. Private, vols., Spanish-American War, 1898-99. Mem. N.E. A., Wisconsin State Teachers' Association (pres. 1925), Phi Delta Kappa, Phi Kappa Phi. Republican. Conglist. Club: University. Author: (with Isobel Davidson), The Lincoln Readers, 1921-25; (with others) Visiting the Teacher at Work, 1925; Reading Objectives, 1925. Co-author: The Triangle Arithmetics, 1927; The Supervision of Rural Schools, 1932; My Government, 1935; The New Curriculum Arithmetics, 1936. Home: Madison, Wis.†

ANDERSON, CLINTON PRESBA, senator; b. Centerville, S.D., Oct. 23, 1895; s. Andrew Jay and Hattie Belle (Presba) A.; student Dakota Wesleyan U., 1913-15, U. Mich., 1915-16; L.H.D. (hon.), Dakota Weslyan U., 1933; D.Agr., N.M. Coll. Agr. and Mechanic Arts, 1946; LL.D., U. Mich., St. Lawrence U., 1946, Mo. Valley Coll., 1949, U. Alaska, 1965; m. Henrietta McCartney, June 22, 1921; children—Sherburne Presba, Nancy (Mrs. Ben L. Roberts). Reporter, editor, Albuquerque, 1918-22; mgr. ins. dept. Loan & Mortgage Co., 1922-24; owner ins. agy., Albuquerque, 1925-63. Treas., State of N.M., 1933-34; mem. 77th to 79th U.S. congresses from N.M. at large; sec. U.S. Dept. Agr., 1945-48; U.S. senator from N.M., 1949-73. Mem. Sears-Roebuck Found. Mem. Delta Theta Phi. Democrat. Presbyn. Mason, Elk, Rotarian (pres. Rotary Internat. 1932-33). Home: Albuquerque, N.M., Died Nov. 11, 1975.

ANDERSON, DILLON, lawyer; b. McKinney, Tex., July 14, 1906; s. Joseph and Elizabeth (Dillon) A.; B.S., U. Okla., 1928; LL.B., Yale, 1929; LL.D., Tex. Christian U., 1954, Allegheny Coll., 1956; m. Lena Carter Carroll, May 30, 1931; children—Susan (Mrs. Charles A. Whiteford, Jr.), Lena (Mrs. Jerry Van Kyle), and Elizabeth (Mrs. Ronald E. Martin). Admitted to Tex. bar, 1929; with firm Baker and Botts, (formerly Baker, Botts, Parker & Garwood), Houston, from 1929, partner from 1940; spl. asst. to Pres. U.S. for nat. security affairs, 1955-56; dir. Westinghouse Electric Corp., Champion Internat., also Fed. Dept. Stores, Inc., Monsanto Co.; cons. Nat. Security council, 1953-60. Trustee Schlumberger Found., Foley Found., Carnegie Endowment Internat. Peace, The Brookings Instn. Mem. U.S. delegation to Summit Conf. at Geneva, 1955. Served to col. U.S. Army, 1942-45. Decorated Legion of Merit, Army Commendation Ribbon. Fellow Am. Acad. Arts and Scis.; mem. Council Fgn. Relations, Inc., Fgn. Policy Assn. (dir. 1966-72), World Affairs Council Houston (adv. bd.), Houston Com. Fgn. Relations (pres. 1950-51), Am. Bar Assn., Am. Law Inst. (council), Tex. Inst. Letters, Tex. Philos. Soc. (pres. 1973). Clubs: Houston Country (pres., dir. 1948-49), Eagle Lake Rod and Gun (Houston); Bayou, Texas, Metropolitan (Washington); Chevy Chase (Bethesda, Md.); The Brook (N.Y.C.). Author: I and Claudie, 1951; Claudie's Kinfolks, 1954; The Billingsley Papers, 1961. Home: Houston Tex. Died Jan. 1974.

ANDERSON, EVA GREENSLIT (MRS. LEONARD O. ANDERSON), journalist, educator, author; b. Surprise, Neb.; d. Walter Henry and Kate (Ammerman) Greenslit; B.A., Neb. Wesleyan U., 1910; M.A., U. Wash., 1926, Ph.D., 1937; postgrad. Columbia U.; m. Leonard O. Anderson, June 10, 1915 (dec. Oct. 1949). Tchr., Neb. and Wash. pub. schs., 1910-15, supt. Douglas County Schs., 1919-21; head English dept. Wenatchee (Wash.) High Sch., 1921-25, supt., girls adviser, 1925-34; state supr. adult edn. Wash. State Dept. Edn., 1934-37; writer, 1937-43; tchr. Chelan (Wash.) Pub. Schs., 1943-49, also regional dir. adult edn. N.W. div. VIII of N.E.A., 1946-47; mem Wash. Ho of Reps., 1949-61; feature writer Wenatchee Daily World from 1961. N.E.A. del. to World Conf. Educators, Edinburgh, Scotland, 1925; pres. Wash. Edn. Assn., 1926-27; faculty U. Ore., summer 1927. Mem. Wash. Gov.'s Com. to Commemorate 1776 Am. Revolution. Bd. curators Wash, State Hist. Soc., also del. to 300th Anniversary Hudson's Bay Exploration, London, 1970; mem. bd. Internat. Christian U., Tokyo; bd. regents U. Wash., 1944-46. Named Wash. State Woman of Year, State Bus. and Profl. Women, 1949; Outstanding Alumna, Neb. Wesleyan U., 1959, Distinguished Citizen, Chelan C. of C., Wenatchee Pioneer Honor Citizen, 1968; recipient award Am. Assn. State and Local History, 1954, pioneer writers' plaque Wash. State Press Women, 1965, author plaque Gov. Dan Evans, 1966, awards for reporting Wash. State Press, 1966-67, Pioneer award Wenatchee YMCA, 1972, also for Service to Youth ann. award, 1972. Mem. Central Wash. Heritage Soc. (sec.), Am. Pen Women, Wash. State Press Women (award 1968), Grange, Am. Assn. U. Women, Phi Lambda Theta, Phi Delta Nu, Alpha Iota, Delta Kappa Gamma (state founder). Republican. Methodist. Club: Soroptomist (Wenatchee). Author: Dog Team Doctor, 1940; Chief Seattle, 1943; A Child's Story of Washington, 1938; (with Dean Collins) Oregon Stories, rev. 1967; The Wenatchee Kid, 1947; George Adams, Indian Legislator, 1956; The Spirit of the Big Bend, 1955; An Orchid for Grandma Little, 1950; Charley Wright-True Pioneer, 1950; E.O. Pybus, Ingenious Pioneer, 1954; Charles Keiser-With a Yen for Work, 1954; Varied and Colorful Career of Jack Rogers, 1947; Dr. Isaac Hubbard-Pioneer Doctor, 1956; Touring Ten Countries of Europe, 1957; Inside-Outside the Iron Curtain, 1958; Inside-Outside Africa, 1960; Round the World, 1962; Down Mexico Way, 1964; Inside-Outside South America, 1966; On to Alaska, 1967; South Pacific Safari, 1968; Europe Again, 1971. Contbr. articles to newspapers and mags. Home: Wenatchee, Wash. Died Dec. 23, 1972.

ANDERSON, FRANK MALEY, historian; b. Omaha, Neb., Feb. 3, 1871; s. Moses Troyer and Ruth Amanda (Thornburg) A.; B.A., U. Minn., 1894, M.A., 1896; studied Harvard, 1896-97; Paris, 1909, 1923; m. Mary Gertrude Steele, Sept. 3, 1898; (died June 1939); children—Troyer Steele (dec.), Gaylord West; m. 2d, Mary Maud Case, Sept. 14, 1944. Instr. history, 1895-96, 1897-98; asst. prof. U. Minn., 1898-1905, prof. 1905-14; prof. history, Dartmouth Coll., 1914-41; later emeritus. Specialist on diplomatic history, 1918, Am. Commn. to Negotiate Peace, Paris, 1919; mem. army ednl. corps, 1919. Mem. exec. com. Mpls. Voters' League, 1908-12, Mpls. Charter Commn., 1911-14. Recipient: Achievement Award, U. Minn., 1953. Democrat. Unitarian. Mem. Am., Miss. Valley hist. assns., Am. Assn. U. Profs., (mem. exec. council 1917-20), Lincoln Group (Boston), Beta Theta Pi, Phi Betta Kappa. Author: Outlines and Documents of English Constitutional History during the Middle Ages, 1895 (joint author); Constitutions and Documents Illustrative of the History of France, 1789-1902, 1904, 2d edit. 1789-1907), 1908; Handbook of the Diplomatic History of Europe, Asia, and Africa, 1870-1914 (joint author); The Mystery of a Public Man, an historical detective story, 1948. Contbr. to periodicals on hist. and polit. subjects. Address: St. Petersburg, Fla.†

ANDERSON, GEORGE LAVERNE, educator; b. Blue Rapids, Kan., Feb. 27, 1905; s. Anders and Mary (Pitman) A.; A.B., U. Kan., 1926, A.M., 1931; Ph.D., U. Ill., 1933; m. Caroline Miek, June 8, 1928; children—Marianne, James LaVerne. Tchr., adminstr. Kan. Pub. Schs., 1926-30; mem. faculty Colo. Coll., 1934-45, No. Mont. Coll., summer 1934, N.M. Highlands U., summers 1939, 40, 42; asso. prof. history U. Kan., 1945-49, prof. history, 1949-71, chmn. dept., 1946-68. Mem. Am., So., Western hist. assns., Orgn. Am. Historians, Agrl. Hist. Soc., Phi Beta Kappa. Lutheran. Author: General William J. Palmer-A Decade of Colorado Railroad Building, 1870-1880, 1936; Kansas West, 1963; The Widening Stream: The History of the Exchange National Bank of Atchison; Variations on a Theme: History as Knowledge of the Past Essays on the History of Banking, Essays on Public Lands; Essays on Railroads in Kansas and Colorado. Editor: Issues and Conflicts: Studies in Twentieth Century American Diplomacy, 1959. Contbr. articles to profl. jours. Home: Lawrence, Kan. Died May 5, 1971.

ANDERSON, JOHN QUNICY, educator; b. Wheeler, Tex., May 30, 1916; s. Albert Slayton and Emily (Grant) A.; B.A., Okla. State U., 1939; M.A., La. State U., 1948; Ph.D., U.N.C., 1952; m. Marie Loraine Epps, Aug. 24, 1946. Asst. prof. McNeese State Coll., 1952-53; faculty Tex. A. and M. U., College Station, 1953-66, prof. English, 1959-66, head dept., 1962-66; prof. English, U. Houston, 1966-74, prof. emeritus, 1974-75. Served to capt. AUS, 1940-46. Decorated French Medaille de la Reconnaissance. Fellow Am. Studies Assn. Tex. (pres. 1963-64), mem. Modern Lang. Assn., S. Central Modern Lang. Assn., Am. Studies Assn. (exec. council 1964-67), Southwestern (editor 1970—), Western Am. lit. assns., Am., Tex. (pres. 1955-56) folklore socs. Author: Brokenburn: The Journal of Kate Stone, 1955; A Texas Surgeon in the C.S.A., 1957; Louisiana Swamp Doctor: The Life and Writings of Henry Clay Lewis, 1962; Tales of Frontier Texas, 1966; Campaigning with Parsons' Texas Cavalry, C.S.A., 1967; John C. Duval, First Texas Man of Letters, 1967; With the Bark On: Popular Humor of the Old South, 1967; Texas Folk Medicine, 1970; The Liberating Gods: Emerson on Poets and Poetry, 1971. Mem. editorial bd. Miss. Quar., 1963-75, Computer Studies in Verbal Behavior and the Humanities, 1966-75, Paisano Books, Tex. Folklore Soc., 1968-75. Contbr. numerous articles to profl. jours. Home: Houston, Tex., Died Feb. 19, 1975.

ANDERSON, JOHN W(ILLIAM), Am. merchant marine officer; b. Jersey City, Feb. 14, 1899; graduated N.Y. State Maritime Coll., 1915; m. Mary Beard; 1 son, Charles. Cadet officer American Lines, 1916-17; served as officer U.S.N., assigned to transport ships, World War I, advancing to rank of second officer of the Westhampton, operated by U.S. Army; ship master, with United States Lines, from 1925; comd. motership, John Ericsson, troop transport, 1942-47, American Merchant, 1947-48, Washington, 1948-49 (superliner) America, 1949-52, (superliner) United States, from 1952; commodore United States Lines fleet, from May 1953. Made mem. Quarter Century Club of United States Lines, 1950; awarded scroll of honor by

Downtown Manhattan Assn. for record-breaking run of liner, United States, 1952. Home: Tenafly, N.J., Died Feb. 15, 1976.

ANDERSON, LEE WILLIAM, educator; b. West Palm Beach, Fla., Nov. 15, 1926; s. Hjalmer Lawrence and Lillian (Betzinger) A.; B.A., Reed Coll., 1952; M.S., Tulane U., 1955, Ph.D., 1956; m. Jacqueline Downing, Apr. 6, 1951; children—Kimberly, Alan, Lars. Asst. prof. U. Ore., 1956-60; asso. prof. U. Ga., 1960-62; asso. prof. Pa. State U., 1962-64, prof. math., from 1964. Math. cons. Naval Ordnance Testing Sta., China Lake, Cal., 1959. Served with USNR, 1944-46. Republican. Episcopalian. Elk. Contbr. sects. to text books, articles to math. jours. Home: State College, Pa. Died Feb. 5, 1973.

ANDERSON, LEROY, composer, conductor; b. Cambridge, Mass., June 29, 1908; s. Brewer A. and Anna M. (Johnson) A.; A.B., Harvard, 1929, M.A., 1930, postgrad., 1930-34; m. Eleanor Jane Firke, Oct. 31, 1942; children—Jane M., Eric R., Rolf F., Kurt A. Tutor div. music Radcliffe Coll., 1930-32; music dir. Harvard Band, 1932-35; organist, choirmaster East Congl. Ch., Milton, Mass., 1929-35; guest condr. own rec. orch., 1950—; guest condr. many symphony orchs. Served as capt. M.I., AUS, 1942-46, 51-52. Mem. A.S.C.A.P., Dramatists Guild, Am.-Scandinavian Found., Assn. Ex-Mems. Squadron A, Am. Guild Authors and Composers, Phi Beta Kappa. Club: Harvard (Boston). Composer: Jazz Pizzicato, Jazz Legato, The Syncopated Clock, Fiddle- Faddle, Irish Suite, Sleigh Ride, Serenata, A. Trumpeter's Lullaby, The Waltzing Cat, A Christmas Festival, Belle of the Ball, Blue Tango, The Typewriter, Bugler's Holiday, Forgotten Dreams, Clarinet Candy, Home Stretch, Arietta, Balladette, The Golden Years, The Captains and the Kings, and others. Home: Woodbury, Conn. Died May 18, 1975; buried New North Cemetery, Woodbury.

ANDERSON, ROY NELS, univ. prof.; born Denver, June 29, 1902; s. Nels J. and Amanda (Hakinson) A.; A.B., U. of Denver (scholarship 1923-26), 1926; M.A., Columbia (fellowship 1928-29), 1928, Ph.D., 1932; m. Beatrice Marie Ewart, Sept. 10, 1929; children—Barbara McVeigh, Douglas Ewart, David Nels. Dir. employment bur. U. of Denver, 1925-26; dir. vocational guidance and placement YMCA, N.Y. City, 1926-27; research asst. in guidance and personnel Teachers Coll., Columbia, 1927-29, asso. in guidance and personnel, 1929-37, asst. prof. edn., 1937-43; dir. ednl. training program S.H. Kress & Co., N.Y. City, 1943-46; prof. of edn., head department occupational guidance information N.C. State U., University of North Carolina, from 1946, acting dean basic div. N.C. State U., 1948-49; also part time, summer positions. Personnel service committee Nat. Council YMCA, 1938-41, from 1948. Mem. Am. Coll. Personnel Assn. (exec. com.), Am. Assn. U. Profs., A.A.A.S., Am. Psychol. Association (member executive committee 1957-60). National Office Management Assn. (pres. Raleigh, 1952-53) Nat. Vocational Guidance Assn. (treas. 1938-41; v.p. 1949-50; pres. N.Y. City br. 1943-45; pres. N.C. br. 1947-49; professional and life mem.), Nat. Assn. Fgn. Student Advisers (dir. 1954-58), Alpha Kappa Delta, Phi Delta Kappa. Lambda Chi Alpha. Baptist. Mason, Rotarian. Club: Torch. Home: Raleigh, N.C. Died July 16, 1973; interred Hamilton, N.Y.

ANDERSON, WALTER WILLIAMS, ednl. adminstr.; b. Arkansaw, Wis., May 13, 1879; s. Walter H. and Mary Hannah (Plummer) A.; B.S. U. of Nev., 1912; grad. study, summers, U. of Ill., 1922, U. of Wis., 1924; m. Hope Viola Bain, of Golconda, Nev., June 26, 1901; children—Walter Lindley, Harry LeRoy, Dorothy Hope (Mrs. Harry Clinton Duncan). In U.S. Reclamation Service, Truckee-Carson project, 1902-06; with Tonopah (Nev.) Extension Mining Co., 1912-13, West End Consol. Mining Co., Tonopah, 1914; teacher of science, high sch., Tonopah, 1914-16; prin. schs., Dayton, Nev., 1916-18, Ely (Nev.) Mining Sch., 1918-19; mill foreman West End Consol. Mining Co., 1919-21; city supt. schs., Tonopah, 1921-25; in charge mining and milling operations, Masonic and Pine Grove, Nev., 1925-26; state supt. pub. instrn., Nev., from 1927. Republican. Mason, Elk, O.E.S. Home: Carson, Nev.†

ANDERSON, WILLIAM, ret. educator; b. Mpls., Oct. 25, 1888; s. Edward and Maren (Olausen) A.; A.B., U. Minn., 1913; A.M., Harvard, 1914, Ph.D., 1917; m. Morgia DeLaittre Mansur, Dec. 28, 1915; children—Morgia Jeanette (Mrs. Howard Pennlman), Marian Ruth (Mrs. Robert L. Olson). Instr. govt. Harvard, 1915-16; successively instr. polit. sci., asst. prof., asso. prof. and prof. U. Minn., 1916-57, chmn. dept. polit. sci., 1927-32, 35-47, dir. Bur. for Research in Govt., 1919-28. Mem. Social Science Research Council, 1932-36; mem. Council's Com. on Pub. Adminstrn., 1933-45, chmn. 1939-45; chmn. Council's Com. on Gov., 1941-45. Mem. Mpls. Charter Commn., 1926-36, 45-48, Minn. State Planning Bd., 1935-38, Minn. Resources Commn., 1939-43; mem. com. on fed.-state relations Commn. on Orgn. Exec. Br. Govt., 1947-48, Commn. on Intergovtl. Relations, 1953-75. Pres., Mpls. Research Bur. 1941-47. Fellow A.A.A.S.; mem. Am. Polit. Sci. Assn. (1st v.p. 1929, pres. 1942). Am. Soc. Pub. Adminstrn., Am. Assn. U. Profs., Phi Beta Kappa. Author: A History of the Constitution of Minnesota, 1921; City Charter Making in Minnesota, 1922; American City Government, 1925; The Units of Government in the United States, 1934, rev. edit., 1943; Local Government and Finance in Minnesota, 1935; American Government, 1938, rev. edit., 1946; Fundamentals of American Government, 1940; The National Government of the United States, 1946; Federalism and Intergovernmental Relations, 1946; The Nation and the States, Rivals or Partners?, 1955; Intergovernmental Fiscal Relations, 1956; Man's Quest for Political Knowledge: The Study and Teaching of Politics in Ancient Times, 1964. Editor: Local Government in Europe, 1939; Intergovernmental Relations Series, 1950-60. Contbr. to Minn. Law Rev., National Municipal Rev., Am. Polit. Science Rev., others. Home: Minneapolis, Minn. Died May 14, 1975.

ANDREW, EDWIN LEE, advertising exec.; b. Washington, Pa., Oct. 28, 1894; s. Charles Baker and Hanna Jane (Day) A.; B.S., U. Wis., 1916; m. Florence Fleming, Dec. 24, 1917; children—Charles F., Jane (Mrs. Sheldon T. Clark), Elizabeth Lee (Mrs. Robert G. Horton). Asst. gen. advt. mgr. Westinghouse Electric Corp., 1916-27, mgr. sales promotion merchandising div., 1923-27; div. sales mgr. Gen. Cable Corp., 1927-31; sales mgr. Dobeckmun Co., Cleve., 1931-33; account exec. Fuller & Smith & Ross, Inc., 1933-35, v.p., 1935-43, exec. v.p., dir., from 1943, chmn. bd., 1954-59; bd. dirs. Cloyes Gear Works. Trustee of Cleveland Council World Affairs, Friends Cleveland Library. Served as comdg. officer 19th aerial photog. sect., U.S. Army, World War I. Mem. C. of C., Cleve. Advt. Club, Newcomen Soc., Sigma Delta Chi, Eta Kappa Nu, Theta Delta Chi. Clubs: Hermit, Country, Rowfant, Midday (Cleve.). Contbr. to profl. publs. Home: Bridgeport, Conn. Died May 26, 1973.

ANDREWES, SIR WILLIAM (GERRARD), British naval officer; b. Winchester, Eng., Nov. 3, 1899; s. Rev. Canon G.T. and Helen Louisa (Kirby) A.; student Twyford Sch., 1909-12, Royal Naval Coll., Osborne, 1912-14, Dartmouth, 1914-15; m. Frances Audrey Welchman, Feb. 26, 1927; children—Gerrard John Michael, Jennifer Mary. Commd. sub lt., Royal Brit. Navy, 1918, advancing through grades to admiral, 1954; served aboard H.M.S. Canada and destroyers, 1915-19, H.M.S. Walrus, Baltic Campaign, 1919-20; specialized in torpedo, torpedo officer submarine flotilla, destroyer flotilla, cruisers and battleships, Far East, Mediterranean, Atlantic, 1920-32; naval staff coll., sea duty, 1932-38; capt. Imperial Def. Coll., 1938-48; comd. H.M.S. Albatross, 1939; with Joint Planning Staff, 1940-42; comd. H.M.S. Uganda, invasions of Sicily and Italy, 1943-44; planning and staff duties for invasion of Normandy, 1944; planning and staff duties for adminstrn. Brit. Pacific Fleet, 1944-45; comd. H.M.S. Indomitable, 1946; chief of staff to comdr.-in-chief, Portsmouth, 1947; sr. naval directing staff officer Imperial Def. Coll., 1948; second-in-command Far East Sta., 1950; comd. Commonwealth and Allied Naval Forces, also Allied Naval Blockade and Support Forces, Korean War; comdr.-in-chief Am. and B.W.I. Sta., 1951-53; deputy supreme allied comdr. Atlantic, 1952-53; became pres. Royal Naval Coll. Greenwich, 1954; ret. from Royal Navy, 1957. Mem. bd. dirs. John I. Thorneycroft Ltd. (shipbuilders), from 1957. Decorated Knight Comdr. of Brit. Empire, Companion of Bath, Companion Distinguished Service Order (Eng.); Legion of Merit, Silver Star (U.S.); Greek War Cross; Knight Comdr. Royal Order of Sword (Sweden); also numerous war and campaign medals. Fellow Instn. Elec. Engrs. London. Clubs: United Service, Pall Mall (London, Eng.). Home: Winchester, Hampshire, Eng. Died Nov. 21, 1974; buried Chilcomb, near Winchester, Hampshire, Eng.

ANDREWS, CHARLTON, author; b. Connersville, Ind., Feb. 1, 1878; s. A.M. and Marie Louise (Newland) A.; Ph.B., DePauw U., Ind., 1898; A.M., Harvard, 1911; m. Maude Cory Smolley, of Fairfield, Ind., May 15, 1901; m. 2d, Azlin Shirley, of Muncie, Ind., Sept. 16, 1925. In newspaper work, Paris, 1898-99, Indianapolis, 1902-04; prin. High Sch., W. Lebanon, Ind., 1904-05; teacher High Sch., LaFayette, Ind., 1905; instr., later asst. prof., State Coll. of Wash., 1906-07; head dept. English, State Normal Sch., Valley City, N.D., 1907-14; editorial staff, New York Tribune, 1914; instructor, New York University and lecturer Brooklyn Polytechnic Institute, 1914-17 teacher of English. Stuyvesant High Sch., New York City, 1915-21; and from 1928. Member Delta Tau Delta. Author: A Parfit Gentil Knight, 1901; The Interrupted Revels, 1910; The Drama To-Day, 1913; His Majesty the Fool (play, prod. at Little Theatre, Phila., 1913); The Technique of Play Writing, 1915; The Torches, play from the French, 1917; Ladies' Night (with Avery Hopwood), 1920; Bluebeard's Eighth Wife, adaptation from the French, 1921; The Dollar Daddy (from the Hungarian), 1922; Sam Abramovitch (from the French), 1926; The Lady of Gestures, 1926; Get Me in the Movies (with Philip Dunning), 1927; The Golden Age (with Lester Lonergan), 1928; Fioretta (with Earl Carroll), 1929; Don't Believe It, 1930; He Got the Job, 1932; The Butterfly Murder, 1932; Chin-Music, 1935; A Night at Valley Forge, 1935; The Affair of the Malacca Stick, 1936; The Affair of the Syrian Dagger, 1937; Murder at the Class Reunion, 1938. Contbr. to mags. Deceased.†

ANDREWS, DONALD HATCH, chemist; b. Southington, Conn., June 11, 1898; s. Russell Gad and Mary Boies (Hatch) A.; grad. Phillips Acad., Andover, Mass., 1916; B.A., Yale, 1920, Ph.D., 1923; m. Josephine Adair Veeder, June 20, 1939 (div. 1950); m. 2d, Elizabeth Howland, Sept. 23, 1950; 1 son, Donald Hatch. Research asst. in chemistry, Yale, 1923; nat. research fellow U. Cal. at Berkeley, 1924-25; internat. research fellow U. Leiden, 1925-26; research fellow Bartol Research Found., 1926-27; with Johns Hopkins U., Balt., from 1927, prof. chemistry, from 1930, chmn. dept., dir. chem. laboratory, 1936-44, dir. Cryogeny Lab., 1943-48. B. N. Baker prof. chemistry, 1957-63, prof. emeritus, from 1963; prof. chemistry Fla. Atlantic U., Boca Raton, 1963-64, distinguished prof. chemistry, 1964-67, distinguished prof. emeritus, from 1967. Mem. div. chemistry NRC, 1933; chmn. Calorimetry Conf., 1957-58. Mem. 1st sci. commn. L'Inst. Internationale de Froid. Fellow Royal Chem. Soc. (Eng.), N.Y. Acad. Scis., A.A.A.S., Am. Philos. Soc., mem. Am. Chem. Soc. (sec. div. phys. and inorganic chemistry, 1932, vice chmn., 1933, chmn. 1934), Am. Math. Soc., Am. Math. Assn., Am. Phys. Soc., Philosophy of Sci. Assn., Brit. Assn. Philosophy of Sci., Phi Beta Kappa, Sigma Xi. Republican. Episcopalian. Club: Appalachian Mountain. Author: Fundamental Chemistry, 1962; Quimica Fundamental, 1964; Symphony of Life, 1967; Quimica Geral., 1968; Notions Fondamentales de Chimie 1968; Introductory Physical Chemistry, 1970. Home: Boca Raton, Fla. Died June 3, 1973.

ANDREWS, JOHN WILLIAMS, writer, editor, lawyer; b. Bryn Mawr, Pa., Nov. 10, 1898; s. Charles McLean and Evangeline (Walker) A.; ed. Taft Sch., Watertown, Conn.; A.B., Yale, 1920, J.D., 1926; m. Elizabeth Robert, July 14, 1934 (div. 1953); 1 son, John Douglas Walker; m. 2d, Miriam Benton Wise, Oct. 30, 1953. Mgr. Chung Mei News Agency, Internat. News corr., Peking, China, 1921-22; legislative corr. New Haven (Conn.) Journal Courier, 1922-23; admitted to N.Y. State bar, 1927, practiced with firm Root, Clark, Buckner & Ballatine, N. Y. City, 1926-32; free-lance writer since 1932; asso. with history dept. Yale, 1938-40, special instr. honor students in thesis writing; asst. to adminstr. Conn. State Defense Council, 1940-42; chief Fed. State Relations Sect., U.S. Dept. Justice, Washington, 1942-48; adminstrv. vice chmn. Nat. Conf. on Prevention and Control of Juvenile Delinquency, 1947-48; trial atty., Anti-Trust Division Dept. Justice, Washington, 1948-50; cons. N.P.A. 1952; with Hill & Knowlton, Inc., pub. relations council 1952-53; pres. Andrews Assos., Inc., 1954-62; pres. Lit. publs. Found., Boston. Dir. Cooper Hill Writers' Conference, East Dover, Vermont. Served as 2d lt. Army Air Service, World War I. Co-recipient Robert Frost Narrative Poetry award, 1963. Fellow Timothy Dwight Coll. (Yale U.), 1938-40. Vice chmn. and mem. bd. trustees Lingnan U., Canton, China. Vice pres. and mem. bd. dirs. Washington Housing Assn., 1947-52, pres., 1952; dir. Washington Inst. Mental Hygiene, 1951-52. Member Poetry Soc. Am., Catholic Poetry Soc. of Am., Alpha Delta Phi, Wolf's Head. Clubs: Aviation Country of Long Island; Elizabethan (Yale U.); Cosmos (Washington); Rowfant (Cleve.); Yale (N.Y.C.). Author: History of the Founding of Wolf's Head, 1934; Prelude to "Icaros." 1936; Georgia Transport (verse play for radio), 1938; A Ballad of Channel Crossings, 1940; First Flight, the Story of the Wright Brothers at Kitty Hawk, N.C.; Hill Country North, a Vermont Cycle, 1965; A.D. Twenty-One Hundred, A Narrative of Space, Legends of Flight, Triptych for the Atomic Age. Editor-in-chief Poet Lore. Editor St. Lawrence Sea Way Fact Sheet, 1958-61. Contbr. articles and poems to various publs. Home: Westport, Conn. Died Apr. 1975.

ANDREWS, MARIE SCHERER, nursing educator; b. Boston, Sept. 12, 1914; d. William Francis and Elizabeth Theresa (Fitzgerald) Scherer; R.N., Mass. Gen. Hosp., 1936; student Simmons Coll., Boston, 1937-39; B.S. in Edn., Boston U., 1941, M.S., 1949, fellow Sch. Nursing, 1947-49; m. Joseph William Andrews, Feb. 20, 1943; 1 son, William Richard. Mem. staff Mass. Gen. Hosp. and Mass. Eye and Ear Infirmary, 1936-41, supr., instr. nursing and nursing edn., 1937-41, pvt. duty nurse, 1941-42; pub. health nurse, summer 1941; part-time instr. nursing Bouve Sch. Phys. Therapy, Tufts U., 1941-44; instr. nursing supr. field practice and teaching Boston U. Sch. Nursing, 1943-48; mem. faculty Boston Coll. Sch. Nursing, from 1948, prof. nursing edn., from 1960. Mem. Watertown (Mass.) Bd. Health, from 1956, sec., 1956-58, chmn., 1958-62; chmn. nursing edn. com. Nat. Found. Infantile Paralysis, from 1956; civilian cons. to surgeon gen. U.S. Navy, 1962-70; lectr. Walter Reed Army Hosp., 1962-64; civilian cons. Murphy Army Hosp., from 1944; clin. cons. VA Hosps., from 1956; cons. to trustees Boston City Hosp., from 1962; tech. cons. Mass. State Hosp. Sch., Canton, from 1952; cons. Nat. Soc. Prevention Blindness, from 1967; cons. schs. nursing Peter Bent Brigham, Worchester City, Cambridge-Mt. Auburn, New Eng. Bapt. hosps.; mem. Mass. Bd. Registration in Nursing, from 1970. Trustee Met. State Hosp., Boston, 1963-70; bd. dirs. Mass. Mental Health Center Region III, from 1971. Recipient citation Nat. Found. Infantile Paralysis, 1950-59; named Nurse of Year, Archdiocesan Council Catholic Nurses, Boston, 1960; recipient 150th Anniversary medal and citation Mass. Gen. Hosp., 1961; 25th Anniversary Alumnae award Boston Coll.

Sch. Nursing, 1972. Mem. Am., Mass. (pres. 1958-62, bd. dirs. from 1962) nurses assns., Nat. League Nursing, A.R.C. Nurses Assn., Northeastern Assn., Bds. of Health, Boston U., Mass. Gen. Hosp. (bd. dirs.) alumni assns., Nat. Council Cath. Nurses, Mass. Cath. Women's Guild, Mass. Heart Assn. (mem. exec. com from 1967, chmn. profl. edn. com.), League Cath. Women, Sienna Soc. (hon.), Sigma Theta Tau. Contbr. articles to profl. jours. Co-editor Cardio-vascular Nursing, 1963-70; 1st editor Am. Heart Nursing Jour., 1964-70. Home: Watertown, Mass. Died Apr. 14, 1973; interred St. Patrick's Cemetery, Watertown, Mass.

ANDREWS, MARSHALL, operations analyst; born Memphis, Tenn., June 15, 1899; s. Daniel Marshall and Adeline Baker (Van Court) A.; student Ala. Poly. Inst., 1917, 1919-20; m. Cora Wells Means, June 21, 1926; children—Cora, Adeline, Marshall; m. 2d, Patricia Wilson Angelo. Reporter, editor newspapers and press services in Midwest and South, 1920-37; aviation editor Washington Post, 1928-31; mil. writer, 1939-50; corr., Washington, from 1928; operations analyst Johns Hopkins Univ. Served as pvt. to sgt., U.S.A.S., 1917-19; 2d lt. Air Corps Res., 1930-35; served as 1st lt. to maj., inf. AUS, 1943-46. Mem. Am. Hist. Assn., Co. Mil. Collectors and Historians. Author: Our New Army, 1942; Disaster Through Air Power, 1950. Home: Sterling, VA. Died Aug. 1, 1973.

ANDRIC, IVO, novelist; b. 1892; ed. univs. Zagreb, Vienna, Cracow; Doctorate in Philosophy, Graz U. Former mem. Young Bosnia, Yugoslav revolutionary nat. movement; mem. Diplomatic Service, World War I to World War II, ambassador to Berlin at outbreak World War II; writer numerous books on history and conditions of Bosnia and the struggle of the Serbian people against Turkish occupation. Recipient the Nobel prize for literature in 1961. Mem. Serbian Acad. Belgrade, Yugoslav Acad. Zagreb, Slovenian Acad. Ljubljana. Author: The Spinster (English transl. The Woman from Sarajevo), 1965; Bosnian Story, English transl., 1959, Bridge on the Drina, English transl., 1959, Devil's Yard, English transl., 1962, The Vizier's Elephant, English transl., 1962, The Pasha's Concubine and Other Tales, English transl., 1968, others. Address: Belgrade, Yugoslavia. Died Mar. 13, 1975.

ANGEL, FRANZ, educator; b. Urfahr-Linz/Donau, Austria, Jan. 1, 1887; s. Franz and Anna Maria (Palmy) A.; Ph.D., U. Graz, 1909, dozent mineralogy, 1920; also studies U. Vienna; m. Johanna Zangger, Nov. 11, 1911; 1 son, Harold. Prof. natural history, math., physics Higher Sch., Austria, 1909-31; asst. U. Graz, 1910-11, dozent, 1920-25, extraordinary prof., 1925-31, ordinary prof., dir. inst., 1931-48; expert mineralogy and potrography Austro-Am. Magnesit A.G. Mem. Geol. Assn. U.S.A., Natural Sci. Assn. Sierra and Carpathia; corr. mem. Austrian Acad. Scis. Contbr. articles to profl. jours. Address: Graz, Austria. Deceased.

ANGELL, EMMETT DUNN, physician, writer; b. Mooers, N.Y., Apr. 25, 1879; s. Richard H. and Mary Anne Jeanette (Dunn) A.; study Springfield (Mass.) Y.M.C.A. Coll., 1899, Harvard Summer Sch. Physical Edn., 1903, Yale Summer Sch. Physical Edn., 1905; M.D., Marquette U., Milwaukee, Wis., 1916, B.S., 1917; hon. diploma, Battle Creek Normal Sch., 1913; m. Rose Zander, of Mishicot, Wis., Aug. 12, 1905; children—Ralph, Allen, Emmett, Robert, Caroline, Frances. Physical dir. State Normal Sch., Plattsburg, N.Y., 1901-03; instr. in physical edn., U. of Wis., 1903-06, asst. prof., 1906-08; prof. physical edn. and hygiene, Ore. Agrl. Coll., 1908-10; prof. physical edn. and physiology, State Normal Sch., Milwaukee, 1911-16; extension lecturer, U. of Wis.; pres. Angell Games, Inc.; organized recreation and health plan for ships of United States Lines, 1924-27; on clin. staff New York Post-Grad. Hosp., 1929; mem. staff West Side Hosp., N.Y. City, 1930. Lt. M.C., U.S.N., Apr. 9, 1917-Apr. 19, 1921; med. officer Camp Decatur, Great Lakes Naval Tr. Sta., Camp Logan (Ill.), Pelham Bay Tr. Sta., Wards Island Naval Hosp., and U.S.S. Gold Shell. Mem. Am. Physical Edn. Assn., A.M.A., Alpha Kappa Kappa. Club: Civic (New York), Author: Play-A Book of Games, 1910; History of the University of onsin,$ 1912; Basket Ball for Men, 1917; The Story of a Tanker, 1918; Real Games for Real Kids, 1923. Contbr. on athletic games to Ency. Britannica, 14th edit. Home: Wood Glen, N.J.†

ANGLE, PAUL MCCLELLAND, historian, writer; b. Mansfield, O., Dec. 25, 1900; s. John Elmer and Nellie Laverne (McClelland) A.; student Oberlin Coll., 1918-19; A.B., Miami U., Oxford, O., 1922, Litt.D., 1966; A.M., U. Ill., 1924; Litt.D., Augustana Coll., 1941; LL.D., Knox Coll., 1944; L.H.D., Ill. Coll., 1947; LL.D., Lake Forest, 1965; m. Vesta Verne Magee, June 17, 1926; children—Paula, John Edwin, Rep., Am. Book Co., 1924-25; exec. sec. Abraham Lincoln Assn. (formerly Lincoln Centennial Assn.), 1925-32; historian Ill. State Hist. Library and sec. Ill. State Hist. Soc. 1932-45; dir. Chgo. Hist. Soc., 1945-65, sec., 1965-70. Mem. Am., Mississippi Valley hist. assns., Phi Beta Kappa, Sigma Chi. Clubs: Tavern (Chicago). Author: (with Carl Sandburg) Mary Lincoln, Wife and Widow, 1932; Lincoln—1854 to 1861, 1933; Here I Have Lived—A History of Lincoln's Springfield, 1935; (with Richard L. Beyer), Handbook of Illinois History, 1943; A Shelf of Lincoln Books, 1946; The Lincoln Reader, 1947; Bloody Williamson, 1952; By These Words, 1954; (with Earl S. Miers) The Living Lincoln, 1955; The Chicago Historical Society, 1856-1956, 1956; Created Equal?, 1958; The Complete Lincoln-Douglas Debates, 1958: The American Reader, 1958; (with Earl Schneck Miers) Tragic Years 1860-1865, 1960; Crossroads; 1913, 1963; The Civil War Years in Pictures, 1967; A Portrait of Abraham Lincoln in Letters by his Oldest Sons, 1968; Prarie State, 1968; First in the Hearts of his Countrymen, 1970; The Great Chicago Fire, Oct. 8-10, 1871, 1971; Pioneers: Narratives of Noah Harris Letts and Thomas Allen Banning 1825-1865, 1972; On a Variety of Subjects, 1974; Philip K. Wrigley: A Memoir of a Modest Man, 1975. Home: Chicago, Ill. Died May 11, 1975.

ANISFELD, BORIS, artist; b. Russia, Oct. 2, 1879; s. Israel and Augusta A.; grad. Petrograd Acad. of Fine Arts, 1908; m. Frida Anisfeld, Petrograd, 1904 (died 1933); 1 dau., Morella (Mrs. Otis Chatfield-Taylor). Came to U.S., 1918, naturalized, 1924. Painted scenery for Mariinsky Theater, Petrograd Diagileff Opera Russe, Paris; with Diaghileff's Ballet Russe, 1907-12; engaged by Metropolitan Opera, N.Y. City, 1918-25, to design costumes and scenery for La Rene Fiomet, Blue Bird, Le Roide Lahore, Mephistopheles, Snow Maiden; designed costumes and scenery for opera Love of Three Oranges presented by the Chicago Opera Co.; prof. of advanced drawing and painting Chicago Art Inst., from 1928. Exhibited at Petrograd World of Art (1904), Salon d'Automme, Paris (1906), Malmo North Exhibition, Sweden (1914), Milan, Italy, 1914; one-man traveling exhbn. of leading museums in U.S., 1918-19; exhibited in Phila. Sesqui-centennial (gold medal), Chicago World's Fair, San Francisco World's Fair; exhibited Lincoln Center Astor Gallery, 1968, Nat. Collection of Fine Arts, Smithsonian Instn., 1971. Represented in Brooklyn Museum, Gardner Museum (Boston), Buffalo Museum, Chicago Art Inst., also museums in principal cities of Russia, including the Russian Mus., Hermitage Mus. (both Leningrad). Home: Stonington, Conn. Died Dec. 4, 1973.

ANOKHIN, PETR KUSMICH, physiologist; b. Jan. 27, 1898; grad. Leningrad Inst. Med. Knowledge, 1926; D. Med. Sci. With Pavlov's Lab., 1926-30; prof. physiology Gorky Med. Inst., 1930-35; head dept. gen. physiology of higher nervous system All Union Inst. Exptl. Medicine, 1934-46; head chair physiology of higher nervous system Central Postgrad. Med. Inst., 1936-40, 53-55; dir. Inst. Physiology, USSR Acad. Med. Sci., 1946-49; head chair physiology Vishnevsky Inst. Surgery, USSR Acad. Med. Sci., 1950-56; head Sechenov Inst. Physiology, 1955-74; head Lab. Human Embryogenesis, Inst. Midwifery and Gynecology, RSFSR Ministry Health. Del., Internat. Congress Physiologists, Brussels, 1956, Buenos Aires, 1959, Paris, 1960. Mem. USSR Acad. Scis., USSR Acad. Med. Sci., Internat. Orgn. for Brain Research (exec. com.). Co-author: The Problem of the Central and Peripheral Nervous System in the Physiology of Nervous Activity, 1935; author: Problems of Higher Nervous Activity, 1949; Neuroplasty for Battle Injuries of the Peripheral Nervous System, 1944; Systemogenesis as a General Patern of the Evolutionary Process, 1948; The Problem of Cortical Inhibition and Its Place in the Study of Higher Nervous Activity, 1946; General Principles of the Compensation of Functional Disturbances and their Physiological Basis, 1955; Electroencephalograph Analysis of the Conditioned Reflex, 1958; Internal Inhibition as a Problem of Physiology, 1958; A New Conception of the Architecture of the Conditioned Reflex, 1961; Systemogenesis as a General Regular of Brain Development, 1964; Biology and Neurophysiology of Conditional Reflex, 1968; Biology and Neurophysiology of the Conditioned Reflex and Its Role in Adaptive Behavior, 1973; The Principal Questions of General Theory of the Functional Systems, 1973; Systems Analysis of Integrative Activity of a Neuron, 1974. Mem. editorial bd. Sechenov Physiol. Jour. of UUSR; editor Physiology sect. Large Med. Ency., 2d edit. Developer secretary-motor method of conditioned reflexes, 1930; formulated functional system theory as unit of intergrative brain activity, 1935, including idea of systemogenesis as new form of devel. of functions in evolutionary process; proposed physiol. theory of neutral cicatrix, theory of pathogenesis of amputation pains and theory of pathogenesis of central paralyses; formulated neurogenic theory of arterial hypertension; elaborated original concept of mechanism of selective effect of narcotics and psychotropic drugs on cortico-subcortical interactions. Address: Moscow, USSR., Died Mar 6, 1974.

ANSLINGER, HARRY JACOB, U.S. commr. of narcotics; b. Altoona, Pa., May 20, 1892; s. Robert J. and Christina (Fladtt) A.; student Pa. State Coll., 1913-15; LL.B., Washington Coll. Law, 1930; LL.D., U. Md.; m. Martha Denniston; 1 son, Joseph. Attached to Am. Legation, The Hague, 1918-21; vice-consul, Hamburg, Germany, 1921-23; consul, La Guaira, Venezuela, 1923-25, Nassau, Bahamas, 1926; chief div. of foreign control, Treasury Dept., 1926-29; asst. commr. of prohibition, 1929-30; U.S. commr. of narcotics, 1930-62. Mem. efficiency bd., Ordnance Div., War Dept., 1917-18. Del. of U.S. to Conf. on Suppression of Smuggling, London, 1926, Paris, 1927, to Internat. Congress against Alcoholism, Antwerp, 1928, Conf. to Revise Treaty with U.S., Ottawa, Can., 1928, Conf. of Limitation of Mfr. of Narcotic Drugs, Geneva, 1931; co-observer of U.S. at League of Nations Opium Adv. Com., 1932, 33, 34, 36, 37, 38, 39; U.S. del. Internat. Conf. for Suppression Illicit Traffic in Narcotic Drugs, League of Nations, Geneva, 1936; U.S. rep. commn. on Narcotic Drugs of U.N. Recipient Pa. Ambassador, Proctor Gold Medal Awards, 1952; One of ten outstanding career men, Federal Govt., Nat. Civil Service League, 1958; Alumni Recognition award Am. U., 1959; Distinguished Alumnus award Pa. State U., 1959; Alexander Hamilton medal, Remington medal, Presdl. Citation. Mem. Com. drug addiction NRC. Hon. mem. Terre Haute Acad. Medicine; asso. mem. Internat. Police Chief Assn.; mem. adv. com. Internat. Cooperation Criminal Law, Am. Bar Assn.; life mem. Pa. and Blair County Pharm. Assn.; adv. bd. Mil. Police Assn. Mem. Am. Fgn. Service Assn., Diplomatic and Consular Officers Ret. (bd. govs.), Sigma Nu Phi. Co-author: The Traffic in Narcotics, The Murderers, The Protectors. Address: Holidaysburg, Pa., Died Nov. 14, 1975.

ANSPRENGER, ALOYS GEORGE, physician; b. Munich, Germany, Feb. 18, 1905; s. Franz Xaver and Katharina Ansprenger; came to U.S., 1936, naturalized, 1944; M.D., U. Munich, 1932; m. Ellen Madeleine Oppler, Aug. 21, 1937; 1 dau., Susan (Mrs. Chester Clark Wood). Intern, St. Hedwig's Hosp., Berlin, Germany, 1931-32, asst. roentgenologist, 1932; asst. roentgenologist Univ. Clinic, Charite Hosp., Berlin, 1933; asst. and head dept. roentgenology Charite Policlinik, Berlin, 1934-35; spl. fellow in roentgenology Mayo Found., Rochester, Minn., 1936-37; attending radiologist New Haven Grace Hosp., 1947-59; chief radiology U.S. Naval Hosp., Newington, Conn., 1947-50, Westerly Hosp., 1952-72; asst. clin. prof. radiology Yale Med. Sch., 1947-55. Served to lt. comdr., M.C., USNR, 1945-46. Diplomate Am. Bd. Radiology. Fellow Am. Coll. Radiology; mem. Radiol. Soc. N.Am., Mayo Found. Alumni Assn. Home: Masons Island, Mystic, Conn., Died Dec. 20, 1972.

ANTHONY, DONALD ELLIOT, educator; b. Oakland, Cal., Nov. 30, 1899; s. Arthur Kellog and Minnie (Buckelew) A.; B.A., Leland Stanford U., 1922, Ph.D., 1928; M.A., Cornell, 1923; student U. Cal., 1923-25; m. Arvella M. Coffin, June 24, 1929; 1 son, Donald Bruce. Instr. econs., bus., sociology U. Nev., 1926-28; asst. prof. econs. Lehigh U., 1928-29; asst. prof. dept. econs. U. Akron, 1929-34, asso. prof., 1934-35, prof., head dept., 1935-36; prof., head dept. bus. adminstr. Kent State U., 1936-65, asst. dean Coll. Bus. Adminstrn., 1965-70, prof. mgmt. emeritus, 1970-74. Chmn. Portage County chpt. A.R.C., 1951. Mem. Am. Econ. Assn., Indsl. Relations Research Assn., Am. Arbitration Assn., Soc. Advancement Mgmt., Omicron Delta Gamma, Beta Gamma Sigma, Delta Sigma Pi. Episcopalian (lay reader). Kiwanian (hon.). Club: Torch (Akron). Contbr. articles profl. publs. Home: Kent, O. Died Sept. 5, 1974; interred Macon, Ga.

ANTIN, MARY (MARY ANTIN GRABAU), author; b. Polotzk, Russia, 1881; d. Israel and Esther (Weltman) A.; came to America, 1894; ed. pub. schs. and Girls's Latin Sch., Boston, to 1901; non-matriculated student, Teachers' Coll. (Columbia), 1901-02, Barnard Coll., 1902-04 (no degree); m. Prof. Amadeus W. Grabau, of Columbia U., 1901; 1 dau., Josephine. Author: From Polotzk to Boston, 1899; The Promised Land, 1912; They Who Knock at Our Gates, 1914. Home: Great Barrington, Mass.†

ANTON, ROBERTA CHARLOTTE WEISS (MRS. AARON ANTON), electronic instrument mfg. co. exec.; b. Phila., Apr. 21, 1929; d. Maurice Philip and Esther (Margulies) Weiss; A.B., U. Pa., 1949; postgrad., 1949-51; m. Aaron Anton, Feb. 4, 1949; children—Aimee S., Leslie J. Substitute tchr. Phila. Pub. Schs., 1949; research asst., asst. instr. dept. psychology U. Pa., 1949-51; treas. Deltron, Inc., North Wales, Pa. from 1953, dir., from 1969. Mem. Cheltenham Art Centre, Cheltenham Twp. Library, North Penn C. of C., Phi Beta Kappa, Pi Gamma Mu. Home: Elkins Park, PA. Deceased.

ANTONIEWICZ, WLODZIMIERZ, archeologist; b. Sambor, Poland, July 15, 1893; s. Karol and Wanda (Kurowska) A.; ed. U. Lvov, 1912, U. Cracow, 1914, U. Vienna (Austria), 1919, U. Paris (France), 1923; Ph.D., 1918; D.Sc. (hon.) U. Riga, 1938; m. Mary Szymczak, Aug. 15, 1919. Prof., U. Warsaw (Poland), 1920-63, Free U., Warsaw, 1919-39; prof., mem. senate Clandestine U., Warsaw, 1940-44; pres. medieval researches U. and Poly. Warsaw; dir. archeol. mus. Warsaw Sci. Soc., 1924-45, dep. dir., 1945-47. Decorated Polonia Restituta, Legion D'Honneur, Merites Civils, others. Mem. Polish Acad. Scis., Swedish Acad. History, Archeology and Arts, German Acad. Natural Scis. Author: Foundations Prehistoric Archeology Poland, 1926; Polish Archeology, 1928; Museum Affairs, 1933; History of Primitive Art, 1958; Pastoral and Shepherd's Life in Tatra Mountains, 1959-69; others. Home: Warsaw, Poland. Died May 20, 1973.

APGAR, VIRGINIA, physician; b. Westfield, N.J., June 7, 1909; d. Charles Emory and Helen (Clarke) Apgar; A.B., Mt. Holyoke Coll., 1929; M.D., Columbia, 1933; M.P.H., Johns Hopkins, 1959; Med.Sc.D.,

Womans's Med. Coll., 1964, N.J. Coll. Medicine and Dentistry, 1967; Sc.D., Mt. Holyoke Coll., 1965, Boston U., 1969. Intern in surgery Presbyn. Hosp., N.Y.C., 1933-35; resident anesthesiology U. Wis. and Bellevue Hosp., N.Y.C., 1937; clin. dir. dept. anesthesiology Columbia-Presbyn. Med. Center, 1938-59; prof. anesthesiology Columbia, 1949-59; med. staff Nat. Found., March Dimes, from 1959, chief div. congenital malformations, 1959-68, v.p. for med. affairs, 1968-73, sr. v.p. med. affairs, from 1973; lectr. pediatrics (teratology) Cornell Med. Sch., 1965-71, clin. prof. pediatrics, from 1971; lectr. genetics Johns Hopkins, 1973. Mem.-at-large Methodist Bd. Hosps. and Homes, 1965-71; alumnae trustee Mt. Holyoke Coll., 1965-71. Recipient Alumnae award Mt. Holyoke Coll., 1954, Elizabeth Blackwell award, 1960. Diplomate Am. Bd. Anesthesiology. Fellow Am. Coll. Anesthesiology (chmn. bd. govs. 1950-52), N.Y. Acad. Medicine, Am. Acad. Pediatrics (hon. asso.), Am. Coll. Obstetrics and Gynecology (asso.), N.Y. Acad. Scis.; mem. Am. Pediatric Soc., A.A.A.S., Am. Eugenics Soc., Cong. Anomalies Research Assn. Japan, Catgut Acoustical Soc. (v.p.), Am. Soc. Human Genetics, Teratology Soc., Am. Pub. Health Assn., Pan-Am. Soc. Anesthesiology (hon.), Am. Soc. Anesthesiology (treas. 1939-45, distinguished service award 1961, hon. mem.), Harvey Soc., A.O. Whipple Surg. Soc., 25 Year Club Presbyn. Hosp., Amateur Chamber Music Players, Am. Philatelic Soc., Ubiquiteers (treas. 1959), Alpha Omega Alpha; hon. mem. N.Y. State Soc. Anesthesiology, Wash. State Obstet. Soc., Alaska Med. Soc., Irish-Am. Pediatric Soc., Alumni Soc. Sloane Hosp., Pediatric Soc. Dominican Republic. Home: Tenafly, N.J. Died Aug. 7, 1974; interred Fairview Cemetery, Westfield, N.J.

APPEL, LEON HOWARD, clergyman, coll. pres.; b. Volga, S.D., Nov. 1, 1921; s. Harve E. and Erva Vida (Leavitt) A.; student Ia. Central Coll., 1939-40, Butler Sch. Religion, 1947-48; A.B., Minn. Bible Coll., 1943, D.D., 1962; m. Veva Mae Crooks, Dec. 22, 1942; children—Gloria (Mrs. Timothy F. Fry), Glenda (Mrs. James Allison), Gail (Mrs. Norman D. Clark), Gregg, Gene, Michael. Ordained to ministry Ch. of Christ, 1943; minister Ch. of Christ, Sheldon, Wis., 1940-44, Toluca, Ill., 1944-50, Christian Ch., Lincoln, Ill., from 1950; v.p. Lincoln (Ill.) Coll. and Sem., 1970-72, pres., from 1972. Mem. City Park Commn., Lincoln, 1960-61. Chmn. trustees Lincoln Christian Coll. and Sem., 1960-67, exec. v.p., from 1970; ministerial rep. dir. Abraham Lincoln Meml. Hosp., 1959-63; pres. N.Am. Christian Convention, 1964; trustee Minn. Bible Coll., from 1950; mem. exec. com. N.Am. Christian Convention, 1954, 58, 65, 66, 67; chmn. Christian Loan Fund, 1963-67; mem. pub. com. Standard Pub. Co., Cin., from 1956. Mem. Lincoln Ministerial Assn. (pres. 1954, 66). Mason, Kiwanian. Contbr. articles to profl. jours. Home: Lincoln, Ill. Died Aug. 1, 1974; interred Union Cemetery, Lincoln, Ill.

APPLBAUM, KARL, rabbi, lawyer, social scientist; b. Hungary, Feb. 10, 1910; s. Rabbi Emanuel and Goldie (Eckstein) A.; B.S., State Tchrs. Coll., California, Pa., 1932; M.S., Coll. City N.Y., 1935; LL.B., St. Lawrence U., 1937, J.S.D., 1939; M.A., N.Y. U., 1952; D.H.L., Yeshivah U., N.Y.C., 1957; Ph.D., St. Andrews' Ecumenical U. Coll., London, Eng., 1956, D.D. with honors, 1956; LL.D. Honoris Causa, Phoenix Acad., Bari, Italy, 1957; J.D., Bklyn. Law Sch., 1967; m. Helen Siegel, June 9, 1934; children—Elaine Claire (Mrs. I. David Feldman), Florence Rene (Mrs. Ephraim Laifer), Joseph Stewart. Came to U.S., 1922, naturalized, 1922. Ordained rabbi, 1936; rabbi Avenue M Jewish Center, Bklyn., 1938-50, from 1957, Jewish Community, Bayside, L.I., 1950-53; interim rabbi Garden Jewish Center, Flushing, N.Y., 1971-72; prof. practical rabbinics, history various theol. sems., 1950-56; chaplain 307th Gen. Hosp., Jamaica, L.I.; spiritual adviser Assn. Jewish Employees of N.Y.C. Dept. Social Services. Admitted to N.Y. bar, 1939, Fed. Dist. Cts. So. and Eastern dists., 1955, U.S. Supreme Ct., 1956, Ct. Mil. Appeals, 1956; practice of law, 1938; spl. dep. attorney general State of N.Y., from 1958. Active United Jewish Appeal, Fedn. Jewish Philanthropies, Young Israel of Kew Gardens Hills; chaplain, trustee Ind. Buakrester Sick Aid Assn.; trustee Sherishower Benevolent Assn. Chmn., The Queens Civic Improvement Council; treas. Community Local Sch. Bd. 25, Queens, from 1970. Served as 1st lt. Chaplains Corps., AUS, 1945; col. Res., ret. Mem. Hapoel Hemizrachi Am., Am. Legion, Acad. Scis., Zionist Orgn. Am., Royal Arcanum, Am. Pub. Welfare Assn., N.Y. State Welfare Conf., Queens County Bar Assn., Rabbinical Alliance Am., Jewish War Vets (state chaplain), Affiliated Young Democrats, Mil. Chaplains Assn. U.S., Res. Officers Assn., (state chaplain, v.p., nat. chaplain 1965-66, 70-71, exec. v.p. Queens chpt. 1970), Navy League U.S., Mil. Order World Wars, Assn. U.S. Army (pres. L.I. chpt., chaplain 1st region), Hon. Order Ky. Cols., Internat. Platform Assn., N.Y. State Bar Assn., Am. Acad. Polit. and Social Sci., Amvets, N.A.A.C.P., Assn. Jewish Chaplains Armed Forces, Am. Judicature Soc., Assn. Orthodox Jewish Scientists. Odd Fellow, K.P. (past chancellor); mem. B'nai B'rith, Sinai Fraternal Order. Clubs: Democratic; American Israeli; Roslyn Country; Forest Hills County. Home: Flushing, N.Y. Died Aug. 1974.

APPLETON, FRANCIS RANDALL, JR., lawyer; b. Lenox, Mass., July 9, 1885; s. Francis Randall and Fanny (Lanier) A.; grad. Groton Sch., 1903; A.B. cum laude, Harvard, 1907, LL.B. cum laude, 1910; m. Joan Mary Egleston, May 29, 1935. Admitted to N.Y. bar, 1911; asso. firm Winthrop & Stimson, 1910-16; mem. firm Appleton, Rice & Perrin, 1916 — (both N.Y.C.). Hon. life pres. Ipswich (Mass.) Hist. Soc., 1943-74; pres. N.Y. Farmers, Inc., 1940-47; bd. mgrs. Am. Soc. Prevention Cruelty to Animals, N.Y.C., 1922-43. Commd. capt., inf. O.R.C., 1916; active duty U.S. Army, 1917-19, A.E.F., 1918-19; advanced from capt. to lt. col., inf.; lt. col. inf. Res., 1919-46; Officers' Hon. Ret. List, 1946, ret., 1952. Mem. Assn. Bar City N.Y., N.Y. State Bar Assn., N.Y. Soc. Colonial Wars, S.R., Am. Legion (founder mem.). Mem. Ascension Meml. Ch. (Vestryman 1929-70, churchwarden 1942-71). Clubs: Meadow Brook (past v.p., treas., sec.) (Westbury, L.I.); Racquet and Tennis, Westminster Kennel, Harvard (N.Y.C.); Somerset, Myopia (Boston); Porcellian (Harvard); Army and Navy (Washington); White's (London, Eng.). Breeder registered Guernsey and Polled Hereford cattle and Shropshire sheep at Appleton Farms, Ipswich, Essex County, Mass., a 1000 acre farm granted to ancestor Samuel Appleton, 1638; owner Barberry Kennels (registered Am. Kennel Club, 1899), breeders of Smooth Fox Terriers; horse trainer, fox hunter. Home: New York City, N.Y. Died Aug. 4, 1974.

ARENDT, HANNAH, author, polit. scientist; b. Hannover, Germany, Oct. 14, 1906; d. Paul and Martha (Cohn) Arendt; B.A., Königsberg Pr., 1924; student univs. Marburg, Freiburg; Ph.D., Heidelberg U. (Germany), 1928; H.L.D., Bard Coll., 1959, Goucher Coll., 1960; hon. degree Smith Coll., 1966, York U., Toronto, 1968, Loyola U., Chgo., 1970, Yale, 1971, Princeton, Notre Dame, 1972; m. Heinrich Bluecher, 1940 (dec.). Came to U.S., 1941, naturalized, 1951. Social worker, Paris, France, 1934-40; research dir. Conf. on Jewish Relations, 1944-46; chief editor Schocken Books, Inc., 1946-48; exec. dir. Jewish Cultural Reconstrn., N.Y.C., 1949-52; vis. prof. U. Cal. at Berkeley, 1955, Princeton, 1959, Columbia, 1960, others; prof. U. Chgo., 1963-67; univ. prof. New Sch. for Social Research, N.Y.C., 1967-75; lectr. Recipient award Nat. Inst. Arts and Letters, 1954; Lessing Preis, Hamburg, 1959; Freud preis Deutsche Akademie für Sprache und Dichtung, 1967. Guggenheim fellow, 1952-53. Rockefeller fellow, 1959-60, 69-70. Fellow Am. Acad. Arts and Scis. (Emerson-Thoreau medal 1969); mem. Am. Acad. Polit. Sci., Am. Soc. Polit. and Legal Philosophy, Nat. Inst. Arts and Letters, mem. Deutsche Akademie für Sprache und Dichtung (corr. mem.). Author: The Origins of Totalitarianism, 1968; Rahel Vornhagen, 1957; The Human Condition, 1958; Between Past and Future, 1968; On Revolution, 1963; Eichmann In Jerusalem, 1964; Men In Dark Times, 1968; Crises of the Republic, 1972; others., Died Dec. 4, 1975; interred Bard Coll., Annandale-on-Hudson, N.Y.

ARMITAGE, MERLE, writer; b. Mason City, Ia., Feb. 12, 1893; s. Elmer E. and Lula May A.; ed. pub. schs.; m. 2d, Elsa Stuart, 1943; 1 dau., Chama Armitage; m. 3d, Isabelle Heymann, 1953; stepchildren—Agnes, Marc. Engaged civil engring., then designer of modern stage decorations until 1911; impresario, asso. with Charles L. Wagner, 1911-15; publicity dir. Diaghilev Ballet, 1915; asst. to pres. Nat. Soc. for Broader Edn., 1916-17; managed tours of Scotti Grand Opera Co., Russian Grand Opera Co., The Beggars Opera, concert courses of leading artists, 1919-21; mgr. Fitzgerald Concert Direction, Los Angeles, 1921; a founder, Los Angeles Grand Opera Assn., 1924, gen. mgr., 1924-30; mgr. Philharmonic Auditorium, from 1933; editorial and art dir. Look mag. Commd. lt. col. AAF, World War I. Decorated Legion of Merit; recipient Cordon Bleu from Wine and Food Soc. Regional chmn. PWA Project. Author-designer many items, from 1929; works produced include among others: Burro Alley (Corle), Saints and Saint Makers (Boyd), First Penthouse Dwellers of America (Underhill), 1946; Merle Armitage Dance Memoranda, Paintings of Russell Cowles, 1947; Smile at the Foot of the Ladder (Miller), 1948; Operations Santa Fe, 1948; Murder and Mystery in N.M., 1948; Paul Klee, 1950; Claude Debussy, 1950; Gershwin, man and legend, 1958; Fit for a Queen; Stella Dysart of Ambrosia Lake; Railroads of America, Dynamic Dissonance (Danz), Operatic Masterpieces (Downs), 1952; Neighborhood Frontiers, 1954; Photographs of Brett Weston, 1956; two books on Igor Stravinsky, 1956. Home: Santa Fe, N.M. Died Mar. 1975.

ARMSTRONG, BARBARA NACHTRIEB, prof. of law; b. San Francisco, Calif., Aug. 4, 1890; d. John Jacob and Anna (Day) Nachtrieb; A.B., U. of Calif., 1913, J.D., 1915, Ph.D., 1921; m. Ian Alastair Armstrong, 1926; 1 dau., Patricia. Admitted to Calif. bar, 1915; exec. sec. Calif. Ins. Commn., 1915-19; lecturer in law and economics, U. of Calif., 1919-22, instr., later prof., of law and economics, 1922-29, prof. of law from 1929; consultant on unemployment and old age ins. to President's Com. on Econ. Security (on leave from U. of Calif.), 1934. Mem. Order of Coif, Phi Beta Kappa, Alpha Phi. Democrat. Club: Women's Faculty (U. of Calif.). Author: Insuring the Essentials—Social Insurance Plus Minimum Wage, 1932; The Health Insurance Doctor—His Role in Great Britain, Denmark and France, 1939. Contbr. to law reviews. Home: Berkeley, Cal., Died Jan. 18, 1976.

ARMSTRONG, CLYDE ALLMAN, lawyer; b. New Kensington, Pa., June 14, 1898; s. Ulysses S. and Anna M. (Allman) A.; A.B., Westminster Coll., 1919, hon. doctorate, 1972; LL.B., U. Pitts., 1922; m. Ethlyn W. Logan, Dec. 27, 1923; children—Dale L., Clyde W., Carolyn Lee. Admitted to Pa. bar, 1922, practiced in Pitts., mem. firm Thorp, Reed & Armstrong; prof. comml. law Carnegie Inst. Tech., 1923-30. Dir. Nat. Storage Co. Past pres. Columbia Hosp.; past dir. Hosp. Service Assn. Pitts. (Blue Cross); v.p., past pres. bd. trustees Westminster Coll.; pres. United Presbyn. Bds. Served as 2d lt. F.A., U.S. Army, 1918. Mem. Am., Pa., Allegheny County bar assns., Am. Judicature Soc., Am. Coll. Trial Lawyers, Acad. Trial Lawyers Allegheny County, Delta Theta Phi. Republican. Mason. Clubs: Duquesne, Fox Chapel Golf, Williams Country (Pitts.). Home: Pittsburgh, Pa. Died Feb. 24, 1975; interred Allegheny Cemetery, Pittsburgh, Pa.

ARMSTRONG, HARRIS, architect; b. Edwardsville, Ill., Apr. 6, 1899; s. Henry Clair and Leone (Weir) A.; spl. student Ohio State U., 1924-25; grad. Washington U.; m. Louise McClelland, Jan. 1, 1926; children—Joan, Jeffrey, John Harris. Pvt. practice architecture, Kirkwood, Mo., 1931-69; executed Shanley Bldg.; 1934, Grant Med. Clinic, 1938, Am. Stove Co. Administrn. Bldg., 1948, Cancer Research Labs., Clayton br. dept. store, adminstrv. group for McDonnell Aircraft Corp., St. Louis Airport, U.S. Consulate at Basra, Iraq, Epiphany Episcopal Ch., Lutheran Ch. Atonement, St. Andrew Presbyterian Ch., Ethical Soc. Meeting House, Kirkwood Community Center. Design cons. G.S.A. Bldg., Kansas City, Mo. Chmn. St. Louis County Bldg. Com.; mem. architect's adv. council Porcelain Enamel Inst., 1966-68. Recipient silver medal Paris Expn., 1936, award of merit Epiphany Ch., Kirkwood, Mo., 1961; Alumni citation Washington U., 1963. Fellow A.I.A. Home: St. Louis, MO. Died Dec. 15, 1973.

ARMSTRONG, HERBERT DEUEL, oil co. exec.; b. San Rafael, Cal., Sept. 20, 1907; s. Thomas S. and Nancy E. (Deuel) A.; J.D., U. Cal., 1933; m. Muriel H. Cunningham, June 27, 1931; 1 dau., Alice Lynn. Admitted to Cal. bar, 1933; asso. Agnew & Boekel, San Francisco, 1934-39; mgr. credit dept., asst. cashier Fed. Res. Bank, San Francisco, 1939-43, dir., from 1966; asst. treas. Standard Oil Co. of Cal., 1943-47, asst. to chmn. bd., 1947-59, treas., until 1971. Home: Woodside, Cal. Died Nov. 8, 1973.

ARNDT, ROBERT NORTON DOWNS, advt. exec.; b. Phila., Sept. 11, 1904; s. Charles H. and Helen (Flakner) A.; grad. Germantown Friends Sch.; A.B., Kenyon Coll., 1927; m. Alice Sumner, June 7, 1929; children—Robert Ewins Sumner, Thomas Moore, Judith Channing (Mrs. Theodore S. Ingalls). Partner, account exec. Arndt, Preston, Chapin, Lamb & Keen, Inc., advt., Phila., 1928-65, exec. v.p., 1929-65. Trade adviser to govt. and people Poland in collaboration with U.S. Dept. State, auspices Dept. Commerce, 1959. Former publicity chmn., regional chmn. Phila. United Fund; mem. Nat. Council Protestant Episcopal Ch. Am.; chmn. gen. div. 3d province, Episcopal Laymen's Work; chmn. dept. communications. Episcopal Diocese Pa.; vestryman St. Stephen's Episcopal Ch., Cohasset, Mass.; dir. parish relations, asst. promotion dir. Episcopalian Mag. Chmn., Republican Town Finance Com. Bd. dirs. Neighborhood League, Wayne, St. Davids, Ithan Civic Assn.; mem. exec. council Brotherhood St. Andrews. Recipient certificiate of service U.S. Dept. Commerce. Mem. Nat., Eastern (past. dir.) indsl. advertisers assns., Phila. Jr. C. of C. (past pres.), Nat. Sales Execs. Assn., Newcomen Soc., Cohasset Hist. Soc. (dir.), Psi Upsilon. Clubs: Church, Union League (Phila.) Editor: The Citizen, Hanover, Mass. Contbr. articles to trade jours. Home: Cohasset, Mass. Died Aug. 16, 1975; interred Orr's Island, Me.

ARNHEIM, RALPH LEROY, financial cons.; b. Chgo., July 17, 1891; s. Benjamin and Henrietta (Berger) A.; student Northwestern U., 1919-24; m. Catherine Louise Baum, Mar. 3, 1929; children—Barbara Jean (Mrs. Frank Lieber), Ralph L. Clk., Aldens Inc. (name now changed to Gamble Skogmo) Chgo., 1908-10, exec., 1919-22, asst. treas., 1922-35, sec., 1924-35, sec.-treas., 1935-43, v.p., treas., 43-57, dir., 1943-64, mem. finance com., 1924-64, chmn. profit sharing com., 1942-64; bookkeeper, salesman Louis Stern & Co., Chgo., 1912-18; financial cons., from 1957; v.p., dir. Morgan Wrightman Supply Co., Nathan Rubel & Co. Served as lt. USAAF, World War I. Mem. Financial Execs. Inst., Nat. Assn. Accountants Retail Mchts. Assn., Ill. Mfrs. Assn. Jewish religion. Republican. Mason. Clubs: Standard, Economic (Chgo.); Northmoor Country (trea., pres., bd. dirs. Highland Park, Ill); Ravisloe Country (v.p., bd. dirs. Homewood, Ill.); Racquet (Palm Springs, Cal.) Home: Glencoe, ILL. Died Sept. 11, 1974.

ARNHOLTZ, ARTHUR, educator; b. Copenhagen, Denmark, Nov. 28, 1901; s. Sören Peter Lauritz and Anna (Willumsen) Sorensen; grad. U. Copenhagen, 1920, Phil. Dr., 1938; postgrad. Cambridge (Eng.) U., 1924; postgrad. U. Freiburg (Germany), 1925, M.A., 1928; m. Karen Marie Beenfeldt, Sept. 8, 1928;

children—Ilse Ulrike, Jan Ditlev. Lectr., Abenra Gymnasium, 1928-33, U. Berlin, 1933-38, Lyngby Gymnasium, 1938-49; lectr. recitation, metrics U. Copenhagen, 1939-49, prof., 1949-70; lectr. Pastoral Seminar, Copenhagen, 1943-72. Mem. com. for Support Old People, 1949-73. Decorated knight Order of Danebrog lü, 1963; recipeint prize Soc. for Promotion Fine and Useful Arts, 1952. Mem. Vernacular Soc. (chmn. 1966), Soc. Speech Therapists (com.), Student's Choral Union (com.), Royal Danish Acad. Scis. and Letters. Author: (with C.A. Reinhold) Einfuehrung in das danische Lautsystem mit Schallplatten, 1936; Rhythmical Studies in Poetry and Music, 1938; The Sapphical Form, 1946; Elements of Delivery, 1954; Handbook of Danish Metrics, I-II, 1966, 72. Co-editor: Old Danish Songs, I-V, 1941, 44, 47; Danish Metrists, I-II, 54, 1953; Danish Metrics I, 1966, II, 1972. Writer poems, songs, 1958-73. Home: Lyngby, Denmark. Died Oct. 16, 1973; interred Sorgenfri Churchyard.

ARNOLD, CHARLES, educator; b. Ashland, Mo., May 26, 1879; s. George and Samantha Isabell (Manaugh) A.; A.B., U. Mo., 1907, B.S. in Journalism, 1909 A.M., 1925; grad. study in English 5 quarters, U. Chgo.; m. Ethlynn Mitchell, Nov. 14, 1908. Corr. Kansas City Star and St. Louis Post-Dispatch, Columbia, Mo., 1906-10; reporter, pub. and pres. Columbia Herald, 1906-10; copy reader St. Louis Globe-Democrat and St. Louis Star, 1910-14; instr. journalism U. Pitts., 1914-16, asst. prof., 1916-20, prof. 1920-21, asst. prof. English 1921-40, asso. prof., 1940-44, prof., 1944 until retirement, later prof. emeritus, Mem. Am. Assn. U. Profs., Acacia, Kappa Tau Alpha, also member of Sigma Delta Chi. Democrat. Presbyterian. Mason (32°), K.T., Shriner). The first grad. of world's first sch. of journalism U. Mo. Address: Columbia, Mo.†

ARNOLD, JOHN A., ins. exec.; b. Lake Geneva, Wis., Oct. 2, 1890; s. Clifton S. and Anna E. (Alfred) A.; student Middlebury Coll., 1913, M.A., 1954; m. Lucy M. Kelley, Dec. 22, 1917 (dec. Nov. 1969); 1 son, John A.; m. 2d, Grace M.K. Swenson, Oct. 30, 1971. Spl. agt. Fitchburg Mut. Fire Ins. Co. (Mass.), 1915-17; sec. Mut. Ins. Agy., Inc., Fitchburg, 1917-23, Merrimack Mut. Ins. Co., Andover, Mass., 1923-32; sec. Fed. Mut. Fire Ins. Co., Boston, 1932-37, v.p., dir., from 1937, gen. mgr., 1952-56, sr. v.p., 1956-70; v.p. Am. Mfrs. Mut. Ins. Co., N.Y.C., 1941-70, exec. v.p., 1953-56, sr. v.p., 1956-70; treas., dir. Am. Mut. Reins. Co., Chgo., 1941-65; pres., dir. Mut. Loss Research Bur., 1946-60; v.p. Lumbermens Mut. Casualty Co., 1948-58, sr. v.p., 1963-70; v.p. Am. Motorists Ins. Co., 1949-65, sr. v.p., 1963-70; exec. asst. to chmn. bd. Kemper Ins. Group; dir. Asso. Mutuals, Inc.; mem. council Braniff Internat. Mem. exec. com. Transp. Ins. Rating Bur., 1946-66. Past trustee Middlebury Coll. Mem. Mut. Ins. Inst. (pres., dir. 1962-70) Mut. Ins. Adv. Assn. (dir.), Asso. Alumni Middlebury Coll. (past pres.), Delta Kappa Epsilon. Republican. Conglist. Mason (32 deg., K.T., Shriner). Club: Tower (Chgo.). Contbr. to profl. jours. Home: Bangor, Me. Died Nov. 1, 1973.

ARNOLD, JOHN HAMPTON, pediatrician, pediatric virologist; b. Port Arthur, Tex., Nov. 26, 1921; s. Jesse Hampton and Amy Arnold; M.D., Tulane U., 1951; M.A. ad eundem, Brown U., 1967; m. Mary Louise Bertucio, July 28, 1956; children—John Hampton, Mark McKay, Matthew Baylor. Intern Med. Coll. Va., 1951-52; resident in pediatrics Tulane unit Charity Hosp. of La., New Orleans, 1952-53, chief resident, 1953-54; research fellow in pediatrics Children's Med. Center, Boston; fellow in pediatric infectious diseases Children's Hosp., Boston, 1954-57; practice medicine, specializing in pediatrics, from 1956. Instr. pediatrics Tulane U., 1954-55; asst. prof. pediatrics U. N.C., 1957-65; asso. prof. pediatrics Brown U., Providence, R.I., 1965-72. Served as capt. USAAF, 1942-46. Decorated D.F.C., Purple Heart. Diplomate Am. Bd. Pediatrics. Mem. Am. Acad. Pediatrics, A.A.A.S., A.M.A., R.I., Providence med. socs., New Eng. Pediatric Soc., Am. Heart Assn., So. Soc. Pediatric Research, Sigma Xi. Clubs: University (Providence); Barrington (R.I.) Yacht. Contbr. numerous in field of virology and pediatrics to med. jours. Home: Barrington, R.I. Died Apr. 14, 1972.

ARNOLD, RALPH, cons. geologist, petroleum engr.; b. Marshalltown, Ia., Apr. 14, 1875; s. Delos and Hannah R. (Mercer) A.; Throop Poly. Inst., Pasadena, Calif., 1896; A.B., Stanford, 1899, A.M., 1900, Ph.D., 1902; Sc.D., U. of Pittsburgh, 1921; D. Eng., U. of Southern Calif. 1925; m. Frankie Winninette Stokes, July 12, 1899 (died Jan. 17, 1946); children—Winninette (Mrs. Richard M. Noyes), Elizabeth (Mrs. W. R. McKee). Assistant in geology, Stanford, 1899-1903; instructor in chemistry and physics, Hoitt's School, Menlo Park, California, 1899-1900; field assistant, 1900-03, geologic aid, 1903-05, palentologist; 1905-08, geologist, 1908-09, U.S. Geol. Survey; consulting petroleum engineer, U.S. Bur. Mines, 1911-22; in pvt. practice since 1909. Was in charge paleontologic and petroleum investigations U.S. Geol. Survey in Calif., 1903-09; made investigations in oil fields of Tex., Wyo., Mexico, Trinidad, B.W.I., Venezuela, and elsewhere, also exploration for oil Calif., Utah and Texas. Cons. geologist and engr. Trindad Lake Petroleum Co., etc.; dir. extensive explorations for oil in Venezuela, for Caribbean Petrol. Co. Pres. Calif. Central Oil Co., 1922-23; trustee Snowolene Oil Co. from 1923; cons. geologist Atlantic-Pacific Gas and Oil Co.; pres. Arnold Corp., Ltd., 1933-34. Organizer and mem. adv. council Filmoteeas Internacionales, semi-official organization for introducing visual, audio and technical education into schools of Mexico. Fellow Geol. Soc. America, Paleontol. Soc. America (v.p. Pac. Coast Sect., 1915-16), A.A.A.S., Royal Geog. Soc., Geol. Soc. London, Calif. Acad. Science; mem. Geol. Soc. Washington (sec. 1907-09), Nat. Geog. Soc., Le Conte Geol. Club (sec. 1901-02), Cooper Ornithol. Soc., Geol. Soc. Am. Univs., Am. Assn. Petroleum Geologists, Astron. Soc. Pacific, Mining and Metall. Soc. (v.p. 1921-23), Seismol. Soc. America (v.p.), Malecolog. Soc. of London, Paleontologischen Gesellschaft, Nat. Research Council (chmn. finance com. of sect. geol. and geog., 1919), Am. Soc. Econ. Geologists, Academy of Natural Science of Philadelphia; formerly member of American Institute Mining and Metall. Engrs. (chmn. petroleum com. 1919-23), Made important geologic investigations in oil, Fla., Cal., Ala. and Honduras, in tin, Ore. and Ariz., in gold, Wyo. Address: Santa Barbara, Cal.†

ARNSTEIN, KARL, design and constrn. of airships; b. Prague, Bohemia (now Czechoslovakia), Mar. 24, 1887; s. Wilhelm and Ida (Feigl) A.; Dr. Tech. Sciences, U. of Prague, 1912; hon. Dr. Engring., U. of Aix-La-Chapelle, 1927; D.Sc. (hon.), U. of Akron, 1967; m. Bertl Maria Jehle, Sept. 18, 1919; children—Marian Renee, Ruth Suzanna, Karl Frank, William Gerald. Came to U.S., 1924, naturalized 1930. Asst. prof. bridge design U. of Prague, 1912; designed reconstruction of found. of Cathedral of Strassburg; with engring. staff of Zeppelin Co., builders of aircraft, Friedrichshafen, Germany, 1914-24; designed about 70 mil. and comml. airships, including the American ship, Los Angeles, supervising constrn. and participating in major trial flights of most of the ships; tech. dir. aircraft constrn. Goodyear Tire & Rubber Co., Akron, O., 1924; v.p. and chief engr. Goodyear-Zeppelin Corp., 1925-39; v.p. and chief engr., Goodyear Aircraft Corp., 1940-57, cons., 1957-59; engaged in practice as independent cons., from 1959. Developed designs for two mil. rigid airships of 6,500,000 cubic feet capacity for U.S. Navy, directed design and construction of U.S.S. Akron and U.S.S. Macon, Large airship dock near Goodyear factories, pressure type airships, stratosphere balloons, lightweight streamline train and heavier-than-air craft. Recipient Distinguished Pub. Service award USN, 1957, Naturalized Am. award Akron Bar Assn., 1959. Registered profl. engr., State of Ohio. Fellow Am. Soc. Mech. Engrs., Am. Inst. Aeros. and Astronautics; mem. Soc. Automotive Engrs., Soc. Exptl. Stress Analysis, Sigma Tau. Club: Exchange. Author: Einflusslinien, 1912. Co-Author: Joseph Melan. 1923; Aerodynamic Theory, Vol. 6. Contbr. to Th. von Karman Applied Mechanics Anniversary Volume, 1941; also numerous articles to Am. and European tech. mags. on theory of structures and gen. engring. subjects, particularly on airships. Home: Akron, O. Died Dec. 12, 1974; interred Akron, O.

ARONOVICI, CAROL, city planner; b. Roumania, Sept. 18, 1881; s. Julius and Peppi (Segala) A.; B.I., Roumania, 1898; studied, Paris, 1898; B.S.A., Cornell, 1905; Ph.D., Brown, 1911; m. Florence Rosmand Parsons, July 1906; children—Carol Parsons, Vladimir Stanwood. Came to U.S., 1900, naturlaized citizen, 1906; head Union Settlement, Providence, R.I., 1907-09; dir. Bur. Social Research, N.E., 1909-11; sec. Suburban Planning Commn., Phila., 1912-14, Bur. Social Research, 1914-17; dir. Wilder Charity Foundation, St. Paul, Minn., 1917-19; dir. of housing, Calif. State Commn. on Immigration and Housing, 1919-20; lecturer extension div., U. of Calif., lectured at Brown U., U. of Pa., U. of Minn., U. of Wash., Columbia U., New York U., etc.; dir. Columbia U. Housing Study, Chmn. Americanization Com. of Minn., World War; studied social conditions in more than 60 cities; consultant on city planning and housing and housing legislation. Author: Nativity and Race Factors in Rhode Island, 1910; The Social Survey, 1916; Americanization, 1919; Housing and the Housing Problem, 1920; Architectural Control, 1928; Catching Up with Housing (with Elizabeth McCalmont), 1936; Housing The Masses, 1939; A plea for Civic Art, 1943; Civic Art, 1944; The Public Fountain in Civic Art, 1946; also is author of various brochures, articles and reports on sociol. topics as well as comprehensive city plans for many cities. Editor: The Community Builder. In Europe studying housing and city planning, 1 yr. Home: Greenwich, Conn.†

ARTHUR, FRANKLIN KILNORE, JR., newspaperman; b. Redlands, Cal., June 27, 1910; s. Franklin K. and Helen (Williams) A.; A.B., U. Redlands, 1931; m. Mardelle Ann Simpson, Apr. 12, 1946; children—Rita, Franklin Kilnore III. Successively sports writer, reporter, polit. reporter, night city editor San Bernardino (Cal.) Sun, 1931-38; reporter, city editor A.P., Los Angeles, 1938-53, news editor Newsfeatures, N.Y.C., 1953-58, adminstrv. asst. to gen. mgr. A.P., 1958, chief bur., N.Y.C., 1958-63; editor, pub. Monterey (Cal.) Peninsula Herald, 1936-71; editor Toledo Times, from 1971. Mem. Pulitzer Prize bd., 1964-66, 71. Served to lt. comdr. USNR, 1942-45. Mem. Cal.-Nev. A.P. Assn. (pres. 1968-69), Cal. Newspaper Pubs. Assn. (chmn. Central Coast Counties unit 1968-69), Sigma Delta Chi (pres. No. Cal. profl. chpt. 1969-70). Baptist. Rotarian. Clubs: Los Angeles Press (dir., treas. 1951-53); Deadline (treas. 1959-60), Dutch Treat (N.Y.C.); Old Capitol (Monterey); Beach (Pebble Beach). Home: Sylvania, O. Died 1974.

ARTHUR, JOHN MORRIS, biochemist; b. Paris, Ill., Nov. 12, 1893; s. Daniel and Charity (Morris) A.; B.S., U. Chgo., 1919, Ph.D., 1926; m. Ruth Mallory, Nov. 10, 1918; children—Ruth A. (Mrs. Stanley Banker), Martha A. (Mrs. Herbert Fischer), Joan A. (Mrs. Myles S. Richmond). Asst. plant physiology Ia. State U., 1916, U. Chgo., 1919-21, Md. Agr. Expt. Sta., College Park, 1917; biochemist Boyce Thompson Inst. Plant Research, Yonkers, N.Y., 1921-59, sec., 1942-59, dir., from 1942; dir. Boyce Thompson Southwestern Arboretum, Superior, Ariz. Served to lt. San. Corps, U.S. Army, 1918-19. Mem. A.A.A.S., N.Y. Acad. Sci., Am. Chem. Soc., Optical Soc. Am., Bot. Soc. Am., Am. Soc. Hort. Sci., Am. Inst. N.Y., Torrey Bot. Club, Sigma Xi. Home: Paris, Ill. Died Mar. 12, 1975; interred Edgar County Cemetery, Paris, Ill.

ARTHUR, WILLIAM REED, educator; b. Warfordsburg, Pa., Warfordsburg, Pa., Aug. 4, 1876; s. Rev. Richard and Ruth Ann (Barnett) A.; student Coll. Emporia, Kan., 1895-96; A.B., Washburn Coll., 1899; LL.B., Northwestern U., 1908; student U. Chgo., summer 1916; m. Winifred Blanchard, Sept. 19, 1905; children—William Reed (dec.), Helen B., (Mrs. Joe V. Adair). Dean, prof. law Washburn Coll., 1909-15, vis. prof. law, 1946-47; prof. of real property U. Colo., 1915-46, prof. law emeritus from 1946; vis. prof. law Northwestern U., summer 1929, U. Kansas City, 1947-49, John B. Stetson Law Sch., 1949-50; prof. Law St. Louis U., 1950-54. Member city council, Boulder. Trustee City and Co. Hosp., Boulder, 1940-46, Colo. Consistory Bldg., Denver, 1941-46. Mem. American, Colorado, Illinois bar associations, Bar Assn. of State of Kan., Acacia, Sigma Phi Epsilon, Phi Alpha Delta, Order of Coif. Mason (33°, grandmaster Colo., 1936; Shriner). Author: The Law of Newspaper (with Dean Crosman), rev. edit. 1940; Manual on Drug Laws (with Dean Washburn), 2d edit., 1940; Law of Drugs and Druggists (4th edit.), 1955. Compiler; Road Laws of Kansas, 1911; Election Laws of Kansas, 1913, Address: Boulder, Colo.†

ARTOM, EUGENIO, ins. co. exec.; b. Italy, 1896; LL.D.; me. Giuliana Treves, 1927. Pres., mng. dir. La Fondiaria Vita Ins. Co., La Fondiaria Incendio Ins. Co., hon. pres. Associazione Nazionale Imprese Assicuratrici; v.p. La Previdente Ins. Co., La Consorziale Reassurance Co. Bd. dirs. Unione Italiana Riassicurazione. Mem. Soc. Gen. Immobillare, Mem. Italian Liberal Party. Clubs: Rotarian, Soc. Leonardo da Vinci, Toscana Soc. per la Storia del Risorgimento (pres.). Home: Florence, Italy. Died July 17, 1975.

ASBURY, WILBUR FRANCIS, diversified industry exec.; b. Winslow, Ariz., Nov. 13, 1911; s. Harry Wilber and Fannie May (Klooz) A.; B.S., U. Ariz., 1933; m. Angela Lane, July 5, 1949; children—Harry W., Frank B., Craig T., Wilbur Francis, Donald James; Richard L. Beck, Robert Beck (foster sons). With City Products Corp., Phoenix, 1933-72, mgr. Western div., 1941-72, v.p., 1957-72; dir. Valley Nat. Bank, Phoenix. Chmn. Maricopa County Better Govt. Assn., 1956; co-dir. civil def., Maricopa County-City Phoenix, 1950-60; mem. Ariz. Hwy. Commn., 1959-64. Mem. Aircraft Owners and Pilots Assn., Phoenix C. of C. (past pres.), Thunderbirds, Sigma Chi. Episcopalian. Mason (Shriner) Clubs: Phoenix Country, Kiva (Phoenix). Home: Phoenix, Ariz. Died Sept. 10, 1972.

ASCHER, ABRAHAM HARRY, physician; b. N.Y.C., Apr. 3, 1906; s. Alter and Elka (Witkend) Ashkewitz; Licentiate, Royal Coll. Physicians, U. London (Eng.), 1931; m. Dorothy Svigals, July 26, 1929; children—Susan (Mrs. Vincent Joseph Valentine Naimo), Rose (Mrs. Jack Davis). Intern, N.Y.C. Hosp., 1932-33, resident in neuropsychiatry, 1933; postgrad. courses in neuroanatomy and neuropathology Mt. Sinai Hosp., N.Y.C., 1945-46; asso. in neuropsychiatry Sanitarium for Chronic Disease, Jewish Hosp., Bklyn.; examiner neuropsychiatry induction centers SSS, 1941-46. Recipient Selective Service medal, 1946. Diplomate Am. Bd. Psychiatry and Neurology. Fellow Am. Psychiat. Assn. Jewish religion. K.P. Home: Brooklyn, N.Y. Died Feb. 2, 1973; buried Beth David Cemetery, Elmont, N.Y.

ASHBY, WINIFRED MAYER, med. biologist; b. London, Eng., Oct. 13, 1879; d. George Mayer and Mary-Ann (Brock) A.; B.Sc., U. Chgo., 1903; M.S., Washington U., St. Louis, 1905; Ph.D., U. Minn., 1921. Came to U.S., naturalized, 1892. Fellow Immunology Mayo Found., 1917-24; med. bacteriologist, health officer St. Elizabeth Hosp., Washington, 1925-48, vol. researcher, 1948-58. Mem. Am. Assn. Immunologists, Am. Soc. Bacteriologists, Soc. Biol. Psychiatry, Am. Soc. Pub. Health, Soc. for Exptl. Biology and Medicine, Mayo Found. Contbg. author: George R. Minor Symposium of Hematology, 1949; Carbon Dioxide Therapy, 1958; also numerous articles. Pioneered technique for studying life tranfused blood cells; demonstrated that essential factor in pernicious anemia was not blood destruction; research on relationship between quantitative distbn. enzyme and functioning brain. Address: Lorton, Va., Deceased

ASHMAN, JAMES ERNEST, corp. ofcl.; b. East Palestine, O., July 19, 1902; s. Jacob and Camella (Atchison) A.; student Geneva Coll., Beaver Falls, Pa., 1920-21, U. N.C., 1922-23; m. Lena Frances Core, Dec. 5, 1925. Salesman, Ashman Coal Co. East Palestine, 1924-29; salesman, sales promotion mgr. Burroughs Adding Machine Co., Detroit, 1929-40; procedures dir. U.S. Steel & Carnegie Ill. Steel Corp., Pitts., 1940-46; controller Rockwell Mfg. Co., 1948-51, v.p., 1951, exec. v.p., 1952; pres., dir. Air Assos., Inc., Teterboro, N.J., 1953-56, Ultrasonic Corp. (now Advance-Wilson Industries, Inc.), Cambridge, Mass., 1956-62; chmn. bd., pres., chief exec. officer Gray Mfg. Co., N.Y.C., from 1962; chmn. bd. Quaker City Industries, Inc., Saddle Brook, N.J., from 1970. Mem. A.I.M. (pres.'s council). Clubs: Farmington County (Charlottesville, Va.); Mt. Kenya Safari. Home: Shadwell, Va. Died Oct. 23, 1973.

ASHMORE, FRANK LEON, univ. ofcl.; b. Greenville, S.C., Dec. 12, 1925; s. Frank Little and Lemma Leone (Burdette) A.; student Duke, 1943-44; A.B., Furman U., 1947; student Candler Sch. Theology, Emory U., 1950-53; m. Nancy Price Hall, Sept. 4, 1948; children—Elaine Anne, Hall Burdette, Louise Leona. Asst. news editor Greenville News, 1947-49; life ins. salesman, 1949-50; theol. student assigned also to churches in S.C. Ann. Conf., 1951-53; copy editor Atlanta Jour., 1953; staff pub. relations and devel. Emory U., 1953-57, asst. dir. devel. and pub. relations, 1956-57; dir. devel. and pub. relations Randolph-Macon Woman's Coll., 1957-59; exec. dir. Am. Coll. Pub. Relations Assn., Washington, 1959-61; asst. v.p. for devel. Duke, Durham, N.C., 1961-63, v.p. instl. advancement, from 1963. Mem. nat. adv. com. Council Advancement Small Colls.; pub. relations adv. com. So. Regional Edn. Bd., 1959-62, chmn., 1961-62. Trustee Bennett Coll., Paine Coll.; trustee N.C. Symphony. Served to ensign USNR, 1943-45. Mem. Am. Coll. Pub. Relations Assn., Am. Alumni Council, Delta Tau Delta. Democrat. Methodist. Kiwanian. Contbr. articles to profl. publs. Home: Durham, N.C. Died May 28, 1973.

ASHTON, ALBERT A., mech. engr.; b. Adana, Turkey, Feb. 16, 1908; s. Hampar H. and Esther (Haleblian) Ashjian; student Am. U. Beirut, 1924-26, Los Angeles Poly. U., 1926-30; m. Elizabeth Carson Leland, May 16, 1934; children—Denis Leland, Bruce Leland. Engr., Hallet Mfg. Co., Los Angeles, 1930-32; engr. Emsco Derrick & Equipment Co., Los Angeles, 1936-52; chief engr. Emsco Mfg. Co., Houston, 1942-52; dir. engring. Continental-Emsco, Dallas, 1952-73, cons., 1973-75. Lectr. oilwell drilling machinery U. Tex. Extension Div., 1952-56, Tex. A. and M. U., 1961-62. Recipient Spl. Citation for Meritorious Service, Am. Petroleum Inst., 1961. Mem. Am. Soc. M.E. (named engr. of year N.Tex. sect. 1973), Am. Gear Mfg. Assn. (chmn. oilfield gears com. 1958-66), Am. Petroleum Inst. (chmn. mfrs. sub.-com. 1954-68), Am. Inst. Mining, Metall. and Petroleum Engrs., Am. Ordnance Assn., Am. Inst. Aeros. and Astronautics, Am. Soc. Metals (Quarter Century of Service award 1970). Republican. Conglist. Patentee in field. Home: Dallas, Tex. Died Feb. 14, 1975; interred Hillcrest Meml. Park, Dallas.

ASHTON, RAYMOND J., architect; b. Salt Lake City; s. Edward T. and Effie (Morris) A.; student sch. engring. U. Utah, Ecole des Beaux Arts Sch. Archtl. Design; m. Winnie Richards, June 18, 1913; children—Yvonne R. (Mrs. Richard Willey), Joy R., Leila R. (Mrs. J.P. Collier), Janet R. (Mrs. Wesley J. Gransden). Traveled in Europe, 1909-12; archtl. draftsman, 1913-16; architect Rutherford & Ashton, 1918; formed partnership with Raymond L. Evans, 1922. Pres. bd. Utah Symphony; mem. bd. Utah Art Inst. Fellow A.I.A. (past pres.; past pres. jury of fellows); mem. Am. Archtl. Found. (pres.), Utah Bldg. and Constrn. Congress (pres. 1933-54). Mem. Church of Jesus Christ of Latter-day Saints. Clubs: University, Alta (Salt Lake City). Home: Prescott, Ariz. Died Apr. 7, 1973; buried Mountain View Cemetery, Prescott.

ASKEW, RALPH KIRK, JR., art dealer; b. Kansas City, Mo., Nov. 19, 1903; s. R. Kirk and Marion (Ess) A.; grad. Phillips (Andover) Acad., 1921; student architecture Mass. Inst. Tech., 1921-23; B.S., Harvard, 1925, postgrad. history of art, 1926-27; m. Constance Atwood, May 18, 1929; children—Pamela, Phoebe (Mrs. Des Marals), Atwood (Mrs. Charles Allaire). Agt., Durlacher Bros., art dealers, London and N.Y.C., 1927-37, owner, from 1937; specialized in old and modern paintings and drawings. Publisher: Oedipus by Meyer Schapiro with original etchings by Kurt Seligmann, 1944; also definitive catalogues on loan exhbns. of Tintoretto, Poussin, Claude, Magnasco, Caravaggio and the Caravaggisti, Domenico Fetti, others. Home: East Greenville, Pa. Died Mar. 30, 1974.

ASKEY, EDWIN VINCENT, surgeon; b. Sligo, Pa., Aug. 15, 1895; s. Edwin Nelson and Pauline (Williams) A.; B.S., Allegheny Coll., 1917, D.Sc., 1958; M.D., U. Pa., 1921; L.H.D., Cal. Coll. Medicine, 1963; m. Martha Kirk Nebinger, July 10, 1923; children—Jane Elizabeth (Mrs. Walter Edwin Moore, Jr.), Edwin Vincent, David Harrison. Surgeon, Los Angeles, from 1924. Mem. bd. edn., Los Angeles, 1937-43, pres., 1941. Diplomate Am. Bd. Surgery. Fellow A.C.S.; mem. A.M.A. (speaker ho. of dels. from 1955, nat. pres. 1960-61), Cal. (past pres.), Los Angeles County (past pres.) med. assns., Los Angeles Surg. Soc., Alpha Omega Alpha, Delta Tau Delta, Alpha Chi Sigma, Nu Sigma Nu. Methodist. Home: Los Angeles, Cal. Died Dec. 11, 1974.

ASPINALL, RICHARD, educator; b. Bolton, Eng., Dec. 1, 1881; s. Archibald James and Catherine (Barlow) A.; m. Anne Maude Rusmisell, June 11, 1912; children—Catherine Virginia, Samuel Rusmisell. Pres. Western State Coll., Gunnison, Colo., 1927-30; prof. of philosophy and biblical lit., W.Va., Wesleyan Coll., 1914-23; dir. of student affairs, dir. of university extension, asst. to pres., West Va. U., 1930-48; supt., Mooseheart Home and School, Mooseheart, Ill., 1948-53. Mem. Kappa Delta Pi, Phi Delta Kappa, Phi Kappa, Sigma. Mason (32°; K.C.C.H.), Moose, Clubs: Rotary (dist. gov., 1920-21). Contbr. various mags. Ph.D. dissertation: Legal Phases of Religious Edn. Pub. Schs. of U.S. Address: Ft. Lauderdale, Fla.†

ASPLUNDH, E. T., business exec.; b. Philadelphia, Pa., Aug. 12, 1888; s. Carl H. and Emma (Steiger) A.; B.S. in C.E., Pa. State Coll.; m. 2d, Marion Pendleton, Jan. 10, 1942; children—Carolyn, Joan, Elsa. Became v.p. and gen. manager Pitcairn Aircraft, Inc., Phila., 1929; also v.p. Autogiro Co. of America to 1934; asst. v.p. Pittsburgh Plate Glass Co., 1934-40, v.p., 1942-57, chmn. 1957-75; v.p. Southern Alkali Corp., 1944; pres. Columbia-Southern Chemical Corp., 1951-75; chmn. bd. Pitts Plate Glass Co., 1957-75. Clubs: Portgage Country (Akron); Huntingdon Valley Country (Phila.); Edgeworth; Rolling Rock Country (Ligonier, Pa.); Alleghany Country, Duquesne, University (Pitts.). Home: Sewickley, Pa. Died Apr. 1975.

ASSUM, ARTHUR LOUIS, univ. dean; b. Cin., June 10, 1917; s. Clifford John and Jeannette (Purves) A.; student U. Cin., 1935-36; B.Sc. cum laude, Miami U. (O.), 1939; M.A., Ohio State U., 1944; student U. Chgo., 1945-47. Instr. math. Roosevelt Jr. High Sch., Middletown O., 1939-42, Miami U., 1942-45; asst. prof. psychology, dir. counseling and testing service Roosevelt U., Chgo., 1947-54; faculty U. Rochester, 1954-67, asso. prof. edn., dean Univ. Sch., dir. evening and summer sessions, 1959-67; dean curriculum and instrn. Monroe Community Coll. Pres. Chgo. Film Council, 1953-54, Rochester Personnel and Guidance Assn., 1956-57; chmn. Am. Film Soc., 1954-55. Mem. Am. Psychol. Assn., Modern Lang. Assn., Gesellschaft der Freunde von Bayreuth. Democrat. Home: Victor, N.Y. Died June 23, 1970.

ASTAUROV, BORIS LVOVICH, biologist; b. Kazan, Russia, Oct. 27, 1904; s. Lev Mikhailovich and Olga Andreyevna (Teeckenko) A.; grad. Moscow U., 1927, Cand. Biol. Sci., 1936, D.Biol. Sci., 1938; m. Tatiana Michailovna Yakovleva, Jan. 15, 1936; 1 dau., Olga; m. 2d, Natalia Sergeevna Skadovskaya, Jan. 8, 1944; 1 dau., Natalia. Asst. genetics lab. Inst. Exptl. Biology, Moscow, 1924-26, sci. worker lab. developmental mechanics, 1935-47; sci. worker genetics dept. Commn. for Investigation Natural Resources, USSR Acad. Scis., Moscow, 1926-30, with Inst. Cytology, Histology and Embryology, from 1939, head Filatov Lab. Developmental Mechanics, 1947-48, sci. worker, 1948-55, head Filatov Lab. Exptl. Embryology, Severtzov Inst. Animal Morphology, 1955-74, head lab. developmental cytogenetics Inst. Biology of Devel., 1967, dir. Inst., 1967-74; sci. worker dept. genetics and breeding Middleasian Inst. Sericulture, Tashkent, 1930-36. Recipient Silver medal for invention heat shock method for thermic cure of silkworm nosema disease All-Union Exhbn. Achievements of Nat. Economy, 1963, G. Mendel 100th Anniversary Meml. medal Czechoslovak Acad. Sci., 1965, I.I. Mechnikov Gold medal, 1970. Fellow Internat. Inst. Embryology; mem. Internat. Soc. for Cell Biology, Moscow Soc. Naturalists (chmn. genetics sect.), Am. Soc. Zoologists (corr.), USSR Acad. Scis. (academician), Genetics and Breeding Soc. USSR (pres. from 1966). Mem. editorial Cytology, from 1959, div. biology Bull. Moscow Soc. Naturalists, from 1962, Genetics, from 1965, Priroda, from 1965. Research and numerous publs. on cytogenetics and developmental biology of Drosophila and silkworms; developer method of thermal artificial parthenogenesis in unfertilized silkworm eggs, 1934, complete androgenesis for 1st time in animals especially for 1st time of interspecific androgenesis—devel. of adult exclusively male progeny from enucleated egg cytoplasms taken from one species with nucleus taken from another species; proved by means of androgenesis the nuclear versus cytoplasmic control of specific differences and nuclear versus cytoplasmic localization of injuries caused by ionizing irradiation, 1947, prodn. of exptl. tetraploid bisexual strain for 1st time in animal (silkworm), 1957-66. Home: Moscow, USSR., Died June 21, 1974.

ASTURIAS, MIGUEL ANGEL, author; b. Oct. 19, 1899; ed. Inst. Nacional de Guatemala, U. de Guatemala, also U. de Paris a la Sorbonne. Founder Gen. Students Assn. Guatemala, also U. Popular de Guatemala; founder periodical El Diario del Aire; cultural attache Guatemalan embassy, Mexico, 1946-47; minister-counsellor embassy, Buenos Aires, 1947-52; minister, Paris, 1952-53; ambassador to El Salvador, 1953, to France, from 1966. Lectr. on lit., S. Am. and Europe. Recipient Prix Sylla Mnosegur, Paris, 1931; Pris du Meilleur Roman Etranger, Paris, 1952; Lenin Peace prize, 1966; Nobel prize in lit., 1967. Author: El Problema Social del Indio, 1923 (lectures) Argultecture de la Vida Nueva, 1928; Leyendas de Guatemala, 1930; El Senor Presidente, 1946; (poetry) Sien de Alondra, 1948; Hombres de Maiz, 1949; Viento Fuerete, 1950; El Papa Verde, 1953; Week-End en Guatemala, 1955; Los Ojos de los Enterrados, 1960; El Alha Jadito, 1961; Mulata de Tal, 1963; Antologia Teatral, 1964; (poem) Clarivigilia Primaveral, 1965; Le Miroir de Lida Sal, 1967; Mulata, 1967; Strong Wind, 1969; Talking Machine, 1970; (essay) Latinoamerica y otros. ensayos, 1968. Home: Paris, France. Died June 1974.

ATKESON, CLARENCE LEE CONNER, naval officer; b. Columiba, Ala., Oct. 27, 1899; s. Clarence Lee Crawford and Annie May (Conner) A.; B.S., U.S. Naval Acad., 1922; m. Mary Paulding Breed, Dec. 19, 1925; children—Timothy, Edward, George. Commd. ensign, U.S.N., 1922, promoted through grades to rear adm., 1951; comdg. officer U.S. Steamships, Pope, 1939-40, Patoka, 1943, Ashland, 1943-44, Olmsted, 1944-45, Albany, 1948-49; staff, comdr. in chief Pacific, 1945-46, staff, chief naval operations, 1946-48, then comdr. naval base, Guantanamo Bay, Cuba. Home: Washington, D.C. Died Sept. 1975.

ATKINS, ARTHUR KENNEDY, naval officer; b. Charlotte, Mich., Oct. 4, 1881; s. Charles Morton and Maria Theresa (Kennedy) A.; grad. high sch., Butte, Mont., 1899; grad. U.S. Naval Acad., 1905; post-grad. course, same acad., 1913; m. Frances Griswold Terry, of Annapolis, Md., Oct. 24, 1907; children—Griswold Terry, Barry Kennedy, Janet Wolcott. Promoted through various grades to comdr., 1917. Assigned to duty Navy Dept., Washington, March 1917; apptd. mem. Aircraft Bd., Joint Army and Navy Tech. Bd., Joint Army and Navy Airship Bd. and mem. sub-com. Nat. Advisory Com. on Aeronautics; later served as chmn. Army-Navy Helium Bd., tech. asst. Army-Navy Aeronautics Bd., European dir. of constrn. and repair, 1920, European operating mgr., 1921, asst. European dir., 1922, U.S. Shipping Bd.; mgr. U.S. Navy Yard, Charleston, S.C., 1923-26; asst. U.S. Naval Attaché, attached to Am. embassies, London, Rome, Paris and Berlin, and to Am. Legation, The Hague, from 1926. Episcopalian. Home: Hasitings, Mich.†

ATKINS, JOSEPH ALEXANDER, army officer; b. Atlanta, Ga., Nov. 13, 1879; s. Elisha Clay and Alice (Alexander) A.; B.S., Emory Coll., 1898; B.S., U.S. Mil. Acad., 1904; attended Gen. Staff Coll., Langres, France, 1918, Army War Coll., 1929-30, Field Officers Course, Chem. Welfare Service Sch., 1930; m. Nancy Winchester, Oct. 18, 1904; 1 dau., Harriotte W. Commd. 2d lt., Inf., U.S. Army, 1904, and advanced through grades to col. Inf., 1935; brigadier gen., 1940; asst. chief of staff, 3d and 36th Divs., A.E.F., 1918-19; with War Dept. Gen. Staff, 1920-23, sec., 1925-29; chief of staff, 2d Div., 1940, 8th Army Corps, 1940; chief of staff, 3d Army, 1940; retired, Oct. 31, 1941. Awarded D.S.M., 1920; Victory medal (four major engagement clasps), 1918. Methodist. Clubs: Army and Navy, Army, Navy and Marine Country (Washington, D.C.). Home: San Antonio, Tex.†

ATKINS, JOSEPH PRESTON, physician, educator; b. Red Lion, Pa. Sept. 16, 1909; s. Joseph C. and Ella (Donohoe) A.; A.B., Dickinson Coll., 1930; M.D., U. Pa.; 1934, M.Sc. in Medicine, 1941; m. Genevieve Knaus, July 17, 1937 (dec. May 1975); children—Mary Lou, Joseph, Barbara, Paul, John, Steven, Catherine, William, Robert. Intern U. Pa. Hosp. 1934-36; surg. resident Western Res. U., 1936-37; preceptee broncho-esophagology U. Pa. Clinics, 1938-41, mem. staff clinics, from 1941; chief service broncho-esophagology U. Pa. Hosp., from 1946; chmn. dept. bronchology, esophagology and laryngeal surgery Grad. Sch. Medicine, U. Pa., from 1954, also acting chairman dept. otolaryngology; mem. staff Bryn Mawr, Children's, Phila. Gen., VA hosps. Diplomate Am. Bd. Otolaryngology. Mem. A.M.A., Am. Broncho-Esophagological Association (pres. 1962-63, Chevalier Jackson award 1969), Am. Coll. Chest Physicians, Am. Acad. Otolaryngology and Ophthalmology (pres. 1971-72), Am. Laryngol. Assn., Laennec Soc. (pres. 1960-61), Coll. Physicians Phila., John Morgan Soc., Pa., Phila. County med. socs. Presented sci. papers in field before societies. Home: Wynnewood, Pa. Died Mar. 2, 1974; buried Calvary Cemetery, Villanova, Pa.

ATWOOD, ALBERT WILLIAM, writer; b. Jersey City, Feb. 25, 1879; s. William Henry and Elizabeth (Havens) A.; student Fredonia (N. Y.) State Normal Sch.; A.B., Amherst, 1903; A.M. (hon.), 1920. L.H.D. (hon.). 1953; A.M. (hon.) Princeton, 1920; LL.D., Gallaudet College, 1951; m. Sarah Edwards Pratt, Sept. 15, 1906 (dec. 1971); children Albert William, Elizabeth Havens (Mrs. Charles Cornell Bemsen Jr.) Sarah Vanderlip (Mrs. James Wallace Dailey). Minor Giles (dec.), Reporter N.Y. Sun, 1903-06; financial editor N.Y. Press, 1904-12; contbr. Financial News for Investors, Rev. of Revs., 1912-16; asso. mem. faculty Sch. Journalism Columbia, 1915-22; lectr. on finance N.Y.U., 1908-15; financial and ins. editor McClure's mag., 1913-17; financial editor Harper's Weekly, 1913-

14, Every Week and Asso. Sunday mag., 1913-17; contbr. articles on finance, econs. and govt. Sat. Eve. Post, 1914-37, editorial writer, 1919-37, from 1957; contbr. Nat. Geog. mag., 1941-55. Dir. Washington Gas Light Co. Trustee Gallaudet Coll. (chmn.), Madeira Sch., Sidwell's Friends Sch., D.C. Pub. Library (president). Secretary of President Hoover's Citizens Conference on Crisis in Education, 1933. Mem. Washington Lit. Soc., Social Hygiene Soc. (trustee), English-Speaking Union (past pres. D.C.), Order of St. John, Phi Beta Kappa, Alpha Delta Phi. Sr. warden St. Albans Ch. Clubs: Century, University (N.Y.C.); Cosmos (past pres.), Rotary (past president), Metropolitan (Washington). Author or co-author 13 books, 1911-69, including The Mind of the Millionaire, 1926; The Great Stewardship: A Story of Life Insurance, 1945. Editor: Growing with Washington, 1943; Gallaudet College: Its First 100 Years, 1964. Home: Washington, D.C. Died Jan. 23, 1975; buried Union Cemetery, Chatham, Mass.

ATWOOD, FELIX, lawyer; b. Ennis, Tex., Mar. 4, 1908; s. Harry and Bessie (Craig) A.; A.B., Tex. Christian U., 1931; LL.B., Tex. U., 1931; m. Martha Ellen Templeton, Aug. 4, 1934; 1 son, Felix Michael. Admitted to Tex. bar, 1931, practiced in Ennis, 1931-39, city atty., 1936-39; spl. atty. Bur. Internal Revenue, Washington, 1939-42, counsel charge tech. staff, St. Louis office, 1946; pvt. practice specializing in fed. income taxation, Dallas, 1946-74; lectr. tax matters Southwestern Legal Inst., former chmn. 4th ann. inst. U. Tex. Law Sch. Served as lt. col. judge Adv. Gen's. Dept., AUS, 1942-45. Mem. Am. (tax sect.), Fed., Tex., Dallas bar assns., Sigma Alpha Epsilon. Presbyn. Woodman of World, Mason. Club: Engineers (Dallas). Lectr. before various bar, accountants assns. Home: Ennis, Tex. Died Apr. 7, 1974; interred Myrtle Cemetery, Ennis.

AUB, JOSEPH CHARLES, physician: b. Cin., May 13, 1890; s. Samuel and Clara (Shohl) A.; A.B., Harvard, 1911, M.D., 1914; ScD., Jefferson Med. Coll., 1956; m. Elizabeth Francis Cope, June 27, 1925; children—Elizabeth Francis, Frances, Nancy Cope. Med. house officer Mass. Gen. Hosp. Boston, 1914-15, med. resident, 1916-17, asst. medicine, 1921-22, asso., 1922-25, asso. physician, 1925-28, physician, from 1942; asst. physician Russell Sage Inst. Pathology, N.Y.C., 1915-16; instr. physiology Harvard Med. Sch., 1919, asst. prof., 1920-24, asst. prof. medicine, 1924-28, asso. prof., 1928-43, chmn. dept., 1943-56, prof. research medicine, 1948-56, now emeritus; sr. asso. physician Peter Bent Brigham Hosp., 1928-40, physician, 1940-42; physician-in-chief Collis P. Huntington Meml. Hosp. of Harvard, 1928-43, dir. med. labs., 1943-56; expert cons. sec. def., 1949-60; med. cons. Palmer Meml. Hosp., Beth Israel Hosp. South County Hosp. Wakefield, R.I. Mem. com. on growth NRC, 1950-53; mem. Nat. Adv. Cancer Council, 1951-55; mem. sci. adv. com. Detroit Inst. Cancer Research, 1952-58; mem. Unitarian Service Com. Teaching Mission to India, WHO, 1953; nat. sci. council City of Hope, 1954-57. Pres. Ella Sachs Plotz Found.; bd. trustees Worcester Found. Exptl. Biology, 1954-65, pres., 1955-59. Served as lt., M.C., U.S. Army, 1917-19. Decorated Order White Lion (Czechoslovakia); recipient Bertner award M.D. Anderson Hosp., Houston; medal Charles U.; Kober medal Assn. American Physicians, 1966; recipient medal Endocrine Society, 1967. Member of A.M.A., Soc. Clin. Investigation, Am. Physiol. Soc., Assn. Am. Physicians, Am. Acad. Arts and Scis., Meml. Found. Neuroendocrine Research (v.p.), Soc. Endocrinology (pres. 1931), Am. Cancer Research (v.p. 1948-49, pres. 1949-50), Am. Gerontol. Soc. (pres. 1948-49), New Eng. Cancer Soc. (pres. 1945-46), Mass. Med. Soc., Endocrinol. Soc. Czechoslovakia, Am. Cancer Soc. (bd. dirs. 1951-60, pres. Mass. div. 1957), Nat. Acad. Scis. Clubs: Harvard (Boston and N.Y.C.); Aesculapian; St. Botolph (Boston). Home: Belmont, Mass. Died Dec. 30, 1973.

AUDEN, WYSTAN HUGH, poet; b. Feb. 21, 1907; s. George Augustus A.; ed. Gresham's Sch., Holt, and Christ Ch., Oxford; Litt.D. (hon.), Swarthmore Coll. Author: Poems, 1930; Orators, 1932; Dance of Death (play), 1933; (with Christopher Isherwood) Dog Beneath the Skin, 1935, Ascent of F. 6, 1936, Journey to a War, 1939, On the Frontier, 1939; (with Louis MacNeice) Letters from Iceland, 1937; Spain, 1937; On This Island, 1937; Selected Poems, 1938; (with T. Worsley) Education Today-and Tomorrow, 1939; Some Poems, 1940; Another Time, 1940; Double Man, 1941; For the Time Being, 1944; Collected Shorter Poems, 1930-44, 1950; Enchafed Flood, 1950; R. Hoggart (An Introduction Essay), 1951; Nones, 1952; The Dyer's Hand and Other Essays, 1962; About the House, 1966. Editor: (with John Garrett) Poets Tongue, 1935; Oxford Book of Light Verse, 1938; Selections from Tennyson, 1944; Nineteenth Century Minor Poets, 1967; Secondary Worlds, 1968; City Without Walls (poems), 1969. Recipient Rollingen prize for poetry, 1953; National Book award for vol. poetry The Shield of Achilles, 1956; Times Three, 1960; Alexander Droutsky Meml. award, 1959; Guinness poetry award, 1959; Nat. Medal for Lit., 1967. Home: New York City, N.Y. Died Sept. 29, 1973

AUDY, JACK RALPH, educator, med. ecologist; b. Eng., Dec. 24, 1914; s. Alphonse William and Hannah (Whitemore) A.; L.M.S.S.A., Guy's Hosp. Med. Sch., U. London, 1937, M.B., B.S., 1939, Ph.D., 1952, M.D., 1971; m. Catherine Florence Murray, Mar. 26, 1947; 1 dau., Helen M. Intern Hull (Eng.) Royal Infirmary, 1937-39, E. African Med. Service, Brit. Somaliland, 1940; head div. virus research and med. zoology Inst. Med. Research, Kuala Lumpur, Malaysia, 1947-59; dir. George Williams Hooper Found. Med. Research, U. Cal. at San Francisco, 1959-74, prof. internat. health and human ecology, chmn. dept. internat. health, 1967-74; program dir. U. Cal. Internat. Center Med. Research and Tng., 1960-74; Heath Clark lectr. U. London. Served to lt. col. M.C., Brit. Army, 1940-47. Fellow Am. Pub. Health Assn., Cal. Acad. Sci., Royal Entomol. Soc., Royal Soc. Tropical Medicine and Hygiene (Chamler's Meml. award 1959); mem. A.A.A.S., Am. Soc. Parasitologists, Am. Soc. Tropical Medicine and Hygiene, Brit. Ecol. Soc., N.Y. Acad. Sci., Royal Soc. Medicine, Sigma Xi. Author: Red Mites and Typhus, 1968. Editor: Malaysian Parasites I-XV, 1953, XVI-XXXIV, 1957; Public Health and Medical Sciences in the Pacific, 1964. Home: San Francisco, Cal. Died Mar. 1974.

AUER, HARRY ANTON, lawyer, author; b. Washington, May 10, 1878; s. P. A. and Emma L. (Patterson) A.; ed. Washington pub. schs.; grad. Sch. of Law, Columbian (now George Washington) Univ., LL.B., 1898, Sch. of Comparative Jurisprudence and Diplomacy, Same, LL. M., 1899; unmarried. Admitted to bar, 1899, later engaged in corp. practice. Chief dir. of final review, office Sec. of Treas., during issue of U. S. Gov't bonds for war loan, 1898; Republican. Author: The North Country, 1906-63; contbr. short stories to mags. Home: Cleveland, O.†

AUSE, ORVAL HOPE, dairy co. exec.; b. Kenyon, Minn., Aug. 15, 1909; s. Oscar A. and Anna (Hope) A.; student St. Olaf Coll., 1928-29; B.S., Ia. State U., 1932; M.S., U. Minn., 1934; m. Maurine Brogmus, Sept. 17, 1932; children—Orval Craig, Robert G., Marianne (Mrs. Alan Mitchell), Carol (Mrs. Thomas Nelson). Instr. dairy industry Ia. State U., 1934-35; butter insp. Dept. Agr., 1935; with H.C. Christians Co., Chgo., 1935-70, pres., 1960-70; pres. Gt. Lakes Packing Co. Internat., from 1970. Pres. West Suburgan council Boy Scouts Am., 1959-60, mem. exec. com. Region XII; pres. Oak Park (Ill.) Elementary Sch. Bd., 1945-48, Hinsdale (Ill.) Community Chest, 1953-55, Hinsdale Community House, 1955-60; v.p., mem. council Suburban Community Chest; mem. Hinsdale Plan Commn., 1962-64, Hinsdale Zoning Bd. Appeal, 1965-70. Bd. govs. Ia. State U. Found.; trustee Chgo. Met. Crusade of Mercy. Mem. Nat. Dairy Council (dir. 1963-67), Am. Butter Inst. (dir. 1962-68), Chgo. Dairy Tech. Soc. (pres. 1942), Am. Dairy Sci. Assn., Chgo. Assn. Commerce and Industry, Chgo. Merc. Exchange, Audubon Soc., Wilderness Soc., Sierra Club, Izaak Walton League, Alpha Sigma Phi, Alpha Zeta. Republican. Lutheran. Clubs: Hinsdale Golf; Dairymens Country (Boulder Junction, Wis.). Home: Hinsdale, Ill. Died Aug. 7, 1974; buried Bronswood Cemetery, Oak Brook, Ill.

AUSLEY, CHARLES SAXON, lawyer; Tallahassee, Jan. 15, 1907; s. Charles Merit and Elizabeth (Saxon) A.; LL.B., U. Fla., 1930; m. Loranne DuBose, June 28, 1933; children—Anne (Mrs. Ryals Lee), Charles DuBose, Nancy Mitchell (Mrs. Joe Hannon). Admitted to Fla. bar, 1930, Since Practiced in Tallahassee, Sr. mem. firm Ausly, Ausly, McMullen, McGehee & Carothers and predecessors, 1935-72. Dir. Capital City 1st Nat. Bank, Capitol City 2d Nat. Bank, Tallahassee. Mayor, Tallahassee, 1937-42. senator, 1943-45. Fellow Am. Bar Found.; mem. Am. Bar Assn., Am. Coll. Trial Lawyers, Internat. Acad. Trial Lawyers. Presbyn. Home: Tallahassee, Fla. Died May 16, 1972.

AUSTELL, ADELAIDE ROBERTS, (Mrs. Charles Benjamin), club woman; b. Shelby, N.C., Aug. 16, 1905; d. William Joshua and Frances (Eskridge) Roberts; Mus.B., Converse Coll., 1926; m. Charles Benjamin Austell, July 26, 1933; 1 dau., Mary Adelaide. Tchr. piano, voice, music theory Shelby (N.C.) pub. schs., 1926-41. Pres., Cecilia Music Club, Shelby, 1959-60. Shelby Opera Guild, 1960-61, Contemporary Book Club, 1961-62; mem. Shelby Beautification Com., 1959-60; charter mem. Jr. Charity League; patron Womens Hosp. Auxiliary; chmn. Cleveland County United Arts Council, 1969. Mem. N.C. Soc. for Preservation of Antiquities (life), N.C. Roanoke Island Hist. Soc., Am. Assn. U. Women, N.C. Soc. County and Local Historians, N.C. Art Soc., Pi Kappa Lambda (v.p. 1960-61). Democrat. Baptist Clubs: North Lake Country; Cleveland Country; Blowing Rock (N.C.) Country. Composer piano composition Ballade, vocal solo Spring. Research on history Cleveland County, N.C. Home: Shelby, N.C., Died Nov. 24, 1975.

AUSTIN, CHARLES BURGESS, coll. pres. b. Wabash, Ind., Apr. 11, 1879; s. Thomas Benton and Kate Elizabeth (Eltzroth) A.; A.B., Indiana U., 1907, A.M., 1908; grad. student in sociology, Columbia, 1915-18; m. Gertrude Bishop Phillips, Apr. 3, 1914. Teacher pub. schs., Ind., 7 yrs.; fellow in economics, U. of Wis., 1908-09, asst., 1909-10; in charge work in economics and sociology, Grinnell (Ia.) Coll., 1901-11; instr. economics, U. of Tex., 1911-12; head div. of pub. welfare, dept. extension, U. of Tex., 1912-15; mem. Am. Commn. for Study of European Credit and Cooperation, 1913; instr. Ind. U., summers 1914, 15; asst. prof. sociology, Coll. City of New York, 1917-18; pvt. research and business, 1919-31; mem. adminstrative com. Am. Missionary Assn., 1927-31; pres. Straigh Coll., New Orleans, 1931-1935, also acting pres. Tougaloo (Miss.) Coll., 1933-1935. Mem. Nat. Guard, Ind., 18 mos. Mem. Am. Economic Assn., Am. Sociol. Soc. Congregationalist. Home: Los Angeles, Calif.†

AUSTIN, EDWARD THOMPSON, pub. relations exec.; b. Loudon, Tenn., Dec. 2, 1897; s. William Thompson and Hassie (Wilkerson) A.; ed. Manitou, Okla. High schs.; m. Florence Prairie, Mar.18, 1922; 1 daughter, Maryann (Mrs. Fred C. Sisty). Began as apprentice printer, Sept. 1916; successively reporter, city editor and Sunday editor Daily Oklahoman, Oklahoma City, 1919-23; rewrite and copyreader Chicago Herald-Examiner, 1924-26; mng. editor Cleveland Press, 1926-28; mng. editor San Diego Sun, 1928-31; editor Toledo News-Bee, 1931-32; editorial writer Santa Barbara News-Press, 1933-34; dir. mag. publicity Calif. Pacific Internat. Expn., San Diego, 1935-36; editor-in-chief San Diego Union and Tribune-Sun, 1937-50; exec. editor Copley Newspapers, 1944-50; past director public relations, Rohr Corporation, Chula Vista, Cal.; public relations dir. Lane & Huff, advt., San Diego, California, 1966-75. Served with U.S. Army 1917-19. Mem. Am. Inst. Aeros., Inst. Aero. Scis. Aviation Writers Assn. Republican. Clubs: Cuyamaca, San Diego Rowing; The National Press (Washington); La Jolla (Cal.) Beach and Tennis. Author: Rhor, The Story of a Corporation. Free lance magazine writer. Home: San Diego, Cal., Died Dec. 5, 1975.

AUSTRINS, EMILIJA PONE (MRS. PETERIS AUSTRINS), dentist; b. Naudite, Latvia, May 11, 1908; d. Karlis and Angelike (Irbe) Pone; D. Dental Disease, U. Latvia, Riga, 1934; D.D.S., U. Pitts., 1957; m. Peteris Austrins, June 19, 1932; children—Andrievs, Girts, Mikelis, Silvija (Mrs. Janis Meija). Came to U.S., 1949, naturalized, 1956. Sch. dentist City of Riga, also pvt. practice, 1935-44; pvt. practice dentistry, Würzburg, Germany, 1945-49, Kalamazoo, Mich., 1957. Mem. Kalamazoo Latvian Assn., Am. Latvian Assn. U.S., Kalamazoo Valley Dental Soc., Imeria. Lutheran. Home: Kalamazoo MI. Died May 1973.

AVERBACH, ALBERT, lawyer, author, lectr.; b. Benoer Bessarabia, Feb. 22, 1902; s. Matus and Eva (Kirchen) A.; LL.B., Albany Law Sch., Union U., 1923. Admitted N.Y. bar 1924; mem. firm Freshman & Averbach, Syracuse, 1924-30; Averbach & Goldstein, 1930-32; pvt. practice 1932-41; Averbach & Bonney, Seneca Falls, 1941-55; mem. firm Gair, Finley, Averbach, Mahley & Hoffmann, Syracuse, Seneca Falls, N.Y.C., 1955-62, Gair and Averbach, 1962-75; pvt. practice Syracuse, Seneca Falls, N.Y.C., Buffalo, 1955-75; v.p., gen. counsel to Rumsey Mfg. Corp., also Rumsey Products, Inc., 1941-47. Asso. editor personal injury and and tort law Nat. Assn. Claimants Compensation Attys. law jour. Hon. fellow Am. Coll. of Legal Medicine; fellow of Internat. Acad. Law and Sci.; mem. Am. Trial Lawyers Assn. (past v.p., bd. govs.), Internat. Acad. Trial Lawyers (pres. bd. dirs.), Legislative Com. N.Y. State Assn. Plaintiffs Trial Lawyers, Inc. (bd. dirs.), Federal bar assns. of N.Y., N.J., Conn., Am., Internat., Onondaga County, N.Y. State (trial lawyers sect.) bar assns., Am. Judicature Soc., Justinian Legal Soc., Soc. Med. Jurisprudence Scribes. Author numerous profl. publs., including: Handling Accident Cases, 8 vols.; Handling Automobile Cases, 2 vols., Tort and Medical Yearbook (co-editor with M. M. Belli), 2 vols. Mem. legal adv. bd. Traumatic Medicine and Surgery for the Attorney, 10 vol. ency. Asso. editor Internat. Jour. Law and Sci. Lectr. numerous law instrns. Home: Auburn, N.Y., Died May 10, 1975.

AVERY, WILLIS FRANK, lawyer, business exec.; b. Manchester, N.H., Jan. 31, 1881; s. Frank Winfield and Hannah (Quinn) A.; student Brown U., U. Me.; LL.B. Washington Coll. Law, 1920; m. Annice Robinson Hill, Aug. 25, 1904 (died Sept. 11, 1949); children—Mrs. Dorothy A. Campbell, Frank W., Mrs. Edythe A. Warburton, and Mrs. Mary Elizabeth Coates; m. second, Mildred Priscilla Bell on December 30, 1950 (dec. Mar. 26, 1962). Prin. Westmoreland (N.H.) High Sch., 1904-05, Wiscasset (Me.) Acad., 1905-06, Limington (Me.) Acad., 1906-15; asst. examiner U.S. Patent Office, 1915-20; mem. legal staff Westinghouse Electric & Mfg. Co., South Philadelphia, Pa., 1920-24; patent atty. The B.F. Goodrich Co., Akron, O., 1924-36; asst. sec., patent counsel, 1936-44, gen. counsel, 1944-48, sec., 1944-49, retired 1950; entered pvt. practice law, Project Research Service, Rubber Industry Problems, 1950-71; v.p., gen. mgr. Industry Inventions Inc. Trustee Sr. Citizens Center of Summit County, Inc. Mem. Am., Ohio, Akron bar assns., Bar Assn. D.C., Cleve. Patent Law Assn., (hon.), Ohio, D.C., U.S. Supreme Ct. bars, S.A.R. Republican. Episcopalian. Mason, Rotarian. Clubs: Akron City, Franklin (Akron). Address: Akron, O. Died Aug. 27, 1971.

AVINOAM, REUBEN, author, educator; b. Chgo., Aug. 12, 1905; s. Aaron Leib and Miriam (Gorenstein) Grossman; student Columbia U.; B.A., in English lit., psychology, N.Y. U., 1929; m. Anna Shaffer, June 20, 1925; children—Noam (dec.), Ednl. Tchr. Bible, Herzila Hebrew Acad., N.Y.C., 1923-25; lectr. lang. and style Tarbuth Tchrs. Sem., N.Y.C., 1925-29; instr. English, English lit. Herzila Coll., Tel-Aviv, Israel, 1929-49; supr. English Instrn. Israeli Ministry Edn. and Culture, 1950-52; editor lit. works deceased soldiers Israeli Def. Forces, 1950-74; ednl. lectr. tours. Australia, U.S., 1951, 63. Recipient Tchernichowsky prize for Hebrew Anthology of English Verse, 1958; prize for lit. achievements N.Y. U., 1973. Mem. PEN (past sec. del. internat. congress 1947, 49, 53), Israeli Writers Assn. (past mem. exec. bd.). Author: Father and Daughter, 1934; (poem collections) Shirim, 1930, Idylis, 1934, Leaves of Woe, 1948, Poems, 1951, A Tree I Planted, 1958, Images of Yore, 1964, Along My Lanes, 1971. Translated various works English, Am. authors, from 1930; editor, translator Hebrew Anthology English Verse, 1958, Hebrew Anthology Am. Verse, 1953; co-editor Shakespeare's Tragedies, 1950, translator Romeo and Juliet, King Lear, Anthony and Cleopatra. Home: Tel-Aviv, Israel., Died Sept. 2, 1974.

AVRAM, MOIS H(ERBAN), engineer; b. Roumania, Dec. 15, 1880; s. Herban and Rebecca A.; came to U.S., 1899; B.S., New York U., 1904, M.E., 1905; m. Ernestine Kaunitz, of Tampa, Fla., Sept. 6, 1906. Formerly consulting engring. practice; later pres. M. H. Avram & Co., Inc. Lecturer on industrial engring., New York U. Holder of many patents. Mem. Am. Soc. M.E., Soc. of Industrial Engrs., Soc. for Promotion Engring. Edn., Acad. Polit. Science, A.A.A.S., Royal Soc. of Arts, Mfg. and Commerce (London). Clubs: Bankers', Faculty of New York U. Author: Patenting and Promoting Inventions, 1918; The Rayon Industry, 1927, 2d edit., 1929; also many papers on industrial engring. Home: New York City, N.Y.†

AXELRAD, SIDNEY, social psychologist; b. N.Y.C., May 25, 1913; s. Harris and Bessie (Ehrenworth) A.; B.S.S., Coll. City N.Y., 1933; M.A., N.Y.U., 1937; D.S.S., New Sch. Social Research, 1943; postgrad, N.Y. Psychoanalytic Inst., 1948-52; m. Sylvai Brody, May 11, 1949. Research asso. N.Y.U., 1933-34, N.Y. State Tng. Sch. Boys, 1934-48; supr. N.Y.C. Bd. Child Welfare, 1938-41; fellow Rockefeller Found., 1941-42; staff Research Project on Totalitarian Communications, 1942-43; from tutor to vis. prof. grad. faculty New Sch. Social Research, 1946-54; from instr. to asso. prof. Queens Coll., 1948-60, prof., 1960, chmn. anthropology-sociology dept., 1950-64, dir. grad. studies, 1962-67, dean of grad. studies, 1967-76; asso. dean grad. studies City U. N.Y., 1962-76; research cons. Social Work and Mental Health Agys., 1946-76; psychol. pediatric psychiatry service Lenox Hill Hosp., 1961-67, co-dir. child devel. research project, 1963-76. Served with USAAF, 1943-46. Decorated knight Order Merit Republic Italy. Fellow Am. Social Assn., Royal Soc. Health, A.A.A.S.; mem. Am. Psychol. Assn., Sigma Xi. Author: (with others) German Radio Propaganda, 1944; Occupational Choice, 1950; Anxiety and Ego Formation in Infancy, 1970; also articles in profl. jours. Asso. editor: Psychoanalysis and the Social Sciences, 1954-58; editorial bd. Am. Jour. Orthopsychiatry, 1957-62; co-mng. editor Psychoanalytic Study of Society, 1958-70. Home: New York City, N.Y., Died Jan. 1976.

AXELROD, LEONARD RICHARDSON, biochemist, educator, govt. ofcl.; b. Bklyn., Mar. 31, 1927; s. Philip and Rose (Richardson) A.; B.S., Coll. City N.Y., 1948; Ph.D., U. Rochester (N.Y.), 1951; m. Phyllis Thelma Seiden, Aug. 18, 1951; children—Douglas Wayne, Judith Ellen, Mitchell Brian, Janet Ann. Cons. Atomic Energy Project AEC, Rochester, 1951-55; chmn. dept. biochemistry S W Found. Research and Edn., 1955-65, dir. of div. biol. growth and devel., 1965-73; research prof. chemistry St. Mary's U., 1961-75; dir. div. criteria and evaluation Office Pesticide Programs, Environmental Protection Agy., Washington, 1973-75. Mem. Am. Mus. Natural Histroy, N.Y.C.; mem. nat. adv. bd. Cystic Fibrosis Found. Fellow Am. Inst. Chemists, Chem. Soc. (London); mem. Am. Endocrine Soc., Am. Chem. Soc., N.Y. Acad. Scis., Soc. Nutrition and Endocrine-Mexico, Internat. Soc. Reproduction and Fertility, Sigma Xi. Contbr. articles to profl. jours. Patentee in field. Home: Annandale, Va. Died July 30, 1975.

AXTELLE, GEORGE EDWARD, educator; b. Crandall, Tex., Nov. 28, 1893; s. James Monroe and Marie Edith (Haney) A.; student Reed Coll., 1912-15; B.S., U. Wash., 1923; M.A., U. Hawaii, 1928; Ed.D., U. Cal., 1935; m. Jeanne B. Hauser, May 28, 1916 (died May 28, 1925); m. 2d, Margaret Brown, Mar. 31, 1926 (dec.); 1 son, George Edward. Tchr., adminstr. Hood River Co., Ore., 1920-24; adminstr. pub. schs., Hawaii, 1924-30; prin. Jr. High Sch., Oakland, Cal., 1930-35; faculty Northwestern U., 1935-42; labor relations shipbldg. stblzn. com. W.P.B., 1942-45; dir. employee relations O.P.A., 1945-46; prof. edn. N.Y.U., 1946-59, chmn. dept. history and philosophy of edn., 1959; prof. edn. So. Ill. U., from 1959; faculty Mich. State U., summer 1959; lecturer, Yale Univ., 1956-57; Fulbright lecturer Egypt, 1952-53. Vice chairman New York Committee to Abolish Capital Punishment. Vice chairman N.Y. Liberal Party. Mem. Conf. of Method in Science and Philosophy, League for Industrial Democracy (executive board), National Soc. Coll. Tchrs. Edn., American Humanist Assn. (pres. 1959-62), Middle Atlantic States Philosophy Edn. Soc. (pres. 1957-59), Am. Fedn. Tchrs. (v.p., exec. council 1937-42,) Commn. Ednl. Reconstrn., Philosophy Edn. Soc. (past pres.). John Dewey Soc. (exec. com., pres. 1962-64), N.E.A., A.A.A.S., Am. Democratic Action, League Indsl. Democracy, Kappa Delta Pi (laureat chpt.). Author: The Improvement of Practical Intelligence (with Raup et al.), 1950. Editor: Collected Works of John Dewey, 1961. Co-editor: Teachers for Democracy, 1940. Contbr. to profl. jours. Home: Carbondale Ill. Died Aug. 1, 1974.

AYER, FRED CARLETON, educator; b. Greene, Ia., Oct. 29, 1880; s. Joseph Perkins and Josephine (Short) A.; B.S., Upper Ia. U., 1902; M.S., Georgetown U., Washington, D.C., 1905; Ph.D., U. of Chicago, 1915; m. Annes E. Keating, Sept. 5, 1907; children—Nona Marie (Peggy), Jack Keating, Instr. high sch., Marion, Ia., 1903; prof. biology, S. Dak. State Normal Sch., 1904, Ariz. State Normal Sch., Tempe, Ariz., 1905-10; prof. edn., U. of Ore., 1912-16, State U. of Ia., 1917, U. of Washington, 1918-26; also dir. research dept., pub. schs., Seattle; prof. ednl. administration, U. of Tex., from 1927, distinguished prof. from 1940. Dir. various sch. surveys since 1915; dir. dept. of research, sect. of superintendence, Tex. State Teachers Assn., 1931-35; gen. curriculum consultant, Tex. Curriculum Revision Program, from 1934. Mem. N.E.A. (mem. of Yearbook Commn. Am. Assn. School Adminstrs., N.E.A., 1938), Nat. Soc. for Study of Edn., Nat. Soc. Coll. Teachers of Education, Ednl. Research Assn., Soc. for Curriculum Study (exec. com.), Phi Delta Kappa. Presbyterian. Clubs: University, Austin Country. Author: A Study of High School Spelling Vocabulary, 1945; Gateways to Correct Spelling, 1946; Check List for Planning and Appraising Supervision, 1948; Practical Child Acctng., 1949. Editor: (with Fred Englehard) Educational Administration Series. Home: Austin, Tex.†

AYER, NATHANIEL FARWELL, corp. exec.; b. Boston, Mass., June 24, 1879; s. James B. and Mary E. (Farwell) A.; B.S., Harvard, 1900. Formerly mfr. of rayon, later retired; dir. Boston Safe Deposit & Trust Co., Boston Mfrs. Mutual Fire Ins. Co., Dwight Mfg. Co., Whitin Machine Works. Trustee Suffolk Savings Bank. Dir. Boys Clubs of Boston. Home: Boston, Mass.†

AYERS, JOSEPH BURTON, steamship exec.; b. Dayton, Oct. 8, 1881; s. Joseph G. and Alice A.; ed. pub. schs.; m. Flora Sayle, Jan. 11, 1911; children—Joseph Burton. Chmn. bd. the Great Lakes Steamship Company, Incorporated, Cleveland. Republican. Clubs: Union, Cleveland Country, Pepper Pike. Home: Shaker Heights, O.†

AYERS, WILLIAM P(ENDERGAST), meat packer; b. Brookline, Mass., Feb. 28, 1905; s. Thomas J. and Ellen (Pendergast) A.; B.B.A., Boston U., 1927; m. Grace Epperson, July 27, 1930 (dec. Mar. 1962); children—Susan Ann, William Pendergast, Grace Janet m. 2d, Jessie L. Rhamstine, Nov. 1963. With Swift & Co., Chgo., from 1926, mgr. South Fulton (Ky.) dairy and poultry plant, 1932-34, Lexington dairy and poultry plant, 1934-35, mgr. Chgo. ice cream plant, 1935-38, mgr. Chgo. dairy and poultry, 1938-51, asst. to vice pres., 1952-53, v.p., dir., from 1953. Home: La Grange Park, Ill. Died Mar. 4, 1974; interred Queen of Heaven Cemetery.

AYUB KHAN, MOHAMMED, pres. Pakistan; b. Rehana, West Pakistan, 1907; student Aligarh Moslem U., also Royal Mil. Coll., Sandhurst, Eng.; married; four sons, three daus. Commd. officer Royal Fusilers, 1928, advanced through grades to gen. Pakistan Army, 1951; bn. comdr. 14th Punjab Regt., Brit. Indian Army, World War II; comdr. brigade Brit. Indian Army, in Waziristan, then East Pakistan; comdr. East Pakistan div. Pakistan Army, 1948-50, Pakistan comdr. in chief, 1951-58; minister of def., Pakistan, 1954-55; chief adminstr. martial law, supreme comdr. all armed forces, 1958; pres. Pakistan, 1958-69. Moslem. Address: Islamabad, Pakistan. Died Apr. 20, 1974; buried Rehana.

BABBS, CHARLES FREDERICK, lawyer; b. Brandon, O., July 25, 1903; s. Carl R. and Maude L. (Conaway) B.; Ph.B., Denison U., 1925; J.D., Ohio State U., 1928; m. Mary E. Bitner, Aug. 17, 1935; 1 son, Charles Frederick. Admitted to Ohio bar, 1928; asso. firm Tracy, Chapman & Welles, Toledo, 1928-35, Welles, Kelsey & Coburn, 1935-37; partner firm Welles, Kelsey, Cobourn & Harrington, 1937-45, Welles, Kelsey, Fuller, Cobourn & Harrington, 1945-49, Fuller, Harrington & Seney, 1949-53; asst. gen. counsel Owens-Ill. Glass Co. (name changed to Owens-Ill. Inc. 1965), Toledo, 1953-68, sec. 1958-69, v.p., 1963-69; counsel Fuller, Seney, Henry and Hodge, 1969-71, Fuller, Henry, Hodge & Snyder, Toledo, 1971. Served from capt. to maj. Judge Adv. Gen.'s Dept., AUS, 1943-45. Mem. Am., N.Y. State, Ohio, Fed., Inter-Am., Toledo bar assns., Am. Judicature Soc., Judge Advs. Assn., Am. Soc. Corporate Secs., Order of Coif, Delta Theta Phi. Unitarian. Clubs: Toledo, Toledo Country. Home: Toledo, O. Died Sept. 5, 1973; buried Ottawa Hills Meml. Park, Toledo.

BABCOCK, JAMES CHESTER, educator; b. Fayetteville, Ark., Feb. 25, 1908; s. George Edward and Hannah (Muncy) B.; A.B., U. Ark., 1929; M.A., State U. Ia., 1930, Ph.D., 1934; M.A. (hon.), Dartmouth, 1951; studied at Centro de Estudios Históricos, Madrid, Spain, 1932, Sorbonne, Paris, 1933; m. Helen Alberta Wood, June 2, 1930 (div. 1961); children—Janet Elizabeth, James Stephen, Arthur E., Helen L.; m. 2d, Sandra Eileen Scharff, Dec. 30, 1961. Instr. Romance langs. U. Chgo., 1936-43, asso. prof., 1943-50; vis. prof. of the humanities Dartmouth, 1949, prof. Romance langs., 1950-57, chmn. dept., 1953-57; professor Romance langs., Ohio State U., Columbus, 1957-74, chmn. dept. of Romance languages, 1957-65. Mem. of Modern Language Assn. Author: (with P.K. Hartstall) Sinous écrivions, 1937: (with S.N. Trevino) Introduction to Spanish, 1944; also contbr. book chpt. Editor: (with M.B. Rodriguez) Amilia, 1949; Contigo pay y cebolla, 1953. Editorial adviser in Spanish for Houghton Mifflin Co., 1945-74. Home: Columbus O. Died Jan. 16, 1974.

BABCOCK, WINNIFRED EATON (ONOTO WATANNA), author; b. Nagasaki, Japan, 1879; d. Edward and Grace (Trepesis) Eatoa; ed. Montreal, Can., and course in English, Columbia; m. B. W. Babcock, July 16, 1901. Writer short stories for leading mags. from 1893; first story, "A Poor Devil," appeared as serial in Metropolitan Magazine, Montreal; went to West Indies, 1895, and worked as gen. writer and reporter on Jamaica News Letter; first Japanese stories and a serial, "The Old Jinrikisha," appeared in Conkey's Magazine, Chicago, 1895; also contbr. serials or short stories to Woman's Home Companion, Good Housekeeping, The Electric, Harper's, Century, Ladies' Home Journal, Munsey's, Frank Leslie's, Saturday Evening Post, etc. Author: Miss Numé of Japan, 1899; A Japanese Night ingale, 1901; Wooing of Wistaria, 1902; Heart of Hyacinth, 1903; Daughters of Nijo, 1904; Love of Azalea, 1904; A Japanese Blossom, 1906; Diary of Delia, 1908; Tama, 1910; The Honorable Miss Moonlight, 1912; Chinese-Japanese Cook Book (with Sara Bosse), 1914. A dramatic version of A Japanese Nightingale was prod. at Daly's Theatre, New York, with Margaret Illington in the leading role.*†

BABLER, BERNARD JOSEPH, chemist, educator; b. Humbird, Wis., Mar. 19, 1914; s. John and Mary (Benish) B.; B.S. in Chemistry, U. Wis., 1935; M.S., 1936; Ph.D., La. State U., 1940; m. Berenice A. Brunk, June 9, 1942; children—Susan M. (Mrs. Robert W. Powers), James Harold, Maribeth Ann, Pamela Jane. Asst. in limnology U. Wis., 1935-36; teaching fellow La. State U., 1936-39; from instr. chemistry to prof., chmn. dept. DePaul U., 1940-47; faculty U. Ill. at Chgo. Circle, 1947-74, prof. chemistry, 1957-74, acting head div. phys. sci., 1961-62, exec. sec. Chemistry Dept., 1965-74. Cons. in field, 1941-74. Mem. Am. Chem. Soc., Alpha Chi Sigma, Phi Eta Sigma, Phi Lambda Upsilon, Omega Beta Pi. Elk. Home: Chicago, Ill. Died June 10, 1974; interred Queen of All Saints Cemetery, Des Plaines, Ill.

BACH, HARRY, coll. librarian; b. Laupheim, Germany, Mar. 23, 1922; s. Hugo and Selma (Stiefel) B.; came to U.S., 1938, naturalized, 1943; A.B., U. Cal. at Berkeley, 1943, B.L.S., 1947, postgrad., 1955-56; m. Grace A. Jones, Jan. 12, 1952; children—Michele Elizabeth, Claudine Olivia. With staff U. Ore. Library, Eugene, 1947-50; staff U. Neb., Lincoln, 1950-52; head acquisitions and serials depts. U. Ia., Iowa City, 1952-55; head acquisitions dept. San Jose (Cal.) State Coll. Library, 1956-62; coll. librarian Riverside (Cal.) City Coll., 1962-74. Surveyed Ia. State Reformatory Library, Anamosa, 1953, 54. Mem. Riverside Urban Coalition, 1968-74. Served with AUS, 1943-46. Mem. Am. Civil Liberties Union (pres. Riverside chpt. 1967-70, mem. bd. So. Cal.), Cal. Library Assn. (chmn. regional resources coordinating com., 1964-66). Contbr. articles in field to profl. jours. Home: Riverside, Cal. Died Jan. 24, 1974.

BACHE-WIIG, JENS, corp. exec.; b. Eidsvold, Norway, Nov. 15, 1880; s. Hartvig and Amalie (Holth) Bache-W.; student engring., U. Karlsruhe; m. Tordis Micholaysen, Dec. 8, 1916; children—Per, Jens Hartvig, Knuth Frithjof. Elec. engr., Germany, 1902-06; asso. Westinghouse Corp., Pitts., 1906-12; prof. elec. engring. Norwegian Tech. U., 1912-17; mng. dir. A/S Elektrisk Bureau, Oslo, Norway, 1917-27. Standard Elektrizitets A.G., Berlin, 1930-36; v.p. Internat. Standard Electric Corp., N.Y., 1930-36, from 1946; chmn. bd. Standard Telefon og Kabelfabirk A/S, Oslo. Mem. Norwegian Adminstrn. Bd., German Occupation, 1940; past pres. Royal Norwegian Council Scientific and Industrial Research. Honorary member Norwegian Engineering Society, Norwegian Electrical Engrs. Soc.; mem. Norwegian Acad. Sci. and Letters, Royal Norwegian Sci. Acad. Author articles, books on elec. engring. Home: Oslo, Norway†

BACHMAN, INGEBORG, writer; b. 1926; ed. Innsbruck, Graz, Vienna. Staff, Rot-Weiss-Rot radio sta., Vienna, 1950's; vis. prof. poetry U. Frankfurt, 1959-60. Recipient Buchner prize, 1964. Author:

(poetry) Die gestundete Zelt, 1953; (radio play) Zikaden, 1954: (poetry) Anrufung des grossen Bären (Bremer Lit. prize), 1956; Der gute Gott von Manhattan (Hörspielpreis der Kriegsblinden), 1958 (short stories) Das dreissigste Jahre (Deutscher Kritikerpreis), 1961; Ein Ort für Zufälle, 1965; also librettos for ballet, operas. Address: Munich Federal Republic of Germany., Died Oct. 17, 1974.

BACHOUR, RAFIC JIBRAIL, lawyer; b. Safita, Syria, 1901; s. Jibrail B.; Licentiate Law, U. Damascus (Syria); Barrister; adminstr. Der Ez Zor, 1953-54; dep. Safita (Syria), 1954-63; pres. Syrian delegation, Moscow, 1955; v.p. Chamber Deputies, 1954-62; minister culture and pub. orientation, 1962-63. Home: Damascus, Syria. Died Apr. 13, 1973; interred Safika, Syria.

BACK, ERNEST ADNA, entomologist; b. Northampton, Mass., Oct. 7, 1880; s. Adna and Mary Elizabeth (Young) B.; B.Sc., Mass. Agrl. Coll. (now Mass. State Coll.), 1904, Ph.D., 1907; B.Sc., Boston U., 1904; m. Clara Winifred Newcomb, Sept. 29, 1919; children—David Newcomb, Richard Chapell. Instr. entomology, Mass. Agrl. Coll., 1904-06, instr. botany, 1906-07; state nursery insp., 1902-06; agt. expert citrus insect investigations, U. S. Dept. Agr., 1907-10; entomologist and plant pathologist, Va. State Crop Pest Commn., and entomologist Va. Agrl. Expt. Sta., 1910-12; fruit fly investigations, H.I. and Spain, for U.S. Dept. Agr., 1912-16; entomologist in charge stored products and household insect investigations, Bur. of Entomology, U.S. Dept. Agr., 1916-34; prin. entomologist, research, div. of insects affecting man and animals, Bureau of Entomology and Plant Quarantine, U.S. Dept. Agr., since 1934. Mem. Am. Assn. Econ. Entomologists, Am. Entomol. Soc., Biol. Soc. Washington, Entomol. Regional Soc. Washington, Phi Kappa Phi, Alpha Sigma Phi; fellow A.A.A.S., Nat. Acad. Sciences, Am. Inst. Geneology. Republican. Conglist. Club: Cosmos. Author many tech. govt. publs., etc. Home: Washington, D.C.†

BACKER, GEORGE, newspaperman: b. New York, N.Y. Jan. 18, 1903; s. Sarah (Baverman) and George Backer, Sr.; student Barnard Sch. for Boys and U. of Pa.; m. Dorothy Schiff, Oct. 21, 1932 (div. 1943); 1 dau., Sarah-Ann; m. 2d, Eve Weil (dec. 1971). Pres. and editor of the New York Post, 1939-42. Trustee University of Exile and Chatham Square Music School. Decorated Chevalier of Legion of Honor (France). Author: The Deadly Parallel: Stalin and Ivan the Terrible, 1950; Appearance of a Man, 1966. Home: New York City N.Y. Died May 1, 1974.

BACKUS, LOUISE BURTON LAIDLAW (MRS. DANA CONVERSE BACKUS), author; b. N.Y. City, Oct. 24, 1906; d. James Lees and Harriet Davenport Wright Burton Laidlaw; A.B., Barnard Coll., 1929; student Oxford U.; m. Dana Converse Backus, 1933; children—Mary Louise Burton Backus Rankin, Janet Graham Backus Stason, Elizabeth Backus Laidlaw Girard, Harriet Merideth Backus Todd, Anne Converse (dec.). Contbg. editor Voices, poetry mag., from 1930. Bd. dirs., pres., chmn. Inst. World Affairs; bd. dirs. Christadora House; mem. Com. to Defend Am. by Aiding Allies, 1939-41; sec., editor, mem. Women's Action Com. for Victory and Lasting Peace, 1939-48, rep. to UN orgn. conf., San Francisco, 1946; mem. ednl. com., and nat. exec. com. UN Assn. U.S.A.; mem. U.S. Nat. Commn. for UNESCO 1951; chmn. com. Am. Com. of Pan-Pacific Women's Assn. 1951. Trustee Barnard Coll. Mem. Author's League of America, National Inst. of Soc. Sci., Poetry Soc. of Am. Women Poets, Huguenot Soc., D.A.R., Nat. Soc. of Colonial Dames, Order of the Lords of Manors in America, Daughters of Holland Dames, Junior League, League of Women Voters. Clubs: Woman's City, Cosmopolitan, Colony, Women's University (N.Y. City). Author: Wishing on a Comet, 1931; Traveler of Earth 1937. Contbr. verse and essays to mags. Home: Sands Point, L.I. N.Y. Died July 5, 1973.

BACON, MARY ELIZABETH (MRS. PHILIP BACON), polit. worker; b. El Cajon, Cal., Apr. 11, 1898; d. John A. and Minna J. (Roeder) McDonald; B.S., Washington U., 1954; m. Philip Bacon, June 7, 1919; children—Edith M., Harry P., Margaret Ann (Mrs. Leon Smith). Tchr. social studies, English, journalism Crestview Jr. High Sch., Glencoe, Mo., 1955-65. Del. Democratic Nat. Conv., Atlantic City, 1964, Chgo., 1968; Dem. Central Com., 1936-74; vice chmn. St. Louis County Dem. Com., 1936-38, sec. 1944-46, sec. 12th Congl. Dist. Mo., 1940-42, 8th Congl. Dist. Mo., 1968-72; state committeewoman 2d Dist., 1958-60, 64-68, 8th Dist., 1968. Mem. Internat. Program Assn., Nat., Mo., County tchrs. assns., Bus. and Profl. Women's Club. Am. Ordnance Assn. Baptist. Home: Chesterfield, Mo. Died Aug. 6, 1974; interred Antioch Cemetery, Chesterfield.

BADER, RICHARD GEORGE, educator; b. N.Y.C., Aug. 1, 1920; s. Charles Emil and Dorothy (Vogler) B.; B.S. in Botany, U. Me., 1948; B.S. in Geology, U. Chgo., 1949, M.S. in Paleoecology, 1950, Ph.D. in Geology-Geochemistry (Rollin B. Salisbury fellow), 1953; postgrad. U. Wyo., 1949; postdoctorate Oak Ridge Inst. Nuclear Studies, 1957; m. Anitra L. Thorhaug. Research asst. U. Chgo., 1950-52, Bermuda Biol. Sta., 1952; research asso. dept. oceanography U. Wash., 1953-55; asso. prof. oceanography and meteorology Tex. A. and M. U., College Station, 1955-58, prof., 1958-61; asso. dir. phys. sci. NSF, 1961-62, program dir. geochemistry, asso. program dir. oceanography, 1962-63, program dir. oceanography, 1963-65; prof., chmn. dept. oceanography U. Hawaii, 1965-67, also head div. oceanography Hawaii Inst. Geophysics; prof. geochemistry U. Miami, 1967-74, asso. dir. Inst. Marine Sci., 1967-69, asso. dean Sch. Marine and Atmospheric Sci., 1969-74, dir. sea grant program, 1969-71, acting chmn. div. chem. oceanography Sch. Marine and Atmospheric Sci., 1970, 72, chmn. Research Coordination Council, 1971-72, dir. sea grant program, 1973-74. Cons. Am. Council on Edn., 1958-61; participant several internat. expdns., 1953; mem. Tex. Water Com., 1959-60; mem. panel on utilization radioisotopes AEC, Tex. A. and M. U., 1960; alternate mem. interagy. com. oceanography Fed. Council Sci. and Tech., 1964-66; mem. U.S. delegation to UNESCO, Paris, 1963, chmn. 1965; bd. advisers U.S. Oceanographic Data Center, 1963-65; nat. coordinator Indian Ocean Expdn., 1963-65; chmn. com. on oceanography Internat. Coop. Year, 1965; mem. Hawaii Gov.'s Com. on Sci. and Tech., 1965-67, chmn. Gov's Commn. Marine Resources, 1966-67; adviser fellowships NSF, Nat. Acad. Scis., 1966-67; mem. com. oceanography Nat. Acad. Scis., 1967-71; mem. U.S. com. Sci. Com. on Ocean Research, 1967-71; chmn. Nat. Acad. Scis., Facilities Utilization Panel, 1971; mem. panel on conservation of ecosystems Nat. Acad. Scis., 1973; sci. adviser to U.S. delegation UN Com. on Peaceful Uses of Sea Bed. Trustee, Gulf Univs. Research Consortium, 1972. Fellow Tex. Acad. Sci.; mem. Geochem. Soc. (chmn. 1966), Am. Chem. Soc., A.A.A.S., Am. Geog. Union, Geol. Soc. Am., Arctic Inst. N. Am., N.Y. Acad. Sci., Internat. Sediment Soc. Editor, Jour. Marine Chemistry, 1971-74. Contbr. articles to profl. jours. Home: Miami Beach Fla. Died Oct. 31, 1974; cremated.

BAER, ARTHUR A., banker; b. Chgo., 1896; grad. U. Chgo., 1918. Chmn. bd. Beverly Bank, Chgo.; chmn. Riverdale Bank, Gary-Wheaton Bank, Mt. Greenwood Bank, Alsip Bank. Home: Chicago, Ill., Died Oct. 24, 1975.

BAER, JEAN HITCHCOCK, educator; b. Peking, China, Nov. 15, 1918 (parents Am. citizens); d. Allison Harvey and Lillian Elizabeth (Cozier) Baer; B.A., U. Ida., 1939; postgrad. Stanford, 1939-41; (scholar) Harvard, 1955; certificate U. Colo., 1944; M.A., Columbia U., 1947; Ph.D. (fellow), U. Ia., 1958. Asst. instr. Stanford, 1939-41; lang. tchr. Kellogg (Ida.) High Sch., 1941-43, Nampa (Ida.) High Sch., 1941-43; counselor Stephens Coll., Columbia, Mo., 1947-49; counselor and instr. U. Ia., Iowa City, 1949-51, asst. prof., 1951-53, adminstrv. asst., asso. prof., 1953-56, research asso. Office of Admissions, 1956-58; mem. faculty U. Ill. at Chgo. Circle, 1958—, counselor, 1958-60, adminstrv. asst., 1960-71, asso. dir. counseling service, 1971—, asso. prof. edn., 1963-68, prof. edn., 1968—; vis. prof. U. Ill. at Urbana, summer 1959, 60; Ill. State U. at Normal, summer 1966, 67; vocational cons. Social Security Disability Program, U.S. Dept. Health, Edn. and Welfare, 1962—. Served to lt. (j.g.) USNR, 1944-46. Mem. Ill. Vocational Guidance Assn. (charter, pres. 1971-72), Ill. Psychol. Assn. (chmn. acad. sect. 1972-73), Chgo. Guidance and Personnel Assn. (sec. 1963-64, dir. 1969-72, 73-74), Nat. Vocational Guidance Assn. (program chmn. 1972, nat. sec. 1973-75), Am. Psychol. Assn., Am. Coll. Personnel Assn. (commn. chmn. 1967-69), A.A.U.P., A.A.U.W. (chpt. sec. 1962-63, chpt. v.p. 1953-55), Phi Beta Kappa (v.p. chpt. 1955-57), Pi Lambda Theta, Alpha Lambda Delta, Delta Gamma (chpt. pres. 1954-56, 62-64). Editorial bd. The Vocational Guidance Quar., 1972—. Contbr. articles to profl. jours. Home: Palos Hills Ill., Died Sept. 14, 1974.

BAER, JOSEPH AUGUSTUS, army officer; b. Kutztown, Pa., Apr. 29, 1878; s. Samuel Adams and Clara (Hartman) B.; B.S., U.S. Military Acad., 1900; Sch. of the Line, 1922, Command and Gen. Staff Sch., 1923, Army War Coll., 1921; m. Lelia Skipwith Lee, Apr. 28, 1906; 1 dau., Lelia Lee (Mrs. Tibor Borgida). Commd. 2d lt., 1900, and advanced through grades to brig. gen., 1943; served in Spanish-Am. War, 1898, Boxer Uprising in China, 1900-01, Philippine Insurrection, 1901-03; instr. U.S. Mil. Acad., 1903-07; Moro Campaign, Philippines, 1907-10; asst. prof. U.S. Mil. Acad., 1911-15; Plattsburg Training Camps, 1915-17; asst. to Inspector Gen., A.E.F., 1918; Army of Occupation, Germany, 1919; instr. Army War Coll., 1923-24; War Dept. Gen. Staff, 1924-27; military attache to Austria, Czechosloviakia and Hungary, 1929-33; chief of staff, 3rd Corps Area, 1935-39; chief of staff 2d Corps Area and 2d Service Command from 1941. Awarded D.S.M., Silver Star, Order of Merit (Hungary). Dir. Pearson Foundation for Cancer Research, Vienna and London. Mem. Vienna Cancer Soc. (hon. mem.). Clubs: Army-Navy, Chevy Chase (Washington), Home: Governors Island, N.Y.†

BAER, TOWNSEND W., dermatologist; b. Finleyville, Pa., Dec. 1, 1903; s. John M. and Emma (Wilkoff) V.; M.D., U. Pitts., 1928; m. Rowena Goldstein, Oct. 21, 1937; children—Ellen Sue (Mrs. Stephen Monheim), Barbara. Intern, Montefiore Hosp., Pitts., 1928-29; postgrad. tng. Skin and Cancer Unit, N.Y.U., 1939-40; pvt. practice medicine specializing in dermatology, Pitts.; mem. staff South Side Hosp.; cons. dermatology VA Regional Office, Pitts.; asso. prof. U. Pitts. Med. Sch. Served to capt., M.C., AUS, 1942-44. Mem. A.M.A., Am. Acad. Dermatology, Pitts. Dermatol. Soc. (pres.), Pi Lambda Phi, Phi Delta Epsilon. Author: A Primer of Skin Diseases, 1963. Home: Pittsburgh, Pa. Died Aug. 25, 1974; buried Rodef Shalom Temple Cemetery, Pittsburgh, Pa.

BAGWELL, PAUL D(OUGLAS), investment firm exec.; b. Hendersonville, N.C., Aug. 24, 1913; s. Vollie Vernon and Nancy Margaret (Brown) B.; B.S., U. Akron, 1937; M.A., U. Wis., 1938, student, summers 1939-40-41; D.Lit. (hon.), Yankton Coll., 1960; m. Edith Harriet Clark, Feb. 1, 1938, (dec. Nov. 1973); children—Paul Timbrelle, Judith Naomi. Tchr., high sch., Akron, O., 1937; dir. religious edn. Congl. Ch., Stoughton, Wis., 1937-38; instr. speech, dramatics, radio, Mich. State U., 1938-40, asst. prof., 1941-42, asso. prof., 1942-43, prof. and head dept. of speech, radio, dramatics, 1942-47, head dept. and prof. Written and Spoken English, 1944-52, head dept., prof. communication skills, 1952-59, dir. scholarships and admissions, 1959-61; pres., dir. K-S Funds, Inc., Detroit, 1961-67; pres. chmn. bd. Royal Resources Exploration, Inc., Royal Resources Corp. 1967-69, chmn. bds., 1969-73, pres., 1971-73. Mem. U.S. Commn. UNESCO, 1949-56; state chmn. citizens for Eisenhower, 1954-56. Active in Community Chest, Boy Scouts Am.; pres. Ohio Assn. Physically Disabled; bd. dirs. Mich. Soc. Mental Health, 1957-67, v.p., chmn. exec. com., 1967-68, pres., 1969-70; mem. President's com. Employment of Physically Handicapped, 1950-55; state chmn. March of Dimes, 1951-63; mem. Mich. Higher Edn. Assistance Authority, 1964-68; pres. Mich. State U. Friends of Library, 1959-60. Trustee Mich. State U., 1963-67, Cumberland U., 1967-71, Kirwood Gen. Hosp., 1965-70, Alvin M. Bentley Found., Mich. Jaycee Found. (chmn. bd. 1966-67), Hampton Inst., 1970-72, Detroit chpt. UN Assn. of U.S., Nat. Found., N.Y. City. Republican nominee for auditor general State of Mich., 1956, for governor, 1958, 60. Recipient Freed Forum award, 1951; Silver Beaver, Boy Scouts, 1959; Gallantry award. Nat. Soc. Crippled Children and Adults, 1959. Mem. National Rep. Com. on Program and Progress. Fellow Internat. Inst. Arts and Letters; mem. Nat. Artists Found. (pres. 1956-60), Nat. Acad. Polit. Sci., Mich. Grange, Mich. Jr. C. of C. (pres. 1943-44; state vice pres. 1944-45), U.S. Jr. C. of C. (nat. dir. 1945-46; v.p. 1947-48; pres. 1948-49), U.S. C. of C. (nat. dir. 1949-50), Speech Assn. Am. (exec. council 1946-49; exec. v.p. 1951-54), Nat. Soc. Study Communication (pres. 1950-51), Atlantic Union Com. (nat. council 1948-52), Nat. Council Tchrs. English, Mich. Assn. Tchrs. Speech (exec. council 1940), Mich. Edn. Assn., Am. Acad. Arts and Letters, Internat. Acad. Arts, Scis. and Letters, Am. Assn. U. Profs., Lansing Civic Players Guild (dir.), Mich. Schoolmasters Club Mich., Ill. Gas and Oil Assn., Ind. Petroleum Assn. Am., Am. Petroleum Inst., numerous fraternities. Mason, Rotarian, Elk. Clubs: Detroit, Detroit Athletic, Press, Economic (Detroit); Grosse Pointe. Home: Grosse Pointe Park Mich. Died Oct. 23, 1973.

BAHR, WALTER JULIEN, physician; b. Des Moines, Nov. 21, Walter C. and Sara (Julien) B.; M.D., U. Okla., 1955; m. Carman E. Bloedow, Aug. 31, 1968. Intern, St. Mary's Group of Hosps., St. Louis, 19 resident, 1956-57; resident U. Okla. Med. Center, 1957-59, VA Hosp City, 1959-60; practice medicine specializing in internal medicine, Oklahoma City, 1962-71; staff physician, chief outpatient dept. VA Hosp.; asso. prof. medicine U. Okla. Med. Sch. Moderator TV program Medicine and You. Served with USCGR. Mem. A.M.A., Sigma Chi. Roman Catholic. Home: Oklahoma City, Okla. Died Sept. 24, 1971; interred Rose Hill Burial Park, Oklahoma City.

BAILEY, ERVIN GEORGE, mech. engr.; b. Damascus, O., Dec. 25, 1880; s. George W. and Ruthetta (Butler) B.; M.E., Ohio State U., 1903, D. Engring., 1941; Engring., Lehigh U., 1937; Sc.D., Lafayette Coll., 1942; m. Carrie Huntington, Aug. 23, 1904 (dec. March 1966); children—George Huntington (dec.), Mrs. Katharine Bailey Hoyt. Asst., chief testing dept. Consol. Coal Co., Fairmont, W.Va., 1903-07; in charge coal dept. Arthur D. Little, Boston, 1907-09; mech. engr., partner Fuel Testing Co., Boston, 1909-15; founder, pres. Bailey Meter Co., mfrs. fluid meters, automatic combustion control devices, Cleve., 1916-44; chmn. Bailey Meter Co., 1944-56; pres. Fuller Lehigh Co., mfrs. pulverized coal equipment, water cooled furnaces, 1926-36; v.p., dir. Babcock & Wilcox Co., N.Y.C., 1930-52, cons., dir., 1952-56; pres. Bailey Inventions, Inc., Easton, Pa., from 1962. Clayton lectr. Inst. Mech. Engrs., London, 1949. Life trustee Lafayette Coll., 1943-65, emeritus, from 1965. Recipient Longstreth medal Franklin Inst., 1930; Lamme medal Ohio State U., 1936, Distinguished Service award, 1952; Percy Nicholls award, fuels div. Am. Soc. M.E. and coal div. Am. Inst. Mining and Metall. Engrs., 1942; Fritz medal, 1952. Mem. Am. Inst. Mining, Metall. and Petroleum Engrs., Cleve. Engring. Soc. (meritorious mem.), Ohio State U. Assn. (life), Franklin Inst., Am. Soc. M.E. (hon., pres. 1948), Inst. Mech. Engrs. London (hon.), Am. Soc. C. E. (hon.), Instrument Soc. Am. (hon.), Sigma Xi, Pi Tau

Sigma, Tau Beta Pi. Republican. Presbyn. Club: Northampton Country (Easton, Pa.); Engineers (N.Y.C., Lehigh Valley), Patentee, inventor in field. Address: Easton, Pa.†

BAILEY, HAROLD HARRIS, naval architect, ornithologist, mammalogist; b. East Orange, N.J., Oct. 13, 1878; s. Harry Baulch and Lillie Adams (Taylor) B.; ed. pvt. and pub. schs., N.J. and Va.; studied naval architecture in London; m. Ida Margaret Eschenburg, Nov. 1, 1906 (died 1936); children—Harold Whitney, Elizabeth Eschenburg (Mrs. Ralph Carlson). Merritt Palmer, Dorothy Munson (Mrs. J. E. Flowers); married 2d, Laura Beatty Law, August 7, 1937. Employed with various shipyards, Newport News Shipbldg. & D.D. Co., Union Iron Works, San Francisco. With U.S. Biol. Survey 4 yrs.; U.S. Navy, Dept. C. & R., twice. Student of natural history, especially of ornithology, mammalogy and oölogy; owns private collection of over 35,000 specimens, also notable library. Mem. Fla. Soc. Natural History (pres.), Audubon Soc., Am. Soc. Mammalogists, Wilson Ornithol. Club, Cooper Ornithol. Club. Va. Ornithol. Soc. Democrat. Unitarian. Author: The Birds of Virginia, 1913; Birds of Florida, 1924-25. Home: Goshen, Va.†

BAILEY, HAROLD WOOD, educator; b. Chgo., Oct. 16, 1901; s. John William and Celestine Marcella (Wood) B.; B.S., Ottawa U., 1921, LL.D., 1941; A.M., U. Ill., 1924, Ph.D., 1926; m. Marian A. Kinney, Aug. 31, 1926; children—Marjory Elizabeth, Mary Virginia. Instr. math. Ottawa U. 1921-22; asst. math. U. Ill., 1922-25, fellow, 1925-26, instr., 1926-28, asso., 1928-31, asst. prof., 1931-42, asso. prof., 1942-49, prof. 1949-71, emeritus, 1971-74, exec. sec. dept. math., 1934-38, acting dir., 1938-39, dir. 1939-46, student counseling bur., asso. dean, liberal arts and scis. Chgo. Undergrad. Div., 1946-63, asst. v.p., 1963-66, asst. chancellor, 1966-67, asso chancellor, 1967-71; vis. lectr. math. Va. Union U., 1971-74; curriculum cons. Chgo. Bd. Edn., 1937-39. Civilian ednl. adv. Army Tng. Program, 1943-44; treas. Ill. League for Nursing, 1955-61. Fellow A.A.A.S.; mem. Am. Math. Soc., Math. Assn. Am., Am. Coll. Personnel Assn., Council of Guidance and Personnel Assns. (treas. 1948-50), Phi Eta Sigma. Pi Kappa Delta, Pi Mu Epsilon. Baptist. Home: Richmond Va. Died Jan. 24, 1974.

BAILEY, JESSIE EMERSON, author; b. Fredonia, N.Y., Aug. 22, 1880; d. Edward Randolph and Idanthea (de Lacey) Emerson; ed. pub. schs. and pvt. tutors; m. Joseph Alpheus Moffat, Sept. 11, 1898; 2d, Francis Duncan Bailey, of London, Eng., June 8, 1911. Extensive traveler in U.S., Canada and Europe. Mem. D.A.R., Daughters of Empire State, Actors' Ch. Alliance. Clubs: Woman's Press, New Yorkers (pres.), Athenia (Washingtonville, N.Y.). Congregationalist. Contbr. short stories to mags. Author: A Friend at Court, 1904; The Mirror of Miyama (play prod. Herald Square Theatre, New York, 1907). Address: New York City, N.Y.†

BAILEY, JOHN MORAN, chmn. Democratic Nat. Com.; b. Hartford, Conn., Nov. 23, 1904; s. Michael and Louise (Moran) B.; A.B. in Sci., Cath. U., 1926; LL.B., Harvard, 1929; m. Barbara Leary, Aug. 1, 1933; children—Louise (Mrs. Conrad Kronholm), Barbara (Mrs. James Kennelly), Judith and John (twins). Admitted to Conn. and Mass. bars, 1929, also U.S. Dist. Ct.; exec. sec. to mayor of Hartford, 1931-33; judge, Hartford Municipal Ct., 1933-35, 39-41; law clk. judiciary com. U.S. Senate, 1937; commr. statute revision Conn., 1941-46; exec. sec. gov. Conn., 1946; sr. partner Bailey & Wechsler, Hartford. Mem. Democratic Party, 1925-75; mem. Conn. Central Com., 1932-75; chmn., 1946-75; chmn. Dem. Nat. Com., 1961-75; Vice chmn. Met. Dist. Commn. within County of Hartford, 1951-75; Greater Hartford Flood Commn., 1955-75; mem. Conn. Fiscal Study Com., 1957; commr. Promotion Uniformity of Legislation in U.S., 1957-75; mem. Conn. Econ. and Planning and Devel. Com., 1956-75; Dir. New Amsterdam Casualty Co., South End Bank, Hartford, Bd. dirs. St. Francis Hosp., Hartford; mem. founders com. U. Hartford. Mem. Am. Bar Assn., Harvard U. Alumni Assn., Cath. U. Alumni Assn. (bd. govs.), Hartford C. of C. (dir.). Roman Catholic. K.C. (4°), Elk. Clubs: Wethersfield (Conn.) Country; Wampanoag Country (West Hartford, Conn.); Burning Tree Country (Bethesda, Md.). Home: Hartford, Conn. Died Apr. 10, 1975.

BAILEY, LEWIS W.;, b. Spring Arbor, Michigan, July 18, 1880; s. Alfred Edgar and Ida (Bell) Bailey; graduate Waldron (Michigan) High School, 1897; m. Minnie Ila Smith, December 31, 1901; children—Russell O., Claribel (Mrs. Thomas R. Thompson), Grace Louise (Mrs. Tom Neighbors), Barbara (Mrs. M. D. Sparks). Pub. Waldron Recorder, 1898-1903; held various positions in news depts. Grand Rapids Herald, Detroit Journal, Grand Rapids Press, Lansing State Journal, 1903-18; editor Dallas (Tex.) Dispatch, 1919-38, Dispatch-Journal, 1938-39, Dallas Journal, 1939-42; with Office of Price Adminstrn., 1943-43; v.p. Dallas Rupe & Son, from 1943. Democrat. Congregationalist. Clubs: Town and Gown, Bonehead, Dallas Athletic. Home: Dallas, Tex.†

BAILEY, PERCIVAL, neurologist; b. Mt. Vernon, Ill., May 9, 1892; s. John Henry and Mattie Estella (Orr) B.; student Southern Ill. State Teachers Coll., Carbondale, Ill., 1908-12; S.B., U. of Chicago, 1914, Ph.D., 1918; M.D., Northwestern U., 1918; m. Yevnigé Bashbazirghanian, Oct. 25, 1923; children—Irene Anahid, Norman Alishan. Surg. house officer Mercy Hosp., Chicago, 1918-19; asst. resident surgeon Peter Bent Brigham Hosp., Boston, 1919-20; resident physician neurol. and psychopathic services, Cook County Hosp., Chicago, 1920-21; asst. á la Salpêtrière, 1921-22, l'hospice St. Anne (both of Paris), 1925-26; asso. in surgery Peter Bent Brigham Hosp., 1922-25; attending neurologist New England Deaconess Hosp. and Boston Dispensary, 1926-28; neurosurgeon Albert Merritt Billings Hosp., Chicago, 1928-39; neurologist Univ. of Chicago Clinics, 1933-39; teaching for different periods in various capacities, Univ. of Chicago, Northwestern Univ. and Harvard until 1928; asso. prof. surgery, Univ. of Chicago, 1928-29, prof. surgery, 1929-39, prof. neurology, 1933-39; prof. neurology and neurosurgery, U. Illinois; director Illinois State Psychopathic Institute; dir. research Ill. State Psychiat. Inst., Chicago, 1959-69. Mem. Am. Med. Assn., Chicago Medical Society, Chicago Neurological Society, Institute of Medicine of Chicago, Central Neuropsychiatric Assn., Am. Assn. Anatomists, Am. Assn. Pathologists and Bacteriologists, Am. Neurol. Assn., Soc. Neurol. Surgeons, and other American and foreign societies. Club: Chicago Literary. Home: Evanston, Ill. Died Aug. 10, 1973.

BAILEY, RALPH EMERSON, congressman; b. Harrison Co., Mo., July 14, 1878; grad. S.E. Mo. State Teachers Coll., Cape Girardeau, Mo.; spl. study, U. of Mo.; m. Agnes Williams. Admitted to Mo. bar, 1907; mem. 69th Congress (1925-27), 14th Mo. Dist. Mem. Bd. Regents S.E. Mo. State Teachers Coll. Republican. Home: Sikeston, Mo.†

BAIN, JARVIS JOHNSON, army officer; b. Martinsville, Ind., May 2, 1880; s. James Gallagher and Sallie (Johnson) B.; prep. edn., high sch., Martinsville; grad. U.S. Mil. Acad., 1905; grad. Garrison Schs., U.S. Army, 1907, Engr. Sch., 1908, Sch. of The Line (distinguished grad.), 1921, Gen. Staff Sch., 1922, Army War Coll., 1923; m. Edith Ralston, of Nineveh, Johnson Co., Ind., Dec. 25, 1905; children—James Gallagher, Joan Botsford. Commd. 2d lt. C.E., June 13, 1905; promoted through grades to lt. col. Duty with engr. troops, Ft. Leavenworth, Kan., and Ft. Mason, Calif., 1905-07; at Camp Columbia, Cuba, 1908-09; with troops, and fortification work, P.I., 1909-12; in charge water supply, Dist. of Columbia, defenses of Washington, etc., 1912-13; river improvements, Tenn. and Cumberland rivers, 1913-17; with engr. troops, U.S., France and Germany, 1917-19; sec. Mississippi River Commn., St. Louis, June-Sept., 1919; duty Camp Grant, Ill., 1919-20; mem. War Plans Div. Gen. Staff, 1923-27; U.S. dist. engr. river improvements Pittsburgh, 1927-31; member faculty Command General Staff School Fort Leavenworth Kan., Aug. 1, 1931-35; mem. Miss. River Commn., 1929-30; comdg. 2d U.S. Engrs., Port of Ft. Logan, Colo. also Colo. Dist. Civilian Conservation Corps, from 1935. Served as private, Spanish-Am. War.; duty earthquake and fire, San Francisco; Army of Cuban Pacification; in World War as div. engr. 84th, 90th and 6th divs., and as chief engr. 7th Army Corps in Germany, Feb.-June 1919. Mem. Soc. Am. Mil. Engrs., Assn. Graduates U.S. Mil. Acad. Republican. Protestant. Clubs: Bennie Havens, Keystone Athletic (Pittsburgh). Address: Washington, D.C.†

BAIRD, DAVID W. E., physician; b. Baker, Ore., Oct. 21, 1898; s. David W. E. and Mamie (Berntson) B.; M.D., U. of Oregon, 1926; LL.D., University of Portland, 1946; m. Mary Alexander, September 27, 1925; children—Mary, David Michael. Interne Multnomah Hosp., Portland, Ore., 1926-27, resident in medicine, 1927-28; practiced medicine, Portland Ore., from 1928; asst. in anatomy, Med. Sch. U. of Ore., 1923-28, clin. instr. medicine, 1929-32, asst. clin. prof. medicine, 1932-38, med. dir. hosps. and clinics, 1935-43, asso. clin. prof. med., 1938-43, asso. dean, 1937-42, acting dean, 1942-43, dean and prof. med. from 1943. Mem. A.M.A., Ore. State Med. Soc., Multnomah Co. Med. Soc., Am. Coll. Physicians, N.W. Soc. Internal Medicine, Clinical Interurban Club, Assn. Am. Med. Colls., Sigma Xi, Alpha Omega Alpha, Republican. Protestant. Clubs: University, Waverly Country. Home: Portland Ore. Died July 28, 1974.

BAIRD, EDWARD ROUZIE, lawyer; b. Norfolk, Va., Nov. 20, 1909; s. Edward R. and Katharine (Michaux) B.; grad. Woodberry Forest Sch., Orange, Va.; LL.B., U. Va., 1933; m. Eleanor Gray Perry, Apr. 23, 1934, (div. 1958); children—Edward Rouzie, Eleanor Gray; m. 2d, Mary L. Riggan, Feb. 23, 1963. Admitted to Va. bar, 1933, practiced in Norfolk. Past sec.-treas., mem. bd., gen. counsel Atlantic & Danville Ry. Former adviser to bd. Norfolk Seaman's Aid Soc. Past v.p., bd. mem. Tidewater Legal Aid Soc.; past bd. dirs. Norfolk Zool. and Aquarium Soc.; past pres., hon. mem. bd. trustees Norfolk Acad.; past pres., dir. Norfolk Soc. for Prevention Cruelty to Animals; past trustee Ballentine Home. Served as lt. comdr. USNR, 1942-46. Mem. Am. Bar Assn. (past mem. maritime law com., past mem. ho. of dels.), Va. State (past pres., mem. council, chmn. com. legal ethics), Va., Norfolk, Portsmouth (pres. 1954) Cin. Soc., Va. Hist. Soc., Ducks Unltd. (past chmn. Norfolk chpt). Presbyn. Clubs: Virginia (pres. 1960), Norfolk Yacht and Country. Home: Norfolk, Va. Died Dec. 4, 1974.

BAITY, HERMAN GLENN, engring. educator; b. Davie County, N.C., Sept. 2, 1895; s. George Wesley and Sarah Elizabeth (Sprinkle) B.; A.B.; Univ. of N.C., 1917, B.S. in C.E., 1922; studied at Sorbonne, Paris, 1919; M.S. in Sanitary and Municipal Engrings., Harvard, 1925, Sc.D., Engring., 1928; m. Elizabeth Chesley, Mar. 15, 1930; children—William Anthony, Philip Chesley. Asst. in physics U. N.C., 1915-17, instructor in mathematics, 1920-22, associated prof. sanitary and municipal engring., Univ. of N.C., 1926-29, prof., 1929-36, head dept. civil engring., 1928-36, dean of engring., 1931-36, prof. san. engring. Sch. Pub. Health, 1936-55, professor emeritus sanitary engring., 1955-75; acting dean public health, 1946-47; vis. prof. san. engring. Univ. of Tehran, 1964-65. Assistant sanitary engineer N.C. State Board Health, 1922-24, associate sanitary engineer, 1926-31, member board, 1931-43. Served as mem. State Advisory Bd., and state engr. for N.C. of Fed. Emergency Adminstrn. of Public Works, 1933-35, state dir. same, 1935-36, special engr., 1938; cons. practice in engring.; water consultant Nat. Resources Planning Bd., 1937-43; special asst. to commr. of publ works, Federal Works Agency, 1941; spl. consultant U.S. Public Health Service, 1941-49; designer of sewage treatment works, Chapel Hill; project mgr. air base Walterboro, S.C., 1942; chief sanitary engr. for Brazil, Office Coordinator of Inter-American Affairs, Rio de Janeiro, 1943-44; cons. Inst. Inter-Am. Affairs, 1944-52; cons. World Health Orgn., Geneva, Switzerland, 1950-51, 62-65, dir. div. environmental sanitation 1952-61; com. on sanitary engring. Nat. Research Council, 1949-52; mem. adv. bd. on health services Am. Red Cross, 1945-50; cons. German Found. for Developing Countries, 1963. Served as 2d and 1st lt. Ordnance Corps, U.S. Army, 1917-19; with 1st Army, A.E.F., in charge ammunition supply and demolition units. Mem. Am. Soc. C.E., Am. Pub. Health Assn., Am. Water Works Assn., Water Pollution Control Federation, Institute of Sewage Purification (British), Inter-Am. Assn. Sanitary Engring. (pres. 1950-52), N.C. Water and Sewage Works Assn. (pres. 1936-37), Sigma Xi, Phi Beta Kappa, Tau Beta Pi, Delta Omega, Sigma Chi. Democrat. Episcopalian. Mason. Clubs: Harvard of N.C. (pres. 1936-37), Chapel Hill Country. Home: Geneva, Switzerland. Died Apr. 6, 1975.

BAKER, DANIEL CLIFTON, JR., physician; b. Phila., Dec. 19, 1908; s. Daniel Clifton and Anna (Golden) B.; student U. Pa., 1929; M.D., Jefferson Med. Sch., 1933; Med. Sc.D. in Otolaryngology, Columbia, 1939; m. Geraldine Dieck, June 23, 1938; children—Geraldine, Daniel Clifton III, Judith, Marianne, Elizabeth. Intern, Jefferson Med. Coll. Hosp., 1933-35, fellow bronschoscopy and laryngeal surgery, 1935-37; fellow otolaryngology dir. otolaryngol. service Presbyn. Hosp., N.Y.C., 1964. Served to lt. commdr. USNR, 1942-46. Diplomate Am. Bd. Otolaryngology (dir.). Mem. A.C.S. (bd. govs.), Am. Acad. Ophthalmology and Otolaryngology (v.p.), Am. Laryngol. Soc., Am. Bronch-Esophagological Assn., Am. Triological Soc., Am. Coll. Chest Physicians, Am. Soc. for Study Headache. Home: Demarest N.J. Died June 1, 1974.

BAKER, EDGAR CAMPBELL, radiologist; b. Harrisburg, Pa., Nov. 20, 1895; s. Almon Green and Sarah Elizabeth (Croft) B.; A.B., Hiram Coll., 1917; M.D., Western Res. U., 1921; m. Mary B. Blades, May 28, 1921; children—Elizabeth N., Robert B. Intern, Youngstown (O.) Hosp. Assn., 1926-27, attending radiologist 1934-67; attending radiologist Mahoning Co. Sanitarium 1946-67; pres. staff Youngstown Hosp. Assn., South Side Unit, Youngstown, O. Life bd. trustees Ohio div. Am. Cancer Soc. Diplomate Am. Bd. Radiology. Fellow Am. Coll. Radiology; mem. Radiol. Soc. N.Am., Am. Roentgen Ray Soc., Am. Radium Soc., A.M.A., Ohio, Mahoning County med. assns., Welcome Society of Pa., Ohio (past president), Pa. (past pres.) radiol. socs., A.A.A.S. Elk. Club: Youngstown Country. Home: Youngstown, O. Died Dec. 22, 1973.

BAKER, ERIC WILFRED, clergyman; b. Birmingham, Eng., Feb. 17, 1899; s. Alfred and Elize (Farmer) B.; M.A., Christ's Coll. Cambridge U., 1925; Ph.D., U. Edinburgh (Scotland), 1941; D.D. (hon.), Randolph-Macon Coll., 1956; LL.D., Mt. Union Coll., 1968; m. Winifred Mary Throne, Aug. 15, 1934; children—Derek, Susan (Mrs. David Bruce Payne). Ordained to ministry Meth. Ch., 1926; circuit minister, 1923-46; sec. Meth. Edn. Com., 1946-51; sec. Meth. Conf., 1951-71, pres., 1959-60; moderator Free Ch. Fed. Council, 1964-65; del. assemblies, Brit., World council chs. Bd. govs. Leys Sch., Cambridge, Farringtons Sch., Chislehurst, Eng., Kingswood Sch., Bath, Eng., Queenswood Sch., Hatfield, Eng. Served with Royal Army, 1914-18. Mem. Brit., Fgn. Bible Socs. Author: He Shall Suffice Me, 1947; A Herald of the Evangelical Revival, 1948; From the Church in the Orchard, 1949; Belief and Behavior, 1950; Preaching Theology, 1954; John Scott Lidgett, 1957; The Faith of a Methodist, 1958; The Neglected Factor, 1963. Home: Eastbourne, Sussex, England. Died Sept. 19, 1973; cremated.

BAKER, ERNEST HAMLIN, artist; b. Essex, N.Y., May 5, 1889; s. Clarence Hamlin and Jane Martha (Roberts) B.; A.B., Colgate U., 1912; m. Ernestine Herder Pendorf, June 14, 1913; 1 dau., Jean Ernestine (Mrs. Leonard Nagel Henrich). Free lance artist from 1905; polit. cartoons for Dutchess County Democrat and Peoples Plain Spokesman, Poughkeepsie, N.Y., 1905-07, for Evening Enterprise, Poughkeepsie, 1912-14; cover designs for B.R.T. Monthly, 1915-19; designed Christmas seals for Nat. Tuberculosis Assn., 1919, 20, 31, 35; created giant figure symbolizing Telephone Co. service, used in 12 large paintings for N.Y. Telephone Co., 1928-30; painted small mural "Colonial Williamsburg," for West Va. Paper Co., 1937; drew "profiles" for New Yorker, 1926-42; covers for Fortune, 1931-38; mural, "Economic Activities . . . of the Narragansett Planters," for Wakefield, R.I., Post Office, 1938-39; wrote series of articles, illustrated by diagrams, analyzing old master paintings for Am. Artist, 1940-41; cover portraits for Time 1939-56; also 4 special war maps for Time, 1940; 12 war propaganda posters (with Frances O'Brien Garfield), from 1942; one man shows include Walle Studio, N.Y.C, 1940, N.Y. Guild Free Lance Artists, 1943, Colgate U., 1944, Charles Francis Press Gallery, N.Y.C., 1947, Flat Rock (N.C.) Playhouse, 1953, Civic Art Gallery, Greenville, S.C., 1953, Asheville (N.C.) Art Mus. Assn.; 1954, Rowlands Traveling Exhbns., 1957-60. Fellow Internat. Inst. Arts and Letters (life); mem. N.Y. Guild Free Lance Artists. Asheville Art Mus. Assn., Skull and Scroll, Theta Nu Epsilon, Phi Gamma Delta. Address: Hendersonville, N.C., Died Nov. 17, 1975.

BAKER, GEORGE, cartoonist; b. Lowell, Mass., May 22, 1915; son of Harry and Mary (Portman) B.; married Brenda Emsley, May 29, 1946 (divorced 1947). Commercial artist in Chicago, 1935; went to Hollywood, 1937, to work for Walt Disney as animation artist working on such pictures as "Pinnochio," "Dumbo," "Bambi," and "Fantasia." Inducted into the Army in 1941; transferred to staff of Yank, the Army's weekly newspaper in 1942, to do the cartoon strip, "The Sad Sack," created six months previously, which has appeared in every issue of Yank since the first edition; joined Bell Syndicate, 1946, to do the "Sad Sack." Awarded Legion of Merit. Mem. Nat. Cartoonists Soc. Author: The Sad Sack, 1944; The New Sad Sack, 1946, also periodical booklets. Sad Sack radio program, 1947, motion picture, 1957. Home: Beverly Hills, Cal. Died May 1975.

BAKER, GEORGE CLAUDE, JR., educator, clergyman; b. Atlanta, Aug. 23, 1904; s. George Claude and Willia Tallulah (Walters) B.; B.Ph., Emory U., 1925; B.D., 1938; B.D., Union Theol. Sem., N.Y., 1934, S.T.M., 1936; Ph.D., Columbia, 1941; D.D. (hon.), Southwestern U., Georgetown, Tex., 1946; m. Lovell Roena Wright, Feb. 2, 1948; children—George Leonard, George Claude III, Randolph Monroe, Lovell Jeannine, Merrimon Walters. Dir. student activities Wesley Found., U. Tex., 1928-31; ordained to ministry Meth. Ch., 1930; asst. minister Travis Park Meth. Ch., San Antonio, 1931-33; minister Asbury Community Meth. Ch., Mt. Vernon, N.Y., 1934-37, First Meth. Ch., Laredo, Tex., 1937-41, Harlingen, Tex., 1941-43, San Angelo, Tex., 1937-41, Harlingen, Tex., 1941-43, San Angelo, Tex., 1943-46, Laurel Heights Meth. Ch., San Antonio, 1946-49; chaplain Southern Meth. U., also prof. homiletics, 1949-55, McCreless prof. Evangelism Perkins Sch. Theology, 1955, also dir. Perkins Outreach; staff Lakewood United Methodist Church, 1968-70; asso. minister Kessier Park United Meth. Ch., 1970-74; Deceli lectr. Millsaps Coll., 1953; lectr. Methodist Mission Centers in Africa, 1960; lecture tour to Meth. Sems. in South Am., 1967. Fraternal del. Meth. Centennial Conf., Foochow, China, 1947; del. jurisdictional conf. South Central Jurisdiction Meth. Ch., 1948; fraternal del. Diamond Jubilee of Methodism in Mexico, 1949; mem. Inst. World Meth. Theol. Studies, Oxford U., 1958. Commd. 2d lt., R.O.T.C., 1925; missioner to Air Force and Navy bases. Mem. Nat. Assn. Coll. Chaplains, Omicron Delta Kappa. Author: Early New England Methodism, 1941; Bible Lectures, 3 vols., 1944, 45, 46; Biography of Boldness, 1952. Editor: The Church and Evangelism, 1960. Contbr. lessons Adult Student. Home: Dallas, Tex., Died Oct. 6, 1974.

BAKER, GEORGE MERRICK, educator; b. Hartford, Conn., July 10, 1878; s. George Luther and Laura Ann (Marcy) B.; A.B., Yale, 1900 (Phi Beta Kappa), Ph.D., 1905; studied univs. of Berlin and Munich; m. Grace Edith Mahl, Apr. 8, 1903. Instr. German, Yale, 1901-10; German master, Penn Charter Sch., Phila., 1910-14; prof. Germanic langs. from 1914, dean coll. arts and scis., 1920-52, Univ. of the South. Served as capt. gen. staff, in France, World War. Republican. Episcopalian. Home: Sewanee, Tenn.†

BAKER, GLADDEN WHETSTONE, bus. exec.; b. Fall River, Mass., Jan. 11, 1898; s. Marion Whetstone and Emma (James) B.; A.B., Washburn College, 1916, LL.D. (hon.), 1954; M.A., Yale, 1920, Ph.D., 1922; LL.D. (hon.), Trinity College, 1965; m. Marion Julia Williams, Oct. 11, 1923; children—Janet Williams (Mrs. J. Baker Tenney), Shepard Williams. Statistician N.Y. State Dept. Health, Albany, 1919; instr. econs. Yale, 1920-21; agts. dept. Fed. Res. Bank of N.Y., 1923-24; with Internat. Telephone Securities Corp., N.Y.C., 1925-26; joined Travelers Ins. Co., Hartford, Conn., 1926, asst. treas., 1930-34, treas., 1934-41, v.p., treas., 1941-55, director, mem. finance com., 1945-64, chmn. finance com., 1955-64; chmn. Broadcast-Plaza, Inc., 1964-68; spl. partner Wood, Struthers & Winthrop, 1965-69. Corporator St. Francis Hosp., Hartford Hosp., Mt. Sinai Hosp.; trustee, treas. Kingswood Sch., West Hartford, 1943-58, Boys' Club; chmn. Com. for Hartford Redevel. Trustee Washbrun Coll., 1962-71. Recipient Distinguished Pub. Service award Conn. Bar Assn., 1963; Nathan Hale award, 1970; Yale medal, 1971; Wilbur Lucius Cross medal, 1971. Asso. fellow Silliman Coll.; mem. Yale Grad. Sch. Assn. (pres. 1965-70). Conglist. Clubs: Graduates (New Haven); Recess, Yale (N.Y.C.); Hartford (Hartford, Conn). Home: West Hartford, Conn. Died July 4, 1974; interred Fairview Cemetery, West Hartford, Conn.

BAKER, HERBERT MADISON, lawyer; b. Greeley, Colo., Mar. 18, 1879; s. Edwin Eaton and Charlotte Adelle (Smith) B.; U. of Denver Law Sch., 1906-07; m. Mary Salmon Ware, June 21, 1914. Dep. clk. Dist. Court, Weld Co., Colo., 1901-06; began law practice, 1908, specializing in irrigation law; judge County Court of Weld Co., 1913-21. Mem. Am. Bar Assn., Colo. State Bar Assn., Boulder Co. Bar Assn., Am. Sociol. Society. Democrat. Unitarian. Elk. Author: The Farm and the School, 1918. Made retardation and attendance surveys of pub. schs. of Weld Co., while on bench, in order to handle juvenile cases scientifically, and pamphlets published by the court have been extensively distributed. Lecturer and contbr. to mags. on juvenile delinquency problems. Home: Longmont, Colo.†

BAKER, JAMES ANDREW, educator, animal virologist; b. Garland, La. Dec. 16, 1910; s. William Benjamin and Mary (Baldridge) B.; B.S. La. State U., 1932, M.A., 1934; Ph.D., Cornell U., 1938, D.V.M., 1940; m. Hallie Dudley Dodson, Nov. 27, 1934; 1 son, Andrew Lindsay. Fellow, Rockefeller Inst. Med. Research, Princeton, N.J., 1940, asst., 1941, asso., 1946; prof. virology Cornell U., 1947-75, dir. Vet. Virus Research Inst., 1950-75; cons. virology and immunology to hosps., govt., industry. Mem. adv. com. Office of Dir. Def. Research and Engring., Dept. Def., 1962-75. Named Veterinarian of Year, 1951, Dogdom's Man of Year, 1956, Gaines Poll. Mem. Am. Vet. Med. Assn., N.Y. Acad. Scis., Soc. Exptl. Pathology, Soc. Exptl. Biology and Medicine, Soc. Microbiology, Acad. Microbiology, U.S. Animal Health Assn., Conf. Research Workers. Contbr. articles profl. jours. and Ency. Brit. Research on viruses animals devel. into vaccines. Address: Ithaca N.Y. 14850 Died Apr. 14, 1975.

BAKER, JAMES CHAMBERLAIN, bishop; b. Sheldon, Ill., June 2, 1879; s. Benjamin Webb and Martha Frances (Henry) B.; A.B., Ill. Wesleyan U., 1898, D.D., 1913; S.T.B., Boston U., 1905; LL.D., Ill. Wesleyan U., 1928; Cornell Coll., 1930, Ohio Wesleyan U., 1931, College of the Pacific, 1934, U. of Southern Calif., 1940; L.H.D., Boston U., 1943; m. Lena Benson; children—Lois Benson, Elizabeth Benson (dec.). Prof. of Greek, Mo. Wesleyan Coll., Cameron, 1898-1902; entered M.E. ministry, 1900; pastor Ashland, Mass., 1903-05, McLean, Ill., 1905-07, Trinity Ch., Urbana, 1907-28; organizer and head of Wesley Foundation, U. of Ill. (the first Wesley Foundation in the country); elected bishop of M.E. Ch., 1928, assigned to supervision of work in Japan, Korea and Manchuria, assigned to San Francisco area, 1932, Cal., 1939, Los Angeles, 1940-52; vis. prof. Sch. of Religion, U. So. Cal. Del. Gen. Conf. M.E. Ch., 1916, 20, 24, 28, Oxford Conf., 1937, Madras Conf., 1938; v.p. Internat. Missionary Council since 1838, chmn., 1941-47, chmn. Whitbey Conf., 1947, International Missinary Council, 1941-47; mem. 4 man del. from Protestant Chs. of Am. to Japan, Oct. 1945; mem. Cambridge, Eng., conf. on ch. and internat. affairs, August 1946; mem. program committee organization meeting World Council of Churches, summer 1948, also mem. 1st Assembly and com. of 90; member Board of Foreign Mission, 1916-20; Member Joint Committee on State University Work; member University Senate of M.E. Church, 1920, also of Bd. of Edn., 1920-28; formerly mem. Student-Dept. Com. of Nat. Council Y.M.C.A.; chmn. Advance Program Com. Y.M.C.A. and mem. Constl. Conv. Y.M.C.A.; chmn. Div. of Educational Institutions, Meth. Bd. Education, since 1944; trustee U. of Southern Calif., Coll. of Pacific, Goodwill Industries; cons. U.N. Conf., San Francisco, 1945. Pres. Council of Meth. Bishops, 1948-49. Mem. Acacia Fraternity. Mason (32°). Hon. mem. A.K.L. Home: San Marino, Cal.†

BAKER, JOHN HOPKINSON, assn. exec.; b. Cambridge, Mass., June 30, 1894; s. George Pierce and Christina (Hopkinson) B.; student Cambridge Latin Sch., 1908-11; A.B., Harvard, 1915; m. Elizabeth Dabney, Mar. 2, 1921; children—Barbara C., Joan P. With fgn. sales dept. Nat. Cash Register Co., Dayton, O., 1915-17; accounting dept. Am. Internat. Corp., N.Y. City, 1919-21; with White Weld & Co and other investment bankers N.Y.C., 1921-34; chmn. bd., exec. dir. and pres. Nat Audubon Soc., N.Y.C. 1933-59; owner Blackbriar Farm, Dutchess Co., N.Y., breeder Aberdeen-Angus beef cattle, since 1932. Served as 1st lt., A.S., A.E.F., 1917-19. Mem. adv. com. to sec. of interior, from 1948, also chairman. Member board trustees National Parks Association. Member Audubon Society of Canada (pres.), Nat. Audubon Soc. of Greenwich, Inc. (pres.), Nat. Resources Council America (exec. com.), Am. Geog. Soc., Calif. Acad. Scis., Am. Mus. Natural History, Friends of the Land, Am. Ornith. Union, Linnaean Soc. of N.Y., Am. Soc. Mammalogists, Save-the-Redwoods League, Wilson, Cooper and Nuttall ornith. clubs, Sierra Club. Republican. Club: Century Assn. (New York). Editor: Audubon Guide to Attracting Birds, 1941. Home: Dover Plains N.Y. Died Sept. 21, 1973.

BAKER, JOSEPHINE, singer; b. St. Louis, June 3, 1906; d. Louis Baker; ed. Phila. schs.; m. Pepito Abbltano (dec.); m. 2d, Jean Lion; m. 3d, Jo Bouillon (div.); 12 adopted children. Appeared as singer in Harlem nightclubs at age 8, later chorine in Broadway musical, Shuffle Along; appeared in Paris in Le Revue Negre, later starred in Folies Bergeres, Casino de Paris, L'Olympia de Paris, other French revues; stage appearances Broadway's Carnegie Hall, also on Boardway's Brooks Atkinson Theater, N.Y.C.; star operattas, including La Creole; motion picture appearances include Zouzou, Princesse Tam-Tam, Fausse alerte. Decorated chevalier Legion of Honor, Croix de Guerre, Rosette de la Resistance (France). Mem. Internat. League Against Racism. Author: Les Memoires de Josephine Baker; La Tribu Arc-en-Ciel. Home: Dordogne, France. Died Apr. 1975.

BAKER, MORTON, radiologist; b. Chgo., 1913; M.D., Loyola U., 1936. Intern, Cook County Hosp., Chgo., 1937-38, resident, 1938-42; practice medicine specializing in radiology, Chgo., 1942-72; radiologist Walther Meml. Hosp. Mem. A.M.A. Home: Chicago, Ill. Died Feb. 1972.

BAKER, SAMUEL GARLAND, chemicals exec.; b. Tacoma, Oct. 19, 1902; son Samuel Garland and Ingeborg Marie (Paulson) B.; student U.S. Naval Acad., 1919-20; B.S., U. Wash., 1925; m. Frances Edith Buzard, July 25, 1929; children—Mary Elizabeth (Mrs. Robert Bacon), Janet Ellen (Mrs. Donald Vassallo). Gen. mgr. photo products dept. E. I. du Pont de Nemours & Company, 1950-56, general mgr. organic chems. dept., from 1956. Vice pres. U. Del. Research Found., Inc., 1960. Mem. Am. Petroleum Inst. (dir.), Color Assn. U.S. (pres. 1961), Synthetic Organic Chem. Mfrs. Assn. (pres. 1959-60), U. Wash. Alumnus, Summa Laude Dignatus, Alpha Sigma Phi, Phi Lambda Upsilon, Tau Beta Pi. Clubs: Wilmington, Wilmington Country; Chemists (N.Y.C.). Home: Wilmington, Del. Died July 10, 1974.

BAKER, WALTER BROWNE, banking and real estate cons.; b. Houston, Jan. 23, 1900; s. James A. and Alice (Graham) B.; grad. Hill Sch., Pottstown, Pa.; grad. Princeton, 1921; m. Adelaide Lovett, Dec. 23, 1922; children—W. Browne, Lovett Graeme. With Tex. Nat. Bank (formerly S. Tex. Comml. Nat. Bank), Houston, 1917-66, clk. proof dept., 1921-23, asst. cashier, 1924-25, sr. v.p., dir., 1945-66 (now Tex. Nat. Bank of Commerce of Houston); cons. banking and real estate, Houston, 1966-68; asst. nat. bank examiner, 1923-24; v.p., trust officer, dir. Guardian Trust Co., 1925-45; dir. Graham Realty Co., Oriental Textile Mills, Heitman, Bering-Cortes Co., Houston, York Royalty Co. Bd. dirs., v.p. Houston Met. YMCA. Served with USN, World War I; chief negotiation div. Office Sec. Navy, World War II. Recipient Distinguished Civilian Service award USN, 1945. Mem. Houston Com. Fgn. Relations, Philos. Soc. Tex., English Speaking Union, Newcomen Soc. N.Am., Friends of Rice. Episcopalian. Clubs: Ramada, River Oaks Country, Princeton (N.Y.C.); Cottage (Princeton); Greater Houston Gun. Home: Houston Tex. Died Nov. 17, 1968.

BAKER, WILDER DUPUY, ret. naval officer; b. Topeka, July 22, 1890; s. Isaac Newcomb and Mary Richards Haskins (DuPuy) B.; B.S., U.S. Naval Acad., 1914; m. Constance Metcalfe, 1916 (died July, 1925); 1 dau., Constance Kathryn (wife of Comdr. Harold G. Bowen, Jr., U.S.N.); m. 2d, Cora Barry, Jan. 1, 1930; 1 son, Wilder DuPuy. Commd. ensign, U.S. Navy, 1914, advancing through the grades to rear adm., 1942, now vice adm. U.S.N. ret.; with Solar Aircraft Co., San Diego. Decorated Navy Cross, Silver Star, Legion of Merit, Bronze Star, Clubs: Chevy Chase, Army and Navy. Home: La Jolla, Cal., Died Nov. 10, 1975.

BAKER, WILLIAM REGINALD, JR., advt. agency exec.; b. Madison, N.J., Oct. 13, 1898; s. William Reginald and Margaret (Decker) B.; Litt.B., Princeton, 1919; m. Ruth Kinnicutt, June 23, 1923; children—William Kinnicutt, Bruce Kinnicutt. Began in retail grocery work, 1919-20; production, Batten, Barton, Durstine & Osborn, Inc., 1920-22, asst. to mgr., account representative, Boston office, 1922-26, account group head, handling large and small food accounts, 1926-32; with Benton & Bowles, Inc., 1933-65, account rep. for General Foods products, 1933-37, mgr. Hollywood office and supervisor four radio programs, 1937-39; supr. account Gen. Foods, 1939-56, exec. v.p., 1943-50, pres., 1950-52, chmn. bd., 1952-61, hon. chairman board, 1961-65; director Advt. Council, from 1943, chairman, 1963-65. Director, former president Nat. USO; director N.Y. Travelers Aid Society; vice president of National Travelers Aid Society. Apprentice seaman, Wissahickon Barracks, N.J., USNR, 1918. Mem. Am. Assn. Advt. Agencies (former chairman),

National Outdoor Advt. Bur. Inc. (dir.). Clubs: Oyster Harbors (Osterville, Mass.); Princeton, University, India House (N.Y.C.); Wianno (Mass.); Burnam Wood Golf (Montecito, Cal.). Home: New York City, N.Y. Died Mar. 11, 1975; interred Beechwood Cemetery, Centerville, Mass.

BAKWIN, HARRY, pediatrician; b. Utica, N.Y., Nov. 19, 1894; s. Simon and Emma (Nadel) B.; B.S., Columbia, 1915, M.D., 1917; postgrad. Berlin and Vienna univs., 1924-25; m. Ruth Morris, 1925; children—Edward Morris, Barbara Swift (Mrs. W.S. Rosenthal), Patricia Anne (Mrs. F.R. Selch), Michael. Interne, Bellevue Hosp., 1917-18, asst. vis. physician, 1925-30, asso. attending physician, 1930-43, vis. physician children's med. service, from 1943; research asst. N.Y. Nursery and Childs, 1919-24; asst. instr. pediatrics Cornell Med. Coll., N.Y.C., 1919-24; instr. pediatrics Columbia, 1925-30; asst. prof. pediatrics N.Y.U., 1939-40, asso. prof., 1940-49; asso. prof. pediatrics N.Y.U.-Bellevue Med. Center, 1940-50, prof. clin. pediatrics, from 1950; courtesy staff Univ. Hosp., N.Y.C.; cons. Norwalk (Conn.) Hosp., Elizabeth A. Horton Meml. Hosp., Middletown, N.Y. Infirmary, N.Y.C., Bayonne (N.J.) Hosp. and Dispensary, Newark, Beth Israel Hosp., Mt. Vernon (N.Y.) Hosp., Phelps Meml. Hosp., Tarrytown, N.Y. Served as 1st lt. M.C., AUS, 1918-19. Fellow Am. Pub. Health Assn.; mem. N.J. Soc. Dentistry Children (hon.), Am., World med. assns., Am. Soc. Human Genetics, Am. Acad. Pediatrics (pres. 1955-56), Am. Pediatric Soc., N.Y. Acad. Medicine, Soc. Exptl. Biology and Medicine, N.Y. State, N.Y. County med. societies, Soc. for Research in Child Devel., Brit. Pediatric Assn. (corr.), Sociedad Antioquena de Pediatria (hon.), Sociedad Ecuadorana de Pediatria (hon.), Associaciòn Pediatrica de Guatemala (hon.), Sociedad Peruana de Pediatria (hon.), Sociedad de Puericultura y Pediatria (hon.), Sociedad Argentina de Pediatria (hon.), Brazilian Pediatric Soc. (hon.), South African Pediatric Assn. (hon.), Alpha Omega Alpha. Author: Psychologic Care during Infancy and Childhood, 1942; Clinical Management of Behavior Disorders in Children, 1953, 60, 66, 72; also numerous articles on growth and devel. of children. Home: New York City N.Y. Died Dec. 25, 1973.

BALASSONE, FRANCIS SALVATORE, state ofcl.; b. Thomas, W.Va., Feb. 5, 1915; s. Joseph and Anna (La Civita) B.; B.S., U. Md., 1940; m. Dolores R. Bond, July 3, 1945; children—Francis Salvatore II, John J., Michael T., Paul L. Chemist Standard Pharm. Corp., Balt., 1940-41; gen. mgr., exec. v.p. Yager Drug Co., Balt., 1941-51; instr. U. Md. Sch. Pharmacy, 1946-51; owner Overlea Pharmacy, Balt., 1951-56; commr. Md. Bd. Pharmacy, 1955-72, sec.-treas., 1955-72; chief div. drug control Md. Dept. Health and Metal Hygiene, 1955-72, acting dir. Bur. Consumer Health Protection, 1970-72; cons. FDA; chmn. com. Nat. Assn. Bds. Pharmacy on Status Pharmacists in Govt. Service; mem. com. Revision Model Food and Drug Act; del. Office Emergency Planning, Exec. Office Pres., 1963; cons. pharmacy services com. med. care Md. Health Dept.; mem. Gov.'s Commn. Revise Food, Drug, Poison Laws. Served to capt. USMCR, 1942-46. Recipient Honored Alumnus award Sch. Pharmacy, U. Md., 1965, Meml. Lecture Hall dedicated in his honor, 1973. Mem. Am. (pres. Balt. br.), Md., Balt. Met. pharm. assns., Nat. Assn. Bds. Pharmacy (pres. 1965-66), Assn. Food and Drug Ofcls. U.S. (pres. Central Atlantic States 1966-67, H.W. Wiley award 1971), Am. Pub. Health Assn. (chmn. program area com. on drugs 1967—), Internat. Narcotics Enforcement Officers Assn., Am. Council Pharm. Edn., National Drug Trade Conf., Md. Pub. Health Assn., Md. Soc. Hosp. Pharmacists (W. Arthur Purdum award 1976), Md. Soc. Med. Research, Phi Delta Chi. Democrat. Roman Catholic. K.C. Home: Baltimore, Md. Died Jan. 2, 1972; interred Dulaney Valley Meml. Gardens, Timonium, Md.

BALCHEN, BERNT, air force officer; b. Tveit, Topdal, Norway, Oct. 23, 1899, s. s. Lauritz and Dagny (Dietrichson) B.; ed. Oslo and Horten, 1918-21, Advanced Forestry Engring. Sch., Sweden, 1921; D.Sc., Tufts Coll., 1953, U. Alaska, 1954; m. Emmy Soerlie, Oct. 18, 1930 (separated 1941); 1 son, Bernt; m. 2d, Inger Engelbrethsen, Feb. 26, 1948; 1 son, Lauritz; m. 3d, Audrey Schipper, Nov. 30, 1966. Came to U.S., 1926, declared citizen, 1931. Served with White Army, Finland, 1918, Royal Norwegian Naval Air Force, 1921-26. Pilot engr. Roald Amundsen, Svalbard, 1925-26: test pilot Fokker, Northrop aircraft corps., 1926-33; with Western Can. Airways, Ft. Churchill ops., 1927; piloted Adm. Byrd across Atlantic, 1927; pilot of Bremen relief expdn. to Greenly Island, Laborador, 1928; chief pilot Adm. Byrd's Antarctic Expdn. (piloted first flight over South Pole Nov. 29, 1929), 1928-30; pilot Viking Rescue Expdn. to Nfld. (Can.), 1931; chief pilot Ellsworth Antarctic Expdn., 1933-35; chief insp. Norwegian Airlines, Oslo, 1935-40, mng. dir., 1946-48; served with RAF Ferry command as pilot-navigator, 1940-41, head first flight from San Diego to Singapore, joined U.S. Air Force, 1941. Builder secret airbase Bluie West 8 on Greenland, comdg. officer of sta., 1941-43; leader bombing missions out of Iceland; chief Allied A.T.C. for Norway, Sweden, Denmark, Finland, USSR in Stockholm, Sweden, 1943-45; also support Norwegian underground resistance against German occupation forces, comdg. officer air operations against German forces in no. Norway, 1944-45, evacuation of 70,000 Russians from slave labor camp no. Norway; spl. missions 8th Air Force U.S.S.T.A.F.-O.S.S. (Scandinavia), 1943-45; comdr. 10th Rescue Squadron, Alaska; stationed Ft. Richardson, Alaska, 1948-50; pilot first flight from Alaska across North Pole, 1949; assigned Hdqrs., Air Force, 1951-56; pioneered building air base, Thule, Greenland, 1953. Cons. Gen. Precision Labs., Inc., Tarrytown, N.Y., Gen. Dynamics Corp., N.Y.C. Decorated Congressional medal, D.S.M., Legion of Merit, D.F.C., Air medal with 5 silver oak leaf clusters, Soldiers medal with oak leaf cluster, 2 medals of Valor, City of N.Y., King Albert's Flying Cross, City of Paris Gold medal, Leiv Erickson medal, Medaille de Merit, King Christian X medal of freedom, comdr. 1st class Order of St. Olav with Swords and Stars; recipient Explorers Club's medal Harmon Trophy, 1953; comdr. 1st class Royal Order of Sword, Sweden. Mem. Quiet Birdmen, Norwegian Geog. Soc. Am., Norwegian Polar Soc., Am. Legion (comdr.), Nat. Pilots Assn., Norwegian Air Force Officers Assn. (hon.), Order Daedalians. Mason. Clubs: Explorers (hon.), Lotos, Wings (N.Y.C.); Aero (Norway); Adventurers; Camp Fire Am. Author: Next Fifty Years of Flight, 1954; Come North With Me, 1958. Exhibited paintings, 3d watercolor show Grand Central Galleries, 1955. Home: Chappaqua N.Y. Died Oct. 17, 1973; buried Arlington Nat. Cemetery.

BALDES, EDWARD JAMES, biophysicist; b. Fairfield, Neb., July 5, 1898; s. Joseph James and Margaret (Lenzen) B.; B.A., U. Sask., 1918, LL.D., 1955; M.A., Harvard, 1920, Whiting Fellow, 1922, Ph.D., 1924; Ph.D., Univ. Coll., London U. (Eng.), 1936; m. Mary Cooney, June 27, 1934; children—Joseph James, Mary Margaret, Honora, Elizabeth Louise. Asst. physics U. Sask., 1918-19, Radcliffe Coll., Cambridge, Mass., 1921-24; instr. physics Harvard, 1923-24; asso. div. physics and biophys. research Mayo Clinic, 1924-63, chmn. sect. biophysics, 1948-58; vice chmn. Mayo Aero Med. Unit, 1942-63; prof. biophysics Mayo Found. Grad. Sch., U. Minn., 1943-63; with sci. analysis br., life sci. div. U.S. Army Research Office, 1963-67, sci. adviser U.S. Army Aeromed. Research Lab., Fort Rucker, Ala., 1967-72, cons., 1973-75. Cons. council on phys. medicine and rehab. A.M.A., 1946-56; mem. council Am. Electroencephalographic Soc., 1947-51; chmn. panel on aviation medicine Research and Devel. Bd., Nat. Mil. Establishment, 1946-53; mem. panel on aero. medicine Sci. Adv. Bd., Chief Staff USAF, 1948-54; alternate mem. Aero Space Med. Panel Adv. Group, Aero. Research and Devel.-NATO, 1960-64, mem. com. biodynamics, 1970-75; adv. panel sci. and tech. Ho. Reps. com. sci. and astronautics, 1960-69; mem. subcom. acceleration NRC, 1942-46, com. aviation medicine 1946-49, com. hearing, bioacoustics and biomechanics; spl. cons. Aero Med. Lab., Wright-Patterson AFB, 1942-49; mem. adv. panel physiology Office Naval Research, 1947-51; mem. adv. com. Stapp Car Crash Confs.; chmn. symposium Linear Acceleration of Impact Type, 1971. Decorated chevalier Legion of Honor (France); knight St. Gregory the Great; recipient of War Dept. Commendation and Medal for Exceptional Civilian Service in aviation medicine to USAF, 1945; presdl. citation for work in aviation medicine, 1948; Eric LilJencrantz award Aerospace Med. Assn., 1968. Fellow Aerospace Med. Assn. (exec. council 1953-56), Am. Phys. Soc.; mem. Am. Inst. Aero. and Astronautics, Am. Physiol. Soc., A.A.A.S., Biophys. Soc., Minn. Acad. Sci. (pres. 1956-57), Am. Minn. heart assns., Air Force Assn., Internat. Soc. Med. and Biol. Engring. Sigma Xi (hon.). Author of over 150 sci. papers in field of biophysics, physiology, aviation medicine. Editorial bd. Internat. Jour. EEG and Clin. Neurophysiology, 1947-54, Jour. Physiology, Jour. Applied Physiology, 1956-63; adv. editorial bd. Aerospace Medicine, Aerospace Med. Assn., 1957-75. Home: Vista, Cal. Died May 11, 1975; buried Valley Oaks Meml. Park, Westlake Village, Cal.

BALDWIN, CALVIN BENHAM, assn. exec.; b. Radford, Virginia, Aug. 19, 1902; s. William Thomas and Lizzie (Worth) B.; student Va. Poly Inst. 1920-23; m. Louise Delp, June 25, 1924 (div. 1948); children—Calvin Benham, Sally Worth; m. 2d, Lillian H. Traugott, June 11, 1948. Shop insp. N. & W. Ry., Roanoke, Va., 1923-25, asst. to gen. foreman, 1925-28; mgr. and owner Electric Sales & Service Col, East Radford, 1928-33; asst. to U.S. sec. of agr., Washington, D.C., 1933-35; asst. adminstr. Resettlement Adminstrn. and Farm Security Adminstrn., Washington, D.C., 1935-40; adminstr. Farm Security Adminstrn., Oct. 11, 1940-Sept. 1943; apptd. coordinator State Department, Italy, 1943. Del. Pan-American Housing Conf., Buenos Aires, 1939; asst. chmn., C.I.O. Polit Action Com., Nov. 1943-May 1945; executive vice chmn. Progressive Citizens of Am. 1947-48; nat. sec. Progressive Party since 1948; campaign mgr. for Henry A. Wallace, Progressive Party candidate for pres., 1948. Presbyn. Home: Greenwich, Conn. Died May 12, 1975.

BALDWIN, JOHN THOMAS, JR., botanist; b. Chase City, Va., Sept. 5, 1910; s. John Thomas and Lona Earle (Price) B.; A.B., Coll. William and Mary, 1932; Ph.D., U. Va., 1937; Gen. Edn. Bd. fellow Cornell U., 1937-38. Asst. prof. biology Coll. William and Mary, 1937-39; instr. in botany U. Mich., 1939-42; agt. (asso. cytologist) Rubber Plant Investigations, U.S. Dept. Agr., Amazon Valley, 1942-44; mgr. Blandy Exptl. Farm, also asst. prof. U. Va., 1944-46; prof. biology Coll. William and Mary, 1946-74, chmn. dept. biology, 1952-62. Horticulturist U.S. Econ. Mission to Liberia, U.S. Dept. of State, 1947-48; prin. botanist Div. Plant Exploration and Introduction, U.S. Dept. of Agr., in Africa and Mexico, 1949-50. Mem. Va. State Parks Study Com. Exec. dir. William and Mary participation in Va. 350th Anniversary Year; mem. adv. com. Orland E. White Research Arboretum, Blandy Exptl. Farm, Boyce, Va. Recipient Alumni medallion Coll. William and Mary, 1971, award Council Williamsburg Garden Clubs, 1971. Fellow A.A.A.S.; mem. Boxwood Soc. Am. (dir. 1960-64, 1st v.p. 1964—), Am. Soc. Naturalists, Am. Assn. Bot. Gardens and Arboretums (dir.), Am. Genetic Assn., Am., New Eng., Cal. bot. socs., Association pour l'Etude Taxonomique de la Flore d'Afrique Tropicale, Am. Soc. Plant Taxonomists, Soc. Study Evolution, Soc. Venezolana de Ciencias Naturales (hon.), Torrey, South Appalacian bot. clubs, Phi Beta Kappa (v.p. Alpha of Va. 1960-62), Phi Kappa Phi, Sigma Xi, Phi Sigma. Club: Cosmos (Washington). Contbr. papers to tech. jours. Home: Williamsburg Va. Died Sept. 3, 1974.

BALDWIN, MARSHALL WHITHED, ret. educator; b. New Haven, Mar. 30, 1903; s. Charles Sears and Gratia Eaton (Whithed) B.; B.A., Columbia, 1924; Ph.D., Princeton, 1934; m. Helen Muhlfeld, June 18, 1936 (dec.); children—Mary, Margaret (Mrs. Roland Walters). Instr. in history N.Y.U., 1932-34, asst. prof., 1935-45, asso. prof., 1945-54, prof., 1954-73. Mem. Am. Hist. Assn., Am. Cath. Hist. Assn. (pres. 1941), Mediaeval Acad. Am. Author: Raymond III of Tripoli, 1936; Pope Alexander III and the Twelfth Century, 1969, The Mediaeval Church, 1953; (with C. H. Hayes, C. W. Cole) History of Western Civilization, 1962. Editor: Christianity Through The Thirteenth Century, 1970; (with K. M. Setton) History of the Crusades, 1955. Died 1975.

BALDWIN, WESLEY MANNING, anatomist; b. Troy, N.Y., Aug. 18, 1879; s. Melvin Cornelius and Helen Smith (Capron) B.; A.B., Cornell U., 1907, A.M., 1909; M.D., Cornell U. Med. Coll., 1911; candidate for Ph.D. at Bonn, 1911-12, Würzburg, 1913; Sorbonne, 1925; married Helen Patton Bullard, February 11, 1925; 1 daughter, Cynthia J. Assistant demonstrator, instructor in anatomy, Cornell University Medical Coll., Ithaca, 1904-09; instr. anatomy, 1909-14, asst. prof., 1914-15, Cornell U. Med. Coll., N.Y. City; prof. anatomy, Albany Med. Coll. (Union U.), 1915-36; anatomist to Albany Hosp., 1929-1936. Mem. Am. Assn. of Anatomists, Deutsche Anatomische Gesellschaft, Sigma Xi, Alpha Omega Alpha, Nu Sigma Nu, Gamma Alpha; fellow A.A.A.S., Mason. Contbr. articles to anat. and biol. jours. in U.S., Germany and Switzerland. Special studies on biol. effects of X-ray energy, studies on muscle structure, and on the ducts of the pancreas in man, various physical forces on cells. Home: York Beach, Me. Died June 16, 1975; buried Troy, N.Y.

BALL, HELEN ELIZABETH VOELLMIG, Mrs. Robert Tyler Ball), office supply co. exec.; b. Detroit; d. William and Ida (Slinger) Voellmig; A.B., Wayne State U., 1929, M.A., 1936, also tchrs. life certificate; studied voice and piano at Detroit Inst. Mus. Art; m. Robert Tyler Ball, June 20, 1936. Tchr. English, Western High Sch., Detroit, 1936-41; sec., buyer Ball Office Supply, Inc., Ann Arbor, Mich., 1953-74. Meml. library given to Grace Bible Ch., Ann Arbor, Mich. Mem. Am. Assn. U. Women, Alpha Gamma Delta. Clubs: Zonta, Ann Arbor Garden, Women's City (charter mem.) (Ann Arbor). Home: Ann Arbor, Mich., Died Aug. 1974; buried Woodmere Cemetery, Detroit, Mich.

BALL, ROBERT BRUCE, ry. official; b. Huntsville, Mo., Dec. 17, 1878; s. James Harris and Sallie (Davis) B.; A.B., Stanford U., 1904; m. Mabel G. O'Brien, Oct. 15, 1909; children—Mary Davis (Mrs. John Blair Crawford), Eileen Mable (Mrs. Robert Biering). Held various position in engring. dept., Santa Fe Ry., 1904-10, div. engr., 1910-12, dist. engr., 1912-19, chief engr., 1919-29, asst. chief engr. of system, 1929-36, asst. gen. mgr., 1936-39; v.p. and gen. mgr. G.C.&S.F.Ry. (Santa Fe) from 1939; dir. Dallas Union Terminal, Ft. Worth Union Depot, Texas City Terminal, All Tex-Santa Fe subsidiaries. Home: Galveston, Tex.†

BALLER, STUART TAYLOR, ednl. adminstr.; b. De Witt, Nebr., July 19, 1903; s. Albert H. and Mary (Taylor) B.; A.B., Neb. Wesleyan U., 1924; A.M., U. Nebr., 1932, Ph.D., 1950; student George Peabody Coll., 1937; m. Mabel B. Lake, July 25, 1926; children—Richard H., Robert S. Coach, tchr. Exeter (Neb.) High Sch., 1924-25; head coach Univ. Place High Sch., Lincoln, Neb., 1925-30; head coach Lincoln High Sch., 1930-1936; coach, asst. dir. phys. edn. Peru (Neb.) State Tchrs. Coll., 1936-38; coach, dir. phys. edn. U. Omaha, 1938-44; dir. recreation Martin Aircraft Co., 1944-45; supt. schs., Wayne, Neb., 1945-49; dean Carthage (Ill.) Coll., 1949-61; acad. v.p., 1961-64; dean acad. affairs Robert Morris Jr. Coll. of Carthage, 1965-66; prof. edn. and psychology, asso. dean for research and grants William Penn Coll., Oskaloosa, Ia., 1966-67, asso. dean, 1967-75. Named Ark. Traveler, 1967, adm. Neb. Navy, 1969. Mem. N. Central Academic Deans Assn. (pres. 1956-57), Phi Delta Kappa. Mason; mem. Order of

Eastern Star (worthy patron 1961-62). Kiwanian. Contbr. articles to ednl. publs. Home: Oskaloosa, Ia. Died Aug. 24, 1975; interred Lincoln, Neb.

BALLINGER, CHARLES L., med. assn. ofcl., osteo. physician; b. East Liberty, O., Aug. 20, 1899; s. Amer Jesse and Anna (Morse) B.; B.A., Ohio Wesleyan U., 1922; D.O., Kirksville Coll. Osteo. Medicine, 1925; m. Mildred Elizabeth Bowling, Sept. 2, 1922; children—Richard, Bowling, Robert Morse, Lucy Ann (Mrs. Robert Craig), Larson. Intern Delaware Springs Hosp., Delaware, O., 1925-26, gen. practice of osteo. medicine and surgery, Medina, O., 1926-35, Akron, O., 1935-43, Toledo, 1943-59. Trustee Parkview Hosp., Toledo, 1939-74, sec., treas., 1943-74. Fellow Am. Coll. Osteo. Surgeons (gov. 1942-58, sec. 1953-74, exec. sec. 1960-74, pres. 1950-74, Orel F. Martin medal 1968), Ohio Assn. Osteo. Physicians and Surgeons (pres. 1948-74). Methodist (trustee 1930-49). Kiwanian (pres. 1936). Home: Coral Gables, Fla. Died June 15, 1974.

BALLINGER, JOHN H., business exec.; b. Keokuk, Ia., 1879; grad. George Washington U., 1910. Mem. Venables, Ballinger & Clarke, Seattle; dir. Seattle-First Nat. Bank, Gen. Am. Corp., Centennial Flowing Mill Co., McKesson & Robbins, Inc. Home: Seattle, Wash.†

BALLINGER, ROBERT IRVING, architect; b. Md., May 22, 1892; s. Walter F. and Bessie M. (Connell) B.; grad. Germantown (Phila.) Acad., 1910; Pratt Inst., 1915; m. Frances Taylor, May 17, 1917; children—Robert I., Jean B. Rauch, Dr. Walter F. Practiced in Phila., from 1915; ret. sr. mem. firm The Ballinger Co., architects and engrs., Ballinger Assos.; pres., dir. Balcom Realty Corp. Designed plants of Atwater Kent Mfg. Co., Budd Mfg. Co., Victor Talking Machine Co., etc., also many chs., office bldgs., hosps. and apt. houses in eastern U.S.; designed reconstruction of Phila. Quartermaster Depot, and other bldgs. for Army, Navy and the Defense Corp.; bldgs. for bd. dirs. of City Trusts of Philadelphia; asso. in design U.S. Fed. Bldg., Philadelphia. Mem. Am. Inst. Architects. Republican. Methodist. Former pres. trustees Meth. Home for Aged. Club: Union League. Home: Alden Park, Phila. Pa. Died Aug. 18, 1974.

BALUTIS, BRONIUS KASIMIR, diplomat; b. Seirijai, Lithuania, Dec. 27, 1879; s. Ipolitas and Ursulé (Zidanavicaite) B.; grad. Sch. of Surveying, Pskov, 1904; LL.M., Coll. of Law, 1916; m. Mary Rechen, of Pskov, Sept. 3, 1910; 1 dau., Ada. Editor and lawyer, 1912-1919; del. to Peace Conf., Paris, 1919; dir. polit. dept., Foreign Office, Lithuania, 1920-27, undersec., 1927; E.E. and M.P., Washington, D.C., from 1928. Decorated Knight of Grand Duke of Lithuania Gediminas; Knight, Corona d'Italia. Roman Catholic. Address: Washington, D.C.†

BANCROFT, PHILIP, farmer; b. San Francisco, Calif., June 30, 1881; s. Hubert Howe and Matilda Colley (Griffing) B.; prep. edn. Phillips Exeter Acad., 1894-95, and Browne and Nichols Sch., 1895-98; A.B., Harvard, 1903, A.M., 1904; LL.B., Hastings Coll. of Law, University of California, 1905; married Nina Otis. Eldred, June 30, 1905; children—Anne Bancroft, Lucy Eldred (Mrs. John Alden Redfield), Philip Bancroft, Jr. Admitted to California bar, 1905. and practiced in San Francisco, 1905-17; farming in Contra Costa Co., Calif., since 1919; active in local and statewide farmer activities. Pres. West Am. Finance Co.; dir. Tech. Oil Tool Co. Rep. nominee for U.S. Senator, 1938. Served in 1st R.O.T.C., San Francisco, 1917; served with U.S. Army, with A.E.F., 1917-19; disch. as 1st lt. Mem. Am. Legion, Farm Bur., Asso. Farmers (pres.), Grange. Clubs: Commonwealth, Harvard, Family (San Francisco); Rotary (Walnut Creek); Pi Eta (Harvard). Radio speaker on public questions, Address: Walnut Creek, Cal.†

BANDY, ORVILLE LEE, geologist, educator; b. Linden, Ia., Mar. 31, 1917; s. Alfred Lee and Blanche (Meacham) B.; B.S., Ore. State U., 1940, M.S., 1941; Ph.D. (Shell Oil fellow), Ind. U., 1948; m. Alda Ann Umbras, June 10, 1943 children—Janet Lee, Donald Craig. Mem. faculty geology U. So. Cal., Los Angeles, 1948-73, prof., 1954-67, chmn. dept. geol. scis., 1967. Bd. dirs. Cushman Found. for Foraminiferal Research. Fellow Geol. Soc. Am.; mem. A.A.A.S., Soc. Econ. Paleontologists and Mineralogists (counselor 1963-64, v.p. 1969-70, pres. 1971-72), Am. Assn. Petroleum Geologists (trustee research fund 1960-64, distinguished lectr. 1963-64), Am. Soc. Limnology and Oceanography, Ecol. Soc. Am., Schweiz. Geologische Gesellschaft, Sigma Xi. Contbr. articles to profl. jours. Home: Los Angeles, Cal. Died Aug. 2, 1973; cremated.

BANKER, WALTER, b. Wilkes-Barre, Pa., Mar. 13, 1881; s. Charles Henry and Emily (Campsen) B.; ed. pub. schs. m. Edna Seward, of Luzerne, Pa., Oct. 23, 1907; children—Elizabeth Martha, Marjorie Jean, Philip Walter. Druggist since 1894. Pres. and chmn. exec. com. Luther League of America from 1922. Mem. Nat. Assn. Retail Druggists, Luzerne County Pharm. Assn. Odd Fellow, Kiwanian. Home: Kingston, Pa.†

BANNERMAN, ARTHUR MARLING, coll. pres.; b. Juneau, Alaska, May 26, 1900; s. William S. and Grace (Mitchell) B., A.B., Lafayette Coll., 1922, L.H.D., 1945; A.M., U. N.C., 1940; LL.D., Berea Coll., Johnson C. Smith U., Warren Wilson Coll., 1972; student U. Wis., Middlebury Coll.; m. D. Lucile Patton, Nov. 27, 1930; children—Janet Patton, Mary Mitchell. Instr. Asheville (N.C.) Farm Sch., 1928-42, prin., 1930-38, supt., 1940-42; pres. Warren Wilson Coll., Swannanoa, N.C., 1942-71, pres. emeritus, 1971-76. Dir. Swannanoa Bank & Trust Co. Mem. adv. bd. Asheville County Day Sch. Trustee James G. K. McClure Devel. and Ednl. Fund. Pres. Swannanoa Community Council, Greater Asheville Council; pres. bd. dirs. United Fund of Asheville and Buncombe County, 1957-58; mem. Buncombe County Planning Council; Commr. Hosp. Authority Buncombe County; treas. N.C. Found. Ch. Related Colls., 1959-60; pres. N.C. Council Ch. Related Colls., 1959-60; trustee Asheville City Libraries. Recipient Award of Merit, Asheville Sch., 1971. Mem. So. Mountain Workers (past pres. council), United Church Men (bd. mgrs.), Nat. Council Presbyn. Men (pres.), Sigma Alpha Epsilon. Presbyn. Clubs: Civitan of Asheville (past pres.); Biltomore Forest Country. Address: Swannanoa, N.C., Died Jan. 16, 1976.

BANNING, WILLIAM VAUGHN, physician; b. Mt. Vernon, O., July 13, 1906; s. William McCreary and Edna Lula (Vaughn) B.; B.S., Denison U., 1930; M.D., Ohio State U., 1931; postgrad. course in radiology U. Pa., 1948-49; m. Edna Roth, Aug. 10, 1946; 1 son, Jon Willroth. Intern, City Hosp., Akron, O., 1931-32, Womens and Childrens Hosp., Toledo, 1932-33; resident Peoples Hosp., Akron, 1949-50, Aultman Hosp., Canton, O., 1950-51, Strong Meml. Hosp., Rochester, N.Y., 1951-52, Miami Valley Hosp., Dayton, O., 1952-53, Caylor-Nichol Clinic, Bluffton, Ind., 1953-56; mem. staff Licking County Meml. Hosp., Newark, O., dir. dept. nuclear medicine, 1970-72; mem. staff Coshocton (O.) Meml. Hosp., Mercy Hosp.; mem. staff Martin Meml. Hosp., Mt. Vernon, dir. dept. nuclear medicine, 1970-72. Served as capt., M.C., AUS, 1942-46. Diplomate Am. Bd. Radiology. Mem. Am. Coll. Radiology, Radiol. Soc. N.Am., Ohio, Central Ohio radiol. socs., A.M.A., Ohio Med. Assn., Licking County Med. Soc., Newark Area C. of C. Presbyn. Home: Newark, O. Died Dec. 5, 1972; buried Mound View Cemetery, Mt. Vernon, O.

BANNISTER, ROBERT JAMES, lawyer; b. Ottumwa, Ia., Sept. 2, 1878; s. Dwight and Lavinia (Murdoch) B.; A.B., State U. Ia., 1900; LL.B., 1903; m. 1st, Lucille Thomas, June 2, 1909 (died 1943); m. 2d, Helen S. Shoak, Mar. 3, 1945. Admitted to Ia. bar, 1903, since practiced Des Moines; mem. firm Stipp Perry Bannister & Storgright, Carpenter Ahlers & Cooney; assistant attorney Chicago, Rock Island & Pacific Ry. Company, 1911-16; gen. counsel Des Moines & Central Ia. Ry. Co.; pres. Pushing Fuel Co., 1918-47. Mem. Des Moines Bd. Edn., 1916-20. Mem. Am., Ia. State and Polk Co. bar assns., Phi Beta Kappa. Home: Des Moines, Ia.†

BANNON, JOHN JOSEPH, JR., business exec.; b. Labadie, Mo., June 14, 1896; s. John Joseph and Annie (Schmonskie) B.; student evening coll. Tex. Christian U.; m. Helen K. Holmes, Sept. 11, 1941; 1 dau., Johanna Frances. Ins. salesman, 1922-26; dist. mgr. Reliable Life Ins. Co., Ft. Worth, Dallas, and Waco, Tex., 1926-49; pres. Capitol County Mut. Fire Ins. Co., Ft. Worth, 1949-67, dir., chmn. bd., chief exec. officer, 1967-69; asso. Steve Murrin Co., comml. real estate, 1969-73; dir. Capitol Town Mut. Ins. Co., St. Louis. Served with U.S. Mcht. Marine, 1918-22. Mem. Ft. Worth Life Mgrs. Assn. (past pres.), Ft. Worth Life Underwriters Assn. (past pres.), Ft. Worth C. of C., Tex. Christian U. Ex-Students Assn., Holy Name Soc. Roman Catholic. Lion. Home: Fort Worth Tex. Died Mar. 25, 1973.

BANOV, LEON, physician; b. Suwalki, Poland, July 5, 1888; s. Alexander and Sonia (Danielewicz) B.; M.D., Med. U. S.C.; m. Minnie Monash, Oct. 8, 1912; children—Leon, Morton Ira, Roslyn Desiree (Mrs. George Elbert Wyman). Operator Pharmacy, Charleston, S.C., 1909-12; asst. bacteriologist City of Charleston, 1913-18, chief food insp., 1918-20, health officer, 1926-36; health officer Charleston County, 1920-36, dir. health, 1936-62, spl. cons., 1962-71; instr. pharm. Latin and arithmetic, comml. pharmacy Sch. Pharmacy, Med. Coll. S.C., 1913-17, instr. bacteriology, 1917-18; asst. prof. pub. health and preventive medicine Med. U. S.C., 1920-26, asso. prof., 1926-46, prof., 1946-62, prof. emeritus, 1962-71; spl. cons. div. chronic diseases USPHS, 1950-62, spl. cons. on prevention accidental poisoning, 1962-71; spl. cons. pub. health adminstrn. S.C. Bd. Health, 1962-71. Exec. sec. Charleston County Tb Assn., 1925. Recipient Service to Mankind award Sertoma Internat., 1961, Citizens award Sta. WCSC-TV, 1966, James A. Hayne award S.C. Pub. Health Assn., 1970; named Man of Year, Charleston Rotary Club, 1970. Diplomate Am. Bd. Preventive Medicine. Fellow Am. Pub. Health Assn., Am. Coll. Preventive Medicine; mem. A.M.A., So. Med. Assn., Am. Assn. Pub. Health Physicians, Internat. Soc. Med. Health Officers (past pres.), Alpha Omega Alpha. Author: As I Recall—The Story of the Charleston County Health Department, 1971. Home: Charleston, S.C., Died Nov. 3, 1971; buried K.K. Beth Elohim Cemetery, Charleston, S.C.

BARAKAT, MOHAMMAD ZAKI TAHA IBRAHIM, educator; b. Cairo, Egypt, June 7, 1914; s. Taha Ibrahim and Dawiat (Hassny B.; Bachelor Pharmacy, Cairo U., 1935, M.Sc., 1940, Ph.D., 1949; m. Safia Saber El Hamalawi, Apr. 8, 1948; children—Amina, Amine. Pharmacist, Egyptian Ministry Public Health, 1935-37, chemist, 1939-42; demonstrator chemistry, faculty of sci. Cairo U., 1942-47, lectr. Higher Tng. Coll., 1947-49; lectr. biochemistry Faculty Medicine Abbassia, 1949-52; asst. prof. biochemistry Ain Shams U., Cairo, 1952-57; prof. biochemistry Faculty Vet. Medicine Cairo U., 1957-65; prof., head dept. Faculty Medicine Azhar U., Cairo, 1965-74. Mem. vis. staff radiotherapeutic dept. Cambridge (Eng.) U., 1951-52. Fellow Chem. Soc. London; mem. Egyptian Acad. Pharmacy (vice prin. 1966-74). Author: (with R. Moubasher) Theoretical Organic Chemistry, 1947. Contbr. profl. articles. Editorial bd. Jour. Vet. Medicine, 1960-65 Research in food sci., radio-biology, biol. fluids, deficiency diseases. Home: Cairo, Egypt., Died June 12, 1974.

BARBER, MURIEL V. (MRS. J.S. BARBER), artist; b. West Orange, N.J.; ed. Fawcett Art Sch., Newark, Wayman Adams Sch. Art; student Hubert DeGroat Main, Michael Lenson, Stanley Marc Wright, others. Exhibited in shows at Drew U., 1959, N.J. Fedn. Water Colorists, 1959, Art Center of Oranges, 1959, 60, Maplewood Art Gallery, 1959, Newark Library, 1960, Newark Mus., 1960, 64, Papermill Playhouse, 1965, Sarasota Art Assn., 1967, 68, Seton Hall U., 1964, numerous others; represented in permanent collections at Davis Elkins Coll., W. Va., others. Recipient numerous art prizes. Mem. Essex Watercolor Soc., Maplewood Watercolor Club, South Orange-Maplewood Art Assn., Art Center of Oranges. Address: Sarasota, Fla. Died Nov. 29, 1971; interred Sarasota, Fla.

BARBER, WILLIAM HARLEY, educator; b. Black Earth, Wis., Aug. 28, 1878; s. David A. and Martha Elizabeth (Wilson) B.; B.S., U. of Wis., 1901, A.M., 1909; grad. student in physics, U. of Chicago, summers, 1911-13 and year 1913-14; m. Esther Ellen Darrow, July 24, 1919; children—Jane Cornwell (Mrs. M.P. Emerson), Anne Homewood. Assistant principal Ripon High School, 1901-04, principal, 1904-05; with Bureau of Standards, United States Dept. Commerce and Labor, 1905-06; prof. physics Ripon Coll., 1906-46, prof. emeritus from 1946, registrar, 1910-15, and 1940-46, dean, 1915-24, acting president, 1917 and 1921; instr. in physics, U. of Wis., 1924-26. Mayor of Ripon, 1936-40. Coordinator, Ripon College, for Army Specialized Training Reserve Program for Service Unit 3657, 1944 Trustee League of Wisconsin Municipalities, 1939-40; sec. Wisconsin State Board of Examiners in the Basic Sciences. Recipient Oersted medal, 1947. Member Am. Physical Soc., Wis. Acad. Sciences, Arts and Letters, Am. Assn. of Univ. Profs., Wis. State Hist. Soc., Sigma Xi, Acacia Fraternity. Conglist. Mason. Home: Ripon Wis. Died 1973.

BARCELLA, ERNEST LAWRENCE, automotive co. exec.; b. Hamden, Conn., June 7, 1910; s. Battista J. and Ernesta R. (Casella) B.; A.B., Dartmouth, 1934; m. Louise Marian Berniere, June 18, 1935; children—Andrea Louise (Mrs. Bruce M. Kelleher), Ernest Lawrence. Reporter, sports writer New Haven Register, New Haven Times, 1928-30; with United Press Assn., 1930, successively staff New Haven, Hanover, N.H., Phila., Albany, N.Y., New Eng. sports editor and night mgr., Boston, central div. night mgr., Chgo., 1930-40, staff Washington bur., 1940, Pacific War Theater, 1945, bur. mgr. U.P.I., Washington, 1953-61; pub. relations exec. Gen. Motors Corp., 1961-65, dir. communications, pub. relations, 1963-65, Washington mgr., 1965. Washington trustee Fed. City council Dartmouth Alumni Council; bd. dirs. Washington Heart Assn., Washington Bd. Trade. Recipient Nat. Headliners award for fgn. coverage, 1960. Mem. White House Corrs. Assn., Am. Baseball Writers Assn., Sigma Chi, Sigma Delta Chi. Club: Nat. Press (Washington); Kenwood Country (Bethesda, Md.); Gridiron. Contbr. articles nat. mags. Home: Chevy Chase, Md. Died Jan. 19, 1974; interred North Haven, Conn.

BARD, RALPH A., former under-sec. Navy; b. Cleveland, O., July 29, 1884; s. George M. and Helen (Norwood) B.; B.S., Princeton U., 1906; m. Mary Hancock Spear, Feb. 23, 1909; children—Ralph A. Jr., Mrs. Thomas J. Johnson, Jr., Mrs. Martin E. Manulis, George M, II. Salesman Eversz & Company, investments, Chicago, 1906; Kennett Cown & Co., 1908-09; organizer and mem. Hitchcock, Bard & Co., Inc., 1919-25; formed and became pres. Ralph A. Bard & Co., later Bard & Co., 1925; became pres. Chicago Corp. 1932, vice president and director until 1934; organized Ralph A. Bard & Co., Chicago, Ill., 1934, president, 1934-41. Appointed assistant secretary of the Navy, Feb. 1941; under-secretary of the Navy, June 1944-July 1945; apptd. deputy to U.S. representative, U.N. Commn. on Conventional Armament, Mar. 1947. Served as vice pres. Chicago Council, Boy Scouts of America, Director of Military Relief, Central Div. Am. Red Cross, World War I. Trustee, Northwestern U. Clubs: Chicago, Coleman Lake, Old Elm, Attic, Commercial (Chicago); Princeton, Army and Navy, Chevy Chase (Washington, D.C.). Home: Lake Forest, Ill. Died Apr. 1975.

BARDEN, RODERICK DUDLEY, educator; b. Shreve, O., Mar. 26, 1900; s. Edwin A. and Izena M. (Stough) B.; B.S., Ohio State U., 1923, M.S., 1938; m. Frances Janney, June 15, 1929; 1 dau., Marilyn Lee. Sales staff Internat. Harvester Co., 1923; specialist Agrl. Extension Service, Ohio State U., 1924-46, faculty agrl. engring. dept., 1946-51, dir. Sch. Aviation and U. Airport, 1951-55, chmn. dept. agrl. engring., 1955-75; propr. Outdoors Store, Inc., 1934-75. Recipient distinguished service award U.S. Power Squadron; named prof. of the year, 1955. Mem. U.S., Columbus power squadrons, Am. Soc. A.E. Mason. Club: Sandusky Yacht. Home: Columbus, O. Died Mar. 15, 1975.

BARDO, AUGUST JOHN, govt. ofcl; b. Detroit, July 29, 1917; s. August J. and Catherine (Stahl) B.; A.B., U. Rochester, 1940; J.D., Union U., 1968; m. Beatrice F. Varney, Apr. 3, 1943; children—John Barry, Pamela Diane, Deborah Lynne, Lisa Anne. Mgr., operator Elmwood Restaurant, 1936-40; edn. contract officer VA, 1947-49; legal cons. for vet. affairs State U. N.Y., 1949-67; dept. commr. N.Y. State Liquor Authority, 1949-50; dir. div. profl. conduct N.Y. State Edn. Dept., 1950. Justice of Peace, Town of Somers, 1958; mem. faculty St. Bernardine of Siena Coll., Dept. Bus. Adminstrn., 1949; pvt. practice part time, from 1947. Cons. Joint Legislative Com. to Revise and Simplify Edn. Law State N.Y. Vice pres., dir. Cancer Detection Services, Inc., N.Y.C., 1969-71; trustee Psychoendocrine Research Found., Manhasset, N.Y. Served to 2d lt. AC, AUS, 1943-45. Mem. Am., N.Y. State, Westchester County bar assns. Republican. Episcopalian. Mason. Home: Katonah N.Y. Died July 17, 1972.

BARGER, FLOYD, newspaper editor; b. Boardman, O., Oct. 26, 1906; s. Emery and Susan (Nelson) B.; B.A., Wittenberg U., 1927, LL.D., 1969; m. Elizabeth Chick, Dec. 28, 1928; 1 son, Bruce. With Flushing (N.Y.) Jour., 1927-28, Bklyn. Eatle, 1928-40; with N.Y. Daily News, 1941-75, mng. editor, 1966-68, asso. editor, 1968-69, exec. editor, 1969-75; sr. v.p., dir. N.Y. News; dir. Tribune Co., Chgo. Tribune-N.Y. News Syndicate. Mem. Silurians, Lutheran. Clubs: Nat. Press (Washington); Garden City (N.Y.); Dutch Treat. Home: Garden City, N.Y. Died Aug. 1975; buried Rosehill Cemetery, Springfield, N.Y.

BARING, WALTER STEPHAN, congressman; b. Goldfield, Nev., Sept. 9, 1911; s. Walter Stephen and Emilie Louise (Froehlich) B.; B.S., B.A., U. Nev., 1934, high sch. tchrs. certificate; m. Alma Geraldine Buchanan, Jan. 31, 1942; children—Walter Stephan III, William Robert, John Buchanan, Thomas Jefferson. Elected chmn. Dem. Central Com. of Washoe County, 1936; assemblyman from Washoe County to Nev. Legislature, 1936, 1942; councilman 6th Ward, Reno City Council 1947; asso. with father in Sierra Furniture Co., Reno, 1945-48; mem. 81st-82nd Congress, 85th-93d Congresses, Nev. at large, chmn. pub. lands subcom. of interior com., mem. vets. affairs com. Served with USNR, 1942-45. Mem. Am. Legion. Democrat. Mason (32°, Shriner), Eagle; mem. Order Eastern Star. Club: Sertoma. Home: Reno, Nev. Died July 13, 1975.

BARKER, B(URRILL) DEVEREUX, lawyer, corp. officer; b. Sept. 2, 1878; s. William G. and Alice I. (Miller) B.; A.B., Harvard, 1901, LL.B., 1903; m. Irene Fitch Shepard, Jan. 16, 1907; 1 son, B. Devereux. Began practice at Boston, 1903; treas., dir. Boston Storage Co., Knitted Padding Co.; dir. Internat. Hydro Electric System. Republican. Episcopalian. Clubs: Union, Tennis and Racquet (Boston); Eastern Yacht, New York Yacht. Home: Boston, Mass.†

BARKER, BURT BROWN, lawyer; b. Waitsburg, Wash., Nov. 3, 1873; s. William Clement and Elvira Chadwick (Brown) B.; student Williamette U., Salem, Ore., 1889-93; A.B., U. of Chicago, 1897; LL.B., Harvard, 1901; LL.D., Linfield Coll., Ore., 1935; Litt.D., Pacific Univ., Forest Grove, Ore., 1964; m. Ella Starr Merrill, June 15, 1904; 1 dau., Barbara (Mrs. John A. Sprouse). Began practice of law, Chicago, 1901; mem. Wolseley & Barker, 1902-15; practiced alone in Chicago, 1915-17; practiced in N.Y. City, 1917-29; vice-pres. University Oregon, 1928—; member of the board of directors First Nat. Bank (Portland). Mem. Legal Advisory Bd. N.Y. City during period of World War, also sec. War Work Com. of Chicago Bar Assn. during same period. Trustee, dir. Salem Art Assn.; trustee Catlin Sch.; dir. Multnomah Co. Chpt. A.R.C., McLoughlin Meml. Assn.; chmn. liaison com. Ore. Hist. Soc. for Ore. history and mem. exec. com. Oregon Territorial Centennial Commission; president Herbert Hoover Foundation. Pres. Doernbecker Children's Hosp. Guild; chancellor Columbia Basin Session of Inst. of Internat. Relations, 1932; president dir. Ore. Hist. Soc.; chmn. Northwest Regional Committee of Advisory Committee to Treasury Dept. on Fine Arts; regional art dir. Federal Works of Art Projects, Ore., Wash., Idaho and Mont., 1935-36; state dir. for Ore. and regional advisor Fed. Art Project from 1936; chmn. Ore. Com. to place statues in Nat. Statuary Hall, Washington; chmn. Ore. Lewis and Clark Sequicentennial Celebration. Mem. Am. Bar Assn. com. of Am. Inst. for Endowments; chmn. Portland Advisory com. of 2d Am.-Japan Student Conf., 1935, 4th Conf., 1937, 6th Conf., 1939. Recipient of U. Chgo. Alumni Assn. citation for pub. service as useful citizen, Edith Knight Hill Meml. award for distinguished service in field of edn. and hist. research, award of distinction for services in scholarly fields and contbn. hist. materials American Association for State and Local History. Member American, New York State and Illinois State bar assns., U. of Chicago Alumni Assn., Delta Sigma Rho (charter mem.); life mem. Chicago Alumni Assn., Delta Sigma Rho (charter mem.); life mem. Chicago Bar Assn., sec. 2 terms; pres. Henckel Family Assn.; mem. S.A.R. (vice president general 1954-56), Sons and Daughters Ore. Pioneers, Native Sons and Daughters of Ore., Patrons and Friends of the U. of Ore. Library (pres.). Republican. Baptist. Clubs: University, City (Portland); Montclair (N.J.) Art Assn.; Nantucket (Mass.) Yacht. Author: Letters of Dr. John McLoughlin; Financial Papers of Dr. John McLoughlin; The Dr. John McLoughlin House; Ore., Prize of Discovery, Exploration and Settlement; Introduction—Ogden's Snake Country Journals; Vol. 13 Hudson's Bay Record Society Publications; Oregon and Statuary Hall; Oregon Territorial Centennial (chpt. IV); Nation Claims in Old Oregon; McLoughlin Empire and Its Rulers; The Henckel Geneology; other hist. and geneal. publs. Donor bronze statue Pioneer Mother to University of Oregon, 1935. Home: Portland, Ore.†

BARKER, HARRY, cons. engineer; b. Rutland, Vt., July 19, 1881; s. Barney and Hannah Estelle (Coburn) B.; B.S., U. of Vermont, 1904, Doctor of Engineering (honorary) 1954; m. Marion I. Booth, Apr. 21, 1909; children—Samuel Booth, Ruth Elizabeth. Instr. in engring., U. of Vt., 1903-05; asst. engr., Vt., Ariz., Calif. and Nev., 1904-07; asso. editor Engring. News and Engring. News-Record, 1907-17; cons. engr. from 1919; mem. Barker & Wheeler, engrs., N.Y.C., Albany, 1919-59, Barker, Karolyi & Thomason, engrs., N.Y.C., from 1960; cons. engr. to Vt. Public Service Commn., 1925-39; advisory engr., Municipal Electric Utility Assn. of N.Y., from 1935; cons. engr. Tenn. Valley Authority, 1936-39. Lecturer on practice of engring., U. Vermont, Trustee U. Vt., from 1956. Served as capt. Engr. Corps, U.S. Army, 1917-18. Mem. Am. Soc. Mech. Engrs., American Institute Electrical Engineers, S.A.R., Phi Beta Kappa, Tau Beta Pi, Sigma Nu. Republican. Conglist. Author: Public Utility Rates, 1917; also brochures and booklets. Contbr. articles to tech. publs. Home: Montclair, N.J.†

BARKER, JAMES L(OUIS), phonetician; b. Ogden, Utah, July 27, 1880; s. Henry and Margaret (Stalle) B.; A.B., U. of Utah, 1901; licencié és lettres, U. of Neuchatel, Switzerland, 1911; student Inst. Catholique and Collége de France, 1911-13; m. Kate Montgomery, May 30, 1906; children—Dr. Nancy Montgomery (dec.), Margaret Montgomery (wife of Dr. Albert O. Mitchell), James Louis Montgomery. Instr., Ogden (Utah) High Sch., 1904-06; chmn. dept. modern langs. Brigham Young U., 1907-13; pres. Weber Normal Coll., Ogden, Utah, 1914-17; head department of modern languages, University of Utah, 1917-46; vis. prof. phonetics, U. of Chgo, summer 1922; lecturer and demonstrator on the eradication of accent, U.S. Immigration and Naturalization Service, 1935-36. Pres. Latter Day Saints (Mormon) Argentine Mission, 1942-44. Pres. French Mission, 1946-50. Recipient of subventions for research in phonetics for modern foreign language study, Am. Council of Edn., Paris, 1924-25, Commonwealth Fund of Modern Lang. Assn. of America, Europe, 1926-27; opening lecturer, University of Geneva, summer session, 1927. Decorated Officier d'Académie. Member Society de Linguistique de Paris, Modern Lang. Assn. America (chmn. phonetics sect.). Author: The Divine Church. Contbr. articles, publs. of Modern Lang. Assn., Jour. of Speech Disorders, Modern Philology, Modern Lang. Notes, Protestors of Christendom, and other professional publs. Home: Salt Lake City, Uath†

BARKER, JAMES MADISON, retail exec.; b. Pittsfield, Mass., Mar. 13, 1886; s. Charles T. and Emma J. (Burke) B.; S.B., Mass. Inst. Tech., 1907; D.Sc., Middlebury Coll., 1939; LL.D., Westminister Coll., 1964; m. Margaret Clark Rankin, April 13, 1914; children—Robert Rankin, Hugh, Cecily Helen (Mrs. R.W. Finley), Ralph. Asst., Mass. Inst. Tech., 1907-09; draftsman, designer Am. Bridge Co., 1909-10; engr. Canadian Pacific Ry., Montreal, Que., Can., and Bur. Engring. Statistics, N.Y., 1910-12; with E.A. Tucker Co., Boston, 1912-13; instr. Harvard, 1914-15; instr., asst. prof. structural engring., cons. structural engr. Mass. Inst. Tech., 1914-19; cons. engr. Div. Constrn. and Repair Dept. Navy, 1918; with 1st Nat. Bank, Boston, 1919-20, mgr., Buenos Aires, Argentina, br., 1920-28; with Sears, Roebuck & Co., from 1928, successively regional mgr., Phila., eastern v.p., retail adminstr. v.p., v.p. and treas., v.p., treas., controller, dir., 1930-68, named hon. dir., 1968; dir. Allstate Ins. Co., 1935-68, chmn. finance com., 1956-60, chmn. bd., 1943-60, subsequently hon. dir., dir. Harris Trust & Savs. Bank, Chgo., 1939-56. Mem. Price Adjustment Bd., Chgo. Ordnance Dist., War Dept., 1942-47; mem. reorgn. com. C.M.S.P. & P. Ry. Co., 1945-46, voting trustee, 1946-50, mem. finance com., dir., 1946-69; chmn. Savs. and Profit Sharing Pension Fund Sears, Roebuck & Co. Employees, 1956-60, trustee, chmn. investment com., 1956-66. Life trustee Northwestern U.; life mem. corp. Mass. Inst. Tech.; hon. trustee Newberry Library, Mus. Sci. and Industry, Chgo.; governing life mem. Art Inst. Chgo. Participant missions to Iran, 1948-49; chief econ. mission to Turkey, Internat. Bank for Reconstrn. and Devel., 1949-51; mem. Real Property Task Force Hoover Commn. on Orgn. Exec. Br. Govt. Engring. library Mass. Inst. Tech. named for him, 1970. Clubs: Chicago, University, Commercial, Wayfarers (Chgo.); Century, University, Brook (N.Y.C.); jockey (Buenos Aires, Argentina). Home: Chicago Ill. Died July 3, 1974.

BARKER, JOSEPH WARREN, engineering cons.; b. Lawrence, Mass., June 17, 1891; s. Frederick and Alice Ann (Alletson) B.; student U. of Chicago, 1909-10; B.S. in E.E., Mass. Inst. Tech., 1916, M.S., 1925; student U.S. Coast Arty. Sch., 1916-17 and 1923-24; LL.D., Bucknell U., 1940; Sc.D., Northeastern U.; 1940; D.Eng., Case Sch. Applied Science, 1942; LL.D., Union College, 1944; D. Eng., Univ. of Rochester, 1944; L.H.D., Muhlenberg College, 1945; married Mary Metcalf Perin, June 17, 1916 (died Sept. 30, 1937); children—Beatrcie Perin (Mrs. Sidney L. Hall), John Perin; m. 2d, Mary Casey Mallon, Dec. 11, 1943; 1 son, Michael Mallon. Prof. elec. engring. Mass. Inst. Tech., 1925-29; professor and head dept. elec. engring., Lehigh U., 1929-30; dean of faculty engring., Columbia, 1930-46; on leave to serve as special asst. to Sec. of Navy, 1941-45; pres., Research Corp., Research Constrn. Co., Inc., 1945-47, chmn. bd. 1945-59, dir.; chmn. bd. Research-Cottrell, Inc., 1945-47, dir. Cons. NASA, 1963-75. Commissioned 2d lt., U.S. Army, 1916, advanced to maj., Sept. 26, 1925; with A.E.F. in France and Germany, 1918-22. Decorated Victory Medal (U.S.); Order of Prince Danilo (Montenegro) received U.S. Navy Distinguished Civilian Service Award. Fellow Am. Inst. Elec. Engrs. (v.p. 1940), A.A.A.S. (mem. exec. com. 1941, Am. Soc. M.E. (pres. 1957); mem. Bus. Equipment Mfrs. Inst. (cons. 1960-75, exec. v.p. 1961-62), Am. Soc. C.E., Am. Inst. Mining and Metall. Engrs., Illuminating Engrs. Soc. (pres. 1932-33); Am. Society Engring. Education, Tau Beta Pi, Sigma Xi (acting pres. 1954, pres. 1955-56), Phi Kappa Sigma, Theta Tau. Episcopalian (warden). Mason. Clubs: Cosmos (Washington); University (New Rochelle, N.Y.); Century, (N.Y.), Westchester Country. Home: New Rochelle, N.Y., Died Dec. 10, 1975.

BARKER, LEBARON R., JR., editor; b. Plymouth, Mass., Jan. 13, 1904; s. LeBaron Russell and (Hutchins) B.; A.B., Harvard, 1926; m. Mary Pope, June 28, 1926 (div. Apr. 1933); children—LeBaron Russell III, Randolph; m. 2d, Leslie Greenough, Sept. 14, 1934 (dec. Aug. 1939); 1 dau., Leslie Lindsay; m. 3d, Eileen Lange, Apr. 10, 1941 (div. 1950); children—Jeffery, Stephanie; m. 4th, Adeline Crankshaw, Jan. 17, 1952. Worked in advt., sales, editorial departments Houghton Mifflin & Co., 1927-43, New York editor, 1937-43; trade advt. mgr. Doubleday Doran, 1943, editor-in-chief, 1943-45, exec. editor, 1945-69, sr. editor, 1969-71, sr. con. editor, 1971-73. Pres. Publishers Ad Club, 1941-43; chmn. radio com., Council on Books in Wartime, 1942; v.p. Am. Inst. Graphic Arts, 1947-52. Club: Dutch Treat (N.Y.C.). Co-author: (pseud. Admiral Jettison) Addelgrams, 1934. Home: New York City N.Y. Died July 2, 1973; buried Plymouth, Mass.

BARKSDALE, ETHELBERT COURTLAND, educator; b. Athens, La., Oct. 24, 1905; s. Ethelbert Courtland and Eliza (Wellborn) B.; B.A., U. Tex., 1928, M.A., 1931, Ph.D., 1941; m. Marjorie Miller, June 12, 1937; children—Ethelbert Courtland, Stephen Webb. Tchr., Tex. Pub. Schs., 1926-39; tchr. U. Tex., Austin, 1940-41, prof. history, Arlington, from 1942, head dept. history, govt., sociology, philosophy, 1954-71. Mem. adv. com. Civil War, 1961-65. Kennedy U.S. Senate com. selection outstanding U.S. Senators, 1958. Pres. San Antonio Young Democrats, 1934, Baytown (Tex.) Young Democrats, 1937. Mem. Orgn. Am. Historians, Acad. Am. Polit. Social Sci., Am., So., Western, Tex. hist. assns., Southwestern Social Sci. Assn. (gen. program chmn. 1964-65, mem. exec. bd. 1965-67). Methodist. Author: Financing a System of State Highways, 1935; The Art and Science of Speech, 1937; Genesis of Texas Aviation, 1957; The Meatpackers Come to Texas, 1959; The Power Structure and Southern Gubernatorial Conservatism, 1969; Duncan Robinson, The Story of a Teacher, pub. posthumously 1975. Editor: History as High Adventure, 1969. Mem. editorial bd. Texana, 1967; mem. adv. editorial bd., contbr. articles Ency. Brit. Home: Arlington, Tex. Died Sept. 4, 1974.

BARNARD, HARRY ELIOT, ret. lawyer; b. Denver, July 11, 1892; s. Henry F. and Eugenia (Buffum) B.; A.B., Oberlin Coll., 1915; LL.B., U. Mich., 1920; m. Helen L. Coleman, Dec. 6, 1922 (died 1945); children—Robert C., Margaret A. (Mrs. Robert Edgar Maxwell), Mary L. (Mrs. George Yannopoulos); m. 2d, Mrs. Erma S. Boulton, April 10, 1948. Admitted to Mich. bar, 1920; former pros. atty., Jackson County; formerly mem. Mich. State Legislature. Trustee Oberlin Coll. Served with U.S. Army, World War I. Mem. Am., Mich. State, Detroit bar assns., Baronial Order Magna Charta. Presbyn. Clubs: Circumnavigators, Detroit, Grosse Pointe Yacht. Home: Grosse Pointe Farms, Mich. Died Aug. 20, 1973; interred Woodlawn Cemetery, Detroit.

BARNARD, KATE, sociologist; b. Geneva, Neb., 1878; d. John P. (lawyer and civ. engr.) and Rachel (Shiell) B.; ed. pub. schs., and St. Joseph's Acad., Oklahoma

City, Okla.; unmarried. Began as teacher, pub. schs., Okla.; represented Okla. as commr. at World's Fair, St. Louis, 1903; upon returning to Okla. devoted attention to assisting immigrants, then entering Okla. by the thousand; in 3 yrs. provided for 3,000 destitute families and placed many children in pub. schs., also organizing the unemployed; made tour of inspection through factories and slums of large eastern cities, and entered into systematic campaign, securing child labor, compulsory edn. and dept. of charities planks in new Okla. state constitution; now commr. of charities and corrections, Okla. Active in securing prison laws, juvenile court laws, etc., along advanced lines, also in effecting prison reform in Kan. and Ariz. and in restoring $572,000,000 to Indians of Okla. from which they had been illegally deprived. Delivered addresses before Internat. Tuberculosis Congress, Washington, 1908, Governors' Congress, Richmond, Va., 1913, and before many univs., colls. and socs. Democrat. Hon. mem. Am. Acad. Polit. Science. Home: Okalhoma City, Okla.†

BARNES, DONALD C., utility exec.; b. Cambridge, Mass., Sept. 14, 1880; s. Albert Mallard and Emily Leighton (Carter) B.; A.B. cum laude, Harvard Coll., 1902; B.S. magna cum laude, Harvard U., 1904; m. Helen Hayden Brooks, May 1, 1912; 1 son, Albert Mallard. Meter man and gen. mechanic Birmingham Ry. Light & Power Co. and Little Rock Ry. & Electric Co., 1904-05; statistician Stone & Webster, Boston, 1905; salesman Electric Light & Power Co. of Abington and Rockland, Mass., 1906-07; salesman Edison Electric Illumination Co. of Brockton, 1908-09; lighting supt. Pawtucket Electric Co., R.I., 1909-11; mgr. Everett Ry. Light & Water Co. & Pacific N.W. Traction Co., Wash., 1911-19; mgr. Central Dist. Puget Sound Power & Light Co., Seattle, 1919-24; div. mgr. Southeast and Northwest Properties, S. & W., Boston, 1924-31; vice pres. Engrs. Public Service Co., N.Y., 1931-33; vice pres. Stone & Webster Service Corp., N.Y., 1934-37; pres. Engrs. Public Service Co., N.Y., 1937-47; chmn. bd. Va. Electric & Power Co., Charlottesville, Va. from 1947. Home: Charlottesville, Va.†

BARNES, DONALD LEE, JR., finance co. exec.; b. Springfield, Ill., July 11, 1917; s. Donald Lewis and Dorothy (Ide) B.; B.S.C., St. Louis U., 1939; m. Leslie Jane Newell, Nov. 8, 1939; children—Donald Leslie III (dec.), James D., Barbara Ann, Dennis N., L. Neil, Donna Lynn. With Am. Investment Co., St. Louis, exec. v.p., 1959-64, pres., 1964-75, chmn. bd., 1967-75, also dir.; pres., dir. Charter Nat. Life Ins. Co., 1962-67, chmn. bd., 1967-75; pres., dir. Clarkson Valley Estates, Inc., 1962-75; Charter Nat. Ins. Co., 1964; chmn. bd. Am. Nat. Stores; dir. St. Louis County Nat. Bank, Mo. Portland Cement Co. Trustee St. Louis U., Cardinal Glennon Meml. Hosp. Children, Boys Town, Mo., Calvary Cemetery Assn., Govt. Research Inst., St. Louis Found. for Alcoholism; chmn. adv. bd. Mo. Colls. Fund, St. Louis. Served to lt. (j.g.) USNR, 1944-46; PTO. Recipient Alumni Merit award St. Louis U., 1962. Mem. Alpha Sigma Nu (hon.). Knight of Malta. Clubs: Forest Hills Golf and Country, St. Louis (charter), Mo. Athletic, Old Warson Country, St. Louis Stadium (founding mem., dir.)(St. Louis). Home: Ladue, Mo. Died Jan. 23, 1975.

BARNES, HOWEL HENRY, JR., electrical engr.; b. New York, Dec. 15, 1875; grad. in Elec. Engring., Technische Hochschule, Stuttgart, Germany; unmarried. With Siemens & Halske, Berlin, Germany, 1897-99; supt. Mexican Electric Works, City of Mexico, 1899-1901; staff engr., Stanley Electric Mfg. Co., Pittsfield, Mass., 1902-06; consulting and dist. engr., Gen. Electric Co., 1907-27, asst. dist. mgr., 1920-28; district manager, 1928-30, commercial vice-president, 1931-41, ret. Dec. 31, 1941. Industry member, Nat. War Labor Bd., Region 2, 1943-45. Trustee United Engineering Society, New York, 1912-17 and 1921-27; fellow American Institute Elec. Engrs. (mgr. 1910-13, v.p. 1913-15), N.Y. Elec. Soc. (pres. 1913-14); mem. Elec. and Gas Assn. of New York (pres. 1936), Am. Soc. Mech. Engrs. Mem. Hoover Medal Bd. of Award, 1936-47. Clubs: Engineers (pres., 1929-31), Explorers, Union, Century, Bankers, Mohawk. Address: New York City, N.Y.†

BARNES, JAMES PHILLIPS, ry. exec.; b. Syracuse, N.Y., Jan. 26, 1881; s. James and Ida E. (Breed) B.; spl. student in music, Syracuse U., 2 yrs.; B.S. in E.E., Mass. Inst. Tech., 1905; m. Merriam Ernhout, of Syracuse, Jan. 3, 1906; children—James Merriam, Mary Ann. Connected in engring. capacities with various rys. in N.Y. State, 1905-12; gen. mgr. Syracuse and Suburban R.R. Co., 1913-14, Buffalo, Lockport and Rochester R.R. Co., 1914-17, Schenectady Ry. Co., 1917-20; pres. Louisville (Ky.) Ry. Co. and affiliated cos., 1920-31; v.p. and gen. mgr. Mobile Light & R.R. Co. Lt. col. Special Res. Mem. advisory coms. Dept. of Elec. Engring. of Mass. Inst. Tech. and Speed Scientific Sch. of U. of Louisville. Fellow Am. Inst. E.E.; mem. Am. Electric Ry. Assn. (pres. 1928-29), N.Y. Elec. Ry. Assn. (ex-pres.), Central Electric Ry. Assn. (ex-pres.), Ky. Assn. Pub. Utilities (ex-pres.). Presbyn. Mason (32°, K.T., Shriner). Home: Mobile, Ala.†

BARNES, NATHAN, Liberian diplomat; b. Cape Palmas, Liberia, Apr. 14, 1914; s. Nathan and Elizabeth (Knight) B.; ed. Cape Palmas Sem.; m. 2d, Josephine Brewer, Nov. 15, 1950. With Liberian Revenue Service, 1937-44; admitted to bar; county atty. Maryland County, Liberia, 1944; circuit judge 4th Jud. Circuit Liberia, 1945-56; Liberian minister to Italy, 1956, Liberian ambassador, 1956-60; permanent rep. from Liberia to UN, N.Y.C., 1960-75. Chmn. Liberian delegation to 1st UN Conf. of Law of Sea, Geneva, 1958, 2d conf., 1960, UN Conf. Diplomatic Intercourse and Immunities, Vienna, 1961; pres. UN trusteeship council, 1963; chmn. 1st com. UN Conf. on Consular Relations; chmn. UN com. defining aggression; rubber-planter in Liberia. Decorated knight Grand Bank Humane Order African Redemption; grand condr. Star Africa (Liberia); cavalier Order Merit (Italy). Mem. Am. Soc. Internat. Law. Mason. Odd Fellow. Mem. United Bros. of Friendship. Home: New Rochelle, N.Y. Died July 1975.

BARNETT, CHARLES CONDITT, ch. worker, ret. utilities exec.; b. Dermott, Ark., Aug. 14, 1915; s. Uzal Conditt and Alma (Daniels) B.; B.S. in Civil Engring., U. Ark., 1937; m. Mary Lee Mitchell, Feb. 7, 1942. With United Gas Pipe Line Co., Shreveport, La., 1937-73, engr. 1937-41, gas engr., 1946-55, v.p., dir., 1955-69, sr. v.p., 1969-73; bus. mgr. First Presbyn. Ch., Shreveport, La., 1973-75. Served as maj. C.E., AUS, 1941-46. Mem. Am. Gas Assn., Am. Petroleum Inst. Presbyn. Home: Shreveport La. Died March 9, 1975.

BARNETT, JOSEPH W., textile mfg. co. exec.; b. 1902; ed. Ga. Mil. Acad., U. Ga.; m. Elfrieda Ankerson; 1 son, Joseph W. With Cannon Mills, Inc., Kannapolis, N.C., 1929-67, v.p., 1946-60, pres., 1960-67, also dir., vice chmn. Mem. Assn. Cotton Textile Mchts., Textile Export Assn., Assn. Cotton Mfrs. Inst., Am. Textile Mfrs. Inst., Arbitration Council N.Y. Home: Rye N.Y. Died Aug. 12, 1974.

BARNHILL, JOHN HENRY, univ. athletic dir.; b. Savannah, Tenn., Feb. 21, 1903; s. James Monroe and Alice (Bryan) B.; B.S.A., U. Tenn., 1928; m. Katherine Peeler, Aug. 28, 1930; 1 dau., Nancy (Mrs. Ellis Trumbo). Coach, Bristol (Tenn.) High Sch., 1928-31; athletic dir., football coach U. Tenn., 1931-46; athletic dir., football coach U. Ark., Fayetteville, 1946-49, dir. athletics, 1949-70. John Barnhill Fieldhouse named in his honor at U. Ark., 1958. Mem. Alpha Tau Omega. Methodist. Mason (Shriner), Rotarian. Home: Fayetteville Ark. Died Oct. 21, 1973.

BARNWELL, HENRY STEPEHN, clergyman; b. Charleston, S.C., Aug. 1, 1881; s. William and Mary (Weston) B.; Talladege Coll., 1903; m. Augusta Lillian Bibb, of Uniontown, Ala., Aug. 28, 1907. Ordained Congl. ministry, 1904; pastoral supply, Battery Ch., Charleston, S.C., 1903-04, Beaufort, N.C., June-Oct., 1904; asso. pastor Talladega Coll., Ala., 1904-06; pastor Woodburv Ch., Lake Charles, La., 1906-11, Bethany Ch., Thomasville, Ga., 1911-15; prin. Fessenden Acad. Republican. Address: Fessenden, Fla.†

BARR, ROY EVAN, ry. official; b. Mechanicsburg, O., July 20, 1883; s. Edgar and Ada Belle (Comstock) B.; grad. high sch., Mechanicsburg, 1901, Met. Business Coll., Lima, O., 1902; m. Ruth D. Jocelyn, Dec. 3, 1910 (dec.); 1 son, Robert Comstock; m. 2d, Frances Rycroft Clarke, Apr. 12, 1947. Employed by Am. Express Co., Chicago, July-Oct. 1902; with traffic dept., I.C. R.R., 1902-17; sales mgr. Edwards & Bradford Lumber Co., Chicago, 1917-20; v.p. Great West Coal & Lumber Co., 1920-25, pres., 1925-26; northwestern mgr. Knox Consolidated Coal Co., Chicago, 1926-30; mgr. Consolidation Coal Co., Chicago, 1930-32; coal traffic mgr. I.C. R.R., 1932-39, freight traffic mgr., 1939-42, v.p. from 1942. Mem. Nat. Freight Traffic Golf Assn., Indiana Society of Chicago. Republican. Methodist. Mason. Clubs: Chicago, Union League, Traffic, New York Traffic, South Shore Country, Missouri Athletic, Chicago Athletic Assn.; Boston (New Orleans, La.); Mountain Brook (Birmingham, Ala); International House (New Orleans); Duquesne (Pittsburgh). Home: Chicago, Ill. Died Dec. 16, 1974; buried Oak Woods Cemetery, Chicago, Ill.

BARRETT, ALVA PEARL, lawyer; b. Gibson County, Tenn., Apr. 12, 1878; s. Marcus Lafayette and Sarah Amelia (Burns) B.; B.S., East Tex. Normal Sch.; LL.B., U. of Tex., 1905; m. Frances Steiner, Oct. 23, 1912 (dec.); 1 dau., Frances Virginia; m. 2d, Hazel Hunter, Dec. 7, 1921; children—Richard Hunter, Bruce Robert, Barbara Amelia. Teacher Fannin County (Tex.) schs., 1899-1900; prin. Gober Pub. Sch., Fannin County, 1900-02; admitted to Tex. bar, 1905, and began practice at Bonham; moved to San Antonio, 1908, Fort Worth, 1919. Mem. Tex. Ho. of Rep., 1902-04, Tex. State Senate, 1904-08 (pres. pro tem.). Pres. Southwestern Gas, Light and Power Co. and Continental Gas, Light and Power Co., 1924-25, Tex.-La. Power Co. of Chicago, 1926-28, Southwest Broadcasting Co., 1930-31; pres. and chmn. bd. Tex. Air Transport, Inc., Dixie Motor Coach Corp., 1928-30. Mem. Phi Gamma Delta. Baptist. Mason (32°). Home: San Antonio, Tex.†

BARRETT, WILLIAM HENRY, Salvation Army leader; b. Cardiff, S. Wales, Mar. 3, 1881; s. Henry and Charlotte B.; grad. Internat. Training Coll., London, Eng.; m. Lydia Harriet Paul, May 11, 1903; children—William J., Mrs. Carl Warner, Alfred H., Mrs. J. Machold, Mrs. A. Gray, Mrs. Ray Ogg. Came to U.S., naturalized. Commd. Salvation Army; Commr. Salvation Army for Western States, Alaska, Hawaii, P.I., since 1943; travelled with Gen. Evangeline Booth as asst.; prin. Officers Training Coll., New York, N.Y. Interested in youth work and as adminstr. held positions as div. comdr., field sec., chief sec., asst. nat. sec. Salvation Army, N.Y., helped formulate Army's war service program, evangelist. Mem. San Francisco Chamber of Commerce. Club: Rotary. Home: Millbrae, Cal.†

BARRIGER, WILLIAM LILLARD, army officer; b. Shelby Co., Ky., Feb. 1, 1897; s. William Shelby and Ida Alma (Lillard) B.; B.S., U.S. Mil. Acad., West Point, N.Y., 1918; grad. Command and Gen. Staff Sch., Ft. Leavenworth, Kan., 1937; m. Helen Conway Bryant, July 10, 1968; 1 son, William Lillard. Commd. 2d lt. Cav., U.S. Army, 1918, advanced through grades to maj. gen., 1952; served southwestern U.S., also P.I., 1918-24; instr. English U.S. Mil. Acad., 1924-28; gen. staff 1st armored div. and armored force; gen. staff 1st and 12th Army groups, 1941-45; chief staff Panama Canal Dept. and U.S. Army, Caribbean, 1946-49; asst. div. comdr. 9th inf. div., 1949-50; Dept. Army gen. staff, 1950-51; chief staff 1st Army, Governors Island, N.Y., 1951-52; gen. staff Far East Command, Tokyo, 1952; chief of staff Army Forces Far East, 1952-53; comdg. gen. 2d inf. div. with attached UN troops, 1953-54; office, Secretary of Defense, from 1954. Decorated Legion of Merit with 2 Oak Leaf clusters, Bronze Star medal; Order Brit. Empire; Officer Legion of Honor, Croix de Guerre with Palm (France); D.S.M.; Korean Presdl. Unit Citation; Knight Comdr. Order White Elephant; Grand Officer Order of Orange of Nassau. Club: Army-Navy Washington. Home: McLean, Va., Died Feb. 29, 1976; interred Arlington Nat. Cemetery.

BARRON, MINERVA CROWELL ROGERS (MRS. ROBERT EGLINTON BARRON), educator, artist; b. Asbury Park, N.J., June 30, 1902; d. Arthur Garfield and Mary Anne (Shaftoe) Rogers; B.S., Columbia, 1924, M.A., 1943; m. Robert Eglinton Barron, Sept. 7, 1929; children—Orlyn Rae (Mrs. Richard La Brake), Ona Lee (Mrs. David L. Bickelhaupt), Robert Bruce. Tchr. art and indsl. art Horace Mann Sch., N.Y.C., 1923-24; faculty art Skidmore Coll., Saratoga Springs, N.Y., 1924-30, 1933-34, 39-67, prof. emeritus art, 1967-72; exhibited in one-man shows Skidmore Art Gallery, 1926, 40, 45-46, 59, 65, Stratford Conn. Sterling House, 1932, 35, Katring Trash House Gallery, 1939, 42, 45, Schenectady Mus., 1964; exhibited in group shows Downtown Gallery, 1942, Bklyn. Mus., 1943, Westchester Art Show, 1949, Skidmore Coll.; represented in pvt. collections; executed murals Saratoga Hosp., Hallmark Nursing Home, Holly Home for Children, Saratoga Springs. Mem. Nat. Soc. Interior Designers, Am. Assn. U. Women (pres. 1945-47, mem. bd. 1925-72, arts chmn.), Nat. Interior Designers Educators Council, Nat. Interior Designers (chmn. edn. work 1965-69, bd. dirs. 1963-72), Delta Phi Delta. Episcopalian. Club: Faculty Staff (pres. 1948-50 Skidmore Coll. Home: San Miguel de Allende Mexico. Died Nov. 1, 1972; interred Parkview Cemetery, Schenectady, N.Y.

BARROWS, WAYNE GROVES, author; b. at Chicago, May 12, 1880; s. George Groves and Martha Wayne (Thompson) B.; ed. pub. schs. and bus. coll.; m. Clara Stehlin, of Chicago, Apr. 16, 1904. Bookkeeper Nat. Bank of America, Chicago, 1897-98; resigned and went West on account of inflammation of the eyes; spent several years on ranch; in banking and lumber business, 1906-09; farming, from 1911. Congregationalist. Author: The Law of the Range, 1909; A Child of the Plains, 1911. Address: Crystal Lake, Ill.†

BARRY, MAURICE JOSEPH, physician; b. Indianapolis, Ind., Dec. 31, 1880; s. Maurice Joseph and Emma Frances (Holmes) B.; M.D., Indiana U., 1908; m. Mary Hazlett Michie, July 8, 1911; 1 son, Maurice Joseph. Prof. clin. medicine, Sch. of Medicine, Indiana U.; commd. lt. col., U.S. Pub. Health Service, 1943. Mem. A.M.A., Ind. State Med. Assn., Indianapolis Med. Soc. Democrat. Roman Catholic. Home: Indianapolis, Ind.†

BARTHOLD, ROBERT M., fruit packing co. exec.; b. Livermore, Calif., Jan. 4, 1879; s. H. F. and C. H. (Jessen) B.; ed. pub. schs.; m. Augustine C. Aubin, Aug. 6, 1902; children—Aubin, Marion, Robert. Began as accountant, San Francisco, 1899; became mgr. Central Calif. Canneries, San Francisco, 1901; elected v.p. Calif. Packing Corp., 1920; pres., 1930, chmn. bd., 1931-46, retired; dir. Calif. Packing Corp., Alaska Packers Assn. Lutheran. Clubs: Pacific Union, Olympic, Golf. Home: San Francisco, Cal.†

BARTHOLOMAY, ANTHONY FRANCIS, educator; b. Utica, N.Y., Aug. 11, 1919; s. James A. and Grace D. (Abbate) B.; A.B., Hamilton Coll., 1940; M.A., Syracuse U., 1942; S.D., Harvard, 1957; m. Priscilla Millicent Upham, Jan. 3, 1944; children—Alan L., Marsha L., James A., Andrea F. Instr. math. Syracuse U., 1940-42, Brown U., 1942-45; asst. prof., chmn. depts. math. and physics, Keuka Coll., 1945-46; instr. math. Rensselaer Poly. Inst., 1946-47; instr. math.

Rutgers U., 1947-51; mathematician Lab. Electronics, Boston, 1951-52; mathematician Lincoln Lab., Mass. Inst. Tech., 1952-54; staff Biophysics Research Lab., Peter Bent Brigham Hosp., Harvard Med. Sch., Boston, 1954-62, asso. staff medicine, 1954-67, asst. prof. math. biology, 1960-67, dir. div. math. biology and biomath. lab., 1962-67; asst. prof. math. biology, dept. biostatistics Harvard Sch. Pub. Health 1957-60; prof. biomath. N.C. State U., Sch. Medicine and Pub. Health U.N.C., 1967-69; prof., chmn. dept. math. medicine Med. Coll. Ohio, Toledo, 1969-72; prof. math. medicine Dept. Community Medicine, prof. biomath. Dept. Surgery, Rutgers Med. Sch., 1972-75; ind. investigator Howard Hughes Med. Inst., 1957-67; dir. research and tng. grants biomath. NIH, 1962-67; mem. Pres. Adv. Bd. Biometric Soc., 1966-69; lectr. in field. Mem. Am. Math. Soc., Am. Statis. Assn., Soc. Indsl. and Applied Math., Soc. Gen. Systems Research, Biometric Soc., Am. Inst. Biol. Scis., A.A.A.S., Assn. Am. Med. Colls., Am. Pub. Health Assn., Math. Assn. Am., N.Y. Acad. Sci., Soc. Math. Biology (founder), Ohio Pub. Health Assn. Mng. editor Bull. Math. Biology. Asso. editor Computers in Medicine and Biology, Internat. Jour. Gen. Systems. Contbr. articles to profl. jours., books. Home: Somerset, N.J. Died Mar. 21, 1975; buried Riverside Cemetery, Pawtucket, R.I.

BARTKY, ADOLPH JOHN, educator; b. Chgo., Apr. 10, 1899; s. Adolph and Louise (Schaar) B.; student Ill. Inst. Tech., 1915-17; M.S., U. Chgo., 1923; A.M., Northwestern U., 1933, Ph.D., 1935; LL.D., Golden Gate Coll., 1965; m. Ruth Ashworth, Dec. 21, 1929; children Johanna Louise, Judith, Joyce, Janet, Jill. Asst. prof. engring. mathematics Ill. Inst. Tech. (then Lewis Inst.), 1921; prin. elementary schs., Chgo., 1925-33, Calumet High Sch., Chgo., 1933-37; dist. supt. of schs., Chgo., 1938-39; pres. Chgo. Teachers Coll., 1939-42; also dean Woodrow Wilson Jr. Coll.; prof. emeritus Stanford U. Sch. Edn., dean, 1946-53; distinguished prof., trustee Golden Gate Coll., San Francisco. Served with U.S. Army, World War I; in tng. as officer in charge, instr. training and asst. dir. Standards and Curriculum Div., with rank of capt. USNR, World War II. Decorated Legion of Merit. Mem. Phi Delta Kappa. Author: Supervision as Human Relations; Administration as Educational Leadership Social Issues in Education. Co-Author: The High School Teacher and His Job. Contbr. to Saturday Evening Post, and ednl. jours. Home: San Francisco, Cal. Died Sept. 4, 1974.

BARTLE, H(AROLD) ROE, lawyer, youth leader; b. Richmond, Va.; s. Samuel Dunn and Ada Mae (Roe) B.; student Fork Union Mil. Acad.; LL.B., Chattanooga Coll. Law, 1920; J.D., Hamilton Coll. Law, 1921; LL.D. (hon.), Mo. Valley Coll., 1943; Dr. Humane Letters (hon.), Center Coll. Ky., 1949; D.Sc., Salem Coll., 1951; D.Litt., Kirksville College, 1955; LL.D., William Jewell College, 1956; married Margaret Jarvis Rains, Sept. 26, 1923; 1 dau., Margaret Roe (Mrs. John James Taylor). Admitted to Ky. bar, 1920, Mo. bar, 1921, since practiced in K.C.; adminstr. Am. Humanics Found. 1947; chmn. bd. Visa-Meter Corp., 1957; dir. Mercantile Bank & Trust Co.; dir., chmn. finance committee Milgram Super Markets, Inc.; pres. R-B-T Investment Co.; dir. Bond Stores, Inc., Kansas City Mdse. Mart, Inc. Mayor, Kansas City, Mo., 1955; president Missouri Munical League, 1958. Mem. W.L.B., region 9 Loyalty Bd.; regional dir. Region 9 Econ. Stablzn. Agy. Vice pres. Mo. Municipal League, 1956. Director Rockhurst College, President of the Missouri Valley College, Marshall, Mo., 1948-51, pres. bd. trustees, 1945; trustee Fork Union Military Academy; national exec. director Am. War Dads, 1942-50; chmn. Co. Bd. Visitors; chmn. bd. merit Juvenile Ct. of Jackson Co., Mo.; mem. bd. govs., trustee Menninger Found.; mem. nat. bd. Nat. Council Chs. of Christ in U.S.A.; gen. chmn. K.C. Community Chest, 1948. Exec. K.C. area council Boy Scouts Am. Decorated Medal for Service (Gt. Britain). Citation for distinguished and meritorious citizenship, Cath. Community Service, 1947; Knight of St. Patrick, U. Mo., 1948; named Man of the Month, Aug. 1948, Man-of-the-Month Club; Toast of 1950, Delta Theta Phi; Kansas City's Most Distinguished Citizen, Am. Legion, 1939; Man of the Year, Vets. Fgn. Wars, 1953; citizenship award, Nat. Conf. Christians and Jews, 1953; Silver Beaver, Silver Antelope and Silver Buffalo awards Boy Scouts Am.; Order of Santiago, Chile; Medal of Honor, Uruguay; Order Simon Bolivar, Peru; Distinguished Service award Boys Club; Order of Merit (Republic Ecuador); H. Roe Bartle Conv. Center dedicated posthumously in his honor, 1976. Mem. Nat. Assn. Coll. Deans (life), Nat. Conf. Christains and Jews s (nat. exec. com.), Alpha Phi Omega (nat. pres. 1931-47). Presbyn. (mem. bd. annuities and relief; exec. com. man United Churchmen). Mason (33 deg., Shriner, Jester, Knight Comdr. Ct. of Honor, Knight of Constantine); mem. Order of DeMolay (founders' medal, legion of honor, mem. supreme council). Rotarian (pres. K.C. (Mo.) 1936, dist. gov. 1940, internat. com. man 1939). Home: Kansas City, Mo. Died May 9, 1974; buried Forest Hill Cemetery, Kansas City, Mo.

BARTMAN, RUSSELL C(LYDE), lawyer; b. Collegeville, Pa., May 29, 1897; s. John H. and Catherine (Bechtel) B.; B.A., Ursinus Coll., 1918; LL.B., Temple U., 1934; m. Mary A. Saylor, Feb. 4, 1920; 1 son, James Saylor. Enlisted as seaman U.S. Navy, 1918; commd. ensign U.S.N.R.F., 1919; trans. to regular Navy, 1920, commd. capt., 1942, chief staff 8th Naval Dist., New Orleans, 1941-42, served in Atlantic, World War I, Atlantic, Pacific, Far Eastern Waters, World War II; ret. from active duty, 1947; admitted to Pa. bar, 1934; practice Barnard & Bartman, Norristown, Pa. from 1947. Exec. dir. Pa. State Pub. Sch. Bldg. Authority, 1948-61. Mem. Engrs. Soc. Pa., Pa. and Montgomery bar assns., Am. Legion, V.F.W., Pa. Soc. of N.Y. Y.M.C.A. Presbyn. Mason (32°). Clubs: Army-Navy Country (Washington); West Shore Country, Executives (Harrisburg); Kiwanis. Home: Harrisburg, Pa. Died Jan. 19, 1975; buried Arlington Nat. Cemetery.

BARTON, JOSEPH WESLEY, prof. psychology; b. Greenville, Utah, Apr. 28, 1881; s. Joseph Alma and Sarah Maria (Horton) B.; prep. edn., Murdock Acad., Beaver City, Utah; B.S. in Edn., U. of Utah, 1915; post-grad. study, U. of Minn., 1916-19; Ph.D., Peabody Teachers Coll., Nashville, Tenn., 1923; m. Hannah Elizabeth Greenhalgh, of Meadow, Utah, July 11, 1900; children—Wesley Austell, Hannah Editha, Eva (dec.), Byron Bowider (dec.), Instr. in psychology and edn., Branch Normal Sch., Cedar City, Utah, 1910-14, U. of Utah, 1914-16; supt. schs., Elk River, Minn., 1917-20; prof. psychology, U. of Ida., from 1920. Mem. Am. Psychol. Assn., Northwest Scientific Assn., Am. Assn. Univ. Profs., Sigma Xi, Sigma Chi, Phi Delta Kappa. Elk. Rotarian. Contbr. Jour. Ednl. Psychology, Pedagogical Seminary, Psychological Monographs, etc. Discoverer of an original method of learning typewriting. Home: Moscow, Idaho.†

BARWELL-WALKER, FRANCIS JOHN, clergyman; b. London, England, Oct. 25, 1881; s. Thomas and Catherine (Barwell) Walker; studied arts and theology, U. of Durham, Eng.; came to America, 1909; A.B., Oskaloosa Coll., Ia., 1910, B.D., 1912, S.T.D., 1913; A.M., Highland U., Kan., 1912, Ph.D., 1913; (D.D., Campbell U., Kan., 1914; Litt.D., U. of South Minn., 1914; M.A., Muskingum Coll., Ohio, 1915); m. Amy Louisa Largen, of London, Eng., July 8, 1908. First took up pharmacy and medicine, later drugless healing; organist and lay preacher, 1896-11, deacon, 1911, priest, 1912, P.E. Ch.; rector Ascension Ch., Ontonagon, and St. George's Ch., Hancock, Mich., 1911-15; rector St. Mark's Ch., Chester, and vicar Holy Trinity Ch., Murphysboro, Ill., from 1915. Prof. of Oskaloosa Coll., from 1915. Founder, 1910, and superior gen. Am. branch Guild of the Holy Ghost. Fellow Philos. Soc. England, 1914. Mason. Address: Murphysboro, Ill.†

BASILE, ANTHONY ROBERT, lawyer; b. Chgo., Mar. 13, 1918; s. Raffael and Carnela (D'Urso) B.; A.B., U. Chgo., 1939, M.B.A., 1940, J.D., 1943; m. June Crezsic, July 28, 1944. Admitted to Ill. bar, 1943; pvt. practice law, from 1943; exec. v.p., dir. Schneck Aviation Inc., Rockford, Ill. and San Antonio, Tex., 1970-73, Schneck Internat. Sales, Rockford, 1972-73, Brigance Chevrolet Sales, Oak Park, Ill., 1970; dir. ABET Industries, Inc., Broadview, Ill. Served with USAAF, 1942-46. Decorated Silver Star. Mem. A.I.M. (mem. pres.'s council), Phi Alpha Delta. Home: Highland Park, Ill. Died Oct. 28, 1973; buried Woodlawn Cemetery, Forest Park, Ill.

BASSETT, LOUIS D., city ofcl., tax cons.; b. Hubbell, Neb., Aug. 26, 1904; s. David Marcus and Grace (Napier) B.; student Kan. Wesleyan U., 1923-25; m. L. Daphne Worland, June 3, 1933; children—Daphne Darlene (Mrs. Brian Emlyn Davies), Robert Louis. With Skaggs Stores, Denver, 1926-28; supt. Young & Hall Constrn. Co., Maywood, Neb., 1928-31; asst. resident engr. Kan. Hwy. Commn., Osage City, Kan., 1931-36, asso. engr., 1936-43, dist. hwy. supr., 1943-70; owner Osage Tax Service, 1970-72; mayor of Osage City, 1971-72. Mem. Kan. Hwy. Suprs. Assn. (pres. 1959-69). Methodist (mem. Bishop's com. of 50 for reconciliation). Mason; Order Eastern Star, Kiwanian (pres. 1957-58, dist. com. hwy. safety 1960-61, lt. gov. 1962). Home: Osage City, Kan. Died Sept 22, 1972; interred Osage City, Kan.

BASSLER, RAY SMITH, paleontologist; b. Philadelphia, Pa., July 22, 1878; s. Simon Stein and Allie (Smith) B.; B.S., U. of Cincinnati, 1903; A.M., George Washington U., 1903, Ph.D., 1905; m. Clara M. Bloom, November 24, 1902; 1 son, Robert Stein; married second, Alida Baker, September 5, 1939. Aid in department of geology, U.S. National Museum, 1901-04, asst. curator, div. of invertebrate paleontology, 1904-08, curator, div. invertebrate paleontology, 1908-11, curator paleontology, 1911-29, head curator, dept. of geology, 1929-48; asst. prof. and prof. geol., George Washington U., 1904-43. Fellow Geol. Soc. of America, Paleontol. Soc. of America, Geol. Soc. of America. Paleontol. Soc. of America, Wash. Acad. of Science, Geol. Soc. of Washington; corr. mem. Geol. Soc. of London, Acad. of Sciences (Philadelphia); mem. Sigma Xi, Sigma Gamma Epsilon; hon. mem. Soc. Natural History of Tartu. Club: Cosmos (Washington). Author of about 200 monographs, papers and bibliographies on invertebrate paleontology and stratigraphy, dealing chiefly with micro-organisms. Home: Washington, D.C.†

BASTIAN, WALTER MAXIMILLIAN, judge; b. Washington, D.C., Nov. 16, 1891; s. Charles Sandal and Katherine (Draeger) B.; LL.B., Georgetown U., 1913; LL.D., Nat. U., 1953, George Washington U., 1958; m. Eva E. Alger, July 3, 1914; children—Walter M., David C. Admitted to D.C. bar, 1913, practiced in D.C., 1915-50; U.S. dist. judge U.S. Dist. Ct. for D.C., 1950-54; U.S. circuit judge Ct. of Appeals, 1954-68, sr. judge, 1968-75; lectr. Nat. U. Sch. of Law, 1918-48. Served as 1st lt. chem. warfare service, World War I. Trustee George Washington U. Mem. Bar Assn. D.C. (treas., past pres.), Am. Bar Assn. (treas. 1945-50, ho. of dels. 1936-53, from 1956), Order of Coif. Republican. Methodist. Mason (past master). Clubs: Metropolitan, Columbia Country, Lawyers, Alfalfa (Washington); University (Winter Park, Fla.). Author legal articles. Home: Alexandria Va. Died Mar. 12, 1975.

BATES, HARRIET HEGAR, physician; b. Danville, Ill., Dec. 10, 1921; d. Francis A. and Lee (Ewald) Hegar; M.D., U. Tex., 1943; m. Charles Richard Bates, May 19, 1944; children—Richard Stephen, Jeffrey Lee, Leslie Ann. Intern, Jefferson Davis Hosp., Houston, 1943-44; resident in pediatrics Charity Hosp. of La., New Orleans, 1944-45, Univ. Hosp., Ann Arbor, Mich., 1945-47; active staff Children's Med. Center, Dallas; attending pediatric staff Parkland Hosp., Dallas; dir. pediatric unit Wichita Falls (Tex.) State Hosp.; instr. pediatrics U. Tex., Dallas, 1948-52. Diplomate Am. Bd. Pediatrics. Mem. A.M.A., Am. Acad. Pediatrics. Home: Wichita Falls, Tex. Died Dec. 14, 1974; buried Wichita Falls, Tex.

BATES, HERBERT ERNEST, author; b. Rushden, Eng., May 16, 1905; s. Albert Ernest and Elizabeth (Lucas) B.; m. Marjorie Cox, July 18, 1931; children—Ann, Judith, Richard, Jonathan. Novelist, short story writer, playwright and critic, 1926-74. Served with RAF, 1941-46. Decorated comdr. Order Brit. Empire. Fellow Royal Soc. Lit. Author: The Two Sisters, 1926; Country of White Clover; Face of England; Fair Stood the Wind for France, 1944; The Purple Plain, 1947; The Jacaranda Tree, 1949; Scarlet Sword, 1951; Love for Lydia, 1952; The Feast of July, 1954; The Sleepless Moon 1956; Death of a Huntsman; The Darling Buds of May, 1958; The Cruise of the Breadwinner; Daffodil Sky, Country Heart; A Breath of French Air, 1959; An Aspidistra in Babylon, 1960; When the Green Woods Laugh, 1960; The Day of the Tortoise; Hark, Hark the Lark, 1960; The Grapes of Paradise, 1960; The Golden Oriole, 1962; A Crown of Wild Myrtle, 1962; Oh! to Be in England, 1963; Seven by Five, 1963; A Moment in Time, 1964; The Wedding Party, 1965; The Distant Horns of Summer, 1967; The Four Beauties, 1968; The Triple Echo (novella), 1969; The Vanished World (autobiography), 1969; A Little of What You Fancy, 1970; (autobiography) The Blossoming World, 1971, World in Ripeness, 1972; also short stories, essays, criticism. Home: Little Chart, Kent England. Died Jan. 28, 1974; inurned Charing Crematorium, Kent, England.

BATES, LEWIS ELON, editor; b. Rawlins, Wyo., Sept. 27, 1910; s. Charles Emerson and Edith May (Magor) B.; A.B., U. Wyo., 1933; m. Helen Elsie Lang, June 5, 1937; children—George Lang, Dana Magor. Reporter Republican-Boomerang, Laramie, Wyo., 1929-32, Laramie Bulletin, 1933-34, Wyoming Eagle, Cheyenne, 1936-40; news editor Wyo. State Tribune, 1941-44, mng. editor, 1944-48, editor, 1948-61; Wyo. pub. relations dir. Sperry and Hutchinson Co., from 1962. Chmn. Keep Wyo. Green Assn., Laramie County Cancer Crusade, Mem. Wyo. Press Assn. (dir.), Sigma Alpha Epsilon. Republican. Home: Cheyenne, Wyo. Died Sept. 7, 1972; interred in Lakeview Cemetery, Cheyenne.

BATES, MARSTON, naturalist; b. Grand Rapids, Mich., July 23, 1906; s. Glenn Freeman and Amy Mabel (Button) B.; B.S., U. Fla., 1927; A.M., Harvard, 1933, Ph.D., 1934; D.Sc., Kalamazoo Coll., 1956; m. Nancy Bell Fairchild, Jan. 11, 1939; children—Marian Hubbard, Sally Norton, Barbara Fairchild, Glenn Peregrine. Entomologist, advancing to dir. Servicio Técnico de Cooperación Agricola, United Fruit Co., 1928-31; Sheldon traveling fellow Harvard, 1934-35; research asst. Mus. Comparative Zoology, 1935-37; staff internat. health div. Rockefeller Found., 1937-50, spl. asst. to pres., 1950-52; prof. zoology U. Mich., 1952-71 (on leave 1956-57, 70); dir. research U. Puerto Rico, 1956-57; Timothy Hopkins lectr. Hopkins Marine Sta., Stanford U., 1954. Mem. div. com. biol. and med. scis. Nat. Sci. Found., 1952-58, chmn., 1956-58; adv. bd. Guggenheim Found., 1955-58; fellow Center for Advanced Studies, Wesleyan U., spring 1961; Phi Beta Kappa vis. scholar, 1962-63, 68-69. Trustee Cranbrook Inst. Sci., 1955-62. Recipient Daly medal Am. Geog. Soc., 1967. Mem. Pacific Sci. Bd., Am. Soc. Naturalists (pres. 1961), Council Fgn. Relations, Am. Acad. Arts and Scis., many sci. socs. Club: Cosmos (Washington). Author: The Natural History of Mosquitoes, 1949; The Nature of Natural History, 1950; Where Winter Never Comes, 1952; The Prevalence of People, 1955; The Darwin Reader, 1957; Coral Island, 1958; The Forest and the Sea, 1960; Man in Nature, 1960; Animal Worlds, 1963; The Land and Wildlife of South America, 1964; Gluttons and Libertines, 1968; A Jungle in the

House, 1970. Editorial bd. Am. Scholar, 1955-58. Contbr. to publs. Home: Ann Arbor, Mich. Died Apr. 3, 1974.

BATES, PHAON HILBORN, chemist; b. Sipesville, Pa., Aug. 1, 1879; s. William Harrison and Margaret (Peterman) B.; B.A., Central High Sch., Phila., 1898; B.S., U. of Pa., 1902; m. Helen Bell Graham, Jan. 1, 1904; children—Dorothy Hilborn (Mrs. James King), Marion Margaret (Mrs. Eugene B. Daniels). Chemist with Pa. R.R. Co., 1902-06; with U.S. Geol. Survey, 1906-10; Nat. Bur. Standards, Wash., D.C., from 1910, chief, Div. Clay and Silicate Products from 1919. Fellow A.A.A.S., Am. Ceramic Soc.; mem. Am. Concrete Inst. (pres. 1934-36), Am. Soc. for Testing Materials (pres. 1944-45), Am. Chem. Soc. Republican. Presbyterian. Club: Cosmos. Contbr. many papers giving results of research in cements, concrete and ceramics. Home: Washington, D.C.†

BATES, RICHARD WALLER, naval officer; b. San Francisco, Jan. 16, 1892; s. Henry Lesley Alexander and Rebecca Helen (Rixon) B.; B.S., U.S. Naval Acad., 1915, postgrad., 1920-21; M.S., Columbia, 1922; postgrad. Naval War Coll., 1940-41; Litt.D., L.I. U., 1958. Commd. ensign U.S. Navy, 1915, advanced through grades to rear adm., 1949; exec. officer U.S.S. Cincinnati, 1918-19; comdg. officer U.S.S. Buchanan, 1932-33, U.S.S. Ramapo, 1933, U.S.S. Long, 1934-35, U.S.S. Clark, 1938-40, U.S.S. Minneapolis, Pacific, 1943-44; on staff comdr. in chief Pacific Fleet, 1944; chief staff Bombardment and Fire Support Group, 3d Fleet, Palau, 1944, and 7th Fleet, 1944-45, participating in battles Leyte Gulf and Surigao Strait; chief staff Battleship Squadron 1, Lingayen and Okinawa, 1945; comdr. motor torpedo boats Pacific Fleet, 1945; chief staff Philippine Sea Frontier, 1945-46; mem. staff Naval War Coll., 1941-42, chief of strategy, 1942-43, head dept. analysis, 1946-49, later lectr.; ret. for phys. disability, 1949; recalled and served on active duty as head of World War II Battle Evaluation Group, 1949-58. Vice pres. Naval War Coll. Found., Inc., 1969-72, pres., 1972-73. Decorated Navy Cross, Legion Merit with 2 gold stars, Navy Unit citation, Victory Medal World War I (with star), Mexican Campaign, Yangtze Service, Am. Def., Am. Area Campaign, Asiatic-Pacific Area Campaign (with 10 bronze stars), Philippine Liberation, Nat. Def. medals, Victory Medal World War II. Episcopalian. Clubs: N.Y. Yacht (N.Y.C.); Army-Navy Country, University (Washington); Bohemian (San Francisco); Reading Room, Clambake, Ida Lewis Yacht (Newport, R.I.); Army-Navy (Manila, P.I.). Author numerous analysis of major naval battles of World War II. Contbr. to Colliers Ency. Home: Newport R.I. Died Dec. 27, 1973; interred Mountain View Cemetery, Oakland, Cal.

BATTLE, KEMP DAVIS, lawyer; b. Rocky Mount, N.C., Oct. 9, 1888; s. Thomas Hall and Elizabeth (Mershon) B.; A.B., U. N.C., 1909, LL.D., 1960; LL.B., U. Denver, 1914; m. Laura Maud Bunn, Oct. 30, 1917; children—Elizabeth Mershon (Mrs. Irving Grossberg), Laura (Mrs. Emerson C. Winstead, Jr.). Admitted to N.C. bar, 1910, practiced in Rocky Mount; mem. firm Battle, Winslow, Merrell, Scott & Wiley, from 1911; judge municipal ct., Rocky Mount, 1918-20. Vice pres., dir. Rocky Mount Mills; dir. Carolina Tel. & Tel. Co. Pres. N.C. Tb Assn., 1949; del. triennial con. Episcopal Ch., mem. exec. council, chancellor Diocese N.C., 1954-57. Bd. dirs., sec. Nat. Tb Assn., 1952-55; trustee Rocky Mount pub. schs., 1923-44, Braswell Meml. Library, Rocky Mount, 1925-40, U. N.C., 1927-59, Park View Hosp., Rocky Mount, from 1927. Recipient Will Ross medal Nat. Tb Assn., 1956. Mem. Am., N.C. (pres. 1932-33) bar assns., N.C. State Bar (council 1933-41). Democrat. Kiwanian. Club: Benvenue Country (Rocky Mount). Contbr. N. C. Law Rev. Home: Rocky Mount, N.C. Died July 3, 1973.

BATTS, WILLIAM OSCAR, educator; b. Cedar Hill, Tenn., Nov. 27, 1880; s. Oscar Llewellyn and Frances Jane (Jackson) B.; grad. Branham & Hughes Sch., Spring Hill, 1902; B.A., Vanderbilt U., 1908; m. Beulah Frances Featherston, June 30, 1909; children—Elizabeth Featherston, Margaret Jackson, William Oscar, Jane Hamblin. Prin., Cedar Hill Inst., 1902-08. Vanderbilt Training Sch., Elkton, Ky., 1908-17; headmaster Branham & Hughes Mil. Acad., Spring Hill, 1917-19, supt., 1919-31; supt. Columbia (Tenn.) Mil. Acad., from 1931. Mem. Tenn. Alcoholism Commn.; dir. United Tenn. League. Mem. Headmasters Assn., Vanderbilt (U.) Alumni Assn. (dir.), Beta Theta Pi. Mem. Gen. Conf. M.E. Ch., S., 1930, 1938; lay leader Tenn. Conf. of M.E. Ch., S. Mem. Uniting Conf. Meth. Ch., 1939; mem. Gen. Conf. Meth. Ch., 1940. Democrat. Methodist, K.P. Clubs: University (Nashville); Kiwanis. Home: Columiba, Tenn.†

BAUER, EUGENE CASPER, mfg. exec.; b. Chgo., Jan. 23, 1891; s. Emil J. and Augusta (Wolters) B.; student Chgo. Bus. Coll., Internat. Corr. Schs.; m. Helen K. Tschappat, June 19, 1915; children—Eugene Casper, Margaret H. (Mrs. Leland C. Oliver). Vice pres. Inland Engring. Co., 1923-26; v.p. Kensington Steel Co., 1926-30, pres., chmn. bd., 1930-45; v.p. Poor & Co., Chgo., 1945-50, exec. v.p., 1950-51, pres., 1951-56, chmn. bd., 1956-58; dir. Union Nat. Bank, Chgo. Dir. Kendall Coll. Mem. Kenilworth Union Ch. (trustee). Clubs: Chicago, Chgo. Athletic Assn.; Westmoreland Country (Wilmette, Ill.). Home: Kenilworth, Ill. Died Dec. 13, 1973.

BAUER, FRANZ KARL, physician, coll. dean; b. Vienna, Austria, Jan. 29, 1917; s. Julius and Marianne (Jokl) B.; student U. Vienna, 1934-38, U. Geneva (Switzerland), 1938-40; M.D., La. State U., 1941; m. Marjorie Frantz Bauer (Frantz), May 29, 1943; 1 dau., Anne Kathryn. Came to U.S., 1940, naturalized, 1943. Intern Charity Hosp. La., New Orleans, 1941-42, resident, 1942; resident Los Angeles County Gen. Hosp., 1946-48, chief med. resident, 1949-50; dir. radioisotope service VA Center, Los Angeles, 1951-56; mem. faculty Sch. Medicine, U. Cal. at Los Angeles, 1951-56, 60-65, asso. clin. prof., 1954-56, prof. medicine, 1960-65; mem. faculty, adminstrn. Sch. Medicine, U. So. Cal., 1956-60, 65-76, prof., 1965-76, also dean Sch. Medicine, 1969-74; chief outpatient clinics Los Angeles County Gen. Hosp., 1956-60, chief med. service Harbor Gen. Hosp., Torrance, Cal., 1960-65; vis. prof. Commissariat a l'Energie Atomique, dept. biology Service Hosp. Frederic Joliot, Orsay, France, 1967, Alexandra Hosp., Athens, Greece, 1962; cons. Oak Ridge Inst. Nuclear Studies, 1955. Bd. dirs. Profl. Staff Assn. of Los Angeles County, U. So. Cal. Med. Center, Children's Hosp. Los Angeles and Charles R. Drew Postgrad. Med. Sch., Los Angeles, 1965-71, v.p., 1972—; bd. dirs. Barlow Sanitorium, Los Angeles, Hosp. Good Samaritan Med. Center, Los Angeles. Served to maj. M.C., USAAF, 1942-46. Diplomate Am. Bd. Internal Medicine, Am. Bd. Nuclear Medicine. Fellow Soc. Tropical Medicine and Hygiene, A.C.P.; mem. Am. Fedn. Clin. Research (sec. Western sect. 1953), Soc. Nuclear Medicine (v.p. 1958), Pacific Interurban Clin. Club (chmn. 1971-72), Los Angeles Soc. Internal Medicine (pres. 1966), Western Assn. Physicians, Western Soc. Clin. Research, Soc. Exptl. Biology and Medicine, A.M.A., World Fedn. Nuclear Medicine and Biology, Alpha Omega Alpha (mem. faculty). Home: Los Angeles Cal., Died Feb. 1976.

BAUKHAGE, HILMAR ROBERT, radio commentator, writer, lectr., newspaperman; b. LaSalle, Ill., Jan. 7, 1889; s. Frederick Robert and Alice (Blood) B.; Ph.B. in Lit., U. Chgo., 1911; student Univs. of Bonn, 1933, Kiel, 1912, Jena, 1912, Freiburg, 1913, Sorbonne, 1913; m. Marjorie Collins, Nov. 8, 1922. With Chautauqua Daily, 1908; with Paris bur. London Pall Mall Gazette, 1913, Washington bur. Asso. Press, 1914; asst. mng. editor Leslie's, 1916; with Consol. Press, 1919-32, as supt. Washington and San Francisco, and supt. and bus. mgr., Chgo.; with U.S. News, 1932-37, N.Am. Newspaper Alliance, 1937; Washington corr. Western Newspaper Union, 1940-45; news commentator Farm and Home Hour NBC, 1934-42; broadcast outbreak, of World War II from Berlin for NBC, 1939; cons. editor Army Times Pub. Co.; columnist Army Navy Air Forces Register, 1955-62; spl. writer U.S. News and World Report, 1963. First Person to give news broadcast from White House (Pearl Harbor attack, 1941); Washington commentator ABC Network, 1942-51; commentator MBS 1951-54. Enlisted as pvt. CAC, AUS, 1918, commd. 2d lt., F.A., and served with A.E.F.; covered Peace Conf., Paris, for Stars and Stripes after Armistice. Recipient Nat. Headliners Club Award, 1945, for best domestic broadcast of the year, award for Pub. Service by U. Chgo. Alumni Assn., 1946, Poor Richard Citation for Merit. Mem. Overseas Writers, Radio Corrs. (pres. 1941-42), Radio News Analysts Assn., S.A.R., Am. Legion, Owl and Serpent, Mil. Order World Wars, Delta Upsilon. Mason. Clubs: National Press, Cosmos (Washington). Author: (with C.L. Baldridge) I Was There, 1919; also several translations from German and French. Co-author, editor: American Military Leaders WWI; American Military Leaders WWII; Tangled Web; Yanks Are Coming Pershing (biography); McArthur (biography). Home: Washington, D.C., Died Jan. 31, 1976; interred Balt. Nat. Cemetery.

BAUM, MARY HELEN, home economist; b. Frankfort, Ind., Oct. 19, 1920; d. Henry Millenberg and Anna Michael Baum; B.S., Purdue U., 1948. Exec. sec. Hicks Body Co., Lebanon, Ind., 1943-46; sr. home economist So. Cal. Gas Co., Hollywood, Cal., 1953-54, consumer specialist, Monterey Park, 1972-74; tech. adviser TV commls., 1966-75. Recipient Spl. commendation Industry-Edn. Council So. Cal., 1966. Mem. Am. Cal., Los Angeles Dist. (pres. 1961-62) home econs. assn., Los Angeles Home Economists in Bus. Assn. (chmn. 1954-55). Mem. Order Eastern Star. Home: Inglewood, Cal., Died Sept. 25, 1975.

BAUMANN, GUSTAVE, artist, engraver; b. Magdeburg, Germany, June 27, 1881; s. Gustav and Pauline (Nagel) B.; came to U.S., 1891; ed. Art Inst. Chicago, Kunst Gewerbe Schule, Munich, Germany; m. Jane Devereux Henderson, June 25, 1925; 1 dau., Ann. Rep. in Met. Mus. Print Room; New York Public Library; Boston Museum; Nat. Gallery, Washington; Nat. Gallery, Toronto; Hibbard Memorial Collection, Chicago Art Inst., etc. Marionette Theatre Plays and Productions from 1931. Book, Frijoles Canyon Pictographs, selected for fifty books of the year, 1939. Awarded gold medal for engraving, San Francisco Expn., 1915. Home: Santa Fe. N.M.†

BAUMBERGER, JAMES PERCY, physiologist; b. San Leandro, Calif., Sept. 17, 1892; s. James and Elise Marie-Louise (Deprez) B.; B.S., U. Cal., 1914; M.S., Harvard, 1916, Sc.D., 1918; m. Alberta Loraine Jackson, Dec. 22, 1914. Asst. or teaching fellow in entomology, zoology, botany, or physiology at Harvard or Radcliffe, 1914-18; instr. natural scis. Lowthorpe Hort. Sch., Groton, Mass., 1915-18; mem. faculty, dept. physiology Stanford Medical School, from 1919, professor physiology, 1935-58, professor emeritus, from 1958; senior research associate with the Palo Alto Medical Research Foundation, from 1961; research associate, department of medicine Collis P. Huntington Cancer Hosp., Harvard Med. Sch., 1932-33; vis. prof. anatomy dept. Washington U., 1941, also research asso. Barnard Free Skin and Cancer Hosp., St. Louis; vis. prof. aviation physiology U. So. Cal. Sch. Medicine, 1943 (working on O.S.R.D. project on explosive decompression); spl. cons. Aero. Med. Lab., Army Air Force, Wright Field, Dayton, O., 1944; responsible investigator Office Naval Research project on field physiology, 1952-53, on bird migration, 1953-55; prin. investigator project oxygen delivery rate of erythrocytes, other projects for Air Force. Served with M.C., AUS, AEF, in traumatic shock lab., 1918. Held Commn. for Relief in Belgium Ednl. Found. Fellowship, Bruxelles, 1925-26; Am. Scandinavian Fellowship, Lund, Sweden, and Copenhagen, Denmark, 1926; Rockefeller Table, Naples Biol. Sta., 1926. Fellow A.A.A.S.; mem. Am. Physiol. Soc., Am. Assn. U. Profs., Soc. Exptl. Biology and Medicine (chmn. Pacific coast section 1956-58), Am. Association Cancer Research, Soc. Gen. Physiol., Western Soc. Naturalists, Sigma Xi, Cercle des Alumni de la Foundation Universitaire. Club: Commonwealth of Cal. (San Francisco). Asso. editor Physiol. Revs., 1945-52; Ann. Reviews Physiology, 1952-58. Contbr. to sci. jours. Home: Palo Alto, Cal. Died June 21, 1973.

BAUMGARDNER, EVELYN JULIA GROVES (MRS. CHARLES ERNST BAUMGARDNER), artist; b. San Francisco; d. Oliver Henry and Carrie (Scheihing) Groves; student U. Cal. at Berkeley, 1943-44, Cal. Coll. Arts and Crafts, 1950-53, Art Workshop, Mexico, 1964-66, 70, Art Workshop, South Seas, 1965, Caribbean, 1969, El Salvador, 1972, Guatemala, 1972, Portugal, 1972; pvt. study art various Cal. artists; m. Charles Ernst Baumgardner, June 29, 1928; 1 dau., Lynne Mari. Exhibited in group shows at De Young Mus., San Francisco, Oakland Art Mus., Richmond (Cal.) Art Center, Crocker Art Gallery, Sacramento, Haggin Gallery, Stockton, Setay Gallery, Beverly Hills; represented in permanent collections Exec. Suites Kaiser Industries, Oakland, Bank of Cal., Berkeley, Bank Am., Golden Pacific Airways, also pvt. collections. Art juror, moderator, demonstrator, from 1954. Recipient oil and watercolor painting awards; first award for miniatures, 1969; 1st awards abstract painting, 1971, 72; Purchase award El Cerrito, 1970. Mem. Nat. Assn. U. Dames (chpt. pres. 1942-43), Nat. League Am. Pen Women (br. pres. 1960-62). Club: The Thinkers (San Francisco pres. 1928). Address: Berkeley, Cal. Died Aug. 31, 1973.

BAUMGARTNER, JOSEPHINE MAE, educator, journalist; b. nr. Garner, Ia.; d. August E. and Bertha (Schmolke) Baumgartner; B.S., Drake U., 1957, M.S., 1960; postgrad. Northwestern U. Tchr. high sch., jr. high sch. and Grand View Coll., Des Moines, from 1957; free lance journalist, 1936-70. Active YWCA. Jour. clk. Ia. Gen. Assembly, 1947; pub. relations dir. for women Republican State Central Com., 1940. Mem. Philos. Soc. Am., Am. Assn. U. Women, Ia., Nat. fedns. press women, Theta Sigma Phi (pres. local alumni group 1968-69; Service award 1949, 69). Methodist (officer Ia. conf. 1966-68). Clubs: Internat. Press, Audubon (conservation programming). Home: Des Moines, Ia. Died May 28, 1973; buried Garner Evergreen Cemetery.

BAXTER, JAMES PHINNEY, 3D, educator; b. Portland, Me., Feb., 15, 1893; s. James Phinney, Jr., and Nelly Furbish (Carpenter) B.; A.B., William Coll., 1914, A.M., 1921; A.M., Harvard, 1923, Ph.D., 1926; LL.D., Harvard and Amherst, 1938, U. of Me. and Wesleyan U., 1939, Hobart Coll., 1942; Bowdoin College, 1944; Litt.D., Syracuse University, 1945, L.H.D., Case Institute of Technology, 1948, American International College, 1954; LL.D., Williams College, 1947, Kenyon College, 1949, Columbia Univ., 1954, Brown U., 1956, U. Rochester, 1960; D.Sc., Union Coll., 1949; m. Anne Holden Strang, June 21, 1919 (dec. May 1962); children—James Phinney IV, Arthur Brown, Stephen Bartow. With Indsl. Finance Corp., New York City, 1914-15; instr. history, Colo. College, 1921-22; Harvard traveling fellow, 1924-25; instr. history, Harvard, 1925-27, asst. prof., 1927-31, asso. prof., 1931-36, prof., 1936-37, master of Adams House, 1931-37; president of Williams Coll., 1937-61, pres. emeritus, 1961-75; educational adviser U.S. Military Academy; lecturer, Lowell Inst., Boston, 1931, Naval War Coll., since 1932, Cambridge U., 1936. Dir. research and analysis for Coordinator of Information, Washington, D.C., August 1941-June 1942; deputy director, Office of Strategic Services, June 1942-43; historian Office of Scientific Research and Development, Washington, D.C., 1943-46. Pres. Assn. of American Colls., 1945. Trustee Williams Coll., 1934-37, World Peace Found., Phillips Acad.; member board of overseers Harvard University;

dir. State Mutual Life Ins. Co. (Worcester, Mass.). Term trustee Mass. Inst. Tech., 1956-61; trustee Tchrs. Ins. and Annuity Assn., 1955-59. Presdl. Certificate of Merit. Fellow A.A.A.S., Council on Foreign Relations (Senior); mem. American Council Education (1st vice chmn. 1954-55), Am. Historical Association (executive committee, 1937-38), Am. Antiquarian Soc., Am. Soc. Internat. Law, Am. Polit. Science Assn., Council on Foreign Relations, Colonial Soc. of Mass., Mass. Hist. Soc., Soc. of Am. Historians (pres., 1945-46), Gargoyle Soc., Phi Beta Kappa, Kappa Alpha. Republican. Episcopalian. Clubs: Harvard, Tavern (Boston, Mass.); Century, Williams (New York City, New York). Author of the Introduction of the Ironclad Warship, 1933 (translation, Naissance du Cuirassé, Paris, 1935); Scientists Against Time, 1946 (translation, Secrets de la Science Americaine, Paris, 1947). Winner 1947 Pulitzer prize in history. Contbr. to hist. and law jours. Home: New York City, N.Y. Died June 17, 1975.

BAYNE, STEPHEN FIELDING, JR., bishop; b. N.Y.C., May 21, 1908; s. Stephen Fielding and Edna Mabel (Ashley) B.; A.B., Amherst Coll., 1929, D.D. (hon.), 1948; S.T.B., Gen. Theol. Sem., 1933, S.T.M., 1934, S.T.D., 1947; LL.D., Mills Coll., 1951; D.D., Whitman Coll., 1952, Anglican Theol. Coll., 1954; S.T.D., Columbia, 1952; D.Litt., Hobart Coll., 1957, Kenyon Coll., 1960; L.H.D., U. Puget Sound, 1959; D.D., St. Paul's (Rikkyo) Tokyo, 1960, Harvard, 1961, Australian Coll. Theology, 1962, Huron Coll., 1963, Cuttington Coll., 1967, Trinity Coll., 1969; m. Lucie Culver Gould, June 19, 1934; children—Stephen Fielding, Maurice Philip Gould, Duncan A., Lydia L., Bruce G.C. Fellow and tutor Gen. Theol. Sem., 1932-34; ordained diaconate P.E. Ch., 1932, priesthood, 1933; rector Trinity Ch., St. Louis, 1934-39, St. John's Ch., Northampton, Mass., 1939-42; chaplain Columbia U., 1942-47 (on leave serving as chaplain USNR, 1944-45); bishop Diocese of Olympia, 1947-59; Anglican exec. officer, 1960-64; 1st v.p. exec. council P.E. Ch. U.S.A., 1964-70, dir. overseas dept., 1964-68, dep. for program, 1968-70; prof. Christian mission Gen. Theol. Sem., from 1970, dean, 1972-73, dean emeritus, from 1973. Chmn. com. on the family Lambeth Conf., 1958. Mem. Theta Delta Chi. Clubs: Century (N.Y.C.); University (Seattle); Athenaeum (London, Eng.). Author: The Optional God, 1953; Christian Living, 1957; In The Sight of the Lord, 1958; Enter with Joy, 1961; Mindful of the Love, 1962; An Anglican Turning Point, 1964. Home: New York City, N.Y. Died Jan. 18, 1974.

BEACH, EARL EDWARD, educator, musician; b. Crestline, O., May 22, 1909; s. Carl Theodore and Arzona (Zellner) B.; B.S., Capital U., 1931; postgrad. Ohio State U., 1931, U. Pitts., 1935, U. Mich., 1936, U. Ga., 1951; M.A., Western Res. U., 1948; m. Vivian Frances Stout, Apr. 28, 1945; children—Theodore Wayne, Marcia Rae. Supervising instr. music, Bellaire, O., 1931-40, Alliance, O., 1940-43; dir. bands, instr. music Mt. Union Coll., 1941-43; dir. sch. and community music, Charlevoix, Mich., 1943-44; dir. instrumental music South High Sch., Cleve., 1944-45; chmn. music edn., dir. bands and symphonette Ohio Wesleyan U., 1945-50; chmn. grad. and undergrad. divs. music edn. U. Ga., 1950-58; dir. dept. music East Caroline Coll., Greenville, N.C., 1958-62, dean Sch. Music, from 1962. Organizing dir. Ogelby Park High Sch. Music Camp, 1937, Ohio Wesleyan Summer Music Camp, 1946-50, U. Ga. Music Festival, U. Ga. Summer Youth Camp, from 1951. Named Outstanding Music Educator, N.C. Music Educators Assn., 1970. Fellow Inst. Arts and Letters; mem. Nat. Council Coop. Tchrs. Edn. (rep. Music Educators Nat. Conf. 1961-63), N.C. Music Educators Conf. (life mem.; pres. 1967-69), Music Educators Nat. Conf. (research council 1952-58, nat. chmn. music in higher edn. 1952-54, pres. So. div. 1957-59, mem. exec. com. 1958-60, nat. chmn. Go Project 16; mem. commn. on reorgn. and devel. 1970—), Ga. Music Assn. (dir.), Phi Mu Alpha, Pi Kappa Lambda, Phi Beta Mu (pres. N.C. chpt., nat. dir.), Beta Theta Pi, Phi Delta Kappa. Editorial bd. Music Educators Jour., 1950-58, 70-74, Jour. Research Music Edn., 1952-58; chmn. editorial bd. Ga. Music mag., 1950-56; editor Triad pub. Ohio Music Edn. Assn., 1947-49. Editor Bibliography of Music Edn. Materials, 1958. Home: Greenville, N.C. Died Apr. 16, 1974.

BEAMER, GEORGE NOAH, judge; b. Bowling Green, Ind., Oct. 9, 1904; s. Jasper F. and Frances M. (Roush) B.; LL.B. U. Notre Dame, 1929; LL.D., Ashland Coll., 1971; m. Charlotte L. Hoover, May 14, 1932; children—George Noah, Judith Ann. Admitted to Ind. bar, 1929, practiced in South Bend; mem. firm Crumpacker, May, Beamer, Levy & Searer, 1939-62; U.S. dist. judge, Hammond, Ind., 1962-73, South Bend, Ind., 1973-74, chief judge, 1972-74; pros. atty., 1937-38; atty. gen., Ind., 1941-42. Trustee Ashland Coll.; mem. South Bend Sch. Bd., 1957-62. Fellow Am. Coll. Trial Lawyers; mem. Am., Ind., St. Joseph County (pres. 1957) bar assns., C. of C. (pres. 1951-52). Democrat. Mem. Brethren Ch. Club: Optimist (dist. gov. 1951). Home: South Bend, Ind. Died Oct. 21, 1974.

BEAN, RICHARD, banker; b. Mt. Sterling, Ky., May 13, 1879; s. Robert Thompson and Pauline (Summers) B.; grad. Louisville Male High Sch., 1899; student Y.M.C.A. night sch. 3 yrs.; m. Rella C. Bourne, of Louisville, Ky., Oct. 17, 1911; children—Alice Goodridge, Robert Thompson, Richard, Bourne. Began in employ of Ballard & Ballard Co., flour millers, advancing to sec.; then with Louisville Nat. Bank & Trust Co., advancing to pres.; pres. Louisville Trust Co. since Feb. 1, 1929; v.p. Banco-Kentucky Co.; v.p. Louisville Bedding Co.; dir. Ky. Oxygen Co., Brandeis Machinery Co., Brinly-Hardy Co., The Helium Co., The Girdler Corpn., J.V. Pilcher Mfg. Co. Served as pvt., Co. C., 1st Ky. Inf., Spanish-Am. War; chmn. Jefferson County Council of Defense, World War. Mem. bd. dirs. Louisville Conv. and Publicity League, Louisville Safety Council. Republican. Baptist. Mason. Clubs: Pendennis, Country. Home: Louisville, Ky.†

BEAN, WILLIAM (GLEASON), educator; b. Heflin, Ala., Dec. 26, 1891; s. Jesse Coleman and Louise (Moore) B.; A.B., U. of Ala., 1913; A.M., Harvard, 1916; Ph.D., 1922; m. Lucy B. Marstellar, May 27, 1927; children—Jesse Coleman, II, William Gleason, Jr. Teacher Blount Co. (Ala.) Sch., 1913-15; Austin teaching fellow in history, Harvard, 1920-22; asst. prof. history Washington and Lee U., Lexington Va., 1922-23, asso. prof., 1923-29, prof., 1929-30, head dept. history, from 1930, prof. history Thomas Ball Found., from 1947, Douglas Southall Freeman prof. history, from 1958; instr. summer sessions, Tulane U., U. of Va. and U. of Ala. Mem. of Va. Civil War Centennial Commn. Served as 2d lt. A.E.F. 1917-19. Mem. So. Hist. Assn., Acad. Social Sci. of Va., Phi Gamma Delta, Phi Beta Kappa. Democrat. Presbyterian. Author: Stoneman's Man: Sandie Pendleton, 1959; Party Transformation in Massachusetts with Special Reference to the Antecedents of the Republican Party, 1848-60 (unpublished dissertation); contbr. to hist. jours. and dictionary of American Biography. Home: Lexington, Va., Died May 24, 1974.

BEASLEY, JEAN TALLMAN, physician; b. N.Y.C., Nov. 14, 1921; d. John and Olga (Edwards) Tallman; M.D., N.Y.U., 1948; m. Albert Sidney Beasley, Aug. 21, 1942; children—Scott Albert, Jean Marion. Intern children's med. service Bellevue Hosp., N.Y.C., 1948-49; asst. resident children's service N.Y. Hosp., N.Y.C., 1951-52, fellow in pediatrics outpatient dept., 1952-53, pediatrician outpatient dept., 1953-58, instr., 1956-62; attending pediatrician Norwalk (Conn.) Hosp., 1954-73, dir. adolescent clinic; courtesy pediatrician Bridgeport (Conn.) Hosp., 1954-73; pediatrician outpatient dept. Grace-New Haven Community Hosp., 1962-69; clin. instr. pediatrics Yale, 1962-69; sch. physician, Westport, Conn., 1954-56; physician Intercommunity Camp, Westport, 1968-71. Mem. Westport Community Council, Conn. Mental Health Planning Assn. Diplomate Am. Bd. Pediatrics. Fellow Am. Acad. Pediatrics; mem. Soc. for Adolescent Medicine (charter). Home: Westport, Conn. Died Jan. 24, 1973; buried Westport, Conn.

BEATTIE, FOUNTAIN FOX, banker; b. Greenville, S.C., July 29, 1878; s. John Edgeworth and Mary Caroline (Mays) B.; student Furman U., Greenville, and U. of Mich.; LL.B., Columbian (now George Washington) U., 1902; m. Janell Cobb Arnold, Nov. 12, 1912; children—Fountain Fox, Jane Arnold, Dannitte Mays. Admitted to S.C. bar, 1902, and began practice at Greenville; entered banking business as sec.-treas. Piedmont Savings & Investment Co., Greenville, became pres., 1914 (absorbed by 1st Nat. Bank); v.p. 1st Nat. Bank, 1916, pres. from 1946, retired as pres., later chmn. bd. Mem. S.C. Ho. of Rep., 1906-08. Mem. Am. Bankers Assn. (mem. exec. council 1931), S.C. Bankers Assn. (v.p. 1927; pres. 1928), Am. and S.C. bar assns., Chi Psi, Democrat. Episcopalian. Address: Greenville, S.C.†

BEATTIE, RONALD HANNA, govt. ofcl.; b. nr. Oregon City, Ore., Sept. 5, 1903; s. William Gilbert and Willametta (Hanna) B.; B.A., U. Ore., 1926, J.D., 1928, M.A., 1932; m. Inez B. Morris, July 15, 1931; children—Alan G., Dwight M., Robert T. Admitted to Ore. bar, 1928; research asst. U. Ore. Law Sch., 1929-32; research asso. Bur. Pub. Adminstrn., U. Cal., Berkeley, 1932-36; regional dir. Atty. Gen.'s Survey of Release Procedures for Ariz., Cal. and Nev., Berkeley, 1936; crime statistician U.S. Bur. Census, 1937-40; statistician Adminstrv. Office U.S. Cts., Washington, 1940-45, chief div. procedural studies and statistics, 1961-65; chief Bur. Criminal Statistics, Sacramento, 1945-61, 65-72. Fellow Am. Statis. Assn. Home: Sacramento, Cal. Died Mar. 18, 1974.

BEATTY, MORGAN, news analyst; b. Little Rock, Sept. 6, 1902; s. Hugh Mercer and Caroline Sarah (Morgan) B.; ed. pub. and high schs., Ft. Smith, Ark., also Centre Coll., Danville, Ky., and Washington U., St. Louis, Mo.; m. Mary Virginia Garwood, Oct. 15, 1928 (dec. May 1957); children—Hugh (dec.), Morgan Mercer, Stephen Garwood; m. 2d, Kathryn Josephine Ring, Apr. 13, 1958. Reporter, Ft. Smith Southwest Am., 1920; news editor Ft. Smith Southwest Times-Record, 1922-23; telegraph editor Little Rock Gazette, 1923-27; wire editor A.P., Atlanta, 1927-28, N.Y.C., 1928-31, asst. news supr., N.Y.C., 1931-32, fgn. cable editor, 1932-33, bur. chief, Cleve., 1933-34, asst. feature editor, N.Y.C., 1934-35, bur. chief, Albany, N.Y., 1935-36, chief feature editor, Washington, 1936-42; NBC fgn corr., London, 1942-43, news analyst, Washington, 1941-56, Chgo., 1959, N.Y.C., 1958-61; war corr. ETO, London, 1943; radio corr. representing all Am. networks, Berlin Big Three Conf., 1945. Recipient Dupont award, 1949, Headliner's award, 1948, Dell radio Excellence award, 1959, American Legion award, 1961. Mem. Overseas Writers' Assn., Kappa Alpha. Clubs: Nat. Press (Washington); London Press (hon.); Overseas Press (N.Y.C.). Author: Our Nation's Capital. Home: New York City, N.Y. Died July 1975; buried Antigua.

BEATTY, PAUL COUSART, realtor; b. Beverly, N.J., Mar. 1, 1918; s. Albert Edwin and Florence (Perkins) B.; T.E., Phila. Textile Inst., 1939; grad. Advanced Mgmt. Program, Harvard, 1954; m. Moselle Olive Butterworth, Dec. 4, 1943; children—Sherryl Ann, Paul Craig. Mgr. Watertown Woolen Mills, Millbury, Mass., 1940-41; woolen supt. Beacon Mfg. Co., Swannanoa, N.C., 1941-42; instr. Phila. Textile Inst., 1942-43; technician Am. Viscose Corp., Marcus Hook, Pa., 1943-46; mgr. Pacific Mills, Halifax, Va., 1946-59; v.p. Record Advertiser, South Boston, Va., 1959-60; gen. mgr. Halifax Cotton Mills, South Boston, 1960-62; pres. Danville Industries, Inc. (Va.), 1963-71, also dir.; salesman McDaniel Realty, Richmond, 1972-73; also dir. Pres. Halifax United Fund, 1960-61; chief Halifax Vol. Fire Dept., 1947-52. Chmn. Halifax County Sch. Bd., 1966-70; mem. Halifax Town Council, 25 yrs. Bd. dirs. Red Cross Bloodmobile, Halifax County Little Theatre. Recipient Outstanding Citizen award Woodmen of the World, 1951; named Outstanding Citizen of Halifax County, Boston Jaycees, 1960. Mem. Nat. Assn. Hosiery Mfrs. (dir. 1967-73), The Carded Yarn Assn. (dir. 1966-70) Newcomen Soc. N. Am. Episcopalian (vestryman 1959-68). Lion (pres. 1952-53), Rotarian. Club: Sportsmen (dir.) (Halifax). Home: Halifax, Va. Died June 26, 1973; buried St. Johns Episcopal Ch. Cemetery, Halifax Va.

BEATY, JULIAN BONAR, lawyer; b. Conway, S.C., Dec. 10, 1880; s. Edgar Robert and Emma Jane (Collins) B.; student Princeton Prep. Sch., 1901-02; A.B. with honors, Princeton, 1906; LL.B., N.Y. Law Sch., 1908; m. Constance Saltonstall Dawbarn Peck, Apr. 6, 1915; children—Julian Bonar, John Thurston, Richard Norton, Nancy Lee, David Collins. Accountant, Georgetown, S.C.; sec. to former Pres. Grover Cleveland, 1902-06, then Woodrow Wilson, pres. of Princeton, 1905-06; law clk., stenographer; admitted to N.Y. bar, 1908; sec. to pres. Borough of Manhattan, 1910-12, supt. pub. bldgs., 1912, sec. to mayor, 1913; pvt. practice oflaw with Hedges, Ely & Frankel, 1914; partner, sr. partner, Reeves, Todd, Ely & Beaty, N.Y.C., from 1925; asst. to gen. counsel Am. Metal Co., Ltd., N.Y.C., 1914-23, dir., 1917-23, sec.-treas., 1918-23; v.p., dir., gen. counsel Nichols Copper Co., 1923-26, counsel, 1926-30; assisted consolidated Nicols Copper Co., Phelps Dodge Refining Corp., 1930-58, sec., dir., gen. counsel Phelps Dodge Refining Corp., 1930-58, dir., spl. counsel, from 1958; sec. dir., gen. counsel Nichols Engring. & Research Corp., from 1931; counsel dir. N.Y. and Honduras Rosario Mining Co.; dir. Granby Consol. Mining, Smelting & Power Co., Ltd., Vancouver, D.C., 1929-59, v.p., 1937-39, pres., chmn., 1939-55; dir., counsel Rio Blanco Copper Corp., Ltd., 1923-60; incorporator Am. Business Shares, Inc., investment trust, 1930, dir.; dir. Affiliated Fund, mut. investment trust; dir., counsel Ore & Chem. Corp.; spl. counsel Internat. Minerals & Metals Corp., Am. Dutch Trading Co. Past trustee Village of Rye, mem. common council, mayor, Rye. Past pres. Rye Community Chest; active Boy Scouts, YMCA; dir., counsel Valeria Home, Nichols Found.; past v.p., trustee Rye Country Day Sch. Mem. N.Y. (past gov.), Westchester (pres. 1930) Southern socs., U.S. Seniors Golf Assn., Assn. Bar City N.Y., Phi Beta Kappa. Democrat. Presbyn. (past trustee). Clubs: Lawyers, Princeton, University (N.Y.C.); Apawamis, Manursing (Rye); Cap and Gown (Princeton, N.J.).†

BEAUBIEN, DE GASPE, cons. engr.; b. Outremont, Can., May 18, 1881; s. Honr. Louis and Lauretta (Stuart) B.; B.Sc., McGill U., 1906; D.Sc., U. Man., 1945; m. Gabrielle Dandurand, Oct. 1910 (dec.); children—Jacques, Claire, Andrée; m. 2d, Angeline Rodier, May 10, 1934. Asst. to constrn. engr. Montreal Light, Heat & Power, 1903; demonstrator McGill U., 1907; apprentice Westinghouse Electric & Mfg. Co., Pittsburgh, 1908; ind. cons. engr., 1908-22; cons. engr. Beaubien, Busfield & Co., 1922-27, De Gaspe, Beaubien & Co., from 1927; pres. Beaubien, Ltd.; dir. W. Can. Collieries, Ltd., Dominion Ltd. Formerly nat. joint chmn. War Savs. Com.; mem. Nat. War Finance Com. Decorated comdr. Order Brit. Empire. Mem. Canadian Standards Assn., Engring. Inst. Can. (past pres.), Asst. Cons. Engrs. (hon.), Am. Inst. E.E., Corp. Profl. Engrs. of Que. Roman Catholic. Clubs: Canadian (past pres.); Rotary (past pres.); Montreal, University: Cercle Universitarie (past pres.); Royal Automobile of Can. (past pres.) (Mt. Royal); Laval sur-lelac Golf. Home: Que., Canada.†

BEAUMONT, ANDRE ALDEN, educator; b. Wilkes-Barre, Pa., Apr. 3, 1900; s. Andre and Elsie (Butler) B.; A.B., Yale, 1921; A.M., Princeton, 1922, Ph.D., 1925; m. Cecelia M. Casserly, June 25, 1929 (deceased August 28, 1951). Member faculty Washington Square Coll., New York University from 1923, professor history from 1945. Member Am. Hist. Assn., Mediaeval

Acad., Am. Assn. U. Profs. Clubs: University (N.Y. City); Wilton (Conn.) Riding. Home: New York City, N.Y. Died Jan. 21, 1974.

BEAZLEY, GEORGE GRIMES, JR., clergyman, ch. orgn. ofcl.; b. Danville, Ky., Feb. 13, 1914; s. George Grimes and Hettie Page (Miller) B.; B.A., Centre Coll. of Ky., 1935, D.D., 1965; B.D., Coll. of Bible, 1938; postgrad. U. Chgo., U. Mo., Union Theol. Sem.; D.D., Culver-Stockton Coll., 1964; m. Charlotte Strother Holman, June 24, 1939. Ordained to ministry Christian Ch., 1938; pastor in Richmond, Mo., 1938-47, Bartlesville, Okla., 1947-60; pres. Council on Christian Unity, Christian Church (Disciples of Christ), Indpls., from 1960. Del. 3d assembly World Council Chs., 1961, del. 4th assembly, 1968, mem. faith and order commn., 1962-; secretary com., from 1968; del. 4th World Conf. Faith and Order, 1963; mem. gen. bd. Nat. Council Chs., from 1961, adv. com. faith and order, from 1962, sec. Unity Commn. Christian Ch., from 1961, mem. central com. on restructure Disciples, from 1961; sec. Consultation on Church Union, 1966-68, vice chmn., then chmn., 1968-71; elder Northwood Christian Ch., Indianapolis, Ind. Board dirs. Ecumenical Inst., Chateau de Bossey, from 1961. Mem. Soc. Bibl. Lit. and Exegesis, Am. Sch. Oriental Research (asso.), N. Am. Acad. Ecumenists, Soc. Ky. Cols., Theta Phi, Omicron Delta Kappa. Home: Indianapolis, Ind. Died Oct. 1973; interred Danville, Ky.

BECH, JOSEPH, diplomat; b. Diekirch, Luxembourg, 1887; grad. in law and admitted to bar. Mem. of Parliament of Luxembourg from 1914; minister of justice and home affairs, 1921-25; prime minister and minister of foreign affairs, 1926-37; minister of foreign affairs, since 1937, confirmed in this office on return after liberation of the Grand Duchy of Luxembourg; prime minister, minister of fgn. affairs, from 1954; represented Luxembourg at Assemblies of League of Nations, 1926-40; led delegations of Luxembourg to San Francisco Conf., 1945, and Gen. Assembly of the U.N., London, 1946; chmn. NATO Conf., from 1957. Died Mar. 11, 1975.

BECHET, PAUL ESNARD, physician; b. New Orleans, La., July 28, 1881; s. Alphonse A. and Pauline (Claudel) B.; ed. Univ. Sch., New Orleans, La.; M.D., Tulane U. (La.), 1903; License, La., 1903, N.Y., 1910, N.J., 1941. Acting asst. surgeon U.S. Pub. Health Service in New Orleans yellow fever epidemic, 1905; received spl. official citation from the Surgeon-Gen.; asst. demonstrator anatomy, Tulane U., 1903-07; asst. physician N.Y. Skin and Cancer Hosp., 1909-25, several different staff assignments in both dermatology and syphilology, N.Y. area, from 1925; cons. dermatologist, Hospital for Special Survey, from 1918; cons. N.Y. Post Grad. Hosp. and Skin Cancer Unit; Alexian Bros. Hosp.; St. Elizabeth's Hosp., both Elizabeth, N.J.; New York University-Bellevue Medical Center, and others. Diplomate (founders group) Am. Bd. Dermatol. and Syphilology. Corr. mem. Societe Francaise de Dermatologie et de Syphilligraphie, Paris, France, Hungarian Dermatol. Soc., Budapest, Austrian Dermatol. Soc., Vienna, Argentine Assn. Dermatol. and Syphilol., Buenos Aires; hon. mem. de la societe de Prophylaxie Sanitaire et Morale, Fournier Inst., Paris, France, Montreal Dermatological Society; mem. nat., state and local gen. and spl. med. assns. and socs., has served as officer of several particularly in spl. fields. Roman Catholic. Author: History of the American Dermatological Association in Commemoration of its Seventy-fifth Anniversary, 1952. Contbr. med. and hist. papers on dermatology and syphilology. Home: Elizabeth, N.J.†

BECKER, ARTHUR CHARLES, musician, educator; b. Louisville, Sept. 20, 1895; s. John Philip and Mary Margaret (Schmitt) B.; grad. St. Xavier's Coll., Louisville, 1917; Mus.B., Sherwood Music Sch., 1921, Mus. M., 1922; Mus.D., Boguslawki Coll. Music, 1936; hon. Mus.D., Chgo. Musical Coll., 1942; student organ with Widor and Dupre, Paris; composition with Roussell; m. Barbara Sieben, May 16, 1936; 1 son, Arthur John. Composer, Roman Cath. Masses for four voices, numerous organ compositions, motets both sacred and secular, sextet for brass instruments; dean Sch. of Music, De Paul U., Chgo., 1922-76, organist, choirmaster Univ. Ch. of St. Vincent De Paul, 1918-76; conductor all Cath. High Sch. chorus of Chgo. Mem. Am. Guild of Organists, Soc. Am. Musicians, Nat. Assn. Sch. Music. Club: Cliff Dwellers. Home: Chicago, Ill., Died Feb. 9, 1976.

BECKER, HARRY J., hosp. ins. cons., educator; b. Lincoln, Neb., Oct. 3, 1909; s. Harry J. and Julia (Hotaling) B.; A.B., U. Neb., 1933, A.M., 1941; student Columbia, 1940, N.Y. Sch. Social Work, 1937, Yale, 1940; children (by previous marriage)—Harry J. Ruth M., Martha Jane. Spl. asst. to state dir. Kan. Emergency Relief Adminstrn., hdqrs. Topeka, 1935-37; state dir. Neb. State Child Health and Welfare Services, Lincoln, 1937-41; cons. med. care adminstrn. N.Y. City Dept. Health, 1940-41, USPHS, 1941-42; dir. adminstrv. methods, med. care adminstrn. cons. Fed. Security Agy., Washington, 1942-48; dir. social security dept. United Automobile Workers-C.I.O., Detroit, 1948-57; also dir. Commn. on Financing Hosp. Care; now hosp.-med. program cons.; tchr. hosp. econs. and prepayment plan adminstrn., program in hosp. adminstrn. Northwestern U.; exec. sec. com. on spl. studies N.Y. Acad. Med.; v.p. Nat. Blue Cross Assn., also mem. faculty Sch. Adminstrv. Medicine Columbia, 1957-75; prof. community medicine Albert Einstein Medical Coll.; prof. New Sch. for Social Research. Cornell Inst. Adminstrv. Med.; cons. Health Services Adminstrn., N.Y.C. Mem. pension research council Wharton School of Finance. Dir. United Automobile Workers-C.I.O. Health Inst.; labor rep. bd. trustees Mich. Hosp. Service (Blue Cross), Mich. Med. Service (Blue Shield); mem. com. pensions 20th Century Fund. Author: Financing Hospital Care in the U.S.; Prepayment and the Community; Financing Care for Non-Wage and Low Income Groups; also contbr. various publs. Editor: Expanding Ambulatory Services, others. Home: Brookfield Center, Conn., Died Dec. 23, 1975.

BECKER, RAYMOND HERMAN, banker; b. Chicago, Dec. 1, 1903; s. Herman M. and Ione (Schermerhorn) B.; student U. of Chicago, 1922, Northwestern U. Sch. of Commerce (evenings), 1931-37; m. Grayce V. Baier, Apr. 26, 1926. Clerk, The First Nat. Bank of Chicago, 1922, teller, 1924-31, asst. cashier, 1931-41, assistant vice president, 1941-45, vice president, 1945-58, v.p., cashier, 1958-62, exec. v.p., cashier, 1962-75. Trustee Glenwood (Ill.) Sch. for Boys. Mem. Ill. State C. of C., Assn. Res. City Bankers. Clubs: The Attic, Bankers, Executives, University (Chicago); Glen Oak Country (Glen Ellyn, Ill.). Home: Elmhurst, Ill., Died Nov. 14, 1975.

BECKETT, PETER GORDON STEWART, physician; b. Dublin, Ireland, Oct. 11, 1922; came to U.S., 1949, naturalized, 1954; s. Gerald Paul Gordon and Margaret Robinson (Collen) B.; B.A., Trinity Coll., Dublin, 1943, M.B., 1945, M.D., 1960; m. Victoria Ling, Jan. 9, 1954; 1 son, Paul T. Intern, Dublin, 1946, London, 1948, Overlook Hosp., Summit, N.J., 1949-50; fellow in psychiatry, asst. to staff Mayo Clinic, Rochester, Minn., 1950-55; staff psychiatrist, chief adult inpatient service Lafayette Clinic, Detroit, 1955-60 research dir., 1960-69, chief adolescent service, 1962-69, asst. dir., 1960-69; prof. psychiatry Wayne State U., Detroit, 1960-69; chmn., acad. prof. psychiatry Trinity Coll., U. Dublin, 1969-74, dean faculty of medicine Vet. and Dental Schs., 1972-74, mem. univ. council and bd., 1972-74, fellow, 1972; cons. psychiatrist St. Patrick's Hosp., Dublin, 1969-74; chief professorial unit psychiatry St. James's Hosp., Dublin, 1969-74; mem. central council, med. com. Federated Dublin Vol. Hosps., 1972-74. Mem. com. for cons. selection, postgrad. edn. council Med. Social and Research Bd., 1972-74. Mem. Detroit Youth Commn., 1966-69. Served as capt. Royal Army Med. Corps, 1946-48. Diplomate Am. Bd. Psychiatry and Neurology (examiner, 1962-74). Fellow Am. Psychiat. Assn. (nat. com. on research 1965), Am. Coll. Psychiatry, Royal Coll. Psychiatry, Royal Coll. Physicians Ireland; mem. A.M.A., Brit., Irish med. assns. Author: Adolescents Out of Step—Their Treatment in a Psychiatric Hospital, 1965; (with T. H. Bleakley) A Teaching Program in Psychiatry, vol. 1, 1968, (with E. F. Domino and T. H. Bleakey), vol. 2, 1969; contbr. chpts. to textbooks. Contbr. numerous articles to profl. jours. Research in biol. aspects of schizophrenia, applications of computers to psychiatry, adolescent psychiatry. Home: Dublin, Ireland., Died Feb. 13, 1974; buried St. Fintan's Cemetery, Sutton, County Dublin, Ireland.

BECKHART, BENJAMIN HAGGOTT, economist; b. Denver, Nov. 9, 1897; s. William Edmund and Jessica (Haggott) B.; A.B., Princeton U., 1919; M.A., Columbia, 1920, Ph.D., 1925; m. Margaret Good Myers, June 18, 1921; 1 son, Gordon Haggott. Instr. econs. and social instns. Princeton, 1920-21; instr. banking, Columbia, 1921-24, asst. prof., 1924-31, asso. prof., 1931-39, prof., 1939-63. Ednl. supr. N.Y. chpt. Am. Inst. of Banking, 1927-36; sec. bd. trustees Banking Research Fund Assn. of Reserve City Bankers, 1938-45; dir. research The Chase Nat. Bank, 1939-49, econ. cons., 1949-54; econ. cons. Equitable Life Assurance Soc., 1954-61. Dir. research Am. Assembly's project on inflation, 1951-52; del. internat. Credit Conf. Rome, 1951; del. Internat. Conf. Bank Economists, 1947, 50, 53, 56; vis. prof. univs. Melbourne and Sydney, 1957, Australian Adminstrv. Staff Coll., 1960; vis. prof. Kobe U., Japan, 1967. Pres. Dutchess Sr. Citizens Housing Corp., 1968-73. Japanese banking research fund named in his honor, 1956. Recipient distinguished citizens' award Denver, 1959. Mem. Am. Finance Assn. (pres. 1948), Conf. Bus. Econ. (chmn. 1953), Am. Assn. U. Profs., Am. Econ. Assn., Phi Beta Kappa, Delta Sigma Rho, Beta Gamma Sigma. Clubs: Men's Faculty (Columbia U.); Nassau (Princeton); Princeton (N.Y.); Amrita (Poughkeepsie). Author: The Discount Policy of the Federal Reserve System, 1924; The Federal Reserve System, 1972 (trans. into Japanese 1975); co-author: Foreign Banking Systems, 1929; co-author, editor The New York Money Market, 4 vols. 1931-32; Business Loans of American Commercial Banks, 1959. Editor: Banking Systems, 1954 (trans. into Japanese 2 vols.), 1956, 57, Spanish edit. 1958, Indian edit., 1967. Contbr. articles to profl. jours. Home: Poughkeepsie, N.Y. Died Mar. 21, 1975; buried Poughkeepsie Rural Cemetery.

BECKWAY, HARVEY GEORGE, packaging co. exec.; b. Chgo., Mar. 17, 1898; s. George and Francis (Johnston) B.; student pub. schs., Chgo., Can.; m. Margaret Pamela Nicodemus, Aug. 11, 1934; children—Bruce C., Diane Camille (Mrs. Robert H. deGroot). With Foreman Bros. Bank, Chgo., 1926-28; engaged in real estate bus., Chgo., 1928-30; sales mgr. Odman Paper Co., Chgo., 1930-33, Mchts. Paper Co., Chgo., 1933-47; founder, pres., chmn. bd. Packing Materials Corp., Chgo., 1947-72. Served with U.S. Army, World War 1. Mem. Nat. Geog. Soc., Nat. Rifle Assn. Republican. Home: River Forest, Ill. Died Oct. 8, 1972.

BECKWITH, EDWARD ANSON, state dir. Selective Service for S.D.; b. Titusville, Pa., Dec. 19, 1879; s. Edward Hill and Emma Izena (Cole) B.; ed. Pierre pub. sch., 1890-98; m. Amalia Barbara Brandhuber, Sept. 25, 1917. Entered service as pvt. with Nat. Guard, 1896; commd. 1st lt., cav., 1901, and advanced through the grades to col., 1939; appt. brig. gen. by gov. of S.D., 1946; dir. Selective Service for South Dakota, 1940-47; in command 147th F.A., 1938-39; adj. gen. of S.D., Jan. 9, 1939-Jan. 20, 1947; retired, Feb. 25, 1947. Decorated Spanish Am. War Medal, Philippine Insurrection Medal, Philippine Congressional Medal (Spanish-Amer. War), Mexican Border Medal (Mexican War), Victory Medal, Silver Star (World War I), Legion of Merit, Army Commendation, American Defense, American Theater, Victory Medals (World War II). Address: Rapid City, S.D.†

BECKWITH, FREDERICK DOWNEY, physician; b. Hartford, Conn., Jan. 17, 1926; s. Frederick Ryan and Elizabeth (Downey) B.; M.D., Georgetown U., 1952; M.P.H., U. Cal. at Berkeley, 1964; m. Faith Milikowski, Aug. 10, 1946; children—Sharon Jane, Barbara Ann. Rotating intern U.S. Naval Hosp., San Diego, 1952-53, resident in dermatology, 1955-56; basic flight surgeon's course U.S. Navy Sch. Aviation Medicine, Pensacola, Fla., 1952-53, resident in aviation medicine, 1962-64, instr. survival tng., 1963-64; sr. med. officer in U.S.S. Enterprise. Served with UNSR, 1943-46; to capt. M.C., 1952-71. Diplomate Am. Bd. Preventive Medicine. Mem. A.M.A., Aerospace Med. Assn. Home: La Jolla, Cal., Died Jan. 13, 1971; buried at sea.

BÉDARD, PIERRE (PIERRE-ARMAND BÉDARD DE LA PERRIERE), cultural consultant; born in Lynn, Mass., May 23, 1895; son of J. Armand and Rose Louise Chandler (Valiquet) B.; A.B., Harvard University, 1917; LL.D., Ripon College, 1949; Doctor of Letters, Middlebury College, 1954; married Caroline Baker Pryor, June 30, 1932; m. 2d, Gertrude King Winter, January 10, 1948. With American Shipping Board, Marseille, Bordeaux, 1920; asst. bunkering mgr., London, 1921-22; auditor, Rotterdam, 1922-23; The Bankers Trust Company, New York City, 1923-25; business mgr. Famous Players Lasky, 1925-27; asst. treas. and production mgr. Gloria Swanson Productions, 1927-29; producer educational and scientific films, Harvard Film Foundation, 1929; dir. French Inst. U.S. 1929-52; pres. Parsons Sch. Design, 1952-58, cons., 1958-63; dir., chmn. exec. com. French & Co., 1959-68; chmn. exec. com. Cartier, Inc., 1963-67, radio news analyst France, CBS, 1937-40; Am. counselor to French Mil. Mission, Washington, 1943-44. Mem. hon. bd. advisors Ft. Ticonderoga Mus.; mem. adv. bd., sec. adv. com. on arts for the John F. Kennedy Center for the Performing Arts, Washington; chairman executive com. Nat. La Fayette Bicentennial Com., 1957; pres. P.R. Cultural Center. Dir., secretary gen. and dir. lectures Fed. of French Alliances in U.S. and Canada, 1935-42; sec. 6th Cong. of French Lang. and Lit., N.Y. City, Apr. 1936, 7th Congress, N.Y. World's Fair, 1939. Served with Batt. A, Mass. N.G., Mexican Border, 1916; American Field Service, Apr.-Oct. 1917; 2d lt., O.R.C. later 1st lt. U.S. Army, 1917-19; assistant secretary and member of staff of Gen. Tasker H. Bliss, Am. mil. rep., Supreme War Council, Versailles, France. Decorated Commander French Legion of Honor. Mem. national selection com. on Fulbright Awards (1951-54). One of founders, treas., Lycee Francais de New York, 1935-40; mem. exec. com., bd. trustees Free Europe Univ. in Exile. Former pres., chmn. exec. com. France-America Soc.; hon. chmn. bd. dirs. Fedn. French Alliances in U.S. Mem. Order of Lafayette (charter mem., dir.), Council on Fgn. Relations, Soc. Les Amis d'Escoffier (pres. found.), Am. Inst. Interior Designers, Am. Soc. French Legion of Honor, Am. Legion (Paris post). Clubs: Century, Knickerbocker (N.Y.C.); Newport Reading Room, Clambake (Newport R.I.). Home: New York City, N.Y. Died Dec. 2, 1970.

BEDELL, ARTHUR J., ophthalmologist; b. Waterford, N.Y., Dec. 16, 1879; s. Albert Pomeroy and Jane Vian (Mors) B.; M.D., Albany Med. Coll., 1901; grad. work in European clinics, 1906, 09, 10, 14, 25, 29, 34, 37, 38, 39; LL.D., St. Bonaventure Coll., 1940; D.Sc., Hobart Coll., 1941, U. of Colorado, 1941, U. of the South, 1950; m. Bessie Wilson, February 12, 1913; children—Arthur Willson, Albert Pomeroy, Wallace Canaday. Ophthalmologist from 1901; resident Ellis Hosp., Schnectady, N.Y., 1 year; resident surgeon Wills Hosp., Phila., 2 years; teacher of ophthalmology, Albany Med. Coll., 1907-27, head of dept., 1913-27, emeritus prof. of ophthalmology from 1941; attending opthalmologist Albany Guardian Soc.; honorary consulting surgeon to Wills Eye Hospital; consulting ophthalmologist Anthony N. Brady Maternity Hosp., Vassar Brothers Hosp. (Poughkeepsie, N.Y.). Del. A.M.A., to Brit. Med Assn., 1936, 56, 62. Lectr.

Oxford, 1935 (Eng.), Ophthal. Congress, 1937, 38, 62. Ophthal. Soc. of United Kingdom, London, 1939. Received silver medal for scientific exhibit, A.M.A., 1928; Herman Knapp gold medal, from Ophthal. Sect., A.M.A., for outstanding work in ophthalmology, 1929; Lucien Howe prize for research in ophthalmology, from N.Y. State Medal Society, 1922, 24, 27, 36, 38; gold medal for outstanding work in ophthalmology A.M.A., 1952, Howe medal U. Buffalo. Chnn. Medical Advisory Board. Certified by American Board Ophthalmic Examinations, 1919. Hon. Fellow Internat. Coll. Surgeons. Fellow American Coll. Surgeons, N.Y. Acad. Medicine, A.M.A. (chmn. sect. on ophthalmology 1934), Acad. Ophthalmology and Otolaryngology (former councillor); mem. N.Y. State Med. Soc. (mem. house of dels from 1913; pres. 1935), Am. Ophthal. Soc., Med. Soc. of Albany County (president 1909), Association of Military Surgeons; also ophthal. socs. of several World countries and U.S. cities; corresponding mem. La. Sociedad Mexicanade Optalmologia, Sociedade De Medicina e Cirurgia de Sao Paulo, Brazil, Organo de la Sociedad Peruana de Otorrinolaringologia y Oftalmologia; mem. S.A.R., Nu Sigma Nu, Sigma Xi., Alpha Omega Alpha. Republican. Episcopalian. Mason (K.T., 32°, Shriner). Clubs: University, Torch (both Albany). Author: Photographs of the Fundes Oculi, 1929; Clinical Ophthalmoscopy, 1946. Contbr. numerous monographs, articles, chpts. in several textbooks. Formerly asso. editor Annals of Ophthalmology. Address: Albany, N.Y.†

BEDFORD, HOMER F., state ofcl.; b. Balltown, Mo., Mar. 16, 1880; s. John Franklin and Eliza Ann (Summers) B.; m. Stella V. Cornell (dec.); children—Lloyd E., Amy. Postmaster, Platteville, Colorado, 1914-21; assessor Weld County, Colo., 1923-33; Colo. state treas. or state auditor, 1933-48; Colo. state treas. from 1948. Presbyn. Odd Fellow, Elk, Woodman. Mason. Address: Denver, Colo.†

BEDSOLE, JOSEPH LINYER, dry goods co. exec.; b. Clarke County, Ala., Aug. 7, 1881; s. Travis L. and Martha (Goodman) B.; ed. pub. schs.; m. Phala Bradford, Aug. 10, 1910; 1 son, Joseph Linyer (dec.). With Bedsole Dry Goods Co., Thomasville, Ala., from 1902, chmn. bd., from 1946; pres. Bedsole-Colvin Drug Co., Mobile, 1919-28; v.p., dir. McKesson & Robbins, Inc., 1928-46; v.p. S. B. Adams Lumber Co., Inc., Mobile, 1927-39, pres., 1939-51, chmn. bd., 1951-68; pres. Bedsole Surg. Supply Co., Inc., Mobile, from 1957; Mobile Fixture & Equipment Co., Inc., from 1927, Bedsole Trading Co., Mobile, from 1952; pres. Alco Land & Timber Co., Mobile, 1951-68, chmn. bd., from 1968; pres. Bedsole Investment Co., Mobile, from 1928. Vice-pres. Ala. War Chest, 1942. Chmn. bd. Mobile Coll., 1962-67, hon. chmn., from 1967; trustee Mobile Infirmary, Mobile United Fund, So. Research Inst. Mem. Newcomen Soc. Baptist. Mason (Shriner). Clubs: Athelstan, Bienville (Mobile). Home: Mobile, Ala.†

BEEKEY, CYRUS EZRA, ret. coll. pres.; b. Myerstown, Pa., Mar. 29, 1906; s. Samuel Peter and Elvy (Kilmer) B.; B.S., Albright Coll., 1927, LL.D., 1968; M.S., Cornell U., 1934, Ph.D., 1940; postgrad. Temple U., 1929-30; m. Viola B. Sweigart, June 25, 1932; children—Lois Elva, Sara Ann, Cyrus Ezra. Tchr. math. pub. schs., Reading, Pa., 1927-29, tchr. biology, 1931-43; instr. physics Commonwealth Pa. State Tchrs. Coll., 1943-44, prof., dept. head biology, 1944-56, dean instrn., 1956-64, dean acad. affairs, 1964-67; pres. Kutztown (Pa.) State Coll., 1967-69. Mem. Pa. Acad. Sci. (pres. 1954-55), Phi Kappa Phi, Kappa Delta Pi, Phi Delta Kappa, Kappa Mu Epsilon. Home: Kutztown, Pa., Died Oct. 11, 1974; interred Mt. Hope Cemetery, Myerstown, Pa.

BEELER, HELEN MARION, psychologist; b. N.S., Can., Sept. 13, 1907; d. James Frederich and Mary Jane (Potter) Beeler; R.N., Faulkner Hosp. Nurses Sch., 1932; postgrad. Johns Hopkins Hosp., 1933; A.B., U. Cal., Santa Barbara, 1949; M.A., Claremont Grad. Sch., 1952. Sch. tchr., N.S., 1927-29, pvt. duty nurse, 1932-41; sch. psychologist Redlands (Cal.) Pub. Schs., 1953-68; pvt. practice psychology, Redlands, Cal. from 1968, psychologist research project on epilepsy in San Bernardino County, Cal. Dept. Pub. Health, 1961-63. Served with Nurse Corps, AUS, 1942-46. Mem. Am., Western, Cal. psychol. assns., Cal. Ednl. Research Assn., Cal. Assn. Sch. Psychologists, A.A.A.S. Am. Acad. Polit and Social Sci., Am. Mus. Natural History, Nat. Audubon Soc., Nat. Soc. for Crippled Children and Adults, San Bernardino Area Mental Health Assn. Democrat. Home: Rialto, Cal. Deceased.

BEELEY, ARTHUR LEWTON, educator; b. Manchester, Eng., Aug. 28, 1890; s. John William and Elizabeth Ann (Lawton) B.; came to U.S., 1908; A.B., Brigham Young U., 1913; A.M., U. Chgo., 1918, Ph.D., 1925; LL.D., U. Utah, 1955; m. Glenn Johnson, June 6, 1916; children—Mary (Christensen), Stephen. Prin. Emery Acad., Castle Dale, Utah, 1917-18; asst. prof. psychology U. Utah, 1919-21; research asso. Ill. state criminologist, 1924-25; asst. prof. social economy U. Chgo., 1925-26; prof. sociology, dir. Bur. Student Counsel, U. Utah, 1927-47, dean Grad. Sch. Social Work, 1937-56, dean, prof. emeritus, from 1956; dir. Inst. World Affairs, 1946-56; vis. prof. U. Chgo., summers 1928, 29, 31, U. So. Cal., 1936, U. Minn., 1938, San Francisco State Coll., 1954; lectr. Nat. Police Acad., 1943-45; adviser War Relocation Authority, 1943; educational cons. 9th Service Command, 1943-46. Mem. Utah Council Criminal Justice Adminstrn., from 1961; del. Internat. Congress Mental Hygiene, London, 1948; mem. White House Conf. Child Health and Protection, 1929-30. Criminol. research in England, 1932-33, under grant from Am. Social Scl. Research Council; recipient award distinguished service to social science Utah Acad. Scis. Arts and Letters, 1954. Fellow Am. Ortho-Psychiat. Assn., A.A.A.S.; mem. Am. Sociol. Soc., Nat. Assn. Social Workers, Am. Correctional Assn., Am. Soc. Criminology (August Vollmer award 1965), Am. Judicature Soc., Nat. Conf. Bail and Criminal Justice Adminstrn. (exec. bd. 1964—), English-Speaking Union U.S., Utah Soc. Mental Hygiene (pres. 1928-29), Utah Conf. Social Work (pres. 1929-30), Phi Beta Kappa, Phi Kappa Phi. Author: An Experimental Study of Left-Handedness, 1918; The Bail System in Chicago, 1927; Boys and Girls in Salt Lake City, 1929; Community Health and Hygiene (with L. L. Daines), 1935; Outlines of Social Psychology, 1949; also articles. Home: Salt Lake City, Utah. Died Sept. 23, 1973.

BEESLEY, EUGENE NEVIN, found exec.; b. Thorntown, Ind., Jan. 29, 1909; s. Ralph N. and Della Mae (Rinehart) B.; A.B., Wabash Coll., 1929; LL.B., Ind. U., 1943; LL.D., DePauw U., 1956, Wabash College, 1959; D.Sc., U. Toledo, 1957; Doctor of Humanities, Ind. Central Coll., 1964; D.H.L. Butler U., 1966; LL.D., Ind. U., 1966, Franklin Coll., 1973; D.B.A., Marian Coll., 1973; m. Marian L. Crehore, Oct. 23, 1931; children—Mary Louise (Mrs. Needham S. Hurst), Mark Crehore. With Eli Lilly & Co., Indpls., 1929-76, various sales, personnel and adminstrv. positions, 1929-51, v.p., 1951-52 exec. v.p., dir., 1952-53, pres., 1953-69, chmn. bd., 1969-73, now dir.; dir. Lilly Endowment, Inc., 1951-76, v.p., 1960-73, pres., 1973-76; dir. Procter & Gamble Co., Am. Fletcher Corp., Gen Motors Corp., Pub. Service Ind. Admitted to Ind. bar, 1943. Pres., United Presbyn. Found. Bd. govs. Asso. Colls. Ind.; bd. dirs. Radio Free Europe Fund, Inc., Ind. U. Found., United Fund Greater Indpls., Inc.; v.p. bd. trustees Wabash Coll. Mem. Am. Ind. bar assns., James Whitcomb Riley Meml. Assn., Bus. Council, Beta Theta Pi, Presbyn. (elder). Mason (33 deg., Shriner). Clubs: Indpls. Athletic, Meridian Hills Country, Columbia (Indpls.); Links (N.Y.). Home: Indianapolis, Ind., Died Feb. 8, 1976.

BEESON, MALCOLM ALFRED, agronomist; b. Gadsden, Ala., June 20, 1879; s. William Baker and Mary Ann (Sibert) B.; B.Sc., Ala. Polytechnie, Auburn, Ala., 1900; student Johns Hopkins, 1901-03; hon. D.Sc., Meridian (Miss.) Coll., 1910; LL.D., Oklahoma City (Okla.) U., 1933; m. Effie Harrison, July 14, 1904; children—Evelyn, Wilamina, William Malcolm. Prof. science East Miss. Female Coll., 1900-01; pres. and owner Meridian Male Coll., 1903-14; prof. agronomy and agronomist, Okla, Agrl. and Mech. Coll., 1915-21, dean Agrl. Div. and dean Sch. of Agr., 1921-23, also dir. Experiment Sta., 1923; pres. B., K. & T. Co., 1923-31; pres. Central State Teachers Coll., Edmond, Okla., 1931-35; field rep. George Peabody Coll. for Teachers, Nashville, Tenn., 1935-37; private business enterprises from 1937. Fellow A.A.A.S.; mem. Kappa Delta Pi. Pi Kappa Delta, Alpha Phi Sigma, Kappa Sigma, Kappa Tau Pi, Pi Gamma Mu, Sigma Tau Delta. Methodist. Home: Stillwater, Okla.†

BEFFA, HARVEY ARTHUR, brewery exec.; b. St. Louis, June 19, 1900; s. Anton and Mary (Degan) B.; student pub. schs. St. Louis; m. Henrietta Stahl, June 24, 1922; children—Harvey Arthur, Helen, Mary Etta, Daniel. Clk. Anton Beffa & Son Wrecking & Supply Co., St. Louis, 1915-20, gen. mgr., 1920-32; sec. Falstaff Brewing Corp., St. Louis, 1933-35, v.p., dir. 1935, later exec. v.p., gen. mgr., then chmn. bd., 1962-69, later chmn. exec. com.; dir. Merc. Commerce Nat. Bank. Bd. dirs. Midwest Polio Assn.; chmn. bd. trustees Shriners Hosps. for Crippled Children, also chmn. emeritus St. Louis unit. Recipient St. Louis Humanities award, 1964; named Big Brother of Year, St. Louis, 1966. Mem. Master Brewers Assn. Am. Republican. Presbyn. Mason (33 deg., Shriner; past imperial potentate). Clubs: Missouri Athletic, Glen Echo Country, St. Louis. Home: Normandy, Mo., Died Oct. 20, 1975.

BEGG, JOHN ALFRED, artist, book designer; b. New Smyrna, Fla., June 23, 1903; s. John Alfred and Rose (Gradick) B.; student U. Fla., 1920-21; B.S., Columbia, 1924; m. Miriam Mendelsohn, Mar. 3, 1934; children—John Alfred, Barbara Jane. Free lance artist, Fla., 1924-25; advt. mgr. Taylor-Alexander Properties, Inc., Winter Haven, Fla., 1925-26; art dir. Anderson Advt. Agy., Tampa, 1926-27, Madison Square Press, N.Y.C., 1927-31, Union Lithograph Co., San Francisco, 1931-32; art editor, book designer Am. Book Co., N.Y.C., 1932-37; free lance book designing, N.Y.C., 1937-39; prodn. mgr. Oxford U. Press, N.Y.C., 1939-68, asst. sec., 1956-60, v.p., 1960-68; instr. typography and design N.Y. U., 1950-57. Exhbn. book work Am. Trade Book Designers, 1945; books designed ann. textbook exhbns. sponsored by Am. Inst. Graphic Arts, in the Fifty Books of the Year and in Artes del libros los Estados Unidos; one-man show, sculpture, water colors Wakefield Gallery, N.Y.C., 1942, Friedman Gallery, 1947, Feist Gallery; 1969; exhibited group shows Whitney, Worcester, Bklyn., Riverside, Albany museums; retrospective exhbn. (with wife) Hudson River Mus., 1962, sculpture show 1967; represented Addison Gallery Am. Art, N.Y. Pub. Library, pvt. collections. Bd. dirs. Am. Inst. Graphic Arts, 1942-44, 51-54. Recipient 1st prize in sculpture Hudson River Mus., 1958, 59, 64, purchase award, 1970. Mem. Yonkers Art Assn. (chmn. bd. 1972-73). Club: Typophiles. Home: Hastings-on-Hudson, N.Y. Died Dec. 20, 1974.

BEGG, ROBERT BURNS HALDANE, civil engr.; b. Campbell County, Va., Jan. 4, 1880; s. James Beveridge and Janet (Haldane) B.; B.S., Va. Poly Inst., 1899, C.E., 1901; m. Adah Mann., Sept. 5, 1907; 1 son, James Currie. Began as civil engr., 1899; railroad and highway work, 1901-05; successively instr., asst. prof., and asso. prof. civil engring., Syracuse U., 1905-10; prof. civil engring., Pa. Mil. Coll., 1910-12; prof. sanitary and hydraulic engring., U. of Kan., 1912-13; prof. civil engring., Va. Poly. Inst., from 1913; in charge inspection of all construction Resettlement Adminstrn., 1935-36. Served as capt. Engrs., U.S. Army, 1917-19; major Engrs. Reserves, 1919-23; major Cavalry Reserves, 1923-30, lt. col. from 1930; aide on staff of Gov. of Va., 1938-42; lieut. col., commanding 12th Bn., Va., Protective Force from 1941. Dir. Southwestern Virginia, Inc. Mem. Am. Soc. Civil Engrs., Soc. for Promotion Engring. Edn., Nat. Soc. Professional Engrs., Tau Beta Pi., Chi. Epsilon. Democrat. Club: Rotary (Christiansburg, Va.). Home: Blacksburg, Va.†

BEGGS, LYALL T., lawyer; b. Plainfield, Wis., Nov. 9, 1899; s. Charles A. and Mavorite (Booth) B.; student Eau Claire State Teachers Coll., 1922; grad. U. Wis., 1925, LL.D., 1966; m. Christine C. Kaether, June 25, 1927; children—Geraldine Ann, Robert Kaether, Nancy Belle. Admitted to Wis. bar, 1926; mem. firm Beggs & Assos., from 1928. Elected dist. atty. Dane County, 1936, 1940; elected mem. legislature, 1940, 42, 44, 46; served as county pub. adminstr. Recipient Distinguished Service award Eau Claire State Tchrs. Coll., 1965. Mem. V.F.W. (comdr. post 1918, 39; Wis. dept. comdr. 1941; nat. legislative com. 1942-46; nat. judge adv. gen. 1945; nat. jr. vice-comdr. in chief 1946; nat. comdr.-in-chief 1948, Distinguished Service medal 1966), Am., Wis. (gov., pres. 1964), Dane County (pres. 1957) bar assns., Am. Legion, Gamma Eta Gamma. Republican. Lutheran. Eagle, Elk. Mason (32 deg., Shriner). Home: Oregon, Wis. Died May 14, 1973.

BEGLEY, JOHN PATRICK, educator; b. Omaha, Feb. 11, 1894; s. Michael James and Catherine (Lafferty) B.; B.S.C., Creighton U., 1926, M.A., 1928; Ph.D., U. Ia., 1933; student U. Chgo., summers 1927-30. Accountant, Swift & Co., 1911-24; admitted to La. bar, 1940; mem. faculty Creighton U., 1924-74; prof. accounting, 1947, head dept., 1947-65; cons., pub. accountant, 1924-74; sr. partner Begley, Herbert, Graham & Waring, C.P.A.'s, Omaha, 1962-72; dir. Begley Realty, Heafey & Heafey, Andersen Fire Equipment Co., Begley Investment Co. Mem. Neb. Bd. C.P.A. Examiners, 1942-61. Served with U.S. Army, World War I. Recipient Bene Merenti medal Pope John XXIII, 1959; Alumni Merit award Creighton U., 1973; decorated knight of St. Gregory, 1966. C.P.A., Neb., Ia. Mem. Neb. Soc. C.P.A.'s, Am. Inst. C.P.A.'s, Am. Accounting Assn., Nat. Assn. Accountants, Holy Name Soc. (pres. Met. council 1956), Delta Sigma Pi, Omicron Delta Epsilon, Beta Gamma Sigma, Alpha Sigma Nu, Beta Alpha Psi. Democrat. Roman Catholic. K.C. Home: Omaha, Neb. Died Oct. 25, 1974; interred St. Mary's Cemetery, Omaha, Neb.

BEHAN, HELEN PETERS, social worker; b. Troy, N.Y., Feb. 24, 1904; d. Joseph C. and Helen P. (Peters) Behan; student Manhattanville Coll., 1922-23; B.A., St. Rose Coll., 1935; M.S.W., Fordham U., 1951; postgrad. Columbia, 1953. Psychiat, social worker N.Y. State Dept. Mental Hygiene, Albany, 1947-74; supr. social work N.Y. Cath. Charities Guidance Inst., 1952-55, St. Vincent's Hosp., N.Y.C., 1957-59; asst. dir. Rensselaer County Mental Health Bd., Troy, N.Y., 1961-74. Cons. St. Colman's Home, Watervliet, N.Y., 1961-74. Rensselaer County Mental Health Assn., 1961—. Asso. prof. pediatrics Albany Med. Sch., 1955-56. Bd. dirs. Kenwood Alumnae Assn., 1960-66, pres., 1947-49; asst. dir. Rensselear County Community Comprehensive Mental Health Center, 1968-74, mem. adv. com., 1968-74, bd. dirs. Kenwood Braille Assn., 1949-74, Sunnyside Day Camp, Troy, N.Y., 1955-16. Home: Troy, N.Y., Died Dec. 28, 1974.

BEHAN, RICHARD JOSEPH, surgeon; b. Pittsburgh, Pa., 1879; s. John and Annie (O'Donnell) B.; M.D., U. of Pittsburgh, 1902; studied in Europe, 1910-14; m. Esther H. Hrubesky, Jan. 20, 1914. Resident, Mercy Hosp., Pittsburgh, 1902, South Side Hosp., 1903; pathologist, St. Francis Hosp., 1904-05, asst. surgeon, 1906; asst. to chair of physical diagnosis, U. of Pittsburgh School of Medicine, 1903-08, asso. prof. same, 1908; vol. asst., Royal Surg. Clinic, Berlin, 1912-13; surgeon, St. Joseph's Hosp., from 1914, City Hospital for Tuberculosis, 1916-42, City Hospital, Mayview, 1922-43; president of Pan Am. Cooperative Foundation, Pittsburgh Skin and Cancer Foundation, Capt. Medical Corps, U.S. Army. Surgeon 4th Reserve Hosp., Nish, Serbia, 2d Balkan War. Mem. A.M.A., Am. Coll. Surgeons (ex-gov.), Internat. Coll. Surgeon's Pan American Medical Association, American

Therapeutic Society, Allegheny County Medical Society (past pres.), etc. Decorated Order of San Savar (Serbian). Member Knights of Columbus., Am. Assn. Mil. Surgeons, Am. Acad. Dental Medicine. Author: Pain, 1913; Cancer, 1938; Relation of Trauma to New Growths, 1939. Contributor of sect. "Tumors" to American Medical Encyclopedia; sect. "Head Pain" to Dental Diagnosis; also numerous monographs on surgery and cancer. Home: Pittsburgh, Pa.†

BEHOUNEK, FRANTISEK, radiol. scientist, educator; b. Prague, Czechoslovakia, Oct. 27, 1898; s. Frantisek and Antoine (Prochazkova) B.; Dr. Res. Nat., Charles U., Prague, 1922; attended Sorbonne, Paris, France, 1920-22; D.Sc., Czechoslovak Acad. Scis., 1964; m. L. Fellixova, 1928. With State Radiol. Inst., 1921-46; participant Gen. Nobile's Polar Expdn., 1928; prof. Faculty Natural Scis. and Faculty Tech. and Nuclear Physics, Charles U. to 1958; prof. Faculty Tech. and Nuclear Physics, Czech Tech. U., Prague, 1958-73; with Oncological Inst. Prague, 1946-55; with Inst. Nuclear Research, Czechoslovak Acad. Scis.; mem., head sci. council Czechoslovak Acad. Scis. and Czechoslovak Com. for Atomic Energy, 1956-73. Mem. UN Atomic Com.; cons. WHO; participant internat. radiol. congresses, symposia and panels Internat. Atomic Energy Agy., Vienna. Recipient Order of Labour, 1955, Silver medal Paris, 1957, Silver plaque Czechoslovak Acad. Scis. for services to sci. and mankind, 1963, Hon. Mem. J.E. Purkyne Med. Soc., 1964, Order of Republic Golden Felber medal, 1968, Golden plaque Czechoslovakian Acad. Scis. Author: The Problems of Potassium, 1927; Artificial Disintegration of Radioactive Bodies, 1930; Atmospheric Electricity and radioactivity in the Region of the North Pole, 1930; Determination of Natural Radioactive Aerosols, 1965; Accidents of Nuclear Power Plants, 1968. Home: Prague, Czechoslovakia., Died Jan. 1, 1973.

BEHREND, GENEVIEVE A. (MRS. HUGO W. BEHREND), educator, author; b. Paris, France, Sept. 5, 1881; d. Charles and Janette (de Guise) Moore; brought to U.S. in infancy; pvtly. ed.; m. Hugo W. Behrend, of Copenhagen, Denmark, 1918. Founder and prin. School of The Builders, N.Y. City. Author: Your Invisible Power, 1921; also (brochures) Love—How to Obtain It and How to Retain It; How to Heal by Mental Science; Freedom through Visualizing. Lecturer on powers of the mind. Home: Yonkers. N.Y.†

BEHRENS, CHARLES FREDERICK, radiologist; b. Phila., Mar. 18, 1896; s. Charles William and Augusta Emelia (Hulsman) B.; M.D., U. Pa., 1920; postgrad. radiology Cornell U. Med. Center, 1936-37; m. Emma G. Spencer, May 30, 1920 (dec. May 1964); children—Eleanor (Mrs. John E. Parker), Diana E. (Mrs. M.J. Swann), Charles Frederick, Sylvia M. (Mrs. Richard P. Ellison). Served with S.A.T.C., Army Med. Res., World War I; entered U.S.N. as lt. (j.g.), 1920, advanced through grades to rear adm., 1951; specialist radiology, from 1925; dir. atomic def. div. Bur. Medicine and Surgery, also comdg. officer Naval Med. Research Inst., 1948-51; med. officer staff Eastern Sea Frontier, N.Y.C., 1951-53; dist. med. officer 6th Naval Dist., 1953-56; ret., 1956; radiologist Yater Clinic, Washington, 1956-66; cons. in radiology Naval Hosp., Bethesda, 1957-67. Mem. Baruch Com. Phys. Medicine, 1943-51. Diplomate Am. Bd. Radiology, Am. Bd. Internal Medicine. Fellow Am. Coll. Radiology. Mem. Radiol. Soc. N.A., Assn. Mil. Surgeons, N.Y. Acad. Scis., A.M.A., Radiation Research Soc. Editor: Atomic Medicine, 5th edit., 1969; After the A Bomb, 1951. Contbr. articles to profl. jours. Aided in establishing photofluorographic chest survey procedure, U.S.N., World War II. Home: Tracys Landing, Md. Died Mar. 21, 1974; interred Arlington Nat. Cemetery, Arlington, Va.

BEHRMAN, SAMUEL NATHANIEL, playwright; b. Worcester, Mass., June 9, 1893; s. Joseph and Zelda (Feingold) B.; student Clark Coll., 1912-14, LL.D., 1949; A.B., Harvard, 1916; A.M., Columbia, 1918; m. Elza Heifetz, 1936; 1 son, Arthur David. Trustee Clark Coll. Mem. Nat. Inst. Arts and Letters. Contbr. The New Yorker. Author screenplays in Hollywood including Queen Christina Greta Garbo and Tale of Two Cities for Ronald Colman; also Me and the Colonel for Danny Kaye, 1958. Author: (plays) The Second Man, 1927, Serena Blandish, 1928, Meteor, 1929, Brief Moment, 1932, Biography, 1933, Love Story, 1934, Rain from Heaven, 1935, End of Summer, 1936, Amphitryon 38 (adapted from French), 1937, Wine of Choice, 1938, No Time for Comedy, 1939, The Talley Method, 1941, The Pirate, 1942, Jacobowsky and the Colonel (with Franz Werfel), 1944, Dunnigan's Daughter, 1945, Jane (from Somerset Maugham), 1946, I Know My Love (from Achard), 1949, Fanny (with Joshua Logan), 1954, The Cold Wind and The Warm, 1958, Lord Pengo, 1962, But For Whom Charlie, 1964; (books) Duveen (biography), 1952, The Worcester Account, 1954, Portrait of Max, 1960, The Suspended Drawing Room, 1965, The Burning Glass, 1968, People in a Diary-A Memoir, 1972. Recipient Brandeis U. Creative Arts award-Theatre medal, 1962. Home: New York City N.Y. Died Sept. 1973.

BEILSTEIN, EDWARD HENRY, ophthalmologist and otolaryngologist; b. Mansfield, O., Sept. 23, 1913; s. Henry A. and Caroline Ann Beilstein; M.D., Western Res. U., 1943; m. Phyllis J. Egner, Nov. 7, 1942; children—Douglas Edward, Kathryn Ann, Stephen Henry. Intern St. Luke's Hosp., Cleve., 1944, resident in eye, ear, nose and throat, 1944-46; practice medicine, specializing in ophthalmology and otolaryngology, Mansfield, O., 1951-73; mem. staff, treas. Mansfield Gen. Hosp.; founder bd. dirs. Richland County Hearing and Speech Center (now North Central Ohio Rehab. Center); adv. com. North Central Ohio Rehab. Service. Served to capt. M.C., AUS, 1946-48. Diplomate Am. Bd. Otolaryngology. Mem. A.M.A., Ohio Richland County, med. socs., Acad. Ophthalmology and Otolaryngology. Lutheran. Home: Mansfield, Ohio., Died Jan. 22, 1973; buried Mansfield (O.) Meml. Park Cemetery.

BEIRNE, JOSEPH ANTHONY, labor union ofcl.; b. Jersey City, Feb. 16, 1911; s. Michael Joseph and Annie T. (Giblin) B.; evening student Hudson Coll. of St. Peter, Jersey City, 1933-37, N.Y. U., 1937-39; LL.D., Merrimack Coll., 1968, U. Notre Dame, 1968; m. Anne M. Abahaze, July 2, 1933; children—Carole Anne (Mrs. James McDonald, III), Maureen Anne (Mrs. Clifford Houston), Bren Anne (Mrs. Robert Leiss). Utilities, instrument repairman Western Electric Co., N.J. and N.Y., 1928-39; organized Nat. Assn. Tel. Equipment Workers, 1937, nat. pres., 1938-45; v.p. Nat. Fedn. Tel. Workers, 1940-43, pres., 1943-47, pres. Communications Workers Am. (successor union), 1947-74; v.p. CIO, 1949-55, mem. exec. council AFL-CIO, 1955-74; pres. Postal, Tel. and Tel. Internat., 1969-74; sec,-treas. Am. Inst. for Free Labor Devel., 1961-74, African-Am. Labor Center, 1964-74; mem. exec. bd. Internat. Confedn. Free Trade Unions, 1966-74. Catholic. Elk. Author: New Horizons for American Labor, 1962. Home: Chevy Chase, Md. Died Sept. 2, 1974.

BEITLER, HAROLD BORNEMANN, lawyer; b. Phila., Pa., Dec. 31, 1880; s. Abraham Merklee and Julia Louise (Bornemann) B.; ed. Eastburn Acad., 1891-97, under pvt. tutors, 1897-1901; student Law Sch., U. of Pa., 1898-1901; m. Ethel Haffline Eisenbrey, Oct. 16, 1906; children—Abraham Merklee, Eleanor, Anita Barbara. Admitted to Pa. Bar, 1902, and since practiced in Philadelphia; partner Maxwell & Beitler, 1908-15, Dickson, Beitler & McCouch, 1915-31, later Beitler, Burns & Rosenberger. Chmn. Four Minute Men, Pa., and 3d Federal Res. Dist., 1917-19. Dir. Sleighton Farm Sch. for Girls. Mem. Am. Bar Assn., Pa. Bar Assn., Phi Delta Theta. Republican. Episcopalian. Mason. Clubs: Union League, Constitutional, Keystone Automobile (v.p.); Edgemere (Pike County, Pa.). Home: Bryn Mawr, Pa.†

BELAVAL, JOSÉ S., M.D., b. San Juan, P.R., Jan. 14, 1879; s. José S. and Concencion (Veve) B.; B.S., Universidad central de Madrid, Spain, 1897; student Coll. Phys. and Surg., Baltimore, 1899-1902; M.D., Jefferson Med. Coll., Phila., 1904; post-grad. work, New York, 1909-11; m. Mary Ritter, Oct. 1905; children—Joseph Herman, Edgard Franklin, Lister Noel, Maria Ester. Began practice at Yauco, P.R., 1905; health officer, San Juan, 1911; dir. Municipal Hosp., 1912-14; chief of staff, University Hosp. of Porto Rico; mem. Pension Bd.; attending obstetrician Mimiyas Hosp. and Auxilio Mutuo Maternidad; clin. prof. tropical medicine, Sch. of Tropical Medicine. Club: Union. Home: San Juan, P.R.†

BELCHER, WALLACE EDWARD, structual engr.; b. Medford, Mass., Oct. 4, 1879; s. Edward Wheatcroft and Mary Frances (Camp) B.; B.C., University of Maine, 1899, C.E., 1902, Eng. D., 1949; A.M., Harvard Universify, 1904; married to Elisabeth Holden, Nov. 23, 1909; children—Mary Elisabeth (Mrs. T. G. A. Henstridge), Ralph Holden, Wallace Edward. Was designing engineer of industrial and pub. utility structures, with J. G. White Engring. Co., 1906-08, H. M. Byllesby & Co., 1909-13, Westinghouse Church Kerr Co., 1915-16, Stone and Webster, 1916-19; structural engr. Dwight P. Robinson & Co. (supervising engr. Hotel Statler, Boston, Mass.; designing and supervising engr. North Station Development and Coliseum, B. & M. R.R., Boston) from 1919; structural engineer United Engineers & Constructors. Mem. American Society Civil Engineers, Colonial Society of Pennsylvania, Harvard Engineering Soc., Beta Theta Pi, Tau Beta Pi, Phi Kappa Phi. Republican. Episcopalian. Mason. Clubs: Harvard, Engineers (Phila.); Bala Golf.†

BELDING, ANSON WOOD, editor; b. Troy, N.Y., June 2, 1881; s. Rufus Elisha and Martha Ann (Seymour) B.; student Syracuse U., 1900-01; A.B., Harvard, 1904; m. Mary Allison Miller, Jan. 2, 1908; children—Harwood Seymour, Robert Edward, John Miller, Mary Alison; married 2d, Florence Haskin, July 9, 1955. Began as teacher Hazen Sch., Morristown, N.J., 1904; prin. high schs., Simsbury (Conn.), 1905-09, Claremont (N.H.), 1909-12; editor and pub. Claremont Eagle (weekly), 1912-18; founder, and pub. Claremont Daily Eagle, 1914-18; with personnel and advt. depts., William Filene's Sons Co., Boston, 1918-19; chief editorial writer Boston Traveler, 1919-30; asso. editor Jour. of Edn., 1925-33, editor-in-chief, 1933-52. Dir. Watertown Fed. Savings Bank. Instr. in current history, Mass. Univ. Extension, 1932-41. Mem. Phi Beta Kappa. Conglist. Author: The Truth About New England, 1930. Home: Watertown, Mass.†

BELIN, FERDINAND LAMMET, fgn. service officer; b. Scranton, Pa., March 15, 1881; s. Henry and Margaretta Elizabeth (Lammot) B.; Hotchkiss School, Lakeville, Connecticut, 1896-98; Ph.D., Sheffield Scientific Sch. (Yale), 1901; m. Frances Jermyn, Jan. 17, 1912; 1 son, Peter. Foreign service with State Dept., U.S., 1917-31; A.E. and M.P. to Poland, 1932-33; retired, 1933. Commr. City of Scranton, 1909-14; trustee and v.p. Nat. Gallery of Art, Washington, D.C. Presbyterian. Clubs: University, The Brook (New York); Metropolitan, Burning Tree, Chevy Cahse (Washington, D.C.). Home: Washington, D.C.†

BELKNAP, PAUL EDWARD, ret. bus. exec.; b. Bay City, Mich., Mar. 17, 1910; s. Joseph Howard and Ida (Dell) B.; B.S., Northwestern U., 1936; m. Mary Elizabeth Givv, July 28, 1936; children—Gail (Mrs. Robert A. Nelson), Michael Howard Paul. Writer, Bauer & Black, Chgo., 1936-37; advt. mgr. Gibb Mfg. Co., Chgo., 1937-38; asst. advt. mgr. Standard Oil Co. (Ind.), 1938-43; advt. mgr. Atlas Supply Col, Newark, 1943-51; dir. marketing, account exec. McCann-Erickson, N.Y.C. and Chgo., 1951-54; exec. v.p., mng. dir. NY div. Needham, Harper & Steers, Inc., 1954-67, also dir., mem. exec. com.; partner Gibb Groves, Clermont, Fla., 1955-70, Group Six Assos., citrus groves, Winter Park, Fla., 1969-75; dir. Financial Data Scis., Inc., Winter Park, 1970-74. Mem. Am. Assn. Advt. Agys. (dir. Chgo. 1953), Fla. Citrus Mut., Sigma Delta Chi. Republican. Episcopalian. Mason. Club: University (Winter Park). Home: Winter Park, Fla. Died Apr. 8, 1975.

BELL, ALFRED LEE LOOMIS, physician; b. East Hampton, N.Y., Apr. 15, 1890; s. James Finley and Elizabeth Cordelia (Mayes) B.; M.D., Columbia, 1916; m. Grace Seidel, Jan. 1, 1920; children—James Finley II, Alfred Lee Loomis, Nancy Bell Gosch. Intern, Babies Hosp., N.Y.C., 1916-17, St. Lukes Hosp., N.Y.C., 1917-18; postgrad. in mil. roentgenology Cornell U., 1917, instr., 1917-18; attending radiologist L.I. Coll. Hosp.; cons. Caledonian Hosp., Prospect Heights Hosp., St. Giles Hosp., Lutheran Med. Center, Coney Island Hosp.; emeritus prof. L.I. Coll. Medicine, State U.N.Y. at Bklyn., 1922-56; practiced in Bklyn., until 1974. Served to 1st lt. M.C., AUS. Diplomate Am. Bd. Radiology. Fellow Am. Coll. Radiologists; mem. Am. Roentgen Ray Soc., Radiol. Soc. N.Am., A.M.A., Acad. Compensation Medicine, Sigma Chi. Republican. Episcopalian. Rotarian. Home: Birdsboro, Pa., Died July 8, 1974; buried St. Michael's Ch. Cemetery, Birdsboro, Pa.

BELL, HENRY GOUGH, agronomist; b. Orangeville, Ont., Can., May 24, 1880; s. Emanuel and Martha (Hannam) B.; B.S.A., Ont. Agrl. Coll., 1905; Toronto U.; post-grad. studies, U. of Me.; m. Lueva Patterson, of Orangeville, Can., Dec. 25, 1906. Asst. experimentalist, Ont. Agrl. Coll., 1905-07; asst. prof. of farm corps, Ia. State Coll., Ames, Ia., 1906-09; prof. agronomy, U. of Me., 1909-11; agronomist Soil Improvement Com. of Nat. Fertilizer Assn. from 1911. Mem. Am. Soc. Agronomists. Am. Genetic Assn. Republican. Presbyn. Mason. Author of numerous pamphlets and bulletins on soil improvement and crop production. Speaker before agrl. orgns. Home: Evanston, Ill.†

BELL, JACK L., newspaperman; b. Yates Center, Kan., July 24, 1904; s. John H. and Anna J. (Peterson) B.; A.B., U. Okla., 1925; m. Helen Morey, Aug. 21, 1926; 1 son, Stratton Morey. City editor Daily Oklahoman and Times, 1929-37; chief polit. writer, head Senate staff Asso. Press, 1937-69; columnist for Gannett Newspapers. Mem. Phi Beta Kappa, Pi Kappa Alpha. Clubs: Nat. Press, Gridiron, Internat., Chevy Chase. Author: The Splendid Misery; Mr. Conservative: Barry Goldwater; The Johnson Treatment; The Presidency: Office of Power. Home Washington, D.C. Died Sept. 15, 1975.

BELL, JOHN CROMWELL, JR., judge; b. Phila., Oct. 25, 1892; s. John Cromwell and Fleurette deBenneville (Myers) B.; grad. Episcopal Acad., 1910; A.B., U. Pa., 1914, LL.B., 1917; m. Sarah Andrews Baker, June 29, 1918; children—John Cromwell, Louis Baker, George deBenneville, Sarah (Mrs. Lyman Greenleaf Bullard), Sophie Shepley. Admitted to Pa. bar, 1917; asst. city solicitor, Phila., 1919-22, asst. dist. atty., 1922-25; sec. banking Commonwealth of Pa., 1939-43; lt. gov. Pa., pres. State Senate, chmn. Pa. Bd. Pardons, 1943-47; gov. Pa., Jan. 2-21, 1947; justice Supreme Ct. Pa., 1950-72, chief, 1961-72. Mem. Am., Pa., Phila. bar. assns., Colonial Soc. Pa., Soc. S.R., Crusaders Pa. (past comdr.), Delta Psi. Clubs: Racquet (past pres.), Rittenhouse, Gulph Mills Golf, Merion Cricket (Phila.) Ranked In 1st 10 Am. Lawn Tennis Doubles, 1920; finalist U.S. Ct. Tennis Doubles Championship, 1926, 29, 31, 32, 34. Home: Bryn Mawr, Pa. Died Mar. 19, 1974.

BELL, L. NELSON, surgeon, editor; b. Longdale, Va., July 30, 1894; s. James Harvey and Ruth Lee (McCue) B.; student Washington and Lee U., 1911-12; M.D., Med. Coll. Va., 1916; LL.D., King Coll., Bristol, Tenn.,

1964; m. Virginia Myers Leftwich, June 30, 1916; children—Rosa (Mrs. C. Donald Montgomery), Ruth (Mrs. Billy Graham), L. Nelson (dec. 1925), Virginia (Mrs. John N. Somerville), Benjamin Clayton. Chief surgeon Tsingkiangpu (China) Gen. Hosp., 1916-41; surg. fellowship grant Rockefeller Found., 1922-23; practice surgery, Asheville, N.C., 1941-56; sec. staff Meml.-Mission Hosp., Asheville, 1942-46, asst. chief staff, 1947-48; retired from surgery, 1956; a founder Christianity Today, 1955, exec. editor, from 1955, also dir.; founder, dir. Presbyn. Jour.; dir. Blue Ridge Broadcasting Corp., Christian Broadcasting Assn., Honolulu. Del. meeting Royal Coll. Surgeons, Geneva, Switzerland, 1956. Bd. dirs. Billy Graham Evangelistic Assn., Mountain Retreat Devel. Corp.; trustee King Coll., Bristol, Tenn. Recipient Editorial award Freedoms Found., 1954, 57, 58, 59, 60, 65, 67; subject of biography A Foreign Devil in China, 1971. Fellow A.C.S.; mem. A.M.A., N.C. Med. Soc. Author: Convictions to Live By, 1966; While Men Slept, 1970. Contbr. numerous articles, editorials to med., secular, religious mags. Home: Montreat, N.C. Died Aug. 2, 1973.

BELL, REASON CHESNUTT, judge; b. Webster County, Ga., Jan. 28, 1880; s. Reason Alexander and Martha (Elliott) B.; LL.B., Mercer U., 1902, hon. LL.D., 1936; m. Jennie Vereen, Jan. 28, 1908; children—Vereen M. (lt. U.S.N.R.; killed in action, Philippines, Oct. 26, 1944), Martha Alexandria (Mrs. J. T. Daniel, Jr.). Admitted to Ga. bar, 1902; practiced at Sylvester, 1904-05, Cairo, 1905-21; solicitor gen., Albany Jud. Circuit, 1913-21, and judge, same circuit, 1921-22; judge, Ga. Ct. of Appeals, 1922-32; justice Supreme Court, Ga., 1932-49, chief justice, 1943-46, justice emeritus from 1949. Democrat. Presbyn. Clubs: Capitol City, Athletic (Atlanta) Home: Thomasville, Ga.†

BELL, ROBERT EDWARD, pathologist; b. Edmonton, Alta., Can., Jan. 5, 1918; s. Irving Robert and Emilie (Graydon) B.; M.D., U. Alta., 1942; postgrad. Hammsersmith, Eng.; m. Mary A. Wholey, Oct. 11, 1948; children—James Edward, John Irving, Robert Bruce. Intern. Univ. Hosp., U. Edmonton, later dept. clin. pathology; fellow in medicine Univ. Hosps., Mpls.; clin. prof. pathology U. Alta. Served to capt. M.C., Royal Canadian Army, 1942-46. Mentioned in despatches. Diplomate Am. Bd. Pathology. Fellow Royal Coll. Pathology, Can. Assn. Pathologists, Internat. Soc. Hematology; mem. Can. Med. Assn. Home: Edmonton, Alta., Canada., Died May 30, 1973; cremated.

BELL, STOUGHTON, lawyer; b. Newton, Mass., June 28, 1874; s. Albert D. S. and Susan Laura (Stoughton) B.; A.B., Harvard, 1896, LL.B., 1899; m. Mabel A. Lewis, June 8, 1908; children—Lewis Stoughton, Mabel, Madelene. Began practice of law with Putnam & Putnam, Boston, 1899, admitted to firm, 1908; named changed to Putnam, Putnam & Bell, 1911, to Putnam, Bell Dutch & Santry, 1918, to Putnam, Bell, Santry and Ray, Boston, from 1953. Mem. Common Council, Cambridge, 1900, 01; mem. Cambridge Bd. of Alderman, 1902, 03; mem. bd. trustees Dowse Inst.; mem. advisory council Cambridge Found.; chmn. Cambridge chapter Am. Red Cross, 1920-42, past mem. board trustees Moutn Auburn Hosp. Member Ameria American (past vice-pres. for Mass.) and Mass. State (past sec. and pres.) bar assns., Bar Associaiton of the City of Boston, Am. Academy Arts and Sciences, Cambridge Historical Society, Phi Delta Phi. Rep. Episcopalian (past chancellor, diocese of Mass.; past mem. Nat. Council P. E. Church). Club: Harvard, Harvard Faculty (Boston). Contbr. law jours. Home: Cambridge, Mass.†

BELLAH, MILDRED MARIE, editor; b. N.Y.C.; d. Harry Bolton and Teresa V. (Lynch) Finn; student Speyer Sch., Brentwood Acad., Columbia Sch. Journalsim. With promotion dept. N.Y. Am., 1926-28; with McNaught Syndicate, Inc., N.Y.C., 1928-75, exec. editor, 1942-75, sec. corp., 1938-75. Clubs: Women's Nat. Press; Advertising (N.Y.C.). Author articles trade mags., newspapers. Home: Mount Vernon, N.Y. Died Feb. 22, 1975.

BELLAMY, GLADYS CARMEN, educator; b. Bay City, Tex., Mar. 9, 1904; d. Orlando Rollin and Pearl (Cunningham) Bellamy; student Okla. Coll. for Women, 1923-25; B.A., U. Okla., 1932, M.A., 1938, Ph.D., 1946. Treas., Roger Mills County (Okla.), 1925-26, municipal accountant, 1927-29; instr. Cheyenne (Okla.) High Sch., 1932-35; instr. English, N. Tex. State Coll., 1944, U. Okla., 1944-49; prof. English, head dept. Southwestern State Coll., Weatherford, Okla., 1949-67, chmn. div. lang. arts, 1957-67. Rockefeller grantee, 1948. Mem. Am. Assn. U. Profs., Am. Assn. U. Women (past br. pres.), Okla. Council Tchrs. English (state pres. 1952, recipient Ann. State award in 1968), S. Central Modern Lang. Assn., Phi Beta Kappa, Sigma Kappa, Kappa Kappa Iota, Chi Delta Phi, Kappa Phi. Methodist. Club: Probieren Civic Study (pres. 1969-70). Author: Mark Twain as a Literary Artist, 1950. Mark Twain editor Eight American Writers, 1963. Contbr. articles to profl. jours. Home: Weatherford, Okla. Died Aug. 3, 1973.

BELLMAN, RUSSELL, retail furniture exec.; b. Louisville, June 29, 1896; s. John Hutchins and Mary (Theobald) B.; M.E., Lehigh U., 1920; m. Katharine Haverty, May 1, 1926; children—John, Ann. Sales engr., asst. dist. mgr. Elliott Co., 1920-28; sec. Haverty Furniture Cos., 1928-38, sec.-treas., 1938-46, v.p., treas., 1946-48, exec. v.p., 1948-55, vice chmn., 1955-61, chmn. bd., 1961-74, also dir.; dir. Fulton Nat. Bank Atlanta. Bd. dirs. YMCA, Atlanta Symphony Guild; chmn., trustee St. Joseph's Infirmary. Served as ensign USN, World War I. Mem. Atlanta Art Assn. (exec. chmn. exec. com.), U.S. C. of C., Kappa Sigma, Tau Beta Pi. Club: Atlanta Civitan (dir., past pres.). Home: Atlanta, Ga. Died Oct. 2, 1974.

BELNAP, LAMONTE JUDSON, paper corp. exec.; b. Burr Oak, Mich., Nov. 7, 1877; s. I. Judson and Ella I. (Burtch) B.; B.Sc., U. Neb., 1898, D. Engring., 1939; m. Lillian Young, Jan. 5, 1901 (dec. 1949); children—Jane I. (widow of H. W. von Eicken), Celeste (Mrs. Gordon C., Liersch). Div. engr., dist. mgr., mgr. Allis-Chalmers B., Ltd., Montreal, Can., 1902-11; v.p. Rudel-Belnap Co., Ltd., Montreal, 1911-17; asst. dir. war supplies British War Mission, Washington and Montreal, 1917-19; pres. Rolls-Royce of Am., Springfield, Mass., 1919-25, Worthington Pump & Machinery Corp., N.Y.C., 1925-31; pres. Consol. Paper Corp., Ltd., Montreal, 1931-47, chmn. bd., 1947-64, hon. chmn., from 1964 dir. Consolidated Paper Sales, Ltd.; pres., dir. Anticosti Shipping Co. (both Montreal); chmn., dir. Dominion Glass Co., Ltd., Montreal; chmn. of exec. com., dir. Worthington Corporation, N.Y.C.; mem. exec. com., director Canadian Pacific Railway Co., Dominion Bridge Co., Ltd., Ogilvie Flour Mills Co., Ltd. (Montreal); director Consol. Mining & Smelting Co. of Can. Ltd., Glenora Securities, Inc., Ogilvie Grain Co., Ltd., Seaforth Milling Co. Royal Trust (hon. dir.) (all Montreal). Member National Industrial Conf. Bd., N.Y.C. Member Engineering Institute of Canada, Sigma Chi. Clubs: St. Jame's Mount Royal, Laval-sur-le-Lac Golf (Montreal); Canadian (New York City). Home: Montreal, Que., Can.†

BELTZ, WILLIAM RAY, data processing mgr.; b. Canton, O., Dec. 19, 1936; s. John William and Genevieve Grace (Sponseller) B.; student evening schs. Malone Coll., 1960, 62-65, U. Ky., 1962; m. Judith Ruth Kogel, Sept. 14, 1958; children—Lisa Ann, John Fredrick. Asst. mgr. comml. loan dept. Harter Bank & Trust Co., Canton, 1954-59; mgr. data processing Perry Rubber Co., Massillon, O., 1960-69; mgr. data processing Crown Divs. of Allen Group, Orrville, O., 1969-73. Dir. Props of Canton, Inc., v.p., 1971-73. Served with AUS, 1961-62. Mem. Data Processing Mgmt. Assn., Archeol. Soc. Ohio. Republican. Mem. United Ch. of Christ. Mem. Ind. Order Foresters. Home: Massillon, O. Died Nov. 3, 1973; interred Sunset Hills Memory Gardens, Canton, O.

BELZ, MRS. HENRY (DOROTHY PERSHALL BELZ), ins. exec.; b. East St. Louis, Ill., Apr. 24, 1913; d. Estes Edward and Leita (Horton) Pershall; student Ohio State U., 1931-33, Washington U., St. Louis, 1936; m. Kenneth Dillman, June 3, 1932 (dec.); 1 dau., Nancy Wade (Mrs. William Peck); m. 2d, Frederick Carson Jones, Jan. 2, 1939 (div. Oct. 1949); children—Judith Pershall (Mrs. Louis Humes), Cynthia Pedley (Mrs. Michael Todorovich); m. 3d, Henry Belz, June 23, 1952; stepchildren—Henry III, Margartha Hager (Mrs. Alfred Kerth), John Ralph B. Spl. agt. Gen. Am. Inst. Co., St. Louis, 1959-74; spl. rep. Gen. Am. Life Ins. Co. Mem. citizens com. St. Louis U. Expansion Fund, 1959-74, women's com. Mo. Botan. Garden; city co-chmn. A.R.C. drive, 1952; maintenance fund chmn. St. Louis Symphony, 1940-41, now dir.; mem. promotion com. Art Mus. Ballot; mem. spl. gifts com. United Fund, Fine Arts Drive; mem. Camelot Auction Com. Bd. dirs. Washington U. Women's Assn. Mem. Women's Leaders Round Table, Life Underwriters Assn. (chmn. women's assn. 1962, mem. exec. com. Mo. assn.), Playgoers (dir.), Jr. League Tea room Womens Assn. (v.p.), St. Louis Symphony Assn., Nat. Quality Club, Qualified President's Club, Kappa Kappa Gamma. Methodist. Club: Clayton for Women. Home: St. Louis, Mo. Died Nov. 2, 1974.

BEMIS, SAMUEL FLAG, educator; b. Worcester, Mass., Oct. 20, 1891; s. Charles Harris and Flora M. (Bemis) B.; A.B., Clark U., 1912, A.M., 1913, hon. D.H.L. 1937; A.M., Harvard, 1915, Ph.D., 1916; grad. study in Eng. and France, 1915-16; Litt.D., Williams Coll., 1953; L.H.D., Yale, 1963; m. Ruth M. Steele, June 20, 1919 (dec. Oct. 1967); one daughter, Barbara. Instructor in history, Colo. Coll., Colorado Springs, 1917-18, asso. prof., 1918-20; prof. history, Whitman Coll., Walla Walla, Wash., 1920-23; research asso., Carnegie Instn. of Washington, 1923-24; prof. history, George Washington U., 1924-34; director European mission of Library of Congress, 1927-29; lecturer at Harvard, 1934-43; Farnam professor of diplomatic history at Yale, 1935, professor of inter-American relations, 1945, Sterling professor diplomatic history, inter-American relations emeritus, 1960; Carnegie visiting professor to Latin American Universities, 1937-38, Cuba, 1945, 1956. Member American Historical Association (pres. 1961), American Academy Arts and Sciences, Am. Antiquarian Soc., Colonial Soc. of Mass., Mass. Historical Soc., Sociedad Geograficia y Estadistica Mexico). Unitarian. Club: Cosmos. Author historical volumes including: Pinckneys Treaty: A Study of America's Advantage from Europe's Distress 1783-1800, 1926 (Pulitzer prize in letters, 1927); John Quincy Adams and the Foundations of American Fgn. Policy, 1949 (received the Pulitzer award for biography in 1950); John Quincy Adams and the Union, pub. 1956. Editor: The Am. Secretaries of State and their Diplomacy (part author), 10 vols., 1927-29. Contributor to reviews, newspapers, etc. Home: Bridgeport Conn. Died Oct. 1973.

BEMIS, THOMAS FREDERICK, rancher; b. Hays, Kan., June 28, 1925; s. Lawrence Allen and Irma Clio (Hatcher) B.; student Kan. U., 1943, Colo. U., 1944; m. Melva Mae Weber, Oct. 31, 1947; children—George, Ann, William. Draftsman, Internat. Engr. Co., Denver, 1945-47; farmer and rancher, Plainville, Kan., 1957-72; founder, pres., dir. Bemis, Inc., Plainville, Kan., 1967-74. Trustee Bemis Land Trust, Hays. Recipient 2d prize 1st Ann. Conv. Kan. Inventors, 1965. Mem. Am. Soc. Agrl. Engrs., Nat. (nat. councilman 1962), Kan. (sec.-treas. 1961-64), Ellis County (supt. 1955-72) assns. soil conservation dists., Ellis County Taxpayers Assn. (chmn. 1969), Delta Tau Delta. Methodist (dir. 1961-62). Mason, Rotarian. Patentee in field. Home: Hays, Kan. Died Nov. 24, 1974.

BENDELARI, ARTHUR ENRICO, exec. com. The Eagle-Picher Lead Co.; b. Toronto, Can., Nov. 23, 1879; s. Enrico and Mary Olivia (Worthington) B.; student Upper Canada Coll.; came to U.S., 1897, naturalized, 1913; m. Grace Full Hutson, Nov. 17, 1923. Sec. to pres. Cleveland Stone Co., 1897-1900; operator lead and zinc mines, Joplin, Mo., 1900-11; mgr. Underwriters' Lead Co., 1911-15; pres. Eagle-Picher Lead Co., Cincinnati, 1928-37; dir. and mem. exec. com. Eagle-Picher Lead Co.; dir. Am. Mining Congress, Am. Zinc Inst., Lead Industries Assn.; mem. The Newcomen Society, Lexington Club. Republican. Episcopalian. Mason (32°). Home: Lexington, Ky.†

BENDER, JOHN FREDERICK, prof. ednl. adminstration; b. Kansas City, Kan., Nov. 24, 1879; s. Theodore and Gertrude (Schuch) B.; A.B., U. of Kan., 1906; A.M., Columbia, 1922, Ph.D., 1926; m. Margarethe von Unwerth, July 14, 1909; children—John B. (dec.), Herman Robert, William Alfred. Tchr., rural schs. of Kan., 1900-02; fellow in German, U. of Kans., 1905-06; supt. schs., Arkansas City, Kans., 1907-15, Pittsburg, Kan., 1915-24; mem. ednl. survey staff, Watertown, N.Y., 1924-25; instr. Hunter Coll., New York, 1925-26; prof. ednl. adminstration, U. of Okla., since 1926; instr. Mount Allison U., Sackville, N.B., summer 1926, David Ross Boyd prof. ednl. adminstrn. emeritus; cons. Okla. State dept. pub. instruction from 1951. Life mem. N.E.A. (Dept. Superintendence); fellow A.A.A.S.; mem. Nat. Soc. for Study of Edn., Okla. Acad. Science, Okla. Edn. Assn., Phi Beta Kappa, Phi Delta Kappa, Kappa Delta Pi. Methodist. Mason. Author: The Functions of Courts in Enforcing School Attendance Laws, 1927; Purcell, Oklahoma, Survey, 1933; Problems in Financing the Common Schools of Oklahoma, 1941. Contbr. Am. Sch. Bd. Journal, Social Sciences. Home: Norman, Okla.†

BENEDICT, CRYSTAL EASTMAN, social investigator; b. Marlborough, Mass., June 25, 1881; d. Rev. Samuel E. and late Rev. Annis (Ford) Eastman; A.B., Vassar, 1903; M.A., Columbia, 1904; LL.B., New York U. Law Sch., 1907; m. Wallace J. Benedict, of Milwaukee, Wis., May 5, 1911. Admitted to N.Y. bar, 1907; conducted accident investigation in Pittsburgh Survey, 1907-09; apptd. by Gov. Hughes mem. N.Y. State Employers' Liability Commn., 1909, and elected sec.; drew up report same, 1911; campaign mgr. Woman's Suffrage Campaign, Wis., 1911-12. V.-chmn. N.Y. br. Woman's Peace Party, since May, 1915. Author: Work Accidents and the Law, 1910. Home: New York†

BENESCH, ALFRED ABRAHAM lawyer; b. Cleve., Mar. 7, 1879; s. Isidore Julius and Bertha (Federman) B.; A.B. magna cum laude, Harvard, 1900, A.M., 1901, LL.B., 1903; LL.D., Fenn College, 1955, Western Reserve U., Cleveland, 1965, H.L.D. (hon.), Hebrew Union College, 1962; married to Helen Newman, Nov. 29, 1906. Admitted to Ohio bar, 1903, practiced law in Cleveland, Ohio; with firm of Benesch, Friedlander, Mendelson & Coplan. Mem. Cleve. City Council 1912-13, dir. Pub. Safety, 1914-15; dir. commerce State of Ohio, 1935-39; area rent dir. Northeastern Ohio, 1942-45; mem. Bd. Edn., 1926-63, pres., 1933-34. Presdl. elector Democratic Party, 1941. Vice pres. Nat. Jewish Hosp.; trustee Cuyahoga County Hospital; member bd. of trustees Mt. Sinai Hospital; member Bur. Jewish Edn., Jewish Community Fedn.; v.p. Cleve. Jewish Orphan Home. Recipient Distinguished Service awards Cleve. Community Fund, 1951, Citizens League, 1952, Cleve. C. of C., Jewish Welfare Fedn., Jewish Nat. Fund. Bd. Edn. Mem. Phi Beta Kappa. Mem. B'nai B'rith (past pres. Grand Lodge 2). Clubs: Commerce, Oakwood (Cleve.). Author articles. Home: Cleveland, O.†

BENGTSON, NELS AUGUST, geographer, geologist; b. Morkhult, Sweden, May 22, 1879; s. August and Hanna (Johnson) B.; grad. Peru (Neb.) State Normal Sch., 1902; student Cornell U., 1904; A.B., U. of Neb., 1907, A.M., 1908; Ph.D., Clark U., 1927; m. Iva Maxey,

June 14, 1902; children—Juanita L., Paulus A., Rowena S., Ruth J., Martha Ann. Prin. high sch., St. Paul, Neb., 1902-03; prof. geography, Peru State Normal Sch., 1904-06, U. of Neb., from 1908, dean univ. jr. div. from 1940; prof. geography, summer sessions, Cornell U., 1912, U. of Va., 1913, U. of Wis., 1925, Columbia, 1929-39, 47; petroleum geologist, summer 1917. Commodity expert, War Trade Bd., 1918; U.S. trade commr. to Norway, 1919; geologist in Honduras, 1920, Ecuador, 1922, Venezuela, 1927-28. Mem. Assn. Am. Geographers (v.p. 1923 and 1942), Nat. Council Geography Teachers (pres. 1929), Am. Soc. Professional Geographers, Nebraska Acad. of Science (pres. 1935), Sigma Gamma Epsilon, Sigma Xi, Phi Delta Kappa, Sigma Phi Epsilon, Phi Beta Kappa. Mason, Unitarian. Author: Physical Geography Manual, 1913; Geography of Nebraska, 1917; Norway—Commercial and Industrial Handbook, 1920; Student's Workbook in the Geography of Nebraska, 1925. Senior Author: The Wheat Industry, 1915; Fundamental of Economic Geography, 1935, rev. edit., 1942, 3d edit., 1949; Economic Geography Manual, 1937, rev. edit., 1943. Wrote various brochures, articles and reports. Home: Lincoln, Neb.†

BEN-GURION, DAVID, Israeli statesman; b. Plonsk, Poland, Oct. 1886; educated privately and at U. Constantinople; D.H.L., Jewish Theol. Sem. Am., 1952; Ph.D., Hebrew U., Jerusalem, 1957; LL.D., Brandeis U., 1960, Rangoon U., 1961; D.Architecture, Israel Inst. Tech., Haifa, 1962; m. 1917; 3 children. Went to Palestine, then under Turkish rule, 1906; became active in Palestine Labor Party and editor of its jour., 1915; exiled by Turkish govt.; came to U.S. and helped organize pioneers for settlement in Palestine; helped organize and extend Jewish Legion (Am., Brit. and Palestinian vols.) for service in World War I; served as pvt. with 39th Bn., Royal Fusiliers, in Gen. Allenby's operations against Turks; became mem. Gen. Council of Zionist Orgn., 1920; gen. sec. Gen. Fedn. Labor, 1921-35; mem. exec. bd. Jewish Agy. for Palestine, 1933, chmn. bd., 1948; proclaimed Independence of Israel, May 14, 1948; head provisional govt. and minister of def., 1948-49; prime minister of Israel and minister of def., 1949-53, 55-63. Leader of Mapai (Labour) Party. Recipient Bublick prize Hebrew U., 1949; Bialik Lit. prize for Judaica, 1952; Henrietta Szold award Hadassah Women's Zionist Orgn. Am., 1958. Author: Palestine A Historical, Economic and Geographical Research Survey, 1917; We and Our Neighbors, 1930; From The Working Class To a Nation, 1933; Mimaamad Leam, 1933; The Struggle (5 vols.), 1949; Israel at War, 1950; Vision and Implementation, 5 vols., 1951-57; Rebirth and Destiny of Israel, 1954; The Sinai Campaign, 1959; Eternity of Israel, 1963; Israel-Years of Challenge, 1963; Ben-Gurion Looks Back, 1965; Dvarim Kehavayatam; Talks with Arab Leaders; Michtavim LePaula, 1969; The Restored State of Israel, 2 vols., 1969; Iyunim Batanach, 1969; Memoirs, 1971; and others. Home: Sdeh Boker Negev Israel Died Dec. 1, 1973.

BENHAM, ALLEN ROGERS, educator; b. St. Peter, Minn., Jan. 1, 1879; s. Charles Merton and Emma (Rogers) B.; B.A., U. of Minn., 1900 M.A., 1901; Ph.D., Yale, 1905; m. Agnes Isabel Rich, of Minneapolis, July 9, 1902; children—Dorothy, Merton R., Caroline, Ruth. With U. of Wash. from 1905, prof. English from 1916. Visiting prof. English, New York U., 1929-30. Mem. Modern Lang. Assn. America, Western Philos. Assn., Medieval Acad. of America, Phi Beta Kappa, Lambda Alpha Psi, Phi Sigma Kappa, Soc. Colonial Wars, Modern Humanities Research Assn., Alumni Assn. A.E.F. Univ., etc. Author: English Literature from Widsith to the Death of Chaucer, 1916; A Bibliography of Fifteenth Century Literature (with Lena L. Tucker), 1928. Editor: Specimen Letters (with A.S. Cook), 1905; The Voice of Carlyle (with Prof. H. G. Pearson), 1923; Selections from the Writings of Thomas Carlyle, 1928. Contbr. mags. and tech. jours. Home: Seattle, Wash.†

BENKEN, EUGENE EDWIN, lawyer, accountant; b. Savannah, Ga., Dec. 9, 1889; s. Eugene Edwin and Effie (Strobhar) B.; grad. Walton Sch. Commerce, Chgo., 1924; LL.B., Blackstone Coll. Law, 1935; m. Elsie Ehler, Sept. 15, 1932. Accounting dept. So. Cotton Oil Co., Savannah, 1911-24; certified pub. accountant, Savannah, from 1925; admitted to Ga. bar, 1936; practice law, Savannah, from 1937; partner Thompson & Benken, from 1967. Mem. Civil Service Bd. City of Savannah. Served in Armed Forces, World War I. C.P.A., Ga., Ind., Tenn. Mem. Am. Inst. C.P.A.'s, Ga. Soc. C.P.A.'s (v.p. 1930-31), Ga. Assn. Atty.-C.P.A.'s, Am. Ga., Savannah bar assns., Telfair Acad. Arts and Scis., S.R. (treas., bd. mgrs.), Am. Legion, S.C.V., Ga. Hist. Soc., Soc. Colonial Wars. Baptist. Mason (32 deg., Shriner), Elk. Home: Savannah, Ga. Died May 2, 1974.

BENNETT, ARTHUR LAWTON, ophthalmologist; b. Buffalo, N.Y., Nov. 25, 1898; s. Arthur George and Alice Emma (Ross) B.; M.D., U. Buffalo, 1928; m. Sara Frances Minard, June 28, 1930. Intern Buffalo Gen. Hosp., later sr. ophthalmologist; practice medicine, specializing in ophthalmology, Buffalo, 1932-74; attending ophthalmologist Children's Hosp.; cons. ophthalmologist Lafayette Gen. Hosp., Buffalo, Columbus and Gowanda state hosps. Asst. prof. ophthalmology State U. N.Y. at Buffalo. Served to comdr. M.C., USNR, World War II. Diplomate Am. Bd. Ophthalmology. Mem. A.M.A. Home: Buffalo, N.Y., Died Apr 13, 1974; buried Lakeside Cemetery, Hamburg, N.Y.

BENNETT, EARL WILLARD, chem. co. exec.; b. White Cloud, Mich., Jan. 18, 1880; s. Frank and Eudorah (Ostrander) B.; student pub. schs., Grand Rapids, Mich., 1897; D.Eng. (hon.), Mich. Sch. Mines and Tech., 1953; m. Eva V. Barclay, Aug. 9, 1905; children—Vada L. (Mrs. Alden B. Dow), Helen L. (Mrs. Alden B. Hanson), Willard V., Grace E. (Mrs. Charles E. Reed), Barbara, Robert B., David, Thomas J. Clk., Marshall Field & Co., 1897-1900; with Dow Chem. Co., from 1900, beginning as clerk, became v.p., 1931, treas., 1930, dir., from 1927, chmn. bd., 1949, then hon. chmn.; dir. Dow Corning Corp., Dow Chem. Co. Can., Cliffs Dow Chem. Co., Chem. State Savs. Bank. Mem. light metal com. NRC, World War II. Republican. Baptist. Clubs: Midland Country; Saginaw Bay (Mich.) Yacht. Home: Midland, Mich. Died Sept. 19, 1973.

BENNETT, GEORGE KETTNER, psychologist; b. N.Y.C., Feb. 26, 1904; s. Walter Taylor and Henriette Charlotte (Kettner) B.; A.B., Yale, 1928, Ph.D. in psychology, 1935; m. Marjorie Gelink; children—George Kettner, Deborah Swan. Dir. test div. The Psychol. Corp., 1936-44, v.p., dir., 1944-47, pres., 1947-70. Mem. applied psychol. panel OSRD, 1943-45; mem. com. on service personnel NRC, 1942-45, vice chmn. div. anthropology and psychology, 1947-48. Diplomate in indsl. psychology Am. Bd. Examiners in Profl. Psychology. Fellow Am. Psychology Assn.; mem. N.Y. State Assn. for Applied Psychology (pres. 1947-48), Sigma Xi. Republican. Episcopalian. Clubs: N.Y. Yacht; Larchmont Yacht. Author or co-author: Test of Mechanical Comprehension, Differential Aptitude Tests, Short Employment Tests, Stenographic Aptitude Test, Stenographic Proficiency Test. Home: Bronxville, N.Y. Died Feb. 2, 1975; interred Ferncliff, Hartsdale, N.Y.

BENNETT, HOWARD FRANKLIN, educator; b. Worcester, Mass., Jan. 3, 1911; s. Edwin Harlan and Abbie Minerva (Flagg) B.; A.B. magna cum laude, Amherst Coll., 1933; A.M. in Teaching (Homes fellow teaching 1937-38), Harvard, 1939, Ph.D. in Am. History (Edward Austin fellow history 1938-39), 1951; m. Elizabeth Maurine Hoover, Feb. 10, 1951. Tchr., Worcester High Sch., 1933-35, W. Hartford (Conn.) High Sch., 1935-37; asst. history Harvard, 1939-42, asst. Dean's Office, 1939-42; mem. Faculty Northwestern U. Sch. Bus., after 1946, prof. bus. history, after 1960, chmn. dept. bus. history and environment, after 1955, faculty Inst. Mgmt., after 1961, pres. Student Pub. Co., Inc., Northwestern U.; dir. Bus. History and Econ. Life Program, Inc.; mem. staff exec. and mgmt. devel. program Bell Telephone System, 1959-60; faculty Gen. Electric Advanced Mgmt. Program, after 1964, Ill. Bell Telephone Mgmt. Program, after 1961; cons. Field Enterprises Ednl. Corp., after 1963. Served with USNR, 1942-46, 51-53; capt. Res. Mem. Am., Miss. Valley hist. assns., Econ. History Assn., Am. Econ. Assn., Soc. History Tech., Naval Res. Assn., Navy League U.S., Am. Assn. U. Profs., Phi Beta Kappa, Theta Delta Chi. Clubs: Harvard of Chicago; Chicago Amherst (past pres.). Author: Precision Power: The First Fifty Years of Bodine Electric Co., 1959; also articles. Home: Wilmette, Ill. Died Sept. 21, 1974; interred Arlington Nat. Cemetery.

BENNETT, JAMES MURRELL, architect; b. Dallas, Aug. 22, 1904; s. Edward C. and Maude (Ramsey) B.; B.A., So. Meth. U., 1923; B. Arch. with honors, Washington U., St. Louis, 1927; m. Juanita Morgan, Jan. 2, 1926; children—Elizabeth (Mrs. David Schultz), Edward. With archtl. firms, St. Louis, 1926-37; partner charge design Gill & Bennett, Dallas, 1938-42; archtl. rep. in Dallas and Houston, J. Gordon Turnbull, Inc., Cleve., 1942-44; partner Bennett & Crittenden, Dallas, 1945-64; partner Bennett & Bennett, Dallas, 1965-73; specializing in design of churches; prin. works include Fain Meml. Presbyn. Ch., 1948, Floral Heights Meth. Ch., Wichita Falls, Tex., 1949, Flow Meml. Hosp., Denton, Tex., 1950, Highland Park Meth. Ch., 1951, Kessler Park Meth. Ch., 1952, Restland Mortuary, 1957, Lovers Lane Meth. Ch., 1958, Zion Luth. Ch., Dallas, 1958, Rowsev Meml. Chapel, Muskogee, Okla., 1960, 1st Presbyn. Ch., Irving, 1st Meth. Ch., Alexandria, La., 1968, Trinity Meth. Ch., Ruston, La., 1971. Mem. city plan commn., University Park, Tex., 1956-73, chmn., 1962-73; mem. city zone commn., University Park, 1956-62. James Harrison Steedman travelling fellow, Europe, 1928. Fellow A.I.A. (pres. N. Tex. chtp. 1946, Dallas chpt. 1947); mem. Tex. Soc. Architects (chmn. com. archtl. practice 1953-58). Methodist. Lion. Home: Dallas, Tex. Died July 28, 1973.

BENNETT, MAILLARD, hotel exec.; b. Berkeley, Cal., Sept. 9, 1904; s. Oscar M. and Bertha (Olsen) B.; B.S., U. Cal. at Berkeley, 1926; m. Gladys Comstock, Dec. 25, 1932 (dec. Jan. 1961); children—Ardys C., Jane; m. 2d, Mary Carrell, Oct. 22, 1963. Truck, bus tire sales mgr. Firestone Tire & Rubber Co., San Francisco, 1926-36; mgr. Brockway Hot Springs, Lake Tahoe, Cal., summers 1936-75, Ariz. Inn, Tucson, winters 1936-75; pres. Brockway Hotel Co., Brockway Land & Water Co., Oakwood Investment Co.; dir. Hotel Red Book Corp. Mem. hotel adv. com. NPA; v.p., trustee Am. Hotel and Motel Assn. Ednl. Inst.; mem. adv. com. Cal. Dept. Parks and Recreation. Named Compagnon de Bordeaux, Le Grand Counceil L'Académie du Vin de Bordeaux; recipient Distinguished Service award Tex. Hotel Assn.; Distinguished Order Dinnergong. Am. Hotel and Motel Assn. (past pres.), Ariz. (dir., past pres.), No. Cal. (hon. dir.), Cal. (hon. dir.) hotel assns., Okla. Univ. Hotel and Restaurant (life), Internat. Platform Assn., Hotel Greeters Internat., Confrerie de la Chaine des Rotisseurs, Delta Phi Epsilon. Rotarian. Clubs: President's (U. Ariz.); Old Pueblo (pres. 1972-75), Tucson Country, Tucson Sunshine Climate (dir.)(Tucson); Tavern (N.Y.C.); Incline Village (Nev.) Golf and Country; Brockway Country (Lake Tahoe, Cal.); Soc. for Pi-eons, (N.Y.C.). Home: Tucson, Ariz. Died Feb. 22, 1975.

BENNING, BERNHARD, banker; b. Munich, Germany, Sept. 17, 1902; s. Karl Wilhelm and Margarete (Bergdolt) B.; Diploma Volkswirt, U. Munich, 1927, Dr. oec. publ., 1928; m. Ilse Gussow, Aug. 7, 1939; children—Glsela (Mrs. Freisenhahn), Birgit (Mrs. Christians). With Bay. Hypoteken-und Wechsel Bank, Munich, 1923-28, Statistisches Reichsamt, Berlin, 1928-33; dir. econ. dept. Reichs-Kredit-Gasellschaft, Berlin, 1933-45; Interned in Russian concentration camps, 1945-50; bd. mgrs. Bank deutscher Lander March, 1950-57; bd. mgrs. Zentralbank-rat Deutsche Bundesbank, 1957—; dept. chmn. bd. Deutsche Verkehrs-Kredit-Bank AG, Lastenausgleichsbank, Deutsche Gesellschaft f. offentliche Arbeitan. Decorated Grosses Verdienstkreuz mit Stern der Bundesrepublik Deutschland. Clubs: Frankfurter Gesellschaft fur Handel; Industrie und Wissenchaft (Frankfurt am Main). Author: Der Schwarze Freitag; Elna Untersuchung des Borsenzusammenbruchs vom, 1927; Kapitalbildung und Investition in dar Deutschen Volkswirtschaft, 1931. Home: Frankfurt/Main Federal Republic of Germany., Died Dec. 19, 1974.

BENNY, JACK (STAGE NAME OF BENJAMIN KUBELSKY), entertainer; b. Waukegan, Ill., Feb. 14, 1894; s. Meyer and Emma (Sachs) Kubelsky; ed. Waukegan High Sch.; m. Mary Livingstone (actress), Jan. 25, 1927; 1 adopted dau., Joan Naomi. Began as violinist, 1912; featured player on vaudeville stage; star in motion pictures 1939; radio entertainer, from 1932, also on TV as guest artist and in own programs; recent pictures: To Be or Not to Be, George Washington Slept Here, The Horn Blows at Midnight. Served in U.S. Navy, World War I; spent summers 1943, 44, 45, entertaining armed forces overseas during World War II. Recipient award for best continuing performance by a male entertainer Nat. Acad. Television Arts and Sci., 1957, Spl. award. Club: Friars. Home: Beverly Hills, Cal. Died Dec. 26, 1974.

BENSEL, FRANCIS SCOTT, lawyer; b. N.Y.C., Oct. 2, 1905; s. Charles E. and Julia (Smith) B.; LL.B., Fordham U., 1926; m. Nora Murphy, Aug. 31, 1929, children—Irene (Mrs. Leland Markley), Francis P., Joan. Admitted to N.Y. bar, 1927, practiced in N.Y.C.; mem. firm Kelley Drye, Warren, Clark Carr & Ellis and predecessor, from 1936. Trustee Marymount Manhattan Coll. Fellow Am. Bar Found.; mem. Am., N.Y. bar assns., Assn. Bar City N.Y., N.Y. County Lawyers Assn. (pres. 1960-62), Am. Judicature Soc., Cath. Lawyers Guild, Soc. Friendly Sons of St. Patrick. Clubs: Lake Placid (N.Y.); St. Andrews Golf (Hastings-on-Hudson, N.Y.). Home: New York City, N.Y. Died May 12, 1973.

BENSON, ELIZABETH ENGLISH, educator; b. Frederick, Md.; d. Harry and Minnie (English) Benson; B.S., George Washington U., 1931; M.A., Gallaudet Coll., 1932; LL.B., Washington Coll. Law, 1937. Tchr. rural pub. schs., Woodsboro, Md., 1924-25; mem. faculty Gallaudet Coll., Washington, 1926-70, prof., 1950-70, dean women, 1950-70; served to 2d lt. AUS, 1943-46. Recipient award for outstanding achievement Alumni Assn. State Tchrs. Coll., Towson, Md., 1962; named Alumnae of Distinction, Columbian Women George Washington U., 1956. Mother of Year, Alpha Sigma Pi, 1963, Woman of Year Frederick Bus. and Profl. Womens Club and Western Dist. Md. Fedn. Bus. and Profl. Womens Clubs, 1965. Mem. N.E.A., Nat. Assn. Women Deans and Counselors, Delta Kappa Gamma. Club: D.C. Zonta. Author: A Survey of the Occupations of the Graduates and Ex-Students of Gallaudet College, 1932. Asso. editor: American Annals of the Deaf, 1964-67. Home: Frederick, Md. Died Dec. 13, 1972.

BENSON, ROBERT LOUIS, physician; b. Flint, Mich., May 30, 1880; A.B., U. Mich., 1902, M.A., 1904; M.D., U. Chicago, 1910; m. Hazel Altman, Sept. 8, 1915; children—Patricia (Mrs. Ralph Altman), Nancy (Mrs. Donald E. Drake), Robert. Bacteriologist, Fla. State Bd. Health, 1910-12; asst. prof. anatomy U. Ore. Med. Sch., 1912-13, prof. pathology, 1913-29, asso. clin. prof. medicine, 1929-47, clin. prof. medicine and chief division of allergy, 1947-51, emeritus prof. medicine from 1951; consultant regional office V.A., Portland, 1949-51, area consultant in internal medicine and allergy, San Francisco area, 1949-51. Chmn. Gov.'s. Interim Commn. for study of pub. health and welfare, 1933; mem. State Bd. Health, 1933-40, pres., 1935;

mem. State Pub. Welfare Commn., 1934-41. Served as 1st lt. to maj., active service Med. Res. Corps, U.S. Army, 1917-19. Diplomate Am. Bd. Internal Medicine (Allergy). Fellow A.M.A., A.C.P., Am. Acad. Allergy; mem. Am. Heart Assn., N. Pacific Soc. Internal Medicine, Portland Acad. Medicine, City and Co. med. socs., A.A.A.S., Phi Beta Pi, Sigma Xi, Alpha Omega Alpha. Republican. Roman Cahtolic. Club: Pacific Interurban Clinical. Home: Portland, Ore.†

BENTHALL, MICHAEL PICKERSGILL, theatre producer; b. London, Feb. 8, 1919; s. Edward Charles and Ruth McCarthy (Cable) B.; student Christ Church, Oxford U. Actor, 1938; with Old Vic and Open Air Theatre, London, 1939; with Old Vic tours of Australia, 1955, U.S., Can., 1955, 58, 60; tours Europe, Middle East, USSR, 1916, Australia, 1961, N. Am., S. Am., 1962; dir. Old Vic, 1953-62, gov. Old Vic Trust, 1962; prin. prodns. include Hamlet, 1944, 48, 53, 59; The Merchant of Venice, 1947; King John; The Taming of the Shrew; Aida, 1948; A Midsummer Night's Dream, 1949, 54; Cymbeline, 1949; As You Like It, 1950; Antony and Cleopatra, Caesar and Cleopatra, The Tempest, 1951; The Millionairess, 1952, Macbeth, Henry V., Twelfth Night, The Cenci, The Double Dealer, The Importance of Being Ernest, 1959; Man and Boy, 1963; MacBeth, 1964; Romeo and Juliet, 1965; Coco, N.Y.C., 1969. Dir. Bird and Co. (London) Ltd., Trevor Prodns. Ltd., Popinjay Ltd. Served to maj. Royal Arty., 1939-46. Address: London, England., Died Sept. 1974.

BENTON, MARGARET PEAKE, artist; b. South Orange, N.J.; d. James October and Elizabeth Maude (Peake) Benton; student N. Toronto Collegiate Inst., 1925, (assn. Ont. Coll. Art scholar), Ont. Coll. Art, 1925-30, Victoria Coll., 1929-30. Exhibited in group shows Ont. Soc. Artists, Toronto, 1933, Royal Can. Acad. Art, 1938-40, 42, 45, 49, Royal Acad. London, Eng., 1950, Pa. Soc. Miniature Painers, 1940, 41, 45-51, Miniature Painters, Sculptors and Graver's Soc. Washington, 1943, 45-47, 51-73, Nat. Soc. Miniature Painters, N.Y.C., 1949, Miniature Art Soc. N.J., 1971-74, Frame House Gallery, Louisville, 1973; exhibited one-man shows in Victoria Coll. Library, Toronto, Eaton's Coll. St. Gallery, Toronto, Odeon Carlton, Toronto, St. Catherines (Ont.) Pub. Library, Oak Hall, Niagara Falls, Ont., Courthouse, Niagara-On-The Lake, Ont.; represented in permanent collections Queen's Pvt. Collection, Eng., King's Coll., Halifax, N.S., Can., United Ch. Bldgs., Toronto, Nurmanzil Psychiatric Clinic, Punjab, India, Pa. Acad. Art, Phila. Recipient Elizabeth Muhlhofer award Miniature Painters, Sculptors and Gravers Soc. Washington, 1962, Levantia White Boardman Meml. 2d prize, 1970, 72, R.V. Shope award Miniature Art Soc. N.J., 1971, 72, First award First Nat. Bank N.J., 1973. Mem. Miniature Painters, Sculptors and Gravers Soc. Washington, D.C., Minature Art Soc. N.J., Internat. Platform Assn., World's Woman's Christian Temperance Union, Women's Aux. Can. Bible Soc., Aux. Brit. and Fgn. Bible Soc. Home: Niagara-On-The-Lake, Ont., Canada., Died Feb. 3, 1975.

BENTON, RITA, playwright; b. St. Louis, Mo., Oct. 24, 1881; d. William Henry and Kate (Sturges) B.; A.B., Vassar, 1903; course in stagecraft, Little Theatre, Art Ins. of Chicago. Has specialized since 1906 in story telling, dramatizing stories and working them out in church and settlements. Author: The Star-Child and Other Plays, 1921; Shorter Bible Plays, 1922; Bible Plays, 1922; Bible Play Workshop, 1923; Franklin and Other Plays, 1924; The Elf of Discontent and Other Plays, 1927. Home: Chicago, Ill.†

BENTON, THOMAS HART, artist; b. Neosho, Mo., Apr. 15, 1889; s. Maecenus E. and Elizabeth (Wise) R.; ed. Western Mil. Acad., Alton, Ill., 1906; student Art Inst. Chgo., 1906-07, Academie Julien, Paris, France, 1908-11; A.F.D. (hon.), U. Mo.; m. Rita Piacenza, Feb. 19, 1922; children—Thomas Piacenza, Jessie Piacenza. Began as cartoonist Joplin (Mo.) Am., 1906, and as profl. painter, 1912; dir. dept. painting Kansas City (Mo.) Art Inst., 1935-41; executed murals New Britain (Conn.) Mus., New Sch. Social Research, N.Y.C.,; murals for states Ind. and Mo., Power Authority State N.Y. (2 murals), River Club, Kansas City, Truman Library, Independence, Mo., City of Joplin. Served as pvt. U.S. Army, World War I. Recipient gold medal Archtl. League, 1933. Hon. mem. Academia de Bellas Artes (Argentine Republic), Academia Sienesa deglia Intronatl (Siena, Italy), Academia Fiorentina della Artl del Disegno (Florence, Italy); mem. Am. Acad. Arts and Scis., N.A.D., Phi Beta Kappa. Democrat. Author: An Artist in America, 1937; An American in Art; Benton Essays. Home: Kansas City, Mo. Died Jan. 19, 1975.

BENTONELLI, JOSEPH, (Joseph Horace Benton), lyric tenor; b. Kansas City, Sept. 10, 1898; s. Oliver Horace and LaMiza (Seawell) Benton; A.B., U. Okla. 1920, Mus.B., 1921, M.A. in Modern Langs., 1941; studied with Jean De Reszk. Debut in Don Giovanni, Nice, France, Dec. 1924; created world-premieres two different operas Il Vassallo of Smareglia, Trieste, Nov. 1930, and Cecilia of Refice with soprano, Claudia Muzio, at Royal Opera House, Rome, Feb. 1934; with Chgo. Civic Opera Co., 1934; debut with Met. Opera Co., N.Y.C., Jan. 10, 1936, taking place (on 33 hrs. notice) of Richard Crooks because of latter's sudden illness, and subsequently performed many roles inculding first Am. presentation Puccini's Gianni Schicchi in English; entor Met. Opera Quartet, from 1936. Chmn., adviser dept. of voice U. Okla., Norman, 1944-69. Voted by Italian Fascist Soc. of Musicians one of Italy's Four most popular tenors during 1934 season; elected Olka. Hall of Fame, 1951. Fellow Am. Inst. Vocal Pedagogy of Nat. Assn. Tchrs. of Singing (Geneva); mem. Internat. Inst. Arts and Letters (asso.), Am. Hist. Soc., Am. Biol. Assn., Am. Nat. Opera Assn. (dir.), Pi Kappa Alpha, Phi Beta Kappa, Phi Beta Kappa Assos., Phi Mu Alpha, Phi Delta Kappa, Kappa Delta Pi, Kappa Tau Pi (one of founders). Presbyn. (elder). Mason (32 deg.), Lion. Star on 3 major radio hours of NBC, 1934 and guest on 7 other radio hours, NBC and CBS; gave yearly coast-to-coast concert tours and lecture-recitals; made first English translation of Clovis Nogueira de Sa's Brazilian novel No Delirio da Vida (In the Delirium of Living), summer 1942; on commn. from novel's author, first translation into Italian as Nel Delirio della Vita, 1943. Hon. Col. on staff of gov. of Okla. Author: Oklahoma Tenor (autobiography), 1973. Home: Norman, Okla., Died Apr. 4, 1975.

BENTSUR, SHMUEL, Israeli diplomat; b. Cluj, Rumania, July 15, 1906; ed. Cluj (Rumania) Acad. Commerce and Polit. Economy; m. Sara Weinstein, 1930; 1 son. Consul, Budapest, 1948-49, consul, first sec., 1949-50; charge d'affaires, 1950-52, in Sofia, 1952; dir.-adjoint Eastern European div. Ministry Fgn. Affairs, Jerusalem, 1952-53, dir., 1953-56; minister to Austria, 1956-58; dep. dir. gen. Ministry Fgn. Affairs, Jerusalem, 1958-62; ambassador to Switzerland, 1962-67, insp. gen. fgn. service, from 1967. Address: Jerusalem, Israel., Died 1973.

BENZ, ALEXANDER OTTO, orgn. exec.; b. Mayville, Wis., July 17, 1880; s. Otto W. and Elise (Schoen) B.; grad. Dr. Martin Luther Coll. Tchrs. Sem., 1902; m. Lina M. Glasow, Aug. 19, 1902; children—Leona (Mrs. Douglas Barkelew), Alex W., Walter H., Herbert G., Bernice (Mrs. Louis Getschow). Tchr. schs., Wis., 1902-18; successively treas., credit and sales mgr., general mgr. Glasow-Tubbs Co., wholesale grocers, 1918-26; v.p. Aid Assn. for Lutherans, 1926-34, pres., 1934-53, chairman, 1953-63, mem. adv. council, from 1963. President, Nat. Fraternal Flag Day Found. Progressive Party candidate, gov. Wis., 1944. Mem. C. of C. (past pres.), Nat. Fraternal Congress Am. (past pres.). Republican. Lutheran. Clubs: Kiwanis (past pres.); Valparaiso (Ind.) University. Home: Appleton, Wis.†

BERDIE, RALPH FREIMUTH, psychologist, educator; b. Chgo. June 21, 1916; s. Sidney S. and Enid (Freimuth) B.; B.A., U. Minn., 1938; M.A., 1939; Ph.D., 1942; m. Frances Warren Strong, Aug. 6 1942; children—Phyllis (Mrs. Immre Somlai), Douglas, Carl. Teaching asst. U. Minn., Mpls., 1938-41, counselor 1941-46, prof. psychology, dir. Student Counseling Bur., 1947-65, prof. psychology, dir. student life studies, 1965-71, univ. coordinator admissions, registration and records, 1971-74; asso. prof. George Peabody Coll., Nashville, 1946-47; Ford Found. cons. U. Calcutta, 1962; summer teaching appointments Harvard, Stanford, U. Cal. at Berkeley, U. Mont., U. Utah, U. So. Cal., U. Pitts.; lectr. in Tokyo, Bangkok, Edinburgh, Stockholm, Paris, Melbourne, Sydney, Perth, Can.; mem. exec. com. Internat. Roundtable for Advancement Counseling. Precinct chmn. Minn. Democratic Party, 1960-68. Pres. E.K. Strong Meml. Found. Served to lt. USNR. 1943-46. Recipient award of profl. achievement Am. Bd. Psychology, 1968; Interest Measurement award, 1972. Fulbright research scholar in Australia, 1956-57. Mem. Am. (past pres. div. counseling psychology), Minn. (past exec. sec.) psychol. assns., Am. Coll. Personnel Assn. (past pres.) Am. Personnel and Guidance Assn. (past pres.). Author: After High School-What?, 1954; (with Albert, Hood) Decisions for Tomorrow, 1965, The Minnesota Counseling Inventory, 1956, The Revised Strong Vocational Interest Blank, 1968-74. Editor: Jour. of Counseling Psychology, 1970-74. Contbr. articles profl. jours. Home: St Paul Minn. Died Aug. 21, 1974.

BERGER, ANITA LOUISE FREMAULT (MRS. HENRY BERGER), actress; b. N.Y.C.; d. Louis and Michelan (Beresford) Fremault; grad. high sch.; m. Buddy Adler, May 18, 1940 (dec. July 1960); children—Melanie, Anthony; m. 2d, Henry Berger, Apr. 21, 1962. Actress, 1935-70; appeared in theatre prodns. including Mr. and Mrs. North, The Swan, Kiss the Boys Good Bye; appeared in motion pictures including Midsummer's Night Dream, Green Light, Bandit of Sherwood Forest; appeared as Nell, tv series, My Friend Flicka, 1956; tv appearances include Mannix, 1969, Movie Game, 1970. Pres. U. Cal. Los Angeles Womens Aux., 1956-59; bd. dirs. George Jr. Republic, N.Y.C., 1963-70; mem. nat. bd. govs. Nat. Conf. Christians and Jews, 1967-70. Named Woman of Year B'nai B'rith, 1958, City of Hope, 1959. Address: Los Angeles Cal. Died Apr. 25, 1970.

BERGER, GEORGE WILLIAM, mfr.; b. N.Y.C., Oct. 7, 1880; s. George Albert and Isabelle (Keene) B.; m. Mabel Sims, Nov. 5, 1907. Co-founder Berger Bros. Co., New Haven, 1904. now chmn., also dir. subsidiaries other countries; dir., mem. exec. com. First New Haven Nat. Bank, New Haven, Connecticut. Organized New Haven (Conn.) Community Chest after World War I; active fund-raising activities hosps., YMCA, YWCA, similar agencies, New Haven. Past mem. Rep. Statñ Finance Com. Dir. Grace-New Haven Community Hosp.; trustee The Children's Center, New Haven. Conglist. Mason (32°). Clubs: Quinnipiac (New Haven); Preston Mountain (Kent, Conn.); Mountain View Golf (Whitefield, N.H.); Bath, Indian Creek Country (Miami Beach, Fla.). Home: New Haven, Conn.†

BERGERMAN, MELBOURNE, lawyer; born in Pueblo, Colo., Sept. 21, 1900; s. Ben and Setta (Hirsh) B.; B.A., U. Wis., 1922; LL.B., Harvard, 1925; S.J.D., 1926; m. Dorothea Davis, June 24, 1929; children—George M., Anne D. Admitted to N.Y. bar, 1927; asso. firm Root, Clark Buckner & Ballantine and predecessor firms, N.Y.C., 1926-35; mem. firm. Lauterstein, Spiller & Bergerman, N.Y.C., 1935-46; v.p., gen. counsel, dir. C.I.T. Financial Corp., N.Y.C., 1946-62, also of Comml. Investment Trust, Inc., C.I.T. Corp., Universal C.I.T. Credit Corp., Service Fire Ins. Co., N.Y. Service Casualty Co. N.Y., Patriot Life Ins. Co.; dir. N. American Accident Ins. Co., The N. Am. Co. for Life, Accident and Health Ins., Picker X-Ray Corp. Member Am., N.Y. State bar assns., Am. Law Inst., Am. Judicature Soc., N.Y. County Lawyers Assn., Assn. Bar City N.Y. (treas. 1960-64). Home: New York City, N.Y. Died July 8, 1973; interred Roselawn Cemetery, Pueblo, Colo.

BERGIDA, JEROME JACOB, physician; b. Bklyn., Feb. 18, 1907; s. Adolf and Anne (Roth) B.; M.D., L.I. Coll. Medicine, 1932; m. Fannie Geshwind, Mar. 21, 1933; children-Joanne (Mrs. Laurence Norman Smith), Amy Lynn (Mrs. Michael Arnold Sobel). Intern, Med. Center, Jersey City, N.J., 1932-34; postgrad. work in otolaryngology, Postgrad. Hosp. of Columbia Coll. Phys. and Surgs., 1935-36; resident in otolaryngology Bklyn. Jewish Hosp., 1936-37; cons. in otolaryngology Bklyn. Jewish Hosp. and Med. Center, Unity Hosp.; attending in otolaryngology Kingsbrook Med. Center, Adelphi Hosp., Kings Hwy. Hosp., Flatbush Gen. Hosp. Served with M.C., USNR, 1942-46; capt. Res. ret. Diplomate Am. Bd. Otolaryngology. Fellow Am. Acad. Ophthalmology and Otolaryngology; mem. A.M.A., Assn. Mil. Surgeons U.S., Pan. Am. Med. Assn., Beta Sigma Rho, Phi Lambda Kappa. Jewish religion (trustee congregation). Co-author: Group Medicine and Health Insurance in Action, 1949; Understanding Surgery, 1955. Home: Brooklyn, N.Y. Died Mar. 11, 1974; buried Washington Cemetery, Brooklyn, N.Y.

BERGLAND, JOHN MCFARLAND, physician; b. West Point, N.Y., Mar. 5, 1879; s. Eric and Lucy Scott (McFarland) B.; B.S., Princeton, 1900; M.D., Johns Hopkins Univ., 1904; m. Alice Lloyd Pitts, June 5, 1902; children—John McFarland, Eric Lloyd. Interne and asst. resident in obstetrics, Johns Hopkins Hosp., 1904-06; interne, asst. and resident Hosp. for the Women of Md., Baltimore, 1910-11; pvt. practice in obstetrics, Balt., from 1911, partnership with Dr. Geo. W. Dobbin, 1915-26; asso. prof. of obstetrics, Univ. of Md. Sch. of Medicine from 1920; acting prof. of obstetrics and acting chief of service Johns Hopkins Univ. and Hosp., 1931-35, lectr. in clin. obstetrics from 1935; vis. obstetrician Johns Hopkins Hosp., Hosp. for the Women of Md., Union Memorial Hosp., Sinai Hosp., Ch. Home and Infirmary, from 1910; cons. obstetrics St. Joseph's Hosp. from 1935. Diplomate of the Am. Bd. of Gynecology and Obstetrics. Fellow Am. Coll. Surgeons, Assn. Obstetricians, Gynecologists, and Abdominal Surgeons, A.M.A. Mem. Southern Med. Assn., Med. and Chirurgical Faculty of Md. and Baltimore City Med. Soc. Democrat. Episcopalian. Clubs: Bachelors Cotillon, Maryland. Home: Baltimore, Md.†

BERGLUND, EVERETT RUDOLPH, dentist; b. nr. Haxtun, Colo., Aug. 3, 1915; s. J. Alfred and Hattie (Munson) B.; B.S., U. Colo., 1940; D.D.S., U. Kansas City, 1950; m. Gwendolyn B. Snyder, Jan. 3, 1948 (div. 1960); children—Allen Andrew, Karen Jay (Mrs. Michael E. Downing); m. 2d, Virginia I. Scheehser, Sept. 10, 1970. Practice dentistry, specializing in oral surgery, Denver, from 1946. Served to capt. AUS, 1940-46, U.S. Army, 1950-54. Mem. Am. Dental Assn., Pierre Fauchard Acad., Rocky Mountain Soc. Oral Surgeons, Am. Soc. Oral Surgeons, Psi Omega. Mason (Shriner). Home: Denver Col. Died Nov. 10, 1971.

BERITASHVILI, IVANE, (Beritov Ivan Solomonovich), physiologist; b. Village of Veczhini, Georgia, USSR, Dec. 29, 1884; grad. natural sci. dept. Physics and Math. Faculty, St. Petersburg U., 1910. With natural sci. dept. chair physiology St. Petersburg U., 1910-14; on sci. mission to Holland, worked in lab. of R. Magnus, 1914-15; sr. asst., dozent Novorosslysk U., Odessa, 1915-19; sci. leader Physiology Research Inst. of Georgian Acad. Sci.; dir. Physiol. Research Inst., Georgian Acad. Sci., 1941-51, also head dept. gen. physiology Inst. Physiology; prof. Tbilisi U., 1919—, head chair human and animal physiology, 1919-60, founder physiol. lab., 1920-22. Decorated Order of Lenin; recipient Pavlov prize, 1938, State prize, 1941; Sechenov prize, 1962. Mem. USSR, Georgian, N.Y. (hon.) acads. sci., Am. EEG Soc., Internat. Brain Orgn. (UNESCO), Soc. Biol. Psychiatry, Collegium Internationale Activitaties Nerrosae Superioris. Author over 300 works including The Theory of the Labyrinths and Cervical Tonic Reflexes, 1915; Essential Features of the Skeletal Musculature, 1916; Individually Acquired Activity of the Central Nervous Systems, 1932; General Physiology of the Muscular and Nervous Systems, 1922, rev., 1937, 2 vols., 1947-48, latest edit. pub. as Muscular System, Peripheral System (Somatic and Vegetative), Vol. 1, 1959, Spinal Cord and Brain Stem, Vol. 2, 1966, Structure and Function of the Cerebral Cortex, Vol. 3, 1969; Basic Forms of Nervous and Neuro-Psychic Activity, 1947; The Morphological and Physiological Principles of Temporary Connections in the Cortex of the Hemispheres, 1956; Neural Mechanisms of Spatial Orientation in High Vertebrate Animals, 1959; Neural Mechanisms of Higher Vetebrate Behavior, 1961; Memory of Vertebrate Animals, Its Characteristcs and Origin, 1968, rev. edit., 1974. Research on forms of nervous and psychic activity, muscular coordination, and physiological mechanism of behavior in higher vertebrates. Home: Tbilisi Georgian SSR, USSR., Died Dec. 29, 1974.

BERKE, MARK, hosp. adminstr.; b. London, Eng., Dec. 6, 1914; s. Morris and Miriam (Schwartz) B.; B.A., London U., 1935; m. Marcia Menchik, Aug. 4, 1940; children—David, Cynthia. Accountant, Hosp. for Joint Disease, N.Y.C., 1943-45; asst. dir. Mt. Sinai Hosp., Cleve., 1945-50; dir. Mt. Sinai Hosp., Phila., 1950-52; dir. Mt. Zion Hosp. and Med. Center, San Francisco, 1952-60, exec. v.p., from 1960. Cons., Council Hosp. Dental Services, Am. Dental Assn., from 1968; mem. adv. com. USPHS, from 1966. Fellow Am. Coll. Hosp. Adminstrs., Am. Pub. Health Assn.; mem. Am. Hosp. Assn. (past pres.), Assn. Western Hosps., Internat. Hosp. Fedn., Royal Soc. Health. Contbr. articles to profl. jours. Home: San Francisco, Cal., Deceased.

BERKELEY, BUSBY (WILLIAM BERKELEY ENOS), dance dir.; b. Los Angeles, Nov. 29, 1895. Started career on N.Y. stage, later joined Warner Bros.; joined MGM, 1939. Pictures include: 42nd Street, Footlight Parade, Hollywood Hotel, Men Are Such Fools, Broadway Serenade, Strike Up The Band, Fast and Furious, Ziegfeld Girl, For Me and My Gal, Gang's All Here, Cinderella Jones, Take Me Out to the Ball Game, Two Weeks with Love, Call Me Mister, Two Tickets to Broadway, Million Dollar Mermaid, Small Town Girl, Easy to Love, Rose Marie; supr. revival of No No Nanette, N.Y.C., 1971. Address: Palm Desert, Cal. Died Mar. 14, 1976.†

BERKELEY, JAMES PERCIVAL, clergyman; b. Salt Lake City, Utah, Jan. 21, 1879; s. James Eli and Annie Louise (Means) B.; B.A., Marietta (Ohio) Coll., 1905; B.D., Newton Theol. Instn., 1908; postgrad. work at same instn., Free Ch. Coll., Glasgow, Scotland, Manchester U., England Manchester Coll. (Oxford U.), and Harvard; D.D., Colby Coll., 1922, also from Marietta Coll. in 1935; m. Grace Isabel Lane, Oct. 28, 1908; children—James Lane, Austin West, Flinor Grace. Ordained Bapt. ministry, 1908; instr. N.T. dept., 1909-14, Turner fellow in Eng. and Scotland, 1914-15, asst. prof. O.T. and N.T. depts., 1915-19; instructor religious edn. Andover Newton Theol. School, 1919-51, prof. O.T., 1942-51, emeritus. Member Delta Upsilon, Phi Beta Kappa, Republican. Author: Jesus Our Leader; The Torch Bearers; The Two Ways; You Can Teach. Home: Newton Center, Mass.†

BERKMAN, ANTON HILMER, coll. dean; b. Round Rock, Tex., Apr. 10, 1897; s. Gustav August and Hilda Antionetta (Forsman) B.; B.A., U. Tex., 1924, M.A., 1926; Ph.D., U. Chgo., 1936. Asst. prof. biology Tex. A. and M. Coll., 1926-27; instr. botany U. Tex., summer 1927; asso. prof., head dept. biol. sci. Tex. Coll. Mines, 1927-35, acting dean arts and scis., 1934-45; faculty Tex. Western Coll. of U. Tex., 1935-72; prof. head. dept. biol. scis., 1935-61, acting dean grad. div., 1958-59, dean arts and scis., 1959-63, acting pres., summer 1960. Pres. El Paso Community Concert Assn., 1943-44. Bd. dirs. Tex. League Nursing, 1956-60. Served with U.S. Army, 1918-19. Recipient Minnie Stevens Piper Prof. award, 1966. Fellow A.A.A.S. (pres. S.W. and Rocky Mountain div. 1961-63); hon. life mem. Tex. Acad. Scis.; mem. Am. Bot. Soc., Soc. Am. Bacteriologists, Internat. Soc. Plant Morphologists, Am. Water Works Assn., N.E.A., Gamma Alpha, Phi Beta Pi, Phi Mu Alpha. Episcopalian. Home: Round Rock, Tex. Died May 14, 1973; buried Palm Valley Lutheran Cemetery, Round Rock.

BERKSON, MAURICE, lawyer; b. Rock Island, Ill., Jan. 15, 1880; s. Simon and Hannah (Sternberg) B.; student Chgo. Coll. Law, 1901; m. Maude May Gelder, July 28, 1907; children—Ethel May, John Stephen. Admitted to Ill. bar, 1901; partner Fishell & Berkson, Chgo., 1903-06, Sonnenschein, Blumenthal & Berkson, 1906-09, Sonnenschein, Berkson, Lautmann, Levinson & Morse, and predecessor, from 1909. Mem. Am., Ill. State, Chgo. bar assns. B'nai B'rith, Mason. Home: Encino, Cal.†

BERLA, JULIAN EMERSON, architect; b. Newark, Apr. 7, 1902; S.B., Mass. Inst. Tech., 1923. Draftsman, Bertram Goodhue & Assos., 1922, designer, 1925-29; draftsman Edward S. Hewitt, 1924-25; with U.S. Resettlement Adminstrn., 1936-37; with Berla & Abel, Washington, 1941—; cons. architect Dept. Commerce, 1937-39, U.S. Housing Authority, 1938-40, U.S. Golden Gate Commn., 1939, Bldg. Ministry, Kingdom of Denmark, 1951-52, 53-54; cons. Denmark embassy Washington, 1954-76, lectr. N.Y.U., 1930-32, N.Y. Met. Mus. Art, 1931; archtl. critic Mass. Inst. Tech., 1958-63; archtl. lectr. and critic U. Va., 1963-76. Mem. design adv. panel Dept. Housing and Community Devel., Bait. Fellow A.I.A. (pres. Washington chpt. to 1948). Address: Washington, D.C., Died Feb. 16, 1976*

BERNARD, JOSEPH ALPHONSUS, govt. ofcl.; born Sea Cow Pond, P.E.I., Mar. 27, 1881; s. Theodore and Ann (Perry) B.; student Chrisitian Bros., Amawalk, N.Y.; Union Comml. Coll., Charlottetown, P.E.I., 1906; m. Zoe Chiasson, Sept. 21, 1909; children—Letitia. R.N. (wife of Eric C. Loth, M.D.), Joan of Arc (wife of James Higgins, D.V.S.), Marcelia (Mrs. J. A. Gallant), Gloria, Edith, R.N., Norma, R.N. Streetcar conductor, Boston, 1906-09; retail bus. Tignish, P.E.I., 1911-45; bookkeeper, Morris Bernard & Co., 1940, pres., 1940-45; lt. gov., Canada, 1945-50; mem. Parliament, 1943-45. Mem. St. Thomas Aquinas Soc., Liberal Assn. (v.p., 1920-43). K.C. Club: Charlottetown. Home: Tignish, Prince Edward Island, Can.†

BERNARDY, AMY ALLEMAND, author; b. at Florence, Italy, Jan. 16, 1880; d. Hon. S. and Rosine (Allemand) B.; ed. univs. of Florence and Rome, Italy; Litt.D., 1901, Dr. of Palaeography and Diplomatics, 1902, U. of Florence); unmarried. Prof. Italian, Smith Coll. from 1903. Contbr. various newspapers and mags., U.S. and Italy and to encys. Identified with emigration and immigration study movement in Italy and U.S. Translater: (into Italian) Carnegie's Gospel of Wealth, 1903; Empire of Business, 1903. Author of several books in Italian. Address: Northampton, Mass.†

BERNET KEMPERS, KAREL PHILLIPUS, musicologist; b. Nijkerk, Netherlands, 1897; ed. U. Munich; m. Gertrude D. Boursse, 1934; 2 daus. Prof. history of music Royal Conservatory, The Hague, 1929-49; prof. Amsterdam Conservatory, 1934-53; pvt. tchr. U. Amsterdam, 1929-37, lectr. musicology, 1937-46, prof., 1946-68; sec. Royal Netherlands Soc. Musicians, 1934-41, chmn., 1945-65, hon. pres., 1965; v.p. Netherlands Council Musicians, 1950-65; mem. council Concertgebouw Orch., 1956-68. Decorated officer Order Oranje Nassau, knight Order Netherlands Lion. Mem. Internat. Musicological Soc. (pres. cons. com.), Mahler Soc. (pres. Dutch sect.), Dutch Mozart Soc. (hon.). Author: Jacobus Clemens non Papa und seine Motetten, 1928; De Italiaanse Opera van Peri tot Puccini, 1929; Muziekgeschiedenis, 1932; Muziek in de ban der letteren, 1935; Beknopte geschiedenis van het kerklied (with G. v. d. Leeuw), 1948; Meesters der muziek, 1948. Editor: Complete works of Clemens non Papa, 21 vols., 1972; (with Chris Maas) The Leyden Choirbooks, 1970. Address: Amsterdam, Netherlands. Died Sept. 30, 1974; interred The Hague, Netherlands.

BERNO, JACK CHARLES, physician; b. Cuyahoga Falls, O., Sept. 3, 1920; s. Robert J. and Helen (Frank) B.; M.D., Western Res. U., 1945; m. Marilynn Miller, June 12, 1945; children—Jack, Melissa. Intern, Cleve. City Hosp., 1945-46, asst. resident, 1948-49; jr. resident Crile VA Hosp., Cleve., 1949-50, asst. resident, 1950-51, resident, 1951-52, chief resident, 1952-53; mem. surg. staff, sec. Chillicothe (O.) Hosp., also chief staff. Served as lt. (j.g.), M.C., USNR, 1946-48. Diplomate Am. Bd. Surgery. Fellow A.C.S.; mem. A.M.A., Chillicothe C. of C. (past pres.). Episcopalian. Club: Sunset. Home: Chillicothe, O. Died Mar. 20, 1973; buried Grandview Cemetery, Chillicothe, O.

BEROL, ALFRED C., pencil mfr.; b. N.Y.C., Oct. 5, 1892; s. Emil and Gella (Goldsmith) B.; student Phillips Exeter Acad., 1909; A.B., Harvard, 1913; m. Madeleine Rossin, May 4, 1922; 1 son, Kenneth. Chmn., dir. Berol Corp., Eagle Pencil Co., N.Y.C., London, Eng., Mexico City, Montreal, Que., Can., Bogata, Colombia, Caracas, Venezuela, Danbury, Conn., Blaisdell All-Rite, Fair-Lawn, N.J.; chmn., dir. Elkins Sawmill, Inc., Anderson, Cal., Hudson Lumber Co., San Leandro, Cal. Mem. Pencil Makers Assn. (pres.). Home: New York City NY. Died June 14, 1974.

BERRETH, HERBERT RAYMOND, optometrist; b. Selby, S.D., Jan. 27, 1931; s. Gottfried and Josephine (Bohle) B.; B.A., Whitman Coll., 1956; O.D., Pacific U., 1960; m. Marjorie Putman, Feb. 7, 1960; children—Suzanne, Sandra. Clin. asst. Pacific U. Coll. Optometry, Forest Grove, Ore., 1961; asso. practice optometry, Corvallis, Ore., 1962-64, Albany, 1965; partner, Astoria, Ore., 1966, owner, from 1967. Served with USCGR, 1951-54. Mem. Am., Ore. (Pres.'s award 1970) optometric assns., Assn. Optometric Editors (past pres.), Astoria Regatta Assn., Toastmasters, C. of C. (sr. v.p., George award 1971). Presbyn. (elder). Republican. Lion. Editor Ore. Optometrist, 1963-68. Home: Astoria Ore. Died Feb. 2, 1972.

BERREY, RHODES CLAY, bldg. materials co. exec.; b. Mexico, Mo., Apr. 24, 1911. Vice pres. transp. and phys. distbn. U.S. Gypsum Co., Chgo. Home: Palatine, Ill. Died Aug. 29, 1973; interred Elm Lawn Cemetery, Elmhurst, Ill.

BERREY, RUTH ROBERTSON, physician; b. Clayton, Ala., Aug. 29, 1906; d. William Henry and Mary (Foster) Robertson; student Judson Coll., 1921-22; A.B., U. Ala., 1926; M.D., Tulane U., 1928; m. Ivan C. Berrey, Aug. 27, 1928; children—Anne (Mrs. McKeller Townes), William Selden, Alice (Mrs. James D. Pruett). Intern Charity Hosp., New Orleans, 1928-29; physician outpatient dept. Children's Hosp., Buffalo, 1932-37; med. supr. Ala. Nat. Youth Adminstrn., 1940-41; asst. prof. biology Howard Coll., Birmingham, Ala., 1943-45; asst. prof. pediatrics U. Ala. Med. Coll. at Birmingham, 1948, asso. prof., 1948-63; asso. missionary So. Bapt. Conv., Nigeria, 1958-61, 63-66; county health officer Barbour and Macon counties, Clayton, Ala., from 1966; cons. child health Jefferson County Health Dept., Birmingham, 1941-63; mem. staff Children's Hosp., Univ. Hosp., Bapt. Hosp. (all Birmingham). Diplomate Am. Bd. Pediatrics. Fellow Am. Acad. Pediatrics; mem. Ala. Pediatric Soc. (pres. 1947), Chi Omega. Baptist. Club: Zonta (Birmingham). Home: Clayton Ala. Died July, 23, 1973.

BERRY, CHARLES SCOTT, univ. prof.; b. Hamlin, Brown Co., Kan., May 23, 1875; s. Joseph Festus and Julia Maria (Parmley) B.; A.B., Hiram (O.) Coll., 1903; A.M., Harvard, 1905, Ph.D., 1907; studied U. of Berlin, 1907-08; m. Edna May Reed, Aug. 25, 1917; 1 son, Reed Parmley. Traveling fellow Harvard, 1907-08; asst. prof. end., U. of Mich., 1908-15, asso. prof., 1915-19, prof. ednl. psychology, 1919-30; dir. psychol. clinic, Detroit pub. schs., 1919-20, dir. spl. edn., 1920-29; consultant in spl. edn., Detroit, 1929-30; now dir. Bur. of special and Adult Education and prof. psychology, Ohio State U. Chmn. Com. on Special Classes, White House Conf., 1930. Served as capt., later major Sanitary Corps, U.S. Army, Nov. 1917-Oct. 1, 1919. Fellow A.A.A.S.; mem. Am. Psychol. Assn., N.E.A., Nat. Com. for Mental Hygiene, Am. Assn. Social Workers, Nat. Soc. for Study of Edn., Phi Delta Kappa. Mem. Christian (Disciples) Ch. Home: Columbus, O.†

BERRY, JAMES BERTHOLD, educator; b. Edwardsville, Ill., Aug. 2, 1880; s. James Frederick and Fanny (Meyer) B.; grad. Sch. of Agr., U. of Minn., 1908; B.S.F., U. of Minn., 1910; M.S.A., Pa. State Coll., 1913; studied U. of Munich, Mich. Agrl. Coll., Cornell U.; m. Gladys Elizabeth Jones, of Wilkes Barre, Pa., Dec. 26, 1914; 1 son, James B. Farming, 1897-1901, 1905-08; with St. Paul (Minn.) Rubber Co., 1901-05; forest asst., U.S. Forest Service, 1910-11; instr. in forestry, Pa. State Coll., 1911-13; prof. forestry, 1914-17, prof. plant pathology and forestry, 1917-20, U. of Ga., also dir. Ga. State Forest Sch., 1914-20; state leader of extension projects in forestry and plant pathology; county vocational supervisor, Pa. State Dept. Pub. Instrn. from 1920. Collaborator of U.S. Plant Disease Survey; collaborator Botanical Abstracts. Sec. for Ga. of Wood Fuel Dept., U.S. Fuel Adminstration, 1917-19. Pres. Dept. of Vocational Edn., Pa. State Edn. Assn., 1925. Mem. A.A.A.S., Am. Soc. Genetics, Am. Forestry Assn., Am. Phytopathol. Soc., Nat. Soc. for Vocational Edn. Progressive. Presbyn. Mason, Odd Fellow. Author: Farm Woodlands; Northern Woodlot Trees; Southern Woodland Trees; Western Forest Trees; Methods of Teaching Agriculture. Home: Meadville, Pa.†

BERRY, JOSEPH FRANCIS, lawyer; b. Boston, Feb. 13, 1880; s. Charles F. and Emily C. (Morgan) B.; A.B., Tufts Coll., 1901; LL.B., Harvard, 1904; m. Mildred E. Fowle, Dec. 5, 1908; 1 son, Richard Francis. Admitted to Mass. bar, 1904, and practiced Boston, asso. Choate, Hall & Stewart, 1904-07; atty. for N.Y., N.H. & H. R.R. Co. and subsidiaries, New Haven, Conn., 1907-19; gen. practice, mem. firm Day, Berry & Howard, Hartford, Conn., from 1919. Mem. Am. Bar Assn. (bd. govs. 1942-45), Am. Judicature Soc. (bd. dirs.). Home: West Hartford, Conn.†

BERRY, MARK PERRIN LOWREY, college pres.; b. Blue Mountain, Miss., Aug. 22, 1878; s. William Edwin (D.D.) and Modena (Lowrey) B.; student Blue Mountain Coll., 1896-98; Ph.B., Mississippi Coll., 1903; m. Mary Wyatt Gregory, of Prentiss, Miss., Sept. 7, 1903; children—Lowrey Halbert (dec.), Edwina (Mrs. William Harold Cox). Began as mgr. brick yard, 1900; bus. mgr. Blue Mountain Coll., 1903-08, teacher, 1905-08; registrar Miss. Coll., 1908-11; registrar Hillman Coll., 1911-15, v.p., 1915-23, pres. from 1923. Pres. State Bd. of Ministerial Edn.; ex-pres. Miss. Assn. of Colleges. Democrat. Home: Clinton, Miss.†

BERRY, MERVIN ALBERT, physician; b. Pampa, Tex., Jan. 14, 1940; s. Albert Eura and Bessie Mae (Chatwell) B.; B.S., W. Tex. State U., 1962; M.D., U. Tex., 1965; m. Kathleen Ann Knox, Dec. 27, 1966; 1 son, Robb Marvin. Intern, John Peter Smith Hosp., Fort Worth, 1965-66; gen. practice resident, 1966-67; gen. practice medicine Pampa (Tex.) Clinic, 1967-68, Lubbock, Tex., from 1971; dir. dept. gen. practice and emergency services John Peter Smith Hosp., Fort Worth, 1968-71. Mem. Fort Worth Emergency Med. Services Com., 1970; med. cons. Fort Worth Fire Dept., 1970-71; coordinator emergency med. technician-ambulance course Tarrant County Jr. Coll., 1970-71; instr. cardiopulmonary resuscitation Lubbock Dept. Pub. Safety and Fire Dept., 1971. Served to capt. M.C., USAFR, 1966-71. Recipient award for leadership S.A.R., 1961. Service award Fort Worth Fire Dept., 1971. Diplomate Am. Bd. Family Practice. Mem. Am. Acad. Family Practice, A.M.A., Am. Coll. Emergency Physicians, Tex. Acad. Gen. Practice, Tex. Med. Assn., Tarrant County, Lubbock-Garza-Crosby med. socs.,

Am. Rifle Assn., Red Helmets, Kappa Alpha, Phi Chi, Alpha Chi. Mem. Ch. of Christ. Home: Lubbock Tex. Died Sept. 8, 1971.

BERRY, NIXON T., lawyer; b. Caledonia, Ont., Can., Oct. 15, 1905; grad. U. Toronto, Osgooode Hall. Admitted to Ont. bar, 1931; partner frim McMillan, Binch, Toronto. Mem. Canadian Bar Assn. Home: Toronto, Ont., Can. Died Jan. 2, 1975.

BERTALANFFY, LUDWIG VON, biologist; b. Atzgerdorf, Austria, Sept. 19, 1901; s. Gustav and Charlotte (Vogl) von B.; student U. Innsbruck Vienna, Austria; Ph.D., U. Vienna, 1926; m. Maria M. Bauer, 1925; 1 son, Felix D. Faculty, U. Vienna, 1934-48; prof., dir. biol. research dept. U. Ottawa (Ont., Can.), 1949-54; dir. biol. research Mt. Sinai Hosp., vis. prof. U. So.Cal., Los Angeles, 1955-58; Sloan vis. prof., mem. research dept. Menninger Found., Topeka, 1958-60; prof. theoretical biology, then Univ. prof. U. Alta., Edmonton, Can., 1961-69; Faculty prof. State U. N.Y. at Buffalo, 1969-72. Fellow, Notgemeinschaft der Deutschen Wissenschaft, 1930-32, Rockefeller Found., 1937-38, Lady Davis Found., 1949, Center for Advanced Study in Bahavioral Scis., Stanford, Cal., 1954-55, others. Fellow Am. Psychiat. Assn. (hon.), Internat. Acad. Cytology, A.A.A.S.; mem. Soc. for Gen. Systems Research (founder, life mem., v.p. 1956-60), Canadian Physiol. Soc. (emeritus), Deutsche Akademie der Naturforscher. Author numerous books including: Modern Theories of Development, 1928, 33, 62; Theoretische Biologie, 2 vols., 1932, 42, 51; Problems of Life, 1949, 52, 60; Robots, Men and Minds, 1967; General System Theory, 1968. Editor: Handbuch der Biologie, 1942; (with A. Rapoport) General Systems, 1956. Contbr. articles to sci. jours. on gen. and theoretical biology, physiology, cytology, behavior, system theory, history and philosophy of sci. Home: Williamsville, N.Y. Died June 12, 1972; buried Notre-Dame de Neiges Cemetery, Montreal, Que., Can.

BERWIN, FRANKLIN, steamship exec.; b. Boston, Dec. 3, 1881; s. Jacob and Mathilde (Aborn) B.; student pvt. schs., Boston, also Eng.; m. Irma Freeman, Feb. 25, 1902; 1 dau., Virginia (Mrs. Jose David). Member of the board directors Colorado Fuel & Iron Corp. Clubs: Deepdale Golf (gov., Manhasset, L.I.); National Golf Links of America (Southampton, L.I.); Downtown Athletic (life mem. N.Y.C.); Seminole (Palm Beach, Fla.). Home: New York City, N.Y.†

BESOSA, HARRY FELIPE, lawyer; b. Brooklyn, N.Y., Apr. 24, 1881; s. Manuel and Fruta (Melero) B.; grad. common schs., Brooklyn, 1897; m. Maria Caballero, Sept. 15, 1900; children—Harry Manuel, Nydia Maria, Howard Manuel. Interpreter to chief Quartermaster, United States Army, Puerto Rico, 1898; mgr. Ponce office Dooley, Smith & Co., 1900-02; in brokerage business, 1902-06; sec. Chamber of Commerce of P.R., 1906-12; gen. agent Nat. Surety Co., 1907-33, resident v.p. and counsel, 1921-33; admitted to P.R. bar, 1910; gen. agent and resident vice pres. Am. Surety Co., 1933. Mem. Rep. Nat. Com., 1928-32; U.S. dist. atty. for P.R., 1932-33; atty. city of San Juan, April 1937-April 1939. Rep. cdidate for P.R. Senate, 1924; apptd. State dir. Selective Service for Puerto Rico by President Roosevelt, Oct. 16, 1940. Called to active service as lt. colonel, Judge Advocate Gen., AUS, and assigned to duty with Selective Service as state dir. for Puerto Rico, 1942; promoted to grade of col., 1943. Commd. 1st lieutenant U.S. Army, 1918; maj. judge adv. P.R. Nat. Guard. Mem. Am. Bar Assn., P.R. Bar Assn. (treas. 1920), Federal Bar Assn. of P.R. (v.p. 1919), Res. Officers Assn., Am. Legion (an organizer; comdr. P.R. Post 1919), Ateneo Puertorriqueno. Protestant. Elk. Clubs: Casino de P.R., Union, Rotary, Optimist Club (pres. 1943-44). Wrote "Brief Outline of Procedure of Trials before Summary Courts" for Nat. Guard of P.R. Home: Santurce, San Juan, P.R.†

BETELLE, JAMES O., architect; b. Wilmington, Del., Apr. 1, 1879; s. John W. and Annie (Barton) B.; ed. in pub. schs. and by pvt. instrn., U.S. and Europe; m. Marie Louise Cohan, 1932. Began independent practice of architecture with firm Guilbert & Betelle, 1910; specialized in design of schs., pub. bldgs.; served as cons. architect for schs. erected in Charleston, S.C., Augusta, Ga., Berkeley, Calif., Westbury, L.I., Scranton, Pa.; mem. adv. bd. of architects which passed on bldgs. erected for Institutions in State of N.J.; designer and supervisor building of 56 high schs., including Greenwich, Conn., New Rochelel, N.Y., Baker, Tuxedo Park, N.Y., Great Neck, L.I.; disigner 9 state colls., including Trenton, N.J., New Britain, Conn., also 300 grade schs., including 125 in Del. (gift of Pierre S. Dupont). Trustee Newark Mus. of Art., 1926-39. Fellow A.I.A. (dir. 1932-35); mem. Newark C. of C. (pres. 1926-27). Author numerous mag. articles and pamphlets on sch. bldg. design and architecture.

BETHEA, OSCAR WALTER, physician; b. Marion County, S.C., Apr. 27, 1878; s. William Walter and Sallie Eugenia (Morrison) B.; Ph.G., Atlanta College Pharmacy, 1901; M.D., Tulane U., 1911; Ph.M., Phila. Coll. Sci. and Pharmacy, 1934; m. Ruby Mae Hardee, Aug. 28, 1907; children—Theodore Wood, June Hardee, Ruby Mae (wife of Rev. Leland W. Kuns). Prof. pharmacology Miss. Med. Coll., 1906-09; began practice at New Orleans, 1911; prof. med. emeritus Sch. of Medicine, Tulane U.; sr. physician So. Bapt. Hosp. New Orleans; cons. physician Charity Hosp. Mem. revision com., United States Pharmacopoeia, 1930-40. Contract surgeon and examiner, Selective Draft, World War I; member Appeal board No. 1, World War II. Diplomate Am. Bd. Internal Medicine. Fellow A.C.P., A.A.A.S., Chem. Soc. (Great Britain), Am. Therapeutic Soc. (past pres.); mem. A.M.A., Am. Heart Assn., So. Med. Assn., New Orleans Academy Internal Medicine, La. Med. Soc., Orleans Parish Medical Soc., New Orleans Acad. Sci., Alpha Omega Alpha, Alpha Kappa Kappa, Beta Phi Sigma. Rotarian. Mem. Presbyn. Mason (32°, Shriner). Author: Materia Medica, Drug Adminstration and Prescription Writing, 1915, 5th edit., 1938; Clinical Medicine, 1928. Editor: Year Book of Therapeutics, 1940-48. Pub. over 100 med. papers including the presentation of new instruments, original diagnostic measures, etc. Home: New Orleans, La.†

BETTS, ROME ABEL, health assn. exec.; b. Summit, N.J., Aug. 17, 1903; s. Romeo Thompson and Eva Marion (Abel) B.; A.B., Amherst Coll., 1925; M.A., Columbia, 1929; m. Ruth Robbins, Oct. 1, 1927; children—Eve Robin, Priscilla. Tchr. Lance Sch., Summit, 1930-33, Summit High Sch., 1933-36; sec. Am. Bible Soc., 1936-42, gen. sec., 1942-48; exec. dir. Am. Heart Assn., 1949-68; exec. v.p. Internat. Cardiology Found., N.Y.C., 1969-70; sec.-gen. Internat. Fedn. Multiple Sclerosis Socs., N.Y.C., from 1970. Pres. Protestant Film Commn., 1946-51; pres. broadcasting, film commn. Nat. Council Chs., 1958-59, chmn. finance com., 1960-68; pres. YMCA, Summit, 1943, United Campaign, Summit, 1942. Mem. Common Council, Summit, 1940-49, pres., 1947-48. Mem. Nat. Health Council (sec. 1953-54, chmn. exec. com. 1958-59, pres. 1963-64), Am. Bible Soc. (bd. mgrs.) Delta Upsilon. Republican. Baptist. Home: Summit, N.J. Died May 10, 1973; buried Meml. Garden of Christ Ch., Summit, N.J.

BETTY, FRANK F., lawyer; b. Rock Island County, Ill., July 22, 1880; student Normal Sch., Valparaiso, Ind.; LL.B., U. Mich., 1906. Admitted to Mich. bar, 1906, Ia. bar, 1906; partner firm Betty, Neuman, Heninger, Van Der Kamp & McMahon. Davenport, Ia.; city atty., Davenport, 1918-20. Mem. Am., Ia., Scott County bar assns.†

BEVAN, RALPH HERVEY, publicist; b. Providence, R.I., July 21, 1881; s. Alexander and Emma Rosanna (Mason) B.; descendant of Roger Williams; A.B., Brown University, 1904; Rhodes scholar from Rhode Island, at Oxford University, 1904-07, B.C.L. in Jurisprudence, Roman and English law, 1906; student Am. law, 1907-14; has specialized in application of reason in faith, religion and philosophy, and in progressive interpretation of unifying principles fof the promotion of peace and happiness among men. Advocate for scientific measures for progress, especially of internat. universities for the fraternizing and professional training of prospective world leaders; had papers read on international universities at first world conference on education,1923. Mem. Com. on Feasibility of a World Univ. of World Federation of Edn. assns., 1924-25; mem. Phi Beta Kappa, Delta Upsilon. Contbr. to Outlook, Advocate of Peace (Am. Peace Soc.), Forum, Am. Ednl. Digest, etc. Address: Providence, R.I.†

BEYMER, WILLIAM GILMORE, author; b. Chambersburg, Pa., Aug. 14, 1881; s. Hervey Winthrop and Mary H. (Nixon) B.; ed. pub. schs., Allegheny and Parnassus, Pa.; student Chambersburg (Pa.) Acad., 1897-98, Stanford U., 1903-05, N.Y. Sch. of Art (William M. Chase Sch.), 1905-07; m. Jean M. Hayward, June 18, 1907; children—Jean Gilmore (wife of Lt. Comdr. George Cook, U.S.N.R.), Marybel (Mrs. Malcolm Hall). As artist, exhibited at Nat. Acad. of Design and at Kensington Garden, London, Eng., 1906-07; staff writer, especially Civil War articles and period fiction, Harper's Mag., 1909-11; lecturer on short story and scenairo writing, U. of Calif. extension div., Los Angeles, 1920-25; city editor Los Angeles bureau Associated Press, 1928; tech. adviser for Am. hist. and period pictures to major motion picture studios, 1933-42; instr. Army Air Force Tech. Training Sch. (civilian contract sch.), 1943; Lockheed P-38 assembly line, 1943-44. Republican. Presbyterian. Club: Authors (Hollywood). Author: On Hazardous Service, 1912; 12:20 P.M. (also serialized in Saturday Evening Post), 1944; The Middle of Midnight (novel), 1947 (Armed Forces edit.). Contbr. of Civil War fiction and general fiction to nationally known mags. for many years. Home: Los Angeles, Cal.†

BEZANSON, PHILIP THOMAS, educator, composer; b. Athol, Mass., Jan. 6, 1916; s. Claude Edward and Blanche (Redden) B.; Mus.B., Yale, 1940; M.A., U. Ia., 1948, Ph.D., 1951; m. Lillian Elizabeth Carlson, Nov. 28, 1940; children—Carol Ann (Mrs. William Arthur Garrabrant), Thomas Edward. Instr., U. Ia., 1948-51, asst. prof., 1951-54, asso. prof., 1954-61, prof. composition, 1961-64; head music dept. U. Mass., Amherst, 1964-73, prof., 1964-75. Chmn. music screening com. Internat. Exchange of Persons, Washington, 1968-70. Mem. Mass. Council on Arts and Humanities, 1966-69. Served with USNR, 1945-46. Bezanson Recital Hall U. Mass. named in his honor. Guggenheim fellow, 1967-68. Mem. Am. Composers Alliance, Yale Sch. Music Alumni Assn. (certificate of merit award 1974). Publns. include: Prelume and Dance for Brass Sextet, 1961; String Quartet No. 1, 1965; Diversion for Brass Trio, 1968. Composer: Piano Concerto, N.Y. Philharmonic Symphony Orch., 1953; Opera, Golden Child, NBC-TV, Hallmark Hall of Fame, 1960; Sinfonia Concertante commd. by U. Ia., 1972; also solo, chamber, vocal, orchestral works. Home: Hadley, Mass. Died Mar. 11, 1975; buried Hadley.

BIANCHI-BANDINELLI, RANUCCIO, archeologist; b. Siena, Italy, Feb. 19, 1900; s. Mario and Lily (von Korn) B.; Dr. Humanities, U. Rome, 1923; Dr.H.C., U. Berlin, U. Jena, U. Brussels; m. Maria Garrone, Mar. 2, 1924; children—Martha (Mrs. Cy David Steg), Sandra (Mrs. Ruggero Boscu). Prof. classical archeology U. Groningen (Netherlands), 1931-33, U. Pisa (Italy), 1934-37, U. Florence (Italy), 1938-45, 50-56, U. Rome (Italy), 1957-64; dir. gen. Antiquities and Arts, 1945-48; pres. Instituto Antonio Gramsci, Rome, Studies Marxism, 1960-71. Decorated chevalier de la Legion d'Honneur. Author: Hellenistic-byzantine Miniaturns of the Iliad, 1955; Archeologia e Cultura, 1961; The Buried City; Leptis Magna, 1964; Rome, le Centre du Pouvoir, 1969; La Fin de l'Art de l'Antiquitié, 1970, Les Etrusques et l'Italie avant Rome, 1973, L'Italia Storica e Artistice allo Sbaraglio, 1974. Editor: Enciclopedia dell'Arte Antica, 1958-66, Dialoghi di Archeologia, 1967-75. Address: Rome, Italy. Died Jan. 17, 1975.

BIANCO, MARGERY WILLIAMS (MRS. FRANCESCO BIANCO), author; b. London, Eng., July 22, 1881; d. Robert and Florence (Harper) Williams; ed. pvtly. and at Sharon Hill, nr. Phila., Pa.; m. Francesco Bianco, of Turin, Italy, 1904; children—Cecco Marco, Pamela. Author: The Late Returning, 1902; The Price of Youth, 1904; The Bar, 1906; (books for children) The Velveteen Rabbit, 1922; Poor Cecco, 1925; The Little Wooden Doll, 1925; The Apple Tree, 1926; The Skin Horse, 1927; The Adventures of Andy, 1927.†

BICKEL, ALEXANDER MORDECAI, educator, lawyer; b. Bucharest, Rumania, Dec. 17, 1924; s. Solomon and Yetta (Schafer) B.; brought to U.S., 1939, naturalized, 1943; B.S., Coll. City N.Y., 1947; LL.B., Harvard, 1949; M.A. (hon.), Yale, 1960; m. Josephine Ann Napolino, Oct. 17, 1959; children—Francesca Ann, Claudia Rose. Admitted to Mass. bar, 1950, U.S. Supreme Ct. bar, 1959; law clk. to chief judge U.S. Ct. Appeals, Boston, 1949-50; law officer State Dept., 1950-52; law clk. to U.S. Supreme Ct. Justice Frankfurter, 1952-53; spl. asst. to dir. policy planning staff State Dept., 1953-54; research asso. Harvard, 1954-56; faculty Yale Law Sch., 1956-74, prof., 1960-66, also mem. history faculty and Chancellor Kent prof. law and legal history, 1966-74, William Clyde DeVane prof., 1971-74. Cons. sub-com. on separation powers Senate Com. on Judiciary, 90th-93d Congresses; Holmes lectr. Harvard Law Sch., 1969. Served with AUS, 1943-45. Guggenheim fellow, fellow Center for Advanced Study in Behavorial Scis., 1970-71; decorated Combat Infantryman's badge. Mem. Am. Acad. Arts and Scis. Author: The Unpublished Opinions of Mr. Justice Brandeis, 1957; The Least Dangerous Branch, 1962; Politics and the Warren Court, 1965; The Supreme Court and the Idea of Progress, 1970; Reform and Continuity, 1971. Contbg. editor New Republic, 1957-74. Home: New Haven Conn. Died Nov. 7, 1974.

BICKNELL, WARREN, JR., ret. constrn. exec.; b. Wheaton, Ill., Sept. 5, 1902; s. Warren and Anne Sabra (Guthrie) B.; A.B., Williams Coll., Williamstown, Mass., 1925; m. Kate Benedict Hanna, Nov. 4, 1931; children—Constance Hanna (Mrs. Reynolds), Kate Hanna (Mrs. Kirkham), Wendy Hanna, Warren III. Pres., The Cleve. Constrn. Co., 1940-71; dir. Soc. Nat. Bank of Cleve., Hanna Mining Co. Trustee, pres. Cherokee Found.; trustee John D. Archibald Hosp., Western Res. Acad., Hudson, O., Greater Cleve. council Boy Scouts Am. Mem. Delta Kappa Epsilon. Clubs: Fifty (Cleve.); Glen Arvin Country (Thomasville, Ga.); Chagrin Valley Hunt, Union, Tavern, Kirtland Country, Killearn. Home: Chardon, Oh. Died Apr. 23, 1975; interred Thomasville, Ga.

BIDDLE, GEORGE, painter, sculptor; b. Phila., Jan. 24, 1885; s. Algernon Sydney and Frances (Robinson) B.; grad. Groton Sch., 1904; A.B., Harvard, 1908, LL.B., 1911; m. Anne Coleman, 1917 (div.); m. 2d, Jane Belo, 1925 (div.); m. 3d, Helene Sardeau, Apr. 1931; 1 son. Michael John. Over 100 one-man shows Paris, Vienna, Rome, Mexico City, Tokyo, New Delhi. Bombay, Calcutta, most Am. cities; commd. with Helene Sardeau to execute fresco and sculpture Supreme Ct. Bldg., Mexico City; commd. to execute fresco Nat. Library, Rio de Janeiro; assisted inauguration fed. art projects, 1933; executed murals Justice Bldg., Washington; chmn. art adv. com. War Dept., sent to N. Africa to assist with pictorial war record, 1943; painter-mem. art adv. com. State Dept.; mem. Fine Arts Commn., 1950; retrospective exhbn. of prints circulated by U.S. Information Agy., Japan, Italy, India, other European countries; works in permanent collections, museums U.S., Berlin, Mexico City, Modern Mus., Tokyo, Butler Inst. Am. Art, Fogg Art Mus., Corcoran Gallery Fine Arts, Walter E. Chyrsler collection. Mem. Nat. Coms. for an Effective Congress. Served from 1st lt. to capt.

U.S. Army, World War I. Recipient art award, fellowship Huntington Hartford Found., 1954; art award Edward MacDowell Colony, 1956; purchase prize Brandeis U. Mem. Soc. Painters, Gravers and Sculptors (v.p. 1934), Nat. Soc. Mural Painters (pres. 1935), Mural Artists Guild (pres. 1937-38), Nat. Soc. Arts and Letters (v.p. 1962). Club: Century. Author: (text and illustrations) Green Island, 1930; American Artist's Story. 1936; Artist at War, 1944; George Biddle's War Drawings, 1944; The Yes and No of Contemporary Art, 1957; (text and drawings) Indian Impressions, 1960; Tahitian Journal, 1968. Contbr. to mags. Home: Cronton-on-Huston N.Y. Died Nov. 6, 1973.

BIENSTOCK, DAVID PAUL, mus. curator; b. N.Y.C., June 27, 1943; s. Abraham and Charlotte (Panish) B.; B.A., Coll. City N.Y., 1965; M.A., N.Y. U., 1968. Ind. filmmaker, N.Y.C., 1966-68; tchr. English and drama Brandels High Sch., N.Y.C., 1968-70: prof. film Pace Coll., N.Y.C., 1970; curator film Whitney Mus. Am. Art, N.Y. C., 1970-73. Dir. films Nothing Happened This Morning, 1965, Brummer's, 1967. Recipient 1st prize exptl. film Chgo. Film Festival, 1965, 1st prize Ann Arbor (Mich.) Film Festival, 1965. Home: New York City N.Y. Died July 24, 1973.

BIGELOW, ALBERT FRANCIS, lawyer, trustee; born Oct. 4, 1880; s. Albert S. and Mary (DeFord) B.; A.B., Harvard, 1903, LL.B., 1906; m. Gwladys Williams, Feb. 18, 1903; children—Martha W., Albert S., Jr., Hugh W., Gladys. Admitted to Boston bar, 1906; practiced Boston, 1906-14; indsl. management, 1914-18; asst. to pres. Ludlow Mfg. & Sales Co. from 1920. Served as capt. U.S. Air Service, 1918-19. Rep. Mass. Legislature, 1927-46, chmn. ways and means com., 1931-44; overseer Harvard College, 1934-40; v.p., trustee Bd. of Investment, Franklin Savings Bank; pres. Boston Legal Aid Soc., 1923-44; trustee Brookline Public Library; mem. Brookline Limited Town Meeting from 1916. Chmn. Brookline Branch Boston Chapter Am. Red 1943-47. Club: Tavern. Mason. Home: Chestnut Hill, Mass.†

BIGELOW, JOHN OGDEN, judge; b. Newark, Sept. 30, 1883; s. Moses and Lila R. (Fowler) B.; A.B., Princeton, 1905; m. Elizabeth Simpson, Aug. 15, 1918; children—John Ogden (killed in action, 1944), Elizabeth (Mrs. J. Keith Stewart), William Simpson. Admitted to N.J. bar, 1908; in practice at Newark, 1908-29; prosecutor of pleas, Essex County, 1922-26; counsel Pub. Utility Commn. of N.J., 1927-29; vice chancellor of N.J., 1930-48; judge of appellate div., Superior Ct., N.J., 1948-53. Served A.U.S., World War I, retiring with rank of capt. Mem. Bd. Foreign Missions, Mem. Am. Law Inst., N.J. Hist. Soc. (trustee). Democrat. Presbyn. Club: Essex (Newark, N.J.). Home: Newark, N.J. Died Feb. 5, 1975; buried Princeton (N.J.) Cemetery. N:M:1917:1974:L02

BIGGAR, FRANK, Irish diplomat; b. 1917; ed. Blackrock Coll., Dublin. Third sec. Dept. External Affairs, 1941-43; 3d sec., vice consul, N.Y.C., Washington, San Francisco, 1943-46; 2d sec., Rome, 1946-48; 1st sec., counsellor Econ. Div., Dublin, 1948-54; counsellor, London, 1954-59; minister to Portugal, 1959-60; ambassador to Belgium, 1960-66; head Irish Mission to EEC, 1961-66, ECSC, 1963-66; minister, then ambassador to Luxembourg, 1961-1966; ambassador to Switzerland, from 1966, to Austria, from 1967; resident to Iaea, from 1970. Decorated grand croix Order Couronna (Belgium); grand cross Order du Chene (Luxembourg). Address: Dublin, Ireland., Died May 1974.

BIGGERS, JOHN DAVID, glass mfr.; b. St. Louis, Mo., Dec. 19, 1888; s. William David and Emma Melvina (Fisse) B.; prep. edn., Smith Acad., St Louis; student Washington U., 1905-06; A.B., U. of Mich., 1909; LL.D., U. Toledo, U. Mich., Defiance Coll.; D.C.S., N.Y.U.; H.H.D., Ohio Northern University, 1960; m. Mary Isobel Kelsey, October 22, 1912; (died Aug. 15, 1942); children— Reeve Kelsey, Mary Sherret (Mrs. Sprague H. Gardiner), Jane Lowry (Mrs. Corwin Lockwood Jr. (dec.); m. 2d, Frances Morrison Doyle, June 24, 1944; step-children—Dr. Henry W. Doyle, Cynthia Doyle (Mrs. James R. MacColl, III), Mary Frances Doyle. Advertising mgr. Larned, Carter & Co., Detroit, 1909; assistant secretary Detroit Board of Commerce, 1910-11; sec. Toledo (O.) Chamber Commerce, 1911-14; successively asst. treas., treas., asst. gen. mgr., v.p. Owens Bottle Co., Toledo, 1914-26; mng. dir. Dodge Bros. Britain, Ltd., London, 1926-27; v.p. Graham Bros. Corp., 1927-30; vp.p Graham-Paige Internat. Corp., N.Y. City, 1929-30; president and director Libbey-Owens-Ford Glass Co., Toledo, 1930-53, chmn. chief exec. officer, 1953-60, dir., chmn. finance com., 1960-64, honorary member of bd. of directors, from 1967; dir. Toledo Scale Co., Selas Corporation of America, also dir. B. & O. R.R. Company, Bendix Corp., Worthington Corp., Toledo Edison Co., Toledo Trust Co. (emeritus). Public governor N.Y. Stock Exchange, 1957-60. Director production Office Production Management, 1941; minister to Great Britain in charge of coordination of war production, 1941. Administrator census of U.S. unemployed, 1937-38. Trustee Toledo YMCA; chairman of executive committee Toledo Museum of Art; member board of trustees Endowment Funds of Toledo Hosp.; emeritus bd. dirs. Toledo U.; dir. U. Toledo; mem. citizens com. Community Chest, Toledo Labor-Mgmt.-Citizens Com., 1945-66. Chairman of the business advisory council Dept. Commerce, 1954. Recipient President's Medal of Merit, 1946; decorated Comdr. Cross Order Orange-Nassau, 1956. Mem. Am. Ordnance Assn. (adv. bd.), Sigma Alpha Epsilon. Conglist. Clubs: Toledo, Toledo Country; Links (N.Y.); Rotary. Home: Perrysburg O. Died Dec. 13, 1973; buried Woodlawn Cemetery, Toledo, O.

BIGGS, KATE BRITT (MRS. FURNAM KENNETH BIGGS), genealogist, historian; b. Lumberton, N.C., Sept. 7, 1899; d. Angus Isley and Florence (Townsend) Britt; student Campbell Coll., 1917, Chowan Coll., 1918-19; m. Furman Kenneth Biggs, Feb. 16, 1921; children—Furnam Kenneth, I. Murchison, John Duckett. Farmer, Lumberton, from 1955; pres. Katy Did Farms, Inc., from 1968. Chmn. Robeson County campaign A.R.C., Lumberton, N.C., 1944; chmn. bond sales, Lumberton, 1942-43; chmn. Robeson County Cancer Dr., 1953-54; mem. Robeson County Centennial Com. Mem. Am. Legion Aux. (N.C. v.p. 1947-48, dist. committeewoman 1944-46, pres. unit 42 1942-44, unit historian 1940-67, recipient 1st history prize N.C. 1956), U.D.C. (chmn. hist. markers N.C. 1948-54, historian 1950-67). D.A.R. (regent Col. Thomas Robeson chpt. 1950-52, geneal. chmn. 1944, recipient N.C. prize for records 1944, historian 1952-67), Colonial Dames 17th Century, Daus. Am. Colonists, Nat. Soc. Magna Charta Dames, Am. Camellia Soc. Baptist (historian 1950-67). Club: Pine Crest Country (chmn. local beautification 1930-54, bridge chmn. 1954). Author: Progress on the Lumbee Since 1787, 1952 (pageant); The History of First Baptist Church, Lumberton, 1832-1955, 1955; The History of Lumberton's American Legion and Auxiliary, 1919-1955, 1955; The Musselwhites and Allied Families, 1961; Biggs-Britts and Allied Families, 1970. Home: Lumberton N.C. Died Nov. 24, 1972; buried Meadowbrook Cemetery, Lumberton.

BIGGS, WILLIAM RICHARDSON, banker, economist; b. Islip, L. I., N.Y., Sept. 9, 1901; s. Hermann Michael and Frances (Richardson) B.; A.B., Yale, 1922; postgrad. Trinity Coll., Cambridge U., 1922-23; m. Georgene Williams, Nov. 1, 1929; children—Barton M., Jeremy H., Christopher N. Employee Seaboard Nat. Bank (merged with Equitable Trust Co.), N.Y.C. 1923-31; joined Bank of N.Y., 1931, v.p., 1935-64, trustee, exec. v.p., 1964-66, hon. trustee, econ. cons., from 1966; dir. Am. Security Trust, Washington, N. Am. Reassurance Co., N. Am. Reins. Corp. N.Y., Dome Mines, Ltd., Peoples Life Ins. Co., Washington, Rand McNally and Co., Julius Garfinckel Co.; trustee Atlantic Mut. and Centennial Ins. Cos., N.Y.C. Trustee, mem. finance com. retirement system Nat. A.R.C.; chmn. Brookings Instn. Vice chmn. War Dept. Price Adjustment Bd., 1944-45; pub. rep. U.S. del. to UN Econ. and Social Council, Geneva, 1954. Presbyn. Clubs: Cosmos, Chevy Chase, Metropolitan, University (Washington). Home: Washington D.C. Died Oct. 9, 1974.

BILDER, NATHANIEL, lawyer, b. New York, N.Y., May 1, 1881; s. Levy and Amalia (Garfunkel) B.; LL.B., Kent. Coll. of Law, Chicago, 1905; m. Zerlina Hirsch Bilder, 1907; 1 son, Robert Martin. Admitted to N.J. bar, 1906, and practiced in Paterson, later forming partnership with David H. Bilder; sr. partner firm Bilder, Bilder & Freeman, Newark, from 1907; vice pres. counsel Bank of Commerce, Newark, A. W. Faber, Inc. Trustee Y.W.H.A. Mem. American Bar Association, New Jersey State Bar Association, New Jersey State Chamber of Commerce, Essex County Bar Assn., New York County Lawyers Assn. Clubs: Downtown (Newark); hon. pres. Mountain Ridge Country (West Caldwell, N.J.). Home: Mountainside, N.J.†

BILL, HARRY LEON, machine tool exec.; b. Hartford, Conn., 1881; v.p., gen. mgr. and dir., Greenfield Tap & Die Corp., Greenfield, Mass.; pres. and dir. Geometric Tool Co. Home: Greenfield, Mass.†

BILLINGS, JOHN SHAW, former editor; b. Beech Island, S.C., May 11, 1898; s. John S. and Katharine (Hammond) B.; grad. St. Paul's Sch., Concord, N.H., 1916; student Harvard, 1916-17, 1919-20; m. Frederica Washburn Wade, Apr. 19, 1924 (dec.); 1 dau., Frederica Wade (dec.); m. 2d, Elise Lake Chase, Sept. 10, 1963. Reporter Bklyn. Daily Eagle, 1921, Washington Corr., 1921-29; nat. affairs editor Time, 1929-33, mng. editor, 1933-36; mng. editor Life, 1936-44; editorial dir. all Time Inc. publs., Time, Life, Fortune, 1944-54. Served as ammunition truck driver French Army, 1917; 2d lt. Air Service, U.S. Army, 1918-19. Home: Redcliffe Beech Island, S.C. Died Aug. 25, 1975; buried Hammond Cemetery, Beech Island.

BILLINGS, THOMAS HENRY, clergyman; b. Lyn, Ont., Can., Mar. 22, 1881; s. Bruce and Mary Catherine (McCready) B.; grad. Brockville (Can.) Collegiate Inst., 1898; M.A., Queen's U., Kingston, 1902; certificate, Wesleyan Theol. Coll., Montreal, 1910; Ph.D., U. of Chicago, 1915; m. Grace Elvina Hadley, of North Grafton, Mass., July 31, 1912; children—Bruce Hadley, Frances Catherine. Tutor in Latin, Queen's Univ., 1901-03, Wesleyan Theol. Coll., 1903-05, McGill U., 1905-07, also lecturer in classics same univ.; traveling sec. student dept. Internat. Committee, Y.M.C.A., 1907-10; mem. Gen. Com. of World's Christian Fed. 1907-10; lecturer in classics, Wesley Coll., Winnipeg, Can., 1910-16; prof. classical lit., U. of Chattanooga, Tenn., 1916-19, also dean Coll. Liberal Arts, 1918-19; prof. classics, Carleton Coll., Northfield, Minn., 1919-21; study and lecturing in England, 1921-22; minister Unitarian Ch., Woburn, Mass., 1922-25, First Ch., Salem, Mass., 1925-34; prof. of history, Edgewood Park, Briarcliff Manor, N.Y., from 1934. Del. to World's Student Christian Fed., Tokyo, Japan, 1907, Oxford, Eng., 1909, World's Y.M.C.A. conf., Barmen, Germany, 1909. Ordained ministry Canadian Methodist Ch., 1910. Address: Briarcliff Manor, N.Y.†

BILLMAN, CARL, assn. exec.; b. Winchester, Mass., June 23, 1913; s. Christopher Lewis and Lilian (Livermore) B.; A.B., Harvard, 1935, M.A., 1936. Asst. in history Harvard, 1937-41; instr. St. Marks Sch., 1941-42; tariffs and schedules analyst Am. Airlines, Inc., 1942-46; asst. sec. United Chpts. of Phi Beta Kappa, 1946-47, exec. sec., 1948-74. Died Jan. 26, 1974.

BILLOCK, GEORGE D(ONALD), bus. exec.; b. Pitts., Mar. 25, 1909; s. John J. and Julia (Conick) B.; B.S., U. Pitts., 1930; m. Genevieve Judge, Dec. 1, 1943; children—George Donald, Robert J., John K., Elise J. With Nat. Steel Corp., Pitts., 1931-46, successively asst. chief accountant, supr. tax div., asst. to controller; sec.-treas. Unity Land Co., Latrobe, Pa., 1946-55; asst. treas. Latrobe Steel Co. (Pa.), 1946-55; successively v.p., treas., v.p. asst. to pres. and mem. mgmt. bd. Hubbard & Co., Pitts., 1955-58; v.p., treas., dir. mem. exec. com. McCall Corp., N.Y.C., 1958-64; sec.-treas., dir. Vulcan, Inc. Latrobe, from 1964; sec., treas. Unity Market, Inc., Latrobe, 1950-55; mem. faculty Robert Morris Sch. Bus. Adminstrn., Pitts., 1940-46. Mem. Financial Execs. Inst., Am., Pa. Insts. C.P.A.'s, Sigma Alpha Epsilon. Republican. Episcopalian. Clubs: Duquesne, University (Pitts.); Latrobe Country. Home: Greensburg, Pa. Died June 19, 1973; interred St. Michaels of the Valley, Rector, Pa.

BILLUPS, RICHARD ALPHONZO, lawyer; b. Jefferson, Carroll Co., Miss., Apr. 24, 1878; s. William and Irene (Kimbrough) B.; pub. sch. edn.; LL.B., Cumberland U., Tenn., 1899; m. Beatrice Tyler, of Duck Hill, Miss., Mar. 30, 1902. Located in practice of law, Mountain View, Okla., Aug., 1899; elected probate judge, 1899, re-elected, 1901; mem. Okla. Senate; author of Billups prohibition enforcement law, that has made Okla. a prohibition state. Sec. Dem. Com., 1902, chmn. Co. Com., 1904; mem. Dem. Nat. Com., 1904-08. Baptist. Address: Cordell, Okla.†

BILTZ, JOHN FREDRIC, radiologist; b. Mpls., Sept. 15, 1936; s. Francis Julius and Mavis (Olene) B.; M.D., U. Minn., 1962; m. Hannelore Helen Odorff, Nov. 20, 1960; children—Kristina J., Rebecca E., Fredric J. Intern, Gorgas Hosp., C.Z., 1962-63; resident Wilford Hall USAF Hosp., Lackland AFB, Tex., 1965-68; course in radioisotope physics Mt. Sinai Hosp., N.Y.C., 1966; pvt. practice medicine specializing in radiology; mem. med. staff St. Mary's Hosp., Mpls., 1971-73; chief of radiology St. John Hosp., Red Wing, Minn., 1971-73. Served to maj., M.C., USAF, 1963-71. Mem. Bavarian Am. Radiol. Soc., Radiol. Soc. N.Am., Christian Med. Soc., A.M.A. Home: Red Wing, Minn. Died June 13, 1973; buried Haycreek Cemetery, Red Wing, Minn.

BILTZ, NORMAN HENRY, realtor, cattle raiser; b. Bridgeport, Conn., July 6, 1902; s. Charles F. and Lucie B. (Kingman) B.; student Peekskill Mil. Acad., 1920; m. Esther J. Auchincloss, June 2, 1930; children—Jeanne A. (Mrs. William L. McLaughlin), Sheila (Mrs. Biltz O'Brien), Esther A. (Mrs. Paul Langham). Pres., dir., Greenridge Mgmt. Corp.; partner Red Rock Ranch, Ltd., Heizer-Biltz Exploration; v.p. Nevada Properties Corp., Donner Lake Utility Co.; dir. Donner Lake Devel. Co. Elk. Clubs: Bohemian (San Francisco); Prospectors (Reno). Home: Reno Nev. Died July 3, 1973.

BINFORD, THOMAS HOWELL, naval officer; b. Durant, Miss., Aug. 25, 1896; s. John Alexander and Elizabeth (Lowrance) B.; student Miss. A. and M. Coll., 1914-15, Marion (Ala.) Mil. Inst., 1915-16; B.S., U.S. Naval Acad., 1919; m. Helen Geary, Mar. 31, 1928. Commd. ensign U.S. Navy, June 1919, advanced through grades to vice adm., 1954; service on destroyers, battleship, cruisers; signal officer, chief engr., navigator, damage control officer, exec. officer; command destroyers div., Asiatic Fleet (participated entire Java Sea campaign), 1942; comdg. officer Destroyer U.S.S. Clark, 1940; comdg. cruiser U.S.S. Miami (participated in first strikes on Tokyo, raids on Chichi Jima, Iwo Jima, Kyushu, Okinawa, and bombardment of Okino Daito Jima), 1945; comdr. cruiser div. one, U.S. Pacific Fleet, 1949-54, ret. Recruiting duty, student at Naval War Coll., Bur. of Navigation; personal aide to comdt. Ninth Naval Dist., Great Lakes, Ill., 1938-40; asst. to exec. officer enlisted sect. Bur. Naval Personnel, 1934-35; dir. enlisted personnel, 1942-44; chief of staff and aid to comdt. 14th Naval Dist., Pearl Harbor, T.H., 1948-49; comdt. Armed Forces Information Sch. Assisted in establishing Enlisted Wave Program, 1942. Decorated Navy Cross, First Legion of Merit, Silver Star, Order William of

Netherland (presented in person by Queen Wilhelmina in Washington, 1942), 2d Legion of Merit, Bronze Star. Campaign medals World Wars I and II, Am. Defense, 2d Nicaraguan campaign, Am. Area, Pacific Area, 4 stars, Occupation Medal, World War II, China Service, Philippine Defense. Mem. Newcomen Soc. N. Am., Naval Order U.S., Mil. Order World Wars. Clubs: Army-Navy Country (Washington); New York Yacht; La-Jolla Beach and Tennis. Home: La Jolla Cal. Died Aug. 27, 1973.

BINGHAM, ALBERT YOUNG, portfolio mgr., b. Chgo.; s. Horace W. and Amy M. (Young) B.; A.B., U. Ill.; m. Helen M. Worst, 1932; children—Poppy (Mrs. Quattlebaum), Albert Y. II. Asso. Continental Ill. Nat. Bank & Trust Co., 1927-36; with Walter P. Murphy, 1936-42; financial v.p. Chgo. Title & Trust Co., 1942-67, chmn. finance com., 1968-69, dir., from 1954; chmn. exec. com. Halsey, Stuart & Co., 1968-69, dir., from 1967; dir. Am. Ins. Co., 1960-69, Nat. Survey Corp., 1960-69, Transatlantic Reins. Co., 1960-69. Life-term trustee Highland Park Hosp.; bd. dirs. Sarah Hackett Stevenson Meml. Home. Founder Financial Analysts Fedn. (former dir.), Investment Soc. Chgo. (pres. 1946-47). Republican. Clubs: Zeta Psi, University, Chicago, Attic, Commercial (Chgo.). Home: Winnetka Ill. Died June 15, 1973.

BINGHAM, JOSEPH WALTER, lawyer, publicist; born in the city of Indianapolis, Indiana, December 5, 1878; son of Joseph West and Achsah Dollie (Brough) B.; A.B., U. of Chicago, 1902, J.D., cum laude, 1904; m. Florence M. Cornell, June 24, 1907; 1 son, Rodman. Admitted to Ill. bar, 1904; practiced at Chicago, 1904-05; act. asst. prof. law, Cornell U., 1905-07; same, Stanford U., 1907-08, asst. prof., 1908-09, associate professor, 1909-12, professor, 1912-44, professor of law emeritus since 1944; visiting prof. of law, Columbia, 1926-27. Acting prof. law, summers, U. of Chicago, 1916, U. of Mich., 1923, U. of Cal., 1925, U. of Wis., 1927. Asst. dir. Bur. War Trade Intelligence, War Trade Bd., 1918, Mem. Calif. and Ill. state bars, bar of Supreme Court of U.S. Mem. Am. Bar Assn., Am. Law Inst., Am. Academy Political and Social Science, American Academy Political Science, American Judicature Society Inter-Am., Fed. bar assns., Inst. World Policy, National Planning Assn., Am. Assn. U. Profs., Nat. Geog. Assn., Am. Civil Liberties Union, Phi Gamma Delta, Delta Chi, Phi Alpha Delta, Order of Coif. Democrat. Episcopalian. Clubs: Commonwealth of Cal., Sierra. Olympic (San Francisco, California); Cosmos, National Lawyers (Washington, D.C.); Stanford Faculty, Author: Cases on Law of Water Rights, 1916; Draft Treaty on Piracy and Comment (Harvard Research in Internat. Law); Report on the Internat. Law of Pacific Coastal Fisheries; Costigan's Cases on Wills, 3d edit.; also articles, reports, editorials and other writings in legal and other periodicals. Home: Palo Alto Cal. Died Dec. 15, 1973.

BINGHAM, THEODORE CLIFTON, ombudsman; b. Bklyn., Mar. 29, 1925; s. Arthur Clifton and Dorothy (Roelker) B.; B.A., Ind. U., 1949; m. Mildred McMurray, Sept. 12, 1947; 1 son, Timothy. Mng. editor Bloomington Star-Courier, Bloomington, Ind., 1948; reporter, editorial writer The Springfield (O.) Sun, 1949-59; Washington corr., asst. city editor, editorial writer, editor of editorial page, The Journal Herald, Dayton, 1959-71; dir. Joint Office of Citizen Complaints, 1971-73. Mem. exec. bd. Health & Welfare Planning Council, Greene-Montgomery Counties, 1967-73. Served with AUS, 1944-45. Decorated Purple Heart. Mem. Nat. Conf. Editorial Writers, Am. Soc. Pub. Adminstrs., Sigma Delta Chi. Republican, Episcopalian. Home: Dayton O. Died July 3, 1973.

BIOSSAT, BRUCE, journalist; s. Harry Biossat; m.; 1 dau., Mrs. Susan Patton. Early career with U.P.I., Chgo. Daily News; Washington columnist Newspaper Enterprise Assn. Home: Washington D.C. Died May 27, 1974.

BIOW, MILTON H., bus. exec.; b. N.Y.C., July 24, 1892; s. Harry L. and Lena (Deckinger) B.; H.H.D., Wilberforce U., 1958; m. Sophie Taub, July 5, 1917; children—Richard M., Patricia; m. 2d, Melise Banning, Jan. 9, 1944. Advt. bus., 1917-76; pres. The Biow Co., Inc., N.Y.C., 1918-53, chmn. bd., 1953-76. Mem. Eisenhower's Com. Govt. Employment Policy. Recipient Cuban Cross, Carlos Finley Inst., 1942. Home: Ridgefield, Conn., Died Feb. 1, 1976.

BIRCH, ALEXANDER CLITHERALL, lawyer; b. Opelika, Ala., Jan. 21, 1878; s. George Anthony and Allie Burgwyn (Clitherall) B.; B.S., U. of Ala., 1896; LL.B., Washington and Lee U., 1898; m. George Weatherly, Nov. 6, 1907 (now dec.); 1 dau., Florence Milner (Mrs. Leslie A. Stradley); m. 2d, Marion Madel; 1 stepdaughter, Rosemary S. von Wiesel (Mrs. John Enright Kack, II). Admitted to Ala. Bar, 1898; began practice in law department L.&N. R.R.; with Thomas G. and Charles P. Jones, Montgomery, Ala., 1898-1902; U.S. commr., Birmingham, 1903-06; U.S. referee in bankruptcy, Birmingham, 1906-14; mem. firm Banks, Deedmeyer & Birch, 1914-16, Weatherly, Deedmeyer & Birch, 1917-20, Weatherly & Birch, 1920-23, Weatherly, Birch, McEwen & Hickman, 1923-27; U.S. dist. atty., Southern Dist. of Ala., 1927-35; spl. asst. to Atty. Gen. of U.S., from 1934; practiced at Montgomery; member faculty, Birmingham School of Law. Member Rep. State Exec. Com. of Ala.; del. to Rep. Nat. Conv., 1912, 28; Rep. nominee for U.S. senator, 1924. Mem. Am. and Ala. State bar assns., Sigma Nu, Pi Gamma Mu. Episcopalian. Clubs: Rotary, Athelston, Country (Mobile); Country (Birmingham); Beauroir Country (Montgomery). Home: Montgomery, Ala.†

BIRCH, FRANK VICTOR, advt. and pub. relations exec., mfr.; b. Stevens Point, Wis., Dec. 14, 1894; s. Albert V. and Helen (Church) B.; A.B., U. Wis., 1918; m. Marion Yost, July 5, 1919 (div.); children—Frank Victor, John Richard, Richard, Thomas Merrill; m. 2d, Roa Kraft, Nov. 24, 1943. Newspaper editorial writer, 1913-18; editor The Badger, U. Wis., 1918; export advt. J. Roland Kay, 1919; copy dir. Klau-Van Pietersom-Dunlap, Inc., 1919-23, account exec., 1923-39, exec. v.p., 1935-51, pres., 1951-54, chmn. bd., 1954-57, chmn. spl. projects, 1957-60; pres., treas. BirchKraft, Inc., Milw.; dir. Hilldale Shopping Center, Madison; v.p., sec. ROA's Films, Milw., 1960-71; dir. Green Bay Packers. Pres. U. Wis. Found., 1956-62, chmn. bd., 1962-66, hon. v.p., 1966-73, mem. President's Club, 1966-73; mem. Nat. Boys' and Girls' Week Com.; vice chmn. Milw Community Chest, 1956; bd. dirs. Milw. Civic Progress Commn., 1955-57. Served as 2d lt. USAAF, 1918. Decorated Carlos Manual de Cespides (Cuba), 1938; named Hon. Conch, Fla. Keys. Mem. Wis. Alumni Assn. (dir. 1938-39), Am. Legion, Acadia, Order of Good Time of N.S., Sigma Delta Chi, Beta Gamma Sigma. Presbyn. (deacon 1971-73). Mason (32°). Clubs: University, National W (pres. 1955-56), Advertising (pres. 1956-57), Milwaukee Press, Lions (pres. Milw. 1927-28 Wis. dist. gov. 1929-30, internat. internat. dir. 1931-33, v.p. 1934-37, internat. pres. 1937-38; life dir. Milw.; chmn. pub. relations and publicity com. Internat. 1958-68); Rosarians (Portland, Ore.); Islamorada (Fla.) Fishing. Home: Milwaukee, Wis. Died Aug. 8, 1973; buried Meml. Park, Milw.

BIRCH, RAYMOND RUSSELL, veterinarian, animal husbandman; b. Zeandale, Kan., Mar. 30, 1881; s. Francis Asbury and Alice Victoria (Anderson) B.; B.S., Kan. State Agrl. Coll., 1906; D.V.M., Cornell U., 1912, Ph.D., 1916; m. Olive McKeeman, June 21, 1911; children—Frank McKeeman, Juanita Rae. Agrl. insp. and specialist in animal industry, Philippine Bureau Agr., 1906-09; with Cornell U. from 1912, research prof. of vet. medicine, Vet. Exptl. Sta., now emeritus; vet. mem. Procurement of Assignment Service, 2d Corps Area, U.S. Army, 1942. Cons. Orgn. European Econ. Coop., hdqrs. Paris, 1950-51. Mem. American Vet. Med. Assn., N.Y. State Vet. Med. Soc., U.S. Livestock Sanitary Assn., Omega Tau Sigma, Sigma Xi. Republican. Methodist. Mason; mem. Acacia, Rotary Club. Author: Hog Cholera, 1922; also numerous papers on infectious diseases of animals and articles on research in Bang's disease in cattle. Awarded Rockefeller fellowship for European study, 1926. Home: Ithaca, N.Y.†

BIRD, RICHARD ELY, lawyer; b. Cincinnati, O., Nov. 4, 1878; s. Nicholas and Laura Cordelia (Wilder) B.; moved to Kan. with parents, 1887; ed. pub. schs. of Kan.; m. Gertrude M. Hacker, May 21, 1903; children—Margaret Cordelia (wife of Capt. Hugh L. Hixon), Richard Ely. Admitted to Kansas bar, 1901, and began practice in Wichita; judge District Court, 18th Judicial District of Kansas, 1st Division, 1917-20; member 67th Congress (1921-23), 8th Kan. Dist., served on Judiciary Com. Republican. Presbyterian. Mason (K.T., 33°, Scottish Rite Shriner); grad master A.F.and A.M. of Kan., 1923-24. Home: Long Beach, Calif.†

BIRDZELL, LUTHER EARLE, lawyer; b. St. Joseph, Ill., Dec. 1, 1880; s. Eathan A. and Mahalah O. (Koch) B.; LL.B., U. of Ill., 1903; LL.D., U. of N.D., 1948; married Bessie Leola Perring, Dec. 28, 1904; children—Robert Allen, Dorothy, John Perring, Luther Earle, Floyd Douglas. Practiced in Chicago, 1903-04; instr., 1904-06, asst. prof., law, 1906-07, prof., 1907-17 (except. 1912-14), of N.D.; chmn. 1st N.D. Tax Commn., 1912-14 (resigned to resume law professorship); justice Supreme Court of N.D., 1917-33 (chief justice, 22, 27, 33); general counsel Fed. Deposit Ins. Corp., Washington, D.C., 1933-40; v.p. and sr. trust officer, Bank of Am. Nat. Trust & Savs. Assn., San Francisco, from 1940. Chmn. Dist. Bd. for N.D., World War. Democrat. Conglist. Mem. Am. Bar Assn., Am. Econ. Assn., Order of Coif (U. of Ill.). Home: San Francisco, Cal.†

BIRNBAUM, NATHAN, chemist; b. N.Y.C., July 14, 1907; s. Jacob and Sarah (Schutzberger) B.; B.A., cum laude, Coll. City N.Y., 1929; M.A., Columbia, 1932, Ph.D., 1937; m. Jeanne D. Pancoast, Jan. 16, 1931. Mem. faculty dept. chemistry Coll. City N.Y., 1929-73, beginning as fellow, successively tutor, instr., asst. prof., asso. prof., 1929-56, prof., 1956-72, chmn. dept., 1954-69. Mem. Nat. Def. Research Com., Columbia, 1941; mem. radiol. safety sect. Bikini atomic weapons test, 1946; civilian cons. to Chem. Corps, U.S. Army, 1947-49, 52-65; cons. FDA, 1965-67; mem. Nat. Com. Radiation Protection, 1950-51; chief Chem. Corps group Operation Greenhouse, Eniwetok, 1951. Served from capt. to lt. col. AUS, 1942-47, 49-52; col. Res. Decorated Army, Navy Air Force commendation ribbons. Mem. Am. Chem. Soc., A.A.A.S., Phi Beta Kappa, Sigma Xi, Phi Lambda Upsilon. Home: St. Petersburg, Fla., Died Dec. 9, 1975.

BISGYER, MAURICE, social work exec.; b. Bklyn., Aug. 28, 1897; s. Joseph and Sara (Flaumenhaft) B.; B.A., N.Y.U., 1918, M.A. with honors, 1919; L.H.D., Hebrew Union Coll. Jewish Inst. Religion; m. Hoda Adele Rosenberg, July 7, 1925; children—Jay Lewis, Doris, Instr. N.Y. U., 1918-19; exec. dir. Jewish Ednl. Alliance, Balt., 1919-22; dir. YMHA, Trenton, N.J., 1922-23; dir Jewish Community Center, Washington, 1923-37; sec. B'nai B'rith (Internat), Washington, 1937-56, exec. v.p., 1956-66, hon. exec. v.p., from 1966; pres. Nat. Assn. Jewish Center Workers; mem. Nat. Adv. Com. on Edn. apptd. by presidents Herbert Hoover and Franklin D. Roosevelt; sec.-gen. Coordinating Bd. Jewish Orgns. to ECOSOC; exec. com. U.S. nat. commn. for UNESCO. Exec. com., later budget com., Community Chest, Washington; mem. presdl. inaugural com., 1929, 1948; mem. atty. Gen.'s com. on Juvenile Delinquency, v.p. Nat. Citizenship Conf. Fellow N.Y. U.; bd. govs. Nat. Jewish Ednl. Assn., Nat. Conf. Jewish Social Welfare, Zionist Orgn. Am. (editorial bd.), Phi Beta Kappa. Jewish religion. Author: Henry Monsky — The Man and His Work (with Daisy Monsky), 1947; also series for N.Y. Daily Mirror, 1948; Challenge and Encounter, 1967. Home: Chevy Chase Md. Died Aug. 12, 1973; buried Adas Israel Cemetery, Washington, D.C.

BISHOP, INEZ SHANNON, (Mrs. Carroll W. Bishop), librarian; b. Parsons, Kan., Nov. 12, 1892; d. Rolf and Lenora Katherine (Eistertz) Shannon; L.S., La. U., 1939; L.S. Sp., Columbia, 1942; certificate spl. study, U. Chgo.; m. Carroll Wood Bishop, Apr. 14, 1915. Head librarian Pine Bluff and Jefferson County (Ark.) Library, 1919-39; exec.-sec., librarian Ark. Library Commn., 1939-42; acting librarian Ark. Tchrs. Coll., 1943-44; asst. librarian, Muskogee, Okla.; asst. cataloguer, pub. relations dir. Oklahoma City Pub. Library, 1945-46; librarian Ark. Coll., 1946-52, Searcy and White County (Ark.) Pub. Library, 1952-74. Mem. Am., Southwestern, Ark. (pres. 1927) library assns., Bus. and Profl. Women's Club, White County Hist. Assn., Women's Nat. Book Club, Delta Kappa Gamma (pres. Alpha Xi chpt. 1959-61). Presbyn. Home: Searcy, Ark., Died July 31, 1974.

BISHOP, MORRIS GILBERT, educator, author; b. Willard, N.Y., Apr. 15, 1893; s. Edwin Rubergall and Bessie (Gilbert) B.; A.B., Cornell U., 1913, A.M. 1914, Ph.D., 1926; Dr. honoris causa, U. Rennes, 1948; D.Litt., Union Coll., 1953, U. Laval, 1954, Hofstra Coll., 1956, Colgate U., 1959; Litt.D. (hon.) Trent U., 1969; m. Alison Mason Kingsbury, June 14, 1927; 1 dau., Alison. Instr. Romance langs. Cornell U., 1921-26, asst. prof., 1926-36, prof., 1936-60, faculty trustee, 1957-60, curator Cornell ú Dante and Petrarch Coll., from 1970; vis. prof. Am. civilization U. Athens, 1951-52. Mem. Am. Relief Adminstrn. Mission to Finland, 1919. Served as lt. in inf. U.S. Army, World War I; with O.W.I., N.Y. and London, 1942-44, Psychol. Warfare div. AUS 1944-45. Decorated Order White Rose (Finland); Officier d'Academie, Chevalier Legion D'Honneur (France). Fellow A.A.A.S.; mem. Modern Lang. Assn. Am. (pres. 1964), Nat. Inst. Arts and Letters, Am. Assn. Tchrs. French, Phi Beta Kappa (senator 1958-64). Unitarian. Club: Century (N.Y.C.). Author: Champlain, The Life of Fortitude, 1948; The Life and Adventures of La Rochefoucauld, 1951; A Bowl of Bishop, 1954; College Survey of French Literature, 1955; White Men Came to The St. Lawrence, 1961; A History of Cornell, 1962; Petrarch and His World, 1963; Blaise Pascal, Life and Works, 1966; Letters from Petrarch, 1966; The Horizon Book of the Middle Ages, 1968; The Exotics, 1969; Francis of Assisi, 1974. Editor; A Medieval Storybook, 1970; A Classical Storybook, 1970; A Renaissance Storybook, 1971; A Romantic Storybook, 1971. Translator: Eight Plays of Moliere, 1957. Home: Ithaca N.Y. Died Nov. 20, 1973.

BISSELL, HILLARY RARDEN (MRS. WADSWORTH BISSELL), human relations adviser; b. Greenville, Mich., Dec. 24, 1912; d. W. H. and Nelle (Crowell) Rarden; A.B., U. Mich. (Earhart scholar 1933-34), 1934; postgrad. Ariz. State Coll., 1937-38, Mich. State U., 1958; m. Wedsworth Bissell, May 9, 1936; children—Brereton, Torre, Trim. Social work Kent County (Mich.) Emergency Relief, 1934-35; supr. social research Nat. Youth Adminstrn., Grand Rapids, Mich., 1935-36. Mem. interracial com. Grand Rapids Council Social Agys., 1949-58; Grand Rapids bd. Mich. Com. on Civil Rights, 1952-58; exec. sec., 1958-75; mem. City of Grand Rapids Human Relations Commn., 1955-62; mem. casework com. Family Service Assn., 1956-58; mem. state steering com. Mich. Coordinating Council for Civil Rights, 1958-75. Asso. mem. Nat. Council for Social Action, Congl. Christian Chs., 1946-54, mem. nat. race relations com. Bd. Home Missions, 1952-54; state chmn. race relations Social Action Com., Mich. Congregation Christian Conf. Chs., 1949-53; del. Fed. Council Chs. Nat. Conf. on ch. and Econ. Life, 1950; vice chmn. social action dept. Mich. Council Chs., 1950-51, chmn. human relations, 1951-52. Candidate for Mich. Legislature, 1952; sec. Dem. State Central Com., 1952-54; mem. Dem. county exec. com., 1960-75; candidate county treas., 1960; mem. Mich. Livil

Service Commn. Hearing Bd., 1960-75. Mem. YWCA pub. affairs com. Recipient spl. achievement award Mich. Conf. N.A.A.C.P. Branches, 1959; Dale Carnegie Alumni Assn. honor citation, 1962; Lambda Kappa Showcase award, 1968. Mem. Nat. Assn. Intergroup Relations Ofcls., League Women Voters (dir. Grand Rapids 1939-42, Edgerton, Wis., 1944-46), N.A.A.C.P. (dir. Grand Rapids, 1949-75; v.p. Grand Rapids 1955-57, state treas 1952-55, mem. nat. youth com. 1957-58, adviser Grand Rapids youth council, 1956-59, mem. Mich. youth work com., 1957-59, state v.p. 1959-62), Urban League, Women's Internat. League for Peace and Freedom, Am. Civil Liberties Union (dir. West Mich. chpt. 1970), Kappa Kappa Gamma. Club: Nautico (Boqueron, P.R.). Home: Middleville Mich. Died Mar. 1, 1975; cremated.

BISSET, ANDREW G(USTAVE), naval officer, engr.; b. Washington, D.C., Oct. 4, 1893; s. Peter and Maria (Anderson) B.; C.E., Lafayette College, 1915; D.Eng. (hon.), 1945; m. Helen Boas Walzer, July 2, 1917; children—Andrew W., Helen Ann (Mrs. James Maher), Sarah Maria (Mrs. James Douglas). Elizabeth Ruth (Mrs. Lawrence T. Simmelink). Jacqueline Boas. Engr. Pa. R.R., Phila., 1915-16, Geo. Fuller Construction Co., Washington, 1916-17; commd. lt. (j.g.), Corps of Civil Engrs., USN, 1917, and advanced through grades to rear adm., 1947. ret. rank vice admiral July 1950; treaty engr. to Republic of Haiti, 1924-28; officer charge constrn., U.S. Naval Acad., 1936-39; pub. works officer, Navy Yards, Portsmouth, N.H., 1939-41, Norfolk, Va., 1941; commd. of Sea Bees in South Pacific and Okinawa operations, World War II; dist. civil engr., 5th Naval Dist., 1948-50; recalled to active duty as dir. Pacific division Bureau Yards and Docks USN, hdqrs. Hawaii, 1954. N.H. State dir. Civil Defense, 1951-52; dir. Indsl. Park Authority, N.H. Decorated D.S.M. (Army), Legion of Merit, Navy Expeditionary medal, Republic of Haiti Order of Honor and Merit, Victory medal, World War I, Am. Defense Service medal, American Area Combat medal, Asiatic-Pacific area campaign medal with five stars, Japanese Occupational medal. Registered engr., N.H. Mem. Am. Soc. C.E. Newcomen Soc. of England, Phi Beta Kappa, Tau Beta Pi, Chi Epsilon, Chi Phi. Club: Rotary (Conway, N.H.). Republican. Episcopalian. Mason. Home: Madison, N.H., Died Jan. 23, 1976.

BISSET, GEORGE, utilities exec.; b. Washington, Mar. 3, 1899; s. Peter and Marie (Anderson) B.; student George Washington U., 1917-19; m. Lynda Seaman, June 16, 1920 (dec.); children--Lynda Almetta, George; m. 2d, Mary Osborne Bass. With United States Bureau Standards, 1917-19; with Potomac Electric Power Co., 1919-63, successively asst. supt. sub-sta. dept., asst. to chief engr., operations asst. to gen. mgr., gen. supt. elec. system, chief operations engr., v.p. operations, 1919-54, sr. v.p., 1954-63; also dir., mem. exec. com.; trustee Power Reactor Development Co., Inc.; bd. Atomic Power Development Co., Inc., The Liberty Savs. & Loan Assn. Mem. Washington Board Trade, Washington Bldg. Congress (board member), Am. Inst. E.E. Episcopalian. Clubs: Columbia Country (Chevy Chase, Md.); Metropolitan, Engineers (Washington). Home: Washington, D.C., Died Jan. 29, 1976.

BISSHOPP, KENNETH EDWARD, educator; b. Beloit, Wis., July 14, 1909; s. John and Maud Alice (Lufkin) B.; A.B. in Math., U. Ill., 1930; M.S. in Math., Ill. Inst. Tech., 1946, Ph.D. in Mech. Engring., 1954; m. Beatrice Lenora Ortmann, June 16, 1932; 1 son, Frederic Edward. Design calculator Fairbanks Morse and Co., 1930-32, research engr., 1934-44, cons., 1950-55; mech. engr. Sun Shipbldg. & Dry Dock Co., Chester, Pa., 1932-34; research engr. Armour Research Found., Chgo., 1944-48, st. engr., 1948-55; prof. mechanics Hartford Grad. Center, Rensselaer Polytech. Inst., East Windsor Hill. Conn., 1955-57, prof. mech. engring., Troy, N.Y., 1957-75, chmn. dept. mech. engring., 1957-67. Mem. Am. Soc. M.E. (lectr. 1959-60), Am. Math. Soc., Am. Soc. Engring, Edn., Sigma Xi, Tau Beta Pi. Contbr. articles to profl. jours. Home: Troy, N.Y. Died June 19, 1975.†

BITTINGER, CHARLES, artist; b. Washington, June 27, 1879; s. Charles and Isabel (Wilson) B.; student Mass. Inst. Tech., 1897-99; Ecole des Beaux Arts, Paris, 1901-05; m. Edith Gay, Mar. 14, 1904; children—Isabel, Charles, Francis Gay. Has exhibited at Paris Salon (Société Nationale des Beaux Arts), New York, Phila., Washington, etc.; medal, St. Louis Expn., 1904; 2d Hallgarten prize, Nat. Acad. Design, 1909; Clark prize, same, 1912; silver medal, San Francisco Expn., 1915; 1st prize, Duxbury Art Assn., 1919; 1st prize Washington Soc. of Artists, 1925; Ranger Fund, 1932. Works: Entrance Salle des Glaces, Versailles, Allegheny Coll., Pa., 1910; The Boudoir, Nat. Arts Club, New York, 1912; Bibliotheque du Dauphin, Versailles, Art Museum, St. Louis, 1923; The Boston Atheneum, Met. Museum, New York, 1924. Captain, U.S.N.R.; camouflage Sect. World Wars I, II. Legion of Merit, 1946; Ben. West Clinedinet Medal, 1948. N.A., 1937; mem. Ecole des Beaux Arts, American Art Assn. (Paris), Optical Soc. America, Duxbury Art Assn. (pres.), Soc. of Washington Artists (past pres.). Presbyn. Clubs: Arts of Washington (past pres.); Nat. Arts (life), Cosmos Club (Washington). Century Club (N.Y.). Mem. Nat. Geographic Expdn. to Canton Island for 1937 Eclipse; official artist for operation Crossroad, Bikini, 1946. Home: Washington, D.C.†

BIXBY, WALTER EDWIN, ins. co. exec.; b. Champaign, Ill., Aug. 20, 1896; s. Walter Albert and Lizzie (Holmes) B.; student Culver (Ind.) Mil. Acad., 1914-15, Drury Coll., U. Mo.; LL.D., Drury Coll., 1967; m. Angeline I. Reynolds, Apr. 11, 1923 (dec.); children—Joseph Reynolds, Walter Edwin; m. 2d, Louise T. Bogart, Apr. 8, 1964. Field timekeeper Liquified Petroleum Gas Co. of Okla., Tulsa, 1921-23; clk. Kansas City Life Ins. Co. (Mo.), 1923-24, asst. sec., 1924-37, exec. v.p., 1937-39, pres., 1939-64, chmn. bd., from 1964; past Life Ins. Med. Research Fund; past pres. Am. Life Conv.; gov. Am. Royal. Past mem. bd. dirs. Salvation Army, Boy Scouts Am., Jackson County Chpt. A.R.C.; past mem. Kansas City Crime Commn.; trustee Midwest Research Inst., past trustee U. Mo. at Kansas City. Mem. Inst. Life Ins. (past dir.), Sigma Alpha Epsilon. Democrat. Episcopalian. Clubs: Kansas City, University, Country, River, Casper (Wyo.) Tavern (Chgo.) Home: Kansas City, Mo., also Glenrock, Wyo. Died Aug. 16, 1972.

BJERKNES, JACOB AALL BONNEVIE, educator; b. Stockholm, Sweden, Nov. 2, 1897; s. Wilhelm Friman Koren and Honoria Sophia (Bonnevie) B.; Ph.D., U. Oslo, 1924; LL.D., U. Cal., 1967; m. Hedvig Borthen, July 11, 1928; children—Vilheim, Kirsten. Came to U.S., 1939, naturalized, 1946. Meteorologist Meteorol. Obs., Bergen, Norway, 1918-20; supt. Weather Forecast Center, 1920-31; prof. meteorology Geophys. Inst., 1931-40; prof. meteorology U. Cal., Los Angeles, 1940-75. Fulbright & Guggenheim research asso., 1957-58. Lectr. Mass. Inst. Tech., 1933, 34; cons. in weather forecasting, Zurich, Switzerland, 1922-23, London, 1925-26, 1935-36, Toronto, 1933, 39, Washington, 1939, 40, 46; lectr., exchange program Nat. Acad. Scis.-Soviet Acad. Scis., Moscow, Leningrad, 1963. Served as cons. USAAF, Eng., North Africa, Italy, Hawaii, Guam, 1943-45. Recipient Symons medal Royal Meteorol. Soc. , London, 1940, Bowie medal, Am. Geophys. Union, 1942, Vega medal, Swedish Society Anthropology and Geography, WMO medal World Meteorol. Orgn., Losey medal Inst. Aerospace Scis. Decorated Royal Norwegian Order of St. Olav, 1947. Recipient the Nat. Medal Sci., 1966. Hon. mem. Royal Meteorol. Soc. of London; mem. Am. Acad. Arts and Scis., Royal Norwegian, Nat., N.Y., Indian acads. scis. Danish Acad. Tech. Scis., Royal Swedish Acad. Scis., Internat. Assn. Meteorology (pres. 1948-51), Am. Meteorol. Soc. (v.p., hon.), Am. Acad. Achievement. Author: Polar Front theory and initiator of weather map analysis methods based on same, 1920; Theory on Pressure variations as function of flow pattern, 1944; Theory on the gen. circulation of the atmosphere, 1942; research on atmosphere-ocean interaction. Home: Santa Monica, Cal. Died July 1975.

BJORK, ESKIL IVER, utilities exec.; b. Florence County, Wis., Feb. 19, 1896; s. August Frederick and Mathilda (Ericson) B.; student (evenings) Northwestern U., Harvard Grad. Sch. Bus., summer 1927; m. Luella Holgard, Sept. 18, 1920 (dec. 1952); 1 son, Leslie V.; m. 2d, Willie Marcum Lyttle, June 18, 1955. With Peoples Gas Light & Coke Co., Chgo., 1920-63, chmn., 1957-61, dir., mem. exec. com., 1961-63; dir. Chgo. Dist. Pipeline Co., Kimswick Development Co., Natural Gas Storage Co. Ill., Texoma Prodn. Co., Natural Gas Pipeline Co. of Am., Peoples Prodn. Co. Hon. trustee Inst. Gas Technology; trustee Glenwood Sch. for Boys; dir. Travelers Aid Soc. Chgo. Hosp. Planning Council Met. Chgo. Served with 149th F.A., Rainbow Div., AEF, 1917-19. Mem. Ill. C. of C., Am. Gas Assn. (dir.), Nat. Petroleum Council. Clubs: Commercial, Chicago, North Shore Country (Chgo.). Home: Harbor Bluffs Fla. Died Jan. 21, 1975.

BLACHER, BORIS, composer, educator; b. China, Jan. 3, 1903; s. Eduard B. and Helene (Wolff) B.; student of Friedrich E. Koch, also univ. courses in music, m. Gerty Herzog, 1945. Tchr., Dresden Conservatory, later dir. High Sch. for Music, Berlin. Composer; (oratorio) Der Grossinquisitor; (operas) Preussisches Marchen, Romeo and Juliet; Concertante Musik; Variations on a Theme by Paganini; Music for Cleveland; Studie im Pianissimo; Thirteen Ways of Looking at a Blackbird; also ballets, concerti, chamber music, piano works, songs. Home: Berlin Germany. Died Jan. 1975.

BLACHLY, CLARENCE DAN, economist; b. Gunnison, Colo., Dec. 30, 1881; s. Andrew Trew and Mary Adele (Bradley) B.; grad. Grinnell (Ia.) Acad., 1904; Ph.B., Grinnell Coll., 1908; traveled and studied in Europe, 1908-09; Ph.D., U. of Chicago, 1919; m. Margaret Gray Bacon, Sept. 6, 1916. Supt. social surveys, Dept. of Pub. Welfare, Chicago, Ill., 1914-15; asso. prof. sociology, Goucher Coll., Baltimore, Md., 1916-18; research economist, Legislative Reference Service, Library of Congress, 1918-20; economist U.S. Tariff Commn., 1920-49. Member Phi Beta Kappa. Author: Treatment of the Problem of Capital and Labor in Social Study Classes, 1919; also (studies) The Concentration of Misery; Fifty Cheap Lodging Houses; The Function of a Farm Colony in the Repression of Crime; etc.-all in First Semi-Ann. Rept. of Dept. of Pub. Welfare, Chicago, 1915; Poems, 1928; The Ending Year, 1929; Open Ways, 1930; Philosophy for Everyday, 1932; One Year, 1933; Western Trails, 1934; Borderlands, 1935; Overseas, 1936; Autumn Leaves, 1937; Native Notes, 1938; Stubble Fields, 1939; Seasons and Days, 1940; Katahdin, 1943; International Paradoxes, 1943; Oaks, 1944; Sand Dunes, 1945; Carillons, 1946; The High Places, 1947. Principal author of economic articles and the editor in chief of Dictionary of Tariff Information (U.S. Tariff Commn.), 1924. Home: Takoma Park, Md.†

BLACHLY, FREDERICK FRANK, author; b. Salida, Colo., 1880; s. Andrew T. and Mary Adele (Bradley) B.; A.B., Oberlin, 1911; Ph.D., Columbia, 1916; m. Miriam Eulalie Oatman, Nov. 29, 1914; children—Frederick Johnson, Charles Howard, Rachel Ann. With N.Y. Bur. Municipal Research, 1914-16; prof. govt., U. of Okla., 1916-25; pvt. research in Europe on comparative governmental administration, 1924-25; joined sr. staff of Inst. for Govt. Research of Brookings Instn., Washington, D.C., 1925. Co-dir. N.M. State Reorgn. Commn., 1952-53. Mem. Am. Polit. Science Assn., Southwestern Polit. Science Assn.; sec. Okla. Municipal League, 1916-25, also dir. Okla. Bureau of Municipal Research. Author: The Accounting and Reporting System of the State of New York, 1916; Everyday Citizenship, 1920; The Financial System of the State of Oklahoma, 1921; The Government of Oklahoma, 1924; Some Problems in Oklahoma Finance, 1924; The Government and Administration of Germany, 1928; Administrative Legislation and Adjudication, 1934; Comparative Government, 1937 (last 7 books with Dr. Miriam E. Oatman); Working Papers in Administrative Adjudication, 1938; Federal Regulatory Action and Control, 1940; Natural Gas and The Public Interest, 1947 (both with Dr. Miriam E. Oatman). Home: Chevy Chase, Md. Died Mar. 13, 1975; interred Brightwater, Me.

BLACK, BARRON FOSTER, lawyer; b. Norfolk, Va., Nov. 27, 1893; s. Foster and Jennie M. (Tilley) B.; B.A., U. Va., 1917, LL.B., 1920; m. Aileen Pettit Taylor, Nov. 24, 1925; children—Anna (Mrs. C. Randolph Hudgins), Aileen (Mrs. Walter B. Martin, Jr.), Jane (Mrs. David Clark). Admitted to Va. bar, 1920, practiced in Norfolk, mem. Hughes, Vandeventer Eggleston, 1922-25, Vandeventer, Eggleston & Black, 1925-35, Vandeventer & Black, 1935-51, Vandeventer, Black, Meredity & Martin, from 1951; dir. Bank of Va. Rector U. Va., mem. bd. visitors, 1945-56, chmn. Alumni Fund, vice pres. U. Va Law Assn.; chmn. U.S. Savs. Bond Campaign, 1958; overseer Sweet Briar Coll., 1954-56; chmn. Norfolk Pub. Library; chmn. distbn. com. Norfolk Found. Served as sgt. U.S. Army, Am. Field Service, French Army, World War I. Named first citizen of Norfolk, 1959; Mr. Hampton Roads, Hampton Roads Maritime Assn.; recipient Commerce Builder award Hampton Roads Fgn. Commerce Club, 1961, Brotherhood citation Norfolk chpt. Nat. Conf. Christians and Jews. Fellow Am. Bar Assn.; mem. Hampton Roads Maritime Asso. (past pres.), Norfolk, Portsmouth (past pres.) bar assns., Maritime Law Assn. U.S., Raven Soc., Phi Gamma Delta, Omicron Delta Kappa, Phi Beta Kappa. Clubs: Virginia (pres.), German, Norfolk Yacht and Country (Norfolk), Harbor. Home: Norfolk Va. Died Mar. 1, 1974.

BLACK, CARLYLE H., mfg. executive; b. Brooklyn, N.Y., Jan. 3, 1887; s. Alexander and Elizabeth (Helmle) B.; B.S., St. Lawrence U., 1908; m. Louise Fielder, May 15, 1915; children—Fielder, Alexander, Julia C. (Mrs. Malcolm Stearns, Jr.). With Am. Can Co., 1908-52, elected dir., 1941, v.p., 1943-48; pres., 1948-52, retired as chmn. bd. and dir., Apr. 30, 1952. Trustee St. Lawrence U., Canton, New York, Republican. Conglist. Clubs: University (N.Y. City); Cloud; Country Club of New Canaan, Conn.; The Links (N.Y.). Home: New Canaan Conn. Died Aug. 14, 1973.

BLACK, ELI M., corp ofcl. chmn. bd. United Brands Co.; dir. PEC Israel Econ. Co. Trustee Alfred (N.Y.) U. Home: New York City, N.Y. Died Feb. 3, 1975.

BLACK, EUGENE, former judge U.S. Tax Court; b. Blossom, Tex., July 2, 1879; s. Alexander Wesley and Talula Ann (Shackelford) B.; LL.B., Cumberland U., 1905, LL.D., 1937; m. Mamie Coleman, Mar. 15, 1903; children—Margaret, Lyda Gene, Adelle, Rachel, Harold, Barbara. Admitted to Texas bar, 1905, and practiced at Clarksville; mem. 64th to 70th Congresses 1915-29, 1st Texas Dist.; mem. U.S. Board of Tax Appeals now Tax Court of U.S. 1929-66, chmn., 1933-37. Democrat. Methodist. Home: Washington, D.C. Died May 22, 1975; interred Cedar Hill Cemetery, Washington.

BLACK, LEON HAROLD, dental equipment mfr.; b. Kirksville, Mo., Nov. 12, 1918; s. Ernest R. and Letha M. (Scott) B.; grad. Coe Coll., 1941; postgrad. Harvard, 1954, Colgate U., 1958; m. Cheryl J. Hampton, June 12, 1941; children—Karen, Jon, Barbara. With W.A. Sheaffer Pen Co., Ft. Madison, Ia., 1946-69, asst. purchasing agt., 1946-53, exec. v.p., 1957-60, v.p. internat. relations, 1960-69; research analyst Ia. Devel. Commn., 1969-70; gen mgr. Den-Tal-Ez Mfg. Co., 1970-72, v.p. internat. operations, 1972-74; pres. W.A. Sheaffer Pen Co. of Can., Ltd., Goderich, Ont., Can., 1953-57. Chmn. Ia. Regional Export Council, 1969-74; mem. Nat. Export Expansion Council. Served with

USAAF, 1942-45. Recipient certificate for contbns. to internat. mktg. U.S. Dept. Commerce, 1974. Mem. Nat. Stationary and Office Equipment Assn. (v.p., chmn. mfrs. div. 1961-62), Ia. Mfrs. Assn., Greater Des Moines C. of C. (chmn. Internat. Club 1973-74, chmn. world trade council 1973-74). Mason, Lion. Club: Wakonda Golf and Country. Address: Des Moines, Ia. Died Apr. 11, 1974; buried Hillcrest Cemetery, Ft. Madison, Ia.

BLACK, MARIAN WATKINS, educator; b. Arcadia, Fla., Jan. 21, 1905; d. Richard Ellis and Bertha Marian (Parker) Watkins; A.B., Fla. State U., 1926; M.A., U. Fla., 1943; Ph.D., Northwestern U., 1953; m. Robert Franklin Black, Aug. 10, 1927 (dec. 1943). Tchr. pub. schs. Lee and De Soto counties, (Fla.), 1926-42; instr. University Sch., Fla. State Coll. for Women, Tallahassee, 1942-45; gen. supr. schs. Calhoun and Liberty counties, (Fla.), Blountstown, 1945-48; asst. prof. Fla. State U., Tallahassee, 1948-52, asso. prof., 1952-65, prof. ednl. adminstrn., 1965-75, dir. research for doctoral dissertations dept. adminstrn. and supervision, 1970-74. Cons. McPherson Sch. for Delinquent Girls, Ocala, Fla., 1968-72. Recipient Achievement award Fla. chpt. Delta Kappa Gamma, 1971; Appreciation award City of Tallahassee, 1972. Mem. Assn. Supervision and Curriculum Devel. (nat. bd. dirs. 1958-62, 65-66, 69-72), Fla. Assn. Supervision and Curriculum Devel. (bd. dirs. 1957-60, pres., 1965-66, v.p., 1966-67), LeMoyne Art Found., Fla. State U. Alumni Assn., Tallahassee Jr. Mus., Phi Kappa Phi (pres. Fla. State U. chpt. 1963-64), Kappa Delta Pi (nat. presdl. adv. bd. 1964-68, Honor Key 1970), Phi Alpha Theta, Kappa Alpha Theta, Pi Lambda Theta, Delta Kappa Gamma (state parliamentarian 1959-61, pres. chpt. 1962-64, 1st state v.p. 1965-67). Methodist. Clubs: Faculty, Tallahassee Women's. Contbr. articles profl. jours. Home: Tallahassee, Fla., Died June 20, 1975; interred Joshua Creek Cemetery, Arcadia, Fla.

BLACK, NEWTON WADE, labor union exec.; b. Mt. Vernon, Ill., Jan. 6, 1912; s. General Lawrence and Mettie (Lemmons) B.; student Shurtleff Coll., 1930-33; m. Helen Edna Kane, Sept. 1, 1937; children—Michael L., Thomas N., Timothy W. With Owens-Ill. Glass Co., Alton, Ill., 1933-45, shop steward, 1923-24, mem. bus. com. 1935-36, chmn. com., 1936-38, recording sec. of local union, 1936-38, pres. local union, 1943-44, part-time rep. internat. union, 1943-45- mem. exec. bd. Glass Blowers Assn. Am., Phila., 1946-49, internat. sec., 1949-71, pres., 1971-74. Trustee Glass Blowers Assn. Am. Employers Retirement Trust Fund. Vice-pres. Boys Baseball Inc., 1959. Home: Wayne Pa. Died Mar. 8, 1974.

BLACK, ROBERT FAGER, mfr.; b. Harrisburg, Pa., Nov. 2, 1889; s. Alfred T. and Mary Elizabeth (Fager) B.; grad. Mercersburg (Pa.) Acad., 1907; student Princeton, 1907-10; D. Humanities, John Carroll U.; m. Fredonia Frazer, Jan. 12, 1926; children—Robert Fager, Barbara (Mrs. David L. Yeomans), Elizabeth Frazer (Mrs. Alexander C. Vehring), David Fulton. Factory worker, 1910; salesman Mack Truck Co., Inc., N.Y., 1912-16, br. mgr., 1916-18, div. mgr., 1919-21; v.p. Mack Internat. Motor Truck Co., N.Y.C., 1921-30; pres. Brockway Motor Co., N.Y.C., 1930-35; pres. White Motor Corp., Cleve., 1935-56, chmn., chief exec. officer, 1956-59, dir.; former chmn. bd. White Motor Co. Can. Ltd.; trustee, former chmn. 1st Union Realty Co. Trustee, chmn. John Carroll U., former trustee and chmn. Ohio State U.; chmn. bd. Univ. Hosps. of Cleve. Enlisted in 23d Engrs., U.S. Army, 1918; commd. 2d lt. and 1st lt.; served with AEF 18 months; mem. War Labor Bd., World War II. Recipient Distinguished award Ohio State U., Distinguished Service award City of Cleve. Lutheran. Clubs: Union, Chagrin Valley Hunt, Tavern, Cleve. Skating (Cleve.); Princeton (N.Y.C.); Kirtland Country; The Country, The Fifty. Home: Cleveland, O. Died Jan. 25, 1975; buried Lakeview Cemetery, Cleve.

BLACKBURN, WALTER EVANS, coll. dean; b. Marion, Ky., Oct. 21, 1907; s. Walter Ashel and Cora Cynthia (Hurley) B.; A.B., Georgetown Coll., 1927; M.S., U. Fla., 1930; postgrad. La. State U., summer 1939; Ph.D., U. Ill., 1944; m. Virginia Alling Adams, June 1, 1929; 1 son, Walter Evans. Instr. high sch., Somerset, Ky., 1927-29; instr. to asst. prof. Murray (Ky.) State Coll., 1930-43; spl. research asst., group leader U. Ill., Champaign, 1944; tech. cons. Rubber Reserve Co., Washington, 1944; research chemist rayon dept. E.I. duPont de Nemours & Co., Waynesboro, Va., 1944-45; prof. chemistry, head dept. phys. sci. Murray State U., 1945-58, chmn. chemistry dept., 1958-68, dean Sch. Arts and Scis., from 1968, Distinguished prof., 1967, Alpha Chi lectr., 1968. Cons. Union Carbide Nuclear Co., Paducah, Ky., from 1958. Mem. Am. Chem. Soc. (councilor 1959-70), A.A.A.S., Nat. Sci. Tchrs. Assn., Ky. Acad. Sci. (pres. 1949-50), Ky. Assn. Chem. Tchrs. (pres. 1949-51), Am. Assn. U. Profs. (Ky. pres. 1958-60), N.E.A., Sigma Xi, Phi Lambda Upsilon, Kappa Alpha. Mem. Disciples of Christ Ch. Rotarian. Author: Soap Development Program for Government Synthetic Rubber, 1944. Contbr. articles to profl. jours. Home: Murray Ky. Died Sept. 20, 1974; buried Murray City Cemetery, Murray, Ky.

BLACKETT, PATRICK MAYNARD STUART, physicist, b. London, Eng., Nov. 18, 1897; s. Arthur Stuart and Caroline (Frances) B.; grad. Royal Naval Colls., 1914; student Magdalene Coll., 1919-23; fellow King's Coll., 1923-33; D.Sc. (hon.), New Delhi U., 1947, U. Strasbourg, 1947, U. Reading, 1948, Queen's U., Belfast, 1953, Cambridge, 1954; LL.D. Glasgow, 1955, Dalhousie U., Halifax, N.S., 1960; m. Costanza Bayon, Mar. 17, 1924; children—Giovanna, Nicolas Maynard. Prof. physics Brikbeck Coll., 1933-37; Langworthy prof. physics U. Manchester, 1937-53, pro-vice chancellor, 1950-52; prof. physics Imperial Coll. Sci. and Tech., U. London, 1953-65, sr. research fellow, from 1965, pro rector Imperial Coll., 1961-64. Mem. Council Dept. Sci. and Indsl. Research, 1955-60; mem. council and exec. com., Overseas Devel. Inst., from 1960; councillor Inst. for Strategic Studies, 1958-61. Served in the Royal Navy, 1914-19, lt. 1919. Recipient Royal medal Royal Soc., 1940, Copley medal, 1956; Am. medal of Merit, 1947; Nobel Laureate for physics, 1948; hon. fellow Magdalene Coll., 1948, Weizmann Inst. Sci., Israel, 1954. Fellow Royal Soc. (pres. 1965-70); mem. Inst. France, Acad. Scis., Berlin Acad. Sci., Brit. Assn. Advancement Sci. (pres. 1957-58). Club: Athenaeum (London). Author: Military and Political Consequences of Atomic Energy, 1948; Lectures on Rock Magnetism, 1956; Atomic Weapons and East-West Relations, 1956; Studies of War, 1962; also sci. papers in field. Home: London England. Died July 13, 1974.

BLACKMER, SYDNEY, motion picture actor, producer; b. Salisbury, N.C., July 13, 1898; student Mercerburg Acad., also U. N.C. Numerous appearances N.Y. stage, including Little Sheba (Donaldson award, Antoinette Perry award); motion pictures include: Sweethearts and Wives, Count of Monte Cristo, Little Colonel, Duel in the Sun, President's Mystery, Saturday's Hero, In Old Chicago, Song is Born, High and Mighty, High Society, Beyond a Star, other; frequent radio and TV appearances. Address: Hollywood Cal. Died Oct. 15, 1973.

BLACKWELDER, ELLIOT, geologist; b. Chgo., June 4, 1880; s. Isaac Simeon and Alice Gertrude (Boughton) B.; A.B., U. Chgo., 1901, Ph.D., 1914; field study, 1903-04; m. Jean Otis Bowersock, September 26, 1904; children—Margery, Martha Jean, Richard, Gertrude, Lois. Ruth, Justin. Fellow and asst. in geology, U. Chgo., 1902-03; paleontologist, Carnegie Instn. Expdn. to China, 1903-04; instr., asst. and asso. prof. geology, U. Wis., 1905-11, prof., 1911-16; head of geology dept., U. Ill., 1916-19; vis. prof. U. Chgo., 1907, 16. Stanford U., 1919, Harvard, 1921; chief geologist, East Butte Copper Mining Co., Denver, 1919-21; mgr. Teton Syndicate, 1921-22; head dept. geology, Stanford, 1922-45, emeritus prof., from 1945; asst. geologist, Alaska and Southeastern Wyoming, 1906-08, geologist, northern Utah, southeastern Ida. and western Wyo., 1909-13, Alaska, 1915, all U.S. Geol. Survey; mem. Calif. Petroleum Comn., 1917 Chmn. U.S. Delegation to Eighteenth Internat. Geol. Congress, London, 1948. Fellow Geol. Soc. of America (vice pres. 1933, 39; pres. 1940), A.A.A.S. (vice pres. 1921), mem. Nat. Acad. Sciences, Wash. Acad. Sciences, Calif. Acad. Sciences, Am. Philos. Soc., Am. Assn. Petroleum Geologists, Assn. Am. Geographers, Seismological Soc. of America (pres. 1947-48), Commonwealth Club (San Francisco), LeConte Geol. Club (pres. 1924), Am. Ornithologists' Union, Soc. Geol. Belgique, Geol. Soc. China (hon.), Geologische Vereinigung, Bonn (hon.), Peninsula Geol. Soc. (pres. 1955), Geol. Soc. of London (fgn. mem.) Beta Theta Pi, Sigma Xi. Author: Research in China (with B. Willis), 1906; Elements of Geology (with H. H. Barrows), 1911; Regional Geology of the United States, 1912. Contbr. geol. jours. Home: Atherton, Cal.†

BLACKWELDER, PAUL, librarian; b. Hillsboro, Ill., Apr. 7, 1878; s. I. S. and Gertrude (Boughton) B.; U. of Chicago, 1896-98; A.B., Harvard, 1900; m. Maud, d. Alexander Del Mar, Feb. 18, 1908. Teacher English and history, Lyons Tp. High Sch., La Grange, Ill., 1900-02; prin. Laclede and Washington (grammar) schs., St. Louis, 1902-05; asst. librarian, Pub. Library, St. Louis, from 1905. Organized vacation schs. in St. Louis, 1905. Mem. A.L.A., Mo. Library Assn. (pres., 1912), Beta Theta Pi. Progressive. Mem. Artists' Guild, Civic League, Public Question Club, City Club. Home: St. Louis, Mo.†

BLACKWELL, ASHBY CARLYLE, educator; b. Lynchburg, Va., Aug. 4, 1896; s. Samuel Ashby and Minnie Lee (Doyle) B.; A.B., Randolph-Macon Coll., 1918; A.M., 1919; D.Sc., Morris Harvey Coll., 1941; student Princeton U., 1920-21; Ph.D., U. Chgo., 1960, Union Carbide Corporation fellow, 1957-58, 1959-60; U.S. Rubber Co. Institute of Organic Chemistry fellow, 1958-59, Shell fellow in fundamental research, spring 1959; m. Harriett Cazenove Purdy, Apr. 9, 1925; 1 dau., Nancy Purdy (Mrs. John Charles Allan). Instructor of mathematics at Randolph-Macon Coll., 1916-19; instr. mathematics and science, Randolph-Macon Acad., 1919-20; part-time asst. in chemistry, Princeton U., 1920-21; prof. chemistry, Morris Harvey College, after 1921-71, then tchr. phys. sci., 1971-73, v.p., 1933-51, chairman of natural sci. div., 1938-41, dean, 1941-56, dean emeritus, 1956-75. Municipal recorder, Barboursville, W.Va., July 1, 1933-Aug. 31, 1935. Mem. Am. Chem. Soc. (dir. Kanawha Valley Sect., 1939 and 1942, v.chmn. fall 1940, chmn. 1941, councillor 1954-56), A.A.A.S., N.E.A., W.Va. Edn. Assn., W.Va. Assn. Higher Edn. (pres. 1947-48), W.Va. Acad. Sci. (pres. 1955-56), Internat. Platform Assn., Phi Beta Kappa, Chi Beta Phi (nat. pres. 1924-48, hon. dir.; nat. marshal), Sigma Upsilon, Tau Kappa Alpha, Pi Gamma Mu, Sigma Xi, Theta Xi. Democrat. Episcopalian. Mason. Club: Lions. Writers articles in field. contbg. editor in test program Am. Chem. Soc. Home: Charleston, W. Va. Died July 7, 1975.

BLACKWELL, MARY B. (MRS. EDWARD F. JOEHRENDT), airplane pilot; b. San Francisco, Feb. 19, 1924; d. Albert G. and Lucille (Devol) Bates; A.B., Vassar Coll., 1945; student Woods Hole Oceanographic Inst., 1945; m. E. Alston Blackwell, Feb. 9, 1946 (dec. July 1966); 1 son, Stephen D.; m. 2d, Edward F. Joehrendt, July 19, 1969. Flight instr. Orlando Aviation (Fla.), 1960-73, chief flight instr. 1963-73; designated pilot examiner FAA Orlando, 1963-73; designated factory check pilot Mooney MU-2 Twin Prop-Jet Aircraft, 1967-73; chief pilot, dir. tng. Falcon Aviation Corp., Orlando, 1969-73, dir. operations, 1972-73. Mem. Nat. Assn. Flight Instrs., Internat. Assn. Women Pilots (chpt. chmn. 1968), Airplane Owners and Pilots Assn. Episcopalian. Home: Winter Park FL. Died Sept. 28, 1973.

BLAGONRAROV, ANATOLI ARKADYEVICH, Soviet scientist; b. Ankovo, Russia, June 1, 1894; student Mikhailovskaya Sch. Arty., then Higher Sch. Arty.; grad. Military-Tech. Acad., 1929; Dr. Tech. Scis., 1938. Charge dept. small arms Acad. Arty., later founder and dir. Inf. Weapons Research Center, also developed ednl. program for ordnance engrs.; charge Dzerzhinski Mil. Acad., World War II, specializing improvement arty. weapons, instr., research scientist, 1929-46, prof., 1938; head Soviet Acad. Arty. Sci., 1946-64; head Soviet delegation Internat. Congress on Missiles, Paris, 1956; chmn. Soviet delegation Internat. Rocket and Satellite Conf., U.S., 1957; dir. Inst. Study of Machines, Moscow, 1953. Served as comdr. units Red Army, Bolshevik Revolution, lt. gen. arty., World War II. Decorated Order of Lenin (3 times), Order of Red Banner of Labor (3 times); named meritorious sci. and tech. worker Soviet Union, 1940; recipient Stalin prize for contbn. to arty., 1941. Mem. Soviet Acad. Scis. (academician-sec. Dept. Scis. 1957-63; chmn. commn. on study and use of space; v.p. com. space research), Czechoslovak Acad. Scis. Author: Foundations of Design of Automatic Armaments, 1931; also numerous sci. monographs on inf., aviation armanment, ballistics, kinematics, rockets and automatic weapons. Editor-in-chief Mashinovedenie (Study of Machines). Address: care Academy of Science of USSR 14 Lenin Prospekt Moscow USSR. Died Feb. 4, 1975.

BLAIR, PAXTON, lawyer; b. New Orleans, Sept. 30, 1892; s. Joseph Paxton and Eugenie (Kruttschnitt) B.; grad. Lawrenceville (N.J.) Sch., 1910; A.B., Princeton, 1914; J.D., Harvard, 1917; m. Gertrude Hubbard Grosvenor, Dec. 5, 1925 (div. 1938); children—Joan Grosvenor (Mrs. Henry Paul Sullivan), Edwin Augustus Grosvenor, Joseph P.; m. 2d, Edna D. von Rynkofski, Nov. 16, 1940; 1 son, David P. Admitted to N.Y. bar, 1918, began practice in N.Y.C.; asst corp. counsel N.Y.C., 1934-43; justice Supreme Ct. State N.Y., 1945; solicitor gen. State of N.Y., 1957-65. Trustee Child Edn. Found., 1931, pres. 1942-53. Mem. N.Y. State Bd. Social Welfare, 1946-56; dir. Council for Basic Edn., 1956, pres., 1958-59. Dir. N.Y. County Lawyers' Assn., 1958-60. Served as 2d lt., inf., U.S. Army, AEF, World War I. Mem. S.A.R., Am. Jud. Soc., Am., N.Y. State bar assns., Assn. Bar City of N.Y., Pilgrims, Phi Beta Kappa. Republican. Episcopalian. Clubs: Church, University (N.Y.C); Fort Orange (Albany). Author: Breach of Contract Due to War, 1940. Contbr. to Harvard Law Rev., Columbia Law Rev., N.Y. State Bar Bull. Home: Hillsdale N.Y. Died Dec. 25, 1974.

BLAIR, WILLIAM RICHARDS, physicist; b. County Derry, Ireland, Nov. 7, 1874; s. Thomas Wray and Mary (Richards) B.; came to America, 1884; grad. Kan. State Normal Sch., 1895; S.B., U. of Chicago, 1904, Ph.D., 1906; grad. Signal School of U.S. Army, 1923, Command and Gen. Staff Sch. of U.S. Army, 1926; m. Florence Lyon Smith, Oct. 1909; children—William Richards, Thomas Wray, Charles Lyon. Prin. high sch., Pittsburg, Kan., 1897-99; asso. in mathematics, State Normal Sch., Oshkosh, Wis., 1900-02; asst. instr. U. of Chicago, 1903-06; entered govt. service, Oct. 1906; research dir. in charge upper air research, U.S. Weather Bureau, June 1907, and of Physical Lab., June 1910, and exec. officer in charge Mt. Weather Obs., Va., 1912-14; prof. meteorology, in charge aerology, U.S. Weather Bureau, 1915-17; commd. maj. Nat. Army, 1917; and assigned to Aviation Corps, with A.E.F. in France; trans to Signal Corps, July 1918; lt. col., Feb. 1919; major in regular army, Nov. 1921, lt. col., Oct. 1934; col. Oct. 1938; retired Nov. 1938; chief of research and engring. div., Office of Chief Signal Officer, U.S. Army, Washington, D.C., 1926-30; officer in charge Signal Corps Labs., from 1930; tech. cons., from 1929. Chairman technical sub-committee Internat. Commn. for Aerial Navigation; technical advisor Internat. Wireless Commn., Paris, first half 1919; meteorologist for the "World Flight," 1924; mem. Internat. Radiotelegraph Conf., Washington, 1927; mem. Daniel Guggenheim Com. on Aeronautical Meteorology,

1927-30. Fellow Royal Meteorological Soc.; mem. Internat. Com. for Scientific Aeronautics, Am. Phys. Soc., Philos. Soc. Washington, Am. Soc. Aeronautic Engrs. (exec. bd.), Washington Acad. Sciences, Acad. Polit. Science, Inst. of Aeronautical Sciences (founder-mem.), Phi Beta Kappa, Sigma Xi, Alpha Tau Omega, Am. Geog. Union, Am. Radio Union, Nat. Research Council; fellow Am. Meteorol. Soc. Club: Cosmos (Washington, D.C.) Home: Locust, N.J.†

BLAKELOCK, DAVID HAZEN, army officer; b. Washington, D.C., June 1, 1895; s. John W. and Isabell R. (Hazen) B.; C.E., Cornell U., 1923; grad. Cav. Sch., advanced course, 1927, Command and Gen. Staff Sch., 1928, Chem. Warfare Sch., 1935; Army War Coll., 1936; m. Lula Ann Brenner, Sept. 15, 1917; children—Jean E. (wife of Lt. Clifton L. MacLachlan, U.S. Army), John H. (officer U.S. Army Air Corps), David R. (U.S. Army). Enlisted in Dist. of Columbia Nat. Guard; called to active duty as sergt., 3d Inf., 1916; served on Mexican Border; commd. 2d lt., cav., U.S. Army, 1917; promoted through grades to brig. gen., 1945; asst. chief of logistics div. on staff comdr. in chief U.S. Pacific Fleet and Pacific Ocean areas, 1943-44; assigned G-4, Tenth Army, Sept. 1944. Decorated Legion of Merit. Mem. Cornell Soc. Engrs., Tau Beta Pi. Mason (32°). Home: San Clamente, Cal. Died May 26, 1975.

BLAKELY, CHARLES ADAMS, naval officer; b. Whitley County, nr. Williamsburg, Ky., Oct. 1, 1879; grad. Williamsburg Acad., 1897, U.S. Naval Acad., 1903; m. Virginia Allen Lyons, Nov. 15, 1909; children—John Siler, Amelia (dec.), Charles Adams, Jr., Lila Allen. Promoted through grades from midshipman to vice adm.; comd. torpedo boats and destroyers, ensign through lt. comdr.; comd. destroyer O'Brien in European waters, 1917-18, destroyer squad Asiatic, 1926-28, aircraft carrier Lexington, 1932-34; became naval observer, 1932, naval aviator, 1936; comdt. Naval Air Sta., Pensacola, 1936-37, 2d Carrier Div., 1937, All Patrol Plane Squadrons, 1937-39; as vice adm. (temp.), Aircraft Battle Force, 1939-40; comdt. 11th Naval Dist., San Diego, Calif., 1940-41; retired as vice adm., Oct. 1, 1942. Sergt. Co. K, 2d Ky. Vol. Inf., Spanish-Am. War. Participated in Morocco Campaign against Raisuli, 1904. Awarded Distinguished Service Order (British) and Distinguished Service Medal (U.S.) for work against enemy submarines and successful engagement June 17, 1917, while comdg. destroyer O'Brien; campaign medals for Spanish-Am. War, Cuban Pacification, 1906, Mexican, 1914, World War, Yangtze River (China), 1927. Clubs: Army and Navy Country; New York Yacht. Address: Coronado, Cal.†

BLAKELY, EDWARD BRADFORD, headmaster; b. Newport, R.I., Feb. 9, 1878 s. Thomas Edward and Jenney (Briggs) B.; student Harvard, 1898-1901; m. Amandita Rivera, Feb. 4, 1902 (died June 6, 1932); 1 dau., Rosita Rivera; m. 2d, Helene Becker, June 6, 1933. Studied automobile engring. in France, 1903-05; chief engr. Haynes Automobile Co., 1905-07; exptl. engr. Daimler Co., 1907-08; field engr. Internat. Harvester Co., 1908-11; advisory engr. Sears, Roebuck Co., 1911-20; gen. supt. Worthington Pump Works Milwaukee, Wis., 1920-22; teacher St. George's Sch., Middletown, R.I., 1923-28; founded St. Luke's Sch., New Canaan, Conn., 1928, and since pres. and dir.; founded Camp Mechano for Boys, South Caso, Me., 1923, and since proprietor and dir. Civilian engr. in charge spl. engine lab., U.S. Army Civilian engr. in charge spl. engine lab., U.S. Army Barracks, Washington, D.C., World War. Mem. Camp Dirs. Assn., Headmasters Assn. of Conn., Soc. Automotive Engrs., Alpha Tau Omega. Republican. Episcopalian. Mason. Clubs: Harvard (New York and New Canaan). Contbr. articles to mags. and newspapers. Home: New Canaan, Conn.†

BLAKEMAN, EDWARD WILLIAM, cons. religious edn.; B. Gary, Minn., 1880 s. Edward E. and Florence (Long) B.; A.B., Lawrence Coll., Appleton, Wis., 1907, D.D., 1918; student Boston University, 1907-09; A.M. University of Wisconsin, 1911; m. Anna DuPré Smith, Apr. 7, 1915; children—Anna DuPré, William Edward (dec.). Ordained ministry Meth. Ch., 1908; univ. pastor, U. of Wis., 1908-12; pastor Univ. Meth. Ch., 1912-25; dir. Wesley Foundation of Wis., 1915-25; dir. Inter-Ch. Survey of Wis., 1918-19; dir. Wesley Foundation of Calif., 1925-31; dir. Pacific Pastors' Summer Sch., 1929, 30; instr. in polity, Pacific Sch. of Religion, Berkeley, Calif., 1927-31; counselor in religious edn., U. of Mich., 1933-46, consultant, 1947-48; chairman religious edn. Pacific Sch. of Religion, 1948-52; lecturer Williamstown Inst. Human Relations, 1935, 1937-39. Member of the executive board of Michigan Child Guidance Institute, 1938-42. Member General Conf. Meth. Ch., 1920; chmn. Commn. to Survey Week-Day Religious Edn., 1920-24; adviser, Nat. Council on Religion in Higher Edn., 1920-27, Univ. Religious Conf., 1927-31. Mem. Research Sect. Internat. Council Religious Edn., 1940-45; chmn. Higher Edn. Religious Edn. Assn. U.S., Can., 1942-53; mem. Am. Acad. of Polit. and Soc. Sci., Conf. Ch. Workers in State Univs., Nat. Conf. Social Work, Nat. Science, Philosophy and Religion, No. Cal. council of Churches, Phi Beta Kappa, Beta Theta Pi, Tau Kappa Alpha. Mason. Clubs: City Commons, Faculty (U. of Calif.) Author monographs. Contbr. column Dominie Says in Mich. Daily, 1939-47. Home: Berkeley, Cal.†

BLAKLEY, WILLIAM A., lawyer, found. exec.; b. 1898; student U. Okla. Admitted to bar, 1933; part-time lawyer; chmn. bd., dir. Blakley-Braniff Found., Dallas. Trustee Southwestern Med. Found., Inc., Dallas. Mem. Am. Bar Assn. Address: Dallas, Tex., Died Jan. 5, 1976.

BLANCHARD, RALPH HARRUB, economist; b. Plympton, Mass., Dec. 3, 1890; s. Thomas Williams and Clara (Harrub) B.; A.B., Dartmouth, 1911, A.M., 1912; Ph.D., U. of Pa., 1916; unmarried. Asst. in economics Dartmouth, 1911-12; Harrison fellow U. of Pa., 1912-13; asst. and instr. in ins. Wharton sch. finance U. Pa., 1913-17; instr. ins. Columbia, 1917, asst. prof., 1920-23, asso. prof., 1923-27, prof., 1927-57, prof. emeritus, from 1957; ednl. dir. Ins. Inst. of Hartford, Conn., 1917-18; consultant Teachers Ins. and Annuity Assn., 1926; ins. adviser Com. to Study Compensation for Automobile Accidents, 1929-31; consultant Social Security Bd., 1936-37, 1942-55; mem. Advisory Com. on Insurance, U.S. War Dept., 1941-45; mem. Bd. Insurance Advisors, Department of Def., 1950-53; cons. Office Secretary of Def., from 1954; mem. administrative board, S.S. Huebner Foundation for Insurance Education, 1941-55; vice-pres. in charge Insurance Div., Am. Mgt. Assn., 1939-40, dir 1940-43, 1946-49; consultant to the Treasury Department, 1949-53. Adviser Com. on Fire Ins. Rates, 1939-40. Commd. 1st lt. U.S. Army, Apr. 23, 1918; capt., Oct. 23, 1918; served as statis. officer cargo sect. Embarkation Service, 1918-19; chief of shipping sect. Statis. Br. U.S. Army, Apr.-June 1919; spl. expert U.S. Shipping Bd., 1919. Mem. Reunion Internacional de Tecnicos Aseguradores, Spain, 1947. Fellow Casualty Actuarial Society (v.p., 1925-26, 1935-36, pres., 1942-43); mem. Ins. Forum San Francisco, American Arbitration Assn. (nat. panel), Am. Economic Association, Am. Risk and Insurance Assn. (v.p. 1933-34, pres. 1935-36) Ins. Soc. N.Y. (dir. 1929-31, 1946-57), Ins. Library Assn., Ins. Underwriters Assn. of the Pacific (hon.), Insurance Hall of Fame, Alpha Kappa Psi, Phi Kappa Psi, Beta Gamma Sigma. Clubs: Century (New York City); Cosmos (Washington). Author: Insurance (with Albert H. Mowbray), 1955. Prepared reports on nat. revisions of workmen's compensation ins.; survey of Accident and Health Ins. for Soc. Security Adminstrn., 1942-46. Prepared Dictionary of Insurance Terms, 1949. Editor McGraw-Hill Ins. Series, 1922-58. Contbr. articles on ins. to periodicals. Home: Plympton Mass. Died Sept. 28, 1973.

BLANCK, JACOB NATHANIEL, bibliographer, author; b. Boston, Nov. 10, 1906; s. Selig and Mildred R. (Friedman) B.; student Boston schs.; L.H.D. (hon.), Brown U., 1969; m. Stella Balicer, Aug. 28, 1938; 1 dau., Rosamunde. Rare book editor Publishers Weekly and Antiquarian Bookman, 1936-52; bibliographer Americana, Library of Congress, 1939-41; cons. bibliography Ind. Hist. Soc., 1942; editor Bibliography of Am. Lit., from 1943. Mem. Mass Hist. Soc., Bibliog. Soc. Am., Am. Antiquarian Soc., Antiquarian Bookseller's Assn. Am., (hon.), Phi Beta Kappa (hon.). Club: Odd Volumes (Boston). Mason. Author: Peter Parley to Penrod, 1938, rev. edit. 1961; Harry Castlemon, Boy's Own Author, 1941; Jonathan and the Rainbow, 1948; The King and the Noble Blacksmith, 1950. Editor: Merle Johnson's American First Editions, 3d and 4th edits. 1936, 41. Contbr. to Ency. Brit. Year Books, profl. jours. Home: Chestnut Hill, Mass. Died Dec. 23, 1974.

BLANCO, JOSE G., physician; b. San Juan, P.R., 1917; M.D., U. Md., 1941. Rotating intern Jackson Meml. Hosp., Miami, Fla., 1941-42; asst. resident in obstetrics Balt. City Hosps., 1946-47; preceptor in radiology and diagnostic gynecol. cancer with Dr. I. Gonzales-Martinex, 1947; resident in obstetrics and gynecology South Side Hosp., Pitts., 1954-55, St. Margaret's Hosp., Pitts., 1955; resident in pathology VA Hosp., Pitts., 1962-66; pathologist Charleroi-Monessen (Pa.) Hosp., 1966-71; teaching fellow in pathology U. Pitts., 1961-66. Served as capt., M.C., AUS, 1942-46. Diplomate Am. Bd. Obstetrics and Gynecology. Fellow A.C.S., Coll. Am. Pathologists, Am. Soc. Clin. Pathologists; mem. A.M.A., Am. Assn. Blood Banks, Assn. Mil. Surgeons U.S. Home: Charleroi, Pa. Died Mar. 1, 1971.

BLANK, ABE H., business exec.; b. Galatz, Rumania, July 27, 1879; s. Israel and Miriam Greenburg) B.; brought to U.S., 1887, naturalized, 1893; student pub. schs., Council Bluffs, Ia.; m. Anna Levy, Sept. 20, 1905; children—Raymond (dec.), Myron. Partner motion picture theater, Casino, Des Moines, 1911; acquired holdings, constructed theaters, Davenport, Ia., Omaha, Neb., also Des Moines, Cedar Rapids, Waterloo, others, 1913-29; mem. exec. com. First Nat. Pictures Corp., 1916-28; organized Central States Theater Corp., 1929, partner since 1937; organizer, pres. Tri-States Theater Corp., Des Moines, from 1933, partner, from 1937; partner Paramount Pictures, Inc., 1937-51. Leader motion picture theater participation Ia. and Neb. war loan drives, also A.R.C., March Dimes, Russian clothing, Greek war relief, U.S.O. campaigns. Exec. bd. Y.M.C.A., Boy Scouts Am., A.R.C., Am. Soc. Cancer Research, Nat. Found. Infantile Paralysis, Joint Distbn. Com., Ia. Meth. Hosp. Received ann. community award, Des Moines Register and Tribune, 1945; named mem. Meth. Hall Fame in Philanthropy, 1950; named Exhibitor of Year, Look Mag., 1953. Mem. B'nai B'rith (chmn. Ia. chpt.). Mason (Shriner). Clubs: Hyperion Country, Des Moines, Standard (Chgo.), Nat. Variety, Motion Picture Pioneers Am. Home: Des Moines, Ia.†

BLANKINSHIP, LESLIE CHARLES, govt. ofcl.; b. Buckongham, Va., Mar. 23, 1909; s. Herman and Minnie (McCraw) B.; A.B., Lynchburg Coll., 1932; grad. study U. Va., 1936; m. Elizabeth Hoye, June 9, 1934; children—Martha Elizabeth, Leslie Scott. Tchr., coach Gordonsville (Va.) High Sch., 1932-36, Randolph-Macon Acad. Fort Royal, Va., 1936-41, Lexington (N.C.) High Sch., 1941-42; dir. phys. edn. YMCA, Roanoke and Lynchburg, Va., 1946-51; gen. sec. YMCA, Daytona Beach, Fla., 1951-53; pres. Millersburg Mil. Inst., 1953-62; founder, pres., Carolina Mil. Acad., Maxton, N.C., 1962-68; dir. Jarvis Sch. Bur.; Atlanta; 1969-70; program officer U.S. Office Edn., Atlanta, 1970-73. Founder, Vardell Hall, Red Springs, N.C., 1956, Highlands Sch., Avon Park, Fla., 1966. Served with AUS, 1942-46. Presbyn. Mason (32 deg), Rotarian. Home: Stone Mountain, Ga. Died Oct. 29, 1973; buried Fort Hill Cemetery, Lynchburg, Va.

BLANN, JOHN EDWARD, govt. ofcl.; b. Hawthorne, N.J., Dec. 22, 1905; s. John Edward and Tina (Killen) B.; B.S., U. Va., 1931, C.E., 1932; m. Letitia May Wagstaff, July 28, 1934; children—Nancy W., John Edward, Peter C. Page U.S. Senate, 1920-22; clk. Civil Service Commn., 1923-27, position classification analyst, 1934-35, examiner, 1935-42, adv. fed. personnel mgmt., 1946-50, asst. chief inspection div., 1951-52; chmn. bd. appeals and review, 1952-61; personnel cons. U.S. Dept. Army, 1962. Served as col. Specialist Corps, AUS, 1942-43; comdr. USNR, 1943-46. Registered civil engr., Va. Home: Arlington, Va., Died Dec. 9, 1973.

BLAUCH, LLOYD E., educator; b. Meyersdale, Pa., May 26, 1889; s. Elias K. and Ida A. (Maust) B.; A.B., Goshen (Ind.) Coll., 1916; A.M., U. of Chicago, 1917, Ph.D., 1923; m. Mary Augusta Brannock, Aug. 9, 1928; 1 son, James Lloyd. Began career as teacher, principal and superintendent of public schools, 1905-14; spl. agt. U.S. Employment Service, 1920-21; specialist U.S. Bureau of Edn., 1921-23; prof education North Carolina Coll. for Women, 1923-30; staff mem. Survey of Methodist Colls., 1930-31; exec. sec., curriculum com. Am. Assn. Dental Schs., 1931-36; prin. ednl. specialist, advisory com. on edn., 1936-39; consultant on inter-Am. ednl. relations U.S. Office of Edn., 1939-40, sr. specialist higher education, 1940-46, specialist for land grant colls. and univs., 1946-48, chief education health professions 1948-55, asst. commr. higher edn., 1955-59, specialist for grad. edn., from 1959; member summer school faculty U. Md., 1922-40, 52, 59, U. Chgo., 1931. Recipient Superior Service award Dept. Health Edn. Welfare. Mem. Am. Coll. Dentist, Am. Assn. Dental Examiners, N.E.A., Rho Chi. Omicron Kappa Upsilon. Presbyn. Author: Intensive Study of Selected Colleges for Negroes (with Jenkins), 1942; The Pharmaceutical Curriculum (with Webster), 1952; Education for the Professions (with others), 1955, Accreditation in Higher Education (with others), 1959. Home: Washington DC. Died Feb. 20, 1974.

BLAYNEY, LINDSEY, educator; b. Lebanon, Ky., Dec. 3, 1874; s. Rev. John McClusky and Lucy Weisiger (Lindsey) B.; A.B., Centre Coll., Ky., 1894, A.M., 1897; univs. Gottingen, Geneva, Grenoble and Faculty of Lit., Florence; Ph.D., U. Heidelberg, 1904; LL.D., Southwestern U., Loyola University, New Orleans,University of Notre Dame, 1923, Austin (Texas) College, 1926, Centre Coll., Ky., 1947; m. Gertrude South, Sept. 9, 1896 (dec. 1945); children—Lucy L. (dec.), John McC., Lindsey; m. 2d, Dr. Ida Kubitz, 1948. Expdn. interior Morocco, 1899; vice consul, Mannheim, Germany, 1901-04; prof. modern langs., and history European art Central U. Ky., 1904-12; prof. German, William M. Rice Inst., Houston, 1912-24; pres. Tex. State Woman's Coll., 1924-26; dean Carleton Coll., 1926-46; Chmn. first Houston City Planning Commn.; as pres. Houston Art League, planned, negotiated for, present site Houston Mus. Art, and self-perpetuating bd. trustees. Am. Albert Kahn fellow to Orient, 1914-15. Served from maj. to lt. col. AEF, 1917-19. Decorated Croix de Guerre with palm (2). Officer Legion of Honor (France); Hon. Officer Chasseurs Alpins; Order White War Eagle, Serbia; Chevalier Order St. Sauveur (Greece); Comdr. Order Crown of Italy; 6 citations for D.S.M., Order Purple Heart (United States). American Legion del. 17th Congress FIDAC, Warsaw; del. Internat. Ednl. Congress, Heidelberg. Mem., fellow nat. and internat. orgns., Rice U. Alumni Assn. (hon.). Vice pres. Am. Fed. Arts, 1910. Presbyn. Mason, Rotarian (hon.). Author: Thomas Moore, als irisch-galischer Dichter, 1906 Ideals of Orient, 1916; To Our Country (verse series); Am. Ideals and Traditions. Contbr. Am., fgn. and lit. press. Pioneered history of art Am. Colls. and univs. Article on Philippine independence credit with slowing down Congressional action. Home: St. Croix, Minn. Died Mar. 13, 1971; buried Frankfort (Ky.) Cemetery.

BLAZER, REXFORD SYDNEY, oil co. exec.; b. Aledo, Ill., Sept. 1, 1907; s. Frederick B. and Elizabeth E. (Niederlander) B.; U. Ill., 1928; D.Sc., Pikeville Coll., 1969; B.B.A. (hon.), Morehead State U., 1973; m. Mary Elizabeth Vary, 1935 (dec.); 1 dau., Mary Linda; m. 2d,

Frances Montross Green, 1942 (div.); 1 son, Richard; m. 3d, Lucile Thornton Scott, 1954; 1 son, Rexford Sydney; stepchildren—Dan W. III, W. Thornton Scott. Joined Allied Oil Co., Cleve., 1928, dir., 1935-59, v.p., 1938, pres., 1948-59; dir. Ashland Oil & Refining Co. (Ky.) (name now Ashland Oil, Inc.), 1949, pres., 1951-57, chmn. bd., 1957-72, chmn. exec. com., 1972-73; dir. 3d Nat. Bank of Ashland. Mem. Nat. Petroleum Council, 1960-61. Mem. Eastern Ky. Regional Planning Commn., Ky. Indsl. Devel. Bd., 1956-59; mem. adv. com. Ohio Valley Improvement Assn., Nat. Waterways Conf. Dir. Spindletop Research Center, 1962-66; bd. dirs. U. Ill. Found., U. Ill. Pres.'s Club; trustee Ky. Ind. Coll. Found., 1952-64; chmn. exec. com. U. Ky. Devel. Council, also fellow, hon. alumnus U. Ky.; regent, then trustee U. of South. Recipient of Alumni Achievement award U. Ill., 1968. Mem. Am. Petroleum Inst. (v.p. transp. 1971-72, exec. com., dir. 1957-73), Nat. Petroleum Assn. (past pres.), Asphalt Inst. (dir. 1960-68), Nat. (dir., mem. exec. com., finance com. 1960-70), Western (v.p. 1957-61) petroleum refiners assns., Ky. (pres. 1955-56), Ohio (dir. 1960-68) chambers commerce, Ky. Oil and Gas Assn. (dir.), Cleve. Petroleum Club (pres. 1947), 25-year Club Petroleum Industry (pres. 1971-72), Hwy. Users Fedn. for Safety and Mobility (trustee, chmn. 1970-72, exec. com. 1968-73), Psi Upsilon (chmn. bd. govs. Omicron chpt., past v.p., exec. council). Episcopalian. (sr. warden 1959, 73, mem. exec. council Lexington diocese 1958-62). Rotarian. Clubs: Bellefonte Country (Ashland); Pendennis, Filson (Louisville); Keeneland, Idle Hour Country (Lexington); Westwood Country (Cleve.). Home: Ashland, Ky. Died Jan. 2, 1974; buried Rosehill Cemetery, Ashland, Ky.

BLIM, MILES G., coll. pres.; b. Council Grove, Kan., Mar. 23, 1898; s. William Henry and Flora Arrista (Rose) B.; A.B., Coll. Emporia (Kan.), 1919; M.A., U. Kan., 1920; grad. student U. Chgo., U. Colo.; m. Latha Daniels, Sept. 2, 1921; 1 son, Richard Don. Tchr., Atchison (Kan.) High Sch., 1920-21, vice prin., 1921-22; prof. history Jr. Coll. Kansas City, Mo., 1922-37, asst. dean, 1937-53, dean, 1953-64; pres. Met. Jr. Coll., 1964-65, pres. emeritus, 1965-72; dir. higher edn. Kansas City schs., 1957-65. Mem. Bd. Sci. Pioneers, Kansas City; mem. adv. bd. State Commn. on Missouri Higher Education. Mem. Am. Guild Organists, Phi Delta Kappa, Phi Mu Alpha. Presbyn. Rotarian. Home: Leawood, Kan. Died Aug. 27, 1972; interred Meml. Park, Kansas City, Mo.

BLINN, CHARLES PAYSON, JR., banker; b. Boston, Mass., Feb. 5, 1879; s. Charles Payson and Ida Ware (Chadbourne) B.; educated public schools, Boston; m. Etta Gallison, October 11, 1905; children—Marian (Mrs. James Ramsey Ullmann), Marjorie (Mrs. John F. P. Gallagher); m. 2d, Laura Maryland Carpenter, Apr. 13, 1937; 1 dau., Laura Maryland Carpenter, (now Mrs. David Spencer Atkinson). Asst. treas. City Trust Co., Boston, 1905-08; v.p. and dir. Nat. Union Bank, Boston, 1908-16; v.p. Phila. Nat. Bank, 1916-41, exec. v.p., 1941-44, dir., 1926-44; financial v.p., dir., Publicker Industries, Inc. (Phila.). Republican. Episcopalian. Clubs: Union League, Midday (Phila.); Merion Cricket (Haverford, Pa.); Merion Golf (Ardmore, Pa.); Eastern Yacht (Marblehead, Mass.). Home: Ardmore, Pa.†

BLISS, ARTHUR, composer; b. London, Aug. 2, 1891; s. Francis E. Bliss; ed. Rugby, Pembroke Coll., Cambridge, Eng. (hon.) fellow, 1954; Mus.D. (hon.) univs. Edinburgh, 1945, London, 1947, Cambridge, 1964, Bristol, 1954; LL.D., U. Glasgow, 1949; D.F.A., Westminster Choir Coll. Princeton U.; Litt.D., U. Lancaster; m. Gertrude Hoffmann, 1925; children—2 daus. Prof. music Royal Coll. and Royal Acad. Music; dir. music BBC, 1942-44; master Queen's Music, 1953—; composer; Colour Symphony, 1922, Oboe Quintet, 1927, Viola Sonata, 1933, Checkmate (ballet), 1937, Piano Concerto, 1939, The Olympians (opera), 1948, Lady of Shalott (ballet), 1956, Tobias and the Angel (TV opera), 1958, The Beatitudes (cantata), 1961, Mary of Magdala (cantata), 1963, The Golden Cantata, 1964, song cycle Angeles of the Mind, 1968, Concerto for Cello and Orchestra, 1969, music for films including Things to Come, 1935, Beggars' Opera, 1952, Metamorphic Variations, 1973, and others. Chmn. music com. Brit. Council, 1946-50. Decorated knight comdr. Royal Victorian Order, companion of honor, comdr. Order Leopold II; created knight, 1950; recipient Gold medal Royal Philharmonic Soc., 1963. Author: As I Remember (autobiography), 1970. Home: London, England., Died Mar. 27, 1975.

BLISS, MILDRED, philanthropist; b. N.Y.C., Sept. 1879; d. Demas and Anna Dorinda (Blaksley) Barnes; student Miss Porter's Sch., Farmington, Conn., also pvt. sch., Paris, France; m. Robert Woods Bliss, Apr. 14, 1908. Vice pres. Enfants de la Frontier, Franco-Am. orgn. for relief frontier children of World War I, 1914; founder, maintained Am. Distbg. Service, until integrated with A.R.C. in France, 1915-17; assisted Brit.-adminstered mil. hosp. for French wounded, Nevers, France, World War I; contbd. to reconstrn. La Loupe, France, and rehabilitation of inhabitants, end World War II; founder with husband and conveyed to Harvard, 1940, the Dumbarton Oaks Research Library and Collection, with it's gardens, in Washington. Dir. Am. Women's Vol. Services, Santa Barbara Bot. Gardens; trustee Mus. Modern Art N.Y., Washington Housing Assn., Nat. Recreation Assn., Nat. Symphony Assn. Washington, internat. scholarships Am. Field Service. Decorated Cross, Serbian Red Cross, 1915; Cross of Mercy, Serbia, 1919; gold medal of honor with rosette French Ministry Fgn. Affairs, 1915, Chevalier Legion of Honor, 1919, officer Legion of Honor, 1947 (France); medal Queen Elizabeth, 1918; Comdr. Order of Crown (Belgium), 1937; comdr. Royal Order of Welfare (Greece), 1961. Mem. Am. Hort. Soc. (2d v.p.), U.S.-Argentine Soc. (1st v.p.), Atlantique (adv. com.), Am. Soc. Landscape Architects, Nat. Fedn. Music Clubs, Garden Club Am., Mediaeval Acad. Am., Nat. Assn. Gardners, Nat. Assn. Housing Ofcls., Washington Choral Soc., Am. Rose Soc., N.Y., Cal. bot. socs. Clubs: Colony Hroswitha, Needle and Bobbin (N.Y.C.); 1925 F Street, American Newspaper Women's, Sulgrave (Washington). Home: Washington, D.C.†

BLISS, RALPH KENNETH, agrl. educator; b. Diagonal, Ia., Oct. 30, 1880; s. Horace and Mary Ellen (Day) B.; B.S. in Agr., Ia. State Univ., 1905, D.Sc., 1958; m. Ethel Eveleth McKinley, Sept. 14, 1912 (dec. 1945); children—Robert McKinley, William Ralph, Richard Kenneth; married second, Ella Luick, 1957. Farm mgr., 1906; in charge animal husbandry extension, 1906-11, actg. supt. agrl. extension, 1912, Ia. State Coll.; prof. animal husbandry, University Nebraska, 1912-14; driector agricultural extension Ia. State Coll., 1914-46, director emeritus since 1946. Chmn. extension section Am. Assn. Agrl. Coll. and Expt. Stas., 1917, Sec. War Emergency Food Com. of Ia., 1917; state dir. of Boys' Working Reserve, 1917-18; chmn. State Seed Stocks Com., 1917; chmn. com. on extension organization and policy of Land Grant College Assn., 1933 and 1936; mem. Ia. State Corn-Hog adjustment Com., 1933-35; chmn. State Advisory Committee, Soil Conservation Service, 1937-46; chmn. State Land Use and Program Development Com., 1939-42; mem. State Farm Security Advisory Com., 1939-46, State Agrl. Adjustment Com., State Soil Conservation Dist. Law Com., 1939-46, State U.S. Dept. Agrl. War Bd., 1941-46; rep. War Food Administration on State Manpower Priorities Commn. Recipient of National Award for Distinguished Service to American Agriculture from Am. Farm Bur. Fedn., 1943; Alumni Merit Award from Chicago Alumni of Ia. State Coll., 1946; nat. citation for leadership in 4-H Club work, 1950; plaque for outstanding leadership in soil conservation by Ia. State Soil Conservation Com., 1950; hon. award Soil Conservation work, Soil Conservation Soc., 1951; faculty citation Ia. State Coll., 1952; American Country Life Association Award, 1953; Ruby Award, 1958. Member of Epsilon Sigma Phi, Delta Sigma Rho, also Phi Kappa Phi. Republican. Conglist. Author: History of Extension Work in Iowa, 1960; also various bulls. and articles on agrl. subjects. Compiler, editor: Spirit and Philosophy of Extension, 1952. Radio commentator. Home: Ames, Ia. Died Apr. 16, 1972.

BLISS, WILLIAM LANCER, judge; b. Lincoln Twp., Polk County, Ia., Dec. 13, 1876; s. Wentworth Harrington and Ellen (MacDonald) B.; LL.B., Drake U., Des Moines, 1902; m. Margaret A. McGruder, June 6, 1906; children—Helen Frances (Mrs. David V. Temple), Ruth Corinne (Mrs. Milo Jay Conley), Robert Lancer. Admitted to Ia. bar, 1902; began practice with John A. Senneff, at Britt, Hancock County, 1904, continuing to 1914; then became mem. firm Senneff, Bliss & Witwer, later Senneff, Bliss & Senneff, Masson City; apptd. to Ia. Supreme Court, Sept. 1932; defeated at election that fall; elected to Ia. Supreme Court, fall 1938, for term 1939-45; reelected for 1945-51, 51-57, 57-63. Mem. Am., Ia. bar assns. Republican. Home: Mason City, Ia.†

BLOCH, CHARLES JULIAN, lawyer; b. Baton Rouge, Oct. 10, 1893; s. Michel and Lena (Blum) B.; student La. State U., 1909-10; A.B., U. Ga., 1913; student Mercer U. Law Sch., 1913-14; J.D., Suffolk U., 1959; m. Marie L. Klein, Nov. 8, 1917; children—Eleanor (Mrs. Jerome K. Small), Marian (Mrs. Richard A. Hecht). Admitted to Ga. bar 1914, mem. Hall, Grice & Bloch, 1933-54, Bloch, Hall, Groover & Hawkins, Macon, Ga., 1954-68, Bloch, Hall, Hawkins, & Owen, 1968-72; div. counsel (for Ga.), So. Ry. System. Chmn. Rules com. Supreme Ct. of Ga., 1946-74; bd. regents U. System of Ga., 1950-57. Past head Mar. Dimes. Del. Dem. Nat. Conv., 1932, 44, 48, 52, 60. Recipient alumni scroll U. Ga. Fellow Am. Coll. Trial Lawyers, Am. Bar Found.; mem. Am., Ga. (pres. 1944-45), Macon (past pres.) bar assns., Jud. Council Ga. (chmn. 1945-57), Order Sphinx, Phi Delta Phi, Phi Kappa Phi. Jewish religion (past pres. congregation). Elk. Clubs: Commerce (Atlanta, Ga.); Idle Hour Country (Macon, Ga.). Author: States' Rights-The Law of the Land, 1958. Editor: Ga. Bar Jour., 1958-66. Home: Macon, Ga. Died Aug. 27, 1974.

BLOCH, ROBERT GUSTAV, physician, educator; b. Nuernberg, Germany, Mar. 3, 1894; s. Sally Gustav and Gutta (Rosenberg) B.; M.D., U. Munich, 1922, grad. study, 1922-23; m. Lotte Donnerstag, Dec. 28, 1925; children—Francis Adolph, Peter Robert. Came to U.S., 1923, naturalized, 1931. Intern U. Clinics, U. Munich, 1922-23; resident physician, Montefiore Sanatorium, N.Y. City, 1923-25; instr. U. Ill., 1926-27; chief div. pulmonary diseases U. Chicago, 1927, asst. prof., 1928, asso. prof., 1930, prof. medicine, 1942-51; chief div. pulmonary diseases, Montefiore Host., N.Y.C., after 1951; clin. prof. medicine coll. phys. and surg. Columbia University. Served with German Army Service, 1914-19. Fellow American College Physicians; member A.M.A., Nat. Tuberculosis Assn., Am. Soc. Clin. Investigation, Am. Assn. Thoracic Surgery, Soc. Exptl. Biology and Medicine, Am. Thoracic Soc., Acad. Medicine, Sigma Xi. Home: New York City, N.Y. Died Apr. 1975.

BLOCK, RALPH, writer; b. Cherokee, Ia., June 21, 1889; s. Sigfried and Doris (Count) Block.; A.B., U. Mich., 1911; m. Mary Greenacre; children—Beulah (dec.), Bridget. Reporter, Louisville Courier Jour., Detroit News, dramatic editor Kansas City Star until 1917; with N.Y. Evening Sun, dramatic editor N.Y. Tribune, 1917-18; Washington staff New Republic, 1918; Washington corr. N.Y. Tribune, 1918-19; asso. editor Goldwyn Picture Corp., 1919-22; with Paramount-Famous Players-Lasky Corp., 1922-27, editor in chief, 1926-27; became asso. producer Pathe Studios 1927; with Fox Film Corp., 1929; later free-lance writer of screen plays; in Europe observing motion picture prodn., 1936-37; asst. regional dir. 9th Civilian Def. Region, U.S. Office Civilian Def., 1942; spl. asst. to personal rep. U.S. Pres. in India, 1943; gen. rep. in India overseas operations U.S. OWI and spl. asst. to U.S. commr. India, 1944-45; chief pub. affairs officer Am. Mission, New Delhi, India, 1945-46; spl. asst. to dir. Office Internat. Information, U.S. Dept. State, 1947, information policy adviser to asst. sec. state for pub. affairs, 1949-50, acting dir. fgn. information policy staff, 1951-52, dir. gen. staff, policy and plans. div. Internat. Information Administrn., 1952-53; spl. asst. to chief policy and program staff USIA, 1954, spl. adviser information center service, chief bibliog. div., 1954-60. Hon. trustee Motion Picture Relief Fund. Hon. fellow Harry S. Truman Library Inst. Recipient Medal of Freedom, War Dept., 1946; Merit citation Nat. Civil Service League, 1958; Superior Service award USIA, 1959. Mem. Screen Writers' Guild of Authors League Am. (past pres.), Am. Fgn. Service Assn., Phi Beta Kappa, Michigamua. Clubs: Players, Coffee House (N.Y.C), Fossils (Chevy Chase, Md.). Home: Washington DC. Died Jan. 2, 1974.

BLOEDORN, FERNANDO GERMANE, educator, physician; b. Varginha, Brazil, Oct. 12, 1913; s. Reynaldo and Maria (Pasquale) B.; M.D., U. del Litoral, Rosario, Argentina, 1936; m. Nelida Ansaldi, Feb. 10, 1938. Came to U.S., 1951, naturalized, 1957. Instr. anatomy U. del Litoral, 1933-36; intern Hosp. Centenario, Rosario, 1934-36; dir. surgery pvt. clinic, San Pedro, Argentina, 1936-49; asst. surgeon Hosp. San Pedro, 1943-48; scholar Brit. Council in Eng., 1948-51; sr. resident radiotherapy Frances Delafield Hosp., N.Y.C., 1951; asso. radiotherapist M.D. Anderson Hosp. and Tumor Inst., Houston, 1951-55; head div. radiotherapy U. Md. Hosp., 1955-68, asso. prof. radiology Sch. Medicine, 1955-60, prof., 1960-68, chmn., prof. dept. therapeutic radiology at Tufts-New Eng. Med. Center, 1968-75; cons. numerous hosps. in area, 1956-75. Mem. radiation study sect. NIH, 1963-67, 69-73, mem. com. for radiation therapy studies, 1971-75. Diplomate Am. Bd. Radiology. Fellow Am. Coll. Radiology; mem. Inter-Am. Coll. Radiology (sec. 1968-70), Balt. Med. Soc., Med. and Chirurgical Faculty Md., A.M.A., Am. Soc. Therapeutic Radiologists (pres. elect), Am. Radium Soc. (pres. 1969-70, chmn. exec. com. 1972-73), Md. Radiol. Soc., Radiol. Soc. N.Am., Pan Am. Med. Assn., New Eng. Cancer Soc., New Eng. Roentgen Ray Soc.; hon. mem. numerous fgn. med. assns. Contbr. profl. jours. Home: Boston, Mass. Died Sept. 6, 1975; Interred Rosario, Argentina.

BLOOD, ROBERT OSCAR, physician, ex-gov.; b. Enfield, N.H., Nov. 10, 1887; s. William E. and Lorinda (Colby) B.; M.D., Dartmouth Coll., 1913, A.M., 1941; LL.D., Univ. of New Hampshire, 1941; m. Pauline Shepard, June 3, 1916; children—Robert O., Jr. Horace S., Emily. Interne Mary Hitchcock Memorial Hosp., Hanover, N.H., 1913-14; post grad. work in Boston and New York, N.Y.; mem. surg. and obstet. staff Margaret Pillsbury Gen. Hosp., Concord, N.H., since 1916; owner-mgr. Crystal Spring Farm, East Concord, N.H.; president City Realty Co. Governor of State of New Hampshire for term 1941-43, re-elected Governor for the term 1943-45. Served as lieut., later advanced through grades to maj., Med. Corps., U.S.A., 1917-19, with A.E.F. in France; lieut. col. M.O.R.C. since 1927. Decorated with Croix de Guerre (France); 26th Div. Distinguished Service Cross (U.S.). Fellow Am. Coll. Surgeons; mem. Am. Med. Assn., N.E. Obstet. and Gynecol. Soc., N.H. Surg. Soc., N.H. Med. Soc., Am. Legion. Republican. Congregationalist. I.O.O.F. Home: Concord, N.H. Died Aug. 1975.

BLOOM, MELVIN HAROLD, surgeon; b. Des Moines, Jan. 10, 1925; s. Morris and Sadie (Yeglin) B.; M.D., U. Ia., 1954. Intern, Mercy Hosp., Des Moines, 1954-55; resident in gen. surgery Des Moines VA Hosp., 1955-59, asst. sect. chief gen surgery, 1959-74; practice medicine, specializing in surgery, Des Moines, 1960-74; clin. instr. surgery U. Ia., Iowa City, 1971-74, clin. asst. prof. surgery, 1974. Served with AUS, 1943-46; ETO, NATOUSA. Diplomate Am. Bd. Surgery. Mem. A.M.A., Polk County, Ia. med. socs. Home: Des Moines, Ia., Died Dec. 9, 1974; buried Des Moines, Ia.

BLOOMER, MILLARD J., JR., lawyer; b. N.Y.C., June 10, 1899; s. Millard J. and Nellie Adams (Crist) B.; A.B., Columbia, 1920, LL.B., 1923; m. Patricia Foss, Sept. 12, 1962; 1 son by previous marriage, George L. Admitted to N.Y. bar, 1924, practiced in N.Y.C.; asso. Cravath, Swaine & Moore, 1923-40; mem. firm Rand, French & Carpenter, 1940, Bloomer & Jacobi, 1941, Wickes, Riddell, Bloomer, Jacobi & McGuire, 1941. Dir Res. Bank of Peru, Caja de Depositos y Consignaciones Peru. Chmn. Columbia Class of 1920 Reunion Com., 1945-70, chmn. Columbia Law Sch. Fund Class of 1923, 1957-65, mem. Columbia Coll. Council, 1959-63, chmn., 1962-63, exec. com., 1960-62, chmn. com. on budget, 1960-62, chmn. nominating com., 196061; bd. dirs., v.p. Met. Opera Guild, later bd. dirs. Emeritus; v.p., mem. exec. com. Masterpieces of Art Exhibit, N.Y. Worlds Fair, 1939-40. Recipient Columbia Alumni Fedn. Alumni medal, 1961. Mem. Am., N.Y. State bar assns., Assn. Bar City N.Y., N.Y. County Lawyers Assn., Am. Judicature Soc., Acad. Polit. Sci. (life), Municipal Art Soc. N.Y., France-Am. Soc., John Jay Assos., Sr. Soc. Sachems, Kent Moot Ct., Soc. Older Grads., Columbia U. Club Found., Columbia Assos., Down Town Assn., Sigma Sci. Clubs: The Creek (Locust Valley, L.I.). Extensive travel in Europe and S.Am.; mem. Am. Olympic Fencing Team, 1920. Home: New York City, N.Y. Died July 2, 1974.

BLOSSOM, ROBERT ALDEN, pathologist; b. St. Paul, Jan. 29, 1923; s. Frank Edward and Margaret Hilda (Morris) B.; M.D., St. Louis U., 1948; m.; children—Sue Ellen, Robert Alden deCourcy, Randolph Stevens. Intern, Los Angeles County Gen. Hosp., 1948-49, resident, 1949-51, fellow in pathology, 1953-54; practice medicine specializing in pathology, 1954-71; mem. staff Los Angeles County Hosp., Rancho Los Amigos Hosp. for Poliomyelitis; dir. labs. Ventura County Hosp.; instr. pathology U. So. Cal. Med. Sch., 1954-61; pathologist St. John's Hosp., Oxnard, Cal., Community Hosp., Ventura Gen. Hosp., Ventura. Served to lt. (j.g.) M.C., USNR, 1951-53. Diplomate Am. Bd. Pathology. Fellow Coll. Am. Pathologists, Am. Soc. Clin. Pathologists; mem. A.M.A., Ventura County Med. Soc., Ventura County Cancer Soc. (pres.), Phi Chi. Republican. Episcopalian (vestryman). Home: Ventura, Cal. Died Aug. 24, 1971; buried Ivy Lawn Cemetery, Ventura, Cal.

BLOUGH, ELIJAH ROBERT, physician; b. Somerset Co., Pa., Apr. 7, 1878; s. Benjamin and Rachel (Berkey) B.; Pharm. D., Phila. Coll. Pharmacy, 1902; M.D., Eclectic Med. Coll., Cincinnati, O., 1907; m. Catherine E. Bevan, of Parnassus, Pa., June 29, 1910. Began practice at Carrick Borough, now part of Pittsburgh, 1908; owner Carrick Pharmacy, 1908-13. Served as 1st lt., Med. Corps, U.S.A., World War. Mem. Nat. Eclectic Med. Assn. (pres. 1932-33), Pa. Eclectic Med. Assn. (ex-pres.; corr. sec.), Pa. Eclectic Med. Soc., Allegheny Co. Med. Soc., Sigma Theta. Republican. Baptist. Mason (32°), Shriner. Home: Pittsburgh, Pa.†

BLOUNT, GEORGE DEXTER, lawyer; b. Live Oak, Fla., Feb. 16, 1881; s. Judson O'Connor and Rebeccah (Dexter) B.; B.Ph., Emory U., Oxford Ga., 1901; LL.B., U. of Ga., 1903, Yale, 1904; m. Mary Deane, Apr. 24, 1908; children—Deane, Mary Dexter Liscum. Admitted to Georgia bar, 1904, and practiced in Savannah, Georgia, 1904-06; admitted to Colorado bar, 1904, and practiced in Savannah, Georgia, 1904-06; admitted to Colorado bar, 1907; partner in firm of Bicksler, Bennett, Dana & Blount, Denver, 1910-12, Dana & Blount, 1912-18, Dana, Blount & Silverstein, 1918-29, Blount January and Yegge, 1938-42; regional attorney for Rocky Mountain Region War Production Bd., 1942-45; regional counsel War Assets Adminstrn. 1945-49. Captain, artillery, U.S. Army, World War I. Mem. Am. Bar Assn. (mem. gen. council 1934-36, state del., 1936-39; board of govs., 1939-42), Colo. State Bar Assn., (pres. 1938-39), Denver Bar Assn. (pres. 1934-35), Denver Law Club (pres. 1923), Commercial Law League of America (pres. 1935-36), Internat. Assn. of Ins. Counsel, Kappa Alpha, Phi Delta Phi. Democrat. Mason (Shriner). Clubs: Denver, Denver Athletic, Denver Country, Wigwam, Gyro, Rotary. Home: Denver, Colo.†

BLOUNT, ROY A., banker; b. Hosford, Fla., Oct. 9, 1913; s. N.C. and Lou Allie (Wylie) B.; student Ind. U., 1960-61; m. Louise Floyd, June 10, 1938; children—Roy A., Susan Louise. Office mgr. Libby, McNeill & Libby, 1934-66; regional mgr. Packard Motor Car Corp., 1946-56; dist. mgr. Ford Motor Co., 1956-58; with Decatur Fed. Savs. & Loan Assn. (Ga.), 1958-74, pres., 1960-74, also dir. Bd. dirs., Met. Atlanta Rapid Transit Authority, 1965-74, past chmn. Trustee Wesley Woods Home, Decatur, 1964-74. Mem. U.S. (exec. com.), Ga. (past pres.) savs. and loan leagues, Dekalb County C. of C. (pres. 1963). Methodist (chmn. trustee). Rotarian. Home: Avondale Estates, Ga. Died 1974.

BLUM, ELIAS, musician; b. Eisdorf, Hungary, Feb. 22, 1881; s. Elias and Eva (Glaser) B.; came to U.S., 1891; student New Eng. Conservatory, Boston; studied under Dr. Percy Goetschius 2 yrs.; grad. Grand Ducal Sch. of Music, Weimar, Germany, 1908; M. Jenny Hallbauer, Aug. 16, 1910. Début as tenor soloist at Weimar, 1907, also as composer and organist, 1907; concert singer and organist, Boston, 1908-09; dir. Conservatory of Music, Whitman Coll., Walla Walla, Wash., 1909-17; prof. theory of music and singing, Grinnell (Ia.) Coll., from 1917; organist and dir. of music, First Congl. Ch., Grinnell; dean of fine arts Des Moines U., 1926-27. Ex-pres. Northwest Music Teachers' Assn.; colleague Am. Guild organists. Composer of anthems, choruses, songs, choruses with orchestra, piano and organ solos, notably Capriccio in B Minor (piano); Passacaglia in B Minor (organ); The Last Tea of Tsuki; Female Chorus, soil and orchestra; Silverbells and Cockleshells (female chorus, piano, violin, cello and soli); On the Sunset Trail (male chorus, soli and orchestra); Romany Rede (scene for female chorus, soil and orchestra); Symphonic Variations for organ and orchestra. Home: Grinnell, Ia.†

BLUME, CLINTON WILLIS, realtor; b. Bklyn., Oct. 17, 1898; s. Ernest W. and Mary Adelaide (Fairhurst) B.; B.S., Colgate U., 1926: m. Dorothy Chatman Wells Greve, May 20, 1966; children—Clinton Willis, Bradford Longfellow. Pres. Clinton W. Blume Realty Corp., N.Y.C., from 1950; pres., treas. Clinton W. Blume Co., Inc., N.Y.C., from 1950; trustee Lincoln Savs. Bank. Cons., adviser Gt. Atlantic & Pacific Tea Co., from 1939; cons., broker numerous cos., lawyers, estates, banks, financial instns., from 1930; dir. Realty Adv. Bd. on Labor Relations, from 1950; mem. adv. com. FHA, 1954; v.p. Realty Found. N.Y., 1954. Mem. exec. com. Met. Fair Rent Com.; mem. exec. council Joint Conf. for Better Govt. in N.Y.C., 1954; mem. council St. John's U., 1955; chmn. real estate com. Nat. council Boy Scouts Am., 1955. Arthritis and Rhematism Found., 1945; active numerous other civic orgns. Bd. dirs. N.Y. Conv. and Visitors Bur., West Side Youth Found.; trustee L.I. U., 1961-69. Served with USN, 1918. Named Real Estate Man of Year, Real Estate Sq. Center of N.Y., 1954, medal for outstanding accomplishment in keeping N.Y.C. sports capital of world City of N.Y., 1961. Mem. Nat. (dir., exec. com., ethics com.), N.Y. State (dir.), Met. (past pres.) assns. real estate bds., Real Estate Bd. N.Y. (pres. 1954-56, past gov., life mem. sales brokers com.), Am. Soc. Real Estate Counselors (charter, gov.), Nat. Inst. Real Estate Brokers (dir.), Nat. Realty Club (past pres.), West Side Assn. Commerce (v.p., dir.), Am. Irish Hist. Soc. (life), Am. Legion, Delta Kappa Epsilon. Clubs: Union Leagur (N.Y.C.); St. George Golf and Country (Stony Brook, N.Y.); Yale. Home: Islip, N.Y. Died June 12, 1973; buried Ferncliff Cemetery, Westchester County, N.Y.

BLUSTEIN, HERMAN, physician; b. Chgo., Aug. 6, 1916; s. Israel and Bessie Blustein; M.D., U. Ill., 1941; m. Sylvia Andelman, June 8, 1941; children—David Aron, Rachel L. (Mrs. Martin Allen), Marian F. (Mrs. Wallace Lane Peters), Joseph N. Rotating intern Alexian Bros. Hosp., Chgo., 1940-41; clin. tng. Manteno (Ill.) State Hosp., 1941-42; jr. clin. fellow dept. nervous and mental disease Northwestern U. Med. Sch., Chgo., 1941-42; mem. dean's com. on neurology VA Hosp., Hines, Ill., 1946-49, neuropsychiatrist, 1946-54; neurologist VA Regional Office, Chgo., 1954-55; chief neurology service VA Hosp., Downey, Ill., 1955-57, chief phys. medicine and rehab., 1958-62; clin. dir. Ariz. State Hosp., Phoenix, 1957-58; staff psychiatrist VA Westside Hosp., Chgo.; clin. asst. prof. neurology Chgo. Med. Sch.; clin. asst. prof. psychiatry U. Ill. Served to capt., M.C., AUS, 1942-46. Diplomate Am. Bd. Psychiatry and Neurology. Mem. A.M.A., Chgo. Med. Soc., Am. Acad. Neurology, Am. Psychiat. Assn., Assn. Research in Nervous and Mental Disease. Contbr. articles to med. jours. Home: Chicago, Ill., Died Apr. 5, 1970; buried Poale Zedeck Cemetery.

BLYDEN, LARRY (IVAN LAWRENCE BLIEDEN), actor, dir., producer; b. Houston, June 23, 1925; s. Adolph and Marian (Davidson) Blieden; student Southwestern La. Inst., 1943-44; B.S., U. Houston, 1948; studied performing arts with Stella Adler, Ethel Meyers, Frank Wagner, Matt Mattox; m. Carol Haney, Apr. 17, 1954 (div. 1961); children—Joshua, Ellen. Made N.Y.C. debut in Mr. Roberts, 1948; since appeared in N.Y. plays The Miser, 1950, Wish You Were Here, 1952, Oh, Men. Oh, Women, 1953, Italian Straw Hat, 1957, Who Was That Lady I Saw You With? 1958, Flower Drum Song, 1958, Foxy, 1964, Luv, 1965, The Apple Tree, 1968, You Know I Can't Hear You When the Water's Running, 1969; appeared in The Time of Your Life, Brussels World's Fair, 1958, Foxy, Dawson City, Yukon, Can., 1962; dir. Harold, N.Y.C., 1962; appeared in films Bachelor Party, 1957, Kiss Them for Me, 1957, On a Clear Day You Can See Forever, 1969, TV programs What Makes Sammy Run? 1960, Joe and Mabel, 1954, Harry's Girls, 1963, others; master ceremonies TV program Personality, 1967-69, The Movie Game, 1969-71, What's My Line; producer revival of A Funny Thing Happened on the Way to the Forum, 1972. Mem. Actors Equity Assn., Am. Fedn. TV and Radio Actors. Screen Actors Guild. Home: New York City, N.Y. Died June 6, 1975.

BOARDMAN, PAUL LAWRENCE, banker; b. Indpls., Oct 22, 1906; s. Fred Lawrence and Nettie Rae (Beaver) B.; extension student Ind. U.; student Am. Inst. Banking Grad. Sch. Banking, Rutgers U.; m. Mary C. Mackey, Apr. 12, 1928. With Am. Fletcher Nat. Bank Trust Co., Indpis., 1923-71, v.p., 1957-64, sr. v.p., 1964-71, ret., 1971. Mem. Am. Inst. Banking (nat. chmn. pub. relations com. 1954), Ind. Bankers Assn., Indpis. C. of C., Ind. Soc. Pioneers. Mason (Shriner). Club: Hillcrest Country (Indpls.). Home: Indianapolis, Ind. Died Dec. 31, 1974; buried Memorial Park Cemetery, Indianapolis, Ind.

BOBBITT, JOSEPH MATTHEW, psychologist; b. St. Joseph, Mo., Oct. 26, 1908; s. Joseph Matthew and Della Pearl (Carlin) B.; A.B., U. So. Cal., 1931, A.M., 1932; Ph.D., Northwestern U., 1937; m. Katherine C. Long, June 16, 1949; 1 son, Bruce Long. Instr. psychology Mich. State Coll., 1937-41, asst. prof., 1941-42; mem. profl. services br. Nat. Inst. Mental Health, USPHS, 1946-50, acting chief profl. services br., 1950-51, chief, 1951-57, asst. dir. Nat. Inst. Mental Health, 1957-60, asso. dir., 1960-64; asst. dir. manpower devel., acting asso. dir. program planning, acting asso. dir. communications Nat. Inst. Child Health and Human Devel., NIH, USPHS, 1964-66, asst. dir. for behavioral scis. Office Planning and Evaluation, Nat. Inst. Child Health and Human Devel., 1969-75; exec. dir. Joint Commn. on Mental Health of Children, 1966-69. Mem. research com. Adv. Council to Pres.'s Com. on Traffic Safety. Served from lt. (j.g.) to lt. comdr., USCGR, 1942-46. Recipient Harold M. Hildreth Meml. award Div. Psychologists in Pub. Service Am. Psychol. Assn., 1967. Fellow Am. Psychol. Assn.; mem. Eastern, D.C. psychol. assns., Am. Psychopath. Assn., Soc. Research Child Devel., Phi Beta Kappa, Sigma Xi, Psi Chi, Phi Delta Kappa. Club: Cosmos (Washington). Home: Bethesda, Md., Died July 24, 1975.

BOBBITT, MARY LAVINIA REED (MRS. VERNON L. BOBBITT), librarian; b. Blue Point, L.I., N.Y., July 13, 1914; d. William Ebenezer and Emma (DuPuy) Reed; grad. Emma Willard Sch., 1933; student U. Mich., 1934-35; B.A., Vassar Coll., 1937; B.S., Columbia, 1939; m. Vernon L. Bobbitt, Feb. 11, 1942; children—Susan DuPuy (Mrs. Theodore Wells Pietsch III), Cara Lane Hochhaller. Head librarian Central Coll. Library, Pella, Ia., 1939-41; art librarian U. Ia., Iowa City, 1942-43; library staff N.Y. Hist. Soc., N.Y.C., 1943-44; library staff Albion (Mich.) Coll., 1947-48, curator West Mich. Meth. Hist. Collection, 1967-72. Mem. Albion Community Hosp. League, 1969-72. Mem. Am. Assn. U. Women (treas. 1947), Albion Arts Council (bd. mem. 1967-70), Community Arts Program (bd. mem. 1969-72), Gamma Phi Beta. Methodist (mem. exec. bd. 1967-70). Author: A Guide to the Central College Library, 1940; A Bibliography of Etiquette Books Published in America Before 1900, 1947; With Dearest Love to All, The Life and Letters of Lady Jebb, 1960; A Short History of Albion, 1965. Home Albion Mich. Died Dec. 30, 1972.

BOCQUERAZ, LEON EDWARD, banker; b. San Francisco, Calif., Dec. 31, 1871; s. Antoine and Mathilde (Girod) B.; student Lycée Janson de Sailly and Ecole de Droit, Paris; B.Litt. and B.S., U. of Paris; m. Claire Chabot, July 28, 1908; 1 dau., Suzanne (Mrs. Lewis G. Carpenter, Jr.). Secretary of the French American Bank, San Francisco, 1902-07, vice-pres., 1907-17, pres., 1917-27; pres. United Bank & Trust Co., 1927; chmn. bd. Bank of America of Calif., 1928; dir. Bank of America N.T.&S.A.; chmn. bd. Merchants Nat. Realty Corp.; dir. Capital Co., Pacific Nat. Fire Ins. Co., South San Francisco Land and Improvement Co., Cosumnes Gold Dredging Co.; director Pacific Oil & Gas Development Corporation. President Fed. French Alliance, U.S. and Can. Decorated Comdr. Legion of Honor (France). Mem. Calif. Hist. Soc., Am. Soc. French Legion of Honor, France-Amerique, Cal. Acad. of Science. Roman Catholic. Clubs: Pacific Union, Burlingame Country; Union Interalliée (Paris); Press and Union League, Cercel de L'Union, Claremont Country. Home: San Francisco, Cal.†

BODINE, ROY L., dentist, ret. army officer; b. West Manchester, O., Oct. 19, 1883; s. James E. and Catherine (Siler) B.; D.D.S., Ind. Dental Coll., 1903; m. Zelda Hobart Read, June 12, 1907; children—Roy L., Donald R. Prosthodontist, Indpls., 1903-17; commd. 1st lt. U.S. Army Dental Corps, 1917, advanced through grades to col., 1943; dentist Maxilo-Facial Clinic, Walter Reed Hosp., Washington, 1919-22; faculty Army Dental Sch., Washington, 1921-22; prof. George Washington U., Dental Sch., Washington, 1921-22; organizer, 1st comdg. officer Army Dental Tech. Sch. and Lab., Army Med. Center, Washington, 1926-30; organizer, comdg. officer Central Dental Lab., Presidio of San Francisco, 1943-47; ret., 1947. Mem. Am. Dental Assn. (life), Ret. Army Officers of San Francisco (sec. 1950-55, pres. 1957), Delta Sigma Delta. Rotarian. Contbr. articles to profl. jours. Home: Duarte Cal. Died Sept. 28, 1974.

BODMER, WALTER, painter, sculptor; b. Basel, Switzerland, Aug. 12, 1903; s. Gottlieb and Mrs. (Gessier) B.; ed. Ecole des Arts et Metiers, Basel; m. Marthe Eckerie, 1945. Prof. drawing Ecole des Arts et Metiers; mem. commn. Found. Kiefer-Hablitzer, Lucerne Switzerland; mem. Commn. Art Museum, Basel; work represented museums, Basel, Zurich, St. Gall, Bern, Stuttgart, Germany, Modern Art Mus. Paris, Museo civico, Turin, Italy, Middleheim Park, Antwerp, Belgium, Cambridge, Mass.; sculpture exhibited Comml. Univ. St. Gall; executed relief for Swiss Sch. in Rio de Janeiro, 1971; relief for entrance lobby, main office bldg. Hoffmann-La Roche Inc., Nutley, N.J., also relief for entrance main office bldg. Hoffman-LaRoche,

Basel, Switzerland. Recipient Solomon Guggenheim Found. Nat. prize, Art prize City of Basel, 1968. Address: Basel, Switzerland., Died June 3, 1973.

BODY, RALPH C., U.S. judge; b. Yellow House, Pa., Feb. 18, 1903; s. Howard W. and Mary Alice (Esterly) B.; A.B., Pa. State U., 1925; LL.B., U. Pa., 1928; m. Ruth Sproesser, July 26, 1930; children—R. William, Howard E., Ruth Eleanor (Mrs. Terry E. Fetterman). Admitted to Pa. Bar, 1928; asso. Stevens & Lee, 1928-36; partner Body, Muth, Rhoda & Stoudt, 1936-60; judge Court of Common Pleas of Berks County, 1960-62, U.S. Dist. Ct., Eastern Dist. Pa., 1962-73. Solicitor for Recorder of Deeds, 1933-36, HOLC, 1933-41; asst. county solicitor, 1936-38; mem. Berks County Bd. Law Examiners, 1946-60. Mem. exec. bd. Daniel Boone Council Boy Scouts Am. Del. Democratic Nat. Conv., 1952. Served with AUS, 1941-46; lt. col. Res. Fellow Am. Coll. Trial Lawyers, Am. Coll. Probate Counsel; mem. Am. Legion (past comdr.), Fed., Am., Pa., Berks County bar assns., Internat. Assn. Ins. Counsel, Vets. Fgn. Wars, Scabbard and Blade, Phi Kappa Psi, Phi Delta Phi, Pi Delta Epsilon. Mem. Church of Christ. Mason. Clubs: Wyomissing; Hare Law; Endlich Law (past pres.): Rotary (past pres.) (Boyertown). Home: Boyertown Pa. Died June 5, 1973.

BOESEL, FRANK TILDEN, lawyer; b. New Bremen, O., Aug. 2, 1876; s. Charles and Mary (Schroeder) B.; Ph.B., Ohio State U., 1896; LL.B., Harvard, 1899; m. Ella H. Manegold, June 19, 1906; children—Charles M., John P., Marianna (Mrs. Frederick D. Ivins). Admitted to Wis. bar, 1899; practiced law in Milwaukee, in all courts, state and fed., from Aug. 1, 1899; mem. law sch. faculty, U. of Wis. from 1911; apptd. special master in railroad reorganizations for 7th U.S. Circuit, by U.S. Circuit Court of Appeals, 1933; special counsel for Insurance Dept. of Wis. in liquidation of insurance companies; special prosecutor for Milwaukee County Grand Jury, 1922-33. Treas. Nat. Conf. Judicial Councils; mem. Advisory Com. on Rules of Pleading Practice and Procedure to Wis. Supreme Court from 1929. Awarded citation U. Wis., 1948. Member panel of arbitrators, American Arbitration Assn.; compliance commissioner, War Prdn. Bd. Delegate Internat. Congress of Comparative Law, The Hague, 1932, 37, Inter-Am. Bar Assn., Havana, Cuba, 1941, Life mem. Am. Law Inst.; mem. Am. Judicature Soc., Wis. State Bar (past pres.), Milwaukee Bar Assn. (past pres.), Am. Bar Assn. (past mem. bd. of govs.), Order of Coif, Phi Delta Phi, Phi Beta Kappa (pres. Milwaukee chapter). Mason (32°; K.T.; Shriner). Democrat. Conglist. Clubs: Milwaukee, City (past pres.), University, Harvard (all in Milwaukee); University (Madison, Wis.); Union League (Chicago). Author: Cases on Wisconsin Code Procedure, 1926. Co-author: Bryant's Wisconsin Pleading and Practice, 1931. Contbr. law jours. Home: Milwaukee, Wis.†

BOETTGER, THEODORE, chmn. bd. United Piece Dye Wks.; b. Union City, N.J., July 13, 1876; s. Henry William and Pauline (Stoppel) B.; Hoboken Acad., 1883-92, Walworth Business Coll., 1893, Textile Sch., Grefeld, Germany, 1896-98; m. Charlotte Jahns, Feb. 23, 1901; children—Helen Louise, Anna (Mrs. Wolfgang Rudolf Hutz), Charlotte (Mrs. Joseph B. Ryan), Margarita (Mrs. Harold A. Kipp). Office employee, 1894-96; mgr. Boettger Piece Dye Works, Lodi, N.J., 1899; v.p. United Piece Dye Works, 1903, pres., 1922, chmn. bd. of dirs., from 1936; dir. Pub. Service Corp. of N.J. Commissioner Palisade Interstate Park Commn., 1945. Chmn. N.J. Interstate Bridge and Tunnel Com. (built the Holland Tunnel and Camden (Phila.) Bridge), 1922-30. Former v.p. chmn. exec. com. Hackensack Hosp. Elk. Clubs: New York Athletic, Arcola Country, Essex (Newark, N.J.). Home: Hackensack, N.J., Died Oct. 10, 1975.

BOGARDUS, EMORY STEPHEN, sociologist, editor, educator; b. nr. Belvidere, Ill., Feb. 21, 1882; s. Henry Brown and Eliza Maria (Stevenson) B.; A.B., Northwestern U., 1908, A.M., 1909; Ph.D., U. Chgo., 1911; Litt. D., U. So. Cal., 1945, U. Ariz., 1960; L.H.D., U. Redlands, Cal., 1946; LL.D., Boston U., 1950; m. Edith Mildred Pritchard, Aug. 9, 1911; 1 dau., Ruth Mildred. Fellow Northwestern U. Settlement, Chgo., 1908-09; fellow in sociology U. Chgo., 1909-11; asst. prof. sociology and econs. U. So. Cal., 1911-13, asso. prof., 1913-15, prof. sociology, from 1915, also organizer and first chmn. same dept., dir. Social Work div., 1920-37, dean, 1937-39, acting dean Grad. Sch., 1926-27, ann. research lectr., 1937, dean, 1945-49, dean, prof. emeritus. Vis prof. sociology Northwestern U., summer 1926, U. Wash., summer 1928. Regional research dir. (So. Cal.) Pacific Coast Race Relations Survey, 1923-25; social research dir. Boys Work Survey of Los Angeles, 1924-25. Pres. Los Angeles Social Service Commn., 1916-18; mem. bd. Goodwill Industries of So. Cal., 1919-49; trustee All Nations Found., 1940-55. Recipient Merit award Northwestern U., 1933. Registered social worker, Cal. Mem. Am. Assn. Social Workers (pres. Los Angeles chpt. 1923-25), Am. (pres 1931), Pacific (pres. 1929) Sociol. socs., Phi Beta Kappa, Delta Sigma Rho, Phi Kappa Phi, Alpha Pi Zeta, Alpha Kappa Delta (nat. pres., 1924-28, and 1947), Phi Delta Kappa, Editor: Jour. Sociology and Social Research, 1916-61, ann. proceedings, Pacific Sociol. Society, 1930-39; univ. editor U. So. Cal., 1942-45; adv. editor Dictionary of Sociology, 1944; editor Research News, U. So. Cal., 1945-49. Author numerous books, 1912, latest being: Fundamentals of Social Psychology, 4th edit., 1950; The Making of Public Opinion, 1951; Principles of Cooperation, 1952, 3rd edit., 1964 Spanish edit., 1964; Sociology Applied to Nursing (with Brethorst) 3rd edit., 1952; Sociology, 4th edition, 1954; The Development of Social Though, 4th edit., 1960, also Spanish, Indian, Portuguese edits., 1964-65; History of Cooperation, 2d edit., 1965; The Traveler, 1956; Social Distance, 1959; Problems of Cooperation, 1960; The Explorer, 1961; Much Have I learned, 1962; Toward a World Community, 1964; Thrice-Seven Wonders of the World, 1965; The Observer, 1966; A Forty-Year Racial Distance Study, 1967; The Wonderful World of Sonnets, 1968; New Concepts for Sociology, 1969; Personal Tributes to Friends, 1970. Contbr. articles. Address: Los Angeles, Cal. Died Aug. 21, 1973; buried Forest Lawn Meml. Park, Glendale, Cal.

BOHAN, MERWIN LEE, Latin Am. cons., b. Chgo., Jan. 21, 1899; s. Daniel Joseph and Delia (Lee) B.; ed. Am. Grammar Sch., Mexico City, Mexico, 1909-13; grad. Dallas High Sch., 1916; m. Harriet Davis, Feb. 5, 1921; children—Elizabeth Rowe, Harriet Davis. Clk. Pierce Fordyce Oil Assn., Dallas, 1916, Cia. Mex. de Petroleo El Agulia, Mexico City, 1917, Am. consulate, 1919, Am. embassy, Mexico, 1920; asst. mgr. U.S. Rubber Export Co., 1920-22; with Dallas C. of C. (fgn. trade sec. and publicity mgr.), 1922-26; trade commr. U.S. Dept. Commerce, Havana, 1927, asst. comml. attache, 1927; comml. attache Guatemala, San Salvador and Honduras, 1928-31, Peru and Ecuador, 1931-33, Chile, 1933-40, Colombia, 1940-41; chief U.S. Econ. Mission to Bolivia, 1941-42; counselor of embassy for econ. affairs Am. embassy, Buenos Aires, 1942; assigned to Dept. of State, 1944-45; counsellor of embassy for econ. affairs, Mexico City, 1945-49, ret. 1949; prof. internat. relations Am. Inst. Fgn. Trade, Phoenix, 1949-50; mem. U.S. delegation GATT Conf., Torquay, Eng., 1950-51; U.S. ambassador Inter-Am. Econ. and Social Council, 1951-55; U.S. commr. Joint Brazil U.S. Econ. Devel. Commn., 1952-53; ret. 1955; cons. to U.S. and internat. agys., Dept. State, AID, UN, OAS, others, 1955-72. Decorated grand cross Order of So. Cross (Brazil, 1956), grand officer Order of Quetzal (Guatemala) 1962. Mason. Author publ. Investment in Cuba. 1956; Investment in Chile, 1960. Home: Dallas, Tex., Died Nov. 23, 1975.

BOHLEN, CHARLES EUSTIS, investment co. exec., b. Clayton, N.Y., Aug 30, 1904; grad. St. Paul's Sch.; A.B., Harvard, 1927; LL.D. (hon.), Columbia, 1968; m. Avis Howard Thayer; children—Avis T., Charles E., Celestine E. Fgn. service officer, 1929-69; vice consul, Prague, 1929-31, Moscow, 1934; sec. in diplomatic service, 1934; 3d sec., Moscow, 1934; with Dept. State, 1936, 42; sec. U.S. delegation Internat. Sugar Conf., London, 1937; 2d sec., Moscow, 1937; sec. U.S. delegation Conf. of Brussels, 1937; consul, Moscow, 1938; 2d sec., Tokyo, 1940-41; asst. chief Div. European Affairs, 1943; accompanied Sec. of State to Moscow Conf., 1943; attended Tehran Conf., 1943; 1st sec., Moscow, 1942-44; chief Div. Eastern European Affairs, 1944; area adviser U.S. Group, Dumbarton Oaks Conversations on Internat. Orgn., Washington, 1944; asst. to sec. of State for White House Liaison, 1944; accompanied Pres. Roosevelt to Crimea Conf., 1945; polit. and liaison ofcr., U.S. del. U.N. Conf. on Internat. Orgns., San Francisco, 1945; polit. adviser U.S. delegation Berlin Conf., 1945; asst. to U.S. mem. Meeting of Council Fgn. Ministers, London, 1945; detailed to Meeting of Fgn. Secs., Moscow, 1945; polit. adviser U.S. del. 2d session Conf. Fgn. Ministers, Paris, 1946; polit. adviser, U.S. del. Paris Conf., 1946; spl. polit. adviser U.S. del., Paris Conf., N.Y.C., 1946; apptd. spl. asst. to sec. of State, 1946; polit, adviser, U.S. del., 4th session Council Fgn. Ministers, 1947; apptd. counselor Dept. State 1947, 51; adviser, U.S. del. Gen. Assembly, UN, N.Y., 1947; adviser U.S. del. to Council Fgn. Ministers, London, 1947; adviser, U.S. del., Gen. Assembly U.N., Paris, 1948; minister at Paris, 1949; U.S. ambassador to Russia, 1953-57, Philippines, 1957-59. France, 1962-68; spl. asst. to sec. of state for Soviet affairs, 1959-61; dep. under sec. state for polit. affairs, Washington, 1968-69; ret. 1969; pres. Italamerica, S.A., 1969-74. Home: Washington, D.C. Died Jan. 1, 1974; buried Laurel Hill Cemetery, Philadelphia, Pa.

BOHN, ERNEST JOHN, lawyer, univ. lectr.; b. Austria-Hungary, May 12, 1901; s. Frank J. and Juliana (Kiry) B.; came to U.S., 1911, naturalized, 1920; A.B cum laude, Adelbert Coll., Western Res. U., 1924, J.D., Law Sch., 1926, LL.D., 1951. Admitted to Ohio bar, 1926, practiced in Cleve., 1926-38; mem. Ohio Gen. Assembly, 1929-30; mem. Cleve. City Council, 1930-40; mem. Internat. Housing Commn., 1934; archtl. adv. com. Fed. Pub. Housing Authority, 1939; cons. U.S. Housing Authority, HHFA, Resettlement Adminstrn., Def. Housing div. Fed. Works Agy. Pub. Housing Adminstrn., U.S. Dept. Health, Edn. and Welfare; ret. 1st dir. Cleve. Met. Housing Authority; now lectr. urban and environmental studies Case Western Res. U.; dir., organizer Regional Assn. Cleve.; bd. dirs. Nat. Housing Conf.; dir. 2d Fed. Savs. and Loan Assn. Cleve.; former chmn. City Planning Commn. Cleve.; adv. bd. Urban Renewal Agy. Cleve.; organizer chmn. 1st Nat. Conf. Slum Clearance, 1933; mem. Ohio Urban Devel. Commn., Midwest Regional Planning Commn.; mem. policy com., planning com. health goals and central planning bd. Cleve. Welfare Fedn.; mem. Regional Planning Commn. Cuyahoga County (O.); formerly mem. exec. com. Internat. Fedn. Housing and Town Planning, The Hague; exec. com. Pres. Eisenhower's adv. com. housing policies; past exec. com. Am. Council to Improve our Neighborhoods; mem. Nat. Action Council of Urban Am. Nat. Urban Coalition, Nat. Council on Aging, com. on housing for elderly, adv. com. housing and community devel. and housing for sr. citizens HHFA, Washington; adv. com. on retired workers UAW, Detroit; U.S. del. housing com. UN Econ. Commn. for Europe, Geneva, Switzerland, 1959; nat. com. White House Conf. Children and Youth, 1960, panel on phys. environment Pres.'s Commn. Nat. Goals, 1960; adminstrv. com., nat. adv. com. White House Conf. on Aging, 1961; cons. subcom. problems aged and aging U.S. Senate; mem. Ohio Gov.'s Commn. on Aging, also adv. bd. Ohio Adminstrn. Aging; mem. adv. com. Ohio Civil Rights Commn.; panel cons. on aging Dept. Health Edn., Welfare; trustee Better Homes and Neighborhoods Cleve.; mem. Cleve. Met. Services Commn.; adv. bd., past chmn. Cath. Charities Bur.; trustee, mem. exec. com. Cath. Charities Corp.; citizens adv. com. Cuyahoga County Hosp. Bd., DePaul Infant Home, others; mem. council of Civil Def. adv. bd. St. Vincent's Charity Hosp., Garden Center, Cleve.; adv. com. Notre Dame Coll., Cleve.; chmn. Devel. Council Greater Cleve.; mem. Cuyahoga County Govtl. Consol. Com. Past pres. League Rep. Clubs of Cuyahoga County; former mem. Cuyahoga County Republican Exec. Com. Past mem. vis. com. Harvard Grad. Sch. Design; mem. vis. com. Western Res. U. Sch. Applied Soc. Scis.; trustee Goodrich Social Settlement; co-founder, former trustee Golden Age Center, Roadside Council; bd. dirs., past pres. Ohio Planning Conf. Cleve. Forum for Community Devel., Citizen's Action Com. on Nursing Homes; trustee Vis. Nurses Assn. Recipient many awards for pub. service including Archbishop Edward F. Hoban medal for distinguished service, 1964, silver medal Am. Soc. Planning Ofcls., 1966. Gov.'s award for Community action; named Outstanding Alumnus, Case-Western Res. U. Law Sch., 1972, Sr. Citizen of Year, Cuyahoga County Sr. Citizen's Council, 1972; Ernest J. Bohn Center, goldenage center, named in his honor 1968; Ernest J. Bohn Tower, named in his honor, 1972. Mem. Nat. Assn. Housing and Redevel. Ofcls. (a founder, 1st pres.), Am. Soc. Planning Ofcls. (pres. 1951), Adult Edn. Assn., Consumers League, Nat. Conf. Social Welfare, Cleve Bar Assn., Western Reserve U. Law Sch. Alumni Assn. (pres. 1952). Roman Catholic. K.C. (past pres. Cleve. dist.). Club: Mid-Day. Author (with others) A Housing Program for the U.S., 1934. Wrote and obtained passage of Ohio Housing Authority Law (1st in nation), 1933. Home: Cleveland, O., Deceased.

BOHN, FRANK, writer, lectr.; b. Cuyahoga, County, O., Sept. 26, 1878; s. Henry Charles and Charlotte (Emrich) B.; student Baldwin-Wallace Coll., 1894-99; Ph.B., Ohio State U., 1900, M.A., 1901; grad. work, univs. of Mich., Wis. and Columbia; Ph.D., U. of Mich., 1904; m. Grace Roper, July 1, 1935. Engaged in western labor movement, 1904-06, 1911-14; lectr. Columbia U., 1910-11; rep. French labor leaders in Germany and Austria, 1915; in Europe for U.S. Com. on Public Information. 1918-19; toured Can., South Seas. New Zealand and Australia for N. Y. Times, 1923-24; with Pres. Obregon of Mexico as polit. adviser, at hdqrs., Mexican Army, rebellion of 1924; contbr. on internat. relations and economic problems to N.Y. Times and various mags.; lecturer on international relations, U. of Southern Calif., summers, 1931, 32, 37, 39, Rep. of American joint labor com. in France for rescue labor leaders and democratic political leaders various countries after surrender French Army, 1940. Del. Pa. 18th Dist., Dem. Nat. Conv., Chgo., 1956. Corpl. Co. D. 5th O. Vol. Inf., Spanish-Am. War. With Office of Censorship, Washington, D.C., 1942-43; with Civil Service Commission, N.Y. Office, 1943-45. Member Franklin County (Pa.) Citizens Com. on Aid of Delinquent Youth, 1955-65. Mem. Franklin County, So. Pennsylvania District, Blue Ridge Summit Sportsmen's Associations (chairman coms.), Phi Beta Kappa. Democrat. Author: (with Richard T. Ely). The Great Change, 1935. Capt. Baldwin-Wallace football team, 1898, chosen tackle all time team, 1937. Home: Blue Ridge Summit, Pa.†

BOHN, GEBHARD C., mfr.; b. Winona, Minn., Feb. 22, 1878; s. Gebhard and Caroline B.; ed. high sch. and Shattuck Mil. Sch.; m. Janet H. Fishbein, Oct. 1902; children—John G., Gebhard C., Haskell G. Pres. Bohn Refrigerator Co., White Enamel Refrigerator Co. of N.Y., White Enamel Refrigerator Co. of Ill. Clubs: University, Automobile, Town and Country, Somerset Country. Home: St. Paul, Minn.†

BOKAT, GEORGE, govt. ofcl.; b. N.Y.C., Nov. 15, 1904; s. Max and Ida (Levy) B.; student Coll. City N.Y.; LL.B., N.Y.U., 1927; m. Golda Shurack, Nov. 24, 1929; children—Robert Bruce, Stephen Arthur. Admitted to N.Y. bar, 1928; practice, N.Y.C., 1928-37; mem. firm Bokat & Bokat, N.Y.C., 1935-37; with NLRB, 1937-72, chief trial examiner, then chief adminstrv. law judge, 1961-72. Mem. Am. Bar Assn. Home: Bethesda Md. Died Nov. 15, 1973.

BOLAND, GEORGE BERNARD, lawyer, ins. co. exec.; b. Omaha, Aug. 15, 1897; s. Peter G.H. and Alice V. (Cocur) B.; Creighton U., 1920, LL.B., 1923; m. Helen Forster, July 7, 1920. Admitted to Neb. bar, 1923, since practiced in Omaha with firm Boland, Mullin, Walsh & Cooney; dir. Nat. Am. Fire Ins. Co., 1958-60, United Benefit Fire Ins. Co., 1958-61, United Benefit Life Ins. Co., 1963-75. Chmn. adv. bd. Vols. Am.; vice chmn., asso. bd. trustees St. John Vianney Sem.; bd. regents Creighton U. Served to 2d Lt., F.A., U.S. Army, 1918. Fellow Am. Coll. Trial Lawyers; mem. Neb. (v.p. 1947), Omaha (pres. 1943-44) bar assns., 40 and 8 (nat. comdr. 1952, nat. atty. 1951, 54-64), Alpha Sigma Nu. Home: Omaha Neb. Died Jan. 13, 1975.

BOLIN, ROLF LING, ichthyologist; b. N.Y. City, Mar. 22, 1901; s. Jakob and Hermanna Hedwig (Lindbom) B.; A.B., U. of Utah, 1925; A.M., Stanford, 1929, Ph.D., 1934; m. Mary Kathryn Sanders, Mar. 3, 1925; 1 dau., Barbara Noel (Mrs. John Edward Culin). Asst. in oceanography, Hopkins Marine Sta., Stanford, 1930-34, instr. in zoology, 1934-37, asst. prof., 1936-37, asso. prof., 1941-49, prof. since 1949; John Simon Guggenheim fellow, 1947-48; participant Crocker-Stanford Deepsea Expdn. off Southern Calif., 1938, also in first N. B. Scofield Expdn. to Mexico and Central Am., 1939; participant Galathea Expdn. to South Pacific, 1952; chief scientist TE VEGA expeditions, 1962-67 chief scientist emeritus, 1967-73. Recipient Fulbright scholar (Hong Kong), 1957-58. Fellow Calif. Acad. Sci.; mem. A.A.A.S., Am. Soc. Ichthyologists and Herpetologists (v.p. Western div., 1937, pres. 1937), Am. Soc. Limnology and Oceanography, Western Soc. Naturalists, Sigma Xi, Pi Kappa Alpha. Contributor articles to scientific journals. Home: Carmel Cal. Died Aug. 1973.

BOLLENGIER, ALBERT EMILE, JR;, mfg. co. exec.; b. Pawtucket, R.I., June 7, 1913; s. Albert E. and Alice (Bollengier) B.; B.S. in Bus. Adminstrn., U. So. Cal., 1935; m. Edith Lodema Kennerd, Nov. 25, 1936; children—Berta (Mrs. Shaw), William E. With Price Waterhouse & Co., C.P.A.'s, 1936-42; treas., controller Hal Roach Studios, Inc. and Eagle Lion Studios, also Eagle Lion Film Inc., also asst. studio controller Universal Pictures Co., Inc., 1945-51; treas., controller United Artists Corp., 1951-56; financial v.p., treas. United Artists Theatre Circuit, 1956-66; v.p., controller W. R. Grace & Co., 1967-74. C.P.A. Mem. Am. Inst. C.P.A.'s, Cal. Soc. C.P.A.'s, Beta Alpha Psi. Home: Larchmont N.Y. Died Sept. 1974.

BOLSTAD, MILO MYRUM, educator; b. Dawson, Minn., July 17, 1915; s. Alfred Christian and Mertie (Myrum) B.; B.S. in Mech. Engring., U. Minn., 1936, Ph.D., 1949; S.M. in Mech. Engring., Mass. Inst. Tech., 1938; m. Margaret Susan Thomes, Aug. 15, 1938; children—Susan Mertie, William Milo, Sally Elizabeth. Faculty U. Mo., Columbia, 1938-44, 45, prof. mech. engring., 1955, chmn. dept., 1958-67; mem. sci. staff Manhattan Project, Los Alamos, 1944-45. Chmn. water and light adv. bd., City of Columbia, 1962-74. Co-recipient Wolverine award best tech. article Am. Soc. Refrigerating Engrs., 1950. Registered profl. engr., Mo. Fellow Am. Soc. Heating, Refrigerating and Air Conditioning Engrs.; mem. Am. Soc. M.E., Am. Soc. Engring. Edn., Mo. Soc. Profl. Engrs., Sigma Xi, Tau Beta Pi, Pi Tau Sigma. Episcopalian. Editor-in-chief Refrigerating Data Book, Design, vol. 9, 1955. Home: Columbia Mo. Died Apr. 14, 1974.

BOMZE, HENRY DANIEL, publisher, editor; b. N.Y.C., Apr. 30, 1906; s. Herman and Rose (Seidenwurm) B.; ed. N.Y.C. schs.; m. Anne Herman, May 26, 1927; children—Sandra (Mrs. Jay Lawrence Werther), Rosalie (Mrs. Harold Steinberg), Richard, Edward. Founder, editor, pub. Racing Star Weekly, N.Y.C., after 1930, Am. Turf Monthly, N.Y.C., after 1946; pres. Star Pub. Co., Amerpub. Co., N.Y.C. Mem. Hunterdon County Hist. Soc., Clinton Art Center, Hunterdon Watershed Assn. Clubs: Century, Beaver Brook Country (founding mem.). Author: A Treasury of American Turf. Home: Annandale, N.J. Died Aug. 27, 1974; buried Temple-B'nai Abraham Meml. Park, Union, N.J.

BONACCOLTO, GIROLAMO, ophthalmologist; b. Italy, 1899; s. Giuseppe and Anna (Viola) B.; B.S., Coll. City N.Y., 1919; M.D., Royal U., Rome, Italy, 1926; m. Patricia Ethel McKenzie, June 1943. Clin. prof. ophthalmology N.Y. U.; asso. clin. prof. ophthalmology Columbia, 1946-48; cons. ophthalmologist Manhattan Eye, Ear and Throat Hosp.; dir. ophthalmology St. Clare's Hosp., dir. emeritus; attending ophthalmologist Univ. and Bellevue hosps.; cons. ophthalmologist Kings Park (N.Y.) State Hosp., N.Y. Police Dept., 1932, Correction Hosps., N.Y.C., Columbus Hosp., Mother Cabrini Hosp. Mem. bd. SSS, 1941-47. Decorated comdr. Order Merit (Italy), 1966; recipient citation scoll Am. Legion, 1968. Diplomate Am. Bd. Ophthalmology. Fellow A.C.S., Am. Acad. Ophthalmology and Otolaryngology, Internal. Coll. Surgeons, N.Y. Acad. Medicine, Am. Acad. Compensation Medicine, Pan Am. Assn. Ophthalmology, Soc. Francaise d'Optalmologie, Soc. Mexico de Oftal. (hon.), Central Ill. Soc. Ophthalmology and Otolaryngology (hon.), Central N.Y. Eye, Ear, Nose and Throat Soc. (hon.), A.M.A., Assn. Research Ophthalmology, N.Y. Ophthalmological socs. Clubs: Metropolitan, New York University (N.Y.C.). Contbg. author Principles and Practice of Ophthalmic Surgery (Spaeth). Contbr. articles to profl. jours. Translator: Fundus Oculi (di Marzio). Home: New York City N.Y. Died July 21, 1973.

BONCHER, HECTOR PETER, former mfg. exec.; b. Luxemburg, Wis., Apr. 13, 1904; s. Hector and Catherine (Arendt) B.; Comml. Engr., U. Cin., 1928; m. Elizabeth Day, Jan. 27, 1939; children—William H., John D. Sales mgr. Dresser Industries, Inc., Dallas, 1955-59, v.p. marketing, 1959-66, v.p. pub. relations, 1966-69. Home: Dallas, Tex., Died Aug. 3, 1973.

BOND, BEVERLY WAUGH, JR., educator; b. Blacksburg, Va., July 31, 1878; s. Rev. Beverley Waugh and Elizabeth (Lumsdon) B.; student Randolph-Macon Acad., Front Royal, Va., 1892-97; A.B., Randolph Macon Coll., Ashland, Va., 1900, A.M., 1901; Ph.D., Johns Hopkins, 1905; m. Louisa S. Worthington, April 3, 1933. Asst. prof. of history, U. of Miss., 1905-06; prof. English, Southwestern Presbyn. U., 1906-07; instr. in history, Purdue U., 1907-13, asst. prof., 1913-18, asso. prof., 1918-20; asso. prof., U. of Cincinnati, 1920-26, prof., 1926-49, emeritus prof. from 1949; lectr. history U. of Wis., 1919-20, Johns Hopkins, summer 1920, 21, Duke U., summer 1925, U. of W.Va., summer 1927, U. of Mich., summer 1930. Member Am. Hist. Assn., Miss. Valley Hist. Assn. (pres. 1931-32; asso editor, 1925-28, 1937-38) Historical and Philosophical Society of Ohio (curator, 1939-42, president, 1942-45, curator emeritus from 1945), Soc. Colonial Wars in State Ohio, Phi Beta Kappa, Phi Kappa Psi. Awarded Henrico medallion, Johns Hopkins Univ., 1908. Episcopalian. Clubs: University, Cincinnati Country. Author: State Government in Maryland, 1777-1781, 1905; The Monroe Mission to France, 1794-1796, 1907; The Quit Rent System in the American Colonies, 1919. Editor: The Correspondence of John Cleves Symmes, 1926; The Civilization of the Olf Northwest, 1933; History of the State of Ohio, Foundations of Ohio, vol. I, 1941; Thomas Hutchins, Courses of the Ohio, 1766, 1942. Contbr. to Am. Hist. Review, Nat. Dictionary of Am. Biography. Essays in Colonial History, etc. Home: Cincinnati, O.†

BOND, EARL DANFORD, psychiatrist; b. St. Paul, Minn., Jan. 25, 1879; s. Johnathan Danford and Martha (Bunker) B.; A.B., Harvard, 1900, M.D., 1908; m. Grace Lee Newson, Aug. 4, 1909; children—Douglas Danford, Ann Sharpless. At McLean Hosp., 1908-12; instr. in neuropathology, Harvard Med. Sch., 1912-13; clin. dir. and pathologist, Danvers (Mass.) State Hosp., 1912-13; med. dir. dept. for mental and nervous diseases, Pa. Hosp., Phila., 1913-30; prof. psychiatry, Grad. Sch. Medicine, U. of Pa., vice dean, for psychiatry, U. Pa., 1930-39, dir. research, 1939, emeritus. Recipient Phila. Award, 1932. Maj., Med. Corps. U.S. Army, Sept. 1917-Mar. 1919. Mem. bd. Grant Found. Mem. Am. Psychiatric Assn. (pres. 1930), Coll. Phys. Philadelphia, Royal Medical Psychiatric Association (honorary), Alpha Omega Alpha, Phi Beta Kappa. Republican. Unitarian. Clubs: Harvard, Art Alliance, Merion Golf, Divotee Golf. Author: The Treatment of Behavior Disorders Following Encephalitis (with Dr. K. E. Appel), 1931; Dr. Kirkbirde and His Mental Hospital, 1947; Thomas W. Salmon, Psychiatrist, One Mind Common to All, 1957. Home: Bryn Mawr, Pa.†

BOND, GEORGE HOPKINS, JR., lawyer; b. Syracuse, N.Y. Oct. 28, 1909; s. George Hopkins and Florence (Woodford) B.; A.B., Williams Coll., 1933; LL.B., Syracuse U., 1936; m. Margaret Wade, Oct. 22, 1931 (div. 1939); children Suzanne, Margot; m. 2d, Sally Van Santvoord Pyle, May 24, 1940 (dec. Sept. 1947); children—Anita, George, Sari; m. 3d, Ulla Ouchteriony, Aug. 9, 1949 (div. 1972); 1 dau., Margrethe. Admitted to N.Y. bar, 1936, since practiced in Syracuse; partner firm Bond, Schoeneck & King, 1941. Trustee Everson Mus. Served to lt. comdr. USNR, 1942-45. Mem. Am., N.Y. State (head young lawyers sect. 1941), Onondaga County bar assns., S.A.R., Delta Kappa Epsilon, Phi Delta Phi. Mason. Clubs: Century (Syracuse); DKE (N.Y.C.); Church Street Social (Millbrook, N.Y.) Home: Cazenovia N.Y. Died Sept. 27, 1973.

BOND, NELSON L., publisher; b. Caldwell, N.J., June 17, 1903; s. Edwin E. and Marion B. (Chitterling) B.; B.S., Lehigh U., 1926; m. Dorothy L. Minsch, Nov. 18, 1933; children—Nancy L., Nelson L., Sarah (dec.). Salesman Bus. Week, N.Y.C., 1938-45, advt. mgr., 1945-46; dir. advt. McGraw-Hill Pub. Co., Inc., N.Y.C., 1946-58, exec. v.p., 1958-63, exec. v.p. publs. div., 1955-59, pres. publs. div., 1959-63; pres., dir. McGraw Hill Internat. Corp.; 1st v.p. Asso. Bus. Publs., chmn. bd., 1957-58; dir. McGraw Hill Pub. Co., Inc., McGraw Hill Book Co. Mem. advt. adv. com. Sec. Commerce. Mem. Advt. Council (dir., chmn. bus. paper adv. Com., mem. exec. com.), Marketing Execs. Soc., Advt. Fedn. Am. (dir., chmn. finance com., mem. exec. com.), Sigma Phi. Episcopalian. Clubs: Union (Cleve.); University. Home: Orleans Mass. Died Apr. 12, 1974.

BOND, PERRY A(VERY), educator; b. Storm Lake, Ia., July 28, 1878; s. Charles Avery and Alice (Tantlinger) B.; B.S., State U. of Ia., 1901, M.S., 1908, Ph.D., 1918; student U. of Chicago, summer 1906; m. Florence Booth Davidson, Aug. 4, 1909 (dec.); 1 dau., Alice Clara; m. 2d, Helen Elizabeth Judy, June 1, 1931. Teacher high sch., Marengo, Ia., 1901-07; instr. chemistry, Armour Inst. Tech., 1909-11, instr. chemistry, Iowa State Teachers Coll., 1911-18; asst. prof. chemistry, State Univ. of Iowa, 1918-25, asso. prof. from 1925. Served aas vol. Spanish-Am. War. Fellow Am. Inst. Chemists; mem. A.A.A.S., Am. Chem. Soc., Phi Lambda Upsilon, Alpha Chi Sigma, Sigma Xi, Presbyn. Mason (32°, Shriner). Club: Triangle (Iowa City). Author: Fundamentals of General Chemistry, 1935; Laboratory Manual of General Chemistry, 1937. Contbr. to professional jours. †

BOND, THOMAS BURKE, radiologist; b. Hillsboro, Tex., 1889; M.D., Baylor U., 1917. Tng. with Dr. George D. Bond; practice medicine specializing in radiology, Ft. Worth; radiologist Peter Smith Hosp.; clin. prof. radiology U. Tex. Southwestern Med. Sch., Dallas; pres. Radiation and Med. Research Found.; dir. Radiation Center. Diplomate Am. Bd. Radiology. Fellow Am. Coll. Radiologists; mem. Radiol. Soc. Am. (pres. 1955). Home: Ft. Worth, Tex. Died Dec. 7, 1971.

BOND, WALTER HUNTINGTON, lawyer; b. Waltham, Mass., Apr. 6, 1878; s. David Taylor and Emma Gertrude (Bigelow) B.; LL.B., U. of Mich., 1901; m. Mary Madeline Morgan, Apr. 6, 1914 (dec. Sept. 24, 1934); children—David Jameson, Mary Rice, Madeline Morgan; m. 2d, Florence Seward Thompson, April 17, 1941. Admitted to N.Y. bar, 1901; U.S. Supreme Ct. bar; in law office of Judge James B. Dill, New York, 1901-03; sr. mem. Bond & Babson, gen. practice in law and equity. Mem. Order of Founders and Patriots of America (former gov.), Soc. of Colonial Wars, Soc. of Mayflower Descendants, Soc. of the Cincinnati Sons of the Revolution, Soc. of Am. Wars, Loyal Legion, Baronial Order of Runnemede (Magna Charta Barons, Somerset Chapter), The Plantagenet Soc., Colonial Order of the Crown, New England Soc., N.Y. Geneal. and Biog. Soc., Met. Museum of Art, Am. Acad. Polit. and Social Science, N.Y. Law Inst., Am. Bar Assn., N.Y. State Bar Assn., of the City of New York, Nassau County (N.Y.) Bar Assn. Republican. Baptist. Clubs: Union League, Univ. of Michigan (N.Y. City); National Republican; American Alpine Club (Phila.). has traveled in U.S., Can., Europe, and Asia; mountain climber. Home: Franklin Sq., L.I., N.Y.†

BONDS, MARGARET, composer, conductor, pianist; b. Chgo., Mar. 3, 1913; ed. Northwestern U.; B.M., M.M., Juilliard Sch. Music; scholar Nat. Assn. Negro Musicians, Alpha Kappa Alpha, Julius Rosenwald, Roy Harris; pvt. study music. Tchr. Am. Theatre Wing; music dir. Stage for Youth, 52 Assn., East Side Settlement Ho., White Barn Theatre; composer stage background scores Shakespeare in Harlem: U.S.A.; arranger spirituals; dir. pub. relations orch. Nat. Gallery Art, Washington. Composer: The Negro Speaks of Rivers; 3 Dream Portraits; Peter and the Bells; Mass in d: Troubled Island. Also recorded. Home: New York City N.Y. Died Apr. 26, 1972.

BONNER, EMMETT PEYTON, naval officer; b. Macon, Ga., Feb. 27, 1918; s. Emmett Peyton and Bessie (Napier) B.; B.S. in E.E., U.S. Naval Acad., 1939; M. Elizabeth Healy, Sept. 2, 1942; children—Emmett Peyton III, Mark Helay, Vance, Gregory Beauregard. Commd. ensign U.S. Navy, 1939, advanced through grades to rear adm., 1966; served in cruisers and amphibious group staff, World War II; active guided missile devel. program; dir. Terrier Missile Program, 1961-63; comdr. Naval Support Activity, Danang, Vietnam, 1968-70; sr. Navy mem. weapons systems evaluation group Office Sec. Def., Washington, 1970-75. Decorated Legion of Merit, Joint Services Commendation medal, numerous unit and area ribbons. Home: Chevy Chase, Md. Died Aug. 1, 1975.

BONNER, MARY GRAHAM, writer; b. Cooperstown, N.Y.; d. George William Graham and Margaret Cary (Worthington) Bonner; grad. Halifax Ladies' Coll., Halifax. N.S. Episcopalian. Author numerous books, latest publs.: Hidden Village Mystery, 1948; The Mysterious Caboose, 1949; The Winning Dive, 1950; Haunted Hut, 1950; The Base Stealer, 1951; Wait and See, 1952; Dugout Mystery, 1953; Baseball Rookies Who Made Good, 1954; How to Play Baseball, 1955; Wonders Around the Sun, 1957; The Real Book About Crime Detection, 1957; Two-Way Pitcher, 1958; Real Book About Sports, 1958; Spray Hitter, 1959; Real Book About Journalism, 1960; Wonders of Inventions, 1961; Mystery at Lake Ashburn; contributor of children's stories reviews, also special articles and short fiction to mags.; 3000 "Sundown Stories" for children. Reviewer children's books and others. Winner of Constance Lindsay Skinner Award, 1943. Home: New York City N.Y. Died Feb. 1974.

BOOCOCK, CORNELIUS BRETT, educator; b. Jersey City, N.J., Apr. 21, 1898; s. William Henry and Maud (Brett) B.; grad. Nichols Prep. Sch., Buffalo, N.Y., 1916; A.B., Rutgers, 1920; studied Harvard, summer 1923; M.A., U. of Pa., 1940; m. Ruth Allen, June 6, 1925; children—Catharyna Rombout, Cornelius

Brett, Margaret Allen. Instr. Polytechnic Prep. Country Day Sch., Brooklyn, N.Y., 1920-27; headmaster Troy Country Day Sch., 1927-30; headmaster Collegiate Sch., N.Y. City, 1930-34; asso. headmaster Haverford Sch., 1934-37, headmaster 1937-42; headmaster Scarborough Sch., 1945-48; dean of men, Rutgers University, New Brunswick, 1948. Served as lieut. U.S. Naval Reserve, September 1942-45; lt. comdr., comdg. officer Naval Training Sch. (radio), Bedford Springs, Pa. Served in U.S. Navy, 1918. Mem. Country Day Schs. Assn. and Headmasters Assn., Nat Assn. Student Personnel Advisors. Delta Phi. Republican. Mem. Reformed Ch. Home: Mantoloking N.J. Died May 14, 1973.

BOOCOCK, PHILIP MILLEDOLER BRETT, headmaster; b. Bayonne, New Jersey, April 1, 1905; s. of William Henry and Maude Runyon (Brett) B.; A.B., Rutgers U., 1926, Litt.D., 1966; m. Katrina Van Tassel Morey, December 20th, 1929; children—Katrina Van Tassel (Mrs. Michael Hamilton), Roger Brett, Ann Morey (Mrs. Arthur L. Coburn, III). Engaged as teacher of Latin at Nichols School, Buffalo, N.Y., 1926-34; headmaster Rutgers Prep. Sch., 1934-37, Nichols Sch. 1937-69. Received Rutgers U. award, 1937. Mem. Headmasters Assn., Country Day School Headmasters Assn., Delta Phi. Presbyterian. Home: Buffalo, N.Y., Nov. 30, 1975.

BOOGHER, ELBERT WILLIS GRIFFIN, educator; b. Lexington, Va., Sept. 11, 1880; s. Edward Nicholas and Mary Ann (Vanderslice) B.; A.B., Washington and Lee U., 1902, M.A., 1903; A.M., U. Pa., 1925, Ph.D., 1932; m. Elizabeth Louise Reynolds, June 21, 1913; children—Charles R., Elizabeth (Mrs. Edwin B. Benson), Elbert, Jr. Mem. English faculty, Ga. Inst. Tech., 1903-14, asst. prof. of English, 1909-14; leather mfr., Camden, N.J., 1914-24; prof. English, Rider Coll., Trenton, N.J., 1934-46, dean, 1946-49 when ret. Mem. sch. bd., Merchantville, N.J., 1921-42, pres., 1932-42. Mem. N.E.A., Phi Delta Kappa, Kappa Sigma. Author: Secondary Education in Georgia 1732-1858, 1932. Home: Moorestown, N.J.†

BOONE, JOEL THOMPSON, physician, naval officer; b. Saint Clair, Pa., Aug. 29, 1889; s. William Agard and Annie (Thompson) B.; grad. Mercersburg (Pa.) Acad., 1909; M.D., Hahnemann Med. Coll., Phila., 1913, hon. M.A., 1923, LL.D., 1947; grad. study U.S.N. Med. Sch., Washington, 1915; m. Helen Elizabeth Koch, June 20, 1914; 1 dau., Suzanne Boone Heller. Naval medical officer, 1914-50; served combat duty in Haiti, 1915-16, and in France and Germany, World War I; physician to Presidents Harding, Coolidge and Hoover, 1922-33; staff comdr. Base Force, U.S. Fleet, Jan.-Aug. 1940; sr. med. officer U.S. Naval Air Sta. San Diego, 1940-43; comdg. officer U.S. Naval Hosp., Seattle, 1943-45; fleet med. officer, 3d Fleet, 1945; dist. med. officer 11th Naval Dist., 1946; insp. med. activities, Pacific Coast, also insp. med. dept. activities, 1946; exec. sec. Com. on Med. and Hosp. Services, Armed Forces, chief Joint Plans and Action dev., Med. Services, Office of Sec. of Def., 1948-50; insp. gen. Med. Dept., 1950; ret. as vice adm., 1950; med. dir. VA, 1951-55. Bd. regents Mercersburg (Pa.) Acad. Fellow A.C.P. (nat. bd. med. examiners), A.C.S., A.M.A., Internat. Coll. Surgeons (gov.); member Am. Institute Homeopathy, (p.p.), Assn. Mil. Surgeons Army and Navy Legion of Valor, Mercersburg Alumni Assn., Boone Family Assn., Alpha Sigma, Alpha Omega Alpha. Decorated Congressional Medal of Honor, Distinguished Service Cross, Silver Star medal with 5 oak leaf clusters, Purple Heart with 2 oak leaf clusters, Bronze Star with Combat V, Sec. of Navy's Commendation Medal, Army of Occupation Medal, Defense Medal with star, Haitian Campaign Medal, Victory Medal with 6 battle clasps (World War I), Asiatic Pacific Campaign Medal, 2 bronze stars, Am. Area Compaign Medal (World War II), Am. Theatre Ribbon, Croix de Guerre with 2 Palms, Officer Legion of Honor, Order of Fourragere (France), War Cross (Italy). Republican. Presbyterian. Clubs: Army and Navy, Chevy Chase Country; Bohemian (San Francisco). Home: Washington, D.C. Died Apr. 2, 1974; interred Arlington National Cemetery, Arlington, Va.

BOOS, WILLIAM FREDERICK, physician, biological chemist, toxicologist; b. Longwood, Massachusetts, Aug. 2, 1870; s. Gabriel and Theresa Carola (Schraubstaedter) B.; A.B., Harvard University, 1894; Ph.D., in Chemistry, University of Heidelberg, 1896; M.D., Harvard, 1901; Mass. Gen. Hosp., 1902; m. Margaret Theresa Eskridge, Oct. 1, 1902; children—Margaret Theresa, Mimi Eskridge, Anne-Marshall. Instr. in chemistry, Harvard, 1896-97; asst. in hygiene, Harvard Med. Sch., 1898-1901; med. house phys., Mass. Gen. Hosp., 1901-02; Parker traveling fellow, Harvard, at U. of Strassburg, 1902-04; instr. in pharmacology, U. of Strassburg, 1904-06; research chemist, Mass. State Bd. of Health, 1906-07; biol. chemist and pharmacologist, Mass. Gen. Hosp., 1907-13; specializing in internal medicine; consulting physician, Nat. Canners' Assn. Expert in medicine, biol. chemistry and toxicology; expert for U.S. Govt. in pure food and drug prosecutions from 1908; medico legal expert for U.S. Govt., State of Mass., etc. Lecturer on medicine and public health subjects; former lecturer on toxicology, Harvard Med. Sch. Mem. A.M.A., Am. Therapeutic Soc., Am. Chem. Soc., Mass. Med. Soc., Boston Soc. Med. Sciences, etc. Author: Poison Trail, 1939; also many monographs on chem. subjects and subjects relating to internal medicine, occupational poisoning and pub. health.†

BOOTH, CHARLES BRANDON, religious, social welfare exec; b. Brooklyn, Dec. 26, 1887; s. Ballington and Maud (Charlesworth) B.; student Montclair Acad., 1897-1905, Hill Sch., 1905; pvt. tutoring Europe; m. Naomi Bailey, Jan. 1913 (dec. 1925); children—Audrey Charlesworth (Mrs. Arthur E. Ueland), Weldon Sutherland, Carroll (dec.); m. 2d Betsy Irene Ross, Sept. 8, 1927; 1 son, Richard Ross. Gen. sec. Vol. Prison League, 1906-15; nat. field sec. Big Bro. and Big Sister Fedn., 1925-29; v.p. Council Social Agencies, Kansas City, Mo., 1935-37; asst. officer, Vols. Am. posts, Detroit, Pittsburgh, officer charge Kansas City, Mo., 1930-37, Western area sec., 1938-39, nat. field sec., 1939-45, Central area comdr., 1945-49, gen., comdr. in chief 1949-58; lectr. religious, social welfare subjects. Mem. Nat. Correctional Chaplains Assn. (dir.), Am. Correctional Assn., Nat. Parole and Probation Assn., Assn. Ch. Social Workers, Nat. Conf. Social Work, Urban League. Mason (K.T.). Club: Optimist Internat. Home: La Mesa, Cal.

BOOTH, LOUIS WINEERA, educator, musician; b. Paris, Ida., Apr. 19, 1911; s. Louis H. and Phoebe (Price) B.; student New Eng. Conservatory Music, 1929-34; B.A., Brigham Young U., 1943, M.A., 1945; m. Marguerite Jacques, May 14, 1936; children—Colette Jacques (Mrs. Keith Baird), Janine Marguerite (Mrs. David Petersen), Nicole Louise (Mrs. George Ramjoue), Jacques Louis. Instr., asst. prof. Brigham Young U., 1941-47; asst. prof. U. Utah, 1947-54, asso. prof., 1954-64, prof., 1964-74; dir. chamber music dir. fine arts study tours; prin. oboist Utah Symphony Orch., 1939-68, Seattle Symphony Orch., 1945. Dir. music div. Utah State Fair, 1955-74. Mem. Am. Federated Musicians, Phi Kappa Phi. Mem. Ch. of Jesus Christ of Latter-day Saints. Home: Salt Lake City, Utah. Died June 7, 1974; buried Salt Lake City Cemetery.

BOOTH, WILLIAM EDWARD, ins. holding co. exec.; b. Owensboro, Ky., Jan. 8, 1920; s. Henry Overstreet and Elizabeth Rogers (Sweeney) B.; B.A., Vanderbilt U., 1941; m. Jessie Gardner McCracken, Dec. 13, 1941; children—Elizabeth Anne (Mrs. B. Taylor Bennett III), Susan McCracken, Lucinda Forrest, Sales engr. IBM, 1941-46; 1st v.p., co-founder Charokee Ins. Co., Nashville, 1946-64; co-founder v.p., sec. Forrest Life Ins. Co., Nashville, 1964-69; v.p., sec. Synercon Corp., Nashville, 1969-73. Pres., Vanderbilt Alumni Panhallenic Council, 1954-56; bd. dirs. Nashville Police Assistance League, 1965-73, Nashville Mental Health Assn., 1971-73, Davidson County Anti Tb. Assn., 1957-62. Served to maj. AUS, 1942-46. Decorated Legion of Merit; recipient Presdl. award Insurors of Tenn., 1961. Mem. Soc. Chartered Property and Casualty Underwriters (past nat. v.p., chpt. pres.), S.A.R., Phi Beta Kappa, Sigma Nu (past pres., alumni adviser), Omicron Delta Kappa, Omicron Delta Gamma. Club: Wildwood Country. Home: Nashville, Tenn., Died Dec. 25, 1973. Interred Woodlawn Mausoleum, Nashville.

BOOTHBY, EVERETT J., utilities exec.; b. Somerville, Mass., 1893; grad. Tufts Coll., 1915; m. Marion Boothby, 1918. Formerly with Fall River Gas Co. (Mass.), Lowell Gas Light Com. (Mass.); with Washington Gas Light Co., 1932-63, pres., 1949-58, chmn. bd., 1950-60, dir., until 1963; chmn., chief exec. officer greater Washington Indsl. Investments, Inc.; dir. McLachlen Nat. Bank, Acacia Life Ins. Co. Mem. Met. Washington Bd. Trade. Bd. dirs. chpt. A.R.C., trustee Fed. City Council; adviser YMCA, Am. U. Recipient Boss of Year award Jr. C. of C., 1959. Mem. Am. Gas Assn. (pres. 1946), Inst. Gas Tech., Tau Beta Pi. Mason. Clubs: Metropolitan, Columbia Country. Home: Chevy Chase Md. Died Nov. 15, 1973.

BORDEAUX, LE PECQ ANDREE, painter, engraver; b. Laval (Mayenne), France, Oct. 3, 1910; d. Michel Le Pecq and Marie Angele (Regheasse); grad. Oxford U.; m. Rene Jacques Bordeaux De Noyant, Jan. 26, 1935; 1 son, Jean-Luc. Numerous one man shows in France and Paris, also Rome, N.Y.C., Mexico City, Vienna, Tokyo, Rio de Janeiro, Spain, Brussels, Genova, executed murals for French State and tapestries for Mobillier National (Beauvals and Aubusson); Illustrator The Temptation of Grazia Deledda, also L'Equipage of Joseph Kessel; represented in permanent collections Mus. Nat. D'Art Moderne, Paris, other collections in Paris, Tel Aviv, Vienna, Tokyo, Phoenix, Mexico City, Rio de Janeiro, Genova, numerous pvt. collections. Pres. founder Salon Comparisons, 1954-67, hon. pres., 1967—; pres. found. Henri Rousseau Mus. Primitive Art, Laval, 1966—; pres. found. Art et Prospective, 1967; jury mem. Recherches et formes de demain. Recipient Silver medal for arts, scis., letters, honor medal Red Cross, Gold Palm Paris-Critic, Honor Diploma Nika Soc., Tokyo, Grande Vermeli medal of Town, Paris, 1964; decorated chevalier Legion d'Honneur, officer Palmes Academiques. Mem. Action Artistque Francaise, Women's Profl. Union (nat. pres. fine arts sect. 1964-67), Sorpotimist Club. Home: Paris, France., Died Jan. 5, 1973.

BORDEN, SAM WHEATLEY, savs. and loan assn. exec; b. Bethesda, Md., Apr. 22, 1899; s. Thomas Sheppard and Frances Caroline (Wheatley) B.; student George Washington U., 1923-24; m. Ruth Walters, Apr. 1, 1938. With Perpetual Bldg. Assn., Washington, 1921-24; asst. chief clk. Supreme Ct. for D.C., 1924-26; exec. v.p. Loyola Fed. Savs. and Loan Assn., Balt., 1939-48, pres., dir., 1948-67, chmn. bd., chief exec. officer, 1967-74; chmn. bd., dir. Ins. Mgmt. Corp., Balt., 1956-74; chmn. Loyola Financial & Devel. Corp.; pres., dir. Gibson Island Corp. (Md.), 1944-46; dir. 1st Mortgage Ins. Co., Ltd., Australia, 1st Mortgage Ins. Co., Greensboro, N.C., Fed. Home Loan Bank of Atlanta, Security Title & Trust Co., Balt., Md. Marketing Co., Home Protection Life Ins. Co.; mem. exec. com., dir. Blue Ridge Ins. Co., Hagerstown, Md., 1956-61. Mem. Commn. To Modernize Govt. of Md., 1965-74, chmn. natural resources sub-com., 1965-74; mem. adv. com. Balt. Planning Commn.; mem. Charles Center Planning Commn., 1964-66. Bd. dirs. Mt. Vernon Improvement Assn., 1955-67, Charles Street Assn., 1948-50. Served with USAAC, 1918-21; to lt. USNR, 1942-44. Mem. Nat. League Insured Savs. Assn. (exec. com., dir. state govs.), Md. League Bldg. Savs. and Loan Assn. (dir., past pres.), Internat. Union Bldg. and Savs. Socs., Newcomen Soc. N.Am. Episcopalian (past trustee, treas.). Clubs: Chevy Chase (Md.); Maryland, Center, Governors, Merchants (Balt.); Army-Navy; Gibson Island. Home: Gibson Island Md. Died Apr. 10, 1974.

BORELLA, VICTOR, mgmt. cons.; b. Plymouth, N.H., Oct. 13, 1906; s. Gaspar and Giuditta (Moruzzi) B.; student Norwich U., Northfield, Vt., 1926-27; A.B., Dartmouth, 1930; m. Cecelia O'Connell, July 2, 1934 (dec. 1956); m. 2d, Eleanor Dwinell, May 11, 1957-(dec. Nov. 1975). Dir. personnel Terminal Transp. System, 1930-34; with Gen. Motors Corp., 1934-39; asst. coordinator U.S. Office Inter-Am. Affairs, 1942-45; with Rockefeller Center, Inc., 1939-42, 45-65, exec. v.p., 1958-65. Labor adviser to Gov. Rockefeller, 1959-75; bd. dirs. Am. Arbitration Assn., 1962-70, chmn. exec. com., 1965; chmn. Gov. N.Y. Workmen's Compensation Rev. Com., 1962; mem. Presdl. Mission to Latin Am., 1969. Home: Enfield, N.H. Died July 9, 1975; buried Plymouth, N.H.

BORG, ALVIN ANDREW, former drug chain store exec.; b. Ludington, Mich., Apr. 8, 1904; s. Andrew and Ida (Gustafson) B.; A.B., U. Mich., 1927; m. Marjorie Mailler, Mar. 25, 1931; children—Betty (Mrs. Stanley D. Whitford, Jr.), Judith (Mrs. Rody Biggert), Alvin Andrew, Christine (Mrs. James D. Houck). With Walgreen Drug Co. Chgo., 1928, beginning as mfg. supr., successively mgr. constrn., dir. engring. and equipment, 1928-54, dir. 1952-73, dir. engring., 1955-60, v.p., treas. 1961-63, pres., 1963-69, cons., 1969-73. Mem. Tau Kappa Epsilon. Episcopalian. Clubs: Chicago Athletic, North Shore Country (Chgo.). Home: Wilmette Ill. Died May 1973.

BORG, DONALD GOWEN, newspaper editor; b. N. Bergen, N.J., Jan. 19, 1906; s. John and Hazel (Gowen) B.; grad. Hill Sch., 1924; B.A., Yale, 1928; m. Flora B. Austin, Aug. 9, 1935 (dec. 1971); children—Malcolm A., Gregory G. With Bergen County County (N.J.) Record, 1929-75, editor, 1932, pub., 1949-70; pres., Bergen Evening Record Corp., 1949-70, chmn. bd., 1957-75; pres., chmn. bd. Call Printing & Pub. Co., Paterson, N.J., 1964-69. Mem. Palisades Insterstate Park Commn., 1953-75, sec., 1960-70, v.p., 1970-75; pres. Grand Jurors Assn. Assn. Bergen County, 1952-75; mem. exec. bd. N.J. Grand Jurors Assn., 1960-75, pres., 1970, 1970. Bd. mgrs. Bergen Pines County Hosp., 1941-75, pres., 1946-75; bd. dirs., 2d v.p. Bergen County United Fund, 1962-75; bd. govs. Hackensack Hosp., 1945-75; chmn. Bergen County Charter Study Commission, 1967; mem. State Tax Policy Com., 1970. Recipient Good Scout award N. Bergen council Boy Scouts Am., 1964; Howard G. Law medal civic achievement, 1949; brotherhood award Nat. Conf. Christians and Jews, 1964; Citizens award Acad. Medicine N.J., 1969; hon. M.D., Bergen County Med. Soc. Mem. Nat. Parks Assn. (life), Palisades Nature Assn. (life). Home: Hackensack, N.J. Died May 1975.

BORGMEYER, ERNEST, journalist. Bus., finance editor Omaha World-Herald. Office: Omaha Neb. Died Apr. 22, 1974.

BORGQUIST, ERASMUS SWAN, educator, civil engr.; b. Salt Lake City, Apr. 19, 1887; s. Rasmus and Ulrika (Swan) B.; B.S., Univ. of Utah, 1911, C.E., 1917; m. Dora Vance, Aug. 23, 1912; children—Arline, Helen, Neil, Beverly. Jr. engr., U.S. Bur. Reclamation, Provo, Utah, 1911-13; asst. engr., Utah State Engring. Dept., 1913-17; resident engr., Utah State Road Commn., Salt Lake City, 1919-26; prof. civil engring., Univ. Ariz., 1926-42, head dept. civil engring. since 1942. Served as 1st lt., Engr. Corps, U.S. Army, 1917-19, in France, 1918-19. Mem. Am. Soc. C.E. (past pres. Ariz. sec.), Am. Soc. Professional Engineers, Am. Soc. Engring. Edn., Am. Legion. Registered Engr., Ariz. Died June 23, 1974.

BORLAND, ANDREW ALLEN, educator; b. Sandy Lake, Pa., June 11, 1878; s. Adam C. and Sarah Ann (Carmichael) B.; B.S., Pa. State Coll., 1909; M.S., U. of Wis., 1910; m. Jessie E. Canon, Oct. 12, 1910; children—Gerald Canon, Margaret Eleanor. Teacher, pub. schs. in Mercer County, Pa., 1898-1905; asst., dairy husbandry research, Pa. State Coll., 1910-11; prof. animal and dairy husbandry in charge dept. U. of Vt., 1911-15; prof. in charge dairy husbandry extension, Pa. State Coll., 1915-19, prof. dairy husbandry in charge of dept., 1919-48. Served as mem. Bd. of Edn., Burlington, Vt., 1913-15. Mem. Civic Planning Bd., State Coll., Pa., 1930-45. Trustee of Westminster Foundation, State Coll., Pa. from 1939, v.p. from 1941. Mem. Am. Dairy Sci. Assn. (v.p. 1920-22, pres. 1922-24, pres. Eastern Div. 1925; hon. life mem.), Pa. Dairyman's Assn. (pres. 1925-27), Phi Kappa Phi, Gamma Sigma Delta, Delta Sigma Rho, Alpha Zeta, Delta Theta Sigma, Pres. Coll. Feed Conf. Bd., 1931. U.S. and Pa. del. to 8th World Dairy Congress, London, Reading, Edinburgh, Glasgow, 1928; U.S. judge 4H Internat. Dairy Cattle Judging Contest, Kent, Eng., 1928. Presbyterian. Mason Mem. com. of management Jour. of Dairy Science, 1932-44, chmn., 1943-44. Contbg. eidtor Pennsylvania Farmer from 1923. Contbr. many artciles and bulls. on dairy cattle feeding and management. Home: College, Pa.†

BORMAN, ABRAHAM, chmn. exec. com. Borman Food Stores, Inc. Deceased.

BORNHOLDT, WALLACE JOHN, ret. heavy vehicle mfg. co. exec.; b. Peoria, Ill., Dec. 28, 1907; s. John and Barbara Katherine (Kohl) B.; student U. Ill., 1925-28; m. Esteleen M. Allen, June 17, 1939. With Caterpillar Tractor Co., 1928-72, v.p., 1963-72. Mem. Am. Soc. Metals, Am. Ordnance Assn. Mason. Club: Country of Peoria. Home: Peoria Ill. Died Jan. 5, 1974.

BORTHWICK, HARRY ALFRED, plant physiologist; b. Wright County, Minn., Jan. 7, 1898; s. Alfred Ellenwood and Frances Estella (Humphrey) B.; student U. Minn., 1917-19; A.B., Stanford, 1921, M.A., 1924, Ph.D., 1930; m. Myrtis Vietta Hall, June 4, 1923; 1 son, Howard Hall. Research asst. div. botany U. Cal., 1922-30, asst. prof., 1930-36; morphologist Dept. Agr., Beltsville, Md., 1936-44, botanist, 1944-48, plant physiologist, 1948-68, ret., 1968, collaborator, 1968-74. Recipient Distinguished Service award U.S. Dept. Agr. 1959; Charles Reid Barnes Life Membership award in plant physiology, 1960; Norman Jay Coleman award in horticulture, 1962; recipient (with S.B. Hendricks) Hoblitzelle award, Stephen Hales award in plant physiology, 1962; Nessim Habif World prize U. Geneva, 1963. Fellow Am. Acad. Arts and Scis.; mem. Nat. Acad. Scis., A.A.A.S., Am. Soc. Plant Physiologists (pres. 1956), Bot. Soc. Am., Washington Acad. Sci., Washington Biol. Soc., Washington Bot. Soc. (pres. 1952), Am. Soc. Hort. Sci., Academia Nazionale del Lincei (Rome), Sigma Xi, Phi Beta Kappa, Alpha Gamma Rho. Contbr. articles sci. publs. Home: Silver Spring, Md. Died May 21, 1974; cremated.

BORTON, ELON G., assn. exec.; b. Flint, Mich., Mar. 31, 1889; s. Joseph Henry and Emily Jane (Wright) B.; A.B., Greenville (Ill.) Coll., 1910; student Univ. Chicago, 1912-13, Univ. Toulouse, France, 1919; m. Dorothea Boardman, July 5, 1921; children—Glenn Elon, Dona Jeanne, Asst. gen. mgr., Mutual Chautauquas, Chicago, 1919-21; dir. advt., LaSalle Extension Univ., Chicago, 1923-45; pres. and gen. mgr. Advertising Fedn. of Am., N.Y.C., 1945-57; v.p. Internat. Union Advertising. Served as 1st sergt., 108 Engrs., U.S. Army, 1917-19. Finance chmn. West Suburban Council, Boy Scouts of Am., La Grange, Ill., 1943-45. Dir. Chicago Better Bus. Bur., 1931-45. Mem. Advertising Fedn. of Am. (pres. 1940-41, chmn., 1941-43), Am. Legion, Delta Chi, Alpha Delta Sigma (hon. mem.). Republican. Presbyterian. Mason. Clubs: Advt. of New York, Chicago Federated Advt. (hon. mem., pres., 1939-40), Advt. Mgrs. of Chicago (pres. 1934-35). Co-arthor: Advertising Handbook. Author: Some Questions and Answers About Advertising, 1956. Home: Chapel Hill N.C. Died Mar. 5, 1974.

BOSLEY, HAROLD AUGUSTUS, clergyman; b. Burchard, Neb., Feb. 19, 1907; s. Augustus and Effie (Sinclair) B.; A.B., Neb. Wesleyan Coll., 1930, D.D., 1943; D.D., Northwestern U., 1950; B.D., U. Chgo., 1932, Ph.D., 1933; D.S.T. (hon.), Ripon Coll., 1953; L.H.D. (hon.), Cornell Coll., 1953; D.D., Manchester Coll., 1964, Central Methodist Coll., 1972; m. Margaret Marie Dahlstrom, July 21, 1928; children—Paul Shailer, Sidney Stanton (dec.), Norman Keith, Diane Marie, David Merril. Entered ministry Meth. Ch. as local preacher, 1924; ordained elder by Neb. Conf., 1933; dir. religious activities Ia. State Tchrs. Coll., 1934-38; minister Mt. Vernon Place Meth. Ch., Balt., 1938-47; dean Div. Sch., also preacher to Duke U., Durham, N.C., 1947-50; minister 1st Meth. Ch., Evanston, Ill., 1950-62; sr. minister Christ Ch. Meth., N.Y.C., 1962-74. Lectr. at various confs., also religious emphasis weeks at various colls. and univs.; lectr. Earl Found., Pacific Sch. Religion, 1942, Ayer Found., Rochester Colgate Div. Sch., 1944, Russell Found., Tufts Coll., 1948, Carnahan sems. and schs. in Latin Am., 1951, Japan, Korea, 1955; Mendenhall lectr. DePauw U., 1957; Wilson lectr. McMurry Coll., Abilene, Tex., 1959; mem. interfaith team to S.E. Asia, 1965, USSR, 1967, 68, 69, Spain, 1968; del. 2d assembly World Council of Chs., Evanston, Ill., 1954, 3d assembly, New Delhi, 1961, 4th assembly, Uppsala, Sweden, 1968; Chancellor lectr. Queens Coll., Can., 1951; del., mem. central com. World Conf. on Religion and Peace, Kyoto, Japan, 1970, mem. central com. World Conf. on Religion and Peace, Louvain, Belgium, 1974. Mem. Am. Philos. Assn. Author: The Quest for Religious Certainty, 1939; The Philosophical Heritage of the Christian Faith, 1945; On Final Ground, 1946; Main Issues Confronting Christendom, 1948; A Firm Faith for Today, 1950; The Church Militant, 1952 (pub. in Spanish); Preaching on Controversial Issues, 1953; What Did the World Council Say to You?, 1955; Sermons on the Psalms, 1956 (pub. in Korean); Sermons on Genesis, 1958; Doing What is Christian, 1960; He Spoke To Them in Parables, 1963; The Mind of Christ, 1966; The Character of Christ, 1968; The Deeds of Christ, 1969; Men Who Build Churches, 1972. Home: Bronxville N.Y. Died Jan. 21, 1975.

BOSS, LOUIS JOSEPH, accountant; b. Vallejo, Cal., Jan. 16, 1917; s. Louis J. and Ethel (Mathus) B.; B.B.A., Golden Gate U., 1951; m. Marie Anne Cerles, Apr. 18, 1942; children—Judith (Mrs. Richard del Tredici), Monica (Mrs. Thomas A. Sauer), Louis Joseph III, Michael Thomas. Vice pres. Gilbert-Shirley Co., San Rafael, Cal., 1951-57; sr. accountant Webster & Buechner, C.P.A.'s, San Francisco, 1957-59; mgr. Ernst & Ernst, San Francisco, 1959-74; accounting mgr. City of Oakland, 1974. Lectr. govt. acctg. U. San Francisco, 1963-64, Sacramento State Coll., 1966-67. Mem. Cal. Gov.'s Survey on Efficiency and Cost control, 1967. C.P.A., Cal. Mem. Am. Inst. C.P.A.'s, Cal. Soc. C.P.A.'s (chmn. Cal. com. on municipal accounting 1970-71), Am. Accounting Assn. Clubs: San Francisco Commonwealth, Press. Home: Berkeley, Cal. Died Mar. 5, 1975; interred St. Mary's Cemetery, Oakland, Cal.

BOSSART, KAREL JAN, aircraft engr.; b. Antwerp, Belgium, Feb. 9, 1904; s. Louis K. J. and Carolina (Tyck) B.; Mining Engr., Aero. Engr., U. Libre Libre de Bruxelles, Belgium, 1925; M.S., Mass. Inst. Tech., 1927; m. Cornelia Newell Chase, Sept. 24, 1938; children—Karel J., Newell C., Marion C., Alfred T. Newell Chase, Marion Chase. Came to United States, 1925, naturalized, 1936. Chief aerodynamicist Service Technique de l'Aeronautique, Belgium, 1929-30; engr. Skorsky Aircraft Corp., Gen. Aviation Corp., Fleetwings, Inc., Edward G. Budd Mfg. Co., 1930-37; chief research aircarft div. Edward G. Budd Mfg. Co., 1937-39; asst. chief engr. Spencer-Larsen Aircraft, 1940-41; chief structures engr., project engr., asst. chief engr. Consol. Vultee Aircraft Corp., Vultee Field and San Diego divs., 1941-55; chief engr. Convair Astronautics div. Gen. Dynamics Corp., San Diego, 1955-58, tech. dir., 1958-60, asst. to v.p. engring., 1960-75. Recipient Godard Meml. award, 1960. Fellow Am. Rocket Soc.; mem. Am. Ordnance Soc. Address: La Jolla, Cal. Died Aug. 1975.

BOSWELL, CLAY CARLTON, utilities exec.; b. Joplin, Mo., Dec. 7, 1893; s. Ammie Victor and Mattie Pearl (Rickman) B.; B.S., U. Mo., 1915; m. Peggy H., 1 son, Clay Carlton, Jr.; Power sta. operation, maintenance Utah Power & Light Co., Salt Lake City, 1915-16, accountant and statistician, 1916-17, asst. to comml. mgr., 1919-23; operating analyst Electric Bond & Share Co., N.Y.C., 1923-28; asst. chief engr. Minn. Power & Light Co., Duluth, 1929-34, chief engr., 1934-40, dir., 1936-69, v.p., chief engr., 1940-50, v.p., asst. gen. mgr., 1950-53, exec. v.p., 1953-54, pres., gen. mgr., 1954-58, pres., 1958-59, pres., chief exec. officer, 1959-62, chmn. bd. dirs., 1962-66; chief engr. Superior (Wis.) Water Light & Power Co., 1934-54, chmn. bd., dir., 1959-65. Served as 2d lt. C.E., U.S. Army, 1917-19, A.E.F., 11 mos. Registered profl. engr. Fellow Am. Inst. Elec. Engrs.; Mem. Duluth C. of C., I.E.E.E., Am. Soc. C.E., Sigma Nu, Eta Kappa Nu. Clubs: Athletic, Engrs., Duluth, Kitchi Gamma, Northland Country, Rotary (Duluth). Home: Duluth, Minn. Died Dec. 29, 1973; interred Forest Hill Cemetery, Duluth.

BOTEIN, BERNARD, lawyer; b. N.Y.C., May 6, 1900; s. Herman William and Sarah (Leonson) B.; student Coll. City N.Y., 1917-19; LL.B., Bklyn Law Sch., 1924; LL.D., N.Y. Law Sch., 1959, N.Y.U., 1964, Jewish Theol. Sem., 1965, Yeshiva U., 1965, Bklyn. Law Sch., 1966; m. Marian Berman, Oct. 13, 1940; children—Stephen William, Michael Harris. Admitted to N.Y. bar, 1926; practiced, N.Y.C., 1926-41; asst. dist. atty. N.Y. County, 1929-36; justice N.Y. State Supreme Ct., 1941-53, asso. justice appellate div., 1953-57, presiding justice appellate div., 1957-69, ret.; sr. partner firm Botein, Hays, Sklar & Herzberg, N.Y.C., 1969-74. Head N.Y.C. Accident Fraud Investigation, 1936, N.Y. State Ins. Fund Investigation, 1938, N.Y. State Printing Investigation, 1940; Cardozo lectr.; vis. lectr. U. P.R. Law Sch., 1960; Cooley lectr. U. Mich. Law Sch.; chmn. Nat. Conf. on Bail and Criminal Justice; chmn. exec. br. N.Y. State Constl. Conv., 1967. Bd. dirs. Nat. Legal Aid and Defender Assn.; trustee-at-large Fedn. Jewish Philanthropies; trustee William Nelson Cromwell Found., Vera Inst. Justice, N.Y. U. Law Found., N.Y.C. Rand Inst.: mem. Nat. Com. on Jud. Adminstrn.; v.p. YMHA, YWHA, 1949-59. Served with U.S. Army, World War I. Recipient medal Assn. Bar City N.Y., 1963; New Sch. medal for distinguished service to N.Y.C., 1965; Chief Justice Stone award, 1965, Citizens Union award, 1970, Gold medal St. Nicholas Soc. of N.Y., 1970; Meml. awards established in his honor include Nat. Moot Ct. competition Bernard Botein ann. award, Bernard Botein grad scholarship at N.Y. U. Law Sch., Bernard Botein ann. medal for outstanding non-jud. ct. staff employee. Fellow Am. Coll. Trial Lawyers; mem. Am., N.Y. State (Gold medal 1970) bar assns., Assn. Bar City N.Y. (pres. 1970-72), N.Y. County Lawyers Assn., Jud. Conf. N.Y. (mem. adminstrv. bd. 1957-68), Century Assn., Am. Arbitration Assn. (exec. com.), Order of Coif (hon.). Jewish religion (pres. Met. Council Synagogues 1948-50, chmn. bd. trustees synagogue 1942-47). Author: (with Irving W. Halpern) The Slum and Crime, 1935; Trial Judge, 1952; The Prosecutor, 1956; (with Murray A. Gordon) The Trial of the Future, 1963; Our Cities Burn, 1972. Home: New York City N.Y. Died Feb. 3, 1974.

BOTKE, JESSIE ARMS, artist; b. Chgo.; d. William Aldis and Martha (Cornell) Arms: ed. high sch., Art Inst. Chgo.; m. Cornelis Botke, Apr. 15, 1915 (dec. 1954); 1 son, William Arms. Exhibited at Art Inst. Chgo., N.Y. Water Color Club, Am. Water Color Soc., Nat. Acad. (New York), Corcoran Gallery (Washington), also Paris Salon, 1924, Sesqui-centennial, Phila., etc. Represented in Municipal Gallery (Chgo.) Art Inst. Chgo., Neb. Art Assn., Treasure Island, San Francisco Art Collection; mural in Noyes Hall, U. Chgo., Woodrow Wilson High Sch., Ornard, Cal., Oaks Hotel Ojai. Rep. in permanent collection of Los Angeles Co., also Fine Art Gallery, San Diego, Gardena High Sch., Santa Paula High Sch., Santa Paula Meml. Hosp., Dean Dobbs Blanchard Meml. Library, and in collections of Ralph Norton. Mem. Chgo. Soc. of Artists, Women Painters and Sculptors (hon. mention exhibit, 1925), Cal. Water Color Soc., Am. Water Color Soc., Santa Barbara Art Assn. Awarded 1st prize for water color Cal. State Fair, 1947. Clubs: Cordon (Chgo.); California Arts. Home: Santa Paula Cal. Died Oct. 2, 1971.

BOTKIN, BENJAMIN ALBERT, writer, b. Boston, Feb. 7, 1901; s. Albert and Annie (Dechinick) B.; A.B., Harvard, 1920; M.A., Columbia, 1921; Ph.D., U. Neb., 1931, Litt.D. (hon.), 1956; m. Gertrude Fritz, Aug. 30, 1925; children—Dorothy Ann (Mrs. Jerome Alan Rosenthal), Daniel Benjamin. From instr. English to asso. prof. U. Okla., 1921-40; asst. instr. U. Neb., 1930-31; tchr. summer sessions U. Mont., 1932, N.M. Normal U., 1933; Julius Rosenwald fellow, 1937; folklore editor Fed. Writers Project, Washington, 1938-39; chief editor writers unit Library of Congress Project, 1939-41; resident fellow folklore Library of Congress, 1940-42, hon., 1943-55, Guggenheim fellow, 1951. Mem. subcom folk music Office Cultural Presentations, Bur. Ednl. and Cultural Affairs, Dept. State, 1967-70; expert cons. Nat. Com. Folk Arts U.S., 1935-70; mem. nat. adv. council Nat. Folk Festival, 1934-67, bd. dirs., 1967-75; spl. folklore cons., 1971-75; chmn. Workshop for Cultural Democracy, 1956-58; Louis M. Rabinowitz Foundation grant, 1965; sr. fellow Nat. Endowment for the Humanities, 1967. Fellow Am. Folklore Soc. (pres. 1944-45, del. Am. Council Learned Socs. 1951-53); mem. Manuscript Soc., Internat. Folk Music Council, Internat. Soc. Ethnology and Folklore, Folklore Soc. Greater Washington, N.Y. (hon. v.p.), Northeastern forklore socs., The Westerners, Phi Beta Kappa. Author: The American Play-Party Song, 1937, reprint, 1963; editor: Folk-Say, A Regional Miscellany, 4 vols., 1929-32, reprint, 1970; The Southwest Scene, 1931; Space, Vol. I. Nos. 1-12, 1934-35, reprinted 1970; Lay My Burden Down; A Folk History of Slavery, 1945, German version, 1963; A Treasury of American Folklore, 1944; A Treasury of New England Folklore, 1947, rev., 1965; Sidewalks of America, 1954; N.Y.C. Folklore, 1956; (with Carl Withers) The Illustrated Book of American Folklore, 1958; A Civil War Treasury of Tales, Legends and Folklore, 1960; numerous other folklore treasuries. Asso. editor N.Y. Folklore Quar.; contbr. to Ten Eventful Years, Ency. Brit., 1947; Standard Dictionary of Folklore, Mythology, and Legend, 1949-50; Collier's Ency., 1950; The World Book Ency., 1960; The Book of the American West, 1963; The Reader's Adviser, 1969; editorial cons. the Life Treasury of American Folklore, 1961; The Badmen, Columbia Records Legacy Collection, 1963; cons. on games The Random House Dictionary of the English Language, 1966; editor-in-chief Folklore and Soc. and Rediscovering Am. reprints Johnson Reprint Corp., 1966; others. Address: Croton-on-Hudson, N.Y. Died July 30, 1975; interred Sharon Gardens, Valhalla, N.Y.

BOTTS, CLARENCE MILTON lawyer; b. Hancock County, Ill., Jan. 30, 1881; s. Robert Waggoner and Laura Ann (White) B.; student Carthage (Ill) Coll. 2 yrs., D.C.L., 1925; studied law privately; m. Lessie Clara Fletcher, Sept. 1, 1906; children—Robert William, Catherine Mildred, Clarence Milton, Jr. (lt. col., U.S. Infantry, killed in action, Philippines, May 16, 1945). Admitted to New Mexico bar, 1911; general practice in Eddy County, New Mexico, during most of time as member firm Armstrong & Botts, Carlsbad, until 1915; asst. atty. A.,T.&S.F. Ry. Co., for State of N.M., with hdqrs. at Albuquerque, 1915-19; mem. firm Simms & Botts, Albuquerque, 1919-22; asso. justice Supreme Court of N.M., 1923-24; again mem. firm Simms & Botts, 1925-32; mem. Botts & Botts from 1933. Delivered course of lectures at Northestern U. Law Sch., 1924. Republican candidate for gov., N.M., 1930. Mem. bd. of trustees Southwestern Legal Foundation. Mem. N.M. State Bar, pres., 1935-36. Mem. Am. Bar

Assn., N.M. Bar Assn. (pres. 1917), Am. Law Inst. Rep. Mason, Elk. Club: Lawyers. Mem. bd. mgrs. Sch. of Am. Research. Home: Albuquerque, N.M.†

BOUCHER, CARL OPDYCKE, dentist, educator; b. Ft. Wayne, Ind., October 14, 1904; s. Charles Foster and Winifred (Opdycke) B.; student Ohio State U., 1928, D.D.S., 1927; m. Florence Leona Griess, May 9, 1931; 1 son, James Bradford. Asst. prof. Ohio State U., 1939-40, asso. prof., 1940-42, chmn. prosthetic div. Coll. Denistry, 1940-71, prof., 1940-75, chmn. dental lab. tech., 1947-57; gen. practice denistry, Columbus, O., 1927-35, prosthodontist, 1935-75; vis. prof. Nihon U., Matsudo, Japan. cons. AUS, 1942-75, VA, 1950-75, USAF, 1954, Walter Reed Army Hosp. Trustee, Ohio Dental Care Corp., 1961-68; mem. med. adv. bd. Services for Crippled Children, Ohio Dept. Pub. Welfare, 1959-75. Mem. Joint Commn. Accrediation Dental Labs., 1964-68. Recipient Callahan Meml. award (gold medal) Ohio Dental Assn., 1970. Mem. Ohio Dental Assn. (pres. 1963-64), Columbus Dental Soc. (pres. 1946-47), Acad. Denture Prosthetics (pres. 1950-51), Am. Dental Assn. (past sec. prosthetic dental service com.), Am. Bd. Prosthodontics (founder, diplomate, pres. 1952-53), Am. Assn. Cleft Palate Rehab. (past v.p.), Southeastern Acad. Prosthodontics (hon.), Carl O. Boucher Prosthodontic Conf. (hon. pres.), Am. Dental Soc. Europe (hon.), Academia Brasiliera de Odontologia (corr. mem.), Am. Assn. Dental Editors, Am. Equilibration Soc., Pierre Fauchard Acad., Am. Acad. Dental Sci. Internat. Assn. Dental Research, Am. Acad. Maxillofacial Prosthetics (hon.), Am. Prosthodontic Soc. (hon.), Am. Coll. Dentists, Fedn. Dentaire Internat. (recipient Georges Villain prize 1972), Pacific Coast Soc. Prosthodontics (hon.), Fedn. Prosthodontic Orgns. (founder, pres. 1965-67), Prosthodontic Soc. South Africa (hon.), Dental Assn. South Africa (hon.), Am. Acad. Implant Denistry (hon.), Sigma Xi, Psi Omega (supreme grand master 1952-53), Omicron Kappa Upsilon. Author: Dental Prosthetic Laboratory Manual, 1947; co-author: Prosthodontic Treatment for Edentulous Patients; author, editor Glossary of Current Clinical Dental Terminology, 2d edit., 1973; Swenson's Complete Dentures, 5th edit., 1964, 6th edit., 1970. Editor Jour. Prosthetic Denistry 1949-75, Ohio Dental Jour., 1958-60. Home: Columbus, Ohio Died Mar. 11, 1975; interred Shiffler Cemetery, Bryan, Ohio.

BOUDEMAN, ROBERT MEIER, pharm. co. exec.; b. Kalamazoo, June 21, 1917; s. Dallas, Jr. and Freda (Meier) B.; B.A., Kalamazoo Coll., 1939; m. Carol Gilmore, June 14, 1938; children—Sherwood M., Martha (Mrs. Thomas Vander Molen), Carol (Mrs. Donald Coggan), Mary Jane (dec.). With Upjohn Co., Kalamazoo, 1939-69, dir. internat. adminstrn., internat. controller, v.p., exec. v.p., 1966-69, pres., dir., 1966-69; pres. Upjohn Internat. Inc., 1962-68, dir., 1968-74; dir. 1st Nat. Bank and Trust Co., Kalamazoo. Trustee Kalamazoo Coll. Served to lt. (j.g.) USNR, 1943-45. Mem. Pharm. Mfg. Assn., Gull Lake Star Fleet. Clubs: Gull Lake Country (pres., dir.) (Richland, Mich.); Park (Kalamazoo). Home: Kalamazoo Mich. Died Mar. 23, 1974.

BOUGHNER, LEROY JOHN, editor; b. Simcoe, Ont., Can., July 10, 1880; s. Cleveland W. and Frances (Flanagan) B.; U. of Toronto, 1899-01; m. Genevieve Jackson, of Minneapolis, Minn., Mar. 12, 1910. City editor Minneapolis, Minn., Mar. 12, 1910. City editor Minneapolis Tribune, from 1908. Mem. Gov. John A. Johnson Memorial Commn. of Minn.; mem. Am. Civic Assn. (exec. bd.). Pres. Garden Club of Minneapolis; dir. Juvenile Protective League of Minneapolis; dir. Boys' Club of Minneapolis; dir. Infant Welfare Assn. of Minneapolis; Mason, Elk. Clubs: University, Athletic, Automobile, Rotary. Orginator of vacant lot gardening on civil basis. Home: Minneapolis, Minn.†

BOURDIER, LILLIAN BLANCHE (MRS. JAMES BOURDIER), journalist; b. Opelousas, La., Sept. 29, 1907; d. Aaron and Hannah (Hirschman) Jacobs; student La. State U., 1924-27; m. James M. Bourdier, Dec. 9, 1927 (dec. May 1951); 1 son, James A. Editor, Clarion News, weekly newspaper, and Herald, semi-weekly newspaper, Opelousas, 1940-50; city and woman's editor Daily World, Opelousas, 1950-73; corr. New Orleans Times Picavune, Baton Rouge Adv., Beaumont (Tex.) Enterprise. Bd. dirs. United Givers Fund, Opelousas Eunice Pub. Library, Yambilee sweet potato festival. Recipient citizenship award Opelousas C. of C., 1970; first place winner Nat. Press Women, 1970; recipient presidential award of honor Opelousas Jr. C. of C., 1969, certificate of merit V.F.W. Auxiliary, 1966, community service award Theta Sigma Phi, 1959, outstanding publicity award Am. Legion of La., 1969; named La. Press Woman of Yr. for 1971-72. Mem. Theta Sigma Phi, La. Press Woman (past treas.). Clubs: Opelousas Woman's (pres. 1946), Pilot (pres. 1954). Home: Opelousas La. Died May 15, 1973.

BOVARD, JOHN FREEMAN, educator; b. Los Angeles, Calif., Jan. 18, 1881; s. Freeman Daily and Sally (North) B.; B.S., U. of Calif., 1903, M.S., 1906, Ph.D., 1916; m. Camille Carroll, Sept. 1, 1910; children—Jeanne, Freeman Carroll. Asst. zoology, U. of Calif., 1903; instr. zoology, U. of Ore., 1903-08; research asst., San Diego Marine Station, summers of 1903-06; asst. prof. zoology, U. of Ore., 1908-10; prof., 1910-20; investigator, U.S. Bureau of Fisheries, 1910; taught summer session, U. of Washington, Friday Harbor Marine Station, 1918-19; dean, Sch. of Phys. Edn., U. of Ore., 1920-37; taught summer session, U. of Calif., Berkeley, 1928, Los Angeles, 1927-30; dir. phys. edn., Ore. State System Higher Edn., 1932-33; prof. phys. edn., U. Cal., 1937-48, emeritus prof., from 1948, chmn. dept. phys. edn., 1939-48, dean of College of Applied Arts, 1942-46. President Oregon State Phys. Edn. Assn., 1922, 1925, 1933; Pacific Coast Phys. Directors Assn., 1927; pres., Kiwanis Club, Eugene, Ore., 1932-33. Fellow A.A.A.S. (1921-48) Am. Assn. Health, Phys. Edn. and Recreation (pres. northwest dist., 1935-36; pres. southwest dist., 1943-44; contbg. editor research quarterly, 1933-46); Am. Acad. of Phys. Edn. Mem. Am. Assn. U. Professors (pres. U. of Calif. chapter, 1941-42), Sigma Xi, Phi Delta Kappa, Sigma Delta Psi. Home: La Jolla, Cal.†

BOWEN, CATHERINE DRINKER, author; b. Haverford, Pa., Jan. 1, 1897; d. Henry Sturgis and Aimee Ernesta (Beaux) Drinker; student Peabody Inst., Inst. Mus. Art; Litt.D., U. Pa., Temple U., Boston U., Rochester U., Lafayette Coll., Lehigh Coll.; m. Ezra Bowen; children—Catherine Drinker, Ezra; m. 2d, Thomas McKean Downs, July 1, 1939. Author books, including: Free Artist-Anton Rubinstein, 1939; (with Barbara Von Meck) Beloved Friend-Biography of Tchaikowski, 1937 (Book-of-Month); Yankee from Olympus-Justice O. Holmes and His Family (Book of Month), 1944; John Adams and the American Revolution (Book of Month), 1950; The Lion and the Throne, 1956 (History Book Club); Adventures of a Biographer, 1959; Francis Bacon, The Temper of a Man (Book-of-Month), 1963; Miracle at Philadelphia (Book of the Month), 1966; The Craft and the Calling 1968; Family Portrait, 1970. Trustee emeritus Free Library System Phila.; past mem. Nat. Portrait Gallery Commn. Mem. Am. Philos. Soc., Royal Soc. Lit., Phi Beta Kappa (hon.). Home: Haverford Pa. Died Nov. 1, 1973.

BOWEN, RICHARD LEBARON, textile exec., author; b. 1878; student Brown U.; grad. R.I. Sch. Design, 1898. Vice pres. and gen. mgr. O'Bannon Corp., 1912-22; founder Coated Textile Mills, Providence, 1923, pres. and treas. from 1923; founder, pres. and treas. Bowen Mills, Inc., Pawtucket, from 1929. Fellow Am. Soc. Geneal.; mem. New Eng. Hist. Geneal. Soc. (fgn. and English research from 1943, asst. editor Register 1946-47, councilor 1948, v.p. R.I. from 1949), Colonial Soc. Mass., Am. Antiquarian Soc., Mass. (corr. mem.) and R.I. (pres. 1948-50) hist. socs., Soc. Geneal. London. Research on history of Rehoboth; life of Rev. Samuel Newman; history of Swansea. Author: Early Rhode Island Colonial Money and Its Counterfeiting, 1647-1726, 1942; The Providence Oath of Allegiance and Its Signers, 1651-52, 1943; Index to Early Providence Town Records, 1949; Early Rehoboth (4 vols.), 1950; also contbr. various articles. Home: Rehoboth, Mass.†

BOWER, JOSEPH AUGUSTUS, banker; b. Denver, Colo., Sept. 2, 1880; s. William Alexander and Sarah Anne (Berry) B.; grad. Detroit Business U., 1900; m. Emma Anna Wuelfing, Aug. 22, 1906; children—Phyllis Louise (Mrs. Arthur H. Lamborn, Jr.), Robert Alexander, Joseph Wuelfing, Barbara Ann. Admitted to Mich. bar, 1901, and began practice at Detroit; 1st jr. officer, later v.p. Detroit Trust Co., 14 yrs., 1902-1915, pres. Hale & Kilburn Co., mfrs., Phila., 1915-17; v.p. Liberty Nat. Bank (now New York Trust Co.), New York, 1917-29; resigned, pres. Chemical Securities Corp., 1929-32; exec. v.p. Chem. Bank & Trust Co. from 1932; vice chmn. exec. com. Chem. Bank & Trust Co., chmn. Trust Com.; pres. Detroit Internat. Bridge Co.; dir. Safety Car Heating & Lighting Co. Life trustee Rutgers U. (resigned 1944). Decorated Officer of The Crown (Belgium); Master Knight Sovereign Order of Malta (R.C.). Mem. Acad. Polit. Sci., Am. Geog. Soc., Policy Assn. World Peace Foundation, Gen. business mgr., Alien Property Custodian, World War I. Republican. Catholic. Clubs: Recess, Union League (New York); Montclair Assn., Upper Montclair Country. Home: Montclair, N.J.†

BOWERS, ELSWORTH, educator; b. Delaware County, O., Jan. 21, 1879; s. John Henry and Mary E. (Wright) B.; Ph.B., Otterbein Coll., Westerville, O., 1901; A.M., Ohio State U., 1922, Ph.D., 1929; m. Stella B. Martin, June 26, 1912. Teacher pub. schs. in O., 1901-05; supt. schs., Gahanna, O., 1905-09, New Albany, O., 1909-11; science teacher, Newark, O., 1911-16; dist. supt. Scioto County, O., 1916-19; supt. Tippecanoe City, O., 1919-22, Galion, Ohio, 1922-24; professor psychology, Marsahll Coll., Huntington, W.Va., 1924-45, dean Col. Arts and Sciences, 1939-45; acting prof. psychol. U. of Tenn., 1945-46; prof. psychology, W.Va. Wesleyan Coll., 1947-49; promotional service for ch. related colls. from 1949; cons. psychologist from 1949. Member American Psychological Association, Midwestern Psychol. Assn., Kappa Delta Pi. Meth. Mason (32°). Home: Buckhannon, W.Va.†

BOWERS, HENRY SMITH, banker; b. Arlington Heights, Mass., May 7, 1878; s. William Benton and Laura Rebecca (Smith) B.; A.B., Harvard, 1900; m. Margaret Thomas, Oct. 31, 1905; children—William Benton II, Margaret (Mrs. John C. Witt), Paul Sachs. Began with Goldman Sachs & Co., N.Y.C., 1899, partner from 1915; dir. S. H. Kress & Company, The Jewel Tea Company, Inc., Champion Paper and Fibre Co., United Biscuit Co., of Am., Minneapolis-Moline Power Implement Co., Kelsey-Hayes Wheel Co., Detroit, Mich. Trustee Tuskegee Inst.; trustee, Samuel H. Kress Foundation, New York City; mem. bd. mgrs. State Charities Aid Assn. N.Y.; dir. Andrew Freedman Home, N.Y. City. Clubs: Harvard, University (New York); Scarsdale Golf (Hartsdale, N.Y.), University (Chicago); Biltmore (N.C.) Forest Country. Home: Greenwich, Conn.†

BOWERS, WALTER ABRAHAM, abstract co. exec.; b. Chgo., Nov. 19, 1898; s. Abraham and Elizabeth (Scott) B.; Ph.B., U. Chgo., 1920; LL.B., George Washington U., 1937, J.D., 1969; m. Helen Arnold, Aug. 28, 1949; children—Joy Anne (Mrs. James Kenworthy), Jeanine (Mrs. Harry Dodge), Elizabeth (Mrs. Lowell V. Hammer), Walter Abraham, Sally C. (Mrs. Richard W. Kennett), Edward Jones. With Harris Trust and Savs. Bank, Chgo., 1920-27, Halsey Stuart and Co., St. Louis, 1927-29; with U.S. Commerce, Treasury and War depts., Washington, 1929-44; admitted to D.C. bar, 1937, Kan. bar, 1946, also U.S. Supreme Ct. bar, ICC bar, other fed. bars; sr. chief fiscal officer War Dept., 1941-44; v.p., treas. Lawrance Aero. Corp., Linden, N.J., 1944-46; v.p. Indian Motorcycle Co., Springfield, Mass., 1945; v.p., treas. Aireon Mfg. Corp., Kansas City, Mo., 1946; pres. Western Inst. Bus. Mgmt., Eureka, Kan., 1947-51; instr. bus. adminstrn. U. Kan., Lawrence, 1946-47; regional mgr. Burns and Roe, Inc., N.Y.C., 1952-65; pres. Street Abstract Co., Yales Center, Kan., from 1965; dir. commerce and indsl. devel. State of Mo., Jefferson City, 1961-62. Served with AC, U.S. Army, 1917-19. C.L.U. Mem. Phi Gamma Delta, Delta Theta Phi. Presbyn. Mason (32 deg., Shriner), Rotarian. Home: Yates Center Kan. Deceased.

BOWLBY, HARRY LAITY, clergyman; b. nr. Asbury, N.J., Jan. 26, 1874; s. Robert Melroy and Elizabeth (DeHart) B.; A.B., Princeton, 1901, A.M., 1903; grad. Princeton Theol. Sem., 1904; D.D., Washington (Tenn.) Coll., 1917; m. Bertha H. Watson, Nov. 6, 1909; 1 dau., Bertha Virginia. Ordained Presbyn. ministry, 1904; pastor First Ch., Altoona, Pa., 1905-13; gen. sec. Lord's Day Alliance U.S., 1913-54; class of 1901 agent of Princeton U., 5 yr. term. On The Lord's Day Alliance Bd. of Mgrs. Life mem. Oregon Trail Memorial Assn.; mem. bd. dirs. Allied Patriotic Socs. of Am.; founder and life mem. Am. Pioneer Trails Assn.; pres. David Lawrence Pierson Hist. Library Memorial Assn. Service with Y.M.C.A. in mil. camps, 1917-18; visiting speaker by official appointment to U.S. Naval Stations and bases and army forts and camps, from 1941. Recipient award for nat. welfare benefits for postal employees N.Y.C., General Society War of 1812 (chaplain general 1959-60), National and New Jersey Societies S.A.R., Friars Alumni Assn. Princeton Theol. Sem. (pres. bd. trustees), Cliosophic Soc. (Princeton), hon. mem. Federal Employees Soc. of N.Y.; ex-gov. for N.J. of Pi Gamma Nu. Mu. Del. to Fifteenth (Quadrennial) Council of the Alliance of Churches holding the Presbyterian System, 1937; Republican. Mason. Clubs: Clergy, Fraternities, Princeton (New York City). Author numerous articles on Sabbath and Sunday subjects. Contbr. to secular and religious publs. Home: Poughkeepsie, N.Y.†

BOWLER, JOHN POLLARD, surgeon, educator; b. Cambridge, Mass., Jan. 3, 1895; s. John William and Ellen Cecilia (Pollard) B.; A.B., Dartmouth, 1915, M.A., hon., 1935, D.Sc., 1952; student Dartmouth College Medical School, 1915-17; M.D., Harvard, 1919; M.Sc. in Surgery, Mayo Foundation, U. of Minn., 1924; m. Madelaine Gile, May 27, 1928; children—Patricia, Janet. With Dartmouth Med. Coll., 1924-45, prof. surgery, from 1935. Fellow Am. Coll. Surgeons; mem. A.M.A., N.H. State and Grafton County med. Societies, Am. Urol. Assn., New Eng. (pres. 1952-53), Eastern surgical societies, International Society of Surgery, N.H. Surgical Club, Assn. of Ex-Residents of Mayo Clinic (pres. 1934), Am.Goitre Assn., Theta Delta Chi, Alpha Kappa Kappa, Gamma Alpha. Catholic. Club: Graduate. Contbr. on med. subjects. Home: Hanover, N.H. Died Jan. 22, 1974; buried Pine Knoll Cemetery, Hanover, N.H.

BOWLES, FRANK HAMILTON, ednl. adminstr.; b. Taihoku, Japan, Nov. 20, 1907; s. Frank Carroll and Sarah D. (Siceloff) B.; student Central Coll.; A.B., Columbia, 1928, M.A., 1930; Litt.D., Wagner Coll., 1949; LL.D., Providence Coll., 1956; L.H.D., Dickinson, 1957; also other hon. degrees; m. Frances Callaway Porcher, 1939; children—Francis Porcher, Courtney Callaway, Mason Banks. Dir. admissions Columbia U., 1934-48; pres. Coll. Entrance Examination Bd., 1948-63; dir. edn. program Ford Found., 1963-66, adviser to pres. Ford Found. in Internat. Edn., 1966-75; v.p. Fund for Advancement Edn., 1964-67, pres., 1967-75; pres. Fund for Adult Edn., 1965-75. Fulbright Nat. Selection Com., 1949-51; con. U.P.R., 1946-56, Internat. study univ. admissions UNESCO-CEEB. Chmn. Commn. on Instns. of Higher Edn., Middle States Assn. of Colls. and Secondary Schs., 1947-50; mem. bd. visitors U.S. Mil. Acad., 1958-61, Haile Selassie I U., Addis Ababa, Ethiopa, 1966-73, Air U. trustee Nat. Scholarship Service and Fund for

Negro Students, 1951-56, New Lincoln Sch., 1958-61, Inst. Internat.Edn.; mem. adv. com. to study Cath. edn., 1962-65. Served from lt. to comdr. USNR, 1942-45. Mem. Sigma Alpha Epsilon, Phi Delta Kappa. Episcopalian. Clubs: Cosmos, Century, University (N.Y.C.). Author: How to Get Into College, 1958; Access to Higher Education, 1963; Re-founding of the College Board, 1968. Home: Demarest, N.J. Died May 1975.

BOWLIN, WILLIAM RAY, educator, author; b. Somerfield, Pa., May 24, 1881; s. John Howard and Mary (Bradley) B.; Ph.B., U. of Chicago, 1911; m. Cornelia Henderson, of Canton, Mo., Aug. 24, 1903; children—Ellen Bradley, Richard Henderson. Began teaching at 18, later prin. and supt. schs.; instr. English, Englewood High Sch., Chicago, 1908-19; apptd. asst. prin., Lindblom High Sch., 1919; prin. Robert Fulton Pub. Sch. from 1926. Mem. Schoolmasters' Club of Chicago (pres., 1917-18). Democrat. Methodist. Mason. Author: (with George L. Marsh) Vocational English, 1918; A Laboratory Manual of English, 1927; A Book of Treasured Poems, 1928. Conductor of daily column, English Speechcraft, Chicago Daily News, 1925-1926. Home: Chicago, Ill.†

BOWMAN, GUS KARL, JR., advt. agy. exec.; b. Columbus, O., May 23, 1928; s. Gus Karl and Stella M. (Flatau) B.; B.F.A., Ohio U., 1950; m. Evelyn Press, Sept. 16, 1951; children—Debbie Lynn, Gus Karl III, David Lewis, James Arthur. Account exec. Byer & Bowman Advt. Agy., Inc., Columbus, 1952-59, exec. v.p., 1959-64, pres., from 1964; pres. Regional Features, Inc., Columbus, from 1966. Bd. dirs. Better Bus. Bur., Columbus. Publicity chmn. United Appeal, 1970. Served with AUS, 1950-52. Club: Winding Hollow Country (pres. 1971) (Columbus). Home: Columbus, O. Died Jan. 20, 1974.

BOWMAN, HARRY SAMUEL, lawyer; b. Pueblo, Colo., Oct. 20, 1880; s. Samuel H. and Clara (Goldsmith) B.; student U. of Colo., 1900-01; LL.B., U. Mich., 1907; m. Bertha M. Cohn, Sept. 6, 1911; children—Robert D. (dec.), Harold E. Began practice at New York City, 1907; removed to Clovis, N.M., 1909; city atty., 1910-11; asst. dist. atty., 5th Jud. Dist., N.M., 1911; asst. atty. gen., N.m., 1916-17 and 1919-21, atty.-gen., term Jan. 1921-Dec. 31, 1922; asst. U.S. atty. from 1923. Mem. Exemption Bd., Dist. No. 1, during World War, also legal appeal agt., co. food adminstrator, legal advisor Co. Council of Defense, etc. Capt. insp. gen., New Mexico N.G. Mem. Am., N.M. and Santa Fe Co. bar assns., Acacia. Mason (33°), Elk. Home: Santa Fe, N.M.†

BOWMAN, JOHN FIFE, church exec.; b. West Weber, Utah, May 27, 1880; s. of Andrew Gray and Elizabeth (Fife) B.; grad. Weber Acad., Ogden, Utah, 1899; student law, U. of Chicago, 1906-08; m. Edna M. Smith, Jan. 27, 1903; children—Richard, Dorothy, Katheryn, John H., Ruth, Joseph F. Teacher grade sch., Croydon, Utah, 1899; bookkeeper, with Utah Light & Power Co., 1903-05; admitted to Utah bar, 1908, and began practice at Salt Lake City; asst. county prosecutor, Salt Lake County, 1909-12; mem. Stewart, Bowman, Morris & Callister, 1912-17. Mayor of Salt Lake City, term 1928-32. Mem. Draft Bd., Salt Lake City, World War. Pres. Chamber of Commerce of Independence, Mo. Mem. exec. council, Salt Lake City, Boy Scouts America, Am. Red Cross, Travelers Aid Soc. Mem. gen. bd. Young Men's Mutual Improvement Assn., Ch. of Latter Day Saints. State chmn. The Defenders (dry orgns. of Utah); organizer and former pres. Salt Lake County Fish and Game Protective Assn.; pres. of Central States Mission of Latter Day Saints Ch. and mgr. Zion's Printing Co., headquarters at Independence, Mo., from 1939. Clubs: Kiwanis, Exchange. Address: Independence, MO.†

BOWNE, WILLIAM RAINEAR, naval officer; b. Bordentown, N.Y., May 21, 1878; grad. Naval War Coll., 1929. Commd. ensign, U.S. Navy, 1901, and advanced through the grades to commodore, 1945; served in U.S. ships Monocacy, Southery, North Dakota, New York, Maine, Arizona, Huron; transferred to retired list, 1942, but continued on active duty as dist. supply officer, Brooklyn, N.Y., also became inspector Supply Corps activities under cognizance of Chief of Naval Air Primary Training Command within Third Naval Dist., 1944. Decorated Victory and Am. Defense Service medals. Home: North Grafton, Mass.†

BOXER, HAROLD HORTON, lawyer; b. Chgo., Apr. 24, 1907; s. Joseph and Dorothy (Lindner) B.; LL.B., St. John's Coll., 1928; Ph.D. (hon.). Midwestern U., 1932; m. Enid Aussenberg, Mar. 9, 1946. Admitted to N.Y. bar, 1929; mem. firm Boxer & Boxer, N.Y.C., 1930-63; spl. asst. atty. gen. election frauds u.c. N.Y. State, 1932; referee Small Claims N.Y.C. Municipal Ct., 1955-63, N.Y.C. Civil Ct., from 1963; law sec. Supreme Ct., N.Y.C., from 1969. Cons., U. Notre Dame, Levanburg Corner House, Study on Problems of Youth. Del. Keep Am. Beautiful, 1960; rep. council Nat. Orgn. Children and Youth, 1964; nat. financial sec. Union Orthodox Jewish Congregations Am., 1960-62, nat. sec., 1962-64, v.p., from 1964; chmn. Nat. Conf. Synagogue Youth, 1954; chmn. joint youth commn. Union Orthodox Jewish Congregations of Am.-Rabbinical Council Am.-Yeshiva U., 1964; vice chmn. coordinating com. Fedn. Jewish Philanthropies, Queens, from 1954; sec. Synagogue Council Am., from 1970. Del. Democratic Nat. Conv., 1932; pres. Tryion Dem. Assn., 1967-71. Recipient Kather Shem Tov award Union Orthodox Jewish Congregations Am., Mogen Ha Elef Honor award, 1964, 69; award Fedns. Jewish Philanthropies, 1960. Mem. N.Y. County Lawyers Assn., Queens County Bar Assn., Internat. Platform Assn., Hebrew Immigrant Aid Soc., Am. Jewish Congress, Phi Delta Mu. Author: Jewish Aspects of Juvenile Delinquency, 1960. Home: Forest Hills N.Y. Deceased.

BOYCE, WILLIAM A., ophthalmologist; b. Mar. 22, 1881; s. William A. and Elizabeth (Aldredge) B.; M.D., Louisiana School of Medicine, Tulane University, 1905; m. Estelle Merrill Rachal. Prof. emeritus of ophthalmology, Coll. of Medicine Evangelists. Los Angeles, sr. surgeon emeritus in Ophthalmology 1 Hosp.; mem. sr. staff, Calif. Hosp. Fellow Am. Los Angeles Gener Coll. of Surgeons, A.M.A.; mem. Am. Acad. of Ophthalmology and Oto-Laryngology, Am. Bd. of Ophthalmology, Pacific Coast Oto-Ophthalmological Soc., Calif. Med. Assn., Hollywood Acad. of Medicine. Home: Los Angeles, Calif.†

BOYD, BERNARD HENRY, educator, clergyman; b. Mt. Pleasant, S.C., Nov. 16, 1910; s. Frank T. and Eunice (Beaty) B.; A.B., Presbyn. Coll., 1932; Th.B., M.A., Princeton, 1935; Th.D., Union Theol. Sem., 1946; m. Thelma Hicklin, Aug. 5, 1944; children—Donald Beaty, Karen Elizabeth. Ordained to ministry Presbyn. Ch., 1943; prof. Bible Presbyn. Coll., 1936-47, Davidson Coll., 1947-50; James A. Gray prof. Bibl. lit. U. N.C., Chapel Hill, from 1950, chmn. dept. of religion, 1952-60; archaeol. exploration in Israel, summers 1963-72; organizer of expedn. to Lachish, 1966; ednl. dir. Inst. of Mediterranean Studies, 1965-67, archaeol. dir., from 1968; co.-dir. U. N.C.-Hebrew U. expdn. to Tell Arad, 1967, Lynn Prickett archaeol. expdn. to Lachish, 1968; ednl. dir. Archaeol. Expn. to Tell Beer Sheba, 1971-75. Lectr. Served as chaplain USN, Marines, 1943-45. Recipient Tanner Meml. award, Salgo award. Mem. Soc. Bibl. Lit. and Exegesis, Am. Acad. Religion, Am. Schs. Oriental Research, Archaeol. Inst. Am., Order Golden Fleece, Blue Key, Pi Kappa Delta. Omicron Delta Kappa. Home: Chapel Hill, N.C., Died Sept. 28, 1975; buried Chapel Hill, N.C.

BOYD, CHARLES ARTHUR, clergyman; b. Randolph, Mass., Sept. 24, 1878; s. Arthur Augustus and Annie Howard (Smith) B.; prep. edn. Vt. Acad., Saxtons River, Vt.; student Hartford Sch. of Religious Pedagogy, 1907-08; m. Bertha Louise Buffum, May 12, 1903; children—Arthur F., Albert C., Philip S., Alice L. Asst. pastor Worcester, Mass., 1906-07, Central Bapt. Ch., Norwich, Conn., 1907, Second Ch. (now Bapt. Temple), Rochester, N.Y., 1907-10, First Ch., Syracuse, 1911; pastor First Ch., West Hartford, Conn., 1912-13; ordained to Bapt. ministry, 1913; gen. sec. Vt. S.S. Assn., 1914-18; pastor First Ch., Reedsboro, Vt., 1919-; dir. religious edn., Wis. Bapt. State Conv., 1919-23; asso. pastor Temple Bapt. Ch., Detroit, 1923; pastor First Ch., Marquette, Mich., from 1924. Rotarian. Lectr. colls. and summers schs. Author: Perspective Bible Studies, 1913; Worship in Drama, 1924; The Singers of Judah's Hills, 1926. Asso. editor Living Hymns. Home: Marquette, Mich.†

BOYD, FISKE, painter, graphic artist; b. Phila., July 5, 1895; s. Peter Keller and Lydia Butler (Fiske) B.; student Pa. Acad. Fine Arts, 1913-16, Art Students League, N.Y., 1921-24; m. Clare Mary Constance Shenehon, May 1, 1926; 1 dau., Sheila Shenehon (Mrs. S. A. Hoermann). Paintings and prints exhibited 1923-75; represented in collections Met. Mus. Art, Whitney Mus. (N.Y.C.), Philips Meml. Gallery (Washington), Addison Meml. Gallery (Andover, Mass.), Phila. Art Mus., Boston Mus. Fine Arts, Fogg Art Mus. (Cambridge, Mass.), N.Y. Pub. Library, Bklyn. Mus., Gallery Fine Arts (Columbus, O.), Library of Congress, Montclair (N.J.) Art Mus. Served USN, 1917-21. Recipient Boericke prize Phila. Print Club, 1931; Am. Artists Group prize Soc. Am. Graphic Artists, 1947, John Taylor Arms Meml. prize, 1954; Cannon prize N.A.D., 1955; purchase awards Library of Congress, Bklyn. Mus. Mem. Soc. Am. Graphic Artists, Audubon Artists, Nat. Acad. Design (asso.), Xylon. Boston Printmakers, Phila. Print Club. Address: Plainfield, N.H., Died Sept. 21, 1975.

BOYD, FRANCIS R(AYMOND), lawyer; b. Quincy, Mass., Aug. 25, 1881; s. William and Ellen F. (Moriarty) B.; grad. Adams Acad., 1898; A.B., Harvard, 1902; LL.B., 1908; m. Sarah Haynsworth Lyles, Apr. 27, 1915; children—Harriet (Mrs. James B. Sedgwick), Francis Raymond. Admitted to Mass. bar, 1908, practiced in Boston; mem. Gaston, Snow, Rice & Boyd from 1937; gen. counsel several corps. Mem. Am., Mass. State, Boston bar assns. Clubs: Union (Boston); Country (Brookline, Mass.). Home: Cambridge, Mass.†

BOYD-CARPENTER, educator, author; b. North of Ireland, Oct. 1881; s. Sir William (bishop Ch. of England) and Lady Charlotte (Piers) Boyd-Carpenter; B.A., LL.B., Yorkshire U., 1900; M.A., Cambridge, 1903; LL.D., Berlin, 1904; m. Mrs. T. C. Hornbrook, 1917. Active in 5 parliamentary elections for Conservative Unionist Party, 1900-10; examiner for Scotch Bd. of Edn., 1904-09; parliamentary legal counsel, House of Lords, 1907-11; etc.; spent many yrs. in Oriental countries and traveled widely studying conditions there; first came to U.S. in 1915, naturalized, 1920; lecturer at Univ. of Communications, Peking, 1921-24, also at the Law School, Peking, 1923-26, and in Tokyo; lecturer at U. of Va., 1926, Johns Hopkins, 1926-27, Georgetown U., 1927-30; prof. polit. science, Georgetown U., from 1930, also prof. Asiatic langs. and history. Mem. Am. Acad. Polit. and Social Science, Am. Soc. Internat. Law, Japan Asiatic Soc. (life mem.), Chinese Social and Polit. Science Assn., Am. Meteorol. Soc. (life mem.), Academie Diplomatique Internationale. Clubs: Chevy Chase (Md.); Grolier, Town Hall (New York); Royal Socs. (London); Peking Club (Peiping, China); also Stoke Poges Club. Author: Political Background of the French Revolution, 1911; Syndicalism-A Study, 1913; Elements of International Law, 1919; Elements of Political Science, 1920-All pub. in London. Translator: The Leather Seller of Samarcand, 1934; When I to You, 1935; Wayfarers Note Book, annually from 1936; part editor and author of Asiatic Sound and Symbol, Vol. I, 1938. Contbr. to mags. on Oriental and polit. subjects. Home: Chase, MD.†

BOYER, C. VALENTINE, educator; b. Jamestown, N.Y., June 25, 1880; s. Samuel P. and Amelia (Fuller) B.; B.S., Princeton, 1902, M.A., 1909, Ph.D., 1911; student Pittsburgh Law Sch., 1902-04; student Oxford, Eng., Am. Acad., Rome, Am. Acad., Athens, 1906-07; m. Ethel Parkhurst, July 2, 1912. Admitted to Ohio bar, 1905 and practiced at Marietta until 1906; resumed practice at Pittsburgh, 1907; Charles Scribner fellow, Princeton, 1909-11; instr. English, U. of Ill., 1911-14; asso., 1914-21, asst. prof., 1921-26, prof. English and head of department, U. of Ore., 1926-45, dean Coll. of Arts and Letters, 1932-42; acting pres., Jan.-April 1934, pres., 1934-38, prof. English emeritus, from 1945. Named Eugene's "First Citizen" by Eugene Realty Bd., 1938. Mem. Modern Language Assn. Am., Philol. Assn. of Pacific Coast (pres. 1941-42), Am. Assn. Univ. Profs. Club: Elm (Princeton). Author: The Villian as Hero in Elizabethan Tragedy, 1914; also contbr. essays and reviews. Home: Eugene, Ore.†

BOYER, JOHN F., lawyer; b. Seattle, Oct. 28, 1907; s. John E. and Louise (Hutsinpiller) B.; A.B., U. Wash., 1927; LL.B., Harvard Law Sch., 1930. Admitted to N.Y. State bar, 1932; pvt. practice law, N.Y.C., 1932-73; asso. firm Gould & Wilkie, N.Y.C., 1932-60, partner, 1961-73. Served to maj. AUS, 1942-46. Decorated Bronze Star medal. Mem. Am., N.Y. State bar assns., Assn. Bar City N.Y., Phi Beta Kappa, Sigma XI. Republican. Episcopalian. Home: New York City N.Y. Died Apr. 16, 1973.

BOYER, WILLIS BOOTHE, steel co. exec.; b. Pitts., Feb. 3, 1915; s. Pearce F. and Sarah Hester (Boothe) B.; student Mercersburg Acad., 1934-35, Lafayette Coll., 1935-37, Case Inst. Cleve. Coll., 1937-42; advanced mgmt. tng. Harvard, 1951; D.H.L. (hon.), Lafayette Coll., 1965; m. Esther Greenwood, June 25, 1938; children—Willis Boothe, Jonathan Greenwood, Paul Christopher. With Republic Steel Corp., Cleve., 1937, asst. to treas., 1946-51, asst. treas., 1951-53, treas., 1953-60, v.p., treas., 1960-63, v.p. finance, 1963, v.p. finance and adminstrn., 1963-66, dir., 1963-66, exec. v.p., 1966-68, pres., 1968-73, chief exec. officer, 1971-74, chmn. bd., 1973-74; dir. Sherwin Williams Co. Nat. City Bank of Cleve., Procter & Gamble Co., Marathon Oil Co., Met. Life Ins. Co. Trustee charitable, civic and bus. assns. Mem. Am. Iron and Steel Inst. (dir., mem. exec. com.), Conf. Bd. (vice chmn.), chief exec. officer, 1971; Chi Phi. Clubs: Union, Kirtland Country, Pepper Pike Country, Union (Cleve.); Laurel Valley, Rolling Rock (Ligonier, Pa.); Blind Brook (Port Chester, N.Y.); Augusta (Ga.) National; Links (N.Y.C.). Home: Shaker Heights, O. Died Jan. 31, 1974; buried Lakeview Cemetery, Cleveland, O.

BOYKIN, RICHARD MANNING, business exec.; b. nr. Sumter, S.C., Apr. 13, 1878; s. Burwell Henry and Mary (Deas) B.; B.S. and E.E., Ala. Poly. Coll., 1897; m. Caroline J. Morris, Jan. 11, 1909. Vice pres., gen. mgr. North Coast Power Co. Clubs: Multnomah Athletic, University Barge, University, Portland Rowing. Home: Portland, Ore.†

BOYLE, ALBERT CLARENCE, JR., geologist, mining engr.; b. Salt Lake Co., Utah, Mar. 8, 1880; s. Albert Charles and Elizabeth (Boam) B.; diploma, State Normal Sch., Salt Lake City, Utah, 1900; A.B., Utah U., 1901; B.S. in Mining Engring., Utah State Sch. of Mines, 1905; studied Sibley Coll., Cornell, 1905-06; A.M., Sch. of Mines (Columbia), 1910, Ph.D., 1913; m. Meriba May Best, of Mill Creek, Utah, Oct. 1906. Asst. instr. in physics, Utah Sch. of Mines, 1897-1901, asst. instr. in shops, 1901-03, foreman mechanic arts, 1903-07; foreman constrn., Am. Smelting & Refining Co., Murray, Utah, 1904-06; cons. geologist, Bully Hill Mining & Smelting Co. and many oil cos., 1907-20; asst. instr. geology, Columbia, 1907-10; prof. mining engring. and geology, 1910-20, prof. mining, metall. engring. and econ. geology, 1912-20, U. of Wyo.; state assayer and mineralogist of Wyo., 1910-20; chief geologist U. P. System from 1920. Pres. State Coal Miners' Bd., Wyo., 1910-20. Pvt. and sergt. R.O.T.C., U. of Wyo., 1916-17. Mem.Am. Inst. Mining Engrs., Am. Inst. Metall.

Engrs., Am. Assn. Petroleum Geologists, Soc. for Promotion Engring. Edn., N.E.A., Am. Geog. Soc., A.A.A.S., Seismol. Soc. of America, Sigma Xi, Sigma Mu. Home: Laramie, Wyo.†

BOYLE, ANDREW JOSEPH, educator; b. Cannanes, Mex., Dec. 21, 1906; s. Andrew Joseph and Rose Theresa (O'Donnell) B.; B.S., U. Notre Dame, 1928, M.S., 1929, Ph.D., 1931; m. Mary Agnes Harris, June 22, 1935 (dec. Sept. 1953); children—Kathleen, Andrew. Asst. in chemistry U. Notre Dame (Ind.), 1928-31, instr., 1931-34, asst. prof., 1934-37, asso. prof., 1937-41, prof., 1941-72, acting head dept. of chemistry, 1943-46, administry. head, 1946-72, asst. dean Coll. Sci., 1966-68, asst. dean. Freshman Year of Studies, 1968-72. Mem. Am. Chem. Soc., Soc. for Metals, Ind. Chem. Soc., Ind. Acad. Sci. Roman Catholic. Home: South Bend, Ind. Died Mar 18, 1975.

BOYLE, HAROLD VINCENT (HAL), foreign corr.; b. Kansas City, Mo., Feb. 21, 1911; s. Peter Edward and Margaret (Gavaghan) B.; student Kansas City (Mo.) Junior Coll., 1928-30; B.A. and B.J., U. of Missouri, 1932; m. Mary Frances Young, Nov. 6, 1937. Copy boy, Associated Press, Kansas City office, 1928, corr. for A.P., Columbia, Mo., 1933-35, night editor, St. Louis office, 1935, feature editor, Kansas City office, 1936, reporter and editor, New York City staff, 1937-41, night city editor, N.Y. City, 1942; war corr. for A.P. covering allied campaigns in Mediterranean and European areas 1942-74; columnist of daily "Leaves from War Correspondent's Notebook, "pub. by 400 A.P. newspapers; contbr. articles on mil. and journalistic topics to several mags.; writer of Boyles Column for A.P. Awarded Pulitzer prize for Distinguished Correspondence, 1945; listed by Jr. C. of C. in selection of 10 most outstanding young men, 1945. Mem. Am. Newspaper Guild, Sigma Phi Epsilon, Kappa Tau Alpha. Club: Overseas Press. Author: Help, Help, Another Day (collection of columns), 1969. Home: New York City, N.Y. Died Apr. 1, 1974.

BOYLES, AUBREY, lawyer; b. Mt. Pleasant, Monroe Co., Ala., Oct. 9, 1878; s. Andrew Jackson and Minnie (Ferrell) B.; grad. Barton Acad., Mobile, 1895; A.B., U. of Ala., 1901, LL.B., 1904; m. Mary Washington Moody, Nov. 5, 1907. Organized the first high sch. at Lucena, P.I., 1902; began practice of law at Mobile, 1904; spl. counsel Law and Order League, to prosecute liquor violators, 1909-10; U.S. atty. for Southern Dist. of Ala., 1922-26; defeated for Congress, 1926; promoted natural gas line Monroe, La., to Memphis, Tenn., 1927-28; assisted in promoting natural gas line Monroe, La., to St. Louis, 1927-29, and in bringing natural gas from Jackson, Miss., to Mobile, Ala., and Mississippi coast towns, 1929-31. Organizer Mobile Fed. of Ch., 1911; active in all war drives. Mem. Alabama and New York bar assns. Presbyn. While U.S. atty., forced resignation of sheriff of Mobile County; secured conviction ex-sheriff and chief field deputy of sheriff of Mobile County, sheriff of of Washington Co., chief of police of Mobile, chairman Mobile Democratic Exec. Com. and several members-all leading bootleggers at Mobile-and utter destruction of the liquor ring, politically dominant in Mobile for 25 yrs. Home: New York City, N.Y.†

BOYLES, EMERSON R(ICHARD), lawyer; b. Chester Twp., Eaton County, Mich., June 29, 1881; s. William and Emma Jane (Braybrooks) B.; LL.B., U. of Mich., 1903; m. Mabel Casler, June 14, 1905; 1 dau., Mary Frances (Mrs. Henry E. Crouse). Admitted to Mich. bar, 1903, and began practice in Charlotte; pros. atty., Eaton County, 1912-16; probate judge, 1921-26; dep. atty. gen. of Mich., 1927-32; mem. Mich. Pub. Utilities Commn., 1935-36; legal adviser to gov., 1939-40; justice of Supreme Court of Mich., 1940-56; dir. Eaton County Savings Bank, Mem. Mich. Bar Assn. Mason (K.T.). Author: Index of Michigan Criminal Laws, 1909. Edited Michigan Comp. Laws, 1929. Home: Charlotte, Mich.†

BOYNTON, BEN LYNN, physician; b. Chgo., Sept. 3, 1909; s. Melbourne Parker and Hattie (Wells) B.; B.S., U. Chgo., 1932; M.B., Northwestern U., 1936, M.D., 1937; m. Elizabeth Katterjohn, Aug. 19, 1933; children—Lynn William, Irvin Parker, Sylvia Wells, Melbourne Roy, Elizabeth Helen. Intern St. Luke's Hosp., Chgo., 1936-37; instr. phys. therapy U. Wis. Med. Sch., 1937-39; dir. dept. phys. medicine Norfolk (Va.) Gen. Hosp., 1940-42; dir. phys. medicine service Shannon Meml. Hosp., San Angelo, Tex., 1946-47; chief phys. medicine and rehab. div., br. office VA, Dallas, 1947-49; chief phys. medicine and rehab. service VA Hosp., Houston, 1949-52; prof. phys. medicine and rehab. Baylor U. Coll. Medicine, 1949-53; med. dir. Rehab. Inst. Chgo., 1953-56, chmn. dept., prof. phys. medicine, Med. Sch. Northwestern U., 1953-60; dir. phys. medicine and rehab. Oak Forest (Ill.) Hosps., 1957-60; med. dir. Rehab. Center of Summit County, Akron, O., 1960-69; ret., 1970. Served as lt. col., M.C., AUS, 1942-46. Diplomate Am. Bd. Phys. Medicine and Rehab. Meml. Congress Phys. Medicine and Rehab., Am. Acad. Phys. Medicine And Rehab. (nat. pres. 1956). Methodist. Home: Shelby, Mich. Died Mar. 22, 1975; cremated.

BRAASCH, WILLIAM FREDERICK, urology; b. Lyons, Ia., July 6, 1878; s. John and Albertina (Classen) B.; B.S., U. of Minn., 1900, M.D., 1903; m. Nellie Stinchfield, Nov. 11, 1908; children—Marion, Elizabeth, John William. Pathologist, Minneapolis City Hosp., 1903-04; asst. city phys., Minneapolis, 1905-07; mem. staff, Mayo Clinic, Rochester, Minn., since 1907; became prof. urology, Grad. Sch. of Medicine, U. of Minn., 1915, prof. emeritus. Fellow American College Surgeons, Am. Med. Assn. (chmn. urology section, mem. house of dels.; mem. bd. of trustees); mem. A.M.A., Clin. Soc. of Genito-Urinary Surgeons (pres.), Am. Urol. Assn. (pres.), Minn. State (pres.), and Olmstead County med. assns., S. Minn. Med. Assn. (pres.), Minn. Acad. Medicine, Delta Upsilon, Alpha Kappa Kappa, Sigma Xi, Gen. Alumni Assn., U. of Minn. (pres.); corr. mem. Deutsche Gesellschaft für Urologie, Assn. Francaise d'Urologie, Societa Italiana Di Urologia, Asociacion Espanola De Urologia, Sociedad Argentina de Urologia, La Sociedad Urologica de Bogota; corr. mem. Sociedad Venezolana de Urologia, Sociedad Cubana de Urologia, La Sociedad Mexicana de Urologia, Sociedad Chilena de Urologia; hon. mem. British Assn. Urologic Surgeons; sec. Nat. Physicians Com. Clubs: Civic and Commerce, University (Rochester); Minneapolis, Author: (monographs) Pyleography, 1915; Urography, 1927. Home: Rochester, Minn. Died May 1, 1975.

BRADEN, ARTHUR, clergyman, educator; b. Westbromwich, Eng., May 29, 1881; s. William Henry and Seleina (Barton) B.; A.B., Hiram (O.) Coll., 1903; grad. Auburn Theol. Sem., 1909; Ph.D., Syracuse U., 1914; m. Cora G. Yoho, 1904; children—Coral Arta, Norman Adelbert, Donald Dwight, Arthur Wayne, Iril Dale. Ordained ministry Disciples of Christ, 1903; pastor Deerfield (O.) Ch., 1903-05, Auburn, N.Y., 1905-09; pres. Keuka Coll., Keuka Park, N.Y., 1909-10; pastor Central Ch. of Christ, Syracuse, N.Y., 1910-14; dir. Kansas U. Bible Chair, 1914-21, also minister DeSota, Kan., 1915-19; pastor 1st Ch., Kansas City, Mo., 1920-22; dean Kan. Sch. of Religion, Lawrence, Kan., 1922; pres. Calif. Christian Coll., 1922-30; pres. Transylvania Coll. and Coll. of the Bible, Lexington Ky., 1930-37; pastor 1st Christian Ch., Los Angeles, 1938-39; pastor Wilshire Christian Ch., Los Angeles, 1940-44. Author: Religious Revivals and Their After Effects, 1914. Address: Los Angeles, Cal.†

BRADEN, GEORGE WALTER, recreation dir.; b. Waterloo, Ia., Nov. 14, 1879; s. James N. and Ida Bell (Hollenbeck) B.; student Throop Poly. Inst., Pasadena, Calif. and Pacific Coll. Osteopathy, Los Angeles, Calif., 1899-1901, U. of Calif., summer 1903; grad. U.M.C.A. Summer Training Inst., Silver Bay, N.Y., 1909, Nat. Recreation Sch. Short Course, Chicago, Ill., 1920; m. Florence Esther Brent, June 24, 1901; children—Paul Sumner, Dorothy Frances. Dir. physical edn., Throop Poly. Inst. and Y.M.C.A., Pasadena, Calif., also instr. Summer Sch., U. of Calif., 1900-08; dir. physical edn., Occidental Coll., Los Angeles, 1908-11; same and dir. instrn., Central Br. Y.M.C.A., Philadelphia, Pa., 1911-17; Y.M.C.A. rep. and athletic officer, Fort Niagara, N.Y., later Camp Mead, Md., 1917-18; gen. dir. sports and recreation, Italian Army, Jan.-July 1918; asso. sec. and dir. dept. of service, Y.M.C.A., Philadelphia, 1918-20; financial organizer, European relief, Dec. 1920-Feb. 1921; with Playground & Recreation Assn. America (now Nat. Recreation Assn.) from 1921, western rep. from 1923. Made recreational survey of Baltimore for Am. Youth Commn., 1937. Pres. Pacific S.W. Br. of Amateur Athletic Union 3 yrs., Calif. Interscholastic Athletic Assn. 2 yrs., Pa. Y.M.C.A. Physical Edn. Assn. 6 yrs. Charter mem. Art Barn, Salt Lake City, Utah; mem. Welfare Survey Com., Boulder Dam, Colo., 1932. Mem. N.E.A., Am. Acad. Polit. and Social Science, Nat. Probation Assn., Conf. of Social Workers; hon. mem. Circolo Italiano, Philadelphia. Awarded certificate of meritorious service by Italian Govt.; hon. maj. Italian War Coll. Republican. Presbyn. Contbr. articles to recreations and sports to newspapers and mags. Home: Altadena, Cal.†

BRADFIELD, GEORGE HERNDON, justice; b. Delta, La., Mar. 24, 1880; s. George Julius and Lucy Jane (Herndon) B.; Honor grad. W. Tex. Mil. Academy, 1918; LL.B., U. Denver, 1904; m. Bessie Edmonson, Nov. 15, 1904; children—Mary Lucy (Mrs. R. Cecil Montgomery) Betsey (widow Kenneth G. Campbell), George Edmonson. Former rancher, Hereford cattle raiser, farm owner; admitted to Colo. bar, 1904; established and pub. Ault (Colo.) Advertiser, 1904-06; co. and probate judge Weld Co., 1908-12; dist. judge 8th Judicial District, 1918-25, and 1943-53; served as city attorney of Greeley, Colo., 1925-29, compiled ordinances, 1929; county attorney, Weld Co., 1940-42; justice Supreme Ct., Colo. from 1952. Mem. Am., Colo., Weld Co. (past pres.) bar assns., Am. Judicature Soc., Greeley C. of C. (past dir.), Weld Co. Blind Assn. (pres.) Colo. Soc. S.A.R. (pres.), Salvation Army Bd. (dri.), Greeley Y.M.C.A. (pres.), Colo. State Hist. Soc., Phi Delta Phi (hon.). Republican (chmn. Weld Co. central com. 1914-18; chmn. state conv., 1918; candidate for Congress, 2d dist., 1933-36). Methodist (pres. bd. trustees 20 yrs.; Colo. del. gen. conf., 1928; conf. com. to bd. trustees Denver U.). Mason (32°, Shriner), Eastern Star (past patron), K.P. (past grand chancellor, mem. grand tribune and supreme rep.), Elk Odd Fellow. Club: Lions (internat. counsellor). Home: Greeley, Colo.†

BRADFORD, HARRY E., educator; b. Sheboygan, Wis., Feb. 12, 1878; s. DeWitt A. and Almeda V. (Crocker) B.; A.B., U. of Neb., 1904, A.M., 1917; Ph.D., Cornell U., 1931; m. Ethel King, Dec. 27, 1904; 1 dau., Eloise Marguerite (Mrs. W. J. Harding). Formerly chmn. dept. vocational edn. U. of Neb., emeritus; lectr. on ednl. topics. Mem. Alpha Zeta, Phi Delta Kappa, Alpha. Gamma Rho. Republican. Conglist. Mason (32°). Club: Rotary (pres. Lincoln 1938). Home: Lincoln, Neb.†

BRADLEY, DOROTHY WINCHESTER, (Mrs. John D. Bradley), govt. ofcl., social worker; b. Hutchinson, Kan., Feb. 7, 1909; d. Stanley Allen and Edith (Carey) Winchester; A.B., U. Ia., 1932; M.A., U. Chgo., 1938; m. John D. Bradley, Feb. 26, 1946 (dec. Dec. 1968). Social worker Reno County, Hutchinson, 1933-34; supr. Family Transient Service, Kansas City, Kan., 1934-36; child welfare worker, cons., supr. Kan. Dept. Social welfare, 1938-42; dist. child welfare supr. Indpls., Dept. Pub. Welfare, 1942-45; dir. Div. Children, Youth and Their Families, Kan. Dept. Social and Rehab. Services, Topeka, 1945-75. Dir., Winchester Packing Co. Mem. Kan. Gov's. Interagy. Council on Children and Youth, Kan. Gov.'s Adv. Com. on Mental Retardation; mem. Kan. Gov.'s com. attending White House Conf. on Children and Youth, 1950, 60, State White House Planning Com., 1970. Mem. Am. Pub. Welfare Assn., Child Welfare League Am., Nat., State confs. social welfare, Nat. Assn. Edn. Young Children, Nat., Kan. (dir.) rehab. assns., Kan. Council for Children and Youth, P.E.O., Kappa Kappa Gamma. Home: Topeka, Kan., Died July 2, 1975; interred East Side Cemetery, Hurchison, Kan.

BRADLEY, GEORGE EDGAR, educator, physicist; b. Indpls., Feb. 21, 1924; s. George Stanley and Alice (Edgar) B.; A.B., Miami (O.) U., 1945; M.S., U. Mich., 1947, Ph.D., 1952; m. Jean Garee, May 31, 1950; 1 son, John William. Mem. faculty Western Mich. U., Kalamazoo, 1951-75; prof. physics, 1958-75 chmn. dept., 1964-71. Mem. Central States Univs. Adv. Bd.; guest prof. U. Karlsruhe (Germany) and Kernforschungzentrum, 1971-72. Active, National Council on Religion in Higher Edn. Served with USNR, 1945-46. NSF fellow Harvard, 1959-60. Mem. Am. Phys. Soc., Phi Beta Kappa, Sigma Xi. Conglist. Kiwanian. Home: Kalamazoo, Mich. Died Feb. 15, 1975.

BRADLEY, HAROLD CORNELIUS, physiol. chemist; b. Oakland, Calif., Nov. 25, 1878; s. Cornelius Beach and Mary (Comings) B.; A.B., U. of Calif., 1900; Ph.D., Yale, 1905; M. Josephine Crane, 1908; children—Mary Cornelia (dec.), Charles Crane, Harold C., David John. Stephen Crane, Joseph Crane, Richard, William. Asst. in physiol. chemistry, Yale, 1904-05; instr. chemistry, Yale Med. Sch., 1905-06; asst. prof. physiol. chemistry, U. of Wis. Med. Sch., 1906-13; asso. prof. physiol. chemistry, U. of Wis., 1913-19, prof. 1919-49, research dir. Woods Hole Marine Biol. Lab. from 1910. Served as capt., maj. C.W.S., U.S. Army, 1918-19. Mem. Am. Chem. Soc., A.A.A.S., Am. Geog. Soc., Am. Physiol. Soc., Am. Soc. Biol. Chemists, Delta Upsilon, Sigma Xi. Clubs: Sierra, Am. Alpine, Sierra Ski Club. Contbr. articles to Am. Jour. Physiology, Jour. Biol. Chemistry, Am. Ski Annual, Sierra Club Bull, Am. Forestry Mag. Home: Berkeley, Calif.†

BRADLEY, HENRY D., publishing co. exec.; b. Detroit, Mich., Jan. 10, 1893; s. William H. and Bertha W. H. (Schulz) B.; ed. pub. schs.; m. Louise McLendon, Jan. 16, 1926; children—David R., Natalie D. (Mrs. Francis), Ray Louise (Mrs. Cox). With Toledo Blade, 1906-23; gen. mgr. Norristown (Pa.) Times-Herald, 1924-26; pres., gen. mgr. Times-Star, Bridgeport, Conn., 1927-39; pub. News Press and Gazette, St. Joseph, Mo., 1939-56, pres. News Press and Gazette Co., 1950-71; adviser to Lord Beaverbrook, London Express (Eng.), 1923. Former mem. Mo. Hwy. Commn.; former chmn. Nat. Adv. Com. on Scenic Hwys. and Pkwys. Organized St. Joseph Indsl. Devel. Co., Civic Improvements Assns. Awarded citizenship citation V.F.W., 1949. Mem. Internat. Press Inst., Inter-Am. Press Assn., Bridgeport C. of C. (life), Mo. Acad. Squires, Am. Philatelic Soc., Sigma Delta Chi. Republican. Episcopalian. Mason (33 deg., Shriner, Jester); mem. Order of De Molay. Clubs: Country, Benton (St. Joseph). Home: St. Joseph, Mo. Died Dec. 14, 1973; interred Meml. Park Cemetery, St. Joseph.

BRADLEY, JOHN ROBINS, consular service; b. Tupelo, Miss., June 9, 1881; s. Jeptha R. and Tennessee (Whithead) B.; student Henry Kendall Coll., Tulsa, Okla., 1 yr.; m. Mary Elizabeth Orendorff, Dec. 7, 1912. Served in Cuba and Philippines as pvt. 1st U.S. Inf., 1900-02; dep. treas. Leyte Province, P.I., 1905-06; in ry. business and ranching, Okla., 1906-15; postmaster, Alderson, Okla., 1915-17; apptd. consul at Punta Arenas, Chile, Nov. 5, 1917, at Puerto Cortes, Honduras, 1918, resigned; mgr. Cuyamel Fruit Co., Honduras, 1919; consul at Bluefields, Nicaragua, 1920-21, at Cardiff, Wales, 1921-23, at Porto Alegre, Brazil, from 1923. Democrat. Mem. M.E. Ch. S. Mason. Elk. Address: Porto Alegre, Brazil.†

BRADLEY, JOSEPH GARDNER, coal operator; b. Newark, N.J., Sept. 12, 1881; s. William Hornblower and Eliza (Cameron) B.; grad. St. Mark's Sch.,

Southboro, Mass., 1898; A.B., Harvard, 1902, LL.B., 1904; m. Mabel Bayard Warren, Nov. 4, 1905; children—Mabel Bayard, Joseph Gardner. Admitted to bar but has devoted attention to resources of W.Va.; pres. Elk River Coal & Lumber Co. Bank of Widen, and Buffalo Creek & Gauley R.R. Co., 1904-58; now pres. Gauley Coal Land Co.; dir. Dauphin Deposit Trust Co. (Harrisburg, Penn.); trustee J. D. Cameron Trust. Secured the Creation of W.Va. constabulary and the W.Va. gross sales tax law; led coal operators in effecting revision of W.Va. mining law in the interest of safety. Del. Rep. Nat. Conv., Chicago, 1916, Kansas City, Mo., 1928; chmn. Rep. Exec. Com., Clay County, W.Va.; mem. W.Va. Constl. Commn. 1930; mem. W.Va. Library Commn., 1934-35; mem. Nat. Council Y.M.C.A.; chmn. W.Va. State Y.M.C.A., 1919-43; trustee Boston Library Soc.; ex-dir. So. States Indsl. Council. Dir. Nat. Coal Assn., 1917-46 (pres. 1921-22), W.Va. Coal Assn. (pres. 1916-40), Am. Mining Congress (pres. 1927-28), W.Va. C. of C.; mem. Am. Inst. Mining and Metall Engrs., Pa. Bar Assn., W.Va. Bar Assn., Am. Bar Assn., Institute Fiscal and Polit. Education (trustee), Alpha Delta Phi. Episcopalian. Clubs: Somerset, Tennis and Racquet, Brookline Country (Boston); Union, University, Harvard, Racquet (New York); Philadelphia. Home: Lewisburg, W.Va.†

BRADLEY, MARK EDWARD, educator; b. Abbeville County, S.C., May 9, 1878; s. John Edward and Sarah Margaret (Wideman) B.; A.B., Erskine Coll., S.C., 1898; student U. of Chicago, summers 1904, 1910, U. of N.C., summer 1927; m. Mary Elizabeth Morrah, Sept. 5, 1906; children—Mark Edward, Jr., Mary Elizabeth (Mrs. Robert Louis McGarity). Teacher pub. schs. of S.C., 1898-1901; mem. dept. of English, Clemson Coll., from 1901, head English dept., 1941, retired, 1950; pioneered in making radio broadcasts from speech class, 1937. Chmn. local Red Cross, 1918-47. Charter mem. Coll. English Assn.; mem. Nat. Assn. Teachers of Speech. Democrat. Presbyterian. Co-author: Better Speaking (with Dr. D. W. Daniel), 1941. Home: Clemson, S.C.†

BRADMAN, FREDERIC LEISON, officer U.S. Marine Corps; b. Newark, N.J., Jan. 18, 1879; s. Frank Cushing and Helen Mary (English) B.; prep. edn., Friends' Sch., Crosswicks, N.J., and Bordentown (N.J.) Mil. Inst.; grad. Army War Coll., 1928; grad. Navy War Coll., senior course, 1929, advance course, 1937; m. Lydia J. Malowansky, June 9,1906; children—Lyd English (Mrs. Thomas J. Cleere), Frederic Cushing, Helen Elena (Mrs. Harry D. Chamberlin), Mary Josephine (Mrs. William G. Romadka), John. Commissioned 2d lt. U.S. Marine Corps, 1898, and advanced through grades to col., 1920; apptd. brig. gen., 1931; retired, 1939. Awarded medals, Spanish Campaign, 1898; Philippine Campaign, 1903; Mexican Border, 1914; World War, 1919; 2d Nicaraguan Campaign. Presidential Medal of Merit (Nicaragua), 1931, and Nicaraguan Medal of Distinction, 1931. Mem. Royal Arcanum. Clubs: Army and Navy Country (Washington). Address: San Marino, Cal.†

BRADSHER, EARL L(OCKRIDGE), educator, writer; b. Clifton Hill, Mo., Apr. 20, 1879; s. Augustine and Martha Jane (Davis) B.; student William Jewell Coll., 1899-1900; B.A., U. of Mo., 1903; A.M., Columbia, 1904, Ph.D., 1911; student Oxford U., 1907, U. of Berlin, Germany, 1907-08; m. Augusta St. Amant, June 9, 1927; children—Earl Lockridge, Henry St. Amant, Margaret Augusta. Instr. English, U. of Ill., 1908-11, Dartmouth Coll., 1911-13, U. of Tex., 1913-21; mem. faculty comparative lit. La. State U., from 1921, prof. Mem. Authors League of Am., Acad. Polit. Scis. Author: (biography) Mathew Carey, 1911, 66; (poetry) Nothing Is Alien, 1948, From Farce to Tragedy, 1949, In Troubled Years, 1952, On a Chartless Sea, 1958; also profl. articles and numerous short stories. Home: Baton Rouge, La. Died July 17, 1974; interred Greenoaks Meml. Park, Baton Rouge, La.

BRADY, JAMES HARRY, indsl. exec., mgmt. cons.; b. Cleveland, Tenn., June 4, 1925; s. Harry Lee and Edith (Rutherford) B.; student Am. U. With Manhattan Engring. Dist., Oak Ridge, 1943-44; Navy reporter, Army and Navy Jour., 1944-45; reporter Yankee Network, Indpls. Star, 1944-45; with Mil. News Service, Washington editor, 1945-47; asso. Army & Navy Pub. Co., Washington Press Service, 1945-48; author columns Inside Washington, Washington Newsletter, bus. columns, reporting events on Capitol Hill, White House, others; promotion mgr. Knoxville (Tenn.) News Sentinel, 1948-49; asst. to pres. Lancaster Engring. Corp., Daffin Mfg. Co., Lancaster, 1949-56; chmn. Brady Enterprises, Knoxville, Tenn.; mem. exec. com., dir. pub. relations Zimmerman Equipment Co., Inc., Nashville; pres. Motel Mgmt. Inc., Knoxville; merchandising cons. Enterprise Paint Mfg. Co., Chgo., 1954-62, Inertol Co., Inc., Newark. Prepared, issued 1st statis. findings on cost of World War II, 1945; pub. relations asso. Soc. for Advancement Mgmt., 1945, Washington Coll. Law, 1945; officer, dir. several corps. Chmn. exec. com. Serene Manor Med. Center. Mem. White House Corrs. Assn. Republican. Methodist. Kiwanian, Elk, Mason (K.T., Shriner, life). Clubs: National Press, Variety of Am. (Washington); Deane Hill Country, Senators (Knoxville); Lancaster County Riding (Lancaster). Contbr. articles to ednl., sci. jours. Home: Knoxville Tenn. Died Apr. 14, 1974.

BRAGINTON, MARY VICTORIA, educator; b. Manson, Ia., Mar. 15, 1901; d. George Frederick and Anna (Greenside) Braginton; A.B., Grinnell (Ia.) Coll., 1920, L.H.D., 1950; A.M., Yale, 1921, Ph.D., 1923; student univs. of Brussels and Ghent, Belgium, 1925-26; Univ. of Grenoble (France), summer 1925; Am. Sch. of Classical Studies, Athens, Greece, summer 1934; L.H.D. (hon.), Rockford College, 1967. Instr. in Latin, Mount Holyoke Coll., S. Hadley, Mass., 1923-25; fellow Commn. for the Relief of Belgium, Ednl. Found., 1925-26; asst. prof. Latin, Mt. Holyoke Coll., 1926-27; prof. Latin and Greek, Rockford (Ill.) Coll., 1927-67, dir. admission, 1945-47, academic dean, 1949-57, dean of faculty, 1957-63, chmn. dept. fgn. languages, chmn. div. language and lit., 1963-67; vis. prof. classics U. Pacific, Stockton, Cal., from 1967. Bd. dirs. Kobe College Corp., Chicago. Served from lt. (j.g.) to lt. Women's Reserve. USNR, 1943-45, retired. Emerson-Lathrop grantee, Europe, 1961-62. Member of American Philol. Assn., American Classical League, Classical Assn. Middle West and South (1st v.p., 1938, pres., 1949-50). N.E.A., Ill. Classical Conference, (vice pres. 1952-53, pres. 1953-54), American Association Univ. Profs., Am. Assn. U. Women (pres. local br. 1942-43, chmn. Ill. com. status women 1959-61), Classical Soc. Am. Acad. Rome (pres. 1942). Phi Beta Kappa (sec.-treas. east central dist. 1958-64, v.p. 1964-67), Delta Kappa Gamma. Conglist. Clubs: Zonta (Rockford, Ill.); Cercle des alumni de la Foundation Universitaire (Brussels). Author: The Supernatural in Seneca's Tragedies, 1933. Contbr. articles to classical jours. Home: Rockford Ill. Died July 26, 1973; buried Rose Hill Cemetery, Manson Ia.

BRAINARD, NEWTON CASE, printing co. exec.; b. Hartford, Conn., Dec. 26, 1880; s. Leverett and Mary (Bulkeley) B.; A.B., Yale U., 1902; M.A., Trinity College, 1946; married Elsie L. Burks. In printing business from 1902; chmn. Conn. Printers, Inc; pres., trustee Dime Savs. Bank; dir. Smyth Mfg. Co. Hartford Steam Boiler Inspection & Insurance Company, Standard Fire Insurance 2d Plattsburg, T.C., 1917; 2d lt. F.A., N.A., 1917-18. Trustee Trinity Coll., Conn. Republican. Conglist. Home: Hartford, Conn.†

BRAINERD, EZRA, JR., lawyer; b. Middlebury, Vermont, Aug. 26, 1878; s. Ezra and Frances Viola (Rockwell) B.; LL.B., U. of Mich., 1904; LL.D., Middlebury (Vt.) Coll., 1932; m. Edith Maris Hubbard, Apr. 15, 1908; children—Jane, Bettie Maris, Frances Rockwell, Ethel, Edith. Admitted to Mich., Vt., Okla. bars, 1904, D.C. bar, 1934, U.S. Supreme Ct., bar, 1921; practiced at Muskogee until 1927; mem. firm Brainerd, Gotwals & Gibson, 1918-27; formerly gen. counsel and v.p. First Nat. Bank Muskogee; gen. practice of law, Washington, from 1934. Mem. Interstate Commerce Commn., 1927-33, chmn. 1931; cons. counsel B. & O. R.R., 1935-43. Mem. Am. Bar Assn., Chi Psi; hon. mem. Lawyers' Club, U. of Mich. Presbyn. Mason (K.T. Shriner). Clubs: Cosmos (Washington); Michigan Union (Ann Arbor, Mich). Home: Washington, D.C.†

BRAKENSIEK, CLIFTON MACK, surgeon; b. Carthage, Ill., Mar. 15, 1909; s. Albert Simon and Mary (Holmes) B.; A.A., Fullerton (Cal.) Coll., 1929; A.B., Pacific Union Coll., Angwin, Cal., 1935; M.D., Loma Linda U., 1940; m. Joyce Parsonson, Aug. 27, 1939; children—Carlyle Ray, Everett Trent, Warren Niles. Chief of surgery Downey Community Hosp. (Cal.), 1953, chief of staff, 1954-55; chief of staff Bellwood Gen. Hosp. (Cal.), 1956-57; 1st chief staff Woodruff Community Hosp., Long Beach, Cal., 1958; organizer, med. dir. Bellflower Med. Group; chief surgery Bellwood Hosp., 1961-62. sr. surgeon to staffs Downey, Bellwood, Lakewood, Woodruff, Community hosps. Organizer, chmn bd. Bellflower Nat. Bank, 1964-68. Chief area examiner SSS, 4 yrs. Dir. Community Concert Assn.; adv. bd. Cerritos Coll., Bellflower Unified Sch. Dist.; bd. dirs. Better Bus. Bur. of Long Beach (Cal.) Area; active Boy Scouts Am.; organized Sister City program between Los Mochis, Mexico and Bellflower, 1959. Mem. city council, mayor City of Bellflower, 1958-60. Served as 1st lt., Med. Res., 1939-43. Recipient bronze service medal Jr. C. of C., 1952, Outstanding Service award Boy Scouts Am., 1958; Silver Beaver award Boy Scouts Am., 1959. Diplomate Nat. Bd. Med. Examiners. Mem. Am. Soc. Abdominal Surgery, Am., Cal., Los Angeles County med. assns., Am. Acad. Gen. Practice, C. of C. (pres 1953, dir.), Am. Med. Soc. of Vienna (life). Presbyn. (dir.). Elk. Kiwanian. Home: Bellflower, Cal. Died Dec. 2, 1974; interred Rose Hills Memorial Park, Whittier, Cal.

BRAM, JOSEPH, educator; b. Ekaterinburg, Russia, July 17, 1904; s. Nahum and Sophie (Rosenzweig) B.; License es-Lettres, U. Paris (France), 1930; Ph.D., Columbia, 1941; m. Jean Rhys, June 1946; children—Susan, Elizabeth, Margaret. Came to U.S., 1935, naturalized, 1942. Mem. faculty Queens Coll., N.Y.C., 1941-48; mem. faculty N.Y.U., N.Y.C., 1948-71, prof. sociology and anthropology, 1948-71, ret.; prof. emeritus sociology Hofstra U., Hempstead, N.Y., 1971-74. Fellow Royal Anthropol. Inst. Gt. Britain and Ireland. Spl. research Jehovah's Witnesses, Spiritualist cult in P.R., French Canadian separatist movement. Author: An Analysis of Inca Militarism, 1941; Language and Society, 1955. Home: Baldwin N.Y. Died Mar. 20, 1974.

BRAMSON, LEO, mcht.; b. Chgo., Jan. 19, 1902; s. David Leo and Jenny Rose (Edelman) B.; student architecture Armour Inst. Tech., 1927-31, sculpture Art Inst. Chgo., 1922-26; m. Ann Travis, Dec. 25, 1928; children—Joan Davida (Mrs. Samuel Kraus), David Jay. Supervising architect Provident State Securities Corp., 1929-31; organized Bramson, Inc., Chgo., 1931, chief exec. officer, 1931-75; pres. Martha Weathered Shops, Inc., 1954-75; partner, organizer 715 Farms, Pahokee, Fla., Sugar Cane Growers Coop. of Fla., Belle Glade; gen. partner Chiglades Farms, Ltd., Belle Glade, Palm Beach Asparagus Corp. Ltd., Palm Beach, Fla.; sec., treas. Tuscany Devel. Corp., Palm Beach, Fla.; pres. Bueno Farm, Inc., Pahokee, Fla.; partner Banyan Realty Trust, Palm Beach; asso. Chas. Passantino Real Estate, Palm Beach; mem. adv. bd. Commerce Nat. Bank, Lake Worth, Fla. Guarantor, sponsor Lyric Opera of Chgo. Bd. dirs. Palm Beach Habilitation Center. Mem. Chgo. Assn. Commerce, Sigma Alpha Mu. Jewish religion. Kiwanian; mem. B'nai B'rith. Clubs: Standard (Chgo.); Palm Beach (Fla.) Country, Banyan Country (dir.), Palm Beach Golf and Racquet. Home: Palm Beach, Fla. Died Aug. 29, 1975; interred Meml. Gardens, Skokie, Ill.

BRANCH, OLIVER WINSLOW, judge; b. N.Y.C., Oct. 4, 1879; s. Oliver Ernesto and Sarah Maria (Chase) B.; grad. Phillips Andover Acad., 1897; A.B., Harvard, 1901, A.M., 1902; LL.B., Harvard Law School, 1904; m. Isabel Dow Hogle, Nov. 23, 1910; children—Jane B. Sanders, Oliver Winslow Jr., Robert Dow, Elinor B. Nourie, Bartram Chase. Admitted to N.H. bar, 1904, and began practice at Manchester; asso. justice, Superior Court of N.H., 1913-24, chief justice, 1924-26, asso. justice Supreme Court of N.H., 1926-46; apptd. chief justice; mem. National War Labor Bd., Region 1, Feb. 1943-Jan. 1946. Mem. Am. Law Institute. Democrat. Conglist. Club: Rotary. Home: Manchester, N.H.†

BRAND, EDWARD ALEXANDER, commercial expert, lawyer; b. Luray, Va., Mar. 20, 1879; s. Judge Alexander Joseph and Fannie Glenn (Stewart) B.; LL.B., Georgetown U., Washington, D.C., 1909. In service of ry., coal and iron cos., 1899-1905; connected with Bur. of Mfrs., Washington, D.C., 1905-11; asst. dir. Bur. of Foreign and Domestic Commerce, by apptmt. of Pres. Taft, 1912-14; reapptd. by Pres. Wilson, July 29, 1914; asst. to pres. Tanners Council America, 1917-27; adviser for leather, hair garment industries, etc. Pres. New York Soc. Trade Executives, 1923-24. Sent on trade investigation in Europe, in 1916, special diplomatic mission to South America, Mar. 1917. Democrat. Catholic. Frequent lecturer on foreign trade before commercial assns. Author: Community and Trade Organizations; World's Trade in Hides, Skins and Leather. Writer on commercial topics. Clubs: University (Washington); Montgomery Club (Md.). Home: Rockville, Md.†

BRANDENBURG, MORT, pres. Distillery, Rectifying, Wine and Allied Workers Internat. Union, 1958-74. Home: Tenafly N.J. Died Dec. 27, 1973.

BRANDENBURG, SAMUEL J., educator; b. nr. Germantown, O., Jan., 13, 1880; s. Richard Emsley and Emily (Cooper) B.; A.B., Miami U., Oxford, O., 1904; Ph.M., U. of Chicago, 1909; student Library Sch., U. of Ill., 1908-09; Ph.D., U. of Wis., 1922; m. Margaret Johnston, Aug. 5, 1907; 1 son, William J. Librarian and prof. economics, Miami U., 1909-20; asst. in economics, U. of Wis., 1920-22; prof. economics and sociology, U. of Ark., 1922-23, Clark U., 1923-50, now emeritus; vis. lectr. on economics, U. of Texas, summer 1923, Brown U., 1939; visiting prof. economics La. State U., 1952. Dir. County Councils, Ohio Council Nat. Defense, Columbus, O., 1918; ednl. dir. Dist. No. 7, Veterans' Bureau, Cincinnati, O., 1919. President Worcester Peoples Forum. Mem. American Econ. Assn., Am. Sociol. Soc., Am. Acad. Polit. and Social Science, Am. Polit. Science Assn., Delta Kappa Epsilon, Phi Beta Kappa, Tau Kappa Alpha. Conglist. Clubs: Worcester Economic, Appalachian Mountain. Joint Author: Elementary Principles of Economics, 1923. Asso. editor Economic Geography (quarterly mag.). Home: Worchester, Mass.†

BRANDENBURG, WILLIAM AARON, JR., coll. pres.; b. Mason City, Ia., Jan. 26, 1910; s. William A. and Alta A. (Penfield) B.; B.S., Kan. State Coll., Pittsburg, 1930, M.S., 1931; Ph.D., U. Colo., 1946; m. Gwendolyn Bloker, 1941; children—Ann Avery (Mrs. William F. Zeman, II), William Aaron III. Tchr. pub. schs., Tulsa, 1932-38; instr. history Ohio State U., 1939-40; dean faculty William Woods Coll., Fulton, Mo., 1940-50, N.W. Mo. State Coll., 1950-56; pres. Wayne (Neb.) State Coll., 1956-74, prof. history, 1974--. Served to capt. USMCR, 1943-46. Mem. Marine Corps Res. Officers Assn., Am. Hist. Assn., Kappa Delta Pi, Phi Mu Alpha, Phi Sigma Epsilon (past nat. pres.). Presbyn. Mason (33 deg., Shriner), Rotarian (pres. dist. gov., info. counselor). Author publs. in field of polit. philosophy, fgn. lang. instrn. Home: Wayne, Neb. Died Jan. 20, 1975; interred Pittsburg, Kan.

BRANDHORST, OTTO WILLIAM, dentist; b. Nashville, Ill., Mar. 29, 1889; s. August and Caroline (Finke) B.; D.D.S., Washington U., St. Louis, 1915; m. Eunice L. Schroeder, June 10, 1916; children—William

Schroeder, Helen Caroline. Asst. in dental histology, Washington U. Sch. Dentistry, 1915-18, prof., 1918-30, also prof. orthodontia, 1925-30, dean and prof. orthodontics, 1945-52; sec. Am. Coll. Dentists, 1953-69, sec., 1935-53, pres.-elect, 1969-70, pres., 1970-71; in practice of dentistry, specializing in orthodontics, St. Louis, 1918-53. Mem. task force on med. services in fed. govt. Hoover Commn. Orgn. Exec. Br. Govt., 1953-54; mem. Commn. Survey Dentistry in U.S., 1960-61; cons. on Dental Study Bur. Research and Statis., Social Security Bd. and various divs. USPHS, 1945; mem. dental adv. council Com. Econ. Security, 1934; chmn. pub. dental edn. com. St. Louis Dental Soc. Fellow A.A.A.S.; mem. Am. Dental Assn. (pres. 1952-53; mem. council dental edn. 1949-52; chmn. com. survey of dentistry 1952-61), Am. Assn. Orthodontists, Internat. Assn. Dental Research, Am. Soc. Dentistry for Children (mem. publ., editorial and information com. 1936), Mo. Dental Assn. (chmn. program com. 1929; publ. com. 1930; council 1932-38, pres. elect 1943, pres. 1944), St. Louis Dental Soc. (pres. 1931; program com. 1930-46, econ. com. 1932; sec. Study Club bd. 1939-44), St. Louis Soc. Orthodontists, St. Louis Soc. Dental Sci. (council 1935-44), Am. Assn. Dental Editors (hon., sec. 1932-48), Washington U. Dental Alumni Assn. (chmn. 75th Anniversary Com. Washington U. Sch. Dentistry 1940-41; alumni rep. Washington U. Dental Jour. 1935-44). Author: The American College of Dentists History-The First Fifty Years, 1971. Editor: Jour. Mo. Dental Assn., 1932-38; asst. editor Jour. Am. Coll. Dentists, 1935-37, asso. editor, 1938-41. Contbr. dental mags. Home: Webster Groves Mo. Died Nov. 15, 1974; interred Sunset Burial Park, St. Louis, Mo.

BRANDI, HERMANN THEODOR, bus. exec.; b. Dortmund, Germany, Dec. 25, 1908; student Achen Inst. Tech., Berlin-Charlottenburg Inst. Tech., Leoben Inst. Tech.; Dr. Ing. E.h., Dr. Mont. Mem. mgmt. bd. August Thyssen-Hutte A.G., Verein Deutscher Eisenhuttenleute, Wirtschaftsvereiningung Eisen-und Stahlindustrie, Vereinigung Industrieller Kraftwirtschaft, Gesellschaft fur Wasserwirtschaft, Arbeitgeberverband Eisen-und Stanlindustrie, Dusseldorf, Gesellschaft zur Forderung der Spektrochemie und angewnadten Spektroskopie e.V.; chmn. bd. dirs. Linde A.G., Messerschmit-Bülkow-Blohm GmbH., dep. chmn. bd. dirs. Rheinische Kalksteinwerke GmbH; dir. Bergbau A.G., Oberhausen, Blohm & Voss A.G., Bong Mining Co., Brown, Boveri & Cie. A.G., Deutsche Edelstahlwerke A.G., Gelsenberg A.G., Thyssen Niederrhein A.G., Mannesmannrohren-Werke A.G., Stahlwerke Bochum A.G., Westfalische Union A.G., others; pres. Gesellschaft von Freunden der Aachener Hochschule; chmn. Stromausschuss der Gesellschaft fur Stromwritschaft m.b.H.; senator Max-Planck-Gesellschaft. Home: Mulheim-Ruhr-Speldorf Federal Republic of Germany. Died June 1973.

BRANDON, RODNEY HOWE, b. Monroe County, Ind., Sept. 21, 1881; s. Galbraith Lynn and Narcissa Lee (Smith) B.; student Ind. U., 3 yrs.; LL.D., MacMurray Lane, Dec. 6, 1909; children—Adele (dec.), Jean, Nancy. Clk. and auditor Am. Telephone & Telegraph Co., New York, 1900-02; one of the organizers, 1906, of the Loyal Order of Moose, in which served an official, 1906-29; supervised construction of Mooseheart, 1913; sec. Mooseheart Governors; grand regent Mooseheart Legion; established Moosehaven (Fla.), 1922, Pilgrim governor of the Loyal Order of Moose, from 1947. An organizer of Progressive Party in Ind., 1912; moved to Ill., 1913; del. Ill. Constl. Conv., 1919 (chmn. com. on edn. and editor of Conv. Proceedings); sec. Rep. State Central Com., Ill., 1928-30; dir. Dept. of Pub. Welfare, Ill., 1929-33 and 1941-45; mem. Bd. of Pub. Welfare Commrs., State of Ill., 1933-40. Spl. investigator for U.S. Govt. of child welfare conditions in Europe, 1926. Lecturer in criminology, social hygiene and medical jurisprudence, Coll. of Medicine, U. of Ill. from 1933. Dept. comdr. Sons of Union Vets. of the Civil War, 1938-39. Mem. Disciples of Christ. Mason. K.P.; past lt. gov. Kiwanis. Home: Batavia, Ill.†

BRANDT, KARL, agrl. economist; b. Essen, Germany, Jan. 9, 1899; s. Maxmillian and Wilhelma (Troschwitz) B.; grad. Württemberg U., 1921; Dr. Agr., U. Berlin, 1926; Dr. Phil. (hon.), U. Heidelberg, 1951; m. Anitta Hewel-von Lindenfels, Dec. 31, 1932; children—Klaus, Jobst, Goetz, Ralph. Came to U.S., 1933. Dir. Seed Breeding Coop. Assn., Saatzucht Heidesand, Rotenberg, 1921-24; dir. German Farm Tenants Bank, 1925-27; agrl. adviser Central Coop. Bank, Berlin, 1928-29, Trustee, 1929-33; prof. Coll. Agr., Berlin U., dir. Inst. Agrl. Market Research, 1929-33; mem. bd. experts German Bank for Indsl. Obligations, 1929-33; prof. grad. faculty New Sch. Social Research, N.Y.C., 1933-38; vis. research prof. La. State U., 1937-38; cons. to Fed. Land Bank, New Orleans, adviser to Gen. Edn. Bd., 1937-38; prof. agri. econs. Food Research Inst., Stanford, 1938-64, asso. dir., 1954-61, dir., 1961-64, emeritus, 1964-75; econ. adviser to sec. agr., 1942; cons. to War Dept., 1943, War Food Asminstrn., 1944, Farm Credit Adminstrn., 1944-45; econ. adviser on food and agr. to U.S. Milt. Govt. in Germany, 1945-46; guest prof. U. Heidelberg, U. Goettingen, Tech. Coll. Manheim, 1948-49; mem., editor report Joint Tech. Mission of Internat. Bank for Reconstrn. and Devel. and FAO to Uruguay, 1950-51; cons. European econ. cooperation to Ford Found.; initiator C.E.P.E.S., 1951-53; adviser to Belgian Royal Dep. on devel. of Kilombrve Valley (congo), 1954; cons. Stanford Research Inst., 1944-62, sr. econ. cons., 1963-71; mem. Pres.'s Council Econ. Advisers, Washington, 1958-61; mem. econ. adv. mission to Prime Minister of Malaya, 1963; adviser to pres. Di Tella Found., Buenos Aires, Argentina, 1964; cons. to Rockefeller and Ford founds. in Columbia, 1965. Trustee, Found. for Econ. Edn., 1963-72; mem. adv. council Am. Inst. Research on Govt. Affairs, 1958-72. Decorated Bundesverdienstkolne with star (Fed. Republic of Germany); chevalier L'Order Nat. du Merité (France); Order of Brillant Star (Taiwan); recipient Justus von Liebig prize Found. F.V.S. Hamburg-Kiel, 1969; Distinguished Service award William Volker Fund, 1970; elected Old Master, Soc. Polit. Sci., Purdue U., Lafayette, Inc., 1967. Fellow Am. Agrl. Econs. Assn. (pres. 1956), Royal Econ. Assn.; mem. Societe Royale d'Economice Politique de Belgique (hon.), Mount Pelerin Soc., Western Agrl. Econ. Assn. (pres. 1943-44, pres. emeritus 1965-75), Academie d'Agriculture (France), Internat. Conf. Agrl. Economists. Clubs: Cosmos (Washington); Commonwealth of Cal.; University (Palo Alto); Stanford Faculty. Author: The Principles and Theory of Farm Tenancy, 1928; The German Fat Plan and its Economic Setting, 1938; Reconstruction of World Agriculture, 1945; Germany is Our Problem!, 1946; The Management of Agriculture and Food in German Occupied and Other Areas of Fortress Europe, 1959; World Food: Calming the Cassandras, 1967; others. Mem. editorial adv. bd. The Intercollegiate Rev., 1964-75. Home: Palo Alto Cal. Died July 8, 1975.

BRANDT, RAYMOND PETER, ret. newspaperman; b. Sedalia, Mo., June 6, 1896; s. Jacob and Amelia (Sarman) B.; B.J., U. Mo., 1918; B.A., Lincoln Coll., Oxford, Eng., 1922; m. Adele Harrison, Sept. 11, 1926. Reporter St. Louis Post-Dispatch, 1917, 19, corr. Washington bur., 1923, chief Washington bur., 1934-61, contbg. editor, 1962-67; with Am. Relief Adminstrn., Vienna, Austria, 1920, dist. supr., Vitebsk, Russia, 1922-23. Served to 2d lt. U.S.F.A., 1918-19. Recipient U. Mo. Sch. of Journalism medal for distinguished service in journalism, 1939; winner first Raymond Clapper Meml. award for Washington corr., 1945. Mem. Sigma Chi, Sigma Delta Chi, Kappa Tau Alpha. Independent. Methodist. Clubs: Overseas Writers, Gridiron (pres. 1946), Nat. Press (pres. 1933), Metropolitan (Washington); Burning Tree (Bethesda, Md.); Chevy Chase. Visited Russia 1930, 31, 37, 55, for series of articles for St. Louis Post-Dispatch. Home: Washington D.C. Died Mar. 27, 1974.

BRANIGIN, ROGER DOUGLAS, gov. Ind., lawyer; b. Franklin, Ind., July 26, 1902; s. Elba L. and Zula (Francis) B.; A.B., Franklin Coll., 1923, LL.D., 1956; LL.B., Harvard, 1926; LL.D., Butler U., Ind. U., Ind. State U., Vincennes U.; m. Josephine Mardis, Nov. 2, 1929; children—Roger, Robert M. Admitted to Ind. bar, 1926; dep. pros. atty., Franklin, Ind., 1926-29; counsel Fed. Land Bank and FCA, Louisville, 1930-38, gen. counsel, 1932-38; pvt. practice law, 1938-42, 46-65; gov. State ofInd., 1965-69; practiced in Lafayette, Ind., 1969-75. Dir., Nat. Homes Corp., Lafayette Nat. Bank, Gen. Telephone Co. of Ind., Inc., Lafayette Life Ins. Co., Duncan Electric Co., Inc. Past pres. Harrison Trails council Boy Scouts Am.; trustee Franklin Coll., Purdue U., Asso. Colls. Ind., Conner Prairie Farms, Inc.; bd. dirs. Lilly Endowment, Inc. Served to lt. col. AUS 1942-46; chief legal div., transp. corps, 1944-45. Decorated Legion of Merit. Hon. fellow Lilly Library Ind. U. Mem. Harvard Law Sch. Assn., Am. Legion, Ind. (pres. 1951-52), Am. (ho. of dels.) bar assns., Am. Coll. Trial Lawyers, C. of C. (past pres.), Am. Law Inst., Indiana Soc. of Chgo. (v.p.), Am. Coll. Probate Counsel, Am. Counsel Assn., Am. Judicature Soc. (dir.), Newcomen Soc., Ind. Hist. Soc. (trustee), Indpls. Lit. Club, Phi Delta Phi, Phi Delta Theta. Democrat (chmn. Ind. conv. 1948). Mason, Elk. Clubs: Indianapolis Athletic Town and Gown, Press (hon. life) (Indpls.); Sagamore of the Wabash; Legal (hon. life Chgo.); Lawyers (U. Mich.). Home: Lafayette, Ind., Died Nov. 19, 1975.

BRANNER, ROBERT, educator; b. N.Y.C., Jan 13, 1927; s. Martin M. and Edith (Fabbrini) B.; B.A., Yale, 1948, Ph.D., 1953; student Ecole des Chartes and Inst. d'art et d'archeologie, Paris, 1950-52; m. Shirley S. Prager, Jan. 25, 1953; 1 son, David P. Asst. prof. U. Kan., 1954-57; faculty Columbia, 1957-69, prof. art history and archaeology, 1966-69, chmn. dept. art history and archaeology, 1968-69; prof. history art Johns Hopkins, Balt., 1969-71; prof. art history and archaeology Columbia, 1971-73; dir. excavations Bourges (France) Cathedral, 1950-52. Mem. Nat. Com. History Art, 1969-72; mem. adv. com. Medieval dept. Met. Mus. Art, 1972-73; mem. adv. bd. Speculum, 1973. Served with AUS, 1945-46. Fulbright-Hayes grantee, 1950-52; Guggenheim fellow, 1963; recipient Alice Davis Hitchcock award for most distinguished book archtl. history Society Archtl. Historians, 1963; Am. Council Learned Socs. fellow, 1967. Mem. Mediaeval Acad. Am., Coll. Art Assn., Soc. francaise d'archaeologie, Soc. Archtl. Historians (bd. dirs. 1960-63, editor jour. 1964-66), Internat. Center Mediaeval Art (dir. 1966-73), Soc. Nat. des Antiquaires de France. Author: Burgundian Gothic Architecture, 1960; Gothic Architecture, 1961; La Cathedrale de Bourges, 1962; Saint Louis and the Court Style, 1965; Chartres Cathedral, 1969; Manuscript Painting in Paris during the Reign of Saint Louis, 1976. Bibliography and index to his works pub. in Jour. Soc. Archtl. Historians, Oct. 1975. Home: New York City, N.Y. Died Nov. 27, 1973.

BRANSCOMBE, GENA (MRS. JOHN FERGUSON TENNEY), composer; b. Picton, Ont., Can., Nov. 4, 1881; d. Henry W. and Sara (Allison) Branscombe; ed. high sch., grad. Chgo. Musical Coll. (gold medalist); studied with Rudolph Ganz, composition, Felix Borowski, and Prof. Engelbert Humperdinck, in Berlin; M.A. (hon.), Whitman Coll., 1932; m. John Ferguson Oct. 1910; children—Gena, Vivian Allison, Betty (dec.), Beatrice (dec.). Condr. Branscombe Choral N.Y., MacDowell Chorus Mountain Lakes, N.J.; condr. state chorus N.J., 1940-42; condr. first organized Glee Club, Am. Women's Voluntary Services, 1942-44; condr. Contemporary Club Choral, Newark, 1945. Nat. chmn. Am. music and folksong, Gen. Fedn. Women's Clubs, 1930-35. Mem. MacDowell Colony. Bd. dirs. (hon.) N.Y. Fedn. Music Clubs; dir. Nat. Assn. Am. Composers and Conductors (citation 1967). Recipient citation for achievement Beta Sigma Phi, 1958. Mem. numerous profl. assn., A.S.C.A.P. Composer numerous music items, latest being: American Suite (for Ft. horn), 1959; Old Woman Rain (song), Gift at Parting (song), Across the Blue Aegean Sea (song), 1960; Arms That Have Sheltered Us (Navy hymn), 1961, 91st Psalm (for chorus and orch.), 1962; orch. work Procession performed in N.Y.C., San Francisco, Manila, 1962; choral work Prayer for Song performed in Pitts., 1963; orch. manuscripts displayed at N.Y. Pub. Library, 1963; Pilgrims of Destiny (choral drama), 1964, pub. score and orch. parts in Library of Congress; A Joyfull Litany, 1967; Our Canada from Sea to Sea, 1967; Youth of The World (for chorus and orch.); Coventry's Choir, spl. performances, N.Y.C., 1970; Soldier, Soldier, Come From Wars (men's chorus), 1969; I Send My Heart up to Thee (song), 1969; Sleep, Then, Ah Sleep (song), 1969; What Are We Two (song), 1969. Contbr. to Showcase mag. Condr. own compositions in U.S., Can., Eng., 1957. Home: New York City, N.Y.†

BRANSON, FREDERICK PAGE, judge; b. Cassville, Bartow Co., Ga., Mar 1, 1880; s. Levi and Rhoda (Page) B.; grad. Piedmont Inst., Rockmart, Ga., 1898; student Emory Coll. (now Univ.) through jr. yr.; B.L., Mercer U., 1903; m. Eula Jeanes, 1905. Settled at Muskogee, Ind. Ty. (now Okla.), 1904, and served as law clk. of commn. to five civilized Indian tribes; elected mem. 1st State legislative, 1907; chmn. Dem. State Exec. Com., Okla., 1910-12; mem. State at large Dem. Nat. Conv., Baltimore, 1912; pros. atty. Muskogee County, 1912; dist. judge Muskogee and Wagner counties by apptmt., 1913-14; justice Supreme Court of Okla., term 1923-28, inclusive, v. chief justice, 1925, chief justice, Jan. 10, 1928. Delivered course of lectures on Equity Jurisdiction, Northwestern U., summer 1925. Mem. Okla. Bar Assn., Delta Tau Delta. Mason, Elk. Clubs: City, Kiwanis, Cooperative (Oklahoma City). Home: Muskogee, Okla.†

BRANT, GERALD CLARK, army officer; b. Chariton, Ia., June 29, 1880; s. Clark Thompson and Sarah Ellen (Matson) B.; grad. U.S. Mil. Acad., 1904, Sch. of the Line, 1921, Gen. Staff Sch., 1922, Army War Coll., 1923; m. Ethel Cushing, June 18, 1904 (divorced 1927); children—Gerald Clark, Virginia Cushing Freeman, Philip Delano; m. 2d, Elizabeth Daingerfield Jackson, May 25, 1928. Commd. 2d lt. cavalry, 1904, and promoted through all grades to major gen., 1941; comdt. Pa. Mil. Coll., 1911-13; served on Mexican border, later in Philippines, 1913-17; transferred to air service, 1917; chief of operations and asst. dir. mil. aeronautics, 1918; War Dept. Gen. Staff, 1923-27; exec. officer to asst. sec. of war, 1927; comdg. officer 18th Wing Air Corps, 1930-34; comdg. gen. 3d Wing, Air Force, 1935-37, 2d Wing, Air Force, 1937-38; commandant Air Corps Tehcnical Schs., 1938-40; comdg. gen. Gulf Coast Training Center, 1940-41; comdg. Newfoundland base, 1941-43; comdg. gen., Air Force Gulf Coast Training Center from Jan. 1943; retired May 1944. Mem. Am. Legion. Episcopalian. Clubs: Army and Navy, Bohemian, Camp Fire (New York). Address: Mico, Tex.†

BRANZELL, KARIN, singer; b. Stockholm, Sweden, Sept. 24, 1897; d. Anders and Jenny (Pearson) Branzell; attended Stockholm High Sch.; m. Fedya Reinshagen, April 29, 1938; naturalized U.S. citizen. Debut, Royal Opera House, Stockholm, 1915; State Opera, Berlin, 1919-34; leading contralto, Met. Opera, N.Y., since debut there in 1924; has appeared in all leading opera houses in the world. Awarded Litteris et Artibus, Sweden, 1932; apptd. singer of the Royal Court of Sweden, by King Gustaf, 1935. Home: Altadena Cal. Died Dec. 15, 1974.

BRASCH, FREDERICK EDWARD, librarian; b. Mobile, Ala., Dec. 18, 1875; s. Otto Wilhelm and Carolyn E. (Johannsen) B.; special student Stanford U., 1897-99, U. of Calif., 1899-1901; studied privately, 1905-12; Harvard, 1916; hon. M.S., Ramsay Inst. Tech., 1926; m. Winnifred E. Orpin, Aug. 5, 1903 (died June 11, 1938); children—Carolyn Mildred, Maxwell Frederick. Asst. observer, Harvard Coll. Obs., 1903-04; computer, Lick Obs., Mt. Hamilton, Calif., 1905; asst., Library of Stanford U., 1912-16; asst. reference librarian, John Crerar Library, Chicago, 1917-21; reference librarian James Jerome Hill Reference Library, St. Paul, Minn., 1921-22; bibliog. research, Nat. Research Council, Washington, D.C., 1922-23; acting librarian Dept. Terrestrial Magnetism, Carnegie Instn., Washington, 1923-24; sec. history of science section, A.A.A.S., 1920-28; mem. Commn. of Bibliography, Internat. Astron. Union from 1922; sec. Sir. Isaac Newton Commemoration, 1927. Chief scientific collection, Library of Congress, 1925-43; consultant in the history of science, 1944-1948; consultant in bibliography, Stanford Univ. from 1948. Del. of Library of Congress of Tercentenary Celebration of Birth of Isaac Newton, Longon, 1946. Mem. History of Science Soc. (treas.-corr. sec. 1924-37), Am. Astron. Society, Astronomical Society of Pacific, Am. Antiquarian Soc.; fellow A.A.A.S., Royal Astronomical Society (London); honorary member Phi Beta Kappa. Writer and Untarian., bibliographer various articles and bulletins on the history of science. Editor of memorial volume, Sir Isaac Newton 1727-1927; editor Johann Kepler Memorial Volume, 1931. Editor: Portfolio of Newton's Portrait and Statues. Author: The Royal Society of London and its Influence upon Scientific Thought in the American Colonies, Science Press, 1931; Bibliography of Johann Kepler 1571-1630, 1931; Newton's First Critical Disciple in the American Colonies-John Winthrop of Harvard College, 1714-1779, 1928; Newtonian Epoch in the American Colonies, 1680-1783, 1940; James Logan, A Mathematical Scholar and Newton's Principia, 1st edition, in the American Colonies; Bibliography of Sir Isaac Newton.†

BRASHEARS, EDWIN LAWRENCE, hotel exec.; b. Hannibal, Mo., Jan. 6, 1899; s. George W. and Edna (Williamson) B.; ed. U.S. Naval Acad., 1919; m. Katherine Field, Nov. 23, 1922; children—Edwin Lawrence, Charles Walton. With Nat. Realty and Investment Co. becoming pres.; chmn. bd. The Drake Hotel, Chicago; pres., dir. Drake Oakbrook, Inc.; dir. Bank of Oakbrook (Ill.), Lake Shore Trust & Savings Bank. Mem. Chgo. Bd. Trade. Commd. lt. comdr., U.S. Navy, June 1942; assigned to Midshipmen's Sch., Abbott Hall, Northwestern U.; retired from naval service, Sept. 1944. Clubs: Chicago, Chicago Yacht, Indian Hill. Home: Winnetka Ill. Died Sept. 1973.

BRATNEY, JOHN FREDERICK, telephone exec.; b. Preston, Ill., Oct. 8, 1880; s. Theodore Stillman and Sarah (Mitchel) B.; 1899; B.S. in E.E., Washington U., St. Louis, 1903; study Benton Coll. Law, St. Louis, m. Grace Gunn, July 9, 1910 (divorced). Chief engr., Bell Telephone Co. of of Mo., St. Louis, 1905-10; dist. supt. of plant, Mo. & Kan. Telephone Co., Kansas City, Mo., 1910, gen. supt. traffic, 1911-15, gen. commercial supt., 1915-17; asst. to operating vice-pres. Southwestern Bell Telephone System, St. Louis, 1917-20; rate engr., Am. Telephone & Telegraph Co., N.Y. City, 1920-26, comml. results and practices Engr., 1927, gen. commercial problems engr., 1928, asst. tech. rep. in Europe, with hdqrs. in London, for Am. Tel. and Tel. Co. and Bell Telephone Labs., Inc., 1929-34; at New York hdqrs. of Am. Tel & Tel. Co., 1934, and telephone rep. at Washington, D.C., for same, 1935-36. Mem. Am. Inst. E.E., Am. Statis. Soc., Telephone Pioneers of America, Empire State Soc., S.A.R.; former fellow Royal Soc. of Arts (London) and former mem. various coms. of Comite Consultatif International des Communications Telephoniques a Grande Distance, Paris. Republican. Presbyterian. Mason. Clubs: University (New York); Glen Ridge Country (N.J.); Nantucket Yacht, Pacific (Nantucket); Bath and Tennis Club (Palm Beach, Fla.), former mem. various social and civic clubs and Chambers of Commerce in U.S. and England, including Engineers of St. Louis; Engineers (past vice-pres. and sec.), Electric (past dir.), Univ. of Kansas City, Mo., American, Royal Automobile, Woodcote Country, Regency, Gargoyle of London. Home: Glen Ridge, N.J.†

BRATT, ELMER CLARK, prof. economics; b. Arapahoe, Neb., Nov. 12, 1901; s. Reuben Wilkinson and Daisey (Clark) B.; A.B., U. Neb., 1925, A.M., 1926, LL.D., 1955; study U. Cal., 1926-27; Ph.D., U. Wis., 1935; m. Bertha Margaret Brodfuehrer, June 16, 1928; 1 dau., Margaret (Mrs. Wayne Akers). Tchr., Furnas Co., Neb., 1918-20; prin. Stockville (Neb.) pub. sch., 1920-21; supt. Holstein (Neb.) pub. schs., 1921-22; supt. Danbury (Neb.) pub. sch., 1923-24; teaching asst. U. of Calif., 1926-27, U. of Wis., 1927-29; research asst. Nat. Bur. of Econ., 1928-29; asst. prof. of economics Lehigh U., 1929-38, associate professor, 1938-41, professor, 1941-70, head dept. economics, 1958-65, associate dean research, director Business Economic Center, 1966-70 chief econ. analyst Bur. Fgn. and Domestic Commerce, Dept. of Commerce, working on problems of economic reconstruction after the war, 1942-45; prof. of finance, Biarritz Am. Univ. in France and U.S. Army lecturer in Germany, 1945-46; statis. consultant Bethlehem Steel Co., 1930-31, 1949-53; econ. cons. U.S. Govt. Central Statistical Bd., 1934; indsl. economist, Nat. Bur. Econ. Research, 1936; dir. Consumers Mail Order Co., N.Y. 1938-42; consultant Federal Reserve Board, 1954-55 Bur. of Budget, 1956-70; dir. data clearing house project Nat. Assn. Bus. Economists, 1962-70; dir., vice pres. Growth Found. of America, 1964-69. Fulbright research scholar, evaluation rural devel. program Ceylon, 1955-56. Fellow Royal Econ. Soc., Nat. Assn. Bus. Economists (mem. council 1965-67); mem. Am. Econ. Assn., Am. Statis, Assn., Econometric Society, American Finance Association, Omicron Delta Kappa, Beta Gamma Sigma, Alpha Kappa Psi, Pi Gamma Mu, Artus. Republican. Methodist. Club: Cosmos. Author: Problems of Economic Change, 1936; Business Cycles and Forecasting, 1937, fifth revised edition published, 1961; This unbalanced World, 1940; (with others) Econ. Problems of War, 1942; Business Forecasting, published 1958. Contributor articles to American Economic Rev., Jour. Am. Statistical Assn., Management Rev., Journal of Business, also mags. and profl. jours. Home: Bethlehem, Pa. Died Nov. 9, 1970.

BRAU, CHARLES FREDERICK, banker; b. Bklyn., Jan. 4, 1911; s. Charles and Emma G. (Koch) B.; student Am. Inst. Banking, 1927-31, N.Y.U. Sch. Bus. Adminstrn., 1947, Rutgers U. Grad. Sch. Banking, 1949-51; m. Ellen Naekel, Feb. 11, 1937 (dec.); children—Charles A., Jane L. Leonard, George Taylor; m. 2d, Vivian H. Taylor, May 13, 1967. With Kings County Savs. Bank, Bklyn., 1927, pres., 1960-69 (merged with Union Sq. Savings Bank now United Mutual Savings Bank), chmn. bd., 1969; mem. Bklyn. adv. bd. Chase Manhattan. Bank; past pres. Instl. Investors Mutual Fund; former dir. Savs. Banks Trust Co., Instl. Securities Corp. Bd. dirs. Blkyn. A.R.C.; mem. adv. com. supervision mut. inst. N.Y. State State Banking Dept. Dir. L.I. Council of Chs., House of St. Giles, the Cripple. Mem. Investments Officers of Savs. Bank Assn. (pres.), Savs. Banks Assn. (dir., past pres.), Nat. Assn. Mut. Savs. Banks. Baptist (trustee). Home: Garden City, N.Y. Died July 31, 1973; interred Cedar Grove Cemetery.

BRAUN, ARTHUR E., banker; b. Pitts., Nov. 23, 1876; s. Carl J. and Elise (Laube) B.; grad. pub. high sch., 1892; LL.D. (hon.), U. Pitts., 1947; m. Eliza R. Munhall, 1904 (dec. 1950); 1 dau., Elizabeth Munhall (Mrs. Paul B. Ernst). Bank messenger, clk., 1892-96; with Farmers Deposit Nat. Bank of Pitts., 1897-51, pres., 1919-44, chmn. bd., 1944-51; successively v.p., pres., pub. Pitts. Post and Pitts. Sun, 1911-27; former dir. Radio Corp. Am., NBC, Allegheny-Ludlum Steel Co., Duquesne Light Co., Harbison-Walker Refractories Co., Pitts. Consolidation Coal Co.; chmn. adv. com. Mellon Nat. Bank & Trust Co.; ret. from all bus. affiliations in 1951. Hon. pres. Western Pa. Hosp.; mem. bd. dirs. Hosp. Service Assn. Pitts. (Blue Cross); mem. distbn. com. Pitts. Found. Chmn. bd. trustees Chatham College, Winchester-Thurston Sch.; mem. bd. trustees U. Pitts., Carnegie Inst. Tech.; mem. bd. mgrs. Buhl Found., Falk Found. Clubs: Duquesne, University, Fox Chapel, Rolling Rock. Home: Pittsburgh, Pa.†

BRAUNER, JULIUS FREDERICK, lawyer; b. Mt. Vernon, N.Y., June 20, 1909; s. Julius F. and Lillian (Moore) B.; A.B., Cornell U., 1931, LL.B., 1932; m. Ruth E. Gordon, Apr. 16, 1938; children—Julius Frederick, Andrea (Mrs. Edward Hein). Admitted to N.Y. bar, 1932; asso. firm Cravath, deGersdorff, Swaine & Wood (now Cravath, Swaine & Moore), 1932-38; atty. CBS, 1938-42, gen. atty., 1942-74, sec., 1947-74. Mem F.C.C., N.Y. State, Am. bar assns., Assn. Bar City N.Y., Am. Arbitration Assn., Assn. Gen. Counsel, Order of Coif, Phi Beta Kappa, Phi Kappa Phi. Home: Scarsdale N.Y. Died Jan. 5, 1974.

BRAUNSCHWEIGER, WALTER J., banker; b. Wellsville, N.Y., Nov. 19, 1894; s. Christian and Alice (Paulman) B.; children—W. James, Janet; m. Helen Raymond, Apr. 19, 1955. Started in banking with Bank of Wellsville, N.Y. 1912; asst. nat. bank examiner, N.Y. state and Penna.; various exec. positions in banks of these two states until 1922; v.p. and dir. Bank of America, Los Angeles, Calif.; merged with Bank of Italy, becoming Bank of America, N.T. & S.A.; exec. v.p. until 1959, mem. adv. council to bd. dirs., mem. trust com.; ret., 1959; pres. Forest Lawn Co., Am. Fidelity and Security Co.; dir. Charles Luckman Assistants, Waldorf-Astoria Hotel Corporation, N.Y.C. Past chmn. Community Chest Campaign; chmn. Central City Com. of Los Angeles. Past pres. Los Angeles C. of C. Clubs: Stock Exchange, Jonathan (Los Angeles); Bohemian (San Francisco); Thunderbird Country (Palm Springs, Cal.). Home: Los Angeles Cal. Died Nov. 1, 1974.

BRAY, ROBERT STUART, librarian; b. Cin., Sept. 9, 1915; s. Charles Ayers and Helen Mar (Pollock) B.; B.S., George Washington U., 1941; postgrad. library service Catholic U. Am., 1947-50; m. Virginia Elizabeth Ballard, Oct. 2, 1937; children—Robert Stuart, James Sargent, Paul Charles, Philip Austin. Page, D.C. Library, 1935-40; mem. staff Library of Congress, 1940-44, 46-72, chief div. blind and physically handicapped, 1957-72. Mem. adv. bd. Rec. for Blind; chmn. service adv. creditation Council Agys. Serving Blind and Visually Handicapped; chmn. library com. President's Com. Employment Handicapped. Served to lt. (j.g.) USNR, 1944-46. Recipient Migel medal Am. Found. Blind, 1963; Apollo award Am. Optometric Assn., 1968; Francis Joseph Campbell award, 1968. Mem. Assn. Hosp. and Instn. Libraries (pres. 1968), Adult Edn. Assn., Am. Pub. Health Assn., Council Exceptional Children, A.L.A., Nat. Assn. Physically Handicapped, Nat. Braille Assn., Nat. Rehab. Assn., Nat. Soc. Prevention Blindness, Am. Assn. Workers Blind, Am. Assn. Instrs. Blind. Assn. Edn. of Visually Handicapped. Democrat. Episcopalian. Home: Sanibel Fla. Died Nov. 26, 1974.

BRAY, STEPHEN, marketing specialist; b. Knox Co., Ky., Feb. 7, 1878; s. Rev. William F. and Emily Jane (Baker) B.; prep. edn., Sue Bennett Memorial Sch., London, Ky., LL.B., Kansas City (Mo.) Sch. of Law, 1908. Farmer and teacher pub. schs., 1899-1904; with Dept. of Agr. from 1905; with Bur. Animal Industry, at Kansas City, 1905-16; engaged in enforcement of quarantine regulations, with Bur. of Markets, 1916-21, live stock market repts. and investigations, and active in govt. control of live stock markets under food control act, World War; chief of administrative div. Packers and Stockyards Adminstration, 1921-25; now in field div. livestock market reporting service. Baptist. Mason (32°, Shriner). Home: Pittsburgh, Pa.†

BREAN, HERBERT, editor, author; b. Detroit, Dec. 10, 1907; s. Walter Joseph and Eva R. (Dumas) B.; A.B., U. Mich., 1929; m. Dorothy Skeman, Oct. 6, 1934; children—Judith Ann, Martha Elizabeth. Reporter, asst. bur. mgr. U.P.I. Assns., N.Y.C., Detroit; reporter, columnist, feature writer, asst. city editor, picture editor Detroit Times, 1933-43; news bur. chief, Detroit, for Time, Life, Fortune mags., 1943-44, asso. editor Life mag., N.Y.C., 1944, asst. editor nat. affairs, 1953-73, staff writer, 1953-62. Lectr. mystery writing Columbia, N.Y. U.; cons. Gen. Motors Corp., 1966. Fellow Internat. Inst. Arts and Letters; mem. Baker St. Irregulars, Mystery Writers Am. (nat. pres.), Crime Writers Assn., Authors League N.Y. Clubs: Players (N.Y.C.); Scarsdale Golf. Author: Wilders Walk Away, 1948; The Darker the Night, 1949; Hardly a Man is Now Alive, 1950; How to Stop Smoking, 1951; The Clock Strikes Thirteen, 1952; A Matter of Fact, 1956. Editor: The Mystery Writer's Handbook, 1956; The Traces of Brillhart, 1959; The Life Treasury of American Folklore, 1961; The Music of Life, 1962; The Only Diet That Works, 1963; The Traces of Merrilee, 1966. Contbr. fiction to mags., articles to profl. publs. Home: New York City N.Y. Died May 7, 1973.

BREARLEY, HARRY CHASE, author; b. Detroit, Mich., Oct. 2, 1870; s. William Henry and Lina (DeLand) B.; ed. pub. schs., Detroit; m. Grace Musselman, Apr. 9, 1903. With Detroit Evening News until 1890; asst. business mgr. Detroit Journal, 1890-91; mgr. for Eastern Mich. for Mutual Life Ins. Co. several yrs.; New York rep. Exporters and Importers Journal several yrs.; sec. and treas. Search-Light Library until 1914; partner Brearley Service Organization. Republican. Baptist. Author: Animal Secrets Told, 1911; The Problem of Greater New York, and Its Solution, 1914; Fifty Years of Civilizing Force, 1916; Time Telling Through the Ages, 1919; A Symbol of Safety, 1923; The Story of New York, 1929; also various monographs co-economic subjects. Editor: ABC's of Foreign Debts (booklet), 1929. Home: Palisades, N.Y.†

BREED, MARY BIDWELL, educator; b. Pittsburgh, Pa., Sept. 15, 1870; d. Henry Atwood and Cornelia (Bidwell) B.; A.B., Bryn Mawr, 1894 (European fellowship), A.M., 1895, Ph.D., 1901; post-grad. work, U. of Heidelberg, Germany, 1895-96; unmarried. Instr. in science, Pa. Coll. for Women, Pittsburgh, 1897-99; dean of women, and asst. prof. chemistry, Ind. U., 1901-06; adviser of women and head of Read Hall, U. of Mo., 1906-12; asso. head St. Timothy's Sch., Catonsville, Md., 1912-13; dir. Margaret Morrison Coll. of Carnegie Inst. Tech., Pitts., from 1913. Presbyn. Clubs: Twentieth Century, College (Pittsburgh); Bryn Mawr (New York). Home: Pittsburgh, Pa.†

BREED, WILLIAM CONSTABLE, JR., lawyer; b. N.Y.C., Feb. 13, 1904; s. William Constable and Emma (Ryder) B.; student St. Paul's Sch.; A.B., Princeton, 1927; LL.B., Harvard, 1930; m. Ellen Whitman, June 29, 1928 (dec. Oct. 1957); children—Ellen B. (Mrs. F.F. Staniford, Jr.), Jane B. (Mrs. Peter E. Fleming, Jr.), William Constable III; m. 2d, Helen S. Croll, Sept. 25, 1965. Admitted to N.Y. bar, 1931; asso. firm Breed, Abbott & Morgan, N.Y.C., 1930-37, partner firm, 1937-67, counsel firm, 1967-73. Chmn. bd. dirs. Manhattan Eye, Ear and Throat Hosp.; bd. dirs., chmn. bd. Nat. Multiple Sclerosis Soc. Mem. Am., N.Y. State bar assns., Assn. Bar City N.Y., N.Y. County Lawyers Assn., Am. Judicature Soc. Home: New York City N.Y. Died June 1973.

BREITENBACH, EDWARD VICTOR, transp. cons.; b. Bostinin, Russia, Oct. 12, 1896; s. Richard and Bertha (Mueller) B.; came to U.S., 1901; student Nat. U. Law Sch., Washington; m. 2d, Anna Mae Perry, Apr. 10, 1951; 1 son, Edward Darwin. Accountant, C.M.St.P. & P. Ry., Chgo., 1913-18, U.S. R.R. Adminstrn., Washington, 1919-25; accountant ICC, Chgo., 1925-28, sect. chief accounts, Washington, 1935-42; transp. specialist Burroughs Adding Machine Co., Detroit, 1928-35; dir. adminstrn. Iranian Hwy. Transport System, Teheran, 1943-45; chief R.R. br. U.S. Mil. Govt., Berlin, Germany, 1945-48; chief, bur. finance, U.S. Maritime Commn., Washington, 1948-49; transport cons. Civil Transport Tokyo, Japan, 1949-52; adviser Japanese Nat. Rys., Tokyo, 1960-61; part-time cons. World Bank, 1964. Served with USNRF, 1918-19. Home: Boynton Beach Fla. Died Apr. 17, 1974.

BREITHUT, FREDERICK ERNEST, educator; b. N.Y.C., Aug. 15, 1880; s. Frederick and Mary (Neuser) B.; B.S., Coll. City of New York, 1900; Sc.D., New York U., 1909; m. Edith Commander, Apr. 2, 1904 (dec.); 1 son, Richard; m. 2d, Florence Hastings Mar. 20, 1924. Became prof. chemistry, Coll. City of N.Y., 1903; head dept. chemistry, Brooklyn Coll. until Jan. 1938. Maj., Chem. Warfare Service U.S.A., 1917; chmn. chem. div., War Trade Bd., 1918; dir. Bur. Conservation, Federal Food Bd., 1918; later chem. trade commr., U.S. Dept. Commerce, Trustee Student's Aid Fund, Coll. City of New York. Fellow A.A.A.S., Am. Inst. Chemists (pres.); mem. Am. Chem. Soc. Home: Nantucket, Mass.†

BRENDEL, OTTO JOHANNES, educator; b. Nuremberg, Germany, Oct. 10, 1901; s. Randolf and Mathilde (Gareis) B.; Ph.D., U. Heidelberg (Germany), 1928; m. Maria Weigert, Feb. 9, 1929; 1 dau., Cornelia (Mrs. Lukas Foss). Came to U.S., 1938, naturalized, 1943. Docent, Erlangen U., 1931; vis. asst. prof. Washington U., St. Louis, 1939; asso. prof., then prof. Ind. U., 1941, 45-56; prof. art history and archaeology Columbia, from 1956, prof. emeritus, until 1973. Fellow German Archaeol. Inst., Am. Acad. Rome; mem. Archaeol. Inst. Am., Coll. Art Assn., Renaissance Soc. Am. Spl. research Greek, Etruscan and Roman art and archaeology, ancient religion classical survivals in Renaissance and later art. Home: New York City N.Y. Died Oct. 8, 1973.

BRENNAN, ROBERT, Irish diplomat; b. Wexford, Ireland, July 22, 1881; s. Robert and Brigid (Kearney) B.; student Royal U. of Ireland, 1900; m. Una Bolger, July 6, 1909; children—Emer (Mrs. Svend Yort), Deirdre (Mrs. Gilbert Jerrold), Maeve, Robert Patrick. Began as journalist, 1900; dir. publicity for Sinn Fein, 1918-21; undersec. foreign affairs,Irish Govt., 1921-22; freelance journalist, 1922-31; gen. mgr. Irish Press, Dublin, 1931-34; sec. Irish Legation, Washington, D.C., 1934-38; minister of Ireland to U.S. from 1938. Catholic.†

BRENNAN, WALTER ANDREW, actor; b. Lynn, Mass., July 25, 1894; s. William John and Margaret Elizabeth (Flanagan) B.; grad. Rindge Tech. Sch., Cambridge, Mass., 1915; A.F.D. (hon.), Morris Harvey Coll.; LL.D., Stonehill Coll., 1968; m. Ruth Caroline Wells; children—Arthur Wells, Walter Andrew, Ruth Caroline. Motion picture actor, 1924-74; more recent pictures include: Surrender, Best of the Badmen, Across the Great Divide, 1950; Return of the Texan, Lure of the Wilderness, 1951; Sea of Lost Ships, Drum across the River, The Far Country, 1953; Four Guns to the Border, Bad Day at Black Rock, 1954; At Gunpoint, Come Next Spring, Glory, Good Bye My Lady, 1955; The Proud Ones, Tammy, 1956; The Way to the Gold, God is My Partner, 1957; Rio Bravo, 1958; How the West Was Won, 1963; Those Calloways, 1965; The Knomobile, 1966; The Family Band, 1967; Support Your Local Sheriff, 1968; The Over The Hill Gang, 1969; appeared TV series The Real McCoys, The Tycoon, Guns of Will Sonnett, To Rome With Love. Served with 101st F.A., U.S. Army, 1917-19; with A.E.F., 19 mos. Recipient acad. awards as best supporting actor, Come and Get It, 1936, Kentucky, 1938, The Westerner, 1940; Freedoms Found. award, 1965; Horatio Alger award, 1966; Western Heritage Nat. Cowboy Hall of Fame award, 1967; elected to Cowboy Hall of Fame, 1970. Has appeared as guest on TV. Address: Moorpark, Cal. Died Sept. 21, 1974.

BRENNER, RUTH MARIE (MRS. CHESTER T. MELLINGER), physician; b. nr. Lancaster, Pa., Mar. 14, 1913; d. Irvin and Elsie (Brookmyer) Brenner; B.S., Oberlin Coll., 1935; M.D., Women's Med. Coll. Pa., 1939; m. Chester T. Mellinger, Oct. 21, 1950. Intern, resident Lancaster Gen. Hosp., 1939-41, mem. staff; gen. practice medicine, Manheim, Pa., 1941-73; sch. physician, 1945. Mem. Pa. Gov.'s Task Force Comprehensive Health Planning, Commn. Occupational Hazards. Mem. Heart Assn. Lancaster County (pres. 1969-70), Am. Heart Assn., A.M.A., Pa. Med. Soc. Address: Manheim Pa. Died Oct. 8, 1973.

BRENT, MEADE STITH, neurophyschiatrist; b. Healthsville, Va., Sept. 11, 1881; s. Andrew Mason and Robert Andrews (Harper) B.; student William and Mary Coll., 1899-1900, Massey Business Coll., Richmond, Va., 1901; M.D., Med. Coll. of Va., 1908; m. Helen Irving Wilson, Mar. 21, 1918 (died Jan. 6, 1924). Bookkeeper, 1902-04; interne Retreat for the Sick, Richmond, Va., 1908-09; resident physician Central State Hosp., Petersburg, Va., 1909-24, asst. supt., 1924-38, med. supt. from 1938; asso. in nervous and mental diseases, Med. Coll. of Va. Mem. Governor's Advisory Board on Mental Hygiene. Diplomate in pyschiatry, Am. Board of Psychiatry and Neurology. Mem. Med. Soc. of Va., Neuropsychiatric Soc. of Va., Am. Psychiatric Assn., A.M.A., 4th Dist. Med. Soc., Phi Rho Sigma. Democrat. Episcopalian. Club: Rotary (Petersburg).†

BRESKY, OTTO, milling co. exec.; b. Mpls., 1889; ed. Dartmouth. Chmn., chief exec. officer Seaboard Allied Milling Corp., Seaboard Flour Corp. Home: Newton Mass. Died Jan. 25, 1974.

BRETHORST, ALICE BEATRICE, dean sch. nursing; b. Freeport, Ill., Sept. 8, 1879; d. Peter John and Gertie (Wibben) Brethorst; grad. Asbury Hosp Sch. Nursing; grad. work, King County Hosp.; A.B., U. Wash., 1922, A.M., 1923, Ph.D., 1931. Prin. jr. high sch. Tzechow, W. China, 1913-20; lectr. Wash., N.D., S.D., Minn. and Ill., 1920-21, and 1929-30; dean, Women's Coll. Chengtu, W. China, 1923-29; prof. edn. and supervisor practice teachers, Dakota Wesleyan, 1933-45; dean Hamline U. Sch. Nursing,. St. Paul, from 1945, also prof. of nursing edn. Mem. Am. Assn. U. Profs., Am. Assn. U. Women (past state chmn. edn.), Nat. League Am. Women. Minn. State League of Nursing Edn. (pres. 1950), Phi Kappa Phi, Alpha Kappa Delta, Pi Lambda Theta. Author: Sociology for Nurses (with Emory S. Bogardus), 1945; Methods of Teaching in Schools of Nursing, 1948. Home: St. Paul, Minn.†

BREUER, BESSIE, writer; b. Cleveland, O., Oct. 19, 1893; d. Samuel A. and Julia (Bindley) Freedman; ed. pub. schs. of St. Louis, Mo., and Sch. of Journalism, Missouri State U.; m. Henry Varnum Poor, 1925; children—Anne Kahler, Peter Varnum. Author: Memory of Love, 1935; The Daugher, 1938; The Actress, 1957; Take Care of My Roses, 1961. Short stories appeared in New Yorker, Harper's Bazaar and anthologies here and abroad. Volume of short stories. The Bracelet of Wavia Lee, 1947; play, Sundown Beach, directed by Elia Kazan, Belasco Theatre, N.Y. City, 1948. Recipient second prize, O. Henry Memorial Award, 1944. Home: New City, N.Y., Died Sept. 26, 1975.

BREUER, CARL A., steel co. exec.; b. Pitts., Dec. 22, 1911; s. Andrew J. and Emma M. (Becker) B.; B.S. in Mgmt. Engring., Carnegie Inst. Tech., 1933; m. Dolores Marcella Ogden, Oct. 29, 1933; children Carole Ann (Mrs. William K. Sarber), Douglas A., Bruce B. With Am. Rolling Mill., Butler, Pa., 1933-36, William B. Scaife Co., Oakmont, Pa., 1936-37, H.H. Robertson Co., Ambridge, Pa., 1937-38; with Pitts. Steel Co. (now Wheeling-Pitts. Steel Co.), 1938-72, v.p., 1957-68, exec. v.p., 1968-72. Trustee Charleroi- Monessen Hosp., North Charleroi, Pa., 1958-74. Mem. Am. Iron and Steel Inst., Am. Petroleum Inst. Mason, Elk. Home: Belle Vernon, Pa. Died Aug. 12, 1974.

BREUNINGER, LEWIS TALMAGE, mem. Republican Nat. Finance Com., real estate exec.; b. Washington, July 23, 1893; s. Lewis Eugene and Sadie I. (Love) B.; A.B., Johns Hopkins, 1913; LL.B., George Washington U., 1916; LL.D., Southeastern U., 1956; m. Marie L. Ashford, June 28, 1919 (dec. 1959); 1 son, Lewis Talmage. Admitted to D.C. bar, 1916; practice in D.C.; pres. L.E. Breuninger & Sons, Inc., builders and realtors, Washington, 1929—; dir. Nat. Savs. & Trust Co., Dist. Title Co. (both Washington). Active Rep. Party, 1944-74; chmn. D.C. Rep. Finance Com., 1944-60; vice chmn. Rep. Nat. Finance Com., 1956-74; exec. vice chmn., 1957 Inaugural Com.; mem. Rep. Nat. Com. for D.C., 1960-68. Pres. Washington Real Estate Bd., 1944-45, Washington Met. Home Builders Assn., 1956. Pres. Washington Met. YMCA, 1954-56, bd. dirs., 1940-74; Am. dir. Benjamin Franklin Found., coop. with City of Berlin, Germany; bd. dirs. Central Union Mission, Washington. Mem. Am., D.C. bar assns. Kiwanian (pres. Washington 1934). Clubs: Metropolitan, Nat. Press, Capitol Hill (bd. govs.), Congressional Country. Army and Navy (Washington). Home: Washington, D.C. Died Jan. 27, 1974.

BREWBAKER, CASSIE LETA (MRS. WILLIAM STYNE BREWBAKER), clubwoman, educator; b. Calvert, Tex., Mar. 14, 1904; d. Cassie Anthony and Mary (Screws) Garrett; grad. Ward-Belmont, 1923; extension courses U. Ala., Ala. Poly. Inst., Troy Normal Sch.; A.B., Huntingdon Coll.; m. William Styne Brewbaker, June 22, 1929; 1 son, William Styne. Tchr. elementary grades, Montgomery, Ala., 1923-64. Mem. Ala. State Textbook Com., 1957; dist. dir. United Appeal, A.R.C.; mem. Montgomery Hist. Devel. Commn.; mem. bd. Montgomery Landmark Found., Montgomery Civic Ballet, Montgomery Humane Soc.; active Cub Scouts, Boy Scouts. Bd. dirs. Birmingham-Southern Coll., 1955-56; bd. dirs., sec., membership chmn. Montgomery Mus. Fine Arts. Mem. Ala. Edn. Assn. (del. Assembly of Del.), Montgomery Tchrs. Assn. (sch. rep., sec. 1942-50), Classroom Tchrs. Assn. (past pres.), D.A.R. (chmn. Jr. Am. Citizens Club, 1st vice regent), Daus. Am. Colonies, Magna Charta Dames, U.D.C., Jr. League, Antiquarian Soc. (pres.), English-Speaking Union (bd.), Delta Kappa Gamma (state pres. 1955-57, internat. legislative chmn., 1958-70, past state exec. sec., mem. commn. membership). Methodist. Clubs: Literary, Masked. Author: articles profl. jours. Home: Montgomery, Ala. Died Dec. 16, 1970; interred Montgomery, Ala.

BREWER, ARTHUR ALLEN, JR., radiologist; b. St. Joseph, Mo., July 13, 1912; s. Arthur Allen and Vera (Chittenden) B.; M.D., Washington U., St. Louis, 1937; m. Helen Roberta Valentine, Feb. 2, 1941; children—Jane (Mrs. Bond Richard Hattershire), David Kent. Intern, St. Luke's Hosp., St. Louis, 1937-38, resident in radiology, 1939-43; sr. intern St. Louis County Hosp., Clayton, Mo., 1938-39; radiologist Alton (Ill.) Meml. Hosp. Mem. Alton Civic Orch. Diplomate Am. Bd. Radiology. Fellow Am. Coll. Radiology; mem. Radiol. Soc. N.Am., Am. Roentgen Ray Soc., A.M.A. Rotarian. Home: Alton, Ill., Died Sept. 26, 1969; buried Valhalla Cemetery, Alton, Ill.

BREWER, BASIL, newspaperman; b. Rush Hill, Mo., July 22, 1884; s. Addison Lanius and Juliet B.; grad. Mo. State Teachers Coll., Kirksville, 1901; student U. Chgo., 1903-05; Dr. Journalism, Suffolk U., 1951; M.S., New Bedford Inst. Textiles and Tech., 1954; Litt.D., Calvin Coolidge College Liberal Arts. Portia Law Sch., 1957; m. Jean Armor Given, 1913; children—Given, Juliet; m. 2d, Mary Minot Caswell, Jan. 3, 1920; children—John Caswell (dec.), Alice Caswell. With Scripss-Howard newspapers, 1908-21, bus. mgr. Cincinnati (O.) Post, 1916-19; same, Cleveland (O.) Press, 1919-21; editor and pub. Omaha (Neb.) Morning and Evening Bee, 1921-24; editor, pub. and prin. owner Lansing (Mich.) Capital News, 1924-29; now publisher and controlling owner of New Bedford (Mass.) Standard-Times; controlling owner Mass. Air Industries, New Bedford; Cape Cod Standard-Times, Hyannis, Mass., radio station WNBH and WNBH-FM, New Bedford, Mass., WOCB and WOCB-FM, West Yarmouth, Mass., president, treasurer WTEV Television, Inc. Trustee Robert A. Taft Meml. Hosp Found., Inc. Decorated Knight Officer Ancient and Most Noble Mil. Order of Christ (Portugal), 1947; Knight Order So. Cross (Brazil), 1949; Distinguished Service award for gen. reporting, Sigma Delta Chi, 1941; Pedro Francisco award Portuguese Continental Union, 1960; Brewer Hall at No. State Tchrs. Coll. dedicated in his honor, 1958; Basil Brewer Boys Town of Desert, Banning, Cal., renamed in his honor, 1960; recipient Naval Res. Surface Div. award, 1961. Elk (named hon. founder Nat. Found. for Elks 1960), Mason. Clubs: Wamsutta, Country (New Bedford); Racquet, Thunderbird (Palm Springs, Cal.). Home: New Bedford, Mass., Died Oct. 5, 1975.

BREWER, EDWARD VERE, educator; b. Ithaca, Mich., Aug. 27, 1887; s. Edward Franklin and Florence Ruby (Russell) B.; A.B., Stanford, 1911, A.M., 1913; A.M., Harvard, 1919; student U. Munich, 1923-24, 1931-32; m. Susan Louise Fischbeck, Sept. 6, 1917; children—Edward Vere, Janet Louise (Mrs. Frank Forsburg, Jr.). Austin teaching fellow Harvard, 1914-15, instr. German, 1915-18, U. Cal. at Berkeley, 1921-27, asst. prof., 1927-37, asso. prof., 1937-47, prof., 1947-67, chmn. dept., 1945-54. Served as ensign U.S.N.R.F., 1918-19. Mem. Modern Lang. Assn., Phi Beta Kappa, Delta Upsilon. Clubs: Bohemian (San Francisco), Faculty (Berkeley); Meadow (Marin Co., Cal.). Episcopalian. Author publs. in German Romanticism and on Jean Paul Richter. Home: Berkeley, Cal. Died Oct. 21, 1967.

BREWER, F(RANCIS) THRALL, patent lawyer; b. Mpls., Jan. 21, 1906; s. Francis Curtis and Verna (Thrall) B.; B.S. in E.E., U. Ill., 1929, E.E., 1941; J.D., U. Dayton, 1935; m. Anna Bernice Doering, Dec. 29, 1929; children—Ronald Dale, Sharolyn Dell (Mrs. Howard Ray Marr). Admitted to Ohio bar, 1937, Ill. bar, 1938; radio engr. Bremer-Tully Mfg. Co. Chgo., 1929; trainee, engr. Automatic Electric, Inc., Chgo., 1929-30; radio engr. Gen. Motors Radio Corp., Dayton, O., 1930-31; patent solicitor and patent atty., Gen. Motors Corp., Dayton, 1931-38, engr., legal, electro-motive div., La Grange, Ill., 1942-44; patent atty., Williams, Bradbury, McCaleb and Hinkle, Chgo., 1938-39, Jefferson Electric Co., Bellwood, Ill., and pvt. practice, Chgo., 1939-42, patent counsel and exec. engr., 1942; patent lawyer Albert G. McCaleb, Chgo., 1944-56; patent lawyer, partner, Horton, Davis & McCaleb, Chgo., 1956-69, Horton, Davis, McCaleb & Lucas, Chgo., 1969-73. Lectr. photography and color slides, 1956-59. Registered profl. engr., Ill. Mem. Patent Law Assn. Chgo., Chgo. Bar Assn., Ill. Bar Assn., Tau Kappa Epsilon, Am. Radio Relay League. Mason. Patentee in field. Home: Hinsdale Ill. Died Mar. 1, 1973.

BRICKER, GARLAND ARMOR, educator, author; b. Etna, O., Mar. 20, 1881; s. David A. and Christianna A. (Rudolph) B.; B.Pd., Lima (O.) Coll., 1907; A.M., U. of Ill., 1910; B.S., Ohio U., 1918; m. Edith Mabel McClelland, June 12, 1909; children—Paul, Robert (twins); m. 2d, Hazel Louise Baughman, Apr. 24, 1939. Teacher in rural schs. of Ohio unitl 1905; prin. high sch. McArthur. O., 1905-06; supt. schs., New Holland, O., 1906-09; asst. in agrl. edn., 1910-11, asst. prof., 1911-16, Ohio State U.; prof. agrl. teaching and dir. rural extension service, Syracuse U., 1916-19; pres. N.Dak. State Sch. of Science, 1919-21; agrl. training officer U.S. Veterans Bur., 1921-23; dir. N.Y. State Inst. of Applied Apr. on L.I., 19Service 3; pres. Union Christian Coll., 1925-26; asso. examiner U.S. Civil Service Commn., 1927-28; pres. Youth Improvement Schs., 1933-34; pres. Nat. Speakers Assn. from 1926; mgr. Youngstown Book Store from 1937. Editor, The Rural Educator, 1912-16; asso. editor Farm Life, 1924-25; farm editor Toledo News-Bee, 1926; farm editor and special writer, Youngstown Vindicator, 1929-30. Mem. N.E.A., Phi Kappa Phi, Acacia. Methodist. Mason, Odd Fellow. Author: The Teaching of Agriculture in the High School, 1911; Solving the Country Church Problem (with others), 1913; Agricultural Education for Teachers, 1914; Bricker's Agricultural Charts, 1915; The Church in Rural America, 1919; Illustrated Lessons in Agriculture, 1919. Home: Youngstown, Ohio.†

BRIDGE, ANN (LADY O'MALLEY), author; b. Shenley, Harts, Eng., Sept. 11, 1889; d. James Harris and Marie (Day) Sanders; diploma social sci. and adminstrn. London Sch. Econs., 1913; m. Sir Owen O'Malley, Oct. 25, 1913; children—Jane, John Patrick, Kate (Mrs. Paul Willert). Sec. Charity Orgn. Soc., Chelsea, Soho, Whitechapel (London), 1911-13; central pres. Wives Fellowship, 1923-25; mem. prize com. Femina-Vie Heureuse, 1935-39. Brit. Red Cross rep., Hungary, 1940-44; active Polish Red Cross, 1944-45; relief work in France. Fellow Soc. Antiquaries of Scotland, Royal Hort. Soc., Wine and Food Soc. Author: Peking Picnic (Atlantic Monthly prize), 1932; The Ginger Griffin (Brit. Book Soc., choice), 1934; Illyrian Spring (Brit. Book Soc. choice), 1935; The Song in the House (short stories), 1936; Enchanter's Night Shade (Brit. Book Soc. choice), 1937; Four-Part Setting, 1939; Frontier Passage, 1942; Singing Waters (Brit. Book Soc. and Lit. Guild choice), 1945; And Then You Came, 1948; The House at Kilmartin (juvenile), 1950; The Dark Moment (Lit. Guild Choice), 1951; A Place to Stand, 1953; A Family of Two Worlds (autobiography), 1955; The Light-Hearted Quest, 1956; (with Susan Lowndes) The Selective Traveller in Portugal, 1949; The Portuguese Escape (Lit. Guild choice), 1958; The Numbered Account, 1959; The Tightening String, 1962; The Dangerous Islands, 1963; Emergency in the Pyrenees, 1964; The Episode at Toledo, 1966; Facts and Fictions (Literary Recollections), 1968; The Malady in Madeira, 1969; Moments of Knowing, 1971. Home: Oxford, England. Died Mar. 9, 1974.

BRIDGMAN, OLGA LOUISE, physician, univ. prof.; b. Jackson, Mich., Mar. 30, 1886; d. Chester Edwin and Alma Antonia (Goecker) Bridgman; A.B., U. of Mich., 1908, M.D., 1910, A.M., U. of Calif., 1914, Ph.D., 1915; hon. Sc.D., Mills Coll., Oakland, Calif., 1937; unmarried. Resident physician State Sch. for Girls, Geneva, Ill., 1910-12; asst. physician Lincoln State Sch. and Colony, Lincoln, Ill., 1912-13; univ. fellow, U. of Calif., 1914-15; instr. in psychology and pediatrics, 1915-19, asst. clin. prof., 1919-22, asso. prof., 1922-26, prof., 1926-55, prof. emeritus, 1954-74; dir. div. mental hygiene, San Francisco Dept. Pub. Health, 1918-52; psychiatrist, San Francisco Juvenile Ct., 1915-55; chief children's psychiatry clinic U. of Cal. Hosp., 1919-55, cons. mental health unit, 1955-74; hon. staff San Francisco Children's Hosp., 1960-74. Mem. bd. dirs. San Mateo Family Service Agy. Fellow Am. Psychol. Assn., Am. Psychiatric Assn., Am. Assn. on Mental Deficiency, Am. Orthopsychiatric Assn., A.A.A.S.; mem. Am., Cal. med. assns., Cal. Acad. Scis., World Affairs Council, Alpha Epsilon Iota, Sigma Xi. Republican. Episcopalian. Clubs: Women's Faculty and Women's City (Berkeley, Cal.). Contbr. to sci. journals. Home: Hillsborough, Cal. Died Feb. 6, 1974.

BRIEFS, GOETZ A(NTONY), labor economist; b. Eschweiler, Rhinelands, Jan. 1, 1889; s. Francis and Ann (Vieten) B.; student U. of Munich, Bonn and Freiburg, 1908-12; hon. degree in econs. Milan U., Munich U., St. Gall Institute of Commerce; honorary degree St. Mary's College, California; married Ann Stephany Weltmann, February 9, 1919; children—Godfrey, Henry, Angela, Elisabeth; married 2d, Elinor Castendyk Sturve; 1 dau., Regina. Lectr. Freiburg U., 1913-21; asso. prof. Würzberg (Franconia) 1922; prof. economics, U. of Freiburg, 1923-26, U. of Berlin, 1926-34; visiting prof., Catholic U. of America, 1934-37; prof. labor economics, Georgetown U., from 1937, prof. emeritus econs.; lecturer, Columbia U., summers, 1938-49; summer lecturer, U. of Vienna, U. of Berne (Switzerland) and U. of Salzburg. Dir. Inst. Indsl. Relations, Berlin, 1928-34. Recipient Grand Cross of Merit (Fed. Republic of Germany), 1959. Mem. Am. Econ. Association, German Sociological Society, Mont Pelerin Society Economics, Pi Gamma Mu. Roman Catholic. Author: Between Capitalism and Syndicalism, 1952; Trade Unions-Past and Present, Cologne U., 1955. Editor: Economics and Labor (monthly), Berlin. Co-editor: Archives of the Philosophy of Law and Economics, Berlin. Home: Chevy Chase, Md. Died May 16, 1974.

BRIER, ROYCE, author, columnist; b. River Falls, Wis., Apr. 18, 1894; s. Warren Judson and Marion (Royce) B.; student U. Wash., 1914-15; m. Monica Doonan, Oct. 14, 1926 (dec. Feb. 1949); children—Susan and Judith (twins); m. 2d, Crystal Smith, July 1, 1949 (dec. Nov. 1970); 1 son, Royce. Short story writer, 1920-25; studied in Orient, Middle East and Europe, 1925, Europe and Middle East, 1936; reporter San Francisco Chronicle, 1926-36, interpretive news columnist, 1937-75, dir. editorials, 1942-53. Awarded Pulitzer prize for reporting, 1934; lit. gold medal Commonwealth Club of Cal., 1947. Author: Crusade, 1931; Reach for the Moon, 1934; Boy in Blue (Civil War), 1937; Last Boat from Beyrouth, 1943; Western World (history), 1946. Home: San Anselmo, Cal. Died Jan. 10, 1975; cremated.

BRIERLY, JAMES LESLIE, internat. lawyer; b. Hudersfield, England, Sept. 9, 1881; s. Sydney Herbert and Emily (Sykes) B.; B.A., Brasenose Coll., Oxford, 1904, D.C.L., 1931; J.D. (hon.), Oslo U., 1946; LL.D. (hon.), Chicago University 1948, Manchester University, 1953; married Ada Foreman, 1920; 1 son. Professor International law, Oxford Univ., 1923-47; delegate of Oxford U. Press, 1923-50. Mem. Internat. Law Commn., United Nations. Author: Law of Nations (4th ed.). 1947, etc. †

BRIETZKE, JUNE ONESON (MRS. CHARLES H. BRIETZKE), organist, harpist; b. Racine, Wis., June 1, 1917; d. Irvin and Bess (Hannon) Oneson; student Carre Mus. Coll., 1934-36, Chgo. Mus. Coll., 1936-37; Ph.D. (hon.), Colo. State Christian Coll., 1972; m. Charles H. Brietzke, Jan. 25, 1946; Harpist, Racine Symphony Orchestra; organist with the First Presbyn. Ch., Racine. Mem. Guild Organists, Am. Harp Soc., Sigma Alpha Iota. Home: Racine Wis. Died June 14, 1974.

BRIGGS, AUSTIN EUGENE, artist; b. Humboldt, Minn., Sept. 8, 1908; s. Harry and Ethel (Davison) B.; student Wicker Art Sch., Detroit, 1924-26, Art Students League, N.Y.C., 1927-28, Harvey Dunn classes in illustration, 1945; m. Ellen Jeannette Weber, May 12, 1927; children—Austin Eugene, Lorne (Mrs. Sherwood Harris). Illustrator for Henry Ford's Dearborn Independent, 1925-27, also nat. mags.; one of founders, mem. faculty Famous Artists Schs., Westport, Conn., 1950-73; paintings in permanent collections including Bruce Barton sculptures include Bernard Meadows, Alexander Calder, Leonard Baskins. Mem. Westport Artists Group (pres. 1952-53), Soc. Illustrators. Recipient numerous awards including gold medals from Soc. Illustrators, Art Dirs. Club; named to Hall of Fame, Soc. Illustrators, 1969. Club: New York Art Directors (judge 33d annual exhbn. 1954, recipient medal, 1951, award of distinctive merit, 1953, 54, 63, 64, 66, 67-69). Author articles in pop. mags. Home: Paris, France. Died Nov. 1973.

BRIGGS, ELLIS O., writer, former U.S. ambassador; b. Watertown, Mass., December 1, 1899; s. James and Lucy (Hill) B.; A.B., Dartmouth, 1921, LL.D., 1955, Bowdoin Coll., 1959, Colby Coll., 1965, Ricker Coll., 1965, Nasson Coll., 1966; m. Lucy Barnard, May 26, 1928; children—Lucy, Everett. Instr. Robert Coll., Constantinople, 1921-23; contbr. articles mags., 1923-25; joined Fgn. Service, 1925, after jr. service Peru, Liberia, Cuba. Chile and Washington, apptd. ambassador 1945-62, to Dominican Republic, 1944, to Uraguay, 1947, to Czechoslovakia, 1949, to Korea, 1952, to Peru, 1955, to Brazil, 1956, to Greece, 1959, to Spain, 1961; minister-counselor, Chungking, China, 1945; dir. Office Am. Republics Affairs, 1945-47, vis. prof. U.S.C. Inst. Internat. Relations, 1965. Recipient Medal Freedom for meritorious services as ambassador to Korea, 1955; Annual award The Americas Found., 1966. Clubs: Metropolitan. Chevy Chase (Washington); University, Brook, Century (N.Y.C.). Author: Shots Heard Round the World, 1957; Farwell to Foggy Bottom, 1964; Anatomy of Diplomacy, 1968; also numerous mag. articles. Home: Hanover N.H., Died Feb. 21, 1976.

BRIGGS, RAYMOND WESTCOTT, army officer; b. Beaver, Pa., July 19, 1878; s. Joseph Stockdale B.; prep. edn., Central Manual Training High School, Phila.; grad. Mounted Service Sch., 1910; m. Helen Cameron, of Tucson, Ariz., Mar. 4, 1903. Pvt. Hosp. Corps, July 20, 1898-May 25, 1899; pvt. and acting hosp. steward Hosp. Corps, and pvt. unassigned 4th Inf., July 5-Sept. 12, 1900; 2d lt. 25th Inf., Aug. 31, 1900; trans. to Arty. Corps, Apr. 18, 1901; 1st lt., July 5, 1901; capt., Jan. 25, 1907; assigned to 6th Field Arty., June 6, 1907; trans. to 2d F. Arty., June 5, 1911; q.-m., June 12, 1911; assigned to 2d F.A., Oct. 26, 1913; trans. to 6th F.A., July 1, 1914, to 5th F.A., Nov. 27, 1914; maj., May 15, 1917; col. N.A., Aug. 1917; brig. gen. (temp.), Aug. 8, 1918. Went to France with Gen. Pershing as chief of Remount Service; with British army during battle of Cambrai, Nov. 1917; relieved from remount duty and returned to U.S., Dec. 25, 1917; on liaison duty; assigned to comd. 311th F.A., 79th Div., Jan. 14, 1918; returned to France in comd. 304th F.A., 77th Div., Apr. 26, 1918; comdr. 204th Regt. F.A., 152d Brigade, 77th Div., 2d Army Corps, A.E.F., May 2d-Sept 10, 1918; assigned duty Camp Travis, Tex. 1918.†

BRIGHAM, CLAUDE ERNEST, army officer; b. Indianapolis, Ind., Apr. 14, 1878; s. Reeder Smith and Mary (Goe) B.; grad. U.S. Mil. Acad. 1901; hon. grad. Coast Arty. Sch., 1909, grad. advanced course, 1910; m. Eliza Dorr, Oct. 18, 1905; children—Mary Elizabeth, Ernest Dorr (dec.). Commd. 2d lt. Arty. Corps, 1901; promoted through grades to maj. gen. and chief of Chem. Warfare Service, May 24, 1933. Instr. and dir. arty. and submarine mine defense, Coast Arty. School, 1914-17; asst. to chief, Coast Arty., Washington, D.C., 1917-19; lt. col., col. (temp.) Germany, Eng., 1919-20; comdr. Ft. Monroe, officer in office of chief of C.W.S., 1921-29; comdg. officer Edgewood (Md.) Arsenal, and comdt. Chem. Warfare Sch., 1929-33; chief of Chem. Warfare Service, 1933-37; maj. gen., retired, 1937. Clubs: Army and Navy Country (Washington). Address: Carmel, Cal.†

BRIGHT, J(OSEPH) S(HIRLEY), civil engr.; b. San Bernardino, Calif., Aug. 29, 1878; s. Joseph Shannon and Annetta (Daley) B.; B.S., U. of Calif., 1901; m. Mollie Hudson Tyler, May 28, 1907; 1 son, Charles Joseph. With A.T. & S.F. and So. Pacific Rys., 1901-05; dep. county surveyor San Bernardino County, Calif., 1905-09. county surveyor, 1911-15; asst. city engr., San Bernardino, 1909-10; chief engr. Fontana Land and Water Co., Rialto, Calif., 1910-11; chief engr. San Bernardino Highway Commn., 1915-17; with U.S. Pub. Rds. Adminstrn. from 1917, successively as sr. highway engr., Portland, Ore., and Missoula, Mont., dist. engr., Denver, chief constrn. engr., Western Hdqrs., San Francisco, dist. engr. directing Am. and Canadian contractors working on Alaska Highway, dep. commr. in charge of dept. of constrn. and maintenance. Washington. Registered civil engr., Calif. Mem. Am. Assn. State Highway Officials (member maintenance and equipment com.), Am. Soc. C.E. (life), Highway Research Bd., Nat. Research Council (chmn. dept. of maintenance com.), Permanent Internat. Assn. of Rd. Congresses, Calif. Alumni Assn. (life). Republican. Christian Scientist. Mason. Author numerous papers on highway engring. Home: San Bernardino, Cal.†

BRILL, JOSEPH EUGENE, lawyer; b. Warsaw, Poland, Sept. 16, 1903; s. Max and Renie (Silber) B.; came to U.S., Jan., 1904, naturalized, 1917; ed. Coll. Arts and Scis., N.Y. U., 1921-24; LL.B., Fordham U., 1928; m. Doris Wright Sutton; children—Elizabeth, Victoria, Maxine, Walter. Admitted to N.Y. bar, 1930, and began practice N.Y.C.; asso. with Bainbridge Colby, N.Y.C., 1930-31; asst. U.S. atty., So. Dist. of N.Y., 1931-34; spl. asst. U.S. gen., N.Y.C., 1934-37; mem. firm. Brower, Brill & Tompkins, N.Y.C., 1937-38; asst. dist. atty. for N.Y. County by apptmt. of Thomas E. Dewey, 1938; spl. asst. to U.S. atty. gen. in charge Wage and Hour Unit, Dept. of Justice, 1938-40; mem. firm Brower, Brill & Tompkins, name now Brower, Brill & Gaugel, N.Y.C. Commd. 1st lt. U.S. Army Air Corps, 1942, capt., 1943, lt. col., adj. gen. troop carrier command. Decorated Bronze Star Medal, Army Commendation Ribbon, also Conspicuous Service Medal. Fellow Am. Coll. Trial Lawyers, Am. Acad. Matrimonial Lawyers; mem. Nat. Assn. Def. Lawyers in Criminal Cases, Am. Bar Assn., N.Y. County Lawyers Assn. Jewish religion. Home: New York City, N.Y. Died May 20, 1975.

BRIM, KENNETH MILLIKEN, lawyer; b. Mt. Airy, N.C., Jan. 21, 1898; s. Thomas L. and Laura (Payne) B.; student Trinity Park Sch., Durham, N.C., 1914-16; A.B., Duke, 1920, postgrad. law sch., 1920-21; m. Doris Overton, June 9, 1923 (dec. Apr. 1967); 1 dau., Doris (Mrs. Frederick L. Carr). Admitted to N.C. bar, 1921; practiced in Greensboro, 1921-44; mem. firm McLendon. Brim, Brooks, Pierce & Daniels, and predecessors, Greensboro, 1944-74, referee bankruptcy, 1929-44; master chancery, 1930-44; dir., gen. counsel Piedmont Natural Gas Co.; counsel Fed. Home Loan Bank Atlanta, 1955. Chmn. nat. council Duke, 1951, trustee, 1952-71, emeritus, 1971-74, mem. exec. com. bd. trustees, 1962-71. Mem. Am., N.C. bar assns., Duke U. Alumni Assn. (pres. 1954), Mchts. and Mfrs. Club, Order of Coif, Pi Kappa Phi. Republican. Methodist. Rotarian. Home: Greensboro, N.C. Died Oct. 27, 1974.

BRINDLEY, JOHN EDWIN, economist; b. Boscobel, Wis., Mar. 31, 1878; s. William and Jane (Brindley) B.; B.L., U. of Wis., 1902, M.A., 1906; Ph.D., State U. of Ia., 1911; m. Mabel Iverson, June 25, 1908; children—Mary Elizabeth, Edward Charles, John Arthur (dec.). Mem. faculty Ia. State Coll. Agr. and Mechanic Arts from 1907, prof. econ. sci., from 1916. Sec. Ia. Spl. Tax Commns., 1912; tax expert for Ia. Code Commn. in rearranging, codifying and revising laws of the state, 1919; tax expert Joint Legislative Tax Commn., 1923, adviser same from 1929; dir. of research of Okla. Tax Economy Assn., 1932; prepared survey of state finance and preliminary survey of county finance of Okla.; dir. research for Ia. Bd. Assessment and Rev., from 1934. Mem. Am. Econ. Assn., National Tax Assn., Royal Econ. Soc., Phi Beta Kappa. Congregationalist. Author: History of Taxation in Iowa (2 vols.), 1911; History of Road Legislation in Iowa, 1912; Highway Administration and Finance (with T.R. Agg), 1927; also contbr. to economic jours. Home: Ames, Ia.†

BRINEY, PAUL WALLACE, publishing co. exec.; b. Louisville, Mar. 8, 1906; s. William Newton and Claudia (Cantrell) B.; A.B., U. Louisville, 1928; m. Nancy B. Wells, Mar. 31, 1936; 1 son, Timothy. Chief underwriter Ky. Home Mut. Life Ins. Co., Louisville, 1928-38; reins. underwriter Am. United Life Ins. Co., Indpls., 1938-40; spl. agt. Fidelity and Deposit Co., Indpls., 1940-45; personnel and indsl. relations mgr. Electronics Lab., Indpls., 1945-48; personnel mgr. Allstate Ins. Co., N.Y.C., 1948-51, v.p., 1951-66, sr. v.p., 1966-69; pres. Brownstone Press, Inc., 1970-73; founder Fireside Theatre Book Club, 1946. Vice chmn. Gen. R. E. Wood Boys' Club, Chgo. Served to capt. USAAF, 1942-45. Clubs: Yale (N.Y.C.); Barrington Hills Country (Barrington, Ill.); Lyford Cay (Bahamas); Louisville Country. Home: Barrington, Ill. Died May 30, 1973.

BRINK, CHARLES BERNARD, educator; b. Kansas City, July 31, 1910; s. Vincent Bernard and Anne Rae (Linder) B.; A.B., U. Mo., 1932; M.Sc., Western Res. U., 1936, certificate in psychiat. social work, 1937; m. Dorothy Mary Reid, Apr. 21, 1934; children—Sarah Anne, David Vincent, Nancy Patricia, Steven Charles. Caseworker, supr. Family Service Assn., Detroit, 1937-41; exec. dir. Family Service Soc., Lansing, Mich., 1943-44, 46-48; lectr. Mich. State Coll., 1946-48; exec. dir. Family Service Assn., St. Louis County, Clayton,

Mo., 1948-51; dean Sch. Social Work, Wayne State U., Detroit, 1951-63; prof., dean Sch. Social Work, U. Wash., Seattle, 1963-71; dep. sec. Wash. Dept. Social and Health Services, Olympia, 1971-72; prof. social work U. Wash., Seattle, 1972-74. Creator, producer, narrator TV series Troubled Lives, 1959-60. Mem. central office social work adv. com. VA, 1965-70; bd. dirs., v.p. Council on Social Work Edn.; vice chmn. Wash. Gov.'s Com. on Pub. Assistance, 1963-64; mem. Gov.'s Adv. Com. on Health, 1967-71; chmn. program com. Western Interstate Commn. for Higher Edn., 1968-71; cons. Wash. Dept. Pub. Assistance, 1964-71, project on income maintenance Stanford Research Inst., 1969-71. Mem. bd. United Good Neighbors, Seattle, 1968-71, Urban League, Seattle, 1967-71. Served as 1st lt., M.C., AUS, 1944-46. Recipient awards including Distinguished Faculty Service award Wayne State v. Alumni Assn., 1963, Distinguished Alumni award Case-Western Res. U., 1966. Mem. Nat. Assn. Social Workers, Wash. Assn. for Social Welfare (bd. 1965-68), Wash. Assn. for Retarded Children, Council on Social Work Edn., Family Service Assn. Am., Am. Pub. Welfare Assn., Am. Pub. Health Assn., Alpha Kappa Delta, Delta Upsilon. Home: Seattle, Wash. Died Sept. 19, 1974.

BRINLEY, CHARLES EDWARD, corp. exec.; b. Phila., Feb. 25, 1878; s. Charles A. and Mary Goodrich (Frothingham) B.; graduated Groton (Mass.) Sch., 1896; A.B., Yale Univ., 1900; Ph.D., Yale Scientific School, 1901; m. Helen Frazier, June 6, 1908; children—Mary Frothingham, Charles Edward (deceased), William West Frazier, George (dec.). With Am. Pulley Co. from July 1901, beginning as timekeeper, v.p., 1908-19, pres., 1919-39; acting v.p. Baldwin Locomotive Works, Sept.-Dec. 1938, pres. and dir. Jan. 1, 1939-43, chmn. bd. and dir. 1943-50; chmn. exec. com. The Midvale Co.; mem. exec. com., dir. Phila. Electric Co.; dir. Baldwin, Lima-Hamilton Corp.; trustee Penn Mutual Life Ins. Co.; mem. bd. mgrs. Western Saving Fund Soc. Fellow Am. Society Mech. Engrs. Republican. Episcopalian. Clubs: Sunnybrook Golf (Flourtown, Pa.); Philadelphia, Midday (Phila.). Home: Philadelphia, Pa.†

BRINTON, JASPER YEATES, judge; b. Phila., Pa., Oct. 5, 1878; s. John Hill (M.D.) and Sarah (Ward) B.; grad. Episcopal Acad., Phila., 1894; A.B., U. of Pa., 1898, LL.B., 1901; hon. A.M., Washington Coll., 1915; m. Alice B. McFadden; children—John, Pamela; m. 2d, Geneva Febiger, of Palo Alto, Calif., Sept. 10, 1927. Admitted to Pa. bar 1901, and began practice at Phila; mem. firm Conlen, Brinton & Acker, 1901-21. Assistant United States attorney, Eastern Dist. of Pa., 1904-12; sometime counsel Pa. Dept. Labor and Industry; apptd. solicitor U.S. Shipping Bd., 1921; justice Court of Appeals, Mixed Courts of Egypt, since 1921. Maj., judge adv. gens'. dept., O.R.C., 1917, detailed to service in provost marshal gen.'s office, Washington, D.C.; judge adv. and renting, requisition and claims officer, rank of lt. col., France and Eng., Mar. 1918-Aug. 1919; mem. Am. Mil. Mission to Armenia, 1919; lt. col., O.R.C.; certificate meritorious service; Legion of Honor (France). Former mgr. Pa. House of Refuge and pres. Pa. Child Labor Assn. Mem. Am. Bar Assn., Am. Soc. Internat. Law, Internat. Law Assn., Phi Kappa Sigma, Phi Beta Kappa (1933). Republican. Clubs: Coffee House (New York); Alexandria (Egypt) Sporting. Author: The Mixed Courts of Egypt, 1930. Contbr. to Am. Jour. Internat. Law, Current History, etc. Home: Alexandria Egypt. Died Aug. 1973.

BRISSENDEN, PAUL FREDERICK, educator; b. Benzonia, Mich., Sept. 21, 1885; s. James Taylor and Retta Odell (Lewis) B.; prep. edn. Warren Acad., University Park, Colo., 1900-04; A.B., U. of Denver, 1908; A.M., U. of Calif., 1912; Ph.D., Columbis, 1917; m. Margaret A. Geer, Sept. 30, 1924; children—Arik, Hoke, Donald. Spl. agt. U.S. Commn. on Industrial Relations, 1914; spl. agt. U.S. Bur. of Labor Statistics, 1915-20; asst. prof. economics, New York U., 1920-21; lecturer, asso. prof. and prof., economics, Columbia, from 1921; then sr. scholar East West Center, U. Hawaii; vice chmn. Millinery Stabilization Commn., Inc. (N.Y. City), since 1936; impartial chmn. under various labor agreements since 1937; mem. Industrial Tribunal, Am. Arbitration Assn., since 1939; consultant and mem. clothing advisory com., Office Prodn. Management and War Prodn. Bd., 1941-43; spl. consultant U.S. Bur. of Labor Statistics, 1941-43; mediator, arbitrator and referee Nat. War Labor Bd., 1942; vice-chmn. and pub. mem. Regional War Labor Bd. for the Second Region, 1943-45. Chmn. bd. dirs. Nat. Consumers League, 1939-40; mem. bd. dirs. Internat. Rescue and Relief Com. since 1940; mem. Citizens Transit Com., N.Y. City, 1942. Charter mem. Nat. Acad. Arbitrators, since 1947. Mem. Am. Econ. Assn., Sigma Alpha Epsilon, Beta Gamma Sigma. Democrat. Club: Faculty (New York). Author: The I.W.W., a Study of American Syndicalism, 1919, 2d edit., 1920, Russian translation, 1926; Labor Turnover in Industry (with Emil Frankel), 1922; The Great Hawaiian Dock Strike, 1953; The Labor Injunction in Hawaii, 1956; Arbitration in Australia and the U.S., 1960; also reports, monographs, etc. Contbr. to econ. and labor jours. Home: Lemon Grove Cal. Died Nov. 29, 1974.

BRIST, GEORGE LOUIS, consular service; b. Hill Settlement, Monroe Co., Wis., June 29, 1878; s. Fillmore Marion and Ida (White) B., father the youngest federal vol. soldier in Civil War, enlisting as 16 (4 days under 12); ed. pub. schs. and Bayliss Business Coll., Dubuque, Ia.; George Washington U. Coll. of Law (non-grad.); D.C., D.O. and P.C., Riley Coll. of Spinal Therapy, Washington, D.C., 1922; m. Margaret Heeter, Dec. 1, 1902; children—George Louis, Uriah Marion. Civil service appointee to Dept. of State, Mar. 2, 1897; made acting chief Div. of Passport Control, Aug. 17, 1922, and chief of div., 1922-25; assigned on request to consular service. Republican. Methodist. Mason.†

BRITTON, MASON, cons. metal trades industry; b. Petersburg, Va., Aug. 28, 1882; s. Stephen Wells and Richardetta (Marks) B.; m. Anne Hugus, Feb. 4, 1922; children—Mason, Wright. With McCraw-Hill Pub. Co., 1901-44, v.p., 1922-44; chief Tools Div., O.P.M., 1940-41; dir., Advt. Council; former president Associated Business Papers; former chairman board directors Advt. Federation of America. Civilian tech. recruiting officer, 1917-18; chmn. surplus property com., U.S. Army, 1920-24; adminstr. Surplus War Property Adminstrn., 1944, Surplus Property Bd., 1945; cons. F.E.A. Former pres. Metal Cutting Tool Inst.; now cons. Recipient Medal for Merit for services in World War. Mem. Mag. Pubs. Assn. Bus Adv. Council (hon. dir.), S.A.R. Republican. Episcopalian. Mason. Clubs: Boothbay Harbor (Me.) Country; Union League (N.Y.C.); Southport (Me.); Yacht: Home: Delray Beach Fla. Died Mar. 1974.

BROCKWAY, HOBART MORTIMER, JR., physician; b. Beacon, N.Y., Jan. 2, 1920; A.B., Harvard, 1944; M.D., U. Rochester, 1953; m. Elaine Stewart (dec.); children—Hobart, Joan (Mrs. David Gray), Judith (Mrs. Ray Flynn); m. 2d, Mary Mylod Brockway. Intern, Vassar Bros. Hosp., Poughkeepsie, N.Y., 1953-54, attending staff, 1963-73; resident French Hosp., N.Y.C., 1960-63. Served to capt. USAAF, 1942-45; ETO. Decorated D.F.C. with 11 oak leaf clusters. Diplomate Am. Bd. Obstetrics and Gynecology. Fellow A.C.S., Am. Coll. Obstetricians and Gynecologists; mem. A.M.A. Home: Fishkill, N.Y. Died Aug. 23, 1973.

BRODA, FREDERICK MARTIN, ins. co. exec.; b. Canton, O., Jan. 14, 1895; s. Frederick and Katherine (Slusser) B.; A.B., Western Res. U., 1917; m. Amy A. Ash, Mar. 17, 1951. Pres., treas. Webb-Broda & Co., Inc., gen. ins. and surety bonds, Canton, 1921-74. Mem. Stark County Rep. Exec. Com.; del. 16th Congl. Dist., Rep. Nat. Conv., 1952. Trustee Kent State U., 1958-69; mem. Inter-Univ. Council for State Supported Univs., Ohio, 1964-69. Served to 1st lt., inf., U.S. Army, World War I. Recipient Man of Year award Canton C. of C., 1962. Mem. Stark County Hist. Soc. (trustee, past pres.), Ohio (trustee), Canton (pres. 1931-32) chambers commerce, Am. Legion, Delta Upsilon. Baptist. Mason. Club: Canton (dir., v.p.). Home: Canton, O. Died Mar. 1974.

BRODE, WALLACE REED, sci. cons.; b. Walla Walla, Wash., June 12, 1900; s. Howard Stidham and Martha Catherine (Bigham) B.; B.S., Whitman Coll., 1921, D.Sc., 1955; M.S., U. Ill., 1922, Ph.D., 1925; D.Sc., Ohio State U., 1958, Ohio Weslyan U., 1962; D.Textile Sci., Phila. Coll. Textiles and Sci., 1970; m. Ione Sundstrom, Mar. 19, 1941. Grad. asst. dept. chemistry U. Ill., 1922, asst., 1922-24; asst. and asso. chemist U.S. Nat. Bur. Standards, 1924-25, asso. dir., 1947-58; Guggenheim Meml. Found. fellow, Leipzig, Zurich, Liverpool, 1926-28; asst. prof. chemistry Ohio State U., 1928-32, asso. prof., 1932-39, prof., 1939-48; mem. London mission of liaison office OSRD, 1944-45, head Paris office, 1944-45, Alsos Mission, 1944-45; head sci. dept. U.S. Naval Ordnance Test Station, Inyokern, Cal., 1945-47, mem. adv. bd., 1948-58: mem. phys. div. NRC, 1947-54, chemistry div., 1954-60, 69-71. Sci. adviser to sec. of state, 1958-60; sci. cons., 1960-74; fgn. sec. Am. Chem. Soc., 1965-67; co-chmn. People-to-People Com. for Scientists and Engrs., 1957-58, 64-74, pres., 1970-74; mem. Pres.'s Com. Sci. and Engrs., 1957; cons. to Pres.'s Sci. Adv. Com., 1958-60; mem. Sci. Manpower Commn., 1960-74, pres., 1972—; mem. adv. bd. Desert Research Inst., U. Nev., 1964-69; dir. Barnes Engring. Co., 1960—; Am. del. Internat. Union Pure and Applied Chemistry, Zurich, Switzerland, 1936, 55, N.Y.C., 1951, Paris, France, 1957, Internat. Council Sci. Unions, Washington, 1958; mem. Harvard-M.I.T. eclipse of sun expdns. Siberia, 1936; Marburg lectr. Am. Soc. for Testing and Materials, 1950. Bd. overseers Whitman Coll., 1954-74. Mem. Ann. Assay Commn. for U.S. Mint, 1952. Served with U.S. Army, 1918. Recipient Presdl. certificate of merit, 1945; medal Soc. for Applied Spectroscopy, 1958; Exceptional Service medal Dept. Commerce. 1958; Priestley medal Am. Chem. Soc., 1960. Fellow Am. Phys. Soc.; mem. Soc. Applied Spectroscopy (hon.), Am. Chem. Soc. (councilor, chmn. sec. Columbus sect., nat. dir. 1951-60, 68-70, pres. 1969), Optical Soc. Am. (pres. 1960, dir. 1951-60), Am. Inst. Physics (gov. 1948-52, 60-63), Sci. Research Soc. Am. (gov. 1950-58, 60-63, chmn. 1954-57), Am. Assn. U. Profs., Sci. Service (dir., treas. 1958-72), Nat. Acad. Scis., A.A.A.S. (dir. 1953-60, pres. 1958, chmn. bd. 1959), Phi Beta Kappa, Sigma Xi (nat. lectr. 1952, nat. pres. 1961-62), Phi Lambda Upsilon (hon.), Sigma Pi Sigma (hon.), Alpha Chi Sigma, Gamma Alpha, Alpha Epsilon Delta. Club: Cosmos (Washington). Author: Chem. Spectroscopy, 1939, 2d edit., 1943; (with others) Lab Outlines for Organic Chemistry, 1940, 4th edit., 1955; (with Gilman) Organic Chemistry, 1938; Scott's Standard Method of Analysis (with Furman), 1939; Advances in Enzymology (with Nord and Werkman), 1944; Applications of Instruments in Chemistry (with Burk and Grummitt) 1945; Physical Methods in Chemical Analysis (with Berl and Corning), 1960; (with others) Science in Progress, 1956; Roger Adams Symposium, 1955. Editor: Science in Progress, vols. 12-16, 1962-67; Jour. Optical Soc. Am., 1950-60. Home: Washington, D.C. Died Aug. 10, 1974.

BRODERICK, HENRY, business exec.; b. Mpls., Oct. 12, 1880; s. Lawrence and Mary (Cronin) B.; student pub. schs., Mpls.; m. Mary Barclay, Oct. 1901 (dec.). Founder, Henry Broderick, Inc., 1911, pres., from 1911; pres., dir. Henry Broderick Investment Co.; pres. Realty & Leasehold Co., Boston Drug Co.; sec. 1941 Corp.; dir. Seattle 1st Nat. Bank, New World Life Ins. Co., Seattle Baseball Club; trustee J.C. Silverton Trust. Mem. Prison Parole Bd., 1929-33. Trustee Seattle U. Republican. Roman Catholic Clubs: Rainier Tennis, Washington Athletic, Press, Harper. Author: The Shoveler, 1932; The Commandment Breakers of Walla Walla, 1933; Early Seattle Profiles. Home: Seattle, Wash.†

BRODERICK, JOHN P., former public relations and advt. cons.; b. Breckenridge, Minn., June 3, 1904; s. Edward J. and Sarah Elizabeth (Carr) B.; A.B., U. Minn., 1926; m. Lucille Kern, July 1, 1938; children—John Patrick, Stephanie. Editorial asst. Northwestern Miller, 1927-29; reporter Wall Street Jour., 1929-35, editor, 1935-42; v.p., dir. Doremus & Co., 1942-52; partner Broderick & Coleman, financial pub. relations, N.Y.C., 1953-65; v.p., dir. Albert Frank-Guenther Law, Inc., advt.-pub. relations agy., 1966-71. Lectr. English, Columbia, 1956-57. Mem. N.Y. Financial Writers Assn. (charter). Pub. Relations Soc. Am. (charter), Cath. Inst. of Press, Soc. Silurians, N.Y. Soc. Security Zeta Psi, Sigma Delta Chi. Roman Catholic. Clubs: National Press (Washington); Overseas Press, Deadline (N.Y.C.); Bankers Am. Home: Sun City, Ariz. Died Aug. 13, 1973.

BRODIE, ALLAN GIBSON, orthodontist, Educator; b. N.Y. City, Oct. 31, 1897; s. John Ritchie and Jane Cleeland (Brown) B.; D.D.S., U. of Pa., 1919; student Angle Coll. of Orthodontia, Pasadena, Calif., 1925-26; M.S., U. of Ill., 1934, Ph.D., 1940; m. Vera Elizabeth Smock, Apr. 26, 1923; children—Allan Gibson Jr., Donald Herbert, Anna Hopkins. Began practice of dentistry in Newark, 1920; specialized in orthodontia, Newark, 1927-29; removed to Chicago, 1929, and organized dept. of orthodontia in Grad. School of Univ. of Ill., and head dept., prof. orthodonita, emeritus, 1966-76; Fulbright prof. U. Nijmegen, 1966-67; acting, dean Coll. Dentistry, U. of Ill., 1944-47, dean, 1947-55; dental cons. VA; in practice orthodonia exclusively. Member of the board of scientific advisers National Institute of Dental Research; member of research fellowships br. Nat. Insts. Health. Served as hosp. apprentice 1st class, USN, World War. Recipient Geo. Villain prize, Fed. Dentaire Internat., 1947, Callahan medal, Ohio State Dental Soc., 1957; Joske Meml. orator, Melbourne, Australia, 1954; recipient alumni award of merit U. Pa., 1951. Mem. Inst. of Med., Internat. Assn. Dental Research (pres. 1947-48), Ed. H. Angle Soc. of Orthodontia, Chicago Dental Soc., Am. Assn. Anatomists, Xi Psi Phi, Sigma Xi, Omicron Kappa Upsilon. Awarded Certificate of Merit by Am. Med. Assn., 1935. Mason. Presbyterian. Club: of University of Chicago. Home: Glenview, Ill., Died Jan. 2, 1976.

BRODIE, DONALD M., found. exec.; b. Cin., Aug. 31, 1890; s. Andrew M. and Charlotte J. (Moore) B.; A.B., Oberlin Coll., 1911; M.A., Columbia, 1913; grad. study U. Chgo., 1915; m. Marion L. Williams, Jan. 28, 1928. Mem. Am. Commn. to Negotiate Peace, Paris, 1919; sec. Am. Commn. on Mandates in Turkey, 1919; sec. Am. Minister, Peking, China, 1920-21: financial sec. Charles R. Crane, 1922-39; treas. China Inst. in Am., 1939-46; treas. Marine Biol. Lab., Woods Hole, Mass., 1942-52; treas. China Found. (Boxer Indemnity Funds), from 1947; v.p. Am. Bur. Med. Aid to China, 1948-68. Sec.-treas. Inst. Current World Affairs, 1925-55. Served as capt. AEF, France, 1918. Home: New York City, N.Y. Died Feb. 3, 1974.

BRODIE, GANDY, artist; b. N.Y.C., May 20, 1924; s. Max and Minnie (Tau) B.; m. Jocelyn Levine, Jan. 25, 1955; 1 son, Shane. One-man exhbns. include Kootz Gallery, N.Y.C., Durlacher Bros. Gallery, N.Y.C., Saidenberg Gallery, N.Y.C., Zabriskie Gallery, N.Y.C.; represented in permanent collections Met. Mus. Art, Mus. Modern Art, Whitney Mus., Jewish Mus., N.Y.C., Park Ave. Synagogue, N.Y.C., Phillips Collection, Washington, Balt. Mus. Art, Chrysler Mus., Norfolk (Va.) Mus., Mass. Inst. Tech., Sarah Lawrence Coll., Gloria Vanderbitl Mus. (purchase fund), Longview Found. (Purchase award 1960, 61), Mint Mus., Charlotte, N.C.; art faculty New Sch. Social Research, 1967; artist-in-residence Hollins Coll., 1968; vis. scholar Wash. State Colls., 1968-69, Gandy Brodie Sch. Fine Arts, Newfane, Vt.; asso. prof. Carnegie Mellon U., Winner Mark Twain Contest, 1958; recipient Ingram

Merrill Found. award, 1962; Nat. Arts Council award, 1968; Guggenheim fellow, 1968-69. Home: West Townshend, Vt., Died Oct. 22, 1975; buried West Townshend.

BRODNEY, SPENCER, editor; b. Melbourne, Australia, Aug. 29, 1883; ed. Scotch Coll., Melbourne, U. of Melbourne and London Sch. of Economics and Polit. Science, U. of London; m. Edith Siebel, June 22, 1918; children—Kenneth, Richard. Mem. staff various Australian, English and Am. newspapers and mags., 1905-16; asso. editor Current History, 1916-18, 1922-31, editor from 1931 until its sale by The N.Y. Times. In 1937 founded and became editor of Events; merged Events with Current History and Forum, 1941, editor Current History, 1941-43; mem. bd. govs., Spl. Social Services, from 1943. Died May 1973.

BRODSKY, NATHAN, univ. dean; b. Phila., Sept. 22, 1916; s. Alfred and Pauline (Sennett) B.; B.S., with honors, Temple U., 1937; postgrad. U. Pa., 1938-40; Ph.D. in Econs., Am. U., 1959; m. Margaret Sara McStay, Dec. 27, 1946; children—James Alfred, David Arthur, Barbara Ann. Social worker Pa. Dept. Pub. Assistance, 1937-40; successively chief Brit. Dominions and India br. and chief procurement coordination br. UNRRA, 1946-48; chief policy div. office of distbn., dep. chief office of distgn., dep. vice-chmn. for supply mgmt. Munitions Bd., 1948-52; dep. dir. Def. Supply Mgmt. Agy., 1952-53; asst. dir. cataloging, standardization and inspection Dept. Def., 1954-57; dir. research and spl. projects Office Sec. Def., 1957-66, dir. edn. programs and mgmt. tng., 1966-73, acting dep. asst. sec. def. for edn., 1968-70, 72; dean Coll. Continuing Edn., Am. U., Washington, 1973-75; comdg. officer Moblzn. detachment, 1961-63, chmn. Def. Logistics Mgmt. Tng. Bd., 1963-66, chmn. Def. Logistics Research Conf., 1965. Vis. lectr.; cons. intergovtl. relations subcom. U.S. Ho. of Reps., 1949-52; mem. Interagy. Council on Internat. Ednl. and Cultural Affairs, 1966-73, Fed. Interagy. Com. Edn., 1968-73, Nat. Adv. Council on Extension and Continuing Edn., 1966-73; assited Hoover Commn. Task Force and Fed. Supply, 1948. Served as 2d lt. to col., AUS, 1941-46. Decorated Bronze Star medal; recipient Civilian Meritorious Service medal Soc. of Def., 1970, 73. Mem. Am. Econ. Assn., Acad. Polit. Sci., Am. Polit. Sci. Assn. Inst. Mgmt. Sci., Washington Operations Research Council. Contbr. articles in bus. and econ. jours. Home: Arlington, Va., Died Oct. 7, 1975.

BRODY, DANIEL ANTHONY, physician, educator; b. Youngstown, O., June 8, 1915; s. Jacob George and Jenny (Supnik) B.; B.S., Case Inst. Tech., 1936; M.D., Western Res. U., 1940; m. Barbara Elizabeth Murray, Sept. 3, 1943; children—Jennifer Joyce (Mrs. H. William Dornbush, Jr.), Judith Jean (Mrs. David Monen), Jonathan George. Mem. staff and faculty U. Tenn. Med. Units, 1946-75, prof. medicine, 1958-75, prof. physiology and biophysics, chmn. div. clin. physicology, 1968-75. Mem. sci. adv. com. Krannert Inst. Cardiology, Ind. U. Served to maj. AUS, 1943-46. Recipient Research Career award NIH, 1962—. Diplomate Am. Bd. Internal Medicine. Fellow Am. Coll. Cardiology, A.C.P., Am. Coll. Chest Physicians; mem. Assn. Am. Physicians, Assn. Univ. Cardiologists, Am. Soc. Clin. Investigation, Am. Fedn. Clin. Research, Am. Physiol. Soc., Am. Assn. U. Profs., A.M.A., Sigma Xi, Alpha Omega Alpha, Tau Beta Pi. Contbr. med. jours. Mem. editorial bd. Am. Heart Jour., Circulation, Medcom. Home: Memphis, Tenn., Died Sept. 30, 1975.

BROEK, JAN OTTO MARIUS, geographer; b. Utrecht, Netherlands, Dec. 8, 1904; s. Jan and Geertruida Elizabeth Juliana (van Zwicht) B.; student U. Utrecht, 1924-29, Ph.D., 1932; fellow Rockefeller Found., 1929-31; postgrad. London Sch. Econs., 1929, U. Cal. at Berkeley, 1930-31; m. Orletta Ruth Heineck, May 25, 1931; children—Orletta Marianne (Janna) (Mrs. John M. Leffingwell), Gertrude Juliana (Mrs. G.A. Williams), Jan Maarten. Came to U.S., 1936, naturalized, 1942. With Netherlands Inst. Housing and Town Planning, Amsterdam, 1929, Netherlands Rys., Utrecht, 1933-36; vis. lectr. univs. Ia., Ohio, Cal., 1936-37; asst., then asso. prof. geography U. Cal. at Berkeley, 1937-46; prof. geography, dir. Social Geography Inst., U. Utrecht, 1946-48; prof. U. Minn., 1948-70, prof. emeritus, 1970-74, chmn. dept. geography, 1948-57. Vis. prof., adviser U. Indonesia, Batavia, 1947; Fulbright vis. prof. U. Malaya, Singapore, 1954-55; hon. research asso. U. Coll., London, 1961-62; vis. prof. U. Cal. at Berkeley, 1970-72, research asso., 1972-74; cons. geog. br. M.I. Service, 1943; spl. asst. to chief Far Eastern div., Research and Analysis Br., OSS, 1945. Recipient Research award Am. Council Learned Socs.-Social Sci. Research Council, 1961-62. Fellow Am. Geog. Soc.; mem. Alexander Maconochie Found. (hon.), Assn. Am. Geographers (pres. 1960-61), Royal Netherlands Geog. Soc. (corr. mem.), Netherlands Soc. Econ. and Social Geography, S.E. Asia Inst., Inst. Pacific Relations, El Instituto de la Producion (U. Buenos Aires, corr. mem.). Clubs: Campus. Author: The Santa Clara Valley, California, 1932; The Economic Development of the Netherlands Indies, 1942; Geography, its Scope and Spirit, 1965; Compass of Geography, 1966 (transl. into Spanish, Portuguese, Dutch); (with J.W. Webb) A Geography of Mankind, 1968, 2d rev. edit., 1973. Adv. editor Terrae Incognitae, Annals Soc. for History of Discoveries, 1967-74. Contbr. numerous articles to profl. jours. Home: Berkeley, Cal. Died Aug. 23, 1974.

BROGAN, SIR DENIS WILLIAM, educator; Glasgow, Scotland, Aug. 11, 1900; s. Denis and Elizabeth (Toner) B.; m. Olwen Kendall, Aug. 20, 1931; children—Denis Hugh Vercingetorix, Patrick William Kendall, Brian Joseph, Olwen Elizabeth. Lectr., London Sch. Econs.; hon. fellow Corpus Christi Coll., Oxford U., also Peterhouse, Cambridge; prof. polit. sci. Cambridge (Eng.) U., 1939-67, prof. emeritus, 1967-74. Decorated Legion of Honor; comdr. Order of Orange Nassau; created knight. Mem. Institut de France, Brit. Acad., Am. Philos. Soc., Mass. Hist. soc. Clubs: Reform (London); Lotos (N.Y.C.); Nat. Press (Washington). Author: The Free State, 1945; French Personalities and Problems, American Themes, Politics in America, 1954; The French Nation, 1957; American Aspects, 1964. Home: Cambridge England. Died Jan. 5, 1974.

BROGDEN, WILFRED JOHN, psychologist; b. Sydney, Australia, May 6, 1912; s. John and Elsie May (Taylor) B.; came to U.S., 1914, naturalized, 1926; student So. Meth. U., 1929-32; A.B., U. Ill., 1933, Ph.D., 1936; NRC fellow Johns Hopkins Sch. Medicine, 1936-37; m. Elinor Taylor Davis, Sept. 8, 1935; children—Penelope, Ann. Research asst. in psychiatry Johns Hopkins Sch. Medicine, 1937-39; asst. prof. psychology U. Wis., 1939-43, asso. prof., 1944-46, prof. psychology, 1946-73, asst. dean Grad. Sch., 1947, asso. dean, 1951-58. Vis. lectr. U. Rochester, summer 1942, Harvard, summer 1946. Active research applied psychology panel NDRC, 1942-45 (awarded presdl. certificate of appreciation, 1947); expert cons. to sec. nat. def., 1947-54; mem. sub-panel on sensory functions Research and Dev. Bd., 1947-48, chmn., 1948, mem. panel on human engring. and psychophysiology, 1948-54; emm. div. anthropology and psychology NRC, 1948-52, chmn. com. fellowship selection procedures. Mem. profl. adv. com. on human resources USAF, 1948-50. Fellow A.A.A.S., Am. Psychol. Assn. (pres. div. physiology and comparative psychology 1949; sec. div. theoretical and exptl. psychology 1948); mem. Am. Assn. U. Profs., Psychonomics Soc. (organizing com. 1960; governing bd. 1960-63, chmn. 1962), Soc. Exptl. Psychology, Midwestern Psychology Assn., Sigma Xi. Contbr. articles to sci. jours. Home: Madison Wis. Died Feb. 22, 1973.

BROGHAMER, GEORGE P., banker; b. Covington, Ky., July 23, 1909; s. Luke and Catherine Broghamer; student U. Cin., 1930-31; Sch. Banking, Rutgers U., 1946. Nat. bank examiner Treasury Dept., 1937-47; asst. v.p. 2d Nat. Bank of Cin., 1947-51; with First Nat. Bank Cin., 1951-73, sr. v.p., 1971-73; dir. Elmac Corp., Huntington, W.Va. Club: Bankers (Cin.). Home: Fort Wright, Ky. Died Nov. 4, 1973.

BROMILOW, FRANK, coll. dean; b. Lancashire, Eng., May 13, 1916; s. Peter and Jane (Gregory) B.; came to U.S., 1923, naturalized, 1929; B.S. in Civil Engring., U. Pitts., 1937, M.S., 1939; student Carnegie Inst. Tech., 1941-42; m. Dorothy O'Neill, June 10, 1941; children—Margaret, Neil, Mary. Instr., then asst. prof. civil engring. U. Pitts., 1937-46; chief engr. Plasteel Product Co., Washington, Pa., 1946-48; asso. prof. civil engring. U. Fla., 1948-51; head dept. civil engring. N.M. State U., University Park, 1951-61, dean Coll. Engring., dir. Engring. Expt. Sta., 1961-75. Mem. N.M. Bd. Registration Profl. Engrs. Registered profl. engr., N.M., Pa. Mem. Nat., N.M. (past bd. dirs.) socs. profl. engrs., Am. Soc. Engring. Edn. (council, chmn. civil engring. div.), Am. Soc. C.E., Am. Concrete Inst., Sigma Xi, Sigma Tau, Lambda Chi Alpha, Chi Epsilon, Phi Kappa Phi. Rotarian. Home: Las Cruces N.M. Died June 15, 1975.

BRONK, DETLEV W, scientist, educator; b. N.Y.C., Aug. 13, 1897; s. Mitchell and Marie (Wulf) B., A.B., Swarthmore Coll., 1920; postgrad. U. Pa., 1921; M.S., U. Mich., 1922, Ph.D., 1926; recipient over 55 hon. degrees from univs. and colls.; m. Helen A. Ramsey, Sept. 10, 1921; children—John Everton Ramsey, Adrian, Mitchell Herbert. Mem. univ. faculties, 1921-49; pres. Johns Hopkins, 1949-53; pres. Rockefeller U., N.Y.C., 1953-68, pres. emeritus, 1968-75. Coordinator research Air Surgeons Office, Hdqrs. Army Air Forces, 1942-46. Held 12 endowed named lectureships, 1938; dir. Johnson Research Found., U. Pa., 1929-49; chmn. NRC, 1946-50; pres. Nat. Acad. Scis., 1950-62; chmn. bd. NSF, 1956-64; mem. Pres.'s Sci. Adv. Com., 1956-63; cons.-at-large, from 1963; chmn. Panel on Internat. Sci., 1957-63; vice chmn. N.Y. State Sci. and Tech. Found., 1965-68, chmn., from 1968; pres. N.Y. Hall of Sci.; mem. Inter-Am. com. on sci. and tech. OAS, from 1969. Trustee Atoms for Peace Awards, Renssalear Poly. Inst. (chmn. bd. 1966-71), Tulane U., U. Pa., Bucknell U., Marine Biol. Lab., Johns Hopkins, Population Council, Protein Found., Rockefeller Bros. Fund, Sloan-Kettering Inst. Served as ensign U.S. Naval Aviation Corps, 1918-19. Decorated officer Order Brit. Empire; recipient award for exceptional civilian service, 1946, Longacre award Aero. Med. Assn., 1948, Priestley award Dickinson Coll., 1956; Gold medal Internat. Ben Franklin Soc., 1958; medal Soc. Promoting Internat. Sci. Relationships, 1959, Gold medal Holland Soc., 1961, George Washington award Hungarian-Am. Soc., 1962, Franklin medal Franklin Inst., 1962; Presdl. Medal of Freedom, 1964; Pub. Welfare medal Nat. Acad. Scis., 1964; Nat. Sci. medal, 1969. Fellow A.A.A.S. (pres. 1952); mem. or hon. mem. many Am., fgn. profl. socs. (sometime officer several). Baptist. Clubs: N.Y. Yacht, University, Century, Lotos (N.Y.C.); Rittenhouse (Phila.); Maryland (Balt.); Seal Harbour Yacht; Cosmos (Washington); Athenaeum (London, Eng.). Home: New York City, N.Y., Died Nov. 17, 1975.

BRONNER, AUGUSTA FOX (MRS. WILLIAM HEALY), psychologist; b. Louisville, July 22, 1881; d. Gustave and Hannah (Fox) Bronner; grad. Louisville Normal School, 1901; B.S., Teachers College (Columbia U.), 1906, A.M., 1909, Ph.D., 1914; m. William Healy, 1932. Teacher pub. grammer sch., 1901-03; asst. in edn., Teachers Coll. (Columbia), 1911-13; teacher high sch., Louisville, Ky., 1906-11; psychologist, Juvenile Psychopathic Inst., Chicago, 1913-17; asst. dir. Judge Baker Guidance Center, Boston, 1917, dir. 1917-46, now dir. emeritus; asso. dir. Research Inst. Human Relations, Yale, 1929-32; lectr. School Edn., Boston U.; lectr. mental hygiene, Simmons Coll., 1942-49. Fellow Am. Acad. Arts and Sciences; mem. Am. Psychol. Assn., Assn. Clin. Criminologist, Am. Orthopsychiatric Assn., Nat. Conf. of Social Work, Ethical Culture Society. Club: Boston Women's (Boston). Author: Treatmant and What Happened Afterward, 1940. Contbr. numerous articles to psychol. jours. Home: Clearwater Beach, Fla.†

BRONOWSKI, JACOB, mathematician; b. Poland, Jan. 18, 1908; s. Abram and Celia (Flatto) B.; M.A., Jesus Coll., Cambridge (Eng.) U., 1930, Ph.D., 1933; m. Rita Coblentz, Feb. 17, 1941; children—Lisa Anne, Judith Jill, Nicole Ruth, Clare Beth Alice. Came to U.S., 1964. Sr. lectr. Univ. Coll., Hull. Eng., 1934-42; sr. scientist Ministry Home Security, 1942-45; asst. dir. Ministry Works, 1946-50; dir. Coal Research Establishment, Nat. Coal Bd., 1950-59, dir. gen. process devel., 1959-63; research prof., fellow, dir. council for biology in human affairs Salk Inst. Biol. Studies, San Diego, 1964-74. Carnegie vis. prof. Mass. Inst. Tech., 1953; lectr. man and nature Am. Mus. Natural History, 1965; Eastman Meml. vis. prof. U. Rochester, 1965; Condon lectr. Ore. State U., 1967; Silliman lectr. Yale, 1967; Bampton lectr. Columbia, 1969; Meilon lectr., Washington, 1969. Sci. dep., joint target group, Washington, also Brit. chiefs staff mission to Japan, 1945-46; head projects UNESCO, 1947-48. Hon. fellow Jesus Coll., Cambridge U., 1967. Fellow Royal Soc. Lit., World Acad. Art and Sci.; fgn. hon. mem. Am. Acad. Arts and Scis. (Blashfield address 1966). Author: The Poet's Defence, 1939, 66; William Blake, A Man Without a Mask, 1944; The Common Sense of Science, 1951; The Face of Violence, 1954, 67; Science and Human Values, 1958; Selections from William Blake, 1958; (with Bruce Mazlish) The Western Intellectual Tradition, 1960; Insight, 1964; The Abacus and The Rose; A New Dialogue on Two World Systems, 1965; William Blake and The Age of Revolution, 1965; The Identity of Man, 1965; Nature and Knowledge, 1969; The Ascent of Man, 1973. Home: La Jolla Cal. Died Aug. 22, 1974.

BROOK, CLIVE, actor; b. London, Eng., June 1, 1891; s. George Alfred and Charlotte (Melton) B.; ed. under pvt. tutelage; m. Mildred Evelyn, Sept. 26, 1921; children—Faith Evelyn, Clive Lyndon. Served as officer in Machine Gun Corps, British Army, 1914-18, World War. Entered upon stage career in England, 1918; came to U.S., 1924; has appeared in Christine of the Hungry Heart, Enticement, The Mirage, Playing with Souls, Declasse, If Marriage Fails, Woman Hater, The Homemaker, Pleasure Buyers, Seven Sinners, Compromise, Three Faces East, When Love Grows Cold, Why Girls Go Back Home, You Never Know Women, For Alimony Only, Popular Sin, Barbed Wire, Afraid To Love, Underworld, Hula, Devil Dancer, French Dressing, Midnight Madness, Yellow Lily, Perfect Crime, Heliotrope, Interference, Four Feathers, Dangerous Woman, Charming Sinners, Sherlock Holmes, Laughing Lady, Slightly Scarlet, Sweethearts and Wives, Anybody's Woman, East Lynne, Tarnished Lady, The Lawyer's Secret, Silence, 24 Hours, Husband's Holiday, Shanghai Express, Man From Yesterday, The Night of June 13th, Return of Sherlock Holmes, Cavalcade, Midnight Club, If I Were Free, Gallant Lady, Dover Road, Let's Try Again, Loves of a Dictator, Dressed to Thrill. Address: Hollywood Cal. Died Nov. 18, 1974.

BROOKE, JAMES J., banker; b. Russia, Jan. 24, 1879; s. Isidore and Sarah (Bacrack) B.; student New York U. 1900-03; m. Blanche Keiter, Sept. 28, 1909; children—Constance Sarah, Alvin Boris. Came to U.S., 1894, naturalized citizen, 1900. Vice pres. Nat. Title Guaranty Co., Brooklyn from 1924; pres. Elmont Cemetery, Inc., Elmont Monumental Works, Climont Realty Corpn.; v.p. Bedford Nat. Bank; treas. Heights Theatres, Inc., Curtiss Gardens, Inc. Trustee Brooklyn Hebrew Orphan Asylum; dir. Y.M.H.A., Brooklyn Federation of Jewish Charities, United Jewish Aid Socs. Mem. Brooklyn Mus., Bnai Brith, Brooklyn Chamber Commerce. Clubs: Unity, Brooklyn, Economy, Lawyers, Brooklyn Real Estate (pres.), Fresh Meadow Country. Home: Brooklyn, N.Y.†

BROOKEBOROUGH, VISCOUNT (BROOKE), prime minister of Northern Ireland; b. Colebrooke, Brookeborough, Northern Ireland, June 9, 1888 s. Sir Arthur and Gertrude Isabella (Batson) B.; ed. Winchester and Royal Mil. Coll., Sandhurst; married Cynthia Sergison, 1919; children—Basil Julian David (killed in action, 1943), Capt. John Warden, Henry Alan (killed in action, 1945). Fifth baronet, created 1822, created viscount 1952; Privy Councillor North Ireland, 1933. Elected member Parliament North Ireland, 1929; minister agr., 1933-41; minister commerce and prodn., 1941-43; prime minister and minister of commerce and prodn., 1943-45; prime minister, 1943-63. Served in 10th Royal Hussars, World War I, 1914-19. Decorated Comdr. Order of British Empire, Military Cross, Croix de Guerre, Home: Colebrooke, Brookeborough Northern Ireland. Died 1973.

BROOKS, JOHN B., army officer; b. New York, June 8, 1891; grad. Air Service Tactical Sch., 1924. Command and Gen. Staff Sch., 1925, Army War Coll., 1927, Commnd. 2d lt., Cavalry, Nov. 30, 1912; promoted through grades to col., Jan. 1, 1940; apptd. brig. gen., Oct. 25, 1940, maj. gen., Mar. 11, 1943. Served as comdg. gen., Newfoundland Base Command, 1943-44, also as mem. office joint chiefs of staff, 1944-45; commdg. gen., 11th Air Force, Aleutian Islands on V-J Day. Awarded Distinguished Service Medal, Legion of Merit (Navy), Distinguished Flying Cross, Air Medal; Companion of the Most Honorable Order of the Bath. Retired as maj. gen. for physical disability, Sept. 1946. Address: Greenwich, N.Y., Died Dec. 31, 1975.

BROOKS, PHILLIPS, ofcl. USIA; b. Eng. Feb. 28, 1921; A.B., Dartmouth, 1942; m. Carolyn Killary. Info. officer USIA, Washington, 1955; asst. cultural affairs officer, Paris, 1955-59, dir. library sers., 1959-60; dep. cultural affairs officer, Mexico D.F., 1960-62; cultural affairs officer USIA, Beirut, 1967-71, pub. affairs officer, 1971-72; chief publs. div., Washington, 1972-74; cultural affairs officer, London, 1974-75. Died Jan. 10, 1975.

BROOKS, ROBERT PRESTON, educator; b. Miledgeville, Ga., July 23, 1881; s. James Henry and Anna (Moore) B.; grad. Ga. Mil. Coll., 1899; A.B., U. of Ga., 1904; B.A., Oxford Univ., England, 1907; fellow in Am. history, U. of Wis., 1911-12, Ph.D., 1912; m. Josephine Reid, June 25, 1908. Assistant prof. history U. of Ga., 1907-12, asso. prof., 1912-14, prof., 1914-19; mgr. publicity, 4th Nat. Bank, Macon, Ga., 1919-20; dean Coll. of Business Adminstrn., University of Georgia, 1920-45; dean of faculties, 1945-47, dir. Inst. Pub. Affairs, from 1929, prof. econs. emeritus; Kahn traveling fellow, 1930-31; asso. editor Southern Banker, 1924-25. Mem. com. of selection of Rhodes Scholarships for Ga. Mem. Ga. Fact Finding Com. from 1937, and author of its studies on Taxation; dir. Inst. for Assn., Southern Econ. Assn. (pres. 1934), Am. Assn. of Collegiate Schs., of Business (pres. 1938-39), Georgia Historical Society, Alpha Tau Omega, Phi Beta Kappa, Beta Gamma Sigma. Democrat. Methodist. Author: A Bibliography of Georgia History, 1910; A History of Georgia, 1913; The Agrarian Revolution in Georgia, 1914, The Financial History of Georgia, 1732-1950, 1952; Georgia Studies, 1952. Joint editor A Bibliography of the South, 1917; Correspondence Addressed to John C. Calhoun, 1837-1849; The Independence Movement in India, 1931; Financing Government in Georgia, 1850-1944; Supervision of Local Government Finances in Georgia, 1948. Home: Athens, Ga.†

BROOKS, ROELIF HASBROUCK, clergyman; b. Poughkeepsie, N.Y., June 26, 1875; s. John R. and Ann (Ross) B.; B.A., Columbia, 1900, hon. M.A., 1910, S.T.D., 1930; Gen. Theol. Sem., 1903; M.A., King's Coll., N.S., 1921; S.T.D., Hobart Coll., 1924; D.C.L., University of the South, 1935; D.D., from Trinity College, 1940; married Julia Stuart Laing, Jan. 20, 1904; children—Emily Ferris (dec.), John. Deacon, 1902, priest, 1903, P.E. Ch.; asst., St. Michael's, Brooklyn, 1902, Ch. of the Messiah, Brooklyn, 1903-06; rector St. Paul's Ch., Albany, N.Y., 1906-26, St. Thomas' Ch., 1926-54, emeritus, from 1954; arch-deacon of Albany, 1917-26; del. Gen. P.E. Ch., 1919, 22, 27, 40, 43, 46, 49. Chaplain Conv., .. . (col.) 7th Regt. N.Y.; chaplain, assigned, 1941-42, 207th C.A., A.A.A., Camp Stewart, Ga., and Newport, R.I.; chaplain (brig. gen. ret.) 107th Regt. N.Y.; chaplain, N.Y. Chapter Mil, Order World Wars, 1944-46; chaplain. Military Order of World Wars, 1946-47, now chaplain St. Andrew's Soc., N.Y. Trustee Pomfret Sch., 1952-55, Cathedral of St. John The Divine (N.Y.), Gen. Theol. Sem. Trinity Sch., Greer Sch. Hope Farm N.Y.; trustee St. Peter's Ch., Ogunquit, Me., 1926-53, pres. bd., 1936-53. Received King's Medal for Service in Cause of Freedom, Mem. bd. Ho. of Holy Comforter N.Y., Episcopal City Missions. Mem. Newcomen Soc., Delta Kappa Epsilon. Mason (33°); Past Grand Chaplain. Clubs: Columbia Univ., Union (New York); Ft. Orange (Albany); Tuxedo (Tuxedo Park, N.Y.); Knickerbockers-Greys (chaplain); Metropolitan. Home: New York City, N.Y.†

BROOKS, WILLIAM F., editor and writer; b. Kansas City, Mo., Nov. 2, 1902; s. James Lucian and Willa May (McCully) B.; student U. Mo., 1920; m. Louise Daly, July 10, 1944; 1 son, William F. Newspaper work Sedalia (Mo.) Capital, 1917; worked various newspapers in Middle West, including Kansas City Star, 1920-26; joined A.P., 1926, served in Washington and N.Y.C. as exec. editor feature service, 1926-30, exec. asst. to gen. mgr., 1930-33, exec. news editor, 1933-37; mng. dir. The Asso. Press of Great Britain, London, 1937-40; advt. agy. bus., N.Y.C., 1940-41; exec. editor Forbes mag., 1941-42; dir. news and spl. events, also dir. internat. relations, NBC, 1942-46, v.p., 1946-50, chief pub. relations officer, 1950-52; corp. cons., 1953-59; pres. William F. Brooks & Assos., Inc., N.Y.C., 1959-61; nat. news editor N.Y. Daily News, 1961-75. Presbyn. Clubs: Press (Washington); Dutch Treat, Overseas Press (N.Y.C.); Savage (London, Eng.). Author: Radio News Writing, 1948. Home: New York City N.Y. Died Jan. 27, 1975.

BROOKSHER, WILLIAM RILEY, radiologist; b. Yellville, Ark., 1894; M.D., Tulane U., 1919. Intern, Binghamton (N.Y.) City Hosp., 1919-20; practiced medicine specializing in radiology, Ft. Smith, Ark., 1921-71; roentgenologist St. Edward Mercy Hosp., Municipal Hosp., Clarksville, Ark., Meml. Hosp., Mena, Ark.; cons. radiology Atoka Meml. Hosp., Scott County Hosp., Waldron, Ark., Boonville (Ark.) City Hosp., Turner Meml. Hosp., Ozark, Ark. Diplomate Am. Bd. Radiology. Fellow Am. Coll. Radiology (v.p. 1949); mem. A.M.A., Am. Radium Soc., Am. Roentgen Ray Soc., Brit. Inst. Radiology, Radiol. Soc. N.Am., Am. Cancer Soc. (past pres. Ark. chpt.), Ark. (pres. 1954-55), Sebastian County (pres. 1924) med. socs., Kappa Sigma. Editor: Ark. Med. Jour., 20 yrs. Home: Ft. Smith, Ark. Died Sept. 4, 1971; buried Forest Park, Ft. Smith, Ark.

BROREIN, CARL D., telephone co. executive; b. Buckland, O., Nov. 3, 1895; s. Jacob Frederick and Cora I. (Buther) B.; A.B., U. of N.M.; m. Ethel L. Kieke, Feb. 17, 1919; children—Carl D., Jr., William J., Marjorie L., Robert L. Began career with Mentmore (N.M.) Cerillos Coal Co., 1919; sec. Peninsular Telephone Co., Tampa, Fla., 1920-23, asst. to gen. mgr., 1923-26, v.p., gen. mgr., 1926-38, pres., gen. mgr., 1938-57; pres. General Telephone Company of Fla., 1957-61, chmn. bd. consultants, from 1961; dir. Gen. Tel. & Electronics Corp., Marine Bank & Trust Co., First Federal Savings & Loan Assn. (Tampa, Fla.), Gulf Life Ins. Co., 1st Fla. Bancorp., Sunshine State Mortgage Corp., Midway Marine Bank. Mem. regional exec. com., past pres. Gulf Ridge Council Boy Scouts of America. Past president Independent Pioneer Telephone Assn. Served as capt., U.S. Marine Corps, Aviation Sect., 1917-19. Exec. v. chmn., State Defense Council of Fla., 1940-46. Cons. Communications Div., W.P.B., 1942-45. Treasurer and past president of United States Independent Telephone Assn.; dir. (past pres.) Fla. State Chamber of Commerce; past vice pres. Chamber Commerce of U.S., 1942; past mem. adv. bd. Fla. Hist. Research Inst.; Domestic Communications Operating Industry Adv. Com. (NSRB). Pres. Fla. State Fair and Gasparilla Assn.; past. pres. Tampa Urban League; past chmn. Hillsborough County Budget Bd. Chmn. exec. com., trustee U. Tampa. Mem. Golden Eagles. Club: Exchange (past pres.). Home: Tampa, Fla., Deceased.

BROUGHTON, CARRIE LOUNGEE, library exec.; b. Raleigh, N.C., Sept. 16, 1879; d. Needham Bryant and Caroline Rickards (Lewis) Broughton; student N.C. Coll. for Women, Greensboro, 1896-97; Peace Jr. Coll., Raleigh, 1898-99, Meredith Coll., Raleigh, 1899-1901; unmarried. Appointed asst. state librarian, 1902, librarian from 1918 (1st woman in state to hold state office). Chmn. N.C. Library Commn. Mem. A.L.A., N.C. Library Assn., N.C. Hist. Assn., the Y.W.C.A. of Raleigh (life member), Delta Kappa Gamma (hon.). Democrat. Baptist. Compiler: Bibliography of genealogical material in N.C. State Library, 1926; Marriage and Death notices appearing in newspapers from 1799-1856 (to be continued), 1942. Home: Raleigh, N.C.†

BROUGHTON, CHARLES FREDERIC, textile co. exec.; b. Beverly, Mass., Mar. 8, 1878; s. Thomas Payson Bartlett and Emma (Pitman) B.; ed. pub. schs.; Dr. Textile Sci., New Bedford Inst. Tech.; m. Clara Putnam Smith, Sept. 12, 1904 (died Mar. 30, 1947); children—Carolyn (Mrs. Richard Hawkins Gee), Martha (Mrs. Donald Francis Horne); married 2d, Helen L. Horton, April 2, 1948. Clerk Amoskeag Mfg. Co., 1895, purchasing agt., 1906-11, supt. weaving, 1911-13; asst. mgr. N.E. Cotton Yarn Co., 1913-17; asst. treas. Wamsutta Mills, 1917-19, treas., gen. mgr., 1919-48, dir. 1921, pres., 1934-48, chmn. bd. 1948-54, vice chmn. bd., 1954-58, ret.; dir. First Safe Deposit Nat. Bank of New Bedford; mem. dirs.' adv. bd. State St. Bank & Trust Co. (Boston); trustee New Bedford Five Cents Savings Bank. Trustee Swain Sch. of Design, St. Luke's Hosp. Named New Bedford Man of Year, 1956. Unitarian. Mason. Clubs: Wamsutta, Country (New Bedford). Home: South Dartmouth, Mass.†

BROWER, DANIEL, psychologist; b. Bklyn., Mar. 27, 1916; s. William and Edith (Korant) B.; A.B., N.Y.U., 1940, M.A., 1942, Ph.D., 1946; student Columbia, 1940-42, New Sch. for Social Research, 1942-45; m. Judith L. Fagen, Dec. 20, 1942 (div.); 1 son, William Charles. Lectr. psychology N.Y.U., 1943-52; asst. prof. City U. N.Y., 1946-50; asst. med. psychology N.Y.U., Bellevue Med. Center, 1945-46; lectr. Pratt Inst. Tech., 1948-49; asso. prof. dept. psychology Montclair (N.J.) State Coll., 1958-67, prof. psychology, chmn. dept., 1967-74; practice clin. and child psychology, Montclair, 1946-74. Cons. Bellevue Psychiat. Hosp., Essex County Hosp. and Guidance Clinic, St. Barnabas Hosp., Montclair Guidance Center, Kingston Av. Hosp. Served with USAAF, 1942-43. Diplomate Am. Bd. Clin. Psychology. Fellow Am. Psychol. Assn., A.A.A.S., Projective Soc., Am. Orthopsychiat. Assn.; mem. Sigma Xi, Psi Chi. Contbr. articles profl. jours., books. Home: Montclair, N.J. Died Nov. 4, 1974.

BROWER, REUBEN ARTHUR, educator; b. Lanesboro, Pa., May 5, 1908; s. Arthur and Hannah Adeline (Taylor) B.; B.A. summa cum laude, Amherst Coll., 1930, Litt.D., 1964; B.A., Cambridge U., 1932, M.A., 1936; Ph.D., Harvard, 1936; D.Litt., Amherst Coll., 1964; m. Helen Porter, Sept. 12, 1934; children—Jonathan, Richard, Ellen. Tutor English and classics Harvard, Cambridge, Mass., 1932-36, instr. English, 1936-39, prof., 1953-71, Henry B. and Anna M. Cabot prof. English lit., 1971-75, master Adams House, 1954-68; asst. prof. Greek and English, Amherst Coll., 1939-44, asso. prof., 1944-48, class of 1880 prof. Greek and English, 1948-53. Faculty Bread Loaf Sch. Eng., summers 1940, 41, 47, 51; vis. prof., Fulbright fellow Oxford U., 1968-69; Martin Classical lectr. Oberlin Coll., 1970; Phi Beta Kappa vis. scholar, 1971-72. Trustee, Radcliffe Coll., 1963-71, English Inst., 1969-75. Guggenheim fellow, 1956-57, 65-66; fellow Center Advanced study Behavioral Scis., 1961-62; fellow Nat. Endowment for humanities, 1974; overseas fellow Churchill Coll., Cambridge U., 1974. Mem. Classical Assn. N.E., Soc. Fellows of Harvard (sr. fellow), Club of Odd Volumes, Modern Lang. Assn., A.A.U.P., Acad. Arts and Scis., Phi Beta Kappa (Christian Gauss award 1960). Club: Century Assn. (N.Y.C.). Author: The Fields of Light, 1951; Alexander Pope: The Poetry of Allusion, 1959; The Poetry of Robert Frost (Explicator award 1964), 1963; Hero and Saint: Shakespeare and the Graeco-Roman Heroic Tradition, 1971; Mirror on Mirror: Translation, Imitation, Parody, 1974. Editor: On Translation (hon. mention Harvard Faculty prize), 1959; (with R. Poirer) In Defense of Reading, 1962; John Dryden, 1962; Jane Austen; Mansfield Park, 1965; Shakespeare; Coriolanus, 1966; (with W.H. Bond) Pope's Iliad, 1965; Forms of Lyric, 1970; Harvard English Studies, II, 1971; (with H. Vendler and J. Hollander) I.A. Richards: Essays in his Honor, 1973. Contbr. to various books; articles in mags., learned jours. Mem. editorial bd. Harvard English Studies, 1969-75. Home: Belmont, Mass. Died Mar. 27, 1975; interred Lanesboro, Pa.

BROWN, ALICE COOKE, educator; b. Westfield, Mass., Apr. 13, 1913; d. William Alfred and Kate (Gault) Cooke; A.B., Middlebury Coll., 1935; M.A., N.Y.U., 1939, Ph.D., 1948; postgrad. (fellow) Columbia, 1940; m. John Hull Brown, June 30, 1947. Tchr., Rutherford (N.J.) High Sch., 1937-45; tchr. history and English, Fairleigh Dickinson Coll., 1945; dean freshman women, dir. admissions Middlebury Coll., 1945-47; prof., chmn. dept. history and govt. U. Hartford, 1953-63, dean women Hillyer Coll., 1953-62, univ. archivist, 1962-63; faculty Green Mountain Coll., Poultney, Vt., 1963-74, prof. history, 1967-74, chmn. social scis. div., 1966-74. Moderator TV series As We Were, WNBC-TV, 1959, Americana, 1960; exhibited oil paintings group shows, Bridport, Goshen, Vergennes, Chaffee Art Gallery, Rutland, Poultney, Vt., U. Hartford, Green Mountain Coll. Mem. evaluation com. social studies Conn. Dept. Edn., 1959-63; overseer Old Sturbridge Village, 1966-74; mem. Mayor of Hartford Commn. Civil War Centennial; mem. U.S. com. for UN Internat. Children's Emergency Fund. Mem. Am. Assn. U. Women (past pres. Vt. div.; chmn. mass media and edn. com. Conn. div. 1958-60), Soc. for Preservation Indian Lore, Inc., Assn. Higher Edn., N.E.A., U. Hartford Womens Assn., New Eng. Polit. Sci. Assn., League Women Voters, Am. Soc. Pub. Adminstrn. (exec. bd.), Conn. Antiquarian and Landmark Soc., Vt., Conn. hist. socs., So. Vt. Art Center, Hartford Civil War Round Table (bd. govs.), Service Bur. Women's Orgns., Soc. Desc. Founders Hartford, Soc. Founders Norwich (Conn.), Vt. Acad. Arts and Scis. (v.p. 1967-69, trustee), Vt. Council on Arts, Sigma Kappa, Delta Gamma, Pi Lambda Theta. Clubs: Soroptimist (past pres. Hartford, del. nat. conv. N.Y.C. 1956); Faculty Women's Author: History of the University of Hartford, 1959; Connecticut's Role in the Civil War, 1959; Connecticut's Roots, 1963; Mrs. Lincoln's Closest Friend, 1963; Early American Herb Recipes, 1966; Vermont's Role in American Art; also radio and TV scripts; articles in field. Home: Brandon, Vt. Died Nov. 3, 1974; buried East Lawn Cemetery, Williamstown, Mass.

BROWN, BRIAN, author, lecturer; b. Bellivor, Co. Meath, Ireland, Mar. 11, 1881; s. Thomas and Margaret (Smyth) B.; ed. Christian Brothers Acad., Co. Meath; unmarried. Came to U.S. 1898; concert tenor singer. Catholic. Mem. Oriental Soc. Clubs: Authors, Advertising Cleff (New York); Cold Stream Golf (Hempsteda, L.I.). Author: The Dynamic Power of the Inner Mind, 1923. Compiler: The Wisdom of the Chinese, 1920; The Wisdom of the Hindus, 1921; The Wisdom of the Egyptians, 1923; The Wisdom of the Hebrews, 1923; The Story of Confucius—His Life and Sayings; The Story of Buddha and Buddhism; Power and Beauty in the Speaking and Singing Voice (Kavo-Kanto method of voice developemnt), 1929. Lecturer on the history and application of phonology.†

BROWN, DUDLEY B(RADSTREET) W(ILLIAMS), utilities exec.; b. Concord, Mass., June 6, 1908; s. Franklin Q. and Ida (Eldredge) B.; A.B., Harvard, 1932, grad. study, 1932-33; m. Jane S. Acheson, Sept. 1941; 1 son, David Stuart. With Dept. Agr., 1933-36, U.S. Cane Sugar Refiners Assn., 1936-38; v.p. Inland Sugar Co., 1938-40, Columbia Aircraft Corp., 1940-41, Aircraft Service Corp., 1945-48; pres. Bay Colony Co., 1948-49; v.p. Milwaukee Gas Light Co., 1949-50, dir., exec. v.p., 1950-52, pres. 1952-55; vice president, secretary, director Am. Natural Gas Co., 1955-61, dir., consultant, 1961-75. Served from ensign to comdr. USN, 1941-45; comdr. USNR. Mem. Mil. Order World Wars, Soc. Mayflower Descs., Colonial Order of Acorn, Am. Gas Association. Clubs: Nat. Press (Washington), Chevy Chase (Washington); Harvard, N.Y. Yacht (N.Y.C.). Home: Lantana, Fla. Died June 9, 1975.

BROWN, EDWARD FISHER, dairy products exec.; b. N.Y. City, Oct. 2, 1889; s. Samuel and Bertha (Fisher) B.; law student N.Y.U., 1908-10; m. Nathalie Boshko, Mar. 30, 1922; children—David, Carolyn Baily (Mrs. Geoffrey Carpenter Doyle), Edward Fisher II. Field agt., later legislative rep. Nat. Child Labor Commn., 1910-13; asso. with Willard D. Straight of J. P. Morgan & Co. as dir. Bur. Welfare Sch. Children, organizing and dir. N.Y. Sch. Lunch Com., 1913-17, George W. Perkins in development of N.Y.-N.J. Palisades Interstate Park, 1917-21, Thomas W. Lamont in orgn. and direction Diphtheria Prevention Commn., concurrently deputy commr. N.Y. Health Dept., and Div. Noise Abatement and Loose Milk commns., 1928-31; impartial chmn. in labor disputes N.Y. garment industry, 1917-20; field sec. Playground and Recreation Assn. Am., 1921-23; organizer, dir. Santa Barbara (Calif.) Community Arts Assn., 1923-24; exec. dir. Child Welfare Com. Am., Inc., 1925-28; pres. Health News Services Inc., syndicating sci. news, 1932-42; asst. to pres. National Dairy Products Corporation, New York City, 1946-52, v.p., from 1952, ret.; exec. v.p. Milk Research Council, 1932-42. Served from lt. col. to col. transportation corps, AUS, 1942-46, ETO; mem. Res., 1946-50. Decorated Army Commendation Ribbon with cluster (U.S.) Mil. Order of Kutuzov (Russia). Fellow Am. Pub. Health Assn., A.I.M.; mem. Am. Transportation Assn. (dir.). Clubs: Army and Navy (Washington); Metropolitan (N.Y.C.); Beach (Southampton, L.I.). Author several books and articles relating to noise abatement, milk purification, nutrition, pub. health. Home: New York City N.Y. Died May 1973.

BROWN, ERNEST G(AY), business exec.; b. New Haven, Conn., June 22, 1896; s. Frank Martin and Margaret (Donegan) B.; Ph.B., Yale, 1916; student Grad. Sch. of Bus. Adminstrn., Harvard, 1920-21; m. Pearl Van O'Linda Kellam, Apr. 19, 1922; children—Eautha Kellam, Margaret Ernestine (Mrs. Sylvester P. Larkin), Ray Ashbell (Mrs. Norman E. Swanson). Engr. Acme Wire Co., New Haven, Conn., 1917-28; asso. sec. Taylor Soc., N.Y. City, 1929; with U.S. Rubber Co., N.Y.C., from 1929, engr., factory mgr., 1929-41, prodn. mgr., 1941-42, gen. mgr., from 1942, v.p., 1945-57, 59-60; chmn. bd. Texas-U.S. Chem. Co., 1955-59. Served as lt. ordinance, U.S. Army, 1918. Episcopalian. Home: Darien Conn. Died Dec. 21, 1974.

BROWN, FAY (CLUFF), physicist; b. Washington C.H., Ohio, Nov. 23, 1881; s. Argo A. and Jennie Frances (Cluff) B.; A.B., Ind. U., 1904; A.M., U. of Ill., 1906; Ph.D., Princeton, 1908; post-grad. work U. of Ill., U. of Chicago; m. Dora Davidson, July 14, 1908; children—Herman Cluff, Barbara Esther, Robert Bruce, Annabel. Instr. physics, U. of Ill., 1905-07; instr., asst. prof. and asso. prof. physics, State U. of Ia., 1909-19. Capt. and maj. Ordnance Dept. U.S. Army, in charge ballistics and testing airplane bombs, Feb. 1918-Aug. 1919; asst. dir. Bur. of Standards, 1919-23; acting dir. same, Jan.-Apr. 1923, asst. dir., 1923-27; chief examiner Civil Service Commn., 1927; director Museums of the Peaceful Arts, New York, 1927-32, director of annual science exhbn., 1932-38; curator dept. of physics, Museum of Science and Industry, Chicago, 1937-40; staff member of Mass. Institute Tech., 1940-47. Member Interdepartmental Committee on Reclassification of Scientific Employees, 1924; mem. President's Interdepartmental Patent Com., 1924-27; dir. Art Alliance, New York, 1927; mem. Nat. Research Council. Fellow A.A.A.S., Am. Physical Soc. (councillor); member Washington Acad. Sciences, Philos. Soc. Washington, Gamma Alpha, Phi Beta Kappa, Sigma Xi. Representative of Dept. of Commerce on Am. Engring. Standards Com. Conglist. Mason (Shriner). Clubs: Cosmos (Washington, D.C.); Federal (past pres.), Princeton. Writer of numerous papers and articles giving results of researches in pure and applied physics, chemistry, and also on subjects of general interest. Home: Washington, D.C.†

BROWN, FRED, hotel cons., cosmetic co. exec.; b. Coleman County, Tex., Dec. 11, 1902; s. S. E. and Eugenia (Canady) B.; B.A., Abilene Christian Coll., 1923; m. Elnora Dulaney, Jan. 31, 1926 (dec. 1967); m. 2d, Bobbye Bowen Ogden, 1969. Mgr., Baker Hotel, Mineral Wells, Tex., 1938-43, 49-54; v.p. Eastland Nat. Bank (Tex.), 1943-49; mgr. Crazy Water Hotel, Mineral Wells, 1954-57; dir. sales and pub. relations Hotel Adolphus, Dallas, 1957-63, resident mgr., 1961-63; gen. mgr. Inn. of Six Flags, Arlington, Tex., 1963-65; ind. hotel cons., Dallas, 1965-68; exec. v.p. Ind. Innkeepers Internat., Dallas, 1966-68; pres. Innkeepers Mgmt. & Services, Inc., 1967-74; pres., dir. Florence Miller Cosmetics, Inc., 1968-74. Trustee, mem. exec. com. Presbyn. Village Dallas. Mem. Dallas, Mineral Wells chambers commerce. Democrat. Presbyn. (ruling elder). Club: Lakewood Country (Dallas). Home: Dallas Tex. Died Apr. 1, 1974; buried Mineral Wells, Tex.

BROWN, FREDERIC L., school principal; b. Newark, N.Y., May 20, 1878; s. Benjamin Franklin and Mary Louise (Lee) B.; B.S., Syracuse U., 1900; m. Mary Agnes Thompson, of Cazenovia, N.Y., Sept. 12, 1905; children—Alice Winifred, Barbara Charlotte. Teacher, 1900-06; owner and principal Brown School of Tutoring, New York from 1906. Mem. School Masters' Assn. Republican. Methodist. Clubs: Andiron, West Side, Thousand Island Yacht. Home: New York City, N.Y.†

BROWN, FREDERICK RONALD, physician; b. Castlebar, P.Q., Can., Dec. 7, 1890; S. G. Frederick and Violet (Thorburn) B.; student Danville Acad.; A.B., McGill U., 1913; M.D. magna cum laude, Harvard, 1917; m. Florence E. Wilson, Sept. 19, 1922; children—Frederick, Margaret (wife of Lt. Lloyd W. Goddu), Louise, Anne. Came to U.S., 1923. naturalized, 1930. Intern, B.C.H. Hosp., 1917; instr. medicine McGill U., 1920-23, Harvard Med. Sch., 1924-25; vis. physician, Montreal Gen. Hosp., 1920-23; asst. med. dir., New Eng. Mut. Life Ins. Co., Boston, 1928-38, asso. med. dir. from 1938; mem. staff Winchester Hosp. Mem. Town Meeting, Winchester. Served as capt., med. corps Royal Canadian Army, World War I. Mem. A.M.A., Mass. Med. Soc., Life Ins. Med. Dirs. Assn. Republican. Club: St. Botolph (Boston). Home: Winchester, Mass.†

BROWN, HAROLD EUGENE, contractor: b. Salina, Kan., Sept. 19, 1917; s. Herbert Lee and Alfreda Margarita (Sly) B.; B.S., Kan. State U., 1939; m. Mary Alice Arnold, Sept. 6, 1939; children—Gary, Michael, Alan. Trail locator Navajo Service, Indian div. Civilian Conservation Corps, Chinle, Ariz., 1939; jr. engr. Internat. Boundary Commn., Las Cruces, N.M., 1939-41; steel detailer Am. Bridge Co., Trenton, 1941; chief draftsman Wilson & Co., engrs., Colorado Springs, Colo. and Albuquerque, 1941-44; pres. Brown & Brown, Inc., contractors, Salina, Kan., 1946-72; dir. Planters State Bank. Served with USNR, 1944-45. Mem. Nat. Soc. Profl. Engrs., Kan. Engr. Soc., Kan. Contractors Assn., Asso. Gen. Contractors, Salina C. of C. (dir. 1957-60), Am. Legion, V.F.W. Clubs: Elks, Country (dir. 1961-64, pres. 1964) (Salina). Home: Salina, Kan. Died Aug. 12, 1972; interred Gypsum Hill Cemetery, Salina, Kan.

BROWN, HARRY ALVIN, Coll. president; b. Liberty, Me., Aug. 19, 1879; s. Alonzo Alvin and Caroline Betsey (Knowlton) B.; A.B. Bates Coll., Lewiston, Me., 1903; A.B., U. of Colo., 1907, A.M., 1923; Ed.D., Bates Coll., 1925, Miami U., 1925; m. Florence Maria Seaver, Dec. 23, 1908. Teacher rural schs., 1899-1902; supervising prin. schs., Liberty, Me., 1903-04; dist. supt. schs., Salem, and Hudson, N.H., 1904-05; superintendent of schs., Glasgow, Mont., 1907-09; dist. supt. schs., Colebrook and Errol, N.H., 1909-13; instr. psychology and edn., summer session State Normal Sch., Plymouth, N.H., 1912; dep. supt. pub. instrn., N.H., 1913-17, also dir. Bur. Ednl. Research, N.H.; instr. psychology and edn., summer session, State Normal Sch., Keene, N.H., 1916; asso. prof. edn. U. of Chicago, summer 1921; pres. State Teachers College, Oshkosh, 1917-30; pres. Ill. State Normal Univ. from 1930; instr. in edn., State Normal Sch., Keene, N.H., summer 1931. Member N.E.A. (com. on orgn. and adminstration secondary schs., 1916-19), Nat. Soc. for Study of Edn., Nat. Assn. Dirs. Ednl. Research, Am. Assn. Teachers Colleges, (com. on standards and surveys, 1922-26, chmn. 1925-26). Republican. Baptist. Mason. Clubs: Candlelight (pres. 1932-33), Rotary (Oshkosh). Lecturer and contbr. numerous articles on ednl. topics. Author: Latin in Secondary Schools, 1919. Home: Normal, Ill.†

BROWN, HARRY GUNNISON, prof. economics; b. Troy, N.Y., May 7, 1880; s. Milton Peers and Elizabeth H. (Gunnison) B.; B.A., Williams College, 1904; student Ohio State Univ., 1905-06; Ph.D., Yale Univ., 1909; L.H.D., Williams College, 1936; m. Fleda Philips, Aug. 31, 1911 (dec. Feb. 1952); children Cleone Elsa (Mrs. Robert C. Luckey), Phillips Hamlin, Richmond Flint; m. 2d, Elizabeth Read, May 29, 1953. Instr. economics, Yale, 1909-15; asst. prof. economics, 1915-16, asso. prof., 1916-18, prof., 1918-50, emeritus professor of economics U. Mo., after 1950, chmn. dept., 1916-31, 35-40, 42-47, acting dean, 1934-36, 42-46. Mem. Am. Economic Assn., Delta Sigma Rho, Alpha Pi Zeta, Alpha Kappa Psi. Author: Transportation Rates and Their Regulation, 1916; Principles of Commerce, 1916; The Economics of Taxation, 1924; The Economic Basis of Tax Reform, 1932; Basic Principles of Economics, 1942; 3d edit., 1955. Fiscal Policy, Taxation and Free Enterprise, 1946. Editorial bd. Am. Jour. Econs. and Sociology, 1941-75. Contbr. articles to profl. jours. Home: Columbia, Mo. Died Mar. 18, 1975; interred Cleon Cemetery, Pomona, Mich.

BROWN, HOWARD JUNIOR, physician; b. Peoria, Ill., Apr. 15, 1924; s. Frank Howard and Frances (Timmons) B.; B.A., Hiram (O.) Coll., 1945; M.D., Western Res. U., 1948. Intern, Univ. Hosp., Cleve., 1949-50; resident Jennings Meml. Hosp., Detroit, 1950-51, Detroit Receiving Hosp., 1952-54; staff physician UAW-CIO, Clinic, Detroit, 1951-52; dir. profl. services Health Ins. Plan Greater N.Y., 1954-61; med. dir. Gouverneur ambulatory care unit Beth Israel Med. Center, N.Y.C., 1961-66; health services adminstr. N.Y.C., 1966-68; asso. attending 1st div. Bellevue Hosp., N.Y.C., 1954-63; instr. medicine Columbia Coll. Phys. & Surg., 1956-63, lectr. Sch. Pub. Health and Adminstrv. Medicine, 1966-75; asso. prof. clin. medicine N.Y.C. Sch. Medicine, 1964-66, vis. lectr. Sch. Pub. Adminstrn., 1964-75; asso. attending medicine Beth Israel Hosp., 1956-69; asso. prof. community medicine Mt. Sinai Hosp. Sch., 1966-68, Albert Einstein Coll. Medicine, 1968-70; lectr. Yale Coll. Medicine, 1968-75; dir. community medicine Miseri Cordia, Fordham hosps., 1968-70; prof. pub. adminstrn., prof. preventive medicine N.Y. U., 1970-75. Mem. adv. bd. Regional Med. Programs. Served wtih AUS, 1943-44. Recipient citation N.Y. state Optometric Assn., dept. dentistry Beth Israel Hosp., Beth Israel Med. Center, 1966, Apollo award Am. Optometric Assn., 1965. Diplomate Am. Bd. Internal Medicine. Fellow Am. Pub. Health Assn., N.Y. Acad. Medicine; mem. Pub. Health Assn. N.Y.C. (Merit award 1965). Contbr. articles to profl. jours. Home: New York City, N.Y. Died Feb. 1, 1975.

BROWN, HUGH AUCHINCLOSS, elec. engr., author; widower; children—Samuel C., Hugh Auchincloss. Pres., Columbia U.'s Grand Army of the 49th St Era Mem. A.A.A.S. Author: Cataclysms of the Earth, 1967. Home: Douglaston, N.Y., Died Nov. 9, 1975.

BROWN, HUGH B., clergyman; b. Granger, Utah, Oct. 24, 1883; s. Homer Manley and Lydia J. (Brown) B.; student pub. schs., Salt Lake City; legal edn. and tng., mil tng., Alta., Can., Brigham Young U., U. Utah; m. Zina Young Card, June 17, 1908; children—Zina Lydia (Mrs. Guardello Brown), Zola Grace (Mrs. Waldo G. Hodson), LaJune (Mrs. Jerry Hay), Mary Myrtice (Mrs. Edwin R. Firmage), Hugh Card (dec.), Charles Manley, Margaret Alberta (Mrs. Clinton Jorgensen), Carol Rae (Mrs. George Sonntag). Latter Day Saints missionary to Gt. Britain, 1904-06, officers tng. sch., 1910-14; pres. Latter Day Saints Stake, Lethbridge, Alta., 1921-27, Salt Lake City, 1928-36; pres. Brit. Mission, 1937-40, 44-46; prof. Brigham Young U., 1946-50; asst. Council of Twelve, 1953-58; ordained an apostle, 1958, mem. first presidency. Former barrister, solicitor, Alta., 1921-27; practice of law, Salt Lake City, 1927-53; gen. mgr. Richland Oil Devel. Co. of Can., Ltd., 1950-53; lectr. Served to maj. Canadian Army, WWI. Author: Rational Faith, 1949; Eternal Quest, 1956; You and Your Marriage, 1960; Continuing the Quest, 1961; The Abundant Life, 1965; Vision and Valor, 1971. Home: Salt Lake City, Utah., Died Dec. 2, 1975.

BROWN, IVOR JOHN CARNEGIE, author, journalist; b. Penang, Malaya, Apr. 25, 1891; s. William Carnegie B.; ed. Cheltenham Coll., Ballioi Coll., Oxford; LL.D., St. Andrews, Aberdeen, 1950; m. Irene Hantschel, 1916. London drama critic, leader-writer Manchester (Eng.) Guardian, 1919-35; drama critic Saturday Review, 1923-30, Observer, 1929-54, Week End Review, 1930-34, Sketch, 1935-39, Punch, 1940-42; Shute lectr. art Theatre at Liverpool U., 1926; prof. drama Royal Soc. Lit., 1939; dir. drama Council for Encouragement Music and the Arts, 1940-42; editor Observer, 1942-48, asso. editor, hon. dir., 1948-54; chmn. Brit. Drama League, 1954-65; gov. Old Vic, Royal Shakespeare Theatre. Fellow Inst. Journalists. Decorated knight Order of Dannebrog (Denmark); comdr. Order Brit. Empire. Clubs: Garrick, Saville. Author: The Meaning of Democracy, 1919; Masques and Phases, 1926; Parties of the Play, 1928; Brown Studies, 1930; Master Sanguine, 1934; Heart of England, 1935; The Great and the Goods, 1937; Life Within Reason, Amazing Monument (with George Fearon), 1939; A Word in Your Ear, 1942; Just Another Word, 1943; A Book of Words, 1945; I Give You My Word, 1946; Say the Word, 1948; Shakespeare, 1949; Having the Last Word, 1946; Say the Word, 1948; Shakespeare, 1949; Having the Last Word, 1951; Winter in London, 1951; I Break My Word, 1951; Summer in Scotland, 1952; A Word in Edgeways, 1953; The Way of My World, 1954; Balmoral Theater, Chosen Words, 1955; Dark Ladies, 1957; Words in Our Time, A Book of England, 1958; London, 1960; Shakespeare in His Time, 1960; Words in Season, 1961; How Shakespeare Spent the Day, 1963; Dickens in His Time, 1963; What is a Play?, 1964; Bernard Shaw in His Time, History of London, 1965; A Ring of Words, 1966; The Women in Shakespeare's Life, 1967; Rhapsody of Words, 1969; Shakespeare and the Actors, 1970; Old and Young, 1971; A Charm of Names, 1972. Address: London, England. Died Apr. 1974.

BROWN, JOSEPH ex-congressman; b. Jasper, Tenn., Feb. 11, 1880; s. Hon. Foster V. and Lulu (Farrior) B.; B.S., Cumberland U., LL.B., 1904; m. Hester Jefferson McClain, of Lebanon, Tenn., 1904; 1 dau., Farrior. Admitted to Tenn. bar, 1904, and began practice at Chattanooga; jr. mem. firm, Brown, Spurlock & Brown; mem. 67th Congress (1921-23), 3d Tenn. Dist. Chmn. Rep. State Exec. Com. for Tenn. Presbyn. Mem. Am. and Tenn. State bar assns. Mason, Elk. Club: Mountain City. Home: Chattanooga, Tenn.†

BROWN, MONTREVILLE JAY, lawyer; b. Morris, Minn., June 13, 1884; s. Calvin Luther and Annette (Marlow) B.; A.B., U. Minn., 1907, LL.B., 1909; married Minnie Stinchfield, Nov. 19, 1910; children—Alice Katherine (Mrs. Raymond Brown), Louise (Mrs. Robert James Christianson), Margaret Annette (Mrs. Conley Brooks), Joanne (Mrs. Theodore Douglas Wright). AdmitteeAdmitted to Minn. bar, 1909; practiced in Bemidji, 1909-18; city atty., 1917-18; asst. atty. gen. Minn., 1918-23, also mem. State securities Commn., 1918-21; instr. Minn. Coll. Law, 1921-31; mem. Oppenheimer, Hodgson, Brown, Wolff and Leach, St. Paul, 1923-71; counsel Mpls. St. Paul Met. Airports Commn., 1944-71; spl. counsil City of Mpls., 1948-60. Mem. Draft Bd., Beltrami County, World War I; appeal agt. Draft Bd 3, Ramsey County, World War II. Mem. Am., Minn., Ramsey County bar assns., Alpha Delta Phi, Phi Delta Phi. Conglist. Mason (grand master Minn. 1933). Club: Athletic (St. Paul). Home: St. Paul, Minn. Died July 4, 1971.

BROWN, PRENTISS MARSH, elec. co. exec.; b. St. Ignace, Mich., June 18, 1889; son of James John and Minnie (Gagnon) B.; A.B., Albion College, 1911, LL.D., 1937; U. Ill., 1911-12; LL.D., U. Mich., 1952; m. Marion Walker, June 16, 1916; children—Mariana Frances, Ruth Margaret, James John, Barbara Jean, Patricia Jane, Prentiss M., Paul W. Admitted to Mich. bar, 1914, and since in practice at St. Ignace; city. atty. St. Ignace, 1914-33; prosecuting atty. Mackinac County, 1914-26; mem. 73d and 74th Congress (1933-37), 11th Mich. Dist.; apptd. to U.S. Senate to fill unexpired term of late James Couzens, 1936; elected for term 1937-43; adminstr. Office Price Adminstrn., Jan. 20, 1943-Oct. 23, 1943; member of the firm of Brown, Lund & Fitzgerald, Washington, D.C., since 1943; chairman board Detroit Edison Company since May 16, 1944. Pres. 1st Nat. Bank of St. Ignace, Arnold Transit Company; Essex County Light & Power Co., Ltd., Peninsular Electric Light Co., Washtenaw Light and Power Co. (also dir.); v.p. and dir. Edison Illuminating Co., Detroit, St. Clair Edison Co.; v.p. Union Terminal Piers; dir. Great Lakes Sugar Co., Nat. Bank of Detroit, Detroit Fire and Marine Insurance Company. Mem. defense electric power administration Department of Interior; chairman Mackinac Bridge Authority. Dem. candidate for Congress, 1924, for judge Mich. Supreme Court, 1928. Was chmn. Dem. State Conv. 5 times; chmn. Dem. Senatorial Campaign, 1938. Chmn. special Senate Com. on Taxation of Govtl. Securities and Salaries, 1938-40; later chmn. Claims Com. Mem. Mich. Bd. of Law Examiners since 1930-41. Mem. exec. committee Assn. Edison Illuminating Companies; member board of trustees Albion Coll. Mem. Delta Tau Delta, Delta Sigma Rho, Phi Beta Kappa. Clubs: Recess (New York), Detroit, Detroit Athletic, Detroit Yacht, Country (Detroit, Mich.). Methodist. Mason, K.P. Home: St. Ignace Mich. Died Dec. 1973.

BROWN, RAY EVERETT, univ. administr., educator; b. Union, S.C., Sept. 26, 1913; s. Rev. William Thomas and Fan (Casey) B.; student Gardner Webb Coll., 1932-34; S.B., U. of N.C., 1937; M.B.A., U. Chgo., 1943; L.H.D., Wake Forest U., 1958; m. Mary Norvell Witherspoon, Nov. 26, 1937; children—Margaret Witherspoon, Mary Norvell, Barbara Casey. County mgr. Cleveland County, N.C., 1937-40; supt. Shelby (N.C.) Hosp., 1940-42; supt. N.C. Baptist Hosp., Winston- Salem and prof. hosp. administrn. Bowman-Gray Sch. of Medicine, Wake Forest U., 1943-45; supt. U. Chgo. Clinics and Hosps., 1945-61; v.p. for adminstrn. U. Chgo., 1961-64, asso. prof. sch. of bus., 1947-53, prof., 1953-64; asso. dir., grad. program in hosp. adminstrn., 1947-51, dir., 1951-62; prof. adminstrn., dir. grad. program in hosp. adminstrn. Duke, 1964-67; prof. administrn. Harvard, 1967-70, exec. v.p. affiliated hosps., 1967-70; prof. mgmt. Northwestern U., Chgo., exec. v.p. Med. Center, 1970-74. Dir. Am. Sterilizer Corp., Parke, Davis Co. Mem. exec. com. White House Conf. on Health, 1965; trustee U. Chgo. Settlement, 1945-54, pres., 1952-54; cons. surgeon-gen. USAF, 1957-63, surgeon-gen. U.S. Army, 1964-70; trustee Home for Destitute Crippled Children, 1950-64; dir. Chgo. Welfare Council, 1953-59. Mem. Nat. Joint Commn. Accreditation Hosps., 1955-61; chmn. Nat. Joint Council Health Care of Aged, 1960-61; chmn. Nat. Task Force Health Facilities, 1963-66; mem. Nat. Commn. To Study Med. Edn., 1967-68; mem. com. on med. edn. A.M.A., 1967-74; mem. Nat. Commn. on Nursing and Nursing Edn., 1967-70. Bd. dirs. Blue Cross Plan of Chgo., 1960-64, 70-74, Nat. Council on Philanthropy, 1973, Community Fund Chgo., 1959-64 (exec. com. 1961-64), Health Information Found., 1961-68. Recipient Gold Medal award Am. Assn. for Hosp. Planning, 1963; Gold medal award Am. Soc. Hosp. Pharmacists, 1964. Fellow Royal Coll. Health (Eng.), Am. Pub. Health Assn., Am. Coll. Hosp. Adminstrs. (bd. regents 1952-61, pres. 1959-60, Gold Medal award 1969); mem. Am. Hosp. Assn. (pres. 1955-56, trustee 1954-57, ho. of dels. 1954-57, 59-62, Distinguished Service award 1963), A.I.M., Assn. U. Program in Hosp. Adminstrn. (pres. 1966-67), Chgo. Hosp. Council (pres. 1952-53, trustee 1950-63), Ill. Hosp. Assn. (trustee 1953-60, pres. 1958-59, recipient Distinguished Service award 1962), U. Hosps. Exec. Council, U. Chgo. Gen. Alumni Assn. (bd. dirs. 1947-57), Phi Beta Kappa, Beta Gamma Sigma, Baptist. Club: Economics (Chgo.) Author: Hospitals Visualized (with others), 1952; Criteria for Student Selection, 1958, Graduate Education for Hospital Administration, 1959; Judgment in Administration, 1966; also articles on mgmt. and hosps. to profl. jours. Mem. editorial bd. Hosp. Mgmt., Med. World News, Modern Hosp. Mag., Med. Edn. Home: Chicago Ill. Died May 4, 1974.

BROWN, RICHARD EVAN, publisher; b. Bklyn., Aug. 9, 1881; s. Richard Benjamin and Ada McDonough (Denyse) B.; grad. Bklyn. Poly.; m. Leta May Baker, Aug. 13, 1920. Asst. contract agt. Bklyn. Edison Co., 1907-11; asst. mgr. F. W. Dodge Corp., 1912-19; sec., dir. Engring. & Contracting Pub. Co., Chgo., 1920-26; pres., dir. Quinn Brown Pub. Co., Stamford, , 1928-52; pub. Wire and Wire Products, Stamford, from 1928. 1st lt. N.Y. N.G., 1902-09, capt., 1912-16; maj. Signal Corps, U.S. Army, 1931-40. Mem. Am. Iron and Steel Inst., Nat. Assn. Mfrs., Wire Assn. Am. Ordnance Assn., Res. Officers Assn. U.S., Santa Barbara Mus. Art, Am. Legion, S.A.R. Presbyn. Club: Military and Naval (N.Y.C.) Home: Santa Barbara, Cal.†

BROWN, ROBERT MARSHALL, educator; b. Grafton, Mass., Mar. 11, 1870; s. George Roberts and Emily Caroline (Waters) B.; A.B., Brown U., 1893; A.M., Harvard U., 1902; Ed.D., Rhode Island College of Education, 1943; m. Fannie L. Plimpton, Sept. 5, 1905 (died Jan., 1909); m. 2d, Myrtis E. Hyde, Aug. 23, 1910. Instr. sciences, high sch., Portsmouth, N.H., 1894-98, prin. 1898-1900; asst. in geology, Harvard U., 1901-02; instr. sciences and mathematics, New Bedford High Sch., 1902-03; teacher geography, Worcester State Normal Sch., 1903-13; prof. geography and geology, R.I. Coll. of Edn., Providence, from 1913, acting pres., 1939-41, retired; lectr. U. N.C., summer 1903; instr. geography, Martha's Vineyard Summer Institute, 1904; lecturer in geography, Cornell U., summer 1923, 24. Fellow A.A.A.S.; mem. Assn. Am. Geographers, Nat. Council Geography Teachers. Conglist. Co-Author: Teaching the Social Studies, 1927; Teaching of Geography—32 Year Book National Society for Study of Education, 1932; Directed Geography Studies, 3 vols. (with Mary 5. Thorp), 1933; Natural Resources and Conservation, 1936 (with others). Contbr. New Internat. Ency. and many mags. on geographic subjects. Home: West Barrington, R.I.†

BROWN, ROBERT WOODROW, newspaper editor; b. Covington County, Miss., Jan. 3, 1912; s. Emmett Lige and Alma Louise (Garner) B.; grad. high sch.; Nieman fellow Harvard, 1951-52; m. Sarah Elizabeth Wood, Feb. 6, 1936; 1 dau., Barbara. Reporter, Hattiesburg (Miss.) American, 1930-32; mng. editor Greenville (Miss.) Delta Star, 1936-38; staff corr. United Press, New Orleans, 1938; reporter, city editor Times-Picayune and New Orleans States, 1938-42; asst. city editor Washington Daily News, 1942-43; news supr. NBC, 1943-45; exec. editor Internat. News Service, 1945-47; news editor ABC, 1947-48; editor Columbus (Ga.) Ledger, 1948-57; information officer fgn. service USIA, New Delhi, India, 1957-58; asso. editor St. Petersburg (Fla.) Times, 1958-63; mng. editor Delta Democrat-Times, Greenville, 1963; editor Rock Hill (S.C.) Evening Herald, 1964-68; mng. editor Augusta (Ga.) Chronicle, 1968-74; lectr. Am. press freedom, India and Iceland, 1954. Recipient Pulitzer prize for disinterested meritorious pub. service, 1955. Mem. Am. Soc. Newspaper Editors, So. Assn. Nieman Fellows, Inc., Sigma Delta Chi. Methodist. Contbr. articles for Parade mag., Editor and Pub. mag., others. Home: Augusta, Ga. Died Apr. 1, 1974; interred Westover Memorial Park, Augusta, Ga.

BROWN, ROY HOWARD, univ. pres.; b. Girard, Kan., May 2, 1878; s. James and Mercy (Playler) B.; grad. Park Coll. Acad., 1896; B.A., Park Coll., 1900, D.D., 1922; B.D., cum laude, McCormick Theol. Sem., 1903; post grad. work, U. of Chicago; LL.D., from Cedar Coll., 1934; m. Nellie McAfee Pollock, June 4, 1900; 1 dau., Barbara. Ordained Presbyn. ministry, 1903; went to Albay Province, P.I., as a pioneer missionary, 1903, continuing there 18 yrs.; established 79 chs. an received over 2500 members into the communion; pastor Fullerton Av. Ch., Chicago, 1922-25, Central Ch., Des Moines, Ia., 1925-28, Irving Park Presbyn. Church, Chicago, 1928-32; pres. Silliman U. largest evang. ednl. instn. in P.I., 1932-27; head of theol. dept. Union Sem., Manila, P.I., 1932-37; head of theol. dept. Union Sem., Manila, P.I. from Nov., 1939. Interned by Japanese in Manila for 3½ yrs.; rescued by U.S. troops; now lecturing in U.S. Mem. staff Pasadena Presbyn. Ch. Engaged in Y.M.C.A. war work, 1917-18; vice pres. Assn. Evang. Colleges in P.I.; chmn. ednl. com. Nat. Christian Council of P.I.; mem. exec. com. Philippine Mission. Republican. Mason (32°). Translator of Old and New Testament, with cooperation of nationals of P.I., completed in 1921. Writer on mission work of P.I. Public speaker on P.I. questions. Home: Pasadena, Cal.†

BROWN, S(IMPSON) LEROY, physicist; b. Brownsburg, Ind., Nov. 23, 1881; s. John Wiman and Mary Catherine (Huffer) B.; A.B., Ind. Univ., 1905, M.A., 1907; Ph.D., U. of Calif., 1909; m. Josephine Ellen Brown, July 10, 1910; 1 dau., Elizabeth B. (Mrs. James A. Campbell). Asst. instr. Purdue U., 1905-07; instr. Lehigh U., 1909-11; instr. U. of Tex., 1911-13, adjunct prof., 1913-17, asso. prof. physics, 1917-23, prof. physics from 1923; cons. Mil. Physics Research Lab. from 1942. Dir. Fidelity State Bank of Austin. Served as pres. academic bd. U.S. Air Force Radio Sch., Penn Field, Tex., 1917-19. Whiting Research fellow U. of Calif., 1907-09. Fellow A.A.A.S., Am. Phys. Soc.; mem. Sigma Xi, Sigma Pi Sigma, Tau Beta Pi. Contbr. sci. papers to profl. jours. Home: Austin, Tex.†

BROWN, THEODORE HENRY, educator; b. Mystic, Conn., Oct. 5, 1888; s. Herbert Stanley and Emma (Hall) B.; A.B., Yale, 1910; A.M., 1911; Ph.D., 1913; M.A. (hon.), Harvard, 1942; m. Louise Allis Bulkley, July 18, 1914; children—Helen Bulkley, (Mrs. Donald Gilfoy), Margaret Bulkley (Mrs. Buhrman Garland). Instructor mathematics, Yale, 1913-15; mem. research staff, bur. of bus. research, grad. Sch. of Bus. Adminstrn., Harvard, 1925-26; asst. prof. bus. statistics, 1926-27; asso. prof., 1927-32; from 1932, then prof. emeritus; cons. to various corps., including IBM; dir. Am. Textile Co., Investors Trust Co., Providence. Johnston Mutual Fund, Inc. Taught naval training unit, sec. naval training com., Brown, 1918; head consultant, W.P.B., 1941-42; chief consultant, Army Air Forces, 1942-43; chief econ. consultant to v. chmn. in charge of Office of Civilian Requirements, W.P.B., 1943-44. Fellow A.A.A.S., Am. Acad. of Arts and Sciences, Am. Statistical Assn. (chmn. com. on statistics in bus., 1934; v.p., 1935, 38; v.p. Boston chap., 1939-40; pres., 1940-41; director, 1940-44; mem. com. on fellows, 1940-45); mem. Am. Astron. Soc., Am. Econ. Assn., American Marketing Association (member research com., board of dirs., 1940), Society Terminal Engineers, Am. Math. Soc., Econometric Soc., Math. Assn. of Am., Psychometric Soc., Am. Soc. Quality Control, Nat. Association of Cost Accountants, Phi Beta Kappa, Sigma Xi, Alpha Chi Rho. Clubs: Yale (New York); Yale (Boston). Contbr. articles to professional journals. Home: Englewood Fla. Died Dec. 1973.

BROWN, THEOPHILUS, research engr.; b. Worcester, Mass., Apr. 19, 1879; s. William T. and Kate Amelia (Curtis) B.; B.S., Worcester Poly. Inst., 1901; m. Elise A. Koehler, Nov. 29, 1913; children—Elise (Mrs. William M. Cade), William T. Research engr. Deer & Co. from 1911, dir., mem. adv. com.; dir. Iowa-Illinois Gas & Electric Co. Dir. Nat. Safety Council. Mem. Newcomen Soc., Eng., Am. Soc. Agrl. Engrs. Home: Moline, Ill.†

BROWN, VOLNEY MASON, lawyer; b. Oakville, Tex., Oct. 10, 1876; s. Robert H. and Amanda (Buchanan) B.; student Washington and Lee U., 1898-1900; LL.B., U. of Tex., 1902; m. Carrie M. Morton, Mar. 17, 1908. Admitted to Tex. bar, 1902, practiced in El Paso; member law firm, Kemp, Smith, Brown, Goggin & White, counsel for railroads and numerous utilities and corporations; assistant city attorney, El Paso, 1909-15; member Board of Legal Examiners, 4th Supreme Jud. Dist., Tex., 1909-11, 8th Dist., 1911-19. Served in Tex. N.G., 1905-08. Mem. Am., Tex. State and El Paso (ex-pres.) bar assns. K. P. Home: El Paso, Tex.†

BROWN, WALTER L., lawyer; b. Precott, Ark., Oct. 23, 1893; LL.B., George Washington U., 1920. Admitted to Ark. bar, 1921; pros. atty. 13th Jud. dist. Ark., 1920; now mem. firm Brown, Compton & Prewett, El Dorado, Ark. Mem. Ark. Oil and Gas Commn., 1937-39. Chmn. Union County (Ark.) Democratic central com., 1938-50, mem. Ark. Dem. central com., 1939-40. Mem. Union County (pres. 1942-43), Ark., Am. bar assns. Address: El Dorado Ark. Died June 1972.

BROWN, W(ILLIAM) NORMAN, indologist; b. Baltimore, Md., June 24, 1892; s. George William and Virginia Augusta (Clark) B.; student Prep. Sch., Hiram (O.) Coll., 1905-07, Hiram Coll., 1907-08; A.B., Johns Hopkins, 1912, fellow, 1913-15, Ph.D., 1916; Harrison research fellow, U. of Pa., 1916-19, Litt.D. (hon.), 1963; Johnston scholar, Johns Hopkins, 1919-22; studied Sanskrit at Benares, India, 1922-23; D.Litt. (Honorary), University of Madras, 1957, University of Michigan, 1965, Jadavpur U., 1970; Jnana-Ratna-Kara, W. Bengal Government Sanskrit Coll., Calcutta, 1961; m. Helen Harrison, June 29, 1921; children Norman H., Ursula (Mrs. J.H. Perivier). Acting head of Sanskrit dept., Johns Hopkins, 1921-22, asso. in Sanskrit, 1925-26; prof. Sanskrit, U. Pa., 1926-66, prof. emeritus, 1966-75; chairman South Asia regional studies, 1947-66; editor Jour. of Am. Oriental Society, 1926-41; fellow on the John Simon Guggenheim Memorial Foundation, 1928-29; curator of Indian art, Phila. Mus. Art, 1931-54; curator Oriental sect. U. Pa. Museum, 1942-50; pres. Am. Inst. Indian Studies, Poona, India, 1961-71. Successively cadet U.S. Naval Aviation Corps, cryptographer with Mil. Intelligence Bur. and spl. agt.

with U.S. Naval Intelligence, 1918; Office of Strategic Service Wash., 1941-45. Recipient G.V. Watumull Distinguished Achievement award in Indology, 1967. Fellow Royal Asiatic Soc. (London); hon. fellow Asiatic Soc. (Calcutta), Bhandar-Kar Oriental Research Inst. (Poona), Deccan Coll. (Poona), Kuppuswauri Research Inst. (Madras); mem. of the Am. Philosophical Soc., American Oriental Soc. (pres. 1941-42), Linguistic Soc. Am., Assn., Asian Studies (pres. 1960-61), Royal India, Pakistan and Ceylon Soc. (London), Phila. Oriental Club, Phi Beta Kappa, Delta Upsilon. Author: The Story of Kalaka, 1933; Miniature Paintings of the Jaina Kalputras, 1934. Manuscript Illustrations of the Uttaradhyayana Sutra, 1941; The United States and India and Pakistan, 1953, 2d rev. edit., 1963, (with Kitle), 3d edit., 1972; The Saundaryalahari, 1958; The Vasanta Vilasa, 1962; The Mahimnastava, 1965; Man in the Universe, 1966; several other publs. prior to 1940. Editor, part author: India, Pakistan, Ceylon, 1951, 2d rev. edit., 1963. Contbr. to learned and popular publs. Home: Moylan, Pa. Died Apr. 22, 1975.

BROWNE, ALFRED DAVID, educator; b. Belfast, Ireland, May 14, 1879; s. Thompson and Jane (Whiteside) B.; brought to U.S. in infancy; student Springfield (Mass.) Coll., 1900-02 U. of N.C., 1902-05; M.D., U. of Tenn., 1907; grad. study N.Y. Post-Grad. Hosp. Coll., 1907-08, Harvard, 1908, 1911-13, U. of Mich., summer 1912; m. Roberta G. Jones, 1908; children—Herbert Thompson, Robert Alfr 1917-18), Amateur Athletic Union (v.p. Pacific Coast Dist., 1919-21), Am. Health and Physical Edn. Assn. (nat. council), Southern Health and Physical Edn. Assn. (pres. 1928-29), Delta Kappa Epsilon. Phi Chi; mem. White House Conf. for Child Health and Protection. Unitarian. Contbr. to Am. Med. Assn. Jour. Pub. Health, etc. Recipient nat. honor award from Am. Health and Physical Edn. Assn., 1940, for outstanding services to profession. Address: Palo Alto, Cal.†

BROWNE, BEVERLY F(IELDING), army officer; b. Accomac, Va., Mar. 24, 1880; s. T.H. Bayly and Anna (Fletcher) B.; student Episcopal Acad., Phila., 1893-97; B.S., U.S. Mil. Acad., 1901; m. Louise Ingham Adams, July 10, 1907. Commd. 2d lt., Arty. Corps, U.S. Army, Feb. 2, 1901, and advanced through grades to brig. gen., 1918; commanded 166th F.A. Brigade, France, 1918, arty. of the First Corps, France, 1918; attached to 30th regt. F.A., French Army, Orlians, France, 1912-13, P.I., 1913-15, chief F.A., 7th Corps, Germany, 1918-19; asst. chief F.A., Washington, D.C., 1919-20, Hawaii 1921-25, ret., 1928. Pres. and gen. manager The Blue Ridge Distilleries, Inc., Front Royal, Va., from orgn., 1934-43. Decorated D.S.M., Officer Legion of Honor, French; campaign and service medals, Spanish Am. War, Philippine Insurrection, Mexican Border, 1st World War, France and Germany. Mem. Shenandoah Valley, Inc., Horticultural Soc. of Va., Va. Hist. Soc., Soc. of First Div., U.S. Army, Front Royal C. of C. (pres. 1930-33). (vestry from 1928, treas., 1934-48). Clubs: Maryland, Baltimore; an Army and Navy, Washington. Address: Front Royal, Va.†

BROWNE, ROGER J., air force officer; b. Norfolk, Neb., Jan. 5, 1906; s. Ernest Irving and Laura Ruby Elizabeth (Hensley) B.; student State U. Ia., 1923-25; B.S., U.S. Mil. Acad., 1929; grad. AC Advanced Flight Sch., 1930; student Nat. War Coll., 1947-48; m. Charlotte Gregory Decker, Aug. 29, 1929; children—Roger J., Patricia; m. 2d, Edith Elizabeth Joan Morris, July 27, 1946; children—William Nicholas, Jennifer Noble; stepdau., Jane Elizabeth. Commd. 2d lt. USAAF, 1929, advanced through grades to maj. gen., 1952; comdr. 16th and 32d pursuit groups, Panama C.Z., 1939-42; operations div. War Dept. Gen. Staff, 1942-44; chief staff XIX Tactical Air Command, 9th A.F., 1944-46; sr. Air Force instr. U.S. Army Command and Gen. Staff Sch., Ft. Leavenworth, Kan., 1946-47; chief moblzn. div. Office Dept. Chief Staff operations, Hdqrs. USAF, 1948-49, dep. dir. manpower and orgn., 1951, from 1952. Chief A.F. Group, Joint U.S. Mil. Assistance Planning Group to Greece, 1949; U.S. planner North Atlantic Treaty, dep. dir. Joint Am. Mil. Adv. Group, London, Eng., 1949-51. Died 1974.

BROWNE, ROLLIN, lawyer; b. Talladega, Ala., Dec. 30, 1895; s. Cecil and Sara (Booker) B.; A.B., U. of Ala., 1915, LL.B., 1916; LL.B., Columbia U., 1919; m. Doonya de Mitkjewicz Holland, Feb. 12, 1921; 1 son, Cecil. Asso. with law firm Booth & Hewitt, 1919-20, Cutcheon, Taylor, Bowie & Marsh, 1921-26; mem. firm Taylor, Bowie & Marsh, 1926-27, Mitchell, Capron, Marsh, Angulo & Cooney, 1927-43 1945-48; mem. firm Browne Staley, Sanford & Farner, Albany, 1945-61; mem. Saterlee Browne & Dickerson, N.Y.C., 1948-63, Browne, Hyde & Dickerson, N.Y.C., Satterlee, Browne, Carusi & Goodson, Washington, 1963-70; president Woodward Found.; state commr; of taxation, finance and pres. State Tax Commn., State of N.Y., 1943-45. Enlisted in U.S. Army, May 1917, 2d lt. F.A., World War I. Mem. N.Y. State Bar Assn., Bar Assn. City of N.Y. (past chairman com. on taxation), Soc. Mayflower Descs., Kappa Sigma, Phi Beta Kappa. Episcopalian. Clubs: Down Town Association, University (N.Y.C.); Chesapeake Bay Yacht. Writer of articles and papers on tax and other legal subjects. Home: New York City, N.Y. Died Sept. 11, 1970; buried Old Wye Ch., Wye Mills, Md.

BROWNING, ARTHUR MONTCALM, ins. co. exec.; b. Grafton, W. Va., Sept. 4, 1908; s. William L. and Hattie L. (Corpening) B.; A.B., Dartmouth, 1930; LL.B., Harvard, 1933; m. Martha P. Reed, Sept. 1, 1934, children—Reed St. Clair, Simms C., Sandra M. Clk., Equitable Life Assurance Soc., 1934-36, legal asst. president's staff, 1936-39, asst. counsel, 1939-49, asso. group underwriter, 1949, mgr. group casualty coverages, 1949-50; admitted to N.Y. state bar, 1938; exec. asst. N.Y. Life Ins. Co., 1950-51, asst. v.p., 1951-55, 2d v.p., 1955, v.p. charge group ins., 1955-61, v.p. charge group adminstrn., 1961-62, v.p. charge group sales and adminstrn., 1962-63, v.p., 1963-73. Mem. central com. Health Ins. Council, 1957-62, chmn., 1960-61, chmn. N.Y. State com., 1965-72, mem. exec. com., 1969-72, chmn. state council's dept., 1969-71; mem. adv. com. Nat. Health Survey, 1957-61; adviser Nat. Center Health Statistics, 1965-72; N.Y. State coordinator community health action planning Health Ins. Council, 1967-72; mem. N.Y.C. Mayor's Orgn. Task Force for Comprehensive Health Planning, 1968-70; mem. health task force N.Y.C. Urban Coalition, 1969-72. Del. White House Conf. on Aging, 1961, 71. Bd. dirs. Greater N.Y. Safety Council, 1960-72; Comprehensive Health Planning for N.Y.C., 1970-72; trustee L.I. Health and Hosp. Planning Council, 1969-72. Mem. Am. Pub. Health Assn., Am. Judicature Soc., Assn. Life Ins. Counsel, N.Y. State Bar Assn., Health Ins. Assn. Am. (N.Y. legislative chmn. 1968-72), Gamma Delta Chi, Phi Kappa Sigma, Gamma Delta Epsilon. Conglist. Contbr. author: Group Insurance Handbook, Principles of Risk Management. Home: Manhasset, N.Y. Died Apr. 25, 1974; interred Manhasset, N.Y.

BROWNRIGG, DOROTHY RUTH AKIN (MRS. ROBERT CHARLES BROWNRIGG), educator; b. Ft. Collins, Colo., June 3, 1914; d. Abraham I. and Nellie (Taylor) Akin; B.S., Colo. State U., 1935, NSF research grantee summers 1959-60, postgrad., 1962-65; grantee U. Neb., summer 1966; postgrad. Texas Tech University, summer 1969; m. Robert Charles Brownrigg, May 27, 1937; children—Robert Bruce, Charles Stuart. Tchr. chemistry, biology, gen. sci., home econs. Primero High Sch., Weston, Colo., 1935-64; head homemaking dept. Trinidad (Colo.) High Sch., 1964-71; tchr. adult nutrition Trinidad State Jr. Coll. Mem. Stonewall (pres. So. div. 1963-64), Las Animas County (pres. 1962-64) tchrs. assns., Trinidad Edn., Assn. (pres. 1964-65), Homemaking Tchrs. Colo. (pres. 1965-67), Colo. Vocational Homemaking Tchrs. (pres. elect 1968), Gamma Phi Beta (chpt. sec. 1933-34), Delta Kappa Gamma (pres. 1966-68), Colo. Edn. Assn., N.E.A., Colo. Vocational Edn. Republican. Mem. Order Eastern Star. Home: Trinidad Colo. Died Dec. 3, 1971.

BRUCE, GUSTAV MARIUS, theologian; b. Oslo, Norway, Feb. 11, 1879; s. Erik Larson Brunsholdt and Anne Bolette (Anderson) B.; brought by parents to U.S., 1884; B.Pd. and B.S., Fremont (Neb.) Coll. and Normal Sch., 1904; candidate of theology, Red Wing (Minn.) Sem., 1905; A.B., U. of S.D., 1907; A.M., 1909; B.D., Temple U., Phila., 1914, S.T.D., 1916; Ph.D., Hartford Sem. Foundation, Hartford, Conn., 1927; D.D., Luth. Theol. Sem., Chicago, 1928; m. Minnie Jensen, Aug. 27, 1902; 1 dau., Marie Augusta. Teacher, Jewell (Ia.) Coll., 1905-06; ordained ministry Luth. Ch., 1906; pastor Hooker and Dell Rapids, S.D., 1906-10, Pontiac, Ill., 1911; prof. practical theology, Red Wing Sem., 1911-17, prof. N.T. symbolics and ethics, Luther Theol. Sem., St. Paul, 1917-19; v.p. Luther Theol. Sem., 1944-49. now prof. emeritus; editor and publisher Lutheran Intelligencer, 1911-14; editor Little Folks, weekly S.S. paper, 1922-31, Lutheran Teacher, 1926-31, Jour. of Theology of Am. Luth Conf., 1940-41; mem. board dirs. Ministers Life & Casualty Union from 1924, v.p., 1940-46, pres. 1946-50. Mem. bd. dirs. of English work, Hauge's Synod, 1912-14; pres. Young Peoples Fedn. of Hauge's Synod, 1915-17; mem. com. on Ch. Union, 1916-17; v.p. Young People's Luther League, 1917-22; mem. B.d Elementary Christian Education, 1920-30; 2d v.p. Norwegian Luth. Ch. of America 1926-48; delegate to Second Luth., World Conv., Copenhagen, 1929; pres. Bygdelagenes Fellesraad, Inc., 1934-37, and 1938; pres. United Temperance Movement of Minn., 1944-50; mem. Assn. Nordmanns Forbundet (Internat. League of Norsemen); mem. Norwegian-Am. Hist. Soc.; mem. com. on social trends, Nat. Luth. Council, 1935-45; mem. Commn. on Social Relations, Am. Luth. Conf. 1934-46. Mem. of the Acad. of Polit. and Social Science. Republican. Editor: Folkekalenderen, 1916. Contbr. religious and secular press both in English and Norweigian. Address: Minneapolis, Minn.†

BRUCE, JAMES LATIMER, mining engr.; b. Dublin, Ireland, Mar. 20, 1880; s. Stuart and Margaret (Latimer) B.; E.M., Colo. Sch. of Mines, 1901; m. Leah Sidney Hills, Dec. 25, 1915; children—Mary Adaline, Janet, James Stuart, Victor. Came to U.S., 1893, naturalized citizen, 1902. Mining engineer, Cripple Creek, Colo., 1901-03; chief engr. and gen. foreman Federal Lead Co., Flat River, Mo., 1903-07; asst. mgr. Grace Zinc Co., Joplin, Mo., 1907-11; mgr. Continental Zinc Co., Joplin, 1911-13; gen. mgr. Butte & Superior Mining Co., Butte, Mont., 1912-20, Davis-Daly Copper Co., Butte, Mont., 1920-24; vice-president and general manager Cyprus Mines Corporation 1925-47; gen. mgr. Cornoado Copper & Zinc Co., 1942-47, Compania Minera Acme, S.A., 1943-45; vice pres. and cons. engr. Cyprus Mines Corp., cons. engr. Coronado Copper and Zinc Co. and Minera Acme S.A., 1947-53; cons. practice, 1924-25. Mem. Am. Inst. Mining and Metall. Engrs., Am. Mining Congress. Republican. Conglist. Mason. Club: California. Home: San Marino, Cal.†

BRUCE, ROSCOE CONKLING, educator; b. at Washington, Apr. 21, 1879; s. Blanch Kelso and Josephine (Bealle) B.; A.B., Harvard, 1902; m. Clara Washington Burrill June 3, 1903. Dir. acad. dept., Tuskegee Normal and Industrial Inst., 1902-06; supervising prin. 10th div. of pub. schs., Washington, 1906-07; asst. supt. pub. instrn., 1907-21; prin. Brown's Creek Dist. High Sch., Kendall, W.Va., from 1921. Mem. Nat. Assn. Advancement of Colored People, Am. Negro Acad., Phi Beta Kappa, Kappa Delta Pi, Sigma Pi Phi. Republican.†

BRUDNO, EZRA SELIG, author, lawyer; b. Lithuania, June 5, 1878; s. Isaac and Hannah (Model) B.; attended Adelbert Coll. (Western Reserve U.), 1896-97; at Yale U., 1898-1900, reading law and pursuing academic studies; finished law studies at Western Reserve U., 1900; m. Rose Hart Hess, June 2, 1913. Began practice of law in Cleveland, 1901; asst. dist. atty., from 1909. Republican. Author: The Fugitive, 1904; The Little Conscript, 1905; The Tether, 1908; One of Us, 1912; Scribes and Pharisees; The Jugglers, 1920; The Sublime Jester, 1924; Ghosts of Yesterday, 1935. Contbr. to mags. Home: Cleveland Heights, O.†

BRUENING, EDWARD H(ENRY), dentist; b. Montezuma, Ia., Nov. 25, 1881; s. Hans I. and Paulina (Quickenstedt) B.; D.D.S., U. of Omaha, 1903; m. Lottie Frick, 1907. In practice of denistry at Omaha from 1903; instr. dental dept. Creighton U., 1906-07. prof. dental anatomy from 1907. supt. and vice dean of dept. of denistry, 1913-18, prof. histology, 1916-18. Mem. National Com. on Health and Safety. Past pres. Catalina Council Boy Scouts America (mem. at large Nat. Council). Dental examiner, World War; commd., June 1935, lt. comdr. Dental Corps, Volunteer, Special Service, U.S. Naval Res.; retired. Mem. Nat. Rifle Assn. (training men to shoot military rifle). Fellow American Coll. Dentists; mem. Am. Dental Assn. (formerly trustee 11th Dist.; chmn. mil. affairs com.), Neb. State Dental Soc. (ex-pres.), Omaha Odontological Soc. (ex-pres.), Tri City Dental Society (ex-pres.), Am. Dental Foundation, Inc. (past sec.), So. Dist. Dental Soc.; Ariz. State Soc. Clubs: Woodbury Study, Old Pueblo Rifle, Tucson County (Tucson). Contbr. to dental edn. jours. Home: Tucson, Ariz.†

BRUMAGIM, ROBERT SMITH, accountant; b. Amsterdam, N.Y., Dec. 6, 1907; s. Robert B. and Julia (Smith) B.; B.S., Syracuse U., 1930, M.S., 1939; M. Accounts in Govt., Columbus U., 1946; spl. courses, Northwestern U., 1937, 44; m. Eola Floris Williamson, June 7, 1928 (dec. Dec. 1954); m. 2d, Betty Florence Beach, July 23, 1955. Head comml. dept. Mynderse Acad., Seneca Falls, N.Y., 1930-37; accountant Ernst & Ernst, Rochester, N.Y., 1937-40; asst. dir. corp. audits div., asst. chief accounting systems div. U.S. Gen. Accounting Office, Washington, 1945-50; controller Charles Lachman Co., Phoenixville, Pa., 1950; mgr. cost and budget depts. Mohawk Carpet Mills, Amsterdam, N.Y., 1951-53, controller, 1953-55, dir., 1955; dir. Mohasco Industries, Inc., Amsterdam, N.Y., 1955-59, controller, 1955-64, dir. audits, 1965, exec. asst. to controller, 1966-67, accounting cons. to officers and bd., 1968-69. Congl. accounting liaison officer for Comptroller Gen. U.S., 1949-50; prof. govt. corps. Columbus U., 1945-50; accounting cons., adviser investigator for Com. on Appropriations, U.S. Ho. of Reps., 1949, 50; co-author govt. corps. reference manuals; expert examiner U.S. Civil Service Commn. for accounting 1947-50; chmn. adv. group to mayor, Amsterdam, 1958-59. Served from capt. to lt. col., AUS, 1940-45, ret., 1968. Named to Wisdom Hall of Fame, 1970. C.P.A., Ill., N.Y. Mem. Am. Inst. C.P.A.'s (mem. com. fed. budgeting and accounting 1963-64), Inst. Internal Auditors (charter mem., v.p. Capital dist. N.Y. 1966-67, dir. 1968), N.Y. State Soc. C.P.A.'s (adv. com. to comptroller of State N.Y., 1957-58); D.C. Inst. C.P.A.'s, Fed. Govt. Accountants. Assn. (charter), Financial Execs. Inst. (pres. Albany 1964; nat. com. accounting prins. 1963-66), Army Finance Assn., Gamma Rho Tau, Kappa Phi Kappa. Beta Alpha Psi, Alpha Kappa Psi. Mason. Contbr. articles profl. jours. Home: Wells, N.Y. Died Sept. 30, 1974.

BRUNDAGE, AVERY, engr., amateur sportsman; b. Detroit, Sept. 28, 1887; s. Charles and Amelia (Lloyd) B.; B.S. in C.E., U. Ill., 1909; LL.D. and M.P.E. (hon.), Springfield Coll.; m. Elizabeth Dunlap, 1927 (dec. 1971); m. 2d, Mariann Reuss, 1973. Pres. Avery Brundage Co., builders, 1915-47; chmn. Roanoke Real Estate Co., 1932-75; pres. Roanoke Hotel Corp., 1939-45; chmn. bd. Susquehanna Corp., 1957-59. Pres. U.S. Olympic Assn. and Com., 1929-53; v.p. Comite Internationale Olympique, 1945-52, pres., 1952-72, hon. life pres., 1972-75; first pres. Comite Deportive Pan-Am., 1940. Vice pres. Internat. Amateur Athletic Fedn., 1930-52; past pres. Amateur Athletic Union of U.S. (pres. seven terms). Collector of Oriental art; trustee Art Inst. Chgo. Decorated highest civilian orders of many nations; recipient Spl. award Northwestern U., 1951; Excelentisimo Senor Don de Santa Barbara, Cal.;

first Medal of Merit, City Chgo.; Achievement award U. Ill.; 1st John Perry Bowditch Meml. for outstanding service; Key to City and Hon. Citizen of San Francisco, Tokyo, Seoul; Order of Lincoln from the State of Ill.; many other honors. Mem. Sigma Xi, Tau Beta Pi, Sigma Alpha Epsilon. Clubs: Chicago Athletic, Chicago Engineers; Montecito Country (past pres.). Amateur all-around champion of America, 1914, 16, 18. Author numerous articles on amateur sport, Olympic Games. Died May 8, 1975. Address: Garmisch-Portenkirchen, Germany.

BRUNER, HERBERT BASCOM, educator; b. Monserrat, Mo., Dec. 18, 1892; son of Calhoun and Elizabeth (Richardson) B.; A.B., Central Coll., 1913; A.M., Missouri U., 1915; Ph.D., Columbia U., 1925; m. Lucile Munday, June 6, 1918; children—Jean, Beverly. Teacher Mexico (Mo.) high sch., 1913-14; asst. in psychology, U. of Missouri, 1914-16; supt. schs., Lathrop, Mo., 1916-18; acting prof. edn., U. of Ark., 1918; supt. schs., Okmulgee, Okla., 1918-24; asso. curriculum research, Teachers College, Columbia U., 1924-29, prof. edn., dir. Curriculum Lab., 1929-40, prof. edn., head dept. of the exceptional, 1940-43; supt. of schools, Oklahoma City, Okla., 1943-48; supt. of schools, Minneapolis, Minn., 1948-50; prof. sch. of edn., New York University since 1950. Curriculum consultant: Houston Beaumont, Port Arthur, Fort Worth (Tex.), Baltimore, Md., Chester, Pa., and State Dept. Edn., S.D.; dir. Md. State School Survey, 1941; v.p. Nat. Kindergarten Assn.; cons. editor, Internat. Jour. for Exceptional Children. Mem. Aviation Industry Adv. Panel, Air Coordinating Com. of U.S., representing Am. Assn. Sch. Adminstrs. and Nat. Edn. Assn. Mem. Kappa Delta Pi, Phi Delta Kappa Sigma Chi. Meth. Author: What Our Schools Are Teaching (with Evans, Hutchcroft, Wieting, Wood), 1941. Home: Boca Raton Fla. Died Aug. 2, 1974.

BRUNING, WALTER HENRY, food chain exec.; b. N.Y.C., Apr. 1, 1904; s. Charles and Minns (Bunger) B.; student N.Y. U., 1923-26, Acad. Advanced Traffic, 1943-46; m. Gertrude Goossen, June 10, 1927; 1 dau., Joan M. (Mrs. Harold B. Schell). With Gristede Bros., Inc., 1928-69, clk. and store mgr., asst. mgr. produce div., traffic mgr., corp. sec., 1928-61, v.p., sec., dir., 1961-69, chmn. bd., 1965-69; chmn. bd. Charles & Co., 1965-69; dir., mem. exec. com. Yorkville Savs. & Loan, 1960-70; trustee Dollar Savs. Bank, N.Y.C., 1965-74, mem. exec. com., 1973-74; v.p., dir. Brunell Realty Corp. Mem. transp. research adv. com. U.S. Dept. Agr., 1956-63, chmn., 1961-62; mem. Atlantic States Shippers Adv. Bd. Mem. Assn. ICC Practitioners, U.S. Power Squadron, Delta Nu Alpha (pres. Bronx chpt. 1950-54). Home: Lakewood, N.J. Died Oct. 25, 1974; interred Kensico Cemetery, Valhalla, N.Y.

BRUNIS, GEORG (GEORGE BRUNIES), jazz trombonist; b. New Orleans, Feb. 6, 1902; s. Henry and Elizabeth (Lotz) Brunies; m. Chloris Wyckoff. At age 6 played alto horn with Pap Laine's Street Parade Band at Mardi Gras; studied trombone with brother, Henry Brunies; in 1918 went to Chgo. and played jazz on showboats J.S. and President between Davenport, Ia. and St. Louis, with neuleus of future New Orleans Rhythm Kings. The NORK, which included, in addition to Brunis, Paul Mares, trumpet, Leon Rappolo, clarinet, Jack Pettis, sax, Elmer Schiebel, pianist and composer, Arnold Loyocano and later Steve Brown, bass, and Frank Snyder, drums; was organized in Chgo., 1921, for a long engagement at Mike Fritzel's Friar's Inn. The NORK, one of the 1st great dixieland bands in the North, influenced Frank Teschemacher, Bud Freeman and the Austin High Gang, in the devel. of the Chgo. Jazz Style. Known as King of the Tailgate Trombone, Brunis subsequently played with Ted Lewis and Eddie Condon for many years, and more recently with bands in Chgo., including his own-retaining his mellow, vocal tone and hard-driving Chgo. style in disregard of the many shifting trends of jazz and periods of apathy to it. Home: Chicago, Ill. Died Nov. 19, 1974.

BRUNNER, EDMUND DE SCHWEINITZ, sociologist; b. Bethlehem, Pa., Nov. 4, 1889; s. Franklin Henry and Nina (de Schweinitz) B.; B.A., Moravian Coll., 1909, M.A., 1912, Ph.D., 1914, L.H.D., 1935; B.D., Moravian Theol. Sem., 1911; LL.D., U. Natal, S. Africa; m. Mary Vogler, Dec. 16, 1912 (dec.); children—Edmund de Schweinitz, Wilfred Robert; m. 2d, Lousene Rousseau, Nov. 6, 1948. Ordained to ministry Moravian Ch., 1911; pastor, Coopersburg, Pa., 1911-14, 1st Ch., Easton, 1914-18; rural sec. Com. on War Indsl. Communities, 1918-19; dir. Town and County Survey Dept., Interch. World Movement, 1919-20; dir. Town and Country Surveys, Inst. Social and Religious Research, 1921-33; asso. in rural edn. Columbia Tchrs. Coll., 1926-31, prof., 1931-55, grad. faculty polit. sci., 1940-63, chmn. Bur. Applied Social Research 1951-63; lectr. Western Conn. State Coll., 1957-67; lectr. New Zealand and Australia state univs., 1937; collaborator Bur. Agri. Econs., U.S. Dept. Agr., 1936-54; adviser Extension Service, 1942-51; cons. Inst. Social Research, U. Natal 1954. Mem. Am., Rural (pres. 1945) sociol. socs., Am. Philatelic Soc., Am. Philatelic Congress, Fgn. Policy Assn. Author, co-author numerous books, including: Village Communities, 1927; Rural Korea, 1928; Immigrant Farmers and Their Children, 1929; (with J.H. Kolb), Rural Social Trends, 1933; (with Irving Lorge) Rural Trends in Depression Years, 1937, new edit., 1971; American Society: Urban and Rural Patterns (with W.C. Hallenbeck), 1955; 22 vols. of Town and Country Studies; Rural America and the Extension Service (with Hsin-Pao Yang), 1949; Growth of a Science: A History of Rural Sociological Research, 1957; (with Sloane Wayland) The Educational Characteristics of the American People, 1958; (with others) An Overview of Adult Education Research, 1959; As Now Remembered, 1968. Home: Wilton, Conn. Died Dec. 1973. N:M:1878:9999:W26

BRUNS, FRIEDRICH, educator; b. Zwischenahn, Oldenburg, Germany, June 27, 1878; s. Diedrich and Anna (Kahlen) B.; came to U.S., 1887, naturalized, 1893; A.B., Wartburg Coll., Clinton, Ia., 1901; A.M., U. of Wis., 1904, Ph.D., 1909; student Univ. of Leipzig, 1904-05; m. Lydia Dallwig, Aug. 1, 1913; children—Gertrude Elizabeth, Ingeborg Marie. Instr. in German, Williams Coll., 1905-06; instr. in German, 1907-11, asst. prof., 1911-25, asso. prof., 1925-29, prof., 1929-48, U. of Wisconsin, prof. emeritus from 1948; vis. prof. German, Haverford (Pa.) Coll., 1947-48; professor German. Mem. Modern Lang. Assn. Am., Am. Assn. U. Profs., Goethe Soc. Editor: A Book of German Lyrics, 1921; Goethes Gedichte und Spruche in Prosa, 1932; Die Lese der deutschen Lyrik von Klopstock bis Rilke, 1937. Author: Hebbel und Ludwig—Ein Vergleich ihrer Ansichten urber das Drama, 1913; Modern Thought in German Lyric Poets, 1921; Die amerikanische Dichtung der Gegenwart, 1930. Home: Montgomery Co., Pa.†

BRYAN, JULIEN, documentary film maker; b. Titusville, Pa., May 23, 1899; A.B., Princeton, 1921; B.D., Union Theol. Sem., 1926; m. Marian Knighton, Dec. 25, 1936; 1 son, Samuel Knighton. After completing theol. studies, served as dir. boys work, Bklyn. YMCA several years; toured Russia, 1930, on return, gave lectures while showing film; lectured with Burton Holmes 1933; has photographed Russia, Japan, China, Turkey, Poland (notably the bombardment and fall of Warsaw in film), Finland, Nazi Germany (for The March of Time), Afghanistan, S.Am. countries and Mexico; observer for UNRRA, Western Russia, 1946-47; produced over 30 U.S. documentaries for U.S. Dept. State for use fgn. countries; exec. dir. Internat. Film Found., 1945-74. Presbyn. Clubs: University, Coffee House, Explorers, Circumnavigators, Dutch Treat, Princeton (N.Y.C.); Adventurers (Chgo.). Author and photographer: Ambulance 464, Siege, Warsaw, 1960; recent films include: Japan, 1957; Russia, 1958; Middle East, 1959; South America, 1960; Tropical Africa, 1961, Amazon Family, 1961, Yugoslavia, 1962, Turkey, 1962, Africans All, 1963, Ancient Egyptian, 1964, Poland, 1965, Israel, 1965; African Village Life (Mali), 1967; Ancient Peruvian (with Sam Bryan), 1968; Mountain Peoples of Central Asia, 1968; First Americans, 1969; (with Sam Bryan) Ancient Africans, South America Today, 1973; Makiritare Indians (Venezuela), 1971; The Ancient Chinese, 1974; The Changing Middle East, 1975. Home: Bronxville, N.Y. Died Oct. 20, 1974.

BRYAN, O(VAL) N(ELSON), educator; b. Watertown, Tenn. July 4, 1881; s. Joshua Lester and Jennine (Wood) B.; M.D., Vanderbilt, 1907; m. Vance Bogle, Nov. 4, 1913; children—Martha, Jane, Oval Nelson. Began practice, 1907; asso. prof. Medicine, Vanderbilt Sch. Medicine from 1918. Capt. Med. Corps, 1918-19. Pres. Tenn. State Med. Assn., 1943. Fellow Am. Coll. Physicians; mem. A.M.A., Southern Med. Assn., Alpha Kappa Kappa. Christian. Republican. Mason (Shriner). Clubs: Bellemeade Country, Jesters. Home: Nashville, Tenn.†

BRYAN, SHEPARD, lawyer; b. New Bern, N.C., Dec. 8, 1871; s. Judge Henry Ravenscroft and Mary (Biddle Norcott) B.; A.B., U. of N.C., 1891, Law, 1892; m. Florence King Jackson, Jan. 14, 1909; children—Marion (Mrs. W. Colquitt Carter), Florence (Mrs. Bonneau Ansley), Mary (Mrs. William N. Benedict). Judge Superior Court, Atlanta Circuit, 1922; mem. Bryan, Carter, Ansley & Smith; Ga. counsel N.Y. Life Ins. Co., Aetna Life Ins. Co., Aetna Group of cos., U.S. Fidelity & Guaranty Company and other insurance companies; chmn. bd. DeKalb County Federal Savings & Loan Assn. Ex-pres. Atlanta Safety Council. Mem. Legal Advisory Bd. of Fulton Co., Ga., World War; active in Red Cross and Liberty Loan work. Former pres. and mem. Bd. of Control of Eleemosynary Instns. of Ga.; dir. Atlanta Tuberculosis Assn.; former mem. Atlanta Bd. of Edn. Mem. Am. Bar Assn., Georgia Bar Assn. (ex-v.p.), Atlanta Bar Assn. (ex-pres.), Lawyers' Club, Ga. Hist. Soc., Gen. Alumni Assn. U. of N.C., Atlanta Hist. Soc., N.C. Hist. Soc., Assn. of Life Insurance Counsel; former Worthy High Chancellor Alpha Tau Omega, Phi Delta Phi. Ex-pres. Y.M. Democratic League, Episcopalian. Mason. K.P. Clubs: Capital City, Piedmont Driving. Home: Atlanta, Ga.†

BRYAN-JONES, NOEL D., first reader Gen. Orgn. of Ch. of Christ, Scientist. Home: Worthing, Eng. Died Jan. 1974*

BRYANS, WILLIAM REMINGTON, engring. educator; b. New York, N.Y., June 30, 1884; s. Andrew K. and Ida L. (Farrington) B.; B.S., New York U., 1906, M.E., 1909; Dr. Engring. (honorary). New York University, 1949; m. Helen Lockwood Dayton, June 10, 1911; children—Ruth F., Dayton R. Draftsman, S. Vickers, cons. engr., 1906; engaged in part-time engring. work since 1907; instr. engring., Coll. of Engring., New York U., 1907-09, asst. prof. engring. drawing, 1909-13, asso. prof., 1913-18, asso. prof. mechanics and machine design, 1918-24, prof. engring. mechanics, 1924-49, asst. dean, 1933-49, prof. emeritus, 1949-75; adviser Coll. Engring., N.Y.U., 1949-51. Asst. dir. in direct charge of instruction, sect. B, S.A.T.C., New York U., during World War I. Member American Society Mechanical Engineering, Society Promotion Engineering Education, American Assn. Univ. Profs., Tau Beta Pi, Pi Tau Sigma, Scabbard and Blade (hon.). Contbr. tech. articles to engring. publs. Home: Hastings-on-Hudson N.Y. Died May 11, 1974.

BRYANT, DANIEL PENNINGTON, van and storage co. exec.; b. Waukegan, Ill., Sept. 28, 1908; s. Daniel and Emma (Dempcy) B.; A.B., Stanford, 1931, J.D., 1934; m. Noel Walster, Dec. 25, 1932; children—Rachel, Dan W., David W. Admitted to Cal. bar, 1934; mem. firm Chase, Barnes & Chase, Los Angeles, 1934-43; v.p., sec. Bekins Moving & Storage Co., Los Angeles, 1943-45, gen. mgr., 1945-57, pres., 1957-68, chmn. bd., chief exec. officer, 1968-76; chmn. bd. chief exec. officer The Bekins Co., 1968-76; dir. Bank of Am. Nat. Trust & Savs. Assn., Pacific Tel & Tel. Co., Pacific Lighting Co., Olga Co. Bd. dirs. Greater Los Angeles Urban Coalition; trustee Occidental Coll., Los Angeles, Com. Econ. Devel.; regent ct. of honor Forest Lawn Meml. Park, Glendale, Cal.; mem. corp. Conf. Bd. Mem. Nat. Furniture Warehousemen's Assn. (past pres.), Mchts. and Mfrs. Assn. Los Angeles (past pres., dir.), Los Angeles C. of C. (dir., past pres.). Conglist. Clubs: California, Bohemian, Lincoln (past pres.). Home: Pasadena, Cal., Died Feb. 3, 1976.

BRYANT, DONALD H., banker; b. Eaton, O., Mar. 27, 1919; s. Virgil L. and Marquerite (Marker) B.; B.S. in Bus., Miami U., Oxford, O., 1941; grad. Grad. Sch. Banking, U. Wis., 1968; m. Bettijane Pees, Oct. 31, 1942; children— Pamela Jane, William R. With Winters Nat. Bank, Dayton, O., 1946-75; dir. banking offices adminstrn., 1968-75. Served to maj. USMCR, World War II and Korea. Decorated Bronze Star. Mem. Phi Kappa Tau. Home: Dayton, O. Died July 10, 1975.

BRYANT, EMMONS, investment banker; b. Elizabeth, N.J., 1910; s. Emmons Bryant and Dorothy (Lyon) B.; grad. Amherst Coll., 1932; m. Mary Esther Stilwell, Sept. 11, 1937; children—Penelope (Mrs. Hale H. Carey), Mary E., Barbara Ann (Mrs. Neil W. Hller). Vice pres. Thomson McKinnon Auchincloss Inc., 1970-74; dir. Overhead Door Corp., Dallas, World Wide Helicopters, Nassau, Lab. for Electronics, Boston. Home: New York City N.Y. Died Oct. 14, 1974.

BRYANT, SAMUEL HOLLINGER, dentist, educator; b. Chester, Pa., Mar. 25, 1905; s. F. Otis and Mary Elizabeth (Hollinger) B.; A.B., Western Md. Coll., 1928; D.D.S., U. Md., 1932; m. Edna Claire Carmichael, Mar. 22, 1938; 1 son, Robert Samuel. Practice dentistry, Balt., 1933-72; faculty Balt. Coll. Dental Surgery. Dental Sch., U. Md., 1933-72, asst. prof. oral diagnosis, 1946-72. Dental intern Md. Gen. Hosp., 1932-33; dental staff U. Hosp., Balt., 1933-50; dental staff Md. Gen. Hosp., Balt., 1933-72; treas. Md. Dental Service Corp., 1964-72; chmn. dental adv. com. to Selective Service System of Md., 1960-71. Served to lt. col. AUS, 1942-46. Fellow Am. Coll. Dentists (chmn. Md. sect. 1966-67); mem. Am. (ho. of dels. 1963), Md. State (pres. 1963-64) dental assns., Balt. City Dental Soc. (pres. 1960-61, founder-chmn. immediate benefit com. 1966-70), Omicron Kappa Upsilon. Methodist (bd. dirs. 1968-71). Mason (Shriner), Lion. Club: Rolling Road Golf (Catonsville, Md.). Contbr. articles to dental jours. Home: Baltimore Md. Died Dec. 7, 1972; interred Baltimore, Md.

BRYCE, WILSON BARTLETT, printing co. exec.; b. Bay City, Mich., June 3, 1908; s. William James and Mary Ann (Kearney) B.; student Detroit Inst. Tech., 1926, Wayne U., 1930-31; m. Grace Elizabeth Wright, Oct. 24, 1934; children—Wilson David, Robert Terrence, Elaine Angela. Pres. Litho-Art, Inc., Detroit, from 1946, Kingsley Pub. Co., Inc., 1960. Mem. Beta Phi Sigma. Republican. Presbyn. Clubs: Detroit Yacht; Stonycroft Hills Golf. Home: Bloomfield Hills Mich. Deceased.

BUCHANAN, HERBERT EARLE, educator; b. Cane Hill, Ark., Oct. 4, 1881; s. James Albert and Susan Emaline (Clark) B.; A.B., U. of Ark., 1902, LL.D., 1928; A.M., U. of Chicago, 1903, Ph.D., 1909; m. Ada Clementine Tilley, Dec. 29, 1904; children—Herbert Tilley, Forest Christopher, Clara May (wife of Dr. F. W. Ogden), John Andrew. Instr., Ky. Mil. Inst., Lyndon, Ky., 1903-04; prof. mathematics, Lincoln (Ill.) Coll., 1904-07; instr., U. of Wis., 1909-11; prof. math., U. of Tenn., 1911-20, Tulane U., 1920-37, Dinwiddie grad. prof., since 1937, head dept., 1920-47, prof. emeritus, 1947-74. Fellow A.A.A.S.; mem. Am. Math. Soc., Math. Assn. Am. (v.p. 1935-38), Phi Beta Kappa, Sigma Xi. Club: Round Table (New Orleans, La.). Co-author of 6 textbooks in mathematics; also author of numerous research articles in math., astronomy. Home: Fayetteville Ark. Died Jan. 17, 1974.

BUCK, CHARLES HENRY, title ins. exec.; b. Balt., Oct. 18, 1889; s. Charles Henry and Roselia (Robinson) B.; LL.B., U. Md., 1911; m. Adele C. Strauss, June 1, 1914; children—Charles Henry, Frederick R., Adele (Mrs. John A. Ware). Abstractor Title Guarantee & Trust Co., 1911; admitted to Md. bar, 1911; examiner, city solicitor's office, Balt., 1912; title examiner Md. Title Guarantee Co., 1913, active charge mgmt., 1918-71, pres., dir., 1929-60, chairman board and chief executive officer, 1960-62, chairman of the board, 1962-71 (co. merged to form Title Guarantee Co. 1960); v.p. Equitable Trust Co., 1921-40; v.p. Md. Title Securities Corp., 1931-33, pres., 1933-40; dir., mem. exec. com. U.S. Fidelity & Guaranty Co., Maryland National Bank; mem. finance com. U.S. Fidelty & Guaranty Co.; dir. Lyric Co., Fidelity & Guaranty Life Ins. Co., Tower Bldg. Co. (Balt.), Dover Perpetual Bldg. & Loan Assn. Mem. bd., v.p., finance com. Church Home and Hosp.; chmn. exec. com. Greater Balt. Com., Inc., 1957-71; chmn. New Revenue Commn., Balt., 1958; pres. Balt. Real Estate Board, 1932. Mem. Mayor's com. to rep. Balt. at Md. Legislature, 1941, 43 sessions; chairman State Aviation Commission, 1944-46; member Mayor's Alcoholism Task Force Committee, past chairman Dem. candidate for mayor City Balt., 1939. Mem. Md., Balt. bar assns., Am. Title Assn. (chmn. title ins. sect. 1940-41, pres. 1941-42), Maryland Historical Society. Episcopalian. Rotarian. Clubs: Baltimore County (pres. 1963), Center Advertising (Balt.). Home: Baltimore, Md. Died Dec. 2, 1971; interred Balt.

BUCK, CHARLES NEVILLE, author; b. Woodford Co., Ky., Apr. 15, 1879; s. Charles W. and Elizabeth Crow (Bullitt) B.; A.B., U. of Louisville, 1898, LL.B., 1902; studied art, 1898-99; admitted to bar, 1902, but did not practice; m. Mrs. Margaret Field de Motte, June 20, 1918. Cartoonist, Evening Post, Louisville, 1899-1900; on editorial staff Evening Post and Morning Herald, 1900-08. Mem. Ky. Chapter S.A.R. Clubs: Arts, Pendennis (Louisville); Southern (Phila.). Author: The Key to Yesterday, 1910; The Lighted Match, 1911; The Portal of Dreams, 1912; The Call of the Cumberlands, 1913; The Battle Cry, 1914 (last two books dramatized); The Code of the Mountains, 1915; Destiny, 1916; Tyranny of Weakness, 1917; Bearcat Goes Dry, 1918; A Pagan of the Hills, 1919; The Tempering, 1920; The Roof Tree, 1921; Alias Red Ryan, 1923; The Gentleman in Pajamas, 1924; The Rogue's Badge, 1924; Portuguese Silver, 1925; Flight to the Hills, 1926; San Dollar, 1926; Iron Will, 1927; Marked Men, 1929; The Man and the Gun, 1931; Hazard of the Hills, 1932; Mountain Justice, 1935. Contbr. to mags. Home: Orleans, Mass.†

BUCK, ERNEST FERGUSON, clergyman, educator; b. Harrowsmith, Ont., Aug. 14, 1881; s. Danford E. and Mary V. (Westbrook) B.; came to U.S., 1900; A.B., Southwestern Coll., Winfield, Kan., 1908, D.D., 1923; B.D., Drew Theol. Sem., 1912; m. Frances Thomas, Aug. 7, 1906; children—Thomas Maxwell, Marian Louise. Ministry Meth. Ch. from 1901; pastor various chs. in Southwest Kan.; pastor 1st Ch., Winfield, Kan., 1918-21; extension sec. Southwestern Coll., Winfield, Kan., 1921-23; pres. Mo. Wesleyan Coll., Cameron, Mo., 1923-27; pastor First Ch., Ottawa, Kan., 1927-31, First Ch., Abilene, Kan., 1931-36, First Ch., Chanute, Kan., 1936-38; supt. Manhattan Dist., 1938-39, Ottawa Dist., 1939-43; First Ch. McPherson, Kan., from 1943. Republican. Club: Rotary. Home: McPherson, Kan.†

BUCK, JOHN LOSSING, economist; b. LaGrange twp., Dutchess County, N.Y., Nov. 27, 1890; s. Vincent Morgan and Grace Tenhagen B.; B.S., Cornell, 1914, M.S., 1925, Ph.D., 1933; m. Pearl Comfort Sydenstricker, May 30, 1917 (div. 1935); children—Carol, Janice; m. 2d, Lomay Chang, Oct. 11, 1941; children—Rosalind Grace, Paul Lossing. Farm instr. New Hampton Farms, New York, 1914-15; was advisor ministry of finance, Rep. of China, May 1939-Sept. 1940; prof. dept. agrl. econ., U. of Nanking, Oct. 1920-Mar. 1944; monetary advisor to sec. treasury, U.S.A., 1934-35; U.S. Treasury rep., China, 1935-39; chief edn. Nat. Agrl. Engring. Corp., Chungking, Apr. 1944-Mar. 1946; econ. advisor Farmer's Bank of China, Jan. 1945-Mar. 1946; agrl. econ. (tech. advisor) office fgn. agrl. relations, U.S. Dept. of Agr., July 1945-June 1946; mem. China-U.S. Agr. Mission, June 5-Dec. 4, 1946; chief land and water use br. agr. div. FAO, 1947-54; dir. for agr. econs. Council on Econ and Cultural Affairs, 1954-57, research associate, 1958. Member of Ministry of Industry, National Government of China (member com. for establishment of nat. agrl. research bur., 1932; advisory rural rehabilitaion commn., 1935), Chinese Statis. Assn. (mem. com. on population research, 1934), Nat. Econ. Council (mem. tech. com. of Cotton Commn., 1934), Sigma Xi, Phi Kappa Phi. Decorated with White Cravat with Red and Blue Borders of the Order of Brilliant Jade, Chinese Govt., 1938; awarded commendation for book, 1937. Home: Pleasant Valley, N.Y., Died Sept. 27, 1975.

BUCK, WILLIAM BRADFORD, humanitarian; b. Kalamazoo, Mich., Apr. 3, 1874; s. George Machan and Anne (Bradford) B.; A.B., Albion (Mich) Coll., 1895, A.M., 1896; A.M., Harvard, 1898; m. Anna Louise Bacorn, Aug. 27, 1904; 1 son, John Rutledge. Asst. minister Peoples Ch., N.Y. City, 1898-1900; sec. Cuban Orphan Soc., 1900-02, N.Y. County Visiting Com., 1902-04; supt. inspection N.Y. State Bd. of Charities, 1904-06; sec. and supt. Seybert Instn., Phila., 1906-15; supt. N.Y. City Children's Hosp. and Schs., 1915-16; dir. Sea View Farms, Dept. of Pub. Charities, N.Y. City, 1917-18; dir. of refugee relief for Am. Red Cross, Paris, 1918-19; commr. to Serbia, Am. Reconstruction Commn., 1920-21; supt. Speyer Hosp., 1924-25. Vol. sec. Children's Bur. of Philadelphia, 1907-08; mem. White House Conf. on Dependent Children, 1938. Mem. Nat. Conf. Social Work, State Conf. Charities and Correction, Nat. Inst. for Social Service, Am. Alumni Council. Mem. Alpha Tau Omega. Ind. Republican. Home: South Stanton Hill, N.Y.†

BUCKINGHAM, THEOPHILUS NASH, sportsman; b. Memphis, Shelby County, Tenn., May 31, 1880; s. Miles Sherman and Annie Gifford (Nash) B.; student Memphis U. Sch., 1894-98, Harvard, 1898-1901; 4-letter man at U. of Tenn. Law Sch.; m. Irma Lee Jones, June 1, 1910; 1 dau., Irma Jones (Mrs. Roy Edward Witt). Engaged in insurance and as newspaper reporter, 1904-10, writing and ranching, 1910, $2317, insurance, 1917-24; v.p. Buckingham-Ensley-Carrigan Co., sporting goods, Memphis, 1925-28; game restoration dir. Western Cartridge Co., East Alton, Ill., 1928-32; exec. sec. Am. Wildfowlers, Washington, D.C., 1928-33; waterfowl sanctuary examiner, U.S. Biol. Survey, 1935; with Am. Wildlife Inst., 1936; Western mgr. Cross Roads of Sport, N.Y. City, from 1938. Served as sergt., Co. I, 1st Tenn. Inf., 1916. Mem Citizens Federal Com. of Shelby Forest, Tenn.; formerly mem. exec. com. State Wildlife Fedn. Mem. Sigma Alpha Epsilon. Democrat. Episcopalian. Author: De Shootinest Gent'man, 1934; Mark Right, 1936; Ole Miss, 1937; Blood Lines, 1938; also many articles on subject of wildlife restoration. Contbr. to Sportsman, Field and Stream, Am. Forests, Am. Field and many other publs. Collaborator (with Caroline Gordon); "B from Bull's Foot," and other Scribner short stories. Asso. judge national field trial championships from 1932; judge many nat. and internat. field trial stakes. Home: Memphis, Tenn.†

BUCKLEY, HOMER JOHN, adv. agy. exec.; Rock Island County, Ill., Mar. 16, 1879; s. John A. and Mary (Sullivan) B.; ed. St. Ignatius Coll. and Bryant & Stratton Business Coll., Chicago; m. Lucile Kathleen Wallace, Sept. 23, 1908; 1 dau., Marihelyn. Began as messenger, Marshall Field & Co., 1891, mgr. circular advertising and follow up system, to 1905; now chmn. Robertson, Buckley, and Gotsch, Inc., advt. agy.; dir. Binks Mfg. Co. Major spl. sect. Officers Reserve. Dir. Century of Progress Expn., Chicago, 1933. Organizer and first pres. Nat. Assn. Direct Mail Advertisers; dir. Nat. Council of Business Mail Users; dir. Ill Manufacturers' Assn., Civic Fedn. of Chicago; dir., Chicago Tuberculosis Institute; mem. Asso. Advertising Clubs of the World, Chicago Assn. Commerce (exec. com.). K.C. Clubs: Union League, Chicago Advertising, Irish Fellowship, Chicago Athletic Assn., Butterfield Country Club. Author: Science of Marketing by Mail, 1924. Revised edit., 1941. Home: Chicago, Ill.†

BUCKLEY, TIM, composer, vocalist; b. Washington, Feb. 14, 1947; s. Tim and Elaine (Scalia) B. Recorded albums Tim Buckley, Hello and Goodbye, Happy Sad, Greetings from L.A., Lorea, Starsailor, 1966-75; composer (with others) mus. score for film Changes; concert performances include Royal Albert Hall, London, Eng., 1968, appearance with N.Y. Philharmonic, 1969. Lyricist. Contbr. anthologies, poetry books. Home: Santa Monica, Cal. Died June 1975.

BUCOVE, BERNARD, physician, educator; b. South Porcupine, Ont., Can., Nov. 3, 1912; s. Abraham and Sonia (Helperin) B.; M.D., U. Toronto, Ont., 1937, D.P.H., 1946; m. Dorothy Darling Broatch, Oct. 26, 1940; children—Michael A., Gregory O., Rodney I., Jeffrey O. Practice medicine, Rockglen, Sask., Can., 1939-41, Foam Lake, Sask., 1948-49; regional health officer, Sask., 1946-48; health officer Thurston-Mason County Health Dist., State of Wash., 1949-54; chief Div. Local Health, Wash. Dept. Health, 1954-55, dir. Dept. Health, chmn. Bd. Health, 1955-68; health services adminstr. City of N.Y., 1968-70; dir., prof. health adminstrn. Sch. Hygiene, U. Totonto, 1970-73. Mem. Health Ins. Benefits Adv. Council to sec. health, edn. and welfare, 1965-70; mem. Nat. Adv. Health Manpower Council USPHS; mem. Council Against Poverty, N.Y.C., 1968-70; mem. adv. council N.Y. regional med. programs, 1968-70; chmn. N.Y.C. Mayor's Organizational Task Force on Comprehensive Health Planning, 1969-70. Bd. dirs. Health and Hosp. Rev. and Planning Council So. N.Y., 1968-70, Vis. Nurse Service, N.Y.C., 1969-70, Hosp. Ins. Plan Greater N.Y., 1969-70. Served to maj. M.C., Royal Canadian Army, 1941-45; ETO. Fellow Am. Pub. Health Assn. (exec. bd. 1966-73, chmn. 1971-73, governing council 1956-65, 66-73), Royal Soc. Health (Eng.); mem. Ont., Canadian med. assns., Am. Assn. Pub. Health Physicians, Canadian Pub. Health Assn. (exec. com., chmn. com. pub. policy and legislation). Home: Toronto Can. Died Oct. 4, 1973; cremated.

BUDINA, ADOLPH OTTO, architect; b. O'Fallon, Ill., Feb. 25, 1891; s. Gustav W. and Sophia (Tiedemann) B.; B.Sc., U. Ill., 1914; m. Edna McCray Darrow, July 17, 1917; children—Margaret Jane (Mrs. John J. Zenner, Jr.), Barbara McCray (Mrs. William R. L. Smith, III). Draftsman Holabird & Roche, Chgo., 1916, Louis H. Sullivan, Chgo., 1917; office mgr. John Eberson, Chgo. and N.Y.C., 1919-30; pvt. practice architecture, 1930-54, mem. Budina and Freeman architects, Richmond, Va. Mem. Va. Bd. Exam. and Certification of Architects, Profl. Engrs. and Land Surveyors, 1947-52, pres., 1952. Sec.-treas. Va. Found. Archtl. Edn., 1955-57. Fellow A.I.A.; mem. Alpha Rho Chi. Presbyn. Home: Richmond, Va. Died Jan. 11, 1975.

BUEHNER, CARL WILLIAM, ch. ofcl., mfg. exec.; b. Stuttgart, Germany, Dec. 27, 1898; s. Carl Frederick and Anna Bertha (Geigle) B.; brought to U.S., 1901; grad. Granite High Sch.; m. Lucile Thurman, Sept. 26, 1922; children—Ruth (Mrs. Joseph M. McPhie), June (Mrs. Jack Ferrin, dec.) Marilyn (Mrs. John C. Riches), Carl Thurman. Missionary Ch. Latter-day Saints, to Eastern states, 1919-21, now gen. authority the church; pres. Utah Fur Farm, Inc.; sec.-treas., dir. Otto Buehner & Co.; pres., dir. Buehner Block Co.; chmn. bd., dir. Mineral Fertilizer Co.; pres., dir. Brookfield Products Co., Beacon Poultry Farms, Inc.; sec., dir. Sunset Lawn Memorial Corp.; dir. Comml. Security Bank, Sunset Life Ins. Co. Utah rep. Bus. Adv. Com. to Sec. Commerce, 1951-54. Pres. Gt. Salt Lake Council Boy Scouts Am., 5 years. Author: Do Unto Others. Home: Salt Lake City, UT. Died Nov. 11, 1974.

BUEHRER, THEOPHIL FREDERIC, educator; b. Brenham, Tex., Dec. 20, 1891, s. William and Eva (Mehr) B.; A.B., U. of Tex., 1916, A.M., 1918; Ph.D., U. of Calif., Berkeley, 1921; m. Etelka Eva Blumberg, Sept. 25, 1917; children—Ruth Ellen, Ruby May; m. 2d, Rosa Lee Brookes, May 1, 1959. Teacher Tex. pub. schs., 1910-13; instr. chemistry, U. of Ariz., 1921-24, asst. prof., 1924-26, asso. prof., 1926-28, prof., 1928-30; prof. agri. chemistry and physical chemist, Ariz. Agri. Expt. Sta., 1930-64, emeritus professor agricultural chemistry and soils, 1964-74; chmn. dept. agri. chemistry and soils, 1931-55, asso. Coll. Agr., 1954-58, coordinator ICA contract program in Iraq, 1955-59, prof. agri. chemistry and soils, 1959-61, emeritus prof., 1961-74; cons. to faculty agr. U. Shiraz, Iran under Ford Found., 1961-62; adviser in adminstrn. and edn. U. Agri. Scis., Bangalore, India under Univ. Tenn.-India Agri. Program, AID, from 1964; professor soil science Abu Ghraib Coll. Agr., Bagdad, Iraq, under Tech. Coop. Adminstrn., U.S. Dept. of State, 1953. Served as jr. chemist C.W.S., U.S. Army, 1918. Mem. Soil Sci. Soc. Am., Am. Chem. Soc., Theta Chi, Phi Kappa Phi, Sigma Xi, Pi Mu Epsilon, Phi Lambda Upsilon, Alpha Chi Sigma, Gamma Sigma Delta, Alpha Zeta. Democrat. Methodist. Mason, Kiwanian. Contbr. to profl. jours. Home: Sun City Ariz. Died Dec. 5, 1974.

BUELL, MURRAY F., educator; b. New haven, Oct. 6, 1905; s. Charles E. and Elinor (Fife) B.; B.A., Cornell U., 1930; M.A., U. Minn., 1934, Ph.D., 1935; D.Sc. (hon.), Doahe Coll., 1972; m. Helen Foot, Dec. 22, 1902; children—Peter F., Honor M. Teaching asst. U. Minn., 1931-35; instr. N.C. State Coll., 1935-37, asst. prof., 1938-46; asst. prof. Rutgers U., 1946-48, asso. prof., 1948-56, prof., 1956-71, prof. emeritus, 1971-75; vis. prof. U. Minn., 1971, Yale, winter-spring 1972, U. Ga. fall, 1972, U. Ariz., winter-spring 1973 Dir. Hutcheson Meml. Forest. Mem. Torrey Bot. Club (pres. 1954, editor Bull. 1963-69), N.J. Acad. Sci. (pres. 1963-65), Ecol. Soc. Am. (pres. 1961-62 Eminent Ecologist citation 1970), Bot. Soc. Am., Soc. Am. Foresters, Sigma Xi. Died July 1975.

BUFORD, LAWRENCE B., ry. official; b. Washington, D.C., 1879; ed. pub. schs. With Erie R.R. from 1902, successively in clerical positions till 1908, chief of tariff bur., at Chicago, 1908-10, at New York, 1910-11, gen. agt., at Baltimore, 1911-15, asst. to gen. traffic mgr., at New York, 1915-19, to gen. freight agt., at New York, 1919-20, gen. freight and passenger agt. from 1920.†

BUFORD, RIVERS HENDERSON, jurist; b. Pulaski, Tenn., Jan. 18, 1878; s. Albert and Mattie (Rivers) B.; ed. pub. schs. and in law office of Frederick T. Myers, of Tallahassee, Fla., m. Mary C. Munroe, Sept. 14, 1904 (died Sept. 13, 1924); m. 2d, Mary Hollingsworth, Jan. 27, 1926. Admitted to Fla. bar, 1900, and practiced in Wewahitchka, later at Qunicy and Marianna; mem. Fla. Ho. of Rep., 1901; pros. atty. Gadsden County, 1909-11; state's atty. Marianna Jud. Circuit, 1912-21; atty. gen. of Fla., term Jan. 4, 1921-Jan. 1925; reelected atty. gen., term Jan. 1925-29; resigned Dec. 4, 1925, and same day apptd. justice of Supreme Court of Fla.; elected same office for term, 1927-33, chief justice, Mar. 1931-Jan. 1933; designated chief justice for term Jan. 1943-Jan. 1945; justice Supreme Ct., from 1925. Democrat. Baptist. Mason (Shriner), Woodman, Elk. Home: Tallahassee, Fla.†

BUHLER, CHARLOTTE, psychologist; b. Berlin, Germany; d. Hermann and Rose (Kristeller) Malachowski; student U. Freiburg, 1913-14, U. Berlin, 1914-15; Ph.D., U. Munich, 1918; postgrad. U. Vienna, 1923-24, Columbia, 1924-25; m. Karl Buhler, Apr. 4, 1916 (dec. 1963); children—Ingeborg (Mrs. Alf Jorgen Aas), Rolf D. Came to U.S., 1940, naturalized, 1945. Lectr., Sch. Tech. Dresden, 1920-23; lectr. U. Vienna, 1923-29, asso. prof., 1929-38; prof. U. Oslo, Norway, 1938-40, St. Catherine Coll., St. Paul, 1940-43; chief clin. psychologist Mpls. Gen. Hosp., 1943-45, Los Angeles County Gen. Hosp., 1945-53; asst. clin. prof. psychiatry U. So. Cal. Med. Sch., 1950; pvt. practice psychology, Beverly Hills, Cal., 1950-74; vis. prof. numerous univs. Europe, also Columbia, U. Cal. at Berkeley, Hunter Coll., Clark U., Brandeis U. Dir. Child

Guidance Clinics, Vienna, London, Oslo, Worcester, Mass. Recipient Hon. medal city Vienna, 1964. Diplomate Am. Bd. Examiners in Profl. Psychology. Fellow Am. Psychol. Assn. Soc. for Projective Techniques, Am. Orthopsychiat. Assn.; mem. Psychologists for Advancement Psychotherapy (dir.), Am. Assn. Humanistic Psychology (pres. dir.), Am. Assn. Psychotherapy, Am. Assn. Gerontology, Los Angeles Soc. Practicing Psychologists, Am. So. Cal. (Outstanding award 1958, past pres.) group psychotherapy assns. Author: Childhood and Adolescence, 1928; The First Year of Life, 1930; The Human Course of Life as a Psychological Problem, 1933; From Birth to Maturity, 1935; Childhood Problems and the Teacher, 1952; Values in Psychotherapy, 1962; Die Psychologie im Leben Unserer Zeit, 1962; The Human Course of Life in its Goal Aspects, 1968; Humanistic Psychology and Education, 1970; (with F. Massarik) The Human Course of Life: Studies of Goals in the Humanistic Perspective, 1970; (with W. Allen) Intruduction into Humanistic Psychology, 1972. Home: Los Angeles, Cal., Died Feb. 3, 1974.

BUIE, LOUIS ARTHUR, SR., surgeon; b. Kingstree, S.C., July 30, 1890; s. Wilson Robert and Mable (Benjamin) B.; A.B., U. S.C. 1911, D.Sc., 1949; M.D., U. Md., 1915; m. Zelma L. Jones, Aug. 19, 1920; children—Nancy Louise, Louis Arthur. Resident in surgery Univ. Hosp., Balt., 1915; in charge Kernan Hosp., Balt., 1916; chief of dept. proctology Mayo Clinic, 1919-53, sr. cons., 1953-55; fellow Mayo Found., U. Minn., 1917, instr. surgery, 1920, asso. prof. surgery, 1921, prof. surgery (proctology), 1935-55, prof. emeritus U. Minn. Med. Sch., 1955-75; emeritus mem. Mayo Clinic Staff, Rochester, Minn., 1955-75. Nat. cons. to surgeon gen. USAF, 1956-58. Served as 1st lt. M.C., U.S. Army, Base Hosp. No. 102, attached to 4th and 6th Italian armies, No. Italy, 1918-19; received la Croce al Merito di guerra, Italian Govt., 1934. Mem. Gov.'s Adv. Council on Health, Phys. Edn. and Recreation, 1945-47. Mem. central certifying com. Am. Bd. Surgery, 1936-49; mem. Am. Bd. Protology (pres. 1934-35; chmn. bd. 1934-37; sec. 1949-53); sec. emeritus Adv. Bd. for Med. Specialties, 1957-75. Fellow A.C.S.; mem. Am. Proctologic Soc. (pres. 1928, 34-35). Minn. Med. Assn. (pres. 1947). A.M.A. (mem. Jud. council 1945-60), The Nat. Found. (mem. com. on fellowships 1954-62), A.A.A.S., Med. Library Assn.; has been active in state, local and spl. med. socs. and assns., Sigma Xi, Phi Beta Kappa, Nu Sigma Nu. Author: numerous med. books and articles, primarily in field of proctology. Editor-in-chief emeritus: Diseases of Colon and Rectum, 1957. Home: Rochester, Minn. Died July 2, 1975.

BULGANIN, NIKOLAI ALEKSANDROVICH, former premier of USSR; b. Nizhni-Novgorod (now Gorky), 1895. Mem. bd. Goselectrotest, 1923-27; dir. Moscow Elect. Works, 1927; mayor of Moscow, 1931; chmn. Council of People's Commissars, RSFSR, 1937; dep. chmn. Council of People's Commissars USSR, chmn. Gosbank, 1938-41; full gen. of the army, 1944, Marshall, 1947; dept. People's Commissar for Defense, 1944; minister of Armed Forces, 1947; dept. chmn. Council of Ministers of USSR, 1949-55; premier of USSR, 1955-58; mem. Politburo (now Presidium), Central Com. Community Party of Soviet Union, 1948-61. Address: Moscow USSR. Died Feb. 1975.

BULL, WILLIAM RUTLEDGE, corporation exec.; b. N.Y.C., Mar. 1, 1880; s. Charles Pinckney and Frances Margaret (Parrott) B.; educated pub. schs., Plainfield, N.J.; m. Louise Cranford du Moulin, July 28, 1915; children—Frances (Mrs. Sren Sommerfelt), Barbara B. (Mrs. J. H. Cameron Peake), Claire L. (adopted). Clk., U.S. Commr., Caribbean Commn., Sept., June 1947; U.S. Commr., West Indian Conf. (2d session), St. Thomas, Virgin Islands, Feb.-Mar., 1946; director, Div. Trusteeship, U.N., April 1946-Dec. 1948; principal dir. Dept. of Trusteeship from 1948. Prin. sec., U.N. Palestine Commn., 1948; personal rep. of Sec. Gen. with the U.N. Mediator on Palestine, 1948; acting U.N. Mediator on Palestine 1948-49; prof. govt. Harvard. Trustee Oberlin Coll. Awarded Spingarn medal by Nat. Assn. for Advancement of Colored People, 1949; Nobel Peace Prize, 1950. Home: Kew Gardens, N.Y.†

BULMAN, OLVIER MEREDITH BOONE, geologist; b. London, Eng., May 20, 1902; s. Henry H. and Beatrice E. (Boone) B.; ed. Imperial Coll. Sci., London, 1923; Ph.D., U. London, 1925, Sidney Sussex Coll., Cambridge, Eng., 1928, Sc.D., 1936; Ph.D. honoris causa U. Oslo, 1965; m. Marguerite Fearnsides, July 5, 1938; children—Elisabeth Jane (Mrs. C. Graeme Hely), Louisa Mary, Charlotte Anne (Mrs. J.T. Dean), William Henry. Demostrator zoology Imperial Coll. Sci., London, Eng., 1928, geology, 1929-31; demonstrator geology U. Cambridge (Eng.), 1931-34, lectr., 1934-45, reader in palaeozoology, 1945-55, Woodwardian prof. geology, 1955-66, emeritus prof., 1966-74. Trustee Brit. Mus. Natural History, London, 1964-71. Meml. volume pub. Palaeontological Assn. London, 1974. Fellow Royal Soc.; mem. Geol. Soc. London (pres. 1962-64, fgn. sec. 1964-67), Palaeontol. Assn. (pres. 1960-62), Brit. Assn. (sect. pres. 1959), Linnean Soc. (v.p. 1969-70), Palaeontographical Soc. (pres. 1971-74); fgn. mem. Geol. Soc. Stockholm, Roy. Fysiogr. Soc. Lund, Palaeontol. Soc. India. Author: (with W.G. Fearnsides) Geology in the Service of Man, 1944; Graptolithina, In Treatise of Invertebrate Paleontology, part V, 1955, 2d edit. 1970. Editor Geol. Mag., 1933-72. Contbr. articles to profl. jours. Home: Cambridge, England. Died Feb. 18, 1974; interred, Cambridge.

BUMBY, JOHN HAROLD, mfg. co. exec.; b. Juneau, Wis., Aug. 15, 1900; s. John Colley and Olive (Wells) B.; Ph.B., Ripon Coll., 1923; m. Isabel Borthwick Ingram, June 27, 1924; children—Adain James, Severy Bruce, Mary Jane, Beverly Anne (Mrs. Jack Gelst). Pres. Ripon Fed. Savs. & Loan Assn. (Wis.), 1932-42; chmn., dir. Advertisers Mfg. Co., Ripon, 1923-73; v.p., dir. Ripon Foods Inc., 1933-73; pres. Mac Gillis and Gibbs Co., Milw., 1942-67, chmn. bd. dirs., 1967-74; pres. J. Harold Bumby Ltd., Vancouver, B.C., Can. Mayor of Ripon, 1932-36; mem. Ripon Sch. Bd., 1936-42. Mem. Ripon Municipal Hosp. Bd., 1938-42. Mem. English Speaking Union. Republican. Conglist. Mason. Clubs: Milwaukee, University, Farmers, Civil War Round Table, Bookfellows (v.p. 1971-73) (Milw.) Home: Milwaukee, Wis. Died Nov. 4, 1974; interred, Ripon, Wis.

BUMGARDNER, HELEN AYERS, librarian; b. Athens, Ill., May 6, 1929; d. Thomas Hargrave and Elizabeth (Hall) Ayers; B.S., Northwest U., 1951; M.L.S. (Edgar Bergen scholar 1954-58, Sch. Librarians' scholar 1954), U. Wash., 1958; m. Melvin L. Bumgardner, Aug. 2, 1953; children—Thomas Orin, Florence. Tchr. English, Feitshans High Sch., Springfield, Ill., 1951-53; children's librarian Multnomah County Library, Portland, Ore., 1953-57; head librarian Wash. State Hist. Soc., Tacoma, part time, 1959-63; head librarian Clover Park Vocational-Tech. Sch., Tacoma, part time 1963-72. Tchr. library sci. Pacific Luth. U., Tacoma, evenings and summer, 1966-68. Sec., Wash. Jr. Soccer Assn., 1971. Mem. Wash. Assn. Sch. Librarians (pres. elect, 1972), Tacoma Genealogical Soc., N.E.A. (life), U. Wash. Alumni Assn., A.L.A., Wash. Assn. Sch. Librarians, Wash. Edn. Assn., Am. Vocational Tech. Assn. Editor Library Leads, 1968-69. Contbr. to mags., profl. jours. Home: Tacoma Wash. Died Oct. 31, 1972.

BUNCE, EDGAR F., coll. pres.; b. Frewsburg, N.Y., Mar. 21, 1887; s. Lester Fenn and Frances (Rhodes) B.; diploma, Fredonia Normal Sch., 1908, B.S., Teachers Coll. Columbia Univ., 1916, A.M., 1926, Ed.D., New York Univ., 1939; m. Julia Mory, June 22, 1911; children—Lester Mory, Edgar Fenn, Wilma Rhodes. Principal of a grade sch., 1908-10; supervising prin., Lodi, N.J., 1910-18. Mount Holly, N.J., 1918-28, Metuchen, N.J., 1928-30; part-time instr. in edn., Rutgers Univ., 1924-31; v.p. Trenton State Teachers Coll., 1930-31; state dir., Teacher Edn. for N.J., 1931-37; pres. N.J. State Teachers Coll., Glassboro, from 1937, then pres. emeritus. Mem. N.J. Council of Edn., N.E.A., N.J. Edn. Assn. Club: Rotary (Glassboro, N.J.). Home: Glassboro N.J. Died Feb. 20, 1974.

BUNKER, CHARLES C., merchant; b. West Chicago, Ill., Sept. 4, 1880; s. Lewis C. and May D. (Wheeler) B.; student pub. schs.; m. Fay Bailey, Dec. 17, 1907; children—Charles C., Allen B. Began with Marshall Field & Co., 1897; foreign buyer, 1916. dept. mgr., 1919, div. mdse. mgr., 1927; asst. gen. mdse. mgr., 1931, v.p. and asst. gen. mgr., 1935; v.p. and mgr. Eastern Retail Div., 1936; v.p. and gen. mdse. mgr. from 1937. Mason. Clubs: Chicago Athletic Assn., Chicago Golf, Racquet of Chicago. Home: Chicago, Ill.†

BURBANK, WILBUR SWETT, geologist; b. Amesbury, Mass., Mar. 30, 1898; s. Wilbur Augustus and Emma Elizabeth (Swett) B.; S.B., Mass. Inst. Tech., 1919, S.M. 1920, postgrad., 1924-25; m. Beryl Frances Loughlin, Apr. 1, 1933; children—John Francis, Phillip Augustus. With U.S. Geol. Survey, 1920-75, successively mineral resource investigations, gen. geologic mapping, Republic of Haiti, geologic mapping, Mont., studies copper deposits of Mich., fed. and state coop. study geology and mineral resources of Colo., 1926-39, mineral investigations Republic of Haiti, Dominican Republic, strategic mineral investigation minor metal resources of U.S., research volcanism and mineralizing processes ancient volcanic areas, San Juan Mountains, Colo., adminstrv. com. work geologic programs, 1920-58, field research ancient volcanic processes in relation geochemistry, thermodynamics of mineralizing processes, 1958-75. Soc. Econ. Geologists rep. earth scis. div. NRC, 1934-36, exec. com. div. earth scis., 1955-58. Recipient Distinguished Service award Dept. Interior, 1958. Mem. Am. Geophys. Union (v.p. volcanology 1935-38, pres. 1947-50, sec. tectonophysics sect. 1947-53), Soc. Econ. Geologists, Geol. Soc. Am., Mineral. Soc. Am., Geochem. Soc., No. New Eng. Acad. Scis., Colo. Sci. Soc., Geol. Soc. Washington. Unitarian. Clubs: Cosmos, Petrologists (Washington). Contbr. numerous tech. articles profl. publs. Home: Exeter, N.H. Died Apr. 1, 1975; interred Bartlett Cemetery, Amesbury, Mass.

BURCH, GEORGE BOSWORTH, educator; b. Hartford, Conn., July 12, 1902; s. George Washington and Mary Jane (Bosworth) B.; A.B., Harvard, 1923, A.M., 1927, Ph.D., 1939; grad. study U. Geneva, 1933-34, U. Paris, 1935-36; m. Betty Brand, Sept. 25, 1933; children—Jean Brand, Peter George, John Bosworth. Prof. philosophy, psychology Coll. Ida., 1942-46; Fletcher prof. philosophy Tufts U., Medford, Mass., from 1946, then prof. emeritus; vis. scholar Indian Inst. of Philosophy, Amalner, India, 1953-54; vis. prof. philosophy Visvabharati Univ., Santini Ketan, India, 1961. Mem. Am. Philos. Assn., Guild Scholars in Episcopal Church, Metaphysical Society Am. Author: Early Medieval Philosophy, 1951. Editor, translator: The Steps of Humility (Bernard of Clairvaux), 1940. Home: Belmont Mass. Died June 4, 1973.

BURCHARD, JOHN ELY, archtl. historian, critic and cons.; b. Marshall, Minn., Dec. 8, 1898; s. James Clark and Sidonie (Schupp) B.; U. Minn. Coll. Liberal Arts, 1915-17, Coll. Medicine, 1917; S.B. in Archtl. Engring., Mass. Inst. Tech., 1923, S.M., 1925; L.H.D. (hon.), Union Coll., 1953; D. Architecture (hon.) U. Mich., 1956; m. Marjorie Walker Gaines, Sept. 7, 1926; children—John Ely, Marshall Gaines. Prof. and dir. Albert Farwell Bemis Found., Mass. Inst. Tech., 1938-48, became dean sch. humanities and social sci., 1948, dean emeritus, 1964--; Canadian Hazen lectr., 1953; Lowell Inst. lectr. Boston Mus. Fine Arts, 1955; vis. prof. U. Cal., 1954, 55, 64-68, acting head dept. design, 1965-66, acting dean Coll. Environmental Design, 1966-67; Mellon vis. prof. environmental design 1967-68; Thomas Jefferson vis. prof. U. Va., 1969; cons. on aesthetics Bay Area Rapid Transit Dist., lectr., Iran, Pakistan, India, 1962; studied new German architecture as guest of Fed. Republic, 1963; cons. Graham Found. for Advanced Studies in Fine Arts, 1955-60. Various posts OSRD, 1944-46, ending as chief div. 2 and dep. chief Office Field Services; mem. Am. delegation to France and Norway on higher edn., 1957; mem. Kawana (Tokyo) Conf. on Sci. and Modern Civilization, 1960. Mem. adv. bd. U.S. Mcht. Marine Acad., Kings Point, N.Y., 1953-60, chmn., 1956-57; mem. Yale Council Com. on Library, 1949-58, Princeton U. adv. council of library, 1949-55; trustee Mt. Holyoke Coll., 1951-61, mem. exec. com., 1953-61; mem. coml to visit grad. sch. design Harvard, 1953-59; trustee Boston Mus. Fine Arts, 1957-60. Recipient Presdl. medal for Merit, 1948; U. Minn. outstanding achievement award, 1960; Thomas Jefferson Meml. medal Architecture, 1969; decorated officier de lOrdre des Arts et des Lettres (France). Fellow Am. Acad. Arts and Scis. (pres. 1954-57, bd. editors Daedalus 1958-73); mem. A.I.A. (hon.). Author: (with others) The Evolving House, 3 vols., 1933-36; (with Oscar Handlin) The Historian and The City, 1963; (with A. Bush-Brown) The Architecture of America, 1961; The Voice of the Phoenix, Post-war Architecture in Germany, 1966. Editor, annotator: Mid-Century; The Social Implications of Scientific Progress, 1950. Contbr. chpts. to Planning the University Library Building, 1949, Religious Faith and World Culture, 1951, The Individual and Liberal Education, 1952, The Metropolis in Modern Life, 1954, Symbols and Society, 1954, The Metropolitan Enigma, 1967. Home: Boston, Mass., Died Dec. 25, 1975.

BURCHKHARDT, CHARLES JACOB, historian, author; b. Basel, Switzerland, Sept. 10, 1891; s. Charles and Helene Aline (Schazmann) B.; student schs. Basel, Glarlsegg, Munich, Gottingen, Zurich, Paris; Dr. h.C., U. Basel; 1939, U. Lille, 1947, U. Grenobie, 1947, U. Rehovot, 1963; m. Elisabeth de Reynold, Nov. 10, 1926; children—Henriette Chiesa-Gautler-Vignal, Sabine de Murait. Attache, Swiss Legation, Vienna, Austria, 1918-22; chief del. Internat. Com. Red Cross, Turkey, 1923; prof. meodern history U. Zurich, 1923-32; prof. Postgrad. Sch. Internat. Studies, Geneva, Switzerland, 1932; high commr. League of Nations, Free City Danzig, 1937-39; pres. com. Internat. Red Cross, 1944-48, pres. mixed relief com.; Swiss minister, France, 1945-49. Decorated Knight Order Merit (Germany); grand officer Legion of Honor (France); named hon. citizen Lille, 1947, Lubeck, 1950, Vinzel, 1966. Asso. mem. Acad. Salamanca, Inst. des Sciences morales et politiques de l' Acad. Francaise, Bavarian Acad. Fine Arts, Bourges Acad., Berlin Acad. Arts; hon. mem. Austrian Acad. Sci. and Art. Author: Charles Chr. Buckhardt, 1916; Travel in Asia Minor, 1924; Maria Theresa, 1931; Richelleu, 4 vols.; Correspondence H.Von Hofmannsthal-C.J. Burckhardt, 1956; My Mission at Danzig, 1960; Collected Works, 6 vols., 1971; others. Home: Vinzel, Switzerland., Died Mar. 3, 1974.

BURDETTE, FRANKLIN L., educator; b. Huntington, W.Va., Dec. 7, 1911; s. Frank Lee and Laura (Buckner) B.; A.B. summa cum laude, Marshall Coll., 1934; A.M., U. Neb., 1935; postgrad. U. N.C., 1935-36, U. Chgo., 1936; A.M., Princeton, 1937, Ph.D., 1938; LL.D., Marshall Coll., 1959; m. Evelyn Spruill Page, June 28, 1938; children—Franklin Page, Joseph Bryan. Instr. politics Princeton U., 1936-37, 1938-39, fellow, 1937-38; research asso. Princeton Local Govt. Survey, 1939-40; mem. faculty Butler U., 1940-46; asso. prof. govt. and politics U. Md., 1946-47, prof., 1947-75, head dept., 1950-54, dir. bur. govtl. research, 1956-75, on leave as head of overseas book program and related cultural activities U.S. Govt., 1954-56; exec. sec. Nat. Found. Edn. Am. Citizenships, 1940-46, editor publs., 1946-50; editor polit. sci. series D. Van Nostrand Co., 1948-75; bd. dirs. Operations and Policy Research, Inc. Mem. bd. editors Am. Polit. Sci. Rev., 1948-49; lectr. polit. sci. Am. U., 1948-49. Trustee Westminster Choir Coll., Princeton, N.J.; bd. dirs. Council on Islamic Affairs, 1957-60; chmn. Md. Gov.'s. Commn. on Reapportionment of Legislature, 1962-64; mem. Md. State Constl. Conv. Commn., 1965-67; del. Md. Constl. Conv., 1967-68. Sec., mem. bd. trustees Inst. for Am.

Univs., U. Aix-Marseille, France, 1958-75; trustee Montgomery Coll., 1969-75. Mem. ednl. bd. YMCA evening high sch., Indpls., 1941-46; mem. bd. Ind. Merit Assn., 1941-46; mem. Ind. War History Commn., 1943-46; sec. Indpls. br. Fgn. Policy Assn., 1944-46. Mem. Am. Soc. Internat. Law, Am. Hist. Assn., Am. Polit. Sci. Assn. (pres. Washington chpt. 1950-51, mem. nat. council 1962-64), Middle States Council for Social Studies (pres. 1953-54), Am. Soc. Pub. Adminstrn. (ofcl. observer Baghdad Pact in Iraq 1957, pres. Md. chpt. 1958-59), Nat. Civil Service League (mem. council), Nat. Municipal League, S.A.R. (v.p. gen. nat. soc. 1933-38; sec. W.Va. Soc. 1930-38; sec. Ind. Soc. 1943-46), So. Polit. Sci. Assn. (v.p. 1952), Assn. Coll. Honor Socs. (pres. 1969-71), Kappa Delta Pi, Phi Alpha Theta, Phi Kappa Phi, Pi Sigma Alpha (nat. sec., treas. 1946-48, nat. pres. 1956-58, nat. dir. 1960-75). Baptist. Mason. Author: Filibustering in the Senate, 1940; Political Parties: An American Way, 1945; Lobbyists in Action, 1950; Election Practices in Maryland, 1950; The Republican Party: A Short History, 1968, 2d edit., 1972; contbg. author: Maryland, A History, 1632-1974, 1974. Editor: Education for Citizen Responsibilities, 1942; biog. directory of Am. Polit. Sci. Assn., 1945-48, 61; Addresses and State Papers of Spiro T. Agnew, Governor of Maryland, 1967-69. Co-editor hist. monographs on religion and Am. Instn., 1947-49; chmn. bd. editors World Affairs, 1965-75; adv. editor Ency. Americana, 1968-75. Contbr. articles on polit. subjects to publs. Home: Bethesda Md. Died Aug. 8, 1975; buried Yatesmont Cemetery, Ona, W. Va.

BURDICK, HAROLD ORMOND, educator; b. New Market, N.J., June 26, 1897; s. Alberne Hugh and Josephine (Dunham) B.; A.B., Milton College, 1919; M.A., U. Wis., 1926; Sc. D. (hon.), Salem Coll., 1939, Alfred U., 1962; m. Hannah Shaw, June 23, 1919; children—Kenneth, Carol B. Hudson, Judith B. Downey. Instr. Salem Coll. Acad., 1919-20; prof. biology Salem Coll., 1920-29; grad. asst. U. Wis., 1925-27; prof. biology Milton Coll., 1929-31; asso. prof. biology Alfred U., 1931-37, prof. biology, dept. chmn. 1937-62, then prof. emeritus, acting dean coll. liberal arts, 1948-49, dean, 1949-55, dir. summer sch., 1950-53. Field dir. A.R.C., Bengal Province, India, 1945. Dir. Alfred University Research Found. Mem. Endocrine Soc., American Physiol. Soc., Am. Society Zoology, Soc. Exptl. Biology and Medicine, N.E.A., Sigma Xi, Phi Sigma, Lambda Chi. Seventh Day Baptist. Author numerous research articles on reproductive physiology. Home: Alfred, N.Y. Died July 8, 1974; buried Alfred (N.Y.) Rural Cemetery.

BURES, CHARLES EDWIN, educator; b. Cedar Rapids, Ia., Mar. 7, 1910; s. Frank Joseph and Olga (Janda) B.; B.A., Grinnell Coll., 1933; postgrad. Columbia, 1933-34; M.A., U. Ia., 1936, Ph.D., 1938; m. Helen Elizabeth Bonde, June 1, 1948. Prof. philosophy and psychology Coll. Ida., 1938-42; with N.Am. Aviation, Inc., 1943-45; lectr. U. So. Cal., 1947-48; instr. U. Ore., 1948-49; asst. prof. Cal. Inst. Tech., Pasadena, 1949-53, asso. prof., 1953-69, prof., 1969. Fellow A.A.A.S.; mem. Am. Philos. Assn., Am. Math. Soc., Am. Psychol. Assn. Philosophy Sci. Assn., Nat. Audubon Soc., Sierra Club, Phi Beta Kappa. Home: Pasadena Cal. Died Apr. 30, 1974; cremated.

BURKE, ELLEN COOLIDGE, librarian; b. Alexandria, Va., May 10, 1901; d. Henry Randolph and Rosella (Trist) Burke; B.A., Catholic U. Am., 1938, M.A., 1943. With Alexandria Library, 1939-69, successively cataloguer, reference, 1st asst. library dir., 1948-69, Ellen Coolidge Burke Br. Library dedicated in her honor, Alexandria, 1968. Mem. Va. Library Assn., Va. Council Human Relations, Common Cause, League Women Voters, Montecello Assn., Historic Alexandria Found. (charter). Roman Catholic. Club: Zonta. Home: Washington House Alexandria, Va., Died Dec. 29, 1975.

BURKE, RAYMOND H., congressman; b. Nicholsville, O., Nov. 4, 1881; s. Daniel Fletcher and Mary Jane (McNair) B.; student Oberlin (O.) Acad. and Coll., 1900-05; B.S., Univ. of Chicago, 1906, post grad. study, 1907-08; m. Daisy Minnich, June 24, 1908; 1 son, Robert McNair. Instr. in geog. and nature study, Miami, (O.) Univ., 1906-07, asst. prof. of geology, 1907-08, dir. of univ. music, 1908-15; dist. mgr. The Midland Mutual Life Ins. Co., Columbus, O., 1915-18; personnel and employment mgr., The Hooven, Owens, Rentschler Co., Hamilton, O., 1928-23; sec.-treas., dir., mgr., The Fort Hamilton (O.) Automobile Co., 1923-26; dir. The Investors Service and Finance Co., Hamilton, 1922-25; sales rep., The Northwestern Mutual Life Ins. Co. of Milwaukee and other cons., Hamilton, from 1926; mem. 80th Congress (1947-49), 3d Ohio Dist. Mem. charter commn., 1926-27; mem. Hamilton City Council, 1928-42; mayor Hamilton O., 1928-40; state senator 2d and 4th dists., O., 1942-46. Served as chmn. Selective Service Bd. No. 2, Butler County, O., 1939-42. Dir. Hamilton Y.M.C.A. 25 yrs. Served as dir. Presbyn. Ch. choir, Hamilton, 31 yrs. Republican. Clubs: Rotary (pres.), Unity, Round Table, Hamilton. Composer Miami Univ. songs: Alma Mater (Old Miami), 1908, Miami March song, 1907, Miami Scalp song, 1915; (church anthems) Fairest Lord Jesus, 1929, The Radiant Morn, 1929, The Apostles' Creed, 1941. Author: Outline of School Music, 1910. Home: Hamilton, O.†

BURKE, VINCENT JOHN, journalist; b. Chgo., June 17, 1919; s. Victor and Marie (Larke) B.; B.A. in History, U. Chgo., 1941; m. Velma Lois Whitgrove, Dec. 5, 1942; children—Douglas, Barbara, Judith, Patricia. With U.P.I., 1940-42, 46-63, assigned Washington, 1947-63; mem. staff Los Angeles Times, 1964-73, Moscow (USSR) bur., 1965-66, reporter, Washington, 1967-74. Co-author: (with wife) Nixon's Good Deed, Welfare Reform, 1974. Home: Washington, D.C. Died May 7, 1973.

BURKHALTER, EVERETT GLEN, congressman; b. Mulberry, Ind., Jan. 19, 1897; student Purdue U.; m. Velma Proctor, 1923. Various positions copper mines, Bisby, Ariz.; electrician charge unit lighting, motion-picture studio, later became illuminating engr.; mem. Ariz. Assembly, 1942-53, mem. coms. Ways and Means, Edn., Fish and Game, Pub. Utilities and Corps., Social Welfare, Mil. Affairs; mem. 88th Congress, 27th Cal. Dist. Mem. city Council, Los Angeles, 1953-62; chmn. pub. works com., mem. recreation and parks coms., Los Angeles. Democrat. Home: North Hollywood, Cal. Died May 1975.

BURKHALTER, FRANK ELISHA, educator; b. Cotton Gin, Tex., Apr. 19, 1880; s. Pleasant Hill and Sallie (McMillan) B.; Ph.B., Baylor U., 1907; A.B., Columbia, 1908; unmarried. Newspaper reporter, Ft. Worth, Tex., 1908; staff corr. Ft. Worth Record, 1909-11; news editor Waco Tribune, 1912-13; editor Waco Morning News, 1914-15; on editorial staff San Antonio Express, 1916, Houston Chronicle, 1917; editorial and publicity dir. Tex. Agrl. and Mech. Coll., 1918; publicity dir. Southern Bapt. Conv., 1919-29; publicity dir. Baptist World Alliance, Stockholm, 1923, Toronto, 1928; sec. exec. com. Southern Baptist Conv., 1926-29; prof. journalism, Baylor University, 1929-47; teacher, U.S. Army program, Biarritz, Fr., Berlin, Ger., July 1945-46. Awarded 1st prize, $571000, C.E. Palmer Foundation nat. contest for outline comprehensive program for propagating principles of Golden Rule; Silver Keystone award, Boys Club Service Bar, Boys Clubs Am., Inc. for outstanding service to boys. Mem. Southwestern Journalism Congress (pres. 1937), Am. Assn. Teachers Journalism, Texas Press Association, Am. Assn. U. Profs., Sigma Delta Chi. Baptist. Author: Winning the Adolescent Boy, 1935; Living Abundantly, 1942; A World Minded Church, 1945; Intermediate Fishers, 1951. Wrote "Texas Baptist Laymen and Their Work" in Centennial Story of Texas Baptists, 1936. Contbr. to So. Bapt. Ency., religious mags. Home: Waco, Tex.†

BURKHART, SAMUEL ELLSWORTH, physician; b. Pitts., Feb. 8, 1914; s. Ellsworth Raymond and Edna Mae (Crossland) B.; B.S. U. Pitts., 1935; M.D., Hahnemann Med. Coll., Phila., 1939; m. Helen Catherine McKee, May 21, 1941; children—Frederich McKee, Jeffrey Lynn, Gregory James. Intern, Shadyside Hosp., Pitts., 1939-40; resident Huron Rd. Hosp., East Cleveland, O., 1940-43, dir. dept. obstetrics and gynecology, 1955-60, pres. med. staff, 1964-66, later also vis. staff; practice medicine, specializing in obstetrics and gynecology, Cleve.; vis. staff Booth Meml. Hosp., Cleve. Served to lt. M.C., USNR, 1944-46; PTO. Diplomate Am. Bd. Obstetrics and Gynecology. Fellow Internat. Coll. Surgeons, A.C.S.; mem. A.M.A., Am. Coll. Obstetrics and Gynecology, Cleve. Acad. Medicine, Cleve. Obstet. and Gynecol. Soc., Central Assn. Obstetrics and Gynecology (life). Home: Cleveland, O., Died Oct. 24, 1974; buried Lakeview Cemetery, Cleveland, O.

BURKHEAD, MARGARET BRISTOW, library dir.; b. St. Louis, Nov. 5, 1905; d. Harry L. and Mary V. (Safford) Bristow; student Harris Tchrs. Coll., St. Louis, Mt. Holyoke Coll., Ill. U. Library Sch.; grad. Strassburger Conservatory Music; m. Lingurn S. Burkhead, June 24, 1925. Exec. sec. legal firm Thompson, Mitchell, Thompson & Young, St. Louis, 1930-37; tchr. Miss Hickey's Sch. for Secs., St. Louis, 1937-39; pvt. tutor, Little Rock, 1939-42; exec. sec. Little Rock Pub. Library, 1942-56, adminstr., 1956-57, dir., 1957-70. Mem. Ark. Library Assn., Nat. Soc. Arts and Letters, D.A.R. (past regent Little Rock chpt.), P.E.O. (past pres.), Order of Bookfellows (past pres.). Home: Little Rock, Ark., Died Apr. 1975.

BURLING, (FRED) TEMPLE, psychiatrist; b. Chicago, Mar. 22, 1896; s. James Perkins and Terese (Temple) B.; student Grinnel (Ia.) Coll., 1913-15; B.S., University of Chicago, 1920; M.D., Rush Medical College, 1923; married Katherine White, January 30, 1924; children—Robbins, James Perkins, Helen. Interne Los Angeles County Hospital, 1922-23; medical director Providence Child Guidance Clinic, Providence, 1940-47; field director, div. of vocational rehabilitation, Nat. Com. for Mental Hygiene, 1947-48; prof. sch. of indsl. and labor relations, Cornell, 1948-75. Faculty Middle East Tech. U., Ankara, Turkey, 1962-63. Served with Ambulance and San. Corps, U.S. Army, 1917-18. Member A.A.A.S., American Psychiatric Asso. A.M.A., Am. Orthopsychiatric Assn. Author: The Vocational Rehabilitation and Psychiatric Patients (with Thomas A. C. Rennie and Luther E. Woodward), 1950; The Give and Take in Hospitals (with Edith Lentz and R. N. Wilson). Contributor articles on industrial and child psychiatry to professional publications. Home: Trumansburg, N.Y. Died Feb. 16, 1975.

BURNETT, CORDAS CHRIS, ednl. adminstr., assn. exec.; b. Mounds, Ill., Feb. 6, 1917; s. Charistopher prof., Columbus and Lucy Virginia (Cline) B.; student Central Bible Inst., Springfield, Mo., 1934-35, U. Notre Dame, 1942-44; B.A. cum laude, DePaul U., 1948; student Washington U., St. Louis, 1949-50; D.D. (hon.), Southeastern Bible Coll., Birmingham, Ala., 1958; m. Dorothy Charlene Talley, June 3, 1937; children—Barbara Celeste, Marilyn Kay. Ordained to ministry Assemblies of God, 1937; minister in South Bend, Ind., 1940-45, Chgo., 1945-48, Cin., 1952-54; instr. history and philosophy Central Bible Inst., 1948-52, v.p. inst., 1954-58; mem. bd. edn. Assemblies of God, 1958, sec. dept. edn., 1958-59; sec. Nat. Assn. Evangs., 1956-75, mem. bd. adminstrn., 1953-75, treas. commn. on higher edn., 1964-75; pres. Bethany Bible Coll., Santa Cruz, Cal., 1959-72; exec. v.p. Assemblies of God Grad. Sch. Theology and Missions, Springfield, Mo., 1972-75. Mem. exec. com. Accrediting Assn. Bible Colls., 1959-64; treas. N. Am. Assn. Bible Insts. and Bible Colls., 1956-75. Pres. Scotts Valley County Water Dist., 1962-75. Bd. dirs. Berean Sch. Bible, Springfield, 1958-59, Evangel Coll., Springfield, 1958-59. Home: Springfield, Mo. Died Aug. 27, 1975.

BURNETT, LEO, advt. exec.; b. St. Johns, Mich., Oct. 21, 1891; s. Noble and Rose (Clark) B.; A.B., U. Mich., 1914; m. Naomi Geddes, May 29, 1918; children—Peter, Joseph, Phoebe. Founder, pres. Leo Burnett Co., Inc., 1935, founder, chmn. bd. Dir. Advt. Council 1941-71, chmn., 1962-63; trustee, mem. exec. com. Am. Heritage Found., 1953-71; dir. Better Bus. Bur. Met. Chgo., 1950-71; dir. advt. Non-Partisan Register and Vote campaign, 1952. Mem. exec. bd. Com. Econ. and Cultural Devel. Chgo.; bd. dirs Adler Planetarium, Chgo. Received honor award, Wartime Advt., 1945, Freedoms Found., Inc., 1949; Gold Medal award, Printers Ink, 1955; Special Merit award, N.Y. Art Directors Club, 1956; Honor award distinguished service in journalism, Sch. Journalism, U. Mo., 1963; Bus. Statesmanship award Harvard Bus. Sch. Assn. Chgo., 1963; named Mktg. Man of Yr. Chgo. chpt. Am. Mktg. Assn., 1966; Named to Advt. Hall of Fame, 1972 Republican. Clubs: University, (N.Y.); Everglades (Palm Beach, Fla.); Detroit Athletic; Minneapolis; Chicago, Racquet, Tavern, Executives, Economic, Mid America, Commercial (Chgo.). Lake Zurich (Ill.) Golf; University (Indpls.). Author: Communications of an Advertising Man, 1961. Editor, compiler: Good Citizen, 1948. Home: Lake Zurich, Ill. Died June 7, 1971; buried Rosehill Cemetery, Chgo.

BURNETTE, WELLS DEWEY, pub. relations co. exec.; b. San Antonio, Sept. 14, 1915; s. LaSalle Dewey and Margaret (Seits) B.; A.B., U. Chgo., 1937; postgrad. John Marshall Law Sch., 1942-43; m. Cora A. Clauson, Sept. 9, 1939; children—Mark Clauson, James Dewey (dec.), Linnea Margaret. Own bus., Pueblo, Colo., 1933-35; editor U. Chgo. Mag., 1935-36; asst. bus. mgr. Pitts. Sun-Telegraph, 1937; social sci. editor Wonderland of Knowledge Ency., Chgo., 1938; asst. sales promotion mgr. Scott, Foresman & Co., Chgo., 1938-43; asso. dir. Midwest area Nat. Conf. Christians and Jews, Chgo., 1946-49; v.p. Roosevelt U., Chgo., 1950-60; exec. v.p. Charles R. Feldstein Co., Inc., pub. relations, Chgo., 1960-61; pres. Wells Burnette Assos., Inc., pub. relations and fund raising cons. for ednl. and welfare orgns., Chgo., 1961-74; dir. Library of Living Philosophers, Inc. Vice Chmn. Budget rev. com. Chgo. Community Fund, 1960. Served as personnel classification specialist USNR, 1943-46. Mem. Am. Civil Liberties Union, Chgo. Urban League, U.S. Assn. UN (dir. Ill. chpt.), Assn. for Family Living, Kappa Sigma. Unitarian (former ch. chmn.). Editor: Story of the Rights of Man, 1942. Author ednl. monographs, articles. Home: Winnetka Ill. Died Dec. 30, 1974.

BURNIGHT, RALPH FLETCHER, coll. pres.; b. Pasadena, Cal., Jan. 5, 1897; s. Joel M. and Emma Florence (Babcock) B.; A.B., U. So. Cal., 1918, M.A., 1920; LL.D., California College of Medicine, 1957; m. Gladys H. Ogborn, June 17, 1923; children—David Ralph, Frances Ruth, Jean Marie. Instr., Yenching U., Peking, China, 1920-22, Washington Union High Sch., Fresno, Cal., 1922-24, Excelsior Union High Sch., Norwalk, Cal., 1924-27, vice prin., 1927-30, dist. supt., 1930-57; pres. Cerritos College, Norwalk, California, 1955-62, president emeritus, 1962-73. Served with U.S. Army, 1917-19; AEF. Mem. Los Angeles County High Sch. Prin. Assn. (pres. 1934-36), Los Angeles County Sch. Adminstrs. and Suprs. Assn. (pres. 1937-38), Cal. Interscholastic Fedn. (pres. so. sect. 1942-43), N.E.A., Am. Assn. Sch. Adminstrs., Cal. Tchrs. Assn. (council 1939-48), Phi Beta Kappa, Phi Delta Kappa, Alpha Kappa Delta. Presbyn. Rotarian (pres. 1938). Home: Bellflower Cal. Died Dec. 19, 1973.

BURNS, DONALD BRUCE, detective agy. exec.; b. Ossining, N.Y., July 16, 1921; s. William Sherman and Dorothy (Abell) B.; student Union Coll., Schenectady, 1940-42; children—Donald Bruce, Patricia Anne, Sharon Lynne, Diana Sue. With Burns Internat. Security Services, Inc. (formerly William J. Burns Internat. Detective Agy., Inc.), 1942-75, v.p., 1955-64, pres., 1964-70, chmn. bd., chief exec. officer, 1970-72, chmn. exec. com., 1972-75. Served as pilot USAAF, 1942-46, USAF, 1951-52. Mem. Am. Legion (past post comdr.), Quiet Birdmen, Phi Delta Gamma (pres. Chi Assn. 1962). Elk Clubs: Winged Foot Country (Mamaroneck, N.Y.); Sleepy Hollow Country (Scarborough, N.Y.) Home: Briarcliff Manor, N.Y. Died May 4, 1975.

BURNS, JOHN ANTHONY, gov. Hawaii; b. Ft. Assinneboine, Mont., Mar. 30, 1909; s. Harry Jacob and

Anne Florida (Scally) B.; student U. Hawaii, LL.D., Chaminade Coll., 1963; m. Beatrice Majors Van Vleet, June 8, 1931; children—John Anthony, Mary Elizabeth (Mrs. Harry J. Staats, Jr.), James Seishiro. Mem. Honolulu Police Dept., 1934-45, chief espionage bur., 1941-43; retail store operator, 1945-53; adminstr. Oahu Civil Def. Agy., 1951-55; pres., mgr. Burns & Co., Ltd., real estate, 1955-62; Hawaii del to Congress, 1956-59; gov. Hawaii, 1962-74. Presdl. rep. to South Pacific Commn. Conf., 1962; presdl. rep., spl. ambassador, head U.S. delegation to inauguration Korean pres., 1963; presdl. rep. Independence of Botswana, 1966, Independence of Lesotho, 1966; presdl. rep., head U.S. delegation coronation King of Tonga, 1967. Organizer, Democratic party Hawaii; chmn. County Dem. Com., 1948-52, Central Com., 1952-56; del. Dem. Nat. Conv., 1952, 56, 60, 64, 68. Served with U.S. Army, 1927-28. Named Outstanding Cath. Layman, 1959. Mem. Nat. Soc. Crippled Children and Adults (1st pres. Hawaii chpt.), 442d Vets., Honolulu C. of C. (hon.). Clubs: Waialae Country, Mid-Pacific Country, Aloha Civitan (hon.). Lion. Home: Honolulu, Hawaii. Died Apr. 5, 1975.

BURNS, MURRAY EDWIN, ret. constrn. co. exec.; b. Spokane, Wash., Nov. 29, 1898; s. Cyrus R. and Marietta (Tilsley) B.; grad. high sch.; m. Betty Bonnell, Apr. 23, 1921; children—Murray W., Robert N., Bartlett J., Bonny Jean (Mrs. Donald J. Baranco), Mary Ellen (Mrs. Leon W. Nowierski), Betty (Mrs. Charles Holt), Nancy Ann (Mrs. Dan Davis). Successively rodman, levelman, transitman Ore. Hwy. Dept., 1920-22; resident engr. Ida. Hwy. Dept., 1922-23; asst. engr. S.P. Co., 1923-30; constrn. supt. Morrison-Knudsen Co., Inc., 1930-32, dist. mgr., 1932-43, v.p., dir., 1946-69. Mem. lay bd. St. Alphonsus Hosp., Boise. Served with USMC, 1918-19; as col. C.E., AUS, 1943-46. Decorated Bronze Star, Legion of Merit. Mem. Asso. Gen. Contractors (pres. Ida. 1958). Republican. Episcopalian. Mason. Home: Boise, Ida. Died May 7, 1971.

BURNS, RALPH ARTHUR, educator; b. Vinalhaven, Me., Apr. 5, 1897; s. Willie Horace and Carrie (Hopkins) B.; A.B. Bates Coll., 1920; Ed.M., Harvard, 1926; A.M. (hon.), Dartmouth, 1934; LL.D., Farleigh Dickinson Coll., 1968; Ped.D., Franklin Pierce Coll., 1971; m. Ethel Emroye Magwood, July 7, 1920; children Robert Edwin, Elizabeth, William Arthur. Supervising prin. pub. schs., Cornish, Rockport, Me., 1920-24; prin. Am. Sch. Found., Mexico City, 1924-25; instr. Carleton Coll., 1926-27; faculty Dartmouth, from 1927, prof. edn., chmn. dept., 1934-63, emeritus, 1963-75. Dir. evaluation program Commn. on Instns. Higher Edn., New Eng. Assn. Colls. and Secondary Schs., Boston, from 1964; chief cultural affairs br. Edn. and Cultural Relations Div., Office Mil. Govt. U.S., Bad Nauheim, Germany, 1948-49. Chief exchanges div. Office U.S. High Commr. Germany, 1949-52; Am. specialist Dept. State to Nat. U. Asuncion, Paraguay, 1959-60. Served as lt. col. USAF, 1942-45. Recipient Gold medal Paraguay, 1959; Bundesverdienst-Kreuz, Germany, 1960; named hon. prof. Nat. U. Asuncion, 1960. Mem. Am. Legion, N.E.A., Soc. Mayflower Descs., Descs. Colonial Clergy Soc., Hanover Hist. Soc., S.A.R., Internat. Platform Assn., Dragon, Phi Beta Kappa, Phi Delta Kappa, Sigma Phi Epsilon. Mem. Ch. of Christ. Home: Hanover N.H. Died Nov. 4, 1975.

BURROWES, THOMAS, naval officer, b. Bklyn., Oct. 17, 1904; s. Thomas and Mabel Therese (Conover) B.; B.S., U.S. Naval Acad., 1925; m. Jean Archer Randel, June 29, 1931; children—Thomas, Jean Ann. Commd. ensign, U.S.N., 1925, advanced through grades to rear adm., 1953, comdr. various destroyers, 1940-48. Naval Group at Eniwetok A-Bomb tests, 1948, battleship USS Wisconsin, 1951-52. Decorated, Silver Star, Legion of Merit with combat V, Bronze Star with combat V, Commendation Ribbon with combat V. Protestant Episcopalian. Home: Silver Spring Md. Died June 1974.

BURT, GLENN BRIGHAM, JR., plastic surgeon; b. Boston, July 19, 1922; s. Glenn Brigham and Wilma (Ceppi) B.; M.D., Tufts U., 1949; m. Helen Marie Ennis, June 24, 1947; children—Glenn Brigham III, Candie L. (Mrs. Frank H. Owens). Intern, Cambridge (Mass.) City Hosp., 1949-50; resident Fitzsimons Gen. Hosp., Denver, 1952-56, Brooke Gen. Hosp., San Antonio, 1962-63, Barnes Hosp., St. Louis, 1963-64; comdg. officer U.S. Army Hosp., Asmara, Eritrea, Ethiopa, 1959-62; chief plastic surgery service Letterman Gen. Hosp., San Francisco, 1966-69; chief plastic surgery Brooke Gen. Hosp., 1969-72. Served to col. M.D., USA, Decorated Legion of Merit. Diplomate Am. Bd. Plastic Surgery. Mem. A.M.A., Am. Soc. Plastic and Reconstructive Surgery, San Antonio Surg. Soc. Home: San Antonio, Tex. Died Sept. 5, 1972; buried Ft. Sam Houston Nat. Cemetery, San Antonio.

BURTON, SPENCE, bishop; b. Cincinnati, O., Oct. 4, 1881; s. Caspar Henry and Byrd Waithman (Spence) B.; A.B. cum laude, Harvard, 1903, A.M., 1904; B.D., Gen. Theol. Sem., 1907, S.T.D. (hon.), 1939; D.D. (hon.), Nashotah (Wis.) House, 1930; unmarried. Reporter N.Y. Daily News, 1903-04; ordered deacon, Episcopal Ch., 1907; asst. Ch. of St. John the Evangelist, Boston, 1907-08; ordained priest, 1908; novice of Soc. of St. John the Evangelist, Cowley-St. John, Oxford, Eng., 1908-12; professed religious, 1912; master of novices and master of lay brothers, Soc. of St. John the Evangelist, St. Francis House, Cambridge, Msss., 1913-21; superior of Branch House of Soc. of St. John the Evangelist, San Francisco, rector Ch. of the Advent, San Francisco, and chaplain Calif. State Prison, San Quentin, Calif., 1922-24; father superior of Am. Congregation of Soc. of St. John the Evangelist, hdqrs. at Monastery of St. Mary and St. John, Cambridge, Mass., and chaplain gen. Sisters of St. Margaret in U.S.A., Can. and Haiti, 1924-39; consecrated bishop, 1939; suffragan bishop of Haiti and Dominican Republic, 1939, Nassau from 1942. Mem. Am. Ch. U., Clerical Assn. for Maintenance and Defense of Cath. Principles. Republican. Episcopalian. Clubs: Queen City of Caspar Henry Burton, 1921; The Atonement, 1929; also articles in religious jours. Home: Cincinnati, O.†

BUSCH, FRANCIS XAVIER, lawyer; b. Detroit, May 9, 1879; s. Francis Xavier and Carolyn (Van Buskirk) B.; LL.B., Ill. Coll. of Law, Chicago, 1901, LL.M., 1905; LL.D., DePaul U., 1912; m. Jeannette Morrison, June 10, 1903 (died Aug. 12, 1912); children—Helen, Frances, Ruth, Lorraine; m. 2d, Jean Mapes Lucas, Apr. 28, 1933. Admitted to Ill. bar, 1901, and began practice at Chicago; asst. corp. counsel and atty. for Chicago Civil Service Commn., 1904-06; master in chancery, Circuit Court, Cook County, 1920-23; atty. Bd. of Election Commrs., 1923; corp. counsel, Chicago, 1923-27 and Apr.-June, 1931; Dean emeritus DePaul U. Law Sch. Mem. Am. Bar Assn., Ill. State Bar Assn., Chicago Bar Assn. (pres. 1929-30), Law Club of Chicago. Mason, Woodman. Clubs: Union League. Author: In and Out of Court, 1942; Law and Tactics in Jury Trials, 1949; Guilty or Not Guilty, 1952; Prisoners at the Bar, 1952; They Escaped the Hangman, 1953; Enemies of the State, 1954; Case Book of the Curious and True, 1956. Home: Wetumpka, Ala.†

BUSCH, JOSEPH PETER, county dist. atty.; b. Chgo. Feb. 12, 1926; s. Joseph Peter and Clara Henrietta (Schukenecht) B.; B.S., U. Tex., 1947, J.D., Loyola U., Los Angeles, 1951; m. Jennie Frances Roasio, Feb. 22, 1947; children—Joseph, Steven, David. Admitted to Cal. bar, 1952; mem. dist. attys. office Los Angeles County 1952—, chief trial dep., 1965-68, dir. bur. spl. operations, 1968, asst. dist. atty., 1969, chief dep. dist. atty., 1970, dist. atty., 1970-75. Served with USNR, 1944-46. Mem. Nat. Dist. Attys. Assn., Dist. Attys. and County Counsels Assn. Cal. (1st v.p.). Home: West Covina, Cal. Died June 27, 1975; buried Queen of Heaven Cemetery, Rowland Heights, Cal.

BUSH, VANNEVAR, adminstr., elec. engr.; b. Everett, Mass., Mar. 11, 1890; s. Richard Perry and Emma Linwood (Paine) B.; B.S., M.S., Tufts Coll., 1913, hon. Sc.D., 1932; Eng.D., Mass. Inst. Tech., Harvard, 1916; hon. degrees from twenty univs. and colls.; Sc.D., Boston U. 1959; m. Phoebe Davis, Sept. 5, 1916; children—Richard Davis, John Hathaway. With test. dept. Gen. Electric Co., 1913; with inspection dept. U.S. Navy, 1914; instr. math. Tufts Coll., 1914-15, asst. prof. elec. engring., 1916-17; research on submarine detection, with spl. bd. on submarine devices, U.S. Navy, 1917-18; asso. prof. elec. power transmission Mass. Inst. Tech., 1919-23, prof., 1923-32; v.p. and dean engring., 1932-38; pres. Carnegie Instn. of Washington, 1939-55, trustee, 1958-74. Trustee Carnegie Corp. of N.Y., 1939-55, then trustee emeritus. Mem. adv. com. Nat. Security Resources Bd. Trustee Tufts Coll., Johns Hopkins, 1943-55; life mem. Mass. Inst. Tech. Corp., hon. chmn. corp., 1959-74; chmn. bd. Graphic Arts Research Found.; trustee Putnam Funds; regent Smithsonian Instn., 1943-55. Recipient some twenty prizes, awards and medals, 1928, including Founders' medal Nat. Acad. Engring., 1966, Atomic Pioneer award U.S. Govt., 1970; decorated knight comdr. Order Brit. Empire. Mem. numerous adv. coms. and bds., govtl. orgns., research projects including chmn. Nat. Def. Res. Commn., World War II. Fellow or mem., sometime honoree several scientific and profl. socs. Clubs: St. Botolph (Boston). Author: (with W.H. Timbie) Principles of Electrical Engineering, 1922; Operational Circuit Analysis, 1929, Endless Horizons, 1946; Modern Arms and Free Men (book), 1949; Science is Not Enough, 1967; Pieces of the Action, 1970. Was the builder of differential analyzer (machine for solving differential equations). Contributor numerous articles to American Institute Elec. Engring. and other scientific publs. Home: Cambridge Mass. Died June 28, 1974.

BUSHER, GEORGE DEWEY, real estate exec.; b. Bronx, N.Y., Oct. 10, 1898; s. Eugene J. and Anna (Crantz) B.; B.S., Dartmouth, 1922; LL.B., Fordham U., 1926; m. Josephine Lane, Jan. 18, 1929; children—Joan E. (Mrs. Wallace M. Kain), Eugene L. Admitted to N.Y. bar, 1927; v.p., dir. Eugene J. Busher Co., Inc., N.Y.C., 1922; dir., mem. adv. bd. Mfrs. Hanover Trust Co.; trustee Bronx Savs. Bank. Mem. adv. bd. Bronx Community Coll. Hon. trustee Fordham U. Mem. Am. Bar Assn., Bronx Real Estate Bd. (dir., past pres.), Bronx Bd. Trade (dir., past pres.). Clubs: Winged Foot Golf (Mamaroneck, N.Y.); Union League, Dartmouth (N.Y.C.); Rhode Island Country. Home Bronxville N.Y. Died Dec. 8, 1973.

BUSHNELL, ASA SMITH, athletic adminstr.; b. Springfield, O., Feb. 2, 1900; s. John Ludlow and Jessie Manton (Harwood) B.; grad. The Hill Sch., 1917; B.S., Princeton, 1921; student law sch., Columbia, 1922; LL.D., Syracuse U. 1955, Hobart and William Smith Colls., 1965; Ph.D., St. John's U., 1961; m. Thelma Lucille Clark, Feb. 11, 1924; children—Asa S., Barbara C. (Mrs. John C. Leonard). Teller Morris Plan Bank, Springfield, 1922-23, dir., 1924-25; treas., office mgr. Direct Products Co., 1924-25; editor Lagonda Pub. Co., 1924, Princeton (U.) Alumni Weekly, 1925-30; founder Princeton Athletic News, 1932, editor, 1932-37; grad. mgr. athletics Princeton, 1927-37, acting dir. athletics, 1942-44; commr. Eastern Coll. Athletic Conf., 1938-70, cons., 1970-71. Apprentice seaman USNR, 1918. Dir. sports sect. Office Coordinator Inter-Am. Affairs, 1941-42; mem. Nat. Com. on Phys. Fitness, 1942-44; asst. to dir. schs. and tng. br. OSS, 1944; spl. cons. athletic br. Spl. Services Div., U.S. Army, 1944-45. Originator Princeton Invitation Track Meet, 1934, dir., 1934-38. Sports adv. com. N.Y. World Fair, 1939, Sec. Nat. Football Found. and Hall Fame, Inc., 1948-51, 70-75; dir., 1952-75. Recipient Olympic Torch, U.S. Olympic Com., 1966; Austrian Olympic medal, Austria, 1966; Distinguished Service award from Princeton Class of 1921, 1955; Sportsmanship Brotherhood award, 1954; Touchdown Club award, 1957; meritorious service award N.Y. Track Writers Assn., 1958; named to Helms Athletic Found. Rowing Hall Fame, 1958; James Lynah Meml. award Eastern College Athletic Conf., 1959; distinguished service award Del. Valley chpt. Football Found., 1967; Madison Square Garden Hall of Fame, 1967; James Corbett Meml. award Nat. Assn. Coll. Dirs. Athletics, 1969; Helms Athletic Found. Commrs. and Athletic Dirs. Hall Fame, 1970. Mem. Amateur Athletic Union of U.S. (gov.), Nat. Coll. Athletic Assn. (exec. com. 1943-44, 1947-51; dir. TV program 1952-70, cons. 1970-72). Collegiate Commrs. Assn. (pres. 1947-52), S.R., U.S. Olympic Com. (asst. treas. 1936-37, mem. exec. com. 1937-45, 65-71, sec. 1945-65), Order Founders and Patriots Am. Episcopalian (vestryman). Club: University Cottage (gov.). Editor: 1948 and 1952 U.S. Olympic Book. Co-contbr. sects. on football in Ency. Brit. and Collier's Ency. Home: Princeton, N.J. Died Mar. 22, 1975; interred Springfield, O.

BUSHNELL, LELAND DAVID, educator; b. Bronson, Mich., Oct. 19, 1880; s. William Butts and Sarah Maria (Taggart) B.; B.S., Mich. State Coll., 1905; M.S., U. of Kan., 1915; Ph.D., Harvard, 1921; m. Florence Warner, Sept. 5, 1912. Asst. in bacteriology, Mich. State Coll., 1905-07, dairy div., U.S. Dept. Agr., 1907-08, Kansas State College, 1908-09; instr. in bacteriology, same coll., 1909-10, asst. prof. bacteriology, 1910-12, prof. and head dept., bacteriologist in charge Kan. Agrl. Expt. Sta., 1912-46; ret. 1946. Pres. Mo. Valley Branch Soc. Am. Bacteriologists, 1939-40. Fellow A.A.A.S.; mem. Soc. Am. Bacteriologist, Kan. Acad. Science (pres. 1944-45), Sigma Xi, Gamma Sigma Delta, Alpha Zeta, Acacia; hon. mem. Am. Veterinary Med. Association. Republican. Mason. Contributor to Biol. Abstracts, etc. Home: Manhattan, Kan.†

BUSKIN, MARTIN, journalist; b. Bklyn., July 9, 1930; s. Harry and Frances (Drimmer) B.; A.B., N.Y.U., 1951; m. Saundra Rosman, June 3, 1956; children—Linda, Randi. Reporter, Newsday, Garden City, N.Y., 1953-55, copy editor, 1955-59, feature editor, 1959-61, edn. editor from 1962. Cons. U.S. Office Edn. Served with AUS, 1951-53. Recipient 1st prize for outstanding coverage local edn. issues Edn. Writers Assn., 1964, 65, 1st prize for outstanding columns on brotherhood Nat. Conf. Christians and Jews, 1966. Mem. Edn. Writers Assn. (pres.), Nat. Council for Advancement Edn. Writing (vice chmn.). Author: (with Howard Hagler) Great Moments in Sports, 1968. Contbr. to Naked Came The Stranger, 1969. Contbr. articles profl. jours. Home: Commack, N.Y., Died Feb. 8, 1976.

BUSSEY, WILLIAM HENRY, educator; b. Chicago, Ill., Oct. 24, 1879; s. William Henry and Carrie (Sedgwick) B.; A.B., Northwestern U., 1900; A.B., Harvard, 1901, A.M., 1902; Ph.D., U. of Chicago, 1904; m. Marian Alden Smith, Aug. 25, 1915; children—James Alden, Natalie, David Alden. Instr. in mathematics, Northwestern U., 1904-05; tutor in mathematics, Barnard Coll., Columbia U., 1905-07; asst. prof. mathematics U. of Minn., 1907-14, asso. prof., 1914-20, prof. from 1920, asst. dean jr. coll. 1920-45, chmn. dept. math., 1920-26; editor in chief Am. Math. Monthly, 1927-31. Fellow A.A.A.S.; mem. Am. Math. Soc. (mem. council 1923-25), Math. Assn. Am., Phi Beta Kappa, Sigma Xi. Contbr. to Trans. Am. Math. Soc., Bull. Am. Math. Soc., The Mathematics Teacher, Proc. London Math. Soc., The Am. Math. Monthly. Home: Minneapolis, Minn.†

BUTCHER, EDWIN, army officer; b. Staten Island, N.Y., June 28, 1879; s. Daniel and Anna Amelia (Sommer) B.; B.S., U.S. Mil. Acad., 1904; m. Susan Adelaide Downing, April 8, 1915; children—Elizabeth Susan (wife of Lt. Col. Richard C. Hopkins), Edwin Corette. Commd. 2d. lt., Inf., U.S. Army. June 15, 1904 and advanced through the grades to brig. gen., March. 11, 1943; served in P.I., 1905-07, 1936-38, in the Panama Canal Zone, 1915-18; chief of staff, Hdqrs. Third Service Command, Baltimore, Md. Decorated Victory Medal, Army service prior to Pearl Harbor Ribbon; Legion of Merit, 1943. Mason (K.T., Shriner). Club: Army and Navy Country (Arlington, Va.). Home: Baltimore, Md.†

BUTCHER, HOWARD, JR., stock broker; b. Phila., Pa., Dec. 28, 1876; s. Howard and Mary L. (Richards) B.; grad. William Penn Charter Sch., 1893; student U. of Pa., 1894-96; B.A. (honorary), U. of Pa., 1957, as of 1898; m. Margaret Keen, Apr. 10, 1901; children—Howard III, Margaret, Dora (Mrs. J. Hart Hillman, Jr.),

Mary Louisa (Mrs. Julian W. Hill), Wm. Williams Keen, Florence (Mrs. George H. Harris, Jr.). Began career as bond salesman, 1901-10; partner Butcher & Sherrerd from 1916. Mem. bd. govs. Phila. Stock Exchange, 1922-46, v.p., 1929-34, pres., 1934-40; mem. board govs., N.Y. Stock Exchange. Member finance committee Home for Incurables, Philadelphia, Pennsylvania. Served overseas with YMCA in France, 1918. Mem. Zeta Psi. Republican. Episcopalian. Mason. Clubs: University, Union League (Philadelphia, Pa.); Merion Cricket (Haverford, Pa.); Philadlephia Skating Club and Humane Society (Ardmore, Pa.); Appalachian Mountain (Boston). Home: Ardmore, Pa.†

BUTLER, DORIS LANE, mus. adminstr.; b. Aurora, Ill., Nov. 23, 1904; d. Wilfred Emory and Stella (Cooper) Lane; student Sch. of Art Inst., Chgo., 1922-23, U. Ill., 1924-26; m. Eugene Kincaid Butler II, May 28, 1927 (dec. Sept. 1959); children—Shirley Turnbull, Eugene Kincaid, Dana (Mrs. Thomas Carey Strobel). Art critic Chgo. Daily News, 1957-59; Chgo. corr. Art in Am., 1958-65; dir. pub. relations Mus. Contemporary Art, Chgo., from 1937, sec. bd. trustees, from 1964. Mem. adv. com. Ill. Arts Council, from 1966. Mem. woman's bd. Internat. Visitors Center, Chgo., from 1965. Mem. Delta Gamma. Club: Arts of Chicago (dir.). Home: Chicago Ill. Deceased.

BUTLER, MRS. EDWARD H., newspaper exec.; b. Atlanta; d. Augustus Marcellus and Jennie (Maddux) Robinson; student Gunston Hall and France; m. Edward Hubert Butler, Feb. 2, 1909; 1 dau., Kate Robinson (Mrs. Bruce Exton Wallis). Dir. Buffalo Evening News, Inc., 1951-74, pres., 1956-71, pub., 1971-74; v.p. WBEN, Inc., 1956-67, pres., 1967-74. Hon. mem. council U. Buffalo; mem. corp. Am. Hosp. Paris (France); mem. Buffalo Fine Arts Acad. Mem. Frontier of Republican Women Buffalo. Mem. Colonial Dames Am. Presbyn. Clubs: Buffalo Country, Garret, Saturn; Adirondack League (Old Forge, N.Y.). Home Buffalo N.Y. Died Aug. 3, 1974.

BUTLER, GEORGE ALFRED, hosp. dir.; b. San Francisco, Sept. 13, 1911; s. Alfred John and Virginia (Davis) B.; B.A., Coll. of Pacific, 1936, M.A., 1943; M.D., U. Cal., 1947; m. Margaret Lowry Moore, Aug. 1, 1942; children—Alan Moore, Ann Virginia. Intern San Francisco County Hosp., 1947-48; grad. tng. psychiatry Met. State Hosp., 1957-60; dir. health Santa Ana (Cal.) Schs., 1948-57; asso. supt., med. dir. Sonoma State Hosp., Eldridge, Cal., 1963-69, supt., med. dir., 1969. Served with AUS, 1943-46, 51-53. Fellow Am. Assn. Mental Deficiency; mem. A.M.A., Am. Psychiat. Assn. Home: Santa Rosa, Cal. Died Feb. 21, 1974; cremated.

BUTLER, G(ORDON) MONTAGUE, educator, mining engr.; b. Lake Geneva, Wis., Mar. 26, 1881; s. Samuel Marsh and Olive Louise (Montague) B.; E.M., Colo. Sch. of Mines, 1902, Sc.D., 1922; m. Alice Ellen Quick, July 5, 1906; children—Gurdon Montague, Enid Louise. Instr., asst. prof. geology, Sch. of Mines, Ore. Agrl. Coll., 1913-15, also geologist, Sch. Ore. Bur. of Mine and Geology; prof. mining engring. and dean Coll. of Mines and Engring., U. of Ariz., 1915-40, also dir. Ariz. Bur. of Mines, 1918-40; dean engring. U. Ariz. 1940-51, dean emeritus from 1951; geologist Colorado Survey, 1908-13. Former pres. Nat. Council State Boards Engring. Examiners. Fellow Geog. Soc. Am., A.A.A.S., Mineral Soc. of Am.; hon. mem. A.I.A.; Am. Inst. Mining and Metall. Engrs., Mining and Metall. Soc. Am., Soc. Promotion Engring. Edn. (past dir.), Am. Assn. Engrs. (past 1st v.p.), Conn. Soc. Colonial Wars, Conn. Soc. of War of 1812, Conn. Soc. Order of Founders and Patriots, Mass. Soc. Mayflower Descendants, Tau Beta Pi, Phi Kappa Phi, Phi Delta Kappa, Sigma Xi, Theta Tau, Phi Gamma Delta. Mason (33°, past grand master, Ariz.). Rotarian (past dist. gov.). Author numerous books, 1908—; also tech. articles and bulls, Ariz. Bur. Mines. Home: Santa Ana, Cal.†

BUTLER, OVID, editor, forester; b. Indianapolis, Ind., July 14, 1880; s. Scot and Julia (Dunn) B.; A.B., Butler U., 1902; M.F., Yale, 1907; m. Adele McMaster, Nov. 28, 1908; children—Ovid McMaster, Elizabeth Anne, Scot. Mem. editorial staff, Indianapolis Jour., 1903-04, Indianapolis News, 1904-05; was U.S. forester, Boise (Ida.) Nat. Forest, 1907-08; asst. dist. forester, Utah, Southern Ida., 1909-10, 1911-14, Mont., Northern Ida., 1910-11; in charge special study Lumber Distribution in U.S., 1915-16; asst. dist. forester, Ariz., N.M., 1916-17; asst. dir. U.S. Forest Products Lab., Madison, Wis., 1917-22; forester Am. Forestry Assn., 1922-23, exec. sec., 1923-44; exec. dir. 1945-48, exec. dir. emeritus, from 1948; editor-in-chief. American Forests 1922-48; mem. adv. council Nat. Arboretum; editorial adv. com. American Scholar; mem.-at-large, Nat. Council Boy Scouts of Am.; Am. del World Forestry Congress, Budapest, 1936. Fellow Soc. Am. Foresters (pres. 1927-28; mem. Sigma Chi, Sigma Xi. Episcopalian. Clubs: Cosmos, Yale, Wrote: Wholesale Distribution of Lumber in U.S., Retail Distribution of Lumber in U.S. (both pub., U.S. Forest Service). Compiler and Editor; Rangers of the Shield, Youth Rebuilds, American Conservation—In Picture and in Story—All 1935. Home: Chevy Chase, Md.†

BUTTERFIELD, VICTOR LLOYD, educator; b. Kingston, R.I., Feb. 7, 1904; s. Kenyon Leach and Harriet (Millard) B.; grad. Deerfield Acad., 1923; B.A., Cornell U., 1927, M.A., 1928; Ph.D., Harvard, 1936, LL.D., 1961; M.A. (hon.), Wesleyan U., 1942; L.H.D., 1967; LL.D. (hon.), Brown U., 1943, Amherst Coll., 1944, Williams Coll., 1944, Lawrence Coll., 1947, Columbia, 1954, Tulane U., 1957, Mount Allison (Can.), 1958, Dartmouth, 1967; Litt.D., Bowdoin Coll., 1955; L.H.D., Trinity Coll., 1946, U. Hartford, 1959, Boston Coll., 1965; D.Sc., Union U., 1961; m Katharina Geyer, June 11, 1928; children—Margot (Mrs. Robert Siekman), Daniel Kenyon. Tchr. English, Deerfield Acad., 1928-29, Riverdale Sch., N.Y.C., 1929-31; instr. philosophy Lawrence Coll., 1934-35; dir. admissions Wesleyan U., Middletown, Conn., 1935-41, dean freshmen, 1938-41, asso. dean, 1941-42, acting pres., 1942-43, pres., 1943-67, pres. emeritus, 1967-75. Chmn., Conn. Commn. Selection for Rhodes Scholarships, 1946-49; chmn. com. faculty fellowships Fund for Advancement of Edn., Ford Found., 1951-54, study assignment ednl. situation in Near East, 1952-53; mem. coll. grants adv. com. Ford Found., 1955; mem. New Eng. Bd. Higher Edn., 1955-61; mem. vis. com. Harvard Divinity Sch., 1956-61, Philosophy Dept., Harvard, 1962-65; v.p. New Eng. Colls. Fund, Inc., 1958-60; cons. Ford Found. Humanities and Arts Program, 1960; mem. com. plans and objectives for higher edn. Am. Council of Edn., 1962-65; mem. adv. council Danforth Grad. Fellowship Program, 1963-65; mem. Nat. Com. on Accrediting Adv. Commn. to Study Influence on Higher Edn., 1963; mem. commn. coll. and soc. Assn. Am. Colls., 1966-69, mem. com. on liberal learning, 1966-69, chmn. spl. com. liberal studies, from 1965; chmn. bd. selection E. Harris Harbison Award for Gifted Teaching, Danforth Found., 1967-69; cons. liberal studies Ford Found., from 1969; mem. council Coll. Arts and Scis., Cornell U., from 1958; cons. Acad. for Ednl. Devel., 1969-70; pres. Nat. Council on Religion in Higher Edn., 1949-56, fellow, 1927-75. Alumni trustee Cornell U., 1946-51; trustee Edward W. Hazen Found., 1947-67; bd. regents U. Hartford, 1959-63; trustee Deerfield Acad., from 1956, Wilbraham Acad., 1957-65, New Coll., 1965-75. Carnegie Corp. grantee, 1939, 52. Fellow Soc. for Religion in Higher Edn. (bd. dirs. 1962—); mem. Am. Acad. Arts and Scis., Phi Beta Kappa, Beta Theta Pi. Club: University. Author: The Life of the Teacher, 1954; The Faith of a Liberal College, 1955; Counter Attack in Liberal Learning, 1966; numerous essays. Home: Middletown, Conn., Died Nov. 19, 1975; buried Wildwood Cemetery, Amherst, Mass.

BUTTERWORTH, WILLIAM WALTON, foreign service officer; b. New Orleans, La., Sept. 7, 1903; s. Dr. William Walton and Maud Ravencamp (Campbell) B.; student New Orleans Acad., 1909-16, Lawrenceville Sch., 1916-21; B.A., Princeton U., 1925; Rhodes Scholar, Oxford U., 1925-27; m. Virginia Parker, Nov. 10, 1928; children—Cynthia, John Blair. Foreign service officer, since May 1928; Dept. of State, 1928-29; vice consul, Singapore, 1929-31; Dept. of State, 1931-32; 3d sec. Am. Legation, Ottawa, Can., 1932-34; 2d sec. Am. Embassy, London, 1934-41, also financial attache, 1935-41; temp. detailed as spl. asst. to under-secretary of commerce, Washington, D.C., 1941-42; mem. Advisory Com. of Trade Policy in Relation to Lend-Lease; 1st sec. Am. Legation, Lisbon, Portugal and 1st sec. Am. Embassy, Madrid, Spain, also dir. gen. for operations in the Iberian Peninsula of the U.S. Commercial Co. (Govt.-owned corp. engaged in preclusive buying of strategic materials), 1942-44; counselor of Embassy, Madrid, Spain, 1944-46; counselor of Embassy with rank of Minister, Nanking, China, 1946-47; asst. sec. for Far Eastern Affairs, Dept. of State 1947-49, asst. sec. 1949-50; ambassador to Sweden, 1950-53; minister and dep. chief of mission, London, 1954-55; U.S. rep. to European Coal and Steel Community with rank of ambassador, 1956-62, to European Econ. Community, European Atomic Energy Community, 1958-62; U.S. ambassador to Can., Ottawa, Ont., 1962-68. Clubs: Metropolitan (Washington); Writers, Whites (London); Cottage (Princeton), Boston (New Orleans); Century (N.Y.C.). Rideau (Ottawa). Home: Princeton, N.J. Died Mar. 31, 1975.

BUXTON, FRANK W., editor; b. Woonsocket, R.I., Oct. 24, 1877; s. Parker Jonas and Elizabeth (Byrne) B.; A.B., Harvard, 1900; m. Grace M. Cushing; 1 son, Francis Cushing. Sunday editor, mng. editor Boston Herald, editor, 1929-47, retired. Winner Pulitzer editorial prize, 1923. Trustee Five Cents Savings Bank of Boston, Tabor Acad., Boston Pub. Library, N.E. Conservatory of Music, N.E. Deaconess Hosp., Museum of Fine Arts (ex-officio). Clubs: Union Boat, Harvard (Boston); Examiner. Home: Boston Mass. Died Sept. 1974.

BYERS, CLOVIS E., army officer, corp. exec.; b. Columbus, O., Nov. 5, 1899; s. William Ethelbert and Minnie (Potter) B.; student Ohio State U., 1917-18; B.S., U.S. Mil. Acad., 1920; student Cav. Sch., 1920-21, 30-31, Signal Sch., 1923-24; grad. Command and Gen. Staff Sch., 1936, Army War Coll., 1940; m. Marie Richards, July 14, 1921; 1 son, Clayton Potter. Commd. 2d lt. cav., U.S. Army, 1920, advanced through grades to lt. gen., 1955; chief staff 77th Div., 1942, 1st Corps, 1942-43, 8th Army, 1944; comdg. gen. 82d Airborne Div., 1948-49; dep. asst. chief staff G-1, Dept. of Army, 1949-51; comdg. gen. X Corps, Korea, 1951, XVI Corps, Japan, 1952; chief staff Allied Forces So. Europe, 1952-54; dep. comdg. Nat. War Coll., 1954-55; comdt. NATO Defense Coll., Paris, 1955-57; mil. adviser asst. sec. def. for internat. security affairs, 1957-59; ret., 1959; exec. v.p. Council Econ. Growth and Security, Inc., N.Y.C., 1960-61, now mem. bd. dirs.; v.p. Gen. Telephone & Electronics Corp., Washington, 1961-68. Decorated D.S.C., D.S.M. with oak leaf cluster, Silver Star with oak leaf cluster, Legion of Merit with oak leaf cluster, Bronze Star with two clusters, Air medal, Presdl. Unit citation with oak leaf cluster; comdr. mil. div. Order Brit. Empire; officer Legion of Honor (France); grand cross King George I (Greece); commendater Order Italian Republic; Mil. Merit medal Philippine Republic; grand officer Order Leopold II with palm; Croix de Guerre with palm (Belgium); Presdl. Unit citation (Korea). Mem. Washington Inst. Fgn. Affairs, Phi Gamma Delta. Episcopalian, Mason. Clubs: Army and Navy, Chevy Chase, 1925 F Street, Carlton (Washington). Home: Washington, D.C. Died Dec. 1973.

BYERS, GORDON LESLIE, lawyer; b. Coalport, Pa., Mar. 27, 1898; s. Thomas V. and Laura (Thompson) B.; student San Diego Tchrs. Coll., 1926-27; B.S., U. Cal. at Berkeley, 1929, J.D., 1942; m. Helen Binder, Sept. 2, 1922; 1 dau., Carol Lynn (Mrs. Lorin H. Soderwall). Admitted to Cal. bar, 1942; auditor Strouss-Hirshberg Co., dept. store, Youngstown, O., 1919-25; sr. accountant Price Waterhouse & Co., San Francisco, 1929-33, Pitts., 1933-36; atty. Pillsbury, Madison & Sutro, San Francisco, 1942-44; sr. partner Byers, Howell & Elson, Berkeley, Cal., 1944-64; lectr. U. Cal. at Berkeley, 1944-47. Dir. Standard Process & Engraving Co., J.F. Hink & Son Dept. Store, Berkeley, Cal. Served with Med. Dept., U.S. Army, 1917-19. Mem. Am. Inst. C.P.A.'s Am., Cal., Berkeley, Alameda County bar assns., Assn. or Atty. C.P.A.'s Los Angeles. Home: Berkeley, Cal. Died Dec. 7, 1973.

BYRD, ELON EUGENE, biologist; b. Richton, Miss., June 9, 1905; s. Henry Webster and Eleanor Elizabeth (Hinton) B.; B.S., Miss. A. and M. Coll., 1929; M.S., Miss. State Coll., 1931; Ph.D., Tulane U. 1934; m. Margaret Elizabeth Powell, Sept. 3, 1938. Instr., Miss. State Coll., 1929-32; faculty U. Ga., Athens, 1934-74, prof. zoology-parasitology, 1945-72, prof. emeritus, 1972-74. Spl. cons. filarial studies USPHS, 1951-62; cons. parasitology Southeastern Coop. Wildlife Disease Study, 1968-74. Trustee, exec. com. Highlands Biol. Lab., 1950-74, Highland (N.C.) Biol. Sta., 1957-74. Served to lt. Med. Service Corps, USNR, 1942-45; capt. Res., ret. 1965. Decorated Bronze Star medal. Recipient Michael award for research in parasitology, 1948. Fellow A.A.A.S.; mem. Am. Micros. Soc., Am. (editorial bd. 1949-55, mem. council 1952-55), Southeastern (pres. 1970) socs. parasitologists, Am. Soc. Tropical Medicine, Assn. Southeastern Biologists (sec.-treas. 1947-49, pres. 1950), Am. Soc. Systematic Zoology. Club: Men's Garden (organizer, pres. Athens). Asso. editor: Am. Midland Naturalist, 1960-66. Contbr. articles to profl. jours. Home: Athens, Ga. Died Mar. 3, 1974; interred Oconee Hill Cemetery, Athens, Ga.

BYRD, WILLIAM CLIFTON, music dir., condr.; b. Cin., Sept. 6, 1926; s. William Clifton and Alverta Ellen (Frazee) B.; Mus.B., Coll. Music of Cin., 1950, M.Mus., 1953; m. Margaret Margaret Sutton, May 1, 1954 (div. Aug. 1972); children—Alesia, Belinda; m. 2d, Susan Marie Diebel, June 23, 1973. Condr., Cin. Music Drama Guild, 1947-53; music dir. Cin. Little Symphony, 1949-56; condr. orch., chorus and opera Cin. Coll. Music, 1951-53; tchr. advanced conducting Cin. Coll. Conservatory of Music, 1954-56; mus. dir., condr. Lima (O.) Symphony Orch., 1956-66, Flint Symphony Orch. (Mich.), 1966-74; artistic dir. Flint Inst. Music, 1971-74; mus. dir. Overture to Opera, Detroit, 1970-74; guest condr. BBC, London, 1954, 55, 57-59, 62, 64, 66, 67, Danish State Radio, Copenhagen, 1953, 54, 56-59, 62, 64, 66, 67, 70, 72, Norwegian State Radio, 1956-59, 61, 62, 64, 69, 72, 73, Swedish Radio, Goetborg, 1961, 62, 62, 69, 72, 73. Bd. dirs. Flint Arts Council Frank Huntington Beebe grantee New Eng. Conservatory of Music, 1953-54. Mem. Phi Mu Alpha Sinfonia, Phi Kappa Lambda. Presbyn. (ruling elder 1971-73). Kiwanian. Author: (with J. Anderson, M. Gminder, W. Sonntag) Music, A Wonder World of Sound, 1964, rev., 1965. Home: Flint Mich. Died July 8, 1974.

BYRNE, CORNELIUS JAMES, dept. store exec.; b. Kansas City, Mo., July 18, 1907; s. Frank P. and Agnes (Smith) B.; B.S., U. Ill., 1929. With Mandel Bros., Chgo., 1929-43, mdse. mgr., 1934-39, 41-43; with Famous-Barr, St. Louis, 1939-41; with Frederick & Nelson, Seattle, 1946-70, v.p., gen. mgr., 1954-61, pres., gen. mgr., 1962-70; v.p. Marshall Field & Co., Chgo.; chmn. News Pub. Co. Trustee Central Assn.; v.p., trustee Greater Seattle; bd. dirs. Seattle chpt. A.R.C.; trustee World Trade Center; bd. govs. Am. Nat. Red Cross, 1963-66; bd. regents Seattle U. Served with USNR, 1943-46. Mem. Nat. Retail Mchts. Assn. (dir., v.p.), Seattle Municipal League. Clubs: Wash. Athletic, Rainier, Golf (Seattle). Home: Seattle, Wash. Deceased.

BYRNE, EMMET FRANCIS, congressman; b. Chgo., Dec. 6, 1896; s. James Patrick and Mary Alice (Murphy) B.; student Loyola U., 1916; LL.B., DePaul

U., 1920; m. Mary Margaret Farrell, Feb. 6, 1928; children—Sally, Mary Dugan, Barbara, Patrice, Emmet, Judith, Helen, Thomas. Admitted to Ill. bar, 1919, U.S. Supreme Ct., 1925; asst. corp. counsel City of Chgo., 1921-23; asst. state's atty. Cook County, 1923-29; nominated for judge Municipal Ct., 1934-36; pvt. practice of law, Chgo., 1929-74; mem. 85th Congress, 3d Ill. Dist. Mem. Am. Legion. 40 and 8, Phi Alpha Delta. K.C. Clubs: Lake Shore (Chgo.); Capitol Hill (Washington). Home: Evanston Ill. Died Sept. 1974.

BYRNE, HARRY VINCENT, ophthalmologist; b. Lawrence, Mass., Mar. 17, 1904; s. Joseph H. and Margaret (Young) B.; m. Elizabeth G. Gallagher, June 27, 1932; children—Donn B., Stephen R., Cynthia L. (Mrs. Doyle). Practiced medicine, specializing in ophthalmology, 1958-70. Diplomate Am. Bd. Ophthalmology. Home: Andover, Mass. Died Dec. 9, 1970.

BYRNE, WILLIAM MATTHEW, judge; b. Bakersfield, Cal., July 10, 1896; s. John Joseph and Mary Ellen (Mills) B.; LL.B., Loyola U. of Los Angeles, 1929; m. Julia Ann Lamb, June 2, 1925; children—Margaret Moira, William Matthew. Admitted to Cal. bar, 1929; mem. Cal. State Legislature, 1925-31, speaker pro tem State Assembly, 1927-31; judge Los Angeles Municipal Ct., 1943-48, Superior Ct. of Cal., 1948-50, U.S. dist. judge, 1950, chief judge, 1964-67. Mem. Los Angeles Bar Assn., Phi Alpha Delta, Alpha Sigma Nu. Home: Los Angeles Cal. Died Mar. 1974.

BYRNES, CLIFFORD HAMILTON, lawyer; b. Mpls., Sept. 8, 1893; s. Timothy Edward and Clara M. (Goodrich) B.; grad. Phillips Exeter Acad., 1911; B.A., Yale, 1915; LL.B., Harvard, 1919; m. Blanche Edith Trainor, Aug. 1, 1925 (dec. Nov. 1973). Admitted to Mass. bar, 1920; spl. asst. U.S. atty. gen., Washington, 1922-26, 27-31; asst. U.S. atty., Boston, 1926-27; partner firm Hale, Sanderson, Byrnes & Morton, Boston, 1927-72, of counsel, 1972-74. Served to 2d lt., inf. U.S. Army, 1917-19. Mem. Alpha Delta Phi. Republican. Unitarian. Mason. Clubs: Cohasset; Laurel Brook; Union (Boston); Yale (N.Y.C., Boston). Home: Hingham Mass. Died Jan. 19, 1974. /7502329

CABELL, EARLE, former congressman; b. nr. Dallas, Oct. 27, 1906; s. Ben E. and Sadie (Pearre) C.; student Tex. A. and M. Coll., 1925-26, So. Meth U., 1926; m. Elizabeth Holder, Feb. 22, 1932; children—Elizabeth Lee (Mrs. Pulley), Earle. Salesman, Morning Glory Creameries, Houston, 1926-28; plant supt. Mistletoe Creameries, Amarillo, Tex., 1928-30; owner Cabell's Dairy, Pine Bluff, Ark., 1930-32; with Cabell's Inc., 1932-75, successively sec.-treas., exec. v.p., 1932-52, pres., 1952-75, chmn. bd., 1961-64; chmn. bd. Cabell's Dairies, Dallas; dir., exec. com. Grand Av. State Bank, 1945-65; mayor City of Dallas, 1961-64; mem. 89th-92d congresses 5th Dist. Tex. Pres. Dallas Crime Commn., 1954-56; mem. Gov.'s Econ. Adv. Commn., 1954-56; adv. bd. Tex. Indsl. Commn.; active Boy Scouts Am.; sec., mem. exec. com. Tex. Law Enforcement Found. Bd. dirs., Jr. Achievement. Served from capt. to lt. col., Tex. State Guard, 1941-46. Mem. Southwestern Law Enforcement Inst. (exec. com.), East Tex., Dallas chambers commerce, Dallas Sales Execs. Club (past pres.), Dairy Products Inst. Tex. (past pres.), Tex. Mfrs. Assn. (past pres.), Dallas Salemanship Club, Dallas Sales Execs. Clubs: Dallas Country, Dallas Athletic (past dir.), McKinney Lake (past pres.), City. Home: Dallas, Tex. Died Sept. 24, 1975.

CABOT, HENRY B., univ. trustee; b. Boston, Dec. 7, 1894; s. Henry B. and Anne M. (Codman) C.; A.B., Harvard, 1917, LL.B., 1922; L.H.D. Tufts U.; m. Olivia Ames, June 18, 1927; 1 son, Henry B. Practicing lawyer, Boston, 1922-30; research asso. Harvard Law Sch., 1930-38, trustee, 1938-74. Mem. bd. overseers Harvard, 1954-60; trustee emeritus Boston Symphony Orch. Author: (with S.B. Warner) Judges and Law Reform, 1937. Home: Dover, Mass. Died Sept. 11, 1974.

CADBURY, HENRY JOEL, educator; b. Phila., Dec. 1, 1883; s. Joel and Anna Kaighn (Lowry) C.; A.B., Haverford Coll., 1903, Litt.D., 1933; A.M., Harvard, 1904, Ph.D., 1914; D.D., U. Glasgow, 1937; LL.D., Whittier Coll., 1951, Swarthmore Coll., 1954; L.H.D., Howard U., 1959, Earlham Coll., 1967; m. Lydia Caroline Brown, June 17, 1916; children—Elizabeth (Mrs. John K. Musgrave, Jr.), Christopher Joel, Warder Henry, Winifred (Mrs. Martin M. Beer). Asso. with Haverford Coll. 1910-19, Harvard, 1919-26, Bryn Mawr Coll., 1926-34; Hollis prof. divinity Harvard, also Dexter lectr. Bibl. lit., 1934-54, now emeritus; lectr. Pendle Hill, Wallingford, Pa., 1954-72, Haverford Coll., 1954-63; adj. prof. Temple U., 1962-66; sec. Am. Schs. Oriential Research, 1934-54; dir. Andover-Harvard Theol. Library, 1938-54; Lowell lectr., Boston, 1935, 53, Carew lectr. Hartford Sem., 1935; Shaffer lectr. Yale Div. Sch., 1946; Samuel A. Crozer lectr. Crozer Sem., 1953; Edward Cadbury lectr. U. Birmingham, 1956; Swarthmore lectr. at London Yearly Meeting, 1957. Chmn. bd. dirs. Bryn Mawr Coll., 1956-68. Mem. Am. Friends Service Com. (chmn. 1928-34, 44-60, hon. chmn. 1960-74, engaged child-feeding in Germany, summer 1920, commr. to Eng., winter 1941; mem. Am. Standard Bible Com., 1930-72. Recipient Nobel Peace prize on behalf of Am. Friends Service Com., 1947. Fellow Am. Acad. Arts and Scis.; hon. mem. Oxford Soc. Hist. Theology; mem. Am. Oriental Soc., Soc. Bibl. Lit. (sec. 1916-33, pres. 1936; del. Am. Council Learned Socs., 1929-50), Am. Antiquarian Soc., Am. Philos. Soc., Studiorum Novi Testamenti Societas (pres. 1958-59), Phi Beta Kappa. Mem. Soc. of Friends. Pacifist. Author books including: The Making of Luke-Acts, 1927; George Fox's Book of Miracles, 1948; Letters to William Dewsbury, 1948; The Book of Acts in History, 1955; John Woolman in England, 1971; Friendly Heritage, 1972; Narrative Papers of George Fox, 1972; also articles on history of Quakerism, Bibl. subjects. Editor: Annual of Am. Schs. of Oriental Research, 1927-32. Home: Haverford, Pa. Died Oct. 7, 1974; interred Philadelphia, Pa.

CADDOO, WILLIAM HENRY, carton co. exec.; b. Yonkers, N.Y., July 18, 1908; s. William A. and Nettie Cole (Jones) C.; B.S., Colby Coll., 1932; grad. Advanced Mgmt. Program, Harvard, 1957; m. Barbara Louise King, Dec. 11, 1948. From chemist to v.p. boxboard div. Robert Gair, Inc., 1937-56; co. merged with Continental Can Co., Inc., 1956, v.p., gen. mgr. boxboard and folding carton div., 1958-60, gen. mgr. mfg. boxboard until 1970, ret., 1970. Club: Wee Burn Country. Home: Darien, Conn. Died Apr. 12, 1974.

CADORIN, ETTORE, sculptor; b. Venice, Italy, Mar. 1, 1878; s. Vincenzo and Matilde (Rocchin) C.; art edn., Royal Acad. Fine Arts, Venice (awarded 2 first medals and scholarships) Sch. of Applied Arts, and in studio of father; m. Lovie Mueller, of Bendigo, Austrailia, Apr. 25, 1912. Came to U.S., 1915. Prof. lit. and art, Columbia, 1915-17; official rep. of Italian Govt. in U.S.A. as lecturer in art, 1918-19; teacher of sculpture, Santa Barbara (Calif.) State Teachers Coll., 1926-29. Prin. owrks: Statues for Library Bldg., St. Mark Sq., Venice; protrait in ivory of royal princesses of Italy, Caruso, Etc.; War Memorial, Edgewater, N.J.; statuary for court house, Santa Barbara, for building of Christian Brothers, Napa, Calif.; bronze statue of Father Serra, for Nat. Statuary Hall, Washington, D.C.; 3 statues in stone for Washington (D.C.) Cathedral- St. Peter, St. Paul and St. John, patrons of the Cathedral; bronze replica of statue of Junipero Serra, of Washington, erected in Plaza Sq., Los Angeles; works for Golden Gate Expn., San Francisco, 1939: The Evening Star (fountain). The Moon and the Dawn (a group in the South Gardens), The Earth (statue); 4 statues in stone for the Church of St. Peter and St. Paul of San Francisco symbolizing the four evangelists; statue of "Our Lady" for San Mateo, Calif. Served as lt., Italian Army, World War. Mem. Nat. Sculpture Soc., Beaux Arts Inst. Design. Chevalier Officer of Crown (Italy). Home: Sonoma, Cal.†

CADY, CLAUDE E., ex-congressman; b. Lansing, Mich., May 28, 1878; married; children—Stanley W., Clella E. Owner of 3 theaters in Lansing; also intersted in various Mich. corpns. Alderman of Lansing, 1910-17; mem. Police and Fire Commn., 1918-28; mem. 73d Congress (1933-35), 6th Mich. Dist.; then postmaster of Lansing. Democrat. Home: Lansing, Mich.†

CAFFERY, ELDON LEE, urologist; b. Athensville, Ill., Feb. 23, 1924; s. Robert Lee and Leah (Walkington) C.; M.D., U. Tenn., 1947; m. Nellie Mae Tombs, Dec. 19, 1947; children—Dawn Michelle, Michael Shawn. Intern, Wayne County Gen. Hosp., Eloise, Mich., 1947-49, resident, 1949-53; practice medicine specializing in urology, Jonesboro, Ark., 1958-72; chief of staff St. Bernard's Hosp.; asst. prof. urology Med. Coll. Ga., 1956-58. Trustee 1st Nat. Bank, 1968-72. Served to lt., M.C., USN, 1954-56. Diplomate Am. Bd. Urology. Fellow A.C.S.; mem. A.M.A. Home: Jonesboro, Ark. Died Sept. 7, 1972; buried Jonesboro Meml. Park, Jonesboro, Ark.

CAFFERY, JEFFERSON, diplomat; b. Lafayette, La., Dec. 1, 1886; s. Charles Duval and Mary Catherine (Parkerson) C.; B.A., Tulane U., 1906, LL.D., 1968; LL.D., Cath. U. Am., 1941, U. Lyon (France), 1947, Seattle U., 1955, U. Southwestern La., 1971; J.S.D., Holy Cross Coll., 1955, Ph.D. (hon.), U. Brazil, 1943; m. Gertrude McCarthy, Nov. 20, 1937. Admitted to La. Bar, 1909; sec. U.S. legation, Caracas, Venezuela, 1911-13, followed by various fgn. service appointments (including Paris, 1917-19), 1913-19; assigned Dept. State for U.S. visits King of Belgian and Prince of Wales, 1919; various assignments abroad, 1919-24; E.E. and M.P. to Salvador, 1926-28, to Columbia, 1928-33; spl. presdl. rep. wtih rank of ambassador, at inauguration Pres. Herrera of Columbia, 1930; spl. rep. Dept. State, Salvador, 1931-32; apptd. asst. sec. state, 1933, mem. personnel bd. Fgn. Service, personal presdl. rep. to Cuba, with rank of ambassador, 1933; A.E. and P. to Cuba, 1934-37; ambassador to Brazil, 1937-44; U.S. rep. with rank of ambassador to de facto French authority, 1944; ambassador to France, 1944-49, to Egypt, 1949-55; ret., 1955. Personal rep. of Pres. Eisenhower for inauguration Pakistan Republic and 1st Pakistan pres., Karachi, 1956; rep. U.S. Senate spl. com. to study fgn. aid programs in France, Italy, Spain, Portugal, U.K., 1956; U.S. rep. numerous confs., delegations; signer for U.S. internat. agreements, treaties. Recipient Cath. Action medal, 1944, State Dept. Distinguished Service award, 1950, Laetare medal, 1954, Bellarmine Coll. medal, 1955, Pres.'s medal Canisius Coll., 1955, Am. Fgn. Service Cup, 1971, Meml. Placque, U. Southwestern La. Alumni Assn., 1971; named hon. papal chamberlain (Pius XII, John XXIII, Paul VI); decorated grand cross Legion of Honor (France); Roman Cath. Grand Cross Pius IX; Order of Cordon of Egypt 1st class; grand cross of Carlos Cespedes Cuba Order Prder of Boyaca (Columbia); Order of Simon Bolivar (Venezuela); honored with establishment Jefferson Caffery Chair polit. sci. S. Western La. U., also Jefferson Caffery La. Room; numerous fgn. honors; made hon. citizen numerous French cities; hon. mem. Egyptian tribes. Mem. Am. Fgn. Service Assn., Brazilian Bar Assn. (hon.), S.A.R. Roman Catholic. Knight of Malta. Clubs: Metropolitan (Washington); Jockey (Paris); Boston (New Orleans). Home: Lafayette, La. Died Apr. 13, 1974; interred St. John's Cathedral Cemetery, Lafayette, La.

CAKE, WALLACE ELLWOOD, chemist; b. Lake Linden, Mich., Oct. 24, 1897; s. Henry Wallace and Mabelle E. (Bennallack) C.; student U. Mich.; m. Ilene Fischer, Nov. 23, 1922; children—Arthur F., W. Ellwood, Sara Anne. Vice pres. U.S. Rubber Co., N.Y.C. Home: Greenwich, Conn. Died Feb. 16, 1973.

CALDERON, LUIS, ambassador; b. Madrid, Spain, Sept. 17, 1881; s. Antonio and Paulina Martin (Almayer) C.; student U. of Madrid; m. Annina Schiaffino, Mar. 1921; children—Paulina, Elena. Began as vice consul, Montreal, Canada, 1907; consul, Southampton, 1910-19, Salonica, 1919-21, Glasgow, 1921-26; consul in the ministry of State of Madrid, 1926, rep. before the Central Bd. of Ports, 1926; mem. commn. of Officers of Ministry of State to study and coordinate its legislation, 1927; mem. delegation form Spain to draft a treaty with Italy about the fiscal regime of the mercantile socs., 1927; consul gen., Manila, 1929; comml. counselor of Spanish Embassy, Washington, with juridiction in U.S., Mexico and Cuba, 1930; consul gen., chief of the commerical sect., Ministry of State, Madrid, 1931; consul gen., London, 1932; ambassador to U.S., Washington, D.C., since 1934. Awarded Cross of Naval Merit, gold medals of Brihuega and Villaviciosa, and silver medal of Astorga (Spain); Grand Official of Order of Leopold 11 (Belgium); Commander of the Crown (Italy). Home: Washington, D.C.†

CALDWELL, JOHN KENNETH, foreign service officer; b. Piketon, Ohio, Oct. 16, 1881; s. James Oscar and Leila Ada (Cox) C.; B.S., Berea (Ky.) Coll., 1905; m. Grace Colquhoun Thompson. d. Am. missionaries, of Tokyo, June 16, 1908; children—David Kenneth, Margaret Colquhoun, James Thompson, John Rea. Employed in laboratory of surpervising architect of the Treasury Dept., Washington, D.C., 1906; apptd. student interpreter in Japan, 1906; vice and de. consul-gen., also interpreter at Yokohama, 1909; asst. Japanese sec. to Embassy to Japan, 1909-14; vice consul at Dalny temporarily, Jan. 17-Feb. 17, 1911; consul at Vldadivostok, 1914-20, Kobe, Japan, Sept. 11, 1920; apptd. Japanese sec. Am. Embassy at Tokyo, July 1921; spl. duty at Chita, Siberia, 1921; apptd. consul gen., June 1924, asst. chief Div. of Far Eastern Affairs, Dept. of State, Nov. 19, 1925, later acting chief; lectr. on Far East, Georgetown Univ. Foreign Service Sch., 1926-27. Rep. of sec. of state on Federal Narcotics Control Bd., 1925-30; attended meetings of League of Nations Opium Ad. Coin. in Geneva as tech. expert on behalf Dept. of State, 1928-31; del. of U.S. to Preliminary Narcotics Conf., 1930; chmn., U.S. delegation and v.p. Conf. on Limitation of Mfr. of Narcotic Drugs, Geneva, Switzerland, 1931; Am. observer at conf. on Suppression of Opium Smoking, Bangkok, Siam, 1931; consul gen. at Sydney, Australia, 1932-35, at Tientsin, China, 1935-42; assigned to Dept. of State, Washington, D.C., 1942-43; E.E. and M.P. to Ethiopia, 1943-45; retired from fgn. service, 1945; asst. diplomatic adviser to U.N.R.R.A., 1946. Mem. Asiatic Society of Japan. Club: Columbia Country (Washington). Home: Robles Del Rio, Cal.†

CALDWELL, ROBERT TATE, lawyer; b. Taylor County, Ky., May 7, 1882; s. James Thomas and Annie (Read) C.; B.S., Centre Coll., Danville, Ky., 1903; student Centre Coll. Law Sch., 1906-08; m. Virginia B. Hoge, Dec. 27, 1916 (dec. 1962)); m. 2d, Ruth Turner, 1963. Admitted to Ky. bar, 1908; instr. and coach Selma Mil. Inst., 1908-10; practiced in Louisville, 1910-14; asst. atty. gen. for Ky., 1914-16; chmn. Ky. Workmen's Compensation Bd. (author of Ky. Workmen's Compensation Act), 1916-18; pvt. practice, Ashland, Ky., 1919; mem. firm Caldwell, Van Antwerp, Welch & Hughes. Enlisted Field Arty., 1918, commd. capt., Nov. 1918. Adviser U.S. delegation Internat. Labor Conf., 1935; mem. Nat. Conf. of Commrs. Uniform State Laws (1944-50). Trustee Pikeville Coll. Mem. regional adv. conf. NLRB; mem. Ky. All Industries Wage Bd., Ky. Adv. Com. on Nuclear Energy. Mem. Am., Ky. (pres. 1934, 35), Boyd County bar assns., Order of Coif, Kappa Alpha (So.). Democrat. Presbyn. Home: Ashland, Ky. Died Apr. 25, 1973; buried Danville, Ky.

CALFEE, ROBERT MARTIN, lawyer; b. Pulaski, Va., Apr. 13, 1876; s. Lee S. and Ella (Martin) C.; A.B., Roanoke Coll., 1893; LL.D. (hon.), 1955; LL.B., George Washington U., 1901; LL.M., Nat. U., 1902; m. Alwine Haas, June 27, 1906 (died Mar. 1937); children—Robert M., John B., William L. Admitted to Ohio bar, 1902, then practiced in Cleve., head firm Calfee & Fogg, 1908-45, Calfee, Fogg, McChord & Halter, after 1945. Acted as syndicate agt. in raising funds to asst. Col. Isaac N. Lewis in devel. his machine gun, and took gun to Eng., 1910, rep. Am. owners arranged for sales of fgn. patents to Belgian group, 1912; asst. contract adjustment div., U.S. War Dept., 1918-19, (asst. in drafting Declaration of Independence for Rep. of Czechoslovakia, 1918). Legal mem. Ohio Pub. Health Council, 1916-36; mem. bd. trustees Cleveland Asso. Charities (now Family Welfare Assn.), since 1920, pres., 1926-34. Mem. bd. trustees Roanoke Coll., pres., bd., 1948-53. Mem. bd. trustees Roanoke Coll., pres. bd., 1948-53. Mem. Am., Ohio and Cleveland bar assns., Sons Am. Revolution. Presbyterian. Clubs: Union, Mayfield Country, Pepper Pike Country (Cleveland); University (New York, Washington), Home: Cleveland Heights, O.†

CALKINS, ALLARD A., bank cons.; b. San Francisco, Apr. 26, 1889; s. John U. and Harriet L. (Bates) C.; B.L., U. of Calif., Berkeley, 1911, grad. student, 1912; special study mil. science; m. Persis N. Bunker, Jan. 21, 1929; children-Allard A., Jr., Persis M., Elizabeth N. Admitted to Calif. bar, 1914. Asst. law dept. Asso. Oil Co. (now Tidewater Asso. Oil Co.), San Francisco, 1912-14; private practice of law, 1914-17; teacher in English dept., U. of Calif., 1914-16; bank officer (all depts.) Security Trust and Savings Bank (now Security First Nat.), Los Angeles, 1919-28; analyst in security field, 1928-30; v.p. Pacific Nat. Bank, San Francisco, 1930-32; mgr. San Francisco Loan Agency, R.F.C., 1932-40; chairman of the board Anglo California National Bank of San Francisco (now Crocker-Anglo Nat. Bank), 1951-54, dir., mem. exec. com., 1941-58; dir., mem. operating exec. com. Pickering Lumber Corp., 1938-59; cons. on constrn. and campuses. Trustee St. Helena Unified Sch. Dist. Pres. San Francisco Clearing House Assn., 1949-51, Trustee Coro Found. Served in Officers' Reserve Corps, Cal. N.G., 20 years; chmn. adv. com. 6th Army, San Francisco. Member of American Legion, Phi Kappa Sigma, Phi Delta Phi. Clubs: Commonwealth, Pacific Union (San Francisco); Faculty (U. Cal.), Kiwanis. Home: St. Helena, Cal. Died May 20, 1973.

CALKINS, HOWARD W., advt., pub. relations exec.; b. Cortland, N.Y., May 30, 1902; s. Chauncey E. and Minnie L. (Lang) C.; B.S., U. Pa., 1924; m. Mary Ellen McGovern, Aug. 21, 1932; children—Carole E., Howard W. Reporter, financial writer, N.Y. News, bur. assn. pub. Wall Street News, 1924-35; financial writer N.Y. Times, 1935-45; became v.p., dir., dir. publicity dept. Albert Frank-Guenther Law, Inc., 1945, chmn. bd., 1951-70, pres., 1958-60, chmn. emeritus, 1970-73. Served with USNR, 1942-45; disch., lt. comdr. Home: Yonkers, N.Y. Died Aug. 25, 1973.

CALL, CHARLES WARREN, JR., food co. exec.; b. Hackensack, N.J., Sept. 25, 1925; s. Charles Warren and Ruth (Adelsperger) C.; A.B., Harvard, 1949; LL.B., Northeastern U., 1954; m. Eloise Faxon, June 16, 1953; 1 son, Charles Bradford. Pres., dir. Noma Corp., N.Y.C., 1963-66; pres., chief exec. officer Ward Foods, Inc., 1966-71, chmn., chief exec. officer, 1971-75. Mem. nat. adv. com. N.Y.C. Hall of Sci.; mem. Northeastern U. Corp.; trustee Worcester Acad. Served with Inf. AUS, 1943-46. Mem. Am. Bakers Assn. (gov.). Home: Morristown, N.J. Died Jan. 2, 1975.

CALL, LELAND EVERETT, agronomist; b. Kent, O., Feb. 9, 1881; s. Charles Augustus and Olive (Prior) C.; B.S. in Agr., Ohio State U., 1906, M.S. in Agr., 1912; m. Clara Willis, 1910 (died July 17, 1944); 1 dau., Marjorie; m. 2d, to Mary Eck Holland, Mar. 2, 1946. Teaching fellow in agricultural chemistry, Ohio State University, 1906; asst. in agronomy, Kansas State College, 1907-08, asst. prof. soils, 1908-11, asso. prof., 1911-13, prof. agronomy and in charge dept., 1913-25, dean agr. and dir. Agrl. Expt. Sta., 1925-46, dean and director emeritus and prof. of rural investigations since 1946; agrl. research advisor Mut. Security Agy., Manilla, since 1952; dir. of Fed. Land Bank, Wichita, 1930-42, pres., 1934. Served in France, World War, in Y.M.C.A., and Army Ednl. Corps, in charge farm crop instructional work, and at A.E.F. University, Beaune, France, 1919. Fellow American Soc. Agronomy (president 1922), A.A.A.S.; member Kansas Crippled Children's Commission since 1945, Sigma Xi, Alpha Zeta, Phi Kappa Phi, Gamma Sigma Delta and Delta Tau Delta. Congregationalist. Rotarian. Author agrl. lab. manual, text book, numerous bulls, and papers on agrl. subjects. Home: Manhattan, Kan.†

CALL, MARGARET FLEMING, (Mrs. Asa V. Call), civic worker; b. Los Angeles; d. Thomas J. and Ella (Thompson) Fleming; student pub. schs.; m. Asa V. Call, May 23, 1917; children—Thomas Fleming, Richard William, Janet Call (Mrs. William Burby, Jr.). Sponsor, Thomas J. Fleming Poison Information Center Children's Hosp. Vice pres., bd. dirs. Children's Hosp., Los Angeles; bd. dirs. Girls Collegiate, Ely Ct. Sch. for Girls. Recipient Outstanding Achievement award for exceptional service to safety Nat. Safety Council, 1966; Pro Ecelesia medal Pope John XXII. Mem. Town and Gown Soc. U. So. Cal. Home: Beverly Hills, Cal., Died Dec. 29, 1975.

CALL, NORMAN, ry. pres.; b. Richmond, Va., Mar. 29, 1880; s. Manfred and Elizabeth (Watt) C.; ed. high sch. and Va. Mechanics/23 Inst.; m. Eileen Hearon, September 30, 1903 (deceased); children—Norman (deceased), Eileen Hearon (Mrs. J. Downman Mitchell, Jr.), Daniel Hearon, Clara Hearon (Mrs. Charles William Frazier, Jr.); m. 2d, Anne Murray, Apr. 6, 1942. Stenographer and clk. Richmond Locomotive Works, 1897-99, mgr. purchasing dept., 1900-01; sec. to pres. Richmond, Fredericksburg & Potomac R.R., 1901-10, sec., 1910-17, asst. to pres., 1917-19, v.p., 1920-32, pres. and dir. after 1932; pres., dir. Richmond Terminal Ry. Co., Richmond Land Co.; dir. Fruit Growers Express Co., First & Merchants Nat. Bank of Richmond, Richmond-Greyhound Lines, Inc. Mem. Bd. Visitors, Mt. Vernon. Mem. Am. Ry. Engr. Assn., Am. Soc. Mech. Engrs., Newcomen Soc. of England, S.A.R. Ind. Democrat. Mason (K.T., Shriner). Clubs: Commonwealth, Country Club of Va. (Richmond); Corinthian Yacht (Washington, D.C.). Home: Richmond, Va.†

CALLOWAY, THOMAS CLANTON, composer; b. Troy, Ala., Mar. 1, 1878; s. Robert and Martha Ann C.; mus. edn. New England Conservatory of Music. Composer, tchr. of music after 1898. Composer: (songs) There Are No Eyes Like Thine, Down in the Jeweled Deep; The Green Kentucky Pastures; Loves Dreaming Song; Eventide; Whar de Watermilyuns Grow; On the Sands When Starlight Shone; The White Rose; The Pink Carnation; Where the Shady River Deepens; All Thy Works Shall Praise Thee; Elder Blooms; The Tale of the Humming Bird. Instrumental: Storm on the Ocean; Gaiety Gallop; Love's Vision Waltzes; The Debutant Two-Step; Daughters of the Confederacy March; Montgomery Advertiser March; An Idyl; A Summer Dream; An Autumn Deram; A Winter Dream; An Evening Reverie; At Twilight; Moonbeams; Grande Gallop Brilliante; The Violet; The Hyacinth: The Lily; I Love Only You; I'm Dreaming of You; A Song of Spring; My Love Is Like the Rose; Love's Meldoy; An Evening Serenade. Home: Montgomery, Ala.†

CAMAK, DAVID ENGLISH, clergyman, educator; b. Winnsboro, S.C., July 26, 1880; s. Thomas Charles and Lou Emma (Meadors) C.; student Mt. Zion Inst., Winnsboro, 1897-98; A.B., Wofford Coll., 1903, D.D., 1921; m. Lottie Elizabeth Blair, Oct. 8, 1903; children—Anna Lou (dec.), Pascal Meadors, Mariana, David English (dec.), Blair. Admitted into S.C. Conf. M.E. Ch., South, 1903, ordained deacon, 1905, elder, 1907; pastor Green St. Ch., Union, S.C., 1903-04, Jonesville, 1904-07, Saluda, 1907-09; agt. Southern Industrial Inst., 1909-10; pastor Duncan Memorial Ch., Spartanburg, S.C., 11; founded Textile Indsl. Inst. (now known as Spartanburg Jr. Coll.), Spartanburg, S.C., Sept. 5, 1911, pres., 1911-23; pastor Ware Shoals, S.C., 1923-25, St. Paul Ch., Greenville, 1925-29, Grace Ch., Union, 1929-33, St. Johns Ch., Rock Hill, 1933-34, Canton, N.C., 1934-38, First Meth. Ch., Hendersonville, N.C., 1938-42; pastor First Meth. Church, Marion, N.C., since 1942. Pioneer in part-time edn., having gained wide notice for operation of a plan of study at Textile Industrial Institute, whereby pupils alternately studied a week (later 2 weeks) in sch. and then exchanged places for a like period with workers in cotton mills, and other industrial plants, thus earning expenses of edn. Author and pub. June of the Hills, ¾ 0 prize in novel writing contest of Womans Club, Lake Juneluska, N.C. Author of plays and pageants; contbr. to periodicals. Home: Marion, N.C.†

CAMERON, AUGUSTUS GARFIELD, business exec.; b. Knightstown, Ind., Mar. 21, 1880; s. John Duncan and Martha Anne (Fort) C.; grad. Knightstown Acad., 1898; student various extension courses; m. Sarah Dorothy Fleener, Nov. 14, 1900; children—Evelyn May (Mrs. Samuel B. Boudreau), Leone (Mrs. Karl Linwood Lange). Vice pres. The August M. Kuhn Co., wholesale grocers, Indpls., 1910-13; truck tire rep., Goodyear Tire & Rubber Co., 1913-14, dist. mgr., 1914-18, mgr. Australasian Div., Goodyear Tire & Rubber Export Co., 1919-23, sales mgr. Goodyear Export, 1923-25; vice president and general mgr. Goodyear Fgn. Operations, Inc., since 1939, vice pres. Goodyear Tire & Rubber Export Company, after 1925. Member National Foreign Trade Council, Inc. (dir.). Rubber Export Assn. (mng. dir.). Republican. Presbyterian. Mason. Clubs: Portage Country, Akron City. Home: Akron, O.†

CAMERON, DONALD FORRESTER, librarian; b. Glasgow, Scotland, May 29, 1901; s. Alexander Forrester and Marion Cooper (Stark) C.; B.S., Union Coll., 1924; A.M., Princeton University, 1925; Litt.D., Rutgers University, 1956; m. Donna Priest, June 28, 1929; children—Donald Forrester, Alan Edward, Sarah Priest. Instr. English, Union Coll., 1925; instr. English, Rutgers U., 1929-34, asst. prof., 1934-41, associate professor, 1941-45, professor from 1945, also associate librarian, later being librarian, 1945. Mem. Am. and N.J. library assns., Bibliog. Soc. Am., St. Andrew's Soc., Phi Gamma Delta. Clubs: Grolier, Phi Gamma Delta (N.Y.C.). Editor: Rutgers University Press, 1943-45. Home: Highland Park, N.J. Died Aug. 27, 1974.

CAMERON, FRANCIS, mining geologist; b. Washington, Mar. 14, 1902; s. Frank K. and Katherine (Boyle) C.; A.B., Leland Stanford U., 1924; D. Engring. (hon.), U. Mo., 1961; m. Louise Lang, Mar. 5, 1932; children—Frank K., William L. Asst. foreman, engr. Chief Consol. Mining Co., Eureka, Utah, 1924-25; asst. geologist Internat. Smelting Co., Salt Lake City, 1926-28; geologist Anaconda Copper Mining Co., N.Y.C., various U.S., fgn. cities, 1928-45; adviser Metals Res. Co., Washington, 1942-45; asst. to exec. v.p. St. Joe Minerals Corp., N.Y.C., 1945-46, v.p., 1946-60, pres., 1960-67, chmn. 1967-71; retired, 1971, dir.; dir. St. Joseph Explorations Ltd., P. & L.E. R.R., Jododex Australia Pty. Ltd. Fellow Geol. Soc. Am.; mem. Am. Inst. Mining and Metall. Engrs., Mining and Metall. Soc. Am., Canadian Inst. Mining and Metallurgy, Soc. Econ. Geologists. Clubs: Sharon (Conn.) Country; University, Mining (N.Y.C.); Cosmos (Washington). Home: Lakeville, Conn. Died Feb. 27, 1975.

CAMERON, J. WALTER, fruit canner; b. Canton, Mass., June 6, 1895; s. Colin Campbell and Mary E. (Pond) C.; student pub. schs., Brookline, Mass.; m. Frances H. Baldwin, July 19, 1924; children—Colin Campbell, Mary Ethel. With Street & Smith Pub. Co., Honolulu, T.H., 1923-24; foreman Haleakaia Ranch, Maui, T.H., 1924-26; mgr. Haleakala Pineapple Co., 1926-33; chmn. dir. Maui Pineapple Co. Ltd., 1933-76; pres., pub. Maui Pub. Co., 1939-76; pres., dir. Haleakala Ranch Co., Ltd., Maui Electric Co., Ltd., Maui Pub. Co., Ltd.; dir. Hawaiian Telephone Co., Sheraton Corp. Hawaii, Hawaiian Airlines Ltd. Served from 2d lt. to capt. U.S. Army, 1917-19. Mem. Hawaiian Sugar Planters Assn. (exec. com.). Clubs: Maui Country; Pacific (Honolulu); Pacific Union (San Francisco). Address: Kahului, Hawaii., Died Jan. 2, 1976.

CAMERON, THOMAS BROWN, educator, chemist; b. Newburgh, N.Y., Mar. 22, 1916; s. T. Brown and Rose Ethel (Taylor) C.; B.S. in Chemistry, Rensselaer Poly. Inst., 1937, M.S., 1938, Ph.D. in Inorganic Chemistry, 1942; m. Virginia Leggett, June 24, 1944; children—Ann Leggett, Beth Leggett, John Taylor. Mem. faculty Rensselaer Poly. Inst., 1941-46, instr. chemistry, 1942-46; mem. faculty U. Cin., 1946-73, prof. chemistry, 1956-73, dir. undergrad. studies in chemistry, 1959-62, chmn. dept., 1962-66. Asso. chemist Argonne Nat. Lab., 1948-49. Area radiol. officer Ohio Civil Def. Orgn., 1950-56: faculty chmn. com. coll. work P.E. Diocese So. Ohio, 1954-59. Recipient of Cinn. Chemist award, 1966. Mem. Am. Chem. Soc. (chmn. Cin. Sect. 1956-57, nat. councillor 1951-53, 61-72), A.A.A.S., Ohio Acad. Sci., Am. Assn. U. Profs., Sigma Xi, Phi Lambda Upsilon (nat. pres. 1960-63). Home: Cincinnati, O. Died Mar. 2, 1973.

CAMP, CHARLES LEWIS, educator; b. Jamestown, N.D., Mar. 12, 1893; s. Edgar Whittlesey and Theodosia Irvin (Baird) C.; student Throop Polytechnic Inst., 1906-10; A.B., U. of Calif., 1915; M.A., Columbia, 1921, Ph.D., 1923; m. Jessie Margaret Pratt, Mar. 7, 1924; children—Charles MacLeod, Nancy Jean, Patsy Ann, Roderick Edgar. Asst. to Museum Vertebrate Zoölogy, 1908-15; asst. dept. of zoölogy, Columbia, 1916-17, 1919-21; asst. in Am. Museum Nat. History, 1919-21; research asso. U. of Calif. 1922-24, asst. prof., asso. prof., 1924-39, prof. and chmn. of dept. paleontology, 1940-49; dir. Museum of Paleontology, 1931-49; fellow John Simon Guggenheim Foundation 1935, travel in Europe, S. Africa and China. 1st lt. A.E.F., 1918-19, F.A. Reserve, 1922-30; Coast Guard Reserve Temp. Service, 1943. Awarded Croix de Guerre. Fellow A.A.A.S.; member Geol. Soc. Am., Calif. Acad. Sciences (corr. sec.), Paleontology Society, Am. Hist. Assn., Am. Society Herpetol.-Ichthyology, Calif. Hist. Soc., Calif Folklore Soc., E. Clampus Vitus, Sigma Xi, Phi Beta Kappa. Clubs: Faculty, Roxburghe, Cooper, Grinnell, History of Science, Cosmos, Commonwealth Club of San Francisco. Author, editor books on frontier history of Am.; also papers. Home: Berkeley, Cal. Died Aug. 14, 1975.

CAMP, HUGH DOUGLAS, paper products mfg. exec.; b. Franklin, Va., Apr. 4, 1903; s. James Leonidas and Caroline Fountain (Savage) C.; student Wake Forest Coll., U. Va., Phila. Textile Sch.; m. Ada Norris Coleman, 1927; 1 dau., Caroline (Mrs. Leonidas A. Karafylakis). Vice pres. Roanoke Mills Co., Roanoke Rapids, N.C., 1926-37; v.p. Camp Mfg. Co., 1937-54, exec. v.p., 1954-56, pres., Franklin, Va., 1956-73; exec. v.p. Union Camp Paper Corp. (now Union Camp Corp.), N.Y.C., 1956-60, chmn. bd., 1960-73, also dir. Bd. dirs. Camp Found. Rotarian. Clubs: Ridgewood Country, Commonwealth, Union League, (N.Y.C.). Home: New York City, N.Y. Died Apr. 17, 1974; buried Poplar Springs Cemetery, Franklin, Va.

CAMP, THOMAS JAMES, army officer; b. Seymour, Conn., Nov. 10, 1886; s. Lewis Abel and Elizabeth (James) C.; Manlius Sch., 1903-04, B.A., Yale U., 1908, M.A., 1915; m. Mary Mattis, Oct. 7, 1915; children—Major Thomas James, Jr., Lt. Ross Mattis, Julie (Mrs. John R. McLean) Instr. at Manlius Sch., 1909-12; commd. 2d lt., U.S. Army, 1912, assigned to 2d Inf., Hawaii, 1912-17; instr. First Officers Training Camp, 1917; battalion comdr., France, 1918; honor grad. Command and Gen. Staff Sch., 1926, instr., 1926-30; grad. Army War Coll., 1931, Naval War College, 1935; War Dept. Gen. Staff, 1937-41; organized 51st Armored Inf. Reg., 1941; temp. brig. gen., 1942. Mem. Phi Beta Kappa, Beta Theta Pi. Mason. Clubs: Chevy Chase, Army-Navy (Washington). Edited Infantry Jour., 1931-34. Home: Champaign, Ill. Died Dec. 23, 1974.

CAMP, WILLIAM BACON, govt. ofcl.; b. Greenville, Tex., Nov. 25, 1913; s. William Hille and Marguerite (Bacon) C.; student Tex. Mil. Coll., 1932, Baylor U., 1933; m. Lida Eileen Conner, Nov. 23, 1947. With U.S. Office Comptroller, 1937-73, comptroller of currency, 1967-73; mem. faculty Stonier Sch. Banking, Rutgers U., from 1962. Mem. Christian Ch. (chmn. trustees, elder). Rotarian. Home: Rockville, Md., Died Nov. 13, 1975.

CAMPBELL, ARCHIBALD DUNCAN, educator, economist; b. Glasgow, Scotland, Jan. 22, 1919; s. Duncan Alexander and Catherine Anne (Ferguson) C.; M.A., U. Glasgow, 1940; m. Mary Elizabeth McFarlane Wilson, Aug. 29, 1950; children—Duncan, Janet, Gillian. Lectr., U. Glasgow, 1945-52, sr. lectr., 1952-55; prof. applied econs. U. St. Andrews (Scotland), 1955-67, dean Faculty Social Sci., 1961-65; prof. applied econs. U. Dundee (Scotland), 1967-75. Econ. cons., sec. of state for Scotland, 1962-75. Dir. Sidlaw Industries Ltd., Dundee. Mem. Scottish Gas Bd., 1966-72, Brit. Gas Corp., 1973-75. Served to maj. Royal Engrs., 1940-45. Decorated comdr. Order Brit. Empire. Home: Dundee, Scotland. Died Jan. 6, 1975; interred Western Cemetery, St. Andrews, Fife, Scotland.

CAMPBELL, DAN HAMPTON, scientist, educator; b. Freemont, O., Jan. 18, 1907; s. Ralph and Edna Catherine (Moses) C.; A.B., Wabash Coll., 1930, Sc.D., 1960; M.S., Washington U., St. Louis, 1932; Ph.D., U. Chgo., 1935; m. Margaret Kathryn Dorr, May 12, 1930; 1 son, John Hampton. Instr. comparative anatomy and embryology, Washington U., r 1930-33; research fellow U. Chgo., 1933-37, instr. bacteriology and immunology, 1937-39, asst. prof. immunology, 1940-42; asst. prof. immunochemistry Cal. Inst. Tech., 1942-45, asso. prof., 1945-50, prof. immunochemistry 1950. Mem. research adv. bd. City of Hope Med. Center, 1952-60, Nat. Nephrosis Found., 1954-58, Los Angeles Children's Hosp., 1955-57; mem. Com. Advanced Advanced Sci. Tng., 1957-74; served as responsible investigator of plasma substitute program for Com. of Med. Research, World War II; cons. for Manhattan project and AEC, 1943-45, 48-49; responsible investigator for U.S. Pub. Health Research program on chemistry of blood and plasma substitute and for Office of Naval Research program for immunochem. research of Arctic animals, 1948-74; cons. NIH on immunochem. problems, 1957-74; chmn. com. standardization allergen Nat. Inst. Allergy and Infectious Diseases, 1959-74; mem. sci. adv. council St. Jude Hosp.; mem. sci. adv. bd. Hastings Found., chmn. bd. for research and devel.; dir. Internat. Chem. and Nuclear Corp., 1962-74. Fellow Rockefeller Found. Ednl. Bd., 1940-41. Fellow N.Y. Acad. Sci., Am. Acad. Allergy (hon.; distinguished service award), Internat. Soc. Hematology, A.A.A.S.; mem. Am. Assn. Immunologists (council midwinter conf.; pres. 1972-73), Coll. Physiol. Chemistry and Physics, Am. Chem. Soc., Soc. Exptl. Biology and Medicine, Arctic Inst. N.A., Pan Am. Med. Assn., Sigma Xi, Phi Chi, Tau Kappa Epsilon. Author: Principles of Immunology, 1957; co-author Methods in Immunology, 1963, 70. Adv. editor Jour. Infectious Diseases, 1941-48; asso. editor Jour. of Immunology, 1953-58, mem. editorial bd., 1960; chmn. editorial bd. Immunochemistry, 1964-74. Contbr. articles to profl. jours. Home: Altadena, Cal. Died Sept. 16, 1974.

CAMPBELL, GORDON HENSLEY, b b. Wakeeney, Kan., Aug. 16, 1880; s. Donald Kennedy and Margaret (McGilvary) C.; prep. edn., high sch., Pontiac, Ill.; student Lake Forest (Ill.) Coll., 1898-1900, U. of Chgo., 1901; m. Alice Robinson, Oct. 14, 1908; children—O. P. Robinson, Margaret McGilvary, Laura Pemberton, Elizabeth Kennedy. Gen. agt. Aetna Life Ins. Co. for Ark. and Southeast Missouri since 1909; dir. several companies. Chmn. bd. of trustees Little Rock Museum of Fine Arts; sec. Arkansas War Memorial Stadium Commn.; member Kappa Sigma. Republican. Presbyterian. Mason (31°. Shriner). Clubs: Rotary. Little Rock Country. Home: Little Rock, Ark.†

CAMPBELL, JOHN A(RTHUR), JR., banker; b. Asheville, N.C., Sept. 17, 1903; s. John Arthur and Mary Duff (Robinson) C.; student Peirce Sch. Bus. Adminstrn., Phila., m. Elizabeth McMorine Folk, Nov. 12, 1930. Clk., teller, Asheville, 1922-23; asst. cashier, later cashier, Marion, N.C., 1924-26; examiner banks in N.C., State Banking Dept., Raleigh, 1927-30; asst. sec., treas. Am. Trust Co., Charlotte, N.C., 1930-33; mgr. loan agy. R.F.C., Charlotte, 1933-47; v.p. S.C. Nat. Bank, Columbia, 1947, 1st v.p., 1948-50, pres., dir., 1951-56; sr. v.p., dir. Branch Banking & Trust Co., Wilson, N.C., 1956-60, executive vice president, director, 1960-74. Pres., dir. S.C. Tb Assn., 1950-55; dir. Carolinas United Community Services; mem. N.C. USO com.; mem. loan com. Bus. Development Corp. of N.C. Mem. S.C. (pres. 1952-53), N.C. bankers assns., Newcomen Soc., Am. Inst. Banking. Club: Wilson (N.C.) Country. Home: Wilson, N.C. Died Dec. 15, 1974; buried in Edenton, N.C.

CAMPBELL, KATHLEEN ROSEANNE, librarian, educator; b. Salt Lake City, Dec. 15, 1903; d. James Michael and Mary Ellen (Logue) Campbell; certificate in library sci., U. Denver, 1933, B.S., 1934, M.S., 1939. Sec. to librarian Denver Pub. Library, 1924-33, exec. sec., 1933-39; librarian and prof. library econ. Mont. State U. from 1939. Chmn. Mont. State Library Commn., 1939-75; mem. exec. board Pacific N.W. Bibliog. Center, 1959-64. Member Mont. State Library Assn. (pres. 1946-47), Pacific N.W. Library Assn. (pres. 1947-48; exec. com. library development project 1956-58, chmn. library edn. div. 1961-63), Am. Library Assn. (council 1948-52, 61-65), Phi Chi Theta. Clubs: Missoula Country. Contbr. library publs. Home: Missoula, Mont. Died Feb. 25, 1975.

CAMPBELL, M(ARY) EDITH, social edn.; b. Ripley, O., Dec. 27, 1875; d. William Byington and Mary (Leavitt) C.; B.A., U. of Cin., 1901, M.A., 1906, L.H.D., 1931. Asst. dept. economics, U, of Cincinnati, 1907-08; mem. State Bd, of Women Visitors; mem.-at-large Bd. of Edn., Cin., 1912-16; mem. State Commn., Ohio Sch. Survey, 1913; v.-chmn. com. women in industry of Nat. Council Defense, 1917; supervisor in industrial relations service, Ordnance Dept., 1918; federal dir. woman's div. U.S. Employment Service for Ohio, 1918; mem. exec. com. Nat. Conf. Social Work; dir. Schmidlapp Fund for Girls; dir. Vocation Bur. Cincinnati Pub. Schs., 1921-40, asso. dir., dept. of personnel service, since 1940; mem. bd. Ohio Inst. for Pub. Efficiency, Cincinnati Community Chest (chmn. 1943). Cincinnati Municipal Reserach Bureau League of Women Voters; mem. com. on Vocational Guidance and Child Labor of White House Conf. on Child Health and Protection, also chmn. vocational guidance div. of this com.; mem. Com. on Child Welfare, Dept. of Superintendence, N.E.A.; mem. The Governor's Com. on the follow-up program of the White House Conf. in Ohio, 1941; chmn. bd. trustees Ohio State U., 1939; pres. Ohio Welfare Conf., 1931-33; com. mem. Ohio Children's Code Commn., 1942-43; mem. exec. bd. and chmn. Social Planning Com., Mayor's Friendly Relations Com.; sec. Council on Racial Adjustments within the Public Sch., since 1942; mem. Scholarship Found. of Public Schools; chmn. Samuel Ach Memorial Com. Hon. mem. Delta Kappa Gamma. Presbyterian. Clubs: Cincinnati College, Woman's City (pres. 1914). Home: Cincinnati, O.†

CAMPBELL, PERSIA (MRS. EDWARD RICE, JR.), educator; b. Australia, Mar. 15, 1898; d. Rodolphe A. and Beatrice (Hunt) Campbell; B.A., Sydney U., 1918, M.A., 1920; M.Sc., London Sch. Econs., 1923; grad. certificate in social economy, Bryn Mawr Coll., 1923; Ph.D., Columbia, 1940; m. Edward Rice, Jr., Oct. 1931 (dec.); children—Sydney Campbell, Edward Boyden. Came to U.S., 1930, naturalized, 1936. Asst. editor Australian Ency., 1924-26; research economist New South Wales govt., Australia, 1926-31; faculty Queens Coll. of City U., N.Y., 1940-65, prof. econs., 1959-65, chmn. div. social sci., 1959-61, chmn. dept. econs., 1961-65, prof. emeritus econs. City U., N.Y., 1965; K. P. Bryan prof. econs. U. N.C., Greensboro, 1965-66; consumer counsel N.Y. Gov., 1955-58; bd. dirs. Consumers Union of U.S.; mem. Pres. Kennedy's Consumer Adv. Council, Pres. Johnson's Com. on Consumer Interests; mem. Nat. Adv. Com. on Internat. Trade; consumer cons. N.Y.C. Anti-Poverty Com., 1966; chmn. internat. aid com. U.S. Internat. Orgn. Consumers Unions; consumer cons. N.Y.C. Community Devel. Agy., 1966-74; dep. rep. to UN for Internat. Fedn. U. Women. Adviser, U.S. delegation Internat. Confs. FAO, 1948, 49, 51; former v.p., observer at UN for Nat. Assn. Consumers Traveling fellow to London, 1921-23, Bryn Mawr fgn. fellow, 1923, Rockefeller internat. fellow to U.S., 1930-32. Mem. Am. Econs. Assn. Am. Assn. U. Women, Nat. Council Women, Pan-Pacific and S.E. Asia Women's Assn. (past chmn. U.S. group, leader Am. Delegation to confs. Tokyo 1958, Australia, 1961). Author: Chinese Coolie Immigration, 1923; American Agricultural Policy, 1933; Consumer Representation in the New Deal, 1940; The Consumer Interest, 1949; Mary Williamson Harriman, a biography, 1960. Co-editor: Studies in Australian Affairs, 1927. Conducted series weekly programs on consumer econs. local ednl. TV sta., 1962-63. Columnist on UN econ. and social documents for Internat. Devel. Rev., 1966. Home: Flushing, N.Y. Died Mar. 2, 1974.

CAMPBELL, ROBERT MORRELL, ceramic engr.; b. Passaic, N.J., Jan. 27, 1899; s. John McAllister and May (Northrop) C.; B.S., Alfred U., 1923, Ceramic Engr., 1950; m. Anna Merrill, Apr. 6, 1926; children—Merrillyn Anne, Robert Merrill. Ceramic engr. J. L. Mott Co., Trenton N.J., 1923, plant supt., 1926-30; ceramic engr. Trenton Potteries Co., 1930-33; prof. ceramic tech. Alfred U. Coll. Ceramics, 1933-44, prof., chmn. dept. ceramic engring., 1944-64, professor of ceramic engring., 1964-75; president of Alfred Atlas Gravel & Sand Corp., 1953-75; dir. Alfred Mut. Savs. & Loan Assn., 1953-75. Served as seaman signalman 1st class USNRF, 1918-19. Profl. engr., N.Y. Fellow Am. Ceramic Soc. (chmn. whiteware div.); mem. Nat. Inst. Ceramic Engrs. (pres. 1956-57, A. F. Greaves Walker award 1967), Am. Soc. Engring. Edn. (gen. council 1956-59, chairman mineral engineering division 1963-64, mem. exec. council tech. divs., 1964-65), N.Y. Soc. Profl. Engrs., Am. Legion, Delta Sigma Phi, Keramos. Mason. Contbr. profl., tech. jours. Home: Alfred, N.Y. Died Jan. 5, 1975.

CAMPBELL, ROY HILTON, clergyman; b. Benecia, Calif., Nov. 19, 1879; s. Alfred Hilton and Emmeline (Burroughs) C.; A.B., Pomona Coll., Claremont, Calif., 1903; A.M., U. of Calfo., 1906; B.C., Pacific Sch. of Religion, 1910, D.D., 1924; m. Mary Elizabeth Burleigh, Apr. 9, 1902 (died Jan. 1938); 1 son, Royal Hilton; m. 2d, Abigail Swisher Martin, June 25, 1939. Ordained minstry Congl. Ch., 1910; boys' work sec., Y.M.C.A., Portland, Ore., 1902-03; gen. Sec., Y.M.C.A., San Diego, Calif., 1904-05; same, U. of Calif., 1908-09; pastor Palo Alto, Calif., 1910-15, Calvary Congl. Ch., Oakland, Calif., 1915-17; dir. Pacific Coast religious activities, Y.M.C.A., huts in cantonments, 1917-19; pastor Pilgrim Congl. Ch., Seattle, Wash., 1919-20, 1st Congl. Ch., San Diego, 1920-40, Central Congl. Church, La Mesa, 1940-45. Leader San Diego Community Chest; pres. Calif. Conf. of Social Work; trustee Pacific Sch. of Religion; chaplain Greenwood Mem. Park. Republican. Kiwanian. Author: Three Vital Questions, 1926; Learning to Live, 1939; The Turn to Religion, 1940. Feature writer San Diego Evening Tribune. Radio lecturer. Home: La Mesa, Cal.†

CANNON, JIMMY, columnist; b. N.Y.C., Apr. 10, 1909; s. Thomas J. and Loretta (Monahan) C. Reporter, N.Y. Daily News, 1927-1930, N.Y. World-Telegram, 1930-34; feature writer, Internat. News Service, 1935-36; sports writer, N.Y. Jour. Am., 1936-39; columnist (specializing in sports, also covering other important nat. events), N.Y. Post, 1946, also war corr. in Korea; now columnist N.Y. Jour. Am. Served with AUS, 1941-45; 3d Army corr. for Stars and Stripes in 4 campaigns. Recipient Dutton award 3 times. Author: The Sergeant Says, 1942; Nobody Asked Me, 1950; Who Struck John?. Home: New York City, N.Y. Died Dec. 5, 1973.

CANTACUZENE, MME, writer, lecturer; b. The White House, Washington, D.C., June 7, 1876; d. Maj. Gen. Frederick D. (U.S. Army) and Ida (Honore) Grant; ed. at home; m. Prince Cantacuzene, Sept. 25, 1899; children—Michael, Mrs. W. D. Siebern, Lady Hanbury-Williams. Member Rep. State Com. of Fla. since 1944, Sarasota County Rep. Com. since 1944, Rep. Woman's Nat. Council since 1936, Women's Nat. Rep. Club, Women's Rep. League of Washington, D. C. Mem. D.A.R. (nat. vice chmn. of nat. defense, 1933-34), Am. Coalition (v.p., 1934-36), Dames of Loyal Legion (nat. pres. 1935-37), Daughters of 1812 (nat. officer), Daughters of Founders and Patriots (nat. officer), many other hereditary socs. Episcopalian. Clubs: Governor, Sulgrave. Author: My Life Here and There, Revolutionary Days, Russian People; numerous articles for Saturday Evening Post, Ladies Home Journal; columnist for N.Y. Evening Post and Phila. Ledger. Home: Washington, D.C.†

CAPOGROSSI, GUISEPPE, painter; b. Rome, Italy, Mar. 7, 1900; s. Gugliemo Capogrossi Guarna and Beatrice Tacchi Venturi; classical diploma, Inst. Massimo, Rome, 1917; M.A. in Jurisprudence, U. Rome, 1921; m. Costanza Mennyey, June 2, 1959; children—Beatrice, Olga. Engaged in painting, 1921—; a founder Roman Sch., 1932, Origine Group, 1950; prin. works in abstractionism, 1949—; pvt. shows include Rome, Milan, Venice, Florence, Trieste, Leghorn, Frankfort, N.Y.C., Paris, Berlin, London, Lausanne, Brussels, Dusseldorf, Sao Paulo; group shows include Pitts., Johannesburg, Tokyo. Recipient 1st certificate, Kassel, 1955, 2d certificate, 1959. Author: (monographs) Michel Sauphor, 1954; Michel Tapie, 1962; G.C. Argan-Capogrossi, 1968. Home: Rome, Italy., Died Oct. 9, 1972.

CAPPELLUCCI, GABRIEL ORAZIO, educator; b. Amsterdam, N.Y., Apr. 1, 1935; s. Concezio and Concetta Ann (Marinelli) C.; A.A., Mater Christi Sem., 1959; B.A., St. Bernard's Sem., 1961; M.A., Coll. St. Rose, 1967; m. Mary Ann Spelta, June 25, 1966; 1 son, John. Tchr., English and Latin, Cath. Central High Sch., Troy, N.Y., 1964-65; tchr. English and humanities Fonda-Fultonville High Sch., Fonda, N.Y., 1965-66; instr. English and philosophy Broome Community Coll., Binghamton, N.Y., 1966-67, asst. prof., 1967-71, asso. prof. philosophy, 1971-75. Mem. N.Y. Assn. Jr. Coll., State Tchrs. Assn., N.Y. State Philos. Assn. Club: Creighton. Home: Binghamton, N.Y. Died Mar. 4, 1975.

CARBAJÀL, FERNANDO, Peruvian engr.; corp. exec.; b. Lima, Peru, Mar. 1, 1880; grad. Peruvian Sch. of Engring. and Mining, 1900. Apptd. govt. engr. and explorer; engr. Panama Canal Constrn.; state engr. of Peru, in charge of public works, 1909-12; headed commn. to settle Peru-Bolivia boundary dispute, 1912-13; again state engr., and in charge construn., repair and maintenance of Peruvian coastal docks, 1913-20; gen. mgr., Peruvian Telephone Co., 1920, now v.p.; dir. Industrial Bank of Peru; v.p. Crandall Engring. Co., Boston, Mass. Organized Rotary Club, Lima, Peru, 1921, now its past pres.; ed. mag. The Peruvian Rotarian; held Rotary offices of v.p., dist. gov., chmn. convention com., 1939-40; mem. 1939-41 and chmn. 1939-40, South Am. Com. of Collaboration Among Rotary Clubs; also mem. other coms. and of Relief to Rotarians com., especially formed to relieve Rotary Internat. families in need due to war; pres. Rotary Internat., 1942. Mem. Am. Soc. of Civil Engrs., Pan Am. Soc. of U.S. Decorated Officer of the Order of Carlos Manuel de Cespedes (Cuba); Order of the Sun (Peru); Orfer of the Eagle of the Andes (Bolivia). Home: Lima, Peru.†

CARDER, EUGENE CLAYTON, clergyman; b. Liverpool, N.S., Dec. 11, 1881; s. Richard and Maria Elizabeth (Leadbetter) C.; grad. Colby Acad., New London, N.H., 1903; Ph.B., Brown U., Providence, R.R., 1907, D.D., 1935; D.D., Colgate U., 1928; student Rochester Theol. Sem., 1907-10; m. Jean DeWitt Bergfels, Sept. 19, 1910; 1 dau., Doris Bergfels (Mrs. Henry Horns). Came to U.S., 1885, naturalized, 1911. Ordained ministry Bapt. Ch., 1910; pastor Cuba, N.Y., 1910-17, 1st Ch., Morristown, N.J., 1917-19; asso. pastor Fifth Av. Ch., N.Y. City, 1919-22 (ch. moved in 1922, and named Park Av. Ch., again moved 1930, named Riverside Ch.); Riverside Ch., 1930-43. Trustee Colgate-Rochester Divinity Sch.; dir. N.Y. Bapt. City Mission Soc.; pres. bd. dirs., Wiltwyck School for Boys, Inc.; mem. bd. edn., Northern Baptist Convention. Republican. Club: Men's Faculty (Columbia U.). Home: Greensboro, Vt.†

CARDEW, EMILY CRASKE, univ. dean; b. Scranton, Pa Mar. 22, 1907; d. Henry and Evelyn Chandler (Frear) Cardew; student Rochester Gen. Hosp. Sch. Nursing, 1926-29; B.S., U. Chgo., 1943, M.S., 1946, Ph.D., 1956. Supr., instr. Rochester Gen. Hosp., 1929-32, 1935-39, Grace Hosp., New Haven, 1932-35; asst. dir., instr. Michael Reese Hosp. Sch. Nursing, Chgo., 1942-46; ednl. dir. St. Luke's Hosp. Sch. Nursing, 1946-49; asst. prof. nursing U. Ill., 1949-56, dean, asso. prof., 1956-74. Mem. Am. Nurses Assn. (chmn. adminstrv. sect., dir. 1948-50), Nat. League Nursing Edn., Ill. League Nursing Edn. (pres. 1949-53, dir. 1953), Am. Cancer Soc., Pi Lambda Theta. Author: Instructors' Manual, 1955. Editor, contbr.: Study Guide for Clinical Nursing, 1953. Contbr. profl. publs. Home: Chicago, Ill. Died Sept. 10, 1974.

CAREY, JAMES BARRON, labor exec.; b. Phila., Aug. 12, 1911; s. John and Margaret (Loughery) C.; student Drexel Inst., evenings, 1929-31, Wharton Evening Sch., U. Pa., 1931-32; LL.D., Rollins Coll., 1947; m. Margaret McCormick, Jan. 8, 1938; children—James Barron, Patricia Ann. Elec. worker, radio lab. Phila. Storage Battery Co., 1929-34; nat. pres. Radio and Allied Trades, 1933-40; apptd. gen. organizer for U.S. by A.F. of L., July 1934; nat. sec. Congress Indsl. Orgn., 1938-73, sec.-treas., 1942-73; gen. pres. United Elec., Radio and Machine Workers Am., 1936-41; pres. Internat. Union Elec., Radio and Machine Workers, AFL-CIO, 1950-65; v.p. AFL-CIO, 1955-65, sec.-treas. Indsl. Union Dept.; apptd. mem. prodn. planning bd. Office Prodn. Mgmt., Washington, 1941; exec. officer Utility Workers Organizing Com.; chmn. Congress Indsl. Orgn. Comm. to Abolish Discrimination; del., London, 1945, Paris, 1945, Moscow, 1946, Paris, 1947, Rome, 1948, meetings of World Fedn. Trade Unions; del founding meeing Internat. Confedn. Free Trade Unions, London, 1949; worker del. ILO, Geneva, 1956; mem. presdl. commn. on civil rights, 1946; presdl. non-partisan (Harriman) Commn., 1947; mem. adv. com., ECA, 1948; labor rep. Commn. on Jud. and Congl. Salaries, 1953; mem. labor adv. com. FOA, 1954, Dept. Labor, 1955; mem. Commn. on White House Fellows, 1964-65; dir. labor participation UN Assn. U.S. Mem. fgn. policy and labor policy adv. coms. Dem. Nat. Com., 1958; mem. nat. bd. Ams. for Dem. Action. Recipient award for service to youth Parent Mag., 1940; Quadragesimo Anno award Assn. Catholic Trade Unionists, 1961; James B. Carey Labor Library, Rutgers U., named in his honor, 1962. Mem. Am. Arbitration Assn. (dir.), Workers Def. League (v.p.), League for Indsl. Democracy (nat. council), Nat. Planning Assn. (trustee). Contbr. to labor jours. Home: Silver Spring, Md. Died Sept. 11, 1973.

CAREY, LAWRENCE BERNARD, banker; b. Bklyn., Feb. 7, 1892; s. Michael F. and Eliza (Byron) C.; student Fordham U., 1915-17, also Columbia and N.Y.U.; m. Agnes Monetti, Sept. 15, 1920 (dec. Nov. 1946); m. 2d, Francesca Ferris, July 31, 1954. With Irving Trust Co., N.Y.C., 1920-35, asst. v.p., 1929-35; pres. First Nat. Bank, Plainfield, N.J., 1936-39, Plainfield Nat. Bank, 1939-45; commr. banking and ins. N.J., 1945-48; exec. v.p. The Trust Co. of N.J., 1948-58, pres., 1958-64, chmn. bd., 1964-70; cons., 1971-73. Served with U.S. Navy, World War I. Mem. Fordham Alumni Assn., Club: Plainfield Country (treas. 1941-43). Home: Plainfield, N.J. Died Jan. 19, 1973; buried Holy Cross Cemetery, Bklyn.

CARHARDT, RAYMOND T., educator, audiologist; b. Mexico City, Mexico, Mar. 28, 1912; s. Raymond Albert and Edith (Noble) C.; A.B., Dak. Wesleyan U., 1932; M.A., Northwestern U., 1934, Ph.D., 1936; m. Mary Ellen Westfall, Aug. 2, 1935; children—Richard Alan, Robert Noble, Raymond Edgar; m. 2d, Jeanette Davis Grunig, Mar. 31, 1973; Instr. speech re-edn. Northwestern U., 1936-40, asst. prof., 1940-43, dir. Edn. Deaf and Hard of Hearing, 1942-55, asso. prof., 1943-47, prof. audiology 1947-75, asst. prof. otolarynology, 1948-52, prof., 1952-75; instr. 1st Internat. Course in Audiology, Stockholm, 1950; cons. U.S. Army, 1946-52; com. on hearing NRC, 1948-52; cons. com. on conservation of hearing Am. Acad. Opthalmology and Otolaryngology, 1944-65; cons. audiology VA, 1955-61. Mem. nat. adv. council Nat. Inst. Neurol. Diseases and Stroke, NIH, 1965-69; dir. Am. Bd. Examiners in Speech Pathology and Audiology, 1960-61. Served as capt. Med. Adminstrv. Corps, U.S. Army, acoustic physicist, Deshon Gen. Hosp., Pa., 1944-46. Recipient award of merit Am. Acad. Opthalmology and Otolarynology, 1960; Research Career award Nat. Inst. Neurol. Diseases and Stroke, 1963. Fellow Am. Speech and Hearing Assn. (pres. 1957), Am. Acad. Ophthalmology and Otolaryngology (hon.), Acoustical Soc. Am., Otosclerosis Study Group, Am. Triological Soc., Am. Otol. Soc. Author articles in profl. publs. Research on psychophysis of hearing loss, hearing aids edn. of the acoustically handicapped, training non-med. specialists in audiology. Home: Wilmette, Ill., Died Oct. 3, 1975.

CARIANI, ANTHONY, educator; b. Boston, June 13, 1918; s. Walter and Elena (Govoni) C.; A.B., Boston U., 1953, M.A., 1954, Ph.D., 1958; m. Vanda Bertazzoni, June 18, 1949; children—Peter, Karen. Asst. prof. geology U. Miss., 1956-58, asso. prof., 1958-64; prof. geology Memphis State U., 1964-66, chmn. dept., 1966-74. Served with AUS, 1942-45. Fellow Geol. Soc. Am. Home: Memphis, Tenn. Died Apr. 4, 1974.

CARIS, ALBERT GARFIELD, college pres.; b. nr. Cardington, Morrow Co., O., Sept. 13, 1881; s. Squire A. and Frona E. (Warner) C.; A.B., Defiance Coll., 1907, A.M., 1908; studied U. of Chicago and Columbia; Litt.D., Elon Coll., 1914; m. Mary Gertrude Jennings, of Raymond, O., Dec. 27, 1904; children—Mary Alberta, Ruth Lillian (dec.), Stuart Alan, Frona Elizabeth, Gertrude Jean, Albert Garfield, Paul Robert. With Hocking Valley Ry., Columbus, O., 1903-04; instr. mathematics and phys. dir., 1907-08, prof. mathematics, 1908-17, dean, 1911-17, actg. pres., 1917-18, pres. after June 1918, Defiance Coll. Pres. Ohio Coll. Assn., 1926-27. Mem. Math. Assn. America, N.E.A. Mem. Christian Ch. Rotarian. Mason (K.T.). Home: Defiance, O.†

CARLE, E. E., orgn. exec.; b. Knoxville, Ia., June 4, 1880; s. Eber S. and Nancy Jane (Cooley) C.; ed. Knoxville High Sch., Highland Park Sch. Pharmacy; m. Myrtle McCasheu, Aug. 26, 1903; children—Lois (Mrs. Casey), Col. Donald E. Began as pharmacist; later traveling salesman; became dept. adjutant, United Spanish War Vets., Washington, now adjutant gen. in charge nat. hdqrs. Mem. Travelers Protective Assn. United Comml. Travelers, United Spanish War Vets., Elk. Mason (Shriner). Club: Knife and Fork. Home: Washington, D.C.*†

CARLETON, EDWARD HERCULES, physician; b. Ayer, Mass., Oct. 25, 1904; s. Phillips Alexander and Susan Lillian (Smith) C.; M.D., U. Louisville. 1932; m. Pauline Edmonda Bessire, July 7, 1933; children—Sue (Mrs. Karl H. Brenner), Christy (Mrs. M.L. Sass), Edward Hercules. Intern, Louisville Gen. Hosp., 1932-34; gen. practice medicine, Louisville, 1934-35, practice orthopedic surgery, 1935-37; asst. resident physician Wheelwright (Ky.) Coal Mine, Inland Steel Co., 1937-40; asst. med. dir. Inland Steel Co., East Chicago, Ind., 1940-44, med. dir. 1944-53, gen. med. dir., 1953-69, in charge of health and indsl. hygiene for entire co. and its subsidiaries. Liaison rep. N.W. Ind. area on Chgo. Med. Civil Def. Com.; mem. tech. com. President's Conf. on Indsl. Safety; mem. adv. com. Research Council for Econ. Security. Mem. vis. com. Harvard Sch. Pub. Health; mem. med. com. and research adv. council Mellon Inst. Indsl. Hygiene Found.; mem. profl. adv. com. Portal House, Chgo. Recipient Meritorious Service award Indsl. Med. Assn., 1952. Diplomate Am. Bd. Preventive Medicine. Fellow Central States Soc. Indsl. Medicine and Surgery; mem. Am. Coll. Preventive Medicine, Med. Dirs. Club Chgo., Am. Med. Writers Assn., Am. Foundrymen's Soc., A.M.A., World (mem. U.S. com.), Ind., Lake County med. assns., Order Ky. Cols., Am. Acad. Polit. and Social Scis., N.A.M. (mem. subcom. on indsl. health industry liaison group), Am. Forestry Assn., Chgo. Assn. Commerce and Industry (mem. cleaner air com.), Am. Assn. Indsl. Physicians and Surgeons (pres. 1950-51), Occupational Health Inst. (trustee), Assn. Am. Phys. and Surgs., Am. Indsl. Hygiene Assn. (dir. Chgo. sect.), Am. Pub. Health Assn., A.A.A.S., Am. Iron and Steel Inst., Nat. Safety Council, NRC, Am. Inst. Biol. Scis., C. of C., Ramazzinian Soc. Republican. Mason. Contbr. articles on indsl. health. Address: Solvan Cal. Died Apr. 19, 1975.

CARLETON, PHILIP GREENLEAF, lawyer; b. Lawrence, Mass., Feb. 7, 1878; s. Charles Greenleaf and Frances Ellen (Putnam) C.; grad. Phillips Acad., Andover, Mass., 1895; A.B., cum laude, Harvard, 1899, LL.B., 1905; m. Sarah Swift Schaff, June 19, 1915. Tutor in English, Columbia 1899-1901; instr. in English, Harvard, 1901-05; admitted to Mass. bar, 1905, and began practice with Walter I. Badger, Boston; with Currier, Young & Pillsbury, 1909-19, mem. firm, 1917-19; gen. counsel Pub. Trustees of Eastern Mass. Street Railway Co., 1919-46, vice pres. and gen. counsel, 1946-49, retired; pres. Eastern Mutual Ins. Co., Boston. Served as govt. appeal agt. on legal advisory bd. of Selective Draft, World War. Mem. Am. and City of Boston bar assns. Democrat. Conglist. Clubs: Union, Harvard (Boston); The Country Club (Brookline); The Cambridge Club. Home: Cambridge, Mass.†

CARLETON, ROBERT ANDREW WOOD, b. b. New York, N.Y., 1881; grad. Columbia Univ., 1904. Gen. chmn. Engring. Center Development Fund Com. of Columbia since 1953. Home: Garrison, N.Y.†

CARLETON, SPRAGUE, urologist; b. N.Y. City, May 6, 1881; s. Bukk G. and Sarah (Robinson) C.; student Rutgers, 1900-02, A.M. (hon.), 1918; summer sch. Oberline, 1904; M.D., N.Y. Med. Coll., 1906; m. Mabel C. Snider, Nov. 27, 1912; 1 dau., Jane (wife George R. Santoro, M.D.). Intern, Grace Hosp., New Haven, 1906-07; pvt. practice medicine since 1908, specialist in urology, N.Y. City, after 1908; head dept. urology Flower Fifth Av. and Met. hosps., 1914-49; prof. N.Y. Med. Coll. Maj., U.S. Army Med. Res., 1925-40. Diplomate Am. Bd. Urology. Fellow A.C.S. Home: New York City, N.Y.†

CARLSON, ALBERT SIGFRID, educator; b. Worcester, Mass., July 4, 1907; s. Albert and Anna (Norling) C.; B.A., Clark U., 1929, M.A., 1931, Ph.D., 1939; m. Mildred Swenson, June 10, 1933; children—Russell Albert, Betty Ann, Warren Herbert. Instr. geography Dartmouth, 1929-37, asso. prof., 1937-44, prof., 1944-72, prof. emeritus, from 1973; pres. Lebanon (N.H.) Coll., evenings 1970-71, dean faculty, 1971-72. Econ. cons. New Eng. region Nat. Resources Planning Bd., 1942-43; exec. sec. Dartmouth-Lake Sunapee Region Assn., 1945-74; 1945; mem. indsl. devel. com. New Eng. Council. Mem. Assn. Am. Geographers, Nat. Council Geography Tchrs., New Eng. Geog. Conf., Am. Geog. Soc. Editor in chief: Industrial Economic Geography, 1956. Contbr. geog. publs. Home: Hanover, N.H. Deceased.

CARLTON, ROMULUS LEE, physician, health officer: b. Wilkes Co., N.C., Mar. 17, 1881: s. Joel A. and Sarah L. (Ferguson) C.; prep. edn., Oak Ridge (N.C.) Inst.; M.D., U. of Md., 1906; m. Elizabeth Lancaster, of Oak Ridge, June 6, 1906; children—Joseph L., Romulus L., Frances E. (dec.). Began practice at Kermersville, N.C., 1906; moved to Winston-Salem, 1916,, in gen. practice until 1917; city health officer, Winston-Salem, after 1917. Mem. Am., N.C. State and Forsythe Co. med. assns., Nat. Tuberculosis Assn. (dir.), Am. Pub. Health Assn., Am. Child Health Assn., Nu Sigma Nu. Democrat. Baptist. K. of P. Clubs: Rotary, Automobile. Home: Winston-Salem, N.C.†

CARMICHAEL, FRANCIS ABBOTT, JR., physician; b. Goodland, Kan., June 30, 1909; s. Francis Abbott and Rosemary (McCloskey) C.; A.B., U. Kan., 1930; postgrad. (Oxford exchange scholar) McGill U., 1933; Nuffield Inst., Oxford U., 1942; M.D., U. Pa., 1934; M.S. in Neurol. Surgery, U. Minn., 1938; m. Deloras Van Peyma, Apr. 13, 1935; children—Francis Abbott III, Carol C. (Mrs. Gerald E. Staab). Intern, Kansas City (Mo.) Gen. Hosp., 1934-35; fellow Mayo Clinic, Rochester, Minn., 1935-38, cons. in neurology, 1938-39; practice medicine specializing in neurol. surgery, Kansas City, 1939-60; dir., chief neurosurg. service Kansas City Municipal Hosp., 1939-57; sr. neurosurg. cons. VA Hosp.; sr. attending neurosurg. cons., chief surg. dept. St. Lukes Hosp.; cons. neurosurgeon U.P. R.R.; attending neurosurgeon St. Marys, St. Joseph, Baptist, Menorah hosps. (all Kansas City). Served to maj., M.C., AUS, 1942-46. Diplomate Am. Bd. Neurol. Surgery, Nat. Bd. Med. Examiners. Fellow A.C.S., Internat. Coll. Surgeons; mem. A.M.A., Mo., Jackson County med. socs., Am. Assn. Neurol. Surgeons, Congress Neurol. Surgery, So. Neurosurg. Soc., Southwestern Surg. Congress, Soc. Internationale de Chirurgie, Kansas City Surg. Soc., Kansas City S.W. Clin. Soc., Kansas City Acad. Medicine, Kansas City Anat. Soc. (co-founder), Kansas City Neurosurg. Soc. (founder, past pres.), Mil. Order World Wars, Am. Legion, Am. Radio League, Inernat. Amateur Radio Union, Radio Soc. Great Britain, DX Century Club, Old Timers Club, Sigma Xi, Phi Beta Pi, Sigma Nu. Episcopalian. Contbr. numerous articles to med. jours. Home: Shawnee Mission, Kan. Died Feb. 8, 1973; buried Mt. Moriah Cemetery, Kansas City, Mo.

CARMICHAEL, JAMES VINSON, bus. exec.; b. nr. Smyrna, Ga., Oct. 2, 1910; s. John Vinson and Emma Mae (Nolan) C.; LL.B., Emory U., 1933; m. Frances Elizabeth McDonald, June 3, 1938; children—Mary Emma, James Vinson, Frances Elizabeth. Admitted to Ga. bar, 1933, practiced Marietta, 1933-44; exec. dir. state revenue commn., 1943; mem. commn. to redraft state constn.; gen. mgr., v.p. Bell Aircraft Corp., Marietta, 1944-46; asst. to pres. Scripto, Inc., 1946, pres., 1947-64, chmn. bd., 1964-72; v.p., gen. mgr. Ga. div. Lockheed Aircraft Corp., Marietta, 1951-52, also dir.; dir. Scripto Pens, Ltd., London, Trust Co. of Ga., Southern Co., Ga. Internat. Life Ins. Co.; of counsel Smith, Currie & Hamrock, Atlanta. Former nat. vice chmn. A.R.C. Trustee Com. Econ. Devel., Interdenominational Theol. Center; adv. com. bus. programs Brookings Instn.; grad. mem. The Bus. Council; former chmn. bd. trustees Boys Estate, Ga.; mem. Ga. Sci. and Tech. Commn., Ga. Nuclear Adv. Commn.; trustee, exec. com. Emory U.; regent U. System of Ga.; vice chmn. Atlanta Sch. Art; trustee Atlanta Arts Alliance. Mem. Ga. Legislature, 1936-40; candidate for gov. of Ga., 1946. Decorated Order St. John of Jerusalem (England); recipient Presdl. Citation of Merit; Distinguished Service award Woman's Coll. Ga., 1964; Ga. Medal for Distinguished Pub. Service, 1964. Mem. Atlanta Art Assn. (past pres.), Atlanta Music/Festival Assn. (v.p.), Atlanta Symphony Guild (past pres.), Nat. Fountain Pen and Mech. Pencil Mfrs. Assn. (past pres.), Am., Ga., Atlanta bar assns., Alpha

Kappa Psi, Sigma Pi, Phi Alpha Delta, Omicron Delta Kappa. Presbyn. Kiwanian (past gov. Ga. dist.). Clubs: Capital City (past pres.), Piedmont Driving (Atlanta); Buck's (London, Eng.); Marietta Country; Century Assn. (N.Y.C.). Home: Marietta, Ga. Died Nov. 28, 1972.

CARMICHAEL, LEONARD, assn. exec.; b. Germantown, Phila., Nov. 9, 1898; s. Thomas Harrison and Emily Henrietta (Leonard) C.; grad. Germantown Friends Sch., 1917; B.S. summa cum laude, Tufts Coll., 1921, Sc.D., 1937; Ph.D. (Sheldon traveling fellow), Harvard, 1924, LL.D., 1952; postgrad. U. Berlin, 1924; LL.D., Boston U., 1938, Colgate U., 1938, Northeastern U., 1941, R.I. State Coll., 1942, St. Lawrence U., 1943, Boston Coll., 1951, Amherst Coll., 1954, U. Mass., 1954, Fairleigh Dickinson U., 1959; Litt.D., Portia, 1939, Clark U., 1953; L.H.D., U. Me., 1949; Sc.D., Brown U., 1952, Lowell Inst. Tech., 1955, George Washington U., 1956, Tulane U., 1958, Trinity Coll., 1960, Worcester Poly. Inst., 1964; D.C.L., Dickinson Coll., 1955; D.Sc., Drexel Inst. Tech., 1959; m. Pearl Kidston, June 30, 1932; one dau., Martha (Mrs. S. Parker Oliphant). Instr. biology Tufts Coll., part-time 1923-24; instr. psychology Princeton, 1924-26, asst. prof., 1926-27; asso. prof. psychology Brown U., 1927-28, prof., 1928-36, dir. psychol. lab., 1927-36, dir. lab. sensory physiology, 1934-36; chmn. dept. psychology, dean faculty arts and sci. U. Rochester, 1936-38; pres. Tufts U., also dir. lab. sensory psychology and physiology, 1938-52; sec. (the seventh) Smithsonian Instn., 1953-64; v.p. for research and exploration, chmn. mus. com. Nat. Geog. Soc., 1964-73; lectr. Harvard, summers 1927-31; vis. prof. exptl. psychology Clark U., 1931-32; vis. prof. psychology Harvard, 1935; vis. prof. Radcliffe Coll., 1935, U. Wash., 1940; lectr. Naval War Coll. to 1952; Arthur D. Little lectr. Mass. Inst. Tech., 1953; Herbert S. Langfeld lectr. Princeton, 1968. Dir. Nat. Roster Sci. and Specialized Personnel, 1940-44; mem. sci. com. Nat. Resources Planning Bd., 1941-43; chmn. com. sci. research personnel War Manpower Commn., 1941-43; chmn. anthropology and psychology div. NRC, 1941-44; mem. applied psychology panel OSRD, 1942-45; mem. adminstr.'s spl. com. on vocational rehab., edn. and tng. problems VA, 1945-52; dir. human resources NSRB, 1948; chmn. com. N.E. Comprehensive Econ. Survey, 1950-54; mem. com. on human resources Research and Devel. Bd., 1952-53, mem. Naval Research Adv. Com., 1947-52; mem. Internat. Union Sci. Psychology, 1948-52; vice chmn. Harvard Found. Advanced Study and Research, 1951-54, 58-64; mem. com. on research Ednl. Testing Service, 1952-57; bd. sci. dirs., trustee Roscoe B. Jackson Meml. Lab., 1952-73. Hon. trustee Brookings Instn.; dir. Research Corp. (N.Y.); trustee Sci. Service, 1955-72, pres. bd., 1955-67, pres. emeritus, 1972-73; mem. NACA, 1952-58, vice chmn., 1956-58; chmn. U.S. delegation Internat. Conf., The Hague, signer for U.S., Treaty for Protection Cultural Property in Time of War, 1954. Trustee Tufts U., George Washington U., Textile Mus., Nat. Trust Historic Preservation; dir. White House Hist. Assn. Mem. bd. sci. dirs. Yerkes Labs. Primate Biology, 1942-69, chmn., 1942-60; sci. adv. bd. Tulane Delta Regional Primate Research Center, 1964-73; chmn. selections com. Time Capsule, N.Y. World's Fair: mem. Army Sci. Adv. Panel, 1956-62, cons., 1963-73. Decorated knight comdr. Order of Alfonso the Wise (Spain); knight comdr. cross with star Order of Merit of Fed. Republic of Germany; comdr. Order of Dannebrog (Denmark); commendatore dell'Ordine Al Merito della Republica Italiana (Italy); Hartley Pub. Welfare medal Nat. Acad. Scis., 1972. Fellow Royal Soc. Arts, Am. Acad. Arts and Scis., A.A.A.S.; mem. Am. Philos. Soc. (pres. 1970-73), Nat. Acad. Sci. (chmn. sect. psychology 1950-53), NRC, Soc. Exptl. Psychologists. Soc. Research in Child Devel., Internat. Primatological Soc. (pres. 1964-68), Nat. Geog. Soc. (trustee), Am. Psychol. Assn. (pres. 1939-40), Soc. Exptl. Biology and Medicine, Internat. Union Biol. Scis. (pres. sect. exptl. psychology and animal behavior 1961-69), Soc. of the Cin., S.A.R., Am. Legion, Newcomen Soc., Lit. Soc. Phi Beta Kappa, Sigma Xi; hon. mem. Ergonomics Research Soc. Eng., Soc. Francaise de Psychologie. Episcopalian. Clubs: St. Botolph (Boston); Century Assn., Princeton (N.Y.C.); Alfalfa, Metropolitan, Chevy Chase, Cosmos (Washington). Co-author books, 1925-73, including Elements of Human Psychology. Editor, contbg. author: Carmichael's Manual of Child Psychology, 3d edit., 1970. Co-editor: The Selection of Military Manpower, 1952; Basic Psychology, 1957. Asso. editor Jour. Genetic Psychology, Genetic Psychology Monographs, Brit. Jour. Ednl. Psychology. Editor Houghton Mifflin Co. series of books on psychology. Contbr. psychol. jours. Home: Washington, D.C. Died Sept. 16, 1973; interred Washington National Cathedral, Washington, D.C.

CARMICHAEL, ROBERT DANIEL, mathematician; b. Goodwater, Ala., Mar. 1, 1879; s. Daniel Monroe and Amanda (Lessley) C.; A.B., Lineville (Ala.) Coll. 1898; Ph.D., Princeton, 1911; m. Eula Narramore, H. Roberts), Erdys Lucile (Mrs. Ernest C. Hartmann), Gershom Narramore, Robert Lessley. Prof. Ala. Presbyn. Coll., 1906-09; fellow Princeton, 1909-10, Jacobus fellow, 1910-11; asst. prof. mathematics, Ind. U., 1911-12, asso. prof., 1912-15; asso. prof. U. of Chicago Summer Sch., 1915; asst. prof. mathematics, 1915-18, asso. prof., 1918-20, prof. since 1920, head of dept., 1929-34, acting dean Grad. Sch., U., of Ill., 1933-34, dean, 1934-47, dean emeritus since 1947. Asso. editor, Annals of Mathematics, 1916-18, Am. Math. Monthly, 1916-17, editor in chief, 1918; editor Transactions Am. Math. Soc., 1931-36. Fellow A.A.A.S. (v.p., Sec. A, 1934j; mem. Am. Math. Soc. (councillor 1916-18, v.p. 1922, chmn. Chicago sect. 1920-21), Math. Assn. American Assn. American (Councillor 1916-18, 20, 24, 25-27; v.p. 1921-22, pres. 1923), Am. Philos. Assn., Kappa Delta Rho. Pi Mu Epsilon, Sigma Xi, Phi Beta Kappa, Phi Kappa Phi. Mem. div. phys. science, Nat. Research Council, 1929-32. Clubs: Chaos, University, Philosophical. Author: What Is Man, 1950. Contbr. numberous articles to profl. jours. Home: Griggsville, Ill.†

CARNEY, HARRY HOWELL, musician; b. Boston, Apr. 1, 1910; s. Harry F. and Jennie (King) C.; ed. high sch.; m. Dorothy Streat, Nov. 4, 1929. Player bass saxophone, bass clarinet Duke Ellington's Orch., 1927-74. Recipient numerous musical awards. Home: New York City, N.Y. Died Oct. 1974.

CARPENTER, ALFRED SAINT VRAIN, horticulturiest, company dir.; b. Colorado Springs, Colo., May 7, 1881; s. Alfred F. and Mary Louise (Dunbar) C.; A.B., Harvard, 1905; m. Helen F. Bundy, Mar. 15, 1922; children—Julie (Mrs. Burton A. Daugherty), Harlow; m. 2d Helene Salade, May 5, 1961. Engaged in pear growing in Rogue River Valley, Ore., after 1910; dir. Pacific Power & Light Corp., Cascade Wood Prod. Corp., Loading Co., So. Ore. Sales, Inc. Chmn. Bd. Rogue Valley Meml. Hosp.; bd. dirs. local A.R.C. Donor Carpenter Center Bldg. for Visual Arts, Harvard, 1957. Address: Medford, Ore.†

CARPENTER, CLARENCE RAY, educator; b. Lincoln County, N.C., Nov. 28, 1905; s. C.E. and Gaddie Lee (Harrelson) C.; B.A., Duke, 1928, M.A., 1929; NRC fellow Yale, 1931-33; Ph.D., Stanford, 1932; D.Sc. (hon.), Bucknell U., 1972; m. Mariana Evans, July 16, 1932 (dec. July 1963); children Richard Lee, Lane Evans; m. 2d, Ruth Jones Chamblee, Oct. 8, 1966. Research asst. Yale, 1931-34; fellow, asst. prof. Bard Coll. Columbia, 1934-38, co-leader Asiatic Primate expdn., Thailand, Sumatra, 1937, comdr. Indian Primate expdn., 1938, asst. prof. Coll. Phys. and Surg., 1938-40; developed Santiago Primate Research Colony, P.R., 1938-40; asso. prof. psychology Pa. State U., 1940-46, prof., 1946-65, research prof. psychology and anthropolog 1965-69, emeritus research prof., 1969-75, dir. div. instructional research and services, 1954-63; mem. bd. control New U. Planning Commn. State of Fla., 1960-62; exec. dir. survey com. Hershey Med. Center, 1963-64; Ford vis. prof. U. N.C., 1964-65; research prof. psychology and anthropology U. Ga., Athens, 1969-73; NSF Lectr., 1971-75; Dir., State Coll. Fed. Savs. & Loan Assn., 1952—; v.p., dir. State Coll. Flying Service, 1958-62; cons. long range devel. com. Pa. U., ednl. products project Gen. Electric, RCA, Holt, Rinehart & Winston, UNITEL, Atlanta; prin. planner Nat. Complement Learning Research Center for U.S. Office Edn.; mem. Community Planning Com; mem. appraisal com. pub. sch., TV project Fund for Advancement of Edn., Ford Found., 1957-58; mem. evaluation com. Midwest Airborne Instrnl. TV Project, 1961-65; dir. Center Applied Ednl. Research, Washington, 1960-65; mem. Joint Council Ednl. Telecommunications, pres., 1968-70; mem. team experts on communications and media advisers Indian Govt. on devel. communication system (Ford Found.-Indian Govt.), 1963; mem. planning meeting-U.S.-Japan Coop. Program in Sci., 1964; mem. adv. com. U.S. Office of Edn., 1966-68; mem. exec. com. Nat. Commn. Instrnl. Tech., 1968-69; mem. EDUCOM: mem. Ga. Instructional Television Adv. Council; mem. sci. adv. com. Yerkes Regional Primate Research Lab., Emory U., 1967-69, chmn., 1969-75; UNESCO lectr., Spain, 1971; NRC lectr., West Coast, 1971, East Coast, 1972-73. Bd. dirs. Internat. Psychiat. Found., 1971-75. Served capt. to maj. USAAF 1943-46, head research sect., dept. psychology and sociology Biarritz Am. Army U., 1945-46; organized German Youth Re-edn. Program; lt. col. USAF Res. Sr. fellow East-West Center, Hawaii, 1972-73. Fellow Animal Behavior Soc., N.Y. Zool. Soc. (research coordinator 1948-50), Nat. Council Religion in Higher Edn.; member A.A.A.S., Am. Soc. Zoologists, Pa. Psychol. Assn., Am. Anthrop. Assn., Nat. Acad. Sci. (del 13th Pacific sci. congress 1966), Am. Assn. U. Profs., Am. Acad. Sci., N.E.A., Internat. Primatological Soc. (Am. sec. 1964-68), Assn. Higher Edn. (pres. 1965-66), Phi Beta Kappa, Sigma Xi. Author: Naturalistic Behavior of Nonhuman Primates. Editor: Telecommunications: Toward a National Policy for Education; Behavioral Regulators of Behavior in Primates; U.S. editor: Behaviour, internat. jour.; Jour. Human Evolution; editorial bd. Ednl. Broadcasting Rev., 1967-73. Address: Athens, Ga. Died Mar. 1, 1975.

CARPENTER, HOMER WILSON, clergyman; b. Flemingsburg, Ky., Dec. 19, 1880; s. John Simon and Julia Anne (Hughes) C.; B.A., Transylvania Coll., 1906, D.D., 1932; student Coll. of the Bible, 1899-1907; m. Lillie Tevis Carpenter, June 30, 1909; 1 dau., Eleanor Tevis (Mrs. Leslie Preston Long). Ordained to the ministry of the Disciples of Christ Ch., June 6, 1906; pastor Louisville, after 1929; chaplain Chautauqua (N.Y.) Inst., 1933-36. Trustee Milligan Coll.; curator Transylvania Coll. Bd. mem. Red Cross Home Bd., Salvation Army, Louisville Council of Chs., State Social Agencies. Engaged in gov. publicity work. World War 1: served as dir. div. of War Drives in Ky., World War 11. Rep. of Disciples of Christ, World Orgn. Chs., 1948. Mem. Internat. Convention, Disciples of Christ (acting pres., 1932, mem. exec. bd., 1931-34), Assn. for Promotion of Christian Unity (pres. 1944-46, mem. exec. bd. since 1930, spl. speaker World's Conv., Leicester, Eng., 1935), United Christian Missionary Soc. (mem. exec. bd.), World Convention Commn. (mem. exec. bd.), Louisville Community Chest Convention of Christian Chs. in Ky. (pres. 1928-29); Emergency Million in Ky. (dir., 1920); Pi Kappa Alpha (nat. chaplain), Theta Phi. Democrat. Clubs: Rotary Internat. (hon. life mem., past pres. Richmond Club). Pendennis, Louisville Country. Author: The Future Is Now. Home: Louisville, Ky.†

CARPENTER, JOHN WILLIAM, pub. utility exec.; b. near Corsicana, Tex., Aug. 31, 1881; s. Thomas Wirt and Ellen Isaphene (Dickson) C.; ed. N. Tex. State Normal Coll., Draughon's Business Coll., Fort Worth, Internat. Corr. Schs.; LL.D., Tex. Tech. Coll., Lubbock, Tex.; hon. Dr. Engring., So. Methodist U.; student course, testing dept., General Electric Company, Schenedtady; m. Flossie Belle Gardner, June 18, 1913; children—Ellen Carolyn (Mrs. Dan C. Williams, Jr.), John William (dec.), Benjamin Howard. Tex. Power & Light Co., The Crockett Co., Trinity Valley Cattle Co., Southland Life Ins. Co.; dir. St. L. S.W. Ry. Co. of Texas, Limestone Products, Inc. Pres. Dallas Plio Inst. Mem. adv. com. National Rivers and Harbors Congress; member rural electrification and adv. coms., Edison Electrical Inst.; mem. adv. bd. Dallas Girl Scout Council (council mem.-at-large); mem. Circle Ten Council Boy Scouts of America; mem. advisory com. Bureau of Business Research, U. of Tex.; mem. adv. com. Tex. branch Reconstruction Finance Corp.; gen. chmn. Nat. Conf. Christians and Jews; mem. utilities div. Nat. Indsl. information Com.; trustee Nat. Com. for Econ. Development; mem. U.S. Chamber of Commerce (S.W. bus. council), dir. Big Bend Nat. Park Assn.; dir. Big Bend Trail Association, Trinity Improvement Assn. Co-chmn. Tex. State Research Found.; dir. Tex. Chemurgic Council; v.p. State Fair of Tex.; v.p. Tex. Safety Assn., Inc.; dir. Bradford Mem. Hosp., Dallas Citizens Council, Dallas Arboretum Foundation, Inc., Intra-Coastal Canal Assn. Tex., La., Tex. Manufacturers Assn., Tex. Forestry Association. Member East Texas C. of C., Dallas C. of C. (mem. arbitration, new industries, agr. coms.); chmn. Trinity River Development Com.; v.p. bd. dirs. Texas Centennial of Statehood Commn.; chmn. com. on pub. bldgs. of Greater Dallas Planning Conf.; mem. S.W. Regional adv. com. of Nat. Assn. Mfrs.; chmn. bd. trustees Southwestern Legal Found.; dir. Dallas Grand Opera Assn.; mem. bd. trustees of National Safety Council. Member Dallas Civic Federation, Civic Music Association, Tex. Water Conservation Assn., A.I.E.E., Dallas Hist. Soc., Tex. State Hist. Assn., North Tex. State Teachers Coll. Ex-students Assn. (adv. bd.); hon. mem. Kappa chapter Phi Psi. Democrat. Presbyterian. Odd Fellow, Elk. Clubs: Dallas Athletic, Dallas Country, Dallas Electric, Critic, City, Dallas Petroleum, Dallas Agricultural, Dallas Automobile, Insurance (Dallas). Home: Dallas, Tex.†

CARPENTER, LESLIE E., newspaper corr.; b. Austin, Tex., Feb. 20, 1922; s. John W. and Edleen (Falwell) C.; B.J., U. Tex., 1943; m. Mary Elizabeth Sutherland, June 17, 1944; children—Scott Sutherland, Christy. Reporter, Austin Am.-Statesman, 1942; Washington corr. Ft. Worth Star-Telegram, Dallas Times Herald, Houston Chronicle, New Orleans States, other newspapers, 1945-51; chief Washington bur. Variety (N.Y.C.), Daily Variety (Hollywood), Ark. Gazette (Little Rock), Beaumont (Tex.) Enterprise and Jour., Abiliene (Tex.) Reporter-News, Lubbock (Tex.) Avalance-Jour., San Antonio Express and Evening News, Corpus Christi (Tex.) Caller-Times, Honolulu Advertiser, Amarillo News-Globe, Austin Am.-Statesman, Waco (Tex.) Tribune-Herald, Wichita Falls (Tex.) Record-News & Times, numerous others, 1951-74; columnist Publishers-Hall Syndicate, 1963-74. Served to lt. USNR, 1943-45. Mem. Sigma Delta Chi. Episcopalian. Club: Nat. Press (Washington). Home: Washington, D.C. Died July 24, 1974.

CARPENTER, MIRIAM FERONIA, educator; b. Mont Vernon, N.H., Sept. 21, 1881; d. Charles Carroll and Nancy Feronia (Rice) C.; student Mount Holyoke Coll., 1899-1900 and 1902-03, Litt.D., 1933; A.B., Colorado Coll., 1905, L.H.D., 1930. Sec. to Dean Briggs, Harvard, 1906-10, to dean, Mount Holyoke Coll., 1910-13, Central Presbyn. Ch., Montclair, N.J., 1914-17; registrar and adviser of women, Grad. Sch. of Edn., Harvard, 1917-29; on leave of absence to act. as dean, Spelman Coll., Atlanta, Ga., 1927-28; dean, Wheaton Coll., Norton, Mass., 1929-44; engaged in special work, reorganization of records, Harvard Law School, 1944-47; spl. work on alumnae records, Bouvé-Boston Sch. Phys. Edn. after 1947. Home: Andover, Mass.†

CARPENTER, W. T. COLEMAN, business exec.; b. Yonkers, N.Y., Apr. 10, 1872; s. Edward O. and Annie (Horton) C.; student pub. schs.; LL.D., Colgate U., 1943; m. Grace Felt Russell, Apr. 21, 1898. Started with J.M. Young & Co., New York, 1888-89; upon orgn. of

Colgate Hoyt & Co., N.Y. City, 1900, became partner, now sr partner; dir. mem. exec. com. U.S. Pipe & Foundry Co., United Concrete Pipe Corporation of California. Trustee emeritus Colgate U. Clubs: Baltusrol Golf (Springfield, N.J.); Downtown Assn. (New York). Home: Summit, N.J.†

CARPENTER, WALTER SAMUEL, JR., industrialist; b. Wilkesbarre, Pa., Jan. 8, 1888; s. Walter S. and Belle (Morgan) C.; prep. edn., Wyoming Sem., Kingston, Pa., 1902-06; student Cornell U., 1906-10; m. Mary Wootten, June 3, 1914; children—Walter Samuel III, John W., Edmund N. II. With E. I. du Pont de Nemours & Co., Wilmington, Del., 1909-75; v.p., 1919-40, pres., 1940-48, chmn., 1948-62, then hon. chmn.; dir. Christiana Securities Co. Trustee emeritus Wyoming Sem., Kingston, Pa.; past pres. U. Del. Methodist. Clubs: Wilmington, Wilmington Country; Fisher's Island (N.Y.); Racquet and Tennis (N.Y.C.). Home: Wilmington, Del., Died Feb. 2, 1976; buried Wilmington and Brandywine Cemetery.

CARR, WILLIAM JARVIS, lawyer; b. Batavia, Ill., Sept. 12, 1879; s. James and Eunice M. (Burton) C.; B.Litt., U. of Wis., 1901; unmarried. Admitted to Wis. bar. 1902; asst. pros. atty., Manila, P.I., 1903-5; mem. firm of Gibbs, Gale & Carr, Manila, 1905-6; removed to Cal., 1907; city atty., Pasadena, 1910-13; mem. State Senate, Cal., 1913-14; mem. law firm of Heney & Carr. Progressive. Home: Pasadena, Cal.†

CARRINGTON, ALEXANDER BERKELEY, JR., tobacco mcht., banker; b. Danville, Va., Jan. 26, 1895; s. Alexander Berkeley and Mary Miller (Taylor) C.; A.B., Hampden-Sydney Coll., 1915, LL.D., 1942; A.M., U. Va., 1917; m. Ruth Simpson, Oct. 30, 1920. With Dibrell Bros., Inc., Danville, 1919, pres., 1936-51, chmn. bd. dirs., 1951-69; chmn. bd. Am. Nat. Bank & Trust Co., 1949-69; dir. Dan River Mills. Trustee Hampden-Sydney Coll., Stratford Coll., Meml. Hosp., Danville. Served as capt. C.A.C., with AEF, 1917-19. Home: Danville, Va. Died July 20, 1974.

CARRINGTON, FRANCIS LOUIS, clergyman, educator; b. Gibraltar, Apr. 27, 1880; s. Maj. Walter (British Army) and Eva (Worsley) C.; ed. Clifton Coll., Queen's Coll., Oxford U., Eng.; LL.D., St. Mary Coll., Dallas, Tex., 1916; m. Constance Isobel, dau. of late A. R. Dickey, Minister of Justice, Dominion of Canada, Nov. 6, 1909. Deacon and priest P.E. ch., 1909; curate, Denton, Tex., 1909-10; rector High River, Can., and Rual dean, 1910-11, All Saints' Ch., Dallas, 1911-15; dean St. Mary Coll., and prof. natural science, 1915-19; formerly pres. St. Mary's Sch., Knoxville, Ill. Republican. Mason (32°). Home: Onekama, Mich.†

CARRINGTON, HEREWARD (HUBERT LAVINGTON), author; b. Jersey, Channel Islands, Eng., Oct. 17, 1880; s. Robert Charles and Sarah Jane (Pewtress) C.; ed. Sansom's and Philol. schs., London, and Cranbrook, Kent; Ph.D. Came to America, 1899. Editor Street & Smith' novels, 1906-07. Co-author and master ceremonies radio series "Who Knows," Mutual, Station WOR, 1940-41. Am. Permanent del. Internat. Psychic Congresses; founder and dir. Am. Psychical Institute and Lab., N.Y. City. Member Society for Psychical Research (London), etc. Agnostic. Author: The Physical Phenomena of Spiritualism, 1907; Vitality, Fasting and Nutrition, 1908; The Coming Science, 1908; Eusapia Palladino and Her Phenomena, 1909; Death-Its Causes and Phenomena (with J. R. Meader), 1911; Death Tricks, 1913; Side Show and Animal Tricks, 1913; Personal Experiences in Spiritualism, 1913; The Problems of Psychical Research, 1914; True Ghost Stories, 1915; Psychical Phenomena and the War, 1918; Modern Psychical Phenomena, 1919; Boy's Book of Magic, 1920; Your Psychic Powers: and How to Develop Them, 1920; Higher Psychical Development (Yoga Walsh), 1925; Psychical Reserach (2 Vols.); Life-Its Origin and Nature; Great Men of Science; New Discoveries in Science; The Great Pyramid of Egypt; Astronomy for Beginners; Chemistry for Beginners; Psychology for Beginners; Food and Diet; The Nature of Dreams; The Problem of Death; Yoga Philosophy; Fasting for Health; Ventiloquism Self Taught; Gamblers' Tricks Exposed; Magic for Everyone, 1927; Bridge Simplified, 1928; The Projection of the Astral Body (with Sylvan J. Muldoon), 1929; The Story of Psychic Science, 1930; A Primer of Psychical Research, 1932; Houdini and Conan Doyle (with B. M. L. Ernst), 1932; Loaves and Fishes, 1935; The Psychic World, 1937; Indtroduction to The Maniac, 1937; Telepathy and Clairvoyance, 1938; Psychic Science and Survival, 1939; Laboratory Investigations into Psychic Phenomena, 1939; Psychology, in the Light of Psychic Phenomena, 1940; Eusapia Palladino's American Séances, 1946; The Invisible World, 1945; The Phenomena of Astral Projection (with S. J. Muldoon), 1951; Haunted People (with Nandor Fodor), 1951; and numerous other articles. Editor scientific page Leslie's Weekly, Reach Mag., Bulletins of the Am. Psychical Inst., etc. Translator: Flournoy's Spiritism various mags., encyclopedias, etc. Home: Hollywood, Cal.†

CARROLL, JAMES E., lawyer; b. St. Louis, Mo., Sept. 12, 1878; s. Thomas J. and Margaret (Ryan) C.; ed. Central High Sch. (St. Louis), U. of Mo., 1 yr., Christian Brothers Coll. (St. Louis); LL.B., Washington U., 1906; m. Eleanor B. Luth, of St. Louis, June 14, 1911; children—Eleanor, Mary, Virginia Ann, Cathrine, James Thomas. Began practice in St. Louis, 1906, as claims atty. for various ins. cos.; formed law partnership, 1907, with William L. Igoe (later congressman 4 terms to 1920); became U.S. atty. Eastern Dist. of Mo., 1920. Democrat. Me. Am., Mo. and St. Louis bar assns. Club: Mo. Athletic Assn. Home: Webster Groves, Mo.†

CARROLL, JOHN E., equipment co. exec.; b. 1912; married. With Am. Hoist & Derrick Co., St. Paul, from 1937, 1949-74, successively gen. sales mgr., v.p., pres., 1953-73, chmn. bd., 1973-74, chief exec. officer, 1953-74, also dir.; formerly partner, head constrn. div. Harran, Rickard & McCone Co.; dir. Econ. Labs, Inc., Am. Nat. Bank & Trust Co., 1st Midwest Corp., Murphy Motor Freight Lines, Inc., Twin City Area Ednl. TV Corp., Zinsmaster Baking Co. Bd. dirs. Occupational Tng. Center, St. John's U., St. Joseph Hosp. Home: St. Paul, Minn. Died Dec. 7, 1974.

CARROLL, PAUL E., physician; b. Milw., 1925; M.D., Marquette U., 1952. Intern, Columbia Hosp., Milw., 1952-53; resident Milw. Hosp., 1953-56; practice medicine specializing in obstetrics and gynecology, Waukesha, Wis., 1956-72; mem. staff Waukesha Meml. Hosp., 1956-72, chief dept. obstetrics, 1960-72; asst. clin. instr. obstetrics Marquette U. Sch. Medicine, 1956-63. Served with USAF. Diplomate Am. Bd. Obstetrics and Gynecology; mem. A.M.A. Home: Waukesha, Wis. Died May 30, 1972.

CARSON, CALE WELLMAN, banker; b. Ashland, Kan., Nov. 19, 1891; s. Cale Wellman and Mattie (Congelton) C.; A.B., U. Kan., 1915; m. Alice Coors, Nov. 29, 1922 (dec.); children—Kathryn, Cale Wellman; m. 2d, Ruth Eaves, June 6, 1959. Cashier, First Nat. Bank, Spearman, Tex., 1919-25; v.p. First Nat. Bank, Amarillo, Tex., 1925-29; liquidating agt. Nat. Bank of Commerce, 1931; dep. land bank commr., Washington, 1933; pres. First Nat. Bank, Albuquerque, 1933-61, chmn. bd., 1961-69; past dir. Denver br. Fed. Res. Bank Kansas City. State chmn. War Finance Com., World War II; former mem. State Bd. Finance. Trustee emeritus Lovelace Found. for Med. Edn. and Research, S.W. Research Inst., San Antonio; bd. dirs. Presbyn. Hosp. Center. Served as maj. inf. U.S. Army, AEF, 1917-18. Mem. N.M. (past pres.), Am. bankers assns., N.A.M., Albuquerque C. of C. Rotarian. Clubs: Albuquerque Country, Petroleum (Albuquerque). Home: Albuquerque, N.M. Died Aug. 28, 1973.

CARSTENS, HENRY ROHNERT, physician; b. Detroit, Dec. 19, 1888; s. J. Henry and Hattie (Rohnert) C.; A.B., U. Mich., 1909; M.D., Wayne State U., 1911; m. Coral Bremer, Mar. 7, 1947. Grad. study Krankenhaus Friedrichshain, Berlin U., 1911-12; practice medicine specializing in internal medicine, Detroit, 1912-46; physician outpatient dept. to physician div. internal medicine Harper Hosp., Detroit, 1913-46, chief div. internal medicine, outpatient dept., 1927-43; chief dept. medicine Crittenton Gen. Hosp., Detroit, 1920-40, cons., 1940; from instr. medicine to asso. prof. clin. medicine Wayne State U. Sch. Medicine, Detroit, 1914-46; physician Detroit House of Correction, 1913-20; med. dir. Detroit Life Ins. Co., 1920-36; med. dir., 1st pres. Mich. Med. Service (Blue Shield), Detroit, 1940-42; br. med. dir. VA Br. Office, Phila., 1946-49; chief gen. medicine and subspecialities VA Central Office, Washington, 1949-55; chief medicine VA, Springfield, Mass., 1955-58; ret., 1959. Served with U.S. Army, 1916-19; to col. M.C., AUS, 1942-46. Decorated Legion of Merit, Crown of Italy. Diplomate Am. Bd. Internal Medicine; Fellow A.C.P. (gov. 1936-42, 2d v.p. 1942-44); mem. A.M.A., Mich. (pres. 1941-42), Wayne County (pres. 1938-39), West Side (pres. 1936-37) med. socs., Assn. Mil. Surgeons U.S., Internat. Soc. Internal Medicine, Detroit Med. Club (pres. 1927-28), Detroit Acad. Medicine (pres. 1940-41), Mich. Assn. of Professions, Alumni Assn. Wayne State U. Sch. Medicine (pres. 1926-27), Harmonie Soc., Union Interalliee (Paris), Mil. Order World Wars (comdr. Detroit chpt. 1, 1933-36), Am. Legion, Friends of Detroit Pub. Library, Detroit Hist. Soc., Alpha Omega Alpha, Nu Sigma Nu. Republican. Clubs: Detroit Boat, U. Mich. (Detroit); Army and Navy (Washington). Home: Bloomfield Hills, Mich. Died Feb. 5, 1973.

CARTER, ALAN, musician; b. Greenwich, Conn., July 29, 1904; s. Herbert Swift and Mabel (Pettit) C.; student Taft Sch., Watertown, Conn., 1920-22, Mannes Music Sch., N.Y.C., 1922-23, Conservatory of Music, Cologne, Germany, 1923-24; Mus. D. (hon.), U. Vt., 1955; m. Marianne Townsend, May 18, 1926; children—Joan Pettit, Alan Peter; m. 2d, Barbara Kent, July 7, 1934; children—Timothy, Eric, Kent, Thayer. Musician, 1923-75; founder, condr. Vt. State Symphony Orch.; mem. musical faculty Middlebury Coll., 1939-69, chmn. music dept., 1955-69; music dir. Vt. Symphony Orch. Assn., Inc.; dir. Composers' Conf. and Chamber Music Center, Johnson State Coll., from 1946. Served as capt. U.S. Army, music officers Hdqrs. 4th Service Comd., Atlanta, 1942-44; Hdqrs. 1st Service Comd., Boston, 1943-44. Recipient Alice M. Ditson condr.'s award Columbia U., 1968; Gov.'s award for excellence in the arts Vt. Council on Arts, 1972. Contbr. articles on music and music edn. Home: Middlebury, Vt., Died Sept. 21, 1975.

CARTER, ALBERT EDWARD, ex-congressman; b. near Visalia, Cal., July 5, 1881; s. David Francis and Elizabeth E. (Reeves) C.; grad. San Jos State Normal Sch., 1903; LL.B., U. of Calif., 1913; m. Martha Lee Grimsley, Dec. 30, 1905. Teacher pub. schs. 6 yrs.; admitted to California bar, 1913, and has since practiced at Oakland; special representative of the War Dept. Commn. on training camp activities, 1917-1919; atty. for Calif. State Bd. of Pharmacy, 1920-21; commr. City of Oakland, 1921-25; mem. 69th to 78th Congresses (1925-1945), 6th Calif. Dist. Studied harbors and harbor development on Pacific Coast and in U.S., also important ports of world and planned harbor development for east shore San Francisco Bay; formerly pres. and v.p. Pacific Coast Assn. of Port Authorities. Mem. Native Sons of the Golden West, Phi Alpha Delta. Republican. Mason (32°, Shriner), Elk, Moose, Eagles, Woodman. Home: Oakland, Cal.†

CARTER, CREED FULTON, JR., horse farm owner, former merchandising exec.; b. Roxie, Va., May 26, 1909; s. Creed Fulton and Caroline Kyle (Fulton) C.; student McGuire U. Sch., 1927-29, Emory and Henry Coll., 1929-30; Ph.D., Hamilton State U., 1975; m. Mary Virginia Monteiro, June 8, 1929; 1 dau., Evelyn Nan (Mrs. Robert A. Sadler III). Mgr., McCrory Stores, N.J., Conn., Va., 1939-46, dist. mgr., Carolinas, Pa., Tex., 1947-59, gen. supt. McCroroy-McLellan Stores, N.Y.C., 1960, v.p., 1960-64, v.p., East Central regional mgr., 1964-67, v.p. co., 1968-69, ret., 1970; v.p. new stores planning and devel. McCrory, McLellan-Green Stores, 1960-63; treas. Car-Nan-Sa Farms, Inc., Allentown, Pa., 1966-75, chief exec. officer, 1966-72; partner Nanco Corp., 1969-75; dir. Blacks Poultry, Supreme Products Co.; dealer horses, Hereford cattle. Del., Pa. Horsemen's Goodwill People-to-People Travel Program, USSR, Poland, Hungary, Austria and Germany, 1970. Bd. dirs., regent, chmn., pres., life mem. bd. trustees Swain Sch., Allentown; bd. dirs. Allentown Symphony Assn. Mem. adv. bd. on retailing Leigh County Community Coll. Named to Wisdom Hall of Fame, recipient Wisdom award of Honor, 1970; col. W.Va. Centennial, 1965. Mem. Am. Mgmt. Assn., Nat. Steeplechase and Hunt Assn., Northeast Pa. Horse Assn., Pa. Horse Breeders Assn., Pa. Soc., 100,000 Pennsylvanians, Allentown Art Mus., Pa. Chain Store Council, Pa. Retailers Assn., Penn-Jersey Horse Show Assn. (chmn. show com.), Allentown Art Mus., Allentown Civic Little Theatre, Internat. Platform Assn. Methodist (trustee, regent, mem. ofcl. bd.). Rotarian, Mason (32°); mem. Order Eastern Star. Clubs: Lehigh Country, Lehigh Valley; Three Oaks Riding and Hunt (life dir., pres.); Orange County Hunt; United Hunt and Racing; Ridglea Country. Home: Allentown, Pa. Died Apr. 5, 1975.

CARTER, HOMER MUNROE, SR., co. exec.; b. Van Zant County, Tex., Dec. 16, 1901; s. Jessee O. and Mary E. (Barber) C.; B.S., Ga. Sch. Tech., 1923; m. Mary Jane McGinnis, June 30, 1925; 1 son, Homer Munroe. Joined Pepperell Mfg. Co., 1925, gen. mgr. Ala. div., 1931-59, exec. v.p., 1959-61, pres., 1961-66, dir., 1952-65; pres. West Point-Pepperell, Inc., 1965-68, vice chmn., 1968-69, dir., 1965-70; dir. Farmers Nat. Bank, Opelika, Ala. Mem. Phi Delta Theta, Phi Kappa Phi. Methodist. Club: Capital City (Atlanta). Home: Atlanta, Ga. Died June 5, 1974.

CARTER, JOHN, mfg. executive; b. Montclair, N.J., May 31, 1920; s. Paul S. and Mary A. (Suhr) C.; A.B., Lafayette Coll., 1941, Doctor of Humane Letters (honorary), 1964; m. Jane Dill, Oct. 8, 1943; children—John, Stephen, Scott. Prodn. dir. Corning Glass Works of Can., Ltd., Leaside, Can., 1948-73; gen. mgr. New Products Div., Corning Glass Works, Corning, N.Y., 1950-52, gen. mgr. Consumer Products Div., Corning, 1952-54, v.p. and gen. mgr. New Products div., 1955-57; chmn. bd., chief exec. officer, Fairchild Camera and Instrument Corp., Syosset, L.I., N.Y., 1957-73; chmn. Human Resources Corporation. Chairman of the Human Resources School, Albertson, New York. Served USAF, 1941-46. Mem. N.A.M., Inst. Mgmt. Scis., A.I.A., Am. Mgmt. Assn., Nat. Indsl. Conf. Bd., Am. Ceramic Soc. Home: Mill Neck, N.Y. Died Dec. 23, 1973.

CARTER, JOHN WAYN FLETE, bibliographer; b. Eton, Eng., May 10, 1905; s. Thomas Buchanan and Margaret Teresa (Stone) C.; student Eton Coll., King's Coll., Cambridge; m. Ernestine Marie Fantl, Dec. 26, 1936. European rep. rare book dept. Scribners, N.Y.C., 1927-39, mng. dir. Charles Scribner' Sons, Ltd., London, 1946-53 staff Ministry Information, 1939-43; with Brit. Information Services, N.Y.C., 1944-45; counsellor embassy, personal asst. to Brit. ambassador in Washington, 1953-55; asso. for Am. operations Sotheby & Co., auctioneers, London; bibliog. cons., 1956-75; dir. Parke- Bernet Galleries, Inc., N.Y.C. Decorated comdr. Order Brit. Empire, 1956; named Hon. Ky. col., Sandars reader bibliography U. Cambridge, 1947. Fellow Eton Coll., 1967-74 Mem. Arts Council Gt. Britain (mem. council 1951-53), Bibliog. Soc. (pres. 1968-69, Gold Medal 1974). Clubs: Garrick, Double Crown, Eton Ramblers, Beefsteak (London); Grolier; Rowfant. Author: ABC for Book Collectors, 1952, 4th edit., 1966; Taste and Technique in Book Collecting, 1948, enlarged, 1970; (with Graham Pollard) An Enquiry into the Nature of Certain 19th Century Pamphlets, 1934, Books and Book Collectors,

1956. Editor: Selected Prose of A.E. Housman, 1961: (with Percy H. Muir) Printing and the Mind of Man, 1967. Home: London, England. Died Mar. 18, 1975; buried Eton, Windsor, Berkshire, England

CARTER, LOUISE WILSON LAMICA, journalist; b. Supply, N.C., Sept. 21, 1927; d. Frank and Rosa Dewey (Clemmons) Holden; student U. N.C., 1953; m. George Edward Lamica, Feb. 22, 1951; children—Darlene Gail (Mrs. Dale Buck), George Edward, Cathy (Mrs. David Kendrick), m. 2d, Allen Scott Carter, Aug. 1974. With Star-News Newspapers, Inc., Wilmington, N.C., 1947-54, 57-75, edn. editor, 1970-75; operator with Washington Post-Times Herald, 1955-56. Recipient awards N.C. County and Local Historians, 1959, Newspaper Inst. Am., 1962, N.C. Council Chs., 1964, N.C. Assn. Educators, 1970, 73. Mem. Edn. Writers Assn., N.C. Press Assn. (award 1961), N.C. Press Women's Assn. (award 1964). Contbr. articles to various publs. including Wildlife of N.C., State mag., Guideposts, Ladies Circle. Home: Wilmington, N.C. Died Apr. 29, 1975.

CARTER, LYNDALL FREDERIC, mfg. co. exec.; b. Needham, Mass., 1902; s. Horace Albert and Bertha Louise (Manson) C.; grad. Williams Coll., 1924, Harvard Bus. Sch., 1926; m. Margaret Walker, June 29, 1925 (dec. May 1962); m. 2d, Ruth Plummer Reynolds, Sept. 21, 1963; children—Dana Pierce, Mary Lee. With William Carter Co., Needham, Mass., 1926-73; pres., 1959-69, chmn., 1969-73; also dir.; dir. Needham Nat. Bank. Trustee Modern Sch. Fashion Design. Home: Weston, Mass. Died May 14, 1973.

CARTER, MORRIS, museum dir.; b. Woburn, Mass., Oct. 23, 1877; s. John Ruel and Elizabeth Parkinson (Wheeler) C.; A.B., Harvard, 1898, A.M., 1899; m. Beatrice A. Grant, Sept. 17, 1913. Teacher, Robert Coll., Constantinople, Turkey, 1899-1902; asst. Princeton Univ. Library, 1903-04; librarian Museum of Fine Arts, Boston, 1904-13, asst. dir., 1913-19; became asst. to Mrs. Gardner at Isabella Stewart Gardner Mus., 1919, dir., 1924-54,. ret. Mem. Phi Beta Kappa. Author: Isabella Stewart Gardner and Fenway Court, 1925. Address: Boston, Mass.†

CARTER, OMA BELLE BIXLER (MRS. W. TAYLOR CARTER), librarian; b. Burlingame, Kan., Feb. 1, 1913; d. C. Roy and Bessie M. (Conner) Bixler; B.S., Abilene Christian Coll., 1952; M.S., Kan. State Tchrs. Coll., 1955; postgrad. Okla. State U., summer 1965; m. W. Taylor Carter, June 1, 1934; children—Betty Lois (Mrs. Ted W. Colby, Jr.), Patricia Marie (Mrs. James L. Jackson). Acting librarian Abilene Christian Coll., 1933-34; librarian Central Christian Coll., 1953-58, Okla. Christian Coll., 1959-64; librarian Edmond (Okla.) High Sch., 1964-65. Edmond Sch. Dist., 1965-67; dir. Library Cons. Service, Edmond, Okla., 1967-72; cons. dir. dist., 1964-72; cons. library Christian Coll. S.W. Mem. Am. Assn. U. Women, Am., Southwestern, Okla. library assns., N.E.A., Alpha Chi. Mem. Ch. of Christ. Author booklet; How to Organize a Small Library, 1962. Home: Edmond, Okla. Died Jan. 29, 1972; interred Meml. Cemetery, Edmond, Okla.

CARTER, WARREN RAY, diversified co. exec.; b. Ashtabula, O., Apr. 18, 1922; s. Laddie F. and Mary Elizabeth (Brake) C.; B.B.A., Western Res. U., 1950; m. Ruth Lillian Danes, Apr. 10, 1943; children—Gary, Jane. Supr., Thompson Products, Cleve., 1942; with Gen. Motors Corp., Detroit, 1950-53, asst. supr., 1953; plant supt. Borg Warner Corp., Decatur, Ill., 1953-58, works mgr., 1958-60; with Sealed Power Co., Muskegon, Mich., 1960-70, v.p. 1961-69, group v.p., 1970; sr. v.p. Weatherhead Co., Cleve., 1970-71, exec. v.p., 1971, pres., 1971-73, also dir.; dir. East Shore Chem. Co., Muskegon, Mich. Pres., founder Jr. Achievement Muskegon, 1963-70; trustee Jr. Achievement of Cleve.; bd. govs. Asso. Industries of Cleve.; trustee Cleve. Scholarship Programs. Served to 1st. lt. USAAF, 1943-46. Recipient Law Day award Mich. Young Lawyers Group, 1966. Mem. Soc. Automotive Engrs. Mason (Shriner). Clubs: Mayfield Country, Clevelander. Home: Pepper Pike, O. Died Aug. 31, 1973.

CARTER, WILLIAM DANIEL, life ins. co. exec.; b. Reading, Mass., Sept. 16, 1911; s. Frank Clifford and Mary (Daniel) C.; B.A., Amherst Coll., 1933; m. Elizabeth Cooke Alling, May 7, 1938; children—Nancy Chute (Mrs. Joseph C. Miller), Elizabeth C. (Mrs. Michael S. Welch). Clk., Prudential Life Ins. Co. Am., Newark, 1934-40; with Conn. Mut. Life Ins. Co., Hartford, 1940-74, sec., 1958-70, 2d v.p., 1970-72; v.p., 1972-74. Group chmn. Hartford Community Chest, 1959. Mem. Conn. Ho. of Reps. from North Branford, Conn., 1963, 65; mem. Bd. Finance North Branford, 1957-65, chmn., 1966-71. Bd. dirs. North Branford Library, 1953-59. Fellow Life Office Mgmt. Assn.; mem. Alpha Delta Phi. Republican. Conglist. (former deacon, trustee, treas.). Home: Northford, Conn. Died Mar. 6, 1974; buried Northford Cemetery, Northford, Conn.

CARTER, WILLIAM HARRISON, educator; b. Gloucester City, N.J., Apr. 20, 1905; s. William Harrison and Olive Edna (Taylor) C.; A.B., Amherst Coll., 1926; M.A., Harvard, 1930, Ph.D., 1932; m. Joan L. Cooke, Aug. 22, 1931; 1 dau., Alice E. Woods. Instr. econs. Amherst Coll., 1927-28, Brown U., 1930-31; instr. to prof. U. Conn., Storrs, 1931-66, prof., 1942-66, head dept. econs., 1945-54, dean Coll. Liberal Arts and Scis., 1954-66, dean emeritus, 1966-74, coordinator of nat. def. tng., 1954-66. Price economist OPA, Conn., 1943-44; chmn. Conn. Minimum Wage Bd., 1951-52. Mem. Am. Econ. Assn., Phi Beta Kappa. Conglist. Mason. Author: Economic Geography, 1939; Economic Theory, 1948; Economic Analysis, 1952; Intermediate Economic Analysis, 1961. Home: Storrs, Conn. Died June 4, 1974; interred Storrs, Conn.

CARTER, WORRALL REED, naval officer (ret.); b. aboard Storm King, Pacific Ocean, Jan. 11, 1885; s. Charles John and Clarissa (Reed) C.; B.S., U.S. Naval Acad., 1908; A.M., Columbia, 1915; m. Mary Ambler Willcox, July 2, 1912; children—Worrall Reed, Thomas Hamlin Willcox, Charles John (killed in combat, France), Mary Cary. Commd. ensign U.S. Navy 1908, and advanced through grades to commodore, 1944; comdr. U.S. Naval Sta., Guantanamo, Cuba, 1938-40, naval service squadron (Adm. Nimitz's secret floating support of Pacific fleet in drive across central Pacific), World War II; ret. from active duty, 1947. Awarded D.S.M., Legion of Merit, various area medals. Mem. U.S. Naval Inst. Protestant Episcopal. Club: Army Navy (Washington). Home: Norfolk, Va. Died 1975.

CARTLIDGE, HAROLD TYNDALE, fire ins. exec.; b. Lincoln, Neb., Sept. 13, 1878; s. Edward J. and Martha O. (Crane) C.; ed. Topeka High Sch., Kan., 1894-98; m. Genevieve Butterfield, 1900; 1 son, Richard Kingman; m. 2d, Nonna Ostergren Morse, Dec. 1927. State agt., agency supt. Shawnee Fire Ins. Co., Topeka, Kans., 1900-10; agency supt., asst. mgr. western dept., Nat. Fire Ins. Co., 1910-22; western mgr. The Liverpool & London & Globe Ins. Co., Ltd., 1922-31; dep. U.S. mgr., v.p., dir. Royal-Liverpool Groups after 1931. Republican. Presbyterian. Mason. Club: Bankers of America (New York, N.Y.). Address: New York City, N.Y.†

CARTWRIGHT, MORSE ADAMS, educator; b. Omaha, Nov. 3, 1890; s. Theodore Parker and Isabella Titus (Hudson) C.; B.S., U. Cal., 1912; grad. study Sch. Jurisprudence, 1912-13; LL.D., Southwestern at Memphis, 1933; LL.D., Mount Allison U. (Can.), 1938; m. Myrtle Lenore Salsig, Aug. 15, 1914; children—Morse Adams, Catherine Croft. Adminstrv. and teaching asst. U. Cal., 1912-14; newspaper editor Riverside, Cal., 1914-17; mgr. U. Cal. Press, 1917-20, 23-24; instr. journalism U. Cal., 1918-20, asst. to pres. and exec. sec. univ., 1918-23, asst. dir. Extension Div., 1923-24; asst. to pres. Carnegie Corp. N.Y., 1924-26; dir. Am. Assn. for Adult Edn., 1926-49, pres., 1950. Vis. prof. edn., Tchrs. Coll., Columbia, 1932; prof. edn., 1941-51, exec. officer Inst. Adult Edn., 1941-49. Cons., Bur. Spl. Operations, OWI, 1942-43. Mem. Belgian-Am. Ednl. Found. (trustee), Chi Psi, Phi Delta Phi. Republican. Conglist. Editor: Adult Edn. Jour., 1927-49. Author: Marching Home: Educational and Social Adjustment After the War, 1944; (with Glen Burch), Adult Adjustment, 1945, others. Contbr. various publs. Editor and compiler studies and reports. Home: San Marino, Cal. Died 1974.

CARVAJAL, MANUEL, bus. exec.; b. Cali, Colombia, Feb. 20, 1916; student U. del Valle, Cali, Mass. Inst. Tech. Pres. Carvajal & Cia., 1939-71; Colombian del. GAAT Conf., Annency, France, 1949; minister mining and petroleum, 1950-51; pres. Oleoducto del Pacifico, Cali, 1954-71, Hernando Carvajal Found., Cali, 1961-71, Paccios, Cali, 1967; minister communications, 1969. Dir. Cartón de Colombia S.A., Corporación Regional del Cauca C.V.C., Central de Anchicayá, ANDI. Mem. superior council U. de los Andes, U. del Valle. Decorated Cross of Boyaca; knight Order San Gregorio Magno. Address: Cali, Colombia., Died Aug. 30, 1971.

CARY, CHARLES REED, mfg. exec.; b. Balt., Dec. 26, 1881; s. Charles Jackson and Sue B. (Reed) C.; student Westtown Boarding Sch., 1896-99; B.S., Haverford (Pa.) Coll., 1902; S.B., Mass. Inst. Tech., 1904; m. Margaret Morris Reeve, Sept. 7, 1912; children—Barbara Lloyd, Stephen Grellet, Sarah Comfort. Salesman James G. Biddle, 1904-06; engr. Pa. R.R. East River Tunnels, 1906-08; with Leeds & Northrup Co., Phila., 1908-22, v.p. in charge sales, 1922-39, v.p., 1942-51, sr. v.p., 1951-59, chmn. bd., after 1959. Mem. Am. Mgmt. Assn. Home: Philadelphia, Pa.†

CARY, RUSSELL SINGER, assn. exec.; b. Melrose, Mass., May 3, 1932; s. Russell Singer and Mary (Sewall) C.; A.B., Dartmouth, 1954; postgrad. Mass. Inst. Tech., 1954-55; M.S., U. Colo., 1960; postgrad. U. Denver, 1961-64; m. Nancy Nancrede Proctor, June 21, 1960; children—Heidi Lynn, Scott Proctor, Kirsten Charlene. Geologist, Pan Am. Petroleum Corp., Denver, 1959-64; accountant Alexander J. Lindsay & Co., Denver, 1964-67; officer mgr. Am. Assn. Petroleum Geologists, Tulsa, 1967-69; asst. exec. sec. Geol. Soc. Am., Boulder, Colo., 1970-72. Ski instr., Winter Park, Colo., 1957-67; ski conditioning instr. Tulsa S.E. YMCA, 1969-72. Served with AUS, 1955-57, C.P.A., Colo., Okla. Mem. Am. Assn. Petroleum Geologists, Tulsa Geol. Soc. (v.p. 1969-70), Rocky Mountain Assn. Geologists, Am. Inst. C.P.A.'s, Okla., Colo. socs. c.p.a's, YMCA (membership dr. team capt. 1969-72), Jr. C. of C. Sigma Xi. Club: Tulsa Ski. Contbg. author: Oil and Gas Fields of Colorado, 1962; Guidebook to Geology of Southwest Utah, 1963. Home: Boulder, Colo. Died May 1972.

CASALS, PABLO (PAU CARLOS SALVADOR DEFILLO DE), cellist, composer, condr.; b. Vendrell, Spain, Dec. 29, 1876; s. Carlos Casals and Pilar Defillo; studied music under father; later studied in Barcelona and Madrid; hon. degrees, U. Edinburgh, 1934, U. Barcelona, 1939, U. Montpellier, 1946; m. Susan Metcalfe, 1914; m. 2d, Marta Montanez, Aug. 1957. Made profl. debut Crystal Palace, London, and with Lamoureux Orch. Paris, 1898; concert tour, U.S., 1901, N.Y. debut, 1904, last N.Y. recital, 1928; founder, condr. Orquesta Pau Casals, Barcelona, 1920-36; founder Workers Concert Soc., Barcelona, 1923; soloist Brit. Broadcasting Orch., 1945; guest condr. orchs. in capital cities throughout world; last pub. profl. appearance U. Montpellier, 1947; mus. dir. Prades Festival (12 concerts) celebrating Bach bicentenary, June 1950; instr. various colls., univs. Compositions include: oratorios, symphonies, several masses, choral works, string quartets. Made numerous recs. Columbia. Decorated grand officer Legion of Honor (France); Grand Cross Republic of Spain, Rep. of Austria, Grand Cross Isabella the Cath.; hon. citizen many cities. Recipient Beethoven gold medal, 1912, gold medal Worshipful Co. of Musicians (London), 1937; Freedom awards, 1968. Fellow Royal Coll. Music (Eng.); hon. mem. Spanish Acad., Acad. Scis. et Lettres of Montpellier, Royal Philarmonic Soc., Friends of Music Soc. (Vienna). Address: Pyrenees Orientales, France. Died Oct. 22, 1973.

CASAMAJOR, LOUIS, neurologist, psychiatrist; b. Brooklyn, N.Y., Aug. 12, 1881; s. Paul and Louise Jane (Holberton) C.; prep. edn., Adelphi Acad., Brooklyn; A.B., Columbia, 1903, A.M., M.D., 1906; unmarried. Practiced in N.Y. City since 1910; attending neurologist, dir. of child neurology, Neurol. Inst., 1935-51; cons. in neurology Presbyn. Hosp. since 1951; neurologist Knickerbocker, Nassau, Kings Park State, Englewood, Manhattan State and Pilgrim State Hosp. Prof. clin. neurology, Coll. Phsycians and Surgeons, Columbia, 191-48, emeritus since 1948. Fellow A.M.A., A.A.A.S.; mem. (founder) Am. Bd. of Psychiatry and Neurology, 1931-42; mem. Am. Neurol. Assn. (v.p. 1939), American Psychiatric Assn., Assn. Am. Anatomists, Am. Mammalogists, N.Y. Zoöl. Soc., N.Y. Acad. Medicine (chmn. sect. on Hist. and Cultural Medicine, 1939-40), N.Y. Neurol. Assn. (v.p. 1927-29, pres. 1929-30), N.Y. Soc. for Clin. Psychiatry (sec. 1919-26; pres. 1927), N.Y. Psychiatric Soc. (pres. 1936-37), N.Y. Bot. Soc., Am. Geog. Soc., Nu Sigma Nu, Alpha Omega Alpha. Capt. and maj. Med. Corps, U.S. Army, World War; with A.E.F. in France, 1917-18; maj. Med. O.R.C. Awarded Selective Service Medal, 1946. Distinguished Service Medal, Presbyn. Hosp., 1953. Democrat. Club: Columbia Univ., Associate editor Archives of Neurology and Psychiatry, 1929-50. Contbr. on neurology and psychiatry. Home: New York City, N.Y.†

CASE, GEORGE WILKINSON, civil engineer; born Fowler, Ind., Mar. 2, 1880; s. Horace Sanford and Amelia Hurlbut (Wilkinson) C.; B.S. in C.E., Purdue U., 1905; M.C.E., Cornell U., 1912; m. Georgia Browne, Aug. 16, 1903. Engaged as asst. instr. civil engring., Purdue U., 1905-06, instr., 1906-07, asst. prof., 1907-13; asst. prof. sanitary engring., U. of Pittsburgh, 1913-14, asso. prof., 1914-16, rpof., 1916-22; asst. engr. Morris Knowles, Inc., Pittsburgh, 1917-19; chief engr. and exec. officer Am. City Engring. Co., Pittsburgh, 1919-25; prof. and head mech. engring. dept., also dean Coll. of Tech. and dir. Engring. Expt. Sta., U. of N.H., Durham, 1925-45, on leave of absence, 1940-45, dean emeritus, Coll. of Tech., U. of N.H., after 1949; prin. specialist Engring. Defense Training, 1941, prin. specialist and dep. dir., Engring., Science and Management Defense Training, 1941-42, director of Engineering, Science and Management War Training program, U.S. Office of Education, Washington, D.C., 1942-45. Life member American Soc. Civil Engineers, Am. Soc. Engring. Edn. (vice president 1938-39); member Newcomen Soc. England, N.H. Acad. of Science, Phi Kappa Phi, Republican. Conglist. Contbr. papers and articles on engring. subjects to scientfici mags. Home: North Manchester, Ind.†

CASH, JAMES (ROBERT), physician; b. Chattanooga, Tenn., May 2, 1893; s. James Albion and Elizabeth (Cheney) C.; A.B., U. of Va., 1914, A.M., 1915; M.D., Johns Hopkins, 1919; m. Mary Frazier Meade, Sept. 5, 1943. Instr., Johns Hopkins Med. Sch., 1919, asst. prof. pathology, 1922; asso. prof. pathology Peiping (China) Union Med. Coll., 1924-28, prof., 1928; prof. pathology U. Va., 1931-58, 60-63; vis. prof. Basic Med. Sci. Inst., Kaeachi, Pakistan, under Internat. Coop. Adminstrn., 1958-60. Member American Soc. Exptl. Pathology. Specialist in diseases of vascular system; interested in cancer control in Va. Home: Crozet, Va., Died June 1975.

CASLER, LESTER ALONZO, corp. ofcl.; b. Little Falls, N.Y., Nov. 17, 1903; s. Floyd Joseph and Ruby (Hollingsworth) C.; student Valparaiso U., 1923-24; m. Ruth Lindsay Lyon, Oct. 21, 1929; children-Deborah Ann (Mrs. Ira A. Wyant, Jr.), Nancy Jane (Mrs. James Bixby), Susan DeWitt (Mrs. John Sterhan); married second to Esther Boyle, Aug. 21, 1954. Served as vice president Lyddon, Hanford & Frohman, Inc., 1933-35, Stewart, Hanford & Casler, Inc., 1935-43; pres., dir. Casler, Hempstead & Hanford, Inc., 1943-50; exec. v.p., dir. Eureka Williams Corporation, 1950-54; vice president, director M B Mfg. Co., (New Haven); v.p. Textron American, Inc. (Providence), James Street Bldg. Co. (Rochester, N.Y.); treas., dir. Nelson Telephone Directory Advt. Service, Rochester, N.Y.; dir. Fanner Mfg. Co. (Cleve.), partner Little & Casler Financial Cons. Dir. Oil Heat Inst. Am., 1950-54. Mason (Shriner). Home: Warwick, R.I. Died Nov. 17, 1974; interred East Barrington, N.H.

CASSELS, LOUIS WELBORN, newspaperman; b. Ellenton, S.C., Jan. 14, 1922, s. Horace Michael Jr. and Molly (Welborn) C.; A.B., Duke, 1942; m. Charlotte Norling, July 10, 1943; 1 son, Horace Michael IV. Corr., U.P.I., N.Y.C., 1946, mem. staff Washington bur., 1947-74, asst. news editor, 1951-56, feature editor, religious news columnist, 1956-74, Washington news analyst, religion editor, 1964-68, sr. editor, nat. news commentator, religion columnist, 1968-74; owner Cassels Oil Co., Aiken, S.C.; J. Rion McKissick lectr. in journalism U. S.C., 1972-74; Recipient Christopher award, 1956; School Bell award N.E.A., 1960; Faith and Freedom award in religious journalism, 1960; Front Page award best U.S. domestic reporting, 1967; Supple ward best religion writing, 1968; St. Augustine award Villanova U., 1970. Mem. Phi Beta Kappa, Alpha Tau Omega. Episcopalian. Club: Nat. Press. Contbr. articles popular mags., 1948-74. Author: Christian Primer, 1964; What's the Difference?, 1965; Your Bible, 1967; The Real Jesus, 1968; The Reality of God, 1971; Haircuts and Holiness, 1972; A Feast for a Time of Fasting, 1973; This Fellow Jesus, 1973; Forbid Them Not, 1973; Coontail Lagoon; Preludes to Prayer; A Bad Investment, 1974; Faiths of America, 1975. Syndicated columnist. Home: Aiken, S.C. Died Jan. 23, 1974; interred St. Joseph's Columbarium, Washington National Cathedral, Washington, D.C.

CASSIDY, WILLIAM JOSEPH, surgeon; b. Tilbury, Ont., Can., Sept. 4, 1880; s. Alexander and Elizabeth (Palmer) C.; Ph.G., Ont. Coll. of Pharmacy, 1901; Ph.B., U. of Toronto, 1901; M.D., Detroit Coll. of Medicine, 1908; m. Katherine Hamilton, July 12, 1926 (died Feb. 28, 1932). Pharmacist, 1901-08; interne Harper Hosp., 1908-10, chief resident surgeon, 1909-10, jr. surgeon, 1914-20; jr. surgeon Providence Hosp., 1914-15; asst. to Dr. Angus McLean, surgeon, 1910-17; attending surgeon and roengenologist, Children's Hosp., 1916-19; gen. surg. practice, 1910-33; now surgeon in charge, St. Mary's Hosp.; also cons. surgeon Receiving, Grosse Pointe, Wayne, Wyandotte Gen., Wayne County, Delray Gen., Forest, Eastside Gen., St. Joseph's and Gaylord hosps. Lieut. comdr. U.S. Navy, Jan. 1935. Fellow Am. Coll. of Surgeons; mem. Wayne County Med. Soc. (pres.), Mich. State Med. Soc., A.M.A., Detroit Acad. of Surgery, Nu Sigma Nu. Republican. Roman Catholic. Clubs: Athletic, Yacht (Detroit). Home: Detroit, Mich.†

CASSIL, HURD ALEXANDER, ry. official; b. Mt. Vernon, O., Nov. 8, 1878; s. Col. Alexander and Jane (Hunter) C.; ed. pub. schs. and 2 yrs. under pvt. tutor; m. M. Gene Putt, of Mt. Vernon, Oct. 20, 1897; 1 son, Armond. Began in employ of Cleveland, Akron & Columbus Ry., 1898; served successively with Pere Marquette R. R., C., H. & D. Ry., B. & O. Southwestern R. R. and B. & O. R. R. until 1917, including a period with Canadian White Constrn. Co.; again with Pere Marquette R. R. after 1917, chief engr. after 1922. Mem. Am. Ry. Engring. Assn. Republican. Episcopalian. Mason. Club: Lake Shore Country. Home: Detroit, Mich.†

CASSILLY, PHILIP JACQUEMN, govt. ofcl.; b. Louisville, Dec. 23, 1904; s. Louis Vincent and Lillie (Jones) C.; student Notre Dame U., 1922-23; m. Ruth Fisher Erickson, May 8, 1943. With Ford Motor Co., Louisville, 1925-26; engr. dam and levee constrn. U.S. C.E., lower Ohio and Miss. Rivers, 1926-29; constrn. maintenance engr. United Fruit Co., Jamaica, B.W.I., 1930-34; state dir. employment WPA, Phoenix, 1935-42; labor relations rep. Consol.-Vultee Aircraft Co., Tucson, 1942-43; personnel officer War Relocation Auth., Poston, Ariz., 1943-46; adminstrv. officer Southwestern Power Adminstrn., Tulsa, 1946-70, asst. adminstr. for adminstrv. operations, 1967-70. Recipient honor award meritorious service sec. of interior, 1970. Home: Tulsa, Okla. Died Sept. 19, 1973; buried Calvary Cemetery, Tulsa, Okla.

CASSIN, RENE, jurist, human rights advocate; b. Bayonne, France, Oct. 5, 1887; s. Henri and Gabrielle (Dreyfus) C.; M.A. (Licenci es lettres); Dr. Juridical, Econ. and Polit. Scis., law schs., Aix (France) and Paris (France); hon. doctorates univs. Oxford (Eng.), Mainz (Germany), London (Eng.), Jerusalem (Israel), Brandeis U., m. Simone Yzombard, Mar. 29, 1917; m. 2d, Ghislaine Bru. Prof. law univs. Lille (France), 1920, Paris, 1929-60; prof. Nat. Sch. Colonial Studies, 1935-40; faculty Acad. Internat. Law, The Hague, Netherlands, U. Inst. Advanced Studies in Internat. Affairs, Geneva, Switzerland; pres. Nat. Sch. Pub. Adminstrn., 1945-60. French del. League of Nations, 1924-38, UN, 1946-58; French founding mem. UNESCO, 1944, del., 1945-52; past. pres. UN Human Rights Commn., chief recorder Universal Declaration of Human Rights, 1947-48; judge, past pres. European Ct. Human Rights, 1959-76, pres., 1965-68; permanent sec. Def. Council under DeGaulle, 1940-41; nat. commr. justice and edn. French Govt. in Exile, 1941-43; mem. Interallied Commn. of Inquiry on War Crimes, 1943-45; mem. consulative assembly Algiers, pres. juridical com.; v.p. Council of State, 1944-60, subsequently hon. pres., also founder jour. Researches and Documents, 1947; pres. High Ct. of Arbitration, 1945-46; mem. Constl. Council, 1960-71; founder Internat. Inst. Human Rights, Strasbourg, 1968. Served during World War I, World War II. Decorated grand cross Legion of Honor, Companion of the Liberation, Mil. medal, Croix de Guerre, Resistance Rosette (France). Recipient Nobel Peace prize, 1968, UN Human Rights prize, 1968, Bernard Cogan prize. Mem. Institut de France (pres. Acad. Moral and Polit. Sci. 1962-76), Soc. Comparative Legislation (hon. pres.), Assn. Devel. World Law (hon. pres.) Friends of U. Paris (pres.), Inst. Internat. Relations (pres.) Alliance Israélite e Universelle (pres.), Author: L'Exception d'inexécution dans les Contrats. les Droits de l'Etat dans les Successions en Suisse, 1914; Le Domicile dans le Conflit des Lois, 1930; La Déclaration, Universelle et la Mise en Oeuvre des Droits de l'Homme, 1951; Livre Jubilaire du Conseil d'Etat, 1952. Home: Paris, France., Died Feb. 21, 1976.

CASTEN, DANIEL FRANCIS, surgeon; b. N.Y.C., Feb. 9, 1906; c. Charles and Sarah Casten; M.D., L.I. U., 1930; m. Constance Mary Bell; 1 son, Richard Francis. Intern, Hosp. for Joint Diseases, N.Y.C., 1930-31, cons. surgeon; pvt. practice medicine specializing in surgery, N.Y.C.; mem. staff St. Clare's Hosp.; dir. surgery Sydenham Hosp.; asso. clin. prof. surgery N.Y. Med. Sch. Diplomate Am. Bd. Surgery. Fellow A.C.S.; mem. A.M.A., A.A.A.S. Contbr. articles to profl. jours. Home: Croton-on-Hudson, N.Y. Died Aug. 16, 1973.

CASTLE, ALFRED L., lawyer; b. Honolulu, Mar. 18, 1884; A.B., Harvard, 1906, LL.B., 1908. Admitted to Hawaii bar, 1908; mem. firm Anthony & Waddoups, Honolulu. Mem. Territorial Ho. of Reps., 1911-13. Trustee Punahou Sch., 1924-45. Mem. Am. Bar. Assn., Bar Assn. Hawaii. Home: Honolulu, Hawaii. Died Oct. 22, 1972.

CASTLE, EDWARD SEARS, biologist; b. Cambridge, Mass., Dec. 25, 1903; s. William Ernest and Clara (Bosworth) C.; A.B., Harvard, 1925, A.M., 1927, Ph.D., 1929; m. Natalie Watson Berle, June 12, 1930; children—Peter Watson, Philip Sears. Instr. Harvard, 1930-31, asst. prof., 1931-40, asso. prof., 1940-54, became prof. physiology, 1954, prof. emeritus, dir. biology labs., 1940-45. Fellow Fund for Advancement Edn., 1953-54. Mem. Am. Physiol. Soc., Am. Assn. Plant Physiologists, Bot. Soc. Am., Soc. Gen. Physiologists, Soc. Growth and Devel., Am. Acad. Arts and Scis. Contbr. tech. papers to profl. lit. Home: Cambridge, Mass. Died May 19, 1973.

CASTLE, SAMUEL NORTHRUP, cons. engineer; b. Honolulu, T.H., Feb. 6, 1880; student Haile a/d Saale, Oahu Coll.; Hamilton Coll; A.B., Harvard, 1901; grad. work, Cornell U., 1902-04; m. Anna Ellison Haviland, June 3, 1903; children—Anna Haviland (dec.), Northrup Haviland. With Westinghouse Machine Co., 1905, Allis Chalmers Co., 1905-06, constrn. engr., N.Y. Dist., 1906-08; comml. engr. General Electric Co., N.Y., 1909-15, in charge in field, elec. steel furnace work, 1916-18, in office, 1918-19; in pvt. practice, after 1919; dir. Castle & Cooke, Ltd., Hawaiian Pineapple Co., Ltd., Advertiser Pub. Co., Ltd., KGU; dir., v.p. sec. Honolulu Rapid Transit Co., Ltd., dir., v.p. Ewa Plantation Co., Kohala Sugar Co., Waialua Agrl. Co., Ltd.; dir. vice president, Halemano Company, Ltd. Inventor centrifugal oiling device for Corliss engines, entrifugal gas cleaner, non-inductive method of leading in, condrs. on arc furnaces, comml. searchlight, etc. Lecturer, U.S. Army Arty. Sch., Sandy Hook, 1910-14. Vice pres. S. N. and Mary Castle Foundation. Mem. and sec. bd. regents U. of Hawaii, 1941-43. Fellow A.A.A.S., Am. Inst. E.E.; mem. Am. Soc. Mechanical Engineers, American Society of Civil Engrs., Am. Inst. Mining & Metall. Engrs., Soc. Automotive Engrs., Am. Inst. Chem. Engrs., Am. Iron and Steel Inst., Am. Math. Soc., Soc. Am. Mil. Engrs., Am. Ordnance Association, New York Electrical Society (life member, ex-vice president), Harvard Engineering Soc. (life; ex-sec.), Newcomen Soc., Engring. Assn. of Hawaii, Hawaiian Sugar Planters Assn., Soc. of the Cincinnati, Hawaiian Mission Children's Soc., Alpha Delta Phi, Theta Nu Epsilon. Mason (32°, K.T., Shriner). Clubs: Engineers, University (New York); Honolulu Automobile, Cornell of Hawaii, Harvard), Oahu Country, Pacific, University of Hawaii (pres., 1935-). Home: Waimanalo, Oahu, Hawaii.†

CASTLEBERRY, WINSTON, bus. exec.; b. 1912; B.B.A., So. Meth. U., 1934; m. With Southwest Airmotive Co., 1938-71, v.p., treas., 1941-55, exec. v.p., 1955-60, pres., service dir., 1960-67, pres., chief exec. officer, 1967-71, also dir. Served as maj. USAF, 1942-45. Office: Dallas, Tex. Died 1971.

CASTRO, FRANK MONROE, orthodontist; b. Blanchester, O., May 30, 1875; s. James Monroe and Margaret R. (Watkins) C.; student Ohio State U., 1895-1902, D.D.S., 1898, M.D., 1900, Ph.G., 1902; m. Florence May Andrus, Feb. 20, 1902; children—William Andrus, Ruth Amelia, Florence Adele. Practiced orthodontics, Cleveland, O., 1904-37, La Jolla, Calif., since 1937; dean emeritus Sch. of Dentistry and prof. emeritus of orthodontics, Western Reserve U. Lt. comdr. U.S.N.R.F., ret. Ex-v.p., dir. Preparedness League of Am. Dentists; mem. bd. govs., first and hon. v.p. of second Internat. Orthodontic Congress; mem. dental advisory com. President Roosevelt's Com. on Economic Security; former mem. bd. visitors Ohio State U. Mem. bd. trustees La Jolla Town Council. Recipient of Ohio State University alumni award, 1955. Past pres. Am. Bd. of Orthodontia; v.p. Pan-Am. Odontol. Assn. Master Internat. Coll. of Dentists; fellow of the American College of Dentists. Member Soc. for Promotion of Dentistry for Children, American Association Orthodontists (past pres.), Am. Dental Assn. (past pres.), Ohio State (past pres.), Northern Ohio Dental Society (past pres.), Cleveland Dental Soc. (past pres.), Great Lakes Assn. Orthodontists, Eastern Assn. Angle Grads., European Orthodontological Soc., First Dist. Dental Soc. of N.Y., New York Acad. of Dentistry, Chicago Dental Soc., Am. Med. Assn., Calif. Med. Assn., San Diego County Med. Assn., Cleveland Med. Library Assn., San Diego County Golf Assn., Am. Dental Golf Assn., Am. Med. Golf Assn., Pan-Am. Med. Assn., La Jolla Conservation Soc., Mil. Order World Wars, La Jolla Art Center, Nu Sigma Nu, Delta Sigma Delta, Omicron Kappa Upsilon. Presbyn. Mason (32°, K.T., Shriner). Clubs: Big Ten University, Rancho Santa Fe Country, La Jolla Kiwanis. Home: La Jolla, Cal.†

CASTRO, MATILDE (MRS. JAMES H. TUFTS), educator and lecturer; b. Chgo., Ill., Mar. 16, 1879, d. Daniel and Louise (Hager) C.; A.B., Univ. of Chicago, 1900, Ph.D., 1907; m. Dean James H. Tufts, June 18, 1923. Prin. high sch., Morris, Ill., 1901-03; instr. philosophy, Mt. Holyoke Coll., 1904-05; instr. philosophy, 1906-09, actg. head of dept. of philosophy, 1908-09, Vassar Coll.; prof. psychology and edn., Rockford Coll., 1910-12; dir. Phebe Anna Thorne Model School of Bryn Mawr Coll., 1913-, also asso. prof. edn., 1914-16; prof. and head of dept. of edn., 1916-23, Bryn Mawr Coll. Fellow A.A.A.S.; mem. Am. Philos. Assn., Am. Psychol. Assn., Sigma Xi, Phi Beta Kappa. Author: The Respective Standpoints of Psychology and Logic (U. of Chicago contbns. to philosophy No. 4), 1913. Home: Chicago, Ill.†

CASWELL, EDWARD C., illustrator, lecturer; b. New York, N.Y., Sept. 12, 1880; s. Alanson W. and Caroline E. (Schwarz) C.; ed. pub. schs., Brooklyn; m. Laura Rometsch, June 1910; children—Eleanor, Elizabeth. Began as illustrator for newspapers in 1900; with exception of brief service with advt. firms in 1914 and 1917, has been free-lance book and mag. illustratior since 1915 and lecturer after 1924. Teacher book illustration, Washington Irving Evening High Sch., N.Y. City. Decorated Order of White Lion (Czechoslovakia) for drawings in book, "Romantic Czechoslovakia" by Robt. McBride. Illustrated "Old New York" by Edith Wharton and "The Old Cities Series." Home: New York City, N.Y.†

CATON, HARRY ANDERSON, sec. Nat. Grange; b. nr. Fresno. O., Oct. 31, 1881; s. Dr. Franklin and Lucinda (Wilhelm) C.; student village and high schs.; m. Maude Winnifred Norman, Oct. 8, 1902; 1 dau., Beatrice Irene (Mrs. John V. Porter). Formerly farmer; sch. tchr., 1902-18; lectr. Ohio Grange, 1918-21, master, 1921-28; sec. Nat. Grange, after 1928; Grange editor for the National Stockman and Farmer, 1912-28; vice pres., dir. Farmers and Traders Life Ins. Co.; dir. Grange Mut. Casualty Co.; mem. bd. control Ohio Agrl. Export Sta. Trustee Ohio State U., 1925-39. Democrat. Presbyn. Address: Coshocton, O.†

CATTO, THOMAS SIVEWRIGHT, LORD, 1st Baron Catto of Cairncatto, P.C., 1947; born Peterhead, Aberdeen, March 15, 1879; son of William and Isabella (Yule) C.; student Peterhead Academy, Rutherford Coll.; m. Gladys Gordon, 1910; children—Isabel Gordon, Ruth Gordon (Mrs. Ernest Bennett), Gladys Gordon (Mrs. Evan Richmond Watson), Stephen Gordon. With MacAndrews & Forbes Co., merchants, 1898-1904; v.p., N.Y. br., 1909-19; chmn. Andrew Yulae & Co., Ltd., 1919-40; partner Morgan Grenfell and Company, 1919-40; partner Morgan Grenfell and Company, 1919-40; member British Food Mission to U.S.A., 1915-17, chmn. British and Allied Provisions Commn. and British Ministry of Food in U.S. and Can., 1918-19. Mem. Govt. of India Retrenchment Com., 1922-23. Dir. gen. of equipment, Ministry of Supply, 1939-40; financial adviser to Chancellor of Exchequer, 1940-44; governor, Bank of England, 1944-49. Clubs: Athenaeum (London); Reform; Bengal (Calcutta); Oriental. Home: London, Eng.†

CAULFIELD, JOHN FRANCIS, business exec.; b. New York City, Nov. 14, 1878; s. William Austin and Sarah Emma (Nichols) C.; ed. N.Y. U.; m. Helen Harriott Nash, February 15, 1905 (deceased); children—Mrs. Joseph E. Clark, Mrs. Leslie R. Hawkins (deceased), Mrs. J. P. Dorgan, Marjorie Austin and Elizabeth Gascoyne (Mrs. Frederick A. Lory) (twins); married 2d, Margaret Alene Moody, June 2, 1951. Began with Am. Cotton Oil Co., New

York, 1893-1902; sec. to chief accountant Fairmont Coal Co., New York, 1902-05; chief clerk and asst. to sales mgr. Consol. Coal Co., N.Y. City, 1905-13; asst. sec. and asst. treas. Elk Horn Fuel Co., 1913-15; treas. Elk Horn Coal Corp., 1915-19, v.p., treas., dir. and mem. exec. com., 1919-31, treas. for receiver, 1931-35, and since 1940, for trustee, 1935-37, pres. of company after 1940; sec. and treas. Wayland Oil & Gas Co., 1914-20; sec. and treas. West Va. Metal Products Corp., 1920-24; dir. Kentucky River Coal Corp. Mem. Past Masters Masonic Assn. of Essex Co., N.J. Asso. mem. A.I.M.M.E. Mason (past master, K.T., 32°, Shriner). Apptd. aide-de-camp on staff of Gov. Laffoon of Ky., with rank and grad of col., Mar. 12, 1935. Home: Charleston, W. Va.†

CAUSEY, JAMES CAMPBELL, JR., city mgr.; b. Suffolk, Va., Apr. 23, 1902; s. James C. and Marguerite (Crump) C.; B.S., Va. Mil. Inst., 1924; m. Margaret Urquhart Jordan, June 9, 1928; children—James Campbell III, Margaret (Mrs. Bedford Horton Brown). Transitman Bd. Commrs. Everglades Drainage Dist., State Fla., West Palm Beach, 1924-25; asst. engr. Moore Haven (Fla.) Engring. Co., Moore Haven, Fla., 1925-26; engr. Wallis Engring. Co., Tallahassee, 1926; timber surveys Surry Lumber Co., Sedley, Va., 1926-27; engr. R. G. Lassiter & Co., 1927; bridge insp. The Virginian Ry. Co., 1927-32; city engr. City of Suffolk, Va., 1932-42, city mgr., 1942-46, 55-73; sr. engr. Myron Sturgeon Engrs., Norfolk, 1946-53; partner Causey & Weeks, Engrs., 1953-55; dir. A. B. Miner Co. Bd. dirs. Louise Obici Meml. Hosp. Registered civil engr., Va. Mem. Am. Soc. C. E., City Mgrs. Assn., Soc. Am. Mil. Engrs., Nat., Va. fox hunters assns. Episcopalian. Rotarian. Home: Suffolk, Va. Died Jan. 14, 1973.

CAVANAGH, JOHN ALEXIS, banker; b. Des Moines, Ia., July 23, 1878; s. Thomas and Mary Alice (Gibbons) C.; A.B., Creighton U., Omaha, Neb., 1905; post-grad. work, U. of Innsbruck, Austria; m. Mary S. Denman, of Des Moines, Feb. 16, 1915. Pres. Des Moines Nat. Bank since Jan. 13, 1920. Roman Catholic. Contbr. numerous articles to financial mags. Home: Des Moines, Ia.†

CAWLEY, ROBERT RALSTON, educator, author; b. Canasaraga, N.Y., July 18, 1893; s. Frank Edward and Sarah Haseltine (Brown) C.; A.B., Harvard, 1914, A.M. (honors), 1915, Ph.D., 1921; postgrad. (Harvard traveling fellow) univs. of London, Berlin, Paris, 1921-22; m. Elizabeth Hoon, Sept. 18, 1937; 1 dau., Margaret Elizabeth. Tchr. French, German, Spanish, Thacher Sch., Ojai, Calif., 1915-18; instr. French, German, Spanish, Mass. Inst. Tech., 1919-20; instr. English, Princeton, 1922-25, asst. prof. 1925-27, asso. prof. 1927-44, prof., 1944; acting chmn. dept., 1948-49, 1951-52. Distinguished prof. City U. N.Y., 1963. Pres., London Scholars' Group of Am. U. Union. Served as 2d lt. Q.M. Res. Corps. AUS, 1918. Mem. Modern Lang. Assn. Am. (chmn. English sect. I, chmn. adv. bd. 1947, chmn. Milton group 1948, adv. bd. 1949-51), Am. Assn. U. Profs., Alpha Phi Sigma (Harvard). Presbyn. (elder). Club: Princeton (Phila.). Editor: Truth of Our Times (Henry Peacham), 1942. Author: The Voyagers and Elizabethan Drama, 1938; Unpathed Waters; Studies in the Influence of the Voyagers on Elizabethan Literature, 1940; Milton's Literary Craftsmanship, 1941; Milton and the Literature of Travel, 1951; A Brief History of the First Presbyterian Church of Princeton, 1954; (with George Yost, Jr.) Studies in Sir Thomas Browne, 1965; (with Arthur Link), The First Presbyterian Church of Princeton: Two Centuries of History, 1967; Henry Peacham: His Contribution to English Poetry, 1971. Contbr. articles to Am., fgn. jours. Home: Princeton, N.J. Died May 11, 1973; interred Princeton Cemetery.

CEKADA, EMIL BOGOMIR, physician; b. Jelshane, Austria, Oct. 12, 1903; s. John and Rose Serena Cekada; Sc.D., Johns Hopkins, 1926, M.D., 1929; m. Louise Lewis, Sept. 22, 1934; children—Althea C. (Mrs. Charles E. Rowe), Emil Lewis. Intern, Johns Hopkins Hosp., 1929-30; resident Duke Hosp., 1930-33, Watts Hosp., 1933-34; practice medicine specializing in internal medicine, Durham, N.C., 1934-72; mem. staff Duke Hosp., Watts Hosp., Lincoln Hosp., VA Hosp., Columbia, S.C.; instr. internal medicine U. N.C. Med. Sch. Served to lt. col., M.C., AUS, 1942-46. Diplomate Am. Bd. Internal Medicine. Fellow Am. Pub. Health Assn.; mem. A.M.A., So. Med. Assn., A.A.A.S., Assn. Mil. Surgeons U.S., N.Y. Acad. Scis., Durham-Orange County Med. Soc. (pres. 1949-50). Elk. Contbr. articles to profl. jours. Home: Durham, N.C. Died July 17, 1972; buried Raleigh Nat. Cemetery, Raleigh, N.C.

CERF, JAY HENRY, mgmt. cons., polit. scientist; b. Chgo., May 17, 1923; s. Nathan Randolph and Blanche (Ruth) C.; B.A. (Residence Halls fellow), U. Wis., 1948, M.A., 1951; postgrad. Heidelberg U. 1949; M.A., Yale, 1952, Ph.D. (Block fellow, Cowles fellow, Falk fellow), 1957; postgrad. (Fulbright fellow), Free U., Berlin, 1953-54, (Penfield fellow) U. Pa., 1956; m. Carol Montgomery McGovern, June 12, 1951; children—Jay Randolph, Christopher David, William Montgomery. Research analyst U.S. Govt., 1949-51; teaching asst. Yale, 1952-53; guest lectr. Russian Research Center, Harvard, 1955; legislative asst. U.S. Ho. of Reps., U.S. Senate, 1955-56; dir. Fgn. Policy Clearing House, 1957-61; spl. asst. to sec. commerce, 1961; sec. Pres. Kennedy's Cabinet Trade Policy Com., 1961-62; dep. asst. sec. commerce for internat. affairs, 1962; mgr. internat. group U.S. C. of C., 1962-69, sec. U.S.-Can. com. 1962-63, U.S.-Mexico com., 1962-66, fgn. policy com., 1962-64, fgn. commerce com., 1962-64; sec. U.S. Mgmt. Adv. Com. to OECD, 1962-64; sec. ann. U.S. delegation Japan-U.S. Bus. Leader Confs. Keidanren of Japan and U.S. C. of C., 1962-67; exec. dir. Pathfinder Fund, 1969-71; pres. Cons. Internat. of Cambridge, Inc., 1972-74; bd. dirs. Fed. Union, Interlandia Corp., Roadstead Found. Cons. on population policy Harvard, 1970-71. Trustee Internat. Devel. Conf., U.S. Council Internat C. of C.; bd. advisers Council of Latin Am., India Cultural Center. Served with USNR, 1943-46. Am. Polit. Sci. Assn. Congl. fellow, 1955-56. Mem. UN Assn. (dir.), Washington Inst. Fgn. Affairs, Am. Polit. Sci. Assn., Soc. for Internat. Devel. Clubs: Yale, Nat. Press, Federal City, Harvard Faculty, Harvard of Boston, Cambridge Boat, Internat. Center of New Eng. Author: The Intellectual Bases of Nazism, 1951; History of the Free University, 1954; Political Indoctrination of Students in East Germany, 1957; The Alliance for Progress-A Hemispheric Response to a Global Threat, 1965. Editor: Strategy for the '60's, 1961; collaborating editor Europe and America, The Next Ten Years, 1970. Contbr. article to N.Y. Times mag. Home: Cambridge, Mass. Died Aug. 15, 1974.

CERRACCHIO, ENRICO FILIBERTO, sculptor; b. Castel Vetro Val Furtore, Italy, Mar. 14, 1880; s. Memnato and Joseppa (Alterisio) C.; grad. acad. and sculpture courses, Inst. Avellino, Italy, 1898; studied scultpure with Raffaele Belliazzi 2 yrs.; m. Marion Kowalski, of Shamokin, Pa., July 27, 1907; children—Genevieve Josephine, Harold Mennotto. Came to U.S., 1900, naturalized citizen, 1905; settled at Houston, Tex. Prin. works: Gen. John A. Wharton monument, State Capitol, Austin, Tex; The American Doughboy, presented to Gen Diaz and accepted by Italian Govt.; Confederated monument adopted by Confederate vets. at Nat. Conv., 1920; World War monument (à0,000 public subscription), City of Houston; The Am. Doughboy, presented to Gen. Pershing by citizens of Houston; bronze statue of Gen. Sam Houston, Main Boul. and Montrose Av., Houston, financed by State of Tex. and City of Houston; marble bust, Gov. ("Ma") Ferguson, Capitol bldg., Austin, Tex.; bust of Tim Murphy, comedian, etc. Republican. Theosophist. Elk. Home: New York City, N.Y.†

CESTARO, MICHAEL PAUL, assn. exec.; b. June 25, 1907; m. Jennie Gallo, Sept. 22, 1929; 1 son, Joseph Michael. Vice pres., dir. SarJen, Inc., Boynton Beach, Fla.; past pres., dir., chmn. bd. J.E. Hangen, Inc., J.E. Hanger, Inc. N.Y. past dir., pres. Am. Orthotics and Posthetics Assn., Washington; past bd. dirs., treas. Am. Bd. Certification Orthotics and Prosthetics, Washington. Home: Boynton Beach, Fla. Died Oct. 10, 1974.

CHACE, ARTHUR FREEBORN, physician; b. Warren, R.I., May 13, 1879; s. Charles Anthony and Adeline Francis (Slade) C.; B.S., Earlham Coll., Richmond, Ind., 1897; A.B., Harvard, 1899; A.M., M.D., Columbia, 1903; hon. Sc.D., Earlham Coll., 1946; m. Kathleen Stirling Fletcher, Nov. 2, 1911; 3 sons-Arthur F., Jr., James Fletcher, Charles Anthony. Practiced at New York City after 1903; professor medicine, N.Y. Post-Grad. Med. Sch. (Columbia), 1912-38; president New York Academy Medicine, 1942-44 (trustee), N.Y. Post-Grad Med. Sch. and Hosp., 1930-44. Maj. Med. Corps. U.S. Army; chief medical service, Base Hospital, Camp Dix, World War 1. Trustee Paul Smith's College Arts and Sciences. Trustee Byrn Mawr College, 1914-39. Member, A.M.A., New York County Medical Society (pres. 1923), Am. Gastro-Enterol. Assn. (pres. 1924-25), Harvey Soc., Soc. Exptl. Biology and Medicine, Société Internationale de Gasto-Enterologie; fellow Am. Coll. Physicians. Republican. Mem. Soc. of Friends. Clubs: University, St. Regis Yacht. Address: New York City, N.Y.†

CHACE, WILLIAM N(IELS), textile exec.; b. Fall River, Mass., Aug. 25, 1908; s. Leonard Sanford and Laura Eliza (Arnzen) C.; student Phillips Andover Acad., 1923-27, U. Va., 1927-29; m. Isabel Butler Jameson, Oct. 29, 1934; children—Benjamin Cartwright, Niels Jameson, Constance, Carol Margaret. Overseer Standard Oil N.J., Sumatra, East Indies, 1930-31; sales mgr. Lawton Mills Corp., Plainfield, Conn., and N.Y.C., 1933-35; fiber sales mgr. Am. Viscose Corp., N.Y.C., 1938-45; asst. v.p. Burlington Mills, N.Y.C., 1945-46; v.p., dir. Greenwood Mills, Inc., 1947-58; pres. Bondyne Assos., Inc., from 1958; president Fort Church Properties, 1960-76. Member of the coordination committee Industry Adv. Com. to OPS, 1950-51. Mem. Nat. Fedn. Textiles, Inc. (pres. 1953-54). Republican. Conglist. Mason (32°). Died Jan. 19, 1976.

CHADWICK, JAMES, physicist; b. Oct. 20, 1891; s. J.J. Chadwick; ed. Univs. Manchester and Berlin; Ph.D., Cambridge U.; M.Sc., Victoria; D.Sc. (hon.) Oxford, Birmingham, Reading, Dublin, Leeds, McGill, Exeter; LL.D., Liverpool, Edinburgh; m. Aileen Stewart-Brown, 1925; twin daus. Lectr., asst. dir. radioactive research Cavendish Lab. (Cambridge); master Gonville and Caius Coll., Cambridge, 1948-58, fellow, from 1958; Lyon Jones prof. physics U. Liverpool, 1935-48. Recipient Nobel prize (physics), 1935; created knight, 1945; U.S. Medal for Merit, 1946; Faraday medal, 1950, Franklin medal, 1951; elected to Pontificia Academia Scientiarum, 1961; fgn. mem. German Order pour le merite, 1966; companion of honor, 1970. Fellow Royal Soc. (Hughes medal 1932, Copley medal 1950), Am. Phys. Soc. (hon.); fgn. mem. Royal Acad. Brussels, Royal Danish Acad. Sci., Royal Acad. Sci. Amsterdam; corr. mem. Sachsische Akademie der Wissenchaften, Acad. Sci. Leipzig. Author: (with Lord Rutherford, C.D. Ellis) Radiations from Radioactive Substances; 1930; papers on radioctivity. Actively engaged in expts. that led to devel. of atomic bomb; head Brit. delegation to U.S., 1943. Clubs: Athenaeum (London). Home: Cambridge, Eng. Died July 1974.

CHADWICK, JAMES CARROLL, clergyman; b. Carthage, Tex., Jan. 10, 1915; s. William Sandy and Martha Beulah (Ingram) C.; A.A., Marshall Coll., 1935; B.A., Baylor U., 1937; B.Th., Southwestern Theol. Sem., 1940; D.D., E. Tex. Bapt. Coll., 1953; m. Marieta Todd, Feb. 22, 1942; children—Daniel David, Martha Lou, Carleta Louise. Ordained to ministry Bapt. Ch., 1934; student pastor, 1933-40; pastor 1st Bapt. Ch., Leonard, Tex., 1940-42, Center, Tex., 1942-73. Dir. Gt. Commonwealth Life Ins. Co., Dallas, First Home Credit, Jacksonville, Logos Corp., Ft. Worth, Treasure Chest Bookstores, Dallas. Rep., Home Mission Bd. Dept. Evangelism, Alaska, 1954; participant, Bapt. World Alliance meeting, Rio de Janeiro, Brazil, 1960; preacher, Europe, Africa, Asia, Holy Land, 1962; participant New Life Movement, Japan, Hong Kong, 1963. Dir., v.p., chmn. religious awards East Tex. council Boy Scouts Am. Sec., Tex., So. U. Bd. Regents, Houston, 1955-73; trustee E. Tex. Bapt. Coll., Valley Bapt. Acad., Pineywoods Bapt. Encampment; life mem. East Texas Coll. Bd. Mem. So. Bapt. Conv. (state missions commn., mem. exec. bd. 1954-62, annuity bd. 1962-73, nomination bd.), Bapt. Gen. Conv. Tex. (chmn. exec. bd. 1963-65, pres. conv. 1965-67, chmn. state missions commn.). Home: Center, Tex. Died Oct. 8, 1973.

CHADWICK, LEIGH E(DWARD), physiologist; b. Washington, Aug. 9, 1904; s. DeWitt Clinton and Charlotte Alice Rothwell (Pechell) C.; B.S., Haverford Coll., 1925; follow Am.-German student exchange, Phillips-Universitat, Marburg, Germany, 1927-28; M.A., U. Pa., 1929; M.A., Harvard, 1938, Ph.D., 1939; m. Maria Beatrice Kievenaar, Nov. 17, 1941. Instr. French and German, 1925-32; instr. biology Pueblo (Colo.) Jr. Coll., 1939-41; asst. physiology U. Rochester Sch. Medicine and Denistry, 1941-42, instr., 1942-44; chief entomology br. med. labs. Army Chem. Center, Md., 1944-56; prof. entomology U. Ill., 1956-75, former head dept. Mem. Am. Acad. Arts and Sci., A.A.A.S., Am. Physiol. Society, Entomological Society of America, Society of General Physiologists, Sigma Xi, Phi Beta Kappa. Home: Champaign, Ill. Died Feb. 4, 1975.

CHADWICK, STEPHEN FOWLER, lawyer; b. Colfax, Wash., Aug. 14, 1894; s. Stephen James and Emma (Plummer) C.; LL.B., Washington and Lee U., 1914; J.D., U. Wash., 1915; m. Margaret Gardiner Tyler, July 2, 1919; children—Mary T. McCracken, Stephen. Admitted to Wash. bar, 1915; mem. firm Chadwick, Chadwick & Mills, 1929-70, Chadwick, Mills & McLaughlin, 1970-74; counsel LeSourd, Patten, Flemming & Hartung, 1974-75. Democratic candidate Congress, 1st Dist., Wash., 1926; candidate Dem. nomination U.S. Senate, 1932; Republican candidate U.S. Senate, 1940. Mem. Seattle Charter Commn., 1925; nat. judge adv. Forty and Eight, 1922-24; civilian aide to sec. war, 1933-47, sec. army, 1947-54; mem. Civilian War Commn., 1942-46; chmn. U.S.O. Council, 1942-46, Regional Loyalty Bd., 1948-53; pres. Washington div. Am. Cancer Soc., 1947-52, mem. exec. com., 1952—; mem. Mut. Security Adminstrn. evaluation team, Philippines, 1953; del. Atlantic Congress, 1959; Nat. Com. Vets. AEF in Siberia, 1973-74. Trustee Seattle C. of C., 1931-51, v.p., 1936-38, sr. council, from 1951. Served as 1st lt., inf. AEF, Siberia, 1918-19; capt. Judge Adv. Gen. Res., 1922-32. Decorated comdr. Legion of Honor (France). Recipient Distinguished Service medal Am. Cancer Soc., 1953, 72. Mem. Am. Coll. Trial Attys., Am., Wash. State bar assns., Am. Legion (mem. nat. Am. Com. 1929-38, chmn. 1935-38, nat. com. 1938-39), Seattle Hist. Soc. (pres. 1965-67), Omicron Delta Kappa, Phi Delta Phi, Kappa Sigma. Republican. Episcopalian. Mason. Club: University, Rainier, Seattle Tennis (Seattle). Home: Seattle, Wash., Died Aug. 28, 1975.

CHAFFEE, EMORY LEON, physicist; b. Sommerville, Mass., Apr. 15, 1885; s. Emory Franklin and Belle Genevieve (Carter) C.; S.B., Massachusetts Institute Technology, 1907; A.M., Harvard, 1908, Ph.D., 1911 (Bowdoin) Prize), S.D., (hon.) Harvard, 1944; D. Engring. (hon.), Chase Institute Tech., 1955; m. Alice Hampson, March 25, 1924. Instr. physics and elec. engring., Harvard, 1911-17, asst. prof. physics, 1917-23, asso. prof., 1923-26, prof., 1926-35, Gordon McKay prof. physics and communication engring. 1935-46, Gordon McKay professor of Applied Physics 1946-53, professor emeritus, 1953-75, Rumford prof. physics, 1940-53, professor emeritus, 1953-75; dir. Cruft Lab. 1940-46, co-dir. Lyman Lab. of Physics

1947-53, dir. Labs. of Engring. Sci. and Applied Physics, 1948-53. Recipient Medal of Honor, Inst. Radio Engrs., 1959. Fellow Am. Acad. Arts and Scis., Am. Phys. Soc., Am. Inst. Radio Engrs. (v.p. 1925); mem. Tau Beta Pi, Sigma Xi. Author textbooks; articles. co-author: Electronic Circuits and Tubes, 1948. Home: Belmont, Mass. Died Mar. 8, 1975.

CHAFFEE, ROBERT EMORY, law printing co. exec.; b. Belmont, Mass., Jan. 9, 1918; s. E. Leon and Marie (Krautz) C.; B.S. in E.E., Northeastern U., 1941; m. Anne Getchell, Dec. 25, 1941; children—Elsa G., Donald M. Test technician Gen. Radio Co., 1937-41; with Raytheon Mfg. Co., 1945-52, project mgr. submarine signal div., Portsmouth, R.I., 1958-66, div. mgr. night operations, 1966-68, programs mgr., 1968-70; pres., treas. Addison C. Getchell & Son, Inc., Boston, 1970-74; asst. to mgr. tube devel. electronics div. Sylvania Elec. Products, Inc., Woburn, Harry Wolff Co., Inc., Newton, Mass., 1958. Chmn., Wellesley Music Council, 1950-53; mem. Wellesley Spl. Police Assn., 1949-74. Trustee, Mass. Women's Hosp. Served to lt. comdr. USNR, 1941-46; comdr. Res. Mem. Toastmasters Internat., I.E.E.E. (sr.), Am. Phys. Soc., Am. Inst. Physics. Conglist. Mason; mem. Order Eastern Star. Home: Wellesley, Mass. Died Oct. 25, 1974.

CHALLIS, JOHN, harpsichord builder; b. South Lyon, Mich., Jan. 9, 1907; s. Charles and Alice D. (Callen) C.; student Eastern Michigan Univ., 1924-26, Arnold Dolmetsch Haslemere, Eng. (Dolmetsch Found. scholarship), 1926-30, U. Mich., 1933; M.Ed. (hon.), Eastern Mich. U., 1953; H.H.D., Wayne State U., 1958. Harpsichord builder, Ypsilanti, Mich., 1930-46, Detroit, 1946-65, N.Y.C., 1966-74; developed nonwearing, split proof tuning pin blocks, complete aluminum frame, moisture resistant jacks, metal bridge and soundboard for keyboard instruments. Mem. Am. Musicol. Soc. Address: New York City, N.Y. Died Sept. 6, 1974; interred South Lyon, Mich.

CHAMBERLAIN, JAMES MORTIMER WILLS, cons.; b. Akron, O., July 19, 1905; s. John and Elizabeth (Wills) C.; B.S., Mass. Inst. Tech., 1927; m. Florence Scott, 1928; 1 dau., Cynthia Scott; m. 2d, Roberta Wunderlich, June 2, 1945; 1 son, Craig. Devel. engr. Goodyear Tire & Rubber Co., 1927-28, Goodyear Zeppelln, 1928-30; gen. mgr. U.S. Stoneware Co., Akron, 1930-36, chmn., pres., 1936-66; chmn. bd. Intervest, Inc.; pres. Chamberlain Investment Corp., Ensine Corp.; v.p. Hamilton Kent Mfg. Co., Flexlock Corp., Republic Lead Equipment Co.; sec. Hamilton Kent, Ltd., Can., Hamilton Kent of Atlanta, Hamilton Kent of Kan., Freeport Rubber, Freeport, Grand Bahama Islands. Mem. Am. Soc. of M.E., Am. Inst. Chm. Engrs., Nat. Soc. Profl. Engrs., Am. Chem. Soc., Am. Ceramic Soc. Clubs: Aviation Executives (Washington); Union League, Nat. Aviation, Wings, Chemist (N.Y.C.); Portage Country (Akron). Congress Lake Country. Home: Akron, Ohio. Died Apr. 17, 1974.

CHAMBERLAIN, RICHARD HALL, physician, educator; b. Jacksonville, Fla., May 25, 1915; s. Emmett Edward Robinson and Lucille (McKowen) Robinson Chamberlain; A.B., Centre Coll., 1934; M.D., U. Louisville, 1939; postgrad. U. Pa., 1940-42; m. Merle Johnson, Aug. 23, 1941. Asst. instr. radiology U. Pa., Phila., 1940-46, instr., 1946-47, asso., 1947-48, asst. prof., 1948-50, asso. prof. 1950-52, prof., 1952-75, chmn. dept. radiology, 1961-75; cons. in radiology USPHS, 1968-73. Mem. nat. adv. council radiation USPHS, 1958-60, chmn. med. x-ray adv. com., 1964-68; chmn. radiology tng. com. Nat. Inst. Gen. Med. Scis., 1966-69; mem. com. on pathologic effect of atomic radiation NRC-Nat. Acad. Sci., 1957-63; sr. adviser Internat. Commn. on Radiol. Units; mem. Nat. Council Radiation Protection; mem. expert adv. panel radiation WHO, 1964-75; U.S. ofcl. del. UN Sci. Com. on Effects Atomic Radiation, 1963-75. Trustee Asso. Univs., Inc., 1963-70. Diplomate Am. Bd. Radiology, Fellow Am. Coll. Radiology (v.p. 1964-65, Gold medal 1969); mem. A.M.A., Radiol. Soc. N.Am. (Gold medal 1971), Am. Radium Soc., Am., Phila. (past pres.) roentgen ray socs. Home: Philadelphia, Pa., Died Dec. 4, 1975.

CHAMBERLAIN, SAMUEL, etcher, author b. Cresco, Ia., Oct. 28, 1895; s. George Ellsworth and Cora Lee (Summers) C.; student U. Wash., 1913-15, Mass. Inst. Tech., 1915-16, 19-20, Royal Coll. Art, London, 1926-27, M. Edward Leon Paris, 1925; M.A. (hon.), Marlboro (Vt.), Coll., 1968; m. Narcissa Gellatly, Apr. 27, 1923; children—Narcisse, Stephanie. Architect, 1919-25; asst. prof. architecture U. Mich., 1925-26; dir. Am. Scene. Represented in Brit. Mus., Bibliotheque Nationale (Paris), Library of Congress, Boston Mus. Fine Arts, Art Inst. Chgo., N.Y. Pub. Library, Boston Pub. Library. Served as ambulance driver with French Army, 1917-19; served to maj. USAAF, World War II. Decorated Legion of Merit, Bronze Star medal (U.S.); chevalier Legion d'Honneur, Croix de Guerre (France); Italian Star of Solidarity; recipeint hon. mention Paris Salon, 1925, bronze medal, 1928; Field Service traveling fellow, 1923; Guggenheim Meml. fellow, 1926; Kat W. Arms prize Soc. of Am. Etchers Exhbn., 1933, John Taylor Arms prize, 1936; ann. award New Eng. Soc. N.Y., 1955; spl. award Nat. Trust for Historic Preservation. Fellow Am. Acad. Arts and Scis.; mem. A.I.A. (hon.), Photog. Soc. Am. (asso.), Nat. Acad. (Academician 1945), Société de la Gravure Originale en Noir (Paris), Phi Delta Theta. Democrat. Episcopalian. Author: Tudor Homes in England, 1929; A Small House in the Sun, 1936; Cape Cod in the Sun, 1937; Open House in New England, 1937; Beyond New England Thresholds, 1937; Longfellow's Wayside Inn, 1938; Historic Salem in Four Seasons, 1938; Historic Boston in Four Season, 1938; Gloucester and Cape Ann, 1938; Lexington and Concord, 1939; Nantucket, 1939; New England Doorways, 1939; Old Marblehead, 1940; Portsmouth, N.H.; A Camera Impression, 1940; France Will Live Again, 1940; Martha's Vineyard, A Camera Impression, 1941; The Coast of Maine, 1941; Fair Is Our Land, 1942; Historic Cambridge in Four Seasons, 1942; Ever New England, 1944; Springtime in Virginia, 1947; Behold Williamsburg, 1947; Six New England Villages, 1948; Fair Harvard, 1948; Princeton in Spring, 1950; The Yale Scene, 1950; Salem Interiors, 1950; Old Sturbridge Village, 1951; (with Henry N. Flynt) Frontier of Freedom, 1952; (with Mark A. deWolfe Howe) Who Lived Here, 1952; Bouquet de France, 1952; Soft Skies of France, 1953; The Berkshires, 1956; Southern Interiors (with Narcissa Chamberlain), 1956; Italian Bouquet, 1958; Bouquet de France; Mystic Seaport, 1960; The Flavor of France (with Narcissa and Narcisse Chamberlain), 1960; The New England Image, 1962; British Bouquet, 1963; Etched in Sunlight, 1968; A Stroll through Historic Salem, 1969; (with wife) The Chamberlain Selection of New England Rooms, 1639-1863, 1972; numerous on Am., European architecture. Editor: This Realm, This England, 1941. Home: Marblehead, Mass. Died Jan. 10, 1975; buried Waterside Cemetery, Marblehead

CHAMBERLIN, RALPH VARY, zoölogist; b. Salt Lake City, Utah, Jan. 3, 1879; s. William Henry and Eliza Frances (Brown) C.; B.S., University of Utah, 1898, Sc.D. (hon.), 1942; student Stanford, 1902, 09; Ph.D., Cornell University, 1905; studied University of Pennsylvania, 1911-13; m. Daisy Ferguson, July 9, 1899; children—Beth Naneve, Ralph Vary, Della, Ruth; m. 2d, Edith Simons, June 28, 1922; children—Richard Eliot, Arey Frances, Helen, Shirley, Edith, Martha Sue. Goldwin Smith fellow in zoölogy, Cornell U., 1902-04; asst. prof. of biology, U. of Utah, 1904-05, prof., 1905-06, prof. zoölogy and dean Med. Sch., 1906-08; prof. zoölogy, Brigham Young U., 1908-11; Harrison research fellow and lecturer in zoölogy, U. of Pa., 1911-13; curator of Myriapoda, Arachnida and Vermes, Museum Comparative Zoölogy, Harvard, 1913-25; prof. zoölogy, and head div. of biology, University of Utah, 1925-48, professor emeritus biology since 1948. Secretary-treasurer Salt Lake Mosquito Abatement Board, 1930-39. Sect. editor on Myriapoda and on Sipunculoidea, Biol. Abstracts, since 1925. Fellow A.A.A.S., Entomol. Soc. America; mem. Am. Soc. Naturalists, Torrey Botanical Club, Soc. Arthrop. de Argentina (corr.), N.Y. Acad. Sciences, Utah Acad. Sciences. Author: The Lycosidae of North America, 1908; The Meaning of Organic Evolution, 1911; Tropical Pacific Annelida, 1919; The Myriapoda of the Australian Region, 1920; Lithobiomorpha of North America, 1925; The Life and Philosophy of W. H. Chamberlin, 1926; The Mollusca of Utah (with D. T. Jones), 1929; The Gnaphosidae of North America; the Agelenidae, 1939; The Genera of Parajulidae, 1940; The Spiders of Georgia (with W. Ivie) 1944; North American Erigonidae, 1949; also numerous tech. articles. Editor U. of Utah Biol. Series. Home: Salt Lake City, Utah.†

CHAMBERS, SHERMAN DANIEL, engr.; b. Sheffield, O., May 9, 1881; s. Thomas William and Mary Agnes (Conley) C.; B.S., Baldwin-Wallace Coll., Berea, O., 1904, M.S., 1911; C. E., Lehigh U., 1918; m. Helen Grace Ware, Aug. 4, 1909; 1 son, David Ware. Instr. in mathematics U. of Me., 1909-12, Lehigh U., 1916-18; asst. prof. Purdue Univ., 1921-25, asso. prof., 1925-36, rpof. engring. mechanics after 1936. Mem. Acacia, Scabbard and Blade. Presbyterian. Mason. Author: Engineering Mechanics, 1934; Analytic Mechanics (with Prof. V. M. Faires), 1943. Home: West LaFayette, Ind.†

CHANDLER, HENRY PORTER, lawyer, judicial adminstr.; b. Indian Orchard, Mass., Mar. 19, 1880; s. John Henry and Abbie White (Smith) C.; student Leland Stanford Jr. U., 1896-98; A.B., Harvard, 1901; J.D., U. Chgo., 1906; m. Helen Firman Mack, Mar. 24, 1907 (dec. Nov. 1930); 1 dau., Margaret Mack (Mrs. Myles F. Gibbons); m. 2d, Olive Hull, Nov. 28, 1931. Instr. English, U. Chgo., 1901-04, sec. to pres., 1904-06; admitted to Ill. bar, 1906; in practice law, 1906-39; mem. law firm Tolman & Chandler, 1931-39; dir. Adminstrative Office U.S. Cts., 1939-56, ret.; cons. territorial cts. Hawaii, 1957; cons. judical adminstrn., ct. systems, 1957-75; 1st ct. adminstr. State of Ill., 1959-60. Mem. permanent commn. on inter-ch. relations Presbyn. Ch. U.S.A., 1938-53. Mem. Am. Law Inst., Am. (chmn. municipal law sect. 1938-39), Ill., Chgo. (pres. 1938-39), Fed. bar assns., Phi Delta Phi. Clubs: Union League (pres. 1932-33), City (pres. 1923-25), Chicago Literary (Chgo.); Cosmos (Washington). Author: Some Major Advances in the Federal Judicial System, 1922-1947, 1963. Contbr. to legal periodicals. Home: Bethesda, Md., Died Dec. 12, 1975; buried Oak Woods Cemetery, Chicago, Ill.

CHANDLER, NORMAN, pub. co. exec.; b. Los Angeles, Sept. 14, 1899; s. Harry and Marian (Otis) C.; A.B., Stanford, 1922; LL.D., Occidental Coll., 1956, U. So. Cal., 1958; m. Dorothy Buffum, Aug. 30, 1922; children—Camilla (Mrs. Chandler Frost), Otis. With Times Mirror Co., 1922-73, chmn. exec. com., dir., from 1973; v.p., dir. Chandis Securities Co., Chandler-Sherman Corp; dir. Sante Fe Industries, Inc., Buffum's Dept. Store, Long Beach, Cal., Security-Pacific Nat. Bank of Los Angeles. Mem. adv. bd. Am. Mut. Fund, Inc. Trustee Cal. Inst. Tech.; Pfaffinger Found.; pres., bd. dirs. Times Mirror Found. Mem. Delta Kappa Epsilon. Republican. Clubs: Bohemian (San Francisco); California (Los Angeles). Home: Los Angeles, Cal. Died Oct. 20, 1973.

CHAPELLE, HOWARD IRVING, marine architect; b. Tolland, Mass., Feb. 1, 1900; s. Irving and Sarah (Hardy) C.; ed. pub. schs., New Haven and Waterbury, Conn.; m. Alice Zayma Connolly, July 16, 1935. Draftsman and designer, 1919-25 and 1926-31 (at sea 1936). Chmn. tech. com. Restoration of the Niagara (Perry's flagship). Cons. (naval architect) FAO of UN to Turkey, 1956-57; curator transp. U.S. Nat. Mus., Smithsonian Instn., Washington, 1957-67, sr. historian Mus. History, Washington, 1957-67, sr. historian Mus. History and Tech., 1967-71, historian emeritus, 1971-75; cons. for constrn. maritime mus., Singapore, 1973. Commd. capt. U.S. Army Transp. Corps, 1943, maj., Aug. 1944, lt. col., Sept. 1946; chief, marine br. Research and Devel. div. Army Transp. Corps, Apr. 1945-46; Guggenheim Fellowship Marine Hist. Research, 1950; established initial research and devel. program for marine transport equipment for U.S. Army. Recipient secretary's exceptional service award, 1970. Mem. Am. Naval Hist. Found. Soc. Naval Archs. and Marine Engrs. Mem. Western hemisphere com. Internat. Fishing Vessel Congress. Author books including: History of American Sailing Navy, 1949; American Small Sailing Craft, 1951; The National Watercraft Collection, 1962; The Bark Canoes and Skin Boats of North America, 1964; Search for Speed Under Sail, 1967; The Constellation Story, 1970; History of the American Fishing Schooners. Home: Cambridge, Md. Died June 30, 1975. cremated.

CHAPIN, JAMES, artist; b. West Orange, N.J., July 9, 1887; s. James A. and Delia S. (Ryder) C.; ed. pub. schs., West Orange; studied art, Cooper Union and Art Students League (N.Y.C.), Royal Acad. Art, Antwerp, Belgium, 1910-12; m. Mary Fischer; 3 sons. Instr. advanced portraiture Pa. Acad. Fine Arts, Phila., 1935-45. Represented in permanent collection Amherst College, museums and many pvt. collections throughout U.S. Awarded portraiture and purchase prize Art Inst. Chgo., 1927. Temple gold medal Pa. Acad. Fine Arts, 1928; Isaac N. Maynard Award, Nat. Acad. Design, 1956. Home: Glen Gardner, N.J. Died July 1975.

CHAPIN, SAMUEL M., lawyer; b. N.Y.C., June 30, 1902; LL.B., Columbia, 1925. Admitted to N.Y. bar, 1926; sr. partner firm Parker, Chapin and Flattau, N.Y.C. Mem. Assn. Bar City N.Y., Am. Bar Assn. Home: San Diego, Cal., Died June 1, 1975.

CHAPIN, SLOCUM, travel agy. exec.; b. Quincy, Mass., May 12, 1913; s. Charles Mathews and Helen Marguerite (Slocum) C.; student Peoples Acad., Morrisville, Vt., 1928-30, Tilton (N.H.) Sch., 1930-32, Dartmouth, 1932-35; m. Elaine Hunt, Oct. 20, 1933; 1 son, John; m. 2d, Joan Igou Aug. 18, 1937; children—David (dec.), Joan, Michele; m. 3d, Jane Daly, Mar. 4, 1961. Guest relations NBC, N.Y.C., 1933-35; pres. Broadcast Builders, Inc., Hanover, N.H., 1935-36; asst. sales promotion mgr. World Broadcasting System, Inc., N.Y.C., 1936-37; salesman Radio Sta. WOC, Davenport, 1937-41; sales mgr. Radio Sta. WKBN, Youngstown, O., 1941; gen. mgr. Radio Sta. WSTC, Stamford, Conn., 1941-42; with Am. Broadcasting Co. (then Blue Network, Inc.), 1942-66, Eastern sales mgr. for TV, 1948-51, v.p. charge ABC owned TV Stas. 1951, v.p. charge sales TV Network, 1954, v.p. charge sales Western div., 1958-64, v.p. exec. relations, 1964-66; pres. Adventures Unlimited, agts. for travel at Abercrombie & Fitch, N.Y.C., from 1966. Mem. Camp Fire Club Am., St. Hubert's Soc., Broadcast Pioneers, Psi Upsilon. Clubs: Explorers; African Safari. Home: New York City, N.Y., Died Nov. 15, 1975.

CHAPLIN, F(RANCIS) STUART, sociologist; b. Brooklyn, N.Y., Feb. 3, 1888; s. Charles Brookes and Florence Adelaide (Johnson) C.; U. of Rochester, N.Y., 1905-08; B.S., Columbia, 1909, A.M., 1910, Ph.D., 1911; univ. fellow in sociology, 1910-11; m. Nellie Estelle Peck, Sept. 7, 1911 (died Nov. 29, 1925); children—Edward Barton, Francis Stuart, Florence Estelle; m. 2d, Eula Elizabeth Pickard, Feb. 19, 1927. Mem. faculties Wellesley Coll., Smith Coll., Univ. Minn., 1911-53; mem. editorial staffs various publs., 1923-74; editor Harper's Social Science Series 1926-63; mem. adv. board Sociological Abstracts of N.Y., 1957-64. Cons. to Community Assos., 1953-74; North Carolina Board - of Higher Edn., 1963-74; mem. com. hygiene of housing, Am. Pub. Health Assn., 1936-57; chmn. bd. commrs. Asheville Housing Authority, 1962-64. Recipient Alumni Medal, Columbia U., 1940. Pres. Consumer Bahavior, Inc., 1952-62. Chmn. seminar on exptl. methods 4th World Congress Sociology, Stersa, Italy, 1959. Fellow Am. Statis. Assn., A.A.A.S. (v.p.

sect. K 1943), Am. Sociol. Soc. (pres. 1935), Royal Soc. Health (London), Sociol. Research Assn. (pres. 1936); mem. Acad. Certified Social Workers, Am. Assn. U. Profs. (chpt. pres. 1942-43), Nat. Assn. Social Workers (chpt. pres. 1932-33), American Council of Learned Societies (delegate 1939-42), Social Science Research Council. Clubs: Automobile, Campus, Asheville Civitan, Mountain City of Asheville (N.C.). Author books including: Experimental Designs in Sociological Research, 1947, rev. edit., 1955. Editor-in-chief Social Sci. Abstracts, 1928-32. Home: Asheville, N.C. Died July 7, 1974; buried Lewis Meml. Cemetery, Asheville.

CHAPMAN, ALFRED FRANCIS, polit. worker, gen. traffic exec.; b. Milw., Mar. 19, 1900; s. John Stephen and Mary Ann (Meyerhaultz) C.; grad. U. Wis., 1921; m. Lucille E. Palmer, Jan. 26, 1920; 1 dau., Margaret. Efficiency traffic dir. Chgo.-Alton R.R., 1922-28; with Gen. Electric Co., 1928-32; traffic mgr. Louis Marx & Co. of W.Va., 1934-74. Charter mem. Ohio Valley Traffic Club, Wheeling, W.Va.; mem. state adv. council, vice chmn. state council Small Bus. Adminstrn, W.Va., 1962-74, mem. regional adv. bd., Richmond. Mem. Indsl. salvage commn., storage and warehouse facility coms. War Dept., 1942-45. Mem. W.Va. Human Relations Commn., 1942-45. Active Dem. party, Milwaukee County vice chmn., 1924-26, mem. W.Va. state com., 1940-56, sec. W.Va. del. 1960, Dem. del. nat. convs., 1940, 44, 48, 52, 56, 64, Dem. nat. del. at large, 1968-74, state leader, 1938-74, vice chmn., 1972; mem. Ohio Co. Dem. Exec. Com., 1964-74; Presdl. elector for W.Va., 1964. Recipient citation Hon. Citizen Tenn., 1957; hon. citizen City of Goldsboro (N.C.), 1970, hon. citizen Tex., 1971; col. Gov.'s Staff, W.Va., 1957; Ky. Col., 1960; hon. lt. col., a.d.c. Gov. Ala., 1970; lt. col. on staff gov. Ga., 1972, also ambassador of goodwill. Mem. Foresters Am. (hon. life) Civilian Internat. (life), Warwood Vets. Assn. (hon. life), Ohio Valley Bd. Trade, Am. Acad. Polit. and Social Sci. Methodist. K.P., Eagle, Elk, Moose. Clubs: Traffic (Pitts.); Kain (hon. life); The President's (Washington). Home: Wheeling, W.Va. Died Mar. 12, 1974; buried Halcyon Hills Memorial Park, Wheeling, W. Va.

CHAPMAN, EDNA MAE COLEMAN (MRS. BRUCE CHAPMAN), broadcasting co. exec.; b. Marlow, Okla.; d. Richard Harrison and Isabelle Frances (Holt) Coleman; student Columbia, 1920-23, Drew U., 1923; m. Bruce Chapman, June 10, 1931; 1 son, William Brewster, Sec., YWCA, 1920-22; social worker Bd. Meth. Missions, 1922-23; asst. analyst market research J. Walter Thompson Co., 1923-25; analyst food research and copy Batten, Barton, Durstine & Osborn, 1925-27; radio editor Forecast Mag., 1927-29; editor Nat. Homemakers Mag., 1929-31; v.p. Bruce Chapman Co., Grafton, Vt., from 1931. Pres., Edna Coleman Candies, 1924-25; author syndicated newspaper column Here's Howe, from 1945; feature writer N.Y. Herald Tribune, McCalls Mag., others, from 1929. Dir. aux. Rockingham Meml. Hosp., Bellow Falls, Vt., from 1967. Contbr. articles to profl. jours. Office: Grafton, Vt. Died July 26, 1972; interred Grafton, Vt.

CHAPMAN, IONE MINERVIA, librarian; b. Parke County, Ind. Apr. 20, 1900; d. Alfred William and Josa (Rutter) Chapman; A.B., U. Ill., 1925, M.S. in L.S., 1944; M.A., Columbia Tchrs. Coll., 1928. Tchr. rural and high schs., Ind., Ill., Ky., 1918-34; dean women Adrian (Mich.) Coll., 1934-40; head residence Russell Sage Coll., 1940-41; librarian Adrian Coll., 1941-42, Western State Coll., Gunnison, Colo., 1944-46, Morehead (Ky.) State U., 1946-70, dir., until 1970. Mem. Ky. Gov.'s Planning Com. Libraries, 1967-68. Trustee, treas. Rowan County Pub. Library, from 1953. Mem. Am., Southeastern, Ky. (pres. 1960-61), library assns., Am. Assn. U. Women, Beta Phi Mu. Club: Morehead Womens. Home: Morehead, Ky. Died May 18, 1974.

CHAPMAN, JOHN STANTON HIGHAM (PEN NAME MARISTAN CHAPMAN), author; b. London, Eng., May 21, 1891; s. Joseph John and Alice Mary (Williams) C.; ed. privately; m. Mary Hamilton Ilsley, Feb. 26, 1917. Came to U.S., 1917, naturalized, 1926. Aero. engr. Graham-White Aviation Co., Hendon, Eng., 1910; with Aircraft Mfg. Co., Hendon, to 1914; with Dayton Wright Airplane Co., 1914-18; writer of fiction, 1928-72. In Air Service, Brit. Army Res., 1914-17; transferred to U.S. Signal Corps, 1917. Mem. Am. Radio Relay League, P.E.N. Episcopalian. Author (with wife, under pen names including Dent Ilsley, Jane Selkirk, Kirk Connell); Happy Mountain, 1928; Homeplace, 1929; Imperial Brother, 1931; Weather Tree, 1932; Wild Cat Ridge, 1932; Timber Trail, 1933; Glen Hazard, 1933; Eagle Cliff, 1934; Marsh Island Mystery 1936; Rogues on Red Hill, 1937; Girls of Glen Hazard, 1937; Clue of the Faded Dress, 1938; Mystery of the Broken Key, 1938; Flood in Glen Hazard, 1939; Mystery of the Missing Car, 1939; Mystery Dogs of Glen Hazard, 1940; Glen Hazard Cowboys, 1940; Gulf Coast Treasure, 1941; Mountain Mystery, 1941; Mystery on the Mississippi, 1942; Trail Beyond the Rockies, 1942; Blue Smoke Mystery, 1943; Secret of Wild Cat Cave, Treasure Hunters, Mystery of the Jasper Jewel Case, Mystery of the Hectic Holidays, Clue of the Cipher Key, 1944, Green Garnet Mystery, 1945; Mystery of Horseshoe Caves, 1947; Trilogy of Historical Novels About Tennessee, 1948-50; Mystery of Burro Bray Canyon, 1957; Trail of the Cheery Cows, 1958; Laird of Chipping Rock, A Biography, 1957; Doubloons, 1959; The Helpful Treasure, 1959; Devorguilla; A 13th Century Chronicle. Contbr. short stories to mags. Address: Solvang, Cal. Died Oct. 13, 1972.

CHAPMAN, KENNETH MILTON, artist, writer; b. Liogonier, Ind., July 13, 1875; s. John Milton and Mary Cordelia (White) C.; ed. Art. Inst. Chicago, Art Students League, N.Y.C.; hon. Litt. D., U. Ariz., 1951; hon. L.H.D., U. N.M., 1952; Doctor of Fine Arts, Art Inst. Chgo,, 1953; m. Katherine A. Muller, Sept. 30, 1915, (died 1944); children—Frank Springer, Helen Hope (Mrs. Robert K. Potter, Jr.). Mag. illustrator, 1894-99; instr. in art, N.M. Normal University, Las Vegas, 1899-1903; also engaged, 1899-1925, in illustration of works on paleontology. Identified with Sch. of Am. Research and Museum of N.M., 1909-29; exec. sec. Lab. or Anthropology, 1929-35, acting dir., 1936, dir., 1937, dir. Indian art since 1938; instructor in Indian art, U. of New Mexico, 1926-42, prof., 1942-45, emeritus since 1945; special consultant in Indian arts and crafts, U.S. Indian Service after 1932. Author: Pubelo Indian Pottery, Vol. 1, 1933, Vol. 11, 1936; the Pottery of Santo Domingo Pueblo, 1936; Contbr. to art mags. Research on abstract designs of world-wide origin. Home: Santa Fe, N.M.†

CHAPPELL, WILL CHARLES, clergyman; b. Cambrida, Mich., Mar. 6, 1878; s. Judson D. and Julia M. (Henry) C.; B.A., Hillsdale Coll., 1902; post-grad. work, same coll., D.D., 1922; B.D., Union Theol. Sem., 1907; m. Ethel Gurney, 1906 (died 1923); children—Will Judson, Mary Ethel (Mrs. Earl Stephen), Esther Julia; m. 2d, Adda Huntsinger, 1924. Ordained ministry Bapt. Ch., 1907; pastor Danville, N.H., 1907-l0, Buffalo, N.Y., 1910-19; became exec. sec. Pittsburgh Bapt. Assn., 1919; pastor Community Ch., North Danville, N.H., 1932; now pastor First Bapt. Ch., Danville, N.H. Mem. bd. dirs. Rankin Christian Center Welfare Fund of Pittsburgh, Federation of Social Agencies, Pittsburgh Council of Chs., Phi Delta Theta. Moderator Buffalo Bapt. Assn.; mem. exec. com. Pa Bapt. Conv., Bapt. Bd. of Missionary Cooperation. Republican. Mason. Co-Author: Teacher's Manual for Christian Americanization, 1919; Baptist City Planning, 1920. Home: Danville, N.H.†

CHARLESWORTH, JAMES CLYDE, educator; b. nr. Greensburg, Pa., May 21, 1900; s. James and Priscilla (Hawkins) C.; student Carnegie Inst. Tech., 1919-23; A.B., U. Pitts., 1926, A.M., 1927, Ph.D., 1932; postgrad. Harvard, 1928; m. Dorothy Lucille Coy, Aug. 14, 1928 (dec. Sept. 1945); children—Audrey Elaine (dec. 1971), Sylvia Jean; m. 2d, Berenice Louise Steward, July 6, 1946 (dec. Dec. 1969); children—Pamela Steward, Rodney James. Asst. chief engr. Miller Machine Co. Pitts., 1922-24; mem. faculty U. Pitts., 1926-39; faculty U. Pa., 1939, prof. polit. sci., 1945-70, dir. grad. div. Wharton Sch., 1942-43, supr. ednl. program Inst. Local and State Govt., 1939-55. Sec. adminstrn. Commonwealth Pa., 1955-56; exec. dir. Pa. Reorgn. Commn., 1956: comdg. officer Strategic Intelligence Unit, U. Pa., 1946-47; dir. personnel and tng. Phila Regional Civilian Def. Council, 1942. Served from maj. to lt. col. AUS, 1943-46. Decorated Legion of Merit. Mem. Am., Western, So. polit. sci. assns., Am. Soc. for Pub. Adminstrn. (pres. Phila. region 1947-49), Am. Acad. Polit. and Social Sci. (asso. editor Annals 1949-53, acting editor 1950-51, pres. 1953-70), Nat. Parks Assn. (dir.), United World Fedn., Phi Beta Kappa. Author: Governmental Administration, 1951; Governmental Reorganization of the Commonwealth of Pennsylvania, 1957. Editor: American Civilization and Its Leadership Needs, 1959; Behavioralism in Political Science, 1962; Mathematics and the Social Sciences, 1963; Leisure in America, Blessing or Curse? 1964; Ethics in America; Norms and Deviations, 1966; A Design for Political Science, 1966; Contemporary Political Analysis, 1966; The Changing American People: Are We Deteriorating or Improving?, 1968; The Theory and Practice of Public Administration, 1968; Harmonizing Technological Development and Social Policy in America, 1970; America's Most Challenging Objectives, 1971; Integration of the Social Sciences through Policy Analysis, 1972. Contbr. articles to profl. jours. Home: Kirkwood, Pa. Died Jan. 21, 1974.

CHASE, BURR LINDEN, textbook publisher; born Niagara Falls, N.Y., June 11, 1891; s. Adin Burr and Louise F. (Lindenbolt) C.; A.B., Harvard, 1913; m. Helen Josephine Whitney, Oct. 25, 1917; children—Burr Linden, Whitney. Partner Niagara Printing Co., Niagara Falls, N.Y. 1908-13, pres. of co., 1913-16; with Stanhope Press, Boston, 1916-18; asst. prodn. manager for the Silver Burdett Company, Morristown, New Jersey, 1920-24, then production mgr., 1924-42, asst. sec., 1924-28, mem. bd. dirs. 1926-62, sec., 1928-41, v.p., 1941-42, pres., 1942-60, chairman, 1960-62; dir. Franklin Publications, Inc., Madison (N.J.) Nat. Bank. Member book pub. and mfg. industry adv. com., W.P.B., 1942-46; mem. pubs. com. apptd. by State Dept. and Office of Coordinator for Inter-Am. Affairs to survey possibilities of more extensive interchange of culture and information through books, 1943. Trustee of the Morristown Memorial Hospital, Morris Junior Museum. Borough councilman, Madison, New Jersey, 1961-65. Served ensign USNR, 1918-20, lieut. (j.g.), 1920-23. Mem. C. of C. (dir.), Am. Textbook Pubs. Inst. (dir. 1942-48, treas. 1942-46, pres. 1946-48), Soc. Advancement of Edn., Am. Inst. Graphic Arts. Clubs: Harvard, Players (N.Y. City); Madison (N.J.) Golf; Baltusrol Golf. Home: Madison, N.J. Died May 3, 1974; buried Restland Meml. Park, East Hanover, N.J.

CHASE, FREDERICK AUGUSTUS, editor; b. Rahway, N.J., Oct. 1, 1908; s. Edward S. and Ann (Adams) C.; student N.Y. U., 1940-41; m. Lydia Anna Paul, Dec. 23, 1944; children—Paul, Dudley, Martha, Janet, Katharine. With Financial World, N.Y.C., 1945-74, statis. editor, 1968-74. Contbr. articles to Christian Sci. Monitor, Univ. Quar., Sewanee Rev., others. Home: Cranford, N.J. Died Dec. 16, 1974; interred Rahway, N.J.

CHASE, JULIAN, editor, publisher; b. London, Eng., June 21, 1878; s. Julian Augustine and Martha Jenks (Wheaton) C. (parents Am. citizens); Ph.B., Brown Univ., 1899; m. Beulah Dimmick, June 14, 1934; children-by previous marriage, Julian, Jr., Robert Ramsay. Entered automobile business, 1899, participated in numerous automobile endurance contests and races, 1902-04; mng. editor The Horseless Age, automobile mag., 1904, editor Motor and Motor Boating, 1905-15, v.p., editor The Horseless Age, 1915-18; organizer tng. centers for transport drivers, com. on edn. and spl. training, Gen. Staff, War Dept., World War I, 1918; directing editor, Automotive Industries, Motor Age, Motor World, Commercial Car Jour., Automobile Trade Jour., and allied publications, 1919-49; member standardization com. on Motor Vehicle Laws, Dept. of Commerce under Sec. Hoover, 1924-27; patented major improvements in Chase hosp. manikin used in civilian, Army and Navy nurses training schs., 1943; consultant Bd. of Econ. Warfare, World War II, 1942-44; mem. bd. of dirs. Chilton Co., 1934-49, vice pres., 1945-49; pres. M. J. Chase Co. Received commendation of Sec. of War for work done for com. on education and special training, World War I, 1919; citation by Automobile Old Timers for contributions to development of automobile, 1940. Mem. Soc. of Automotive Engrs., Brown Engrng. Assn., Nat. Aeronautic Assn., Nat. Conf. of Business Paper Editors (past pres.), Automobile Old Timers (past mem. bd. of dirs.), Antique Automobile Club. Theta Delta Chi. Author: The Gasoline Engine, Motor Car Operation, The Care of the Car. Special dept. editor: Funk & Wagnall New Standard Dictionary, 1913. Contbr. numerous articles and editorials to technical magazines. Home: Woodbury, Conn. Died Feb. 14, 1974; interred Swan Point Cemetery, Providence, R.I.

CHASE, KELSEY STILLMAN, banker; b. Crookston, Minn., Apr. 15, 1878; s. Kelsey David and Isabel E. (Gardner) C.; student Pa. Mil. Coll., 1895-6, Phillips Acad., Andover, Mass., 189607, U. of Minn., 1897-1903, LL.B., 1903; m. Ruth Law Cole, of Minneapolis, Minn., June 22, 1904. Cashier Chase State Bank, Faribault, Minn., 11, pres. Peoples Bank of St. Paul, 1914-20; elected treas. Rumsey Co., Minn., Feb. 1920. Served in 2d Regiment, Minn. N.G., as pvt., sergt., 2d. lt. and capt., 1899-1903; commd. maj. 6th Regt. Minn. N.G., 1918, resigned Apr. 7, 1919. Mem. Rep. State Central Com., Minn., 1908; supt. banks State of Minn., 1911-14; mem. Am. Bankers Assn., Minn. State Bankers Assn. Conglist. Mason (32°, Shriner), Elk. Clubs: Minnesota, St. Paul Athletic, Automobile, Town and Country. Home: St. Paul, Minn.†

CHEATUM, ELMER PHILIP, biologist, educator; b. Langdon, Kan., July 19, 1901; s. Jasper W. and Grace (Wright) C.; A.B., Southwestern Coll., 1924; M.S., Kan. State U., 1925; Ph.D., U. Mich., 1933; m. Edith Deck, Aug. 8, 1925; children—Don, Dan. Asst. prof. So. Meth. U., Dallas, 1925-31, asso. prof. biology, 1933-41, prof. biology, 1941-67, chmn. biology dept., 1955-64; instr. zoology U. Mich., 1931-33. Mem. Tex. Acad. Sci. (pres. 1941-42), Phi Kappa Phi, Sigma Xi. Author: Common Pests of Garden, Yard, Home and Their Control, 1973; (with R.W. Fullington) The Aquatic and Land Mollusca of Texas, 3 parts. Contbr. articles in aquatic biology, ecology of gastropods, and Pleistocene paleoecology to profl. jours. Home: Dallas, Tex. Died May 1, 1973; interred Restland of Dallas.

CHEEK, ROBERT STANLEY, business exec.; b. Burkesbille, Ky., Jan. 14, 1878; s. Joel Owsley and Minnie (Ritchey) C.; grad., Class of 1900, Vanderbilt U.; m. Helen Pickslay, Apr. 25, 1908; children—Pickslay, Helen, Owsley, Florence. Entered coffee business with father, Nashville, 1900, advancing through positions of responsibility to vice pres., also mgr. hdqrs. plant; business was sold to Postum Co., now Gen. Foods Corp., 1928; bd. dirs., 1929-50; dir. Nat. Life & Accident Ins. Co.; dir., mem. exec. com. Nashville Trust Co.; chmn. bd. dirs. Cumberland Motor Co. Trustee Vandervilt Univ., Joint University Library; mem. adv. com. Old Woman's Home, Junior League Home for Crippled Children. Dir. Y.M.C.A., Salvation Army, Nashville Mus. of Art, Nashville Automobile Club. Episcopalian. Mason (32°). Home: Nashville, Tenn.†

CHEESMAN, WILLIAM JAMES, mfg. co. exec.; b. Barrie, Ont., Can., July 26, 1921; s. James Walter and Fern (Hutton) C.; B.A. Sc., U. Toronto, 1943; m. Suzanne Grasett, Dec. 1, 1945; children—Judith (Mrs. Gary Bray), Pamela, James, Margaret. Lab. engr.

Canadian Gen. Electric Co., 1946-47; research engr. Ont. Hydro Commn., 1947-51; gen. mgr. Westinghouse Can. Ltd., 1951-61, pres., 1967-74, also dir.; gen. mgr. ITT, Can., 1961-64, RCA Victor, 1964-65. Bd. govs., mem. senate McMaster U.; bd. dirs. Hamilton United Appeal. Served with Royal Canadian Navy, 1943-45. Mem. Canadian Nuclear Assn. (v.p., bd. dirs.). Clubs: Hamilton, Hamilton Officers. Home: Burlington, Ont., Can. Died Aug. 28, 1974.

CHENERY, WILLIAM LUDLOW, publisher; b. Caroline County, Va., June 26, 1884; s. James Hollis and Ida Burnley (Taylor) C.; A.B., Randolph-Macon Coll., 1907, LL.D., 1953; fellow sociology, U. Chgo., 1908-09; research fellow Chgo. Sch. Civics, 1909; m. Dai Consuelo Smith, Apr. 30, 1913 (died 1927); children—Elsa Madeira (dec.), Peter Jaspersen, Burnley, Janet; m. 2d, Margaret Elizabeth Miller, May 23, 1928. Reporter and spl. writer Chicago Evening Post, 1910-14; in charge editorial page Rocky Mountain News, 1914, column conductor and editorial writer, Chicago Herald, 1914-18; asso. editor The Survey since 1919; asso. editor New York Globe, 1921-23; editorial writer New York Herald, 1923; mng. editor Telegram-Mail, 1924; editor Collier's Weekly, 1925-43, publisher, 1943-50. In charge of labor publicity for U.S. Committee on Public Information, 1918, and representative at Paris, France, 1918-19; pres., Pelham New York board of education, 1937. Member Phi Delta Theta, Phi Beta Kappa. Independent. Episcopalian. Clubs: Century, University, Dutch Treat (N.Y.C.); Chgo. Literary; Bohemian (San Francisco). Author: Industry and Human Welfare, 1922; So It Seemed, 1952; Freedom of the Press, 1955. Editor: Ideals of America, 1919; Standards of Child Welfare, 1919. Home: Big Sur, Cal. Died Aug. 18, 1974.

CHENEY, FRANK D., mfg. exec.; b. South Manchester, Conn., Oct. 16, 1878; s. Frank Woodbridge and Mary (Bushnell) C.; grad. Hotchkiss Sch., 1896; A.B., Yale, 1900; m. Sara Otis Amory, June 1, 1904; children—F. Dester, Jr., Rosalie (Mrs. Fiske), Amory (Mrs. Marshall), Hope (Mrs. Talcott, dec.), Edward Amory. With Cheney Bros., Manchester, since 1900, now chmn. bd.; dir. and treas. Textile Found. Trustee The Hotchkiss Sch., Deerfield Acad. Mem. Conn. State Council of Defense, World War 1. Home: Manchester, Conn.†

CHERINGTON, PAUL WHITON, educator, railroad exec.; b. Cambridge, Mass., June 16, 1918; s. Paul Terry and Marie Louise (Richards) C.; grad. Phillips Exeter Acad., 1936; B.S., Harvard, 1940, D.B.A., 1956; grad. student Columbia, 1940-41; m. Rita Mary Van Dusen, Jan. 20, 1945 (div.); children—Charlotte Lund, Alexander Whiton, Paul Van Dusen; m. 2d, Dorothea B. Edwards, Aug. 26, 1971; 1 child, Aun ten Cate. With Pan Am. Airways Africa, Ltd., Brit. West Africa, 1942; econ. analyst, surplus property sub-com. U.S. Senate Mil. Affairs Com., 1946; liaison officer Civil Aero. Bd., Washington, 1947-48, exec. asst. to chmn., 1948-50; asst. prof. Harvard Bus. Sch., 1950-53, asso. prof., 1953-58, prof., 1958-63, James J. Hill prof. transp., 1963-74; asst. sec. policy and internat. affairs Dept. Transp., 1969-70; dir. research Aero. Research Found., 1956-58; dir., cons. United Research, Inc., Cambridge, Mass., 1958-67; cons. Harbridge House, Inc., Boston, 1966-69; pres. Transp. Research Found., 1965-67; chmn. bd. Temple, Barker & Sloane Inc., 1970; trustee B. & M.R.R., 1970-71; pres., chief exec. B & M R.R., 1973-74. Mem. Mass. Bd. Econ. Advisers, 1965-67. Served from 2d lt. to maj., USAAF, 1943-45. Mem. Am. Econ. Assn., Am. Statis. Assn., Signet Soc. Author: Airline Price Policy, 1958; (with Ralph Gillen) The Business Representative in Washington, 1962; (with Lewis Schneider) Transportation and Logistics Education, 1967. Clubs: Cosmos, Nat. Aviation (Washington); Harvard (Boston) (N.Y.C.). Home: Boston, Mass. Died Aug. 11, 1974.

CHERNICK, JACK, physicist; b. Newark, Nov. 27, 1911; s. Isadore and Sarah (Tessler) C.; student Rutgers U., 1929-32; B.S. in Math., U. Chgo., 1938; M.S. in Math., Bklyn. Coll., 1941; m. Norma Leonia Weiner, Feb. 19, 1939; children—Irene Alice, Michael Ross, Julian August. Mathematician, Ballistics Research Lab., Aberdeen Proving Ground, Md., 1941-47; physicist Brookhaven Nat. Lab., Upton, L.I., N.Y., from 1947, sr. physicist. Mem. adv. com. for reactor physics U.S. AEC, 1951. Fellow Am. Nuclear Soc. (Spl. award 1966). Editorial com. Nuclear Sci. and Engring. Jour., 1955-71. Research and publs. on theory of reactor Kinetics and resonance absorption of neurtrons in reactors; invented high flux beam reactor. Home: East Patchogue, N.Y. Died Apr. 8, 1971.

CHERRINGTON, VIRGIL ARTHUR, univ. prof., bacteriologist; b. Des Moines, Ia., Jan. 24, 1905; s. Charles and Helen (Miller) C.; B.S., Ia. State Coll., 1928, Ph.D., 1941; Ph.D., 1941; M.S., U. of Ida. 1930; m. Maurine Merwin, Dec. 24, 1928. Successively instr., asst. prof., asso. prof., U. of Ida., 1929-42, prof. and head dept. of bacteriology, 1946-70. Served as 1st lt., capt., and maj., Sanitary Corps, U.S. Army, 1942-46. Mem. Am. Acad. Microbiology, Am. Soc. for Microbiology, Idaho Public Health Assn., Ida. Acad. Sci., Am. Pub. Health Assn., Sigma Xi, Phi Sigma, Alpha Epsilon Delta. Methodist. Home: Moscow, Ida. Died Dec. 29, 1973.

CHERRY, HOWARD H., processing machinery co. exec.; b. Cedar Rapids, Ia., Feb. 24, 1880; s. John and Mary A. (Miles) C.; grad. Cedar Rapids High Sch., 1898; m. Neva W. Verbeck, April 15, 1902; children—John G., Howard H. With Cherry-Burrel Corp. and its predecessor J. G. Cherry Co., after 1898, chairman of board. Republican. Presbyterian. Clubs: Union League (Chgo); Cedar Rapids Country, Elks. Home: Cedar Rapids, Ia.†

CHERRY, LLOYD BENJAMIN, univ. dean; b. Weatherford, Tex., Mar. 1, 1915; s. Benjamin Franklin and Posie Ann (Heifrin) C.; B.A., U. Tex., 1936, M.A., 1937; B.S., Okla. State U., 1951, E.E., 1951; m. Kathryn Ruth Parrott, Nov. 24, 1938; children—Margaret Ann (Mrs. Osborne P. Wiggins, Jr.), Franklin Robinson. Head dept. math. Edinburg Coll., 1941-42; research engr. Brown Instrument Co., 1942-45; asso. prof. physics Hardin-Simmons U., 1945-46; head physics dept. Lamar U., Beaumont, Tex., 1946-51, head elec. engring., 1951-67, dir. research, 1961-67, dean Coll. Engring., 1967-74. Chmn., Jefferson County Welfare Bd., 1963. Recipient award for teaching excellence Piper Found., 1967; named Engr. of Year, Tex. Soc. Profl. Engrs., 1972. Fellow I.E.E.E. (regional dir. 1972-73); mem. Am. Soc. Engring. Edn. (award Western Electric 1964, pres. Houston chpt. 1972-73), Eta Kappa Nu (nat. pres. 1971-72). Methodist (mem. higher edn. com. 1969-74). Rotarian. Patentee in field. Home: Beaumont, Tex. Died Aug. 11, 1974.

CHESEN, DORIS SCHIMMEL, couture buyer; b. Lincoln, Neb., Mar. 10, 1932; d. A. Q. and Marion (Fantle) Schimmel; student Goucher Coll., 1949-51; m. Irwin Somberg Chesen, Dec. 12, 1951; children—Catherine Sue, William Schimmel, Carrie Lynn. With Hovland-Swanson, women's specialty store, Lincoln, 1964-75, couture buyer, 1969-75; profl. organist, 1959-64. Mem. Neb. Arts Council 1968-71; pres. Symphony, 1969-71. Bd. dirs. local Girl Scouts, Child Guidance, Rotary Ann, P.T.A., S. St. Temple Sisterhood, Lincoln Gen. Hosp. Guild. Clubs: Hillcrest Country, Lincoln University, Neb. Home: Lincoln, Neb. Died Jan. 19, 1975.

CHESTER, EDMUND A(LBERT), SR., citrus fruit grower, writer; b. Louisville, June 22, 1897; s. John Fidelis and Margaret (Hennessy) C.; ed. pub. schs. Louisville; m. Enna Rogers Moreno, Sept. 17, 1940; children—Patricia, Cynthia, Edmund A., Carolyn. Asst. auditor Internat. Shipbldg. Co., Pascagoula, Mississippi, 1920; accountant for the Chickashaw Shipbldg. Co., Mobile, Ala., 1921-22; city editor Mobile Register, 1923; exec. sec., nat. comdr. Am. Legion, 1923; exec. sec., McAdoo for President Campaign, 1924; nat. field sec., Am. Legion, 1925; exec. sec. C. of C., Palatka, Fla., 1926-28; reporter Courier-Jour., Louisville, 1929; editor Asso. Press Louisville Bur., 1930-31, Latin-Am. editor, N.Y. City, 1931-32, bur. chief, Havana, Cuba, 1933-35, chief Latin-Am. dept., 1936-40; dir. short wave broadcasting and Latin-Am. relations C.B.S., N.Y. City, 1940-48, dir. C.B.S.-TV News Spl. Events, 1949, dir. C.B.S. News (radio and TV), 1949-51; director of news and public affairs C.B.S. radio network, 1951-52; adviser to Cuban Govt., 1952-59; citrus fruit grower, Mount Dora, Florida, 1959-73; writer. Mem. War Communications Bd., 1943-44. Served as 1st sgt., 63d F.A., U.S. Army, A.E.F., 1916-19. Decorated Order of Merit Carlos Manuel de Cespedes (Cuba); Order of Merit Cristobal Colon (Dominican Republic); Order of Merit (Chile); Cuban Mil. Order of Fourth of Sept.; Medal of Merit (Havana); Order Carlos J. Finlay (Cuba). Mem. Sociedad Colombista Pan American, Am. Legion, Americas Found., Sigma Delta Chi. Roman Catholic. Club: American Club of Cuba. Author: A Sergeant Named Batista. Home: Mount Dora, Fla. Died Oct. 14, 1973.

CHIANG KAI-SHEK (CHIANG CHUNG-CHENG), pres. Republic of China; b. Fenghua, Chekiang Province, Oct. 31, 1887; s. Chiang Suan; ed. Nat. Mil. Acad., Paoting, N. China, and Tokyo Mil. Acad. Coll., Japan; m. Soong May-ling, 1927; 2 sons by previous marriage. Met Dr. Sun Yat-sen (founder Chinese Republic) in Japan, 1906; mem. revolutionary party, 1907-11; joined revolutionary army and displayed mil. ability at capture of Shanghai, 1911; attached to Gen. Hdqrs., Canton, 1917-20; studied mil. and social system in Soviet Russia, 1923; founder and prin. Whampoa Mil. Acad., Canton, 1924; became mem. Central Exec. Com. of Kuomintang chmn. of mil. affairs commn., 1926; comdr. in chief Northward Expeditionary Forces, 1926; chmn. State Council and Generalissimo of all Chinese fighting forces, 1928; resigned all govt. offices in interest of conciliation of groups at Canton and Shanghai, 1931; pres. of Exec. Yun, 1935-38; chmn. Nat. Mil. Affairs Council, 1932-46; chmn. People's Polit. Council, 1939-40; dir.-gen. of Kuomintang Party, Republic of China, 1938, reelected, 1969; elected pres. of China, 1948, 54, 60, 66,72. Supreme comdr. Allied Forces in China Theater, World War II. Author: China's Destiny, 1943; Soviet Russia in China, 1956. Address: Taipel Taiwan Republic of China. Died 1975; interred Tzu Hu, Taiwan.

CHILCOTE, SANFORD MARSHALL, lawyer; b. Nanty-Glo, Pa., May 3, 1905; s. Philip John and Annie (Peters) C.; A.B., Allegheny Coll., 1928; LL.B., U. Pitts., 1931; m. Mildred Vaughn Gilmore, Sept. 2, 1933; 1 son Sanford Marshall. Admitted to Pa. bar, 1934, since practiced in Pitts.; sr. partner firm Dickie, McCamey & Chilcote, 1944-74. Adv. dir. Pitts. Nat. Bank. Mem. Civil Service Commn., Oakmont, Pa., 1940-44. Bd. dirs. George Washington Masonic Nat. Meml., Washington, 1962-74. Fellow Am. Coll. Trial Lawyers, Internat. Acad. Trial Lawyers; mem. Internat. Assn. Ins. Counsel, Fedn. Ins. Counsel, Am. Pa., Allegheny bar assns., Delta Tau Delta, Delta Theta Phi. Methodist. Mason (33). Clubs: Duquesne, Pittsburgh Athletic Assn., (Pitts.); Oakmont Country; Seaview Country (Absecom, N.J.); Country of Florida, Village of Golf (Delray Beach, Fla.). Home: Oakmont, Pa., Died Jan. 11, 1974.

CHILD, ELIAS EARLE, investments; b. Pickens, S.C., May 24, 1880; s. Rufus Alexander, D.D., and Essie (Holcombe) C.; ed. high sch.; m. Nola Klugh, Nov. 2, 1903; children—William Klugh, Earle Holcombe. Commerical banking 1900-12; cotton mfg., 1913-23; financing and investments, after 1924; pres., treasurer Prudence Co., Child & Co.; pres. Aiken 1st Fed. Savs. & Loan Assn., after 1951; dir. Hotel Wade Hampton (Columbia, S.C.), Sequoyah Apartments (Knoxville, Tenn.), Heathwood Courts Apts. (Columbia), Pennsylvania Corp. (Fiduciary M.C.) Philadelphia). Kentucky Corp. (Fiduciary M.C.) (Louisville). Mem. exec. and finance coms. Gen. Bd. Missions. Trustee Textile Industrial Inst. Mason (32°, K.T., Shriner). Home: Aiken, S.C.†

CHILDS, FRANCIS LANE, coll. prof.; b. Henniker, N.H., Dec. 18, 1884; s. Richard Lane and Kate Marion (Gutterson) C.; A.B., Dartmouth Coll., 1906, A.M., 1907; Ph.D., Harvard, 1914; m. Lella B. Kelsey, July 31, 1929. Began as teacher in country school, 1901; instr. English, Dartmouth Coll., 1909-13, asst. prof., 1913-20, prof., 1920-46; chmn. dept., 1943-47, chmn. div. humanities, 1947-51. Winkley prof. Anglo-Saxon and English lang. and lit., 1946-54, emeritus, 1954-74, Mem. Commn. on Ministry Gen. Council Congl. and Christian Chs., 1946-52; mem. Mod. Language Assn. Am., Am. Dialect Soc., Am. Assn. U. Profs., New England Historic Geneal. Soc. (v.p. 1957-74), N.H. Hist. Soc., Phi Beta Kappa. Republican. Conglist. Mason. Home: Hanover, N.H. Died Aug. 1973.

CHILES, WILMA KLEIN, (Mrs. Harrell Edmonds Chiles), oil well servicing co. exec.; b. Oklahoma City, Feb. 13, 1912; d. Jacob Bernard and Wilhelmina (Ashauer) Klein; student Garnder Sch., N.Y.C., 1929-31; B.F.A. in Piano, U. Okla., 1934; m. Harrell Edmonds Chiles, Oct. 12, 1935; children—Carol Ann, Jerry Edmond. Co-founder Western Co., Fort Worth, 1939, treas. sec., 1939-46, dir., 1946-74. Dir. Midland Community Theatre, 1950-52; mem. Tarrant County Assn. Retarded Children. Mem. Ft. Worth Art Assn., Jewel Charity Ball Assn., Internat. Graphoanalysis Assn., Sigma Alpha Iota, Pi Beta Phi (Midland alumni pres. 1951-52). Republican. Episcopalian. Clubs: Minuet (dir.) (Midland, Tex.); Pi Beta Phi Mothers (Fort Worth). Home: Fort Worth, Tex., Died 1974.

CHILTON, J. MATT, lawyer; b. Turners Station, Henry County, Ky., May 18, 1881; s. George Blackwell and Florence N. (Sewell) C.; LL.B., U. of Louisville, 1902. Admitted to Ky. bar, 1902, Supreme Court of the United States in 1910; began the practice of law at Louisville; law clk. to Mayor James F. Grinstead, Louisville, 1908-09; sec., U.S. Senator W. O. Bradley of Ky., 1910-11. Mem. Ky. Rep. State Central Com. after 1912; county atty., Jefferson County, Ky., 1918-27; mem. Rep. National Com. since 1928, for term 1928-36. Apptd. by Gov. Laffoon as the Republican mem. Ky. State Election Commn., July 1935, reappointed 1936, 37, 38, 39, by Gov. Chandler; v.p. New Harmony Realty Corp. Mem. Louisville Bd. Trade. Baptist. Mason (Shriner), Odd Fellow, Elk. Clubs: Pendennis, Audubon Country. Office: Louisville, Ky.†

CHILTON, WILLIAM RANSDELL, banker; b. Ottoman, Va., Jan. 16, 1911; s. William Collin and Kathrine Elizabeth (Kamps) C.; B.S., Va. Mil. Inst., 1931; m. Catherine R. Barham, Jan. 21, 1947; 1 stepson, C. Barham Peirce. Tchr. pub. schs., Lancaster County, Va., 1931-36; dir., asst. mgr. Kilmarnock Fish Products, Inc. (Va.), 1933-41; pres., owner Chilton Fuels, Inc., Kilmarnock, Va., 1938-64; v.p. Peoples Oil Co., Inc., Warsaw, Va., 1956-73; pres. Bank Lancaster, Kilmarnock, Va. 1967-73; chmn. bd. Sylvia Motor Co., Burgess, Va., 1971-73; dir. Tidewater Telephone Co., Warsaw, Va. Mem. Va. Hwy. Commn., 1962-68; mem. No. Neck Regional Planning and Econ. Devel. Com., 1960-70. Bd. dirs. Community Library, Kilmarnock, Found. Historic Christ Ch., Inc., Irvington, Va., Mary Ball Meml. Mus. and Library, Lancaster, Va. Served to lt. comdr. USNR, 1942-46. Mem. Va. State C. of C. (dir. 1969-73), Tidewater Automobile Assn. (dir. 1973). Episcopalian (vestryman 1969-73). Clubs: Indian Creek Yacht and Country (pres. 1961-63) (Kilmarnock); Commonwealth (Richmond, Va.); Chesapeake (Irvington). Home: Lancaster, Va. Died Aug. 1, 1973; buried St. Marys White Chapel, Lively, Va.

CHINOY, ELY, educator, sociologist; b. Newark, Sept. 5, 1921; s. Solomon and Bella (Traskanoff) C.; B.A., U. Newark, 1942; Ph.D., Columbia, 1953; m. Helen Krich, June 6, 1948; children—Michael, Claire Nicole. Instr., Newark Coll. Engring., 1942-44; instr. N.Y. U., 1945-

46; lectr. U. Toronto (Ont., Can.), 1947-51; instr. sociology Smith Coll., Northampton, Mass., 1951-53, asst. prof., 1953-57, asso. prof., 1957-61, prof., 1961-75, Mary Huggins Gamble prof. sociology, 1969-75; Fulbright vis. prof. U. Leicester (Eng.), 1963-64; Fulbright lectr., Philippines, summer 1971. Mem. Am. Sociol. Assn., Eastern Sociol. Soc., Am. Assn. U. Profs., A.C.L.U. Author: Sociological Perspective, 3d edit., 1975; Society; An Introduction to Sociology, 2d edit., 1967; Automobile Workers and the American Dream, 1954; The Urban Future, 1972. Cons. editor Lieber-Atherton Press, 1964-75; asst. editor Am. Sociol. Rev., 1957-60, asso. editor, 1961-64; mem. editorial bd. Cambridge Studies in Sociology, 1972-75. Home: Northampton, Mass. Died Apr. 21, 1975; interred B'nai Israel Cemetery, Northampton.

CHOATE, EMETT CLAY, U.S. judge; b. Columbus, O., May 21, 1891; s. William Clay and Emma Caroline (Brown) C.; LL.B., U. Ind., 1914; m. Margaret Genevieve Merritt, May 31, 1924; 1 son, William Clay. Admitted to Ind. Okla. bars, 1914, N.Y., 1922, Fla., 1925; practiced in Oklahoma City, 1917-21, N.Y.C., 1922-25, Miami, 1925-54; U.S. judge So. Dist., Fla., 1954-74. Mem. Housing Authority, City of Miami, 1952; mem. nat. bd. field advisors Small Bus. Adminstrn., 1954-74. Del. Rep. Nat. Conv., 1952. Served as lt. 1st Okla. Inf., 1914-16; maj. F.A., U.S. Army, 1917-18. Mem. Am. Automobile Assn., Am., Fla., Dade Co. bar assns., Phi Delta Phi. Clubs: Kiwanis (Miami); Surf (Miami Beach. Fla.). Home: Miami Beach, Fla. Died Aug. 14, 1974.

CHOMMIE, JOHN CAMPBELL, educator; b. Thief River Falls, Minn., Sept. 5, 1914; s. Hans D. and Florence (Campbell) C.; student U. Minn., 1932-33, 35-36, U. N.D., 1934-35; LL.B., St. Paul Coll. Law, 1941, B.S.L., 1942; LL.M., U. So. Cal., 1952; LL.M., N.Y. U., 1956, J.S.D., 1960; m. June K. Ray, July 5, 1947; children—Barbara (Mrs. Lloyd Tosse), Frances (Mrs. Phillip Knox), Johanna, Karen (Mrs. Thomas Wyce), John, Catherine. Traffic mgr. Navjo Ordance Depot, 1942-43; prof. law S.W. U., Los Angeles, 1948-53, Dickinson Sch. Law, 1953-56; research asso. Harvard Law Sch., 1957-58; prof. law U. Miami, Coral Gables, Fla., 1956-73, dir. tax program. Law Sch., 1965-73; vis. prof. La. State U., 1965. Mem. Fla. Citizens Com. for Promotion of Humanities, 1971. Served with U.S. Mcht. Marine, 1944-45. Mem. Am. Trial Lawyers Assn., Minn., Interamerican bar assns., Am. Assn. U. Profs., Dade County Bar Assn. (asso.). Author: (with George Eder) Taxation in Columbia, 1964; Federal Income Taxation, 1968; The Internal Revenue Service, 1970. Editor, contbr. El Derecho de Los Estados Unidos, 3 vols., 1963. Home: Miami, Fla. Died May 13, 1973.

CHORLEY, KENNETH, b. Bournemouth, England, May 21, 1893; s. Edward Clowes and Florence (Dover) C.; brought to U.S., 1900; student Manlius (N.Y.) Sch., 1908-13; LL.D., Coll. of William and Mary, 1934; L.H.D., Hobart and William Smith Colls., 1957; H.H.D., Westminster Choir Coll., 1968; m. Elizabeth O'Kane, January 7, 1920 (divorced 1941); children—Kenneth, Edward Clowes, 3d; m. 2d, Jean Travers, Aug. 29, 1941. Asst. to pres. Laura Spelman Rockefeller Memorial, 1923-28; staff mem. Spelman Fund of N.Y., 1928-34; former pres., dir., chmn. finance com., mem. exec. com. Williamsburg Restoration, Inc.; former pres., trustee, chmn. exec., finance coms., trustee emeritus Colonial Williamsburg Found.; dir., Caneel Bay Plantation, Inc.; dir. exec. com. Grand Teton Lodge Company; director Delaware and Bound Brook Railroad Co., Yorktown Sesquicentennial; trustee, mem. exec., finance coms. Jackson Hole Preserve, Inc. Past chmn. bd. trustees Westminster Choir Coll. Decorated comdr. Order of the Brit. Empire. Mem., sometime officer, several hist. socs., Am. Craftsmen's Council (hon. trustee), Am. Conservation Assn. (trustee, exec. and finance coms.), Newcomen Soc. N.Am. (hon.), Am. Inst. Decorators (hon.), Va. C. of C. (spl. award). Republican. Episcopalian. Clubs: University, Bedens Brook, Nassau. Home: Skillman, N.J. Died Mar. 21, 1974; interred St. Philip's Ch.-in-the-Highlands, Garrison, N.Y.

CHOTINER, MURRAY M., lawyer; b. Pitts., Oct. 4, 1909; s. Albert H. and Sarah (Chass) C.; student U. Cal. at Los Angeles, 1925-26; LL.B., Southwestern U., 1929; 1 son, Kenneth L. Admitted to Cal. bar, 1931; practiced in Newport Beach, Beverly Hills and Los Angeles, 1931-69, Washington, 1971-74; gen. counsel Office Spl. Rep. for Trade Negotiations, Exec. Office Pres., 1969-70; spl. counsel to Pres. Nixon, 1970-71. Died Jan. 30, 1974.

CHOU EN-LAI, premier and foreign minister Chinese People's Republic; b. 1898; ed. Nankai U., Tientsin; m. Teng Ying-chao. Active in work of Communist Party, 1921-76; became sec. and chief of polit. dept. Whampoa Mil. Acad., 1924; became polit. commissar First Army (under Chiang Kaishek); joined Communist insurrectionists against First Army, at Shanghai; acted as liaison man between Communists, Nationalists and representatives of Western nations, Chungking, China, 9 yrs.; mem. People's Polit. Council, 1945-76; premier, fgn. minister Chinese People's Republic, 1949-76; rep. of Chinese People's Republic at Geneva Conf., 1954. Died Jan. 8, 1976.

CHOW, BACON FIELD, educator; b. Foo Chow, China, July 22, 1909; s. Yu-Sing and Su-Fong (Liu) C.; came to U.S., 1927, naturalized, 1942; B.S., U. Ill., 1929; Ph.D., Harvard, 1932; m. Idella Tong, June 30, 1931; children—Jean (Mrs. Vernon Wong), Bryant. Asst., Harvard, 1931-33; fellow Rockefeller Hosp., N.Y.C., 1933-35; asso. prof. Peking Union Med. Coll., 1935-38; head phys. chemistry and nutrition dept. Squibb Inst. Med. Research, 1938-48; prof. biochemistry Sch. Hygiene, Johns Hopkins, 1948-73. Mem. Am. Inst. Nutrition, Am. Immunologists, Soc. Internal. Secretions, Am. Soc. Clin. Nutrition, Am. Soc. Biol. chemists, Am. Pub. Health Assn., Paviovian Soc. Home: Baltimore Md. Died Sept. 27, 1973.

CHRISTENBERRY, HERBERT WILLIAM, former U.S. judge; b. New Orleans, Dec. 11, 1897; s. Herbert Aden and Anna (Schmitt) C.; student Soule Coll.; LL.B., Loyola U., 1924; postgrad. N.Y. U., 1927; m. Anna Born, Aug. 5, 1924; children—Carolyn Ann, Herbert William. Pvt. practice, 1924-33; asst. atty. Bd. Commrs. Port of New Orleans, 1933-35; dep. commr. La. Debt Moratorium Commn., 1935; asst. dist. atty. Parish of Orleans, 1935-37; asst. U.S. atty. Eastern Dist. La., 1937-42, U.S. atty. 1942-47; U.S. dist. judge, 1947-75. Instr. Loyola U. of South Sch. of Law. Mem. bd. commrs. City Park, New Orleans, Mem. Fed., La., New Orleans bar assns., Democrat. Club: Young Men's Business. Home: New Orleans, La., Died Oct. 5, 1975.

CHRISTENSEN, ERWIN OTTOMAR, art curator; b. St. Louis, June 23, 1890; s. Otto and Ida (Schnuhr) C.; B.S., U. Ill., 1914; M.Arch., Harvard, 1916, M.A., 1927; m. Edna Florance, Aug. 14, 1937; children—Hilde Marie (Mrs. Edward F. McGrath), Edith Anne (by previous marriage), James Erwin, Judith Florance. Instr. art history Ohio State U., 1915-19, U. N.D., 1919-26, Syracuse U., 1934-36, U. Pa., 1937-39, Am. U., 1945-46; asst. dir. Isabella Stewart Gardner Mus., Boston, 1928-31; dir. edn. work Am. Fedn. Arts, Washington, 1931-34; curator decorative arts and index Am. design Nat. Gallery Art 1940-60; dir. publs. and research Am. Assn. Museums, Washington, 1960, consultant, 1964-76. Served as Aerial Photography, Aero Section, Number 84, 1918-19. Member Washington Ethical Soc. Author: Popular Art in the U.S., 1948; The Index of American Design, 1950, 2d edit. 1959; Early American Wood Carving, 1952; Primitive Art, 1955; The Hist. Western Art, 1959; Am. Crafts and Folk Arts. 1964; A Pictorial History of Western Art, 1964; A Guide to Art Museums of the United States; also articles profl. jours. Home: Lanham, Md., Died Jan. 7, 1976.

CHRISTENSON, CARROLL LAWRENCE, economist; b. Viroqua, Wis., May 9, 1902; s. Christian A. and Louise (Larson) C.; Ph.B., U. Chgo., 1924, Ph.D., 1931; m. Cornelia Vos. June 11, 1929; children—John Martin, Ann Louise. Instr. econs. Ind. U., Bloomington, 1925-27, became asst. prof. econs., 1932, asso. prof., 1935-37, prof., 1937-69, emeritus, 1969-75, chmn. dept. econs.; 1945-50, on leave 1933-34 to act as econ. adviser NRA, on leave to serve with OPA, 1941-43, loaned to Republic of Costa Rica to aid in adminstrn. price control and rationing, 1944; vis. prof. (summer), U. Wis., 1947, U. So. Cal., 1949. Served as impartial arbitrator under various trade agreements, and as panel chmn. War Labor Bd. Fellow Am. Scandinavian Found., 1931-32; Ford Found. research fellow, 1956. Mem. Am. Econ. Assn., Mid-West Econ. Assn. (pres. 1947). Author books including; Economic Redevelopment in Bituminous Coal, 1962; (with Richard Myren) Wage Policy Under Walsh Healey Public Contracts Act, 1966. Contbr. tech. articles to jours. Home: Bloomington, Ind., Died Oct. 11, 1975.

CHRISTIE, AGATHA MARY CLARISSA, author; b. Torguay; d. Frederick Alvah Miller; m. Col. Archibald Christie, 1914 (div. 1928); 1 dau., Rosalind Christie Hicks; m. 2d, Max Edgar Lucien Mallowan, 1930. Decorated Comdr. Order Brit. Empire; 1956, dame Brit. Empire, 1971. Fellow Royal Soc. Lit. Author 80 books including: Murder of Roger Ackroyd, 1926; Mystery of the Blue Train, 1928; Thirteen at Dinner, 1933; Death Comes as the End, 1945; The Hollow, 1946; A Murder is Announced, 1950; They Came to Baghdad, 1951; Mrs. McGinty's Dead, 1952; Murder With Mirrors, 1952; Funerals are Fatal; A Pocketful of Rye, 1954; So Many Steps to Death, 1955; Hickory Dickory Death, 1955; Dead Man's Folly, 1956; What Mrs. McGillicuddy Saw, 1957; The Pale Horse, 1962; The Clocks, 1964; A Caribbean Mystery, 1965; Third Girl, 1966; At Bertram's Hotel, 1966; Crooked House, 1950; Easy to Kill, 1939; And Then There Were None, 1940; Endless Night, 1968; (plays) Alibi, Appointment with Death, Black Coffee, Go Back for Murder, The Hollow Love from a Stranger, The Mousetrap, Murder at the Vicarage, Murder on the Nile, Peril at End House, Witness for the Prosecution, Rule of Three. Address: Oxfordshire, England., Died Jan. 12, 1976.

CHRISTIE, DAN EDWIN, educator, mathematician; b. Dover-Foxcroft, Me., Oct. 11, 1915; s. Dan Foss and Blanche (Hamlin) C.; A.B., Bowdoin Coll., 1937; postgrad. (Henry fellow) St. John's Coll., Cambridge (Eng.) U., 1937-38; A.M., Princeton, 1940, Ph.D., 1942; m. Eleanor Wilson, Aug. 31, 1940; 1 son, Mark Edwin. Instr. math. Princeton, 1939-42; faculty Bowdoin Coll., Brunswick, Me., 1942-75, prof. math. and physics, 1955-65, chmn. math. dept., 1964-72, Wing prof. math., 1965-75. Lectr., USAAF, 1943-44, USN, 1944-46; cons. math. D.C. Heath & Co., 1965-70. Mem. com. advanced math. grad. record exam. Ednl. Testing Service, 1964-65; mem. panel undergrad. math. edn.Com. Support Research Math. Scis., 1966-68; dir. summer insts. and seminars in math. NSF, 1959-71; mem. Com. Undergrad. Program Math., 1963-66, mem. panel coll. tchr. preparation, 1965-69; adv. bd. Sch. Maths. Study Group, 1967-71; mem. com. undergrad. edn., div. math. scis. NRC, 1970-73, chmn., 1972-73; mem.-at-large council Conf. Bd. Math. Scis., 1972. Mem. Bowdoinham Sch. Bd., 1954-59. Ford Found. faculty fellow, 1953-54. Mem. Am. Math. Soc., A.A.A.S., Am. Assn. Physics Tchrs., Math. Assn. Am. (chmn. N.E. sect. 1960-61, nat. bd. govs. 1966-67, 70-73, mem. com. on publs. 1972-75), Nat. Council Tchrs. Math., Phi Beta Kappa, Sigma Xi. Author: Intermediate College Mechanics, 1952; Vector Mechanics, 1964; Basic Topology: A Developmental Course for Beginners, 1976. Home: Brunswick Me. Died July 18, 1975.

CHRISTIE, GEORGE IRVING, college prof.; b. Winchester, Ont., Can., June 22, 1881; s. David and Mary Ann (House) C.; B.S.A., Ontario (Can.) Agrl. Coll., 1902; B.S.A., Ontario (Can.) Agrl. Coll., 1902; B.S.A., Ia. Agrl. Coll., 1903, D.Sc., 1925; m. Ethel Maria Carpenter, of Des Moines, Ia., June 27, 1906; 1 dau., Erminia Margaret. Asst. in Agronomy, Ia. State Coll., Ames, Ia., 1903-05; asst. soils and crops, Purdue U., asso. agrl. extension, 1906-09, supt. agrl. extension after 1909, dir. Agrl. Experiment Station, after 1920, dir. Summer Sch. for Teachers, after 1912. Mem. Ind. Corn Growers' Assn. (sec. after 1906) supt. Ind. agrl. exhibit, Panama Expn.; chmn. agrl. after com. Ind. Centennial Celebration, 1916. State food dir. for Ind., 1917-19; asst. to Sec. of Agr., U.S. Dept. Agr., 1918, asst. sec. agr., 1918-19; mem. War Labor Policiies Bd., 1918, Nat. Com. for Employment of Soldiers and Sailors, 1919. Supt. Internat. Grain and Hay Show from 1919; apptd. mem. Ind. Deep Waterways Commn., 1923; supt. Ind. Agrl. Exhibit, Sequicentennial Expn., Phila., 1926; chmn. exec. com. Internat. European Corn Borer Orgn., 1926. Mem. Am. Land Grand College Assn. (com. on agrl. extension, organization and policy); Am. Acad. Polit. and Social Science, Ind. Acad. Science, Sigma Xi, Alpha Gamma Rho, Alpha Zeta, Sigma Delta Chi. Presbyn. Mason. Clubs: Town and Gown, West Lafayette Country. Rotarian. Home: Lafayette, Ind.†

CHRISTIE, JOHN WATSON, clergyman; b. Frankfort, Ky., Nov. 7, 1883; s. Robert (D.D., LL.D.) and Pauline Clay (Watson) C.; A.B., Princeton, 1904, A.M., 1908; student Western Theol. Sem. 1904-07; postgrad. work Glasgow, Scotland and Marburg, Germany, 1907-08; D.D., College Wooster, 1922; LL.D., University Del., 1951; L.H.D., Washington Jefferson Coll., 1953; m. Ruth Tracy Bigelow, July 28, 1909; children—Catharine (Mrs. Curtis Marshall Dann), Pauline Clay (Mrs. Richard Morris Knapp), Robert, Dana Bigelow, Andrew Dobbie, John Watson. Minister, Nelson Memorial Ch., Columbus, O., 1909-12; Van Wert, O., 1912-18, Mt. Auburn Ch., Cincinnati, O., 1918-31; minister Westminster Presbyn. Church, Wilmington, Del., 1931-56; ret. Formerly vice moderator Gen. Assembly Presbyn. Ch. U.S.A.; formerly moderator Permant Jud. Commn., Synod of Balt. Mem. bd. McCormick and Lane seminaries. Former mem. Wilmington Family Soc. (bd.), Presbyn. Hist. Soc. (pres. Phila.), Hist. Soc., Del. (pres.), Del. Soc. of Cincinnati (hon.), Am. Soc. of Church History. Club: Quill and Grill. Author: (with Dwight L. Dumond) George Bourne and The Book and Slavery Irreconcilable, 1969. Contbr. articles for hist. jours. Home: Wilmington, Del. Died July 8, 1974.

CHRIST-JANER, ALBERT WILLIAM, artist, educator; b. Appleton, Minn., June 13, 1910; s. William Henry and Bertha Wilhelmina (Beckman) C-J.; B.A., St. Olaf Coll., 1931, A.F.D., 1963; postgrad. Sch. Chgo. Art Inst., 1931-32, Yale Div. Sch., 1932-33; M.A., Yale, 1934; postgrad. Harvard, 1939-40; A.F.D., Lake Erie Coll., 1956; m. Virginia Morgan Carpenter, May 28, 1941. Instr. art Stephens Coll., 1934-36, head art dept., 1936-42, dir. summer art school, 1936-39; prof. art Northwestern U., summmer 1937; head art dept. Mich. State Coll., 1942-45; dir. mus. and library Cranbrook Acad. Art, 1945-47; dir. humanities devel. U. Chgo., 1947-51; dir. Arts Center Assos., Inc., 1951-52, office ednl. planning N.Y.U., 1952-56; dir. sch. of arts, prof. art Pa. State U., 1956-58; dean Art Sch., Pratt Inst., Bklyn., 1958-68, dir. Pratt Manhattan Center, 1968-70; Fuller E. Callaway Found. prof. art U. Ga., Athens, 1970-73. Internat. cons. Inst. Internat. Edn. Guggenheim award, 1950, 60. One man shows include Galleries, 1973; exhibited in group shows including Brit. Biennale Exhbn., 1968, 72, Phila. Water Color Club, 1969, Soc. Am. Artists, 1969. Pa. Acad. Fine Arts, 1969, Northwest Printmakers Internat. Exhbn., 1969, Boston Printmakers 22d Ann. Exhbn., 1970, Internat. Graphic Arts Soc., 1970, Weatherspoon Mus., 1971, High Mus. Art, Atlanta, 1971, Mint Mus., Charlotte, N.C., 1971, 72, 73, Nat. Collection Fine Arts, 1973, others; represented in permanent collections Nat. Air and Space Mus., Nat. Collection Fine Arts, Brit. Mus., Victoria and Albert Mus., London, Nat. Gallery, Stockholm, Nasjonalgalleriet, Oslo, Phila. Mus. Art,

Boston Mus. Fine Arts, USIS, Cranbrook Mus., Whitney Mus., Bklyn. Mus., Phillips Gallery, Washington, New York Pub. Library, Library of Congress, Art Inst. Chgo., Met. Mus. Art, others. Served in AUS, 1942-43. Recipient awards including Addie and Herbert Segerman Purchase award, 1968; prizes Print Club Phila., 1968, 69; Purchase prize Auburn U., 1969; Granger Fund Purchase award Audubon Artists, 1969; Am. Philos. Soc. award, 1968, 69; Arthur Judson Found. award, 1968, 69, 70; S.M. Kaplan Fund award, 1969; Tamarind grantee U. N.M., 1972. Mem. Phi Beta Kappa. Club: Century Association. Author: George Caleb Bingham of Missouri, 1940; Boardman Robinson, 1945; Eliel Saarinen, 1948; (with Mary Mix Foley) Modern Church Architecture, 1962; Forms, 1968; George Caleb Bingham Frontier Painter of Missouri, 1975. Contbr. articles to profl. jours. Home: Athens, Ga. Died Dec. 12, 1973.

CHRISTMAN, CHARLES E., compay exec.; b. Ross Twp., Pa., Mar. 19, 1870; s. Dawalt and Maryan (Van Bushkirk) C.; student bus. coll.; m. Edna Mae Dean, Oct. 20, 1926; children—Paul, Isabel, Virginia. Organized, 1892, and then pres., treas. Fed. Enameling & Stamping Co., McFees Rocks, Pa. Home: Pittsburgh, Pa.†

CHRISTOPHER, WILLIAM RODOLPHUS, artist; b. Columbus, Ga., Mar. 4, 1924; s. Ira and Grace (Anglin) C.; student Sorbonne, Paris, France, 1946-47, Acad. Julian, Paris, 1946-48, Ecole des Americaines, Fontainbleau, France, 1947; pupil Ossip Zadkine, Paris, 1947, Amedee Ozenfant, N.Y.C., 1948-50, Hans Hoffman, N.Y.C., 1950. One-man shows include Gallerie du Dragon, Cahier D'Art, Paris, 1947, Palais de Fontainebleau, 1947, Roko Gallery, N.Y.C., 1952, Nexus Gallery, Boston, 1957, 59, 60, Joan Peterson Gallery, Boston, 1961, 62, 65, 66, Amel Gallery, N.Y.C., 1961, Boston Archtl. Center, 1963, Dartmouth, 1964-66, Boston U., 1964, Addison Gallery Am. Art, 1966, Larcada Gallery, N.Y.C., 1968, Drew U., 1968, catalog Kennedy Library, 1968, Nat. Mus. Contemporary Art, Madrid, Spain, 1971, Nat. Mus. Modern Art, Barcelona, Spain, 1971, Galeria Juana Mordó, Madrid, 1972-73, Musee d'Art Moderne, Paris, 1972, Kuntshalle, Kassel, Germany, Galeria Nacional d'Arte, Lisbon, Portugal, 1972; group exhbns. include Whitney Mus., N.Y.C., Bklyn. Mus., Mus. Modern Art, N.Y.C., Fogg Mus., Boston Mus. Fine Arts, Inst. Contl. Arts, Boston, Northeastern U., Boston, Smith Coll., Norfolk Mus., Smithsonian Instn., Corcoran Galleries, Harvard, Providence Mus., Am. Fedn. Arts traveling exhbns., DeCordova Mus., Lincoln, Mass., Am.-Soviet Printmakers, N.Y.C., Larcada Gallery, Joan Peterson Gallery, Park Bernet Gallery, Terrain Gallery, Art at U.S. embassies Program, Boston U., Newport (R.I.) Art Assos., Wellesley Coll., Silvermine Artists Guild, R.I. Sch. Design, Wadsworth Atheneum, N.A.D., U. Tenn., Va. Mus. Art, Inst. Arts and Letters, Swain Sch.; represented in permanent collections Boston Mus. Fine Arts, Whitney Mus., DeCordova Mus., Boston U. Libraries, U. Mass., Dartmouth, Addison Gallery Am. Art, Chase Manhatten Bank, Carroll Reece Mus., U. Tenn., Seattle Art Mus., Wichita Art Mus., Yale, Tate Gallery Art, Inst. Contemporary Arts Library (both London, Eng.), also numerous pvt. collections; tchr. Bklyn. Poly. Inst., 1956-61, Dartmouth, 1966, 68, 69; instr. Dartmouth, 1970. Served with USNR, 1941-44. Schmitz-Hille Found. grantee, 1946-48. Recipient Rosenthal Found. award, 1953-55; Shiva award for drawing Bklyn. Mus., 1956; award for painting Silvermine Artists Guild, 1962; Gold medal merit Boston Arts Festival, 1964; Frank C. Kirk Meml. prize painting N.A.D., 1968; 1st Purchase award Carroll Reece Mus., 1968; award Inst. Arts and Letters, Am. Acad. Arts and Letters, 1969; Childe Hassam Fund purchase award Inst. Arts and Letters, 1968. Mem. So. Christian Leadership Conf., N.A.A.C.P. Home: Malaga, Spain. Died Dec. 5, 1973; buried Cemeterio de San Miguel, Malaga.

CHU, LAN JEN, engr., educator; b. Hweiying, Kiangsu, China, Aug. 24, 1913; s. Shao Wen and Ken C.; came to U.S., 1934, naturalized, 1952; B.S., Chiao Tung U., 1934; S.M., Mass. Inst. Tech., 1935, Sc.D., 1938; m. Grace Yu Ping Feng, Aug. 12, 1939; children—Yuan Bo, Yuan Hou, Yuan Ming. With Mass. Inst. Tech., 1934-73, prof. elec. engring., 1951-73. Recipient Presdl. Certificate of Merit. Fellow Inst. Radio Engrs., Am. Phys. Soc.; mem. Eta Kappa Nu. Home: Lexington, Mass. Died July 25, 1973.

CHURCH, ALOYSIUS STANISLAUS, psychiatrist; b. Detroit, Feb. 4, 1909; S. James J. and Josephine (Suchy) Kostielney; B.A., Wayne State U., 1932, M.B., 1936, M.D., 1937; postgrad. Cath. U. Am.; m. Elizabeth Kormend Kuttner, Sept. 11, 1937; children—Elizabeth Maria, Aloysius Stanislaus, Michael Joseph. Intern, Wayne County Gen. Hosp., Eloise, Mich., 1936-37, resident psychiatrist, 1937-38; fellow psychiatry Child Center (auspices Nat. Com. Mental Hygiene, Rockefeller Found.), Washington, 1938-41; med. dir. Lincoln Hall, Westchester County, New York, 1941-45; med. dir. St. Joseph's Retreat, Dearborn, Mich., 1945-62; psychiatrist Recorder's Ct., Psychiat. Clinic, City of Detroit, from 1962; adminstrv. psychiatrist Detroit Pub. Sch. System, from 1945; cons. psychiatrist, bd. dirs. Sobriety House; cons. Cath. Family Center, Detroit, 1945-53, Youth Service Bur., 1945-53; mem. staff Jennings Meml. Hosp., asso. staff Detroit Meml., Lynn hosps. Mem. Mich. Bd. Alcoholism Dept. Pub. Health; mem. bd. Greater Detroit Council on Alcoholism; mem. internat. council on alcoholism WHO; mem. bd. Nat. Council on Alcoholism. Mem. Nat. Council on Crime and Delinquency; Active Detroit Mus. Art Founders Soc., Detroit Symphony Orch. Trustee Detroit Com. Alcoholism. Fellow Am. Psychiat. Assn., Acad. Psychosomatic Medicine, Am. Geriatric Soc.; mem. Mich. Soc. Gerontology, Am. Soc. Med. Psychiatry, Mich. Soc. Neurology and Psychiatry, Nat. Acad. Religion and Mental Health, Wayne County, Mich. med. socs., A.M.A., Am. Pub. Health Assn., Internat. Council for Exceptional Children, Mich. Soc. Mental Hygiene, Electroshock Research Assn., Med. Correctional Assn., Nat. Conf. Cath. Charities, Guild Cath. Psychiatrists, Nat. Acad. Religion and Mental Health (charter), Am. Forestry Assn., Am. Rocket Soc., Internat. Oceanographic Found., Internat. Brotherhood Magicians, Nat. Med. and Dental Arts Assn., N.Y. Acad. Medicine, Cath. Physician's Guild, Wayne State U., Cath. U. Am. alumni assns., Am. Acad. Polit. and Social Sci., Detroit Players, MacKenzie Honor Soc., Phi Chi. Rotarian. Contbr. articles to profl. jours. Home: Detroit, Mich., Died Feb. 25, 1975.

CHURCH, EDWIN FAYETTE, JR., cons. mech. engineer; b. Elmira, N.Y., Jan. 17, 1879; s. Edwin Fayette and Alberta (Burling) C.; B.S. in Naval Architecture, Mass. Inst. Tech., 1901, M.S. in Mech. Engring., 1909; m. Adelaide Hayes Dovey, Dec. 28, 1904. Began as a draftsman, 1901; instr. in mech. engring. and naval architecture, Lehigh U., 1903-04; asst. prof. machine design, West Virginia Univ., 1904-06, asso. prof., 1906-09, professor, 1909-11, professor machine design and constrn., 1911-18; prof. mech. engring. and head of dept., Poly. Inst. of Brooklyn, 1918-46; cons. mech. engr., after 1946. Mem. Phi Beta Kappa, Tau Beta Pi, Newcomen Soc. Republican. Author: Stream Turbines, 1928. Contbr. of definition sec. to Ency. of Material Handling, 1921. Home: Brooklyn, N.Y.†

CHURCH, ELIHU, civil engineer; b. N.Y. City, 1881; s. Elihu and Anna M. (Cuynyngham) C.; E.C., Columbia, 1904, A.M., 1909; m. Clare Southmayd DeHart, 1915. Specialized in transportation engineering. Now president of Church Freight Service, Inc. Served 10 yrs. 7th Infantry, N.Y. Nat. Guard; Mexican Border, 1916; commd. capt. Engr. R.C.; with A.E.F. in France, 1917-18; commd. maj.; apptd. mem. Gen. Staff. Chevalier Legion d' Honneur (France). Mem. Am. Soc. C.E., Instn. Civ. Engrs. of Great Britain, Soc. of the Cincinnati, Soc. Colonial Wars, The Pilgrims, Sigma Xi. Presbyterian. Clubs: University, St. Nicholas Society, Century Association (New York City); Army and Navy Club (Washington, D.C.). Home: New York City, N.Y.†

CHURCH, GEORGE DUDLEY, educator; b. Providence, May 12, 1878; s. George E. and Abbie Green (Dudley) C.; A.B., Brown U., 1899, hon. A.M., 1913; m. Helen Louise Bigelow, of Worcester, Mass., June 23, 1904; children—Helen Elizabeth, Adelaide Bigelow (dec.). Taught in Abbott Sch. and 2 yrs. in Worcester Acad.; reoganized and incorporated, 1902, owner and head-master, after 1918, the Abbott Sch.; registrar Worcester (Mass.) Acad., 1918-33; and bursar Westminster Sch., Simsbury, Conn., 1933-37; then with Brookmire Corp. Mem. Phi Beta Kappa. Republican, Conglist. Home: West Hartford, Conn.†

CHURCH, RICHARD CASSIUS, musician, educator; b. Belvidere, Ill., May 14, 1907; s. Cassius M. and Minnie E. (Adams) C.; B.A., U. Wis., 1927, Mus. B., 1936, M.A. in Music, 1940; m. Agatha G. McCaffery, June 21, 1928; children—Kathleen Kirwan (Mrs. Stuart W. Wirth), Meredith Ann (Mrs. Joseph L. Rousseau), Julie Adams (Mrs. John Ringer), Richard Anthony. Tchr., orch. condr. Janesville (Wis.) High Sch., 1927-28; dir. instrumental music Central High Sch., Madison, Wis., 1928-30, West High Sch., Madison, 1930-44; faculty dept. music U. Wis., Madison, 1944-76, prof., 1957-76; condr. U. Wis. Symphony Orch., 1944-46, mus. dir. Wis. Players Mus. Prodns., 1935-65. Guest condr. various symphony orchs.; music adjudicator; lectr.; former bassoonist, violist Madison Symphony Orch. Recipient citation for excellence in teaching Midwest Program for Airborne Television Instn. Mem. Music Educators Nat. Conf., Wis. Edn. Assn., Nat. Collegiate Players, Phi Mu Alpha (Sinfonia), Alpha Kappa Lambda. Developer 1st systems approach to teaching violin with firm cartridges and manual. Home: Lodi, Wis., Died Feb. 7, 1976.

CHURCHILL, RALPH LOREN, cooperative marketing; b. Cedar Falls, Ia., Apr. 7, 1880; s. Joshua Perry and Martha (Stamp) C.; ed. pub. schs.; m. Letta King, July 12, 1904; children—Paul King, Edwin Perry, Phoebe May. Began as stenographer and bookkeeper, 1902; with the Limoneira Co. and affiliated corps. Santa Paula, until 1917, treas., 1909-17; sec. and mgr. Calif. Bean Growers Assn., after 1917; dir. Teague-McKivett Co., South Mountain Lemon Co. Pres. Nat. Bean Marketing Assn. Widely known as advocate of cooperative marketing. Republican. Presbyn. Mason. Address: Oxnard, Cal.†

CHWOROWSKY, MARTIN PHILIP, educator; b. San Antonio, Tex., Jan. 28, 1900; s. Frederick J. and Marie (Sussnitz) C.; A.B., Harvard, 1922, LL.B., 1926; A.M., U. Pitts., 1936, Ph.D., 1937; m. Eleanor Weeks, Aug. 21, 1926 (dec. 1965); 1 dau., Jane Lee; m. 2d, Eleanor Dunwoody, July 9, 1966. Tchr., Indian Mt. School, Lakeville, Conn., 1926-29, Community Sch., Pittsburgh, 1929-30; prin. Falk Sch., lectr. in edn., U. Pittsburgh, 1931-39; asso. prof. edn. and psychology, Carnegie Inst. Tech., 1939-46; asso. dir. Commn. Secondary Schs. NCCJ, 1946-48; became prof. edn., coordinator, inter-group relations program. Columbia Teachers Coll., 1948; research prof. human relations U. Pa., Phila., 1951-61, prof. human relations, dir. A.M. Greenfield Center for Human Relations, 1951-66, prof. emeritus, 1968-75; prof. social work Va. Commonwealth U., 1966-67, prof. sociology, 1967-70. Contbr.: Year Book of Edn., 1955; Adult Leadership. Home: Paoli, Pa. Died Apr. 29, 1975; interred Croydon, N.H.

CIANCA, BERNARD JOSEPH, accountant; b. N.Y.C., Apr. 16, 1916; s. Louis and Mary (Datre) C.; B.B.A., Coll. City N.Y., 1937; m. Mary Louise Neary, Oct. 4, 1952 (dec. June 1964); 1 dau., Deborah; m. 2d, Frances J. Peck, July 1, 1966. Jr. accountant H.H. Rieders Assos., N.Y.C., 1937-39; sr. accountant Groger, Kamrass & Schneidman, N.Y.C., 1939-41; partner Touche Ross, & Co., N.Y.C., from 1946. Served with finance dept., AUS, 1941-45. C.P.A., N.Y., Ga., Mich., La., N.J., Va. Mem. Nat. Assn. Accountants, Internat. Council Shopping Center, N.Y. State Assn. Professions, N.Y. Credit and Financial Assn., A.I.M., Am. Inst. C.P.A.'s, N.Y. State Soc. C.P.A's, Am. Accounting Assn., 45th Div. Assn., City Coll. N.Y. Alumni Assn. Club: Whitehall. Roman Catholic. Home: New York City, N.Y. Deceased.

CICOGNANI, AMLETO GIOVANNI, sec. state Pope Paul VI; b. Brisighella, Ravenna, Italy, Feb. 24, 1883; s. William and Ann (Ceroni) C. Ordained priest Roman Catholic Ch., 1905; Ph.D., theology, canon and civil (Roman) law. Adviser, Sacred Roman Rota; ofcl. Sacred Congregation of Sacraments, 1910-14; minutante Sacred Consistorial Congregation, 1914-23; under-sec., 1923-28; assessor Sacred Congregation for Oriental Ch., sec. Commn. for Codification Oriental Canon Law, 1928-33; titular archbishop Laodicea, apostolic del. U.S., 1933-58; consecrated in Rome, 1933; created cardinal, 1958; sec. Sacred Congregation for Oriental Ch., Vatican, 1960-61; sec. state to His Holiness Pope John XXIII, 1961-63; sec. state to Pope Paul VI, 1963-73. Address: Vatican City. Died Dec. 17, 1973.

CINELLI, ALBERT ARTHUR, physician; b. N.Y.C., Mar. 12,1900; s. Pietro and Maria (Severia) C.; B.S., Fordham U., 1922; M.D., Georgetown U., 1926; diploma in rhinotolaryngology N.Y. Postgrad. Med. Sch. and Hosp., 1929; m. Dorothy LaFleur, 1942; children—Albert Burton, Dorothy (Mrs. Thomas P. Powers, Jr.); m. 2d, Veronica Byrnes, Jan. 25, 1956. Intern, St. Mary's Hosp., Bklyn., 1926-28; postgrad. in surgery of ear, nose and throat and facial plastic surgery Veraby Clinic, Budapest, Hungary, 1929-30, U. Vienna, 1930-31; practice medicine specializing in surgery of ear, nose and throat and facial plastic surgery, N.Y.C., 1931-72; asso. vis. surgeon N.Y. Postgrad. Hosp., 1931-41, ear, nose and throat cons. thyroid clinic, 1938-42; asst. surgeon Manhattan Eye, Ear and Throat Hosp., 1940-50; cons. otolaryngologist and facial plastic surgery Nat. Hosp. for Speech Defects, 1942-62; attending ear, nose and throat surgeon St. Clare's Hosp., 1948-50; asso. vis. surgeon Italian Hosp., dir. ear, nose, throat and facial plastic surgery, 1947-72; surg. dir., 1964, pres. med. bd., 1966; cons. dept. otolaryngology N.Y. Polyclin. Hosp., 1970; cons. dept. plastic surgery Columbus Hosp., 1971; lectr. Columbia Coll. Phys. and Surg., 1931-41, State U. N.Y. Med. Sch., Bklyn., 1957; founder Med. and Surg. Plan of Specialists, N.Y.C., 1942, med. dir., 1942-72; founder, pres., chmn. bd. Gen. Health Information Service, Inc., N.Y.C., 1956-72; med. dir. Surg. Assistance Fund, N.Y. Fire Dept., 1942-72; lectr. in U.S. and fgn. countries. Mem. med. div. N.Y. Bd. Trades. Decorated cavilière Ordine al Merito della Republica Italiano; recipient numerous awards. Diplomate Am. Bd. Otolaryngology. Fellow Am. Acad. Ophthalmology and Otolaryngology, Am. Coll. Cardiology, Am. Geriatrics Soc., Am. Soc. Ophthalmologic and Otolaryngologic Allergy, Internat. Coll. Surgeons, Internat. Acad. Cosmetic Surgery, Am. Largyngol., Rhinol. and Otol. Soc.; mem. A.M.A., N.Y. State (life), New York County (life) med. socs., World (U.S. com.), Pan Am. med. assns., A.C.S. (life), Acad. Medicine (life), A.A.A.S., Pan Am. Assn. Oto-Rhino-Laryngology and Broncho-Esophagology, N.Y. Oto-Rhino-Laryngol. Soc., Nat. Soc. for Study Headache, Internat. Corr. Soc. Otolaryngologists, Nat. Found. for Research for Deafness, Am. Acad. Facial Plastic and Reconstructive Surgery (life), Soc. for Cryosurgery, N.Y. State Soc. Surgeons, Royal Soc. Health, Uniformed Fire Officers Assn. (hon.), Philatelic Soc. N.Y. Fedn. Post Office Clks (hon.), N.Y. State Fire Fighters Assn. (hon.), Am. Soc. of Italian Legion of Merit, Am. Council Otolaryngology, Italian Hist. Soc. Am. Mem. editorial bd. Physicians' Drug Manual. Contbr. numerous articles to med. jours., chpts. to books. Home: New York City, N.Y., Died Dec. 28, 1972; buried Woodlawn Cemetery, New York City, N.Y.

CIOBANU, IOAN, educator, scientist; b. Mures, Rumania, Apr. 12, 1910; s. Ioan N. and Marie D. (Murarlu) C.; B.A. in Natural Scis., U. Cluj, 1934, Ph.D. in Biology, 1948, honoured prof., 1969; m. Augusta Gavris, July 29, 1954. Secondary sch. tchr. in Tirgul-Mures, Rumania, 1935-40, Tlmisoara, Rumania, 1940-45; mem. faculty U. Cluj (Rumania), 1942—, prof. plant morphology and palynology, 1959—, dean 1950-53, pro-rector, 1953-56, 66-72, rector, 1960-66. Dist. dep., Cluj, 1950—. Decorated Work Order 3d class, 1965. Mem. Rumanian Communist Party. Author: University Handbook of Morphology, 1971; also articles. Home: Cluj, Rumania., Died Aug. 4, 1974.

CIPOLLARO, ANTHONY CAESAR, physician; b. N.Y.C., Aug. 6, 1900; s. Enrico and Maria (Maucione) C.; B.S., Dartmouth, 1924; M.D., Columbia, 1927; m. Rose Sullivan, July 2, 1925; children—Patricia (Mrs. Joseph Harper), Michael. Intern N.Y. Postgrad. Hosp., 1928-30; practice of dermatology and syphilology, N.Y.C., 1930-75; attending dermatologist Mother Cabrini Hosp., 1934-49, cons., 1949-64; asst. prof. medicine Cornell U., 1948-53, asso. prof., 1953-60; clin. prof., 1961-66, prof. emeritus, 1966-75; prof., dir. dept. dermatology and syphiology N.Y. Polyclinic Med. Sch. and Hosp., 1949-60; dir. dept. dermatology Columbus Hosp., 1940-49, cons., 1949-75; asst. attending physician dept. medicine N.Y. Hosp., 1948-60, asso. attending, 1960-65, attending physician, 1965-66, cons. physician, 1966-75; cons. dermatologist Saranac Lake (N.Y.) Hosp., St. Joseph's Hosp., Far Rockaway, N.Y., 1940-67. Mem. nat. com. on radiation protection U.S. Dept. Commerce, Nat. Bur. Standards, 1947-55; mem. research and grants com., mem. bd. dirs., chmn. com. edn. N.Y.C. cancer com. Am. Cancer Soc., 1950-60, pres., 1960-62, chmn. exec. com., 1962-64, Recipient bronze medal Am. Cancer Soc. for outstanding contbns. to control of cancer, 1959; Clement Cleveland award for contbg. to cancer control N.Y.C. Cancer Com. of Am. Cancer Soc., 1961. Diplomate Am. Bd. Dermatology and Syphilology (pres. 1952). Fellow A.C.P.; mem. A.M.A. (mem. council phys. medicine and rehab. 1936-56, council on med. physics 1956-61; past chmn. dermatology sect.; editorial bd. archieves of dermatology 1949-62), Am. Acad. Dermatology and Syphilology (pres. 1959, dir.), N.Y. State Med. Soc. (past chmn. dermatology sec.), Am. Dermatol. Assn. (pres. 1965-66, dir.), N.Y. (pres. 1958-59), R.I. (hon.), Manhattan dermatol. socs., N.Y. Acad. Medicine (past chmn. sect. dermatology and syphilolgy, chmn. com. on admissions 1960-61, sec. 1963-66); hon. mem. Australian, Venezuelan, Italian dermatol. socs.; corr. mem. Swedish, French dermatol. socs. Roman Catholic. Author: Cutaneous Cancer and Precancer (with G.M. MacKee), 1937; Skin Diseases in Children, rev. edit. 1946; X-Rays and Radium in the Treatment of Diseases of the Skin (with G.M. MacKee), rev. edit., 1946, 5th edit. (with Paul C. Crossland), 1967. Contbr. articles, chpts. med. publs. Home: New York City, N.Y. Died July 5, 1975.

CLAESSENS, MARIA, mezzo-soprano; b. Brussels, Belgium, May 20, 1881; d. Adolph and Clementine (Decrous) C.; ed. in Brussels and Barcelona. Début in Barcelona, as Eleonora in Donizetti's "Favorita," Aug. 15, 1903; sang in Italy and for 5 seasons in Buenos Aires; jointed the Boston and Metropolitan Opera cos., appearing as Amneris, Azucena, etc.; became identified with the Chicago Opera Co., 1916.*†

CLAFLIN, W(ALTER) HAROLD, teacher; b. Newton, Mass., Oct. 20, 1880; s. Charles Henry and Emma Florence C.; A. B., 1902, A. M., 1904, Harvard. Taught in Quincy, Mass., 1905-06. Author: Modern Perisa, 1907. Editor: History of Holland and Belgium, 1907; co-editor History of Turkey, 1907. Home: Newtonville, Mass.†

CLAPP, MARGARET, college president; b. East Orange, N.J., Apr. 11, 1910; d. Alfred Chapin and Anna (Roth) Clapp; A.B., Wellesley Coll., 1930; A.M., Columbia 1937, Ph.D., 1946; LL.D., Litt.D. Tchr. Todhunter Sch., N.Y.C., 1930-39, Dalton Sch., N.Y.C., 1939-41; instr. Coll. City of N.Y., 1942-44, N.J. Coll. for Women, 1945-46, Columbia, 1946-47; asst. prof. Bklyn. Coll., 1947-49; pres. Wellesley Coll., 1949-74. Dir., Gen. Foods Corp. Trustee Walnut Hill Sch., Dana Hall Schools. Awarded the Pulitzer prize for biography. Forgotten First Citizen: John Bigelow, 1947. Fellow Am. Acad. Arts and Scis.; mem. Am. Assn. U. Profs., Phi Beta Kappa. Club: Cosmopolitan (N.Y.C.). Home: Tyringham, Mass. Died May 4, 1974.

CLARK, ANDREW HILL, geographer, educator; b. Fairford, Man., Can., Apr. 29, 1911; s. Jeremiah S. and Belle (Pratt) C.; B.A., McMaster U., 1930; student U. Man., 1931-32; M.A., U. Toronto, 1938; Ph.D., U. Cal. at Berkeley, 1944; m. Louise Sassmann, Dec. 28, 1940; children—Charles D., John R. and Stephen P. (twins)-Mary E. Came to U.S., 1938, naturalized, 1945. Wtih actuarial dept. Mfrs. Life Ins. Co., Toronto, 1932-35; instr. U. Toronto, 1935-38; asst. Dominion Geol. Survey Can., 1936, 37; extension lectr. U. Cal. at Berkeley, 1940; lectr. Canterbury U., Christchurch, New Zealand, 1941, 42; Instr. USAAF, Berkeley, 1943, ASTP, Johns Hopkins, 1943-44; geographer OSS and Dept. of State, 1944-46; asso. prof. geography Rutgers U., 1946-49, prof., chmn. dept., 1949-51; prof. geography U. Wis., Madison, 1951-64, research prof., 1964-66, Vernor Clifford Finch research prof. geography, 1966-75, chmn. dept., 1958-61; fellow in Am. studies U. Dundee, Scotland, 1971-72. John Simon Guggenheim Meml. fellow and Fulbright Research scholar, 1961-62; S.S.R.C. fellow, 1962. Chmn. com. hist. geography NRC, 1949-53. Mem. Am. Geog. Soc., Assn. Am. Geographers (hon. pres. 1961-62, editor Monograph series 1961-63), Canadian Assn. Geographers (award for scholarly distinction 1974), Internat. Geog. Congress (chmn. hist. geography sect. 1964), Agrl. History Soc. Author: The Invasion of New Zealand by People, Plants and Animals, 1949; Three Centuries and the Island, 1959; Acadia: The Early Geography of Nova Scotia to 1760, 1968 (citation Beveridge Award com. Am. Hist. Assn.); (with others) Canada: A Geographical Interpretation, 1968; New Zealand, 1947, American Geography, Inventory and Prospect, 1954. Contbr. to monographs, jours. in field. Co-editor Jour. Hist. Geography, 1973-75; editor series The Historical Geography of North America, Oxford U. Press, N.Y.C. Died May 21, 1975.

CLARK, EDITH KIRKWOOD ORMSBY, educator; b. Washington, D.C., Sept. 7, 1881; d. George W. and Sara Eaton (Robinson) C.; student Des Moines (Ia.) Coll., 1899-1900; Grinnell (Ia.) Coll., 1900-1; U. of Wis., summer, 1901; U. of Wyo., summer, 1913; unmarried. Engaged in teaching in rural and town schs., Wyo., 1906-8; supt. pub. schs., Sheridan Co., Wyo., 1909-14, inclusive; state supt. pub. instrn., Wyo., 1915-18. Trustee U. of Wyo.; mem. State Bd. Edn., State Bd. Charities and Reform, State Bd. Pardons, State Land Bds. Mem. N.E.A., Wyo. State Teachers' Assn., Wyo. Soc. D.A.R. Republican. Episcopalian. Home: Cheyenne, Wyo.†

CLARK, GLENN W(HITMIRE), business exec.; b. Salem, Mo., Dec. 11, 1905; s. Joseph Henry and Rosalie Belle (Marsh) C.; LL.B., Univ. Mo., 1928; m. Helen Durham, 1928; children—Stuart Clive, David Marsh. Admitted to Mo. bar, 1927, Okla. bar, 1928; practice of law, Lebanon, Mo., 1928, Tulsa, 1929; mem. legal dept. Empire Companies, Bartlesville, Okla., 1930-38; gen. atty. Panhandle Eastern Pipe Line Co., Kansas City, Mo., 1938-44; dir. Cities Service Gas Co., Oklahoma City, 1944-56; v.p., gen. counsel, 1944-52, pres., 1952-56; pres., dir. Cities Service Gas Producing Co., 1953-56; pres., dir. Mississippi River Fuel Corp., St. Louis, 1956-65; chmn. bd., chief exec. Northwest Pipeline Corp., 1965-73. Mem. Am. Gas Assn., Ind. Natural Gas Assn. Am. (dir., pres., 1959-60), Am., Mo., Okla., Ark. bar assns. Clubs: Fayetteville Country; Old Warson Country, Racquet (St. Louis). Home: Fayetteville, Ark. Died Oct. 20, 1973.

CLARK, HOMER PIERCE, publisher; b. Boston, Mass., July 6, 1868; s. Charles Henry and Martha Cowper (Pierce) C.; LL.B., University of Minn., 1894; m. Elizabeth Turner Dunsmoor, Jan. 12, 1910; children—Lt. Robert Stuart (killed in action, Feb. 1, 1943), Thomas Kimball, Elizabeth Turner, Catherine Pierce, Helen Dunsmoor. Began as clerk for Finch, Van Slyck & McConville, St. Paul, 1888, continuing until 1890; with West Pub. Co. since 1892, treas., 1902-21, pres., 1921-32, chairman of the board, 1932-50, hon. chairman board, after 1950; hon. chmn. Am. Law Book Co.; dir. Waldorf Paper Products Co., St. Paul Fire & Marine Insurance Co. Vice chmn. Liberty Loan Com. for 9th Dist., World War. Pres. St. Paul Community and War Chest, 1943, 44. Trustee James Jerome Hill Reference Library, St. Paul. Mem. Am. and Minn. bar assns., Soc. Mayflower Descendants. Republican. Unitarian. Clubs: Minnesota, Minneapolis (Minneapolis, Minnesota); Eastern Yacht (Marblehead, Mass.). Home: St. Paul, Minn.†

CLARK, JOHN ALDEN, educator; b. Ahmednagar, India, Aug. 27, 1907 (parents Am. citizens); s. Alden Hyde and Mary (Whitcomb) C.; A.B., Amherst Coll., 1929; M.A., Harvard, 1930, Ph.D., 1935; m. Mary Ann Scott, May 5, 1943; children—Alice (Mrs. Jayant L. Chhaya), Evelyn (Mrs. Marvin R. Farbman), Alden Lee. Instr. philosophy Carleton Coll., Northfield, Minn., 1933-35; asst. prof. Earlham Coll., Richmond, Ind., 1935-37, asso. prof., 1937-39; asso. prof. U. N.C., Greensboro, 1939-41; mem. faculty Colby Coll., Waterville, Me., 1946, prof., 1952-72, chmn. dept. philosophy and religion, 1952-71, prof. emeritus, 1972-74; vis. prof. Unity (Me.) Coll., 1972-74; researcher Columbia, 1941-42, U. Edinburgh (Scotland), 1954-55. Served to 1st lt. AUS, 1942-46. Fulbright lectr. Ahmednagar Coll., U. Poona (India), 1961-62. Mem. Am. Philos. Assn., Soc. Religion Higher Edn. Democrat. Mem. United Ch. Christ. Editor: The Student Seeks an Answer, 1960. Contbr. profl. jours. Home: Waterville, Me. Died Aug. 31, 1974.

CLARK, RICHARD FRANCIS MAPLESTONE, Ins. co. exec.; b. Kew, Victoria, Australia, Mar. 23, 1906; LL.B., Melbourne U.; m. Barbara Shaw, July 9, 1936; 2 daus. Partner, Mallesons, Solicitors, 1946-70, cons., 1970-74. Dir. Containers Ltd., Colonial Mut. Life Assurance Soc. Ltd. Served with Royal Australian Air Force, 1942-45. Clubs: Australian, Royal Melbourne Golf. Address: Melbourne Victoria, Australia. Died May 11, 1974.

CLARK, ROBERT FRY, coll. prof.; b. Galt, Ont., Can., Feb. 10, 1880; s. Robert Allison and Elizabeth (Fry) C.; A.B., Central Coll., Huntington, Ind., 1901; A.B., Oberlin Coll., 1902; A.M., U. of Chicago, 1906; m. Mary Adeline Willard, Sept. 16, 1913; children—Elizabeth (Mrs. C. M. Bunnell), Francis Willard, Florence (Mrs. C. W. Coffman). Came to U.S., 1898, naturalized, 1918. Prof. fgn. langs., Central Coll., 1902-05; prin. Washburn Acad., Topeka, Kan., 1906-11; asso. prof. economics and Sociology Colgate University, 1913-14, dean, prof. economics and sociology Pacific Univ., 1915-17, acting pres., 1917-19, pres., 1919-22; prof. economics and sociology Marietta Coll. after 1922. Mem. Am. Sociol. Soc., Am. Economics Assn. Conglist. Home: Marietta, O.†

CLARK, SAMUEL ORMAN, JR., lawyer; b. Woodbridge, Conn., July 9, 1900; s. Samuel Orman and Pauline C. (Marquard) C.; Ph.B., Sheffield Sci. Sch., Yale, 1921; student Yale Grad. Sch., 1921-22; LL.B., magna cum laude, Yale Law Sch., 1928; m. Charlotte I. Northrop, Jan. 3, 1931. Civil engr. Stone & Webster, Boston, 1922-26; admitted to N.Y. bar, 1929, Conn. bar, Dist. of Columbia bar, bar U.S. Supreme Court; practice with Milbank, Tweed & Hope, and its predecessor, Masten & Nichols, New York, 1938-31; with Chambers & Hesselmeyer, New Haven, Conn., 1932-34; chief atty., protective com. study, Securities and Exchange Commn., Washington, D.C., 1934-38, dir. of reorganization div., 1938-39; asst. atty. gen., Dept. of Justice, in charge of tax div., July 1939-Dec. 1945; partner Hewes & Awalt, Washington, D.C., and Hartford, Conn., 1946-49; partner Awalt, Clark & Sparks, Washington. Mem. Am. Bar Assn., Dist. of Columbia Assn., Alpha Chi Rho, Phi Delta Phi, Order of Coif. Democrat. Clubs: Graduate (New Haven, Conn.); Metropolitan, Yale (Washington, D.C.). Contbr. to legal jours. Home: Bradenton, Fla. Died Jan. 21, 1975.

CLARKE, DAVID ANDREW, JR., educator, agrl. economist; b. Milford, Conn., Feb. 26, 1919; s. David Andrew and Hazel (Munson) C.; B.S., U. Conn., 1940, M.S., 1942; Ph.D., U. Cal. at Berkeley, 1951; m. Dorothy Stoddard Burnap, July 18, 1942; children—Marilyn, David Alan, Sandra S. (Mrs. Steven A. Smith), Margaret Ann. Grad. asst. U. Conn., 1940-42, research instr., 1942-44; faculty U. Cal. at Berkeley, 1946-74, prof. agrl. econs., 1960-74, chmn. dept., 1968-73, dir. Giannini Found. Agrl. Econs., 1968-74. Served to 1st lt. AUS, 1944-46. Mem. Am. (award of merit 1957), Western agrl. econs. assns. Democrat. Conglist. Contbr. profl. jours. Home: Orinda, Cal. Died July 31, 1974.

CLARKE, E(LWYN) L(ORENZO), civil engr.; b. Momence, Ill., June 18, 1879; s. Joseph Lorenzo and Mary Louise (Wooster) C.; B.S., U. of Ill., 1902, C.E., 1931; m. Lucile Anne Wyatt, July 8, 1933; 1 dau., Anne McNeil. Asst. engr. Lackawanna R.R., Hoboken, N.J., 1902-05; resident engr. Big 4 Ry., Lawrenceville, Ill., 1905; instr. Mo. Sch. of Mines, 1905-07; jr. engr. U.S. Engr. Dept., Seatlte, 1907-08; in pvt. practice survey and irrigation, Sheridan, Wyo., 1908-12; engr. Carey Act Dept., State of Wyo., Cheyenne, 1912-16; supt. constrn. Westinghouse, Church, Kerr & Co., N.Y. City, 1916-20; asso. prof. civil engring. U. of S.D., 1920-21; prof. civil engring. and head civil engring. dept. Clemson (S.C.) Coll. 1921-51, then emeritus. Mem. A.S.C.E. (pres. S.C. sect. 1941), S.C. Soc. Engrs. (dir. 1934; v.p. 1941; pres. 1942), Am. Soc. E.E. Mason. Home: Clemson, S.C.†

CLARKE, THOMAS HOWARD, physician, surgeon; b. Ottawa, Ont., Can., June 30, 1909; s. Thomas Enoch and Marie (Rhodes) C.; B.A., U. Western Ont., 1931, M.D., 1935; m. Thelma Dow, Aug. 17, 1940; children—John Thomas, Paul Howard, Gilbert Byron, Robert Burton. Came to U.S., 1937, naturalized, 1942. Fellow pathology U. Western Ont., 1935-36, research asst. pathology, 1937; Intern Royal Victoria Hosp., Montreal, Que., Can., 1936-37; resident surgery, asst. dept. U. Chgo. Med. Sch., 1938-41; faculty Northwestern U. Med. Sch., 1941-71, prof. surgery, 1964-71; prof. surgery U. Ill. Med. Sch., Chgo., 1971-73; sr. attending staff Chgo. Wesley Meml. Hosp., 1941-71, cons., 1971-73; cons. staff VA Research Hosp., Chgo.; civilian cons. U.S. 5th Army, 1959-71; dir. med. affairs Ill. Masonic Med. Center, 1969-73. Trustee U. Western Ont. Found.; bd. dirs. Am. Cancer Soc.; bd. regents Luther Coll., Decorah, Ia. Served to lt. col. M.C., AUS, 1942-46. Fellow A.C.S. (gov.); mem. A.M.A., Central, Western surg. assns., Chgo. (pres. 1964), Ill. surg. socs., Ill., Chgo. med. socs., Am. Thyroid Assn. Contbr. papers to profl. lit. Home: Chicago, Ill. Died May 10, 1973.

CLARKSON, JESSE DUNSMORE, historian; b. Bklyn., Aug. 6, 1897; s. William Kemble and Mary Augusta (Brown) C.; A.B., Williams Coll., 1918; A.M. Columbia, 1920, Ph.D., 1925; m. Mary Griffiths, Nov. 25, 1922; children—Myfanwy G., William K. Mem. faculty Coll. City N.Y., 1922-30; faculty Bklyn. Coll., 1930-67, prof. history, 1945-67, emeritus, 1967-73, chmn. dept. history, 1937-50, sec. faculty council, 1938-50; sometime vis. prof. history Russian Inst. Columbia U., 1952-63; vis. prof. U. Cal. at Berkeley, 1962, Columbia, 1963; lectr. O.W.I. tng. program, 1944-45, staff officers European studies course, 1945-46. Mem. Am. Assn. U. Profs., Am. Hist. Assn. (exec. com. Slavic conf.), Am. Acad. Polit. Sci., Am. Acad. Polit. and Social Sci., Econ. History Assn., Soc. Am. Historians, Phi Beta Kappa. Club: Union League (Bklyn). Author: Labour and Nationalism in Ireland, 1925; A History of Russia, 1961. Bd. editors Jour. Modern History. Contbr. articles to profl. jours. Translator and editor various works. Home: Bay Shore, N.Y. Died Sept. 4, 1973.

CLAUDY, CARL HARRY, writer; b. Washington, Jan. 13, 1879; s. Frank and Mary Josephine Dillon (Catlin) C.; ed. Washington High Sch.; m. Clara Fitch Duvall, Apr. 7, 1902. Prospector and pioneer in Alaska, 1898; editor American Inventor, 1900-04, Prism, 1908-09; editor Cathedral Calendar, 1921-27; asso. editor The Master Mason, 1924-30; freelance writer; aviation corr. N.Y. Herald, at Washington, D.C., 1908-09; dir. publicity, Nat. Highways Assn., since 1911; exec. sec. Masonic Service Assn. since 1929. Formerly maj. Officers Res. Corps. Progressive. Episcopalian. Mason (33°). Author: Press Photography, 1903; Battle of Baseball, 1912; First Book of Photography, 1912; Tell Me Why Stories About Mother Nature, 1912; Making Pictures of Children, 1912; Tell Me Why Stories About Animals, 1914; Tell Me Why Stories About Color and Sound, 1915; Partners of the Forest Trail, 1915; Tell Me Why Stories of Great Discoveries, 1916; Pirates by Force, 1917; Washington, 1923; A Master's Wages, 1924; The Old Past Master, 1924; Old Tiler Talks, 1925 (revised edition, 1949); Foreign Countries, 1925; The Gold He Found, 1928; Dangerous Waters, 1929; The Girl Reporter, 1930; Beginner's Book of Model Airplanes, 1930; Introduction to Freemasonry Airplanes, —1 (3 volumes), 1931; Washington's Home and Fraternal Life, 1931; United Masonic Relief, 1931; Mystery Men of Mars, 1933; Thousand Years a Minute, 1933; Land of No Shadow, 1933; Treasurer of Darkness, 1933; The Unknown Mason 1934; Blue Grotto Terror, 1934; The Master's Book, 1935; Masonic Service Association, 1939; The Lion's Paw, 1944; Where Your Treasure Is, 1946; These Were Brethren, 1947; Masonic Harvest, 1948; (Masonic Plays) Greatest of These, 1934; He That Believeth, 1935; Greater Love Hath No Man, 1936; A Rose Upon the Altar, 1937; Judge Not, 1938; Hearts of the Fathers, 1939; And Not Forsake Them, 1940; To Entertain Strangers, 1941; A Gift in Secret, 1942; Treasurers of Darkness, 1943; He Which Is Accused, 1944; If a Man Die, 1945; also booklets. Editor; Prize Winners Book of Model Airplanes, 1931; Little Masonic Library, 1946. Contbr. to mags. Clubs: Nat. Press, Columbia Country. Home: Washington, D.C.†

CLAUSON, GERARD LESLIE MAKINS, business exec.; b. Apr. 28, 1891; s. John Eugene Clauson; student Eton, Corpus Christi Coll., Oxford U.; m. Honor Emily Mary Husey, 1918; 3 children. Prin. Colonial Office, 1920-24, asst. sec., 1934-40, asst. undersec. of state, 1940-51, ret., 1951; chmn. Pirelli Ltd., 1960-69. Vice pres. Royal Archaeol. Inst. Created knight. Mem. Royal Asiatic Soc. (past pres.). Address: London, Eng., Died May 1, 1974.

CLAWSON, BENJAMIN J., univ. prof.; b. Dixonville, Pa., Jan. 9, 1881; s. Andrew Bingham and Martha Jane (Volvin) C.; B.S., U. of Kan., 1909, M.A., 1911; M.D., Rush Med. Coll., Chicago, 1917; Ph.D., U. of Chicago, 1911; m. Vera M. Jennings, June 22, 1911. Asst. prof. Okla. Agrl. and Mech. Coll., 1911-12; successively instr. and asst. prof. U. of Kan., 1912-17; instr. U. of Chicago, 1917-19; prof. pathology U. of N.D., 1919-21; successively asst. prof., asso. prof. and prof. pathology, U. of Minn., 1921-49, professor emeritus since June 15, 1949. Member American Soc. Bacteriologists, Am. Society Bacteriology and Pathology, Internat. Soc. Med. Museums, Am. Soc. Cancer Research, Minn. Pathol. Soc., Sigma Xi. Republican. Contbr. articles on diseases of heart to professional jours. Home: Minneapolis, Minn.†

CLAY, JAMES LLOYD, lawyer, builder; b. Paintsville, Ky., Oct. 20, 1911; s. J. Lloyd and Grace (VanHoose) C.; A.B., U. Ky., 1937, LL.B., 1940; m. Dorothy Davis, 1932 (div. 1953); children—Robert L., James L., William Wade; m. 2d, Della R. Callahan, Apr., 1968. Admitted to Ky. bar, 1940, since practiced in Lexington; tchr. and prin. Johnson County and Paintsville City Schs., 1931-37; asst. adj. gen. of Ky., 1946-47; individual law practice, from 1947. Dir., sec., treas. J. H. Warrington Co., Inc.; pres. Lansdowne Village Apts., Inc., Delmar Village, Inc., Perma Glaze of Ky., Perma Cement of Ky., Gale Builders; sec. Johnson Electronics Co.; dir. Kadett Equipment Co. Past mem. Lexington-Fayette County Planning and Zoning Commn. Mem. Fayette County Republican Exec. Com. (past chmn.), Citizens for Eisenhower (past dist. chmn.), Woodford County Rep. Exec. Com. Pres. Gardenside Nursing Home, Fayette Nursing Home. Served as lt. comdr. USCGR, 1942-45. Named Ky. Col.; adm. Neb. Navy. Mem. Am., Ky., Fayette County bar assns., Am. Legion (past state exec. com., past post comdr.), Jr. C. of C. (past dir.). U. Ky. Law Coll. Alumni Assn. (past pres.), V.F.W., D.A.V., Order Confederate Cols., Fraternal Order Police, Phi Delta Phi, Methodist, Mason (Shriner). Clubs: Kiwanis, Ky. Mountain (past v.p.), Pyramid; Tates Creek Country; Thoroughbred of Am. Home: Versailles, Ky. Died Feb. 23, 1974

CLAYBERGER, RAYMOND PIERCE, assn. exec.; b. Brandonville, Pa., Nov. 24, 1881; s. Benjamin Franklin and Helen Elizabeth (Sanborn) D.; student Drexel Inst., Phila.; m. Helen M. Adams, Oct. 14, 1914; children—Helen Jane (Mrs. H. George Gelding, 111), Raymond Pierce, Jr. Secretary, treas., and dir., Calkins & Holden, since 1904; pres., dir. Nat. Better Business Bur. since 1932; pres., dir. Winter Golf League of Advt. Interest since 1931; vice president Owen & Chappell; v.p., gen. mgr. Ray McCarthy Advt. Service; dir. Republic Fireproofing Co., The Safety Car Heating & Lighting Co. Pres. Nat. Shrine of Bill of Rights, Mt. Vernon, N.Y. Formerly trustee bd. of edn., Bronxville, N.Y. Rep. Episcopalian. Clubs: St. Andrew Golf, Hastings-on-Hudson, The Canaidan, Waldorf-Astoria Hotel, Pine Valley Golf, Clementon, Shenorock Shore. Home: New York City, N.Y.†

CLAYTON, CLAUDE FEEMSTER, U.S. circuit judge; b. Tupelo, Miss., Aug. 4, 1909; s. Claude and Mary Annis (Feemster) C.; LL.B., U. Miss., 1931; m. Bronson Elizabeth Munday, Oct. 10, 1940; children—Mary Munday (Mrs. Nelson O. Tyrone, Jr.), Bronson, Claude. Admitted to Mississippi State bar, 1931, practiced law in Tupelo; county pros. atty., Lee County, 1935-38; circuit judge 1st Circuit Ct. Dist., 1938-42; pvt. practice of law. 1945-58; U.S. dist. judge No. Dist. Miss., 1958-66, chief judge, 1966-67; U.S. circuit judge, Court of Appeals, 5th Circuit, 1967-69; city attorney for the City of Tupelo, 1949-53. Dist. tng. chmn. Boy Scouts; disaster chmn. A.R.C., Lee County, 1935-36. Dist. commr. Young Democrats, 1936-38; county chmn. Roosevelt Nominators, 1936. Served to col. AUS. World War II; now maj. gen. Miss. N.G. retired. Decorated Legion of Merit, Bronze Star medal, various service medals. Member American Bar Association, Tupelo Chamber of Commerce (secretary 1932-33, v.p. 1933-34), Community Development Found., Lee County Bar Assn. (pres. 1956-57). Am. Legion, V.F.W., Miss. State Bar, Sigma Alpha Epsilon, Phi Alpha Delta Methodist. Clubs: Nettleton Fox Hunting and Fishing, National Lawyers, Tupelo Country; Merigold Hunting, Memphis Press, Top of the 100. Home: Tupelo, Miss. Died July 4, 1969; interred Glenwood Cemetery, Tupelo.

CLAYTON, EVERETT MCCORD, JR., physician; b. Mayfield, Ky., Mar. 9, 1923; s. Everett McCord and Elizabeth (Creason) C.; student Peabody Demonstration Sch.; grad. Vanderbilt U.; M.D., U. Tenn., 1947; m. Ada Page Davidson, 1944; children—Everett McCord III, Elizabeth C. Buchanan, Philip Davidson. Intern in obstetrics and gynecology Vanderbilt U. Hosp., Nashville, 1947-48, asst. resident, then resident, 1948-50; practice medicine specializing in obstetrics and gynecology, Nashville, 1953-74; clin. prof. obstetrics and gynecology Vanderbilt U.; dir. obstetrics and gynecology St. Thomas Hosp., Nashville, 1968-73. Served to lt., M.C., USNR, 1950-52. Diplomate Am. Bd. Obstetrics and Gynecology. Fellow Am. Coll. Obstetricians and Gynecologists; mem. Central Assn. Obstetricians and Gynecologists, South Central Soc. Obstetricians and Gynecologists, Tenn. (charter), Nashville (charter, pres. 1969) obstet. and gynecol. socs. Methodist. Research on Rh factor in childbirth. Pioneer use of ultrasonics for med. diagnosis, intra-uterine transfusions. Home: Nashville, Tenn. Died Oct. 2, 1974; buried Mt. Olivet Cemetery, Nashville.

CLELAND, JOSEPH P., army officer; b. Holdredge, Neb., Mar. 2, 1902; s. Joseph Pringle and Effie Geddes (Reed) C.; B.S., U.S. Mil. Acad., 1925; grad. Inf. Sch., 1933. Command and Gen. Staff Sch., 1939, Airborn Sch., 1950; m. Florence E. Cadotte, June 12, 1931. Commd. 2d lt. inf., U.S. Army, 1925, advanced through grades to maj. gen., 1952; assigned P.I., 1929-31; prof. mil. sci., tactics Kemper Mil. Sch., Mo., 1936; assigned Panama, 1940-42; asst. mil. attache, Bogota, Colombia, 1942; asst. chief staff for supply U.S. Army Forces, South Pacific area, 1942; comdg. officer Provisional Service Command, Guadalcanal, 1943, 103d Inf. Regt., 1944-45; asst. div. comdr. 43d Div., 1945; mil. attache, Santiago, Chile, 1946; instructor Command and Gen. Staff Coll., 1947-50; with 82d Airborne Div., 1950; comdg. ofcr. 504th Inf. Regt., Ft. Bragg, 1950, 508th Regtl. Combat Team, Fort Benning, Georgia, 1951; asst. div. comdr. 82d Airborne Div., Ft. Bragg, 1951; comdg. officer 40th Div., Korea, 1952, 1st Cavalry Div., Hokkaido, Japan, 1953, 18th Airborne Corps, Ft. Bragg, since 1953. Decorated Distinguished Service Medal, Silver Star, Legion of Merit with Oak Leaf Cluster, Soldier's Medal, Bronze Star with Cluster, Combat Inf. Badge; Al Merito Militar, Estrella de Oro (Chile); Comdr. Order Brit. Empire. Master parachutist. Home: Clearwater, Fla. Died Mar. 28, 1975.

CLEMENCE, GERALD MAURICE, astronomer; b. Greenville, R.I., Aug. 16, 1908; s. Richard R. and Lora E. (Oatley) C.; Ph.B., Brown U., 1930; Sc.D., Case Inst. Tech., 1954; Dr., Univ. de Cuyo (Argentina), 1961; m. Edith M. Vail, Aug. 17, 1929; children—Gerald V., Theodore G. Jr. astronomer Naval Obs., 1930-37, asst. astronomer, 1937-40, astronomer, 1940-42, sr. astronomer, 1942-45, head astronomer and dir. Nautical Almanac, U.S. Naval Obs., Washington, 1945-58; sci. dir. Naval Obs., 1958-63; sr. research asso., lectr. astronomy Yale 1963-66, prof. astronomy, 1966-74. Chmn. div. phys. scis. NRC, 1963-66; vis. prof. astronomy Columbia, 1958. Adviser Internat. com. on weights and measures Asso. Royal Astron. Soc., 1952, gold medal, 1965. Recipient USN award for distinguished achievement, 1963, superior achievement, 1964; James Craig Watson Gold medal Nat. Acad. Scis., awarded posthumously 1975. Mem. A.A.A.S. (sect. chmn., v.p. 1954); mem. Inst. Nav. (charter mem., councillor 1945-57), Internat. Astron. Union (pres. commn. on clestial mechanics 1948-55, pres. commn. on ephemrides 1946-67), Academia Nacional de Ciencias Exactas, Fiaicas y Naturales de Buenos Aires (Argentina), Bur. Geophysics, Am. Astron. Soc. (councillor 1949-52, v.p. 1952-54, pres. 1958-60), Am. Acad. Arts and Scis., Nat. Acad. Scis., Paine Brook Assos. (dir.), Royal Astron. Soc. Can. (hon.), Sigma Xi. Author: First-order Theory of Motion of Mars; Standards of Time and Frequency. Joint author: Coordinates of Five Outer Planets 1653-2060; Methods of Celestial Mechanics; Spherical Astronomy. Asso. editor Astron. Jour., 1949-63, joint editor, 1963-66, editor, 1966. Contbr. articles to astron. jours., obs. publs Home: Providence, R.I. Died Nov. 22, 1974; interred Brockway Cemetery, New Brunswick, Canada.

CLEMENT, KENNETH WITCHER, surgeon; b. Pittsylvania County, Va., Feb. 24, 1920; s. Harry Leonard and Inez (Mae) C.; A.B. (Amos Miller scholar), Oberlin Coll., 1942, LL.D., 1968; M.D. with honors (W.K. Kellogg scholar), Howard U., 1945; LL.D., Central State U., 1968; m. Ruth Doss, Aug. 22, 1942; children—Michael Craig, Leslie Denise, Lia Deborah. Intern N.Y.C. Hosp., 1945-46; intern Cleve. City Hosp., 1945, resident surgeon, 1946-50, chief resident surgeon, 1950-51; practice medicine specializing in surgery, Cleve., 1953-74; mem. staff St. Luke's, Forest City, Marymount hosps.; asst. vis. surgeon Met. Gen. Hosp.; sr. clin. instr. surgery Western Res. U., 1959-66, asst. clin. prof., 1966-74. Dir. Mt. Pleasant Med. center, Inc., 912 Galatin Corp., Bardun Investment Corp. Mem. Cleve. Mayor's Com. Employment Physically Handicapped, 1958-74; mem. Nat. Adv. Com. Social Security, 1963-65, med. adv. com. disability operation, 1965-74; mem. Hosp. Ins. Benefit Adv. Council, 1965-74, Nat. Selective Service Bd., 1966-74; cons. Office Tech. Coop. and Research, AID, State Dept., Cleve. Adv. Com. Urban Renewal, 1961-74; com. community resources nursing edn. Cleve. Hosp. Council, 1961-74; mem. Cleve. Community Relations Bd., 1963-66. Team capt. United Appeal Cleve., 1952-63; gen. campaign chmn. Cleve. YMCA, 1959; co-chmn. life membership com. Cleve. and Ohio N.A.A.C.P., 1957-74, v.p. Cleve. br., 1962-74. Bd. dirs. Cleve. Christian Community Center, Greater Cleve. Equal Opportunity Act, Nat. Urban League; bd. dirs., pres. Cleve. Urban League, Cleve. N.A.A.C.P., 1955-74, Cleve. Bapt. Assn., 1956-74, Cleve. and Ohio br. Am. Civil Liberties Union, 1962-74; chmn. planning and devel. com. bd. trustees Howard U. Served to maj., M.C., USAF, 1951-53. Recipient Jesse Green award surgery Howard U., 1945, John Hale award surgery Winston Salem (N.C.) Med. Sch., 1950; merit award for med. bldg. Cleve. C. of C., 1958; Distinguished Service award Cleve. Med. Assn., 1962, 64, Nat. Med. Assn., 1965; New Frontiers award Ams. for Democratic Action. Diplomate Am. Bd. Surgery. Fellow A.C.S.; mem. Am., Nat. (chmn. com. health care aged 1960, pres. 1963-64), Ohio med. assns., Aero-Space Med. Assn., Assn. Mil. Surgeons, Howard U. Sch. Medicine (exec. com. 1962-65), Howard U. (pres. 1965-67) alumni assns., Kappa Pi. Democrat. Baptist. Club: City (Cleve.). Contbr. articles to profl. jours. Home: Shaker Heights, O. Died Nov. 29, 1974.

CLEMONS, HARRY, librarian; b. Corry, Pa., Sept. 9, 1879; s. Henry Dwight and Harriet Eliza (Barber) C.; A.B., Wesleyan U., 1902; post-grad. study same university, 1902-03, A.M., 1905, Litt.D., 1942; Scribner fellow, Princeton University, 1903-04, A.M., 1905; Jacobus fellow of Princeton at Oxford University, England, 1906-07; studied School of Library Service, Columbia, 1927; m. Jeannie Cooper Jenkins, May 21, 1918; children—Henry Jenkins (lieutenant Army Air Corps, died July 31, 1943), Emily Barber (Mrs. George Southall Vest). Began as assistant in library, Wesleyan University, 1902-03; instructor in English, Princeton, 1904-06, 1907-08; reference librarian, same, 1908-13; professor English, U. of Nanking, China, 1913-20, librarian, 1914-27; librarian, U. Va., 1927-50, cons. library resources, 1950-57, librarian emeritus, after 1957. Hon. trustee Woodrow Wilson Birthplace Found. Ofcl. rep. A.L.A. in charge library war service, A.E.F., Siberia, 1918-19; spl. cataloguer Chinese sect., Library of Congress, 1922. Recipient Thomas Jefferson Award, U. Va., 1956. Member Virginia State Board for Certification of Librarians, 1936-48. Member A.L.A., Virginia Library Association (president 1931-32), Raven Soc., Phi Beta Kappa. Omicron Delta Kappa, Pi Delta Epsilon, Psi Upsilon. Presbyn. Clubs: Colonade, Farmington Country. Wrote An Essay Towards a Bibliography of the Published Writings and Addresses of Woodrow Wilson (1875-1910), 1913; The A.L.A. in Siberia, 1919; A Survey of Research Materials in Virginia Libraries, 1936-37, 1938; University of Virginia Library, 1825-1950: Story of a Jeffersonian Foundation, 1954; The Home Library of the Garnetts of Elmwood, 1956; Notes on the Professors for Whom the University of Virginia Halls and Residence Houses are named, 1961. Editor: (with M. W. Croll) Lyly's Euphues, the Anatomy of Wit, Euphues and His England, 1916. Home: Charlottesville, Va.†

CLERKIN, JAMES JOSEPH, JR., telephone co. exec.; b. New Britain Conn., June 4, 1923; s. James Joseph and Lillian (Seipel) C.; B.S. in Mech. Engring., Worcester Poly. Inst., 1944; M.B.A., Harvard, 1947; m. Theresa D. Vadnais, June 30, 1945; 1 dau., Patricia Ann. With Theo. Gary & Co., and subsidiaries, 1947-56; v.p., dir. Continental Telephone Co. and subsidiaries, 1952-56; with Comptometer Corp., 1956-61; pres. Gen. Telephone & Electronics Internat. Corp., N.Y.C., 1961-64; exec. v.p. telephone operations Gen. Telephone and Electronics Corp., 1964-74, also dir.; dir. Allied Products Corp., Genesco, Inc. Trustee Worcester Poly. Inst. Served with USNR, 1944-45. Mem. Harvard Bus. Sch. Assn., Worcester Poly. Inst. Alumni Assn. Clubs: Harvard of New York; Wee Burn Country (Darien, Conn.); University (N.Y.C.). Home: Darien, Conn., Died Nov. 20, 1975.

CLEVENGER, GALEN HOWELL, metallurgist; b. Pike, N.Y., Sept. 1, 1879; s. Galen Smith and Lila Eleanor (Howell) C.; B.S., S. Dak. State Sch. of Mines, Rapid City, S.D., 1901, E.M., 1908; A.M., Columbia U., 1903; Met.E., Leland Stanford Jr. University, 1906; m. Alice Emily Clemens, June 30, 1903; children—Lila Clemens, Galen William, Alice C. (dec.). Proprietor of cyanide process plant, Rapid City, S.Dak., 1899-1901; assayer and chemist Dak. Mining & Milling Co., Deadwood, S.Dak., 1901-02; research metallurgist, Nat. Smelting Co., Rapid City, 1903-04; supt. gold reduction mill, Horseshoe Mining Company, Terry, S.Dak., 1904-05; instr. metallurgy, Stanford U., 1905-06; spl. asst. U.S. Geol. Survey, in charge electric smelting experiments, Portland, Ore., 1905 (leave of absence from Stanford); in practice as consulting metallurgist, San Francisco, 1906-09; sucessively asst. asso. and reserach prof. metallurgy, Stanford U., 1909-18; metallurgist U.S. Bur. Mines in charge coöperative investigation of treatment of manganese-silver ores for U.S. Bur. Mines and Mines Service of Netherlands E. Indies Govt., also in charge metall. investigations for production of war minerals for Bur. of Mines; chmn. sect. on metallurgy, Div. of Engring. Nat. Research Council, Washington, D.C., 1919, v. chmn. Div. of Engring., 1920-23. Consulting metallurgist Cia Real del Monte y Pachuca, Mexico, 1919-20; consulting metallurgist, U.S. Smelting, Refining & Mining Co., since 1921. Mem. exec. bd. Am. Engring. Council, 1922-23; mem. bd. dirs. Engring. Foundation, 1926-31, vice chmn., 1929-30; chmn. advisory com. on nonferrous metallurgy, U.S. Bureau of Mines, 1937-38. Member American Institute of Mining and Metallurgical Engineers (director 1920-26), Mining and Metallurgical Society of America, Am. Chem. Soc., Am. Electro-Chem. Soc., A.A.A.S., Sigma Xi. Awarded gold and silver medals, San Francisco Expn., 1915. Clubs: Engineers' (New York); Chemists' (New York); Cosmos (Washington, D.C.), Contributor of many papers to technical press and trans. of tech. societies; inventor various processes and devices for treatment of ores. Home: Newtonville, Mass.†

CLEVENGER, JOSEPH R., lawyer, author, editor, pub.; b. nr. Excelsior Springs, Mo., May 13, 1884; s. Gordon and Sarah (Sisk) C.; A.B., U. Mo., 1905, LL.B., 1907. Admitted to N.Y. bar, 1912, tried and won N.Y. City Savs. and Loan Fraud cases, 1916-19. Author 92 vols including: Supreme Court Practice, 1921; Rules of Civil Practice, 1922; Surrogate's Court Practice, 1922; New York City Court and Municipal Court Practice, 1922; Annual Practice of New York, 1922-56; Criminal Law and Practice, 1928-53; Parol Evidence, 1928; Applied Law of Automobiles, 1929; Clevenger-Huddy Cyclopedia of Automobile Law, 1932; Automobile Trials, 1935; Annulment of Marriage, 1946. Editor: Gulbert-Bliss Civil Practice, 1940-56; Nichols- Cahill Annotated Civil Practice Acts, 1950-56; pub. propr. Am. Law Pubs. 1922-50. Staff editor Corpus Juris (1908-12). Home: New York City, N.Y. Died Nov. 5, 1974; buried Old New Garden Cemetery, Ray County, Mo.

CLEWELL, EDGAR L., army officer; b. Bethesda, Minn., July 22, 1896; s. Robert Eugene and Mamie Christina (Gillie) C.; grad. Nazareth Hall Mil. Acad., Pa., 1912; A.B., Moravian Coll., Bethlehem, Pa., 1916, LL.D., 1945; A.M. Columbia, 1922; grad Tank Sch., 1923, Signal Sch., 1934, Command and Gen. Staff Sch., 1940; m. Mildred Sager, June 13, 1918. Commd. 2d lt., Inf., U.S. Army, Aug. 15, 1917, advanced through the grades to brig. gen. (temp.), 1942; signal officer 4th Army Corps, 1940; exec. officer Ft. Monmouth, N.J., 1940-42; apptd. comdg. gen. Eastern Signal Corps Replacement Training Center, 1942, Chicago Signal Depot and Assistant Chief, Signal Corps Procurement and Distribution Service for Western Area, and ASF Representative for WPB Region VI, 1943-44; dir. of Signal Supply, ETO, 1944; asst. chief Procurement and Distbn. Service, chief, 1945-46; Office, Chief Signal Officer, Washington, 1945; ret., 1946. Decorated Victory National Defense and Pa. Flood Service and European Theater Service medals; U.S. Army Legion of Merit, Army Commendation Ribbon, and French Legion of Honor; awarded citation, Nat. Com. for Mental Hygiene. Mem. Nat. Com. for Mental Hygiene, National Sojourners, Heroes of '76. Mason (Shriner). Clubs: Army and Navy (Washington); Beaufort Hunt; Country of Harrisburg. Home: Ft. Lauderdale, Fla. Died May 27, 1973.

CLIFFORD, WILLIAM SCHOFIELD, physician; b. Lockhart, Tex., Oct. 10, 1911; s. Forshey Nichols and Emma (Forke) C.; M.D., Med. Coll. Va., 1943; m. Kathryn Perkins (dec. 1958); children—William Dandridge, Sally (Mrs. Stephen Cummings Kelly); m. 2d, June Celeste Dickson, Nov. 26, 1959; 1 son, Charles Nichols. Intern, Jefferson Davis Hosp., Houston, 1943; asst. resident in obstetrics and gynecology U. Mich. Hosp., Ann Arbor, 1946-47, fellow in obstetrics and gynecology, 1947-48, resident in obstetrics and gynecology, 1948-49, instr. gynecology, 1949-50; resident in radiology Baylor U., 1964-67; dir. radiology Montgomery County Hosp., Conroe, Tex., 1967-71; asso. prof. radiology Baylor Coll. Medicine, 1971-72. Served with USNR, 1944-46; PTO. Diplomate Am. Bd. Radiology, Am. Bd. Obstetrics and Gynecology. Fellow Am. Coll. Obstetrics and Gynecology, Am. Coll. Radiology, Phi Beta Pi. Republican. Episcopalian. Mason (32°). Home: Houston, Tex., Died Jan. 29, 1972; buried Rosehill Cemetery, Fort Worth, Tex.

CLIFT, DAVID HORACE, librarian; b. Mason County, Ky., June 16, 1907; s. Charles Lawson and Mary E. (Tomlin) C.; B.S., U. Ky., 1930; B.S. in L.S., Columbia, 1931; m. Eleanore Flynn, Nov. 4, 1933. Student asst. U. Ky. Library, 1927-30, Lexington (Ky.) Pub. Library, summer 1930, Columbia U. Libraries, 1930-31; reference asst. N.Y. Pub. Library, 1931-37; asst. to dir. libraries Columbia, 1937-42; dep., later acting chief Library of Congress Mission to Germany, 1945-46; asso. librarian Yale, 1945-51; instr. New Haven State Tchrs. Coll., summer 1948; exec. sec. Am. Library Assn., 1951-58, exec. dir., 1958-72, exec. dir. emeritus, 1972-73. Head delegation U.S. Librarians to Soviet Union, 1961; study tour libraries Fed. Republic Germany, 1963; bd. visitors Duke U. Library, 1964-73; mem. Librarian of Congress Liaison Com.; del. Internat. Fedn. Library Assns., 1964-72. Hon. trustee Am. Library, Paris, 1969-73; mem. Freedom to Read Found. Served from pvt. to 1st lt. OSS, AUS, 1942-45. Recipient U. Ky. Founders' Day award for distinguished achievement in librarianship, 1957, Joseph W. Lippincott award for notable achievement in librarianship, 1962; Distinguished Alumni Centennial award U. Ky., 1965. A.L.A. travelling fellow, 1972-73. Mem. Conn. Library Assn. (pres. 1950-51; hon. mem.), A.L.A. Club: N.Y. Library (pres. 1941-42). Home: Evanston, Ill. Died Oct. 12, 1973; buried Washington, Ky.

CLINE, GENEVIEVE R., judge; b. Warren, O., July 2, 1879; d. Edward B. and Mary A. (Fee) Cline; student Oberline (O.) Coll.; LL.B., Baldwin-Wallace Coll., 1921. Admitted to O. bar, 1921; apptd. U.S. appraiser of merchandise at Cleveland by President Harding, 1922; apptd. judge U.S. Customs Court N.Y. City, by President Coolidge, 1928 (1st woman U.S. judge). Home: New York City, N.Y.†

CLINE, HOWARD FRANCIS, govt. ofcl., historian; b. Detroit, June 12, 1915; s. Francis E. and Sarah L. (Orr) C.; S.B. magna cum laude in History, Harvard, 1939, A.M. (Frederick Sheldon Prize fellow), 1939-40, Social Sci. Research pre-doctoral fellow 1942-43, 1943, Ph.D. in History, 1947; m. Mary A. Wilson, June 14, 1941; children—Ann E., Sue L. Asst. dean coll. Harvard, 1943-47, registrar coll., 1945, asst. counsellor for vets. univ., 1945-46, Woodbury Lowery traveling fellow, 1946, exec. sec. Com. Internat. and Regional studies, 1946-47, instr. history, 1947; instr. history Yale, 1947-49; asst. prof. history Northwestern U., 1949-52; dir. Hispanic Found., Library Congress, Washington, 1952-71. U.S. Govt. rep. II Internat. Colloquium on Luso-Brazillian Studies, Sao Paulo, 1954; adviser U. S. delegation VI Gen. Assembly, Pan Am. Inst. Geography and History, Mexico, 1955, II Cultural Council, Orgn. Am. States, Lima, Peru, 1956; Am. Council Learned Societies rep. III Internat. Colloquium on Luso-Brazillian Studies, Lisbon, Portugal, 1957; adviser U.S. delegation IV Consultation, Commn. on History, Cuenca, Ecuador, 1959, national mem. Commn. on History, 1959-68; v. chmn. U.S. delegation IV Interam. Cultural Council, 1959; mem. exec. cons. commn. Latin Am. Anthropology NRC, 1956-59. Decorated Commander Order Isabel la Catôlica. Mem. Am. Hist. Assn. (exec. mem. com. guide to hist. lit. 1956-60, com. info. services 1968-71), Anthrop. Soc. Washington, Conf. Latin Am. History (chmn. 1963), Societé des Américanistes (France), Latin American Studies Association (sec. 1966-67), Hispanic Soc. of Am. (corresponding mem.), Am. Acad. Franciscan History (asso.), Phi Beta Kappa. Club: Cosmos. Author: The United States and Mexico, 1953; Mexico: Revolution to Evoluation, 1940-60, 1962; also numerous articles. Editor: Latin American History: its study and teaching, 1967; Handbook Middle American Indians, Guide to Ethnohistorical Sources, vol. 12, 1972, vol. 13, 1973, vols. 14 and 15, 1975. Bd. editors: Hispanic Am. Hist. Rev., 1957-62. Home: Arlington, Va., Died June 1, 1971.

CLINE, JOHN WESLEY, surgeon; b. Santa Rosa, Cal., 1898; A.B., U. Cal., 1921; M.D., Harvard, 1925; D.Sc. (hon.), Cal. Coll. Medicine, 1962; m. Edith Corde, 1925; children—John W. III, Robert C., Janet. Intern, Mass. Gen. Hosp., Boston, 1925-27; resident surgeon Cornell div. Bellevue Hosp., 1927-29; surgeon Hosp. for Children; Stanford Service, San Francisco Hosp.; surg. cons. Biggs-Gridley Meml. Hosp.; expert med. cons. to Surgeon Gen. USAF and USN, 1950-54; cons. for cancer control to surgeon gen. USPHS; asso. clin. prof. Stanford U. Sch. Med.; dir. Citizens Savs. and Loan Assn., United Financial Corp. Cal. Trustee St. Francis Meml. Hosp.; mem. Council on Med. Edn. and Hosps., 1952-59. Diplomate Am. Bd. Surgery. Fellow A.C.S. (chmn. commn. on cancer 1965-69, Distinguished Service award 1973); mem. A.M.A. (del. to World Assn. 1948, 49; pres. 1951-52; chmn. sect. gen. surgery 1964-65), Soc. Head and Neck Surgeons, Cal. Med. Assn. (chmn. cancer commn.), Am. Pacific Coast surg. assns., Cal. Acad. Medicine, San Francisco Surg. Soc., San Francisco County Med. Soc., Am. Cancer Soc. (dir. 1957-59, chmn. med. and sci. com. 1958-59, pres. 1960-61), S.A.R. Clubs: Bohemian, Family, St. Frances Yacht (San Francisco). Contbr papers on surg. subjects. Address: San Francisco, Cal. Died July 10, 1974; interred Cypress Lawn Cemetery, Colma, Cal.

CLINTON, HARRIET PETTIBONE (MRS. FRED DAVIDSON CLINTON), assn. exec.; b. Burlington, Ia., Dec. 29, 1896; d. John Holland and Margaret Cornelia (Danner) P.; B.A., U. Wis., 1919; postgrad. Columbia, 1923-24, U. Queensland, Australia, 1943; m. Fred Davidson Clinton, Apr. 30, 1925. With Milw. Jour., 1920-21, Milw. Sentinel, 1921-23, Milw. Leader, 1926-32; with pub. information dept., div. for children and youth Wis. Dept. Pub. Welfare, Madison, 1949-53; pub. relations cons. Internat. Inst., Milw., 1953-75, Holiday Folk Fair, 1953-75. Dir. Women's and profl. div. WPA, Milw. County, 1934-40, Eastern Wis., 1940-42; club dir. A.R.C., Australia, 1943-45; work relief specialist UNRRA, China, 1946-47; mem. Wis. Bd. Mental Hygiene, 1938-39; mem. Mayor's com. for Observance UN Day, 1962-63. sec. Gov.'s Conf. on Children and Youth, 1952-53. Mem. Women In Communications. English Speaking Union of Wis. (dir. 1964-75). Club: Milw. Press. Home: Milwaukee, Wis. Died 1975.

CLIPPINGER, ARTHUR RAYMOND, bishop; b. Franklin County, Pa., Sept. 3, 1878; s. Harry R. and Harriet Rebecca (Gillan) C.; A.B., Lebanon Valley Coll., Annville, Pa., 1905, D.D., 1918, LL.D., 1940; B.D., Yale Divinity Sch., 1910; m. Ellen Weinland Mills, Oct. 16, 1907; children—Conrad Keister, John Arthur, Malcolm Mills. Ordained United Brethren ministry; pastor New Cumberland, Pa., 1905-07; Euclid Av. Ch., Dayton, O., 1910-18; conf. supt., 1918-21; elected bishop U. B. Ch., May, 1921, sr. bishop Evang. United Brethren Ch., 1946-51, then bishop Trustee Otterbein Home, Otterbein Coll.; del. to World Council of Chs., Amsterdam, 1948. Republican. Mason (33°, K.T.). Home: Dayton, O.†

CLOAK, EVELYN KIMMEL CAMPBELL (MRS. F. THEODORE CLOAK), curator; b. Spokane, Wash., Mar. 9, 1907; d. William Leasure and Lorene (Mills) Kimmel; student U. Wash., 1926-28, U. Geneva (Switzerland), 1948-49; m. Rowland Campbell, Jan. 9, 1930 (dec. October 1943), children—Nancy (Mrs. Danny Wynn-Ye Kwok), Jane (Mrs. Louis de la Boutetiere), Sue (Mrs. Eugene Barna); m. second, F. Theodore Cloak, January 8, 1965. With John Nelson Bergstrom Art Center and Mus., Neenah, Wisconsin, 1959-71, asst. dir., curator paperweights, 1963-71. Commr., Appleton (Wis.) council Girl Scouts U.S.A., 1941-43; 1st pres. Appleton Vis. Nurse Assn., 1947-48. Mem. Kappa Kappa Gamma. Conglist. Founder center for research on glass paperweights Bergstrom Art Center, 1965. Author: Glass Paperweights of the Bergstrom Art Center, 1969. Home: Appleton, Wis. Died Oct. 1, 1971; interred Golders Green, London, England.

CLOKE, HARVEY WALTON, pub. relations and advt. exec.; b. Hazelton, Pa. Aug. 12, 1919; s. Harvey Raymond and Viola Mary (Walton) C.; A.B., Bucknell U., 1942; m. Janet Alden House, July 24, 1943; m. 2d, Marjorie Mithcell, Dec. 1960. Mng. editor Lewisburg (Pa.) Jour., 1940-42; financial writer, legislative corr. Asso. Press, 1943-45; financial corr. N.Y. Times, Phila. and Washington burs., 1945-50; coordinator pub. relations Kaiser Industries Corp. and affiliates, 1950-63; sr. v.p. Barnet and Reef Assos., Inc., N.Y.C., 1963-64; v.p. pub. relations and advt., corporate officer Am. Can Co., N.Y.C., 1964-68; v.p. pub. relations and advt., also corporate officer Rockwell Internat., Pitts., 1968-75; Washington editor Finance mag., 1948-50. Bd. dirs. Advt. Council; mem. Nat. Advt. Rev. Bd. Past exec. bd. U.S. nat. com. UNESCO. Mem. Pub. Relations Soc. Am. (past pres., mem. accreditation bd.), Am. (pres.), Internat. pub. relations assns., Assn. Nat. Advertisers (dir.) Pub. Relations Found. (dir.), N.A.M. (pub. relations council), Aerospace Industries Assn. (exec. com., pub. affairs council), Lambda Chi Alpha, Sigma Tau Delta, Phi Delta Epsilon. Clubs: Nat. Press, Internat. Nat. Aviation (Washington); Fox Chapel, Racquet (Pitts); Overseas Press, Pinnacle (N.Y.C.); Bel Air Country (Los Angeles). Home: Pittsburgh, Pa., Died Sept. 1975.

CLOONAN, JOHN JOSEPH, clergyman, coll. prof.; b. Hancock, N.Y., Mar. 24, 1881; s. Michael and Mary Martha (Warner) C.; student Niagara Univ., 1897-1900, St. Vincent's Sem., Germantown, Pa., 1900-02; S.T.B., Gregorian Univ., Rome, 1905; S.T.D., Univ. of Rome, 1925. LL.D. from Niagara U., 1927. Joined Congregation of the Mission, Lazarist Fathers, 1900;

ordained priest R.C. ch., 1904; prof. English, Niagara U., 1905-06; asst. rector Ch. of Immaculate Conception, Germantown, 1906-08; treas., later v.p., St. John's Coll., Brooklyn, N.Y., 1908-24; pres., 1925-31; also pres. St. John's Theol. Sem., Brooklyn, Sept. 1925-31; pastor St. Vincent's Ch., Germantown, Pa., 1931-33; treas. St. Joseph's Coll., Princeton, N. J., 1933-34; treas. Vincentian Mission House, Bangor, Pa., 1934-39; prof. philosophy, St. Joseph's College, Emmitsburg, Md., 1939-45; prof. philosophy Mary Immaculate Sem., Northampton, Pa., after 1945. Author: History of the Miraculous Medal, 1916; Principles of the Spiritual Life, 1942. Address: Northampton, Pa.†

CLOOS, ERNST, geologist, educator; b. Saarbrucken, Germany, May 17, 1898; s. Ulrich and Elisabeth (Heckel) C.; student univs. Freiburg and Gottingen; Ph.D., U. Breslau, 1923; m. Margret Spemann, Dec. 27, 1923; children—Gisela, Veronica. Came to U.S., 1932, naturalized 1938. Geologist, Selsmos Co., Hannover, Germany, 1924-29, in charge geophys. exploration in Tex., 1924-26, Eng. and Germany, 1927, Iraq, 1927-28; conducted investigation Sierra Nevada granites, 1929-30; lectr. Johns Hopkins U., Balt., 1931-37, asso. prof., 1937-41, prof., 1941-68, prof. emeritus, 1968-74. Chmn. Commn. Md. Geol. Survey, 1962. Guggenheim fellow, 1956-57, Fellow Geol. Soc. London; mem. Nat. Acad. Scis., Geol. Soc. Am., Am. Geophys. Union, A.A.A.S., Am. Philos. Soc., Geol. Soc. Finland, London Geologists Assn., Phi Beta Kappa, Sigma Xi. Condr. research expdns. Mesopotamia, Cal. and Tex. Research in structural geology of Appalachians and Petrofabrics. Home: Towson, Md. Died May 28, 1974; interred Baltimore, Md.

CLOSTERMAN, DONALD FRANKS, physician; b. Jersey City, Aug. 25, 1907; s. John Watt and Adelaide Elizabeth (Franks) C.; M.D., Hahnemann Med. Coll. and Hosp., 1931; m. Elizabeth Charlotte Buckingham, Aug. 27, 1934; children—Donald Franks (dec.), David Malcolm and Elizabeth Adelaide (Mrs. Thomas William Roberts) (twins). Intern, Fitkin Meml. Hosp., Asbury Park, N.J., 1931-32; postgrad. in internal medicine and cardiology Harvard, Columbia Coll. Physicians and Surgeons; chief staff, cardiologist Nesbitt Meml. Hosp., Kingston, Pa.; cons. internal medicine Wyoming Valley Hosp., Wilkes-Barre, Pa. Bd. dirs. Nesbitt Meml. Hosp. Served to capt. M.C., AUS, 1942-46. Diplomate Am. Bd. Internal Medicine. Fellow A.C.P., Am. Coll. Cardiology; mem. A.M.A., Am. Heart Assn. Am. Legion. Republican. Methodist. Mason (Shriner). Home: Kingston, Pa. Died Feb. 22, 1974; buried Fern Knoll Burial Park, Dallas, Pa.

CLOTHIER, WILLIAM JACKSON, coal mcht.; b. Sharon Hill, Pa., Sept. 27, 1881; s. Isaac Hallowell and Mary Clapp (Jackson) C.; A.B., Harvard, 1904; m. Anita Porter, Feb. 21, 1906. Pres. Boone County Coal Corp. Clubs: Harvard Racquet. Merion Cricket (Phila.); Pickering Hunt; Harvard, Racquet & Tennis (New York). Home: Valley Forge, Pa.†

CLOUGH, GEORGE OBADIAH, coll. prof.; b. Feb. 10, 1878; Ben Wheeler, Van Zandt County, Tex.; s. Ancel Cicero Heard and Mary Eveline (Belcher) C.; A.B., U. of Tex., 1908, M.A., 1924; student Teachers Coll., Columbia U., 1928, Ph.D., New York U., 1931; m. Maggie Llewellyn Johnson, aug. 25, 1904; children—Forrest Weldon, Ancel McBridge, Margaret Louise. Rural School teacher and prin., Loli, Tex., 1901-02, Rogers Prairie, Tex., 1904-06; teacher of mathematics at Fort Worth (Tex.) High Sch., 1908-10, head of physics dept., 1910-14; prin. Corsicana High Sch., 1914-18; asst. prin. Ft. Worth Junior High Sch., 1918-20; supt. Tyler Public Sch., 1920-27; pres. Tyler Junior Coll., 1926-27; prof. edn., Southern Meth. U., after 1927, dir. Extension Div., since 1934, Dallas Coll., after 1935; lecturer on edn. in summer schs. U. of Tex., 1921-24 and 1938, Greeley Colo. Teachers Coll., 1925, Tex. Teachers Coll., 1934, Tex. Tech. Coll., 1935, N.Y. Univ., 1937; dir. Dallas Teachers' Credit Union; co-chmn. Texas Inter-professional Commn. on Child Development, 1945. Fellow Tex. Acad. of Science; mem. A.A.A.S., National Society College Teachers of Education, N.E.A., Am. Assn. of Sch. Adminstrs., Tex. State Teachers Assn. (pres. 1924), Tex. Soc. of Coll. Teachers of Edn. (pres. 1939), Tex. Commn. on Corr. and Extension Teaching (chmn. after 1939), Phi Delta Kappa. Mason. Democrat. Mehtodist. Clubs: Paideian, Kiwanis (Dallas). Co-author: Let's Learn to Spell (state adopted text). Home: Dallas, Tex.†

CLOUGH, JOHN H., pres. Gen. Electric X-Ray Corp.; b. July 29, 1892; s. Andrew M. and Elizabeth J. (Vicary) C.; B.S., U. of Rochester, 1912; m. Mrs. Jean Anderson Edwards, Apr. 7, 1934. With Gen. Elec. Co. at Schenectady, N.Y. as asst. cons. engr., asst. dir. research, sect. mgr.; pres. Gen. Elec. X-Ray Corp., Chicago, since 1938; dir. Newton Victor, Ltd., London, Capt. Signal Corps, U.S. Army. Clubs: University, Mohawk (Schenectady); Canadian of New York; Milwaukee County. Home: Milwaukee, Wis. Died Aug. 1, 1975.

CLOVIS, PAUL CURTIS, business exec.; b. Griswold, Ia., Sept. 5, 1902; s. Curtis Brady and Pearl Grace (Salisbury) C.; B.A., Grinnell Coll., 1924; J.D., U. Ia., 1927; m. Lucile Kepford, Sept. 6, 1924; 1 son, Paul Curtis. Admitted to Ill. bar, 1927; with Butler, Lamb, Foster & Pope, 1927-31; v.p. Twentieth Century Press, Inc., Chgo., 1931-38, dir., 1938—, pres., 1938-75; dir. pres. Graphic Arts Assn. Ill., Inc., 1949-52; dir., exec. com. Printing Industry Am. Inc., 1951-54; dir. Lumbermens Mut. Casualty Co., Ill. Mfrs. Co. Co-chmn. gen. campaign Community Fund Chgo., 1947. Former trustee Chgo. Wesley Meml. Hosp., Evanston Hosp. Mem. Am., Ill., Chgo. bar assns., Order of Coif. Clubs: Chicago, Commercial, Mid-Am., Commonwealth, University (Chgo.); Old Elm, Glen View (Winnetka, Ill.). Home: Winnetka, Ill., Died Aug. 28, 1975.

COATES, GRACE STONE, writer; b. Ruby, Kan., May 20, 1881; d. Henry Charles and Olive Sabrina (Sweet) Stone; ed. Normal Sch. (Oshkosh, Wis.), 1897-99, U. of Chicago, 1901-02; m. Henderson Coates, of Butte, Mont., Sept. 14, 1910. Democrat. Order of the Eastern Star. Author: Black Cherries, 1931; Mead and Mangel-Wurzel (verse), 1932; Portulacas in the Wheat (verse), 1033; Riding the High Country (with Patric T. Tucker), 1933. Home: Martinsdale, Mont.†

COATES, ROBERT HARRY, educator; b. Phila., Dec. 4, 1905; s. Robert and Movvanue (Evans) C.; B.S. in Edn., Temple U., 1930, M.S. in Edn., 1937; m. Beatrice Wright, June 25, 1930; 1 son, Robert Harry. Tchr. phys edn. Sch. Dist. Phila., 1927-39, spl. asst. adult edn., 1945-56, dir. adult edn., 1956-73. Mem. Kensington Community Council, Phila., 1929-73; chmn. Philenape Dist. council Boy Scouts Am., 1956-60, mem. Phila. council, 1960-73. Served to lt. comdr., USN, 1942-46. Mem. Nat. Assn. for Pub. Sch. Adult Edn. (pres. 1966-67), Phila. Assn. Health, Recreation and Welfare (pres. 1939-40, 46-48), Fedn. Community Councils (pres. bd. 1956-73). Methodist. Kiwanian. Club: Melrose Country (Cheltenham, Pa.) (pres. 1963-65). Author: Nature and Scope of Adult Education, 1946. Editor revised textbooks on citizenship U.S. Bur. Immigration and Naturalization, 1964. Creator TV edn. programs; Operation Alphabet, High School of the Air, University of the Air. Home: Philadelphia, Pa. Died June 21, 1973; interred Forest Hills Cemetery, Philadelphia, Pa.

COBB, CULLY ALTON, editor, printing corp. exec.; b. Prospect, Tenn., Feb. 25, 1884; s. Napoleon Bonaparte and Mary Agnes (Woodward) C.; B.S., Miss. Agrl. & Mech. Coll. (now Miss. State U.), 1908; D.Sc., Clemson U., 1937; m. Byrdie Ball, Dec. 23, 1910 (dec.); children—Cully Alton, David Alexander; m. 2d, Loise Dowdle, Aug. 24, 1934. Supt. high sch. Buena Vista, Miss., 1908-10; state agt. Miss. Agrl. and Mech. Coll., in charge boys' agrl. club. work, 1910-19, also asst. dir. extension work in Miss.; editor and dir. So. Ruralist, 1919-30; pres. Ruralist Press, Inc., Atlanta. Dir. cotton div. AAA, 1933; served as mem. printing industry com. WPB. Mem. agr. com. U.S.C. of C. Bd. govs. Agrl. Hall of Fame, 1964. Mem. Ash Kahn Crew (hon. soc. printing industry Am.); recipient Distinguished Service award Printing Industry of Atlanta, 1958, citation for distinguished service Printing Industry Am., 1962; Patron Excellence award Miss. State U., 1965. Mem. Nat. Boys' and Girls' Club Com. 1923-75, Unit of Value Stabilization Com. created by Am. Farm Bureau Fed. Mem. Atlanta C. of C. (chmn. agrl. com., livestock com.), Ga. Printers Assn. (pres.), Atlanta Master Printers Club (pres. 1944), Am. Agrl. Editors Assn. (pres. 1923-28), Country Life Assn. (dir.), Printing Industry Am. (past pres. union employer sect.), Omicron Delta Kappa (hon.). Democrat. Baptist. Mason (32°). Rotarian. Organized first sch. of Miss. system of agrl. high schs., and first internat. stock judging contests; as pres. Am. Agrl. Editors' Assn., conducted agrl. study tours to Europe, Can. and Mexico. Home: Decatur, Ga. Died May 7, 1975; buried City Cemetery, Decatur, Ga.

COBB, JAMES HARREL, educator; b. Bloomfield, Ind., Nov. 13, 1906; s. John and Margaret (Harrel) C.; A.B., Ind. State U., 1927, postgrad., 1928-29; M.A., Ind. U., 1930; B.D., Garrett Theol. Sem., 1942; postgrad. U. Utah, 1935-39, U. Chgo., 1942-46, Hebrew Union Coll., 1953-54 Tchr., Princeton (Ind.) High Sch., 1927-28; instr. English, Ind. State U., 1929-30, Mont. State U., 1930-32; supr., state curriculum specialist Adult Edn., Salt Lake City, 1932-39; asso. prof. English dept. Kan. Wesleyan U., 1946-47; asst. prof. Central Coll., 1947-48; asst. prof. Bible and religion U. Toledo, 1948-50; vis. asso. Greek and Hebrew, Vanderbilt U. Div. Sch., 1951-52; prof. Yankton Coll. Sch. of Theology, 1954-60; asst. prof. dept. English, speech S.E. Community Coll., U. Ky., 1960-63; U. Ky. at Lexington, 1963-73. Mem. Am. Acad. Religion, Nat. Assn. Profs. Hebrew, Am. Philos. Assn., Ky. English Assn., Pi Kappa Delta, Kappa Delta Pi, Lambda Iota Tau, Phi Delta Kappa. Republican. Jewish religion. Author: Principles and Concepts of Tanak (Old Testament), 1972; (corr. courses) The Literature of the New Testament, 1972. Home: Lexington Ky. Died Aug. 3, 1973.

COBB, LEE J., actor; b. N.Y.C., Dec. 9, 1911; s. Benjamin Jacob and Kate (Neilecht) C.; student City Coll. N.Y.; m. Helen Beverly, Feb. 6, 1940; m. 2d, Mary Hirsch, July 1957. Actor, dir. Pasadena Community Playhouse, 1931-33; mem. Group Theatre, N.Y.C., 1935-40, appeared Group prodn. Golden Boy, London, Eng., 1938; appeared in title role Broadway prodn. Death of a Salesman, The Emperor's Clothes; on screen 1937-76; numerous motion pictures include: The Moon is Down, 1943; Song of Bernadette, 1945; Anna and the King of Siam, 1946; Boomerang, 1947; Captain from Castile, 1948; Call Northside 777, 1948; But Not For me, 1959; The Trap, 1959; Green Mansions, 1959; Exodus, 1960, How the West Was Won; Come Blow Your Horn, 1963; The Man Who Loved Cat Dancing, 1973; appeared on TV series The Virginian, the Young Lawyers. Mem. Actors Equity Assn., Screen Actors Guild, Am. Fedn. Radio Artists, Nat. Aero. Assn., Aircrafts Pilots and Owners Assn., Civil Air Patrol. Address: Beverly Hills, Cal., Died Feb. 11, 1976.

COBBS, SUSAN PARKER, coll. dean; b. Anniston, Ala., Dec. 9, 1905; A.B., Randolph-Macon Women's Coll., 1927; A.M., N.Y.U., 1930; Ph.D., U. Chgo., 1937. Tchr., Latin High Sch., Alexandria, Va., 1927-28, Phillips High Sch., Birmingham, Ala., 1928-29, Randolph-Macon Woman's Coll., 1930-31, 1932-39, adj. prof., 1939-40; tchr. St. Catherine's Sch., Richmond, Va., 1931-32, Shipley Sch., Pa., 1940-41; asst. prof. Latin and Greek, Agnes Scott Coll., Decatur, Ga., 1941-45; dean Swarthmore Coll., 1945-69, also prof. classics. Mem. Philol. Assn. Address: Greensboro, Ala., Died Sept. 28, 1975.

COBBS, THOMAS HARPER lawyer; b. Lafayette Co., Mo., Aug. 26, 1868; s. Thomas T. and Catherine (Harper) C.; B.S., Odessa (Mo.) Coll., 1889; A.B., Washington U., St. Louis, 1896, LL.B., Yale, 1897; m. Lucie May Jones, Aug. 30, 1898. Admitted to Mo. bar, 1896, Ill. bar, 1897; with Flower, Smith & Musgraves, Chgo., 1897-1900; mem. firm Bishop & Cobbs, St. Louis, 1901-18, Cobbs & Logan, 1919-50, Cobbs, Blake, Armstrong, Teasdale & Roos after 1950; dir., Bank of St. Louis, Washington Fire & Marine Ins. Co., Gen. Grocer Co., Gen. Contracto Corp. and Ins. Co. of St. Louis. Vice pres. Met. Bd. Police Commrs. of St. Louis, 1945-49. Trustee pension & profit sharing fund, Bank of St. Louis; trustee endowment funds YMCA, St. Louis; dir. Scottish Rite Endowment Found., St. Louis; dir., v.p., Lindenwood Ferndale Coll. Presbyn. Mason (33°, Shriner). Club: Missouri Athletic. Home: St. Louis, Mo.†

COBLE, ARTHUR BYRON, mathematician; b. Williamstonw, Pa., Nov. 3, 1878; s. Reuben and Emma Irene (Haegy) C.; A.B., Pa. Coll., 1897; A.M., 1900; Ph.D., Johns Hopkins, 1902; LL.D., Pa. Coll., 1933; m. Abby Walker Adams Whitney, Sept. 19, 1905; children—Mary Whitney (Mrs. Don C. Allen), James Arthur, Roger Whitney, Elinor Newell (Mrs. John Barr). Tchr. pub. schs., 1897-98; student asst. Johns Hopkins, 1900-01, fellow, 1901-02, instr. mathematics, 1904-06, asso., 1906-09, asso. prof., 1909-18, prof., 1927-28; mathematics U. Mo., 1902-03; research asst. Carnegie Instn., at Johns Hopkins and in Germany, 1903-04; prof. mathematics U. Ill., 1918-27, 28-47, head dept., 1935-47, emeritus prof., after 1947; vis. prof. mathematics Haverford College, 1947-49, Phillips lectr., 1952-53; vis. prof. U. N.C., 1952. Mem. Nat. Acad. Sciences, Am. Philos. Soc., Am. Math. Soc., Am. Math. Assn., Phi Delta Theta. Phi Beta Kappa, Pi Mu Epsilon, Sigma Xi, Phi Kappa Phi. Contbr. tech. publs. America and Europe. Home: La Canada, Cal.†

COBURN, ALVIN F., physician; b. Asheville, N.C., Aug. 1, 1899; A.B., Yale Coll., 1921; M.D., Johns Hopkins, 1925; m. Agnes Cooke, Oct. 2, 1934; children—Anne, Peter Dunlop, Timothy Beveridge, Sarah Hastie, Stephen Campbell, Susan. Resident physician. Presbyterian Hospital, New York City, 1927-30; Proudfit fellow, 1930-32; assistant professor of medicine, Columbia, 1937-42; visiting investigator, Rockefeller Inst., 1940-41; dir., rheumatic fever research inst. Northwestern U., 1947-59 with New York Medical College and Hosp., 1959-68; consultant U.S. Naval Hospital, Great Lakes. Served as ensign, naval aviator, U.S. Naval Aviation, World War I; capt., U.S. Navy Med. Corps. World War II. Mem. Assn. of Am. Physicians, Am. Soc. for Clin. Investigation, Am. Assn. of Immunologists, Soc. for Exptl. Biology and Medicine, A.A.A.S. Author: The Factor of Infection in the Rheumatic State, 1931; The Epidemiology of Hemolytic Streptococcus, 1949. Home: Charlottesville, Va., Died Dec. 29, 1975.

COBURN, DONALD ELLSWORTH, physician; b. Hardwick, Vt., Oct. 6, 1909; s. Nelson and Margaret (Wilson) C.; M.D., U. Vt., 1934; m. Marion M. Fitch, June 6, 1936; children—Katherine C. (Mrs. Barry Dyer), David W., Andrew N. Intern, St. Francis Hosp., Hartford, Conn., 1934; resident in pathology Royal Victoria Hosp., Montreal, Que., Can., 1935-36; resident in surgery Fitch Clinic, 1936-41, chief surgeon, 1941-72; attending surgeon Northeastern Vt. Regional Hosp. Chmn., Vt. Commn. on Chronic Illness, 1948-50. Mem. Vt. Boxing Control Bd., 1972. Chmn., St. Johnsbury Republican Town Com. Diplomate Am. Bd. Surgery. Fellow A.C.S.; mem. A.M.A., New Eng. Surg. Soc., New Eng. Cancer Soc., Pan Pacific Surg. Assn., U. Vt. Med. Alumni Assn., Sigma Alpha Epsilon. Roman Catholic. K.C., Elk. Club: U. Vt. Varsity. Home: St. Johnsbury, Vt. Died Oct. 29, 1972; buried Hardwick, Vt.

COBURN, ROBERT D., ins. exec.; b. Pickaway County, O., Aug. 28, 1880; s. Robert Henry and Melvina Isabel (Colegrove) C.; student pub schs. of

Shawnee, O.; m. Hazel Belle Hathaway, Oct. 18, 1917; 1 son, Robert David. Coal miner, 1891-1905; carpenter, 1905-10; mine safety engr., claim adjuster London Guarantee & Accident Co., Ltd., 1910-17; joined Bituminous Casualty Corp. and Bituminous Fire & Marine Ins. Co., Rock Island, Ill., 1918, exec. v.p., dir., after 1930. Pres. Rock Island Community Chest, 1942; co-chmn. War Bond Dr., 1944; mem. bd. Park Commrs., after 1945. Mem. Rock Island C. of C. (pres. 1946), Ill. State C. of C., U.S. C. of C. Elk, Mason. Clubs: Arsenal Golf (bd. govs.), Treadway Rod and Gun, Meredosia Farms Gun (Rock Island). Home: Rock Island, Ill.†

COCA, ARTHUR FERNANDEZ, immunologist; b. Phila., Pa., Mar. 20, 1875; s. Joseph Fernandez and Augustine (Ware) C.; A.B., Haverford (Pa.) Coll., 1896, A.M., 1899; M.D., U. of Pa., 1900; grad. study U. of Heidelberg, Germany, 1905-07; m. Marietta A. Clews, Apr. 27, 1905 (divorced); children—Paul, Augustine Ware (Mrs. John Eugene McCarthy); m. 2d, Ella Foster Low, Aug. 28, 1930. Asst. demonstrator, U. of Pa., 1909-!!1900-03, demonstrator, 1903-05; chem. asst., Cancer Inst., U. of Heidelberg, 1907-09; bacteriologist Bureau of Science, Manila, P.I., 1909-10; instr. in pathology and bacteriology, Cornell U., 1910-19, asst. prof. of immunology, 1919-24, prof., 1924-32; clin. prof. of medicine N.Y. Post Grad. Med. Sch., Columbia, 1931-35; med. dir. Blood Transfusion Assn., New York, 1928-40; founder and editor in chief, Jour. of Immunology, 1916-43; managing editor, 1943-48; med. director Lederle Laboratories, Inc., 1931-48. Mem. Am. Association Immunologists (sec.-treas. 1917-48, hon. pres.), Am. College Allergists (honorary), A.A.A.S., Society American Bacteriologists, American Association Cancer Research, Harvey Society, New Jersey Med. Society, William Pepper Med. Soc. (U. of Pa.), Alpha Omega Alpha. Episcopalian. Author: Essentials of Immunology for Medial Students, 1925; Asthma and Hay Fever in Theory and Practice (with Matthew Walzer and A. A. Thomen), 1931; Familial Nonreaginic Food-Allergy, 1943. Contributor med. jours.; mem. editorial bds. Jour. of Investigative Dermatology and Annals of Allergy. Home: Oradell, N.J.†

COCHRAN, H. MERLE, govt. official; b. Crawfordsville, Ind., July 6, 1892; s. Lewis W. and Martha Frances (Hutton) C.; B.S., U. Ariz., 1913, M.S., 1914; m. Barbara Parnell, Oct. 17, 1917. Apptd. vice and dep. consul, Mannheim, June 1914, Nogales, Dec. 1914; vice consul Nogales by act approved Feb. 5, 1915; detailed to Guatemala, 1916, resigned Aug. 1916; ranching in Mexico, 1916-18, clk. Am. Legation Berne, Feb.-Oct. 1918; vice consul, Lugano, 1918-19, Kingston, Jamaica, Apr.-Oct. 1919; detailed to Port-au-Prince, Feb. 1920; vice consul, Montreal, 1920-23; detailed to dept., 1923-27; consul, Paris, 1927-30, Basel, 1930-32; fgn. service officer Am. Embassy, Paris, 1932; adviser 1st meeting of Experts' Prep. Com. for Internat. Monetary and Econ. Conf., Geneva, 1932, asst., 2d meeting, Geneva, 1933; attended 2d session League of Nations Com. for Study Internat. Loan Contracts, 1937; detailed to dept., 1939, as tech, asst. to sec., Treasury Dept.; spl. mission to China, 1941, to Argentina, 1942; insp. Fgn. Service establishments in Central and S. Am., Africa, Asia and Europe; U.S. rep. UN Good Offices Commn. for Indonesia, 1948; apptd. ambassador to Pakistan, 1949; ambassador to Indonesia, 1949-53; dep. mng. dir. Internat. Monetary Fund, 1953-73. Mem. Acad. Polit. Sci., American Foreign Service Assn., Phi Delta Theta. Clubs: Metropolitan (Washington); Union Inter-aliee (Paris). Home: Washington, D.C. Died Sept. 20, 1973.

COCHRANE, ROBERT HENRY, film exec.; b. Wheeling, W.Va., Dec. 27, 1879; s. Robert Henry and Martha (Dakin) C.; grad. high sch., Toledo, O., 1897; m. Julia Martha Fallis, of Toledo, June 18, 1902; children—Betty (Mrs. John Howard Laeri), Robert Henry. Reporter Toledo Bee, 1897, later city editor (youngest on any Scripps McRae paper), then mng. editor; joined bros. in Cochrane Advertising Agency, Chicago, 1904; joined Laeminle Film Service, 1906; v.p. Film Co., 1909-12; v.p. Universal Film Mfg. Co. . (later Universal Pictures Corpn.), 1912-36, pres. since April 1936; pres. Universal Corpn., Universal Pictures Co., Inc., Universal Film Exchanges, Inc., Universal Canadian Film Co., Ltd.; dir. Motion Picture Producers & Distributors of America; former mem. Code Authority of Motion Picture Industry. Served as maj. Signal Corps Res., U.S. Army. Clubs: Rockefeller Center Luncheon; Orienta Beach (Larchmont, N.Y.). Home: New Rochelle, N.Y.†

COCKE, NORMAN ATWATER, lawyer and business exec.; b. Prince George Co., Va., Nov. 20, 1884; s. John James and Sarah (Atwater) C.; student Petersburg (Va.) Acad., 1898-1902, N.Y. Law Sch., N.Y. City, 1902-05; Dr. Industry, Clemson Agricultural College, 1951; LL.D., Furman University, Greenville, 1960, Davidson (North Carolina) College, 1958, Duke U., 1962; m. Mary Sommers Booth, Nov. 28, 1911; children—Norman Atwater Jr., William Booth, John. Admitted to N.Y. bar, 1906, N.C. bar, 1907, S.C. bar, 1907; law clk. Atwater & Cruickshank, N.Y.C., 1902-06; atty. So. Power Co., Charlotte, N.C., and its successor, Duke Power Co., 1906-59, v.p., dir., 1927-53, pres., 1953-59, now dir.; v.p., dir. Piedmont & Northern Ry. Co., 1921-58, dir. Trustee Duke U., 1947-60, now emeritus, chmn. bd., 1954-60; trustee Converse College, John Motley Morehead Found., Duke Endownment (hon. chmn.). Mem. Newcomen Soc. Democrat. Episcopalian. Clubs: Quail (Charlotte, N.C.); Biltmore Country (Asheville, N.C.); Springdale Hall (Camden, S.C.). Home: Charlotte, N.C. Died Nov. 1974.

COE, CHARLES FREDERICK, aero. corp. exec.; b. Springfield, Ill., Apr. 6, 1910; s. Louis Johnson and Lydia (Williams) C.; B.S., U.S. Naval Acad., 1923; m. Charlotte Sells, July 31, 1931 (dec. Feb. 1976); children—Charlotte Wyman (Mrs. William Harding Jackson, Jr.), Charles Howard. Commissioned ensign in the USN., 1923, advanced through grades to vice adm., 1954, ret., 1954-74; attached to U.S.S. Fla., U.S.S. Litchfield, U.S.S. Saratoga, 1924-29; instr. Naval Air Sta., Pensacola, 1929-32; Fighting Squadron Six. 1932-34; Bur. Aero., 1934-36; staff Comdr. Aircraft Base and Battle Forces, 1936-38; assigned Naval Air Sta., Norfolk, Va., 1939-40; operations officer Comdr. Patrol Wing TWO, Pearl Harber, T.H., 1940-42; chief of staff Comdr. Air Solomons, 1943; in command Naval Air Sta., Memphis, 1943-45, U.S.S. Puget Sound, U.S.S. Hornet, 1945-46; chief of staff, aide to Chief of Naval Air Tng., Pensacola, 1946-48; in command U.S.S. Leyte, 1948-49; asst. dir. Air Warfare Div. Office Chief Naval Operations, 1949-50, dir., 1950-52; mem. mil. liaison com. to AEC, 1950-52; dep. dir. Joint Am. Mil. Adv. Group, London, 1952; Paris rep. to Comdr. in Chief U.S. European Command, 1952-54; asst. to v.p. Ryan Aero. Co., San Diego, Cal., 1956-74. Decorated Legion of Merit (with Oak Leaf Cluster), Air Medal; Comdr. Order Brit. Empire. Asso. fellow, Inst. Aero. Scis. Mem. Soc. Automotive Engrs. Clubs: Nat. Aviation, Army Navy, Army Navy Country (Washington). Home: Alexandria, Va. Died Jan. 1974.

COETZEE, BARZILLAL, South African diplomat; b. Hopetown, South Africa, May 14, 1914; s. Pieter Hermanns Christian and Jamalma (DuPlessis) C.; B.A., U. Stellenbosch, 1935; m. Estelle Helena Pauw, May 19, 1961; children by previous marriage-Jeanette (Mrs. Eric Traverso), Pieter, Hendrik. Polit. organizer, 1936-42; newspaper editor, 1942-44; mem. Provincial Council, 1943-48, mem. exec. com., 1948-53; M.P., 1953—; dep. minister of Bantu Adminstrn., 1966-68; minister Community Devel. and Pub. Works, 1968-72; ambassador to Italy, Rome, 1972—. Mem. Nat. Party. Dutch Reformed Ch. Home: South Africa, Deceased.

COFFIN, JOSEPH HERSCHEL, author; b. Thorntown, Ind., Jan. 12, 1880; s. Thomas Elihu and Ella (Cook) C.; B.S., Penn Coll., Oskaloosa, Ia., 1902; Ph.D., Cornell U., 1908; m. Viva Pearl Dean, Aug. 24, 1904; children—Thomas Erwin, Joseph Herschel. Instr. psychology, 1907-08, prof. philosophy, 1911-23, sec., 1918-23, Earlham Coll., Richmond, Ind.; acting prof. psychology, Mt. Holyoke Coll., 1917; prof. philosophy, Whittier Coll., Calif., since 1923; acting prof. psychology, Swarthmore Coll., 1932-33. Dir. Whittier Inst. of Internat. Relations since 1935. Curriculum coordinator of the seven state colls. of Calif., 1938-1941. Mem. Am. Assn. Univ. Profs., Am. Philos. Assn., Am. Assn. for Applied Psychology. Mem. Soc. of Friends. Author books including: Outline of the Psychology of Personality, 1940. Home: Whittier, Cal.†

COFFIN, PHILLIP O., telephone exec.; b. Brunswick, Me., Nov. 14, 1881; s. Emory A. and Evelyn (Condon) C.; A.B cum laude, Bowdoin Coll., 1903; m. Alice A. Meyer, June 27, 1928. Joined N.Y. Telephone Co., 1904, various positions Bell System, including v.p., sec., treas., dir. Bell cos. operating in Md., Va., W.Va. and D.C., dir. Washington Co. until 1950, retired, 1944. Mem. bd. govs., exec. com. A.R.C. (D.C.). Mem. Loyalty Review Bd. U.S. Civil Service Commn., after 1951. Mem. Zeta Psi Clubs: Metropolitan, Alibi (Washington); Myopia Hunt (Hamilton, Mass.). Home: Washington, D.C.†

COGLEY, JOHN PHILIP, surgeon; b. Council Bluffs, Ia., Mar. 22, 1899; s. Edward F. and Elizabeth G. (Stambach) C.; ed. Creighton Prep. Sch., Creighton Coll.; M.D., Creighton U., 1921; postgrad. J. Pa., 1924; m. Helen Gould Sprague, Aug. 17, 1971, (dec.); 1 dau., Charlotte Ann; m. 2d, Patricia E. Noonen, Dec. 25, 1940; children—Kathleen Ann, John Philip. Clin. prof. surgery Creighton U. Coll. Medicine, 1921-68, surg. dir., 1934-68; mem. exec. staff Mercy Hosp., Council Bluffs; dir. Cogley Clinic, Council Bluffs, asso. Drs. Edwards, Floersch and Mathiasen. Regent, Coll. St. Mary; lay bd. Duchesne College. Served as pvt., inf., U.S. Army, World War I; lt. col., M.C., AUS, World War II. Decorated knight commander st. Gregory the Great. Fellow A.C.S., Internat. Coll. Surgeons v.p., internat. gov.; mem. A.M.A., Ia. Pottawattamie County med. socs., Am. Assn. R.R. Surgeons, Ia. Clin. Surg. Soc., Am. Legion, Vets. Fgn. Wars. Democrat. Roman Catholic. K. C., Knight of Malta. Author articles in field. Home: Council Bluffs, Ia. Died Mar. 13, 1968.

COHEN, NATHANIEL A., physician; b. N.Y.C., July 7, 1912; s. Louis and Anna Cohen; B.S., N.Y.U.; M.A., Columbia; M.D., L.I. U., 1937; m. Mary S. Schasney, Aug. 7, 1941; 1 dau., Anne Louise (Mrs. William P. De Pietro). Intern, Jewish Hosp., Bklyn., 1937-39, resident in medicine, 1939-40; attending physician Queens Hosp. Center; dir. medicine Parkway Hosp., Forest Hills, N.Y. Served to maj., M.C., AUS, 1942-46. Decorated Bronze Star medal. Diplomate Am. Bd. Internal Medicine. Fellow A.C.P.; mem. A.M.A., Am. Heart Assn. Contbr. articles to med. jours. Home: Forest Hills, N.Y. Died Apr. 29, 1974; buried Summit Hill, Pa.

COHEN, SARA BARR, pub. relations exec.; b. Chgo.; d. Joseph and Goldie (Barr) Cohen; B.A., U. Chgo., 1938; M.A., Rosary Coll., 1954. Pub. relations asst. Ill. Nat. Youth Adminstrn., Chgo., 1938-41; asst. pub. relations dir. Chgo. Pub. Library, 1941-51; with Am. Coll. Surgeons, Chgo., 1952-73, dir. pub. information, 1971-73. Judge journalism awards Ill. State Med. Soc., 1972-73. Mem. Pub. Relations Soc. Am. (chpt. dir. 1968-73, sec. 1968-69), Publicity Club Chgo. (dir. 1953-55, sec. 1953, award 1960), Am. Women in Radio and TV, Nat. Assn. Sci. Writers (citation 1969); U. Chgo. Alumni Assn. Home: Chicago, Ill. Died Oct. 9, 1973; interred Waldheim Cemetery, Forest Park, Ill.

COIT, J(OHN) ELIOT, horticulturiest; b. San Antonio, Tex., Mar. 9, 1880; s. William Henry and Anna Maria (Summerell) C.; A.B. Agr., N.C. State Coll., 1903; student Cornell U., 1903-07, M.S. in Agr., 1905, hon. fellow, 1905-06, Ph.D., 1907; m. Emilie Augusta Hanna, of Raleigh, N.C., Aug. 7, 1907 (died 1924); children—Eleanor Mitchell, Frances Eliot, Lucy Catherine Moore; m. 2d, Louise Galt Viney, of Pasadena, September 4, 1926. Asst. in Department of Horticulture, Cornell U., 1906-07; asso. prof. horticulture, U. of Ariz., 1907-09; asst. prof. pomology, 1909-11, asso. prof., 1911-13, prof. citriculture, 1913-20, U. of Calif.; now consulting horticulturist and head of Coit Agrl. Service. Supt. Citrus Expt. Sta., U. of Calif., 1912; county farm adviser, Los Angeles Co., 1917-19. Presbyn. Fellow A.A.A.S.; mem. Am. Genetic Assn., Am. Soc. for Hort. Science, Gamma Alpha, Alpha Zeta. Sigma Xi. Author: Citrus Fruits, 1915. Home: Altadena, Cal.†

COLBERT, JAMES WILLIAM, JR., govt. med. dir.; b. N.Y.C., Dec. 14, 1920; s. James William and Mary (Tormey) C.; A.B., Holy Cross Coll., 1942; M.D., Columbia, 1945; m. Lorna Tuck, Aug. 26, 1944; children—James William, Edward, Mary, William, Margaret, Thomas, John, Andrew, Elizabeth, Paul J., Peter, Stephen. Intern Bellevue Hosp., N.Y.C., 1945-46; resident medicine Grace-New Haven Community Hosp., 1948-49, asso. physician, 1950-53; instr. medicine Yale, 1949-50, asst. prof. Sch. Medicine, 1950-53, asst. dean, 1951-52; clin. dir. U.S. Army Hepatitis Center, Munich, Germany, 1949-50; dir. edn. Middlesex Hosp., 1950-53, cons. physician, 1952-53; asst. prof. internat. medicine St. Louis U., 1953-62, dean sch. medicine, 1953-62; asso. dir. Nat. Inst. Allergy and Infectious Diseases, NIH. Bethesda, Md., 1962-74. Chmn. Montmery Health and Welfare Council. Mem. Washington Acad. Medicine, Sigma Xi, Alpha Sigma Nu, Delta Epsilon Sigma. Home: Bethesda, Md. Died Sept. 11, 1974.

COLBERT, RICHARD GARY, naval officer; b. Brownsville, Pa., Feb. 12, 1915; s. Charles F. and Marie Louise (Benford) C.; B.S., U.S. Naval Acad., 1937; postgrad. Naval War Coll., 1955-56; m. Prudence Ann Robertson, Nov. 15, 1950; children—Melissa Robertson, Richard Gary, Anthony Jonathan, Christopher Mark. Commd. ensign USN, 1937, advanced through grades to adm., 1972; dir. naval command course for Free World Naval Officers at Naval War Coll., Newport, R.I., 1956-58, pres. coll., 1968-71; mem. joint staff Joint Chiefs of Staff, Washington, 1958-60; comdg. officer U.S.S. Altair, 1960-61, U.S.S. Boston, 1961-63; mem. Policy Planning Council U.S. Dept. State, 1963-65; comdr. Cruiser Destroyer Flotilla Six, 1965-66; dep. chief staff, asst. chief staff for policy, plans, operations Supreme Allied Comdr. Atlantic, Norfolk, Va., 1966-68; chief staff Supreme Allied Command Atlantic, NATO Norfolk, 1971-73; ret., 1973. Decorated Joint Service Commendation medal, Legion of Merit. Clubs: New York Yacht; Army and Navy (Washington); Chevy Chase (Md.); Duquesne (Pitts.); Internat. Sportsmens (London, Eng.). Home: Norfolk, Va. Died Dec. 1973.

COLBY, JOSEPH MILTON, mech. engr., army officer; b. Lake Mills, Ia., Mar. 27, 1904; s. Joseph Eli and Millie J. (Eiel) C.; B.S., U. S. Mil. Acad., 1929; M.S., Mass. Inst. Tech., 1935; m. Margaret Capelle Brisley, Aug. 19, 1929; children—Janice Margaret (Mrs. Michele DeAngeli), Carol Capelle (Mrs. Chen Tung Leong). Commd. 2d lt. U.S. Army, 1929, advanced through grades to brig. gen., 1954; chief devel. br. Tank Automotive Center, Detroit, 1942-45; chief indsl. operations, chief engring. and mfg. div. Detroit Arsenal, 1945-46, chief devel. and engring. dept., 1946-51; spl. duty mission to Japan and Korea, 1950-51; adviser to sr. U.S. rep. North Atlantic Def. Prodn. Bd., London, Eng., 1951-52; organized, comdr. Ordnance Procurement Center, U.S. Army Europe, 1952-54; exec. officer then comdg. gen. Frankford Arsenal, 1954-57; comdg. gen. Ordnance Ammunition Command, 1957-58; dep. comdg. gen. Army Ordnance Missile Command, Redstone Arsenal, Ala., 1958-59; ret., 1959; v.p. research, devel. Rockwell Mfg. Co., Pitts., chmn. products com., 1959-66; v.p. tech. growth N. Am. Rockwell Corp., 1967-69, ret. 1969. Bd. dirs. Pitts. Opera. Decorated Legion of Merit with two oak leaf clusters, Bronze Star medal (U.S.); Order Brit. Empire Merit; officer Legion of Honor (France); comdr. Royal Order Phoenix (Greece). Mem. Am. Gas. Assn., Am. Ordnance Assn. Am. Petroleum Inst., Am. Soc. M.E., Assn. Grads. U.S. Mil. Acad. (trustee), Pitts. Athletic Assn., Assn. U.S. Army, C. of C. Greater Pitts., Mil. Order World Wars (vice comdr., past pres. Pitts. chpt.), World Affairs Council Pitts., Army Athletic Assn., Soc. Automotive Engrs., Pa. Soc. V.F.W. Clubs: Steel City Retired Officers (past pres.); Duquesne, Pittsburgh Press (Pitts.); Army-Navy (Washington). Contbr. numerous articles to profl jours. Home: Ft. Lauderdale, Fla. Died Oct. 18, 1974; buried West Point, N.Y.

COLCLOUGH, OTHO THOMAS, fgn. service officer; b. Durham, N.C., Feb. 23, 1907; s. William S. and Mattie E. (Brogden) C.; A.B., Duke, 1928; m. Virginia A. Brown, Oct. 9, 1928; children—Robert L., Andrew E. Elec. design engr. Allied Engrs., Inc., Jackson, Mich., 1928-33; with U.S. fgn. service, 1933-74; assigned Am. Embassy, Ottawa, Can., 1933-50; adminstrv. officer Am. Embassy, Prague, Czechoslovakia, 1950-52; with Bur. European Affairs, Dept. of State, 1952-58; chief internat. activities div. Office of Budget, Dept. of State, 1958, 60, chief policy div., office budget, 1961, chief program review div. office budget, 1962; chief personnel and mgmt. div. Bur. Ednl. and Cultural Affairs, 1963-74; principal officer Am. consulate, Niagara Falls, Canada, 1959-60. Baptist. Home: Arlington, Va. Died May 15, 1974.

COLE, GEORGE LEE, supt. schs.; b. Spearsville, La., July 11, 1910; s. George Lee and Isadora (Waldrop) C.; B.S., La. State U., 1940; M.S., Ark. U., 1953; m. Clyta Holloway, Jan. 10, 1933; 1 son, Herbert Larry. Prin. elementary sch., Cross Roads, La., 1933-39; tchr. agr. pub. schs., Downsville, La., 1940-46; prin. high sch., Spearsville, La., 1946-57; supr. high sch., Union Parish, La., 1957-69; supt. Union Parish Schs., Farmerville, La., 1969-72. Chmn. constrn. Spearsville Drug Co. Chmn. bd. dirs. Office Equal Opportunity Mayor, City of Spearsville, 1969-72. Chmn. bd. dirs. constrn. of Bernice (La.) Clinic and Hosp. Mem. La. Sch. Adminstrs. Assn., La. Tchrs. Assn. Baptist. Home: Spearsville, La. Died May 30, 1972; interred Spearsville Cemetery, Spearsville, La.

COLE, JACK, choreographer, dancer, dir.; b. New Brunswick, N.J., Apr. 27, 1914; student with Ted Shawn, Ruth St. Denis, Charles Weidman, Doris Humphrey, others, ethnic dance forms in Brazil, Cuba, Philippines, Ireland. Made debut as dancer in Job, N.Y.C., summer 1931; toured with Denishawn Concert Dancers, 1930-32, Humphrey-Weidman Dance Group, N.Y.C., 1932-33; Broadway debut as dancer in The School for Husbands, 1933, later danced in Thumbs Up, 1934, May Wine, 1935; appeared with own dance group, 1937, in Keep 'Em Laughing, 1942; dancer the Ziegfeld Follies, 1943; choreographer Something for the Boys, 1943, Allah Be Praised., 1944, Bonanza Bound, 1947, Magdalena, 1948, Alive and Kicking, 1950, Kismet, 1953, Jamaica, 1957, Candide, 1959, Kean, 1961, A Funny Thing Happened on the Way to the Forum, 1962, Foxy, 1964; choreographer, dancer films including Moon Over Miami, 1941, Kismet, 1944, Lydia Bailey, 1952, Designing Woman, 1957; choreographer movies including Eadie Was a Lady, 1945, The Jolson Story, 1945, Tars and Spars, 1946, Down to Earth, 1947, On the Riviera, 1951, David and Bathsheba, 1951, The Merry Widow, 1952, Gentlemen Prefer Blondes, 1953, The Farmer Takes a Wife, 1953, Gentlemen Marry Brunettes, 1955, Les Girls, 1957, Some Like It Hot, 1959, Let's Make Love, 1960; choreographer, dancer TV shows including Perry Como Show, Bob Hope Show, Sid Caesar Show; commentator Tragic Celebration, N.Y.C., 1972; also nightclub work. Recipient award for dancing in Ziegfeld Follies, Dance Mag., 1943; Photoplay award for choreography The Jolson Story, 1945; Donaldson award for choreography and dancing in Alive and Kicking, 1950; Dance mag. award for choreography Three for the Show, 1955. Died Feb. 17, 1974.

COLE, JOHN TUPPER, army officer; b. West Point, N.Y., July 23, 1895; s. James Alfred and Mary (Tupper) C.; B.S., U.S. Mil. Acad., 1917; m. Janet MacKay, Jan. 6, 1927; children—Jean Tupper, Frederick MacKay. Commd. 2d lt., U.S. Army, 1917, and advanced through grades to brig. gen., 1950; Cavalry Sch., 1923, 1929, 1930; student Command and Staff Sch., 1937; served A.E.F., 1917-19; E.T.O., 1942-45; spcl. services, Washington 1946-49; comdg. officer, M.D.W., 1949-50; mem. U.N. Mil. com., 1950; chief Mil. Assistance Adv. Group, Bangkok, Thailand, 1951-52; asst. dir. comdr. 3d Armored Div., Ft. Knox, from 1952. Awarded Legion of Merit, Silver Star, Bronze Star (with four oak leaf clusters), Army commendation ribbon, Purple Heart. Mem. Olympic Equestrian Team, 1930. Mem. Army Athletic Assn., U.S. Armour Assn., U.S. Olympic Com., Nat. Horse Show (dir.). Club: Huntington Country. Home: Boonton, N.J. Died Apr. 17, 1975.

COLE, REDMOND SELECMAN, lawyer; b. nr. Savannah, Andrew Co., Mo., Aug. 22, 1881; s. James Buchanan and Virginia Lee (Bedford) C.; student Kirksville (Mo.) State Normal Sch., 1899-1901; A.B., U. of Mo., 1905, A.M., 1906; studied law, same univ., 1907-09; m. Mary Thompson Cross, of Columbia, Mo., June 11, 1910; children—Olivia Harris, Virginia Bedford. Editor Mo. Univ. Independent (student weekly), 1905-07; asso. editor Sentinel, and editor Herald (both Columbia publs.), 1908; admitted to bar, 1909; county atty. Pawnee County, Okla., 1901-15; registrar Pawnee Co., 1916-17; mayor of Pawnee, 1917; asst. U.S. dist. atty., Western Dist. of Okla., 1917-19; judge 21st Jud. Dist. of Okla., 1919-23; resumed practice at Tulsa. Rep. U. of Mo. in debates, U. of Tex., 1904, Kan., Okla. and Mo. state hist. socs., Delta Tau Delta, Delta Sigma Rho, Phi Alpha Delta, S.A.R. Democrat. Methodist. Mason. Home: Tulsa, Okla.†

COLE, ROY, supt. schs.; b. Detroit, Aug. 30, 1915; s. George and Beatrice (Iles) C.; B.S., Central Mich. U., 1940; M.A., Wayne State U., 1949, Ed.D., 1957; m. Velda Smith, Jan. 24, 1947; children—Martha (Mrs. Stephan Glazek), Roy, Roger. Sch. social worker Dearborn (Mich.) Pub. Schs., 1949-54, elementary prin., 1954-58, secondary prin., 1958-61, area adminstr., 1961-65, supt., from 1965. Served with AUS, 1941-46, 51-52. Mem. Mich. (regional pres.), Wayne County (pres.) assns. sch. adminstrs., C. of C. Mason, Rotarian (dir. 1968), Elk. Home: Dearborn, Mich. Deceased.

COLE, THOMAS (RAYMOND), univ. prof.; b. Colesburg, Ia., Mar. 15, 1881; s. Robert and Mary C.; A.M., Upper Ia. U., 1902; grad. study DePauw U., 1903; m. Apphia Davis, Aug. 20, 1906; children—Raymond, Virginia, Charlotte, Mary. Prin. pub. schs., Ridgeway, Ia., 1902-04; teacher, high sch., Winona, Minn., 1904-06; supt. schs., Minneota, Minn., 1906-07. Wabasha, Minn., 1907-09; prin. Cleveland High Sch., St. Paul, Minn., 1909-10; asst. state supt. schs., Minn., and prin. Central High Sch., St. Paul, 1910-11; prin. Broadway High Sch., Seattle, Wash., 1911-15; asst. supt. schs., Seattle, Washington, after 1930; dir. Washington Mutual Savings Bank. Lecturer, summers; member State Commn. Sch. Accreditation. Active school survey work, Mem. N.E.A., Phi Delta Kappa. Conglist. Club: Rotary, College. Author: Learning to be a Schoolmaster, 1922; Beginning Superintendent (with others), 1937; author bulls. on teacher load, departmentalizing elementary schools, group guidance and rating sheet for teachers. Home: Seattle, Wash.†

COLE, WILLARD W., merchandising exec.; b. Montclair, N.J., 1908. Chmn. bd., dir. Lytton's, Henry C. Lytton & Co., Chgo.; v.p. Cluett Peabody & Co., Inc., N.Y.C.; dir. First Bank Oak Park. Home: River Forest, Ill. Died Oct. 18, 1973.

COLEGROVE, KENNETH WALLACE, educator; b. Waukon, Ia., Oct. 8, 1886; s. Chauncey Peter and Winifred Della (Mack) C.; diploma Ia. State Tchrs. Coll., 1905; A.B., State U. Ia., 1909; Ph.D., Harvard, 1915; Litt.D. (hon.), Columbia, 1945; m. Louise Burrows Funkhauser, Jan. 5, 1923; 1 dau., Marian Louise (Mrs. John H. Blankenship); m. 2d, Gladys Marie Chadsey St. John. Lectr. history Mt. Holyoke Coll., 1913-16; asst. prof. European history Syracuse (N.Y.) U., 1916-19; asso. prof. polit. sci. Northwestern U., 1919-26, prof., 1926-52; prof. polit. sci. Queens Coll., 1953-54; editor-in-chief Inst. Fiscal and Polit. Edn., N.Y.C., 1954-58; prof. history and polit. sci. C.W. Post Coll., L.I. U., 1959-69; sr. research asso. Center for Study of the Presidency, N.Y.C., 1970-75. Mem. Bd. Personnel Examiners, U.S. Dept. Labor, 1933; chmn. Evanston chpt. Com. to Defend Am. by Aiding the Allies, 1940-41; cons. OSS, Washington, 1943-45; polit. cons. Gen. MacArthur Hdqrs., Tokyo, Japan, 1946. Trustee Upper Ia. U. Mem. Am. Soc. Internat. Law, Am. Council Learned Socs. (del. 1952-55), Am. Hist. Assn., Am. Polit. Sci. Assn. (sec.-treas. 1935-47), Alpha Pi Zeta. Methodist. Clubs: Faculty House, Columbia University (N.Y.C.); University (Evanston). Author several books including: International Control of Aviation, 1929; Militarism in Japan, 1936; The American Senate and World Peace, 1944; Democracy versus Communism, 1957; (with Hall Bartlett) The Menace of Communism, 1962. Editor: European Economic and Political Survey (Paris), 1929. Contbr. articles to profl. jours. Address: New York City, N.Y. Died Jan. 3, 1975; interred Wooster Memorial Cemetery, Danbury, Conn.

COLEMAN, ARTHUR PRUDDEN, educator; born in Seymour, Conn., July 19, 1897; s. Michael Lyon and Carrie Augusta (Davis) C.; A.B., Wesleyan U., 1920; A.M., Columbia, 1922, Ph.D., 1925; student univs. of Prague, Warsaw and Krakow; L.H.D. honoris causa, Alliance College, 1962; m. Marion Reeves Moore, July 1, 1922. Asst. prof. modern langs. Columbia, 1928-48; prof. Fairleigh Dickinson Coll., 1948-49; vis. lectr. U. Tex., 1949-50; pres. Alliance Coll., Cambridge Springs, Pa., 1950-62; pres. Alliance Tech. Inst., 1950-62; vis. lectr. Russian, U. Arizona, Tucson, 1962-63; adjunct professor Fordham U., N.Y., 1963-64; master in hist. Cheshire (Conn.) Academy, 1964-74. Mem. Am. Assn. Teachers Slavic and East European Langs. (chmn.), Nat. Fedn. Modern Lang. Teachers Assn. (pres., national foreign lang. achievement award 1961), Modern Lang. Assn. (life), Phi Beta Kappa. Member Cong. Church. Rotarian (president 1954). Author: Humor in the Russian Comedy, New York, 1925; Report on the Status of Russian and Other Slavic and East European Languages, 1948. Co-author: Wanderers Twain, 1964. Home: Cheshire, Conn. Died July 14, 1974.

COLEMAN, JAMES DANIEL STETSON, financial exec.; b. Macon, Ga., Sept. 29, 1904; s. Samuel Taylor and Edith Dean (Stetson) C.; grad. Phillips Exeter Acad., 1923; A.B., Yale, 1927; M.B.A., Harvard, 1929; m. Dorothy Wooden, Dec. 11, 1944. Chmn. bd. Coleman-Meadows Pate Wholesale Drug Co., Macon, 1949-75, Cities Transit Inc. of Fla., Lakeland, 1950-75; chmn. finance com. Fannie May Candy Co., Chgo., 1945-75; part-owner Los Angeles Angels Baseball Team, 1960-75; finance chmn. Pennzoll United, Inc.; dir. Overseas Prt. Investment Corp., Comml. Solvents Corp. Served to maj. USMCR, 1941-45; PTO. Mem. Chi. Psi. Episcopalian. Clubs: Racquet and Tennis, Brook (N.Y.C.); Chevy Chase (Md.); Burning Tree (Washington); Cypress Point (Cal.); Seminole, Indian Creek (Gulf Stream, Fla.); Pacific Union (San Francisco); Links (N.Y.C.). Home: The Plains, Va. Died Aug. 16, 1975.

COLEMAN, ROBERT, drama editor and critic, columnist; b. Bainbridge, Ga., Aug. 6, 1900; s. Robert Bruce and Sarah (Blasingame) C.; student Culver (Ind.) Naval Acad.; U. Ga. and Columbia (B.A.), also 1 year Columbia U. Sch. Journalism; m. Ingrid Hallen, 1946. Reporter, feature writer, columnist, asst. drama editor and critic New York Morning Telegraph, 1924; drama editor, columnist and critic N.Y. Mirror, daily and Sunday, from 1924. Was active in support and encouragement of the summer theater; furthered the careers of many players in radio, pictures and theater as a result of tours of the summer circuits; made systematic coverage summer theater. Lt. (s.g.) U.S.N.R., Served 1934-41. Recipient N.Y. Acad.'s John Golden Cup, 1952. Pioneer radio speaker on photography; exhibited in Internal. Photograph Salons from 1934. Radio commenator on theatre, and master firm ceremonies on variety programs. Hon. overseas mem. London Critics Circle; mem. N.Y. Drama Critics Circle, Ry. and Locomotive Hist. Soc., S.A.R., Alpha Tau Omega. Presbyn. Clubs: Lotos, Stamford (Conn.) Yacht, N.Y. Camera. Office: New York City, N.Y. Died Nov. 27, 1974.

COLEMAN, S. WALDO, investment corp. exec.; b. Grass Valley, Cal., Sept. 7, 1881; s. John Crisp and Persis H. (Sibley) C.; student U. Cal., 1903; m. Margaret Lucille McCormick, Apr. 28, 1909; children—John C., Lewis V., Margaret L. (Mrs. Woodhams). Started career as an apprentice with Gen. Electric Co., Schenectady, 1903-05; master mechanic Petaluma (Cal.) & Santa Rosa R.R. Co., 1905-06; mgr. Union Traction Co., 1906-08, Coast Counties Gas & Electricity, 1908-13, pres., 1913-28 (Santa Cruz); chmn., dir. North Am. Investment Corp., after 1925, Commonwealth Investment Co. after 1932, founder both cos. Clubs: Pacific Union, Bohemian. Home: Woodside, Cal.†

COLEMAN, SIDNEY ANDREW, editor; b. Wichita, Kan., Nov. 3, 1879; s. Thomas Henry and Susan Anne (McBride) C.; student Wichita and Kingman (Kan.) pub. schs.; m. Marie Victoria DeBacker, Oct. 11, 1905. News staff Kingman (Kan.) Jour., 1898-1903; reporter Wichita Daily Beacon, 1903-06, city editor, 1906-12, mng. editor, 1912-28, feature, radio editor, 1928-44; chief editorial writer, 1944-54, bus. and financial editor, 1954-60; asso. market and financial editor, Wichita Daily Eagle, after 1900. Home: Wichita, Kan.†

COLETTI, JOSEPH ARTHUR, sculptor; b. San Donato, Italy, Nov. 5, 1898; s. Dominick and Donata (Cardarelli) C.; came to U.S., 1900; student Mass. Art. Sch., 1915-17, Northeastern Prep. Sch., 1917-19; A.A., Harvard, 1923; m. Miriam Kerruish Whitney, Sept. 28, 1929 (div. 1943); children—Donata (Mrs. Kirke L. Mechem), Miriam Whitney (Mrs. Peter B. Dow). Pupil, became asst. John Singer Sargent. Numerous works including: baptismal font St. John's Episcopal Ch., Westwood, Mass., Henry B. Washburn Meml., Episcopal Sem., Cambridge, Mass., Lt. William F. Callahan, Jr. Callahan Tunnel Entrance, Boston, Albert Schweizer medal; Ferdinand Gagnon Meml. Seminaire St. Hyacinthe, Que., Can.; Gagnon statue, LaFayette Park, Manchester, N.H.; "Mourning Victory," Lafayette Park, Salem, Mass.; Harvard Glee Club medal in collection Bibliotheque Nationale, Paris, France; Senator David I. Walsh Statue, Esplanade, Boston; Orpheus, Nonquitt, Mass.; Gen. Edward L. Logan statue Logan Internat. Airport, Boston: Father Michael Joseph McGivney statue, Waterbury, Conn.; Boston Arts Festival medal; facade and 11 heroic sized panels for Cathedral of Mary Our Queen, Balt.; St. George statue Nat. Gall. Modern Art, Florence, Italy; Paderewski Centennial medal Mus. Treasures Cathedral Wavel Castle, Cracow, Poland; Admiral Samuel Eliot Morison medallion Vatican Collection; Dr. George P. Berry Meml., Countway Med. Library, Boston, Orphens Fountain, Lowell (Mass.) State Coll., Dante Soc. Am. 7th Centennial medal, Dow Meml., Buffalo, Boston Tea Party coin-medal, George Peabody Gardner Meml., Sci. Bldg. Children's Hosp. Boston. Mem. Nat. Humanities Faculty. Decorated cavaliere ufficiale Nell'Ordine al Merito (Italy); recipient 1st prize medal Boston Tercentenary Fine Arts Exhbn., 1932; traveling fellow fine arts Harvard, 1923, Sachs fellow, 1924-25; vis. fellow Am. Academy Rome, 1924-

26. Mem. Boston Hist. Conservation Com.; chmn. Mass. Art Commn., 1960-65; adv. com. Inst. Modern Art; mem. camouflage com. Mass. Com. Pub. Safety, 1939-42; adv. com. Swain Sch. Design. Trustee New Eng. Conservatory Music. Fellow Nat. Sculpture Soc.; mem. Medieval Acad. Am., Am. Federation Arts, Dante Soc. Am., Italian Hist. Soc., Phi Beta Kappa (hon.). Clubs: Saint Botolph, Harvard. Author: Aristide Maillol; articles for Ency. Brit. Home: Boston, Mass. Died May 5, 1973.

COLLAMORE, HARRY BACON, steel co. exec.; b. Middletown, Conn.; s. Harry N. and Matie (Bacon) C.; A.M., Colby Coll., 1939; m. Dorothy H. Rowe, Oct. 24, 1925; children—Harry Bacon, Wallace Rowe, Examiner, Nat. Fire Ins. Co., 1912-16, Conn. spl. agt. for gen. agy., 1916-17; fieldman Nat. Fire Ins. Co., Tex., 1918-21; Pa., 1925, agy., supt. Hartford, Conn., 1925-1926, later asst. sec. advancing to sec. and v.p., dir. and exec. v.p., pres. and chmn. bd., ret. 1956; chmn. bd., dir. Pitts. Steel Co., ret.; dir. Am. Leasing Co., Conn. Bank & Trust Co., Mechanics Savs. Bank. Trustee Rosenbach Found., Phila., Watkinson Library; bd. dirs. Am. Sch. for Deaf. Served with U.S. Army, 1917-18. Episcopalian. Clubs: Hartford, Hartford Golf, Acron (Hartford); Duguesne Club (Pitts.); Lotos, Grolier (N.Y.C.). Author: (with Lawrence R. Thompson) E.A. Robinson-Collection of His Works, 1936. Contbr. to Colophon, Lit. Observer. Home: West Hartford, Conn., Died Sept. 28, 1975.

COLLENS, ARTHUR MORRIS, dir. Phoenix Mut. Life Ins. Co.; b. Cleveland, O., Nov. 4, 1880; s. Rev. Charles Terry and Mary Abbey (Wood) C.; A.B., Yale, 1903; m. Annette Bailey Whipple, Nov. 14, 1906; children—Katherine (Mrs. Jeremiah H. Bartholomew, Jr.), Arthur Morris (died June 27, 1935), William Lette. In investment business, 1903-16, with Ladd & Wood, New York, 1911-16; organized and head of The Investment Bur. for Phoenix Mut. Life Ins. Co., Phoenix (Fire) Ins. Co., and Conn. Mut. Life Ins. Co., 1916-23; financial v.p., Phoenix Mut. Life Ins. Co., 1923-26, v.p., 1926-35, pres. 1935-48, chmn. bd., 1948-50, dir., mem. exec. com. since 1950; dir. Nat. Fire Ins. Co., United Nat. Indemnity Co., Phoenix State Bank & Trust Co., Mechanics & Traders Ins. Co.; trustee Mechanics Savs. Bank. Past pres. Hartford Community Chest; dir. Hartford Hosp., Conn. Institute for Blind; trustee Hotchkiss School in Lakeville; member advisory com. Hartford Art Society; mem. governing body Nat. Indsl. Conf. Board. Mem. Psi Upsilon. Republican. Episcopalian. Clubs: Hartford Golf (past pres.), 20th Century (past pres.), Hartford; Yale (New York). Home: Hartford, Conn.†

COLLETT, ARMAND RENÉ, chemist, educator; b. Hartford City, Ind., Feb. 3, 1895; s. August and Eugenie (Loriaux) C.; A.B., W.Va. U., 1918; Ph.D., Yale, 1923; m. Dorothy May Atwood, Aug. 7, 1922; children—Dorothy May, Armand Joseph, Florence Marie. Instr. chemistry, Yale, 1923-24; with W.Va. U. from 1924, instr., 1924-26, became prof. chemistry, 1939, dean coll. arts and scis., 1951-73. Served as 2d lt., Coast Artillery Corps, U.S. Army, 1918. Mem. Am. Chem. Soc., A.A.A.S., Sigma Xi, Phi Beta Kappa, Alpha Chi Sigma, Gamma Alpha, Phi Lambda Upsilon. Kiwanian. Home: Morgantown, W.Va. Died June 17, 1973; buried Morgantown.

COLLETT, ROBERT ARTHUR, apparel co. exec.; b. Evanston, Ill., Sept. 16, 1922; s. Arthur Barrie and Daisy (Gaunt) C.; student Beloit Coll., 1939-41; B.B.A., Northwestern U., 1947; m. Gwynneth C. Hamilton, Jan. 23, 1951; children—John Frederick, Thomas Arthur, Robert James. Auditor, Touches, Ross, Bailey & Smart, Chgo., 1947-49; auditor, factory comptroller Sears, Roebuck & Co., Chgo., 1949-60, asst. to v.p. in charge mfg., 1960-62; v.p. finance Kellwood Co., St. Louis, 1962-74, treas., 1966, also dir. Served to capt. USMCR, 1942-45, to maj., 1951-53. Decorated D.F.C. with 6 air medals. Mem. Mo. Amateur Ice Hockey Assn. (pres.), Sigma Chi. Episcopalian. Mason. Home: Webster Groves, Mo. Died Oct. 16, 1974.

COLLIGAN, FRANCIS JAMES, specialist internat. relations; b. San Francisco, Dec. 27, 1908; s. Dr. Francis Joseph and Mary Helen (Barrett) C.; A.B., U. San Francisco, 1929; A.M., U. Cal., 1933, Ph.D., 1941; student Latin Am. Inst., Am. Council Learned Socs., 1941; Prof. (hon.), Sch. Letters and Edn., Nat. U. Ecuador, 1944; m. Margaret Clara Haxton, Aug. 1, 1933; 1 son, Francis Sherwin. Jr. employee Bank of Am., 1929; jr. underwriter State Compensation Ins. Fund, 1930; instr. to asst. prof. U. San Francisco, 1931-35; organizer and dir. library services City Coll. San Francisco, 1935-40, chmn. dept. English and speech, 1941; cultural relations attache U.S. Embassy, Quito, Ecuador, 1942-44; sect. chief Div. Cultural Cooperation, Dept. State, 1944-45, asst. chief Div. Exchange of Persons, 1946, chief div., 1947-52, dep. dir. Internat. Ednl. Exchange Service, 1952-58, also exec. sec. Bd. Fgn. Scholarships, 1948-57; dir. Cultural Planning and Coordination Staff, 1958-60; dir. Ednl. and Cultural Plans and Devel. Staff, 1960-64; dir. Cultural Policy and Review staff, exec. dir. Inter-Agy. Council Internat. Ednl. and Cultural Affairs, 1964-70; sr. policy adviser Ednl. and Cultural Affairs, 1970-71; vis. fellow Princeton, fall 1956; U.S. rep. Ad Hoc Com. on Cultural Policy, Southeast Asia Treaty Orgn., 1958; U.S. rep. Commn. on L.S. Rowe Fund, OAS, 1948-50; U.S. mem. com. experts UNESCO, Paris, 1960, 62; U.S. del. Anglo-Am. Conf. on English Lang., Ditchley, 1965; adviser U.S. del. Inter-Am. Cultural Council, Mexico, 1951, P.R., 1959, Inter Am. Conf., Caracas, 1954, Geneva Meeting of Fgn. Ministers, 1955. Mem adv. council Sch. of Langs. and Linguistics, Georgetown U. Recipient Rockefeller Pub. Service award, 1955, Superior Service award U.S. Dept. State, 1966, 71; Distinguished Service award Bd. Fgn. Scholarships, 1971. Mem. Internat. Studies Assn., Am. Fgn. Service Assn., Acad. Polit. and Social Sci., Soc. Internat. Devel., Modern Lang. Assn.; hon. mem. Grupo America, Socledad Juridico-Literarla (Ecuador), Nat. Assn. Univ. Men of Finland. Roman Catholic. Clubs: Bethesda (Md.) Country; Commonwealth (San Francisco); Cosmos, Internat. (Washington). Co-author: Fundamentals of Public Speaking, 1935; The Fulbright Program: A History, 1966; articles on cultural relations. Editor: Guide to U.S. Govt. Agencies in Internat. Ednl. and Cultural Activities, 1968. Home: Chevy Chase, Md. Died June 16, 1974.

COLLINGE, PATRICIA, actress, writer; b. Dublin, Ireland, Sept. 20, 1894; d. F. Channon and Emmie (Russell) Collinge; ed. in Dublin; m. James Nichols Smith, June 10, 1921. Made first appearance in Garrick Theatre, London, as Ching-a-Ling in "Little Black Sambo and Little White Barbara," Dec. 21, 1904; latest stage appearances include Birdie in The Little Foxes, 1939, The Heiress, 1947, I've Got Sixpence, 1952; latest motion picture roles in Teresa, 1950, Shadow of a Doubt, The Nun's Story, 1958; numerous TV appearances. Author: (with Margalo Gillmore) The B.O.W.S., 1945; Small Mosaics of Mr. and Mrs. Engel, 1959. Contbr. to The New Yorker and other mags. Home: New York City, N.Y. Died 1974.

COLLINS, CARTER, indsl. realtor; b. Fairfield, Ia., Dec. 17, 1893; s. Dennis Colfax and Gertrude (Cowen) C.; A.B., Stanford, 1917; m. Clella Reeves, Aug. 16, 1916; children—Betty (Mrs. Frederick Ogden Lyons), Carter Compton. Entered U.S. Army, 1917; chief of staff 11th Army Corps, 1942; comdg. officer, 13th Inf. Regiment, 1943; asst. chief of staff G-2, 2d Army, 1944; post comdr., Ft. Benning, Ga., 1945; ret. as col., 1946; indsl. realtor, Berkeley, Cal. Mem. Cal. Real Estate Assn., Nat. Assn. Real Estate Bds., Chi Psi, Elk. Club: Commonwealth of Cal. Home: Berkeley, Cal. Died May 31, 1973.

COLLINS, CHARLES BERTINE, lawyer; b. Portland, Me., July 20, 1904; s. John Lyon and Aimee R. (Brown) C.; A.B., Rutgers Coll., 1927; postgrad. Harvard Law Sch., 1927-30; m. Marjorie Marten Perine, Mar. 12, 1935; children—Patricia (Mrs. Robert Curry), Charles Bertine, Susan (Mrs. Frederick N. Reidenbach), Marcia (Mrs. J. Stephen Jenkins). Admitted to N.J. bar, 1930, also U.S. Supreme Ct.; practice in Newark, 1959-75; sr. partner Carpenter, Bennett & Morrissey. Referee Maplewood Juvenile Conf. Com., 1964-75. Trustee, counsel Boys Clubs Newark, 200 Club Newark. Mem. Am., N.J., Essex County bar assns., Am. Judicature Soc., Maritime Law Assn. U.S., Harvard Law Sch. Assn. N.J. (pres. 1966), No. N.J. Estate Planning Council, Am. Arbitration Assn. (arbitrator), Lambda Chi Alpha. Republican. Methodist. Mason, Rotarian (pres. Newark 1973-74). clubs: Harvard (N.Y.C.); Essex, Down Town (Newark); Rock Spring (West Orange, N.J.); Merriewold (Forestburg, N.Y.). Author: Foreclosure of Mortgages, Skills and Methods, N.J. Practice, 1960. Asso. editor N.J. Law Jour., 1957-72. Home: Maplewood, N.J. Died July 16, 1975.

COLLINS, CHARLES WALLACE, lawyer, author, farmer; b. Callion, Ala., Apr. 4, 1879; s. Robert Wood and Ann Bates (Allen) C.; B.S., Ala. Poly. Inst., Auburn, 1899; Ph.B., U. of Chicago, 1908, A.M., 1909; fellow Semitic languages, same, 1908-09; student govt. and economics, Harvard Univ., 1910-11; studied law under pvt. tuition, 1899-1901; m. Sue Steele Spencer, July 12, 1933. Admitted to Ala. bar, 1901, to Supreme Court of U.S., 1917; practiced in Birmingham, 1901-06; librarian Haskell Oriental Mus., U. of Chicago, 1909-10; in charge economic section legislative reference service, Library of Congress, 1915-18, dir. same, 1918-20. Mem. Legal Advisory Bd. to Draft Bd., 1918; legal adviser to Senate and House select coms. to devise a budget plan, 1919-20; drafted Senate bill to establish a nat. budget system; advisory com. on econ. sci. to Federal Reclassification Commn., 1919-20; contributing editor Commercial and Financial Chronicle, New York, 1920-23; law librarian of Congress, 1920-21; librarian U.S. Supreme Court; gen. counsel of Bureau of the Budget, Treasury Department, 1921-23, dep. comptroller of the currency, and gen. counsel, 1923-25, 1st dep. comptroller same, 1925-27; counsel merger Bank of America and Bowery & East River Nat. Bank (New York), 1928, merger Blair & Co. and Bancamerica Corp. (New York), 1929 Blair Nat. Bank and the Bank of America N.A. (New York), 1929, Bank of America (Los Angeles) and Bank of Italy Nat. Trust & Savings Assn. (San Francisco), 1930; Counsel Bank of America Nat. Trust & Savs. Assn., 1927-47; Transmerica Corp., 1928-47; drafted McFadden-Pepper nat. bank bill, 1924. Mem. Md. Hist. Soc., Am. Farm Bur., Alpha Tau Omega. Clubs: National Press, Metropolitan. Author: The Fourteenth Amendment and the States, 1912; The Nat. Budget System and Am. Finance, 1917; Plan for Nat. Budget System (House Doc. 1006, 65th Congress), 1918; The British Budget System, 1920; Essential Elements of a National Budget System, 1920; Constitutional Aspects of the President's Veto of the Budget Bill, 1920; The Branch Banking Question, 1926; Rural Banking Reform, 1931; Whither Solid South?, 1947; (brochures) Constitutional Power of Congress to Enforce a Single System of Commercial Banking, 1930; The South and the Electoral Coll., 1944; The South Must Not Surrender, 1948; Constitutional Aspects of the Truman Civil Rights Program, (published) 1949; Peril at Home and Abroad; Estimates, Appropriations and Reports, 1924. Contributor on law, finance and banking to journals. Spl. counsel Am. Bankers Assn., 1933. Home: Oxon Hill, Md.†

COLLINS, ROBERT ALEXANDER, educator; born at Marble Falls, Texas, June 9, 1891; son of Uriah and Ida (Barber) C.; A.B., Simmons Coll., 1912; A.B., U. of Tex., 1921, Peabody fellow, 1922, A.M., 1923, Ph.D., 1935; student Columbia, summers 1926-27, U. of Ia., summers 1928-29, U. of Calif., summer 1930; m. Lily Ada Lanham, August 18, 1915; children—Dorothy Sue, Charlotte Barbara. m. 2d, Bertha Mae Largent, Sept. 26, 1968. Adminstr., teacher Tex. Pub. Sch., 1912-32; instr. Southwest Tex. Teachers Coll., 1933-35; dean of students Hardin-Simmons U., prof. edn., 1935-45, dean, 1945-54, professor education. Served from 1st lt. to capt., USAAF, 1943-45. Mem. Phi Delta Kappa. Democrat. Baptist. Mason. Home: Abilene, Tex. Died July 24, 1972.

COLLINS, ROSS ALEXANDER ex-congressman; b. Collinsville, Miss., Apr. 25, 1880; s. Nathaniel Monroe and Rebecca J. (Ethridge) C.; A.B., Ky. U., 1900; LL.B., U. of Miss., 1901; LL.D., Transylvania U., 1930; m. Alfreda Grant, Nov. 2, 1904; children—Jane (Mrs. Thomas P. Corwin), Madison M. Began practice at Meridian, Miss., 1901; elected atty. gen. of Miss., 1911; reelected, 1915; candidate for gov., Dem. primaries, 1919; mem. 67th to 73d Congresses (1921-35) and 75th, 76th and 77th Congresses (1937-43), 5th Miss. Dist. Candidate for nomination to U.S. Senate, 1934, also for nomination to fill vacancy after death of Senator Pat Harrison, 1941, and for full term following. As chmn. Mil. Appropriation, during early 30's and later, wrote, spoke and fought for mechanized weapons; credited with bringing into being the Flying Fortress. Hon. mem. Am. Library Assn. Club: Cosmos (Washington, D.C.) Episcopalian. Mason. Home: Meridian, Miss.†

COLLINS, WILBUR M(AUSLY), business exec.; b. Cochran, Ga., Dec. 3, 1892; s. Elisha P. and Florell (Sauls) C.; grad. Cochran High Sch., 1908; attended Ga.-Ala. Bus. Sch., Macon, Ga., 1909; m. Mary Naomi, July 12, 1918; children—Ann Valerie (Mrs. Frank J. Van Ulk), Mary Naomi (Mrs. Joseph P. Herr), Laurine Elizabeth (Mrs. Paul F. O'Neil). Bookkeeper, Dannenberg Co., Macon, Ga., 1909-20, gen. mgr. and sec., 1920-29, vice pres. of wholesale co., Dannenberg-Waxelbaum, Inc., 1924-29; in private bus., 1929-31; sales mgr. Happ Bros. Co., 1931-35; gen. sales mgr. Can. Dry Ginger Ale, Inc., N.Y. City, 1935-36, v.p., 1936-58, also dir.; pres. Can. Dry, Ltd., Can. Dry Internat., 1954-58. Alderman, Macon City Council, 1927-29. Served as 1st lt., advancing to capt., 327th Inf., 82nd Div., U.S. Army, 1917-19, World War I; overseas, France. Received Distinguished Service Cross (U.S.), Italian War Cross. Mem. Am. Legion. Democrat. Clubs: Kiwanis (pres. 1927 Macon); Sales Executives, Uptown, N.Y. Advertising (New York); Cherry Valley Inc. (Garden City, L.I.). Home: Garden City, N.Y. Died July 30, 1973.

COLLINS, WILLIAM DENNIS, chemist; b. Malden, Mass., Sept. 4, 1875; s. Dennis and Eliza Jemima (McKinnon) C.; A.B., Harvard, 1895, A.M., 1897; m. Jane Lydia Richards, Apr. 20, 1907 (dec. Jan. 10, 1946). Prof. chem. and physics, Earlham Coll., Ind., 1897-1906; chemist U.S. Geol. Survey, 1906-08, Bur. of Chemistry, U.S. Dept. Agr., 1908-20; chemist in charge div. of quality of water, Geol. Survey, U.S. Dept. Interior, 1920-46. Recipient Dept. of Interior award for distinguished service, 1948. Fuller award, American Water Works Assn., 1951; award for distinguished service to division water sewage and sanitation chemistry Am. Chem. Soc., 1956. Fellow A.A.A.S.; mem. Am. Chem. Soc., Am. Geophys. Union (life member), American Water Works Association (life member). Member Society of Friends. Club: Cosmos (Wash., D.C.). Author of amny papers on chem. character of waters in Geol. Survey Water Supply Papers; reports on standardization of apparatus and reagents; contbr. articles on water problems to tech. jours. Address: Washington, D.C.†

COLLINS, YYVONNE DEAKINS (MRS. CARR P. COLLINS, JR.), investment constrn. co. exec.; b. Midland, Tex.; d. Homer L. and Kathryn Deakins; B.B.A., So. Methodist U., Dallas, postgrad. study law Southwestern Legal Center, Dallas; m. Carr P. Collins, Jr.; children—Mark D. Bond, J. Bradford Bond. Owner Y-V Investments; officer, dir. Investment Trust Co.; constrn. co. exec.; former cattle rancher; vice-consul of Honduras for Dallas; mem. Consular Corps Dallas, Internat. Trade Assn. Dallas, Dallas Council World Affairs, Dallas Theatre Center, Dallas Mus. Fashion, Les Femmes du Monde, Tex. Fine Arts Assn.; active

Easter Seal campaign, Am. Cancer Soc., United Fund. Past officer, bd. dirs. Les Fieures des Jeunes, Dallas Symphony League; trustee Dallas Acad.; v.p. Sangreal Found. Recipient Freedom Medal Douglas MacArthur Acad. Freedom; named Ky. col.; named Ambassador Hemls-Fair, San Antonio, Tex., 1968. Mem. Dallas C. of C. (world trade com.), Delta Delta Delta. Episcopalian (active ch. guild work). Clubs: Dallas Country; Dallas Woman's; Petroleum; Cipango; Pub. Affairs Luncheon (past officer, bd. dirs.). Home: Dallas, Tex. Died May 16, 1974.

COLT, SAMUEL SLOAN, banking; b. N.Y. City, July 13, 1892; s. Richard Collins and Mary (Sloan) C.; prep. edn. Groton Sch.; B.A., Yale, 1914; hon. LL.D., Colgate, 1936; Dr. Comml. Sci. (honorary), N.Y. University, 1950; m. Margaret Van Buren Mason, Jan. 12, 1918; children—Marion (Mrs. McLean Williamson), Catherine S. (Mrs. David W. Yandell), Richard; m. 2d, Anne Weld McLane, Sept. 10, 1945. Began with Farmers Loan and Trust Co., N.Y. City, 1914, vice pres., 1925-29; vice pres. National City Bank, June 1929-Mar. 1930; v.p. and dir. Bankers Trust. Co., 1930-31, pres., 1931-56, chmn. of bd., 1956-57, dir., mem. exec. com., 1957-75; dir. General Foods Corp.; member U.S. adv. com. Royal Exchange Assurance; dir. Provident Insurance Company, Am. Bank Note Co.; trustee Mutual Life Insurance Company of N.Y.; director, member executive committee American Can Company; dir. General Electric Company. Pres. trustee Nat. Fund Med. Edn.; trustee, mem. adv. financial com. Com. for Econ. Development; treas. Eisenhower Exchange Fellowships, Recording for the Blind; dir. and treas., Met. Opera Assn., 1941-57. Nat. chmn. Am. Red Cross War Fund Campaign, 1941-42; dir. and treas. American Red Cross, New York Chapter; chairman of Port of New York Authority; trustee and treasurer, Tax Foundation, Incorporated. Served as corporal, advancing to major, U.S. Army, World War I. Mem. Internat. C. of C. (trustee U.S. council), Scroll and Key Society (Yale University), Delta Kappa Epsilon. Clubs: Yale, University, Links, Rolling Rock, Oneck Gun, Nat. Golf Links, River, Wyandanch. Home: New York City, N.Y. Died May 2, 1975.

COLTON, HAROLD SELLERS, zoologist, archaeologist; b. Philadelphia, Aug. 29, 1881; s. Sabin Woolworth, Jr., and Jessie (Sellers) C.; preparatory education DeLancey Sch., Phila.; B.S., U. Pa.; 1904, A.M., 1906, Ph.D., 1908; LL.D., University Arizona, 1955; D.Sc., Arizona State College, 1957; m. Mary Russell Ferrell, May 23, 1912; children—Joseph Ferrell, Sabin Woolworth (dec.). Asst. in zoölogy, 1909, instr., 1912, asst. prof., 1918, prof. zoölogy, University of Pennsylvania, 1926-54, professor emeritus, after 1954; research in Arizona since 1926; dir. San Francisco Mountain Zoöl. Sta., Flagstaff, Ariz., 1929-54; dir. Museum of Northern Ariz., Flagstaff, 1928-58. Mem. Archeol. Commn. of Ariz., 1929-31. Capt. Mil. Intelligence Div., 1918-19; capt. O.R.C., 1919-26. Trustee (sec. of bd.) Ariz. State Teachers Coll., Flagstaff, 1929-31; trustee Lab. of Anthropology, Santa Fe, 1934-53, Northern Ariz. Society Science and Art. Commr. Flagstaff FHA, 1944-51. Recipient conservation service award U.S. Dept. Interior, 1959. Fellow A.A.A.S. (pres. southwest div. 1935-36), Am. Geog. Soc.; mem. Am. Soc. Zoölogists, Am. Soc. Naturalists, Am. Anthrop. Assn., Am. Genetic Assn., Ecol. Soc. Am., Phila. Acad. Natural Science, Northern Ariz. Soc. Sci. and Art (pres. after 1928), American Microscopic Society, Soc. for Am. Archaeology, Sigma Xi. Republican. Club: U. Pa. Faculty. Author: Selected Readings for Students in Elementary Zoölogy, 1915; Examination-Quiz Questions in General Zoölogy, 1924; Laboratory Guide in Principles of Animal Life, 1925; Days in the Painted Desert and on the San Francisco Mountains (with Frank C. Baxter), 1927, 32; Handbook of Northern Arizona Pottery Wares (with L.L. Hargrave); The Sinagua; Hopi Indian Kachina Dolls; Potsherds; Pottery Types of Southwest; Black Sand, 1960; North of Market Street, 1961; also papers in field. Home: Flagstaff, Ariz.†

COLTON, JAMES HOOPER, business exec.; b. Morganton, N.C., Jan. 31, 1875; s. James Hooper and Eloise (Avery) C.; student pvt.and pub. schs. of Jonesboro, Ga.; m. Charlotte Maydwell, Aug. 8, 1898; children—Roger Maydwell, James Hooper, Eloise A. (Mrs. Karl O. Bohme); m. 2d. Minnie May Campbell, June 1, 1921. Admitted to Ky. bar, 1897, practiced Ky., 1897-99; traveled Wholesale Grocery, Louisville, 1900-01; with Nat. Coal & Iron Co., Pineville, Ky., 1901-02, Old Va. Portland Cement Co., Fordwick, Va., 1903-06; office mgr., asst. to gen. mgr., asst. to pres., gen. supt., v.p. in charge operation Pacific Portland Cement Co., 1906-45. adv. capacity 1945-52; organized Nev. Bldg. Materials, Inc., Reno, 1945, pres. after 1945. Republican. Presbyn. Home: 587 Ridge St. Office: Reno, Nev.†

COLTON, WINFRED RUFUS, college prof., musician; b. Sycamore, Ill., Dec. 27, 1879; s. Arunah C. and Cecile (Wyman) C.; studied music under Arthur Hartmann and Anton Witek, Berlin Germany, 1905-06, under Leopold Auer, Lake George, N.Y., 1918; Mus. M., Gunn Sch. of Music and Dramatic Art, Chicago 1930, Juilliard Sch. of Music, N.Y.; Mus. D., Morningside Coll., Sioux City, Ia., 1948; m. Ella Christenson, June 22, 1915; children—Dorothy Cecile (Mrs. David Pratt), Winifred. Teacher violin and orchestra Simpson Coll., Indianola, Ia., 1902-05, Southwestern State Normal Coll., Weatherford, Okla., 1907; teacher violin and orchestra also conductor, U. of S.D., after 1908, dean Coll. of Fine Arts, 1921-50. Mem. Nat. Assn. of Execs. of Music in State Univs. (pres. 1940). Contbr. articles to Violinist mag. Home: Vermillion, S.D.†

COLWELL, ERNEST CADMAN, educator; b. Hallstead, Pa., Jan. 19, 1901; s. Ernest and Anna (Lantz) C.; Ph.B., Emory U., 1923, Litt.D. (hon.), 1944; B.D., Candler Sch. Theol. 1927; Ph.D., U. Chgo., 1930; LL.D. (hon.), Colby Coll., 1947; S.T.D. (hon.), Harvard, 1947, Ripon (Wis.) Coll., 1962; L.H.D. (hon.), Claremont Coll., 1966; D.Hum.Litt., Hebrew Union Coll.-Jewish Inst. Religion, 1968; m. Annette Carter, May 7, 1925; children—Elizabeth Ann, Carter Colwell. Instr. English lit. and Bible, Emory U., 1924-28; with U. Chgo., 1930-45, asst. prof. of N.T. lit., 1930-38, asso. prof., 1938-39, prof., 1939-51, dean Div. Sch., 1938-43, dean faculties, 1943-45, v.p. univ., 1944, pres., 1945-51; dean faculties, v.p. Emory U., 1951-57; pres. So. Cal. Sch. Theology, Claremont, 1957-68; distinguished prof. N.T., Claremont Grad. Sch., 1968-71; vis. prof. Greek, Stetson U., Deland, Fla., 1969-74. Mem. bd. edn. Meth. Ch., vice chmn. commn. ecumenical consultation, 1963; trustee Blaisdell Inst. Claremont, Cal., 1958-70, Interdenominational Theol. Center at Atlanta, 1961-74. Pres. Soc. Bibl. Lit. and Exegesis, 1947, Am. Assn. Theol. Schs., 1958-60. Recipient Profl. Achievement citation U. Chgo. Alumni Assn., 1973. Hon. fellow Am. Coll. Dentistry; mem. Phi Beta Kappa, Omicron Delta Kappa, Sigma Chi. Methodist. Author: The Greek of the Fourth Gospel, 1931; John Defends the Gospel, 1936; The Study of the Bible, 1937, rev. edit. and paperback edit., 1964; The Four Gospels of Karahissar, Vol. I, 1936; Elizabeth Day McCormick Apocalyse, Vol. II, 1939; An Approach to the Teaching of Jesus, 1947; What is the Best New Testament?, 1952; The Text and Ancient Versions of the New Testament (in The Interpreter's Bible); (with E. Titus) The Gospel of the Spirit, 1953; Jesus and the Gospel, 1963; (with Ernest W. Tune) A Beginner's Reader-Grammar for New Testament Greek, 1965; Studies in Methodology in Textual Criticism of the New Testament, 1969; New or Old? The Christian Struggle with Change and Tradition, 1970. Editor: (with D.W. Riddle) Prolegomena to the Study of Lectionary Text of the Gospels, 1933; (with E.J. Goodspeed) A Greek Papyrus Reader, 1935; (with J.R. Mantey) A Hellenistic Greek Reader, 1939; (with Ralph Marcus and A. P. Wikgren) Hellenistic Greek Texts, 1947. Contbr. to religious jours. Home: DeLand, Fla. Died Sept. 12, 1974; buried Oakdale Cemetery, DeLand

COLWELL, FELTON, printer; b. Excelsior, Minn., Aug. 17, 1902; s. Thomas Henry and Harriet Hortense (Felton) C.; B.A., Carleton Coll., 1925; m. Helen Edythe Graham, Oct. 27, 1928; children—Thomas Graham, John Graham, David Graham, Cynthia Felton. With Colwell Press, Mpls., 1920-74, pres., 1934-65, chmn. bd. 1965-74; pres., treas. Colight, Inc. (formerly Colwell Litho Products, Inc.), 1951-60, chmn. bd., 1960-74; dir. Twin City Fed. Savs. & Loan Assn., Mpls., 1950-74. Mem. exec. com. Ednl. Council of Graphic Arts Industry, Inc., 1954-60, mem. research and engring. council, exec. com., 1960-74; pres. Research and Engring. Council Graphic Arts, Inc., 1956-58. Mem. Bd. Edn., planning commn., Mpls., 1945-51. Alumni trustee Carleton Coll. 1946-54. Gen. campaign chmn. United Fund Hennepin County, 1964; 1st v.p. United Fund Mpls. and Hennepin County, 1965-69; chmn. Mpls. Library Campaign Millage, 1966; del. Minn.-Uruguay Partners Alliance, pres., 1968, chmn. bd., 1969. Recipient A.F. Lewis Meml. award as 1957 Man of Year in the Graphic Arts Industry Mem. Lithographic Tech. Found. (dir. 1951-55, v.p. 1960, pres. 1961-63), Printing Industry Twin Cities (pres. 1961-62), Printing Industry Am. (dir. 1960, nat. sec. 1954), Mpls. C. of C. (dir. 1951-54, pres. 1956-58), Carleton Coll. Alumni Assn. (sec. 1927, pres. 1944), Mpls. Soc. Fine Arts. Conglist. (chmn. bd. trustees 1954). Clubs: Advertising (pres. 1931-32), Breakfast (pres. 1948), Kiwanis (pres. 1960, lt. gov. 1965), Minneapolis, Minikahda, 6 O'Clock, Athletic (dir. 1962-65), Thirteen (chmn. 1964), Dunkers (Mpls.); Alexandria (Minn.) Golf. Home: Minneapolis, Minn. Died Apr. 1, 1974.

COMAR, JEROME MORTON, automotive, textile machinery mfg. co. exec.; b. Chgo., May 20, 1911; s. Samuel R. and Goldie (Maremont) Cohen; B.S. in Mech. Engring., U. Mich., 1933; m. Gertrude Mintz, June 16, 1937; children—Stephen R., Lois D. With Maremont Corp., Chgo., 1933-75, chmn. exec. com. dir. Past pres. Vocational Research Council, Jewish Vocational Service and Employment Center. Bd. dirs. Joint Distribution Com.; past chmn. Chgo. chpt. and mem. Chgo. exec. bd. Am. Jewish Com.; nat. v.p., bd. govs., nat. exec. com. Am. Jewish Com.; bd. dirs., past pres. Jewish Fedn. Met. Chgo.; founding dir., trustee Chgo. Youth Centers. Mem. Am. Mgmt. Assn. Clubs: Standard, Mid-America (Chgo.); Northmoor Country. Home: Winnetka, Ill. Died Sept. 18, 1975.

COMBEST, EARL EDGAR, ins. co. exec.; b. Paducah, Tex., Feb. 5, 1899; s. Obe Jasper and Mollie (Meeks) C.; student Tyler Comml. Coll., 1917-18, Tex. Christian U., 1918-20; m. Erna Williams, June 3, 1937. Gen. ins. bus., 1921-35; v.p., exec. com., dir. Gt. Am. Res. Ins. Co., Dallas, 1935-73; exec. v.p., treas. Home Mortgage & Investment Co., Dallas, 1935-73; v.p., dir., mem. exec. com. Gt. Am. Fire & Casualty Co., Dallas. Trustee Tex. Christian U., Ft. Worth. Served with U.S. Army, 1918. Mem. Nat., Tex., Dallas assns. life underwriters, Am., Tex. life convs., Dallas Ins. Club. Mason (32 deg., Shriner). Club: Lake Wood Country. Home: Dallas, Tex. Died June 1973.

COMBS, PAT (WILLIAM MALONE), city ofcl.; b. Haskell, Okla., June 4, 1908; s. William Eli and Burla (Malone) C.; student U. Ark., 1925-26; m. Frances Harsha, Sept. 2, 1928; 1 son, Bill; m. 2d, Peggy Avis Dugan, Sept. 28, 1963. Teller, Exchange Nat. Bank Tulsa, 1926-34; salesman P. Lorillard Co., Muskogee, Okla., 1934-37; utility clk. Nat. Bank Tulsa, 1937-41; flight instr. Tulsa Aviation, 1941-44; owner, operator Skymerchants Flying Service, Tulsa, 1945-54; contract pilot Union Oil Co. Cal., Tulsa, 1950-55; mgr. airports Tulsa Airport Authority, from 1955. Mgr., Tulsa Municipal Airport Trust, 1967-71, Tulsa Airports Improvement Trust, 1967-71. Bd. dirs. Travelers Aid Soc. Tulsa. Served with USAAF, 1944-45. Mem. Airport Operators Council Internat. (dir. 1962-67, pres. 1965-66), Quiet Birdmen, Sigma Phi Epsilon. Mason. Home: Tulsa, Okla. Died July 18, 1971; buried Rose Hill Mausoleum, Tulsa, Okla.

COMPERE, EBENEZER LATTIMORE, army officer; b. Witcherville, Ark., Feb. 26, 1880; A.B., Ouachita Coll., LL.D., 1947; LL.B., University of Arkansas Law School; m. Emma Lucille Hawkins, Dec. 29, 1914; three sons. Commd. 1st lt., inf., Ark. Nat. Guard. Sept. 1905 and advanced to col., 1917; served World War I, 1918; commd. col. inf., Ark. Nat. Guard, 1919; commd. F.A., 1937, brig. gen., Mar. 1941 to serve as adjutant gen. of Ark.; dir. of selective service for Ark., after 1941. Awarded Legion of Merit with presidential citation, 1946. Home: 615 Champagnolle, El Dorado, Ark. Office: Headquarters Selective Service System Little Rock, Ark.†

COMPTON, RANULF, congressman; b. Poe, Ind., Sept. 16, 1881; s. William Charles and Alice Emily (True) C.; grad. Howe Mil. Sch., 1899; student Harvard, 1899-1901; m. Florence Jane Mabee, May 20, 1907; children—William Ranulf (lt. United States Navy), Douglas Mabee, Alice True (Mrs. Gordon Giffen). With American Can Company, 1902-04; New York Curb Exchange, 1905-09. Adirondack Trust Anthony and Co. (N.Y. Stock Exchange), 1929-30; Cool-Rite Products Corp., New Haven, 1934-36; mem. 78th Congress (1943-45), 3d Conn. Dist. Served as capt. 369th U.S. Inf., 1916-17, capt. Tank Corps and chief instr., A.E.F. Tank Sch., 1918-19, maj. 345th Batn., 1st Brigade, Tank Corps, 1919. Mil. sec. to Gov., N.Y., 1920-21; dep. sec. of state, N.Y., 1921-22; sec. and treas. Hudson River Regulating Dist., 1923-28; major, aide-de-camp, gov. State of Conn., 1939-40. Chmn. Madison (Conn.) United Service Orgns. Awarded N.Y. Conspicuous Service Cross; Purple Heart, Legion of Honor (France). Mem. Forty and Eight, Disabled Am. Vets., Vets. of Foreign Wars, Mil Order of Purple Heart, Am. Legion, Sojourners. Mason (K.T.). Clubs: Harvard (N.Y.), Madison (Conn.) Beach, Actor's Equity Assn. Home: Madison, Conn. Died Jan. 1974.

COMPTON, WILLIAM RANDALL, lawyer; b. Elmira, N.Y., July 9, 1902; s. William R. and Helen R. (Tubbs) C.; LL.B., Albany Law Sch., 1928; M.B.A., Harvard, 1931; J.S.D., Cornell U., 1933; m. Norma E. Haynes, Mar. 27, 1946; children—William Randall, Anne. Prof. bus. adminstrn., dean Green Mountain Jr. Coll., Poultney, Vt., 1931-32; admitted to N.Y. bar, 1933, practiced in Elmira until 1935; professorial lectr. law George Washington U., 1935-52; gen. counsel Q.M.C., Dept. of Army, 1943-56; dep. gen. counsel Dept. of Army, 1956-63; professorial lectr. law Am. U., 1963-65; prof. Utah State U., 1965-68. Served from capt. to lt. col. AUS, 1942-45. Decorated Legion of Merit; recipient Exceptional Civilian Service award, Meritorious Civilian Service award. Mem. Order of Coif. Author: Digest of Safe Deposit Custom, 1933. Editor: Cases on Domestic Relations, 1951; 1965 Supplement to Compton Cases and Materials on Domestic Relations. Co-editor: Cases on Domestic Relations (with Madden), 1940. Home: West Lafayette, Ind. Died May 18, 1974; interred Elmira, N.Y.

COMSTOCK, ADA LOUISE, educator; b. Moorhead, Minn., Dec. 11, 1876; d. S. G. and Sarah A. (Ball) Comstock; student U. of Minn., 1892-94; B.L., Smith Coll., 1897; diploma State Normal Sch., Moorhead, 1898; M.A., Columbia, 1899; Litt.D., Mt. Holyoke Coll., 1912; L.H.D., Smith Coll., 1922; LL.D., U. of Mich., 1921, Boston Univ., 1928, U. of Rochester, 1924. U. of Maine, 1925, Brown U., 1934, U. of Minn., 1936. Goucher Coll., 1938. Western Reserve U., 1938. Williams Coll., 1938, Skidmore Coll., 1942. Harvard 1959; M.A., Oxford University 1949; married Wallace Notestein, June 14, 1943. Asst., instr., asst. prof., prof. rhetoric, dean of women to 1912, Univ. of Minn.; dean Smith Coll., 1912-23; president of Radcliffe College, 1923-43; mem. Commn. on Direction of Investigation of History and Other Social Studies in the Schools under auspices of Am. Hist. Assn., 1929-34; mem. Nat. Commn. on Law Observance and Enforcement, apptd.

May, 1929, by President Hoover. Trustee Teachers Institute and Annuity Association of America, 1940-44; member educational council adv. to Navy on Women's Reserves (WAVES). Decorated Heraldie Order of Christobal Colon, 1940, at legation of Dominican Republic, as mem. Columbus Meml. Lighthouse Com.; recipient Jane Addams medal Rockford, Coll., 1958. Fellow American Academy of Arts and Sciences since 1943; mem. Am. Assn. Univ. Women (pres. 1921-23). Delta Gamma, Phi Beta Kappa. Clubs: Chilton, College (Boston); Cosmopolitan (N.Y.C.). Home: New Haven, Conn.†

CONAGHAN, BRIAN FRANCIS, state legislator; b. Tonkawa, Okla., Feb. 8, 1927; s. Billy Frank and Letha (Siler) C.; grad. No. Okla. Jr. Coll., 1948; B.S. in History, U. Okla., 1951; m. Dorothy Dell Miller, June 10, 1951; children—Joseph Lee, Charles Alan, Roger, Lloyd. Owner, Contractors' Bit Service, Tonkawa, 1956-73; mem. Okla. Ho. of Reps., 1963-73. Active No. Okla. Jr. Coll. Alumni Trust Fund Pres., Kay County Young Republicans, 1957. Served with AUS, 1944-47. Mem. Am. Legion, Tonkawa C. of C., Acacia, Oklahoma Ct. Chevaliers. Republican. Baptist. Mason (32 deg.); mem. Order Eastern Star, Order DeMolay; Elk. Home: Tonkawa, Okla. Died Apr. 1, 1973.

CONAWAY, PAUL BREWER, road constrn. co. exec; b. Chillicothe, O., Aug. 22, 1913; s. Joseph William and Bertha (Brewer) C.; B.A., Ohio Wesleyan U., 1935; postgrad. Ohio State U., 1938, 59, U. Md.; m. Jessie-Louise Franklin, Nov. 26, 1935; children—Paula Louise, Franklin Brewer, Robert Lewis, Constance Martin. Vice pres. Brewer & Brewer Sons, Inc., Chillicothe, 1936-49, pres., 1949-71, chmn. bd., 1967-71. Mem. Chillicothe City Planning Commn., 1938-39; mem. bldg. com. YMCA. Original trustee Felxible Pavements, Inc. Ohio, Roweton Boys Home So. Ohio. Ky. Col. Mem. Ohio Contractors Assn. (legislative com.), Ohio Sand and Gravel Assn. (life pres. 1953-54, dir.), Bituminous Concrete Producers Assn. Ohio (pres. 1961-62), Chillicothe Area C. of C., Internat. Platform Assn., Ross County Hist. Assn., Am. Automobile Assn. (trustee Ross-Highland), Symposiarea, Hon. Order Ky. Cols., Alpha Sigma Phi. Mason (Shriner), Elk, Rotarian. Club: Antique Automobile of Am. (Phila.). Home: Chillicothe, O. Died Sept. 4, 1971.

CONDIT, KENNETH HAMILTON, educator, engr.; b. East Orange, N.J., Mar. 1, 1888; s. Oscar Halstead and Fannie Crane (Harrison) C.; M.E., Stevens Inst. Tech., 1908; student Columbia, 1911; C.E., Princeton, 1931, D.Eng., Stevens, 1940; m. Marjorie Walbridge Brown, June 6, 1916; children—Paul Taylor, Kenneth Walbridge, Anna Ryckman. Draftsman, 1908-10; automobile salesman, 1910-11, instr. in engring., Princeton, 1913-17; asso. editor Am. Machinist, 1919, mng. editor, 1920, editor, 1921-38; editor Product Engineering, 1929-35; consulting editor, Product Development Series, McGraw-Hill Book Company; executive assistant to president, The Conference Board, New York, 1938-40; dean engring. Princeton U., 1940-54, emeritus, 1954-74. Served from 1st lt. to capt. A.S., U.S. Army, 1917-18. Mem. Am. Soc. M.E. (v.p. 1939-41), Sigma Xi, Phi Beta Kappa, Tau Beta Pi, Sigma Nu. Republican. Presbyn. Clubs: Princeton Tower, Nassau (Princeton). Home: Princeton, N.J. Died Dec. 15, 1974.

CONDON, EDDIE (ALBERT EDWIN CONDON), band leader; b. Goodland, Ind., Nov. 16, 1905; s. John Henry and Margaret (McGraw) C.; student pub. schs., Chicago Heights, Ill.; m. Phyllis Smith, Nov. 16, 1942; children—Margaret, Liza. Banjo player Hollis Peavey Orchestra, 1923; club dates, Chgo., 1923-27; musician Bath Club, Stork Club, N.Y.C., 1930-33; 1st appearance Town Hall, N.Y.C., 1942; night club owner, N.Y.C., 1946-73. Mem. Toots Shor Athletic Club. Author: (with Thomas Sugrue) We Called It Music, 1948; (with Richard Gehman) Eddie Condon's Treasury of Jazz, 1954; (with Hank O'Neal) the Eddie Condon Scrapbook of Jazz. Contbr. articles to mags. Home: New York City, N.Y. Died Aug. 3, 1973; cremated.

CONDON, EDWARD U., physicist; b. Alamogordo, N.M., Mar. 2, 1902; s. William Edward and Caroline Barr (Uhler) C.; A.B., U. Cal., 1924, Ph.D., 1926; D.Sc. (hon.), U. Delhi (India), N.M. Sch. of Mines, 1950, Alfred U., Am. U., 1952, U. Chgo., 1972; m. Emilie Honzik, Nov. 9, 1922; children—Caroline Marie, Paul Edward, Joseph Henry. Nat. Research fellow, Göttingen and Munich, 1926-27; lectr. in physics, Columbia U., spring 1928; asst. prof. physics. Princeton U., 1928-29, asso. prof., 1930-37; prof. theoretical physics, U. Minn., 1929-30; asso. dir. Westinghouse Research Lab., 1937-45; dir. Nat. Bur. Standards, Washington, 1945-51; dir. research and devel. Corning Glass Works, 1951-54; cons. physicist, 1954-74; prof. Washington U. at St. Louis, 1956-63; prof. physics, fellow joint inst. for lab. astrophysics, U. Colo., 1963-74; vis. prof. Oberlin (O.) Coll., 1962-63; v.p. Ann. Reviews, Inc.; sci. dir. Air Force financed investigation Unidentified Flying Objects. Mem. NACA, 1945-51; sci. adv., spl. senate com. on atomic energy, 79th congress; pres. Colo. Sci. Devel. Commn., 1966-68. Mem. Am. Philos. Soc., Soc. for Social Responsibility in Sci. (pres. 1968-69), Am. Acad. Arts and Sci., Royal Soc. Arts (London), Societé Francaise de Physique (Paris), Royal Swedish Acad. Engring. Sci. (Stockholm), Royal Norwegian Soc. Scis. (Trondheim), Nat. Acad. Scis., Am. Phys. Soc. (pres. 1946), A.A.A.S. (pres. 1953), Am. Assn. Physics Teachers (pres. 1964), Phi Beta Kappa, Sigma Xi. Clubs: University (Boulder, Colo.); Cosmos (Washington). Author: Quantum Mechanics (with P. M. Morse), 1929; Theory of Atomic Spectra (with G. H. Shortley), 1935. Editor: Handbook of Physics (with Hugh Odishaw), 1958; Revs. of Modern Physics, 1957-68. Home: Boulder, Colo. Died Mar. 26, 1974.

CONDRA, GEORGE EVERT, univ. dean; b. Seymour, Ia., Feb. 2, 1869; s. Isaac N. and Mary A. (Keller) C.; student Western Normal Coll., Shenandoah, Ia., 1889-91, U. of Mich., 1891-92; B.S., U. of Neb., 1896, A.M., 1898, Ph.D., 1902; spl. study, Cornell U., 1902; m. Hattie M. Davenport, Aug. 13, 1893. Head of dept. science, Lincoln (Neb.) Normal Sch., 1892-96, high sch., Lincoln, 1896-1902; instr. in geography and econ. geology, U. of Neb., 1902-03, asst. prof., 1903-04, asso. prof., 1904-05, prof., 1905-08, head of dept., 1908-12, head prof. geography and conservation, 1912-18, dir. conservation survey div. since 1918, dean fron 1929; prof. geography, Cornell, summer sessions, 1905-11; asst. state geologists, Neb., 1902-10; state geologist for Nebraska, after 1910; director Nebraska Conservation and Soil Survey, 1910-18; dir. Neb. Geol. Survey after 1919. Pres. Neb. Conservation and State Development Congress, 1909, 10; chmn. Neb. Conservation Commn., 1908-13; exec. sec. Neb. Conservation and Pub. Welfare Commn., 1913-19; pres. Nat. Assn. State Conservation Commrs., 1910-13; mem. Neb. Rural Life Commn., 1910-12; chmn. exec. com. Nat. Conservation Congress, 1915-16, pres., 1916; mem. Federal Irrigation Readjustment Bd. for Neb., 1926; chmn. Neb. Soil Conservation Com. from 1934; mem. Neb. State Planning Bd. from 1935; consultant United States Soil Conservation Service. Lt. col. Engr. Reserve Corps. Recipient of 1951 award of the Am. Forestry Assn. Dir., v.p. Lincoln Chamber of Commerce, 1922-24. Mem. Gel. Soc. Am., Am. Paleontol. Soc., Am. Assn. for Advancement of Sci., Am. Soil Survey Assn. (pres. 1928), Am. Geophysical Union. Neb. Acad Science (pres. 1909-11), Neb. Science Teachers Assn. (pres. 1898), Am. Assn. State Geologists (pres. 1939), Sigma Xi, Sigma Chi, Acacia; mem. bd. Neb. Reclamation Assn. from 1944; pres. State Irrigation Assn. 1950; pres. Neb. div. Izaak Walton League, 1943, 44; Received Kiwanis award for distinguished service in 1945. Republican. Methodist. Mason, (33°). Author of numerous papers, bulletins and books, chiefly on geology, geography, hydrology and conservation. Home: Lincoln, Neb.†

CONKLING, DONALD HERBERT, newspaper pub.; b. Denton County, Tex., July 11, 1879; s. Richard Adolphus and Ida (Wade) C.; ed. pub. schs.; m. Katherine Agnes Cullinan, Nov. 25, 1903; children—Zoe Agnes, Katherine Dulari, Donald Herbert. Founder of Palm Beach (Fla.) Post, 1911. Commr. Fla. Inland Navigation Dist. Mem. S.A.R. Episcopalian. Mason (K.T., Shriner), Elk. Clubs: Sailfish, Tuscawilla, Circuit Riders', Palm Beach Yacht (ex-commodore). Home: West Palm Beach, Fla.†

CONLEY, CAREY HERBERT, prof. English; b. Tecumseh, Mich., Jan. 29, 1879; s. Rev. Charles Edgar and Emma A. (Mosey) C.; B.A., U. of Mich., 1902; M.A., U. of Chicago, 1912; Ph.D., Yale, 1922; m. Ethel Thomson, Oct. 2, 1911. Prof. English, Grand Island (Neb.) Coll., 1905-07; instr. English, Purdue U., 1907-09; instr. rhetoric, U. of Mich., 1909-13; asso. prof. English, Wesleyan U., 1913-20, prof. after 1920, then emeritus; instr. English, Biarritz Am. U., France, 1945; visiting professor English, U. of Redlands (Calif.), 1947-49; lecturer Calif. Inst. Technology, 1950. Mem. Modern Lang. Assn. of Am., Am. Assn. Univ. Profs., Sigma Chi, Phi Beta Kappa. Author: The First English Translators of the Classics, 1927. Editor: Patterns of Reading and Writing, 1937; The Reader's Johnson, 1940. Home: Alhambra, Cal.†

CONLEY, CLYDE G., business exec., b. Newark, O., Dec. 26, 1879; s. Edmund J. and Leota J. (Beard) C.; B.S., Denison U., Granville O., 1900; C.E., Ohio State U., 1902; m. Elizabeth B. Sperry, Oct. 18, 1905; children—Annis Leota (Mrs. T. Kenneth Miller), Ruth Elizabeth, Evelyn Sperry (Mrs. Keith Allan Karhl), Helen Brooks (Mrs. Nicholas Tiedeman), with The Mount Vernon Bridge Co. after 1902, beginning as draftsman, pres., 1930-51, 53-57, v.p. 1951, chmn. exec. committee after 1957; chmn. Knox County Savs. Bank. Pres. City council Mt. Vernon 3 terms, Govt. appeal agt. for draft bd. Mem. Am. Inst. of Steel Constrn. (hon.), Am. Soc. C.E., Am. Railway Engring. Assn., Soc. Profl. Engrs., Ohio Mfrs. Assn. (trustee), Phi Beta Kappa Assos. Beta Theta Pi, Phi Beta Kappa. Clubs: Columbus, Ohio State U. Faculty (Columbus); Union (Cleveland); Mt. Vernon Rotary (pres.), Mt. Vernon Country. Home: Mount Vernon, O.†

CONLEY, DUDLEY STEELE, surgeon, univ. dean; b. Columbia, Mo., Jan. 26, 1878; s. Sanford Francis and Kate (Singleton) C.; B.L., U. of Mo., 1899; M.D., Columbia 1906; m. Sidney A. Boales, Jan. 2, 1915. In practice surgery, New York, 1909-18; instr. surgery, Columbia, 1912-18, Post Grad. Medical Sch., 1916-18; prof. surgery, Sch. of Medicine, U. of Mo., 1919-33, dean 1933-48, dean and professor emeritus after 1948. Served in Medical Corps, United States Army Reserves, 1917-19. Fellow Am. Coll. Surgeons; mem. A.M.A., mO. sTATE Med. Assn. (v.p. 1935, pres. 1937), Phi Delta Theta. Democrat. Presbyterian. Home: Columbia, MO.†

CONLEY, WILLIAM H., educator; b. Sharon, Wis., Feb. 13, 1907; s. Stephen E. and Agnes (Kinna) G.; B.S.C., Loyola U., 1930, A.M., 1935; M.B.A., Northwestern U., 1932, Ph.D., 1947; LL.D., Seton Hall, 1953, St. Ambrose Coll., 1962; L.H.D., Manhattan Coll., 1963; Marvcrest Coll., 1964; LL.D., Fairfield U., 1965, U. Bridgeport, 1967; m. Evelyn McIntyre, June 20, 1936; children—William H., Mary Cecile, Mary Eileen, Stephen E. Instr., Loyola U., 1930-32, asst. dean, 1932-35; dean, Wright Jr. Coll. (Chgo. Municipal), 1935-46; dean Loyola U. Sch. Commerce, 1946-48; specialist higher edn. U.S. Office Edn., 1948-49; chmn. dept. edn., dean U. Coll. Loyola U., 1949-51; v.p. instruction Seton Hall U., 1951-53; ednl. asst. to pres. Marquette U., 1953-63; on leave, dir. Carnegie Study Cath. Edn., U. Notre Dame, 1962-63; pres. Sacred Heart U., Bridgeport, Conn., 1963-71, chancellor, 1971-74. Regional rep. consumer div., O.P.A., 1941-42; dir. publs. Naval Air Tech. Tng. Center, 1942-44; mem. U.S. Nat. Com. on UNESCO, 1956-74, mem. exec. com., 1957-74; mem. Gov.'s Commn. on Youth; mem. Conn. Commn. in Cooperation with Fed. Authorities in Matters Pertaining to Higher Edn. Pres., Conn. Fedn. Citizens for Ednl. Freedom; mem. Diocesan Sch. Bd., 1968-74. Trustee Coll. Entrance Exam. Bd., 1959; bd. dirs. Center for Study of Liberal Edn. for Adults, 1956. Served as lt. comdr. USNR, officer-in-charge instrn., tng. Service Schs. Bur. Personnel, Navy Dept., 1944-46. Chmn., U.S. Armed Forces Edn. Program Com. 1949-51. Recipient Distinguished Alumni award Loyola U., 1961. Mem. Nat. Catholic Bus. Edn. Assn. (co-chmn. midwest div. 1948), Am. Econ. Assn., N.E.A. (v.p. Assn. for Higher Edn. 1963-64), Am. Assn. Sch. Adminstrs., Am. Ednl. Research Assn., Nat. Cath. Ednl. Assn. (exec. com. 1956, chmn. mid-west coll. and univ. dept. 1956-57, pres. coll. and univ. dept. 1960-62, v.p. gen. 1966). Am. Council on Edn., Cath. Com on Intellectual and Cultural Affairs, Assn. U. Evening Colls. (pres. 1956-57), Serra Internat. Roman Catholic. Clubs: University, Algonquin, Brooklawn. Contbr. ednl. articles to profl. jours. Editor, Cath. Sch. Jour., 1961; Ofcl. Guide to Catholic Educational Instns., 1960. Home: Stratford, Conn. Died July 18, 1974.

CONLIN, EARL EDGAR, business cons.; b. Detroit, July 20, 1906; s. James S. and Nellie (Cowing) C.; A.B., U. Mich., 1933, M.B.A., 1934; m. Annette Pauline Fansler, May 29, 1935; children—James, David, Ann. With Ex-Cell-O Corp., Detroit, 1934-74, successively statistician and analyst, asst. sec., sec. and asst. treas., sec.-treas., sec., 1934-60, v.p. finance, 1960-67, exec. v.p. group operations, 1967-69, became sr. exec. v.p., 1969, dir., 1955; officer, dir. affiliated and subsidiary cos., then cons. Trustee Citizens Research Council Mich.; bd. dirs. Mich. Med. Services, dist. v.p.; bd. dirs. United Community Services. Mem. Financial Execs. Inst., Highland Park (dir.), Detroit bds. commerce, N.A.M., Council Tech. Advancement (financial council), Am. Accounting Assn., Corporate Secs. Am., United Community Services Com., Delta Sigma Pi. Clubs: Economic, Detroit Golf (Detroit); Lost Lake Woods. Home: Birmingham, Mich. Died Mar. 1974.

CONLON, MRS. WILLIAM F. (SARA FRANCES SMITH CONLON), lectr.; b. Waco, Tex., Aug. 15, 1901; d. John E. and Sara (Robertson) Smith; A.B., Manchester Coll., 1923; postgrad. U. Wis., 1924-25, Northwestern U., 1930-31; spl. student U. London (Eng.), 1926-27, U. Geneva (Switzerland), 1926; m. William F. Conlon, Sept. 1, 1928; 1 dau., Ellen Augusta (Mrs. Robert K. Adams). Lectr. ancient methods spinning textile fibres, 1931; tchr., mus. cons. ancient methods and equipment spinning textile fibres. Sec., Alliance Francaise de Chgo., mem. Magna Charta Dames, Antiquarian Soc., D.A.R. Republican. Club: Womans Athletic. Home: Chicago, Ill. Died Dec. 22, 1973.

CONNALLY, BEN C., judge; b. Marlin, Tex., Dec. 28, 1909; s. Tom and Louise (Clarkson) C.; A.B., U. of Tex., 1930, LL.B., 1933; LL.M., Harvard, 1934; m. Sarah Nell Allen, Sept. 27, 1937; children—Tom, Louise. Admitted to bar, Tex., 1933; practiced as mem. firm Sewell, Taylor, Morris & Connally, Houston, 1934-42, Butler & Binion, 1945-49; U.S. district Judge, southern district of Texas, 1949—75. Served with USAAF, 1942-45. Mem. Am., Tex. and Houston bar assns. Methodist. Home: Houston, Tex., Died Dec. 3, 1975.

CONNELL, KENNETH HUGH, educator; b. Southampton, Eng., Sept. 6, 1917; s. James and Susanna (Cambridge) C.; B.Sc. (Econ.) with 1st class honors, London Sch. Econ., Polit. Sci., 1940, Ph.D., London, 1948; M.A., Oxford U., 1950; m. Hanna Schumer, July 3, 1945; children—Myral Caroline, Monica Bridget. Lectr., econ. history U. Coll. Wales, Aberystwyth, 1941, Liverpool (Eng.) U., 1941-45, London Sch. Econs., 1946-49; ofcl. fellow Nuffield Coll., Oxford U., 1949-52; lectr. econs. Oxford U., 1950-52; mem. faculty Queens U., Belfast, No. Ireland, 1953-73, sr. lectr. econ. history, 1953-66, head dept. econ. and social history, 1961-70, reader econ. and social history, 1966-67, prof. econ. and social history, 1967-70, prof. Irish social history, 1970-73; vis. fellow Research Sch. Social Scis., Inst. Advanced Studies, Australian Nat. U., Canberra, 1965-66, All Souls Coll., Oxford, 1970-71; mem. econ., social history com. Social Sci. Research Council, London, 1968-72. Recipient George Unwin Meml. prize London Sch. Econs., 1940, Leverhulme Research student, 1940-41; Madden prize Trinity Coll., Dublin, Ireland, 1951. Fellow Royal Hist. Soc., Econ. History Soc. (council 1951-59, 62-71), Econ. and Social History Soc. Ireland (pres. 1970-73); mem. Royal Irish Acad., Internat. Union Sci. Study Population. Author: The Population of Ireland, 1750-1845, 1950, Irish Peasant Society, 1968. Gen. editor, contbr. projected Oxford Economic and Social History of Ireland; editorial com. A New History Ireland (Royal Irish Acad.), 1964-73. Contbr. profl. jours. Home: Belfast, Northern Ireland. Died Sept. 26, 1973.

CONNER, ALBERT HOLMES, lawyer; b. Cardington, O., Feb. 9, 1879; s. Homer Erasmus and Mary Virginia (Holmes) C.; grad. high sch., Akron, O., 1895; m. Lydia Bartels, 1904 (died 1905); m. 2d, Mabel Glenn Barton, 1932. Admitted to Ida. bar 1907, and began practice at Wallace; moved to Sandpoint, 1909; mem. Ida. Ho. of Rep., 1907-08, 1913-16 (speaker of House, 1915-16); atty. Idaho Public Utilities Com., 1921-23; atty. gen. of Idaho, 2 terms, 1923-26; supt. of prisons, U.S. Dept. of Justice, 1927-29; spl. asst. atty. gen. of U.S., 1929-34; legislative counsel of NRA, 1935; then asso. commr. and general counsel Federal Prison Industries, Inc. Served as capt. 361st Inf., U.S. Army, 1917-20, World War; participated in St. Mihiel and Meuse-Argonne offensives; wounded in Argonne, Mem. advisory bd., Federal Industrial Instn. for Women, U.S. Industrial Reformatory for Men, 1927-29; dir. Penal Industries Assn., 1942-48; mem. Am. Prison Assn.; alternate mem. Fed. Bd. of Hospitalization, 1942-48. Mem. Soc. Amer. Revolution. Home: Alexandria, VA.†

CONNER, BENJAMIN HOWE, lawyer; b. Connersville, Ky., Nov. 28, 1878; s. Dr. Alpheus and Susan Amelia (Reed) C.; B. Letters, Central U. of Ky., 1899; student U. of Va. Law Sch., summer 1901; LL.B., Albany Law Sch., 1902; student U. of Paris (France) Law Sch., 1905-07; m. Maud Burton Swiggette, Oct. 14, 1921. Admitted to N.Y. bar, 1902; practiced in N.Y. City, 1902-04, Paris, France, 1904-37; judge, Mixed Tribunals at Cairo, Egypt, 1937-40; practiced law New York City after December 1940; member law firm Conner, Chopnick, & Garrell. Corporal 2d Ky. Vol. Infantry, Spanisn-Am. War, 1898; major of Inf., U.S. Army, with A.E.F., World War. Pres. Am. Chamber of Commerce in France, 1925-28; past comdr. Am. Legion, Dept. of France; past pres. Nat. Aeronautic Assn. of France; past comdr. United Spanish War Vets. of France; former mem. Arbitration Court, Internat. Chamber of Commerce, Paris; Am. del. of France-Amerique. Decorated Officer French Legion of Leopold I (Belgium); Victory, Verdun, St. Mihiel Internat. Diplomatic Acad., Am. Bar Assn., Assn. of State Society, S.A.R., Va. Soc. of Cincinnati, Am. Legion, Forty and Eight, N.Y. Southern Soc. Independent Democrat. Epsicopalian. Mason. Elk. Clubs: Nat. Sojourners, Travellers, American, Interallied, St. Cloud Country, Golf of Saint-Germain (Paris); Manhattan. Bankers (New York). Contributor articles on law and international problems to jours. Home: New York City, N.Y.†

CONNOLLY, BRENDAN, librarian; b. Boston, Feb. 10, 1913; s. Daniel and Mary Ellen (Keane) C.; A.B., Boston Coll., 1937; M.A., 1938; S.T.L., Weston Coll., 1944; B.S. in L.S., Cath. U. Am., 1946; Ph.D., U. Chgo., 1955. Joined Soc. of Jesus, 1931, ordained priest Roman Cath. Ch., 1943; instr. English, Boston Coll., 1938-40; instr. library sci. Cath. U. Am., 1950-51; librarian Weston Coll., 1951-59, asst. prof. theology, 1951-59; dir. libraries Boston Coll., 1959-74; chaplain Country Day Sch. Sacred Heart, 1959-74. Cons. library adminstrn. and bldg. Mem. Am. Cath., Mass., New Eng. library assns., N.A.A.C.P., Am. Assn. U. Profs., Jesuit Library Conf. Asso. editor: New Testament Abstracts, 1956-60, Writer religious and library articles. Home: Chestnut Hill, Mass. Died Apr. 21, 1974; buried Jesuit Cemetery, Weston, Mass.

CONNOR, CHARLES ASHLEY RICHARD, physician; born N.Y. City, Oct. 12, 1905; s. Joseph P. and Octavia (Willis) C.; A.B., Holy Cross Coll., 1927; M.D., Univ. and Bellevue Hosp. Med. Coll., 1931; D.Sc. med., N.Y.U., 1940; m. Elizabeth R. Prial, Aug. 18, 1934; children—Charles Prial, Irene (Mrs. Timothy Flint), Elizabeth. Intern Bellevue Hosp., 1932-34, resident medicine, 1934-35; pvt. practice limited to cardiovascular diseases, N.Y.C., 1935-74; asst. prof. clin. medicine N.Y.U. Coll. Medicine, 1947-58, associate professor of clinicial medicine, 1958-74; consulting physician cardiovascular diseases Lenox Hill Hosp., 1968-74; attending physician, chief cardiovascular service St. Clare's Hosp., 1951-74; asso. in cardiology VA, 1956-74; cons. physician St. Francis Hosp., Poughkeepsie, N.Y. 1954-74; cons. physician Misericordia Hosp., Bronx, 1961-74. Yonker's General Hosp., Yonkers, N.Y., 1966-74, Maj. U.S.A.A.F., 1942-45; flight Surgeon instructor School Aviation Med., 1942-44; cons. cardiol., 1st A.F., 1944-45; assistant chief medical division Office Air Surgeon, 1945-46. Qualified specialist Am. Bd. Internal Med., Subsplty. Cardiovascular Disease, 1940. Fellow A.C.P., A.M.A., Am. Heart Assn., A.A.A.S., N.Y. Acad. Medicine, Am. Therapeutic Soc. (pres. 1964-65), Knights Malta. Roman Catholic. Author med. pubs. on rheumatic fever, heart disease. Home: New York City, N.Y. Died Sept. 8, 1974; buried Gate of Heaven Cemetery, Hawthorne, N.Y.

CONNOR, CHARLES FRANCIS clergyman; b. N.Y. City, Feb. 8, 1881; s. Charles Augustus and Agnes (Nolan) C.; prep. edn., Xavier High Sch., New York; A.B., St. Francis Xavier's Coll., New York, 1900, A.M., 1907; theol. course, Woodstock (Md.) Coll. Joined Soc. of Jesus (Jesuits), 1900; ordained priest R.C. Ch., 1915; instr. classics and English, Holy Cross Coll. High Sch., 1907-10; instr. freshman classics and English, Holy Cross Coll., 1910-11, St. Francis Xavier Coll., New York, 1911-12; dean, St. Joseph's Coll., Phila., 1919-21, Atenco Di Manila, Philippine Islands, 1921-22; prin. St. Joseph's Coll. High Sch., 1923-24; also served as prof. dialectics and epistemology Holy Cross Coll., and with Fordham U. Extension School; preacher, lectr. as mem. Jesuit Order Missionary Band; mem. Jesuit Mission Band of New York Province. Widely known as speaker on religious and ednl. subjects. Chaplain, U.S. Army, World War; in action St. Die Sector and Meuse Argonne offensive; with Army of Occupation in Germany. Mem. K.C. (4th degree). Chaplain, Legion of Honor, Vasella Post 277, Am. Legion, mem. of Catholic War Vets. Assn. Address: New York City, N.Y.†

CONNORS, JAMES JOSEPH, metal products co. exec.; b. Hartford, Conn., Dec. 11, 1926; s. James Joseph and Catherine Elizabeth (Meshan) C.; student Notre Dame, 1944-45; B.S., U.S. Naval Acad., 1949; m. Lorraine Marie Felice, June 11, 1949; children—Dennis Michael, Peter James. Salesman, Container Corp. Am., Phila., 1955-58, sales mgr., 1958-62, marketing mgr. Haveg Industries, Wilmanston, Del., 1962-64, v.p. marketing, 1964-65, exec. v.p., 1966; v.p. marketing Ametak, Inc., N.Y.C., 1966-67, v.p. operations staff, 1967-68, sr. v.p., 1969-74. Served to capt. USMCR. Decorated Navy Commendation medal. Home: Wayne, Pa. Died Jan. 21, 1974.

CONNORS, JAMES JOSEPH, collector customs; b. Halifax, N.S., Can., Apr. 27, 1878; s. James Joseph and Isabell Louise (Williams) C.; self educated; m. Katherin Ann Collins, of Kent, Wash., July 1907; 1 son, James Joseph. Came to U.S., 1893, naturalized citizen, 1902. Began as flunky in lumber camp, 1893; lineman, Am. Telephone & Telegraph Co., 1895-97; constrn. foreman, N.E. Telephone & Telegraph Co., 1897-1902; engaged in mining, Alaska, 1902-15; proprietor Connors Motor Co., Juneau, Alaska, after 1915. Mem. City Council, Juneau, 1918, 22, 23, 24; mayor of Juneau, 1925, 26; formerly mem. Dem. Nat. Com.; apptd. collector of customs for Alaska, July 1933, reapptd., 1937. Democrat. Catholic. Elk; mem. Pioneers of Alaska. Home: Juneau, Alaska.†

CONRAD, JAMES LAWSON, educator; b. Fitchburg, Mass., Nov. 28, 1900; s. Thomas Harry and Catherine Agnes (Kane) C.; student Fitchburg State Teachers Coll., 1918-19, U. of N.H., Sept.-Dec. 1920, Villanova (Pa.) Coll., 1921-24; B.B.A., Boston U., 1925; m. Annette Bourassa, Sept. 3, 1927; 1 son, James Lawson; married 2d Beulah M. Bruce, 1947. Began in employ Texas Company, Fitchburg, Mass., 1925; mgr. Lincoln Adjustment Co., Fitchburg, 1925; gen. mgr. Patenaude's Auto Sales Co., Fitchburg, 1925; credit mgr. Edward Malley Co., New Haven, Conn., 1925-26; teacher and coach, New Hampton (N.H.) Sch., 1926-27; dir. Jr. Coll., same sch., 1927-29; president Nicholas Junior College, Dudley, Mass., 1930-58; president, Nichols College, 1958-74; exec. dir. Worcester Acad., 1946-74, mem. exec. com., trustee, 1951-52; v.p. N. E. Jr. Coll. Council, 1951-52, pres. 1953; nat. chmn. legislative com. Am. Assn. Jr. Colleges, 1951-52; bd. dirs. Daniel Sch. of Worcester (Mass.) Mus. Nat. History, 1953; chmn. bd. trustees Oakdale State Tng. Sch., 1954-55. Dir. First Nat. Bank, Webster, Mass. Pres. Webster-Dudley Boy's Club. Mem. finance and adv. com. Town of Dudley. Trustee Worcester (Mass.) Mus. Natural History, Mound Park Hosp. Found., St. Petersburg, Fla. Served from capt. to col. U.S. Army, 1941-46. Recipient Outstanding Citizen of the Year award Webster-Dudley, 1957; Golden Deed award Exchange Club, 1959; Keystone award Boys Clubs America, 1960. Member Res. Officers Assn., Mass. Comdry., N.E.Q.M. Assn. (president 1950-51; member bd. govs. 1951-52), Am. Legion, Dudley Vets. Assn., Naval and Mil. Order Spanish-Am. War, Nat. Def. Assn., Council Advancement Small Colls. (dir.). Club: Webster-Dudley Rotary (past pres.). Home: Dudley, Mass. Died Apr. 1974.

CONRAD, LOWELL EDWIN, civil engr.; b. Miles, Jackson County, Ia., June 24, 1879; s. Martin Luther and Marcia Lavina (Caton) C.; S.B., in C.E., Cornell (Ia.) Coll., 1904, C.E., 1906; M.S., Lehigh, 1908; m. Ada Amelia Noyes, of N.H., June 26, 1911; children—Ralph Martin, Marcia Noyes, Mary Martha. With engring. depts. various railways until 1903; insp. on sewer constrn., Ia. Engring. Co., Centralia, Ill., 1904; asst. engr. with S. Pearson & Sons, Ltd., Mexico, 1905-06; instr. and grad. student, Lehigh U., 1906-08; prof. civ. engring., Kan. State Coll. from 1909, head dept. 1909-47, acting dean engring., Dec. 1940-June 1942; cons. practice. In gen. charge investigation of atmospheric resistance of motor vehicles, carried on by U.S. Bur. Pub. Roads and Kan. State Coll., 1926. Mem. Am. Soc. C.E., Kan. Engring. Soc. (ex-pres.), Am. Soc. Engring. Edn. (mem. council, 1931-35; vice pres., 1940-41, mem. council from 1946, representing Kan.-Neb. section), Phi Beta Kappa, Phi Kappa Phi. Sugma Psi, Sigma Tau. Rep. Am. Soc. C.E. on delegatory com. of engrs. council for professional development to accredit engring schs. in Region No. 5 after 1937. Methodist. Mason. Club: Wranglers. Home: Manhattan, Kan.†

CONSIDINE, ROBERT BERNARD, newspaperman; b. Washington, D.C., Nov. 4, 1906; s. James William and Sophie (Small) C.; ed. Gonzaga High Sch., George Washington U.; m. Mildred Anderson, July 21, 1931; children—Michael Riley, Robert Barry, Dennis Joel, Deborah Joan. Corr. sports, drama, writer Sunday features Washington Post, 1930-33; sports editor, editorial and feature writer Washington Herald, 1933-37; syndicated sports columnist, trial reporter, feature writer N.Y. Am., during 1937 was transferred to Mirror and Internat. News Service, 1938; war corr. Internat. News Service, England, 1943, C.B.I. theatre, 1945, Korea. 1950. Member Sigma Alpha Epsilon, Sigma Delat Chi. Roman Catholic Knight of Malta. Clubs Dutch Treat, Overseas Press (past pres.), Nat. Press (Washington); Artists and Writers (pres.). Author: MacArthur the Magnificent, 1942; Thirty Seconds over Tokyo (with Capt. Ted W. Lawson), 1943; Where's Sammy (with Sammy Schulman), 1943; Gen. Wainwright's Story (with Gen. Jonathan M. Wainwright), 1946; The Babe Ruth Story (with Babe Ruth), 1948; Innocents at Home, 1951; Panama Canal, 1952; Man Against Fire, 1955; Christmas Stocking, Jack Dempsey Story (with Bill Slocum); Ask Me Anything-Our Adventures with Khrushchev (with W. R. Hearst, Jr. and Frank Conniff); The Brink's Robbery; It's All News to Me-A Reporter's Deposition; asst. Harold E. Stassen, Stanislaw Mickolajczyk Robert E. Stribling, and Dr. Armand Hammer in preparation their books, 1948; motion picture originals; Church of the Good Thief, Ladies Day, The Beginning or the End, The Babe Ruth Story, Hoodlum Empire. Contbr. fiction and articles to nat. mags., 1944-75. Awarded George R. Holmes Memorial Award, 1947; Catholic Writers Guild and Catholic Inst. of the Press Awards, 1949, Lasker Award 1952; Overseas Press Club awards for best fgn. correspondence, 1957-58. Home: New York City, N.Y. Died Sept. 25, 1975; interred Gate of Heaven Cemetery, Valhalla, N.Y.

CONSTABLE, WILLIAM GEORGE, art historian, author; b. Derby, Eng., Oct. 27, 1887; ed. Slade Sch., London, Eng.; M.A., Cambridge (Eng.) U. Former asst. dir. Nat. Gallery, London, dir. Courtauld Inst. Art, U. London, Slade prof. Cambridge U., curator paintings Boston Mus. Fine Arts, lectr. Yale U. New Haven. Decorated chevalier Legion of Honor; commendatore Crown of Italy; officer Ordre Arts and Lettres, France. Fellow Soc. Antiquaries, Internat. Inst. Conservators (past pres.); mem. Art Workers Guild, Goldsmiths Co., Am. Acad. Arts and Scis. Author: English Painting 17th and 18th Centuries; The Painters Workshop; Canaletto and Art Collecting in the U.S. Contbrs. articles to profl. jours. Address: Cambridge, Mass., Died Feb. 3, 1976*

CONTE, RICHARD, actor; b. Jersey City, Mar. 24, 1916; s. Pasquale and Julia (Fina) C.; scholar Neighborhood Playhouse, N.Y.C.; m. Shirlee Colleen Garner, Aug. 1972; 1 son (by previous marriage) Mark. Appeared on N.Y. stage in Jason and the Family; motion pictures include Guadalcanal Diary, The Purple Heart, Call Northside 777, Cry of the City, House of Strangers, Thieves Highway, Whirlpool, Under The Gun, Sleeping City, Hollywood Story, Raging Tide, The Fighter, Raiders, Desert Legion, Blue Gardenia, Slaves of Babylon, Highway Dragnet, New York Confidential, Big Combo, Target Zero, Big Tip Off, Bengazi, Case of the Red Monkey, I'll Cry Tomorrow, Full of Life, Brothers Rico, Oceans Eleven, They Came to Cordura, Assault on a Queen, The Greatest Story Ever Told, The Godfather; actor, dir. motion picture Operation Cross Eagle; appeared in films in Europe, 1972-73, numerous TV appearances. Address: Beverly Hills, Cal. Died Apr. 15, 1975.

CONVERSE, FLORENCE, author; b. New Orleans, Apr. 30, 1871; d. George T. and Caroline (Edwards) Converse; B.S., Wellesley Coll., 1893, M.A., 1903. Staff, Churchman, 1900-08, Atlantic Monthly mag., 1908-30. Mem. Phi Beta Kappa. Author: Diana Victrix, 1897; The Burden of Christopher, 1900; Long Will (now in Everyman's Library), 1903; The House of Prayer (now Everyman's Library), 1908; A Masque of Sibyls, 1910; The Children of Light 1912; The Story of Wellesley, 1915; The Blessed Birthday (Christmas miracle play), 1917; Garments of Praise, 1921; Into the Void, 1926; Sphinx, 1931; Efficiency Expert (poem), 1934; Collected Poems, 1937; The Madman and the Wrecking Crew (play), 1938; Wellesley College, a Chronicle of the Years, 1875-1938, 1939; Prologue to Peace; The Poems of Two Wars, 1949.†

CONVERSE, MIRIAM SEWALL, educator; b. Rochester, N.Y., Oct. 18, 1880; b. Charles Thomas and Eleanor Sewall (Pray) C.; A.B., Vassar, 1904. Registrar and teacher of English, Wheaton Sem., Norton, Mass., 1905-12; asst. prin., Ferry Hall, Lake Forest, Ill., 1912-

20; prin. Lincoln Sch., Providence, R.I., after 1920. Mem. Head Mistresses' Assn., Nat. Assn. Principals of Schs. for Girls, N.E. Assn. Colls. and Secondary Schs. Conglist. Address: Providence, R.I.†

CONWAY, JOHN SEBASTIAN, engineer; b. Philadelphia, Sept. 16, 1878; s. John J. and Regina K. (Rudolph) C.; B.S. in C.E., U. of Pa., 1900; m. Eleanor M. Gorman, of Phila., Jan. 2, 1907; 1 son, John S. Municipal water supply and reinforced concrete constrn. work Pa. and Mo., 1900-04; irrigation constrn. work, Colo., Mont., Calif. and state of Washington, 1905-10; chief constructing engr., U.S. Lighthouse Service, 1910-12; deputy commr. of lighthouses, 1912-30. Mem. Am. Soc. C.E., Am. Soc. M.E., Washington Acad. Sciences, Washington Soc. Engrs. (pres. 1922), Sigma Xi, Delta Kappa Epsilon. Republican. Catholic. Author: The U.S. Lighthouse Service, 1923. Clubs: Cosmos, Kenwood Golf and Country. Home: Washington, D.C.†

CONWELL, HUGH EARLE, orthopaedic surgeon; b. Oakman, Ala., Dec. 29, 1893; s. Thomas and Catherine (Williams) C.; M.D., U. Ala., 1915. Began practice at Birmingham, Ala., 1915; vis. orthopaedic surgeon St. Vincent's Hosp., South Highlands Infirmary, Children's Hospital, Univ. Hospital, and also Bapt. Hosp.; chief Conwell Orthopaedic Clinic, Birmingham; state orthopaedic cons. and mem. med. adv. bd. Ala. Crippled Children's Services. asso. prof. orthopaedic surgery, U. Ala. Med. Coll.; orthopaedic cons. Vets. Hosp. in Tuscaloosa and Montgomery Ala. Capt. Med. Res. Corps. U.S. Army, 1917-19, attached to Brit. Army Med. Corps, base hosps. London. England and Calais, France, 1917-19. Fellow A.C.S. (nat. fracture com.; chmn. Ala. state regional fracture com.), A.M.A. (mem. adv. com. on fractures); mem. A.A.S., Ala. Acad. Sci., Birmingham Surg. Soc., Ala. State Med. Assn. (life councillor, also chmn. fracture com.), Jefferson County Med. Soc. (pres. 1936), Am. Med. Editors Assn., Am. Orthopaedic Assn. (chmn. orthopaedic sect. 1932). Clin. Orthopaedic Soc. (sec. 1936-37; pres. 1939-40); Am. Acad. Orthopaedic Surgeons (mem. com. on fractures and traumatic surgery, v.p., 1944-45-46), Assn. of Mil. Surgeons, So. Surg. Assn., Southeastern Surg. Congress, Cattahoochee Valley Med. Assn., Pan-Pacific Surg. Assn., Internat. Soc. Traumatic and Orthopedic Surgery, Am. Bd. Orthopedic Surgeons, Sigma Xi, Theta Kappa Psi. Baptist. Mason (Shriner, Jester). Clubs: Sir Robert Jones, Rotary, The Club. Mountain Brook Country. Author: (with Key) The Management of Fractures, Dislocations and Sprains. Co-author of Text-book The Management of Fractures. Dislocations and Springs (textbook). 7th edit., 1961. Asso. editor Southern Surgeon; mem. editorial com. on Progress of Orthopaedic Surgery, Contbr. to Cyclopedia of Medicine, Textbook of Surgery, The Injured Spine, also many papers on fractures. Home: Birmingham, Ala. Died Mar. 18, 1973; interred Elmwood Cemetery, Birmingham.

COOGAN, THOMAS JAMES, physician; b. Lincoln, Ill., Nov. 24, 1900; s. Michael J. and Alice (Ryan) C.; B.A. cum laude, Columbia Coll., 1922; M.D., St. Louis (Mo.) U., 1927; Sc.D., Loras College, 1967; m. Evelyn Bermingham, Apr. 13, 1929; children—Mary Alice, Thomas James, Evelyn Renee. Intern. St. Luke's Hosp., Chgo., 1927-29, asst. physician, 1930-36, sr. attending physician, 1940-57, v.p. staff, 1947-50, chmn. dept. of medicine, 1956-59; asso. attending physician Cook County Hosp., 1932-37; asso. in medicine, instr. Northwestern U., 1936-57; asso. in medicine, prof. medicine U. Ill. Coll. Med., 1958-61, clin. asso. prof. medicine, 1961-68, clin. prof., 1968-74; staff Presbyn.-St. Luke's Hosp., 1957-74, pres. staff, 1960-62, faculty Sch. Medicine. Diplomate Am. Bd. Internal Medicine, Nat. Bd. Med. Examiners. Fellow Am. Coll. Chest Physicains (gov. Ill. 1963-69), A.C.P., Am. Therapeutic Soc. (pres. 1947-48), Am. Coll. Cardiology; mem. Ill. Soc. of Internal Medicine, also St. Luke's Hosp. Interns Alumni Assn. (past pres.), Alumni St. Louis U. Sch. of Medicine (past pres.), Am., Chgo. heart assns., Chgo. Soc. Internat Medicine, Ill State, Chgo. med socs., Am. Chgo diabets assns., World Med. Soc., Internat. Soc. Internal Medicine, Am. Med. Writers Assn., Chgo. Inst. Medicine, Alpha Omega Alpha. Republican. Roman Catholic. Clubs: Glen View, Casino. Home: Chicago, Ill. Died June 29, 1974; interred Holy Cross Cemetery, Lincoln, Ill.

COOK, ARTHUR LEROY, elec. engr.; b. Worcester, Mass., June 10, 1878; s. Leroy and Olive Augusta (Shipman) C.; B.S. Worcester Poly. Inst., 1901, M.S., 1903; m. Florence A. Jones, Apr. 4, 1904 (dec.). Grad. asst., Worcester Poly. Inst., 1902, 03; instr., Pratt Inst., Brooklyn, 1903-07; engr., Westinghouse, Church, Kerr & Co., N.Y.C., 1907-13; head of dept. of industrial elec. engrg., 1918-38, dir. School of Science and Technology, 1938-44, Pratt. Inst. (retired). Mem. Am. Inst. E.E., Am. Society for Engineering Edn. Republican. Baptist. Author: (with Clifford C. Carr) Elements of Electrical Engineering (5th edit., 1947), Electric Wiring for Lighting and Power Installations, 1933. Home: Oak Bluffs, Mass.†

COOK, EVERETT RICHARD, merchant, exporter; b. Indpls., Dec. 13, 1894; s. Jesse Everett and Ollie Belle (Shonacker) C.; ed. Memphis public schs.; LL.D. D. (hon.), Southwestern at Memphis, 1954, Christian Bros. Coll., Memphis, 1971; m. Phoebe Willingham, June 4, 1919; children—Edward (Willingham), Phoebe (Mrs. John L. Welsh, Jr.). Organized own cotton bus., Marianna, Ark., 1916; pres. Cook and Co., Inc., raw cotton, Memphis; chmn. bd. Cook Industries, Inc., Memphis, Bayonne, Peoria, Chgo., Washington, N.Y.C., Kansas City, Mo., Fresno, Portland, Ore., Ft. Worth, Lubbock, Paris, Rotterdam, Tokyo, Osaka, Hong Kong, Mexico City, Marseille, Rome, Madrid, Sydney, Geneva, London, Sao Paulo, Singapore, Winnipeg, 1969-74; chmn. bd. subsidiaries Cook, Treadwell & Harry, Inc., E.L. Bruce Co., Inc., Terminix Internat., Inc., Riverside Chem. Co.; dir. Eastern Air Lines, Schering-Plough Corp. Adviser wartime econ. affairs Dept. State, 1945, cons., 1945-46; spl. asst. war food adminstr. and sec. agr.; nat. chmn. Agrl. War Bd., 1944-45. Mem. U.S. mission to negotiate Peruvian cotton purchase, 1942; v.p. CCC, 1942; mem. Tenn. Constl. Com., 1953, Rubber Producing Facilities Disposal Commn., 1953. Chmn. Cook Found., Memphis, 1954-74; bd. dirs. Falcon Found., US-Air Force Academy, 1966; trustee Air Force Hist. Found. Served as capt., pilot comdg. officer 91st Aero Squadron Army Air Service, France, 1918-19, col., A.A.F., 1942-44; dep. chief staff, 8th, 12th Air Forces, U.K., N. Africa and Italy, 1942-43; Northwest African Air Force, 1943; U.S. Strategic Air Force, E.T.O., 1944; brig. gen., Air Force Researve, 1948-53, ret.; mem. Res. Forces Policy Bd. for Dept. of Defense, 1951-52. Decorated D.S.C., Legion of Merit, Silver Star (U.S.); Croix de Guerre palm; Legion of Honor (France); Master of Free Enterprise award Jr. Achievement, 1968. Mem. Am. Cotton Shippers Assn. (pres. 1949), New York Cotton Exchange, New Orleans Cotton Exchange, Memphis Cotton Exchange (pres. 1931) Cotton Council Internat. (pres. 1957-58), Memphis Cotton Carnival Assn. (pres. 1931), So. Cotton Shippers Assn. (pres. 1931-32), Independent. Episcopalian. Clubs: Memphis Country, Memphis Hunt and Polo (Memphis); Metropolitan (Washington); Boston (New Orleans). Home: Memphis, Tenn. Died Jan. 21, 1974.

COOK, JOHN BELMONT, educator; b. Forestville, Chautauqua Co., N.Y., Nov. 7, 1879; s. Albert Charles and Augusta Ann (Chadsey) C.; grad. Forestville Acad., 1899; B.S., Bucknell U., Lewisburg, Pa., 1903, M.S., 1904; studied U. of Pittsburgh and Potomac U., LL.D., Potomac, 1925; m. Sadie A. Blood, of Lewisburg, June 21, 1905; children—John Belmont, Eugene Marshall, Alice Chadsey. Head of science dept. Keystone Acad., Factoryville, Pa., 1903-08; prin. high sch., Antwerp, N.Y., 1908-10; supt. schs., Canajoharie, N.Y., 1910-17; vice prin. Slippery Rock (Pa.) State Teachers Coll., 1917-23; headmaster Vermont Acad. after 1923, also minister Bapt. Ch. and lecturer on secondary edn. Mem. examining bd. Andover Newton Theol. Sem. Trustee Pub. Library, Bellowa Falls, Vt. Mem. Sons of Vets. Republican. Mason (32°). Club: Men's Home: Saxtons River, Vt.†

COOK, MAY ELIZABETH, sculptor; b. Chillicothe, O., Jan. 1, 1881; d. William Alexander and Anna (Sappington) Cook; student Ohio State U., Academie Colorossi, 1912-14, Ecole des Beaux Arts, 1912-14. Established studio in Columbus, O., 1912; held one-man show, Toledo (O.) Mus., and Columbus, 1915; represented in exhbns. at Nat. Sculpture Soc., Pa. Acad. of Fine Arts, Corcoran Gallery, Phila. Plastic Club, Allbright Gallery, Buffalo (Nat. Sculpture Soc.); Sculpture Exhbn., San Francisco World's Fair. Permanently represented by wax facial models in Med. Mus., Washington, D.C.; memorial in bronze Ohio State Mus.; memorial in Caen stone, 1st Presbyterian Ch., Columbus, O., marble and bronze memorials and bronze portraits in bas-relief, Ohio State U.; bronze and marble fountain, Pub. Library, Columbus, O. Bronze memorials; Garden Figure, St. Augustine, Fla.; The Seasons, Madonna, Pan. Cora Alicia, Mtn. Lake Club, Fla. 1st mention Internat. Painters and Sculptors, and Spring Salon, Paris; War Work medal, U.S., 1922. Served in Med. Dept., U.S. Army, on models for reconstruction of human faces, 1918-22. Life mem. Am. Assn. Univ. Women. Mem. Internationale des Beaux Arts, Nat. Sculputure Soc., Am. Ceramic Soc., Nat. Pen Women of America. Clubs: National Arts (New York); Symphony of Ohio (Columbus). Home: Columbus, Ohio†

COOKE, LUCY FINKEL (MRS. S. JAY COOKE), librarian; b. N.Y.C., Oct. 6, 1918; d. Jack and Lillian (Feldman) Finkel; B.S., Geneseo Coll., 1940; m. S. Jay Cooke, Oct. 10, 1953. Library asst. N.Y. Pub. Library, 1940-43, U.S. Naval Sta., Lido Beach, N.Y., 1943-46; patients' librarian V.A. Northport, N.Y. and Bronx, 1946-48; med. librarian VA Hosp., Bronx, 1948-51; librarian Hahnemann Med. Coll., Phila., 1951-73. Mem. Med. Library Assn. Home: Philadelphia, Pa. Died Sept. 30, 1973; buried Montefiore Cemetery, Philadelphia, Pa.

COOLEY, CHARLES PARSONS, JR., investment banker; b. Hartford, Conn., June 17, 1903; s. Charles P. and Sarah I. (Whitman) C.; grad. Pomfrat Sch., 1922; student Yale, 1922-24; m. Adelaide F. Eberts, June 25, 1930; children—Samuel, Timothy, David E., Robert H. With U.S. Security Trust Co., 1924-26, Thomson Fenn & Co., 1926-30, Francis R. Cooley & Co., 1930-34; sir. partner Cooley & Co., Hartford, 1934-69; with Burnham & Co., N.Y.C., 1970-75; dir. Aetna Ins. Co., Conn. Gen. Life Ins. Co., Conn. Gen. Ins. Corp. Past gov. N.Y. Stock Exchange. Trustee Hartford Hosp. Mem. Assn. Stock Exchange Firms (past gov.), Nat. Assn. Securities Dealers (past gov.). Home: West Hartford, Conn., Died Jan. 27, 1975.

COOLEY, HAROLD DUNBAR, congressman; b. Nashville, N.C., July 26, 1897; s. Roger A. P. and Hattie (Davis) C.; student U. of N.C. and Yale U. Law Sch.; m. Madeline Strickland, June 30, 1923; children—Roger A. P., Harriet Davis. Admitted to N.C. bar, 1918; elected to 73d Congress, July, 1934, to fill unexpired term, reelected 74th to 89th U.S. Congresses from 4th N.C. Dist.; chmn. House Com. Agr. 81st, 82d, 84-89th congresses, Exec. com., council Interparliamentary Union, past pres. Am. group (joint congressional organization); consultant and congressional adviser to UNESCO. Served in Naval Aviation Flying Corps, World War I. Mem. North Carolina Bar Association, Nash County Bar Association (past president), Am. Bar Assn., Phi Delta Theta, Phi Delta Phi. Democrat. Baptist. Jr. Order United Am. Mechanics. Home: Nashville, N.C. Died 1974.

COOLEY, MCWHORTER STEPHENS, accountant; b. nr. Homer, Ga., Jan. 11, 1907; s. William Pledger and Lilly (Rogers) C.; B.S.C., U. Ga., 1928, M.S.C., 1929; m. Thelma Jane Leathers, Aug. 30, 1930; children—Janey Mae, William Leon. Instr. accounting U. Ga., 1929-30; accountant Richardson, Jackson & Davis C.P.A.'s, Atlanta, 1930-38; self-employed as C.P.A., Athens, Ga., 1938—; dir. So. Mut. Ins. Co. Mem. Am. Inst. C.P.A.'s, Ga. Soc. C.P.A.'s, Alpha Kappa Psi, Beta Gamma Sigma, Phi Kappa Phi. Home: Athens, Ga. Died Aug. 19, 1973.

COOLIDGE, EDGAR D., dentist, educator; b. Galesburg, Ill., July 15, 1881; s. James H. and Ellen Frances (Brown) C.; student Knox Coll., 1900-02; D.D.S., Chgo. Coll. Dental Surgery, 1906; B.S., Lewis Inst., 1925; M.S., Northwestern U., 1930; LL.D., Loyola U., 1948; m. Laura M. Richelsen, July 21, 1909; children—Ellen M., Edgar David, John Walter. Began dental career, 1906; instr. operative technics Chgo. Coll. Dental Surgery, 1906-13, prof. oral hygiene, preventive dentistry and therapeutics, 1927-48, chmn. Found. Dental Research; prof. materia medica and therapeutics U. Ill. Coll. Dentistry, 1913-23. Fellow Am. Acad.* Periodontology (past pres.), Am. Coll. Dentists; mem. Internat. Assn. Dental Research (hon. v.p. 1958), Odontographic Soc. Chgo. (past pres.), Inst. Medicine Chgo., Fedn. Dentaire Internationale, Am. Assn. Endodontists, Am. Dental Assn., Ill., Chgo. dental socs., A.A.A.S., Am. Acad. Oral Pathology, Xi Psi Phi (past pres.), Delta Kappa Upsilon. Author: Clinical Pathology and Treatment of Dental Pulp and Periodontal Tissues, reve. edit. 1946; Endondontia, 1950; (with Robert Kesel) Endodontology, 1956; (with Maynard K. Hine) Peridontia, rev. edit. 1958. Home: Evanston, Ill.†

COOLIDGE, WILLIAM DAVID, phys. chemist; b. Hudson, Mass., Oct. 23, 1873; s. Albert Edward and M. Alice C.; B.S., Mass. Inst. Tech., 1896; Ph.D., U. Leipzig, 1899; D.Sc. (hon.) Lehigh, Union Univ., 1927; M.D. (hon.), U. Zurich, 1937; LL.D., Ursinus Coll., 1942; Dr. h.c., U. Sao Paulo, 1945, Nat. Sch. Engring., U. Brazil, 1945; D.Sc., Catholic U. Chili, 1945; D.Eng., Ind. Tech. Coll., 1947; m. Ethel Westcott Woodard, Dec. 30, 1908 (dec. Feb. 1915); children—Elizabeth B., Lawrence D.; m. 2d, Dorothy Elizabeth MacHaffie, Feb. 29, 1916 (dec. Oct. 1969). Faculty, Mass. Inst. Tech., 1897, 1901-05, U. Leipzig, 1899; research in physical-chemistry Gen. Electric Co., Schenectady, 1905-07, asst. dir. research lab., 1908-28, asso. dir., 1928-32, dir., 1932-40, v.p. dir. research, 1940-44, cons. X-rays, 1945-75. Served wih Nat. Def. Research Com., World War II; apptd. to Nat. Acad. Scis. Com. in connection with Atomic Bomb project, 1941, attended first Bikini test as spl. observer for Manhattan Dist. Mem. Nat. Inventors Council, 1940-75. Recipient numerous awards for work in tungsten and on X-ray, inculding Faraday medal Instn. Elec. engrs. Eng., 1939; Franklin medal, 1944, K.C. Li medal and award Columbia, 1952; Henry Spenadel award, 1st Dist. Dental Soc., 1953; Roentgen medal, 1963. Fellow Am. Acad. Arts and Sci., A.A.A.S., Am. Philos. Soc., Am. Inst. Chemists, Am. Acad. Oral Roentgenology, Sigma Psi; mem. Am. Acad. History Dentistry (hon.), Nat., Washington acads. sci., Edison Pioneers, Soc. Non-Destructive Testing, Am. Chem. Soc., Am. Electrochem. Soc., Am. Phys. Soc., I.E.E.E.; hon. or corr. mem. numerous Am., fgn. socs. Unitarian. Clubs: Mohawk, (Schenectady); Engineers (Dayton, (O.). Contbr. results original research to sci. publs. Home: Schenectady, N.Y. Died Feb. 3, 1975.

COOMBES, ETHEL RUSSELL, editor and publisher; b. Plainville, Ill.; d. Albert Alan and Sarah Ann (Haynes) Russell; ed. high schs., by special study and George Washington U., m. David S. Combes; children—David Russell, Edward Raymond. With American Mining Congress, 1913-37; organized national standardization movement to eliminate waste and promote efficiency and economy in mineral Congress; founder, editor The Mining Congress Jour., 1923-37; founder, also conv. and expn. mgr. annual meetings Am. Mining Congress, 1925-37; est. Mechanization, Inc., 1937, publishers of

Mechanization, the Magazine of Modern Coal, and Mechannual, The Book of Mechanization Progress, Utilization, The Magazine of Coal Uses (chmn. bd. publishers). Founder, Energy Reports, 1936; owner, editor newsletter The Energy Report; dir. Nat. Bus. Publs., Inc. Named hon. Ky. Col. Mem. Am. Women's Party. Home: Chevy Chase, Md., Died Oct. 4, 1969.

COOPE, GEORGE FREDERICK, dir. Potash Co. America; b. .Y.C., July 5, 1893; s. Herbert and Catherine (MacDougall) C.; E.M., Columbia U., 1916; m. Jessica Lewis, Dec. 8, 1917; children—George Frederick, Peter MacDougall, Robert Lewis. Mining engr. in Nev., Ariz., Chile and N.M., 1916-36; with Potash Co. of America, Denver, 1936-1958, retired as pres. 1958, dir. Home: Blue Hill, Me. Died Apr. 10, 1972; interred, Blue Hill.

COOPER, ALBERT HUDLBURGH, engring. educator; b. Knoxville, Tenn., Nov. 6, 1906; s. John Hudibrugh and Rubie (Wallace) C.; B.S. in Chem. Engring., U. Tenn., 1929, M.S. in Chem. Engring., 1930; postgrad. Mass. Inst. Tech., 1930-31; Ph.D., Mich. State U., 1933; m. Louise Kaderly, Feb. 20, 1930. Chem. engr. Aluminum Co. Am., 1926-27; asst. editor Chem. and Metall. Engring. mag., 1929; chem. engr. E.I. du Pont de Nemours & Co., 1930; asst. prof. N.C. State Coll., 1935-37; asso. prof. Va. Poly. Inst., 1937-45; chem. engr. U.S. Indsl. Chem. Co., 1945-46; head chem. engring. dept. Bucknell U., 1946-51; mgr. engring. research and devel. Davison Chem. div. W.R. Grace Co., 1951-52; prof. chem. engring. U. Md., 1952-56; prof., head dept. Pratt Inst., 1955-59; gen. mgr. Am. Indsl. Chem. Co., 1956-59; tech. dir. Waverly Chem. Co., 1959-61; prof. chem. engring., head dept. chem., metall. and nuclear engring. U. Conn., 1959-64; dean grad. sch. Tenn. Technol. U., 1964-68; dir. U. Tenn. Grad. Centers, 1968-74; v.p., tech. dir. Chemecon Corp., 1952-60; pres. Pilot Engring. Co., 1947-74; mgr. engring. research and devel. D. M. Weatherly Co., 1967-69. Served to capt., CWS, AUS, 1942-45; lt. col. Res. Registered profl. engr., Conn., Md., Pa., Va. Mem. Am. Chem. Soc., Am. Inst. Chem. Engrs., Am. Soc. M.E., A.A.A.S., Am. Soc. Engring. Edn., Am. Assn. U. Profs., Am. Mgmt. Assn., Electrochem. Soc., Sigma Xi, Alpha Chi Sigma, Tau Beta Pl. Contbr. articles profl. jours. Editor Chem. Engring. Edn., 1946-64. Home: Knoxville, Tenn. Died Apr. 1974.

COOPER, DAVID ACRON, bus. coll. pres.; b. Charlotte, N.C., Oct. 16, 1910; s. David P. and Roberta (Lewis) C.; B.S., U. Tenn., 1931, M.S., 1934; A.M., Columbia, 1938; postgrad. Harvard, 1939, Washington and Jefferson Coll., 1943, Am. U., Biarritz, France, 1945; m. Agnes Pearson, Oct. 15, 1941; 1 son, David A. Tchr., Knoxville (Tenn.) High Sch., 1931-34; spl. cons. bus. edn. Southwestern Pub. Co., Cin., 1935-39; personnel dir. S. H. George & Sons, Knoxville, 1941-48; owner, mgr. Dapco Sales & Services, 1949-74; founder, pres. Coopers' Inst., Inc., 1948-74; pub. acct. personnel cons. Instr. Am. U., Biarritz, France, 1945; vis. asso. prof. bus. Knoxville Coll., 1967-72. Treas., Mental Health Clinic; mem. Com. on Teaching Bible in Pub. Schools; founder, leader Tuesday Evening Bible Conf. Hour. Sec., Bd. Edn. Pres., Asso. Evang. Chs. of Greater Knoxville. Served as tech. sgt. AUS, 1943-46; ETO. Mem. Am. Mgmt. Assn., Adminstrv. Mgmt. Assn., Nat. Soc. Pub. Accountants, Am. Accounting Assn., Nat. Assn. Accountants, Nat. Assn. Tax Consultants, North Knoxville Bus. Men's Club, C. of C., Internat. Platform Assn. Baptist. Kiwanian. Home: Knoxville, Tenn. Died May 2, 1974; buried Greenwood Cemetery, Knoxville,

COOPER, JOSEPH DAVID, educator; b. Boston, May 25, 1917; s. Samuel and Hinde R. (Bryner) C.; A.B., George Washington U., 1944; M.A., Am. U., 1947, Ph.D., 1951; m. Ruth Zeidner, Feb. 11, 1942; children—Lenore, Byron. Employee Fed. Service, 1934-45, 47-58; dep. dir., dir. procedural coordination staff UNRRA, 1945-47; chief procedural coordination br. State Dept., 1947-51, exec. dir. Salary Stblzn. Bd., 1951-53; exec. asst. to dep. postmaster gen., 1953-58; dir. mgmt. engring. div. Corp. for Econ. and Indsl. Research. Arlington, Va., 1958; prof. dept. polit. sci. Howard U., also adj. prof. Am. U., Washington; project dir. conf. series on philosophy and tech. drug assessment Interdisciplinary Communications Program, Smithsonian Instn.; asst. to exec. v.p. Emerson Research Labs., Emerson Radio and Phonograph Corp., 1958-60; dir. pub. relations U.S. Photo Supply Co., Inc., 1961; cons. commn. on research A.M.A., 1965-67. Fellow Royal Soc. Medicine; mem. Am. Soc. Pub. Adminstrn., Am. Polit. Sci. Assn., Am. Acad. Polit. and Social Sci. Author books in field of mgmt., med. econs., also books on photography; How to Communicate Policies and Instructions, 1960; The Minox Manual, 1961; The New Ultra-Miniature Photography 1961; The Art of Dicision-Making, 1961; How to Get More Done in Less Time, 1962, rev. edit., 1971; Organization, 1963, The Nikon F. Nikkormat Handbook of Photography, 1968; The Minolta Systems Handbook, 1971, others. Editor: The Economics of Drug Innovation, 1970; Decision-Making on the Efficacy and Safety of Drugs, 1971; The Quality of Advice, 1971; The Philosophy of Evidence, 1972; The Efficacy of Self-Medication, 1973. Contbr. Modern Photography mag., Med. Tribune, Popular Photography mag.; articles on med. sociology, econs. and politics. Home: Chevy Chase, Md. Died Mar. 25, 1975.

COOPER, LINTON LEANDER, univ. prof.; b. Hope Villa, La., Apr. 5, 1880; s. Henry Montgomery and Stella Breckinridge (Hampton) C.; B.S., La. State U., 1904; m. Lela O'Fallon, Nov. 14, 1906; children—Linton Curtis, Mildred (Mrs. Bain). Instr. mech. arts and drawing, La. State U., Baton Rouge, 1904-09, asst. prof. mech. drawing, 1909-18, prof. and head dept. mech. drawing, from 1918. Maj. and aide-de camp on governor's staff, 1904. Director and asst. training in machine shopwork, S.A.T.C., 1918, A.S.T.P. World War II. Mem. Am. Assn. Univ. Profs., Am. Soc. Engring. Edn., La. Teachers Assn., La. State U. Alumni Fedn., Tau Beta Pi, Phi Kappa Phi. Democrat. Methodist. Club: 25 year (pres. 1946-47). Home: Baton Rouge, La.†

COOPER, PHILIP, physician; b. East Boston, Mass., Nov. 11, 1908; s. Samuel and Ida Cooper; M.D., Harvard, 1934; m. Dorothy Barth, Sept. 16, 1934; 1 son, Nathaniel Warren. Intern, Michael Reese Hosp., Chgo., 1934-35, Boston Tb Sanitarium, 1935; intern in pathology Beth Israel Hosp., Boston, 1935; resident in surgery Mt. sinai Hosp., N.Y.C., 1938-39; surg. staff New Eng. Med Center, 1940-41; chief surg. service VA Hosp., White River Junction, Vt., 1943-47, VA Hosp., Wichita, Kan., 1947-50, VA Hosp., Providence, 1950-57, VA Hosp., Bronx, N.Y., 1957-71; sr. cons. surgeon VA Hosp., Gainesville, Fla., 1971-72; clin. prof. surgery Albert Einstein Coll. Medicine, Yeshiva U., N.Y.C., 1957-71, clin. prof. emeritus, 1971-72; prof. clin. surgery Mt. Sinai Sch. Medicine, N.Y.C., 1968-71; clin. prof. surgery U. Fla., Gainesville, 1971-72. Trustee, N.Y. Found. for Med. Tech., 1963. Served from maj. to lt. col., M.C., AUS, 1944-46. Diplomate Am. Bd. Thoracic Surgery, Am. Bd. Surgery. Fellow Mass. Med. Soc., A.C.S.; mem. Soc. Thoracic Surgeons, N.Y. Surg. Soc., Soc. Surgery Alimentary Tract, Academia Nacional de Medicine (corr.), Brazilian Coll. Surgeons (corr.). Author: Ward Procedures and Techniques, Editor: Surgery Annual, 1969, co-editor, 1970, 71. Home: Gainsville, Fla. Died Oct. 1, 1972; buried Gainesville, Fla.

COOPER, RUSSELL MORGAN, educator; b. Newton, Ia., Dec. 6, 1907; s. William Reupert and Virginia Steele (Russell) C.; A.B., Cornell Coll., 1928, LL.D., 1953; M.A., Columbia, 1929, Ph.D., 1934; postgrad. L'Institut Universitaire des Hautes Etudes Internat., 1932-33; m. Lucile Trump, June 26, 1930; children—Mary Lee, Donald Russell, Julia Ann, Sarah Ruth. State student sec. YMCA, Mich., 1929-31; prof. history, polit. sci. Cornell Coll., 1934-44; chmn. dept. interdisciplinary studies U. Minn., 1944-59, asst. dean coll. sci. lit. and arts, 1945-59; dean liberal arts coll., U. South Fla., 1959-71, asst. to v.p., 1971-73, prof. interdisciplinary social sci., 1973-75; editor gen. edn. books U.S. Armed Forces Inst., 1943-44. Exec. sec. com. liberal arts edn. North Central Assn., 1940-46, chmn., 1946-59, vice chmn. commn. on research and service, 1955-57, sec., 1957-59; mem. Am. Council on Edn. Commn. on Instrn. and Evaluation, 1953-56. Cons. Civil Information and Edn., S.C.A.P., Japan, 1948. Mem. N.E.A. (mem. exec. com. Assn. Higher Edn. 1956-60, pres. 1958-59), Am. Acad. Polit. and Social Sci., Am. Polit. Sci. Assn., Am. Assn. U. Profs., Phi Beta Kappa, Tau Kappa Alpha. Author: American Consultation in World Affairs, 1934; Better Colleges Better Teachers, 1944. Editor: The Two Ends of the Log; Learning and Teaching in Today's College, 1958. Co-editor: Preparation of College Teachers, 1950. Home: Tampa, Fla. Died Mar. 3, 1975.

COOPER, SAMUEL INMAN, architect, engr.; b. Atlanta, Feb. 14, 1894; s. Joseph Walter and Nellie Sue (Inman) C.; student Episcopal Acad., 1906-10; grad. Hotchkiss Sch., 1913; Litt.B., Princeton, 1917; B.Arch., U. Pa., 1921; m. Augusta Skeen, Oct. 14, 1930. Draftsman office A. Ten Eyck Brown, architect, Atlanta, 1922-25; pres. Cooper & Cooper, architects, 1925-42; v.p. Cooper, Bond & Cooper, Inc., architects and engrs., 1945-52, pres., 1952-65; chmn. Cooper, Barrett, Skinner, Woodbury and Cooper, Inc., architects on pub. and residential bldgs., 1965-72, cons., 1972-74; pub. bldgs. include sch., coll., libraries, dormitories, chs., gymnasia, pub. housing and office bldgs. A.I.A. del., State Dept. rep. 6th Pan Am. Congress Architects, Lima, Peru, 1947, 7th Pan Am. Congress, Havana, Cuba, 1950, 8th Pan Am. Congress, Mexico City, 1952; A.I.A. del. 12th Pan Am. Congress, Bogota, Colombia, 1968, 13th Congress, San Juan, P.R., 1970; chmn. A.I.A. delegation 9th Pan Am. Congress, Venezuela, 1955, 10th Pan Am. Congress, Buenos Aires, Argentina, 1960; A.I.A. rep. to V Congress, Union Internat. Architects, Moscow, Russia, 1958, to Assembly, Lisbon, Portugal, 1959, VI Congress, London, Eng., 1961; pres. 11th Pan Am. Congress, Washington, 1965; chmn. Atlanta Civic Design Commn., 1967-70. Bd. visitors Berry Coll. Served as lt. 22d Inf., U.S. Army, 1917-19; as lt. col. C.E., 1942-45. Hon. mem. archtl. faculty U. of Chile. Fellow A.I.A. (chmn. com. on internat. relations 1961-65); mem. Pan Am. Fedn. Assns. Architects (pres. 1960-65, hon. life mem. supreme council), Nat. Soc. Profl. Engrs., Archeol. Inst. Am. (v.p. Ga. chpt. 1951-52), Soc. Colonial Wars in Ga. (dep. gov. 1963), The Newcomen Soc., Atlanta Art Assn. (dir. 1946-48), English Speaking Union, Princeton, U. Pa. alumni assns., Atlanta Hist. Soc. (chmn. 1974, dir.), Phi Kappa Sigma; hon. mem. Brazilian, Chilean, Colombian, Mexican, Venezuelan, Panamanian socs. architects. Presbyn. Mason. Clubs: Charter, Nassau (Princeton); Piedmont Driving, Capital City, Nine O'Clocks, Commerce (Atlanta); Cosmos (Washington). Home: Atlanta, Ga. Died June 7, 1974; buried West Laurel Hill Cemetery, Bala-Cynwyd, Pa.

COOPER, WILLIAM LEE, cons. engr.; b. Saginaw, Mich., July 10, 1878; s. William T. and Emma (Walker) C.; B.S. in M.E., University of Mich., 1899; m. Lillian Weld, July 26, 1904. Cons. engr., 1899-1902; European mgr. and prin. engr. for R.W. Hunt Co. (Chicago), at London, Eng., 1902-17; in business for self, N.Y. City, engr. and purchasing agt. for clients abroad, 1917; dist. mgr., supply div. Emergency Fleet Corp., 1918; cons. engr., purchasing and shipping agent, N.Y. City, in partnership with R. D. McCarter, 1919-26; Am. commercial attaché, Am. Embassy, London, 1931-33; v.p. and dir. of foreign operations, R.W. Hunt Co., Chicago, New York, London. Address: New York, N.Y.†

COPELAND, KENNETH WILFORD, bishop; b. Bexar, Ark., Apr. 3, 1912; s. Rev. John Wesley and Nancy Elizabeth (Hively) C.; student Westminster Coll., Tehuacana, Tex., 1930-32, East Tex. State Tchrs. Coll., 1933-34; B.A., So. Meth. U., 1938; student Garrett Bibl. Inst., 1947; D.D. (hon.), Southwest U., Georgetown Tex., 1951; S.T.D. (hon.), Neb. Wesleyan U., 1961; LL.D., Southern Methodist University, 1964; m. Catherine Andrews, October 5, 1933; children—Patricia Ann (Mrs. Dr. James Wilbur Ard, Jr.), Martha Sue (Mrs. Preston Hastings Dial, Jr.). Ordained to ministry Methodist Ch., 1931; pastor, Corsicana, Tex., 1931-32, Cooper, Tex., 1932-34, Dallas, 1934-38; pres. Tex. Conf. Meth. Portestant Ch., 1938-39; pastor, Wichita Falls, Tex., 1939-40, Haskell, Tex., 1940-44, First Ch., Stillwater, Okla., 1944-49, Travis Park Ch., San Antonio, 1949-60; bishop Neb. area Meth. Ch., 1960-68, Houston area, 1968-73. Alt. del. uniting conf. M.E. Ch., Meth. Protestant Ch., Meth. Episcopal Ch. South, 1939; mem. Jurisdictional confs. 1940, 48, 52, 56, 60, gen. confs., 1952, 56, 60; v.p. Gen. Bd. Missions, pres. joint commn. on edn. and cultivation, 1964-68; pres. World Div. Bd. Missions, 1968-73; mem. Gen. Bd. Christian Social Concerns, 1960-68. Trustee Alaska Methodist University, Southern Methodist Univ., Neb. Wesleyan U., St. Paul Sch. Theology Methodist. Mason (K.T., Shriner), Lion. Author: A Primer of Beliefs for Methodist Laymen, 1959. Home: Houston, Tex. Died Aug. 1973.

COPELAND, MANTON, biologist; b. Taunton, Mass., July 24, 1881; s. Henry Preston and Abby Carver (Dean) Copeland; grad. Bristol and Acad., Taunton, Mass., 1900; S.B., Lawrence Scientific Sch. (Harvard Univ.), 1904; S.M., Harvard Grad. Sch., 1905, Ph.D., 1908; m. Ruth Winsor Ripley, Dec. 20, 1910; children—Preston Sumner, Frederick Cleveland, Manton, Elizabeth Williams. Asst. in zoölogy, Harvard Univ. and Radcliffe Coll., while doing grad. work at Harvard, 1903-08, instr. in biology, Bowdoin Coll., 1908-09, asst. prof., 1909-10, prof. biology, 1910-47, Josiah Little prof. natural science, 1936-47, emeritus from 1947. Lecturer histol. and embryol., Medical Sch. of Me., 1912-13, prof. embryology and histology, 1913-21; spl. lecturer in biology, Bangor Theol. Sem., 1909-12. Mem. Am. Acad. Arts and Sciences, Am. Soc. Zoölogists, Ecological Soc. of America, Biol. Soc. of Washington, Am. Soc. of Mammalogists, etc. Chi Psi. Republican. Episcopalian. Home: Brunswick, Me.†

COPELAND, MELVIN THOMAS, educator; b. Brewer, Me., July 17, 1884; s. Salem Dwight and Livonia Estelle (Pierce) C.; A.B., Bowdoin Coll., 1906, Sc.D., 1931; A.M., Harvard, 1907, Ph.D., 1910; m. Else Helbling, June 25, 1912; children—Elsie Marie (Mrs. Chester Zell Brown), Martha (Mrs. David Richardson Bott). Instr. econ. resources Harvard, 1909-10, instr. comml. orgn., 1912-15, asst. prof. marketing, 1915-19, prof. marketing and bus. adminstrn., 1919-53, prof. emeritus, 1953-75, dir. Bur. Bus. Research, 1916-26, dir. bus. research, 1942-53; instr. econs. N.Y. U., 1911-12. Mem. Mass. Commn. on Cost of Living, 1916-17; sec. comml. econ. bd. Council Nat. Def., Washington, 1917-18; exec. sec. conservation div. War Industries Bd., 1918; chmn. Mass. Com. on Post-War Readjustment, 1941-46; mem. purchase policy adv. com. U.S. War Dept., 1943. Bd. overseers Bowdoin Coll., 1934-47, trustee, 1947-61, trustee emeritus, 1961—. Recipient David A. Wells prize Harvard, 1912, Assn. medal Nat. Assn. Cotton Mfrs., 1921-75; Fellow Am. Statis Assn.; mem. Phi Beta Kappa Assos. (founding mem.), Beta Theta Pi. Republican. Author: Cotton Manufacturing Industry of U.S. 1912; Business Statistics, 1917; Problems in Marketing, 1920; Principles of Merchandising, 1924; Raw Material Prices and Business Conditions, 1933; A Raw Commodity Revolution, 1938; And Mark An Era, 1958. Joint author: Merchandising of Cotton Textiles, 1933; The Board of Directors and Business Management, 1947; The Saga of Cape Ann, 1960. Home: Annisquam Mass. Died Mar. 27, 1975.

COPLEY, JAMES STROHN, publisher; b. St. Johnsville, N.Y., Aug. 12, 1916; s. Ira Clifton and Edith (Strohn) C.; student Phillips Acad., Andover, Mass., 1930-35; B.A., Yale, 1939; m. Helen Kinney, Aug. 16, 1965; 1 son, David Casey. Dir., mem. exec. com. The Copley Press, Inc., Aurora, Ill., 1942-73, 1st v.p., 1945-

52, chmn. corp., 1952-73, pres., 1961-65; dir. Union-Tribune Pub. Co., San Diego, 1947-73, asst. sec., 1947-50, pres., 1950-60, pub., 1950-61, 65-73, asst. treas., 1950-54, treas., 1954-58, chmn. bd., 1958-73, dir. So. Cal. Asso. Newspapers, Los Angeles, 1946-73; v.p., 1948-53, 1st v.p., treas., 1953-57, chmn. bd., 1957-73, pres., 1964; dir. San Pedro (Cal.) Printing & Pub. Co., 1947-73, sec., 1947-53, treas., 1953-58, chmn. bd., 1958-73, pres., 1964; hon. chmn. dir. Copley Internat. Corp., 1965-67; chmn., dir. (Radio Sta. KGU) Communications, Hawaii, Inc., 1966-67; chmn. bd. Copley News Service, 1965-73, Served with USNR, 1942-46; capt. Res. Recipient Maria Moors Cabot award, 1959, 67. Mem. Sigma Delta Chi. Republican. Episcopalian. Elk, Moose. Clubs: Ill. Country, Union League (Aurora, Ill.); Sangamo (Springfield, Ill.); Metropolitan, Nat. Press (Washington); Metropolitan, Yale (N.Y.C.); Yale, Chicago (Chgo.); Cuyamaca, The San Diego, Kona Kai (San Diego); Greater Los Angeles Press, Los Angeles Country (Los Angeles); La Jolla Country, Beach and Tennis (La Jolla, Cal.); Oahu Country (Hawaii); La Costa Country (Carlsbad, Cal.). Home: La Jolla Cal. Died Oct. 6, 1973; buried Aurora, Ill.

COPPOCK, FRED DOUGLASS, san and gravel prodn. exec.; b. Miami County, O., Sept. 14, 1878; s. Allen and Marie (Furnas) C.; student high sch., Ludlow Falls, O., also Columbus; m. Maude E. Miles. May 11, 1898; children—Dorothy (Mrs. Edward Hole), Eugene (Mrs. W. D. Brumbaugh). Pioneered plant prodn. sand and gravel; pres., gen. mgr. Greenville Gravel Co.; pres., gen. mgr., Am. Aggregates Corp., later chmn.; pres. Marine Exhibition Corp., Miami, Fla.; mem. bd. Fourth Fed. Loan Bank, Louisville. Reclaimed gravel pit areas to become Wayne Lakes, nr. Greenville; constructed Anthony Wayne Meml. Park, Greenville; built home for Girl Scouts, Greenville. Recipient award of merit Vets. Fgn. Wars, 1958. Mason (32°), Elk; mem. Red Men. Clubs: Rotary, Miami. Home: Greenville, O.†

COPPOCK, WILLIAM HOMER, educator; b. Lincoln, Neb., June 8, 1911; s. Homer and Carrier (Rowan) C.; B.S., Monmouth (Ill.) Coll., 1933; M.S., U. Ia. 1935, Ph.D., 1939; m. Florence Lundine, June 15, 1937; children—Ted, Kathleen (Mrs. Roland Oberg), Yvonne, Bill. Tchr. chemistry Holdrege (Neb.) High Sch., 1935-37, Eastern Ill. State Coll., 1939-41, U. Notre Dame, 1943, Winona State Coll., 1945-46; asst. chief chemist Sangamon Ordnance Plant, 1941-42; faculty Drake U., Des Moines, 1946—, prof. chemistry, 1949—, head dept., 1949-69. Mem. Am. Chem. Soc., Sigma Xi. Presbyn. Home: Des Moines, Ia., Died Dec. 26, 1975.

CORBETT, GERALD ROBERT, judge; b. Ladysmith, Wis., July 3, 1903; s. John Arthur and Mary Louise (McGee) C.; student U. Cal. at Los Angeles, 1922-23; LL.B., Loyola U., 1926; m. Ann Humphries Johnston, Dec. 15, 1933; 1 dau., Jancy Jean (Mrs. Charles W. Robertson). Admitted to Cal. bar, 1928, Hawaii bar, 1929; gen. law practice Calif, also Hawaii, 1929-33; dep. city atty., Honolulu, 1933-39; controller City and County Honolulu, 1939-44; sec. Territory of Hawaii, 1944-46; judge Juvenile Ct., Honolulu, 1946-66, judge Family Court, Honolulu, 1966-73. Cons., Big Bros. of Hawaii 1964-73, named Big Brother of the Year, 1966; nat. bd. dirs. Family Service Assn., Am., 1958-63; chmn. Hawaii Com. Alcoholism, 1957-59, cons., 1959-73; pres. Child and Family Service of Hawaii, 1956-57, Oahu Health Council, 1956-57, Mental Health Assn. Hawaii, 1954-56, Honolulu Council Social Agys., 1952-54. Trustee Palama Settlement, 1960-73. Mem. Am., Hawaii bar assns. State Bar Cal., Am. Judicature Soc., Nat. Council Crime and Delinquency, Western, Hawaii probation and parole assns., Nat. (exec. com.). Hawaii (pres.) councils juvenile ct. judges. Home: Honolulu Hawaii. Died June 29, 1973.

CORBETTA, ROGER HENRY, constrn. co. exec.; b. N.Y.C., June 9, 1896; s. Joseph and Maria (Vacca) C.; m. Thelma Weiss, Nov. 25, 1961; 1 dau., Marian (Mrs. Francis A. Vitolo). Founder, Corbetta Constrn. Co., Inc., N.Y.C., 1922, chmn. bd., 1962—; founder Corbetta Equipment Corp., N.Y.C., 1935, chmn. bd., 1962—; pres. Roger H. Corbetta Corp., 1966—; dir. Flexicore Corp. Chmn. exec. com. Reinforced Concrete Research Council, 1962-65; founder, pres. Concrete Industry Bd. N.Y., 1947-53, bd. dirs., 1947—; mem. N.Y. Bldg. Trades Employers Assn., 1927-74, bd. govs., 1947-53, pres., 1968-71; pres. Am. Concrete Inst., 1962-63; mem. N.Y. Cement League, 1927-74, pres., 1947-51; mem. N.Y. Bldg. Congress, 1922-74. Chmn. zoning bd. appeals, Washington, N.Y., 1952-72. Trustee Dutchess Community Coll., Poughkeepsie, N.Y., St. Francis Hosp., Poughkeepsie; bd. dirs. Astor Home for Children, Rhinebeck, N.Y., Dutchess County Agrl. Soc.; mem. N.Y. State Guernsey Breeders Co-op., Inc. Served with U.S. Army, World War I. Mem. Nat. Acad. Scis., Am. Soc. Concrete Constructors (founder, pres. 1965-68, chmn. 1968—), Eastern Guernsey Breeders Assn. (pres. 1968-72), The Moles (recipient award 1970). Home: Millbrook, N.Y. Died May 26, 1974; buried St. Joseph's Cemetery, Millbrook, N.Y.

CORBIN, CLEMENT K., lawyer; b. Elizabeth, N.J., Oct. 3, 1879; s. William H. and Clementine (Kellogg) C.; student Princeton, 1898-99; A.B., Cornell U., 1902; LL.B., N.Y. Law Sch., 1904; m. Margaret L. Talcott, Oct. 25, 1906 (dec.); children—Margaret T. (Mrs. Frank W. Dinsmore), William H.; m. 2d, Linda M. Fromer, Feb. 28, 1934. Law clerk Collins & Corbin, Jersey City, N.J., 1902-05; in various capacities Consol. Water Co., Utica, N.Y., 1905-10; law clerk, later mem. Collins & Corbin, Jersey City, 1910-47; practicing in Newark from 1948. President and member Common Council, Summit, New Jersey, 1914-15, city solicitor, 1924-31. Served as private, Essex Troop, New Jersey national Guard, 1897-98. Trustee Kent Place Sch. for Girls. Mem. Am., N.J. and Essex County bar assns. Republican. Episcopalian. Clubs: Essex (Newark); Canoe Brook Country (Summit, N.J.); The Hartwood (Hartwood, N.Y.). Home: Summit, N.J.†

CORBIT, JOHN DARLINGTON, JR., physician, educator; b. Reading, Pa., May 6, 1910; s. John Darlington and Lovinia Adelaide (Garner) C.; M.D U. Pa., 1935; m. Helen Veronica O'Brien, June 7, 1937 (dec. 1968); children-John Darlington III, Nancy Jean (Mrs. Michael Wilson Lewars), Margaret Deborah; m 2d, Dorothy Ann Dickenson Robinson, May 21, 1970. Intern, Phila. Gen. Hosp., 1935-37, resident in obstetrics and gynecology, 1937-39, staff, 1935-73, chief obstetrics and gynecology U. Pa. service, 1953-63, dr. div., 1963-65, cons., 1965-66; research fellow U. Pa., 1939-41, instr. obstetrics and gynecology, 1939-56, asst. prof., 1956-63, asso. prof., 1963-66; asso. attending Hosp. of U. Pa., 1939-47; staff Presbyn. Hosp., Phila., 1941-73, chief obstetrics and gynecology, 1952-54, dir. div women, 1954-66; staff Lankenau Hosp., Phila., 1954-73, chief obstetrics and gynecology, 1964-66, dir., 1966-73; prof. Jefferson Med. Coll., Phila., 1966-73; cons. Haverford State Hosp. Pres., Berks Nurseries; v.p. Reading Flowers, Inc.; dir. Profl. Retirement Orgn., Inc. Human Resources Network, Inc. Bd. dirs. Friends Select Sch., Nat. Council on Alcoholism, Delaware Valley Council on Alcoholism. Served to capt. M.C., AUS, 1939-43. Recipient bronze key award Nat. Council on Alcoholism, 1973. Diplomate Am. Bd. Obstetrics and Gynecology. Mem. A.M.A. (obstetrics and gynecology residency rev. com. 1970-73), Am. Coll. Obstetricians and Gynecologists (com. on continuing edn. 1966-73, health care delivery com. 1967-73, council on resident edn. 1969-73, chmn. subcom. on obstet. utilization 1970-73, v.p. 1972, sect. chmn. 1966-69), Am. Assn. Med. Colls., Assn. for Hosp. Med. Edn. Blockley (pres. 1967-69); Phila. (pres. 1967-68) obstet. soc., Pa., Philadelphia County med. socs., Coll. Phys. Phila., S.A.R., Phila. Art Alliance, Pa. Nurseryman's Assn., Am. (v.p. 1958), Greater Phila. (pres. 1959), Southeastern Pa. orchid socs., Nat., Pa. hort. socs., Huguenot Soc., Colonial Soc. Republican. Mem. Soc. of Friends. Home: Penn Valley, Narberth, Pa. Died Aug. 10, 1973; buried Washington Meml. Chapel, Valley Forge, Pa.

CORBIT, ROSS, distillery exec.; b. Toronto, Ont., Can., Sept. 16, 1899; s. William Joseph and Margaret Euphemia (Conley) C.; student schs. of Toronto; m. Agnes May Miller, Mar. 20, 1928 (dec. Jan. 1, 1954); m. 2d, Shirley Elizabeth Swingle; 1 son, Thomas J. Came to US 1922, naturalized, 1938. Exec. steel industry, 1929-35; with Hiram Walker-Gooderham & Worts Ltd. and or its subsidiaries, from 1935, past v.p., dir. Hiram Walker-Gooderham & Worts Ltd., Walkerville, Ont., Can., ret.; former v.p., dir. Hiram Walker & Sons, Inc., Detroit, Hiram Walker, Inc. Detroit. Served with Canadian Army, World War I; capt. res. Clubs: Detroit Athletic, Detroit Yacht; Lost Lake, La Coquille (Palm Beach, Fla.). Home: Grosse Pointe Woods, Mich. Died Jan. 1974.

CORCOS, LUCILLE, artist; b. N.Y.C., Sept. 21, 1908; d. Joseph and Amelia (Abrams) Corcos; student Art Students League N.Y.; m. Edgar Levy, May 7, 1928; children—David Corcos, Joel Corcos. Commd. paintings include fullpage color reprodns. nat. mags. including Life, Holiday, Vogue, Fortune, etc., U.S. Gypsum Co.; series four painting Upjohn Pharm. Co., 1952; murals include Kaleidoscope, Waldorf-Astoria, 1945, 12 decorative murals in Lounge-Cafe, Waldorf-Astoria, 1940; mural N. Shore Hosp., Manhasset, L.I., 1953; one man shows: Schneider Gabriel Galleries, 1948, N.Y. and Grand Central Moderns, 1948, 1954; Rockland Found., West Nyack, New York; State Dept. Am. Embassy Show, Paris, 1954 paintings exhibited in mus. shows throughout U.S., S.Am., Gt. Britain; Met., Whitney Mus., Audubon Artists, rep. permanent collections: Whitney Mus. Am. Art, Mus. TelAviv, Israel, Shell Oil Co., Naturalizer Shoe Co., Am. Brewers Assn., CBS, R.H. Macy & Co. and in many pvt. collections. Author and illustr.: Joel Gets a Haircut, 1952; Joel Spends His Money, 1954; Joel Gets a Dog, 1958; From Ungskah to Oyaylee: A Counting Book for All Little Indians, 1965; The City Book, 1972. Illustrator: A Treasury of Gilbert and Sullivan, 1941; A Treasury of Laughter, 1946; Chichikov's Journeys, 1945; Little Lame Prince, 1946; Follow the Sunset, 1952; Women Today, 1953; The Picture of Dorian Gray, 1958; Songs of the Gilded Age, 1960; Grimm's Fairy Tales, 4 vols. (for Ltd. Editions Club), 1962. Designer, illustrator multimedia library instrn. programs Libraries are for Children, 1967, Seeking and Finding, 1969, Recipient hon. mention award, 1st portrait of Am. Pepsi-Cola show 1944, Audubon Artists 5th Ann., 1946; Grumbacher purchase award 14th Ann. Audubon Artists, 1956. Mem. Artists Equity Assn. (dir. N.Y. chpt. 1964-66). Home: New City, N.Y. Died Aug. 25, 1973.

CORD, ERRETT LOBBAN, automobile mfr.; b. Warrensburg, Mo., July 20, 1894; s. Charles W. and Ida L. (Lobban) C.; ed. high sch., Los Angeles; m. Helen Marie Frische, Sept. 18, 1914 (dec.); children—Charles Errett, Billy James; m. 2d, Virginia Kirk Tharpe, Jan. 3, 1931; children—Nancy, Sally. Race mechanic, driver, operator garage, stage lines and truck lines, used car stores and new car rental agencies, all Cal.; distbr. automobiles, Chgo.; pres. Cord Corp.; chmn. bd. Auburn Automobile Co. Home: Reno, Nev. Died Jan. 1974.

CORDIER, ANDREW WELLINGTON, univ. dean; b. Canton, O., Mar. 3, 1901; s. Wellington J. and Ida Mae (Anstine) C.; A.B., Manchester Coll., 1922, LL.D., 1946; A.M., U. Chgo. 1923, Ph.D. (fellow), 1926; postgrad. Grad. Inst. Internat. Studies, Geneva, Switzerland, 1930-31; LL.D., Elizabethtown Coll., 1947, Albright Coll., 1953, Kent State U., 1955, MacMurray Coll., 1956, Ind. U., 1957, Oberlin Coll., 1958, N.Y. U., 1959, Fairleigh Dickinson U., 1960, Denison U., 1961, Lewis and Clark Coll., 1961, Haverford Coll., 1962, Western Mich. U., 1962, U. Pa., 1963, Brandeis U., 1966, R.I. Coll., 1967, U. Akron, 1969, Johns Hopkins, 1970, Hamilton Coll., 1970, Manhattan Coll., 1970, Jewish Theol. Sem., 1970, Rider Coll., 1971; D.P.S., Millikin U., 1961; L.H.D., Otterbein Coll., 1952; D.D., Sem., 1966; D.H.L., Susquehanna U., 1968, Internat. Christian U. (Tokyo), 1972; D.L.H., Columbia, 1970; m. Dorothy Elizabeth Butterbaugh, May 23, 1924; children—Lowell, Louise. Asso. prof. history Manchester Coll., 1923-27, chmn. dept. hist. and polit. sci., 1927-44; lectr. social Scis. Ind. U., 1929-44; expert on internat. security Dept. of State, Washington, 1944-46; tech. expert U.S. delegation to U.N. Conf., San Francisco, 1945; chief sect. Prep. Commn. for UN, London, 1945; adviser to exec. sec. Prep. commn.; adviser to all presidents gen. assembly UN, 1946-62; exec. asst. to sec.-gen. UN, 1946-62, held rank under-sec., coordinator U.N. activities with spl. responsibility for Gen. Assembly, spl. rep. Sec.-Gen. to Korea, 1950-52, Mount Scopus, 1958, Congo, 1960; dean Columbia U. Sch. Internat Affairs, 1962-73, dir. devel., cons., 1973-75, acting pres. Columbia, 1968-69, pres., 1969-70. Cons. Dept. State, Ford Found. Trustee Dag Hammarskjold Found., Manchester Coll., Carnegie Endowment for Internat. Peace. Decorated Order of the Sacred Treasure, 1st class (Japan); recipient Charles Evans Hughes medal, Alexander Hamilton medal, U. Chgo. Alumni medal, Ohio Gov.'s award, major; award N.Y.C., others. Mem. Am. Polit. Sci. Assn., Council Fgn. Relations, Fgn. Policy Assn. Clubs: University, Century Assn. (N.Y.C.) Home: Great Neck, N.Y. Died July 11, 1975.

CORDINER, RALPH JARRON, business exec.; born Walla Walla, Wash., Mar. 20, 1900; s. George M. and Mary (Jarron) C.; B.S., Whitman Coll., 1922, LL.D., 1948; LL.D., Union College, Schenectady, New York, 1952; m. Gwyneth Lewis, June 24, 1925; children—Nancy Cordiner Judge, Sallianne Cordiner Lione, Patricia Cordiner Kiley, Jean Cordiner Dougherty. Commercial district manager Pacific Power & Light Co., 1922; with Edison G.E. Appliance Co., 1922-32, at Portland, Ore., 1922-27, northwest mgr., Seattle, 1927-30, Pacific Coast div. mgr., San Francisco, 1930-32; mgr. heating device sect., Gen. Electric Co., Bridgeport, Conn., 1932-34, asst. mgr. appliance sales, 1934-35, mgr. radio div., 1935-36, asst. mgr. appliance and mdse. dept., 1936-38, mgr., 1938-39; pres. Schick, Inc., Stamford, Conn., 1939-42; dir. gen. war production scheduling, War Production Bd., Washington, Dec. 6, 1942-Mar. 1, 1943; vice chmn. War Production Board, Mar.-June 30, 1943; asst. to pres. Gen. Electric Co., 1943-45, vice pres. and asst. to the pres., 1945-49, exec. vice pres. and dir., 1949-1950, president, Gen. Electric Co., N.Y.C., 1950-58, chmn., from 1958, pres. from 1961, chief executive officer, from 1961, also director, Mem. Bus. Council. Served with U.S.N., 1917-18. Fellow Am. Acad. Arts and Scis.; mem. Phi Delta Theta, Delta Sigma Rho. Clubs: Economic (N.Y.C.); University The Links (N.Y.); Mohawk (Schenectady); Blind Brook (Port Chester, N.Y.), Home: New York City, N.Y. Died Dec. 1973.

CORETTE, JOHN EARL, lawyer; b. Grinnell, Kan., June 3, 1880; s. Joseph and MaryEllen (Finley) C.; student Butte (Mont.) pub. and high sch., 1891-98, Butte Business Coll., 1899-1900, Newells Pvt. Sch., 1900; studied law in office of Forbis & Evans, 1901-10; m. Mary T. Driscoll, Sept. 5, 1905; children—John Earl, Robert D., Mary T. (Mrs. John C. Hauck). Margaret D. (Mrs. Walter H. Paul). Admitted to Mont. bar, 1903, and later in practice at Butte; mem. Corette & Corette, attys. for numerous corps., Butte, from 1935; pres. Mayflower Mining Co. from 1935. West Mayflower Mining Co. from 1920, Capital Laundry Co. from 1920; v.p. Interstate Lumber Co., from 1930; v.p. and dir. Butte Daily Post; sec.-treas. R. J. MacDonald Co.; sec. and dir. Largey Estate; dir. Metals Bank & Trust Co. Mem. Rotary (Butte), Am., Mont. and Silver Bow County bar assns. Republican. Roman Catholic. K.C. Clubs: Butte Towne Butte Country. Home: Butte, Mont.†

COREY, LESTER SPAULDING, construction exec.; b. Uintah, Utah, Nov. 20, 1880; s. George L. and Lucinoa (Spaulding) C.; ed. high sch.; m. Kathleen Doherty, Nov. 23, 1940; children (by previous marriage)—Evelyn L., Maxwell E. With Utah Construction Co. from 1910, successively timekeeper, paymaster, foreman, supt. and asst. sec., 1928-30; v.p. and mgr., 1931-40, pres. and mgr. from 1940, also dir.; pres., dir. Utah Constrn., Ltd., Utah Constrn. Co., Ltd., Utah Co. of the Americas, Cia Utah S.A., The Argonaut Co., Ltd., Bonham Mfg. Co., Utah Co. of Panama, Inc., Ucoa, Inc.; v.p., dir. Ore. Ship Builders Co.; dir. Wooldridge Mfg. Co., Consol. Builders, Inc., Permanente Cement Co., Permanente Steamship Co., First Security Corp., Joshua Hendy Iron Works, Pacific Nat. Bank of San Francisco, Daly Acres, Inc., Lewis Acres, Inc., Kirtland Heights, Inc., Sandia Heights, Inc., North Mather Heights, Inc., South Mather Heights, Inc. Mem. Am. Standards Assn. (dir.). Republican. Mason (32°). Clubs: San Francisco Golf, Olympic, The Moles, The Family (San Francisco). Home: San Francisco, Cal.†

CORGAN, JOSEPH ALOYSIUS, govt. ofcl.; b. Luzerne, Pa., Feb. 2, 1907; s. John Bernard and Margaret Elizabeth (Backus) C.; student St. Thomas Coll., Scranton, Pa.; B.S. in Mining Engring., Pa. State U., 1929; m. Katherine Elizabeth Simson, Apr. 11, 1940; children—Kathleen (Mrs. James D. Clements), Margaret (Mrs. Henry C. Kenski), Carolyn (Mrs. William F. Wells), Joseph Aloysius. Anthracite mining activities Hudson Coal Co., Scranton, Pa., 1929-35; combustion engr., D.C. Govt., 936-37; commodity specialist Nat. Bituminous Coal Commn., 1937-40; coal economics br. U.S. Bur. Mines, 1940-45, chief anthracite and coke sect., 1945-54, chief anthracite div., 1955-68, chief, div. environment, 1968-73. Mem. Am. Inst. Mining and Metall. Engrs. Author publs. U.S. Bur. Mines. Contbr. articles on coal research, coal products to trade jours. Home: Chevy Chase, Md., Died July 30, 1975.

CORIELL, LOUIS DUNCAN, periodontist; b. Baltimore, Md., Mar. 25, 1878; s. Alvin and Mary Aurelia (Lawrence) C.; DD.S., Baltimore City Coll., U. of Md., 1899; m. Elizabeth Reid Johnson, Oct. 12, 1904. In practice as periodontist from 1899; lecturer Baltimore Coll. of Dental Surgery; visiting and cons. dental surgeon, Johns Hopkins Hosp. Fellow Am. Coll. of Dentists; mem. Am. Dental Assn., Am. Acad. Periodontology, Md. Acad. Sciences, Mayflower Soc., Soc. of Colonial Wars, Huguenot Soc., S.R., Delta Sigma Delta, Theta Nu Epsilon. Episcopalian. Clubs: University, Johns Hopkins Faculty, Elkridge Kennels (Baltimore). Contbr. to professional jours. Home: Roland Park, Md.†

CORLEY, JAMES HENRY, adminstr.; b. Modesto, Calif., Apr. 18, 1904; s. James Henry and Dora (Pilger) C.; B.S., U. Calif., 1926; m. Marcellene Burns Merrill, Oct. 30, 1926; children—Patricia Ann, James Merrill. Staff, bus. office, U. Calif., Berkeley, since 1928, comptroller, 1939-48, v.p. charge bus. affairs 1948-58, v.p. govt. relations and projects, from 1958, later v.p. emeritus. Bd. mem. Progress Fund, U. Calif., Los Angeles. Mem. Land Grant Coll. Assn., Western and Central assns. of coll. and u. bus. officers, Calif. Alumni Assn. (treas.), Berkeley C. of C. (dir.), Sigma Phi Epsilon, Winged Helmet, Golden Bear, Big "C", Scabbard and Blade, Delta Sigma Phi. Home: Berkeley, Cal. Died Dec. 26, 1974.

CORNEAU, BARTON, lawyer; b. Toledo, O. Sept. 30, 1878; s. William Bonsal and Susan (Addison) C.; ed. pub. and high schs. and by pvt. instrn.; m. Octavia Roberts, Dec. 27, 1913. Admitted to Ill. bar, 1899; connected with law dept. C.&N.W. R.R., 1899-1909; a gen. atty. of the rd. from 1905; spl. asst. to Atty. Gen. of U.S., 1909-13; resumed practice, Boston, Jan. 1, 1913; later ret. Home: Ogunquit, Me.†

CORNELL, KATHARINE, actress; b. Berlin, Germany, Feb. 16, 1893 (parents Am. citizens); d. Peter Cortleyou and Alice Gardner (Plimpton) Cornell; ed. Buffalo, Oaksmere, Mamaroneck, N.Y.; Chancellor's Medal, U. Buffalo, 1935; Litt.D., U. Wis., 1936, Elmira Coll. for Women, 1937, Hobart Coll., 1938, U. Pa., 1938, Middlebury Coll., 1955, Kenyon Coll., 1956; L.H.D., Smith Coll., 1937; Dr. Fine Arts, Clark U., 1941, Ithaca Coll., 1947, Princeton, 1948; H.H.D., Internat. Coll., Springfield, Mass., 1962; m. Guthrie McClintic, Sept. 8, 1921 (dec. 1961). Made debut with Washington Square Players, N.Y.C., 1917; with Jessie Bonstelle Stock Co., 1919-20; traveled with The Man Who Came Back, 1920; appeared in Little Women, London, 1920; with Jessie Bonstelle Stock Co., 1920-21; appeared in N.Y. prodns. of Nice People, A Bill of Divorcement, Will Shakespeare, The Enchanted Cottage, Casanova, The Way Things Happen, The Outsider, Tiger Cats, Candida, The Green Hat, The Letter, The Age of Innocence, and Dishonored Lady. Became actress-mgr. with The Barretts of Wimpole Street, 1931, Lucrece, 1932, Allen Corn, 1933, Romeo and Juliet, 1934, Flowers of the Forest, 1935, Saint Joan, 1936, The Wingless Victory and Candida, 1937, Herod and Mariamne, 1938, No Time for Comedy, 1939-40, The Doctor's Dilemma, 1941, Rose Burke, 1942, The Three Sisters, 1942-43, Lovers and Friends, 1943-44, The Barretts of Wimpole Street, overseas, 1944-45, United States, 1945, 47; Antigone, 1946; Antony and Cleopatra, 1947-48; That Lady, 1949-50; Captain Carvallo, 1950; The Constant Wife, 1951-52; The Prescott Proposals, 1953-54; The Dark is Light Enough, 1954-55; The Firstborn, 1958; Dear Liar, 1959-60; on TV in The Barretts of Wimpole Street, 1956; There Shall be no Night, 1957; narrator full length documentary films Helen Keller in her Story, 1954, This is Our Island. Co-chmn. Plays of Living div. Family Service Assn. Am. Recipient art citation Nat. Conf. Christians and Jews, 1946; Medal of Freedom, 1946; Woman of Year award Am. Friends Hebrew U., 1959; medal for good speech on stage, Am. Acad. Arts and Letters, 1959. Clubs: Colony, Cosmopolitan (N.Y.); Garrett (Buffalo). Author: (autobiography) I Wanted to be an Actress, 1936. Home: New York City, N.Y. Died June 9, 1974; inurned Old Village Cemetery, Vineyard Haven, Mass.

CORNISH, GERTRUDE ELEANOR, educator; b. Worcester, Mass., Jan. 28, 1880; d. Carlos Hiram and Ella Jane (Bryant) C.; grad. Worcester Classical High Sch., 1897; B.S., Middlebury (Vt.) Coll., 1901, honorary A.M., 1927; graduate study Clark University, 1908-09; m. Joseph Knowles Milliken, Sem., Norton, Mass., 1903-08; same, Miss. Porter's Sch., Farmington, Conn., 1909-11; founder, 1911, later prin. House in the Pines, girls' boarding sch., Norton, Mass. Chmn. advisory bd., Women's Coll., Middlebury, Vt. Mem. Am. Assn. Univ. Women, Nat. Assn. Prins. Schs. for Girls, Headmistresses Assn. of the East, Pvt. Schs. Assn. of Boston, Phi Beta Kappa, Kappa Kappa Gamma. Address: Norton, Mass.†

CORNMAN, NOEL, lawyer; b. Bklyn., Feb. 10, 1927; s. David and Sophia (Kaye) C.; student Syracuse U., 1945; A.B., U. Cal. at Los Angeles, 1948, J. D., 1953; B.A., U. So. Cal., 1950; m. Marion T. Tessel, Nov. 26, 1947; children—Robert, Lawrence, Diane. Admitted to Cal. bar, 1954; pvt. practice law, Los Angeles, 1954-58; v.p. Cornman & Co., Inc., Los Angeles, 1958-62, Trans-Pacific Distbg. Co., Inc., Los Angeles, 1958-62; partner Springer, Cornman & King, Los Angeles, 1962-75. Pres. Encino Democratic Club, 1958. Served with AUS, 1945-47. Mem. Am. Bar Assn., Am. Soc. Internat. Law, Am. Polit. Sci. Assn., Am. Judicature Soc., Beta Gamma Sigma, Los Angeles Hillel Alumni Assn. (pres. 1956). Home: Woodland Hills, Cal. Died Mar. 4, 1975.

CORNWELL, FOREST AUGUSTUS, physician; b. Dallas, Feb. 3, 1921; s. Elijah Guy and Edna Pearl (Kuykendall) C.; B.S. in Medicine, U. Kan., Lawrence, 1944, M.D., 1945; post grad. Harvard Med. Sch., 1950. Intern U.S. Naval Hosp., Bainbridge, Md., 1945-46; pediatric resident Children's Mercy Hosp., Kansas City, Mo., 1949; pvt. practice medicine and pediatrics, Dallas, 1951-56. Beckley, W.Va., 1956-70; asso. chief pediatrics Beckley Meml. Hosp., 1956-64, sec.-treas., 1961-62, pres. med. staff, 1962-63; chief pediatric div. Beckley Appalachian Regional Hosp., 1964-70, pres., chief med. staff, 1967-68; pediatric cons. Miners Meml. Hosp. Assn., 1964-65; chief of pediatrics Wyoming Gen. Hosp., Mullens, W.Va., 1956-64; pediatric cons. Raleigh Boone Med. Group, Whitesville, W.Va., Rock Creek Med. Group, Montcalm, W.Va., 1956-64; clin. asso. prof. pediatrics W.Va. U. Sch. Medicine, 1969-73; pres. Mountaineer Family Health Plan, Inc., Beckley, W.Va., 1967-69, project dir., med. dir., 1970-73. Served as lt. (j.g.) M.C. USN, 1946-48, lt. M.C., USNR, 1951-54, now comdr. ret. Mem. governing bd. Raleigh County Community Action Assn., 1968-69; rep. to Joint Council Teaching Hosps., 1969-73; chmn. subcom. on maternal and child health Comprehensive Health Planning Council, Office of Gov. W.Va., 1969-71, mem. subcom. personal health, 1971-73, subcom. health edn., 1972-73; adv. bd. new health rules project Sch. Pub. Health, U. N.C., 1971-73; mem. W.Va. Family Planning Adv. Council, 1971-73; mem. regional adv. group W.Va. Regional Med. Program, 1972-73; Diplomate Am. Bd. Pediatrics. Fellow Am. Acad. Pediatrics (chmn. W.Va. chpt. 1965-73). mem. Raleigh County Med. Soc. (pres. 1969), Am. W.Va. (dir., pres.-elect 1969-70, chmn. research com.), Raleigh County (chmn. pub. service) heart assns., Assn. Am. Med. Colls., World (U.S. com.), Am. So., W.Va. (mem. ho. of dels. 1963-73, com. on md. edn. and hosps., com. on med. econs.) med. assns., Assn. Mil. Surgeons U.S., W.Va. Pediatric Soc. (exec. com.), So. W.Va. Med. Clinic Assn., Raleigh County C. of C., Nu Sigma Nu. Democrat. Methodist (ofcl. bd.). Home: Beckley, W.Va. Died Feb. 24, 1973; buried Sunset Lawns, El Dorado, Kan.

CORP, PAUL METZGER mfg. exec.; b. Madison, Wis., June 21, 1911; s. Charles Ives and Georgia (Metzer) C.; B.S. in Mech. Engring., U. Wis., 1933; m. Helen Mary Bailey, Dec. 29, 1934; children—Charles Ives, Paul Allison, David Owen, Jr. engr. W.G. Kirchoffer, Cons. Engr., Madison, 1933-34; appraisal engr. William Sloan, Chgo., 1934-35; sales, sales demonstrator Lincoln Electric Co., Cleve., 1935-40; welding engr. Heil Co., Milw., 1940-42; chief metallurgist Am. Metal Products Co., Detroit, 1942-44, chief engr., 1944-49, asst. product mgr., 1949-53, v.p. prodn., 1953-56, v.p., 1956-61, dir. from 1955; pres. Alliance Ware, Inc., (O.), 1956-61, chmn. bd., 1958-61; pres., dir. Briggs Mfg. Co., Warren, Mich., 1961-63; pres., treas. PMC Co., mgmt. consulting, Detroit, 1963-69, AAA Leasing dir., 1963-69; chmn. bd., chief exec. officer Pre-Built Homes, Inc., 1971; v.p., exec. dir. Ultec Inc., from 1972. Mem. Am. Ordnance Assn., Soc. Automatic Engrs., Porcelain Enamel Inst., C. of C., Newcomen Soc., Sigma Phi Epsilon, Phi Mu Alpha. Club: Recess (Detroit). Home: Bloomfield Hills, Mich. Deceased.

CORPER, HARRY JOHN, physician; b. Chgo., Mar. 5, 1884; s. Ferdinand and Bertha (Rhoeder) C.; M.D., Rush Med. Coll., 1911; Ph.D., U. Chgo., 1911; m. Margaret Knapp, 1911 (dec.); children—Harry George (dec.), Margaret (Mrs. Gerard James), Marie (Mrs. William Derry), Dorothy (Mrs. Ray Havens); m. 2d, Catherine Clark, May 9, 1960. Intern, Presbyn. Hosp., Chgo., 1912-13; dir. lab. and research City Municipal Tb San., Chgo., 1913-18; dir. research and cons. pathologist Nat. Jewish Hosp., Denver; spl. lectr. Fitzsimons Army Hosp., 1925-52; instr. Yale, 1918-19; asso. prof. medicine U. Colo. Pres., Rocky Mountain Tb Conf., 1936. Served with M.C., U.S. Army, 1918-19. Recipient Useful Citizen award U. Chgo., 1944. Diplomate Am. Bd. Internal Medicine, Am. Bd. Pathology. Fellow A.A.A.S.; mem. Am. Acad. Tb Physicians (Gold medal 1946), A.M.A. (Bronze medal 1938), Am. Soc. Clin. Pathologists (pres. 1930, Ward Burdick medal 1930), Nat. Tb. Assn., Am. Chem. Soc., Am. Legion, Denver Tb Soc. (pres. 1942), Phi Beta Kappa, Sigma Xi, Alpha Omega Alpha. Contbr. to Study of Tuberculosis, vols. 1-19, 1920-53. Mem. editorial bd. Am. Rev. Tuberculosis, 1926-31; editor Tuberculogy, 1937-67; abstrator Chemical Abstracts, 1911-55. Home: Denver, Colo. Died May 12, 1973; buried Ft. Logan Nat. Cemetery, Denver, Colo.

CORRIGAN, LEO FRANCIS real estate, hotel exec.; b. St. Louis, Aug. 30, 1894; s. Dennis J. and Mary (Callahan) C.; student pub. schs. St. Louis; m. Clara Catherine Redman, Dec. 6, 1917; children—Louise (Mrs. Edwin B. Jordan), Leo Francis, Real estate advt. salesman Dallas Dispatch, 1910, advt. solicitor, 1912; asst. advt. mgr. Houston Press, 1911; automotive editor St. Louis Star, 1911, also st. car advt. salesman Western Advt. Co., St. Louis; gen. real estate work, Dallas, 1912; from 1917 engaged in ownership, devel. and mgmt. real estate; controls and operates 5 hotels, some 35 shopping centers, 15 office bldgs. and 15 apt. projects; established Corrigan Ins. Agy., 1942; pres., dir. Los Angeles Biltmore Hotel Co., Dallas Hotel Co., Corrigan Properties Inc., Dallas-Corrigan-Houston, Inc., Houston; pres. Corrigan Co. of Nassau, Ltd.; joint owner C.J.C. Realty Co.; dir. Wynncor Limited, United Fidelity Life Ins. Co. Bd. dirs. Dallas Civic Opera Co. Mem. Dallas, Ft. Worth chambers commerce, Nat. Assn. Real Estate Bds., Nat. Inst. Real Estate Brokers, Dallas Real Estate Bd., Dallas Home Builders Assn., Central Bus. Dist. Association of Dallas. Clubs: Country, Book Hollow Golf, Dallas Country, Dallas, City (Dallas) Home: Dallas, Tex. Died June 12, 1975.

COSTELLO, JOHN A(LOYSIUS), head Govt. of Ireland; b. Dublin, Ireland, June 20, 1891; s. John and Rose (Callaghan) C.; student Christian Bros. Schs.; B.A., Univ. Coll., Dublin, 1911, LL.B., 1914, B.L., 1914, S.C., 1925; LL.D. (honoris causa), U. Montreal, U. Ottawa, Fordham U., Ida Mary O'Malley, July 31, 1919; children—Wilfred, Grace Mary (Mrs. Alexis FitzGerald), Declan, Eavan Leilah, John. Called to Irish Bar, 1914; law practice 1914-76; bencher Hon. Soc. of Kings Inns, 1926; asst. to law officer Irish Free State, 1922; asst. atty. gen., 1923, atty. gen., 1926-32; rep. Irish Free State Imperial Confs., London, 1926, 29, 30. Conf. on Naval Disarmament, 1927, League of Nations, Geneva, 1927-30; entered Dail Eireann. The Irish Parliament, as a Fine Gael (United Ireland) mem. from Dublin County, 1933; Taoiseach (Prime Minister), head of Ireland's 1st inter-party govt., 1948-51; minister for health, 1951; leader of opposition in Dail Eireann, 1951-54, head of Govt. of Ireland, 1954-76. Mem. Dail Eireann Co. Dublin, 1933-37, Dublin Twps., 1937-43, 44-48, Dublin South (East), 1948-76. Mem. Royal Irish Acad. Home: Ballsbridge, Dublin, Ireland. Died Jan. 5, 1976.

COSTELLO, JOHN CORNELIUS, utilities exec.; b. San Francisco, June 15, 1894; s. John and Bridget (Lynch) C.; B.S., U. Cal., 1916; m. Maude Catherine McDougal, Sept. 5, 1929. Power sales engr. Chattanooga Ry. & Light Co., 1916-20, asst. to comml. mgr., 1920-22, Tenn. Electric Power Co., 1922-23, advt. mgr., 1923-36, mgr. securities sales dept., 1928-32; sec.-treas. So. Tenn. Power Co., Chattanooga, 1936; v.p. Tenn. Electric Power Co., 1936-39, dir., 1938-39, sold to Tenn. Valley Authority, 1939; dir. advt. and publicity Ohio Edison Co., Akron, 1939-47, asst. to pres. 1947-62, dir. 1949-62. Vice pres. Ohio Electric Utility Inst., 1960-62, dir. Served as pvt., U.S. Army, World War I. Mem. Newcomen Society of North Am. Roman Catholic, K.C. (4°). Club: Akron City. Home: Akron, Ohio. Died Sept. 23, 1974.

COSTLEY, ELIZABETH CHRISTINE, physician; b. Lamar, Mo., Dec. 23, 1920; d. Vivian and Emma Verla Costley; grad. Burge Hosp. Sch. Nursing, Springfield, Mo., Mercy Hosp. Sch. Anesthesiology, Detroit; B.A. in Nursing, U. Rochester; M.D., Case-Western Res. U., 1958. Intern, Cleve. Met. Gen. Hosp., 1958-59, resident, 1959-61; resident Univ. Hosps. of Cleve., 1961; fell in respiratory physiology cardiovascular Research Inst., U. Cal. Med. Center, 1961-64; head physician acute respiratory disease unit Rancho Los Amigos Hosp., Downey, Cal., 1964-72; pulmonary physiologist Barlow Sanitorium, Los Angeles, 1972-74; pub. health physician Los Angeles County Communith Health Services; staff VA Hosp., Los Angeles, Children's Hosp., Los Angeles; asst. clin. prof. dept. pediatrics U. So. Cal., Los Angeles. Diplomate Am. Bd. Pediatrics. Mem. Am. Thoracic Soc., Am. Coll. Chest Physicians, League Women Voters. Presbyn. Home: Pasadena, Cal. Died Nov. 3, 1974; buried Waters Cemetery, Jasper, Mo.

COTT, TED, radio and television exec.; b. Poughkeepsie, N.Y., Jan. 1, 1917; s. Lewis and Dorothy (Susskind) C.; student College of the City of New York, 1933; m. 2d, Suzanne Oksman, July 1, 1956; one son, James Lloyd; children by Previous marriage—Jonathan H., Jeremy D. Dir. dramatic broadcasts Municipal Broadcasting System, 1935-39; producer radio series So You Think You Know Music, CBS, 1939-44; v.p., program dir. radio sta. WNEW, N.Y.C., 1942-50; instr. radio dramatics and scriptwriting City Coll. N.Y., 1945-47; gen. mgr. WNBC-WNBT, N.Y.C., 1950-53; operating v.p. NBC, 1952-55; v.p., dir., gen. mgr. Dumont Broadcasting Corp., gen. mgr. TV stas. WABD, N.Y.C., WTTG, Washington, 1955-57; v.p. charge WNTA-AM-FM-TV, N.Y.C., KMSP-TV, Minneapolis, from 1957; later chairman of the consulting committee of the French Broadcasting System; author-producer 32 children's albums for Carvan. Karousel and Frolic record Cos. Recipient Nat. Conf. Christians and Jews Brotherhood awards, 1947-48, 51; George Foster Peabody award for fostering internat. relations, 1949; 11 awards from Inst. for Edn. by Radio, Ohio State U., 1945-49; civil rights citations of Freedom House, 1949; Award of Merit, Nat. Safety Council, 1948; Democracy award, Am. Vets. Com.; One World Award for Radio 1952; Variety Show-mgr. of year 1949; Chevalier, French Legion of Honor, 1950; Emmy award for outstanding station operation, 1957; Robert E. Sherwood award, in 1957. Author; Victor Book of Musical Fun, 1945; How to Audition for Radio, 1946; Isn't it a Crime, 1947; A Treasury of the Spoken Word, 1949. Club: Lotos (N.Y.C.). Address: New York City, N.Y. Died June 12, 1973.

COTTAM, CLARENCE, biologist; b. St. George, Utah, Jan. 1, 1899; s. Thomas P. and Emmaline (Jarvis) C.; student Dixie Coll., 1919-20, U. Utah, summer 1923; B.S., Brigham Young U., 1926, M. S., 1927; student Am. U., 1931; Ph.D., George Washington U., 1936; m. Margery Brown, May 20, 1920; children—Glenna Clair (Mrs. Ivan L. Sanderson). Margery B. (Mrs. Grant Osborn), Josephine (Mrs. Douglas Day), Carolyn (Mrs. Dwayne Stevenson). Prin. consol. schs., Alamo, Nev., 1922-25; with Fish and Wildlife Service (formed in 1939 by consol of Bur. of Biol. Survey and Bur. of Fisheries) U. S. Dept. of Interior, 1939—, sr. biologist, 1939-44, in charge food habits research sect., 1939-42, in charge econ. wildlife investigations, 1942-44, asst. to dir., 1944-46, chief div. wildlife research, 1945-46, asst. dir. Fish and Wildlife Service, 1946-54; dean Coll. Biol. and Agrl. Scis., Brigham Young U., Provo, Utah, 1954-58; dir. Welder Wildlife Found., Sinton, Tex., 1955-74. Recipient hon. award Utah Acad. Sci., Arts and Letters, 1948, Laval U., 1952; Conservation award, Aldo Leopold medal, Wildlife Soc., 1955; Distinguished Service award in conservation and forestry Utah State U. of Agr., 1957; Nat. Audubon Conservation Distinguished Service medal, 1961, also other conservation awards; Distinguished Citizen award Sinton, 1958, 67; Poage Humanitarian award Soc. Animal Protection, 1962; Francis K. Hutchenson medal for conservation Garden Club of Am., 1962; Paul Bartsch award for contbn. natural history Audubon Naturalist Soc., 1962, Wisdom award of honor Wisdom Soc., 1970, Distinguished Service award Tex. chpt. Wildlife Soc., 1971, James E. Talmage Sci. Achievement award Brigham Young U., 1971, Alban-Heiser award Houston Zool. Soc., 1974. Fellow A.A.A.S., Am. Ornithol. Union, Tex. (v.p.), Utah acads. sci.; mem. Wilson, Cooper ornithol. clubs, Wildlife Soc. Am. (pres. 1949-50), Am. Wildlife Inst., Am. Fisheries Soc., Wash. Acad. Sci., Wash. Biol. Soc., Wash. Biologists Field Club, Am. Soc. Mammalogists, Ecol. Soc. Am., Internat. Platform Assn., Soil Conservation Soc. Am., Friends of Land, Nat. Audubon Soc., Tex. Ornithol. Soc. (pres. 1957), Soc. Range Mgmt., Nat. Parks Assn. (pres. or chmn. bd. 1960-74), Wilderness Soc., Am. Inst. Biol. Scis., Tex. Philos. Soc., Sigma Xi. Mem. Church of Jesus Christ of Latter-day Saints. Club: Serra. Author: Food Habits of American Diving Ducks, 1939; American Insects, 1950. Co-editor: Whitewings. Contbr. chpts. to books, articles to sci. publs. Address: Sinton, Tex. Died Mar. 30, 1974; interred Orem, Utah.

COTTON, EDWARD HOWE, clergyman, author; b. Boston, Mass., Nov. 21, 1880; s. Edward S. and Addie L. (Howe) C.; grad. Phillips Acad., Exeter, N.H., 1901; A.B., Colby Coll., 1905; grad. Union Theol. Sem., 1908; m. Ruth W. Woodberry, of Beverly, Mass., 1916; children—Estelle W., Edward H., Jr., Webster E. Ordained ministry Congl. Ch., 1909; pastor Ch. of the Pilgrims, Provincetown, Mass., 1909-11, Unitarian Ch., Danvers, Mass., 1912-17; overseas war sec. Y.M.C.A., 1917-18; organized Community Ch. (Unitarian-Universalist), Danvers, 1918-19; associate editor Christian Register, 1921-22; pastor Unitarian Ch., Marblehead, 1922-36, Florence, Massachusetts from 1936. Trustee Abbott Free Public Library. Clubs: Masons Club, Phi Delta Theta, Boston Authors'. Author: The Ideals of Theodore Roosevelt, 1923; Theodore Roosevelt, the American, 1925; The Life of Charles W. Eliot, 1926; William Howard Taft, A Study in Character, 1931; also syndicated articles. Sec. of publicity Am. Unitarian Assn. and editor Unitarian News Letter, 1931-33. Editor: Charles W. Eliot's Talks to Parents and Young People, 1928; Has Science Discovered God?, 1931. Interviewer of notable men and compiler of their expressions. Home: Florence, Mass.†

COTTRELL, LEONARD, author; b. Wolverhampton, Eng., May 21, 1913; s. William Arthur and Beatrice Martha (Tootell) C.; ed. King Edward VI's Grammar Sch., Birmingham, Eng.; m. Doris Swain, May 1940 (div. June 1960); m. 2d, Diana Randolph, Dec. 1965. Free-lance radio writer, dir., 1936-40; staff writer, dir. radio documentaries BBC, London, 1940-55, writer, dir. BBC-TV drama documentary dept., 1955-59; war corr. RAF, 1944-45, seconded to UNESCO as radio writer and dir., Paris, 1951-53; lectr. archaeology on cruises Egypt, Middle East, Aegaean Islands; free lance contbr. TV and radio. Mem. Egypt Exploration Soc., Hellenic Soc., Roman Soc., Inst. Archaeol. Gt. Britain. Clubs: Savile, London. Author numerous books, including: The Lost Pharaohs, 1950; Madame Tussaud, 1951; The Bull of Minos, 1953; One Man's Journey, 1955; Life Under the Pharaohs. 1955; Mountains of Pharaoh, 1956; Seeing Roman Britain, 1956; Lost Cities, 1957; The Anvil of Civilization, 1958; The Great Invasion, 1958; Wonders of Antiquity, 1959; Wonders of the World, 1959; Enemy of Rome, 1960; Land of the Pharaohs, 1960; Land of Two Rivers, 1961; Tiger of Chi'in, 1962; Lost Worlds, 1962; The Lion Gate, 1963; Secrets of Tutankhamun's Tomb, 1964; Crete, Island of Mystery, 1965; Guide to Egypt, 1966; Quest for Sumer, 1966; Queens of the Pharaohs, 1966; The Warrior Pharaohs, 1968; The Mystery of Minoan Civilisation, 1970; Reading the Past, 1970; Up in a Balloon, 1970; also numerous articles and book revs. for Brit. and Am. publs. Editor: Concise Ency. of Archaeology, 1960. Home: Solihull Warwickshire, Eng. Died Oct. 6, 1974.

COTTRELL, SAMUEL, engring. cons.; b. Washington, Oct. 4, 1898; s. Samuel and Ella (Kaufman) C.; Chem. E., Lehigh U., 1922; m. Elise Mardorf, Apr. 22, 1936 (dec. Aug. 1969); children—Susan Elise, Samuel IV: m. 2d, Lucille L. Summers, June 26, 1971. With Trojan Powder Co., Allentown, Pa., 1922-29, where advanced from foreman to supt. acid plants and supt. of a power plant; with Monsanto Chem. Co., 1929-46, advancing from asst. supr. to asst. plant mgr., Monsanto, Ill., plant; with Am. Potash & Chem. Corp., Los Angeles, 1946-49, successively tech. asst. to exec. v.p., v.p. in charge tech. operations; asst. to dir. operations Mathieson Chem. Corp., Balt., 1949-52, v.p., dir. operations, agrl. chems. div., Little Rock, 1952-54; dir. operations, agrl. chems. div. Olin Mathieson Chem. Corp., Little Rock, 1954-61, mgr. prodn. chems. div.-agrl., 1961-63; v.p., gen. mgr. Universal Moulded Fiber Glass Corp., Bristol, Va., 1963-65; adviser engring. World Bank, Washington, 1965-74; cons., 1974. Pres. Little Rock Chamber Music Soc., 1956-57. Served as 2d lt. inf. U.S. Army, World War I. Mem. C. of C., Nat. Safety Council, Am. Chem. Soc., Electrochem. Soc., Am. Inst. Chem. Engrs. (chmn. St. Louis sect.). Unitarina (pres., trustee). Rotarian. Home: Washington, D.C. Died Sept. 8, 1974.

COUCH, GEORGE W., JR., brewery exec.; b. Port Royal, Pa., Oct. 5, 1922; s. George W. and Meryl (Bryner) C.; B.A., U. Md.; m. Geraldine Glockner, July 9, 1945; children—George W., III, Gregory B., Geoffrey A. Vice pres. marketing Anheuser-Busch, Inc., St. Louis. Served to capt. AUS, World War II. Office: St. Louis, Mo. Died Jan. 23, 1973; interred St. Louis, Mo.

COUGHLIN, EDWARD JOSEPH, JR., physician; b. Passaic, N.J., Apr. 17, 1906; s. Edward Joseph and Frances (Hughes) J. C.; grad. Williams Coll.; M.D., Columbia, 1931; m. Ruth Elizabeth Dunlap, Oct. 12, 1934; children—Edward Joseph III, W. David and Cecile (Mrs. T. Craig Renton) (twins). Intern, Presbyn. Hosp., N.Y.C., 1931-33, tng. fracture and tng. service, 1934; clin. tng. St. Agnes Hosp., White Plains, N.Y., 1947; Hosp. for Spl. Surgery, N.Y.C., 1947; dir. orthopedics Putnam Meml. Hosp., Bennington, Vt.; orthopedic surgeon, chief surgery North Adams (Mass.) Hosp., pres. med. staff, 1958; orthopedic surgeon Crippled Children's div. Vt. Dept. Pub. Health; cons. in orthopedics Plunkett Meml. Hosp., Adams, Mass., Crippled Childrens div. Mass. Dept. Pub. Health; cons. orthopedics Williams Coll., Williamstown, Mass., mem. staff infirmary, 1953-73; cons. to surgeon gen. U.S. Army, Germany, 1954; cons. automotive crash research program Cornell U.-State of Vt. Served to maj., M.C., AUS, 1942-45; col. Res. Coughlin trophy named in his honor Williams Coll. Side Line Quarterback Club. Diplomate Am. Bd. Surgery, Am. Bd. Orthopedic Surgery. Fellow Am. Acad. Orthopedic Surgeons, Am. Assn. Surgery of Trauma; mem. New Eng. Surg. Soc., Allen O. Whipple Surg. Soc., A.M.A., Mass. Med. Assn., Pan Am. Med. Assn., Sociedad Latino Americana de Ortopedia y Traumatologia (fgn.), Delta Phi. Republican. Episcopalian. Club: Taconic Golf (v.p. 1950-74) (Williamstown). Contbr. articles to profl. jours. Home: Williamstown, Mass. Died Mar. 2, 1974; buried Arlington Nat. Cemetery.

COULSON, CHARLES ALFRED, educator, chemist; b. Dudley, Worcester, Eng., Dec. 13, 1910; s. Alfred and Annie (Hancock) C.; M.A., Ph.D., Cambridge U.; D.Sc., St. Andrew's U.; m. Eileen Florence Burrett, Aug. 30, 1938; children—Andrew Charles, Martin Geoffrey, Janet Eileen, Wendy Ann, Christopher John (dec.). Fellow Trinity Coll. Cambridge U., 1934-38; lectr. math. U. Coll., Dundee, Scotland, 1938-45; Imperial Chem. Industries fellow Oxford U., lectr. math. Univ. Coll., 1945-47; Wheatstone prof. theoretical physics King's Coll. U. London (Eng.), 1947-52; Rouse Ball prof. math. Oxford U., fellow Wadham Coll., 1952-74, prof. theoretical chemistry Oxford U., 1972-74. Chmn. OXFAM, 1965-71; mem. central com. World Council Chs., 1961-68. Fellow Royal Soc., Royal Soc. Edinburgh. Methodist (lay preacher). Author: Electricity, 1948; Waves, 1941; Valance, 1952 (1st edit.), 1961 (2d edit.); Science and Christian Belief, 1955; Science, Technology and the Christian, 1960; (with A. Streitwieser, Jr.) Dictionary of Pi-Election Calculations, 1965; The Shape and Structure of Molecules, 1973. Contbr. articles profl. jours. Home: Oxford, England. Died Jan. 7, 1974.

COULTER, WILLIAM S(UMMEY), lawyer; born at Newton, North Carolina, Aug. 28, 1886; s. John Summey and Sarah Ann (Herman) C.; grad. prep. dept., Catawba Coll., 1904; A.B., Catawba Coll., 1908; M.A., U. of N.C., 1914; m. Annie Ben Long, Feb. 23, 1921; children—Ann (Mrs. Norman F. Wiss, Jr.), William Herbert, Catherine Long (Mrs. J. Herbert Hattaway). Instr. in Latin, Bennettsville (S.C.) High Sch., 1910-11; supt. Fairview (N.C.) Schs., 1911-13; admitted to N.C. bar, 1914, and practiced in Burlington, 1914-37 with the firms of Vernon & Coulter, Coulter & Cooper, Coulter, Cooper & Carr, Coulter & Allen. City attorney, 1919-33; admitted to bar Supreme Ct., 1931; dir. Burlington Mills Corp. from 1926, sec., 1937-47, treas., 1939-47, v.p., 1947-51, gen. counsel, 1937-52; mem. bd. mgrs. Wachovia Bank & Trust Co., Burlington, N.C. Mem. N.C. Gen. Assembly, 1925-27. Mem. Am. Judicature Soc., Am. and N.C. bar assns., N.C. State Bar, Inc., Newcomen Soc., Sigma Chi. Democrat (mem. state exec. com., 1933-37; del. nat. conv. 1932). Episcopalian. Clubs: Kiwanis (past pres.), Greensboro Country, Merchants and Manufacturers, Bob-White Hunt. Home: Greensboro, N.C. Died May 11, 1975; interred Alamance Meml. Park, Burlington, N.C.

COUNTS, GEORGE SYLVESTER, author; b. nr. Baldwin City, Kan., Dec. 9, 1889; s. James Wilson and Mertie Florella (Gamble) C.; A.B., Baker U., Kan., 1911; Ph.D., U. Chgo., 1916; LL.D., Baker U., Kan., 1935; D.H.L., So. Ill. U., 1971; m. Lois Hazel Bailey, Sept. 24, 1913; children—Esther Mae, Martha Louise. Head dept. of edn. and dir. summer sch., Delaware Coll., Newark, 1916-18; prof. ednl. sociology, Harris Tchrs. Coll., St. Louis, Mo., 1918-19; prof. secondary edn., U. of Wash., 1919-20; asso. prof. Yale, 1920-24, prof., 1924-26; prof. of edn., U. Chgo, 1926-27; asso. dir. Internat. Inst., 1927-32; prof. of edn., Tchrs. Coll., Columbia, 1927-56, prof. emeritus, 1956-74; vis. prof. U. Pitts., 1959, Mich. State U., 1960, So. Ill. U., Carbondale, 1962-74; Horace Mann lectr., 1962; dir. div. founds. edn., 1942-48. Editor of The Social Frontier, 1934-37; mem. Ednl. Policies Commn. of N.E.A., 1936-42. Pres. Am. Fedn. Tchrs., 1939-42; mem. exec. com. of Nat. Com. on Edn. and Def., 1940-42, Nat. Com. Civil Liberties Union, 1940—; mem. Commn. on Motion Pictures in Edn., 1944-48; N.Y. State chmn. Am. Labor Party, 1942-44; N.Y. chmn. Liberal Party, 1955-59. Mem. U.S. Ednl. Mission to Japan, 1946; mem. com. on Internat. Exchange of Persons, 1948-50. Recipient Annual Educator's award B'nai B'rith, 1953; Tchrs. Coll. medal for distinguished service, 1954; award for distinguished service in sch. adminstrn. Am. Assn. Sch. Adminstrs., 1968, Phi Delta Kappa award, 1967, John Dewey Soc. award, 1967. Mem. Nat. Acad. Edn., Soc. Coll. Tchrs. Edn., Nat. Edn. Assn., Am. Assn. U. Profs., P.E.N. Club: Delta Tau Delta, Phi Delta Kappa, Kappa Delta Pi. Author: sixteen books, 1917-42: Education and the Promise of America (Kappa Delta Pi lecture), 1945. Co-translator of New Russia's Primer (M. Ilin), 1931; I Want to Be Like Stalin, 1947; The Country of the Blind: The Soviet System of Mind Control (with N. Lodge), 1949; American Education through the Soviet Looking Glass, 1951; Education and American Civilization, 1952; Decision-Making and American Values in School Adminstration, 1954; The Challenge of Soviet Education ($5,000 Liberty and Justice award A.L.A., 1958), 1957; Khrushchev and the Central Committee Speak on Education, 1959; Education and the Foundations of Human Freedom, 1962; Education and Human Freedom in The Age of Technology, 1958. Home: Carbondale, Ill. Died Nov. 1974.

COURNAND, EDWARD L., perfume co. exec.; b. Paris, France, 1897; ed. Sorbonne, Paris. Pres., dir. Lanvin-Parfums, Inc.; dir. Lavin Boutique, Perfume Atomizers, Inc. Home: New York City, N.Y., Died Nov. 8, 1975.

COURTNEY, LUTHER WEEKS, univ. prof.; b. Aiken County, S.C., June 12, 1880; s. John Calhoun and Sarah Elizabeth (Weeks) C.; A.B., Furman U., 1905; A.M., Baylor U., 1931; grad. student and fellow in English, Yale, 1916-17, University of Iowa, 1924-25; Ph.D., University of Iowa, 1925; Litt.D., Furman Univ., 1944;

m. Estelle McCarley Harris, August 28, 1918; step-children—Frances Elizabeth Harris, Marion Winifred Harris. Supt. schs. Belton, S.C., 1905-08; prof. English and history, Okla. Bapt. Coll., Blackwell, Okla., 1909-11; instr. in English, Baylor U., 1911-14, asst. prof. of English, 1922-25, prof. of English and forensic dir., 1925-34, prof. of English from 1934; headmaster Furman Fitting School, 1914-16; prof. English and head of dept., Okla. Bapt. U., Shawnee, 1917-22. Presidential appointee on fact-finding board, L.A. and L.A.&T. Ry. System, July 1933, and S.P. Lines in La. and Tex., Nov. 1933; neutral arbitrator for S.P. Lines in La. and Tex. and Nat. Brotherhoods in cases pending, Feb. 1934. Mem. bd. dirs. Library Assn., Waco. Chmn. Com. for Civilian Defense for Waco. Pres. Conf. of Coll. Teachers of English of Texas, 1940-41; mem. Nat. Social Science Soc., Am. Assn. of Univ. Profs., Pi Kappa Delta, Pi Gamma Mu. Democrat. Baptist. Rotarian (v.p. Waco Rotary Club, 1937-38; pres. 1939-40). Club: Philosophers (Waco). Author: Suggestions on Debating, 1926; Hannah More's Interest in Education and Govt., 1929; Co-author: Practical Debating 1949. Editor of Types and Times in English literature, 1940. Home: Waco, Tex.†

COUTANT, FRANK RAYMOND, author; b. Jersey City, Aug. 26, 1885; s. Joseph and Nanette (Mayden) C.; D.Comml. Sci., Libertyville U., 1910; m. Dorothy Rolling, Apr. 8, 1933; children by previous marriage Art L., Flora. Stenographer, Standard Oil Co., Bayonne Refinery, 1905-1907; accountant Corn Products Refining, N.Y.C., 1907-12; merchandising pioneer Western Can. frontiers, 1912-1920; mem. creative staff N.W. Ayer & Son, Phila., 1920-25; research dir., v.p. marketing several N.Y.C. advt. agys., 1925-40; founder, pres. Fact Finders Assos., 1940-57; author, lectr., writer. Mem. nat. council Boy Scouts Am., 1958-60; mem. adv. staff Pace U., N.Y.C., 1950-57. Recipient Silver Beaver award Boy Scouts Am., 1957, Good and Faithful Servant award Market Research Council N.Y., 1962, George Washington of Marketing Sci. award U. Fla., 1971. Mem. Am. Marketing Assn. (1st pres. 1937, sr. past pres. 1972). Mason (K.T.). Author: (with others) American Business Practices, 1931; Intimate Glimpses of West Indies, 1957; Hilarious Hawaii, 1958; Alaska Flies to Her Future, 1958; Across Yukon to Alaska, 1961; Yankee Ships on Fraser River, 1963; Cariboo Highway, 1964; The Great North Road of British Columbia, 1967. Home: Monroe, Conn. Died Sept. 1, 1973; interred Stepney Village Cemetery.

COVINGTON, EUCLID M., publishing exec.; b. Bowling Green, Ky., July 8, 1893; s. Robert Wells and Wickliffe (Cooper) C.; student Stanford, 1910-11, U. Va., 1911-14; m. Mary Ingersoll, July 7, 1934; children—Sara Theresa, Mary Wickliffe, Advt. dept. Chgo. Tribune, 1915-19; v.p. Hopper Advt. Agy., N.Y.C., 1921-24; Eastern mgr. Chgo. Herald Examiner, 1927-30; Eastern mgr. This Week mag., 1934-48, advt. dir., 1949-54; dir. United Newspapers Mag. Corp., N.Y.C., 1949-64, pres. 1954-60, chairman board, 1960-64. Served as lt. AS, World War I. Mem. Kappa Alpha. Episcopalian. Clubs: Dutch Treat (N.Y.C.); Fairfield County Hunt (Westport, Conn.); Sharon Country. Home: Sharon, Conn. Died Jan. 4, 1975; interred Boland Dist. Cemetery, Sharon, Conn.

COWAN, CLYDE LORRAIN, educator, physicist; b. Detroit, Dec. 6, 1919; s. Clyde Lorraine and Esther M. (Koenig) C.; B.S., Mo. U., 1940; M.S., Washington U., 1947, Ph.D., 1949; D.Sc. (hon.), U. Dallas, 1962, U. Mo., 1972; m. Betty Eleanor Dunham, Jan. 29, 1943; children—Elizabeth (Mrs. John A. Riordon), Michael (dec. Aug. 1972), Marian, George. Group leader Los Alamos Sci. Lab., 1949-57; prof. physics George Washington U.. 1947, Cath. U. Am., 1948-74; cons. USN, USAF, A.E.C., industry. Served to capt., USAAF, 1942-46. Decorated Bronze Star; Guggenheim fellow, 1957. Fellow Am. Phys. Soc., A.A.A.S.; mem. Sigma Xi. Roman Catholic. Club: Cosmos (Washington). Author: (with Acosta and Graham) Essentials of Modern Physics, 1971; also articles. Patentee in field; discoverer with Reines of the neutrino, 1956. Home: Rockville, Md. Died May 24, 1974; interred Arlington National Cemetery, Arlington, Va.

COWART, HARRY MACIEMORE, corp. exec.; b. Midway, Ala., Aug. 8, 1880; s. William Jacob and Anna Corinne (Smith) J.; student pub. schs., Massey Bus. Coll.; m. Bessie Bishop, Nov. 12, 1902; children—James Harold, William Owen, Anne C. (Mrs. Edmundson). Chief clk., asst. supt. Semet-Solvay Co., 1898-1918; auditor, asst. sec. Ala. By-Products Corp., 1918-35, treas., 1935-49, v.p., 1949-1953, exec. v.p., dir. from 1953; exec. v.p., dir. Smokeless Fuel Co. from 1928. Methodists (steward). Clubs: Birmingham Comml., Uestavia Country. Home: Birmingham, Ala.†

COWDEN, HOWARD AUSTIN, business exec.; b. Pleasant Hope, Mo., May 18, 1893; s. John Porter and Margaret (Burns) C.; ed. Pleasant Hope High Sch., Southwest Mo. Teachers Coll. and U. of Mo.; LL.D. honoris causa, St. Francis Xavier Univ., 1950; m. Thelma Lundy, Nov. 1, 1917; children—Keith Lundy, John Henry; m. 2d, Edna May Reno, Apr. 23, 1932. Began as publ sch. teacher, 1914; mgr. Farm Club Exchange, Bolivar, Mo., 1919-20; sec. Mo. Farmers Assn., Columbia, Mo., 1920-29; pres. and gen. mgr. Consumers Cooperative Association, Kansas City, Mo., 1929-61, also subsidiaries Coop. Refinery Assn. Coops. Farm Chemicals Assn.; cons. Nationwide Mutual Ins. Columbus, O., 1961-69; owner, mgr. farm, Clinton County, Mo. Organizer, dir. Agrl. Coop. Devel. Internat. Sec. Internat. Coop. Petroleum Assn., N.Y.; central com. Internat. Coop. Alliance, London. Pres. Agricultural Hall of Fame, Kansas City, Mo. Breeder registered Herford cattle and imported landrace hogs. Served with S.A.T.C. World War I. Recipient Service to Agr. award Gamma Sigma Delta, 1967, Service to Mankind award Sertoma Internat., 1967, Outstanding Alumnus award S.W. Mo. State Coll., 1969, Citation of Merit award U. Mo. Alumnus Assn., 1972. Trustee Am. Inst. Coop., Ithaca. Mem. Citizens Planning Council (Kansas City, Mo.), Nat. Petroleum Council, Presbyn. (elder). Mason. Author pamphlet, numerous articles in various mags. and periodicals. Home: Kansas City, Mo. Died Dec. 27, 1972; interred Pleasant Hope (Mo.) Cemetery.

COWDERY, ROBERT HOLMES, mfr.; b. Ashtabula, O., Oct. 20, 1881; s. Warren Hervey and Harriet (Kelley) C.; B.S., Case Sch. Applied Science, Cleveland, O., 1903; m. Mabel Ordelia Belden, June 18, 1907; children—Edith, Robert, Richard, Betty. Water boy, later shipping clerk, machinist apprentice Ashtabula (O.) Tool Co., 1893-1903; draftsman Wellman, Seaver Engine Co., Cleveland, 1903-04; draftsman, later foreman, asst. factory mgr. Am. Fork & Hoe Co., mfrs. hand farm tools, sporting goods, railroad supplies, Cleveland, O., 1904-06, factory mgr., later advt. mgr., engr., Cleveland 1906-18, mgr. Geneva (O.) factory from 1918, v.p. and dir. sporting goods div. from 1930-39; v.p. and dir. Champion Hardware Co., Geneva, from 1937; dir. Geneva Savings & Trust Co. Mem. Phi Delta Theta. Clubs: Rotary (Geneva, O.); Golf and Country (Madison, O.); Grand River Yacht Club (Fairport, Ohio). Inventor of multi-blanking process for forks; also of true temper steel golf shaft. Retired from Apr. 1947. Home: Madison, O.†

COWDRY, EDMUND VINCENT, anatomist; b. MacLeod, Alta., Can., July 18, 1888; s. Nathaniel H. and Anna (Ingham) C.; A.B., U. Toronto, 1909; Ph.D., U. Chgo., 1913; D.Sc., Institutum Divi Thomae, Cin., 1957; m. Alice Hanford Smith, Dec. 20, 1916; children—Edmund Vincent, Alice Moira, Margaret Hanford. Came to U.S., 1909, naturalized, 1930. Asst. and asso. anatomy U. Chgo., 1909-13, Johns Hopkins, 1913-17; prof. Peking (China) Union Med. Coll., 1917-21; asso. mem. Rockefeller Inst., 1921-28; prof. cytology Washington U., 1928-41, anatomy, 1941-50; dir. Wernse Cancer Research Lab., 1950-60; dir. research Barnard Free Skin and Cancer Hosp., 1939-48; dir. research Sci. Assos., Inc., 1964; distinguished prof. Institutum Divi Thomae, 1958-75; Harvey lectr., 1923, Gross lectr., 1924, Delamar lectr., 1938, Christian Fenger lectr., 1948; vis. lectr. in oncology U. Cal., 1930. Cons. to USPHS, 1938-46, mem. carcinogenesis panel, 1961; cons. Rand Devel. Corp., 1961-64, Cancer Inst. Miami, 1955-59, VA, 1956-57. Point 4 adviser in cancer Govt. India, also ABMAC adviser Rep. of China, Formosa, 1952. Trustee Bermuda Biol. Sta., 1927-41. Patron, former mem. bd. dirs. Am. Cancer Soc., Nat. Cancer Found., Am. Assn. Cancer Research. Pres. Union Am. Biol. Socs., 1936-38, 4th Internat. Cancer Research Congress, 1947, 2d Internat. Gerontol. Congress, 1951. Am. Assn. Cancer Research, 1951, Gerontol. Soc., 1952, Internat. Assn. Gerontology, 1951-54. Hon. pres. 1st Pan-Am. Gerontol. Congress, 1956, 1st Pan-Am. Cancer Cytology Congress, 1957; pres. Internat. Symposium Cellular Chemistry, 1970. Vice pres. Am. Assn. Anatomists, Am. Soc. Naturalists, Sect. N. of A.A.A.S. Chmn. div. med. sci. NRC, 1930-31, Nat. Sci. Council, City of Hope, 1954-60, VA Adv. Com. on Aging, 1956-57. Mem. adv. com. Fels Inst. Child Devel., Internat. Com. Study Infantile Paralysis, Yellow Fever Commn. Rockefeller Found., Cancer Prevention Com., also various med. and sci. socs. Recipient Bobst award for outstanding work in gerontology, London, 1954, award Gerontol. Research Found., St. Louis, 1956; medal ministry of Edn., Republic China, 1959; Bertner Found. award, research in cancer, 1960, medal 64th meeting Japanese Assn. Anatomists, 1959, mil. decoration comdr.-in-chief Chinese Army, 1959, citation V. Internat. Congress Gerontology, 1960. Hon. fellow Royal Micros. Soc., Soc. de Cancerologia de Guadalajara, Argentine Gerontol. Soc., Soc. Philomanthique de Paris; mem. Nat. Geriatrics Soc. (hon.), Academica Sinica (corr.). Author books including: Cancer Cells, 1958 (Translated into Russian); (with Finerty) Textbook of Histology, 1960; (with Emmel) Laboratory Technique in Biology and Medicine, 1964; (with Lansing and others) Problems of Aging, 1952; Care of Geriatric Patient, 1962 (translated into Spanish); Aging Better, 1972. Editor, author publs. relating to field. Discoverer organism of heartwater, 1924, life cycle of East Coast fever parasite, 1930. Home: St. Louis, Mo. Died June 25, 1975.

COWGILL, GEORGE RAYMOND, physiologist, biochemist, nutritionist; b. St. Paul, Feb. 8, 1893; s. Frank Brooks and Ida Lillian (Hall) C.; student Hamline U., 1911-13; B.A., Stanford, 1916, grad. student, 1916-17; Ph.D., Yale, 1921; Sc.D. (Hon.), U. So. Cal. 1947, Hamline U., 1955; m. Alice May Fesler, Sept. 7, 1922 (dec. Dec. 1957); 1 dau., Barbara (Mrs. A.R. Perrins); m. 2d, Grace C. Deuel, Mar. 31, 1959. Pesearch in physiology and biochemistry, Sch. Medicine, Yale, 1920-60, successively asst. in physiol. chemistry, instr., asst. prof., asso. prof., prof. nutrition, 1944-60, emeritus prof. nutrition, 1960-73; adj. prof. biochemistry, nutrition U. So. Cal., Los Angeles, 1960-73; Smith-Reed-Russell lectr. George Washington U. Sch. Medicine, 1940; De Lamar lectr. Johns Hopkins U. Sch. Hygiene and Pub. Health, 1940. Mem. civilian adv. com. to Sec. Navy, 1946. Served to lt. U.S. Army, 1917-19, AEF. Mem. Conn. Citizens Food Com., 1947-48. Recipient Mead Johnson 1942 award for distinguished researches on vitamin B complex; Sci. award Grocery Mfrs. Am., 1948; Osborne and Mendel award Am. Inst. Nutrition, 1958. Mem. food and nutrition bd. NRC, 1940-46; mem. council on foods and nutrition A.M.A., 1938-59. Fellow A.A.A.S., Am. Inst. Chemists; N.Y. Acad. Sci., Am. Inst. Nutrition, Am. Pub. Health Assn.; mem. Am. Physiol. Soc., Am. Soc. Biol. Chemists, Soc. Exptl. Biol. and Med. (council, 1946), Am. Chem. Soc., Nat. Acad. Medicine Brazil, (hon. fgn.), Inst. Food Technologists, Phi Beta Kappa, Sigma Xi, Alpha Sigma Phi, Phi Chi. Republican. Author: The Vitamin B Requirement of Man, 1934; (with W. L. Marxer, George R. Cowgill) The Art of Predictive Medicine, 1967, also numerous sci. papers reporting researches. Mem. editorial bd. jour. of Nutrition, 1935-39, acting mng. editor, 1935-36, editor, 1939-59. Home: Pasadena, Cal. Died Apr. 12, 1973.

COWLES, DUDLEY REDWOOD, ednl. pub.; b. Cowlesville, Old Plantation home, near Williamsburg, Virginia, March 26, 1872; s. John and Harriet (Spencer) C.; ed. William and Mary Coll., Williamsburg, Va., 1895 (Brafferton medal for highest scholarship); LL.D. (hon.) College of William and Mary, 1948. m. Virginia Alan Spindle, Oct. 29, 1902. Supt. schs., Hampton, Va., 1895-1901; Southern rep. Silver, Burdett and Co., ednl. pubs., 1900-05; agency mgr. New York office same co., 1905-07; advt. mgr. D. C. Heath and Co., 1907-09; Southern mgr. D. C. Heath and Co. (Atlanta, Ga.), 1909-20, Southern mgr. and dir., 1920-27, Southern mgr. and sec., 1927-34, Southern mgr. and vice pres., 1934-37, pres., 1937-46, chmn. bd., 1946-51, hon. chmn., 1952-56, later dir. Pres. Am. Textbook Publishers, 1942-44. Member of staff of governor of Georgia, 1924-28. Recipient medallion from alumni William and Mary Coll., 1952. Member Phi Beta Kappa (president Georgia Association 1930-37), Pi Kappa Alpha, American Geographic Soc. Episcopalian. Mason. Clubs: Piedmont Driving, Capital City (Atlanta); The Country, Rotary (Brookline, Mass.). Home: Brookline, Mass.†

COWLES, PERCIVAL WILLIAM, pres. Automatic Fire Alarm Co.; b. Barton, Vt., Mar. 19, 1880; s. Ashahel Reed and Hattie E. (Titus) C.; B.C.S., New York U., 1911; m. Sarah Banta Cowles, of New York, N.Y., Nov. 10, 1923; children—Richard Carey, David Reed. Began as salesman, 1900; with Nat. Register Co., 1904-07, McCall Co., 1907-09; with Automatic Fire Alarm Co. from 1909, pres. from 1928; also pres. Consolidated Fire Alarm Co., Boston Automatic Fire Alarm Co., Automatic Bldg., Inc., Reeve Electrical Co.; dir. Gen. Fire Extinguisher Co. Trustee Orlean Co. (Vt.) Memorial Hosp. Mem. New York Chamber of Commerce, New York Board of Trade, Merchants Assn. of N.Y., Vt. Soc., Alpha Kappa Psi. Republican. Mem. Scarsdale Community Ch. Mason. Clubs: New York Athletic; Leewood Golf (Scarsdale, N.Y.). Home: New York, N.Y.†

COX, ALLEN, judge; b. Baldwin, Miss., Feb. 16, 1887; s. William M. and Forest (Allen) C.; B.A., Vanderbilt, 1909; m. Louise Norvell Jones, May 3, 1919; 1 dau., Mary Norvell. Admitted to Miss. bar, 1911, and began practice at Baldwyn; chancellor 1st Chancery Court, Dist. of Miss., 1923-29; U.S. dist. judge, Northern Dist. of Miss., 1929-57. Served with U.S. Army, World War. Mem. Beta Theta Pi. Democrat. Mem. Disciples of Christ Ch. Home: Baldwyn, Miss. Died Aug. 28, 1974.

COX, GEORGE BRYAN, educator; b. New Franklin, Mo., Sept. 24, 1896; s. George Barnett and Annie (Faris) C.; B.S., U. of Mo., 1919; grad. work, U. of Ill., summer 1920; U. of Wis., 1923-25; M.S., Ore. State Coll., 1940; m. Josephine Penniman, June 3, 1918; children—Mary Josephine (Mrs. J. H. Capps), George Bryan, Jr. Teacher, Indsl. Arts High Sch., Orange, Tex., 1919-20, Sam Houston State Teachers Coll., Huntsville, Tex., 1920-21; asst. prof. indsl. arts, U. of Wis., 1921-27; mem. faculty, Ore. State Coll., 1927-61, prof. indsl. arts and head dept., 1927-47, prof. indsl. engring. and indsl. arts, and head dept., 1947-61. Mem. Corvallis City Council, 1937-1951; chmn. finance com., 1939-48; mem. Corvallis Airport Commn., 1941-51. Mem. Am. Assn. Sch. Adminstrs., Am. Vocational Assn., Am. Indsl. Arts Assn., Nat. Indsl. Teacher-Trainers, N.E.A. Elk, Pythian. Author: Essentials of Woodworking (with I.S. Griffith), 1931; Woodwork for Secondary Schools, 1937; Carpentry, 1935. Contbr. numerous articles in ednl. and engring. publs. Home: Laguna Hills, Cal. Died Mar. 28, 1973.

COX, HUGH, lawyer; b. Logan, Ia., Sept. 3, 1905; s. William Riley and Caroline (Reel) C.; A.B., U. Neb., 1926; B.A., Christ Church, Oxford (Eng.) U., 1929, B.C.L., 1930; m. Ethelyn Ayres, Oct. 24, 1934. Admitted to N.Y. bar, 1933, lawyer with Root, Clark, Buckner & Ballantine, N.Y., 1930-35; spl. asst. to atty. gen., 1935-43; counsel for Dept. of Justice before Temp.

Nat. Econ. Com., 1938-39; asst. atty. gen., 1943, asst. solicitor gen., 1943-45; gen. counsel Surplus Property Adminstrn., 1945; practicing law, mem. firm Cleary, Gottlieb, Friendly & Cox, 1946, Covington & Burling, 1951. Dir. Chesapeake & Potomac Telephone Co. Mem. Phi Beta Kappa. Clubs: Cosmos, Metropolitan (Washington). Home: Alexandria, Va. Died Oct. 20, 1973; buried Ivy Hill Cemetery, Alexandria, Va.

COX, JAMES FRANKLIN, coll. prof.; b. McLeansboro, Ill., Apr. 2, 1878; s. Van Buren and Julia Minerva (Compton) C.; B.S., U. of Tex., 1904, A.M., 1911; student George Peabody Coll., 1919-20; m. Mary M. Hayes, July 28, 1910; children—Mary Goree, James Franklin, Margaret Minerva. Taught in rural schs., 1896-99; pres. Lingleville Christian Coll., 1904-08; prin. Midway (Tex.) Pub. Schs., 1912-13; pres. John Tarleton Agrl. Coll., 1913-19. pres. Abilene Christian Coll., 1911-12 and 1932-40, prof. of edn., 1920-24, dean, 1924-32, prof. Bible and edn. from June 1940. Mem. Tex. State Teachers Assn., Scholarship Socs. of the South. Democrat. Mem. Ch. of Christ. Home: Abilene, Tex.†

COX, JAMES MIDDLETON, JR., publisher; b. Dayton, O., June 27, 1903; s. James Middleton and Mary Simpson (Harding) C.; student Culver Mil. Acad., 1917-20, Cheshire (Conn.) Acad., 1922-24; Ph.B., Yale, 1928; m. Helen Rumsey, Nov. 21, 1930. Entered newspaper work, Dayton Daily News, 1929, gen. mgr., 1931-38, asst. pub., 1938-39, asst. pub. and v.p., 1939-49, dir., pres., 1949-56; pres. dir. Dayton Journal-Herald, 1948-56; vice chmn., pres. Dayton Newspapers, Inc., 1957-58, chmn., 1958; established Radio Sta. WHIO, Dayton, 1934, WSOC, Charlotte, WSB, Atlanta, WIOD, Miami, consol. with television properties and affiliated holdings to form Cox Broadcasting Corp., chmn., 1964; chmn. Cox Enterprises, Inc., 1968; dir. also numerous newspapers, Ohio, Atlanta, Ga., Miami, Palm Beach. Trustee U. Miami (Fla.). Served as lt. comdr. Naval A.S., U.S.N.R. active duty, 1942-45. Episcopalian. Clubs: Augusta National, Peachtree Golf (Ga.), Indian Creek, La Gorce (Miami); Moraine Country (Dayton, O.). Home: Dayton, O. Deceased.

COX, PHILIP WESCOTT LAWRENCE, educator; b. Malden, Mass., July 25, 1883; s. Alfred Elmer and Annie Adelaide (Bell) C.; B.A., Harvard, 1906, M.A., 1920; Ph.D., Columbia, 1925; grad. student U. of N.H., 1907; m. Ruth Dillaway, July 17, 1909; children—Philip Westcott Lawrence, Edward Dillaway, Nancy Ryder, Kenneth Faulkner (dec.). Asst. instr. in botany Harvard, 1905; tchr., and ednl. adminstrv. positions, 1905-20; headmaster Washington School of N.Y., 1920-22; prin. high sch. dept. Lincoln Sch. of Teachers Coll., New York City, 1922-23; prof. edn. New York Univ., 1923-49, emeritus prof., from 1949. Member National Education Assn. (ex-president dept. elementary education), National Association of Secondary Sch. Principals (ex-v.p.), National Soc. Coll. Teachers of Education (chmn. editorial com. 1937), Teachers' Ins. and Annuity Assn. (nominating com., 1926-27), Boy Scouts America (nat. council from 1930), Marthas Vineyard Assn., Kappa Sigma, Phi Delta Kappa, Kappa Delta Pi, Pi Gamma Mu. Clubs: Harvard (Martha's Vineyard); The Greeks (Maplewood). Author six books, 1925-38; Basic Principles of Guidance (with J. C. Duff and Marie McNamara), 1948. Asso. editor The Clearing House. Contbr. chpts. High School Curriculum (H. R. Douglas, editor), 1947. Home: Vineyard Haven, Mass., Died Nov. 28, 1975.

COXE, LEWIS CROCKER, naval officer; b. Annapolis, Md., Aug. 19, 1912; s. Lewis and Lilian (Crocker) C.; B.S., U.S. Naval Acad., 1934; B.C.E., Rensselaer Poly. Inst., 1938, M.C.E., 1939; m. Nancy Lesh, June 13, 1936; 1 son, Michael Paul Morgan. Commd. ensign, U.S. Navy, 1934, advanced through grades to rear adm. C.E., 1962; assigned Phila. Navy Yd., 1939-43, Naval Air Sta., Coco Solo, C.Z., also Iceland; comdg. officer Navy Advance Base Proving Ground, Davisville, R.I., 1943-44, 81st Naval Constrn. Bn., Okinawa, 1945; design mgr. Bur. Yards and Docks, 1945-49; pub. works officer Naval Shipyard, Long Beach, Cal., 1949-50; asst. dist. pub. works officer 11th Naval Dist., San Diego, 1950-51; comdg. officer Pub. Works Center, Guam, M.I., 1951-53; dist. pub. works officer Severn River Naval Command, 1953-57; asst. chief research, planning and design Bur. Yards and Docks, 1957-60, dir. European Mid-East div., London, 1960-62, insp. gen., asst. chief adminstrn. Bur. Yards and Docks, 1963, dir. Southwest division, dep. comdr. for acquisition Naval Facilities Engring. Command, Yards and Docks Annex, Arlington, Virginia Civil and structural engr., D.C. Mem. Am. Soc. C.E. (past chmn. exec. com., rivers and harbors div.), Soc. Am. Mil. Engrs. (nat. dir.), U.S. Naval Acad. Alumni Assn., Sigma Xi, Tau Beta Pi. Clubs: Army-Navy Country, Kiwanis (San Diego). Contbr. numerous articles profl. gov. publs. Home: Perry Point, Md. Died 1974.

COZART, REED, correctional cons.; b. Normangee, Tex., Apr. 8, 1904; s. William H. and Anna (Reed) C.; B.A., U. Tex., 1926, J.D., 1929; postgrad. St. Mary's U., San Antonio, 1938, Coll. William and Mary, 1939; m. Ruth Mae Bourn, July 17, 1931; 1 son, William Reed. Tchr., Rogers Prairie Sch., Madison County, Tex., 1921-22, Tivy High Sch., Kerrville, Tex., 1924-25; admitted to Tex. bar, 1929; with firm Morriss & Morriss, San Antonio, 1929-32; chief U.S. probation officer, San Antonio, 1932-40; asst. supr. classification Bur. Prisons, Washington, 1940; warden fed. correctional inst., Texarkana, Tex., 1941-42, Seagoville, Tex., 1945-52, LaTuna, Tex., Tex., 1956-57; asso. warden U.S. penitentiary, Leavenworth, Kan., 1942-45; dir. corrections for La., 1952-55; U.S. pardon atty., Washington, 1955-56, 58-68; cons. corrections br. U.S. Army, 1942-46, Sch. Continuing Edn., Am. U., 1966; cons. Am. Correctional Assn., 1968; bd. dirs., cons. Asso. Community Rehab. Enterprises, 1968-70. Chmn. Delinquency Crime Control Conf. Washington. Bd. dirs., pres., v.p. Council Council Chs. Alexandria; bd. dirs. Council Chs. Washington Met. Area, Alexandria Boys Club. Mem. Am. Correctional Assn. (bd. dirs.), Osborne Assn. (bd. dirs), Nat. Council Crime and Delinquency, Tex. Ex-students Assn., Internat. Platform Soc. Presbyn. (elder 1943, past deacon, trustee, chmn. ch. extension com.), Tex. com., Tex. Probation Assn. (pres.). Mason (32), Rotarian (v.p., dir.). Author articles. Home: San Antonio, Tex. Died Oct. 4, 1974; buried Mission Burial Park, San Antonio, Tex.

CRADDOCK, JOHN DERRETT, congressman; b. Munfordville, Ky., Oct. 26, 1881; s. Berry C. and Alice G. (McCarty) C.; ed. high sch.; m. Mary E. Craddock, Sept. 10, 1910; 1 son, John Derrett. Trainman, Panama R.R., 1904-10; farmer, tobacco grower, Hart Co., Ky., 1910-24; pres. Hart Co. Deposit Bank from 1924; dir. Burley Tobacco Growers Co-operative Marketing Served in Spanish-Am. War, Philippines and in Boxer Rebellion, China; chmn., all war activities, Hart Co., World War. Mem. 71st Congress (1929-31), 4th Ky. Dist. Mem. Ky. Mammoth Cave Nat. Park Commn. Mem. United Spanish War Vets. Republican. Methodist. Mason (Shriner). Home: Munfordville, Ky.†

CRAGO, ALFRED, counselor; b. England, Sept. 25, 1879; s. William John and Agnes (Beck) C.; came to U.S., 1881; derivative citizenship; A.B., Univ. Neb., 1905, A.M., 1916; Ph.D., Univ. Ia., 1930; m. Laura Monfort, July 31, 1913; children—Jean Monfort, John Alfred, Anne Elizabeth (Mrs. Rex King), Richard Leon. Supt. of schs., Tobias, Neb., 1905-08, Randolph, Neb.,1908-11; grad. work, U. of Neb., 1911-12; supt. sch. Central City, Nebraska, 1912-16; graduate work; Univ. of Neb., 1916-17; prof. of edn., Peru State Teacher College, Peru, Neb., 1917-28; grad. work, U. of Chicago, summers 1922, 23, 24, U. of Ia., 1928-29, member faculty Univ. of Fla., 1929-50, prof., ednl. psychology and measurements, 1929-50; dir., Univ. Vets. Guidance Center from 1945; counselor in private practice from 1950. Mem. National Society for Scientific Study of Edn., Am. Psychol. Assn. (asso.); Phi Kappa Phi. Presbyn. Club: Kiwanis. Splty.; Personality development in children. Home: Gainesville, Fla.†

CRAIG, ELISABETH MAY, newspaper corr.; b. Coosaw, S.C.; d. Alexander and Elisabeth Anne (Essery) Adams; grad. high sch.; L.H.D. (hon.) U. Me., 1946; m. Donald Alexander Craig (dec.); children—Donald Alexander, Betty (Mrs. Albert A. Clagett). Began regular newspaper writing, 1924; has been corr. for N.Y., N.C. and Mont. newspapers; Washington corr. for Portland (Me.) Press Herald, Evening Express, Sunday Telegram, Waterville Sentinel, Kennebee Jour. (all Me.); Wash. corr. for stas. WGAN, WGAN-TV and radio stas. in Me. War corr., World War II, Korea. Contbr. feature articles to mags. and newspapers. "Meet the Press" program on radio and television. Elected to standing com. Press Galleries, Congress, 1944-46. Recipient Achievement in Journalism. Nat. Council Auxiliaries Am. Med. Center. Denver; Woman of Achievement, Fedn. Soroptimist Clubs; Outstanding Service citation Am. Legion; Distinguished Service award Nat. Fedn. Bus. and Profl. Women's Clubs. Mem. Wash. Newspaper Guild (dir.), Soc. Women Geographers, Nat. Acad. TV Arts and Scis., Theta Sigma Phi. Clubs: Women's Nat. Press (mem. bd. govs., pres. 1943) Overseas Press of Am., American Women in Radio and Television, Inc., Am. Newspaperwomen's. Home: Washington, D.C. Died July 15, 1975.

CRAIG, HARDIN, JR, educator; b. at Fitchburg, Mass., July 17, 1907; s. Hardin and Gertrude (Carr) C.; A.B., Princeton, 1929; A.M., Harvard, 1931, Ph.D., 1937; m. Raemond Wilson, June 11, 1937; children—Greer Wilson, John Hardin. Instr. history Hobart Coll., 1931-33; instr. history Cal. Inst. Tech., 1937-40, asst. prof., 1940-46; asso. prof. history Rice U., Houston, 1946-50, prof., 1950-71, librarian, 1953-68; faculty Munson Inst. Am. Maritime History, Mystic Seaport, Conn., 1968-70. Mem. Am. Assn. U. Profs., Am. Marine hist. assns., A.L.A., U.S. Naval Inst., Navy League U.S. Home: Houston, Tex., Died June 28, 1971; buried Glenwood Cemetery, Ashby, Mass.

CRAIG, JUBAL EARLY, lawyer; b. San Francisco, May 31, 1874; s. William and Ruth Hairston (Thompson) C.; B.L., U. Va., 1895; m. Marie Craig, 1907 (dec. July 10, 1946); children—Lucille M. (Mrs. Malcolm C. Heffelman), Marie Ruth (Mrs. Roy M. Tait), Walter Early; m. 2d, Naomi K. Gibson, Oct. 16, 1954. Admitted to Va. and Cal. bars, 1895, Ariz., 1919; practiced law, San Francisco, 1895-1919, Phoenix, from 1919, with Fennemore, Craig, von Ammon & Udall, from 1927, sr. mem., from 1948. Fellow Am. Bar Found.; mem. Am. Bar Assn. (gen. council, ho. dels, 1935-45); State Bar Cal., State Bar Ariz. (bd. govs. 1933-34). Clubs: Arizona, Phoenix Country, Kiva (Phoenix). Home: Phoenix Ariz.†

CRAIG, LYMAN C., research chemist; b. Palmyra, Ia., June 12, 1906; s. Coy and Anna (Kitchell) C.; B.S., Ia. State Coll., 1928, Ph.D., 1931; Nat. Research fellow Johns Hopkins, 1931-33; D.Sc., Northwestern U., 1973; m. Rachel Parker, Nov. 25, 1937; children—Anna, David, Mary-Elizabeth. Asst. dept. chem. pharmacology Rockefeller U., N.Y.C., 1933-37, asso., 1937-45, asso. mem., 1945-49, mem., 1949-74, also prof. Recipient Lasker award for basic med. research, 1963; Fisher award analytical chemistry Am., Chem. Soc., 1966, Kolthoff medal Am. Pharm. Assn., 1971, Alumni Merit award Ia. State U., 1972, Benedetti-Pichler award Am. Microchem. Soc., 1972, award Soc. Scholars, Johns Hopkins, 1974. Mem. Harvey Soc., Nat. Acad. Scis., Am. Acad. Arts and Scis., Am. Chem. Soc., Am. Assn. Biol. Chem., A.A.A.S., N.Y. Acad. Scis., Am. Inst. Chemists, Sigma Xi, Phi Lambda Upsilon. Contbr. articles to chem. jours. Home: Glen Rock, N.J. Died July 7, 1974; interred Pennsdale, Pa.

CRAIG, PAUL FREDERICK, newspaper editor; b. Worcester, Mass., Feb. 23, 1896; s. Frederick T. and Elizabeth (Shorey) C.; B.S., Wesleyan U., Middletown, Conn., 1918; L.H.D., Am. Internat. Coll., Springfield, Mass., 1957; m. Louise M. Garbe, 1924. With Springfield Union, from 1918, mng. editor, from 1931, editor, from 1940; pres., dir. Springfield Union Publishing Co.; dir. Republican Publishing Co., The Republican Co., Atlas Tack Corp. Pres. Springfield, Adult Edn. Council; incorporator Am. Internat. Coll., Wesson Meml. Hosp. Served to maj. AUS, 1943-46. Decorated Bronze Star. Mem. Am. Soc. Newspaper Editors, N.E. Soc. Newspaper Editors. Republican. Conglist. Club: Longmeadow Country. Home: Longmeadow, Mass. Died Feb. 21, 1974.

CRAIG, ROBERT B., business executive; b. at Scotland, Pa., Oct. 9, 1900; s. William Love and Emma (Kyner) C.; Shippensburg Teachers Coll., 1915-19, B.S. in Edn., Ohio State Univ., 1927, M.A., 1930, post-grad. work, 1931-33; m. Mary Hester Savage, June 15, 1925; 1 dau., Anastasia. Teacher, 1919-21, 1925-26; gen. constrn. work, 1922-23; asst. to dir. of recreation, Columbus, O., 1923-25; with Rural Electrification Adminstrn. as training supervisor, personnel dir., asst. to adminstr., 1936-39, acting adminstr. June-Oct. 1939; deputy adminstr., 1939-43, asso. with Copperweld Steel Co., 1943-46; vice pres. Mannington Pottery Co., 1946; vice pres., treas. Water Systems, Inc., Washington; asst. to pres. Fairbanks, Morse & Co., 1952-54, v.p. 1954-62; dir. sales research Nordberg Mfg. Co., 1962-65. First v.p. Spain-U.S. C. of C., Ind., 1959. Member of Am. Hist. Assn., Phi Delta Kappa. Address: Scotland, Pa., Died Feb. 12, 1973.

CRAIN, G.D., JR., bus. publs. exec. Chmn. bd. Crain Communications, Inc., publishers Advt. Age, Indsl. Marketing, Bus. Ins., Pensions & Investments, Am. Laundry Digest, Am. Drycleaner, Am. Coin-op, Am. Clean Car Automotive News, Rubber and Plastics News, Crain Books. Address: Chicago, Ill. Died Dec. 15, 1973.

CRAIN, JAMES KERR, army officer; b. Hallettsville, Tex., Aug. 28, 1879; s. William Henry and Angeline Genevieve (Mitchell) C.; B.S., U.S. Mil. Acad., 1904; hon. grad. Coast Arty. Sch., 1915; grad. Army War Coll., 1926; m. Catharine Mary Nicholls, Nov. 26, 1912; children—Mary Genevieve, Catharine Barry. Commd. 2d lt., U.S. Army, 1904, and advanced through the grades to brigadier general (temporary), October 1939, major general, November 1942; served in Coast Artillery Corps, 1904-17; served as major, advancing to col. (temp.), with 42d (Rainbow) Div., 1st corps and 2d army, as chief ordnance officer; with A.E.F. and Army of Occupation, 1917-21; commd. Picatinny Arsenal, 1926-30; Office of Asst. Sec. of War, 1930-34; Office Chief of Ordnance, 1939-42; chief, field service, 1940-42; U.S. Exec., London Munitions Assignment Bd., 1942-45. Awarded Distinguished Service medal with oak leaf cluster, Victory medal, Legion of Merit, Companion of the Bath. Home: Washington, D.C.†

CRAMBLET, WILBUR HAVERFIELD, publisher; b. Harrison County, O., July 10, 1892; s. Thomas Ellsworth and Della Stella (Weaver) C.; B.Pd., Bethany (W.Va.) Coll., 1910, A.B., A.M., 1910, D.D., 1952; A.M., Yale, 1911, Ph.D., 1913; LL.D., University of Pittsburgh, 1945, Culver Stockton Coll., 1956; D.D., Drake U., 1955; D.Lit., Texas Christian University, 1958; m. Mildred Margaret Barnacle, Aug. 12, 1914; children—Thomas Ellsworth, Wilbur Haverfield, Joan Anthony. Began as instr. mathematics, U. of Rochester, 1913; prof. mathematics, Phillips U., 1915-17; prof. mathematics, Bethany Coll., 1917-34, dean, 1918-20, treas. 1919-50, sec. bd. trustees, 1929-32; pres. Bethany Coll., 1934-52; pres. Christian Bd. Publ., Disciples of Christ, from 1952. Served in S.A.T.C., Plattsburg, 1918. Pres. Bd. of Higher Edn. Disciples of Christ, 1937-41. Fellow A.A.A.S.; mem. Am. Math. Soc., Alpha Sigma. Phi (past national president). Republican. Member Disciples of Christ Ch. Mason (33°). Club: Missouri Athletic (St. Louis). Died Nov. 5, 1975.

CRANDELL, A. WILLIAM, dean of faculties Coll. of Arts and Sciences, Loyola U., New Orleans. Mem. Soc. of Jesus, ordained priest Roman Catholic Ch. Address: New Orleans, La. Died July 29, 1973.

CRANE, LEO, author, U.S. Indian agt.; b. Baltimore, Md., Feb. 27, 1881; s. William Joseph and Mary (Kailer) C.; ed. pub. schs.; m. Mrs. Walbridge Padgett, mining woman and journalist, of Ariz., Mar. 18, 1922. Commercial work 5 yrs.; newspaper work 2 yrs.; with Indian Bur., Washington, D.C., 7 yrs.; moved to Ariz., 1910; reprsentative Indian Service in settlement of Hopi Indian troubles, at Hotevilla, Ariz., 1911; Indian agt. for Moqui Reservation, Northern Ariz., 1911-19, representing Hopi and Navajo Indians; in charge historic pueblos of Walpi, Oraibi, etc., scene of annual Hopi Snake dances; Indian agt. for the Pueblo Indians of New Mexico, 1919-22, having charge of historic pueblos of Acoma, Laguna, Isleta, Cochiti, Santo Domingo, San Felipe, etc.; Indian agt. for Lower Yanktonai Sioux, S. Dak., 1922; and for Mohave and Chemehuevi Indians of the Colorado River and Ft. Mohave reservations in lower Colorado River Valley, Ariz., 1922-25 (area to be reclaimed under proposed Colorado River development); resigned from Govt. work, June 1925, after 22 yrs'. service, having spent 15 years in Southwest desert region in direct charge of Indians; served as agt. for 6 Indian tribes (14,000 persons) located in five states; exec. sec. Ariz. State Prison, 1931-32; supt. Indian camps, Navajo Desert (Emergency Conservation Work), 1933-35; Library work, U. of Ariz., 1937; Guide Service U.S. Bureau of Reclamation, Boulder Dam, from 1937. Specially known for knowledge of the Navajo and pueblo-type of natives in N.M. and Northern Ariz. Author: Indians of the Enchanted Desert, 1925; Desert Drums, 1928; also author of about 165 short stories and articles invarious Am. mags. Home: Greaterville, Ariz.†

CRANE, VERNER WINSLOW, prof. Am. history; b. Tecumseh, Mich., Aug. 28, 1889; s. Theodore Horace and Bricena (Chadwick) C.; A.B., U. of Mich., 1911; Master of Arts, Harvard, 1912; Ph.D., University of Pennsylvania, 1915. Harrison research fellow, 1916; m. Jane Harris, 1915 (dec. 1953); 1 son, Theodore Rawson; m. 2d Margaret Vining Van Duren, 1958. Instructor in history, Univ. of Mich., 1916-20; asst. prof. history, Brown, 1920-25, asso. prof., 1925-30; prof. Am. history University of Michigan, 1930-59, prof. emeritus, 1959-74. Henry Russel lecturer, 1957-58; visiting lecturer in history, Harvard, 1925-26, 1928-29; Colver lecturer, Brown Univ., 1935; Commonwealth Fund lectr. Univ. Coll., London, 1957; mem. council Inst. Early Am. History, 1958-61. Mem. American Hist. Assn., Miss. Valley Hist. Assn., R.I. Hist. Society, Phi Beta Kappa; corr. mem. Colonial Soc. Mass.; hon. mem. Old Colony Hist. Soc. Author: Southern Frontier, 1670-1732, 1928; Benjamin Franklin: Englishman and American, 1936; Benjamin Franklin and a Rising People, 1954. Mem. bd. editors Am. Hist. Review, 1928-34, Miss. Valley Hist. Review, 1938-39. Editor: Benjamin Franklin's Letters to the Press, 1758-1775, 1950. Contbr. to hist. jours. Home: Ann Arbor, Mich. Died Dec. 11, 1974; buried Botsford Cemetery, Ann Arbor.

CRAWFORD, HARRY CLEMENT, mgr. of transportation; b. South Bend, Ind., Mar. 25, 1881; s. Robert Clement and Mary (Matthews) C.; ed. schools in South Bend, Cleveland High Sch., and business coll.; m. Sarah Hazlette Crawford, Oct. 9, 1912; children—Harry C., Helen (Mrs. Thomas D. Boak), John S., William W. Began with Carnegie Steel Co.; special agent Cambria Steel Co., 1914, eastern traffic mgr. and traffic mgr., 1915; traffic mgr. Midvale Steel and Ordnance Co., 1916; asst. gen. traffic mgr. Bethlehem Steel Co., 1923, traffic mgr., 1927, gen. traffic mgr., 1937, vice pres., 1947 dir. from 1947. Mem. Am. Iron and Steel Inst. (chmn. traffic com. 1934-47) (New York); Racquet, Traffic (Phila.); Duquesne, Traffic (Pittsburgh); Bethlehem and Saucon Valley Country (Bethlehem, Pa.). Home: Bethlehem, Pa.†

CRAWFORD, J(AMES) C(HAMBERLAIN), entomologist; b. West Point, Neb., Aug. 24, 1880; s. James Chamberlain and Katherine (Moore) C.; grad. High Sch., West Point, 1896; student U. grad. High Sch., West Point, 1896; student U. of Neb., 5 ½ years to 1902; (M.Sc., George Washington Univ., 1914); m. Emily Baker, of Washington, D.C., Apr. 30, 1913. Agt. and expert, Bur. of Entomology, U.S. Dept. of Agr., 1904-07; asst. curator, 1911-19; specialist in parasitic hymenoptera. Dept. of Agr., 1919. Fellow A.A.A.S.; mem. Entomol. Soc. America, Entomol. Soc. Washington, Deutsche Entomologische Gesellschaft, Assn. Econ. Entomologists. Club: Cosmos. Author of numerous articles on Hymenoptera; devotes time to parasitic forms and bees, with the Chalcidoidea as a specialty. Address: Washington, D.C.†

CRAWFORD, MILO HICKS, lawyer; b. Crawford Corners, Venango County, Pa., Aug. 12, 1880; s. Carlisle Jennings and Mary Montgomery (McClelland) C.; LL.B., U. of Michigan, 1909; LL.D., Marietta (Ohio) College, 1951; married Maurine Graham, May 27, 1914 (died July 20, 1947); 1 dau., Betty Jane (Mrs. Arthur J. Brandt, Jr.). Bank clerk Peoples Nat. Bank, East Brady, Pa., 1900-02; with Franklin Trust Co., Pa., 1902-06; attended Law School, University of Michigan, 1906-09; admitted to Michigan bar, 1909; connected with Kenna, Lightner & Oxtoby (now Crawford, Sweeny & Dodd), Detroit, head of firm from 1932; secretary and director National Broach & Machine Company (machine tool company) since formation in 1929; trustee and treas. of Mich. Children's Aid Society from 1927. Mem. Am., Mich. State and Detroit bar assns.; mem. Internat. Assn. of Insurance Counsel (pres. 1938-39), Phi Alpha Delta. Republican. Presbyterian. Clubs: Detroit Athletic, Detroit Golf. Home: Detroit, Mich.†

CRAWFORD, WILLIAM WALT, lawyer; b. Louisville, Ky., Sept. 2, 1878; s. William W. and Mary (McCallum) C.; student U. of Louisville, 1899-1901; m. Mary LaClaire Lovelace, Sept. 23, 1903; children—Malcolm, Lorraine (Mrs. M. G. Whitley). Admitted to Kentucky bar, 1901, then in practice of law; mem. Crawford, Middleton, Milner & Seelbach from 1918; pres. Emmart Packing Co.; v.p. and dir. Bourbon Stock Yards, Merchants Ice & Cold Storage Co.; dir. First Nat. Bank, Ky. Title Trust Co. Mem. Am., Ky. State and Louisville bar assns. Republican. Episcopalian. Clubs: Pendennis, Country (Louisville). Home: Louisville, Ky.†

CRAYTON, JENKINS STREET, banker; b. Charleston, S.C., July 29, 1928; s. Maxwell Sloan and Juanita Jenkins (Street) C.; B.S. cum laude, Coll. Charleston, 1949; m. Betty Jane Goldsmith, Oct. 29, 1960; children—Jenkins Street, William G. With Citizens & So. Nat. Bank of S.C., Charleston, 1953-72, pres. computer subisidary, 1968-69, sr. operations officer, v.p., 1969-72. Instr. Am. Inst. Banking, 1961, 69, 70, 71. Chmn. budget com. Charleston United Fund, 1966. Served with AUS, 1950-52. Mem. Alpha Tau Omega, Sigma Alpha Phi. Rotarian. Home: Columbia, S.C., Died June 10, 1972.

CREAN, ROBERT, playwright; m. Kate Crean; 9 children. Author: (plays) A Time to Laugh, 1962; My Father and My Mother, 1968. Address: Larchmont, N.Y. Died May 6, 1974.

CREASEY, JOHN, author; b. Surrey, Eng., Sept. 17, 1908; s. Joseph and Ruth (Creasey) C.; ed. elementary and secondary schs., London; m. Margaret Cooke, 1935 (div. 1939); m. 2d Evelyn Jean Fudge, Feb. 16, 1941 (div. 1970); children—Colin, Martin John, Richard John; m. 3d, Jeanne Williams, 1970 (div. 1973); m. 4th, Diana Hamilton Farrell, May 1973. Author novels, 1932-73, total being 552 pub. in Eng., 250 pub. in U.S.; author Gideon series under pseudonymn J.J. Marric, 1955-73, West Toff series, also series under pseudonymns Anthony Morton, Jeremy York, Gordon Ashe, others; also author motion picture scripts, travel books. Chmn. fund raising coms. for famine relief and refugee orgns. Liberal Party candidate for Bournemouth Constituency, 1950; mem. Brit. Liberal Party Council, 1945-50; founder All Party Alliance Movement Gt. Britain, 1966. Decorated mem. Order Brit. Empire; recipient Best Crime Novel award Mystery Writers Am. (pres. 1966-67). Clubs: Paternosters (chmn. 1960) Nat. Liberal, Royal Automobile (London); Westeners (Tucson). Home: Bodenham, nr. Salisbury, England. Died June 9, 1973; buried Bodenham Churchyard, Eng.

CREASY, WILLIAM NEVILLE, business exec.; b. Bournemouth, Eng., Mar. 8, 1908; s. Frederick Kenwood and Alice Mary (Palethrop) C.; Pharm. B., U. Toronto, 1929; m. Edith Margaret Shore, Aug. 1939; children—William Neville, Robert K. with Burroughs Wellcome & Co. (U.S.A.), Inc., 1938-74, pres., gen. mgr., 1945-68, chmn., 1948-68; mgr. Burroughs Wellcome & Co., Can.. 1942-45; pres. Burroughs Wellcome Fund, 1955-74. Bd. dirs. U. Toronto Assos.; trustee Nat. Kidney Found.; bd. dirs., treas. Royal Soc. Medicine Found.; mem. bd. grants Am. Found. Pharm. Edn.; bd. dirs. Am. Allergy Found. Fellow Royal Soc. Medicine (hon.). Clubs: Saint Andrew's Golf; Canadian (N.Y.C.); Seigniory, Mahopac Curling. Home: Bronxville, N.Y. Died Aug. 27, 1974; interred Avondale Cemetery, Stratford, Ont., Can.

CREEK, HERBERT LESOURD, univ. prof.; b. Yeoman, Ind., Jan. 21, 1879; s. Moses and Martha (LeSourd) C.; student De Pauw U., 1894-95, 1896-98; A.B., A.M., Butler Coll., 1905, Litt.D., 1941; studied U. of Chicago, 1907-08; Ph.D., U. of Ill., 1910; m. Anna LeOne Fisher, Oct. 16, 1901; children—Kenneth Fisher (dec.), Ronald Fisher. Fellow in English, U. of Ill., 1908-10, instr. in English, 1910-14, asso. in English, 1914-19, asst. prof., 1919-20, U. of Ill.; prof. English and head of dept., Purdue U., 1920-49, prof. emeritus from 1949, acting head, 1949-50. Member Modern Language Assn. America, Am. Assn. Univ. Profs., Am. Soc. for engring Edn., College English Assn., Delta Upsilon. Methodist. Club: Optimist. Editor (with Mrs. Alta Gwinn Saunders) The Literature of Business (5th edit., 1946); The Best of Carlyle, 1929. Author: (with H. M. Baldwin and J. H. McKee) A Handbook of Modern Writing, 1930. Home: Lafayette, Ind.†

CRESSON, MARGARET FRENCH, sculptor; b. Concord, Mass., Aug. 3, 1889; d. Daniel Chester and Mary Adams French; ed. Clarke Pvt. Sch., and Brearley Sch. (both N.Y.C.); m. William Penn Cresson, Jan. 10, 1921 (dec. May 1932). Studied under Daniel Chester French, Abastenia St. Leger Eberle and George Demetrios. Works include bronze busts, bronze reliefs, portrait heads, and meml. plaques. Exhibited Paris Salon, N.Y. World's Fair. Mem. N.A.D. Founde Chesterwood Studio Mus., trustee Daniel Cheste French Found.; trustee Chesterwood Studic Stockbridge, Mass., St. Gaudens Meml., Cornish, N.H Berkshire Mus. Pittsfield, Mass. Nat. Academician Fellow Nat. Sculpture Soc. (sec. 1940-41); mem. Archtl League N.Y. (2d v.p. 1944-46), N.A.D., Allied Artist Am., Audubon Artists, Grand Central Art Galleries c N.Y., Winner Shaw Meml. prize N.A.D., 1927; hon mention Jr. League Exhbn., N.Y.C., 1928; Soc Washington Artists. Corcoran Gallery of Art, 1929 Crowninshield Sculpture prize and Popular prize Stockbridge Art Exhbn., 1929; bronze medal Soc Washington Artists, 1937; hon. mention, Stockbridge Art Exhbn., 1938; Popular prize Dublin Hill Art Show 1939; Popular prize Contemporary Am. Masters, 1944 Grand Nat. Gold medal Am. Artist Profl. League, 1959 Author: Journey Into Fame, 1947; Daniel Cheste French, 1949; Laurel Hill, 1953. Contbr. articles on ar and artists to Reader's Digest, Am. Heritage, N.Y Times Sunday mag. Home: Stockbridge, Mass. Diec Oct. 1, 1973.

CRESWELL, MARY E., dean of home econ.; born Ansonville, Pa., Oct. 15, 1879; d. Alexander Evans and Helena (Nevling) C.; student Johnson Inst., 1897-1900, State Normal Sch., 1900-02, Univ. of Chicago, Columbia U., 1936; B.S. in Home Economics, Univ. of Ga., 1919; study tour in Eng., 1929. Public sch. teacher, 1901; critic teacher, Ga. State Normal Sch., 1902-11; extension service Ga. State Coll. of Agr., 1911-13; field agt. for Southern States, U.S. Dept. of Agr., 1913-18; dir. home economics, Univ. of Ga., 1918-32, dir. and dean Sch. of Home Economics 1932-46; dean emeritus and professor, from Sept. 1946; as specialist, conducted a land grant college survey in seven states for U.S. Dept. Interior, Bur. of Edn., summer of 1928; editor, Home Dept., Southern Ruralist, 1922-25. Mem. Nat. Purnell Com. on Research, 1925-26. Del. to White House Conf. on Child Health and Protection; del. to Merrill Palmer Conf. Awarded nat. certificate of recognition Epsilon Sigma Phi, 1936; on founders roll. Associated Country Women of World, London. Mem. State and Nat. home econ. assns., Ga. Edn. Assn., U. Ga. Alumni Soc. (mem. bd. mgrs.), Phi Kappa Phi, Phi Upsilon Omicron, Epsilon Sigma Phi. Contbr. to tech. bulletins and professional jours. Home: Athens, Ga.†

CRIDER, BLAKE, psychologist; b. Personville, Tex., Aug. 7, 1902; s. Allen Blake and Delia (Newsome) C.; B.A., U. No., 1924; M.A., U. Chgo., 1928; Ph.D., Western Res. U., 1933; m. Doris Towne, June 15, 1932; children—Andrew Blake, Harlan Towne. Tchr. Orange (Tex.) High Sch., 1924-26; instr. psychology Albion (Mich.) Coll., 1926-29; psychologist Shaker Heights (O.) Schs., 1929-31; staff psychologist psychiat. pediatric clinics St. Luke's Hosp., Mt. Sinai Mental Hygiene Clinic, Cleve. State Hosp., Windsor Sanitarium, Behavior Day Nursery Assn., Cleve., 1933-50; prof. psychology Cleve. State U., 1934-70, emeritus, 1970-74; pvt. practice psychotherapy. Certified psychologist N.Y., Ohio. Diplomate Am. Bd. Examiners in Psychology, Ohio Psychology Assn., Am. Bd. Examiners in Clin. Hypnosis. Fellow Am. Psychol. Assn.; mem. Internat. Soc. Comprehensive Medicine, Soc. for Sci. Study Sex, Internat. Soc. Clin. and Exptl. Hypnosis, Cleve. Inst. for Gestalt Therapy, Am. Acad. Psychotherapists, Nat. Assn. Standard Med. Vocabulary, Asociacion de Charros de Ajijic (Jalisco, Mexico), Inter-Am. Psychol. Assn., Soc. Clin. and Exptl. Hypnosis, Phi Delta Kappa, Alpha Tau Omega. Contbr. sci. articles to profl. jours. Home: Cleveland, O. Died Jan. 3, 1974.

CRIMI, JAMES ERNEST, coll. pres.; b. Toledo, Aug. 27, 1916; s. Ernest and Bertha (Kraft) C.; B.A., Aurora (Ill.) Coll., 1938; M.A., U. So. Cal., 1941; Ph.D., U. Chgo., 1959; m. Pauline Crouse, Apr. 14, 1943; children—Ann, Martha, Stephen. Mem. faculty Aurora (Ill.) Coll., 1941, successively instr., prof. sociology, registrar, 1946-55, dean of coll., 1955-62, pres., 1962-73. Bd. dirs. W. Suburban Intercollegiate Council, Mental Health and Retardation Services, Inc.; bd. govs. Copley Meml. Hosp. Served to capt. AUS, World War II. Mem. Asso. Colls. Ill. (past chmn.), Aurora C. of C. (past dir.), Am. Sociol. Soc., Adult Edn. Assn., N.E.A. Author: Adult Education in the Liberal Arts Coll. (pamphlet), 1957. Home: Aurora, Ill. Died Sept. 27, 1973; buried Aurora, Ill.

CRISP, ARTHUR, artist; b. Hamilton, Ont., Can., Apr. 26, 1881; s. Alfred C. and Ella (Watkins) C.; ed. Art Students' League, New York, pupil of Bryso Burroughs and F.V. Du Mond; m. Grace Ackerman, Aug. 9, 1922. Instr. in drawing, Cooper Inst., New York; v.p. Art Students' League, 1904. Collaborative prize, Architectural League of New York, 1914; first Hallgarten prize, N.A.D., 1916; bronze medal, Panama P.I. Expn., 1915; gold medal mural painting, Arch. League, 1920. Mem. N.Y.C. Art Commn., 1949-51. Dir. mural painting, Beaux Arts Sch. of Design, 1917, 18, 19; instr. drawing Art Students' League; instr. in mural painting, Nat. Acad. Design. Mem. Nat. Soc. Mural Painters (v.p.), Architl. League N.Y. (v.p., 1918-20), Am. Water Color Soc., New York Water Color Club, Nat. Arts Club, Nat. Acad. of Design. Pres. Artists for Victory. Club: Lotos (N.Y.C.). Home: Biddeford, Me.†

CRISP, DONALD, actor; b. London, Eng.; ed. London, and Oxford U. Came to U.S., 1906. Appeared in grand opera, 1 yr.; became stage dir. for Cohan and Harris; began screen career with Biograph, actor, 2 yrs., later being asst. to David Wark Griffith; appeared in Birth of a Nation and in Broken Blossoms; dir. The Cop, Stand and Deliver, Dress Parade, The Runaway Bridge; had roles in The River Pirate, The Pagan, Trent's Last Case, The Return of Sherlock Holmes, The Laird in "Svengali," with John Barrymore; appeared in The Crime Doctor, The Little Minister, The Life of Vergie Winters, What Every Woman Knows, The Key, 1934; Vanessa, Her Love Story, Mutiny on the Bounty, Laddie, Oil for the Lamps of China, 1935; The White Angel, Charge of the Light Brigade, The Great O'Malley, Mary of Scotland, A Woman Rebels, Beloved Enemy, 1936; Parnell, The Life of Emile Zola, Confession, That Certain Woman, Sergeant Murphy, 1937; The Beloved Brat, Jezebel, The Amazing Clitterhouse, Valley of the Giants, The Sisters, Dawn Patrol, Comet Over Broadway, 1938; Wuthering Heights, Juarez, Daughters Courageous, The Old Maid, Private Lives of Elizabeth and Essex, 1939, How Green Was My Valley, National Velvet. Died May 25, 1974.

CRITES, LOWRY HYER, food mfg. co. exec.; b. Lawton, Okla., July 21, 1906; s. Cloyd Clayton and Jewell (Hyer) C.; student Midwestern U., Wichita Falls, Tex., 1926, U. Okla., 1929; m. Mary Jane Nelson, May 23, 1931; 1 dau., Jane Ann (Mrs. John W. Ellicott, Jr.). With Gen. Mills, Inc., 1929-71, gen. mgr. grocery products div., 1961-71, v.p., 1958-71, administrator consumer food activities, 1964-71, dir., 1965-71. Dir. Cereal Inst. Mem. Kappa Alpha (So.). Clubs: Minneapolis Golf, University. Home: Minneapolis, Minn. Died June 14, 1974; interred Mpls.

CROCKETT, FRANKLIN SMITH, surgeon; b. Logansport, Ind., Mar. 22, 1881; s. Franklin Smith and Sarah Ann (Murdock) C.; Ph.G., Purdue U., 1900; M.D., Ind. Med. Coll., 1903; post grad study, St. Peter's Hosp., London, Eng., 1914; m. Bird Goslee, Dec. 14, 1910 (died Aug. 15, 1932); children—Katheryn Goslee, Nancy Ann; married second, Henrietta Coleman, January 2, 1937 (deceased, February 6, 1951). Interne Indianapolis City Dispensary, 1903-04; physician and surg., Lafayette, Ind., from 1905; meat and milk insp., Lafayette, Ind., 1910-13; mem. Ind. State Bd. med. exam., 1928-34; genito-urinary Ind. State Bd. med. exam., 1928-34; genito-urinary surg., St. Elizabeth's Hosp., 1920, Lafayette Home Hosp., 1920 (pres. staff, 1926); genito-urinary surgeon, Arnett-Crokett Clinic, 1922-37; consultant urology, selective service system, Lafayette, Ind., 1942-45. Dir. Mut. Med. Ins., Inc., 1946. Served as capt., M.C., U.S. Army, World War I. Chmn. com. civic and indsl. relations, gov.'s commn. on Unemployment Relief; mem. adv. com. to Surgeon Gen. Pub. Health Service to adminster Hill-Burton hosp. constrn. law. Dir. med. edn. St. Elizabeth's Hosp.; mem. bd. mgrs. William Ross Sanatorium. Diplomate American Board of Urology. Fellow Am. Coll. Surgeons; mem. Midwestern Agrl. Workers Assn. (pres.), A.M.A. (mem. house of dels. from 1929, mem. coms., chmn. com. rural med. service, 1945), Ind. Med. Assn. (past pres., mem. coms.), Am. Urol. Assn. Tippecanoe Co. Med. Soc. (past pres.), Phi Rho Sigma. Democrat. Presbyterian. Mason. Author numerous articles on sci. and econ. subjects. Home: Lafayette, Ind.†

CROFT, RICHARD GRAHAM, business exec.; b. Pitts. Jan. 18, 1901; s. Harry William and Mary Augusta (Graham) C.; grad. Pomfret Sch.; A.B., Princeton, 1924; m. Jean Brooke Riley, Sept. 25, 1926; children—Joan Struthers (Mrs. William J. Huffer), Richard Graham. With Hayden, Stone & Co., investment bankers and brokers, N.Y.C., 1924-36, mgr. stock dept., 1933-35, mgr. investment dept., 1936; exec. sec. John Hay Whitney, N.Y.C., 1937-41; partner J.H. Whitney & Co., 1946-58; chmn. bd. Gt. No. Paper Co., 1950-66; dir. Gen. Signal corp., Hartford Courant Co. Trustee Am. Mus. Natural History, Pomfret Sch., Manhattan Sch. Music. Served with AUS, 1941-45, Office of Undersec. of War, Washington, 1941-42, Civil Affairs and Mil. Govt., ETO, 1942-45. Presbyn. Clubs: Union, Brook (N.Y.C.). Home: Norfolk, Conn. Died Dec. 29, 1973.

CROMWELL, FRANK H., mayor; b. Kansas City, Mo., Apr. 22, 1878; s. Benjamin H. and Eliza (Hilton) C.; ed. high sch. and business coll.; m. Clara E. Stark, of Kansas City, June 29, 1903. Began in produce business, 1898; now pres. Cromwell Butter & Egg Co. (wholesale); v.p. Fairyland Amusement Co.; dir. Produce Exchange Bank; mayor of Kansas City, Apr. 1922-Apr. 1924. Democrat. Methodist. York and Scottish Rite Mason; Past Potentate Mystic Shrine; Moose, Elk. Clubs: Kansas City, Automobile (pres.), Kansas City Athletic Meadow Lake Golf. Home: Kansas City, Mo.†

CROMWELL, PAUL CRAWFORD, engr. educator; b. Beverly, W.Va., July 12, 1902; s. William Ralph and Stella George (Crawford) C.; B.S. in Elec. Engring., Carnegie Institute of Technology, 1924; M.S. in Physics, New York University, 1935; m. to Owena Margaret Sanderson, June 15, 1929; 1 son, Paul Sanderson. Engr. Westinghouse Electric Corp., 1924-26; engr. asst. Byllesby Engring. and Mgmt. Corp., 1926-28; engr. Arthur Anderson & Co., cons. engr., 1928-30; from instr. to asso. prof. elec. engring. N.Y.U., 1931-47, exec. sec. dept., 1944-47; prof. head dept. U. Tenn., 1947-68. Licensed profl. engr. Tenn., N.Y. Fellow I.E.E.E.; mem. Am. Soc. Engring. Edn., Sigma Xi, Tau Beta Pi, Eta Kappa Nu, Phi Kappa Phi. Presbyn. Home: Knoxville, Tenn. Died Dec. 14, 1974; buried Elkins, W. Va.

CRONIN, RALPH MARVIN, operating co. exec.; b. Dayton, O., Dec. 13, 1907; s. Aaron J. and Esther (Levit) C.; B.Sc., Ohio State U., 1929; Ph.D., U. Mich., 1942; m. Ruthlouise Sachs, Jan. 13, 1939. With Keller Crescent Co., Evansville, Ind., 1930-39, 47-69, v.p., 1955-69; with Jam Handy Orgn., Detroit, 1940-41; dir., v.p. Nat. Industries, Inc., Louisville, 1964-73; v.p., dir. Found. Life Ins. Co., Atlanta, 1964-66; v.p. Lasalle Nat. Ins. Co. Chgo., 1965-69; dir. Computer Research Inc., Pitts., Gen. Nursing Homes, Inc. Pres., Nat. Conf. Christians and Jews, Louisville, 1969-73, nat. trustee, 1971-73. Trustee Old Ky. Home council Boy Scouts Am. Served to lt. with USNR, 1942-46. Recipient Distinguished Selling award, Nat. Sales Execs., 1964. Mem. Sales Execs. (pres. 1960-61), Am. Marketing Assn. (dir., named Man of Yr. 1972), Navy League (pres. Louisville, nat. trustee), Civil War Roundtable. Club: Jefferson. Home: Louisville, Ky. Died Aug. 1973.

CRONKHITE, LEONARD WOLSEY, instrument exec.; b. Maulmein, Burma (parents U.S. citizens), Dec. 11, 1882; s. Rev. Leonard Wolsey and Carrie Sylvia (Foster) C.; student Mass. Inst. Tech., 1901-02; Ph.B., Brown U., 1905; B.Sc., U. Oxford (Rhodes scholar), 1908; grad. study Harvard, 1931-32; m. Mary Hartwell, 1909 (dec.); 1 dau., Elizabeth; m. 2d, Orpha Brewster, 1916; children—Leonard Wolsey, Bayard M.; m. 3d Bernice V. Brown, July 21, 1933. Import, export chem. and mfrs. supplies, 1908-42; past pres. Atomic Instrument Co., Cambridge, Mass.; chmn., dir. Atonium Corp., Waltham, Massacuhusets; member bd. directors Photon, Inc., Atomic Industrial Forum, Regional priorities advisor War Industries Bd., 1914-18, also spl. agt. Dept. Labor and sec. Mass. Bd. Non-War Constrn. Mem. U.N. Assn., Assn. Am. Rhodes Scholars (dir.), Phi Beta Kappa, Delta Upsilon. Contbr. N.Y. Times during World War II. Home: Cambridge, Mass. Died July 16, 1974; buried Mt. Auburn Cemetery, Cambridge.

CRONSTEDT, VAL, cons. engr.; b. Vesterik, Sweden, May 23, 1897; s. Nils Clas A. and Maria (Ingelson) C.; student Orebro Tech. Inst., Sweden, Gottingen U., Germany; Sc. D., Sorbonne, Paris; m. Dorothy Ida Hevner, Oct. 31, 1940; 1 son, George. Chief engr. Avco, Williamsport, Pa., 1928-38; exec. engr. Pratt & Whitney Aircraft, East Hartford, Conn., 1938-51; cons. Swedish Aircraft Industries, 1951-53; dir. engring. AVRO, Can. (Malton. Ont.), 1953-55; sr. partner The Valdor Co.; cons. engr., Williamsport, 1955. Fellow Am. Soc. M.E.; asso. fellow Am. Inst. Aeros. and Astronautics. Clubs: Wings (N.Y.C.); Ross, Williamsport Country (Williamsport, Pa.). Author: Engineering Management and Administration, 1961. Office: Williamsport, Pa. Died Jan. 23, 1974; interred Wildwood Cemetery, Williamsport, Pa.

CROOKS, HARRY MEANS, college pres.; b. Gilman, Ill., Mar. 1, 1878; s. Andrew and Margaret (Armstrong) C.; A.B., Univ. of Wooster (now College of Wooster), 1899, LL.D., 1916; m. Ruth Elliott, of Shreve, O., June 23, 1904; children—Elliott Armstrong, Lee Elliott, Harry Means, Robert Mackenzie. Prin. high sch., 1899-1901, supt. pub. schs., 1902-05, Lisbon, O.; editor Buckeye State, Lisbon, 1901-02; president Albany (Ore.) Coll., 1905-15, Alma (Mich.) Coll., 1915-38; pres. Pikeville (Ky.) College, from 1938, president higher education sect., Mich. State Teachers' Association, 1917-19; pres. Presbyn. Coll. Union, 1922-23; mem. state com. Nat. Econ. League; mem. bd. Presbyn. Theol. Sem., Chicago (chmn. 1926-27); mem. Bd. of Christian Edn. of Presbyn. Ch. in U.S.A., 1928-31; moderator Synod of Mich., 1931; pres. Mich. Council of Chs., 1932-33. Mem. Alpha Tau Omega, Phi Beta Kappa. Republican. Presbyn. K.T. Club: Pine River Country. Home: Pikeville, Ky.†

CROSBY, HENRY LAMAR, prof. Greek; b. Menominee, Mich., May 17, 1880; s. William Henry and Stella Maria (Sexmith) C.; B.A., U. of Tex., 1901; M.A., 1902; A.M., Harvard, 1903, Ph.D., 1905; m. Olive Williams, July 6, 1910; children—Henry Lamar, Oliver Sexmith. Instr. Greek, U. of Pa., 1905-06; asst. prof. Greek, U. of Mo., 1906-09; preceptor in classics, Princeton, 1909-10; asst. prof. Greek, 1910-19, prof. from 1919, dir. summer session, 1918-25, dean of Graduate School, 1928-38, U. of Pa. Annual prof., 1926-27, dir. 1938-39, Am. Sch. of Classical Studies, Athens, Greece. Decorated Comdr. Order of George the First (Greece). Mem. Am. Philol. Assn., Classical Assn. Atlantic States, Archaeol. Inst. America, Phi Beta Kappa, Phi Gamma Delta, Phi Mu Alpha. Episcopalian. Joint author: Introduction to Greek. Translator of Dio Chrysostom (Loeb Classical Library). Home: Philadelphia, Pa.†

CROSS, CLAUDE B., lawyer; b. Enterprise, Miss., Oct. 22, 1893; s. John Clifton and Mary Elizabeth (Killam) C.; A.B., U. Mo., 1914; A.M., Harvard, 1915, LL.B., 1920, J.D., 1969; Dr. Juridical Sci., Suffolk U., 1970; m. Jeannette MacDonald, Apr. 9, 1921. Asst., Office of Pres. N.Y. Central Lines, 1920-21; admitted to Mass. bar, 1922; trial work with Sherman L. Whipple, Boston, 1921-30; sr. partner Withington, Cross, Proctor & Park, and successor firms, including Withington, Cross, Park & Groden, Boston. Chmn. Mass. chpt. Multiple Sclerosis, 1954-56, now hon. chmn. Trustee New Eng. Baptist Hosp.; trustee, mem. exec. com. Andover-Newton Theol. Sch. Served from 2d lt. to capt., 7th F.A., 1st Div., U.S. Army, 1917-19. Fellow Am. Bar Found., Am. Coll. Trial Lawyers; mem. Am. Law Inst., Am., Mass., Boston (pres. 1957-59) bar assns. Club: The Country (Brookline). Home: Brookline, Mass. Died Oct. 16, 1974.

CROSS, LOUIS JOHN, investment banker; b. Chgo., Sept. 10, 1897; s. John Robert and Mary Ann (Barry) C.; student Cathedral Coll., Chgo., 1912-16, Kenrich Sem., St. Louis, 1916-19; m. Gladys B. Boyce, Dec. 31, 1921 (dec. June 1963); children—Louise Robert, Margery (Mrs. William Brice Buckingham); m. 2d, Frances S. Kluck, June 27, 1964. Served as salesman H.T. Holtz & Co., investment bankers, Chgo., 1920-25, sales mgr., 1925-29; Paul H. Davis & Co., 1929-39, partner, mgr. investment dept., 1939; gen. partner Hornblower & Weeks-Hemphill, Noyes, from 1953; dir. and mem. exec. com. Jessop Steel Co., River Forest State Bank; dir., financial cons. Longines-Wittnauer Watch Co., Inc., Vacheron-Constantin Watch Co.; dir. Green River Steel Co., Jessop Steel Ltd., Steel Warehousing div. Jessop Steel Co., House of Vision, Inc., Jessop Steel of Cal., South Shore Oil and Devel. Co. Mem. Chgo. Regional Port Dist. Bd. Citizens bd. Loyola U. Bd. dirs. Cath. Charities, Chgo. Mem. Nat. Assn. Securities Dealers (1st chmn. 8th dist.), Ill. C. of C., Chgo. Hist. Soc. (life), Art Inst. Chgo. (life), Newcomen Soc. of N.A. Republican. Roman Catholic. Clubs: Attic, Economic, The Arts, Bond, Chicago, Chicago Golf, Germania, Yacht, Saddle and Cycle, The Tavern (Chicago, Illinois); Country, Stock Exchange (Los Angeles); The Eldorado Country (Palm Desert, Cal.); Tennis (Palm Springs). Home: Chicago, Ill. Deceased.

CROSS, MILTON, radio announcer; b. N.Y.C., Apr. 16, 1897; LL.D., Ithaca (N.Y.) Coll., 1969, Wagner Coll., 1972; m. Lillian Ellegood, 1925; one daughter, Lillian (dec.). Announcer for the Metropolitan Opera broadcasts, 1931-74, other programs including Information Please, Radio City Music Hall, Town Hall. Recipient gold medal for good diction on radio Am. Acad. Arts and Letters, 1929; George Frederick Handel medallion, City of N.Y., 1969. Hon. life mem. Liederkranz Soc. Home: New York City, N.Y. Died Jan. 3, 1975.

CROSS, MORTON ROBINSON, real estate exec.; b. Wakefield, R.I., Jan. 29, 1879; s. Elisha Watson and Frances Cooper (Wright) C.; student R.I. State Coll.; Burdette Bus. Coll., Boston; m. Mabel Dewar, June 1, 1910; m. 2d, Isabella Wilson, Apr. 20, 1936; children—Victoria Cross (Mrs. John Wilson), Lenore (Mrs. Walter Hutsch), Sec. Tar Klin Zinc Mining Co., Marion Co., Ark., 1900, made mgr., 1901; came to N.Y. in 1902, and entered the real estate business with J. G. Underhill & Co.; became mgr. Gross & Gross Co., 1905, bought that co. out in 1910, and organized real estate firm of Cross & Brown Co., N.Y. City, then serving as pres. and director, later chairman of the board. Organizer, member of the exec. and financial committees and dir. former Gotham Nat. Bank. Mem. Real Estate Bd. of N.Y. Bldg. Co., Inc. Dir. and chmn. of bldg. com. to erect the Real Estate Bd. of New York Bldg., 12 E. 41st St. Incorporator, first treas., v.p. and dir. West Side Assn. Commerce City N.Y., vice president of the executive committee and director of the Am. Arbitration Assn.; mem. exex. com., dir., 2d v.p. Automobile Old Timers, Inc.; bd. mgrs. William Sloane House, Y.M.C.A. Mem. Soc. Colonial Wars in State of N.Y., S.A.R. (Empire State Soc.), Pilgrims in the U.S., Soc. Calif. Pioneers. Clubs: Bankers, Union League, Uptown, Metropolitan Opera (N.Y.C.). Home: New York City, N.Y.†

CROSS, TOM PEETE, prof. English and comparative lit.; b. Farmer's Delight Plantation, Nansemond County, Va., Dec. 8, 1879; s. Thomas Hardy and Eleanor Elizabeth (Wright) C.; prep. edn., Norfolk Acad.; A.B., Hampden-Sydney (Va.) Coll., 1899, S.B., 1900, Litt.D., 1927; A.M., Harvard, 1906, Ph.D., 1909; studied School of Irish Learning, Dublin, 1909; m. Elizabeth Douglas Weathers, June 9, 1914; children—Ellen Elizabeth (Mrs. Storm Bull), Evelyn Douglas (Mrs. Louis S. Baer). Instructor modern languages, Norfolk Academy, 1900-05; instructor Harvard U. and Radcliffe College, 1910-11; professor and head Dept. of English, Sweetbriar Coll., 1911-12; prof. English, Univ. of N.C., 1912-13; asso. prof. Eng. and Celtic U. of Chicago, 1913-20, prof. Eng. and comparative lit., 1929-45. chmn. dept. comparative lit., until 1930. Acting prof. Eng. Stanford, summer, 1920, spring, 1923, Harvard, summer 1927, Colorado, summer, 1929, Calif. (Berkeley), 1930. Instr. mil. camps, 1917. Mem. Am. Council Irish Texts Soc., Modern Lang. Assn. America, Modern Humanities Research Association, Mediaeval Academy of Am. (fellow), Irish Texts Society, American Irish Historical Society (fellow), English Association, Kappa Alpha (Southern) fraternity, Methodist. Club: Quadrangle. Author: Bibliographical Guide to English Studies, 1919, 9th edition, 1947;

Witchcraft in North Carolina (U. of N.C.), 1919; Life and Correspondence of Lodowick Bryskett (with H. R. Piomer), 1927; Heath Readings in the Literature of England (with C. T. Goode), 1927; Lancelot and Guinevere (with W. A. Nitze), 1930; Good Reading for High Schs. (with E. Stauffer, Reed Smith and E. Collette), 4 vols., 3 edn., 1945-47; Harper and Bard, 1931; Heath Readings in the Literature of Europe (with C. H. Slover), 1933; Ancient Irish Tales (with C. H. Slover), 1936; Self-Expression in English (with C. T. Goode and R. A. Law), 1932; Milton's Minor Poems, 1936; Motif-Index of Early Irish Folk-Literature, 1949. Contbr. articles dealing with Celtic and comparative lit.; former publishing editor Modern Philology. Address: King William County, Va.†

CROSSMAN, RICHARD HOWARD STAFFORD, Brit. govt. ofcl., writer; b. London, Eng., Dec. 15, 1907; s. Stafford and Helen (Howard) C.; ed. Winchester Coll., 1919-25; New Coll., Oxford U.; m. Anne McDougall, June 2, 1954; children—Patrick, Virginia. Fellow, New Coll., Oxford, Eng., 1930-37; leader Labour group Oxford City Council; asst. editor New Statesman, 1936-52; asst. dir. psychol. warfare AFHQ Algiers, 1942-43; SHAEF, 1944-45; M.P., 1945-74; minister in Labour Govt., 1964-70, editor New Statesman, 1970-72. Decorated Knight Order Bit. Empire. Clubs: Athenaeum; Garrick, Farmers. Author; Plato To-day; Palestine Mission; Charm of Politics; Government and Governed, Nation Reborn; Planning for Socialism; Inside View; Diaries of a Cabinet Minister. Home: Banbury, England. Died Apr. 5, 1974.

CROTTY, HOMER DANIEL, lawyer; b. Oakland, Cal., March 15, 1899; s. Daniel and Mary Francis (O'Connor) C.; A.B. U. Cal., 1920, J.D., 1922; LLM., Harvard, 1923; LL.D., U. Dublin, 1960; L.H.D., Cal. Western U., 1964; m. Ida Hull Lloyd, May 12, 1934; children—Daniel Lloyd, Mary Elizabeth, Anne Lloyd, Peter Lloyd. Asst. to dir. Chabot Obs., Oakland, 1917-22; with Gibson, Dunn & Crutcher, lawyers, Los Angeles, 1923-72, mem. firm, 1930-72, specializing in corp. and reorganization; dir. Lloyd Corp. Ltd. Mem. com. to revise corp. laws Cal., 1930-35; mem. Cal. com. of Bar Examiners, 1942-47, chmn., 1947. Trustee Claremont U. Center; bd. trustees I.N. and Susanna H. Van Nuys Found; chmn. bd. turstees Henry E. Huntington Library and Art Gallery; mem. council Fellows Pierpont Morgan Library, 1959-62; bd. govs. State Bar Cal., 1948-51, pres., 1950-51; mem. council sect. of legal edn. and admissions to bar, Am. Bar Assn., 1952-62, chmn., 1959-60; mem. com. 22 Am. Bar Assn. and Am. Law Inst. on continuing legal edn.; pres. and dir. Southwest Mus., 1947-70. Fellow Am. Bar Found.; mem. Am. Bar Assn. (chmn. sect. legal edn. 1958-59, mem. legal profession survey group), Cal., Los Angeles County bar assns., A.A.A.S., Am. Law Inst. (mem. legal edn. com. 1948-57; mem. council), Am. Soc. Internat. Law, Internat. Bar Assn., Am. Judicature Soc., Council Fgn. Relations, Inc. (N.Y.), Los Angeles Com. on Fgn. Relations, Fgn. Policy Assns., Am. Acad. Social Sci., Am. Mus. Natural History, Cal., So. Cal. hist. socs., Astron. Soc. Pacific. Selden Soc. London (mem. council), Stair Soc. Edinburgh, Order Coif (hon.). Clubs: California, Chancery, Harvard of N.Y., Grolier (N.Y.C.); Sunset, Stock Exchange, Town Hall, Zamorano, Jonathan, Athenaeum; Valley Hunt (Pasadena). Republican. Author: Glimpses of Don Quixote & La Mancha; also many articles and revs. on legal subjects; co-editor, The Zamorano Eighty. Home: San Marino, Cal. Died Mar. 29, 1972; buried Forest Lawn Cemetery.

CROTTY, SISTER M. MADELEINE, coll. pres.; b. Jersey City, Apr. 11, 1916; d. John J. and Mary Ellen (Finn) Crotty; B.A., Notre Dame Coll, 1937; M.A. Seton Hall U., 1948; Ph.D. Fordham U., 1962. Instr. Seton Hall U., N.J., 1950-62; pres. Englewood Cliffs (N.J.) Coll., 1962-73. Del. gen. chpt. congregation, 1964, 68, 69, 70, Eng., Scotland, Germany, France, Italy, Ireland, Switzerland, Israel; radio-TV personality; mem. Englewood Cliffs Coll. Speakers Bur. Trustee Englewood Cliffs Coll. Press. Mem. Assn. Higher Edn., Clairvaux Speakers Bur. (chmn. 1960), Modern Lang. Assn., N.J. Assn. Tchrs. English. Author: Nun-Sense, 1963, 2d edit., 1972; Chasing Rainbows, 1973. Home: Englewood Cliffs, N.J. Died Aug. 10, 1973.

CROUCH, COURTNEY CHET, lawyer; b. Collins, Mo., June 23, 1912; s. William Edward and Lura V. (Heare) C.; LL.B., U. Mo. at Kansas City, 1933; m. Marie E. Loftis, May 24, 1936; children—Courtney Chet, Michael E., James E. Admitted to Ark. bar, 1933; practice in Springdale, 1933-38, 47-75; with Braun and Co., mgmt. cons., Los Angeles, 1938-47; sr. mem. firm Crouch, Blair, Cypert's Waters; dir. First Nat. Bank. Mem. Ark. Bd. Law Examiners. 1955-58. Mayor Springdale, 1936-38. Bd. dirs. Springdale Meml. Hosp.; trustee U. of Ark. Law Sch. Found., 1965—, trustee Southwestern Legal Found. Dallas, 1968—, mem. exec. com. lawyers, Am. Bar Found. Fellow Am. Coll. Trial Lawyers; mem. Am., Ark. (exec. com. 1961-67, pres. 1965-66) bar assns., Am. Judicature Soc. Methodist (trustee). Home: Springdale, Ark. Died May 7, 1975.

CROUCH, RALPH B., prof. math., head dept. Drexel Inst. Tech., later v.p. acad. affairs. Home: Las Cruces, N.M. Died Apr. 5, 1975.

CROUNSE, ROBERT MABIE, lawyer; b. Mpls., Feb. 18, 1893; s. Avery and Hannah (Seabury) C.; B.A., U. Minn., 1914; LL.B., 1916; m. Lura Mai Harper, Jan. 17, 1933. Admitted to Minn. bar, 1916, since practiced in Mpls., specializing in real estate and probate law; mem. firm Mackall, Crounse & Moore, 1922-74. Dir. Pub. Markets, Inc. Past mem. adv. bd. Mpls. Salvation Army. Served with U.S. Army, 1918. Mem. Am. Legion (past comdr. Lufbery post). Republican. Methodist. Kiwanian. Clubs: Minneapolis, Minneapolis Athletic, Six O'Clock (past pres.) (Mpls.). Home: Edina, Minn. Died Oct. 27, 1974; buried Lakewood Cemetery, Minneapolis, Minn.

CROWLEY, PATRICK F., lawyer; b. Chgo., Sept. 23, 1911; s. Jerome J. and Henrietta Louise (O'Brien) C.; A.B., U. Notre Dame, 1933; J.D., Loyola U., Chgo., 1938; m. Patricia Caron, Oct. 16, 1938; children—Patricia Ann, JoAnn (dec.), Mary Anne, Catherine, Patrick, Theresa. With trust dept. Chgo. Title & Trust Co., 1933-38; admitted to Ill. bar; mem. firm Barry & Crowley, Chgo., 1938-43; gen. atty. Office Alien Property Custodian, 1943-44; mem. firm Crowley, Sprecher, Barrett & Karaba, and predecessors, Chgo., 1944-74; sec., gen. counsel, dir. Caron Internat. Inc.; dir. Mut. Estate Investment Trust, KAR Products; v.p., treas., gen. counsel O'Brien Corp. Pres., Internat. Confedn. Christian Family Movements; chmn. Family Inst. Chgo.; treas. Found. for Internat. Cooperation; sec. Little Brothers of Poor; Pope's Commn. to Study Population Problems. Trustee Calvert Found.; bd. dirs. Marillac House, Fund for Republic, Center for Study Democratic Instns., Cath. Scholarships for Negroes, Gt. Books Found., Immaculate Heart Coll., Bus. Opportunities for Blind, adv. council UN Assn. Chgo., Columbia Coll., St. Scholastica President's Council, Notre Dame Law Sch. Recipient Pro Ecclesia medal Pope Pius XII; Laetare medal, 1966; award Chgo. Commn. Human Relations, 1970; Brotherhood award Nat. Conf. Christians and Jews, 1970. Mem. Am., Chgo., Ill. bar assns. Home: Chicago, Ill. Died Nov. 20, 1974; buried Calvary Cemetery, Chicago, Ill.

CROWN, EDWARD A., phys. and surg., corp. exec.; b. Mar. 10, 1905; s. Arie and Ida (Gordon) C.; A.S., Crane Coll., 1926; B.S., Loyola U., 1928, M.D., 1929. Intern St. Catherine's Hosp., 1928; staff Oak Park Hosp., 1929; resident in charge Bridewell Hosp., 1929, Edgewater Hosp., 1930; faculty Chicago Med. Sch., 1932-42; resident obstetrics Cook County Hosp., 1932-33; cons. gynecology State of Ill. Women's Prisons, 1942-45; charge obstetrics clinics Bd. Health, City of Chgo., 1952-54; dir. med. dept. Material Service Corp., 1933—. staff Columbus Hosp., Am. Hosp., Cuneo Hosp.; cons. obstetrics Am. Hosp. Pres., Stearns Lime & Stone Co., 1932; 50; v.p., dir. Material Service Corp., 1934—; chmn., pres. Rite Way Products Co., 1947-53, G & D Mfg. Co., 1950-57; v.p., dir. Garden City Sand & Fuel Co., 1950-75; pres., dir. Framont Corp., 1953-75; v.p., dir. Trimco Corp.; dir. in charge farm operations material service div. Gen. Dynamics Corp.; me. dir. Freeman Coal Co. v.p., dir. Arie and Ida Crown Memorial, Mt. Sinai Med. Research Found. Founding fellow Am. Coll. Obstetricians and Gynecologists; fellow Internat. Coll. Surgeons; mem. A.M.A., Ill. Chgo. med. socs. Home: Chicago, Ill. Died Sept. 30, 1975; buried Rosehill Cemetery.

CROWNHART, CHARLES HENRY, lawyer; b. Superior Wis., Oct. 2, 1905; s. C.H. and Jessie (Evans) C.; LL.B., U. Wis., 1931; m. Marion A. Palmer, May 19, 1934; children—Maryann (Mrs. Warren F. Turner, Jr.), Sally (Mrs. Theodore S. Hegley), Virginia Jean (Mrs. C. B. Brenneis), Gretchen Jane. Admitted to Wis. bar, 1931; private law practice, Madison, 1932-42; sec. Wis. Med. Soc., Madison, 1942-70, cons., 1970-74, mng. editor Wis. Med. Jour., 1942-70. Dir. Nelson Muffler Corp. Bd. dirs. Wis. Bar Found., 1961. Fellow Am. Pub. Health Assn.; mem. Am., Dane County bar assns., State Bar Wis., Am. Judicature Soc., Wis. Law Alumni Assn., Phi Alpha Delta. Chi Phi. Home: Madison, Wis. Died Jan. 21, 1974.

CROZIER, JOHN, petroleum co. exec.; b. Blyth, Northumberland, Feb. 18, 1911; s. J.T. Crozier; ed. Westoe Coll., Eng., Marine Sch. Eng.; E.D., Sydney Tech. Coll.; m. Elizabeth T. Davidson, Sept. 23, 1939; 3 daus. Estimating engr. A.C.I. Group, 1937-50; operations mgr. Boral Ltd., 1950-54; mgr. Queensland Oil Refineries Pty. Ltd., 1954, dir., 1962, gen. mgr., 1965-69, dep. chmn., 1969-71; dep. chmn. Boral Group, Queensland, 1969-71; dir. Queensland Ind. Concrete Group, 1968-71, Steelbar (Queensland) Pty. Ltd., 1970-71, Brittains Bricks & Pipes Group, 1970-71, Moreton Tug & Lighter Group, 1971, Q.O.R. Rd. Services Pty. Ltd., Gas Supply Co., Queensland. Served with Australian Imperial Forces, 1939-45. Fellow Australian Inst. Mgmt. (pres. 1964), Am. Inst. Finance; mem. Inst. Dirs. Clubs: United Services, Brisbane, Royal Queensland Golf, Q.L.T.A. (life mem.). Home: Brisbane, Australia. Died Sept. 1971.

CRUMMEY, JOHN D., corp. exec.; b. Chgo., Mar. 18, 1878; son David C. and Addie (Bean) C.; ed. Stanford Univ.; LL.D., Coll. of the Pacific, 1951; m. Vivan Gelatt, Mar. 26, 1901; (deceased); children—Beth C. (Mrs. Chinchen), Faith C. (Mrs. Paul L. Davies), D. Clifford, Marie C. (Mrs. R. F. Foster), J. Delbert; m. second, Caroline Hughes Harban, Jan. 2, 1952. Asso. FMC Corp., San Jose, Cal., and predecessor cos., from 1901, pres., dir., 1928-40, chmn. bd., 1940-56, hon. chmn., from 1956, also dir. pres., later hon trustee U. of Pacific; bd. dirs., hon. pres. San Jose YMCA. Methodist (bd. publs. 1936-60, hon. mem. bd.). Mason, Rotarian. Home: San Jose, Cal.†

CSANÁDI, GYÖRGY, hungarian govt. ofcl.; b. Leibach (now Ljubljana), Yugoslavia, July 28, 1905; s. András and Flóra (Fekete) C.; Dr. Civil Engring., U. Tech. Scis.; m. Magda Juhász. Ry. engr., 1929-45; head Ry. Directorate, 1945-47; head tech. dept. rys. Ministry Communications and Posts, 1947-48, 1st dep. minister, 1957-63, minister, 1963-74; dir. gen. Hungarian State Rys., 1949-59; prof. tech. scis. Budapest Tech. U. Constrn. and Communications, 1951-74. Mem. (corr.) Hungarian Acad. Scis. Decorated Labor Order Merit, Golden Degree, 1970; State prize Hungarian People's Republic, 1973. Home: Budapest, Hungary. Died Apr. 27, 1974.

CULBERTSON, WILLIAM H(OWARD), banker; b. Zanesville, O., Mar. 2, 1903; s. Claude L. and Mabel (Cosgrave) C.; B.S., U. Pa., 1926; m. Eleanor Beattie; children—Patricia, Phyllis, Eleanor, Nancy. With Harris Forbes & Co., 1926-31, Chase Harris Forbes Co., 1931-33; dist. sales mgr., partner Starkweather & Co., 1933-37; mgr. Buffalo office, F.S. Moseley & Co., 1937-45; partner Merrill Lynch, Pierce, Fenner & Beane 1945, exec. v.p., dir. Merrill Lynch, Pierce, Fenner & Smith, Inc.; chairman board Merrill Lynch, Pierce, Fenner & Smith, International, Limited, 1961-66. Lt. Col., U.S. Army, 1942-46. Clubs: Bond (N.Y. City); Siwanoy Country (Bronxville); Downtown Assn. (N.Y.C.). Home: Kent, Conn. Died May 1973.

CULLEN, JAMES ALOYSIUS, super market exec.; b. Syracuse, N.Y., July 27, 1912; s. Michael Joseph and Nan (Danaher) C.; ed. pub. schs.; m. Florence Hanrahan, Sept. 3, 1935; children—Michelle (Mrs. John Del Ponti), Mary Ann (Mrs. Walter Miller), Patricia (Mrs. William Groom), Carolyn (Mrs. Vincent Garrish), James Aloysius, Kathleen, Michael, Thomas, Brian. With King Kullen Grocery Co., 1930-74, gen. mgr., 1936-60, pres., 1960-71, chmn. bd., 1964-74, chief exec. officer, 1971-74. Republican. Roman Catholic. Home: Bellport, N.Y. Died Oct. 1974.

CULLEN, WILLIAM GEORGE, physician; b. Ayr, Ont., Can., June 5, 1907; s. David and Florence (Woolcott) C.; M.D., U. Toronto, 1932; postgrad. course in anesthesiology McGill U., 1945-46; children by previous marriage-David McMurchy, James Barry, Donald Gordon; m. 2d, Amy Eleanor Anderson, Dec. 15, 1945; children—Nancy Elizabeth, Judith Marie, George Thomas. Intern, Toronto Western Hosp., 1932-33; anesthesiologist-in-chief Queen Elizabeth Hosp., Montreal, Que., Can., chief anesthesiologist Cornwall Gen. Hosp., 1968-72; asst. prof. anesthesiology McGill U., Montreal. Diplomate Am. Bd. Anesthesiology. Fellow Am. Coll. Anesthesiologists. Royal Coll. Physicians and Surgeons Can., Royal Coll. Surgeons (Eng.); mem. Can. Med. Assn., Can. Anesthesiology Soc., Am. Soc. Anesthesiologists. Home: Lancaster, Ont., Can. Died June 6, 1973; buried Meml. Gardens, Kitchener, Ont., Can.

CULPEPPER, JAMES HENRY, chem. and fertilizer co. exec.; b. Norfolk, Va., Mar. 15, 1914; s. James Henry and Otey (Minor) C.; B.S. in Elec. Engring., Va. Mil. Instr., 1936; m. Frances Baldwin, Apr. 22, 1939; children—Robert Stuart, James Henry; m. 2d, Marian Mish Ganong, Dec. 1, 1969; stepchildren—Jay, Stuart Wentworth Ganong. With Chesapeake & Potomac Telephone Co., 1936-38; with Smith-Douglass Co., Inc. (now Smith-Douglas div. Borden Chem. Co.) Norfolk, 1938-66, v.p. farm fertilizer and specialty fertilizer div., 1957-62, exec. v.p., 1962-66, also dir.; pres. C.A. Nash & Son, Inc., Norfolk, Va., 1968-70; dir. Seabord Citizens Nat. Bank. Finance com. Tidewater div. Girl Scouts U.S.A., trustee Norfolk Acad., Bonney Home for Girls, Norfolk; bd. dirs. Va. Found. Ind. Colls., Norfolk Gen. Hosp., United Communities Fund; dir. Navy YMCA, Norfolk; alumni sec. Va. Mil. Inst., 1937-38; chmn. bd. Research Found. of Old Dominion Coll. Served to maj. AUS, 1943-46; mem. Norfolk C. of C., Va. Mfrs. Assn. (dir.), Va. Mil. Inst. Alumni Assn. Clubs: Norfolk Yacht and Country, Virginia, Harbor, Norfolk (Va.) German; Princess Anne Country (Virginia Beach, Va.). Home: Millboro Springs, Va. Died July 27, 1974.

CULVER, CHARLES AARON, prof. physics, cons. engr.; born Fillmore County, Minn., September 22, 1875; s. Warren and Mary (Crum) C.; B.S., Carleton Coll., Northfield, Minn., 1902; Ph.D., U. of Pa., 1907; m. Gertrude Helen Powell, June 17, 1908 (died 1926); m. 2d, Ruth Evelyn Peterson, June 18, 1927. High sch. teacher, 1902-05; instr., later prof. physics, Beloit (Wis.) Coll., 1907-20; chief high frequency engr. Canadian Radio Corporation, 1920-23; professor physics, Carleton College, 1923-46, Park College, 1947-51; sr. physicist S.W. Research Inst. 1951; served as consulting acoustical engineer; granted various United States and foreign patents pertaining to communication engineering. Served as capt., later maj. on staff of chief officer, U.S. Signal Res. Corps, World War. Fellow Am. Inst. E.E., Inst. Radio Engrs.; mem. Acoustical Soc. Am., Sigma Xi, Phi Beta Kappa, Delta Sigma Rho.

Republican. Conglist. Author several books, including: Theory and Applications of Electricity and Magnetism, 1947; also contbr. papers tech. jours. Address: Claremont, Cal.†

CUMMINGS, GEORGE BAIN, architect; b. New Ipswich, N.H., Feb. 11, 1890; s. John Wyman and Harriet Angeline (Boyce) C.; B.Arch., Cornell U., 1912; m. Aura Marie Butler, Nov. 9, 1912; children—Barbara Joy (Mrs. A. Ward West), Jean Marie (Mrs. Robert W. Storandt), John Butler. Employee Carrere and Hastings, architects, N.Y.C., 1912-17; head draughtsman Trowbridge and Ackerman, N.Y.C., 1919; partner Lacey Schenck and Cummings, Binghamton, N.Y., 1920; own practice, Binghamton, 1921-23; partner Cummings and Starbuck, Binghamton, 1924-25, conrad and Cummings, asso. architects, 1926-61; dir. Columbian Mutual Life Ins. Co., Binghamton; cons. to commr. housing, N.Y. on state bldg. code, 1960. Mem. N.Y. State Bd. of Examiners Architects, 1938-50, pres., 1948-50; vice chmn. N.Y. State Bldg. Code Commn., 1949-59, acting chmn., 1950-52; insp. FHA, 1932-35. Chmn. Binghamton Planning Commn., 1936-38; exec. sec. Broome Co. Planning Board, 1944. Served as 1st lieutenant A.S., U.S. Army, 1917-19. Fellow A.I.A. (regional dir. 1943-44, 48-49; sec. 1953-54, 54-55; pres. 1955-56; chairman of the jury of fellows of the inst., 1960); honorary corresponding mem. Royal Architectural Inst. of Canada, Royal Institute of British Architects, Philippine Int. Architects, El Colegio Nacional De Arquitectos; mem. Am. Legion, Tau Beta Pi. Presbyn. Clubs: Cornell (Broome County); Rotary (Binghamton). Home: Binghamton, N.Y. Died Mar. 28, 1974.

CUMMINS, WILLIAM TAYLOR, physician; b. Media, Pa., May 17, 1879; s. Joseph Grubb and Sarah Jane (Otley) C.; grad. Biol. Dept. U. of Pa., 1902, M.D., Med. Dept., 1902; m. Josephine Widdicombe, Sept. 9, 1908 (died 1932); m. 2d, Laura E. Anderson, Sept. 28, 1938. Asst. demonstrator of pathology, U. of Pa., 1902-11; demonstrator of pathology. Woman's Med. Sch., Phila., Pa., 1907-10; physician Henry Phipps Inst., Phila., 1907-10; bacteriologist, Dept. of Health, N.Y. City, 1911; dir. labs., Southern Pacific Gen. Hosp., San Francisco, Calif., from 1911. Mem. A.M.A., Am. Assn. Pathologists and Bacteriologists, Am. Soc. Clin. Pathologists, Alpha Kappa Kappa. Republican. Presbyterian. Clubs: Commonwealth, Olympic. Author: Syllabus of General Pathology, 1908; Syllabus of Special Pathology, 1909 Home: San Francisco, Cal.†

CUNNINGHAM, CHARLES BARNARD, physician; b. Wheeling, W.Va., July 22, 1906; s. Samuel and Iva (Holiday) C.; M.D., U. Mich., 1934; m. Elizabeth Hill Duncan, Sept. 1, 1941; children—Stella Gates (dec.), Edward Gould. Sr. intern, asst. resident, resident in obstetrics and gynecology Harper Hosp., Detroit, 1934-39; practice medicine specializing in obstetrics and gynecology, Virginia, Minn., until 1948, St. Petersburg, Fla., 1948-72; active staff St. Anthony Hosp., Bayfront Med. Center, Palms of Pasadena Hosp. (all St. Petersburg). Served with M.C., USAAF, 1943-46. Diplomate Am. Bd. Obstetrics and Gynecology. Fellow A.C.S., Am. Coll. Obstetricians and Gynecologists; mem. South Atlantic Assn. Obstetricians and Gynecologists. Clubs: St. Petersburg Yacht, Dragon, Quarterback, Sun Coasters (St. Petersburg). Home: St. Petersburg, Fla., Died Apr. 15, 1972; buried St. Matthews Episcopal Ch. Moritorium, St. Petersburg, Fla.

CUNNINGHAM, FIRMAN, dean Sch. Bus. and Industry, Middleton Tenn. State Univ. Murfreesboro. Home: Murfreesboro, Tenn. Deceased.

CUNNINGHAM, GUSTAVUS WATTS, prof. philosophy; b. Laurens, S.C., Nov. 14, 1881; s. William Lawrence and Kate Elizabeth (Langston) C.; M.A., Furman Univ., Greenville, S.C., 1902, hon. D.Litt., 1916, LL.D., 1935; Ph.D., Cornell Univ., 1908; m. Mattie Cleveland Hipp, June 30, 1909. Prof. of English, Howard Coll., Birmingham, Ala., 1902-05; scholar and fellow, Sage School of Philosophy, Cornell U., 1905-08; instr. philosophy, Middlebury (Vt.) Coll., 1908-09, asst. prof., 1909-15, prof., 1915-17; asso. prof. Philosophy, U. of Tex., 1917-19, prof., 1919-27; prof. philos. Cornell, 1927-42, Sage prof. philos. from 1942, prof. emeritus from 1949, dean Grad. Sch. from 1944. Lectr. Inst. Philosophy, Bowdoin Coll., 1937. Mem. Am. Philos. Assn. (Western and Eastern divs.; pres. Western div. 1930, pres. Eastern div. 1937), Am. Assn. Univ. Professors, Phi Kappa Phi, Phi Beta Kappa. Baptist. Author: Thought and Realty in Hegel's System, 1910; A Study in the Philosophy of Bergson, 1916; Problems of Philosophy, 1924, rev. edit. 1935; Five Lectures on the Problem of Mind, 1925; The Idealistic Argument in Recent British and American Philosophy, 1933; Perspective and Context in the Meaning-Situation (Howison lecture U. of Calif.), 1934. Contbr. to Philosophical Essays in honor of James Edwin Creighton, 1917; Contemporary American Philosophy, 1930; contemporary Idealism in America, 1932. Co-editor: The Philosophical Review from 1930. Home: Laurens, S.C.†

CUNNINGHAM, HARRISON EDWARD, university exec.; b. Hoosick Falls, N.Y., July 29, 1877; s. Charles Edwin and Minnie (Potter) C.; B.A., U. of Vt., 1904; student University of Illinois, 1911-13; married Ethel Lord, Aug. 18, 1906 (deceased March 1960). Reporter and editor of various newspapers, 1904-06; instructor modern langs. and asst. registrar, U. of Vt., 1906-10; asst. registrar, U. of Ill., 1910-18, sec. bd. trustees, 1914-51, secretary committee of the emeriti from 1951, dir. Univ. Press 1918-47, later director with rank of professor emeritus. Book designer and typographer. Mem. editorial board Illinois. Studies in Language and Literature. Mem. Am. Inst. Graphic Arts, Soc. for Promotion Byzantine and Modern Greek Studies, Phi Beta Kappa, Phi Delta Theta. Republican. Conglist. Club: University (Urbana). Translator vita Aesopi vulgaris, Pierpont Morgan codex 397. Home: Urbana, Ill.†

CUNNINGHAM, WALLACE MCCOOK, prof. of economics and finance; b. Lisbon, Ohio, March 23, 1881; s. Hamilton Ferrell and Binney McCook (Wallace) C.; A.B., Roanoke Coll., Salem, Va., 1902; A.M., Princeton University, 1903; Ph.D., Univ. of Pennsylvania, 1922; unmarried. Instructor finance Wharton School of Commerce, Univ. of Pa., 1908-09; ranching, real estate and townsite management, British Columbia, 1909-17; again instr. finance Wharton Sch. of Finance, 1917-21; asst. mgr. ednl. dept. Guaranty Trust Co., New York, summer 1921; asst. prof. finance, Wall Street div. and in Grad. Sch. Business Adminstration, New York U., 1921-24; asso. prof. finance U. of Southern Calif., 1924-25, prof. and acting dean, 1925-27; prof. finance and dean of Lowry Sch. of Banking and Commerce, Oglethorpe U., Ga., 1931-33; prof. economics, Webber Coll. and research with Babson Statistical Orgn., 1933-37; writing and research, from 1937. Mem. Am. Econ. Assn., Beta Gamma Sigma, Delta Phi Epsilon, Phi Gamma Delta, Alpha Kappa Psi. Episcopalian. Club: Phi Gamma Delta (New York). Address: Glendale, Cal.†

CURIE, ROBERT JAMES, paper co. exec.; b. Wooster, O., May 9, 1930; s. Irvin H. and Ebony (Steiner) C.; student Ohio State U., 1948-52; m. Jane Louise Davis, Feb. 25, 1956; children—Christe R., Robert D. (dec.). With Corco, Inc., Columbus, O., 1956-74, dir., 1964-74, pres., 1970-74, chief exec. officer, 1972-74; dir. State Savs. Bank, 1972-74. Trustee Columbus Town Meeting, 1968-74, pres., 1973-74; trustee Riverside Methodist Hosp., 1974; bd. dirs. Center Sci. and Industry Franklin County Hist. Soc., 1974. Served with USAF, 1952-56. Mem. Ohio C. of C. (dir. 1973-74), Young Presidents Orgn. United Methodist (trustee 1972-74, vice-chmn. 1973-74). Clubs: Presidents (Ohio State U.); Columbus Athletic, Columbus Rotary, Scioto Country. Home: Columbus, O., Died Dec. 1, 1974; interred Union Cemetery, Columbus, O.

CURLESS, HOWARD MARION, printer, publisher; b. Blanchester, O., Oct. 12, 1903; s. Elmer J. and Margaret (Higgins) C.; student Whittenberg Coll., Springfield, O., 1922-23; m. Mary Elizabeth Brown, June 23, 1928. Owner, Curless Printing Co., Star-Republican Newspaper, from 1953; dir. First Nat. Bank; pres. Peoples Bldg. and Loan Assn.; owner, mgr. 407 acre farm nr. Blanchester. Pres. Blanchester Pub. Library Bd. Mem. Ohio Printers Assn., Ohio Newspaper Assn., Nat. Editorial Assn., C. of C. Republican. Mason, Rotarian. Home: Blanchester O. Deceased.

CURRAN, EDWARD LAWRENCE, sociology; b. East Bridgewater, Mass., Feb. 14, 1879; s. Bartley John and Ann (Costello) C.; grad. Mass. State Normal Sch., Bridgewater, 1901; spl. student harvard, 1907-12, Sch. for Social Workers, Boston, 1911; A.B., Boston Coll., 1913, A.M., 1914, Philosophy Licentiate, 1917; Ph.D., Fordham, 1930; unmarried. Teacher pub. schs., E. Bridgewater, 1901-02; prin. Bird. Sch., E. Walpole, Mass., 1902-04; prin. Reform Sch., Boston, 1904-08; teacher pub. schs., Boston, 1908-10; supt. Boston Newsboys Club, 1910-23; sales mgr. Am. Oil Co., Cambridge, Mass., 1923-26; registrar, School Social Service, Fordham, from 1934, prof. of group work; sec. bd. Rindge Oil & Gas Co. Sec. Federated Boys Clubs of America, 1913-15; pres. Citizens Pub. Celebrations Assn. of Boston, 1926-27. Mem. Charitable Irish Soc., Kappa Delta Phi. Democrat. Knight of Columbus. Clubs: Boston College, Woolsack (Boston); Boston College, Fordham University (New York). Contbr. articles on edn. Home: New York City, N.Y.†

CURRAN, PETER FERGUSON, educator, biophysicist; b. Waukesha, Wis., Nov. 5, 1931; s. Peter Hugh and Norma (Ferguson) C.; A.B., Harvard, 1953, Ph.D., 1958; M.S. (hon.), Yale, 1969; m. Barbara Jean Werra, July 7, 1956; 1 dau., Maura Elizabeth. NSF post-doctoral fellow U. Copenhagen (Denmark), 1958-60; asso. biophysics Harvard Med. Sch., 1960-63, asst. prof. biophysics, 1963-67; mem. faculty Yale Sch. Medicine, 1967-74, prof. physiology, 1969-74, dir. div. biol. scis., 1972-74. Mem. molecular biology panel NSF, 1968-71; biophys. sci. tng. com. NIH 1968-70, physiology study sect. 1971-74. Recipient Research Career Devel. award NIH, 1962-67. Mem. Biophys. Soc. (council 1970-73), Am. Physiol. Soc. (Bowditch lectr. 1967, chmn. publs. com. 1971-72), Soc. Gen. Physiologists (council 1968-70, pres. 1972). Author: (with A. Katchalsky) Nonequilibrium Thermodynamics in Biophysics, 1965; also numerous articles. Mem. editorial bd. Biophys. Jour., 1967-70, Jour. Gen. Physiology, 1972-74, Biochimica Biophysica Acta, 1973-74; editorial bd. Am. Jour. Physiology, 1964-68, sect. editor, 1968-71. Home: North Haven, Conn. Died Oct. 16, 1974; interred Waukesha, Wis.

CURRY, JOHN FRANCIS, air force officer; b. N.Y.C., Apr., 1886; s. James Francis and Mary (McKinnon) C.; student Coll. City N.Y., 1901-04; B.S., U.S. Mil. Acad. 1908; grad. Signal Corps Aviation Sch., 1915. Air Corps Engring. Sch., 1924, Air Corps Tactical Sch., 1928, Command and Gen. Staff Sch., 1929, Army War Coll., 1936; m. Eleanor Montgomery, Jan. 4, 1921; children—Sheila (Mrs. Duane De Kalb), Joan. Commd. 2d lt. infantry U.S. Army, 1908, promoted through grades to maj. gen., 1940; jr. mil. aviator, 1916, mil. aviator, 1919, pilot, command pilot, combat observer; member 1st Aero Squadron, Pershing Expdn. into Mexico, 1916; with aviation sect. Signal Corps, 1915-20; chief staff A.S. 2d Army, 1918; with A.C., 1920-45, chief air service, engring. div., Dayton, O., 1924-27, comdt. A.C. Tactical Sch., 1931-35; mem. Gen. Staff War Dept., 1936-38; comdg. gen. N.W. Air Dist. and 2d Air Force, 1940-41; head Civil Air Patrol, Washington, Dec. 1941-Mar. 42; comdg. gen. 4th dist. Tech. Tng. Command and Western Tech. Tng. Command, 1942-44; pres. A.A.F.-M.T.O. Evaluation Bd., 1944-45. dir. aeronautics Colo. 1946; dir. aviation, Denver, 1947. Chmn. Red Rocks Music Festival with Denver Symphony Orchestra, 1947-49. Decorated Officer de l'Etoile Noir, Officer Legion of Honor (France); D.S.M. Legion of Merit; V.F.W. Citizenship medal, 1954; Citation, Civil Air Patrol, 1951; special citation City of Denver, 1964; Early Birds of Aviation Plaque, 1965; Aerospace plaque Pioneer Hawaiian Aviation., 1965. Officially credited destruction one German balloon, 1918. Mem. Denver C. of C. (chmn. aviation com.), Aero Club Am. (expert aviator 1916), Early Birds of Aviation (trustee), Daedalians, Am. Legion, Alliance Francaise, English Speaking Union (pres., v.p., dir. Denver), Am. Meteorol. Soc. Am. Ordnance Assn., Air Force Assn., Denver Research Inst. (adv. panel), Alpha Delta Phi. Roman Catholic. Clubs: Army-Navy (Washington); Denver, Mile High, City (Denver); Marines Memorial (life mem. San Francisco). Home: Denver, Colo. Died Mar. 4, 1973; buried Fort Logan National Cemetery, Denver, Colo.

CURTIS, EARL A., exec. v.p. Security Pacific Nat. Bank, Los Angeles. Home: Los Angeles, Cal. Died Mar. 20, 1973.

CURTIS, NATHANIEL CORTLANDT, architect; b. Smithville (now Southport), N.C., Feb. 8, 1881; s. Walter Gilman (M.D.) and Margaret Johnson (Coit) C.; Ph.B., U. of N.C., 1900; B.S. (architecture), Columbia, 1904; m. Elizabeth Thach, June 15, 1913; children—Eleanor Coit (Mrs. Richard Page), Nathaniel Cortlandt, Charles Thach. Instructor drawing and geometry, University of North Carolina, 1904-07; professor and head school of architecture. Alabama Polytechnic Institute, 1907-12, same sch. of architecture, Tulane University, 1912-17; associate professor design, school of architecture, University of Ill., 1917-20; with Moise H. Goldstein and associates, architects from 1920; asso. architect Magnolia St. low rent housing project for New Orleans and U.S. housing authorities; lecturer sch. of architecture, Tulane University, 1921-37, asso. prof. of architecture 1937-48, prof., 1945, retired 1948. Fellow American Institute of Architects (pres. La. chapter); vice chmn. Vieux Carré Commn., New Orleans (a commn. apptd. by the mayor to regulate and preserve the architecture of the "French Quarter", 1938-43); Art Association of New Orleans, New Orleans Academy of Sciences, Alpha Tau Omega. Democrat. Episcopalian. Author: Architectural Composition, 1923, 2d edit., 1928, 3d. edit., 1936; Elements of Graphics, 1924; New Orleans—Its Old Houses, Shops and Public Buildings, 1933; articles, papers, book reviews, etc. in technical jours.; The Creole City of New Orleans—An Historical and Decorative Map, 1933. Editor The Ricker Library of Architecture (U. of Ill.), 1920, Contbr. to American Year Book, 1943, 44, 45. Collaborator: Built in U.S.A., 1932-44, publication of Museum of Modern Art, N.Y. Home: New Orleans, La.†

CURTIS, WILLIAM RODOLPH, govt. ofcl.; b. Franklinville, N.C., Oct. 27, 1908; s. Rodolph Clinton and Ora Alma (Bray) C.; A.B., U. N.C., 1930, M.A., 1931; Ph.D., U. Ill., 1935; m. Luceil May Hamilton, June 22, 1935; children—Margaret Lucille, Aletha Estelle, William Edward. Tchr. econs. U. Ill., 1931-35, U. Ala., 1935-36; economist WPA, Washington, 1936-37; chief research, dir., acting chmn. Unemployment Compensation Commn. of N.C., 1937-45; chief adminstrn. standards div. Bur. Employment Security, Social Security Bd., 1945-48; exec. sec. Interstate Conf. Employment Security Agys., 1948-58; dep. adminstr. bur. employment security Dept. Labor, Washington, 1958-69, regional manpower adminstr., Phila., 1969-70, dep. asso. manpower adminstr., Silver Spring, Md., 1970-73. Mem. Social Security tech. staff ways and means com. Ho. of Reps., 1945-46; U.S. del. 3d session adv. com. Salaried Employees and Profl. Workers ILO, Geneva, 1954; alternate mem. study Commn. on Inter-Govtl. Relations, 1954-55. Mem. Am. Econ. Assn., Internat. Assn. Personnel in Employment Security, Phi Beta Kappa, Phi Kappa Phi, Phi Eta, Delta Sigma Pi.

Baptist. Mason. Author articles on labor subjects. Home: Falls Church, Va. Died Oct. 13, 1974; interred Nat. Meml. Park, Falls Church.

CURTS, MAURICE EDWIN, naval officer; b. Flint, Mich., Mar. 25, 1898; s. Edwin James and Minnie Elwood (Quirk) C.; B.S., U.S. Naval Acad., 1919; S.M. in Elec. Engring., Harvard, 1928; m. Nina Irvine, Aug. 16, 1919 (dec. Nov. 1965); children—Robert, Daniel; m. 2d, Fayette Purcell Hobbs, Jan. 1967 (dec. Nov. 1970). Commd. ensign U.S. Navy, 1919, advanced through grades to adm., 1955; with Naval Research Lab., 1936-38, comdr. U.S.S. Case, 1938-39; communication officer U.S. Fleet, 1939-44; comdr. U.S.S. Columbia, 1944-45; chief of staff 1st Carrier Task Force, Pacific Fleet, 1945; comdr. Cruiser Div., 1946; chief Navy Gen. Plans, 1947-48; comdr. operational devel., 1949-50; asst. chief of Naval operations, 1951-53; comdr. cruisers, destroyers, Pacific, 1953-55; dep. comdr. in chief Pacific Fleet, 1955-57, comdr. in chief, 1958; comdr. Western Sea Frontier, comdr. Pacific Res. Fleet, 1958-60; dir. telecommunications policy Dept. Def., Washington, 1960-65; ret., 1965. Decorated Navy Cross, Silver Star, Bronze Star, Purple Heart; recipient Commendation for Radar Devel. Home: Coronado, Cal., Died Feb. 15, 1976.

CUSHING, CHARLES PHELPS, writer, photographer; b. Mendota, Ill., Oct. 21, 1884; s. Willard Edward and Ada Clara (Phelps) C.; A.B., U. of Mich., 1907; m. Alice Connolly Campbell, July 24, 1937. Reporter Kansas City Star, 1907-09; writer for mags., 1910-12; on editorial staff Literary Digest, 1912; news editor Collier's, Jan. 1913-June 1914, then, for a short time, acting managing editor. Commd. 2d lt., U.S. Marine Corps Reserve, Apr. 11, 1917, and assigned to duty in Marine Corps' recruiting publicity bureau, N.Y. City; transferred, July 1917, to the Marine O.T.C., Quantico, Va.; assigned, Oct. 1917, to active service with the A.E.F., in France; commd. 1st lt., and made regtl. intelligence officer of 6th Regt. U.S. Marines, Jan. 11, 1918; with the Stars and Stripes, newspaper of the A.E.F., first as managing editor, then as corr. at the front until May 1918; photo news editor of A.E.F. (attached to U.S. Signal Corps), May 1918-May 1919, furnishing photographs to O.W.L., in World War II; owner Charles Phelps Cushing Photographic Illustration. Mem. Second Div. Assn., Mo. Writers Guild, Phi Beta Kappa, Sigma Delta Chi. Club: Quadrangle (Univ. of Mich.). Author: If You Don't Write Fiction (book on magazine writing), 1920. Contbr. to mags. and news weeklies, both in text and photographic illustrations; Ozark hill region of Mo. and Ark. and photographic themes favored as specialties. Home: Bronx, N.Y. Died Aug. 13, 1973; buried St. Charles Cemetery, Farmingdale, N.Y.

CUSHWA, CHARLES B., JR., metal products mfg. exec.; b. Youngstown, O., Apr. 30, 1909; s. Charles B. and Mary (Coll) C.; A.B., U. Notre Dame, 1931; m. Margaret Hall, Oct. 15, 1932; children—Charles, William W., Mary Ellen. Chmn., pres. Comml. Shearing, Inc., Youngstown, O.; dir. Union Nat. Bank; v.p., dir. Watson Terminal & Warehouse Co.; dir. Home Savs. & Loan Co., Youngstown Bldg. Material and Fuel Co. Mem. sci. and engring. bd. U. Notre Dame; trustee St. Elizabeth Hosp.; trustee, treas. Youngstown Ednl. Home: Youngstown, O., Died Apr. 25, 1975.

CUSICK, JAMES FRANCIS, educator; b. Gardiner, Me., Sept. 9, 1898; s. Thomas Francis and Mary (Thooel) C.; A.B., Amherst Coll., 1921; Ph.D., Harvard, 1934; m. Margaret Theresa Ronzone, June 29, 1931; 1 dau., Jean Frances. Prin. Freedom (Me.) Acad., 1922-22; head history dept. Winchester (Mass.) High Sch., 1923-28; instr. econs. Amherst (Mass.) Coll., 1930-35; faculty Dartmouth, from 1935, asst. prof., 1937, prof., from 1944, edn. dir. Alumni Coll., 1964-66. Mem. nat. adv. com. Consumers' Union of U.S. Mem. sch. bd., Hanover, N.H., 1944-53, chmn., 1947-53; mem. exec. com. N.H. Sch. Bd. Assn., 1947-53; mem. N.H. Commn. on Tchr. Tng., 1950-55; chmn. Post War Planning Com., Hanover, 1947-48, chmn. Zoning Com., 1948. Cons. to Fund for Advancement of Edn., 1956-57, Mem. Am. Econ. Assn., American Assn. U. Profs. Home: Hanover, N.H., Died Sept. 29, 1975.

CUSUMANO, STEFANO, painter; b. Tampa, Fla., Feb. 5, 1912; s. Ignazio and Rosa (Albano) C.; student Cooper Union, 1928-29, Met. Art Sch., 1930-32; m. Antoinette Ferrari, Aug. 16, 1939; children—Noelle (Mrs. Louis Marak), Peter Anthony. Tchr. painting, drawing Cooper Union, from 1954, N.Y. U., from 1951; one-man shows include Montross Gallery, N.Y.C., 1942, George Binet Gallery, N.Y.C., 1946, 47, 48, 50, Passedoit Gallery, N.Y.C., 1953, 56, 57, 59, Mari Gallery, Woodstock, N.Y., 1962, Gallery 63, N.Y.C., 1963, 64, Phila. Art Alliance, 1948, Woodmere Art Gallery, Phila., 1950, Tampa Art Inst., 1949, Ore. State Coll., 1951, Wash. State U., 1951, Gallery 63, Rome, Italy, 1964, T. Dintenfass Gallery, N.Y.C., 1967; Tweed Mus. Art, Duluth, Minn., 1971, 72; Pa. Acad. Fine Arts, Phila., 1972; nat. exhbns. include Mus. Modern Art, Whitney Mus., U. Ill. Pa. Acad., Corcoran Gallery, Carnegie Inst., Am. Inst. Arts and Letters, numerous others; represented in permanent collections Nat. Gallery, Met. Mus. Art, Whitney Mus., Bklyn. Mus., Phila. Mus., Newark Art Mus., Pensacola (Fla.) Art Mus., U. Ill., Wesleyan U. Ill., Johns Hopkins, Joslyn Art Mus., Omaha, Tweed Mus. Art, Albrecht Mus. Art, St. Joseph, Mo., Butler Inst. Am. Art, Youngstown, O. Recipient Ford Found. Purchase prize, 1962; Childe Hassam award Am. Inst. Arts and Letters, 1968, 71; Dillard Purchase award, Weatherspoon Mus., 1969. Address: New York City, N.Y., Died Nov. 18, 1975.

CUTLER, ROBERT, banking exec.; b. Brookline, Mass., June 12, 1895; s. George Chalmers and Mary Franklin (Wilson) C.; A.B., cum laude, Harvard, 1916, LL.B. cum laude, 1922; LL.B., Trinity Coll., 1943, Norwich Coll., 1948, Northeastern U., 1949, Colby Coll., 1951, Clark U., 1955, Springfield Coll., 1955, Wesleyan U., 1956; L.H.D., Boston U., 1952, Tufts U. 1953, U. N.H., 1963; D.Sc., Lowell Technol. Inst. 1956. Instr. Harvard, 1916-17; editor Harvard Law Rev., chmn. bd. advisers Harvard Law Sch., 1919-22; admitted to Mass. bar, 1922, practiced in Boston, 1922-42, asso. firm Herrick, Smith, Donald & Farley, 1922-28, partner, 1928-40; corp. counsel City of Boston, 1940-42; pres., dir. Old Colony Trust Co., 1946-53, chmn., 1953, 55-57, 58-60; U.S. exec. dir. Inter-Am. Devel. Bank, 1960-62; spl. asst. to sec. of treasury, 1960-62; spl. asst. to Pres. U.S. for nat. security affairs, 1953-55, 57-58; mem. operations coordinating bd., mem. council on fgn. econ. policy, chmn. Nat. Security Council Planning Bd., 1953-55, 57-58, trustee Boston Five Cent Savs. Bank; now ret. Served to 1st lt. inf., A.E.F., U.S. Army, 1917-19; with A.E.F., France, 1918; adj. 3d Army Mil. Police, Germany, 1919; commd. col., U.S. N.A., 1942 and advanced through grades to brig. gen., 1945; asst. dep. dir. Army Specialist Corps, 1942; chief procurement div. Officer Procurement Service, 1942-43; with gen. staff corps office of Sec. of War, 1943-45; coordinator for soldier voting for army, 1944-45; exec. officer U.S. War Ballot Commn., 1944-45. Awarded D.S.M., Legion of Merit, Medal of Freedom. Gen. chmn. Greater Boston 1937 Community Fund Campaign and div. chmn., 1936, 1939 and 1940 campaigns; chmn. adv. bd. Pub. Welfare Dept. of Mass., 1940-42; trustee and officer Peter Bent Brigham Hosp., 1936-74; bd. overseers Boston Sympnohy Orch.; bd. advisers Nat. Fund for Med. edn.; chmn. Citizens Com. to Survey Health, Social and Welfare Agys. of Greater Boston, 1957-59; nat. treas. Nat. Security Com. Trustee Brookline (Mass.) Public Library, 1932-38; pres., dir. Community Chests and Councils, Inc., 1939-42, Nat. Commn. Financing Hosp. Care 1951-52. Fellow Am. Acad. Arts and Scis., Am. Coll. Hosp. Adminstrs. (hon.), A.C.S. (hon.); mem. Greater Boston C. of C. (v.p.), Phi Beta Kappa. Episcopalian. Clubs: Somerset, Tavern, Harvard (Boston); Harvard (N.Y.C.). Author: Louisburg Square, 1917; The Speckled Bird, 1922; No time for Rest, 1966. Home: Boston, Mass. Died May 8, 1974.

CUTTER, ROBERT KENNEDY, pharm. mfr.; b. Fresno, Cal., May 23, 1898; s. Edward A. and Margaret (Kennedy) C.; B.A., M.A., U. Cal.; M.D. cum laude, Yale, 1923; grad. study allergy Cornell div. N.Y. Hosp.; m. Virginia White, Sept. 9, 1922 (dec. July 1969); children—Robert Kennedy, Richard White, David Lee; m. 2d, Alice Knapp, June 10, 1971. Intern San Francisco Hosp., 1923-24; practice of medicine specializing in allergy, Oakland, Cal., 1924-26; asst. med. dir. Cutter Labs., Berkeley, Cal., 1924-28, asst. to pres., 1928-30, chief exec. officer, 1930-45, pres., 1945-62, chmn. bd., 1963-73. Bd. dirs. Trustees for Conservation. Mem. Am. Pharm. Mfrs. Assn. (pres. 1956-57), Cal. Mfrs. Assn. (pres. 1952-53), Delta Sigma Phi, Nu Sigma Nu. Patentee disposable syringes, intravenous injection equipment, snake bite kits. Home: Berkeley Cal. Died Aug. 9, 1973.

CUTTS, RICHARD MALCOLM, inventor, Marine Corps officer; b. Mare Island Navy Yard, Calif., Jan. 9, 1903; s. Col. Richard M. and Margaret Marie (Pitts) C.; B.S., U.S. Naval Acad., 1923; grad. Marine Corps Sch.; m. Dorothea Lane, Sept. 12, 1934; 1 dau., Dorothea Lane. Commd. 2d lt. U.S.M.C., June 1923, advanced through grades to brig. gen., 1946; served in various marine corps posts and naval stations, U.S., Cuba, Haiti, Santo Domingo, China; White House aide, 1933-34; with Office of Naval Intelligence, 1941; comdr. Marine Corps base, Guantanamo Bay, Cuba, and 13th Anti-aircraft Bn., 1943-44; comdr. 2d Marines, 1944-45, participated in Saipan and Okinawa operations and occupation of Japan; ret. from active duty, Sept. 1946. Awarded Bronze Star with combat V, China Service, Marine Corps Expeditionary and other service medals. Mem. Mil. Order of Carabao, Nat. Rifle Assn. Episcopalian. Clubs: Metropolitan, Army Navy (Washington). Inventor-owner of Cutts Compensator; asso. with Philip Quayle and Col. Richard Cutts developed 1st practical application of photography to projectiles in flight, 1926; inventor in fields of ordnance and lubrication. Nat. Rifle champion, 1926, 27. Home: The Plains Va. Died June 14, 1973; buried Arlington National Cemetery, Arlington, Va.

CYBIS, JAN, painter; b. Wróblin, Upper Silesia, Feb. 16, 1897; s. Jan and Maria (Hajda) C.; student Sch. Arts and Crafts, Breslau, 1919-21, Cracow Acad. Fine Arts, 1921-24, br. Cracow Acad. Fine Arts, Paris, France, 1924-30; m. Helena Zaremba; children—Jacek, Jan. Works exhibited Venice Biennall, 1936, 48, Galerie Zak, Paris, Galerie Moos, Geneva, Switzerland, Carnegie Inst., Pitts., Mus. Modern Art, N.Y.C., Edinburg, Scotland, Moscow, U.S.S.R., Rome, Italy, Sao Paulo, Brazil, Warsaw, Poland, others; permanent exhibits nat. museums Warsaw, Cracow, Jan Cybis Mus., Glogowek. Prof. Warsaw Acad. Fine Arts, 1945-50, 57-68. Recipient Polish State Prizes, 1955, 66; Guggenheim Found. prize, Paris, 1956. Leader Polish colorists group. Home: Warsaw, Poland. Died Dec. 13, 1972; buried Powazki Cemetery, Warsaw, Poland.

CYBULSKI, WACLAW BOLESLAW, mining engr.; b. Warsaw, Poland, Oct. 6, 1901; s. Stefan and Kamilla (Filipowska) C.; Chem. Engr., Tech. U., Warsaw, 1925; D.Sc., Mining Acad., Cracow, Poland, 1937; m. Ruta Krzystolik, May 1952; children—Krzysztof, Wl adyslaw. Sr. asst. Tech. U., Warsaw, 1924-25; dir. Exptl. Mines, Barbara, Mikolow, Poland, 1925-39, 46-73; sci. officer Safety in Mines Research Bd., 1942-46; prof. Mining Acad., Cracow, Poland, 1930-39, 48-52; prof. chair dust explosions and safety in mines Tech. U., Gliwice, Poland, 1952-73. Councilor, Katowice Volvodeship Council, 1954-58. Served to lt. Polish Army, World War II. Decorated comdr.'s cross Order Polonia Restituta with Star; Banner of Labor 1st and 2d class; Silesian Partisan Cross; recipient State Prize 2d class, twice. Mem. Polish Acad. Scis., Miners Union. Research on safety of mining explosives, fundamental parameters of coal-dust and firedamp explosions, stone dust and water barriers for stopping explosions, gassy coal seams. Home: Mikotow, Poland. Died Mar. 31, 1973.

CZERNIK, STANISLAW, author; b. Zochcin, Poland, Jan. 16, 1899; s. Wojciech and Maria (Cieszkowska) C.; M.A. in Econs., U. Poznan (Poland), 1925; m. Sulikowska, Dec. 23, 1930; children—Maria, Mieczyslaw. Decorated knight's cross, officer's cross Polonia Restituta Order. Mem. Polish Writer's Union. Author various publications including: Poezje (Lector prize), 1923, Z Trzydziestu (City of Lodz prize), 1955; Reka (prize of Minister of Culture and Art), 1963; Trzy Zorze (prize Nat. Festival of Poetry), 1969. Home: Lodz, Poland. Died Dec. 3, 1969.

DABNEY, FRANCIS LEWIS, mgmt. cons.; b. Seattle, Dec. 13, 1907; s. John Pomeroy and Beatrice Mildred (Gunter) D.; B.S. in Mech. Engring. and Bus. Adminstrn. cum laude, Harvard, 1931; m. Helen Wheeler Baldwin, Sept. 9, 1933; children—John Baldwin, Sally (Mrs. Everett H. Parker), Stephen Francis. With Great Atlantic & Pacific Tea Co., Boston, 1931-34; with Charles F. Rittenhouse & Co., Boston, 1934-37; with Landers, Frary & Clark, New Britain, Conn., 1937-51, controller, 1941-42, sec.-treas., 1942-51; financial v.p. Fairmont Foods Co., Omaha, Neb., 1951-53; with Bullard Co., Bridgeport, Conn., 1953-68, sec.-treas., 1955-58, v.p., 1958-59, exec. v.p., 1959-68, also dir.; mgmt. cons., 1968-74. Mem. Nat. Machine Tool Builders' Assn. (1st v.p. 1966-67, pres. 1967-68, dir.), Financial Execs. Inst. Club: Harvard (N.Y.C.). Home: Fairfield Conn. Died Nov. 10, 1974.

DACSO, MICHAEL MIHALY, physician, eductor; b. Tovaros, Hungary, June 25, 1909; s. Laszlo and Hedvig (Bauer) D.; M.D., Royal Hungarian U. of Budapest, 1934; m. Magda Rona, June 6, 1936 (dec. Oct. 1975); 1 son, Clifford. Came to U.S., naturalized. Research asso. Municipal Research Inst. for Rheumatic Diseases, Budapest, 1934-40; intern, then resident Goldwater Meml. Hosp., N.Y. U. Med. Div., 1941-44, asso. vis. physician in medicine, 1945-52, dir. Rehab. Medicine Service, 1949-68, cons., 1968-75, pres. med. bd., 1967-68; cons. Manhattan State Hosp., Wards Island, N.Y., 1964-67; vis. physician Bellevue Hosp., N.Y. U. div., 1947-68; attending physician Univ. Hosp., N.Y. U. Med. Center, 1945-68, staff physician Inst. Rehab. Medicine, 1948-65; cons. Mary Manning Walsh Home, from 1951; mem. med. adv. bd. Peabody Home, from 1962; attending physiatrist Mt. Sinai Hosp., 1968-72; med. dir. Daus. of Jacob Geriatric Center, from 1972; clin. asst. in medicine N.Y. U. Sch. Medicine, 1944-47, asst. prof. clin. rehab. medicine, 1948-54, asso. prof., 1954-58, asso. prof. rehab. medicine, 1958-63, prof., 1963-68; prof. health scis. Hunter Coll., City U. N.Y., 1968-73, dean Inst. Health Scis., 1968-72; prof. rehab. medicine Mt. Sinai Sch. Medicine, City U. N.Y., 1968-72, prof. community medicine, 1969-75. Chmn. sub-com. on med. care Mayor's Adv. Com. for Aged, N.Y.C., 1955-58; mem. Nat. Adv. Com. on Chronic Disease and Health of Aged, 1957-59; cons. gerontology br. Dept. Health, Edn. and Welfare, 1963-64, cons. rehab. medicine div. direct health services, 1967-68, chmn. med. research study sect. Social and Rehab. Service, 1969—; mem. adv. com. on health careers City U. N.Y., from 1966; cons. City U. N.Y. Feasibility Study on Proposed Inst. Health Scis. in cooperation with Hunter Coll. and Mt. Sinai Sch. Medicine, 1967-68; mem. Health Resources Commn. Task Force, N.Y. Dept. Health, Albany, from 1968; mem. Nat. Joint Practice Commn., 1973-75. Mem. med. adv. com. N.Y. County chpt. Nat. Multiple Sclerosis Soc.; mem. tech. adv. com. Community Service Soc., 1955; mem. adv. com. Pub. Health Nursing Project, 1959; co-chmn. health exec. com. on aging Community Council Greater N.Y., 1960; mem. tech. adv. com. Found. for Med. Tech., 1962; mem. project adv. bd. Goodwill Industries Greater N.Y., from 1968. Vice pres., bd. dirs. Nat. Council on Aging; trustee Sirovich Day Center; bd. govs. Human Resources Center, Albertson, N.Y. Recipient AFL-CIO Dist. 65 award for services to aged, 1959, Japan Rehab.

Assn. scroll for contbn. to process in rehab. medicine in Japan, 1966, Meritorious Services diploma City of N.Y. Dept. Hosps., 1969. Diplomate Hungarian Bd. Phys. Medicine, Am. Bd. Phys. Medicine and Rehab. Fellow A.C.P., Am. Pub. Health Assn., Health Assn.; mem. Am. Congress Rehab. Medicine, Am. Acad. Phys. Medicine and Rehab., Internat. Soc. Electromyographic Kinesiology, Am. Geriatric Soc., Assn. Tchrs. Preventive Medicine, Asso. editor Am. Lecture Series. Editorial bd. jour. Chronic Diseases, 1954. Contbr. articles to profl. jours. Home: Roslyn, N.Y., Died Oct. 11, 1975.

DADOURIAN, HAROUTUNE MUGURDICH, physicist; born Everek, Armenia, Dec. 5, 1878; s. Mugurdich and Ezgule (Kalaijian) D.; came to U.S., 1900; Ph.B., Yale, 1903, M.A., 1905; Ph.D., 1906; m. Ruth McIntire, Dec. 28, 1918. Loomis fellow, Yale, 1903-05, instr. physics Sheffield Scientific Sch. (Yale), 1906-17; lecturer Yale Grad. Sch., 1907-17; aeronautical engr. U.S. Govt., 1917-19; asso. prof. physics, Trinity Coll., 1919-23, Seabury prof. mathematics and natural philosophy, 1923-49, prof. emeritus, 1949-74. Fellow American Physical Society; member American Math. Soc., A.A.A.S., American Math. Assn., Sigma Xi. Author: Analytical Mechanics, 1913; Graphic Statics, 1919; Analytical Geometry and the Calculus, 1949; Plane Trigonometry, 1950; How to Study-How to Solve, 1950. Contbr. to Philos. Mag., Phys. Rev., Am. Jour. Science, Le Radium, Phys. Zeitschrift, etc., papers on electrons, elasticity, radioactivity, sound ranging, X-rays, relativity, etc. Home: West Hartford, Conn. Died June 1, 1974.

DAFOE, CARMIE R., JR., lawyer; b. Portland, Ore., June 22, 1920; B.A., Reed Coll., 1946; J.D. cum laude, Harvard, 1949. Admitted to Ore. bar, 1949; now mem. firm Lindsay, Nahstoll, Hart, Dafoe & Krause, Portland. Mem. Am., Multnomah County bar assns., Ore. State Bar, Phi Beta Kappa. Office: Portland, Ore., Died June 28, 1975.

DAGUE, PAUL BARTRAM, congressman; b. Whiteford, Pa., May 19, 1898; s. William James and Lydia (White) D.; student West Chester (Pa.) State Teachers Coll., 1916-17; student of engring., Drexel inst., 1919-29; m. Mary Virginia Williams, Sept. 16, 1925. Employed in signal dept., Pa. R.R., Paoli, Pa., 1920-21; prin. asst., supt. Pa. Dept. of Highways, hdqrs., West Chester, Pa., 1925-35; dep. and chief dep. sheriff Chester County, Pa., 1936-43, sheriff, 1944-46; mem. 80th-89th U.S. Congresses, from 9th Pa. Dis. State chmn. Pennsylvania Rep. Vets. League, 1944-47. Pvt. 1st class, 1st Regt. U.S.M.C., 1918-19. Mem. Am. Legion (past dept. finance officer, Pa., mem. nat. pubs. commn. after 1944), C. of C., YMCA, Grange. Rep. Presbyn. Mason. Home: Downingtown, Pa. Died Dec. 2, 1974; interred Northwood Cemetery, Downingtown.

DAHLQUIST, JOHN E., ret. army officer, corp. ofcl.; b. Mpls., March 12, 1896; s. Eric Magnurs and Charlotte (Swenson) D.; student University of Minnesota, 1914-17, M.A. (honorary), 1954; Infantry School, 1923-24, 1928-29; Command and General Staff Sch., 1929-31; Army War Coll., 1935-36; Air Corps Tactical Sch., 1936-37; m. Ruth Charlotte Dampier, Oct. 21, 1922; children—Carl Erik, Donald John. Commd. 2d lt., U.S. Army, 1917, and advanced through the grades to brig. gen., 1942, maj. gen., 1943, lt. gen. 1953, gen., 1954; on War Dept. Gen. Staff, 1937-41; comdg. div. overseas, 1943-45; comdg. V Corps, 1951-53; Fourth Army, 1953; comdg. Field Forces and Continental Army Comd., 1953-56; ret. Dir. Armed Forces Dept. Harris, Upham & Co., 1956-58. Decorated D.S.M. with cluster, D.S.C. Mem. Delta Sigma Rho. Mason. Clubs: Army and Navy (Washington); Army and Navy Country (Arlington, Va.). Home: Ft. Lauderdale, Fla. Died 1975.

DAICOVICIU, CONSTANTIN, educator; b. Cavaran, Rumania, Mar. 1, 1898; s. Damaschin and Sofia (Dragan) D.; Dr., docent, U. Cluj (Rumania), 1928-29; M. Lucia Bugnariu, Dec. 17, 1931; children—Hadrian, Constantin. Asst., U. Cluj. 1927-32, reader, 1932-38, prof., 1938-73, rector, 1956-68; dir. History Inst. and Mus., 1949-73. Dep. Rumanian Grand Nat. Assembly, 1948-73; mem. State Council, 1960-73. Mem. Vienna Acad., German Inst. Archeology, Rumanian Acad. Mem. Rumanian Communist Party. Address: Cluj-Napoca, Rumania. Died May 27, 1973.

DALE, ESSIE ROCK, mem. Dem. Nat. Com.; born Mankato, Kan., Feb. 1, 1881; d. John and Harriette (Stone) Rock; student U. Wyo., 1936-37; m. Ford J. Dale, June 1, 1909; children—Inez (Mrs. John A. Ferguson), Dorothy Shannon, Henri Ford. Tchr. pub. schs., Kan., 1901-07; editor Beaver Co. (Okla.) Republican, 1907; editor, pub. The Lower Valley Live Wire, Thayne, Wyo., 1924-25; organizer, lectr. W.C.T.U., Kan., 1907-15; prin. pub. schs., Wyo., 1920-30, co. supt., Teton Co., 1930-38; founder, sr. partner, gen. mgr. Dale Enterprises, Fairbanks, Alaska from 1939. Mem. Fairbanks City Planning Bd., 1946. Mem. Dem. Nat. Com. for Alaska, 1948-52, mem. Central Com., 1944-52, del. Nat. Conv., 1948; pres. Dem. Women Teton Co., 1936-38; elected member Alaska Territorial Legislature, 1948; active supporter statehood for Alaska, appearing before Senate Com. on Territorial and Insular Affairs, 1950. Mem. Fairbanks Retail Mchts. Assn. (pres.), Salvation Army (adv. bd. Fairbanks). Rebecca. Clubs: Soroptimist, Women's (Fairbanks); Author's (Kan.). Author: The Charm String, 1930; Alaska corr. for mag. Listen. Home: Fairbanks, Alaska.†

DALE, NELSON CLARK, geologist; b. Newport, R.I., Aug. 9, 1880; s. Thomas Nelson and Margaret (Brown) D.; B.Sc., Middlebury (Vt.) Coll., 1903; A.M., Brown U., 1910; Ph.D., Princeton, 1914; m. Marion Ethel Norris, Dec. 23, 1916; children—William Norris Dale, Clark Dale (dec.). Instr. geology, Brown U., 1910-12; asst. state geologist, R.I., 1909-12; asst. prof. geology, Hamilton Coll., 1914-16, prof. 1917-50; with N.Y. State Museum from 1926; also director of Knox Museum of Natural History; chmn. Dept. Geography for Mil. Programs, 1942-44. Fellow Geol. Soc. America; fellow Am. Geographical Soc., A.A.A.S.; mem. Sigma Xi, Phi Beta Kappa, Delta Upsilon. Republican. Presbyn. Clubs: Fort Schuyler and Utica; Cosmos (Washington). Author geol. publs. Mem. Internat. Geol. Congress, 16th session, 1933. Home: Washington, D.C.†

DALEY, ARTHUR JOHN, sports writer; b. N.Y.C., July 31, 1904; s. Daniel M. and Mary (Greene) D.; B.A., Fordham U., 1926; grad. spl. courses Columbia, N.Y.U.; m. Betty Blake, Nov. 28, 1928; children—Robert, Kevin, Patricia, Katharine. Sports writer N.Y. Times, 1926-74, writer column Sports of the Times 1942-74. Recipient Pulitzer prize, 1956; Grantland Rice award, 1961; Sportswriter of the Year award, 1963; Prof Football Writers' Distinguished Writing award, 1970. Roman Catholic. Author: Times at Bat, 1950; Sports of the Times, 1959; Knute Rockne, Football Wizard of Notre Dame, 1960; Kings of the Home Fun, 1962; Pro Football's Hall of Fame, 1963; (with John Kieran) Story of the Olympic Games, 1969. Home: Greenwich, Conn. Died Jan. 1974.

DALLAPICCOLA, LUIGI, composer; b. Pisino, Istria, Austro-Hungarian Empire (now Italy), Feb. 3, 1904; s. Pio and Domitilla (Alberti) A.; Masters degree in Piano, Conservatory of Forence, Italy, 1924, in Composition, 1931; D. Muc. h.c., U. Mich., 1967, Durham U., 1973, Edinburgh U., 1973, U. Bologna, 1976; m. Laura Coen Luzzatto, Apr. 30, 1938; 1 dau., Annalibera. Tchr., Conservatory of Florence, 1934-67; composition tchr. Berkshire Music Center, Tanglewood, Mass., summers 1951, 52; vis. prof. Queens Coll., 1956-57, 59-60, U. Cal. at Berkeley, 1962-63. Hon. mem. acads. Munich, Rome, Berlin, Stockholm, Buenos Aires, Graz; mem. Am. Acad. Arts and Letters, Nat. Inst. Arts and Letters, Institut de France, Royal Acad. Music (Eng.) Composer: (operas) Nightflight 1937-39; The Prisoner, 1944-48, Ulysses, 1968; (ballet) Marsyas, 1942-43, (sacred) Job, 1950; (choruses) Six Choruses by Michelangelo Buonarroti the younger 1933-36, Songs from Captivity, 1938-41, Songs from Liberation, 1952-55, Requiescant, 1957-1958, Tempus Destruendi-Tempus Aedificandi, 1970-71; (voice, chamber orch.) Three Laudi, 1936-37, Greek Poems, 1942-45, Tre Poemi, 1949, Goethe-Lieder, 1953, Cinque, Canti, 1956, Concerto per ia notte di Natale, 1956; Prayers, 1962, Parole di San Paolo, 1964, Sicut Umbra, 1970, Commiato, 1972; (orchestral works) Two Pieces for Orchestra, 1946-47, Piccola Musica Notturna, 1954, Variations, 1954; Tartiniana I, 1951, Tartiniana II (violin, orch.) 1956; Dialoghi (cello, orch.), 1960; (chamber music) Music for three pianos, 1935, Sanatina canonica (piano), 1943, Ciaccona, Intermezzo, Adagio (unaccompanied cello), 1945, Rencesvals (voice, piano), 1946, Due Studi (violin, piano), 1946-47, Machado Songs (voice, Piano), 1948, Quaderno Musicale di Annalibera (piano), 1952-53, Tartiniana II (violin, piano), 1955. Author: Appunti, Incontri, Meditazioni, Address: Florence, Italy. Died Feb. 19, 1975; buried Florence.

DALSIMER, PHILIP T., lawyer; b. Far Rockaway, N.Y., June 18, 1913; s. Philip T. and Florence (Furth) D.; B.S., U. Mich., 1934; LL.B., Columbia, 1936; m. Dorothy Williams, May 30, 1935; children—William Robert, Nan (Mrs. Glen A. Corliss). Admitted to N.Y. bar, 1937; asso. Edwards, Bower & Poole, 1936-37, Duell & Kane, 1937-45; partner firm Kane, Dalsimer, Kane, Sullivan & Kurucz, N.Y.C., 1945—; dir. North European Oil Co. Mem. Am., N.Y. patent law assns., Am. Bar Assn., U.S. Trademark Assn., Columbia Law Sch. Alumni Assn. (dir.). Clubs: U. Mich. of N.Y.; Columbia U. Home: New York City, N.Y., Died July 18, 1975.

DALTON, JOHN HENRY, b. Santos, Brazil, Apr. 16, 1881; s. William Henry and Mary Emma (Cook) D.; came to U.S., 1893; ed. Princeton and Egn.; unmarried. Head of Dalton family, Thurnham Hall, nr. Lancaster, Eng., and owner of family estate and lands and coal mines in Tex., Fla. and S. A.; student, traveler and writer on Anglo-Am. federation. Episcopalian. Address: Navasota, Tex.†

DALY, DAVID, pub. utility exec.; b. Boston, Mass., Oct. 16, 1878; s. Timothy and Catherine Alice (Hagerty) D.; grad. Latin Sch., Boston, 1897; A.B., Harvard, 1901; m. Gertrude Hyde Paine, Jan. 12, 1910; children—Gertrude Paine (Mrs. Theodore R. Heyck), David, Susan Duncan (deceased). Began with Stone and Webster, Incorporated, engineers and mgrs. pub. service corps., Boston, 1910; mgr. Co., 1903-05, Houston (Tex.) Electric Co., and Galveston, Houston Electric Ry. Co., 1905-19; dist. mgr. Middle West Dist., Stone & Webster (v.p. Miss. River Power Co., Keokuk Electric Co., Paduach Electric Co., Houghton County Electric Ligh Co., Houghton County St. Ry. Co. and pres. Hotel Iowa Co.), 1919-24; pres. and dir. Blackstone Valley Gas & Electric Co., 1924-57, chmn. bd., dir., chmn. exec. com., 1957-64, honorary chairman of the board, from 1964; bd. dirs. Montaup Electric Co. Clubs: To Kalon, Pawtucket Golf, Rhode Island Country; Harvard (N.Y.); U. (Boston); Houston (Tex.) Club. Home: Barrington, R.I.†

DALY, IVAN DE BURGH, physiologist; b. Leamington, Warwickshire, Eng., Apr. 14, 1893; s. James Thomas and Amy (Pritchard) D.; ed. Gonville and Caius Coll., Cambridge, St. Bartholomew's Hosp., London, Eng., B.A., 1923; M.D., U. Cambridge, 1922; m. Beatrice Mary Daly, Nov. 1, 1920; children—Michael de Burgh, Peter de Burgh (dec.). Asst. lectr. Univ. Coll., London, 1919-23; Beit Meml. research fellow, 1920-24; lectr. physiology U. Wales, Cardiff, 1923-27; prof. physiology U. Birmingham (Eng.), 1927-33; prof. physiology U. Edinburgh (Scotland), 1933-48; 1st dir. Agr. Research Council Inst. Animal Physiology, Babraham, Cambridge, 1948-58; Sr. Wellcome Trust Research fellow U. Oxford (Eng.), 1958-61; vis. research worker, 1958-69. Fellow Royal Soc., 1943; Royal Coll. Physicians (Baly medal 1959); hon. mem. Physiol. Soc., mem. Path. Soc., Biochem. Soc., Thoracic Soc. (past pres.). Decorated Comdr. Brit. Empire. Author: (with Catherine Hebb) The Bronchial and Pulmonary Circulations, 1966; also numerous articles. Research on relation between pulmonary circulation and ventilation; demonstrated active control of lung blood vessels by nervous system. Home: Long Crendon, Bucks, England., Died Feb. 8, 1974; cremated.

DALY, JOHN FRANCIS, banker; b. Cresco, Ia., Nov. 7, 1879; s. Matthew W. and Mary Frances (Fitzgerald) D.; ed. State Normal Sch., Madison, S.D., and Notre Dame U. (non-grad.); m. Marguerite Wiley, of Portland, Ore., June 2, 1909; children—John F., Mary Margaret, James Wiley, Catherine. Entered banking business, Madison, S.D., 1894; moved to Portland, Ore., 1904; pres. Security Abstract & Trust Co., Portland, 1905-08; organizer, and pres. Title & Trust Co., 1908-19; pres. Hibernia Commercial & Savings Bank from 1919; pres. Portland Clearing House Assn., 1927; dir. Portland Br. Federal Res. Bank of San Francisco, Title & Trust Co., Mortgage Guarantee Co., Portland Remedial Loan Assn. Mem. hdqrs. staff Liberty Loan drive, 1917-18. Dir. Portland Chapt. Am. Red Cross. Mem. Am. Bankers Assn. (exec. council), Ore. Bankers Assn. (pres.). Republican. Catholic. Clubs: Arlington (v.p. 1926), Waverly, Multnomah Athletic. Home: Portland, Ore.†

DALY, KAY FRANCES, (Mrs. Warren Leslie), advt. exec.; b. County Tyrone, Ireland, Jan. 8, 1919; d. Joseph and Margaret (Kelly) Daly; brought to U.S., 1922; B.A., Rosary Coll., River Forest, Ill., 1939; m. Richard Patterson Bradford, Apr. 6, 1953 (div. Dec. 1960); children—Kelly, Peter, Richard Patterson; m. 2d, Warren Leslie. Started career as copywriter Gimbels, Milw., 1940-43; fashion and beauty editor Chgo. Herald American, 1943-47; account exec. Foote, Cone & Belding, advt. agy., 1947-49; v.p. Norman Craig & Kummel, Inc., N.Y.C., 1949-61; v.p. creative services Revlon, Inc., N.Y.C., 1961-75. Mem. Fashion Group, Inc. Home: New York City, N.Y., Died Oct. 16, 1975.

DANA, CHARLES ANDERSON, mfr.; b. Apr. 25, 1881; s. Charles and Laura (Parkin) D.; A.B., Columbia University, 1902, A.M., 1904, LL.D. (honorary), 1956; married Agnes Ladson; children—Charles A., Agnes L., Ann, David S.; married 2d, Eleanor Naylor. Chmn. of board and dir. Dana Corporation; president and trustee Coralitos Co.; dir. Mfrs. Trust Co. (N.Y.C.), Kelsey-Hayes Co., Curtiss-Wright Corp. Clubs: University, Down Town. Home: Wilton, Conn., Died Nov. 27, 1975.

DANDY, JOHN PERCY, bus. exec.; b. Morrisburg, Ont., May 19, 1902; s. William Percy and Anna Bethune (Parker) D.; student Harbord Collegiate, 1913-19; B.A., U. Toronto, 1923; fellow Acturarial Soc., Am. Inst. Actuaries. 1927; m. Dorothy Camille Davidson, July 30, 1925; children—William Bethune, Thomas Gordon. Came to U.S., 1942, naturalized, 1948. Asst. actuary Confederation Life Assn., Toronto, Can., 1930-35; asso. actuary Nat. Life Assurance Co. Can., 1935-37, actuary, 1937-42; asso. actuary Occidental Life Ins. Co. Cal., 1942-45, asso. actuary, 1945-46, actuary, 1946-48, v.p., 1948-66, sr. v.p., 1966-67; cons. actuary, 1967-73. Fellow Soc. Actuaries. Club: Gakmont Country. Home: La Canada, Cal. Died Oct. 30, 1973.

DANFORD, ROBERT MELVILLE, army officer; b. New Boston, Ill., July 7, 1879; s. Melville and Dora (Noble) D.; B.S., U.S. Mil. Acad., 1904; grad. Mounted Service Sch., Ft. Riley, Kan., 1907; hon. A.M., Yale, 1917; grad. Command and Gen. Staff Sch., Ft. Leavenworth, 1924, Army War Coll., 1929; m. Katherine Van de Carr Hyde, Oct. 7, 1909; 1 dau., Janet Van de Carr (wife of James B. Wells, U.S. Army). Commd. 2d lt., U.S. Army, 1904, and advanced through the grades to maj. gen., 1938; temp. brig. gen. comdg. F.A. Replacement Depot, Camp Jackson, S.C., 1918;

with A.E.F., France and Germany, 1919; chief of F.A., 1938-42; ret. from active service, Feb. 28, 1942. Comdt. City Patrol Corps (Civilian Defense Police Auxiliary) N.Y. City 1942-45; pres. Assn. of Grads. U.S. Military Academy 1942-44 and 1945-47; sec.-treas. and exec. mgr. West Point Alumni Foundation, Inc., and editor Register of Graduates and Former Cadets, U.S. Military Academy, since Jan. 1946. Decorated D.S.M., 1918. Methodist. Mason. Clubs: Yale (New York); Army and Navy, Army and Navy Country, Chevy Chase (Washington). Home: Darien, Conn. Died Sept. 12, 1974; interred West Point Memorial Cemetery, West Point, N.Y.

DANFORTH, DONALD, bus. exec.; b. St. Louis, Mo., Nov. 12, 1898; s. William H. and Adda (Bush) D.; ed. Smith Acad., St. Louis, Mo., 1916; A.B., Princeton University, 1920; married Dorothy Claggett, March 3, 1925; children—William H., II, Dorothy (Ifrs. Jefferson Lewis Miller), Donald, John Claggett. With Ralston Purina Co., St. Louis, from 1920. various positions, 1920-25, sec.-treas., 1925, elected v.p., treas., 1929, pres., 1932-56; chmn. bd., 1956-63, also dir.; dir. First Nat. Bank in St. Louis, St. Louis Union Trust Company, General American Life Ins. Company. Dir. United Fund Greater St. Louis; v.p., dir. St. Louis Christmas Carols Assn. Pres. Danforth Found., later v.p., sec. bd. dirs.; pres. Am. Youth Found. of St. Louis; trustee Berea Coll., Berea, Ky. Charter trustee, Princeton U. Clubs: Round Table, St. Louis Country, Stack, Noonday, Log Cabin. Home: Clayton, Mo. Died July 14, 1973.

DANGERFIELD, ROYDEN (JAMES), educational administrator; born Provo, Utah, Dec. 31, 1902; s. Jabez William and Alice (Dixon) D.; B.S., Brigham Young U., 1925; Ph.D., U. of Chicago, 1931; student London Sch. of Economics, 1927; m. Helen Morrison, Mar. 30, 1931; children—Helen Kay, Karen. Asst. prof. U. of Okla., 1928-30, asso., prof., 1934-38, prof., also asst. dean of Grad. Sch., 1938-42, dean of faculty, 1942, adminstrv. asst. to pres., 1945-47, exec. v.p. 1947-48; prof. U. of Wis. 1948-50; prof. polit. sci. U. Ill., 1950-69; dir. Inst. Govt. and Pub. Affairs, 1950-58, asso. provost, dean adminstrn., 1957-67, dir. internat. programs, 1962-67; president and exec. director of Midwest Universities Consortium for International Activities 1964-69; civilian professor at National War Coll., lst semester 1948-49, 49-50; professor Tokyo U., 1951, Kyoto U., 1952. Chief internat. law officer Office Judge Adv. Gen., Navy Dept., 1944-45; asst. chief, div. research and publs., Dept. State, 1945; cons. Bur. Budget, 1948, ECA, 1948,51, Mut. Security Agy., 1952,53. Served as lt. comdr., U.S. N.R., 1944-45. Mem. Council Fgn. Relations, Am. Soc. Internat. Law (exec. council 1946-49), Am. Polit. Sci. Assn., Phil Deta Kappa, Tan Kappa Alpha. Democrat. Co-author: In Defense of the Senate, 1933; The Hillen Weapon 1947; The New Japan, 1954. Home: Champaign, Ill. Died Nov. 1, 1969; interred Norman, Okla.

DANHOF, JOHN JAMES, lawyer; b. Grand Haven, Mich., July 15, 1884; s. John and Anna (Medema) D.; A.B., U. Mich., 1907, J.D. with distinction, 1912; J.D. (hon.), Detroit Coll. Law, 1948, LL.D., 1971; m. Erma Mueller, Feb. 14, 1914; children—Rosemary (Mrs. George I. Hammerschmidt), John James, Annabel (Mrs. Samuel A. Hess). High sch. prin., 1907-11; admitted to Mich. bar, 1912; atty. in office of Campbell, Bulkley & Ledyard, Detroit, 1912-13; atty. M.C. R.R. solicitor U.S. R.R. Adminstrn., 1919-20; atty., 1913-19, asst. gen. atty. M.C. R.R., Co., 1920-30; gen. atty. N.Y.C. R.R. Co., jurisdiction over M.C. R.R., 1930-31; gen. counsel N.Y.C. R.R. Co., jurisdiction over M.C. R.R., M.C. R.R. Co., 1931-51, Detroit Terminal R.R. Co. 1932-51, ret. 1951; counsel Mich. Railroads Assn., chmn. exec. com., ret., 1952. Mem. exec. com. Detroit Tomorrow Com. Pres., trustee Detroit Coll. Law, until 1971, pres. emeritus, cons., 1971-73. Mem. Am. Bar Assn. (chmn. coms. on cooperation, 1938-40), State Bar of Mich. (chmn. com. Legal Edn. and Admission to Bar, 1938-39), Detroit Bar Assn. (chmn. Integration Bar com., 1934-35, Legislative com., 1937-38), Assn. ICC Practitioners past v.p.; chmn. Mich. Regional com. on admission to practice 1941-53), U. Mich. Alumni Assn. (past v.p., past dir., recipient Distinguished Alumni Service award 1961, past chmn. class affairs council), Am. Juricature Soc., Newcomen Soc., UN Assn. Am., Internat. Platform Assn., Phi Alpha Delta, Delta Sigma Phi., Order of Coif. Republican. Conglist. Mason (K.T., Shriner). Clubs: Detroit (past pres.) Prismatic (past pres.), Detroit Golf (past dir.), Economic (dir.), Spring Lake Country; University (Washington); Lawyers (Ann Arbor, Mich.). Home: Detroit, Mi. Died Aug. 1973.

DANIEL, CULLEN COLEMAN, clergyman, educator; b. Highland Home, Ala., Aug. 29, 1879; s. Coleman Franklin and Frances Jane (Stough) D.; A.B., Southern U., Greensboro, Ala., 1905; Vanderbilt U., 1907-9; m. Margaret Estelle Elliott, of Moundville, Ala., Dec. 29, 1909. Ordained ministry M.E. Ch., S., 1900; pastor Florala, Ala., 1901, Opp and Red Level, 1906-7, Uniontown, 1910-12, Ft. Deposit, 1913, Wetumpka, 1914-16, Brewton, 1917; pres. Birmingham Southern Coll. from Aug. 17, 1917. Mem. Bd. of Sigma Alpha Epsilon. Royal Arch Mason, K.P. Address: Birmingham, Ala.†

DANIEL, WALTER FLETCHER, air force officer; b. Fletcher, Okla., Sept. 12, 1925; s. John Spencer and Vivian Prentice (Britton) D.; B.S. in Aero. Engring., U. Okla., 1954; M.S., George Washington U., 1967; grad. Advanced Mgmt. Program, Harvard, 1970; distinguished grad. Air Force War Coll., 1967; m. Barbara Jean Mills, Apr. 12, 1949; children—Diana M., Danny B., Dale S. Commd. 1st lt. USAF, 1951, advanced through grades to brig. gen., 1972; reconnaisance pilot, 100 missions over Korea, 1952-53; exptl. test pilot, 1953-66; comdr. 75 missions Fighter/Reconnaisance Wing, N. Vietnam, 1968-69; insp. gen. Air Force Systems Commamd, 1972; asst. dir. Tactical Systems Test and Evaluation, Office of Dep. Dir., Washington, 1973-74. Mem. council U. Tex., Austin, 1971-74. Trustee Austin United Fund. Served with USAAF, 1943-48. Decorated D.F.C. with 2 oak leaf clusters, Air medal with 4 oak leaf clusters, Legion of Merit with 1 oak leaf cluster; recipient (with Col. R. Stephens) MacKay trophy USAF, 1965. Fellow Soc. Exptl. Test Pilots. Established 4 world time-to-climb records in Northrop T-38, 1962, 6 world speed and altitude records in Lockhead YF-12, 1965. Home: Falls Church, Va. Died Sept. 13, 1974.

DANIELIAN, NOOBAR RETHEOS, economist, b. Constantinople, Turkey, Sept. 12, 1906; s. Réthéos and Anne (Papazian) D.: A.B., Harvard, 1928, M.A., 1929, Ph.D., 1932; m. Grace A. Apelian, Aug. 28, 1936; children—Sandra Elizabeth, Ronald Lawrence. Came to U.S., 1923, naturalized, 1928. Instr. dept. econs. Harvard, 1929-35; financial, utility expert FCC, 1935-38; dir. St. Lawrence survey U.S. Dept. Commerce, 1939-43; dir. program staff Fgn. Econ. Adminstrn., 1934-44 cons. Office Sec. Commerce, Office Undersec. State, 1944-45; v.p. Gt. Lakes-St. Lawrence Assn., 1949-52, pres., 1952-65; mem. adv. bd. U.S. St. Lawrence Seaway Devel. Corp. 1961-66; editor, pub. The Heartland, 1953-56, Port Cons., Detroit, 1955-56; econ. adviser Lorain, O. 1955-59; mem. President's Nat. Tourism Resources Rev. Commn., 1971-73. Receipient Certificate of Merit, Amvets, 1955. Mem. Internat. Econ. Policy Assn. (founder, pres. 1957-74, chmn. 1974), Am. Econ. Assn., Am. Acad. Polit. Sci., Nat. Assn. Bus. Economists, Phi Beta Kappa. Episcopalian. Clubs: Congressional Country (Bethesda, Md.); Detroit: Harvard (N.Y.C.); Harvard, National Press, Metropolitan and International (Washington). Author: The St. Lawrence Survey (7 vols.), 1941. Editor: U.S. Balance of Payments, an Appraisal of U.S. Economic Strategy, 1966; U.S. Balance of Payments, A Reappraisal, 1968; United States Balance of Payments, from Crisis to Controversy, 1972. Contbr. articles to profl. publs., mags. Home: Potomac, Md. Died May 12, 1974.

DANIELS, MARK (ROY), architect, landscape architect; b. Spring Arbor, Mich., July 14, 1881; s. Philander Emergene and Julia Frances D.; B.S., U. of California, 1905; grad. work, 1911-12; student city planning and landscape architecture, Harvard, 1913; m. Ruth Glassman Anderson, September 22, 1939. Chief engineer for M.,F.&E. Railroad during its location, 1906-07; town planner, engr., Weyerheuser Lumber Co., 1906; mem. Mark Daniels & Co., Inc., 1906-12; apptd. landscape engr. Yosemite Nat. Park, 1914; gen. supt. and landscape engr., U.S. Nat. Parks, 1914-16; senior architect United States Housing Adminstration, Chinatown bldgs., San Francisco, Calif. Principal works; Mount St. Mary's College and Chapel; estate of John McCormick, Hollywood; Adminstration Bldg., Bel-Air; Bel-Air Bay Club, Los Angeles. Chinese Bldgs., Horticultural Bldg., and landscape architect for State of Calif. at Golden Gate Internat. Expn.; Municipal Auditorium, Santa Cruz, Calif.; The Riviera, Los Angeles, and Pebble Beach, Calif. Asso. mem. Am. Society of Civil Engrs.; mem. Am. Civic Assn., Am. Inst. of Architects, Sigma Alpha Epsilon, Skull and Keys. Served as capt. engrs., U.S. Army, 1918-19; maj. Engr. R.C., from 1919. Clubs: Bohemian, Family (San Francisco). Author: Hillside Homes and Gardens (monograph), 1913; Planning Residential Subdivision (monograph), 1915; Coming Back (1 act play), 1915; Birth of a Notion (1 act play), 1916; Green Symbols, 1921; The Cycle (3 act play), 1933; Running Fire (a column). Editor Architect and Engineer. Pres. San Francisco Art Commission, 1945. Home: San Carlos, Calif.†

DANTON, GEORGE HENRY, prof. German; b. N.Y. City, May 31, 1880; s. Henry and Lucinda (Dollinger) D.; A.B., Columbia, 1902, Ph.D., 1907; m. Annina Periam, of Newark, N.J., June 20, 1907; children—J(oseph) Periam, (Elinor) Adrienne (Mrs. Edwin Oldfather Reischauer). Grad. student and asst. in comparative lit., Columbia, 1902-03; Austin teaching fellow, Harvard, 1903-04; Ottendorfer memorial fellow from New York U. to Berlin and Munich, 1904-05; instr. German Western Reserve U., 1905-07; acting asst. prof., Stanford U., 1907-10; Armstrong prof. German, Butler Coll., Indianapolis, 1910-14; prof. German, Reed Coll., Portland, Ore., 1915-16, Columbia, summer, 1915; prof. German Nat. Tsing Hua U., Peking, China, 1916-27; exchange prof. N.Y. U., 1920-21; visiting prof. U. of Leipzig, 1925-26; spl. lecturer, U. of Berlin, 1926; prof. German and head dept., Oberlin Coll., 1927-35, prof. of German in charge of the Dept. of Modern Langs., Union Coll., 1935-47, prof. emeritus from 1947; visiting prof. Coll. Mines and Metallurgy, El Paso, 1947-48, U. of Ariz., 1948-50. Lecturer; Graduate Sch., Western Reserve Univ., 1931-32. Field agent Simplified Spelling Bd., on Atlantic Coast, 1914-15, Pacific Coast rep., 1915-16, advisory council. Mem. Phi Beta Kappa Fraternity (president New York Alpha 1939-41), Modern Language Assn. America, Andiron Club of N.Y., Am. Assn. of Teachers of German (pres. Hudson Valley Chapter, 1936-39; dir. from 1939; nat. pres., 1941-42). Democrat. Unitarian. Decorated with the Order of Chia Ho. by the President of the Chinese Republic, 1919. Author: The Nature Sense in the Writings of Ludwig Tieck, 1907; Tieck's Essay on the Boydell Shakspere Gallery, 1912; Germany Ten Years After, 1928; The Culture Contacts of the U.S. and China, 1784-1844, 1931; Wie sagt man das suf deutsch?—A Practical Guide to Spoken German (with wife), 1936; The Chinese People, New Problems, Old Backgrounds, 1938. Editor: Gillparzer's Die Ahnfrau (with F. W. J. Heuser), 1907; Schäfer's Stories of the Rhine, 1935; Hausmann' Abel mit der Mundharmonika, 1937; Keller's Der Schmied Seines Glückes, Hauff's Die Karawane, 1939; Four German Stories (with M. W. Pfaffie), 1947. Translator: Grillparzer's Jewess of Toledo (with Annina Periam Danton), 1914; R. Wilheim's Confucius and Confucianism, with translator's notes and bibliography (with same), 1931. Contbr. to periodicals on German Philology and lit., also on Chinese ednl. and social conditions. Address: Tucson, Ariz.†

DANTZIG, HENRY POINCARE, electronics co. exec.; b. Bloomington, Ind., Aug. 4, 1918; s. Tobias and Anna G. (Ourison) D.; B.S. in Physics and Math., U. Md., 1939, teaching fellow, 1946-49; m. Mildred Betty Krieger, Nov. 1, 1941; children—Sharon H., Jonathan A. With communications div. Bendix Corp., Towson, Md., 1950-73, mgr. elec. engring., 1962-73. Cons. shaped beam antenna and microwave design. Served with USAAF, 1941-45. Mem. I.E.E.E. (sr.), Armed Forces Communications and Electronics Assn. Home: Baltimore, Md. Died Dec. 16, 1973; interred Baltimore, Md.

DANTZLER, LEHRE L(IVINGSTON), univ. prof.; born Bradford Springs, Sumter County, S.C., Aug. 17, 1878; son Rev. Daniel David and Mary Frances (Goggans) D.; A.B., Wofford Coll., Spartanburg, S.C., 1898, A.M., 1900, Litt.D., 1934; A.M. Vanderbilt U., 1902; stn., U. of Leipzig, 1904-06, 1908-12; m. Mary Elizabeth Hawkins, July 23, 1908; 1 dau., Mary Hawkins (Mrs. George T. Skinner). Teacher, Prosperity High Sch., S.C., 1898-99; prin. Lykesland (S.C.) High Sch., 1899-1900, Crowley (La.) High Sch., 1902-04; prof. modern langs., Citadel Mil. Coll. ofS.C., 1906-08; lektor für englische literatur, U. of Leipzig, 1909-12; prof. and head of dept., U. of Ky., 1912-17; retired 1947. Mem. Modern Lang. Assn., Am. Dialect Soc., Am. Folklore Soc., Ky. Edn. Assn., Phi Beta Kappa. Phi Delta Kappa, Kappa Sigma. Democrat. Methodist. Consultant on pronunication. Webster's New International Dictionary. Home: Lexington, Ky.†

DARGUSCH, CARLTON SPENCER, JR., lawyer; b. Columbus, O., Nay 24, 1925; s. Carlton Spencer and Genevieve (Johnson) D.; B.S., Ohio State U., 1948, LL.B., 1951; m. Joyce B. Baltzell, June 5, 1947; children—Carlton Spencer III, William D., Timothy B., Jonathan D. Admitted to Ohio bar, 1951; now partner law firm Dargusch & Day, Columbus. Gen. counsel Ohio Assn. Broadcasters, Columbus; gen. counsel Ohio Dental Assn., Columbus counsel Armco Steel Corp.; v.p., sec., gen. counsel, dir. Copeland Corp., Sidney, O.; dir. Buckeye Union Ins. Cos. div. Continental Corp. Served with USNR, 1943-46; col. Ohio N.G., 1947-72. Mem. Phi Delta Phi, Beta Theta Pi. Republican. Rotarian. Clubs: The Columbus, Golf, Columbus Country, Columbus Athletic; Ft. Henry (Wheeling, W.Va.); Lyford Cay (Nassau, Bahamas). Home: Columbus, Ohio., Died Jan. 25, 1975.

DARIN, BOBBY, singer, songwriter; b. Bronx, N.Y., June 14, 1936; student Hunter Coll. Appeared Dorsey Bros. TV Show, Mar. 1956; first recording Rock Island Line, Dealer in Dreams, 1957; numerous recordings Decca Records; compositions include Splish, Splash, 1958; Dream Lover; That's All; Multiplication; If a Man Answers; others; wrote score film The Lively Set; appeared numerous nightclubs and TV shows. Pres. T.M. Music, Inc. Died Dec. 20, 1973.

DARLING, CHARLES ELLETT, physician; b. Detroit, May 4, 1917; s. Milton Alfred and Winogene (Ellett) D.; M.D., Wayne State U., 1943; m. Jean M. Holdredge, Aug. 30, 1968; children—Charles Ellett, Anne, Barbara L., Martha G. (Mrs. Jay W. Kenyon). Intern, Grace Hosp., 1943, asst. resident in obstetrics and gynecology, 1946-47, resident, 1947-48, chief resident, 1948-49, attending dept. obstetrics and gynecology; sr. attending dept. gynecology Detroit Receiving Hosp.; asso. attending Booth Meml. Hosp.; sr. attending staff Hutzel Hosp.; cons. gynecologist Straith Meml. Hosp., Alexander Blain Hosp. (all Detroit); asst. dept. obstetrics and gynecology Wayne State U., 1950-51, asst. clin. instr., 1951-53, clin. asst. prof., 1959-74. Served from 1st lt. to capt. M.C., AUS, 1944-46. Diplomate Am. Bd. Obstetrics and Gynecology. Mem. Wayne County Med. Soc. (pres.-elect). Home: Detroit, Mich. Died Dec. 26, 1974.

DARLING, CHESTER ARTHUR, prof. biology; b. Leon, N.Y., Oct. 4, 1880; s. Charles D. and Dora R. (Laing) D.; A.B., Albion (Mich.) Coll., 1904, A.M., 1906; Ph.D., Columbia, 1909; Sc.D. honoris causa, Allegheny Colt., 1948; married. Madge Williams, Aug. 5, 1908; 1 son, Richard W. Prof. biology, Definance (Ohio) Coll., 1904-06; asst. in botany, 1906-08, tutor, 1908-10, instr., 1910-23, Columbia; prof. biology and head dept. biol., Allegheny Coll., Pa., 1913-48; acting president, 1947-48, professor emeritus of biology from 1948. Fellow A.A.A.S., member Bot. Soc. Am., American Public Health Assn., Am. Genetic Assn., Soc. Am. Bacteriol., Sigma Xi, Delta Sigma Rho, Phi Gamma Delta, Phi Beta Kappa. Club: Round Table. Author: Handbook of the Wild and Cultivated Flowering Plants, 1915; Spring Flowers, 1913; Learning to Live, 1947. Home: Meadville, Pa.†

DARLING, EDWARD, editor, author; b. Roxbury, Mass., June 19, 1907; s. Charles B. and Effie (MacNaughton) D.; A.B., Dartmouth, 1929; postgrad. Harvard, 1930-31; lf. Dorothea Dane Parker, July 11, 1932; 1 dau., Nancy Joan (Mrs. Carl Hard, Jr.). Head English dept. Yarmouth High Sch., Bass River, Mass., 1934-39; head social scis. dept. Belmont (Mass.) Jr. High Sch., 1940-45; sales mgr. Beacon Press, Boston, 1945-58, dir., 1958-62; dir. dept. publs. Unitarian Universalist Assn., Boston, 1958-69; gen. editor Am. Unitarian Assn. 1969-72; ret., 1972; instr. creative Writing Cape Cod Community Coll., 1972-74. Author: Three Oldtimers, 1936; (documentary novel) How We Fought for Our Schools, 1954; Old Quotes at Home, 1966; (with Ashley Montagu) The Ignorance of Certainty, The Prevalence of Nonsense, 1967; They Cast Long Shadows, 1969; When Sparks Fly Upward, 1970; (with Ashley Montague) The Ignorance of Certainty, 1970. Home: Dennis, MA. Died Dec. 12, 1974.

DARLING, PHILIP GRENVILLE, mechanical engineer; b. Somerville, Mass., May 25, 1878; s. Samuel C. and Anna F. (Boyd) D.; A.B., Harvard, 1901; student Harvard Law Sch., 1902; S.B., Mass. Inst. Tech., 1905; unmarried. with Manning Maxwell & Moore, Inc., 1905-10, as mech. engr.; with E. I. Du Pont de Nemours Powder Co., from 1910, chief engr. Exptl. Sta. Republican. Conglist. Mem. Am. Soc. Mech. Engrs., 1912 (chmn. com. on safety valves), Phi Beta Epsilon. Author of papers on safety valves read before engring. societies. Address: Wilmington, Del.†

DARRAH, WILLIAM LEE, lawyer, oil co. exec.; b. Cody, Wyo., Feb. 8, 1911; s. Hudson W. and Kathleen M. (Talmadge) D.; A.B.; U. Neb., 1931, J.D., 1933; m. Inga Margit Sundheim, Oct. 24, 1943; children—Gary Spencer, Richard W. Admitted to Tex. bar, 1934; asso. firm Madden, Adkins, Pipkin & Keffer, 1935-39; atty. Amarillo Oil Co. (Tex.), 1939-49, v.p., 1949—. Mem. exec. bd. Llano Estacado council Boy Scouts Am. Bd. dirs. Potter County (Tex.) chpt. A.R.C., 1949-50. Mem. Am., Tex., Amarillo, Fed. Power bar assns., Ind. Natural Gas Assn. Am., Chi Phi, Phi Delta Phi. Presbyn. Mason. Kiwanian (former dir. San Jacinto). Home: Amarillo Tex. Died Dec. 29, 1973.

DARSEY, JOSEPH FREDERICK, clothing mfg. exec.; b. Amsterdam, Ga., Apr. 11, 1926; s. Charles H. and Mettie (Connell) D.; B.Indsl. Engring., Ga. Inst. Tech., 1949; m. Parkerlyn Florence, Dec. 27, 1952; children—Laurie, Joseph, Steven, Jonathan. Mgmt. trainee Stockham Valves & Fittings Co., Birmingham, Ala., 1948-49; engr. Jaco Pants, Inc., Ashburn, Ga., 1950, plant mgr., 1951-53; v.p., gen. mgr. Anniston (Ala.) Sportswear Corp., 1954-59; founder, pres., gen. mgr. Darsey Mfg. Co., Tallapoosa, Ga., 1960-74; pres. Darsey Clothing Co., Inc., East Point, Ga. Dir. W. Ga. Bank of Tallapoosa. Mem. exec. bd. Ga. div. Am. Cancer Soc.; mem. adv. bd. Shorter Coll., Rome, Ga.; mem. Atlanta Area council Boy Scouts Am. Named Man of Yr., City of Tallapoosa, 1969. Served with AUS, 1944-46. Mem. Ga. Inst. Tech. Alumni Assn. (trustee), Tau Beta Pi, Alpha Tau Omega. Presbyn. (elder). Home: Atlanta, Ga. Died Aug. 27, 1974; interred Forest Lawn Meml. Gardens, College Park, Ga.

DART, EDWARD DUPAQUIER, architect; b. New Orleans, May 28, 1922; s. Henry Plauche and Suzanne (Dupaquier) D.; student U. Va., 1940-42; B.Arch., Yale U., 1949; m. Wilma Cornelia Piansoen, Jan. 19, 1946; children—Elaine Dupaquier, Philip Edward. Pres. Edward D. Dart & Assos., Chgo., 1950-65; v.p. Loebl Schlossman, Bennett & Dart, Chgo., 1965-69, pres., 1969-75; asso. prof. arch. U. Ill., 1963-64. Served to capt. USNR, 1942-45. Fellow A.I.A. Home: Barrington, Ill. Died July 9, 1975; interred Barrington.

DART, RAYMOND OSBORNE, ret. army officer; b. Kansas City, Kan., July 5, 1890; s. Ernest Clinton and Jenny (Osborne) D.; A.B., U. of Kan., 1914; M.D., Rush Med. Coll., 1916; Sternberg medalist and hon. grad. Army Med. Sch., 1921, grad. basic course Med. Field Service Sch., Carlisle Barracks, Pa., 1921; m. Mary Eleanor Thomas, Sept. 8, 1917; children—Raymond Thomas, Robert Clinton, William Carleton. Interne, Presbyterian Hosp., Chicago, 1916-17, resident in gen. surgery Wichita (Kan.) Hosp., 1917 (7 mos.); commd. 1st lt., M.C., U.S. Army, 1917, and advanced through grades to brig. gen., 1948; asst. bn. surgeon, 814 Pioneer Engr. Bn., Rimacourt and Dijon, sanitary officer Dijon dist., asst. dist. surgeon, 1918-19; san. officer, Brest, France, 1919; ward surgeon and mess officer, sta. hosp., Coblenz, Germany, 1919-21; pathologist 3d Army Area, Camp Meade, Md., 1922; pathologist Army Med. Mus., instr. Army Med. Sch., 1923-27, 1932-36, curator, 1935-36; asst. chief preventive medicine div., Office Surgeon Gen., 1924-26; pathologist bd. health lab., Ancon Canal Zone, 1928-32; chief of lab. service Letterman Gen. Hosp., 1936-42; comdg. officer, 105th Gen. Hosp. Unit, S.W. Pacific Area, 1942-43, surgeon Base Sect. 3, Feb.-Sept. 1943, Advanced and Intermediate sect., Services of Supply, New Guinea, Sept. 1943-Mar. 1944, dept. chief surgeon, Apr. 1944-Oct. 1945; dir. Army Inst. of Pathology, Wash., 1946-50; cons. in pathology to surgeon gen., Dept. of Army, 1946-50; dir. Washington Regional Blood Center, A.R.C., Washington, 1954-65, ret.; cons. Armed Forces Inst. Pathology, Washington. Decorated Bronze Star Medal, Legion of Merit (U.S.), Medal of Epidemics for work on influenza (France). Fellow A.M.A., Am. Soc. Clin. Pathologist. A.A.A.S., Am. Coll., Physicians, Coll., Am. Pathologists; asso. Am. Urol. Assn.; mem. Internat. Acad. Pathology, Am. Assn. Pathologists and Bacteriologists, Medical Society of District of Columbia, Am. Acad. Oral Pathology (hon.), Assn. Mil. Surgeons, Am. Acad. Ophthalmology and Otolaryngology (hon.), Mil. Order of Carabao, Academy of Medicine of Washington, Washington Soc. Pathologists (charter mem.), Nu Sigma Nu. Mason. Home: Falls Church Va. Died Feb. 2, 1974.

DARVAS, LILI, actress; b. Budapest, Hungary, Apr. 10, 1902; d. Sandor and Berta (Frieberger) D.; came to U.S., 1938, naturalized, 1944; grad. High sch.; m. Ferenc Molnar, June 9, 1926. Appeared in numerous stage plays, 1922—, including Romeo and Juliet, Budapest, 1922; joined Max Reinhardt's repertory theatre appearing in Vienna, Austria, Berlin, Germany, 1926-38, Salzburg Festivals, summers 1926-29; appeared in German lang. prodns. A Midsummer Nights Dream, 1927, Everyman, 1927, Danton's Death, 1927, Servant of Two Masters, 1928; appeared in New York stage plays The Criminals, 1941, Soldiers Wife, 1944, Hamlet, 1945, Bravo, 1948, Cry of the Peacock, 1950, Hidden River, 1957, The Waltz of the Toreadors, 1958, Cheri, 1959, A Far Country, 1961, First Love, 1961, My Mother, My Father and Me, 1963, Happiness, 1967, The Miser, 1969, Les Blancs, 1970; motion pictures include title role of Marie Baskirchev, Germany, 1936, Meet Me in Las Vegas (MGM), U.S., 1956, Cimarron (MGM), 1961, Love (Szerelem), 1971; appeared in numerous television prodns., 1950 , last being Rachel, La Cubana, WNET Opera Theater, 1974. Mem. Actors Equity Assn., A.F.T.R.A., Screen Actors Guild. Home: New York City N.Y. Died July 22, 1974.

DARWIN, SIR ROBIN (ROBERT VERE DARWIN), artist; b. May 7, 1910; s. Bernard Darwin; student Eton Coll., Slade Sch. Fine Arts, U. London; D.Litt. (hon.), Newcastle U., 1964, Birmingham U., 1966; m. Yvonne Darby, (div.); m. 2d, Ginette Hewitt. Asst. master Eton Coll., 1933-38; comouflage directorate Ministry Home Security, 1939-44; mem. staff Council Indsl. Design, 1945-46, mem. council, 1947-55, 62-67; prof. fine art U. Durham (Eng.), 1946-47; prin. Royal Coll. Arts, London, 1948-67, rector, vice-provost, 1968-71. Exhibited in one man shows at Redfarm Galleries, 1933, 44, Messrs. Agnews, 1935, 38, 40, 51, 52, 55, 61, 64, Leicester Galleries, 1946; mem. Sci. Mus. Adv. Council, 1951-59, Nat. Adv. Council on Art Edn., 1959-69, Nat. Council for Diplomas in Art and Design, 1961-69, Royal Mint Adv. Com. Bd. govs. Imperial Coll. Sci. and Tech. Recipient Bicentenary medal Royal Soc. Arts, 1962. Fellow U. Coll. Hon. fellow Soc. Indsl. Artists; mem. Inst. Dirs. (mem. arts adv. council), Royal Soc. Arts (mem. council 1954-59). Address: England Died 1973.

DAS, RAJANI KANTA, economic advisor, author; b. Demra Dacea; India, May 9, 1881; s. Chamaru and Nandarani Das; B.S. in Agr., Ohio State; M.S. in Agr., U. of Missouri; M.A. in Biology, U. of Wisconsin, Ph.D. in Economics, 1916; m. Sonya Ruth Sklar, June 7, 1922. Chemist, 1917-19; lecturer in economics, Northwestern U., 1919-20, New York U., 1920-22; special agent of U.S. Bureau of Labor Stat., 1921-22; sec. mem. (princ. economist), Internat. Labor Office, Geneva, Switzerland, 1925-40; chief, Resources Adjustment Sect., Fgn. Economic Adminstrn. and State Dept., U.S. Govt., 1942-46; economic advisor to Mil. Govt. on Nat. Econ. Bd., Seoul, Korea, 1946-47; spl. lecturer Calcutta U. Readership, 1937, Batna U. Bennili Readership, 1941; read treatises on Indian population at World Population Congress, Geneva, 1927, Rome, 1932, Paris, 1937. Mem. Am. Econ. Assn. Unitarian. Club: Cosmos (Washington). Author: Factory Labor in India, 1923; Labor Movement in India, 1923; Hindustani Workers on the Pacific Coast, 1923; Production in India, 1924; Industrial Efficiency in India, 1930; Plantation Labor in India, 1931; Woman Labor in India, 1931; Child Labor in India, 1933; Principles and Problems of Indian Labor Legislation, 1938; Industrial Labor in India, 1938; History of Indian Labor Legislation, 1941; India and a New Civilization, 1942; Wartime Labor Conditions in India, Bulletin No. 755, U.S. Bur. of Labor Statisics, 1943. Contbr. of many important treatises and articles on economic subjects for various jours.; these and similar other studies, partly subsidized and published by U.S. Bureau of Labor Statistics, U. of Calcutta and Internat. Labor Office, were undertaken to develop India's economic potential, to build India' labor economics, and to outline, jointly with Mrs. Das, a program for India's rising new civilization. Home: Washington, D.C.†

DASHIELL, JOHN FREDERICK, educator; b. Indpls., Apr. 30, 1888; s. John William and Fannie Sophia (Myers) D.; B.S., Evansville (Ind.) Coll., 1908, B.Litt., 1909, Sc.D., 1961; A.M., Columbia, 1910, Ph.D., 1913; m. Clara Sylvia Knowles, Sept. 17, 1912 (dec. May 1948); children— Frederick Knowles, Dorothy Ann (Mrs. Adrian Waddell Smith); m. 2d, Thelma Hill Smith, Sept. 5, 1950 (dec. Nov. 1970). Instr. history Evansville Coll., 1908-09; ast. philosophy Columbia, 1910-13; prof. philosophy and biology Waynesburg Coll., 1913-14; instr. philosophy Princeton, 1914-15; instr. philosophy U. lfinn., 1915-16, instr. psychology, 1916-17; asst. prof. psychology Oberlin Coll., 1917-19; mem. faculty U. N. C., 1919-75, Kenan prof. psychology, 1935-58, emeritus, 1958-75; prof. psychology Wake Forest Coll., 1958-61; vis. prof. Syracuse U., summer 1925, Clark U., summer 1926, U. Tex., summer 1927, Columbia summer 1928, U. So. Cal., summers 1930-32, U. Ore., summers 1939-40, U. Wis., summer, 1945, Duke, summer 1946, U. Wyo., summer 1947, U. Cal. at Los Angeles, fall 1949-50, U. Fla., spring 1950, U. Rochester, summer 1961, Fla. State U., 1961-62, U. Del., summer 1962, Emory U., 1962-63, Fla. Presbyn. Coll., 1964-65. lfem. fellowship com. NRC, 1937-38. Mem. So. Soc. Philosophy and Psychology (pres. 1924), Soc. Exptl. Psychologists (pres. 1937), A.A.A.S. (v.p. sect. I, 1939), Am. (pres. 1937, past chmn. com. sci. and profl. ethics), N.C. Acad. Sci. (pres. 1960). Author: Fundamentals of Objective Psychology, 1928; An Experimental Manual in Psychology, 1931; Fundamentals of General Psychology, 2d edit., 1949. Cons. editor McGraw-Hill, 1931-50; contbg. editor Ency. Americana, 1957-75. Home: Alexandria, Va. Died May 3, 1975.

DAUGHERTY, JAMES HENRY, artist; b. Ashville, N.C., June 1, 1889; s. Charles M. and Susan Peyton (Telfair) D.; prep. edn., Central High Sch., Washington, D.C.; student Corcoran Sch. Art, Washington, Pa., Acad. Fine Arts, Phila. pupil Frank Brangwyn, London, Eng.; m. Sonia Medwedeff, 1913; 1 son, Charles M. Represented at Yale Mus. Art, Mus. Modern Art, N.Y.C., Whitney Mus. Am. Art, N.Y.C., Mus. Legion of Honor, San Francisco, Spencer collection N.Y. Pub. Library, Smithsonian Inst., Washington, Montclair (N.J.) Mus.; executed mural paintings, Lowes State Theatre, Cleve., Sesquicentennial Exposition, Phila., Stamford High Sch., Ship camoufleur, designer war posters for U.S. Navy and Shipping Bd., World War I. Recipient Newberry medal for most distinguished contribution to Am. literature for children, 1939. Mem. Authors Guild, Silvermine Guild Artists, P.E.N. Illustrator numerous books. Author and illustrator: Of Courage Undaunted, 1951; A. Lincoln; Daniel Boone; Poor Richard; Andy and the Lion; The Magna Charta; The Picnic, 1958; William Blake, 1961; Walt Whitman's America, 1964; others. Home: Westport, Conn. Died Feb. 21, 1974.

DAVES, JESSICA, editor; b. Cartersville, Ga.; d. Walter and Annie (Hopkins) Daves; m. Robert Allerton Parker, Dec. 20, 1930. Fashion mdse. editor Vogue (Conde Nast Publs., Inc.), 1933-36, mng. editor, 1936-46, editor in chief, 1946-63. Decorated Italian Star of Solidarity; French Legion of Honor. Mem. Fashion Group Am. (pres.), MacDowell Assn. (bd. dir.), Women Poets N.Y., English Speaking Union. Clubs: Cosmopolitan (N.Y.C.); Nat. Press (Washington). Author: Vogue Book of Menus; Ready-Made Miracle. Co-author: The World in Vogue. Home: New York City, N.Y. Died Sept. 1974.

DAVIDOFF, LEO MAX, neurol. surgeon; b. Talsen, Latvia, Jan. 16, 1898; s. Israel and Libbe (Lemkus) D.; brought to U.S., 1905, naturalized, 1921; M.D., Harvard, 1922; L.H.D. (hon.), Yeshiva U., 1952; m. Ida Fisher, Oct. 3, 1926; children—Helen, Leonore, Frank, Mary. Interne Peter Bent Brigham Hosp., 1923-26; Surgeon Byrd-Macmillan Arctic expdn., 1925; chief dept. neurol. surgery, attending neurol. surgeon Jewish Hosp. of Bklyn., 1937-45; attending neurological surgeon Montefior Hosp., N.Y.C., 1945-49; professor of clinical neurological surgery, Coll. Phys. & Surg., Columbia U., 1945-49; neurosurg. to Mt. Sinai Hospital, N.Y.C., 1951-57; professor, chairman department of neurological surgery, associate dean of college, Albert Einstein College of Medicine of Yeshiva University, until 1966, professor emeritus, 1966-75; dir. neurosurgery Bronx Municipal Hosp. Center, Chmn. medical mission to Finland, 1948, Israel and Iran, 1951 (auspices Unitarian Service Committee and W.H.O.). Surgeon to Byrd Macmillan Arctic Expedition, June-Oct. 1925. Mem. Unitarian Service Com. Med. Mission Czechoslovakia, summer, 1946. Awarded Charles U. of Praha, hon. medal, Order White Lion, Fourth Class (Czechoslovakia). Diplomate Am. Bd. Neurological Surgery. Fellow A.C.S.; mem. A.M.A., Med. Soc., Am. Neurol Assn., Soc. Neurol. Surgs., (pres. 1951), Harvey Cushing Soc. (pres. 1957), Harvey Soc., Research Assn. for Nervous and Mental Diseases, A.A.A.S., Am. Assn. Neuropathology, N. Y. Acad. Medicine. Author 4 books and 200 papers in field. Home: New Canaan, Conn., Died Dec. 24, 1975.

DAVIDSON, DE WITT A., mfg. jeweler; b. New York, N.Y., Oct.17, 1878; s. Aaron Davidson and Isabella (Schiele) D.; ed. pub. schs.; m. Josephine Lehman, of New York, N.Y., Jan. 6, 1908; children—Elinor B., De Witt Sanger. Began in mfg. jewelry business and importing precious stones New York, 1908; pres. and treas. DeWitt A. Davidson Co.; retired. Mem. Liberty Loan, Red Cross and other drives, World War. Former pres. and dir. Nat. Jewelers Bd. of Trade, Jewelry Crafts Assn. of N.Y., 24 Karat Club of New York. Life mem. Nat. Rifle Assn. (Washington, D.C.). Republican. Christian Scientist. Elk. Clubs: Colonial Yacht, 24 Karat Club, City. Home: New York, N.Y.†

DAVIDSON, HENRY ALEXANDER, physician; b. Newark, May 27, 1905; s. Louis L. and May (Tannenbaum) D.; M.D., Jefferson Med. Coll., Phila., 1928; M.Sc. in Neuropsychiatry, U. Pa., 1931; m. Adelaide Heyman, Oct. 20, 1936; children—Laurence J., Ellen M. Supt. Essex County Hosp., Cedar Grove, N.J., 1954-69; mem. staff VA Hosp.; lectr. in psychiatry Columbia, 1954-73. Bd. dirs. Mental Health Assn. Essex County. Served to maj., M.C., AUS, 1942-45. Diplomate Am. Bd. Psychiatry and Neurology. Mem. Am. Psychiat. Assn. (parliamentarian), N.J. Neuropsychiat. Assn. (pres.). Author: Forensic Psychiatry, 1952, 2d edit., 1965; Short History of Chess, 1949; Handbook of Parliamentary Procedure, 1955; Guide to Medical Writing, 1957. Editor: Jour. Med. Soc. N.J., 1941-73. Home: East Orange, N.J. Died Aug. 23, 1973.

DAVIDSON, THOMAS WHITFIELD, judge; b. Harrison County, Tex., Sept. 23, 1876; s. John Ransom and Sarah Josephine (Daniels) D.; spl. course study Columbia and U. of Chicago; studied law privately; m. Asenath Burkhart, 1902; m. 2d, Mrs. Constance Key Wandel; April 12, 1936 (deceased July 7, 1948); m. 3d, Beulah Rose, Sept. 4, 1949. Admitted to Texas bar, 1903; practiced in Marshall; city atty., 1907-14; state senator, 1920-22; lt. gov. Tex., 1922-24; U.S. dist. judge No. District Texas, 1936-65, sr. Fed. dist. judge, 1965-74. Mem. Dem. Nat. Conv., 1912, 32. Mem. Am., Tex. (pres. 1927), and Dallas bar assns.; pres. Harrison County Bar Assn., 1916. Mem. S.A.R. Democrat. Episcopalian. Odd Fellow (past grand master Tex.). Club: Town and Gown. Author books on hist. and legal subjects. Home: Ennis, Tex. Died Jan. 25, 1974.

DAVID-WEILL, PIERRE SYLVAIN DESIRE GERARD, banker b. Paris, France, lfar. 8, 1900; s. David and Flora (Raphael) David-Weill; Ph.B., Paris Academie, 1916; m. Berthe Haardt, Feb. 17, 1931; children—Michael Alexandre, Elaine Francoise Louise. Entered banking bus. with Lazard Freres & Co., N.Y.C., 1944-75; dir. Lazard Bros. & Co., Ltd., London, Banque de Paris et des Pays Bas, Cie. Financiére de Paris et des Pays-Bas, Rhone Poulenc S.A., Péchiney Ugine Kuhlmann. Pres., Conseil Artistique de la réunion des Musées Nationaux de France; mem. l'Istitut de France (Acaémie des Beaux Arts). Lt. 4 Rt. d'Auto-Mitrailleuses, French Army, 1940. Decorated Croix de Guerre, Officer Legion of Honor. Club: Travellers (Paris). Home: Paris France Died Jan. 1975.

DAVIE, PRESTON, lawyer; b. Louisville, Ky., Jan. 31, 1881; s. George Montgomery and Margaret Howard (Preston) D.; A.B., Harvard, 1904, Harvard Law School, 2 years; LL.D., University of North Carolina, 1946. Married Emily Bedford, January 4, 1910; m. 2d, Eugenie Mary Ladenburg, May 31, 1930. Member Humphrey, Davie & Humphrey, Louisville, Ky., 1907-09, O'Brien, Boardman & Platt, New York, 1910-13, O'Brien, Board, Harper & Fox, 1913-17; member board of directors Universal Pictures, Inc. Apptd. assistant director Council National Defense, April 1917; chmn. remount committee of Council Nat. Defense; lt. col. Gen. Staff U.S. Army; hon. disch. Aug. 8, 1919; col. O.R.C. Chevalier Order Crown (Belgium), Distinguished Service Medal, Grand Officer, Order White Rose (Finland). Mem. Soc. of the Cincinnati, Soc. Colonial Wars. Clubs: Knickerbocker, Brook, Metropolitan. Home: New York City, N.Y.†

DAVIES, JOHN NEWTON, prof. N.T. Greek Exegesis; b. Denbigh, N. Wales, Feb. 25, 1881; s. David H. and Catherine Lloyd (Hughes) D.; A.B., U. of Wales, 1902; B.D., Didsbury Wesleyan Coll., 1905; S.T.D., Syracuse U., 1926; m. Sarah Ann Parry, of Barmouth, N. Wales, Aug. 24, 1909. Ordained ministry Wesleyan. Meth. Ch., 1909; pastor Cardiff, Wales, 1907-13, Lanceston, Eng., 1913-16, Liverpool, 1916-19; visiting prof. N.T. Greek Exegesis, Drew Theol. Sem., 1919-26, prof. from 1926. Home: Madison, N.J.†

DAVIES, MARTIN, mus. ofcl.; b. London, Eng., Mar. 22, 1908; s. Ernest and Eleanor (Taylor) D.; B.A., King's Coll., Cambridge, Eng., 1930; hon. D.Litt., U. Exeter, 1968. With Nat. Gallery, London, Eng., 1932-, dir., 1968-73. Decorated comdr. Brit. Empire; created knight. Fellow Brit. Acad., Soc. Antiquaries of London, Museum Assn. Home: London, England. Died Mar. 7, 1975.

DAVIES, PAUL LEWIS, banker; b. Cozad, Neb., July 27, 1899; s. Robert and Emma Estella (Bennison) D.; student U. Cal. at Berkeley, 1917-21, Harvard Sch. of Bus., 1921-22; m. Faith Crummey, Oct. 2, 1926; children—Paul Lewis, Nancy (dec.), Judith. Clk., Nat. Bank of Commerce, 1922; asst. cashier, asst. v.p., and v.p. Am. Trust Co., 1923-28; v.p., treas., exec. v.p. and treas., pres. Food Machinery & Chem. Corp. (now FMC Corp), 1928-56, chmn. bd., chief exec. officer, 1956-66, dir., chmn. exec. com., 1966-67, sr. dir. and dir., 1967-72, sr. dir. emeritus, 1972; sr. mng. dir. Lehman Bros., N.Y.C., 1966-75; dir. Lehman Corp., IBM; adv. com. Export-Import Bank, 1971. Mem. Bus. Council; hon. trustee Com. Econ. Devel. Founding dir. Stanford Research Inst.; adv. bd. U. Cal. Sch. Bus. Adminstrn. Served U.S. Army, 1918. Mem. Smithsonian Inst. Assos. (dir.), Alpha Sigma Phi. Methodist. Mason. Clubs: Sainte Claire (San Jose, Cal.); Pacific Union, Bohemian (San Francisco); Links, Recess (N.Y.C.); Cypress Point (Pebble Beach, Cal.); Cotton Bay (Eleuthera Island, Bahamas). Home: San Jose, Cal., Died Nov. 25, 1975.

DAVIES, RODGER PAUL, fgn. service officer; b. Berkeley, Cal., May 7, 1921; s. John Leslie and Catherine Paul (Rodgers) D.; B.A., U. Cal. at Berkeley, 1942; student U.S. Army War Coll., 1958-59; m. Sarah Ann Burgess, Sept. 29, 1948 (dec. 1973); children—Ann Dana, John Burgess. Joined U.S. diplomatic service, 1946; 3d sec. and vice counsul, Jidda, Saudi Arabia, 1946-48; assigned Fgn. Service Inst. for Arabic tng., 1948-49, 2d sec. and consul, Damascus, 1949-51; 2d sec. and consul, Beirut, Lebanon, and Amman, Jordan, 1950-51, also consul, Jerusalem, 1950-51; dep. chief Near East, South Asia and Africa div., Internat. Broadcasting Service, 1951-54; prin. officer Am. Embassy, Benghazi, Libya, 1954-56; counselor of embassy and dep. chief of mission Am. Embassy, Tripolli, Libya, 1956-58; with U.S. Army War Coll., 1958; became counselor Embassy and dep. chief Mission at Baghdad, Iraq, 1959; dir. Office Near Eastern Affairs, Dept. of State, 1962-65; dep. asst. sec. state for Near Eastern and South Asian affairs, 1965-74, career minister, 1969. Home: Berkeley, Cal. Died Aug. 19, 1974; interred Berkeley, Cal.

DAVILA, CÉLEO, Honduras diplomat; b. Trujillo, Honduras, 1880; LL.B., U. Honduras. Secretary of pub. edn., then sec. treasury; sec. Honduran legation, Washington, became minister plenipotentiary, now ambassador to U.S. Dir. La Tribuna, daily. Contbr., El Cronista, Tegucigalpa. Home: Washington, D.C.†

DAVIS, ADELLE (MRS. FRANK V. SIEGLINGER), nutritionist, author: b. Lizton, Ind., Feb. 25, 1904; d. Charles Eugene and Harriet (McBroom) Davis; A.B., U. Cal. at Berkeley, 1927; M.S., U. So. Cal. 1939; D.Sc., U. Plano, 1927; m. Frank V. Sieglinger, Apr. 23, 1960; children—George D. Leisey, Barbara A. Leisey. Supr. nutrition Yonkers Pub. Schs., 1928-30; cons. nutritionist, Oakland, Cal., 1931-33; author, lectr., cons. nutritionist, Los Angeles, 1934-74. Dir. West, Insts. for Achievement Human Potential. Recipient Raymond Dart award, 1972, Brazilian Honor of Merit, 1971. Hon. fellow Internat. Coll. Applied Nutrition. Author: Let's Cook It Right, 1947, rev. edit., 1964; Let's Have Healthy Children, 1951, rev. edit. 1973; Let's Eat Right To Keep Fit, 1954; Let's Get Well, 1965. Home: Palos Verdes Estates, Cal Died May 31, 1974.

DAVIS, BRUCE GREGORY, civil engr.; b. Kansas City, Mo., Nov. 24, 1908; s. Herbert Rowan and May (Merritt) D.; B.S., Antioch Coll., 1932; grad. Insl. Coll. Armed Forces, 1954; m. Ruth Penfield Hollenbeck, June 14, 1934; children—Susan (Mrs. David Pearce Snyder), Margaret (Mrs. Rudolph Jaskar). Engr. constrn. Boulder Canyon Project, Nev., 1934-40; area engr. Gatum Third Locks, Panama, C.Z., 1941-45; constrn. contract adminstrn. Bur. Reclamation, Denver, 1945-49, chief schedules br., Washington, 1950-57, chief div. program coordination and finance, 1958-67; irrigation engr. Internat. Bank Reconstrn, and Devel., 1968-75. Registered profl. engr., D.C. Mem. Am. Soc. C.E. Home: Bethesda, Md. Died May 8, 1975.

DAVIS, CHAMPION MCDOWELL, ry. ofcl McDowell ; b. Hickory, N.C., July 1, 1879; s. Robert Burns and Cornelia (Nixon) D.; ed. pub. schs.; ScD., The Citadel, 1952. Beginning as messenger Wilmington & Weldon R. R. (now S.C.L.R.R.), 1893, became successively clk., stenographer freight rate clk., chief rate clk., to 1902, chief clk. traffic dept., 1902-06. asst. gen. freight agt., 1906-11, gen. freight agt. lines south of Charleston, S.C., 1911-16, gen. freight agt. entire system, 1916-18; mem. so. freight traffic com. U.S.R.R. Adminstrn., 1918-20, so. freight rate com., representing so. rail and water carriers, 1920; asst. freight traffic mgr. A.C.L.R.R., 1921-25, freight traffic mgr., 1925-28, v.p., traffic, 1928-39, v.p. all depts., 1939, exec. v.p., 1940-42, pres., 1942-57, ret., 1957; former dir. Jefferson Standard Life Ins. Co. Dir. U.S. C. C., 1949-52, former mem. governing bd. Nations Business. Mem. nat. council P.E. Ch., 1946-52; trustee cape Fear Tech. Inst., Wilmington, N.C.; former trustee Episcopal Radio-TV Found., P.E. Theol. Sem. Va., N.C. Ednl. Radio and Television Commn; chmn. bd. trustees Cape Fear Meml. Hosp., Inc., Wilmington, N.C.; dir. emeritus Episcopal Ch. Found.; founder and prin. donor Champion McDowell Davis Charitable Found., 1963, Cornelia Nixon Davis Nursing Home, Porter's Neck Plantation. Served as pvt. and cpl. 2d Regt., N.C. Inf., - Porter's Spanish—Am. War, 1898, later with 2d N.C. State Guard; resigned as capt., 1901. Mem. United Spanish War Vets. (vice comdr.), N.C. Soc. Cin., N.Y. So. Soc., Am. Soc. Traffic and Transp. (charter mem.), Am. Ry. Engring. Assn., Am. Assn. Passenger Traffic Officers (hon.) Transp. Assn. Am. Newcomen Soc. Episcopalian. Clubs: Cape Fear, Cape Fear Country (Wilmington, N. C.); Surf (Wrightsville Beach, N.C.0: Wilmington Press. Home: Wilmington NC. Died Jan. 28, 1975; interred Porters Neck Plantation, Wilmington.

DAVIS, CHARLES HUBBARD, state supreme ct. justice; b. Fairfield, Ill., Jan. 7, 1906; s. Horace Hubbard and Helen M. (Decker) D.; A.B., U. Ill., 1928; J.D., U. Chgo., 1931; m. Ruth Peugh, Oct. 19, 1935; children—Jean, Joan, Martha (Mrs. Russell Dearing), Mary (Mrs. John Daday). Ruth (Mrs. Thomas Hazen), John Jay, and Thomas C. Admitted to Ill. bar, 1931. practiced in Rockford, 1931-55, mem. firm Thomas & Davis, 1945-55; justice Ill. Supreme Ct., 1955-60, 70-76; chief justice, 1957-58; mem. firm. Thomas, Davis and Kostantacos, 1960-65; justice 2d Dist. Ill. Appellate Ct., 1965-70. Past. pres., dir. Winnebago Farm Sch. for Boys. Mem. Am., Ill., Winnebago County bar assns., Am. Coll. Trial Lawyers, Phi Delta Phi. Republican. Conglist. Mason (Shriner). Home: Rockford, Ill., Died Feb. 22, 1976.

DAVIS, CHESTER CHARLES, consultant; born near Linden, Dallas County, Ia., November 17, 1887; son of William Highland and Elizabeth E. (Johnson) D.; B.A., Grinnell (Ia.) Coll., 1911, LL.D., (hon.) 1935; D.Sc. (hon.) Clemson (S.C.) Coll., 1937; LL.D., (hon.), U. Ark., Washington U., St. Louis, 1951, Montana State U., 1951; m. Helen Smith, Aug. 14, 1913; children—Chester Smith, Norman Hall. Newspaper work, S.D. and Mont., 1911-17; editor, mgr. The Montana Farmer, 1917-21; commr. agr. and labor, Mont., 1921-25; dir. grain marketing, Ill. Agri. Assn., 1925-26; agrl. service for farm orgns., 1926-28; exec. v.p. Maizewood Products Corp., 1929-33; dir. prodn. div. A.A.A., U.S. Dept. Agr., May 15-Dec. 15, 1933, adminstr. A.A.A., 1933-36; bd. govs. Fed. Reserve System 1936-41; pres. Fed. Res. Bank of St. Louis 1941-51; associate dir. Ford Found., 1951-54; study and report on Rural Credit in India for govt. of India, 1953-54; regents prof. agri. econs. University of Cal. at Berkeley, 1955. Dir. Citizens Comml. Trust & Savs. Bank, Chmn. bd. consultants Cal. Dept. Water Resources, 1958-59; member board of govs. Agri. Hall of Fame. Member Nat. Def. Adv. Commn., 1940-41; mem. Com. for Eco. Development; former pres., chmn. bd. Friends of the Land; chmn., public policy com., Advt. Council, Inc. Trustee Grinnell College, 1941-51, the J.N. Darling Foundation. Recipient of the medal for distinguished service to agr. Am. Farm Bur. Fedn., 1939. Mem. Phi Beta Kappa. Independent Democrat. Home: U1Winston-Salem, N.C. Died Sept. 25, 1975.

DAVIS, CLARENCE ALBA, lawyer; b. Beaver City, Neb.; s. Thomas Milburn and Nannie (Gelvin) D.; A.B., Nev. Wesleyan U., 1913; student U. Neb., 1911-13, LL.D.: LL.B., Harvard, 1916; LL.D., Lincoln Meml. U.; L.H.D., Neb. Wesleyan U.; m. Florence Wells, Aug. 2, 1916; 1 son, Thomas Milburn. In practice at Omaha, Neb. 1916-17; moved to Holdrege, Neb., 1917; atty. gen. of Neb., 1919-13; solicitor Dept. Interior, 1953-54, undersec. Dept. of Interior, 1954-57; now in law practice, Washington, Lincoln, Neb.; mem. firm Davis, Thone, Bailey. Pols. Counsel to Neb. interstate water litigation, and in preparation Neb.-Colo. Compact reference South Platte River, 1923; counsel to Mo. Valley Devel. Assn., 1945-46. Lectr. on adminstrv. law, U. Neb., 1943. Mem. commn. compiling Neb. statutes, 1922. Del. Rep. Nat. Conv., 1928, 32. Trustee Neb. Wesleyan U., 1923-27. Mem. Am. (ho. dels. 1951-58; gov. 1965-), Fed. (pres. 1955-56), Neb. (pres. 1950-51), Lincoln bar assns., Nat. Conf. Bar Assn. Presidents (council 1951-53), Inst. Jud. Administrn., Am. Law Inst., Neb. Hist. Soc. (gov.), Am. Judicature Soc., Order of Coif (hon.), Pi Kappa Delta. Republican. Episcopalian. Mason (33, Shriner). Mem. adv. bd. editors Am. Bar Assn. Jour., 1948-52. Clubs: University, National Lawyers, Cosmos, Metropolitan (Washington); Lawyers (N.Y.C.); University (Lincoln). Tennis champion of Neb., 1912-16. Contbr. law reviews. Home: Lincoln, Neb. Died May 1974.

DAVIS, FREDERICK BARTON, psychologist; b. Boston, Mass., Aug. 27, 1909; s. Ernest Lewis Frederick and Dorothy (Barton) D.; B.S., Boston U., 1931; Ed.M., Harvard, 1933, Ed.D., 1941; m. Charlotte W. Croon, Oct., 1940; 1 dau., Dorothy Barton (Mrs. James Franklin Truitt, Jr.). Psychologist Avon (Conn.) Old Farms Sch., 1936-39; editor, Co-operative Test Service, N.Y.C., 1939-42; prof. psychology and head dept. psychology George Peabody Coll. Tchrs., Nashville, 1947-49; prof. edn. Hunter Coll., 1949-64; prof. edn., dir. Center for Research in Evaluation and Measurement, U. Pa., 1964-75; lectr. Wellesley Coll., 1936-37, Univ. Cal., 1947, 56, 57, Harvard 1948, Tchrs. Coll. Columbia U., 1953-54, 60-62, 67-68, Syracure U., 1965; Fullbright prof. U. Amsterdam, 1957-58; vis. research prof. Rutgers U., 1970-71; dir. Test Research Service, 1947-75. Cons. Am. Council on Edn., 1947; spl. cons. Sec. of War. 1941-42, Sec. of Air Force, 1947-51; research cons. Philippine Center Lang. Study, Manila, 1959-66, Edn. Records Bur., 1964-72, Ford Found., 1967, Getulio Vargas Found., Rio de Janeiro, 1968-74, Coll. Entrance Exam. Bd., 1970-71. Served as aviation psychologist USAAF, 1942-47; discharged as maj. Decorated Legion of Merit. Fellow Am. Psychol. Assn.; mem. Psychometric Soc. Unitarian. Author: The AAF Qualifying Examination, 1947; Utilizing Human Talent, 1947; Item Analysis Data, 1946; Davis Reading Tests, 1958, 62; Educational Measurements and Their Interpretation, 1964; Item Analyse (Dutch), 1964; Analyse des Items (French), 1966; The Philippine Language-Teaching Experiments, 1967; Comprehension Skills of Mature Readers, 1967; Measurements of Mental Capability through Research in Reading, 1971. Editor Am. Edn. Research Jour.; Psychometric Monographs. Home: Bronxville, NY. Died Mar. 2, 1975; interred Brookdale Cemetery, Dedham, Mass.

DAVIS, GEORGE ARTHUR, army officer; b. Lynn, lMass., Dec. 19, 1892; s. Arthur and Jennie Florence (Holmes) D.; grad. Inf. Sch., 1925, Command and Gen. Staff Sch., 1933, Army War Coll., 1936, Army Indsl. Coll., 1937; B.S. in Foreign Service, Georgetown U., Washington, D.C., 1937; m. Mary Josephine Whittaker, Aug. 7, 1920 (div.); children—George (killed in action Korea); m. 2d Alice M. Havey, Aug. 18, 1947. Private and corpl., 1st Inf., Schofield Barracks, Hawaii, 1912-15; commd. 2d lt., Aug. 15, 1917, and advanced through the grades to brig. gen., Mar. 17, 1943; participated in ops. Chateau Thierry & Aisne Marne offensive with 2d Div. in China, 1929-31; chief of staff 10th Corps, 1942-43; chief staff 3d Army, Feb. 1943-Apr. 1944; asst. div. comdr. 28th Inf. Div., Normandy, Northern France, Germany, Ardennes, Colmar; now brig. gen., U.S. Army, ret. Asst. prof. mil. science Boston U., 1920-24; prof. mil. sci. Ripon Coll., Wis., 1933-35; instr. and asst. dir. training, Inf. School, 1937-41. Decorated Legion of Merit with oak leaf cluster, Silver Star with oak leaf cluster, Bronze Star with 2 oak leaf clusters, Legion of Honor, Croix de Guerre with Palm, Croix de Guerre with two citations (France), Chateau-Thierry Medal, Heroes de la Cote 204 (Villa de Chateau- Thierry, 1918), Citoyen d'Honneur de la Commune Libre de Centreville, Villa de Chateau-Thierry (France); recipient Minute Man award S.A.R., 1963. Mem. S.A.R. (past pres. Me.; nat. trustee 1959-64, v.p. gen. New Eng. dist. 1961-63), Soc. Colonial Wars (dep. gov. gen. 1962-67), Founders and Patriots Am., New England Hist. and Geneol. Soc., Baronial Order Magna Charta, Mil. Order Crusades, Four Chaplains Legion of Honor, Colonial Clergy, Order Crown Charlemagne U.S.A., also mem. Augustan Society. Author, pub.; Davis and Fifty Allied Colonial Families of New England; 1956; Some Royal, Noble, and Colonial Ancestors, 1959; Descent From a Hundred Kings, 1964, 2d edit., 1965. Home: Southport, Me. Died Jan. 10, 1969; interred Ipswich, Mass.

DAVIS, HAROLD THAYER, educator; b. Beatrice, Neb., Oct. 5, 1892; s. Harry Watson and Hellen Thayer (Moulton) D.; A.B., Colo. Coll., 1915; A.M., Harvard, 1919; Ph. D., U. Wis., 1926; LL.D., Colo. Coll. 1949; m. Agnes Marie Holm, Sept. 3, 1921; children—Hellen Dagmar (Mrs. Leon Little), Donald Holm, Harold Moulton. Instr. math. U. Wis., 1920-23; asst. prof. math. Ind. U., 1923-29, asso. prof., 1929-34, prof., 1934-37; acting prof. econometrics Colo. Coll., 1936-37; prof. math. Northwestern U., 1937-60, chmn. dept., 1942-55; prof. math. Trinity U., San Antonio, 1962—, chmn. dept., 1963-65; asso. Southwest Found., 1960-74; dir. Mind Sci. Found., San Antonio, 1960-62. Asso., Cowles Commn. for Research in Econs. Mem. Math. Assn. Am. (sec.-treas. Ind. sect. 1924-33), Econometric Soc., Phi Beta Kappa, Sigma XI, Delta Epsilon, Tau Kappa Alpha. Republican. Club: University (Evanston, Ill.). Author sci. publs. including: Political Statistics, 1948; Essays in the History of Mathematics, 1948; The Differential Equations of Mathematical Physics, 1949; (with Vera Fisher) Index and Bibliography of Mathematical Tables, 1949; Quantitative Aspects of the Action of Carcinogenic Substances, 1951; Quantitative Aspects of the Carcinogenic Radiations, 1952; Philosophy and Modern Science, 1953; The Fine Art of Punning, 1954; Alexandria, The Golden City, 1956; Studies in Differential Equations, 1956; Nonlinear Differential and integral Equations, 1961; (with M.G. McCown) General Mathematics, 1962; Summation of Series, 1962; vol. 3, Mathematical Function (with Vera Fisher), 1962; Adventures of an Ultra-Crepidarian, 1962; The Spectral Santa Claus, 1967; (with G. L. Holcomb) Moliere Resumes, 1971. Contbr. to sci., math. assns. jours. Translator: (with J.J. Buchanan) Zosimus' Historia Nova, 1967; (with G. Holcomb) Moliere Resumes, 1971. Home: San Antonio, Tex. Died Nov. 14, 1974; interred Evergreen Cemetery, Colorado Springs, Colo.

DAVIS, HOWARD CLARKE, musician; b. Lynn, Mass., May 4, 1881; s. Charles E. and Elizabeth (Clarke) D.; prep. edn., Vt. Mil. Acad., Saxtons River; student Colgate, 1899-1900; spl. student Boston U., 1913-14; B.Mus., Cincinnati Conservatory, 1930; Mus.D., Chicago Conservatory, 1931; M.A. from the University of Pittsburgh, 1933; m. Ottilie Czerny, Sept. 30, 1922. Formerly voice teacher, Lawrence, Chelsea, Boston, Yonkers, N.Y., and N.Y. City; choral condr., Lawrence, Chelsea, Andover, Malden, Newburyport, Watertown, Boston, 1905-17, Yonkers and Fredonia, N.Y., from 1917; dir. Sch. of Music, Chelsea, 1913-17, Yonkers, 1917-21; head of dept. music, State Normal Sch., Fredonia, 1924-31; prof. voice and head of sch. music dept., Villa Maria Coll., Erie, Pa., from 1931; v.p. Chicago Conservatory; dir. extension work, Nat. Acad. Music, N.Y. City, 1921-24, Founder, 1925, later dir. Western N.Y. Music Festival (6 days). Mem. Music Supervisors Nat. Conf., Music Teachers Nat. Assn., Eastern Music Supervisors Assn. (founder). Republican. Mason. Co-Author: University Course of Music Study (10 vols.). Contbr. to The Musician (formerly asso. editor). Home: Erie, Pa.†

DAVIS, JEANNE FRANCES WEST, (Mrs. Wayne Pitman Davis), newspaper editor; b. Charlton, Ia., Oct. 3, 1922; d. Thomas Francis and Maude (Baxter) West; B.A., Drake U., 1944; m. Wayne Pitman Davis, May 28, 1944; children—Kenneth Wayne, Polly Jeanne. Editor, co-pub. Seymour (Ia.) Herald, 1947-75. County pres. Wayne County Republican Women's Club, 1957-59; co-chmn. Wayne County Rep. Central Com., 1970-75. Named Ia. master editor-pub., Ia. Press. Assn., 1971. Mem. Wayne County Federated Women's Clubs (county pres. 1949-50), Bus. and Profl. Women's Club (pres. 1952-53, 56-57), Mortar Bd., Nat. TTT Soc. (chpt. pres. 1966-68), P.E.O. Home: Seymour, Ia., Died June 21, 1975.

DAVIS, JOE LEE, educator; b. Lexington, Ky., Feb. 22, 1906; s. Robert Lee and Jo (Greene) D.; A.B., U. Ky., 1926, A.M., 1927; Ph. D., U. Mich., 1934; D.Litt., No. Mich. U., 1971; m. Lorene Elizabeth Burke, June 10, 1929; 1 dau., Shirley Jo. Instr. in English, U. Ky., 1927-30; mem. faculty U. Mich., 1930-74, prof. English, 1948-74, acting chmn. dept., summers, 1957, 69, chmn. program in American culture, 1952-69; vis. prof. English, U. Minn., summer 1949, No. Mich. U., summers 1945, 53, 61. Mem. Modern Lang. Assn. of Am., Cabell Soc. (pres. 1968-69), Phi Beta Kappa. Author: Boyhood Dreams (poems), 1917; James Branch Cabell in Twayne U.S. Author Series, 1962; The Sons of Ben: Jonsonian Comedy in Caroline England, 1967. Editor: Am. Lit.; An Anthology and Critical Survey, 2 vols. (with John T. Frederick and Frank Luther Mott), 1948-49; Charlotte Bronte's Jane Eyre in Rinehart edits., 1950. Adv. coll. edn. Charles Scribner's Sons, 1949-59. Home: Ann Arbor, Mich. Died Feb. 19, 1974; buried Lexington, Ky.

DAVIS, JOHN KENNERLY, SR., utilities exec.; b. Bristol, Tenn., Oct. 5, 1906; s. John Fletcher and Caroline Frances (Bosang) D.; B.S., in Elec. Engring., Va. Mil. Inst., 1929; m. Ruth Addington Powers, July 11, 1931; children—John Kennerly, Dorothy Gordon. Engr. Pub. Service Co. Colo., Denver, 1929-30; engr. East Tenn. Light & Power Co., Bristol, 1930-36, supt., Greeneville, 1936-41, mgr., Erwin, 1941-42; personnel dir. Toledo Edison Co., 1946-49, v.p., dir., 1949-55, v.p., asst. gen. mgr., 1955-57, exec. v.p., asst. gen. mgr., dir., 1957-59, pres., dir., 1959-74, mem. exec. com., 1950-74; dir. Ohio Valley Electric Corp., Atomic Power Devel. Assos., Ohio Citizens Trust Co., Power Reactor Devel. Co. Active Toledo Mus. Art, East Central Area Reliability Group, Toledo Hosp., Masonic Toledo Trust, devel. council Med. Coll. Ohio, Boys' Club Toledo, Toledo Soc. for Crippled Children. Mem. Toledo Zool. Soc., Edison Electric Inst., Ohio, Toledo chambers commerce, I.E.E.E., Tech. Soc. Toledo, Am. Mgmt. Assn., Assn. Electric Illuminating Cos., Central Area Power Coordinating Group, A.I.M., Am. Legion, Newcomen Soc. N. Am., Eta Kappa Nu, Beta Gamma Sigma. Republican. Methodist. Rotarian. Clubs: Inverness; Belmont Country, Belmont Gun, Toledo. Home: Toledo, O. Died May 27, 1975; buried Shelby Hills Cemetery, Bristol, Tenn.

DAVIS, JOSEPH STANCLIFFE, economist; b. Frazer, Pa., Nov. 5, 1885; s. William Harmar and Mary Charles (Siddall) D.; grad. State Normal Sch., West Chester, Pa., 1902; A.B., Harvard, 1908, Ph.D., 1913; Doctor Letters of Humanity, Columbia, 1954; married Florence Harris Danielson, Aug. 31, 1916; children—Christine, Amy Barbara (dec.), Robert Danielson, Joseph Stancliffe, Jr. Tchr. pub. schs., Pa., 1902-04; dir. Food Research Inst., Stanford, 1921-52, prof. econ. research, 1938-52, emeritus, 1952-75; mem. Presiden's Council of Econ. Advisers, 1955-58. Asst. statistician Am. Shipping Mission, London, 1918-19; Statistican, Allied Maritime Transport Council, London, 1918-19; mem. Food and Nutrition Bd. Nat. Research Council, 1940-45, mem. Agrl. Bd., 1945-48; mem. bd. dirs. Social Sci. Research Council, 1924, 1946-48. Mem. Am. Econ. Assn., Am. Statis. Assn., Am. Farm Econ. Assn., Inter Am. Statis. Inst., Royal Econ. Soc. Phi Beta Kappa, Delta Upsilon, Delta Sigma Rho. Conglist. Clubs: Cosmos (Washington); Sierra. Author: The Population Upsurge in The United States, 1949; others. Contbg. editor Rev. Econ. Statistics, 1919-25, Wheat Studies of Food Research Inst., 1924-44. Home: Los Altos, Cal. Died Apr. 23, 1975.

DAVIS, MERVYN, life ins. exec.; b. England, Feb. 18, 1881; s. David and Sarah (James) D.; A.B., Cambridge (Eng.) U., 1903; m. Dorothy Lowrey, Oct. 7, 1912; children—Mervyn L., James Keith. Came to U.S., 1906. With actuary's dept. Conn. Gen. Life Ins. Co., 1906-09; actuary Equitable Life of Iowa, 1912-18; asst. actuary Equitable Life Assurance Soc. of U.S., N.Y. City, 1918-28, group underwriter, 1928-36, vice president, 1936-50, executive vice president from 1950. Fellow Actuarial Society of America. Home: Upper Montclair, N.J.†

DAVIS, NORAH, author; b. Huntsville, Ala., Oct. 20, 1878; d. Zebulon Pikeand Williametta (Eason) D.; descendant of George Reade (mem. of her Majesty's Council and sec. of state for province of Va.) and in direct line from the famous Harry Hotspur and from 4 of the Magna Charta barons; ed. pvt. tutors at home. Taught in pub. schs., Ala., Fla., Miss., Tenn., Ark., 1893-1900; became stenographer, newspaper writer and held several govt. positions; deputy clk. U.S. Dist. Ct., northern dist., Ala., 1901. Author: The Northerner, 1905; The World's Warrant, 1907; Wallace Rhodes, Address: Huntsville, Ala.†

DAVIS, ROBERT, b. Beverly, Mass., July 29, 1881; s. William Henry (D.D.) and Emma Prescilla (Meacham) D.; A.B., Dartmouth, 1903; grad. study, Harvard, 1903-04; A.M., Columbia, 1908; S.T.B., Union Theol. Sem., 1908; D.D., Kingfisher Coll., 1915; m. Louise Post Corwith, Jan. 1, 1911; children—Corwith, Robert (dec.); m. 2d, Kathleen Johnston, Oct. 20, 1920; children—Marie Francoise, Noelle, Elizabeth. Teacher English, Dartmouth, 1904-05; asso. minister Brick Presbyn. Ch., N.Y. City, 1908-10; minister Englewood (N.J.) Presbyn. Ch., 1910-17; served as maj. Am. Red Cross, with A.E.F., 1917-18; commr. Am. Red Cross to Cossack States, 1919, to Austria and Hungary, 1920; engaged in wine and cattle business, Margaux, Gironde, France, from 1920; mng. dir. Am. Hos;. of Paris, 1931-33; chief editorial writer N.Y. Herald, Paris edit., 1931-34; dir. Am. Library in Paris, 1931-35; chmn. French Wine Growers Marketing Com., from 1935; instr. Biblical lit., Middlebury (Vt.) Coll. from 1936; acting pastor Union Ch., Proctor, Vt., from 1942. Mem. jury Inter-Colonial Expn., Paris, 1931; v.p. Am. Chamber of Commerce in France. Republican. Conglist. Club: American of Paris (v.p.). Author: Mopping Up Bolshevism, 1919; Diary with Denekine, 1919; Unfeathered Eagle of Austria, 1920; Poems of an Old French Northern Vermont, 1937; A Vermonter in Spain, 1938; Padre Porko, 1939; All Gaul is Divided, 1940; Pepperfoot of Thursday Market, 1941; Hudson Bay Express, 1942; Gid Granger, 1944. Home: Harwichport, Mass.†

DAVIS, ROBERT FISHER, lawyer; b. Indpls., Nov. 14, 1905; s. Samuel Newsom and Bertha (Baldwin) D.; LL.B., Ind. U., 1927; A.B., George Washington U., 1930, M.P.L., 1930, J.D., 1930; lM.A., Am. U., 1932; m. lMargaret Louise Warren, Jan. 14, 1943 (dec.); children—Robert Warren, Steven Lamont. Admitted to Ind. bar, 1927, N.Y. bar, D.C. bars, 1932, also U.S. Supreme Ct.; founder, partner firm Stevens, Davis, Miller & Mosher, and predecessor, Washington from 1933. Mem. Fairfax County Sch. Bd., 1952-60, chmn. 1964. County and state rep. Democratic Conv., 1952; alternate del. Va. Dem. Conv., 1952. Served as aviator USNR, World War II. Mem. Am. Bar Assn., Am. Patent Law Assn., Am. Chem. Soc., Chemists Club. Mason. Author: Flight Through Instruments, 1943. Contbr. articles to profl. Jours. Home: Boca Raton, Fla. Died July 8, 1974; buried Arlington Nat. Cemetery.

DAVIS, ROLAND PARKER, civil engr.; b. Beverly, lMass., Aug. 2, 1884; s. Parker Stephen and Julia Etta (Andrews) D.; B.S., Mass. Inst. Tech., 1906; M.C.E., Cornell U., 1908; Ph.D., 1914; m. Bessie Belle Strentzsch, June 16, 1910. Draftsman Am. Bridge Co., 1906-07; instr. civil engring., Cornell U., 1908-11; engr. with Eastern Bridge & Structural Co., summer, 1908, Am. Bridge Co., summer, 1910; asso. prof. W.Va. U., 1911-12, prof. head dept. structural and hydraulic engring., 1912-30; prof. structural engring, since 1930; assistant dean College of Engineering, 1930-32, dean, 1932-September 1944, acting dean, 1945-50, dean from 1950; bridge engr. West Virginia State Commn., 1914-19, now consultant engineer same; division engineer Camp Eustis, 1918. Mem. Am. Soc. C.E. (dir., 1937-39, Vice-pres., 1939-40), Am. Railway Engring. Asso. (com. on iron and steel structures, and cooperative relations with universities), Am. Society for Testing Materials, Association of Land-Grant Colls. and Univs., Newcomen Soc., Am. Society for Engring. Education, Sigma Xi, Tau Beta Pi. Republican. Clubs: Faculty, Kiwanis. Author, editor tech. publs. Home: Morgantown, W.Va. Died Dec. 11, 1974.

DAVIS, ROY TASCO, diplomatist, ambassador, educator; b. Ewing, Mo., June 24, 1889; s. John A. and Bessie (White) D.; A.B., LaGrange (Mo.) Coll., 1908; Ph.B., Brown U., 1910; m. Loyce Enloe, Aug. 16, 1913; children—Roy T., Mercedes. Statistician Mo. Bur. Census and Labor, 1911; clk. to commn. that built Mo. State Capitol, 1912, 13; sec., also bus. mgr. Stephens Coll., Columbia, Mo., 1914-21, asst. to pres., also dir. pub. relations, 1933-37; minister to Guatemala, 1921-22, Republic of Costa Rica, 1922-29, Republic of Panama, 1930-33; chmn. Honduran-Guatemalan Boundary Commn., 1928; mediator Panamanian revolution, 1931; del. of U.S. govt. to North Am. Radio Conf., Mexico City, 1933; pres. Nat. Park Coll. (formerly Nat. Park Sem.), Forest Glen, Md., 1937-42, when coll. was taken over by Govt. for a hosp. under war emergency act; spl. field rep. in Latin Am. for RFC, 1942-43; dir. Inter-Am. Schs. Service of the Am. Council on Edn., 1943-53; chmn. commn. making ednl. survey of Bolivia, 1943; U.S. ambassador, Haiti, 1953-57, ret. Dir. Latin-Am. Orientation Program, Dept. State, 1959. Mem. Md. Senate, 1946-50; mem. Md. Adv. Council for Higher Edn., 1964. Decorated Order

Vasco Nunez de Balboa (Panama); National Red Cross (Costa Rica). Clubs: Union (Panama); Cosmos (Washington). Home: Chevy Chase, Md., Died Dec. 27, 1975.

DAVIS, THOMAS HAROLD, banking; b. Centreville, Md., Jan. 28, 1880; s. Thomas and Susan Frances (Baynard) D.; ed. pub. schs., Queen Anne's County, Md.; m. Estella May Stack, Feb. 26, 1908. Began as bank clerk, and advanced to asst. cashier, Centreville Nat. Bank of Maryland, 1899-1918; apptd. asst. nat. bank examiner, 1918. commd. nat. bank examiner, 1919; apptd. pres. Nat. Mechanics Bank, Newport News, Va., for purpose of perparing for liquidation, 1923; again bank examiner, 1925-30; vice pres. Peoples State Bank, Charleston, S.C., 1930-31; became examiner, Reconstruction Finance Corp., 1932, assigned to bank adminstrn. sect., 1934, adminstrative asst. in charge of the sect. from 1939, also asst. chief of examining div. from 1941. Rejected for mil. service because of physical disability, World War I. Home: Washington, D.C.†

DAVIS, WHITMAN, librarian; b. Kosciusko, Miss., Jan. 9, 1881; s. William V. and Sue M. (Porter) D.; B.S., Miss. State Coll., 1904, M.S., 1916; B.L.S., U. Ill., 1933; m. Jennie Featherstone, Dec. 22, 1909; children—Mary Winifred, Katharine, Jennie. Librarian Miss. State Coll., 1905-18, 21-28, U. Miss. from 1928. Mem. library adv. com. U.S. Office Edn., making survey of land grant colls.; state dir. library war work, 1917; organizer Camp Shelby library, served as librarian 2 mos., 1917. Chmn. Miss. Library Commn., 1926-33. Mem. Am., Southeastern (v.p. 1926-28, mem. policy commn. 1929), Miss. (pres. 1910-11, 16-18, 21-23) library assns., Pi Gamma Mu. Methodist. Mason. Author pamphlet. Home: Oxford, Miss.†

DAVISON, FRANCIS LYLE, engr. and surveyor, twp. govt. ofcl.; b. Mantua, O., Apr. 4, 1911; s. John Henry and Lucy (Wragg) D.; B.A., Coll. Wooster, 1932; m. Grace M. Davison, 1965; children—Mary Williams, Sam, Ethel McConnell. Engaged in practice of surveying in Ohio, 1939-73; pvt. practice civil engring., Ohio 1945-73; also engaged in federal income tax service. Zoning insp., Gustavus Twp., 1958-73; justice of peace, Gustavus Twp., 1940-48. Profl. engr., Ohio. Mem. Nat. Soc. Profl. Engrs., Knox Area Sr. Citizens, Damascus Ruritan club, Theta Chi Delta, Sigma Phi Nu. Methodist (treas., 1972-73). Home: Damascus, O. Died Aug. 6, 1973; interred Presbyterian Cemetery, Kinsman, O.

DAVISON, F(REDERICK) TRUBEE, pres. Am. Mus. Natural History; b. N.Y.C., Feb. 7, 1896; S. Henry Pomeroy and Kate (Trubee) D.; A.B. honoris causa, Yale, 1918, M.A.; LL.B., Columbia, 1922; LL.D., Syracuse Univ., 1933; LL.D., New York Univ., 1935; m. Dorothy Peabody, April 16, 1920; children—Frederick Trubee (dec.), Endicott Peabody, Daniel Pomeroy, Gates. Admitted to N.Y. bar, 1922, and began practice in N.Y. City; mem. N.Y. Assembly from Nassau County, 1922-26; asst. sec. of War (air), 1926-1932; pres. Am. lMus. Natural History, 1933-51, then emeritus. Trustee Mutual Life Ins. Co.; mem. bd. Matinecock Bank Locust Valley, Mem. bd. Hofstra Coll.; mem. bd. mgrs. Meml. Hosp.; governing bd. Yale Corp., 1931-53. Served as lt. (j.g.) U.S. Naval Air Service, World War. Serving as col., U.S. Army Air Forces, since June 1941, deputy chief of staff, Air Force Combat Command, June-Dec. 1941, asst. chief of air staff, A-1, from December, 1941; brigadier general A.A.F., June 3, 1945; awarded Distinguished Service Medal Navy Cross. Chairman Nat. Crime Commn., Aug. 1925-July 1926. Trustee American Museum Natural History Nat. Playground and Recreation; mem. bd. Theodore Roosevelt Memorial Association. Member American Legion. Member Episcopal Church. Mason. Clubs: Yale, Creek, Boone and Crockett. Seawanhaka-Corinthian Yacht. Explorers. Links. Wyandanch; Wings (Washington). Home: Locust Valley, N.Y. Died Nov. 14, 1974.

DAVISON, SARAH MARGARET, educator; b. Chester Twp., Dodge Co., Wis., Mar. 16, 1880; d. James and Sarah (Weimer) D.; prep. edn. high sch. and Wayland Acad., Beaver Dam, Wis., student U. of Wis., 1899-1901, Colorado Coll., Colorado Springs, Colo., 1901-02. Founder, 1910, and propr. Hillcrest School, boarding sch. for girls from 5 to 15 yrs. of age. Mem. Am. Univ. Women, O.E.S., Am. Legion Auxiliary, P.E.O. Republican. Presbyn. Clubs: Women's (Beaver Dam); Contemporary (Colorado Springs). Address: Beaver Dam, Wis.†

DAWKINS, BENJAMIN CORNWELL, b. Ouachita City, La., July 19, 1881; s. Edward A. and Caroline (Shute) D.; student La. Poly. Inst., Ruston, La., 1899-1902; LL.B., Tulane U., 1906; m. Alice Ashley McLeod, July 27, 1910; children—Benjamin Cornwell, Jane Gordon. Admitted to La. bar 1906, and began practice at Monroe, as mem. Lamkin, Millsaps & Dawkins until 1909; mem. Munholland & Dawkins, 1909-12; dist. judge State Court, 1912-18; asso. justice Supreme Court of La., 1918-24; mem. La. Constl. Conv., 1921; judge U.S. Dist. Court, Western Dist. of La., 1924-53 (resigned, continuing to give service in Eastern District and other parts of state). Mem. La. N.G., 1903-06; chmn. Legal Advisory Bd. to Registrants, World War; four-minute man. Mem. La. Bar Assn. Democrat. Methodist. Home: Monroe, La.†

DAWSON, (FRANCIS) WARRINGTON, author; b. at Charleston, S.C., September 27, 1878; s. Capt. Francis W. (founder Charleston News and Courier) and Sarah (Morgan) D.; ed. Ecole St.Thomas d'Aquin, Paris, Univ. Sch., Charleston, Coll. of Charleston, 1893-95; unmarried. Began literary career 1888, writing revs. of children's books for his father's paper; spl. newspaper corr. Spain, 1898, Russia, 1904, Anglo-Russian North Sea Tribunal, Paris, 1905, 2d Hague Conf., 1907, and spl. missions to French Armies, 1914-18; Am. war corr., 1917; confidential adviser, Sept. 17, 1917, and spl. asst. American Embassy at Paris, 1919-1937; Honorary Citizen of Versailles, France. Head of French research dept. for reconstrn. Williamsburg, Va., 1928-32; hon. trustee Yorktown Sesquicentennial Assn., 1931. Hon. pres., Charleston Council, Boy Scouts America, from 1924. Democrat. Sec. to Theodore Roosevelt in E. Africa and Uganda, 1909. Lectured Europe and America various seasons, 1907-15. Sec.-treas. Urgent Fund for Serbian Wounded, 1914-15; mem. 1st neutral commn. sent by French Ministry of War to investigate use of asphyxiating gases by Germany army on Anglo-French front, Apr. 1915. Sec.-gen. Paris Assn. de la Presse Etrangere, 1905-08; foundation mem. Fresh Air Art Soc., London, and Astron. Soc. of France; mem. Authors' League America, British Soc. Authors (v.p.). Société des Américanistes dé Paris, Société Honore de Balzac, Poetry Soc. of S.C., Phi Beta Kappa; mem. exec. com. Sons of Revolution in France, Troop 2 of Paris Boy Scouts of America, Soc. of Am. Friends of La Fayette; hon. mem. Institut Napoleon. Decorated Officer of Legion of Honor (French), 1925, Commander, 1930; hon. Citizen of Versailles, France, 1931; Comdr. Royal Order of St. Sava (Jugoslavia), 1932. Laureate of Académie Francaise, Paris, gold medal, 1926; gold medal of Arts, Sciences et Lettres, 1934. Author: The Scar, 1906; The Scourge, 1908; Le Negre Aux Etats Unis, 1912; The True Dimension, 1916; The Gift of Paul Clermont, 1921; The Sin, 1923; Theodore Roosevelt, 1923; Adventure in the Night, 1924; The Green Moustache, 1925; The Crimson Pall (with letters from Joseph Conrad), 1927; Paul Clement's Story and My Own, 1929. Edited with introd., A Confederate Girl's Diary by Sarah Morgan (Dawson), 1913; The Speeches of Ambassador Wallace, 1921. Inpreparation: Memoirs—Forty Years of a Life, 1898-1938. Address: Versailles, France†

DAWSON, J. DOUGLAS, traffic mgr.; b. Glasgow, Scotland, Feb. 3, 1906; s. Thomas S. and Jean (Thompson) D.; student Harvard Bus. Sch.; m. Ina M. Campbell, Sept. 26, 1933. Clk., Charles E. Vose, traffic cons., Boston; traffic mgr. Ind. Coal Tar Co., Boston; asst. traffic mgr. Norton Co., Worcester, Mass., 1940-44, asst. supt. 1944-46, traffic mgr., 1946-51, gen. traffic mgr., 1951-71. Mem. Worcester Area C. of C., Nat. Freight Traffic Assn., Nat., N. E. indsl. traffic leagues, N. E. Shippers Adv. Bd., Worcester Traffic Assn., N.E. Council, Assoc. Industries Mass. Clubs: New England Traffic; Boston Traffic; Traffic of N.Y.; Norco; Worcester Country. Home: Worcester, Mass. Died Nov. 22, 1971.

DAWSON, JOHN CHARLES, educator; b. Huntsville, Ala., 1876; s. Granville J. and Alice (Roberts) D.; A.B., Georgetown (Ky.) Coll., 1901; A.M., Howard Coll., Birmingham, Ala., 1910, LL.D., 1917; Ph.D., Columbia, 1921; LL.D., Georgetown College, 1927; m. Fletcher Stinson, 1906 (died Oct. 26, 1927); 1 dau., Dorothy (Mrs. Whitley McCoy); m. 2d, Avis Marshall, Dec. 25, 1930 (died May 25, 1938). Began as prof. modern langs., Howard Coll., 1903, dean, 1917, actg. pres., 1917-19. pres., 1921-31; head dept. Romance langs., Univ. of Alabama, Feb. 1930-July 1947, prof. emeritus from July 1947; vis. prof. French, Howard Payne College, Texas, 1947-48; professor modern languages, summer session, Univ. of Alabama, 1911; instr. in French, summer session, Columbia, 1920; prof. history of edn., Western State Coll. of Colo., summer session, 1923. With Ednl. Corps, U.S. Army, as Am. dean of student detachment, U. of Toulouse, France, Mar.-July 1919. Mem. edn. bd. Southern Baptist Conv., 1922-28; mem. bd. trustees Colonial Research Foundation, Inc., Mobile, 1947-47. Pres. S. Atlantic Modern Lang. Assn., 1935; mem. Kappa Phi Kappa, Phi Beta Kappa (pres. Ala. Alpha, 1942-43). Decorated Officier d'Académie (France), 1936. Democrat. Baptist. Club: Authors' (London). Editor; Picard's La Petite Ville (college edit.), 1911. Author: Toulouse in the Renaissance, 1921-23; A French Regicide in Alabama. 1939; Lakanal the Regieide, 1948. Editor Howard College Studies in History and Literature, 1921-30. Contbr. to Romanic Rev. and Modern Language Notes, Home: Tuscaloosa, Ala.†

DAWSON, JOSEPH MARTIN, clergyman; b. Maypearl, near Waxahachie, Tex., June 21, 1879; s. Martin Judy and Laura (Underwood) D.; A.B., Baylor U., 1904, D.D., 1916; LL.D., Howard Payne Coll., 1936; m. Willie Turner, June 3, 1908; children—Alice Elizabeth, Leighton Brooks, Joseph Turner, Ralph Matthew, Donna Booch. Licensed ministry Bapt. Ch., 1899; successively pastor Lampasas, Hillsboro, Temple, Tex., until 1914, First Church, Waco, 1915-46; now doing research and writing. Founder Baylor U. Daily Lariat; editor Baptist Standard; state publicity dir. Southern Bapt. O,000,000 Drive, 1919-24; a dir. Tex. Bapt. Conquest Campaign. Mem. Draft Com., World War I; camp pastorand four-minute speaker, Chmn. Southern Bapt World Peace Com. and rep. of Baptists of the U.S. at San francisco Conference of U.N.; executive director Baptist Joint Committee on Public Affairs; mem. religious adv. com. Office of Civil Def., 1951-53; mem. Secretary Forrestal's Civilian Advisory Committed to the Navy, 1946. Recipient elder statesman award by Tex. Bapt., 1959. Mem. Am. Soc. Internat. Law. Democrat. Author several books, latest: Separate Church and State Now, 1948; The Liberation of Life, 1951; America's Way in Church, State and Society, 1953. East Texas: Its History (Section on Protestant Religion); also features and articles in mags. and sect. on Missions in Tex. Bapt. Centennial History Organizer Protestants and Other Americans for Separation of Church and State, 1948; Baptists and the American Republic, 1956; High Quest; also newspaper, mag. articles. Kiwanian. Home: Austin, Tex.†

DAY, ALBERT EDWARD, clergyman; b. Euphemia, O.; s. Elam Mansfield and Mary Ellen (Bright) D.; A.B., Taylor U., 1904, D.D., 1918; A.M., U. of Cincinnati, 1916; D.D., Ohio Wesleyan U., 1926, Allegheny Coll., 1936; Litt.D., University of Southern Calif., 1939; m. Emma Reader, Sept. 28, 1904; children—Ruth Lucile, Helen McKay, Dorothy, Benjamin Wilson, Mary Ellen. Ordained ministry M.E. Ch., 1904; pastor Mount Vernon Place Church, Baltimore, 1932-37, and since 1948; 1st Meth. Ch. Pasadena, 1937-45; English lectr. Preaching, Andover Newton Theol. Sch., 1949; lectr. preaching Union Theol. Sem., Richmond, Va., 1951. Served as chaplain, 117th Field Signal Bn., A.E.F., World War I. Mem. Bd. Fgn. Missions, 1924-36, M.E. Ch.; del. Gen. Conf. M.E. Ch., 1924, 32, 44, 52, 56, S. Am. Conf. Montevideo, 1925; v.p. Fed. Council Chs. Christ Am., 1942-44: dir. New Life Movement of Meth. Ch. Am., 1945-47; mem. Gen. Bd. Evangelism, 1944; founder Disciplined Order of Christ, 1945; chmn. Nat. Conf. on Ch. and War, 1949-50. Spl. examiner Nat. War Labor Bd., 1942. Shepard lectr. on preaching, Bangor Sem., 1933; Lyman Beecher lectr. Yale, 1934; lectr. Earl Found., Pacific Sch. Religion, 1937; Gates lectr. Grinnell Coll., 1938; Jones lectr. Emory U., 1939; Fondren lectr. So. Meth. U., 1940; English lectr. preaching Andover-Newton Theol. Sch., 1949; S. Wernecke lectr. Eden Theol. Sem., 1955. Mem. Sigma Alpha Epsilon. Mason (32°). Author several books, latest are: The Faith We Live, 1940; Discipline and Discovery, 1946; An Autobiography of Prayer, 1952. Editor New Life Magazine, 1945-47. Chosen 1 of 6 leading preachers of Am. by Christian Century poll, 1940, one of ten most influential living Meths. by Christian Adv. poll, 1947. Home: Front Royal, Va. Died Oct. 12, 1973.

DAY, WILLIAM L., banker; b. Jenkintown, Pa., Dec. 5, 1907; s. Charles and Margaret (Dunning) D.; B.S., U. Pa., 1931; m. Marcella Morgan, Oct. 25, 1935; children—Charles, Louise M. (Mrs. Leon R. Cook), Margaret D. (Mrs. Hugh F. Jones), Patricia L. (Mrs. Finley H. Perry, Jr.), Susan C. Engr., Day & Zimmerman, Inc., Phila., 1931-36; statistician Morgan Stanley & Co., N.Y.C., 1936-41; partner Drexel & Co., 1941-48; exec. v.p., dir. First Pa. Banking & Trust Co., Phila., 1948-52, pres., dir., 1952-55, chmn., 1955-72; chmn. Old Phila. Devel. Corp.; dir. 1st Pa. Corp., John Wanamaker Stores, Mut. Assurance Co., Rorer-Amchem Inc.; bd. mgrs. Phila. Savs. Fund Soc. Chmn. bd. trustees U. Pa. Clubs: Philadelphia, Racquet, Mid Day (Phila.). Home: Devon PA. Died Dec. 31, 1973.

DEAM, ARTHUR FRANCIS, educator, architect; b. Springfield, O., Oct. 1, 1895; s. Charles Henry and Delia (Finn) D.; B.Arch., Ohio State U., 1921, Columbia, 1923; m. Thyra C. Soderberg, Mar. 10, 1927; children—Edward Lee, Martha (Mrs. Roger William Severt), Norman Arthur. Draftsman, H.D. Smith, Columbus, O., 1920-21; archtl. draftsman, N.Y.C., 1919-20; designer Helmet and Corbett, N.Y.C., 1922-23; fellow Am. Acad. in Rome, 1923-26; designer N. Max Dunning, Chgo., 1926; D.H. Burnham and Co., Chgo., 1926-30; asst. prof. arch. Armour Inst. Tech., 1928-29; prof. arch. in charge design U. Ill., 1930-45; prof. arch. U. Pa., from 1945, chmn. dept., 1945-50, prof. emeritus, from 1956; vis. prof. Am. Acad. in Rome, 1939. Pres., bd. dirs. Summer Sch. Painting, Saugatuck, Mich.; hon. life mem., patron, design critic Archtl. Sketch Club Chgo. Served with USNR, 1917-18. Bd. dirs. Am. Swedish Hosp., Phila. Recipient Prix de Rome, 1923. Fellow A.I.A.; mem. Phila. Art Alliance, Scarab, Gargoyle, Alpha Rho Chi, Pi Kappa Alpha. Epsicopalian. Clubs: Lenape (U. Pa.); Critic T Square (Phila.). Patentee constrn. and steel fabrication. Home: Deland, Fla. Deceased.

DE AMORIM FERREIRA, HERCULANO, physicist, educator; b. San Miguel, Azores Islands, Oct. 22, 1895; s. Joao Baptista and Isabel de (Amorim) Ferreira; C.E., U. Lisbon, 1916, D.Sc., 1930; postgrad. U. London, 1929-30; m. Jorgina Monjardino, Jan. 3, 1934; children—Ana-Maria ((Mrs. Antonio de Sousa Moniz), Joao-Antonio, Jose Manuel, Maria Augusta (Mrs. Reis Leal). Lectr. physics U. Lisbon (Portugal), 1920-30, prof. engring. 1928-37, prof. phsyics, 1930-65; pres. sci. div. Acad. Scis., Lisbon, 1960-74. Vis. prof. U. London, 1932-34; dir.-gen. Nat. Meteorol. Service,

1946-65. Mem. Portugal House of Reps., 1925-36, 42-57; undersec. of state for nat. edn., 1944-46. Served as lt. engrs. Portuguese Army, 1917-18. Decorated War Cross and Distinguished Services; comdr. Order of Brit. Empire; Grand Cross Civil Merit (Spain), 1962; Grand Cross Infante Dom Herique (Portugal), 1971; recipient Sci. merit award, 1945. Mem. World Meteorol. Orgn. (v.p. 1955-59), Acad. Scis. of Lisbon (pres.), Royal Acad. Scis. Madrid and Cordoba, Briazilian Acad., Buenos Aires Acad. Roman Catholic. Research on thermionics, dynamic climateology, geomagnetism. Home: Estoril Portugal Died May 18, 1974.

DEAN, EDWARD N., chmn. bd. First Nat. Bank Jersey City, 1968-71. Home: Roslyn, N.Y. Died Oct. 24, 1974.

DEAN, GRAHAM M., newspaper pub.; b. Lake View, Ia., Aug. 10, 1904; s. William M. and Ellen C. Dean; A.B. in Journalism, U. Ia., 1929; m. Ruthe S. Wheeler, Apr. 16, 1928; 1 dau., Elizabeth W. Mng. editor Iowa City Press-Citizen, 1925-35, bus. mgr., 1935-36; pub. Saliness (Cal.) Index-Jour. and Morning Post, 1936-39, Reno Evening Gazette, Nev. State Jour., 1939-51, Western Horseman, 1943-46; owner, pub. Ashland (Ore.) Daily Tidings, 1951-60, Siskiyou Daily News, Yreka, Cal., 1951-70; pres. So. N.M. Newspapers, Inc., pub. Artesia (N.M.) Daily Press, 1957-70, Porterville (Cal.) Evening Recorder, 1960-74. Deming (N.M.) Newspapers, 1966-70. Mem. Am. Soc. Newspaper Editors. Author 32 books for boys and girls. Home: Porterville, Cal. Died Nov. 20, 1974; interred, Porterville.

DEAN, MYRON E., ins. co. exec.; b. Blue Mound, Kan., June 25, 1914; s. John W. and Jennie C. (Chapman) D.; B.A., Hendrix Coll., 1933; grad. Ark. State Tchrs. Coll., 1935; m. Martha E. Brickhouse, Aug. 30, 1935; 1 dau., Patricia Ellen (Mrs. Bruce Vergeer). Credit mgr. dept. store, 1935-38; agt. Met. Life Ins. Co., 1939-42; home officer supr. Union Life Ins. Co., 1945-49; sr. cons. Life Ins. Agy. Mgmt. Assn., 1949-52; v.p., regional v.p. State Farm Ins. Co., Salem, Ore., from 1953. Mem. adv. com. for recodifying Ore. Ins. Code. Bd. dirs. Salem chpt. A.R.C.; trustee Salem Hosp. Served to lt. USCGR, 1941-45. C.L.U., Ore. Kiwanian. Home: Salem, Ore. Deceased.

DEAN, SAMUEL E., JR., chmn. Dean Foods Co., 1946-69. Chmn. Ill. Polit. Action Com., 1972. Mem. Ill. C. of C. (pres. 1963). Home: Oak Brook, Ill. Died Mar. 12, 1975.

DEAN, SIDNEY BUTLER, business exec.; b. St. Paul, Apr. 23, 1879; s. William Blake andMary Catherine (Nicols) D.; A.B., Yale, 1900; m. Marjorie Northup, 1905; children—Marjorie, Virginia Grant-Lawson; m. 2d, Marjorie Bemis West, June 10, 1944. With Gen. Trading Co., and predecessor companies St. Paul, 1902, pres., 1941-52, chmn. bd., 1942-56, ret., later dir.; dir. La. Crosse Auto Supply (Wis.), Clemons Auto Supply (Eau Claire, Wis.), Mpls. Iron Store, Minot Supply Co. (N.D.), Grand Forks Supply Co. (N.D.) Empire Supply Co. (Fargo, N.D.), Faeth Co. (Kansas City, Mo.). Republican. Presbyn. Club: Minn. Home: St. Paul, Minn.†

DE ARAUJO CASTRO, JOAO AUGUSTO, Brazilian diplomat; b. Rio De Janeiro, Brazil, Aug. 27, 1919; s. Raimundo and Carmen (Viveiros De Castro) De Araujo Castro; LL.B., Niteroi Sch. Law (Rio de Janeiro), 1941; Honoris Causa Degree, Nat. War Coll. (Brazil), 1963; m. Miriam Saint-Brisson, July 1, 1943; children ' Carmen Saint-Brisson, Luiz Saint-Brisson, Silvia Saint-Brisson. Vice counsul Brazilian Consulate., San Juan, P.R., 1943-44, Miami, 1944, N.Y.C., 1944-48; assigned ministry external affairs, 1949-51; 2d Sec. Brazilian permanent mission to UN, N.Y.C., 1951-53; 1st Sec. Brazilian Embassy, Rome, Italy, 1953-57; head polit. cultural dept. ministry external relations, govt. Brazil, 1957-58, head dept. internat. orgns., 1961, minister external relations, 1963-64; minister counselor Brazilian Embassy, Tokyo, Japan, 1959-61; Ambassador to Greece, Athens, 1964-66, to Peru, Lima, 1966-68, to U.S., Washington, 1971-75; Perm. Rep. to UN, N.Y.C., 1968-71. Chmn. delegation to Conf. on Trade and Devel., UN, 1964, to Conf. of 18 Nations Com. on Disarmament, Geneva, Switzerland, 1968. Served to 2d lt. Brazilian Army, 1940-41. Decorated Grand Officer Decorations Army, Navy, Aeronautical Merit; Grand Cross Mexico, Bolivia, Peru, Greece, Yugoslavia; Grand Cross Order Rio Branco, Brazil; Grand Officer Order Orange Nassau, Netherlands, Order Merit (Italy), Rising Sun (Japan). Home: Washington, D.C., Died Dec. 9, 1975.

DEARING, FRED MORRIS, diplomatic service; v. Columbia, Mo., Nov. 19, 1879; s. George M. and Marian Elvira (Mathews) D.; A.B., U. of Mo., 1901; M. Dip., Columbian (now George Washington) U., 1904, LL.D., 1932; m. Dorothy Sittenham, of New York, N.Y., Oct. 16, 1915; 1 son, Donn. Apptd. 2d sec. of Legation, Havana, Cuba, July 30, 1906, Peking, China, Apr. 6, 1907; secretary of Legation, Havana, Cuba, 1909-10; 2d sec. American Embassy, London, 1910; sec. Embassy, Mexico City,1910-11; asst. chief Div. Latin Am. Affairs, Dept. of State, 1911-13; sec. Legation, Brussels, Belgium, 1913-14; 1st sec. Embassy, Madrid, 1914-16, conselor Embassy, Petrograd, 1916-17; with Am. Internat. Corpn., New York, 1917-21; asst. sec. of State, 1921-22; E.E. and M.P. to Portugal, Feb. 10, 1922-Jan. 1930; A.E. and M.P. to Peru, 1930-37; E.E. and M.P. to Sweden, 1937-38; retired June 17, 1938. Club: Metropolitan (Washington, D.C.). Address: Wilmington, N.C.†

DEAVER, GEORGE GILBERT, physician; b. Baltimore, Md., July 19, 1890; s. Thomas A. and Augusta (Hartung) D.; B.P.E., Springfield (Mass.) Coll., 1912; M.D. University of Pennsylvania, 1917; married Helen Henry; 1 dau., Elizabeth Jane. Recreational dir., Ch. of Holy Apostles, Philadelphia, Pa., 1912-14; phys. dir., Central Y.M.C.A., Philadelphia, 1915-17; reconstruction and med. work, Egyptian Expeditionary Force, Egypt, 1917-20; dir. phys. edn. Y.M.C.A., Turkey, 1920-21; metropolitan phys. dir., Y.M.C.A., Philadelphia, Pa., 1922-24; prof. hygiene and med. officer, George Williams Coll., Chicago, Ill., 1924-33; instr. in phys. therapy, Northwestern U. Med. Sch., Chicago, Ill., 1932-33; instr. dept. phys. edn. and health, New York U., 1933-34, asst. prof. edn., 1935-44, prof. clin. rehabilitation and phys. medicine Coll. of Medicine since 1944; med. dir. Inst. for Crippled and Disabled, N.Y. City, 1938-46; med. cons. in phys. medicine Hackensack (N.J.) Gen. Hosp. since 1940; physician in charge phys. medicine Bellevue Hosp. from 1944, Lenox Hill Hosp. from 1946; attending physician Willard Parker Hosp. from 1946; cons. U. Hosp., 1949, St. Charles Hosp., Port Jefferson, N.Y., 1951, New York U. Bellevue Inst. of Rehabilitation from 1948, dir. children service from 1950. Special consultant to air surgeon, U.S.A.A.F., 1944-46; phys. medicine cons. to Vets. Adminstrn. and Office of Surgeon Gen., 1946. Received Medal of Merit from the President for pioneer work in the field of rehabilitation. Mem. Am. Med. Assn., New York County Med. Soc., Am. Congress of Phys. Medicine, N.Y. Soc. Phys. Medicine, Y.M.C.A. Phys. Edn. Society. Contbg. editor Y.M.C.A. Journal of Physical Education. Author: Safety in Athletics, 1936; Fundamentals of Physical Examinations, 1939. Home: Paramus, N.J. Died Sept. 1973.

DEBEVOISE, KENDALL BUSH, lawyer; b. Bklyn., Dec. 13, 1913; s. Charles L. and Marguerite R. (Bush) DeB; B.A., Amherst Coll., 1935; LL.B., Yale, 1938; m. Elizabeth Watson, May 18, 1940; children—Kendall W., Susan W., Malcolm B. Admitted to N.Y. bar, 1938, since practiced in N.Y.C.; partner firm Breed, Abbott & Morgan, 1947-73; lectr. antitrust law N.Y. Practising Law Inst. Dir. Union Camp Corp., Montclair Savs. Bank. Mem. Montclair (N.J.) Bd. Ed., 1954-57, pres., 1956-59. Alumni trustee Amherst Coll., 1951-57, life trustee, 1959-73. Mem. Am. N.Y. State (chmn. antitrust sect. 1963) bar assns., Bar Assn., City N.Y., Phi Beta Kappa. Street, Delta Kappa Epsilon. Clubs: Wall University (N.Y.C.); Montclair Golf. Contbr. articles to profl. jours. Home: Montclair, N.J. Died July 2, 1973.

DE BOER, SACO RIENK, city planner, landscape architect; b. The Netherlands, Sept. 7, 1883; s. Rienk Kornelis and Asselina (Rinsma) De B.; student Engring. Inst., The Netherlands, 1900-03; spl. studies in Germany, 1903-05, and in Eng., 1922; m. Anna Sophie Elizabeth Koster, Feb. 24, 1910; children—Elizabeth Thelma, Richard James. Came to U.S., 1908, naturalized, 1914. Engaged in engring., Colo., 1909-10; landscape architect for numerous instns., pvt. estates, subdivs. and schs. landscape architect and city planning cons., Denver, 1910—; city planning cons., Boulder, Colo., 1928-74; city planning for Greeley, Colo., Johnstown, Colo., Grand Junction, Colo., Albuquerque, Cheyenne, Wyo., 1927-34, Englewood, Colo., Sidney, Neb., Las Cruces, N.M.; studies for Douglas and Arapahoe counties, Colo.; regional plan, Grand Junction, 1928, Denver, 1930; cons., planner State of Wyo., 1927-34; Boulder City nr. Hoover Dam, U.S. Bur. Reclamation, 1930-31; cons. planner for Dept. Agr., 1928-32; Nat. Park Service, 1933; cons. (Wyo.) Mountain Park System; state planner Nat. Resources Bd., N.M., Wyo. and Utah, 1934—; studies for Ogden, Utah, Provo, Utah, Salt Lake City, 1942-43; city plans for Aurora, Golden, Boulder, Greenwood Village, Cherry Hills Village (Colo.), Moscow, Ida.; park system, Colorado Springs, Colo.; city plans Brainerd, Minn., Scottsbluff, Neb., Idaho Falls, Ida., Grand Island, Neb., Trinidad, Colo., Glenwood Springs, Colo., Glendive, Mont., Bozeman, Mont.; mil. posts at Fort Bliss, Tex., White Sands Proving Grounds and Holliman Air Base, New Mexico Park and Recreation Plan for Ft. Collins, Colo.; Central Bus. Dist. Plan Ft. Collins; city plans Carriczo, N.M., Arvada, Colo., Kimball, Neb.; landscape plan Interstate Hwy. 70 (Colo.). Fellow Am. Soc. Landscape Architects; mem. Colo. State Planning Bd., Colo. Soc. Engrs. (life), Am. Inst. Planners (pres. Colo.), A.I.A. (hon.), Am. Soc. Planning Ofcls. (hon.), Am. Inst. City Planning, Netherlands Inst. for City Planning and housing. Clubs: Rotary (Denver); Netherlands-America Found. (N.Y.); 100,000 Miles by Air Club. Author: Studies in City Planning-Shopping Districts; Around the Seasons. Contbr. to jours. Home: Denver, Colo. Died Aug. 16, 1974.

DEBOEST, HENRY FRULAN, pharm. mfg. co. exec.; b. Portland, Ore., Oct. 21, 1907; s. Henry and Lusette (Frulan) D.; B.S. in Pharmacy, Ore. State U., 1930; m. Katherine Dearborn, Sept. 5, 1930; children—Richard. Henry, John. Pharmacist, Capitol Drug Store, Salem, Ore., 1930-32; salesman Eli Lilly & Co., Eugene, Ore., 1932-39, dist. mgr., Portland, 1939-47, asst. dir. prodn. control div., Indpls., 1947-51, dir. sales, central and eastern regions, 1951-58, exec. dir. sales, 1958-64, v.p. sales, 1965-66, v.p. corporate affairs, 1966-73, also dir.; dir. Eli Lilly Internat. Corp. Vice pres. Greater Indpls. Progress Com., Inc.; bd. dirs. Nat. Pharm. Council, Inc., Nat. 4-H Service Com., Inc., Ind. Symphony Soc., Inc., Ind. Goodwill Industries Found.; bd. dirs., pres. United Fund Greater Indpls.; pres. bd. trustee Indpls. Mus. Art; trustee Hanover Coll., Christian Theol. Sem., Phila. Coll. Pharmacy and Sci. Served to lt. col. Chem. Corps, AUS, 1942-45. Decorated Purple Heart, Bronze Star with oak leaf cluster (U.S.); Croix de Guerre (France). Mem. Am. Pharm. Assn., Alpha Sigma Phi. Episcopalian. Mason. Clubs: Meridian Hills Country, Columbia, Indianapolis Athenaeum, University (Indpls.); Trader's Point Hunt, Crooked Stick Golf. Home: Indianapolis, Ind. Died Dec. 22, 1973.

DE CARVALHO, ESTEVAO LEITAO, Brazilian army officer; b. Penedo, Estado de Alagoas, Brazil, Apr. 6, 1881; s. Francisco and Maria (Cerqueira) Leitao de Carvalho; ed. Colégio Carneiro, Salvador, Baia, Brazil; Escola Militar do Realengo, Rio de Janeiro; Escola Militar de Engenharia (military engr.), Rio de Janeiro; Escola de Estado Maior, Rio de Janeiro; m. Laura Costa, Nov. 11, 1909; children—Laura (wife of Cap. Ten. Didio Bustamente), Beatriz (wife of Maj. Severino Sombra de Albuquerque), Ruth (wife of Cap. Ten. Ernani Jayne Lima), Eleonora (wife of Dr. Ruy Mello Carvalho), Commd. 2d lt., Army of Brazil, 1907, and advanced through the grades to maj. gen., 1941. Asst. to minister of war, 1914-18; mil. attaché in Chile, 1918-21; mem. Brazilian delegation to Fifth Pan Am. Conf., 1922-23; Brazilian Army rep. to advisory military commn. League of Nations, 1923-26; comdg. officer Inf. Regt., 1928-30, also teacher, Command and Gen. Staff Sch., 1929; head, Office of Chief of Staff, 1932-32; comdg. officer Command and Gen. Staff Sch., 1934-35; chief Brazilian delegation to Neutral Mil. Commn. of the Chaco (Bolivia), 1935; comdg. officer 9th Inf. Brigade, 1936-37; dep. chief, Gen. Staff of the Army, 1937-39; spl. ambassador to Chile, 1938; comdg. officer Third Mil. Dist., 1939-42; inspector, First Group of Mil. Dists., 1942; chief, Brazilian delegation to Joint Brazil-U.S. Defense Commn., 1942; military attaché to U.S. from Aug. 1944. Decorated Comendador of Orden do Mérito Militar do Brazil, medal of 40 years of good military service, Silver medal commemorating Proclamation of the Republic (Brazil), Gran Cruz of Order Al Mérito, medal commemorating IV Centenary of Discovery of Straits of Magellan (Chile), Officer Legion of Honor (France), Grande Official of Orden do Condor dos Andes (Bolivia), Grande Official of Orden Nacional del Mérito (Paraguay), First Class of Order of Abdon Calderon (Ecuador). Mem. Instituto de HistOrio e Geografia Militar, Instituto HistOrica e Geogràfico do Rio Grande do Sul, Instituto Histórica e do Sul, Instituto Histórica e Geografico do Brasil (hon.), Caballeros de la Paz American. Author: Na Revolucao de 30, 1933; a Conferencia do Desarmamento, 1937. One of founders of military review, A Defesa Nacional, which successfully fought for reform of Brazilian Army. Home: Rio de Janeiro, Brazil.†

DE CARDENAS Y RODRIGUEZ DE RIVAS, JUAN FRANCISCO, ambassador; b. May 5 1881; married. In Spanish Diplomatic Service from 1904; apptd. diplomatic attaché to Embassy, Lisbon, 1904; mem. delegation to Internat. Joint Commn. for the Pyrenees, 1906; sec. to Spanish delegation, same, 1910; sec. in Ministry of Foreign Affairs, 1907; sec. of Legation, Havana, Cuba, 1910-14; commr. to Spanish residents of El Paso, Tex., 1914-15; sec. of Legation, Mexico City, 1915-17; counselor to Embassy, Washington, D.C., 1917-23; same, Berlin, Germany, 1923-24; chief of div. in foreign office, Madrid, 1924-26; minister to Bucharest, 1926-30, M.P., 1930; M.P. to Tokyo, Japan, 1930-31; A. E. and P. to U.S., 1932-34; ambassador to France, 1934-36 (resigned post when Spanish Civil War started); rep. Nationalist Spain in New York, Nov. 1936-Apr. 1939; ambassador to U.S. from 1939. Awarded Grand Cross of Isabella the Catholic (Spain); Grand Cross Legion of Honor, France: Grand Cross Star of Rumania; Civil Merit, Hungary; Sacred Treasury, Japan; Knight Order of Savior of Greece; Knight de Cristo de Portugal; Knight Order of North Star (Sweden); etc. Address: Spain†

DECASTRO, JOSUE, scientist, physician, author; b. Recife, Pernambuco, Brazil, Sept. 5, 1908; s. Manoel and Josefa (Barbosa) deC.; M.D., U. Brazil, 1929; Prof. honoris causa, U. Santo Domingo, 1945, U. San Marcos, 1950; m. Glauce Pinto, Apr. 11, 1935; children—Ana Maria, Josue Fernando, Sonia Maria. Physician, specializing in nutrition, 1929-73; prof. human geography liberal arts coll. U. Brazil, 1940-73; dir. Nat. Inst. Nutrition, Brazil, 1946-73. Exec. v.p. Nat.

Commn. for Social Welfare, 1951-73; chmn. exec. council Food and Agr. Orng., U.N., 1951-73, chmn. Brazilian nat. com., 1950-73; pres. Com. of Health, Brazilian Parliament, 1955. Recipient Roosevelt award of the Academy of Political Sciences, 1954. Internat. Prize of Peace, 1955. Mem. Brazilian Inst. Edn., Sci. and Culture (UNESCO), Am. Acad. Polit. and Social Sci., Interamerican Soc. Anthropology and Geography, Brazilian Soc. Biology (hon.), Nutrition Found. (corr. mem. N.Y.C.), Italian Com. for Study Population Problems (corr. mem. Rome), Acad. Medicine (hon., Lima, Peru). Author: O Problema da Alimentacao no Brasil, 1939; Condicoes de Condicoes de Vida da Classes Operarias no Recire, 1935; Salario Minimo, 1935; Alimentacao e Raca, 1936; Dorumentario do Nordeste, 1937; Alimentacao Brasileira a Luz da Geografia Humana, 1937; Basal Metabolism in Tropical Climates, 1938; O Problema da Alimentacao no Brasil, 1939; Geografia Humana, 1939; La Physiologie des Tabous, 1939; Alimentazione ed Aclimatazione Umana nei Tropici, 1939; La Fisiologia de los Tabous, 1940; Fisioogia dos Tabus, 1941; La Alimentacion en los Tropicos, 1946; Geografia da Fome, 1946; La Geographie de la Faim, 1950; La Geografia del Hambre, 1950; Geopolitiea de Fome, 1951; Geography of Hunger, 1952. Home: Rio de Janeiro, Brazil. Died Sept. 1973.

DECHANT, JOHN ALOYSIUS, govt. ofcl., author; b. Milw., June 21, 1917; s. John Henry and Frances Irene (McGee) DeC.; Ph.D. in Journalism, Marquette U., 1939; m. Mary Elizabeth Knoernschild, May 30, 1944; children—John David, Robert Thomas, Michael Patrick, Richard Dennis, James Francis. Publicity dir. Milw. Counc. of Cath. Charities, 1939-40; news editor, columnist, editorial writer The New World, 1940-41; asst. dir. pub. relations Nat. Cath. Community Service, Washington, 1941-42; chief field information War Assets Adminstrn., 1946; dir. community relations Aircraft Industries Assn., Washington, 1946-47, Hill & Knowlton, Inc. N.Y.C. 1947-49; field counseling officer office small bus., ECA Washington, 1949; sr. pub. relations cons. Office Civil Def., NSRB, 1950-51; dir. pub. affairs FCDA and adminstr. Nat. Civil Def. Pub. Edn. Program, Washington, 1951-54; exec. dir. Am. Heritage Found., N.Y.C., 1954-55; v.p. Crusade for Freedom, 1956; established pub. relations counseling firm under own name; head John A. De Chant & Assos., 1957-64; dir. information Bur. Employment Security, Dept. Labor, 1965-68; spl. asst., manpower information dir., 1969-74. Mem. Nat. Def. Exec. Res., Office Emergency Planning, 1962-65. Vice pres. Marine Corps War Meml. Found.; chmn. Fed. Service Overseas Fund Campaign and Washington dir. Crusade for Freedom. Served as capt. USMCR, 1942-46; PTO.; Res. ret. Decorated Navy Ribbon with 4 battle stars; recipient Nat. Air Council fellowship, 1947; Distinguished Service award, FCDA; gold medal, Swedish Civil Def. League. Mem. Pub. Relations Soc. Am., Marine Corps Res. Officers Assn. (exec. council 1950-54), Am. Legion, Sigma Delta Chi. Club: Nat. Press (Washington). Author: (with Richard Hubler) Flying Leathernecks, 1944; Devilbirds-Marine Aviation in World War II, 1947; Modern U.S. Marine Corps, 1966. Home: Bethesda, Md. Died Oct. 1974.

DECHERT, ROBERT, lawyer, govt. ofcl.; b. Phila., Nov. 29, 1895; s. Henry Taylor and Virginia Louise (Howard) D.; grad. Lawrenceville (N.J.) Sch., 1912; A.B., U. Pa., 1916, LL.B., 1921, LL.D. (hon.), 1958; U.S. Army student, St. John's Coll., Oxford (Eng.) U., 1919; m. Helen Hope Wilson, May 24, 1922 (dec. Oct. 1950); children—Peter, Hope (Mrs. Michael C. Mitchell), Marian Godey (Mrs. Donald F. Dixon); m. 2d, Helen Branson, Dec. 1, 1951. Admitted to Pa. bar, 1921, and began practice at Phila.; asso. Hepburn, Dechert & Norris, 1921-27; mem. faculty U. Pa. Law Sch., 1923-42; v.p., counsel Penn Mut. Life. Ins. Co., 1927-30, counsel, 1930-48, gen. counsel, 1949-56, 59-65, trustee, 1959-69; mem. firm Dechert, Price & Rhoads, Phila., 1930-68; dir. Fidelity Bank, Phila., 1932-57, 59-71; gen. counsel Dept. Def. Washington, 1957-59. Cons. Office Gen. Counsel, ECA, 1949-50; mem. Pa. Bd. Law Examiners, 1933-39, 70-72. Trustee U. Pa., from 1928; mem. Bd. of Law, from 1928, chmn., 1952-56, mem. library adv. bd., from 1956, chmn., 1956-65, mem. Bd. of Social Work 1945-68, chmn., 1945-52, chmn. Ednl. Policy Com., 1959-67, mem. Bd. Wistar Inst. of Anatomy and Biology, 1967-72; trustee Lawrenceville (N.J.) Sch., 1929-71; bd. dirs. YMCA Phila., from 1936, pres. 1947-50; bd. dirs. United Fund Phila. 1930-72, gen. campaign chmn. 1942; chmn. Asso. Services for Armed Forces, Inc., 1950-51; mem. bd. govs., mem. corp. U.S.O., 1951-70, chmn. exec. com., 1951-55; bd. dirs., mem. exec. com. United Def. Fund, 1951-55; chmn. J. C. Brown Library Assos., Providence, 1962-65; pres. World Affairs Council Phila. 1963-65. Served to capt., U.S. Army, World War I. Decorated D.S.C. Mem. Am. (ho. dels. 1948-49, 51-55), Pa. (ho. dels. 1966-69), Phila. bar assns., Ins. Fedn. Pa. (dir., pres. 1947-49). Assn. Life Ins. Counsel (pres. 1946-47), S.R., Order of Coif, Phi Beta Kappa, Delta Psi. Republican, Episcopalian. Club: Philadelphia. Contbr. articles publs. in field of law, ins. and rare Am. books. Home: Gladwyne, Pa., Died Nov. 8, 1975.

DEEB, PAUL HAROLD, radiologist; b. Tonawanda, N.Y., June 2, 1917; s. Joseph and Elizabeth Deeb; B.S., Columbia Union Coll., Takoma Park, Md., 1937; M.D., Loma Linda (Cal.) U., 1942; m. Helen Abraham, June 2, 1949; children—Paul Harold, Daniel Peter. Intern White Meml. Med. Center, Los Angeles, 1941-42, resident in radiology, 1942-43, 46-47, staff radiologist, later asso. prof. radiology Sch. Medicine, 1946-55; chief radiology Loma Linda U., 1955-65, asso. clin. prof. radiology Sch. MediMedicine, 1965-74; chief radiologist Cornoa (Cal.) Community Hosp., 1965-74, chief of staff, until 1974, chmn. staff, 1967-70, chmn. adminstrv. council, 1970-74; chmn. bd. Hialeah (Cal.) Hosps. Cons. numerous hosps., also San Bernardino County Dept. Health. Bd. dirs. San Bernardino chpt. Am. Cancer Soc., 1957-74, also past pres., mem. coms.; bd. dirs. San Bernardino County TB and Health Assn. Served with M.C., AUS, 1943-46; PTO. Diplomate Am. Bd. Radiology. Mem. A.M.A., Cal. Med. Assn., San Bernardino County Med. Soc., Radiol. Soc. N.Am., Am. Roentgen Ray Soc., Soc. Nuclear Medicine, Los Angeles County Radiol. Soc., Am. Coll. Radiology, Loma Linda U. Alumni Assn. (governing bd., pres. elect 1974). Contbr. articles to profl. publs. Home: Redlands, Cal., Died Mar. 2, 1974; buried St. George's Cemetery, Bridgeville, Pa.

DEFORD, MIRIAM ALLEN, author; b. Phila., Aug. 21, 1888; d. Moise and Frances (Allen) deFord; student Wellesley Coll., 1907-08; A.B., Temple U., 1911; postgrad. U. Pa., 1911-12; m. W. Armistead Collier, Feb. 14, 1915 (div.); m. 2d, lMaynard Shipley, Apr. 16, 1921 (dec. 1934). Staff writer Phila. N.Am., 1906-07, 08-11, Asso. Advt., Boston, 1912-13; reporter Ford Hall Open Forum, Boston, 1912-15; pub. stenographer and writer house organs, San Diego and Los Angeles, 1915-17; editor house organ, Balt., 1917; ins. claim adjuster, Balt., Chgo., San Francisco, 1918-23; editor WPa Writer' Project, 1936-39; pub. relations writer, 1943-45; staff corr. Federated Press, 1921-56, Labor's Daily, 1956-58, San Jose Reporter, 1959; contbr. biog. dictionaries British Authors of 19th Century, American Authors, 1600-20th Century Authors; British Authors to 1800, European Authors, 1000-1900. Recipient Essay award Com. Econ. Devel., 1958. Fellow Am. Humanist Assn.; mem. Mystery Writers Am., Sci. Fiction Writers Am., Rationalist Press Assn. (London, Eng.), Authors Guild, Poetry Soc. Am., Nat. Orgn. Women, Secularist. Author: Love Children (biog.), 1931; Children of Sun (poems), 1939; Who Was When? A Dictionary of Contemporaries, 1940, rev. edit., 1949; Shaken with the Wind (Novel), 1942; Psychologist Unretired; Lillien J. Martin (biography), 1948; Up-Hill All the Way; Maynard Shipley (biography), 1956; The Overbury Affair (Edgar award Mystery Writers of Am.), 1960; Penultimates, (poetry) 1962; Stone Walls; Prisons from Fetters to Furloughs 1964; Murderers Sane and Mad (award Mystery Writers Am.), 1965; The Theme is lMurder (stories), 1967; Thomas Moore, 1967; The Real Bonnie and Clyde, 1968; Xenogenesis (sci. fiction), 1969; On Being Concerned (biography), 1969; The Real Ma Barker, 1970; Elsewhere, Elsewhen, Elsehow (sci. fiction), 1971. Contbr. stories, articles, verse to mags.; stories in O. Henry Meml. Prize Vol., The Silver Knight, 1930; Pride, 1934; verse included in over 50 anthologies; also numerous short stories in anthologies. Publ. asso.; The Humanist. Editor: Anthology, Space, Time and Crime, 1964. Home: San Francisco, Ca. Died Mar. 22, 1975.

DEIGERT, ROBERT CAMPBELL, architect; b. St. Louis, June 15, 1908; s. Edward Frederick and Agnes (Kludt) D.; student U. Mich., 1928-29; B.F.A., Yale, 1933; m. Joan Lozier Thomas, Dec. 19, 1943; children—Robert Campbell, Alison Lozier, Joan Braddock. Chief architect Yale Expdn. to Doura Europos, Mesopotamia, 1931-32; indsl. design asso. Harold Van Doren Assos., 1934-37; individual practice architecture, Detroit, Toledo, 1937-42, Washington, 1945-46; sr. partner Deigert & Yerkes Assos., architects and engrs., Washington, Asheville, N.C., 1946-74. Chmn. bd. dirs. Primary Day Sch., Washington. Served to lt. col. USAAF, 1942-45. Decorated Legion of Merit. Mem. A.I.A., Acoustical Soc. Am. Clubs: Biltmore Forest Country; Mountain City (Asheville); Kenwood Country (Washington). Important works include Royal Netherlands Chancery, Washington, Water Pollution Lab. Center U.S. Dept. Health, Edn. and Welfare, Narragansett, R.I., Fed. Narcotics Labs., Lexington, Ky., Hdqrs., Studios, Program Recording and Distbn. Center, Voice of Am., Washington, Audio Visual Communication Center Ohio State U., Electronics Lab., Cheltenham, Md. army, navy bldgs., U.S. Embassy, Mogadiscio, Somalia, hdqrs. Nat. Arboretum, Washington. Home: Asheville, N.C. Died Nov. 21, 1974.

DEILY, CURTIS R., banker, Cashier, Nat. savs. & Trust Co., Washington, D.C. Deceased.

DEITRICK, WILLIAM HENLEY, architect; b. Danville, Va., Mar. 5, 1895; s. William H. and Lito (Townes) D.; A.B., Wake Forest Coll., 1916; student Columbia, 1922-24; m. Elizabeth Hunter, Nov. 27, 1920. Prin. Newnan (Ga.) High Sch., 1916-17; bldg. contractor, 1919-22; architect, N.C., 1927-59; projects Western N. C. San., N.C. State Fair Arena, N.C. State Coll. Student Union Bldg., elementary and high schs.; architect Wake Forest Coll., 1931-50; asso. with John A. Park, Jr. & Co., from 1967; bus. broker, from 1969. Pres. N. C. Design Found., N.C. State Coll., 1959-62; chmn. Raleigh Hist. Sites Com., 1965-68; pres. Raleigh Hist. Sites Found., 1965-68, chmn., 1967; mem. exec. com. Keep N.C. Beautiful, from 1972. Gov's Com. Beautification, treas., 1967, 68, 69—. Served as 2d lt. F.A., AUS, 1917-19. Co-winner gold medal in engring. from N.Y. Archtl. League, 1953, first honor award in merit, 1955, 2 awards of merit, 1957. Fellow A.I.A. (chmn. South Atlantic regional conf. 1956), N.C. State Art Soc. (chmn. bd. 1949). Home: Raleigh, N.C. Deceased.

DEJONG, YVONNE GERMAINE, social worker; b. Antwerp, Belgium; d. Jacques and Estelle (Philipse) DeJong; diploma Sch. Social Work, Brussels, 1939; Master degree in Criminology, U Brussels, 1939; M.S.W., U. Mich., 1953. Came to U.S., 1951, naturalized, 1956. Social worker Mental Hygiene Clinic, also Juvenile Ct., Brussels, Belgium, 1938-39, ambulance driver Motor Corps unit Belgian Red Cross, 1940-44; internat. work with UNRRA and Internat. Relief Orgn. in occupied territories in Europe and liberated countries, 1945-50; with S. Fla. State Hosp., Hollywood, 1957-73, asst. dir., casework supr., 1961-73. Decorated govt. medals (2) (Belgium). Mem. Nat. Assn. Social Workers, Acad. Certified Social Workers. Club: Altrusa (Hollywood, Fla.). Home: Hollywood, Fla. Died May 2, 1973.

DEKNATEL, FREDERICK BROCKWAY, art historian; b. Chgo., Mar. 9, 1905; s. Frederick H. and Wilfreda (Brockway) D.; A.B., Princeton, 1928; Ph.D., Harvard U., 1935; L.H.D., Alfred U., 1966; m. Virginia Herrick, June 22, 1931; children—John H., William B., Charles Y. Instr., tutor Harvard, 1932-40, asso. prof. fine arts, 1940-46, prof., 1946-73, William Dorr Boardman prof., 1955-73, emeritus, 1973, chmn. dept., 1944-49. Pres. Coll. Art Assn., 1947-48. Decorated knight 1st class Order St. Olaf (Norway). Author: Edvard Munch, 1950. Home: Cambridge, Mass. Died Nov. 3, 1973.

DEKNATEL, WILLIAM FERGUSON, architect; b. Chgo., May 29, 1907; s. Frederick H. and Wilfreda (Brockway) O.; A.B., Princeton, 1929; Taliesin fellow, Ecole des Beaux Arts, Paris, France, 1932, Diplome parle Gouvernment, 1936; m. Geraldine Eager, Apr. 17, 1930; children—Diane (Mrs. Emery Plerson). Frederick Henry II. Architect, 1936—; dir. Mackie-Lovejoy Co., Chgo., 1932-60, pres., 1949-60; dir. Setwell Co., Chgo., 1932-72, chmn., treas., 1949-72, pres., 1967-72; chmn., treas. Elting, Deknatel & Assos., Inc., 1960-62; co-principal Urban Renewal Planning Assos., 1961-67; v.p. The Clearing, 1951-56, dir., 1951-58. Chmn. planning for services com. Welfare Council Met. Chgo., 1956-59; dir. Nat. Fedn. Settlements and Neighborhood Centers, 1959-67, v.p., 1964-67, chmn. civil rights com., 1964-67; chmn. Near West Side Planning Bd., 1949-50, vice chmn., 1950-56, exec. com., 1956-62; vice chmn. West Central Planning Assn., 1954-64; mem. bd. Gt. Lakes Regional Planning Commn., 1956-69. Trustee Hull House Assn., 1939—, pres., 1953-56, 61-62, hon. pres., 1964. Registered architect, Ill., Wis., Mich. Mem. A.I.A., Soc. Contemporary Am. Art (pres. 1951-53), Lambde Alpha. Clubs: University (Chgo.); Anglers (N.Y.); Arts. Home: Sarasota, Fla. Died Feb. 16, 1973.

DELANEY, GEORGE A., engr.; b. Centerview, Mo., Feb. 11, 1895; s. John and Jessie (Hering) D.; B.S., U. Mo., 1917; m. Barbara A. Stoye, June 30, 1945. Draftsman Savage Arms Corp., Sharon, Pa., 1919-20; product engr. Paige-Detroit Motor Car Co., 1920-23, exptl. engr., 1923-25, asst. chief engr., 1925-27; exptl. engr. Graham Motors Corp., Detroit, 1927-34; elec. engr. Pontiac Motor div. Gen. Motors Corp., Pontiac, Mich., 1934-39, asst. chief engr., 1939-42, 45-47, chief engr., 1947-56; cons. Automobile Mfrs. Assn., Inc., 1959-65, Pioneer Engring. and Mfg. Co., 1965-72; supervising engr. aircraft Fisher Body div. Gen. Motors Corp., Detroit, 1942-45. Served as 1st lt. F.A., U.S. Army, 1917-19. Recipient honor award for distinguished service in engring. U. Mo., 1956. Mem. Am. Standards Assn. (dir. 1953-56), Soc. Automobile Engrs. (pres. 1956), Am. Ordnance Assn., Engring. Soc. Detroit. Home: Pleasant Ridge, Mich. Died July 15, 1974.

DELL'AGNESE, F., v.p. Hilton Hotels in charge Waldorf Towers, 50th and Park Av., N.Y.C. Home: New York City N.Y. Died Nov. 15, 1971.

DEL MAR, WILLIAM ARTHUR, elec. engr.; b. San Francisco, Dec. 15, 1880; s. Alexander and Emily D.; ed. Brizton Sch. of Chemistry, London, Eng.; Asso. of City and Guilds' Inst., City and Guilds' Coll., London, 1900, Fellow, 1952; m. Breta Longacre, Jan. 31, 1918 (died 1923); children—Emily Anne, Breta Eleanor, John Longacre; married 2d, Dorothy Ochtman, Jan. 20, 1945. With General Electric Company, Schenectady, N.Y., 1900-01; Manhattan Ry. Co., 1902-04, N.Y.C.&H.R. R.R. Co., 1904-15, Interborough Rapid Transit Co., 1915-17; served as chief engineer Habirshaw Cable and Wire Corp. from 1917. Active in standardization of elec. apparatus from 1908. Chmn. com. Am. Inst. Elec. Engrs. apptd. at request of U.S. Govt. to assist the Navy and War depts. during World War I, in solving engring. problems respecting elec. wires and cables; also mem. com. through which War Dept., obtained engring. personnel during the war. Fellow Am. Inst. Elec. Engrs. (ex-v.p.). Former pres.

Insulated Power Cable Engrs. Assn. Protestant, Club: Engineers'. Author 2 books contbr. others. Asso. editor in chief Elec. Engrs. Handbook, 1949. Home: Greenwich, Conn.†

DELOUGAZ, PINHAS PIERRE, educator, archaeologist; b. Russia, July 16, 1901; s. Simon and Zipporah (Silverman) D.; student U. Paris (France) 1922-26, U. Chgo., 1939-42; m. Nathalie Poliakoff, May 23, 1943. Came to U.S., 1938, naturalized, 1944. Archtl. asst. Harvard-Baghdad Sch. Expdn., Nuzi, Iraq, 1928-29; field asst. Oriental Inst. Iraq Expdn., 1929-31, dir. excavations at Khafaje, Iraq, 1931-37, field dir. Iraq Expdns., 1948-75, dir. Israel Expdn., 1952-75, dir. Iran Expdn., 1961-75, curator inst. mus., 1944-67, dir. archaeol. reconaissance expdn., 1961-62; field dir. U. Mus. of U. Pa.-Am. Sch. Oriental Research joint expdn., Khafaje, Iraq, 1937-38; faculty U. Chgo., 1949-67, prof. archaeology, 1960-67, chmn. com. archaeol. studies, 1950-67; prof. archaeology U. Cal. at Los Angeles, 1967-75, initiator, dir. Mus. Cultural History at univ., 1969-75. Mem. Am. Oriental Soc. (past mem. exec. com.), Archaeol. Inst. Am., Am. Assn. Museums, Internat. Inst. Conservation, Am. Assn. U. Profs. Author: The Temple Oval at Khafajah, 1940; Pottery from the Diyala Region, 1952; Piano-Convex Bricks and the Methods of Their Employmemt and The Treatment of Clay Tablets in the Field, 1933; (with S. Lloyd) Pre-Sargonid Temples in the Diyala Region, 1942; (with R.C. Haines) A Byzantine Church at Khirbat al-Karak, 1960; (with Hill, Lloyd) Private Houses and Graves in the Diyala Region, 1967; also articles. Address: Los Angeles, Cal. Died Mar. 29, 1975; interred Tel-Aviv, Israel.

DEL SESTO, CHRISTOPHER, gov. of R.I.; b. Providence, Mar. 10, 1907; s. Eraclio and Rose (Geremia) Del S.; B.B.A. cum laude, Boston U., 1928; LL.B., cum laude, Georgetown U., 1939; grad. student N.Y.U., U. Miami, Practicing Law Inst. of N.Y., m. Lola Elda Faraone, Oct. 12, 1933; children—Christopher T., Ronald W., Gregory T. Admitted to D.C. bar, 1937, R.I. bar, 1940, also U.S. Treasury Dept., Fed. Cts., Tax Ct., U.S. Supreme Ct.; with Del Sesto & Biener, Providence, specializing taxation and finance; instr. Taunton (Mass.) High Sch., Boston U., Northeastern U.; adv. com. taxation lectures U. R.I., also Brown U.; chief accountant State Treasurer's Office; judget dir. State of R.I., 1933, finance dir., 1935; staff of chief accountant SEC; spl. asst. to atty. gen., anti-trust div. Dept. Justic, 1937-40; state dir. OPA. World War II; gov. of R.I., 1958-60; asso. judge R.I. Superio Ct., 1966-73. Mem. state unemployment relief commn., state emergency pub. works commn. state retirement bd.; candidate for mayor of Providence, 1952; candidate for gov. of R.I., 1956. Trustee R.I. State Coll. Recipient citation for civilian contbn. war effort Providence Jour., 1944 C.P.A., Rhode Island, 1932. Mem. Am., R.I. bar assns., R.I. Soc. C.P.A.'s, Am. Inst. Accountants, St. Liberato Cath. Soc., Nat. Assn. Cost Accountants. Republican. Clubs: Dunes (Narragansett, R.I.); Italo-American of Rhode Island. Home:U1Providence, R.I. Died Dec. 27, 1973.

DEL SOLAR, JUNE ECKART DE GONZALEZ, orgn. exec.; b. Broadway, Va., June 5, 1918; d. Alejandro Carmen and Linnie E. (Chambers) Eckart; student Radcliffe Coll; N.Y. Sch. Social Research; m. Julio C. Gonzalez del Solar, Nov. 8, 1941 (div. Aug. 1947). Exec., office of financial counselor Argentine embassy, 1936-41; sec.-treas., dir. C. Alonso Irigoyen & Co., N.Y.C., 1946-54; exec. sec. to dir. Population Reference Bur., Washington, 1955-62, asst. sec., 1962-69; administrv. asst. Nat. Parks Assn., Washington, from 1970. Active various local civic orgns. Mem. Population Assn. Am., D.C. Sociol. Soc. Club: Soroptimist (S. Atlantic regional chmn. for sister clubs 1966-68). Home: Washington, D.C. Died Jan. 9, 1972; interred Cedar Hill Cemetery, Washington, D.C.

DE MARE, JEANNE, lectr.; b. Paris, France, Jan. 21, 1884; d. Tiburce and Agnes (Healy) de Mare; student Les Ruehes and Sorbonne, 1900-02, Coll. of Spiritual Sci., 1926-31. Lectr. on The Coming Age, 1931-74; appeared before various clubs throughout U.S., France, Eng., Switzerland; lectr. and writer on metaphysics, art and lit. Mem. English-Speaking Union, New Thought Alliance, Anthoposophical Soc., Nat. Soc. Arts and Letters, Internat. Platform Assn. Club: Lexington Democratic (N.Y.C.). Home: New York City, N.Y. Died Feb. 1, 1974.

DEMBO, LEON H., physician; b. 1895; M.D., Jefferson Med. Coll., 1920. Cons. in pediatrics St. Anns Maternity Hosp., Polyclinic Hosp.; vis. pediatrician St. Luke's Hosp.; asso. pediatrician Babies and Children's Hosp.; cons. De Paul Infants Home; pediatrician Curtiss Clinic; asst. clin. prof. pediatrics emeritus Western Res. U. Sch. Medicine. Diplomate Am. Bd. Pediatrics. Home: Cleveland, O., Died July 12, 1973.

DE MENIL, JOHN, corp. exec.; b. Paris, France, Jan. 4, 1904; s. Georges Menu and Madeleine (Rougier) de M.; B.A., U. Paris, 1922, grad. Sch. Polit. Sci., 1925, B.Law, 1935; m. Dominique Schlumberger, May 9, 1931; children—Christophe (Mrs. Enrique Castro-Cid), Adelaide, Georges, Francois, Philippa (Mrs. Francesco Pellizzi). Came to U.S., 1941, naturalized, 1962. Vice pres. Banque Nat. pour le Commerce et l'Industrie, Paris, 1932-38; pres. Schlumberger Overseas and Schlumberger Surenco, Houston, 1941-57; chmn. exec. com., dir. Schlumberger Ltd., Houston, 1958-68, chmn. bd., 1968-70; dir. Bank of S.W., Istel Fund, Inc. Trustee Mus. Primitive Art, N.Y.C., Mus. Modern Art, Inst. Internat. Edn.; v.p. internat. council Mus. Modern Art; v.p. Menil Found. Clubs: Ramada, River Oaks Country, Petroleum (Houston). Home: Houston, Tex. Died June 1, 1973.

DE MERRALL, LEO CYRIL, business exec.; b. London, Eng., July 31, 1880; s. Albert Edward and Clara (Elizabeth) de M.; m. Harriet Ann Sykes, 1906; children—Elaine, Patricia Clara. Pres. Martin Semour Co., Winnipeg Paint and Glass Co., Harris Paint and Wallpaper Co.; vice pres. Sherwin Williams Co. of Can. from 1935, also dir.; dir. Internat. Varnish Co., Carter White Lead Co. Home: West Vancouver, B.C.†

DE MERRY DEL VAL, ALFONSE, Spanish diplomat; b. Bilbao, Spain, July 24, 1903; s. Alfonso and Maria de Alzola (y G.de Gastejon) de M.; grad. Stonyhurst Coll., Eng., 1913; certificate Oxford and Cambridge Sch., 1921; Licenciate Law, U. Deusto (Spain), 1925, U. Valladolid (Spain), 1925; m. Mercedes de Ocio, May 27, 1936. Joined Spanish Diplomatic Service, 1929; 2d sec., London, Eng., 1929-30; 2d sec., Prague, Czechoslovakia, 1930-31; dep. pvt. sec. to King Alfonso XIII, 1931-32; 2d sec. Washington, 1932-34, Asuncion, Paraguay, 1934-36, Secretariat Fgn. Affairs, Salamanca, Spain, 1936, Ministry Fgn. Affairs, Burgos, Spain, 1936; liaison officer British Commn. exchange prisoners war, 1936, Internat. Commn. Non-Intervention, 1937; 2d sec., Rome, Italy, 1938-39; 2d sec., Bucharest, Rumania, 1939-44, lst sec., 1944; 1st sec. Ministry Fgn. Affairs, 1944-45, Buenos Aires, Argentina, 1945-49; Counselor of embassy, Brussels, Belgium, 1949-53; minister counselor embassy, Lima, Peru, 1953-54; ambassador to Dominican Republic, 1954-56, to Denmark, 1956-58, to Lebanon, 1958-61, to Peru, 1961-64, to U.S., 1964-71. Created marquis; decorated Medal of Civil War, knight grand cross order Civil Merit, knight Order Charles III, knight comdr. Order Isabel the Catholic (Spain); comdr. Order King Leopold (Belgium); knight commdr. Order Oak Leaf (Luxemburg); knight grand cross Order Cedar (Lebanon); knight grand cross Order Duarte (Dominican Republic). Clubs: Real de Puerta de Hierro, Royal Automobile (Madrid); Metropolitan (Washington). Home: Marbella, Spain. Died Jan. 9, 1975.

DEMOREST, WILLIAM JENNINGS, real estate exec.; b. N.Y.C., Apr. 18, 1890; s. Henry C. and Annie (Lawrie) D.; student Trinity Sch.; M.E., Columbia, 1913; Dr. Humanities, Piedmont Coll., 1961; m. Wealthy Albro Lewis, June 29, 1918; children—Dilys (Mrs. Samuel F. Peirce), William Jennings, Annie Lawrie (Mrs. Spence M. Hurtt), Carolyn A. (Mrs. T.H. Tenney, Jr.). With Whitney Co., 1914; sec., v.p. Cushman & Wakefield, Inc., 1919-30; v.p. Wm. A. White & Sons, N.Y.C., 1939-43, pres., 1943-63, vice chmn., chmn. exec. com., 1964-72; v.p., dir. Coliseum Exhbn. Corp., 1955-72; past dir., mem. finance com. Home Life Ins. Co.; past trustee, mem. mortgage com. Greenwich Savs. Bank of N.Y. Past Gov., sec., v.p. Real Estate Bd. of N.Y., pres., 1935-36; dir. Citizens Housing and Planning Council Realty Adv. Bd. on Labor Relations, 1934-37, Citizens Budget Com., 1935; vice chmn. adv. com. World's Fair, 1939; gen. chmn. Met. Fair Rent Com., 1945-48; chmn. bldg. com. Interch. Center, 1955-59; mem. finance com. Com. Econ. Devel., 1962. Chmn. Community Chest drive, Rye, N.Y., 1937. Mem. zoning bd. appeals, Rye, 1944-56; past mem. Mayor's Com. for Removal Elevated Structures, N.Y.C.; mem. finance com. Bd. Nat. Missions, United Presbyn. Ch. U.S., 1933-55; past gov. 42d Street Property Owners Assn. Bd. mgrs. Jerry McAuley Cremorne Mission; trustee Columbia U. Club Found., Univ. Devel. Com., Columbia. Served to capt. U.S. Army, World War 1. Mem. Inst. Real Estate Appraisers, Soc. Older Grads. Columbia U. (Pres.), Laymen's Movement for a Christian World (dir.), C. of C. State N.Y., Huguenot Soc., Pilgrims U.S., St. Andrews Soc., Psi Upsilon. Presbyn. (elder; pres. bd. trustees). Clubs: University, Columbia University (gov.) (N.Y.C.); Apawamis; Misquamicut (Watch Hill, R.I.). Home: Rye N.Y. Died Jan. 2, 1975.

DEMPSEY, EDWARD WHEELER, anatomist; b. Buxton, Ia., May 15, 1911; s. Ald Sell and Julia (Wheeler) D.; A.B., Marietta Coll., 1932, D.Sc., 1954; Sc.M., Brown U., 1934, Ph.D., 1937; A.M., Harvard, 1946; m. Betsey Mills Beach, June 13, 1936; children—Charles Gates, Julia Wheeler, Richard Clinton. Fellow NRC, NRC, Harvard Med. Sch., 1937-38, instr. physiology, 1938-41, asso. in anatomy, 1941-42, asst. prof., 1942-46, asso. prof., 1946-50; prof. anatomy and head dept. Washington U., St. Louis, 1950-66, dean sch. medicine, 1958-64; prof. anatomy, chmn. dept. Coll. Phys. and Surg., Columbia, 1966-75; spl. asst. sec. Dept. Health, Edn. and Welfare, 1964-65; mem. Pres.' Commn. Heart Disease, Cancer, Stroke, 1964; mem. Nat. Adv. Health Council, 1961-64, Nat. Adv. Council Gen. Med. Scis., 1966-70. Mem. Am. Assn. Anatomists, Am. Physiol. Soc., Assn. for Study Internal Secretions, Soc. Exptl. Biology and Medicine, Am. Acad. Arts and Scis., Biol. Stain Commn., Histochem. Soc. Contbr. articles med. and biol. jours. Asso. editor Endocrinology Mag., 1943-44, mng. editor, 1945-52. Home: New York City, N.Y. Died Jan. 9, 1975.

DEMPSEY, F(RANCIS) KENNETH, judge: b. South Bend, Ind., May 16, 1906; s. John Francis and Rose (Mathis) D.; J.D., Georgetown U., 1931; m. Grace A. McLaughlin, June 28, 1932; children—F. Kenneth, Mary Ellen (Mrs. Gerald Kettelkamp), Sheila Maureen (Mrs. Richard Eage), John Dennis, Susan Marie (Mrs. John Donahue), Patricia Rose (Mrs. Gerald Kinyon). Admitted to the State of Ind. bar, 1931; pvt. practice law, South Bend, 1931-54; mayor South Bend, 1945-48; judge St. Joseph Superior Ct., 1954-73. Mem. Am., Ind., St. Joseph County bar assns., Am. Judicature Soc. Democrat. Roman Catholic. Home: South Bend, Ind. Died Apr. 25, 1973.

DEMPSEY, K. MARY, librarian Hist. Soc. Mont., 1960-69. Address: Helena, Mont. Died Feb. 6, 1973; interred Tacoma, Wash.

DEMPSEY, MICHAEL RYAN, bishop Chgo.; b. Chgo., Sept. 10, 1918; s. Edward A. and Mary C. (Ryan) D.; M.A., St. Mary Lake Sem., Mundelein, Ill., 1942, S.T.L., 1943. Ordained priest Roman Cath. Ch., 1943; asso. pastor St. Mary Lake Ch., Chgo., 1944-62; tchr. theology Mundelein Coll., Chgo., 1946-58; asso. pastor St. Francis de Paula Ch., Chgo., 1962-64; pastor Our Lady of Lourdes Ch., Chgo., 1965-74; vicar delegate Archdiocese Chgo., 1966-74, aux. bishop, 1968-74, coordinator inner city apostolate, 1967-74. Nat. dir. Campaign for Human Devel., 1970—. Home: Chicago, Ill. Died Jan. 9, 1974; interred St. Joseph Cemetery.

DENHAM, WILLIAM ERNEST, clergyman, educator; b. Swansea, South Wales, Jan. 4, 1881; s. Frederic Charles and Emeline (Jenkins) D.; student U. of Louisville; M.A., Tulane U.; grad. Moody Bible Inst., Chicago, 1909; M.Th., Southern Bapt. Theol. Sem., Louisville, 1914, D.Th., 1916; m. Myrtle Lane, June 15, 1910; children—William Ernest, Richard Lane, Frederic Charles, Bonnie Lenore. Came to U.S., 1905, naturalized citizen, 1925. Educated as surveyor, in England; with M.,St.P.&Saulte Ste. Marie R.R. until 1907; ordained Bapt. ministry, 1911; pastor successively Mitchell, Ind., Finchville and Simpsonville, Ky., 2d Ch, Columbia, S.C., Coliseum Pl. Ch., New Orleans, until 1919, Carrolton Av. Ch., 1921-29; prof. O.T. exposition, Bapt. Bible Inst., New Orleans, Church, St. Louis, Mo., 1929-40. In fields of evangelism and Bible teaching, 1940-42; acting pastor, 1st Bapt. Ch., Montgomery, Ala., 1942-43; pastor 1st Baptist Church, Miami, Fla., 1943-49; dean Bapt. Bible Inst., Lakeland Fla., from 1949. Author: Synthesis, 1922; Introducing the New Testament, 1925; New Testament Studies, 1934; The Comforter, 1935. Home: Lakeland, Fla.†

DENISON, JAMES HENRY, univ. cons.; b. Mt. Sterling, D., Jan. 8, 1907; s. George and Margaret Olive (Warren) D.; A.B., Defiance Coll., 1928; m. Mary Kendrew, Apr. 3, 1937 (dec. Aug. 1972); 1 dau., Jane Kendrew. Mem. editorial staff Toledo Times, 1928-31, Detroit Free Press, 1931-40; dir. information Mich. War Council, 1940-43; adminstrv. asst. to gov. Mich., 1945-47; asst. pres., dir. univ. relations Mich. State U., 1947-69, cons. to pres., 1969-72, ret., 1972, cons. in univ. archives, 1972-75 asso. prof., 1947-49, prof., 1949-72, prof. emeritus, 1972-75. Mem. Joint Council Ednl. TV, 1950-59, vice chmn., 1952-59; mem. information com. Joint Office instl. Research, 1958-64, chmn., 1960-64; cons. Dept. Def., 1953-54. Mem. nat. budget com. Community Chests and Councils Am., 1953-57; mem. East Lansing Planning Commn., 1958-69, chmn., 1962-68. Bd. dirs. Mich. United Fund, 1953-68. Served to capt. AUS, 1943-45. Decorated Bronze Star medal. Mem. Assn. State Univs. and Land-Grant Colls. (chmn. information com. 1957-61), Am. Coll. Pub. Relations Assn. (trustee-at-large 1962-64, exec. com. 1962-66, pres. 1964-65), Pub. Relations Assn. Mich., Newbury (Eng.) Operatic Soc. (v.p. 1966-75), Fusalier, Mil. Order Fgn. Wars, Sigma Delta Chi. Author: (with A.L. Hunter) Administration and Financing of Educational Education, 1958. Club: University (East Lansing). Home: Lansing, Mich. Died Mar. 6, 1975.

DENNEY, CHARLES EUGENE, railway official; b. Washington, D.C., Oct. 18, 1879; s. William H. and Sarah E. (Talbert) D.; ed. Pennsylvania State Coll.; m. Mrs. Irene S. Sickels, Ohio, April 23, 1919; children—Clark, Charles Eugene. With Union Switch & Signal Co., 1899-1905; asst. signal engr., and signal engr. L.S.&M.S. Ry., 1905-13; spl. engr. to v.p. N.Y.C. Lines West of Buffalo, 1913-14; with Union Switch & Signal Co., 1914-16; with N.Y., Chicago & St. Louis R.R., 1916-27, consecutively spl. engr. to pres. until Jan. 1, 1918, asst. to pres., Jan.-Nov. 1918, asst. federal mgr., 1918-20, v.p. and gen. mgr., 1920-27; v.p. Erie R.R., 1927-29, pres., 1929-39; pres. N.P. Ry. Co., 1939-50. Served as gen. agt. Am. Ry. Assn. in charge Transp. and Constrn. Div., U.S. Army, 1917, 18, 19. Mem. Ry. Engring. Assn., Phi Kappa Sigma. Republican. Address: New York City, N.Y.†

DENNIS, EDWARD WIMBERLY, physician; b. Macon, Ga., July 31, 1923; s. John Cobb and Helen (Wimberly) D.; B.S. in Medicine, Emory U., 1947, M.D., 1949; m. Beatrice L. Forrest, May 28, 1948; children—Sara Margaret, Edward Forrest, Kathleen

Laurie, Kenrick Johnson. Life Ins. Med. Research Fund student fellow, 1946-48; intern, then resident medicine U. Mich. Hosp., 1949-53; mem. faculty Baylor U. Coll. Medicine, Houston, 1954-75, prof. medicine, 1967-75; chief med. cardiology service, also sr. attending physician, also dir. electroencephalograph dept. Meth. Hosp., Houston. Mem. planning com., conf. program dirs. Nat. Heart Inst., 1956-59. Bd. dirs. Houston Heart Assn. Diplomate Am. Bd. Internal Medicine. Fellow A.C.P., Am. Coll. Cardiology, Am. Heart Assn. (council clin. cardiology), Am. Coll. Angiology; mem. Am. Fedn. Clin. Research (councillor 1956-59, vice chmn. 1959-60, chmn. So. sect. 1960-61), Tex. Club Internists, Nat. Acad. Medicine Brazil (hon.). Author articles, chpts. in books. Home: Houston, Tex., Died Aug. 11, 1975; buried Houston.

DE NOGALES, PEDRO RAFAEL (Y MENDEZ), b. San Cristobal, Venezuela, Oct. 14, 1879; s. Gen. Pedro Felipe and Dona Josefa (de Mendez) de Ynchauspe (Basque equivalent to de Nogales); reared in Germany; studied Gymnasium and univs. of Barcelona, Brussels and Louvain; military instruction under pvt. tutors in Belgium. Has served as soldier under many flags; cowboy, miner, world-traveler and explorer; 2d lt. in Spanish Army, Spanish-Am. War; exile from Venezuela from 1910, except when fighting the govt.; with Turkish Army in many battles, World War, advancing to divisional comdr.; was last Turkish mil. gov. (Montacacomandane) of Egyptian Sinai, and comdr. (vekile) 1st Reg. Imperial Lancers in Constaninople. Awarded Iron Cross, 1st Class and 2d lass (Germany); Knight Comdr. Order of Mejedieh with golden swords (Turkey), etc. Fellow Am. Geog. Soc., Royal Geog. Soc. (Eng.), Die Gesellschaft fuer Erdkunde ze Berlin, etc. Roman Catholic. Author: Four Years Beneath the Crescent, 1926; The Looting of Nicaragua, 1927; Memoirs of a Soldier of Fortune, 1931; Silk Hat and Spurs, 1933. Contbr. to Am. and foreign mags. Addesss: Schloss Dilborn bei Brueggen, Niederrhein, Germany; also Authors' League of America, New York, N.Y.†

DENSMORE, HARVEY BRUCE, prof. Greek; b. Stanton, Neb., Sept. 9, 1881; s. Charles Mather and Lucy Elizabeth (Murphy) D.; A.B., U. of Oregon, 1904, Oxford U., 1970; m. Ruth Fisk Anderson, Aug. 1, 1917 (dec.). Instr. in Greek, U. of Washington, 1907, advancing to full prof., 1933, chmn. general studies from 1938, chmn. dept. of classics from 1942. Rhodes Scholar, 1904-07. Mem. Classical Assn. Pacific Coast, Am. Philol. Assn., Am. Assn. Univ. Profs., Archaeological Inst. of Am., A.A.A.S. Phi Beta Kappa (pres. Wash. Alpha). Editor: Ten Greek Plays, 1929. Home: Seattle, Wash.†

DENSTEDT, ORVILLE FREDERICK, educator, biochemist; b. Blyth, Ont., Can., Mar. 2; B.Sc., U. Man., 1929; Ph.D. in Biochemistry, McGill U., 1937; m. 1938; 2 children. Asst., Pacific Fisheries Expt. Sta., 1929-32; mem. faculty McGill U., 1937-68, Gilman Cheney prof. biochemistry, 1965-68, emeritus prof. biochemistry, 1968-75. Fellow N.Y. Acad. Sci.; mem. Am. Soc. Biol. Chemists, Chem. Inst. Can.; emeritus mem. Canadian Physiol. Soc. (past pres.), Canadian Fedn. Biol. Socs., Canadian Biochem. Soc. (past pres.), Canadian Nutrition Soc., Internat. Soc. Hematology, Am. Soc. Hematology, Canadian Inst. Food Tech. (past pres.), Corp. Profl. Chemists Province of Que. Address: Montreal, Que., Canada., Died Mar. 2, 1975.

DENT, JOHN MARSHALL, JR., physician; b. Waynesboro, Ga., Apr. 29, 1937; s. John Marshall and Novine (Holcombe) D.; M.D., Med. Coll. Ga., 1963; m. Mary Widener, Apr. 10, 1960; children—John Marshall III, Sandra Elizabeth, Michael Thomas. Rotating intern Macon (Ga.) Hosp., 1963-64, resident in obstetrics and gynecology, 1964-67; resident in obstetrics and gynecology Talmadge Meml. Hosp., 1965; chief obstet. service, mem. exec. com. Tift Gen. Hosp., Tifton, Ga., 1971-72, chief staff, 1973-74. Chmn., Coastal Plain Maternal and Infant Health Care Task Force, 1974. Served as maj., M.C., AUS, 1967-69. Diplomate Am. Bd. Obstetrics and Gynecology. Fellow Am. Coll. Obstetricians and Gynecologists; mem. A.M.A., Am. Fertility Assn., Am. Assn. Gynec. Laparoscopists, Ga. Wildlife Fedn., Tifton C. of C., Sigma Alpha Epsilon. Home: Tifton, Ga. Died Oct. 4, 1974; buried Oakridge Cemetery.

DE PAULA GUTIERREZ, DON FRANCISCO, ambassador Costa Rica to U.S.; econ. scis., Columbia. Sec. of Treasury, 1937-39, 1943-44; chmn. delegation Monetary Conf., Bretton Woods; twice elected to Congress, representing the Province of Limon; vice pres. Chamber of Deputies, 1932-34; apptd. Sec. of State for Industrial Development, 1943; represented Costa Rica at various internat. confs., including U.N.R.R.A. Conf., Atlantic City, 1944, San Francisco Conf., 1945; ambassador of Costa Rica to U.S. from 1944. Address: Costa Rica.†

DEPINET, NED E., motion picture exec.; b. Erie, Pa., Sept. 9, 1890; s. John and Jessie (Densmore) D.; grad. Erie (Pa.) High Sch., 1909; m. Alida Livingston Cammack, May 7, 1914. Salesman Gen. Film Co., New Orleans, La., 1907-11; dist. sales mgr. Southern Dist., Universal Film Co., Dallas, Tex., 1911-24, gen. sales mgr. New York, 1924-25; v.p. First Nat. Pictures, Inc., 1925-31; v.p. RKO Radio, Inc., 1931-42, pres., 1942-52; pres. RKO Pictures Corp., 1951-52; v.p. Radio-Keith-Orpheum Corp., pres., 1948-52; pres., chmn. bd. RKO Theatres, 1950-52. Pres. Will Rogers Meml. Fund, 1962-74, Will Rogers Meml. Hosp., 1962-74; v.p. Children's Village, Dobbs Ferry, N.Y. Mem. Motion Picture Pioneers (pres. 1960-63). Republican. Mason (32°, K.T., Shriner). Clubs: Variety, Elks (New York); Westchester Country. Home: New York City, N.Y. Died Dec. 29, 1974.

DERBY, ASHTON PHILANDER, chair mfr.; b. Gardner, Mass., Feb. 5, 1878; s. Arthur Philander and Lucy Arvilla (Brown) D.; student Williams Coll., 1895-97; m. Eva May Greenwood, of Gardner, Sept. 26, 1900; children—Stephen A., Philander G., Virginia. Mfr. of chairs from 1897; vice pres. P. Derby Co., Gardner, Mass.; trustee Gardner Savings Bank. Mem. Nat. Council Furniture Assns. (chmn. 1921-23), Nat. Assn. Chair Mfrs. (pres. 1915-1924), Delta Kappa Epsilon. Republican. Conglist. Mason (K.T.). Clubs: Oak Hill Country, Gardner Boat. Home: Gardner, Mass.†

DEROULET, VINCENT W., ambassador; b. Cal., Sept. 16, 1925; B.A., Claremont Men's Coll., 1949; m. Lorinda Payson. Real estate property mgr., 1950-55; chmn. bd. marketing co., 1955-75, investment co., 1958-75; ambassador E. & P. to Jamaica, from 1969. Served with AUS, 1943-46. Home: Falmouth Foreside, Me. Died Aug. 1975.

DERUJINSKY, GLEB W., sculptor; b. Smolensk, Russia, Aug. 13, 1888; s. Wladimir F. and Sophia A. (Artzimovitch) D.; ed. Imperial Acad. of Art, St. Petersburg, Russia; grad. in law U. Petrograd, 1912; m. Alexandra N. Michailoff, May 7, 1924 (dec. Aug. 1956); children—Gleb, Natalie; m. 2d, Natalie Tarby. Nov. 21, 1956. Came to U.S., 1919, naturalized, 1933. Began as sculptor in St. Petersburg, 1915; exhibited in Russia, London, Brussels, Paris, and under auspices of N.A.D. (N.Y.C.), and Art Inst. Chgo. Works in permanent colls. of Met. Mus. Art, San Diego Mus., Toledo, N.Y. Hist. Soc. Represented by fountain (Europa), N.Y. World Fair, 1939; 14 stas. of cross at Cardinal Hayes Meml. Chapel, 1942; 8 medallions carved in wood Postmaster Gen.'s office, Washington; 3 reliefs Chem. Engring. Bldg., Cornell U.; 4 wood statues Ch. of Assumption, Westport, Conn.; meml. bust Franklin D. Roosevelt for Hyde Park Library Court, 1945; Crucifixion (in wood) Kent Sch., Conn.; Madonna and Child in mahogony for Jesuit Ch., India; bronze bust of Dr. Charles May at N.Y. Med. Acad.; teak wood carving meml., Harvard Club, N.Y.; bronze group (Ecstasy) Brookgreen Gardens, South Carolina, also stone carving Samson and the Lion, Diona hunting with dog in bronze; 14 stas. of cross for private chapel for Cardinal Spellman, N.Y.C.; bronze busts Theodore Roosevelt, Theodore Roosevelt House, N.Y.C., 1920, Roosevelt Hunting Lodge, Can., Panama Law Adminstrn. Bldg., Canal Zone, 1958; 28 stas. of cross and crucifixion House of Theology, Cin., 1958; 4 statues for Ch. of St. Vincent Ferrer, N.Y.C.; terra-cotta stas. of cross, 1 wood crucifixion, St. Joseph in wood for St. Mary's Ch., Flushing, N.Y., 1965; 3 statues in marble Cathedral of Immaculate Conception, Washington; St. Bonaventura, Ignatius Loyola, St. Cupertino; Franz Liszt statutte in bronze Haifa (Israel) Music Museum; Torso Okla. Mus. Art, 1970; many others. Recipient numerous awards, most recent: Sculpture prize Am. Artists Profl. League, Allied Artists; Henry Hering medal, 1960, 61; Daniel Chester French Prize, 1962, Bronze Medal of Honor, Nat. Arts Club, 1961, 64, Gold medal Allied Artists Am., 1966, 69, Pauline Law prize, 1968,74; Theresa Richard award Allied Artists Am., 1972; Anna Hyatt Huntington award Am. Artists Profl. League, 1972; Meml. award given in his honor, 1975. N.A. Mem. Nat. Acad. Fine Arts, Nat. Sculpture Soc. (spl. citation, emeritus mem.), N.A.D., Allied Artists (emeritus) Am. Artists Profl. League (medal for sculpture). Mem. Greek Orthodox Ch. N.A. Home: New York City, N.Y. Died Mar. 9, 1975.

DE SANTILLANA, GLORGIO DIAZ, historian of science; b. Rome, Italy, May 30, 1902; s. David and Emilia (Maggiorani) de S.; grad. Rome U., 1925; m. Dorothy Hancock Tilton, Sept. 1, 1948. Came to U.S., 1936, naturalized, 1945. Instr. Rome U., 1929-32; lectr. New Sch. for Social Research, 1936-37; vis. lectr. Harvard, 1937-39; mem. faculty Mass. Inst. Tech., 1941—, prof. history and philosophy of sci., 1954-74, now emeritus; Fulbright fellow in Italy, 1945-55. Mem. Am. Acad. of Arts and Sciences, History of Sci. Soc. Club: Somerset (Boston). Author: Aspects of XIX Century Rationalism, 1941; Galileo's Dialogue of the Great World Systems, 1953; The Crime of Galileo, 1955; The Age of Adventure, 1956; The Origins of Scientific Thought, 1961; Reflections and Ideas, 1968; Hamlet's Mill, 1969. Home: Beverly, Mass. Died June 8, 1974.

DE SAUZE, EMILE BLAIS, educator; b. Tours, France, Dec. 7, 1878; s. Eugéne B. and Marie (Beaubeau) deS.; grad. Collège de Montmorillon, 1898, U. of Poitiers, 1900; A.M., Ph.D., St. Joseph's Coll., Phila., 1907-08; m. Mélanie Philips, 1903; 1 dau., Marcelle. Came to U.S., 1905, naturalized citizen, 1917. Head dept. of Romance langs., Temple U., 1905-16; prof. of French U., of Pa., 1916-18; dir. fgn. langs. Cleveland Bd. of Edn., 1918-49; prof. emeritus French. Grad. Sch., and head dept. Romance langs. Cleveland Coll.; dir. Maison Francaise, Western Res. U., 1919-50; prof. French summer sch. Laval U., Que., from 1950. Editor in chief Fgn. Lang. Series, J.C. Winston Co., 1919-50. Mem. Nat. Fedn. Modern Lang. Teachers of U.S. (pres. 1925), Am. Assn. Tchrs. of French (pres. 1933—), Modern Lang. Assn. America, Am. Classical Assn., Am. Archaeol. Soc., Ohio Coll. Assn. (pres. modern lang. sect. 1939), Central West and South Modern Lang. Teachers Assn. (pres. 1939). Republican. Club: City. Author numerous French texts; (latest) Using French, 1945; Nouveau Cours Pratique, 1946. Home: Cleveland, O.†

DESCHAMPS, PAUL, art critic; b. Paris, France, Sept. 19, 1888; student Ecole Nationale des Chartes (France). Mem. Inst. de France, Decorated comdr. Legion d'Honneur. Author: French Sculpture of the Romanesque Period, 1930; Les chateaux des Crolses en Terre Sainte, vol. 1, 1934, vol. 2, 1939, vol. 3, 1973; La Peinture Murale en France, vol. 1, 1951, vol. 2, 1963; Terre Sainte Romane, 1964; Au temps des Croisades, 1971. Address: Paris, France. Died Feb. 25, 1975.

DE SCHWEINITZ, KARL, social worker, author; b. Northfield, Minn., Nov. 26, 1887; s. Paul and Mary Catherine (Daniel) de S.; A.B., Moravian Coll., 1906, L.H.D., 1932; A.B., U. of Pa., 1907; m. Jessie Logan Dickson, Oct. 4, 1911; children—Mary, Karl; m. 2d, Elizabeth McCord, Aug. 29, 1937. Newspaper reporter, later in publicity work, 1907-11; sec. Pa. Tuberculosis Soc., 1911-13; mem. exec. staff N.Y. Charity Orgn. Soc., 1913-18; gen. sec. Family Soc. of Phila., 1918-30; exec. sec. Community Council of Phila., 1930-36; sec. Phila. Com. for Unemployment Relief, 1929-32; exec. dir. Pa. State Emergency Relief Bd., 1936-37; sec. of Pub. Assistance of Pennsylvania, 1937; director School of Social Work, Univ. of Pa., 1933-36, 1938-42; training consultant, Social Security Bd., 1942-44; dir. Com. on Edn. and Social Security, Am. Council of Edn., 1944-50; vis. prof. Sch. Social Welfare, U. Cal., 1950, prof. social welfare, 1951-58; chief social security mission under Point 4 to the Egyptian Ministry of Social Affairs, 1951; UN cons., 3d Social Welfare Seminar, Arab States, 1952. Sr. Fulbright scholar, London, 1956-57. Democrat. Moravian. Author: The Art of Helping People Out of Trouble, 1924; Growing Up, 1928, 4th rev. edit. 1965; England's Road to Social Security, 1943; People and Process in Social Security, 1948; Social Security for Egypt, (Arabie and Am. edits), 1952; Interviewing in Social Security, 1961. Home: Highstown, N.J. Died Apr. 20, 1975.

DE SICA, VITTORIO, actor, director; b. Sora, Caserta, Italy, July 7, 1902; m. Giuditta Rissone, 1937; m. 2d, Maria Mercader Forcada; 3 children. Appeared first in revues; in films, 1917, plays, 1923-33; own film company, 1933-74; dir. films Red Roses, 1939, Our Children are Watching, 1942, Shoe Shine, 1946, The Bicycle Thief, Miracle in Milan, Umberto D, Indiscretion of an American Wife, The Roof, Neapolitan Gold, The Bigamist, Bocaccio 70, 1962; Anatomy of Love, Bay of Naples, Two Women, Yesterday, Today and Tomorrow (Acad. award as best fgn. lang. film 1965), Marriage Italian Style, Woman Times 7, The Biggest Bundle of Them All, A Place for Lovers, A Young World, 1966, After the Fox, 1966; appeared in The Amorous Adventures of Moll Flanders, 1965; comedy actor Bread, Love and Dreams, 1954. Died Nov. 1974.

DESSEZ, MRS. ELIZABETH RICHEY, ednl. motion pictures; b. Berryville, Va., Oct. 26, 1879; d. John Sinnard and Ellen Marshall (Locke) Richey; ed. pvtly.; m. George A. Dessez, Sept. 8, 1904; children—Minna (wife or Paul Gassard, U.S.N.), John Richey. Dir. pub. relations, motion picture div. Thomas A. Edison, Inc., 1917-18; asso. editor Community Motion Picture Bur., motion picture div. War Work Council Y.M.C.A., 1918-21; dir. ednl. dept. Pathe Exchange, Inc., 1921-29; dir. pub. relations, Beacon Films, Inc., 1931; editor of Lumatone Production Co. from 1932; asst. dir. Motion Picture Research Council, from 1933. Member motion picture com. of White House Conf. on Child America, N.E.A., Internat. Ednl. Cinematographic Inst. Democrat. Christian Scientist. Contbr. to mags. and newspapers and writer of motion picture continuities. Home: New York City, N.Y.†

DETRE, LÀSZLÒ, astronomer; b. Szombathely, Hungary, Apr. 19, 1906; s. Jànos and Gizella (Beczkay) Dunst; D.Sc., Friedrich Wilhelms U., Berlin, 1929; m. Julia Balazs, Sept. 1938; children—Csaba, Villö, Szabolcs, Zsolt. Asst., Budapest Obs., 1929-43, dir., 1943-74; dir. Konkoly Obs., 1943-74; prof. Budapest U., 1963-68. Decorated Order of Labour; recipient Hungarian State Prize I. Mem. Internat. Astron. Union (pres. commn. 1967), Hungarian Acad. Scis. Editor: Information Bull. on Variable Stars (Internat. Astrn. Union), 1961-74, Non-Periodic Phenomena in Variable Stars, 1969. Contbr. articles profl. jours. Died Oct. 15, 1974.

DEUEL, WALLACE RANKIN, newspaper corr.; b. Chicago, Ill., June 14, 1905; s. Duncan MacArthur and Sadie Agnes (Rankin) D.; A.B., U. of Ill., 1926; m. Mary Virginia Smock, Nov. 30, 1929; children—Peter MacArthur, Michael McPherson. Instr. in polit. science and internat. law, Am. U., Beirut, Syria, 1926-29;

editorial writer and asst. to foreign editor of Chicago Daily News, 1929-30, in charge of New York cable office, 1930-31, Washington corr., 1931-32, Rome corr., 1932-34, Berlin corr., 1934-41; spl. asst. to Maj. Gen. William J. Donovan, dir. Office of Strategic Services, 1941-45; on loan to State Dept. as spl. asst. to Ambassador Robert Murphy, political adviser on Germany to Gen. Eisenhower, 1944-45; Washington corr. Chicago Daily News, 1945-49; Washington corr. St. Louis Post-Dispatch 1949-54; with U.S. Govt., Washington, 1954-72. Mem. Phi Beta Kappa, Phi Gamma Delta. Author People Under Hitler, 1942. Home: Chicago, Ill. Died May 10, 1974.

DEUPREE, RICHARD REDWOOD, corp. exec.; b. Norwood, Va., May 7, 1885; s. Richard Overton and Susan Elizabeth (Redwood) D.; ed. pub. schs., Covington, Ky.; m. Martha Rule, Oct. 18, 1913 (died Aug. 1943); children—Richard Redwood, John Rule, James Young, Elizabeth Deupree Goldsmith; m. 2d, Emily Powell Allen, Dec. 26, 1944; stepchildren—Emily A. Laffoon, Susan Elsas. Clerk S. Cincinnati & Covington St. Ry. Co., 1901-05; with The Procter & Gamble Co., 1905, pres., 1930-48, chmn. bd., 1948-59, hon. chmn. bd., 1959-74; dir. Cin. Bell Inc.; mem. dirs. adv. council Morgan Guaranty Trust Co.; trustee Equitable Life Ins. Co. Ia. Hon. trustee Children's Hospital; co-chmn. War Chest, 1942, gen. chmn., 1945. Civilian chmn. Army-Navy Munitions Bd., 1946-47; apptd. mem. President's Com. on Fgn. Aid, 1948; chmn. United Community Campaigns of Am., 1959; mem. Citizens Adv. to Pres. on Mut. Security Program; hon. mem. Bus. Council. Former mem. vis. com. Harvard Bus. Sch.; mem. Cin. Music Hall Assn. Mem. Christian Ch. Clubs: Queen City, Commerical, Commonwealth, Camargo, Cincinnati Country (Cin.). Home: Cincinnati, O. Died Mar. 14, 1974.

DE URSO, JAMES JOSEPH, advt. exec.; b. Bklyn., Nov. 22, 1933; s. Vincent and Jennie (Gallo) DeU.; B.A., Bklyn. Coll., 1959; m. Roberta Zelikowitz, Feb. 5, 1955; children—Michael, Darren. Nat. advt. specialist N.Y. Times, 1951-62; coordinator N.Y. World's Fair advt. Wall St. Jour., N.Y.C., 1962-64, coordinator internat. advt., 1964-65, mgr. liquor industry advt., 1965-66; advt. staff Glamour mag., N.Y.C., 1966-69; account exec. Walston & Co., 1969. Served with AUS, 1955-57. Named Ky. Col.; named to Nat. Football Found. and Hall of Fame, 1960. Mem. Assn. Indsl. Advertisers, L.I. Assn., N.Y., L.I. (treas. 1964-65, pres. 1965-66) advt. clubs, Internat. Platform Assn. Clubs: Touchdown of N.Y., Pro Quarterback, Lambs. Home: Brooklyn, N.Y. Deceased.

DEUTSCH, ADOLPH, banker; b. Budapest, Hungary, Oct. 25, 1881; s. Bernard and Mary (Adelberg) D.; A.B., U. Budapest, 1900; m. Erzsi Sugar; children—Robert St., Alfred L., Charles L. Pres. Am. Savs. & Loan Assn., Detroit, 1947-62, chmn. bd., dir.; pres., dir. Moore, Deutsch & Co., Detroit, from 1931; v.p., dir. Citizens Mortgage Corp., Detroit. Mason (Shriner). Club: Knollwood Country. Home: Detroit, Mich.†

DEVALERA, EAMON, pres. of Ireland; b. New York City, Oct. 14, 1882; s. Vivion and Catherine (Coll) De V.; ed. National Sch., Bruree, Christian Brothers' School, Charleville, Blackrock Coll. and National U. of Ireland; degrees conferred; B.A., B.Sc., H.Dip. in Edn., LL.D., Ph.D., Sc.D. H.C.; m. S. Ni Flhannagain, Jan. 8, 1910; children—Vivion, Máirin Eamonn, Brian (dec.), Ruaidhri, Emer (wife of Briano Cuiv), Toirleach. Joined Irish Vols. at Found., 1931, served as pres., 1917-21; adj. Dublin Brigade, 1915-16, and comdt. in Irish Nat. Insur., 1916; sentenced to death, sentence commuted to penal servtude for life, released in Gen. Amnesty, June 1917, again imprisoned, May 1918; escaped from Lincoln Gaol. Feb. 1919; vis. U.S. and raised loan of six million dollars for Irish Republican Govt., 1919-20; pres. of the Irish Republic, 1919-22; pres. Sinn Féin, 1917-26 (when Fianna Fáil was founded); pres. Fiana Fáil 1926-59, leader opposition Irish Free State Parliament, 1927-32; Parliamentary representative for Clare, 1917-59, also for East Mayo, 1918-21, M.P. for Down (Northern Ireland), 1921-29, South Down (Northern Ireland), 1933-37; president Exec. council, Irish Free State, and minister for external affairs, Mar. 1932-Dec. 1937; Taoiseach (theOshek)O(Head of govt.), 1937-48, 1951-54, 57-59; pres. of Ireland, 1959-73; minister for external affairs, Govt. of Ireland, 1937-48; minister for edn., 1939-40; leader of opposition in Dail Eireann, 1948-51, 54-57. Pres. of council League Nations sessions, Sept. and Oct. 1932; pres. Assemby of League of Nations, 1938. Chancellor of Nat. U. of Ireland, 1921-75. Recipient Grand Cross of the Order of Pius IX, 1933, also Grand Cross of the Order of Charles, 1961; also Supreme Order of Christ, 1962. Rejected Anglo-Irish Treaty in Dail Eireann, Dec. 1921-Jan. 1922. Address: Dublin, Ireland. Died Aug. 30, 1975.

DE VAULT, SAMUEL H., prof. agrl. economics; b. Jonesboro, Tenn., July 1, 1889; s. Fred W. and Laura (Martin) DeV.; A.B., Carson-Newmann Coll., 1912, A.M., U. of N.C., 1915; student U. of Mo., 1916-17; Ph.D., Mass. State Coll., 1931; m. Bess A. Hershey, Feb. 17, 1940. Prin. Conkling High Sch., Telford, Tenn., 1912-14; investigator in food products, U.S. Dept. Agr., 1918; special agt., Bureau of Census, 1919-22; specialist in transportation, U.S. Dept. Agr., June-Aug., 1922; prof. and head dept. of agrl. econ., Univ. of Md., from 1922; spl. investigator in econ. studies, U.S. C. of C., 1923; mem. Governor's Tax Survey Commn. Md., 1931-32, 1938-39; chmn. special advisory com., Census of Agr., from 1939; mem. Maryland State Nutrition Committee from 1940; mem. Joint Land Grant College, Bur. Agrl. Economics Com. on Land Use Planning for Maryland, 1939-43; mem. Ednl. Com. of the National Broadcasting Co. from 1939; sec. Md. Farm Labor com. from 1940; mem. Gov.'s Market com., from 1943; head State Dept. Markets, 1944-46. Served with 89th San. Corps U.S. Army, Camp Meade, Md., 1918-19. Mem. Nat. Assn. Mktg. Ofcls., Am. Farm Econ. Assn., A.A.A.S., Am. Assn. Univ. Profs., Grange, Am. Farm Bureau, Pi Gamma Mu, Alpha Gamma Rho. Democrat. Baptist. Co-author: Vol. Vi, 1920 Census Reports on Agr.; author of many agrl. bulletins. Home: Silver Spring, Md. Died June 22, 1974.

DEVEREAUX, HELENA TRAFFORD, (Mrs. James Fentress), educator; b. Phila., Feb. 2, 1885; d. Arthur Trafford and Betsy (Blyton) Devereaux; ed. Phila. Normal Sch., Temple U., U. Pa.; m. James Fentress (dec.). Founder, dir. Devereux Schs., in Devon, Berwyn, Paoli, Malvern, Glenmore (all Pa.), Santa Barbara, Cal., Atlanta, Ga., Tex., Mass., Conn. and Ariz.; adminstrv. cons., trustee, bd. cons. to Devereux Found., which operates Devereux Schools for Dynamic Edn., also Dr. G. Henry Katz Research and Tgn. Dept. and Dr. Clinton P. McCord Psychiat. Library. Named hon. citizen Tex. Hon. fellow Am. Psychiat. Assn. (life mem.), Phila. Assn. Psychoanalysis (affiliate), Psychoanalytic Soc. Phila. (affiliate), Am. Assn. Mental Deficiency (hon. life), P.E.O. Sisterhood, Delta Kappa Gamma (hon.). Address: Devon, Pa., Died Nov. 17, 1975.

DEVINE, DAVID FRANCIS, ret. electronic and automotive parts exec., financial cons.; b. Bklyn., June 15, 1903; s. David T. and Margaret V. (Hall) D.; ed., Pace Coll.; m. Dorothea Tracy, Aug. 31, 1929; 1 dau., Anne (Mrs. John W. Meyer). Internat. auditor Bell Aircraft, Buffalo, 1942-43, div. controller, 1943-45, comptroller, 1945-52; v.p. finance Am. Bosch Arma Corp. (name changed to Ambac Industries, Inc.), 1952-61, v.p., sec., treas., 1961-68, chmn. finance com. Ambac Internat. Corp., 1968-69; financial cons., 1970-73; dir. Long Island Trust Co., Garden City, N.Y. Treas., mem. Dormitory Authority State N.Y., 1963-73. C.P.A., N.Y. Mem. Financial Execs. Inst., A.I.A., N.Y. State Soc. C.P.A.'s. Home: East Williston, N.Y. Died Jan. 5, 1973.

DEVRIES, LOUIS, coll. prof.; b. Bremen, Germany, May 21, 1885; s. Edward and Gesine (Dauelsberg) DeV.; came to U.S., 1891, naturalized, 1901; A.B., Central Wesleyan Coll., 1907; A.M., Northwestern U., 1908, Ph.D., 1918; student U. of Berlin, U. of Leipzig, U. of Ill., Columbia U., U. of Mich., U. of Chicago; m. Anna Brahms, July 11, 1912; children—Margaret Elizabeth, Donald Ketchem, Louise, Harold Arvidson. Professor of modern languages, Iowa State College, Ames, Iowa, from 1913. Member Phi Kappa Phi fraternity. Author: German for Chemists, 1929; German English Science Dictionary, 1939 (2d edit., 1946); French English Science Dictionary, 1940; Introduction to German, 1943; German English Medical Dictionary, Spanish English Dictionary, German English Technical and Engineering Dictionary, Guide to Scientific German, 1947; A Contemporary German Science Reader, 1948. Editor: Sandeau, Mademoiselle de la Seigliére, 1924; Bordeaux, La Maison, 1930; (with Laura Towne) Mérimée, Carmen, 1932; (with H. E. Biester) Poultry Diseases, 1943. Home: Ames, Ia., Died Jan. 22, 1976.

DEWAR, HENRY HAMILTON, investment banker; b. Chgo., Mar. 26, 1902; s. Hamilton and Mary (Kinney) D.; A.B., U. Tex., 1923; m. Hallie Ball, Oct. 14, 1927; children—Robert Ball, Hallie Ball (Mrs. George Heyer), Marion Cooke (Mrs. Michael Bell). Engaged as employee of Guaranty Co. of N.Y., 1923-24, J.E. Jarratt Co., San Antonio, 1924-29; mgr. bond dept. Alamo Nat. Co., 1929-31; partner Dewar, Robertson and Pancoast, San Antonio, 1932-67, Hornblower & Weeks-Hemphill, Noyes, San Antonio, 1967-72. Chmn. Tex. Dist. Investment Bankers Conf., 1938-39; mem. Nat. Com. of Securities Industry for War Financing, 1942; mem. financial adv. com. Com. for Econ. Devel., 1945. Mem. N.Y. Stock Exchange, gov., 1958-61; mem. Am. Stock Exchange, 1949-67; mem. Assn. Stock Exchange Firms (bd. govs. 1950-52); mem. finance dept. com. U.S. C. of C.; mem. investment banking div. Voluntary Credit Restraint Com. Trustee, mem. bd. govs. S.W. Research Inst., 1954-75, vice chmn., 1962-66. Pres. United Fund of San Antonio, 1957; mem. Tex. Commn. on Higher Edn. (vice chmn. 1956-60); mem. Tex. Bd. of Edn. Investment Adv. Com., 1960; mem. Commn. on Goals for South Higher Edn., 1961; mem. So. Regional Edn. Bd., 1966-75. Mem. Investment Bankers Assn. Am. (v.p. 1944-48, pres. 1948-49, gov. 1943-50), Tex. Investment Bankers Assn. (pres. 1931-32), Nat. Assn. Securities Dealers (mem. bd. govs. and exec. com. 1940-42, chmn. 1942), Delta Tau Delta, Beta Gamma Sigma, Clubs: San Antonio Country, Order of Alamo, Argyle (San Antonio), Racquet and Tennis (N.Y.C.); Bohemian (San Francisco). Home: San Antonio, Tex. Died July 2, 1975.

D'EWART, WESLEY ABNER, congressman, govt. ofcl.; b. Worcester, Mass., Oct. 1, 1889; s. William J. and Mary Elizabeth (Barnard) D'E.; ed. schools in Worcester, Mass., and at Wash. State Coll.; m. Marjorie Cowee, Apr. 3, 1915; 1 son, William Frank. Forest ranger, U.S. Forest Service, 1912-18; rancher, Park County, Mont., from 1918; mem. Mont. legislature, 1937-45; mem. 79th to 83rd U.S. congresses, from 2d Mont. Dist.; spl. asst. to sec. of agr., 1955; asst. sec. of interior, 1955-56. Mem. bd. dirs. Nat. Park Bank. Republican. Mason (32°, Shriner), Elk, Kiwanian. Home: SWilsall, Mont. Died Sept. 2, 1973; buried Mountain View Cemetery, Livingston, Mont.

DEWEY, BRADLEY, cons. engr.; b. Burlington, Vt., Aug. 23, 1887; s. Davis Rich and Mary (Hopkins) D.; A.B., Harvard, 1908; B.S., Mass. Inst. Tech., 1909; D.Sc., U. Akron, 1944, Northeastern U., 1945; LL.D., Harvard, 1945; m. Marguerite Mellen, Apr. 17, 1915; children—Bradley, Davis Rich II, Marguerite, Ann. Research chemist, later dir. research lab. Am. Sheet & Tin Plate Co., 1909-17; entered Army as 1st lt. 1917, later col. Chem. Warfare Service charge gas def. div.; co-founder Dewey and Almy Chem. Co., Cambridge, 1919, pres., 1919-52, chmn. bd., 1952-54; cons., dir. W. R. Grace & Co.; chmn. bd. Hampshire Chem. Corp., Nashua, N.H., 1958-65. Dep. rubber dir. WPB, 1942-43, dir., 1943-44; cons. Q.M.C., cons. to dir. OSRD; cons. D-M Research Corp.; mem. Am. Chem. Soc. adv. com. to Chem. Warfare Service, 1945-46: chmn. joint chiefs of staff, Guided Missiles Com., 1945-46; mem. Presdl. Evaluation Commn., Joint Chiefs of Staff Evaluation Bd. of atomic bomb tests. Life mem. corp. Mass. Inst. Tech., mem. adv. council Sch. Indsl. Mgmt. Awarded D.S.M., Medal for Merit; medal Soc. Chem. Industry, 1944. Fellow Am. Acad. Arts and Scis.; mem. Soc. Chem. Industry, Am. Philos. Soc., Inst. Food Technologists, Newcomen Soc. (Eng.), U. Notre Dame Adv. Council for Science and Engring., A.A.A.S., Am. Chem. Soc. (past pres.), Am. Inst. Chem. Engrs., Chi Phi. Clubs: Commercial (Boston); Mass. Inst. Tech. Faculty, Country (Brookline); Chemists (N.Y.C.); Cosmos (Washington). Home: New London, N.H. Died Oct. 14, 1974.

DEWEY, CHARLES SCHUVELDT, banker; b. Cadiz, O., Nov. 10, 1880; s. Albert B. and Louise (Schuveldt) D.; student St. Paul's Sch., Concord, N.H., 1896-1900; Ph.B., Yale, 1904; m. Suzette deM. Hall, Dec. 20, 1905 (dec. Dec. 1956); children—Suzette D. (Mrs. Frederick Alger), Charles S., Louise (Mrs. Edward B. Smith), A. Peter; m. 2d, Elizabeth Zolnay Smith, June 3, 1959. Vice pres. No. Trust Co., Chgo., 1920-24; asst. sec. treasury charge fiscal affairs, 1924-27; financial adviser Republic Poland, 1927-31; dir. Bank of Poland, 1927-31, hon. life dir.; v.p. Chase Nat. Bank, 1945-50; agt. gen. Joint Congl. Com. Fgn. Econ. Cooperation, 1946-50; mem. Washington Nat. Monument Soc., from 1960. Nat. treas. A.R.C., 1927, chmn. D.C. chpt., 1957-61, now mem. exec. com.; pres. Washington Hosp. Center, 1951-57; mem. adv. com. Export-Import Bank of Washington, 1947. Mem. U.S. Ho. of Reps. from 9th Ill. Dist., 1941-45. Served with USNRF, 1917-19. Decorated grand officer Legion of Honor (France); grand comdr. Polonia Restituta (Poland); grand comdr. Crown of Rumania; grand comdr. Order St.Sava (Yugoslavia). Mem. S.A.R., Delta Psi. Republican. Episcopalina. Clubs: Chicago, Society of Cincinnati, Metropolitan (Washington). Home: Washington, D.C.†

DEWEY, CHESTER ROBERT, banker; b. Mazon, Ill., Aug. 21, 1888; s. Robert Hall and Ida Josephine (Burleigh) D.; A.B., U. Ill., 1908, LL.B., 1909; m. Helen L. Capron, Feb. 1, 1913; children—Chester Robert (dec.), Frederick Capron (dec.), Helen Elizabeth (Mrs. Harlan P. Wallingford), Priscilla Anne (Mrs. Eugene S. Dewey). Admitted to N.Y. bar, 1910, and began practice with Wilmer, Canfield & Stone, later Satterlee, Canfield & Stone, N.Y.C.; moved to Utica, N.Y., 1913; mem. Dunmore & Ferris, 1916, Dunmore, Ferris & Dewey, 1917-32; pres. Citizens Trust Co., Utica, 1928-31; vice chmn. First Citizens Bank & Trust Co., Utica, 1931-33; pres. Grace Nat. Bank of N.Y., 1933-54; partner Ferris, Hughes, Dorrance & Groben, 1954-74; pres. Homestead Aid Assn., Utica, 1929-33; pres. Trust Co.'s Assn. N.Y., 1930-33; pres. Utica Fire Ins. Co., 1955-71, chmn. bd., 1964-74. Trustee Hamilton Coll. Mem. Venezuelan C. of C. (past pres.), Am. Arbitration Assn., S.A.R., Am., N.Y. State bar assns., N.Y. State Bankers Assn. (past pres.). Republican. Presbyn. Mason (32 deg., Shriner). Clubs: Illini, India House (N.Y.C.); Fort Schuyler (Utica); Scarsdale Golf; Yahnundasis Golf. Home: Utica, N.Y. Died Mar. 13, 1974; buried Forest Hill Cemetery, Utica, N.Y.

DEWEY, MALCOLM HOWARD, prof. fine arts; b. Meadville, Pa. Sept. 6, 1881; s. Edward Hooker (M.D.) and Helen (Couch) D.; B.A., Allegheny Coll., 1904; M.A., Harvard, 1911; Ph.D., U. of Chicago, 1918; m. Maybelle Jones, Aug. 20, 1927. Instr. Allegheny Prep. Sch., 1904-05; prin. high sch., Irwin, Pa., 1905-12; instr. German, Allegheny Coll., 1912-14; prof. Romance languages Emory Univ., 1919-27, head department of fine arts, 1927-50, ret., fir. of music from 1950; Rosenwald traveling fellow, 1932. With Am. Red Cross, Ft. Oglethorpe, Ga., 1918; nat. field secretary American Red Cross, 1919. Mem. Delta Tau Delta, Phi Beta

Kappa, Omicron Delta Kappa fraternities. Methodist. Mason (32°). Dir. Emory U. Glee Club and Orchestra (European tour, 1926, 28). Home: Atlanta, Ga.†

DEWITT, WALLACE, army officer; b. Fort Steele, Wyo., June 1, 1878; s. Calvin and Josephine (Lesesne) D.; student Princeton, 1894-95; M.D., U. of Pa., 1900; m. Bessie S. Foster, Sept. 27, 1904; 1 son, Wallace. Began as contract surgeon with U.S. Army, 1900 and advanced through grades to col., 1927; brig. gen. asst. to surgeon gen., 1935-39. Fellow Am. Coll. of Surgeons, A.M.A.; mem. Am. Hosp. Assn., Alpha Mu Pi Omega. Clubs: Graduate (New Haven); Army and Navy (Washington, D.C.). Address: San Francisco, Cal.†

DEXTER, BYRON, editor; b. Newark, Dec. 9, 1900; s. James Leonard and Mary Gordon (Bourne) D.; A.B., Princeton, 1923; m. Jeannette Thurber Pruyn, 1927 (div.); children—Joan Gordon (Mrs. D. Blackmer), Dierdre Pruyn (Mrs. S. Maiarkey); m. 2d, Jane Wilson, 1940 (div.); m. 3d, Lorraine Le Huray Commons, 1944. Reporter, Atlanta Jour., 1923; staff mem. Charles Scribner's Sons, 1924-27; circulation mgr., asst. editor, New Republic, 1928-31, 34-42; asst. editor Fgn. Affairs, 1943, mng. editor, 1949-55; editor Let's Talk About, monthly discussions of fgn. affairs, 1952-55; editor Vermonter mag., 1966. Mem. Council Fgn. Relations. Clubs: Century, Woodstock Country, Princeton of N.Y. Editor: The Arabs: (with Philip K. Hitti) A Short History, 1943. Author: The Years of Opportunity: The League of Nations 1920-26, 1967. Contbr. to Clausewitz and Soviet Strategy in the Soviet Union 1922-62 (editor Philip E. Mosely), 1962. Contbr. to periodicals. Home: South Woodstock, Vt. Died Aug. 2, 1973.

DEY, BENJAMIN CLIFFORD, lawyer; b. Oregon City, Ore., Dec. 29, 1879; s. Thompson and Mary Ellen (Lamphere) D.; A.B., Stanford, 1905; m. Hazel Sobey, Nov. 15, 1911; children—Dorothy, Benjamin Clifford, Franklin Herrin, Marilyn. Admitted to Ore. bar, 1906, and began practice at Portland; mem. law firm of Dey Hampson & Nelson, Portland, 1918-30; gen. counsel S. P. Co., 1930-47, ret. 1947), dir. from 1934. Mem. Kappa Sigma, Phi Delta Phi. Republican. Home: Los Altos, Calif.†

DEY, WILLIAM MORTON, university prof.; b. Norfolk, Va., June 23, 1880; s. George Walters and Mary Jane (Toy) D.; student Univ. of N.C., 1897-98; A.B., Univ. of Va., 1902; A.M., 1902; A.M., Harvard, 1904; Ph.D., 1906; student Univ. of Paris, 1920-21; m. Ellen Alice Old, Dec. 28, 1910. Austin teaching fellow Harvard, 1905-06; asst. prof. romance langs. Univ. of Mo., 1906-09; prof. romance langs., Univ. of N.C., 1909-34, Kenan prof. romance langs., from 1934, chmn. div. of humanities, 1935-40. Decorated Chevalier Legion of Honor (France), 1949. Mem. Modern Lang. Assn. of Am., South Atlantic Modern Lang. Assn., Am. Assn. Teachers of French, Delta Kappa Epsilon, Phi Beta Kappa. Dem. Protestant Episcopalian. Edited Benjamin Constant's Adolphe, 1918; edited and collaborated on Beziat's French Grammar, 1927. Author: Alfred de Vigny, Romantic Poet, 1946. Mem. editorial bd. and contbr., Studies in Philology. Home: Chapel Hill, N.C.†

DEYO, MORTON LYNDHOLM, naval officer; b. Poughkeepsie, N.Y., July 1, 1887; s. Peter and Ida Florence (Woolsey) D.; student Yale; B.S., U.S. Naval Acad., 1911; grad. Naval War Coll., 1932, Staff Naval War Coll., 1934; m. Maria Ten Eyck Decatur Mayo, Nov. 15, 1916; 1 dau., Maria Lila (Mrs. J.H.P. Garnett). U.S.S. Allen out of Queenstown, World War I; comd. U.S.S. Morris in Europe; staff comdr. in chief of U.S. Fleet; staff Naval War College; operations officer Asiatic Fleet, 1936-39; naval aide to Sec. of Navy, 1940-41; comd. Destroyer squadron Atlantic 1941; comd. U.S.S. Indianapolis, Pacific, 1942; rear admiral, 1942; comd. destroyers Atlantic Fleet, 1943; dep. comdr. U.S. Naval Forces, Invasion of Normandy, comdg. Naval Bombardment Groups; comd. Task Force bombardment of Cherbourg; comd. bombardment group, Southern France; comd. bombardment group, Iwo Jima; prin. task comdr. Okinawa, dir. naval occupation forces Kyushu Island, naval task forces in demilitarization No. Japan.; comdt. First Naval Dist., ret., 1949. Decorated with D.S.M., Legion of Merit (combat; twice); Hon. Distinguished Service Order (with bar, twice) (British); Legion of Honor (officer) and Croix de Guerre with palm (France); Expeditionary and other service medals. Mem. Naval inst., Am. Newcomen Soc. Clubs: Somerset (Boston); Metropolitan, Army and Navy (Washington). Retired as vice admiral, 1949. Home: Kittery Point, Me. Died Nov. 10, 1973.

DIBARTOLOMEO, ROBERT EDWARD, mus. exec.; b. Steubenville, O., Feb. 13, 1933; s. Antonio and Rose (Presutti) DiB.; student Coll. Steubenville, 1950-52; B.A., Ohio State U., 1955, M.A., 1957; postgrad. U. Wis., 1956-60; m. Cherry Anne Greve, June 10, 1956; children—Elizabeth Anne, Robert Antonio. Dir. Rock County Hist. Soc., Janesville, Wis., 1960-63; dir. Mus. and Hist. Soc., Janesville, 1960-63; mus. dir. Oglebay Inst., Oglebay Park, Wheeling, W.Va., 1963-74. Mus. cons. Mem. Wis. Civil War Centennial Commn., 1962-63; lectr. Midwestern and Wheeling glass. Mem. Ohio County Hist. Soc., Haklyut Soc., Phi Alpha Theta, Alpha Phi Delta. Democrat. Roman Catholic. Club: Blue Pencil of Wheeling. Editor: American Glass: Pressed and Cut. Contbr. articles to mags., newspapers; book revs. Home: Wheeling, W.Va. Died Apr. 10, 1974.

DICE, CHARLES AMOS, univ. prof.; b. Strasburg, O., Nov. 5, 1878; s. John and Catherine (Amos) D.; A.B., Ohio Northern U., Ada, 1905; B.D., Drew Theol. Sem., Madison, N.J., 1908; student Columbia, 1907-08, Boston U., 1908-09; A.M., Harvard, 1911; student U. of Wis., 1915-16, Ph.D., 1924; m. Anna Mary Schlott, of Louisville, O., Jan. 1, 1914 (died June 28, 1933) Taught in country schs. for 3 yrs.; prin. Richville, O., 2 yrs.; prof. Ohio Northern U., 1911-14, Rockford (Ill.) Coll., 1916-17, Colorado Coll., 1917-19, Ohio State U., 1919-26, prof. business organization, Coll. of Commerce and Adminstrn., Ohio State U., from 1927. Mem. advisory bd. dirs. Ohio Nat. Bank, Columbus. Mem. Am. Econ. Assn., Beta Gamma Sigma, Alpha Kappa Psi, Tau Kappa Epsilon. Republican. Methodist. Club: Faculty. Author: The Stock Market, 1926; New Levels in the Stock Market, 1929. Home: Columbus, O.†

DICKEY, LLOYD BLACKWELL, educator, physician; b. Racine, Wis., Apr. 7, 1894; s. George Harry and Agnes Margaret (Thomson) D.; A.B., Fargo Coll., 1915; M.A., U. Ill., 1917; B.S., U. Minn., 1921, B.M., 1922, M.D. cum laude, 1923; m. Marion Marie Treadwell, Mar. 16, 1935; children—Barbara Marie (Mrs. Michael Driskill), Thomas Lloyd, Patricia Marion (Mrs. William Hubenette). Instr. anatomy U. Minn., 1919-21; asst. in morphology Marine Biol. Sta., U. Wash., summer 1921; chief Children's Clinic, Stanford U. Med., 1928-49; vis. pediatrician in Tb, San Francisco Hosp., 1928-59; vis. physician Arequipa Sanatorium, 1934-57; intern Stanford U. Hosp., 1923-24, asst. resident pediatrics, 1924-25, resident pediatrics, instr., 1925-26, asst. prof. pediatrics, 1926-28, asso. prof., 1928-52, prof., 1952-59, prof. emeritus, 1959-74, acting exec. head dept. pediatrics, 1955. Cons. pediatrics Presbyn. Med. Center and Children's Hosp., San Francisco, Kaiser Hosp., San Rafael, Cal., also Permanente Medical Group, 1959-71, Marin County Health Dept., 1971-74. Served as pvt. with U.S. Army, 1918; 1st lt. M.C., 1929; surgeon Fed. Health Service, World War II. Fellow emeritus Am. Thoracic Soc., Am. Acad. Pediatrics, Am. Coll. Chest Physicians, A.M.A.; mem. Gamma Alpha, Sigma Xi, Alpha Omega Alpha, Pi Gamma Mu, Sigma Chi, Nu Sigma Nu. Author numerous papers in field. Home: San Rafael, Cal. Died July 18, 1974.

DICKINSON, LEVI CALL, lawyer; b. Algona, Ia., June 7, 1905; s. Lester Jesse and Myrtle (Call) D.; LL.B., George Washington U., 1930; m. Marion Carmichael, June 8, 1929; children—Levi Call, Roderick C., Nancy Jane. Admitted to Ia. bar, 1930, practiced in Des Moines, 1930-74; sr. partner Dickinson, Throckmorton, Parker, Mannheimer & Raife; instr. taxation Drake U., 1941-42. Mem. Am., Ia., Polk County bar assns., Sigma Chi. Conglist. Club: Des Moines. Home: Des Moines, Ia. Died June 19, 1974.

DIDUSCH, JOSEPH STEPHEN, educator; b. Baltimore, Nov. 25, 1879; s. Joseph M. and Catherine R. (Doetsch) D.; A.B., Loyola Coll., Baltimore, 1898; A.M., Woodstock (Md.) Coll., 1910. Entered Order of Jesuits, 1898; ordained priest, Roman Catholic Ch., 1912; prof. of biology, St. Joseph's Coll., Phila., 1915-25; regent of med. and dental schs., Georgetown U., 1925-26; dean philosophy dept. and prof. of empirical psychology and biology, Woodstock Coll., 1927-30; rector, Jesuit Novitists, Warnersville, Pa., 1930-35; prof. of biology, Loyola Coll., Baltimore, from 1935, chmn. biology dept. from 1935, trustee of coll. from 1935. Mem. A.A.A.S., Genetic Assn. of Am., Ecological Soc. of Am., Am. Inst. of Biol. Sciences, Am. Mus. Nat. History, Nat. Assn. Biology Teachers, Am. Assn. Jesuit Scientists, Cath. Round Table of Science; Md. Acad. of Sciences, Nat. Hist. Soc. of Md. Author: Biology Syllabus for High Schools, 1923. Contbr. articles on hemoglobin, plant pigments, allergenic pollens, parthenogenesis, anthropoid fossil remains in various publs. Address: Baltimore, Md.†

DIEDERICH, JOHN THOMAS, lawyer; b. Newport, Kentucky, Mar. 10, 1888; s. Frederick and Minnie (Diederich) D.; LL.B., Centre Coll., 1910; m. Ada Murphy, July 18, 1917. Admitted to Ky. bar, 1910, Supreme Ct., 1928; practice of law, Ashland, Ky., 1910-74; city atty., 1912-18, city solicitor, 1922-34. Pres. Ashland Indsl. Corp.; chmn. Third Nat. Bank, Ashland, Del. Republican Nat. Conv., 1932, 52, 68, 72; Rep. state chmn., 1955-56; mem. Rep. Nat. Com. for Ky., 1956-65. Chmn. adv. bd. Our Lady of Bellefonte Hosp. Served from pvt. to lt. U.S. Army, 1918-19. Mem. Ky. Oil and Gas Assn. (pres. 1949-50), Am., Ky., Boyd County bar assns. Presbyn. Mason (Shriner). Home: Ashland, Ky. Died Sept. 10, 1974.

DIEHL, HAROLD SHEELY, physician, pub. health adminstr.; b. Nittamy, Pa., Aug. 4, 1891; s. William Kleinfelter and Annie Belle (Sheely) D.; B.A., Gettysburg (Pa.) Coll., 1912, Sc.D., 1935; postgrad. Syracuse U., summer 1914; M.D., U. Minn., 1918, M.A., 1921; m. Julie Louise Mills, Sept. 7, 1921; children—Annabelle Louise, Antoni Mills. Asst. prin., tchr. math. high sch., Fulton, N.Y., 1912-14; asst. prof. preventive medicine, pub. health U. Minn., 1921-24, asso. prof., 1924-29, prof., 1929-58, dean med. scis., 1935-58; sr. v.p. for research and med. affairs, dep. exec. v.p. Am. Cancer Soc., 1958-68, spl. cons. med. and sci. affairs, from 1968. Dir. no. div. A.R.C. Commn. to Poland, 1919-20; mem. sub-com. on med. edn. Nat. Def. Council, 1939-40; mem. directing bd. Procurement and Assignment Services for Physicians, Dentists and Veterinarians, War Manpower Commn., 1941-46; mem. med. adv. com. United Mine Workers Welfare Fund, 1947-57; mem. adv. com. on health resources Office Def. Mobizn., 1950-57, vice chmn., 1953-57; mem. nat. adv. com. Selective Service on Physicians, Dentists, and Allied Specialists, 1950-57; mem. med. adv. com. U.S. Office Vocational Rehab., 1954-58; hon. cons. Surgeon-Gen. Navy, 1955-58; mem. U.S.A. com. Internat. Union Against Cancer, 1958-64; mem. adv. com., cancer control USPHS, 1958-64; mem. pres.'s com. on Heart Disease and Cancer, 1961; vice chmn. Nat. Interagy. Council on Smoking and Health, 1964-68; mem. Nat. Adv. Food and Drug Council, 1964-67. Mem. U.S. delegation to World Health Assembly, 1954, 55, 58. Bd. dirs. Planned Parenthood, N.Y.C., 1970-74. Served with M.C., U.S. Army, 1918-19. Decorated Medal of Polonia Restituta, 1921. Recipient Ed Hitchcock award Am. Coll. Health Assn., 1961; Diehl Hall (bio-med. library) at U. Minn. named in his honor, 1962; recipient Nat. Distinguished Service award Am. Cancer Soc., 1971. Fellow Am. Pub. Health Assn. (gov. council 1946-50), A.M.A. (chmn. sec. preventive, indsl. medicine and pub. health 1939-40); mem. Assn. Am. Med. Colls. (exec. council 1938-40, 1946-47, v.p. 1955-56), Minn. Med. Assn. (chmn. com. on med. edn. and hosps. 1940-58), Minn. Pub. Health Conf. (hon. life), Central Soc. Clin. Research, A.A.A.S., Minn. Acad. Sci., Minn. Acad. Medicine, Am. Student Health Assn. (pres. 1927-29; sec.-treas. 1934-35), Phi Beta Kappa, Sigma Xi, Phi Delta Theta, Nu Sigma Nu, Alpha Omega Alpha. Republican. Conglist. Clubs: University (N.Y.C.); Campus (U. Minn., pres. 1934-35). Author: (with R.E. Boynton) Healthful Living for Nurses, 1944; Personal Health and Community Hygiene, 1951; (with Anita Laton, Franklin Vaughn, John Lampe) Health and Safety for You, 3d edit., 1969; Healthful Living, 9th edit. (with Willard Dalrymple), 1973; Tobacco and Your Health-The Smoking Controversy, 1969. Editorial bd. Jour. Lancet, 1930; adv. editorial bd. Med. World News, 1962-71. Home: New York City, N.Y. Died July 1973.

DIEHL, WILLIAM WELLS, journalist; b. Newark, O., Oct. 14, 1916; s. Grover Louis and Ruby Moore (Wells) D.; student Kent State U., 1936-37; m. Betty Creusere, June 25, 1948. With Ashtabula (O.) Star Beacon, 1939-40, Newark (O.) Advocate, 1940-42, 43-48, Providence Jour., 1948-49, Toledo Blade, 1949-50; mgr. pub. relations accounts for P.R., Haiti, Hamilton Wright Orgn., 1950-51; adminstrv. asst. press information Mutual Broadcasting System, N.Y.C., 1951-53; editor TV Guide, Detroit, 1953-54; editor, pub. T.V. Today, Detroit, 1955-59; editor Dodge News, mag., Detroit, 1959-62; free lance journalist, editorial cons., Detroit, 1962-74. Lectr. Am. Press Inst., Columbia U., 1948-49; mem. adv. council news photo short course Kent State U., 1942-48. Press sec. to State Auditor Joseph T. Ferguson, Ohio, 1942-43. Recipient medal Nat. Headliners Club, 1946, George Washington honor medal Freedoms Found., 1950, honor certificate Freedoms Found., 1963; numerous journalism awards for writing, editing and photography. Mem. National Headliners Club. Democrat. Conglist. Author: (with Barbara Powers) Spy Wife, 1965. Home: Detroit, Mich. Died Sept. 1, 1974.

DIETL, ERNEST LAWRENCE, physician; b. Lakeville, Ind., June 25, 1909; s. Lawrence Adam Dietl; M.D., Ind. U., 1933; m. Esther Louise Fereira, July 19, 1943; children—Sandra (Mrs. Eugene F. McGuire), Ernest Lawrence. Mem. exec. staff St. Joseph Hosp., Epworth Hosp.; head dept. ear, eye, nose and throat Gen. Hosp., South Bend, Ind. Served to maj., M.C., AUS, 1941-45; ETO. Diplomate Am. Bd. Otolaryngology. Mem. A.M.A., Am. Brocho-Esophago. Broncho-Esophagol. Assn., Ind. Opthalmology and Otolaryngology Assn. (past pres., pres. 3d Dist. 1961). Delta Upsilon. Republican. Presbyn. Club: South Bend Country. Contbr. articles to med. jours. Home: South Bend, Ind. Died Sept. 25, 1974; buried St. Joseph Valley Meml. Park-Garden Mausoleum, Granger, Ind.

DIETRICH, JOHN HASSLER clergyman; b. Chambersburg, Pa., Jan. 14, 1878; s. Jerome and Sarah Ann (Sarbaugh) D.; A.B., Franklin and Marshall Coll., 1900, A.M., 1902; student Ref. Theological Sem., Lancaster, Pa., 1902-05; D.D., Meadville. Theol. School, 1933; m. Louise Erb, Aug. 25, 1912 (died Feb. 22, 1931); children—John Erb, William Erb; m. 2d, Mrs. W. O. Winston, Jr., January 30, 1933. Supt. Ashford Hill Retreat, Ardsley, N.Y., 1900-02; mgr. Life's Fresh Air Fund, N.Y. City, 1903; private secretary to Jonathan Thorne, New York, 1903-05; ordained ministry Reformed Church, 1905; pastor St. Mark's Church, Pittsburgh, Pa., 1905-11, First Unitarian Society, Spokane, Washington,1911-16, First Unitarian Society, Minneapolis, Minn., 1916-38, pastor emeritus from 1938. Mem. board dirs. Minneapolis Open Forum. Mem. Am. Unitarian Assn. (life), Am. Sociol. Soc., Phi Kappa Sigma. Clubs: The Gain for

Religion in Modern Thought, 1908; The Religion of a Skeptic, 1911; Substitutes for the Old Beliefs, 1914; From Stardust to Soul, 1916; The Religion of Evolution, 1917; The Religion of Humanity, 1919; Do We Need a New Moral Outlook? 1922; The Present Crisis in Religion, 1923; Humanism Pulpit (7 vols.), 1926-33; The Fathers of Evolution, 1927; also more than 200 published lectures. Home: Berkeley, Calif.†

DIETRICK, CHARLES ROBERT, propane co. exec.; b. Bayonne, N.J., Aug. 28, 1920; s. Charles J. and Inez M. (Jones) D.; B.S. in Mech. Engring., Pa. State U., 1943; M.S. in Econs., Stevens Inst. Tech., 1954; m. Marion A. Shelley, Nov. 2, 1946; children—Carol Ann, Charles Robert, Janet, Judith. Student engr. Gen. Motors Corp., 1946-48; sales engr. Phillips Petroleum Co., 1948-50; with Suburban Propane Gas Corp., Whippany, N.J., 1950-73, v.p., gen. mgr. oil and gas div., also dir. Served to lt. (j.g.) USNR, 1943-46; PTO. Registered profl. engr., N.J., R.I. Mem. Natural Gas Processors Assn. (dir. 1970), Am. Soc. M.E., Soc. Profl. Engrs., Am. Petroleum Inst. Club: Beaverbrook Country (Clinton, N.J.). Home: Plainfield, N.J. Died Apr. 17, 1973.

DIETSCH, C(LARENCE) PERCIVAL, sculptor, painter; b. New York, N.Y., May 23, 1881; s. Maurice and Clara M. (Henry) D.; studied painting at N.Y. Sch. of Art, under William M. Chase; sculpture with Attilio Piccirilli, N.Y. City; Am. Acad. in Rome, 1906-10, fellow, 1910; unmarried. Exhibited in Italy, France and U.S.; awarded Am. prize and Rinehart prize in sculpture, 1906; hon. mention, San Francisco Exposition, 1915. Awards: John Elliott Memorial prize, Dr. Humphreys Memorial prize. Served as aid to Miss Winifred Holt, pres. Comité Franco-American pour les Aveugles de la Guerre (com. for Men Blinded in Battle). Awarded medal for work with blind soldiers, World War I. Mem. Nat. Sculpture Soc., Archtl. League of New York; v.p. Soc. of Four Arts. Hon. mem. Norton Gallery. Episcopalian. Clubs: Everglades, Palm Beach. Home: Palm Beach, Fla.†

DIKE, GEORGE PHILLIPS, patent lawyer; b. Randolph, Vt., Jan. 30, 1876; s. Samuel Warren and Augusta Margaret (Smith) D.; A.B., Williams Coll., 1897; student Mass Inst. Tech., 1897-98; LL.B., Harvard, 1902; m. Elita Caswell Roberts, Apr. 30, 1907. Admitted to Mass. bar, 1902, Mich. bar, 1936, U.S. Supreme Court, 1915; practiced law with firm Macleod, Calver & Randall, Boston, 1902-05; mem. firm Macleod, Calver, Copeland & Dike, Boston, 1905-34, Dike, Calver, & Gray, Boston and Detroit, 1934-41, Dike, Calver & Porter, Boston, 1941-50, Dike & Sanborn, 1950-51, now Dike, Thompson & Bronstein; pres. H.L. Hildreth Co., Boston, 1913-21; dir. Prophylactic Brush Co., 1928-34. Trustee, dir. Roscoe B. Jackson Meml. Lab. for Cancer Research, Bar Harbor, Me. Mem. spl. com. to advise Secs. of War and Navy on patent royalties, 1917, 18. Mem. Nat. Council of Patent Law Assns., Am. Bar Assn., Law Soc., Am. Judicature Society, American Patent Law Assn., Internat. Assn. for Protection of Indsl. Property (mem. internat. executive com.), Brookline Town Meeting, 1922-47. Republican. Unitarian. Clubs: Williams (N.Y.); Union, Harvard (Boston); Country (Brookline); Kebo Valley (Bar Harbor). Author: The Trial of Patent Accountings in Open Court, 1922; also legal articles. Home: Brookline, Mass.†

DILL, LEONARD CARTER, JR., ednl. adminstr.; b. Phila., Aug. 3, 1906; s. Leonard Carter and Amanda (Vansant) D.; A.B., U. Pa., 1928; m. Helen L. Richardson, Sept. 24, 1929; children—Leonard Carter III, Julie D. with E.W. Clark & Co., Phila., 1929-33, L.C. Dill Jr. & Co., investments, 1933-40; pres., also dir. Beaver Constrn. Co., 1935-45, exec. sec. Gen. Alumni Soc., U. Pa., 1940-65, dir. alumni relations, 1960-65, asst. to pres. com. relations; pub., bus. mgr. Pa. Gazette, Phila., 1945-65, Gen. Mag. and Hist. Chronicle 1940-58; chmn. bd. Bailey, Banks & Biddle Co., Phila.; dir. Cons. Mut. Project dir. Peace Corps, India; dir. spl. projects WHYY, Phila., 1971-74. Pres. Organized Classes, U. Pa., 1938; chmn. Lower Merion Twp. (Pa.) Republican Com., 1960-64; pres. Am. Alumni Council, 1952-53; exec. bd. CARE, Phila; bd. West br. YMCA. Trustee Phila. Community Coll., Brandywine Battle Field Park Comm. Mem. Hist. Soc. Pa., Zool. Soc. Phila., Pa. Acad. Fine Arts, Phila. Museum of Art, Franklin Inst., Beta Theta Pi, Alpha Beta Chi. Presbyn. Clubs: Midday (pres.) (Phila.); Merion Cricket (Haverford, Pa.); University (N.Y.C.). Home: Wynnewood, Pa. Died Nov. 4, 1974; buried Westminster Cemetery, Bala-Cynwyd, Pa.

DILLARD, GEORGE HENDERSON LEE, physician; b. Bluefield, W.Va., Sept. 5, 1915; s. George Lee and Florence Louise (Echols) D.; M.D., Med. Coll. Va., 1943; m. Jeanne Alexander, Nov. 25, 1944; children—Jeanne, George, David. Intern, Lakeside Hosp., Cleve., 1944; resident Med. Coll., Va., 1944-45, fellow, 1947-48; resident Vanderbilt U.-Thayer Hosp., 1952-45; fellow in biochemistry U. Va. Hosp., Charlottesville, 1948-49; pvt. practice medicine specializing in internal medicine; physician Nat. Bur. Standards; 1964-74, asst. prof. pathology U. Va., 1949-50; instr. in internal medicine Vanderbilt U. Sch. Medicine, 1953-54. Served to capt., M.C., USA, 1945-47; with USPHS, 1965-74. Diplomate Am. Bd. Internal Medicine. Mem. A.M.A. Episcopalian. Home: Gaithersburg, Md. Died Sept. 28, 1974; buried Rock Creek Cemetery, Washington, D.C.

DILLINGHAM, W. O., brewery exec.; b. Buffalo, July 22, 1901; s. James B. and Lydia O. (Johnson) D.; student Columbia; m. Loretta B. Bulger, Nov. 22, 1924; children—James B., Jean Smyth, Robert B. With Best Foods, 1925-51; gen. mgr. Newark div. Pabst Brewing Co., 1951-55, exec. v.p., Chgo., 1955-67; exec. v.p. subsidiary Hoffman Beverage Co., 1951-55, pres., 1957-67; dir. Grocery Mfrs. Am., Inc., Topics Pub. Co. Home: Boca Raton, Fla., Died Dec. 20, 1975.

DILWORTH, RICHARDSON, lawyer; b. Pitts., Aug. 29, 1898; s. Joseph R. and Annie H. (Wood) D.; student St. Marks Sch., Southboro, Mass., 1911-17; A.B., Yale, 1921, LL.B. cum laude, 1926; hon. degrees U. Pa., Temple U., Yale, Haverford Coll., LaSalle Coll., Pa. Mil. Colls., Hahnemann Med. Coll., Pa. Med. Coll., Swarthmore Coll.; m. Elizabeth Brockie, May 20, 1922; children—Patricia Anne, Brockie, Warden; m. 2d, Ann K. Hill, Aug. 6, 1935; children—Deborah, Richardson. Admitted to Pa. bar, 1927, practiced in Phila., 1927-74; partner Dilworth, Paxson, Kalish, Levy & Coleman, 1938-55; specialist trial law; dist. atty. Phila., 1952-55. Dir. Lincoln Nat. Bank, Phila. Democratic candidate for gov. Pa., 1950, 62; mayor Phila., 1955-62. Pres., Phila. Bd. Edn., pres. U.S. Conf. Mayors, 1960. Trustee Pa. State U.; bd. dirs. Phila. Contributionship. Served with USMC, A.E.F., 1918, to maj. USMCR, World War II. Decorated Purple Heart, Silver Star. Recipient Phila. award, 1968. Mem. Phila. Bar Assn. (past gov., past chmn. disciplinary com.), Scroll and Key Soc., Order Coif, Delta Kappa Epsilon. Clubs: Philadelphia, Racquet, Rabbit (Phila.); Racquet and Tennis (N.Y.C.). Home: Philadelphia, Pa. Died Jan. 1974; interred Christ Church, Philadelphia, Pa.

DINERMAN, HELEN SCHNEIDER, sociologist; b. N.Y.C., Dec. 25, 1920; d. Maurice and Lillian (Blau) Schneider; A.B., Hunter Coll., 1940; M.A., Columbia, 1948; m. James Dinerman, May 20, 1945; children—Robert, Alice. Analyst for OWI, 1942-44; with Bur. Applied Social Research, Columbia, 1944-47; sci. dept. Am. Jewish Com., 1947-48; chmn. Internat. Research Assos., Inc.; dir. Internat. Research Assos. Compania Anonima (Venequela), 1957. Mem. World (past officer), Am. (past officer) assns. pub. opinion research, Soc. Psychol. Study Social Issues, Am. Sociol. Soc., Phi Beta Kappa. Author: The New Men of Power (with Mills and Schneider), 1949; also articles Public Opinion Quar., chpt. Research for Action, chpt. The Corporation and Its Publics. Home: New York City, N.Y. Died Aug. 14, 1974.

DINES, THOMAS A., banking; born Macomb, Ill., Jan. 31, 1880; s. Charles Wesley and Alta (Hopper) D.; ed. high sch., Springfield, Ill.; m. Frances White Allen, 1907; children—Donna Virginia (Mrs. Andrew W. Cruse), Thomas Marshall (lt. U.S.N.R.). Vice pres. Midwest Refining Co., 1921-24; pres., 1924-30; vice pres. Standard Oil Co. of Indiana, 1930-31; pres. Midwest Oil Co., 1930-36, U.S. Nat. Bank, Denver, 1936, later bd. chmn.; dir. Colo. & So. Ry. Co., Fed. Reserve Bank Kansas City, Denver Union Stockyards Co., Denver Tramway Co., Daniels & Fisher Store Co.; v.p. Utah Oil Refining Co. Clubs: Denver Country, Denver, Mile High. Home: Denver, Colo.†

DINGER, HAROLD EUGENE, radio engr.; b. Barberton, O., May 7, 1905; s. Edwin Clare and Nellie Elizabeth (Thompson) D.; student U. Akron, 1930-31, U. Md., 1947-51, Grad. Sch. U.S. Dept. Agr., 1947-51; m. Edith Elizabeth Cramer, July 27, 1929; children—Marilyn Ruth (Mrs. Kenneth Davis), Barbara Jean (Mrs. Richard Hubbard). Chief instr. McKim Tech. Inst., Akron, O., 1929-38; transmitter engr. Ohio Broadcasting Co., Canton, O., 1938-40; radio engr. Naval Research Lab., Washington, 1940-69, ret., 1969. U.S. del. to Internat. Electrotech. Commn., Lucerne, 1947, Paris, 1950, to Internat. Sci. Radio Union, Sydney, 1952, Boulder, 1957; chmn. U.S. Commn. IV, Internat. Sci. Rad. Union, 1951-53, mem. U.S. nat. com., 1951-57; State Dept. del. Internat. Radio Cons. Com., London, 1953, Warsaw, 1956. Recipient Meritorious Civilian Service Award, USN, 1945. Profl. engr., D.C. Mem. exec. com. Internat. Radio Consultative Com. Fellow A.A.A.S., Inst. Radio Engrs.; mem. Am. Inst. E.E., Sci. Research Soc. Am. Mason. Home: Washington, D.C. Died Feb. 3, 1975.

DINGLE, JOHN HOLMES, physician, educator; b. Cooperstown, N.D., Nov. 24, 1908; s. John Geech and Harriet (Holmes) D.; Ph.C., B.S., U. Wash., 1930, M.S., 1931; Sc.D., Johns Hopkins, 1933; M.D., Harvard (James Jackson Cabot fellow 1936-39, Francis Weld Peabody fellow in medicine 1940-42), 1939; m. Doris V. Brown, Jan. 18, 1946; children—Eva M., David R. Asst., McDermott Found., U. Washington, 1929-31; asst. bacteriologist State Dept. Health, Md., 1933; bacteriologist Upjohn Co., Kalamazoo, 1933-35; house officer in medicine Infants and Children's Hosp., Boston, 1939-40; asst. depts. of medicine, bacteriology and immunology Harvard, 1940-41, instr. bacteriology and immunology, 1940-42, instr. dept. medicine, 1941-42, asso. medicine, 1942-46; asst. physician Boston City Hosp., 1941-46; Elizabeth Severance Prentiss prof. preventive medicine Sch. Medicine, Western Res. U., 1946-74, asso. prof. medicine, 1946-65, prof. medicine, 1965-74, asso. physician Univ. Hosps., Cleve., 1946-68, physician, 1968-74. Cons. to Sec. of War on epidemic diseases, 1941-44; mem. Commn. on Acute Respiratory Diseases, Armed Forces Epidemiol. Bd., 1942-55, dir., 1942-55, asso. mem., 1955-72; mem. Armed Forces Epidemiol. Bd., 1951-67, pres., 1955-57; mem. bd. cons. med. and pub. health Rockefeller Found., 1952-55; mem. Cleve. Health Council, 1946-68. Served from maj. to lt. col. M.C., AUS, 1944-46. Decorated Legion of Merit; recipient Albert Lasker award, 1959; James D. Bruce Meml. award, 1960; Outstanding Civilian Service award Dept. Army, 1967, certificate of appreciation, 1973. Mem. A.A.A.S., Am. Assn. Immunologists (v.p. 1956, pres. 1957), Am. Soc. Microbiology, Assn. Tchrs. Preventive Medicine, Am. Fedn. Clin. Research, Am. Soc. Clin. Investigation, Soc. Exptl. Biology and Medicine, Assn. Am. Physicians, Central Soc. for Clin. Research (v.p. 1958, pres. 1959), Am. Epidemiol. Soc. (pres. 1958), Am. Clin. and Climatol. Assn., Harvey Soc., Nat. Acad. Scis., Phi Beta Kappa, Sigma Xi, Alpha Omega Alpha. Home: Cleveland Heights, O. Died Sept. 15, 1973.

DINSMORE, FRANK F., lawyer; b. Cincinnati, O., Dec. 22, 1869; s. Henry and Rebecca Jane (Watkins) D.; LL.B., Cincinnati Law Sch., 1891; Doctor of Laws from University of Cincinnati, 1948; m. Mary E. Campbell, June 24, 1896 (died July 28, 1940); children—Joseph D., Mrs. Jane D. Comey (dec.), Campbell. Admitted to Ohio bar, 1891, then practiced at Cincinnati; mem. Dinsmore & Sohl, 1912-21, Dinsmore, Shohl, Dinsmore & Todd and predecessors from 1921; served as asst. corp. counsel, City of Cincinnati, 1894-97; asst. solicitor, Hamilton Co., 1897-1900. Mem. Am. Ohio State and Cincinnati bar assns., Am. Law Inst. Republican. Presbyterian. Mason (32°). Clubs: Queen City, Commercial, Cincinnati Country. Home: Cincinnati, O.†

DIPALMA, JOSEPH ALFRED, architect; b. Phila., Feb. 1, 1928; s. Alfred and Vienna (DeMarco) DiP.; B.S. in Architecture, U. Pa., 1952; m. Irene Tonzello, June 7, 1957; children—Diane, Donna, David. Designer-draftsman Cons. Architects and Engrs., Phila., 1952-53, Harry SternFeld, architect, Phila., 1953, Howell Lewis Shay, architect, Phila., 1953-54, Harold E. Wagoner, architect, Phila., 1954-60; partner DiPalma & Grass, architects, Phila., 1960-64; pvt. practice, Cherry Hill, N.J., from 1964. Recipient Speath-Lercaro award for bronze metal, 1961. Mem. A.I.A., Am. Soc. Ch. Architecture. Home: Cherry Hill, N.J. Deceased.

DITTENHAVER, SARAH LOUISE, composer, educator; b. Paulding, O., Dec. 16, 1901; d. Harry Steadman and Dorothea (Rupright) Dittenhaver; Mus.B., Oberlin Conservatory Music, 1924. Tchr. Smead Sch., Toledo, 1924-27; ofcl. accompanist Toledo Choral Soc., 1926-27; dir. music in schs. Wyandotte, Mich., 1927-28; pvt. tchr. piano, Asheville, N.C., 1943-73; numerous compositions pub., 1940-73, songs include Lady of the Amber Wheat, 1944, Passage, 1946, Once More Beloved, 1947, others; piano books Let's Play Duets, 1947, Pick aTune, Books I & II, 1954, 55; My Piano Sketchbook, vols. I, II, 1968; piano solos Where Go the Clouds, 1945, Lyric to the Moon, 1946, 56, Mardi Gras, 1947, Dream Waltz, 1955, Toccata in DMinor, 1953, Starlight Lullaby, 1960, Carolina Cakewalk, Under the Tent of the Sky, Rain Drops are Waltzing, Buckboard Ride, Smoky Mountain Trail, Call of the Waves, Sleepy Wind, Aboard the Santa Fe, At The Craftsman's Fair, Puppet Ballet, Snow Poem, Spring Poem, Autumn in the Smokies, Carousel Gardens, Appalachian Reverie, Circus Day, Spring Breezes, Whirling Dancers, and others; choral music, including Trust In The Lord; athems Bless The Lord, O My Soul, Alleluia, Jesus Child, Light of the Lonely Pilgrim's Heart; Sea Fantasy; piano duets, concert songs. Recipient 1st place award for song N.C. Profl. Composers' Contest, 1944, 45, 59; 1st and 2d place for piano compositions N.C. Fedn. Music Clubs, 1962, 1967, 1968, award, 1968; award for piano composition Nat. League Am. Pen Women, 1963, 1966, 1st place award for anthem, 1969; two awards in 1968; also others. Mem. Nat. League Asheville Music Club, Nat. Guild Piano Tchrs. Democrat. Presbyn. Home: Asheville, N.C. Died Feb. 4, 1973.

DIXON, JOSEPH ANDREW, ex-congressman; b. Cincinnati, June 3, 1879; s. Andrew and Bridgett (Barnable) D.; ed. St. Patrick's Sch. and St. Xavier U., Cincinnati; m. Clara Ann Partridge, of Cincinnati, June 20, 1900; children—Edward Andrew, Joseph Arthur, Blanche Elizabeth (Mrs. Nelson Thomas Corcoran). Mem. 5th Congress (1937-39), 1st Ohio Dist. Hon. mem. exec. bd. Boy Scouts of America. Democrat. Catholic. Elk, Eagles, Moose. Club: Congressional Country (Washington, D.C.). Home: Cincinnati, O.†

DIXON, RUSSELL ALEXANDER, dentist, educator; b. Kansas City, Mo., Feb. 24, 1898; s. William James and Lillie Belle (Tribue) D.; student Hampton Inst., 1918-19, Ferris Inst., 1920-24; D.D.S., Northwestern University, 1929, Rosenwald fellow, 1930-32, M.S.D., 1933, Doctor of Laws (honorary), 1964; Doctor of Science (hon.), Ferris State Coll., 1965; m. Carolyn Isabelle Kealing, on June 11, 1930; children—Russell Alexander, Don Kealing. With Howard U., from 1929, beginning as instr., successively asst. prof., asso. prof.,

1929-34, prof. operative dentistry, from 1934, dean Coll. Dentistry, from 1931. Bd. dirs. Nat. Health Council, from 1964; spl. med. adv. group dept. medicine and surgery VA, from 1964. Mem. bd. regents, Nat. Library Medicine, from 1963. Hon. v.p. odontostomatology 12th Internat. Dental Congress, Rome, Italy, 1957. Gen. chmn. Middle Atlantic Conf. com. on higher edn. fund Congregational Christian Chs. (United Ch. of Christ); bd. dirs. Wash. Area Council on Alcoholism. Mem. bd. overseers of vis. com. Harvard Univ. Served with S.A.T.C., U.S. Army, 1918. Recipient award of merit Northwestern U. Alumni Assn., 1955. Fellow A.A.A.S., Am. College of Dentists; member Maimonides Society (hon.), Nat. Assn. Standard Medical Vocabulary (hon.), Am. Assn. Dental Schs. (sr. dean, chmn. com. on teaching), N.Y. Acad. Sci., Robert T. Freeman Dental Soc., Nat. Dental Assn. (past pres.), Pan Am. Odontological Assn. (past pres.), D.C. Dental Soc., Am. Dental Assn., Odonto-Chirurgical Soc. Phila., Old Dominion Dental Soc., Fedn. Dentaire Internat., Omicron Kappa Upsilon, Sigma Pi Phi, Alpha Phi Alpha. Conglist. (chmn. Missions Council 1954-56). Contbr. articles profl. jours. Home: Washington, D.C., Died Jan. 3, 1976.

DIXON, SHERWOOD, lawyer, ex-lt. gov.; b. Dixon, Ill., June 19, 1896; s. Henry S. and Margaret (Casey) D.; LL.B., U. Notre Dame, 1920; m. Helen Cahill, July 1933; children—Henry, Mary, William, Louise, James, Patrick, David. Admitted to Ill. bar, 1919; practiced law, Dixon, 1920-73, Chgo., 1950-73. Mem. Dixon, Dixon & Wynne. Lt. gov. Ill., 1948-52. Served as sgt., A.E.F., U.S. Army, 1917-19; col. Inf., 1941-46; comdg. officer, 129th Inf. Regt., Ill. N.G. Mem. Am. and Ill. bar assns., Am. Legion, Vets. Fgn. Wars, K.C., Elk. Home: Dixon, Ill. Died May 17, 1973.

DOAN, LELAND IRA, chem. co. exec.; b. North Bend, Neb., Nov. 9, 1894; s. Ira and Hester (Spencer) D.; student U. Mich., 1913-16; D.E. (hon.), Case Inst. Tech., 1952; LL.D., Kalamazoo Coll., 1955, Central Mich. Coll., 1956, Earlham Coll., 1957, Alma Coll., 1963, Northwood Inst., 1967; D.Sc. in Bus. Adminstrn., Cleary Coll., 1957; D.H.L., Findlay Coll., 1962; m. Ruth Alden Dow, Apr. 7, 1917 (dec.); children—Leland Alden, Dorothy (Doan) Arbury, Herbert Dow; m. 2d, Mildred Mellus, 1950. With Dow Chem. Co., 1917, beginning in sales dept., successively asst. sales mgr. and gen. sales mgr., v.p. and sec., 1938-49, pres., 1949-62, chmn. exec. com., 1962-70, dir., 1935-72; past dir. Nat. Bank Detroit, Mich. Bell Telephone Co. Mem. Nat. Indsl. Conf. Bd. Recipient Chem. Industry medal Am. sect. Soc. Chem. Industry, 1964. Mem. Mfg. Chemists Assn., Sigma Chi. Presbyn. Mason (33 deg.). Clubs: Detroit Athletic; Chemists (N.Y.C.); Bohemian (San Francisco); Surf (Miami, Fla.); Midland. Home: Midland, Mich. Died Apr. 4, 1974; interred Midland, Mich.

DOBZHANSKY, THEODOSIUS, educator; b. Nemirov, Russia, Jan. 25, 1900; s. Gregory and Sophie (Voinarsky) D.; grad. U. Kiev, 1921; D.Sc. (hon.), U. Sao Paulo, Brazil, 1943, Coll. Wooster (O.), 1945, U. Munster (Germany), U. Montreal (Can.), 1958, U. Chgo., 1959, U. Sidney, Australia, 1960, Oxford (Eng.) U., 1964, Louvain U., 1965, Columbia, 1964, Kalamazoo Coll., 1965, Clarkson Coll. Tech., 1965, U. Mich., 1966, U. Syrcause, 1967, U. Cal. at Berkeley, 1968, U. Padua (Italy), 1968, Northwestern U., 1968; D.H.L. (hon.), U. Cal., 1968, Wittenberg U., 1970, St. Mary's Coll., 1971; m. Natalie Sivertzev, Aug. 8, 1924; 1 dau., Sophie. Came to U.S., 1927, naturalized, 1937. Asst. prof. zoology Polytechnique Inst., Kiev, 1921-24; lectr. genetics U. Leningrad, 1924-27; fellow int. edn. bd., 1928-29; asst. prof. genetics Cal. Inst. Tech., 1930-36; prof., 1936-40; prof. zoology Columbia, 1940, later DaCosta prof. zoology; prof. Rockefeller Inst., N.Y.C., 1962-71; adj. prof. U. Cal. at Davis, 1971-75; exchange prof. U. Sao Paulo, Brazil, 1943, 48-49. Recipient G. Elliott prize and medal Nat. Acad. Sci., Kimber prize, 1958; Guggneheim fellow, 1959; recipient Nat. Medal of Science, 1964; Addison Emery Verrill medal, 1966; Distinguished Achievement in Sci. award Am. Mus. Natural History, 1969. Mem. Nat. Royal Danish, Royal Swedish, Brazilian acads. scis., Academia dei Lincei, Italy, Royal Soc., London, Eng., Am. Philos. Soc. (past pres.), Am. Soc. Zoologists, Am. Soc. Genetics, Am. Soc. Naturalists, Am. Soc. for Study Evolution. Author: Genetics and Origin of Species, 1937, 3d edit., 1951; Evolution, Genetics and Man, 1955; Mankind Evolving, 1962; Biology of Ultimate Concern, 1967; Genetics of the Evolutionary Process, 1970. Home: Davis, Cal., Died Dec. 19, 1975.

DOCKERAY, FLOYD CARLTON, prof. psychology; b. Kent Co., Mich., May 15, 1880; s. Albert A. and Annie Isabelle (Hutchings) D.; Grand Rapids, Mich., public schools; A.B., U. of Mich., 1907, A.M., 1909, Ph.D., 1915; m. Katharine C. Eddy, of Grand Rapids, Mich., 1906; children—James Carlton, Robert MacIntyre. Instr. psychology, U. of Kan., 1910-13; asst. prof., 1913-16, asso. prof., 1916-20; prof. psychology, Ohio Wesleyan U., 1920-29; prof. psychology, Ohio State U. from 1929. Capt. World War, 1918-19; reserve mil. aviator; psychologist, Med. Research Lab. France. Fellow A.A.A.S., Ohio Acad. Science; mem. Am. Psychol. Assn., Midwestern Psychol. Assn., Southern Soc. Philosophy and Psychology, Soc. for Research in Child Development, Phi Beta Kappa (U. of Mich.), Sigma Xi (U. of Kans.). Address: Columbus, O.†

DODD, CHARLES HAROLD, Brit. theologian; b. Wrexham, Denbighs, Apr. 7, 1884; s. Charles and Sarah (Parsonage) D.; student Univ. Coll., Oxford, 1902-06, Magdalen Coll., Oxford, 1907-11, Mansfield Coll., Oxford, 1908-12, U. Berlin, 1907; M.A., Oxford, 1911, also D.D., D.Litt.; M.A., Cambridge, 1936, also D.D., M.A., Manchester U., 1930, also D.D.; D.D., U. London, Glasgow U., Aberdeen U., U. Wales; S.T.D., Harvard; d. Theol., U. Oslo; Docteur h.c., U. Strasbourg, m. Phyllis Mary Terry Stockings, 1925; children—Rachel Mary, Mark Wilson. Ordained to ministry Congl. Ch., 1912; minister Independent or Congl. Ch., Warwick, 1912-15, 18-19; Yates lectr. in New Testament Greek and exegesis Mansfield Coll., 1915-30; Univ. lectr. New Testament studies Oxford, 1927-30; Grinfield lectr. on Septuagint, Oxford, 1927-31; Rylands prof. bibl. criticism and exegesis Manchester, 1930-35; Speakers lectr. bibl. studies U. Oxford, 1933-37; Shaffer lectr. Yale, 1935; Ingersoll lectr. Harvard, 1935, 50; Norris-Hulse prof. div. Cambridge, 1935-49; fellow Jesus Coll., Cambridge, 1936-49; Hewett lectr. Episcopal Theol. Sem., Cambridge, Mass., 1938; Olaus Petrl lectr. U. Uppsala, 1949; Bampton lectr. Columbia, 1950; Stone lectr. Princeton Theol. Sem., 1950; vis. prof. bibl. theology Union Theol. Sem., N.Y.C., 1950; gen. dir. New Translation of Bible (N.E.B.), 1950-65, joint dir., 1966-70; editor Texts and Studies, 1953-62; Sarum lectr. Oxford, 1954-55. Hon. Freeman, Wrexham, 1964. Hon. fellow Jesus Coll., Cambridge, 1949-73, Univ. Coll., Oxford, 1961-73. Author: The Meaning of Paul for To-day, 1920; The Gospel in the New Testament, 1926; The Authority of the Bible, 1928; Ephesians, Colossians and Philemon, 1929; The Bible and Its Background, 1931; The Epistle to the Romans, 1932; There and Back Again, 1932; The Bible and Greeks, 1935; Parables of the Kingdom, 1935; The Apostolic Preaching and its Developments, 1936; The Present Task in New Testament Studies, 1936; History and the Gospel, 1937; The Johannine Epistles, 1946; The Bible To-day, 1946; Benefits of His Passion, 1947; About the Gospels, 1950; The Coming of Christ, 1951; Gospel and Law, 1951; Christianity and the Reconcillation of the Nations, 1952; According to the Scriptures, 1952; The Interpretation of the Fourth Gospel, 1953; New Testament Studies, 1953; Historical Tradition in the Fourth Gospel, 1963; More New Testament Studies, 1968; The Founder of Christianity, 1970. Address: Oxford, England. Died Sept. 1973.

DODD, VERNE ADAMS, surgeon; b. Waterville, O., Feb. 21, 1881; s. Elijah and Frances Jane (Downing) D.; student Ohio Wesleyan U., 1 yr., M.D., Ohio Med. U., 1903; Doctor of Laws (hon.), Ohio State U., 1948; m. Nellie Jacobs, Oct. 16, 1906; children—Verne Adams, Jane Eleanor. Began practice at Columbus, O., 1903; chief of staff University Hosp., 1922-51, ret.; prof. surgery Ohio State U., 1921-51, emeritus professor of surgery from 1951. Commd. lt. M.C., U.S. Army Reserve, Mar. 5, 1912; called to active duty, Apr. 19, 1917; capt., May 10, 1917; resigned, Aug. 21, 1917; lt. comdr. U.S. Navy Reserve, Aug. 22, 1917; active duty, Oct. 15, 1917-Apr. 12, 1919; commander July 1919; capt. M.C., U.S.N.R.F., July 1, 1938. Pres. Columbus Academy of Medicine, 1934. Fellow Am. Coll. Surgeons; mem. A.M.A., Ohio State and Franklin Co. med. socs., Phi Rho Sigma, Alpha Omega Alpha. Mason. Club: Faculty. Home: Lantana, Fla.†

DODGE, KERN, engineer; b. Chicago, July 20, 1880; s. James M. and Josephine (Kern) D.; grad. Germantown Acad., 1899, Drexel Inst. Tech., Phila., 1901; m. Helen Peterson Greene, Nov. 16, 1904 (dec.); children—Dorothy (dec.), Donald, Jane (Mrs. J.A. Barnett, Jr., dec.), Robert Mapes; m. 2d Helen McCracken (Fessenden). June 28, 1952. Partner, Dodge & Day, 1901-12; cons. engr. in pvt. practice from 1912; dir. Link Belt Co. Dir. pub. safety, Phila., 1932-33. Trustee Germantown Acad. Member Am. Soc. M.E., Am. Inst. E.E., Franklin Inst. Clubs: Keystone Automobile (dir.), Engineers, Union League (Phila.); Aero of Pa. Home: Philadelphia, Pa.†

DOERFLINGER, JON ARNO, sociologist; b. Milw., 1924; s. Arno and Elsa (Solomon) D.; B.A., Ia. State Coll., 1949; M.A., U. Wis., 1957, Ph.D., 1962. Teaching asst. U. Wis., 1951-53, research asst., 1956-57, project asst., 1959, project asso., 1960-61; asso. Ia. State U., 1961, asst. prof. sociology, 1962-67, asso. prof., 1967-68; prof., chmn. dept. sociology U. S.D., Vermillion, 1968-71. Fellow, preceptor Midwest Council for Social Research on Aging, 1964-73; project leader Ia. AHEES Project Changing Communities, 1965-73; project leader Ia. AHEES Project Ia. Coop. Study Post High Sch. Edn. Served with AUS, 1943-46; ETO. Decorated Purple Heart, Combat Inf. badge. Mem. Population Assn. Am., Am., Midwest sociol. assns., Alpha Kappa Delta, Phi Kappa Phi. Home: Kansas City, Mo. Died 1973.

DOERSCHUK, ANNA BEATRICE, ednl. adminstr.; b. Shanesville, O., Aug. 1879; d. John and Mary Catherine (Zahner) Doerschuk; A.B., Oberlin (O.) Coll., 1906; student Columbia, 1916-18. Teacher Oxford (O.) Coll., 1907-11; asst. dean women, Oberlin (O.) Coll., 1911-16, asst. dir. Bur. Vocational Information, 1918-27; director edn. Sarah Lawrence College, Bronxville, N.Y., 1928-46. Trustee Oberlin Coll.; sponsor Vocational Advisory Service. Received Adelia A. Field Johnston Fellowship, Oberlin Coll., 1916. Mem. Am. Edn. Fellowship, Am. Assn. Univ. Women, Phi Beta Kappa. Club: Town Hall (N.Y.). Editor: Opportunities for Wartime Training for Women in New York City, 1918; Women in Law, 1920; Women in Chemistry, 1922; Training for the Professional and Allied Occupations, 1924. Home: Bronxville, N.Y. Died Apr. 18, 1974.

DOHERTY, EDWARD J., clergyman, editor, author; b. Chgo., Oct. 30, 1890; s. James E. and Ellen (Rogers) D.; ed. pub. and parochial schs., Chgo., St. Philip's Acad., Granville, Wis.; m. Marie Ryan, Dec. 15, 1914 (dec. Oct. 1918); 1 son, Edward J.; m. 2d, Mildred Frisby, July 16, 1919 (dec. Mar. 1939); 1 son, Jack Jim; m. 3d, Baroness Catherine de Hueck, June 25, 1943. Asso. with Chgo. newspapers, 1906-24 (with interludes in Tampico, Mex., and Hollywood, Cal.); mem. staff N.Y. Daily News, formerly city editor N.Y. Am.; staff writer Liberty Mag.; war corr.; editorial writer Chgo. Sun, 1941-46; ordained priest Byzantine Rite Catholic Ch., 1969; editor Restoration, publ. of Madonna House, Combermere, Ont., Can. Author: Broadway Murders; Gall and Honey (autobiography), 1941; Splender of Sorrow, 1946; Tumbleweed, 1947; Martin, 1948; Captain Marooner (with Louis B. Davidson), 1952; True Devotion to Mary, a Nun with A Gun, 1959; I Cover God, 1962; King of Sinners, 1963; others. Home: Combermere, Ont., Canada. Died May 4, 1975.

DOLAN, MARGARET BAGGETT (MRS. CHARLES E. DOLAN), nursing educator; b. Lillington, N.C., Mar. 17, 1914; d. John Robert and Allene (Keeter) Baggett; A.A., Anderson Coll., 1932; diploma in nursing Georgetown U., 1935; B.S., U. N.C., 1944; M.A., Columbia, 1953; LL.D., Duke, 1970; D.Sc., U. Ill., 1973; m. Charles E. Dolan, June 3, 1941. Staff nurse Instructive Vis. Nurse Soc., Washington, 1935-36; epidemiol. nurse Tb studies USPHS, 1936-41; staff nurse supr. City Health Dept., Greensboro, N.C., 1941-43; Tb nursing cons. USPHS, 1945-46; supr., spl. cons. Baltimore County Health Dept., Towson, Md., 1947-50; asso. prof. U. N.C. Sch. Pub. Health, 1950-59, prof., head dept. health nursing, 1959-73, prof. emeritus, 1973. Mem. N.C. Med. Care Commn.; mem. Pres.'s Adv. Com. Health Resources, 1962-68; com. social ins. and taxes Pres.'s Commn. Status Women, 1962-64; mem. Nat. Adv. Council for Nurse Tng., 1964-68; mem. Nat. Commn. to Study Nursing Edn.; pres. Nat. Health Council, 1969-70; mem. health ins. benefits adv. council Social Security Adminstrn., 1968-72. Bd. dirs. Nat. Assembly Soc. Policy and Devel., 1968-72 Nat., N.C. Tb assns. Past pres. Am. Jour. Nursing Co. Fellow Am. Pub. Health Assn. (mem. governing council, mem. exec. bd. 1968-72, pres. 1972-73); mem. Am. (pres. 1962-64, dir. 1964-68), N.C. (bd. dirs.) nurses assns., Nat. League Nursing, Am. Assn. U. Profs., Am. Nat. Council Health Edn. of Pub. (dir.), League Women Voters, Phi Theta Kappa, Kappa Delta Pi, Delta Omega, Sigma Theta Tau (nat. treas. 1968). Democrat. Episcopalian. Home: Chapel Hill, N.C. Died Feb. 27, 1974; interred Lillington, N.C.

DOLLARD, STEWART EDWARD, coll. ofcl.; b. Chgo., Sept. 14, 1905; s. Joseph A. and Josephine (Kelley) D.; student St. Mary of the Lake Sem., Mundelein, Ill., 1924-25; A.B., St. Louis U. 1928, A.M., 1930, Ph.D., 1934; S.T.L., St. Mary's Coll., St. Marys, Kan., 1937. Entered Soc. of Jesus, 1925. Instr. in philosophy, West Baden Coll., West Baden Springs, Ind., 1937-42, asso. prof., 1942-46, asso. dean, 1941-46; dean Grad. Sch., Loyola U., Chgo., 1946-65; dir. grad. students, 1965-75. Mem. Jesuit Ednl. Assn., Nat. Cath. Ednl. Assn., Assn. Am. Colls., Am. Cath. Philos. Assn. Home: Chicago, Ill., Died Dec. 9, 1975.

DOLLIVER, GEORGE BENTON, editor; b. Battle Creek, Mich., Mar. 13, 1880; s. John Benjamin and Amy (McCamly) D.; ed. Sorbonne, Paris; m. Mabelle A. White, Oct. 22, 1902; children—Lieut. George Benton (killed in action, Saipan, 1944), John Clark. Editor of Battle Creek Enquirer-News; copublisher Traverse City Record-Eagle, Manistee News-Advocate, Big Rapids (Mich.) Pioneer, Cheboygan, (Mich.) Tribune. Past pres., Chamber of Commerce, Rotary and Community clubs, Battle Creek; pres. Mich. Masonic Home Bd. Mem. Nat. Editorial Assn. (pres., 1930-31). Republican. Conglist. Mason (K.T., Shriner; past grand Master, Mich.; mem. Supreme Council, 33°); Royal Order of Scotland; Elks. Clubs: Athelstan, Battle Creek Country. Home: Battle Creek, Mich.†

DOMERATZKY, LOUIS, federal civil service; b. Raigrod, Russian Poland, Sept. 10, 1881; s. Leo and Dalia D.; student Columbia, 1902, George Washington U., 1905; m. Gladys B. Partridge, Mar. 4, 1922; 1 son, Louis Martin. Began as translator, 1905; asst. chief div. fgn. tariffs, U.S. Dept. of Commerce, 1911-16, chief, 1916-21; asst. dir. Bur. Fgn. and Domestic Commerce, U.S. Dept. of Commerce, 1921-26, chief div. of regional information, 1926-41; chief of European Unit, Div. of Internat. Economy, 1941-47; retired; expert Am. delegation to the World Econ. Conf., Geneva, 1927; asst. to U.S. delegation to the Experts Preparatory Com. for the Internat. Monetary and Econ. Conf., Geneva, 1932; mem. Joint Prep. Com. on Philippine Affairs,

1937. Author: International Cartel Movement, 1928; American Branch Factories Abroad, 1931; Recent Trends in British Industrial Reorganization, 1941; Price Control in Germany—Policy and Technique, 1941. Contributor articles on world economics to jours. Home: McLean, Va.†

DOMONOSKE, ARTHUR B(OQUER), prof. mech. engring.; b. Germantown (now Artois), Calif., Jan. 1, 1884; s. Henry and Clara Jane (Price) D.; B.S., U. of Calif., 1907, M.S., 1909; m. Gladys Eloise Boydstun, June 5, 1912; children—Henry Arthur, Merton Elzwick. Instr. mech. Engr., U. of Calif., 1907-10, 1911-13; with Pacific Telephone & Telegraph Co., 1910; instr. machine design, U. of Ill., 1913-15; engring. draftsman Holt Mfg. Co., Stockton, Calif., 1915-16; with U.S. Shipping Bd. and U. of Calif., 1918-21; asst. prof. mech. engring., U. of Calif., 1919-22; chief engr. Doble Steam Motors, San Francisco, Calif., 1922-23; asso. prof. exptl. engring. and dir. of shops, U. of Calif., 1923-26; prof. mech. engring. and head mech. engring. dept., Stanford U., 1926-45, on leave, 1940, and 1942-44; engineer Westinghouse Electric & Mfg. Co., Deere & Co., and others, summers; cons. engr. Commd. lt. col. Ordnance Reserve and col. U.S. Army, on active duty in the office of Chief of Ordnance, Washington, 1940-41; Office Chief of Ordnance, Washington, and Tank Automotive Center, Detroit, Mar. 1942-Jan. 1944. Certificate of Commendation, Ordnance Dept. 1946. Reg. mech. engr. in Calif. Mem. American Soc. Mech. Engrs., Soc. Automotive Engrs., Am. Soc. for Engineering Education, A.A.A.S., Army Ordnance Assn., Scabbard and Blade, Sigma Xi, Tau Beta Pi. Republican. Author: Aircraft Engines (with V. C. Finch), 1936. Address: Davis, Cal., Died Jan. 5, 1975.

DONAGHY, WILLIAM ANDREW, clergyman; b. New Bedford, Mass., Nov. 13, 1909; s. James J. and Rose (King) D.; student Holy Cross Coll., 1927-29, St. Stanislaus Novitiate, Lenox, Mass., St. Louis U., 1935-36; M.A., Weston (Mass.) coll., 1935; L.H.D., Georgetown U., 1956. Entered Soc. of Jesus, 1929, ordained priest Roman Cath. Ch., 1941; instr. poetry Holy Cross Coll., 1937-38; asso. editor America, 1942; ascetical studies Our Lady of Martys Tertianship, Auriesville, N.Y., 1943; retreat master Campion Hall, North Andover, Mass., 1944-46; spiritual dir. Theologians Weston Coll., 1946-48; superior Campion Hall, 1948-54; pres. Holy Cross Coll., 1954-60; later engaged in spiritual retreat work; became prof. theology Boston Coll., Chestnut Hill, Mass., 1961. Mem. Cath. Poetry Soc. Am. (v.p. 1956). Author: Hear Ye Him, 1948; That We May Have Hope, 1954. Contbr. America, Thought, Rev. for Religious. Home: Worcester, Mass. Died Jan. 24, 1975.

DONALDSON, ALBERT EELEY, lawyer; b. Baltimore, Dec. 17, 1876; s. Thomas William and Ellen Howard (Thompson) D.; LL.B., U. Md., 1899; m. Katharine Gray Blackshere, Feb. 8, 1911. Admitted to Md. bar, 1899, since practiced in Baltimore; mem. Crain & Hershey, 1905-16, Hershey, Donaldson, Williams & Stanley, and predecessors, from 1916. Chmn. Legal Adv. Bd. No. 13, Baltimore, World War I. Mem. Am., Md. State, Baltimore City (1st v.p. 1942-43) bar associations. Clubs: Baltimore Country, The Merchants (Baltimore). Home: Baltimore, Md.†

DONALDSON, ALLYN CAPRON, govt. ofcl.; b. Richmond, Va., Sept. 16, 1898; s. Edward Justus and Mary Ella (Nixon) D.; LL.B., N.Y. Law Sch., 1922; m. Henrietta Mackenzie, Feb. 16, 1924; children—Virginia Henrietta (M.D.), Allyn Capron. With J. P. Morgan & Co., N.Y.C., 1915-27; admitted to N.Y. bar, 1925; partner Baar, Bennett & Donaldson, N.Y.C., 1926-28; office mgr., partner, cons., member firms N.Y. Stock Exchange, 1927-42; successively sr. div. asst., econ. analyst, liaison officer, spl. asst., fgn. affairs officer, dir. office spl. consular services Dept. State, 1942-68. Mem. Nat. Bd. Sponsors Inst. Am. Strategy, 1972. Pres. Civil Service Commn., Glen Cove, N.Y., 1938-41. Recipient Meritorious Service award Sec. State, 1968. Mem. Am. Legion (past post comdr., past department vice commander; mem. nat. exec. com.). American, Federal, D.C. bar assns., Inter-American Bar Assn. American Fgn. Service Association, Diplomatic and Consular Officers Ret., Am. Soc. Internat. Law, Nat. Lawyers Club, Delta Theta Phi, Tau Kappa Epsilon. Mason 33°, K.T. Shriner). Clubs: Post Mortem, Nat. Lawyers. Home: Arlington, Va. Died Dec. 11, 1974; interred Rock Creek Cemetery, Washington.

DONALDSON, CHARLES M., clergyman, educator; b. High Forest, Minn., Aug. 26, 1879; s. George W. and Mary E. (Hoag) D.; Ph.B., Hamline U., 1905; grad. Boston U. Sch. of Theology, 1910; m. Mabel Joyce King, Caledonia, Minn., June 20, 1909. Ordained M.E. ministry, 1910; pastor Ft. Benton, Mont., 1910-13, Lewistown, 1913-18, Helena, 1918-19; pres. Mont. Wesleyan Coll., from 1920. Mem. council Am. Red Cross, for Fergus Co., Mont., World War. Mason. Home: Helena, Mont.†

DONALDSON, JAMES RIDER, orthopedic surgeon; b. Foochow, China, Feb. 4, 1920; s. Frederic Frow Goodhue and Elaine (Strang) D.; M.D., Western Res. U., 1947; m. Mary Ruth Reeder, Mar. 18, 1944; children—Sue (Mrs. William Hawkins Wood), Stephen R., Barbara, Rachel (Mrs. Andrew Yankama), James A., Deborah. Intern, St. Luke's Hosp., Cleve., 1947-48, resident in orthopedic surgery, 1948-51; practice medicine specializing in orthopedic surgery, 1957-72; head dept. orthopedic surgery Wanless Hosp., Miraj, India; cons. orthopedic surgery Richardson Leprosy Hosp., Miraj, Sir William Wanless Tb San., Miraj. Diplomate Am. Bd. Orthopedic Surgery. Fellow Am. Acad. Orthopedic Surgery, A.C.S.; mem. Indian Med. Assn., Assn. Surgeons India (orthopedic sect.). Presbyn. Contbr. articles to profl. jours. Home: Miraj, India., Died Oct. 11, 1972; buried Miraj, India.

DONALDSON, WALTER FOSTER, physician; b. Bridgeville, Pa., Sept. 13, 1873; s. John Boyce and Elizabeth (Foster) D.; student Jefferson Acad., 1889-91; M.D., Northwestern U., 1898; m. Nan Swearingen, June 19, 1913; children—Walter Foster, Sarah (Mrs. Robert R. Stoll), Joseph Van Swearingen, John Boyce, Nancy E. (Mrs. Clarke), William P. Asst. on staff Western Pa. Hosp., 1902-08; mem. staff South Side Hosp., 1906-12; asst. on staff Presbyn. Hosp., from 1912, Woman's Hosp., Pittsburgh, from 1939; medical dir. Standard Life Insurance Co. of America from 1919, president from 1946. Dir. Allegheny County Medical Soc. from 1921 (pres. 1923); sec. Med. Soc. State of Pa. from 1918, treasurer from 1944; sec. Pennsylvania Com. on Med. Preparedness for Nat. Defense World War II. chmn. health com. Pittsburgh C. of C. Fellow A.M.A. (mem. judicial council from 1931, mem. council on med. edn. and hosps, 1924-31; mem. Nat. Health Program, Federal Conf. Com., 1938-40; chmn. com. on war participation, 1942-45), Pittsburgh Academy of Medicine, Am. Coll. of Physicians; mem. Nu Sigma Nu. Republican. Presbyterian. Mason. Editor Pittsburgh Med. Bulletin, 1928-47, Pa. Med. Jour from 1940. Home: Pittsburgh, Pa.†

DONALSON, ERLE MELDRIM, lawyer; b. Bainbridge, Ga., June 11, 1878; s. John Earnest and Amelia Pauline (Pohlman) D.; ed. Ga. Mil. Acad., Edgewood; Gordon Inst., Barnesville, Ga.; Georgetown U., Washington, D.C.; LL.B., U. of Ga., 1902; post-grad. work, U. of Chicago; m. Linda Gordon, niece of Gen. John B. Gordon, of Atlanta, Ga., Nov. 21, 1906. Gen. counsel Ga., Fla. & Ala. R.R. Co. Mem. Ga. Ho. of Rep., 1904-07; U.S. atty. for Southern Dist. of Ga., 1914-19; resigned. Democrat. Presbyn. Mem. Kappa Alpha. Address: Miami, Fla.†

DONATI, PINE, musician; b. Verona, Italy, May 9, 1907; s. Felice and Dorina (Maceri) D.; student Liberal Arts Sch., Verona, Italy, Verdi Conservatory of Milan; protege Riccardo Zandonai; m. Maria Canigila, Sept. 3, 1939; 1 son, Paolo. Gen. mgr. Teatro Arena, Verona, Italy; gen. mgr. Teatro Communale, Bologna; artistic dir. Teatro San Carlos, Lisbon, Portugal; musical asst. to gen. mgr. Lyric Opera, Chgo., 1958, artistic co-dir., 1958-75; conducted operas, Italy, France, Spain, Portugal, S.A., Egypt; composer symphonic music, chamber music; composer opera in two acts Corradino lo Svevo, 1932, three acts Lancilotto del Lago, 1939. Served with Italian Army, 1927. Recipient Commendatore dell'Italia, King Umberto of Italy, 1937; Cavaliere della Cultura, Lisbon, 1946. Contbr. articles Italian newspapers. Address: Rome, Italy. Died Feb. 24, 1975.

DONEHUE, FRANCIS MCGARVEY, surgeon; b. Clemons, N.Y., Aug. 17, 1895; s. Michael Cornelius and Maria Louise (Beckett) D.; grad. Dartmouth, 1917; M.D., Columbia, 1919. Intern, Lenox Hill Hosp., N.Y.C., 1919-21, cons., 1921-73; dir. surgery Lenox Hill Hosp., 1947-60. clin. prof. surgery N.Y.U. Served to capt., M.C., USNR, 1941-46. Diplomate Am. Bd. Surgery (founder's group). Fellow A.C.S.; N.Y. Acad Medicine; mem. N.Y. Surg. Soc. Home: Albany, N.Y. Died Aug. 27, 1973; buried St. Patrick's Cemetery, West Granville, N.Y.

DONNELLEY, ELLIOTT, pub. exec.; b. Chgo., Feb. 28, 1903; s. Thomas E. and Laura (Gaylord) D.; Class of 1928, Dartmouth Coll.; m. Ann Steinwedell, Sept. 12, 1928; children—Thomas E., James R., Robert G., David E. Vice chmn. R. R. Donnelley & Sons Co., Chgo., exec. v.p., 1953-55, dir. R. H. Donnelley Corp. 1955-75, Modern Controls Corp. Vice pres. Chgo. Area Project. Trustee Union League Boys Club, Lake Forest U., King Home; chmn. bd. Chgo. Youth enters. Republican. Clubs: Union League, Chicago, Commercial, Economic, Caxton. Wayfarers' Camp Fire (Chgo.); Onwentsia, Shoreacres, Old Elm (Lake Forest); Coleman Lake (Goodman, Wis.); Dartmouth, New York Athletic (N.Y.C.). Home: Lake Forest, Ill., Died Dec. 29, 1975.

DONNELLY, HORACE JAMES, lawyer; b. Washington, Oct. 24, 1879; s. John J. and Juliette S. (Newman) D.; LL.B., Georgetown U., 1909, LL.M., 1910; m. Mary Alice Whitzell, 1901; 1 son, Horace James. Mgr. Curtis Pub. Co., Washington, 1901; mgr. W. F. Burns Co., 1902; admitted D.C. bar, 1909; atty. U.S. Post Office Dept., 1910-19, asst. solicitor, 1919-25, solicitor 1925-33, spl. counsel 1934; partner Nash & Donnelly, from 1934. Club: University. Author, compiler official legal opinions relating to Post Office Dept. while solicitor. Home: Washington, D.C.†

DONOVAN, RICHARD JOSEPH, lawyer, municipal ct. judge; b. New Rochelle, N.Y., Feb. 24, 1926; s. Richard J. and Ethel (Sherwood) D.; grad. Augusta Mil. Acad., 1943; student San Diego State Coll., 1954-55; LL.B., U. San Diego, 1959; m. Peggy Pearse, Dec. 17, 1950; children—Elizabeth Ann, Roxanne. With police dept. National City, Cal., 1950-56; mem. staff Marshall's Office, South Bay (Cal.) Jud. Dist., 1956-57; clk. Municipal Ct., South Bay, 1957-60; admitted to Cal. bar, 1960; since practiced in National City; mem. Cal. Assembly, 1963-66, mem. joint legislative com., gen. adv. com.; judge Municipal Ct., San Diego Jud. Dist., 1966-71. Mem. Trafficc Safety Council, Am. Cancer Soc., United Team, Chula Vista P.T.A. Mem. San Diego bd. Vols. Am. Served with USNR, 1943-47; MTO. Mem. National City C. of C., S.A.R., V.F.W., Am. Legion. Conglist. K.P., Elk, Kiwanian. Home: Chula Vista, Cal. Died Dec. 21, 1971.

DONOVAN, THOMAS LEROY, civil engr.; b. New Cumberland, W.Va., July 19, 1898; s. Ira Delos and Ida Marie (Cassidy) D.; student Washington and Lee U., 1920-22, Colo. Sch. Mines, 1922-23. Jr. engr. W.Va. Rd. Commn., 1924-27, Pa. Hwy. Dept., 1927-28; transitman Montour R.R. Co., 1928; field engr. Venezuelan Petroleum Co., 1928-34, supervising engr., 1935-39; field engr. Venezuela Gulf Oil Co., 1934-35; chief engr. Tex. Petroleum Co., 1939-47; chief engr. Sinclair Petroleum Co., Ethiopia, 1947-52, asst. to pres. Sinclair Somal Corp., 1952-57; asst. to pres. Sinclair Petroleum Co., Algiers, Algeria, 1957-58, spl. duty Sinclair Venezuelan Oil Co., 1958-62; project engr. W.Va. Dept. Hwys., from 1964. Registered profl. engr., W.Va. Life mem. Am. Soc. C.E.; Am. Congress Surveying and Mapping; mem. Kappa Sigma. Democrat. Presbyn. Mason (32°, Shri ner). Home: New Cumberland W.Va. Died Dec. 6, 1975; buried New Cumberland Cemetery.

DOOLEY, VIRGINIA PERRIN CORTTIS, librarian; b. Dudley, Mass.; d. Elmer Japheth and Edith (Perrin) Corttis; A.B., Wheaton Coll., 1931; B.S., Simmons Coll., 1948; m. C. Vincent Dooley, Aug. 13, 1943 (div. Sept. 1944); 1 son, Jay C. Tchr. Wellfleet (Mass.) High Sch., 1932-33; librarian Bartlett High Sch., Webster, Mass., 1933-43, Concord (N.H.) Sr. High Sch., 1944-46, Lyman Hall High Sch., Wallingford, Conn., from 1946. Pub. library cons. Bur. Library Services, Conn. Dept. Edn., Hartford, summers 1960-64. Participant New Eng. Sch. Library Leadership Conf. Com., 1966-70. Mem. A.L.A., New Eng. (1st v.p. 1965-67, pres. 1967-68), Conn. (1st v.p. 1952-54, pres. 1954-56) sch. library assns., N.E.A., Conn., Wallingford edn. assns., Am. Assn. U. Women, Delta Kappa Gamma. Home: Wallingford, Conn. Deceased.

DORETY, FREDERIC GERBER, lawyer; b. Boston, Mass., July 20, 1878; s. Joseph Henry and Rose Elizabeth (Gerber) D.; B.L., U. of Calif., 1900; LL.B., Harvard, 1903; m. Mary Frances French, Sept. 6, 1904 (died Mar. 21, 1929); children—Lawrence Gerber, Ruth Frances (dec.); m. 2d, Marie Catherine Spellman, Mar. 7, 1931; 1 dau., Margaret Marie. Admitted to Calif. bar, 1903; began practice in San Francisco, 1903; instr. in law. U. of Calif., 1903-05; practiced Seattle, Wash., 1905-08; asst. U.S. atty., Seattle, 1907-08; atty. G.N. Ry. for Ore. and Western Wash., 1908-18; asst. gen. counsel G.N. Ry., St. Paul, Minn., 1918-22, gen. solicitor, 1922-26, v.p. and general counsel, 1926-45. Mem. Am. Bar Assn., and general counsel, 1926-45. Mem. Am. Bar Assn., Kappa Sigma. Order of Golden Bear (U. of Calif.). Republican. Home: Lake North, Fla.†

DORMER, CHARLES JOSEPH, civil engr.; b. N.Y.C., July 10, 1924; s. Charles J. and Aline (Eveno) D.; B.C.E., Manhattan Coll., 1944; m. Eleanor A. Jurcyk, July 6, 1946; children—Robert W., Kenneth C. Civil engr. City Engr's. Office, San Diego, 1947-48, Western Elec. Co., N.Y.C., 1948-49, Div. Hwys., Babylon, N.Y., 1949-50, Voorhees, Walker, Foley & Smith, N.Y.C., 1950-51, Ayers-Hagan-Booth, Providence, 1953-56, 59-60, C.A. Maguire & Assos., Providence, 1956-59; partner Dormer & Mulcahy, Cons. Engrs., Providence, 1960-69; sr. v.p. MacLellan, Dormer & Mulcahy, Inc., 1969-73. Served to lt. C.E., USNR, 1943-46, 51-53. Registered profl. engr., R.I., N.Y., Mass., Vt., N.H. Mem. Nat. Soc. Profl. Engrs., Providence Engring. Soc. Club: Potowomut Golf. Home: Warwick, R.I. Died Dec. 30, 1973.

DORN, JOHN EMIL, educator; b. Chgo., Apr. 10, 1909; s. John and Augusta (Reindl) D.; B.S., Northwestern U., 1931, M.S., 1932; D.Sc. (hon.), 1971; Ph.D., U. Minn., 1936; m. Virginia Alice Henneman, Feb. 22, 1937; children—John Robert, Michael Raymond. Research asst. chemistry Northwestern U., 1931-32; teaching asst. U. Minn., 1932-36; postdoctoral research fellow Battelle Meml. Inst., 1936-38; asst. prof. mech. engring. U. Cal., 1938-41; asso. prof. phys. metallurgy, 1942-48, prof. materials sci. 1949-71; research metallurgist Dow Chem. Co., 1941-42; speaker sci. confs. Recipient Charles B. Dudley medal Am. Soc. Testing and Materials, 1958, Henry Marion Howe medal Am. Soc. Metals, 1959, Albert Easton White distinguished tchrs. award Am. Soc. Metals, 1964, medal Societe Francaise de Metallurgic, 1968, also Joint Army and Navy award, Distinguished Teaching award U. Cal., others. Miller research prof., 1962-63. Fellow Am. Inst. Mining and Metall. Engrs., Am. Soc. Metals (chmn. Golden Gate chpt. 1945, 46, nat. trustee 1947-49); mem. Sigma Xi. Editor: The Mechanical Behavior of Metals at Elevated Temperatures, 1961. Contbr. articles to profl. jours. Home: Orinda, Cal. Died Sept. 24, 1971.

DORR, CARL E., lawyer; b. DePauville, N.Y., Dec. 25, 1879; s. Charles E. and Julia A. (Lee) D.; grad. Canton (N.Y.) Union Sch., 1894; A.B., Syracuse U., 1900, LL.B., 1902; m. Amelia Morgan, Dec. 26, 1903; children—Janice Morgan (Mrs. Theodore H. Fossieck), Barbara Eloise (Mrs. Richard D. Greene), Lois Miriam (Mrs. Robert G. Sharpe). Admitted to N.Y. bar, 1902, and practiced in Syracuse, 1902-45, ret., 1945; mem. Hancock, Dorr, Ryan & Shove, 1937-45; asst. corp. counsel City of Syracuse, 1917-21. Mem. N.Y. State and Onondaga Co. bar assns., Onondaga Hist. Assn., Delta Upsilon. Republican (state com. 1917-34). Mem. United Church of Fayetteville, Mason (32°). Home: Fayetteville, N.Y.†

DORROH, JOHN HAZARD, coll. prof.; b. Madison, Miss., Apr. 29, 1878; s. William Gayle and Eliza (Robinson) D.; student Millsaps Coll., Jackson, Miss., 1897-98, U. of Miss., 1898-1900; B.E., Vanderbitl, 1903, C.E., 1913; m. Lewise L. Dawson, Feb. 8, 1915 (now deceased); children—Mary Louise, John Hazard; m. 2d, Mrs. Mattie C. Thompson, 1926. With U. of Miss., 1906-30, as asst. prof. civ. engring., prof. municipal engring., 1906-15, prof. civ. engring. and dean Sch. of Engring., 1915-30; head dept. civil engring., U. of N.M., 1930-43; practiced as consulting, designing and constructing engr.; later retired. Formerly chmn. N.M. State Bd. of Registration for Engrs. and Land Surveyors; v.p. Nat. Council of State Boards of Engring. Examiners. Mem. Am. Soc. C.E. Presbyterian. Address: Biloxi, Miss.†

DORSEY, CHARLES HOWARD, JR., newspaper editor; b. Balt., May 2, 1904; s. Charles Howard and Leila Risteau (Walter) D.; grad. Balt. City Coll., 1923; A.B., Johns Hopkins, 1927; m. Emma Beck Deputy, Nov. 21, 1933; 1 son, John Russell. Instr. philosophy Johns Hopkins Coll. for Tchrs., 1930-31; reporter Balt. Evening Sun, 1931-32, 33-42, acting asst. city editor, 1942; asst. mng. editor Balt. Sun (morning), 1942-47, mng. editor, 1947-66, asso. editor, 1966-69; v.p. A.S. Abell Co., pub. Balt. Sun papers, 1956-69. Mem. Kappa Alpha. Democrat. P.E. ch. Clubs: Maryland, Tudor and Stuart (Balt.); National Press (Washington). Home: Baltimore, Md. Died Oct. 17, 1973; buried Old St. Paul's Ch., Kent County, Md.

DORSEY, JACK SIDNEY, naval officer; b. Gainesville, Ga., Apr. 5, 1907; s. John William and Marie Theresa (Shanahan) D.; B.S. in Engring., U.S. Naval Acad., 1930; grad. U.S. Naval Postgrad. Sch., 1938; m. Marie Smith, Sept. 19, 1931; 1 dau., Leila Marie (Mrs. William Summers Thompson). Commd. ensign U.S. Navy, 1930, advanced through grades to rear adm., 1958; comdr. destroyer, also destroyer div. in Pacific, World War II; dep. dir. communications Joint Chief Staff, 1958-60; dir. naval communications Navy Dept., 1958; comdr. Destroyer Flotilla 6, also Destroyer Force Atlantic Fleet, 1969-61; dep. dir. Def. Communications Agy. for Satellite Communications, 1962-63; chief staff Def. Communications Agy., 1963-65; commandant 6th Naval Dist., Charleston, 1965-68, ret., 1968. Decorated Legion Merit (2), Bronze Star. Mem. Navy Hist. Found., Naval Inst., Naval Acad. Alumni Assn., Armed Forces Communications-Electronics Assn. Home: Jacksonville, Fla. Died Nov. 8, 1974.

DORSEY, LEO PATRICK, lawyer; b. Towanda, Pa., s. Patrick D. and Margaret M. (Moore) D.; A.B., U. Pa., 1920; LL.B., Harvard, 1923; m. Ruth E. Knickerbocker, Oct. 25, 1923; children—L. L. Dean, John D., Robert K. Admitted to N.Y. bar, 1925, since practiced in N.Y.C.; mem. firm Dorsey, Burke & Griffin, and predecessors; now counsel Boal, Doti, Fitzpatrick & Hart, N.Y.C.; N.Y. State counsel HOLC, 1933-37; mortgage commr. N.Y. State, 1937-39. Bd. dirs. Queens council Boy Scouts Am. Mem. Am. Internat., N.Y. State bar assns., Bar Assn. City N.Y. Home: Tucson, Ariz. Died Dec. 24, 1973.

DORWIN, OSCAR JOHN, lawyer; b. Minocqua, Wis., Jan. 2, 1897; s. Arthur O. and Caroline (O'Leary) D.; Ph.B., U. of Notre Dame, 1917; LL.B., Harvard, 1920; m. Olive McKay Hedge, Feb. 5, 1927. Admitted to Ill. bar, 1921, N.Y. bar, 1935; in gen. law practice, Chicago, 1921-26; counsel Indian Refining Co., Lawrenceville, Ill., 1926-33; atty., Texaco, Inc., Chgo. and N.Y., 1933-42, asso. gen. counsel 1942-44, gen. counsel, 1944-51, v.p., gen. counsel, 1951-58, sr. v.p., gen. counsel, 1958-62, ret., now dir. Chmn. Am. Petroleum Industries Com., 1949-51. Pres. Ambraw-Wabash area council Boy Scouts Am., 1930-31. Mem. bd. supervising trustees Parker Endowment; trustee Parker Sch. Fgn. and Comparative Law, Columbia U., Am. U, in Cairo; mem. adv. council Law Sch., U. Notre Dame; mem. Harvard Alumni Bd., 1958-60. Mem. Am., N.Y. bar assns., Assn. Bar City N.Y., Notre Dame Alumni Assn. (nat. dir. 1956-59). Clubs: Round Hill (Greenwich, Conn.); Augusta (Ga.) Nat., Blind Brook (Port Chester, N.Y.); Burning Tree (Bethesda, Md.); Harvard, Cloud, Special Car Associates, Links (N.Y.C.); Pine Valley Golf (Clementon, N.J.); Honourable Company of Edinburgh Golfers (Muirfield, Scotland); Royal and Ancient Golf (St. Andrews, Scotland); Chicago. Home: Greenwich, Conn. Died Nov. 4, 1974.

DOTSON, GEORGE EDGAR, educator; b. Milton, Ore., Sept. 15, 1904; s. Eli E. and Dora E. (Edgar) C.; A.B., San Diego State Coll., 1926; A.M., Stanford, 1927, Ed.D., 1939; m. Gladys Aileen Fisher, Aug. 15, 1931; 1 son, Robert E. Instr. phys. edn. La Jolla Jr.-Sr. High Sch., San Diego, 1927-30; dir. activities Oceanside-Carlsbad Union High Sch., 1930-35; registrar, dir. student personnel San Diego State Coll., 1936-42; pres. Long Beach City Coll., 1942-64, asst. supt., 1951-61; dir. ednl. services, prof. edn. Cal. State Coll. at Long Beach, 1964-67, prof. edn., 1964-70, prof. emeritus, 1970-74; dep. supt. Long Beach Unified Sch. Dist., 1962-64; on leave to Stanford, 1935-36. Rotarian. Home: Long Beach, Cal. Died Nov. 22, 1974; interred Sunnyside Memorial Park, Long Beach, Cal.

DOTY, CARL BABCOCK, chemist; b. Custer Park, Ill., Sept. 30, 1901; s. Frank Hunter and Clara Jane (Babcock) D.; B.S., Monmouth (Ill). Coll., 1926; m. Elizabeth B. Jenkins, June 16, 1929 (dec. Nov. 1968); m. 2d Gaynelle McClintic, Jan. 11, 1970. Asst. to librarian, John Crerar Library, 1926; chemist, B.H. Wilson Inspection Bur., 1927; research chemist Superior Marking Equipment Co., 1928-43, dir., asst. sec., treas., 1943; research chemist, Eversharp Inc., 1944-47; owner, mgr. Chgo., Ink & Research Co., 1947-60; pres. Chgo. Ink & Research Co., 1960-74. Mem. Marking Device Assn., Chgo. Marking Device Club, Am. Assn. Engrs., Am. Inst. Chemists. Home: Antioch, Ill. Died Nov. 18, 1974.

DOTY, JOHN WILLIAMS, pres. The Foundation Co.; b. Toronto, Can., Jan. 15, 1879; s. Fred W. and Mary E. (Williams) D.; came to U.S., 1897; C.E., Rensselaer Polytehhnic Institute, 1902, Doctor of Engineering (honorary), 1950; married Clara S. Spooner, June 14, 1905; 1 dau., Eleanor Rosamond. Draftsman, The Foundation Co., 1903-07, asst. chief engr., 1907-11, chief engr., 1911-12, v.p. and gen. mgr., 1912-19, pres., 1919-26, chmn. bd., 1926-28, again pres. from 1929. Hon. trustee Renssaelaer Polytechnical Institute. Member American Society C.E., Engring. Inst. Canada. Inst. Civ. Engrs. (London), Soc. Mayflower Descendants, Nat. Soc. Puritan Descendants, Pilgrims of U.S., Chi Phi. Awarded McDonald prize, Rensselaer Poly. Inst., 1902. Mason. Home: New Canaan, Conn.†

DOTY, MADELEINE ZABRISKIE (MRS. ROGER N. BALDWIN), reformer; b. Bayonne, N.J., Aug. 24, 1879; d. Samuel W. and Charlotte G. (Zabriskie) D.; B.L., Smith Coll., 1900; LL.B., New York U., 1902; m. Roger N. Baldwin, Aug. 9, 1919. Admitted to N.Y. bar, 1903; teacher, Mary Haskell's Sch., Boston, 1904, 05; practiced law in New York 4 yrs.; prepared Children's Court exhibit for Child Welfare Exhibit, New York, 1909; apptd. sec. Children's Court Com. of Russell Sage Foundation; apptd. member Prison Reform Commn. of N.Y., 1913; voluntarily spent one week in prison to investigate conditions and make report; went to Europe, 1915, 16, 18, 19, twice traveling through England, France, Germany, Holland, Switzerland, Norway and Sweden, Russia, Austria Hungary and contbr. articles on warring countries of Europe to English and Am. newspapers and mags. Sec. Women's Internat. League for Peace and Freedom, Geneva, 1925-27, editor "Pax," organ of the League, 1925—. Unitarian. Author: Society's Misfits, 1916; Short Rations—an American Woman in Germay, 1917; Behind the Battle Line, 1919.†

DOTY, ROBERT CLARK, fgn. corr.; b. Evanston, Ill., Apr. 7, 1915; s. Samuel Stranahaan and Helen Douglas (Clark) D.; student Northwestern U., 1933-34; m. Mary Woodward Warner, July 16, 1935; children—Elizabeth (Mrs. E. R. Speare), Mark Woodward. With City News Bur., Chgo., Ill. 1937-39; staff Courier Jour., Louisville, 1939-42, Ky. state capital bur., 1946, Washington bur., 1947; dir. pub. relations Internat. Refugee Orgn., Geneva, Switzerland, 1947-50; with N.Y. Times, 1950-70, staff, N.Y.C., 1950-51, Paris bur., 1951-53, chief corr. Middle East, 1953-55, chief corr., Paris, 1958-63, chief corr., Rome, 1964-70, ret., 1970. Served as capt. AUS, 1942-45. Mem. Sigma Chi. Died Nov. 26, 1974.

DOUDOROFF, MICHAEL, educator; b. Petrograd, USSR, Nov. 14, 1911; s. Boris and Natalie (Shulgin) D.; came to U.S., 1923, naturalized, 1928; A.B., Stanford, 1933, M.A., 1934, Ph.D., 1939; m. Mary Gottlund, July 15, 1934 (div. 1944); 1 son, Michael John; m. 2d, Rita Whelton, Oct. 10, 1944 (dec. 1951); m. 3d, Olga Lott, Aug. 15, 1952. Mem. faculty U. Cal. at Berkeley, 1940-75, prof. bacteriology, 1952-75, research prof. Miller Inst., 1960-62, prof. molecular biology, 1964-75; spl. research microbiol. physiology and metabolism, enzymology. Recipient Sugar Found. award, 1947; Guggenheim fellow, 1949-50; spl. fellow NIH, 1963. Mem. Nat. Acad. Scis., Am. Soc. Biol. Chemists, Soc. Am. Microbiologists, Soc. Gen. Physiologists. Died Apr. 4, 1975.

DOUGHERTY, LEE J., life insurance exec.; b. Davenport, Ia., Jan. 29, 1881; s. Edward J. and Alice (Glynn) D.; student St. Ambrose Coll., 1895-99, St. Joseph's Coll., 1899-1902; A.B., Creighton U., 1902; m. Regene b. Hanon, June 15, 1920; 1 dau., Alice Ann. Began as life ins. agent, 1903; sec. Guaranty Life Ins. Co., Davenport, Ia., 1903-20, pres. from 1920; v.p. Occidental Life Ins. Co. of Calif. from 1937; dir. Am. Trust Co., United Realities Co., Iowa State Bldg. Co., Am. Service Bureau, Miss. Valley Fair. Chmn. Davenport 1st, 2d, 3d, Liberty Loan Drives. Mayor of Davenport 1918-20. Mem. Am. Life Convention (dir.), Davenport Chamber of Commerce (ex-pres.). Democrat. Catholic. Elk, K. of C. Clubs: Outing, Rotary (Davenport); Union League (Chicago); Davenport Country. Home: Davenport, Ia.†

DOUGHERTY, THOMAS FRANCIS, histologist; b. Forman, N.D., Mar. 27, 1915; s. Thomas Francis and Mary (Brandenburg) D.; B.S., U. Minn., 1936, A.M., 1937, Ph.D., 1942; fellow Donner Found., 1942-43; m. Jean Ann Hay, Apr. 5, 1941; children—Michael Bruce, Ann Marie. Instr. in anatomy Yale Sch. of Medicine, 1943-47; prof. anatomy (histology) U. Utah, 1947, now chmn. dept. anatomy, dir. radiobiology lab., 1954-74; cons. Surgeon Gen. of U.S. Army. Mem. Reticulendothelial Soc. (pres. 1957), Am. Assn. Cancer Research, Am. Assn. Study Internal Secretions, Am. Assn. Anatomists, Internat. Soc. Hematology, Soc. Exptl. Biology and Medicine, Phi Sigma Kappa. Democrat. Home: Salt Lake City, Utah. Died Feb. 6, 1974.

DOUGHERTY, WILLIAM H., lawyer; b. Independence, Ia., Nov. 9, 1880; s. Michael J. and Mary D.; grad. high sch., Janesville, Wis.,1899; studied law in office of Jackson & Jackson, Janesville; m. Margaret J. Dougherty, Feb. 3, 1904; 1 dau., Catherine. Began law practice at Janesville, 1901; city atty., Janesville, 1913-16; mem. firm Nolan, Dougherty, Grubb & Ryan; U.S. atty., Western Dist. of Wis. by apptmt. of President Harding, 1921-27. Republican. K.C. Club: Madison. Home: Janesville, Wis.†

DOUGLAS, DONALD B., business exec.; b. Cedar Rapids, Ia., Sept. 27, 1892; s. James H. and Inez (Boynton) D.; ed. Princeton, 1914; m. Martha Clow, Oct. 20, 1917. Dir. Quaker Oats Co., Chgo., 1927-57, v.p. charge advt., until 1952; dir. James B. Clow & Sons Co. Home: Lake Forest, Ill., Died Oct. 1, 1975.

DOUGLAS, GRACE PARSONS, educator; b. Cambridge, Mass., Oct. 25, 1881; d. Alexander and Ellen (Hill) Parsons; ed. Sargent Sch. of Physical Edn., Cambridge, U. of Calif., at Los Angeles and U. of Southern Calif.; m. Ernest Douglas, Oct. 2, 1900; children—Marjorie, Barbara, Jean, Shirley. Supervisor physical edn., Winchester, Mass., 1903-05; teacher, pub. schs., Los Angeles, 1920-24; dir. Douglas Schs. and Camps, Pebble Beach, Calif., from 1923. Mem. Camp Dirs. Assn. of Calif. Republican. Episcopalain. Clubs: Ebell, Friday Morning (Los Angeles). Home: Pebble Beach, Calif.†

DOUGLAS, JAMES MARSH, lawyer; b. St. Louis, Jan. 6, 1896; s. Walter Bond and Francesca (Kimball) Douglas; LL.B., Washington U., St. Louis, 1921, LL.D., 1968; LL.D., Westminster Coll., 1958; m. Mary Lumaghi, Aug. 5, 1939; 1 son, James Kimball. Admitted to Mo. bar, 1917, U.S. Supreme Ct. bar, 1932; began practice in St. Louis, 1921; asso. with law firm Nagel & Kirby; city councilor, Florissant, Mo., 1933-35; judge Circuit Ct., St. Louis, 1935-37; apptd. judge Supreme Ct. of Mo., 1937, to fill unexpired term, elected, 1938, for term expiring 1944, reelected under Non-Partisan Ct. Plan known as Mo. Plan of Jud. Tenure for a term expiring 1954, chief justice, 1943-45, resigned, 1949; re-entered law practice as partner Thompson & Mitchell, and predecessors, St. Louis; chmn. Jud. Conf. of Mo., 1943-45; chmn. Appellate Jud. Commn. of Mo., 1943-45; lectr. med. jurisprudence Washington U. Med. Sch., 1929-37; spl. counsel to atty. gen. Mo. on edn. beyond high sch., 1962-64. Orgn. dir. St. Louis Ednl. TV Commn. KETC, 1955-57; Mo. chmn. Nat. Library Week. Pvt. Battery A, Mo. N.G. 1913-17; Mexican border service, 1916; entered 1st O.T.C., Ft. Riley, Kan., 1917; 1st lt. 342d F.A., 89th Div. AEF (St. Mihiel sector, Army of Occupation). Mem. Mo. Def. Council, 1941-45; bd. dirs. St. Louis Crime Commn.; chmn. task force on legal services and procedure 2d Hoover Commn., 1954-55; sponsor mem. Civic Progress, Inc. of St. Louis; mem. orgn. com., bd. mem. United Fund of St. Louis, 1955; bd. dirs. St. Louis Symphony Soc.; Trustee Washington U., 1950-66, chmn. bd., 1954-61, 1st vice chmn. 1961-66, life trustee, 1967-74; trustee St. Louis Children's Hosp., 1951-55; mem. U.S. Territorial Expansion Meml. Commn., 1950-74, chmn. exec. com.; trustee Jefferson Nat. Expansion Meml. Assn. Recipient citation merit U. Mo. Alumni Assn., 1966; hon. col. on staff gov. Mo., 1953-57, 61-65. Fellow Am. Bar Found.; mem. Am. (chmn. sect. jud. adminstrn. 1950-51; ho. of dels. 1952-54; chmn. jud. selection 1950-59; adv. bd. Am. Bar Jour.), Mo. (dir. dept. judiciary 1956-57), St. Louis bar assns., Lawyers Assn. St. Louis (award of honor 1951), Am. Judicature Soc. (dir. 1955-57), Am. Law Inst. (life), Mo. Hist. Soc. (pres. 1940-44; trustee 1950-59; life mem.). Inst. Jud. Adminstrn., Assn. Bar City N.Y. (asso.) Omicron Delta Kappa (hon.), Order of Coif, S.R., Alpha Tau Omega, Phi Delta Phi (nat. pres. 1931-33). Episcopalian. Mason

(32°). Clubs: Round Table, University, Noonday. Author articles legal mags. Home: St. Louis Mo. Died Dec. 3, 1974.

DOUGLAS, JOHN GRAY, geologist, educator; b. Balt., Aug. 1, 1900; s. Eugene and Ethel (Gray) D.; A.B. in Biology, Johns Hopkins, 1921, Ph.D. in Geology and Paleontology, 1928; m. Violet Anath Marshall, May 28, 1936. Geologist, Venezuela Gulf Oil Co., 1924-25, 26-27; paleontologist Lago Petroleum Corp., Venezuela, 1928-31; asso. prof. geology U. N.C. 1931-34; petroleum geologist Mene Grande Oil Co., Venezuela, 1934-55, dist. geologist in charge Western Venezuela, 1939-55; asso. prof. geology U. Miss., 1955-56, prof., 1956-70, prof. emeritus, 1970-74, chmn. dept. geology, 1956-65. Fellow Geol. Soc. Am., A.A.A.S.; mem. Am. Assn. Petroleum Geologists, Miss. Geol. Soc., Am. Assn. Engring. Edn., Scabbard and Blade, Sigma Xi, Gamma Alpha, Sigma Gamma Epsilon. Episcopalian. Contbr. articles to profl. jours. Home: Oxford, Miss., Died Nov. 30, 1974.

DOUGLAS, KENNETH WALLACE, hosp. adminstr.; b. Cando, N.D., Sept. 13, 1912; s. Harry John and Sena (Johnson) D.; B.A., St. Olaf's Coll., 1935; B.S., U. Minn., 1937, M.D., 1939; m. Florence Anna Bostrom, Jan. 22, 1949; children—John Wallace, Harry Greg. Intern, Tacoma Gen. Hosp., 1940; practice medicine, Tacoma, 1940-49; clin. dir. Wilmar (Minn.) State Hosp., 1950-52, acting supt., 1953-54; supt. Sandstone (Minn.) State Hosp., 1952-57, Mt. Pleasant (Mich.) State Home & Tng. Sch., 1957-61; asst. supt., dir. clin. services Eastern State Hosp., Medical Lake, Wash., 1961-67; supt. Interlake Sch., Medical Lake, 1967-74; acting supt. Hastings (Minn.) State Hosp., 1954. Guest lectr. U. N.D., 1953-54. Central Mich., U., 1959-60. Served to lt. AUS, 1940. Fellow Am. Acad. Med. Adminstrs. (dir. Wash.); mem. Spokane County Med. Soc., Mich. Assn. Professions Mich. Soc. Psychiatry and Neurology, Medical Lake C. of C. Presbyn. Rotarian (pres. 1967-68). Home: Spokane, Wash. Died Mar. 13, 1974; interred Spokane, Wash.

DOUGLAS, LEWIS WILLIAMS, ambassador; b. Bisbee, Ariz., July 2, 1894; s. James Stuart and Josephine Leah (Williams) D; B.A. cum laude, Amherst Coll., 1916, LL.D., 1933; postgrad. Mass. Inst. Tech., 1916-17; LL.D., Harvard, 1933, Queens Coll., Princeton, Brown, N.Y. and Wesleyan univs., 1938, U. Ariz., 1940, U. Leeds (Eng.), 1948, Univs. Bristol, St. Andrews, London, 1949, Edinburgh, Birmingham, Glasgow, 1950, U. Cal., McGill U., Columbia, Dalhousie U., 1951; D.C.L., Oxford (Eng.) U., 1948; m. Peggy Zinsser, June 19, 1921; children—James Stuart, Lewis Williams, Sharman (Mrs. Andrew M. Hay). Instr. Amherst Coll., 1920; mem. Ariz. Ho. Reps., 1923-25; mem. 70th to 73d Congresses (1927-33), at large, Ariz.; dir. budget, 1933-34; v.p., dir. Am. Cyanamid Co., 1934-37; prin., vice chancellor McGill U., Montreal, Que., Can., 1938-40; pres. Mut. Life Ins. Co. N.Y., 1940-47, trustee, 1940-72, chmn. bd., 1947-59, chmn. exec. com., 1959-72, hon. trustee, 1972; cons. chmn. bd., dir. So. Ariz. Bank and Trust Co., 1949-66, hon. chmn., cons., 1966; chmn. bd., dir. Western Bankcorp. Internat. Bank, 1962-67, dir., mem. exec. com.; pres. United Cal. Bank Internat., 1967-73, hon. chmn., dir., 1973; dir. Internat. Nickel Co., Ltd., 1951-71, mem. exec. com., 1955-59, alternate mem. exec. com., 1960-71, mem. adv. com., 1971-74; dir. Union Corp., 1951-73, Verde Exploration Ltd., Newmont Mining Corp.; dir. Tech. Studies, Inc., rep. supervisory bd. channel tunnel study group. Dep. war shipping adminstr., 1942-44; mem. Combined Shipping Adjustment Bd.; spl. adviser to Gen. Clay, German Control Council, 1945; ambassador to Gt. Britain, 1947-50; mem. U.S. Adv. Com. on Weather Control, 1953-57; pres., chmn. Nat. Policy Bd., Am. Assembly; chmn. govt. study fgn. econ. problems, 1953; mem. nat. emergency council Nat. Council on Crime and Delinquency; mem. Indian Econ. Devel. Adv. Group for Ariz.; adminstrv. cons. dir. Inst. Atmospheric Physics, U. Ariz. Pres. Winston Churchill Found. U.S., Ltd.; chmn. Founding Friends Harvey Mudd Coll.; hon. pres. Nat. Soc. Prevention Blindness; hon. chmn. Friends Benjamin Franklin House. Bd. dirs. All Hallows Found., St. Luke's Hosp., Ariz., Atlantic Council U.S., Inc.; hon. bd. dirs. Acad. Polit. Sci.; bd. govs. Arctic Inst. North Am., Royal Shakespeare Theatre, Eng.; trustee Thunderbird Grad. Sch. Internat. Mgmt., Neurological Scis. Found., Sam Rayburn Found.; hon. trustee Am. Mus. Natural History, Am. Shakespeare Festival Theatre and Acad.; bd. visitors Honnold Library Soc.; mem. adv. com. to bd. dirs. George C. Marshall Research Found., adv. council on Marshall scholarships; adv. mem. bd. mgrs. Meml. Hosp. for Cancer and Allied Diseases; mem. trustees adv. com. Alfred P. Sloan Found.; mem. adv. council Am. Ditchley Found., Internat. Movement for Atlantic Union, Inc., Am. Mus. in Britain, Internat. Students Trust, London; mem. adv. com. Child Adoption Services; mem. internat. sponsoring com. World Center for Exploration; mem. adv. bd. Claremont Coll., Ariz. Livestock Show. Served to 1st lt. F.A., U.S. Army, World War I; AEF in France. Decorated Croix de Guerre, Grand Croix de l'Order de la Couronne (Belgium); Grand Croix de la Legion d'Honneur (France); hon. knight grand cross Order Brit. Empire; citation from Gen. Pershing; named Freeman City of Edinburgh, Scotland. Benjamin Franklin fellow Royal Soc. Arts of Eng.; mem. English Speaking Union U.S. (pres. 1946-47, chmn. 1951-59, hon. chmn.), Am. Philos. Soc., Grant Monument Assn., Nat. Inst. Social Scis. (pres.), Pilgrims U.S., Council on Fgn. Relations (dir. emeritus), Ariz. Heritage Council (regional dir.), U.S. C. of C. (finance com., internat. com.). Democrat. Episcopalian. Clubs: Angler's, Links, Metropolitan (Washington); Mining, Inc., Mining of the Southwest, Nat. Press, Old Pueblo, Wyandanch; Angler's Co-operative Assn., Athenaeum, Houghton, The Other, White's (London), The Thirty of London; Union Interalliee (France), Balboa de Mazatlan (Mexico). Home: Tucson, Ariz. Died Mar. 7, 1974.

DOUGLAS, WALTER JOHN, cons. engr.; b. New Britain, Conn., Aug. 3, 1922; s. Stanley John and Nora Anna (Yaross) D.; student U. Ala., 1940-42, Wittenburg Coll., 1942; B.S. in Civil Engring., Rensselaer Poly. Inst., 1947; m. Constance Ann Douglas, Aug. 1, 1958; children—Jeffrey Richard, Mark Walter. Founder Walter J. Douglas Assos., Architecture and Engring., West Hartford, Conn., 1951, partner 1951-74; sec., dir. Connie's of Hartford. Mem. West Hartford Sch. Bldg. Commn., 1958-74. Served with USAAF, 1942-45. Decorated Air medal, D.F.C. Registered profl. engr., Conn., Fla., Me., N.H., Mass., N.J., N.Y., R.I., Vt. Fellow Civil Engr. Soc. Nat., Conn. socs. profl. engrs. Home: West Hartford, Conn. Died Oct. 2, 1974.

DOUGLASS, JOSEPH HENRY, govt. ofcl.; b. Washington, June 26, 1917; s. Haley George and Evelyn (Dulaney) D.; A.B., Fisk U., 1937, M.A., 1941; Ph.D., Harvard U., 1946; m. Katherine Washington, Nov. 19, 1938; children—Betty, Jo Ann. Dean Fayetteville State Coll., 1947-54; Fullbright lectr. Cairo Sch. Social Work, Cairo, Egypt, 1952-53; spl. rep. of sec., asst. to asst. sec. Program Analysis Office, Dept. Health, Edn. and Welfare, Washington, 1954-61; program policy coordinator chief interagy. br. Nat. Inst. lMental Health, Bethesda, Md., 1961-68; exec. dir., policy adviser White House Conf. on Children and Youth, 1968-70; exec. dir. President's Com. Mental Retardation, 1971-74. Sr. cons. Acad. for Ednl. Devel., N.Y.C. Bd. dirs. Human Resources Found. N.Y., Nat. Childrens' Clubs D.C.; profl. bd. Acad. Religion and Mental Health; trustee African Art Mus., Washington, Nat. Conf. Christians and Jews. Fellow Am. Sociol. Soc., Royal Geog. Soc.; mem. Royal Acad. Promotion Health (London, Eng.). Author: Racism in America, 1965. Home: Washington, D.C. Died Oct. 23, 1974.

DOW, BLANCHE HINMAN, educator; born Louisiana, Mo., Feb. 9, 1893; d. Ernest Wentworth and Carrie Ann (Reneau) D.; A.B., Smith Coll., 1913; diploma Boston Sch. Expression, 1917; A.M., Columbia, 1925, Ph.D., 1936; Litt.D., Culver-Stockton Coll., 1953; D.Sc. in Edn., Ia. Wesleyan Coll., 1959; L.H.D., Missouri Valley College, 1959; LL.D., Western Coll. Women, U. Mo., 1965. Instr. speech, dramatics Milwaukee-Downer Seminary 1913-14; instructor dramatics, French, Grand River Coll., 1914-18; instr., Northwest Mo. State Coll., 1919-49, asst. prof., asso. prof., prof. French, humanities; pres. Cottey Coll. 1949-65. Exec. com. Mo. Coordinating Council UNESCO, 1948-52; chmn. Mo. Commn. on Status of Women, from 1964; mem. Nat. Com. on Community Relations; mem. U.S. Nat. Commn. for UNESCO, 1965-68, Member of Am. Assn. U. Profs. (mem. nat. council 1937-40, pres. Mo. chpt. 1940-41), Am. Assn. U. Women (pres. Mo. div. 1937-39, v.p. S.W. central region 1949-53, 1st v.p. 1953-57, pres. 1963-67), International Fedn. U. Women (treas. 1950-59), Delta Kappa Gamma, Chi Delta Phi. Author: The Changing Attitude Toward Women in Fifteenth Century French Lit., 1936. Collaborator; Meditations for Women, 1949. Contributor articles, poems, profl. jours. Home: Liberty, Mo. Died May 24, 1973.

DOW, JOHN RENEAU, bakery exec.; b. Oak Bluffs, Mass., May 3, 1898; s. Ernest Wentworth and Carrie Ann (Reneau) D.; A.B., William Jewell Coll., 1922; m. Marjorie Reed, June 1, 1923, Comml. air pilot, 1920-21; mgr. Grennal Bakers, Inc., St. Louis, 1925-26; gen. supt. prodn. Schulze Baking Co., Kansas City, Mo., 1927-35; gen. mgr. sales, prodn. Inter-state Bakeries Corp., 1935-39, v.p., 1940-47, dir., 1943-73, exec. v.p., 1940-57, pres., 1957-64, vice chmn., chief exec., 1964, chmn. bd., chief exec., 1956-73, chmn. exec. com., 1967-73; chmn. bd., dir. Interstate Brands Corp., 1970-73; dir. Starlight Theater Assn. (Kansas City), Commerce Trust Co. (Kansas City). Vice pres., mem. exec. com. Am. Royal. Served as 2d lt. AUS, U.S. Army, 1918-19. Dir. Midwest Research Inst., Kansas City; trustee U. Mo. at Kansas City. Mem. N.A.M., Am. Bakers Assn. (bd. dirs., chmn. bd. govs., exec. com.), Am. Inst. Baking (Chgo. bd. dirs., exec. com.), Kansas City Crime Commn. (bd. dirs.), Phi Gamma Delta. Conglist. Clubs: Saddle and Sirloin (bd. dirs.), Kansas City (v.p.), U. (Kansas City, Mo.); Rancheros Visitadores (Santa Barbara, Cal.); Kansas City 711, River; Mission Hills Country. Home: Shawnee Mission, Kan. Died 1973.

DOWD, FRED A., banker; b. Owen County, Ky., 1906. Former chmn. bd., dir. First Nat. Bank of Cin.; dir. Midland Guardian Co., Cin. Gas & Electric Co., Vulcan Corp., CNO and Tex. Pacific R.R., William Powell Co. Curator, Transylvania U., Lexington, Ky. Clubs: Cin. Country, Queen City, Bankers. Home: Cincinnati O. Died July 9, 1974.

DOWELL, CARR THOMAS, b. Mt. Sylvan, Tex., Dec. 3, 1878; s. William Carr and Nannie (McAdams) D.; B.A., Tex. Christian U., 1901; B.S., U. of Tex., 1902; post-grad. work, U. of Tex., 1902-04; Ph.D., U. of Calif., 1915; m. Jessie Flora Cady, Feb. 22, 1905. With Okla. Agrl. and Mech. Coll., 1917-28, dir. expt. sta., 1921-28, dean of agr., 1923-28; dean Coll. of Agr. and dir. of expt. stations, La. State U., 1928-31, dir. expt. sta., 1928-42; prof. agronomy, La. State U., from 1942. Mem. Phi Beta Kappa, Sigma Xi, Phi Kappa Phi. Democrat. Presbyterian. Home: Baton Rouge, La.†

DOWLING, EDDIE, actor, producer, dir.; b. Woonsocket, R.I., Dec. 9, 1894; s. Charles and Bridget Goucher; ed. pub. schs.; D.H.L., Mt. Mary Coll., Cath. U., Washington; m. Ray Dooley; children—John G., Mary Maxine. Sang with St. Paul's Cathedral Choir on world tour; first stage appearance New England Stock Co.; appeared in She Took a Change, Velvet Lady, Ziegfeld Follies, 1918, 19, 20; The Girl in the Spotlight, Blaze of Glory, Love's Old Sweet Song, Purple Dust, Our Town; produced and palyed in Thumbs Up, Here Come the Clowns, The Time of Your Life; produced His Double Life, Big Hearted Herbert, Richard II, Shadow and Substance, Madame Capet, The White Steed. Wrote and played in Girl Behind the Gun, Rainbow man; Wrote and produced Sidewalks of New York; Wrote, produced and played in Sally, Irene and Mary and Honeymoon Lane; producer, dir. The Righteous are Bold, 1956; star and dir. Mr. Dooley, 1957; prod. plays by new authors for various univs. and colls.; pres. Eddie Dowling Prodns., Eddie Dowling, Inc. Recipient Drama Critics' award for Shadow and Substance, 1938, The White Steed, 1939, both Pulitzer prize and Drama Critics' award for The Time of Your Life, 1940; Critic's Circle Award for The Glass Menagerie, 1943; directed The Iceman Cometh. Organizer, 1st pres., U.S. Camp Shows, Inc. Discovered Kate Smith, Maurice Evans, Paul Vincent Carroll. Also produced, wrote and directed Chrysler-Ziegfeld Radio Follies. Chmn. State and Screen Div. of Nat. Dem. Party, 1932, 36, 40. Roman Catholic. Clubs: Lambs, Dutch Treat; Savage (London); Chinese (Hong Kong). Seven new plays to be produced for a new circuit, Coll. Theatre in Fla. and Ga., 1961. Home: New York City, N.Y., Died Feb. 18, 1976.

DOWLING, EDWARD C., mayor; b. Morocco, Ind., Nov. 5, 1900; s. John E. and Margaret (Meadows) D.; student pub. schs.; m. Opal M. Hendryx, Sept. 27, 1923; children—James, William, Robert, Edward, Theresa, Margaret. Machinist apprentice, 1919-23; locomotive machinist Ind. Harbor Belt R.R., 1925-35; supt. Hammond (Ind.) Water Works, 1936-48; supt. Wicker Park, Ind., 1949-50; registration officer, county commr. Lake County, Ind., 1951-55; mayor, Hammond, 1955-67. Precinct committeeman Democratic Party, city chmn., del. Dem. nat. convs., 1956, 60. K.C., Moose, Eagle. Clubs: Lions, Elks, Exchange. Home: Hammond, Ind. Died Feb. 20, 1974; buried Kentland (Ind.) Cemetery.

DOWLING, JUDSON DAVIE, M.D., b. Daleville, Dale Co., Ala., Apr. 30, 1880; s. Samuel Lawson and Sarah Jane (Windham) D.; grad. Dale Co. High Sch., 1897; M.D., U. of Ala., 1910; m. Lillian Alice MacKenzie, of Nova Scotia, Can., Nov. 17, 1914; children—Judson Davie, Mary MacKenzie, William MacKenzie. Began practice at Birmingham, Ala., 1910; health officer, Jefferson Co. and City of Birmingham, from 1917. Judge, Municipal Court, St. Augustine, Fla., 1905-07. Mem. A.M.A., Am. Pub. Health Assn., Southern Medical Assn., Medical Assn. Ala., Jefferson Co. Med. Soc., Ala. Tuberculosis Assn. (dir.). Democrat. Presbyn. Mason. Home: Birmingham, Ala.†

DOWLING, ROBERT WHITTLE, real estate exec.; b. N.Y.C., Sept. 9, 1895; s. Robert Emmet and Minetta (Link) D.; ed. Cutler Sch., N.Y.C., D.F.A., Adelphi Coll., 1961, Fairleigh Dickinson U., 1963; L.H.D., Dowling Coll., 1969; LL.D., Ithaca Coll., 1970; m. Ethel Robertson, June 1920 (div. 1931); m. 2d, Alcie Bevier Hall, Jan. 5, 1934 (div. 1968); 1 dau., Ruth Alice; m. 3d, Audrey A. Reber, Feb. 9, 1968. Engaged in real estate and bldg. bus., N.Y.C., 1918-73; with firms including U.S. Realty & Improvement Co., N.Y. Dock Co., Starrett Bros. & Eken, Inc., 1943; pres., dir. City Investing Co., 1943-60, chmn., 1966-70, chmn. exec. com., 1970-73; chmn. Pierre Hotel, 1967-73; housing and planning cons. real estate projects, Parkchester (mem. bd. design), Stuyvesant Town, Clinton Hill, Peter Cooper Village, Fordham Hill; dir. Gen. Devel. Corp., United Artists Corp., Knickerbocker Investing Co., French & Co., Hotel Waldorf-Astoria Corp., Chemway Corp., N.Y. Airways, Ednl. Broadcasting Corp., 1st Nat. City Bank Trust Bd., Xicom Inc., Home Ins. Co., R. H. Macy & Co., Inc., Hilton Hotels Internat., trustee Emigrant Savs. Bank; owners rep., Pitts., Gateway Center; cons. Canadian Pacific Ry., Penn Central Company. Hom. chmn. N.Y. Bd. of Trade, Chmn., dir. Citizens Budget Commn.; mem. N.Y.C. Off-Track Betting Corp., N.Y. State Commn. on Powers Local Govt.; vice chmn. D.C. Auditorium Commn.; hon. trustee Nat. Urban League; mem. Am. Com. To Preserve Abu-Simbel; co-chmn., dir. Nat. Conf. Christians and Jews; nat. chmn. fund raising campaign Urban League, 1948; chmn. Borough of Manhattan Planning Bd. Dir. UN Assn. U.S.; member Mayor's Com. Off Street Parking. Trustee St. Johns Guild. Dir.

Regional Plan Assn., Commerce and Industry Assn., Am. Arbitration Assn., Boy Scouts Am. Mem. nat. shriners adv. bd. Dept. Interior; chmn. adv. com. arts John F. Kennedy Center for Performing Arts, 1959-67, trustee, 1968-73; chmn., trustee Dowling Coll. (formerly Adelphi-Suffolk, endowed by, and named for him), 1968-73. Inst. on Man and Sci., 1968-73; hon. chmn. ANTA Bd. overseers Harvard Coll.; chmn. bd. design Penn Central Park, Pitts.; co-chmn. trustee Inst. Internat. Edn.; chmn. exec. com. chmn., founder Fed. Hall, N.Y.C.; preserved and established Ft. Clinton, N.Y.C.; trustee Carnegie Hall Corp., Carnegie Hall Soc. Balloon tng. corps Columbia U. unit, U.S. Army, World War I, on spl. assignment by naval cons. bd., USN; served as first frogman of U.S. Navy, Decorated Cross of Chevalier of Legion of Honor; Order of Merit, Republic of Germany; Brazilian Order of So. Cross; recipient Medal of City of N.Y.; medal for invention of all-glass doors by Glass Inst.; spl. award Nat. Conf. Christians and Jews; Antionette Perry award; Lambs club award for achievements in theatre; certificate of merit C. of C. U.S. Mem. Nat. Inst. Social Sci. (v.p.). Democrat. Clubs: N.Y. Athletic, Knickerbocker, Racquet and Tennis, Tuxedo. Am. Nat. long distance swimming champion, 1916. Home: New York City, N.Y. Died Sept. 1973.

DOWNES, DENNIS SAWYER, educator; b. Derby, Conn., Nov. 15, 1879; s. William Howe and Helen Louise (Sawyer) D.; A.B., Harvard, 1902; post-grad. work in history, 1915-17; m. Marion Pearl Lee, of Searsport, Me., Dec. 5, 1906. In ednl. dept. Little Brown & Co., pubs., Boston, Mass., later engaged in orange raising, Pasadena and Glendora, Calif.; headmaster, also trustee Glendora (Calif.) Foothills Sch., from 1924. Served with Am. Red Cross, Neuilly, France, 1917. Republican. Episcopalain. Home: Glendora, Calif.†

DOXIADIS, CONSTANTINOS APOSTOLOS architect-planner; b. Stenimachos, May 14, 1913; s. Apostolos and Evanthia (Mezeviri) D.; grad. architect-engr., Tech. U. Athens, 1935; Dr. Ing. Mit Auszeichnung, Berlin-Charlottenburg (Germany) U., 1936; LL.D., Swarthmore Coll., 1962, Mills Coll., 1964, U. Mich., 1967, Tulane U., 1968, Kalamazoo Coll., 1968; D.Sc., Detroit Inst. Tech., 1966, U. Pitts., 1967, Marietta Coll., 1969; D.F.A., U.R.I., 1966; D.H., Wayne State U., 1964; L.H.D., No. Mich. U., 1965, Case Western Res. U., 1969; m. Emma Scheepers, Apr. 30, 1940; children—Evanthia, Calliope, Eufrosyne, Apostolos. Chief town planning officer Greater Athens Area, 1937-38; head dept. regional and town planning Greek Ministry Pub. Works, 1939-45; lectr., acting prof. town planning Tech. U., Athens, 1939-43; prof. ekistics Grad. Sch. Ekistics, Athens Tech. Inst., also chmn. bd., 1958-75; minister, permanent sec. Greek Housing Reconstrn., 1945-48; minister-coordinator Greek Recovery Program, 1948-51; pres. Doxiadis Assos., cons. devel. and ekistics, Athens, 1951-72, chmn., 1973-75; vis. lectr. U. Chgo., Yale, Harvard, Princeton, Swarthmore Coll., Mass. Inst. Tech., Ga. Inst. Tech., Dublin, Mich., N.Y., Oxford, Trinity colls. Participant numerous internat. dels., also cons. Decorated Greek Mil. Cross, 1941; officer Order Brit. Empire, 1945; mem. Order Cedar (Lebanon), 1958; Royal Order of Phoenix (Greece), 1960; Yugoslav Flag Order with Golden Wreath, 1966; recipient Sir Patrick Abercrombie prize Internat. Union Architects, 1963; Cali de Oro award Soc. Mexican Architects, 1963; award of excellence Indsl. Designers Soc. Am., 1965; Aspen award humanistic studies Colo., 1966; Gold medal Royal Archl. Inst. Can., 1976. Mem. Soc. Internat. Devel., Am. Mgmt. Assn., Am. Soc. Testing and Materials, Internat. Fedn. Housing and Planning, Am. Inst. Planners, Am. Soc. Planning Ofcls., Greek Tech. Chamber, Inter-Am. Planning Soc.; hon. corr. fellow Royal Incorp. Architects of Scotland; hon. corr. mem. Town Planning Inst. Gt. Britain. Author: Raumordnung im greichieschen Städtebau, 1937; A Simple Story (in Greek), 1945; Ekistic Analysis (in Greek), 1946; Destruction of Towns and Villages in Greece, 1946; A Plan for the Survival of the Greek People (with others), 1947; March of the People (in Greek), 1948; Our Capital and its Future (in Greek), 1960; Architecture in Transition (in English), 1963; Urban Renewal and the Future of the American City (in English), 1966; Between Dystopia and Utopia (in English), 1966; Ekistics, an Introduction to the Science of Human Settlements (in English), 1968; The Two-headed Eagle, from the past to the future of Human Settlements (in English), 1972; Architectural Space in Ancient Greece (in English), 1972; The Great Urban Crimes we permit by law (in English), 1973; Anthropopolis, city for Human Development (in English), 1974; (with J. Papaioannou) Ecumenopolis, the inevitable City of the Future (in English), 1975; Building Entopia (in English), 1975; Action for Human Settlements (in English), 1976; reports problems of devel. and ekistics in 36 countries. Home: Athens, Greece. Died June 28, 1975.

DOZIER, JAMES CORDE, army officer, b. Gallivants Ferry. S.C., Feb. 17, 1885; s. John Henry and Julia Marie (Best) D.; student Wofford Coll., 1 yr.; m. Margaret Tallulah Little. June 10, 1920; children—James C., Donald Preston. With Butler Brothers. N.Y.C., 1908; with Nat. Union Bank, Rock Hill, S.C., later sec. State Bd. Pub. Welfare, Columbia; adj. gen. S.C., 1926-59, also dir. civil defense under act of Gen. Assembly. Mem. bd. visitors The Citadel. Served on Mexican border with S.C. Nat. Guard. 1916; from 2d lt. to 1st lt., 118th Inf., 30th Div., U.S. Army, 1917-19. AEF 11 mos. Cited for conspicuous gallantry and intrepidity above and beyond the call of duty. Decorated Congressional Medal of Honor, Purple Heart (U.S.); Military Cross (Gt. Britain); Croix de Guerre and medal. Chevalier Legion of Honor (France); War Cross (Italy); medal (Portugal); medal (Montenegrin). Motion picture, The Price of Peace, made under auspices U.S. Govt., shows Lt. Dozier in act of charging a nest of machine guns. Mem. Am. Legion, 40 and 8. Disabled Am. Vets. Vets. Fgn. Wars. Democrat. Presbyn. Mason. Rotarian. Home: Columbia, S.C. Died Oct. 25, 1974.

DRAA, CHARLES CLIFTON, pianist, music educator; b. Niles, O., May 13, 1871; s. Samuel Perry and Mary Delmere (Ball) D.; Mus.B., Adrian (Mich.) Coll., 1891; Mus.D., 1928; studied piano under Dr. William Mason, N.Y. City, Jose Vianna da Motta, Berlin, and Harold Bauer, Paris; unmarried. Teacher of piano, Adrian Sch. of Music, 1891-93; dir. music, Wilder (Minn.) Coll. (Episcopal), 1893-95; teacher piano, Atlanta, N.Y. City; same in Berlin, 1905-10; located at Los Angeles from 1911. Mem. exec. staff Nat. War Savings Com. for California (South), organizer and mgr. U.S. Govt. War Savings Concert Bur., World War I. State dir. publicity, Calif. Fed. Music Clubs, 1918-22, and founder, Feb. 1920, editor unitl 1922, Fedn. Official Bulletin. Aided Am. Com. for Devastated France, 1919. Waged successful campaign for the repeal of the Los Angeles Music Teachers' occupational tax, 1923. Audition chmn. Hollywood Bowl Summer Concerts, 1924; California del. and speaker at meeting of Music Teachers' Nat. Assn., Rochester, N.Y., 1926. Mem. Music Teachers' Nat. Assn., Music Teachers's Assn. of California (pres. 1926-27), Los Angeles County Music Teachers' Assn. (pres. 1924-25), Pro-Musica (charter mem. Los Angeles chapter), MacDowell Club of Allied Arts, Minn. Masonic Vet. Assn., Sigma Alpha Epsilon Fraternity and Los Angeles Alumni Assn. Same; founder mem. Hollywood Bowl Assn., Los Angeles Civic Grand Opera Assn., Pacific Geog. Soc.; charter mem. Los Angeles Bach Festival Foundation. Chmn. guarantor's com. for Los Angeles Oratorio Soc., 1927-29; mem. Federal Music Projects Advisory Bd. for Los Angeles, 1936-39, same Work Projects Adminstrn. for So. Calif., 1939-42. Republican. Episcopalain. Mason. (32°; K.C.C.H.; K.T., p.c.; Shriner). Clubs: Gamut (pres. 1928-29), Musicians Guild, Los Angeles Opera and Fine Arts (pres. 1930-31). Home: Los Angeles, Calif.†

DRABKIN, STELLA MOLLY FRIEDMAN (MRS. DAVID L. DRABKIN), artist, printmaker, mosaicist; b. N.Y.C.; d. Carlaman and Francesca (Seandel) Friedman; student N.A.D., N.Y.C., Graphic Sketch Club, Phila; m. David L. Drabkin, May 1, 1926. Exhibited in one man shows at Carlen Gallery, 1938, 39, Mus. N.M., 1947, Phila. Art Alliance, 1944, 50, Prints with Poems, 1969, Meml. Exhibit, 1972, Pa. Acad. Fine Arts, 1952, Print Club, Phila., 1960, Phila. Water Color Club, Phila. Art Alliance, 1965; exhibited in group shows at Phila. Acad. Fine Arts, Phila. Mus. Art, Met. Mus. Art, Chgo. Art Inst., Carnegie Inst., N.A.D., Nat. Gallery Art, Mus. San Francisco, City Art Mus. St. Louis, Japan Print Assn.; numerous others; represented in permanent collections at Pa. Acad. Fine Arts, Pa. Mus. Art, Nat. Gallery Art, Met. Mus. Art, Library of Congress, Rosenwald Collection, Tel Aviv Mus., Dagonia, Israel, Boston Library, Yale Library, N.J. State Mus.; permanent exhibit biblical mosaics and multitypes Phila. Free Library; designer UNICEF Calender, 1966. Recipient 1st prize for painting Gambel Competion, 1933, Am. Color Print Soc. prize, 1944, Katzman prize Print Club Phila., 1955, N.J. State Mus. Purchase prize, 1967. Mem. Phila. Art Alliance (past com. chmn., dir.), Soc. Am. Graphic Artists, Audubon Artists, Artists Equity Assn. (hon. dir.), Am. Color Print Soc. (v.p., Stella Drabkin meml. prize and medallion given in her honor), Phila. Water Color Club (dir.). Author: Prints With Poems, 1969. Home: Philadelphia Pa. Died Aug. 11, 1971.

DRAGSTEDT, LESTER REYNOLD, educator; b. Anaconda, Mont., Oct. 2, 1893; s. John A. and Caroline (Selene) D.; B.S., U. Chgo., 1915, M.S., 1916, Ph.D., 1920; M.D., Rush Med. Coll., 1921; Doctor honoris causa, U. Guadalajara, 1953, U. Lyon (France), 1950, U. Uppsala (Sweden), 1973; D.Sc., U. Fla., 1969; m. Gladys Shoesmith, 1922; children—Charlotte Gladys (Mrs. Thomas E. Jeffrey), Carol Maxine (Mrs. Robert N. Stauffer), Lester R. II, John. Instr. pharmacology State U. Ia., 1916-17, asst. prof. physiology, 1917-19; asst. prof. physiology U. Chgo., 1919-23; prof. physiology and pharmacology Northwestern U. Med. Sch., 1923-25; asso. prof. surgery U. Chgo., 1925-30, then Thomas D. Jones Distinguished Service prof., past chmn. dept., later prof. emeritus; research prof. surgery U. Fla., 1960, prof. physiology, 1968-75; hon. prof. surgery U. Guadalajara, 1953; attending surgeon, Billings Hosp., 1927-60; surgeon res. USPHS; pres. Chgo. Surg. Soc., 1944-45. Served to lt., M.C. U.S. Army, 1918-19. Decorated Royal Order of North Star (Sweden); recipient Distinguished Service award, gold medal A.M.A., 1963; Julius Friedenwald medal Am. Gastroenterol. Assn., 1964; gold medal Malmo Surg. Found., Sweden, 1st Distinguished award Alumni Assn. Rush Med. Coll., others. Fellow Royal Coll. Physicians and Surgeons of Can. (hon.), Internat. Coll. Surgeons (hon.), Royal Coll. Surgeons Eng. (hon.), Internat. Surg. Soc. (hon.); mem. Nat. Acad. Scis., A.C.S., Am. Gastroenterol. Assn., A.M.A. (gold medal, 1950; chmn. sect. on physiology and pathology 1960-61), A.C.P., Internat. Surg. Soc., Am. Physiol. Soc., Soc. for Exptl. Biology and Medicine, Nat. Soc. for Med. Research (pres.), Inst. Medicine Chgo., Am. Surg. Assn. (1st Distinguished Service award and gold medal 1970), Soc. for Clin. Surgery, Nat. Acad. Medicine Mexico, Gastroent. Assn. Mexico, Phi Beta Kappa, Sigma Xi, Phi Chi, Alpha Omega Alpha. Club: Quadrangle. Contbr. articles to sci. jours. Developed and introduced operations of vagotomy; discovered a hormore, lipocaic, also cause of duodenal and gastric ulcers. Home: Gainesville, Fla. Died July 16, 1975; buried Wabigama, Rapid City, Mich.

DRAIN, JESSE CYRUS, army officer, b. Braddock, Pa., Sept. 25, 1883; s. William Henry and Caroline (Eppert) D.; B.S., U.S. Mil. Acad., 1907; honor grad. Command and Gen. Staff Sch., 1922; grad. Staff Sch., Ft. Leavenworth, 1923, Army War Coll., 1926; m. Clara Hoey Sarratt, June 7, 1910; children—Jesse Cyrus, Ann Irvine. Commd. 2d lt. inf., U.S. Army, 1907, and advanced through the grades to brig. gen., Jan. 29, 1941; served in Cuba, China, Mexican Border and World War; instr. and dir. Inf. Sch., 4 years; instr. Command and Gen. Staff Sch., 1926-34; gen. staff, War Dept., 1 year; comd. 8th Inf., Ft. Screven, Ga., 2 years; comd. 31st Inf. and Post of Manila, P.I., 2 years.; comd. 81st Inf. Brig., 41st Div., and Mobile Force, Caribbean Dept., Panama; chmn. Field Sect. WDMB, Office C. of S. and mem. C. of S. group for survey of manpower, Mediterranean and European theaters. Decorated Victory medal and campaign badges for Cuban Pacification and Mexican Border, Am. Defense, Am. and European-African campaigns. Methodist. Mason. Clubs: Army and Navy, Army and Navy Country. (Washington), Army and Navy (Manila). Author: War Dept. pamphlets, Grenade Training Manual, Hand to Hand Fighting. Contbr. to mil. jours. Home: Braddock Pa. Died Jan. 12, 1974.

DRAKE, HELEN VIRGINIA FREDERICK, (Mrs. L. Rodman Drake), concert pianist; b. Terre Haute, Ind.; d. Guy W. and Viola (Wagman) Frederick; studied piano with Robert Schmitz, Alicia de Larrocha; m. L. Rodman Drake, June 4, 1938; children—Rodman L., Joan F. Concert pianist, Town Hall, N.Y.C., Washington, Hollywood, Montreal, Mexico City, Bogota, Lima, Caracas, Santiago, Montreal, Buenos Aires, Manila, Rio de Janeiro, Florence, Italy; toured countries of S.Am., 1966. Bd. dirs. Colorado Springs Symphony Orch. Decorated Medal of Bernardo O'Higgins 1st class (Chile). Mem. Fine Arts Center. Clubs: Broadmoor Golf (Colorado Springs); Cheyenne Mountain Country. Home: Colorado Springs, Colo., Died 1974.

DRAKE, J(AMES) FRANK, mfr.; b. Pittsfield, N.H., Sept. 1, 1880; s. Nathaniel Seavey and Mary A. R. (Green) D.; prep. edn., Kimball Union Acad., Meriden, N.H.; A.B., Dartmouth, 1902; Master Comml. Sci., Amos Tuck Sch., 1903, LL.D., 1952; married Mildred Chase, July 25, 1907 (dec. Aug. 1954); children—Ruth, Virginia, James Frank, Constance. Sec. Bd. of Trade, Springfield, Mass., 1903-08; sec. Phelps Pub. Co., Springfield, Mass., 1903-08; sec. Phelps Pub. Co., Springfield, 1908-14, treas. and dir., 1914-18; asst. to pres. Gulf Oil Corp., Pittsburgh, Pa., 1919-23; pres. Standard Steel Car Co. and subsidiary companies, 1923-30; chmn. bd. Pullman, Inc., 1930-31; prs. Gulf Oil Corporation, 1931-48, chairman bd., 1948-53, chmn. exec. com., 1953-55, past director; pres. dir. Standard Car Finance Corporatiom dir. Rockwell Manufacturing Company. Director Nat. Indsl. Conf. Board (chmn. 1945-47); mem. Petroleum Industry War Council, 1941-45; Common Council, Springfield, 1908-12, pres. 1910-12. Commd. maj. Ordnance Dept., U.S. Army, June 1918; served as comdg. officer finance div. Pittsburgh Dist.; lt. col. Mar. 25, 1919; hon. disch., June 3, 1919. Mem. Am. Philatelic Soc., S.A.R., Soc. Colonial Wars, Order of Founders and Patriots of America, Am. Legion, Military Order World War, American Society of the French Legion of Honor, Theta Delta Chi. Republican. Episcopalian. Clubs: University, Duquesne, Pittsburgh Golf, Fox Chapel Golf (Pittsburgh); Rolling Rock (Ligonier, Pa.); Cosmos (Washington); University (N.Y.C.). Home: Pittsburgh, Pa.†

DRAPANAS, THEODORE, educator, physician; b. Buffalo, Feb. 20, 1930; s. Thomas and Anastasia (Tsiros) D.; M.D., U. Buffalo, 1952; m. Arlene Ann Thrun, June 25, 1954; children—Carol Ann, Mark Thomas, Wendy. Intern, resident surgery E.J. Meyer Meml. Hosp., Buffalo, 1952-58; asst. prof. surgeryState U. N.Y., Buffalo, 1959-64; prof. surgery U. Pitts. Sch. Medicine, 1964-68; Henderson prof., chmn. dept. surgery Tulane U. Sch. Medicine, 1968-75; practice medicine, specializing in surgery, New Orleans, 1968-75; surgeon-in-chief Tulane div. Charity Hosp. of La. Mem. bd. examiners Am. Bd. Surgery; mem. com. on trauma Nat. Acad. Scis.-NRC, 1969; mem. surgery study sect. NIH, 1969-73; mem. adv. com. on trauma Surgeon Gen.'s Office, Dept. Army, 1970-75; mem. surgery adv. com. FDA, 1971. Served with M.C., U.S. Army, Res. Recipient Gold Key award as outstanding man of year Buffalo Jr. C. of C., 1961. Mem. A.C.S., Am., Central,

So. surg. assns., Soc. U. Surgeons (pres.), Soc. Clin. Surgery, Soc. Vascular Surgery, Am. Assn. Thoracic Surgery, Am. Assn. Surgery of Trauma, A.A.A.S., Internat. Soc. Surgery, James IV Assn. Surgeons, Assn. Am. Med. Colls. (rep.), Phi Beta Kappa. Editor: Surgery, 1971-75. Contbr. articles profl. jours. Home: New Orleans, LA. Died June 24, 1975.

DRAPER, WILLIAM HENRY, JR., investment banker, corp. exec., govt. ofcl.; b. N.Y.C., Aug. 10, 1894; s. William Henry and Mary Emma (Carey) D.; A.B., N.Y. U., 1916, M.A., 1917, LL.D. (hon.), 1949; LL.D., U. Louisville, 1948, Duke, 1950; m. Katharine Louise Baum, Sept. 7, 1918 (dec.); children—Dorothy H. (Mrs. Phillips Hawkins), Katharine L. (Mrs. George Haimbaugh), William Henry III; m. 2d, Eunice Barzynski, Mar. 12, 1949. With Nat. City Bank, N.Y.C., 1919-21; asst. treas. Bankers Trust Co., 1923-27; joined Dillon, Read & Co., investment bankers, N.Y.C., 1927, v.p. 1937-53; trustee L.I. R.R., 1950, chmn. L.I. Transit Authority, 1951; exec. officer, chmn. bd. Mexican Light & Power Co., 1954-59; partner firm Draper, Gaither & Anderson, 1959-67. Chmn. bd. Combustion Engring., Inc., 1960-64; dir. U.S. Leasing Corp. Mem. Pres.'s Adv. Com. Selective Service, Washington, 1940; mem. Joint Army and Navy Com. Welfare and Recreation, 1941; chmn. Pres.'s Com. on Fgn. Aid, 1958-59. Hon. chmn. Population Crisis Com.; spl. cons. Internat. Planned Parenthood Fedn.; U.S. rep. UN Population Commn., also spl. cons. UN Fund for Populations Activities, 1969-74. Mil. govt. adv. Sec. State, Moscow Conf. Fgn. Ministers, 1947; under sec. army, 1947-49; U.S. spl. rep. Europe with rank ambassador, also U.S. mem. NATO Coucil, 1952-53. Trustee The Kosciuszko Found. Served as maj. Infantry, U.S. Army, World War I; chief staff, 77th div. O.R.C., 1936-40; active duty inf. Gen. Staff, U.S. Army, Washington, 1940-41; comd. 136th Inf. Regt., 33d Inf. Div., 1942-44. P.T.O., 1943-44; in charge contract termination War Dept., 1944; chief econ. div. Control Council for Germany, 1945-46; econ. adv. to comdr. in chief EUCOM, 1947; now maj. gen. USAR. Decorated Legion of Merit, 1943 (Navy), 1945; Selective Service medal, 1946; D.S.M. (U.S.), 1948; Order of Orange Nassau (Netherlands), 1949; Medal for Freedom, (U.S.), 1953; Great Cross Order of Merit (Italy), 1954; Order Sacred Treasure 1st class (Japan), 1973. Mem. Council Fgn. Relations, Acad. Polit. Science, Am. Legion (co. comdr. 1932-34), Planned Parenthood Fedn. (vice chmn.), Soc. Am. Magicians. Psi Upsilon. Republican. Presbyn. Clubs: Downtown Athletic, Brook (N.Y.C.); Army and Navy, Metropolitan (Washington); Port Royal Beach (Naples, Fla.). Home: Naples Fla. Died Dec. 26, 1974.

DRAYER, CLARENCE EARL; b. Kenton, O., Nov. 18, 1880; s. George Wesley and Amanda Jemima (Potterf) D.; A.B., Western Reserve U., 1902; hon. D.Sc., Ohio Northern U., 1921; m. Edna Isabelle Lambert, of Cleveland, O., 1905; children—Jean L., Ruth L. Various engring. positions with Pa., R.I., U.P. and "Nichel Plate" rys., 1902-18; sec. Am. Assn. Engrs., and editor Professional Engineer, 1918-25; later vice president Bills Realty, Inc. Mem. Phi Gamma Delta, Sigma Tau, Phi Beta Kappa. Republican. Conglist. Mason. Author: (with F. H. Newell) Engineering as a Career, 1919; many mag. articles. Home: Wilmette, Ill.†

DREYER, RUSSELL PAUL, physician; b. Cleve., May 15, 1916; s. Paul Albert and Emma (Reichert) D.; M.D., Ohio State U., 1943; m. Janet Lee Foster, Mar. 20, 1943. Extern, Mercy Hosp., Columbus, O., 1954; intern Starling Livong Hosp., Columbus, 1942; intern St. Francis Hosp., Columbus, 1943, asst. resident in surgery, 1944, chief resident, 1944-45; resident, chief resident in obstetrics and gynecology St. Johns Hosp., Cleve., 1947-49, active staff, dir. obstetrics and gynecology, dir. med. edn., 1959-64; active staff Lakewood (O.) Hosp., dir. obstetrics and gynecology, 1971-72; courtesy staff Fairview Park Hosp. Leader, Scarlet Mask Band, jazz band. Served to capt., M.C., AUS, 1945-47. Diplomate Am. Bd. Obstetrics and Gynecology. Mem. A.M.A., Am. Coll. Obstetricians and Gynecologists, Nu Sigma Nu, Pi Kappa Alpha. Republican. Club: Westwood Country (Cleve.). Home: Cleveland, O. Died Mar. 19, 1974; buried Lakewood Park Cemetery, Lakewood O.

DREYFOUS, FELIX JULIUS, architect; b. New Orleans, Oct. 21, 1896; s. Felix J. and Julia (Seeman) D.; student Tulane U., 1914-15; B.S. in Architecture, U. Fa., 1917; m. F. Vera Scherck, Nov. 15, 1922 (dec. Aug. 1943); children—Carol (Mrs. Fred Eisenman, Jr.), Felix John III; m. 2d. Ruth Simon, June 28, 1947 (dec. July 1961); m. 3d, Rosetta Hirsh, Apr. 24, 1964 (dec. July 1971). Practiced architecture, La., Georgia, Texas, Fla., Miss., Ala., 1919-20; Partner Weiss, Dreyfous, 1920-23, Weiss, Dreyfous and Selferth, 1924-42, Weiss, Dreyfous and Selferth, 1945-52, Dreyfous and Selfeth, 1952-60, Dreyfous, Selferth and Gibert (all New Orleans); engaged in private practice, 1960-75; architect for Louisiana Capitol, Baton Rouge, Charity Hosp., La. State U. Med. Sch., Touro Infirmary, Jung Hotel, Fed. Land Bank, Clairborne Elementary Sch. and L.B. Landry High Sch. (all New Orleans), bldgs. for La. State U., La. Creamery, Inc. (both Baton Rouge). Mem. New Orleans Bd. Park Commrs., 1920-. Hon. mem. bd. adminstrs. Touro Infirmary, 1935-; mem. bd. adminstrs. Isaac Delgado Mus. Art, 1924-75, pres., 1964. Served with U.S. Army, 1918; from capt. to lt. col., E.E., AUS, 1942-46. Mem. A.I.A. (pres. La. 1937), Community Concert Assn. New Orleans. Home: New Orleans, La. Died Jan. 24, 1975.

DREYFUS, LOUIS GOETHE, JR., fgn. service officer; b. Santa Barbara, Cal., Nov. 23, 1889; s. Louis G. and Constance (Auerswald) D.; B.A., Yale, 1910, M.A., 1911; m. Grace Hawes, June 14, 1917. Apptd. consular asst., 1910; dep. consul gen., Berlin, Germany, 1911, v.p., dep. consul gen., 1914, vice consul, 1915; vice consul, Callao, Peru, 1912; consular agr., Quibdo, 1913; vice consul, Budapest, 1915; consul in charge, Sofia, 1916; consul assigned to Sivas, 1917, to Malaga, Spain, 1917, Paris, France, 1919, Palermo, Italy, 1920; consul, Dresden, Germany, 1921-24, consul gen., 1924; fgn. service insp. Dist. Western Europe, 1925-29; consul gen., Naples, Italy, 1929-31, Copenhagen, Denmark, 1931-33; counselor of Embassy, Lima, Peru, 1933-39; E.E. and M.P., Iran, 1939-44, Afghanistan, 1940-42, Iceland, 1944-46; spl. rep. of Pres. with rank of ambassador, ceremonies incident to inauguration 1st pres. Republic Iceland; E.E. and M.P. Sweden, 1946-47; acting chief Fgn. Service Inspection Corps, 1947-48; Am. ambassador to Afghanistan, 1949-50. Mem. Santa Barbara Com. on Fgn. Relations. Chmn. bd. Santa Barbara chpt. A.R.C., 1960, 61, bd. dirs.; bd. dirs. Iran-Am. Soc. of Washington, Santa Barbara Found. Mem. Union Interalliée (Paris), Montecito Protective Assn. Episcopalian. Clubs: Valley, Santa Barbara, Channel City (bd. dirs.). Home: Santa Barbara, Cal. Died May 1973.

DREYFUS-BARNEY, LAURA (MME. L. DREYFUS-BARNEY), lectr., con.; b. Cin. (Nov. 30, 1879; d. Albert Clifford and Laura Alice (Pike) Barney; ed. by pvt. tutors; m. Hippolyte Dreyfus (Cordozo), Apr. 1911. Served with Am. Ambulance at Lycée Pasteur as auxiliary night nurse, Paris, France, 1914-15; engaged in reeducation of mentally and physically handicapped, Mil. Hosp., Marseilles, France, 1915-16; A.R.C., del. Refugee and Repartriate Service for 3 depts. of Southern France, 1916-18; co-founder first children's hosp., L'Avenir des Enfants de Vaucluse, Avignon, France, 1918; formed under aegis League of Nations, Liaison com. major internat. orgns. to promote better understanding between peoples & Classes, 1925-47; apptd. by council of the League of Nations to consultative com. Organization of Intellectual Cooperation, 1926-39, active in establishment of Nat. Agrl. Center, Salon, France (nr. Marseilles), 1928; oragnized for Internat. Council of Women, under auspices Internat. Inst. Ednl. Cinematography of League of Nations, first congress of women specializing in study of motion pictures and their effect upon human relations, Rome, Italy, 1931; expert of Intnl. Inst. Edn. Cinematography of League Nations, 1931-37; elected mem. bd. of the congress, Rome, 1934; mem. com. of experts of League of Nations, dealing with internat. radio broadcasting problems and relationships between peoples, 1937-38; served on Com. Women's Internat. orgns. for control & reduction of Armaments as vice chmn., Geneva, 1931-46; mem. U.S. delegation 2d Am. Conf. Nat. Coms. of Intellectual Cooperation, Havana, Cuba, 1941; sponsor, mem. Inst. on World Orgn., Washington, D.C., 1941-61. Adv. chmn. and dir. of training information service War Hospitality Com., Washington, D.C., 1942-45; also rep. Nat. Council of Women on Coordinating Com. for Better Race Understanding, 1946; sr. liaison officer Internat. Council Women with UN and its specialized agencies; sometime accredited various internat. organizations from non-governmental orgns.; sometime chmn. study groups and orgns. of internat. assns. Founder Alice Pike Barney Meml. Trust Smithsonian Inst., 1951, for development of art in United States; honorary pres. Barney Neighborhood Settlement. Washington. Mem. Am. Soc. French Legion of Honor; officer French Legion of Honor. Author or co-author books, articles and monographs. Address: Washington, D.C.†

DRINKER, HENRY SANDWITH, lawyer; b. Phila., Pa., Sept. 15, 1880; s. Henry S. and Aimee Ernesta (Beaux) D.; student Haverford Sch., 1892-96; A.B., Haverford Coll., 1900, Harvard, 1901; student Harvard Law Sch., 1902-03; LL.B., U. of Pa., 1904, Mus. Doc., 1942; Litt.D., Oberlin College, 1944, Haverford College, 1949; married Sophie Lewis Hutchinson, May 16, 1911; children—Henry Sandwith, Cecilia, Ernesta, Pemberton H. Admitted to Pennsylvania bar, 1904, associated Dickson, McCouch & Glasgow, later Dickson, Beitler & McCouch; admitted to partnership, 1917; sr. mem. Drinker, Biddle & Reath, attorneys, Philadelphia, 1932. Associate trustee U. of Pa., Juilliard Sch. of Music; mgr. Phila. Savings Fund Soc.; v.p. Pa. Acad. Fine Arts (was interim pres. after resignation of J. F. Lewis, Jr.), Settlement Music Sch.; dir. Westminster Choir Coll., Acad. Natural Science (Phila.); chmn. Am. Bar Assn. Com. on Professional Ethics. Mem. Am. Philos. Soc., Phi Beta Kappa. Rep. Presbyterian. Clubs: Philadelphia (Phila.); entury (N.Y.); Wilderness (pres. 1946-48) Author vocal texts in English transl. of Brahms, 1945, Schumann, 1948, Hugo Wolf, 1949, M. Medtner, 1948, M. Moussorgsky, 1950; Fr. Schubert, 1951, H. Schutz, 1952; Legal Ethics, 1953. Home: Philadelphia, Pa.†

DRIPPS, ROBERT DUNNING, physician; b. Phila., June 19, 1911; s. Robert Dunning and Madge (Heron) D.; A.B., Princeton, 1932; M.D., U. Pa., 1936; m. Diana Rogers, Feb. 11, 1939; children—Robert Dunning III, Susan Adair. Intern U. Pa. Hosp., 1938; instr. pharmacology U. Pa. Sch, Medicine, 1938-40, asso., 1942-45, asso. prof. surgery (anesthesia), 1943-49, prof., chmn. dept. anesthesia, 1949-72; dir. anesthesia Hosp. of U. Pa., 1943-72; v.p. for health affairs U. Pa., 1971-73. Commonwealth Fund fellow in anesthesiology U. Wis., 1941; mem. med. teaching mission to Greece and Italy, 1948; civilian cons. Army Med. Service Grad. Sch., 1949; mem. surgery study sect. USPHS, 1951-56, mem. nat. adv. resources com., 1963-67; sr. instr. internat. course anesthesiology WHO, Denmark, 1952; sr. civilian cons. anesthesia Surgeon Gen. of Army, 1953-73; chmn. com. anesthesia NRC, 1954-62; civilian cons. anesthesia U.S. Naval Hosp., Phila.; mem. subcom. trauma Office Surgeon Gen., U.S. Army; mem. med. bd. Project HOPE, 1968-73; chmn. com. on anesthesia NIH, 1967-73, pharmacology research tng. grant com. USPHS. Dir. Narco Sci. Industries, Inc. Trustee Agnes Irwin Sch., 1961-64, Princeton U., 1967-71; pres. U. Pa. Senate, 1965. Recipient Distinguished Achievement award Modern Mechanics, 1973. Diplomate Am. Bd. Anesthesiology (dir. 1956-67). Fellow Royal Coll. Physicians (London), Royal Coll. Physicians (Ireland); mem. Am. Soc. Clin. Investigation, Am. Coll. Anesthesiologists, Am. Soc. Anesthesiologists (Distinguished Service award 1965), Am. Physiol. Soc., Pharmacology, A.M.A., Am. Surg. Assn., Assn. Am. Physicians, Pa. Soc. Anesthesiology (pres. 1950), Assn. U. Anesthetists (founders group pres. 1957), Halsted Soc. (pres. 1957), Phi Beta Kappa, Sigma XI, Alpha Omege Alpha. Republican. Presbyn. (elder 1971-73). Clubs: Philadelphia; Merion Cricket (Haverford; Phila.). Author: Physiological Basis for Oxygen Therapy, 1950; Introduction to Anesthesia, 1967. Mem. revision com. U.S. Pharmacopela, 1950-56; mem. editorial bd. Digest of Treatment, 1946-62, Jour. Pharmacology and Exptl. Therapeutics, 1953-57, Jour. Surg. Research, 1963-68, Rev. Surgery, 1964-73; nat. editorial bd. Modern Medicine, 1954-56; cons. editor Survey of Anesthesiology. Home: Haverford, Pa. Died Oct. 30, 1973.

DRISCOLL, ALFRED E., govt. ofcl.; b. Oct. 25, 1902; A.B., Williams Coll.; LL.B., Harvard; 19 hon. degrees; m. Antoinette Ware Tatem, 1932; 2 sons, 1 dau. Admitted N.J. bar, 1929; mem., partner Starr, Summerill, Lloyd, 1929-47; state senator, N.J., 1938-41; gov. of N.J., 1947-54; dir., mem. exec. com. Warner-Lambert Co., Inc., 1954-71, pres., 1954-67, chmn., 1967, hon. chmn. bd., dir., 1967-71; dir. Chem. Fund. Vice chmn. Pres.'s Commn. on Intergovtl. Relations, 1954-55; pres. Nat. Municipal League, 1963-67; chmn. N.J. Turnpike Authority, 1969-75; mem. N.J. Tax Policy Commn., 1969-75, N.J. Hist. Commn., 1971-75. Trustee Williams Coll., Samuel H. Kress Found., Fairleigh Dickinson U.; bd. dirs. Harvard Law Sch. Council, Friends of N.J. Pub. Broadcasting, N.J. Audubon Soc., N.J. Hist. Soc. Mem. S.A.R. Republican. Clubs: Taconic Country, Williams, Metropolitan. Home: Haddonfield, N.J. Died Mar. 9, 1975.

DRISCOLL, DONALD GOTZIAN, bus. exec.; b. St. Paul, Minn., Feb. 20, 1897; s. Arthur Brown and Helen Evelyn (Gotzian) D.; Ph.B., Yale, 1920; m. Elizabeth Hotchkiss Aull, Dec. 29, 1920; children—Robert Aull, David Aull. Purchasing dept. Sorg Paper Co., Middletown, O., 1920-33, sales dept. 1933-38, sec., 1927-38, exec. v.p., 1938-44, pres., 1944-65, 72-74, chmn., 1965-74. Served as gunnery sgt. Marine Corps Aviation, U.S. Army, 1918. Mem. Book and Snake Soc. (Yale). Republican. Episcopalian. Home: Sea Island Ga. Died Mar. 21, 1974.

DRIVER, GODFREY ROLLES, educator; b. Oxford, Eng., Aug. 20, 1892; s. Samuel Rolles and Mabel (Burr) D.; M.A., Winchester Coll., 1911; New Coll., Oxford, 1911-15; D.D. (hon.), U. Aberdeen, 1946, U. Manchester, 1956; D.Litt., U. Durham, 1948, Oxford; Litt.D., Cambridge U., 1964; m. Madeleine Mary Goulding, Dec. 18, 1924; children—Mary Madeleine, Susanna (Mrs. Hugh Charman) and Joanna (twins). Fellow Magdalen Coll., Oxford, Eng., 1919-62, hon. fellow, 1962-75; hon. Fellow New Coll., Oxford; prof. Semitic philology U. Oxford (Eng.), 1938, prof. emeritus, 1962-75, hon. fellow Sch. Oriental and African Studies, U. London, 1963-75. Vis. prof. U. Chgo., 1925, U. Louvain (Belgium), 1950; Grinfield lectr. Oxford U., 1935-39; Cadbury lectr. U. Birmingham (Eng.), 1958; Walker lectr. Queen's U., Belfast, Ireland, 1961. Joint editor New English Bible, Oxford and Cambridge U. Presses, 1947-70. Served with M.I., 1915-19, 40-42. Decorated Mil. Cross (Eng.); comdr. Order Brit. Empire; knight Bachelor, 1967. Fellow Brit. Acad. (Schweich lectr. 1944, Burkitt medal 1953, 59); mem. Soc. for Study of O.T. (pres. 1937), Soc. Hist. Theology (pres. 1950-51). Author: Nestorious, 1925; Letters of the First Babylonian Dynasty, 1925; Grammar of Colloquial Arabic, 1925; Assyrian Law, 1935; Hebrew Verbal System, 1936; Semitic Writing, 1945, 54, 73; Babyionian Laws, 2 vols., 1952-55; Canaanite Myths and Legends, 1955; Aramaic Documents, 1955; Judaean Scrolls, 1965. Home: Oxford, England. Died Apr. 22, 1975.

DRURY, PHILO WALKER, clergyman; b. Toledo, Ia., Jan. 16, 1876; s. Marion Richardson and Lucinda (Denny) D.; A.B., Western College (consol. with Coe College) 1897; A.B., Yale, 1898; B.D., United Theol. Sem., Dayton, O., 1901; D.D., Coe Coll., 1921; m. Julia Overholser, July 23, 1901; children—Helen (Mrs. Ralph Cole Knight), Marion, Josephine (Mrs. John L. Crawford). Ordained to ministry, U.B. Ch., 1901; missionary in P.R., 1901-06; supt. U.B. Mission, P.R., 1907-30; business mgr. P.R. Evangelico 1912-40 (editor 1912-15); exec. sec. Evang. Union, P.R., 1916-31; missionary service in Santo Domingo, 1920-21; rep. in P.R. of Com. on Cooperation in Latin America, 1916-38. Sec. Fed. Evang. Chs., P.R., 1905-15; treas. United Evang. Ch., P.R., 1930-40; mem. Panama Evang. Congress, 1916, gen. conf. U.B. Ch., 1913, 17, 29, 33, Hispania-Am. Congress, Havana, Cuba, 1929; exec. sec. Assn. of Evang. Chs. of Puerto Rico, 1934-36; supervisor of work of Foreign Mission Bd. of U.B. Ch., Puerto Rico, 1940-44, retired Mar. 31, 1944. Address: Santa Cruz, Cal.†

DRYER, JOSEPH EDWARD, mfr.; b. Bay City, Mich., Aug. 3, 1881; s. Albert A. and Fanny (Schroeder) D.; ed. schools of Mich., Iowa and Minn.; m. Helene Ruth Keefer, Aug. 16, 1915; children—Ruth Helene (Mrs. William R. Dick, Jr.), Sally (Mrs. Douglas Young, Jr.). Past pres. San Diego Council Navy League of U.S. Organized San Diego Industries, 1927. (now hon. mem.) and served as its 1st pres.; mem. San Diego C. of C. (pres. 1932); dir. and v.p., Calif.-Pacific Internat. Expn., San Diego, 1934-36; past pres. Better Business Bur., San Deigo Advt. Club. Founder, 1936. hon. pres. San Diego Heavon on Earth Club (to promote civic development and advertise San Diego's year-round climate). Past pres. San Diego Convention and Tourist Bur. and San Diego Co. Development Fedn. Honorary life member Hotel Greeters of America. Mason (32°), life mem. Shriner), Elk (life), Sciots (life), Fraternal Order of Eagles (life). Clubs: San Diego (life mem.), San Diego Press (hon. life mem.), Lions (hon. life mem.), Cuyamaca (San Diego). Active in civic affairs as writer, speaker, etc. Pub. community lit., songs, etc. Creator weekly community radio program, from 1936. Home: San Diego, Cal.†

DUBOSE, MARION, univ. prof.; b. Warrenton, Ga., March 19, 1878; s. Charles S. and Louise D. (Wellborn) DuB.; A.B., U. of Ga., 1897; A.M., Princeton, 1900; student, Freiburg, Germany, 1910; m. Lalage Darwin, Nov. 4, 1914; 1 son, Marion Derrelle. With Germanic langs. dept., U. of Ga., 1902-17; dir. of edn., Camp Gordon, Ga., under auspices of Y.M.C.A., 1917-18; with Fed. Bd. for Vocational Edn., 1918-20; successively teacher and pres., N. Ga. Agrl. Coll., 1920-23; prof. German. U. of Ga. from 1925 (on leave 1930-31). Mem. Kappa Alpha, Phi Beta Kappa, Sphinx. Democrat. Baptist. Author: Deutsch, 1931. Home: Athens, GA.†

DUCKWORTH, ROY DEMAREST, radiologist; b. N.Y.C., 1899; M.D.; m. Beatrix Gibson, May 22, 1914; 1 son, Roy Demarest. Dir. radiology emeritus White Plains (N.Y.) Hosp.; cons. radiology Westchester div. N.Y. Hosp., Phelps Meml. Hosp.; hon. staff radiology Grasslands Hosp. Diplomate Am. Bd. Radiology. Fellow Am. Coll. Radiology; mem. Radiol. Soc. N.Am., Am. Roentgen Ray Soc. Home: White Plains, N.Y., Deceased.

DUDA, HERBERT WILHELM, author, orientalist; b. Linz, Austria, Jan. 18, 1900; s. Johann and Paula (Binder) D.; student univs. Prague, Vienna, Leipzig, Paris, Berlin; Ph.D., U. Leipzig, 1925; diplome, Ecole Nat. des Langues Orientales Vivantes, Paris, 1926; m. Felicia Lerm, Aug. 30, 1935; children—Dorothea, Sibylle. Lectr., U. Leipzig, 1932; asso. prof. U. Breslau, 1936; vis. prof. State U. Sofia (Bulgaria), 1941-43; prof. U. Vienna, 1943-70, dir. Oriental Inst., 1946-70, dean Philosophy Faculty, 1947-49. Decorated Austrian Great Silver Honour Sign; Austrian Honour Cross of Litteris et Artibus 1st class; comdr. Royal Bulgarian Order Civil Merits; comdr. Imperial Iranian Order Humayun; Golden medal Honour Fed. Capital Vienna. Mem. Austrian Acad., German Archeol. Inst., Türk Dil Kurumu (Ankara), German Orient Soc. (hon.). Author: Ahmed Haschim, Ein turk. Dichter der Gegenwart, 1929; Die Sprache der Qyrg Vezir-Erzahlungen, 1930; Ferhad und Schirin, Die literar. Geschichte eines persischen Sagenstoffes, 1933, Vom Kalifat zur Republik, Die Turkei im 19.u.20.Jh, 1948; Balkantürkische Studien, 1949; Die Seltschukengeschichte des Ibn Bibi, 1959. Home: Vienna, Austria. Died Feb. 16, 1975.

DUDLEY, CARL WARD, motion picture producer; b. Little Rock, Ark., Dec. 31, 1910; s. Arthur Ward and Nettie (Wilson) D.; student Grinell Coll., 1928-29; A.B., U. Cal. at Los Angeles, 1935; m. Eleanor Murphy, Aug. 17, 1939; children—Carol, Eleanor, Deborah, Diana, Jennifer, Barbara. Writer, Cinesound Studio Pty. Ltd., Sydney, Australia, 1936, Metro-Goldwyn-Mayer, Culver City, Cal., 1937-42; writer, producer Warner Bros., Burbank, Cal., 1943-44; pres. Dudley Pictures Corp., Beverly Hills, Cal., 1944-63; pres. Dudley Prodns. Ltd., Beverly Hills, 1965-74, Travel 8, Inc., 1965-74, pres. Leisure World Enterprises, Ltd. Mem. Pacific Area Travel Assn., Explorers Club, Sigma Alpha Epsilon. Home: Beverly Hills, Cal. Died Sept. 2, 1973; buried Ivy Lawn Cemetery, Ventura, Cal.

DUDLEY, HENRY H(OLDEN), assn. exec.; b. Helena, Mont., Feb. 1, 1891; s. John Wesley and Minnie (Clark) D.; ed. Armour Tech. Inst., Chicago, 1910-11; m. Helen L. Weeks, Feb. 7, 1923. With Western Union Telegraph Co., 1912-17 and 1920; partner, constrn. bus., 1921-23; field rep. Am. Red Cross, 1924; with Am. Legion since 1925, adj. Omaha Post, 1925-29, dept. adj., Neb., 1930-36, nat. field rep., 1937-40, dir. defense div., 1941-43, asst. nat. adj., 1943-48, nat. adj. 1948-57, ret., 1957. Served as 1st lt., C.W.S. World War 1; capt., inf., World War II; on loan from Am. Legion to Office of Civilian Defense, 1941-43. Mem. Indianapolis C. of C. Republican. Roman Catholic. Clubs: Columbia, Service (Indianapolis). Home: Indianapolis, Ind. Died 1974.

DUFFELL, WILLIAM R(AYMOND), pub. accountant; b. Phila., Sept. 18, 1898; s. John Harvey and Mary E. (Wilson) D.; student U. Pa., 1924. Asst. treas. Fidelity-Phila. Trust Co., 1924-53; pvt. practice Duffell, C.P.A., Phila., 1953-73; sec. Sovereign Investors, Inc., Phila. Mem. exec. bd. Phila. council Boy Scouts Am., also mem. Nat. council, hon. mem. exec. bd. Minsi Trails council; bd. dirs., treas., chmn. personnel com. Pearl S. Buck Found.; trustee Chapel of Four Chaplains, Pop Warner Little Scholars; patron Am. Humanics Found.; mem. medallion club Douglas MacArthur Found.; mem. com. 1000, Freedoms Found. at Valley Forge; treas., bd. govs. Invest-in-Am. Nat. Council, Inc. Recipient Silver Beaver award Boy Scouts Am., 1963, C.P.A., Pa. Mem. Nat. Assn. Cost Accountants, Am. Accounting Assn., Nat. Assn. Accountants, Pa. Soc., Pa. (exec. com. Pa. 1955-57), Am. insts. C.P.A.'s, A.I.M. (asso.), Am. Mgmt. Assn., Tax Inst. Am., Internat. Platform Assn. Mason (Shriner, K.T.). Clubs: Union League, Anglers (Phila.); Forest Lake; Penn; Confrerie de la Chaine des Rotisseurs; Skytop. Home: Merion Station Pa. Died Sept. 20, 1973.

DUFFEY, GEORGE WALLACE, physician; b. Ritchie County, W. Va., Mar. 17, 1912; s. Charles and Hester Delia (Ankrom) D.; B.S., Akron U.; M.D., Ohio State U.; m. Marilyn M. Schlaffer, Sept. 28, 1946; children—Jeff, Pam (Mlrs. Louis Brunyansky), C. Suzzanne (Mrs. Harry Skinner), David, Maureen, Terrence, Amy. Intern, Akron City Hosp.; attending chief dept. family practice; practice medicine specializing in family practice; instr. medicine Ohio State U. Coll. Medicine. Active Boy Scouts Am. Served with AUS. Family Practice Center of Akron dedicated to his memory, 1971. Diplomate Am. Bd. Family Practice. Mem. Phi Beta Kappa, Phi Chi. Mason (32°). Home: Cuyahoga Falls, O. Died Mar. 2, 1971; buried Chestnut Hill Cemetery, Cuyahoga Falls, O.

DUFFIELD, EUGENE SCHULTE, publishing exec.; b. Denver, July 10, 1908; s. Carroll Hogue and Mary Josephine (Schulte) D.; A.B., U. Wis., 1929, A.M., 1931. Asst. to dean, U. Wis., 1929-30, instr. in history, 1930-31; reporter U.S. Daily, 1931-33; with Washington bur. Chgo. Tribune, 1933-35; with Washington bur. Wall Street Jour., 1935-38, 40-42, chief of bur., 1941-42; asst. to sec. of treasury, 1938-39; asst. to under sec. of Navy, 1942-44; asst. to sec. of Navy, 1944-46; officer and dir. McGraw-Hill Pub. Co., 1946-50; asst. pub. Cin. Enquirer, 1950-56; v.p. Federated Dept. Stores, Inc., 1956-59; pres. Popular Sci. Pub. Co., 1959-73, then dir.; chmn. Select Mags., Inc., 1964-66. Mem. Mag. Pubs. Assn. (chmn. 1970-72), Phi Beta Kappa, Sigma Delta Chi, Chi Phi. Clubs: Pinnacle, University, Dutch Treat (N.Y.C.). Collaborated in editing The Forrestal Diaries. Home: Saratoga Springs, N.Y. Died Sept. 20, 1974.

DUFFY, JAMES PATRICK BERNARD, congressman, judge; b. Rochester, N.Y., Nov. 25, 1878; s. Walter Bernard and Teresa Helen (O'Dea) D.; A.B., Georgetown, 1901; LL.B., Harvard, 1904; unmarried. Clk. law office Foote, Perkins & Havens, Rochester, 1904, Perkins & Havens, 1905-07, Perkins, Duffy & McLean, 1907-12, Duffy & McLean, Duffy & Kaelber, 1918-37, and from 1938; trustee Rochester Savings Bank; mem. 74th Congress (1935-37), 38th N.Y. Dist.; justice New York State Supreme Court, 1937. Chairman State Appeal Bd. No. 22, 1940-44; coordinator, 3 panels of Appeal Bd. No. 22; Washington liaison officer U.S.O., 1941-44. Mem. School Bd., Rochester, 1905-32 (resigned); director Rochester Home Unit, American Red Cross, World War I; director Rochester Chapter American Red Cross, Rochester Community Chest; trustee Rochester C. of C., St. Patrick's Church Soc. Mem. Am., N.Y. State and Rochester bar assns., Georgetown U., Alumni Soc., Harvard U. Alumni Soc. Democrat. Knights of Columbus (Council 178). Pontifical decorations; Knight of the Order of St. Gregory the Great, Knight of Malta (Am. chapter). Clubs: Harvard, Georgetown Univ., Rochester Automobile (past president and dir. Roch. Automobile Club), Humdrum and Kent (all of Rochester); Harvard Varsity (Cambridge, Mass.); Harvard (New York), University (Washington, D.C.). Home: Rochester, N.Y.†

DUFFY, PHILLIP B., paper co. exec.; b. Pitts., Jan. 1, 1909; s. Phillip B. and Helen (Crowley) D.; m. Marjorie Krons, June 2, 1951; children—Pebble, Shawn, Pamela. Formerly with F. J. Kress Box Co.; sr. v.p. St. Regis Paper Co., 1967-72. Home: Fox Chapel Manor Pa. Died June 23, 1973.

DUGGAN, SHERMAN, lawyer; b. Honey Creek, Ia., Feb. 19, 1879; s. John Henry and Ellen (Carey) D.; student S. Dak. Agrl. Coll., 1900-05; LL.B., U. of S. Dak., 1906; m. Iva McKennett, of Webster, S. Dak., Oct. 21, 1915. Began practice at Waubay, S. Dak., 1907; county judge, Day Co., S. Dak., 1909-13; became U.S. atty., Dist. of Alaska, Aug. 21, 1921; dir. First Nat. Bank, Anchorage, Alaska. Republican. Christian Scientist. K.P., Elk. Home: Valdez, Alaska.†

DUKE, WILLIAM MARK, clergyman; b. Saint John, N.B., Can., Oct. 7, 1879; ed. Cath. schs., Saint John; A.B., St. Joseph's U., Memramcook, N.B., 1902, M.A., 1928; D.S.T., Grand Seminary, Quebec, 1928. Ordained priest Roman Cath. Ch., 1905; consecrated archbishop, 1928; asst. in parishes of Diocese of St. John, including Moncton, Chediac, Buctouche, and Cathedral of St. John; apptd. rector Cathedral of Immaculate Conception, St. John, 1913-17, parish priest of Cathedral Parish, 1927-28; titular archbishop of Fasis and coadjutor archbishop of Vancouver, 1928-31, archbishop See of Vancouver from 1931. Home: Vancouver, B.C.†

DULL, FLOYD NORMAN, business exec.; b. Toledo, Dec. 17, 1883; s. Norman R. and Elva F. (Brailey) D.; student pub. schools, Toledo; m. Daisy Myrtle Gordon, Feb. 23, 1904; children—James G., Helen Esther (Mrs. Franklin A. Seward), Lola Myrtle (Mrs. Charles P. Woods), Virginia Marie (Mrs. Malcolm Poignand), Floyd Norman, Office boy, later ckerk Kirk Mfg. Co., Toledo, 1894-1900; clerical work Home Telephone Co., 1900-07, sec., later purchasing agent, Detroit, Mich., 1907-12; special agent, Detroit and Cleveland, later asst. mgr., mgr. Travelers Insurance Co., New York City, 1912-22; resident v.p. Commercial Casualty Co., 1922-30; became v.p. Eastern dept. N.Y. City Continental Casualty Co., Chicago, Ill., 1930; dir. and mem. exec. com. N.Y. Board of Trade (past pres.); became v.p. Best Bldg. Co., New York City, 1932; pres. Preferred Accident Insurance Co. of N.Y., 1947-51; rep. Orvis Bros. & Co. investments, 1951. Director Greater New York Safety Council. Member Ins. Fedn. N.Y., N.Y. State Chamber of Commerce, Insurance Soc. of N.Y. Republican. Mason. Elk. Clubs: Bankers, Drug and Chemical (N.Y. City), Home: Rutherford N.J. Died Mar. 1957; buried Hillside, N.J.

DUMONT, PAUL EMILE, prof. Sanskrit and Indology; b. Brussels, Aug. 27, 1879; s. Constant and Hermine (De Vos) D.; student U. of Brussels, 1897-99; Ph.D., U. of Bologna, 1903; m. Marie Marguerite Howard, Dec. 27, 1937. Charge de cours, U. of Brussels, 1924-29; vis. lectr. in Indology, Johns Hopkins, 1929, research prof. Sanskrit and Indology, from 1931. Mem. Am. Oriental Soc., Linguistic Soc. America, Société Belge des Etudes orientales, Provincial Utrechtsch Genootschap van Kunsten en Wetenschappen. Decorated Chevalier Order of Leopold (Belgium). Author books including: The Horse-Sacrifice in the Taittiriya-Brahmana, 1948; The Special Kinds of Agnicayana in the Taittiriya-Brahmana, 1951. Home: Baltimore, Md.†

DUNBAR, SAIDIE ORR (MRS.), club woman; b. Granger, Mo., June 23, 1880; d. Robert Perry and Katharine Isora (Lindsey) Orr; ed. Portland (Ore.) U., hon. L.H.D., Linfield Coll., McMinnville, Ore., 1937; m. Jesse Austin Dunbar, Sept. 7, 1905 (died Jan. 1, 1928); children—Kathryn (Mrs. William D. Winter), Allen. Began as teacher Portland Pub. Schs.; exec. sec. Ore. Tuberculosis Assn. from 1915; lecturer in community orgn., U. of Ore. Extension; pres. Gen. Fed. Women's Clubs, 1938-41. Life mem. Nat. Orgn. for Pub. Health Nursing; mem. nat. sponsoring com. of Nat. Com. for Mental Hygiene; mem. nat. citizens' com. White House Conf. on Children in a Democracy; mem. adv. com. Allied Youth, Inc.; mem. women's adv. com., War Manpower Commn., com. for study of voluntary health agencies, Nat. Health Council, adv. com., Social Work Publicity Council, Inc. Asso. adminstr. Ore. War Savings Staff (dir. Women's Div.); dir. Ore. Mobilization of Women. Mem. N.E.A., D.A.R., P.E.O., League of Women Voters, Am. Assn. Social Workers, Am. Pub. Health Assn. (fellow). Alpha Kappa Delta. Republican. Presbyterian. Clubs: Portland Woman's (Portland, Ore.), Town. Home: Portland, Ore.†

DUNCAN, ALEXANDER EDWARD, comml. banker; b. nr. Louisville, May 27, 1878; s. John Thomas and Ida (Smith) D.; ed. Louisville Male High Sch.; m. Flora Ross, Apr. 11, 1900 (died June 20, 1936); 1 dau. Elizabeth Duncan Yaggy; m. 2d. Mrs. E. Everett Gibbs (Anne Ranson), Mar. 16, 1940. Began as bank clk. at Louisville, 1896; clerk Jungbluth & Rauterberg, Louisville, 1897-99; mem. Ross & Duncan, Crestwood, Ky., 1900-02; spl. and gen. agt. Ocean Accident & Guaranty Corp., Cincinnati, 1903-06; gen. agent at Baltimore for Am. Credit-Indemnity Co., 1907-09; organized, 1909, and pres., dir. until 1912, Manufacturers' Finance Co., Balt., Md. Organized, 1912, and pres., dir. Comml. Credit Co., Balt., chmn. bd., 1916-54, founder chairman, 1954-64, ret. member. Robert Garrett & Sons, investments, 18 mos., 1916-17; reorganized Humpherys Mfg. Co., Mansfield O., 1917, merged 1956 into and dir. Borg Warner Co., Mansfield, O., 1917, merged 1956 into and dir. Borg Warner Corp., Chicago; director Am. Credit Indemnity Co. N.Y., Mercantile Safe Deposit & Trust Co. (both Baltimore, Md.). Gen. chmn. YMCA War Work campaign (Baltimore), 1917, and for United War Work campaign, 1918; pres. Community Fund of Baltimore, 1929-31; gen. chmn. Balt. Red Cross War Fund, 1943. Adv. bd. Women's Hosp., Children's Hosp., Inc., Keswich-Home for Incurables. Republican. Episcopalian. Clubs: Bachelors Cotillon, Maryland. Eldridge. Merchants. Center (Balt.). Home: Baltimore, Md.†

DUNCAN, EDWIN, banker, state senator; b. Sparta, N.C., June 25, 1905; s. David C. and Della L. (Woodruff) D.; A.B., U. N.C., 1925; m. Katherine R. Reeves, Aug. 31, 1926 (div. 1934); 1 son, Edwin; m. 2d, Bessie L. Wellborn, June 29, 1935; children—Jane C., David C. (dec.). Cashier Bank of Sparta, 1926-37; exec. v.p. Northwestern Bank, North Wilkesboro, N.C., 1937-58, pres., 1958-70; pres., dir. Northwestern Financial Corp., 1970-73; sec.-treas. Northwestern Finance Co., North Wilkesboro, 1940-73; chmn. bd. Lowe's Cos., Inc., 1963-73; partner Wythe Finance Co., Wytheville, Va., 1949-70; pres. Allegheny Devel. Corp., Sparta, N.C., 1953-73; dir. Brad Ragan Enterprises, Floyd Pike Electric Co., Northwestern Financial Investors, Holly Farms Poultry Industries, Wilkesboro; mem. N.C. Senate, 1953-55, 58-60. Mem. N.C. Banking Commn. Chmn. Northwestern Devel. Corp., Industrial Com. N.C. Mem. election com. 9th Dist. N.C. Chmn. finance com. Allegheny County Dist. N.C. Chmn. finance com. Allegheny County Hosp. Mem. Cattle and Dairy Assn. Am. Democrat. Clubs: Roaring Gap (N.C.), Twin City (Winston-Salem, N.C.). Home: Sparta N.C. Died Oct. 7, 1973.

DUNCAN, RICHARD M., judge; b. Nov. 10, 1889; s. Richard F. and Margaret (Meloan) D.; student Christian Brothers Coll., St. Joseph, Mo., 1907-09; m. Glanna Davenport, June 4, 1913; 1 son, Richard D. Deputy circuit court clerk, 1911-17; admitted to practice of law, 1916; city counselor, St. Joseph, 1926-30; mem. 73d Congress (1933-35), Mo. at large, 74th to 77th Congresses (1935-43), 3d Mo. Dist.; appointed judge of U.S. Dist. Court for Eastern and Western Dists. Mo., 1943, ret., 1965, attained sr. status. Mem. Bench and Robe (hon.), Phi Delta Phi (hon.). Presbyn. Home: Kansas City, Mo. Died Aug. 1, 1974; buried Meml. Park Cemetery, St. Joseph, Mo.

DUNHAM, CHARLES LITTLE, physician; b. Evanston, Ill., Dec. 28, 1906; s. William Huse and Margeret (Little) D.; B.A., Yale, 1929; M.D., U. Chgo. (Rush), 1934; m. Lucia Elizabeth Jordan, June 22, 1932; children—George Stuart, Carol Jordan, Sara Gale. Intern internal medicine U. Chgo. Clinics, 1933-34; asst. resident medicine New Haven Hosp., 1934-35; asst., sch. medicine, U. Chgo., 1936-42, instr., 1942-46, asst. prof. medicine, 1946-49; asst. chief med. br. AEC, 1949-50, chief med. br., div. biology and medicine, 1950-54, dep. dir. div., 1954, dir., 1955-67; chmn. div. med. scis. Nat. Acad. Scis.-NRC, Washington, 1967-72. Mem. Nat. Council on Radiation Protection, 1965-73, WHO Expert Adv. Panel on Radiation; primate research adv. com. NIH, 1971-75; vis. com. med. dept. Brookhaven Nat. Lab., 1969-73. Served as capt. M.C., U.S. Army, 1943-46. Recipient U.S. AEC Distinguished Service award, 1957. Mem. Soc. Nuclear Medicine, A.M.A., N.Y. Acad. Sci., Am. Nuclear Soc., Health Physics Soc., Radiol. Soc. N. Am., Am. Rheumatism Assn., A.A.A.S., Radiation Research Soc. (pres. 1969-70), Acad. Medicine Washington, Inst. Medicine Chgo., Sigma Xi, Nu Sigma Nu, Delta Kappa Epsilon. Clubs: Cosmos, Internat. (Washington); Elizabethan (Yale U.). Home: Washington, D.C., Died Dec. 7, 1975.

DUNHAM, HOWARD POTTER, ins. exec.; b. Bennington, Vt., Aug. 14, 1878; s. Isaac Watson and Martha A. (Lindley) D.; A.B., Union Coll., Schenectady, N.Y., 1900, L.H.D., 1940; m. Jane Johnson Robbins, Oct. 22, 1907. Chief office dep. Dept. Internal Revenue, Hartford, Conn., 1920-22; state commr. ins., Conn., 1923-35; v.p., trustee Am. Surety Company, New York City, from 1935; chairman of the advisory board of Wethersfield br. Conn. Bank & Trust Co. Mem. Conn. Legislature, 1919-21. Mem. Assn. Supts. Ins. of Can. (hon.), Vt. Assn. Ins. Agts., Assn. Casualty and Surety Execs., Wethersfield Hist. Soc. (pres.), Am. Trails Assn., S.A.R., C. of C. N.Y. (exec. com.), Commerce and Industry Assn. N.Y., Underwriters Golf Assn., Saints and Sinners, Pi Phi, Delta Phi. Conglist. Mason, Odd Fellow Clubs: Hartford Golf. University, Conn. Field (Hartford, Conn.) Beach; Aetna Life (hon.). Compiler: The Business of Insurance (3 vols), 1913. Home: Wetnersfield, Conn.†

DUNLAP, ARTHUR RAY, educator; b. Sydney Mines, N.S., Can., June 24, 1906; s. Frank Burns and Flora Laleah (Whitman) D.; came to U.S., 1927, naturalized, 1939; B.A., Acadia U. (Can.), 1926; M.A., Harvard, 1928; Ph.D. (Univ. fellow), Yale, 1934; m. Elinore Gertrude Morey, Sept. 2, 1936; 1 dau., Laura Ellen (dec. 1972). Mem. faculty U. Del., Newark, 1928-31, 35-71, prof. English, 1951-71, chmn. dept., 1958-61. Dir. Nat. Def. Edn. Act. Inst., U. Del., 1966-67. Mem. Am. Assn. U. Profs., Am. Dialect Soc., Archeol. Soc. Del., Am. Name Soc. (bd. mgrs. 1970-72), Modern Lang. Soc., Phi Kappa Phi. Author: (with C.A. Weslager) Indian Place-names in Delaware, 1950; (with Weslager) Dutch Explorers in the Delaware Valley, 1961; Dutch and Swedish Place-names in Delaware, 1956. Editor Del. Folklore Bull., 1951-74; adv. bd. Am. Speech, 1947-48, 56-57. Home: Newark, Del. Died Aug. 2, 1974; buried Old St. Anne's Cemetery, Middletown, Del.

DUNLAP, FREDERICK, forester; b. Ross County, O., June 17, 1881; s. Philip Marion and Mary E. (Lutz) D.; student Ohio State U., 1899-1901; F.E., Cornell U., 1904; student George Washington U., 1907-09, U. of Wis., 1909-10; m. Florence Hallowell, Oct. 20, 1906; children—Nathan Hallowell (dec.), Lawrence Hallowell, Marion (Mrs. Edward Rochie Hardy, Jr.), Richard Morris. In employ as timber estimator, Cape Breton Island, Can., 1904, with U.S. Forest Service, 1904-13, successively as forest asst., forest examiner and physicist in Forest Products Lab.; lecturer in forestry, U. of Wis., 1910-13; prof. forestry, U. of Mo., 1913-21; prof. Univ. Internat. of Brussels, 1921-25; cons. forester, 1921-25; editor "Conservation Advocate," 1924-25; state forester, State of Mo., 1925-33; extension forester in Mo. Agrl. Extension Service, 1925-27; cons. forester Springfield City Water Co. and others, 1933-35; in charge management Ottawa Nat. Forest, 1935-37, writing the first option prescribing selective logging practices for govt. purchase of residual stands of growing timber; mem. first bd. of editors, Forestry Quarterly, 1902-16. Scoutmaster Boy Scouts of America, Madison, Wis., 1911-13; charter member Scout Council, Columbia, Mo. (3 times pres.). Listing officer 20th Engrs. (Forest), 1917-18; in charge Govt. black walnut survey West of Mississippi River, 1918; sec. Mo. Wood Fuel Com. of U.S. Fuel Adminstration, 1918. Fellow A.A.A.S., Royal Soc. Arts; sr. mem. Soc. Am. Foresters; mem. Am. Forestry Assn., Central States Forestry League, Nat. Assn. of State Foresters (1925-33), Mo. Corn Growers Assn. (1929-35), Farm Bur. (v.p. 1931-35), Midwest Wool Growers Assn., Pereheron Horse Assn. (breeder), Biol. Soc. Wash., Sigma Xi, Gamma Sigma Delta. Del. U. of Mo. to Nat. Conservation Congress, 1913; del. from Mo. to first four Southern Forestry Congresses, 1916-22. Charter mem. reorganized Southern Forestry Congress, 1923, charger mem. Missouri Assn., 1923; organized, 1921, and sec. Mo. Forestry Assn.; an organizer, Central States Forestry Congress, 1930, and mem. bd. dirs. same. Mem. Central States Forest Research Council, 1929-32; mem. Columbia Park Bd. (pres. 1933-35); mem. City Planning Commn., Columbia. Mem. Bd. Religious Education, Diocese of Mo., 1921-25; an organizer, director and secretary-treasurer Guardian Rock Wool, Inc., of Columbia, 1939. Episcopalian. Club: Players (Columbia, Mo.). Orginated coöperative forest protection policy for Mo., in Ozark region. Purchased "Belleforest," 1928, and started there an aboretum and expts. in forestry. Contbr. to farm papers. Home: Columbia, Mo.†

DUNLAP, JOHN T., supt. schs.; b. Pueblo, Colo., Dec. 25, 1903; s. Theodore A. and Mabel (Winters) D.; B.S., Colo. A. and M. Coll., 1927, M.S., 1939; m. Mary Snider, May 19, 1929; 1 dau., Dorothy Ann. Tchr. high sch., Mead, Colo., 1927; prin., 1928; prin., Woodrow, Colo., 1929-30; tchr. Central High Sch., Pueblo, 1931-36, elementary prin., 1937-45, prin. Central High Sch., 1946-52; asst. supt. schs., Pueblo, 1953-56, supt. schs., 1956-69. Mem. Colo., Nat. edn. assns., Colo., Nat. assns. sch. adminstrs. Home: Pueblo, Colo. Died May 9, 1973; buried Mountain View Cemetery, Pueblo.

DUNLOP, WALTER SCOTT, clergyman; b. at Ayrshire, Scotland, Feb. 23, 1878; s. Walter and Margaret (Kennedy) D.; came to U.S., 1901, naturalized, 1920; A.B., Waynesburg (Pa.) Coll., 1908, D.D., 1929; B.D., Crozer Theol. Sem., Chester, Pa., 1911; studied U. of Pa., 1910-11; m. Elsie Rae Wolf, of Harrisburg, Pa., Aug. 19, 1908; children—Walter Scott, Bonnie St. Clair, Margaret Jean, Jack Grenfell. Ordained Bapt. ministry, 1911; pastor chs. in Pa., Washington, D.C., and W.Va. until 1929; pres. Alderson (W.Va.) Jr. Coll., 1929-32; pres. Alderson-Broaddus Coll., 1932-36; pastor North Baptist Ch., Camden, N.J., 1936-39; retired. V.p. Am. Bapt. Publication Soc.; mem. bd. W.Va. Bapt. State Conv. Republican. Mason. Home: Alderson, W.Va.†

DUNMIRE, GLENN DEWITT, surgeon; b. Duquesne, Pa., Oct. 14, 1893; M.D., U. Pitts., 1921. Intern, Western Pa. Hosp., Pitts., 1921-22; practiced medicine specializing in surgery, Pitts., 1922-71; surgeon emeritus Western Pa. Hosp. Diplomate Am. Bd. Surgery. Fellow A.C.S.; mem. A.M.A. Home: Pittsburhg Pa. Died Dec. 3, 1971; buried Homewood Cemetery, Pittsburgh, Pa.

DUNN, ALAN, writer, cartoonist; b. Belmar, N.J., Aug. 11, 1900; s. George Warren and Sarah Benton (Brown) D.; student Columbia, 1918-19, N.A.D., 1919-23, L. Fontainebleau (France) Ecole des Arts, summer 1923, L.C. Tiffany Found., Oyster Bay, L.I., summers 1921-28; hon. vis. fellow Am. Acad. in Rome, 1923-24; m. Mary Petty, Dec. 8, 1927. Staff contbr. New Yorker mag., 1926-74; editorial cartoonist Archtl. Record, 1936-74; paintings, cartoons exhibited nat., internat. exhbns.; works in permanent collections at various museums; comprehensive collections in Library of Congress, Alan Dunn Manuscript collection Syracuse U. Recipient Architecture Critic's citation A.I.A., 1973. Mem. Authors Guild, Phi Gamma Delta. Club: Century Assn. Author: Rejections, 1931: Who's Paying for this Cab?, 1945; The Last Lath., 1947; East of Fifth, 1948; Should It Gurgle? 1956; Is There Intelligent Life on Earth?, 1960; A Portfolio of Social Cartoons-1957-1968 by Alan Dunn, 1968; Architecture Observed, 1971. Office: New York City N.Y. Died May 20, 1974.

DUNN, LESLIE CLARENCE, geneticist; b. Buffalo, Nov. 2, 1893; s. Clarence Leslie and Mary Eliza (Booth) D.; B.Sc., Dartmouth Coll., 1915, D.Sc. (hon.), 1952; M.Sc. in Zoology, Harvard, 1917, D.Sc., 1920; m. Louise Porter, May 2, 1918; children—Robert Leslie, Stephen Porter. Asst. in zoology, Harvard, 1915-17, 19; geneticist Conn. (Storrs) Agrl. Expt. Sta., 1920-28, cons. genticist, 1930-74; prof. zoology, Columbia, 1928-62, emeritus prof., 1962-74, research asso. Nevis Biol. Sta., 1962-74; dir. Inst. Study Human Variation, 1952-58, exec. officer dept. zoology, 1940-46; vis. lectr. in biology Harvard, 1949-50; research asso. Galton Lab., Univ. Coll., London, 1960-61. Served as 1st lt. infantry, U.S. Army, 1917-19, World War; with A.E.F., 1918-19. Fellow Am. Acad. Arts and Scis.; mem. Am. Soc. Human Genetics (pres. 1961), Accademia Patavina, Fedn. Am. Scientists, Am. Soc. Zoologists (sec.-treas. genetics sect. 1925-28), Am. Soc. Naturalists (pres. 1960), Genetics Soc. Am. (pres. 1932), Norwegian Acad. Scis., Am. Philos. Soc., Nat. Acad. Sci., Phi Beta Kappa. Mem. editorial bd. Genetics 1935-62, also served as mng. editor. Editor: The Am. Naturalist, 1950-60, Genetics, 1936-41. Author: Principles of Genetics (with E.W. Sinnott), 1925, 32, 39, 51, 58; Heredity and Variation, 1932; Heredity, Race and Society (with T. Dobzhansky), 1946; Biology and Race, 1951; Genetics in the 20th Century, 1951; Heredity and Evolution in Human Populations, 1958; A Short History of Genetics, 1965. Home: New York City N.Y. Died Mar. 1974.

DUNN, R. ROY, utility exec; b. Cleve., 1901. Dir. Potomac Electric Power Co.; dir. Acacia Mut. Life Ins. Co., Riggs Nat. Bank of Washington. Home: Phoenix, Ariz. Died June 12, 1974.

DUNN, RAY A., army officer; b. N.Y., Oct. 26, 1892; grad. Air Corps Flying Sch., 1928, Army Indsl. Coll., 1929, Air Corps Tactical Sch., 1937, Babson Inst., 1933; rated comdr. pilot, combat observer, tech. observer, aircraft observer. Commd. 1st lt. Aviation Sect., 1917, advanced through grades to brig. gen., 1943; vice comdr. 14th Air Force, then insp. gen. Air Tng. Command, after World War II; ret. from army, then with J.D. Marsh & Assos., Washington. Died July 1974.

DUNNING, HARRISON F., paper co. exec.; b. West Hartford, Conn., Aug. 12, 1908; s. Stewart Northrop and Hazel (Case) D.; A.B., Dartmouth, 1930. M.A. (hon.), 1969; m. Kathleen Mulligan, Oct. 10, 1933; children—Harrison Case, Stephen Northrop, Kathleen Byron. Real estate broker, West Hartford, 1930-34; salesman and dist. mgr. Fuller Brush Co., Camden, N.J., 1934-35; with Scott Paper Co., 1935-71, exec. v.p., 1960-62, pres., 1962-68, chief exec. officer, 1966-71, chmn., 1969-71, dir., 1955-71, also dir. various fgn. affiliates; dir. Nat. Biscuit Co., Bell Telephone Co. Pa. Trustee Dartmouth Coll., 1968-74. Mem. Phi Delta Theta. Home: Moylan Pa. Died Aug. 31, 1974.

DUNNING, JOHN RAY, physicist; b. Shelby, Neb., Sept. 24, 1907; s. Albert Chester and Josephine (Thelen) D.; A.B., with highest honors, Neb. Wesleyan U., 1929, D.Sc., 1945; Ph.D., Columbia, 1934; LL.D., Adelphi Coll., 1951; D.Sc. in Edn., Coll. Puget Sound, 1957; Sc.D., Temple U., 1955; Sc.D., Whitman Coll., Trinity Coll., 1958, U. Jacksonville, 1965, Marquette U. 1967; LL.D., Phila. Coll. Osteopathy, 1961; m. Esther Laura Blevins, Aug. 28, 1930; children—John Ray, Ann Adele. Began as physicist-radio engr., 1927; with Columbia, 1929-75, asst. in physics, 1929-35, Univ. fellow, 1932-33, instr. physics, 1933-35, cutting traveling fellow Europe, 1935-36, asst. prof., 1935-38, asso. prof., 1938-46, prof., 1946-75, dean faculty engring. and applied sci., 1950-69, Lindsley prof. applied sci., 1969-75; dir. div. I, SAM Labs., 1942-45, dir. research Div. War Research, 1945-46, sci. dir. atomic energy Office Naval Research, 1946-75. Dir. Vitro Corp., Nuclear Energy Corp., Oak Ridge Inst. of Nuclear Studies. Pres. Inst. Applied Sci., 1969-75. Ofcl. investigator, OSRD, 1941-46; sci. adv. panel Dept. of Army; chmn. adv. commn. on sci. manpower N.Y.C. Bd. Edn., mem. congl. panel Impact of Peaceful Uses of Atomic Energy, 1955; mem. sci. adv. com. Dept. Def., 1954-75; adv. com. Nat. Urban League, 1958-75; chmn. nuclear program Empire State Atomic Devel. Assos.; chmn. N.Y. State Sci. Adv. Council to Legislature. Pres. Museum of Sci. and Tech., 1965-67. Bd. visitors U.S. Mil. Acad., West Point, 1953-75, chmn., 1954; dir. Fund for Peaceful Atomic Development, 1954-75, chmn., 1954; dir. Fund for Peaceful Atomic Development, 1954-75, chmn. N.Y.C. Adv. Council Sci. and Tech., 1965-75; pres. Hall Sci., N.Y.C., 1965-75; dir. City Investing Corp.; trustee Armstrong Meml. Research Found., Sci. Service. Mem. div. com. for math., phys. and engrings scis. NSF. 1958-75, adv. com. for instl. programs, 1961-75; mem. adv. council for advancement indsl. research and devel. N.Y. State, 1959-75; chmn. atomic power study Empire State

Utilities Power Resources Assn., 1960-75; chmn. Basic Sci. Found., Nuclear Energy Policy Bd.; adv. com. Thomas A. Edison Found.; adv. council Am. Student Found., 1962-75. Recipient Presdl. Citation, Medal for Merit, 1946; Stevens award, Stevens Inst. Tech., 1958; Pupin medal, 1959, Pegram medal, 1964, Grad. Faculties Alumni award Columbia, 1967; Outstanding Alumnus award Upsilon chpt. Phi Kappa Tau, 1967; AEC spl. recognition citation and award, 1971. Chmn. Mayor's Com. for Atomic Energy , N.Y. Golden Anniversary. Chmn., Am. Soc. M.E. and Nat. Research Council Com. on Nuclear Energy Glossary. Fellow Am. Phys. Soc., N.Y. Acad. Sci., A.A.A.S., (dir.), Am. Soc. M. E., Am. Nuclear Soc.; mem. Soc. History of Tech., Am. Assn. Physics Tchrs., Am. Inst. Mining and Metall. Engrs., Optical Soc. Am., Nat. Acad. Scis. (chmn. pres.'s com. super sonic transport), Am. Soc. for Engring. Edn., Mining and Metall. Soc. Am., Newcomen Soc., Sigma Xi (Nat. lectr., 1948), Sigma Pi Sigma, Phi Kappa Phi, Phi Kappa Tau, Tau Beta Pi. Clubs: Columbia University, Cosmos, Engineers, Men's Faculty, University, Key Biscayne Yacht. Author books including: Matter: Energy and Radiation (a text with H.C. Paxton), 1941. Contbr. to various publs. Pioneered (with colleagues) 1st neutron expts. in U.S., from 1932; conducted research in plasma physics applying to coal. Home: Sherman, Conn. Died Aug. 25, 1975; interred Sherman North Cemetery, Sherman, Conn.

DUNNINGER, JOSEPH, conjurer, author, inventor; b. N.Y.C., Apr. 28, 1896; s. Nicholas and Caroline (Gottchalk) D.; grad. DeWitt Clinton High Sch., N.Y.C.; married. Began as conjurer, illusionist, telepathist, 1902. Author: Dunninger-Houdini Spirit Exposés, 1928; Inside the Medium's Cabinet, 1935; How to Make a Ghost Walk, 1936; Popular Magic, vols. I, II, III; Universal Second Sight; Tricks De Luxe; Tricks Unique; What's On Your Mind?, 1944; Dunninger Explains, 1950; Dunninger's Book of Magic, 1952; 101 Houdini and Dunninger Tricks You Can Do, 1954; You Too Can Read a Mind, 1956; also articles in field, also syndicated series on telepathy. Chmn. Universal Council for Psychic Research; chmn. psychic investigating com. Sci. Am.; chmn. investigating com. of psychic com. Gernsback Publs. Inventor telepathiscope. Home: Cliffside Park, N.J. Died Mar. 9, 1975.

DUNOYER DE SEGONZAC, ANDRE, French painter; b. 1884; ed. Lycee Henri IV, also Ecole des Beaux Arts, Paris. Many paintings exhibited in museums. Served with French Army, 1914-18. Decorated chevalier Legion of Honor; recipient Carnegie prize, 1933, Grand Prix Biennale, Venice, 1934. Hon. mem. Am. Inst. Arts and Letters, royal acads. London and Belgium. Illus.; Georgics, Sonnets (Ronsard), La Trielle Muscate. Address: Paris, France. Died Sept. 17, 1974.

DUPIUS, CHARLES W(ILLIAM), banker; b. Cincinnati, O., June 25, 1876; s. William and Ottilie (Albrecht) D.; ed. Coll. of Commerce, U. of Cin.; hon. M.A., U. Cin., 1922, D.S.C., 1956; m. Lillie Deremo, Aug. 23, 1904; children—John D., Betsy (Mrs. E.L. Hill). Began as messenger Western Bk., Cincinnati, 1892; cashier and v.p. 2d Nat. Bank of Cincinnati, 1913-18; pres. Citizens Nat. Bank, 1920-27; pres. Central Trust Co., 1927-49, chmn. of the bd. from 1949; chmn. bd. Cincinnati Unio n Stock yard Co.; dir. Cin. & Suburban Bell Telephone Co., Cin. Milling Machine Co., F. H. Lawson Co., Union Central Life Ins. Co., The Kroger Co., Mfrs. and Merchants Indemnity Co. Pres., trustee Endowment Fund Assn. U. Cin. One of organizers of Am. Inst. Banking and Cin. Coll. of Finance, Pres. Ohio Bankers Assn. Episcopalian. Mason (33°). Clubs: Queen City, Bankers, Commercial, Commonwealth, Cincinnati, Cincinnati Country. Home: Cincinnati, O.†

DUPONT, EMILE FRANCIS, business exec.; b. Wilmington, Del., May 20, 1898; s. Francis Irenee and Marianna (Rhett) duP.; student Kent (Conn.) Sch., 1914-17, U.S. Naval Acad., 1918-20, Sheffield Scientific Sch., Yale, 1920-22; m. Sarah Townsend, Jan. 31, 1925 (div.); children—Francis Irenee II, Sarah Townsend, Peter Rhett; m. 2d, Margaret Dick Marvel, May 1950. Nitrating house operator, Arlington plant E.I. du Pont de Nemours & Co., 1923-25, with operating dept. Du Pont Rayon Co., Buffalo, 1925-31, asst. plant mgr., cellophane div. du Pont Co., Richmond, Va., 1931-34, mgr. personnel div., Wilmington, 1934-38, plant mgr. Seaford plant, nylon div., 1938-41, dir. prodn., nylon div., 1941-44, asst. mgr. acetate div., Wilmington, 1944-45, dir. employee relations, service dept. Wilmington, 1945-51, dir. employee relations dept. Wilmington, 1951-63, dir. of co., 1944-74, mem. finance com., 1944-74; chmn. bd. benefits and pensions, 1950-64, mem. bonus and salary com., 1964-74; dir. Del. Trust Co., duKane Corp.; pres. bd. trustees Eleutherian Mills, Hagley Found. Chmn. bd. Nat. Safety Council, 1952-55; chmn. Del. Safety Council. Trustee Episcopal Ch. Sch. Found., Inc., Wilmington. Mem. Delta Psi. Clubs: St. Anthony (N.Y.C.); Wilmington, Wilmington Country; Vicmead Hunt. Home: Wilmington, Del. Died Dec. 1974.

DUPUY, R(ICHARD) ERNEST, ret. army officer, author: b. N.Y.C., Mar 24, 1887; s. George Marie and Katharine Pauline (Chute) D.; grad. Augustinian Acad., S.I., N.Y., 1905, Field Arty. Sch., 1924, Command and Gen. Staff Sch., 1933; m. Laura Elizabeth Nevitt, June 1, 1915; 1 son, Trevor Nevitt. Reporter, spl. writer Evening Telegram, N.Y. Herald, N.Y.C., 1909-17. Mem. N.Y. N.G., 1909-17; entered fed. service as 1st lt. C.A., 1917; served with A.E.F. as capt. 57th Arty., C.A.C., U.S. Army, comdg. Hdqrs. Co., adj., operations officer; capt. C.A.C., 1920; maj. F.A., 1935; lt. col., 1940, col., 1941; U.S. Mfil. Acad., 1938-41; chief, news div. War Dept., Bur. Pub. Relations, 1941-43; pub. relations officer Supreme Hdqrs., Europe, 1943-45; acting dir. War Dept. Bur. Pub. Relations, 1945; ret., 1946; bd. govs. Hist. Evaluation and Research Orgn., 1962—; gen. editor Mil. History of U.S., Hawthorn Books, Inc. 1963—. Decorated Legion of Merit with oak leaf cluster; Order Brit. Empire (Britain); Croix de Guerre with palm, Commemoratif, Verdun (France). Mem. West Point Soc. N.Y., Acad. Polit. Sci., Am. Mil. History Found., Assn. AUS, Armed Forces Pub. Relations Assn., Soc. Silurians Silurians, Fellowship U.S. Brit. Comrades, Soc. First Div., U.S. Naval Inst. (Asso.) Roman Catholic. Clubs: Army and Navy, Cosmos, National Press (Washington); Military-Naval (N.Y.C.). Author: With the Fifty-Seventh in France, 1929; (with G.F. Eliot) If War Comes, 1937; World in Arms, 1939; Perish by the Sword, 1939; Where They Have Trod, 1940; (with Hodding Carter) Civilian Defense of the U.S., 1942; (with T.N. Dupuy), To the Colors 1942; St. Vith: Lion in the Way, 1949; Men of West Point, 1952; Compact History of the United States Army, 1956. Co-author: Contemporary World Politics (a symposium), 1939; Contemporary Europe, 1941; (with T.N. Dupuy) Military Heritage of America, 1954, Brave Men and Great Captains, 1959, Compact History of the Civil War (Fletcher Pratt Meml. award Civil War Round Table N.Y.), 1960, Compact History of the Revolutionary War, 1963; Compact History of World War II, 1965; (with T.N. Dupuy) Encyclopedia of Military History, 1970; Five Days to War, 1967; (with W.H. Baumer) Little Wars of the United States, 1968; Compact History of the National Guard, 1971. Compiled Govs. Island, 1637-1937. Asso. editor Army, Navy, Air Force Register, 1957-62. Contbr. articles to Am. periodicals, mil. jours., fiction to popular mags. Home: Arlington, Va. Died Apr. 25, 1975.

DUPUY, SAMUEL STUART, pediatrician; b. Parral, W.Va., Feb. 10, 1912; s. Elbert Stephenson and Lillian (Dixon) DuP.; grad. Va. Mil. Inst., 1932; A.B., Duke, 1934; B.S., W.Va. U., 1936; M.D., Med. Coll. Va., Richmond, 1938; m. Helen Elizabeth Baker, June 1, 1940; children—Nancy (Mrs. James E. Fisk), Samuel Stuart, David Norris. Intern Charleston (W.Va.) Gen. Hosp., 1938-39; resident in pediatrics U. Miami-Jackson Meml. Hosp., 1957-59; practice medicine specializing in pediatrics, 1964-74; attending staff Variety Children's Hosp.; attending physician in pediatrics Mercy Hosp., Miami, Fla. Instr. U. Miami, 1962-74. Recipient pub. service commendations Pres. Roosevelt, 1944, Pres. Truman, 1945. Diplomate Am. Bd. Pediatrics. Fellow Am. Acad. Pediatrics, Assn. Pan Am. Physicians; mem. A.M.A., So. Med. Assn., Phi Chi, Sigma Alpha Epsilon. Republican. Presbyn. Mason, Elk. Home: Coral Gables, Fla., Died Nov. 5, 1974; buried Beckley, W.Va.

DURAND, JAMES HARRISON, lawyer; b. N.Y.C., Nov. 4, 1934; s. Harrison Fisher and Anne (Sawyer) D.; A.B., Harvard, 1956; LL.B., Cornell U., 1961; m. Edna Louise Mottshaw, July 27, 1963; children— Carolyn Louise, Julia Sara. Admitted to N.Y. bar, 1961; law asst. to sr. asso. judge N.Y. Ct. Appeals, 1961-63; with firm LeBoeuf, Lamb, Leiby & MacRae, N.Y.C., 1963-74, partner, 1972-74. Vice pres. Washington Av. Parent Tchr. Orgn., 1972. Trustee Chatham (N.J.) Fish and Game Protective Assn. Served with AUS, 1956-58. Mem. Assn. Bar City N.Y., N.Y. State Bar Assn. Home: Chatham N.J. Died Feb. 4, 1974.

DURAS, VICTOR HUGO, counsellor; b. Wilber, Neb., May 6, 1880; s. Cenek and Marie (Spirk) D.; LL.B., U. of Neb., 1902; LL.M., Columbian U., 1903; D.C.L., and M. Diplomacy, George Washington U., 1905; post-grad. work in internat., constl. and mil. law, univs. of London and Paris. Admitted to bar of Neb., N.Y., and Supreme Court of U.S.; judge U.S. Court, Canal Zone, Panama, 1906; Rep. candidate for Congress, 12th N.Y. Dist., 1908, and 14th N.Y. Dist., 1910. Sec. to Am. delegation to 20th Internat. Parliamentary Conf., The Hague, 1913; del. Internat. Arbitration and Peace Congress, The Hague, 1913; rep. N.Y. State, at dedication of Palace of Peach, The Hague, 1913; A.m v. consul to Liege, Belgium, 1913-14; v. consul to Petrograd, Russia, 1914-15. Col., a.d.c. and mem. staff of gov. of Neb., 1916. Was asst. editor. The "Americana" Jours of History (New York). The Common Cause (Now York), The Peacemaker (Phila.). A founder mem. Ecole de la Paiz Paris; mem. Nat. Assn. on Constl. Govt. (Washington, D.C.). Am. Soc. Judicial Settlement and Internat. Disputes, Nat. Economic League, Nat. Civic Alliance; Am. Red. Cross, Nat. Alumni, Federal Bar Assn. of Washington, D.C. (a founder), Internat. Law Assn. (London, Eng.). Clubs: Nat. Press (Washington, D.C.), Beaux Arts, Aero of America (New York). Author: Panama, West vs. East; Universal Peace by International Government; La Paiz par l'Organisation Internationale; The story of American Diplomacy; Evolution vs. Revolution; Our Ideal Republic; The Peace Maker; The Fine Arts. Historian of Am. Group of the Interparliamentary Union, 1912. Home: Mt. Washington, Va.†

DURBROW, CHANDIER WOLCOTT, lawyer; b. in San Francisco, California, January 28, 1876; son of Elbridge and Gertrude (Chandler) Durbrow; student Yale; m. Marion K. Coffey; children—Elbridge, Elsie D. (Mrs. Shelby Curlee). Admitted to Cal. bar, 1900; praticed law Washington, D.C., state and fed. cts. in San Francisco from 1900; with S.P.R.R.R. Co., 1903-45, gen. solicitor 1939-45; dir., S.P.R.R. Co., San Diego & Ariz. Eastern Railway Company, Central Pacific Railway Company. Repbn. Unitarian. Clubs: Pacific Union, Bohemian, Olympic. Home: San Francisco, Cal.†

DURFEE, WALTER HETHERINGTON, coll. provost; b. Geneva, N.Y., Jan. 31, 1889; s. William Pitt and Charlotte Elizabeth (Racao) D.; A.B., Hobart Coll., 1908; M.C.E., Harvard, 1911; Ph.D., Cornell U., 1930; m. Mabel Keith, Apr. 18, 1914; children—William Hetherington, Kate Keith, Mary, Horton Keith. Draftsman and designer structural and hydraulic engring. projects, 1911-21; with Hobart and William Smith Colls., from 1921, asst. prof. math., 1921-29, prof., from 1930, acting dean Hobart Coll., 1937-38, dean, 1938-48, from 1955, acting pres., 1947-48, provost, from 1948, then dean, prof. math. emeritus. Mem. A.A.A.S., American Mathematical Society, Mathematical Association of Am., Phi Beta Kappa, Phi Kappa Phi, Sigma Phi. Republican. Episcopalian. Home: Geneva, N.Y. Died Dec. 21, 1974.

DURHAM, CARL THOMAS, congressman; b. Chapel Hill, N.C., Aug. 28, 1892; s. Claude Peter and Delia (Lloyd) D.; student U. of N.C., 1917-18, LL.D., 1958; LL.D., High Point College, 1958; m. Margaret Whitsett, Dec. 30, 1918; children—Celia Donnell, Macy Susan, Carl Thomas, Margarett Whitsett, Eulalia Ann. Pharmacist, Chapel Hill, N.C., 1912-38; mem. 76th to 86th Congresses from 6th N.C. District. Member Orange County Commn., 1932-38; mem. Chapel Hill Sch. Bd., 1924-38; mem. Bd. of Aldermen, Chapel Hill, 1924-32. Trustee U. of N.C. Served in U.S. Navy, 1918. Mem. Am. Legion, Alpha Kappa Psi. Democrat. Baptist. Mason. Home: Chapel Hill, N.C. Died Apr. 1974.

DURR, CLIFFORD JUDKINS, former lawyer; b. Montgomery, Ala., Mar. 2, 1899; s. John Welsey and Lucy (Judkins) D.; A.B., U. Ala., 1919; B.A. in Jurisprudence, Oxford (Eng.) U., 1922, M.A., B.C.L., 1964; m. Virginia Heard Foster, Apr. 5, 1926; children—Ann Patterson (Mrs. Walter A. Lyon), Lucy Judkins (Mrs. F. Sheldon Hackney), Virginia Foster (lMrs. Frank R. Parker III), Lulah Johnston (Mrs. Richard V. Colan). Admitted to Ala. bar, 1923, Wis. bar, 1924, D.C. bar, 1948; mem. firm Rushton, Crenshaw & Rushton, Montgomery, 1922-23, Fawsett, Smart & Shea, Milw., 1923-24, Martin, Turner & McWhorter, Birmingham, Ala., 1925-33; asst. gen. counsel RFC, 1933-41; gen. counsel, dir. Def. Plant Corp., v.p., dir. Rubber Res. Corp., 1940-41; commr. FCC, 1941-48; pvt. practice law, Washington, 1948-50, Montgomery, 1952-64. Lectr., Am., Brit. univs.; Regents lectr. theatre arts U. Cal., Los Angeles, 1966. Served with U.S. Army, 1918. Rhodes scholar, 1918; recipient Variety award, 1946, Sch. Broadcaster award, 1947, Page One award Am. Newspaper Guild, 1948, Lasker Civil Liberties award N.Y. Civil Liberties Union, 1966. Life mem. Inst. Edn. by Radio; mem. Phi Beta Kappa, Sigma Alpsh Epsilon. Democrat. Presbyn. Contbr. articles to profl. jours.; contbr. books. Home: Wetumpka, Ala. Died May 12, 1975; buried Greenwood Cemetery, Montgomery, Ala.

DUSHAM, E(DWARD) H(ENRY), entomologist; b. Amesbury, Mass., Sept. 1, 1887; s. Peter and Katherine (Murphy) D.; A.B., Dartmouth Coll., 1910; M.S., Pa. State Coll., 1915; Ph.D., Cornell U., 1924; m. Mary E. Atkinson, Oct. 1, 1912; 1 dau., Sara C. (Mrs. James C. Beveridge). Asst. in zoology and physiology, Ia. State Coll., 1910-12; instr. in zoology, Pa. State Coll., 1913-15, asst. prof., 1915-16; instr. in natural history, Cornell U., 1917-18; head dept. zoology and entomology Pa. State U., from 1918, later prof. emeritus entomology. Fellow A.A.A.S.; mem. Am. Entomol. Soc., Am. Assn. Econ. entomologists, Entomological Society of Pennsylvania, Pennsylvania Academy of Sci., Sigma Xi, Gamma Sigma Delta, Sigma Phi Epsilon, Alpha Epsilon Delta. Republican. Methodist. Home: State College Pa. Died Sept. 25, 1974.

DUTCHER, FRANCIS EDWARD, bldg. products co., exec.; b. Vancouver, B.C., Can., Oct. 24, 1909; s. Bert Elroy and Eva (McQuay) D.; student St. Petersburg Jr. Coll., 1929-30; B.S. in Bus., Miami U., Oxford, O., 1932; m. Nancy Jane Callander, Mar. 6, 1937; children—Barbara Ann (Mrs. Justin Kimball), Nancy Odette (Mrs. Peter Strohmeier). Came to U.S., 1914, naturalized. With Johns-Manville Sales Corp., 1933-73, v.p., sales mgr. dealer bldg. products, N.Y.C., 1958-59, v.p., gen. mdse. mgr. bldg. products div., 1959-61, sr. operating v.p. bldg. materials divs. Johns Manville Corp., N.Y.C., 1961-73, also dir., pres. Johns-Manville Products Corp.; mem. adv. com. Chem. Bank, N.Y.C. Bd. dirs. Producers Council. Served to lt. USNR, 1943-46. Mem. Nat. Mineral Wool Assn. (pres. 1961),

Mineral Fibre Asbestos-Products Bur. (chmn. exec. com.), Asphalt Roofing Mfrs. Assn. (past chmn. exec. com.). Clubs: Union League (N.Y.C.); Tokeneke (Darien, Conn.). Home: Darien Conn. Died May 26, 1973.

DUTRA, EURICO GASPAR, pres. Brazil; b. Cuiabe, Mato Grosso, Brazil, S.A., May 18, 1885; s. Jose Florencio and Maria (Justina) D.; m. Carmela Leite, Feb. 19, 1914; children—Emilia, Joao. Minister of War, Brazil, 1936-45; pres. Republic of the U.S. of Brazil, 1945-51. Home: Rio de Janeiro Brazil. Died June 1974.

DUTROW, HOWARD VICTOR, oculist, aurist; b. Charlesville, Md. Dec. 30, 1880; s. Clinton J. and Mary O. D.; M.D., U. of Md., 1904; m. Emma Agnes Thomas, Dec. 14, 1905; 1 dau., Mary Katherine (Mrs. II Leigh Derby, Jr.). Interne at Univ. Hospital of Baltimore, Md., 1904-05; mem. med. dept., Isthmian Canal Commn., advancing to chief eye, ear, nose and throat clinic, Colon Hosp., Canal Zone, 1905-13; in practice at Dayton, O., specializing on diseases of eye, ear, nose and throat from 1913; oculist and aurist B.&O. R.R. and State Indsl. Commn. Ohio, now ret.; mem. cons. staff Miami Valley Hosp. (ex-chief of staff); now hon. member ex-chief of staff Miami Valley Hosp.; vis. oculist and aurist St. Elizabeth and Good Samaritan Hospitals Dayton, Ohio. Member Medial Advisory Bd., District 10, State of Ohio World War; maj. Med. O.R.C., 1924-54; active duty as maj. Med. Corps, U.S. Army, Station Hospital, Borinquen Field, Puerto Rico, from Feb. 6, 1941); lt. colonel, post surgeon, July 15, 1942-May 23, 1943, chief med. inspector, Army Air Forces Tech. Training Command, Miami Beach, Fla., June-Aug., 1943, chief, Ear, Nose and Throat Service, Nautilus Hosp., Unit No. 1, Aug. 1943-Mar. 1944; retired from active duty with rank of lt. col., Mar.2, 1944. Founder's diplomate Am. Bd. of Otolaryngology. Fellow Am. Coll. Surgeons. Am. Acad. Ophthalmology and Otolaryngology (mem. com. for hard of hearing); mem. A.M.A., Ohio State Med. Assn., Dayton Acad. Med. (ex-pres.), A.A.A.S., Montgomery Co. Med. Soc. (ex-pres),, M. Assn. Isthmian Canal Zone (life). Rep. Evang. Reformed. Mason (32°, K.T., Shriner). Clubs: Dayton City, Dayton Country, Dayton Bicycle. Contbr. many papers to med. jours. Home: Dayton O.†

DUTTON, CLAIR C., banker; b. Elba, O., Oct. 31, 1884; s. Jasper O. and Frances L. (Unger) D.; student Mountain State Coll., Parkersburg, W. Va.; m. Kathryn R. Bohn, May 17, 1905; 1 son, Harold H. chmn. bd. Community Savs. & Loan Co. (became Community Savs. Bank), Parkersburg, W.Va. Past pres. Bd. Commerce, Community Chest; dir. YMCA. Mem. C. of C. (life), Am. Indsl. Bankers Assn. (past pres.). Democrat. Methodist. Mason, Elk, Odd Fellow, Moose. Home: Parkersburg, W. Va. Died Nov. 30, 1973.

DVORNIK, FRANCIS, clergyman, educator; b. Chomyz, Czechoslovakia, Aug. 14, 1893; s. Francis and Frances (Tomeckova) D.; student Classical Gymnasium, Kromeriz, Moravia; D.D., Faculty of Theology, Olomouce, 1920; student Charles U., Prague; diploma Ecole des Sciences Polit., Paris, 1923; D.ès Lettres, Sorbonne, Paris, 1926; D.Litt. (hon.), London, St. Procopius Coll., Fairleigh Dickinson U. Came to U.S., 1948, naturalized, 1954. Ordained priest, 1916; prof. ch. history Charles U., Prague, 1928; dean faculty theology, 1935; Schlumberger lectr. Coll. of France, Paris, 1940; Birbeck lectr. Cambridge U., 1946; prof. Byzantine history, Dumbarton Oaks, Harvard U., 1949-64. Decorated knight French Legion of Honor. Fellow Brit. Acad., Am. Acad. Arts and Scis. of Boston; mem. Royal Hist. Soc. London, Am. Medieval Acad., Royal Belgian Acad. Author: Les Slaves, Byzance et Rome an IXs., 1926; St. Grgoire el Decap, et les Slaves, 1926; St. Wenceslas, Duke of Bohemia, 1929; Les Légendes de Constantine et de Méthode, 1933; National Churches, 1944; The Photian Schism, 1948, French edit., 1950, Italian edit., 1952; The Making of Central and Eastern Europe, 1949; The Slavs, Their Early History and Civilization, 1956; The Idea of Apostolicity in Byzantium, 1958; The Ecumenical Councils, 1961; The Slavs in European History and Civilization, 1962; Byzance et la Primunaté Romaine, 1964, English, German edit., 1966; Early Christian and Byzantine Political Philosophy, 1966; Byzantine Missions Among the Slavs, 1970. Home: Kromeriz, Czechoslovakia., Died Nov. 4, 1975.

DWYER, P. FLORENCE, congressman; b. Reading, Pa., July 4, 1902; m. M. Joseph Dwyer (dec. 1968); 1 son. Mem. N.J. legislature, 1950-56; mem. 85th-92d congresses from 12th N.J. Dist. Republican. Home: Elizabeth, N.J., Died Feb. 29, 1976.

DYE, JOHN WALTER, consul; b. Winona, Minn., Feb. 4, 1878; s. Walter Godfrey and Mary Calantha (Belshaw) D.; grad. Pillsbury Acad., Owatonna, Minn., 1900; A.B., U. of Minn., 1904; studied George Washington U., 1905-06; m. Margherita Anna Marcella Pellegrini Tibaldi, Nov. 7, 1912; children—Willard James, John Paul, George Walter, Philip Godfrey. Apptd. consular clk., July 21, 1906; dep. consul gen. at Berlin, Germany, 1906-08, vice and dpe. consul gen., Genoa, Italy, 1908-10; at Boma, Congo, 1910-11, Smyrna, Turkey, 1911-13; consular agt. at Damascus, 1913-14; vice and dep. consul gen., Cape Town, S. Africa, 1914-15, vice consul, at Johannesburg, 1915, Cape Town, 1915-16; consul at Cape Town, 1916-17, Port Elizabeth, Cape of Good Hope, 1917-20, Cindad Juarez, Mexico, 1920-29, Montreal, Quebec, Canada, 1929-30, Wellington, New Zealand, 1931, Melbourne, 1931-36, Nassau, Bahamas, 1937-42, consul gen., Nassau., 1942; retired from fgn. service, Feb. 28, 1943. Tech. adviser. Conf. with Mex. to Prevent Smuggling, El Paso, Tex., 1925, and Conf. for Formation of Regulations under Smuggling Conv. of 1925, Washington, 1926. Apptd. sec. in diplomatic service, 1937. Mem. Am. Philatelic Soc., Philatelic Soc. of Washington, D.C. (hon.), Phi Beta Kappa, Kappa Sigma. Republican. Baptist. Western Intercollegiate gymnastic champion, 1903. Home: Santa Barbara, Cal.†

DYER, ALBERT JOSEPH, educator; b. Amity, Mo., Mar. 23, 1910; s. Albert Henry and Cora (Dieter) D.; M.S., U. Mo., 1939, Ph.D., 1949; m. Annabel McCallister, Dec. 17, 1935; children—JoAnn (Mrs. Anthony J. Ramos), Larry Manning. Tchr., Mo. rural sch., 1927-29; county extension agt., Carrollton, Mo., 1935-38; asst. animal husbandry U. Mo. at Columbia, 1934-35, mem. faculty, 1938-43, 46—75, prof. animal husbandry, 1954—75, chmn. dept., 1957—75; mktg. and livestock cons., cons. ICA, Chile, 1961; U.S. rep. Feed Grain Council, Eng., 1963. Served to capt. AUS, 1943-46. Named Livestock Man of Year U. Mo. Block and Bridle Club, 1975. Fellow Am. Soc. Animal Sci.; mem. Block and Bridle (nat. treas.), Sigma Xi, Gamma Sigma Delta. Baptist. Author research papers. Home: Columbia Mo. Died Feb. 24, 1975; buried Meml. Park Cemetery, Columbia.

DYER, EVERETT R., assn. exec.; b. Falconer, N.Y., July 26, 1907; s. George Frederick and Katherine (Tanner) D.; A.B., Houghton (N.Y.) Coll., 1929, Pd.D., 1956; M.A., U. Rochester, 1938; student Alfred U., N.Y.U.; m. Bernice May Spangler, Nov. 25, 1931; 1 dau., Joanne Carol. Tchr. mathematics Friendship (N.Y.) Central Sch., 1929-37; prin. Belfast (N.Y.) Central Sch., 1937-47; supervising prin. Richfield Springs (N.Y.) Central Sch., 1947; exec. dir. N.Y. State Sch. Bds. Assn., Inc., 1948-72, emeritus, 1972-74. Charter mem. adv. bd. N.Y. State Office Local Govt.; mem. comptroller's com. Local Finance Law; mem. adv. com. Hudson River Valley Commn.; adv. Council N.Y. Employees Retirement System. Nat. Field scout commr. Boy Scouts Am., recipient Silver Beaver award. Trustee Green Mountain Coll., Poultney, Vt.; bd. dirs. Blue Cross Northeastern N.Y. Recipient Chartered Assn. Exec. award Am. Soc. Assn. Execs., 1962. Mem. Am. Assn. Sch. Administrs., Ednl. Press Assn., Am. Soc. Assn. Execs., N.Y. State Council Sch. Dist. Adminstrs., Nat. Assn. Exec. Secs. of State Sch. Bds. Assn. (pres.), Central Sch. Prins. Assn. N.Y. State (life), N.Y. State Congress Parents and Tchrs. (hon.), N.Y. Assn. Elementary Sch. Prins. (hon.). Methodist. Phi Delta Kappa. Mason. Clubs: Country, University (Albany). Home: Latham N.Y. Died Mar. 24, 1974.

DYER, SALLIE, (Mrs. Robert Francis Dyer), genealogist, club woman; b. Washington, Oct. 16, 1891; d. Nathaniel Talmadge and Emma (Hutchins) Worley; student Cazenovia Jr. Coll., 1908-12, George Washington U., 1912-13, Strayer's Bus. Coll., 1914; m. Robert Francis Dyer, Jan. 1, 1926; children—Robert F., Nancie (Mrs. Edward C. Santelmann), Richard Hutchins, David Marcus. Sec., Brit. Embassy, Washington, 1914-15, Adj. Gen.'s Office, War Dept., 1915-16; owner Dyer's Geneal. Office, Washington, 1914-26. Pres. Washington alumnae club Pi Beta Phi, 1946-47; vice-regent Dorothy Hancock chpt. D.A.R., 1945-75, mem. Eastern Shore Va. chpt., del. to Continental Congress, 1950-73; mem. spl. com. U.S.O., 1941-45, mem. Belasco Theater, 1942-45; nurse's aid A.R.C., 1943-45; mem. Woman's bd. George Washington U. Hosp., 1946-56; mem. George Washington U. Alumni Assn. Recipient service award A.R.C., 1945, Golden Arrow award Pi Beta Phi. Mem. So. Dames Am. (charter mem. nat. soc.; state v.p.), Tex. State Geneal. Soc., Md. Hist. Soc. Clubs: Washington, Chevy Chase Woman's, Arts, Army and Navy. Home: Washington, D.C., Died Oct. 28, 1975; interred Arlington Nat. Cemetery, Arlington, Va.

DYER, SAMUEL EUGENE, dentist; b. Madison, Ill., Jan. 31, 1930; s. Garvey and Nellie Marie (Brown) D.; B.S., U. Ill., 1956; D.D.S., U. Ill. at Chgo., 1960; m. Jewel Carlene Bonds, Mar. 13, 1954; children—Laura Kay, Michael Garvey, Mary Beth. Individual practice dentistry, Maywood, Ill., 1960-67, Glen Ellyn, Ill., 1967-72; chief dental staff, cons. modernization dental dept. Dixon (Ill.) State Sch., 1972-73. Served with USNR, 1948-52, USMCR, 1950-51; Korea. Mem. Am. Dental Assn., Am. Soc. Clin. Hypnosis, World Mental Health Soc. (asso.), Theta Xi, Psi Omege. Home: Dixon, Ill. Died 1973.

DYHRENFURTH, GUNTER OSKAR, author, educator, geologist; b. Breslau, Germany, Nov. 12, 1886; s. Oskar and Katherine (Bayer) D.; baccalaureat U. Breslau, 1904, Ph.D., 1909; postgrad. U. Freiburg i.Br. (Germany), 1904; U. Vienna (Austria), 1905-06; m. Hettie Heymann, 1911 (div. 1947); children—Harold, Norman D.; m. 2d, Irene Klar, 1948; 1 son, Eberhart. With Geol. Survey Switzerland, Grisons, 1909-15; prof. geology and palaeontology U. Breslau, 1919-33; tchr. geography St. Gall, Switzerland, 1939-54. Leader, Internat. Himalayan Expdn., 1930, Internat. Karakorum Expdn., 1934, chronicler of both, 1950—75; adviser mountaineering, sci. expdns., 1947—75. Recipient Prix d'Alpinisme (Olympic Golden medal), 1936. Clubs: British Alpine (hon.); Swiss Alpine (hon.); Alpino Italiano; (hon.) Osterreichisher Alpenklub (hon.). collaborator Brockhaus Enzyklopadie, 1966—. Author: Himalaya, 1931; Baltoro, 1939; To The Third Pole, 1952; The Book of Nanga Parbat, 1954; The Book of Kangchenjunga, 1955; Everest, 1959; The Third Pole, 1960. numerous Contbr. sci., alpinistic articles and essays to profl. jours., mags. Home: Ringgenberg, Switzerland. Died Apr. 14, 1975.

DYKSTRA, RALPH, veterinarian; b. Groningen, The Netherlands, Sept. 24, 1879; s. Jan and Geertje (Smilde) D.; brought by parents to U.S., 1881; D.V.M., Ia. State Coll., 1905; m. Cecelia Welch, Oct. 12, 1910. Asst. prof. anatomy and obstetrics, Ia. State Coll., 1905-07, asso. prof., 1907-09, prof., 1909-11; vet. insp., U.S. Bur. Animal Industry, summer, 1911; asst. prof. vet. medicine, Kan. State Coll., 1911-13, prof., 1913-19, prof. vet. surgery from 1919, head dept. vet. med., Apr.-July 1919, dean sch. vet. med., 1919-48, dean emeritus from 1948. Mem. Am. Vet. Med. Assn. (pres. 1931-32), U.S. Live Stock Sanitary Assn., Kan. Vet. Med. Assn. (pres. 1917). Gamma Sigma Delta, Phi Kappa Phi, Sigma Xi, Phi Zeta; hon. mem. Ia. State Vet. Med. Assn., Neb. Vet. Med. Assn., Eastern Ia. Vet. Med. Assn. Mason. Author: Animal Castration, 1914; Animal Sanitation and Disease Control, 1942. Home: Manhattan, Kan.†

DYSON, VERNE, author, lecturer; b. Rolla, Mo., Jan. 25, 1879; s. Rev. S. A. and Henrietta L. (Singleton) D.; A.B., Central Coll., Fayette, Mo., 1905; m. Nannie May Hubbard, June 21, 1905; children—William V. Dyson, Mrs. E. B. Mullaney. With Kansas City Star, 1906-11, Los Angeles Times, 1912-18; and Politics, and asst. prof. English, U. of Philippines, Manila, 1928-33; dir. Inst. Chinese Studies, New York, 1933-45. Occupational instructor and manager printing plant, Pilgrim State Hospital, Brentwood, 1945-50. Dramatic critic, Manila Daily Bulletin; contbg. editor Philippine Social Science Review (a founder 1930); editor Brentwood Bulletin (monthly) from 1951, Deer Park-Wyandanch News (weekly) from 1952. Del. from P.I. to Institute Pacific Relations. Banff, Canada, 1933. Member Chinese Social and Political Science Assn., Royal Asiatic Society, China Soc. Science and Arts, Philippine Acad. Social Sciences. Clubs: Am. University, Short Story, Lions. Author books including: A Century of Brentwood, 1950. Editor of Shanghai Stores, 1925. Home: Brentwood, L.I., N.Y.†

EAGLE, VERNON AINSWORTH, found. exec.; b. Britt, Ia., Aug. 2, 1919; s. Frank and Mary (Ryan) E.; m. Ann Richmond Sickels, June 28, 1947; children—Vernon Ainsworth, Mary Stuyvesent, Susan Van Houtan; m. 2d, Brenda Hughes Campbell, May 31, 1972. Officer fgn. div. Hanover Bank, N.Y.C., London, Eng., 1944-56; exec. dir., treas. New World Found., N.Y.C., Chgo., 1957; treas., dir. Harrison-Blaine, Inc., N.Y.C., Harrison-Blaine N.J., Inc. Nat. bd. Am. Vets. Com., 1944-59, nat. treas., 1945-50; dir. Ill. br. Am. Civil Liberties Union, 1957-60. Sec., bd. dirs. Old Republic Charitable Found.; treas., bd. dirs. Initial Teaching Alphabet Found., Coop. Assistance Fund; bd. dirs. Austen Riggs Center. Served with Brit. Commandos, 1939-43; ETO. Decorated Mil. Cross, Order Purple Heart. Mem. Council Fgn. Relations, Inst. Internat. Edn. Clubs: Century Assn. (N.Y.C.); Tavern (Chgo.); American (London, Eng.). Office: New York City, N.Y. Died Apr. 1974.

EAMES, ARTHUR JOHNSON, prof. botany; b. Framingham, Mass., Oct. 10, 1881; s. Charles Alexander and Rozella Mary (Johnson) E.; A.B., Harvard, 1908, A.M., 1910, Ph.D., 1912; m. Marguerita Hope Ballard, June 3, 1916; 1 son, David Ballard. Asst. in botany, Harvard, 1906-10, 11-12; instr. botany, 1912-14, asst. prof., 1914-20, prof., 1920-49, prof. emeritus Cornell U.; now consultant to U.S. War Dept. Mem. A.A.A.S., American Academy Arts and Sciences, Botanical Society of America (pres. 1938), Phi Beta Kappa, Sigma Xi, Phi Kappa Phi, Phi Kappa Sigma. Home: Ithaca, N.Y.†

EAMES, EDWARD WILLIAMS, educator; b. Buffalo, N.Y., Aug. 14, 1900; s. Edward Ashley and Isabel Ransom (Morey) E.; grad. Nichols Country Day Sch., Buffalo, 1917; A.B., Amherst, 1922, L.H.D. (hon.), 1955; M.A., Harvard, 1929; L.H.D., Bowdoin Coll., 1944; m. Eleanor Kimball, June 1926; children—Elizabeth Tower, Edward Ashley. Tchr. Deerfield (Mass.) Acad., 1923-24, 25-30; headmaster Gov. Dummer Acad., South Byfield, Mass., from 1930. Trustee Essex County YMCA, Amherst Coll., 1945-51, Internat. Coll., Beirut. Mem. Headmasters's Assn. (pres. 1957-58), Beta Theta Pi, Phi Beta Kappa. Conglist. Clubs: Odd Volumes, Union, Harvard (Boston); Century Assn. (N.Y.C.). Home: Newburyport, Mass., Died Mar. 11, 1975.

EARLE, GEORGE HOWARD, diplomat; b. Devon, Pa., Dec. 5, 1890; s. George Howard and Catherine Hansell (French) E.; grad. Delancey Sch., Phila., student Harvard, 1909-11; LL.B., Temple U., LL.D.; L.H.D., Waynesburg (Pa.) Coll., D.C.L., Susquehanna U., Selinsgrove, Pa., and LL.D., La Salle Coll., Phila. (all

1935); m. Huberta Potter, Jan. 20, 1916 (divorced, 1945); children—George Howard, Hubert, Lawrence Ralph; m. 2d, Jacqueline Germaine M. Sacré, December 1945; children—Jacqueline, Anthony. Was associated with father in the sugar industry, Phila.; later engaged in business in Chicago; after World War founded Flamingo Sugar Mills, Phila.; occupied with various business activities until apptd. E.E. and M.P. to Austria, 1933; resigned 1934, to become Dem. candidate for gov. State of Pa.; elected 1st Dem. gov. of Pa. in 44 yrs. for term, 1935-39; minister to Bulgaria, 1940-41; asst. naval attaché, Elk. Istanbul, Turkey, 1943; asst. gov. Samoa, 1945. Chmn. finance com. Fla. for Eisenhower. Enlisted as pvt. 2d Pa. Inf., 1916; served as 2d lt. on Mexican Border; enlisted in U.S. Navy, 1917, as lt. (j.g.), became comdr. U.S.S. Victor, submarine chaser; awarded Navy Cross for service thereon; comdr., World War II. Trustee U. of Pa., U. of Pittsburgh, State Coll. of Pa. Decorated Great Cross of White Rose of Finland, Great Cross of Northern Star of Sweden; awarded Meritorious Service Medal, Commonwealth of Pennsylvania. Member Tall Cedars of Lebanon, Soc. Friendly Sons of St. Patrick. Episcopalian. Mason (Shriner), Elk. Clubs: Racquet, Harvard, Penn. Athletic (Phila.); Merion Cricket (Haverford); Whitmarsh (Pa.) Valley Country; Leash (New York). Home: Coral Gables, Fla. Died Dec. 30, 1974.

EARLE, SAMUEL BROADUS, mech. engring.; b. Gowensville, S.C., Mar. 11, 1878; s. Thomas John and Eliza Jane (Kennedy) E.; A.B., Furman U., 1898, A.M., 1899, hon. LL.D., 1932; M.E., Cornell, 1902; m. Susan Hall Sloan, Dec. 22, 1908; 1 son, Samuel Broadus. Mem. faculty Clemson (S.C.) Agrl. Coll. from 1902, asst. prof. mech. engring, 1902-03, asso. prof. 1903-10, prof. and dir. engring. dept., 1910-24, dir. engring. dept. and Engring. Expt. Sta., 1924-33, dean Sch. Engring. and director Engineering Experimental Station, 1933-50, dean emeritus from 1950, acting pres., 1919, 24-25. Fellow A.A.A.S., S.C. Acad. Sci., A.S.M.E.; mem. S.C. Soc. Engr. (pres. 1933), Am. Soc. for Engring. Edn. (pres. 1937-38), Nat. Soc. Profl. Engrs., Newcomen Soc. (Am. br.), Chi Psi, Tau Beta Pi, Phi Kappa Phi. Democrat, Baptist. Clubs: Rotary (pres. Anderson 1933, gov. 58th Dist. 1936); Boscobel Golf. Contbr. profl. articles to jours. Home: Clemson, S.C.†

EARLE, SWENSON, hydrographic engr.; b. Queen Anne Co. Md., Aug. 3, 1879; s. William Brundige and Louisa (Stubbs) E.; ed. high sch. and business coll.; engring. course, U. of Va.; m. Mabel Streett, of Bel Air Hartford Co., Md., June 4, 1902 (dec.); children—Juliet Gover Streett, Louise Shepherd, Elizabeth Swenson. With U.S. Coast and Geod. Survey, 1899-1903; Office of U.S. Lighthouse Bd., Washington, D.C., 1903-06; hydrographic engr. Md. Shell Fish Commn., 1906-16; made oyster survey of Md. waters, 1906-12; chief engr. Conservation Commn., 1916-17, now commr. Conservation Dept. of Md. Yeoman, U.S.N., at 18; ensign, U.S.N.R.F., Apr. 1, 1917; comdr. U.S.S. McLane; range officer Naval Proving Grounds, Dahlgren, Va.; constructed range for big navy guns on Lower Potomac River; promoted lt. (j.g.) and sr. lt. during World War, and placed on inactive list, July 1, 1919. Ex-pres. Nat. Assn. Fisheries Commrs.; mem. S.R., Mil. Order World War. Democrat. Episcopalian. Clubs: Engineers', Elkridge Kennels (Baltimore), Author: Maryland's Colonial Eastern Shore (with P.G. Skirven), 1916; The Chesapeake Bay Country, 1923, 24, 3d edit., 1929; also Md. Supplement to Frye-Atwood Geography. Inventor of continuous sounding machine for measuring depth of water, also the Amphibious Tank. Home: Baltimore, Md.†

EASTMAN, NICHOLSON JOSEPH, obstetrician; b. Crawfordsville, Ind., Jan. 20, 1895; s. Thomas Barker and Ota (Nicholson) E.; A.B., Yale U., 1916, M.D., Ind. U. Sch. of Medicine, 1921; D.Sc. (honorary), University of Chicago, 1958; m. Lo Retta Bernice Rutz, July 7, 1925; children—Elizabeth, Thomas Barker. Instr. obstetrics, Indiana U. Sch. of Medicine, 1922-24, asso. in obstetrics and gynecology, Peiping Union Med. Coll., 1924-28; instr. and asso. in obstetrics, Johns Hopkins U., 1928-33; prof. obstetrics and gynecology, Peiping Union Med. Coll., 1933-35; prof. obstetrics Johns Hopkins U., 1935-60, obstetrician-in-chief Johns Hopkins Hosp., 1935-60; vis. prof. obstetrics Univ. Hong Kong, 1955-56, U. Minn., 1962-63; cons. Ford Found., N.Y.C., 1963-73. Chairman Advisory Committee on Maternal and Child Health Services, Childrens Bur., 1943-46; chmn. World Health Orgn. expert com. on maternity care, also chairman expert committee on midwife tng.; dir. Passano Found. Editor-in-chief, Obstetrics and Gynecology Survey. Member of American Gynecological Society (president 1964), Am. Assn. Obstetricians and Gynecologists (pres. 1953), Am. Acad. Cerebral Palsy (pres. 1957), A.M.A., Edinburgh Obst. Soc., S. Atlantic Asso. Obst. and Gynec. (hon.), Balt. City Med. Soc., Soc. Exptl. Biology and Medicine, Am. Gynecology Club, Sigma Xi. Author: Williams Obstetrics, 1950; Expectant Motherhood, 1940, 47; co-author (with L. Zabriskie), Nurses Handbook of Obstetrics, 1943; numerous articles on obstetrical subjects. Republican. Meth. Clubs: Seigniory (P. Q. Canada); Elkridge (Baltimore). Home: Baltimore Md. Died Sept. 28, 1973; buried Druid Ridge Cemetery, Baltimore, Md.

EASTON, ROBERT EASTMAN, corp. exec.; b. Santa Cruz, Cal., Sept. 15, 1875; s. Alexander Giles and Mary Esther (Gushee) E.; A.B., U. Cal. at Berkeley, 1897; m. Ethel Olney, Apr. 14, 1914; 1 son, Robert Olney. Supt., sec., mgr. Sisquoc Ranch Co., Santa Barbara, 1900-50; dir. Gen. Telephone Co. Cal., and predecessors, Santa Monica, 1939—, also Home Telephone Co., Santa Barbara, Santa Barbara Telephone Co. & Asso. Telephone Co. Cal., 1907-44; pres., sec., dir. Santa Maria Realty Co.,1908-55; v.p., sec., dir. 1st Nat. Bank Stant Maria, 1910-28; dir. Crocker 1st Nat. Bank San Francisco, 1922-47. Dir. Santa Barbara Meml. Cancer Found.; trustee Santa Barbara Sch. Manual Arts and Home Econs., 1909-11, Church Divinity Sch. Pacific; trustee, mem. finance com. Santa Barbara Found. Mem. Cal. Cattlemen's Assn., Cal. Farm Bur., Taxpayers Assn., Ind. Telephone Pioneers Assn., Barbara County Hist. Soc., Pioneers of Cal., Delta Kappa Epsilon. Clubs: Channel City, University (Los Angeles); Santa Barbara, Santa Maria, Santa Maria Country. Home: Santa Barbara, Cal.†

EATON, JOHN DAVID, business exec. Dir. Dominion Bank; pres., dir. T. Eaton Co., Ltd., T. Eaton Realty Co., Ltd., Canadian Dept. Stores, Ltd., T. Eaton Life Assurance Co., T. Eaton Co., Western Ltd., T. Eaton Co., Saskatchewan Ltd., T. Eaton Drug Co., Ltd., T. Eaton Co., British Columbia, Ltd., T. Eaton Co., Ltd., Montreal, T. Eaton Co., Maritimes, Ltd. Home: Toronto, Ont., Can. Died Aug. 1973.

EBBERT, FRANK BAKER, lecturer Anti-Saloon League, lawyer; b. Cincinnati, O., June 30, 1879; s. Jonathan and Rebecca (Parke) E.; Ohio Wesleyan U., 1899-1903; A.B., De Pauw, 1904; LL.B., Chicago Law Sch., 1911; m. Mayme M. McMillan, June 5, 1906; children—Elizabeth Gae, Anne. Admitted to practice in Ill., 1911, later in Ida., Calif. and federal courts; practiced at Boise, 1912-13; prof. law of contracts, Chicago Law Sch., 1913-20; gen. counsel and legislative supt. Ill. Anti-Saloon League, 1913-20; asso. gen. counsel and legislative supt. Nat. Anti-Saloon League of America, Washington, D.C., 1919-20; gen. counsel and legislative supt. same for Pacific Coast, 1921-24; state supt. Ill. Anti-Salon League, 1924-25; nat. lecturer Anti-Saloon League of America, 1926-33; gen. counsel Bd. of Temperance M.E. Ch., 1933-. Served in Spanish-Am. War, 1898; capt. C.W.S., World War; lt. col. (Res.). Mem Delta Tau Delta. Republican. Mason. Methodist. Club: Deauville. (Santa Monica, Calif.)†

EBBOTT, PERCY JOHN, banking exec.; b. Fort Atkinson, Wis., Oct. 23, 1887; s. Harry M. and Lucretia Caroline (Edwards) E.; B.A., Oberlin Coll., 1910; LL.D. (hon.), Lawrence College, Appleton, Wis.; m. Elizabeth Camp, Jan. 1, 1923; children—John Percy, Peter Camp. Asst. cashier Nat. Park Bank, New York, 1913-17, asst. v.p., 1919-22; v.p. Seaboard Nat. Bank, 1923-29, Equitable Trust Co., 1929-30; sr. v.p. Chase Nat. Bank, 1930-49, pres., dir., 1949-55; vice chmn. bd. dirs. Chase Manhattan Bank, 1955-56, chmn. trust adv. bd., dir., 1956-75; dir. emeritus Internat. Paper Co., Allied Stores Corp.; dir. Moore-McCormick Lines, Inc., Revlon, Inc. Chmn. United Hosp. Fund. Trustee Oberlin Coll. Member of American Historical Association (trustee). Clubs: University, Wall Street, Bankers, Bedford Golf and Tennis. Home: New York City, N.Y. Died June 1975.

EBLE, FRANK XAVIER A., vice pres. Made in America Foundation, Inc.; b. Milnesville, Pa., Dec. 1, 1879; s. George and Henrietta (Diehl) E.; grad. Holy Trinity Sch., Hazleton, Pa., 1893; special course internat. law, George Washington U., 1921-22; m. Barbara E. Swinger, 1917 (died 1922); m. 3d, Hattie Redel, Aug. 19, 1926; children—(by 1st marriage) Marie Gertrude, Francis A. (dec.), (by 3d marriage) Frank Adolph, Carolyn Jane. With Hosp. Coprs, Med. Dept. U.S. Army, 3 yrs., 1900-02; mem. Eble & Haines, druggists, Hazleton, 1902-11; financial sec. Ad Club, Salt Lake City, Utah, 1914-15; Rep. Candidate for Utah Ho. of Rep., 1916; capt. 361st Inf., U.S. Army, Camp Lewis, 1917-18; capt. Service Batt., A.E.F., 1918; mem. War Loan Staff, Office of Sec. of Treasury, 1919-21; mem. staff Inst. Govt. Research, Washington, D.C., 1921-22; U.S. Treasury attaché, Berlin, 1923-29 and Jan. to Nov., 1933; mem. Kemmerer Commn. of Financial Advisers to Govt. of Poland, 1926; commr. of customs, U.S., 1929-33; now mng. dir. Made in America Foundation, Inc. and editor of Made in America Monthly; on leave to do govt. work in Washington, D.C., from Nov. 1942. Del. to Pan-Am. Commn. on Customs Procedure and Port Formalities, Washington, D.C., 1929. Decorated Order Polonia Restituta (Poland.) Mem. Am. Acad. Polit.and Social Science, Mu Sigma. Mason, Elk. Clubs: Federal Square (hon.), Nat. Republican (New York). Author: The Bureau of Internal Revenue, Its History, Activities and Organization (with L. F. Schmeckebier), 1923. Home: Washington, D.C.†

EBRIGHT, HOMER KINGSLEY clergyman, educator; b. Hartford, Ky., Aug. 30, 1878; s. Alpha Omega and Araminta (Philbrick) E.; A.B., Baker U., Baldwin, Kan., 1900; B.D., Drew Theol. Sem., 1904, Th.D., 1916; A.M., New York U., 1904; student Columbia, summer, 1914, U. of Chicago, summers, 1909, 15; D.D., Southwestern-Coll., 1923; m. Marie Moorhead, June 6, 1905; 1 dau., Elizabeth. Licensed M.E. Ministry, 1898; pastor Lakin, Kan., 1898, Linwood, Kan., 1899, Rockaway Valley, N.J., 1902, Weehawken and Grantwood, N.J., 1903, Argentine Ch., Kansas City, Kan., 1904; prof. Greek, 1905-17 prof. Bibl. lit. from 1917, dean, 1924-35, Baker U. Member Am. Assn. of Univ. Profs., Delta Tau Delta, Nat. Assn. Bibl. Instructors. Republican. Club: Rotary (dist. gov., 1943-44). Author: The Petrine Epistles, 1917; Two Letters for You, 1919; Recreation for Young and Old, 1920; Three Voices, 1934. Home: Baldwin, Kan.†

ECKART, CARL, physicist; b. St. Louis, May 4, 1902; s. William E. and Lilly (Hellwig) E.; B.S., Washington U., 1922, M.S., 1923; Ph.D., Princeton, 1925. NRC fellow, 1925-27, Guggenheim fellow, 1927; faculty U. Chgo., 1928-46, asst. prof., 1928-36, asso. prof., 1936-46; prof. Scripps Inst. Oceanography, 1946-70, emeritus, 1971-73; vice chancellor U. Cal., San Diego, 1965-67. Mem. A.A.A.S., Am. Phys. Soc., Nat. Acad. Sci., Acoustical Soc. Am., Am. Acad. Arts and Scis., Sigma Xi. Home: La Jolla, Cal. Died Oct. 23, 1973.

ECKENRODE, HAMILTON JAMES, author, editor; b. Fredericksburg, Va., Apr. 30, 1881; s. Hamilton John and Mary Elizabeth (Myer) E.; Ph.D., Johns Hopkins U., 1905; unmarried. Va. State archivist, 1907-14; prof. economics U. of Richmond, 1914-16. Apptd. historian of Va., 1927. Mem. Va. Hist. Soc., Southern Hist. Soc. (sec.), Sons Confederate Vets. (historian-gen. 1929-30). Presbyterian. Club: Commonwealth. Author: History of Virginia During the Reconstruction, 1904; Separation of Church and State in Virginia, 1911; The Revolution in Virginia, 1916; Life of Nathan B. Forrest, 1918; Told in Story (textbook), 1922; Jefferson Davis, 1923. Co-author: Rutherford B. Hayes (with P. W. Wight), 1930; Story of the Campaign and Siege of Yorktown, 1931; E. H. Harriman (P. W. Edmunds), 1933; Bottom Rail on Top, a Novel of the Old South, 1935; James Longstreet (with Bryan Conrad), 1936; George B. McClellan (with Byron Conrad), 1941; The Randolphs, 1946. Editor Southern Hist. Papers, vols. 43 to 47; compiler lists of Colonial and Revolutionary soldiers of Va. Home: Richmond, Va.†

ECKMANN, JANOS, educator; b. Keszthely, Hungary, Aug. 21, 1905; s. Janos and Martha (Nagy) E.; student Budapest U., 1925-27, 28-29, Vienna U., 1927-28; Ph.D., Budapest U., 1937; m. Gertrude Riedinger, Aug. 3, 1962. Came to U.S., 1961, naturalized, 1966. Lectr., Ankara U., 1945-48, Istanbul U., 1952-61; asso. prof. U. Cal. at Los Angeles, 1961-66, prof. Turkish, 1966-71. Mem. editorial bd. Turk Ansiklopedisi, 1946-61. Mem. Turkish Lang. Soc., Am. Oriental Soc., Mediaeval Acad. Am., Societas Uralo-Altaica, Middle East Studies Assn. Co-author: New Redhouse Turkish-English Dictionary, 1968. Contbr. articles to profl. jours.; also books. Home: Los Angeles, Cal. Died Nov. 22, 1971; interred Woodlawn Mausoleum Santa Monica, Cal.

ECKRICH, RICHARD P., meat packing co. exec.; b. Fort Wayne, Ind., 1914; grad. Notre Dame U., 1936. Chmn. bd. Peter Eckrich & Sons, Inc., subsidiary Beatrice Foods, Fort Wayne. Home: Fort Wayne, Ind. Died Nov. 5, 1973.

EDDLEMAN, THOMAS STRICKER, physician; b. Charlotte, N.C., Nov. 6, 1905; s. John Louis and Emma Jane (Stricker) E.; M.D., U. S.C., 1935; M.Sc., U. Tenn., 1940; m. Dolly Ann Wilson, Feb. 14, 1946; children—Thomas Stricker, William Loy, John Luther, Nancy Ann (Mrs. Joseph Robert Doss). Intern, Roper Hosp., Charleston, S.C., 1935-36, resident in surgery, 1936-37; fellow in orthopaedic surgery Willis C. Campbell Clinic, Memphis, 1937-40; orthopaedic staff Miss. Baptist Hosp., Jackson, St. Dominic's Hosp., Jackson, Doctors Hosp., Jackson. Served to lt. col., M.C., AUS, 1941-46. Diplomate Am. Bd. Orthopaedic Surgery. Mem. A.M.A., Miss., Central med. socs., A.C.S., Am. Acad. Orthopaedic Surgeons, Jackson C. of C., Alpha Kappa Kappa, Pi Kappa Phi. Presbyn. Home: Jackson, Miss. Died Jan. 9, 1974; buried Lakewood Meml. Cemetery, Jackson, Miss.

EDDY, LEE MOIN, pres. of Capital Development Corp.; b. Cass Co., Mich., Sept. 5, 1881; s. Lawrence and Rosetta (Lundy) E.; grad. high sch., Cass County, Mich.; m. Kathryn Bristol Wells; 1 son, Roger McCully. Sec., mgr. Marcellus (Mich.) Supply Co.; telegrapher, 1904-13; gen. chmn. Order R.R. Telegraphers, G.T. Ry., 1913-19, v.p., 1919-34; dir. Telegraphers Nat. Bank, St. Louis, 1927-35; pres. Member U.S. R.R. Retirement Bd. from 1934 (instrumental in establishment of bd.); pres. Capital Development Corp., N.J., from 1945. Mason. Home: St Petersburg, Fla.†

EDDY, PAUL DAWSON, univ. pres.; b. Montgomery, Ala., Feb. 18, 1895; s. Edgar Dawson and Stelle J. (Phillips) E.; student Des Moines Coll., 1915-17; A.B., University of Pennsylvania, 1921, A.M., 1924; B.D., Crozer Theol. Sem., 1924; LL.D., Adelphi College, 1944; Litt.D. (honorary), Long Island University, 1963; m. Isabel Vane Kinnison, June 25, 1924; 1 son, Paul Dawson. Ordained to ministry of Methodist Church; pastor Parkside Meth. Ch., Chester, Pa., 1920-24; dir. Meth. home missionary work, South Phila., 1924-25; asso. gen. dir. Christian Assn. of U. of Pa., 1925-29; dir. Wesley Foundation, Philippine Islands, and pastor Central Univ. Ch., Manila, 1929-30; dir. vacation and weekday church schs., Internat. Council of Religious Edn., and exec. dir. Religious Edn. Foundation, 1931-37; pres. Adelphi U., Garden City, L.I., N.Y., from 1937. Dir. Nassau Co. chpt. A.R.C., L.I. Assn. Served in USN, 1917-19. Fellow Royal Soc. Arts. Mason. Clubs: Garden City Golf, Rotary. Home: Ft. Pierce, Fla. Died June 30, 1975.

EDELMAN, MAURICE, mem. Brit. Parliament, author; b. Cardiff, Wales, Mar. 2, 1911; s. Joshua and Ester (Solomon) E.; B.A., Trinity Coll. Cambridge U., 1932, M.A., 1941; m. Matilda Yager, 1932; children—Sonia, Natasha. Supr. research devel. timer and plastics, 1932-41; war corr. Picture Post, 1943-45; elected Labour mem. Parliament representing Coventry West, 1945-50, Coventry North, 1950; del. Anglo-French Parliamentary Relations Com., 1948; House of Commons del. consultative assembly, Council of Europe, mem. econ. com., Strasbourg, France, 1949, Parliamentary del., 1950, U.K. del., 1951, 65, 70; vice chmn. Franco-Brit. Parliamentary Relations Com., 1950-53, chmn., 1953. Decorated Coronation medal, 1953; officier Legion of Honor (France). Jewish religion. Author: G.P.U. Justice, 1938; Production for Victory, Not Profit, 1941; How Russia Prepared, 1942; France: The Birth of the Fourth Republic, 1944; A Trial of Love, 1951; Who Goes Home, 1953; A Dream of Treason, 1955; The Happy Ones, 1957; A Call on Kuprin, 1959; The Minister, 1962; The Fratricides, 1963; The Prime Minister's Daughter, 1964; Ben Gurion: A Political Biography, 1964; The Mirrow: A Political History, 1966; Shark Island, 1967; All on a Summer's Night, 1969. Contbr. polit. jours. and mags. Died Dec. 14, 1975.

EDGAR, ALVIN RANDALL, educator; b. Eldora, Ia., Jan. 11, 1903; s. Fred John and Blanche (Foster) E.; B.A., Upper Ia. U., 1924, Mus.D. (hon.), 1948; M.A., State U. Ia., 1935; m. Mildred Lane, Nov. 7, 1925; children—Joyce Elaine (Mrs. Alvin F. Bull), Margaret Ann (Mrs. Donald McWilliams). Tchr. instrumental music pub. schs., Ia., 1924-35; condr. symphony orch. Ia. State U., 1935-72, band dir., 1935-48, prof. music, 1948-73, emeritus, 1973-75, head dept. music, 1948-61; frequent vis. prof. clinics and music festivals; adjudicator music contests. Recipient Faculty citation Ia. State U. Alumni Assn., 1962. Mem. Ia. Bandmasters Assn. (pres. 1938), Coll. Band Dirs. Nat. Assn. (pres. 1949), Music Educators Nat. Conf., Ia. Music Educators Assn., Ia. Music Tchrs. Assn. (pres. 1958-60), Phi Mu Alpha (province gov., exec. com. 1948-58). Rotarian (dist. gov. 1948). Home: Ames, Ia., Died Oct. 26, 1975.

EDGE, ROSALLE (MRS. CHARLES NOEL), conservationist; b. New York, N.Y., Nov. 3, 1881; d. John Wylie and Harriett Bowen (Woodward) Barrow; ed. in private schools; Litt.D. (honorary), Wagner College, 1948; m. Charles Noel Edge, May 14, 1909. Organized Emergency Conservation Com. 1929, one of leading conservation orgns. in U.S.; active campaigns for virgin forests, birds of prey, antelopes, mountain sheep, etc.; est. world's first hawk sanctuary known as Hawk Mountain Sanctuary Assn.; initiated campaign to save sugar pines in Yosemite Park; leader of campaign inestablishment Olympic Nat. Park of Washington State, and Kings Canyon Nat. Park, also other conservation projects in U.S. Alaska. Author and editor numerous pamphlets publs. by the Emergency Conservation Com. Home: New York City, N.Y.†

EDGERLY, BEATRICE (MRS. J. HAVARD MACPHERSON), artist, author; b. Washington; d. Webster and Edna Reed (Borgts) Edgerly; ed. Corcoran Gallery Sch. of Art, Pa. Acad. Art; m. J. Havard MacPherson, Oct. 22, 1922; children—Donald Edgerly, J. Havard (dec.). Author: From the Hunter's Bow, 1942. Home: Tucson, Ariz. Died June 13, 1973.

EDGERTON, EDWARD KEITH, wholesale co. exec.; b. Des Moines, Feb. 21, 1925; s. Orlando V. and Lena Mae (Hobson) E.; B.A., Cornell Coll., 1948; m. Margaret Miriam Frost, Aug. 26, 1948; children—Darcy (Mrs. Douglas Brian McManus), Deborah Dawn, Scott Keith. Salesman, McKesson & Robbins, Rock Island, Ill., 1948-53, Ervin Motors, Mt. Pleasant, Ia., 1953-55, McKesson & Robbins, Sioux City, Ia., 1955-60; with Brown Drug Co., Sioux Falls, S.D., 1960-74, gen. mgr., 1965-74, v.p., 1966-74, treas., 1972-74. Pres., Mankato Brown Drug (Minn.), 1973-74. Bd. dirs. Traffic Bur. Sioux Falls, 1972-74. Served with USNR, 1943-46. Mem. Am. Legion, Nat. Wholesale Druggists Assn. (chmn. merchandising com. 1972), Sioux Falls C. of C., Sales and Marketing Execs. Sioux Falls (v.p. 1972-73). Presbyn. (deacon, elder). Elk. Clubs: Knife and Fork (pres. 1970-71), Metropolitan Dinner (v.p. 1972). Home: Sioux Falls, S.D. Died Feb. 12, 1974.

EDMISTER, FLOYD (HARRIS), univ. prof.; born Canaseraga, N.Y., Oct. 30, 1881; s. Winchell and Cornelia Maria (Harris) E.; student Mount Hermon (Mass.) Sch., 1908-09; B.S., Syracuse U., 1912, Ph.D., 1918; M.S., La. State U., 1913; m. Lida Cleveland, June 27, 1916. Instr., Clemson Coll., 1913-15; prof. sci., U. of Puerto Rico, 1918-23; asst. prof. U. of N.C., 1923-27, asso. prof., 1927-47, prof. of chemistry from 1947, adviser in Gen. Coll. from 1939. Mem. Am. Chem. Soc., Sigma Xi, Alpha Chi Sigma. Presbyterian. Home: Chapel Hill, N.C.†

EDMONDS, IRA CLEMENT, livestock dealer; b. Clinton, Ia., Oct. 1, 1880; s. Edward J. and Frances (Shade) D.; prep. edn. Shattuck Mil. Sch.; student Wheaton (Ill.) Coll.; m. Mabelle Glos, of Wayne, Ill., Sept. 3, 1900. In gen. produce, lumber, feed, hardware and livestock business from 1896; breeder of registered Hereford cattle and Belgian horses; pres. Edmonds Land & Cattle Co. and the Edmonds Co., in Ia. and Minn.; chmn. Exchange State Bank, Hills, Minn.; dir. Western Mut. Fire Ins. Co. Republican. Mason (32°), K.T., Shriner, Elk. Address: Marcus, Ia.†

EDMONDS, JAMES E., army officer, journalist, author; b. New Orleans, La., Dec. 17, 1879; A.B., U. of Miss., 1900. Capt. to lt. col., F.A., Fed. Service, 1916-19; col. to maj. gen., 23d Cavalry Div., Nat. Guard, U.S., 1923-40; comdg. gen., Camp Lee, Va., 1941-43; inactive status from 1943. Awarded Legion of Merit. War correspondent, N.Y. Herald; founder, Baton Rouge (La.), State Times; mng. editor, New Orleans Times-Picayune; mil. analyst, internat. news commentator, WLW and NBC programs. Author: Fighting Fools, 1938. Contbr. Current History, Sat. Evening Post, Liberty and other mags. Address: Cincinnati, O.†

EDMONDS, THOMAS SECHLER, lawyer; b. Chgo., Oct. 21, 1899; s. Howard Owen and Mary Addison (Sechler) E.; student Phillips Exeter Acad., 1914-18, Northwestern U. Law Sch., 1922-23; A.B., Harvard, 1922; J.D., U. Chgo., 1925; m. Elizabeth Fenley, Feb. 1, 1930; 1 son, Howard Owen. Admitted to Ill. bar, 1925; law clk. McCulloch & McCulloch, Chgo., 1925-26; partner firm Gordon, Buckley & Edmonds, 1941-53, Edmonds & Linneman, 1953-56. Ashcraft, Ashcraft and predecessor, 1957-75. Member Am., Ill. (pres. 1955-56), Chgo. bar assns., Delta Tau Delta. Republican. Episcopalian. Clubs: Indian Hill (Winnetka, Ill.); University, Attic, Law, Legal (Chgo.). Home: Wilmette, Ill., Died Jan. 25, 1976.

EDWARDS, RONALD STANLEY, economist, accountant; b. May 1, 1910; s. Charles and Alice E.; B.Com., D.Sc., U. London; LL.D., U. Edinburgh, 1966, U. Strathclyde, 1973; D.Sc. (hon.), U. Bath, 1966; D.Litt., U. Warwick, 1973; m. Myrtle Violet Poplar, 1936; 2 daus. Profl. accountancy, 1926-35; asst. lectr., lectr. bus. adminstrn. London Sch. Econs., 1935-40; dep. dir. Labour, asst. sec. Ministry Aircraft Prodn., 1940-45; Sir Ernest Cassel reader in commerce U. London, 1946-49, prof. econs. (indsl. orgn.), 1949-76; dep. chmn. Electricity Council, 1957-61, chmn., 1962-68; chmn. Beecham Group, 1968-76, Beecham Inc., 1972-76; dir. I.C.I., 1969-76, Brit. Airways Bd., 1972-76, Hill Samuel Group, 1974-76. Mem. Univ. Grants Com., 1955-64, N.E.D.C., 1964-68; gov. Adminstrn. Staff Coll., Henley, 1962-70, London Grad. Sch. Bus. Studies, 1964-76, London Sch. Econs., 1968-76; mem. Govt. Com. Appointment Advt. Agys., 1970, chmn., 1972; pres. Market Research Soc., 1965-76; chmn. Com. Inquiry into Civil Air Transport, 1967-69. Mem. adv. council Dept. Sci. and Indsl. Research, 1949-54. Created knight Brit. Empire, 1963. Mem. Brit. Clock and Watch Mfrs. Assn. (hon. pres. Watch Sect.). Author: Cooperative Industrial Research, 1950; Industrial Research in Switzerland, 1951; Business Enterprise, 1958; (with H. Townsend) Studies in Business Organization, 1961; (with H. Townsend) Business Growth, 1966; (with R.D.V. Roberts) Status, Productivity and Pay: A Major Experiment 1971. Contbr. articles to profl. jours. Home: London, England., Died Jan. 18, 1976.

EDWARDS, WILLARD ELDRIDGE, originator The Perpetual Calendar; b. Chatham, Mass., Dec. 11, 1903; s. Arthur Robbins and Mabel Hallett (Eldridge) E.; student Mass. Inst. Tech., 1922-26; B.S., U. Okla., 1929; M.S., Litt.D., Jackson Coll., 1960, M.A., 1961; m. Dorothy L. Shiell, June 13, 1942; children—Willard Eldridge, Annabelle (dec.), Arthur, Geraldine (Mrs. John C. Josephson). Orginator The Perpetual Calendar, 1919, officially endorsed by Legislature, Hawaii, 1943, Commonwealth Mass., 1952, introduced in each Congress, 1943-75, in 350 cities in 100 fgn. countries, on 9 world tours 1928, 52, 56, 60, 62, 66, 68, 72, 74; proposed by Congl. resolution and bill as ofcl. calendar U.S., also for adoption by all nations; writer, lectr., 1922-75; research engr. Radio Corp. Am., N.Y.C., 1926-28; elec. engr. Alexander Aircraft Co., Colorado Springs, 1929; radio engr. trans-Pacific radio-telephony Am. Tel. & Tel. Co., Denver, also Dixon Cal., 1929-33; readio engr. radio stas., KFI-KECA, 1933-40; elec. engr. Lockheed Aircraft Co., Burbank, Cal., 1940-41; elec. engr. 9th region CAA, Honolulu, 1946-49, 14th Naval Dist., Pearl Harbor, 1949-65; ret., 1965; corrosion cons., 1953-75. Served as lt. comdr. USN, 1942-46; electronics engr. Pacific Islands, USN, ret. Registered profl. engr. Mem. Internat. Platform Assn., Soc. Am. Mil. Engrs., I.E.E.E., A.A.A.S., Nat. Assn. Corrosion Engrs., Hawaiian Astron. Soc., Honolulu Meml. Soc. (pres.), Sigma Chi, Tau Omega, Alpha Sigma Delta, Alpha Eta Rho. Mason (32 deg.). Clubs: Kokua, Toastmasters, Pearl Harbor Officers, Wollaston (Mass.) Yacht, Los Serranos (Cal.) Country. Author: The Perpetual Calendar, 1943; American Samoa, 1949; For Perpetual Generations, 1951; Origin of Christian Time, 1955; Underground Corrosion and Cathodic Protection, 1956; Time and the Calendar, 1961; Logic in a Sea of Unreason, 1964; New-Year Days are Anniversaries, 1973. Contbr. profl. publs. Licensed comml. airplane pilot. Home: Honolulu, Hawaii., Died Aug. 15, 1975; buried Nat. Cemetery of Pacific, Honolulu, Hawaii.

EDWARDS, WILLIAM CUNNINGHAM, newspaper pub.; b. Courtland, Ala., Aug. 1, 1878; s. James Randall and Elizabeth (Cunningham) E.; prep. edn., high sch., Denton, Tex.; student U. of Tex., 1894-96; m. Nettie Williams, Nov. 30, 1899; children—James Lawrence, Virginia Lee (Mrs. Grant Bush), William Cunningham, Isabel Cunningham (Mrs. J. Weldon Thomas); m. 2d, Mary Booth Schweer, Dec. 31, 1932. Owner and publisher of Denton (Tex.) Record-Chronicle, 1899-1927; pub. Washington (D.C.) Herald, 1927, Atlanta Georgian-American, 1927-28; dir. Texas Pub. Service Information Bur., 1929-31; mng. dir. Progressive Texans, Inc., 1931-36; editor Hidalgo County News, 1939; bus. mgr. Odessa (Tex.) American, 1940-41; gen. mgr. Hidalog County News, Edinburg, Tex., 1941-45, editor from 1946. Member of Texas Ho. of Reps., 1922-24; member Texas State Teachers' Edn. Commn., Tex. State Dem. Exec. Com., Internat. Public Relation Com., R.I., 1927. Mem. Tex. Press Assn. (ex-pres.), Tex. Daily Press League (ex-pres.), N.W. Tex. Press Assn. (ex-pres.), Valley Press Assn. (ex-pres.), Rotary Internat. (gov. 41st dist. 1926-27). Presbyterian. Home: Edinburg, Tex.†

EGAN, JOSEPH B(URKE), editor, educator, author; b. Omaha, Neb., Oct. 11, 1879; s. Michael B. and Josephine (Godola) E.; A.B., Creighton U., 1899, A.M., 1900, LL.D., 1936; A.B., Harvard, 1904; m. Grace Robinson, Sept. 30, 1905; 1 son, Robert Burke. Submaster Washington Sch., Boston, 1904-14; master Harvard Sch. Dist. (6 schs.), Boston, from 1914. Editor Educational Standards, Citizenship Through Character Development, The Monthly Journal of Character Training (seven years); now pres. Character Building Publications; editor World Horizon (national youth mag.) and 4-H Horizons; organizer Nat. Radio and Sch. Inst.; author of plan: Edn. Through Power Development. Vice-pres. Anti-Cigarette Alliance America. Catholic. Clubs: Boston Authors. Author: Little People of the Dust, 1913; The Beaten Path, 1918; Citizenship in Boston, 1925; Character Chats, 1926; The Wonder Book (with L. J. Wood). 1928; Wings of Flame, 1930; New Found Tales, 1930; Character Training through Story, Study, Work and Play, Book I, 1932, Book II, 1934; The Talking Statues, 1934; Prairie Days, 1935; Character and Power, 1936; Studio and School Series of Radio Plays (4 vols.) 1936 and (4 vols.) 1937; The History of U.S. in 28 Radio Plays, 1937; Diagnostic Remedial Reading Charts, 1936; Pathway to Power, 1937; Character Building in Primary Grades (8 vols.), 1939; Donn Fendler, Lost on A Mountain in Maine, 1940; The Civil War—Its Photographic History (2 vols.), 1941. Contbr. "Character Chats," syndicated weekly articles, also "Character Workshop" in Jour. of Edn., Weekly radio broadcasts of character building dramatics, 1934-37; "Spotting a Racket," weekly syndicated articles, 1939. Home: Wellesley Hills, Mass.†

EGGERS, ALBERT HERMAN, mfr.; b. Cin., Mar. 23, 1892; s. Albert George and Helene (Hillman) E.; student Cin. Tech. Sch., 1906-09, Cin. U., 1910-12; m. Grace Garrett, Nov. 21, 1917; children—Albert Herman, Joan (Mrs. Edward Flint Seaton), Gordon G. Machinist. Steptoe Shaper Co., Cin., 1913; foreman Moderon Machine Tool Co., 1914; joined Greenlee Bros. & Co., Rockford, 1915, beginning as foreman, ret. as chmn. bd.; dir. Protection Mut. Fire Ins. Co. Mem. Sigma Alpha Epsilon. Republican. Presbyn. Mason. Clubs: Union League (Chgo.); Rockford Country. University, Mid-Day. Home: Rockford, Ill. Died Nov. 20, 1974; buried Greenwood Cemetery.

EGTVEDT, CLAIRMONT LEROY, aircraft mfr.; b. Stoughton, Wis., Oct. 18, 1892; s. Sever Peter and Mary (Rublee) E.; grad. U. of Wash., 1917; m. Evelyn S. Wayland, Oct. 14, 1926. Began as designer and stress engr. Boeing Airplane Co., Seattle, Wash., 1917, chief engr., 1918, sec., 1922, v.p. and gen. mgr., 1926, pres. and gen. mgr., 1933-39; pres. and gen. mgr. Boeing Aircraft Co. until Sept. 1939, chairman; member board dirs. Pacafic Nat. Bank, Washington Mutual Bank (Seattle). Fellow Inst. Aeronautical Sciences; mem. Royal Aeronautical Soc., Theta Xi. Clubs: College, Rainier, Seattle Golf, Seattle Yacht. Home: Seattle, Wash., Died Oct. 19, 1975.

EHLERS, HENRY EDWARD, cons. engr.; b. Phila., Pa., Jan. 25, 1879; s. Peter and Helen (Collins) E.; B.S. in M.E., U. of Pa., 1900; m. Eliza Estelle Bradley, July 18, 1907; children—Peter, Henry Edward, Harriet Elizabeth. With New York Ship Bldg. Co., 1900-02, Am. Hawaiian Steamship Co., 1902-03; instr. in mech. engring., U. of Pa., 1903-06, asst. prof., 1906-11, prof., 1911-15; asst. chief engr. Pub. Service Commn. of Pa., 1914-24; dir. city transit, City of Phila., 1924-28; v.p. Day & Zimmermann, cons. engrs. from 1928. Mem. Am. Soc. M.E. (ex-president Philadelphia Sect.), Am. Soc. C.E.; ex-pres. Engrs. Soc. of Pa. Republican. Episcopalian. Club: Engineers (pres. 1932-33). Home: Philadelphia, Pa.†

EHRENZWEIG, ALBERT ARMIN, educator; b. Herzogenburg, Austria, Apr. 1, 1906; s. Albert and Emma (Bachrachova) E.; Dr. Jtr. Jur., U. Vienna

(Austria), 1928; J.D., U. Chgo., 1941; LL.M., Columbia, 1942, J.S.D., 1952; hon. doctorate, U. Stockholm, 1969; m. Erica Mitrofsky, Apr. 9, 1933; children—Elizabeth (Mrs. David T. Steffen), Joan (Mrs. Egon von Kaschnitz). Came to U.S., 1939, naturalized, 1945. Clk., asst. judge Austrian Cts., 1929-38, judge, 1933-38; research asst. N.Y. State Law Revision Com., 1942-44; admitted to N.Y. bar, 1945; asso. firm Cravath, Swaine & Moore, N.Y.C., 1944-48; Walter Perry Johnson prof. law U. Cal. at Berkeley Law Sch., 1948—; hon. prof. pvt. internat. law U. Vienna, 1960-74. Mem. adv. com. Commn. Internat. Rules Jud. Procedure. Guggenheim fellow, 1952; Fulbright prof. U. Tokyo (Japan), 1956, U. Pavia (Italy), 1960, U. Rome (Italy), 1966; NATO prof. U. Leyden (Netherlands), 1964; hon. senator U. Vienna, 1965—. Deutsche Forschungsgemeinschaft grantee, 1972. Mem. Am., N.Y. State bar assns., Am. Law Inst., Internat. Assn. Ins. Law (hon. pres. 1966—). Author: Schuldhaftung, 1936; Negligence Without Fault, 1952; Full-Aid Insurance, 1954; Treatise on Conflict of Laws, 1962; Conflicts in a Nutshell, 3d edit., 1973; Private International Law, 2 vols., 1967, 73; Psychoanalytic Jurisprudence, 1971, German edit., 1973. Contbr. numerous articles to prof. jours. Asso. editor Am. Jour. Comparative Law, 1954-71, cons., 1971-74. Home: Berkeley, Cal. Died June 4, 1974.

EHRICH, WALTER LOUIS, art dealer; b. N.Y. City, July 9, 1878; s. Louis R. and Henriette (Minzie) E.; Ph.B., Yale, 1899; Stanford U., 1899-1900; E.M., Colo. Sch. of Mines, 1902; m. Adelaide Wallach, of N.Y. City, May 27, 1913. Asst. mgr. mines in Chihuahua, Mexico, later mgr. Bonanza Belt Mining Co., Johnson, Ariz.; sec., treas. The Ehrich Galleries, New York from 1908. Trustee Hebrew Tech. Sch. for Boys. Republican. Mem. Delta Upsilon. Mason. Club: Yale. Author: One Hundred Early American Paintings (with Harold L. Ehrich), 1918. Home: New York City, N.Y.†

EHRMAN, FREDERICK L., investment banker; b. San Francisco, Jan. 3, 1906; s. Albert L. and Mina Louise (Schwabacher) E.; B.A., U. Cal. at Berkeley, 1927; m. Edith Koshland, June 25, 1929; children—Edith, Anita (dec.). Partner, Lehman Bros., 1941-74; chmn. exec. com., dir. Lehman Corp.; dir., mem. exec. com. Greyhound Corp.; dir. Lehman Bros. Internat., Medallion Ins. Co., Beckman Instruments, Inc., Travelers Express Co., Inc., 20th Century Fox Film Corp., Gen. Fire & Casualty Co. Vice chmn. Presdl. Com. for Observance 25th Anniversary UN; U.S. nat. chmn. UN Day, 1970. Chmn., mem. bd. N.Y.U. Med. Center; trustee Inst. for Crippled and Disabled, Ernest Lawrence Hall of Sci., at U. Cal.; trustee, mem. exec. com. N.Y. U. Served as comdr. USNR, 1941-45. Clubs: Bond (N.Y.); Petroleum (Los Angeles) Duchess Valley; Nimrod Valley; Century Country; Sky; Sleepy Hollow Country, Board Room. Home: Armonk, N.Y. Died Jan. 1974.

EHRMANN, HERBERT BRUTUS, lawyer; b. Louisville, Ky., Dec. 15, 1891; s. Hilmar and Ernestine (Heissman) E.; A.B., Harvard, 1912; LL.B., Harvard Law Sch., 1914; m. Sara Emelie Rosenfeld, May 12, 1917; children—Hilmar Bruce, Robert Lincoln. Admitted to Mass. bar, 1915, and began practice at Boston; mem. Goulston & Stores from 1921. Board of directors U.S. Trust Company, Boston. Chmn. Woman's Clothing Wage Bd. of Mass., 1915-19; mem. War Labor Policies Bd., 1918-19; dir. Industrial Relations Div. U.S. Shipping Bd., 1919; counsel (with Wm. G. Thompson) for Sacco and Vanzetti, 1926-27; pres. Hale House Assn., Greater Boston Fedn. Neighborhood Houses, 1934-37; trustee Mass. Training Schs., 1933-37; mem. Mass. Jud. Council, 1934-37. Mem. Mass. Civil Service Commn., 1939-45; referee and panel chmn. N.W.L.B.; arbitrator Am. Arbitration Assn. Trustee of Social Law Library, Boston. Mem. Am. Jewish Com., (pres. 1959-61, hon. pres. from 1961), Am., Mass., Boston (council) bar associations, Old South Assn. (mgr.), C. of C., Delta Sigma Rho. Jewish religion. Club: Harvard. Author several books and plays including: The Case That Will Not Die, 1969; Commonwealth vs. Sacco and Vanzetti (Edgar Allen Poe award 1969). Home: Brookline, Mass. Died June 17, 1970.

EICHELBRENNER, ERNEST A., educator, physicist; b. Rustringen, Germany, June 28, 1913; s. Ernst C. and Katharina (Koehn) E.; student univs. Hamburg, Germany, Rome, Italy, 1931-37; Staatsexamen, Hamburg, 1938, Dipl.-Math., 1943; Dr. es Sc., Paris, France, 1955, Lic. es Lettres, 1956; m. Emilie M. Martin, Aug. 16, 1939; children—Hans-Michael, Detlef, Ursula, Etienne. Research engr. Deschimag, Bremen, Germany, 1938-45; asst. U. Hamburg, 1946; research engr. Onera, Chatillon-sous-Bangneux, France, 1947-58, cons., 1958-65; maitre de conf. U. Poitiers (France), 1958-60, prof. without chair, 1961-62, titular prof. 1962-65; titular prof. mech. engring. Laval U., Quebec, Can., 1965-74. Cons. BTZ, Brunoy, France, 1958-63. Recipient Henry Bazin prize and medal French Acad. Scis., 1965. Fellow Am. Acad. Mechanics (founding mem.); asso. fellow Am. Inst. Aeros. and Astronautics; mem. Am. Soc. Mech. Engrs., Math. Soc. France, other profl. socs. Reviewer Zentralblatt fur Mathematik, 1958—. Research in fluid mechanics particularly boundary layer theory; 3-dimensional (laminar and turbulent) boundary layers, characteristics and criteria of separation and reattachment of 3-dimensional boundary layers; problems of heat transfer in 3-dimensional flow. Home: Que., Can. Died July 1, 1974.

EICHENLAUB, FRANK JOSEPH, physician; b. Erie, Pa., Dec. 4, 1894; s. Frank Joseph and Mary (Sieverding) E.; M.D., Georgetown U., 1918; m. Dorothy Mae Fisk, Dec. 30, 1945; children—Frank Joseph, John, Jane E. (Mrs. William C. Sunier). Intern, St. Elizabeth's Hosp., Youngstown, O., 1918-19; cons. in dermatology Columbia Hosp. Women, Doctors Hosp., D.C. Gen. Hosp., Georgetown U. Hosp.; cons. dermatology and syphyllis Army Med. Center, USPHS, NIH, prof. emeritus in dermatology and syphyllis Georgetown U. Recipient Emeritus award Walter Reed Army Med. Center. Diplomate Am. Bd. Dermatology. Mem. A.M.A. (life), Am. Dermatology Assn., D.C. (life), So. (life, past chmn. dermatology and syphyllis sect.) med. socs. Republican. Lutheran. Club: Farmington Country (Charlottesville, Va.). Home: Westmoreland Hills, Md. Died Feb. 13, 1972; buried Prospect Hills Cemetery, Washington, D.C.

EINUM, LUCILLE GRACE JOHNSON, (Mrs. Elmer John Einum), civic worker; b. New Richmond, Wis., Aug. 13, 1907; d. Willard Joseph and Nora (Unseth) Johnson; grad. Wis. State U., 1926; student U. Minn.; pvt. study voice; m. Elmer John Einum, June 2, 1936; children—Catherine Ann (Mrs. John P. Eimerman), Victoria Lou (dec.). Pres., Wis. Fedn. Music Clubs, 1964-68, bd. dirs., 1947-74, adv. chmn., 1968-72; chmn. TV program Starring Young Wis. Artists, 1968-74; sec.-treas. nat. Council dists. and state presidents Nat. Fedn. Music Clubs, 1966-68, nat. vice-chmn. nat. music week, 1967-69, nat. chmn. nat. music week, 1969-73, nat. bd. dirs., 1971-73, nat. chmn. TV com., 1973; gov.'s appointee to bd. dirs. Wis. Arts Found and Council, 1965-73; 1st state pres. Young Audiences of Wis., from 1968; Midwest regional dir. Nat. Young Audiences, 1970-73; mem. panel Nat. Conf. on Continuing Adult Edn. in Music, U. Wis., from 1967; chmn. 1st Angel Ball Benefit Stout Found., 1968-69; mem. Mayors Adv. Com., from 1968; chmn. Wonderful Wis. Week, Rice Lake, 1971. Pres. Barron County Republican Women's Club, 1969-72. Bd. dirs. Wis. Youth Symphony. Adv. chmn. bd. trustees Stout State U. Found. Barron County Campus; bd. govs. Florentine Opera Co., Milw., from 1972. Named Woman of Year, Rice Lake, Fedn. Woman's Clubs, 1966-67; recipient award for support of arts Gov. Wis., 1972; Distinguished Citizens award Am. Assn. U. Women, 1973. Mem. Civic Concert Assn. (bd. dirs. 1951-73, pres. from 1969), Wis. P.T.A. (bd. dirs. 1959-61), Rice Lake Fed. Music Club (life). Delta Omicron. Republican. Presbyn. (choir dir.), Club: Fortnightly Woman's (life, past pres.). Address: Rice Lake, Wis., Deceased.

EISEMAN, FREDERICK BENJAMIN, dry goods exec.; b. St. Louis, Feb. 28, 1881; s. Benjamin and Mattie (Butzel) E.; A.B., Yale, 1901; m. Justine Godchaux, June 1, 1910; children—Justine (Mrs. Dr. Paul Mecray), Mary (Mrs. Ben Harris), Eleanor (Mrs. Henry Putzel, Jr.), Ben, Fred Benjamin. Sr. v.p. Rice-Stix, Inc. and predecessor, St. Louis; mem. advisory board of R.F.C. in St. Louis; director First Nat. Bank, St. Louis. Pres. bd. trustees David Ranken, Jr. Sch. Mech. Trades. Club: University (St. Louis). Home: Calyton, Mo.†

EISENBERG, DAVID BERTON, editor; b. Sheboygan, Wis., July 1, 1892; s. Max and Natalie (Fradkin) E.; student Milw. State Norman Sch., 1912-13, Marquette Coll., 1913-14, Armour Inst. Tech., 1915-16; Ph.B., U. Chgo., 1918; m. Natalie Marcus, Jan. 10, 1915 (dec.); 1 son, Leland. Book prodn. mgr. A.C. McClurg & Co., pubs., Chgo., 1919-22, advt. mgr., 1923; advt. mgr. Ben Franklin Monthly, 1923-24, Ben Franklin & Western Printing Co., 1924-28; advt. mgr. Graphic Arts Monthly, Chgo., 1929-33, editor, from 1933; president Graphic Arts Publishing Company, 1929-58. Executive chairman of Printing Week in Chicago, 1950. Mem. Chicago advisory bd. Am. Med. Center, Denver; dir. Bus. Opportunities for Blind. Served from pvt. to cpl., U.S. Army, 1918-19, with AEF, France. Mem. Chgo Club Printing House Craftsmen, Soc. Typographic Arts, Am. Legion, Am. Inst. Graphic Arts, Chgo. Press Vets. Assn., Zionist Orgn. Chgo., Vets. Fgn. War, Am. Jewish Congress, Sigma Delta Chi. Jewish religion. Mem. B'nai B'rith. Clubs: Chicago Press, Cliff Dwellers, Caxton. Home: Chicago, Ill. Died July 27, 1975; buried Memorial Park, Skokie, Ill.

EISENDRATH, MAURICE NATHAN, rabbi; b. Chgo., July 10, 1902; s. Nathan Julius and Clara (Oesterreicher) E.; A.B., U. Cin., 1925, LL.D., 1957; rabbi, Hebrew Union Coll., Cinc., 1926, D.D., 1945; LL.D., Brown U., 1964; m. Rosa Brown, Nov. 24, 1926 (dec. July 1963); m. 2d Rita Hands, June 1964; stepchildren—Linda, Charles. Rabbi, Charleston, W.Va., 1926-29, Holy Blossom Temple, Toronto, Cincinnati, O., 1943-46; pres. Union Am. Hebrew Congregations, 1946-52, pres. for life, 1952-73; rep. to Synagogue Council Am. Bd. govs. Hebrew Union Coll.-Jewish Inst. Religion; bd. dirs. Nat. Jewish Welfare Bd; vice chmn. Am. bd. World Jewish Congress; mem. theologian's com. Am. Assn. for Internat. Office of Edn.; v.p. World Union for Progressive Judaism; nat. co-chmn. commns. on religious orgns. Nat. Conf. Christians and Jews; mem. nat. council Joint Distbn. Com. Campaign; mem. Nat. Community Relations Adv. Council; mem. exec. bd Central Conf. Am. Rabbis. Author: The Never Failing Stream, 1939; Can Faith Survive, 1958. Contbr. to Dimensions, American Judaism, Jewish Layman. Died, Nov. 10, 1973.

EISENHART, MARTIN HERBERT, mfr.; b. York, Pa., Sept. 16, 1884; s. Charles Augustus and Emma (Pfahler) E.; B.S., Princeton, 1905; B.S. in Chem. Engring., Mass. Inst. Tech., 1907; LL.D., Syracuse University, 1951; D.Sc., Gettysburg College, 1958; was married to Elsa M. Bausch, April 28, 1914; children—Richard Henry, Eleanor Ann (Mrs. William H. Morris), Edward Charles. Chemical engineer Eastman Kodak Co., Rochester, N.Y., later became asst. supt., then supt.; asst. gen. mgr., Bausch & Lomb Optical Co., Rochester, then gen. mgr. and v.p., pres., gen. manager, 1935-50, chairman bd., 1950-54, hon. chmn., 1954-56; dir. dir. Taylor Instrument Companies; trustee Rochester Savings Bank; dir. Rochester Gas and Electric Co., Rochester Telephone Corp., Security Trust Co. Trustee University of Rochester (ex-chmn. bd.), Eastman Dental Dispensary, Rochester Inst. Tech.; director Rochester Community Chest, Rochester Red Cross; bd. mgrs. Eastman Sch. of Music. Mem. Rochester Chamber of Commerce (trustee), Rochester Museum Assn. (Civic Medalist, 1944), Optical Soc. Am., Rochester Engring. Soc., Newcomen Soc. Eng., Rochester Chem. Soc., Am. Ordnance Assn. Republican. Presbyterian. Clubs: Princeton, University New York; University, Rochester, Genesee Valley, Rochester Country, Rotary (hon.) (Rochester). Home: Rochester, N.Y. Died Jan. 7, 1975.

EISNER, MONROE, business exec.; b. Red Bank, N.J., Jan. 14, 1893; s. Sigmund and Bertha (Weis) E., student Phillips Exeter Acad., 1910; A.B., Harvard, 1914, M.B.A., 1915; m. Winone Jackson, Sept. 16, 1916; 1 son, Robert; m. 2d, Frances Lewis, 1965. With Sigmund Eisner Co., 1915—, now pres.; pres. Sego Trading Co., 1935-73. Bd. dirs., officer Monmouth County chpt. A.R.C., Monmouth County Orgn. Social Service; v.p. Monmouth County Aid Soc.; bd. dirs. Monmouth Med. Center, pres. 1960-73. Mem. Monmouth County Hist. Soc. Clubs: Harvard, Nat. Republican (N.Y.C.); Harvard (N.J.); Hollywood Golf; Palm Beach (Fla.) Country; Elberon Beach, Ocean Beach (Elberon, N.J.). Home: Red Bank, N.J. Died May 2, 1973.

EKEBERG, LARS BIRGER, pres. Nobel Found.; born Uppsala, Sweden, Aug. 10, 1880; s. Alexander and Hilma (Lemke) E.; LL.D., U. Uppsala, 1907; LL.D. (hon.), Heidelberg U., 1921, Copenhagen, 1945; Ph.D. (hon.), Stockholm U., 1953; LL.D. (honorary), Helsinki University, 1955; married Brita Swartz, Aug. 10, 1911; children—Lars-Olof, Dagmar (Mrs. Hesser). Asst. prof. law Uppsala U., 1904-07; prof. law Stockholm U., 1907-25; mem. Civil Legislation Com., 1910-25, pres., 1927-31; minister justice, 1920-21, 1923-24; judge Swedish Supreme Ct. Justice, 1925-27; pres. Svea Ct. Appeal, 1931-46; Marshall of the Realm, after 1947. Swedish del. 6th Hague Conf., 1928, Geneva Conf., 1930, 31; mem. permanent arbitration ct. The Hague 1937-55; pres. Swedish Com. Internat. Relief work, 1944-56. Vice president Nobel Found., 1943-47, pres. after 1947. Pres. bd. Stockholm U., 1928-58, Stockholm High Sch., Economics, 1940-57. Mem. Swedish Acad., Acad. Sci., Acad. History, Acad. Agr. Home: Stockholm, Sweden†

EKIN, JOHN JAMISON, ry. official; b. Whitestown, Pa., June 8, 1873; s. Robert Findley and Mary Jane (Brenneman) E.; grad. Elwood City (Pa.) High Sch., 1895; m. Estelle Huntley, June 8, 1903; children—John Jamison, Jr., Kenneth Huntley, Robert Lee, Charles William. Warehouseman and yardman Pittsburgh & Western R.R. Co. (now B.&O. R.R.), Elwood City, 1895-96, clerk, Mar.-Aug. 1896, clerk accounting dept., Pittsburgh, 1896-1901, chief clerk accounting dept., Pittsburgh, 1901-02, bookkeeper, 1902-03; chief clerk to auditor subsidiary lines, B.&O. R.R. Co., Baltimore, 1903-08; auditor Washington (D.C.) Terminal Co., 1908-13; gen. accounting B.&O. R.R. Co., Baltimore, 1913-15, gen. auditor, 1915-18; federal auditor Allegheny Region, U.S. R.R. Adminstrn. Baltimore, 1918-20; comptroller B.&O. R.R., Baltimore, 1920-36; vice-president and comptroller, 1936-43, v.p., 1943-46, retired from June 1946. President Railway Accounting Officers Assn., 1942. Republican. Presbyterian. Clubs: Scimiter, Maryland (Baltimore); Rotary (Towsen, Md.). Home: Baltimore, Md.†

ELDER, ALFONSO, coll. pres.; b. Sandersville, Ga., Feb. 26, 1898; s. Thomas Jefferson and Lucy Lillian (Phinizy) E.; A.B. magna cum laude, Atlanta U., 1921; A.M., Teachers Coll., Columbia U., 1924, Ed.D., 1938; m. Louise Holmes, Aug. 29, 1931, Teacher mathematics, Bennett Coll., Greensboro, N.C., 1921-22, Elizabeth City (N.C.) State Teachers Coll., 1922-23; dean, N.C. Coll. for Negroes, Durham, 1924-43; dir. grad. sch. of edn., Atlanta U., 1943-47; pres., N.C. Coll., Durham, from 1948. Mem. mayor's com. on human relations, Durham, N.C.; member Bd. of Control for Southern Regional Education. Member of board of dirs. Mutual Building and Loan Association. Member bd. directors Lincoln Hospital, Durham, N.C. Mem. N.C. Negro Teachers Assn. (treas., 1941-43), Alpha Phi

Alpha. Democrat. Author: Culture and the Curriculum (with R.O. Johnson), 1946; A. Manual for Students on the Process of Developing a Plan of Action for Promoting Sch. Improvements (with H. C. Hamilton); A Study of Long Range Needs at North Carolina College, 1958. Home: Durham, N.C. Died Aug. 7, 1974; buried, Durham, N.C.

ELDRIDGE, MURIEL TILDEN (MRS. RICHARD BURDICK ELDRIDGE), advt. agy. exec., musician; b. Malden, Mass., July 22, 1893; d. Bert Olin and Mary Abby (Mayo) Tilden; A.B., Vassar Coll., 1914, M.A., 1921; Ph.D., U. Pa., 1958; grad. Inst. Applied Music, N.Y., 1926; m. Richard Burdick Eldridge, Jan. 28, 1922; children—David Rogers, Robert Tilden. Tchr. piano, 1916-42; tchr. music Prospect Hill Sch., Trenton, N.J., Friends Sch., Fallsington, Pa., 1917-30; Eldridge, Inc., Advt. Agy., Trenton, N.J., 1930-72. Lectr., writer on music and literature, 1915-72. Mem. Trenton Symphony Assn. (past sec.), D.A.R. (past treas.), Lawrenceville Colony New Eng. Women (past pres.). Presbyn. Clubs: Trenton College (past pres.), Zonta (past pres.), Opti-Mrs. Club (past pres.). Author: Thomas Campion: His Poetry and Music. Composer children's songs. Home: Trenton, N.J. Died June 1972.

ELLICKSON, RAYMOND THORWALD, educator; born Charlson, N.D., Mar. 5, 1910; s. John and Christine (Quale) E.; A.B., Reed Coll., 1935; A.M., Ore. State Coll., 1936; Ph.D., U. of Chicago, 1938; m. Loene Gibson, June 17, 1938; children—Bryan, Mary, James. Instr. physics, Poly. Inst., Brooklyn, 1938-41, asst. prof., 1941-46; asso. prof. physics, becoming prof. and head physics dept., Reed Coll., Portland, Ore., 1946-48; professor of physics University of Oregon, 1948-70, head of physics department, 1948-60, asso. dean grad. sch., 1948-55, acting dean, 1955-58; sr. physicist Chgo. Midway Laboratories, 1952; active in research for United States Signal Corps. Office Sci. Research and Development. Pratt & Whitney Aircraft and R.C.A. Communications. Writer, cons. elementary sci. program A.A.A.S., 1964-70, v.p. Pacific Athletic Conf., 1968-69. Mem. Am. Assn. Physics Teachers (pres., Ore. Sect.), Assn. Portland Scientists, Am. Phys. Soc., A.A.A.S., Nat. Collegiate Athletic Assn. (v.p. 1969-70), Am. Assn. Univ. Profs., Optical Soc. of Am., N.Y. Acad. Scis. Kiwanian. Club: Eugene Country. Home: Eugene, Ore. Died May 30, 1970.

ELLING, CHRISTIAN, educator; b. Nov. 14, 1901; M.A., Copenhagen U., Ph.D., Lectr., Copenhagen (Denmark) U., 1932-39, provost dept. art history, 1939-74, prof. history art, from 1949, dean faculty letters, 1944-45. Bd. dirs. Nat. Mus., Fredericksborg, from 1951, Danish Acad. in Rome, 1954-57. Decorated knight comdr. Swedish Order Polar Star, Italian Order Merit, officer Order Dannebrog, Italian Gold Medal Merit. Fellow Royal Danish Acad. Scis. and Letters, Royal Danish Hist. Soc., Danish Acad. Address: Copehagen, Denmark. Died 1974.*

ELLINGTON, EDWARD KENNEDY (DUKE), composer, arranger; b. Washington, Apr. 29, 1899; student pub. schs. Washington; studied music with Henry Grant; hon. degrees Wilberforce U., 1949, Milton Coll., 1964, Coll. Arts and Crafts, 1966, Morgan State, 1967, Yale, 1967; m. Edna Thompson, 1918. First profl. appearance as jazz player, 1916, N.Y.C., 1922; engaged Cotton Club, N.Y.C., 1927-32; toured Europe, 1933, 38, 50, 58, 60, 62-67, 69-71, Eng. and France, 1948, Japan, 1964, 66, 70, Latin Am., 1968, 71, Far East and Australia, 1970, 72, USSR, 1971; appeared ann. concerts Carnegie Hall, 1943-50, Met. Opera House, 1951; appeared motion picture Check and Double Check, 1930; compositions and recordings include Mood Indigo, Solitude, Sophisticated Lady, Caravan, I Let a Song Go Out of My Heart, Do Nothing Till You Hear From Me, Don't Get Around Much Any More, In a Sentimental Mood, Black and Tan Fantasy, Creole Love Call; composed motion picture scores for Anatomy of a Murder, Paris Blues, Assault on a Queen, Change of Mind; pioneered in wordless use of voice as mus. instrument in orchestration, also use of miniature concerto form in bldg. jazz arrangements around a soloist; pioneered in extended orchestral jazz compositions and suites including Reminiscing in Tempo, 1935, Black, Brown and Beige (a tone parallel to the history of the American Negro), 1943, New World A-Coming, 1945, Liberian Suite, 1948, Harlem, 1950, Suite Thursday, 1960, Latin American Suite, 1968, New Orleans Suite, 1970, Goutelas Suite, 1971; Togo Brava Suite, 1971; Uwis Suite, 1972; conceived and wrote A Concert of Sacred Music, premiered Grace Cathedral San Francisco, 1965, Cathedral Ch. St. John the Divine, N.Y.C., 1968; ballet score The River for Am. Theater Ballet, 1970. Recipient numerous mag. poll awards including readers poll Down Beat, Internat. Jazz Critics Poll, Grammy Nat. Acad. Rec. Arts and Scis., 1967, 73. Spingarn medals N.A.A.C.P., 1959; Medal of Freedom presented by Pres. Nixon on 70th birthday, 1969; decorated Legion d'Honneur (France), 1973. Author: Music is My Mistress, 1973. Home: New York City, N.Y. Died May 1974.

ELLIOTT, CHARLES HERBERT, commr. of edn.; b. Normal, Ill., Aug. 2, 1878; s. David Spangler and Emily Alberta (Muilberger) E.; B.S., McKendree Coll., 1907; A.M., Columbia, 1908, fellow in edn., 1909-10, Ph.D., 1914; LL.D., John Marshall Coll. of Law, 1933; Litt.D., Rutgers U., 1937; m. Helen Peters, Aug. 24, 1912; children—Mary Peters, Kathryn Helen. Teacher, prin. and supt. pub. schs., 1899-1906, 1908-09; instr., Southern Ill. Normal Sch., 1910-13; prof. edn. and dir. training sch., N.C. State Coll. for Women, 1914-15; prof. edn. and head of dept., Rutgers, 1915-23, dean of Sch. of Edn., 1923-27, dir. Summer Session, 1915-27, dir. extension courses, 1916-27; commr. of edn., State of N.J., after 1927; sec. N.J. State Bd. of Edn. after 1927. Mem. and sec. Ednl. Survey Commn. of N.J., 1927-31; mem. N.J. State Bd. of Regents (sec. 1929-30), N.J. State Pub. Library Commn., N.J. State Commn. for Rehabilitation of Handicapped Persons, N.J. Conf. on Child Health and Protection (exec. com. after 1931), N.J. Washington Bi-Centennial Com.; mem. White House Conf. on Child Health and Protection (sub com. on spl. classes), 1929-30; mem. N.J. Sch. Survey Commn., 1932-34; one of organizers N.J. State High Sch. Conf. in 1918 (mem. gen. conf. com. 10 yrs.); chmn. sub-com. on state activities Child Edn. Sect., Nat. Safety Council, after 1936; hon. mem. N.J. United States Constitution Commn., 1936-39. Mem. N.J. Council after 1937, Gov.'s. Emergency Com., 1939-40, State Defense Council of N.J. from 1940. Trustee Rutgers U. Mem. N.E.A., Am. Assn. Sch. Adminstrs., Am. Inst., Ednl. Research Assn., Am. Acad. Polit. and Social Science, Nat. Soc. Coll. Teachers of Edn., Nat. Soc. for Study of Edn., N.J. Council of Edn. (chmn. com. on pedagogics, 1920-25), N.J. Edn. Assn. N.J. Science Teachers' Assn., N.J. Schoolmasters Club, N.Y. Science Teachers' Assn., N.J. Schoolmasters Club, N.Y. Schoolmasters Club, Phi Beta Kappa, Sigma Xi, Phi Delta Kappa; fellow A.A.A.S. Presbyn. Club: Newark Athletic. Home: New Brunswick, N.J.†

ELLIOTT, HAROLD HIRSCH, mfg. exec.; b. Rockford, Ill., Aug. 12, 1886; s. James Hirsch and Anna (Fox) E.; student Lewis Inst., 1900-03, St. John's Mil. Acad., Delafield, Wis., 1904-06; m. Hazel Goss, Oct. 30, 1915; children—Louise Caroline, Harold H. Salesman James H. Hirsch & Co., Chgo., 1907-10; exec. Ill. Life Ins. Co., 1910-17; pres., treas. Halsam Products Co., mfrs. toys, embossed wood products, Chgo., 1917-46, chmn., dir., 1946-73; chmn. Goss Printing Press Co., 1937-55. Comdg. officer Lake Mich. area Temp. Res., USCG, 1942-45. Republican. Mason (K.T., Shriner). Clubs: Chicago Athletic, Sheridan Shore Yacht, Chicago Yacht (Chgo.); Glen View (Ill.) Golf; Key Largo Anglers. Home: Gencoe, Ill. Died 1973.

ELLIOTT, WILLIAM JOHN, church official; b. Grundy County, Ia., Sept. 11, 1878; s. George B. and Susan (Weedon) E.; student Cornell Acad., Mount Vernon, Ia., 1899-1901; A.B., Cornell Coll., 1904; LL.D., Dakota Wesleyan U., 1936; m. Emma Cora Bruett, Oct. 10, 1906; children—George Bruett, Orlo John, Duane William (dec.). Bookkeeper and asst. cashier Hubbard (Ia.) State Bank, 1896-99; bookkeeper 1899-1919; nat. treas. Bd. of Home Missions and Ch. Extension of Methodist Ch., 1919-49 and of the Division of Home Missions and Church Extension of the Methodist Church, 1940-49; spl. rep. Div. Home Missions and Ch. Extension, Methodist Ch. from 1949; treasurer and dir. Robert Morris Hotel Co., Phila., 1934-49; vice-pres. and dir. 22d and Arch St., Inc., Phila. 1938-48; director and treasurer National Association of Goodwill Industries, 1920-48. Del. to Gen. Conf. M.E. Ch., 1916; del. Uniting Conf. of Cornell Coll., Mount Vernon, Ia., 1914-19; trustee and treas. Lansdowne Meth. Ch., 1924-48. Mem. Phi Beta Kappa. Republican. Mason. Home: St. Petersburg, Fla.†

ELLIS, CARLYLE, ednl. film producer; b. Toronto, Can., Aug. 17, 1878; s. Robert Baldwin and Adelaide Almina (Callender) E.; ed. high sch., Toronto; m. Elizabeth R. Purdon of New Orleans, La., 1902. Came to U.S., 1900, naturalized citizen, 1917. Began as reporter, British Columbia, Can., 1894; with New York Sunday World, 1901-06; free lance writer, 1906-10; editor Alaska-Yukon Mag., 1910-12; contributing editor Everybody's Mag., 1912; asso. and mng. editor Delineator, 1913-14; West Coast rep. Triangle Corpn., motion picture producers, 1915, eastern scenario editor, 1916; with Div. of Films, U.S. Com. on Pub. Information, 1917; independent producer of ednl. films for U.S. Children's Bur., U.S. Women's Bur., Y.W.C.A., N.Y. State Dept. of Health, N.Y. Tuberculosis Assn., etc., 1918-29; dir. of sound pictures for Am. Telephone and Telegraph Co., 1929-34; dir. pub. relations Central Casting Corpn., Hollywood, Calif., 1934-35, staff contbr. The Spur, N.Y., and other mags. Clubs: New York Camera; Nat. Press (Washington, D.C.). Home: Palmdale, Cal.†

ELLIS, GORDON, food co. exec.; b. Black Rock, Ark., Feb. 6, 1915; s. Harry and Pauline (Creager) E.; corr. student Alexander Hamilton Inst.; student Advanced Mgmt. Program, Harvard Bus. Sch., 1960; m. Marion Louise Jacobs, Dec. 25, 1938; children—Richard Gordon, Emily Ann, Susan Lee, David Edward Store mgr. Kroger Co., 1937-38; salesman Gen. Mills, 1938-40; salesman Pet Inc., 1940, through various positions to dir. merchandising, 1952-57, asst. v.p. marketing, 1957-59, v.p. marketing, 1959-60, exec. v.p. Milk Products div., St. Louis, 1960-61 pres., div., 1961-62, exec. v.p. operations, 1962-66, pres., chief operating officer, 1966-68; pres., chief exec. officer Fairmont Foods, Omaha, 1968-71; exec. v.p., chief operating officer Interstate Brands Corp., Kansas City, Mo., 1971-73; sr. v.p. Wetterau, Inc., 1973; dir. Alcon Labs., Leonard's Pit Barbecue, Inc., Wetterau Foods, Inc. Mem. Am. Mgmt. Assn., President's Assn., Newcomen Soc., Harvard Business Sch. Club. Methodist. Home: Chesterfield, Mo. Died Sept. 12, 1973; interred Valhalla Mausoleum, St. Louis, Mo.

ELLIS, JAMES, engr.; b. Memphis, Dec. 22, 1898; s. S. J. and Elise (Crockett) E.; student Memphis pub. schs.; m. Josephine Morris, Oct. 16, 1928. With Comml. Chem. Co., Memphis, 1922-25; draftsman Tenn. Eastman Co., div. Eastman Kodak Co., Kingsport, 1925, since mech. engr., supt. engring. div., gen. supt. in charge engring., constrn. and power; dep. works mgr. Clinton Engr. Works, Oak Ridge, Tenn., 1943-45; asst. v.p. Tenn. Eastman Co., Kingsport, 1958-64, ret. Profl. engr., Tex., Tenn. Named Engr. of Yr., Tenn. Soc. Profl. Engrs., 1963. Fellow Am. Soc. M.E.; mem. Am. Legion, V.F.W., Tau Beta Pi. Episcopalian. Mason (Shriner). Contbr. articles to tech. jours. Home: Tenn. Died Nov. 3, 1972; interred, Harriman, Tex.

ELLIS, JOHN HENRY, newspaperman; b. New Hope, Tex., Sept. 29, 1894; s. Frank and Sarah Elizabeth (Jones) E.; student U. Tex., 1913-17; m. Jeannette Baxter, Apr. 21, 1926; children—Sarah Jeannette (Mrs. John Mort), John Baxter. Reporter Fort Worth Record, 1921-23; with Dallas News, Houston Chronicle, New Orleans Item, 1923-26; city editor Fort Worth Star-Telegram, 1927-29, news editor, 1929-55. mng. editor, 1955-56, editor, 1956-63. Mem. Nat., Tex. Asso. Press mng. editors, Am. Soc. Newspaper Editors, Sigma Delta Chi. Methodist. Mason. Club: Ft. Worth. Home: Fort Worth, Tex. Died June 28, 1975; buried Greenwood Cemetery, Fort Worth, Tex.

ELLIS, KATHARINE RUTH, author; b. Charles City, Ia., May 31, 1879; d. Charles Daniel and Flora Ann (Wilbur) E.; A.B., Vassar, 1901; Wis. Library Sch., Madison, 1912; unmarried. Later engaged in library work. Author: The Wide-Awake Girls, 1908; The Wide-Awake Girls in Winsted, 1909; The Wide-Awake Girls at College, 1910. Home: Charles City, Ia.

ELLSWORTH, JOHN ORVAL, educator, former mission adminstr; b. Providence, Utah, November 15, 1891; s. Asa Charles and Emily Elizabeth (Theurer) E.; B.S., Utah State Agr. Coll., Logan, Utah, 1917; M.S., Cornell U., 1924, Ph.D., 1926; student Columbia, summer 1925; m. Annie Merrill, Oct. 21, 1914. Teacher of science and agr., Ricks Coll., Rexburg, Ida., 1915-17; county agrl. agent, Gooding, Ida., 1917-19; asst. state leader of county agents, Ida., 1919-21; county agrl. agent, Idaho Falls, Ida., 1921-23; instr., Cornell U., 1925-26, asso. prof., Okla. Agrl. and Mech. Coll., 1926-28; prof. and head of agrl. econ., Tex. Tech. Coll., 1928-36, prof. and head of dept. of econ. and bus. adminstrn., 1937-42, dean of commerce and prof. of marketing, 1942-46; prof., head div. of distribution, U. of Denver, 1946-50. Chief farm management sect., region XII, U.S. Resettlement Adminstrn., 1936-37; pres. Ch. of Jesus Christ Latter Day Saints Mission, 1950-54; professor religion and bus. Brigham Young U., from 1954. Boy Scout Adult Leader for 30 years (Silver Beaver award for Boy Scout leadership). Mem. Am. Econ. Assn., Am. Farm Econ. Assn., Am. Assn. Univ. Profs., Southwestern Social Science Assn., Tex. Acad. Science, A.A.A.S., Phi Delta Kappa. Alpha Phi Omega. Club: Knife and Fork. Author of poems and composer of songs; also author bulletins of experiment sta., Okla. Agrl. and Mech. Coll. Author: Our Ellsworth Ancestors, 1956. Died Sept. 11, 1974.

ELMHIRST, LEONARD KNIGHT, agrl. economist; b. Howden Yorkshire, Eng., June 6, 1893; s. William and Mary (Knight) E.; M.A. cantab., Trinity Coll., Cambridge U., 1919; B.S., Cornell U., 1921; Dr. Polit. Sci. (hon.), U. Freiburg (Germany), 1953; Litt. D. (hon.) U. India, 1960; U. Exter (Eng.), 1972; D. Civil Law, U. Durham, 1962, U. Oxford, 1970. m. Dorothy Whitney Straight, Apr. 3, 1925; children—William, Ruth (Mrs. Maurice Ash). Dir. Inst. Rural Reconstrn., Bengal, India, 1921-24; founder, pres. Internat. Assn. Agrl. Economists, 1929; staff Joint Brit.-Am. agrl. mission Middle East, 1942; chmn. Polit. and Econ. Planning, 1939-53; devel. commr., 1949-65; cons. in field Bd. dirs., chmn. Dartington Hall, trust, 1931-72. Council mem. Exeter U. Author: Robbery of Soil, 1922; Rural Reconstruction, 1923; Application Economic Research Village Bengal, 1930; Trip to Russia, 1933; Social Trends Rural Areas, 1938. Contbr. articles profl. jours. Address: Totnes, Devonshire, England. Died Apr. 16, 1974.

ELOESSER, LEO, surgeon; b. San Francisco, Calif., July 29, 1881; s. Arthur and Molly (Heyneman) E.; B.S., U. of Calif., 1900; M.D., Heidelberg, 1907; unmarried. Vol. asst. surg. clinic, Heidelberg, 1906, asst. Cancer Inst., 1906-07; vol. asst. Royal Surg. Clinic, Kiel, 1908-09, Augusta Hosp., Berlin, 1909; asst. in surgery, U. of Calif., 1910-12; surgeon to Reserve Hosp., Ettlingen, and Reserve hosps. at Karlsrube, 1915-16; maj. M.C., U.S. Army, 1918-19; clin. prof. surgery, Stanford, 1913-46, emeritus clin. prof. after 1946; specialist (surgery) in charge medical training, health div. China Branch, U.N.R.R.A., 1945-47; surg. U.N. World Health Orgn. (China Mission) from 1947; exchange prof. surg., U. of Buenos Aires, Argentina, 1943; consulting surgeon, U.S. Veterans Bureau, U.S. Marine Hosp.; formerly chief of Stanford surgical service at San Francisco Hosp.; chief Mobile Surg. Unit, 7B, Surgeon General's Office, Spain, 1937-38. Mem. A.M.A., Am. Assn. Thoracic Surgery (pres. 1934), Am. Surg. Assn., Am. Coll. Surgeons; mem. sub. com. Thoracic Surgery, Nat. Research Council, Deutsche Gesellschaft for Chirurgie, Alpha Omega Alpha, Sigma Xi. Clubs: San Francisco Yacht, St. Francis Yacht. Contbr. to periodicals. Home: San Francisco, Cal.†

ELSENBAST, ARTHUR S., chemist, corp. exec.; b. N.Y.C., July 16, 1890; s. George J. and Wilhelmina Nickle (Reinhardt), E.; B. Chem., Cornell U., 1912; m. Dorothy Evelyn Chisholm, Apr. 18, 1940. Analytical chemist Nichols Copper Co. (now Phelps Dodge), Long Island City, N.Y., 1912-15; works chemist Central Dyestuff & Chem. Co., Newark, 1915-16, Dr. A. Gessler, S.I., N.Y., 1916; plant chemist Seydel Chem. Co., Jersey City, 1917; joined Johns-Manville Corp., N.Y.C., 1917, gen. mgr. Celite div., 1946-56, v.p. 1951-56; v.p. Johns-Manville Sales Corp., 1937-56, Johns-Manville Products Corp., 1946-56, ret.; cons. Treas., dir. YMCA, Greenwich, Conn., 1958. Mem. Am. Chem. Soc., Am. Inst. Chemists. Clubs: Chemist, Cornell, N.Y. Athletic (N.Y.C.); Greenwich Country. Home: Greenwich, Conn. Died Dec. 31, 1973.

ELSEY, CHARLES, b. Oakland, Calif., 1880. Former pres. Western Pacific R.R. Co., Western Realty Co.; former v.p. Alameda Belt Line, Salt Lake City Union Depot & R.R. Co., retired, 1948; dir. Am. Trust Co. Home: San Francisco, Cal.†

ELSSFELDT, OTTO HERMANN WILHEIM LEONHARD, clergyman; b. Northelm, Hanover, Germany, Sept. 1, 1887; s. Otto and Luise (Wedemeyer) E.; D.D., Berlin U. 1922; Ph.D., Göttingen U. (Germany), 1916; m. Hildegard Kullrich, Mar. 21, 1914. Ordained to ministry Evang. Ch., 1912; preacher, Berlin, 1912; lectr. theology Berlin U., 1913-22; prof. Bibl. sci. Halle U., 1922-73. Mem. Brit. Soc. D.T. Study, Am. Soc. Bibl. Lit. and Exegesis, Saxon, East German acads. sci., Acad. Sci. and Lit. Mainz, Acad. Inscriptions at Belles-Lettres, Brit. Acad., German Archeol. Inst. Kungl. Humanistiska Vatenskapsamfundet 1 Lund. Author: Der Maschal im Alten Testament, 1913; Israesis Geschichte, 1914; Krieg und Bibol, 1915; Erstlinge und Zehnten lm Alten Testament, 1917; Hexateuch-Synopse, 1922, 2d edit., 1962; Die Quellen des Richterbuches, 1925; Die Komposition der Samuelisbucher, 1931; Baal Zaphon, 1932; Einieltung in dos Alte Testament, 1934, 3d edit., 1964; Molk als Opferbegriff, 1935; Phillster und Phönizier, 1936; Ras Schamra und Sanchunjaton, 1939; Tempel und Kulte syrischer Sta dte in hellenistisch-römischer Zeit, 1941; Dia ältesten Traditionan Israels, 1950; El lm ugaritischen Pantheon, 1951; Der Gott Karmel, 1953; Die Genesis der Genesis, 1958, 2d edit., 1961; Das Lied Moses Deuteronomium 32, 1958; Kleine Schriften I-V, 1962 ff.; The Old Testament-an Introduction, 1965; Neu kellaphabetische Texto aus Ras Schamra-Ugarit, 1965; Franz Delitzsch und Wolf Graf Baudissin, 1966; Die Komposition der Sinai-Erzählung Exodus, 19-34, 1966; Adonis und Adonaj, 1970; Bibilography in: Kleine Schriften V; others. Address: Halle, German Democratic Republic. Died Apr. 23, 1973.

ELTON, FREDERIC GARFIELD, educator; b. Boston, Apr. 30, 1881; s. Phineas and Annie Elizabeth (Johnson) E.; grad. Mass. State Normal Sch., 1904; certificate Mass. Inst. Tech., 1906; student Boston U., 1907, Bentley Sch. of Accounting, 1909; pvt. study art; m. Ella Wesley Smith, Aug. 15, 1906; children—Wallace, Roger, Richard, Elizabeth (Mrs. Robert J. Hardy), Jean (Mrs. James B. Moran). Sub-master Brockton (Mass.) High Sch., also prin. Brockton Eve. High Sch., 1904-17; prodn. supt. Marsh Motor Co., Brockton, 1917-18; supr. advisement and tng. Soldier and Sailor Rehabilitation, 1918-20; Fed. Bd. of Vocational Edn., 1920-21; dist. sup., founder civilian rehabilitation N.Y. State Edn. Dept., 1921-51; dir. Am. Rehabilitation Commn., Inc., from 1951; instr. orthopedic dept. Post Graudate Hosp., 1927-34; lectr. Harvard, Columbia, N.Y.U. Founder Rehabilitation Center for Disabled, 1924, N.Y. Convalescent Center, 1926. Received citations from Am. Rehibilitation Commn., Inc., N.Y. State Edn. Dept., Nat. Commn. for Mental Hygiene, Nat. Rehabilitation Assn., Men's Group U. of State N.Y. Mem. Nat. Rehabilitation Assn. (founder, charter mem.), Assn. for Personality Tng. (charter), Internat. Soc. for Welfare of Cripples, N.Y. Personnel Management Assn. Club: Kiwanis. Editor Rehabilitates, Rev., 1927-38, from 1952. Home: Cliff., N.Y.†

ELWELL, CLARENCE EDWARD, bishop; b. Cleve., Feb. 4, 1904; s. George John and Josephine (Messer) E.; B.A., John Carroll U., 1925, LL.D., 1959; student theol. faculty U. Innsbruck (Austria), 1925-29; M.A., Western Res. U., 1934; Ph.D., Harvard, 1938. Ordained priest Roman Cath. Ch., 1929; dir. high schs. and academies Cleve. Diocese, 1938-46; prof. edn. grad. div. St. John Coll., 1938-48; asst. supt. schs., Diocese Cleve., 1933-38, supt. schs., 1946-73; bishop of Columbus, 1968-73. Author: Our Quest for Happiness, 4 vols., 1945; Our Holy Faith, 8 vols., 1959; New Catholic, Speller, 8 vols., 1963; Christian Child Reading Series, 1959-64; New Ways with Numbers, 8 vols, 1964. Home: Columbus, O. Died Feb. 16, 1973.

ELWELL, HERBERT, musician, critic; b. Minneapolis, May 10, 1898; s. George Herbert and Belle (Horn) E.; student U. Minn., 1916-19; pvt. study in composition with Ernest Bloch, N.Y. City, 1919-21, Nadia Boulanger, Paris, France, 1922-27; Doctorate (hon.), Western Res. U., 1946, U. Rochester, 1954; m. Maria Cecchini, July 27, 1927. Head composition dept. Cleve. Inst. Music, 1928-45; music critic Cleve. Plain Dealer 1932-65; program note editor Cleve. Orchestra, 1930-36; tchr. composition Oberlin Conservatory Music 1945-74, Eastman Summer Sch., Rochester, N.Y., 1940-74. Performance of prin. compositions; Ballet Suite, Happy Hypocrite, Charles Weidman, Dance Repertory Theatre, N.Y.C., 1931; Introduction and Allegro, N.Y. Philharmonic, 1942; Quintet for strings and piano, Paris, 1925; String Quartet, N.Y.C., 1944; Blue Symphony, N.Y.C., 1946; Lincoln Requiem, Oberlin (internat, radio broadcast N.B.C.), 1946; Pastorale for voice and orchestra, Cleve. Orchestra, under Szell, 1948; Violin and Piano Sonata, Chgo, 1948; Ode for Orchestra, under Stokowski, Houston, 1953; The Forever Young for voice and orchestra, under Stokowski, St. Louis, under Szell, Cleveland, 1954; Suite for Violin and Orchestra, Louisville, 1957. chmn 1952 Yaddo Festival, mem. Yaddo Corp. Fellow Am. Acad. in Rome, 1923-26. Awarded Paderewski prize, 1945; Ohioana Library Assn. award, 1947. Mem. Phi Delta Theta, Pi Kappa Lambda. Home: Cleveland, O. Died Apr. 17, 1974.

ELWELL, RICHARD E., lawyer, aerospace cons.; b. Leistershire, Eng., May 11, 1895; s. William Elwell-O'Nions and Elizabeth (Kennedy) E.; came U.S. 1910, naturalized 1919; A. B., U. of Calif., 1924; LL.B., George Washington U., 1925; m. Anne Brans, Jan. 21, 1928; children—Richard Brans, Robert Gregory. Law clerk in office of member of Congress, 1924-25; attorney, Office Alien Property Custodian, 1925-27; special asst. to attorney gen., 1928; staff mem. Fokker Aircraft Corp., 1928-30, Gen. Aviation Corp., 1929-30; dir. Myers Patents Corp., 1929-30; Aircraft Engine Development and Accessory Corp., 1929-30; private practice, Washington, 1930-34, 60-74; div. counsel, N.R.A., 1934-35; gen. counsel, Prison Industries Reorganization Adminstrn., 1935-38; 1st asst. to gen. counsel of joint commn. investigating Tenn. Valley Authority, 1938-39; special asst. to solicitor, Dept. of Interior, 1939-40; chief counsel div. of compliance Civil Aeros. Adminstrn., 1941, gen. counsel, 1941-53, chief I.C.A. O. Mission to Turkish Govt., 1953-54; special advisor to adminstr. of Civil Aeros, 1954-60. Served with Medical Detachment, 33d Division, A.E.F., 1917-19; World War II, Army Air Force, 1942-46; col. USAF, ret. Awarded Victory medal with 3 clasps, Occupational medal, Pacific Theater medal with 1 star, European Theater medal with 1 star, Am. Theater and Occupation of Germany medals, Commendation Medal, Silver Star. Member of the United States National Commission of Permanent American Aero. Commn., 1942-43; apptd. mem. U.S. sect. Comite Internat. Technique d'Experts Juridique Avions, 1946, del. to conf., Cairo, 1946; adviser U.S. delegation to Provisional Internat. Civil Aviation Orgn., 1946. del. to 1st session legal com., Internat. Civil Aviation Orgn., Brussels, 1947, mem. and chmn., U.S. delegation, 2d session, Geneva, 1948, member and del., 3d session, Lisbon, 1949, advisor to U.S. delegation, Montreal, 1950, mem. and del. 6th session legal com. Montreal, 1950, 7th session, Mexico City, 1951, Rome, 1952. Alternate mem. Air Staff Com. on Res. Policy USAF. Mem. Lambda Chi Alpha. Pvt. pilot. Home: Washington, D.C. Died Apr. 7, 1974.

ELWOOD, EVERETT SPRAGUE, editor and consultant; born Ft. Plain, New York, July 1, 1881; son of Philip Henry and Alice Viola (Dolan) E.; ed. U. of Mich., 1904-05; Syracuse U., 1905-08 (Ph.B.); m. Olive Louise White, July 1, 1908; children—Margaret Alice (Mrs. John Y. Mohler), Everett Sprague, Barbara Louise (Mrs. George F. Gruschow). Prin. Penn Yan (N.Y.) Acad., 1908-10. Exec. sec. Com. on Mental Hygiene of N.Y. State Charities Aid Assn., 1910-15, also asst. sec. N.Y. State Charities Aid Assn., 1912-15; sec. N.Y. State Hosp. Commn., 1915-21; mng. dir. Nat. Bd. Med. Examiners, 1915-28, exec. sec. and treas., 1928-51, editor and cons., 1951-53, cons., after 1953. Member Mayor's Com. on Survey of Phila. Mental Hosp., 1931; chmn. Governor's Com. on Survey of Pa. State Mental Hosps., 1932-33. Trustee Laurelton (Pa.) State Village for Mental Defectives, 1924-27; trustee Norristown (Pa.) State Hosp., 1931-35; past dir. Armstrong Assn. Phila. Fellow A.A.A.S., Am. Public Health Assn.; hon. mem. Am. Psychiatric Assn.; mem. Am. Occupational Therapy Assn. (v.p. 1931-38; pres. 1938-46), New York State Com. on Mental Hygiene, National Committee for Mental Hygiene, Public Charities Association of Pennsylvania (president 1945-49), Alpha Omega Alpha, Delta Sigma Rho, Pi Kappa Alpha. Republican. Methodist. Mason. Clubs: National Republican (N.Y. City); St. Bernard Fish and Game Club (Canada). Contbr. to med. jours. Editor of The Diplomate (pub. by Nat. Bd. Med. Examiners), 1928-53. Home: Philadelphia, Pa.†

ELY, THOMAS SOUTHGATE, physician; b. Jonesville, Va., June 8, 1914; s. Thomas Bascom and Jennie (Edds) E.; A.B. magna cum laude, Emory and Henry Coll., 1935; M.D., Med. Coll. Va., 1939; m. Barbara Ellen Dixon, Sept. 7, 1940; children—Thomas Harrison, Maria Jane. Intern hosp. div. Med. Coll. Va., 1939-40; practice gen. medicine, Jonesville, 1945-74; med. examiner, coroner Lee County, Va. Pres. Jonesville Drug Co., Inc., 1951-74; dir. Powell Valley Nat. Bank, Jonesville, Lee Farmers' Tobacco Warehouse, Pennington Gap, Va. Chmn. Jefferson Forest dist. Boy Scouts Am., commr. Wilderness Rd. dist., 1970-74, Silver Beaver award, 1972, Pioneer award, 1973. Chmn. Jonesville Town Planning and Zoning Com., Lee County Sch. Electoral Bd.; med. adviser Lee County Selective Service Bd., from 1964. Bd. trustees Holston Conf. Colls., from 1961; exec. com. Emory and Henry Coll., 1962-70. Served to maj. M.C., AUS, 1941-46; ETO, N. Africa. Decorated N. Africa-ETO medal with 7 battle stars; recipient De Molay Legion of Honor, 1970. Fellow Am. Acad. Gen. Practice; mem. Am. Legion (local post positions to dept. comdr., dept. rehab. chmn., nat. med. adv. bd., vice chmn. nat. legislative Commn.; nat. exec. committeeman from Va.), 40 and 8 (life, cheminot nat. 1958-59), Lee County C. of C. (organizer, pres. pro-tem., dir.), Lee County Med. Soc. (past sec.-treas., (past pres.), Med. Soc. Va., A.M.A., Emory and Henry Alumni Assn. (pres. 1963-69), The Cabiri, Blue Key, Tau Kappa Alpha, Pi Gamma Mu, Kappa Phi Kappa, Theta Kappa Psi, Sigma Zeta. Methodist (chmn. bd. stewards, lay leader, chmn. bd. trustees, pres. dist. laymen's orgn. 1959-60, mem. bd. hosps. and instns. Holstein Conf.). Mason (K.T., 32°, Shriner, Jester), Odd Fellow, Woodman of World; mem. Order Eastern Star (past patron). Club: Lions (past pres. Jonesville; zone chmn. 1959-60; dist. gov. 1961-62; internat. counsellor 1962-74, Lion of Year, Achievement award). Address: Jonesville, Va. Died Sept. 21, 1974.

EMERICH, IRA, former newspaper exec.; b. Balt., Apr. 11, 1894; s. David and Adeline (Sulzbacher); E.; m. Cornelia Watts Van Siclen, Oct. 17, 1958. Sales dir. Esquire Features, Inc., 1934-41, Chgo. Sun Syndicate, 1941-42; sales dept. Hall Syndicate, 1946-55, sales dir., 1955-56, exec. v.p., 1956-67, dir., 1958-67; dir. newspaper relations Pubs.-Hall Syndicate, 1967-68. Chief press distbn. sect. OWI, 1942-44; newspaper liaison officer War Finance Program, Treasury Dept. 1944-46. Master ceremonies Washington Stage Door Canteen, 1943-45. Served with F.A., U.S. Army, World War I. Recipient Distinguished Service citation Treasury Dept., 1945. Clubs: Nat. Press (Washington); Forty Plus (dir. 1971-73) (N.Y.C.). Home: New York City, N.Y., Died Oct. 22, 1975.

EMERMAN, DAVID, mfg. co. exec.; b. Akron, O., Sept. 18, 1896; s. Solomon and Deborah (Rudd) E.; student Case Sch. Applied Sci., 1916-17, U. Mich., 1918-19; m. Edith Bergman, Dec. 17, 1939; children—Denise (Mrs. Donald Schmerin), Nancy, Laurie Ann. Chmn. bd., dir. Unit Crane and Shovel Corp., Milw., 1948-74, Davis & Thompson, Milw., 1948-74, Allied Products Corp., Detroit, 1962-74, chmn., 1963-74. Active fund raising drives United Founds., Brandies U., United Jewish Appeal. Served with USNR, 1917. Home: Franklin, Mich. Died Oct. 1974.

EMERSON, CHESTER BURGE, clergyman; b. Haverhill, Mass., July 28, 1882; s. John A. and Abbie Jane E.; A.B., Bowdoin, 1904, D.D., 1919; B.D., Union Theol. Sem., 1909; D.D., Kenyon Coll., 1933; unmarried. Ordained Congl. ministry, 1909; pastor First Parish, Saco, Me., 1909-13, North Woodward Ch., Detroit, 1913-32; canon residentiary Trinity Cathedral (Episcopal), Cleveland, Jan.-Nov. 1933, dean, 1933-51, dean emeritus from 1951; lectr. Gen. Theol. Sem., N.Y.C., 1951-52; locum tenens Calvary Ch., Pitts., 1951-52, St. Peters, Albany, N.Y., 52-53, Ashtabula, O., 1953-54, St. Marks, Toledo, 1955, Christ Ch., Hole Sound, Fla., 1957, St. Michaels in the Valley, Ligonier, Pa., 1959, St. Pauls, Delray, Fla., 1961. Priest-in-charge St. Anne's. Kennebunkport, Me., summers from 1942. Mem. Diocesan Council, deputy, General Convention, October 1940, 1943, September 1946, 1949; member Standing Committee of Diocese, Ohio, 1943-51, diocesan council 1935-41, 42-48. Served under YMCA in France, 1917-18; chaplain Gen. Hosp. No. 36 R.C. Formerly corporate mem. A.B.C.F.M.; mem. exec. Com. State Bd. Congl. Chs.; pres. bd. trustees Mich. Conf., 1919-29; moderator State Conf., 1925; mem. exec. com. Commn. on Missions of Nat. Council Congl. Chs., 1919-28. Overseer Bowdoin Coll.; trustee Hampton Inst.; sometime trustee Olivet Coll., Chgo. Theol. Seminary, Mem. Arts and Crafts Soc., Founders Soc. of Art Museum of Detroit, Detroit Symphony Orchestra (dir., 1920-33), Fine Arts Soc., Alpha Delta Phi. Republican. Mason (32°, K.T., Shriner, also 33° from Grand Council of Greece, Athens, also from Northern Jurisdiction U.S. 1932; Grand Prelate of K.T. of the U.S.). Clubs: Union (Cleve.); University (N.Y.C.); Bath & Tennis, Coral Beach. Lectr. in homiletics. Address: Palm Beach, Fla., Died Aug. 5, 1973.

EMERSON, SAM W., bldg. contractor; b. Cleveland, 1881; s. James and Kate (McKnight) E.; B.S. and C. E., Case Inst. Tech., 1902, D. Eng., 1941; m. Florence Taylor, 1909. Held subordinate positions with engring. and constrn. cos., 1902-11; organized Sam W. Emerson

Co., building contractors, in 1912, chmn. bd., after 1912; dir. Columbia Vise & Mfg. Company, National Acme Co., White Sewing Machine Co. Past chmn. bd. trustees Case Inst. Tech. Recipient Gold Medal, Cleve. C. of C., 1956. Mem. Builders Exchange (past pres.), Cleve. C. of C. (pres. 1944). Clubs: Union, Shaker Heights (past pres.). Home: Cleveland, O.†

EMERY, ALDEN H(AYES), chemist, administrator; b. Lancaster, N.H., June 2, 1901; s. Vernon and Caroline (Hayes) E.; A.B. magna cum laude. Oberlin (O.) Coll., 1922; A.M., Ohio State University, 1923; D.Sc. (honorary), Dickinson College, 1957; m. Dorothy Radde, June 16, 1924; children—Alden Hayes, Robert Wilson. Chemist U.S. Bur. of Mines, Pittsburgh and Washington, D.C., 1923-36; asst. mgr. Am. Chem. Soc., Washington, D.C., 1936-45, asst. sec., 1943-45, sec. and bus. mgr., 1946-47, exec. sec. from 1947. Fellow A.A.A.S., Am. Inst. Chemists; mem. American Chemical Society, Society Chem. Industry, Washington Acad. Scis., Phi Beta Kappa, Sigma Xi, Alpha Chi Sigma, Gamma Alpha. Clubs: Cosmos, Torch, University (Washington); Chemists (N.Y.C.). Asst. editor Chem. Abstracts, 1930-37; sect. editor Metallurgical Abstracts, 1931-39. Home: Silver Spring, Md. Died Mar. 14, 1975.

EMERY, JOHN GARFIELD, past nat. comdr. Am. Legion; b. Grand Rapids, Mich., July 4, 1881; s. John and Mary Ann (Roberts) E.; grad. high sch., Grand Rapids; m. Ethel May Bailey, of Traverse City, Mich., June 20, 1906; children—Jane, Esther. Sec. Chase Constrn. Co., Detroit, Mich., 1898-1903; cashier Antrim Iron Co., Mancelona, Mich., 1904-09; pres. Wolverine Farms Co., Grand Rapids, 1909-17; now in real estate business; president Emery Realty Corporation, Grand Rapids. Entered the O.T.C., Illinois, Aug. 1917; commd. capt. inf.; went to France, Dec. 24, 1917; assigned as capt. Co. F, 18th Inf., later promoted maj.; participated in capture of Cantigny, 2d Battle of the Marne, St. Mihiel, Meuse-Argonne offensive; wounded Oct. 9, 1918, in Argonne and invalided home; hon. discharged Mar. 31, 1919. Awarded D.S.C., Silver Star Medal with Palm, and Order of Purple Heart (U.S.); Croix de Guerre with palm (French); Comdr. Order of Leopold, Militaire (Belgian), Order of the Crown (Italian), Legion of Honor, and Fourragere Croix de Guerre (French). Elected City Commr., Grand Rapids, and reelected to same office, but resigned June 14, 1921, upon election as nat. comdr. Am. Legion for term ending Nov. 2, 1921. Ex-pres. Grand Rapids Real Estate Bd. Commr. of Insurance, State of Michigan. 1940. Republican. Conglist. Mason (Shriner). Home: Grand Rapids, Mich.†

EMIL, ALLAN D., lawyer; b. N.Y.C., Mar. 25, 1898; s. Morris and Rose (Dlugasch) E.; student Erasmus Hall High Sch., N.Y.C., 1911-15; student Columbia U. Extension, 1915-16, N.Y. Law Sch., 1916-18; LL.B., Bklyn. Law Sch., 1919; m. Kate Silverman, June 26, 1921; children—Arthur D., Judy Anne. Admitted to N.Y. bar, 1920, practiced in N.Y.C.; partner law firm Roseman, Colin, Kaye, Petschek, Freund & Emil; dir. Square D. Co., Phillips-VanHeuson Co., Walter Reade Orgn., Midland Glass Co., Guardian Mut. Fund. Asso. chmn. Fedn. Jewish Philanthropies, N.Y.C., 1965-66, fund raising campaign chmn., 1966-68. Trustee Albert Einstein Coll. Medicine, Austin Riggs Center, Inc. Bennington Coll.; v.p., dir. Psychoanalytic Found.; exec. v.p. Montfiore Hosp. and Med. Centre: Served with U.S. Navy, 1917-18. Spl. hon. mem. Am. Inst. Aeros. and Astronautics. Dir. George Jr. Republic. Mem. Assn. Bar N.Y.C., N.Y. County Lawyers Assn., Am. Fedn. Arts (trustee). Clubs: Sands Point (L.I.) Golf (hon., trustee); Glen Oaks Golf (Great Neck, N.Y.) (hon., trustee); Harmonie, Grolier. Home: New York City, N.Y., Died Feb. 4, 1976.

ENDALKACHEW, MAKONNEN, Ethiopian govt. ofcl.; b. Addis Ababa, Ethiopia, 1927; M.A., with honours in Polit. Economy, Oxford (Eng.) U.; married; 3 sons, 4 daus. Attaché, Ministry Fgn. Affairs Ethiopia, 1951-52, chief protocol, 1952-53, dir. gen. charge polit. affairs, 1953-54, vice minister fgn. affairs, 1954-55; mem. Ethiopian delegation to Bandung Conf., 1955-56, to London Conf. and Suez Canal, 1956, to Menzies Com. on Suez Canal, 1956-57; vice minister social affairs and edn., 1957-58; ambassador to Eng., 1959-60; minister commerce and industry, also chmn. Nat. Coffee Bd., 1961-66; permanent rep. Ethiopia to UN, 1966-69, mem. Security Council, 1967-69, pres.; minister communications, telecommunications and posts, 1969-74; prime minister, 1974. Vice pres. Trade to Devel. Conf., Geneva, Switzerland; chmn. bd. Econ. Commn. Africa. Pres., Alliance of YMCA, 1973. Address: Addis Ababa, Ethiopia., Executed by military regime, 1974.

ENGELHARDT, WILLIAM R., lawyer; b. Chgo., June 24, 1909; s. William M. and Louise (Steinke) E.; Ph.B., U. Chgo., 1930, J.D., 1932; m. Doris R. Rickard, Jan. 18, 1936; children—Robert Rickard, Margo Louise. Admitted to Ill. bar, 1932, since practiced in Chgo.; partner law firm Norman & Billick, and predecessors, from 1938. Dir. Cook County (Ill.) Sch. Dist. 17, 1942-45; treas. Tri-County Schs. Bd. of Ill. Assn. Sch. Bds., 1943-45; pres. Inverness (Ill.) Assn., 1953. Trustee Village Inverness, 1962-65, mayor, 1965-69. Mem. Am., Ill., Chgo. bar assns., Phi Beta Kappa, Order of Coif, Phi Alpha Delta (pres. Marshall chpt. 1931-32). Clubs: University, Executives, Legal (Chgo.); Inverness Golf (bd. dirs. 1947-55). Home: Palatine, Ill. Deceased.

ENGELMORE, IRWIN B., advt. exec.; b. N.Y.C., Mar. 22, 1910; s. Abraham Paul and Minnie (Esserman) E.; student Cooper Union, 1927-28, Grant Central Sch. Art, 1929-30, U. So. Cal., 1936-37, N.Y. U., 1944-45; m. Clair Ornstein, June 15, 1933; children—Robert Searl, Anthony Richard. Advt. mgr. Broadway Dept. Stores, Los Angeles, 1935-41; exec. v.p. Sterling Advt. Agy., N.Y.C., 1941-54; chmn. bd. Engelmore Advt. Inc., and predecessor, N.Y.C., 1954-74. Active fund raising advt. div. B'nai B'rith. Served to 1st lt. Civil Air Patrol, 1942-45. Mem. N.Y.C. Advt. Club, Aircraft Owners and Pilots Assn., Nat. Aero. Club. Republican. Clubs: Nat. Republican (N.Y.C.); Shinnecock (L.I., N.Y.) Anglers. Home: Hollywood, Fla. Died June 5, 1974.

ENGSTROM, ADOLPH (HJAIMAR), musician; born Fredrickstad, Norway, Sept. 2, 1880; s. Andreas and Amanda (Petterson) E.; voice student Cosmopolitan Sch. Music, Chicago, 1904-13; m. Gretchen Louise Bueckling, July 26, 1910; 1 son, Dr. Ralph W. Came to U.S. 1885, naturalized 1900. Studied voice with noted teachers in Minneapolis, Chicago, N.Y.; tenor soloist in churches Minneapolis, 1900-04, Chicago, 1904-06. Evanston, 1906-11, Minneapolis and St. Paul, 1917-19; with Innes Orchestral Band 1911, Lyceum Tour 1911-12; concerts, oratorios, and with N.Y. Symphony, 1915; prof. voice, Benton Harbor, Mich. Sch. of Music, 1911-12, Grinnell Coll., Ia., 1913-17, Minneapolis Northwestern Conservatory and Minn. Coll., Minneapolis, 1917-19, St. Olaf Coll., Northfield, Minn., 1919-48. Lutheran. Home: Lancaster, Pa.†

ENGSTROM, WILLIAM WEBORG, educator, physician; b. Milaca, Minn., June 29, 1915; s. Otto and M. Caroline (Weborg) E.; B.S. with distinction, U. Minn., 1935, M.D., 1940, M.S. in Biochemistry and Medicine, 1944; m. Elizabeth G. Wulf, July 12, 1943; children—Ann Rigby (Mrs. Charles Reydel), Frederick William, Sara Elizabeth (Mrs. Douglas Geske). Intern Johns Hopkins Hosp., 1939-40; fellow Mayo Found., 1941-44; instr., then asst. prof. medicine Yale Sch. Medicine, 1946-50; mem. faculty Marquette U. Sch. Medicine, 1950-74, prof., chmn. dept. medicine, 1958-74; med. dir. Milw. County Hosp., 1958-74. Mem. Am. Field Service Com., Elm Grove, Wis., 1960—. Served to capt., M.C., AUS, 1944-46. Recipient Teaching award Phi Chi, 1957; Distinguished Achievement award U. Minn., 1964; Tri-State Teaching award, 1971. Diplomate Am. Bd. Internal Medicine. Mem. Assn. Am. Physicians, Am. Soc. for Clin. Investigation, Central Soc. Clin. Research, A.A.A.S., Am. Coll. Physicians, Endocrine Soc., Am. Thyroid Soc., Am. Fedn. Clin. Research, Am., Wis. diabetes assns., Milw. Acad. Medicine, Milw. Internists Club, Am. Goiter Assn., Assn. Profs. Medicine, Royal Soc. Medicine (London), Sigma Xi, Alpha Omega Alpha. Author articles on metabolis diseases, internal medicine, med. philosophy. Home: Elm Grove, Wis. Died Jan. 22, 1974; interred, Milaca, Minn.

ENRIETTO, JOHN, lawyer; b. Piedmont, Italy, June 20, 1900; s. Joseph and Cecilia (Vallero) E.; brought to U.S., 1904, naturalized, 1923; A.B. magna cum laude, Harvard, 1922, LL.B., 1925; m. Marion Ray Bulmer, Sept. 5, 1928; children—James J., Mary C. (Mrs. David L. Shover). Admitted to Ill. bar, 1925, D.C. bar, 1929; asso. firm Hopkins, Starr, Hopkins & Hamel, Chgo. and Washington, 1925-29; partner Hamel, Park, McCabe & Saunders, specializing in fed. taxation, departmental and govt. claims, Washington, 1929-53, resident partner, Chgo., from 1953. Served as pvt. U.S. Army, 1918; as lt. col. AUS, 1943-46; legal officer SHAED Mission (Norway), 1944-45, legal div. Office Mil. Govt. U.S. (Germany), 1945-46; col. USAR 1953. Decorated Bronze Star medal; King Haakon medal (Norway). Mem. Fed., Am., Ill., D.C., Chgo. bar assns., Harvard Law Sch. Assn., Mil. Govt. Assn., Res. Officers Assn., Am. Arbitration Assn., Phi Beta Kappa Assos. Mason. Clubs: Executives, Ill. Athletic, Nat. Press (Washington). Collaborator in various publs. and articles on procedure and taxation. Home: Wheaton, Ill. Died Mar. 17, 1975; interred Spring Valley, Ill.

ENSIGN, MARY JANE (MRS. DWIGHT CHESTER ENSIGN), club woman; b. Kalamazoo, Apr. 28, 1916; d. Clarence Merton and Alice (Thackeray) Field; B. Design, U. Mich., 1939; m. Dwight Chester Ensign, Oct. 1, 1940; 1 dau., Mary Jane (Mrs. Robert W. Bednas). Interior decorator J. L. Hudson Co., Detroit, 1938-40. Past leader Girl Scouts U.S.A. Mem. St. Dunstan's Guild of Cranbrook (dir. 1957-59), Episcopal Ch. Woman (past chmn. Oakland convocation pres. Christ Ch., Cranbrook, Mich., 1955-56), U. Mich. Alumni Assn., Am. Assn. U. Women, D.A.R., Woman's Aux., Wayne County Med. Soc., Alpha Chi Omega. Republican. Episcopalian (Altar Guild). Clubs: Village Woman's of Birmingham and Bloomfield Hills (mem. bd. dirs., chmn. house and grounds com. 1960-62); Henry Ford Hospital Staff Wive's (Detroit); Little Garden (Birmingham, Mich.). Home: Franklin, Mich., Died Oct. 23, 1975.

ENSIGN, WILLIS LEE, lawyer; b. Binghamton, N.Y., Apr. 5, 1922; s. Willis Lee and Willnita (Strider) E.; A.B., Southwestern U., 1942; LL.B., Harvard, 1948; m. Jule K. Donald, June 13, 1953; children—Donald W., John S. Admitted to N.Y. bar, 1948, Ala. bar, 1953; atty. Western Union Telegraph Co., 1948-50; atty. Ford Motor Co., 1950-52; asso. firm Carter, Ledyard & Milburn, 1953-59, partner, 1959-73. Mem. N.Y. State Bar Assn., Assn. Bar City N.Y., Am. Bar Assn. Home: Short Hills, N.J. Died Sept. 28, 1973.

ENSOR, LOWELL SKINNER, clergyman, coll. pres.; b. Balt., May 15, 1907; s. John T. and Birdie (Skinner) E.; A.B., Johns Hopkins, 1928; B.D., Drew U., 1931; D.D. (hon.), Western Md. Coll., 1944; L.H.D. (hon.), U. Md., 1950; LL.D., Am. U., 1963, Coll. Notre Dame of Md., 1968; m. Eloise Bittner, May 28, 1931; 1 dau., Caryl Jeanne (Mrs. James Lewis). Ordained to ministry Meth. Ch., 1931; pastor Calvert M.E. Ch., Prince Frederick Md., 1931-34, Ames Ch., Pikesville, Md., 1934-40, Westminster Ch., 1940-47; pres. Western Md. Coll., 1947-72, pres. emeritus, 1972-75; dir. Carroll Co. Bank and Trust Co., Balt. Fed. Savs. and Loan Assn. Pres. Assn. Ind. Colls. of Md., 1953-55, mem. Gov's. Commn. to Study Needs of Higher Edn. in Md., 1953-55; mem. So. Regional Edn. Bd., from 1967. Trustee Asbury Meth. Home, Gaithersburg, Md., Balt. Cont. Pensions Fund, Inc., v.p., from 1958; bd. mgrs. Md. Gen. Hosp., mem. univ. senate Meth. Ch. 1952-72; mem. Jurisdictional Conf., 1952-64. Kiwanian. Home: Westminster, Md., Died Oct. 9, 1975.

ENTIZMINGER, LOUIS, clergyman; b. Blythewood, Fairfield Co., S.C., June 28, 1878; s. Rev. John Nelson and Catherine (Rice) E.; A.B., S.C. Co-Educational Inst., Edgefield, S.C. (now Bailey Mil. Inst., Greenwood, S.C.), 1901; m. Ada Violet Frier, of Kathleen, Fla., Dec. 28, 1903. Mercantile and mfg. business until 1906; S.S. sec. Fla. Bapt. Conv., 1909-10; S.S. sec. Gen. Assn. Baptists of Ky., 1911-13; dir. religious work, First Bapt. Ch., Ft. Worth, Tex., 1913-16 and co-pastor same ch., 1918 (built up attendance at S.S. from 249 to 2,000); instr. S.S. orgn. and adminstration, Southwestern Bapt. Theol. Sem., 1917; pastor Lakeland, Fla., and First Ch., New Orleans, until 1922; in S.S. and evangelistic work, 1922-26; pastor Calvary Ch., St. Petersburg, Fla., 1926-27; evangelistic and S.S. work, 1927-31; then pastor Tabernacle Bapt. Ch., San Antonio, Tex.; later pastor Temple Ch., Detroit. Pres. Great Lakes Bible Inst., Detroit. Democrat. Mason. Kiwanian. Author: Seeking the Lost, 1916; The Sunday School Transformed, 1925; The Whole Bible for the Whole Bible School, Vol. I, Genesis-Leviticus, Vol. II, Numbers-Ruth. Originator of the Entzminger S.S. Record System. Home: Detroit, Mich.†

ENTZ, JOHN A., coll. pres.; b. Loyalsock, Pa., Jan. 2, 1880; s. Mathias Walter and Mary Elizabeth (Fullmer) E.; B.S., Litt.D., Albright Coll., 1906; Univ. of Pittsburgh, 1916-36; M.A., New York University, 1929; LL.D., Grove City College, 1944; m. Margaret Rebecca Follmer, July 2, 1913. Rural School teacher, Lycoming County, Pennsylvania, 1897-99; elementary teacher, Port Allegheny, Pa., 1902-04; prin. Coudersport, Pa., 1906-16; teacher, State Normal, California, Pa., 1916-19; prin., Smethport, Pa., 1917-18; prin. State Normal, 1919-28; dean, instr., State Teachers Coll., Slippery Rock, Pa., from 1929, pres., 1942-46. Mem. N.E.A., Pa. State Edn. Assn., Phi Sigma Pi. Mason. Club: Rotary International (Slippery Rock, Pa.). Home: Slippery Rock, Pa.†

EPPERLY, JAMES MELVIN, army officer; b. Duncan's Bridge, Mo., July 5, 1900; student U. Mo., D.D.S., St. Louis U.; student Army Dental Sch., Med. Field Service Sch., 1926. Commd. 2d lt., U.S. Army, advanced through grades to maj. gen., 1956; attached Fitzsimons Army Hosp., Denver, 1924, 51-53; duty, P.I., 1926-28, Presidio of San Francisco, then Letterman Army Hosp., 1928-35; staff U.S. Mil. Acad., 1935-42; chief dental service, Camp Breckinridge, Ky., 1942-44; dental surgeon 9th Army, Ft. Sam Houston, later Eng., France, Germany, 1944-46; dental surgeon 2d Army, Memphis, 1946; chief dental service br. Surgeon General's Office, 1946-51, chief dental div., Washington, from 1956; adviser dental service Greek Army, 1953-54; dir. dental activities Brooke Army Med. Center. Ft. Sam Houston, 1954-56; ret., 1960. Decorated Legion of Merit Bronze Star medal. Home: Ocean City Md. Died Nov. 1973.

EPSTEIN, STEPHAN, educator, physician; b. Nuremberg, Germany, Mar. 14, 1900; s. Ernst and Margaret (Scharbel) E.; M.D., U. Erlangen (Germany), 1925; m. Elsbeth Lauinger, May 27, 1926; children—Ernst, Wolfgang. Came to U.S., 1936, naturalized, 1941. Intern City Hosp., Nuremberg, Germany, 1925; resident U. Breslau (Germany) Skin Clinic, 1926-30, chief radiotherapy dept., 1930-35; dermatologist Marshfield (Wis.) Clinic, 1936-65; pres. Marshfield Clinic Found. Med. Research and Edn., 1960-65; clin. asso. prof. dermatology U. Minn. Med. Sch., 1946-68; clin. prof. dermatology U. Wis. Med. Sch., Madison, 1965-73. Mem. A.M.A., Am. Dermetol. Soc., Am. Acad. Dermatology, Am. Coll. Allergists, Wis. Med. Soc. Author numerous articles on photosensitivity, contact allergy. Editor, transletor: Atlas and Manual of Dermetology and Venerology (Burckhardt), 2d edit., 1965. Home: Madison, Wis. Died June 30, 1973.

ERDMAN, HELGA MAE, physician; b. N.Y.C., Oct. 28, 1929; d. Addison and Helga (Wikander) Erdman; grad. Barnard Sch. for Girls, N.Y.C., 1946; B.A., U. Pa., 1950; M.A., Wagner Coll., 1953; M.D., Howard U. Coll. Medicine, 1958. Intern Meth. Hosp. Bklyn., 1958-59; resident gen. surgery Harlem Hosp., 1959-61, 62-64, gen. surgery N.Y. Polyclinic Hosp., 1961-62; asst. attending in gen. surgery Harlem Hosp., Italian Hosp., Prospect Hosp., 1964-68; practice gen. surgery, 1964—; vol. physician for Viet Nam under the auspices of Am. Med. Assn., 1968, 69. Mem. A.M.A., Am. Coll. Emergency Physicians, Am. Med. Women's Assn., Alpha Omicron Pi. Home: New York City, N.Y. Died May 28, 1972.

ERICKSON, ARVEL BENJAMIN, educator; b. Eveleth, Minn., Sept. 15, 1905; s. Gust and Anna (Mallom) E.; B.A. U. Minn., 1929; M.A., U. Wash., 1933; Ph.D., Western Res. U., 1939; m. Alva C. Roslund, June 9, 1931; 1 dau., Lynn G. (Mrs. Thomas Burnett). Instr., Case Inst. Tech., 1937-40; instr. history Western Res. U., 1940-42, faculty, 1944-74, prof. history, 1952-74, regional economist OPA, 1942-44. Vis. summer prof. U. Man., 1962, U. Victoria, 1963. Recipient Distinguished Tchr. award Western Res. U., 1964; research grantee Social Sci. Research Council, 1953, Am. Philos. Soc., 1953, 61. Mem. Am. Hist. Assn., Ohio Acad. History, Midwest Conf. Brit. Historians, Phi Alpha Theta, Omicron Delta Kappa. Author: The Public Career of Sir James Graham, 1952; Edward Cardwall: Paelite, 1959. Co-author: Reedings in English History, 1967; England: Prehistory to the Present, 1968; The Paelites, 1846-1857, 1972. Contbr. numerous articles to profl. jours. Asso. editor: Jour. Social History. Home: Cleveland Heights, O. Died Nov. 24, 1974.

ERICKSON, CHARLES WATT, educator; b. at Richmond, Jefferson Co., O., Sept. 16, 1881; s. Oliver and Sarah Louisa (Johnson) E.; B.S., Washington and Jefferson Coll., Pa., 1905, M.S., 1914; LL.B., Detroit Coll. of Law, 1911; m. Jane, d. Col. J. B. R. Streator, of Washington, Pa., Jan. 1, 1906. Began teaching in Pa., 1906; practiced law in Detroit, Mich., 2 yrs.; chancellor Cotner U., Bethany, Neb., after August 1916, Mem. N.E.A., Phi Kappa Sigma. Republican. Mem. Christian Ch. Mason. Home: Bethany (Lincoln) Neb.†

ERICKSON, E(DWIN) R., coll. prof.; b. Biggsville, Ill., Nov. 3, 1900; s. Aron H. and Anna (Matson) E.; student Augustana Coll., 1919-20, 1921-22; A.B., Carthage Coll., 1931; A.M., U. Buffalo, 1933, Ph.D., 1937; m. Waneta Howell, June 2, 1926; 1 son, Richard Paul. Instr. in chemistry Carthage (Ill.) Coll., 1933-34, asso. prof., 1934-35, prof., 1937-40; research chemist Mathieson Alkali Works, Inc., Niagra Falls, N.Y., 1941-45; supervisor of plastic research Armour Research Foundn., Chicago, 1945-46; chmn. dept. of chemistry, science division, Augustana Coll., from 1946, then prof. emeritus chemistry; asso. dir. research, Augustana Research Foundation. Mem. Am. Chem. Soc., Ill. Acad. Sci., Am. Assn. Men of Sci., Am. Assn. Univ. Profs., Sigma Xi, Theta Chi Delta. Republican. Lutheran. Mason. Holder 5 patents. Home: Moline Ill. Died Jan. 16, 1974; buried Carman Cemetery, Henderson County, Ill.

ERICKSON, PETER W., clergyman; b. Grotan, Norway, Sept. 14, 1880; s. Sigvard and Caroline (Lokken) E.; brought to U.S. by parents, 1881, naturalized, 1901; A.B., Macalester Coll., 1903, also D.D.; student McCormick Theol. Sem., Chicago, 1903-04, San Anselmo (Calif.) Sem., 1905-06; m. Emma Blair Jamieson, Oct. 14, 1907 (dec.); 1 son, Donald Fergus; m. 2d, Carrie Mae Erickson, June 26, 1918. Ordained to Presbyn. ministry, 1906; pastor Drayton, N.D., 1906-10, Minot, N.D., 1910-25, Wausau, Wis., 1925-33, Univ. Ch., Seattle Wash., 1933-47, ret. 1947. Home: Seattle, Wash.†

ERNEST, JOHN HENRY, univ. adminstr.; b. Swanwick, Ill., Sept. 11, 1905; s. John Albert and Susan Ellen (Kelly) E.; B.S. in Bus. Adminstrn., Washington U., St. Louis, 1930. M.S., 1932; m. Flossie Anna Logan, May 1, 1932. Mem. staff Washington U., 1932-72, treas., 1956-64, vice chancellor bus. and finance, 1961-64, sec. to bd. dirs. 1961-64, prof. accounting, 1964-72, financial adviser to chancellor, 1964-72. Mem. Am. Accounting Assn. Mason. Home: Palm Springs Cal. Died Oct. 20, 1974; buried, Swanwick, Ill.

ERSKINE, GEORGE CHESTER, penologist; b. Jefferson, Me., Aug. 13, 1881; s. George B. and Myra L. (Poland) E.; grad. Farmington (Me.) Normal Sch., 1899; m. Iva Louise McArdle, Dec. 10, 1907; children—George Randolph, John McArdle. Began prison work at South Boston House of Correction, 1900; supt. Prison Camp and Hosp., West Rutland, Mass., 1907-16; supt. Conn. Reformatory from 1916. Capt. q.m. 2d Co., Governor's Foot Guard, Mem. Prison Assn. (pres. 1929, now treas.), Conn. Soc. of Executives (pres. 1925), Waterbury Field Trial Club (pres. 1925-29). Republican. Mason (K.T., Shriner), Woodman. Clubs: Southington Golf, Cheshire Rotary. Home: Cheshire, Conn.†

ERSKINE, GRAVES BLANCHARD, asst. to sec. of def., marine corps officer; b. Columbia, La., June 28, 1897; s. Benjamin and Daisy Laura (Graves) E.; grad. La. State U., 1917; m. Margaret Spratling, 1920 (div.); children—Margaret, Maureen, Bonnie; m. 2d, Constance Caraway Yeatman, Oct. 10, 1954. Entered USMC, 1917, and advanced through grades to gen. (4 stars); served at Pearl Harbor; chief of staff Amphibious Corps, Decorated D.S.M., Legion of Merit with Combat V, Purple Heart, silver star, others; recipient numerous civilian awards, Mem. V.F.W. Clubs: Army-Navy (pres. 1963), Army-Navy Country, City Tavern, Internat., George Town (Washington); Marine Memorial (San Francisco); Metropolitan (N.Y.C.) Atlantic Fleet, other related duties; led assault on Iwo Jima, 1945;; served in Guam 1945; comdr. Camp Pendleton, Cal., 1950; comdg. gen. Fleet Marine Force, Atlantic, 1951-53; ret. 1953; asst. to sec. of def., 1953-61. D.C. Died May 21, 1973; buried Arlington Nat. Cemetery, Arlington, Va.

ERVIN, PAUL REVERE, lawyer; b. Mt. Mourne, N.C., Apr. 7, 1908; s. James Osborne and Stella (Conger) E.; A.B., Duke, 1928, LL.B., 1931; LL.D., High Point (N.C.) Coll., 1964; m. Dorothy Denton, Mar. 28, 1936; children—Diana (Mrs. Gerald C. Strickland), Paul Revere, Sarah Ruth, James Everett. Admitted to N.C. bar, 1930, practiced in Charlotte; sr. partner firm Ervin, Horack & McCartha, from 1961; public guardian, pub. adminstr. Mecklenburg County, N.C., 1936-50. Dir. Carolina Transfer & Storage Co., United Select Foods, Inc., McEwen Funeral Service, Inc. Del. Southeastern Jurisdictional Conf. Methodist Ch., 1944, 48, 52, 56, mem. Gen. Conf., 1948, 52, 56, mem. Jud. Council, from 1956, v.p., 1960-64, pres., from 1964; mem. Charlotte Bd. Health, from 1956; chmn. Citizens Ednl. Commn. Eliminating Obscenity, from 1964; mem. N.C. Adv. Com. Civil Rights, 1958-62. Mem. N.C. Ho. of Reps. from Mecklenburg County, 1935-37. Trustee Pfeiffer Coll., Misenheimer, N.C., from 1956; chmn., from 1959. Mem. Am., N.C. bar assns., Bar 26th Jud. Dist. N.C., Order of Coif, Tau Kappa Alpha, Omicron Delta Kappa. Democrat. Clubs: Civitan (past pres., past internat. judge advocate, Myers Park Country (past pres.) (Charlotte). Author articles. Home: Charlotte, N.C. Died Dec. 21, 1970.

ESCHOLIER, RAYMOND, writer; b. Dec. 25, 1882. Sec. dir. fine arts; keeper Victor Hugo Mus., 1913-33; chef de cabinet to Briand, 1921-22; keeper Petit Palais, 1933, hon. keeper, 1943; conseiller culturel de la Ville de Paris, 1957. Decorated grand officier Legion d'Honneur, medaille Militaire, Croix de Guerre; recipient Grand prize for Lit., Acad. Francaise, 1931. Author: (novels) Cantegril, 1921, La Nuit, 1923, Le Sel de la Terre, 1924, Mahmadou Fofana, 1929, L'Herbe d'amour, 1931; (essays) Daumier, 1932, Delacroix, 1926, Greco, 1937, La peinture francaise au XIX siecie, 1940, Marquid de Gascogne, 1946, Victor Hugo, cet inconnu, 1951, Le Secret de Mont-Segur, 1952, Un Amant de Genie: Victor Hugo, 1953, Matisse, ce vivant, 1956, La Neige qui bruie: Marie Noel, 1957, Mes. Pyrenees, 1958, Eugene Delacroix, 1963. Delacroix et les Femmes, 1963, Daumier et son Monde, 1965, Briand Secret, 1965; Hugo, rio de son siécie, 1970. Address: U1Paris, France., Deceased.

ESHELMAN, ELMER T., banker; b. Niagara Falls, N.Y., May 15, 1877; s. Samuel B. and Harriet (Metz) E.; ed. high sch., Niagara Falls; m. Helen L. Prime, of Niagara Falls, Sept. 12, 1906 (died Dec. 22, 1928). Asst. city treasurer, Niagara Falls, 1899-1909; chief examiner N.Y. State Banking Dept., 1909-17; v.p. Syracuse Trust Co., Syracuse, N.Y., 1917-20; 1st v.p. First Trust & Deposit Co., Syracuse, 1920-23; pres. City Bank & Trust Co., 1923-29; chmn. bd. First Trust Deposit Co., Syracuse, 1929-30; organized Eshelman-Harder Co. Inc., investments, Aug. 1930, and then pres.; v.p. State Bank, Skaneateles, N.Y.; treas. Great Northern Warehouses; dir. Excelsior Ins. Co., Pierce, Butler & Pierce Mfg. Co., Unity Life Ins. Co., Central N .Y. Securities Corpn., Onondaga Guaranty Title Co. Mem. bd. Y.W.C.A.; treas. Onondaga Pub. Health Assn., Milbank Fund. Republican. Conglist. Mason. Clubs: Citizens, Century, Rotary, Tuscarora, Bellevue Country (pres.), Skaneateles Country. Home: Syracuse, N.Y.†

ESHLEMAN, CHARLES L(EVERICH), physician; b. New Orleans, La., May 18, 1880; s. Benjamin Franklin and Fanny Hampton (Leverich) E.; A.B., Tulane Univ., 1900, M.D., 1904; m. Anais Legendre, June 25, 1915; children—Kathleen (Mrs. Donald Maginnis, Jr.), Anais (Mrs. Sidney Bezou), Charles Leverich. Intern, Charity Hosp., New Orleans, 1902-04; practice of internal med., after 1904; part-time instr., Med. Dept., Tulane U., 1904-12, asst. prof., 1912-36, mem. bd. Adminstrs., 1936-59, chmn. med. com., 1945-59, advisory mem. after 1959; cons. on medicine, staff of Touro Infirmary, also Eye, Ear, Nose and Throat Hosp., New Orleans, from 1941; pres., Ochsner Found. Hosp., New Orleans, 1947-50. Mem. and examining physician, Selective Service bds., World Wars I and II. Mem. A.M.A., So. La. med. assns., Newcomen Soc. N. Am., Alpha Tau Omega, Alpha Omega Alpha, Nu Sigma Nu. Democrat. Episcopalian. Club: Boston (pres. 1950-52). Contbr. articles in field to profl. publs. Home: New Orleans, La.†

ESPELAGE, BERNARD THEODORE, bishop; b. Cincinnati, O., Feb. 16, 1892; s. Bernard J. and Clara (Schottelkotte) E.; student St. Francis Coll., 1905-10, Franciscan Sem., 1911-18, Catholic U. of Am., 1925-26 (J.C.L.). Entered Franciscan Order, 1910. Ordained priest Roman Catholic Ch., 1918; nominated Bishop of Gallup, N.M., July 23, 1940, consecrated, Oct. 9, 1940; installed as first bishop, Gallup, Oct. 30, Titiel Bishop, Gallup. Home: Gallup, N.M. Died 1971.

ESTABROOK, ROBERT FRANCIS, communication exec.; b. Fitzwilliam N.H., June 18, 1880; s. George William and Laura (Simonds) E.; ed. Dartmouth Coll., 1902; m. Ethel Pedrick, July 28, 1921; children—Marjorie, Marian Fay. Asso. with New England Telephone & Telegraph Co., Boston Mass., after 1902, now dir. Club: Union. Home: Newton, Mass.†

ESTABROOKS, GEORGE HOBEN, educator; b. St. John, New Brunswick, Can., Dec. 16, 1895; s. Leander E. and Henrietta Rebecca (Hoben) E.; A.B., Acadia U., Wolfville, Nova Scotia, 1920; student Oxford Univ., Eng. (Rhodes scholar), 1921-24; Ph.D., Harvard, 1926; m. Maude Martha Juvet, July 20, 1933; 1 dau., Elizabeth Doreen. Came to U.S., 1924, naturalized 1931. Prof. of psychology, Springfield College, 1926-27; asso. prof. of psychology, dir. placement, Colgate University, 1927-38, prof. psychology, chmn. dept., from 1938, then prof. emeritus. Mem. Am. Psychology Assn., Am. Assn. U. Profs., Mid-State Soc. for Clin. Hypnosis, Theta Chi. Baptist. Mason. Club: Torch (Utica). Author: Man, the Mechanical Misfit, 1941; Hypnotism, 1943; Death in the Mind (with Richard Lockridge), Spiritism, 1947; Future of the Human Mind, 1961. Editor: Hypnosis: Current Problems, 1962. Contbr. profl., popular jours. Home: Hamilton N.Y. Died Dec. 30, 1974.

ESTES, LUDWELL HUNTER, clergyman; b. Memphis, Tenn., Dec. 27, 1879; s. Ludwell Hunter and Esther Taylor (Daman) E.; ed. pub. schs. of Memphis; grad. McTyeire Inst., McKenzie, Tenn., 1906; m. Sarah Lee Powell, June 11, 1907; 1 dau., Virginia (Mrs. J. Rochester Busby). Secretary boys' dept. Y.M.C.A., Memphis, Tenn., 1899, night secretary railraod br., Chicago, 1900; ordained Meth. ministry, 1906; sec. Memphis Annual Conf. M.E. Ch., South, 1914-42; asst. sec. Gen. Conf. M.E. Ch., S., 1922-26, sec., 1930, 34, 38; sec. Uniting Conf. M.E. Ch., M.E. Ch. South, and Meth. Protestant Ch., Kansas City, Mo., 1939; sec. Gen. Conf. The Meth. Ch.; sec. Southeastern Jurisdictional Conf. of the Meth. Ch.; district superintendent Dyersburg Dist., Memphis Annual Conf. The Methodist Ch., 1942; pastor 1st. Meth. Church, Milan, Tenn. after 1948. Sec. board trustees and bd. mgrs. Methodist Hosp., Memphis, from 1921; recording sec. Bd. of Edn. of The Meth. Ch., 1940. Mason (Scottish Rite, Shriner). Democrat. Address: Milan, Tenn.†

ESTES, MAURICE JAMES, ready-mix concrete co. exec.; b. Harpursville, N.Y., May 7, 1910; s. James B. and May (Fuller) E.; student N.Y.U., 1929-30; m. Marian B. Nesbitt, June 29, 1940; children—Lynn A., Mark A. Insp. U.S. Corps of Engineers, 1935-49; pres. Estes Ready-Mix Concrete Co., Inc., Oneida, 1949-72, Plattsburg Ready-Mix Concrete Co., Inc., 1954-72, Structural Founds., Inc., 1959-72, Whiteface Ready-Mix Corp., 1961-72, chmn. bd. dirs. above corps. Served with AUS, 1943-45. Elk, Lion. Home: Sylvan Beach, N.Y. Died Oct. 28, 1972.

ESTREM, HERBERT WILLIAM, lawyer; b. Clinton, Ia., Feb. 18, 1902; s. Andrew and Caroline (Nerge) E.; J.D., U. Minn., 1924, B.A., 1925; m. Hazel A. Yost, Aug. 18, 1928; 1 dau., Carolyn W. Admitted to Minn. bar, 1925, since practiced in Mpls.; judge municipal court Mpls., 1961-70, referee, 1971-72. Govt. appeal agt. SSS, 1941-46. Mem. adv. Commn. to Redraft Criminal Laws State of Minn., 1956-63. Mem. Nat. Conf. State Trial Judges, Am. (recipient Merit awards 1963, 1968). Minn. (gov. 1945-47, chmn. law improvement com. 1952-64), Hennepin County (pres. 1944-45) bar assns., Theta Chi. Republican. Lutheran. K.P. (mem. Supreme Tribunal 1964-73). Contbr. articles to bar assn. jours. Home: Minneapolis Minn. Died Dec. 14, 1973.

ETHRIDGE, GEORGE H., lawyer; b. Kemper County, Miss., Feb. 26, 1871; s. Mark D. and Virginia (White) E.; ed. Iron Springs Inst. (Java, Miss.), Linden (Tenn.) Acad.; m. Lula Tann, Sept. 28, 1904; children—George D., Alice Virginia, Edna M., Thomas Tann, Mark, Doris White. Admitted to Miss. bar, 1894, and practiced at DeKalb and Meridian. Mem. Miss. Ho. of Rep., 1904-06; asst. atty. gen. of Miss., 1912-17; justice Supreme Court of Mississippi, 1917-41; asst. attorney general of Mississippi after Jan. 1, 1941. Democrat. Methodist. Mason (32°). Author: Essays and Poems, 1924; Mississippi Constitutions. 1928; Mississippi History, 1940. Home: Jackson, Miss.†

ETLER, ALVIN DERALD, composer, educator; b. Battle Creek, Ia., Feb. 19, 1913; s. Henry Peter and Mary (Smith) E.; student U. Ill., 1930-31, Western Res. U., 1931-33; Mus.B., Yale, 1944; m. Nancy Jean Cochran, May 28, 1967; children by previous marriage—Margo Turner (Mrs. Thomas D. Doyle), David Christian, Margaret Mary (Mrs. James A. Homola); children—Susan Lee, Cynthia Drew. Free-lance oboist, 1933-38; oboist Indpls. Symphony Orch., 1938-40; instr. Yale, 1942-46; asst. prof. Cornell U., 1946-47; asso. prof. U. Ill., 1947-49; prof. music Smith Coll., 1949-73, Henry Dike Sleeper prof. music, 1968-73, Andrew W. Mellon prof. humanities, 1973; vis. prof.

Mt. Holyoke Coll., 1952-53, 59-60, Yale, 1965-66; artist in residence U. Wis. at Milw., summer 1960, 72; tour Latin Am. with N. Am. Woodwind Quintet, 1941; an inaugurater, planner Festival Contemporary Music, U. Ill., 1948, Yaddo Festival Contemporary Music, 1952; judge student composer awards Broadcast Music, Inc., 1963, 67, young composer awards Am. Fedn. Music Clubs, 1954, 55; com. Mary Duke Biddle scholarship awards, 1966. Recipient 4th award Concours Mus. Internat. Reine Elisabeth de Belgique, 1953; Guggenheim fellow, 1940-41, 63. Mem. Phi Mu Alpha. Composer: Woodwind Quintet I, 1955, II, 1957; Concerto in One Movement for Orchestra, 1957; Sonata for Viola and Harpsichord, 1959; Ode to Pothos for Mixed Chorus, 1960; Concerto for Woodwind Quintet and Orchestra; Triptych for Orchestra, 1961; Concerto for Clarinet and Chamber Group, 1962; Quintet for Brass Instruments, 1963; Quartet I for Strings, 1963, II, 1965; Onomatopoesis for Male Chorus, Winds, Brass and Percussion, 1965; Concerto for Brass Quintet, String Orchestra and Percussion, 1967; Concerto for String Quartet and Orchestra, 1967; Convivialities for Orchestra, 1967; Sonata II for Clarinet and Piano, 1969; XL Plus One for Percussion, 1970; Concerto for Cello and Chamber Group, 1970. Author: Making Music: An Introduction to Theory, 1974. Home: Florence, Mass. Died June 13, 1973.

ETLING, CARL D., dist. judge; b. Corbett, Ore., Mar. 3, 1911; s. Frederick and Martha (Miller) E.; J.D., Northwestern Law Sch., 1934; m. Thelma Fern Davies, Nov. 21, 1940; children—Carl D., Marilee Kay. Admitted to Ore. bar, 1936; individual practice law, Portland, Ore., 1936-60; dist. judge Ore., Multnomah County, 1960-73, presiding judge, 1968-69. Mem. Jud. Conf. Ore. (exec. com. 1966-68), Izaak Walton League Am. (pres. Ore. div. 1961, nat. dir. 1964-73, Thompson award 1961-62). Mason. Home: Portland Ore. Died Feb. 13, 1973; buried Rose City Cemetery, Portland, Ore.

ETZELL, GEORGE FERDINAND, mem. Republican Nat. Com.; b. Clarissa, Minn., Feb. 1, 1909; s. George A. and Ida (Hammer) E.; student pub. schs., Clarissa; m. Ione Margaret Koch, Oct. 4, 1934; children—Peter, Gretchen, Paul, Mary, Martha. Pub. Clarissa Independent, 1940-72; state printer, Minn., 1939-43; spl. adviser Gov. C. Anderson, 1951-52; pres. Etzell Publs., Inc.; mem. Rep. Nat. Com. from Minn., 1952-71. Dist. chmn. Young Rep. League, 1937-38; chmn. Rep. com. 6th Congl. Dist., 1945-52; chmn. rules com. Rep. nat. conv., 1960, 64. Mem. Nat., Minn. newspaper assns., Sigma Delta Chi. Roman Catholic K.C. Clubs; Minneapolis Athletic, Minn. Press. Home: Clarissa Minn. Died June 17, 1975.

EUBANKS, ELINOR MAE, answering service exec.; b. Park Falls, Wis., Dec. 24, 1911; d. Jay H. and Mabel Edith (Pinkerton) Eubanks; student Northland Coll., Ashland, Wis., 1929-31, U. Minn., 1931-32; B.E., Central State U., Stevens Point, Wis., 1934; postgrad. U. Wis., summer 1935. Tchr. English, Ladysmith (Wis.) High Sch., 1934-37; payroll clk. Dept. Agr., Indio, Cal., 1937; sec. United Date Growers of Cal., Indio, 1937; cashier Cal. Electric Power Co., Indio, 1937-42; social worker Riverside County Welfare Dept., Indio, 1942-46; office mgr. Lone Palm Hotel, Palm Springs, Cal., 1946-47, Wonder Palms Hotel, Palm Springs, 1947; social worker Riverside County Gen. Hosp., Arlington, Cal., 1948; classified advt. mgr. Indio Daily News, 1948-52; sec. Planning Commn., Indio, 1948-54, Indio Merc. Co., 1952-54; owner, mgr. Coachella Valley Answering Service, Indio, 1955-75. Mem. Asso. Telephone Answering Exchanges, Inc., Telephone Answering Services of Cal., Answer Am., Order Eastern Star, Sigma Tau Delta, Tau Gamma Beta. Democrat. Presbyn. Home: Indio, Cal. Died Feb. 21, 1975.

EULER, RALPH STAPLETON, banker; b. Howell, Mich., June 10, 1888; s. Frederick C. and Ella (Stapleton) E.; student Howell pub. schs., 1895-1905, U. of Mich., 1907-08; m. Bertha Bragg Gray. Began business in investment securities, 1911; mgr. investment dept. Colonial Trust Co., Pittsburgh, 1913-18; with Federal Reserve Bank, Cleveland, 1917-18; began with The Union Trust Co. of Pittsburgh, 1918, v.p., 1920-46, upon merger with Mellon Nat. Bank, Pitts., became sr. v.p., mem. exec. com., dir. Mellon Nat. Bank and Trust Co., ret. 1957; dir. Shamrock Oil & Gas Corp., Lone Star Gas Co.; dir., finance com. Am. Airlines, Inc.; dir., exec. com. Harbison-Walker Refractories Co. Clubs: Allegheny Country, Duquesne, Edgeworth (Pittsburgh, Pa.). Home: Edgeworth PA. Died Jan. 24, 1972; interred Temple of Memories, Allegheny Cemetery, Pittsburgh, Pa.

EUNSON, ROBERT CHARLES ROMAINE, newspaperman, writer; b. Billings, Mont., July 23, 1912; s. Robert Strong and Jessie (Romaine) E.; student Va. Mil. Inst., 1931-32; B.A. in Edn., Ariz. State Coll., Flagstaff, 1936, LL.D., 1961; m. Katherine Raboglìatti, Feb. 22, 1935; children—Eve Anne (Mrs. Jackson R. Rannells), Dale Ellen (Mrs. Richardson Morse), Lisa Kei, Editor, Holbrook (Ariz.) Tribune-News, 1936-41; with AP, 1941-75, chief bur. Japan, Korea and Okinawa, 1950-56, chief bur. San Francisco, 1956-63, gen. exec. for Asia, 1963-65, asst. gen. mgr., N.Y.C., 1965-69, asst. sec. in charge broadcasting div., 1965-75; dir. AP of Can. Vice pres. Press Assn., 1965-75; pres. Fgn. Corr. Club Japan, 1956, San Francisco Press and Union League Club, 1962. Mem. Radio Television News Dirs. Assn., Nat. Assn. Broadcasters. Clubs: Overseas Press (N.Y.C.); National Broadcasters (Washington); Apawomis (Rye, N.Y.). Author: The Pearl King, 1954; Mig Alley, 1958; Trial at Odawara, 1964. Home: Bronxville, N.Y. Died May 22, 1975.

EUSTIS, ALLAN CHOTARD, JR., investment banker; b. New Orleans, Aug. 28, 1904; s. Allan Chotard and Adele (Brittin) E.; B.S., Sheffield Sci. Sch., Yale, 1925; m. Ann Hyde, Nov. 6, 1947; children—Annette C. (Mrs. Rufus E. Jarman, Jr.), Allan Chotard, III, Brittin Cartwright II, Adele Brittin. With Spencer Trask & Co., N.Y.C., 1925-74, partner, 1947-74. Served to lt. col. USAAF, 1942-46. Mem. Nat. Assn. Securities Dealers (bd. govs. 1964-66, chmn. 1966). Home: Wilton, Conn. Died Dec. 1974.

EVANS, ALICE CATHERINE, bacteriologist; b. Neath, Bradford Co., Pa., Jan. 29, 1881; d. William Howell and Anne B. (Evans) E.; prep. edn. Susquehanna Collegiate Inst., Towana, Pa.; B.S., Cornell Univ., 1909; M.S., Univ. of Wis., 1910; grad. study Univ. of Chicago, George Washington Univ.; hon. M.D. Women's Med. College of Pa., 1934; hon. D.Sc., Wilson College, 1936; unmarried. Dairy bacteriologist, U.S. Dept. Agr., 1910-18; bacteriologist, U.S. Pub. Health Service, 1918-45; later pres. Inter-Am. Com. on Brucellosis for 11 years. Del. First Internat. Microbiol. Congress, 1930. Fellow Am. Assn. for Advancement of Science; mem. Washington Acad. Sciences, Soc. Am. Bacteriologists (pres. 1928), Am. Assn. Univ. Women, Sigma Delta Epsilon, Sigma Xi. Unitarian. Contbr. to Jour. Infectious Diseases, Jour. Agrl. Research, Jour. Immunology, Jour. Bacteriology, Pub. Health Reports, etc. Discovered that undulant fever may be contracted from cattle and swine. Home: Washington, D.C. Died Sept. 5, 1975.

EVANS, CECIL EUGENE, educator; b. Bowdon, Ga., Jan. 21, 1871; s. Hiram Martin and Georgia (Striplin) E.; B.A., Oxford College, Ala., 1888; M.A., Univ. of Tex., 1906; LL.D., Southwestern U., 1923; m. Allie Maxwell, May 18, 1809; 1 dau., Mrs. Bernice Soyars. Clerk Probate Office, 1888-89; prin. schs. in Ala., 1889-93; asst. High Sch., Mexia, Tex., 1894-95; supt. pub. schs., Anson, 1895-1902, Merkel, 1902-05, Abilene, Tex., 1906-08; gen. agent The Conf. for Edn., in Tex., 1908-11, conducting successful campaigns for 3 school amendments to State Constitution; pres. Southwest Tex. State Teachers Coll., Aug. 1911-Sept. 1942, pres. emeritus after 1942. Mem. State Textbook Bd., 1912-13. State Textbook Commn., 1917-27, Tex. Accrediting Com., 1921-41. Mem. N.E.A. Democrat. Methodist. Mason. Home: San Marcos, Tex.†

EVANS, FREDERICK WALTER, clergyman; b. Corsica, Pa., July 17, 1880; s. William Betts and Josephine (DeHaven) E.; student Eldersridge Acad., Pa., 1897-99; A.B., Washington and Jefferson Coll., 1902, A.M., 1906; LL.D., 1946; student Western Theol. Sem., 1902-04, Princeton Theol. Sem., 1904-05; D.D., Bellevue Coll. (now with U. Omaha), 1915; m. Grace T. Mathers, June 1, 1923; children—Frederick Walter, Grace Elisabeth. Ordained ministry Presbyn. Ch., 1905; pastor Union Ch., Oxford, Pa., 1905-06, First Ch., Steubenville, O., 1906-11, Montview Blvd. Ch., Denver, 1911-14, First Ch., Council Bluffs, Ia., 1914-19, Harlem-New York Ch., N.Y. City, 1919-26. Ch. of the Redeemer, Paterson, N.J., 1926-28, Second Ch., Troy, N.Y., 1929-48; eastern rep. bd. pensions, Presbyn. Ch., 1945-50; interim pastor Presbyn. Ch., Drexel Hill, Pa., 1951, Ardmore, Pa., 1952, Chestnut Hill, Pa., 1953. Commr. to General Assembly, 1928, 37; moderator 158th Gen. Assembly the Presbyn. Ch. in the U.S.A.; chmn. gen. council, Presbyn. Ch. U.S.A., 1946-47. Mem. S.A.R. Ind. Republican. Mason. Contributor religious magazines and church publs. Home: Springfield, Pa.†

EVANS, GEORGE L., physician; M.D., Western Res. U., 1932. Intern, resident in obstetrics and gynecology U. Hosps., Cleve. Diplomate Am. Bd. Obstetrics and Gynecology. Fellow A.C.S., Am. Coll. Obstetricians and Gynecologists. Home: Mansfield, O. Died Apr. 9, 1973.

EVANS, GRIFFITH CONRAD, mathematician; b. Boston, Mass., May 11, 1887; s. George William and Mary (Taylor) E.; A.B., Harvard, 1907, A.M., 1908, Ph.D., 1910; University of Rome, 1910-12; LL.D., University of California, 1956; m. Isabel Mary John, June 20, 1917; children—Griffith Conrad, George William, Robert John. Instr. mathematics, Harvard, 1906-07, 1909-10; Sheldon fellow, in Italy, 1910-12; asst. prof. mathematics, 1912-16, prof., 1916-34, Rice Inst.; prof. math. U. Cal., 1934-55, then emeritus, chmn. dept., 1934-49, faculty research lectr., 1950; Walker Ames professor, U. of Wash., summer 1941. Editor Am. Jour. Mathematics, 1927-35. Mem. Nat. Research Council, 1927-31, 1940-43, 1950-53. Tech. consultant, Ordnance, War Dept., 1943-47. Commd. capt. Air Service, U.S. Army, Feb. 23, 1918; scientific and exptl. work in Europe; hon. disch., June 10, 1919. Fellow Econometric Soc.; mem. Nat. Acad. Sciences, Am. Acad. Arts and Sciences, Am. Philos. Soc., Am. Math. Soc. (v.p. 1924-26; pres. 1938-40), Math. Assn. of America (v.p. 1932), A.A.A.S. (v.p. 1931, 36). Catholic. Author: Functionals and Their Applications, Part 1 of Cambridge Colloquium, 1918; The Logarithmic Potential, Colloquium Series Am. Math. Soc., Vol. 6, 1927; Mathematical Introduction to Economics, 1930; Stabilité et Dynamique de la Production dans l'Économie Politique (Mémorial des Sciences Math., 56); also tech. papers. Home: Walnut Creek, Cal. Died Dec. 8, 1973.

EVANS, HARRY MARSHALL ERSKINE, business exec.; b. Toronto, Ont., Can., 1876; grad. Toronto U., 1897. Pres. dir. H.M.E. Evans & Co., Ltd., Edmonton, Alta., Can.; pres., dir. Revillon Freres Alta., Ltd., Revillon Wholesale Ltd.; pres., mng. dir. Brit. Alta. Investors, Ltd.; chmn. bd. mng. dir. Hemevans Investments, Ltd. Office: Edmonton, Alberta, Canada. Died 1973.

EVANS, HIRAM WESLEY, imperial wizard Ku Klux Klan; b. Ashland, Ala., Sept. 26, 1881; s. Hiram Martin and Georgia (Striplin) E.; grad. high sch., Hubbard, Tex.; studied under tutor 2 yrs.; studied dentistry, Vanderbilt U.; m. Bam Hill, of Royce, Tex., Feb. 5, 1903; children—Cecil Roy, Martha Virginia, Ellen Bam. Licensed to practice dentistry in Tex., 1900; practiced in Dallas until 1920, and has devoted attention to Knights of Ku Klux Klan; imperial wizard (pres.) same from Dec. 1, 1922, also mgr. associated enterprises. Democrat. Mem. Christian (Disciples of Christ) Ch. Mason, Maccabee; mem. O.E.S. Clubs: City (Atlanta, Ga.); Congressional Country (Washington, D.C.). Author: Menace of Modern Immigration, 1923; The Klan of Tomorrow, 1924; Alienism in the Democracy, 1927; The Rising Storm, 1929. Home: Atlanta, Ga.†

EVANS, JOHN HENRY, telephone co. exec.; b. Patterson, Cal., Sept. 16, 1919; s. John Henry and Estella (Collins) E.; B.S., U. Cal., Berkeley, 1940; postgrad. San Francisco Coll. Mortuary Sci., 1941; m. Jane Blair, Oct. 18, 1947; children—John Henry, Danna Jane, Cynthia. Pres., Evans Telephone Co., Patterson, 1941-73; pres. Evans Funeral Chapel, Patterson, 1941-73, Livingston Telephone Co. (Cal.), 1969-73, Evans-Kreiger Funeral Chapels, Newman-Gustine, Cal., 1967-73. City councilman, Patterson, 1948-71; mayor, Patterson, 1953-60. Served to lt., Supply Corps, USNR, 1942-46; ETO, PTO. Mem. U.S. (bd. 1969-71), Cal. (pres. 1964-65) independent telephone assns., Cal. Funeral Dirs. Assn. (pres. 1965-66), Cal. (exec. bd. 1963-67), Patterson (pres. 1954) chambers commerce, Patterson 20-30 (pres. 1951), Central Valley Dist. League Cal. Cities (pres. 1957), Sigma Phi Epsilon. Republican. Mason (Shriner), Rotarian. Club: Commonwealth of Cal. (San Francisco). Office: Patterson, Cal. Died Mar. 4, 1973.

EVANS, THOMAS, civil engr.; b. Rasalpura, India, May 13, 1916; s. Thomas Aneurin and Mary Darling (Fairbank) E.; brought to U.S., 1920, naturalized, 1928; B.S., Mass. Inst. Tech., 1938; m. Jean Gleich Mateer, Dec. 21, 1940; children—Ann Fairbank (Mrs. Robert Burroughs), Eleanor Jean (Mrs. Gregroy Egor). Jr. engr. Wininger & Selby, N.Y.C., 1938; field engr. Dravo Corp., Neville, Ia., and Pitts., 1940; stress analyst Curtiss-Wright Co., Buffalo, 1940-42, chief structures, Louisville, 1942-46, asst. chief structures, Columbus, O., 1946-48; chief engr. B.F. Avery & Sons, Louisville, 1948-51, Mpls.-Moine Co., Louisville, 1951-55, Hopkins, Minn., 1955-58; chief engr. J.I. Case Co., Bettendorf, Ia., 1958-66, mgr. harvesting engring., 1967-70, chief engr., 1970-73. Mem. Am. Soc. Agrl. Engrs. Soc. Automotive Engrs., Davenport, Bettendorf chambers commerce, Tau Beta Pi, Chi Epsilon. Presbyn. (deacon). Patentee in field. Home: Bettendorf, Ia. Died 1973.

EVANS, TITUS CARR, educator, radiobiologist, b. Lorena, Tex., Dec. 9, 1907; s. Charles William and Virginia (Whitsett) E.; B.A., Baylor U., 1929; M.S., State U. Ia., 1931, Ph.D., 1934; m. Mertie Ellen Jahnke, June 1, 1935 (dec. Nov. 1968); children—Titus Carr, Susan Ellen, Lucy Virginia; m. 2d. Phyllis Allison, Aug. 9, 1971. Asst. prof. Tex. A. and M. U., 1936-38; research asst. prof. U. Ia., Iowa City, 1938-42, research prof. radiology and radiobiology, 1948-75, head Radiation Research Lab., 1948-75; asst. prof. Columbia Coll. Phys. and Surg., 1942-48; cons., mem. policy adv. bd. Argonne (Ill.) Nat. Lab., 1964-68. Mem. Nat. Council Radiation Protection, Soc. Nuclear Medicine (past pres.), Radiation Research Soc., Soc. Nuclear Medicine, Biophysics Soc., Am. Physiol. Soc., Am. Roentgen Ray Soc., Radiol. Soc. N.Am., Cancer Research Soc., Soc. for Exptl. Biology and Medicine, Am. Soc. Zoology, Am. Cancer Soc. (pres. Ia. 1965, mem. ho. dels., bd. dirs., 1971-75; award distinguished service cancer control 1966), Health Physics Soc., Sigma Xi. Mng. editor Radiation Research, 1952-72; asso. editor Nuclear Medicine, 1960-69. Research, numerous publs. on effects X-ray on cell div. and embryonic devel. in invertebrates, radio-protective effect anoxia in mammals, relative effectiveness fast neutrons devel. techniques for radiosotopes in biol. and med. research, effects X-rays on ascites tumor cells. Home: Iowa City, Ia. Died Apr. 8, 1975; buried Lone Tree, Ia.

EVANS, WALKER, photographer, educator; b. St. Louis, Nov. 3, 1903; s. Walker and Jessie (Crane) E.; student Phillips Acad., Andover, Mass., 1922, Williams Coll., 1923, Sorbonne, Paris, France, 1926; Litt.D., Williams Coll., 1968. Contbg. editor Time mag., 1943-45; asso. editor Fortune mag., 1946-65; prof. emeritus graphic arts Sch. Art Yale; artist-in-residence Dartmouth Coll., 1972; exhbns. include Mus. Modern Art, 1938, 17, Art Inst. Chgo., 1942; represented permanent collections Smithsonian Inst., Met. Mus., Mus. Modern Art, Nat. Gallery Can., Ottawa, Art Inst. Chgo., Yale Art Gallery. Guggenheim fellow, 1941; Mark Rothko Found. grantee, 1973. Recipient award Carnegie Corp., N.Y.C., 1962. Fellow Am. Acad. Arts and Scis. Clubs: Century Assn., Yale (N.Y.C.). Author: American Photographs, 1962; (with James Agee) Let Us Now Praise Famous Men, 1941; Message from the Interior, 1966; Many are Called, 1966; Walker Evans, 1971. Home: Old Lyme, Conn. Died Apr. 1975.

EVANS, WILLIAM NEY, former commr. U.S. Ct. Claims; b. West Plains, Mo., June 18, 1898; s. William Nelson and Sarah Annis (Smith) E.; A.B., Duke, 1920; LL.B., Harvard, 1923; m. May Alcott Thompson, July 26. 1930. Admitted to Mo. bar, 1923; practiced in West Plains and Houston, Mo., 1923-25; prof. law U. Ark., 1925-27, U. N.C., 1927-28; admitted to N.C. bar, 1928; practiced in Greensboro and High Point, N.C. 1928-34; asst. gen. counsel Textile Labor Relations Bd., 1935; atty. Dept. Labor, 1936; atty. U.S. Maritime Commn., 1936-40, legislative counsel, 1940-42; asst. gen. counsel War Shipping Adminstrn., 1943-45; commr. U.S. Ct. Claims, 1942, 45-69, chmn. com. rules, 1960-69. Served with U.S. Army, 1918; to lt. comdr. USNR, 1942-45. Mem. Am., Fed., N.C. bar assns., Order of Coif, Sigma Chi, Democrat. Methodist. Mason. Club: Cosmos. Contbr. articles to profl. jours. Home: Alexandria, Va. Died Oct. 2, 1973.

EVANS, WILMOTH DUANE, economist; b. Watertown, N.Y., June 10, 1909; s. Albert Leslie and Leah Frances (Craig) E.; B.S., Clarkson Coll. Tech., 1930; m. Edna Blanchard, Oct. 19, 1939; children—Patricia, Craig. Engr., statistician, economist various govt. agys., 1930-40; chief productivity and tech. devel. div. U.S. Bur. Labor Statistics, 1941-47, chief div. interindustry econs., 1948-53, chief statistician, 1954-55, asst. commr., 1955-62, asso. commr., 1962-64; prof. econs. and statistics Cornell U., Ithaca, N.Y., 1964-74; cons. Anglo-Am. Council Productivity, 1948-52; faculty econs. and polit. sci. Cambridge U., 1953-54. Recipient Rockefeller Pub. Service award, 1953, Distinguished Service award, Dept. of Labor, 1953. Fellow Am. Statis. Assn., A.A.A.S. (v.p. 1972, council 1972-73); mem. Am. Econ. Assn., Econometric Soc., Conf. on Research in Income and Wealth. Home: Ithaca, N.Y. Died May 25, 1974; buried Oak Point, N.Y.

EVENS, ALFRED, lawyer; b. Greencastle, Ind., Jan. 28, 1881; s. John Wooster and Margaret (Callahan) E.; Ph.B., DePauw U., 1902; LL.B., Ind. Law Sch., 1907; m. Kathleen Lindley, Oct. 2, 1912. Supt. schs., Monrovia, Ind., 1902-05; admitted to Ind. bar, 1907; practice of law, Indianapolis, 1907-10; asst. to Ind. state atty. Frankfort Gen. Ins. Co., 1910-14; partner Wood & Evens, Lafayette, Ind., 1914-20; gen. atty. C.I.&L.Ry., 1920-28; prof. of law, Ind. U. Sch. of Law, from 1928; dir. City Nat. Bank of Lafayette Ind., 1916-21. Mem. Am. Bar Assn., Ind. State Bar Assn., Sigma Nu, Order of Coif, Phi Delta Phi. Republican. Methodist. Club: Columbia. Editor: Indiana Law Jour., 1935-40. Contbr. of articles to law jours. Home: Bloomington, Ind.†

EVERETT, FRANCIS DEWEY, investment banker; b. Worcester, Mass., Feb. 13, 1889; s. Oliver H. and Sarah Frances (Dewey) E.; student St. Marks Sch.; A.B., Harvard, 1911, M.E.E., 1913; m. Marion Alice Lesher, Oct. 10, 1914; m. 2d, Mildred W. Ordway, July 17, 1954; m. 3d, Hertha Jordan, Dec. 1, 1962. With Westinghouse, Church, Kerr, engrs., N.Y.C., 1913-14; asst. Harvard Grad. Sch. Engring., 1914; at Saranac Lake and Ariz. (for health), 1914-18; asst. to Dr. Kennelly, Mass. Inst. Tech., 1918; with Hornblower & Weeks, N.Y.C., 1919-73, head statis. dept., 1924, head buying dept., 1927, partner, 1929-73. Gov. N.Y. Stock Exchange 1937-38; gov. Investment Bankers Assn., 1938-41; gov. Assn. of Stock Exchan ge Firms, 1945-51. Served in USNRF, World War I. Home: New York City, N.Y. Died Apr. 9, 1974.

EVERSMAN, ALICE, musician, writer; b. Effingham, Ill., d. John Caspar and Frances (Gibbons) Eversman; ed. Georgetown Visitation Convent, and Fairmont Sem., Washington, D.C., and Peabody Conservatory, Baltimore, Md.; studied with George Ferguson, (Berlin), Vincenzio Sabatini (Milan, Italy), Mme. Arthur Nikish (Berlin), Emma Thursby (N.Y. City), Herr Braunschweig (Berlin); Mus.D. Mem. Chgo. Opera Co., 1910-13; concert tour of Russia with Elena de Sayn, violinist, 1913; European opera debut, Karlsruhe, Germany, 1913; sang with Montreal, Century and San Carlo opera companies; toured with Victor Herbert and Sousa; mem. Metropolitan Opera Co., New York City, 1916-18; toured with Sonora Opera Co. in Cuba and British West Indies; founder and dir. European Concert Bureau, Paris, 1927-32; music editor and critic, Washington (D.C.) Evening Star, 1932-54. Mem. White House Corrs. Assn., Am. Newspaper Womens Club (pres. 1942-45, bd. govs. 1945, mem. past pres.'s com.), Women's Nat. Press Club. Home: Washington, D.C. Died Feb. 1974.

EVETT, ROBERT, composer, critic; b. Loveland, Colo., Nov. 30, 1922; s. Charles Emery and Sarah (Warnock) E.; student Colo. Coll., 1941-46, Juilliard Sch. Music, 1951-52. Chmn. music dept. Washington Inst. Contemporary Arts, 1947-51; music editor New Republic, Washington, 1952-68, asst. lit. editor, 1952-54, books and arts editor, 1954-68; asso. editor Atlantic Monthly, 1968-69; contbg. critic Washington Star, 1964-65, 69-75, book editor, 1971-75. Mem. Am. Composers Alliance, Nat. Assn. Am. Composers and Condrs., Music Critics Assn. Composer: Cello Concerto, No. 1, 1954; Piano Concerto, 1957; Harpsicord Concerto, 1961; Symphony 1, 1963; Anniversary Concerto, 1964; Lauds, 1964; Symphonies 2 and 3, 1965; The Greater Trumps, 1966; Vespers, 1967; Prime, 1968; Mary Dyer, 1968; Bassoon Concerto, 1970; Cello Concerto No. 2, 1971. Home: Takoma Park, Md. Died Feb. 1975.

EVISON, FRANCES MILLICENT MARION (MRS. FRANK D. MCENTEE), author; b. Leicester, Eng., July 7, 1880; d. Henry and Elizabeth Jane (Samwell) E.; educated in pub. schs., Collingwood, Ont., Can., and under private tutors, Toronto, Ont.; m. Frank D. McEntee, of N.Y. City, Aug. 18, 1902; 1 dau., Helen Margaret. Came to United States, 1901. With Ben Greet Players, appearing in roles of Puck, Ariel, Juliet, Ophelia, etc., 1903-11; appeared in Henry V with Lewis Waller, Daly's Theatre, N.Y. City, 1912 gold medal for piano playing, Metropolitan Sch. Music, Toronto, 1897. Episcopalian. Author: Rainbow Gold, 1920; Peggy Pretend, 1922; The Good-For-Nothing Graysons, 1928. Home: Montague, Mass.†

EVITT, JAMES EDWARD, JR., telephone co. exec.; b. Ringgold, Ga., Sept. 1, 1912; s. James E. and Annie (Ward) E.; grad. McCallie Sch.; student U. Ga., 1929-33, U. Chatanooga, 1931; 1 dau., Alice Lee. Druggist, Ringgold Drug Co., 1934-53; owner, mgr. Ringgold Telephone Co., 1948-58, pres., 1958-73; treas. Catoosa Industries, Inc., 1967-73; dir. Bank of Ringgold. Chmn. Ga.-Tenn. Regional Health Com., 1970-73; mem. Catoosa County Bd. Health; dir. Chattanooga Full Employment Com., Inc., 1969-73; treas. Hutchinson Meml. Tri-County Hosp., Ft. Oglethorp, 1947-67, vice chmn., 1967-73; treas. Ga. Hosp. Indigent Care Council, 1957-59. Dep. clk. superior ct., Catoosa County, 1933-44; mem. Ga. Ho. of Reps., 1945-51; pres. Ga. Young Democratic Club, 1945-46. Bd. dirs Chattanooga Met. Council for Community Services, 1966-73, Coosa Valley Planning Com., YMCA of Ga., Mem. Ga. Telephone Assn. (pres. 1961-62), Nat. REA Telephone Assn. (dir.), Greater Chattanooga C. of C. (dir. 1969-71), Ind. Pioneer Telephone Assn. Clubs: Rotary, Quarterback. Home: Ringgold, Ga. Died Nov. 15, 1973; buried Anderson Cemetery, Ringgold, Ga.

EWELL, GLENN BLACKMER, educator; b. Warsaw, N.Y., Feb. 26, 1880; s. Rev. Jirah B. and M(ary) Florine (Mallory) Ewell; A.B., Colgate U., 1903, M.A., 1927, D.D., 1936; diploma from Rochester Theol. Sem., 1911, B.D., 1912; m. Ada Delamater, Apr. 17, 1906; children—G. Paul Brownell, Jean Helen, Marjorie Adelaide, Roger Allen Blackmer. Ordained Bapt. ministry, 1911; student of library methods, 1911-12; asst. librarian Rochester Theol. Sem., 1912-13; librarian same, also mem. faculty and registrar; asso. dean and registrar Colgate-Rochester Div. Sch., 1928-37; dean adminstration and registrar, 1927-45; emeritus after 1945. Eastern N.Y. director for World Mission Crusade, N.B.C., 1945-47. Recording sec. board trustees New York Baptist Union for Ministerial Edn., 1918-28; sec. Bapt. Edn. Soc. of N.Y. and of bd. of trustees and exec. com. 1925-45; mem. board mgrs., N.Y. Bapt. State Conv., 1928-38; 1st v.p., 1929-30, pres. 1930-32; mem. Nat. Bd. Missionary Co-operation (Bapt.), 1929-34, com. of 15, Northern Bapt. Conv., 1933-34; sec. budget research com., Northern Baptist Conv. from 1934, chmn. from 1945, mem. Nat. Council 1936-42. Second chmn. exec. com., Roger William Fellowship, Northern Bapt. Conv.; interim dir. of bus. affairs. Detroit Council of Churches, 1948-49. Lecturer on the Rural Church 1933-48. Mem. Phi Beta Kappa, Delta Upsilon. Republican. Home: Rochester, N.Y.†

EWING, ALFRED CYRIL, philosopher; b. Leicester, Eng., May 11, 1899; s. Harry Frank and Emma (Zwiki) E.; B.A., U. Coll. Oxford, 1920, D.Phil., 1923; Litt.D., Cambridge, 1933. Asst. lectr. philosophy Univ. Coll. Swansea (Wales), 1927-31; lectr. Cambridge U., 1931-54, reader, 1954-66, chmn. philosophy dept., 1957-59, 64-66; fellow Jesus Coll., Cambridge U., 1962-66, hon. fellow, from 1966; Brit. editor Internat. Bibliography Philosophy, from 1953; vis. prof. U. Mich., 1926, Princeton, 1949, Northwestern U., 1949, U. So. Cal., 1961, U. Colo., 1963, San Francisco State Coll., 1967, U. Del., 1971, schs. India, 1951, 59, schs. S. Am., 1961. Fellow Brit. Acad. (chmn. philos. sect. 1953-61); mem. Internat. Fedn. Philos Socs. (treas. 1953), Inst. Philosophy. Author: Kant's Treament of Causality, 1924; The Morality of Punishment, 1929; Idealism, 1934; A Short Commentary on Kant's Critique of Pure Reason, 1938; The Individual, the State and World Government, 1947; The Definition of Good, 1947; Ethics, 1953; The Fundamental Questions of Philosophy, 1957; Second Thoughts in Philosophy, 1959; Non-Linguistic Philosophy, 1968; Value and Realty, 1973. Home: Manchester, England., Died 1973.

EWING, CHARLES A., live stock; b. Decatur, Ill., Apr. 18, 1878; s. Charles A. and Mary Giselle (Palmer) E.; student Lake Forest (Ill.) Acad., 1893-96, Princeton, 1899-1900; grad. Ill. Wesleyan U. Law Sch., Bloomington, 1903; m. Idelle Kerrick, Apr. 14, 1904; children—Sally E., Mary Idelle. On ranch in Tex. Panhandle, 1898; engaged in farming in Ill. after 1900; in practice of law at Decatur, 1903-07; mem. 1st bd. dirs., 1921, Nat. Live Stock Marketing Assn., nucleus of present assn. of same name, of which is pres.; dir. Chicago Producers Commission Assn. 8 yrs.; pres. Nat. Live Stock Pub. Co., Nat. Feeder & Finance Corpn., 1930-36. Former v.p., now dir. Decatur Water Supply Co. Chmn. nat. live stock advisory com. Coll. of Agr., U. of Ill., Decatur Chamber Commerce (pres. 1914-16). Mem. exemption bd., Decatur, World War. Democrat. Presbyn. Clubs: Decatur, Decatur Country. Home: Decatur, Ill.†

EWING, MAURICE, geophysicist; b. Lockney, Tex., May 12, 1906; s. Floyd Ford and Hope (Hamilton) E.; B.A., Rice Inst., 1925, M.A., 1927, Ph.D., 1931, Hohenthal scholar, 1923-26, fellow in physics, 1926-29; D.Sc. (hon.), Washington and Lee U., 1949, U. Denver, 1953, Utrecht, 1957, Lehigh U., 1957, U. R.I., 1960, U. Durham, 1963, U. Del., 1968, L.I. U., 1969, U. Nacional de Colombia, 1969, Centre Coll. Ky., 1971; LL.D., Dalhousie U., 1960; m. Avarilla Hildenbrand, Oct. 31, 1928 (div. 1941); 1 son, William M. (dec.); m. 2d, Margaret Sloan Kidder, Feb. 19, 1944 (div. 1965); children—Jerome, Hope, Peter, Margaret; m. 3d, Harriett Greene Bassett, May 6, 1965. Instr. physics Pitts. U., 1929-30; faculty Lehigh U., Bethlehem, Pa., 1930-44; asso. prof. geology Columbia, 1944-47, prof., 1947-49, Higgins prof. geology, 1959-72, Higgins prof. emeritus, 1972-74; Cecil H. and Ida Green prof. marine scis., chief earth and planetary div. Marine Biomed. Inst. U. Tex., 1972-74; on leave, 1940-44, from Lehigh U., and Columbia, 1944-45, to act as research asso. on NDRC, projects, Woods Hole (Mass.) Oceanographic Inst., 1940-44, dir. research physics, 1940-45; dir. Lamont-Doherty Geol. Obs., Columbia, 1949-72. Leader, Nat. Geog. Soc.-Columbia Woods Hole Oceanographic Inst. Expdns., 1947, 48, Columbia Expdns., 1953-73, IGY Expdn., 1957-58, NSF Deep Sea Drilling Project, 1968; mem. U.S. com. IGY, 1955-59. Decorated comdr. Order Naval Merit (Argentina); recipient Distinguished Pub. Service award USN, 1955; Vetlesen prize, 1960; John Fleming medal Am. Inst. Geonomy and Natural Resources, 1960; medal of honor Rice U., 1962; Alumni gold medal, 1972; Joseph Priestley award Dickinson Coll., 1961; Collum Geog. medal Am. Geog. Soc., 1961; John J. Carty medal Nat. Acad. Scis., 1963, Agassiz medal, 1965; Vega medal Swedish Soc. Anthropology and Geography, 1965; gold medal Royal Astron. Soc., 1964; Sidney Powers Meml. medal, 1968; Sesquicentennial medal St. Louis U., 1969; Wollaston medal Geol. Soc. London, 1969; Nat. Medal Sci. 1973; Robert Earll McConnell award Am. Inst. Mining, Metall. and Petroleum Engrs., 1973, Distinguished Achievement award Offshore Tech. Conf., 1974. Fellow Indian Geophys. Union (hon.); mem. Academia Nacional de Ciences Exactas Fisicas y Naturales (corr.), A.A.A.S., Geol. Soc. London (fgn. mem.), Am. Assn. Petroleum Geologists (hon.), Am. Geophys. Union (William Bowie medal 1957, Walter Bucher medal 1974, v.p. 1953-56, pres. 1956-59), Soc. Exploration Geophysicists (hon.), Seismol. Soc. Am. (v.p. 1952-54, pres. 1955-57), Royal Netherlands Acad. (fgn.), Royal Soc. New Zealand (hon.), Nat. Acad. Sci., Geol. Soc. Am. (A.L. Day medal 1949, Penrose medal 1974), Am. Acad. Arts and Scis., Am., Houston philos. socs., Royal Soc. London, Royal Astron. Soc. (asso.), Canadian Soc. Petroleum Geologists (hon.) Clubs: Century Assn., Explorers (N.Y.C.); Cosmos (Washington); Galveston Artillery. Author: (with J.L. Worzel and C.L. Pekeris) Propagation of Sound in the Ocean, 1948; (with W. Jardetzky, F. Press) Elastic Waves in Layered Media, 1957; also numerous papers in field. Editorial bd. several publs. Home: Galveston, Tex. Died May 4, 1974; buried Rockland Cemetery, Sparkill, N.Y.

EWING, SHERMAN, lawyer, author, theatrical producer; b. Yonkers, N.Y., May 26, 1901; s. Thomas and Anna Phillips (Cochran) E.; ed. St. Paul's Sch., 1912-19; Peter House, Cambridge, Eng., 1919-20; A.B., Yale, 1924; LL.B., Harvard, 1927; m. Mary Peavey Heffelfinger (div. 1934); children—Sherman, Lucia (Mrs. John Steidl), Anna (Mrs. David Bull), Frank Heffelfinger; m. 2d, Marjorie Wallace Hughes Walsh, Apr. 18, 1938. Dairy Farmer Woodchuck Hill Farm Am.; dir. Vivian Beaumont Theatre. Author: (plays) Wild Swans; Voltaire. Producer (with Marjorie H. Ewing) Angel in the Wings, 1947-48; The Rape of Lucretia (opera by Benjamin Britten), 1948-49. Dir. Mohasco Industries, Inc. Trustee Manhattan Sch. Music; bd. dirs. N.Y. Hort. Soc. Home: New York City, N.Y. Died May 15, 1975; cremated.

EXMAN, EUGENE, book publisher; b. Blanchester, O., July 1, 1900; s. Emmet and Mary Etta (Smith) E.; Ph.B., Denison U., 1922; M.A., U. Chgo., 1925; D.R.E., Middlebury Coll., 1952; m. Gladys Miller, June 6, 1929;

1 adopted son, Frank Walker; children—Wallace Miller, Judith. With U. Chgo. Press, 1925-28, mgr. religious book dept. Harper & Bros., N.Y.C., 1928, dir., 1944, v.p., 1955; later archivist and historian Harper & Row Pubs., Inc. Trustees Wainwright House Inc., chmn., 1960-65; trustee Denison U., from 1944; trustee Sturgis Library, pres., 1968-73. Club: Century Assn. (N.Y.C.). Author: The World of Albert Schweitzer, 1955; The Brothers Harper, 1965; The House of Harper, 1967. Contbr. articles to periodicals, books. Home: Barnstable Mass., Died Oct. 10, 1975.

EYSTER, JOHN AUGUSTINE ENGLISH, physiologist; b. Augusta Co., Va., July 31, 1881; s. George H. and Josephine (English) E.; B.Sc., Md. Agrl. Coll., 1899; Johns Hopkins Grad. Sch.; M.D., Johns Hopkins, 1905; m. Mary Elizabeth Adams, of Loudoun Co., Va., Aug. 8, 1906; 1 son, John English; m. 2d, Alice Brownell, Boston, Dec. 15, 1928. Fellow, asst. instr. and asso. in physiology, Johns Hopkins U., 1905-08; prof. pharmaeology and toxicology, U. of Va., 1908-10; prof. physiology, U. of Wis., after 1910. Fellow Am. Assn. Advancement Science, American Coll. Physicians; mem. Am. Physiol. Soc. (mem. Council), Am. Soc. Pharmacology and Exptl. Therapeutics, Soc. Exptl. Biology and Medicine, Assn. Am. Physicians, Beta Theta Pi, Phi Rho Sigma, Sigma Xi. Club: University. Contbr. articles on physiology and exptl. medicine to scientific jours. Home: Madison, Wis.†

EZEKIEL, MORDECAI JOSEPH BRILL, economist; b. Richmond, Va., May 10, 1899; s. Jacob Levy and Rachel (Brill) E.; B.S., U. of Md., 1918; M.S., U. of Minn., 1924; Ph.D., Robert Brookings Grad. Sch. of Economics and Govt., Washington, D.C., 1926; m. Lucille Finsterwald, Dec. 24, 1927; children—David Finsterwald, Jonathan, Margaret. Statistical asst. in agr., U.S. Census Bur., 1919-22; with div. farm management, U.S. Dept. Agr., 1922-30; asst. chief economist Federal Farm Bd., 1930-33; econ. adviser to the Secretary of Agriculture, 1933-44; econ. adv. bureau of agrl. economics, U.S. Dept. of Agr., 1944-46; asst. to exec. vice chmn., War Prodn. Bd., 1942-43; economist, Food and Agr. Orgn. of U.N., 1947-50, deputy director economic div., 1951-58, head econ. dept., 1959-60, asst. dir. gen., 1961-62; chief UN division of Program Control Staff, Agy. International Development, Department of State, Washington, 1962-67; economic cons., 1967-74. Guggenheim Fellowship for Economic Study, 1930. Mem. Food and Agr. Orgn. Mission for Greece, 1946, Poland, 1947. Developed methods of analyzing data; pioneered in curvilinear multiple correlation and in price forecasting for farm products; assisted in formulating plans for farm relief and in drafting A.A.A. Served as 2d lt. inf. U.S. Army, World War I. Fellow Am. Statis. Assn., Econometric Soc., Am. Farm Econ. Assn; mem. Am. Econ. Assn., Internat. Conf. Agrl. Economists. Mem. Jewish Ref. Ch. Author: Methods of Correlation Analysis, 1930; $2,500 a Year — from Scarcity to Abundance, 1936; Jobs for All, 1939; Use of Agricultural Surplus to Finance Economic Development in Underdeveloped Countries — A Pilot Study in India, 1955. Co-author and editor: Toward World Prosperity, 1947. Contributor articles to jours. Home: Green Acres, Md. Died Nov. 1974.

FABRI, RALPH, artist; b. Budapest, Hungary, Apr. 23, 1894; s. Henrik L. and Helen (Fisher) F.; A.B., Royal State Gymnasium, Budapest, 1912; student Royal Inst. Tech., Budapest, 2 years; prof.'s degree, Royal Acad. Fine Arts, Budapest, 1918. Came to U.S. 1921, naturalized, 1927. Asso. prof. Coll. City N.Y., until 1967; rec. sec. Nat. Acad., 1950-53; instr. Nat. Acad. Sch. of Fine Arts. Paintings and etchings exhibited at Nat. Acad., N.Y.C.; Pa. Acad. Fine Arts, Phila.; Art Inst., Chgo., etc.; one-man shows in N.Y.C., and many other U.S. cities; Budapest, 1946; participated in many internat. exhbns. Works owned by Library of Congress, Met. Mus. Art. N.Y.C., Smithsonian Inst., Honolulu Acad., others. Hon. life pres. of Audubon Artists. Recipient numerous prizes including: Ringius Prize, Hartford, Conn., 1945. Benjamin Franklin fellow Royal Soc. of Arts. London; mem. Soc. Am. Graphic Artists. Am. Assn. U. Profs., Knickerbocker Artists, Painters and Sculptors Soc. N.J. Am. Watercolor Soc., Nat. Acad. Design (treas. 1962-68), Am. Soc. Contemporary Artists, Audubon Artists and Nat. Soc. Painters in Casein (hon. life pres.), Allied Artists Am. (pres.), Authors Guild. Author: Learn to Draw, 1945; Oil Painting, 1966; Color, a Complete Guide for Artists, 1967; Flower Painting, a History of the American Watercolor Society, 1968; Outdoor Painting; Painting Cityscapes, 1969; Artist's Guide to Composition, 1971. Editor Today's Art. Contbr. articles to art mags. Address: New York City N.Y. Died Feb. 12, 1975.

FAGAN, IRVING, labor editor; b. Minsk, Russia, Sept. 30, 1897; s. Louis and Bertha (Faivishov) F.; brought to U.S., 1905, naturalized, 1911; student U. Mo., 1915-17; m. Frances Rosenthal, Dec. 5, 1926; children—Nancy (Mrs. Stanley Schiffman), Judith (Mrs. Alan I. Burbank). With the St. Joseph (Missouri) Gazette, St. Louis (Missouri) Republic, Oklahoma City Oklahoman, St. Louis Times, Washington Herald, Phila. Daily News. Phila. Record, 1917-46; sec. C.I.O. Council, Phila., 1937-47; on panel Regional War Labor Bd., Phila., 1945; editor, mgr. Labor Press Asso., 1949-54; asst. to president C.I.O. Electrical Workers, 1954; now associate editor International Union of Electrical Radio and Machine Workers, AFL-CIO. Cadet Marine Flying Sch., Mass. Inst. Tech., 1918. Mem. Phila. Newspaper Guild (adminstrv. officer 1947-49; established 1st Guild sch., Phila., 1934); Washington Newspaper Guild. Home: Washington D.C. Died Sept. 21, 1974.

FAIRCHILD, HOXIE N., educator; b. N.Y.C., Sept. 7, 1894; s. Jarvis Rose and Sarah Lenita (Plumb) F.; grad., Hackley Sch., 1912; A.B., Columbia, 1917, Ph.D., 1928; m. Mary Creusa Tanner, July 28, 1919; children—Hoxie Mary (died 1930), Anne. Instr. in English, Columbia, 1919-28, asst. prof., 1928-34, asso. prof., 1934-40; prof. English, Hunter Coll., 1940-60, prof. emeritus; vis. lectr. Faculty of English, Cambridge, 1958; guest speaker at meetings and convs., 1935. Past pres., mem. exec. com., English Grad. Union of Columbia U.; founding mem., past pres. Guild of Scholars of Episcopal Church; trustee Church of St. Mary the Virgin; founding mem. Conf. on Science, Philosophy, and Religion. Decorated Croix de Guerre (with palm), 1918; Chevalier de l'Ordre de la Couronne, 1st class, Belguim, 1920. Mem. Modern Language Assn. of Am. (group sec., chmn. com.). Clubs: Hunter College Humanities (past pres.), Faculty of Columbia University. Author: Religious Trends in English Poetry, 1939, Vol. IV, 1957, Vol. V, 1962, Vol. VI, 1968. Editor, co- author: Religious Perspectives in College Teaching, 1952. Contbr. articles to publs. Home: New York City N.Y. Died Oct. 23, 1973.

FAIRES, VIRGIL MORING, educator; b. Gainesville, Fla., Dec. 8, 1897; s. Carl Franklin and Nevada (Moring) F.; student Ga. Sch. Tech., 1916-17, U.S. Naval Acad., 1917-20; B.S. U. Colo., 1922, M.E., 1926, M.S., 1927; 1 dau., Virginia Lee (Mrs. E. W. Merris); m. 2d, Lucile Haley Orr, Oct. 5, 1951. Instr., U. Colo., 1922-25; asst. prof. mech. engring. U. Vt., 1925-26; asst. prof. mech. engring. Tex. A. and M. Coll., 1926-29, asso. prof., 1929-30, prof. 1930-51, head mgmt. engring. dept., 1941-50, dir. A.S.T.P., 1943-46, head dept. postgrad. studies, 1948-51; chief engring. sect. Am. U., Biarritz, France, 1945-46; prof. mech. engring. N.C. State Coll., 1952-58, U.S. Naval Postgrad. Sch., Monterey, Cal., from 1958. Mem. Am. Soc. M.E. (chmn. S. Tex. sect. 1944-45; Worcester Warner Reed Medal 1962), Am. Soc. Engring. Edn. (chmn. machine design div. 1940, past mem. council), Tau Beta Pi, Phi Kappa Phi, Pi Tau Sigma. Author: (with Grinter, et al), Engineering Preview, 1945; (with Chambers) Analytic Mechanics, rev. edit., 1952; Design of Machine Elements, rev. edit., 1965; Elementary Thermodynamics, rev. edit., 1957; Thermodynamics of Heat Power, rev. edit., 1958; Kinematics, 1959; (with Keown) Mechanism, rev. edit., 1960; Thermodynamics, 1962; (with Simmang Brewer) Problems on Thermodynamics, 1962; (with Wingren) Problems on Design Machine Elements, 1965. Home: Carmel, Cal. Died Apr. 28, 1969.

FAISAL, IBN ABDUL AZIZ AL SAUD, king of Saudi Arabia b. Riyadh, Nejd, Arabia, 1905; 2d son of Ibn Saud (Abdul Aziz al Saud), King of Saudi Arabia. As officer in army participated in battles that established kingdom, an absolute monarchy formed of Kingdom of Hejaz and Sultanate of Nejd, under reign of Ibn Saud, 1920-25; apptd. viceroy of Nejd, 1926; became sec. of state, Saudi Arabia, 1932; signed treaty confirming ofcl. relations between U.S. and Saudi Arabia, 1933; became minister fgn. affairs, 1934; upon death of father and elder brother's accession to throne was declared Crown Prince, 1953; prime minister and fgn. minister, 1953-64, minister def., 1958-64; in 1958 King Saud transferred to Faisal a large part of his absolute powers, including control of interior, fgn. and financial affairs; king of Saudi Arabia, 1964-75. Del. San Francisco Conf. on Internat. Orgn., 1945; chmn. Saudi Arabia delegation to UN Gen. Assembly. Recipient Hon. Knight Grand Cross Order Brit. Empire, Hon. Knight Comdr. St. Michael and St. George (Gt. Britain). Address: Riyadh, Saudi Arabia. Assassinated Mar. 5, 1975.

FAITH, PERCY, musician, condr., arranger; b. Toronto, Can., Apr. 7, 1908; s. Abraham and Minnie (Rotenberg) F.; ed. Lansdowne Grammar Sch. and Jarvis Coll. Sch., Royal Conservatory of Music, Toronto; m. Mary Palange, July 17, 1929; children—Marilyn, David Peter. Began as pianist in theatre and hotel work; arranger and condr. for Canadian Broadcasting Corp., 1933-40; performed on Music by Faith program, 1937-40, condr. Carnation radio program, Chgo., 1940, The Pause that Refreshes, The Woolworth Hour; eastern musical dir. Columbia Records Inc., 1957-60, western music dir. popular div., 1960-76. Recipient 1953 Record of Year with gold award for song from Moulin Rouge, Gold award for recording Summer Place, 1960, My Heart Cries for You, (albums) Viva and Bouquet, 1964. Jewish religion. Club: Arts and Letters (Toronto). Composer and arranger of songs and other works, and known for musical backgrounds and arrangements for radio. Recent recordings include: Time for Love, Raindrops Keep Fallin', Love Story, Joy, Jesus Christ Superstar, Day by Day. Died Feb. 9, 1976.

FAJANS, KASIMIR, chemist, educator; b. Warsaw, Poland, May 27, 1887; s. Herman and Wanda (Wolberg) F.; student Univ. of Leipzig, 1904-07; Dr. Nat. Phil., Heidelberg, 1909; research work, Zurich, 1909-10, Univ. of Manchester, 1910-11; m. Salomea Kaplan, 1910; children—Edgar, W. Stefan S. Asst., Technische Hochschule, Karlsrube, 1911-17, privat. dozent phys. chemistry, 1913-17; asso. prof. U. of Munich, 1917-25; prof. 1925-35; dir. of Inst. for Physical Chemistry, 1932-35; prof. chemistry, U. of Michigan, Ann Arbor, 1936-57. Non-resident lecturer in chemistry, Cornell Univ., 1930; lecturer, Austria, Canada, Denmark, England, Germany, Holland, Norway, Poland, Russia, Spain, Sweden, Switzerland, U.S.A., Belguim; cons. Owens Ill. Glass Co., Toledo, 1948-55. Establishment Kasimir Fajans award in chemistry, U. Mich., 1956. Recipient Victory Meyer prize, Heidelberg, 1909; medal of U. Liege, 1948. Fellow Am. Phys. Soc.; mem. Faraday Soc., Am. Chem. Soc. (exec. com. div. phys. and inorganic chemistry 1942-44; council 1944), A.A.A.S., Am. Crystallographical Assn., Soc. Freedom in Sci., Leningrad, Munich and Cracow acads. of sci., Polish Inst. Arts and Scis. in Am. Sigma Xi, hon. mem. chem. Soc. Karlsrube, Soc. Doctors of Madrid, Spanish Soc. for Physics and Chemistry, Royal Institution Great Britain, Phi Lambda Upsilon. Member Council of Deutsche Chem. Gesellschaft, 1921-22, Council of Bunsengesellschaft, 1928-32. Author books Radio elements and Isotopes: Chemical Forces and Optical Properties of Substance, 1931; Quanticule Theory of Chemical Binding, 1961, also articles in books and jours. including: Refractometry in Physical Methods of Organic Chemistry (with N. Bauer), 1945. Editor various publs.; co-editor: Zeitsch fü Kristallographie, 1924-39. Asso. editor: Jour. Physical and Colloid Chemistry 1948-49. Contbr. articles to jours. Home: Ann Arbor, Mich. Died May 18, 1975.

FALAYI, SAMUAL OLADEIE, librarian; b. May 6, 1925; student Igbobi Coll., Yaba, 1941-48, Sch. Agr., Ibadan, 1947-48, Loughborough Coll., Leicester, Eng., 1956-57, Columbia, 1963. Treasury clk., 1946; agrl. asst., 1947-49; marine clk., 1950; library asst. Fed. Ministry Health, 1950-60, med. librarian, 1960-64; med. librarian U. Lagos Coll. Medicine, from 1964; librarian Central Med. Library Fed. Lab. Service, Yaba. Mem. Com. on Internat. Cooperation, 1969, 70; 6th session 2d Internat. Congress Med. Librarianship, Washington, 1963, mem. Internat. liaison com. 3d Congress, 1969, mem. organizing com. 4th Congress. Fellow U.S. Med. Library Assn., 1962-63. Mem. Nigerian Library Assn. (past sec., chmn., councillor, pro tem v.p.). Author: History of Medical Organization in Nigeria, 1959; Book Acquisition Problems in Nigeria, 1963; Problems of Medical Information Systems and Centres in the Developing Countries of Africa, 1969. Address: Lagos, Nigeria., Deceased.

FALK, ELMER M., fgn. service officer; b. New Bedford, Mass., May 6, 1911; s. Elmer H. and Selma P. (Larsen) F.; B.S. in Econs., Wharton Sch. U. Pa., 1931, M.S. in Edn., 1933; m. Margaret Fulton, Nov. 9, 1940; children—Christine M., Martin E. With Pa. Dept. Pub. Assistance, 1934-43, 46; dir. assembly center UNRRA, Salsburg, Austria, 1945-46; with Vocational Rehab. and Edn. Office, VA, Phila., 1946-48; dep. dept. chief, then dept. chief Internat. Refugee Orgn., Germany, 1948-51; dep. European coordinator, then coordinator U.S. Displaced Persons Commn., Frankfurt, Germany, 1951-52; chief U.S. escapee program for Germany, Dept. of State, FOA/ICA, 1952-54; dep. chief intergovtl. refugee program div. ICA, Washington, 1954-56; with Office Internat. Adminstrn., Dept. of State, Washington, 1956-62; dir. office of refugee and migration affairs, 1962-68. Recipient Superior Honor award Dept. State, 1966. Home: Alexandria, Va. Died Aug. 19, 1968.

FALLERS, LLOYD ASHTON, JR., educator; b. Nebraska City, Neb., Aug. 29, 1925; s. Lloyd A. and Fannie (Lincoln) F.; Ph.B., U. Chgo., 1946, M.A., 1949, Ph.D., 1953; student London (Eng.) Sch. Econs., 1949-50; m. Margaret Elinor Chave, June 18, 1949; children—Winnifred Mary, Beth Laura. Lectr. anthropology Princeton, 1953-54; fellow E. African Inst. Social Research, 1950-52, 54-56, dir. inst., 1956-57; asst., then asso. prof. anthropology U. Cal. at Berkeley, 1957-60; mem. faculty U. Chgo., 1960-74, prof. anthropology, 1963-70, prof. anthropology and sociology, 1970-74. Fellow Center Advanced Study Behavioral Scis., 1958-59. Mem. Am. Anthrop. Assn., African Studies Assn., Assn. Social Anthropologists (Great Britain), Internat. African Inst., Royal Anthrop. Inst. (Great Britain). Democrat. Episcopalian. Author: Bantu Bureaucracy, 1956; Law Without Precedent, 1969; Inequality, 1973; The Social Anthropology of the Nation State, 1974. Editor, joint author: The King's Men, 1964. Asso. editor anthropology Internat. Ency. Social Scis., 1962-74. Home: Chicago, Ill. Died July 4, 1974.

FALLIS, LAURENCE SIDNEY, ret. surgeon; b. Millbrook, Ont., Can., Jan. 29, 1894; s. Albert James and Mary Jane (Larmer) F.; M.D., C.M., Queen's U., Kingston, Ont., 1919; M.R.C.S., L.R.C.P, St. Bartholomew's Hosp., London, Eng., 1922; postgrad. univs. London, Edinburg (Scotland), Vienna (Austria); m. Dorothy Marie Moloney, Aug. 16, 1930; children—Laurence Sidney, Richard James. Came to U.S., 1925, naturalized, 1943. Resident Ministry of Pensions Hosp., Toronto, 1919-21; house surgeon Royal Hosp., Portsmouth, Eng., 1921-24; med. dir. Campanhia Ford Indsl. do Brasil, Para, 1928-29; mem. staff Henry Ford

Hosp., Detroit, 1925-28, 30-71, surgeon-in-chief, 1952-66, cons. surgeon, 1966-74; chief surgeon Detroit, Toledo & Ironton R.R., 1951. Served with Canadian Army Med. Corps, 1915-18. Recipient plaque Davis & Geck, Inc., 1956. Diplomate Am. Bd. Surgery (a founder). Fellow Am., Royal colls. surgeons; mem. Am., World, Pan. Am. med. assns., Wayne County, Mich. med. socs. Am., Central (councillor 1960-63), Detroit (pres. 1951-52), Pan Pacific (v.p. 1963-66) surg. assns., Internat. Soc. Surgery, Assn. Francais de Chirugia de Cuba, Surg. Soc. Guadalajara (Mexico), Soc. Surgery Alimentary Tract, Detroit Acad. Surgery (pres. 1945-46), Detroit Acad. Medicine, Detroit Surg. Soc., Detroit Inst. Cancer Research (trustee 1945-74; sec. 1956-58, pres. 1959-61), Mich. Assn. Professions, Assn. Am. Railroads, Internat. Congress Gastroenterology, Internat. Congress Nutrition; hon. mem. Flint Acad. Surgery, Cin., Surg. Soc., Spokane Acad. Gen. Practice, Soc. Chilena de Gastro-Enterologia, Soc. Argentina de Proctologia, Detroit Econ. Club. Clubs: Detroit; Los Buenos Vecinos (Detroit); Nat. Travel (N.Y.C.) Home: Lighthouse Point, Fla. Died Mar. 18, 1974; buried Millbrook, Ontario, Canada.

FALLIS, WILLIAM DAVID, utility exec.; b. Neepawa, Man., Can., Mar. 14, 1909; s. Allan Benjamin and Minnie (Sutherland) F.; m. Donalda Christine Fallis, Sept. 26, 1936; 1 dau., Roberta (Mrs. Jacob Popoff). With Man. Power Commn. (merged with Man. Hydro-Electric Co. 1961), Winniepeg, Man., 1930-74, comptroller, 1944-46, gen. mgr., 1946-74; dir. Atomic Energy Can. Ltd., Ottawa. Mem. Civil Service Superannuation Bd., 1948-73. Mem. Canadian (dir.), Man. elec. assns. Rotarian, Mason (Shriner). Clubs: Griffons, Canadian, Manitoba, Winter (Winnipeg). Home: Winnipeg, Man., Canada. Died Aug. 21, 1974; buried Gary Meml. Gardens, Winnipeg, Man., Can.

FALLS, FREDERICK HOWARD, physician; b. Chicago, Ill., Dec. 14, 1885; s. Samuel Kemp and Florence Mary (Church) F.; prep. edn., Lewis Inst., Chicago, 1900-06; S.B., U. of Chicago, 1909; M.D., Rush Med. Coll., 1910; M.S., U. of Ill., 1916; m. Margaret Haseltine, June 18, 1920; children—Frederick H., Richard H., John L., William H., Hugh C., David C. Private practice, Chicago, 1911-13; research at U. of Ill., teaching and practice, 1913-18; with Chicago Lying-In Hosp., and in private practice, 1919-21; prof. obstetrics and gynecology, U. of Ia., 1921-26; prof. and head dept. of obstetrics and gynecology, University of Illinois College of Medicine, 1926-54, prof. emeritus, 1954-74, also in private practice; chief of obstetrical and gynecological staff West Suburban Hosp.; cons. West Lake Hosp., Maywood, Ill., Ill. Dept. Pub. Welfare; consultant, staff Augustana Hosp., Norwegian and Grant Hosp. Diplomate Am. Bd. Obstetrics and Gynecology. Fellow A.C.S., Internat. Coll. Surgeons; mem. A.M.A. (chairman obstetrics and gynecology 1955), Illinois State and Chicago med. socs., Am. Assn. Obstetricians, Gynecologists and Abdominal Surgeons (pres. 1941), Chicago Gynecol. Soc., Am. Gynecol. Soc., Ill. Obstet. and Gynecol. Soc. Episcopalian. Republican. Author: Atlas of Obstetric Complications. Home: River Forest, Ill. Died Feb. 1, 1974.

FANNING, RAYMOND JOSEPH, editor; b. Waterbury, Conn., Apr. 2, 1893; s. Richard J. and Mary (McEvoy) F.; grad. Danbury Tchrs. Coll., 1916; m. Helen C. Cassin, July 16, 1928; children—Nancy Marie (Mrs. John Rabbott), Richard DeLowry. Began as principal of school Glastonbury, Conn., 1916; reporter Waterbury Republican Am., 1918-30, city editor, 1930-36, mng. editor, 1936-48, exec. editor 1948-61. Agent Bronson Library. Served with U.S.N., 1917-18. Mem. Nat. Assn. Press Mng. Editors Assn., Conn. Circuit of Assn. Press (chmn. 1953-55). Roman Catholic Club: Waterbury. Juror for Pulitzer Prize awards in journalism, 1955, 56, 57. Home: Waterbury, Conn., Died Feb. 8, 1976.

FANT, CLYDE EDWARD, mayor Shreveport, ins. co. exec.; b. Linden, Tex., Oct. 18, 1905; s. John Preston and Rosa Lee (Owen) F.; student Coll. Marshall. 1923-25; LL.D. (hon.), East Tex. Bapt. Coll., 1960; m. Margaret Elizabeth Moos, Sept. 3, 1927; children—Clyde Edward, John Frank. Mayor, City of Shreveport. 1946-58, 58-70; pres. Fant, Chase & Kline, Inc., Shreveport, 1954-58, chmn. bd., 1972-73. Mem. La Tax Commn., 1971-72. Pres., La. Municipal Assn., 1951, 52, 53, life mem. bd. dirs., 1954-73; trustee, mem. exec. bd. U.S. Conf. Mayors, 1960-70. Named Mayor of Yr. in La., 1958; Mr. Shreveport. Civic Clubs of Shreveport, 1963; recipient Shreveport's Best Ad award Shreveport Advt. Club. 1954; Shreveport Outstanding Salesman award Sales Execs. Club, 1962. Baptist (past pres. bd. dirs.). Democrat. Mason (33 deg.), Lion. Home: Shreveport, La. Died July 6, 1973; interred Forest Park Cemetery, Shreveport La.

FARDWELL, HARRY R(INGGOLD), company exec.; b. St. Louis, Jan. 24, 1902; s. Harry Ringgold and Mary Elizabeth (Lewis) F.; student U. Pa., 1920-24; m. Anne M. Peterson, Aug. 14, 1930. Joined Otis Elevator Co., 1924, asst. sec., asst. treas., 1945-51, treas., 1951-73, sec., 1964-73; dir. Blackstone Mutual Ins. Co. Mem. Newcomen Soc. in N.Am., The Treasurers Club. Sigma Phi Sigma. Clubs: Wall Street and Union League (N.Y.C.). Home: New York City, N.Y. Died July 24, 1973.

FARGO, LUCILE FOSTER, librarian, author; b. Lake Mills, Wis., Oct. 18, 1880; d. Joseph Eliot and Emily Francina (Foster) Fargo; student Yankton (S.D.) Coll., 1899-1901; B.A., Whitman Coll., 1903, M.A., 1904; certificate N.Y. State Library School, 1908. Library asst., Walla Walla (Wash). Pub. Library, 1906; 1st asst., catalog and reference departments, Portland (Ore.) Library Assn., 1908-09; librarian N. Central High Sch., Spokane, 1909-26; summers, and leaves of absence, asst. Calif. State Library, Seattle Pub. Library, classifier A.L.A. War Service, Honolulu, T.H., etc.; mem. staff Am. Library Assn., Chicago, 1926-27; A.L.A. curriculum study, U. of Chicago, 1927-28; school library adviser, Akron, O., 1929-30; asso. dir. Library Sch., George Peabody Coll. for Teachers, 1930-33; research asso. Columbia U. Sch. of Library Service, 1933-36; asso. prof. library science, Western Reserve Univ., 1937-45. Mem. adv. com. U.S. Survey of Secondary Edn., 1929-31; sec. of Pacific Northwest Library Assn., 1911-13; dir. A.L.A. and Am. Assn. of Teachers Colls. Joint Com. Tng. Study. Mem. Am. Assn. U. Women, Conglist. Wrote: The Library in the Sch.; The Program for Elementary Sch. Library Service; Preparation for Sch. Library Work; Marian-Martha; Prairie Girl; Activity Book for School Libraries; Activity Book No. 2; Come, Colors, Come; Treasure Shelves; Prarie Chautauqua; Spokane Story, 1950; articles and pamphlets on sch. libraries. Address: Berkeley, Cal.†

FARILL, JUAN SOLARES, physician; b. Mexico City, Mexico, Feb. 11 1902; s. Jaime V. and Manuela (Solares) F.; M.D., Nat. U. Mexico, 1926; postgrad. State U. Ia., (Guggenheim fellow), U. Vienna; m. Ines Novelo, Aug. 17, 1927 (dec. June 1966); children—Eugenia, Jaime, Lourdes (Mrs. Jaime Pastor). Chief dept. orthopaedic surgery Gen. Hosp., Mexico, 1933-43; chief surgeon Shriners Hosp. for Crippled Children, Mexico City 1945-64, cons.; prof. orthopaedic surgery Nat. U. Mexico, 1942-48; hon. prof. orthopaedic surgery U. Guadalajara, 1943-73, U. Zulia State, Venezuela, 1962; gen. dir. Mexican Inst. Rehab., 1960-67; officer council Gen. Pub. Health of Mexico, 1965-73. Pres., 1st Pan Am. Congress Rehab., Mexico, 1948. Recipient Lasker Found. award 1954; comdr. Order of Daniel A. Carrion of Lima, Peru, 1965. Hon. fellow Internat. Coll. Surgeons; mem. Internat. Soc. for Welfare of Cripples (v.p. 1937-42, pres. 1942-48), Sociedad Amigos del Nino Lisiado (founder 1935), Latin Am. Soc. Orthopaedics and Traumatology (founder, pres. 1948-50, later hon. pres.), Mexican Nat. Acad. Medicine, Am., Brit. (corr.) orthopedic assns., Am. Acad. Orthopaedic Surgeons, Nat. Soc. Surgery Cuba, Argentina-Am. Fracture Assn., Internat. Acad. Medicine, Internat. Soc. Orthopaedic Surgery and Traumatology (pres. congress 1969); hon. mem. Academia de Medicina del Brasil, Sociedad Brasilena de ortopedia y Traumatologia, Sociedad Latino Americana de Medicina Fisica y Rehabilitacion, Assn. Bone and Joint Surgeons, Chilean, Spanish orthopaedic assns., Translator: A Primer of the Prevention of Deformity in Childhood (by Shands and Raney), 1946; Strike Back at Stroke (Internat. Soc. Welfare of Cripples), 1960. Mem. editorial bd. Orthopaedic Audio-Synopsis Found. corr. editor Jour. Bone and Joint Surgery, Clin. Orthopaedics, Révue d'Orthopédie et de Chirurgie de l'Apparell Moteur. Devel., publs. on techniques for treatment club foot and congenital hip dislocation, otho-radiographic measurement of shortening of lower limbs. Address: Narvarte, Mexico City, Mexico. Died June 24, 1973.

FARLEY, EUGENE SHEDDEN, educator; b. Phoenixville, Pa., Sept. 29, 1899; s. Robert and Sarah (Shoemaker) F.; B.S., Penn State, 1921; A.M. U. Pa., 1927, Ph.D., 1932; D.H.L., Alliance Coll.; Litt.D., Lafayette Coll.; D.Sc., Wilkes Coll.; LL.D., Seton Hill Coll., Bucknell U.; m. Eleanor Coates, Aug. 24, 1921 (dec.); children—Ethel (Mrs. Walter L. Douglass), Robert Coates, Eugene Shedden. Tchr. Germantown (Pa.) Acad., 1922-25; instr. Univ. of Pa., 1927-29; dir. research Bd. of Edn., Newark; 1929-36; dir. Bucknell Univ. Jr. Coll., Wilkes-Barre, Pa., 1936-47; pres. Wilkes Coll., 1947-70, chancellor, 1970-73. Dir. Pa. Power & Light Co.; dir. Pa. Millers Mutual Ins. Co. Mem. Govs. Com. 100 for State Constl. Revision; past pres. Pa. Commn. Ind. Coll., bd. dirs. Osterhout Library, Greater Wilkes-Barre Indsl. Fund, Wyo, Valley Hosp., former mem. Found. Ind. Colls., Kosciuszko Found. Pa. State Council Edn. Mem. Am. Assn. Jr. Colls. (pres. 1947), Pa. Assn. Jr. Colls. (pres. 1945), Jr. Coll. Council of Middle States and Md. (pres. 1940), Middle States Commn. on Secondary Schs., Phi Delta Theta, Phi Delta Kappa. Republican. Mem. Soc. of Friends. Clubs: Torch, Kiwanis, Westmoreland, Home: Wilkes-Barre Pa. Died Sept. 17, 1973.

FARLEY, JOSEPH FRANCIS, coast guard officer; b. Oxford, O., June 22, 1889; s. Joseph Francis and Sarah (Foote) F.; grad. U.S. Coast Guard Acad., New London, Conn., 1912; m. Routh Bridgers, July 7, 1915; children—Emily Bridgers (Mrs. Albert Francis Wigglesworth), Betty Haywood. Cadet, U.S. Coast Goard, 1909-12, commd. officer, 1912; served on various cutters and destroyers; signal officer on cutter Yamacraw on convoy duty out of Gibraltar, during World War I; served as alternate mem. Bd. of War Communications; chairman U.S. delegation, v.p. of conf., Internat. Conference on Safety of Life at Sea, London, 1948. Assigned as dist. Coast Guard officer, 8th Naval Dist., 1942; commd. commodore, June 1943, rear admiral, Dec. 1943, and assigned asst. chief operations officer, Coast Guard Headquarters, Washington, D.C.; assigned as chief personnel officer, Dec. 1944; made commandant, with rank of Admiral, 1946, ret. 1950. Awarded Victory medal (with excort clasp), Am. Defense Service Medal, Legion of Merit Medal. Mem. Soc. Naval Engrs., Soc. Naval Architects and Marine Engrs., Newcomen Soc., Naval Inst., Am. Rifle Assn. (life), Am. Legion, Am. Geophysical Union, Am. Polar Soc., Soc. Am. Wars, Naval Hist. Found., Naval Order of U.S., Military Order of World Wars. Clubs: Cape Fear (Wilmington, N.C.); Belle Haven Country (Alexandria, Va.); Army-Navy, Metropolitan (Washington). Home: Alexandria, Va. Died Nov. 25, 1974.

FARNSWORTH, HELEN ELLIOTT CHERINGTON, educator; b. Columbus, O., Jan. 23, 1903; d. Lemuel Bundy and Mae Florence (Elliott) Cherington; B.S., M.A., Ohio State U., 1924; Ph.D., Stanford, 1930; m. Paul Randolph Farnsworth, Aug. 31, 1926; children—Elliott Cherington, Susan March Cherington Caron. Teaching asst., Ohio State U., 1924-26, Stanford, 1927-29; research asst. Food Research Inst., Stanford, 1929-32, jr. research asso., 1932-36, asso. economist, 1936-45, econs. and asso. prof., 1945-50, prof. 1950-68, prf. emeritus, 1968, asso. dir., 1960-62. Mem. Am. Econ. Assn., Am. Farm Econs. Assn. and Pacific Coast brs., Alpha Phi, Mortar Board, Pi Lambda Theta, Beta Gamma Sigma. Author: Wartime Food Developments in Germany, 1942; Livestock in Continental Europe During World War II, 1944; World Grain Review and Outlook (with V.P. Timoshenko), 1945; Wheat Growers and the Tariff, 1946; Grain Saving for United States Export, 1947; Internat. Wheat Agreements and Problems, 1949-56, 1956; Multiple Pricing of American Wheat, 1958; American Wheat Exports, Policies and Prospects, 1960; Determinants of French Grain Production, Past and Prospective, 1964; (with K. Friedmann) The West German Grain Economy and The Common Market, 1966; (with Friedmann) French and EEC Grain Policies and Their Price Effects, 1920-1970, 1967. Home: Stanford, Cal. Died Feb. 23, 1974; buried Greenfield, Mass.

FARQUHAR, FRANCIS PELOUBET, accountant; b. Newton, Mass., Dec. 31, 1887; s. David Wabber and Grace Thaxter (Peloubet) F.; A.B., Harvard, 1909; L.H.D., U. Cal., 1967; m. Marjory Bridge, Dec. 21, 1934; children—Peter, Suzanne, David Bridge, Roger Peloubet. Practice pub. accounting, Boston, 1909, 12-14, San Francisco, 1911-12, 15-59; ret., 1959; spl. accountant U.S. Nat. Park Service, 1922-25; lectr. U. Cal., Davis Dir., Varian Assos., Palo Alto, Cal., 1948. Mem. Cal. State Bd. of Accountancy, 1951-59, pres., 1953-54. Served as lt. USNRF, 1917-19. C.P.A., Cal. Fellow Am., Royal geog. socs.; mem. Am. Inst. Accountants, Cal. Soc. C.P.A.'s (past pres.), Cal. Acad. Sci. (hon. trustee, past pres.), Cal. Hist. Soc. (past pres., recipient Wagner Meml. medal 1966), Am. Antiquarian Soc., Arctic Inst., Polar Soc., Save-the-Redwoods League, Greek Mountaineering Soc. (hon.). Christian Scientist. Mason (32 deg.). Clubs: Alpine (London); American Alpine, Sierra (past pres., editor Bull., 1926-46, recipient John Muir award for conservation 1965); Bohemian (San Francisco); California (Los Angeles); Appalachian (Boston); Cosmos (Washington); Explorers (N.Y.C.); Alpin Hellenique (Greece). Author: Place Names of the High Sierra, 1926; Mount Olympus, 1929; Yosemite, the Big Trees and the High Sierra, a Selective Bibliography, 1948; The Books of the Colorado River and the Grand Canyon, 1953; History of the Sierra Nevada, 1965. Contbr. to Ency. Brit., 1940. Editor: Up and Down California in 1860-1864, 1930; Am. Alpine Jour., 1956-59. Made expdns. to Mt. Olympus, Greece, 1914, 51, North Pole, 1949. Home: Berkeley, Cal. Died Nov. 21, 1974.

FARRAND, ROY FELTON, educator, soldier; b. Onalaska, Wis., May 9, 1875; s. Ira Smith and Elizabeth Maud (Fahey) F.; grad. St. John's Mil. Acad., Delafield, Wisconsin, 1894; Litt.B., U. of Wis., 1900; LL.D., Kenyon College, 1934; m. Elizabeth Ross Smythe, Aug. 15, 1901 (dec.); 1 dau., Dorothy Elizabeth Ross; married 2d, Nita Smith Walker, Oct. 30, 1947. With St. John's Mil. Acad., from 1894, except when in Coll. and in the U.S. Army, and pres. same from 1923. Apptd. comdt. cadets and instr. in mil. drill. St. John's Mil. Acad., 1894, also was mem. Wis. Nat. Guard, advancing to brign gen., 1940; resigned commn. after outbreak World War I and entered O.T.C., Ft. Sheridan, Ill., as pvt., graduating from 1st T.C. as maj. inf.; served with French Army 12 mos.; hon. discharged, 1919; col. O.R.C., U.S. Army, comdg. 403d U.S.R. Inf., 1921-39, retired. Decorated Order of The Black Star (French), Knight 1st Class, Order of the White Rose of Finland; citation from Department of the Army, 1953; Good Citizenship Gold medal, Nat. Soc. S.A.R., 1955. Pres. Wis. Roadside Development Council, 1940-48. Mem. Wis. State Council of Defense. Chmn. Selective Service Bd. Member exec. com. Association Military Colls. and Schools of U.S. (pres., 1930-32), Am. Legion (dept. comdr. 1930-31), Mil. Order of World Wars, Theta Delta Chi, 40 and 8, Military Order of Foreign Wars (dept. comdr. 1939), Sojourners Club. Episcopalian. Mason. Writer and lecturer on edn. of boys and mil. training, Americanism and preparedness. Home: Delafield, Wis.†

FARRAR, JOHN CHIPMAN, publisher, author; b. Burlington, Vt., Feb. 25, 1896; s. Edward Donaldson and Sally (Wright) F.; A.B., Yale, 1918; m. Margaret Petherbridge, 1926; children—John Curtis, Alison, Janice. Reporter, N.Y. Sunday World, 1919-21; editor The Bookman, 1921-27; became editor George H. Doran Co., 1925; dir. Doubleday, Doran and Co., 1927; editor, v.p., then chmn. bd., Farrar & Rinehart, Inc., 1929-44; lectr., Columbia, 1945-47; chmn. bd., Farrar, Straus & Giroux, 1946-74. Served as 1st lt., U.S. Air Service, 1917-19; with Overseas Publs., O.W.I., 1943-45. Mem. Nat. Conf. Christians and Jews (chmn. mag. com. 1948-49), Fed. Grand Jury Assn. (exec. com. 1949); v.p. Am. Center of P.E.N., 1952-74; exec. bd., Poetry Soc. Am., 1959-74. Clubs: Century, Elizabethan (New Haven, Conn.). Author: Forgotten Shrines, 1919; Songs for Parents, 1921; The Magic Sea Shell, 1923; The Middle Twenties, 1924; Songs for Johnny Jump-Up, 1930; Indoor and Outdoor Plays for Children, 1933; For the Record, 1943. Home: New York City, N.Y. Died Nov. 5, 1974.

FARREL, FRANKLIN, JR., business exec.; b. Ansonia, Conn., Aug. 17, 1881; s. Franklin and Lillian (Clarke) F.; Hopkins Grammar Sch. (New Haven); St. Paul's Sch. (Concord, N.H.); B.A., Yale University, 1903; m. Marian Vincent Brown, 1906. Continuously identified with Farrel-Birmingham Co., Inc., in various capacities, from 1903. Chmn. bd. Farrel-Birmingham Co., Inc. 1927-45, cons. dir. Served from ensign to lt. (s.g.) U.S. Navy, World War I. Honored by spl. letter of commendation with silver star for services, from Sec. of Navy. Mem. Soc. Colonial Wars, Sons of Am. Revolution, Delta Kappa. Epsilon. Mason (32°). Clubs: Yale of New York; Elihu, Graduates of New Haven, New Haven Lawn. Address: New Haven, Conn.†

FARRELL, FRANCIS DAVID, agriculturist; b. Smithfield, Utah, Mar. 13, 1883; s. George Lionel and Amanda (Steele) F.; B.S., Utah State College, 1907; Agr.D., University of Nebraska, 1925; LL.D., Washburn University, 1943; m. Mildred Jenson, September 16, 1913; children—Frances, James David. Scientific assistant in cereal investigations, U.S. Dept. of Agri., Washington, 1907-10; associate prof. irrigation and drainage, U. of Ida., 1910-11; agronomist in charge of cereal cultivation experiments, 1911-12, asst. agriculturist in western irrigation agr. investigations, 1912-14, agriculturist in charge of agrl. development on govt. reclamation projects, 1914-18, U.S. Dept. of Agriculture; dean div. of agr., and dir. Agrl. Experiment Station, Kansas State College, 1918-25, president of the coll. 1925-43, pres. emeritus and prof. of rural instns., from July 1, 1943; consultant on agricultural education, Univ. of Minnesota, 1944-45, Univ. of Calif., 1946-47. Chairman Kansas Committee on the Relation of Electricity to Agr., 1925-49. Member Kansas State Bd. of Edn., 1925-41; mem. Kan. State Sch. Bk. Commn., 1925-33, and 1937-41; mem. agrl. advisory council Am. Bankers Assn., 1925-43; mem. adv. council Nat. Broadcasting Co., 1926-45; chairman Nat. Land Use Planning Com., 1932-33; trustee The Farm Foundation, 1933-54; past president Kansas State Coll. Research Found.; pres. Assn. of Land-Grant Colleges and Univs., 1939-40. Mem. adv. com. on national affairs, C. of C. of U.S., 1947-49. Fellow A.A.A.S.; mem. Kansas State Historical Soc. (president, 1954-55), Phi Kappa Phi, Alpha Zeta, Sigma Xi. Club: Rotary. Author of numerous bulletins and papers on agrl. and ednl. subjects. Home: Manhattan, Kan., Died Feb. 13, 1976.

FARRINGTON, DORA DAVIS, prof. English; b. of Am. parents, Secunderabad, India, Nov. 30, 1880; d. Rev. Franklin Grasson and Mary Frances (Cary) Davis; grad. high sch., Asbury Park, N.J., 1897; A.B., Wesleyan U., Conn., 1902; A.M., Columbia, 1908; m. Harry Webb Farrington, of Interlaken, N.J. June 1920. Teacher, Clark U., Atlanta, Ga., 1902-03; asst. prof. English, Hunter Coll., 1906-28, then for a time asso. prof. Conducted survey on weekday religious instrn. in U.S. for Religious Edn. Assn., 1918. Treas. Suffrage Party, 17th Assembly Dist., N.Y. City, 1910-14; del. Progressive Party Conv. of N.Y., Syracuse, N.Y., 1912; chmn. mil. census 20th and 21st Assembly dists., World War. Mem. Am. Assn. Univ. Women, Phi Beta Kappa, D.A.R., League of Women, Voters. Episcopalian. Author: The Essay—How to Study and Write It, 1924; Projects in Description and Narration (text book). Editor: Valleys and Visions (by H. W. Farrington—for adults); The Land of Only If (by H. W. Farrington—for children). Address: Pasadena, Cal.†

FASSÒ, GUIDO, educator; b. Bologna, Italy, Oct. 18, 1915; s. Ernesto and Cesarina (Sarbieri) F.; grad. law U. Bologna, 1936, grad. philosophy, 1940; m. Margherita Ostl, Apr. 16, 1942; children—Alberto, Andrea, Silvia, Federico. Prof. philosophy of law U. Parma (Italy), 1949-63, U. Bologna, 1963—. Author: I quattro autori del Vico, 1949; La storia come esperienza giuridica, 1953; Cristianesimo e società, 1956, 69; La democrazia in Grecia, 1959, 67; La legge della ragione, 1964, 66; Il diritto naturale, 1964, 72; Storia della filosofia del diritto, 1966-70, 70-72, Vico e Grozio, 1971; Società, legge e ragione, 1974. Home: Bologna, Italy., Died Oct. 30, 1974.

FATH, EDWARD ARTHUR, astronomer; b. Rheinbischofsheim, Baden, Germany, Aug. 23, 1880; s. Jacob and Bertha Louisa (Judiesch) F.; brought to America in infancy; B.S., Carleton College, Northfield, Minnesota, 1902, D.Sc., 1950; University of Ill., 1905-06; U. of Calif. and Lick Obs., 1906-09; Ph.D., U. of Calif., 1909; Morrison fellow at Lick Observatory, 1933-34; m. Rosina Kiehlbauch, June 1, 1909 (died November 26, 1939); children—Catherine Bertha, Miriam Rosina; m. 2d, Olive M. Hawver, Dec. 19, 1942. Instructor mathematics, Wilton College, 1902-04; President of Redfield College, 1914-20; professor mathematics and astronomy, 1920-26, prof. astronomy and dir. Goodsell Obs., Carleton Coll., Northfield, Minn., 1926-50, ret. Fellow A.A.A.S., Royal Astronomical Soc. London; mem. Am. Astron. Soc., Société Astronomique de France. Sigma Xi, Phi Beta Kappa, Delta Sigma Rho. Author books. Contbr. various papers. Asso. editor Popular Astronomy, 1920-28. Home: Denver, Colo.†

FAUST, CLARENCE HENRY, found. exec.; b. Defiance, Ia., Mar. 11, 1901; s. Henry John and Wilhelmina (Mueller) F.; student Drake U., Des Moines, 1918-19; B.A., North Central Coll., Naperville, Ill., 1923; B.D., Evang. Theol. Sem., Naperville, 1924; MA., U. Chgo., 1929, Ph.D., 1935; LL.D. (hon.), U. Louisville, 1956; L.H.D., Berea Coll., 1958; m. Gladys Lang, June 1924; children—Wm., Dale Henry, Franklin Paul. Ordained ministry of Evang. Ch., 1924; clergyman, 1924-28; instr. Eng., University Ark., 1929-30; inst. English, U. of Chicago, 1930-35, asst. prof., 1935-39, asso. prof., 1939-41, prof., 1941-47, dean of the coll., 1941-46, dean of grad. library school, 1946-47; dir. of libraries, Stanford U., 1947-48, dean humanities and scis., 1948-51, acting pres. Jan.-Apr. 1949. Apptd. head Fund for Advancement Edn., Ford Found., 1950, pres., 1951-57; v.p. Ford Found., from 1957. Club: Century. Co-author; Jonathan Edwards, Selections with Bibliography, Introduction and Notes, 1935; The Decline of Puritanism, 1954. Home: Pomona, Cal. Died May 1975.

FAVILLE, ALPHEUS DAVIS, animal husbandman; b. Lake Mills, Wis., Feb. 27, 1880; s. Stoughton Wheaton and Emma (Myers) F.; B.S., Lawrence Coll., Appleton, Wis., 1902; spl. work in animal husbandry, U. of Wis., 1906-08, M.S., 1915; m. Jean Douglas, July 22, 1913. Prof. animal husbandry, U. of Wyo., Aug. 1908-Jan. 1918, and dean Agrl. Coll. and dir. Expt. Sta., 1918-22; state commr. of agr., 1923-28. Mem. Am. Soc. of Animal Production; mem. Beta Theta Pi, Alpha Zeta, Phi Beta Kappa. Address: Wheatland, Wyo.†

FAWCETT, HAROLD PASCOE, educator; b. Upper Sackville, N.B., Can., July 20, 1894; s. George Albert and Agnes (Carey) F.; A.B., Mt. Allison U., 1914; tchr. certificate, U. Cal., 1916; A.M., Columbia, 1924, Ph.D., 1937; m. Frances Muriel Harper, Dec. 30, 1919; children—Dorothy (Mrs. Leon Zechiel), Winifred (Mrs. William Slocum), Helen (Mrs. Cody Hall). Tchr. high sch., 1914-16, home study div. YMCA Schs., 1919-24; instr. Columbia, 1924-32; asst. prof. mathematics Ohio State U., 1932-37, associate professor, 1937-43, professor, 1943-64, emeritus professor, 1964-76; associate dir. U. Sch., 1938-41, chmn. dept. edn., 1948-56; vis. prof. Northwestern U., 1935-40, Columbia, 1947, U. Va., 1954, U. Michigan, 1955, University of Utah, 1956; director workshops mathematics edn.; lectr., cons.; ednl. adviser Coronet Instructional Films. Served from pvt. to 2d lt., F.A., U.S. Army, 1917-19, France. Recipient Ohio State U. Alumni award for distinguished teaching, 1916. Mem. N.E.A., Nat. Council Tchrs. Mathematics (bd. dirs. Yearbook com. 1952-55, pres. 1958-60), Ohio Edn. Assn., Math. Assn. Am., Ohio Council Tchrs. Math., John Dewey Soc., Phi Delta Kappa. Club: Torch (v.p.) (Columbus). Author: The Nature of Proof, 1938; (with others) Mathematics in General Education, 1940, Mathematics Texts for Secondary School, 1961. Contbr. ednl. jours., chpts. in books. Home: Columbus, O., Died Jan. 6, 1976.

FAXON, NATHANIEL WALES, hosp. adminstr.; b. South Braintree, Mass., Aug. 12, 1880; s. William Otis and Susan Reed (Wales) F.; grad. English High Sch., Boston, Mass., 1896, Hopkinson Sch., Boston, 1898; A.B., Harvard, 1902, M.D., 1905; m. Marie Bassett Conant, Sept. 22, 1905; children—Nathaniel Conant, William Otis II, Herbert Wales. Surg. house officer Mass. Gen. Hosp., Boston, 1905-06; gen. practice, Stoughton, 1906-17; asst. dir. Mass. Gen. Hosp., 1919-22; dir. Strong Memorial Hosp., 1922-35, Mass. Gen. Hosp. and Mass Eye & Ear Infirmary, 1935-49. Served as 1st lt., Med. R.C. and maj. Med. Corps, U.S. Army, World War. Mem. A.M.A., Am. Hosp. Assn. (pres. 1933-34), Mass. Med. Soc. Republican. Clubs: Harvard, Aesculapian (Boston); The Country (Brookline). Home: Boston, Mass.†

FEATHERSTONE, ROBERT MARION, educator, pharmacologist; b. Anderson, Ind., Dec. 24, 1914; s. Marion L. and Adah Mary (Brown) F.; B.A., Ball State U., 1940, LL.D., 1962; M.S., U. Ia., 1942, Ph.D., 1943; m. Joyce Amanda Byrum, Aug. 31, 1940; children—David Byrum, Jean, James Byrum, Judith Ann. Instr. biochemistry Med. Coll. S.C., 1943-44; asst. prof., asso. prof., then prof. pharmacology U. Ia. Coll. Medicine, 1944-57; prof. U. Cal. Sch. Medicine, San Francisco, 1957-74, chmn. dept. pharmacology and extpl. therapeutics, 1957-73. Vis. prof. physiology dept. U. Geneva, Switzerland, 1973-74. Chmn. pharmacology tng. program com. NIH, 1963-67; pres. 5th Internat. Congress Pharmacology, 1972; mem. council Internat. Union Pharmacology, 1969-74; Mem. Am. Inst. Biol. Scis. Physiology Adv. Panel to Office Research, USN, 1973-74. Commonwealth Fund fellow U. London (Eng.), 1965-66. Mem. Am. Soc. Pharmacology and Exptl. Therapeutics (council 1958-61, 64-67, pres. 1968), Soc. Exptl. Biology and Med., Royal Soc. Medicine, Japanese Nat. Pharmacology Soc., Am. Chem. Soc. (chmn. Ia. 1947, nat. council 1972-75), Western Pharmacology Soc. (pres. 1960), Sigma XI. Author, editor (with A. Simon): A Pharmacologic Approach to the Study of the Mind, 1959; (with J. Hidalgo) Farmacologia del Sistema Nervioso Autonomo, 1963; A guide to Molecular Pharmacology, 1973. Editorial cons. Sci., Biochem. Pharmacology, Molecular Pharmacology. Contbr. research papers to profl. lit. Home: Hillsborough, Cal. Died May 1974; interred San Mateo, Cal.

FEIBUS, ARTHUR, otolaryngologist; b. 1899; M.D., Jefferson Med. Coll., Phila., 1922. Practice medicine, specializing in otolaryngology, 1937-72; emeritus staff Lankenau Hosp.; asso. in otolaryngology U. Pa. Hosp. Diplomate Am. Bd. Otolaryngology. Mem. Am. Laryngol., Rhinological and Otological Soc. Home: Philadelphia, Pa., Died Nov. 21, 1972; buried Philadelphia, Pa.

FEINBERG, LOUIS, physician; b. Chgo., Nov. 7, 1909; s. Joseph and Bessie (Ferdinand) F.; B.S. in Chemistry, U. Chgo., 1930, M.D., Rush Med. Coll., 1934. Intern St Anthony's Hosp., Chgo., 1934-35; vol. asst. U. Chgo., 1935; resident in opthalmology Ill. Eye and Ear Infirmary, 1936; resident in otolaryngology, 1937; resident in otolaryngology U. Ill., 1938; eye, ear, nose and throat specialist, Chgo., from 1948; asst. prof. ophthalmology U. Ill., 1955-63. Dir. Jefferson State Bank Chgo., from 1972, vice chmn. bd., from 1973. Served as capt. M.C., AUS, 1942-46. Diplomate Am. Bd. Ophthalmology and Otolaryngology. Mem. A.M.A., Chgo., North Side med. socs., Internat. Coll. Ophthalmologists and Otolaryngologists, Am. Soc. Ophthalmology and Otolaryngology, Phi Beta Kappa, Sigma Xi, Alpha Omega Alpha. Jewish religion (congregation trustee). Mem. B'nai B'rith. Home: Chicago, Ill. Deceased.

FEINBERG, SAMUEL MAURICE, physician; b. Russia, Mar. 28, 1895; s. George and Anna (Shulman) F.; brought to U.S., 1907, naturalized, 1918; B.S., U. of Wis., 1917; M.D., Rush Med. Coll., 1919; m. Cecile Stern, Mar. 19, 1922; children—Alan Richard, Robert Herman and Ruth Ann (twins), Helene Rose (Mrs. Gene Pier). Intern, Cook County Hosp., Chgo., 1920-21, attending physician, 1926-38; practice medicine specializing in internal medicine and allergy; emeritus prof. medicine Northwestern U.; attending physician, dir. Allergy Research Lab., Evanston (Ill.) Hosp. Served with U.S. Army, 1918-19. Diplomate Am. Bd. Internal Medicine. Fellow A.C.P., Internat. Assn. Allergology (past pres.), Am. Acad. Allergy; mem. A.M.A., Ill., Chgo. med. socs., Nat. Inst. for Allergy and Infectious Diseases (past tng. grant com.), Am. Soc. for Study Allergy (past pres.), Chgo Soc. Internal Medicine, Central Soc. Clin. Research, A.A.A.S., Am. Assn. Immunologists, Peruvian Allergy Assn. (hon.), Chgo. Soc. Allergy, also hon. mem. Argentine, Spain, France, Scandinavian, Cuban allergy assns., Phi Beta Kappa, Sigma Xi, Phi Delta Epsilon. Jewish religion. Author: Asthma, Hay Fever and Related Disorders—A Guide for Patients, 1933; Allergy in General Practice, 1934; Allergy in Practice, 1944; The Antihistamines, 1950; Allergy: Facts and Fancies, 1951; Living with Your Allergy, 1958. Mem. editorial bd. Modern Medicine, Clinica Europea. Contbr. articles to med. jours. Home: Highland Park, IL. Died July 10, 1973; buried Shalom Meml. Park, Palatine, Ill.

FELD, JACOB, civil engr.; b. Austria, Mar. 3, 1899; s. Israel and Gussie Rachel (Haarzopf) F.; U.S. citizen by derivation; B.S., Coll. City N.Y., 1918; C.E., U. Cin., 1921, M.A., 1921, Ph.D., 1922; LL.D., City U. N.Y., 1927; m. Ethel Gold, Jan. 26, 1928; 1 dau., Judith (Mrs. David E. Marrus). Engr. with Dr. D.B. Steinman, Henry Goldmark, Turner Constructors, also L.I. R.R., 1922-26; pvt. practice as cons. engr., from 1926; designer engr. N.Y. Coliseum, Guggenheim Museum, Yonkers Raceway, Bellevue Hosp. Center, Lincoln Center structures, Hudson River Water Pollution Control Plant; vis. prof. Purdue U., Northwestern U., N.C. State U. Spl. engring. cons. USAF, Hdqrs. Civil Engring. Directorate; mem. engring. panel USAF Sci. Adv. Bd., 1965-67; mem. Hwy. Research Bd., from 1930; partner firm Feld & Timoney, 1945-68, Feld Kaminetzky & Cohen, from 1966. Chmn. constrn. economy com., N.Y. Citizens Housing Council, 1936; delegate internat. engring. congresses, from 1966. bd. govs. Technion Israel Sch. Tech., Haifa, from 1936. Decorated Order of Merit (France), 1963; recipient silver medal Soc. Encouragement Progress, France, 1966; Distinguished Engring. Alumnus award Coll. City N.Y., 1969; Distinguished Engring. Coll. Alumnus award U. Cin., 1969; named Met. Engr. of Year, Am. Soc. C.E., 1956, Bklyn. Engrs. Club, 1959. Fellow Am. Soc. C.E., A.A.A.S., N.Y. Acad. Sci. (chmn. div. engring. 1960-61, councillor 1962-63, v.p. and pres. 1964-66), World Acad. Art and Sci.; mem. Cons. Engrs. Council, Phi Beta Kappa, Sigma Xi, Tau Beta Pi, Chi Epsilon.

Author: Radio Telescope Structures, 1957; Lessons from Concrete Failures, 1964; Construction Failure, 1968. Home: Yorktown Heights, N.Y. Died Aug. 16, 1975; interred Mt. Pleasant Cemetery, Hawthorne, N.Y.

FELDMAN, A. HARRY, corp. exec. Pres., dir. United Factors Corp., N.Y.C.; director United Mchts. & Mfrs., Inc.; treas., dir. United Internat. Corp.; dir. Birstol Supply Co., Glasgo Finishing Co., Homestead Draperies, Inc., Langley Engraving Co., Langley Processing Co., Seminole Mills, Statistics, Inc., Union Mfg. & Power Co., United Mchts. Lab., Inc. Home: Philadelphia, Pa., Died Nov. 7, 1975.

FELDMAN, WILLIAM H(UGH), pathologist; born Glasgow, Scotland, Nov. 30, 1892; s. Victor William and Isabella (Gunn) F.; came to U.S., 1894, naturalized, 1922; D.V.M., Colo. State Coll., 1917, M.S., 1926. D.Sc., 1945; student in pathology U. of Mich. Med. Sch., 1920; m. Esther Dickinson, Dec. 26, 1917 (died September 1932); 1 dau., Esther (Mrs. John F. Connelly, Jr.) (dec.); m. 2d, Ruth Elaine Harrison, Aug. 15, 1934; 1 son, William Harrison. Asst. prof. pathology Colo. State Coll., and asst. pathologist Exptl. Sta., 1917-27; asso. in div. exptl. medicine Mayo Foundation, 1927-57, instr. in comparative pathology Mayo Foundn. Grad. Sch., U. of Minn., 1927-32, asst. prof., 1932-36, asso. prof., 1936-44, prof. 1944-57; chief lab. research pulmonary diseases, Vets. Adminstrn., 1957-67. Delivered Bell lectr. in tuberculosis, Minn., 1942, Harben lectures, Roy. Inst. Pub. Health and Hygiene, London. 1946; guest lectr., Pasteur Inst., Paris, and med. socs., Lisbon, Copenhagen, Stockholm, Olso, Edinburgh, Oxford, 1946, Paris, 1951, Dublin, 1951. Wartime cons. Nat. Acad. Sci., 1942-45; mem. Gov.'s commn. Study Tb facilities Minn., 1953-54. Mem. med. adv. bd. Leonard Wood Meml. (Am. Leprosy Found.; past. chmn.); adv. council Webb-Waring Inst. Med. Research. Mem. sci adv. bd. Armed Forces Inst. Pathology, 1947-74; sci. cons. on Tb, VA, Wash.; mem. com. sci. advisers Inst. Biomed. Research, A.M.A. Gold Medal (with H.C. Hinshaw and F. C. Mann) for exhibition chemotherapy of tuberculosis, A.M.A., 1944; Alvarenga prize, Coll. Phys. of Phila. for studies on chemotherapy of tuberculosis, 1946; Pasteur Medal Pasteur Inst., Paris, 1946; Alumnus Achievement award, Colo. State Coll., 1950; Dearholt Medal, Miss. Valley Conf. on Tb, 1953; Trudeau medal, 1955; 12th International Veterinary Congress Prize, 1959. Del. Fifth International Congress on Leprosy, Havana, Cuba, 1948. Mem. Am. Vet. Med. Assn.; Am. Coll. Vet. Pathologists (pres. 1949), Am. Thoracic Soc., Conf. Research Workers in Animal Diseases (sec., treas. 1936-48, pres. 1952), Am. Assn. Pathologists and Bacteriologists (pres. 1952-53), Am. Cancer Soc. (past com. on instnl. grants), Sociedad Peruana de Tisiologia (hon.), Societa Italiana delle Scienze Veterinaire (hon.), Royal Soc. Medicine (London) (hon.), Sigma XI, Sigma Nu, Alpha Psi, Unitarian. Mason. Club: Cosmos. Author: Neoplasms of Domesticated Animals, 1932; Avian Tuberculosis Infection; contbr. articles to profl. jours. Home: Rochester, Minn. Died Jan. 15, 1974.

FELDMANN, CHARLES RUSSELL, industrialist; b. Phila., Feb. 8, 1898; s. Charles H. and Eva Adele (Stringfield) F.; ed. N.Y.C. high schs. and evening schs., m. Charlotte M. Vega, June 14, 1919; children—Carolyn J.A. (Mrs. John F. Otto), Phyllis M. (Mrs. Joseph V. McKee, Jr.), Barbara Jane (Mrs. Spyros S. Skouras). From office boy to service dept. employee auto dealer, N.Y.C., 1913-17; traveling accounting expert installing cost systems in leather cos., 1917-19; owner leather-belting repair and mfg. bus., 1919-25; indsl. real estate operator, 1925-27; purchased, reorganized and sold Winton Engine Co., Henney Motor Co., Victor Penninsular Co., 1928; founder, pres., dir. Transitone Automobile Radio Corp., 1928-37, sold controlling interest to Philco Corp., 1930; purchased control Simplex Radio Corp., Sandusky, O., 1937, sold to Philco Corp., 1938, pres., dir., 1937-40; purchased control Foster Machine Co., Elkhart, Ind., 1940, co. purchased Internat. Machine Tool Co., Indpls., 1940, Detrola Corp., 1943, co. assumed name Internat. Detrola Corp., 1943; acquired Newport Rolling Mill, Ky., 1946, assumed name Newport Steel Corp., 1949, pres., dir., chmn. bd., 1940-50, holdings sold, 1950; chmn. bd. Strong, Carlisle and Hammond Co. Cleve., 1942-56, pres., 1951-56, interest sold, 1956; chmn. Nat. Union Electric Corp., 1946-73, pres., dir. 1954-73, acquired by merger, 1960 Eureka Williams Corp., Bloomington, Ill., div. Nat. Union Electric Corp.; chmn. bd. Napco Plastics, Inc., Napoleon, O., wholly owned subsidiary acquired 1960, div. Nat. Union Electric Corp., 1960; pres., chmn. Durham Mfg. Corp., Muncie, Ind., 1960-64; acquired Emerson Radio and Phonograph Corp. (through merger), 1966; dir. Ultra Electric (Holdings), Ltd. Mem. pres.'s com. Notre Dame U., 1949, Methodist, Clubs: CLoud. Metropolitan (N.Y.C.), Detroit Athletic; Indian Creek Country, Key Largo Anglers, Jockey, Surf (Miama). Home: Greenwich, Conn. Died Dec. 13, 1973.

FELDMANN, ROBERT LINCOLN, physician; b. N.Y.C., Apr. 25, 1906; s. William H. and Margaret (Mencken) F.; B.A., Yale, 1929, M.D., 1933; m. Ruth Thomas, Nov. 16, 1935; children—Gretchen (Mrs. Fredrich H. Bierman), Edith Ann, Thomas Lewis, Sallie Joan. Intern, City Hosp., Cleve., 1933-34, Norwegian Hosp., Bklyn., 1934-35; resident in ear, nose and throat Manhattan Ear Nose and Throat Hosp., N.Y.C., 1939-41; asst. in ear, nose and throat St. Mary's Hosp., Mary's Help Hosp., San Francisco, 1941-42; staff York (Pa.) Hosp., 1942-73, mem. Cleft Palate Clinic, former chief staff for ear, nose and throat dept.; practice medicine specializing in otolaryngology, York, 1942-73. One-man show York Coll. Diplomate Am. Bd. Otolaryngology. Fellow A.C.S.; mem. A.M.A. (Nat. Physicians' Art Competition awards), Pa. Med. Assn., York County Med. Soc. (past pres.), Am. Acad. Ophthalmology and Otolaryngology. Lutheran (past deacon, Sunday Sch. tchr.). Home: York, Pa. Died Nov. 30, 1973.

FELDSTEIN, DAVID, automotive co. exec., b. Detroit, Sept. 14, 1909; s. Jacob Harry and Sarah Ida (Chadwick) F.; student U. Mich., 1927-28; m. Rose Jacob, Aug. 5, 1934; children—Esther (Mrs. Ronald Cohen), Richard. Owner Reliable Auto Salvage, Detroit, 1935-39; pres. Automotive Transmission Co., 1939-56; pres., chmn. bd. Automotive Transmission & Gear Co., 1956-72. Mem. War Prodn. Bd., 1941-45; liason officer WPB, 1942-45. Active Shriners Crippled Childrens Found., 1950-56; life mem. bd. govs. Young Israel Center, Oak Woods. Mem. Inst. Transmission Engrs. Democrat. Odd Fellow (past grand, past dist. dep. grand master), Mason. Home: Oak Park, Mich. Died Oct. 26, 1972.

FELITTO, RAYMOND NICHOLAS, consumer products co. exec.; b. Utica, N.Y., May 5, 1921; s. Joseph A. and Rose (Fragetta) F.; B.S., Fordham U., 1943; m. Santa Cl. DiLorio, Dec. 12, 1943; children—Raymond Nicholas, Bradley, Valerie. Salesman, Am. Home Foods Co., 1946-48, various positions to nat. sales mgr., 1948-66; v.p., dir. sales Boyle-Midway div. Am. Home Products Corp., N.Y.C., 1969-71. Served to sgt. AUS, 1943-45; ETO. Club: Burning Tree Country (Greenwich, Conn.). Home: Coscob Conn. Died June 1, 1971.

FELLERS, BONNER FRANK, army officer; b. Ridge Farm, Ill., Feb. 7, 1896; s. Frank and Florence (Newlin) F.; student Earlham Coll., 1914-16, U.S. Mil. Acad., 1916-18 (B.S., 1918); grad. Coast Arty. Sch., 1920, Command and Gen. Staff Sch., 1935, Army War Coll., 1939; m. Dorothy Dysart, Nov. 25, 1925; 1 dau., Nancy Jane. Commd. 2d lt., U.S. Army, Nov. 1, 1918, and advanced through the grades to brig. gen., Dec. 1942; mem. Gen. Douglas MacArthur's staff in Philippines, 1936-38; mil. observer with British forces in Africa, 1940-42; mem. staff Gen. Douglas MacArthur, 1943-46. Sec. Gen. Allied Council for Japan, Tokyo, Jan.-Aug. 1946; retired from active duty, U.S. Army, Nov. 30, 1946; chief pub. relations cons. for Vets. of Fgn. Wars of U.S. until 1947; asst. to chmn. of Rep. Nat. Com. since 1947. Decorated Distinguished Service Star of the Philippines with anahau leaf, D.S.M. with Oak Leaf Cluster, Legion of Merit. Home: Washington, D.C. Died Oct. 7, 1973.

FELLOWS, EUGENE HILPERT, editor; b. Scranton, Pa., Dec. 29, 1879; s. Eugene D. and Iola (Seagreaves) F.; grad. Sch. of the Lackawanna, Scranton, 1899; A.B., Cornell U., 1902; m. Anne Edwards, Apr. 9, 1908; children—Eugene Edgar, Anne Edwards, Mary, Margaret Frances. Teacher of history, high sch., Scranton, 1902-05; prof. history and polit. science, Tech. High Sch., Scranton, 1905-18; farming, 1923-25; editorial writer, Scranton Republican, 1925-26, editor from 1926. Served as sergt. Pa. Vols., Spanish-Am. War; sec. and dir. war work, Council Nat. Defense, Scranton, 1918-19; dir. Americanization, Lackawanna Co., Pa., 1920-21; field work, Pa. State Dept. Pub. Instr., 1921-23. Mem. Kappa Sigma. Republican. Presbyn. Home: Clarks Green, Pa.†

FELTIN, MAURICE, clergyman; b. Delle, France, May 15, 1883. Ordained priest, Roman Catholic Ch., 1909; bishop of Troyes, France, 1929-32; archbishop of Sens, France, 1932-35, of Bordeaux, France, 1935-49, of Paris, France, 1949-66. Created cardinal, 1953. Home: Paris, France. Died Sept. 27, 1975; interred Cathedral Ch., Paris, France.

FENNELL, EARLE JAMES, civil engr., assn. exec.; b. Velva, N.D., Dec. 8, 1905; s. James and Oleanna (Finstad) F.; B.S. in Civil Engring., U. N.D., 1933; m. Helen Ann Holm, Feb. 11, 1931; 1 dau., Susan Earle (Mrs. Richard K. Bambach). With U.S. Geol. Survey, 1925-67, asso. chief topographic engr., Washington, 1960-67; exec. dir. Am. Congress on Surveying and Mapping, Washington, 1968-71; editor ACSM Bull., 1971-72. Recipient Distinguished Service award U.S. Dept. Interior, 1965. Mem. Am. Soc. C.E. (chmn. exec. com. surveying and mapping div. 1960-61), Am. Congress on Surveying and Mapping (pres. 1966-67, chmn. delegation to permanent com. meeting Yugoslavia 1966), Assn. Am. Geographers, Am. Soc. Photogrammetry, Explorers Club, A.A.A.S., Am. Polar Soc., Canadian Inst. Surveying, Lambda Chi Alpha. Conglist. (deacon, moderator). Mason. Contbr. articles to profl. publs. Home: Chevy Chase Md. Died Jan. 22, 1972; interred Velva, N.D.

FENNELLY, JOHN FAUNTLEROY, investment banker; b. New Orleans, July 18, 1899; s. John Joseph and Alice Janney (Fauntleroy) F.; A.B., Princeton, 1920, A.M., 1925, Ph.D., 1928; m. Martha Davis, Dec. 11, 1931 (div. 1955); children—Alison, Anne, Richard; m. 2d, Barbara Potter, May 1957. Reporter, Kansas City (Mo.) Star, 1920; with Hall Baker Grain Co., Kansas City and St. Louis, 1921-23; instr. econs. Columbia U., 1927-20; economist Nat. City Co., N.Y.C., 1929-31; vice chmn. requirements com. and dir. program bur. WPB, Washington, 1942-43; with Glore, Forgan & Co. and predecessor Field, Glore & Co., 1931-65, partner, 1935-65; chmn. policy com. Glore Forgan, Wm. R. Staats, Inc., 1965-70; vice chmn. F.I. duPont Glore Forgan, Inc., 1970-74; dir. Stewart-Warner Corp. Exec. dir. Com. Econ. Devel., 1943-44. Chmn. citizen's adv. bd. U. Chgo., 1954-56; pres. bd. trustees Lake Forest Acad., 1945-49. Served as flying cadet USAAF, 1918-19. Vice pres. Investment Bankers Assn. Am., 1948-51. Clubs: Chicago, Commonwealth, Commerical, Attic, LaSalle Street (Chgo.); Old Elm, Onwentsia (Lake Forest, Ill.); Links, Anglers' (N.Y.C.); Flyfishers' (London). Author: (with W.L. Crum) Fiscal Planning for Total War, 1942; Steelhead Paradise, 1963; Memoirs of a Bureaucrat, 1965; Twilight of the Evening Lands-Oswald Spangler A Half Century Later, 1972. Home: Lake Forest, Ill. Died Dec. 27, 1974.

FENWICK, CHARLES GHEQUIERE, polit. scientist; b. Baltimore, Md., May 26, 1880; s. Henry Martin and Gay (Tiernan) F.; A.B., Loyola Coll., Baltimore, 1907; Ph.D., Johns Hopkins U., 1912; hon. LL.D., Marquette Coll., 1930. Holy Cross Coll., 1948; m. Maria Jose Lynch of Rio de Janeiro, July 25, 1942; children—Charles Henry, Francis Edmund. Law clerk division of International law, Carnegie Endowment for Internat. Peace, 1911-14; lecturer on internat. law, Washington Coll. of Law, 1912-14; asso. in polit. science, 1914-15, asso. prof., 1915-18, prof., 1918-45, Bryn Mawr College U.S. del. to Inter-American Conf. for Maintenance of Peace, Buenos Aires, 1936; del. to 8th Internat. Conf. of Am. States, Lima, 1938, 9th conference, Bogota, 1948; mem. Inter-American Neutrality Committee, 1940-42, mem. Inter-Am. Juridical Com. 1942-47; dir. dept. international law and organization, Pan-American Union, from 1948. Mem. American Political Science Assn., American Soc. Internat. Law, Am. Acad. Polit. and Social Science, Internat. Law Assn. Associate editor Internat. Law Journal. Catholic. Author: The Neutrality Laws of the United States (Carnegie Endowment for Internat. Peace), 1913; Political Systems in Transition, 1920; (with W.W. Willoughby) Types of Restricted Sovereignty and of Colonial Autonomy (Govt. Printing Office), 1919; International Law, 1924, 34, 38; Cases on International Law, 1935; Cases on Constitutional Law, 1938, 1942; Am. Neutrality; Trial and Failure, 1940. Translator of Vattel's Droit des Gens. 1914; Schucking's Der Staatenverband der Haager Konferenzen, and also of Wehberg's Das Problem eines internationalen Staatengerichtshofes, 1915. Home: Washington, D.C.†

FERENBAUGH, CLAUDE BIRKETT, army officer; b. Dresden, N.Y., Mar. 16, 1899; B.S., U.S. Mil. Acad., 1918; grad. Inf. Sch., basic course, 1920, Signal Sch., communications officers course, 1932, Command and Gen. Staff Sch., 1937, Army War Coll., 1940. Commd. 2d lt., U.S. Army, 1918, and advanced through the grades to brig. gen. 1944, later lt. gen.; mem. enlisted branch, G-1 Div. (personnel), War Dept. Gen. Staff, 1941-42, in charge procurement and discharge section, Dec. 1941-Apr. 1942; later became asst. to asst. chief of staff, G-3, Hdqrs, II Corps, Jacksonville, Fla., then asst. chief, North African Theater of Operations; chief, European-North African Theater of Operations Div., War Dept. Gen. Staff, Washington, D.C., Jan.-July 1943, chief of North African section, July 1943-Jan. 1944; became asst. div. comdr. 83d Inf. Div., Jan. 1944; comdg. gen. 7th Inf. Div., Far East Command during Korean conflict; assigned med. holding detachment Walter Reed Army Med. Center, 1955, ret., 1955. Decorated Legion of Merit with oak leaf cluster, D.S.M. with oak leaf cluster, Silver Star with oak leaf cluster, Air medal with oak leaf cluster. Home: Kenwood Park, N.Y. Died Sept. 10, 1975.

FERGER, ROGER H(ENRY), ret. newspaper pub.; b. Cin., O., Jan. 5, 1894; s. August and Margaret (Henry) F.; grad. Franklin Prep. Sch.; Cincinnati, O., Class of 1912; ed. U. of Pennsylvania, Class of 1916; m. Claire Virginia McCartney, June 17, 1933; 1 son by previous marriage, Roger Hutton. Advertising agency exec., 1916-20; advt. mgr. Cincinnati (O.) Enquirer, 1920-33; dir. sales Pacific Railways Advt. Co., San Francisco, Calif., 1933-36; bus. mgr. Milwaukee (Wis.) Sentinel, 1936-39, Pittsburgh (Pa.) Post-Gazette, 1939-40; asst. publisher Cincinnati Enquirer, 1940-44, pub., 1944-65, pres., 1952-65, dir.; dir. Union Central Life Ins. Co., Cin., C. & O. Ry., U.S. Playing Card Co., Diamond Internat. Corp., N.Y.C.; mem. sr. adv. bd. McCormick & Co., Balt.; mem. past pres. Cincinnati So. Ry. Trustee Cin. Bur. Govtl. Research; hon. trustee Cin. Mus. Natural History; past chmn. Ohio Newspaper Assn.; past dir. Inter-Am. Press Assn. Mem. President's council Xavier U. Mem. Cin. Music Hall Assn. Navy League U.S. (past pres. Cin. council), Mem. Sigma Delta Chi, Sigma Chi. Republican. Episcopalian. Mason. Clubs: Queen City, Optimists, Commercial (Cin.); Everglades, Bath and Tennis, Coral Beach (Palm Beach, Fla.). Home: Palm Beach, Fla. Died Apr. 10, 1974.

FERGUSON, CHARLES, physican; b. Parma, Ida., Dec. 30, 1894; s. Charles and Josephine Ferguson; A.B., Coll. of Ida., 1918; M.D., U. Ore., 1922; m. Beatrice Elizabeth McParland, Sept. 11, 1945. Intern, Multnomah Hosp., Portland, Ore., 1922-23; extern Brady Urol. Inst., Johns Hopkins Hosp., Balt., 1924; commd. asst. surgeon USPHS, 1925, advanced through grades to med. dir., 1959; assigned to U.S. Coast Guard, Anacortes, Wash., 1925; chief urology, proctology, venereal diseases, asst. in gen. surgery U.S. Marine Hosp., Ellis Island, N.Y., 1925-36; chief urology and proctology USPHS Hosp., S.I., N.Y., 1936-50, chief venereal diseases, gynecology and obstetrics, 1936-44, chief gen. surgery, 1942-44, chief urology, 1950-59; ret., 1959; clin. prof. urology U. Ore. Med. Sch.; mem. staff Physicians Surgeons Hosp., Portland, also chmn. exec. bd. of library. Served with USN, 1918-19. Charles Ferguson Med. Library, USPHS Hosp., S.I., named in his honor, 1960. Diplomate Am. Bd. Urology. Fellow A.C.S.; mem. A.M.A., Assn. Mil. Surgeons U.S., Am. Urol. Assn., Ret. Officers Club, Commd. Officers Assn. USPHS (life), USPHS Clin. Assn., Alpha Kappa Kappa. Republican. Mason (32°, Shriner). Contbr. articles to med. jours. Inventor surg. and urol. instruments, mobilizer attachment for Stryker frame. Home: Milwaukie, Ore. Died June 12, 1973; buried Mt. Scott-Willamette Nat. Cemetery, Portland, Ore.

FERGUSON, ROY KING, business exec.; b. Paterson, N.J., Dec. 7, 1893; s. Peter Guthrie and Jennie (King) F.; ed. Central High School, Paterson, N.J.; m. Kathleen McMurray, 1916 (dec. 1932); children—Audrey Kathleen (Mrs. James E. Kussmann). Mary (Mrs. Stephen P. Kaptain), Grace (Mrs. Donald K. Hawes), John (dec.), Betty Ann; m. 2d, Leah Conrad, 1944 (dec. 1963); m. 3d, Frances Hurst Mahaffy, 1966. Asst. mgr. Lake Placid Club, N.Y., 1912-17; v.p. Northern N.Y. Securities Co., Watertown, New York, 1917-21; v.p. F. L. Carlisle and Co., N.Y., 1921-32; v.p. and treas., United Corp., N.Y., 1933-34; pres. St. Regis Paper Co., New York, 1934-57, chmn., chief exec. officer 1957-63; dir. St. Regis Paper Co. (Canada) Ltd. Eastern States Corp. Mem. Am. Mus. Natural History, N.Y., Economic Soc., N.Y. Republican. Clubs: Union League, Metropolitan (New York); Manhasset Bay Yacht (Port Washington); Creek, Pinnacle, North Hempstead Country. Home: Oyster Bay, N.Y. Died Dec. 15, 1974.

FERGUSON, WILLIAM BLAIR MORTON (WILLIAM MORTON) author; b. Belfast, Ireland, Feb. 4, 1881; s. Robert Lamont and Rachel (Morton) F.; brought to U.S., 1888; ed. privately, New York; m. Elsie Hubbard, June 2, 1909; children—Robert Lamont. Elsie. Began lit. work, 1904. Mem. Authors' League of America. Republican. Presbyterian. Author: Garrison's Finish, 1907; Zollenstein, 1909; A Man's Code, 1915; The Black Company, 1924; Other Folk's Money; Masquerade, 1925; The Edged Tool; The Clew in the Glass, 1926; The Dumb-bell, 1927; The Riddle of the Rose, 1929; Lightnin' Calvert, 1930; Little Lost Lady, 1931; Mystery of the Human Bookcase, 1931; Murder of Christine Wilmerding, 1932; Pilditch Puzzle, 1932; Black Bread, 1933; Reckoning, A Sequel to Lightnin' Calvert, 1933; Singing Snake, 1935; Vanishing Men, 1935; Wyoming Tragedy, 1935; Crackerjack, 1936; Island of Surprises, 1935; Somewhere Off Borneo, 1936; Bobo Marches, 1937; Dog Fox, 1938; London Lamb, 1939; Sally, 1940; Escape to Eternity, 1944.†

FERM, VERGILIUS TURE ANSELM, educator; b. Sioux City, Ia., Jan. 6, 1896; s. Olof Wilhelm and Mathilda (Slattengren) F.; A.B., Augustana Coll., Rock Island, Ill., 1916; B.D., Augustana Theol. Sem., 1919; postgrad. Ia. State U., 1919-22; A.M., Yale, 1923, Ph.D., 1925, postgrad., 1926; m. Nellie Agnette Nelson, June 25, 1919; children—Verginia Annette (dec.), Vergilius Nelson (dec.), Vergil Harkness, Deane William, Jules Robert Livingston. Ordained to Luth. Ch., 1919; pastor, Cedar Rapids, Ia., 1919-22, St. Paul's Ch., Ansonia, Conn., 1922-26; First Ch., West Haven, Conn., 1924-26; prof. philosophy and social scis. Albright Coll., Reading, Pa., 1926-27; asst. prof. philosophy Coll. of Wooster (O.), 1927-28, prof. 1928-64, Compton prof. philosophy, head dept., 1938-64, prof. emeritus, 1964-74, dean of the Coll. summer session, 1940-42, 44; leave for research and writing, 1946-47, 52-53, 56-57, 61-62; vis. prof. philosophy Sweet Briar (Va.) Coll., 1964-65; vis. prof. Wake Forest (N.C.) U., 1965-68, acting chmn. dept. philosophy, 1966-68; prof. philosophy Ashland (O.) Coll., 1968-72; vis. prof. Heidelberg Coll., Tiffin, O., 1966. Elected affiliate mem. Wooster Presbytery, 1949, mem. Lutheran Ministerium of Augustana Synod (now Synod Ohio, United Luth. Ch. Am.). Mem. Am. Philos. Assn., Am. Assn. U. Profs., Am. Theol. Soc. (v.p. 1943-44; pres. 1944-45), Am. Soc. Ch. History, Authors Guild, Phi Beta Kappa. Author of 30 books including: The Crisis in American Lutheran Theology, 1927; First Adventures in Philosophy, 1936; First Chapters in Religious Philosophy, 1937; What Can We Believe?, 1948; A Protestant Dictionary, 1951; Their Day Was Yesterday, 1954, Pastoral Psychology, 1955; Pictorical History of Protestantism, 1957; A Brief Dictionary of American Superstitions, 1959; Inside Ivy Walls, 1964; Toward an Expansive Christian Theology, 1964; Basic Philosophy for Beginners, 1969; Memoirs of a College Professor, 1971; Cross-Currents in the Personality of Martin Luther, 1972; So . . . You're Going to College, 1972; Philosophy Beyond the Classroom, 1974. Editor: Ency. of Religion, 1945; Religion in the Twentieth Century, 1947; Forgotten Religions, 1949; A History of Philosophical Systems, 1950 (trans. into Japanese, 1956); The American Church, 1952; The Protestant Credo, 1953; Puritan Sage; The Collected Writings of Jonathon Edwards, 1953; Ency. of Morals, 1956; Classics of Protestantism, 1959. Contbg. editor: Dictionary of Philosophy; Philosophic Abstracts; Introduction to A Doctor's Soliloquy, 1953; Questions That Matter Most, 1954; Introduction to the Last Analysis, 1956; other vols. Contbr. to religious and philos. jours. Home: Wooster O. Died Feb. 4, 1974.

FERMAN, JOSEPH WOLFE, publisher; b. N.Y.C., June 8, 1906; s. Wolfe and Esther (Little) F.; B.C.S., N.Y.U., 1927; m. Ruth L. Eisen, Jan. 29, 1931; 1 son, Edward Lewis. Circulation mgr. Am. Mercury, N.Y.C., 1926-39, bus. mgr., 1939- 44, dir., 1940-50, v.p. sec., 1944-50; dir. Jonathan Press Inc., N.Y.C., 1942-56, v.p., sec., 1944-56; v.p., dir. Fantasy House, Inc., 1949-54, pres., 1954-58, Casebook Publs., Inc., 1950-53; pres. Mercury Publs., N.Y.C., 1954-74; pub. mag. Fantasy and Science Fiction, editor, pub. Bestseller Mystery mag., Mercury Mystery mag., 1958-61; treas., dir. Leasehold Assos., 1958-61; dir. Chapin Jr. Corp., 1958-74; editor No Limits, 1964; pub. P.S. mag., 1966, Inner Space, Mag. of the Psychic and Occult, 1970; dir. Monroe Gas System. Mem. exec. com. Com. for World Human Rights. Mem Mag. Pubs. Assn. Clubs: Hundred Million, Nassau County Unity. Home: Rockville, N.Y. Died Dec. 29, 1974.

FERREE, JOHN WILLARD, physician; b. Marion, Ind., Aug. 26, 1904; s. John Daniel and Mary A. (Heaston) F.; A.B., U. Pa., 1925; M.D., Ind. U., 1932; M.P.H., Johns Hopkins, 1939; m. Robert North, June 10, 1930; children—Barbara, John Daniel, Rebecca. Intern Harper Hosp., Detroit, 1932-33; resident Passavant Meml. Hosp., Chgo., 1933-34, Evanston, (Ill.) Hosp., 1934-35; dir. local health adminstrn. Ind. State Bd. Health, 1936-40, state health commr., 1940-42; dir. ednl. services Am. Social Hygiene Assn., 1946-47; asso. dir. Nat. Health Council, 1947-49, sec., 1961; dir. community service and edn. Am. Heart Assn., 1949-57, asso. med. dir., 1957-59; exec. dir. Nat. Soc. Prevention Blindness, 1959-69. Sec. for Western Hemisphere, Internat Assn. Prevention Blindness, 1959-69, sec. gen., 1968-69; mem. nat. adv. eye council NIH, 1968-70. Bd. dirs. Am. Found. Overseas Blind, from 1968, Nat. Accreditation Council for Agys. Serving Blind and Visually Handicapped, from 1967, Illuminating Engring. Research Inst., from 1960. Dir. 1st Nat. Conf. on Cardiovascualr Diseases, 1950. Trustee Mt. Pleasant Library, from 1970. Served from lt. comdr. to comdr. M.C., USNR, 1942-46. Diplomate Am. Bd. Preventive Medicine And Pub. Health. Fellow N.Y. Acad. Medicine, Am. Coll. Preventive Medicine; mem. A.M.A., S.A.R., Alpha Omega Alpha, Beta Theta Pi, Nu Sigma Nu. Presbyn. Home: Pleasantvile, N.Y., Died Oct. 24, 1975.

FERRI, ANTONIO, educator, engr.; b. Norcia, Italy, Apr. 5, 1912; s. Giovanni B. and Iginia (Sparvieri) F.; Dr. Elec. Engring., U. Rome (Italy), 1934, Dr. Aero Engring., 1936; m. Renata Mola, July 12, 1937; children—Paul, Rose Marie, Joseph. Came to U.S., 1944, naturalized, 1952. Assigned to Direzione Superiore Studied Esperienze, Italian Air Ministry, 1935, head supersonic wind tunnel, Guidonia, Italy, 1937-40, head aerodynamics br., 1940-43; asso. prof. U. Rome, 1940-43; head Partisan Brigade Spartaco, 1943-44; with OSS, NACA, 1944-46; research transonic testing techniques, supersonic aerodynamics NACA, 1946-49, head gas dynamics br., Langley Field, Va., 1949-51; prof. aerodynamics Poly. Inst. Bklyn., 1951-54, dir. aerodynamics lab. Poly. Inst. Bklyn., Freeport, N.Y., 1954-63, head dept. aerospace engring. applied mechanics, Bklyn., 1957-63; exec. v.p. Gen. Applied Sci. Labs., Inc., 1958-60, pres., 1960-67; Astor prof. aerospace scis., dir. Aerospace Lab., N.Y. U., 1964. Mem. adv. group for aero. research and devel. propulsion and energetics panel NATO; mem. research adv. com. on air-breathing propulsion systems NASA: mem. research adv. group engring. scis. Air Force Office Sci. Research; mem. Army Sci. Adv. Panel Recipient Premio dell'Accademia d, for Science, 1938; sci. achievement award Columbia Civic Clubs N.J., 1954; Akroyd Stuart prize Royal Aero Soc., 1965; Outstanding Achievement award office Aerospace Research, Dept. Air Force, 1970. Fellow Inst. Aero. Scis.; mem. Nat. Acad. Engring., Accademia delle Scienze di Torino of Italy, Internat. Acad. Astronautics. Author: Elements of Aerodynamics of Supersonic Flows, 1949. Author numerous sci. articles. Home: Woodbury, N.Y., Died Dec. 30, 1975.

FERRIS, JOEL EDWARD, banker; b. Cathage, Ill., Jan. 2, 1874; s. Hiram Gano and Julia (Holton) F.; student Carthage (Ill.) Coll., 1890-94; A.B., U. of Ill., 1895; LL.D. (honorary), State College of Washington; m. Clara Hughes, Apr. 14, 1914; children—Sarah Elizabeth (Mrs. Sarah Ferris Fuller), Phoebe Arnold (Mrs. Philip J. McCoy). With the firm of John A. Prescott & Company, investment bankers, Kansas City Mo., 1900-04; sales exec. 1904-08; treas. Union Trust Co., Spokane, Wash., 1908-13; partner, later pres., Ferris & Hardgrove, 1913-31; pres. Spokane & Eastern Trust Co., 1931-35; exec. v.p., dir. Seattle First Nat. Bank, 1936-46; exec. v.p., mgr. Spokane & Eastern div. Seattle First Nat. Bank, 1936-46, chmn., from 1946; dir. General Telephone Company of the Northwest, Columbia Electric Company, Sunshine Mining Co., Great Northwest Life Ins. Co. Chairman War Savings Com. for State of Washington, dist. chmn. Victory Fund Com. Member bd. Salvation Army, Hutton Settlements. Camp Fire Girls, Spokane Council. Trustee St. Luke's Hospital; mem. board of overseers Whitman College. Member Eastern Washington State Hist. Soc. (pres.), S.A.R., Washington State Bankers Assn. (past pres.). Clubs: Rotary, City, University (Spokane); Rainier (Seattle), LL.D., Whitman College. Home: Spokane, Wash.†

FERRIS, JOHN WALLACE DE BEQUE, Canadian senator; b. White's Cove, N.B., Can., Dec. 3, 1878; s. Lauchlin P. and Mary Louise (Hay) F.; B.A., Acadia U., N.S., 1899; LL.B., U. Pa., 1920; D.C.L., LL.D.; m. Evelyn F. Kierstead, Aug. 16, 1905; three sons, one dau. Read law with Weldon & McLean, St. John, N.B.; called to B.C. bar, 1903; created King's Counsel, 1917; mem. Constituency of Vancouver City, 1916; pres. of council, 1917; atty.-gen., minister of labor, 1917; re-elected for Vancouver, 1921; resigned as atty.-gen., 1922; partner firm Farris, Farris, Vaughn, Taggart, Wills and Murphy, Vancouver, from 1922; mem. Canadian Senate, from 1937. Counsel for B.C. Telephone Co.; solicitor Bank of Toronto, Mem. Law Soc. B.C. (treas. 1933-38), Canadian Bar Assn (pres. 1937-38). Clubs: Vancouver; Capilano Golf and Country; Union (Victoria); Rideau (Ottawa). Home: Vancouver, B.C. Canada †

FETHERSTON, EDITH HEDGES, artist; b. Lewisburg, Pa., June 21, 1885; d. Joel Curtis and Minora Alta (Meixell) Kelly; student Bucknell Sem., 1902; Ph.B., Bucknell U., 1905, A.M., 1908, student, 1940-45; student U. Berlin, 1908, Columbia, 1918, Carnegie Inst. Tech., 1931-32; student of Edmund W. Greacen, 1932-36; m. John Turney Fetherston, June 14, 1917. Exhibited 22d Ann. Exhbn. Asso. Artists of Pitts., 1932; one man shows, Ferargil Galleries, 1933, Bucknell U., 1949, 54; exhbn. garden art by Garden Club of Allegheny County, Carnegie Inst., 1934, Garden Club Am., 1935; exhbn. paintings, Arden Gallery, 1935, Garden of Nations, 1935, The Allied Artists Am., Inc., N.Y. 1935, 36, 37; exhibit, Arden Galleries, 1936, Lewisburg, Pa., 1936, Northumberland, Pa., 1937, 2d ann. exhbns. paintings of Central Pa. Artists, Pa. State Coll. Dept. Architecture, 1937; exhibited Bucknell U., 1938, 39, 40, 45, 46, 49, 51, 52, 53, 55, 56-72, Pa. Acad. Fine Arts, 1951. Made plant discovery which was named Hydrocotyle Fetherstoniana; designed and planted two Chinese Gardens; owner Packwood House Mus. Patron mem. Archaeol. Inst. Mem. Mus. Modern Art, Bot. Soc of Western Pa., The Sullivant Moss Soc., Central Pa. Art Assn., (v.p.), Artists Equity Assn., Nat. Trust for Historic Preservation, Am. Assn. U. Women, D.A.R., Phi Beta Phi. Roman Catholic. Clubs: Rochester Garden, Genessee Valley Hunt, Century (Rochester); Twentieth Century (Pitts.) Author articles in bulls, and mags. Home: Lewisburg Pa. Died Feb. 15, 1972.

FETTER, ELIZABETH LEAN FIELDS HEAD (MRS. FERDINAND FETTER), author; b. Phila., Sept. 6, 1904; d. Joseph and Annie (Wilkinson) Head; student Vassar Coll., 1922-25; B.A., U. Colo., 1927; m. Ferdinand Fetter, June 18, 1930; children—Alexander Lees, Ann Lindsay. Advt. copywriter Strawbridge and Clothier, Blum Store, Phila., 1928-30, 33-34; lectr. exptl. writing Bryn Mawr Coll., 1953-56, Mem. Phila. City Commn. on Human Relations, 1952-59. Dir. Phila. telephone campaign for Clark-Dilworth Reform Democratic ticket, 1951. Nat. bd. dirs. Planned Parenthood-World Population, 1962-68. Mem. Phila. Art Alliance, Soc. Mag. Writers, Authors League. Club: Cosmopolitan. Author: (as Hannah Lees) Women Will Be Doctors, 1939; Prescription for Murder, 1941; Death in the Doll's House, 1942; Till the Boys Come Home, 1944; The Dark Device, 1946; Help your Husband Stay Alive, 1957; The Sweet Death of Candor, pub. 1969; also articles and short stories pub. in mags., including Sat. Eve. Post, Ladies' Home Jour., McCall's, Reader's Digest, Reporter, Atlantic Monthly, others. Home: Philadelphia Pa. Died Jan. 21, 1973.

FETTERMAN, JOHN DAVIS, journalist; b. Danville, Ky., Feb. 25, 1920; s. John Lawrence and Zora (Goad) F.; B.S., Murray (Ky.) State U., 1948; postgrad. U. Ky., 1949-50, LL.D., U. Louisville, 1974; m. Evelyn Alline Maner, Nov. 2, 1944; children—Phyllis Lee (Mrs. John Terry), Mindy Nelle. Editor Murray Ledger & Times, 1946-47; tchr. Ill. pub. schs., 1948-50; with Nashville Tennessean, 1950-57; writer- photographer Louisville Courier-Jour., 1957-69. Served with USNR, 1942-45. Recipient Pulitizer prize in journalism, 1969; Nat. Headliner award, 1969; named Outstanding Alumnus, Murray State U., 1971. Author: Stinking Creek, 1967; also articles, photos. Home: Louisville, Ky. Died June 21, 1975; buried Meml. Gardens East.

FETZER, LEWIS WILLIAM, physician; b. Bklyn., Oct. 3, 1878; s. Albert and Johanna Barbara (Dull) F.; grad. in chemistry, Cooper Union, 1900; Ph.D., U. of Munich, 1902; M.D., George Washington U., 1910; Sc.D., U. Dallas, 1920; graduate Sch. of Aviation Medicine, U.S. Army, 1925, also grad. Med. Field Service Sch., 1928; m. Charlotte C. Kumberger, Aug. 14, 1904; children—Edwin Lewis, Lewis Albert Jacob.

Sanitary engr. and technical biologist, 1903-06; physiol. chemist, Md. Agrl. Expt. Sta., 1906-09; instr. chemistry, George Washington U., 1907; specialist in biol. chemistry, Office of Expt. Stas., U.S. Dept. Agr., 1909-15; asso. prof. pathol. chemistry, Georgetown U. Sch. of Medicine, 1912-15; prof. physiology and biochemistry, Fordham U., 1915-16; prof. pharmacology, later also physiology and biochemistry and dir. of the combined depts., Baylor U. Sch. of Medicine, 1916-1920; prof. physiology, pharmacology, therapeutics, Baylor U. Coll. of Dentistry, 1918-20; prof. physiology, Baylor U. Coll. of Pharmacy, 1918-20; prof. biology, U. of Dallas, 1919-25; med. consultant for disorders of digestion and diseases of nutrition and metabolism, from 1921. Del. to U.S. Pharm. Conv., 1920; mem. 8th Internat. Congress of Applied Chemistry. Fellow A.A.A.S., A.M.A.; mem. Am. Chem. Soc., Am. Pub. Health Assn., Dallas Co. (Tex.) Med. Soc., Tex. State Med. Assn.; mem. com. on occupational diseases in chem. trades, Am. Chem. Soc., from 1919, chmn. 1921-27; chmn. com. industrial toxicology, Am. Chem. Soc., 1927-28. Major M.O.R.C., 1924. Contributor on tehcnical and scientific subjects to New International Ency., and scientific jours. Edited Agrl. Chemistry and Medicine, Expt. Sta. Record, U.S. Dept. Agr.; transls. for Kober and Hanson's Diseases of Occupation and Vocational Hygiene, Kober and Hayhurst Industrial Health. Home: Dallas, Tex.†

FEURT, SELDON DICK, coll. dean; b. Wichita, Kan., Oct. 21, 1923; s. Seldon Ernest and Alice Bouton (Martin) F.; B.S. in Pharmacy, Loyola U., New Orleans, 1949; M.S., U. Fla., 1951, Ph.D. in Pharmacology, 1953; m. Joella Ann Connor, Aug. 8, 1943; children—Dian B., Andi Lee. Instr. pharmacy U. Fla., 1950-53; asso. prof. pharmacology and pharmacognosy U. Ga., 1953-57, prof., 1958-59; dir. research De Leon Labs., Atlanta, 1954-58; dean Coll. Pharmacy, U. Tenn., 1959-75. Mem. Am. Pharm. Assn., Blue Key, Sigma Xi, Phi Kappa Phi, Rho Chi. Mason (Shriner). Co-inventor tranquilizer gun. Author profl. authors. Home: Memphis, Tenn. Died Jan. 19, 1975; interred Hickory Creek Cemetery, Jameson, Mo.

FEYERHERM, HARVEY AUGUST, educator, biologist; b. West Point, Neb., Apr. 27, 1919; s. Frederick Wilhelm and Ida (Kuester) F.; A.B., Neb. Wesleyan U., 1940; M.S., Ia. State U., 1942, Ph.D., 1950; NSF fellow State U. Ia., 1960; m. Ruth Brown, Jan. 17, 1944; children—William H., Ann E., James F. Instr., then asst. prof. zoology Ia. State U., 1942-50; mem. faculty No. Ill. U., DeKalb, 1950-73, prof. zoology, 1956-73, head dept. biol. scis., 1964-69, dir. sch. allied health, 1972-73. Served to capt. San. Corps, AUS, 1943-46. Mem. A.A.A.S., Inst. Biol. Scis., Am. Zool. Soc., Am. Physiol. Soc., Am. Assn. U. Profs., Midwest Coll. Biology Tchrs., Phi Kappa Phi. Home: DeKalb Ill. Died Sept. 24, 1973; interred Fairview Meml. Park, DeKalb, Ill.

FICKEN, CLARENCE ELWOOD, coll. dean; b. Huntingburg, Ind., May 3, 1894; s. August and Sophia (Hauswald) F.; A.B., Baldwin-Wallace Coll., Berea, O., 1916; A.M., Northwestern U., 1917; Ph.D., U. Wis., 1937; student U. Chgo., U. Minn., summers, also student U. Paris, France, 1919; m. Elma Michel, June 21, 1921; children—Ruth Ann (Mrs. John Gustad), Elma Louise (Mrs. Edward DeHart). Tchr., English and French, Van Wert (O.) High Sch., 1917-18; tchr. French, Kiskiminetas Springs Sch., Saltsburg, Pa., 1919-20; tchr. French and German, Culver Mil. Acad., 1920-24; asso. prof. French, Macalester Coll., St. Paul, 1924-27, asso. prof., dean men, 1927-37, prof., dean of coll., 1937-46, acting pres., 1943-44; dean of coll. Ohio Wesleyan U., 1946-47, acting pres., 1947-48, v.p., dean, 1948-58, pres. ad. interim, 1953-55, prof. French, 1958-60, dean emeritus, 1958-75; dean, prof. French, Meth. Coll., Fayaetteville, N.C., 1960-62; staff associate Baldwin-Wallace Coll., Berea, O., 1963; exec. sec. O. Commn. on Edn. Beyond the High Sch., 1957-58, Ohio Council on Tchr. Edn., 1959-60. Alumni trustee Baldwin Wallace Coll., 1959-62. Served with U.S. Army, 1918-19; AEF. Mem. Modern Lang. Assn. Am., Am. Assn. U. Profs., Assn. Higher Edn., Phi Beta Kappa, Kappa Delta Pi, Omicron Delta Kappa. Methodist. Kiwanian. Author: Building a Faculty, 1956. Contbr. articles ednl. publs. Home: Delaware, O. Died Jan. 4, 1975.

FIEDLER, EDWARD HENRY, lawyer, brewery exec.; b. Chgo., May 7, 1895; s. Henry Fred and Anna Maria (Bittel) F.; LL.B., Chgo.-Kent Coll. Law, 1917; m. Rose Rolleri, June 7, 1924; children—Celeste Bristol, Joan Potts, Barbara Hill, Edward Henry. Admitted to Ill. bar, 1917; with Sears, Meagher & Whitney, 1911-14, Meagher, Whitney, Ricks & Sullivan, 1914-19, Cooke, Sullivan & Ricks, 1919-24; partner Cooke, Sullivan & Ricks, and Daily, Dines, White & Fiedler, 1924-42; v.p., gen. counsel, dir, Pabst Brewing Co., 1942-57, counsel, dir., 1957-68; v.p., counsel, dir. Hoffman Beverage Co., 1945-57. Pres., dir. Pabst Breweries Found., 1945-68. Pres., dir. Ill. Beer Industry Com., 1953-68. Mem. Am., Chgo. bar assns., Phi Delta Phi. Address: Oak Park, Ill. Died June 6, 1973.

FIELD, BETTY, actress; b. Boston, Feb. 8, 1918; d. George Baldwin and Katherine Frances (Lynch) Field; student, Am. Acad. Dramatic Art; m. Elmer Rice, Jan. 12, 1942 (div. 1956); children—John Alden, Judith, Paul; m. 2d, Edwin J. Lukas, 1957 m. 3d, Raymond L. Olivere, Mar. 22, 1966. Made first acting appearance on London stage in, She Loves Me Not, 1935; 1st N.Y. appearance, Page Miss Glory, 1934; appearances include: Three Men on A Horse, 1935; The Voice of the Turtle, 1944; Dream Girl, 1945; The Rat Race, 1949; Not For Children, 1951; The Four Poster, 1952; Festival Ladies of Corridor; The Sea Gull, 1953-54, 56; Waltz of the Toreadors, Touch of Poet, Loss of Roses, 1959; The Birthday Party, Landscape, 1970; All Over, 1971; appeared Actor's Studio Revival Strange Interlude; nat. tour The Little Foxes, The Price; appeared in numerous films including Seventeen, The Great Gatsby, Tomorrow the World, What a Life; Picnic, 1955; Bus Stop, 1956; Butterfield 8, 1960, Birdman of Alcatraz, Seven Women, Of Mice and Men, King's Row, Blues in the Night, Shepherd in the Hills, Band of Gold, How to Save a Marriage and Ruin Your Life, Are Husbands Necessary?, Coogan's Bluff; TV appearances Dr. Kildare, Ben Casey, Route 66, Naked City, Perry Mason, The Defenders, Judd for the Defense, Alfred Hitchcock, others. Recipient N.Y. Critic's award for best performance on Broadway stage, 1946. Died Sept. 13, 1973.

FIELD, CYNTHIA, lawyer; b. Peabody, Mass. Sept. 5, 1926; d. Robert and Ida (River) Field; student Boston Coll. Intown, 1944-46; LL.B., Boston Coll. Law, 1950; postgrad. Staley Coll. Spoken Word, 1958 File clk. Hale & Door, Boston, 1946-47, tax clk., 1947-55; asst. to head probate dept. Nutter, McClennan & Fish, Boston, 1955-56; admitted to Mass. bar, 1951; juvenile parole agt. Youth Service Bd., Mass. Youth Authority, Boston, 1956-59, asst. supr. girls' parole, 1961-62, acting supr. girls' parole, 1962-64; staff atty. Boston Legal Aid, 1964-67; asso. firm Parker, Coulter, Daley & White, 1967; probation officer Salem (Mass.) Dist., Ct., 1959-61. Mem. exec. com. Peabody Poverty Commn., Mass. Commn. on Narcotics and Drug Abuse; mem. Peabody (Mass.) Sch. Com., 1958-61; mem. exec. bd., past pres. Salem Community Council; mem. Area Bd. Mental Health and Retardation Planning; vice chmn. Mass. Adv. Council on Developmental Disabilities, 1971-73. Bd. dirs., pres. Salem Mental Health Assn., North Shore Cerebral Palsy Assn., Salem; bd. dirs. Mass. Mental Health Assn. Named Lynn Item Woman of Year, 1968. Mem. Am., Boston, Peabody (treas.) bar assns., Nat. Council Crime and Delinquency, Salem Bus. and Profl. Women's Club, Internat. Platform Assn. Home: Peabody, Mass. Died Mar. 29, 1973; interred Maple Hill Cemetery, Peabody, Mass.

FIELD, EDWARD DAVENPORT, ins. exec.; b. Rutland, Vt., Jan. 13, 1879; s. Fred A. and Lillie (Clark) F.; student Rutland High Sch. and Phillips Andover Acad.; m. Grace Harriman, 1918; children (by previous marriage)—Mrs. Catherine F. Cherry, Mrs. Josephine F. Morgan, Mrs. Viriginia F. Hasbrouck, Clerk in actuarial dept., National Life Ins. Co., Montpelier, Vt., 1897, various positions with same to 1911, supt. agencies, 1911-22, 2d. vice-pres., 1922-34, v.p. from 1934; dir. Vt. Mut. Fire Ins. Co.; Montpelier Savings Bank & Trust Co. Representative general assembly, Vermont, 1921-22. School commr., Montpelier, ten years. Republican. Congregationalist. Mason (Shriner). Clubs: Country, Apollo. Home: Montpelier, Vt.†

FIELD, F(RANCES) BERNICE, librarian; b. Mankato, Minn., Mar. 7, 1906; d. Merton and Carrie Eva (Tambling) Filed; student Am. U., 1925-26; B.A., Carleton Coll., 1927; B.S. in L.S., U. Ill., 1930; M.A. in L.S., U. Mich., 1944. Asst. librarian, cataloger Am. U., 1927-30; cataloger Queens Borough Pub. Library, Jamaica, N.Y., 1930-31; asst. cataloger Vassar Coll. Library, 1939-44; serial cataloger Yale Library, New Haven, 1931-39, sr. cataloger, 1944-47, asst. head cataloger in charge serial dept., 1947-52, asst. head catalog dept., 1952-55, head dept., 1955-63, asst. librarian cataloging and classification, 1963-65, asso. librarian tech. services, 1965-74. Recipient Distinguished Alumnus award U. Mich. Sch. Library Sci., 1971. Mem. A.L.A. (chmn. serials round table 1952-54, pres. resources and tech. services div. 1958-59, chmn. descriptive cataloging com. 1960-66, editorial com. 1963-66; rep. joint com. on union list serials 1957-66; Margaret Mann citation 1966), N.Y. Tech. Services Librarians (pres. 1953-54), Conn. Library Assn., Phi Beta Kappa. Home: New Haven, Conn. Died Oct. 14, 1974.

FIELDING, WILLIAM JOHN, author, editor; b. Wharton, N.J., Apr. 10, 1886; s. William and Mary (Mitchell) F.; ed. pub. schs.; m. Elizabeth C. Veale, June 20, 1910 (dec.); children—Elsie (dec.), John Carbis; m. 2d, Mary Burns Cameron, Aug. 29, 1942. Editor Newark Leader, 1915-18; lit. editor N.J. Leader, 1919-22; editor Know Thyself, 1923-24; dramatic editor Golden Rule Mag., 1925-27, Sketch Book Mag., 1927-43; sec.-treas. Louis Comfort Tiffany Found., 1942-68, trustee, 1946-68, hon. life trustee, 1968—; pres. Thomas Paine Found., 1960-70. Named humanist of yr. Humanist Soc. Greater N.Y., 1970. Mem. A.A.A.S., Am. Social Hygiene Assn., Am. Birth Control League, Soc. for Constructive Birth Control and Racial Progress (London), Freethinkers Am. (hon. pres. from 1970), Euthanasia Soc. of Am. (adv. council), Inst. Literaire et Artistique de France, Am. Acad. Polit. and Social Sci., Authors League Am., Ethical Humanist Soc. L.I. (sec. 1950-55), Pi Gamma Mu. Author: Pebbles from Parnassus, 1917; Sanity in Sex, 1920; Psychoanalysis—The Key to Human Behavior, 1921; The Puzzle of Personality, 1922; The Caveman Within Us, 1922; Health and Self-Mastery through Psycho-Analysis and Autosuggestion, 1923; Autosuggestion—How It Works, 1923; Rejuvenation, 1924; Rational Sex Series, 13 Vols., 1924-25; Teeth and Mouth Hygiene (collaboration), 1925; Dual and Multiple Personalities, 1925; The Cause and Nature of Genius, 1926; Sex and the Love-Life, 1927, rev. 1959; Woman—The Eternal Primitive, 1927; Sex and the Eternal Primitive, Woman—The Criminal, 1928; Woman—The Warrior, 1928; Unconscious Love Elements in Psycho-Analysis, 1929; How the Sun's Rays Give Health, 1930; The Marvels and Oddities of Sunlight, 1930; Boccacio-Lover and Chronicler of Love, 1930; The Art of Love, 1931; Love and the Sex Emotions, 1932; Sex in Civilization (symposia), 1929; The Shackles of the Supernatural, 1938, rev. 1969; Strange Customs of Courtship and Marriage, 1942; Strange Superstitions and Magical Practices, 1945, Self-Mastery Through Psychoanalysis, 1952; Auto-suggestion You Can Use, 1961; All the Lives I Have Lived, 1972. Contbr. poems to anthologies. Home: North Rockville Centre, N.Y., Died Dec. 21, 1973.

FIELDS, DOROTHY, song writer; b. Allenhurst, N.J., July 15, 1905; d. Lew Fields. Writer songs for show at Cotton Club, N.Y.C., with Jimmy McHugh wrote for Lew Leslie's Blackbirds, 1928; including I Can't Give you Anything But Love, On the Sunny Side of the Street, Don't Blame Me, Lovely to Look At, I'm in the Mood for Love, Exactly Like You; writer scenarios, musical shows with her brother Herbert including Let's Face It, Something for the Boys, Mexican Hayride, Up In Central Park, Annie Get You Gun, Arms and the Girl (words only). Winner Acad. Award for song The Way You Look Tonight (with Jerome Kern), 1936; (play) Sweet Charity, 1966. Died Mar. 28, 1974.

FIFE, JAMES, naval officer; b. Reno, Jan. 22, 1897; grad. U.S. Naval Acad., 1917; LL.D., U. Nev., 1946. Commd. ensign, U.S. Navy, 1917, and advanced through the grades to admiral, 1955; served in U.S. ships Tacoma, Chicago, Sea Gull, Beaver, Elcano, Monocacy, Idaho, Leary, Hatfield; comdr. U.S.S. Nautilus, 1935-37, and submarine Div. Twelve, 1937; officer in charge Submarine Sch., New London, Conn., 1938-40; asst. naval attache, Am. Embassy, London, Eng., 1940, assigned to submarine service with Birt. Navy in Eng. and Mediterranean; comdr. Submarine Div. Sixty-two, 1941; chief of staff to comdr. submarines, Asiatic Fleet, 1941 (force operating against Japanese attacks in Philippines Islands and Netherlands East Indies); comdr. submarine squadron, also asst. operating officer on staff of comdr. Southwestern Pacific Force, 1942; comdr. of task force, 1942-44; fellowing duty at hdqrs. comdr. in chief U.S. Fleet, returned to Pacific area as comdr. Submarine 7th Fleet; mem. joint strategic survey com. Joint Chiefs of Staff, Washington; dep. chief U.S. Naval Operations, 1951-53; naval dep. to Comdr. in Chief, Allied Forces, Mediterranean, 1953-55; ret. Decorated D.S.M. with 2 gold stars, Army Distinguished Unit Badge, Navy Unit Commendation, Victory medal with escort claps; Yangtze Service, Navy Expeditionary, Am. Def. Service with fleet clasp, Asiatic-Pacific Area Campaign and Philippines Def. and Liberation medals; hon. comdr. Military Div., Order Brit. Empire; Grand Officer of Order of Orange-Nassau with Swords (Netherlands). Mason (33°). Home: Stonington, Conn., Died 1975.

FIGGATT, TINNEY CAVENAUGH, cotton broker; b. Fincastle, Va., Dec. 6, 1882; s. Moncure Taylor and Catherine (Cavenaugh) F.; m. Violet Guild, Feb. 14, 1912; children—Violet (Mrs. J. H. Escher), Marshall. Engaged in cotton bus., 1900-73; mem. N.Y. Cotton Exchange, 1915-73, v.p., 1948-49, 58-60. bd. mgrs., 1938-73, pres., 1960, chmn. bd., 1960-73. Republican. Episcopalian. Author articles. Home: Fairfield, Conn. Died Sept. 20, 1973.

FIGGE, FRANK HENRY JOHN, scientist, anatomist; b. Silver Cliff, Colo., Dec. 23, 1904; s. John and Maria Barbara (Schwab) F.; A.B., Colo. Coll., 1927, D.Sc. (hon.), 1968; student Colo. U. Med. Sch., 1928-29; Ph.D., U. of Md. Med. and Grad. Schs., 1934; m. Rosalie Mary Yerkes, June 25, 1932; children—Rosalie Ann (Mrs. Robert H. Beasley, Jr.), Barbara (Mrs. George Fox). Asst. in biology Colo. Coll., 1925-26, head asst. in biology and comparative anatomy, 1926-28; asst. in anatomy Colo. U. Sch. of Medicine, 1928-29; asst. in anatomy U. Md. Sch. of Medicine, 1929-30, instr., 1930-34, asso., 1934-35, asst. prof., 1935-36, asso. prof., 1936-47, prof. exptl. anatomy, 1947-49, prof. anatomy, 1949-73, head dept., 1955-72; chmn. Anatomy Bd. Md., 1955-72; vis. prof. anatomy U. Pa., 1948-49; Rockefeller fellow Yale Univ. Med. Sch., 1940-41. Trustee Biol. Stain Commn., 1947, pres., 1954-56. Smith, Kline and French Research grantee, 1953. Fellow A.A.A.S.; mem. Am. Assn. Anatomists (exec. com. 1953-57), Am. Cancer Soc. (v.p. 1952-56; Md. div. bd. dirs., mem. exec. com. 1948-72, pres. 1956-62), Am. Soc. Naturalists, Histochem. Soc., Soc. Exptl. Biology and Medicine, Am. Assn. for Cancer Research, Marine Biol. Corp., Am. Assn. Med. Colls., So. Soc. Cancer Cytology, Sigma Xi, Delta Epsilon. Club: Torch (pres. Balt. chpt. 1953-54). Author of articles med.

subjects to tech. jours. Asso. editor Stain Technology, 1958-65. Am. editor Atlas of Human Anatomy. Died Oct. 25, 1973.

FIHN, JOSEPH ADAM, educator; b. Bac, Austria-Hungary, Apr. 19, 1918; s. Frank and Apollonia (Brochert) F.; student U. Toronto, 1938-39, 43-44; B.A. (hon.), U. Western Ont., 1946; M.A., U. Mich., 1947, Ph.D., 1954; m. Catherine Jean Brunner, Aug. 4, 1945; children—Joseph Thomas, John Michael, Cynthia Ann, Katherine Jean. Mem. faculty U. Detroit, 1947, prof. Germanic langs., from 1961, chmn. modern lang. dept., 1961-65. Bd. dirs. Modern Lang. Conf. Mich., 1955-60, chmn., 1958-60. Mem. Am. Assn. Tchrs. German (pres. Mich. 1955-56), U. Detroit Acad. Arts and Scis. (pres. 1953-54), Modern Lang. Assn. Am. Contbr. articles on contemporary German lit. Home: Detroit, Mich. Died July 26, 1973; buried St. Hedwig's Cemetery, Dearborn Heights, Mich.

FILBEY, EMERY THOMAS, educator; b. Cambridge City, Ind., Dec. 23, 1878; s. Henry and Parintha (Lowry) F.; grad. Ind. State Normal Sch., 1907; Ph.B., U. of Chicago, 1917, M.A., 1920; m. Lena Leora Chance, June 16, 1909. Teacher pub. schs., Ind., 1901-08; with U. of Chgo., from 1909, successively instr. lab. schs., instr., asst. prof., asso. prof. and prof. Dept. of Edn., dean Univ. Coll., 1923-27, prof. Sch. of Commerce and Adminstration, 1927-29, asst. to pres., 1930-33, dean of faculties, 1933-37, v.p., 1937-44; v.p. emeritus from 1945, adviser on special projects from 1947. Home: Chicago, Ill.†

FILLEY, HORACE CLYDE, agrl. economist; b. Filley, Nebraska, Dec. 27, 1878; s. Elmer C. and Annette (Foster) F.; student Peru (Neb.) State Teachers Coll., 1896-99; A.B., Univ. of Neb., 1903, A.M., 1911; grad. student Univ. of Chicago, summer 1929; Ph.D., Univ. of Minn., 1934; m. Creta Warner, Oct. 11, 1911; children—Vernon Warner, Marjorie (Mrs. John Stover), Edith (Mrs. C. L. Garey), Dorothy (Mrs. Ed. Schwartzkopf). Prin., Staplehurst, Neb. 1899-1900; instr. farm management, U. Neb. Coll. of Agr., 1911-12, asst. prof., 1912-14, prof. and chmn. dept. of farm management, 1914-19, prof. rural econs. and chmn. dept. of rural economics, 1919-49; cons. economist for Farmers National Grain Dealers Assn. Comm., Chicago, Ill. (on leave of absence from Univ. of Neb.), Dec. 1934-Apr. 1935, interest in farm near Beatrice, from 1910; economist Union Nat. Life Insurance Co. from 1949, Dir. Union Nat. Life Ins. Co., exec. com. from 1940. Mem. Neb. Legislature, 1911. Member bd. trustees, Bryan Memorial Hosp., Lincoln, Mem. Am. Interprofessional Inst., Am. Economic Assn., Am. Farm Economic Assn., Neb. Hall of Agrl. Achievement (sec.), Neb. Writers Guild, Nebraska State Grange (master), American Assn. Univ. Profs., Lincoln C. of C., Alpha Zeta, Gamma Sigma Delta. Republican. Methodist, Mason. Author books including: The Wealth of the Nation, 1945; Every Day Was New, 1950; also expt. sta bulls., mag. articles. Home: Lincoln, Neb.†

FINCH, OPAL CLAIR LANE (MRS. RALPH FINCH), nurse; b. Mena, Ark., Jan. 31, 1907; d. William Emmet and Lena (Little) Lane; diploma St. Edwards Mercy Hosp., 1928; student Incarnate Word Coll., 1960-61, 61-62; m. Ralph Finch, May 11, 1932; children—Fredrick Lane, Ralph W., Joseph Luther. Nurse, Army and Navy Hosp., Hot Springs, Ark., 1950-55, Brooks Gen. Hosp., Ft. Sam Houston, Tex., 1955-67, ret., 1967. Served with Army Nurse Corps, 1928-32. Mem. D.A.R., Women's Overseas Service League, Am. Nurses Assn., Nat. League Nursing. Home: San Antonio, Tex. Died Apr. 6, 1974.

FINDENEGG, INGOMAR, biologist; b. Villach, Austria, Jan. 29, 1896; s. Hermann and Berta (Satter) F.; Ph.D., U. Graz, 1927; m. Else Gertrud Hempel, Apr. 24, 1936; children—Waltraut (Mrs. Lorenz Sertl), Gert F., Gunter F. Tchr., Gymnasium Klagenfurt, 1927, Kustos Landesmuseum Klagenfurt, 1929; prof. U. Graz, 1955; dir. Biol. Sta. Lunz, 1957; head IBP-Lab. sect. PF, Austrian Alpine Lakes, Klagenfurt, 1967—. Served with infantry military, 1915-19, 39-45. Hon. mem. U. Innsbruck, 1943; recipient Einar-Naumann medal Internat. Vereinigung Limnologie, 1953. Mem. Internat. Vereinigung Limnologie (past v.p.), Austrian Acad. Scis., Am. Soc. Limnology and Oceanography. Contbr. articles profl. jours. Address: Klagenfurt, Austria., Died Feb. 18, 1974.

FINDLEY, THOMAS PALMER, JR., physician; b. Chgo., Apr. 15, 1901; s. Thomas Palmer and Lyda (Hanna) F.; A.B., Princeton, 1923; B.S., U. Minn., 1925; M.D., U. Chgo., 1928; m. Jean Kver, Apr. 11, 1940; children—Susan, Margaret. Intern U. Hosp., Phila., 1927-29; instr. medicine U. Mich., 1929-32; research fellow pharmacology U. Pa., 1932-35; asst. prof. clin. medicine Washington U., 1935-40; head sect. internal medicine Ochsner Clinic, New Orleans, 1952-54; prof. clin. medicine Tulane U., 1942-54; prof. medicine, dir. Ga. Heart Assn. Lab. for Cardiovascular Research, Med. Coll. Ga., 1954-57, chmn. dept. medicine Med. Coll. Ga., 1957-66, emeritus prof. medicine, 1967-74; pvt. practice medicine, specializing in internal medicine, Atlanta, 1971-74; now area coordinator Regional Med. Program; attending physician VA Hosp.; vis. prof. medicine Nat. Def. Med. Center, Taipei, Taiwan, 1968-74. Diplomate Am. Bd. Internal Medicine (sec.-treas. 1955-60). Master A.C.P. (gov. for La. 1950-54, regent 1958, 2d v.p. 1965); mem. Assn. Am. physicians, Am. Clin. and Climatol. Assn., Am. Soc. Clin. Investigation, Central, So. (sec.-treas. 1947-49, pres. 1950) socs. clin. research. Home: Pinehurst, N.C. Died Oct. 18, 1974.

FINE, BENJAMIN, educator; b. N.Y.C., Sept. 1, 1905; s. Charles and Rebecca (Gulden) F.; B.S., R.I. State Coll., 1928; M.S., Sch. Journalism, Columbia, 1933; M.A., 1935, Ph.D., 1941; Ed.D., Bryant Coll., R.I., 1946, R.I. State Coll., 1950; L.H.D., Yeshiva U., 1949; LL.D., Lebanon Valley Coll., 1951; D.Litt., U. Toledo, 1951; Litt.D., Union Coll., 1952; D.So., Tampa, 1953; m. Lillian Rose Chafetz, Oct. 11, 1936; children—Ellen Sydney, Jill Barbara, Carla Coleman, Janet Eva. Asst., Pulitzer Sch. Journalism, 1932; reporter N.Y. Post, 1933; asst. in pub. relations Tchrs. Coll., Columbia, 1933-36; edn. reporter N.Y. Times, 1937-41, edn. editor, 1941-58; dean Grad. Sch. Edn., Yeshiva U., 1958-60; dean Sch. Journalism, Point Park Coll., 1960-62; headmaster Sands Point (N.Y.) Acad. and Country Day Sch.; head Horizon Sch., Miami, Fla., edn. editor N.Am. Newspaper Alliance, Bell-McClure Syndicate, 1960-75; lectr. edn. Coll. City N.Y., 1944, New Sch. for Social Research; lectr. U. Kansas City, U. Houston, Cornell U., Stetson U., Fla. State U. Past pres. Edn. Writers Assn., Am. Assn. for U.N., exec. council of Ednl. Forum. Recipient Frederick Z. Lewis medal Tchrs. Welfare League of N.Y. State, N.Y. State Tchrs. Assn. commendation, 1948; Pulitzer award N.Y. Times, 1944; Nat. Sch. Bell award for edn. reporting, 1963; others from profl. ednl. assns., orgns. for work in ednl. and sociol. fields. Dir., trustee numerous civic orgns. Mem. Soc. Am. Historians, N.Y. Acad. Pub. Edn., Sigma Delta Pi, Phi Delta Kappa, Kappa Delta Pi. Mason. Author: A Giant of the Press, 1933; College Publicity in the United States, 1941; Educational Publicity, 1943; Democratic Education, 1945; Admission to American Colleges, 1946; Our Children Are Cheated, 1947; Opportunities in Teaching, 1952, Fine's American College Counsellor and Guide, 1955; One Million Deliquents, 1955; The School Administrator and the Press, 1956; The School Administrator and His Publications, 1957; How to be Accepted by the College of Your Choice, 1957; How to Get the Best Education for Your Child, 1958; Modern Family Guide to Education, 1962; Teaching Machines, 1963; Stretching Their Minds, 1964; Profiles of American Colleges, 1964; Your Child and School, 1965; Underachievers-How to Help Them, 1966; also numerous articles and series. Home: Rockville Center, N.Y. Died May 16, 1975.

FINESILVER, BENJAMIN, physician; b. N.Y.C., Jan. 19, 1898; s. Aaron and Hattie Finesilver; M.D., L.I. U., 1921; m. Miriam Scheiner, July 16, 1932. Intern, Mt. Vernon Hosp., 1921-23, Montefiore Hosp. for Chronic Disease, 1923-24; asso. attending in neuropsychiatry Sydenham Hosp.; asso. neuropsychiatrist Flower-Fifth Avenue Hosps.; attending neurologist Met. Hosp., Welfare Island, N.Y.C.; attending neurologist and psychiatrist Cedars of Lebanon Hosp., Los Angeles; vis. psychiatrist Los Angeles Psychiat. Service, Gateways Psychiat. Hosp., Los Angeles; instr. neurology N.Y. Med. Coll. Diplomate Am. Bd. Psychiatry and Neurology. Author: Normal Facts in Diagnosis, 1930. Contbr. articles to med. jours. Home: Hollywood, Fla. Died Sept. 15, 1969; buried Brooklyn, N.Y.

FINK, FRANK WOLFE, aero. engr.; b. Phila., Jan. 13, 1905; s. Elwood and Gertrude (Wolfe) F.; B.S., U. Colo., 1928; D.Sc., Northrup Inst. Tech., 1963; m. Janet Glendinning, Sept. 12, 1929; children—James Elwood, John Dillon, Susan F. Farrar. Designer, aerodynamicist, project engr. airplane div., Curtiss-Wright Corp., 1928-35; designer, group engr., project engineer, chief prodn. engr., chief engr. Convair div. Gen. Dynamics Corp., 1935-55; v.p. engring. Ryan Aero Co., San Diego, 1955-65; pres. San Diego Aircraft Engring., Inc., 1965-74; dir. Air Logistics Corp., Pasadena, Cal. Cons. tech. adv. panel aeros. Dept. Def. Bd. dirs. San Diego Soc. Crippled Children, San Diego Child Guidance Clinic, So. Cal. Industry-Edn. Council, U. Colo. Engring. Devel. Found. Registered profl. engineer, State of Cal. Fellow Inst. Aero. Scis.; mem. Am. Rocket Soc., Am. Ordnance Assn., Nat. Mgmt. Assn., Soc. Automotive Engrs. (pres. 1962, bd. dirs.), Aerospace Industry Assn., Nat. Aero. Assn., Army Aviation Assn., Am. Mgmt. Assn., San Diego C. of C. Prebyn. (elder). Clubs: San Diego Yacht, San Diego Lions, San Diego. Contbr. articles engring., trade jours. Home: San Diego, Cal. Died Feb. 12, 1974.

FINK, HOMER BERNARD ry. exec.; b. Willard, O., Oct. 3, 1881; s. Daniel Buchanan and Martha Anne (Nesbitt) F.; student pub. schs., Topeka, Kan.; m. Mattie Virginia McNair, Mar. 26, 1903; children—Nesbitt Clyde, Harry Bernard, Ella Virginia (Mrs. Franklin C. Reamon), Ruth Loraine (Mrs. Albert Henry). Clerk accounting dept. A., T. & S.F. Ry. Co., Topeka, 1899-1901, clerk treasury dept., 1901-06, asst. cashier treasury dept., 1906-14, asst. paymaster treasury dept., 1914-16, gen. cashier treasury dept., 1916-23, asst. treas., 1923-35, sec. and treas. from 1935; v.p., sec., treas. and dir. N.M. Central Ry. Co.; sec., treas. and dir. Clinton & Okla. Western R.R. Co., Dodge City & Cimarron Valley Ry. Co., Santa Fe Pacific R.R. Co., Garden City, Gulf & Northern R.R. Co., Healdton & Santa Fe Railway Co., Kansas Southwestern Railway Co.; sec. and treas. St. Joseph Terminal R.R. Co., Wichita (Kan.) Union Terminal Ry. Co.; asst. sec. Kansas City, Mexico & Orient Ry. Co. of Tex. Mem. Topeka C. of C. (dir.), Assn. of Am. Railroads (adv. com. treasury div.), A.T.&S.F. Hosp. Assn. (sec. and treas., Topeka, from 1935). Democrat. Presbyterian. Mason. Clubs: Traffic (dir.) Topeka Country. Home: Topeka, Kan.†

FINKELSTEIN, JACOB JOEL, educator, Orientalist; b. Bklyn., Mar. 22, 1922; s. Morris and Augusta (Liebhart) F.; B.A., Bklyn. Coll., 1948; Ph.D., U. Pa., 1953. Research asst. Near Eastern langs. Yale, 1953-55; from asst. prof. to prof. Assyriology, U. Cal. at Berkeley, 1956-63, chmn. dept. Near Eastern langs., 1961-65; William Laffan prof. Assyriology and Babylonian lit. Yale, 1965. Served with AUS, 1943-46. Guggenhelm fellow, 1955-56; fellow Am. Council Learned Socs., 1963-64; sr. fellow Nat. Endowment for Humanities, 1970-71. Mem. Am. Sch. Oriental Research, Am. Oriental Soc. (asso. editor jour., 1961-64). Author Late Old Babylonian Documents and Letters, 1972, articles ancient Mesopotamian law, legal history, religion and historiography, also publ. Cuneiform texts. Home: New Haven, Conn. Died Nov. 28, 1974.

FINLEY, HAROLD EUGENE, educator, zoologist; b. Palatka, Fla., Nov. 30, 1905; s. Eugene and Lugenia (Bryant) F.; B.S., Morehouse Coll., 1928; M.S., U. Wis., 1929, Ph.D., 1942; m. Eva Elizabeth Browning, Aug. 30, 1929 (dec. 1954); children—Harold Eugene, Eva Kathleen (Mrs. Selvin F. Gumbs); m. 2d, Irene Sealy Pope, Jan. 5, 1957. From instr. to asso. prof. biology W.Va. State Coll., 1929-38; prof. biology, head dept. Morehouse Coll., 1938-47; exchange prof. biology Atlanta U., 1938-47; prof. zoology Howard U., 1947-75, head dept., 1947-69; ind. research investigator Marine Biol. Lab., Woods Hole, Mass., 1930-33; postdoctoral fellow Johns Hopkins, 1955; vis. prof. Ind. U., 1958, U. Wash., 1968, 70, U. Brasilia (Brazil), 1970. Prin. investigator USPHS research grants, from 1953; dir. NSF-Undergrad. Sci. Edn. research participation program, from 1959; U.S. del. IUBS, Montreaux, 1967, Washington, 1970. Active Boy Scouts Am. Fellow A.A.A.S., Washington, N.Y. acads. scis.; mem. Am. Microscopical Soc. (pres. elect 1971-72), Washington Electron Microscope Soc. (pres. 1963-64), Soc. Protozoologists (v.p., 1964, pres. 1967), Am. Soc. Zoologists, Nat. Inst. Sci., Electron Microscope Soc. Am., Soc. Gen. Microbiology, Sigma Xi, Beta Kappa Chi, Phi Sigma. Editor trans Nat. Inst. Sci., 1943-53; editorial bd. Jour. Protozoology, 1957-61, Oualified Zool. Taxonomist, 1961-75. Ency. Brit. Home: Washington, D.C. Died July 19, 1975; buried Palatka, Fla.

FINLEY, LORRAINE NOEL (MRS. THEODORE FRANK FITCH), composer, author; b. Montreal, Que., Can., Dec. 24, 1899; d. William Copeland and Thora Douglas (Clerk) Finley; student Juilliard Sch. Music, 1917-23, Columbia, 1925-26; student pvt. tchrs. violin, piano, voice, composition, 1910-30; m. Theodore Frank Fitch, Aug. 17, 1938. Came to U.S., 1938, naturalized, 1957. Composer numerous songs, words and music including Dreaming, Hoping Dreaming, 1924, Every Year Will Have its May, 1958, Mountain Song, 1968; composer many chamber works including Sonata for Clarinet and Piano, Sonata in G for Violin and Piano; composer orchestral suites including Persian Miniature, 1935, Three Theatre Portraits, (premiere USAF Symphony Orch.), 1960; author more than 600 translations pub. with music including Voices of Freedom (choral series), 1943, Milhaud's opera Le Pauvre Matelot, Broadway premiere, 1937; performer in concerts, radio recitals poetry with music, with husband as Mr. and Mrs. Composer, Municipal Broadcasting System, N.Y.C., 1952-72; faculty Nat. Assn. Am. Speech, 1925-27. Recipient numerous 1st prizes for songs, instrumental, choral, orchestral compositions; awards of merit for participation in Parade of Am. Music, Nat. Fedn. Music Clubs, 1964, York Club, Delta Omicron, Pen and Brush. Mem. Canadian Authors, N.Y. Browning Soc., Beethoven Assn. (dir. 1937-40), Oratorio Soc. N.Y. (dir. 1949-52), Drama League N.Y. (dir. 1950-72, v.p. 1955-62), Composers Group N.Y. (dir. 1959-64), A.S.C.A.P., (recipient ann. awards 1965), Sorosis (chmn. music 1970-72; recipient gold medal poetry, 1969, dir.), Nat. Assn. Am. Composers and Condrs., Nat. League Am. Pen Women (Edna St. Vincent Millay Sonnet 1st prize 1952, nat. chmn. music 1962-64, nat. music bd. 1964-72, chmn. music N.Y. 1966-72); N.Y. State Fedn. Music Clubs (dir. 1961-72). Republican. Author books: (poems) John Comes First; Forever In Eden. Contbr. poems, articles to mags., newspapers. Home: Greenwich, Conn. Died Feb. 13, 1972; buried Putnam Cemetery, Greenwich, Conn.

FINNEGAN, JAMES FRANCIS, radiologist; b. N.Y.C., Dec. 23, 1893; s. James and Victoria (Shannon) F.; M.D., Fordham U., 1916; m. Aileen Chang-Tung, Dec. 9, 1941. Pvt. practice medicine specializing in radiology; physician, clinic dept. Tb Bur. of Hawaii, 1944-63; lectr. safety engring. U. Hawaii. Served to lt. comdr. M.C., USN, 1917-23, 44. Diplomate Am. Bd. Radiology. Mem. A.M.A., Soc. Radiologists, Ret.

Officers Assn., D.A.V. Republican. Roman Catholic. Home: San Francisco, Cal. Died Nov. 13, 1971; buried Nat. Cemetery of the Pacific, Hawaii.

FIORIO, FRANCO EMILIO, Italian diplomat; b. Milan, Italy, June 2, 1912; s. Giovanni B. and Maria (Civita) F.; M.A. in aeroballistics, Politecnico Torino, 1937; Ph.D. in Mech. Engring., Politecnico Milano, 1934; m. Maria Lanzillotto, Sept. 12, 1946; children—Gianfranco, Maurizio, Alessandro, Livio. Commd. lt. Italian Air Force, 1936, advanced through grades to col., 1957; tech. asst. to air attache Italian embassy, Washington, 1949-55; head tech. services. Italian Air Fighters Force, 1943-49; retired, 1957; mem. Italian delegation UN Gen. Assembly, sci. adviser to Italian permanent mission, 1958-71; mem. spl. group to investigate Argentine Rocket Range, 1969; consul gen. Republic of San Marino, Washington, 1957-68; sci. counsellor Italian embassy, Washington, 1968. Dep. head Italian delegation UN Vienna Space Conf., 1968; mem. Italian delegation Conf. Prevention Surprise Attacks, 1959, Disarmament Negotiations, 1960-63; head Italian delegation INTELSAT Preparatory Conf., 1969, dep. head Italian delegation INTELSAT Plenipotentiary Conf., 1969-71; co-founder allied group for aerospace research and devel. NATO, 1952; columnist, 1962-71; corr., 1949-70. Mem. Am. Inst. Aeros. and Astronautics, Am. Astron. Soc. (sr.), A.A.A.S., Am. Space Pioneers Group, Italian Research Nat. Council (rep.), Internat. Astron. Fedn. (com. on application's satellites). Author: Aviazione Moderna, 1964. Editor Italian Missiles and Rocket Mag., 1957-61, Notiziario Fiorio, 1965-71. Contbr. profl. jours. Address: Arlington, Va., Died May 12, 1975.

FIRESTONE, CHARLES E., banker, Sr. v.p., also cashier City Nat. Bank, Beverly Hills, Cal. Office: Beverly Hills, Cal. Deceased*

FISCHEL, WALTER JOSEPH, univ. prof.; b. Frankfurt am Main, Germany, Nov. 12, 1902; s. Hugo and Zerline (Kahn) F.; student U. Heidelberg, 1921-22; Dr. Rer. Pol., U. Frankfurt, 1924; Ph.D., U. Giessen, 1925; m. Irene Markrich, June 1954; 1 dau., Corinne. Tchr. and lectr. Rabbinical Coll., Frankfurt, 1922-24; asst., research fellow and lectr. Hebrew U., Sch. Oriental Studies, Jerusalem, 1926-73; mem. sci. expdns. Syria, Turkey, Iraq, Kurdistan, Persia, 1930, 36; guest lectr. various univs. S.A., 1938, S. Africa, 1940, in U.S. and Can., 1943-44; vis. prof. Semitic langs. and lit. U. Cal. at Berkeley, 1945-46, prof. Semitic langs. and lit. 1946-73, chmn. dept. Nr. Eastern langs., 1948-58. Participant Internat. Congress Iranian Scholars at 2500 Anniversary of Persian Empire under Cyrus the Great, 1971. Mem. 18th, 19th, 21st, 23d, 25th Internat. Orientalists' congresses. Guggenheim Fellow, 1959-60; Fulbright fellow 1963-64; 71. Recipient awards N.C. Humanities Inst., 1968, 70. Fellow Am. Acad. Jewish Research, Royal Asiatic Soc. Gt. Brit. and Ireland; mem. Soc. Bibl. Lit. Pacific Coast (pres. 1948-51), Am. Oriental Soc., Soc. Bibl. Research and Lit., Am. Assn. Jewish Edn. (bd. govs.). Author numerous books, most recent being: Ibn Khaldun in Mamluk Egypt, 1951; Semitic and Oriental Studies, 1951; Ibn Khaldun and Tamerlane, 1952; The City in Islam, 1955; New Light on the Dead Sea Scrolls, 1956; Studies on the History of Jews in Persia, 1956; Ibu Khaldun's Autobiography, 1956; The Jews in India, Their Contribution to the Economic and Political Life, 1960; also articles sci. and learned jours. Mem. editorial staff Middle Eastern Affairs chmn. editorial bd. U. Cal. publs. in Semitic Philology. Home: Berkeley, Cal. Died July 14, 1973.

FISCHER, ANN KINDRICK (MRS. JOHN L. FISCHER), educator; b. Kansas City, Kan., May 22, 1919; d. Thomas W. and Gertrude (Miller) Kindrick; A.B., U. Kan., 1941; Ph.D., Radcliffe Coll., 1957; m. John Lyle Fischer, July 9, 1949; children—Nikko, Mary Anne. Tchr., U.S. Govt., Trust Ter., Micronesia, 1951-53; research asst. Harvard, Cambridge, Mass., 1953-56; research asso. Children's Hosp., Boston, 1956-58; faculty Tulane U., New Orleans, 1959-71, asso. prof. anthropology, 1963-68, prof., 1968-71. Cons., VA Mental Hosp., Gulfport, Miss., 1964-66. Fellow Am. Anthrop. Assn., Am. Social Assn. Author: (with John L. Fischer) The New Englanders of Orchard Town, 1965. Book rev. editor Am. Anthropologist, 1970-71. Editor Current Directions in Anthropology, 1970. Contbr. articles to profl. jours. Home: New Orleans, La. Died Apr. 22, 1971.

FISCHER, FREDERIC PHILIP, elec. engr., eductor; b. N.Y.C., June 1, 1908; s. Jacob and Emma L. (Kinkel) F.; B.Sc. summa cum laude, Rutgers U.; M. Sc. (research fellow), Lehigh U., 1935; grad. student, Mass. Inst. Tech.; m. Muriel W. Johnson, July 3, 1940; children—Frederic Philip, Robert E., Carol A. Instr. Mass. Inst. Tech., 1935-39; asst. prof. Rutgers U., 1939-42, Lehigh U., 1942-44; asso. prof. U. Conn., 1944-50; prof., head dept. U. Buffalo, 1950; cons. engr. Cornell Aero. laboratory, 1953-57; cal esearch U.S. Air Force, 1957-61. Recipient numerous awards Excellence in Teaching award Tau Beta Pi, 1975. Registered engineer Ins. Radio Engrs.; mem. I.E.E.E. (life), Am. Soc. Engring. Edn., Phi Beta Kappa, Sigma Xi, Tau Beta Pi, Eta Kappa Nu. Contbr. to profl. jours., bulls. Home: Williamsville, NY. Died June 23, 1975; interred Williamsville.

FISCHER, HERMAN ARTHUR, lawyer; b. Wheaton, Ill., Aug. 25, 1882; s. Herman A. and Julia Waters (Blanchard) F.; A.B., Wheaton Coll., 1903; LL.B., Harvard, 1908. Admitted to Ill. bar, 1908, since practiced in Chgo.; mem. firm Fischer, Guy & Jacobson, and predecessor law firms, 1915-73. Pres. Gary-Wheaton Bank, 1931-52, chmn. bd., 1952-66. Trustee emeritus Wheaton Coll. Mem. Am., Ill., Chgo., DuPage County bar assns., Am. Legion. Republican. Congilst. Club: Union League. Home: Wheaton, Ill. Died Apr. 25, 1974; buried Wheaton Cemetery.

FISCHER, MAURICE RITZ, newspaperman, editor, pub. relations cons., b. Chgo., Mar. 22, 1903; s. Abraham and Anna (Silverberg) E.; B.A., U. Ill., 1924; m. Elvera Mary Lampe, Sept. 1, 1942. Staff, City News Bur., Chgo., 1925-27; with Chgo. Daily News, 1927-68, beginning as financial news asst., successively real estate editor, night city editor, asst. day city editor, 1927-58, city editor, 1958-64, asst. mng. editor, 1964-65, asst. to editor, 1966-68; asst. mgr. met. dept. Field Newspapers, 1965; mng. editor Arlington Day, 1965; pub. relations cons, 1968-74. Lay trustee, v.p. Mundelein Coll.; bd. dirs. Cath. Charities Chgo., Citizenship Council Met. Chgo.; mem. Mayor's Commn. for Rehab. of Persons. Served with USAAF, 1942-43. Mem. Chgo. Press Vets. Assn. (dir., chmn. 1973-74), Pan Am. Council Chgo. (pres. 1969-73), Japan Am. Soc. Chgo (dir.), Sao Paulo-Ill. Partners of Ams. (dir.), Sigma Delta Chi. Clubs: Chicago Headline (exec. sec.), Chicago Press (pres. 1965), Ill. Athletic, City (v.p., bd. dirs.). Home: Chicago, Ill. Died Dec. 23, 1974; buried Calvary Cemetery, West Point, Ia.

FISH, MAYER ALVIN, dentist; b. Newark, July 17, 1905; s. Louis and Ida (Redlich) F.; D.D.S., U. Pa. 1926; m. Margaret Powers, July 17, 1939 (div. Jan. 1965); children—Susan Leslie, Michael Jonathan. Practice gen. dentistry, Newark, 1926-52, South Orange, N.J., 1952-73; instr. N.Y. U. Dental Coll., 1935-41. Mem. Am. Dental Assn., Essex County Dental Soc., Newark Dental Club, Sigma Epsilon Delta. Mem. B'nai B'rith. Home: South Orange, N.J. Died Nov. 21, 1973; interred Mt. Lebanon Cemetery, Iselin. N.J.

FISHER, CHARLES WILLIS, naval officer; b. New York, N.Y., Oct. 27, 1880; s. Charles Willis and Eliza Longworth (Flagg) F.; M.S., U.S. Naval Acad., 1897-1901; B.S., Mass. Inst. Tech., 1907; m. Una Gielow, June 4, 1905. Commd. ensign, U.S. Navy, 1901; commd. captain, 1925, rear admiral, Oct. 1941; became director of Shore Establishments, Navy Dept. 1939. Decorated Spanish War medal, Cuban campaign medal, Navy Cross, Chevalier French Legion of Honor, Victory medal (World War I). Legion of Merit. Home: Oakland, Cal.†

FISHER, GENEVIEVE, home economist; b. Lovington, Ill., Aug. 24, 1879; d. George Thomas and Laura (Ricks) Fisher; diploma, U. of Chicago, 1912; B.S., Columbia U., 1914, A.M., 1927; unmarried. Teacher pub. schs., Springfield, Ill., 1899-1903, Southeastern Mo. State Teachers Coll., 1903-05, Ill. State Normal U., Normal, Ill., 1905-07, Eastern Ill. State Normal Sch., Charleston, Ill., 1909-10, Sch. of Edn., U. of Chicago, 1911-13; teacher, Ia. State Coll. 1914-19, head home economics edn. dept., 1916-19; spl. agent home economics edn., Federal Bd. for Vocational Edn., Washington, 1919-22; prof. and head home econs. edn., Carnegie Inst. Tech., Pittsburgh, 1922-27; dean and prof. home economics div., Ia. State Coll., 1927-44, retired. Vice pres. Am. Vocational Assn., 1926-30; mem. N.E.A., Am. Home Econ. Assn., Am. Assn. Univ. Women, Phi Kappa Phi. Omicron Nu (nat. pres. 1924-26), Phi Upsilon Omicron. Sigma Delta Epsilon, Kappa Delta Pi, Mortar Board. Unitarian. Home: Black Mountain, N.C.†

FISHER, HAROLD HENRY, author; b. Morristown, Vt., Feb. 15, 1890; s. Henry Jonas and Elizabeth Malona (Cole) F.; grad. Peoples Acad., Morrisville, Vt., 1907; A.B., Univ. of Vermont, 1911, L.H.D., 1936; m. Helen C. Dwight, May 14, 1917; 1 son, Anthony Henry Dwight. Teacher Black Hall (Conn.) Sch., 1912, Mercersburg (Pa.) Acad., 1912-14, Hill Sch., Pottsdown, Pa., 1914-17; chief of hist. dept., Am. Relief Adminstrn., 1920-24; lecturer in history, 1924-33; vice chmn. Hoover War Library, 1924-44, chmn. from 1944; dir. Russian Rev. Inst., 1930-42, asso. prof. history Stanford, 1933-36, prof., 1936-55, chmn., 1944-55, emeritus, 1955; prof. internat. relations San Francisco State Coll., 1955-60; vis. professor Columbia Univ., 1940, 57, Tokyo U., 1954; vis. prof. polit. sci. U. Cal. at Berkeley, 1960-61, Mills Coll., 1961-64. Dir. Civil Affairs Tng. Sch., 1943-45; dir. Civil Communications Intelligence Sch. 1946; dir. School Naval Adminstration, 1946-48; dir. Belgian-American Educational Foundation, 1943-64. Served as 1st lt., capt., F.A., A.E.F., 1917-19; relief work for Am. Relief Adminstrn. in Russia, 1922. Mem. Am. Hist. Assn., Institute Pacific Relations (chmn. Pacific council 1953-61), Soc. Am. Historians, Am. Polit. Sci. Assn., Delta Psi. Author books including: American and Russia in the World Community, 1946; The Communist Revolution, 1955; Soviet Russia and the West, 1957. Editor publs. including: Life of a Chemist: Memoirs of V. N. Ipatieff, 1946; Am. Research on Russia, 1959. Home: Palo Alto, Cal., Died Nov. 15, 1975.

FISHER, HERMAN GUY, ret. toy mfg. co. exec.; b. Unionville, Pa., Nov. 2, 1898; s. Elwood and Mary (Zimmerman) F.; B.A., Pa. State U., 1921; m. Suzanne Edwina Greist, Sept. 24, 1932 (dec.); children—Susan (Mrs. Victor W. Lavenstein), Rachel (Mrs. J. Steven Renkert), John Burgis; m. 2d, Elizabeth F. Abbott, Feb. 1, 1969. Vice pres., gen. mgr. All Fair, Inc., Churchville, N.Y., 1926-30; pres., gen. mgr. Fisher-Price Toys, Inc., East Aurora, 1930-66, chmn. bd., 1964-69. A founder, former pres. and bd. dirs. Boys' Club, East Aurora. Home: East Aurora, N.Y. Died Sept. 1975.

FISHER, LAWRENCE FREDERICK, radiologist; b. Baraboo, Wis., Jan. 24, 1890; B.A., U. N.D., 1911; M.D., Rush Med. Coll., 1914; m. Irma Jane Mallory, Sept. 4, 1915 (dec. Jan. 1963); children—Lawrence Frederick, Gerald Mallory, Frank Edwin; m. 2d, Viola Pearl Vincent Lybarger, Dec. 31, 1965. Intern Children's Meml. Hosp., Chgo., 1914, Cook County Hosp., Chgo., 1914-16; resident in radiology Stark Meml. Hosp., Knox, Ind.; roentgenologist St. Joseph Hosp., Mishawaka, Ind., Sturgis (Mich.) Meml. Hosp., Three Rivers (Mich.) Hosp., Goshen (Ind.) Gen. Hosp., Dowiagiac (Mich.) Hosp.; radiologist Murphy Med. Center, Warsaw, Ind., 1957-61; head x-ray dept. Starke Meml. Hosp.; cons. radiology St. Joseph's Hosp., South Bend, Ind. Diplomate Am. Bd. Radiology. Mem. A.M.A, Radiol. Soc. N.Am., Am. Coll. Radiologists, Ind. Med. Assn., Ind. (pres. 1930), Chgo Roentgen socs. Methodist. Mason (K.T., Shriner). Clubs: University; Knife and Fork; Exchange. Home: South Bend, Ind., Died June 13, 1969; buried Highland Cemetery, South Bend, Ind.

FISHER, LINDALE CARSON, banker; b. Wyoming, Del., Jan. 16, 1899; s. William Lindale and Grace May (Carson) F.; student U. Del., 1918-20; B.S., U. Pa., 1923; grad. Army Finance Sch., 1943; m. Mary Valliant Short, June 28, 1924. Accountant James L. Wilson & Co., Phila., 1923-26; accountant balance sheet div., accounting dept. E.I. duPont de Nemours & Co., Wilmington, Del., 1926-29; bank examiner State Banking Dept. of Del., 1929-36, dep. bank commr. of Del., 1936-37, chief dep. bank commr., 1941-42, 44-46; asst. to v.p. Union Nat. Bank, Wilmington, 1937-41; v.p., dir. Farmers Bank State of Del., Dover, 1946-66, also sr. v.p. and pres. Georgetown office. Dir. Milford (Del.) Meml. Hosp. Served as capt., finance dept., AUS, 1942-44. Mem. Am., Del. (mem. exec. com.; pres. 1966) bankers assns., Am. Inst. Banking, Kappa Alpha (So.), Episcopalian (past sr. warden, vestryman, treasurer). Clubs: Sussex Pines Country (Georgetown, Del.); Georgetown-Millsboro Rotary (pres. 1954-55). Home: Georgetown, Del. Died 1973.

FISHER, LYLE HARRIS, mfg. exec.; b. Gilby, N.D., Dec. 8, 1912; s. Henry Aiken and Anna Rebecca (Pratt) F.; B.S., Northwestern U., 1935; m. Shirley Ann Larson, July 31, 1937; children—Susan (Mrs. David Ristau), Katherine (Mrs. James Hunter III), Ann (Mrs. David Pheil). With Minn. Mining & Mfg. Co., St. Paul, 1942, dir. indsl. relations, 1942, dir. personnel relations, 1954-74, v.p. personnel and indsl. relations, 1958-70, v.p. pub. affairs and personnel relations, 1970-74; chmn. bd. Eastern Heights State Bank; dir. Mut. of Omaha Growth Fund, Mut. Omaha Income Fund. Mem. adv. council Minn. Dept. Employment Security; steering com. Minn. Businessmen in Govt. Program; adv. council mgmt. personnel Conf. Bd.; employer adviser for U.S., Internat. Labor Conf., Geneva, Switzerland, 1969. Past pres. Greater St. Paul United Fund, Inc. Trustee Mounds Park-Midway Hosp., Children's Hosp. Recipient citation for community service; N.D. Sci. and Industry award, 1965. Mem. N.A.M. (indsl. relations adv. conf.), Am. Mgmt. Assn. (v.p. at large, exec. com., personnel planning council, bd. dirs.), U.S. (labor relations com.), St. Paul (pres., dir.) chambers commerce, St. Paul Employers Assn. (past pres.), Labor Policy Assn. (dir., exec. com.), Machinery and Allied Products Inst. (pub. affairs council), Delta Tau Delta. Presbyn. Clubs: Gyro, Somerset Country, St. Paul Athletic, Minn. (past pres.); Royal Poinciana Golf (Naples, Fla.). Home: St Paul, Minn. Died Dec. 22, 1974.

FISHER, ROBERT JOHN, sugar co. exec.; b. Buffalo, May 23, 1915; s. Albert J. and Elizabeth (Kulow) F.; B.S., Southeastern U., 1940; student econs., grad. sch. Dept. Agr., 1940-43; m. Alice Lindhurst, June 22, 1940; children—Linda, Janet, Norman, Elizabeth, Judith. Sports writer Buffalo Courier-Express, 1932-34; agrl. economist Dept. Agr. and War Food Adminstrn., Washington, 1934-44; asst. to pres. Gt. Western Sugar Co., Denver, 1945-50, treas, 1950-66, v.p., 1961-73, sr. v.p., 1973-74; v.p. No. Ohio Sugar Co., Denver. Treas., Am. Sugar Beet Industry Policy Com., 1946-74. Treas., Colo. Council Chs., 1950-52. Bd. dirs. Luth. Hosp. of Wheatridge, Colo. Mem. Denver C. of C. (dir. 1951-53), Colo. Assn. Commerce and Industry (dir. 1973-74). Office: Denver, Colo. Died Dec. 28, 1974.

FISHER, STANLEY ROSS, clergyman; b. Cleveland, O., Nov. 12, 1880; s. Rev. Oren D. and Mary Lucretia (Noble) F.; spl. student Boston U.; Bach. Sacred Music, Yale Div. Sch., 1905; studied voice, organ, and composition under various masters; m. Estelle Lindell Coleman, Jan. 13, 1906; children—Lindell Ross, Stanley Nathan, Robert Previtt (dec.). Ordained Congl. ministry, 1905; asso. pastor Central Presbyn. Ch.,

Denver, 1904, 05; pastor Ramona, Calif., 1905-06; founder, and pastor Ch. of the Messiah (Congl.), Los Angeles, Calif., 1907-15; pastor First Congl. Ch., Fall River, Mass., 1915-19; co-pastor, Am. Ch. in Paris, 1919-21, pastor Wellesley Congl. Ch., Wellesley, Mass., 1921-30; became connected with China staff of Laymen's Foreign Missions Inquiry of the Inst. of Social and Religious Research, New York, 1930, and visited China and the Far East; ordained to ministry P.E. Ch., 1932; spl. preacher St. Paul's Cathedral, Boston; rector St. Andrew's Ch., Hanover, Mass. Served with Y.M.C.A. and with mil. intelligence dept. U.S.A., in Europe, 1918, 19. Mem. Am. Guild Organists, University Club (Boston). Home: Hanover, Mass.†

FISHER, WALTER KENRICK, zoölogist; b. Ossining, N.Y., Feb. 1, 1878; s. Albert Kenrick and Alwilda (Merritt) F.; A.B., Stanford U., 1901, A.M., 1903, Ph.D., 1906; m. Evlyn Anne Benson, Sept. 2, 1922. Special field naturalist, U.S. Biol. Survey, 1897-1901; asst., U.S. Fish Commn. Steamer "Albatross," 1902, 1904; asst. in zoölogy, instr., asst. prof., asso. prof., 1920-25, professor, 1925-43, Stanford University, professor emeritus from 1943; asso. in zoölogy, Smithsonian Instn., 1943. Director Hopkins Marine Station, Stanford, 1917-43. Fellow A.A.A.S., American Ornithologists' Union; mem. Cooper Ornithol. Club (Calif.), Sigma Xi. Editor The Condor, 1902-06. Author: Birds of Laysan and the Leeward Islands, Hawaiian Group, 1903; New Starfishes from West Coast of North America, 1905; Starfishes and Holothurians of Hawaii, 1906, 07; Asteroidea of the North Pacific, and Adjacent Waters, vol. 1, 1911, vol. 2, 1928, vol. 3, 1930; Starfishes of Philippine Waters and Adjacent Seas, 1919; Hydrocorals of The North Pacific, 1938; Asteroidea of the Discovery Expedition, 1940; Echiuroid Worms of the North Pacific Ocean, 1946. Contbr. to jours. Home: Pacific Grove, Cal.†

FISHER, WILLIAM ALEXANDER, publisher; b. Ethel, Ont., March 20, 1879; s. George Franklin and Isabel Mitchell (Imlay) F.; educated high sch., Hamilton, Ont.; m. Alice Cary Bradshaw, Dec. 25, 1900; 1 dau., Helen Reed (Mrs. Irvin George Henderson). Came to U.S., 1898, naturalized citizen, 1917. Began on staff Hamilton Times, 1893; mem. Staff Ram's Horn (religious weekly), Chicago, 1898-1904; treas. and asso. editor Pluck (monthly juvenile mag.), 1904-05; mgr. New York plant, Rand McNally & Co., 1905-24; asst. mgr. Biola Press, Los Angeles (Calif.), 1924-25, mng. editor The King's Business (monthly), 1925-26, 1928-29, dir. of publ., Bible Inst. of Los Angeles, 1926-27, exec. sec., 1928-29, treas., 1928-30, also exec. vice-pres., 1929-30; sec.-treas. F. W. Getchel & Son, Inc., 1931-45. Republican. Home: Roscoe, Cal.†

FISHER, WOOLF, steel co. exec.; b. 1912; s. Michael Fisher; m. Joyce Paykel, 1935. Founder, joint chmn., mng. dir. Fisher & Paykel, Ltd., Auckland, New Zealand, 1934-75; chmn. New Zealand Steel Investigating Co., 1960-65, New Zealand Steel Ltd., 1965-75; dir. New Zealand Ins. Co. Ltd., BNZ Finance Co. Ltd., Pacific Steel Ltd. Leader, New Zealand Trade Mission to Australia, 1959; mem. Trade Promotion Council, 1962-63. Pres., Outward Bound Trust New Zealand, 1961-63. Created knight, 1964. Mem. Auckland C. of C. (council 1956-62), Auckland Racing Club (pres. 1973-75), New Zealand Thoroughbred Breeders Assn. (council 1948-75), Auckland Polo Club (pres. 1957-62). Rotarian. Address: Auckland, New Zealand. Died Jan. 12, 1975.

FISHMAN, LEO, educator; b. N.Y.C., Feb. 16, 1914; s. Max and Rebecca (honig) F.; B.A., N.Y. U., 1937, M.A., 1938, Ph.D., 1945; postgrad. U. Wash., 1938-39; m. Betty Goldstein, Nov. 20, 1941; children—Margaret Ellen, Robert Michael. Mem. faculty W.Va. U., Morgantown, 1947-75, prof. econs. and finance, 1952-75, chmn. econs. dept., 1970-75, spl. asst. to pres., 1964-65. Financial adviser Govt. El Salvador, 1962-63; chmn. council econ. advisers Gov. W.Va., 1961-62; vis. asso. prof. N.Y. U., N.Y.C., summers, 1949, 50; vis. prof. U. Wis., Madison, summer, 1971; cons. in field. Served with AUS, 1943. Ford Found. fellow, 1953-54; Ford Found. Research fellow, 1961-62. Mem. Am. Econ. Assn., A.A.A.S., Am. Assn. U. Profs. Mem. Am. Civil Liberties Union. Author: (with Betty G. Fishman) The American Economy, 1962, Employment, Unemployment and Economic Growth, 1969. Editor: Poverty Amid Affluence, 1966. Contbr. to profl. jours. Home: Morgantown, W.Va. Died Apr. 4, 1975.

FISHPAW, KENNETH B., dairy products co. exec.; b. Pickerington, O., Aug. 24, 1910; s. Jesse F. and Cora B. (Lawyer) F.; B.S., Ohio State U., 1932; m. Ednah B. Young, Mar. 28, 1936; 1 dau., Anita (Mrs. Evan Bukey). Accountant, Ernst and Ernst, Cleve., 1932-33; treas. Banks-Baldwin Law Pub. Co., Cleve., 1933-40; with Kraftco Corp. (formerly Nat. Dairy Products Corp.), 1941-75, comptroller, N.Y.C., 1964-71, v.p., comptroller, 1971-74, sr. v.p., 1974-75. Mem. Financial Execs. Inst., Am. Inst. C.P.A.'s. Clubs: Country (Darien, Conn.); Knollwood (Lake Forest, Ill.); Union League (N.Y.C.). Home: Lake Forest, Ill. Died Jan. 18, 1975.

FISKE, AUGUSTUS HENRY, chem. engr.; b. Boston, Mass., May 28, 1880; s. Andrew and Gertrude Hubbard (Horsford) F.; A.B., magna cum laude, final honors in chemistry, Harvard, 1901, A.M., 1902, Ph.D., 1912; m. Esther Wayland Bennett, 1907 (died 1923); children—Andrew II, Eben Horsford, Mary Katharine, Augustus Henry, Jr., Leila Horsford; m. 2d, Ruth Dudley Sterry, 1924. Asst. in chemistry, Harvard, 1900-01, Austin teaching fellow, 1902; wholesale cotton broker, Boston, 1902-09; instr. in chemistry, Harvard, 1909-12; asst. chemist and in research, Rumford (R.I.) Chem. Works, 1912-15, chief chemist, 1915-39. Mem. board trustees Providence Pub. Library, Providence Country Day Sch., Providence Athenaeum, 1923-27; mem. bd. visitors, chem. dept., Brown U. Fellow Nat. Geog. Soc., Am. Inst. of Chemists; mem. Am. Inst. Chem. Engrs., Am. Chem. Soc. (chmn. R.I. Sect. 2 yrs., mem. Senate of Chem. Edn.), Nat. Inst. of Social Sciences, Soc. of Am. Military Engrs., Societe de Chimie Industrielle (Am. Sect.), Am. Electro Chem. Soc., A.A.A.S., Am. Inst. Bakery Engrs., R.I. Hist. Soc., Providence Engring. Soc., Soc. Chem. Industry of England, Audubon Soc. of R.I., N.E. Hist. and Geneal. Soc., Am. Assn. Cereal Chemists, Am. Electroplaters Soc., S.A.R., Huguenot Soc. America; asso. mem. Am. Mus. of Natural History, Republican. Episcopalian. Clubs: Hope, Harvard, Turks Head, Agawam Hunt (Providence); St. Botolph (Boston); Beverly Yacht (mem. racing com.), The Dunes Club, Buzzards Yacht (commodore), Deering Harbor Golf. Author of many papers on chem. subjects. Home: Warren, R.I.†

FITCH, RALPH ROSWELL, orthopedic surgeon; b. Halifax, N.S., Oct. 18, 1878; s. Robert S. and Abbie (Hyde) F.; prep. edn., Boston Latin Sch.; M.D., Harvard, 1903; married Ruth Hart (died 1942); m. 2d, Virginia Ralph Kellogg. Practiced at Rochester 1905-48, ret. Fellow A.C.S.; mem. Am. and N.Y. State med. socs., Am. Orthopedic Assn., Knight Legion of Honor (France), 1917. Home: Northeast Harbor, Me.†

FITZGERALD, A. ANN STRAYER, newspaper editor; b. Omaha, June 29, 1930; d. Weir L. and Louise (Axtell) Strayer; student, Bradley U., 1948-65; m. Dale Fitzgerald, Mar. 1, 1952; children—Shari, Merrie, Lyndon. Acting editor Metamora (Ill.) Herald, 1963; reporter Woodford County Jour., 1963-65; editor, gen. mgr. Beckman Newspapers, Inc., Metamora Herald Washburn Leader, Metamora, Ill., 1965-74. Recipient Gen. Excellence award Ill. Press Assn. Metamora Herald, 1969; Gen. Excellence award So. Ill. Editorial Press Assn., 1970. Mem. Ill. Press Assn. Clubs: Metamora Woman's, Metamora Businessmen's; La Rose, Washburn, Low Point Businessmen's (Washburn, Ill.) Home: Metamora Ill. Died Nov. 17, 1974; buried Oakwood Cemetery, Metamora, Ill.

FITZ-GERALD, DANIEL MICHAEL, agrl. and mdsg. exec.; b. N.Y.C., Feb. 6, 1910; s. Richard and Elizabeth (O'Connor) Fitz-G.; student Walsh Inst. Accountancy, Wayne State U.; m. Grace Elizabeth Prier; children—Eve M. (Mrs. Nick Barris), Sandra L. (Mrs. Walter Pfander), Richard Michael. Staff Lybrand, Ross Bros. & Montgomery, 1930-42; comptroller Wickes Bros., Wickes Boiler Co., 1942-49; treas. Wickes Corp., Saginaw, Mich., 1949-56, exec. v.p., 1956-64, pres., 1964-69, chmn. bd., 1969-75; dir. Mich. Nat. Corp., Mich. Nat. Bank, Consumers Power Co. Vice pres., dir. United Fund of Saginaw County. Mem. Saginaw C. of C., Am. Inst. C.P.A.'s Mich. Assn. C.P.A.'s. Home: Saginaw, Mich., Died July 24, 1975; interred St. Andrew's Cemetery, Saginaw, Mich.

FITZGERALD, JAMES ROBERT, physician; b. Columbus, O., Nov. 15, 1910; M.D., Loyola U., Chgo., 1934; children—Sean, Dennis, Mary Ann (Mrs. Peter Kelly). Intern, Cook County Hosp., Chgo., 1935-36, resident in ophthalmology, 1936-39, sr. attending, cons.; sr. attending surg. ophthalmologist St. Ann's Hosp.; supr. ophthalmology State of Ill.; chief ophthalmology services Hines (Ill.) VA Hosp.; prof. ophthalmology, acting head dept. Stritch Sch. Medicine, Loyola U. Diplomate Am. Bd. Ophthalmology. Mem. A.M.A. Home: River Forest, Ill. Died Mar. 1973.

FITZPATRICK, BENEDICT (JAMES BENEDICT OSSORY), writer; b. Egremont, Eng., Feb. 4, 1881; s. Padraic Edmund Macourt and Sarah Agatha Queen (MacMullen) F.; desc. of MacGiollapatraics of Ossory—name translated to Fitzpatrick, by decree of Henry VIII, in 1537; student Ushaw Coll., Durham, 7 yrs.; Univs. of London and Bonn; LL.D., Holy Cross Coll., Worcester, Mass., 1929. Traveled, studied and taught languages in various European countries, 6 years; corr. and contributing editor London and continental journals; served on staffs Daily Mail (London, Eng.), Illustrated London News, New York Herald (Paris, France), etc. Wrote several volumes on industrial and tech. subjects, pub. in London. Honored by the Italian government for drilling army officers and Guardia Civile in English speech. Author: Ireland and the Making of British, 1922; The Commonwealth of Pennsylvania, 1925; Ireland and the Foundations of Europe, 1927; (part author) History of New York State (4 vols.), 1927; Donjon of Demons, 1930; Frail Anne Boleyn—Henry VIII and Anne Boleyn, 1931; A Literatus in Wonderland: An Expostulation, 1942. Contbr. to encys., mags. and hist. works. Has written several vols. on different periods and regions of Am. history. Wrote on the Austro-Italian campaign in The Story of the Great War (Collier's). Home: New York, N.Y.†

FITZPATRICK, BERCHMANS TANNER, lawyer; b. Washington, July 13, 1907; s. James Frederick and Mary Madeline (O'Brien) F.; A.B., Dartmouth, 1930; LL.B., Harvard, 1933; m. Goergiana Mary DeWolfe, Oct. 10, 1936; children—Barry Morgan, Robert Brian, James Frederick. Atty., PWA, 1933-37; spl. counsel Mpls.-St. Paul San. Dist. Project, 1935-37; regional atty. U.S. Housing Authority, 1938-42; asst. and asso. gen. counsel Nat. Housing Agy., 1942-46, gen. counsel, 1947; asst. adminstr. and gen. counsel HHFA, 1947-49, dep. adminstr., gen. counsel, 1949-54, gen. counsel, 1954; vice chmn., dir. Fed. Nat. Mortgage Assn.; v.p., dir. Def. Homes Corp.; gen. counsel First Nat. Redevel. Corp.; counsellor at law and housing cons., 1955-73. Dir. Natl. Housing Conf.; exec. sec. Mayor's Com. for Better Housing of City N.Y.; sec. McNamara's Com. on Mil. Housing Policy and Programs, 1967; cons. to various groups. Recipient Honor award HHFA, 1955; Honor award Nat. Housing Conf., 1970. Mem. Alpha Tau Omega. Democrat. Roman Catholic. Home: Chevy Chase, Md. Died Aug. 19, 1973.

FITZPATRICK, CLYDE J., railroad exec.; b. Centralia, Ill., Dec. 7, 1908; s. Franklin A. and Jeanette (Hafeli) F.; student pub. schs., Centralia; m. Beth Condit. Oct. 27, 1941; children—Barry, Brian. With I.C. R.R., 1925-55, beginning as telegraph operator, successively train dispatcher, St. Louis and Wis. divs., train dispatcher and operator Springfield div., laborer and carman helper, Centralia, Ill., chief clk. locomotive dept., Markham, telegraph operator, Chgo., station insp. Chgo. Terminal, acting asst. gen. yardmaster, asst. gen. yardmaster, clk. superintendent's office, telegraph operator exec. office, asst. trainmaster, trainmaster Freeport, Ill. and McComb, Miss., supt. Springfield div., also Ia. div., gen. supt. transportation, Chgo. gen. mgr. No. Lines, 1951-53, v.p. operations, 1953-55; pres., dir. C. & N.W. Ry., 1956-74; pres., dir. C., St.P., M.&O. Ry., dir. subsidiary and affiliated ry. orgns. Mason (Shriner). Clubs: Chicago Athletic Assn. (dir.), Chicago, Chicago Traffic, Western Railway (Chgo.); N.Y. Traffic; Glen View Country (Ill.). Home: Winnetka, Ill. Died Nov. 19, 1974.

FITZPATRICK, RAY ERIAN, realtor; b. Gardner, Ill., June 25, 1912; s. Ray Harvey and Pearl Adele (Jeffers) F.; student Crane Coll., 1930; m. Stella Marie Baker, July 21, 1945; 1 dau., Susan Adele. With U.S. Govt. Civil Service, 1935-66, indsl. specialist U.S. Dept. Commerce, Washington, 1951-66; realtor Tucker Agy., Abingdon, Va., 1969-74. Asso. prof. mil. sci. and tactics Va. Poly. Inst., 1944. Served to maj. AUS, 1942-46. Mem. Res. Officers Assn., Ret. Officers Assn., Nat. Assn. Ret. Civil Employees, Va. State (dir. 1972-74), Washington-Smyth (pres. 1971) bds. realtors. Kiwanian. Home: Abingdon, Va. Died Sept. 19, 1974; buried Knollkreg Meml. Park, Abingdon, Va.

FLAGG, BURTON SANDERSON, insurance exec.; b. Littleton, Mass., Nov. 10, 1873; s. Charles Francis and Elizabeth Webster (Sanderson) F.; grad. Worcester (Mass.) Acad., 1892; A.B., Brown U., 1896; married Anne Frances, September 19, 1901; children—Dorothea (Mrs. Frederick W. Smith), Elizabeth (Mrs. Sterling Dow), Frances (Mrs. George Knight Sanborn). Began in ins., Fitchburg, Mass., 1897; pres. and treas. Merrimack Mut. Fire Ins. Co., Mut. Fire Ins. Co. (Reading, Pa.); pres. and gov. Fed. Mut. Fire Ins. Cos.; pres. and treas. Cambridge Mut. Fire Ins. Co.; pres. Andover Savings Bank; dir. Andover Nat. Bank, Salem Mutual Fire Ins. Co., Boston Protective Dept. Chmn. Andover, Liberty bond issues. World War I. Chmn. Commrs. Am. Mutual Alliance; member school board and finance com. Andover; chmn. assessors South Parish; pres. Andover Guild. Trustee Memorial Hall Library, South Parish Funds, Inc., American Institute for Property and Liability Underwriters, Abbott Academy (treasurer), Mutual Reinsurance Bureau of Chicago, Mutual Adjustment Bureua, Ministerial Funds South Parish; Mass. Congregational Conf.; dir. Congl. Bd. of Pastoral Supply. Pres. Nat. Assn. Mutual Fire Ins. Cos.; mem. Mutual Fire Ins. Assn. of New Eng. (pres.), U.S. Chamber Commerce (councillor), Mass. chapter of Descendants of the Mayflower, Delta Upsilon. Republican. Conglist. Mason (32°, K.T., Shriner). Clubs: Square and Compass. Appalachian Mountain, Andover Country; Arundel Golf (Kennebunkport, Me.). Home: Andover, Mass.†

FLAHERTY, J.L., bishop; b. Norfolk, Va., May 13, 1910; s. Charles E. and Mary (Ferris) F.; A.B., Holy Cross Coll., 1922; S.T.L., U. Gregoriana, Rome, 1937; Ph.D. in Edn., Cath. U. Am., 1950. Ordained priest Roman Cath. Ch.; supt. schs. Diocese Richmond, Va., 1949-61; founding pastor St. Luke's Parish, McLean, Va., 1961-62; rector St. John Vianney Sem., 1963-65; aux. bishop of Richmond, 1966-75. Served as chaplain AUS, World War II. Decorated Silver Star; recipient Nat. Brotherhood citation Nat. Conf. Christians and Jews, 1967. Mem. Am. Legion (chaplain Va. 1946-47), Cath. War Vets. (nat. chaplain ladies aux. 1952-53). Home: Norfolk, Va. Died Aug. 9, 1975; buried St. Mary's Cemetery, Norfolk, Va.

FLANDERS, MICHAEL, author, actor; b. London, Eng., Mar. 1, 1922; s. Peter Henry and Laura (O'Beirne) F.; grad. Westminster Sch., 1940; M.A., Christ Ch. Oxford, 1941; m. Claudia Cockburn Davis, Dec. 31, 1959; children—Laura, Stephanie. Author: (plays) Penny Plain, 1951; Airs on a Shoestring, 1953; Fresh Airs, 1955; contbr. to many other revues; author, co-performer (with Donald Swann) At The Drop of a Hat, 1956, At The Drop of Another Hat, 1961; author English version Badingk's opera Orestes, 1952, Stravinski's Soldier's Tale, 1953; opera libretti Hopkin's Three's Company, 1953, A Christmas Story, 1954, others; (verse) Creatures Great and Small, 1964; Captain Noah and his Floating Zoo, cantata with Joseph Horovitz, 1971; actor, 1948-75, appeared in The Caucasian Chalk Circle Royal Shakespeare Co., 1961; radio and TV Work especially as commentator documentaries including The Royal Family, 1969; The Tribe that Hides from Man, 1970, (film) The Raging Moon, 1970; many record albums. Served with Royal Navy, 1941-43. Address: London, England. Died Apr. 14, 1975; interred Colwyn Bay, North Wales.

FLANDERS, RUTH STONE (MRS. PHILLIP RAY FLANDERS), clubwoman; b. Breckenridge, Mich.; d. Arlan Warren and Lillie (Clemens) Stone; grad. Mt. Ida Sch., 1924; m. Phillip Ray Flanders, Nov. 14, 1934. First v.p. Sch. Govt. of Detroit, 1971-72, pres. 1972-75. Mem. Mich. Fedn. Music Clubs (life, dist. pres. 1966-70), Detroit Fine Arts Soc. (treas. 1942-45, historian 1961-75), West Oakland Hills Lawyers Wives (pres. 1968-69), Fedn. Womens Clubs Met. Detroit (editor Club Womens Bulletin, 1962-66), Womens Assn. Detroit Symphony Orch. (editor Symphony Notes 1957-59, dir. 1966-68, 70-72, hon. life v.p. 1971-75). Clubs: Village Womans (editor Villager 1964-65 Bloomfield Hills, Mich.); Womens City (Detroit dir. 1966-69). Detroit Colony Town. Home: Bloomfield Hills, Mich. Died Feb. 16, 1975.

FLANNELLY, JOSEPH F., bishop; b. N.Y.C., Oct. 22, 1894; ed. Cathedral Coll., N.Y.C., St. Joseph Sem., Dunwoodie, Yonkers, N.Y. Ordained priest Roman Cath. Ch., 1918; adminstr. St. Patrick's Cathedral, N.Y.C., from 1939; named titular bishop of Metelis, auxiliary bishop of N.Y., 1948; consecrated, 1948. Home: New York City, N.Y. Died May 23, 1973.

FLANNERY, HARRY WILLIAM, writer, lectr.; b. Greensburg, Pa., Mar. 13, 1900; s. John V. and Catherine (Flynn) F.; Ph.B. in Journalism, U. Notre Dame, 1923; m. Ruth Carmody, July 5, 1937 (dec. July 1968); 1 dau., Patricia Ann; m. 2d, Mary Moriarty Heinemann, Aug. 18, 1969, 1 son, William L. Heinemann. Reporter Hagerstown (Md.) Mail, Balt. Sun, Chgo. City News Bur. and Albany Evening News, 1916-25; sec. to J.P. McEvoy, 1925-26; editor Hoosier Observer, Ft. Wayne, Ind., 1931-32; radio news editor WOWO, Ft. Wayne, 1932-33; news editor and analyst KMOX, St. Louis, 1935-40; Berlin corr. CBS, 1940-41; A.T.C. to Europe, Far East and Near East, 1945; news analyst CBS, Los Angeles, 1942-48; makeup editor Los Angeles Examiner, 1948-49; mem. editorial staff Catholic Digest, 1951; editor AFL News Reporter, 1952-56; radio coordinator AFL-CIO, 1956-66; lectr. Inst. Indsl. Relations, U. Cal. at Los Angeles, Mem. Cath. Assn. Internat. Peace (pres. 1956-63), Los Angeles Archdiocesan Com. on Papal Peace Proposals. Nominated for Peabody Award, radio news analysts, S. Cal region, 1946. Mem. council R.W.G., 1948-49; organizer Cath. Labor Inst., Leo XIII Sch. Social Action. Mem. Authors Guild, Broadcast Pioneers. Roman Catholic. Author: Assignment to Berlin, 1942; Off Mike, chpt. on Analyzing Analysts, 1944. Co-author: The Church and the Workingman, 1965; Which Way Germany?, 1967. Editor: Pattern for Peace, 1962. Home: Los Angeles, Cal. Died Mar. 10, 1975.

FLAVEN, ALLAN ERVIN, hosp. adminstr.; b. Reno, July 24, 1910; s. Harry Lee and Jessie (Ervin) F.; certificate pub. adminstrn., San Diego State Coll., 1957; m. Mary Elizabeth Gray Blauvelt, Jan. 29, 1946; children—Ross B., Richard B., 1 step-son, Robert Blauvelt. Welfare worker County San Diego, 1937-40; selection agt. Civilian Conservation Corps., San Diego, 1940-42; county sponsor rep. WPA, also NYA, 1940-42; asst. supt. Geriatric Hops., Santee, Cal., 1952-55, supt., 1955-66. Chmn. adv. bd. Grossmont Sch. Vocational Nursing; bd. dirs. San Diego County Employees Credit Union Lakeside (Cal.) Gardens Retirement Home. Served to lt. (s.g.) USNR, 1942-46. Mem. Nat. Assn. Counties, Hosp. Council San Diego, Santee C. of C. (dir.). Rotarian. (v.p.) Home: El Cajon, Cal. Died Dec. 21, 1973.

FLAVIN, THOMAS J., govt. ofcl.; b. Boston, July 13, 1906; s. John and Bridget (O'Gara) F.; A.B., Boston Coll., 1926, A.M., 1927; LL.B., Georgetown U., 1932; m. Ann E. Jackson, Feb. 1, 1941; children—Thomas J., Patricia Ann, Deborah Peck, Instr., asst. prof. classical lit. Georgetown U., 1927-32; admitted to D.C. bar, 1932, Mass. bar, 1933, practiced in Boston, 1932-34; atty. U.S. Dept. Agr., 1934-42, jud. officer, 1942-73. Mem. Adminstrv. Conf. U.S., 1962, 68-73. Home: Washington, D.C. Died May 16, 1973.

FLEET, REUBEN HOLLIS, aircraft mfr.; b. Montesano, Wash., Mar. 6, 1887; s. David Walker and Lillian (Waite) F.; student Culver Mil. Acad., Culver, Ind., 1902-06; m. Elizabeth Girton, Apr. 29, 1908; children—Phyllis (Mrs. Albin S. Nelson), David Girton; m. 2d, Dorothy Mitchell, July 7, 1931; children—Preston Mitchell, Dorothy Lillian, Nancy. Began as real estate operator, specializing in timber, 1907; organized Consolidated Aircraft Corp., May 29, 1923, pres. and gen. mgr., 1923-41, sr. cons., from 1942. Served as major, U.S. Army Air Forces, 1917-22; officer Nat. Guard of Wash., 1907-17. City clk. and president Chamber of Commerce, Montesano, Wash., 1907; mem. Wash. State Legislature, 1915. Mem. Soc. Automotive Engrs., Inst. Aeronautical Sciences. Republican. Mason, K. P., Elk. Clubs: Cuyamaca, San Diego Country (San Diego). Home: San Diego, Cal., Died Oct. 29, 1975.

FLEMING, HENRY CRAIG, physician; b. Philadelphia, Pa., May 25, 1881; s. George Matthew and Caroline Virginia (Singerly) F.; ed. DeLancy Prep. Sch.; travelled in Italy and England with private tutor, 1898-1900; M.D., Jefferson Med. Coll., 1906; student Johns Hopkins, 1906-07; m. Myrtle Esther Wilkins, Aug. 26, 1905. Intern. Mt. Sinai (N.Y.) Hosp., 1907-08; pvt. practice, N.Y. from 1909; consulting phys. Bellevue Hosp., Sydenham Hosp., Riker's Island Hosp., Woman's House of Detention; dir. dept. of medicine, dept. correction of N.Y. City; asso. clin. prof. of medicine, Coll. of Medicine, N.Y. Univ. Fellow Am. Coll. Physicians, A.M.A.; mem. N.Y. County and N.Y. State med. socs., N.Y. Adac. Medicine, S.R., Alpha Kappa Kappa; diplomate Am. Bd. of Internal Medicine. Episcopalian. Club: The Metropolitan. Home: New York City, N.Y.†

FLEMING, JAMES R., lawyer, pub.; b. Henry Co., Ind., Nov. 8, 1881; s. George R. and Sarah (Cummins) F.; LL.B., U. of Mich., 1904; m. Jennie Adair, Dec. 24, 1906; children—Marian (Mrs. James Abromson), Virginia. Pros. atty. 58th Jud. Circuit, Ind., 1906-10; U.S. dist. atty. for northern Dist. of Ind., 1933-41; resigned to enter private practice, 1941; chmn. bd., pres., pub. Ft. Wayne Journal-Gazette. Mem. Ind. Ho. of Reps., 1913-15, Ind. Senate, 1915-19; mem. Dem. State Central Com., 1922-26. Chairman Governor's Commission on the Arts; mem. UN Ednl., Scientific and Cultural Orgn.; mem. Mayor's Youth Council, Ft. Wayne, Ind. Mem. Am., Ind., Allen County bar assns., Ind. Soc. of Chgo., Ind. Hist. Soc., Am. Soc. Newspaper Editors. Presbyterian. Mason. Elk. Clubs: Nat. Press (Washington); Fort Wayne Country, Press (Ft. Wayne, Indiana); Olympia; Columbia (Indpls.); Indianapolis Athletic. Home: Fort Wayne, Ind. Died June 1973.

FLEMING, MATTHEW JOHN banker; b. New Albany, Ind., June 4, 1879; s. Charles Oliver and Caroline Mary (Myers) F.; student Franklin High Sch., Pittsburgh, Pa., 1895-97; m. Edna Jessie Sias, June 28, 1904; children—Chapman Charles, Edna Virginia (Mrs. Paul Apthorp Lytle), Matthew John. Began as bank messenger, 1898; clk. Farmers Deposit. Nat. Bank, Pittsburgh, 1903-08, asst. auditor, 1908-09, auditor, 1909-14; auditor Federal Res. Bank of Cleveland, O., 1914-20, dep. gov., 1920-35, pres., 1935-46, retired. Republican. Presbyterian. Mason (32°), Club: Union. Address: St. Petersburg, Fla.†

FLERSHEM, RUDOLPH BYFORD, business exec.; b. Chicago, Ill., Dec. 23, 1876; s. Lem Whitney and Mary Sophie (Greiner) F.; student University Sch., Chicago, 1890-94; A.B., Harvard, 1898; m. Lucy M. Garrett, 1912 (died 1918); children—Jane F. (Mrs. George Marshall Drake), Robert Garrett; m. 2d, Alice H. Jamieson, Mar. 27, 1920; 1 dau., Anne D. (Mrs. Harvey Gaylord). With Am. Raditor Co. 1901-26, v.p. sales, 1918-26; v.p. Marine Trust Co., 1927-42, dir. from 1942; pres. Buffalo Bolt Co., North Tonawanda, N.Y., from 1942. dir. from 1930; pres., dir. Buffalo-Eclipse Corporation, 1950-57, chmn., chief exec. officer, 1957-59, vice chmn., dir., from 1959; dir. Garlock, Inc., Kirkeby-Natus Corporation, Patriotic Education, Incorporated. Gen. chmn. Buffalo Community Fund, 1927; treas. and mem. exec. committee Buffalo Joint Charities and Community Fund, 1927; organization chmn. Univ. Buffalo Endowment Fund Campaign, 1929; chmn. British War Relief Soc., 1942. Trustee Gen. Hosp., Buffalo, 1933; dir. Millard Fillmore Hosp., 1927-30; trustee U. Buffalo. Mem. C. of C., S.A.R. (life mem.), Soc. Colonial Wars (p.p. Western N.Y.). Republican. Presbyn. Mason (32°). Clubs: Saturn (dean 1951), Harvard (president 1928), Country of Buffalo (Buffalo); Harvard (N.Y.C.); Athletic Assn. (Chgo.). Home: Buffalo, N.Y.†

FLETCHER, JOHN, banker; b. Williamsburg, Ia., Sept. 13, 1879; s. Charles and Jennie E. (Hughes) F.; ed. pub. schs.; m. Laura Deacon Fletcher, Apr. 28, 1903. Began in banking business with Cedar Rapids Nat. Bank, 1896; asst. cashier Drovers Nat. Bank, Chicago, 1907-12, pres., 1912-14; v.p. Ft. Dearborn Nat. Bank, Chicago, 1914-22; v.p. Continental & Commercial Nat. Bank, which absorbed Fort Dearborn Nat. Bank, from 1922; treas. Briscoe Motor Corpn., Chicago Bearing Metal Co.; dir. Burnside Steel Co., Piggly Wiggly Central Co., Englewood State Bank, Drovers Nat. Bank. Mem. Chicago Assn. Commerce (chmn. ways and means com.). Republican. Mason. Evangelical. Clubs: Chicago, Union League, Bankers, Mid-Day, Saddle and Sirloin, Kenwood. Home: Chicago, Ill†

FLETCHER, LOUIS DUBOIS, lawyer; b. Newburgh, N.Y., June 29, 1899; s. Louis DuBois and Clara Louise (Smith) F.; E.E., Rensselaer Poly. Inst., 1922; LL.B., George Washington U., 1925; m. Louise Ann Thomas, Sept. 27, 1927; children—Linda Louise, Louis DuBois. Asst. examiner U.S. Patent Office, 1922-25; admitted to N.Y. bar, 1928, Supreme Ct. U.S., 1938; asso. Darby & Darby, N.Y.C., 1925-70, mem., 1930-70, sr. partner, 1950-66. Dir. Westchester Heart Assn. Mem. Am. Inst. E.E., Am., N.Y. Patent law assns., Phi Delta Theta, Alpha Tau Omega. Home: Scarsdale, N.Y. Died Aug. 2, 1975.

FLETCHER, (THOMAS) BROOKS, former congressman; b. Mechanicsville, O., 1879; s. Emmett Hiram and Katherine (Culp) F.; ed. high sch., Carrollton, O.; pvt. normal sch.; student speech arts under Prof. Robert Fulton, Ohio Wesleyan U., and Richard Sch. of Dramatic Art, Cleveland; student Mt. Union Coll. 3 1-2 yrs. and grad. business dept. same coll.; spl. course in business psychology under Prof. Aikins, of Western Reserve U.; m. Martha Ethelyn Upton, June 22, 1924. Editor Alliance (O.) Daily Leader; resigned to take position in bus. and editorial depts. Canton (O.) Morning News; eidtor and pub. Marion (O.) Daily Tribune 12 yrs. (newspaper competitor of Warren G. Harding); withdrew from candidacy for gov. of Ohio, 1936, to run for re-election to Congress; mem. 69th and 70th Congresses, (1925-29), and 73d to 75th Congresses (1933-39), 8th Ohio Dist. Nat. speaker and organizer Peoples University Service, Inc. Mem. Nu Sigma Nu. Democrat. Presbyn. Wrote: Why Men Fail; Which Way America. Home: Marion, O.†

FLIEGLER, LOUIS AARON, educator; b. N.Y.C., Sept. 3, 1917; s. Philip and Pearl (Spodek) F.; B.B.A., Coll. City N.Y., 1945; M.A., N.Y. U., 1947, Ph.D., 1954; m. Dorothy Scherr, June 29, 1945; children—Gail, Susan. Tchr., sch. psychologist San Francisco pub. schs., 1947-53; instr. psychology and edn. Wyo. Community Coll., 1954; research psychologist U. Colo. Med. Center, 1954-55; prof. Syracuse U., 1956-60; mem. faculty U. Denver, 1954-56, prof., coordinator spl. edn., chmn. dept. spl. edn., 1960-66; prof., chmn. spl. edn. Kent (O.) State U., from 1966. Adv. bd. Montgomery Inst., Akron, O., from 1966. Served with AUS, 1946-47. Recipient merit award service spl. edn. Colo., 1966. Mem. Am. Edn. Research Assn., Am. Psychol. Assn., Am. Assn. Mental Deficiency, N.E.A., Council Exceptional Children (pres. div. tchr. edn. 1965-66), Assn. Gifted (pres. 1966-67), Phi Delta Kappa. Editor: Curriculum Planning for the Gifted, 1961. Home: Akron, O. Deceased.

FLIKKE, JULIA O., army nurse; b. Viroqua, Wis., Mar. 16, 1879; d. Solfest and Kristi (Severson) Otteson; grad. Viroqua High Sch., 1899; student Augustana Hosp. Training Sch. for Nurses, 1912-15, Columbia U., 1916; m. Arne T. Flikke, Sept. 11, 1901 (died Oct. 15, 1911). Began as nurse, 1912; asst. supt. nurses Augustana Hosp., Chicago, 1917; apptd. nurse in Army Nurse Corps, 1918, promoted to chief nurse, 1918, 1st lt., 1920, capt., 1927, major, 1937, col., 1942; retired due to disability, July 1, 1943. Author: Nurses in Action, 1943. Home: Takoma Park, Md.†

FLINT, KEMP RUSSELL BLANCHARD, polit. scientist; b. Middlesex, Vt., Sept. 1, 1880; s. Leroy Adelbert and Lenette (Kemp) F.; B.S., Norwich U., 1903, A.M., 1909; grad. student in polit. science, U. of Wis., 1914, 15; m. Lena Bernice Thomas, Sept. 12, 1905; 1 son, Winston Allen. With Norwich U. from 1907, prof. polit. sci., head dept. of social scis.; lectr. Redpath Chautauqua, summer, 1920; mem. teaching staff N.Y. State Coll. for Teachers, summers 1922, 23, in charge summer session courses in polit. science, 1928; conferee, session on internat. law, University of Mich., 1935 by appointment of Carnegie Endowment for Internat. Peace. Comdt. Norwich Univ. Mil. Training Camp, 1917; pres. Vt. Conf. Social Work, 1918-20; mem. Vermont House of Rep., 1921-22; pres. Vt. Forestry Assn., 1925-27; mem. advisory com. Eugenics Survey of Vt.; exec. sec. and dir. research Vt. State Commn. to Investigate the Taxation of Pub. Utilities, 1932; an organizer and mem. exec. com. New Eng. Regional Planning Conf. Chmn. Admiral Dewey Centennial Commn., 1937. Mem. Am. Polit. Science Assn., Gen. Alumni Assn. of Norwich Univ. (pres. 1927-30), Northfield Chamber Commerce (ex-pres.), Sigma Alpha Epsilon; hon. mem. N.E. City Mgrs'. Assn. Republican. Universalist. Mason (32°, Shriner). Club: Green Mountain (charter member). Author: Pour Relief in Vermont, 1916; Military Law in Vermont, 1917; Town Planning, 1919; also bulls. on municipal problems. Home: Northfield, Vt.†

FLINTOFT, JAMES, paper co. exec.; b. Montreal, Can., Nov. 18, 1919; s. Edward Percy and Felicia (Howitt) F.; B.Sc., Bishop's U., 1940; LL.B., Osgoode Hall Law Sch., 1948; m. Joan Baird Mitchell, Dec. 27, 1946; children—Sandra Felicia, Virginia Frances, Jane Mitchell. Called to Ont. bar, 1948, created Queen's counsel, 1966; asst. solicitor C.P. Ry., 1948-54; legal officer Abitibi Paper Co. Ltd., 1954-65, sec., 1965-72, v.p., sec., 1973-75. Bd. govs. Lakefield Coll. Sch., 1955-75, chmn. sch. bd., 1970-72; bd. dirs. Bishop Strachen Sch., 1966-75. Served with Canadian Army, 1941-45; ETO. Decorated Mil. Cross. Mem. Can. Pulp and Paper

Assn. (industry devel. sect., chmn. 1974-75), Can. Mfrs. Assn. (chmn. legis. com. 1973-75, exec. com., exec. council), Ont. Assn. Governing Bodies Ind. Schs. (pres. 1974-75), Canadian Bar Assn., Alpha Delta Phi. Mem. United Ch. (chmn. bd. mgrs. 1969, mem. com. 1969 75). Clubs: Toronto Golf, University (pres. 1964) (Toronto). Home: Toronto, Ont. Can. Died June 9, 1975.

FLOCKS, RUBIN H., urologist, educator; b. N.Y.C., May 7, 1907; s. Morris and Rose (Blackman) F.; A.B., Johns Hopkins, 1926, M.D., 1930. Resident house officer Johns Hopkins Hosp., 1930-31; practice of medicine, urology, Iowa City, 1932-75; asst. instr., asso. in urology U. Ia., 1932-37, asst. prof. urology, 1949-74, prof. emeritus, 1974-75. Mem. NRC, 1965-75, Nat. Adv. Cancer Council, 1965-69. Diplomate Am. Bd. Urology (pres. 1963). Fellow A.C.S.; mem. A.M.A. (sec. urology sect. 1954), Am. Urol. Assn. (sec. 1962, pres. N. Central sect. 1954; pres. 1967-69), Johnson County Med. Soc. (pres. 1944), Clin Soc. Genito-Urinary Surgeons, Am. Assn. Genitro-Urinary Surgeons, Phi Beta Kappa, Alpha Omega Alpha, Sigma Xi. Author: Surgical Urology, 1954. Contbr. sects. med. books. Home: Iowa City, Ia. Died May 17, 1975.

FLOETE, FRANKLIN G., business exec.; b. Armour, South Dakota, May 30, 1889; son Charles and Caroline (Grotewohl) F.; A.B., University Wisconsin, 1908; Bachelor of Laws, Harvard, 1912; m. Mildred Swain, Jan. 25, 1929; 1 dau., Kathe (Mrs. Jorgen Hedegaard). Pres. The Floete Land & Loan Co., Armour, S.D., 1912-73; pres. Floete Lumber Co., Spencer, Ia., 1925-32; comptroller, later pres. Woods Bros. Co.'s, Lincoln, Neb., 1932-41; pres. Ia. Ford Tractor Co., Ia. Body and Equipment Co., Des Moines, 1942-52; asst. sec. def. Dept. Def., Washington, 1953-56; adminstr. Gen. Services Adminstrn., 1956-61. Served as capt. F.A., 89th Div., AEF, 1917-19. Mem. Delta Kappa Epsilon. Clubs: Des Moines, Wianno. Home: Osterville Mass. Died Sept. 21, 1973.

FLORIO, LLOYD JOSEPH, physician, fgn. service officer; b. Batavia, N.Y., Mar. 9, 1910; s. Flavio and Ida (Lindinann) F.; A.B., Cornell U., 1931; M.D., U. Rochester, 1935; Dr. P.H., Harvard, 1941; fellow tropical medicine Tulane U., 1942; study tissue culture U. Toronto, 1948; D.Sc. (hon.), Far Eastern U., Manila, P.I., 1966; m. Madeline Carey, June 24, 1937; children—Barbara, Marcia, David. Intern Buffalo Gen. Hosp., 1935-36; fellow W.K. Kellogg Found., Battle Creek, Mich., 1937-40; asso. prof. pub. health U. Colo. Sch. Medicine, 1941-46, prof. pub. health, 1946-47, prof., head dept. preventive medicine and pub. health, 1947-57, mgr. health and hosps., 1952-59, clin. prof., 1957-59; fellow tropical medicine, Costa Rica, 1941, WHO, 1949; cons. USPHS Communicable Disease Center, Atlanta, 1948-57, pub. health in Korea, Am.-Korean Found., 1954, medicine Denver Gen. Hosp., to 1959, pub. health Children's Hosp., Denver, to 1959; chief health div. U.S. Operations Mission, Manila, 1959-66; hon. prof. U. San Tomas, Manila, 1966; regional health adviser Near East and S. Asia, AID, 1967-68, human resources officer, Lima, Peru, 1968-69, asst. dir. (pub. health), Saigon, Vietnam, 1969-71; sr. health adviser Tech. Assistance Bur., AID, 1972. Mem. bd. Nat. Tb Assn., 1947-59, v.p., 1956-57. Diplomate Am. Bd. Preventive Medicine and Pub. Health, 1949. Mem. Assn. Profs. Preventive Medicine (pres. 1950-53), Am., Colo. (pres. 1945-47) pub. health assns., A.M.A., Colo., Denver med. socs., A.C.P., Soc. Exptl. Biology and Medicine, A.A.A.S., Sigma Xi. Contbr. Profl. Publs. Home: Reston, Va., Died Oct. 18, 1975; interred Lancaster, N.Y.

FLÜGGE-LOTZ, IRMGARD, educator; b. Hameln, Germany, July 16, 1903; d. Oscar and Dora (Grupe) Lotz; Diplom-Ingenieur, Tech. U. Hannover (Germany), 1927, D.Engring., 1929; m. Wilhelm Flügge, June 4, 1938. Came to U.S., 1948, naturalized, 1954. Chief asst. applied math. Tech. U. Hannover, 1927-29; from research scientist to head dept. theoretical aerodynamics Aerodyn. Versuchsanstalt (AVA), Göttingen Germany, 1929-38; sci. adviwer Deutsche Versuchsanstalt Für Luftfahrt Berlin-Adlershof, 1938-45; head research group Office Nat. d'Etudes et de Recherches Aéronautiques, Paris, France, 1946-48; mem. faculty Stanford, 1949-74, prof. engring. mechanics, aero. and astronautics, 1960-74. Fellow Am. Inst. Aero and Astronautics; sr. mem. I.E.E.E.; mem. Soc. Indsl. and Applied Math., Sigma Xi. Author: Discontinuous Control, 1953; also articles. Mem. adv. bd. Jour. Nonlinear Mechanics, 1966. Home: Los Altos, Cal. Died May 22, 1974.

FLUHRER, JOHN JAMES, physician; b. Red Lodge, Mont., July 22, 1919; s. Alphaeus and Margaret (Eberly) F.; M.D., U. So. Cal., 1943; m. Eileen Le Quesne, Feb. 5, 1943; children—Catherine (Mrs. Richard Frank Williams), Patricia Lee. Intern, U.S. Naval Hosp., Oakland, Cal., 1943-44; resident in urology Los Angeles County Gen. Hosp., 1948-51, attending staff urologist; cons. staff urologist Alhambra (Cal.) Community Hosp.; cons. and active staff Community Hosp., San Gabriel, Cal.; asst. clin. prof. surg. urology U. So. Cal. Served to lt., M.C., USNR, 1943-47. Diplomate Am. Bd. Urology. Mem. A.M.A., Am. Urol. Assn., Am. Urol. Assn.-Western Sect. Home: San Gabriel, Cal. Died Oct. 24, 1973; buried Forest Lawn Meml. Park, Glendale, Cal.

FLUOR, JOHN SIMON, business exec.; b. Oshkosh, Wis., Apr. 22, 1902; s. John Simon and Emma (Sonnenberg) F.; grad. Poly. Coll. Engring., Oakland, Cal., 1921; m. Mildred Warner, Jan. 15, 1927; 1 son, John Simon; married second Marjorie L. Wade, Aug. 17, 1956. With Fluor Corp., Ltd., 1921-74, exec. v.p., 1931-52, pres., chmn., dir.; dir. Beckman Instruments, Inc. Dir. Los Angeles br. Am. Cancer Soc. Home: Santa Ana Cal. Died Sept. 10, 1974; buried Fairview Cemetery, Santa Ana, Cal.

FLYNN, FRANCIS MARION, newspaper exec.; b. Mt. Ayr, Ia., Jan. 25, 1903; s. John F. and Sara (Long) F.; B.J., U. Mo., 1924, LL.D., 1962; m. Margaret Barnes, July 21, 1924 (dec.); children—Jack Francis Arthur (dec.), Margaret Maureen. Advt. mgr. E.W. Stephens Pub. Co., Columbia, Mo., 1924-26; gen. mgr. Japan Advertiser Press, also corr. for London Express and rep. N.Y. Times World Wide Photo Service, Tokyo, Japan, 1926-29; asst. to bus. mgr. N.Y. News, 1929-31; bus. mgr. Detroit Mirror, 1931-33: asst. bus. mgr. N.Y. News, 1933-38, bus. mgr., 1938-46, dir., 1941-74, gen. mgr., 1946-55, pres., 1947-73, pub., 1955-73, chmn. bd., 1973-74; chmn. bd., dir. TV sta. WPIX, Inc., Conn. Broadcasting Co.; sr. v.p., dir. Tribune Co.; v.p., dir. N.Y. News Charities, Inc.; dir. Chgo. Tribune Co., WGN Continental Broadcasting Co., Ill. Atlantic Co., Ont. Paper Co. Ltd., Quebec North Shore Paper Co., Manicouagan Power Co., Gore Newspapers Co., Sentinel Star Co. Mem. Alpha Tau Omega, Sigma Delta Chi, Kappa Tau Alpha. Clubs: Union League, Pinnacle (N.Y.C.); Pelham (N.Y.) Country; Lyford Cay (Nassau, Bahamas). Home: Pelham Manor, N.Y. Died Nov. 15, 1974; interred Columbarium of Ch of Christ The Redeemer, Pelham Manor, N.Y.

FLYNN, JOSEPH ANTHONY, actor; b. Youngstown, O., Nov. 8, 1924; s. Joseph Anthony and Grayce Ann (McGraw) F.; student U. Notre Dame, 1942-43; A.B., U. So. Cal., 1950; m. Shirley J. Haskin, Nov. 12, 1955; children—Tony, K. C. Appeared motion pictures including The Love Bug, 1968, The Barefoot Executive, 1970, The Million Dollar Duck, 1971, Now You See Him, Now You Don't, 1972; star television series McHale's Navy, 1962-66. Art commr. State of Cal., 1966-68; mem. Mayor's Community Adv. Com., Los Angeles, 1962-74. Bd. dirs. Cal. Epilepsy Soc. Served with AUS, 1943-46. Mem. Screen Actors Guild (dir.). Democrat. Home: Bel Air, Cal. Died July 19, 1974; buried Holy Cross Cemetery, Culver City, Cal.

FOELSCH, CHARLES BEREND, clergyman; b. Ottumwa, Ia., Mar. 31, 1891; s. Rev. Henry and Caroline (Wagner) F.; A.B., Wartburg Coll., 1909; grad. Chgo. Luth. Sem., 1915; Ph.D., U. Pitts., 1924; D.D. (hon.), Newberry Coll., 1934, Carthage Coll., 1943; m. Pauline Gray, May 4, 1920; children—Carolyn, Charles Berend (M.D.), Donald. Ordained to ministry, Luth. Ch., 1915; pastor, Wilkinsburg, Pa., 1920-27, Charleston, S.C., 1927-34, Sunbury, Pa., 1934-40, Washington, 1940-42; pres. Chgo. Luth. Theol. Sem., 1942-47; pastor Holy Trinity Ch., N.Y.C., 1947-52; pres. Pacific Luth. Theol. Sem., Berkeley, Cal., 1952-61, pres. emeritus, 1961-74; pastor Christ the King Luth. Ch., Chgo., 1961-63; co-pastor Seamen's Center, N.Y.C., 1963-66; minister-in-charge Christ Ch., N.Y.C., 1966-74. Chmn. com. on moral and social welfare United Luth. Ch., 1932-36, chmn. dept. evangelism, 1938-40, mem. bd. Am. missions, pres. bd., 1952-56; mem. exec. bd. United Luth. Ch. in Am., 1940-48, 56-62, Sec. of Court of Adjudication, 1962-74; councilor Nat. Luth. Council, 1950-60. Mem. Hymn Soc. Am. (chmn. exec. com. 1968-74), Soc. Luther Research. Author: A Mighty Fortress, 1924; His Word for My Way, 1962; also monthly essay, Landmark Churches of our Faith, in the L.B. Bond, 1956-74. Co-author: Epistle Messages, 1934. Editor: The Day's Worship Book of Devotions, 1935; The New Day's Worship, 1966. Address: New York City, NY. Died Jan. 20, 1974.

FOLEY, HAROLD SCANLON, mfg. exec.; b. Mpls., Sept. 9, 1900; s. Jeremiah and Marie (Scanlon) F.; B. Commerce, U. Notre Dame, 1921; LL.D., U. B.C., 1957, St. Mary's U., 1958; m. Frances C. Burrowes, Sept. 29, 1927; two daughters. Salesman Brooks-Scanlon, Inc., Eastport, Fla., 1922-25; part owner Dunan Lumber Co., Brandenton, Fla., 1925-28; pres. Foley Lumber Co., Jacksonville, Fla., 1928-29; v.p. Brooks-Scanlon, Inc., Foley, Fla., 1929-36; exec. v.p. Powell River Co., Ltd., Vancouver, B.C., 1936-40, pres., 1940-55, chmn. bd., 1955-74, also dir.; chmn., dir. Powell River Sales Co., Ltd., 1938-74; vice chmn. bd., dir. MacMillan, Bloedel & Powell River, Ltd., 1960-61; v.p., dir., mem. exec. com. Bank of Montreal; dir. Union Oil Co. of Can. (Calgary), Harbor Park Devels. Ltd. (Vancouver), Bank of Montreal (Cal.), San Francisco. Hon. pres. B.C. Cancer Found.; hon. chmn. B.C. and Yukon div. Canadian Cancer Soc.; hon. v.p. Red Cross Soc. Bd. dirs., Nat. Heart Found.; bd. lay trustees, finance com. U. Notre Dame. Decorated Knight of St. Gregory; recipient Human Relations award Can. Council Christians and Jews, 1958. Mem. Canadian Assn. Sovereign Order Malta. Roman Catholic. Clubs: Vancouver, Shaughnessy Golf and Country, Faculty (Vancouver); Bohemian (San Francisco); Mount Royal (Montreal). Home: Vancouver BC, Canada. Died Mar. 21, 1974.

FOLEY, RAYMOND MICHAEL, administrator; b. Wayne County, Mich., May 17, 1890; s. Michael J. and Caroline E. (Salliotte) F.; ed. pub. schs. of Detroit, Utica and Mt. Clemens; LL.D. (honorary) University of Detroit, 1948; married Mary C. Hautekeur, Sept. 25, 1912; children—Paul Emmet, Dorothea Hope (Mrs. James E. Brophy), Robert Charles. Reporter, Detroit Free Press, 1908-09; reporter and gen. agent, Detroit News, Pontiac, 1909-11; city and mng. editor Daily Press, Pontiac, 1911-25; editor Mich. Councillor, Detroit, and special pub. Contractor (house organs, etc), 1925-33; established pub. relations div. for various depts. State Govt. of Mich., chmn. Employment Recovery Commn., mem. Tourist and Resort Commn. of Mich., 1933; State dir. for Mich., Fed. Housing Adminstrn., Detroit, Oct. 1934-July 1945; commr. Fed. Housing Adminstrn., Washington, 1945-53, adminstr. Nat. Housing Agy., 1946-47, adminstr. Housing and Home Finance Agency, and chmn. Nat. Housing Council, mem. execs. com., Office of Defense Mobilization. Chmn. bd. dirs. Federal Nat. Mortgage Assn.; mem. bd. govs., Nat. Assn. Housing Officials. Democrat. Catholic, Mem. K.C. (past grand knight. dist. dep., life mem.). Club: National Press (Washington). Contributor general and technical articles to gen. and professional publs. Home: Grosse Pointe, Mich. Died Mar. 2, 1975.

FOLEY, ROGER T., U.S. dist. judge; born Sioux City, Ia., May 25, 1886; s. Thomas L and Mary (McNamara) F.; student St. James Parochial Sch., Chicago, 1897-1901; student St. Vincents Coll., Los Angeles, Calif., 1901-03, Chicago Law Sch., 1908; m. Helen Drummond, July 10, 1913; children—Roger D., Thomas A., George W., Joseph M., John P. Admitted to State Bar Nev., Calif., 1911, in practice of law, Goldfield, Nev., 1911-25; district attorney, Goldfield, Nev., 1917-25; dist. atty., Las Vegas, Nev., 1934-38; dist. judge Clark and Lincoln Counties, 1939-41; U.S. dist. judge, Dist. of Nev., since May 15, 1945. Mem. Am. Bar Assn. Democrat. Roman Catholic, K.C., Elk. Club: Lions (Reno). Home: Las Vegas, Nev. Died Oct. 1974.

FOLGER, JOHN HAMLIN, congressman; b. Rockford, N.C., Dec. 18, 1880; s. Thomas Wilson and Ada Dillard (Robertson) F.; student Guilford Coll., 1898, U. of N.C., 1901; m. Maude Douglas, Nov. 5, 1899; children—Fred, Nell (Mrs. Bailey Glenn), Henry, Frances. Practiced law, Dobson, Surry County, N.C., 1901-05, Winston-Salem, 1905, again in Surry County, at Mount Airy, from 1905. Mayor, Mt. Airy, N.C., 2 terms; mem. N.C. Ho. of Reps., 1926-27, N.C. State Senate, 1930-31; elected mem. 72d Congress, 5th N.C. Dist., June 14, 1941, to fill unexpired term of his brother; mem. 78th to 80th Congresses (1943-49), 5th N.C. Dist. Mem. Am., N.C., Surry Co. bar assns. Democrat. Mason (Shriner); Jr. Order United Am. Mechanics. Home: Mount Airy, N.C.†

FOLSOM, DAVID MORRILL, mining engr.; b. White Sulphur Springs, Mont., Feb. 24, 1881; s. David E. and Lucy T. (Jones) F.; A.B., Stanford, 1902, E.M., 1904; studied Sch. of Mines (Columbia), 1902-03; m. Clinton E. Stone, Jan. 25, 1911. With Boston & Mont. Copper Co., 1904-10; asst. prof. mining, 1910-11, asso. prof., 1911-17, prof., 1917-19, Stanford. Consulting engr. Elkoro Gold Mines Co., 1916; mem. com. on petroleum, Calif. State Council of Defense, 1917; federal oil dir. for Pacific Coast under the oil div. of U.S. Fuel Adminstration, 1918; mgr. land dept. and dir. Gen Petroleum Corpn. Mem. Am. Inst. Mining and Metall. Engrs., Mont. Soc. Engrs. Republican. Clubs: Engineers, University, Commonwealth (San Francisco). Home: Palo Alto, Cal.†

FOLSOM, MRS. ELIZABETH IRONS, writer; b. Peoria, Ill., Sept. 8, 1878; d. Charles David and Etta M. (English) Irons; grad. high sch., Bloomington, 1895. Court reporter the Pantagraph, Bloomington, 14 yrs.; moved to N.Y. City, 1915, to write fiction; contbr. many short stories and several serialized novels; twice named in E. J. O'Brien's honor roll for best stories of the year; winner of O. Henry memorial award for best short story under 3,000 words, 1923. Republican. Club: Pen and Brush. Author: Free, 1925; Mad Rapture, 1926. Address: New York, N.Y.†

FOOTE, NORMAN LANDON, ret. clergyman; b. Saratoga Springs, N.Y., Nov. 30, 1915; s. Leroy H. and Amy V. (Close) F.; A.B., Princeton, 1937; S.T.B., Gen. Theol. Sem., 1940, S.T.D., 1957; D.D., Church Div. Sch. Pacific, 1957; m. Carolyn H. Swayne, June 1, 1940; children—Margaret, Judith, Leroy, Ralph. Ordained to ministry P.E. Ch., deacon, priest, 1940; missionary, Mont., 1940-43, archdeacon, 1943-50; dir. Nat. Town and Country Church Inst. Parkville, Mo., 1950-57; bishop of Ida., 1957-72. Home: Boise Ida. Died May 12, 1974.

FOOTE, WILDER, govt. official; b. Montrose, Pa., Aug. 30, 1905; s. Henry Wilder and Eleanor T. (Cope) F.; A.B. magna cum laude, Harvard, 1927; A.M. (hon.), Middlebury Coll., 1942; m. Marcia Noyes Stevens, Oct. 22, 1928; children—Wilder, Judith. Editorial chmn., Harvard Crimson, 1927; staff writer, Associated Press, Boston, 1928-30, night editor, 1930-31; editor and publisher, Brandon (Vt.) Union, Middlebury (Vt.) Register, Bristol (Vt.) Herald, 1931-41; information officer Office of Emergency Management and Office of War Information, in charge Lend-Lease information, 1941-44; spl. asst. to Foreign Economic Adminstr., 1944-45; asst. to sec. of State, 1945; officer of U.S. Mission to United Nations, 1945-47; dir. press and publications, UN, 1947-75. Home: New York City, NY. Died Feb. 14, 1975.

FORBES, MYRON E., corp official; b. Jarvisburg, N.C., Mar. 15, 1880; s. Andrew Jackson and Margaret Daily (Jarvis) F.; ed. Atlantic Coll. Inst., Elizabeth City, N.C.; m. Janie Sparrow Grimstead, Nov. 6, 1901; children—Helen A. (Mrs. James A. Reeves), Margaret E. (Mrs. S. C. Turner). Treas. Pierce Arrow Motor Car Co., 1919-21; vice pres. and gen. mgr., 1921-22, pres. and gen. mgr., 1922-29; v.p. Oliver Farm Equipment Co., Chicago, 1931-32; now pres. and treas. Walbridge Operating Co., Inc.; also business counselor, Buffalo, N.Y.; dir. and chmn. exec. com. Lincoln-East Side Nat. Bank. Mem. Met. Museum Art (New York). Republican. Methodist. Mason (32°). Clubs: Buffalo Athletic, Wanakah. Home: Buffalo, N.Y.†

FORBES, ROGER SAWYER, clergyman; b. Westboro, Mass., Oct. 24, 1878; s. John Perkins and Maria Almy (Sawyer) F.; A.B., Harvard, 1900; S.T.B., Harvard Theol. Sch., 1903; m. Mary Angeline Low, Nov. 13, 1907; children—John Low, Nathaniel Frothingham, Eleanor, David Low. Ordained Unitarian ministry, 1903; pastor First Parish, Dedham, Mass., 1903-1908; First Parish, Dorchester, Mass., 1908-17, Unitarian Ch., Germantown, Phila., from 1917. Republican. Mason. Club: City (Phila.), Home: Philadelphia, Pa.†

FORD, FRANCIS J.W., judge; b. Boston, Mass. Dec. 23, 1882; s. Cornelius J. and Josephine (Murphy) F.; grad. Boston Latin Sch. 1900, Harvard Coll. 1904, Harvard Law Sch., 1906; m. Ann Cresswell, Mar. 6, 1916; 1 dau., Barbara Ford Carter. Admitted to Mass. bar, 1906, since practiced in Boston; mem. Boston City Council, 1917-22, pres. 1919; U.S. dist. atty. for Mass., 1933-38; U.S. dist. judge for Mass., 1938-72, sr. judge, 1972, ret., 1975. Mem. Am., Boston bar assns., Am. Judicature Soc., Jud. Conf. U.S. Democrat. Catholic. Clubs: Harvard Varsity, Harvard (Boston). Home: Boston, Mass. Died May 26, 1975.

FORD, HOWARD EGBERT, utility exec.; b. Chgo., May 26, 1906; s. Reginald and Maude (Egbert) F.; B.S., U. Ill., 1927; m. Mary Dixie Brown, Mar. 16, 1946; children—Mary Dixie, Leslie Bearden. With No. Ill. Gas Co., and predecessors, Aurora, Ill., 1927-71, v.p., 1958-69, sr. v.p., 1969-71. Served from lt. (j.g.) to lt. USNR, 1943-45. Club: River Forest Tennis. Home: River Forest, Ill., Died Dec. 21, 1975.

FORD, JOHN, (SEAN O'FEENEY), dir. motion pictures; b. Cape Elizabeth, Me., Feb. 1, 1895; s. Sean and Barbara (Curran) O'Feeney; Dr. Fine Arts, U. Me., 1939; M.A., Bowdoin Coll., Brunswick, Me., 1947; L.H.D., Brandeis U.; m. Mary McBryde Smith, July 3, 1920; children—Patrick Roper, Barbara Nugent. Began as property man, Universal City, Cal., 1914; later became dir.; has directed more than 80 pictures for Universal-Fox, Metro-Goldwyn-Mayer, United Artists, Radio-RKO, latest being How the West Was Won, Seven Women. Served from lt. comdr. to capt., USNR, World War II, to rear adm., Korean War. Recipient N.Y. Critics Award 1935, 39, 40, 41; Acad. Motion Picture Arts and Sci. directorial award, 1935, 40, 41, 53; Acad. Awards for two documentaries made for Govt, while in Navy, "Midway," "December 7th." Decorated Legion of Merit, Purple Heart, Air medal; Chevalier Crown of Belguim; Knight Comdr. Italian Republic; Knights of Malta Legion of Honor. Democrat. Catholic. K.C. Clubs: Army and Navy (Washington and Manila, P.I.). Address: Beverly Hills, Cal. Died Aug. 31, 1973.

FORD, MARY ELIZABETH FORKER (MRS. HARLAND B. FORD), author; b. nr. Albion, Ind.; d. Simon Edward and Mina Mae (Bowen) Forker; grad. Newspaper Inst. Am.; m. Harland B. Ford, Feb. 11, 1932 (dec. Sept. 1961); 1 dau., Jane Leigh (Mrs. Ira Carlton Crandall). With Lincoln Nat. Life Ins. Co., Ft. Wayne, Ind., 1924-32. Mem. Mystery Writers of Am., Nat. League Am. Pen Women, Internat. Platform Assn., Alpha Gamma. Methodist. Club: South Side Reading. Author: Murder, Country Style, 1964; The Silent Witness, 1964; The Dude Ranch Murders, 1965; Shadow of Murder, 1965; The Long Journey Home, 1966; The Roswell Heritage, 1968; Journey Into Danger, 1971; Harvest of Years, 1972; Terror in Technicolor, 1972. Home: Fort Wayne, Ind. Died Mar. 11, 1973.

FORD, NIXOLA GREELEY-SMITH (MRS. ANDREW WATRES FORD), writer; b. Chappaqua, N.Y., 1880; d. Col. Nicholas and Ida (Greeley) Smith; ed. Convent of Sacred Heart, N.Y. City, and in Belgium; m. Andrew Watres Ford, Apr. 1, 1910. Spl. writer on staff New York Evening World. Contbr. of poems and prose to mags. Home: Orange, N.J.†

FORD, WILLIAM JESSE, physician; b. Chgo., Oct. 31, 1908; s. Zachary D. and Adeline (Smith) F.; M.D., Northwestern U., 1934; m. Jane Marie Williams, July 18, 1942; children—Barbara J., William D., Brian R., Ann R. Intern, Cook County Hosp., Chgo., 1933-34; resident Chgo. Municipal Tb Sanitarium, 1938-39, Morgan Heights Sanitarium, Marquette, Mich., 1941-43; attanding physician in medicine St. Joseph Hosp., Chgo., to 1953; staff physician VA Hosp., Dwight, Ill., 1953-60; asst. chief of staff VA Westside Hosp., Chgo., 1960-61; chief staff VA Hosp., Saginaw, Mich., 1961-64, VA Hosp., Buffalo, 1964-70, VA Hosp., Des Moines, 1970-72; instr. medicine Northwestern U., to 1953. Diplomat Am. Bd. Internal Medicine. Fellow A.C.P.; mem. A.M.A., Am. Assn. Hosp. Adminstrs. Contbr. articles to profl. jours. Home: Chicago, Ill., Died Mar. 23, 1972; buried Chicago, Ill.

FORDYCE, JAMES PAUL, life ins. exec.; b. Wichita, Kan., Aug. 1, 1892; s. Jesse Harvey and Lucy (Allen) F. m. Roberta Leonard, Jan. 21, 1915 (div. 1933); 1 dau., Audrey Marie; m. 2d, Margaret Monahan, June 15, 1935; 1 son, Donald Michael. Salesman Western Union, Spokane, Wash., 1911-14; dir. agencies New World Life Ins. Co., Seattle, Wash., 1915-22; gen. agent State of Wash., Lincoln Nat. Life Ins. Co., 1923-29; v.p., dir. agys. United Pacific Life Ins. Co., 1930-31; agy. supt. No. Life Ins. Co., 1932-33; dir. agys. Manhattan Life Ins. Co., N.Y. C., 1934-36, v.p., dir. agys., 1936-39, pres., 1939-50, chmn. bd., 1950-66, chmn. exec. com., 1966-70, hon. chmn. bd., 1970-75. Dir. N.Y. Bd. Trade. Lay trustee Gilmour Acad., Gates Mills, O. Mem. U.S., N.Y. State chambers commerce, Am. Life Conv., Life Presidents Assn. Republican. Club: Metropolitan. Home: Fort Lauderdale, Fla. Died Feb. 14, 1975; buried Fort Lauderdale Meml. Park.

FORGAN, JAMES RUSSELL, investments exec.; b. Evanston, Ill., Mar. 12, 1900; s. David Robertson and Agnes (Kerr) F.; grad. St. Mark's Sch., Southboro, Mass., 1918; B.A., Princeton, 1922; m. Ada Rand Johnson, Dec. 2, 1922; children—Joan Berwick (Mrs. Joan Parks), Florence (Mrs. Henry P. Wheeler), James Russell, Ada J. (Mrs. Whitney Addington). Clerk, Nat. City Bank Chgo., 1922-24, asst. cashier, 1924-25, asst. v.p. Nat. Bank Rep. Chgo., 1925-27; v.p. Brokaw & Co., 1927-30; partner Glore, Forgan & Co. (formerly Field, Glore & Co.,) Chgo. and N.Y.C., 1931-65; chmn., chief exec. officer Glore, Forgan, Wm. R. Staats Inc., 1965-70; chmn. du Pont Glore Forgan, Inc., 1970-74; dir. Interco, Inc., Borg Warner Corp., Nat. Distillers & Chem. Corp.; mem. adv. com. Bankers Trust Co. Vice chmn. Joint Emergency Relief Fund, Chgo.; vice chmn. U.S. Navy Relief Soc. Past trustee Princeton U. Served from lt. col. to col. AUS, World War II; comdg. officer OSS, E.T.O., 1945. Decorated D.S.M., Legion of Merit, Legion of Honor; Croix de Guerre with palm; Order British Empire; Order of Leopold (Belgium); comdr. Order Dannebrog (Denmark); Cross of Liberation (Czechoslovakia); Gen. Wm. J. Donovan award, Vets. Strategic Services. Presbyn. Clubs: Links, Racquet and Tennis, Recess, Princeton (N.Y.C.); Links Golf; Travellers (Paris); Buck's, Special Forces (London); Lyford Cay (Nassau). Home: New York City, N.Y. Died Jan. 31, 1974.

FORKNER, HAMDEN LANDON, univ. prof.; b. Stevensville, Mont., Mar. 10, 1897; s. Allen and Lucy Adeline (Irvine) F.; A.B., U. of Calif., 1929, M.A., 1936, Ph.D., 1939; m. Marjorie L. Moore, Nov. 29, 1917; children—Hamden Landon, Irvine Hugh, Marjorie Lucynthia. Instr. Healds Bus. Coll., 1919-21; several other positions 1921-37; head of dept. of vocational and business edn. and prof. edn., Teachers Coll., Columbia U., from 1937; mem. Teachers Coll. Columbia U., School survey staff; dir. Study of Tech. Edn., in Mexico, 1955-56; pres. Forkner Publishing Company, Inc. Served in U.S. Army, 1917-18. Consultant to U.S. Armed Forces Institute Testing Program; asso. Inst. Adult Edn.; mem. Nat. Council for Business Edn. (pres. 1940-44); mem. Nat. Assn. Business Teacher-Training Instns. (pres. 1945-46), Future Bus. Leaders Am. (nat. chairman, 1940-49), United Bus. Edn. Assn. (pres. 1946-48), National Council for Business Edn. (pres. 1946-48; member Nat. Assn. Secondary Sch. Prins., Am. Assn. Sch. Adminstrs., Nat. and Eastern Business Teachers Assn., So. Business Edn. Assn., Comml. Edn. Assn. of N.Y.C. National Edn. Research Assn., Phi Delta Kappa, Delta Pi Epsilon. Mem. Dewey Society Yearbook Com., 1944-45. Co-author: Several textbooks. Inventor Forkenr alphabet shorthand. Home: New York City, N.Y., Died Nov. 25, 1975.

FORSCH, ALBERT, mfr.; b. N.Y. City, May 22, 1880; s. Ferdinand and Rebecca (Schiffer) F.; student Columbia Coll., 1901, Columbia Law Sch., 1903; married; 3 children. Admitted to N.Y. State bar, 1903, and practiced in N.Y. City as mem. firm of Cooke & Forsch, 1903-08; mem. of partnership of Pelgram and Meyer, mfrs. of textiles, 1908-28, and banking firm of Lazard Freres & Co., 1928-38; dir., mem. exec. com. Asso. Dry Goods Corp.; dir. Gen. American Investors. Co., Lord & Taylor, Hehne & Company, James McCreery & Company. Served in U.S. Army, 1917-20, (ret. rank of lt. col.), Ordnance Dept., 1940-43, as adminstr. dir. Propellant Charge Plants and mem. Safety Bd. Home: New York City, N.Y.†

FORSTER, WILLIAM BLAIR, hosp. cons.; b. Martin's Ferry, O., July 1, 1911; s. Emmett Reed and Pearle (Stewart) F.; A.B., Mt. Union Coll., 1933; m. Christeen Lanning, Mar. 6, 1938. Bookkeeper, Alliance (O.) City Hosp., 1929-33; asst. adminstr. Elyria (O.) Meml. Hosp., 1933-38; asst. adminstr. St. Lukes Hosp., Cleve., 1938-42, Akron (O.) City Hosp., 1942-56; adminstr. Bexar County Hosp. Dist., San Antonio, 1956-67; adminstr. Harris County Hosp. Dist., Houston, 1967-69; adminstrv. cons. Methodist Hosp. Houston, 1969-75. Mem. adv. council on health aspects of civil def. Tex. Dept. Health, 1964-75; past pres. Greater Houston Hosp. Council. Recipient Modern Hosp. Gold medal for significant contbn. to hosp. lit., 1942. Fellow Am. Coll. Hosp. Adminstrs. (life); mem. Am., Tex. (past pres.) hosp. assns., Nat. League Nursing (past Tex. bd.). Contbr. articles to profl. jours. Home: Houston, Tex. Died Mar. 26, 1975.

FORT, CARL ALLEN, pub. co. exec.; b. Kenney, Ill., Apr. 23, 1916; s. Carl Everett and Hazel (Burns) F.; B.S., Ill. Wesleyan U., 1939; M.A., U. Ill., 1947; m. Dorothy May Keys, Sept. 12, 1941; children—Allen Keys, Darwin Dale. Supt. schs. Libertyville (Ill.) High Sch., 1952-59; dir. finance and statistics Office of State Supt. Pub. Instrn., Springfield, 1959-63; v.p. adminstrn. L.W. Singer pubs., Syracuse, N.Y., 1963-67; v.p. editorial Follett Ednl. Corp., pubs., Chgo., 1967-73. Served with USMCR, 1942-46. Mem. Am. Assn. Sch. Adminstrs., Assn. Supervision Curriculum Devel., Nat. Council Tchrs. English, Nat. Assn. Elementary Sch. Prins., Theta Xi. Methodist. Elk. Home: Glen Ellyn Woods, Ill. Died 1973.

FORT, GEORGE HUDSON, naval officer; b. Lumpkin, Ga., Aug. 23, 1891; s. George and Martha Rebecca (Carter) F.; B.S., U.S. Naval Acad.; 1912; m. Edythe Nevins McQuade, Nov. 6, 1915; 1 dau., Betty Carter. Commd. ensign, U.S. Navy, 1912, advancing through the grades to rear adm., 1942, later to vice adm.; comdt. 13th Naval Dist., Seattle, Washington, 1946-48; office of Sec. Navy and chmn. gen. bd., 1948-51; comdt. Potomac River Naval Command 1951-53. Decorated Navy Cross, Legion of Merit, Distinguished Service Medal; Order Orange Nassau with sword (Netherlands). Clubs: Chevy Chase (Md.); Army and Navy (Washington). Home: Washington, D.C. Died July 21, 1975; buried Arlington Nat. Cemetery.

FORTIER, LOUIS J., army officer, ret.; b. Gretna, La., Apr. 8, 1892; s. Joseph E. and Estelle Marguerite (Le Beuf) F.; B.C.E., Tulane. U., 1913, D.Sc., 1942; M.S. summa cum laude (in international relations), Ala. Poly. Inst., 1923; grad. F.A. Sch., 1927, Command and Gen. Staff Sch., 1933, Army War Coll., 1936, Ecole Superieure de Guerre, Paris, France, 1939; m. Solidelle Felicite Renshaw, Sept. 5, 1918; children—Solidelle Felicite, Louis Renshaw, Margot Helene. C.E., Rivers and Harbors, 1913-17; commd. 2d lt., F.A., U.S. Army, Aug. 8, 1917, and advanced through the grades to brig. gen., Aug. 1942; served with 17th F.A., 2d Div., A.E.F., 1917-18; mil. attaché, Belgrade, Yugoslava, 1939-41; comd. 94th Div. Arty., 1942-45; mem. mil. staff com. U.N., 1945-46, asst. dir. central intelligence group, Feb.-July 1946; dir. intelligence div. Armed Forces Staff Coll., Norfolk, Va., 1946-49; dir. Theater intelligence div., Far East Command, 1949-50, retired Dec. 1950; writer and lectr., 1951-74; contbr. N. Am. Newspaper Alliance, 1954-58; dep. state dir. La. Civil Defense Agency, 1955; director Louisiana Survival Project, 1956-59. President Vieux Carre' Property Owners, 1960-61; dir. of Mid-Southern Life Insurance Company. Decorated D.S.M., Legion of Merit, Bronze Star Medal (United States), Victory Medal, 3 stars, European Theater, 4 stars. Comdr. Order of Karageorge, Order White Eagle (Yugoslavia), George I (Greece), Legion of Honor, Croix de Guerre with palm and bronze star (France), Comdr. Order White Lion, War Cross (Czechoslovakia), Croix de Guerre with palm (Belguim). Registered professional engineer. Mem. S.A.R. (v.p. La. society), Military Order World Wars (chmn. legislative com.), Soc. War 1812, Assn. des Amis de l'Ecole Superieure de Guerre, Am. Legion, C. of C., Sons and Daus. Founders New Orleans (charter), Phi Delta Theta. Clubs: Army and Navy, Carabao (Washington); Boston (New Orleans); Fairfax (Va.) Hunt. Home: New Orleans, La. Died Nov. 1974.

FORTMILLER, HUBERT CLARE, dentist; b. Portland, Ore., Aug. 3, 1901; s. Fred and Annie Laurie (Lee) F.; D.M.D., U. Ore., 1924; postgrad. Forsythe Dental Infirmary, 1925; m. Laura Eve Pollina, Jan. 29, 1926; children—Frederick Vincent, Hubert Clare. Clin. work Hull St. Med. Mission, Boston, 1925-27; individual practice dentistry, Brookline, Mass., 1927-68, Wellesley, Mass., from 1968. Mem. Am., Mass. dental assns., Brookline Dental Soc. (past pres.), Xi Psi Phi (nat. supreme pres.), Omicron Kappa Upsilon. Mason (32 deg.). Club: Brae Burn Country (West Newton, Mass.). Home: Wellesley, Mass. Deceased.

FOSCO, PETER, union exec.; b. Russia, May 13, 1892; s. Vincent and Antonia Fosco; student U. Ill.; m. Carmela Stantucci, Dec. 3, 1916; children—Angelo, James. Financial exec. sec. Local Union 2 Laborers' Internat. Union of North Am., Chgo., 1916-20, pres., 1920-38, mgr. Chgo. regional office, 1936-68, gen. sec.-treas., 1950-68, gen. pres., Washington, 1968-75; v.p. AFL-CIO, 1st v.p. Bldg & Constrn. Trades Dept. Democratic ward committeeman, Chgo., Democratic commr. Cook County, 1938-46. Named Man of the Year, Amerita Soc., 1972. Mem. Italian Soc., K. of C. Democratic. Roman Catholic. Club: Democratic. Home: Chicago Ill., Died Oct. 26, 1975.

FOSS, MARTIN MOORE, publisher; b. Lewiston, Me., June 3, 1878; s. Savillian Fuller and Nellie Juliet (Moore) F.; prep. edn. Thornton Acad., Saco, Me.; A.B., Harvard, 1900; grad. work same univ., 1900-01; m. Sara Bush Bullard, June 1, 1929. In charge pub. dept. Baker & Taylor Co., New York, 1901-07; manager book dept. Hill Pub. Co., 1907-09; organizer, and sec. McGraw-Hill Book Co., Inc., 1909-17, v.p., 1917-27, pres. Jan. 1, 1927-Feb. 19, 1944; vice chmn. bd., 1944; dir. McGraw-Hill Pub. Co. Mem. Delta Upsilon. Republican. Clubs: Players, University, Engineers, Sleepy Hollow Country (New York). Home: New York, N.Y.†

FOSTER, ADRIANCE S., educator; b. Poughkeepsie, N.Y., Aug. 6. 1901; s. Raymond and Alice (Adriance) F.; B.S., Cornell U., 1923; S.M., Harvard, 1925, Sc.D., 1926; m. Helen N. Vincent, July 29, 1930; 1 son, Richard V. Asst. prof. U. Okla., 1928-34; prof. botany U. Cal. at Berkeley, also chmn. dept. botany, prof. botany emeritus 1968-73. NRC fellow, 1926-28; NSF fellow, 1963-64; Guggenheim fellow, 1941, 48. Mem. Internat. Soc. Plant Morphologists (pres. exec. council 1970-73), Am. Inst. Biol. Sci., A.A.A.S., Bot. Soc. Am., Acad. Arts and Sci., Cal. Acad. Scis., Cal. Native Plant Soc., Zoologische Botannical Gesellschaft (hon.), Sigma Xi. Author: Practical Plant Anatomy, 1942, 2d edit.; 1974; (with E.M. Gifford, Jr.) Comparative Morphology of Vascular Plants, 1959. Contbr. articles to sci. jours. Home: Berkeley, Cal. Died May 1, 1973.

FOSTER, CEDRIC, pub. relations exec.; b. West Hartford, Conn., Aug. 31, 1900; s. Arthur Leon and Josephine (Wilkinson) F.; student Dartmouth Coll., 1920-21, 1922-23; D.Litt., Southwestern U., Georgetown, Tex., Carthage (Ill.) College; LL.D. (hon.), John Brown U.; m. Marguerite Lane, Dec. 12, 1921; children—Shirley Plummer (Shirley Foster Fields), Sarah Ann H. (Mrs. Peter Carpenter). With Hartford (Conn.) Courant and Asso. Press, San Francisco, 1923-25; Conn. mgr. United Press, 1925-26; with New Britain (Conn.) Herald, Waterbury (Conn.) Am. and Providence Jour., 1926-29; financial editor Hartford (Conn.) Times, 1929-35; mgr. radio sta. WTHT, Hartford, 1935-41; news commentator MBS, 1940-67; news commentator radio sta. KTLN and Intermountain Network, Denver, 1967-69, KFML, 1969-70; pub. relations Farland-Buell Chrysler Plymouth, Denver, also Glenco Devel. Corp., Evergreen and Glenwood Springs, Colo., 1970-75. Decorated Comdr. of the Royal Order Phoenix, comdr. of the Royal Order of King George I (Greece); Order of Homayoun (Iran); officer of the Royal Order Orange-Nassau (The Netherlands); recipient plaque for 25 years distinguished service to broadcasting Nat. Assn. Broadcasters, 1963. Mem. Phi Sigma Kappa, Sigma Delta Chi, Order Ahepa. Club: Denver Press. Home: Denver, Colo. Died Mar. 1975.

FOSTER, CLYDE TANNER, bus. exec.; b. Cleveland, Feb. 9, 1893; s. Henry E. and Julia (Tanner) F.; A.B., Western Res. U., 1917, LL.D., 1950; LL.B., Cleveland-Marshall Law School of Baldwin-Wallace College, 1922, LL.D., 1966; LL.D., Fenn College, Cleveland, 1958; married Lyla Coleman, June 19, 1926; children—Coleman A., Byron T. Employe trust dept. Garfield Bank & Cleveland Trust Co., 1919-22; asst. mgr. credit dept. The Higbee Co., 1922-23; admitted to Ohio bar, 1922, and practiced as asso. law firm of Friebolin & Byers, 1923-29; mgr. service stations, mgr. operations, mgr. marketing research, asst. to v.p. sales Standard Oil Co. (O.), 1929-42; asst. to pres., 1942, asst. to pres. and mgr. indsl. relations, 1943-46, vice pres. finance and accounting, 1946-48, dir., 1946-63, exec. vice pres., 1948, pres., 1949-57, chmn. 1956-60, ret. as chmn., now hon. chmn. and cons.; dir. Ferro Corp. (Cleve.). Trustee YMCA (life), Fairview Park Hosp., Children's Aid Soc., Zoological Soc.; chmn. board trustees Western Reserve University; pres. United Appeal, 1959; member of advisory board Salvation Army (all Cleveland). Served as 1st lt. infantry U.S. Army, 1917-19. AEF. Member American Petroleum Institute (hon. director 1960), Phi Gamma Delta. Clubs: Union, Westwood Country, Pepper Pike Country, Clifton, Fifty (Cleve.). Home: Lakewood, Ohio. Died June 23, 1975.

FOSTER, JOHN WINTHROP, stock broker; b. Boston, Sept. 15, 1880; s. Hatherly and Emma (Bickford) F.; B.S., Harvard, 1903; m. Ruth C. Thomas, Sept. 1, 1906; children—Sumner Hatherly, Helen Carolyn (Mrs. William F. Watkins). Mgr. Nyala Farm, Greens Farms, Conn., from 1941; partner Paine, Webber, Jackson & Curtis, stock brokers, N.Y. City, from 1942. Mem. N.Y. Stock Exchange. Home: Greens Farms, Conn.†

FOSTER, JOSEPH C., mfg. co. exec.; b. 1906; married. Pres., chief exec. officer Foster Grant Co. Inc., Leominster, Mass., 1943-69, chmn. bd., chief exec. officer, from 1969, also dir. Office: Leominster, Mass., Deceased.*

FOSTER, JOSEPH FRANKLIN, biochemist, educator; b. Marion, Ind., May 17, 1918; s. DeWitt L. and Grace (Cameron) F.; B.S., Ia. State U., 1940, Ph.D., 1943; m. Ruth E. Hobson, June 8, 1940; children—Ann E. (Mrs. Harald L. Lohn), Gregory H., Michael C. Postdoctoral fellow Med. Sch., Harvard, 1943-45; research chemist Am. Maize Products Co., Roby, Ind., 1945-46, cons., 1948-59; faculty Ia. State U., 1946-54; mem. faculty Purdue U., Lafayette, Ind., 1954-75, prof., 1957-75, head dept. chemistry, 1967-75. Cons. Central Research Labs. Gen. Foods Corp., 1960-63, NIH, 1962-66, Army Q.M.C., 1963-64, Dow Biol. Labs., 1972-75. Mem. Am. Chem. Soc. (Joseph F. Foster Meml. Symposium 1976), Am. Soc. Biol. Chemists, Biophys. Soc., A.A.A.S., Am. Assn. U. Profs., Sigma Xi, Phi Lambda Upsilon, Phi Kappa Phi. Author: (with S.W. Fox) Introduction to Protein Chemistry, 1957. Contbr. articles to profl. jours. Home: West Lafayette, Ind., Died Oct. 6, 1975; interred Tippecanoe Memory Gardens, West Lafayette, Ind.

FOSTER, TED, univ. dean; b. Seward, Neb., Dec. 23, 1903; s. Charles Delmer and Bertha Hope (Daves) F.; LL.B., Oklahoma City U., 1937; LL.D., Cleveland-Marshall Law Sch., 1962; m. Alma Bernice Collier, Oct. 11, 1924; children—Ted, Olive Hope (Mrs. Dan T. Gray). Dept. sheriff Okla. County, 1928-38; admitted to Okla. bar, 1937; practice in Oklahoma City, 1938-56; instr. Office Civil Def., 1940-45; prof. Sch. Law, Oklahoma City U., 1956-60, dean from 1968. Dir., v.p. Air Center, Inc. Chmn. Oklahoma City Bd. Adjustment; mem. Oklahoma County Excise and Equalization Bd., 1970; mem. Gov. Okla. Adv. Com. Law Enforcement, 1934-36. Mng. trustee Meml. Park Cemetery Assn., 1950-76. Mem. Am., Okla., Oklahoma County (bd. dirs. 1948) bar assns., Am. Judicature Soc., Am. Civil Liberties Union, UN Assn. Mason (32°, Jester). Author-editor: Municipal Taxation, 1965. Home: Oklahoma City, Okla., Died Jan. 30, 1976.

FOSTER, VERNON WHIT, lawyer; b. Norwalk, O., Jan. 16, 1881; s. John Whitbeck and Clara (Morehouse) F.; LL.B., Chicago-Kent Coll., Law, 1902; m. Emilie Flanley, Oct. 24, 1908; children—Jane (Mrs. C. V. Wisner, Jr.), John Whitbeck; m. 2d, Elizabeth Bern, Dec. 6, 1924. Admitted to Ill. bar, 1902, and began practice at Chicago; trial atty. Ill. Central R.R. Co., Chicago, 1906-28, dist. atty., 1928-31, general attorney, 1932-33, general solicitor, 1933-42; general counsel and director 1942-45; vice pres., gen. counsel and dir., 1945-51; chmn. Ill. R.R. Assn., from 1951. Mem. Am., Ill., Chgo. bar Assns., Am. Judicature Soc., Assn. Am. Railroads (law com.); past pres. Western Conference Railway Counsel, Ohio Soc. of Chicago, Delta Chi. Republican. Episcopalian. Mason (K.T. Shriner), Elk. Clubs: Chicago, Chicago Athletic, Traffic (Chicago). Home: Chicago, Ill.†

FOSTER, WALTER HERBERT, lawyer; b. LaGrange, Me., Mar. 31, 1880; s. Ernest Montgomery and Caroline (Banton) F.; ed. Harvard Coll.; LL.B., U. of Me., 1905, LL.M., 1914; m. Gertrude Sullivan, Brookline, Mass., Oct. 23, 1909; children—Daphne (Mrs. George Maes Henderson), Walter Herbert Jr., Richard Channing. Mem. law firm MacPherson & Foster, also atty. for Boston Elevated Ry. Co., 1907-10; mem. firm Foster & Colby, 1910-18; practiced alone, Boston, 1919-42; associated with Robert J. Holmes, 1936-42; acted as spl. asst. to atty. gen. of Mass.; chmn. Center Boston Cancer Control Com. (affiliated state bd. of health), 1940-42; mem. Draft Advisory Bd.; Chief Compliance Commr. W.P.B., Washington, 1942-45, Civilian Prodn. Adminstrn., 1945-46, Office of Housing Expediter, 1946-47; resumed practice of law, Boston, 1948; asst. atty. gen. Commonwealth of Mass., and counsel to State Housing Bd. Veterans Housing Program, 1948-49; chief hearing commissioner, NPA, Washington, 1951-53; private practice law, Boston, from 1958. Mem. Soc. Colonial Wars. Republican. Episcopalian. Clubs: Union, Harvard (Boston). Author Administrative Procedure WPB; Promoters' Liability to the Corporation. Home: South Lyndeborough, N.H.†

FOWLER, LAURA, educator; b. Baltimore Co., Md., Apr. 1878; d. Frederick and Mary Hanson (Rosseter) F.; grad. Bryn Mawr Sch., Baltimore, 1897; B.A., Bryn Mawr Coll., 1901; studied Columbia. Teacher Springside Sch., Chestnut Hill, Mass., 1901-02, high sch., Parkersburg, W.Va., 1903-05; asst. to prin. Shipley Sch., Bryn Mawr, Pa., 1908-15; teacher Bryn Mawr Sch., Baltimore, 1916-24; prin. St. Margaret's Sch., Tappahannock, Va., 1924-26; prin. Hannah More Acad., Reistertown, Md., from 1926. Democrat. Episcopalian. Home: Reistertown, Md.†

FOWLER, WILLIAM ERIC, b. Roswell, Ga., Sept. 28, 1874; s. John Calhoun and Emma (Paden) F.; ed. pub. schools, Md. Inst.; studied law, U. of Md. (non-grad.); m. Mrs. Edwin T. Earl, July 27, 1921. Banking business, Va., W.Va. and Washington, D.C.; was v.p. Va. Bankers Assn., 1908, and v.p. W.Va. Bankers Assn., 1909. Served at lt. col., Ordnance Dept., U.S. Army, World War: asst. comdg. officer Port of Boston; later mem. Ordnance Dept. Claims Bd., Washington, D.C., after the war, assisting in settling claims amounting to some $2,000,000,000. Apptd. by President Harding mem. U.S. delegation to 5th Pan-Am.Conf., Santiago, Chile, Mar.-Apr. 1923; del. to Rep. Nat. Conv., 1928, 32; chmn. Los Angeles County Rept. Com. Mem. S.A.R. Republican. Episcopalian. Clubs: Army and Navy, University (Washington). Address: Miami, Fla.†

FOX, AUGUSTUS HENRY, educator; b. Mansfield, O., Sept. 28, 1902; s. Ferdinand Henry and Mary Josephine (Troll) F.; A.B., Adelbert Coll., Western Res. U., 1925; M.A. in Physics, Oberlin Coll., 1927; M.A. in Math., Harvard, 1929; Ph.D., Yale, 1935; m. Katharine Bird Eckert, Sept. 8, 1928; 1 dau., Yvonne Elizabeth (Mrs. Norman Lester Dobyns). Instr., Oberlin Coll., 1925-27, Harvard, 1927-29, Yale, 1931-32; prof. Union Coll., Schenectady, 1929-68, chmn. dept. math., 1958-67. Trustee Dudley Obs. Mem. Am. Math. Soc., Am. Rocket Soc., Am. Assn. U. Profs., Fedn. Am. Scientists (chmn. 1958-59), Math. Assn. Am., Am. Nuclear Soc., Phi Beta Kappa, Sigma Xi, Phi Gamma Delta. Mem. Reformed Ch. (elder). Club: Edison (Schenectady). Author: (with others) Applied Atomic Power, 1946; Fundamentals of Numerical Analysis, 1963. Home: Silver Spring, Md. Died June 15, 1975.

FOX, CHARLES WELFORD, naval officer; b. Balt., Dec. 5, 1894; s. Henry William and Mary Ella (Gressit) F.; ed. in pub. schs., Balt., m. Aida Moore Smith, Apr. 30, 1919; children—Virginia Rachael (Mrs. K.C. Wydler), Mary Ellen, Charles Welford. Enlisted in U.S. Navy, 1913, apptd. pay clk., 1917; commd. ensign supply corps, Dec. 12, 1918, advanced through grades to vice adm.; served at Naval Air Sta., Moutchic, Lacanau, 1918, also with No. Bombing Group, Autiques, Pas de Calais, U.S. Naval Tng. Camp, Deer Island, Mass., 1918-19, Naval Air Sta., Cape May, N.J., 1919-20; charge aviation supply div. Bur. Supplies and Accounts, Washington, 1942-44; asst. aviation supply officer Aviation Supply Office, Phila., 1944-45; supply officer in command Navy Supply Depot, Mechanicsburg, 1945-48; apptd. dep. and asst. chief Bur. Supplies and Accounts, Navy Dept., 1948, chief and paymaster gen., 1949-51, chief of naval materiel, 1951-53, ret. Pres. emeritus bd. trustees St. Luke's and Children's Med. Center, Phila. Decorated Legion of Merit (with gold star). Republican. Episcopalian. Home: Silver Spring, Md., Died Nov. 4, 1975.

FOX, DONALD L., wholesale grocery co. exec.; b. Newport, Ky., Feb. 20, 1921; s. Stuart Charles and Eleanor (Pfirrman) F.; B.A., Va. Mil. Inst., 1943; m. Elizabeth Ann Berry, May 23, 1943; children—Donald L. (dec.), Stuart Charles II, Marion Berry. Asst. to pres. Duffy Mott Co., N.Y.C., 1948-49; v.p. Stuart Fox Food Brokers, Inc., Dayton, O., 1946-47, partner, 1950-66, pres., dir., 1967; chmn. bd. Fox-King Oil Co., 1955-57; pres. Marketing Corp., Columbus, O., 1964; exec. cons., dir. Super Food Services, Inc., Chgo., 1967, vice chmn., 1967-68, chmn., chief exec. officer, Dayton, 1968-72; chmn. Schaefers' Bakery Co., Springfield, O., 1968, Foodway Properties, Inc., 1968-69, Foodway Corp., 1968-69, F.H. Cobb Co., Syracuse, N.Y., Fame Marketing Corp., Dayton; dir. Grocers' Corp., Chgo., Ind. Grocers' Alliance, Distributing Corp., Marvin Burick Advt. & Pub. Relations, Inc., Dayton, Creative Marketing Corp., Indpls., Venice Maid Co., Inc., Vineland, N.J., N.Am. Sounds Co., Las Vegas, F.L.D. Corp., Dayton, Delhi Discount Foods, Inc., Cin., others; partner Lakeview Ranch Coachella Valley, Cal., 1969-70; dir. Fisher Cheese Co., Wapakoneta, O. Cons. Ted Gotthelf & Assos., N.Y.C., 1968-69, Nysco Labs., Inc., Long Island, N.Y., 1968-69, Grocer's Graphic Publ., N.Y.C., 1968-69, Lennen & Newell Advt. Agy., N.Y.C., 1968-70; adviser to chmn. and pres. Mut. Broadcasting Corp., Beverly Hills, Cal., 1968-71. Mem. Pres.'s Com. Mental Retardation, 1970-72. Campaign chmn. Republican Finance Com., Montgomery County, O., 1952-53; dist. chmn. Citizens for Eisenhower Congressional Com., 1954, Citizens for Eisenhower-Nixon, 1956; mem. Citizens Com. for Hoover Commn. Report, 1956-57; mem. Ohio Republican Resources Com., 1969; mem. Ohio Rep. Finance Com., 1969-70; Rep. finance chmn. Montgomery County, O., 1969-70, mem. exec. com., 1969-70. Trustee, v.p. Loren M. Berry Found., IGA, Inc.; trustee, pres. Found. for a Better Am., Dayton. Served to capt. AUS, 1943-46. Mem. UN Assn. Episcopalian. Clubs: Hundred, Dayton (O.) Country; Racquet Internat. (Miami Beach, Fla.); Runaway Bay (Harbour Island, Fla.); Palm Bay (Miami, Fla.); Surf (Surfside Fla.); Executive's, Bay Hill (Orlando, Fla.); Le Club internat. (Fort Lauderdale). Home: Oakwood, O. Died Nov. 9, 1972.

FOX, DONALD RICHARD, pathologist; b. Moscow, Ida., Jan. 16, 1927; s. James H. and Margaret (Russell) F.; M.D., Loyola U., 1952; m. Mary Lu Erhard, Jan. 27, 1951; children—Margaret, Martin J., Nora M., Julie A., Mary P., Kathleen M., Patrick V., Michael T. Intern, Cook County (Ill.) Hosp., Chgo., 1952-53, resident in pathology, 1953-54, asst. in pathology, 1954-56; asst. in pathology Hines VA Hosp., Maywood, Ill., 1956-57, St. Joseph., Chgo., 1957-58; pathologist Highland Park (Ill.) Hosp., Lake Forest (Ill.) Hosp., Lake County Tb San., Waukegan, Ill., 1958-63; dir. lab. Alexian Bros. Hosp., Chgo., 1963-68; dir. lab. Alexian Bros. Med. Center, Elk Grove Village (Ill.), 1966-73, chief of staff, 1966-67. Instr. pathology Northwestern U., 1958-71; instr. med. tech. Harper Coll., 1972-73. Bd. dirs. North Suburban unit Am. Cancer Soc., North Suburban Blood Center; mem. bd. councilors St. Alexis. Served with AUS, 1944-47. Diplomate Am. Bd. Pathology. Fellow Am. Soc. Clin. Pathologists; mem. Coll. Am. Pathologists Assn. Clin. Scientists, A.M.A. Home: Barrington Hills, Ill., Died July 24, 1973; buried All Saints Cemetery, Des Plaines, Ill.

FOX, ROBERT MYRON, educator; b. Detroit, Apr. 23, 1876; s. William Henry and Caroline Amanda (White) F.; B.S. in civil engring., So. Calif., 1927; m.

Susan J. Dorrance, Aug. 26, 1902 (died Aug. 7, 1947); m. 2d Rachel Gilmore Head, May 20, 1949. Computer U.S. Deep Waterways, N.Y., 1898-99; asst. engr. Chicago & West Mich. Ry., Mich., 1899-1900; asst. bridge engr., M.C. R.R., 1900-11; cons. engr., Phoenix, Ariz, 1911-12; structural engr., smelters, Ariz., 1912-18, 1920-22; asst. prof. of civil engring., U. of Southern Calif., 1922-27, chmn. dept. from 1923, prof., from 1927; cons. engr., from 1945. Served as capt. C.E., U.S. Army. 1918-20; capt. Reserves until 1929. Mem. Am. Soc. C.E., Am. Assn. U. Profs., Sigma Phi Delta, Chi Epsilon. Conglist. Home: Laguan Beach, Cal.†

FRACHON, BENOIT, union ofcl.; b. Chambon-Feugerolles, Loire, France, May 13, 1893; s. Jean Benoit and Claudine (Drevet) F.; student elementary sch.; m. Marie Louise Pealat, Apr. 21, 1925; 1 son, Henri. Metall. worker; militant unionist; mem. Socialist party, 1919; sec. Metal Workers Union Chambon-Feugerolles, 1922-24; sec. Dept. Loire Fedn. Trades-Union, 1924-26; regional organising sec. Communist party, 1926-28, mem. central com., 1926-75, nat. sec. party, 1928-33, 39; sec. Confedn. Gen. du Travail Unitaire, 1933-36; sec. Confedn. Gen. du Travail, 1936-39, 44-45, sec. gen., 1945-67, pres., 1967-75. Address: Paris, France. Died Aug. 4, 1975.

FRAME, NORMAN RENVILLE, electric exec.; b. N.Y. City, 1895; s. William H. and Emily I. M. (Frame) F.; grad. N.Y. Law Sch., 1918; m. Dorothy Livingston, June 6, 1922; children—Norman Renville, Henry Livingston. Pvt. practice law, 1920-23; atty. Western Electric Co., Inc., 1923-25, 28-32, 36-43, asst. sec., 1943, sec. after 1943; atty., sec. Graybar Electric Co., Inc., 1926-27; atty. Elec. Research Products, Inc., 1932-36. Material insp. U.S. Army Signal Corps, 1918-19. Home: New York City, N.Y., Died Feb. 22, 1976.

FRANCE, MARY ADELE, educator; b. Chestertown, Md., Feb. 17, 1880; d. Thomas Dashiell and Emma Price (deCorse) F.; grad. Washington Coll. Prep. Sch., Chestertown, Md., 1896; B.A., Washington Coll., 1900, M.A., 1902; M.A., Teachers Coll. (Columbia), 1923. Teacher in own pvt. sch., 1901-07; tchr. sci. and math. St. Mary's Sem., Md., 1900-13; Bristol Sch., Washington, 1913-14, St. Mary's Sem., 1917-18; supervisor elementary schs., Kent Co., Md., 1918-20, Shelby Co., Tenn., 1920-22; prin. St. Mary's Sem., 1923-37, name changed to St. Mary's Female Sem.-Junior Coll., 1937, pres. from 1937. Mem. Am. Assn. Univ. Women, Am. Assn. Sch. Adminstrs., Jr. Coll. Council of Middle States, Assn. Deans of Women and Advisers of Girls, N.E.A., Teachers College Alumni, D.A.R. Ind. Democrat. Episcopalian. Home: St. Mary's City, Md.†

FRANCIS, WARREN BRIGGS, writer; b. Taunton, Mass., July 15, 1908; s. Percy Franklin and Alice (Warren) F.; A.B., Brown U., 1929; m. Lorania Carrington King, Aug. 31, 1929; 1 dau., Janet (Mrs. Robt. P. Midgett). Reporter Taunton Gazette, 1923, and worked during high sch. and coll. on Gazette, Providence (R.I.) Tribune, Providence Journal; mem. suburban staff Provicence Journal and Bulletin, 1929-30; member staff U.S. Daily, Washington, 1930-31; member Washington Bureau, Detroit Free Press, 1932-32; publicity work, 1932; Washington corr. Los Angeles Times, 1932-54; mem. staff Senator Thomas H. Kuchel (Cal.), from 1954. Mem. Phi Beta Kappa, Phi Kappa Psi, Sigma Delta Chi. Clubs: Nat. Press (pres. 1947), Brown (Washington). Author articles miscellaenous publs. Home: Washington, D.C., Died Oct. 20, 1975.

FRANCISCO, DON, advertising and public relations; b. Lansing, Mich., Oct. 18, 1891; s. Will and Lillian (Burgdorf) F.; B.S., Mich. State Univ., 1914. A.M. (hon.), 1923, Sc.D. (hon.), 1949; m. Constance Little, Oct. 27, 1915; 1 son. Don. Fruit inspector, Chicago office of California Fruit Growers Exchange (name now changed to Sunkist Growers), 1914-15, assistant advertising manager, 1915-16, advertising mgr., Los Angeles, 1916-21; with Lord & Thomas, advt. agency, 1921-40, as co-mgr. Los Angeles office, 1921-24, v.p. and Pacific Coast mgr., 1924-38, pres., N.Y.C., 1938-40; dir. Radio div. Office of Coordinator of Inter-American Affairs, Washington, 1940-43, organized Voice of Am. in Eastern hempisphere, 1940-45, asst. co-ordinator, 1943-45; v.p., director J. Walter Thompson Co., N.Y.C., 1945-56, retired Mar. 31, 1956; vis. lecturer Michigan State University, 1956-57; radio cons. State Department, 1945-46; cons. Dept. Commerce, 1957. Vice chairman, dir. Brand Names Found., 1952-55, pres. Hollywood Baseball Club, 1937-38. Trustee Mich. State U. Developemnt Fund, 1956-58, Internat. House (N.Y.C.), 1959-73. Mem. U.S. Com., mass media UNESCO, 1945-46; treas., dir. Nat. Com. on Alcoholism; has served as pres. of Pacific Advt. Clubs' Assn., 1923-24; pres. Advertising Club of Los Angeles, 1920-21; pres. Pacific Advt. Agencies Assn., 1927-28; vice pres. Asso. Advertising Clubs of the World, 1921-23; mem. Bd. of Govs. of Am. Assn. Advertising Agencies, 1937-39, 1940-41; dir. Assn. Nat. Advertisers, 1920-21; dir. Advertising Fedn. of America, 1928-32; dir. Nat. Outdoor Advt. Bur., 1925-30. Mem. Pacific Advt. Assn. (hon. life mem.), Scabbard and Blade, Alpha Delta Sigma, Alpha Zeta Alpha Omega, Republican, Episcopalian, Club: Advertising of Los Angeles (hon. life mem.); University, Cloud (N.Y.C.); Amagansett (L.I.) Beach, Maidstone (East Hampton. L.I.). Contbr. articles on advt., pub. relations, distrn. and co-operative marketing to bus. publs. Home: Amagansett NY. Died Oct. 24, 1973.

FRANCO BAHAMONDA, FRANCISCO, head of Spanish State; b. El Ferrol, Prov. of Corunna, Spain, Dec. 4, 1892; s. Nicolas Franco Salgado-Araujo and Piler Bahamonde Pardo; grad. Inf. Acad., 1907; attended course for officer of various nations, Paris and Verdun, France, 1930; m. Carmen Polo y Martinez de Valdes, Oct. 16, 1923; 1 dau., Carmen (Marquesa de Villaverde). Entered mil. career with rank of 2d lt. inf.; advanced to brig. gen., 1926; served with distinction in Africa; pres. of commn. which organized Gen. Mil. Acad. of Saragossa, 1927, dir. of the acad., 1928-31 (with it was suppressed by the Republic); comd. 15th Inf. Brigade, Corunna, 1932; apptd. mil. comdr. of the Balearies, 1933; promoted maj. gen., 1934; comdr. in chief of the forces in Morocco, Feb.-May 1935, chief of gen. staff, May 1935, comdr. in chief Canary Islands, 1936. Assumed leadership of mil. forces in Africa which rebelled against the Republican govt. in Spain, and conducted campaign in continental Spain 1936; by decree of Council of Nat. Def., apptd. head of Spanish State and Generalissimo of Land, Sea and Air Forces, Sept. 1936, and served as such during Spanish Civil War, 1936-39 and 1940-75; reorganized parliament under name of Cortes Espanolas, 1942; approved Spain's Constl. Charter, 1945; by general referndum the law of succession to headship of the state was approved, 1947. Decorated Gran Cruz Laureado de San Fernando, Medalla de Sufrimientos por la Patria, Cruz del Mérito Naval con distinivo rojo, Cruz del Mérito Militar con distintivo rojo, Cruz y Placa de la Real y Military Order de San Hermenogildo, and numerous other mil. and civil awards (Spain); also decorations and high honors from the govts. of other countries throughout the world. Address: Madrid, Spain., Died Nov. 20, 1975.

FRANK, HELEN SOPHIA, artist; b. Berkeley, Cal.; d. Oskar and Ada Sophia (Matson) Frank; certificate in Fine Arts, Cal. Coll. Arts and Crafts, 1937-41; student Art Students' League 1944-45; pvt. study theatre design Joseph Paget-Fredericks, painting Glenn Wessels. One-man shows Crocker Art Gallery, Sacramento, Cal., 1942, Pinacotheca, N.Y., 1943, Santa Barbara (Cal.) Mus., 1947, San Francisco Mus., 1947, Vancouver (B.C.) Art Gallery, 1949, Curacao Mus., Willenstad, N. W.I. 1949, Parson's Gallery, London, 1954, Chase Gallery, N.Y.C., 1958, Washington County Mus., Hagerstown, Md., 1961, St. Lawrence U., Canton, N.Y., 1962, Spencer Meml. Presbyn. Ch., N.Y.C., 1965, Central Unitarian Ch., Peramus, N.J., 1970, Am. Bible Soc., N.Y.C., 1972; exhibited in group shows, including San Francisco Mus. Art, Oakland (Cal.) Art Gallery, Los Angeles County Mus., Art Inst. Chgo., Milw. Art Inst., Internat. Platform Assn., Washington, Washington Cathedral, 1969. Designer dance costumes, 1940-68, costumes for Oedipus, Roundabout Theatre, N.Y.C., 1970. Illustrator for various books and publs. Address: New York City, NY. Died June 15, 1973.

FRANK, NELSON, government official; b. Buffalo, Feb. 10, 1906; s. Sigmund H. and Hattie (Friend) F.; student Coll. City of N.Y., 1925-26, U. Cal., 1927, New Sch. for Social Research; m. Tillie Miller, June 30, 1935; children—Johanna, Suzanne, William Miller. Various positions newspapers, book pubs.; book firms; joined N.Y. World-Telegram and Sun, 1944, labor columnist, 1949-56; cons., mem. staff internal security subcom. Judiciary Com. of U.S. Senate. Served as spl. agt. Office Naval Intelligence, USN, 1941-43. Home: Long Island City, NY. Died Mar. 3, 1974.

FRANK, SELBY HARNEY, army officer; b. Louisville, Aug. 15, 1891; s. Louis and Elizabeth (Harney) B.; B.S., U.S. Mil. Acad., 1913; grad. Command and Gen. Staff Sch., 1931; m. Mary McKay, Nov. 26, 1913 (dec.); children—Selby McKay, Janet Imrie (Mrs. Hugh D. Wallace), John Harney (dec.); m. 2d, Boneta Sager, Nov. 30, 1937; stepchildren Barbara Pratt (Mrs. Edward L. Jones), Jane Pratt (Mrs. Donald V. Rattan). Commd. 2d lt., U.S. Army, 1913, and advanced through the grades to brig. gen., 1945. Decorated Legion of Merit, Bronze Star Medal; Legion of Honor, Croix de Guerre (France); Comdr. British Empire. Mason. Home: San Antonio, Tex. Died Sept. 3, 1974;interred Louisville

FRANKE, ANN, indsl. designer; b. Bound Brook, N.J., Oct. 29, 1897; d. Otto M. and Marie (Lehn) Franke; student N.Y. Sch. Applied Design for Women, 1916-19, Winold Reiss Sch. Art, 1919-21, N.Y. Textile Eve. Sch., 1931-33; m. Pedro Manuel Gonzalez, Aug. 18, 1923 (dec.); 1 dau., Anita. Designer Willich Embroidery Studios, 1919-22; partner, designer Willich-Franke Studios, from 1922; instr., mem. bd. trustees Design Lab., 1934-36; instr. Cooper Union, 1936-52; cons., designer manual industries div. P.R. Indsl. Devel. Corp., 1945-46; stylist, designer upholstery div. Cohn Hall Marx, 1949-50, Golding Decorative Fabrics, 1951-53; stylist furniture fabrics Collins & Alkman, 1953-73. Exhibited works N.Y. World's Fair, San Francisco Fair, Met. Mus., Toledo Mus., Cleve. Mus., N.Y. Mus. Sci. and Industry, Phila. Art Alliance, Grand Central Palace; mem. adv. bd. N.Y. State Inst. Applied Arts and Sci., 1949-50. Recipient medal for excellence in Textile design, Am. Designer Inst. (nat. bd. trustees, treas. N.Y. chpt. chmn. membership and competitions com., nat. sec.), Indsl. Designers Assn. Am., Manhattan Miniature Camera Club. Contbr. articles profl. publs. Home: New York City, NY. Died Sept. 7, 1973.

FRANKEL, JOSEPH JEROME, hosp. dir.; b. Phila., Aug. 4, 1912; s. Victor and Rebecca (Gross) F.; B.S., Temple U., 1933, M.D., 1936; m. Reba Robins, July 8, 1937; children—Marsha (Mrs. Malcolm N. Blumenthal), Sheila (Mrs. Robert Goldman). Intern Mt. Sinai Hosp., Phila., 1936-37; asst. physician Pa. Tb Sanitarium, Mt. Altom, 1937-38; pvt. practice, Phila., 1938-39; tng. VA Hosp., Oteen, N.C., 1939-40; ward officer VA Hosp., Outwood, Ky., 1940; from ward officer to asst. chief medicine Hines VA Hosp., 1940-50; chief medicines VA Hosp., Wilkes-Barre, Pa., 1950-53; chief staff West Side VA Hosp., Chgo., 1953-59, Hines VA Hosp., 1959-61; dir. West Side VA Hosp., 1961-63, Coral Gables (Fla.) VA Hosp., 1963-64, Indpls. VA Hosp., 1964-67, West Side VA Hosp., 1967-75; prof. medicine Chgo. Med. Sch., 1954-69; lectr. medicine U. Ill., 1967-69, prof. medicine, asst. dean for Vet. Hosp. affairs, Abraham Lincoln Sch. Medicine, 1969-75. Mem. Council Teaching Hosps., Ill. Regional Med. Program, 1967-75; mem. ad hoc planning com. West Side Hosp., 1968-75; mem. Fed. Exec. Bd. and Commn. Intergovtl. Relations, 1967-75. Served to lt. col. M.C., AUS, 1942-46. Diplomate Am. Bd. Internal Medicine. Fellow A.C.P., Am. Coll. Hosp. Adminstrs., Inst. Medicine Chgo.; mem. A.M.A., Ill., Chgo. med. socs., Chgo. Soc. Internal Medicine, Assn. Mil. Surgeons, Chgo. Heart Assn., D.A.V. Mason (Shriner). Home: Chicago, Ill., Died Nov. 30, 1975.

FRANKEL, RUDOLF, architect, city planner; b. Neisse, Germany, June 14, 1901; s. Louis and Ida (Schurgast) F.; B.D.A., Tech. U. Berlin, Germany, 1923; m. Eva R. Tarrasch, June 22, 1922. Came to U.S., 1950. Ind. architect, city planner, Berlin, 1924-33, Bucharest, Rumania, 1933-37, London, Eng., 1937-50, Oxford, O., 1968-74; prof. architecture Miami U., Oxford, O., 1950-68, prof. emeritus, 1968-74; design cons. FHA, 1964. Recipient numerous awards for designs. Fellow Royal Inst. Brit. Architects; mem. Am. Inst. Planners, Am. Assn. U. Profs. Introduced and directed 1st grad. program in city design in U.S., 1954. Address: Oxford, O. Died Apr. 1974.

FRANKENBERG, LLOYD, poet, critic; b. Mt. Vernon, N.Y., Sept. 3, 1907; s. Henry and Helen (Conklin) F.; student Columbia, 1924-29; m. Loren MacIver. Mem. editorial bd. Decision, 1942, Tiger's Eye, 1947-48; dir. poetry readings Mus. Modern Art, 1950-52; mem. poetry jury Nat. Book Award, 1951; Fulbright lecturer in France, 1961-62. Recipient Spenser award, 1938, Guggenheim Found. fellowship, 1940, Carnegie grant, 1942, Acad. Arts and Letters award, 1947, Rockefeller Found. fellowship, 1952. Author: The Red Kite (poems), 1939; Pleasure Dome: On Reading Modern Poetry, 1949; Invitation To Poetry, 1956; A Round of Poems (recording), 1956. Editor: Pleasure Dome (audible anthology modern poetry, read by its creators), 1949; A James Stephens Reader, 1962; James Stephens: a Selection, 1962; James Seumas and Jacques: Unpublished Writings of James Stephens, 1964; Poems of William Shakespeare, 1966; Poems of Robert Burns, 1967; (collected poems) The Stain of Circumstance. Contbr. articles, poems, profl. and popular publs. Home: New York City, N.Y. Died Mar. 12, 1975.

FRANKENFELD, FREDERICK, clergyman; b. Concordia, Mo., Jan. 1, 1878; s. George Frederick and Louise (Stoenner) F.; student Elmhurst (Ill.) Coll., 1894-97, Eden Theol. Sem., St. Louis, Mo., 1897-1900, LL.D., 1927; m. Louise Kramer, Sept. 10, 1902; children—Helen Louise (Mrs. J. C. Slater), Alma Hildegard (Mrs. Clarke W. O'Brien), Lydia Lenore (Mrs. Merrill Lenox), Hubert Frederick. Ordained ministry Evang. Synod, 1900; missionary, Springfield, Ill., 1900-02; pastor Salem Evang. Ch., New Orleans, La., 1902-10, Salem Evang. Ch., Rochester, N.Y., 1910-34, St. Peters Evang. Ch., Elmhurst, Ill. from 1934. Home: Elmhurst, Ill.†

FRANKLIN, CHARLES THOMAS, physician; b. Niagara Falls, N.Y., Feb. 16, 1927; s. James Agustus and Sarah (Agnas) F.; M.D., Georgetown U., 1949; m. Margaret Ann Cherry, Sept. 3, 1949; children—Barbara, Peggy, James J., Mary Elizabeth, Charles Martin. Intern, Queen of Angels Hosp., Los Angeles, 1949-50; resident in obstetrics and gynecology Mercy Hosp., San Diego, 1950-61, mem. staff, 1961-71; resident in obstetrics and gynecology U.S. Naval Hosp., San Diego, 1951-52, U.S. Naval Hosp., Coronado, Cal., 1952-53; preceptorship with Dr. Purvis Martin, San Diego, 1953-55; sr. staff obstetrics and gynecology Grossmont Hosp., La Mesa, Cal.; mem. staff obstetrics and gynecology Sharp Meml. Hosp., San Diego, San Diego County Hosp., Scripps Hosp., La Jolla, Cal., College Park Hosp.; med. dir. Andy Williams Golf Tournament, 1968-71. Active Big Bros. Little League. Bd. dirs. Bayside Settlement Hosp., Salvation Army Hosp. for Unwed Mothers, Greater Sports of San Diego; trustee Century Club. Dr. Charles T. Franklin Favorite Fan award presented annually by San Diego Chargers. Served as lt. (j.g.) USNR, 1951-53. Mem. A.M.A., Southwest Obstet. and Gynecol. Soc. (past pres.), San Diego County Obstetrics and Gynecology Soc. (past pres.), San Diego Med. Soc. Home: La Mesa, Cal. Died Aug. 28, 1971; buried Holy Cross Mausoleum, San Diego.

FRANKLIN, EZRA THOMAS, college pres.; b. nr. Glensboro, Ky., Feb. 24, 1881; s. Benjamin and Katherine (Petty) F.; A.B., Asbury Coll., Wilmore, Ky., 1903; B.Pd., Valparaiso U., 1905; A.B., Ind. U., 1906, A.M., 1910; research scholar, Columbia, 1913-14; D.D., Union Coll., 1928; m. Grace Ralston, June 4, 1907; children—William Ralston, Mildred Gail, Bruce Charlton (dec.), Ezra Thomas, Mariam Josephine. Teacher in graded schs. 2 yrs. and supt. schs. 2 yrs.; dean and prof. philosophy, Asbury Coll., 1908-10; prof. of theology and philosophy, also dean and acting pres., Olivet Coll., 1910-11, pres., 1911-12; v.p. and prof. philosophy and systematic theology, Asbury Coll., 1912-15; pres. Union Coll., Barboursville, Ky., 1915-28 (developed the instn. from a primary and high sch. to a standard college); pres. Southwestern Coll from 1928. Ordained ministry M.E. Ch., 1918. Mem. Phi Delta Kappa. Republican. Methodist. Rotarian. Home: Winfield, Kan.†

FRANKLIN, JOHN MERRYMAN, steamship exec.; b. Cockeysville, Md., June 18, 1895; s. Phillip Albright Small and Laura (Merryman) F.; B.A., Harvard University, 1918; married Emily Hammond, September 7, 1922; children—Emily S., Laura M. Manager India Dept., Norton Lilly Col. 1919-27; v.p. Roosevelt Steamship Co., 1927-31; became dir., v.p., Internat. Mercantile Marine Co., 1931; pres. U.S. Lines Col., 1936-42; reentered active service as Col., 1942, promoted to maj. gen., June 1945; transportation officer in Office of Q.M. Gen., Washington, D.C., 1942; chief, Water Div., Chief of Transportation, 1942; asst. Chief of Transportation, War Dept., June 1943. Pres. U.S. Lines Co., 1946-60, chairman and chief executive committee, 1960-67, chairman, emeritus, dir., 1967-75; pres., dir. U.S. Lines (Canada), Ltd., U.S. Lines Operations, Inc., Number One Broadway Corp., Roosevelt S.S. Co.; dir. Mfrs. Trust Co., Worthington Corp., Am. S.S. Owners Protective and Indemnity Assn., Atlantic Transport Co., Ltd., Home Ins. Co., Am. Bur. Shipping, Continental Can Co., Inc. Trustee Presbyn. Hosp. Awarded Mil. Cross (Brit.); Victory Medal; D.S.M., Bronze Star Medal, European theatre, 1944. Clubs: Harvard, Racket & Tennis, Brook, Links (N.Y.C.); Piping Rock (N.Y.). Home: New York City, N.Y., also Cockeysville, Md. Died June 1975.

FRANTZ, OSWIN STRICKER clergyman, educator; b. Trumbauersville, Pa., Dec. 14, 1880; s. Alfred Singmaster and Sarah Jane (Stricker) F.; grad. Perkiomen Sem. Pennsburg, Pa., 1902; A.B., Franklin and Marshall Coll., 1905. D.D., 1925; grad. Theol. Sem. Ref. Ch. in U.S., Lancaster, Pa., 1908; B.D., Union Theol. Sem., New York, 1922; m. Alice Brubaker, Oct. 7, 1908; children—Harold Melvin, Clair Gordon, Miriam Elizabeth, Robert Oswin. Ordained ministry Ref. Ch. in U.S., 1908; pastor Memorial Ch., Easton, Pa., 1908-12, Christ Ch., Altoona, Pa., 1912-21; prof. N.T. Science, and registrar, Theol. Sem. Evangel. and Reformed Ch., Lancaster, 1922-50, prof. emeritus, from 1950. Bd. visitors Theol. Sem. Evangel. and Reformed Ch. Mem. Phi Beta Kappa, Sigma Pi, Cliosophic Society, Lancaster. Democrat. Mason. Rotarian. Home: Millersville, Pa.†

FRANTZ, VIRGINIA KNEELAND, physician; b. N.Y.C., Nov. 13, 1896; d. Yale and Anna (Ball) Kneeland; B.A., Bryn Mawr Coll., 1918; M.D., Columbia Phys. and Surg., 1922; m. Angus Macdonald Frantz, Dec. 29, 1920; children—Virginia (Mrs. Angelo Moriconi), Angus Macdonald Jr., Andrew Gibson. Successively surg. intern, attending surgeon in pathology, cons. surgeon Presbyn. Hosp., N.Y.C.; prof. emeritus surgery Columbia Phys. and Surg. Responsible investigator for devel. oxidized guase Office Sci. Research and Devel., 1942-45. Trustee Bryn Mawr Coll. Recipient Elizabeth Taylor Blackwell award N.Y. Infirmary, 1957; Janeway medal Am. Radium Soc., 1962. Diplomate Am. Bd. Pathology. Mem. N.Y. Path. Soc. (pres. 1949-51), Am. Thyroid Assn. (pres. 1960-61), A.M.A. Republican. Episcopalian. Clubs: Colony, Cosmopolitan (N.Y.C.). Author: (with Harold D. Harvey) An Introduction to Surgery, 1943; (monograph) Tumors of the Pancreas, 1959. Contbr. numerous articles to profl. jours. Major research contbns. in field of thyroid cancer, pancreatic cancer. Home: New York City, N.Y., Died Aug. 23, 1967; buried Clarendon, Vt.

FRASER, HUGH WILSON, JR., banker; b. Monticello, Fla., Feb. 4, 1904; s. Hugh Wilson and Katherine Archer (Parkhill) F.; B.S., U. of South, 1924; m. Nancy Foster, June 18, 1932; children—Nancy (Mrs. Hugh O. Pearson), Hugh Wilson III. With Citizens & So. Nat. Bank, Atlanta, 1924-70, successively asst. cashier, Savannah, Ga., asst. comptroller, Atlanta, asst. to pres., v.p. and comptroller, 1938-59, v.p. Citizens & So. Nat. Bank, exec. v.p. Citizens and So. Holding Co., pres. Citizens and So. Capital Corp., gen. v.p., 1960-70, ret., 1970; dir. Citizens & So. Nat. Bank, Citizens & So. Bank of Albany, Dublin, Newman, LaGrange, Thomaston; dir. Pamlico, Inc. Mem. Financial Execs. Inst. (nat. dir. 1962-64, So. Area v.p. 1964), Council of Profit Sharing Industries (nat. dir. 1966-67), Soc. Colonial Wars, Kappa Sigma. Clubs: Capital City, Commerce (Atlanta); Oglethorpe (Savannah, Ga.); Plantation (Hilton Head, S.C.). Home: Hilton Head Island, S.C. Died Dec. 1973.

FRASER, WILLIAM JOCELYN IAN, (Baron Fraser of Lonsdale), mem. House of Lords; b. EastBourne, Eng., Aug. 30, 1897; s. William Percy and Ellen maude (Cook) F.; student Marlborough Coll., Royal Mil. Coll., Sandhurst; m. Irene Gladys Mace, July 23, 1918; 1 dau., Jean (Hon. Mrs. Arthur Edward McDonald). Called to English bar, 1932; M.P., 1924-58, House of Lords, 1958-74; pres. Frasers Ltd., Johannesburg, S. Africa; chmn. bd. dirs. Bass Charrington Vintners Ltd. Eng., London, West End. br. Sun Alliance Ins. Group Ltd.; dir. Thomson Newspapers, S. Africa, Ltd. Chmn., St. Dunstan for Blinded Ex-Servicemen, from 1921. Served with Brit. Army, 1915-16. Named Companion of Honour; comdr. Brit. Empire, Order of Crown Belgium, Order Leopold Belgium; officer Legion of Honor; created life peer, 1958. Coubs: Flyfishers, Bath (London); Rand (Johannesburg). Author: Whereas I Was Blind, 1942; My Story of St. Dunstan's 1961. Editor: Conquest of Disability, 1956. Home: London, England., Died Dec. 29, 1974.

FRASIER, WALDO, farm bur. exec.; b. nr. Charleston, Ark., July 1, 1902; s. George Washington and Ollie Mae (Covey) F.; B.S. in Agr., U. Ark., 1924; postgrad. U. Wis., 1929-30; m. Callie Malinda Cox, Nov. 25, 1942. Instr. vocational agr., Vanndale, Ark., 1925-26; asst. county agt., Pine Bluff, Ark., 1926-27; county agrl. agt., Mena, Ark., 1927-30, Lonoke, Ark., 1930-35; exec. v.p. Ark. Farm Bur. Fedn., Little Rock, 1935, Farm Services, Inc., Farm Bur. Bldg., Inc. Member Supplies, Inc., Farm Bur. Mut. Ins. Co. Ark., Inc., Ark. Farm Bur. Investment Corp., Ark. Casualty Investment Corp. Ins. Brokerage, Inc.; dir., mem. exec. com. So. Farm Bur. Life & Casualty Ins. Cos., Jackson, Miss., Coastal Chem. Corp., Yazoo City, Miss. Exec. sec. Romco Ennis Short Meml. Found.; chmn. bd. Ark. Blue Cross and Blue Shield, Inc.; bd. dirs. Ark. chpt. Arthritis and Rheumatism Found., Asso. Industries Ark., S.W. Animal Health Research Found. Named Man of Year in Agr. for Ark., Progressive Farmer mag., 1950; recipient Distinguished Alumnus award U. Ark., 1957. Mem. Ark., Little Rock chambers commerce, Kappa Alpha, Gamma Sigma Delta. Democrat. Methodist. Home: Little Rock, Ark. Died Feb. 19, 1972.

FRASSINELLI, ATTILIO, lt. gov. Conn.; b. Stafford, Conn., Aug. 7, 1908; s. John D. and Josephine (Agnese) F.; ed. LaSalle U.; m. Mildred M. McLagan; five children. Engaged in ins. and real estate bus.; mem. Stafford Sch. Bd., 1940-48; chmn. Stafford Town Com., 1944-48; mem. Conn. Ho. of Reps., 1946-50; selectman, Stafford, 1947-59; commnr. food and drugs Conn., 1955-59; commnr. consumer protection Conn., 1959-66; lt. gov. Conn., 1966-70. Democrat. Address: Stafford Springs, Conn., Died Feb. 8, 1976.

FRAUDENDORFER, ALFRED, art dealer; b. Vienna, June 8, 1903; s. Joseph and Lina (Kainrath) F.; ed. univs. Vienna, Leipzig, Zurich; m. Jeanne Rey, 1949. Apprentice to Messrs. V.A. Heck, Vienna, antiquarian booksellers; lectr. U. Vienna; with C.G. Boerner's of Leipzig, in Zurich, from 1929; dir. L'Art Ancien SA. Mem. Antiquarische Ges., Kunsthistoriker Vereinigung, Zurcher Kunstgesellschaft, Schweizer und Zurcher Buchhäandlerverein, Vereinigung der Buchantiquare und Kupferstichhändler in der Schweiz (past pres.). Author numerous catalogues. Contbr. articles to periodicals. Address: Zurich, Switzerland. Died May 1971.

FRAZER, OSCAR BRYANT, lawyer; b. Rock Island, Ill., May 3, 1886; s. Edwin G. and Mary Elizabeth (Bryant) F.; A.B., U. of Ill., 1908; LL.B., Harvard, 1911; m. Grace Churchill, July 12, 1926; children—Edwin Churchill, Grace Elizabeth. Admitted to New York bar, 1912; practiced in N.Y. City, 1912-13 and 1930-42, San Juan, Puerto Rico, 1913-30; v.p. and attorney South Puerto Rico Sugar Co. 1942-54. Mem. Am. Bar Assn. Republican. Presbyterian. Clubs: Knickerbocker Country (Tenafly, N.J.); Englewood (N.J.); Skytop (Pa.); India House (N.Y. City. Home: Englewood, N.J. Died July 5, 1973; interred Brookside Cemetery, Englewood, N.J.

FRAZER, SPAULDING, lawyer; b. Brooklyn, N.Y., Oct. 7, 1881; s. David R. and Rose (Thompson) F.; student Newark (N.J.) Acad., 1891-97; B.S., Princeton, 1901, A.M., 1904; LL.B., N.Y. Law Sch., 1904; m. Olive Lord Hollister, Oct. 24, 1906; m. 2d, Anne Bunner Ingham, June 23, 1928. Admitted to N.Y. and N.J. bars, 1904; in pvt. practice, 1904-07; mem. firm Riker & Riker, Newark, N.J., 1907-18, Frazer & Trimble, 1926-31, Frazer, Stoffer & Jacobs from 1934; corpn. counsel City of Newark, 1915-17; has also served as counsel on numerous N.J. coms. and commns.; asso. counsel Port of N.Y. Authority (transit div.), 1928; dean Sch. of Law, U. of Newark also trustee Univ. Mem. Am., N.J. Essex Co. bar assns., American Judicature Soc., Newark Music Festival Assn. (ex-pres.). Republican. Clubs: Essex, Downtown, Carteret. Home: Bernardsville, N.J.†

FRAZIER, FRED BRENNINGS, lawyer; b. Dayton, Tenn., Sept. 2, 1880; s. Samuel and Josephene (Locke) F.; student Peabody Coll. for Teachers, Nashville, 1898-1900; LL.B., U. of Tenn., 1908; m. Virginia Benham, October 15, 1919; children—French B., Virginia Jo. Teacher, and superintendent, public schs., Rhea County, Tenn., 1900-08; admitted to Tenn. bar, 1908, and practiced at Dayton; state supervisor elementary schs., Tenn., 1910-14; practiced at Chattanooga from 1914; mem. Frazier & Roberts; spl. master in U.S. Ct. for Eastern Tenn. So. Div. City commr. of edn., Chattanooga, 1919-27. Mem. Chattanooga C. of C., Kappa Alpha. Democrat. Mason (Shriner). Clubs: Mountain City, Fairyland. Home: Chattanooga, Tenn.†

FREDERICKS, MARY PATE (MRS. GEORGE W. FREDERICKS), librarian; b. Elizabethton, Tenn., Oct. 11, 1912; d. George W. and R. Charlotte (Bozart) Pate; B.S., E. Tenn. State U., 1936; m. George W. Fredericks, July 15, 1932; 1 son, George W. III. Head librarian Mayne Williams Pub. Library, Johnson City, Tenn., 1940-72. Mem. Boone Tree Library Club (past sec.), Am., Southeastern, Tenn. library assns. Club: Johnson City Altrusa. Home: Unicoi, Tenn. Died Dec. 31, 1972.

FREDRIKS, GERRITT JAMES, lawyer; b. Cincinnati, May 24, 1882; s. Gerritt Jacobis and Sophia Emily (Oehlmann) F.; student U. Cin., Solomen P. Chase Coll.; m. Texanna Peacock, Jan. 1, 1908; children—Ruth Arkana (Mrs. Arwood Liggett), Ella Emily (Mrs. Robert D. Williamson). Admitted to Ohio bar, 1907, since practiced in Cin.; with Throndyke, Frederiks & Cappelle, 1907-12, Fredriks & Huffman, 1912-16; pvt. law practice from 1916; sr. mem. firm Fredricks & Liggett, Cin.; title officer Title Guaranty & Trust Co., 1908-09; gen. mgr. Bankers Surety Co., 1907-17. Pres. Federated Civic Assns. Hamilton Co.; chmn. bd. Food and Home Show. Lt. Inf., U.S. Army, World War I. Mem. Am. (past mem. house of dels.), Ohio State (pres. 1939-40) Cin. bar assns., Zool. Soc. Cin. (trustee, past pres.). Republican (past sec. Blaine club and past pres. Federation Republican clubs, Hamilton Co.). Mason (Shriner; past monarch, past thrice potent master; hon. mem. Sovereign Grand Insps. Gen. of 33). Club: Hyde Park Businessmen's (past pres.). Home: Cincinnati, O. Died Jan. 8, 1975.

FREE, JOSEPH PAUL, educator, archeologist; b. Cleve., Oct. 1, 1911; s. Joseph LaVerne and Enna Edith (Lamb) F.; A.B., Princeton, 1932, A.M., 1933, Ph.D., 1935; postgrad. student Oriental Inst. U. Chgo., 1940-48; m. Ruby Aldrich, Aug. 20, 1935; children—Alice Anita, David Paul. Asst. prof. archeology Wheaton Coll., 1935-40, asso. prof., 1940-43, prof. archeology, dir. archeol. studies, 1943-66, Fred McManis prof. archeology, 1955-67; staff Am. Sch. Oriental Research, excavating at Dibon in Arab Palestine, 1951, 52; dir. Wheaton archeol. expdn., excavating site of ancient Dothan in Arab Palestine, 1953-60, 62, 64; exec. dir. Nr. E. Sch. Archaeology, Mt. of Olives, Jerusalem, Jordan, 1960, 62, 64; archeol. editor Sunday School Times, 1942-64; prof. archaeology and history Bemidji State Coll., Minn., 1966-74. Member Soc. Bibl. Lit., Nat. Assn. Bible Instrs., Nat. Soc. Arts and Letters (nat. lit. chmn. 1966), Evangel. Theol. Soc., Near East Archaeol. Soc. (founder 1960), Am. Schs. Oriental Research. Author: Archeology and Bible History, rev. edit., 1969. Author articles on Bibl. archeology. Home: Freehaven Park Rapids, Minn. Died Oct. 12, 1974; buried Greenwood Cemetery, Park Rapids, Minn.

FREEBURNE, CECIL MAX, educator; b. Sublette, Kan.; Aug. 19, 1918; s. Cecil Stanley and Beatrice Montez (McCollum) F.; B.S. in Edn., Emporia (Kan.) State Tchrs. Coll., 1940; M.A., State U. Ia., 1941, Ph.D., 1948; m. Edna Louise Fleming, Aug. 10, 1941; children—Anne-Kathleen, Brian Craig. Profl. musician full time, 1936-41, part-time, 1941-58; prin., band instr., Andrew, Ia., 1941-42; supr. instrumental music, Washburn, Wis., 1942; teaching asst. psychology State U. Ia., 1946-48; mem. faculty Bowling Green State U., 1948-74, prof. psychology, 1961-74, chmn. dept., 1960-64; lectr. Ohio Acad. of Sci. vis. Scientist Program. Served with USAAF, 1942-46. Mem. Philosophy Sci. Assn., Am. Assn. of U. Profs., Am., Midwestern, Ohio psychol. assns., Sigma Xi, Psi Chi, Phi Kappa Tau. Contbr. articles profl. jours. Home: Bowling Green O. Died Feb. 19, 1974; interred Oak Grove Cemetery, Bowling Green, O.

FREED, FRED, TV news producer; b. Portland, Ore., Aug. 25, 1920; s. Edgar and Ellse (Oberdorfer) F.; B.A., Princeton, 1941; children—Lisa, Kayce. With Esquire mag., 1946-48, CBS, 1948-56, 57-61; with NBC, 1956-57, 61-75, exec. producer NBC News, 1961-75. Served USNR, 1942-46. Recipient Emmy awards, 1963-64, 65-66, 67-68, 70-71, 72-73, Peabody award, 1966, 70; Dupont Columbia award, 1969-70, 72-73. Author: (with Len Giovannitti) The Decision to Drop the Bomb, 1965. Home: New York City, N.Y. Died Mar. 31, 1974.

FREED, NETTIE S(CHWER), educator; b. Cin., July 21, 1881; d. August and Minnie (Blittersdorf) Schwer; A.B., U. of Colo., 1903; m. Charles E. Freed, Dec. 21, 1907 (died July 29, 1927); children—Charles G., Janet (Mrs. Leo Biele), Robert L., John M., Kathryn (Mrs. W. H. Stallings) Public sch. teacher, Fruita, and Pueblo, Colo., 1903-07; owned and operated Aetna Ins. Agency, Pueblo, Colo., 1927-31; county supt. of schs., Pueblo. Colo., 1931-47; state commr. of edn., State of Colo., from 1947. Mem. N.E.A., Colo. Edn. Assn., Delta

Kappa Gamma. Kappa Kappa Gamma, Adminstrv. Women in Edn. Clubs: Business and Professional Women, Zonta. Home: Denver, Colo.†

FREEDMAN, M. JOEL, dentist; b. Brest Litovsk, Russia, Oct. 15, 1903; s. Nathan David and Tonia (Charlop) F.; student Coll. City N.Y., 1921-22; D.D.S., N.Y. U., 1927; m. Florence Bernstein, June 29, 1930; children—Joanthan, Eric, Matthew. Pvt. practice dentistry, N.Y.C., 1927; faculty N.Y. U. Coll. Dentistry, 1945-73; sec., dir. Med. Letter. Mem. Protestant Welfare Council, Am. Jewish Com., Am. Jewish Congress. Fellow Am. Coll. Dentistry, Internat. Coll. Dentistry, N.Y. Acad. Dentistry, Am. Pub. Health Assn., A.A.A.S.; mem. Am. Acad. Dental Medicine, Am., N.Y. State socs. dentistry for children, others. Jewish religion. Club: City Club of N.Y. Home: New York City NY. Died Feb. 23, 1973.

FREEMAN, ARTHUR MERRIMAN, clergyman; b. Gadsden, Ala., Nov. 7, 1881; s. John W. and Mary A. (Melver) F.; A.B., Birmingham-Southern Coll., 1907, D.D., 1927; B.D., Vanderbilt U., 1911; student U. of Chicago, 1910, 18, 27, Columbia, 1929; m. Dora Newell, June 30, 1915; children—Arthur Merriman, Miriam. Teacher in normal schs., 1907-08; ordained to ministry, M.E. Ch., S., 1913; pastor First M.E. Chs. at Gadsden, Talladega, Huntsville, Tuscaloosa and Florence, Ala., 1920-34; pastor Norwood, Birmingham, 1934-39; pastor First Meth. Ch., Monroe, La., 1939-42; dist. superintendent Shreveport Dist., 1942-48; pastor 1st Methodist Church, Homer, La., 1948-50, Ponchatoula, La., from 1950. Chmn. La. Conf. World Service and Finance Commn. from 1948; vice chmn. La. Moral and Civic Found., from 1942. Mem. So. Interracial Commn.; del. Uniting Conf. Am. Methodism, Kansas City, 1939, Ecumenical Meth. Conf., Springfield, Mass., 1947. Trustee Birmingham Southern Coll., 1920-40, chmn. of bd., 1930-33; trustee Centenary Coll. of La., 1942-48. Mem. Tau Kappa Alpha, Omicron Delta Kappa, Phi Beta Kappa. Mason. Home: Ponchatoula, La†

FREEMAN, FULTON, coll. pres.; b. Pasadena, Cal., May 7, 1915; s. Robert and Margery (Fulton) F.; student Lingnan U., 1934-35; A.B., Pomona College, 1937, LL.D., 1963; postgrad. Princeton, 1937-38, Nat. War Coll., 1950-51; LL.D., Occidental Coll., 1966, Monmouth Coll., 1967; H.H.D., U. of Americas, Mexico City, Mexico, 1967; m. Phyllis Towne Eaton, Oct. 8, 1938; children—Margery Ellen, Carol, Jean. Apptd. fgn. service officer, vice consul, career sec. diplomatic service, 1939; vice consul, Mexico City, 1939; assigned Fgn. Service Sch., Dept. State, 1949; lang. officer, Peiping, China, 1940; interned Dec. 1941-June 42; spl. study U. Cal., 1942, 3d sec., Chungking, China, 1943, 2d sec., 1945; consul, Peiping, 1946; assigned Dept. State, asst. chief div. Chinese affairs, 1948; 1st sec., Rome, Italy, 1951-55; dir. politico-mil. affairs Hdqrs. Supreme Allied Comdr. Atlantic, Norfolk, Va., 1955-57; sr. fgn. service insp., 1957-58; dep. chief mission, Brussels, Belgium, 1959-61; U.S. ambassador to Colombia, 1961-64, Mexico, 1964-69; pres. Monterey (Cal.) Inst. Fgn. Studies, 1969-74. Home: Carmel Cal. Died Dec. 14, 1974.

FREEMAN, JOHN D., JR., clergyman; b. Alleene, Ark., Feb. 25, 1884; s. John D. and Mecha Catherine (Wright) F.; A.B., U. Ark., 1910; A.M., Trinity Coll., Durham, N.C., 1913; Th.M., So. Baptist Theol. Sem., 1916; D.D., Union U., Jackson, Tenn., 1925, Ouachita Coll., Arkadelphia, Ark., 1935, Georgetown Coll., Ky., 1944; L.H.D., U. Ark., 1950; m. Landis Barton, Oct. 9, 1918; children—Georgia May (Mrs. C. Frank Fielden, Jr.), Lucy Katherine (Mrs. Perry M. White, Jr.). Tchr. sci. and history, Warren (Ark.) High Sch., 1910-11; prin. Ashdown (Ark.) High Sch., 1911-12; ordained to ministry So. Bapt. Ch., 1914; missionary S.W. Ark., 1916-18; pastor, Springfield, Ky., 1918-23, Belmont Heights Ch., Nashville, 1923-25; editor Baptist and Reflector, Nashville, 1925-33; exec. sec., treas. Tenn. Bapt. Conv., 1933-42; editor Western Recorder, Louisville, 1942-46; sr. minister Belmont Heights Bapt. Ch., 1960-74. Field sec. rural dept. So. Bapt. Home Mission Bd., 1946-50; recording sec. So. Bapt. S.S. Bd., 1936-42; pres. Nashville Bapt. Hosp. Bd., 1925-28; v.p. bd. dirs. Union U., 1927-33; rec. sec. Am. Bapt. Theol. Sem., Nashville, 1924-42; pres. So. Bapt. Press Assn., 1928-33; del. Bapt. World Congress, Toronto, 1929, Berlin, Germany, 1934, Atlanta, 1939; v.p. United Dry Forces Tenn., 1934-38; chmn. Tenn. Interracial Com., 1937-42; past mem. bd. dirs. Nat. Temp. Movement, So. Bapt. Hosp., Tenn. Temperance League; rec. sec. bd. dirs., Ky. Bapt. Found., 1944-46; field sec. rural life dept. Bapt. Home Mission Bd., 1946-50; instr. Bapt. Bible Inst., Graceville, Fla., 1952-54; mem. Mid-Tenn. Bapt. Historic Soc. (chmn. 1966-67). Mason (32 deg. Shriner, K.T.). Chaplain Nashville Club, 1969. Author: When The West Was Young (novel); The Mystic Symbol (theology); More than Money; the Country Church, Its Problems and Their Solution; Time's Character Gauge; Buried-Living; Death Loses The Game; Shadow Over America, 1956; co-author: Zondervan's Pictorial Bible Dictionary, 1963; Acorns to Oaks, 1971. Address: Nashville, Tenn. Died Oct. 11, 1974; interred Mt. Olivet Cemetery, Nashville, Tenn.

FREEMAN, JOHN WILLIAM, banker; b. Dublin, Ireland, Nov. 30, 1900; s. Richard B. and Alice (Goodbody) F.; student Trinity Coll. Dublin, 1919-22. Partner, Goodbody and Webb, Stockbrokers, Dublin, 1928-68, cons., 1968; local dir. Allied Irish Banks Ltd., Dublin; chmn. Provincial Bank Ireland Ltd., Dublin; dir. Brittain Group, Ltd., Allied Irish Investment Bank Ltd. Home: County Kildare Ireland. Died June 1973.

FREEMAN, LEWIS RANSOME, author; b. Genoa Junction, Wis., Oct. 4, 1878; s. Otto and Maria (Clary) F.; Stanford U., 1896-98; unmarried. Travel and exploration, 1899-1912, in N. and S. America, Asia, Africa, Islands of the Pacific, etc.; corr. Russo-Japanese War, 1905; mem. commn. of Associated Chambers of Commerce of Pacific Coast sent to China, 1910; corr. British, French and Italian armies, 1915-17; lt. Royal Naval Vol. Reserve, 1917-18; corr. attached to Grand Fleet during the war; mem. staff Allied Naval Armistice Commn. sent to Germany, 1918. Spl. corr. with U.S. Fleet on cruise to Australasia, 1925; spl. Naval corr., U.S. fleet maneuvers, 1929. Made expdn. to Andes in Bolivia and Peru, also to tributaries of upper Amazon River, 1941; expdns. through Paraguay, British Guiana, Venezuela, Argentina and other countries, 1941-47; Gran Chaco, 1948. Mem. Sigma Rho Eta. Rep. Author: Many Fronts, 1918; Stories of the Ships, 1919; Sea Hounds, 1919; To Kiel in the Hercules, 1919; In The Tracks of the Trades, 1920; Hell's Hatches, 1921; Down the Columbia, 1921; Down the Yellowstone, 1922; When Cassi Blooms, 1922; The Colorado River—Yesterday, Today and Tomorrow, 1923; Down the Grand Canyon, 1924; On the Roof of the Rockies, 1925; By Water Ways to Gotham, 1926; Waterways of Westward Wandering, 1927; The Nearing North, 1928; Afloat and Alfight in the Caribbean, 1932; South America—Airwise and Otherwise, 1933; Marquesan Nocturne, 1936; Discovering South America, 1937; Many Rivers, 1937; Arizonas, God's Gift of a Garden, 1951; Dicto-Cholos, 1952; Beach Combings (verse), 1951; Trade Tracks Traffic (verse), 1951. Boatman and photographer for United States Geological Survey party traversing Grand Canyon of the Colorado, 1923; illustrated with photographs special edit. Kipling's The Feet of the Young Men, 1923; airplane and motorboat expdn. to Central and S. America, 1930-31; special naval corr. U.S. Fleet nameuvers, 1932; series of airplane flights, coastal and interior, South America, 1933; spl. naval corr. U.S. Fleet Pacific Maneuvers, 1935; Cruises to Juan Fernandez and Tierra del Fuego and expdn. to head waters Amazon, Ecuador, 1936; expdn. to highlands of Southern Mexico and Guatemala, 1938; cruise Galapagos and West Coast of Colombia, 1939; Brazil's Deserved Destiny, 1941. Clubs: Explorers, Ends of the Earth (New York). Home: Pasadena, Cal.†

FREIBERG, JOSEPH ALBERT, orthopedic surgeon; b. Cincinnati, O., Oct. 3, 1898; s. Albert Henry and Jeannette (Freiberg) F.; A.B., Harvard, 1920; A.M., U. Cin., 1922, M.D., 1923; m. Louise Rothenberg, Oct. 6, 1928 (dec. Jan. 1961); children—Richard Albert, Elinor (Mrs. Elliott Meyer). Intern Cin. Gen. Hosp., 1923-24, assistant surgical resident, 1924-25; graduate in orthopedic training, Boston Children's Hosp. and Mass. Gen. Hosp., 1925-27, British and Continental orthopedic clinics, 1927; asso. with Dr. Albert H. Freiberg in practice of orthopedic surgery, 1928-40, asso. with Richard A. Freiberg, 1963-73; instr., assistant prof., in orthopedic surgery, Coll. of Medicine, U. of Cincinnati, 1928-39, asso. prof. surg. and dir. orthopedic div. 1939-62, prof. surgery, orthopedic div., 1962-73, mem. faculty council; area cons. orthopedic surgery Veterans Administration; dir. orthopedic service Cincinnati Gen. Hospital, Holmes Hosp., Cin. Children's Hosp.; consultant in orthopaedic surgery at the Jewish Hospital; orthopedic cons. V.A. Hosp., Cin., Hamilton Co. Tuberculosis Sanatorium (Dunham Hosp.). Served with S.A.T.C., U. of Cincinnati, 1918. Orthopedic consultant Selective Service Bd. No. 1, Cincinnati. Dir. Brace Shop, Incorporated; member of the medical adv. com., Infantile Paralysis Com. of Hamilton County. Fellow Am. Coll. surgeons; diplomate and past member board of American Bd. of Orthopedic Surgery; mem. Am. Orthopedic Assn. (pres. 1962), American Academy of Orthopedic Surgeons (v.p. 1949), World Medical Assn. (U.S. com.), American Rheumatism Association, Orthopedic Forum, Clin. Orthopedic Soc. (pres. 1945), Am. and Ohio med. assns., Cincinnati Acad. Medicine, Sigma Xi, Alpha Omega Alpha. Author numerous scientific articles on orthopedic surgery; contbr. chapters to Nelson's Looseleaf Surgery, Bancroft's Surgery. Jewish religion. Clubs: University. Harvard (Cincinnati); Losantville Country. Home: Cincinnati O. Died May 1, 1973.

FREMONT-SMITH, FRANK, physician; b. St. Augustine, Fla., Mar. 19, 1895; s. Frank and Dorothea M. (Grossman) F.-S.; grad. Groton (Mass.) Sch., 1913; student Mass. Inst. Tech., 1915-16; M.D., Harvard, 1921; m. Frances Eliot, June 5, 1920 (div. 1935); children—Paul, Kenneth, Eliot; m. 2d, Hazel Crockett, July 25, 1935; 1 son, Nicholas. Intern, Peter Bent Brigham Hosp., Boston, 1921-22; mem. dept. neuropathol. Harvard Med. Sch., 1925-36; instr., 1926-29, asst. prof., 1929-36; med. dir. Josiah Macy, Jr., Found., 1936-60; vis. prof. clin. psychiatry Temple U., 1962-70; dir. inter-disciplinary conf. program Am. Inst. Biol. Scis., 1960-64; dir. inter-disciplinary communications program N.Y. Acad. Sci., 1964-68; spl. cons. Nat. Inst. Child Health and Human Devel., 1963-66; cons. Dept. Def., 1958-74; adviser to surgeon-gen. U.S. Army; co-chmn. World Mental Health Yr., 1960. Cons. sec. of war, assigned office insp. gen., 1944-45; sr. monitor Radiol. Safety Sect., Operation Crossroads, Bikini, June, July, 1946; cons. mental health, gerontol., surg.-gen. USPHS, 1946-47; expert cons. to air surgeon in psychology and neurology, 1948-51. Trustee Communication Research Inst., St. Thomas, V.I., 1961-65, Acad. Religion and Mental Health, 1961; mem. corp. Congress Scientists on Survival, 1963-65; bd. dirs. Scientists on Survival, 1963-65. Served with USNR, 1917-18. Fellow N.Y. Acad. Sci., N.Y. Acad. Medicine, Royal Soc. Medicine (London), Am. Psychiat. Assn. (life); mem. Am. Orthopsychiat. Assn., World Med. Assn. (U.S. com.), Group for Advancement of Psychiatry, A.A.A.S. (com. cooperation among scientists), A.M.A., Am. Neurol. Assn., World Fedn. Mental Health (past pres., chmn. gov. bd. 1960-74; incorporator 1962), Acad. Psychoanalysis (asso.), Nat. Assn. Sci. Writers (hon.), Am. Soc. Clin. Investigation, Assn. Am. Physicians, Assn. Research in Nervous and Mental Diseases, Mass. Med. Soc., Soc. Study Growth and Devel., Soc. Research in Child Devel., N.Y. Acad. Medicine, Am. Soc. Research in Psychosomatic Problems, Nat. Com. Mental Hygiene (v.p., 1944-50 chmn. joint adv. com. with Am. Assn. Psychiat. Social workers to War Office Psychiat. Social Work 1945-46), NRC (com. on selection and tng. aircraft pilots, bd. on clin. psychology, com. on mental hosps.), Am. Hosp. Assn., N.Y. Psychiat. Soc., Am. Psychonalytic Assn. (hon.), Gerontological Soc. Inc. U.S. vice pres. Internat. Com. for Mental Hygiene, 1947-48. Club: Cosmos. Co-author: Cerebro-Spinal Fluid, 1937. Address: Massapequa, NY. Died Feb. 27, 1974.

FRERKING, HERBERT WILLIAM, physician; b. Alma, Mo., July 14, 1915; s. Fred August and Christine J. (Kiehl) F.; M.D., Washington U., St. Louis, 1942; m. Sara Louise Hays, Jan. 26, 1940; children—William Preston, Sally (Mrs. Donald F. Beckley), Christine Anne. Intern, St. Luke's Hosp., St. Louis, 1942-43, resident in phys. radiology, 1946-49, chief dept. radiology, 1955-73, mem. med. exec. com. Served to maj., M.C., AUS, 1943-46. Diplomate Am. Bd. Radiology. Fellow Am. Coll. Radiology; mem. Mo., St. Louis radiol. socs., St. Louis, Mo. med. socs., Radiol. Soc. N.Am., A.M.A. Lutheran. Home: St. Louis, Mo. Died July 11, 1973; buried Tipton Masonic Cemetery, Tipton, Mo.

FREVERT, HARRY LOUIS, b. Dayton, O., June 21, 1881; s. George Louis and Bertha (Prass) F.; A.B., Harvard, 1905, Ph.D., 1908; m. Josephine Bate, Sept. 1, 1913. Assistant in chemistry, Harvard, 1903-04, Austin teaching fellow in physical chemistry, 1904-05, instructor in physical chemistry, 1905-09; chemist, later chief chemist, Midvale Steel Co., 1909-13, Superintendent armor and ordnance, 1931-21; general superintendent Midvale Steel & Ordnance Co., 1921-23; dir. and vice-pres. in charge operations The Midvale Co., 1923-31, president 1931-43, chmn. of board, 1943-44; retired April, 1944; dir. Baldwin Locomotive Works. Member Metall. Advisory Bd., U.S. Army and mem. advisory bd. Phila. Ordnance Dist., U.S. Army. Mem. advisory bd. to Sch. of Mines and Metallurgy, Pa. State Coll.; mem. advisory com. John Scott Medal and Award, Bd. of City Trustees, Phila. Mem. Newcomen Soc., Am. Iron and Steel Institute, Mining and Metallurgical Engrs. Clubs: Germantown Cricket, Harvard, Pohoqualine Fish Assn. (Phila.). Home: Philadelphia, Pa.†

FRIDAY, CHARLES BOSTWICK, educator; b. Fort Collins, Colo., Aug. 6, 1921; s. Carl Bostwick and Cleta Mae (Rubart) F.; B.A., U. Colo., 1943, M.A., 1947, Ph.D., 1950; m. Jean Brewer, July 23, 1944; children—Kathryn Ann, Deborah Jean, John Charles. Instr. econs. U. Colo., 1947-50; faculty Ore. State U., 1950-75, prof. econs., chmn. dept., 1957-67. Mem. adv. council Small Bus. Adminstrn., Fed. Govt., 1962-68. Served with AUS, 1943-45. Mem. Am., Western (mem. exec. com. 1963-75, pres. 1970) econs assns., Econ. History Assn., Am. Studies Assn., Am. Assn. U. Profs., Assn. for Evolutionary Econs., Phi Beta Kappa, Pi Gamma Mu. Author: (with B.H. Wilkins) The Economists of the New Frontier, 1963, Home: Corvallis Ore. Died Apr. 16, 1975.

FRIEBOLIN, CARL D(AVID), lawyer; b. Owatonna, Minn., Jan. 19, 1878; s. William and Kate (Donnerline) F.; LL.B., Western Reserve U., Law School, Cleveland, 1899, LL.D., (hon.), 1944; LL.D., Fenn College, 1960; married to Florence Brookes, June 30, 1906; 1 son, Brookes. O. State rep., 1911-13; state senator, O., 1913-14; judge Common Pleas Ct., Cuyahoga Co., O., 1914; U.S. referee in bankruptcy, from 1916; mem. Friebolin & Byers, 1901-47; instr. Law Sch. Western Res. U. from 1934. President, Cleveland City Club, 1917-18; president Cleveland Citizens Bur., 1935-53; trustee Western Reserve U., 1928-36; Kent State Coll., 1933-36; pres. Cleveland Law Library, from 1942; trustee sinking fund commn. of Cleveland Bd. of Edn., 1939-49. Awarded Pub. Service Medal, Cleveland C. of C., 1943. Mem. Am., O., Cleveland bar assns., Cleveland Americanization Council (pres., 1918-26), Cleveland Citizens League (pres., 1923-24; dir. from 1923),

Adelbert Coll. Alumni Assn. (pres., 1928-31), Cleveland C. of C. (dir., 1931-35), Nat. Assn of Referees in Bankruptcy (pres., 1931-32), Cleveland Adult Edn. Assn. (pres., 1933-40), City Club Forum Foundation (pres., from 1940), Nat. Bankruptcy Conf., A.R.C. (trustee, Cleveland, 1922-28), Phi Gamma Delta, Delta Sigma Rho. Phi Delta Phi. Unitarian. Democrat. Clubs: City, University, Canterbury, Mid-day, Nisi Prius. Author: City Club Anvil Revues, 1914-65. Contbr. of articles on bankruptcy to jours. Home: Cleveland, O.†

FRIEDENBERG, ALBERT MARX, lawyer, author; b. New York, Jan. 9, 1881; s. Leopold and Fannie (Stern) F.; ed. pub. schs., Coll. City of New York, B.S., 1900, Columbia Univ. Law Sch. LL. B., 1903; unmarried. In law practice from 1903. New York corr. Jewish Comment of Baltimore, 1902-05; contbr. to Jewish Ency., author of monographs in Publs. of Am. Jewish Hist. Soc., and mem. of its Com. on Indexing Am.-Jewish Periodicals, 1904. Author: Zionist Studies; 1904 B50; Two Mediaeval Jewish Poets, 1905 X1. Address: New York City, N.Y.†

FRIEDLANDER, JACKSON H., hosp. adminstr.; b. N.Y.C., 1909; M.D., L.I. U., 1934. Intern L.I. Coll. Hosp., 1934-35; inter Kings County Hosp., Bklyn., 1935-36, resident in medicine, 1936-39, asso. vis. physician, later asso. Cardiology Dept.; later chief med. services Northport Hosp., L.I., N.Y.; later chief, resident and internship div. VA, Washington, also dir. edn., also area med. dir.; dir. VA Center, Bay Pines, Fla. Served to maj. AUS, 1942-46. Diplomate Am. Bd. Internal Medicine. Fellow Am. Coll. Cardiology, A.C.P.; mem. A.M.A., Am. Heart Assn. Office: Bay Pines, Fla. Died June 30, 1972.

FRIEDMAN, JACOB HENRY, neuropsychiatrist; b. N.Y.C., July 17, 1903; s. William and Sadie (Kleinman) F.; B.S., City Coll. N.Y., 1925; M.D., Tulane Med. Sch., 1929; postgrad. N.Y. Psychoanalytic Inst., 1936-42; m. Ida Seloff, Sept. 4, 1936 (dec. 1953); 1 dau., Alice Sue (Mrs. Gerald B. Appel); m. 2d, Ida Simon, Nov. 3, 1954. Intern Conemaugh Valley Meml. Hosp., Johnstown, Pa., 1929-30, intern in psychiatry Worcester (Mass.) State Hosp., 1931-32; resident Stetson Hosp., Phila., 1930-31, asst. resident neurology Mt. Sinai Hosp., N.Y.C., 1932-33, resident psychiatry Hillside Hosp., Glen Oaks, N.Y., 1933-34; pvt. practice medicine specializing in neuropsychiatry, Bronx, N.Y., 1934-67; clin. asst. Mental Hygiene Clinic, Mt. Sinai Hosp., N.Y.C., 1934-40; chief Mental Hygiene Clinic, Lebanon Hosp., Bronx, 1936-42, 1946-58, dir., 1958-64; neuropsychiatrist Fordham Hosp., Bronx, 1935-64, dir. neuropsychiatry, 1950-64, chief neuropsychiat. sect., 1964-70; cons., 1970-73; clin. dir. geriatric service Bronx State Hosp., 1967-73; asst. clin. prof. psychiatry Albert Einstein Coll. Medicine, Bronx, 1967-73. Served from maj. to lt. col., M.C., AUS, 1942-46. Jacob H. Friedman Fund established in his honor Tulane U. Sch. Medicine. Diplomate in neurology and psychiatry Am. Bd. Psychiatry and Neurology. Fellow Am. Psychiat. Assn. (dist. pres.; del. 1967-69 life fellow), Assn. Advancement of Psychotherapy, A.A.A.S.; mem. Bronx County Soc. Mental Health (dir. 1953-73, mem. exec. bd. 1957-63; chmn. profl. adv. com. 1958-63), Am. Geriatrics Soc., Am. Soc. Psychoanalytic Physicians, N.Y. Soc. Clin. Psychiatry, Assn. for Research in Nervous and Mental Disease, A.M.A., N.Y. Acad. Sci., Am. Group Psychotherapy Assn. Contbr. articles to profl. jours. Home: Bronx, N.Y. Died Jan. 27, 1973; buried Mt. Ararat Cemetery, East Farmingdale, N.Y.

FRIEDRICH, FERDINAND AUGUST, newspaper editor; b. Easton, Pa., July 15, 1871; s. Dr. Gustave Ludwig and Christina Sophia (Frenz) F.; ed. Paterson (N.J.) High Sch., 1883-85,and private study; m. Minnie A. LaRue, Apr. 12, 1909; children—Ferdinand LaRue, Robert Alexander. Began as printer's apprentice on Morning Call, 1886; successively journeyman printer, proofreader, sporting editor, gen. reporter, political writer, telegraph editor, city editor, mng. editor, editor: associated with the Call, 1886-88 and from 1893; editor Call Printing and Pub. Co., pub. Paterson Morning Call, 1917-50. Mem. Passaic County (N.J.) Planning Comm. (former pres.) Mem. North Jersey Newspapermen's Orgn. Republican. Mem. Reformed Ch. Club: Pica. Home: Hawthorne, N.J.†

FRIEES, HORACE LELAND, educator; b. N.Y.C., Mar. 4, 1900; s. Louis G. and Louise S. (Jagle) F.; A.B., Columbia, 1918, Ph.D., 1926; Cutting Travelling fellow, Heidelberg U., 1924-25; m. Ruth Adler, June 25, 1923; 1 dau., Anne. Instr. philosophy Columbia, 1921-26, asst. prof., 1926; asso. prof. 1936-46, prof. philosophy, from 1946, Joseph L. Buttenwieser prof. emeritus human relations; exec. officer, dept. of religion, Barnard Coll., 1940-47, chmn. dept. of religion, Columbia, 1962-65. Guggenheim fellow, 1942-43. Bd. leaders N.Y. Soc. for Ethical Culture, from 1950. Mem. Am. Philos. Assn., Am. Ethical Union, Phi Beta Kappa. Ethical Culture religion. Author books including: (with H. W. Schneider) Religion in Various Cultures, 1932; Our part in this world (edited selections from Felix Adler), 1946. Editor The Review of Religion, 1942-58. Contbr. articles. Home: New York City, N.Y., Died Oct. 12, 1975.

FRIENDLY, OSCAR NATHAN, mining engr.; b. Corvallis, Ore., Aug. 24, 1884; s. Max and Adolphina (Simon) F.; B.S., U. Cal., 1907; m. Carrie Sappington, Aug. 29, 1923 (dec. Oct. 1962 Mine engr. and geologist, Daly Judge Mining Co., 1909-13; engr. in charge Snake Creek Mining & Tunnel Co., 1909-18; gen. supt. Daly Judge Mining Co., 1913-17, Judge Mining and Smelting Co., 1917-22, Daly West Mining Co., 1918-22; gen. mgr. Park City Mining and Smelting Co., 1922-25; chief engr. and asst. gen. mgr. and treas. Park Utah Consol. Mines Co., 1925-34; cons. mining, v.p., gen. mgr., 1934-46, v.p., cons. engr., 1946-52; pres. Park City Utah Mines Co. Gov. Utah chpt. Am. Mining Congress, 1936-37, chmn. bd. govs. Western div., 1937. Dir. Childrens Service Soc. of Utah. Mason (32 deg., Shriner). Clubs: Alta, North Fork. Home: Salt Lake City, Utah. Died Feb. 11, 1975; interred Mt. Olivet Cemetery, Salt Lake City Utah.

FRISHMUTH, HARRIET WHITNEY, sculptor; b. Phila, Pa., Sept. 17, 1880; d. Frank B. and Louise Otto (Berens) Frishmuth; studied art in Paris, France, under Rodin and Injalbert, in Berlin under Porf. Cuno Von Enchtetiz, Art Students League, New York, under Borglum and McNeil, and was awarded the St. Gaudens 1st prize. Exhibited at Nat. Acad. Design, Architectural League, Nat. Assn. Women Painters and Sculptors, Acad. Fine Arts (Phila.), San Francisco Expn., Salon, Paris. Awarded Helen Foster Barnet prize; Nat. Arts Club prize, 1921; Watrons gold medal, Nat. Acad., 1922; Julia A. Shaw memorial prize, Nat. Acad., 1923; Joan of Arc silver medal, Nat. Assn. of Women Painters and Sculptors, 1924, sketch exhbn. for speed; hon. mention, San Francisco Expn., 1928; Garden Club of America gold medal, 1929; Irving T. Bush prize, Grand Central Art Gallery, 1928. Prin. works: "Joy of the Waters," fountain, Mus. of Fine Arts, Dayton, O.; memorial sundial, Englewood, N.J.; "Slavonic Dance," Met. Mus., New York; "Vine," Metropolitan Mus.; "Play Days," Dallas (Tex.) Mus.; Morton memorial, Windsorville, Conn. N.A., 1929; portrait bust of President Woodrow Wilson, for Capitol at Richmond, Va. Designed medals for New York Acad. Medicine and Garden Club of America (Fenwick medal). Mem. Nat. Acad. of Design, Nat. Sculpture Soc., Allied Artists America, League Am. Artists, Art Alliance America. Archtl. League of N.Y. Republican. Episcopalian. Address: New York City, N.Y.†

FROST, HILDRETH, lawyer, corp. official; b. Newton Upper Falls, Mass., June 22, 1880; s. Walter Clarence and Mary Ella (Hildreth) F.; A.B., Colo. Coll., 1901; LL.B., Harvard, 1904; m. Bertha K. Marcum, Oct. 1, 1914 (dec.); children—Hildreth, Walter Jefferson, Richard Edmund (dec.), Mary Catherine (DePola), Robert Marcum; married 2d, Josephine Welon Justice, Oct. 19, 1947. Admitted to Colo. bar 1905, practiced in Colorado Springs, Cripple Creek mining district; pres. and gen. mgr. Joe Dandy Mining Co.; mgr. Cripple Creek Trading & Mining Co.; pres. and mgr. Teller Co. Land & Development Co., Ophir Gold Mines Co., Des Moines Gold Mines Co.; mng. dir., agt. cos. Mem. Colo. and El Paso County Bar Assn., Colo. Bar Assn., Phi Gamma Delta. Republican. Unitarian. Elk. Contbr. articles on legal and mining subjects. Home: Colorado Springs, Colo.†

FROST, NORMAN BURKE, lawyer; b. Montgomery County, Md., Oct. 4, 1897; s. Edward Halleck and Elizabeth (Burke) F.; LL.B., Georgetown U., 1921; m. Mary Demova King. Apr. 27, 1918; children—Betty, Demova, Norma. Admitted to D.C. bar, 1921; Law clk. Supreme Ct. U.S., 1921-22; asso. counsel Landreau Arbitration, U.S.-Peru at London, 1922-23; mem. Frost & Towers, 1922-33, 48-73, Frost, Myers & Towers, 1933-48; pres. Gen. Hydraulic Co., 1935-41, The Rennart Corp., Balt.; dir. Nat. Bank Wash., Financial Gen. Bankshares, Inc., Sperry Rand Corp., Textron. Inc., Nat. Mortgage & Investment Co., Financial Securities Corp. Chmn. U.S. Air Force Price Adjustment Bd., 1944-45. Trustee James F. Mitchell Found.; chmn. bd. trustees James M. Johnston Trust for Charitable and Ednl. Purposes. With AEF, 1918-19; attached to staff Hon. Henry White Peace Commn., Paris, 1919. Recipient Exceptional Civilan Service award, 1945. Mem. Internat. Ins. counsel, Am. Bar Assn., Bar Assn. O.C. Episcopalian. Clubs: Barristers, University, Columbia Country, Burning Tree, Chevy Chase (Washington); Everglades. Seminole (Palm Beach, Fla.). Home: Chevy Chase, Md. Died Aug. 22, 1973.

FRUMESS, GERALD MYRON, physician; b. Denver, 1906; s. Harry H. and Fannie (Breitman) F.; M.D., U. Colo., 1929; m. Lois Isobel Fisher, Nov. 25, 1933; children—Robin (Mrs. Stuart Seiler), Gerald Myron. Intern, Michael Reese Hosp., Chgo., 1930-32; postgrad. studies N.Y. Postgrad. Hosp., N.Y.C., 1933-34, N.Y. Skin and Cancer Hosp., 1933-34; attending dermatologist Denver County and Mercy Hosps., Gen. Rose Hosp., Children's Hosp.; attending dermatologist, past pres. Beth Israel Hosp.; cons. in dermatology Nat. Jewish Hosp., Jewish Consumptive Relief Soc.; asso. attending dermatologist St. Joseph's Hosp., Presbyn. Hosp.; asso. prof. dermatology and syphyllis U. Colo. Mem. Denver, Mayor's Commn. on Human Relations, 1950-57; founder Denver Chamber Music Soc. Served to lt. col., M.C., AUS, 1942-45. Diplomate Am. Bd. Dermatology. Fellow A.C.P., Am. Soc. Internal Medicine; mem. A.M.A., Am. Acad. Dermatology (charter), Rocky Mountain (founder), Southwest, Pacific (v.p.) dermatology socs., Sigma Xi, Alpha Omega Alpha. Jewish religion. Contbr. articles to profl. jours. Home: Denver, Colo. Died Aug. 30, 1971; buried Fairmount Cemetery.

FRY, SHERRY EDMUNDSON, sculptor; b. Creston, Ia., Sept. 29, 1879; s. John Wesley and Ellen (Green) F.; Art. Inst. Chgo., 1900; Academie Julian. Paris, 1902; Ecole des Beaux Arts, Paris, 1903; Florence, Italy, 1904; pupil of Frederick MacMonnies, Barrias, Verlet, and Lorado Taft; unmarried. Traveled and studied in Italy, Greece and Germany, 1908-11; hon. mention, Salon, Paris, 1906, gold medal, 1907; Nat. Roman prize, 1908 (held for 3 yrs.); silver medal, Panama P.I. Expn., San Francisco, 1915; Elizabeth Watrous gold medal, N.A. exhbn., 1917; William M. R. French gold medal, Art Inst., Chgo., 1923. Prin. works; reliefs on Grant Memorial, Washington, D.C.; fountains for William A. Clark, Jr., and Walter B. James; pediments. Frick House (N.Y.C.), mausoleum (Los Angeles); pediment for Labor and Interstate Commerce Bldg.; statues, Ira Allen. U. of Vt.; Capt. Abbey, Enfield, Conn.; Indian Chief, Oskaloosa, Ia.; pediment, Labor & Commerce Bldg., Washington, 1936; etc. N.A., 1931; mem. Nat. Sculpture Soc. Enlisted as pvt. U.S. Army, Sept. 5, 1917; served in Camouflage Corps; 1 yr. as liaison officer, camouflage sect., French Army. Club: Century. Home-Studio: Kent Conn.†

FRY, WILLIAM H., lawyer; b. Cin., Oct. 20, 1905; A.B. cum laude, Ohio State U., 1927; LL.S., Xavier U., 1933. Admitted to Ohio bar, 1933; now partner firm Rendigs, Fry, Kiely & Dennis, Cin. Served to lt. col. AUS, 1942-45. Fellow Am. Coll. Trial Lawyers; mem. Am., Ohio, Cln. bar assns., Internat. Assn. Ins. Counsel, Phi Beta Kappa. Home: Cincinnati, Oh. Died Feb. 11, 1975.

FRYDLER, WILLIAM WLADYSLAW, travel agy. exec.; b. Dabrowa, Upper Silesia, Dec. 23, 1906; (came to U.S. 1941, naturalized 1942); s. Saul and Salomea (Zilberberg) F.; student Oberrealschule-Kattowitz, 1924; Polytechnical Inst. (Warsaw, Poland), 1929-31; m. Antonina T. Goldberg, Aug. 1, 1932; children—Irene Susan, Eric Scott. Tour dir. First Ofcl. Polish Pilgrimmage to the Holy Land, 1932-35; in charge U.S. Embassy Pilgrimage to Cracow, Poland, 1935-39; observer to U.N. on behalf of Polish London Govt., 1945-50; organized language seminars for students in Europe, 1950-54; expanded student travel to Europe motivated to learn fgn. languages, 1954-69; established for Berlitz Sch. the Live and Learn Programs, 1969-71; organized with Pan Am Airlines Club, Ltd., Forest Hills, N.Y., 1965-74. Served with AUS, 1942-43. Mem. Fifth Av. Travel Post Am. Legion (comdr. 1964). Rotarian. Home: Forest Hills Gardens, N.Y. Died Aug. 15, 1973.

FRYE, WILLIAM WESLEY, physician, educator; b. North English, Ia., July 26, 1903; s. Cyrus Alexander and Martha E. (Sheetz) F.; B.S., Ia. Wesleyan Coll., 1926; M.S., Ia. State Coll., 1927, Ph.D., 1931; M.D., Vanderbilt Univ., 1939; Sc.D., Iowa Wesleyan Coll., 1957; m. Lillian Emily Brown, Apr. 5, 1929; children—William Wesley, Emily Ann, Cynthia Brown, Martha Lois, Jane Ellen. Instr. zoology, entomology Ia. State Coll., 1928-31; research asst. dept. preventive medicine, pub. health Vanderbilt U., 1931-37, instr., 1937, intern pediatrics Commonwealth Fund fellowship, 1939-40, asst. prof. dept. preventive medicine, pub. health, asst. clin. medicine, 1940-42, asso. prof., asst. clinical obstet., 1942-45, prof., head dept. preventive medicine, pub. health, 1945-48, dir. Sch. Pub. Health, 1946-48; asst. dean, dir. div. grad. medicine, prof. tropical medicine, pub. health, Tulane U., 1948-49; dean, prof. tropical medicine, pub. health, La. State U., 1949-59 v.p., dean School of Medicine, 1959-65, chancellor La. State U. Medical Center, 1965-69, chancellor emeritus, 1969-75; spl. cons. Tex. Tech. U. Sch. Medicine, Lubbock, 1970-73, dean, 1973-75; field trip tropical diseases Central Am., 1943; mem. Cholera Commn. China, 1945; spl. cons. USPHS, 1946—, chmn. tropical disease study sect., research grants div., 1951-56, chmn. advisory com. Epidemiology and Biometry, 1956-75; chmn. combined deans com. VA Hosp., New Orleans, 1949-75; dep. dir. commn. enteric infections Armed Forces Epidemiol. Bd., 1950-56; net. adv. allergy and infectious diseases council of Nat. Insts. Health, Bethesda, Md., 1958-75. Awarded Ben Witt Key prize by Vanderbilt U., 1939. Diplomate Am. Bd. Preventive Medicine and Public Health. Fellow A.M.A., Am. Pub. Health Assn., Am. Coll. Physicians, 1951; mem. Am. Soc. Tropical Medicine and Hygiene (pres. 1960-61), So. Medical Assn., Louisiana State, Orleans Parish medical societies, Louisiana State Public Health Assn., Am. Gastroenterological Assn., New Orleans Acad. Internal Medicine, New Orleans Grad. Med. Assembly, Am. Cancer Soc. (mem. adv. com. Institutional Grants 1958-60). Am. Soc. of Parasitologists, Louisiana Mental Health Assn. (pres. 1957-59), Am. Acad. Preventive Medicine, Omicron Delta Kappa, Delta Omega, Sigma Xi, Phi Kappa Phi, Alpha Omega Alpha. Author articles on med. subjects in profl. jours. Co-author tropical medicine manual. Home: Lubbock, Tex., Died Dec. 3, 1975.

FRYER, EUGENIE MARY, author; b. Phila., Pa., Sept. 17, 1879; d. Greville E. and Elizabeth P. (Frost) F.; grad. the Misses Hayward's Sch.; certificate electic courses, Drexel Inst., Phila.; studied Grad. Sch., U. of Pa., 1914, 15; unmarried. Contbr. stories, essays, travel and biog. sketches, etc., to mags., from 1900. Librarian Phila. Mus. Sch. of Industrial Art. Republican. Episcopalian. Clubs: Phila. Art Alliance, Automobile (Phila.); American Women's (London). Author: The Hill-Towns of France, 1917; A Book of Boyhoods, 1920; Unending Quest (poems), 1932. Home: Philadelphia, Pa.†

FRYXELL, ROALD H., geologist, educator; b. Moline, Ill., Feb. 18, 1934; s. F.M. and Regina (Holmen) F.; A.B., Augustana Coll., 1956, D.Sc., 1972; postgrad. Wash. State U., 1956-60; Ph.D., U. Ida., 1971; m. Helen Anne Broberg, June 2, 1956; children—Jenny Christine, Tom Douglas. Curator, Gingko Petrified Forest State Mus., Vantage, Wash., 1960-61; staff geologist dept. anthropology Wash. State U., Pullman, 1962-65, instr., 1966-68, asst. prof., 1968-71, asso. prof., 1971-74. Teaching cons., ind. research in France, Spain, Can., Mexico, Alaska, Hawaii, western U.S. Recipient hon. sci. award Bausch & Lombe, 1951; named Distinguished Citizen, Wash. Senate, 1969. Fellow Geol. Soc. Am.; mem. N.W. Sci. Assn., Am. (councilor 1973-74), Internat. assns. for Quaternary research, A.A.A.S., Nat. Assn. Geology Tchrs., Sigma Xi, Phi Kappa Phi. Co-dir. Ozette Sci. Expdn., 1967-68; discoverer Marmes Man, dir. Marmes Salvage Project, 1968-69; mem. NASA Lunar Sample Preliminary Exam. Team, Apollo 11-17, Manned Spacecraft Center, Houston, also mem. subcom. on lunar core samples, 1971-72. Contbr. articles to profl. jours. Home: Pullman Wash. Died May 18, 1974.

FTHENAKIS, EMMANUEL, civil engr., Greek govt. ofcl.; b. Athens, Greece, Aug. 4, 1921; s. Anastasios and Irene (Magoulakis) F.; ed. Nat. Tech. U. Athens, Mass. Inst. Tech.; M.S.; m. Alkystis Kassandras, 1955; 2 daus. Pvt. practice civil engring., 1946-50; testing and research engr. bldg. materials lab. Greek Ministry Pub. Works, Athens, 1950-56; exec. Doxiades Assos., 1956-65, dir. research, bd. dirs., 1963-65; founder, dir. Bldg. Materials and Methods of Constrn. Research Center, Iraq, 1957; cons. to Govts. Ghana and Nigeria, dir. ops. and projects in field of housing planning, town, regional and Nat. phys. and econ. planning and devel., 1959-63; founder, dir. Doxiades Assos. Computer Center, 1963-65; mng. dir. own Internat. cons. firm, planning and devel. cons. to govts. of Nigeria, Ghana, Sierra Leons, internat. orgns., including FAO, banks; minister Communications, 1969; alternate minister Econ. Coordination, 1969; gov. for Greece, Internat. Bank Reconstrn. and Devel., 1969; minister without portfolio, 1971-72. Mem. Am. Concrete Inst., World Soc. Ekistics, A.A.A.S. Home: Athens, Greece., Died Dec. 18, 1972; buried 1st Cemetery, Athens, Greece.

FUESS, JOHN CUSHING, ret. fgn. service officer; b. Andover, Mass., Apr. 13, 1912; s. Claude Moore and Elizabeth (Goodhue) F.; grad. Phillips Acad., Andover, Mass., 1931; B.A., Harvard, 1935, M.A., 1936; m. Cora Frances Henry, Jan. 6, 1943; children—James Henry, David Cushing. Tchr., Brooks Sch., N. Andover, Mass., 1937-39; fgn. service officer, vice consul, Mexico City, 1939-40; assigned Dept. State, 1940-41, Belfast, N. Ireland, 1942-43; consul, prin. officer, Auckland, N.Z., 1944-46; consul, Capetown, S. Africa, 1947-49, Milan, Italy, 1949-50; European specialist Office Internat. Labor Affairs, Dept. Labor, 1951-54; labor attache, 1st sec. Am. embassy, Santiago, Chile, 1955-57, Rome, Italy, 1957-62; dep. dir. Office Internat. Confs., Dept. State, 1962-65; consul gen., Trieste, Italy, 1965-70. Mem. Cal. com. Common Cause, 1972-74; chmn. Carmel Americans Abroad com. Am. Field Service, 1972. Decorated commendatore Ordine al Merito della Repubblica Italiana. Mem. S.A.R., Soc. Colonial Wars. Mason. Clubs: D.U. (Harvard); Monterey Peninsula Country, Old Capital (Monterey). Home: Carmel, Cal. Died Oct. 15, 1974.

FULCHER, GEORGE CORDON, publisher; b. Naples, Tex., Aug. 24, 1909; s. Henry Clarence and Emma Kate (Baker) F.; student Wichita Falls Jr. Coll., 1927-28, U. Tex., 1928-31; m. Ruth M. Moore, Apr. 4, 1931; children—Ruth (Mrs. Julian L. Biggers, Jr.), Todd Moore (dec.). Reporter, Wichita Falls Record News, 1927-28; news editor Austin (Tex.) Am., 1928-36, mng. editor, 1936-41; editor Austin Am.-Statesman, 1941-45; pub. Atlanta (Tex.) Citizens Jour., 1945-71; pub. Texas Star, Austin, 1971-74; contractor Gordon Fulcher Constrn. Co., Austin, 1945-63. Mem. Tex. Water Quality Bd., 1968-69, chmn., 1969-74. Mem. Tex., N. and E. Tex. press assns., Advt. Club Dallas, Phi Kappa Psi. Democrat. Methodist. Clubs: Indian Hill Country (Atlanta); Headliners, Citadel (Austin). Home: Austin, Tex. Died June 24, 1973.

FULDA, CARL HERMAN, educator; b. Berlin, Germany, Aug. 22, 1909; s. Ludwig and Helen (Hermann) F.; Dr. Law, U. Freiburg (Germany), 1931; student U. Geneva (Switzerland), 1927, U. Berlin, 1928-30; LL.B., Yale, 1938; m. Gaby Gros, Feb. 28, 1935; children—Thomas Richard, John Anthony. Came to U.S., 1936, naturalized, 1941. Law clk., Berlin, Germany, 1931-33; with Victoria Ins. Co., Paris, France, 1934-35; research asst. N.Y. State Law Revision Commn., 1938-41, cons., 1949, 52, 55; atty. Treasury Dept., 1942, OPA, 1942-46; from asst. to prof. law Rutgers U., Newark, 1946-54; prof. law Ohio State U., Columbus, 1954-64; prof. law U. Tex., Austin, 1964-75, Hugh Lamar Stone prof. law, 1965-75. Vis. prof. Columbia Law Sch., 1952, La. State U. Law Sch., 1962, U. Frankfurt (Germany), 1962, U. ubingen (Germany), 1964, 70, orientation program Am. law Princeton, 1965, Salzburg Seminar Am. Law, 1960, Osgoode Hall Law Sch., York U., Toronto, Ont., Can., 1970, Hastings Coll. Law U. Cal. San Francisco, 1972, Inst. on Comparative and Internat. Law, Paris, France, 1973; vis. lectr. U. Trieste (Italy), 1964,65; mem. White House Task Force on Antitrust Policy, 1968; pub. mem. gov. N.J. Com. Pub. Utilities Labor Disputes Legislation, 1954; cons. AID, India, 1967. Mem. Am. Bar. Assn. (mem. commn. to study Fed. Trade Commn. 1969; chmn. subcom. fgn. antitrust laws, sect. antitrust law 1968-70), Tex. State Bar, Am. Soc. Internat. Law, Am. Fgn. Law Assn., Am. Assn. U. Profs., Am. Civil Liberties Union. Author: Competition in Regulated Industries, Transportation, 1961; (with Warren F. Schwartz) Cases and Materials on the Regulation of International Trade and Investment, 1970; Introduction to American Law (in German), 1966; also numerous articles. Bd. editors Am. Jour. Comparative Law; editorial adv. bd. Jour. Air Law and Commerce, Transp. Law Jour.; reporter Internat. Ency. Comparative Law. Home: Austin, Tex. Died Jan. 5, 1975.

FULLER, ALFRED CARL, brush mfr.; b. Weisford, Kings County, N.S., Jan. 13, 1885; s. Leander Joseph and Phebe Jane (Collins) F.; ed. common sch.; M.A., Trinity Coll.; A.F.D., Hartt Coll. Music, 1952; D.C.L., Acadia U., Wolfeville, N.S., 1958; D.C.L. Bates Coll., 1963; m. Evelyn W. Ells, Apr. 8, 1908; children—Alfred Howard, Avard Ells; m. 2d, Mary Primrose Pelton, Oct. 21, 1932. Naturalized citizen, 1918. Established Fuller Brush Co., Somerville, Mass., 1906, pres. and chmn. bd; ret. Trustee U. Conn.; chmn. bd. trustee Hartt Coll. of Music; life trustee Kingswood Sch.; bd. regents U. Hartford. Recipient Horatio Alger award, 1959. Mem. Conn. Mfrs. Assn. (pres. 1942-46). Republican. Christian Scientist. Mason (32, K.T., Shriner). Clubs: Hartford, Hartford Golf. Home: West Hartford, Conn. Died Dec. 1973.

FULLER, EDGAR, educator; b. La Crosse, Wis., Mar. 23, 1904; s. Ernest Edgar and Mary (Wise) F.; A.B., Brigham Young U., 1927; J.D., U. Chgo., 1932; Ed.D., Harvard, 1940; m. Alta Pamela Call, Sept. 10, 1926 (dec. 1972); children—Mary Margaret, Kathryn Jean (Mrs. L.S. Reid, Jr.), Carol Yvonne (Mrs. John H. Hinrichs, Jr.); m. 2d, Blanche E Crippen, 1973. Laborer in timber woods and mills, 1919-23; mucker and miner, 1923-27; supt. schs., Virden, N.M., 1929-31, 32-33; pres. Gila Jr. Coll., Thatcher, Ariz., 1933-39; lectr. on ednl. adminstrn. Harvard, 1940-42; prin. educationist and acting chief aviation edn. div. U.S. CAA, Washington, 1942-46; commr. edn. State of N.H., 1946-48; exec. sec. Council Chief State Sch. Officers, 1948-69, exec. sec. emeritus, 1969-73. Mem. Pres.' Nat. Com. for Devel. Scientists and Engrs.; mem. various ednl. bds. and commns. Recipient Brewer trophy Nat. Aeros. Assn. for outstanding contbn. to air youth edn. Mem. N.E.A., Am. Assn. Sch. Adminstrs., Nat. Joint Com. Ednl. TV, Horace Mann League (pres. 1959); chmn. com. constnl. law 1962-73). Unitarian. Author, editor numerous books and articles on pub. law, ednl. finance and adminstrn. and aviation edn., contbr. Harvard Law Rev., Harvard Ednl. Rev., Am. Sch. Bd. Jour., Nat. Aeros., and similar periodicals; also bulls. and pamphlets on these subjects, 1932-73. Home: Silver Spring, Md. Died Aug. 4, 1973; buried Utica, N.Y.

FULLER, HARRY JAMES, botanist. educator, assn. exec.; b. St. Louis, Oct. 8, 1907; s. Henry Lyman and Lydia (Musberg) F.; B.S., Washington U., 1929. M.S., 1930. Ph.D. 1932; m. Mary Ledgerwood, Oct. 1. 1931; 1 dau., Pamela (Mrs. Frederick D. Rawles). With U. Ill., 1932-73., successively instr. botany, asso., asst. and asso. prof., 1932-45, prof. botany, 1945-73. Rubber specialist U.S. Govt. in S.A., 1942-45. Mem. Bot. Soc. Am. (national treas., Award of Merit, honorary president 1958). A.A.A.S., Venezuelan Acad. Sci., Nat. Assn. Biology Tchrs., Phi Beta Kappa, Sigma Xi, Phi Sigma. Author: The Plant World, 3d edit., 1955; Outlines of General Botany. 3d edit., 1955; (with Oswald Tippo) College Botany, 1953. Editor Plant Sci. Bull., 1955-73; Am. Jour, of Botany, 1957-58. Contbr. profl. jours. Home: Champaign, Ill. Died Aug. 24, 1973; buried Mount Hope Cemetery, Urbana, Ill.

FULLER, WARREN GRAHAM, orgn. exec.; b. Bangkok, Thailand, July 30, 1920 (parents Am. citizens); s. Graham and Geraldine (Emerson) Fuller; grad. Mt. Hermon Sch. for Boys, 1938; student Princeton, 1938-40; B.A., U. Ill., 1942; m. Edith McKlarty Barbee, Sept. 10, 1949; children—Emerson Graham, Elizabeth Lyle. With displaced persons operations UNRRA, Germany, 1945-47; with Internat. Refugee Orgn. in Germany, 1947-48, dep. dir., dir. resettlement hdqrs. Geneva 1949-52; dep. chief operations Intergovtl. Com. for European Migration, Geneva, 1952-55, chief of mission, Brazil and Paraguay, Rio de Janeiro, 1955-59, Rome, Italy, 1959-62; dep. dir. Latin Am. programs Peace Corps, Washington, 1962-64, dir. for Brazil, Rio de Janeiro, 1964-67; asst. sec. gen. Internat. Secretariat for Vol. Service, Washington, 1967-70; dir. financial devel. Internat. Planned Parenthood Fedn., London, 1970; later dep. dir. UNICEF in India, until 1975. Served with Am. Field Service with Brit. forces in Middle East, , N. Africa, ETO, 1942-45. Decorated Brit. campaign medals; Medaglia Ricordo (Italy), 1958; cross with crown Order of Merit (Sovereign Order Malta), 1961; recipient Honor certificate for service to Hungarian refugees Brazilian Red Cross, 1958. Clubs: Princeton (Washington); American (v.p. Rome 1961-62); International (Rio de Janeiro). Home: Washington, D.C. Died May 8, 1975.

FULTON, WALLACE H., assn. exec.; b. Oakland, Calif., Mar. 16, 1896; s. Wallace Henry and Catherine (MacMahon) F.; student U. Calif, Farm Sch., Davis, 1915-16, U. Calif., 1920; U. Minn., 1920-22; m. Elizabeth Calkins, Jan. 29, 1925; children—David, Martha (Mrs. Beshers), Miriam (Mrs. Block). Employed as secretary of Walker's Manual, Inc., 1925-27, v.p., 1927-30, president 1930-33; sec. Dist. 1 (Calif.), Investment Bankers Code Com., Apr. 1934-Jan. 1935; dir. of compliance (nat. office), Investment Bankers Code Com., Jan.-May 1935; sec. Calif. Security Dealers Assn., June 1935-July 1936; dir. Investment Bankers Conf. Com., July-Aug. 1936; dir. Investment Bankers Conf., Inc., 1936-39; exec. dir. Nat. Assn. Securities Dealers, Inc., Washington, from 1939. Served as pvt., U.S. Army, 1918-19. Mem. Beta Theta Pi. Clubs: Metropolitan (Washington); Chevy Chase (Md); Lunch (N.Y. City); Bohemian (San Francisco). Home: Napa, Cal. Died Jan. 22, 1974.

FUNDERBURK, JAMES ERNEST, ret. dentist; b. Pageland, S.C., Nov. 24, 1887; s. James Thomas and Mary (Welch) F.; D.D.S., U. Md., 1908, postgrad. degree in Oral Surgery and Anesthesia, 1910; m. Mary Eliza Sellers, Dec. 29, 1909 (dec. Apr. 1934); children—James Ernest, Jullia Sellers, Benjamin Jackson, Thomas Alexander, George Wilson (dec.), Louise (Mrs. Harry Willis), Mary Sinclair (dec.), Eugenia (Mrs. Harry Smoak), Nancy (Mrs. Edwin Waterman Robeson); m. 2d, Effie Ingram Wall, Aug. 29, 1936; 1 son, Ervin. Practice dentistry, Cheraw, S.C., 1908-66. Chmn., Chesterfield County Dept. Welfare, 1945-54. Precinct pres. Cheraw Democratic Com., 1954-70. Recipient citations for doing free dental work for mil. conscripts from Pres. of U.S., 1941, 45. Fellow S.C. Dental Assn. (hon., exec. bd. 1908-66, past chmn. numerous coms. mem. Am. Dental Assn. (life), Pec Dee Dental Soc. (charter), Psi Omega (citation for distinguished service to fraternity and dentistry 1966). Presbyn. (ruling elder 1964-68). Mason (Shriner, K.T.), Kiwanian. Address: Cheraw, S.C. Died Oct. 3, 1972.

FUNKE, ERICH (ALFRED), Germanist; b. Rogaetz-Elbe, Germany, Dec. 11, 1891; s. Wilhelm and Anna (Boeis) F.; student Real-gymnasium Magdeburg, Abitur, 1903-12; student U. of Leipzig, 1912-14, U. of Munich, 1914, U. of Zurich, 1918-19; Ph.D., U. of Halle, 1921; m. Lydia Gunzenhauser, June 12, 1937; children—Thomas, Elizabeth, Barbara. Came to U.S., 1931, naturalized, 1937. Teacher of languages. German high schs., Bitterfeld, 1924-26, Halle-Saale, 1927-31; asst. abt. f. Sprechkunde U. of Halle, 1928-31; guest lecturer in phonetics State U. of Ia., summer 1931; asst. prof. German, U. of Ia., 1931-32; asso. prof. German, State U. of Ia., 1932-37, prof. and head dept. German, 1937-60, professor emeritus, 1960-74, in charge foreign language phonetics laboraory, 1942-60; vis. prof. Knox Coll., 1961-64, Cornell Coll., 1965-68, U. So. Ill., summers 1966-69. Member of American Modern Lang. Assn., Am. Assn. Teachers German (exec. council 1946-48), American Association U. Profs., Delta Phi Alpha (national vice pres. 1947-52). Club: Triangle (pres. 1945). Author books including: Die Umgangssprache, 1945. Co-author: Kriegsdeutsch, 1942; Gesprochenes Deutsch, 1953; Translingua Script, 1957, Translingua-English Dicitonary English-Translingua Dictionary, German-Translingua Dictionary. Co-editor: The Philol. Quar., from 1932. Phonetic and artistic speech records. Contbr. articles. Home: Iowa City, Ia., Died Nov. 5, 1974.

FUNKHOUSER, JOHN WILLIAM, educator; b. Beaverdam, Va., Aug. 28, 1926; s. Joseph Alfred and Mary Gordon (Radd) F.; B.A. magna cum laude, Washington and Lee U., 1948; Ph.D. (Atomic Energy fellow), Stanford, 1951, postgrad., 1953-54; student Richmond Profl. Inst., 1966-67; m. Anne Black, July 8, 1950; children—Susan (Mrs. Donald Patterson), William. Instr. Stanford (Cal.) U., 1951-52, research asso., 1952-54; research geologist Jersey Prodn. Research Co., Tulsa, 1954-63; sr. paleontologist Int. Petroleum, Ltd., Bogota, Colombia, 1963-66; asst. mgr. Concurso de Chivor Emerald Mines, Bogota 1966; mem. faculty John Tyler Community Coll., Chester, Va., 1967-74, prof. geology, 1971-74. Lectr. on environment to clubs, schs., others, 1969-74. Mem. Internat. Com. Bot. Nomenciature, Netherlands, 1959-74. Served with USNR, 1945-46. Recipient Robinson award, 1948, Herndon library award 1948 (both Washington & Lee U.). Mem. Va. Acad. Sci. (sect. chmn. 1973-74), Geol. Soc. Am., Am. Inst. Biol. Sci., Inter-Am. Philatetic Soc., Internat. Assn. Plant Taxonomy, Internat. Assn. Paleobotanists, A.A.A.S., Smithsonian Assos., Sigma Xi, Phi Beta Kappa, Tau

Kappa Iota, Phi Eta Sigma. Clubs: Sierra (San Francisco); Camera (Richmond, Va.). Home: Chester, Va. Died Dec. 3, 1974.

FUQUA, ISHAM W., petroleum co. exec.; b. Downey, Calif., July 13, 1879; s. John M. and Sarah Arminta (Neighbours) F.; ed. grammar sch. and business coll., m. Winnie May West, Apr. 22, 1903. Began in oil fields at Fullerton, 1898; went to Coalinga fields for Am. Petroleum Co., 1908, and was apptd. asst. supt. same yr.; trans. to Am. Oilfields Co., Midway, Calif., as gen. field supt., 1911, to Los Angeles as asst. gen. mgr., 1917; elected pres. and gen. mgr. Calif. Petroleum Corpn. (parent holding co.), May 1918; also pres. and gen. mgr. Am. Oilfields Co., Am. Petroleum Co., Petroleum Midway Co., Ltd., Midland Oilfields Co., Ltd., Niles Lease Co. (all subsidiary cos.); pres. and gen. mgr. Red Star Petroleum Co., Maricopa Star Oil Co.; v.p. and gen. mgr., Calif. Star Oil Co., Coalinga Star Oil Co.; pres. Chamber Mines and Oil, Los Angeles, from 1921. Republican. Mason. Club: Los Angeles Athletic. Home: Los Angeles, Cal.†

FURBERSHAW, VIRGINIA LAWTON, comml. artist; b. Chgo.; d. Walter Louis and Georgia (Schmitt) Furbershaw; B.S., Northwestern U. Art dir., Chgo., 1949-52. Creative artist, art dir., Phila., 1952-57; art dir. Bestwall Certain-teed Sales Corp., Ardmore, Pa., 1957-58; free lance art dir. for periodical advertisements, booklets, TV and sales promotion slides and filmed commls., scale models for exhibits, 1958-65; art dir. Kampmann & Bright Advt., 1965-66; asst. art dir. Calvin Corp., 1966-67; free lance designer, 1967-70; creator exptl. art dept. Indsl. Valley Bank, 1970-71; various creative free-lance positions. Exhibited paintings at Phila. Sketch Club, others. Mem. Soc. Cinema Arts and Scis., Artists Guild, Phila., Alpha. Phi. Clubs: Charlotte Cushman, Plays and Players (Phila.). Home: Evanston Ill. Died Dec. 21, 1972; interred Calvary Cemetery, Evanston, Ill.

FURLONG, WILLIAM REA, ret. naval ofcr.; b. Washington County, Pa., 1881; s. William Allen and Ethel A. (Grant) F.; Ed. M.E., Teachers College, California, Pa., 1898; B.S., U.S. Naval Academy, 1905; M.A., Columbia, 1914; Naval War College, 1933; m. Cora Glover, 1910; 1 son, William Rea Jr. Ensign U.S. Navy, 1907, and advanced through the grades to rear adm., 1937; on staff of Adm. Fletcher after landing at Vera Cruz, 1914; gunnery officer U.S.S. South Carolina, 1916, and U.S.S. Nevada, 1917; attached to Brit. battleship Ramailies, 1918; during World War I served as gunnery officer Atlantic Fleet and as gunnery dobserver in Grant Fleet of Brit. Navy in North Sea, at Scapa Flow and Firth of Forth; also on staff of Adm. Sims at London hdqrs.; in charge design and procurement navy fire control, 1919-20; sent to Germany to investigate German ordnance materials and methods; introduced into U.S. Navy, Synchronous fire control system and remote control of guns by power; fleet gunnery officer U.S. Pacific Fleet, 1921-23; in charge of Island Govts. under the Navy, 1923-26; comdg. officer of Chicago (cruiser), Nechez (oil tanker), div. destroyers; comd. Marblehead, 1932-33, Naval Proving Ground, 1934-35; captain West Virginia (flagship), 1936; on staff commander-in-chief United States Fleet, Admiral Hepburn, 1937; rear admiral and chief Bureau of Ordnance, Washington, D.C., Aug. 1937-February 1941; comdr. Minecraft Battle Force, April 1941; engaged in defense of Pearl Harbor, Dec. 7, 1941, when his flagship, U.S.S. Oglala, was sunk by torpedo; comdt. Navy Yard, Pearl Harbor, 1941-45, in charge salvage operations on ships sunk during Japanese attack. Also of repairs on ships of Pacific Fleet engaged in North and South Pacific actions. Decorated Legion of Merit and gold star; recipient Freedoms Found. award, 1950. Member of the Am. Legion, Vets. Fgn. Wars, S.A.R., Mil. Order of World Wars (nat. comdr. 1949). Clubs: Army and Navy, Chevy Chase. Author articles on history and origin of U.S. Flag. Home: Washington, D.C.†

FURR, ROY, chain grocery exec.; b. McKinney, Tex., Sept. 18, 1904; s. Crone W. and Annie Furr; student Clarendon Jr. Coll., U. Okla.; L.H.D., McMurry Coll., 1962; m. Lela Close, Dec. 27, 1923; children—Don G., Shelly Rose (Mrs. Jack Hall), Roy K. With Furr Food Stores, Amarillo, Tex., 1927, then mgr. 6 stores, Lubbock, Tex.; pres. Furr's Super Markets, Inc., 70 stores in 3 states, Lubbock; chmn. bd. Furr's Cafeterias, Inc., Lubbock Packing Co.; dir. Southwestern Bell Telephone Co.; 1st Nat. Bank of Lubbock. Bd. dirs. Tex. Technol. Coll.; Methodist Hosp., Lubbock, Boys Ranch, Amarillo, McMurray Coll. Mem. Lubbock C. of C., Phi Delta Theta. Methodist (steward). Rotarian. Home: Lubbock, Tex. Died June 1975.

FURTSEVA, YEKATERINA ALEKSEEVNA, Soviet govt. ofcl.; b. Kalinin Oblast, USSR, 1910; grad. Moscow Inst. Fine Chem. Tech., 1942, Higher Course Acad. Civil Air Fleet, Leningrad, 1935, Corr. Dept. Higher Party Sch., Central Com. All-Union Communist Party, 1948. Weaver, Bol'shevicka Plant; sec. Korenevo Rayon Komomol com., Kursk Oblast, then sec. Feodosiya City Com., later dept. head Crimena Oblast Com. All-Union Komsomol, 1930—; asst. head polit. dept. Aeroflot Aviation Technicum, 1935-36; instr. central com. All-Union Komsomol, 1936-37; mem. party bur., then sec., party organ Moscow Inst. Fine

Chem. Tech., 1937-42; sec., 2d sec., then 1st sec. Moscow Frunze Rayon Com. All-Union Communist Party, 1942-50; 2d sec., Moscow City Com. Communist Party Soviet Union, 1950-54, 1st sec., 1954-57, sec., central com., 1956-60, mem., 1956—, mem. presidium, 1957-61; with USSR Ministry Culture, 1960-75, minister culture; mem. USSR Party and govt. delegation to Peking, 1954, Soviet govt. delegation to India and Austria, 1960; head delegation to Mongolia, 1966; dep. USSR Supreme Soviet, 1950, 54, 58, 66, mem. delegation to Yugoslavia, 1965, head delegation to Eng., 1956; dep. and mem. presidium Russian Soviet Federative Socialist Republic Supreme Soviet, 1955, 59; mem. Communist Party, 1930—. Decorated Order Lenin (2), Order Red Banner Labor, Badge of Honor, medals. Visited France, Denmark, Gt. Britain, 1961, Denmark and Italy, 1964, Finland and Gt. Britain, 1963, Poland, Rumania, Eng., France, 1965, Bulgaria, Japan, 1966. Address: Moscow USSR., Died Oct. 25, 1975.

GABLE, WILLIAM RUSSELL, ednl. adminstr.; b. Columbia, Miss., Oct. 14, 1924; s. Harvey Russell and Gladys (East) G.; B.A., La. State U., 1949, M.A., 1949; Ph.D. in Polit. Sci., U. Chgo., 1953; m. Audrey Elaine Lanoux, Jan. 30, 1949; children—William Russell, Gwendolyn Leah, Bradley Walter. Asst. prof. social sci. Ga. Inst. Tech., 1953-56: research asso. U. Mich. Inst. Pub. Adminstrn., Ann-Arbor, 1956-60, asst. dir., 1963-67, asst. prof. polit. sci. U. Mich., 1960-63, asso. prof. polit. sci., 1963-67; prof. polit. sci., dir. Inst. Pub. Adminstrn., Ariz. State U., Tempe, 1967-71, 72-73, dir. Inst. Pub. Adminstrn., 1972-73; exec. coordinating officer Ariz. Bd. Regents, Phoenix, 1971-72; dean Sch. Urban Life, Ga. State U., Atlanta, 1973-75. Chief-of party U. Mich.-AID, Nat. Chengchi U., Taipei, Taiwan, 1962-63. Exec. sec. Gov. G. Mennen Williams' Study Commn. Met. Area Problems, Mich., 1959-60; active various county, municipal, state orgns. Served to lt. C.E., AUS, 1943-46; col. Res. Mem. Am. Polit. Sci. Assn., Ariz. Finance Officers Assn., Internat. City Mgmt. Assn., Res. Officers Assn., Am. Soc. Pub. Adminstrn. Contbr. articles profl. jours. Home: Atlanta Ga. Died May 11, 1975; buried Nat. Cemetery, Biloxi, Miss.

GABUZDA, GEORGE JOSEPH, JR., physician, educator; b. Freeland, Pa., Jan. 26, 1920; s. George Joseph and Anna Mary (Silvasi) G.; B.A. magna cum laude, Lehigh U., 1941; M.D. cum laude, Harvard, 1944; m. Marion E. Jarvis, Apr. 2, 1946 (dec. Oct. 1968); children—Anne T., George Joseph III, Denise C. Intern, Pa. Hosp., Phila., 1944-45; resident medicine Mary Fletcher Hosp., Burlington, Vt., 1945-46; mem. dept. medicine Thorndike Meml. Lab., Boston City Hosp., from instr. to asso. medicine Harvard Med. Sch., 1948-54; faculty Case Western Res. U. Med. Sch., Cleve., 1954-75, prof. medicine, 1964-75; asso. dir. dept. medicine Cleve. Met. Gen. Hosp., 1966-75; cons. Cleve. VA, Luth. hosps. Sec. sci. adv. com. Cleve. Diabetes Fund, 1965-72; sec. adv. com. liver Office Surgeon Gen., 1955-65; mem. sci. adv. com. United Health Founds., 1964-72. Served to capt. M.C., AUS, 1946-48. Mem. Am. Soc. Clin. Investigation, Central Soc. Clin. Research, Am. Assn. Study Liver Diseases (pres. 1960-61), Soc. Exptl. Biology and Medicine, Am. Fedn. Clin. Research, A.A.A.S., Am. Inst. Nutrition, Am. Soc. Clin. Nutrition, Internat. Assn. Study Liver. Contbr. papers on metabolic abnormalities in liver disease with spl. reference to hepatic coma, ascites, renal function, nutrition in man to profl. jours. Home: South Euclid, Ohio. Died May 16, 1975; buried St. Albans, Vt.

GADSBY, EDWARD NORTHUP, lawyer; b. North Adams, Mass., Apr. 11, 1900; s. Herbert H. and Sigma Mirta (Northup) G.; A.B., Amherst Coll., 1923, M.A. (hon.), 1958; J.D., N.Y.U., 1929; LL.D., Suffolk U., 1959; m. Isabelle H. Halsey, Dec. 29, 1934; children—Edward Northup, Susan Elizabeth. Admitted to N.Y. bar, 1929, Mass. bar, 1937; with firm Rushmore, Bisbee & Stern, N.Y.C. 1929-37; pvt. practice, N. Adams, Mass., 1937-47; with firm Sullivan and Worcester, Boston, 1956-57; commr. Mass. Dept. Pub. Utilities, 1947-52, chmn., 1947-49, counsel, 1952-56; mem. chmn. SEC, 1957-61; partner firm Gadsby and Hannah, Boston and Washington, 1961-73. Recipient presdl. citation N.Y.U., 1960. Mem. Am., Fed. bar assns., Phi Beta Kappa, Chi Phi. Author: 11A Business Organizations, Federal Security Exchange Act. Home: Cambridge, Mass. Died June 12, 1973.

GAERTTNER, ERWIN RUDOLF, educator, research scientist; b. Denver, Feb. 27, 1911; s. Rudolf and Pauline Karoline (Groezinger) G.; B.S. in Elec. Engring., U. Denver, 1932; Ph.D. in Physics, U. Mich., 1937; m. Dorothy Mary Polcar, Dec. 21, 1940; children—Robert E., Martin R. NRC fellow physics Cal. Inst. Tech., 1937-38, Horace H. Rackham fellow physics, 1938-39; from instr. to asst. prof. physics Ohio State U., 1939-46; on leave to radition lab. Mass. Inst. Tech., 1942-46; research asso. research lab. Gen. Electric Co., 1946-51, Knolls Atomic Power Lab., 1951-58; prof. physics Rensselaer Poly. Inst., Troy, N.Y., 1958-60, dir. Linear Accelerator Lab., 1958-74, prof. nuclear engring. and sci., head dept., 1960-74. Recipient U. Denver Distinguished Alumni award, 1965. Fellow

Am. Phys. Soc., Am. Nuclear Soc.; mem. Phi Beta Kappa, Sigma Xi. Presbyn. Home: Troy, N.Y. Died Nov. 19, 1974.

GAGE, JOHN BALLEY, lawyer; b. Kansas City, Mo., Feb. 24, 1887; s. John Cutter and Ida (Bailey) G.; A.B., U. of Kan., 1907; LL.B., Kansas City Sch. Law, 1909; m. Marjorie Hires; children—Betty (Mrs. H. W. Jensen), John C., Frank H., Anne (Mrs. Revis C. Lewis). Admitted to Mo. bar, 1909; mem. Gage, Hodges, Kreamer & Varner, Kansas City; lecturer on law Kansas City Sch. of Law, 1915-38; dir. Traders National Bank, also Gas Service Company, Safety Federal Savings and Loan Association. Mayor of Kansas City, 1940-46. Chmn. bd. of adv. bond trustees of Kansas City, Mo.; regional vice president Nat. Municipal League, Trustee U. Kansas City. Mem. Am. (chmn. adminstrv. law sect.), Mo. State Kansas City bar assns., Am. Royal assn., (pres., chmn. bd.), Midwest Research Inst. (v.p.) C. of C., Lawyers Assn. of Kansas City, Sigma Alpha Epsilon, Phi Alpha Delta. Democrat. Episcopalian. Clubs: Kansas City, Kansas City Country, Saddle and Sirloin, Rotary. Editor and compiler: Kelly's Missouri Probate Law. Home: Kansas City, Mo., Died Jan. 15, 1970.

GAILLARD, WILLIAM DAWSON, lawyer; b. N.Y.C., Aug. 29, 1906; s. William Dawson and Marie (Planten) G.; grad. Hotchkiss Sch., 1922; A.B., Princeton, 1926; LL.D., Harvard, 1929; Katharine Miller, Sept. 6, 1930; children—William Dawson, Peter Saxton, Katharine Saxton (Mrs. John E. Strong). Admitted to N.Y. bar, 1929; partner Milbank, Tweed, Hadley and McCloy, N.Y.C., 1938-75. Clubs: Princeton (N.Y.C.); St. Andrews Golf (Hastings-on-Hudson, N.Y.). Home: Scarsdale, N.Y. Died Aug. 8, 1975; buried Fisher's Island, N.Y.

GAINER, DENZIL LEE, state govt. ofcl.; b. Mt. Zion, W.Va., Sept. 12, 1913; s. Lee and Laura (Elliott) G.; student LaSalle U., 1936-38, Morris Harvey Coll., 1943-44; m. Lucille Reading, Mar. 9, 1935; children—Phillip Lee, Kenneth Lee, Karen Reading, m. 2d, Betty Kathleen Wise Butler, June 10, 1972; stepchildren—David Timothy Butler, Joel Daniel Butler. Chief office dep. sheriff Calhoun County W.Va., 1934-36; city recorder Grantsville, 1936-37; dep. chief insp. pub. offices State Tax Commrs. Office, 1939-41; asst. state budget dir. W. Va., Charleston, 1941-46, dir. budget, 1947-57, asst. legislative auditor, 1957-60, state auditor, 1961-72. Served with USMCR, 1944-46. Democrat. Methodist. Mason. (Shriner). Home: Charleston, W. Va. Died Nov. 1, 1972; buried Cunningham Meml. Park, Charleston, W.Va.

GAINES, JAMES MARSHALL, business exec.; b. Poughkeepsie, N.Y., May 8, 1911; s. Marshall Venable and Alice C. (Hawkins) G.; ed. high sch.; m. Eugenia M. Keller, June 14, 1941; children—Richard M., Susan H., Betsy, Eugenia, Christopher. Personal rep. Maj. Edward Bowes, 1935-41; v.p. NBC, 1942-53, Gen. Teleradio, Inc. after 1953, dir. from 1953; dir. MBS, Peoples Nat. Bank of Lynbrook. Trustee North Shore Hosp., L.I., N.Y., L.I. Symphony Orchestra. Mem. Radio and Television Execs. Soc. (pres., mem. bd.) Home: Port Washington, L.I., N.Y., Died Feb. 17, 1976.

GAINES, RUTH, author, social worker; b. Litchfield, Conn., 1879; A.B., Smith Coll., 1901; postgrad. student, Yale, 1901-02. Author: Little Light, 1911; Treasure Flower, 1916; Village Shield (with Georgia Willis Read), 1917; A Village in Picardy, 1918; Helping France, 1919; Ladies of Grécourt, 1920. Dir. publicity for the Smith Coll. Relief Unit in the Somme, 1917-19. Home: Chicago, Ill.†

GAISMAN, HENRY JACQUES, inventor; b. Memphis, Dec. 5, 1869; s. Jacques and Sarah (Kaufman) G.; ed. pub. schs. Cin.; hon. M.E., Stevens Inst. Tech., 1932; m. Catherine A. Vance, Apr. 18, 1952. Founder, pres., chmn. bd. Auto-Strop Safety Razor Co., 1906-30; chmn. bd. Gillette Safety Razor Co., 1930-38; inventor of many articles, especially relating to photography, cutlery and machines to produce same. Founder of Inventors Found., Inc., non-profit orgn. for furthering edn. and guidance of students interested in inventions and to prepare courses for promoting inventions in tech. schs.; founder Gaisman Found., charitable orgn. Mem. bd. N.Y. State Reformatories, 1911-19. Served as expert with chief of Bur. of Research of the Gen. Staff, with Port of N.Y. War Bd., also chmn. safety razor div. War Industries Bd., during World War. Clubs: Lotos (N.Y.C.); Westchester Country (Rye, N.Y.). Home: Hartsdale, N.Y. Died Aug. 6, 1974.

GALE, RICHARD PILLSBURY, congressman; b. Minneapolis, Minn., Oct. 30, 1900; s. Edward Chenery and Sarah (Pillsbury) G.; B.A., Yale U., 1922; student Minn. Agrl. Sch., Minneapolis, 1923; m. Isobel Rising, Aug. 8, 1923; children—Richard Pillsbury, Alfred Gale. Began farming, 1923. Mem. Minn. state legislature, 1939-40; mem. 77th and 78th Congresses (1941-45), 3d Minn. Dist. Mem. Mound Sch. Bd., 8 yrs. Trustee Blake Sch., Hopkins, Minn. Mem. Minn. Farm Bur., Zeta Psi. Republican. Conglist. Home: Mound, Minn. Died Dec. 4, 1973.

GALLAGHER, EDWARD GEORGE, advt. exec.; b. Lancaster, Pa., Aug. 15, 1922; s. John L. and Louise (Rohr) G.; grad. Lancaster Catholic High Sch., 1939; m. Rosa Hamaker Heckel, Dec. 27, 1945; children—Brian, Bruce, Daniel David. Retail clk. Kirk Johnson & Co., Lancaster, 1940-42; advt. mgr. Steinman Hardware Co., Lancaster, 1945-50; with CBS-TV, 1953-54; with N. W. Ayer & Son, Inc., Phila., 1951-53, 55-75, exec. v.p. creative services, 1967-75, also dir. Served with AUS, 1942-45. Home: Springfield, Pa. Died Jan. 2, 1975.†

GALLEN, JOHN JAMES, coll. dean; b. Phila., Nov. 21, 1905; s. Harry S. and Kathryn M. (Stewart) G.; B.S. in Civil Engring., Villanova U., 1927, C.E., 1929, Dr. Engring., 1968; M.S. in Civil Engring., U. Pa., 1947; m. Frances L. Fitzgerald, May 1, 1937; children—John J., Robert M., Frances L., Kevin P., Kathyn M., Raymond J., Elaine A. Constrn. engr. Pa. R.R., 1927-32; instr. math. Roman Cath. High Sch., Phila., 1932-35; sr. engr. WPA, 1936; maintenance supr., purchasing agt. to supt. schs., Diocese Phila., 1936-40; mem. faculty Villanova (Pa.) U., 1940-75, prof. civil engring., 1949-75, dean Coll. Engring., 1961-75. Cons. engr., Phila., 1946-60. Exec. sec. John McKee Scholarship Com., 1957-75. chmn. United Fund drive Villanova U., 1963. Recipient Lindbach Distinguished Teaching award Villanova U., 1961. Registered profl. engr., Pa. Fellow Am. Soc. C.E. (pres. Phila. 1961-62); mem. Franklin Inst., Engrs. Club Phila., Am. Soc. Engring. Edn., Nat., Pa. (Engr. of Year, Delaware County 1968) socs. profl. engrs. Home: Havertown, Pa., Died Jan. 17, 1976.

GALPIN, PERRIN C., educator; b. New Haven, Conn., Aug. 11, 1889; s. Samuel A. and Clara (Larned) G.; A.B., Yale, 1910; A.M., 1912; grad. study, Oxford U., Eng., 1913-14; hon. Dr. U. of Louvain, Belgium, 1928, U. of Brussels, 1930; m. Stephanie K. English, May 10, 1917; children—Anne Perrin (Mrs. Sheldon Judson, Jr.), Stephen Kellogg, Lucy G. (Mrs. William S. Moorhead, Jr.). Teacher Saint Paul's School, Concord, New Hampshire, 1910-11; instructor history and economics, Union College, Schenectady, New York, 1916-17. Secretary Commission for Relife in Belgium, Brussels, 1914-15, Lille, 1918-19. Commissioned second lieutenant Field Artillery, August 15, 1917, honorably discharged as capt., May 5, 1919. Original incorporator Belgian-Am. Ednl. Found., 1920, pres., until 1963; sec. Am. Relief Adminstrn., 1919-23; incorporator Am. Children's Fund, 1923, v.p. 1936-50; president Pelham Community Chest, 1936-38; member School Bd., Pelham, 1933-44; mem. Francqui Foundation of Belgium since 1932; mem. Council of Administration, Fondation Universitaire of Belgium since 1945. Director W. T. Grant Co., 1945-55; exec. dir. The Grant Found., 1947-55. Trustee Inst. for Advanced Study, Princeton, New Jersey, Mem. Herbert Hoover Food Mission to Europe and Asia, 1946. Decorated Commander Order of Leopold, Belgium, 1951. Mem. Boy Scouts America (chmn. nat. health and safety com., 1943-52; recipient Silver Buffalo award 1947). Mem. Phi Beta Kappa, Zeta Psi. Republican. Presbyn. Clubs: Men's of Pelham (pres. 1933-34); Century, Yale (N.Y.C.): Elizabethan (New Haven); Fondation Universitaire (Brussels). Editor: Hugh Gibson, 1883-1954 (book). Home: Pelham Manor, N.Y. Died Aug. 11, 1973.

GALT, ARTHUR THOMAS, lawyer, financier; b. Chgo., Sept. 8, 1876; s. Azariah T. and Isabelle A. (Mason) G.; A.B., Yale, 1898; LL.B., Northwestern U., 1901; m. Ida May Cook, June 25, 1907; children—Arthur T., Raymond M. (M.D.), William C. Admitted to Ill. bar, 1901; practice of law, Chgo. Bd. govs. Art Inst. Chgo. Mem. Phi Beta Kappa, Order of Coif. Home: Chicago, Ill.†

GALVIN, JOHN E., steel co. founder; b. Chattanooga, Jan. 9, 1878; s. John William and Elizabeth (Murray) G.; student Wittenberg U., 1900; m. Florence Cole Fetter, May 10, 1905 (dec); children—Robert F., Virginia Cole (Mrs. John L. Crouse.) Founder, Ohio Steel Foundry Co., Lima, Springfield. O., 1907, then chmn. bd.; dir. Fed. Res. Bank of Cleve., 1930-40. Vice chmn. Ohio Republican Finance Com., 1940-50. Mem. Steel Founders' Soc. Am. (past pres.). Home: Lima, O. Deceased.

GAMBLE, MILLARD GOBERT, ind. consultant; born Louisville, Ga., May 24, 1894; s. Millard Gobert and Fannie (Hunter) G.; B.S., U.S. Naval Acad., 1915; m. Rose McGowan Cantey, 1917; children—Millard Gobert, John Hunter (dec.), Gloria (Mrs. Chastine Walton Jones, Jr.); m. 2d, Doris De Peyster Burger, May 31, 1936; 1 son, William Lawson; m. 3d, Inga Sonja Keventer, Dec. 4, 1959; 1 dau., Sonja. Commd. ensign USN, 1915, and advanced through grades to lt. comdr. (U.S.N.R.); served as U.S. naval officer, 1915-19; joined Standard Oil Co. (N.J.), 1919, served in constrn., operations and traffic divs., 1919-38, mgr. Caribbean div., N.Y. City, 1938-39, marine mgr. for affiliated companies, Aruba and Venezuela, Aruba, N.W.I., 1939-41, asst. gen. mgr., Marine dept., N.Y., 1942-45, gen. mgr. marine operations, 1945-50, pres. and dir. Esso Shipping Co. (co. acquired tanker fleet and marine personnel of Standard Oil Co., N.J. 1950), 1950-58; cons. bd. dirs. Standard Oil Co. (N.J.), 1958-59 (when Esso Shipping Co. merged with Esso Standard Oil Co. (chmn. U.S. delegation to 1st session of assembly Intergovtl. Maritime Consultive Orgn., 1959; now an independent consultant. Consultant transportation, chairman tanker group NSRB; member tanker and barge committee Mil. Petroleum Adv. Bd.; mem. transportation council U.S. Dept. Commerce; mem. of Am. Bur. Shipping, Am. com. Lloyd's Register of Shipping. Dir. United Def. Fund, Inc.; U.S. State Department, Shipping Liaison Com.; trustee United Seamen's Service; member hon. nat. com. Merchant Marine Meml. Chapel, Kings Point. Dir., chmn. exec. com. Am. Mcht. Marine Library Assn.; hon. dir. Transportation Association of America. Appointed Knight Commander of The Order of the Republic of Italy, 1956; recipient of The American Legion Citation for Meritorious Service, 1955. Member National Petroleum Council (chmn. tanker steel requirements group), Permanent Internat. Assn. Nav. Congresses (Am. nat. com.), Nat. Fgn. Trade Council, U.S. C. of C., Navy League U.S. (dir.), Soc. Naval Architects and Marine Engrs., Am. Legion, Naval Athletic Assn., N.Y. Soc. Mil. and Naval Officers World Wars. Clubs: Propeller, The University, New York Yacht (New York City); Circumnavigators. Contributor of many articles to various shipping and petroleum journals. Special interest in rural wild life and vegetation. Home: Wynnewood, Pa. Died Nov. 5, 1974.

GAMBRELL, MARY LATIMER, educator; b. Belton, S.C., Jan. 14, 1898; d. Enoch Pepper and Macie (Latimer) Gambrell; A.B., Greenville Woman's Coll. (now Furman U.), 1917, Litt.D., 1951; A.M., Columbia, 1931, Ph.D., 1937; L.H.D., Queens Coll. (N.C.), 1958. Instr. history New Haven State Tchrs. Coll., 1932-37; lectr. dept. edn. extension State of Conn., 1934; instr. history Hunter Coll., N.Y.C., 1937-43, asst. prof., 1944-48, asso. prof., 1949-53, prof., 1953-74, chmn. dept. history, 1948-62, dean faculties, 1961-66, acting pres., 1965, 66, pres., 1967, pres. emeritus, 1968-74; cons. to profl. orgns. Mem. legislative conf. City Colls., 1946-48; mem. council Furman U., 1972-74. Bd. dirs. N.Y.C. br. YWCA, 1971-72. Named to Furman U. Hall Fame, 1970; recipient Pres.'s medal Hunter Coll., 1971. Mem. Am. Hist. Assn., Am. Assn. U. Women (named Woman of Year, N.Y.C. chpt. 1967; bd. dirs. 1968-72), Berkshire Hist. Conf. (pres. 1946-49), English-Speaking Union, Phi Beta Kappa Assos., Phi Beta Kappa. Presby. Club: Cosmopolitan. Author: Ministerial Training in Eighteenth Century New England, 1937. Contbr. to profl. jours. Home: New York City, N.Y. Died Aug. 19, 1974.

GAMLEN, JAMES ELI, chem. mfg. co. exec.; b. Victoria, B.C., Can., Nov. 22, 1918; s. Harry and Sarah Jane (Chester) G.; Cal. Poly. Coll., San Francisco, 1937; m. Doris Jean Wayland, Sept. 25, 1965; children—James Eli, Thomas Chester. Wtih Gamlen Chem. Co., South San Francisco, Cal., 1933—, v.p. Gamlen Chem. Co. Internat. div. Sybron Co., 1945-73; pres., owner Western Polymer Corp., Burlingame, Cal., 1969-73. Fund raiser San Francisco Children's Hosp., San Francisco Ballet, San Francisco Opera, San Francisco Symphony; charter mem. Internat. Support Worthy Instns. Bd. dirs. Mental Health Recovery, Inc. of San Mateo County, San Francisco Internat. Music Competition Found., Enthusiastic 100 for San Francisco Internat. Film Festival. Served to capt., inf., AUS, 1942-47, 50-52. Mem. San Francisco Annex (charter), San Francisco Mus. Art, Children's Home Soc. Mason. Home: Hillsborough, Cal. Died Aug. 2, 1973.

GAMMON, BURTON OSMOND, cattle breeder; b. Harlan, Ia., Mar. 26, 1881; s. Warren and Anna Elvina (Pickett) G.; B.S., Drake U., Des Moines, Ia., 1903; m. Edith Vivian Koons, Nov. 23, 1904. Associated with Warren Gammon at Des Moines, Ia., in origin and development of Polled Hereford breed of cattle, 1900-18. Sec. Am. Polled Hereford Breeders Assn., 1910-46; then sec. emeritus. Mem. Gen. Board Lay Activities. Methodist Ch. Mem. Block and Bridle Club (hon.). Phi Beta Kappa. Republican. Methodist. Home: Des Moines, Ia.†

GAMMON, GEORGE DAVIS, physician, educator; born Waxahachie, Texas, Apr. 26, 1902; s. John Lea and Quincy (Browning) G.; A.B., U. Texas, 1924; M.D., U. Pa., 1927; m. Audrey Zimmermann VonClemm; children—Audrey VonClemm, George Davis, John Lea, Alma Linda. Intern U. Pa. Hosp., 1927-29, instr. neurology, 1933, prof. clin. neurology, acting head dept., 1944-53, chairman department of neurology, 1953-61; chief of neurology section VA Hosp., Ann Arbor, Michigan, 1962—; teaching assistant department of neurology U. Mich., 1962—; professor neurology department psychology U. Pa., 1948-53; Johnson Foundation, Univ. Pa., 1933-40; instructor medicine Baylor University, 1930-32; clerk National Hospital for Nervous Diseases, London, England, 1938; neurologist in charge out-patient department, consultant wards Children's Hospital, Phila., 1938-58; consultant to the neurological div., 1958—; cons. U.S.P.H.S.; chairman med. adv. bd. Myasthenia Found., 1956-57. Served as mem. Neurotropic Virus Commn., U.S. Army, 1941-45. Fellow A.C.P.; mem. Am. Med. Assn., Society Multiple Sclerosis (mem. med. adv. bd.), John Morgan Soc., American Clinical and Climatological Assn., Assn. for Research in Nervous and Mental Diseases, Soc. for Clin. Investigations, Pa. State Med. Soc., Coll. Physicians Phila., Phila. Neurological Soc. (past. pres.), Am. Physicians Art Assn. Am. Neurological Soc., Am. Acad. Neurology, Delta Tau Delta, AMPO. Home: Phila. Pa. Died May 10, 1974.

GAMMON, LANDON HAYNES, lawyer; b. Saltville, Va., Sept. 28, 1896; s. Landon Haynes and Rosa Cabell (Miller) G.; A.B., U. Va., 1918; LL.B., Harvard, 1922; m. Katherine C. Conn, June 30, 1926. Admitted to Tenn. bar, 1922, practiced in Chattanooga; mem. Goins, Gammon, Baker & Robinson and predecessor firms, 1925-75; spl. judge Ct. Appeals, Tenn., 1959-60. Trustee Chattanooga Pub. Library. Served in U.S. Army, World War I; mem. Selective Service Bd., World War II. Mem. Am., Tenn., Chattanooga bar assns., Selden Soc., Am. Legion. Democrat. Presbyn. Contbr. articles law jour. Home: Chattanooga Tenn. Died Apr. 28, 1975.

GANDEK, CHARLES, physician; b. Thompson, Pa., Oct. 30, 1917; s. Stanley and Agnes (Worek) G.; B.A., Morningside Coll., 1942; M.D., Creighton U., 1945; m. Ruth Louise Hayward, June 22, 1941; children—Judith Anne (Mrs. G. J. DeFranceaux), Linda Jean (Mrs. Thomas McCulston), Susan Ruth (Mrs. John Hicks). Intern, Mountainside Hosp., Montclair, N.J., 1945-46; resident Elizabeth Buxton Gen. Hosp., Newport News, Va., 1948-49; gen. pvt. practice, Newport News, 1949-51, Piscatawaytown, Edison, N.J., 1951-73; mem. staff St. Peters Gen., Middlesex Gen. hosps., New Brunswick, N.J., Middlesex Rehab. Hosp.; plant physician Revlon, Edison, 1960-73; me. dir. Edison Schs., 1952-72; med. dir. N.J. Turnpike Authority, 1968-73. Served from 1st lt. to capt. AUS, 1946-48. Fellow Am. Acad. Family Physicians (past pres. Middlesex County chpt.), A.M.A., Middlesex County Med. Soc. (pres. 1967-68, chmn. bd. trustees 1968-69), N.J. Assn. Sch. Physicians, N.J. Med. Assn., Soc., Nat. Rifle Assn. (life), Am. Coll. Sports Physicians, Am. Legion, Edison C. of C. Methodist. Mason. Clubs: Field Trial; Jockey Hollow Field Trial; Lake Island Gun; Pennsylvania. Home: Edison, N.J. Died Apr. 30, 1973; buried Piscatawaytown Cemetery, Edison.

GANDY, HARRY L., congressman; b. Churubusco, Ind., Aug. 13, 1881; s. W. S. and Ella J. (Matthews) G.; grad. Tri-State Coll., Angola, Ind., 1901; m. Frances Keiser, of Rapid City, S.D., Oct. 30, 1909. Began in newspaper business and ranching, Wasta, S.D., 1910. Mem. S.D. Senate, 1911; receiver, pub. moneys, U.S. Land Office, Rapid City, July 16, 1913-Mar. 3, 1915; mem. 64th and 66th Congresses (1915-21) from 3d S.D. Dist. Democrat. Home: Rapid City, S.D.†

GANGEL, MARTHA O'DONNELL (MRS. ALEXANDER GANGEL), educator, sculptor; b. San Francisco; d. Frank Harte and Sarah (Mallin) O'Donnel; B.S., Columiba, 1933; M.A., N.Y.U. 1946; student Art Students League Cooper Union, Pratt Inst., Traphagen, Clay Arts Club; m. Alexander Gangel, July 10, 1950. Tchr. sculpture and fine arts, N.Y.C. High Schs., 1938-57; exhibited N.A.D., 1964, Nat. League Am. Pen Women, Smithsonian, Tulsa, Stamford, Bruce museums, Hudson Valley Art Assn., Am. Artists Profl. League. One-woman shows sculpture and water color paintings in Mexico, N.Y.C., Westchester County. Chmn. art and promotion Mayfair fund raising United Hosp., 1970-72. Bd. dirs. Genarians of Larchmont, Sr. Citizens Group, 1956-66, Huguenot Young Men's Assn., New Rochelle, N.Y., 1966-73. Founder, organizer Larchmont Outdoor Art Show, 1957-62. Mem. New Rochelle Art Assn. (founder, organizer Anniversary Nat. Art Shows 1963, 64, 65, 66; dir. 1960-67, pres. 1964-66), Nat. League Am. Penwomen (past pres. Westchester br., mem. bd.; parliamentarian Conn. Pioneer br.), Westchester Fedn. Women's clubs (art project chmn. 1964-73, mem. bd. 1970-73, Larchmont Women's Club (chmn. art coms., mem. bd.). Address: Larchmont, N.Y. Died May 30, 1973; interred Mount Hope Cemetery, Westchester County, N.Y.

GANGEWERE, EARNEST PAUL, r.r. exec.; b. Bethlehem, Pa., Nov. 17, 1900; M.E., Lehigh U.; children—Dana Wayne, Martha LaDell (Mrs. Snyder). With Reading R.R. Co., 1922—, asst. gen. mgr., 1949-50, asst. v.p. operations and mgmt., 1949-50, vice president operations and mgmt., 1950-60, pres., 1960-64, chmn., from 1964, dir. B. & O. R.R.; chmn. exec. com. Central R.R. Co. of New Jersey. Fellow Am. Soc. M.E.; mem. Reading C. of C., Phi Beta Kappa, Tau Beta Pi. Mason (Shriner), Elk. Home: Jenkintown, Pa. Died May 1973.

GANNON, FRED HALL, banker; b. Eaton Rapids, Mich., Sept. 18, 1881; s. William Henry and Mary Ellen (Hall) G.; grad. high sch., Ellendale, N.D.; m. Edith Elizabeth Mather, of Groton, S.D., June 1907; children—Frederick Mather, John William, Richard Hall. Began as clerk with First Nat. Bank, Aberdeen S.D., 1899, pres. from 1927; mem. exec. com. and dir. Home Bldg. & Loan Assn.; dir. Aberdeen Finance Co. Mem. Aberdeen Chamber Commerce. Republican. Mason, Elk. Club: Aberdeen Country. Home: Aberdeen, S.D.†

GANTT, NICHOLAS JOURDAN, JR., lawyer; b. Magnolia, Ark., July 13, 1879; s. Nicholas John and Laura (Browning) G.; B.A., Hendrix Coll., Conway, Ark., 1898; M.A., Vanderbilt U., 1901, LL.B. (now J.D.), 1903; m. Clara McRae, Apr. 28, 1915. Admitted to Ark. bar, 1903, since practiced in Pine Bluff; mem. firm Coleman, Gantt, Ramsay & Cox and predecessor firms, after 1904; Pres., dir. Nat. Credit Corp., Reliable Abstract & Title Co., Coca-Cola Bottling Co. of S.W. Ark.; v.p., dir. First Fed. Savs. & Loan Assn.; sec., dir. Ark. Oak Flooring Co., S. Ark. Livestock Corp., Ark.-Ga. Co. Mem. Jefferson County Bd. Health, after 1925;

city atty., Pine Bluff, 1929-32. Recipient Outstanding Lawyer awards Ark. Bar Assn. and Ark. Bar Found., 1916. Mem. Ark. Bar Assn. (pres. 1940, chmn. past presidents), Sigma Alpha Epsilon. Democrat. Methodist (trustee). Mason (Shriner, 33, K.T.). Home: Pine Bluff, Ark.†

GANTT, ROBERT ANDERSON, engr.; b. Falls City, Neb., Sept. 15, 1881; s. Judge Amos E. and Emma (Miller) G.; grad. St. Johns Mil. Acad., 1900; B.S. in E.E., U. Neb., 1909. hon. E.D., 1937; m. Zola Dellecker, Nov. 12, 1912; 1 dau., Nancy (Mrs. John M. H. Lindbeck). Joined Am. Telephone & Telegraph Co., 1909, chief engr. Northwestern Bell Telephone Co., Omaha, 1919-23, So. Calif. Telephone Co., Los Angeles, 1923-25; gen. mgr. Pacific Telephone & Telegraph Co., San Francisco, 1925-28; v.p. Internat. Telephone & Telegraph Corp., 1928, Eastern European resident v.p., hdqrs. Bucharest, Rumania, 1939-42, operating v.p. in charge telephone and radio operations, 1944-47, v.p., cons. after 1947; operating v.p. Postal Telegraph Cable Co., (subsidiary Internat. Telephone & Telegraph Corp.), 1928-39, retired Sept. 1947; v.p. U.S. Comml. Co., Washington, 1942-44; dir. Gen. Telephone Corp., Gen. Telephone Service Corp., Gen. Telephone Directory Co., Internat. Standard Electric Corp. Pres. Jackson Lab. Assn.; trustee Roscoe B. Jackson Meml. Lab. (Bar Harbor, Me.), U. Neb. Found. Mem. Phi Delta Theta. Club: Bankers of America, Ridgewood Country (Danbury, Conn.). Home: New Fairfield, Conn.†

GARAND, JOHN C., ordnance design engr.; b. St. Remi, Que., Can., Jan. 1, 1888; s. Jean Baptiste and Elizabeth Edwidge (Oligny) G.; Dr. Engring. (hon.), Lehigh U., 1949; m. Nellie B. Shepard, Sept. 6, 1930; children—Janice Kay, Richard Norman. Began at age of 12 yrs. to repair, design and fabricate machines and machine parts, 1900-18; engaged in ordnance design engring., specializing in light arms, from 1918; inventor of Garand rifle, standard equipment of U.S. Army. Mem. Jewett City Council. Recipient of William Pynchon award, 1939; Modern Pioneer in Frontier of American Industry award from N.A.M., 1940; Holley medal from Am. Soc. M.E., 1941; first Gen. John H. Rice medal from Army Ordnance Assn., 1941; Lord and Taylor American Design award, 1942; special award Am. Soc. for Metals, 1942; John Scott medal City of Phila., 1943; Medal for Merit from U.S. Govt., 1944; Franco Am. Hist. Soc. award, 1945; Am. Ordnance Assn. medal, 1969; Elected to Hall of Fame Mus., Aberdeen, Md., 1973. Mem. Am. Soc. Metals, Nat. Assn. Ret. Civil Employees; hon. mem. Rotary Internat.; Springfield Armory Hist. Assn.; life mem. Army Emergency Relief. Home: Springfield, Mass. Died Feb. 16, 1974.

GARDINER, ARTHUR Z., govt. officer; b. Garden City, N.Y., Oct. 31, 1901; s. Clement E. and Mary Helen (Zimmermann) G.; A.B., Harvard, 1922; m. Emily D. Floyd, Dec. 7, 1929; children—Helen Floyd Garrison, Arthur Z., John Rolfe, Frederick Prime. Employed as clerk, 1923; pres. Booth Am. Shipping Corp., 1934-41; treas. Surpass Leather Co., 1937-41; vice pres. U.S. Comercial Co., 1944-47; trade adviser, office Coordinator of Aid to Greece and Turkey, 1947-48; sr. adviser Greek-Turkish affairs, Econ. Cooperation Adminstrn., Washington, 1948-49; spl. asst. bur. Near Eastern, S. Asian and African Affairs, Dept. of State, 1949, politico-econ. advisor, 1951-64, minister-counselor, U.S. Embassy, Karachi, Pakistan, 1955; econ. counselor U.S. Embassy and dir. ICA Mission Vietnam, 1958-62; econ minister Am. Embassy, Tokyo, Japan, 1962-64. Mem. Council on Fgn. Relations. Clubs: Harvard (N.Y.C.); Cosmos (Washington). Home: McLean Va., Died Dec. 4, 1975.

GARDNER, DONFRED HUBER, coll. dean; b. Massillon, O., Feb. 16, 1900; s. Daniel Sylvester and Elinor (Huber) G.; student Amherst Coll., 1918, Western Reserve U., 1918-21; A.B., Princeton, 1922, A.M., 1923; m. Margaret Doyle Wilcox, Aug. 22, 1925; children—Ann Margaret, Virginia Eleanor. Teacher pub. schs., Lisbon, O., 1923-24; instr. Prudue U., 1924; instr. history U. of Akron, 1924-26, asst. prof., 1926-31, asso. prof., 1931-36, dean of men, 1926-36, prof., from 1936, dean of students, 1936-55, dean of administration, 1955-59, vice president and dean of administration, from 1959. Member the survey staff N. Central Assn. of Colls. and Secondary Schs., 1931-35; adv. mem. Cooperative Study of Secondary Sch. Standards; ednl. adviser Nat. Interfraternity Conf., 1935-38, Dir. Family Service Soc., Akron Hosp. Service. Served in inf., U.S. Army, 1918; lt. col. Adj. Gen.'s Dept. AUS, 1942-44. Mem. Nat. Assn. Deans and Advisers of Men. (sec. 1931-37, pres. 1937-38); Am. Assn. U. Profs., Council Social Agencies, Beta Theta Pi, Omicron Delta Kappa. Clubs: University, Portage Country. Author: Student Personnel Service, 1936. Contbr. articles and revs. to jours. Home: Akron, O. Died May 11, 1975.

GARDNER, ERLE STANLEY, author, lawyer; b. Maldon, Mass., July 17, 1889; s. Charles Walter and Grace Adelma (Waugh) G.; ed. high sch.; m. Natalie Talbert, Apr. 9, 1912 (dec. Feb. 1968); 1 dau., Natalie Grace (Mrs. Toby Naso); m. 2d, Jean Bethell, Aug. 7, 1968. Admitted to Cal. bar, 1911; in practice at Oxnard, 1911-16; pres. Consol. Sales Co., 1918-21; former mem. firm Sheridan, Orr, Drapeau and Gardner, Ventura. Mem. Am. Bar Assn., Am. Judicature Soc., Harvard Assos. Police Sci., N.H. Medico. Soc., Elk; Hon. Life Mem.; Acad. Sci. Interrogation and Kansas Peace Officers Assn. Adviser, Texas Law Enforcement Found. Club: Adventurers (Chgo., N.Y.). Author several travel and exploration books; The Land of Shorter Shadows, 1948, Neighborhood Frontiers, 1954; Hunting the Desert Whale, 1960; Hovering Over Baja, 1961; The Desert Is Yours, 1963; The Hidden Heart of Baja 1962; The World of Water, 1964; Hunting Lost Mines by Helicopter, 1965; Off the Beaten Track in Baja, 1967; Gypsy Days on the Delta, 1967; Drifting Down the Delta, 1969; Mexico's Magic Square, 1968; Host with the Big Hat, 1969; (non-fiction) the Court of Last Resort, 1952, Cops on Campus and Crime in the Street, 1970; over one hundred detective stories under own and pen names. Principal character, Perry Mason. Latest books: The Case of the Waylaid Wolf, The Case of the Duplicate Daughter, 1960; The Case of the Spurious Spinster; The Case of The Bigamous Spouse, 1961; also The Case of the Mischievous Doll, 1963; The Case of the Troubled Trustee, 1965; The Case of the Phantom Fortune, 1964; The Case of the Daring Divorcee, 1964; The Case of the Amorous Aunt, 1963; The Case of the Beautiful Beggar, 1965; The Case of the Worried Waitress, 1966; The Case of the Queenly Contestant, 1967; The Case of the Carless Cupid, 1968; The Case of the Fabulous Fake, 1969; pub. posthumously The Case of the Fenced - In Woman, The Case of the Postponed Murder, The Case of the Crimson Kiss, The Case of the Crying Swallow, The Case Irate Witness. His principal characters under the pen name A. A. Fair; Donald Lam, Bertha Cool; books include: Cut Thin to Win, 1965; Widows Wear Weeds, 1966; Traps Need Fresh Bait, 1967; All Grass Isn't Green, 1970. Mem. of Paisano Prodns., Inc.; engaged in TV activities at Hollywood, Cal. Contbr. to popular fiction mags. Address: Temecula, Cal. Died Mar. 11, 1970; cremated.

GARDNER, MATTHIAS BENNETT, naval officer; b. Washington, D.C., Nov. 28, 1897; s. Frank Duane and Ellen (Crum) G.; student Tenn. Mil. Inst., 1913-14, Pa. State Coll., 1914-15; B.S., U.S. Naval Acad., 1918; m. Mrs. Helen Shippey Grant, July 22, 1929. Commd. ensign, U.S. Navy, 1918, and advanced through the grades to vice adm., 1950; in naval aviation from 1922; served in Office of Chief of Naval Operations, Navy Dept., Washington, D.C., 1938-40; in U.S.S. Wright, 1940-41; chief of staff Aircraft South Pacific, 1942; comd. U.S.S. Enterprise, 1943-44, Carrier Div. 11, 1944, Carrier Div. 7, 1944; staff comd. in chief U.S. Fleet, 1945; Office of CNO, 1946, 48; comdr. Naval Air Bases, 14th ND, 1947; Office CNO, 1948-50; commander of Second Fleet, 1950-51; commander of Sixth Fleet, 1951-52; deputy chief of naval operations (air) from 1952. Mem. National Advisory Committee for Aeronautics. Decorated Legion of Merit (2), Bronze Star, Victory Medal with star, Am. Defense Medal with star, Pacific Medal with silver star, Distinguished Service medal (Navy). Club: Chevy Chase (Washington). Address: Washington, D.C. Died Aug. 1975.

GARDNER, WRIGHT AUSTIN, prof. botany; b. Tyrone, Livingston Co., Mich., June 6, 1878; s. Austin Wightman and Julia Ella (Wright) G.; B.S., Albion (Mich.) Coll., 1902; A.M., U. of Mich., 1915; Ph.D., U. of Chicago, 1916; m. Mabel A. Anderson, of Hartford, Mich., Dec. 27, 1899; children—Harmon Austin, Louis Wright, Mabel Grace, Donald Anderson. Began teaching at Mich. State Coll., 1902; asso. prof. botany, U. of Ida., 1916-17; head Dept. of Botany, Ala. Poly. Inst., after 1917, also in charge of botany in Ala. Expt. Sta. Mem. Bot. Soc. of America, Phytopathological Society of America, Am. Soc. Plant Physiologists (sec. 1925 and after 1930; v.p. 1926), A.A.A.S., Ala. Acad. Science (pres. 1924-25), Phi Kappa Phi, Gamma Sigma Delta. Methodist. Mason (K.T.); Past H.P. Auburn Chapter, R.A.M. Home: Auburn, Ala.†

GARIBI Y RIVERA, JOSE, clergyman; b. Guadalajara, Mexico, Jan. 30, 1889; s. Miguel and Joaquina (Rivera) G.; grad. Guadalajara Sem.; D.D., Gregorian U., Rome, Italy, 1916. Ordained priest, Roman Catholic Ch., 1912, consecrated bishop, 1930; apptd. titular bishop of Rhosus, aux. bishop of Guadalajara, 1929; apptd. titular archibishop of Bizya and coadjutor of Guadalajara, 1934, archbishop of Guadalajara 1936-72. Address: Guadalajara, Mexico. Died May 27, 1972.

GARLAND, JOSEPH, physician, author; b. Gloucester, Mass., Jan. 1, 1893; s. Joseph E. and Sarah M. (Rogers) G.; A.B., Harvard, 1915, M.D., 1919; D.Sc. (hon.), Boston U., 1955, Tufts U., 1955; m. Mira W. Crowell, Sept. 20, 1921; children—Joseph E., Anne Kimball. Instr., Harvard Med. Sch., 1922-47; practice medicine, specializing in pediatrics, Boston, 1922-48; staff Mass. Gen. Hosp., 1923-73. Pres. bd. Boston Med. Library. Hon. fellow Royal Soc. Medicine; mem. Mass. Med. Soc. (sec. 1947), Am. Acad. Arts and Scis., A.M.A., N.E. Pediatric Soc., Am. Acad. Pediatrics, Aesculapian. Club: St. Botolph (Boston). Author: The Story of Medicine, 1949; All Creatures Here Below, 1954. Editor N. E. Jour. Medicine, 1947-67, editor emeritus, 1967-73, editor The Physician and His Practice, 1954, Harvard Med. Alumni Bull., 1967-73; cons. editor in U.S. for The Practitioner, 1953-68. Home: Chestnut Hill, Mass. Died Aug. 4, 1973.

GARMAN, HARRY OTTO, cons. engr.; b. Rolling Prairie, Ind., Feb. 7, 1880; s. Noah Webster and Rosa Bell (Teeter) G.; B.S., Purdue U., 1902, C.E., 1904; m. Ethel E., d. Gov. J. Frank Hanly, of Ind., Dec. 19, 1904; children—Esther Hanly (dec.), Harry Franklin (dec.), Harry Hanly, Helen Louise. Mem. civ. engring. faculty, Purdue Univ., 1902-13; cons. engr. Ind. R.R. Commn., 1907-13; chief engr. Ind. Pub. Service Commn., 1913-21. Dir. investigations of service standards, rates and evaluations of 410 electric light and power utilities, 650 telephone utilities, 165 municipal and private water works utilities, 145 artificial gas and 28 natural gas utilities, 18 electric street rys., 22 electric interurban rys., 44 central station heating utilities, and several indsl. properties. Wrote rules and standards of service for Ind., covering elec. utilities, artificial gas utilities and central station hot water heating plants. Private cons. practice from 1921. Federal engr. examiner Pub. Works Adminstrn., State of Indiana. Special engineer U.S. Quartermaster General, 1941; member State Office Building Commission, 1946. Mem. American Society for Promotion Engring. Edn., Am. Railway Engring. Assn. (life), Am. Assn. Engrs. (pres. 1913-36), Ind. Soc. Professional Engrs., Am. Soc. C.E. (life), Am. Inst. E.E., Ind. Hist. Soc., (life), Soc. Ind. Pioneers, Ind. Soc. S.A.R. (historian), Ind. Soc. S.R. (sec.-treas.). Methodist. Mason. Clubs: Scientech, Rotary, Conglist. Home: Indianapolis, Ind.†

GARNER, HARRY HYMAN, physician, educator; b. Chgo., Jan. 19, 1910; s. Louis and Clara (Barasch) G.; B.S., U. Ill., 1932, M.D., 1934; m. Eleanor Hetherington, Apr. 5, 1940; children—Larry, Edward. Intern, Cook County Hosp., Chgo., 1935-36; resident Chgo. State Hosp., 1936-39, clin. dir., 1939-41; cons. neurologist and psychiatrist Oak Forest Infirmary, Chgo., 1945-73; supt. Community Clinics Ill., 1945-47; attending neurologist Cook County Hosp., Chgo., 1946-52, attending psychiatrist, 1956-73; chief neuropsychiat. service br. 7, VA, 1947-48; attending psychiatrist, chmn. dept. psychiatry and neurology Mt. Sinai Hosp., Chgo., 1952-70, chmn. dept. psychiatry and behavioral scis. Med. Center, 1970-73; attending physician in psychiatry, cons psychiatrist Hines(Ill.) VA Hosp., 1970-73; asst. prof. psychiatry U. Ill., 1945-48; prof., chmn. dept. psychiatry and neurology Chgo. Med. Sch., 1948-70, prof. chmn. dept. psychiatry and behavioral scis., 1970-73. Mem. Gov. Ill. Psychiat. Adv. Council, 1950-73. Served to lt. col. M.C., AUS, 1941-46. Decorated Bronze Star medal with cluster; co-recipient St. Guthiel - Von Domarus award. Diplomate Am. Bd. Psychiatry, Am. Bd. Neurology. Fellow Am. Psychiat. Soc.; mem. Acad. Psychoanalysis, Central Neuropsychiat. Assn., Chgo. Neurol Soc., Acac. Neurology, A.M.A., Assn. Advancement Psychotherapy. Author: Psychosomatic Management of Patient with Malignancy; Psychotherapy and a Confrontation Problem-Solving Technique; also articles, sects. in books. Home: Chicago, Ill. Died Oct. 3, 1973; interred The Garner Farm, McHenry, Ill.

GARNER, ROBERT LIVINGSTON, former internat. banker; b. Bolton, Miss., Aug. 7, 1894; s. Robert V. and Lillian (Hardgrave) G.; B.S., Vanderbilt U., 1916; student Columbia U. Sch. Journalism, 1916-17; m. Ellen Wright, Sept. 4, 1926 (dec.); children—Robert W. (dec.), Joan F. (Mrs. Stanley Reid McCampbell). With ednl. dept. Guaranty Trust Co. of N.Y., 1919, transferred to Guaranty Co., 1920; with financial dept. Continental Ins. Co., 1925-26; asst. treas. Guaranty Trust Co. of N.Y., 1926-28, treas., 1928-29, v.p. and treas., 1929-43; financial v.p., dir., Gen. Foods Corp., 1943-47; v.p. Internat. Bank for Reconstrn and Devel., 1947-56; pres. Internat. Finance Corp., 1956-61; dir. Am. Security and Trust Co., Washington, Hewlett-Packard Co., Palo Alto, Cal. 1961-68; Banking Bd. State N.Y., 1944-47. Mem. exec. council Boy Scouts Am., 1965—. Trustee Vanderbilt U. Served as capt. 305th Inf., 77th Div., World War I. Clubs: University, Links (N.Y.C.); Chevy Chase (Md.); Metropolitan (Washington). Home: Washington, D.C., Died Dec. 13, 1975.

GARRARD, JEANNE, editor, educator, writer; b. Birmingham, Ala., Apr. 9, 1923; d. Oscar and Jeanne (Holoman) Garrard; student Stetson U., 1940-42; postgrad. Lindsey Hopkins Hotel Sch., 1959; m. Huber S. Ebersole, Oct. 1, 1957 (div. Nov. 1960). Radio dir., writer, commentator radio sta. WDBO, WLOF, Orlando, Fla., 1942-43; columnist Sentinel-Star, Orlando, 1943; radio commentator, writer for Burdine's, Palm Beach, Fla., 1943, Miami, Fla., 1943-44, radio Sta. WKAT, Miami Beach, Fla., 1944-45; commentator Sta. WIOD, Miami, Fla., 1944, commentator, writer Sta. WGBS, 1945; program dir. Melody, Inc., Miami Beach, 1945-48; writer Grant Advt., Inc., 1946; columnist Miami Beach (Fla.) Sun Star, 1946; writer for sta. WVCG, Coral Gables, Fla., 1949-50; columnist Miami Beach, 1950, Riviera-Times, Coral Gables, Fla., 1950, Miami Daily News, 1950-51; writer for Sta. WIOD, Miami, 1951; feature editor Miami Visitor Publ. Co., Miami Beach, 1952-55, mng. editor, 1955-56, editor, 1956-58; later cons. exec. editor Vis. Pub. Co.; free-lance writer, photographer with work appearing in various publ. including Am. Home mag., Stag mag., numerous newspapers; scout asst. to Better Homes & Gardens, Des Moines, 1959—; asst. mgr., housekeeper Anson Hotel, Surfside, Fla., 1959; asst. to editor, photographer Meredith Pub. Co., Des Moines, 1961; instr. writing adult edn. North Miami (Fla.) High Sch., 1956—; editorial asst. Ortho Garden Guide, Cal. Chem. Co., San Francisco, 1964; exec. editor Beach and Town, Visitor Pub. Co., Miami Beach, from 1964; also writer and pub. relations counselor; sometime lectr. Bd. dirs. Miami Beach Garden Center and Conservatory. Recipient Nat. Lit. Horticulture award Nat. Council Garden Clubs, 1967. Mem. S. Fla. Orchid Soc., Met. Miami Flower Show Assn., Gold Coast Unlimited Orchid Soc. (hon. life mem.), Naples Orchid Soc. (hon. mem.), Theta Sigma Phi (chpt. pres. 1966-67), Pi Beta Phi. Club: Miami Beach Garden (pres. 1966-68). Author: Growing Orchids for Pleasure (Nat. Garden Club Hort. award); Potted; Tropical Flowers of Florida, 1970; Flowers of the Caribbean, 1970; Flowers of the Bahamas, 1970; Flowers of Bermuda, 1970; Fairchild Tropical Garden, 1971; Tropical Flowers, 1973. Contbr. articles to pictorial mags. Home: Miami Beach, Fla., Deceased.

GARRETSON, OLIVER KELLEAM, educator; b. Fort Smith, Ark., Jan. 12, 1896; s. Henry David and Anna Rosa (Bonner) G.; A.B., U. Okla., 1918; A. .M., U. Tex., 1926; Ph.D., Columbia, 1929; m. Mary M. Davis, Apr. 24, 1926; children—Henry David, John Thomas, Walter Herman. Pub. sch. tchr. 1919-26; instr. U. Tex., 1926-27; asst. prof. Okla. A. and M. Coll., 1929-30; successively asst., asso. and prof. secondary edn. U. Ariz., from 1930, asst. dean summer session, 1947-50, dean from 1950, dean coll. edn. 1950-59, dean emeritus, prof. end., from 1959; vis. prof. William and Mary Coll. summers 1928, 29, U. Mo., 1937, 38, 39, U. W.Va., 1942. Member nat. adv. com. White House Conf. on Aging Member North Central Assn. Colls. (exec. com. 1940-47, sec. commn. secondary schs.), Phi Kappa Phi, Phi Delta Kappa, Kappa Delta Pi. Democrat. Episcopalian. Mason (K.T.). Author: Relationships Between Preferences and Abilities 1929. Home: Tucson, Ariz., Died Dec. 21, 1975.

GARRETT, CLYDE D., lawyer, ins. exec. banker; b. Washington, Oct. 25, 1887; s. John P. and Emma (Caywood) G.; LL.B., George Washington U., 1910; m. Verda Jones, Nov. 14, 1911 (dec. Aug. 1942); 1 son, Marshall Jones; m. 2d, Belle Hoagland, Sept. 13, 1941. Admitted to D.C. bar, 1911, also U.S. Supreme Ct. bar; dir. Equitable Life Ins. Co., 1933-74, gen. counsel, 1944-68, v.p. 1961-68, legal cons. 1968- 74, dir. McLachlen Nat. Bank, 1937-74, gen. counsel, 1951-68. Atty. in SSS, World War I, govt. appeal agt., World War II. Mem. Republican Nat. Com., D.C., 1948-60. Mem. Met. Washington Bd. Trade, Am. Bar Assn., Bar Assn. D.C., Theta Delta Chi. Episcopalian. Mason. Clubs: University, Capitol Hill (Washington); Columbia Country (Chevy Chase, Md.); Farmington Country (Charlottesville, Va.). Home: Washington, D.C. Died July 3, 1974.

GARRETT, EDWARD ISAIAH, corp. official; b. Vienna, La., Nov. 26, 1877; s. Judge Thomas Abel and Jessie Emma (Simonton) G.; student at Seattle (Wash.) High Sch., 1892-95; m. Jessie C. Ring, Nov. 6, 1941 (dec. 1947); children—Rose Ring, Edward Peter; m. 2d, Cecille D. Lander, July 10, 1952. Began as office boy with Puget Sound Machinery Depot, 1895; chmn. bd. dirs. Garrett & Shafer Engineering Works; partner, Merrill & Ring; dir. mem. exec. com., investment com., trust com. (vice chairman) Peoples National Bank; dir. General American Corp., General Ins. Co. of America. Member board dirs. National Assn. Mfrs., several yrs. Republican. Clubs: Ranier (ex-pres.), Seattle Golf (ex-pres.) (Seattle); The Highlands (p.p.), Country (p.p.); Bohemian (San Francisco); Union (Victoria, B.C.). Home: Seattle, Wash.†

GARRETT, HENRY E(DWARD), psychologist: b. Halifax County, Va., Jan. 27, 1894; s. John Thomas and Virginia Orr (Heidleberg) G.; A.B., U. of Richmond. 1915; M.A., Columbia U., 1921. Ph.D., 1923; D.Sc. (honorary) University of Richmond. 1954; m. Mildred Graham Burch, June 5, 1924. Mathematics teacher, Richmond High Sch., 1915-17 and 1918-19; instr. psychology, Columbia U., 1923-26, asst. prof., 1926-35, asso. prof., 1935-43, prof. since 1943; head of dept. 1941-56, emeritus, 1956; was visiting prof. at U. of Cal. U. of So. Cal., U. Cal. at Los Angeles, U. of Hawaii, U. N.M., U. Fla.; visiting professor, University of Virginia, 1956-64. Master gunner, C.A.C., 1917-18; expert consultant, Sec. of War, 1940-44, 3d Army Orientation Course, Ft. Leavenworth, 1943; mem. commn. Classification Mil. Personnel, advisor to Adj. Gen.'s. Office, 1940-45. Fellow, A.A.A.S. (v.p. sec. I, 1942); mem. Eastern Psychological Assn. (director, 1943, president, 1944). Psychometric Society (pres. 1943), N.Y. State Assn. Applied Psychology (president 1940), National Institute Psychology, American Psychological Association (member council 1933-35 and 1939-41; pres. 1945), Nat. Research Council (div. psychology and anthropology vice chmn. 1940); Phi Beta Kappa, Sigma Xi. Club: Colonnade, Farmington. Author: Statistics in Psychology and Education, 1926, 37, 47, 53, 58; Great Expts. in Psychol., 1930, 41, 51; Psychological Tests. Methods and Results, 1933; Psychology, 1950; General Psychology, 1955; Testing 1959. Gen. editor Am. Psychology Series; mem. editorial bd. Psychometrika. Writer of articles and monographs. Home: Charlottesville, VA. Died June 26, 1973.

GARRETT, ROBERT EDWIN, mfg. exec.; b. Saginaw, Ala., Dec. 13, 1908; s. John Allen and Lena Jane (Nalsh) G.; student U. Ala., 1926-27; m. Annie Cole Smith, Aug. 8, 1931; children—Robert Michael, Joan Elizabeth. Office boy Sloss-Sheffield Steel & Iron Co., 1929, exec. asst., 1945-52, asst. to pres., 1952; v.p. U.S. Pipe & Foundry Co., Birmingham, Ala., 1952-59, exec. v.p., 1959-60, pres., 1960-70, chmn. bd., 1964—, dir., mem. exec. com., 1954—; dir. Jim Walter Corp., Jefferson Fed. Savs. & Loan Assn., Birmingham. Methodist. Clubs: Vestavia Country, Downtown, Country (Birmingham). Home: Birmingham, Ala. Deceased.

GARRISON, LLOYD AMOS, educator; b. Denver, May 20, 1903; s. William arthur and Clara Aleda (Peterson) G.; A.B., Colo. State Coll. of Edn., 1926, A.M., 1932; student u. Chicago, summer 1935; Ph.D., Yale, 1940; m. Hildred Struck, May 26, 1928; children—Geraldine, Kenneth, Lorene, Eleanor, Lon. Sci. teacher and coach, Bent Co. High School, Las Animas, Colo., 1926-29; high sch. prin., Ault, Colo., 1929-30; high sch. prin., Bent County High Sch., 1930-32; dean, Scottsbluff (Neb.) Jr. Coll., 1932-38; research asst. Conn. State Dept. Edn., 1940-41; specialist in school facilities U.S. Office Edn., 1941-43; supt. edn. War Relocation Authority, Granada, Colo., 1943-45; chief ednl. officer U.S. Office Edn., Denver, 1943-46; summer lecturer U. Conn., 1939, Clark U., 1940; mem. faculty U. Denver, 1946-69, dean Grad. College, 1948-60, chmn. U. Research Board, 1948-60; regional rep. U.S. Office Edn., Office of Commissioner, 1960-64, regional representative, Denver, 1964-69; Fulbright lectr. higher edn. Colombia, S.A., 1958; chief edn. advisor Agy. Internat. Devel., Bogota, Colombia, 1962-63; chief human resources development division AID mission de Colombia, 1963-64; cons. in field. Pres. Englewood (Colo.) Sch. Bd., 1953-57. Decorated Order San Carlos (Colombia). Mem. N.E.A., Am. Assn. Sch. Adminstrs., Colo. Assn. Sch. Adminstrs., Colo. Edn. Assn., Phi Delta Kappa. Speaker and cons. in several workshops and confs. Contbr. to ednl. jours. Home: Littleton, Colo. Died Jan. 7, 1975; interred Littleton.

GARY, J. VAUGHAN, congressman; b. Richmond, Va., Feb. 25, 1892; s. T. Jack and Mary Harris (Vaughan) G.; B.A., U. Richmond, 1912, LL.B., 1915, LL.D., 1954; m. Eunice Croswell, Nov. 23, 1918; children—Carolyn (Mrs. Laurence V. Hugo), J. Vaughan. Tchr. Blackstone (Va.) Acad. for Boys, 1912-13; asst. counsel Va. Tax Bd., 1916-18. sec. Nat. Agrl. Adv. Com., Washington, 1918; claims examiner Va. Indsl. Commn., Jan.-July 1919; exec. sec. Nat. Com. on Inheritance Taxation, 1925-26; mem. Va. House of Dels. (rep. City of Richmond), 1926-33; mem. 79th-88th Congresses, from 3d Va. Dist. Served in U.S. Army World War I. Pres. Richmond Stadium. Dir. State Dem. Speakers Bur. Presidential Compaigns, 1936, 1944; Va. Democratic presidential elector, 1968. Mem. Va. World War II History Commn.; chmn. Va. Post-war Employment Com., 1943-45, War Bond Com., 1941-43. Bd. dirs. Va. Coop. Ednl. Assn.; bd. trustees U. Richmond, Fork Union Mil. Acad.; chmn. mayor's com. Richmond Juvenile and Domestic Relations Ct., 1943. Recipient Distinguished Service award U.S. Treasury Dept., 1964. Mem. Va. State of C. of C. (pres. 1944-45), Va. Tb Assn. (pres. 1938-40), Am., Richmond (pres. 1941), Va. (chmn. exec. com. 1941-42) bar assns., Am. Legion, Phi Beta Kappa, Sigma Phi Epsilon, Delta Theta Phi, Omicron Delta Kappa. Democrat. Baptist. Mason (33, Shriner). Home: Richmond Va. Died Sept. 6, 1973.

GASKILL, HAROLD VINCENT, banker, scientist; b. Fayette County, O., Feb. 3, 1905; s. Ralph Pern and Elta (Scott) G.; B.A., Ohio State U., 1926, M.A., 1927, Ph.D., 1930; m. Pauline Ellen Pinnick, July 21, 1926; children—Harold Vincent, Ellen Jane, Charles Shreve. Asst. dept. psychology Ohio State U., Columbus, 1925-27, instr., 1927-30; asst. prof. Ia. State U., 1930-31, asso. prof., 1931-35, prof. psychology, 1935-75, dean sci., 1938-75, dir. Indsl. Sci. Research Inst., Ia. State U., 1938-75, also dir. war research, 1941-75, chief scientist U.S. Army, dep. chief research and devel., Pentagon; v.p. planning Collins Radio Co., Cedar Rapids, 1956-62; v.p. Financial Gen. corp., 1962-75; v.p. planning Internat. Bank Washington, 1962-75; Mem. NRC; chmn. NAS-NRC Com. Hwy. Safety Research. Fellow A.A.A.S., Ia. Acad. Sci., Am. Assn. Applied Psychology (charter mem.); mem. Am., Midwestern pyschology assns., Am. Council on Edn. (liaison officer coop. study, gen. end.), A.L.A. (psychology com.), I.R.E., Am. Statis. Assn., Ia. Hist. Soc., Sigma Xi, Kappa Sigma, Alpha Psi Delta, Phi Kappa Phi, Phi Delta Kappa (Cardinal Key). Episcopalian (vestryman). Mason (32°). Rotarian. Club: Des Moines. Author: Personality, 1936; collaborator and contbr. Handbook of Chemistry and Physics, 1930-55; contbr. psychol. and endl. jours. Home: Delray Beach, Fla. Died Apr. 19, 1975; inurned St. Peter's Episcopal Ch., Arlington, Va.

GASKINS, LOSSIE LEONARD, ednl. adminstr.; b. nr. Sparks, Ga., May 25, 1925; s. Joseph Leonard and Sallie Mae (Thornton) G.; diploma Middle Ga. Coll., 1946; B.S., Ga. Tchrs. Coll., 1954; M.A., Ga. Peabody Coll. for Teachers, 1962; m. Eleanor Hambrick, June 11, 1967. Tchr.-coach Nashville (Ga.) High Sch., 1946-51; prin. New River Jr. High Sch., Nashville, 1951-54; tchr. English dept. head Berrien County High Sch., 1954-59; asst. prof. Abraham Baldwin Coll., Tifton, 1959-64; county sch. supt. Berrien County, Nashville, 1964-75. Active Boy Scouts Am. Served with USNR, 1944. Mem. N.E.A., Ga., Berrien County assns. educators, Ga. Assn. Sch. Supts. Baptist (deacon; Sunday Sch. supt.). Clubs: Civitan (past sec.), Rotary (past pres.), Exchange (charter). Home: Nashville, Ga. Died Jan. 4, 1975; buried Westview Cemetery, Nashville, Ga.

GAST, PAUL FREDERICK, physicist; b. St. Paul, May 29, 1916; s. Gustav Carl and Alma My (Young) G.; student Capital U., Columbus, 1933-35; A.B., Ohio State U., 1937; Ph.D., U. Wash., 1941; m. Virginia Holt, June 15, 1941; children—Barbara Lee, Cynthia Ann. Physicist research lab. Remington Arms Co., Bridgeport, Conn., 1941-43; engaged in tech. liaison and devel. work in connection with design of nuclear reactors, for DuPont Co., Hanford Works of Manhatten Project, 1943-44; chief of physics sect. Hanford Works, for Gen. Electric Co., Richland, 1946-56, mgr. physics and instrument research and devel., 1956-64; faculty Gen. Electric Sch. Nuclear Engring., 1956-64; sr. scientist Argonne (Ill.) Nat. Lab., 1964-66, then asso. dir. liquid metal fast breeder reactor program office. Mem. reactor physics planning group AEC, mem. U.S. delegation Internat. Conf., Switzerland, 1955, mem. tech. mission to U.K., 1956. Mem. Am. Nuclear Soc. (dir. 1964-67), Am. Phys. Soc., Am. Inst. Physics. A.A.A.S., Phi Beta Kappa. Contbr. articles to Phys. Rev. on cosmic rays and on nuclear fission. Mem. editorial bd. Reactor Handbook for AEC com. on reactor reclassification. Home: Oak Brook, Ill. Died May, 1974.

GATENBY, JOHN WILLIAM, JR., indsl. designer, illustrator; b. Cicero, Ill. Feb. 16, 1906; s. John W. and Meta (Hering) G.; student J. Sterling Morton Jr. Coll., Cicero, 1923-25, Sch. of Art Inst. Chgo., 1925-26, Chgo. Acad. Fine Arts, 1926-28, Am. Acad. Art, 1927-29; m. Florence Louise Kennedy, May 19, 1928. Indsl. designer, illustrator, 1928-75; designer various projects and campaigns U.S. Steel Corp., Heating Equipment Corp. Am., William Wrigley, Jr., Co., Bausch & Lomb Optical Co., Halliburton Oil Well Drilling Co., Morrisey Oil Burner Co., Abbott Labs., William S. Merrell Co., Frederick Stearns & Co.; owner John W. Gatenby Studios; cons. Arvid Casler Studio Indsl. Design, Standard Ednl. Soc.; founder, owner, dir. Gatenby Estudio De Arte, Recipient Medinah Legion of Merit. Mem. Soc. Typographic Arts, Palette and Chisel Acad. Fine Arts, Chgo. Guild Free Lance Artists, Nat. Soc. Modern Art (charter) Tucson Fine Arts Assn., Marengo, Ill. C. of C. (charter). Lutheran. Mason (32 deg., Shriner), Kiwanian, Elk. Clubs: Men's Garden (Tucson); Palette and Chisell (Chgo.); Belmar Country; Elgin Shrine; McHenry Shrine (pres. 1953); Belvidere Shrine; Tucson Shrine (pres. 1960). Art editor: The Child's World. A founder, editor Artists Guild Bull. El Jardinero. Address: Tucson, Ariz. Died Feb. 17, 1975; cremated.

GATES, MOODY BLISS, publisher; b. Annville, Pa., Oct. 15, 1879; s. Rev. Martin Luther and Margaret A. (Heagy) G.; B.S., New York U., 1897; m. Eleanor Abrams of Staten Island, N.Y., Nov. 28, 1910. In publishing business, N.Y. City, from 1900; pres., dir., F.M. Lupton, publisher, Inc., Periodical Press, City Hall Place Realty Co., Sember Realty Co.; treas., dir., The People's Home Journal Pattern Co.; dir. Nat. Publishers' Assn. Mem. Zeta Psi (New York), Clubs: Univ. (Brooklyn), Richmond Co. Country. Home: Brooklyn, N.Y.†

GATES, SYLVESTER GOVETT, lawyer; b. banker; b. Richmond, Surrey, Eng., Sept. 2, 1901; s. Walter George and Beatrice Helen (Govett) G.; ed. New Coll., Oxford (Eng.) U., 1920-24, Harvard U., 1925-27. Practiced law, London and Western Circuit, 1928-39; controller home publicity Ministry Information, 1941-44; with Office Minister Reconstrn., 1944; chmn. Brit. Film Inst., 1956-64; mem. Port of London Authority, 1958-64; dep. chmn. Nat. Westminster Bank Ltd., 1968—; chmn. Internat. Comml. Bank Ltd., 1967—, Tecalemit Ltd., 1940—; dep. chmn. Standard Bank Ltd., Westminster Fgn. Bank, Ltd. Bank of W. Africa. Mem. Royal Commn. on Taxation, 1953. Decorated comdr. Brit. Empire. Office: London, England. Died Nov. 1972.

GATES, WILLIAM BYRAM, JR., educator, economist; b. Indpls., Oct. 18, 1917; s. William Byram and Margaret (Detrick) G.; student U. Geneva (Switzerland), 1935-36; A.B., Williams Coll., 1939; M.A., Ph.D., U. Chgo., 1947; m. Sylvia Clack, July 24, 1953; children—Barbara (by previous marriage), William Mark, Nicola. With tax research div. Treasury Dept., 1941-42; mem. faculty dept. econs. Williams Coll., 1947-50, 1954-75, Kenan prof., chmn. dept., 1961-75, exec. com. Williams Center Devel. Econs., 1960-75; economist Export-Import Bank, 1950-54; Brookings Nat. Research prof., Port-au-Prince, Haiti, 1957-58; dep. project mgr., chief devel. specialist Devel. Projects Cons. Service, Indonesia, 1962-63; project dir. Devel. Adv. Service, Malaysia, 1966-68; cons. Devel. Adv. Service, Internat. Bank. Served with USNR, 1942-46. Mem. Am. Econ. Assn., Econ. History Assn., Phi Beta Kappa. Author: Michigan Copper and Boston Dollars, 1951. Home: Williamstown, Mass., Died Dec. 22, 1975.

GATTS, ROBERT ROSWELL, educator, mech. engr.; b. Berlin Heights, O., Mar. 2, 1925; s. Christian Peter and Blanche (Derby) G.; student Kent State U., 1946-47; B.M.E., Ohio State U., 1950, M.Sc., 1951, Ph.D., 1959; m. Donna Ellen Wertman, May 14, 1949; children—Robert Kent, Gail Ann, Roslyn Ruth, Maryl Jan, Christian Peter. Engr. Visking Corp., Terre Haute, Ind., 1951-53; research asso. Ohio State U., 1953-58, asst. prof., 1958-59; engr. mechanics and materials Gen. Elec. Corp., Schenectady, 1959-63; prof., chmn. dept. mech. engring. U. Kan., 1963-74; sr. mech. engr. Nat. Bur. Standards, Washington, 1972-74; cons. in field. Trustee U. Kan. Center Research, Inc., 1968—. Mem. Am. Soc. M.E., Am. Soc. Engring. Educators, Am. Soc. Testing and Materials, Soc. Automotive Engrs., Soc.

Exptl. Stress Analysis, Soc. Mfg. Engrs., Newcomen Soc. Home: Lawrence, Kan. Died Dec. 8, 1974; interred Oak Park Cemetery, Lawrence.

GAUCH, DONALD EUGENE, owner machinery mfg. co.; b. Marshaltown, Ia., Jan. 14, 1937; s. Elmer Raymond and Helen Marie (Phillips) G.; B.S., Ia. State U., 1960; M.S., State U. Ia., 1961; m. Judith Ann McKay, July 21, 1962; children—Matthew Donald, Catherine Ann. Owner, partner Mid Equipment Corp., Grundy Center, Ia., 1961-74. Mason. Club: Community (pres. 1970). Patentee in field. Home: Grundy Center, Ia. Died Oct. 19, 1974; interred Grundy Center, Ia.

GAUCHAT, ROBERT DAVID, physician; b. Warren, O., Nov. 27, 1922; s. Paul Crankshaw and Alta J. (Neidlinger) G.; M.D., Harvard, 1951. Intern dept. pediatrics U. Minn. Hosp., Mpls., 1951-52; resident in pediatrics State U. Ia. Hosps., Iowa City, 1952-54, research asso. in pediatrics, 1954-55; fellow in pediatrics U. Ia., 1953-54, Helen Hay Whitney fellow in pediatric research, 1954-57, instr. pediatrics, 1955-56, asso. in pediatrics, 1956-57, asst. prof., 1957-62, asso. prof., 1962-68, prof., 1968-73. Served with AUS, 1943-46. Diplomate Am. Bd. Pediatrics. Fellow Am. Acad. Pediatrics; mem. A.M.A., Am. Rheumatism Assn., Am. Assn. for History Medicine. Home: Iowa City, Ia. Died Feb. 18, 1973; buried Oakwood Cemetery, Warren, O.

GAUDIN, ANTOINE MARC, metallurgist; b. Smyrna, Turkey, Aug. 8, 1900; s. Paul Augustin and Marie Eleonore G.; B.S., Paris and Aix en Provence, France, 1917; E.M., Columbia, 1921; Sc.D. (hon.) Mont. Sch. of Mines, 1941; m. Anna G. Brooks, Dec. 24, 1926; children—Paul Brooks, Elinor Ruth, Robert Morris. Came to U.S., 1917, naturalized, 1926. Asso. prof. metall. research, Univ. of Utah, 1926-29; research prof. mineral dressing, Montana Sch. of Mines, 1929-39; Richards prof. mineral engring. Mass. Inst. Tech., from 1939, cons. metallurgist. Sir Julius Wernher lectr. Instn. of Mining and Metallurgy, 1952. Past chmn. bd. Engineering Foundation. Recipient Robert Hallowell Richard award Am. Inst. Mining Metallurgical and Petroleum Engineers, 1957. Fellow Am. Acad. Arts and Scis.; mem. Am. Inst. Mining Engrs., Nat. Acad. Engineering (founding mem.), Mining and Metall. Soc., Can. Inst. Mining Engrs., Societe des Ingenieurs Civils de France, etc. Episcopalian. Mason. Author: Flotation, 1932; Principles of Mineral Dressing, 1939. Contbr. technical articles in engring. pubs. Home: Newtonville, Mass. Died Aug. 23, 1974; buried West Laurel Hill Cemetery, Cynwood, Pa.

GAULT, ARTHUR EUGENE, coll. dean; b. Kecksburg, Pa., Sept. 9, 1888; s. Robert Frank and Mary Jane (Trump) G.; B.S., Grove City (Pa.) Coll., 1914; M.S., U. of Chicago, 1921; m. Gwendoline Gurnett, June 14, 1924. Instr. rural schs., Westmoreland County, Pa., 1907-09; prin. schs., Greensburg, Pa., 1909-11; coach athletics, Beaver Falls (Pa.) high sch., 1914-15; instr. and coach athletics, Pa. State Normal, Slippery Rock, 1915-17, prof. mathematics and dean. Bradley U., Peoria, Ill., from 1921. Served as 1st lt. O.M.C., 1917-19. Mem. Math. Assn. Am. (bd. govs.), A.A.A.S., Nat. Council Tchrs. Mathematics. Presbyterian. Mason (32°). Club: Rotary. Home: Peoria, Ill. Died Aug. 31, 1973; buried Parkview Cemetery, Peoria.

GAVER, JACK, drama critic; b. Tolono, Ill., 1906; s. Hayden and Drusilla (Sanders) G.; student U. Ill.; mem. Jessyca Russell, 1945; 1 dau., Claudia. Staff various newspapers, Middle West, 1922-29; with United Press Assn. since 1929, drama critic, amusements columnist since 1930. Mem. N.Y. Drama Critics Circle. Author: Laughter in the Air, 1940; Curtain Calls, 1949. Home: New York City, N.Y. Died Dec. 16, 1974.

GAW, ESTHER ALLEN, univ. dean; b. Hudson, O., Dec. 28, 1879; d. Clarence Emir and Corinne Marie (Tuckerman) Allen; A.B., Western Reserve U., 1900; certificate, Stern Conservatory of Music, Berlin, Germany, 1906; Ph.D., State U. of Iowa, 1919; m. Henry Clinton Gaw, Feb. 25, 1910; 1 son, Emir Allen. Teacher in high schools, Ohio and Utah, 1900-15; instr., State U. of Iowa, 1919; teacher, San Francisco (Calif.) Teachers Coll., 1920-22; asso. dean, Mills Coll., Oakland, Calif., 1922-27; dean of women, Ohio State U., 1927-44, emeritus dean from 1944; visiting prof. Univ. de Chile, Santiago, Chile, 1938, Univ. de Costa Rica (Escuela de Pedagogia), 1942. Testing with Stanford-Binet in Spanish, El Salvador Schs., 1947. Fellow A.A.A.S.; mem. Am. Psychol. Assn., Nat. Assn. Deans of Women, Am. Assn. Univ. Women, D.A.R., Phi Beta Kappa, Sigma Xi, Pi Lambda Theta, P.E.O. Asso. editor of Jour. of Higher Education. Home: Shattuck, Berkeley, Cal.†

GAYLEY, HENRY CLIFFORD, corp. exec.; b. N.Y.C., Feb. 22, 1901; s. Henry Bell and Estelle (Canda) G.; student St. Paul's Sch., Concord, N.H., 1915-18; B.S., Mass. Inst. Tech., 1922, M.S., 1923; m. Sarah V. Gordon, June 22, 1929; children—Oliver, Mary. With Chrome Steel Works, Carteret, N.J., 1923-32, prodn. mgr., then treas., 1929-32; treas. Canda Realty Co., 1932-34; with Schenley Industries, Inc., 1934-55, successively accountant, budget dir., 1948-52, treas., 1952-55; v.p., dir. Lumber Fabricators, Inc., Fort Payne, Ala, 1956; cons. to the IBM Corporation, after 1957. Served as lt. col. Q.M.C., AUS, 1942-45. Decorated Legion of Merit. Clubs: Rockaway Hunting; University (N.Y.C.). Home: New York City, N.Y. Died Oct. 19, 1974; buried Wood Nottingham Presbyn. Ch. Cemetery, Colora, Md.

GAYLORD, EDWARD KING, editor; b. Muscotah, Kan., Mar. 5, 1873; s. George Lewis and Eunice M. (Edwards) G.; grad. Cutler Acad., Colorado Springs, Colo., 1892; student Colo. Coll., 1894-97, LL.D., 1936; studied law at Colorado Springs, 1900-02; m. Inez Kinney, Dec. 29, 1914; children—Edith Kinney, Edward Lewis, Virginia Elizabeth. Clk. Dist. Ct., Colorado Springs and Cripple Creek, 1897-1900; telegraph editor and editorial writer Colorado Springs Telegraph, 1901; bus. mgr. St. Joseph Gazette, 1902; gen. mgr. Daily Oklahoman, Oklahoma City Times; pres. Okla. Pub. Co., 1918-74, Mistletoe Express Co.; chmn. bd. WKY Television Systems, Inc.; dir. Southland Paper Mills, Inc., Lufkin, Tex. Mem. commn. in charge constrn. Okla. State Capitol, 1918. Bd. dirs. Oklahoma City YMCA; trustee Midwest Research Inst., Kansas City, Mo., Southwest Research Inst., San Antonio. Mem. Asso. Press, Am. Newspaper Pubs. Assn., So. Newspaper Pubs. Assn. Okla. City C. of C. (pres. 1915). Democrat. Conglist. Mason. Home: Oklahoma City, Okla. Died May 30, 1974.

GAYNOR, PAUL, SR., advt. pub. relations exec.; b. Battan, Conn., Oct. 13, 1920; s. Harry and Estelle (Seale) G.; student N.Y.U., 1938-39; m. Jean Watters, Dec. 19, 1941; children—Anne, Paul. Account exec. Marschalk & Pratt Co., advt., 1948-50; v.p. CBS-Columbia, 1950-51, Buchanan & Co., Inc., 1951-53; pres., chmn. bd. Gaynor & Co., Inc., 1953-75, Gaynor & Ducas, Inc., N.Y.C., 1955-75, PR Assos., Inc.; pres. Columbia Devel. Corp., 1958-75. Cons. to sec. def., 1950-52, Exec. Office Pres., 1952, sec. air force, 1953; coordinator Nat. Blood program, 1952-53. Served to col. USAAF, 1941-48. Decorated Air Medal, Bronze Star. Mem. Pub. Relations Soc. Am. Clubs: Wings, N.Y. Athletic (N.Y.C.); Army-Navy, Nat. Press, Nat. Aviation (Washington). Home: New York, City, N.Y. Died Aug. 1975.

GEARHART, EPHRAIM MACLAY, clergyman; b. Sunbury, Pa., Dec. 25, 1880; s. Robert Harris and Mary (Cornman) G.; A.B., Susquehanna U., 1903, grad. theol. dept. same, 1906, A.M., 1906, D.D., 1920; m. Minnie Louise Kline, Dec. 19, 1905; 1 son, Ephraim Maclay; m. 2d, Bessie Alice Leonard, July 8, 1911; children—Robert Paul, Gordon Cornman. Ordained Luth. ministry, 1906; pastor Luther Memorial Church, Erie, Pennsylvania, 1922-51, pastor emeritus from 1951. Physical dir. for Y.M.C.A. at U.S. Naval Air Sta., U.S. Navy Yard, Pensacola, Fla., World War. Mem. Nat. Commn. Boy Scouts America from 1919. Chmn. com. on ministerial edn. of Pittsburgh Synod United Luth. Ch. Am., 1945, mem. examining com. Mem. Am. Philatelic Soc., Pi Gamma Mu fraternity; corr. member Académie Latine, Arts, Sciences and Belles Lettres, Paris, Accademia Internazionale di Lettere e Scienze, Naples. Mem. bd. trustees Thiel Coll.; trustee Edinboro Teachers Coll., 1924-26; mem. bd. dirs. Lutheran Home for the Aged from 1950. Awarded Second Class Order of Red Cross at Japan, also title of "The Silver Bearer," by Nat. Com. Boy Scouts America. Republican. Mason (K.T., 32°, Shriner). Clubs: Kiwanis (Erie). Collectors (N.Y.C.). Lectr. on Indian mythology; field researcher; author. Home: Erie, Pa.†

GEBHARD, HEINRICH, pianist; b. Sobernheim, Rhein Province, Germany, July 25, 1878; s. Phillipp and Katharina (Moog) G.; m. Doris E. Sleeper, of Lancaster, N.H., June 30, 1920. Settled in Boston, Mass., 1899; studied pianeforte, theory and composition under Clayton Johns, Boston, and at Vienna under Leschetizky, 1895-99; returned to Boston, 1900; professional debut with Boston Symphony Orchestra, 1900; has appeared in the prin. cities of U.S. with Kneisel Quartet, Longy Club, and in recitals of his own, also with many orchestras. Home: Brookline, Mass.†

GEDDES, ROSS CAMPBELL, 2d Baron Geddes shipping exec.; b. Edinburgh, Scotland, Licencié 20, 1907; s. Auckland (Lord Geddes) and Isabella Gamble (Ross) G.; student Rugby Sch.; M.A., Gonville and Calus Coll., Cambridge (Eng.) U.; m. Enid Mary Butler, 1931; 1 son, 1 dau. With Shell Group Oil Cos., 1931-46; partner Chr. Salvesen & Co., Leith, Edinburgh, 1946-50; chmn. Admiralty Fuels and Lubricants Adv. Com., 1951-57; dir. Peninsular and Oriental Steam Navigation Co., 1957-72; chmn. Trident Tankers Ltd., 1963-71, Limmer & Trinidad Co., 1964-69, Gen. Reversionary & Investments Co., Monks Investment Trust Ltd.; dir. Minerals Separation Ltd., Brixton Estate Ltd., Cambridge Petroleum Royalties Ltd., So. Pacific Properties Ltd., Tech. Investment Trust Ltd. With Brit. Mcht. Shipping Mission, Washington, 1942-44, dep. dir. tanker div. Ministry of War Transport, 1944-45; pres. Inst. Petroleum, 1956-58; chmn. Ministry of Transport Com. on Carriers Licensing, 1963. Decorated knight comdr. Order Brit. Empire. Mem. Chamber of Shipping of U.K. (pres. 1968), Brit. Travel Assn. (chmn. 1964-70), Clerical, Med. and Gen. Life Assurance Soc. (chmn.). Home: Lymington, Hampshire, England. Died Feb. 2, 1975.

GEE, A.M., lawyer; b. Francisville, Ill., March 29, 1889; s. Sylvester Judd and Mary Belle (Weyl) G.; student Miami U., Oxford, O., 1909-12; Ph.B., U. of Chicago, 1913, J.D., 1915; m. Dorothy Irene Sloane, Sept. 23, 1915; 1 son, John Willard. Admitted to Ill. bar, 1915, Wyo. bar, 1920, Okla. bar, 1927, Ohio bar, 1932; and practiced at Lawrenceville, Ill., 1915-20; atty. The Ohio Oil Co., Casper, Wyo., 1920-27, Mid-Kan. Oil & Gas Co., Tulsa, Okla., 1927-32; gen. counsel, The Ohio Oil Co., Findlay, O., 1932-54, dir., 1941-54, ret.; private practice of law, Findlay, from 1954. Former member city planning commn., board of zoning appeals, Findlay. Trustee Westminster Foundation, Inc., Columbus, Ohio. Mem. Old Guard Soc. (Palm Beach) (v.p), Am., Ohio and Okla. bar assns., Am. Petroleum Inst., Mid-Continent Oil and Gas Assn., Ohio golf Assn. (member of board governors), Phi Delta Theta, Phi Alpha Delta. Republican. Mason (32°, Shriner), Elk. Clubs: Findlay (O.) Country; Inverness Country (Toledo); Everglades (Palm Beach, Fla.). Home: Findlay, Ohio. Died Nov. 17, 1974.

GEHRES, LESLIE EDWARD, corp. exec.; b. Newark, N.Y., Sept. 23, 1898; s. Charles Peter and Phoebe Ann (Thomas) G.; B.S., U.S. Naval Acad., 1918; m. Rhoda Elizabeth Cooley, June 16, 1923; 1 dau., Leslie (Mrs. Peter Francois Girard). Commd. ensign USN, advanced through grades to rear adm., 1949; commdr. Fleet Air Wing 4, North Pacific, 1941-44; comdg. officer C-13-U.S.S. Franklin, 1944-45, U.S. Naval Air Sta., San Diego, 1945-49, ret., 1949; personnel dir. Ryan Aero Co., San Diego, 1953-61; pres. Nat. Marine Terminal, San Diego, 1961-62; pres. Yellow Cab Co., San Francisco, 1962-63; pres. Westgate Terminals, Inc., San Diego, 1963-71; v.p. indsl. relations Westgate-Cal. Corp., San Diego, 1971-75. Vice chmn. Nat. Conf. Christians and Jews, 1970-72; mem. Am. Battle Monuments Commn., 1969-75. Chmn. Republican County Central Com., San Diego, 1962-74; mem. Cal. Presdl. Electoral Coll., 1968. Trustee Cal. Maritime Acad., Vallejo, Cal., 1965. Decorated Navy Cross, Legion of Merit with oak leaf cluster, D.F.C., Air medal, Purple Heart. Mem. Cal. Assn. Rep. County Chairmen (pres. 1968-71). Kiwanian. Home: La Mesa, Cal. Died May 15, 1975.

GEIGER, C. HARVE, educator; b. Milford, Ind., June 22, 1893; s. John Henry and Mary Ann (Riggenberg) Geiger; student Manchester Coll., Manchester, Ind., 1915-19; Ph.B., University of Chicago, 1922; Ed.M., Harvard, 1928; Ph.D., Columbia Univ., 1938; m. Velma Beatrice Sprigg, July 6, 1914. Teacher rural sch., Milford, Ind., 1916-17; prin. Winona Lake (Ind.) Pub. Schs., 1917-22; instr. Kankakee (Ill.) High Sch., 1922-23; prin. Beardstown (Ill.) High Sch., 1923-25; asst. prof. edn., Iowa Wesleyan Coll., 1925-27; asso. prof. edn., U. of Dubuque, 1927-28; prof. edn., Coe Coll., 1928-46, dean of College, 1933-46, acting president, 1944-45; president North Central College 1946-60. Member N.E.A., American Assn. Sch. Adminstrs., Iowa Acad. Science, Phi Kappa Phi, Pi Kappa Delta, Sigma Phi Epsilon. Republican. Evangelical. Mason, Rotarian. Author: The Program of Higher Education of the Presbyterian Ch. in the U.S. of Am. 1940. Contbr. to mags. Home: Naperville, Ill., Died Oct. 20, 1975; entombed Chapel of Memories, Cedar Meml. Cemetery, Cedar Rapids, Ia.

GEIGLE, FRANCIS R., educator; b. Trevorton, Pa., Nov. 7, 1906; s. Charles W. and Daisy May (Swinehart) G.; student Lycoming Coll., 1924-26, L.H.D., 1960; student Bucknell U., 1926-27, Ind. State Coll., 1927-30, Bloomsburg State Coll., 1931; B.S., Susquehanna U., 1933; M.A., N.Y. U., 1936, Ed.D., 1941; postgrad. Harvard, 1934; m. Helen Dickert, Nov. 27, 1935. Tchr. bus. Trevorton High Sch., 1926-29; head dept. bus. adminstrn. Lycoming Coll., 1929-35; head dept. bus. edn. Montclair (N.J.) State Coll., 1935-45; asst. v.p. Montclair 1st Nat. Bank & Trust Co., 1945-51; mem. faculty No. Ill. U., 1951-70, head, organizer dept. bus. edn., 1951-53, adminstrv. asst. to pres., 1953-57, v.p., 1957-59, exec. v.p., 1959-63, exec. v.p., provost, 1963-69, exec. v.p., 1969-70, acting pres. Ill. State U., Normal, 1970-71; coordinator exec. activities Coll. Bus. No. Ill. U., DeKalb, 1971-72, v.p. devel. and alumni relations, 1972-74. Mem. Am. Assn. Sch. Adminstrs., Civil War Roundtable, Chgo. Planetarium Soc., Am. Philatelic Soc., Nat. Audubon Soc., Am. Inst. Banking (nat. edn. adv. bd.). Phi Delta Kappa. Rotarian (past pres.). Home: DeKalb, Ill. Died Nov. 15, 1974; buried Wildwood Cemetery, Williamsport, Pa.

GEISLER, JOHN GEORGE, educator; b. Baltimore, Oct. 13, 1886; s. Michael and Margaret (Gruenewald) G.; B.S., U. Dayton, 1918, Lic. Sc., U. Fribourg, 1924. Entered Soc. Marianists, 1900; head chem. dept. Our Lady of the Lake Sem., Cleveland, 1927-31, Trinity Coll., 1931-41, U. Dayton, 1941-50, Universidad de Santa Maria, from 1951. Mem. Am. Chem. Soc., Ohio Acad. Sci. Home: Dayton, O., Died Feb. 3, 1976.

GENGLER, LEONARD, sec. Land O'Lakes Creameries, Inc. Home: Minneapolis, Minn. Died Oct. 1973.

GENNETT, NATHANIEL CHAPMAN WEEMS, JR., lawyer, lumber mfr.; b. Franklin, N.C., Aug. 10, 1915; s. N. C. W. and Nina Burdick (Porter) G.; B.S., Yale, 1936; LL.B., U. Va., 1940; m. Matilann Thoms; children—Virginia (Mrs. Leverett S. Miller), Nathaniel Chapman Weems III, Matilann Selene. Admitted to N.C. bar, 1941, N.Y. bar, 1943; legal tng. Cravath, de Gersdorff, Swaine & Wood, also Fulton, Walter & Halley, N.Y.C., 1942-46; asso. counsel Com. on Mcht. Marine and Fisheries, Ho. of Reps., 79th Congress; partner, gen. counsel Gennett Lumber Co., N.C., S.C., Tenn., N. Ga., 1947—; dir. Gennett Oak Flooring Co., Winnett, Inc., W & G Enterprises Inc. Clubs: University (N.Y.C.), Everglades (Palm Beach, Fla.), Biltmore Forest Country (Biltmore, N.C.), Country of Asheville (N.C.). Home: Asheville, N.C. Died Dec. 1973.

GENSMAN, LORRAIN M., ex-congressman; b. Sedgwick Co., Kan., Aug. 26, 1878; s. Nicholas and Kansas (Osborne) G.; ed. commercial coll., normal sch. and U. of Kan.; m. Lucia Evalena Van Cleef, of Perry, Okla., Apr. 6, 1904. Admitted to Kan. bar, 1901; settled in Okla., 1901; extensively identified with oil development in Okla. Referee in bankruptcy, Western Dist. of Okla., 1902-07; co. atty., Comanche Co., Okla., 1918-20; mem. 67th Congress (1921-23), 6th Okla. Dist.; Republican. Presbyn. Mason (32°, Shriner), K.P., Elk. Home: Lawton, Okla.†

GEORGE, JOSEPH JOHNSON, meteorologist; b. West Plains, Mo., June 20, 1909; s. William and Bess (Johnson) G.; student U. Cal. at Los Angeles, 1926-29, Cal. Inst. Tech., 1933-34; m. Mary Beale Sasscer, Oct. 16, 1937; children—Mary B., Margaret Lynn, Penelope, Joseph Sasscer. Weather and dispatch dept. Western Air Express, Los Angeles. 1929-34; supt. meteorology Eastern Airlines, Atlanta, 1934-41, 46-64, dir. meteorology, 1964-75. Chmn. adv. com. on weather services Dept. Commerce, 1953-75; mem. President's Adv. Com. on Weather Control, 1953; mem. NACA sub. com. Meterorol. Problems, 1946-56; mem. tech. adv. bd. to adminstr. FAA; mem. Pres.'s Adv. Com. on Oceans and Atmosphere, 1971-74. Served from capt. to col., weather service, USAAF, 1942-46, brig. gen. Res. Recipient Meisinger award for aero. research Am. Meteorol Soc., 1941; Losey award Inst. Aero. Scis., 1944; Am. Meteorol. Soc. award, applied meteorology, 1955. Fellow Am. Meteorol. Soc. (v.p. 1950-52); mem. Nat. Acad. Scis. (mem. panel on rivers and weather services, 1968-69). Author: Weather Forecasting for Aeronautics; also numerous papers on weather forecasting. Home: Coral Gables, Fla. Died Aug. 14, 1975; buried Arlington (Va.) Nat. Cemetery.

GEORGE, W. KYLE, ch. ofcl., pharmacist; b. West Point, O., May 6, 1881; s. William and Ida (Wilcoxen) G.; student Westminster Coll., 1898-1901. LL.D., 1953; Ph.G., Ohio No. U., 1902; m. Helen Andrews, June 3, 908; children—William Andrews, Willard K. Pharmacist various drug stores, Cleveland, Lisbon, East Liverpool, O., New Brighton, Pa., 1903-08; owner, operator drug store, Oil City, Pa., 1908-21; asso. Averbeck Wholesale Drug Co., 1921-31, Laeri's Ethical Apothecary Shoppe, Youngstown, O., from 1944. Moderator United Presbyn. Ch. N.Am. from 1951. Trustee Westminster Coll. Mem. Mahoning Valley Druggists Assn. Mason (K.T.). Home Youngstown, O.†

GEPSON, JOHN MORGAN, telephone co. exec.; b. Omaha, Feb. 13, 1913; s. Edward D. and Mae (Morgan) G.; A.B., U. Neb., 1934; LL.B. cum laude, Creighton U., 1937; m. Elizabeth Shearer, Oct. 26, 1938; children—John Edward, Mary Elizabeth. Atty. Northwestern Bell Telephone Co., 1939-43, Am. Tel. & Tel. Co., 1946-51; with New Eng. Tel. & Tel. Co., 1951-73, v.p., gen. counsel, 1956-73. Served to lt. USNR, World War II. Mem. Am., Boston bar assns. Club: Union (Boston). Home: Wellesley Hills Mass. Died Dec. 7, 1973.

GERARD, RALPH WALDO, educator; b. Harvey, Ill., Oct. 7, 1900; s. Maurice and Eva (Teitelbaum) G.; B.S., U. Chgo., 1919, Ph.D., 1921; M.D., Rush Med. Coll., 1924; D.Sc., U. Md., 1952; LL.D., U. St. Andrews (Scotland), 1964; Litt.D., Brown U., 1964; D.Sc., McGill University, Montreal, Que., Can.; M.D. (hon.), U. Leiden, 1962; m. Margaret Wilson, June 15, 1922 (dec. Jan., 1954); 1 son, James; m. 2d, Leona Bachrach Chalkley, Jan. 1955. Prof., chmn. dept. physiology, biochemistry and pharmacology S.D. U., 1921-22; nat. research fellow, Europe, 1925-27; asst. prof. physiology U. Chgo., 1927-29, asso. prof. 1929-41, prof., 1941-52, prof. behavioral sci., 1954-55; prof. neurophysiology and physiology, dir. labs. Neuropsychiat Inst., coll. med. U. Ill., 1952-55; prof. neurophysiology and psychiatry Mental Health Research Inst., U. Mich., 1955-64, cons. sr. scientist, 1964-74; dir. special studies, prof. biol. scis., dean grad. div. U. Cal. at Irvine, 1964-74, special adviser academic affairs, until 1970. Praelector U. St. Andrews, 1958; Lowell lectr., 1958, Robert Johnson, Jr. meml. lectr., 1958, Lakeside lectr., 1960, Stanley R. Dean lectr., 1964; adviser Rockefeller Found., 1935, Unitarian Service-UNRRA Med. Mission, Czechoslovakia, 1946, Greece, 1948; cons. in field. Dir. spl. war research; chmn. physiol. adv. panel, Office Naval Research, 1947-53; chmn. VA com. on problems aging, 1955-60; mem. exec. com., div. biology and agr. NRC, after 1960. Awarded medal Charles U. (Prague), Order White Lion (4th class), Czech govt.; recipient Wilson prize Eastern Psychiat. Research Assn., 1960, Alumni Assn. award, 1974. Fellow Center for Advanced Studies in Behavioral Scis., 1954-55. Fellow Royal Soc. Edinburgh (hon.); mem. Nat. Acad. Scis. (editor Proc.), Am. Acad. Arts and Scis., Am. Psychiat. Assn. (hon.), Physiol. Soc. (pres. 1951-52), Assn. for Research in Nervous and Mental Disease, Chgo. Inst. Medicine, Brit. Physiol. Soc., Biochem. Soc., Am. Neurol. Assn., Am. Naturalists, A.A.A.S., Pan Hellenic Med. Assn. (hon.), A.A.U.P. (pres. chpt. 1948), Soc. Exptl. Biol. and Medicine, Soc. Gen. Physiol., Nat. Soc. Med. Research (sec. treas. 1955-57), Soc. Electroencephalography. Internat. Brain Research Orgn. (council 1962-64), Acad. Psychoanalysis, Internat. Soc. Neurochemistry, Pan Hellenic Med. Assn., Acad. Neurology, Soc. Biol. Psychiatry (pres. 1967), Soc. Neurosci. (hon. pres. 1970-72), Operations Research Soc. Am., Phi Beta Kappa, Sigma Xi, Alpha Omega Alpha. Clubs: Cosmos, Quadrangle, Chicago Literary. Author: Unresting Cells, 1940; The Body Functions, 1941; Food for Life, 1952; Mirror to Physiology; A Self-Survey of Physiological Science, 1958; Computers and Education, 1967. Editor: Methods in Medical Research, 1950; Concept of Biology, 1958; (with Cole) Psychopharmacology, Problems in Evaluation, 1959; (with Duyff) Information Processing in the Nervous System, 1964. Editorial bd. Currents in Modern Biology; asso. editor Jour. Math. Bioscis., Jour. Neurophysiology. Contbr. jours. Editor Behavioral Sci., Jour. Electroencephalography. Home: Corona del Mar, Cal. Died Feb. 1974.

GERBER, DANIEL F., business exec.; b. Fremont, Mich., May 6, 1898; s. Frank and Dora Pauline (Platt) G.; student St. Johns Mil. Acad., Delafield, Wisconsin, (co-author) Pharmacy, 1913-16, Babson Institute, Wellesley Hills, Mass., 1919-20; married Dorothy Marion Scott, January 18, 1923; children—Dorothy S. (Mrs. Ralph K. Merrill, Jr.), Sally Scott (Mrs. R.H. Phinny), Paula P. (Mrs. David Warm), Arabella G. (Mrs. H.M. Cummings), Daniel F. Entire career with Gerber Products Company (formerly Fremont Canning Company), Fremont, Michigan, salesman, 1920-21, dir., 1926-28, asst. gen. mgr., 1926-28, 1st vice president, 1928-45, pres., dir., 1945, president, 1945-64, then chairman board, chief executive officer; dir. Old State Bank of Fremont. Served in United States Army 1917-19; served as head fruit and vegetable sect. food price div., Office Price Adminstrn., 1942-43. Awarded Cross of War (France), 1918. Mem. Mich. Canners Assn. (past pres.), Grocery Association of Am. Member of Babson Inst. Republican. Mem. Christian Science Ch. Home: Fremont, Mich. Died Mar. 16, 1974.

GERE, BREWSTER HUNTINGTON, mathematician, educator; b. Syracuse, N.Y., Dec. 5, 1910; s. William Peck and Gertrude (Gardner) G.; B.A., Yale, 1930; M.A. (grad. Scholar 1933-34), Syracuse U., 1934; Ph.D., Mass. Inst. Tech., 1938; m. Margaret Jewitt Chamberlain, July 31, 1937; children—Judith Chamberlain, Brewster Huntington, Margaret Lynn, Grad. asst. Syracuse U., 1934-35; instr. Mass. Inst. Tech., 1936-39, Herzl Jr. Coll., Chgo., 1939-42; asst. prof. math. and mechanics U.S. Naval Postgrad. Sch., 1946-47, vis. prof. mathematics and mechanics, 1962-63; mem. faculty Hamilton Coll., 1947-73, prof. math., 1953-73, chmn. dept., 1950-69, dir. summer Insts., 1959-62, 64, 67—, now also Samuel F. Pratt prof.; vis. prof. dept. statistics U. N.C., 1970-71. Served to lt. comdr. USNR, 1942-46; comdr. Ret. Res. Mem. Am. Math. Soc., Math. Assn. Am. (dir. Programed Learning Project com. on ednl. media 1965-68), Nat. Council Tchrs. Math., Am. Assn. U. Profs. Home: Clinton, N.Y. Died July 13, 1973.

GERITY, JAMES, JR., corp. exec.; b. Toledo, Jan. 5, 1904; s. James and Mary (Kelley) G.; student Toledo U., 1921-23; LL.D., U. Notre Dame, 1973; m. Virginia Boland, Aug. 11, 1927. Pres. Gerity-Whitaker Co., 1930-37, Gerity Adrian Mfg. Corp., 1937-45; pres., gen. mgr., dir. Gerity Mich. Corp., Adrian, from 1938, chmn. bd., 1946-56, chmn. bd. Gerity Mich. Die Casting Co., 1945-46, pres., 1946-47; owner, pres. Gerity Broadcasting Co., Gerity CableVision, Bay City, Mich., Lee Travel Bur., Bay City and Midland, Mich., Gerity Products, Inc., Toledo; a founder Schultz Die Casting Co., Toledo (became Gerity-Schultz Corp. 1963), chmn. bd., maj. stockholder, pres. Time and Space, Inc. Miami Beach, Fla. Bd. dirs. Heart Inst. Miami Beach; mem. adv. council Coll. Commerce, U. Notre Dame; bd. dirs. Toledo Clinic Found., St. Francis Hosp. (Miami Beach). President Com. 100, Miami Beach, Fla. Hon. del. Mich. State Med. Soc. Recipient Air Force Exceptional Service award, 1963; decorated Knight Comdr. Equestrian Order Holy Sepulchre Jerusalem. Mem. Am. Legion. Elk. Clubs: Athletic, Detroit (Detroit); Key Largo (Fla.); Bath, La Gorce Country, Surf, Indian Creek Country (Miami Beach); Palm Bay, Jockey (Miami); Chicago Press, Chicago Athletic assn. (Chgo.); Detroit (Mich.) Press; Inverness, Belmont Country, Toledo, Adrian (Toledo); Bloomfields Country (Detroit); Metropolitan, Advertising, Canadian (N.Y.); New York Athletic; Nat. Press, Broadcasters (Washington); Lenawee Country; Bloomfield Country; Ocean Reef, Key Largo Anglers (Fla.); Two Hundred; Confrerie des Chevaliers du Tastevin. Home: Adrian, Mich. Died Nov. 1973.

GERMANN, FRANK E(RHART) E(MMANUEL), educator; b. Peru, Ind., Dec. 6, 1887; s. Gustave A. and Mary (Miller) G.; A.B., Ind. U., 1911; student U. of Wis., Lausanne and Neuchâtel, Switzerland, and U. of Berlin; hon. fellow, U. of Berlin, summer, 1912; Dr. és Sc., U. of Geneva, Switzerland, 1914; Carnegie research fellow, Cornell U., 1915-18 (part time); m. Martha M. Knechtel, 1916; children—Richard Paul, Lois Marie. Instr. physical chemistry, U. of Geneva, 1912-13; instr. French, Ind. U., 1913-14; instr. physics, Cornell U., 1914-18; prof. in charge depts. physics and elec. engring., Colo. Sch. of Mines, 1918-19; asso. prof. physical chemistry, U. of Colo., 1919-20, prof. after 1920; on leave doing research work in cooperation with Carnegie Institute, 1925-26. Fellow A.A.A.S. (member council since 1930; vice-pres. S.W. div. 1932-34; pres. 1936-38; exec. sec.-treas. since 1940), Colo.-Wyo. Acad. Science (exec. com. 1927-30; pres. 1930-31); mem. Am. Chem. Soc. (mem. council 1936-38; v.p. Colo. Sect. 1933; pres. 1934-36), Am. Assn. Univ. Profs. (pres. U. of Colo, chapter 1928-30; regional director after 1936; member council since 1943), Colorado Engineering Council; mem. Kansas Academy Science, Société Francaise de Physique, Association des Chimistes de Genéve, Société Suisse de Chimie, Société de Chimie Physique, Phi Beta Kappa (sec.-treas. Western Dist. since 1940), Sigma Xi (pres. U. of Colo. chapter 1926-27), Alpha Chi Sigma. Chmn. Rocky Mountain Regional Com. Am. Petroleum Inst. on Development and Production Research since 1929. Clubs: Town and Gown, Cosmopolitan, University (Colorado) Faculty Club. Author: Line Coördinate Charts for Boiling Points (with O. S. Knight), 1934; Causes d'Erreur Affectant les Détermination de Poids Atomiques (with Ph.A. Guye), 1923; also over 65 papers presenting results of original researches, in various Am. and European phys., chem. and indsl. jours. Editor of Jour. Colo-Wyo. Acad. Science, 1927-31. Home: Boulder, Colo. Died Feb. 27, 1974.

GERSHOY, LEO, historian, educator; b. Krivol Rog, Russia, Sept. 27, 1897; s. Morris and Miriam (Lioubarski) G.; came to U.S., 1903, naturalized, 1913; A.B., Cornell, 1919, A.M., 1920, Ph.D., 1925; m. Ida Elizabeth Prigohzy, Sept. 14, 1924. Social Science Research Council fellow, 1927-28; asst. prof. history L.I. U., 1929-30, asso. prof., 1930-38; mem. social sci. dept. Sarah Lawrence Coll., 1938-46; prof. N.Y. U. 1946-69, emeritus, 1969. Vis. prof. Columbia, 1947-48, 51-52, U. Cal., 1953-55, summer 1966, summer U. Chgo., 1938, Cornell U., 1932-34, 1936. U. Cal., 1948; fellow Center Advanced Study Behavioral Scis., 1963-64. Cons. OSS, 1942, prin. analyst Fgn. Broadcast Intelligence Service, 1943-44; chief regional specialist for France overseas br. OWI, Washington, 1944-45. Fulbright grantee for research, France, 1952-53; Guggenheim Found. fellow, 1936-37, 39, 46, 59. Fellow Am. Acad. Arts and Scis.; mem. Am. Hist. Assn., P.E.N., Société des Etudes Robespierristes (com. dir.), Société d'histoire Moderne, Soc. French Hist. Studies, Am. Soc. Eighteenth-Century Studies, Phi Beta Kappa. Author: The French Revolution, 1789-99, 1932; The French Revolution and Napoleon, 1933; From Despotism to Revolution, 1763-1789, 1944; The Era of the French Revolution, 1789-1799, Ten Years That Shook the World, 1957; Bertrand Barére: A Reluctant Terrorist, 1962. Bd. editors Am. Hist. Rev., 1959-63. Contbr. articles to profl., other jours. Home: New York City, N.Y. Died Mar. 12, 1975; cremated.

GERTKEN, SEVERIN (JAMES), abbot-ordinary; b. Richmond, Minn., July 26, 1881; s. Luke and Margaret (Schneider) G.; Ph.B., St. John's Univ., Collegeville, Minn., 1904; grad., St. John's Univ. Sem., 1907; S.M., Univ. of Chicago, 1924. Ordained priest (Benedictine order), Roman Catholic Ch., 1907; head, dept. of chemistry, St. John's Univ., 1907-23, 1924-26; elected abbot-ordinary, St. Peter's Abbey Nullius, Muenster, Saskatchewan, Can., Sept. 8, 1926, and continued since in that position. Address: Muenster, Sask., Can.†

GETTY, GEORGE FRANKLIN, II, business exec.; b. Los Angeles, July 9, 1924; s. J. Paul and Jeannette (DeMont) G.; student Princeton, 1942; m. Gloria Alice Gordon, June 29, 1951 (div.); children—Anne C., Claire E., Caroline M. m. 2d, Jacqueline M. Riordan, May 20, 1971. Ind. oil operator, Cal., Tex., 1947-48, discovered South Crane oilfield, W. Tex., 1948; mgr. Saudi Arabian div. Pacific Western Oil Corp., 1949-50, mgr. Mid-continent div., 1951-53; v.p., dir., Spartan Aircraft Co., Tulsa, 1953-55; pres. Minnehoma Ins. Co., Minnehoma Financial Co., 1953-56; exec. v.p. Pacific Western oil Corp. (Getty Oil Co.), 1955-56; dir., v.p., gen. mgr. eastern div. Tidewater Oil Co., 1956-58, pres., 1958-67 (merged into Getty Oil Co. 1967), exec. v.p., chief operating officer, dir. Getty Oil Co., 1967-73; dir. Bank of Am., N.T. & S.A., Mission Corp. Mem. 1st U.S. Petroleum Industry delegation inspecting Soviet oil industry, 1960. Bd. dirs. So. Cal. Symphony-Hollywood Bowl Assn. Served as 1st lt. AUS, 1942-47, PTO. Recipient Gold medal of merit V.F.W.; 1964. Mem. Los Angeles World Affairs Council (dir.), Nat. petroleum Council (exec. com., nominating com., com. on factors affecting U.S. Petroleum), Am. Petroleum Inst. (exec. com., dir.). Clubs: The Los Angeles (dir. 1963—, pres. 1964-65), Wilshire Country (Los Angeles); Beach (Santa Monica, Cal.), California. Home: Los Angeles, Cal. Died June 6, 1973.

GETTY, JEAN PAUL, business exec.; b. Mpls., Dec. 15, 1892; s. George Franklin and Sarah McPherson (Risher) G.; student U. Cal. at Los Angeles, U. Cal. at Berkeley; grad. in econs. and polit. sci. Oxford (Eng.) U.; LL.D., Ohio No. U., 1966; m. Jeannette Dumont, 1923 (div.); 1 son, George Franklin II (dec.); m. 2d, Allene Ashby, 1926 (div.); m. 3d, Fini Helmle, 1928 (div.); 1 son, Jean Ronald; m. 4th, Ann Rork, 1932 (div.); children—Jean Paul, Gordon Peter; m. 5th, Louise Dudley Lynch, Nov. 14. 1939 (div.); 1 son Timothy Christopher (dec.). Ind. oil producer, 1914-76; pres. gen. mgr. George F. Getty, Inc., 1930-33; dir. Petroleum Corp., 1932-34; dir. Tidewater Asso. Oil Co., 1932-36; pres., gen. mgr. Minnehoma Financial Corp. (formerly Spartan Aircraft Co.). 1942-61, prin. owner, 1942-76; pres. Mission Devel. Co., 1948-67, Mission Corp.; pres., prin. owner Getty Oil Co., 1956-76. Founder, trustee J. Paul Getty Mus., 1953-76. Mem. N.Y., Cal. chambers commerce. Clubs: Explorers

(N.Y.); Beach (Santa Monica, Cal.); Los Angeles Athletic; Nouveau Cercle (Paris). Author: History of the Oil Business of George Franklin and J. Paul Getty, 1903-39, 1941; Europe in the 18th Century, 1947; Collector's Choice (with Ethel LeVane), 1956; My Life and Fortunes, 1963; The Joys of Collecting, 1965; How To be Rich, 1966; The Golden Age, 1968; How to be a Successful Executive, 1971. Home: Malibu, Cal. Died June 6, 1976.

GIACCONE, JOHN S., physician; b. N.Y.C., Mar. 4, 1915; s. Leonard and Maria (Monteleone) G.; M.D., Marquette U., 1943; m. Evelyn Bernardine Ruffino, Oct. 21, 1945; children—John S., Janice Maria (Mrs. Napolitani), Peter John, Phyllis Christine, Michael John. Intern, Fordham Hosp., Bronx, N.Y., 1943-44; resident in obstetrics and gynecology, 1946-73; attending in obstetrics and gynecology, lectr. Fordham Hosp., Misericordia Hosp.; attending in obstetrics and gynecology St. Francis Hosp., Bronx; attending in obstetrics Mother Gabrini Meml. Hosp., N.Y.C.; lectr. N.Y. Med. Coll. Diplomate Am. Bd. Obstetrics and Gynecology, Internat. Bd. Surgery. Fellow A.C.S., Am. Coll. Obstetrics and Gynecology, Internat. Coll. Surgery, Bronx Obstet.-Gynecol. Soc. (past pres.), N.H. Acad. Medicine. Contbr. articles to profl. jours. Home: Mt. Vernon, N.Y. Died Sept. 11, 1973; buried St. Raymond's Cemetery, Bronx, N.Y.

GIBBS, ROSWELL CLIFTON, physicist; b. at Hume, N.Y., July 1, 1878; s. Orlando Charles and Frances E. (Beaderslee) G.; Buffalo Normal Sch., 1895-97; A.B., Cornell, 1906, A.M., 1908, Ph.D., 1910; m. Clara Laura Davis, Aug. 21, 1901; children—Ruth Carrier (Mrs. Charles W. Jones), Marjorie Jeannette (Mrs. John W. Roehl), Elinor Frances. Teacher and principal pub. and high schs. until 1903; instr. physics, 1906-12, asst. prof., 1912-18, prof. after 1918 and chmn. dept. after 1934, Cornell U., also acting dean, Coll. of Arts and Sciences, second term, 1926-27; research asso. in physics, Calif. Inst. of Technology, 1923-24. Asso. editor Physical Rev., 1931-34. U.S. del. 5th Inernat. Congress on Electricity, Paris, 1932. Fellow Am. Physical Soc., A.A.A.S.; mem. N.Y. State Sciene Teachers' Assn. (pres, 1917), Optical Soc. of America (v.p. 1935-37, pres. 1937-39), Am. Assn. Univ. Profs., Phi Beta Kappa, Sigma Xi, Specialized in spectroscopy, luminescence, study of the absorption spectra of organic compounds in solution, extreme ultra-violet spectra, spectra of isoelectronic Sequences, multiplet and hyperfine structure of spectra, fine structure of hydrogen and deuterium spectra, e ration from such spectra. Home: Ithaca, N.Y.†

GIBSON, NORMAN ROTHWELL, engr.; b. Guelph, Ont., Can., Mar. 23, 1880; s. Theron and Mary Jean (Holmwood) G.; prep. edn. Harbord Street Collegiate Institute; Bachelor Applied Science, Univ. of Toronto, 1904; Dr. Engring. from same univ., 1931; m. Margaret Cecelia Graham, Nov. 4, 1908; children—Mary Marjory Graham (dec.), Grace Eleanor (Mrs. G. E. Ellsworth). In charge constrn. 1st Street Bridge across Assiniboine River, Brandon, 1908; associated with Smith, Kerry & Chace in design and constrn. hydro-electric power developments, 1908-13; with Ontario Power Co. and Electric Power Co., Ltd., 1913-15; partner Kerry & Chase, Ltd., cons. engrs., Toronto, 1913-16; chief engr. Electric Power Co., Niagara Falls, 1916-17; hydraulic engr. Hydraulic Power Co., Niagara Falls, 1918-25; exec. engr. Niagara Falls Power Co., 1925-26, chief engr., 1926-27, v.p. and chief engr., 1927-45, vice pres., 1945-47; chmn. bd. Canadian Niagara Power Co., 1946-47, retired June 1, 1947; dir. Canadian Power Co., Ltd., Buffalo & Niagara Electric Corp. Fellow, Royal Soc. Arts (Eng.); mem. A.A.A.S., Am. Soc. C.E., Am. Soc. Mechanical Engrs., Am. Inst. E.E., Engineering Soc. Canada; non-resident mem. Franklin Institute. Presbyterian. Clubs: Niagara Falls Country, Buffalo. Contributor papers on water measurement, etc. Awarded Elliott Cresson Gold Medal by Franklin Inst. for invention of Gibson method and apparatus for measuring flow of fluids in closed conduits, 1930; awarded Holley Medal by Am. Soc. Mech. Engrs., 1946. Home: Lewiston, N.Y.†

GIBSON, THOMAS L., judge; b. Stanton, Tenn., Sept. 3, 1881; s. James Knox and Rosa Claiborne (Somervell) G.; A.B., U. of Tenn., 1902; studied law pvtly.; m. Nell Buzzard, July 12, 1910; children—Thomas L., Mary S. Admitted to Okla. bar, 1910, and since practiced at Muskogee, becoming partner Gibson, Maxey, Holleman & Gibson, specializing in corp., oil and gas law and land titles; justice Supreme Court of Okla., 1935-53, chief justice, 1946-47. Mem. Am., Okla. State and Muskogee bar assns., Sigma Alpha Epsilon, Phi Delta Phi. Democrat. Methodist. Club: Town and Country. Home: Oklahoma City, Okla.†

GIEGENGACK, AUGUSTUS E., manufacturer; b. N.Y. City, April 19, 1890; s. A.E. and Mary C. (Fitzgerald) G.; M. Margaret A. Morrison; 1 dau., Margaret Mary. Served apprenticeship in printing shops in N.Y. City, becoming journeyman printer; was in charge of printing Charles William Stores, Brooklyn; later with DeVinne Press (New York), Burkhardt Linotype Co.; then treas. Whittaker-Giegengack-Irapp comml. printers; public printer of U.S., 1934-48; now vice pres. charge eastern div. Electrographic Corp.; dir. Bank of Commerce and Savings; chmn. bd. First Fed. Savings & Loan Assn. of Washington. Enlisted in U.S. Army and apptd. mech. supt. of Stars and Stripes, official newspaper of A.E.F. in Paris. Served as pres. N.Y. Club Printing House Craftsmen, Internat. Assn. Printing House Craftsmen, Typographers Assn. of N.Y., also as code dir. of latter; pres. and dir. Nat. Graphic Arts Expns.; mem. Nat. Foundation for Infantile Paralysis (D.C. chapter), Washington Board of Trade. Member of American Inst. Graphic Arts, Am. Soc. Mech. Engrs., U.S. Vets. of Am. Wars, Am. Legion, 40 and 8, Stars and Stripes Assn., Vets. of Foreign Wars, Knights of Columbus, Elks, Washington Club of Printing House Craftsmen, Printing Supply Salesmen's Guild, Columbia Typographical Union Internat. Printing Pressmen and Assts. Union. Printing Industry of Am., Inc., Internat. Trade Composition Assn., N.Y. Employing Printers Assn., Graphic Arts Assn. of Ill. Clubs: National Press (Washington); New York Athletic, Advertising (N.Y.C.); Lake Shore (Chgo.); Quinnipiack (New Haven). Address: New Haven, Conn. Died June 21, 1974.

GIERULA, JERZY KAZIMIERZ, educator; b. Cracow, Poland, Feb. 20, 1917; s. Kazimierz and Zofia (Romanowska) G.; ed. Jagielionian U., 1935-39, Ph.D., 1951; m. Julia Joanna Majdak, Feb. 19, 1944; children—Anna Danuta, Jerzy Filip. Asst., Phys. Inst., Jagielionian U., 1945; asso. prof. Inst. Nuclear Research, Cracow, 1961, prof., 1969-75, chmn. sci. council, 1967; chief chair physics Mil. Tech. Acad., Warsaw, 1952. Served to lt. col. Polish Armed Forces, 1955. Decorated Knight's and comdr.'s cross Polonia Restituta; recipient 1st Grad. prize in Physics, 1963-68. Mem. Am., Polish phys. socs. Polish Acad. Sci. Co-developer fireball model of multiple meson prodn., 1958. Home: Cracow, Poland., Died Jan. 14, 1975.

GILBERT, CAROL JEANNE, theatre mgr.; b. Camden, N.J., Feb. 13, 1943; d. Ross Oswald and Jeanne Marie Gilbert (Porr) Fuller; B.S., Millersville (Pa.) State Coll., 1965; postgrad. Temple U. Tchr. English and drama Woodrow Wilson High Sch., Levittown, Pa., 1965-68; dir. pub. relations Theatre-in-the-Park, Trenton, N.J., summers 1967-69; tchr. English and drama Penn Manor High Sch., Millersville, 1968-69; mem. staff Bucks County Theatre Co., Bucks County Playhouse, New Hope, Pa., 1969-75, asst. mng. dir., dir. ednl. projects, sec.-treas., 1972-75. Mem. New Hope C. of C. Home: Lahaska, Pa. Died May 8, 1975.

GILBERT, FREDERICK AUGUSTUS, ret. chem. exec.; b. Buffalo, May 2, 1912; s. Lester F. and Josephine (Hoyt) G.; grad. Taft Sch., Phillip Exeter Acad.; A.B. Harvard, 1934; m. Nancy Porter, June 17, 1937; children—Samuel L., Nancy P. With Buffalo Electro-Chem. Co., Inc., 1935-52 (merged with Food Machinery & Chem. Corp. 1952, co. now known as FMC Corp.), div. mgr., 1956-58, v.p., 1958-73, ret., 1973. Home: Darien, Conn. Died Aug. 18, 1974; interred Buffalo.

GILBERT, JAMES HENRY, prof. economics; b. Erwin, Tenn., Mar. 9, 1878; s. Isaac Wilson and Nancy (Clouse) G.; A.B., U. of Ore., 1903; Ph.D., Columbia, 1907; m. Isolene Shaver, June 28, 1911; children—Madeleine, Robert Wilson (dec.), Walter M. With U. of Ore., 1907-47, then retired; prof. economics, 1945-47, acting dean Coll. of Literature, Sciences and the Arts, 1925-27, dean, 1927-32, dean Coll. of Social Sci., 1932-42; dean of Liberal Arts Coll., 1942-47. Economic adviser Ore. Tax Investigating Com., 1922-23; mem. Spl. Legis. Com. on Taxation of Municipal Utilities, 1932-33; mem. State advisory com. on Public Works Adminstrn., 1933-34; spl. rep. U.S. Employment Service, Merit Exam., Ore., 1935; mem. Legislative Interim Commn. on Taxation and Industry, 1941-42. Mem. Pacific Coast Assn., Phi Beta Kappa, Baptist. Clubs: Rotary, Round Table. Author: Trade and Currency in Early Oregon, 1907; Tax Systems of Australasia, 1943. Home: Eugene, Ore.†

GILBERT, WILLIAM MARSHALL, prof. home missions; b. Monmouth, Ill., Aug. 24, 1879; s. Abram V. T. and Maria M. (Gaylord) G.; A.B., Cornell Coll., Mt. Vernon, Ia., 1904, D.D., 1920; S.T.B., Boston U. Sch. of Theology, 1909; m. Harriet Harmon Herrick, Dec, 31, 1908; children—Harmon, George, Harriet. Ordained deacon, 1906, elder, 1908, M.E. Church; entered Central Ill. Conf., 1904; pastor Fairview, Ill., 1904-05, Peoria, 1905-06, Cliftondale, Mass., 1909-13; Morgan Memorial Ch., Boston, 1913-18, First Ch., 1918-21; dir. Bur. of Foreign Speaking Work, Bd. of Home Missions and Ch. Extension, 1921-23; prof. home missions and dir. of field supervision, Drew U., since 1923. Mem. Home Missions Council; sec. Commn. of Foreign Language Work of the Gen. Conf. M.E. Ch., 1920-24. Republican. Club: Rotary; dist. gov. 36th Dist., Rotary Internat., 1935-36. Editor: Social Pioneering, 1928. Home: Madison, N.J.†

GIL-BORGES, ESTEBAN, lawyer; b. Caracas, Venezuela, Feb. 8, 1879; s. Esteban Gil Bassalo and Josefa Borges de Gil; LL.D., U. of Caracas, 1899; hon. LL.D., Georgetown U., 1921; m. Matilde Martinez, of Caracas, 1907; children—Josée, Maria, Alberto. Counselor on internat. law, to Venezuelan-Colombian Mixed Frontier Commn., 1900; commr. Supreme Court, later pres., 1902; prof. U. of Caracas, 1903-09; counselor of Legation, Washington, D.C., 1909-14, France, England and Germany, 1914-19; rep. of Venezuela at Internat. Conf. for Suppression of Opium Traffic, at The Hague, 1917; minister of foreign affairs, Venezuela, 1919-21; spl. envoy to unveiling of statue of Bolivar, presented by Govt. of Venezuela to City of New York, 1921; specialist with Breckinridge Long, in European and S. Am. law, 1921-23; asst. dir. Pan Am. Union, 1924. Mem. Am. Acad. Polit. and Social Science, Venezuelan Nat. Acad., Royal Spanish Acad. (corr.). Awarded Great Cross Order of Isabel la Católica. Catholic. Author: Filosofia de la Historia del Derecho, 1912; La Vida del Derecho y sus Formas Primitivas, 1917; Derecho Internacional y Derecho Interno, en Codificacion y Unificacion, 1919; Lecturas Académicas, 1920. Home: Chevy Chase, Md.†

GILBRETH, LILLIAN MOLLER, cons. engr.; b. Oakland, Cal., May 24, 1878; d. William and Annie (Delger) Moller; B.Litt., U. Cal., 1900, M.Litt., 1902, LL.D., 1933; Ph.D., Brown U., 1915, Sc.D., 1931; M. Engring., U. Mich., 1928; D. Engring., Rutgers Coll., 1929, Stevens Inst. Tech., 1950, Syracuse U., 1952; Sc.D., Russell Sage Coll., 1931, Colby Coll., 1951, Lafayette Coll., 1952; LL.D., Smith Coll., 1945, Mills Coll., 1952; L.H.D., Temple U., 1949, Alfred U., 1948; Dr. Indsl. Psychol., Purdue U., 1948; hon. degrees from Milw. Downer Coll., Washington U., Princeton, Skidmore Coll., U. Wis., Pratt Inst., U. Mass., Western Coll. Women; LL.D., Ariz. State U., 1964; m. Frank Bunker Gilbreth, Oct. 19, 1904; children—Anne Moller (Mrs. Robert E. Barney), Mary Elizabeth (dec.), Ernestine Moller (Mrs. Charles E. Carey), Martha Bunker (dec.; Mrs. Richard E. Tallman), Frank Bunker, William Moller, Lillian Moller (Mrs. Donald D. Johnson), Frederick Moller, Daniel Bunker, John Moller, Robert Moller, Jane Moller (Mrs. G.Paul Heppes, Jr.). Pres. Gilbreth, Inc., cons. engrs. in mgmt., Montclair, N.J., 1924—; dir. courses in motion study, 1925-32; prof. mgmt. Purdue U., 1935-48; chmn. dept. personnel relations Newark Coll. Engring., 1941-43; univ. teaching P.I., Formosa, 1953-54; prof. mgmt. U. Wis., 1955; lectr. tech. and human relations problems in mgmt. in Asia, Australia, Can., Europe, Mexico, U.S.A., after 1955. Mem. U.S. Govt. coms. on civil def., also state and local coms. Mem. Essex County Vocational Bd. Trustee Montclair Library, 1944-54. Recipient Henry Lawrence Gantt medal (with Frank Gilbreth) Nat. Inst. Social Scis.; Wallace Clark Internat. award; gold medal Comite Internat. de l'Orgn. Scientifique; Washington award; Allan R. Cullimore medal, 1959; Hoover medal Am. Soc. C.E., 1966. Hon. mem. mgmt. socs. in U.S.A. and fgn. countries. Mem. Nat. Acad. Engring., Internat. Acad. Mgmt. Author: (with Frank B. Gilbreth) Fatigue Study, 1911, Applied Motion Study, 1917, Motion Study for the Handicapped, 1919; The Psychology of Management, 1921; Living with Our Children, 1928; Normal Lives for the Disabled (with Edna Yost), 1945; The Foreman and Manpower Management (with Alice Rice Cook), 1947; Management in the Home (with O. M. Thomas, Eleanor C. Clymer), 1954, 59. Contbr. Indsl. Engring. Handbook. Home: Montclair, N.J.†

GILCHRIST, CLARENCE THOMAS, sales exec.; b. Cleve., Aug. 8, 1893; s. David and Anna Lavera (Church) G.; student pub. schs. Cleve.; m. Florence E. Schnell, Jan. 1, 1918; 1 dau., Norma Joan. With Am. Steel & Wire Co., Cleve., 1907-59, successively salesman, asst. mgr. sales Cleve. office, mgr. mfrs. products div. Chgo. office, asst. gen. mgr. sales Chgo.-Milw., area mgr. sales Western area, 1949-59. Clubs: Chicago Athletic Assn., Executive (Chgo.); Skokie Country (Glencoe, Ill.). Home: Glencoe, Ill. Died Feb. 15, 1974.

GILCHRIST, HUNTINGTON, born in Boston, Massachusetts, on November 16, 1891; son of John and Martha Hyde (Huntington) G.; A.B., Williams Coll., 1913; A.M., Harvard, 1916; Ph.D., Columbia, 1918; m. Elizabeth Brace (Bryn Mawr, 1920), d. Charles Loring Brace, of N.Y. City, Oct. 1, 1920; children—John Huntington, Charles Loring, Elizabeth Brenda. Instr. Anglo-Chinese College, Foochow, China, also Peking U., 1913-15; sr. officer Internat. Secretariat for Internat. Administrn. and Mandated Tys. and liaison between secretary-general, League of Nations and U.S. Govt., 1919-28; exec. chem. industry, U.S.A. and Europe, 1928-55; manager dir. Cyanamid Products Ltd., London, 1935-40; became exec. Am. Cyanamid Co., N.Y., 1940; on leave to serve as dir. industry div. European hdqrs. Marshall Plan, Paris, France, 1949-50, mission chief for Belgium Luxembourg, and Belgian Congo, as minister, Brussels, Belgium, 1950-55; resident rep. for Pakistan with rank of minister Technical Assistance Bd., UN, Karachi, Pakistan, 1955-57. Organizer 1st conf. of coll. newspaper editors Columbia School of Journalism, 1913. Board of trustees Columbia School of Social Work, chairman adv. council, 1959-62. Secretary-general U.N.R.R.A. Council, Montreal, 1944. Exec. officer U.N. Conf. on Internat. Orgn., San Francisco, 1945. Trustee Woodrow Wilson Found., 1948-51; trustee Brookings Instn., from 1943, (v.p. 1949-55), Belgian-Am. Ednl. Found., from 1953, International Schs. Found., 1955-65 (chmn. bd. dirs. 1960-63); hon. treas. Royal Inst. Internat. Affairs, N.Y.C., 1946-57. Decorated Sitara in Order of Quaid-i-Azam (Pakistan). Mem. council Fgn. Relations, Am. Soc. Internat. Law, Kappa Alpha, Gargoyle. Conglist.

Clubs: Pilgrims Century, Union Interallie (Paris); Cosmos (Washington). Home: Ridgefield, Conn. Died Jan. 13, 1975.

GILL, WILLIAM HANSON, college president; b. Unison, Loudoun County, Va., Aug. 7, 1886; s. John Love and Sudie Victoria (Leith) G.; B.S., Va. Mil. Inst., 1907; grad. Inf. Sch., 1924; honor grad. Command and Gen. Staff Sch., 1925; grad. Army War Coll., 1930; LL.D. (honorary), University of Denver, 1950; m. Elizabeth Grady, Oct. 21, 1913; 1 dau., Elizabeth Suzanne (wife of Col. Frank P. Norman, Jr.). Served as capt. Va. Nat. Guard, 1910-12; commd. 2d lt., U.S. Army, Apr. 24, 1912, advanced through grades to maj. gen., 1942; with 8th Inf., Philippines, 1915-17; capt. and maj., 5th Div., with A.E.F., France, Apr., 1918-July 1919; participated in St. Mihiel and Meuse-Argonne campaigns; instr. Va. Nat. Guard, 1919-23; instr. Command and Gen. Staff Sch., 1925-29; mem. War Dept. Gen. Staff, 1931-35; exec. officer, 27th Inf., Hawaii, 1936-38; prof. mil. tactics, U. of Calif., 1938-40; instr. Army War Coll., 1940; chief of staff, 8th Div., 1940-41; comdg. gen., 55th Brig., 28th Div., Oct. 1941-Apr. 42; comdg. 89th Div., July 1942-Feb. 1943; comdg. 32d Div. in Southwest Pacific, Feb. 1943-Sept. 1945; pres. Colo. Coll. from 1947. Decorated D.S.C., D.S.M., B.S.M., Silver Star (oak leaf cluster), Legion of Merit. Home: Colorado Springs, Colo., Died Jan. 18, 1976.

GILLETTE, GENE, newspaperman; b. Norfolk, Neb., Oct. 29, 1907; s. Elmer and Mary (Ely) G.; student U. Neb., 1927-28; m. Josephine Threlkeld, May 5, 1927; children—Joan (Mrs. David Totton), Patricia (Mrs. Bradford Claxton), Gene E. Mgr. United Press bur., Lincoln, Neb., 1927-28, Milw., 1928-29, Des Moines, Ia., 1930-32, news editor Central div., Chgo., 1933-35, day news mgr., Washington, 1935-38, news editor Southwest div., Kansas City, 1939-42, night bur. mgr., N.Y.C., 1943-45, night news mgr., 1946-48, day news mgr., 1949-59, central div. news mgr., 1959-65, central div. news and picture mgr., 1965-75. Home: Winnetka, Ill. Died Feb. 3, 1975.

GILLETTE, GUY MARK, senator; born Cherokee, Ia., Feb. 3, 1879; s. Mark Dennis and Mary (Hull) G.; LL.B., Drake U., 1900; LL.D., Drake University, St. Ambrose Coll.; m. Rose Freeman, June 17, 1907; 1 son, Mark Freeman. Admitted to Ia. bar, 1900, and began practice at Cherokee; city atty., Cherokee, 1906-07; county atty., Cherokee County, 1907-09. Served as sergt. U.S. Vol. Inf. Spanish-Am. War; capt. inf., U.S. Army, 1917-19. Mem. Ia. State Senate, 1912-16; mem. 73d and 74th Congresses (1933-37), 9th Ia. Dist.; elected U.S. Senate to fill unexpired term of Louis Murphy, 1936, term expiring, 1939; reelected to Senate of U.S. for term, 1939-45; re-elected Nov. 1948, for 6-yr. term; chairman Surplus Property Board, 1945. President Am. League for Free Palestine, 1945. Member Spanish War Vets., Vets Fgn. Wars, Am. Legion. Democrat. Presbyterian. Mason, K.P. Home: Cherokee, Ia.†

GILLIE, GEORGE W., congressman; b. Berwickshire, Scotland, Aug. 15, 1880; s. James and Janet (Taylor) G.; came to U.S., 1882, naturalized, 1890; student Purdue U., 1899-1901; D.V.M., Ohio State U., 1907; m. Grace Merion, 1908; children—Charlotte (Mrs. John Strawbridge), Jean (Mrs. Elton Marquart). Meat and dairy inspector, Allen County, Ind., 1908-14; began practice of vet. medicine, Allen County, Ind., 1914; sheriff of Allen County, 1917-20, 1929-30, 1935-36; mem. 76th to 80th Congresses (1939-48), 4th Indiana District. Capt., Reserve Officers Corps. Mem. Am. Veterinary Med. Assn., Ind. Veterinary Assn., U.S. Livestock San. Assn., Ft. Wayne Am. Red Cross and Y.M.C.A. Republican. Conglist. Mason (Scottish Rite, Shriner), Odd Fellow, Modern Woodman, Moose. Club: Kiwanis (Fort Wayne). Home: Fort Wayne, Ind.†

GILLIGAN, EDMUND, novelist; b. Waltham, Mass., June 7, 1899; s. John and Ellen (Dillon) G.; grad. Harvard, 1926; m. Marjorie Cook (died 1929); 1 dau., Joy; m. 2d, Nancy Rittenhouse, 1933; children—Judith, Edmund, Stephen. Reporter, Boston Globe, 1926, 30, N.Y. Sun, 1930-39; asso. editor Fortune Mag., 1939-42; rod and gun editor N.Y. Herald Tribune since 1949. Seaman, U.S. Navy, World War I. Author: One Lives to Tell the Tale, 1937; Boundary Against Night, 1938; White Sails Crowding, 1939; Strangers in the Vly, 1941; The Gaunt Woman, 1943; The Ringed Horizon, 1943; Voyage of the Golden Hind, 1945: I name Thee Mara, 1946; Storm at Sable Island, 1948. Home: Woodstock, N.Y. Died Dec. 29, 1973.

GILLILAND, CHARLES EDWARD, JR., coll. dean; b. Austin, Tex., Mar. 2, 1916; s. Charles Edward and Olive May (Wiley) G.; B.S., Harvard, 1938; M.S. in Bus. Adminstrn., Washington U., St. Louis, 1947, Ph.D., 1956; m. Flora Reller Smith, June 12, 1948; children—Thomas Lee, Susan Virginia. Asst. to dean Washington U. Sch. Bus. and Pub. Adminstrn., 1948-54; exec. sec. Am. Assn. Collegiate Schs. Bus., 1949-53; dean U. Kansas City (Mo.) Sch. Bus. Adminstrn., 1954-58; chief party Washington U. ICA project, Korea, 1958-60; prof. econs. Ariz. State U., 1960; dean Temple U. Sch. Bus. Adminstrn., 1960-65, prof. finance, 1960-68; dean Coll. Bus. Adminstrn., Fla. Tech. U., 1969-75; U.S. aid Temple U., adviser Inst. Bus. Adminstrn., U. Karachi, 1965-66. Served with USAAF, 1941-45. Mem. Acad. Mgmt. Beta Gamma Sigma (nat. treas. 1963-65), Omicron Delta Epsilon. Home: Orlando, Fla. Died Mar. 16, 1975.

GILLILAND, EDWIN R., educator, chem. engr.; b. El Reno, Okla., July 10, 1909; s. Owen Edwin and Elsie (Kelly) G.; B.Sc., U. Ill., 1930; M.Sc., Pa. State Coll., 1931; Sc.D., Mass. Inst. Tech., 1933; D. Engring., Northeastern U., 1948; m. Ann. F. Miller, June 15, 1938; 1 dau., Gail Ann (Mrs. Corbett). Instr. chem. engring. Mass. Inst. Tech., 1934-36, asst. prof., 1936-39, asso. prof., 1939-44, prof., 1944, dep. dean engring., 1945-46, chmn. faculty, 1952-54, acting head dept., 1951-53, 55-56, 60, head dept., 1961-69, Warren K. Lewis prof. chem. engring., 1969-71, Inst. prof., 1971-73. Asst. rubber dir. charge research and devel. Office of Rubber, 1942-44; dep. chmn., mem. div. 11, NDRC, 1944-45; mem. Pres.' Sci. Adv. Com., 1960-65; dep. chmn. guided missiles com. Joint Chiefs Staff, 1945-46; vice chmn. fuels and lubricants subcom. NACA, 1946-47; cons. Office Sci. and Tech., 1965-73. Recipient Profl. Progress award 1950, William H. Walker award, 1954, Warren K. Lewis award chem. engring. edn., 1965, all from Am. Inst. Chem. Engrs.; Baekland award Am. Chem. Soc., 1945, Indsl. and Engring. Chemistry award, 1959. Fellow Am. Inst. Chemists, Am. Inst. Chem. Engrs. (dir. 1958-60, Founders award 1971); mem. Nat. Acad. of Engring., Am. Chem. Soc., Nat. Acad. Scis., A.A.A.S., Am. Soc. for Engring. Edn., Am. Acad. Arts and Scis., Sigma Xi, Tau Beta Pi. Republican. Presbyn. Co-author: 3d edit. Principles of Chemical Engineering; author: 4th edit. Elements of Fractional Distillation. Author numerous articles on chem. engring. and related subjects. Home: Belmont Mass. Died Mar. 10, 1973.

GILLIN, JOHN P(HILIP), anthropologist; b. Waterloo, Ia., Aug. 1, 1907; s. John Lewis and Etta (Shaffner) G.; A.B., U. Wis., 1927, A.M., 1930; postgrad. U. Berlin, U. London Sch. Econs., 1928; A.M., Harvard, 1931, Ph.D., 1934; m. Helen Norgord, Mar. 29, 1934; 1 son, John Christian. Anthrop. field work in Algeria, Europe, 1930, N.M., 1931, Brit. Guiana, 1932-33, Ecuador and eastern Peru, 1934-35, Utah, 1936-37, Wis., 1938-39, Guatemala, 1942, 46, 48, Peru, 1944-45, Colombia, 1946, Cuba, 1948, various parts Latin Am., Europe, 1958-73; staff Peabody Mus., 1934-35; faculty Sarah Lawrence, 1933-34, U. Utah, 1935-37; Ohio State U., 1937-41, Duke, 1941-46; prof. anthropology and research U. N.C., 1946-59; dean div. social scis., prof. anthropology U. Pitts., 1959-62; research prof. anthropology Nat. Inst. Mental Health Career, 1962-72. Vis. prof. Columbia, 1957-58, U. Hawaii, summer 1956; hon. fellow in psychology Yale, 1940-41: mem. bd. of econ. warfare, U.S. embassy, Lima, Peru, 1942-44; Smithsonian rep., Peru, 1944-45; research asso. Carnegie Instn. Washington, 1942, 46. Center for Advanced Study in Behavioral Scis. fellow, 1954-55. Fellow A.A.A.S., Am. Anthrop. Assn. (exec. bd. 1949-52, pres. 1965-66), mem. Am. Sociol. Soc., Nat. Research Council (chmn. com. Latin Am. 1945-51), Soc. for Applied Anthropology (pres. 1959-60), Phi Beta Kappa, Sigma Xi, Phi Kappa Phi, Alpha Kappa Delta, Alpha Kappa Lambda. Unitarian. Clubs: Torch; University; Faculty; Harvard (Pitts.). Author various books, latest being: The Ways of Men, 1948; Moche: A Peruvian Coastal Community, 1947; (with J.L. Gillin) Cultural Sociology, 1948, The Culture of Security in San Carlos, 1951; (with others) Integration Social de Guatemala, 1957; San Luis Jilotepeque, 1958; (with others) Social Change in Latin America Today, 1961; Human Ways, 1969. Editor, co-author: For A Science of Social Man, 1954. Contbr. articles to profl. jours. Address: Chapel Hill, N.C. Died Aug. 4, 1973; buried Madison, Wis.

GILLINGHAM, ANNA, educator; b. Batavia, Ill., July 12, 1878; d. Theodore Tyson and Elizabeth (Heacock) Gillingham; A.B., Swarthmore Coll., 1900, Radcliffe Coll., 1901; M.A., Tchrs. Coll. Columbia, 1910. Tchr. elementary dept. Friends Central Sch., Phila., 1901-05; sch. psychologist Ethical Culture Sch., N.Y.C., 1905-36; dir. remedial reading Punahon Sch., Honolulu, T.H., 1936-38; sch. cons. remedial reading, various schs., after 1938. Mem. Am. Civil Liberties Union, Nat. Assn. Advancement Colored People, League Women Voters, Am. Friends Service Com., Nat. Urban League. Mem. Community Ch. Author: (with Stillman) Remedial Training for Children with Specific Disability in Reading and Spelling and Penmanship, revised edit., 1956. Home: Bronxville, N.Y.†

GILLS, JOE PITZER, power co. exec.; b. Marion, Va., July 18, 1913; s. Henry Pitzer and Mary (Gilliam) G.; B.S., in Elec. Engring., Va. Poly. Inst., 1934; grad. Advanced Mgmt. Program, Harvard, 1958; m. Ruth Alice Waller, July 1, 1937; children—Richard H., Cynthia. With Appalachian Power Co., Roanoke, Va., 1934-69, asst. gen. mgr., 1954-62, v.p., gen. mgr., exec. v.p., 1962-69; exec. v.p. Ohio Power Co., Canton, 1969-74, Ohio Electric Co., 1972-74; v.p. Beach Bottom Power Co., Franklin Real Estate Co.; v.p., dir. So. Ohio Coal Co., Cardinal Operating Co., Central Coal Co., Central Ohio Coal Co., Central Operating Co., Windsor Power House Coal Co.; dir. Am. Electric Power Service Corp., Ohio Valley Electric Corp., Harter Bank & Trust Co. Past pres. Pub. Utilities Assn. Virginias; dir. Ohio Electric Utility Inst.; trustee East Central Nuclear Group; dir. Ohio Coal Assn. Bd. visitors Emory and Henry Coll.; adv. bd. Malone Coll.; mem. exec. bd. Buckeye council Boy Scouts Am. Served to maj. AUS, 1942-46. Mem. Ohio, Canton chambers commerce, Va. Poly. Inst. Alumni Assn. (dir.), Baptist. Elk. Clubs: Brookside Country, Canton, Columbus Athletic. Home: Canton, O. Died Sept. 13, 1974.

GILMAN, ANDREW L., lawyer; b. Scottsburg, N.Y., Apr. 28, 1886; A.B., Cornell U., 1908; LL.B., Albany Law Sch., Union U., 1910. Admitted to N.Y. bar, 1911; mem. firm Woods, Oviatt, Gilman, Sturman and Clarke, Rochester, N.Y. Bd. dirs. Rochester Gen. Hosp., 1944-63, pres., 1947-50. Mem. Am., N.Y. State, Monroe County (pres. 1929) bar assns. Home: Rochester, N.Y. Died Dec. 13, 1973; buried Scottsburg, N.Y.

GILROY, WILLIAM EDGAR, editor; b. Mt. Forest, Ont., Can., Feb. 10, 1876; s. William John and Margaret (Ellis) G.; A.B., Toronto U., 1897; grad. in theology, Victoria U., 1900, D.D., 1938; D.D., Ripon (Wis.) Coll., 1923; Litt.D., Syracuse Univ., 1926; D.D., Victoria Univ., Toronto, 1938; m. Annie Elizabeth McKichan, 1901; 1 son, John. Came to U.S., 1919, naturalized, 1925. Meth. itinerary, 1897-99; ordained Congl. ministry, 1900; pastor Broadview Av. Ch., Toronto, 1900-06, also editor Canadian Congregationalist, 1904-06; pastor Brantford Ch., 1906-11, First Ch., Hamilton, 1911-19, Plymouth Ch., Fond du Lac, Wis., 1919-22; acting pastor, Congl. Ch., Barrington, R.I., during absence of its pastor on naval service, during World War II; became editor The Congregationalist, 1922, and after its merger with Herald of Gospel Liberty continued as editor of the renamed monthly, Advance, until 1943; since retirement from editorship engaged in various journalistic activities and writing books, also in syndicated work with Newspaper Enterprise Assn. Clubs: Monday, Winthrop, Fortnightly. Home: Newton Center, Mass.†

GINGER, RAY, author, editor. Author: The Bending Cross: a Biography of Eugene Victor Debs, 1949; Six Days or Forever?: Tennessee versus John Thomas Scopes, 1958; Altgeld's America, 1958; Age of Excess, 1965; Ray Ginger's Jokebook about American History, 1974; People on the Move, 1975. Editor Business History Review, 1952-53; Spectrum: the World of Science, 1959; American Social Thought, 1961; Spectrum: The World of American Life, 1965; William Jennings Bryan: Selections, 1967; Modern American Cities, 1969. Home: Canmore, Alta., Canada., Died Jan. 3, 1975.

GINOTT, HAIM G., psychologist, author; b. Aug. 5, 1922; B.S., Columbia Tchrs. Coll., 1948, M.A., 1949, Ed.D., 1952. Chief clin. psychologist Jacksonville (Fla.) Child Guidance Clinic, 1952-60; lectr. Jacksonville U., 1955-58; supr. tng. and research Fla. Council Tng. and Research Mental Health, 1956-59; group therapist Fla. Alcoholic Rehab. Program, 1958-60; sr. ú psychologist ICD, N.Y., 1960-61; tng. surpr. L.I. Cons. Center, 1961; cons. group psychotherapist Adelphia U., 1960-63, guest lectr. Postgrad. Center Mental Health, 1961-63, cons. child psychotherapist Family Service Assn. Five Towns, Woodmere, 1962-63; cons. group counsellor Long Branch Bd. Edn., 1963-64; expert guidance and cons. UNESCO, Israeli Govt., 1965-66; group therapist N. Shore Child Guidance Center, Manhasset, L.I., 1960-61, chief psychologist, 1961-62, cons. child phychotherapist, 1962-73; asso. clin. prof. postdoctoral program Adelphia U., 1966-73; ind. cons. in field, 1960-73. Author: Group Psychotherapy Children, 1961; Between Parent and Child, 1965; Between Parent and Teenager, 1969. Address: New York City, N.Y. Died Nov. 4, 1973.

GIPSON, LAWRENCE HENRY, historian; b. Greeley, Colo., Dec. 7, 1880; s. Albert Eugene and Lina Maria (West) G.; A.B., U. Ida., 1903, LL.D., 1953; Rhodes Scholar, Oxford U., Eng., 1904, B.A., 1907; Farnham fellow Yale, 1910-11, Bulkley fellow, 1917-18, Ph.D., 1918, L.H.D., 1955; U. Chgo., summers 1912-16; Litt.D., Temple U., 1947; M.A., Oxford, 1951; L.H.D., Lehigh U., 1951, Kenyon College, 1961; Doctor of Laws, Moravian College, 1962, Wabash College, 1963; married to Jeannette Reed, Oct. 8, 1909. Asst. in history, U. Ida., 1903-04; prof. history, College of Ida., 1907-10; prof. history, 1911-17, prof. history and polit. sci., 1918-24, Wabash College; professor history and head dept. history and govt. Lehigh U., 1924-46; reserach, prof. history, 1946-52, now emeritus; Harmsworth prof. Am. history and fellow of Queen's Coll., Oxford, 1951-52. Past Pres. Conf. on British Studies, 1959-61. Past pres. Pa. Historical Soc. Mem. council Inst. Early Am. History and Culture, 1956-58. Recipient Justin Winsor prize 1922; Hillman Award of Lehigh University, 1947; Loubat Prize, 1948; Bancroft Prize, 1950; Athenaeum Award, 1953; others. Author of numerous books in the field of early American history, 1918—; including: The British Empire in the Eighteenth Century, its Strength and its Weakness, 1952; The Great War for the Empire: The Culmination, 1760-1763, 1954; The Coming of the Am. Revolution, 1763-1775, 1954; series on The British Empire before The American Revolution, vols. 1-14, 1936—, and vols. I-III, rev., 1958-60; The Triumphant Empire: Thunder-Clouds Gather in the West (winner of Pulitzer Prize for history 1962). Bd. editors Am. Historical Rev., 1946-52. Contbr. portion relating to U.S. The Expansion of the

Anglo-Saxon Nations. London, 1920; also various hist. articles in jours. and revs. Conglist. Club: Franklin Inn (Phila.). Home: Bethlehem, Pa.†

GIRVETZ, HARRY KENNETH, educator, philosopher; b. Jeannette, Pa., Feb. 17, 1910; s. Jacob and Freda (Silver) S.; A.B., Stanford, 1931, M.A., 1933; Ph.D., U. Cal. at Berkeley, 1937; m. Bertha Wise, July 3, 1931; children—William Basil, Jon Eric. Faculty, U. Cal. at Santa Barbara, 1944-74, prof. philosophy, 1952-74, chmn. dept., 1958-64; research sec. to gov. Cal., 1959-60. Vice-pres. Santa Barbara County Citizens Planning Assn., 1961-74. Mem. Cal. Dem. Central Com., 1948, Santa Barbara County Dem. Central Com., 1939-74. Mem. Am. Philos. Assn., Am., Assn. U. Profs., Am. Polit. Sci. Assn. Author: From Wealth to Welfare, 1950; Evolution of Liberalism 1962. Editor: Contemporary Moral Issues, 1963; 2d edit., 1968, 3d edit., 1974; Literature and the Arts-The Moral Issues, 1971; Beyond Right and Wrong, 1973. Editor, contbr.: Science, Folklore and Philosophy, 1965; Democracy and Elitism, 1966. Editor: Moral Issues Today, 1963. Home: Santa Barbara, Cal. Died Sept. 27, 1974; interred Santa Barbara Cemetery.

GITCHELL, MAZIE, lawyer; b. Evart, Mich., Apr. 16, 1894; s. Benjamin Franklin and Mary Elizabeth (Smith) Gitchell; student Mich. State U., 1910-11, 26, Mich. Central U., 1912-13; LL.B., Wayne U., 1936. Tchr. Jr. High Sch., Dimondale, Mich., 1913-15; asst. to pres. Grange Life Ins. Co., Lansing, Mich., 1915-30; actuarial, statis. work Maccabees Life Ins. Co., Detroit, 1930-32; admitted to Mich. bar, 1936, later practiced in Detroit and Hartland; also small farm operator; adjudicator, mortgage loan examiner for VA, purchasing agent, and claims officer Dept. of Army, Detroit and Centerline, Mich., 1944-60. Mem. Mich. Bar Assn., Alpha Sigma Tau, Kappa Alpha Theta. Home: Hartland, Mich., Died Mar. 23, 1974.

GITT, JOSIAH WILLIAM, editor, pub.; b. Hanover, Pa., Mar. 28, 1884; s. Clinton Jacob and Emma (Koplin) G.; A.B., Franklin and Marshall Coll., 1904; postgrad. U. Pa., 1904-05; m. Elizabeth Moul, June 12. 1913; children—Charles M., Eleanor (Mrs. George Taylor), Marian (Mrs. Michael B. Rebert), Susan Elizabeth (Mrs. Edmund Gordon). Admitted to Pa. bar, 1908, practiced in York, 1908-15; editor and pub. York (Pa.) Gazette and Daily, 1915-70. Democrat. Unitarian. Home: Hanover Pa. Died Oct. 7, 1973.

GIVAN, THURMAN BOYD, physician; b. Alexandria, Tenn., Oct. 3, 1888; s. Henry Clay and Ellen (Luck) G.; A.B., Union U., Jackson, Tenn., 1910; M.D., Vanderbilt U., 1914; m. Dorothy Jagles, June 28, 1922; children—Joan (Mrs. Herbert Kritzlerj, Doris, Thurman Boyd; m. 2d, Marian Goebel Klein, July 14, 1951. Intern, St. Thomas Hosp., Nashville, 1914-16; resident pediatrics L.I. Coll., Hosp., 1919-20; practice medicine, Bklyn., 1920-69; lectr. pediatrics, L.I. Coll. Hosp. and Med. Sch., 1919-23, asst. clin. prof., 1925-26, clin. prof., 1927-49; clin. prof. pediatrics Downstate Med. Sch., State U. N.Y., 1950-58, clin. prof. pediatrics emeritus, 1958-75. Chmn. coordinating council Five County Med. Socs. of N.Y.C., 1949-52; mem. Gov.'s Com. to End Poliomyelitis in N.Y. State, 1957-60. Served as 1st lt. M.C., U.S. Army, 1917-19. Mem. Med. Soc. State N.Y. (chmn. sect. pediatrics 1950, council 1951-58, pres. 1957-58), A.M.A. (council constn. and by-laws, 1963-72, chmn., 1970-72, ho. of dels 1952-68), Bklyn. Pediatric Soc. (pres. 1925), Am. (N.Y. state chmn. 1947-53), Bklyn. (pres., founder 1932) acads. pediatrics, Med. Soc. County of Kings (pres. 1946, chmn. bd. trustees, 1961-67, then hon.), Am. Assn. Med. Milk Commns. (pres. 1950j, Am. Legion, 50-Yr. Club Am. Medicine (pres. 1972-73), Sigma Alpha Epsilon, Alpha Kappa Kappa. Rotarian, Mason. Clubs: Medical, Brooklyn, Rembrandt, Ihpetonga (Bklyn.). Home: Hilton Head Island, S.C., Died Oct. 20, 1975.

GLASGOW, BENJAMIN BASCOM, clergyman, educator; b. Birmingham, Ala., June 2, 1880; s. Marcus Alexander and Phoebe Olivia (Samples) G.; A.B., Birmingham Vanderbilt Coll., 1902; student and U. of Chicago, 1902-04; mem. U. of Chicago traveling class, Egypt, Palestine, Europe, 1911; D.D., Birmingham Coll., 1917; m. Signa E. Shroyer, Nov. 20, 1907; 1 dau., Signa Shroyer (Mrs. J. William Irwin). Ordained ministry M.E. Ch., S., 1904; pastor Owenton, Birmingham, 1905-07, 1st Ch., Ensley, Ala., 1907-09; presiding elder, Albertville (Ala.) Dist., 1909-12, Athens Sta., 1912-16, Talladega Dist., 1925-29, Tuscaloosa Dist., 1929-33; pastor, Avondale-Grove Park Ch., Birmingham, Ala., 1933-36, First Ch., Huntsville, Ala., from 1936; pres. Athens (Ala.) Coll. for Young Women, 1916-25. Mem. N. Ala. Conf. M.E. Ch., S. Trustee Birmingham-Southern College from 1930; pres. Ala. Assn. Colleges, 1920. Mem. Omicron Delta Kappa. Mason. Kiwanian. Home: Athens, Ala.†

GLASS, MARVIN, toy designer; b. Chgo. Designer children's toys Marvin Glass & Assos., Chgo.; ann. exhibits Am. Toy Fair, N.Y.C. Holder numerous patents. Home: Evanston, Ill. Died Jan. 7, 1974.

GLEASON, ARCHIE LELAND, physician; b. Glenville, Minn., June 5, 1891; s. Eugene Watson and Elizabeth (Brady) G.; M.D., Rush Med. Coll., 1918; m. Solveig Moe, Sept. 28, 1920; children—Eugene Watson, David Solberg. Intern, Passavant Meml. Hosp., Chgo, 1917-18, City and County Hosp., St. Paul, 1918-19; postgrad. in pediatrics Washington U., St. Louis, 1928, Harvard, 1932; practice medicine specializing in pediatrics, Gt. Falls, Mont., 1919-72; Asso., later partner Gt. Falls Clinic; attending pediatrician Mont. Deaconess Hosp.; vis pediatrician Columbus Hosp. Diplomate Am. Bd. Pediatrics. Fellow A.C.P.; mem. A.M.A., Am. Acad. Pediatrics. Republican. Home: Great Falls, Mont. Died Jan. 12, 1972; buried Acacia Meml. Park, Mendota, Minn.

GLEASON, RALPH JOSEPH, journalist, critic; b. N.Y.C., Mar. 1, 1917; s. Ralph A. and Mary (Quinlisk) G.; student Columbia, 1934-38; m. Jean Rayburn, Oct. 12, 1940; children—Bridget, Stacy, Toby. Jazz and popular music critic San Francisco Chronicle, 1950-75, also now daily columnist; former contbg. editor Down Beat, 1948-60, Hi/Fi Stereo Rev.; contbg. editor Scholastic Roto; writer numerous album liner notes for recording cos.; writer nationally syndicated jazz column; producer-host Jazz Casual, TV program, 1962-75; lectr. in jazz U. Cal. Extension, 1960-63; lectr. music dept. Sonoma State Coll., 1965-67. Mem. adv. vis. bd. jazz Lenox Sch. Jazz, Inst. Jazz; adviser Stanford Jazz Jr., Stanford U., 1965, U. Cal. Jazz Festival, 1967-68. Served with OWI, 1942-44. Author: The Jefferson Airplane and the San Francisco Sound, 1969. Editor: Jam Session, Anthology of Jazz, 1957; Jazz, A Quar. of Am. Music, 1957-58. Contrbr. articles to publs. including New Statesman, Am. Scholar, Esquire, Show Bus. Illustrated, Saturday Rev.; cons. editor Rolling Stone; former mem. editorial bd. Ramparts. Home: Berkeley, Cal. Died June 3, 1975.

GLEASON, SARELL EVERETT, govt. ofcl.; b. Bklyn., Mar. 14, 1905; s. Sarell Everett and Florence Agalia (Sellon) G.; A.B.; Harvard, 1927, A.M., 1928, Ph.D., 1934; postgrad. U. Paris, Ecole des Chartes, Paris, 1931; m. Mary Eleanor Abbott, June 19, 1937; children—Abbott, Ellen Richmond (Mrs. Philip V.R. Tilney). Instr. history Harvard, 1930-38; asst., asso. prof. history Amherst (Mass.) Coll., 1938-46; with OSS, Washington, 1943-45; with Dept. State, Washington, 1945, 1962-72, historian, 1962-72; historian Council Fgn. Relations, 1946-50; dep. exec. sec. NSC, Washington, 1950-59; cultural attache Am. Embassy, London, 1959-61; Served as lt. col. joint intelligence com. Joint Chief of Staff, AUS, 1943-45. Decorated Legion of Merit; recipient Bancroft Prize, 1954. Mem. Am. Hist. Assn. Mass. Hist. Soc., Council Fgn. Relations, Colonial Soc. Mass. Clubs: Athenaeum (London, Eng.); Century (N.Y.C.); Cosmos (Washington). Author: An Ecclesiastical Barony of the Middle Ages, 1937; (with W. L. Langer) The Challenge of Isolation, 1952, The Undeclared War, 1953; also articles, revs. profl. jours. Home: Washington, D.C. Died Nov. 20, 1974.

GLEASON, WILLIAM THOMAS, army officer, engr.; b. Ely, Nev., June 30, 1917; s. William Thomas and V. Hazel (Woodcock) G.; B.S., U.S. Mil. Acad., 1941; student Command and Gen. Staff Sch., 1944; The Armed Forces Staff Coll., 1956; Indsl. Coll. Armed Forces, 1959; m. Karma Hill, June 12, 1941; children—Susan (Mrs. James P. Avett), Emilie (Mrs. Melvin A. Marini), Elizabeth Anne (Mrs. Basil S. Norris), William Thomas, Jr. Commd. 2d lt. U.S. Army, 1941, advanced through grades to brig. gen., 1967; dep. asst. chief staff logistics Material Assistance Command, Vietnam, 1967; asst. div. comdr. 25th Inf. Div., Vietnam, 1967-68, comdg. gen. U.S. Army Element, Allied Forces Central Europe, The Netherlands, 1968-71; chmn. Central Europe Pipeline Orgn.; ret., 1971; engr. Cavanagh Communities Corp., Miami Beach, Fla., from 1971. Chmn. Com. on Youth, from 1970. Decorated D.S.M., Silver Star, Legion of Merit with oak leaf cluster, D.F.C., Bronze Star with oak leaf cluster, Air medal with 9 oak leaf clusters, Combat Inf. badge with star. Mem. U.S. Armed Forces Mgmt. Assn., West Point Soc. So. Fla., Assn. Grads. U.S. Mil. Acad., Netherlands Am. Inst. Lions. Home: North Miami Beach, Fla., Died May 6, 1975; buried Arlington National Cemetery.

GLEDHILL, FRANKLIN, business exec.; b. Jersey City, N.J., July 29, 1898; s. Henry and Ella Pitney (Dalrymple) G.; student Newark Acad., 1910-14, Episcopal Acad., Phila., 1914-16; B.S., Yale, 1923; m. Martha Stout, Sept. 2, 1926. Mining engr. Crowe Coal Co., Kansas City Mo., 1923-26; supt. bldg. constrn. The Whitney Co., N.Y. City, 1927-28; gen. purchasing agt. Pan Am. Airways, 1929-40, vice pres. 1940-65, dir. from 1946; vice pres. and gen. mgr. Pan Am. Airways-Africa Ltd., 1941; v.p. Pan Am. Air Ferries, Inc., 1941. Served with 1st Pa. Cav., Mexican Border Service, 1916; 2d lt., pilot, U.S. Army Air Service, 1917-19. Mem. Aviators Post of Am. Legion. Republican. Episcopalian. Clubs: Yale, St. Anthony. Cloud, Seawanhaka Corinthian Yacht (N.Y.C.); Cotton Bay (Bahamas). Home: New Hartford, Conn. Died Jan. 2, 1975.

GLENN, OLIVER EDMUNDS, educator, author; b. Moorefield, Ind., Oct. 3, 1878; s. James Drummond and Jane Harvey (Culbertson) G.; A.B., Ind. U., 1902, A.M., 1903; Ph.D., U. of Pa., 1905; m. Alice Thomas Kinnard, of Pendleton, Ind., Aug. 18, 1903; children—William James, Robert Culbertson. Instr. U. of Ind., 1902-03; acting prof. mathematics, Drury Coll., Springfield, Mo., 1905-06; instr. in mathematics, 1906-10, asst. prof., 1910-14, prof., 1914-30, U. of Pa. Mem. Am. Math. Soc. (councilor 1914-17), Ind. Academy of Science, Sigma Xi, Kappa Sigma. Author: A Treatise on the Theory of Invariants, 1915; The Mechanics of the Stability of a Central Orbit, 1933; The Sources of Error (essays), 1933; contbr. from 1905 numerous memoirs in math. and other scientific jours.; also scientific biography in Poggendorff Biographical Dictionary of the Exact Sciences (Leipzig.) Home: Lansdowne, Pa.†

GLICKSMAN, HARRY, coll. prof.; b. Chippewa Falls, Wis., Aug. 25, 1882; s. Morris and Lana (Jacobs) G.; A.B., Yale 1904, Ph.D., 1918; LL.B., U. of Wis., 1907; m. Edna Kerngood, Mar. 2, 1908 (died Mar. 5, 1923); 1 dau., Marjorie (Mrs. David Grene); m. 2d, Margaret Pryor, Aug. 11, 1934. Admitted to Wis. bar, 1907, and practiced in Milwaukee, 1907-15; instr. in English, U. of Wis., 1918-21, asst. dean. Coll. of Letters and Sci, also lecturer in English, 1921-27, jr. dean, 1927-44, prof. after 1936. Club: University. Contbr. articles to prof. jours. Home: Madison, Wis. Died July 16, 1975.

GLINSKY, VINCENT, sculptor; b. Russia, Dec. 18, 1895; s. Wolf and Sonia (Sherfman) G.; ed. pub. high schs., Syracuse, N.Y., Columbia U., Coll. City N.Y., Beaux Arts Inst. Design; m. Cleo Hartwig, 1951; 1 son, Albert Vincent. Naturalized citizen of U.S. One-man show, Paris, 1929-30, N.Y.C., 1931, 56; exhibited group shows including Expn. Artists Americans de Paris, 1932, Nat. Gallery Art, Washington, 1932, Internat. Water Color Exhbn., Art Inst. Chgo., 1935, Contemporary Art, Golden Gate Expn., San Francisco, 1939, N.Y. World's Fair, 1939-40, Sculpture Internat., Phila. Museum Art, 1940, 1949, Am. Sculpture, Carnegie Inst., 1941, Contemporary Am. Art, London, 1941, First Annual Exhbn. Contemporary Am. Drawings; Nat. Acad., 1945, Met. Mus. Art, Bklyn. Mus., Detroit Inst. Arts, Whitney Mus. Am. Art, Mus. Modern Art, 150 Years of Am. Sculpture, Westbury Gardens, N.Y., 1960, World's Fair, 1964, Pa. Acad. Fine Arts, 1964, So. Vt. Art Center, 1964-73, also traveling shows; represented in collection Brookgreen Gardens Outdoor Mus., Norfolk (Va.) Mus., Wiltwyck Sch. for Boys, N.Y.C., Dept. Labor, Washington, Am. Cancer Found., N.Y.C., All Faiths Meml. Tower, Paramus, N.J., Bethesda (Md.) Health Center, St. Paul's Coll., Washington, Nat. Commemorative Soc., N.Y.U. Hall Fame, USAF Acad.; Lenox Hill Hosp., N.Y.C.; represented in many pvt. collections; commd. execute sculptures for govt., pub., other bldgs., portrait Wilbur Wright N.Y.U. Hal Fame Great Ams., Theodore Roosevelt coin-medal Nat. Commemorative Soc. Recipient awards Arts and Letters Grant from Am. Acad. Arts and Letters and Nat. Inst. Arts and Letters, 1945; George D. Widener gold medal Pa. Acad. Fine Arts, 1936, Dr. Herbert M. Howe Meml. prize Pa. Acad. Fine Arts, 1948; First prize Adelphi Coll. Trophy Competition, 1956, Avery award Archtl. League N.Y., 1956, medal of hon. Nat. Arts Club, 1958; Silver Anniversary medal for sculpture Audubon Artists Ann., 1967; Gold Medal Nat. Sculpture Soc., 1967, C. Percival Dietsch prize Seventy-Fifth Annual Exhbn., 1968; Ellin P. Speyer prize N.A.D., 1970. Guggenheim fellow, 1935-36. Engaged in war work with Diesel design sect. U.S.N., 1943-46. N.A. Fellow Nat. Sculpture Soc. (Bronze medal 1972); mem. Sculptors Guild (exec. sec. 1955-60), Audubon Artists, Archtl. League N.Y.C. (v.p. 1956-58). Instr. Beaux Arts Inst. Design, 1931-32, 40-41, Bklyn. Coll., 1949-55, Columbia, 1957-61; adj. asst. prof. N.Y.U. Sch. Continuing Edn., 1950-75. Home: New York City, N.Y. Died Mar. 19, 1975.

GLOVER, W(ARREN) IRVING, b. Brooklyn, N.Y., Oct. 2, 1879; s. Thomas and Mary Frederica (Fisk) G.; ed. pub. schs.; m. Anna Bell, d. John Englis, shipbuilder, Brooklyn, Oct. 29, 1908 (died 1932); children—Thomas, Warren, Frances. Began as a boy with James Talcott, commn. mcht. New York, and continued as distributor in woolen trade until 1906; organizer, 1906, Afton Holding Corpn., real estate; sec. Sussex Holding Co., Inc.; sec. and treas. The Edwards Co., Sanford, N.C. Mem. Bd. of Freeholders, Bergen Co., N.J., 1915; mem. N.J. Assembly, 1916-21 (speaker 1920); 3d asst. postmaster gen., 1921-25, 2d asst., 1925-33. Mem. Englewood (N.J.) Hosp. Society. Republican. Presbyterian. Clubs: National Republican (New York); Columbia, Congressional Country (Washington, D.C.); Gibson Island Club (Md.). Home: Sanford. N.C.†

GOBETZ, WALLACE, educator, psychologist; b. Bklyn., Dec. 18, 1916; s. James I. and Annie (Ackerman) G.; B.A. summa cum laude, N.Y.U., 1938, M.A., 1940, Ph.D., 1952; m. Ida Bordoff, Mar. 21, 1942; children—Jay Russell, Audrey Claire. Instr. Bklyn. Coll., 1942; mem. faculty N.Y.U., from 1946, prof. psychology, after 1963, sr. psychologist Testing and Advisement Center, 1946-52, after dir., 1952. Dir. testing and counseling div. Personnel Psychology Center, N.Y.C., 1970—; supr. counseling Retirement Inst., Inc., N.Y.C., 1972—; area cons., counseling psychology VA, N.Y.C., 1959-70. Served to 2d lt. AUS, 1942-46. Fellow Am. Psychol. Assn.; mem. N.Y. State Psychol. Assn. (recipient Distinguished Service award 1969), Soc. Clin. Psychologists (exec. sec. 1959-61, pres. 1962-63), N.Y.C. Personnel and Guidance Assn. (pres. 1955-57), A.A.U.P., Nat. Soc. Study Edn., Phi

Beta Kappa, Beta Lambda Sigma, Mu Chi Sigma. Contbg. author: Handbook of Applied Psychology, 1950; President's Guide, 1958. Contbr. articles to profl. jours. Home: Brooklyn, N.Y. Died July 5, 1973; buried Beth Israel Meml. Park, Woodbridge, N. J.

GODOLPHIN, FRANCIS RICHARD BORROUM, educator; b. Del Rio, Tex., Apr. 8, 1903; s. Francis Richard and Alma (Borroum) G.; A.B., Princeton, 1924, Ph.D., 1929; M.A., N.Y. U., 1926; m. Isabelle Simmons, July 25, 1925 (dec. Dec. 1964); children—Jeane, Thomas (dec.); m. 2d, Catherine V. Clark, June 19, 1965. Instr. in classics N.Y. U., 1924-26, N.J. Coll. for Women, 1926-27; instr. classics Princeton, 1927-30, asst. prof., 1930-40, asso. prof., 1940-45, prof., 1946-74, acting chmn., 1941-42, chmn., 1942-45, dean coll., 1945-55; asst. editor Classical Weekly, 1937-39. Commd. lt. USMCR, 1942; promoted capt., 1944; inactive duty, Sept. 1945; service in Pacific with 4th Marine Div., Jan.-Sept. 1944, 1st Marine Air Wing, Sept. 1944-Apr. 1945. Decorated Bronze Star medal. Mem. Am. Philol. Assn., Classical Assn. of Atlantic States, Am. Assn. Univ. Profs. Democrat. Editor: The Greek Historians, 1942; The Latin Poets, 1949; Great Classical Myths, 1964. Contbr. to Am. Jour. Philology, Classical Philology. Home: Princeton, N.J. Died Dec. 1974.

GOEBEL, JULIUS, JR., b., Menlo Park, Calif., Dec. 3, 1892; s. Julius and Kathryn (Vreeland) G.; A.B., U. of Ill., 1912; A.M., 1913; Ph.D., Columbia, 1915; LL.B., Columbia; Doctor of Laws, Trinity College, 1954; married Dorothy Burne, June 27, 1925. Legal adviser to Legaion of Switzerland, at Washington, 1917-22, also law practice; acting adj. prof. law, U. of Va., 1920-21; lecturer on internat. law, Columbia, 1921, asso. internat. law, 1923-25; associated in law, Columbia University School of Law, 1925-28, assistant professor of law, 1928-31, professor of law, 1931, now George Welwood Murray professor emeritus of legal history. Served as pvt. 13th Co., Gen. Service Inf., U.S. Army, 1918. Dir. Foundation for Research in Legal History. Mem. District of Columbia Bar, Hispanic Soc. of America (asso.), Phi Eta, Phi Delta Phi. Club: Cosmos. Author books including: Generals in the White House (with D. B. Goebel), 1945; Cases on Demestic Relations (with A. C. Jacobs), 1961; History of the United States, Volume I. Contributor of articles. Editor; Publs. of the Found. for Research in Legal History; History of Columbia Law School, 1955; Legal Papers of Alexander Hamilton, 1961. Winner of the Harris politicial science prize, 1911. Home: New York City, N.Y. Died Aug. 4, 1973.

GOEBEL, LOUIS WILLIAM, clergyman; b. Carlinville, Ill., June 8, 1884; s. George and Emilie (Haeberle) G.; student Elmhurst (Illinois) College, 1899-1903, D.D., 1946; graduate Eden Theological Seminary, St. Louis, Mo., 1906; graduate study Hartford (Connecticut) Theological Seminary; D.D., Franklin and Marshall Coll., 1935; LL.D. Catawba Coll., 1939; m. Edith Roesche, June 26, 1912; children—Louis Henry, Ruth Louise, Edith Jane. Ordained ministry Evang. Synod of N.A., 1907; pastor Bellevue, Ky., 1907-11, First Eng. Evang. Ch., Chicago, 1911-38. Vice-pres. Evang. Synod of N.A., since 1929; v.p. Evang. and Reformed Ch., 1934-38, pres., 1938-53, ret. Member gen. bd. Nat. Coun. Chs.; mem. central com. World Council Chs. Home: Webster Groves, Mo. Died Oct. 22, 1973.

GOERKE, LENOR STEPHEN, univ. dean; b. Hitchcock, Okla., Jan. 22, 1912; s. Leonard H. and Nellie (Bradon) G.; B.S., Southeastern State Tchrs. Coll., Okla., 1931; B.S., M.D., U. Okla., 1936; M.S. in Pub. Health, U. Cal. at Berkeley, 1938; m. Evelyn M. Foster, May 17, 1938; children—William S., Susan K. Intern, Good Samaritan Hosp., Portland, Ore., 1936-37; county health officer Astoria and McMinnville, Ore., 1938-39, Woodland, Cal., 1940; dir. med. bur., med. dir. also dir. dist. services Los Angeles City Health Dept., 1946-54; clin. asso. prof. preventive medicine and pub. health Coll. Med. Evangelists, 1947-50; asso. clin. prof. medicine U. So. Cal., 1951-54; faculty U. Cal. at Los Angeles, 1950-72, prof. pub. health Sch. Pub. Health, 1954-72, dean Sch. Pub. Health, chmn. dept. preventive medicine and pub. health Sch. Medicine, 1956-72. Mem. Cal. Bd. Health, Los Angeles City Bd. Health; chmn. So. Cal. adv. com. to SSS and Armed Forces, 1955-72. Served to col. M.C., AUS, 1940-46; ETO. Mem. Am. Coll. Preventive Medicine (bd. regents 1955-72), Am. (governing council 1955-58, pres. Western br. 1953), So. Cal. (Pres. 1954) pub. health assns., Assn. of Schs. Pub. Health (pres.), Am., Cal. (chmn. pub. health sect. 1954-55, sec. 1953-54), Los Angeles County med. assns., Hollywood Acad. Medicine (exec. com. 1954-55), Cal. Acad. Preventive Medicine (pres. 1957). Editorial cons., contbr. The New Physician, 1958-72. Home: Pacific Palisades, Cal. Died Sept. 29, 1972.

GOETTE, JOHN, newspaper corr., author, lectr.; b. Phila., Dec. 3, 1896; s. Gustave and Irene (Jackson) G.; ed. Central High Sch., Law Sch., Temple U.; unmarried. Student, writer in India and Peking, China, 1920; with China Famine Relief, A.R.C., 1921; corr. Assembly League of Nations, Geneva, 1926; mem. suite of Queen Marie of Rumania, Paris to N.Y., 1926; roving corr., U.S., Europe, Palestine, Egypt, Java, 1928-29; war corr. with Chinese Army, Manchuria-Russian crisis, 1929; with Japanese Army, Sino-Japanese Shanghai warfare, 1932, Manchukuo, 1932; with Chinese Army, Sino-Japanese fighting inside Great Wall, 1933; chief China corr. Internat. News Service, 1923-41; corr. London Daily Express, 1927-39; with Japanese Army, N. China campaign, 1937-41; Japanese prisoner of war, Dec. 1941-June 1942, repatriated aboard S.S. Gripsholm, 1942; corr., Japan, Korea, China, Manchuria, 1946, Europe, 1951, 56, 60, 62-65, 66, Australia, 1954, Far East, 1959, S.Am., 1961; mem. editorial staff King Features Syndicate, 1949-70. Testified for U.S. War Dept. at trial of Japanese war criminals, Tokyo, 1946. Served with USNR 1917-19; France and England, 1918-19. Recipient Chinese decoration, Chiao Ho. Mem. Am. Oriental Soc., Am. Platform Guild, Sigma Delta Chi. Clubs: Peking, Peking Golf; National Press; Overseas Press, Shanghai Tiffin; The Banshees. Specialist in Chinese jade. Author: Jade Lore, 1936; Japan Fights for Asia, 1943, London edit., 1945. Contbr. Am. periodicals. Book reviewer, radio commentator and lectr.; also war speaker for U.S. Treasury Dept. and United China Relief. Address: Malaga, Spain. Died Oct. 27, 1974; interred Malaga, Spain.

GOFF, CHARLES WEER, orthopedic surgeon; b. Rock Island, Ill., June 4, 1897; s. Edward L. and Cora (Weer) G.; student Augustana Coll., 1916; B.S., U. Ill., 1920, M.D., 1923; spl. orthopedic student European clinics, 1937-39; student anthropology Columbia, 1945-46, Yale, 1946-49, Harvard, 1949-51; m. Fern Harper, 1921; 1 son, Michael Harper; m. 2d, Mary Magdalen Lachkareff, Sept. 4, 1934; 1 stepson, George deHahn. Intern. Kings County Hosp., Bklyn., 1923-26; with traumatic clinic, South Manchester, 1926-28; surgeon, Hartford, Conn., 1928-30; asst. orthopedic surgeon St. Francis Hosp., Hartford, 1930-42, asso., 1943-48, vis., 1949-55, cons., 1956-75; asst. orthopedic surgeon Newington (Conn.) Home and Hosp. for Crippled Children, 1931-42, attending orthopedic surgeon, 1943-63, cons., 1963-75, chmn. med. staff, 1948-50; asst. clin. prof. orthopedic surgery Yale, 1948-55, asso. orthopedic surgeon, lectr. anatomy, 1956-65, emeritus, 1965-75; anthropologist, adj. prof. anthropology U. Hartford, 1964-75; cons. orthopedic surgeon div. crippled children State Conn., 1949-55, Bristol, Backus Meml., Manchester Meml., Day-Kimball, Bradley Meml. hosps.; orthopedic surgeon Nat. Found. Infantile Paralysis, Hartford; attending orthopedic surgeon Vets. Home and Hosp., 1950-55. Co-chmn. Rehab. Work Shop, 1948-58. Served as 2d lt. F.A., U.S. Army, 1917-19, pvt. 101st Cav., N.Y. N.G., 1923-25, capt. Conn. N.G., 1927-33. Recipient Kappa Delta award for orthopedic research, 1955. Diplomate Am. Bd. Orthopedic Surgery. Fellow A.C.S. (chmn. regional com. on trauma 1949-59, Med. Records award 1936), A.A.A.S., Am. Assn. Phys. Anthropology, Am. Assn. Anthropology, Am. Assn. Med. Writers, Am. Acad. Orthopedic Surgery (lectr.); mem. Assn. Bone and Joint Surgeons, Boston Orthopedic Club, Conn. Archeol. Soc. (past pres.), A.M.A., Hartford Med. Soc. (past sec.), Orthopedic Guild, Orthopaedic Research Soc., Soc. Internat. Surgery and Orthopaedics, Surg. and Orthopedic Soc. Guatemala, Archeol. Inst. Am. (chpt. pres.), Delta Kappa Epsilon, Nu Sigma Nu. Club: Golf (Hartford). Author: Legg-Calve-Perthes Syndrome, 1954; (with Phelps, Kiphuth) Diagnosis and Treatment Postural Defects, rev. edit., 1956; The Ruins of Zaculeu, Guatemala, 1954; Surgical Treatment of Unequal Extremities, 1960; Traumatic Cervical Syndrome and Whiplash, 1964. Asso. editor Clinical Orthopedics. Contbr. articles to profl. jours. Home: West Hartford, Conn. Died May 18, 1975.

GOLDBERG, ABRAHAM ISAAC, retired newsman; b. Pitts., July 30, 1904; s. Nathan and Fannie (Schmidt) G.; student Ohio State U., 1923-24; m. Victoria Beebe, Nov. 20, 1933; children—Joel H.Z., Ethan. Reporter, Steubenville (O.) Gazette, 1922-25; news editor Steubenville Herald-Star, 1925-33; mem. staff A.P., 1933-70, chief Prague (Czechoslovakia) bur., 1947-49, mem. UN staff, 1947-56, mem. fgn. news desk, N.Y.C., 1956-59, mem. Moscow (USSR) bur., 1959-60, mem. UN bur., 1960-65, editor AP Log, 1965-69. Mem. Sigma Delta Chi. Mason. Club: Deadline. Home: Rhinebeck, N.Y. Died Aug. 30, 1973.

GOLDBERG, REUBEN LUCIUS (RUBE), sculptor; b. San Francisco, July 4, 1883; s. Max and Hannah G.; B.S., U. of Cal., 1904; m. Irma Seeman, Oct. 17, 1916; children—Thomas Reuben, George Warren. Cartoonist on San Francisco Chronicle, 1904-05, Bulletin, 1905-07, N.Y. Evening Mail, 1907-21; cartoons syndicated 1921-64; sculptor, 1964-70; retrospective show Smithsonian Instn., 1970. Dir. cartoon course Farmous Artists Sch. Winner 1948 Pulitzer Prize, best editorial cartoon; Reuben Nat. Cartoonists Soc. Award of Yr., 1968. Mem. Soc. Illustrators, Nat. Cartoonists Society (hon. pres.), Clubs: Coffee House, Dutch Treat, also Artists and Writers Golf Association. Author books including: Soup to Nuts (motion picture), 1930; Rube Goldberg's Guide to Europe, 1954; How to Remove Cotton from Bottle of Aspirin; I Made My Bed; Rube Goldberg vs. The Machine Age, 1968. Creator of Boob McNutt, Mike and Ike, Lucifer Butts, A. K. polit. cartoons. Home: New York City, N.Y. Died Dec. 1970.

GOLDBERG, SAMUEL AURON, lawyer; b. Phila., June 2, 1898; s. Louis and Jennie (Gaber) G.; B.A., U. Pa., 1920, LL.B., 1923 J.D., 1970; m. Elizabeth Orowitz, Aug. 12, 1925; 1 dau., Leone Eve (Mrs. Malcolm L. Schoenberg). Admitted to Pa. bar, 1923, since practiced in Phila.; partner Wolf, Block, Schorr & Solis-Cohen, 1936-66; counsel Wolf, Block, Schorr and Solis-Cohen. Dir. emeritus Continental Bank & Trust Co., Phila. Lectr. for Bar and Title Assns. Past pres. Fedn. Jewish Charities, Jewish Family Service; former dir. United Fund; trustee Fedn. Jewish Agencies Greater Phila. Company comdr. Phila. Port Security Force, USCG, 1942-45. Mem. Am., Phila. Pa. bar assns., Am. Law Inst., Order of Coif. Author: Sales of Real Estate in Pennsylvania, 1958; Sales of Real Property, 1971; also monograph. Asso. editor: Law Notes. Mem. adv. com. that drafted Pa. Mechanics's Lien Law of 1963. Home: Phila. Pa. Died Feb. 16, 1974.

GOLDEN, ROSS, physician, educator; b. Iowa Center, Ia., Sept. 30, 1889; s. A. Lincoln and Jennie (Funk) G.; A.B., Cornell Coll., 1912, D.Sc. (hon.), 1947; M.D., Harvard, 1916; m. Hazel D. Smith, Oct. 29, 1923 (dec. Mar. 1957); children—Mary Jean Hamilton, Joann Limbacher; m. 2d, Frances L. Kraft, Dec. 30, 1961. House officer med. service Peter Bent Brigham Hosp., Boston, 1916-17, asst. resident physician, 1921-22; resident physician, radiol. service dept. Mass. Gen. Hosp., Boston, 1920-21; asst. prof. medicine Columbia, 1922-28, dir. radiol. service, 1928-34, asso. prof., 1929-34, prof. radiology, 1934-54, prof. emeritus, 1954-75; vis. prof. radiology U. Cal. at Los Angeles, 1954-67; cons. Presbyn. Hosp., N.Y.C., 1954-69, Wadsworth VA Hosp., Brentwood, Cal., 1954-68, VA physician-in-residence program, Washington, 1958-67, Armed Forces Inst. Pathology, Washington, and U.S. Naval Hosp., San Diego, 1959-61. Chmn. Internat. Commn. Rules and Regulations of Internat. Congress Radiology, 1959-69. Served with MC, U.S. Army, World War I, disch. as maj. Recipient gold medal Am. Coll. Radiology, 1958. Diplomate Am. Board Radiology. Hon. fellow Inter-Am. Coll. Radiology; hon. fellow faculty radiologists Royal Coll. Surgeons Ireland, mem. Am. Roentgen Ray Soc. (pres. 1945-46), Am. Coll. Radiology (pres. 1943-44), Radiol. Soc. N.A. (Carman lectr. 1940, Gold medal 1952), A.M.A. (past chmn. radiology sect.), N.Y. Acad. of Medicine (trustee); hon. mem. Indian Radiol. Assn. (Sir Jagdish Bose Medal, 1956), Accademica Medica di Roma, Brit. Inst. Radiology, Deutsche Röntgen-Gesellschaft, Radiol. sect. Royal Soc. Medicine London, also six Latin Am. radiol. socs. Author: The Radiologic Examination of the Small Intestine, 1945, revised edit., 1959; Roentgen-Ray Examination of the Digestive Tract, 1949; Roentgenology of the Abdomen, 1961; (with others) The Digestive Tract, pub. as sect. 5 Golden's Diagnostic Radiology, 1969. Ross Golden lectureship established by Columbia U. and N.Y. Roentgen Soc., 1954. Home: Laguna Hills, Cal. Died Jan. 10, 1975.

GOLDFORB, ABRAHAM JULES, biologist; b. London, Eng., Mar. 13, 1881; s. Morris and Anna (Goldforb) G.; brought ot U.S. at age of 3; B.S., Coll. City of N.Y., 1900; Ph.D., Columbia, 1909; m. Frances Shostac, Aug. 1915; 1 dau., Miriam. Instructor biology, Boys' High School, Brooklyn, 1907-10; with Coll. City of N.Y. after 1910, asso. prof. biology, 1920-26, prof. after 1926. Fellow A.A.A.S. (sec. sect. med. sciences, 1921-28, chmn. 1928-29); mem. Am. Soc. Zoologists, Am. Soc. Naturalists, Soc. Exptl. Biology and Medicine (sec. and treas after 1924); editor-in-chief Proceedings after 1924. Mem. Marine Biol. Lab., Bermuda Marine Biol Lab., Am. Soc. Physiologists, Am. Naturalists, Am. Geneticists, Sigma Xi; fellow N.Y. Acad. Medicine, N.Y. Acad. of Sci. Extensive researches in regeneration, growth, physiology and exptl. embryology. Mem. Carnegie Instn. Expdn. to Porto Rico, 1916, to Dry Tortugas, 1913-20. Republican. Jewish religion. Home: New York City, N.Y.†

GOLDMAN, ALFRED, physician; s. Louis and Addie Goldman; B.A., Washington U., St. Louis, 1916, M.D., 1920, M.S. in Medicine, 1922; m. Miriam Londy, July 2, 1936; children—Alan, Roger, Thomas. Resident pathologist Barnes Hosp., 1920-21, asst. resident medicine, 1922-24, resident medicine, 1922-24, now cons. chest diseases; dir. chest clinic Washington U. Med. Sch., from 1930, prof. emeritus clin. medicine; cons. chest diseases Jewish Hosp., Koch Hosp., Homer Phillips Hosp., VA Hosp., St. Louis; area cons. chest diseases area A, VA; sr. physician Jewish Hosp. Diplomate Am. Bd. Internal Medicine. Mem. Am., So., Mo. med. assns., St. Louis Med. Soc., A.C.P., Central Soc. Clin. Research, Am. Coll. Chest Physicians (pres. 1964-65), St. Louis Soc. Internal Medicine (past pres.), Phi Beta Kappa, Sigma Xi. Home: St. Louis, Mo. Died Nov. 25, 1973.

GOLDMAN, ALVIN D(AMASCUS), business exec.; b. St. Louis, Jan. 31, 1881; s. Jacob D(amascus) and Sarah (Hirsch) G.; grad. Phillips Exeter Acad., 1899; A.B., Harvard, 1903; student Washington U. Law Sch., St. Louis, 1904-05; m. Blanche Lesser, June 3, 1907; children—J. Lesser, Lenore (Mrs. J. S. Myer, Jr., died Aug. 26, 1940), Jacob D. Entered Lesser Goldman Cotton Co., 1904. pres., 1922, name of co. changed to Lesser Goldman Co., pres. until liquidation, 1945; dir. May Dept. Store Co., St. Louis, dir. Traders Compress Company, Ft. Worth, Tex.; former dir. and mem. exec.

com. Fed. Compress & Warehouse Co., Memphis, Tenn.; former dir. Mercantile Commerce Bank & Trust Co., St. Louis; dir. St. Louis Cotton Compress Co., dir. and officer of numerous cotton interests enterprises in Mo., Ark., Okla., Tenn. Mem. Selective Service Draft Bd. 6, Clayton, Mo., 1943-46; hon. mem. and dir., mem. exec. bd. Jewish Hosp. of St. Louis, Jewish Fedn. of St. Louis (treas. 1928-43;) trustee St. Louis Country Day Sch., St. Louis Pub. Library; former dir., hon. mem. Y.M.H.A.; mem. St. Louis Symphony Soc., Mo. Hist. Soc., Navy League of U.S., St. Louis. Jewish Reformed. Clubs: Westwood Country (former dir.), Columbia, Harvard (St. Louis). Home: St. Louis, Mo.†

GOLDMAN, LEON, educator, physician; b. Cin., Dec. 7, 1905; s. Abraham and Fannie (Friedman) G.; M.D., U. Cin., 1929; m. Belle Hurwitz, Aug. 23, 1930; children—John Steven, Carol (Mrs. Edward Schechter). Intern, resident internal medicine and dermatology clin. Gen. Hosp., 1929-37; research fellow Dermatologische Poliklinik, U. Zurich (Switzerland), 1932-33; mem. faculty U. Cin. Coll. Medicine, 1933-75, prof. dermatology, 1948-75, chmn. dept., 1948-75; dir. dermatology Cin. Gen. Hosp., 1948-75; dermatology Cin. Children's Hosp., 1948-75, dir. Laser Labs., 1960-75. Pres. Cin. Cancer Control Council; cons. USPHS. Mem. Cin. (pres. 1937, 63), Chgo. (pres. 1960) dermatol. socs., Cin. Soc. History Medicine (pres. 1966), Sigma Xi, Alpha Omega Alpha. Author: Laser Cancer Research, 1966; Introduction to Laser in Biology and Medicine, 1967; also articles. Co-author: Lasers in Medicine, 1969; Medicine and Science in Art, 1969. Home: Cincinnatti, O. Died Mar. 4, 1975.

GOLDMAN, MORRIS H., lawyer; b. Phila., Mar. 30, 1906; s. Abraham and Annie (Doskow) G.; LL.B., Temple U.; Litt.D., Delaware Valley Coll.; m. Rose Ellman, June 26, 1932; children—Benjamin Donald, Andrew A. Admitted to Pa. bar, 1927, practiced in Phila.; sr. partner Wolf, Block, Schorr and Solis-Cohen, 1955-73. Chmn. trustees Delaware Valley Coll. Sci. and Agr.; trustee, sec. Fedn. Jewish Agys. Greater Phila.; trustee, chmn. exec. com. Pierce Jr. Coll. Served with AUS, 1943-45. Mem. Am., Pa., Phila. bar assns., Am. Coll. Probate Counsel (chmn. Pa. chpt.), Am. Judicature Soc. Home: Cheltenham, Pa. Died Dec. 24, 1973; interred Mt. Sinai Cemetery, Philadelphia, Pa.

GOLDSMITH, GRACE ARABELL, physician; b. St. Paul, Apr. 8, 1904; d. Arthur William and Arabell Louise (Coleman) Goldsmith; B.S., U. Wis., 1925; M.D., Tulane U., 1932; M.S. in Medicine, U. Minn., 1936; D.Sc., Woman's Med. Coll., 1962. Intern Touro Infirmary, New Orleans, 1932-33, now cons. med. staff; fellow internal medicine Mayo Clinic, Rochester, Minn., 1933-36; instr. medicine Tulane U., New Orleans, 1936-39, asst. prof., 1939-43, asso. prof., 1943-49, prof. medicine, 1949-67, dean Sch. Pub. Health and Tropical Medicine, 1967-75, prof. medicine and nutrition pub. health, 1967-75, dir. div. nutrition, metabolism, 1946-67; cons. physician Charity Hosp., New Orleans. Mem. food and nutrition bd. NRC, 1948-69, chmn., 1958-68; mem. nutrition study sect. USPHS, 1959-63, mem. gastroenterology and nutrition tng. com., 1966-70; mem. panel world food supply Pres.'s Sci. Adv. Com., 1966-67; mem. food and nutrition research adv. com., agrl. research service USDA, 1951-63; chmn., 1954-56; sci. adv. com. Nutrition Found., 1948-64, 72-75; cons. La. Bd. Health, 1962-67; panel chmn. advanced acad. teaching of nutrition White House Conf. on Food, Nutrition and Health, 1969; mem. nat. adv. arthritis and metabolic diseases council NIH, 1970-73. Mem. corp. vis. com., dept. nutrition and food sci. Mass. Inst. Tech., 1964-65; mem. Com. Etiology and Epidemiology Anemas-Interna Union Nutritional Scis. 1967-75; mem. tech. adv. com. Inst. Nutrition C. Am. and Panama, 1967. Recipient Outstanding Achievement award U. Minn., 1964; Goldberger award clin. nutrition A.M.A., 1965; Axson-Choppin award La. Pub. Health Assn., 1970; Seale-Harris award So. Med. Assn., 1970. Diplomate Am. Bd. Internal Medicine, Am. Bd. Nutrition (pres. 1966). Fellow A.C.P., Am. Pub. Health Assn. (mem. council food and nutrition sect. 1964-67, mem. governing council 1969-75, A.A.A.S., N.Y. Acad. Sci.; mem. A.M.A. (mem. council foods and nutrition 1958-63, 65-75, chmn. 1970-72), Assn. Am. Physicians, Am. Dietetic Assn. (hon.), Pan Am. Med. Assn., Am. Diabetes Assn., Am. Inst. Nutrition (Osborne and Mendel award 1959, pres. 1963), Fedn. Am. Socs. for Exptl. Biology (dir.; adv. com. 1962-65), Internat. Union Nutrition Scis. (U.S. nat. com. 1960-68), Am. Soc. Clin. Nutrition, Am. Soc. Clin. Investigation, Internat. Soc. Hematology, So. Med. Assn., So. Soc. Clin. Research, Soc. Exptl. Biology and Medicine, Sigma Xi, Alpha Omega Alpha, Delta Omega, Alpha Gamma Delta, Alpha Epsilon Iota. Episcopalian. Author: Nutritional Diagnosis, 1959; chpts. in books, articles profl. jours. Editorial bd. Am. Jour. Clin. Nutrition, 1952-63, Physiol. Revs., 1961-67, Jour. Atherosclerosis Research 1962-68, Archives Internal Medicine, 1966-69. Home: New Orleans, La. Died Apr. 28, 1975.

GOLDSTEIN, BENJAMIN FRANKLIN, lawyer; b. St. Louis, June 16, 1895; s. Julius and Naomi (Goldstein) G.; A.B., Washington U., St. Louis, 1914; LL.B., Harvard, 1917; m. Wilda Carsten, Sept. 4, 1964. Admitted to Ill. bar, 1917, practiced in Peoria, 1917-20, Chgo., 1920—; mem. firm Haight, Goldstein & Hobbs, 1938-49, Haight, Goldstein & Haight, 1949-55; head own law firm, 1956-57, 60-74; mem. firm Goldstein & Wahlen, 1958-60. Mem. bd. overseers vis. com. Harvard Law Sch., 1952-57; trustee Marquis Biog. Library Soc. Served with AEF, 1917-19. Mem. Am., Inter Am., Ill., Chgo. bar assns., Ill. Harvard Law Sch. Assn. (council 1958-62), Phi Beta Kappa, Delta Theta Phi. Clubs: Harvard, Economic. Author: Marketing-A Farmer's Problem, 1928. Address: Phoenix, Ariz. Died May 14, 1974; interred Greenlawn Mausoleum, Springfield, Mo.

GOLDSTON, ELI, indsl. exec.; b. Akron, O., Mar. 8, 1920; s. Issachar Jacob and Gertrude (Robins) G.; A.B., Harvard, 1942, M.B.A., 1946, LL.B., 1949; LL.D. (hon.), Babson College, 1969, Bates Coll., 1970, Boston Coll., 1971; m. Elaine Friedman, Oct. 20, 1943; children—Dian Barbara, Robert James. Admitted to Ohio bar, 1949; with firm Hahn, Loeser, Keough, Freedheim & Dean, Cleve., 1949-62, partner, 1955-62; with Midland Enterprises Ind., Cin., 1954-62, pres., 1961-62; exec. v.p. Eastern Gas and Fuel Assos., Boston, 1962, pres., 1962-74, chief exec. officer, 1963-74, also trustee; dir., chmn. Ohio River Co., Boston Gas Co., Boston Tow Boat Co., Castner, Curran & Bullitt, Inc., Eastern Asso. Coal Corp., Eastern Asso. Properties Corp., Midland Enterprises Inc., Mystic Steamship Corp., Ohio River Corp., Orgulf Transport Co., Red Circle Transport Co.; dir. Arthur D. Little Inc., 1st Nat. Bank Boston, Raytheon Co., John Hancock Mutual Life Ins. Co., Algonquin Gas Transmission Co. Mem. White House Conf. Fulfill These Rights; chmn. Boston Kyoto Sister City Com. Trustee Hebrew Union Coll., Cin., Combined Jewish Philanthropies Greater Boston, New Eng. Aquarium, World Peace Found.; bd. dirs. Internat. Center New Eng.; chmn. Boston project Joint Center Urban Studies, Mass. Inst. Tech. and Harvard; chmn. Boston Winterfest, 1966, 67. Served with USNR. 1943-46. Mem. Am. Acad. Arts and Scis., Am., Ohio, Mass., Cleve. bar assns., C. of C. (dir. greater Boston), mem. Am. Law Inst. Clubs: Harvard, St. Botolph, Cambridge Boat. Contbr. Articles law revs. and other periodicals. Home: Cambridge, Mass. Died Jan. 21, 1974.

GOLDSWORTHY, WILLIAM ARTHUR, organist, conductor, composer; b. Cornwall Eng., Feb. 8, 1878; s. Thomas and Mary Jane (Rogers) G.; came to U.S. 1888; ed. grammar and high schs., Kingston, N.Y.; studied music under masters in U.S., London and Paris; m. Elsie Gage, of Kingston, N.Y., Apr. 15, 1903; 1 son, Edwin Arthur. Organist successively 1st Bapt. Ch. (Kingston), St. Ann's on the Heights (Brooklyn), St. Andrew's Ch. (N.Y. City); organist and dir. St. Mark's Ch. in the Bouwerie after 1927; recital organist Bd. of Edn., N.Y. City, 1907-17, Waldorf Astoria Hotel, 1932-35; dir. Rubinstein Club, 1934. Mem. Am. Guild of Organists, Soc. Am. Composers, organists and Publishers. Progressive in politics. Episcopalain. Composer of all the music for services of St. Mark's Ch. and of many compositions, among them: Majesty, Scherzo for organ, 1921; Te Deum, 2 Anthems, 1928-29; Eight Male Choruses, 1929-34; The Vision in the Wilderness (oratorio), 1931; The Last Wish (chorus and solos), 1934; opera for women's voices, The Queen of Sheba, 1935; The Prophet, A Mystical oratorio, 1936. Contbr. many articles to Am. Organist. Home: New York City, N.Y.†

GOLDWYN, SAMUEL, (surname adopted), motion picture producer; b. Warsaw, Poland, 1882; s. Abraham and Hannah Goldfish; came to U.S., 1896, naturalized, 1902; ed. night sch.; married. Organized Jesse Lasky Feature Photoplay Co., 1913, Goldwyn Pictures Corp., 1916, Eminent Authors Pictures, Inc., 1919, also Samuel Goldwyn, Inc., Famous Players-Lasky Corp.; dir. United Artists Corp. until 1940; chmn. bd. Samuel Goldwyn Prodn., Inc. A pioneer in inducing eminent authors to work actively in writing for motion pictures; introduced Vilma Banky, Eddie Cantor, Gary Cooper, Dana Andrews and Danny Kaye to the screen. Recipient Motion Picture Acad. award for prodn., The Best Years of Our Lives, 1974; Irving Tholberg Award for consistent high quality. Home: Beverly Hills, Calif. Died Jan. 31, 1974.

GOMBERG, MORRIS, educator, musician; b. Chgo., Jan. 15, 1909; s. Samuel and Bella (Mitchell) G.; Mus.M., DePaul U., 1933; grad. Juilliard Sch. Music, 1930; m. Helen Winner, Dec. 5, 1937; children—David, Joel. Mem. faculty string instrument dept. DePaul U., Chgo., 1934-50; vis. prof. Ottumwa Coll., Ia., 1941; prof. violin Chgo. Musical Coll., Roosevelt U., 1951-74; chmn. string instrument dept., 1951-74. Condr. Chgo. Chamber Players. Home: Chicago, Ill. Died Mar. 4, 1974.

GOMORL, PAL, physician; b. Budapest, Hungary, Feb. 26, 1905; s. Gyozo and Erzsebat (Kolhanek) G.; M.D., U. Sci., 1930; m. Katalin Kelen, Feb. 17, 1949; children—Zsuzsi (Mrs. S. DeBoer), Krisztina; m. 2d, Rosa Walter, Jan. 21, 1972. Head dept. Budapest Med. Sch., 1945-50, prof. medicine, 1950-73, also dir. med. sch. Recipient Gold medals Hungarian People's Republic, Labor medal for Services to Country; Gold Order Hungarian People's Republic, Kossuth prize. Mem. Hungarian Acad. Sci. (sec. med. sect. 1955—), Nat. Inst. Internal Medicine (head), Fedn. Hungarian Med. Socs. (pres.), Brit. Renal Assn., Internat. Soc. Internal Medicine, Internat. Soc. Angeiology (hon.), Acad. Med. Sci. USSR (fgn.), Purkyne Soc. (hon.), Internat. Nephrology Soc. (exec. com.). Contbr. articles to profl. jours. Home: Budapest, Hungary., Died Sept. 20, 1973.

GONZALEZ, MARIO FLORES, architect; b. San Antonio, Mar. 4, 1925; s. Braulio Garcia and Arcenia Ancira (Flores) G.; student Bradley U., 1946-48; B.Arch., U. Ore., 1952; m. Consuelo Carvajal, June 15, 1959; children—Mario Flores, Teresa, Sonia. Architect, Hesson & May & Assos., architects, San Antonio, 1952-56; self-employed as architect, San Antonio, 1956-73. Mem. Bd. Housing Appeals, San Antonio, 1962-65; chmn. San Antonio Fine Arts Commn., 1966-69. Served with USAAF, 1943-45. Mem. A.I.A., Tex. Soc. Architects, Mexican, San Antonio chambers commerce. Roman Catholic. Club: Optimist (v.p. 1966) (San Antonio). Prin. archtl. works include Eastside Pub. Health Center, City of San Antonio, Tex., Anthony Margil Elementary Sch., San Antonio Ind. Sch. Dist., Gus. Garcia Jr. High Sch., Edgewood Ind. Sch. Dist. Home: San Antonio, Tex. Died Jan. 16, 1973.

GOOD, JOHN WALTER, college prof.; b. nr. Fayetteville, Lincoln Co., Tenn., Feb. 13, 1879; s. James Alexander and Martha Minerva (Jones) G.; A.B., Erskine Coll., Due West, S.C., 1902, A.M., 1904; grad. Erskine Theol. Sem., 1904, Pittsburgh Theol. Sem., 1905; Ph.D., U. of Ill., 1913; studied Columbia, summers 1917, 18; m. Estelle Beulah Alexander, of Huntersville, N.C., Aug. 1, 1906. Ordained ministry U.P. Ch., 1905; pastor Corsicana, Tex., and Birmingham, Mich., 1905-08; supt. schs., Albion, Ill., 1908-10; grad. scholarship, U. of Ill., 1910-11, fellowship, 1911-13; asst. prof. English lit., Kan. State Agrl. Coll., Manhattan, Kan., 1913-16; head dept. of edn. Muskingum Coll., New Concord, O., 1916-18; head dept. of English, Ga. State Coll. for Women, 1918-24, sec., 1919-24, and dir. Summer Sch., 1921-24; head dept. of English, Agnes Scott Coll., Decatur, Ga., 1924-27. Mem. Modern Lang. Assn. America Soc. Coll. Teachers of Edn., N.E.A., Southern Edn. Soc., Am. Acad. Polit. and Social Science, A.A.A.S., Royal Soc. Arts (London), Phi Kappa Phi. Democrat. Club: Kiwanis. Author: Studies in the Milton Tradition, 1915; The Jesus of Our Fathers, 1923. Home: Moultrie, Ga.†

GOODALE, HUBERT DANA, zoologist; b. Troy, N.H., June 5, 1879; s. David Wilder and Mary Lydia (Reed) G.; A.B., Trinity Coll., Conn., 1903, A.M., 1904; Ph.D., Columbia, 1913; m. Lottie A. Merrell, of Suffield, Conn., June 20, 1906; children—Hazel Margaret, Marion Putnam, Wendell Merrell (dec.). Research work, Stamford, Conn., 1907-11; resident investigator Expt. Station, Cold Spring Harbor, L.I., 1911-12; research prof. Mass. Agrl. Expt. Sta., Amherst, Mass., 1913-22; research work, Mt. Hope Farm, Williamstown, Mass., after 1922. Mem. A.A.A.S., Am. Soc. Naturalists, Am. Zool. Soc., Poultry Science Assn., Genetics Soc. of America, Phi Gamma Delta, Sigma Xi. Republican. Conglist. Author: Gonadectomy in Relation to the Secondary Sexual Character of Domestic Birds, 1916; also papers on genetics, selective breeding and evolution. Home: Williamstown, Mass.†

GOODEN, ROBERT BURTON, clergyman, educator; b. Bolton, Eng., Sept. 18, 1874; s. James and Hannah (Burton) G.; came to U.S., 1888; B.A., Trinity Coll., Conn., 1902, M.A., 1904, D.D., 1922; B.D., Berkeley Div. Sch., 1904, D.D., 1931; Dr. Canon Law, Ch. Div. Sch. Pacific, 1966; m. Alice Leonard Moore, Nov. 7, 1904; children—Alice Mary, Carolyn Frances, Robert Burton, Reginald Heber, Muriel Margaret. Ordained deacon P.E. Ch., 1904, priest, 1905; rector St. Paul's Ch., Ventura, Cal., 1904-06, Trinity Ch., Escondido, 1906-07, St. Luke's Ch., Long Beach, 1907-12; headmaster Harvard Sch., 1912, v.p. bd. trustees, 1937-49; pres. Province of Pacific, 1946-50; v.p. bd. trustees Bishop's Sch., LaJolla Cal.; suffragan bishop of Los Angeles, 1930-47, acting bishop, 1947-48. Sec. standing. com. Diocese of Los Angeles, 1910-29, pres. standing com., 1929-30, exam. chaplain, 1907-30, pres., 1929-30, mem. bd. Christian Edn., Diocese Los Angeles; mem. bd. Episcopal Home for Aged. Elected pres. bd. trustees, hon. life mem. Ch. Div. Sch. of Pacific, Berkeley, 1941; hon. life trustee Bishop's Sch., LaJolla, Cal.; trustee Bishop Godden Home Alcoholic Men, Pasadena, Cal. Mem. Phi Beta Kappa, Alpha Chi Rho. Democrat. Contbr. P.E. Ch. Congress papers, 1927, P.E. Church press, 1928—. Home: Glendale, Cal.†

GOODFELLOW, MILLARD PRESTON, publisher; b. Bklyn., May 22, 1892; s. George and Elizabeth (Dowling) G.; ed., N.Y. U. Sch. Journalism; m. Florence Haeussler, June 29, 1917; children—Alice, Millard Preston. Reporter, Bklyn. Eagle, 1907; successively dist. reporter, ct. reporter, sports writer, telegraph editor, copy reader, city editor and war corr., Bklyn. Times; asst. city editor N.Y. Evening Mail and spl. corr. on Mexican Border, N.Y. Times until 1919; successively circulation dir., advt. mgr. Bklyn. Eagle; asst. pub. N.Y. Am.; pres., pub., trustee Bklyn. Daily Eagle, 1932-38; pres., dir. Bklyn. Pub. Corp., B.D.E. Broadcasting Co., B.D.E. Properties Corp., Tri-County Pub. Corp., 1932-38, also M. P. Goodfellow & Co.; pres. Newspapers, Inc., Overseas Reconstrn. Inc., also pub. Pocatello (Fl.) Tribune. Bd. dirs. Boys Clubs Am. Served as 2d lt., S.C.,

World War I; col., Army of U.S., General Staff G-2, World War II; dep. dir. OSS, Washington, 1942-46; polit. adviser to comdg. gen., Korea, 1946. Decorated Mexican Border Service and World War I and II medals; hon. officer, mil. div. Most Excellent Order Brit. Empire; chevalier Order Polonia Restituta; officer's cross; comdr. Crown of Italy. Episcopalian. Mason. Clubs: Army and Navy (Washington); Society Old Brooklynites. Home: Washington, D.C. Died Sept. 5, 1973.

GOODHARTZ, ABRAHAM SAMUEL, coll. dean; b. Bklyn., Oct. 14, 1910; s. Jacob and Ida (Dudowitz) G.; A.B., Coll. City N.Y., 1932; M.A., Columbia, 1939; Ph.D., N.Y.U., 1951; m. Zena Frank, Dec. 29, 1934; children—Natalie Ruth, Dorothy Ann, Sima Beth. Tchr. English, Townsend Harris High Sch., N.Y.C., 1933-37; faculty Bklyn. Coll., 1938-73, dean studies, 1960-71, emeritus, 1971, dir. div. grad. studies, 1960-63; vis. prof. higher edn. N.Y.U., 1953-61. Bd. dirs. Pride of Judea Children's Services, 1964-73; exec. com. Nat. Hillel Commn., 1966-73. Recipient Gold Service award Hillel Found., 1958; Gold medal Bklyn. Coll., 1970; Plaque State of Israel Bonds, 1970. Mem. Modern Lang. Assn., A.A.U.P., Kappa Delta Pi. Contbr. profl. jours. Editor: A Commitment to Youth, 1960. Home: Brooklyn, N.Y. Died Sept. 3, 1973; interred Beth David Cemetery, Elmont, N.Y.

GOODHUE, EVERETT WALTON, economist; b. West Barnstable, Mass., Mar. 17, 1878; s. Henry Anthony and Mary Isabelle (Perkins) G.; A.B., Dartmouth, 1900, A.M., 1905; Dartmouth fellow in sociology, 1900-02, resident at South End House (social settlement), Boston; grad. student, Cornell U., 1911-12; m. Mary Julia Taylor, June 27, 1911. Special lecturer in sociology, Dartmouth, 1901, 02; teacher history and economics, Montepelier (Vt.) Meth. Sem., 1902-03; instr. economics and sociology, 1903-05, asso. prof., 1905-08, prof., 1908-21, Colgate U.; acting prof. economics, Cornell U., 1920-21; prof. economics, Dartmouth, 1921-48, professor emeritus, 1948; prof. economics, Principia Coll. after 1948. Christian Scientist. Fellow Royal Economic Soc., Eng.; mem. Am. Econ. Assn., Nat. Geog. Soc., Chi Phi. Contbr. on economic and sociol. topics. Home: Elsah, Ill.†

GOODLOE, DON SPEED SMITH, educator; b. Lowell, Ky., June 2, 1878; s. Don and Amanda (Reed) G.; student Berea Coll., Ky., until 1899; grad. Meadville (Pa.) Theol. Sch., 1906; A.B., Allegheny Coll., Meadville, 1906; m. Fannie Lee Carey, of Knoxville, Tenn., June 9, 1899; children—Don Burrowes, Wallis Anderson, Reid Carey. Teacher and prin. Normal Dept., Greenville (Tenn.) Coll., 1899-1903; teacher, and in business, Danville, Ky., 1906-10; vice prin. Manassas Industrial Sch., 1910-11; prin. State Normal Sch. No. 3, of Md., 1911-21; engaged in lit. work after 1921. Mem. Am. Acad. Polit. and Social Science. Mason. Home: Bowie, Md.†

GOODRICH, ALVA CURTIS, lawyer; b. Yamhill, Ore., May 14, 1912; s. Alva Curtis and Rachel Jane (Rose) G.; B.S., Linfield Coll., McMinnville, Ore., 1933; LL.B., U. Ore., 1935; m. Grayce Barendrick, Sept. 12, 1937; children—Gretchen (Mrs. Sterling Williver), Rachel (Mrs. L. A. Baker), Sylvia (Mrs. R.S. Radabaugh), Sarah (Mrs. Patrick R. Taylor). Admitted to Ore. bar, 1936; gen. law practice, Bend, 1937-73; former mem. firm DeArmond, Goodrich, Gray, Fancher & Holmes; now in individual practice; municipal judge City of Bend, 1945-50; asso. bd. dirs. Equitable Savs. & Loan Assn., Portland, Ore. Mem. Ore. Bd. Aeros., 1962-67. Bd. dirs. Central Ore. Hosp. Found. Rep. Ore. State Legislature from 28th Dist., 1950-54. Mem. Deschutes County Republican Central Com. Mem. Bend C. of C., Deschutes County Vets. Council, Am., Deschutes County bar assns. Oregon State Bar (v.p. 1950-51, gov. 1948-51), Ore. Hist. Soc. (dir. or sec. 1952-58), O.R.C., Am. Legion, 40 and 8. Republican. Mem. Christian Ch. K.P. Clubs: Lions, University (Portland). Home: Bend, Ore. Died Apr. 19, 1973.

GOODRICH, CARTER, economist; b. Plainfield, N.J., May 10, 1897; s. Rev. Charles Lyman and Jeannette Margaret (Carter) G.; A.B., Amherst Coll., 1918, L.H.D., 1958; Ph.D., U. Chgo., 1921; m. Florence Perry Nielsen, Aug. 4, 1921; children—Janet Carter (Mrs. John W. Chapman). Barbara Nielsen (Mrs. Stuart H. Schulberg), Laurance Villers. Hitchcock fellow and mem. faculty Amherst Coll., 1919, 1921-24, faculty U. Mich., 1924-31; prof. econ. Columbia, 1931-63, prof. emeritus, after 1963; Mellon prof. history U. Pitts., after 1963; exec. officer dept. econs., Columbia, 1946-49, rep. grad. sch. business at Univ. of Buenos Aires, 1961-62; Sidney Hillman Found. lectr., Cornell Univ., 1955; dir. study of population distbn., Wharton School, U. of Pa., 1934-36; cons. Resettlement Adminstrn., 1936, Social Security Bd., 1937; U.S. Labor Commr., Geneva, Switzerland, 1936-37, 1938-40; U.S. Govt. member, governing body International Labor Office, 1936-46, chmn., 1939-45; mem. U.S. govt. del., Internat. Labor Conf., 1937, 38, 39, 41, 44, 45; member of the delegation on economic depressions, League of Nations, 1938-45; special asst. to Am. Ambassador to Great Britain, 1941; chmn. preparatory com. and program dir. U.N. Sci. Conf. on the Conservation and Utilization of Resources, 1948-49; consultant United Nations, 1948-51; spl. rep. of Sec.-Gen. UN in Bolivia, 1952-53; chief UN Economic Survey Mission, Viet Nam, 1955-56. Adv. com. Eleutherian Mills-Hagley Found., 1966-69. Henry Russell award U. Mich., 1926; Order of Condor of the Andes (Bolivia), 1953. Fellow Am. Acad. Arts and Scis.; mem. Am. Philos. Soc. (councillor 1956-59), Am. Econ. Assn. (bd. editors, 1931-34, exec. com. 1937-40, v.p. 1946). Acad. Polit. Sci., Council on Fgn. Relations, Econ. Hist. Assn. (pres. 1954-56), Beta Theta Pi, Phi Beta Kappa. Clubs: Century. Adirondack Mountain. Author several books including; The Frontier of Control, 1920; Government Promotion of American Canals and Railroads, 1960; sr. author: Migration and Economic Opportunity, 1936; Canals and American Economic Development, 1961. Editor: The Government and the Economy, 1783-1861, 1967. Contbr. jours., Ency. Social Scis. Address: Pittsburgh, Pa. Deceased.

GOODRICH, PIERRE FRIST, lawyer; b. Winchester, Ind., Sept. 10, 1894; s. James Putnam and Cora (Frist) G.; A.B., Wabash Coll., 1916, LL.D., 1949; LL.B., Harvard Law Sch., 1920; m. Dorothy Dugan, 1920; 1 dau., Nancy; m. 2d, Enid Smith, Feb. 1941. Admitted to Ind. bar, 1920, began practice at Winchester; mem. Macy & Goodrich, 1920-23, Mote & Goodrich, 1923-25, Goodrich, Emison & Campbell, 1928-39, Goodrich & Campbell, 1939-52, Goodrich, Campbell & Warren, 1952-61, Goodrich & Warren, Indpls., 1961-73; pres., dir. Ind. Telephone Corp., 1935-73, Peoples Loan & Trust Co.; chmn. Liberty Fund, Inc., 1960-73, Thirty-Five Twenty, Inc., 1965-73; dir. Pub. Telephone Corp. Served as 2d lt. U.S. Army, 1917-18. Trustee Found. for Econ. Edn., Inc. Mem. Mont Pelerin Soc., Am., Ind., Indpls. bar assns., Indpls., Ind. chambers commerce, Am. Legion, Athenaeum Turners, Phi Beta Kappa, Phi Beta Kappa Assos., Phi Gamma Delta. Republican. Presbyn. Clubs: University (N.Y.); Columbia; Woodstock. Home: Indianapolis, Ind. Died Oct. 25, 1973; interred Winchester, Ind.

GOODRICH, RALPH DICKINSON, dean engring., retired; b. Manchester, Mich., Mar. 18, 1878; s. Edward Payson and Mary Isabelle (Hall) G.; B.S. in C.E., University of Michigan, 1903, C.E., 1913; m. Margaret Knight, 1908; children—Margaret, Ralph Dickinson, Edward, Mary (Mrs.Robert K. Pittman), John. Asst. engr. Toledo Urban and Interurban Ry., 1903, Marine Basin Co., Bklyn., N.Y., 1904; inspector East River Tunnels, Pa. R.R., 1904-05; asst. state engr., Cheyenne, Wyo., 1906. dep. state engr. in charge irrigation projects, 1907-09, chief engr. Buffalo Basin irrigation projects, 1910; gen. practice as irrigation engr., 1911; city engr., Cheyenne, Wyo., 1911-15; city engr. and mgr. pub. utilities, Ypsilanti, Mich., 1916; city engr., Lansing, Mich., 1917-18; hydrographer, Grand Canal, Shantung, and Chihli, Grand Canal Improvement Bd., Tientsin, China, 1918-19; engr. flood relief and river regulating works, Chihli River Commn., Tientsin, 1919-27; asso. prof. civil engring., U. of Wyo., 1927-28, prof. from 1928, head civil engring. dept. 1928-35, acting dean. 1934-35, dean 1936-48, ret.; chief engr. Upper Colorado River commn. 1950-55; on leave as sr. hydraulic engr. for flood control problems, U.S. Engr. Office, Sacramento Dist., 1930-31; cons. engr. N. Pacific Div., U.S. Engrs. Office, 1935-37; coordinator of civilian pilot training, U. of Wyo., 1940-44, instl. dir. engr. defense tng., 1940-41. Member American Geophysical Union, American Society Civil Engineers, American Water Works Assn., Wyo., Engrs., Soc., Sigma Xi, Phi Kappa Phi, Sigma Tau, Tau Beta Pi, Phi Gamma Delta. Clubs: Rotary, Newcomen Society of Eng. Episcopalian. Mason. Contbr. to engring. jours. Home: Grand Junction, Colo.†

GOODSELL, FRED FIELD, ch. official; b. Montevideo, Minn., Sept. 21, 1880; s. Dennis and Abby Manchester (Field) G.; A.B., U. of Calif., 1902; B.D., Hartford (Conn.) Theol. Sem., 1905, William Thompson fellow same at Univ. of Marburg and Berlin, 1905-07; D.D., Pacific Sch. of Religion, 1926; m. Lulu K. Service, June 29, 1905; children—Lynda Irene (Mrs. Everett Carll Blake), Lincoln Service, Caroline Service (Mrs. Richard Bonsall Smith). Ordained ministry of the Congregational Church, 1905; missionary A.B.C.F.M., Turkey, 1905. Aintab, Turkey, 1907-11; dir. Bentral Turkey Coll., 1908-10; prin. Marash (Turkey) Theol. Sem., 1911-14; service with Laymen's Missionary Movement, Missionary Edn. Movement, 1914-16, Y.M.C.A. war service, Russia, Rumania and Siberia, 1916-19; in Turkey, 1919-29; organizer and exec. sec. Stamboul Branch Y.M.C.A.; founder and prin. Am. Bd. Lang. Sch., Constantinople; founder, 1922, prin. until 1925, Sch. of Religion, Constantinople; pres. and mem. bd. mgrs. Constantinople City Y.M.C.A., 1924-29; mem. exec. com. Near East Christian Council, 1927-29; field sec. Near East Mission, 1925-29; exec. v.p. A.B.C.F.M., Boston, 1930-49, historian and research asso. from 1949; spl. commr. for A.B.C.F.M. in Near East 1949-50. Member faculty and Earle Foundation lecturer, Pacific School of Religion (on furlough), 1926-27. Trustee Constantinople Woman's College, Internat. College, Beirut, Syria; trustee American Hospital, Istanbul, Turkey; del. Internat. Missionary Council, Jerusalem, 1928, Madras, India, 1938; mem. Internat. Missionary Council, 1935; chmn. exec. com. Foreign Missions Conference North America, 1935-37; chmn. Fgn. Mission Conf., 1947-48. Delegate of Congl. and Christian chs. to Universal Conf. on Life and Work, Oxford, Eng., 1937. Fellow American Geographical Soc.; member American Oriental Soc., Phi Beta Kappa. Clubs: Boston Congregational, Winthrop, Rotary. Author: Inductive Turkish Lessons, 1926. Contbr. chapter in "Constantinople Today," 1929; John Service Pioneer, 1945; also numerous articles in religious jours. Home: Boston, Mass.†

GOODSELL, HENRY GUY, clergyman; b. Platteville, Wis., Jan. 20, 1880; s. Henry and Sarah (Savidge) G.; student Lawrence Coll., Appleton, Wis., 1902-04, D.D., 1919; A.B., Northwestern U., 1905; Boston U. Sch. of Theology, 1908-09; m. Anna C. Tyler, Nov. 27, 1909; children—Helen, Nan, James Warren; married 2d, Mrs. Ina Penwarden Awl, June 25, 1946. Ordained ministry M.E. Ch., 1907; pastor Platteville, Wis., 1914-16, First M.E. Ch., Madison, Wis., 1917-20, Warren Memorial Ch. Denver, Colo., 1921-23; supt. Denver Dist., 1926-28; pastor First M.E. Ch., Colorado Springs, Colo., 1928-34, First M.E. Church, Portland, Ore., 1934-41; dist. supt. Portland Dist. Methodist Church 1941-47, ret. Trustee U. of Denver, Willamette U., Beth El Hosp., Colorado Springs. Mem. Bd. of Edn., M.E. Ch.; del. to Meth. Ecumenical Conf., Atlanta, Ga., 1931; dean of Estes Park Epworth League Inst. 3 yrs.; Denver area rep. on World Service Commn. of M.E. Ch., term 1932-36; del. from Oregon Conf. Methodist Ch. to Gen. Conf. Methodist Ch., Kansas City, 1944. Club: City (Portland). Address: Portland, Ore.†

GOODWIN, ANGIER LOUIS, congressman; b. Fairfield, Me., Jan. 30, 1881; s. Albert Bates and Ruby Augusta (Hoxie) G.; A.B., Colby College, 1902; Harvard Law Sch., 1905; m. Eleanor Hardy Stone, 1905; children—Roger L., Mary E. (Mrs. Robert Culver), Barbara (Mrs. A. E. Flint). Admitted to Me. bar, 1905, Mass., 1906; practiced Boston from 1906. Mem. Melrose (Mass.) Bd. of Alderman, 8 years, pres., 1920; mayor of Melrose, 1921-23; mem. Mass. House of Reps., 1925-28, Mass. State Sentate, 1929-41, pres., 1941; mem. 78th to 83d Congresses, 8th Dist. Massachusetts. Republican. Served as trustee Melrose Pub. Library; member Planning Board and chairman Board of Appeal, Melrose; chairman Massachusetts Commission on Adminstration and Finance, 1941-42. Member Massachusetts State Guard and legal advisory to aid draft registrants, World War I. Chmn. Mass. 1939-40. Mem. Zeta Psi. Mason (32°), Odd Fellow, Commn. on Participation in New York World's Fair, K.P., Elk. Grange. Home: Melrose, Mass.†

GOODWIN, FRANCIS M., lawyer; b. Allegany County, Md., June 15, 1871; s. James and Henrietta (Barnes) G.; grad. Milton Acad., Baltimore, 1891; grad. U. of Md., 1896; m. Margaret Cecelia Carnan, Nov. 6, 1901; children—James Carnan, Margaret Ridgely (Mrs. Edward B. Williams), Francis M. Editor and manager Baltimore Jour. of Commerce, 1896-1898; practiced law at Baltimore, 1898-1901; spl. agt. and chief of field div., Gen. Land Office, Interior Dept., 1901-07; spl. asst. to U.S. atty. gen. in land fraud cases, 1907; chief asst. prof. atty.'s office, Spokane, Wash., 1913-14; moved to Spokane, Wash., 1904; resumed the gen. practice of law in 1907; asst. sec. Dept. of the Interior, 1921-25; in practice of law after 1925. Presbyn. Mason. Clubs: Cosmos, Congressional Country. Home: Washington, D.C.†

GOODWIN, ROBERT ELIOT, lawyer; b. Cambridge, Mass., Oct. 27, 1878; s. Frank and Mary G. (Buttrick) G.; A.B., Harvard, 1901; LL.B., Boston U. Law Sch., 1903; m. Elsie T. Wainwright, Oct. 3, 1922 (dec. 1948); m. 2d, Marguerita S. Putnam, June 25, 1950. Admitted to Mass. bar, 1903, then practiced in Boston; jr. asso. Carver & Blodgett, 1903-06; pvt. law practice, 1906-07; partner Carver, Wardner & Goodwin, 1907-12, Goodwin, Procter & Hoar, and pedecessor, after 1912; referee in bankruptcy, Middlesex Co., Mass., 1921-27. Chmn. Mass. Bd. Probation, 1943-53. Col. 101st F.A., 26th Div., A.E.F., 1918-19. Decorated D.S.M. Mem. Harvard Fund Council, 1930-42, bd. dirs. alumni assn., 1943-46, v.p., 1944-45. Mem. Am., Mass. State, Boston bar assns., Boston C. of C. Clubs: Union, Somerset, Harvard (Boston). Home: Boston, Mass.†

GOODWIN, WILLIAM N., judge; b. McKenna, Wash., Aug. 17, 1909; B.A., Wash. State Coll., 1931; LL.B., U. Ore., 1934. Admitted to Ore. bar, 1934, Wash. bar, 1937; practice of law, Tacoma; mem. firm. Gordon, Goodwin, Sager & Thomas; later U.S. dist. judge, chief judge Western Ind. Dist. Mem. bd. regents Wash. State U., 1957-75. Fellow Am. Coll. Trial Lawyers; mem. Am., Wash. State, Tacoma bar assns. Address: Tacoma, Wash.

GORDON, CHARLES A., pulp and paper; b. Thorold, Ont., Canada, Apr. 14, 1879; s. Charles G. and Mary (Skinner) G.; student pub. schs.; m. Lily M. Kuhnle, Sept. 5, 1907. Sales mgr. Street Ry. Advt. Co. of New York, 1902-12; treas. and gen. mgr. Perry Dame & Co., 1912-17; exec. v.p. Oxford Paper Co. and Oxford Miami Paper Co., N.Y. City, from 1917 to retirement, then dir.; was executive v.p. Nashwaak Pulp & Paper Co. Home: New York City, N.Y.†

GORDON, COLLN STUART, company exec.; b. Chgo., Apr. 23, 1904; s. Robert and Jessie C. (Macdonald) G.; student U. Chgo., 1923-25; m. Marietta Puerner, Feb. 26, 1929 (dec.); m. 2d, Mary E.

Walling, 1969. Joined Quaker Oats Co., 1927, v.p. 1940-52, then vice chmn., pres., also dir. Chmn. Chgo. Crime Commn. Trustee Ill. Inst. Tech. Home: Chicago, Ill. Died May 5, 1975; interred Forest Home, Milwaukee, Wis.

GORDON, PETER BENJAMIN, engr.; b. Montclair, N.J., Aug. 15, 1907; s. Louis and Fannie (Mattises) G.; B.C.E., Rutgers U., 1928; m. Alice I. Wylie, 1946 (dec. 1973). Engr. George E. Gibson Co., 1929-36; engr. Wolff & Munior, Inc., 1936-73, treas., 1939-51, dir., 1940-73, v.p., 1951-66, exec. v.p., 1966-72, v.p. spl. projects, 1972-73. Lectr. air conditioning Bklyn. Eve. Tech. High Sch., 1934-38; instr. air conditioning evening div., coll. engring. N.Y. U., 1937-42, adj. asso. prof. mech. engring. grad. div., 1946-52; assisted in design gaseous diffusion plant, Oak Ridge, 1943-46; vis. lectr. mech. engring. Princeton, 1946-47. Bd. dirs. Bldg. Research Inst., 1957-67, v.p., 1957-73, pres., 1966-67; v.p. C.H. Cronin of N.Y., Inc., 1962-66, Wolff & Munior-Cronin, Inc., 1970-73; dir. Bldg. Research Adv. Bd., 1959-63. Trustee, pres. John B. Pierce Found., 1959-73. Recipient Distinguished Service award Mech. Contracotors Assn. Am., 1956; F. Paul Anderson Medal award Am. Soc. Heating, Refrigerating and Air Conditioning Engrs., 1960. Fellow Am. Soc. Heating, Refrigerating and Air Conditioning Engrs. (mem. council 1952-58, pres. 1957); mem. Am. Soc. M.E., Phi Epsilon Pi. Home: N.Y.C., N.Y. Died Dec. 14, 1973.

GORDON, THURLOW MARSHALL, lawyer; b. Methuen, Mass., Nov. 20, 1884; s. Albert Brigham and Elizabeth Jane (Hamlet) G.; A.B. summa cum laude, Dartmouth, 1906; LL.B. cum laude, Harvard, 1911; m. Pauline Sawyer, Nov. 12, 1912; children—Thurlow M., Frances. Admitted to Mass. bar, 1911, U.S. Supreme Ct. bar, 1914, N.Y. Bar, 1918; spl. asst. Atty.-Gen. U.S., 1912-16; atty. FTC, 1916-17; asso. Spooner & Cotton, N.Y., 1917; partner McAdoo, Cotton & Franklin then Cahill, Gordon, Sonnett, Reindel & Ohl. Trustee Mt. Desert Island Hosp. Mem. Am., N.Y. State, N.Y. City bar assns., Soc. Bus. Adv. Professions, Soc. Colonial Wars, English Speaking Union, Pilgrims, Acad. Polit. Sci. Republican. Episcopalian. Clubs: Century, University, Harvard, Down Town, Economic (N.Y.C.); Cosmos (Washington); Harbor (Seal Harbor, Me.); Bar Harbor, Pot and Kettle (Bar Harbor, Me.). Author various articles and speeches relating to fed. anti-trust laws. Home: Methuen, Mass. Died Aug. 14, 1975; buried Ferncliffe Cemetery, Hartsdale, N.Y.

GORE, ROBERT HAYES, newspaper editor, publisher; b. Knottsville, Ky., May 24, 1886; s. Joseph Henry and Mary (Carrico) G.; B.A., St. Mary's Coll., 1904; LL.D., U. Notre Dame, 1958; m. Lorena Haury, Oct. 3, 1907; children—Robert Hayes, Edward F., Dorothy (Mrs. Jack Firlit), Mary (Mrs. Charles Palmer), John W., Frederick P., Joseph A., George H., Theodore T. Mng. editor Evansville (Ind.) Press, 1909-16; editor, pub. Terre Haute (Ind.) Post, 1916-21; owner, operator R. H. Gore Co., Ins., Chgo., 1921-68, Ft. Lauderdale (Fla.) News, 1929-63; hon. chmn. Gore Newspaper Co., 1963-72; builder Gov.'s Club Hotel, Ft. Lauderdale, 1935, Sea Ranch Resort Hotel, Ft. Lauderdale, 1939, Park Hill Hotel, Hendersonville, N.C., 1948-55, Franklin Hotel, Brevard, N.C., 1949-55, Green Park Hotel, Blowing Rock, N.C., 1947-55, Algren Hotel, Asheville, N.C., 1954-59; gov. P.R., 1933-34; pres., chmn., dir. R. H. Gore Co., Bardstown, Ky., 1949-68, Home Owners Life Ins. Co., Ft. Lauderdale, 1954-61, Instnl. Ins. Co. Am., Chgo., 1955-70, Gore Pub. Co., Ft. Lauderdale, 1929-63, N.A. Co., Ft. Lauderdale, 1931—, Gore-Milkon Mortgage Co., Ft. Lauderdale, 1958-62, Gore-Calder Investments, Inc., Ft. Lauderdale, 1927-72, Fla. Industries and Warehousing, Inc., Ft. Lauderdale, 1955-72. Writer scenarios Edison, Essanay, Biograph, 1909-10. Mem. Fla. Bd. Control, 1938-42, 56-59. Mem. Nat. Democratic Exec. Com. Campaign, 1932-33. Author: Wampus Cat, 1918; Newsboys' Mystery Novels, 1918. Inventor exercising bed, Ready-Lady chair. Home: Ft. Lauderdale, Fla. Died Dec. 26, 1972.

GORRELL, FAITH LANMAN, prof. home economics; b. New London, Conn., Nov. 21, 1881; d. John Trumbull and Charlotte Elizabeth (Stilwell) Lanman; B.S., Ohio State U., 1903, B.S., Columbia Univ., 1907, M.A., 1924; student U. of Mich., 1931-32; m. Edmund Morgan Gorrell, Dec. 23, 1932. Teacher, St. Petersburg, Fla., 1903-06; dir. home economics, Columbus O., 1907-18; asst. state leader of home demonstration work, Ohio State U., 1918-19, state leader, 1919-20; head of dept. of home economics Ohio State U., 1920-29, dir. Sch. of Home Economics, 1929-44; chief, Dept. of Home Economics, Ohio Agrl. Experiment Station 1926-45. Chmn. Ohio Nutrition com. of Ohio State Council of Defense, 1943-July 1944. Mem. Am. Home Economics Assn., Am. Dietetic Assn., Phi Upsilon Omicron, Omicron Nu. Author: (with H. McKay and F. Zuill) The Family's Food, 1931, revised 1937; (with H. McKay) Foods Workbook, 1939, rev., 1945 (with H. McKay and F. Zuill) Food and Family Living, 1942, rev., 1947. Home: Columbus, O.†

GOSA, ROBERT EARL, civil engr., contractor; b. Eutaw, Ala., Apr. 26, 1891; s. Wilson Coleman and Margaret (Lamb) G.; student Marion Inst., 1908-09; C.E., U. Ala., 1913; m. Grace Mary Bell, June 30, 1924 (dec). Insp. locks and dam constrn., U.S. Govt., 1913-15; layout engr. Hardaway Contracting Co., 1916-17; field engr. Doullut & Williams Co., Inc., 1920. mgr. bridge and hwy. dept., 1921-22, supt. wharf constrn., Houston, 1923-24; v.p. W. Horace Williams Co., Inc., New Orleans 1924-40, partner, 1940-49, v.p., 1950. pres., 1951-55; exec. v.p., dir. Williams-McWilliams Industries, Inc., New Orleans, 1956-58, dir., vice chmn., cons., 1958-59, ret., 1960. Served pvt. to co. comdr. C.E., AUS, 1917-19. Mem. Am. Soc. C.E. (asso.), La. Engring. Soc. (dir.), New Orleans Engrs. Club (dir.), Internat. House. Club: New Orleans Country. Home: New Orleans, La. Died Oct. 29, 1974.

GOSLING, GLENN DONALD, univ. ofcl.; b. Overisel, Mich., Sept. 29, 1909; s. Edward and Berendiena (Fynewever) G.; student Grand Rapids Jr. Coll., 1925-27; A.B., U. Mich., 1931, M.A., 1931; B.A. (Rhodes scholar), Oxford (Eng.) U., 1933, M.A., 1938; m. Laura Marshall, Mar. 24, 1942 (dec.); 1 dau., Anne Laura. Tchr. writing, English lit. Olivet (Mich.) Coll., 1934-41, mem. staff Olivet Writers Conf., summers 1936-41; editor trade dept. Henry Holt & Co., N.Y.C., 1941-50; editor-in-charge U. Cal. Press, Los Angeles, 1950-56, sr. editor, Berkeley, 1956-62; dir. U. Mich. Press, 1962-72; cons. to dean Horace H. Rackham Sch. Grad. Studies, U. Mich., 1972-74. Served with CIC, AUS, 1942-46. Mem. Am. Assn. Rhodes Scholars, Phi Kappa Phi, Kappa Tau Alpha. Home: Ann Arbor, Mich. Died Nov. 9, 1974.

GOTSHALK, DILMAN WATER, educator; b. Trenton, N.J., Sept. 11, 1901; s. William Calvin and Josephine (Walters) G.; A.B., Princeton, 1922; Ph.D., Cornell, 1927; m. Naomi Irene Smith, Oct. 17, 1930; children—Richard Allan, Mary Laine, Instr. English lit. Mohegan Lake Sch., N.Y., 1922-24; acting prof. philosophy Colgate U., 1927; instr. philosophy U. Ill., Urbana, 1927-30, asst. prof., 1930-36, asso. prof., 1936-43, prof. philosophy, 1943-65, prof. philosophy emeritus, 1965-74, chmn. dept., 1951-61. Fellow A.A.A.S.; mem. Am. Philos. Assn. (v.p. Western div. 1947-48, 49-50, pres. 1950-51, chmn. nat. bd. officers 1951, Carus lecture com. 1952, chmn. 1953-65), Am. Soc. Aesthetics (trustee 1952-55, pres. 1957-59, del. soc. to Am. Council Learned Socs. 1959-61), Am. Assn. U. Profs. Author: Structure and Reality, 1937, 68; Metaphysics in Modern Times, 1940; Art and the Social Order, 1947, 51, 62; The Promise of Modern Life, 1958; Patterns of Good and Evil, 1963; Human Aims in Modern Perspective 1966; The Structure of Awareness, 1969; Twentieth Century Theme, 1971. Contbr. to Heritage of Kant, 1939. Ency. of the Arts, 1946, P.F. Collier's Gen. Ency., 1951, A Modern Book of Esthetics, 1952, 60, Problems of Aesthetics, 1953; also other books and various philos. periodicals. Home: Olney, Ill. Deceased.

GOTTLIEB, ADOLPH, artist; b. N.Y.C., Mar. 14, 1903; s. Emil and Elsie (Berger) G.; student, Europe, 1921-22; m. Esther Dick, June 12, 1932. One man shows various pvt. galleries, 1930-74; P.O. mural, Yerrington, Nev., 1939; ten year retrospective exhbn. Bennington Coll., Williams Coll., 1954; retrospective exhbn. Jewish Mus., 1957; exhbns. Paris, 1947, 52, 59, Tokyo, 1952, London, 1959; designer Ark curtains Congregation B'nai Israel, Millburn, N.J., 1952, Congregation Beth El, Springfield, Mass., 1953; designer stained glass facade Park Av. Synagogue, N.Y.C., 1954; one-man shows at Guggenheim Mus., Whitney Mus. Am. Art, 1968, series one-man shows Marlborough Galleries in Rome, London, Zurich, N.Y.C., 1970-72; represented permanent collections Met. Mus. Art, Mus. Modern Art, Whitney Mus. Am. Art, Tel Aviv Mus., Bklyn. Mus., U. Neb., Soc. Four Arts, Isaac Dalgado Mus., Smith Coll., Guggenheim Found., U. Miami, Detroit Inst., others. Winner mural award for Nev., U.S. Treasury competition, 1939, 1st prize Bklyn. Soc. Artists, 1944, Purchase award U. Ill., 1951, Carnegie Internat. 3d prize, 1961, Grand Prix, Sao Paulo Bienal, 1963. Mem. Nat. Inst. Arts and Letters. Home: Hampton, N.Y. Died Mar. 4, 1974.

GOTTLIEB, JAMES E., dept. stores co. exec.; b. Mpls., 1924; B.S., U. Minn., LL.B., 1949; married. Admitted to Minn. bar; exec. v.p. Equity Capital Co., 1950-66; with Gamble-Skogmo Inc., Mpls., 1968-69; sr. v.p. real estate, Nat. Tea Co., Chgo., 1969-75; 1969-75; dir. Red Owl Stores, Inc., Gamble Alden Life Ins. Co. Home: St. Paul, Minn. Died Jan. 28, 1975.

GOTTLIEB, POLLY ROSE (MRS. ALEX GOTTLIEB), author, artist; b. N.Y.C.; d. David and Fannie (Wernick) Rosenberg; student N.Y. U.; m. Alex Gottlieb, Sept. 29, 1964. Actress appearing in mus. comedies with Bert Lahr, Beatrice Lillie, 1935-37; one-woman show Gregg Juarez Galleries, Los Angeles, 1966; exhibited in group shows Newport (Cal.) Art Festival, Barnsdall Park Municipal Art Festival, Los Angeles. Mem. Orgn. for Rehab. through Tng. (chpt. pres. 1958-60). Author: The Nine Lives of Billy Rose, 1968. Address: Beverly Hills, Cal. Died Feb. 1971.

GOTTSCHALK, ALFRED, biochemist; b. Aachen, Germany, Apr. 22, 1894; s. Ben Carl and Rosa (Kahn) G.; student U. Munich (Germany), 1912-13, U. Freiburg (Germany), 1913; M.D., U. Bonn (Germany), 1920; postgrad. Kaiser-Wilhelm Inst. Biochemistry, Berlin, Germany, 1921-26; M.D. (hon.), U. Muenster (Germany); m. Elizabeth Orgler, Aug. 2, 1923; 1 son, Rudolf. Dir. biochem. dept. Gen. Hosp., Stettin, Germany, 1927-35; sr. biochemist Walter and Eliza Hall Inst. Med. Research, Melbourne, Australia, 1939-59; hon. fellow Australian Nat. U., Canberra, Australia, 1959-63; guest prof. Max-Planck Inst. Virus Research, Tübingen, Germany, 1963-73; hon. prof. U. Tübingen, 1966-73. Lectr., U. Melbourne, 1949-59. Recipient David Syme prize, also medal U. Melbourne, 1950. Fellow Royal Inst. Chemistry, Royal Australian Chem. Inst. (H.G. Smith Meml. medal 1952), A.A.A.S., Australian Acad. Sci., Max Planck Inst. (fgn. sci. mem.). Author: Chemistry and Biology of Sialic Acids, 1960; Glycoproteins: Their Composition, Structure and Function, 1966, 2d rev. edit., 1972; also numerous articles. Research, publs. on chemistry and metabolism of carbohydrates, molecular structure neuraminic acid, reaction mechanism enzyme neuraminidase, molecular structure glycoproteins, especially carbohydrate group, elucidation chemistry underlying initial phases influenza virus infection. Home: Tübingen, Germany. Died Oct. 4, 1973.

GOTTSCHALK, LOUIS, educator; b. Bklyn., Feb. 21, 1899; s. Morris Frank and Anna (Krystall) G.; A.B., Cornell U., 1919; A.M., 1920, Ph.D., 1921; D.Litt. (hon.), Augustana Coll., 1954; Doctor honoris causa, U. Toulouse (France), 1957; D.H.L., Hebrew Union Coll., 1963; LL.D., U. Louisville, 1960; m. 2d, Fruma Kasdan, Dec. 16, 1930; children—Alexander, Paul Abo. Asst. in history Cornell U., 1919; instr. history U. Ill., 1921-23; asst. prof. history U. Louisville, 1923-25, asso. prof., 1925-27; asso. prof. modern history U. Chgo., 1927-35, prof., 1935-59, Gustavus F. and Ann M. Swift Distinguished Service professor, 1959-64, prof. emeritus, 1964-75, chmn. dept. history, 1937-42; vis. prof. U. Ill., Chgo. Circle, 1966-75, asso. dir. honors program, 1968-75; summer appointments univs.; Fulbright Distinguished lectr., Japan, 1968. Pres. Chgo. Bd. Jewish Edn., 1942-45; chmn. B'nai B'rith Hillel Commn. 1963-69, hon. chmn., 1969-75. Col. a.d.c. to gov. of N.M., 1966-75. Apprentice seaman, USNRF, 1918. AAF Com. Historians, 1943-44. Mem. Social Sci. Research Council, 1955-63. Fellow Center for Advanced Study Behavioral Scis., 1957-58. Mem. Am. Hist. Assn. (pres. 1953), Am. Assn. Univ. Profs., Am. Friends of Lafayette (exec. com.), Am. Acad. of Arts and Scis., Am. Philos. Soc., Société des Etudes Robespierristes, Société d'Histoire Moderne, Conf. on Jewish Relations (mem. council), Am. Council Learned Socs. (vice chmn. 1965-67), Phi Beta Kappa, Zeta Beta Tau (hon.). Recipient Guggenheim fellowship, 1928-29, 54-55; medal of merit Union Fédérale des Anciens Combattants de France, 1938; Princeton Bicentennial Medal, 1946; Newberry Library fellowship, 1946; U. Louisville Sesquicentennial, 1948; James H. Hyde Prize, 1948; Chevalier Legion of Honor, 1953; Fulbright research award, 1954-55, 68; award by Am. Council Learned Societies, 1959. Club: Quadrangle. Author books including: The Letters of Lafayette to Washington, 1945; Lafayette between the American and the French Revolution (1783-1789), 1950; Understanding History, 1950, 2d edit., 1969. Editor: Generalization in the Writing of History, 1963. Author, editor: Vol. IV UNESCO Scientific and Cultural History of Mankind. Co-author publs. including: Europe and the Modern World, 2 vols. 1951-54; Lafayette in the French Revolution, 1969; contbr. articles to mags. Asst. editor Jour. Modern History, 1929-43, acting editor, 1943-45; asso. editor several hist. periodicals. Participant in radio and public forums. Home: Chicago, Ill. Died June 23, 1975.

GOURLEY, ROBERT JOHN, lumber exec.; b. Brampton, Ont., Can., Feb. 20, 1878; s. William and Mary Jane Gourley; ed. pub. schs., Birtle, Manitoba; m. Laura Lyle Bary, 1903; 5 children. With R. W. Gibson, Birtle, Manitoba, also lumberman, Wolsely, Saskatchewan, 1893-1903; mgr. Union Bank of Can., Souris and Carberry, Manitoba, 1903; sec.-treas. Beaver Lumber Co., Ltd., Winnipeg, Manitoba, 1907-08, gen. mgr., 1908-43, pres. after 1943; dir. Empire Sash and Door Company Limited. Monarch Life Assurance Company, Toronto-Dominion Bank, Manitoba Bridge and Engineering Works, Limited, also Westeel Products, Ltd. Mem. Strathcona Curling Soc. Independent. United Church of Can. Clubs: Manitoba; St. Charles Country; Granite (Toronto). Home: Winnipeg, Can.†

GOVE, GEORGE, corp. exec.; b. Milwaukee, Feb. 18, 1881; s. George William and Anna Elizabeth (Wise) G.; A.B., U. of Wis., 1904; post grad. student Stanford, 1905-06; m. Marguerite Pannill, Dec. 21, 1911. Asst. sec. Merchants and Manufacturers Assn., Milwaukee, Wis., 1907-10; asst. to sec. of interior, 1911-13; engaged in planning and organization of large scale low rental housing developments, East Walpole, Mass., and Bridgeport, Conn., 1914-17, in New York City after 1926; with Am. City Bureau, 1918-20, vice-pres. and gen. mgr., 1920-22; dir. N.Y. State Commn. of Housing and Regional Planning, 1923-25; exec. sec., N.Y. State Bd. of Housing, 1926-37; mgr. housing projects Metropolitan Life Ins. Co., 1938-44, 3d v.p. charge housing projects, 1944-52; v.p., dir. Fred F. French Investing Co., Inc.; v.p. Stuyvesant Town Corp. Pres. Nat. Assn. Housing Officials, 1937. Mem. Sigma Alpha Epsilon. Home: New York City, N.Y.†

GOW, ARTHUR SIDNEY, publishing co. exec.; b. Upson, Wis., Dec. 16, 1892; s. Arthur Hill and Jennie (Kelly) G.; LL.B., U. Minn., 1916; m. Lila Reeves, Feb. 23, 1919; children—Arthur Sidney, Dorothy B. (Mrs. Donald B. Stroetzel), Neale A. With Am. Relief Adminstrn., Paris, 1919; br. mgr. advt. sales Curtis Pub. Co., Phila., 1937-42, v.p., 1954-73. Dir. Met. YMCA, 1949, mem. internat. com., 1950-51. Served as maj. F.A., U.S. Army, 1916-19; comdr. USCG T.R., 1942-45. Decorated Purple Heart; Legion of Honor (France). Mem. Sales Mgrs. Assn. (past pres.). Clubs: Rotary, Right Angle (past pres.), Automobile (dir.), Racquet, Down Town (Phila.). Home: Ithan, Pa. Died Nov. 11, 1973.

GOWEN, SAMUEL EMMETT, author; b. LaVergne, Tenn., Sept. 10, 1902; s. George Washington and Nona Elizabeth (Duffel) G.; ed. pub. sch., LaVergne; m. Claire Loeb, May 31, 1941. Reporter Memphis News Scimitar, Memphis Comml. Appeal, 1922-25; field sec. Fla. Lumber & Millwork Assn., winter 1925; reporter Bronx Home News, 1926; editor The Fourth Estate, 1927; publicity dir. Better Bus. Bur. N.Y., 1927-29; mng. dir. Emmett Gowen Ltd., Belize, Brit. Honduras; expdns. in Mexico And Central Am. Served as pvt. USMC, 1919-23. Mem. Authors League Am., Outdoor Writers Assn. Am. Author: Racketeers, an Expose, 1930; Mountain Born, 1932; Dark Moon of March, 1933; Old Hell, 1937; The Joys of Fishing, 1961; Expedition Holy Book, 1967; One Man and the Good Life, 1974; short stories in Yale Review, Atlantic Esquire and others; articles in Americas, True, Field and Stream, Outdoor Life, Sports Afield, Sports Illustrated, others Mem. Adv. council Who's Who in Am. Home: LaVergne, Tenn. Died July 3, 1973; buried LaVergne.

GRAHAM, ARTHUR BUTLER, lawyer; b. N.Y. City, July 10, 1878; s. Henry Sylvester and Charlotte Emme (Porter) G.; student New York University College of Arts, 1901-03, LL.B., 1904; m. Linda Fraissinet, of N.Y. City, June 22, 1910; children—John Fraissinet, Frederick Lorimer. Admitted to N.Y. bar, 1905, and began practice at N.Y. City; member firm of Laughlin, Gerard, Bowers & Halpin; pres. of the Allied Mutuals Liability Ins. Co. Organizer Community Assn. of Bay Shore, 1916, Visiting Nurse Assn. of Bay Shore, 1917; pres. Southside Hosp., 1920-23; mem. council New York U.; chmn. com. on centennial celebration, New York U. Mem. Am. Bar Assn., N.Y. State Bar Assn., Los Angeles Bar Assn., Assn. Bar City of N.Y. (mem. com. on professional ethics and mem. com. on courts of superior jurisdiction), New York Co. Lawyers Assn., Soc. of the Cincinnati, Huguenot Soc., Soc. Colonial Wars, S.R., Founders and Patriots America, Soc. War of 1812, Geneal. and Biog. Soc. N.Y., N.Y. Hist. Soc., St. Nicholas Soc., Delta Phi, Delta Chi. Democrat. Episcopalian. Clubs: Church, Manhattan. Home: New York City, N.Y.†

GRAHAM, DONALD EARL, tool co. exec.; b. Northampton, Mass., Mar. 28, 1926; s. Gerald S. and Clara A. (McKelligott) G.; student U. Cal. at Los Angeles; m. Charlotte D. Smith, Mar. 30, 1952; children—Diana D., Steven S., Trina D. With Smith Tool Co. (formerly H.C. Smith Tool Oil Co.), Compton, Cal., 1952-74, exec. v.p., 1959-60, pres., 1960-74, also dir.; pres. Smith Industries Internat., Inc. 1961-74. Served with USMCR, 1944-46. Republican. Clubs: Jonathan (Los Angeles); Hacienda Golf (La Habra, Cal.). Home: Whittier, Cal. Died May 15, 1974.

GRAHAM, FREDERICK J., lawyer; b. Stockbridge, Mich., Mar. 30, 1881; s. Benjamin and Helen M. (Kellogg) G.; grad. Manual Training Sch., Ellendale, 1902; LL.B., Univ. of N.D., 1906; M. Ina E. Randall, Jan. 24, 1912; children—Gordon M., Helen, Randall, Benjamin. Admitted to N.D. bar, 1906, and practiced then at Ellendale. States atty., Dickey County, N.D., 1915-16; judge, N.D. Dist. Court, 3d dist., 1919-20; mem. Rep. Nat. Com., 1928-32, 1944-48; mem. Platform Com. Rep. Nat. Conv., Cleveland, O., 1936; mem. House of Rep., 1943, 1945, 1947, 1949, floor leader. Mem. Am. and N.D. State bar assns. Republican. Methodist. Mason (32°, Shriner). Home: Ellendale, N.D.†

GRAHAM, JOHN JOSEPH, mfg. and financial co. exec.; b. Phila., July 18, 1915; s. Walter Thomas and Laura Cecilia (McGowan) G.; grad. Wharton Sch., U. Pa., grad. Advanced Mgmt. Program, Harvard, 1955; m. Kathryn Mary Brady, Nov. 28, 1942; 1 dau., Elaine Marie. With RCA, 1947-61, div. v.p., gen. mgr. RCA, 1959-61; v.p., area gen. mgr. N. Am., also dir. Internat. Tel. & Tel. Co., 1961-64; v.p. Curtiss-Wright Corp., also pres., gen. mgr. Wright Aero. div., 1964-66; group v.p. Gen. Dynamics Corp., N.Y.C., 1966-69; pres., chief exec. officer, dir. DCL, Inc., Saddle Brook, N.Y., 1969-74. Recipient Distinguished Alumni award Wharton Sch., U. Pa. Mem. I.E.E.E. (sr.), Navy League, Newcomen Soc., Pa. Soc., Sigma Kappa Phi. Club: Union League (N.Y.C.). Home: Saddle River, N.J. Died Jan. 15, 1974; interred Washington Meml. Park, Paramus, N.J.

GRAHAM, JOHN WILLIAM, JR., coll. chancellor; b. Dayton, O., May 25, 1915; s. John William and Louise (Whipps) G.; B.C.E., Ohio State U., 1939; C.E., Princeton, 1940; D.Sc., Carnegie Inst. Tech., 1950; L.H.D., St. Lawrence U., 1968; m. Ruth E. Orr, Feb. 7, 1942; children—Judith Ann (Mrs. William Lucianovic), Kathleen (Mrs. David Williams), John William III, Margaret Louise, Engr. fabricated steel constrn. div. Bethlehem Steel Corp., Rankin, Pa., 1940-42, 45-46; instr. to asso. prof. civil engring., dean Coll. Engring. and Sci., dean students Carnegie Inst. Tech., Pitts., 1946-56; v.p. Cooper Union, 1956-59; dean engring. U. Rochester, 1959-66; pres., chancellor Clarkson Coll. Tech., Potsdam. N.Y., 1966-74. Dir., Marine Midland Bank-No. Served from 2d lt. to maj. C.E., AUS, 1942-46. Registered profl. engr., Pa., N.Y. Mem. Rochester Engring. Soc., Am. Soc. Engring. Edn., Sigma Xi, Tau Beta Pi, Chi Epsilon, Phi Kappa Phi. Home: Potsdam, N.Y. Died Sept., 1974.

GRAHAM, WALTER WAVERLY, JR., educator; b. College Grove, Tenn., Dec. 1, 1906; s. Walter Waverly and Bettie (Hatcher) G.; B.A., Vanderbilt U., 1929, M.A., 1930; Ph.D., George Peabody Coll., 1943; m. Irene Turner, Aug. 6, 1931; children—Walter Waverly III, Jane Turner. With Vanderbilt U., 1930—, instr. math., 1930-41, asst. prof., 1941-43, asso. prof. applied math., 1946-50, prof., 1950-51, prof. head dept., 1951-69, prof., 1969-74. Served from lt. (j.g.) to lt. USNR, 1943-46; tchr. math. U.S. Naval Acad., 1943-46. Mem. Am. Math. Assn., Am. Soc. Engring. Edn., Tenn. Acad. Sci., Sigma Xi, Omicron Delta Kappa. Methodist. Mason. Home: Nashville, Tenn. Died Nov. 13, 1974.

GRAIG, FRANK ANDREW, physician; b. Vienna, Austria, Nov. 8, 1914; s. Emil and Elizabeth (Pfeifer) Gyori; came to U.S., 1947, naturalized, 1952; M.D., U. Budapest (Hungary), 1940; m. Edna R. Berman, Jan. 12, 1951 (div.); 1 son, Eric. Intern, Met. Hosp., N.Y.C., 1947-48, research fellow, 1948-51, clin. asst., 1950-52, asst. vis. physician, 1953-58; asst. attending physician nepolastic div. Montefiore Hosp., Bronx, N.Y., 1951-53, asst. attending physician med. div., 1952-53, adj. attending physician, 1953-60, course in radioisotopes, 1957; dir. div. medicine Grasslands Hosp., Valhalla, N.Y., 1966-74; cons. in endocrinology United Hosp., Port Chester, N.Y.; cons. in medicine Mt. Vernon (N.Y.) Hosp.; asst. clin. instr. N.Y. Med. Coll., 1951-58, prof. medicine, 1970-74; asso. in clin. medicine Albert Einstein Coll. Medicine, 1966-67, asst. clin. prof., 1967-70. Mem. med. adv. com. Westchester Heart Assn. Diplomate Am. Bd. Internal Medicine. Fellow A.C.P.; mem. Endocrine Soc., Soc. Nuclear Medicine, A.A.A.S., Am. Physiol. Soc., Harvey Soc., Am. Thyroid Assn., A.M.A., Westchester County Med. Soc., Westchester Acad. Medicine, Am. Diabetes Assn. Contbr. articles and abstracts to med. jours. Home: White Plains, N.Y., Died June 12, 1974; buried New York City, N.Y.

GRAMLICH, FRANCIS W(ILLIAM), educator; b. Buffalo, N.Y., Oct. 12, 1911; s. William Francis and Christine (Egeling) G.; A.B., Princeton, 1933, A.M., 1934, Ph.D., 1936; m. Caro MacArthur, June 22, 1940; children—Francis, Carolyn MacArthur. Clin. psychologist Buffalo Public Sch. System, 1937-40; asst. prof. Grad. Sch., Canisius Coll., Buffalo, 1937-40; asst. prof. of philosophy, Dartmouth Coll., 1940-46, prof. of philosophy since 1947, chmn. dept. of philosophy, 1947-51. Served with USNR, 1942-46; disch. as lt. H(S) (clinical psychologist). Mem. Am. Philos. Assn., Am. Psychol. Assn., Phi Bets Kappa. Home: Hanover, N.H. Died June 4, 1973.

GRANDJANY, MARCEL, harpist, composer; b. Paris, France, Sept. 3, 1891; s. Eugene and Marie Jeanne (Hugo) G.; mus. edn. Nat. Conservatory Music, Paris, 1900-12; studiéd composition with Taudou and Vidal, harp with Renié and Hasselmans; m. Georgette H. Boulanger, May 20, 1919; 1 son, Bernard. Came to U.S., 1936, naturalized, 1945. Debut as concert artist on harp, Paris, Jan. 24, 1909; played in recitals and with orchs. throughout France; London debut, 1922; N.Y. debut at Aeolian Hall, 1924, later soloist with N.Y. Symphony Orch.; annual tours, Europe, U.S. and Can.; head harp dept. Fontainebleau (France) Summer Sch., 1921-35; head harp dept. Juilliard Sch. Music, N.Y.C., 1938-75; gave Master Classes Conservatoire de Musique, Province Que., Montreal, 1943-63; mem. faculty Manhattan Sch. Music, 1956-66. Founder Am. Harp Soc., 1962. Mem. A.S.C.A.P. Club: Bohemians. Prin. compositions include: Aria in classic style for harp and string orch.; Poem for harp, horn and orch.; Rhapsodie for harp; The Colorado Trail, Fantaisie on a Theme of Haydh for harp; Children's Hour, suite for harp; Fughetta and Divertissement for harp; Cadenza for the Handel harp Concerto in B flat; Cadenza for the Mozart Concerto for Flute and Harp; Realization of the Sonata for Harp by C. Ph.E. Bach, 1964. Address: New York City, N.Y. Died Feb. 24, 1975.

GRANGER, AMÉDÉE, radiologist; b. New Orleans, La., Mar. 23, 1879; s. Jules and Cora (Bercier) G.; M.D., Tulane U., 1901; D.Sc., La. State U., 1935; m. Imelda Smith, Apr. 29, 1903; children—Amédée Pierre, Carroll Jules; m. 2d, Corinne Pruitt, Aug. 15, 1917. Began practice at New Orleans, 1901; prof. radiology, Grad. Sch. of Medicine, Tulane, 1916-31, Med. Center, La. State U., from 1931; chief of service of radiology, Charity Hosp., 1905-21, dir. of dept. from 1921. Served in Hosp. Corps, U.S. Army, Spanish-Am. War. Mem. Radiological Soc. N. America (v.p. 1929; mem. com. on internat. relations), Coll. of Radiology (chancellor 1923-26), French-Speaking Doctors of N. America (v.p. 1934), La. State Soc. Radiology (pres. 1918), Orleans Parish Med. Soc. (pres. 1908), Am. Roentgen Ray Soc., Tex. Roentgen Ray Soc. (hon.), New Orleans Eye, Ear, Nose and Throat Club (hon.), Am. Med. Assn., Alpha Omega Alpha. Decorated Knight, French Legion of Honour; Knight Belgian Order of the Crown; Knight, Italian Order of the Crown; Gold Palmes Universitaires (France); awarded gold medal, Radiological Soc. N. America, 1926, 1st prize for best scientific exhibit, 1927. Club: Round Table. Author: Radiographic Atlas of the Pathological Changes of Bones and Joints, 1911; Radiological Study of the Para Nasal Sinuses and Mastoids, 1932. Discoverer of Granger's Sign and Granger's Line. Home: New Orleans, La.†

GRANGER, LESTER B., social service adminstr.; b. Newport News, Va., Sept. 16, 1896; s. William Randolph and Mary (Turpin) G.; grad. Dartmouth, 1918; postgrad. N.Y. U., 1921; profl. studies, N.Y. Sch. Social Work, 1925; D.H.L. (hon.), Dartmouth, 1946, Wilberforce U., 1947; LL.D., Oberlin Coll., 1952, Morris Brown Coll., 1952, Va. State Coll., 1953; D.H.L., Columbia, 1954; m. Harriet Forrester Lane, Aug. 11, 1923. Extension worker N.J. State Manual Sch., Bordontown, 1922-34; workers' ednl. sec. Nat. Urban League, 1934-38; sec. on Negro welfare Welfare Council of N.Y.C., 1938-40; asst. exec. sec. Nat. Urban League, 1940-41, exec. dir., 1941-61; Edgar B. Stern distinguished vis. prof. Dilliard U., New Orleans, 1962-66, vis. prof. urban sociology, 1966-76. Mem. President's com. on Equal Opportunity in Armed Services; chmn. Fed. Adv. Council on Employmeny Security. Decorated comdr. Royal Order of Phoenix (Greece); recipient Navy Medal for Distinguished Civilian Service, Pres.'s Medal for Merit. Vice pres. Am. Assn. Social Workers, 1942; pres. Nat. Conf. Social Work, 1952, Internat. Conf. Social Work, 1961; hon. pres. Internat. Council Social Welfare, 1964; bd. dirs. Council Social Work Edn. Home: New Orleans, La., Died Jan. 9, 1976.

GRANT, AMY (ALLISON), dramatic reader; b. Chicago, 1880; d. Samuel Veal and Dorcas Emma (Hill) G.; abroad 1905, 1907; Stanhope-Wheatcraft Dram. Sch., New York, 1898; U. of Chicago, 1899-1901; Chicago Mus. Coll., Dept. of Acting, 1 yr., 1901-02; Oxford U., Eng., 1 term, 1906; B.S., Columbia, 1908. Developed art of reciting with mus. accompaniment, having in her repertory "Enoch Arden" and about 100 other poems with musical setting, as well as the standard operas, which has arranged as readings with accompaniment from the vocal scores, making her own translations of the libretti; gives weekly recitals at Aeolian Hall, New York, following the repertory of the Met. and Chicago opera cos. Home: New York City, N.Y.†

GRANT, CHARLES LEON, ret. govt. ofcl.; b. Chester, S.C., June 14, 1915; s. Leon Mills and Janie Ethel (Lee) G.; student George Washington U., 1936-37, Grad. Sch. U.S. Dept. Agr., 1938-40; m. Nellie Flora Oliver, Sept. 18, 1940; children—Phy)lis Anne (Mrs. Bobby Edward Childers), Elizabeth Jane (Mrs. Jesse Landrum Kelly, Jr.), Charles Wayne. Accountant U.S. Weather Bur., 1935-41; fiscal accountant, budget analyst, asst. to dir. finance and chief div., Office Budget and Finance, Dept. Agr., 1941-53, dep. dir. finance, 1953-57, dir. finance, 1957-72. Consultant: Executive Management Services, Inc. 1973-74. Recipient Superior Service Award, USDA 1962, Distinguished Service Award, 1965. Baptist. Home: Arlington, VA. Died July 10, 1974; interred Meml. Park Cemetery, Falls Church, Va.

GRANT, DUNCAN CAMPBELL, railway exec.; b. Toronto, Can., June 1, 1880; s. Robert and Annie (Coulson) G.; ed. in public schools, high school and bus. college, Toronto; m. Mary L. McGlade (died 1942); children—Catherine May (Mrs. R. F. Daniels), Duncan Coulson, Mary Louise, (Mrs. C. V. W. Vickers). With Bank of Toronto, holding various positions, 1897-1924; vice pres. in charge finance and accounting Canadian Nat. Railways, Montreal, from 1924. Home: Montreal, Que., Can.†

GRANT, FREDERICK CLIFTON, clergyman, author; b. Beloit, Wis., Feb. 2, 1891; s. Frank Avery and Anna Lois (Jack) G.; ed. Lawrence Coll., Nashotah (Wis.) House; B.D., Gen. Theol. Sem., 1913, S.T.D. (honorary), 1952; S.T.M., Western Theol. Sem., 1916; Th.D., 1922, S.T.D., 1958; D.D., Nashotah House, 1927, Garrett Bibl. Inst., 1938; D.S. Litt., Kenyon Coll., 1939; L.H.D., U. Chgo., 1953; S.T.D., Gen. Theol. Sem., 1953, Va. Theol. Sem., 1959; D.C.L., Bishop's U., 1948; Litt.D., Princeton U., 1958; L.H.D. (honorary), Hebrew Union College, 1962; sr. Fulbright scholar Oxford U., 1959-60; married to Helen McQueen Hardie, June 24, 1913; children—Robert McQueen, Eleanor Jean. Deacon 1912, priest, 1913, P.E. Church; president Seabury-Western Theol. Sem., Evanston, 1927-38; prof. Biblical Theology, Union Theol. Sem., 1938-59, and director of graduate studies 1945-54; visiting prof., Univ. Chicago, 1928, 37, 63. Mem. Soc. Bibl. Lit. and Exegesis (pres., 1934), Chicago Soc. Bibl. Research (pres. 1924, 29). Mem. Gen. Conv. P.E. Ch. 1928, 31, 34, 37, and mem. commn. on marriage and divorce, 1928-40; commn. on hymnal, commn. on Constitution and Canons of P.E. Church, and commn. on ministry; chmn. com. on Christian edn., Diocese of Chicago, 1928-38; vice-pres. Am. Assn. Theol. Schools,

1936-38; mem. com. on revision of American Standard Revised Version of the Bible since 1937; mem. versions com. Am. Bible Soc., 1944-54. One of three observers Anglican Communion at Vatican Council, Rome, 1962-63. Author books including: The Practice of Religion, 1946; An Introduction to New Testament Thought, 1950; Commentaries, in Harper's Annotated Bible, 1952; Commentary on Mark, Interpreter's Bible, 1951; Hellenistic Religions, 1953; How to Read the Bible, 1956; Ancient Roman Religion, 1957; The Gospels, Their Origin and Growth, 1958; Ancient Judaism and the New Testament, 1959; Basic Christian Beliefs, 1959; Translating The Bible, 1961; Roman Hellenism and the New Testament, 1961; Banton Books New Testament, 1962; Dictionary of the Bible, 1963. Editor: Rev. Standard Version Bible Commentary, 1962. Editor in chief Anglican Theol. Rev., 1924-55. Chairman editorial bd. The Witness (weekly) 1941-45, book editor, 1945-52. Home: N.Y.C., N.Y. Died July 11, 1974.

GRANT, WALTER SCHUYLER, army officer; b. Ithaca, N.Y., Jan. 24, 1878; s. Chauncey Lewis and Martha (Schuyler) G.; B.S., U.S. Mil. Acad., 1900; grad. Army Sch. of the Line, Ft. Leavenworth, Kan., 1914. Gen. Staff Sch., 1915, Army War Coll., Washington, 1924; m. Marjorie Commiskey, Mar. 29, 1910; children—Walter Schuyler, Francis Commiskey, Marjorie Louise (wife of Hugh McClellan Exton, U.S. Army), Philip Schuyler. Commd. 2d lt., U.S. Army, 1900, and advanced through the grades to maj. gen., 1938; served in Boxer uprising, China, 1900; Philippine Insurrection, 1900-02, Mexican Border, various times, 1911-17; dep. chief of staff, 1st Army and chief of staff, 1st Army Corps, with A.E.F., France, Sept. 1918-Jan. 1919 (recommended by Gen Pershing to grade of brig. gen. for efficiency); Instr. Gen. Service Schools, 1921-23; instructor and dir. Army War Coll., 1923-27, asst. comdt. and comdt., 1935-37; chief of staff 1st Corps Area, 1931-33; comd. New York Port of Embarkation, 1937-38; comdr. Philippine Dept., 1939-40; comd. 3d Corps Area, Baltimore, Oct. 21, 1940-Aug. 22, 1941; retired, Jan. 31, 1942; recalled to active duty Feb. 1, 1942, and assigned on a continuing bd. of Gen. Officers, War Dept., Washington, relieved from active duty May 16, 1946. Decorated D.S.M., Legion of Merit (U.S.), Officer Legion of Honor (France), Officer Order of Leopold (Belgium). Roman Catholic. Home: Washington, D.C.†

GRANT, WILLIAM DANIEL, physician; b. Pueblo, Colo., Nov. 9, 1918; s. Oliver Spencer and Pauline Erma (McDowell) G.; M.D., U. Colo., 1943; m. Loraine R. Dahlen, Sept. 11, 1948; children—Katherine, William Daniel. Intern, U.S. Naval Hosp., Long Beach, Cal., 1944; resident in ophthalmology VA Hosp., Cleve., 1949-51; practice medicine specializing in ophthalmology, Pueblo, 1946-49. 51-55, Cleve., 1955-73; mem. med. staff Euclid (O.) Gen. Hosp., dir. ophthalmology, 1971-73. Bd. dirs. Sight Center. Served with M.C., USNR, 1944-46. Diplomate Am. Bd. Ophthalmology. Mem. A.M.A., Am. Acad. Ophthalmology and Otolaryngology. Home: Euclid, O. Died Jan. 7, 1973; buried Cleveland, O.

GRANVILLE-SMITH, WALTER, JR., ret. advt. exec.; b. Bellport, N.Y., June 20, 1905; s. Walter and Jessie May (Stout) Granville-S.; B.S. summa cum laude (Rufus Choate scholar), Dartmouth, 1926; m. Jean Masson, Apr. 5, 1930; children—Walter III, Beverly (Mrs. George A. Bullwinkel). With Young & Rubicam, Inc., 1928-33; v.p., media dir. Ruthrauff & Ryan, Inc., 1934-47; v.p., dir. media planning Biow Co., Inc., 1947-55; v.p. William Esty Co., Inc., 1955-65. Mem. Phi Beta Kappa, Zeta Psi. Republican. Episcopalian. Clubs: Larchmont Yacht, Dartmouth; Coral Beach (Bermuda). Home: Harrison, N.Y. Died Feb. 1, 1974.

GRASSIE, HERBERT J., naval officer; b. Cohasset, Mass., Dec. 12, 1894; s. John Jason and Caroline Elizabeth (Neagle) G.; B.S., U.S. Naval Acad., 1916; student Naval War Coll., Newport, R.I., 1923-24; m. Angela Sullivan, Mar. 21, 1923; 1 son, Herbert John. Commd. ensign, U.S.N., 1916, and advanced through grades to commodore, 1945; served on transports and destroyers, World War I, on gunboats, Asiatic waters, 1924-26; instr., dept. seamanship and navigation, U.S. Naval Acad., 1931-34; comdr. destroyers, U.S.S. Humphreys and McDonough, 1935-37; in Navy Dept., Washington, 1937-40, 1942-44; exec. officer, U.S.S. Nevada, 1940-41; comdr. attack transport, U.S.S. J. Franklin Bell, 1941-42; comdr., U.S.S. Idaho, at Guam, Pellieu, Iwo Jima, Okinawa, 1944-45; comdr., Naval Training Center, Great Lakes, Ill., 1945-49, retired as rear admiral, 1949; pres. Lewis Coll. of Science and Tehcnology 1949-54. Awarded Bronze Star (with 1 star for second award), Legion of Merit, World War I Victory Medal (with 1 star and transport clasp), Am. Defense Ribbon (1 star), Am. Theater Ribbon, Asiatic-Pacific Theater Ribbon (with 4 stars), World War II Victory Ribbon, Philippine Liberation Ribbon. Mem. U.S. Naval Inst., Am. Legion, Roman Catholic. Club: Army-Navy Country (Washington). Address: Coronado, Cal. Died Oct. 1973.

GRATON, L(OUIS) C(ARYL), mining geologist; b. Parma, N.Y., June 10, 1880; s. Louis and A. Ella (Gould) G.; B.S., Cornell U., 1900, Ph.D., 1930, A.M., (hon.), Harvard, 1941; LL.D., University of California, 1964; postgraduate work, McGill Univ., Can.; m. Josephine Edith Bowman, June 30, 1906 (dec. Feb. 3, 1952); children—Louis Bowman, Josephine Gould (Mrs. Philip W. Chase); m. 2d, Mrs. Marion Petitpain Hart, Mar. 5, 1953. Mem. U.S. Geological Survey, 1903-09; secretary-treasurer Copper Producers' Assn., New York, 1909-15; prof. mining geology, Harvard, 1912-49, emeritus, after 1949; former hon. fellow in geology Yale Sec. Copper Producers' Committee for War Service, 1917-19; charge copper mine valuation, U.S. Revenue Bur., 1919-20; cons. engr. U.S. Bur. Mines, 1930-31; mem. com. on mineral resources Nat. Sci. Found., 1952-60; cons. geologist various mining companies; director, member policy committee Cerro Corporation, Cerro de Pasco Corp. Recipient Penrose Gold Medal from Soc. Econ. Geologists, 1950. Fel. Am. Acad. Arts and Scis.; fgn. asso. Mex. Nat. Acad. Scis.; hon. mem. Geol. Soc. Belgium, Geol. Soc. Peru; fgn. mem. Geol Soc. London; mem. Geol. Soc. Can., Am. Inst. Min. and Metall. Engrs., Canadian Inst. Mining and Metall. Engrs., Geol. Soc. America, Geol. Soc. Washington, A.A.A.S., Washington Acad. Sci., Mining and Metall. Soc. Am., Soc. Econ. Geol. (pres. 1931), Geochem. Soc., Am. Geophys. Union, S. African Instn. Mining and Metallurgy, Geol. Soc. S. Africa, Mineral Soc. Am. Author reports on geology of mining dists. and principles of ore deposition. Asso. editor: Economic Geology. Home: Orange, Conn.†

GRAVATT, JOHN JAMES, bishop; b. Hampton, Va., Oct. 3, 1881; s. John James and Indie Wray (Jones) G.; student McGuire's Sch., Richmond, Va., 1893-1900; A.B., U. of Va., 1903; student P.E. Theol. Sem., Alexandria, Va., 1905-08, hon. D.D., 1932; D.D., U. of the South, 1939; m. Helen Stevens, April 19, 1922 (deceased); children—Helen Stevens, George Stevens (deceased). Teacher McGuire's School, 1903-05; ordained deacon, P.E. Church, 1908, priest, 1909; assistant secretary Church Students Missionary Association, 1908-09; student sec. Bd. Missions Episcopal Ch., 1909-11; rector Slaughters Parish, Rapidan, Va., 1911-13, Ch. of the Ascension, Frankfort, Ky., 1913-18; chaplain, U.S. Army, with A.E.F., 1918-19; rector Trinity Ch., Staunton, Va., 1919-39; bishop Upper South Carolina from 1939; pres. Trustees of P.E. Ch. in Upper S.C.,; pres. Episcopal Ch. Home for Children, York; pres. P.E. Soc. for Advancement of Christianity in Upper S.C. Trustee U. of the South; mem. board of directors Kanuga Conferences, Inc. Received Beaver award, Boy Scouts America, Member Delta Tau Delta. Mason, Club: Rotary (Columbia, S.C.). Home: Columbia, S.C.†

GRAVEN, BRUCE, lawyer; b. Trinity, N.C., May 14, 1881; s. J. L. (M.D.) and Nannie (Bulla) C.; g.s. Braxton Graven, D.D., LL.D., founder and 1st pres.-Trinity Coll., N.C.; educated at Duke University; m. Clara Chaffin, of Mocksville, N.C., Nov. 5, 1901; 1 son, Braxton Craven (lawyer). Was superintendent of schs., and newspaper editor 9 yrs.; admitted to N.C. bar, 1909, and practiced at Trinity, specializing in municipal bonds. Maj. judge advocate, U.S.A.; connected with Bd. of Review of court martial proceedings, later with Legal Advisory Bd. of War Dept., Washington, D.C.; hon. discharged, Sept. 4, 1919. Methodist. Democrat. Mason. Author: Torrens Land Title System, 1914; Federal Income Tax, 1916. Contbr. to mags. and newspapers. Home: Trinity, N.C.†

GRAY, DANIEL THOMAS, agrl. educator; b. Harrison Co., Mo., Jan. 27, 1878; s. William L. and Miriam (Crews) G.; A.B., B.S., U. of Mo., 1904; M.S., U. of Ill., 1905; m. Lillian Dale Hardin, of Stanberry, Mo., Sept. 5, 1901; children—Daniel T. (dec.), Emily Dale, Lillian Vera. Prof. animal industry, Ala. Poly. Inst., 1905-13; prof. same, State Coll. Agr. and Engring., Raleigh, N.C., 1913-20; in charge U.S. Govt. live stock extension work in the South during World Wars; dean Agrl. Coll. and dir. Expt. Sta., Ala. Poly. Inst., 1920-23; dean Agrl. Coll. and dir. Expt. Sta. and extension service, U. of Arkansas, 1924-35, dean and director College of Agriculture, 1935-39, retired July 1, 1939; then farmer; leave of absence, 1934-35, as regional dir. of 5 states, U.S. Dept. Agr. Mem. Assn. Agrl. Workers (sec. 1913-20; pres. 1920-21), Ark. State Planning Bd., State Forestry Commn. of Ark., Sigma Xi, Alpha Zeta, Alpha Gamma Rho. Sigma. Delta. Animal industry editor Southern Ruralist, Protestant. Author of numerous agrl. bulls. Home: Fayetteville, Ark.†

GRAY, ERNEST WESTON, educator; b. Scituate, Mass., Dec. 19, 1902; s. Ernest Weston and Dora Frances (Harwood) G.; student Northeastern U., 1919-22; Ph.B., Brown U., 1924, A.M., 1926; Ph.D., Harvard, 1931; m. Gladys Margaret Bauer, June 24, 1926; 1 dau., Anne Harwood. Instr. English, Brown U., 1925-28; asst. prof. English, asso. prof., prof. Coll. William and Mary, Norfolk (Va.) div., 1931-47; prof. English, U. Toledo, 1947-74, chmn. dept. English, 1949-60, dir. honors program, 1965-70, ret., 1970. Mem. Coll. English Assn., Nat. Council Tchrs. English, Am. Assn. U. Profs., Phi Beta Kappa, Phi Kappa Phi. Home: Attleboro, Mass. Died Apr. 21, 1974; buried Hillside Cemetery, Attleboro, Mass.

GRAY, LEWIS CECIL, economist; b. Liberty, Mo., Dec. 2, 1881; s. Lewis Pressley and Elizabeth (Chambliss) G.; B.A., William Jewell Coll., Liberty, 1900, M.A., 1903; student Univ. of Chicago, summers, 1907-08; Ph.D., U. of Wis., 1911; LL.D., William Jewell College, 1927; m. Pearl B. Patterson, 1905; children—Mrs. Marceline E. Eder, Emily Belle, Lois Cecilia, John Lewis. Prof. history and economics, Okla. Agrl. and Mech. Coll., 1905-08; instr. economics, U. of Wis., 1910-13; prof. economics, U. of Saskatchewan, 1913-15; prof. rural economics, George Peabody Coll. for Teachers, Nashville, Tenn., 1915-19; became economist in charge div. of land economics, U.S. Bur. Agrl. Economics, Apr. 1919, then asst. chief of Bureau; asst. adminstr., Resettlement Adminstration, Dec. 1935; later became asst. to sec. of state. Special agent Bureau of Census, 1911; in charge price fixing div., U.S. Food Adminstration, State of Tenn., 1918; chmn. special com. on land utilization apptd. by Sec. of Agriculture; dir. of land use section, Nat. Resources Com.; mem. President Roosevelt's Great Plains Com. and executive secretary President's Farm Tenancy Committee. Mem. Am. Econ. Assn., Am. Farm Econ. Assn. Represented U.S. Dept. Agr. at meeting of Internat. Inst. Agr., Rome, 1922, 28. Democrat. Christian Scientist. Club: Cosmos. Author: An Introduction to Agricultural Economics; History of Agriculture in the Southern United States to 1860; also numerous articles and bulls. Home: Chevy Chase, Md.†

GRAY, RALPH WELD, architect; b. Boston, Mass., Jan. 19, 1880; s. Samuel Shober and Caroline Balch (Weld) G.; student Noble & Greenough Sch., 1891-97; A.B., Harvard, 1901; studied Ecole des Beaux Arts, Paris, 1904-07; m. Georgiana Hemingway, Dec. 26, 1921. Architect after 1907; prin. works: River Street Bridge, Boston, Monument in Memory of Governor John Endicott. Capt. inf., A.E.F., U.S. Army, 1917-19; detached to French Army for liaison duty, 1918-19. Awarded Croix de Guerre. Fellow Am. Inst. Architects; mem. Boston Soc. of Architects (ex-pres.), Am. Water Color Soc., Guild of Boston Artists, Boston Soc. of Water Color Painters. Unitarian. Clubs: Tavern, Somerset (Boston); Harvard (New York). Home: Boston, Mass.†

GRAY, WALTER H., bishop; b. Richmond, Va., Aug. 20, 1898; s. William Cole and Irena Hanswood (Talley) G.; student Coll. William and Mary, U. Richmond Law Sch.; B.D., Va. Episcopal Theol. Sem., 1928 (hon.), D.D., 1941; hon. S.T.D., Berkeley Divinity Sch., 1940, Trinity Coll., Hartford, Conn., 1941; D.D., U. Richmond, 1954, Wycliffe Coll., Toronto, Can., 1962; D.C.L., U. of South, 1960; L.H.D., U. Hartford, 1962; D. Canon Law, Berkeley Div. Sch., 1969; m. Virginia Stuart Hutchinson, Feb. 4, 1933; children—Agatha Ashton (Mrs. J. T. Cabaniss, Jr.), Parke Hanswood. Admitted to Va. bar, 1925; ordained deacon, P.E. Church, 1928, priest 1929; asst. rector St. John's Ch., West Hartford, Conn., 1928-32; dean Nativity Pro-Cathedral, Bethlehem, Pa., 1932-36; dean Christ Ch. Cathedral, Hartford, 1937-40; suffragan bishop Diocese of Conn. 1940-45, bishop coadjutor, 1945-51, bishop, 1951-69, bishop emeritus, 1969-73. Pres. Province of New Eng., P.E. Ch. Chmn. 3d Lambeth Conf. Com., Nat. Council. P.E. Ch., 1958; chmn. com. arrangements Anglican Congress 1954. Pres. Ch. Missions Pub. Co.; trustee Trinity Coll., Hartford, St. Stephen's Sch., Rome, Italy; corporator Inst. of Living, Mt. Sinai Hosp., Hartford. Served with 29th Div., U.S. Army, 1917-19, AEF; 2d lt. inf., later 1st lt., Cav., O.R.C. to 1933. Pres. Trustees of Colt Bequest, St. Margaret's Sch., Episcopal Acad. of Conn. Brewster Mem. Corp., Trustees of Donations and Bequests, Glebe House Soc., Ch. Home of Hartford, Ch. Scholarship Soc. Mem. S.R. in Va., Soc. Colonial Wars (Conn. chaplain, chaplain gen.), Soc. Cincinnati (Conn. chaplain), Kappa Alpha, Delta Theta Phi. Clubs: Farmington (Conn.) Country; University, Hartford (Hartford); Graduates (New Haven); Commonwealth (Richmond) Editor: Pan Anglican. Author: Our Belief, 1945; Faith in the Right (anthem), 1945; Future Course of the Anglican Communion, 1946; A Bishop's Carol, 1966. Home: Hartford, Conn. Died Dec. 4, 1973.

GRAY, WILLARD FRANKLIN, univ. adminstr.; b. Flint, Tex., Dec. 25, 1913; s. John Franklin and Leona (Booth) G.; B.S. in Elec. Engring., Tex. Tech. Coll., 1934; M.S. in Elec. Engring., Tex. A. and M. U., 1940; m. Clotyde Roberts, Jan. 2, 1937; children—Jay Willard, Paula Kay (Mrs. Clyde Samuel Precise). Jr. engr. Tex. Power and Light Co., Dallas, 1934-37; mem. faculty Tex. Tech. Coll., 1937-46, asso. prof. elec. engring., 1943-46; asst. prof. elec. engring. Mass. Inst. Tech., 1946-47; mem. faculty U. Ala., 1947-73, prof. elec. engring., head dept., 1959-66, asst. v.p. acad. affairs, 1966-68, asst. v.p. adminstrn., 1968-71, asso. acad. v.p., dean adminstrn., 1971-73; cons. to bus. and industry, 1950-73. Mem. panels evaluation applications for undergrad. instructional equipment NSF, 1965-66; mem. Charles LeGeyt Fortescue fellowship panel I.E.E.E. 1966-73. Mem. Am. Soc. Engring. Edn. (chmn. elec. engring. div. 1964-65, chmn. prizes and award div. elec. engring. 1967-73), I.E.E.E., Nat. Soc. Profl. Engrs., Am. Assn. U. Profs., Tau Beta Pi, Eta Kappa Nu. Theta Tau, Pi Tau Chi, Omicron Delta Kappa. Methodist. Registered profl. engr., Ala. Home: Tuscaloosa, Ala. Died July 7, 1973.

GREAVES, FREDERICK CLARENCE, naval med. officer; b. Ladora, Ia., Nov. 11, 1896; s. Frederick and Magdalene (Bergman) G.; M.D., State U. Ia., 1920; m. Rose Torbol, Aug. 11, 1923; children—Richard F.,

Thomas F., Bobbe (Mrs. E. W. Cooke). Intern Northern Pacific Hosp., Brainerd, Minn., 1920-21; asst. surgeon, med. corps, U.S. Navy, 1923, advanced through grades to rear adm., 1950; fleet med. officer 8th Fleet, Mediterranean, 1943-45, Pacific Fleet, 1947-49. Inspector Naval med. activities, Pacific Coast, and dist. med. officer Twelfth Naval Dist., 1954-58; ret., 1958. Fellow A.C.P.; mem. A.M.A. Home: San Francisco, Cal. Died Died May 20, 1973.

GREELEY, MELLEN CLARK, architect; b. Jacksonville, Fla., Feb. 14, 1880; s. Jonathan Clark and Leonora (Keep) G.; student Lawrenceville (N.J.) Sch., 1893-97; m. Alice Driggs Seeley, June 23, 1904; children—Barbara (Mrs. Frank O. Miller Jr.) Phyllis (Mrs. Richard S. Paine Jr.). Studied in archtl. offices in Jacksonville (Fla.) and New York City, 1901-09; pvt. practice under own name, Jacksonville, from 1909; among clients are U.S. Treasury Dept. (remodeled U.S. Post Office and Custom House, St. Augustine, Fla.), Fed. Pub. Housing Adminstrn., State of Fla., several counties in Fla., City of Jacksonville, Ch. of Good Shepherd, Jacksonville (with J.W.C. Corbusiev, Cleveland, O.) Woman's Club of Jacksonville and others. Served with 3rd U.S. Volunteer Engrs. with service in Cuba, Spanish-Am. War, 1898-99; mem. Fla. Nat. Guard, 1899 to 1910, capt. Q.M. Corps, 1918-19. Fellow A.I.A. (charter mem. and past pres. Fla. chapter, 1921 and Fla. north chapter 1928 and 1946); mem. bd. supervising architects Fla. Hotel Commn., 1928-38; pres. Nat. Council Archtl. Registration Bds. 1939-42. Mem. Fla. state bd. of architecture, (sec.-treas. from 1923), Jacksonville planning adv. bd. (sec.-treas. 1928-47). Democrat. Episcopalian. Findings of studies and research relative to damage to bldgs. by termites and fungi, pub. by A.I.A. in The Octagon, Mar., 1931. Home: Arlington, Fla.†

GREELY, ANTOINETTE, industrial service expert; b. Washington, D.C., June 2, 1879; d. Maj. Gen. Adolphus W. (U.S.A.) and Henrietta H. C. (Nesmith) G.; edn. finished by course of 1 yr. at Convent of Assumption, Paris, France. Investigated working conditions and housing methods in France and in England; began in employ Curtis Pub. Co., Phila., 1906, seeking improvement of labor relations, later with John Wanamaker (Phila.), Bryan, Marsh & Co. (now Gen. Electric Co.), and with the Bush Terminal Co. (New York), where she initiated conf. that ended the strike of ry. trainmen; employed by Nashua Mfg. Co., Nashua, N.H., 1916; organizing employment bureaus for corpns. with war orders, Washington, 1917-18; with Henry Disston & Sons, Tacony, Pa., Oct. 1919; now in employ Dolphin Jute Mills, Paterson, N.J. Mem. Nat. Soc. Colonial Dames of America. Episcopalian. Home: Washington, D.C.†

GREEN, ABEL, editor of Variety; b. N.Y.C., June 3, 1900; s. Seymour A. and Berta (Raines) G.; student N.Y. U.; m. Gracelyn Adele Fenn, June 3, 1921. Organizer theatrical news coverage European, N. African, S. Am. capitals for Variety mag., 1929-30; as theatrical trade reporter, writer, editor; recognized as an authority on contemporary film, TV, radio, state, music, nightclub, concert, Tin Pan Alley, vaudeville 1921—; editor of Variety —. Co-author, producer Philco-Variety Radio Hall Fame, coast-to-coast, Blue Network radio hour. Author: Mr. Broadway, Warner Bros. film saga of Variety's founder-editor-publisher, the late Sime Silverman, 1947; Tin Pan Alley; Outward Bound and Gagged; Show Biz (From Vaude to Video) (with Joe Laurie, Jr.), 1952. Editor: Variety Music Cavalcade, 1952, latest rev. edit., 1971; The Spice of Variety, 1953; ann. anthologist, Show Biz, Am. Peoples Ency.; contbr. articles on theatrical world to nat. mags. Decorated medal of Merit (Italy). Mem. Motion Picture Pioneers, Skeeters, A.S.C.A.P. Club: Variety (N.Y.C.). Home: N.Y.C. N.Y. Died May 10, 1973; cremated.

GREEN, CONSTANCE MCLAUGHLIN, author; b. Ann Arbor, Mich., Aug. 21, 1897; d. Andrew Cunningham and Lois Thompson (Angell) McLaughlin; student U. Chgo., 1914-16; A.B., Smith Coll., 1919, Litt.D., 1963; M.A., Mt. Holyoke Coll., 1925; Ph.D., Yale, 1937; m. Donald Ross Green, Feb. 14, 1921 (dec. 1946); children—Lois Angell (Mrs. Jack Ladd Carr), Donald Ross, Elizabeth L. Faculty, U. Chgo., 1919-20, Mt. Holyoke Coll., 1925-32, Smith Coll., 1939-47; historian Army Ordnance Dept., Springfield, Mass., 1942-45, A.R.C., Washington, 1947-48; chief historian ordnance Army Hist. Div., Dept. Def.; 1948-51; historian research and devel. bd. Office Sec. Def., 1951-54; dir. Washington History Project, Am. U., 1954-60. Commonwealth Fund lectr. Univ. Coll., U. London, 1951. Grantee Rockefeller Found., Chapelbrook Found. Recipient Pultizer prize for History, 1963. Mem. Am. Hist. Assn., Econ. History Assn., U.S. Capitol Hist. Soc., Washington Lit. Soc. Author: Washington, Village and Capital, 1800-1878, Vol. 1, 1962; Washington: Capital City, 1963; American Cities in the Growth of the Nation, 1957; Eli Whitney and the Birth of American Technology, 1956; The Rise of Urban America, 1965; The Secret City: A History of Race Relations in the Nations Capital, 1967; others. Contbr. to various jours., books, Ency. Brit., Ency. Am., book revs. Home: Washington, D.C., Died Dec. 5, 1975.

GREEN, CRAWFORD RICHMOND, physician; b. Troy, N.Y., Sept. 8, 1881; s. Arba Read and Lydia (Richmond) G.; prep. edn. Troy Acad.; A.B., Brown U., 1902; M.D., N.Y. Medical College and Flower Hosp., 1906; m. Helen Waterman, 1907 (died, 1944); children—Carleton, Warren James; m. 2d, Janet Greenhill Parker, 1946. Practiced at Troy from 1907; specialized in internal medicine; now consulting phys., Samaritan Hosp.; mem. dir. James A. Eddy Memorial Foundation. Trustee Troy Pub. Library, Russell Sage Coll. Fellow Am. Coll. Phys.; diplomate Am. Bd. Internal Medicine; mem. A.M.A., N.Y. State Med. Assn. Homoe. Med. Soc. State of N.Y., Am. Inst. Homoeopathy, S.R., Delta Phi, Phi Alpha Gamma, Phi Betta Kappa. Club: Troy. Home: Troy, N.Y.†

GREEN, DWIGHT PHELPS, lawyer; b. Fulton, Ill., Oct. 13, 1886; s. Nathaniel and Elizabeth (Baker) G.; grad. pub. schs., Fulton, 1904; grad. Morgan Park Acad., 1905; A.B., Princeton, 1909; J.D., U. of Chgo. Law Sch., 1912; m. Ella K. Porter, Oct. 10, 1914; (dec. 1970); 1 son, Dwight Phelps; m. 2d. Elizabeth Earle. Admitted to Ill. bar, 1912, and since practiced in Chicago; asso. with firm of Kirkland, Ellis, Hodson, Chaffetz & Masters and its predecessors from beginning of practice, admitted as partner, 1919, and to firm name in 1928, retired, 1958, now counsel to the firm. Member of Am. Ill. State and Chicago bar assns., Phi Delta Phi. Democrat. Baptist. Clubs: Law, Legal, University, Indian Hill Country, Chicago, Mid Day. Home: Winnetka, Ill. Died Aug. 1975.

GREEN, EDWARD AVERILL, actuary; b. Morgantown, W.Va., May 14, 1907; s. Robert Rodman and Mary Lyon (Purinton) G.; student Rutgers U., 1925-28; A.B., Yale, 1930; m. Doris Harriette Hinman, Aug. 12, 1933; children—Deborah (Mrs. William D. Morrison), Martha (Mrs. David K. Cuthbert). With actuarial dept. State Mut. Life Assurance Co., Worcester, Mass., 1930-41, asst. actuary, 1941-46, asso. actuary, 1946-48; 2d v.p. John Hancock Mut. Life Ins. Co., Boston, 1948-54, v.p. 1954-56, v.p., group actuary, 1956-69, sr. v.p., group actuary, 1969-72, cons., 1972-75. Instr. bus., statistics and forecasting Worcester br. Northeastern U., 1939-42. Mem. joint group com. Life Ins. Assn. Am. and Am. Life Conv., 1946-57. Mem. budget com. Newton (Mass.) Community Chest, 1956-57, chmn., 1958; gov's com. studying pension laws of Mass., 1954-55. Trustee Newton-Wellesley Hosp., 1966--, bd. govs., 1969-74, chmn. personnel com., 1970-75, chmn. task force devel. ambulatory care services, 1974-75. Fellow Soc. Actuaries; mem. Boston Actuaries Club. Club: Brae Burn Country (West Newton, Mass.). Home: West Newton, Mass., Died Aug. 12, 1975; interred Fairview Cemetery, North Stratford, N.H.

GREEN, ESTILL I., elec. engr.; b. St. Louis, Nov. 24, 1895; s. John F. and Eleanor (Ibbotson) G.; A.B., Westminster Coll., 1915; B.S., in Elec. Engring., Harvard, 1921; Sc.D. (honorary), Westminster College, 1956; married Sara V. Grant, Jan. 5, 1918; 1 dau., Wanda Mae. With dept. development and research Am. Tel. & Tel. Co., 1921-34; with Bell Telephone Labs., Murray Hill, N.J., 1934-74, dir. transmission apparatus devel., 1948-53, dir. mil. communication systems, 1953-55, v.p., 1955-58, exec. v.p., 1959-60, dir.; dir., research cons. United-Carr Fastener Corp., Xerox Corp., 1960-74; research cons. IBM Corp., 1960-74. Trustee Westminster Coll. Served as capt. inf. U.S. Army, 1917-19. Fellow Am. Inst. E.E. (dir.), I.R.E., Acoustical Soc. Am., A.A.A.S.; mem. Torrey Bot. Club, Nat. Audubon Soc. Address: Short Hills, N.J. Died June 24, 1974; buried Bellfontaine Cemetery, St Louis, Mo.

GREEN, GARNER LELAND, educator, poet; b. Franklin, Vt., Apr. 22, 1883; s. Lucius Davis and Cora Belle (Chamberlin) G.; B.S., U. of Vt., Coll. of Agr., 1906; hon. Pd.D., Univ. of Georgia, 1928; Ed.D., Univ. of Vt., 1936; m. Flora Gertrude Humphrey, July 10, 1907; children—Gardner H., Gordon L., Randolph B., Virginia B. Teacher of science, Thetford (Vt.) Acad., 1906-07; prin. high sch., Highgate, Vt., 1907-08, Franklin, 1908-09, Richford, 1909-11; prin. Vt. State Sch. of Agr., Randolph Center, Vt., Aug. 1, 1911-20, except Y.M.C.A. work in France, 1918; prin. The Berry Schools, Mount Berry, Ga., 1920-31; pres. Berry Coll., Mount Berry, 1931-1944; chairman of the division of education 1944-54. Specialty was rural organization and cooperation; ednl. bldgs. named in his honor at Randolph Centre, 1969, Berry Coll., Mount Berry. Winner Kaleidography poetry mag. quatrain prize, 1939; Page poet American Bard poetry magazine 1950 (1st prize winner Peace and Unity poetry contest). Member Vt. State Teachers' Assn. (v.p. and chmn. 1919 conv.), Civil Legion, Ga. Edn. Assn. (v.p. 1939), Ga. Teachers Edn. Council (chmn. div. edn. and instructor creative writing from 1944), Poetry Soc. Am., American Poetry League, Acad. of Am. Poets, Poetry Soc. of Ga., Bookfellows Club, Midwest Poetry League, Pi Gamma Mu, Omicron Delta Kappa, Kappa Sigma, Phi Beta Kappa. County dir. Boys's Working Reserve; mem. Pub. Safety Com.; "4-minute man." Democrat. Mason. Clubs: University (Randolph, Vt.); Kiwanis of Rome (pres. 1939); The Upward Quest (verse), 1943; These Will Remain (verse), 1948. Contbr. verse to anthologies, magazines and newspapers. Lecturer on agrl. topics and rural betterment. Home: Rome, Ga., Died Mar. 6, 1971; interred Berry Coll. Chapel, Mount Berry, Ga.

GREEN, HAROLD ROY, dentist; b. Bridgeport, O., Sept. 1, 1921; s. James W. and Helen (Davis) G.; B.S., Muskinqum Coll., 1943; D.D.S., O. Pitts., 1945; postgrad. U. Mich., 1950-60; m. Dorothy Smith, Oct. 18, 1945; children—Sue Lorraine (Mrs. Ferris L. Grooss), Margaret-Ruth, Patricia-Lee. Pvt. practice children's denistry, Wheeling, W.Va., 1947-72. Asso. prof. dental materials West Liberty (W.Va.) Coll., 1958-65. Pres. Mental Health, Belmont County, O., 1964-65. Served to lt. (j.g.) USNR, 1945-47; now comdr. Res. Fellow Internat. Coll. Denistry, Am. Coll. Denistry; mem. W.Va. State Dental Assn. (pres. 1963), Am. Legion, Psi Omega. Republican. Methodist. Mason (Shriner), Eagle. Editor W.Va. Dental Jour., 1959-72. Home: Clairsville, O. Died Mar. 16, 1972.

GREEN, HARRY E., cement mfr.; b. Linton, Ind., May 17, 1907; s. William Miller and Fanny Pearl (Foulke) G.; grad. Browns Bus. Coll., Terre Haute, Ind., 1925; extension student Ind. U.; m. Lucile Dyar, Aug. 9, 1930; 1 son, Harry Thomas; m. 2d, Freda Oddo Byrnes, Oct. 8, 1968. With Lone Star Cement Corporation, N.Y.C., 1925—, v.p., treas., 1958-65, exec. v.p. adminstrn. and finance, 1965-66, exec. v.p., 1966-67, pres., chief exec. officer, 1967-69, chairman of the board, 1968-69, also director. Member of Portland Cement Assn., Financial Execs. Inst. Am. Mining Congress. Methodist. Clubs: Union League (N.Y.C.); Siwanoy Country (Bronxville, N.Y.); Scarsdale Golf (Hartsdale, N.Y.). Home: White Plains, N.Y. Died Aug. 14, 1973.

GREEN, JOHN M., newspaper editor. Editor, L.I. Daily Press Pub. Co., Jamaica, N.Y. Office: Jamaica, N.Y. Deceased.

GREEN, JOSHUA, banker; b. Jackson, Miss., Oct. 16, 1869; s. William Henry Harrison and Bentonia (Johnston) G.; student pvt. schs.; m. Laura Moore Turner, Apr. 24, 1901; children—Bentonia Johnston (Mrs. A. G. Rez), Frances Turner (Mrs. C. P. Burnett, Jr.), Joshua, Jr. Clerk in post office, Jackson, 1883; purser on S.S. Henry Bailey, 1888-90; mate on S.S. Fannie Lake, 1890; master of S.S. T. W. Lake and other vessels, 1891-96; pres. LaConner Trading & Transportation Co., 1896-1901; Puget Sound Nav. Co., 1901-28; chmn. bd. Peoples Nat. Bank of Washington, Seattle, Wash., 1926-62 hon. chairman of the board, 1962-74; dir. C.M. St.P.&P. Ry. Co., Elec. Products Consol., Seattle Brewing & Malting Co., No. Life Ins. Co., Gen. Am. Ins. Co., Puget Sound Power & Light Co. Chmn. bd. Riverton Gen. Hosp.; dir. Pioneer Assn. State of Wash.; curator, Washington Historical Society; director Seattle C. of C. Mem. Newcomen Soc., S.A.R., Puget Sound Maritime Hist. Soc., Seattle Hist. Soc. Vestryman St. Mark's Episcopal Cathedral. Clubs: Propeller of U.S. (Port of Seattle); Rainier, Washington Seniors Golf Assn., Washington Athletic, Seattle Tennis, Seattle Golf and Country; Seniors Northwest Golf Assn., Union (Victoria, B.C.). Home: Seattle, Wash. Died Jan. 1975.

GREEN, LESLLE H., automotive materials co. exec.; b. Detroit, June 18, 1886; s. Edmund Henry and Caroline M. (Betz) G.; ed. pub. schs. of Detroit; m. Edith M. Cornyn, Sept. 28, 1907; 1 son, Robert Newton. Pres. Automotive Materials Corp., 1921-48, chmn. bd., 1948-73; chmn. bd. Standard Cotton Products Co., Flint, Mich.; dir. Detroit Bank & Trust Co. Trustee Brighton (Mich.) Hosp., Detroit Mus. Art Founders Soc., St. Peter's Home for Boys, Detroit. Mem. Detroit Zool. Soc. Episcopalian. Clubs: Detroit, Detroit Athletic, Recess; Bloomfield Hills Country, Forest Lake Country (Bloomfield Hills, Mich.). Home: Bloomfield Hills Mich. Died Aug. 10, 1973.

GREEN, PAUL MARTIN, coll. dean.; b. East Liverpool, O., Apr. 26, 1902; s. Edward Lawrence and Annie J. (Martin) G.; A.B., Miami U., 1926, LL.D., 1952; M.S., U. Ill., 1927, Ph.D., 1933, postgrad. law, 1933-34; m. Hilda Jane McCoy, Sept. 9, 1930; 1 dau., Jane Ellsworth. Prof. accounting U. Fla., 1934, 41; head research accountant FHA, 1934-37; dep. adminstr. charge accounting OPA, 1941-47; controller AEC, 1947-50; professorial lectr. George Washington U., 1949; controller ECA, 1950-52; asst. dir. charge accounting OPS, 1951-52; instr. accounting, finance U. Ill., 1926-34, asst. prof. econs. in charge corp. finance, 1937-41, prof. head div. mgmt., 1949-51, dean Coll. Commerce and Bus. Adminstrn., 1952-67, emeritus, 1967-74, prof. mgmt., 1952-57, prof. bus. adminstrn., 1957-67, emeritus, 1967-74, dir. Grad. Sch. Bus. Adminstrn., 1952-54, 59-67, emeritus, 1967-74; dean Coll. Bus. Adminstrn., prof. Fla. Tech. U., 1967-68; exec. dean for bus. schs., prof. bus. and econs. Stetson U., Deland, Fla., 1968-69. Cons. accounting and mgmt. govt. agys.; dep. asst. sec. def., 1961-62. Pres., Council for Profl. Edn. for Bus., 1959-60. Mem. Am. Econ. Assn., Am. Accounting Assn., Royal Econ. Soc., Fed. Govt. Accountants Assn., Am. Statis. Assn., Am. Assn. Collegiate Schs. Bus. (pres. 1957-58), Am. Finance Assn., Phi Beta Kappa, Phi Kappa Phi, Delta Sigma Pi (scholarship key 1926), Beta Alpha Psi, Phi Delta Phi, Beta Gamma Sigma, Artus, Beta Nu Kappa, Sigma Iota Epsilon, Pi Gamma Mu, Sigma Alpha Epsilon. Presbyn. Club: Union League (Chgo.). Contbr. articles to tech. publs. Home: Urbana, Ill. Died May 12, 1974.

GREEN, WYMAN REED, prof. biology; b. Moultrie County, Ill., June 1, 1881; s. John Rogers and Mary Jane (Jones) G.; life diploma, State Teachers' Coll., Alva, Okla., 1907; A.B., A.M., U. of Kan., 1911; Ph.D., U. of Chicago, 1919; m. Frances La Vergne Powers, June 16, 1920 (died Aug. 1922); 1 son, Francis Powers; m. 2d, Sophie Anna Bachofen, June 2, 1929; children—Wyman Reed, Henry Albert. Assistant in biology, State Teachers' Coll., Alva., 1908-10; head dept. biology, Wichita (Kansas) High Sch., 1911-12; fellow U. of Chicago, 1912-14; instr. zoology, Carleton Coll., Northfield, Minn., 1914-19, Northwestern U., 1919-20; head dept. biology, U. of Chattanooga, 1920-31; head dept. biology, Drew U., after 1931. Mem. Sigma Xi. Presbyn. Home: Madison, N.J.†

GREENBAUM, DAVID, musician; b. Glasgow, Scotland, Mar. 29, 1908; s. Barnet and Annie (Wasserstrum) G.; ed. Scottish Nat. Acad., Royal Coll. Music London; m. Hilda Feinblatt, Apr. 29, 1938; children—Joan (Mrs. William Goldsmith), Marvin. Studied wtih W. E. Whitehouse, London; cellist Scottish Nat. Symphony, London Philharmonic Orch. at Covent Garden, 1937, BBC recitals, N.Y. Philharmonic Orch., 1941-46; mem. Cleve. Orch., 1940-44, Metropolitan Opera Co., 1944-48, Chgo. Symphony Orch., 1948-74; solo cellist Russian Ballet, N.Y.C., 1939, Tommy Dorsey Orch., 1944; faculty Settlement Sch. Music, Cleve., 1940, Roosevelt U., Chgo., 1957. Named Chicagoan of Year for Outstanding Cultural Achievement from Mayor Daley, 1971; recipient Dir.'s scholarship Royal Coll. London, 1928-30. Home: Chicago, Ill. Died Apr. 1974; buried Shalom Meml. Park, Palatine, Ill.

GREENBERG, SARAH K., physician; b. Russia, 1884; M.D., Eclectic Med. Coll., N.Y.C., 1908. Intern outpatient dept. Mt. Sinai Hosp., N.Y.C., 1908-09; asso. obstetrician Jewish Hosp., Bklyn. Diplomate Am. Bd. Obstetrics and Gynecology. Mem. A.M.A., Womans Med. Soc. Home: Brooklyn, N.Y. Died Dec. 5, 1971.

GREENBIE, MARJORIE BARSTOW, writer; b. Jersey City, N.J., Aug. 4, 1891; d. Edward and Mary Francis (Latta) Barstow; A.B., Cornell U., 1912; fellow Yale, 1913-14, 1915-16, Ph.D., 1916; m. Sydney Greenbie, May 24, 1919 (dec.); children—Barstow, Alison. Instr., U. of Kan., 1912-13, Vassar Coll., 1914-15, Conn. Coll., 1916-17; dir. of pageantry, Methodist Centenary, editor World Outlook and contributing editor Green Book, 1917-19; asst. prof. English and dir. publicity, Mount Holyoke College, South Hadley, Mass., 1924-28; pres., chmn. bd. Traversity Press; dir. publicity, mem. nat. council Nat. Woman's Party. Dir. Margaret Brent Fellowship. Cons. OWI, New Zealand, 1944-45. Member of Phi Beta Kappa. Author: Memories (Yale prize poems), 1914; and others, latest being: Castine a Dramatized Biography of a Town (with husband), 1948; The General Was a Lady (play) (with Sydney Greenbie) 1949; Devil Take the Dream Girl (play), 1950; Anna Ella Carroll and Abraham Lincoln (with husband), 1951; Count Philippe's Wild Orange Tree (with Sidney Greenbie), 1953; This We Inherit, 1953; Hoofbeats to Heaven (with husband), 1954; (with husband) The Aunty Mar Books for Children, 1954; Grow Up But Don't Grow Old, 1958; Hoof Beats in the Canebrake, 1962; Leaves of the Lotus (poems), 1966; (with husband) Breath of the Lotus, 1963; Hoff Beats Down the River, 1966. Dir. drama workshop U. Tampa (Fla.), 1950-52; dir. Open Sky theatres, Clearwater, Fla., and Castine, Me., 1952-53. Dir. Margaret Brent Fellowship. Home: Castine, Me., Died Jan. 28, 1976.

GREENBLATT, JACOB, physician; b. 1915; M.D., La. State U., 1939. Intern, Beth El Hosp., Bklyn., 1939-40, resident in pediatrics, 1940-41; intern Kingston Av. Hosp., Bklyn., 1941; resident in pediatrics Grasslands Hosp., Valhalla, N.Y., 1943; pediatric intern Bellevue Hosp., N.Y.C., 1942; resident med. dir. Irvington House, N.Y.C., 1943-44; attending pediatrian, asso. dir. pediatrics Stamford (Conn.) Hosp.; dir. pediatrics St. Joseph's Hosp. Diplomate Am. Bd. Pediatrics. Home: Stamford, Conn. Died Sept.25, 1972.

GREENE, ANNE BOSWORTH, author, artist; b. Chippenham, Wiltshire, Eng., 1878; d. Homer Lyman and Delia Evelyn (Rood) Bosworth; ed. pvtly.; student of art of Eric Pape Sch. of Art (Boston), Boston Mus. Sch.; m. Dr. Harrie William Greene, 1900; 1 daughter, Lorna (deceased.) Brought to United States, 1885; water color artist; has exhibited in Boston, New York, Chicago, etc. Owner of dairy and beef-cattle farm. Episcopalian. Clubs: P.E.N., Pen and Brush (New York, N.Y.); League of Vermont Writers, Lanier (Tryon, N.C.). Author: The Lone Winter, 1923; Greylight, 1924; Dipper Hill, 1925; White Pony in the Hills, 1927; Lambs in March, 1928; Lighthearted Journey, 1930; Sunshine and Dust, 1936; Punch, the Cruising Dog, 1939; also preface to "Morning Moods" (poems), by Lorna Green, 1929. Home: South Woodstock, Vt.†

GREENE, CONDON LORNTZ, dentist; b. Lake City, Tenn., Apr. 12, 1895; m. Thomas Wiley and Mary Frances (Pebley) G.; student Carson-Newman Coll., 1916; U. Tenn., 1918-19; D.D.S., U. Tenn. Coll. Dentistry, 1924; m. Gladys Irene Hill, June 29, 1926; 1 dau., Frances Hill (Mrs. Benjamin A. Morton, Jr.) Pvt. practice dentistry, Clinton and Lake City, Tenn., 1924—. Chmn. Anderson County Red Cross, 1942; chmn. Crippled Children's program for Shriners, 1930; active Great Smokey Mountain council Boy Scouts Am.; chmn. Anderson County Youth for White House Program, 1958. Recipient Silver Beaver award Boy Scouts Am. Mem. Anderson County Fair Assn. (pres. 1926), Am., Tenn. dental assns., Clinton Literary Soc. (pres. 1941). Methodist. Mason, Lion. Clubs: Civitan, Knoxville Executive, City. Home: Clinton, Tenn. Deceased.

GREENE, LAURENCE WHITRIDGE, physician; b. Hutchinson, Minn., June 13, 1895; s. William Whitridge and Caroline (Schleuter) G.; student U. Minn., M.D., U. Colo., 1922; m. Freda Schmitt, Jan. 15, 1921; children—Laurence Whitridge, Charlotte (Mrs. Richard Danforth Horton). Cons. staff Denver Gen. Hosp., St. Lukes Hosp., Childrens Hosp., Colo. Gen. Hosp.-U. Colo. Med. Center; asso. clin. prof. otolaryngology, acting head dept. orolaryngrhinology U. Colo., 1958-59. Served to lt. U.S. Army, World War I. Decorated Silver Star. Diplomate Am. Bd. Otolaryngology. Fellow A.C.S.,; mem. Am. Acad. Ophthalmology and Otolaryngology, Sigma Xi, Alpha Kappa Kappa. Democrat. Episcopalian (vestryman 1928-32). Mason (K.T.). Clubs: University (Denver); Wigwam Fishing. Contbr. numerous articles to med. jours. Home: Denver, Colo. Died Aug. 24, 1971; buried St. John's Cathedral Columbarium, Denver.

GREENEBAUM, SAMUEL LEWIS, lawyer; b. Louisville, Nov. 20, 1902; s. Samuel Lewis and Cora (Popper) G.; A.B. cum laude, U. Mich., 1924; J.O., Harvard, 1927; m. Rita Levine, Jan. 29, 1956; children—John S., Jane (Mrs. Richard Eskind). Admitted to Ky. bar, 1927, D.C. bar; practiced in Louisville; sr. mem. firm Greenebaum, Doll Matthews & Boone; asst. county atty. Jefferson County, Ky., 1930-33. Pres., Community Chest of Louisville and Jefferson County, 1948-49. Mem. Am., Ky., Louisville bar assns., Assn. Bar City N.Y., Zeta Beta Tau. Home: Louisville, Ky. Died Dec. 28, 1973.

GREENFIELD, ERIC VIELE, prof. modern langs.; b. Williamstown, N.Y., Jan. 30, 1881; s. Melvin L. and Julia (Viele) G.; A.B., Colgate, 1902; A.M., Harvard, 1907; grad. study, U. of Marburg, Germany, 1 semester 1908, U. of Poitiers, France, summer 1925, U. of Madrid and U. of Grenoble, France, 1925-26; m. Gudrida Buck, Sept. 12, 1907; 1 son, Lyman Buck; m. 2d, Elizabeth Storrie, June 12, 1931; 1 son, Eric Storrie. Teacher Mt. Pleasant (Pa.) Inst., 1902-03, Jackson (Mo.) Mil. Acad., 1903-05, Trinity Hall, Washington, Pa., 1905-06; instr. in modern langs., Purdue, 1908-14, asst. prof., 1914-19, asso. prof., 1919-31, prof. after 1931. Pres. of Indiana Assn. of Teachers of German, 1939-40; mem. Modern Lang. Assn. America. Am. Assn. Univ. Profs., Phi Beta Kappa, Phi Gamma Delta. Republican. Baptist. Mason. Club: Brookston (Ind.) Country. Author: Brief Summary of German Grammar, 1914; Technical and Scientific German, 1916, 22; Introduction to Chemical German, 1918; Industrial and Scientific French, 1925; Parmi les Conteurs Modernes, 1929; Spain Progresses, 1932; Brief Summary of French Grammar, 1935; Outline of German Grammar, 1940; Outline of Spanish Grammar, 1942; Outline of Portuguese Grammar (d'Eca and Greenfield), 1944. Home: West Lafayette, Ind.†

GREENFIELD, JOSEPH A., banker; b. St. Joseph, Mo., May 10, 1879; s. James Alexander and Julia (Dowling) G.; student Christian Brothers Schs., St. Joseph, Mo., 1886-93; m. Florence Stinehilver, June 29, 1914; children—Julia Elizabeth (Mrs. Chas. Aikin Hauber), Florence Bertha, Office boy R. L. McDonald & Co., wholesale dry goods, 1893-95; with Central Savings Bank, 1895-98; Nat. Bank of St. Joseph, 1898-1900; with First St. Joseph Stock Yards Bank (formerly St. Joseph Stock Yards Bank) from 1900. v.p. from 1918. Republican. Catholic. Mem. K.C., Elk. Clubs: St. Joseph Country, East Hills Country (St. Joseph). Home: St. Joseph, Mo.†

GREENHILL, J P, gynecologist, obstetrician; b. N.Y.C., Feb. 28, 1895; s. Charles and Fanny (Pearl) G.; B.S., Coll. City N.Y., 1915; M.D., Johns Hopkins, 1919; m. Olga B. Hess, Mar. 16, 1929. Recipient house officer Johns Hopkins Hosp., 1919-20; asst. resident Sinai Hosp., Balt., 1920-21; first resident Chgo. Lying-In Hops., 1921-23, later sr. attending obstetrician; sr. attending obstetrician, gynecologist Michael Reese Hosp., Chgo., 1931—; attending gynecologist Cook County Hosp., Chgo., 1925-75, chmn. dept., 1941-47; prof. gynecology Cook County Grad. Sch. Medicine, 1936—; asso. obstetrician Northwestern U., 1922-32; prof. obstetrics, gynecology, vice chmn. dept. Loyola U., Chgo., 1933-47; hon. prof. Nat. U., Peru. Mem. White House Conf. Com., 1930. Decorated chevalier Legion of Honor, 1957, conseiller d'Honneur, Inst. Endocrinologie, Haiti, 1960; recipient Fulbright Travel award, 1962. Diplomate Am. Bd. Obstetrics and Gynecology (charter). Fellow A.C.S. (life), Am. Coll. Obstetrics and Gynecology (charter), Am. Acad. Psychomatic Medicine, Chgo. Inst. Medicine; hon. fellow Internat. Coll. Surgeons (treas., trustee), Internat. Fertility Soc. (charter, v.p.); mem. Am. Med. Writers Assn., A.M.A. (chmn. com. female gential system for standard nomenciature diseases and operations), Ill., Chgo. med. socs., Am. Pub. Health Assn., Central Assn. Obstetrics and Gynecology (charter), Am. Geriatric Soc., Chgo. Gynecol. Soc. (pres. 1954-55), A.A.A.S., Am. Assn. Antomists, Venereal Disease Assn., Johns Hopkins Med. and Surg. Assn., Ill., N.Y. acads. scis. Am. Assn. Study Internal Secretions, Am. Soc. Cancer Control, Soc. Sci. Study Sex (charter), Am. Soc. Abdominal Surgeons, Pan-Pacific Surg. Assn.; hon. mem. obstet. and gynecol. socs. S. Africa, Dominican Republic, Chile, Argentine, Panama, Brazil, Uruguay, Venzuela, Portugal, Algeria, Turkey, Guatemala, Hawaii, Philippines, Cuba, W.Va.; gynecol. socs. France, Germany, Brazil, S.W., Med. Assn. Maternity Hosp. Lima, Peruvian Acad. Surgeons, Hollywood Acad. Medicine, fertility socs. Brazil, Argentina, Portugal. Author: Obstetrics for the General Practitioner, 1935; Office Gynecology, 9th edit., 1965; Obstetrics in General Practice, 4th edit., 1948; Obstetrics, 13th edit., 1965; Surgical Gynecology, 4th edit., 1969; Analgesia and Anesthesia in Obstetrics, 2d edit., 1962 (trans. Japanese, Spanish, Portuguese, Italian, Serbian); The Miracle of Life, 1971. Editor: (with J.B. DeLee) Year Books of Obsettrics, 1923-31; Year Book of Gynecology, 1931-42; 1931-42; Year Book of Obstetrics and Gynecology, 1942—; book rev. editor Fertility and Sterility, 1949-67. Book reviewer, mem. editorial bd. numerous med. jours. U.S. Europe, S.Am. Editor: Hosp. Publs., Inc., 1964. Home: Chicago, Ill., Died Dec. 22, 1975.

GREENLEE, JOHN REECE, mining co. exec.; b. Bellaire, O., Apr. 29, 1916; s. James Ross and Catherine Adella (Thomas) G.; grad. high sch.; m. Viola Caroline Blaess, Sept. 14, 1946; children—Sally Kaye, James Ross. Accountant Paul W. Conrad, Inc., Cleve., 1933-38, Scovell, Wellington & Co., C.P.A.'s, Cleve., 1938-42; dir. taxes Hanna Mining Co., Cleve., 1942-75. Served with AUS, 1943-46. C.P.A., Ohio. Mem. Financial Execs. Inst. (chmn. tax com. 1970-71), N.A.M. (vice chmn. tax com. 1973-75), Tax Council (chmn. tax policy com. 1968-75), Am. Iron Ore Assn. (chmn. tax com. 1968-75), Internat. Econ. Policy Assn. (chmn. tax com. 1969-75), Am. Mining Congress (mem. tax com. 1955-75). Republican. Presbyn. (elder 1961-75). Clubs: Shaker Heights Country, Cleve. Athletic. Home: Shaker Heights, O. Died Jan. 25, 1975.

GREENOUGH, ALLEN JACKSON, ret. railroad exec.; b. San Francisco, Sept. 20, 1905; s. Ernest Allen and Nellie (Jackson) G.; B.S. in Civil Engring., Union Coll., Schenectady, 1928, Dr. Engring. (hon.), 1960; m. Jean Lytel, Apr. 8, 1933; children—Allen Lytel, Norman Jackson; m. 2d, Julie McCormack Waterman, Oct. 29, 1966. With Pa. R.R., 1928-68, engring. dept., 1928-45, operating dept., 1945-53, v.p. 1953-59, pres., 1959-68, ret., 1968; dir. Lehigh Valley R.R. Co., Merchants Warehouse Co., Raymond Internat., Inc.; trustee Penn Mut. Life Ins. Co. Trustee Union Coll. Mem. Soc. Colonial Wars, Chi Psi, Sigma Xi. Clubs: Round Hill (Greenwich); Pine Valley Golf. Home: North Salem, N.Y. Died Sept. 21, 1974.

GREER, ISAAC GARFIELD, supt. orphanage, teacher; b. Zionville, N.C., Dec. 4, 1881; s. Philip and Mary G.; ed. diploma, Appalachian Training Sch., Boone, N.C., 1906; student Univ. N.C., 1906-08; Columbia Univ., 1915; LL.D., Wake Forest (N.C.) Coll., 1944; m. Willie Spainhour, Aug. 10, 1916; children—Isaac Garfield, Joseph Philip. Taught in public schools, 1900; prin. Walnut Grove High Sch., 1908-10; teacher of history and citizenship, Appalachian State Teachers Coll., 1910-32; gen. supt. Baptist Orphanage of N.C., at Thomasville, from 1932. Pres. North Carolina Bapt. State Conv. Nov. 1942. City alderman, Boone, N.C., 1922-26; mem. Ho. Rep. in N.C., 1925. Pres. Tri-State Orphanage Conf., 1937-38; mem. Child Welfare League of America; mem. White House Conf. on Youth and Democracy, 1940 and 1941. Chmn. Red Cross and Liberty Loan drives in Watauga County during World War I. Vice pres. N.C. Assn.; v.p. United War Fund Drive, N.C.; mem. Governor's Commn. on Hospitalization and Medical Care in N.C. Trustee Baptist Orphanage of N.C., 1928-32, Watauga Hosp. from 1930. Pres. Allied Ch. League of N.C., 1942. Republican. Club: Rotary (Thomasville, N.C.). Home: Thomasville, N.C.†

GREGG, EARL LAMONT, head master; b. Warren Co., O., May 6, 1878; s. Jonan R. and Ella S. G.; A.B., U. of Mich., 1904; m. Bertha Maude Mills, of Lincoln, Ill., June 12, 1900. Instr., Racine (Wis.) Coll., 1899-1905; head master, Racine Coll., Grammar Sch., 1905-09, Nat. Cathedral Sch. for Boys, Washington, 1900—. Republican. Episcopalain. Asso. sec. Washington Branch Archaeol. Inst. America; mem. Nat. Geog. Soc. Clubs: Cosmos, University. Home: Washington, D.C.†

GREGG, FLORENCE CLARA, govt. ofcl.; b. Nevada, Mo.; d. Harry J. and Florence (Edmondson) Gregg; student S.W. State Coll., Springfield, Mo., 1930-32; B.S., Tex. Christian U., 1950. Adminstrn. clerical asst. TVA, Knoxville, Chattanooga, Tenn., 1935-44; adminstrv. asst. UNRRA, Washington, Rome, Italy, 1944-46; adminstrv. officer Chgo.-Cook County Health Survey, 1946; exec. asst. San Antonio Health Dept., 1946-47; sr. analyst, adminstrv. asst. Ft. Worth Health Dept., 1947-74. Mem. Am., Tex. pub. health assns., Am. Acad Health Adminstrs., Alpha Chi. Methodist. Home: Fort Worth, Tex. Died Jan. 3, 1974.

GREGG, GODFREY ROBERT, metal co. exec.; b. Shanghai, China, Dec. 14, 1923; s. Robert Joseph and Gwendoline Irene (Godfrey) G.; came to U.S., 1941, naturalized, 1944; B.S. in Chem. Engring., Stanford, 1948; m. Elizabeth Anne Allan, July 14, 1945; children—Peter, Christopher. With Am. Can Co., Los Angeles, 1948-65; pres. C.T. Supply Co., Fremont, Cal., 1965-73. Served with M.C., AUS, 1943-46. Mem. Sigma Nu. Home: Menlo Park, Cal. Died Dec. 27, 1973.

GREGG, JOHN WILLIAM, landscape architect; b. Weare, N.H., Jan. 8, 1880; s. Frank Pierce and Ruth Adelia (Sleeper) G.; B.S., Boston U., and Univ. of Mass., 1904; m. Mary Jennings, Jan. 27, 1906; children—John Jennings, Ruth Greenwood, Donald Franklin. Began with Dept. of Horticulture, St. Louis Expn., 1904; practiced in Neb., 1904-07; prof. and head dept. horticulture, Baron de Hirsch Agrl. Sch., Woodbine, N.J., 1907-10; asst. prof. horticulture, Pa. State Coll., 1910-13; prof., chief of division and consultant in landscape design U. of Calif., 1913-47; emeritus prof. of landscape design from June 30, 1947. Developed parks and park system of Berkeley, campus of U. of Calif. at Berkeley, Los Angeles, Riverside, Davis and La Jolla sch. grounds, parks and pvt. estates in various parts of Calif. Mem. University Landscape Architects' Society, Assn. Landscape Architects, Am. Society Landscape Architects (fellow), Alpha Sigma Phi, Delta Tau Sigma, Phi Phi. Presbyterian. Home: Berkeley, Cal.†

GREGG, RUSSELL TAAFFE, educator; b. Fairfield, Ill., July 24, 1903; s. John Lewis and Bertha Lee (Taaffe) G.; B.S., U. Ill., 1928, M.A., 1929, Ph.D., 1934; m. Genevieve Catherine Owen, June 7, 1930; children—Jane Gregg Steinhauer, Richard Owen. Rural sch. tchr., Wayne County, Ill., 1923-24; elementary sch. tchr., Fairfield, 1924-25; asst. in edn. U. Ill., 1928-33; instr. edn., asst. prin. U. Ill. High Sch., 1933-36, supr. visual aids library, 1933-36; asst. prof. edn. Syracuse U., 1936-39, asso. prof. edn., 1939-42, dir. curriculum workshops, 1939-42, supr. ednl. film library, 1938-42; asso. prof. edn. U. Wis.-Madison, 1945-48, prof. ednl. adminstrn., 1948-73, chmn. dept. ednl. adminstrn., 1967-70, dir. Fellowship Porgram in Urban Sch. Adminstrn., 1968-70, dir. Research Tng. Program for State Dept. Edn. Personnel, 1967; vis. prof. U. So. Cal., 1950, U. Cal., Berkeley, 1955, U. Cal., Los Angeles, 1960. Cons. Pa. Gov.'s Com. on Edn., 1960; participant Wilton Park (Eng.) Internat. Conf., 1971; cons., coordinator Nat. Project Staff Devel. in State Ednl. Agencies, 1971-72. Pres. Shorewood Hills (Wis.) Bd. Edn., 1952-58. Trustee Univ. Council for Ednl. Adminstrn., 1958-61. Served to lt. comdr. USNR, 1942-45. Decorated Navy Commendation medal. Mem. Am. Assn. Sch. Adminstrs., Internat. Com. on Ednl. Adminstrn., Am. Ednl. Research Assn., Am. Friends of Wilton Park, Nat. Conf. Prof. Ednl. Adminstrn. (dir. 1946-49, pres. 1948-49), Am. Assn. U. Profs., N.E.A., Nat. Soc. for Study Edn., Wis. Edn. Assn., Acacia, Phi Kappa Phi, Phi Eta Sigma, Phi Delta Kappa, Kappa Delta Pi. Conglist. Rotarian. Clubs: University (Madison), Blackhawk Country (Shorewood Hills, Wis.). Co-editor, author: Administrative Behavior in Education, 1957. Author: (with others) A Functional Program of Teacher Education, 1941, Schools in Our Democratic Society, 1951, Personal Expenditures for High School Education, 1951, The County Superintendency in Wisconsin, 1957, Instructional Change and Its Relationship to Decision Making in School Systems, 1966, The School Board as an Agency for Resolving Conflicts, 1967, Wisconsin Educational Assessment Study, 1969. Mem. editorial adv. bd. Sch. Exec. mag., 1955-60. Home: Madison, Wis. Died Sept. 13, 1973.

GREGORY, L.H., journalist; Sports editor Portland Oregonian, to 1973. Home: Portland, Ore. Died Aug. 1975.*

GREGORY, MAURICE CLINTON, marine officer; b. Cresco, Ia., Oct. 9, 1881; s. Isaac and Anna B. (Allen) G.; grad. Cresco High Sch., 1897; student, U.S. Army Subsistence Sch., 1926-27; Marine Corps Officer' Schs., 1922-23, 1931-32; m. Edith Wanless, July 21, 1903 (dec. Sept. 4, 1904); 1 dau., Edyth (Mrs. William M. Vibre); m. 2d Mary A. McGraw, May 21, 1909; children—Loraine Agnes (Mrs. William Huffman), Noel Clinton, Marshall Coleman. Enlisted in U.S.M.C., Feb. 23, 1905; commd. 2d lt., June 15, 1917, and advanced through grades to brig. gen., May 7, 1944; served in Philippines, Nicaragua, Caribbean area, U.S., 1905-40; head, indsl. and supply depot, U.S.M.C., Phila., 1940-46; ret. from active service, Apr. 1, 1946. Awarded Legion of Merit, campaign, expeditionary and defense medals, commendation letters from Sec. of Navy, Sec. of Treasury and Marine comdg. gen., Medal of Merit (Nicaragua), World War I and II medals, Good Conduct medal. Mem. Mil. Soc. of Am. Engrs., Mil. Order of World War, Marine Corps League, Am. Legion, U. League. Club: Rotary. Address: Philadelphia, Pa.†

GREGORY, VIRGINIA WHITNEY, (Mrs. Linwood E. Gregory), clubwoman; b. Pittsfield, Mass., July 10, 1912; d. Laurence Haines and Frances (Taylor) Whitney; A.B., Smith Coll., 1934; Ph.D. (hon.), Colo. State Christian Coll., 1973; m. Stephen W. Irwin, Aug. 1, 1939; m. 2d, Linwood E. Gregroy, Sept. 23, 1950. Sec., Wise, Hobbs & Seaver, Boston, 1935-37, Clarke & Co., Boston, 1937-39, Mass. Women's Def. Corps, Boston, 1941-44, New Products Research Corp., 1945-50, also dir. Bd. dirs., 2d v.p. charge vis. nurses Women's Civic Club, 1957-59; regent Jane McCrea chpt. D.A.R., 1959-61, pres. Capital Dist. Council, 1970-72, N.Y. State chmn. mag. advt. com., 1971-75; pres. Glens Falls Colony Nat. Soc. New Eng. Women, 1966-68, corr. sec. Glens Falls Colony New Eng. Women, 1970-72; pres. Welcome Wagon, Newcomers Club, 1953-54, Hosp. Guild, 1951-71; sponsor N.Y. State Assn. Crippled Children, Glens Falls Operetta Club, Glens Falls Concert Assn.; 1st v.p. Glens Falls Club Coll. Women, 1955-56; sec. bd. dirs. Health Assn., Warren County, 1958-64; 1st v.p. Am. Assn. U. Women, 1952-54; pres. Camera Club, 1961-62; bd. dirs. League Women Voters, 1957-60; pres. Alumni Couples Club, Presbyn. Ch., 1954-55; mem. N.Y. Huguenot Soc. (chmn. membership com. to 1975), Glens Falls Hist. Assn. (sponsor), Nat. Soc. Daus. of Founders Patriots of Am., Smithsonian Instn. (charter), Boston Smith Coll. Club, Glens Falls Country Club. Recipient award for work with Mass. Def. Crops from gov. Mass., 1943, certificate Palomino Horse Breeders Assn. Am., Inc., Commendation N.Y. Civil Def. Commn., certificate Nat. Police Officers Assn. Am. Home: Glens Falls, N.Y., Died June 28, 1975; interred Pittsfield, Mass.

GRENFELL, NICHOLAS PIRIE, JR., physician; b. Douglas, Ariz., May 6, 1920; s. Nicholas Pirie and Margarite Grenfell; M.D., U. Tenn., 1944; m. Laura Grenfell, May 6, 1955; children—Nicholas Pirie, Jeffrey Gregory. Teaching fellow in pharmacy U. Tenn., 1941-42; intern John Gaston Hosp., Memphis, 1944, Mpls. Gen. Hosp., 1946-47; asst. resident in pathology Lane Hosp., 1954-55, Stanford, 1954-55; fellow in pathology San Francisco City and County Hosp., 1955-56; resident in pathology St. Luke's Hosp., San Francisco, 1956-58; resident in clin. pathology Good Samaritan Hosp., Phoenix, 1958-59; dir. labs. Maricopa County Gen. Hosp., Phoenix, 1959-70. Pathologist, Maricopa County Office Med. Examiners, 1965-70. Bd. dirs. So. Nev. Meml. Hosp., S.W. Blood Bank, 1960-65. Served with AUS, 1942-43. Diplomate Am. Bd. Pathology. Home: Phoenix, Ariz. Died Oct. 25, 1970.

GRESHAM, THOMAS DEW, lawyer; b. Galveston, Tex., Feb. 12, 1879; s. Walter and Josephine Carey (Mann) G.; LL.B., U. of Tex., 1901; m. Loraine V. Milliken, Sept. 16, 1916; children—Margaret, Marianne. Practiced in Dallas, Tex., 1901-02; asst. gen. atty. M.K.&T. Ry. of Tex., 1903-05, gen. practice, Dallas, 1906-24; gen. atty. T.&P. Ry. Co., 1924-33, gen. counsel, 1933-37, became v.p. and gen. counsel, 1937; also gen. counsel various other rys.; v.p. Eagle Ford Land & Industrial Co.; resigned ry. work to engage in gen. practice law. Commd. 1st lt. Vols., Va., and 2d lt. in Spanish-Am. War (no active service). Mem. Am., Tex. State and Dallas bar assns., Kappa Sigma. Democrat. Episcopalian. Mason. Home: Dallas, Tex.†

GRIDLEY, MARION ELEANOR (MRS. ROBINSON JOHNSON), author; b. White Plains, N.Y.; d. William Thomson and Ada A. (Robertson) Gridley; student Northwestern U., 1954-55; m. Robinson Johnson, May 15, 1932 (div.). Free-lance writer, 1957—. Dir. pub. relations for Children's Meml. Hosp., Chgo. YWCA, Ill. Heart Assn., Chgo. Med. Sch., Nat. Soc. for Med. Research, Francis W. Parker Sch.; exec. sec. Indian Council Fire, 1923—. Named Woman of Year award Ill. Woman's Press Assn., 1965. Mem. D.A.R., Geog. Soc. Chgo., Midland Authors, Childreú ú Reading Round Table, Ill. Women's Press Assn., (past 3d v.p.), Nat. Fedn. Press Women (past regional dir.). Republican. Episcopalian. Author: Indians of Today, 1936; Indians of Yesterday; 1940; Pocohontos, 1948; Hiawatha, 1950; Indian Legends of American Scenes, 1959; Jamie's Dog, 1961; The Iroquois, The Navajo, The Seminole, The Sioux, The Haida (All 1968). Editor, pub. The Ameri-indian, 1952. Home: Chgo, Ill. Died Oct. 31, 1974.

GRIER, BOYCE MCLAUGHLIN, coll. pres.; b. Mecklenburg Co., N.C., Aug. 9, 1894; s. John Owen and Mary Alice (Hunter) G.; A.B., Erskine Coll., 1916, Litt.D., 1942, M.A., U. Ga., 1928; Ph.D., Peabody Coll., 1947; m. Lois Johnson, June 5, 1924. Supt. schs., Elberton, Ga., 1920-29; mem. faculty summer sch. U. Ga., 1928-36; supt. schs., Athens, Ga., 1929-48; pres. Lander Coll., Greenwood, S.C., 1948-66, pres. emeritus, 1966-74. Chmn. Greenwood plan Crusade for Freedom, Inc., S.C. state chmn. Crusade for Freedom. Served with USMC, World War I. Mem. S.A.R., Am. Legion, N.E.A. Am., S.C. assns. sch. adminstrs., Ga. Edn. Assn. (past pres.), Ga. Assn. Sch. Adminstrs. (past pres.), S.C. Edn. Assn., S.C. Coll. Assn. (past president), S.A.R. (past pres. South Carolina; past nat. vice president gen.), C. of C. (past pres.), Kappa Delta Pi, Pi Kappa Delta. Presbyn. (elder). Rotarian (pres. Elberton, Athens, Ga.; dist. gov.; pres. Greenwood, S.C.). Home: Greenwood, S.C. Died Nov. 18, 1974; buried Edgewood Cemetery, Greenwood.

GRIER, HARRY DOBSON MILLER, art museum exec.; b. Phila., Jan. 23, 1914; s. Edwin Stanley and Ethel Milnor (Miller) G.; B.S. in Architecture, Pa. State U., 1935; postgrad. art, archaeology Princeton, 1935-38; postgrad. Inst. d'Art et d'Archeologie, U. Paris (France), summer 1936, N.Y. U. Inst. Fine Arts, 1939-41. Architect, archaeol. field asst. Princeton Expdn. for Excavation Antioch and Vicinity, 1937; lectr., later asst. to dean, dept. edn. Met. Mus. Art, 1938-46; asst. dir. Mpls. Inst. Arts, 1946-51; asst. dir. Frick Collection, 1951-64, dir., 1964-72. Adv. council Princeton Art Mus. Trustee Internat. Exhbns. Found., Amon Carter Mus. Western Art, Ft. Worth; bd. dirs. Am. Friends Attingham, sponsors Nat. Trust Summer Sch. for study historic Houses Eng. Served to maj. AUS, 1941-46; ETO. Decorated Bronze Star with oak leaf cluster; officer Order of Leopold II. Mem. Museums Council N.Y.C. (chmn. 1962-64), Nat. Com. Drawing Soc., Am. Inst. Interior Designers, Coll. Art Assn., Am. Italy Soc. (dir.), Internat. Council Museums, Am. Assn. Museums, Assn. Art Mus. Dirs. (pres. 1968-69, trustee, treas. 1970—). Home: New York City, N.Y., Died 1972.

GRIER, ROBERT MAXWELL, physician; b. Evanston, Ill., 1898; M.D., Northwestern U., 1925. Intern, Evanston Hosp., 1924-25, attending gynecologist and obstetrician; resident Lying-In Hosp., N.Y.C., 1926, Chgo. Lying-In Hosp and Dispensary, 1927; asso. prof. gynecology and obstetrics Northwestern U. Med. Sch., Chgo. Diplomate Am. Bd. Obstetrics and Gynecology. Fellow A.C.S.; mem. A.M.A., Central Assn. Obstetricians and Gynecologists. Home: Lake Chapala, Guadalahara, Mexico. Died Oct. 7, 1973; buried Lake Chapala, Guadalahara, Mexico.

GRIEST, THEODORE REED, architect; b. Cheyenne Wells, Colo., Aug. 14, 1898; s. John E. and Annie (Campbell) G.; B.S. in Architecture, Kan. State U., 1923; postgrad. Harvard, 1929-30; m. Frances H. Crarey, Jan. 24, 1931. Archtl. draftsman and designer, Chgo., Boston, Topeka, 1923-33; practicing architect, Topeka, 1933-56; cons. architect, Topeka, 1956-74. Mem. Topeka City Planning Com., 1957-59; planning cons. Topeka Urban Renewal, 1962-70; mem. Kan. Registration and Examining Bd. for Architects, 1949-58; engring. adv. council Kan. State U. 1959-62. Bd. dirs. Topeka YMCA. Served with the U.S. Army, 1918. Recipient Distinguished Service award Sch. Engring. and Architecture, Kan. State U., 1960. Fellow A.I.A. (regional jud. com.; pres. Kan. 1946-47), Sigma Tau. Address: Topeka, Kan. Died Apr. 19, 1974; inurned Mount Hope Cemetery, Topeka, Kan.

GRIFFIN, EMMET D., business exec.; b. Dover, O., Oct. 4, 1880; s. Michael E. and Margaret (Doyle) G.; grad. public high school; m. Blanche Cuyler, Jan. 18, 1906; children—Thomas V., Helen M. (Mrs. H. H. Ayers), Emmet D. Chmn. Koppers Pitts. Co.; dir. Pitts. Plate Glass Co. Clubs: Duquesne (Pitts.); Oakmont (Pa.) Country. Home: Pittsburgh, Pa.†

GRIFFIN, EUGENE LEONARD, physician; b. Augusta, Ga., Feb. 14, 1912; s. Ralph Leonard and Corrie (Merritt) G.; M.D., Emory U., 1936; m. Joan Miller, Dec. 15, 1945; children—Ralph DeWitt, Stephen Leonard. Intern Grady Hosp., 1936-37, later clin. asst. prof.; asst. resident, then resident N.Y. Lying-In Hosp., 1937-42; practice medicine specializing in obstetrics and gynecology, Atlanta, 1947-73; vis. obstetrician and gynecologist Crawford W. Long Meml. Hosp.; asso. staff obstetrics and gynecology St. Joseph's Infirmary; courtesy staff Emory Hosp. (all Atlanta). Asso. in obstetrics and gynecology Emory U. Mem. Ga. Gov.'s Spl. Council on Family Planning, 1973. Served to maj. USAAF, 1942-46. Recipient Outstanding Clin. Prof. award Dept. Gynecology and Obstetrics, Emory U., 1968. Diplomate Am. Bd. Obstetrics and Gynecology. Fellow Am. Coll. Obstetrics and Gynecology; mem. A.M.A., So. Med. Assn., Med. Assn. Ga. (chmn. maternal and infant welfare com. 1959-73), Alpha Tau Omega. Episcopalian. Home: Atlanta, Ga., Died Sept. 2, 1973; buried Atlanta, Ga.

GRIFFIN, ROBERT MELVILLE, naval officer; b. Washington, May 23, 1890; s. Robert Stanislaws and Helena (Laube) G.; student Swavely Prep. Sch., 1906-07, B.S., Naval Acad., 1911, post-grad. work, 1916-17; m. Mary McKay Hemming, Dec. 16, 1924; children—Patricia Hemming (Mrs. Frank Gum Sterrett), Robert M. Commd. and advanced through the grades to v. adm. as comdr. Naval Forces Far East; ret. 1951; pres. Pa. Hosp., Phila., from 1951. Awarded Navy Cross, World War (service overseas); Legion Merit with star for second award. Officer, Order of the Crown (Belgium). Club: Chevy Chase. Home: Washington, D.C., Died Jan. 30, 1976.

GRIFFIS, STANTON, investment banker; b. Boston, Mass., May 2, 1887; s. William Elliot and Katharine Lyra (Stanton) G.; A.B., Cornell U., 1910; LL.D., Union College, 1944; m. Dorothy Nixon, June 19, 1912; children—Theodora, Nixon. Fruit grower, Medford, Oregon, 1910-14; partner Hornblower & Weeks-Hemphill, Noyes, investment bankers, N.Y.C., 1914-74. On govt. bus. Eng., Sweden, Finland, Spain and Portugal, 1942-43; chief Motion Picture Bur. (domestic br.) O.W.I., 1943-44; special rep. U.S. Govt. to Sweden, Apr. 1944; ambassador to Poland, 1947, Egypt, 1948, Argentine, 1949, Spain, 1951-52. Commr. Am. Red Cross, Pacific Ocean Areas, 1944-45. Trustee Cornell U., Am. Hist. Soc.; bd. dirs. Meml. Hosp., Nat. Hosp. for Speech Disorders. Recipient Medal for Merit, Medal of Freedom, Treasury Medal for War Bond work; Motion Picture Assn. Medal. Served to capt. U.S.

Army, World War I. Clubs: Cornell, Links Golf, Recess, Racquet and Tennis, Links (New York); Everglades, Seminole (Palm Beach). Author: Lying in State, 1952. Home: New York City, N.Y. Died Aug. 29, 1974.

GRIFFITH, GEORGE CUPP, physician; b. Meyersdale, Pa., Apr. 12, 1898; s. Harvey L. and Linda (Cupp) G.; A.B., Juniata Coll., Huntingdon, Pa., 1921; M.D., Jefferson Med. Coll., 1926; D.Sc., University of Southern California, 1961; div.; children—Paul H., George G.; m. 2d, Leona A. Moore, June 24, 1945. Interne Presbyn. Hosp., Phila., 1926-28; physician, Phila. area, 1929-46; attending physician Los Angeles County Gen. Hosp., 1946-64, now hon. emeritus staff; prof. medicine U. of So. Cal., 1946-64, emeritus prof., 1964-75; med. dir. Good Hope Med. Found., 1950-58; sr. med. staff Hosp. Good Samaritan, St. Vincent's Hosp.; cons. physician Cedars-Sinai Med. Centers, Hollywood Presbyn., Huntington Meml., St. Luke, San Antonio Community, VA hosps.; mem. med. adv. com. div. indsl. accidents State of Cal.; vis. prof., Eberhard Found. lectr. Hahnemann Med. Coll. and Hosp., 1965. Active duty lt. comdr. U.S. Naval Med. Corps Reserves, 1943-46. Recipient Letter of Commendation, Chief of Med. Bur., 1946, numerous other awards. Trustee Juniata Coll., 1930-46. Diplomate Am. Bd. Internal Medicine. Fellow A.C.P. (regent), N.Y. Acad. Scis., Alpha Omega Alpha; mem. A.M.A., Am. (dir., awards of merit), Cal. (past pres.), Los Angeles heart assns., A.A.A.S., Western Soc. Clin. Research, Los Angeles Soc. Internal Medicine, Med. Research Assn. Cal., Inter-Am. Soc. Cardiology, Am. Coll. Cardiology (pres. 1963-64, chmn. postgrad. edn. com., Gifted Tchr. award 1967). Republican. Contbr. articles pertaining to cardiology in med. publs. Home: LaCanada, Cal., Died Oct. 26, 1975.

GRIFFITH, M. DISON, business exec.; b. Seaford, Del., Aug. 12, 1887; s. Abraham Dison and Margaret Virginia (De Shields) G.; Litt.B., Princeton, 1907; student Univ. of Pa. Law Sch.; m. Julia Angier, Oct. 31, 1934; 1 dau., Julia Ann. Instr. Robert Coll., Constantinople, Turkey, 1911-13; asso. with Philadelphia Chamber of Commerce, 1915-17; sec. Beaver Falls, Pa., C. of C., 1917-19; sec. Elizabeth, N.J., C. of C., to 1928; exec. v.p., N.Y. Bd. Trade, 1928-58, sr. v.p. 1958-64. Spl. civilian work for U.S. Army in small war plants div. Army Service Command, World War I. Organized Charities Bur.; organized Nat. Assn. Stevedores. Republican. Protestant. Home: Westport Conn., Died Oct. 13, 1975.

GRIFFITH, PAUL HOWARD, corp. exec., bus. cons.; b. Uniontown, Pa., Apr. 8, 1897; s. David Ambrose and Annie May (Fleegle) G.; student Salem Coll.; m. Pearl Jennewine, June 30, 1920 (dec.); children—Nancy Lee (Mrs. Robert R. Seeeney), Paul Howard. Partner, D.A. Griffith & Son, wholesale dairy products, Uniontown, 1919-32, Hutchinson-Griffith Motor Co., Brownsville, Pa., 1928-30; owner Paul H. Griffith Industries, Washington, 1940—; chmn. bd. Militronics, Inc., Alexandria, Va.; pres. Creative Chems., Ins., C.D. Distbrs., Inc., Potomac, Md.; exec. v.p. Buchart, Inc., architects and engrs., York, Pa., 1956—; now with Buchart-Horn, cons. engrs.; asst. sec. def., 1949-50. Pres., U.S. Small Bus. Council, 1954-55; exec. mem. Nat. Selective Service (Presdl.) Appeal Bd., 1949-59; mem. Am. tech. mission to India, also asst. to Louis Johnson, personal rep. of Pres. in Middle and Near East, 1942; served as mem. bd. to establish essential activities and critical occupations War Manpower Commn. and SSS; chief Vets. Personnel div. SSS; adminstr. Retng. and Reëmployment Adminstrn., Office Manpower Moblzn.; asst. exec. Office Undersec. of War; chmn. Pa. Vets. Commn. Pres., Religious Heritage Am. Bd. Pres. Arms of Friendship. Served U.S. Army, World War I; to col. AUS. Decorated U.S. France, Belgium (World War 1), U.S., France, Greece, Italy (World War II). Mem. Soc. Am. Mil. Engrs., Engrs. Soc. Pa., Am. Rd. Builders Assn., Am. Legion (nat. comdr. 1946-47). Republican. Mem. Christian Ch. (elder, trustee, mem. bd.). Club: Army and Navy (Washington). Home: Potomac, Md. Died Dec. 29, 1974.

GRIFFITHS, EDWIN PATTERSON, lawyer; b. Pittsburgh, Pa., Aug. 26, 1880; s. Wilson Edwin and Katherine Ensell (Patterson) G.; A.B., Bucknell U., Lewisburg, Pa., 1904; LL.B., U. of Pittsburgh, 1907; m. Luvisa Moore, June 21, 1911 (died Mar. 19, 1937); children—John Edwin, Wilson Arnold (dec.), David Patterson (lieut. U.S. Air Corps, deceased), Rachel Luvisa; m. 2d, Maude E. Lamm, Dec. 2, 1939. Admitted to Pa. bar, 1907; with law dept., Pittsburgh Coal Co., 1907-08; in gen. practice, Muskogee, Okla., 1908-12, Pittsburgh, 1912-20; with law dept., Phila. Co., and affiliated corps., Pittsburgh, 1920-38, gen. atty., 1927-39; atty., mgr. real estate div., Calif.-Ore. Power Co., Medford, Ore., 1938-40; engaged in gen. practice of law at Pittsburgh with firm Reed, Smith, Shaw & McClay. Member American and Pa. State bar assns., Phi Gamma Delta. Republican. Protestant. Club: University (Pittsburgh). Home: Pittsburgh, Pa.†

GRIGGS, DAVID TRESSEL, geophysicist, educator; b. Columbus, O., Oct. 6, 1911; s. Robert F. and Laura (Tressel) G.; A.B., Ohio State U., 1932, A.M., 1933; postgrad. (jr. fellow), Harvard, 1934-41; m. Helen Avery, May 4, 1946; Children— Nicola F., Stephen F. Research asso. radiation lab. Mass. Inst. Tech., 1941-42; chief nuclear energy sect. Project RAND, 1946-48, cons., 1948—; prof. geophysics Inst. Geophysics and Planetary Physics, U. Cal. at Los Angeles, 1948-74; cheif scientist USAF, 1951-52, sci. adv. bd., 1952-72; chmn. ballistic systems div. adv. group USAF, 1963-65; cons. Army Forces Spl. Weapons Proj., 1951-56; cons. various govtl. agys., also AEC; mem. Nat. Geog. Soc. Expdn. to Valley 10,000 Smokes, 1930; lectr. Lowell Inst., 1938; dir. FMA, Inc., Inglewood, 1960-67. Expert cons. Office Sec. of War, 1942-46; chief sci. adv. group Far East Air Forces, 1945; sci. adv. group U.S. Strategic Air Force, 1944-45; mem. Def. Sci. Bd., 1964-72, Army Sci. Adv. Panel, 1965—, OST Panel for Earthquake Prediction, 1965-66; asso. sci. adviser COMUSMAC, Vietnam, 1968. Decorated Purple Heart, 1944, President's Medal for Merit, 1946; USAF award for exceptional civilian service, 1953; Bucher medal Am. Geophys. Union, 1970; Centennial Achievement award Ohio State U., 1970. Fellow Geol. Soc. Am., Am. Phys. Soc.; mem. Nat. Acad. Sci., Am. Geophys. Union (pres. sect. tectonophysics 1964-68), Am. Acad Arts and Scis., Phi Beta Kappa, Sigma Xi. Clubs: Cosmos (Washington); Riviera Country (Los Angeles). Author: Rock Deformation, 1960. Home: Los Angeles, Cal. Died Dec. 31, 1974; interred Valley of 10,000 Smokes, Mt. Griggs, Katmi, Alaska.

GRIMES, FERN EDITH MUNROE (MRS. WILLIAM SCHUYLER GRIMES), librarian; b. Ladysmith, Wis., June 24, 1915; d. Frank Ellsworth and Crystal Belle (Ensign) Munroe; B.A. summa cum laude (scholar), Lawrence U., 1938; certificate in library sci. with honors Washington U., St. Louis 1964; m. William Schuyler Grimes, Nov. 5, 1938; children—Steven Munroe, Warren Schuyler, Marcia Ellen. Asst. librarian Ladysmith, Wis., 1934-35; sec. to pres. Lawrence U., 1938-40; children's service, later cataloger St. Louis County Library, 1960-62; rare books asst. Washington U., St. Louis, 1962-64; tech. librarian, head cataloger Alpena (Mich.) Community Coll., Besser Tech. Sch., 1965-75. Active A.R.C., adminstrv. com. and Gray Ladies, St. Louis. Recipient Lewis prize and Commerce and Industry prize Lawrence U., 1938. Mem. N.E.A., A.L.A., Spl. Libraries Assn., League Women Voters (officer), Am. Assn. U. Women, P.E.O., Civic League, Phi Beta Kappa, Pi Beta Phi. Republican. Conglist. Clubs: Shakespeare, Garden, College (St. Louis), Associated Women's (Alpena). Home: Alpena, Mich. Died May 25, 1975; cremated.

GRIMES, J. FRANK, pres., dir., Independent Grocers Alliance; b. Chicago, Dec. 17, 1881; s. Joseph Lawrence and Mary Ann (Mapes) G.; ed. Chicago pub. schools; m. Barbara C. Adam, Jan. 28, 1903 (dec. Mar. 1951); children—John Franklin, Donald Robert, Douglas Adam, Helen Margaret; m. 2d, Alice Curry Burton, June 1954. Began Marshall Field & Co., Chgo., in charge group of cash boys, 1896; became accountant Corbin & Sons Co., Chgo.; paymaster Armour & Co., Chicago; accountant and dept. mgr. Tolerton & Warfield Co., wholesale grocers, Sioux City, Ia., 1906-13; sales mgr., Baker-Vawter Co., Benton Harbor, Mich., and Chicago, 1913-17; partner William W. Thompson & Co., certified public accountants, Chicago, 1917-33; founded, 1926, pres. Independent Grocers Alliance (IGA) of Am., 1926-52; pres. subsidiary distributing companies of Wash., Calif., N.Y., Can.; pres. Marketing Specialists, Inc.; in 1952, ret. as pres. Market Specialty Co. Food Products Co. of Am., Neighbor Products Co., Chicago Offset Printing Co.; dir. Progressive Wholesale Grocery Co., Northern New York Grocery Co., Western N.Y., Grocery Co. Formerly chairman of Independent Food Distbrs. Council; dir. Nat. Vol. Group Inst. President of the Great Lakes Foundation, Inc. Mem. Illinois State Food Marketing Com., adv. com. surplus foods War Food Adminstrn., food adv. com. O.P.A. Mem. Chicago Art Inst. (life), Chicago Farmers. Clubs: Union League, Illinois Atheltic, Westmoreland Country; Beach and Tennis (La Jolla, Cal.). Home: La Jolla, Cal.†

GRIMKE, ANGELINA WELD, writer; b. Boston, Mass., Feb. 27, 1880; d. Archibald Henry and Sara Eliza (Stanley) G.; student Carleton Acad., Northfield, Minn., Cushing Acad., Ashburnham, Mass., and Girls' Latin Sch., Boston; grad. Boston Normal Sch. of Gymnastics, 1902. Began as teacher Armstrong Manual Training Sch., 1902; teacher Dunbar High Sch., Washington, D.C., after 1916. Author: Rachel (3-act play), 1920; also short stories in Birth Control Rev. Home: Washington, D.C.†

GRIMSTON, JOHN (6TH EARL OF VERUIAM), metal co. exec.; b. St. Albans, Eng., July 17, 1912; s. James Walter and Lady Violet Brabazon (dau. Earl of Meath); student Christ Ch. Oxford U., 1930-36; m. Marjorie Ray Duncan, June 2, 1938; children—Elizabeth (Viscountess Pollington), Hermione (Lady Thompson), Lady Romayne Bockstoce, Iona Charlotte, Viscount Grimston. Chmn., mng. dir. Enfield Rolling Mills, Ltd., 1938-60; chmn. Delta Metal Co., London, 1968-73. Conservative mem. Parliament for St. Albans, 1943-45, 50-59. Served with RAF, World War II; hon. air commodore County Hertford Maritime Hdqrs. Unit Royal Aux Airforce, 1963-73. Mem. London C. of C. (past pres.), Internat. Wrought Copper Council (past chmn.) Home: Saint Albans, Hertfordshire, England. Died Apr. 15, 1973; buried Saint Albans, Hertfordshire, England.

GRINER, JOHN F., labor union ofcl.; b. Camilla, Ga., Aug. 7, 1907; s. Will and Dollie (Shiver) G.; LL.B., Columbus U., Washington; m. Claranell Nicholson, Nov. 27, 1936; children—John F., Remer Will. With various railroads, 1925-36; adjudicator, liaison officer, labor relations officer U.S. Railroad Retirement Bd., 1936-62; nat. pres. Am. Fedn. Govt. Employees, 1962-72. Mem. Order R.R. Telegraphers, Am. Train Dispatchers Assn.; hon. mem. Brotherhood R.R. Trainmen, R.R. Yardmasters Am., Brotherhood R.R. Signalmen. Democrat. Baptist. Mason (Shriner). Home: Cairo, GA. Died Apr. 22, 1974; interred Cairo, Ga.

GRISSOM, PINKNEY, lawyer; b. Tippah County, Miss., July 7, 1897; s. James Henry and Charlotte Anna (Mathis) G.; student North Tex. State Coll., 1916-17; LL.B., Washington and Lee U., 1920; m. Karl Ruth Simmons, Jan. 1, 1921; children—Pinkney, John, David. Tchr. rural sch., 1917-18; admitted to Tex. bar, 1920; asso. Thompson, Knight, Wright & Simmons, Dallas, 1921-34, a sr. partner, 1934-68, of counsel, 1968—; atty. specializing trial practice, 1921—; lectr. on malpractice, other medico-legal problems of physicians Research fellow, mem. medico-legal com., chmn. ins. div. (1957) Southestern Legal Found. Fellow Am. Coll. Trial Lawyers, Internat. Acad. of Trial Lawyers, Am. Bar Found.; mem. Am. and Dallas (chmn. 1955) bar assns., Tex. State Bar, Internat. Assn. Ins. Counsel. Fedn. Ins. Counsel, Order of Blue Goose Internat., Engr. Club of Dallas, Phi Delta Phi, Phi Sigma Kappa. Mason (Shriner). Clubs: Dallas Exchange (pres. 1940), Insurance (Dallas); The Carriage. Home: Dallas, Tex. Deceased

GRISSOM, RICHARD H., state ofcl.; b. Columbia, Ky., Sept. 28, 1881; s. Benjamin B. and Martha Sue (Staples) G.; School, Bowling Green, Kentucky, Lindsey Wilson College, Columbia, Kentucky; m. Lillian D. Robertson, July 13, 1913 (dec. 1952); children—Maxine (Mrs. Arnold Schempp), Richard H; m. 2d, Janet T. Cooper, August 29, 1954. Ednl. budget auditor of N.M. for 22 yrs.; treas. State of N.M. Mem. Nat. Assn. State Auditors, Comptrollers and Treasures; N.E.A. Mason. Home: Sante Fe, N.M.†

GROEL, FREDERICK HENRY, lawyer, ins. exec.; b. Newark, Jan. 15, 1899; s. Charles and Augusta N. (Schiener) G.; A.B., Princeton, 1921; LL.B., Harvard, 1914; m. Audrey Berdine, June 21, 1929; children—Marjory Eve (Mrs. James S. Ward), Berdine. Admitted to N.J. bar, 1924, practiced in Newark, 1924-40; asst. corp. counsel City Newark, 1927-33; with Prudential Ins. Co. of Am., 1940-65, v.p., sec., 1948-61, exec. v.p., 1961-65; asso. prof. Rutgers U., 1926-38; dir., chmn. trust com. 1st Nat. State Bank of N.J.; dir. Triangle Industries Inc. Mem. N.J. Legislature, 1926-27. Mem. bd. United Hosps. (Newark), Newark Mus., N.J. State Safety Council, N.J. Econ. Devel. Council; mem. N.J. Tercentenary Commn.; pres., mem. Newark Indsl. Devel. Corp.; pres. Newa,k 300 Anniversary Com. Served as seaman USN, World War I. Mem. Am., N.J., Essex County bar assns., N.J. C. of C. (pres.), N.J. Hist. Soc. (mem. bd.). Republican. Clubs: Princeton, Essex (Newark); Advertising (mem. bd.), Harvard (N.Y.); Short Hills, Baltusrol Golf; Bay Head Yacht. Home: Springfield, N.J. Died Oct. 31, 1974.

GROEZINGER, LELAND BECKER, lawyer; b. San Francisco, June 17, 1907; s. Emile August and Emma (Becker) B.; A.B., U. Cal. at Berkeley, 1927; J.D., Harvard, 1930; m. Clara-Catherine Hudson, Sept. 30, 1939; children—Leland Becker, Marlene Margaret (Mrs. James S. Doak). Admitted to Cal. bar, 1930; dep. legis. counsel State of Cal., 1930-31; practice in San Francisco, 1931-75; asso. Pillsbury, Madison & Sutro, 1931-46; mem. firm Allan, Miller & Groezinger, 1946-55, Allan, Miller, Groezinger, Keesling & Martin, 1955-66, Miller, Groezinger, Pettit, Evers & Martin, 1966-69, Miller, Groezinger, Pettit & Evers, 1970-73, Pettit, Evers & Martin, 1973-75. Mem. Am. Bar Assn. (chmn. sect. ins. and negligence law, state del.). Home: San Francisco, Cal., Died July 28, 1975; inurned Groezinger Niche, San Francisco Meml. Collumbarium, San Francisco, Cal.

GROGAN, STARKE MCLAUGHLIN, statistician; b. Elbert County, Ga., Feb. 15, 1880; s. George Calvin and Addie Harvey (Starke) G.; grad. Elberton (Ga.) Sem., 1897, m. Aileen Harper, of Elberton, Ga., Oct. 3, 1900, 1 son, Samuel Starke. Mem. Co. F, 3d Ga. Regt., Spanish-Am. War; in banking business, 1899-1900; apptd. clk. Bur. of the Census. Washington, D.C., 1900; chief statistician Financial Statistics of States and Cities, same, 1914-35, and of Territorial Insular and Foreign satistics from 1935. Mem. Internat. Assn. of Comptrollers and Accounting Officers, Nat. Assn. of State Auditors, Comptrollers, and Treasurers. Democrat. Methodist. Mason (Shriner). Club: Manor Golf. Home: Washington, D.C.†

GRONDAHL, LARS OLAI, consultant in research; born at Hendrum, Minn., Nov. 27, 1880; s. Peder Elias and Herborg (Huglen) Larson; student Concordia Coll., Moorhead, Minn., 1897-99; B.S., St. Olaf Coll., Northfield, 1904, M.S., 1905; Ph.D., Johns Hopkins, 1908; hon. D.Sc., St. Olaf Coll., 1940; student U. of Chicago, summers 1903, 09, U. of Berlin, spring semester, 1914; m. Grace Elizabeth Fuller, Sept. 11, 1970; 1 son, Martin (dec.) Prof. Spokane (Wash.) Coll.,

1908-09; instr. physics, U. of Wash., 1909-12; instr. physics, Carnegie Inst. Tech., 1912-14, asst. prof., 1914-17, asso. prof., 1917-20; dir. research Union Switch & Signal Co., 1920-37; director research, engring., 1937-47; cons., 1947-49; independent cons. after 1950. Section member Nat. Defense Research Committee, 1940-42, chief of section 5.2, 1942-45. Awarded Howard N. Potts medal by Franklin Inst., 1938, Modern Pioneer award, Nat. Assn. of Mfrs., 1940; George R. Henderson medal by Franklin Inst., 1947; President's Medal for Merit, 1948. Commd. captain United States Army, later released for service with Naval Cons. Bd., World War I. Mem. bd. dirs. Pittsburgh Acad., 1934-36; mem. Nat. Research Council, 1933-36; chmn. of exec. com. of Advisory Council on Applied Physics of Am. Inst. of Physics, 1936. Fellow A.A.A.S., Am. Inst. Elec. Engrs., Am. Phys. Soc. (mem. council 1933-36); mem. Am. Electrochem. Soc., Franklin Inst., Phys. Soc. of Pittsburgh (organizer and past pres.), Pittsburgh Chamber of Commerce, Sigma Xi, Sigma Alpha Epsilon. Unitarian. Clubs: University, Discoverer of copper-copperoxide rectifier and inventor various headlight, train control and signal devices. Home: Pittsburgh, Pa.†

GROSS, CHARLES PHILIP, born Brooklyn, N.Y., March 14, 1889; son of Frederick Charles and Elizabeth (Stoetzer) G.; M.E., Cornell U., 1910; B.S., U.S. Mil. Acad., 1914; grad. Engr. Sch., 1916, Command and Gen. Staff Sch., 1927, Army War Coll., 1932; m. Eleanore Marion Hubach, June 30, 1914; children—Lucy Helen (wife of Lt. Col. John S. B. Dick), Dorothea Katherine (wife of Lt. Col. Walter Swank), John Edward, Nancy Ellen (wife of Capt. Heston Cole), Sheldon Harley. Commd. 2d lt. U.S. Army, June 12, 1914, and advanced through the grades to major general, Aug. 1942; with 2d battalion engineers, 1914-15; comd. 318th Engineers, A.E.F. (Gerardmer Sector and Meuse Argonne), World War I; engineer Sixth Army Corps., 1941; General Staff, G-4, transportation, 1941; became chief of transportation Army Service Forces, War Dept., 1941; on Harriman Mission to London and Moscow 1941; member combined staff conferences in London, 1942; duty at Combined Chiefs of Staff Conferences, Washington, Quebec, Malta, Yalta and Potsdam. Chmn. Board of Transportation, New York N.Y., 1945-47; chief Transport Group, O.M.G.U.S., 1948; Military Gov., Wuerttemberg, Baden, 1949; land commr. Wuerttemberg, Baden, 1949-52. Decorated Purple Heart; Army of Occupation in Germany medal; 2d Marine Nicaraguan Campaign medal; Victory medal (World War I); Presidential Medal of Merit (Nicaragua), Legion of Merit, Distinguished Service Medal, Commander Order of British Empire. Honorary member American Society C.E.; mem. Am. Soc. M.E. Club: Army and Navy (Washington, D.C.). Died July 1975.

GROSS, MYRA GERALDINE, author; b. Newburg, N.Y., Jan. 14, 1872; d. William Tremaine and Harriet Newell (Coddington) FitzGerald; moved with parents to Baltimore, at 4yrs. of age; grad. Western Female High Sch., Baltimore, 1889; course in physical geography and geology, Johns Hopkins; m. Francis Harry Gross, of Baltimore, June 12, 1906. Teacher pub. schs., Baltimore until 1906. Methodist. Author: The Star of Valhalla, 1907. Home: Emmitsburg, Md.†

GROSS, NELS, corp. exec.; b. Oscarshamn, Sweden, Sept. 14, 1887; s. William Nelson and Clara Cecelia (deBiale) G.; student Inst. Tech., Stockholm, Sweden, 1905; m. Wilhelmina Boon, Aug. 1, 1924; children—Leonora, George'Ann, Marilyn, Nelson Boon. With Stewart Blast Furnace Co., 1906-10; mgr. N.Y. office Stewart & Clark Mfg. Co., 1910-13; v.p., gen. mgr. Stewart Mfg. Co., Chgo., 1913-20; pres., gen. mgr. L. Wolff Mfg. Co., Chgo., 1920-24, Pacific Seaboard Corp., Los Angeles, 1924-28, Dist. Bond Co., Los Angeles, 1928-45; pres. Gross, Rogers & Co., 1946-52; pres. Gross & Co., 1959-70; chmn. bd. Fiduciary Capital Co., 1960-70; pres. Fiduciary Retirement Fund, Inc., 1961-65; chmn. bd. Business Developers, Inc., 1960-65, Indsl. Mgmt. Corp., 1932-39, Tetco Co., 1939-59, Roadmaster Products Co., Los Angeles and Chgo., 1936-52; dir. Consol. Rock Products Co. Mem. Am. Chem. Soc., Engrs. and Architects Assn., A.A.A.S. Republican. Episcopalian. Mason. Clubs: Engineers, Stock Exchange, Wilshire Country, Jonathan; Bankers (N.Y.C.); Lake Shore (Chgo.). Address: Los Angeles, Cal. Died Nov. 13, 1970.

GROSSI, CARMINE JAMES, steam generating and fuel burning co. exec.; b. Paterson, N.J., Apr. 1, 1913; s. Carmine and Lucia (Luce) G.; B.S. in Mech. Engring., Ga. Inst. Tech., 1935; m. Elinora Barrett, Nov. 6, 1936; children—Michael Barrett, Anthony Frederick, Patrick. With Combustion Engring., Inc., N.Y.C., from 1936, export sales mgr., 1955-61, v.p., from 1961; chief heavy power equipment br. NPA, 1951-53; dir. Wayne State Bank (N.J.), 1962-63. Mem. exec. reserve bus. and defense services adminstrn. Dept. of Commerce, Washington. Served to lt. comdr. USNR, 1942-46; ETO. Decorated Commendation medal; recipient Commendation, Dept. Commerce, 1953. Clubs: Engineers (N.Y.C.); N.J. Country (Preakness, N.J.); Indian Trail (Franklin Lakes, N.J.); Manhattan (N.Y.C.). Home: Stanford, Conn., Deceased.

GROSSMAN, MARY BELLE, judge; b. Cleve., June 10, 1879; dau. Louis and Fannie (Engle) Grossman; student Euclid Avenue Business Coll., Cleveland, 1895-96; LL.B., Baldwin Wallace Coll., Berea, O., 1912; LL.D., Cleveland-Marshall Law School, 1959; unmarried. Admitted to the bar of Ohio, 1912, to Dist. Court of U.S., 1913, to U.S. Supreme Court, 1932; pvt. practice in Cleveland, 1912-23; judge, Municipal Court of Cleveland, 1923-59; judge, Traffice Court of Cleveland, 1925-59; judge Morals Court (an organizer), 1926-59. Mem. Four Minute Man during World War I; served as chmn. O.P.A., Ration Bd., 34-18-10, World War II. Trustee, mem. bd. Diabetes League of Greater Cleve.; member hon. board, Phillis Wheatley; chmn. bd. of Alta House Settlement. Recipient Inter-Club Council Award, Woman of Achievement, 1954, Award of Merit, Alumni Assn. of Baldwin-Wallace Coll., 1956. Mem. Cancer Control Assn. (mem. adv. bd. Woman's Field Army), Nat. Probation Assn. (bd.), Am. Ohio (hon.), Cleve. (hon.), Cuyahoga County bar assns., Am. Adjudicature Soc., Nat. Assn. Women Lawyers, Ohio Citizens' Council for Health and Welfare, Nat. Bus. and Profl. Women's Club, N.A.A.C.P., Council for Retarded Children (adv. bd.), Am. Jewish Congress, League Women Voters, Council Jewish Women, Baldwin Wallace Coll. Alumni Assn. (hon.), Kappa Beta Pi (hon.), Alpha Epsilon Phi (hon.). Republican. Clubs: Women's City of Cleveland, Altrusa (hon.). Home: Cleveland, O.†

GROTHJEAN, FRANCESCA C. R., artist; b. nr. Hamburg, Germany, Apr. 12, 1871. Pupil of Courtois, Girard, Paul J. Blanc, Pierre Fritel, and A. J. Delécluse. Has exhibited in most important exhibitions in Europe and America. Exhibited in Paris Exp'n, 1900. Home: New York City, N.Y.†

GROVE, PHILIP HARVEY, constrn. engr.; b. Atlantic City, N.J., Oct. 4, 1904; s. Philip Bruner and Mignon (Lee) G.; C.E., Rensselaer Poly. Inst., 1925; m. Harriet Flaherty, July 17, 1926; (died 1973); children—Barbara (Mrs. Guy P. Simoni), Jane (Mrs. George F. Pritchard), Winthrop Denison, Elizabeth (Mrs. Frederick W. Schweizer); m. 2d. Birgit Groendahl. Founder, chmn. bd., pres., chief exec. officer Grove, Shepherd Wilson & Kruge Inc., N.Y.C., 1929-51, also dir.; founder, chmn. bd. MacLean-Grove & Co. Inc., N.Y.C., 1951-75; also dir., also chmn. bd., dir. Grove Internat. Corp. Trustee Rensselaer Poly. Inst. Mem. Am. Soc. C.E., Soc. Am. Mil. Engrs., Delta Kappa Epsilon. Clubs: Metropolitan, Canadian, Yale, N.Y. Yacht (N.Y.C.); Ft. Orange (Albany, N.Y.). Home: Skaneateles, N.Y. Died Aug. 16, 1975.

GROVE VALLEJO, MARMADUKE, Chilean aviator and army officer; b. Copiapó, 1878; s. José Marmaduke Grove and Ana Vallejo; ed. Naval School, 1892-94; Superior School of Engineering, 1895-96; Military School, 1897-98; m. Rebeca Valenzuela; children—Marmaduek, Rebeca, Elvira, Blanca, Elena, Hirma, Ana Rosa, Amaro. Officer, Field Artillery Regt., 1898; capt. "maturana" Artillery Regt., 1911-12; major of artillery and gen. staff officer, 1918; commander-in-chief, Air Service, 1925-26; military and aeronautical attaché in London, 1927-28; political prisoner on island of Pascua, 1931, then went to France; proclaimed candidate for presidency of Republic by Workers' Party, 1933; leader of Socialist Party; pres. of Popular Front Party (Frente Popular). Mem. Centro Mentalista "armonia," Awarded sword of honor. Author on military and political subjects. Address: Santiago, Chile.†

GRUENBERG, SIDONIE MATSNER (MRS. BENJAMIN C. GRUENBERG), writer, lecturer; b. in Austria, June 10, 1881; d. Idore and Augusta Olivia (Bassechés) Matzner; ed. Höhere Töchterschule, Hamburg, Germany, 1894; Ethical Culture Sch., N.Y., 1897, spl. student, normal tng. dept., same, 1905-06; grad. student Techrs. Coll., Columbia 1906-10; m. Benjamin C. Gruenberg, Ph.D., June 30, 1903; children—Herbert M., Richard M., Hilda (Mrs. David Krech), Ernest M. With Child Study Assn. Am. (formerly Fedn. for Child Study) 1906—, dir. 1923-50, spl. cons., 1950—; chmn. Nat. Council for Parent Edn., 1947-51; lectr. in parent edn., Tchrs. Coll. (Columbia), 1928-36, 47, N.Y. U. 1936-37, 40; U. Colo., 1940, 42. Chmn. sub-com. of White House Conf. on Child Health and Protection, 1930; mem. White House Conf., 1940, Pres.' Conf. on Home Building and Home Ownership, 1931, adv. commn. on children in wartime, U.S. Children's Bur., 1942; mem. com. communications, Mid-Century White House Conf., 1950. Mem. editorial bd. Jr. Lit. Guild 1929-74, Parents Mag., 1926-43; "Child Study"; editorial cons. to Fawcett Publs., 1943-45; cons. on family relationships, Woman's 1947-49; Spl. cons. Doubleday & Co., 1950—. Fellow A.A.A.S.; mem. Am. Social Hygiene Assn. (hon. life), Assn. Childhood Edn., Nat. Assn. for Nursery Edn., Campfire Girls, Pub. Edn. Assn., Nat. Pub. Housing Conf., N.Y. State Conf. on Marriage and the Family, Nat. Orgn. for Pub. Health Nursing. Dir. Pub. Affairs Com., 1947—; dir. Social Legislation Information Service, 1947-61. Author many books for children and parents, 1914—, later ones: The Wonderful Story of How You Were Born, 1952, rev., 1959, new rev. edit., 1970, trans. into Japanese, Norwegian, Swedish; Parents' Guide to Everyday Problems of Boys and Girls: Guiding Your Child from Five to Twelve, 1958. Co-author: Parents, Children and Money, 1933; (with Hilda Sidney Krech) The Many Lives of Modern Woman, 1952; (with Benjamin C. Gruenberg) Children for the Childless, 1954; (with Benjamin C. Gruenberg) The Wonderful Story of You, 1960. Editor: Our Children: A Handbook for Parents, 1932; Parents Questions, 1936, rev. edit. 1948; The Family in a World at War, 1942; Favorite Stories Old and New, 1942, rev. edit. 1955; More Favorite Stories Old and New, 1948, rev. 1960; Let's Read a Story, 1957; Let's Read More Stories, 1960; Let's Hear a Story, 1961; Kinds of Courage, 1962; The Encyclopedia of Child Care and Guidance, 1953, rev. edit., 1967. Home: N.Y.C. N.Y. Died Mar. 1974.

GRUENING, ERNEST, U.S. senator, editor, author; b. N.Y. City, Feb. 6, 1887; s. Emil and Phebe (Fridenberg) G.; grad. Hotchkiss Sch., Lakeville, Conn., 1903; A.B., Harvard, 1907, M.D., 1912; LL.D., U. Alberta, 1950, U. Alaska, 1955, Brandeis U., 1958; L.H.D., Wilmington Coll.; m. Dorothy E. Smith, Nov. 19, 1914; children—Ernest (dec.), Huntington Sanders, Peter B. (dec.). Reporter, spl. article writer, editor various newspapers, 1911-20; mng. editor The Nation, 1920-23, and editor, 1933-34; nat. dir. of publicity, LaFollette Progressive Presidential Campaign, 1924; founder Portland (Me.) Evening News, 1927, editor until 1932, contbg. editor, 1932-37; editor N.Y. Evening Post, Feb.-Apr. 1934, mem. Cuba Commn. Fgn. Policy Assn., 1934; dir. Div. Territories and Island Possessions, U.S. Dept. Interior, 1934-39, adminstr. P.R. Reconstrn. Adminstrn, 1935-37; fed. emergency relief adminstr. P.R., 1935-36; mem. Alaska Internat. Hwy. Commn. 1938-42. Gov. of Alaska, 1939-53; keynoter, Alaska Constnl. Conv., 1955; elected provisional U.S. Senator from Alaska, 1956-58, Senator 1958-69. Gen. adviser to the U.S. delegation to 7th Pan Am. Conf., Montevideo, 1933. Cons. Population Crisis com., 1968-74. Recipient Hadassah award, Geo. W. Norris award, Herbert H. Lehman award, Margaret Sawyer award; decorated Order of Aztec Eagle, Mexico, Mem. Phi Beta Kappa. Clubs: Harvard (N.Y.); Cosmos (Washington). Rotarian. Editor: These United States. Author: Mexico and Its Heritage, 1928; The Public Pays, 1931; The State of Alaska, 1954; An Alaska Reader, 1967; The Battle for Alaska Statehood, 1967. Contbr. various books and mags. Home: Washington, D.C. Died June 26, 1974.

GRUMBINE, GRANT BARTHOLOMEW, educator; b. Hastings, Neb., Aug. 24, 1879; s. Henry B. and Sarah A. (Gessner) G.; B.S., Central Coll., Fayette, Mo., 1903, M.S., 1904; m. Mary E. Cox, Dec. 23, 1903; children—Grant B., Levi C., Mary E., Nathan G., Pres. Woodson Inst., Mo., 1904-07; prof. mathematics, Epworth U., Oklahoma City, Okla., 1908-10; pres. Northwestern State Normal Sch., Alva, Okla., July 1, 1910-July 1, 1916; pres. Central State Normal Sch., Edmond, Okla., July 1916-Sept. 1917; field supt. North American Oil & Refining Corpn., Burkburnett Dist., 1917-19; supt.S. Okla. Dist., 1919-22; rotary drilling contractor, 1922-27; prof. mathematics, Okla. A. & M. Coll., 1923-24; supt. production, Cromwell-Franklin Petroleum Co., 1930-31. Mem. Okla. Bar, S.A.R. Mem. 17th Quadrennial Conf. M.E. Ch., South, Oklahoma City, 1914. Democrat. Mason (K.T.), Home: Oklahoma City, Okla.†

GRUNERT, GEORGE, army officer; b. White Haven, Pa., July 21, 1881; s. David and Henrietta (Holman) G.; student Command and Gen. Staff Sch., Ft. Leavenworth, Kan., 1930-32; m. Florence I. Reynolds, Oct. 22, 1907; children—George Reynolds, Mary Clark. Enlisted as pvt., U.S. Army, 1898, advancing through the grades to lieut. gen., 1943; served in Spanish-Am. War, Philippines Campaign, Mexican Border, A.E.F. in France and Army of Occupation, Germany; prof. mil. sciences and tactics, Shattuck Sch., Faribault, Minn., 1912-16; instr. Army War Coll., Washington, D.C., 1919-20, dir., 1932-36; Philippine Islands, 1936-38; Vancouver Barracks, 1938-39; comdg. gen., Philippine Department, 1940-41; comdg. gen. 6th Army Corps, 1941-42, 6th Service Command, 1942; deputy chief of staff, Army Service Forces, Sept. 1942-43; comdg. gen. First Army and Eastern Defense Command, Oct. 1943-July 1945. Decorated with medals of Span.-Am. War. Army of Cuban Pacification, Philippine Campaign, Army of Cuban Occupation, Mexican Border Service, World War Campaign (with 6 battle clasps and silver star). D.S.M., Order of Purple Heart, French Legion of Honor, Distinguished Service Medal with Oak Leaf Cluster, Legion of Merit. Lutheran. Clubs: Army and Navy, Army and Navy Country (Washington, D.C.); Fort Sam Houston Officers and Golf. Wednesday Luncheon (San Antonio, Tex.). Retired. Home: San Antonio, Tex.†

GRUNSFELD, ERNEST ALTON, JR., architect; b. Albuquerque, N.M., Aug. 25, 1897; s. Ernest Alton and Theresa (Nusbaum) G.; S.B., Mass. Inst. Tech., 1918; certificate in naval architecture, same, 1919; studied Ecole des Beaux Arts, Paris, 1920-22, Am. Acad. in Rome, 1921; m. Mary-Jane Loeb, 1926; children—Esther, Ernest Alton III; m. 2d, Maurine G. McCormick, 1943. Architect Whitehall Hotel, 1926; Michigan Blvd. Apts. (Negro housing project founded by Julius Rosenwald), 1928; Jewish People's Inst., 1925; Stephen A. Douglas Branch Library (Chicago), 1928; Infirmary, Mass. Inst. Tech. (with C. Butler), 1927; Adler Planetarium, 1930; Terrazo Promenade, and Lumber House Exhibit for Nat. Lumber Mfg. Assn. at

A Century of Progress Expn., 1933; main broadcasting studio WGN, 1935; Chicago Bar Assn., 1937; Alverthorpe (residence and gallery for L. J. Rosenwald, Jenkintown, Pa.), 1939; Max Straus Community Center, Chicago, 1941; Bachelor Officers Quarters, Great Lakes, Ill. 1942; various war housing projects. Consulting architect. Sinai Temple. Also many residences and misc. work, Cincinnati, Phila., Columbus, Detroit, Savannah, New York. Visiting lecturer U. Illinois, 1950, Leland Stanford, 1951, 52. Exhibited paintings Salon d'Antomne, Paris, 1956, 57, 58, 59. Pres. Ernest A. Grunsfeld Fund. Awards; gold medal Societé des Architectes, par le Gouvernement Francais, 1917; student medal Am. Inst. Architects, 1918; gold medal Chicago Chapter, same for Alder Planetarium, 1931; Rotch prize, 1918; silver medal and diploma Pan-American Architectural Congress, Montevideon, 1939; Gold Medal Order of Civic Merit (France); Chevalier Legion of Honor (France). Member of the Illinois Housing Commission, 1931; cons. Housing Div., P.W.A. Member archtl. groups for design of Jane Addams Trumbull. Cabrini and Brooke and other housing projects. Served in United States Navy, 1918-19. Fellow A.I.A. Clubs: Tavern; American (Paris). Contbr. to profl. mags. Address: Chicago, Ill. Died Aug. 12, 1970; buried Tallories, France.

GRUZEN, BARNETT SUMNER, architect; b. Riga, Latvia, July 25, 1903; s. Max and Ida (Friedman) G.; came to U.S., 1905, naturalized, 1925; B.Arch., Mass. Inst. Tech. 1926, M.Arch., 1928; grad. work, Ecole des Beaux Arts, Paris, France, 1930; m. Ethel Brof, Aug. 7, 1930; children—Jordan Lee, Maxson Stewart. Rotch travelling scholar in Europe. 1930-32; now prin. Gruzen and Partners, Architects-Engrs., N.Y.C. and Newark, 1932—; prin. works include U.S. mission to UN bldg., 1959, Albert Einstein Coll. Medicine, 1954, Rutgers U. dormitories and related facilities, 1954, VA Hosp., Wilkes-Barre, Pa. (Nat. Honor award A.I.A. 1951), 1952, Canton (O.) City Hall, 1960, N.Y. Sch. Printing, N.Y.C., 1955, Passaic (N.J.) High Sch. (one of five 1st prizes for sch. design Sch. Exec. mag. 1955), 1949, monument and park for Theodore Herzl (3d prize World Zionist Orgn. 1951). 1951, also other high schs., shopping centers, mil. installations; new campus for State U. N.Y., Rutgers U.; new police headquarters for N.Y.C. Bd. dirs. Israel Inst. Tech., Haifa, 1935—; chmn. archtl. div. United Jewish Appeal, N.Y.C., 1951, Fed. Jewish Philanthropies, N.Y.C. 1952-53. Recipient 1st prize archtl. competition for development new state capitol, N.J., from A.I.A., 1945. Registered profl. engr., N.J. Fellow A.I.A.; mem. Nat. Council Archtl. Registration Bds., Nat. Soc. Profl. Engrs., N.J. Soc. Architects, N.Y. State Assn. Architects, Soc. Am. Mil. Engrs., Am. Hosp. Assn., Archtl. League of N.Y., Am. Technion Soc., Am. Arbitration Assn. Club: Mass. Inst. Tech. (N.Y.C.). Author articles, papers, also chpt. in book. Home: N.Y.C., N.Y. Died Sept. 27, 1974.

GUASTI, SECONDO, III, vineyard exec.; b. Los Angeles, Oct. 13, 1925; s. Secondo and Gertrude (Orcutt) G.; student Hill Sch., Gunnery Sch., U. Cal. at Los Angeles, 1946-48; m. Martha Outlaw Huntington, Apr. 17, 1954; stildreHenry Edwards Huntington III, Edward Outlaw Huntington. Self-employed, Los Angeles, 1948-55, 58-62; with Willis & Christy, investment counsel, Los Angeles, 1955-57; mgr. So. Cal. area, 1962—; Ind. oil and gas producer, 1958—; pres. Cal. Vineyard; pres. Montecito Minerals Corp.; dir. Ajax Internat. Corp., Five Wines of Am. Served as pilot USAAF, 1942-46. Clubs: California (Los Angeles); Valley of Montecito (Santa Barbara). Home: Santa Barbara, Cal. Died Aug. 16, 1973.

GUDEMAN, EDWARD, investment banker; b. Chgo., Oct. 9, 1906; s. Edward and Clara (Asher) G.; B.A., Harvard, 1927; m. Frances Alschuler, Oct. 12, 1932; children—Jon Edward, Stepehn Frederick. Formerly v.p., dir. Sears, Roebuck & Co.; formerly dir. One William Street Fund, Inc., Brunswick Corp., Globe Union Corp., Whirlpool Corp., Warwick Corp., Schnadig Corp.; under-sec. commerce, 1961-63; partner Lehman Bros., investment bankers, 1963-69, ltd. partner, 1969-73; bd. dirs. Marcor, Inc., Esquire Corp., Montgomery Ward & Co., Duplan, Inc. Former exec. dir. Pres.'s Adv. Com. on Labor Mgmt. Policy. Bd. dirs. Lenox Hill Hosp., N.Y.C., Nat. Com. Against Crime and Delinquency. Mem. adv. council U. Chgo. Grad. School Bus. Clubs: Lake Shore Country (Glencoe, Ill.); Montego Bay Tennis (Jamaica), Mid America, Harvard (Chgo.); Bath and Racquet (Sarasota, Fla.). Home: Sarasota, Fla. Died Aug. 12, 1974.

GUDGEN, MARJORIE GLORIA, art edn. dir.; b. Independence, Kan.; d. Herbert Truman and Emma (Billington) Gudgen; bB.S., Kan. State Tchrs. Coll., 1936; M.S., U. Kan., 1952; postgrad. West Tex. State U., 1958. Art instr., prin. art supr. Coffeyville (Kan.) pub. schs., 1929-52; art cons. Galveston (Tex.) Ind. Sch. Dist., 1952-57; dir. art edn. Amarillo (Tex.) Ind. Sch. Dist., 1957-74. Chmn. adv. com. local Scholastic Art Awards contest, Amarillo, 1964-74, mem., 1974-75. Bd. dirs. Amarillo Art Center. Mem. Amarillo C. of C. (mem. fine arts council 1963-75), N.E.A., Tex. State Tchrs. Assn., Nat. Art Edn. Assn., Tex. Art Edn. Assn. (life mem., pres. 1962-64), Amarillo Fine Arts Soc., Delta Kappa Gamma, Pi Lambda Theta, Kappa Delta Pi. Methodist. Selected to participate in Programa De Educacion Interamericana, 1968. Home: Amarillo, Tex., Died Mar. 17, 1975; interred Coffeyville, Kan.

GUESS, WALTER EUGENE, lawyer, state legislator; b. Tutwiler, Miss., Dec. 30, 1932; s. Thomas L. and Ralda (Bailey) G.; B.A. in Econs., Coll. William and Mary 1955; LL.B., U. Va., 1959; m. Carolyn Bailey Suber, July 14, 1956; children—Carl Thomas, John Bailey, Philip Mosby, Gretchen Gene. Asst. field solicitor, 1959-61; admitted to Alaska bar, 1961, practiced in Anchorage; pres. Ely, Guess, Rudd, Inc., 1961-75; mem. Alaska Ho. of Reps., 1965-72, chmn. judiciary com., 1965-66, vice chmn. commerce com., 1965-66, mem. spl. house com. on Pub. Service Commn. legislation, 1965, House minority whip, 1967-68, chmn. Minority Caucus, 1967-68, chmn. Alaska State Legislative Council, 1969-71, vice chmn., 1971-72, majority floor leader, 1969-70, chmn. local govt. com., 1969-70, spl. com. on monetary policy, 1969-70, speaker house, 1971-72. Vice chmn. Gov.'s Adv. Com. on Econ. Devel., 1962-64; spl. asst. to Gov. Post Alaska Earthquake of 1964 as liaison to Anchorage Banking Community; mem. Alaska Export Expansion Council, Dept. Commerce, 1966-75. Mem. Alaska devel. council Alaska Meth. U.; participant Eagleton Inst. Polit. Sci. Served to capt., arty. AUS, 1963. Mem. Fed. (past pres.), Va., Alaska, Anchorage bar assns., Alaska (mem. Alaska Nippon Kai), Anchorage chambers commerce, Alaska Arts Council. Home: Anchorage, Alaska., Died Mar. 13, 1975.

GUEVARA, PEDRO, Philippine commr.; b. Santa Cruz, Laguna Prov., P.I., Feb. 23, 1879; s. Miguel and Maria (Valenzuela) G.; coll. grad.; studied law at La Jurisprudencia, Manila; admitted to bar, 1909; m. Isidra Baldomero, of San Felipe Nery, Rizal, 1901. Officer with Filipino forces throughout Spanish-Am. War and Philippine Insurrection; served 5 yrs. with organization to maintain peace; was editor newspapers devoted to Philippine independence; served in Philippine Ho. of Rep., 1909-16, Senate, 1916-23 (chmn. com. on pub. instrn. chmn. com. on finance, 1922-23); resident commr. at Washington, D.C., 4 terms 1923-35. Mem. bd. regents U. of Philippines, 1916-22. Chmn. Philippine delegation to Internat. Bar Assn. Conf., Peking, 1921; mem. and acting chmn. on part of Senate, Philippine Parliamentary Mission to U.S., 1922. Home: Washington, D.C.†

GUFLER, BERNARD, fgn. service officer; b. Lawrence, Kan., June 1, 1903; s. Otto Bernard and Myrtle (Kelsey) G.; student U. Kan., 1921-22; A.B., Princeton, 1925; student Harvard Bus. Sch., 1925-26; m. Dorothy Van Ness, Dec. 9, 1937. Entered fgn. service, 1929; vice consul, Vancouver, B.C., 1930, Riga Latvia, 1930-33; sec. of Embassy, Warsaw, 1933-34; political desk officer, Div. of European Affairs, Dept. of State, 1934-38; sec. of legation and consul, Kaunas, Lithuania, 1938-40; sec. of Embassy, Berlin, Germany, 1940-41; asst. chief spl. war problems div., Dept. of State, 1941-45, mem. policy planning staff, 1948; mem. staff, U.S. polit. adviser in Germany, 1948-49; chief fgn. relations div. Office U.S. Polit. Adviser to U.S. High Commr., 1949-51; counselor of embassy Am. Embassy, Colombo, Ceylon, 1951-54; fgn. service inspector, 1954-55, asst. chief of Mission, also dep. comdt., Berlin, 1955-59; Am. ambassador to Ceylon, 1959-61, Finland, 1961-63, assigned Dept. State, 1963-66, then mem. exam. panels, bd. examiners for fgn. service, Broker, Seattle, 1945-47. Dept. State Superior service award, 1960. Mem. Phi Delta Theta. Roman Catholic. Club: Metropolitan (Washington). Home: Topeka, Kan. Died Sept. 6, 1973.

GUGLER, ERIC, architect; student Armour Inst. Tech. and Art. Inst. Chgo.; A.B., Columbia, 1911; McKim fellow, Am. Acad. in Rome, 1911-14. Architectural works include Exec. Office Bldg. of The White House Washington, Oval Room, Office of the Pres. of U.S., cabinet room, The White House Piano for the East Room, and Adams inscription for dining room; Forman Schools, Litchfield, Conn.; meml. to Harvey Firestone, Akron, O., to Drs. William and Charles Mayo, Rochester, Minn., Anzio-Nettuno Meml., Italy, Am. Battle Monuments Commn.; bldgs. Wabash Coll., Crawfordsville, Ind.; mural decoration, chronological tables, historical geography (in assn. with historians and other mural painters), the Ednl. Bldg., Capitol Park, Harrisburg, Pa.; houses for Katharine Cornell, others; memls. to Waldo Hutchins, Theodore Roosevelt, Franklin D. Roosevelt, Anna Eleanor Roosevelt. Recipient 1st prize Chgo. War Meml., 1929. Fellow A.I.A.; mem. N.A.D., Nat. Inst. Arts and Letters. Archtl. League N.Y. Club: Century Assn. (N.Y.C.). Home: Palisades, N.Y. Died May 16, 1974.

GUILD, WILLIAM ALVA, physician, surgeon; b. Carlisle, Ia., June 7, 1879; s. Jonathan Ellis and Elizabeth (Bartholomew) G.; B.S., Des Moines (Ia.) Coll., 1900, M.S., 1903; Drake U., 1901; M.D., Chicago Homoe. Med. Coll., 1903, Hahnemann Med. Coll., Chicago, 1905; B.S., Sioux Falls Coll., 1939; m. Leonora Campbell, Mar. 16, 1904. Asst. police surgeon, Des Moines, 1904; prof. physiology and bacteriology, Des Moines Coll., 1905-06, city chemist and bacteriologist, 1906-08; prof. bacteriology and hygiene, Drake U. Dental Dept.; lecturer on forensic medicine, hygiene and sanitary science, Des Moines Hosp. Training Sch.; sec. Des Moines Gen. Hosp. Assn.; pres. and dir. Sch. of Orificial Surgery; pres. and chief of staff Northwest Hosp., 1925-32; organizer Professional Ins. Corp. and pres., 1924-33. Trustee Allied Hosp. Unit. Settled in Chicago, 1925. Served in French mil. hosps., 1914-15. Officer or mem. Am. Inst. Homoeopathy, A.M.A., Ill. State Homoe. Soc., Chicago Homoe. Mem. Soc. (ex-pres.), Homoe. Med. Soc. of Fla., Southern Homoe, Med. Assn., Ill. Med. Soc., Chicago Med. Soc., Surg. and Gynecol. Soc., Hahnemann Institute, Central States Homeo, Council, American Assn. Orificial Surgeons, National Soc. Physical Therapeutics, Acad. of Science (Mexico), Mexican Homoe. League (hon.), Am. Legion (Med. Post), S.A.R., Sioux Falls Alumni fo Chicago (pres.), etc. Hon. pres. and exec. sec. Pan-Am. Homoe. Med. Congress; delegate Internat. Congress of Social Hygiene, Brussels, 1916; World's Purity Federation, Louisville, Ky., 1917; 1st Internat. Congress of Mental Hygiene, Washington, D.C., 1932; held surg. clinics in London, 1924; apptd. under Wickersham Com. to investigate physical causes of habitual criminality in federal penitentiary, 1932; spent winters, 1929-32, in St. Petersburg, Fla., on staff Faith Hosp.; introduced cecal surgery in treatment of epilepsy and dementia praecox; introduced autogenous vaccines in Paris mil. hosps. and elsewhere; operated and lectured many hosps., U.S., Can., Mexico, eng. and European countries; has made extensive researches in cancer, the relation of physical defects to incorrigibility, delinquency, habitual criminality, functional insanities, etc. Baptist. Mason. Elk. Author of Defects of Right Lower Quadrant, Penoplasty, Vulvaplasty, Orgin of Symptoms, Puritis Ani, Course in Orificial Surgery. Co-author of Course in Homoeopathy; editor "The Orificialist," 1919-29; contbr. to med. and scientific jours. Home: Chicago, Ill.†

GUILLE, FRANCES VERNOR, educator; b. Atlanta, Mar. 1, 1908; d. B. Frank and Margaret Davis (Baker) Guille; student Muskingum Coll., 1926-27; B.A., Coll. of Wooster, 1930; M.A., Western Res. U., 1936; postgrad. Middlebury Lang. Sch., summers 1934, 38, Ohio State U., summer 1940; Docteur de l'Université, U. Paris, 1949. Tchr., Fairview High Sch., Cleve., 1930-37; tchr. French, Coll. of Wooster, O., 1937-75, prof., 1955-75, chmn. dept. French, 1969-72, acting dean women, 1944-46; instr. math. and geopolitics Naval Flight Prep. Sch., 1943-44; tchr. Central Mich. Coll., summer 1950, Western Res. U., summer 1955; dir. Wooster-in-Paris Summer Program, 1951-59, Crossroads-Africa group to Sénégal, summer 1960. Corr. Bur. for Students of French, from 1953.Research grantee Gt. Lakes Coll. Assn., 1967, 68; decorated chevalier des Palmes Académiques; French Govt. scholar, 1947-49, Vis. scholar Radcliffe Coll., 1961-62. Mem. Am. Assn. Tchrs. French (past pres. Ohio chpt.), Modern Lang Assn., Am. Assn. U. Women (past pres. local chpt.), Midwest, Ohio modern lang. assns., Am. Council on Teaching Fgn. Langs., Assn. Depts. Fgn. Lang., Phi Beta Kappa, Phi Sigma Iota, Delta Sigma Rho. Presbyn. Author: Francios-Victor Hugo et son Oeuvre, 1950; (with Bonthius, Davis, Drushal and Spencer) Independent Study Programs in the U.S., 1957. Editor: Le Journal d'Adéle Hugo, Vol. I, 1968, Vol. II, 1971. Asso. editor Wooster Alumni Mag., 1941-44. Home: Wooster, Ohio., Died Oct. 22, 1975.

GULICK, LEE NELSON, univ. adminstr.; b. Northumberland, N.Y., Sept. 11, 1893; s. Nelson Joseph and Harriet Helena (Lee) G.; B.S., U. Pa., 1916. M.E., 1927, M.A., 1930; m. Frances Reynolds Graham, June 12, 1920; children—Graham Lee, Robert Reynolds, Richard Wallace, Jane Lee. Supvr. Midvale Steel Co., Phila., 1916-20; instr. mech. engring. U. Pa., 1920-22, asst. prof., 1922-27, prof., 1927-64, emeritus professor of mechanical engineering, 1964—, dir. sch. mech. engring., 1951-57, sr. research engr. inst. coop. research, 1954-58, asst. dean Towne Sci. Sch., 1946-50, dean, 1950-54, asst. v.p. engring. undergrad. affairs, 1962-63; inventor improvements two-stroke cycle internal combustion eng. Profl. engr., Pa. Mem. Am. Soc. M.E. (chmn. nat. admissions com. 1952), Am. Soc. Engring. Edn., Alpha Chi Rho. Conglist. Home: Bala-Cynwyd, Pa. Died Oct. 23, 1973.

GULLIVER, ASHBEL GREEN, educator, lawyer; b. N.Y.C., Nov. 23, 1897; s. William Curtis and Louisa (Green) G.; student Groton (Mass.) Sch., 1910-15; B.A., Yale, 1919, LL.B., cum laude, 1922, M.A. (hon.), 1935; m. Eugenia B. Porter, Dec. 18, 1926; children—William Curtis, Anne Porter, Ashbel Green. Admitted to N.Y. bar, 1923, engaged in gen. practice law, N.Y.C.; asso. with Alexander & Green, 1922-27; mem. faculty Yale U. Sch. Law, 1927-74, asst. prof. law, 1927-31, asso. prof. law, 1931-35, prof. law, 1935-65, Garver prof. law emeritus 1965, 74, asst. dean, 1934-39, acting dean, 1939, dean, 1940-46. Fellow Timothy Dwight Coll., Yale, 1935-48. Served to 2d lt. F.A., U.S. Army, 1918, Mem. Conn. State Bd. Pardons, 1936-59, Alien Enemy Hearing Bd. of Dist. Conn., 1942-45, Conn. Post-War Planning Bd., 1943-45; chmn. Conn. State Bd. Labor Relations 1945-55, 64; arbitrator labor, motion picture and contract cases. Mem. Wolfs Head of Yale, Beta Theta Pi. Author: Future Interests, 1959; (with Clark, Lusky and Murphy) Gratuitous Transfers, 1967. Contbr. to legal periodicals. Home: Norwich, Vt. Died July 3, 1974.

GUNN, GEORGE PURNELL, bishop; b. Winona, Miss., Oct. 11, 1903; s. Elijah Steirling and Susan Ellwood (Carter) G.; grad. Portestant Episcopal Theol. Sem., Alexandria, Va., 1930, D.D., 1948; student Va. Episcopal Sch., Lynchburg, 1921-23; U. Va., 1924-27; m. Frances Hawkins Purnell, Sept. 3, 1930; children—George Purnell Jr., James Steirling. Carter Tredway. Ordained deacon Protestant Episcopal Ch., 1929, priest, 1930; consecrated bishop, 1948; rector Moore Parish, Altavista. Va., 1930-32, Ch. of the Good Shepherd, Norfolk, Va., 1932-48; bishop coadjutor Diocese So. Va., 1948-50, diocesan (sr. bishop), Apr. 1950-71. Dean Tidewater Convocation. Pres. bd. turstees St. Paul's Poly. Inst. Lawrenceville, Va.; trustee P.E. Theol. Seminary, Chathan Hall, Episcopal H.S., Stuart Hall, Boy's Home, Jackson-Field Home. Bd. dirs. Travelers Aid; bd. dirs., mem. exec. com. Tidewater council Boy Scouts Am., Norfolk chpt. A.R.C. Mem. Order First Families of Va., Phi Delta Theta. Mason, Rotarian (bd. dirs.). Home: Norfolk, Va. Died June 16, 1973.

GUNN, GLENN DILLARD, pianist, conductor; b. Topeka, Kan., Oct. 2, 1879; s. John Donald and Liela Salome (Collins) G.; ed. pub. schs., Evansville, Ind.; Royal Conservatory of Music, Leipzig, 1894-99, grad. 1896; apptd. asst. to Robert Teichmuller, 1896; m. Bernya Bracken, June 23, 1903. Lecturer in music, U. of Chicago extension faculty, 1905; mem. faculty Am. Conservatory, Chicago, 1901, Chicago Mus. Coll., 1901-06; founded, 1906, Glenn Dillard Gunn Piano Studios. Has appeared as soloist with Chicago Symphony Orchestra, New York Symphony Orchestra, Minneapolis Symphony Orchestra, Boston Opera Orchestra, Detroit Symphony Orchestra, New York Civic Orchestra; concert tour, Europe, 1898-99. Mus. editor Chicago Journal, 1902-04, Chicago Inter-Ocean, 1904-10, Chicago Tribune, 1910-14, Chicago Herald and Examiner, 1922-37; lecturer in music, U. of Chicago, U. of Notre Dame, 1908-28. Director piano department Catholic University of Am., 1943-46; faculty member, American University, 1948. Conducted series of American concerts, 1911-17, Chicago and American Symphony orchestras; music editor Washington Times-Herald Mem. (hon.) American Federation of Musicians. Author of a course of lessons on History and Enjoyment, 1939. Clubs: Cliff Dwellers (emeritus). Bohemian. Home: Washington, D.C.†

GUNSETT, HELEN TOSSEY, (Mrs. Luther Gunsett), mem. Democratic Nat. Com.; b. Van Wert, O., Oct. 5, 1909; d. Ira and Lucy (Stuckey) Tossey; student Ohio State U., 1927-29; m. Luther Gunsett, Feb. 2, 1936. Mem. Ohio Dem. Exec. Com., 1950-70; charter mem. Ohio Young Dem. Exec. Com.; mem. Ohio Dem. Central Com. from 5th Dist., 1950-70; trustee Federated Dem. Women Ohio, 1955-57; vice chmn. Van Wert County Dem. Exec. Com., 1956-58; mem. Dem. Nat. Com. from Ohio, 1956-68; alternate at large Dem. Nat. Conv., 1956, del. at large, 1960, 64, 68, co-chmn. credentials com., 1964, 68. Mem. Van Wert Bd. Health, 1956-71; mem. Presdl. bd. advisers Fed. Reformatory for Women; vice chmn. Van Wert Civic Planning Com. Incorporator Van Wert County Hist. Soc.; mem. twig group Van Wert Hosp.; dir. women's aux. Ohio br. Starr Commonwealth Sch. Boys, local A.R.C., YWCA and Am. Heart Assn. Mem. League Women Voters, D.A.R., Columbus Urban League, UN Assn., Federated Dem. Women of Ohio (life), Kappa Delta. Clubs: Van Wert Country Democratic Women's (pres.), Van Wert Woman's (pres. 1954-56). Address: Columbus, O., Died Dec. 17, 1971; interred Woodland Cemetery, Van Wert, O.

GUNTER, RICHMOND BAKER, church executive; b. Zion, Leake Co., Miss., Sept. 3, 1880; s. George Aaron and Mary Ellen (Philips) G.; grad. Miss. Central Normal Sch., Walnut Grove, Miss., 1904; Ph.B., Mississippi Coll., Clinton, Miss., 1907, D.D., 1921; Th.M., Southern Bapt. Theol. Sem., Louisville, Ky., 1912; m. Tyna Amelia Pate, of Coffeeville, Miss., Oct. 1, 1912 (died Feb. 25, 1931); children—Charles Pate, Mary Jessie; m. 2d, Katie South, Aug. 31, 1932. Teacher pub. and high schs., 3 yrs.; ordained minstry Southern Bapt. Ch., 1908; pastor Laurel, later Louisville, Miss., unitl 1917; sec. Miss. Bapt. Edn. Commn., 1917-19; pastor Carthage, Miss., 1920; corr. and exec. sec., also treas. Miss. Bapt. State Conv. Bd., 1920-38; now engaged in evangelistic work. Home: Jackson, Miss.†

GUNTHER, JOHN, writer; b. Chgo., Aug. 30, 1901, s. Eugene McClellan and Lisette (Schoeninger) G.; Ph.B., U. Chgo., 1922; D.Litt., Gettysburg Coll., 1955; m. Frances Fineman, 1927 (div. 1944); 1 son, John (died 1947); m. 2d, Jane Vandercook, 1948; 1 son, Nicholas. Reporter, Chgo. Daily News, 1922, asst. London corr., 1924-26, corr. in Paris, Moscow, Berlin, Rome, Scandinavia, Geneva, Spain, Near East, 1926-29, Central European and Balkan corr., Vienna, 1930-35, London corr., 1935-36. Has interviewed Lloyd George, Pres. Masaryk of Czechoslovakia, King Carol, Rumania, Gandhi, Trotsky, De Valera, Dollfuss, Generalissimo and Madame Chiang Kai-shek, Pres. Quezon, P.I.; presidents Cardenas, Avila Camacho, Mexico; Vargas, Brazil; Marshal Tito, Yugoslavia; Pope Plus XII; Premier de Gasperi, Italy; Nehru, Emperor Hirohito of Japan, Gen. MacArthur, Prime Minister MacMillian, DeGaulle, Dr. Almah, Ghana, others. Covered numerous important world events, 1926-70; including evacuation of Rhineland, 1930; sino-Japanese break at Geneva, 1931; Spanish revolution, 1932; Germany's departure from League Nations, 1933, fgn. corr. N. Am. Newspaper Alliance 1937-38, NBC, summer 1939; covered outbreak of war, London, 1939; war corr., London, 1941, Gen. Eisenhower's Hdqrs., Malta; Sicily, 1943; spl. cons. U.S. War Dept., 1942-44, corr. Look Mag., 1948; also covered Summit Conferences. Mem. Assn. Radio News Analysts N.Y., N.Y. Council Fgn. Relations. Clubs: Bucks (London); Century (N.Y.C.). Author: Inside Europe, 1936, rev. edits., 1937, 38, 39, 40; Inside Asia, 1939, rev. edit., 1942; The High Cost of Hitler, 1940; Inside Latin America, 1941; D-Day, 1944; The Troubled Midnight, 1945; Inside U.S.A., 1947, rev. edit. 1951; Death Be Not Proud, 1949; Behind the Curtain, 1949; Roosevelt in Retrospect, 1950; The Riddle of MacArthur, 1951; Eisenhower; The Man and the Symbol, 1952; Alexander the Great, 1953; Inside Africa, 1955, Days to Remember (with Bernard Quint), 1955; Meet North Africa (with Sam and Beryl Epstein), 1957; Inside Russia Today, 1958; Meet South Africa (with Sam and Beryl Epstein), 1958; Meet the Congo, 1959; Julius Caesar, 1959; The Golden Fleece, 1959; Taken at the Flood, the story of Albert D. Lasker, 1960; Inside Europe Today, 1961, A Fragment of Autobiography, 1962; Meet Soviet Russia, 2 vols., 1962; The Lost City, 1964; Procession, 1965; Inside South America, 1967; Chicago Revisited, 1968; Twelve Cities, 1969; also articles in periodicals. Commentator on internat. affairs for radio, TV. Editor: Mainstream of Modern World history series. Address: New York City, N.Y. Died May 29, 1970.

GUNTHROP, HORACE, zoologist; b. Holbeach, Lincolnshire, Eng., Aug. 28, 1881; s. Charles and Mary Elizabeth (Bambridge) G.; brought by parents to U.S., 1882; Ph.B., Hamline U., 1905; A.B., Stanford, 1909; A.M., U. of Kan., 1912, Ph.D., 1923; grad. study U. of Minn., 1917-18; m. Maude Amy Robson, of Red Wing, Minn, Aug. 15, 1906; 1 son, Charles Lawrence. Prof. biology, Southwestern Coll., Winfield, Kan., 1909-11; instr. in zoology, U. of Kan., 1911-12; prof. biology. Monmouth (Ill.) Coll., 1912-16; prof. zoology, Washburn Coll., Topeka, Kan., 1918-20; asst. prof. zoology, U. of Wash., 1920-24; prof. zoology, Mills Coll., Oakland, Calif., 1924-27, dir. science, 1927; prof. biology, U. of Ariz., 1927-30, prof. zoology after 1930. Mem. Kan. State Biol. Survey, 1910. Fellow A.A.A.S.; mem. Am. Assn. Univ. Profs., Nat. Assn. Audubon Socs. (mem. advisory bd. after 1932), Am. Ornithol. Union, Cooper Ornithol. Club, Western Soc. Naturalists, Acacia, Beta Kappa (founder nat. orgn.; grand arkon 1923-25; grand scribe 1925-29), Sigma Xi; asso. mem. Am. Zool. Soc. Republican. Methodist. Mason (Shriner). Contbr. scientific and ednl. articles. Home: Tucson, Ariz.†

GUREWITSCH, ARNO DAVID, physician, educator; b. Zurich, Switzerland, Oct. 31, 1902; s. Aron David and Maria (Markovitch) G.; student Berlin (Germany) U., 1921-23, 27-29; M.D., U. Basel (Switzerland), 1933; postgrad. tng., Basel, Vienna, London and N.Y.C.; m. Nemone Balfour, Aug. 13, 1937; 1 dau., Grania Marion; m. 2d, Edna Perkel, Feb. 23, 1958; 1 dau., Maria Anna. Came to U.S., 1935, naturalized, 1943. Intern, Jeusalem; resident Hadassah Hosp.; asst. pathology Mt. Sinai Hosp., N.Y.C., 1935-36, asst. hematology, 1937-39; attending physician, dir. phys. therapy N.Y. State Rehab. Hosp., West Haverstraw, N.Y., 1942-47; attending physician phys. therapy Polio Service Knickerbocker Hosp., N.Y.C., 1945-49; mem. faculty Columbia Coll. Physicians and Surgeons, 1939—, clin. prof. rehab. medicine, 1964-68, prof. emeritus, spl. lectr., 1968—; attending physician Columbia Presbyn. Med Center, 1962—; 1st med. officer UN Secretariat, 1949-51; physician Mrs. Eleanor Roosevelt, 1945-62; med. dir. Blythdale Children's Hosp., Valhalla, N.Y., 1951-68, med. dir. emeritus, 1968—; med. dir. Inst. for Crippled and Disabled, 1956-59; charge phys. medicine and rehab. service S.S. Hope, 1962-63. Mem. adv. council edn. and vocational rehab. Dept. Health, Edn. and Welfare, 1963-66; mem. med. adv. bd. Medico, U.S. del. Am. Assn. UN to World Fedn. UN Assns. at Bangkok, 1954; Geneva, 1955, Brussels, 1958, Warsaw, 1961, N.Y.C., 1963, New Delhi, 1965. Fellow Am. Acad. Phys. Medicine and Rehab.; mem. A.M.A, Am. Congress Rehab. Medicine. Contbr. med. jours. Home: N.Y.C., N.Y. Died Jan. 30, 1974; interred Ferncliff Cemetery, Hartsdale, N.Y.

GURLEY, BOYD, editor; b. Sandusky, O., Feb. 23, 1880; s. William Fletcher and Mary Eunice (Richards) G.; prep. edn., high sch., Sandusky; student Ohio Wesleyan U. and Western Reserve Law Sch. (non-grad.); m. Eleanor Huffman, Jan. 29, 1927; 1 dau., Eleanor. Editor Sandusky Star, 1900; in newspaper work, Columbus, Cleveland (O.) and Los Angeles (Calif.), 1900-06; editor Denver (Colo.) Express, 1906-13, Kansas City (Mo.) Post, 1914-19, News-Times, South Bend, Ind., 1921-26, Indianpolis Times, 1926-33. Mem. Sigma Chi. Clubs: Indianapolis Athletic; University (South Bend). Home: Indianapolis, Ind.†

GURNEY, E. FLOYD, v.p., sec. N.J. Bank and Trust Co. Address: Passaic, N.J. Died Dec. 26, 1969; buried George Washington Meml. Park, Paramus, N.J.

GURWITSCH, ARON, educator; b. Wilna, Russia, Jan. 17, 1901; s. Meyer and Eva (Bloch) G.; student U. Berlin, 1918-21, U. Frankfurt, 1921-28; Ph.D., U. Goettingen, 1928; m. Alice Stern, Apr. 1929. Came to U.S., 1940, naturalized, 1946. Research fellow Prussian Ministry Scis., Arts and Pub. Instrn., Berlin, Germany. 1929-33; lectr. Institut d'Histoire des Scis. Sorbonne, Paris, 1933-40; research fellow Caisse Nationale de la Recherche Scientifique, Paris, 1939-40; vis. lectr. philosophy Johns Hopkins, 1940-42; instr. physics Harvard, 1943-46; vis. lectr. math. Wheaton Coll., Norton, Mass., 1947-48; asst. prof. math. Brandeis U., 1948-51, asso. prof. philosophy, 1951-59; prof. philosophy Grad. Faculty Polit. and Social Sci. New Sch. for Social Research; N.Y.C., 1959-73. Fulbright Exchange prof. philosophy U. Cologne (Germany), 1958-59; vis. prof. philosophy Columbia, 1962, U. P.R., 1963, U. Mainz (Germany), 1968. Mem. Am. Assn. U. Profs., Am. Philos. Assn., Internat. Phenomenological - Soc. (mem. council), Soc. Phenomenology and Existential Philosophy, History of Sci. Soc., Société Francaise de Philophie. Author: Théorie du Champ de la Conscience, 1957; The Field of Consciousness, 1964; Studies in Phenomenology and Psychology, 1966. Mem. editorial bd. Philosophy and Phenomenological Research, 1940; Social Research, 1964. Cons. editor: Studies in Phenomenology and Existential Philosophy, 1963; Phenomenologica, 1966; Conscientia, 1966; Phenomenology and the Theory of Science, 1974; Leibniz Philosophie des Panlogismus, 1974; Das Bewnsstiseinsfeld, 1975; mem. editorial bd. Man and World, 1968. Contbr. articles to profl. jours. Home: N.Y.C., N.Y. Died June 25, 1973.

GUSTAFSON, WESLEY A., neurosurgeon; b. Waukegan, Ill., Mar. 5, 1909; s. Axel and Victoria (Johnson) G.; M.D., U. Ill., 1934; m. Jennie Robinson; 2 sons, 1 dau. Intern, Ill. Research and Edn. Hosp., Chgo., 1933-34, resident neurosurgery, 1934-35, resident gen. surgeon, 1935-37, asso. neuro-surg.; fellow neuro-pathology Albert Merritt Billings Hosp., Chgo., 1937-38; clk. Nat. Hosp., London Eng., 1938; fellow neuro-surgery, Lahey Clinic, Boston, 1938-39; attending neurosurgeon Henrotin, Augustana, Garfield Park, Ravenswood hosps., Chgo.; attending neurosurgeon McAllen Municipal Hosp.; cons. neuro-surgeon Gt. Lakes Naval, U.S. Marine, Bethany Meth. hosps.; later clin. prof. neurosurgery U. Ill. Del. surgery Internat. Congress Neurosurgeons. Served as lt. M.C., AUS, 1946. Specialist nerve surgery of heart disease. Diplomate Pan Am. Med. Assn. Mem. A.M.A., Warren Cole Soc., Am. Acad. Neurol. Surgery, Chgo. Surg. Soc., Harvey Cushing Soc., Inst. Medicine Chgo., Miss. Valley Med. Soc., Interurban, So., Chgo. neurol. socs., So. Neurosurg. Soc., Nu Sigma Nu, Sigma Xi. Club: University. Contbr. articles in field to profl. jours. Home: Jensen Beach, Fla., Died July 16, 1975.

GUSTAV, ADOLF, VI, King of Sweden; b. Stockholm, Sweden, Nov. 11, 1882; s. King Gustaf V and Victoria, Princess of Baden; ed. pvt. tutors; student U. Uppsala, 1902-03, U. Oslo, 1903-04; hon. degrees, U. Lund, 1918, Princeton, Yale, Clark, Chgo. univs., 1926, Cambridge U., 1929, Dorpat U., 1932, Harvard, 1938, Stockholm U., 1944, Helsingfors U., 1952; Oxford, 1955; m. Margaret, Princess of Great Britain and Ireland, June 15, 1905 (dec. 1920); children—Gustaf Adolf, Duke of Vasterbotten (dec., 1947); Sigvard; Ingrid, Queen of Denmark; Bertil, Duke of Halland, Carl Johan; m. 2d, Lady Louise Mountbatten, former Princess of Battenberg, Nov. 3, 1923 (dec. 1965, Crown Prince, 1907-50, King of Sweden, 1950-73. Commd. to Army, 1902, advanced through grades to gen., 1932. Promoter humanistic research in general in Sweden; an organizer Swedish humanistic scholarship; a founder and pres. Swedish Archaeol. Inst. in Rome, 1925, in Athens, 1948; pres. Humanistic Research Fund, 1928-50. royal Acad. Hist. and Antiquities, 1945-50, Swedish-Chinese Research Com. from its foundation 1922; of Swedish Cyprus Com., 1926-73. Active part in archaeol. excavations in Sweden, Greece, Cyprus and China. Pres. Swedish Olympics Com., 1912. Mem. Swedish Sports Fedn. (pres. 1908-39), Central Assn. Promotion Athletics (pres. 1907-33), Nat. League Against Tuberculosis (hon. pres.). Swedish Export Assn. (hon. pres.); fgn. mem. Académie des Inscriptions et Belles Lettres; mem. numerous other Swedish, fgn. socs., Archeol. Inst. d.deutschen Reiches, British Acad. clubs. Interested in archaeology and art, particularly ancient Chinese art. Address: Stockholm, Sweden. Died Sept. 15, 1973.

GUSTAVSON, REUBEN GILBERT, univ. prof.; b. Denver, Colo., Apr. 6, 1892; s. James and Hildegard Charlotte (Silen) G.; A.B., U. of Denver, 1916, A.M., 1917; Ph.D., U. of Chicago, 1925; D.Sc., Regis Coll., James Millikan U., Doan Coll., U. Me., U. Fla., Ripon Coll., Knox Coll., U. Colo., Colo. State U.; L.H.D., Nat. Coll. Edn., U. Denver; Litt.D., Cedar Crest Coll.; LL.D., Colo. Coll., U. Maine, Creighton University, U. Pitts.; H.H.D., U. Neb.; m. Edna Marie Carlson, June 15, 1918; children—Charlotte Marie, Russell Gilbert. Instr. in chemistry, Colo. Agrl. Coll., 1917-18, asst. prof., 1918-19, asso. prof., 1919-20; asst. prof., U. Denver, 1920-21, asso. prof., 1921-27, prof., 1927-37, prof. chemistry and chmn. dept. U. Colo., 1937-45; prof. chemistry and dean of graduate sch., 1942, president, U. of Colo., 1943-45; vice pres., and dean of faculties, U. of Chicago, 1945-46; vis. prof., 1929-30; chancellor

U. Neb., 1946-53. Bd. govs. Argonne Nat. Lab., 1945-50; pres., exec. dir. Resources for the Future, Inc. 1953-58; prof. chemistry, Univ. of Ariz., 1959—. Decorated Knight Order of North Star (Sweden). Fellow Chgo. Gynecol. Soc. (hon.); mem. Am. Inst. Chemists, Am. Med. Soc. (asso.), Am. Fedn. Biochemists, Soc., for Study Internal Secretions, Svensk Kemist Samfundent, Phi Beta Kappa, Sigma Xi, Phi Sigma, Phi Lambda Upsilon, Tau Beta Pi, Sigma Phi Epsilon. Clubs: Teknik, Cactus. Contbr. to Jour. Am. Chem. Soc., Jour. A.M.A. Address: Tucson, Ariz. Died Feb. 23, 1974.

GUTHE, CARL EUGEN, anthropologist; b. Kearney, Neb., June 1, 1893; s. Karl Eugen and Clara Belle (Ware) G.; B.S., U. of Mich., 1914; A.M., Harvard, 1915, Ph.D., 1917; m. Grace Ethel McDonald, Sept. 12, 1916; children—Karl Frederick, Alfred Kidder, Marjorie Belle (dec.), James McDonald. Austin teaching fellow, Harvard Univ., 1915-17; asso. dir. Andover-Pecos Expdn., Phillips Acad., Andover, Mass., 1917-21; research asso. in Middle Am. archaeology, Carnegie Instn., Washington, 1921-22; asso. dir. anthropology Univ. Museums, U. of Mich., 1922-29, dir. Mus. of Anthropology, 1929-43; chmn. div. social sciences, U. of Mich., 1935-38; dir. Univ. Museums, U. of Mich., 1936-43; dir. N.Y. State Mus., 1944-53, N.Y. State Sci. Service, 1945-53; research asso. Am. Assn. Museums, 1953-59. Chmn. Com. State Archaeol. Surveys, NRC, 1927-37; chmn. Div. Anthropology and psychology NRC, 1938-41; chmn. board Lab. of Anthropology, Santa Fe, 1936-39; president Midwest Museum Conference, 1940-44. Has made excavations in New Mexico, Guatemala, and Philippine Islands. Fellow Rochester Mus. Arts and Scis., Cranbrook Inst. Sci. Mem. Soc. Am. Archaeology (sec. 1936-40, pres. 1945-46), American Assn. Museums (mem. council 1943-53), Am. Anthrop. Assn. (v.p. central br. 1927-28, pres. 1928-29), N.Y. State Hist. Assn. (hon. trustee), A.A.A.S., Mich.-Ind.-Ohio Mus. Assn. (pres. 1929-33), Mich. Acad. Sci., Arts and Letters (pres. 1935-39), N.Y. State Archaeological Assn. (pres. 1952-53), Sigma Xi, Phi Kappa Phi, Delta Tau Delta. Author: Pueblo Pottery Making, 1925; So You Want a Good Museum, 1957; The Canadian Museum Movement, 1958; The Management of Small History Museums, 1959; also pamphlets and articles in jours. Home: Ann Arbor, Mich. Died July 24, 1974.

GUTHMANN, WALTER S., educator, chemist; b. Chgo., Apr. 3, 1907; s. William B. and Ida (Seligmann) G.; B.S., Yale, 1928, Ph.D., U. Chgo., 1932; m. Edith Greenbaum, Oct. 16, 1940; children—Babette (Mrs. David Steinbrecher), William Alan. Co-founder Edwal Labs., Chgo., 1933, v.p., 1933-41, pres., 1947-53; pres. Ringwood Chem. Co., 1953-58, Morton Chem. Co., 1958-61; mem. faculty Roosevelt U., Chgo., 1961-74, prof. chemistry, 1965-74, chmn. dept., 1966-73, trustee, 1972-74; faculty U.N.C., 1974-76. Cons. in field, 1935-76; dir. Ventron Corp. Mem. Bd. Edn. dist. 111, Highland Park, Ill., 1953-59; chmn. jr. coll. com. Highland Park-Deerfield, 1962-67. Cons. examiner Commn. on Inst. Higher Edn. North Central Assn. Colls. Served to maj., C.W.S., AUS, 1941-45. Mem. Am. Chem. Soc. (chmn. Chgo. sect. 1972—, nat. councilor 1965—), Mfg. Chemists Assn. (chmn. edn. activities com. 1963-65), Soc. Chem. Industry, Sigma Xi, Clubs: Chemists (Chgo.). Contbr. articles to jours. Research in organo-metallic reactions. Home: Charlotte, N.C., Died Mar. 2, 1976.

GUTHRIE, HUNTER, educator, clergyman; b. N.Y.C., Jan. 8, 1901; s. Jacob Francis and Mary (Ross) G.; A.B., Woodstock (Md.) Coll., 1923, A.M., 1924; S.T.D., Gregorian U., Rome, Italy, 1931; student Tronchiennes, Belgium, 1931-32, univs., Berlin, Munich, Freiburg, 1932-37; Dr. de. l'U., Univ. Paris, 1937. Entered Soc. of Jesus, 1917; ordained priest Roman Catholic Ch., 1930, instr. rhetoric, Latin, Vigan Sem., P.I., 1924-25, English, Latin, econ., Ateneo de Manila, P.I., 1925-27; prof. history and philosophy Woodstock (Md.) Coll., 1937-40 prof., head grad. philosophy Fordham, 1940-43; dean grad. sch. Georgetown U., 1943-49, pres., rector, 1949-52; prof. head dept. philosophy St. Joseph's Coll., Phila., 1952-74. Latin American special Dept. State, 1954, 58. Decorated Grand Cross of Alfonso X el Sabio (Spain); officer Legion Honor and Merit (Haiti); recipient Freedom award Valley Forge, 1950; Air U. award, 1958. Mem. Internat. Mark Twain Soc., Cath. Commn. for Intellectual and Cultural Affairs (co-founder), Am. Cath. Philos. Assn., Am. Acad. Polit. and Social Sci., Nat. Cath. Edn. Assn., U.S. Commn. on Reconstrn. Edn., Inst. of Religious Studies (com., guest prof.), Assn. Am. Colls. (vis. prof.), Medieval Acad. Am., Am. Philos. Assn., Nat. Fund Med. Edn. Author: Modern Trends in Am. Culture, 1923; Introduction au probleme de l'histoire de la Philosophie, 1937; Symposium on American Catholic Education, 1941; History of Theology, 1968. Asst. editor Dictionary of Philosophy. Home: Phila. Pa. Died Nov. 11, 1974; buried Jesuit Cemetery, Georgetown U., Washington.

GUTHRIE, JOHN DENNETT, forester; b. Charlotte Court House, Va., July 15, 1878; s. Eppa Dennett and Nancy Katherine (Franklin) G.; Ph.B., Union Coll., Schenectady, N.Y., 1902, M.S., 1932; M.F., Yale, 1906; unmarried. Government forestry work in western part of the United States, 1902-08; forest supervisor Arizona, 1908-17, New Mexico, 1919-20; assistant regional forester, Portland, Ore., 1920-33; liaison officer, 8th Corps Area, Civilian Conservation Corps, Ft. Sam Houston, Tex., 1933-34; general inspector Civilian Conservation Corps, Washington, D.C., 1934-43; retired, 1943; forest travel in Alaska, Mexico, France, Russia, Italy, Switzerland, Germany, Hungary, Austria, Scotland, Finland, Sweden. Commd. capt., Co. C. 10th Engrs. (forestry), A.E.F., June 1917; successively with timber acquisition, central France, staff 14th Batt. 20th Engrs., war damages commn., to Rumania, 310th Engrs., N. Russia (capt.). Gen. W. P. Richarson's staff, Archangel, Russia; hon. disch., July 1919; maj. Engrs., O.R.C. from 1919. Del. to Internat. Forestry Congress, Rome, 1926 Budapest, 1936. Fellow A.A.A.S., Am. Geographical Soc., Soc. Am. Foresters; life mem. Am. Forestry Assn., Finnish Forestry Society, Va. Hist. Society, A.V.P.A.; mem. Military Order World War, American Legion, Sons of American Revolution, S.C.V., Virginia Academy Science, Farm Bureau, Patrick Henry Memorial Foundation (national trustee and vice pres.), Poe Foundation, Institut Francais de Washington, D.C., Sigma Phi. Awarded Merite Agricole (France); Orders of St. Anne, St. Nicholas, and Compassionate Heart (Russia); Pack prize Soc. of Am. Foresters, 1925. Democrat. Presbyterian. Clubs: Army and Navy, National Press (Washington), Ruritan. Author: Forest Ranger and Other Verse, 1919; Forest Fires and other Verse, 1929; Saga of the CCC, 1942; and chapters in "Naturalists Guide to the Americas," "American Conservation" and "The Loop" (novel). Contbr. numerous tech. articles. Home: Charlotte Court-House, Va.†

GUTHRIE, MARSHALL CRAPON, U.S.P.H.S.; b. 1879; M.D., U. of N.C., 1904. Became med. dir. U.S.P.H.S., Ellis Island, now asst. surgeon gen. Fellow A.M.A Address: Washington D.C.†

GUTHRIE, MARY J(ANE), zoologist; b. New Bloomfield, Mo., Dec. 13, 1895; d. George Robert and Lulu Ella (Loyd) Guthrie; A.B., U. of Mo., 1916, A.M., 1918; Fellow in Biology, Bryn Mawr Coll., 1921-22, Ph.D., 1922. Demonstrator in biology Bryn Mawr Coll., 1918-20, instr., 1920-21; asst. prof. zoology U. of Mo., 1922-27, asso. prof., 1927-37, prof., 1937-51, chmn. dept. of zoology, 1939-50; research asso. Detroit Inst. Cancer Research from 1951. Fellow A.A.A.S., Am. Assn. Anatomists, Am. Soc. Naturalists, Am. Soc., Zoologists, Genetics Soc. Am., Am. Assn. U. Profs., Sigma Xi. Author: General Zoology, 1938: Laboratory Directions in General Zoology, 1938. Mem. editorial bd. Jour. Morphology, 1944-47. Died Feb. 22, 1975; buried New Bloomfield, Mo.

GUTHRIE, RAMON, poet; b. N.Y.C., Jan. 14, 1896; s. Harry and May (Hollister) G.; doctorat en droit, U. Toulouse (France), 1922; Litt.D. (hon.), Dartmouth, 1971; m. Marguerite Maurey, Apr. 8, 1922. Asst. prof. U. Ariz., Tucson, 1924-27; prof. Romance langs. Dartmouth, 1930-63. Served with U.S. Army, 1916-19, OSS, 1943-45. Decorated Silver Star. Author: Trobar Clus, 1923, A World Too Old, 1927, Graffiti, 1959, Asbestos Phoenix, 1968, Maximum Security Ward, 1970. Address: Norwich, Vt. Died Nov. 1973.

GUTIERREZ ROSS, FRANCISCO DE PAULA, ambassador from Costa Rica to U.S.; b. San Jose, Costa Rica, Apr. 21, 1880; s. Augustin Gutierrez Yglesias and Julia (Ross) G.; educated in schools and colleges of Costa Rica; married Stella Mangel Rosat, October 5, 1911; children—Francisco de Paula, Margarita (Mrs. George Gutierrez Cooper), Jose Joaquin. Formerly governor of Province de Limon; elected to Congress, 1930, vice president of Congress, 1932-34; mem. Bd. of Control of Exchange, 1935-37; apptd. Sec. of State for Finance and Commerce, 1937-39, and during tenure of office greatly reduced the pub. debt; apptd. pres. Bd. of Control of Exports and Imports, Mar. 1943; recalled to office as Sec. of State for Finance and Commerce, Aug. 1943; appt. Sec. of Pub. Works and Industry, Nov. 1943; resigned all positions, 1944; ambassador to U.S. from June 1944. As farmer is interested in tropical agr., and controls large tract of fertile land in Atlantic Zone of Costa Rica where U.S. Govt. is developing manila hemp, rubber, balsa wood, etc. Address: Home: San Jose, Costa Rica†

GUTMAN, MONROE C., banker; b. N.Y.C. Oct. 15, 1885; s. Sanders and Pauline (Bernstein) G.; A.B. magna cum laude, Harvard, 1905, M.A., 1906; m. Pauline Ehrich, Oct. 8, 1917 (div.); m. 2d, Edna Cullman, Nov. 24, 1932 (dec.). Began in brokerage bus., 1905; with firm Bernhard, Scholle & Co., 1910; joined Lehman Bros., N.Y.C., 1922, partner 1927-74; dir., mem. exec. com. Lehman Corp. Trade distbr. U.S. War Trade Bd., World War I. Hon. chmn. bd. trustees Montefiore Hosp. and Med. Center. Jewish religion. Clubs: Harvard, Harmonie (N.Y.C.). Home: New York City N.Y. Died July 3, 1974.

GUTTMACHER, ALAN FRANK, physician; b. Balt., May 19, 1898; s. Adolf and Laura (Oppenheimer) G.; A.B., Johns Hopkins, 1919, M.D., 1923; D.Sc. (hon.), Brandeis U., Dartmouth Coll., 1970; m. Leonore Gidding, July 22, 1925; children—Ann (Mrs. Robert Loeb), Sally (Mrs. Eric Holtzman), Susan (Mrs. Ben Green). Intern Johns Hopkins Hosp., 1925-26; asst. in anatomy Johns Hopkins, 1923-24, U. Rochester, 1924-25; various positions from resident to asso. prof. obseterics Johns Hopkins. 1926-52; practice medicine, specializing in obstetrics and gynecology, Balt., 1929-52, N.Y.C., 1952-74; former chief obstetrics and gynecology Mt. Sinai Hosp; emeritus prof. obstetrics-gynecology Mt. Sinai Med. Sch.; vis. prof. Einstein Med. Sch. Pres. Planned Parenthood Fedn., 1962; bd. dirs. Margaret Sanger Research Bur. Recipient Lasker award, 1947; Bronfman award, 1970. Diplomate Am. Bd. Obstetrics and Gynecology. Fellow Assn. Obstetrics and Gynecology, N.Y. Acad. Medicine, N.Y. Obstet. Soc. (past pres.). Author: Life in the Making, 1933; Into This Universe, 1937; Pregnancy and Birth, 1957; Babies by Choice or Chance, 1959; (with J. Rovinsky, Williams, Wilkins) Complications of Pregnancy, rev., 1965; Complete Book of Birth Control, 1961; Planning Your Family, 1964; Birth Control and Love, 1969; Understanding Sex, 1970. Home: New York City, N.Y. Died Mar. 18, 1974.

GWATHMEY, EDWARD SMITH, aircarft co. exec.; b. Norfolk Va., Nov. 4, 1909; s. George Tayloe and Margaret Cabell (Smith) G.; B.S., U. Va., 1930, M.S., 1932, Ph.D., 1937; postgrad. Columbia, 1933-36; m. Berwyn Neal Heise, July 11, 1944; children—James Taylor, Anne Temple (Mrs. Maxwell Perrotta). Instr. physics Coll. City N.Y., 1933-37; dir. research Spltys., Inc., Syosset, N.Y., 1945-48; v.p. new devels. Feed Products, Groveland, Fla., 1948-51; dir. research Spltys., Inc., Charlottesville, Va., 1951-64; dir. engring. and research Automated Spltys. div. Teledyne, Inc., Charlottesville, gen. mgr. Teledyne Avonics div., Charlottesville, 1969-73. Served to comdr. USNR, 1937-45. Fellow Am. Inst. Aeros. and Astronautics; mem. A.A.A.S., Raven Soc. Clubs: Colonade, Boarshead (Charlottesville). Home: Boca Raton, Fla. Died Oct. 30, 1973.

GWYN, THOMAS LENOIR, stock raiser; b. Springdale, N.C., Oct. 16, 1881; s. James and Amelia (Foster) G.; Ph.B., U. of N.C., 1903; m. Hilda Way, of Waynesville, N.C., Dec. 20, 1920; 1 dau., Mary Patricia. Prominently identified with development of live stock industry in the South; breeder of Shorthorn cattle; owner Springdale Stock Farms. Pres. Haywood Supply Co., Waynesville, N.C.; dir. N.C. R.R.; chmn. Bd. of Commrs. of Haywood Co., N.C. Mem. Nat. Highway Council, N.C. Good Roads Assn., Western Carolina Good Roads Assn. (pres.), Phi Beta Kappa, Zeta Psi. Mem. State legislature, 1923-24. Democrat. Epsicopalian. Mason. Home: Waynesville, N.C.†

HAAS, HARRY J., banker; b. Luzerne County, Pa., Jan. 20, 1879; s. John and Elizabeth H.; grad. Wyoming Sem. and Coll. of Business, Kingston, Pa. grad. Evening Sch. of Accounts and Finance, U. of Pa., 1910; grad. Am. Inst. Banking, 1910; m. Rufie Watson Sanders, Oct. 28, 1914; 1 son, Joseph Sanders. Salesman and newspaper corr. until 1902; teller Berwick (Pa.) Nat. Bank, 1902-03; asst. treas. Berwick Savings & Trust Co., 1903-07; sec. and treas. Farmers & Mechanics Trust Co., West Chester, Pa., 1907; with Merchants Nat. Bank of Phila. (merged with First Nat. Bank 1910) from 1908, asst. cahsier, 1908-16, v.p., dir. 1924-44; past dir. dir., v.p. Phila. Bourse. Mem. Am. Bankers Assn. (pres. 1931-32), Am. Inst. Banking (hon.), Pa. Bankers Assn. (pres. 1928), Assn. Reserve City Bankers (hon., an organizer). Republican. Presbyn. Clubs: Bank Officers' (hon.), Merion Cricket. Author: Golf Service for Caddies and Members. Home: Haverford, Pa.†

HAAS, LEONARD, lawyer; b. Atlanta, Nov. 20, 1880; s. Aaron and Fanny (Rich) H.; A.B., U. of Ga., 1899; LL.B., Columbia, 1902; m. Beatrice Hirsch, Mar. 31, 1927; children—Leonard, John. Admitted to N.Y. bar, 1902, and practiced in N.Y. City, 1902-04, to Ga. bar, 1904, and then practiced in Atlanta, individually 15 years and in various partnerships, now Haas & Hunt; counsel for numerous insurance and transportation cos., etc. Mem. Am. Bar Assn., Phi Beta Kappa. Jewish religion. Home: Atlanta, Ga.†

HAASE, FERDINAND, JR., med. adminstr.; b. Elmira, N.Y., Jan. 2, 1911; s. Ferdinand and Sarah (Mosher) H.; B.A., Yale, 1934; M.D., Harvard, 1942; m. Eleanor Ruby Nelson, June 17, 1943; children—Ferdinand Carl, Sarah Elizabeth, Christine. Intern, pediatrics Children's Hosp., Boston, 1942-43; asst. resident pediatrics Children's Hosp., Buffalo, 1943-44; asst. dir. Mass. Gen. Hosp., 1944-49; exec. dir. Nathan Littauer Hosp., Gloversville, N.Y., 1949-52; med. dir. Albany Med. Center Hosp., 1952-70; asst. dir., 1970-72; faculty Albany Med. Coll., 1952-72. Dir. Albany Area Chpt. A.R.C. Fellow Am. Coll. Hosp. Adminstrs.; mem. Northeastern N.Y. Hosp. Assn. (pres. 1952-54). Home: Delmar, N.Y. Died Oct. 22, 1972.

HABOUSH, EDWARD JOSEPH, physician; b. New London, Conn., Apr. 15, 1904; B.S. in Medicine, U. Richmond, 1924; M.D., Med. Coll. Va., 1928; m. Donata V. Brosen, Mar. 22, 1972. Rotating intern Kanawah Valley Hosp., Charleston, W.Va., 1928; surg. intern Nassau County Hosp., Mineola, N.Y., 1929; rotating intern Hosp. for Joint Diseases, N.Y.C., 1929-30, resident in orthopedic surgery, 1930-31, then courtesy staff orthopedic surgery; asso. orthopedic surgeon Cumberland St. Host., Bklyn., 1935-52, acting attending orthopedic surgeon, 1942; cons. orthopedic surgeon LeRoy Hosp., N.Y.C., Interborough Gen. Hosp., Bklyn., Prospect Hosp., Bronx, N.Y.; asso.

orthopedic surgeon Columbus Hosp., N.Y.C.; courtesy orthopedic surgeon Hempstead (N.Y.) Gen. Hosp., Madison Av. Hosp., N.Y.C.; clin. instr. N.Y.U., 1951. Orthopedic cons. to dir. SSS, N.Y.C., 1948-73; orthopedic cons. Office Atty. Gen., State of N.Y.; orthopedic impartial specialist N.Y. State Workmen's Compensation Bd. Served to lt. col., M.C., AUS. Diplomate Am. Bd. Orthopedic Surgery. Fellow Am. Acad. Orthopedic Surgeons, A.C.S.; mem. N.Y. County, Nassau County med. socs., A.M.A., Am. Fracture Assn. Contbr. articles to profl. jours. Developer hip replacement with use of acrylic bone cement. Home: New York City, N.Y. Died July 2, 1973; interred L.I. Nat. Cemetery, Farmingdale, N.Y.

HACKETT, CHAUNCEY, lawyer; b. Washington, D.C., May 20, 1881; s. Frank Warren and Ida (Craven) H.; prep. edn. St. Mark's Sch. (Southboro, Mass.), Friends Sch. (Washington, D.C.); A.B., Harvard, 1903, LL.B., 1906; m. Katharine Jennings, May 23, 1914; children—Hennen Jennings, Sylvia Joan; m. 2d, Mary Cleveland Moffett, Jan. 5, 1926; children—Wendy Anne, Thomas Truxton. Admitted to District of Columbia bar, 1906, practiced at Washington; gen. counsel Assn. Against Prohibition Amendment, 1923-26, Capt. Air Service U.S.A., 1917-19. Mem. Am. Bar Assn., Am. Soc. Internat. Law. Republican. Episcopalian. Clubs: Metropolitan, Chevy Chase (Washington, D.C.); Cercle Interalliée (Paris). Author: The Log (with Arthur Guiterman), 1915. Home: Washington, D.C.†

HACKETT, JAMES J., retail co. exec.; b. 1907. With Scheuer & Co., textile brokers, 1936-47; with J.P. Stevens & Co., Inc., 1947-75, exec. v.p., 1968-75, pres. Woolens and Women's Wear div., 1970-75, also dir. Died Nov. 3, 1975.

HACKL, GEORGE F., JR., stock broker; b. Chgo., Sept. 25, 1904; s. George F. and Olga (Hockstrom) H.; student Prince(on, 1926; m. Faith Douglas Severance, Jan. 9, 1929; children—Faith Griswold (Mrs. Donald Ward), George Craig Severance. Partner Laird, Bissell & Meeds, N.Y.C. Bd. govs. N.Y. Stock Exchange. Home: Princeton N.J. Died Mar. 1974.

HACKLER, VICTOR, journalist; b. Gregory, S.D., Feb. 2, 1906; s. Joy M. and Nellie (Tisue) Hackler; B.A., U. Neb., 1927; m. Harriet Corey (div.); children—Robert, Kent (dec.); m. 2d, Mrs. Grethel Crawford Lloyd. Received early training as reporter and corr. on Omaha Bee; with A.P., Press, 1927-71, staff mem. Omaha, Milw., Duluth, Chgo., N.Y., chief of bur., Milw., 1934-36, Chgo., 1937-42, exec. asst. to gen. mgr., N.Y.C., 1942, gen. financial editor, 1943, chief N.Y. Bur., 1944-45, news editor, London, 1945-48, assigned to exec. news staff, N.Y., 1948-50, gen. exec., 1951-71, cons., 1971; editor Asso. Press Mng. Editors Assn. Redbook, 1953-71; nat. coordinator A.P. Election Coverage, 1950-71. Bd. mgrs. Network Election Service, 1964, News Election Service, 1966-71. Mem. Phi Kappa Psi, Sigma Delta Chi. Home: Sanibel Island, Fla. Died Aug. 1975.

HACKMAN, PEARL E(STELLA), physician; b. nr. Sunneytown, Pa.; d. Joseph B. and Jennie V. (Heany) Hackman; student Temple U., 1916-18; B.S., Pa. State U., 1920; M.D., Woman's Med. Coll., 1924. Intern, Reading (Pa.) Gen. Hosp., 1924-25; gen. practice ophthalmology, asst. gen. practitioner, part-time sch. health and san. inspection, Reading, 1926-43; indsl. medicine E. I. duPont deNemours & Co., Penn's Grove, N.J., 1944-45; gen. practice eye, ear, nose and throat, Canton, O., 1945-46; dir. maternal and child welfare, sch. health physician Lansing and Ingham County Health Dept., Lansing, Mich., 1946-49; gen. practice, hosp. adminstrn. U.S. Indian Service, Navajo Indian Reservation in Ariz., N.M., Utah, Colo., 1950-52; physician Milw. Health Dept. Maternal and Child Welfare Dept., 1952; gen. psychiatry State Hosp., Cleve., 1952-53; psychiatrist, acting chief internal medicine, surgery, geriatrics, chief outpatient services and admissions officer VA Neuropsychiat. Hosp., Gulfport, 1953-65, ret., 1965. Diplomate Nat. Bd. Med. Examiners. Fellow Royal Soc. Health; mem. A.M.A., Miss., Coast Counties med. socs., A.A.A.S., Internat. Platform Assn., Am. Assn. Ret. Persons, Airline Passenger Assn., Nat. Hist. Soc., Smithsonian Assos., Defenders of Wildlife, Am. Security Council (adv. bd.), Marquis Biog. Library Soc. (adv. mem.), Nat. Hist. Soc. (founding mem.), Nat. Assn. R.R. Passengers. Address: Gulfport, Miss. Deceased.

HADDOW, ALEXANDER, physician; b. Jan. 18, 1907; s. William and Margaret H.; M.B., Ch.B., U. Edinburgh, 1929, Ph.D., 1937, M.D. (Gold medal), 1937, D.Sc., 1938; D.Sc. (hon.), 1967; M.D. (hon.), U. Perugia, 1957; D., U. Liege, 1967; D. (hon.), U. Helsinki, 1965. m. Lucia Lindsay Crosbie Black, 1932 (dec. 1968); 1 son; m. 2d, Feo Standing, 1969. Carnegie research student, house physician Royal Infrimary Edinburgh; Davidson research fellow, lectr. bacteriology U. Edinburgh; Laura de Saliceto student U. London; prof. exptl. pathology U. London, 1946-72; dir. Chester Beatty Research Inst., Inst. Cancer Research, Royal Cancer Hosp., until 1969; mem. com. mgmt. Inst. Cancer Research. Recipient Katherine Berkan Judd award Meml. Hosp. N.Y., 1948; Walker prize R.C.S. Eng., 1951; Robert Roesler de Villers award Leukemia Soc. N.Y., 1960; Claude Perchot prize Faculty de Medecin, Paris, 1960; Karnofsky Meml. lectr., 1970; Sidney Farber Med. Research award, 1970; Gold medal Worshipful Soc. Apothecaries London, 1963; Internat. Union against Cancer award, 1970; diploma and medal Italian Soc. Toxicology, 1971; officier de l'Ordre de la Sante Publique; croix de Chevalier de la Legion d'Honneur; officer Order Don Carlos Finlay (Cuba). Fellow Royal Soc. Medicine (hon.), World Acad. Arts and Scis., Inst. Biology (hon); mem. Royal Med. Soc. Edinburgh (life), Am. Acad. Arts and Scis. (fgn. hon.), Path. Soc. Gt. Britain and Ireland, Chem. Soc., Genetical Soc., Soc. for Endorinology, Soc. Gen. Microbiology, Soc. Exptl. Biology, Inst. Biology, Acad. Roy. de Med. de Belgique, Ciba Found. (exec. council), Parliamentary Assn. World Govt., Grand Council of Brit. Empire Cancer Campaign, Internat. Union Against Cancer (pres. 1962-66), Soc. Study Growth and Devel., N.Y. Acad. Scis., Am. Assn. Cancer Research, Parliamentary Group for World Govt., B.B.C. Sci. Cons. Group (past chmn.); hon. mem. Czechoslovak Med. Soc., Hungarian Acad. Scis. Club: Chelsea Arts. Contbr. articles to sci., med. jours. Home: Chalfont St Giles, Bucks, England., Died Jan. 21, 1976.

HADER, BERTA HOERNER, (Mrs. Elmer Stanley Hader), writer, illustrator; b. San Pedro, Coahuila, Mexico; d. Albert and Adelaide (Jennings) Hoerner; student, U. of Wash., 1909-12; Calif. Sch. of Design, San Francisco, 1915-18; m. Elmer Stanley Hader, July 14, 1919. Began as fashion designer, 1914; newspaper artist, San Francisco Bulletin, 1916-18; minature portrait painter, 1916-37; illustrator and writer of children's books 1919-76. Author and co-author numerous books including: Little Stone House, 1944; Rainbow's End, 1945; The Skyrocket, 1946; Little Chip, 1958; Reindeer Trail, 1959; Mr. Billy's Gun, 1960; Quack-Quack, 1961; Little Antelope, 1962. Illustrator with Elmer Stanley Hader: Adventures of Theodore Roosevelt, Humpy, Stripey; The Big Snow, 1948 (awarded Caldecott Medal). Author illustrator (with husband): Little Appaloosa, 1949; Squirrely of Willow Hill, 1950; Lost in the Zoo, 1951; Little Whitefoot, 1952; The Friendly Phoebe, 1953; Wish on the Moon, 1954; Home on the Range, 1955; The Runaways, 1956; Ding Don Bell, 1957; Snow in the City, 1963; Two is Company, Three's a Crowd, 1965. Contbr. stories and drawings to mags. Home: Grand View-on-Hudson, N.Y., Died Feb. 6, 1976.

HADJIMARKOS, DEMETRIOS MARKOS, educator; b. Athens, Greece, Mar. 30, 1912; s. Markos G. and Euterpi (Stamatakes) H.; D.D.S. U. Athens, 1931; M.S.D., Northwestern U., 1943; M.P.H., Harvard, 1946; m. Clara Budlong, Sept. 22, 1954; 1 dau., Marcia-Charlotte. Came to U.S., 1940, naturalized, 1948. Asso. prof. Ore. State U., 1946-52; asst. prof. U. Ore. Dental Sch., Portland, 1953-55, asso. prof., 1955-57, prof., chmn., dept. preventive dentistry, 1957-73. Fellow A.A.A.S., Am. Pub. Health Assn. Greek Orthodox. Author: chpts. in books. Contbr. articles profl. jours. Home: Portland Ore. Died Oct. 9, 1973; interred Athens, Greece.

HADLEY, HAMILTON, lawyer; b. New Haven, Jan. 13, 1896; s. Arthur Twining and Helen Harrison (Morris) H.; ed. Groton Sch., 1908-14; B.A., Yale, 1919, LL.B. cum laude, 1923; m. Emily Hammond Morris, July 13, 1929; 1 dau., Anne (Mrs. John Keith Howat). Partner, law firm Winthrop, Stimson, Putnam and Roberts, N.Y.C., 1929-40; trustee U.S. Trust Co., N.Y.C., 1936-68, hon. trustee, 1968-75; v.p., dir. Am. Superpower Corp., 1929-40; in period of orgn. and original financing v.p. Niagara Hudson Power Corp., Commonwealth and So. Corp.; dir. Research Corp., 1930-57. Dir. and trustee The Brearley Sch., 1930-54; asso. fellow Branford Coll., Yale, 1939-75; former councillor Am. Geog. Soc.; gov. N.Y. Hosp., 1947-65, hon. gov., 1966-75, pres., 1953-57. Served as capt. A.E.F., U.S. Air Service, World War I. Life mem. Am. Mus. Natural History, Acad. Polit. Sci., Am. Geog. Soc.; mem. Assn. Bar City N.Y., Am., N.Y. State bar assns. Clubs: Century Assn., Down Town Assn., Yale (N.Y.); New Haven Lawn, Graduates, Elizabethan (New Haven). Author: A Free Order, 1963. Address: Armonk N.Y. Died Mar. 23, 1975; inurned Middle Patent Cemetery, Armonk, N.Y.

HADLEY, PHILIP BARDWELL, bacteriologist; b. Shelburne Falls, Mass., Jan. 10, 1881; s. Edison Parker and Elizabeth (Fairbanks) H.; Ph.B., Brown U., 1903, Ph.D., 1908; m. Ruth Barbara Canedy, May 16, 1908; children—Jarvis Bardwell, Francis Canedy, Barbara; m. 2d, Faith Elizabeth Palmerlee, Aug. 7, 1924. Chief, div. of animal breeding and pathology, R.I. Agrl. Expt. Sta., 1908-20; prof. bacteriology, R.I. State Coll., 1912-20; asst. prof. bacteriology, Sch. of Medicine, U. of Mich., 1920-27, asso. prof. from 1927. Mem. A.A.A.S. Soc. Am. Bacteriologists, Am. Soc. Naturalists, Soc. for Exptl. Biology and Medicine, Mich. Acad. Science, Am. Soc. Experimental Pathology, Am. Soc. Immunologists, Phi Kappa Phi, Sigma Xi, Delta Upsilon. Showed manner of inheritance of plumage color in birds; developed methods of immunication against haemorrhagic septicemia; established role of flagellated protozoa as intestinal and hepatic tissue parasites; established new principle relating to egg production in the domestic fowl; recent studies on bacteriophage and microbic dissociation. Address: Ann Arbor, Mich.†

HAEBERLE, FREDERICK EDWARD, naval officer; b. St. Louis, Mo., July 18, 1893; s. George Frederick and Elizabeth Fay (Corey) H.; student U. of Colo., 1910-12, B.S., U.S. Naval Acad., 1917; M.S., Mass. Inst. Tech., 1921; m. Faye Vivian Davis, Dec. 21, 1918; 1 son, Frederick Roland. Commd. ensign, U.S. Navy, 1917, and advanced through the grades to rear adm., 1945; duty on U.S.S. Wyoming, 1917-18; designer of U.S. ships Lexington and Saratoga and modernization of battleships, Bureau Construction and Repair, 1922-27; design superintendent, New York Navy Yard, designing battleships North Carolina, Washington, Iowa, New Jersey, Missouri, Wisconsin, Kentucky, 1937-42; head design and constrn. branches, Bureau of Ships, 1942-45; mgr. Navy Yard New York, 1945; comdr. New York Naval Shipyard, 1945-49, on duty with Bureau of Ships, 1949-51; adminstr. Webb Institute of Naval Architecture. Awarded Victory Medals, World War I, World War II. American Theatre and European and Mediterranean Theatre ribbons, Defense Medal, Legion of Merit, Gold Star in lieu of second Legion of Merit. Mem. Soc. Naval Architects and Marine Engrs., Am. Soc. of Naval Engrs. Home: Glen Cove, N.Y. Died Feb. 24, 1975.

HAESSLER, CARL, editor; b. Milw., Aug. 5, 1888; s. Herman F. and Lina Elizabeth (Wagner) H.; A.B., U. Wis., 1911; B.A. (Rhodes Scholar), Balliol Coll., Oxford U., Eng., 1914; Ph.D., U. Ill., 1917; m. Mildred Barnes, 1917; two children; m. 2d, Lucy Whitaker, 1940. Fgn. corr. Milw. Leader, 1911-14, mail circulation mgr., 1917-18, staff city room, 1920-21; instr. philosophy U. Ill., 1914-17; lectr. forum groups, labor schs. from 1920; Milw. corr. Federated Press, 1920-21, mng. editor, sec.-treas. from 1922; financial, free lance publicity, Chgo., 1928-37; publicity, editorial work U.A.W. (Flint sitdown strike, 1937), United Rubber Workers C.I.O., 1937. Labor's Non-Partisan League on Supreme Ct. Reform, Washington, 1937, Detroit publicity and editing, U.A.W., C.I.O., 1937-62; v.p. H. F. Haessler Hardware Co., Milw., 1943-51; editor Union Engineer (AFL) Detroit, 1953-65. Detroit corr. The National Guardian, N.Y.C., from 1961. Trustee Inst. Applied Religion, 1942-49. Drafted for U.S. mil. service, 1918 (court-martialed as radical objector, gen. prisoner Ft. Leavenworth, U.S. Disciplinary Barracks, Alcatraz, 1918-20). Mem. Am. Newspaper Guild, Phi Beta Kappa. Club: Nat. Press (Washington). Translator: Oriental Religions in Roman Paganism (Franz Cumont), 1911. Home: Detroit, Mich. Died Dec. 1, 1972.

HAGEMEYER, JESSE KALPER, business exec.; b. Meridian, Miss., July 29, 1908; s. John William and Jessie (Kaiper) H.; student pub. schs., Meridian; m. Juanita Hasty, July 29, 1928; children—Jack W., Juanita C. (Mrs. James R. Bolton), Jesse Kaiper. Mgr. radio and refrigeration dept. Motor Supply Co., 1936-40; owner Radio Supply Co., Meridian, 1940-54; owner J. K. Hagemeyer Co., radio and TV distbr., Meridian, 1954, Radio Supply Bldg., Hagemeyer Bldg. Vice pres. Lamar Sch. Found. Mem. United Comml. Travelors Am., Red Cross of Constantine, Royal Order Scotland. Mason (32D), Lion (dist. gov. 1966-73). Home: Meridian Miss. Died Nov. 17, 1973; interred Magnolia Cemetery, Meridian, Miss.

HAGENAH, WILLIAM JOHN, lawyer, corp. exec., b. Reedsburg, Wis., Jan. 25, 1881; s. John Henry and Catherine (Meyer) H.; B.L., U. Wis., 1903, LL.B., 1905, LL.D., 1956; LL.D. Northland Coll., 1952; m. Florence Doyon, July 26, 1913; children—Florence Catherine, William John. Statistician, Wis. Bur. Labor, 1905; dep. commr. labor, 1906; chief financial and legal depts. Wis. R.R. Commn. 1907-10, cons. expert, 1911; engr. and analyst, specializing in pub. service commn. practice, cons. City of Chgo., 1910-11; made appraisals and rate studies of gas, telephone, traction, electric and water utilities for states, municipalities or corps., covering one or more of such utilities in Akron, Butte, Chgo., Cleve., Dayton, Detroit, Des Moines, Duluth, Indpls., Louisville, N.Y.C., Omaha, Portland (Ore.), St. Louis, Springfield (Mass.), Toronto, Wichita, Birmingham, Columbus, Montreal, Washington, Milw., Houston, Seattle, St. Paul, Los Angeles, Mobile, Jacksonville, Tulsa, Balt., Pitts., Erie, Charleston, Grand Rapids, Cin., San Francisco, Nashville, Chattanooga, also Rio de Janeiro, Sao Paulo and other cities in Brazil, cities in Mexico and W.I., 1911-28, as mem. Hagenah & Erickson, 1916-28; v.p., spl. counsel Byllesby Engring. and Mgmt. Corp., 1928-31; mem. Hagenah & Flynn, counsel for Standard Gas & Electric Co. and subsidiaries, 1931-38; pres. Pub. Utility Engring. and Service Corp., 1938-42; dir. and chmn. bd. Schering Corp., Bloomfield, N.J., 1942-52; dir. Mather Stock Car Co., 1947-56, chmn. bd., 1953-56; dir. Adams and Westlake Co., 1948-65, Aladdin Industries, Ltd. (London, Eng.), Alladin Industries, Inc. (Nashville), N. Am. Car Corp. (Chgo.), 1955-70. Vice pres. Nat. Electric Light Assn., 1932; v.p. Edison Elec. Inst., 1933-35, trustee, 1935-43; chmn. Utilities Publ. Com., Washington. past pres. Glencoe Bd. Trustees; trustee Rush Med. Coll., Chgo., 1937-69, Northland Coll., Ashland, Wis. Seabury-Western Theol. Sem., Evanston, Ill., Alonzo Mather Home for Ladies, Evanston, Ill.

(pres.); v.p., chmn. U. Wis. Found.; chmn. Alonzo Mather Found., Chgo. hon. trustee Rush, Presbyn. and St. Lukes Med. Center, Chgo., 1969. Mem. Am. Ill., Chgo., Wis. bar assns., Wis. Acad. Sci. and Letters, Wis. Soc. (pres.), Phi Alpha Delta, Delta Sigma Rho. Republican. Episcopalian. Mason. Clubs: Chicago, Mid-Day, Union League (Chgo); Skokie County (Glencoe, Ill.). Home: Glencoe, Ill.†

HAGER, ERIC HILL, lawyer; b. Albany, N.Y., Oct. 5, 1918; s. Herman Edward and Irma Adele (Hill) H.; grad. Phillips Exeter Acad., 1935; A.B. summa cum laude, Princeton, 1939; LL.B., Yale, 1942; m. Jean Dutcher, Apr. 1, 1949 (dec. July 1968); children—George Dutcher, Susan Hill, Bruce Linton. Admitted to N.Y. State bar, 1946, D.C. bar, 1960; law asso. Shearman & Sterling, N.Y.C., 1946-52, partner, 1952-59, 61-72; legal adviser Dept. State, 1959-61, mem. adv. panel on internat. law, 1970. Mem. arbitrators panel Internat. Telecommunications Satellite Consortium (Intelsat), 1967-69, adviser U.S. delegation to internat. conf. on Intelsat definitive arrangements, 1969, dep. chmn. delegation, 1970. Dir. Forbes Inc., Howmet Corp., Pechiney Ugine Kuhlmann Corp. Trustee Miriam Osborne Meml. Home Assn., Rye, N.Y. Served to capt. AUS, 1942-46. Decorated Bronze Star medal. Mem. Inter-Am., Am., N.Y. State, Fed. bar assns., Assn. Bar City N.Y., Am. Soc. Internat. Law, Council on Fgn. Relations, Phi Beta Kappa, Order of Coif, Phi Delta Phi. Republican. Episcopalian. Clubs: Links, Princeton, India House, Down Town Assn. (N.Y.C.); Metropolitan (Washington); Belle Haven, Round Hill (Greenwich); University Cottage, Nassau (Princeton). Home: Greenwich, Conn. Died May 1973.

HAGGERTY, JOHN JAMES, government official; b. Houltin, Wis., Apr. 4, 1905; s. Edward Peter and Mary Jane (O'Connell) H.; B.S., Mont. State Coll. Agr., 1933; M.Sc., U. Wis., 1934; m. Alice Leanore Scarseth, Nov. 29, 1934; children—John Scarseth, Edward Denis. Teacher, Mont. rural schs., 1923-27; grain insp. Mont. State Grain Inspection Lab., 1929-31; research in agrl. econs. U.S. Dept. of Agr., 1934-42, chief Latin Am. sect., 1943-45, sec. to U.S. sect. Mexican-U.S. Agrl. Commn., Mexico City and Washington, 1944; sec. to U.S. delegation 3d Inter-Am. Conf. on Agr., Caracus, Venezuela, 1945; advisor to U.S. dels. Inter-Am. Econ. Conf., Bogota, Colombia, 1948; agrl. attache, Am. Embassy, Lima, Peru, 1945-47; appt. fgn. service officer, consul of career, sec. in Diplomatic Service, 1947, 54; detailed to U.S. Dept. Agr., Washington, 1947-48; 1st sec. and consul, agrl. attache, U.S. Embassy, Belgrade, Yugoslavia, 1948-52; dir. office of fgn. agrl. relations, U.S. Dept. of Agr., 1952-53; agrl. attache, Bonn, Germany, 1953-55; dir. Food and Agr. div. U.S. mission to NATO and OEEC, Paris, 1956-57; dir. U.S. Econ. Aid mission to Israel, Tel Aviv, 1957-60; dir. ICA, Athens, Greece; counselor econ. affairs, econ. sect. Am. Embassy, Athens, 1960-72. Vice pres. Agri-Research Inc. until 1965. Rationing executive United States Possessions, OPA, 1942-43. Active Boy Scouts Am., 1947-48. Served as sgt. Mont. N.G., 1928-32. Mem. Alpha Gamma Rho, Alpha Zeta. Home: Vienna Va. Died June 1973; buried Vale Meth. Ch. Cemetery, Oakton, Va.

HAGGERTY, WILLIAM J., ednl. cons.; b. Somerville, Mass., Nov. 30, 1908; s. Melvin Everett and Laura C. (Garretson) H.; student Stanford, 1930-31; A.B., U. Minn., 1930; A.M., U. Chgo., 1938, Ph.D., 1943; m. Marjorie Geraldine Hooper, Aug. 22, 1933; children—Susan Haggerty Vaughn, Sally (Mrs. C. Baker-Carr), James R. Engaged in research for North Central Assn. Colls. and Secondary Schs., 1931-33, 34-40; adult edn. program TVA, 1934; research study on regional devel. Nat. Resources Planning Bd., 1935; research Pres.'s Commn. on Adminstrn. Mgmt., 1936; dir. student personnel U. Conn., 1940-44; pres. State U. Coll., New Paltz, N.Y., 1944-66; v.p., dir. High-Tor Opera Co., 1963-66; mem. staff survey N.Y.C. Colls. for Joint Legislative Commn., 1943; mem. staff Md. Commn. Higher Edn., 1946; rep. N.Y. State Tchrs. Assn., World Conf. Teaching Profession, Endicott, N.Y., 1946; cons. Pa. Study on Post-High Sch. Study, 1948; edn. cons. Govt. India, 1952-53; U.S. Tech. Coop. Adminstrn. del. to UNESCO conf., Bombay, 1952; mem. com. on internat. relations Am. Assn. Colls. for Techr. Edn., chmn. 1952-59; bd. dirs. World Edn., Inc., pres. 1957-59; chmn. Conf. World Affairs, Inc., 1967-75; pres. bd. dirs. Am. Friends of Vidyodaya Girls Sch. India, Inc.; mem. Am. Overseas Educators Orgn. (pres. 1958-59), Internat. Council Edn. for Teaching (pres. 1958-68); adv. com. coll. and univ. pres. Inst. Internat. Edn., 1957-59; edn. com. People to People program; exec. com. Mid-Hudson Sch. Study Council, 1948-66; mem. commn. internat. edn. Am. Council Edn., 1964-66; chmn. Com. on World U., 1965-75; vice chmn., dir. Patterns for Progress, Inc., 1963-67; mem. edn. com. Asia Soc.; chmn., dir. World Tchr. Project, Inc., 1970-75; asso. dir. Ind. Policy Commn. on Post High Sch. Edn., 1968; cons. State U. N.Y., 1967-68; chmn. Citizen Participation in World Affairs. Mem. Am. Acad. Polit. and Social Sci., Am. Edn. Research Assn., Sigma Phi Epsilon, Phi Delta Kappa, Kappa Delta Pi. Author: Manual for Instructors for Engineering, Science Management War Training Program, 1944; Purposes of the University of Chicago, 1943; Higher and Professional Education in India, 1970; An Indiana Pattern for Higher Education, 1968. Home: Ossining, N.Y. Died June 25, 1975.

HAGUE, ELIOTT BALDWIN, physician; b. Rochester, N.Y., Nov. 28, 1902; s. Eliott Moriarity and Harriet (Baldwin) H.; M.D., U. Pa., 1932; m. Dorothy Gnann, June 29, 1947; children—Jill (Mrs. Pedro de Alarcon), Karen (Mrs. Ronald B. Miller), Martje T., Kimsa; children by previous marriage—Allison Harriet (dec.), Thomas Eliott. Intern, Genesee Hosp., Rochester, 1932-33; resident Inst. Ophthalmology, Columbia-Presbyn. Hosp., N.Y.C., 1935-38; attending ophthalmologist Millard Fillmore Hosp., Buffalo, 1938-46, chmn. dept. ophthalmology, 1947-67, cons., 1967-74; practice medicine specializing in ophthalmology and ophthalmic plastic surgery, Buffalo. Founder eye clinic, Vietnam, 1960; with Project Focus, Haiti, 1966. Diplomate Am. Bd. Ophthalmology. Mem. A.M.A., N.Y. State, Erie County med. socs., Am. Acad. Ophthalmology and Otolaryngology, Pan Am. Assn. Ophthalmology, N.Y. Acad. Scis., Peruvian (hon.), Mexican (hon.) socs. ophthalmology, Buffalo Ophthalmologic Club, Wine and Food Soc., Alpha Delta Phi. Presbyn. Contbr. articles to med. jours. Inventor ultraviolet lamp for cataract surgery. Home: Buffalo, N.Y. Died Oct. 29, 1974; buried Forest Lawn Cemetery.

HAHN, CALVIN, physician; b. Phila., July 12, 1925; s. Israel Hahn; M.D., Temple U., 1948; m. Hanna Schorsch, Oct. 1950; children—Jan Theodore, Leslie, David. Intern, Jewish Hosp., Phila., 1948-50; preceptorship Westover AFB Hosp., Mass., 1950-52; postgrad. course U. Pa. Grad. Sch., 1952-53; resident in obstetrics and gynecology Albert Einstein Med. Center, Phila., 1953-55, asst. attending Mo. Div., 1955-58; cons. obstetrician and gynecologist N.J. State Mental Inst., Ancora, 1956-74; chief obstet. and gynecol. staff Newcomb Hosp., Vineland, N.J.; practiced medicine specializing in obstetrics and gynecology, Vineland. Mem. N.J. Health Planning Councils for Maternal and Child Health Services, N.J. Maternal Mortality Com. Bd. dirs. Ellison Pvt. Elementary Sch., Vineland, 1960-65. Served as capt., M.C., USAF, 1950-52. Diplomate Am. Bd. Obstetrics and Gynecology. Fellow A.C.S.; mem. A.M.A., Am. Coll. Obstetricians and Gynecologists. Home: Vineland, N.J., Died Dec. 12, 1974; buried Alliance Cemetery, Vineland, N.J.

HAHN, NANCY COONSMAN, sculptor; b. St. Louis, Mo.; d. Robert A. and Henrietta T. (Hynson) Coonsman; student Washington U., St. Louis, and St. Louis Sch. of Fine Arts, 1910-14; m. Manuel Hahn, May 6, 1918; 1 son, Charles S. Awards: gold medal, St. Louis Sch. of Fine Arts; silver medal, Kansas City Art Museum. Works: Missouri State Memorial (Cheppy-par-Varennes, France); D.A.R. Memorial (Memphis, Tenn.); Kincaid Fountain and Reedy Memorial (St. Louis Art Museum); Daughters Am. Colonists Fountain (St. Louis); Sally Paige Goddard Memorial (Clayton, Mo.); Barclay Memorial (New London, Mo.); "Maidenhood" (Art Museum of Cleveland, St. Louis, etc.); Culver Monument (Culver Mil. Acad.); "Old Voree" Monument Burlington, Wis.), Pick Memorial, Chicago; "Pioneer Woman" (Dakota Wesleyan U.), Joseph Sears Memorial (Kenilworth, Ill.), etc. Mem. North Shore Art League. Clubs: Artists Guild, Wednesday (St. Louis). Home: Winnetka, Ill., Died Jan. 27, 1976.

HAILES, PATRICK BUCHAN-HEPBURN, Brit. govt. ofcl.; b. Preston Kirk, U.K., Apr. 2, 1901; s. Archibald Buchan-Hepburn, 4th Baronet; M.A., Cambridge U. 1925. Attache, Brit. Embassy, Constantinople, 1926-27; M.P. for East Toxteth Div. Liverpool, 1935-50, for Beckenham, 1950-57; parliamentary pvt. sec. to Oliver Stanley, 1931-38; jr. lord of the treasury, 1939, 44-45; dep. Conservative chief ship, 1945, chief whip, 1948-51; parliamentary sec. to Treasury, govt. chief whip, 1951-55; minister of works, 1955-57; gov.-gen. Fedn. W.I., 1958-62; chmn. Historic Bldgs. Council for Eng., 1963-73; privy councillor, 1951. Created baron, 1957; decorated Companion of Honor, knight Grand Cross Order of Brit. Empire. Address: London England. Died Nov. 5, 1974.

HAILE SELLASSIE, Emperor of Ethiopia; original name Ras Tafari Makonnen; b. July 23, 1892; s. Ras Makonnen; LL.D. Cambridge, Columbia, Howard, McGill, Michigan, Athens, Banaras, Bonn. Laval, D.C.L. Oxford Univs.; m. Wolzero Menen, July 30, 1911; children—Princess Tenagne Worg (wife of Bitwoded Anargachew Masai), Crown Prince Mered Azmach Asfa Wosen, Princess Zannaba Worq (dec. 1933), Princess Tsahai (dec. 1942), Prince Mfakonnen (dec. 1957), Prince Sahle Sellassie. Proclaimed heir to throne when Sauditu, dau. Menelik II, was nominated Empress and the Queen of Kings of Ethiopia, 1918; proclaimed king, 1928; proclaimed emperor after death of Empress Zauditu, 1930; appeared before League of Nations, Geneva, to appeal against Fascist aggression, 1938; lived in Eng. during war years until 1941; rallied refugee patriots in Kenya and Sudan, and crossed frontier, Jan. 1941; reinstated in Addis Ababa, May 1941; since has reorganized govt., reopened parliament, reinstituted State Bank of Ethiopia, proclaimed new currency, abolished slavery, reorganized army, air force and navy on modern lines, established modern airlines, opened new road, started indsl. and agrl. projects, est. 450 new schs., 4 colls. and a mil. acad., a first-class post, telegraph and telecommunications system, several well-equipped modern hosps., built up system cts. justice, begun codification of laws, entered into diplomatic relations with most of the important nations of the world, secured reintegration of Eritrea, granted full adult suffrage to his people, 1955. Howard, McGill, Michigan, Athens, Banaras, Bonn. Laval, D.C.L. Oxford Univs.; Decorated Grand Cross of Order Legion d'honeur (France); Orders of Annusiata, Leopole (Belgium); Lion dlor de la Maison de Nassau (Lux.); Orange-Nassau (Neth.); Elephant (Den.); San Sebastian Guillaume (Brazil); Azgec Eagle (Mex.); Mil. Merit (Fed. Republic Germ.); Star (Yugo); Mil. Merit (France); Mohammed Ali (Egypt); Seraphim (Sweden); St. Olaf (Norway); Saviour (Greece). Address: Addis Ababa, Ethiopa. Died Aug. 28, 1975.

HAIN, EDWARD WILES, corp. exec; b. Troy, N.Y., Feb. 14, 1910; s. Andrew Sylvester and Anna (Wiles) H.; student Rensselaer Poly. Inst., 1928-30; m. Marjorie Matthews, July 12, 1944; children—Bruce Wiles, Matthew Edward. Securities analyst Jacob L. Hain & Co., Reading, Pa., 1946-52; sec., treas., dir. Bush Universal, Inc., N.Y.C., 1952-73; dir. Bush Terminal R.R. Co. Trustee Bloomfield Coll. Served to capt. USAAF, 1942-46. Mem. N.Y. Soc. Security Analysts, Am. Soc. Corp. Secs., Bankers Club Am. Lutheran (trustee). Clubs: West Side Tennis (N.Y.C.); Smoke Rise Tennis. Home: Butler, N.J. Died Mar. 9, 1973.

HAINDS, JOHN ROBERT, educator; b. Brookfield, Mo., Sept. 10, 1896; s. Frederick Potts and Jennie E. (Jones) H.; student U. Ill., 1918; Ph.B., Shurtleff Coll., 1925; postgrad. U. Mich., summer 1926; M.A., Northwestern U., 1933, Ph.D., 1939; m. Jeannie Armstrong, May 17, 1916; 1 son, James Armstrong. Instr. English and speech Gladstone (Mich.) Sr. High Sch., 1925-27, Davenport (Ia.) Sr. High Sch., 1927-30, J. Sterling Morton High Sch., Cicero, Ill., 1930-33, Morton Jr. Coll., Cicero, 1933-37, Northwestern U., Evanston, Ill., 1937-40; prof. English, No. Ill. U., DeKalb, 1940-66, mem. adminstrv. council, 1945-51, 53-62, acad. v.p., 1959-63, coordinator research grants, 1963-66, dean Grad. Sch., 1951-59, curriculum cons.; dir. No. Ill. U. Found., 1950-67, v.p., 1962-66, emeritus, 1966-74. prof. English, Friends U., 1967-70; ednl. cons., 1945-74. Mem. N.E.A. (life), Ill. Edn. Assn. (pres. Rock River div. 1954-55). Adult Edn. Con. Greater Chgo., Nat. Council Tchrs. English, Am. Legion, Phi Beta Kappa, Phi Delta Kappa, Alpha Delta, Sigma Tau Delta. Mason (32 deg.,) Editor: (with others) Bibliography of the Published Writings of John Stuart Mill, 1945. Contbr. to Jour. History of Ideas. Home: Ozona, Tex. Died Sept. 13, 1974; buried Elmira, Ill.

HAINES, EDMUND THOMAS, composer, music educator; b. Ottumwa, Ia., Dec. 15, 1914; s. Verlan J. and Edna May (Waters) H.; student U. Kan., 1933-34; B.M., Kansas City Conservatory of Music, 1936; M.M., Eastman Sch. of Music, U. Rochester, 1938, Ph.D., 1941; m. Joyce Williams, Aug. 27, 1939 (div.); m. 2d, Beatrice Thorne, June 2, 1951 (div.); 1 son, David; m. 3d, Lauren Levey, Mar. 30, 1970. Tchr. piano and theory Conservatory of Kansas City, 1936-37; teaching fellow and grad. student Eastman School, 1938-41; apptd. to faculty U. Mich., 1941, Sarah Lawrence Coll., 1948; Guggenheim fellow, 1956-57, 57-58; Ford Found. orchestral commn., 1958; composer-in-residence La Napoule Art Found., France, 1957-58; Fulbright research grant, Spain, 1965-67. Recipient Pulitzer Prize, 1941. Composer of orchestral, choral, keyboard, ballet chamber music; performed in the U.S. and abroad. Home: New York City, N.Y. Died July, 5, 1974.

HAISS, CATHERINE NUGENT (MRS. JOHN D HAISS), lawyer; b. Watervliet, N.Y.; d. William Charles and Loretto (McCarthy) Nugent; B.S., Coll. of New Rochelle, 1932; LL.B., Union U., 1956, J.D., Albany Law Sch., 1968; m. John D. Haiss, Feb. 8, 1942 (dec. Jan. 1957). Sec., Social Service Exchange, Troy, N.Y., 1940-45; tax cons. John D. Haiss Asso., Plattsburg, N.Y., 1946-53; admitted to N.Y. bar, 1956; practiced in Troy, N.Y., 1956-73; law librarian, lectr. legal bibliography and writing Union U. Albany Law Sch., 1958-73. Mem. Am., N.Y., State, Rensselaer County bar assns., Am. Assn. Law Librarians, Am. Acad. Polit. and Social Sci. Home: Troy, N.Y. Died May 1, 1973.

HALDANE, WILLIAM GEORGE, metallurgist; b. Cleveland, O., Nov. 5, 1879; s. William Leon and Margaret (Dobson) H.; B.S. in Mining Engring., Case Sch. of Applied Science, Cleveland, O., 1900; post-grad. work, Columbia, 1908; Sc.D., U. Denver, 1914; m. Lorena Beaver, Feb. 28, 1912. Asst. engr., Am. Steel & Wire Co., Newburg, O., 1900; instr. in mathematics, 1900-03, instr. in Metallurgy, 1903-07, asst. prof., 1907-11, asso. prof., 1911-12, mgr. expt. sta., 1912-13, Colo. Sch. of Mines, also acting pres., May 1913-15; also practices as mining engr. Mem. Am. Inst. Mining Engrs., Colo. Metall. Mining Assn., Tau Beta Pi, Kappa Sigma, Sigma Xi. Presbyn. Mason. Contbr. on mining and metallurgy of the rare metals in southern Colo. Home: Denver, Colo.†

HALE, FRANK J., ballet co. exec.; b. San Francisco, Mar. 26, 1899. Vaudeville dancer; appeared with Dixieland Jazz Vaudeville, Keith-Albee Circuit; prod. Royal Poinciana Playhouse, Palm Beach, Fla.; founder, pres. Palm Beach Ballet Co.; v.p., treas. Internat. Co-Prodns., Inc.; producer films The Princess, Dr. Coppelius; developed Nat. Yeast Corp. (merged with Universal Foods Corp. 1968), now cons. Pres. Am. Soc. Aged. Address: Palm Beach, Fla. Deceased.

HALE, HARRISON, chemist; b. Columbus, Miss., Dec. 27, 1879; s. Moses Artemas and Sue Miller (Cook) H.; A.B., Emory Coll., Oxford, Ga., 1899; M.Sc., U. of Chicago, 1902; Ph.D. Univ. of Pa., 1908; LL.D., Drury Coll., Springfield, Mo., 1928; m. Mabel Hays, Dec. 22, 1904; children—Arthur, Harrison, Mabel Elinor (Mrs. Charles P. Clayton). Assistant principal pub. schs. of Edgewood, Ga. 1899-1901; instr., asst. prof. and prof. ehemistry, Drury Coll., Springfield, Mo., 1902-18; city chemist, Springfield, 1911-14; chemist to state food commr., Mo., 1912, to Springfield City Water Co., 1911-18, to municipal water works, Ft. Smith, Ark., 1923-27, to Fayetteville Water Dept., from 1927; sec. Ark. Water and Sewage Conf. from 1931; head department chemistry, U. of Ark., 1918-45; emeritus Research chemist Bureau of Research, 1945-48; research splist., Institute Science and Tech. 1949-50; head dept. chemistry. So. State Coll., Magnolia, Ark., from 1951. Fellow A.A.A.S.; mem. Am. Chem. Soc. (past councilor Ark. sect., chmn. division of chem. edn., 1936; chmn. division of history of chemistry, 1941-46, Am. Inst. Chemical Engineers, Arkansas Academy of Science, American Association University Professors, Arkansas Ednl. Assn. (pres. science sect. 1925, chemistry sect. 1928), Kappa Alpha, Phi Eta, Alpha Chi Sigma and Phi Beta Kappa fraternities. Pres. Fayetteville Chamber of Commerce, 1921-22, 1925-26; chmn. Fayetteville Centennial Celebration, 1928. Democrat. Presbyterian. Clubs: Fortnightly, Rotary. Author: American Chemistry, 1921; Arkansas City Water Supplies, 1926; Scientific Sidelights on Jesus, 1930; also joint author of General Chemistry (Miner Series), 1927; The Why Book, 1936; Public Water Supplies of Arkansas, 1947; Hist. of University of Arkansas, 1948; also articles in professional jours. Home: Magnolia, Ark.†

HALE, WILLIAM HARLAN, editor, writer; b. N.Y.C., July 21, 1910; s. William Bayard and Olga (Unger) H.; student Riverdale Country Sch., 1924-27; A.B., Yale, 1931; m. Jean Laughlin Barker, Aug. 19, 1941; children—Katherine, Jonathan, Elizabeth. Asso. editor Vanity Fair mag., 1932-33; columnist Washington Post, 1933; editorial asso. Fortune mag., 1934-35; free lance writer for various mags., 1935-41; spl. writer Norman Bel Geddes & Co., 1939; with O.W.I., 1941-45, in charge of radio broadcasts to Germany from N.Y., chief of German propaganda operations for O.W.I., London, chief of Radio Luxembourg for psychol. warfare div., supreme hdgrs. A.E.F.; policy adviser, information control div. U.S. Forces European Theater, Bad Homburg, Germany; sr. editor New Republic, 1946-47; sr. writer The Reporter, 1948-49, contbg. editor, 1954-58; apptd. U.S. Fgn. Service Res. Officer, 1950, press attache and chief information br. Office U.S. High Commr. Am. embassy, Vienna, 1st sec., dir. pub. affairs div., 1952-53; mng. editor Horizon mag., N.Y.C., 1958-61, editor, 1961-63, editor Horizon Books, N.Y.C., 1963-67, sr. writer, 1967-68. Democrat. Episcopalian. Club: Century Assn. (N.Y.C.). Author: Challenge to Defeat, 1932; Hannibal Hooker, 1938; The March of Freedom, 1947, Horace Greeley Voice of the People, 1950; Innocence Abroad, 1957; The Horizon Book of Ancient Greece, 1965; The Horizon History of Eating and Drinking Through the Ages, 1968. Editor: The Horizon Book of Ancient Rome, 1966; Ghosts of Berlin, 1976. Contbr. numerous mags. Home: Weston Conn. Died July 1974.

HALECKI, OSCAR, prof. history; b. Vienna, May 26, 1891; s. Lieut-Field Marshall Oscar de Chalecki-Halecki and Leopoldina de Dellimanich; Ph.D., University of Cracow, Poland, 1913; hon. Dr. University of Lyons, 1934, University of Montreal, 1943, De Paul University, 1945; Litt.D. (hon.), Fordham University, 1961; m. Helen de Sulima-Szarlowska, July 15, 1913. Lecturer in Polish history, University of Cracow, 1916-18; prof. Eastern European History, and dean faculty letters U. Warsaw, 1919-39; Kosciuszko Found. vis. prof. U.S., 1938; pres. Polish U. in Exile, Paris, 1939-40; visiting prof. history, Vassar Coll., 1940-42; dir. Polish Inst. of Arts and Sciences in Am., 1942-53, pres. of bd. since 1953; prof. Eastern European history, Fordham U. (graduate school), 1944-61; professor Slavonic history, U. Montreal, 1944-51; vis. prof. History, Columbia, 1955-56, adjunct prof., 1956-61; vis. prof. Loyola University in Rome, 1962-63, U. Fribourg, 1963, U. Cal. Los Angeles, 1963-64; mem. bd. of governors College of Europe, Bruges, 1950. Fulbright Research Scholar in Italy, 1952-53; Guggenheim research fellow, 1957-58. Fellow Polish Academy (Cracow), Society Sciences and Letters (Warsaw and Lwow); president Polish History Society in Exile, 1950; mem. Royal Hist. Soc. (London), Institut de France (Paris), Société Hist. et Littéraire Polonaise, Paris, 1948, also other European learned societies and Am. Hist. Soc., Acad. Internat. libre des Sciences et des Lettres, Paris (elected president of American Branch in 1959), Mediaeval Academy America, American Academy of Political and Social Science, Am. Cath. Hist. Assn. (pres. 1956), Cath. Com. Intellectual and Cultural Affairs (chmn. 1961). Decorated Commander Polonia Restituta; Commander Saint-Gregory, with Star; Commander Hungarian Croix de Mérite; Officer Legion of Honor (France); Papal Chamberlain; Knight Grand Cross Order of Malta; Roman Cath. Author: Limits and Divisions of European History 1950; Eugenio Pacelli Pope of Peace, 1951; Borderlands of Western Civilization, 1952; History of Poland, 1956; From Florence to Brest, 1958; The Millennium of Europe, published in 1963; other books pub. in Poland and abroad. Mem. editorial bd. Am., Slovic and East Europe Review, 1947; Journal of Central European Affairs, 1950. Contbr. to Polish and other European and Am. mags. Address: New York City, N.Y. Died Sept. 1973.

HALEY, MRS. LOVICK PIERCE;, b. Ripley, Miss., Sept. 7, 1880; d. Frederick Jones and Corra (Gaillard) McDonnell; A.M., Lambuth Coll., Jackson, Tenn., 1901; post- grad. student, U. of Miss., 1902; m. Lovick Pierce Haley, Oct. 26, 1904 (died May 28, 1929); children—Fred McDonnell, Lovick Pierce, Archie McDonnell. Teacher of Latin, French and history, 1902-04 and 1917-20; 1st asst. Miss. Dept., of Archives and History from 1934. Dir. Gen. Fedn. of Women's Clubs, 1928-30; one of five Mississipians chosen to constitute Nat. Dem. Hdqrs. in Miss., 1932-36; mem. State Library Commn., 1928-30; chmn. advisory com. Miss. Fedn. of Women' Clubs, 1930-36; president, 1928-30, state parliamentarian, 1936-40. Mem. Philomathean Soc. Democrat. Methodist. Clubs: Research, Review, Business and Professional Women's Mag. Traveled throughout U.S. and in other countries. Rep. Mothers of the State on Mother's Day, U. of Miss., 1930, and responded to Address of Welcome. Holder for life of state teachers' professional license. Home: Jackson, Miss.†

HALL, ALVIN PERCY MCDONALD, psychiatrist; b. Franklin, O., Apr. 21, 1910; s. Jesse Alvin and Frances Elizabeth (Jackson) H.; A.B., Ohio U., 1932; M.D., Meharry Med. Coll., 1936; m. Ellen F. Talbert, Dec. 30, 1935; children—Dora Ellen, Alvin. Intern Greater Provident Hosp., Chgo., 1936-37; resident Cleve. Psychiat. Inst., Western Res. U.; practice medicine specializing in psychiatry, Ohio, 1948-73; psychiatrist Cleve. Psychiat. Inst., 1948-62; sr. psychiatrist Fairhill Hosp., Cleve., 1962-64, Green-Clin. Guidance Center, Xenia, 1964-70, Columbus Community Mental Health Center, 1970-73. Cons. psychiatrist Wilberforce U., 1967-73, also Antioch Coll., Central State U. asst. clin. prof. psychiatry Ohio State U., 1971-73. Served to capt. USMCR, 1941-46. Diplomate Am. Bd. Psychiatry and Neurology. Fellow Am. Psychiat. Assn.; mem. Am., Ohio Central, Ohio psychiat. assns., Ohio State Med. Soc., Columbus Acad. Medicine, A.M.A., Columbus Soc. Physicians and Dentists, Meharry Alumni Assn., Alpha Phi Alpha. Home: Columbus O. Died Nov. 4, 1973.

HALL, ARTHUR BENEDICT, real estate; b. Mt. Vernon, O., Mar. 27, 1881; s. Russell T. and Mary (Tyler) H.; A.B., Yale, 1902; m. Elsie Springer, Oct. 18, 1910; children—Russell Edward, Barbara; married Louise N. Warren, February 18, 1961. Entered joint office of Bryan Lathrop and Thomas A. Hall & Co. in 1902; became mem. of firm of Thomas A. Hall & Co., 1909; with partner William Marshall Ellis succeeded to the business of Bryan Lathrop and Thomas A. Hall & Co., 1916, adopting Hall & Ellis as the new firm name, retired as active partner, 1965; now president and director of Graceland Cemetery Co. Trustee U. Chgo., Carroll Coll., Orchestral Association, Chicago YMCA. Member Chicago Real Estate Bd., Art Inst. Chicago (life). Republican. Presbyterian. Clubs: University, Yale, City; La Grange Country; Phi Gamma Delta, Phi Beta Kappa. Home: La Grange, IL.†

HALL, COLBY DIXON, clergyman, educator; b. Madisonville, Ky., Dec. 29, 1975; s. Robert Mahlon and Mahala (Pritchet) H.; student Acad. and Coll. Add-Ran U. (now Tex. Christian U.), 1896-99; A.B., Transylvania U., Ky., 1902, also diploma from its Bible Coll.; M.A., Columbia Univ., 1904; student same univ., 1916; LL.D., from Transylvania Univ., 1935; Doctor of Divinity, Texas Christian University, 1951; m. Beatrice Tomlinson, Aug. 19, 1909; children—Bitta May, Colby Dison. Ordained ministry Disciples of Christ, 1898; pastor Hillsboro, Tex., 1904-06; ednl. sec. Tex. Christian U., 1906-09; pastor Waco, Tex., 1909-12; became prof. of English Bible, Texas Christian Univ., 1912, dean of 1912, dean Brite College of the Bible, 1914-47, dean of the university, 1920-43, prof. church history, 1928-50, dean emeritus ad interim teaching and writing. Pres. Tex. Christian Endeavor Union 1905-09; chmn. com. on standards, Assn. Tex. Colleges, 1923-36, pres., 1933-34; v.p. Southern Assn. Colleges, 1934; mem. com. on classified and accredited schs., State Dept. of Education, Tex., 1935-43; pres. Tex. Conv. Christian chs., 1951; pres. Tex. Christian Missionary Soc., 1948-53. Clubs: Kiwanis (pres. 1938), Torch. Author: History of Texas Christian University, 1947; Texas Disciples, 1954; Rice Haggard, American Frontier Evangelist Who Revived the Name Christian, 1957; New Light Christians, Initiators of the 19th Centruy Reformation, 1959. Home: Ft. Worth, ex.†

HALL, LOUIS DIXON, b. Taylorville, Ill., June 13, 1878; s. William W. and Sarah L. (Stewart) H.; B.S. in Agr., U. of Ill., 1899, M.S., 1906; m. Elizabeth C. Wilder, June 13, 1900; children—Dixon W., Charles N., E. Virginia; m. 2d, Juanita M. Fish, Feb. 16, 1929. Mgr. Hall Cattle Co., Hawarden, Ia.,1899-1903; asst. chief animal husbandry dept., Coll. of Agr., U. of Ill., 1903-14; in charge live stock and meat div. Bur. of Markets, U.S. Dept. Agr., 1914-20; v.p. and mng. dir. Pan Am. Cattle Exchange and Trading Co., 1920-21; cons. live stock specialist, 1921-23; agr. orgn., investment and insurance specialist, 1923-33; assistant chief of cattle and sheep section, Agrl. Adjustment Adminstrn., 1934; field rep. Ill. Livestock Marketing Assn. from 1935. Executive sec. Nat. Better Beef Assn., 1926. Organized and developed live stock and meat div., U.S. Bur. Markets; inaugurated daily govt. market reports on live stock and meats; administered federal supervision of stock yards and grading of beef during World War. Fellow A.A.A.S.; mem. Am. Soc. Animal Production, Sigma Xi, Alpha Zeta. Mason. Author of numersous Govt. bulls. and circulars in relation to grades of meat and marketing, etc. Home: Peoria, Ill†

HALL, LUELLA JEMIMA, educator, author; b. Duluth, Minn., Oct. 18, 1890; d. John O. and Jennie (Hillstead) H.; B.A., U. N.D., 1917, M.A., 1919; Ph.D., Stanford, 1938. Elementary tchr., N.D., 1910-11, 12-14; prin., tchr. jr. high sch., Tagus, N.D., 1914-15; teaching fellow history U. N.D., 1917-19, instr. sociology, 1919-21; critic tchr. in jr. high sch. State Tchrs. Coll., Valley City, N.D., 1922-23; head social sci. dept. Union High Sch., Lodi, Cal., 1923-29; instr. social sci., high sch. and jr. coll., Salinas, Cal., 1929-37; instr. social sci. Hartnell Coll., Salinas, 1937-55, dean gen. coll. div., 1938-53; hist. research and writing, 1955-73. Pres., Salinas Library Bd., 1952-53. Mem. Am. Assn. U. Women, League Women Voters, Nat. Ret. Tchrs. Assn., Monterey County Hist. Soc. (v.p. 1952), Nat. League Am. Pen Women, Internat. Platform Assn., Delta Zeta (nat. scholarship chmn. 1924-26), Phi Beta Kappa, Delta Kappa Gamma. Democrat. Unitarian. Author: History of the Formation of Counties in North Dakota, 1933; The United States and Morocco, 1776-1956, 1971; One Man's Family, a genealogy. Contbr. articles to various publs. Home: Seal Beach, Cal. Died June 21, 1973; buried Alta Mesa Meml. Park, Palo Alto, Cal.

HALL, OAKEL FOWLER, educator; b. Crawfordsville, Ind., Dec. 20, 1878; s. James Quincy and Amyann (Cox) H.; A.B., Wabash Coll., 1907, D.D., 1932; S.T.B., Harvard, 1910; m. Edna A. Barker, June 30, 1910; children—Harriet W., James Edward, Helen F., Ruth B. Taught rural sch., 1899-1902; prin. first twp. consolidated school in Ind., 1902-03; ordained Congl. ministry, 1910; pastor Winthrop Congl. Ch., Charlestown Dist., Boston, 1910-14; univ. pastor Purdue U., 1914-17; prof. sociology same univ., 1917-48, now meritus; also chmn. administrative com., dept. of education, 1934-37. Mem. West Lafayette Sch. Bd., 1934-41; mem. bd. of dirs. Indiana Conf. of Social Workers; founder and dir. Ind. Rural Leadership Sch.; pres. Ind. Rural Life Council, from 1939; sec. American County Life Assn., Jan. 1, 1942-46. Mem. exec. com. Ind. Hist. Assn., 1941. Lecturer in Dept. of Agrl. Extension. State lecturer Indiana Grange, 1939-42. Member Ind. Migrant Com., from 1945. Pres. Indiana's Town and City School Adminstrs. Assn., 1938-41, Purdue Bldg. & Loan Assn., 1929-47. Army Y.M.C.A. sec., World War I. Mem. Kappa Delta Pi, Pi Gamma Mu, Alpha Chi Rho. Methodist. Mason. Kiwanian. Home: Louisville, KY. Deceased.

HALL, ROBERT BURNETT, geographer; b. Espanola, N.M., July 18, 1896; s. William and Grace Laura (Burnett) H.; A.B., U. of Mich., 1923, A.M., 1924, Ph.D., 1927; married Pauline Augusta Fead, August 31, 1922; children—Robert Burnett, Joyce Laughlin. Director geographic expeditions to Republic of Haiti, 1924, 25; director geographic field expeditions to Japan, 1928, 29, 31, 33, 35-36; asso. prof. geography, U. of Mich., 1935-38, prof. after 1938, also dir. Center for Japanese Studies, 1947-57; dir. Inst. of Far Eastern Studies, 1937-39. Intelligence officer, World War I. Lt. Col., Army of U.S., and dir. Pacific Coast Office, O.S.S., 1942-43; col. A. U.S. in China and India, 1943-44. Mem. council and dir. Social Sci. Research Council, 1941-55, chmn., 1948; mem. Ethnogeographic Bd., Smithsonian Instn., 1942-44. Field research, countries of Latiin Am., 1941-42. Chmn., com. Joseph R. Hayden Mem. Library, U. Philippines, 1946-55; Japan rep. The Asia Found., Tokyo, 1955-62; vis. prof. Tokyo U., 1956-57. Decorated Order Rising Sun (Japan); Order of Sacred Treasure; recipient silver medal Tokyo Geog. Soc., 1960. Mem. Assn. Am. Geographers, Far Eastern Association (v.p. 1949-50, pres. 1951-52), Research Club (U. Mich.), Michigan Academy of Science, Phi Beta Kappa, Sigma Xi, Phi Kappa Phi, Chi Phi. Club: Cosmos (Washington, D.C.). Author: Area Studies: Implications for Research in the Social Sciences, 1947; Contbr. on Far East topics to jours. Mem. editorial bd. Far Eastern Quarterly 1938-45. Home: Ann Arbor, Mich. Died Apr. 4, 1975.

HALL, WILLIAM O., educator; b. Sylvan, Richland Co., Wis. Oct. 15, 1880; s. Calvin and Mary Elizabeth (Barrett) H.; grad. Milwaukee State Normal Sch., 1904; Ph.B., U. of Wis., 1912; m. Margaret Barnard, July 10,

1913. Teacher rural schs., Richland Co., Wis., 1899-1902; prin. ward sch., Waukesha, Wis., 1904-05; prin. high sch. and supervisor grades, Walworth, Wis., 1905-07; supt. schs., Hayward, Wis., 1908-10; supervisor of dept. Milwaukee State Normal Sch. 1911-13; supt. schs., Roswell, N.M., 1913-16; head of training dept. Milwaukee State Normal Sch., 1916-19; pres. N.M. State Normal Sch., from 1919. Presbyn. Mason Home: Silver City N.M.†

HALL, YOUNG LAFAYETTE, JR., physician; b. Adrian, Ga., Oct. 5, 1910; s. Young Lafayette and Addie Lee (Frentian) H.; M.D., U. Ga. 1934; m. Margaret Davis Griffin, June 1, 1938; 1 son, Young Lafayette III. Intern, Jackson Meml. Hosp., Miami, Fla., 1934-35; resident in anesthesiology Jefferson-Hillman Hosp., Birmingham, Ala., 1949-51; dir. dept. anesthesiology Victoria Hosp., Miami. Diplomate Am. Bd. Anesthesiology. Mem. A.M.A., Am. Soc. Anesthesiologists. Home: Miami, Fla. Died Dec. 6, 1971; buried Woodlawn Park Cemetery, Miami, Fla.

HALLENBORG, CHARLES EDWARD, business exec.; b. N.Y. City, April 12, 1898; s. Axel W. and Emily (Stewart) H.; ed. Newport (Vt.) Public Schs.; m. Dorothy Peck Hopkins; 1 dau., Jane Stewart Hallenborg. Mem. Dictaphone Dept., Columbia Graphophone Co., Boston, 1920-22; Phila. Branch mgr., Dictaphone Corp., 1922-34; asst. gen. sales mgr., New York, 1934-36; sec., 1936-38; gen. sales mgr., 1937; vice pres., 1937-48, exec. vp., 1948-52; pres., dir. Copease Corp., N.Y.C., from 1953, Copease Mfg. Company, Inc., 1954-62. Served as chief Contract Distribution Branch and special asst. to dir. aircraft production, Office of Production Management and W. P.B. at Washington, 1941-42. Republican. Episcopalian. Clubs: Racquet and Tennis (N.Y. City); Metropolitan (Washington). Home: New York City, N.Y.

HALLER, WILLIAM, univ. prof., writer; b. N.Y.C., May 12, 1885; s. Frederick and Anna (Zeip) H.; A.B., L.H.D. Amherst Coll.; Ph.D., Columbia; m. Malleville W. Emerson, Sept. 3, 1913; children—William, Benjamin Emerson, Maria Malleville. Instr., prof. English, Barnard Coll.; mem. faculty of philosophy, Columbia, 1909-50; exec. officer, dept. of English, Barnard Coll., 1925-37. Mem. advisory council Folger Shakespeare Lib., Washington. Formerly mem. Town Planning Bd. and Zoning Commn., Leonia, N.J. Guggenheim fellow, research fellow. Huntington Library, San Marino, Calif. Mem. Modern Language Assn., Am. Assn. Univ. Profs. Am. Church History Soc., Delta Upsilon. Phi Beta Kappa. Author: Early Life of Robert Southey; Writing (with R. P. Baker); Tracts on Liberty in the Puritan Revolution; Rise of Puritanism; The Leveller Tracts (with Godfrey Davies); contbr. numerous articles and reviews to various jours. Home: Washington, D.C. Died May 1974.

HALLGARTEN, GEORGE WOLFGANG FELIX, educator, historian; b. Munich, Germany, Jan 3, 1901; s. Robert (b. N.Y.C.) and Constance (Wolff-Arndt) H.; Ph.D., U. Munich, 1925; m. Katherine MacArthur Drew, Feb. 15, 1941. Came to U.S., 1937. Substitute asst. Inst. for Fgn. Politics, Hamburg, Germany, 1925; pvt. research, 1926-34; lectr. Ecole des Hautes Etudes Sociales et Internationales, 1935, grad. div. Bklyn. Coll., 1938; research asso. history U. Cal. at Berkeley, 1940-41; historian, then sr. research analyst Dept. of Army, 1945-49; guest prof. history U. Munich, 1949-50; lectr., author, 1951-75; lectr. univs. in India and Japan, 1965, Rome and Munich, 1967; vis. prof. history U. N.M., Albuquerque, 1968-69; Pres.'s scholar and vis. prof. history U. Dayton, 1970-71; Robert Lee Bailey prof. history U. N.C., Charlotte, 1972. Co-founder Am. Com. Study War Documents, 1955. Served with AUS, 1942-45. Research grantee Am. Philos. Soc., 1940-41. Mem. Am. Hist. Assn., Societe d'Histoire Moderne. Author: Imperialismus vor 1914, 2 vols., rev. edit., 1963; Why Dictators?—the causes and forms of tyrannical rule since 600 B.C., 1954; Daemonen oder Retter?, 1957, English and French edit., 1960; Das Wettrusten — sein Geschichte bis zur Gegenwart, 1968, Italian edit., 1972; Als die Schatten Fielen-memoirs, 1969; (with Joachim Radkau) Deutsche Industrie U. Politik von Bismarck bis Heute, 1974. Home: Washington, DC. Died May 22, 1975.

HALLIDAY, ERNEST MILTON, clergyman; b. Vienna Twp., Genesee County, Mich., July 26, 1878; s. James D. and Alcina (Colton) H.; A.B., U. of Mich., 1904; LL.B., 1906; A.M., Columbia, 1913; grad. Union Theol. Sem., 1917; D.D., Marietta Coll., 1924; m. Eleanor Armstrong, June 5, 1907; children—Dorothy (Mrs. Ralph F. Hefferline), Lois (Mrs. Lewis C. Clapp), Ernest Milton. Instr. pub. speaking, U. of Ill., 1906-07, asso., 1907-12; Columbia U. Extension, 1912-19, 1921-42; ordained Congl. ministry, 1913; pastor Ocean Av. Ch., Brooklyn, 1913-22; gen. sec. Congl. Ch. Extension Bds., 1922-37; sec. Bd. of Home Missions, and gen. sec. Extension Div., 1937-46; instr. pub. speaking, N.Y. U., from 1946; interim pastor First Congl. Ch., Flushing, N.Y., 1946; Ocean Av. Congl. Ch., Brooklyn, 1947; summer pastor Plymouth Church of the Pilgrims, Brooklyn, from 1947. Pres. Home Mission Council, 1935-36; hon. mem. Home Missions Council; pres. Union Theol. Sem. Alumni Council, 1942-44; trustee Am. and Foreign Christian Union, Mem. Phi Beta Kappa, Delta Sigma Rho. Phi Alpha Delta. Home: Brooklyn, N.Y.†

HALLIGAN, JAMES EDWARD, chemist; b. S. Boston, Feb. 11, 1879; s. John and Margaret Elizabeth (McCarty) H.; B.S., Mass. Agrl. Coll., 1900; m. Eliza Perry Jones, June 30, 1908 (died Sept. 1916). Assistant chemist, Massachusetts Agrl. Experiment Sta., 1900-04, La Sugar Expt. Sta., 1904-05; chemist in charge, La. State Agrl. Sta., Aug., 1905-13. Demonstrator in sugar lab. for U.S. Office Expt. Stas., St. Louis Expn., 1904; referee for Assn. Official Agrl. Chemists on molasses and asso. referee on sugar, 1906-07; referee cattle foods standard's com., same, 1906, etc. Mem. 8 Internat. Congresses of Applied Chemistry, Am. Chem. Soc., Official Agrl. Chemists, Southern Feed Control Officials, Kappa Sigma. Author: Fundamentals of Agriculture, 1911; Elementary Treatise on Stock Feeds and Feeding, 1911; Fertility and Fertilizer Hints, 1911; Soil Fertility and Fertilizers, 1911; also numerous articles, bulls, etc. Mem. firm Allen, Douglass & Halligan, cotton commn., New Orleans, 1915-17; mgr. Barrow Cottonseed Preserver Co., Memphis, Tenn., 1917-19; in charge research and exptl. dept., Internat. Sugar Feed Co., Minneapolis and Memphis, 1919-20; with John Wade & Sons, Inc., July 1, 1920—. Contbr. poems and agrl. articles to Commercial Appeal, Memphis. Address: Memphis, Tenn.†

HALLORAN, EDWARD ROOSEVELT, naval officer, pub. information exec.; b. Washington, Dec. 30, 1895; s. Matthew Francis and Mary Agnes (Beadle) H.; LL.B., Columbus U., Washington, 1932; m. Flavia Griffin, Aug. 15, 1926; 1 dau., Julia Ann (Mrs. Richard H. Rush). Admitted to D.C. bar, 1932; reorganized property and supply dept. Fed. Bd. Vocational Edn., 1921; purchasing agt. Bur. Pub. Roads, 1922-24; bus. mgr. VA Hosp., Jefferson Barracks, Mo., 1924-27; securities counselor Young Bros., St. Louis, 1927-28; pres. Halloran & Thorn, Inc., road building, St. Louis, 1929; spl. agt. Dept. Commerce, 1930-32; information specialist RFC, 1932-33; asst. comptroller, credit mgr. Washington Post, 1933-41; served with Md. N.G. on Mexican Border, 1915-17; served to maj. Signal Corps and inf., U.S. Army Res., 1917-40; commd. lt. (s.g.) USNR, 1941, advanced through grades to rear adm USN, 1958; coordinator press censorship, officer charge overseas telephone communications censorship 12th Naval Dist., 1942-43; served in M.S. Sommels-Dijk, 1943, U.S.S. Rigel, 1943-44; comdg. officer naval beach parties 7th Amphibious Forces, 1944-45; tng. officer, liaison officer Office Pub. Information, Navy Dept., 1946-49; dist. pub. information officer 15th Naval Dist., 1949-52; officer charge fleet home-town news center, Great Lakes, Ill., 1952-57; asst. dir. civil relations Navy Dept., 1957-58; ret., 1958; counselor Richard H. Rush Enterprises, Washington, from 1958. Decorated Legion of Merit with combat V. others: Order of J. Gabriel Duque (Panama). Mem. Gamma Eta Gamma. Clubs: Washington State Press (Seattle); Army and Navy (Washington). Address: Tucson, Ariz. Died Oct. 22, 1975.

HALLOWELL, ALFRED IRVING, anthropologist, educator; b. Phila., Dec. 28, 1892; s. Edgar Lloyd and Dorothy (Edsall) H.; B.S., U. Pa., 1914, A.M., 1920, Ph. D., 1924, D.Sc. (hon.) 1963; m. Maude Frame, Oct. 17, 1942. Social worker, Phila., 1914-22; Instr. anthropology U. Pa., 1923-28, asst. prof., 1928-36, asso. prof., 1936-39, prof., 1939-44, 47-63, now prof. emeritus; prof. anthropology Northwestern U., 1944-47; prof. anthropology in psychiatry U. Pa. Med. Sch., curator of social anthropology U. Pa. Museum. Guggenheim fellow, 1940-41; Viking medalist in gen. anthropology, 1955. Chmn. div. anthropology and psychology NRC, 1946-49. Mem. Am. Philos. Soc., Internat. Congress Anthrop. and Ethnol. Scis. (mem. permanent council), Am. Folk Lore Soc. (past pres.), Am. Anthrop. Assn. (pres. 1949), Nat. Acad. Sci., Soc. for Personality Assessment (past pres.), Sigma XI. Club: Cosmos (Washington). Author: The Role of Conjuring in Saulteaux Soc., 1942; Culture and Experience, 1955. Editor: Viking Fund Publications in Anthropology, 1951-56. Home: Wayne, Pa. Died Oct. 10, 1974; interred Laurel Hill Cemetery, Philadelphia, Pa.

HALSEY, (WILLIAM) FORREST, motion picture writer; b. Roseville, N.J., Nov. 9, 1878; s. Augustus Ogden and Maria Lucas (Whittemore) H.; ed. Newark (N.J.) Acad., Art Students' League, and Artist Artisan's Inst., New York; unmarried. Art dir. Hampton Adv. Agency, 1912, Hampton's Mag., 1913; free lance writer from 1913. Major Officers' Reserve Corps of U.S. Army, 1924-29. Decorated Officier d'Académie Francaise, 1925, by the French govt. in recognition of the adaptation of the motion picture, "%22Madam Sans-Gêene." Author: The Stain, 1910; The Question, 1911; The Bawlerout, 1911. Co-Author: The Wonderful Thing, and his Chinese Wife (plays, prod. New York, 1920); co-author of Eunice (play prod. in London), 1910. Has written more than 20 motion picture plays; adapted Parker's "Disraeli" and "The Green Goddess" for George Arliss. Home: Fredericksburg, Va.†

HALVORSEN, RAYMOND GEORGE, mfg. exec.; b. Manitowoc, Wis., June 15, 1906; s. George J. and Rose P. (Herman) H.; m. Marion Houle, Nov. 17, 1937; children—Morrie E., Brenda Rae. Sales engr. Wiese Mfg. Co., Manitowoc, 1924-29; plant mgr. W. M. Welch Mfg. Co., Manitowoc, 1929-34; dir. sales, lab. equipment div. Hamilton Mfg. Co., Two Rivers, Wis., 1934-42, sales mgr. contract div., 1942-53, v.p. charge sales, 1953-55, exec. v.p., dir., 1955-63, pres., gen. mgr., 1963-66, pres., chief exec. officer, 1966-70, chmn., chief exec. officer, 1970-74; pres. Ray Halvorsen Assos., Two Rivers, 1973- 75. Dir. Camp Manito-Wish YMCA, Silver Lake Coll. Recipient Meritorious Service award N. Central area YMCA, 1958, Silver Knight of Mgmt. award Nat. Mgmt. Assn., 1968. Mem. Assn. Home Appliance Mfrs. (Service Record award 1969), Sci. Apparatus Makers Assn. (pres. 1961-62, dir.; recipient sci. award 1966), Manitowoc-Two Rivers (pres., dir.), Wis. State (dir.) chambers commerce. Mason (32 deg., Shriner), Elk. Clubs: Milwaukee Athletic; Rotary (pres. 1956) (Two Rivers, Wis.); Manitowoc Branch River Country. Home: Two Rivers Wis. Died Nov. 18, 1974.

HALVORSON, HALVOR ORIN, educator; b. River Falls, Wis., Mar. 26, 1897; s. Hallie and Elizabeth (Heyerdahl) H.; B.S., U. Minn., 1921, Chem. E., 1922, Ph.D., 1928; D.Sc. (hon.), St. Olaf Coll., 1948; m. Selma C. Halvorson, Aug. 1922; children—Betty Jean (Mrs. Theodore Caspar), Harlyn, Loren, Gayle Adair (Mrs. John Mosand). Teaching fellow U. Minn., 1922-23, instr., 1923-28, asst. prof., 1928-30, asso. prof., 1930-40, prof., 1940-49; dir. Hormel Inst., 1943-49; prof., head dept. bacteriology U. Ill., 1949-60, dir. Sch. Life Scis., 1959-65; research prof. dept. biochemistry U. Minn., St. Paul, 1965-71. Cons. san. engring. and food tech., from 1928. Civilian with Office Sci. Research and Devel., 1943-45, panel mem. Office Naval Research, 1947-51, NIH, 1949-54, mem. council Inst. of Alleergy and Infectious Diseases, 1954-58; mem. subcom. food stability NRC, 1955-57. Served as 1st lt. C.A.C., U.S. Army, 1917-19. Named Outstanding Am. Investigator Am. Mfrs. Assn., 1940; recipient Pasteur award, 1960. Mem. Soc. Am. Bacteriologists (past pres.), Am. Acad. Microbiology (chmn. bd. govs. 1956-57), Sigma Xi, Phi Kappa Phi, Phi Lambda Upsilon, Alpha Chi Sigma, Gamma Alpha. Author: Quantitative Bacteriology, 1933; articles sci. jours. Contbg. author: The Chemistry and Technology of Food and Food. Home: Minneapolis, Minn., Died Oct. 20, 1975.

HAM, BERTRAM LAMAR, hwy. constrn. co. exec.; b. Kingston Springs, Tenn., Feb. 6, 1910; s. James Davis and Ida Lura (Fulghum) H.; student pub. schs.; m. Loretta Susan Robinson, May 27, 1939. Partner, J.D. Ham & Sons, Nashville, 1929-32; employed with various bridge and bldg. contractors, 1932-37; bridge foreman Rea Constrn. Co., Charlotte, N.C., 1937-40; with Oman Constrn. Co., Inc., Nashville, 1940-74, project mgr., 1945-54, gen. supt. hwy. and r.r. constrn., 1955-74, v.p., 1971-74. Home: Nashville, Tenn. Died Apr. 9, 1974.

HAM, WILLIAM ROSS physicist; b.Lewiston, Me., Feb. 10, 1879; s. John Lowell and Emily (Ford) H.; B.A., Bates Coll., Lewiston, Me., 1901; Ph.D., U. of Chicago, 1909; m. J. Elizabeth Dunmore, July 1908; children—Priscilla, John L. and Frank (twins), Nelson. Prof. physics, Pa. State Coll., 1909-44, also head of dept. Capt. Ordnance Dept., U.S. Army, June 1917-June 1919; lt. col., O.R.C. from 1939. Mem. Am. Phys. Soc., Phi Beta Kappa, Sigma Xi, Phi Kappa Phi, Alpha Tau Omega. Wrote papers on polarization of Röntgen rays, depth of complete scattering of kathode rays, absorption in the ultra violet, relation between vapor tension and temperature, design of stereobinoculars (patents), reflection of electrons, energy of high velocity electrons, variation of photoelectric effect with temperature, equations of thermionic emission, diffusion of gases through metals. Club: Cosmos. Home: Dixfield, Me.†

HAMBER, ERIC WERGE, business exec.; b. Winnipeg. Manitoba, Can., Apr. 21, 1879; s. Eric Frederick March and Ada (Jefferson) H.; student St. John's Coll. Sch., Winnipeg, 1887-93; B.A., classics, U. of Manitoba, 1894-98; fellow St. John's Coll., 1939; LL.D., U. of British Columbia, Can., 1937; m. Aldyen Irene Hendry, May 14, 1912. With The Dominion Bank, Winnipeg, Can., 1898; mgr. Calgary, Can., 1906, mgr. Vancouver, Can., 1907, mgr. The Dominion Bank, London, Eng., 1911, dir. Canada, 1912; pres. and gen. mgr. B.C. Mills, Timber and Trading Co., 1913-35; pres. and gen. mgr. Hastings Sawmill Co., Ltd., from 1935; dir. Canadian Pacific Ry. Co., The Dominion Bank; dir. Toronto General Trusts Corp. (mem. advisory bd.); dir. Pacific Mills, Ltd. Lt.-gov. Province of B.C., Can., 1936-42; chancellor U. of B.C., Vancouver, Can., freeman City of Vancouver. Hon. col. Seaforth Highlanders of Canada. Decorated: Companion of the Order of St. Michael and St. George and Knight of Grace of the Order of St. John of Jerusalem, both presented by King George VI. Life gov. Vancouver Gen. Hosp.; former gov. and life mem. B.C. Cancer Found.; former pres. and life mem. Canadian Red Cross Soc., B.C. Div., 1941-45; mem. Nat. Council, Salvation Army, Canadian Council, Boy Scouts Assn.; hon. v.p. Victorian Order of Nurses for Canada; hon. v.p. Queen Alexandra Solarium for Crippled Children; hon. life mem. Canadian Legion, British Empire Service League, B.C. Acad. of Sciences, U. of B.C.; life mem. Naval Officers Assn. of B.C., B.C. Architects Assn., Vancouver Exhibition Assn.; hon. pres. B.C. br., St. John's Ambulance Assn.; v. chmn. Canadian Com. of Newcomen Soc. of Eng.; former pres. Canadian Mfg. Assn., B.C. div.; mem. Vancouver Bd.

of Trade. Clubs: The Bath, Royal Automobile (London, Eng.); Vancouver, Capilano Golf, Quilchena Golf (Vancouver); Union (Victoria); Rainier (Seattle); Cypress Point Golf (Monterey, Calif.). Home: Vancouver, B.C., Canada†

HAMER, HOMER G., surgeon; b. Bellefontaine, Ohio, May 27, 1880; s. W. Frank and Mary Julia (Pool) H.; M.D., Ind. Univ., 1904; attended N.Y. Post Grad. Med. Sch. and Hosp., 1905; m. Catherine Maone Dolphin, Feb. 7, 1912; children—John Kendrick, Julianne. Interne St. Vincents Hosp., Indianapolis, Ind., 1904-05; pvt. practice of urological surgery, Indianapolis, from 1905; mem. faculty Ind. Univ. Sch. Medicine, from 1905, as clin. lecturer, 1905, lecturer on genito-urinary surgery, 1906, asso. in genito-urinary surgery, 1913, asst. prof., 1916, asso. prof. 1921, clin. prof. urology from 1927; attending urologist Meth. Hosp.; cons. urologist at Indianapolis Gen., Ind. Univ., St. Vincent's Hosps. Served as 1st lt., M.C., U.S. Army, 1918-19. Fellow. Am. Assn. Genito-Urinary Surgeons (pres., 1941-42); mem. A.M.A. (mem. house of dels. from 1933), Am. Urol. Assn. (sec. 1921-28, pres., 1929). Clin. Soc. Genito-Urinary Surgeons, Internat. Soc. Urology, A.C.S., Indianapolis Med. Soc. (pres. 1927), Ind. State Med. Assn., S.A.R. Republican. Methodist. Mason (K.T., Scottish Rite). Clubs: Columbia, Contemporary. Contbr. numerous articles on genito-urinary diseases in med. jours. European travel 1930, 33, 36. Home: Indianapolis, Ind.†

HAMILL, ROBERT LYON, engr.; b. Chgo., Apr. 4, 1899; s. Robert W. and Katharine (Lyon) H.; A.B., Yale, 1920; m. Katharine Porter, Oct. 9, 1920; children—Katharine Delano (Mrs. John F. Garde, Jr.), Ann Porter (Mrs. John L. Koehne, Jr.), Joan (Mrs. Robert H. Porter), Robert Lyon. Partner, chmn. bd. Sanderson & Porter, N.Y.; chmn. bd. Lawrence (L.I)-Cedarhurst Bank, 1933-39; dir. The Liberia Co., Liberian Devel. Corp., Bermuda Properties, Ltd., Pan Am. World Airways; mem. adv. com. The Bank N.Y. Pres. N.Y.C. of C., 1950-52; mem. bus. adv. council N.Y. State Dept. Commerce, 1950-52. Gov., mem. finance and exec. coms. Soc. N.Y. Hosp., 1955-60; pres. bd. trustees Sailors' Snug Harbour, 1950-52. Served as chief boatswains mate, USNRF, 1918; worked on reparations AUS, Japan, 1947, Germany, 1948. Mem. Am. Arbitration Assn., Delta Kappa Epsilon. Clubs: Union, Down Town Assn. (N.Y.C.); Adirondack League (Old Forge, N.Y.); Rockaway Hunting (Cedarhurst); Royal Bermuda Yacht, Mid-Ocean (Bermuda); Lyford Cay (Nassau, Bahamas); Wyandanch Sportsmen's (Smithtown, N.Y.); Sewanhaka Corinthian Yacht (Center Island, N.Y.); Lawrence Beach (Atlantic Beach, L.I.); Cotton Bay (Eleuthera, Bahamas). Home: New York City, NY. Died May 1974.

HAMILTON, DAVID WILEY, educator; b. Florenceville, N.B., Can. Apr. 30, 1878; s. John and Ellen (Dyer) H.; B.A., U. of New Brunswick, 1901, M.A., 1903, Ph.D., 1907; B.S.A., McGill U., 1914; studied U. of Chicago, Cornell U., Columbia, Clark; M.S. in Voc. Edn., Ia. State Coll., 1923; Ed.M., Harvard, 1926; m. Bertella Annie Dayton, Dec. 28, 1904; children—Florence Alberta, Lillian Marguerite. Supt. consolidated rural high sch., Kingston, N.B., 1904-07 (the first consolidated rural high sch. on a vocational basis in America); prof. agrl. edn., Normal Sch., Fredericton, 1907-12, McGill U., 1914-19, State Coll. of Wash. from 1919. Mem. N.E.A., Nat. Soc. for Vocational Edn., Nat. Soc. for Vocational Guidance, Phi Delta Kappa, Phi Kappa Phi, Pi Gamma Mu. Home: Pullman, Wash.†

HAMILTON, DEXTER, lawyer; b. Corsicana, Tex., May 22, 1879; s. N. S. and Mary (Hunter) H.; LL.B., U. of Tex., 1904; m. Alma Grayson, 1904; children—Wm. Dexter, Mabel. Admitted to Tex. bar, 1904, and began practice at Corsicana; city atty., Corsicana, 1905-09; dist. atty., Navarro County, 1910-14; moved to Dallas. Tex., 1920; judge Court of Civil Appeals, Fifth Supreme Jud. Dist. of Tex., 1920-24; resigned to re-enter practice; mem. firm Hamilton, Edwards & Shults; vice pres., general counsel Dallas Nat. Bank; pres. Dallas Title and Guaranty Co. Mem. Am., Tex. State and Dallas bar assns., Nat. Economy League, Am. Acad. Polit. Science, Alumni Assn. of U. of Tex. (pres. 1918). Democrat. Baptist. Clubs: University (pres. 1932), Dallas Country (gov). Home: Highland Park, Tex.†

HAMILTON, HARRY HEBER, coll. pres.; b. Glass, Tenn., Feb. 28, 1878; s. John Tweed and Annie Beatrice (Hadley) H.; student U. of Ark., 1896-99; A.B., Walla Walla Coll., College Place, Wash., 1921; m. Mary Davis, Sept. 8, 1902; children—Evelyn (Mrs. William H. Shephard), John Tweed. Law reporter, Jonesboro, Ark., 1902-06; head of dept. commerce, Southwestern Jr. Coll., Keene, Tex., 1906-18, Walla Walla Coll., 1918-22; prin. Western Wash. Acad., Auburn, 1922-25; pres. Southern Jr. Coll., Collegedale, Tenn., 1925-27; pres. Washington Missionary Coll., 1927-35; pres. Southwestern Junior Coll., Keene, Tex., from 1935. Ordained ministry Seventh-Day Adventist Ch., 1923, Mem. Kappa. Alpha (Southern). Home: Keene, Tex.†

HAMILTON, JOHN DANIEL MILLER, lawyer; b. Ft. Madison, Ia., Mar. 2, 1892; s. John Daniel Miller and Mary (Rice) H.; grad. Phillips Acad., Andover, Mass., 1913; LL.B., Northwestern U., 1916; LL.D. (hon.), Dickinson Law Sch.; m. Rosamond Kittle. Practiced Kansas City, Mo., 1916-18, Topeka, 1918-40, mem. Pepper, Hamilton and Scheetz. Dir. Glenmede Trust Co. Mem. Kan. Ho. of Reps., 1925-28, speaker, 1927-28. Chmn. Rep. State Central Com., 1930-32; mem. Rep. Nat. Com., 1932-40, chmn., 1936-40. Trustee Robert A. Taft Meml. Found. Mem. Am. Pa., Phila., Shawnee Co. bar assns., Bar Assn. State Kan., Phi Alpha Delta. Mason, Elk. Home: Clearwater FLa. Died Sept. 24, 1973.

HAMILTON, J(OSEPH) G(RÉGOIRE) DE ROULBAC, prof. history; b. Hillsboro, N.C., Aug. 6, 1878; s. Daniel Heyward and Frances Gray (Roulbac) H.; M.A., U. of the South, Sewanee, Tenn., 1900; Ph.D., Columbia, 1906, Litt.D., Washington and Lee U., 1942, U. of the South m. Mary Cornelia Thompson, Dec. 22, 1908; children—Joseph Grégoire de Roulhac, Alfred Thompson. Instr. in Horner Mil. Sch., Oxford, N.C., 1901-02; prin. Wilmington (N.C.) High Sch., 1904-06; asso. prof. history, 1906-08, alumni prof. history, 1908-20, Kenan prof. history and government, 1920-48, also dir. Southern Hist. Collection, U. N.C., ret., 1948, cons., from 1948. Awarded Columbia University Medal, 1932. Dist. dir. war issues course, 4th dist., S.A.T.C., 1918; lecturer, citizenship unit, Army Ednl. Corps, A.E.F., 1919; consultant in gen. edn. to war plans div., Gen. Staff, 1920-22; visiting prof., summers, U. of Mich., 1928, Harvard, 1931, U. of Chicago, 1933, 34, 36, U. of Southern Calif., 1939; editor James Sprunt Historical Publs., 1908-24; book review editor, Greensboro Daily News, 1921-25. Democrat. Episcopalain. Mem. Am. Hist. Assn. (mem. council, 1929-33), Southern Historical Association (pres. 1943), North Carolina Literary and Historical Association (pres. 1920), Kappa Alpha, Phi Beta Kappa. Author: Reconstruction in North Carolina, 1914; Our Republic (with F. L. Riley and J. A. C. Chandler), 1910; A Syllabus of North Carolina History (with W. K. Boyd), 1913; Party Politics in North Carolina, 1835-1860, 1916; Life of Robert E. Lee (with Mary Thompson Hamilton); North Carolina since 1860, 1919; Making of Citizens (with E. W. Knight), 1922; Henry Ford, 1927. Editor: The Correspondence of Jonathan Worth (2 vols.), 1909; The Papers of Thomas Ruffin (4 vols.), 1918-21; Selections From the Writings of Abraham Lincoln, 1921; The Best Letters of Thomas Jefferson, 1926; The Papers of Randolph Abbott Shotwell, 1929; Truth in History with Other Essays by William A. Dunning, 1937. Contbr. to mags. and revs. Home: Chapel Hill N.C.†

HAMILTON, KENNETH GARDINER, clergyman; born Bethlehem, Pa., Feb. 20, 1893; s. John Taylor and Cecelia Elizabeth (Beck) H.; student Moravian parochial schs., Bethlehem, Pa., Herrnhut and Niesky, Germany; A.B., Moravian Coll. and Theol. Sem., 1912, B.D., 1914; D.D., 1951; student Livingstone Coll., London, 1922-23; Ph.D., Columbia, 1941; m. Marie Pauline Peterson, Aug. 15, 1923. Ordained deacon, Moravian Ch., 1914, ordained presbyter, 1919, consecrated bishop, Feb. 16, 1947; pastor, West Salem, Ill., 1914-15; sec. Internat. Com., Y.M.C.A. for prisoner of war work in Britain and Switzerland, 1915-18; missionary, pastor, Sandy Bay, Cabo Gracias and Bluefields, Nicaragua, C.A., 1919-37; prof. Moravian Ch. history Moravian Coll. and Theol. Sem., 1937-46; asst. archivist Moravian Ch., North, Bethlehem, 1937-46; advocate Moravian Missions, 1942-46; dean Moravian Theol. Sem., 1946; mem. at large and vice pres. exec. bd. The Moravian Ch., North, Bethlehem, 1946-56, president, 1956-63; exec. officer bd. fgn. missions, 1949-56, chmn, 1956-63, chmn. archives com., 1946-63. Mem. bd. trustees Moravian Coll. and Theol. Sem. Mem. Soc. for Propagating The Gospel (pres.), Moravian Hist. Soc. (vice pres.), Am. Soc. Ch. History. Republican. Club: Torch of Lehigh Valley. Author: Meet Nicaragua, 1939; John Ettwein and the Moravian Church During the Revolutionary Period, 1940; Church Street in Old Bethlehem, 1942. Home: Bethlehem, Pa. Died Feb. 28, 1975.

HAMILTON, LOUIS FRANKLIN, printing co. exec.; b. Mineola, Tex., Jan. 16, 1907; s. Louis Franklin and Ernestine (Clement) H.; student So. Meth. U., 1927-30; m. Ruth Loree Dalton, Dec. 24, 1938. Pres. Litho Offset Supply, Inc., Dallas, 1941-75; v.p. Eldorado Oil and Gas, Inc., Dallas, 1956-75. Methodist. Mason. Club: Glen Lakes Country. Home: Dallas, Tex., Died Feb. 24, 1975.

HAMILTON, WALTER RALEIGH, cons. engr., operator; b. Grayson, Calif., Aug. 10, 1880; s. Henry and Nora (Coughlin) H.; A.B., Stanford, 1904; m. Mattie E. Dunn, May 27, 1905; children—Fay Dunn, Barbara. Supt. cyanide plant, 1904-05; asst. supt. Standard Consol. Mining Co., Bodie, Calif., 1905-06; chemist Ymir (B.C., Can.) Gold Mines, 1906-07; geologist, Associated Oil Co., San Francisco, Calif., 1907-08, chief geologist, 1908-10; v.p. and gen. mgr. Oak Ridge Oil Co., Montebello Oil Co., Ventura Oil Lands Co., Ventura Refining Co., San Francisco, 1910-16; mem. firm Pomeroy & Hamilton, cons. engrs., San Francisco and Tulsa, Okla. 1916-19; v.p. and mgr. Oil Issues Co., Tulsa, 1919-22; pres. Hamilton Oil Co Corpn., Tulsa, 1922-23; asst. to pres. United Central Oil Co., Houston, Tex., 1923-24; cons. engr. and oil operator, Tulsa, from 1924. Mem. nat. bd. Stanford, 1922-28. Mem. Am. Assn. Petroleum Geologists, Am. Inst. Mining & Metall. Engrs., Tulsa. Geol. Soc., Sigma Xi. Republican.*†

HAMLEY, FREDERICK GEORGE, fed. judge; b. Seattle, Oct. 24, 1903; s. Charles E. and Zoe N. (Stetson) H.; LL.B. cum laude, U. Wash., 1932; LL.D. (hon.), Gonzaga U., Spokane, 1967; m. Marjorie E. Wood, Sept. 19, 1932; children—June E., Arlene L. Admitted to Wash. bar, 1932; practiced in Seattle, 1932-38; supt. Seattle Water Dept., 1938; asst. dist. counsel Bur. Reclamation, 1938-40; personal legal adviser Gov. Langlie, 1941; dir. pub. service Wash., 1941-43; asst. gen. solicitor Nat. Assn. R.R. and Utilities Commrs., Washington, 1943-44, gen. solicitor, 1945-49; judge Wash. Supreme Ct., 1949-56, chief justice, 1955-56; judge U.S. Ct. of Appeals, 9th Circuit, 1956-75. Chmn. Gov.'s Statewide Com. on Ednl. TV, 1954-55; chmn. Wash. Jud. Council, 1955-56. Mem. Seattle City Council, 1935-38. Mem. Am. Bar Assn., Am. Judicature Soc., Inst. Jud. Adminstrn., Phi Beta Kappa, Order Coif, Phi Alpha Delta. Home: San Francisco, Cal. Died May 5, 1975.

HAMLIN, CONDE, mgmt. cons.; b. St. Paul, July 1915; s. Condé and Pearl (Terry) H.; grad. Culver Mil. Acad., 1932; m. Dorothy Armstrong. Nov. 22, 1940; children—Condé III, Jane (Mrs. Richard J. Schulten), William A. Regional sales mgr. Ozalid div. Gen. Aniline & Film Corp., 1946-52; v.p. charge sales De Walt Inc., Lancaster, Pa., 1952-54, exec. v.p., 1954, pres., dir., 1955-61; pres., dir. Motors Inc., Lancaster, DeWalt Canada Ltd., Guelph, Ont.; mgmt. and marketing cons., 1962-63; v.p. Chgo. Pneumatic Tool Co., 1963-67; pres. Jay V. Hall & Assos., Inc., N.Y.C., 1968-75. Served from 2d lt. to lt. col. AUS. 1940-46. Republican. Episcopalian. Club: Army and Navy (Washington) Home: Darien Conn. Died June 20, 1975; interred Spring Grove Cemetery, Darien, Conn.

HAMLIN, EDWARD, JR., physician; b. Boston, Nov. 18, 1906; s. Edward and Katharine Brooke (Conrad) H.; grad. Groton Sch., 1925; A.B., Harvard, 1929, M.D., 1933; m. Rose Bryant, June 1930; 1 son, Edward III; m. 2d, Jane Hamlin, Dec. 31, 1942; children—Katherine (Mrs. Robert Zappala), Jane (Mrs. Hilary F. Russell, Jr.), Hilary, Charlotte. Intern, Mass. Gen. Hosp., Boston, 1934-36, resident in surgery, 1937-39, vis. surgeon, mem. bd. consultants; asst. surgery in eye and ear Free Hosp. for Women, Mass. Eye and Ear Infirmary; asso. dir. med. services St. Lukes Hosp., New Bedford, Mass.; clin. asso. prof. surgery, lectr. surgery Harvard. Mem. Dartmouth (Mass.) Conservation Commn., 1971-73, chmn. 1972-73. Bd. dirs. Mass. Charitable Soc., 1942-73, pres., 1972-73. Diplomate Am. Bd. Surgery. Mem. A.M.A., A.C.S., Am. Soc. for Surgery Hand, New Eng. Surg. Soc., Am. Thyroid Assn. Home: South Dartmouth, Mass. Died Oct. 2, 1973; buried Slocum River, South Dartmouth, Mass.

HAMLIN, HUYBERTIE LANSING PRUYN (MRS. CHARLES S. HAMLIN);, b. Albany, N.Y., Apr. 8, 1878; d. John V. L. and Anna Fenn (Parker) Pruyn; ed. St. Agnes Sch., Albany, N.Y.; m. Charles S. Hamlin, June 4, 1898; 1 dau., Anna (dec.). Mem. Panama P.I. Expn. Commn. from Mass., 1915. Episcopalian. Mem. Patrons of Husbandry, Colonial Dames of America. Clubs: Chilton, Woman's Nat. Democratic (ex-pres.). Home: Mattapoisett, Mass.†

HAMMOND, DATUS MILLER, educator; b. Providence, Utah, May 20, 1911; s. Horace E. and Salina (Tibbitts) H.; B.S., Utah Agrl. Coll., 1932; A.M., U. Cal., 1934, Ph.D., 1936; m. Emily Merrill, Dec. 23, 1937; children—Anna Marie, Louise, Betty, Marilyn, Carol. Instr. zoology Utah State U., Logan, 1937-40, asst. prof., 1940-41, prof., head dept., 1945, faculty honor lectr., 1964; asst. protozoologist, zool. div. Bur. Animal Industry, U.S. Dept. Agr., Beltsville, Md., 1941-42, asso. protozoologist U.S. regional lab. for animal disease research, Auburn, Ala., 1942-44; guest prof. U. Bonn, 1970, 72. Fulbright research scholar U. Munich, 1955-56. Fellow A.A.A.S.; mem. Utah Acad. Scis., Arts and Letters (pres. 1972-73), Soc. Protozoologists (sec. 1967-73, pres.-elect 1973-74), Am. Soc. Zoologists, Am. Soc. Parasitol., Am. Micros. Soc., Phi Beta Kappa, Phi Kappa Phi (pres. Utah State chpt. 1963-65), Sigma Xi (pres. Utah State chpt. 1946-47). Mem. Church of Jesus Christ of Latter-Day Saints. Rotarian. Editorial bd. Jour. Protozoology, Zeitschrift fur Parasitenkunde. Contbr. articles to sci. jours. Researcher on coccidia of cattle, other animals. Home: Logan, Utah. Died Mar. 1974.

HAMMOND, DEAN B(URT), corp. exec.; b. Saline, Mich., Dec. 24, 1908; s. Burt David and Mary Emma (Cotton) H.; B.S. in aero. engring. U. Mich., 1931; m. Bertha Cyrena Flo, Sept. 29, 1932; children—Anne Flo, Joan Beth. Pres. Hammond Aircraft Corp., Ypsilanti, Mich., 1932-36; v.p. Stearman-Hammond Aircraft Corp., San Francisco, 1936-39, Hammond Aircraft Co., San Francisco, 1939-44; cons. engr. Henry J. Kaiser Co., Oakland, Cal., 1944-46; cons. engr. Kaiser-Frazer Corp., Willow Run, Mich., 1946-47, chief engr., 1947-51, v.p. engring. from 1951-54; cons. engr. Willys Motors, Inc., 1954-58, v.p., 1958-65; v.p. Kaiser Jeep Corp., 1958-65; exec. asst. to chmn. bd. Kaiser

Industries Corp., 1966-70; cons., 1971-74. Mem. Soc. Automotive Engrs., Delta Phi. Presbyn. Home: Oakland, Cal. Died July 17, 1974.

HAMMOND, LAURENS, inventor, mfr.; b. Evanston, Ill., Jan. 11, 1895; s. William Andrew and Ida Louise (Strong) H.; M.E., Cornell U., Ithaca, N.Y., 1916; m. Mildred Anton-Smith, Sept. 1, 1924 (dec.); children—Mildred, Margaret; m. 2d, Roxana Scoville, Oct. 25, 1955. Founder, Hammond Organ Co., chmn. bd. to 1960; founder Hammond Clock Co. Inventions include differential mercurial barometer, organ, stereoscopic motion pictures, various stage effects for Ziegfeld, electric clock, parts for guided missiles; cons. U.S. Air Corps, 1940-43. Served as capt., engrs., U.S. Army, 1917-19; AEF in France. Recipient Wetherill medal Franklin Inst., 1940. Holder 110 U.S. patents. Home: Chateau de Champremault Meung-sur-Loire Loizet, France Mill Reef Club Antigua British West Indies New York City, NY. Died July 1, 1973.

HAMMOND, WILLIAM, physician, editor; b. N.Y.C., Oct. 17, 1900; s. John and Mary (Corbett) H.; M.D., C.M., McGill U., 1927; m. Shirley Louise Blanchard, Aug. 22, 1931; children—Graeme Lord, Mary Rand (Mrs. Arthur W. Ticknor), Melissa Blanchard (Mrs. Donald H. Lang). Postgrad. tng. Royal Victoria Hosp., Montreal, Que., Can., 1927, Mass. Gen. Hosp., Boston, 1928-29, Johns Hopkins Hosp., 1929-31; pvt. practice internal medicine, Scarsdale, N.Y., 1931-73; cons. physician Grasslands Hosp.; vis. physician White Plains Hosp.; med. cons. Westchester County Dept. Welfare, 1942-62, N.Y. State Dept. Social Welfare, 1962-73. Mem. Scarsdale Non-Partisan Com., 1960-73. Bd. dirs. Physicians Home, N.Y.C., 1963-73. Fellow A.C.P., Am. Geriatrics Soc. (pres. 1965; pres. Research Found). Am. Med. Writers Assn. (pres. Met. chpt. 1964, nat. pres. 1966); mem. N.Y. State (council), Westchester County (historian) med. socs. Clubs: Canadian (N.Y.C.); Shenorock Shore (Rye, N.Y.). Asst. editor N.Y. State Jour. Medicine, 1957-61, editor, 1961-73. Home: Scarsdale, N.Y. Died Dec. 11, 1973.

HAMMONS, PAUL EDWARD, educator; b. Bogalousa, La., June 16, 1925; s. James Clifford and Norma Beatrice (Booty) H.; B.S., Northwestern State Coll., 1949; M.S., U. Ark., 1951; D.D.S., Loyola U., New Orleans, 1954; m. Doris Nell Denham, Sept. 3, 1950; children—Bruce Clifford, Mark Denham. Pvt. practice dentistry, Crossett, Ark., 1954-55; asst. prof. dentistry Sch. Dentistry, U. Ala., Birmingham, 1955-58, asso. prof., 1958-64, prof., 1964-74, dir. aux. research, 1963-69, prof., chmn. dept. operative dentistry, 1968-74. Cons. VA Hosp., Council on Dental Edn. Am. Dental Assn. Served with AUS, 1943-46. Recipient Fuller award, 1973. Fellow Royal Soc. Health; mem. Am. Assn. Dental Schs., Delta Sigma Delta, Omicron Kappa Upsilon, Beta Beta Beta. Contbr. articles profl. jours. Home: Birmingham, Ala. Died Sept. 3, 1974.

HAMPSON, PHILIP F., trust executive; b. Chicago, July 30, 1894: s. John and Olive (Bower) H.; student Evanston Acad., 1909, pub. schs. Chicago; m. Kathryn Mathews, June 1, 1929 (deceased Sept. 1954); m. 2d, Georgina George Finley, June 11, 1955. Librarian Chicago Tribune, 1913-17, reporter 1920-31, financial writer, 1931-56, financial editor, 1951-56; exec. dir. Robert R. McCormick Charitable Trust, Cantigny Trust, Robert R. McCormick Found., Cantigny First Div. Found., 1956-69. Served as sgt. U.S. Army, 1917-19. Mem. Am. Legion, Sigma Delta Chi. Club: Chicago Press. Home: Chicago, Ill. Died May 25, 1974; buried All Saints Cemetery, Des Plaines,Ill.

HANBY, ALBERT THATCHER, lawyer; b. Claymont, Del., Apr. 12, 1881; s. Samuel and Mary (Cherry) H.; B.A., West Chester State Normal Sch., 1906; LL.B., U. of Pa., Law. Sch., 1909; m. Cecil DeClyne, July 3, 1925. Admitted to Pa. bar, 1909. Coordinator for Phila. Draft Appeal Bd., Area No. 1, Right Worshipful Jr. Grand Warden, Grand Lodge Free and Accepted Masons of Pa. Member American, Pennsylvania State, Phila. and United States Supreme Court bar assns., Masonic Vets. of Pa., Masonic Vets. Assn. of D.C., Sons of Del., Joshua Assn., Tri-County Club, Society of the Friendly Sons of St. Patrick, Alpha Chi Rho. Republican. Methodist. Mason (Royal Arch, K.T., 32°, Shriner, Phila. Consistory, Royal Order of Scotland, Priestly Order of the Temple, Order of Knights of St. John the Evangelist, Royal Order of Jesters, Grand Imperial Conclave of Canada, Grand Conclave of Canada, Penn Priory No. 6, Grand Council Royal and Select Masters of Pa.—Grand Rep. to England and Wales, Commandery; holds numerous of highest official and hon. positions all divs. of Masonry, including Past Most Illustrious Grand Soverign of Grand Imperial Council, Knights of the Red Cross of Constantine. Clubs: Shrine, Lawyer's, Pennsylvania Square, Kiwanis (Phila. Pa.); International High Noon (N.Y. City); Yeadon (Pa.) Square; Tri-Square (Dolyestown, Pa.). Home: Philadelphia, Pa.†

HANCHETT, EDWIN LANI, bishop; b. Honolulu, Nov. 2, 1919; s. A. Kaumu and Mary (McGuire) H.; student U. Hawaii, 1937-39; D.D., Ch. Div. Sch. of Pacific, 1969; m. Puanani Akana, June 21, 1941; children—Carolyn (Mrs. James Remedios) Suzanne (Mrs. William Swartman), Stuart, Tiare (Mrs. Richard McIntyre). Ordained priest Episcopal Ch., 1952; vicar Ch. of Holy Innocents, Lahaina, Maui, 1952-59; vicar St. George's Episcopal Ch., Honolulu, 1959-60; rector St. Peter's Episcopal Ch., Honolulu, 1960-67; suffragan bishop Episcopal Ch. in Hawaii, 1967-69, diocesan bishop, 1969-75. Home: Kaneohe, Hawaii. Died Aug. 11, 1975; interred St. Clement Ch., Honolulu.

HANES, P(LEASANT) H(UBER), knitting company exec.; b. Winston-Salem, North Carolina, Mar. 5, 1880; s. Pleasant Henderson and Lizora (Fortune) H.; B.S., Trinity College (now Duke Univ.), 1900; grad. Eastman Business School, Poughkeepsie, N.Y., 1901; m. Evelyn Hazen, Oct. 27, 1909; children—Rosalie Hanes (Mrs. Thomas O. Moore), P. Huber, Jr. Sec.-treas., P.H. Hanes Knitting Co., 1903-17, vice-pres. and treas., 1917-25, pres., 1925-54, chmn. bd. 1954-60, hon. chmn. bd., from 1960; pres., dir. West End Properties, Inc., successor W. End Development Co.; dir. emeritus Security Life & Trust Co., Wachovia Bank & Trust Co. Gen. chmn. Centennial Fund Com., Duke U., 1939; past pres., dir. emeritus Underwear Inst.; trustee emeritus Duke. Regional v.p., dir. N.A.M., 1940. Mem. Newcomen Soc. Eng., Alpha Tau Omega, Omicron Delta Kappa. Democrat. Member Methodist Ch. Mason (K.T., Shriner). Clubs: Ch. Forsyth Country (Winston-Salem); Southern (N.Y.C.); Rotary. Home: Winston-Salem, N.C.†

HANES, RALPH PHILIP, mfg. exec.; b. Winston-Salem, N.C., Feb. 22, 1898; s. John Wesley and Anna (Hodgin) H.; grad. Phillips Acad., 1916; B.A., Yale, 1920; m. DeWitt Thurmond Chatham, Apr. 4, 1923; children—Ralph Philip, Martha T. (Mrs. Calder W. Womble), Anna H. (Mrs. Thomas L. Chatham). With Hanes Dye & Finishing Co., Winston-Salem, N.C., 1925-73, successively v.p., pres., chmn., now chmn. exec. com.; pres. Central Parking, Inc., 1956-63, Old Salem, Inc., 1956-58, chmn. bd., 1963-73; dir. Chatham Mfg. Co. Executive bd. N.C. Dept. Archives and History; pres. Civic Music Assn. of Winston-Salem; past chmn. bd. Pub. Library of Winston-Salem and Forsyth County. Mem. Nat. Trust for Historic Preservation (vice chmn. bd. trustees), Scroll and Key Soc., Delta Kappa Epsilon. Home: Winston-Salem N.C. Died July 1973.

HANES, THOMAS ANDREWS, editor; b. Stevenson, Ala., May 10, 1896; s. Rev. James Oscar and Emma (Barton) H.; student Birmingham-Southern Coll., 1914-17; m. Kathryn Crooks Cornick, Feb. 18, 1922. Sports editor Montgomery (Ala.) Jour., 1919; city editor Montgomery Evening Advertiser, also sports editor Birmingham Ledger, 1919-20; sports editor Norfolk (Va.) Ledger-Dispatch, 1920-36, mng. editor since 1936; war corr., 1943; Va. chmn. Asso. Press, 1943; Va. advisor Office Censorship, 1943-45. Chmn. city recreation commn., 1944-46; bd. mem. Norfolk community chest. Served with U.S.N., 1917-19. Mem. Va. Press Assn. (pres. 1946, hon. life mem.), Res. Officers Assn., Am. Soc. Journalism Sch. Adminstrs. (adv. bd.), Va. Contract Bridge Assn., Am. Soc. Newspaper Editors, American War Correspondents Association, Chamber of Commerce, Am. Legion, Sigma Delta Chi. Ind. Democrat. Methodist. Mason. Clubs: Cosmopolitan Internat. Virginia, Princess Anne Country. Home: Norfolk, Va. Died Oct. 7, 1972.

HANEY, GEORGE JACOB, stock brokerage firm exec.; b. Perth Amboy, N.J., May 15, 1914; s. Frederick and Lillian (French) H.; student Georgetown U., 1935-37; J.D., Rutgers U., 1941; m. Mary H. Hamilton, Apr. 27, 1957. Admitted to N.J. bar, 1941; practiced in Newark, 1941-42, Woodbridge, N.J., 1949-51; mem. firm McCarter & English, Newark, 1940-41; partner Kerbs Haney & Co., mem. N.Y. Stock Exchange, 1952-59; v.p. Auchincloss Parker & Redpath, Newark, 1959-69, Kohlmeyer & Co., mems. N.Y. Stock Exchange, Newark, 1969-70, asso. mgr. A.G. Edwards & Sons, Inc., Clifton, N.J., 1970-72, Halle & Stieglitz, Newark, 1972-73. Chmn., asso. dir. Broad Nat. Bank, Newark, 1963-73; chmn. securities adv. com. Atty. Gen.'s Dept. of State N.J., 1969-71. Asst treas. N.J. region Am. Cancer Soc., 1962-69, mem. dist. bd. trustees, 1962-70; pres. Arthritis Found. N.J., 1972-73; nat. bd. trustees Nat. Conf. Christians and Jews, 1968-73, N.J. sec., 1960-73, mem. N.J. regional exec. com., 1960-73; trustee Nat. Housing Conf., Washington; chmn. bd. Biafran Relief Fund, 1968-70; v.p. Robert Treat Council Boy Scouts Am., 1965-73; mem. exec. com., trustee Leaguers, Newark, 1960-73; No. N.J. com. chmn. John F. Kennedy Meml. Library, Newark, 1965-66; vice chmn. bd. trustees Heart Research Inst., St. Michael's Med. Center, Newark, 1968-73; mem. adv. bd. Inst. Human Relations, Newark Arch-diocese, 1972-73. Served to capt. AUS, 1942-46, 51-52. Decorated Purple Heart, Bronze Star medal; recipient awards including N.J. Catholic Brotherhood award Nat. Conf. Christians and Jews, 1965; named Citizen of Year, Leaguers, 1967; Newarker of Week, Prudential Life, 1968, Man of Year, Nat. Jewish Hosp., 1972. Mem. Am., N.J., Essex County bar assns., Am. Judicature Soc., Ironbound Mfgs. Assn. (pres. 1970-72), Catholic Lawyers Guild, N.J. C. of C., Investment Bankers Am., V.F.W., Ancient Order Hibernians, Advt. Club N.J. (sec. 1968-72, trustee). Patrolmen's Benevolent Assn. (hon. life). Clubs: N.Y. Athletic, Essex, First Friday, Marco Polo (N.Y.); Sales Executive (N.J., exec. bd. 1967-70). Home: Newark N.J. Died Mar. 1, 1973.

HANFORD, A(LFRED) CHESTER, coll. prof.; b. Makanda, Ill., Apr. 12, 1891; s. George Chester and Anna (Pease) H.; B.A., U. of Ill., 1912, M.A., 1913; Ph.D., Harvard, 1923; LL.D., Tulane U., 1938, So. Ill. U., 1952; m. Ruth Hyde, Mar. 23, 1918; 1 son, George Hyde, Asst. in polit. sci., U. of Ill., 1913-15; mem. govt. dept., Harvard from 1915, asst. prof. govt., 1923-27, asso. prof., 1927-30, prof., 1930-57, prof. emeritus, 1957-75; also dean Harvard Coll., 1927-47; dir. Harvard Summer Sch., 1924-27. Lt. (j.g.) U.S. N.R.F., 1917-19; investigator for Ill. Efficiency and Economy Commn., 1915; compiled information for Mass. Constitutional Convention, 1916-17; sec. to com. on new sources of revenue for Boston, Mass., 1920. Trustee, Fessenden Sch., 1930-54, and president of bd. 1933-35; mem. Council for Special Program in the Humanities Princeton University, 1948-52. Member of Special Commission on Legislative System and Procedure of Commonwealth of Massachusetts, 1942-43; vice-president, New England Association of Colleges and Secondary Schools, 1945. Member American Polit. Science Assn., Phi Beta Kappa. Republican. Clubs: Faculty, Harvard (Boston). Author: Problems in Municipal Government, 1926, Book review editor Political Science Review, 1923-33. Home: Ware, Mass. Died Aug. 12, 1975.

HANLEY, DELOSS REED, physician; b. Fairbury, Ill., Oct. 5, 1903; s. Francis James and Laura Edna (Reed) H.; M.D., U. Ill., 1934; m. Lodema Helen Brown, June 23, 1933; children—James Charles, DeLoss Neale. Intern, Detroit Receiving Hosp., 1934-35; resident in radiology Cook County Hosp., Chgo., 1935-36; dir. dept. radiology Fairbury Community Hosp., St. Mary's Hosp., LaSalle, Ill., St. James Hosp., Pontiac, Ill. Bd. dirs. Streator High Sch., 1955-60. Diplomate Am. Bd. Radiology. Fellow Am. Coll. Radiology; mem. A.M.A., Radiol. Soc. N.Am., LaSalle County (past pres.), Streator (past pres.) med. socs., Ill. Radiol. Soc., Sigma Chi, Phi Chi. Republican. Roman Catholic. K.C. (4°) Elk. Contbr. articles to profl. jours. Home: Streator, Ill. Died Mar. 3, 1972; buried St. Mary's Cemetery, Streator, Ill.

HANLEY, JAMES HUGH, federal radio commr.; b. O'Neill, Neb., July 4, 1881; s. Dennis and Mary (Devaney) H.; grad. Fremont (Neb.) Normal Coll., 1903; LL.B. Creighton U., Omaha, 1910; m. May J. O'Brien, Oct. 28, 1913; children—James Francis, John Joseph, Thomas O'Brien. Began as teacher, Neb., 1903; admitted to Neb. Bar 1910, practiced in Omaha; mem. firm Hanley & O'Brien; sec. to late Congressman C. O. Lobeck, 1911-19; federal prohibition dir. for Neb., 1919-21; mem. Federal Radio Commn. from Apr. 1, 1933. Mem. Am., Neb. State and Omaha bar assns., Creighton Univ. Alumni Assn. Democrat. Catholic. Clubs: K.C., Elks, Omaha Athletic, Omaha Field; Congressional Country (Washington, D.C.). Home: Omaha, Neb.†

HANLEY, WILLIAM SCOTT, ry. official; b. Terre Haute, Ind., Sept. 9, 1879; s. John and Margaret (Scott) H.; B.S., in C.E., Rose Poly Inst., Terre Haute, 1905, C.E., 1925; m. Carolyn Louise Bloom, Jan. 24, 1906 (deceased August 12, 1959). Assistant on engineer corps Pennsylvania Railway, Logansport, Ind., 1900-02. C.&E.I. R.R. Co., at Chicago, 1905-06; asst. div. engr. same rd., at Danville, Ill., 1906-07, asst. engr., at Chicago, 1907-12; chief engr. N.O. Gt. Northern R.R. 1912-21 (rehabilitating the system); chief engr. St.L. Southwestern Ry. Lines 1921-50. Served as supt. transportation mechanical and engring. depts. N.O.Gt.Northern R.R., World War, also commn. home service Am. Red Cross. Mem. Am. Ry. Engring. Assn., Am. Soc. C.E., Soc. Am. Mil. Engrs., Tau Beta Pi, Rose Polytechnic Alumni Association (pres. 1951). Democrat. Mem. Knights of Columbus (4th degree). Club: Willowbrook Country. Home: Tyler, Tex†

HANNON, WILLIAM GARRETT, social work exec.; b. Schenectady, Aug. 23, 1919; s. Neil Joseph and Catherine (Lonergan) H.; A.B., Siena Coll., 1952; M.Social Service, Syracuse U., 1960; m. Mary E. Rose, Aug. 14, 1947; children—Neil, Catherine, Mary Anne, William Garrett, John, Brian. Caseworker, Schenectady County Welfare Dept., 1951-54, Hudson River State Hosp., Poughkeepsie, N.Y., 1954-61; psychiat. social worker LaSalle Sch., Albany County Mental Health Assn., Albany, N.Y., 1961-62; dir. social service St. Anne Inst., Albany, 1962-69; supr. child welfare State N.Y. Dept. Social Service, Albany, 1969-71, sr. con. div. for youth, 1971-72; exec. dir. Assn. Child Caring Agys. N.Y. State, 1972-73. Lectr. sociology St. Rose, 1971-73. Lectr. sociology St. Rose Coll., 1965-66, Siena Coll., 1964. Pres., Albany Health, Edn., Welfare Club, 1964-65. Pres. bd. dirs. Albany County Mental Health Assn., 1966-68. Served with AUS, 1942-45. Mem. Nat. Assn. Social Workers, Acad. Certified Social Workers. Home: Schenectady N.Y. Died Nov. 12, 1973.

HANNUM, WARREN THOMAS, army officer (ret.); b. Pottsville, Pa., Mar. 8, 1880; s. Luther Keefer and Isabel (Reiter) H.; B.S., U.S. Mil. Acad., 1902; grad. U.S. Army Engr. Sch.,1908, Command and Gen. Staff Sch., 1916. Army War College, 1926; m. May Josephine Nickeeson, Feb. 21, 1905; children—Charlotte (Mrs. Lewis L. Snider) (U.S. Navy), Warren Thomas (U.S. Army). Commd. 2nd lt. Corps of Engrs., 1902, and advanced through the grades to brig. gen., 1942; served in Philippines, 1902-04, Ft. Leavenworth, 1904-05, Washington Barracks, 1905-06, Cuba, 1906-08; U.S. Engr. Office, Washington, 1908-12; Hawaiian Islands, 1912-15; Mexican Border, 1916-17; organized 6th Engrs., Washington Barracks, 1917; 308th Engrs., Camp Sherman, O., 1917; France, 1918, G-5 Sect., Gen. Staff at Gen. Hdqrs. and on Eastern Front; asst. comdt. Engr. Sch., Ft. Belvoir, Va., 1919; instr. Command and Gen. Staff sch., Ft. Leavenworth, Kan., 1920-22; War Dept. Gen. Staff, 1922-25; comdt. 2d Regt. Engrs., Ft. Sam Houston, Tex., 1926, Ft. Logan, Colo., 1927-29; dist. engr., Baltimore, 1929-31; div. engr., Gulf Mexico Div. 1931-35; asst. to Chief of Engrs., Mil. Div., 1935-38; div. engr., S. Pacific Div., 1938-42, Pacific Div., 1942-44; retired June 1942. active duty to Jan. 1944. Dir. Dept. Natural Resources, State of Calif. from Feb. 1944. Awarded D.S.M.; Legion of Merit; Ordre de L'Etoile Noire (France). Mem. Am. Soc. Mil. Engrs. Clubs: Army-Navy, Army and Navy Country (Washington, D.C.), Engrs. (San Francisco). Home: San Francisco Cal.†

HANSEN, ALVIN HARVEY, educator; b. Viborg, S.D., Aug. 23, 1887; s. Niels and Bergita Mary (Nielsen) H.; B.A., Yankton (S.D.) Coll., 1910, LL.D., 1936; M.A., U. Wis., 1915, Ph.D., 1918; m. Mabel Lewis, Aug. 25, 1916; children—Marian Grace, Mildred Jean. Prin. high sch., Lake Preston, S.D., 1910-12, supt., 1912-13; asst. instr. econs. U. Wis., 1915-16, Brown U., 1916-19; asso. prof. econs. U. Minn., 1919-23, prof., 1923-37; Lucius N. Littauer prof. polit. economy Harvard, 1937, emeritus, 1958-75; vis. prof. U. Bombay (India), 1957-58; William Allan Nielson research Smith Coll., 1960; dir. research, sec. Commn. of Inquiry on Nat. Policy in Internat. Econ. Relations, 1933-34; economist Dept. State, 1934-35; econ. adviser Prairie Provinces before Canadian Royal Commn. in Dominiton-Provincial Relations, 1937-38. Mem. Adv. Council on Social Security, 1937-38; chmn. econ. adv. council Nat. Indsl. Conf. Bd., 1938-39; chmn. U.S.-Can. joint Econ. Coms., 1941-43; spl. econ. adviser Fed. Res. Bd., 1940-45. Guggenheim fellow, 1928-29; recipient Francis A. Walker medal Am. Econ. Assn., 1967; Gold Medal King of Sweden, 1964. Mem. Am. Econ. Assn. (pres. 1938), Am. Statis. Assn. (v.p. 1937), Royal Econ. Soc., Econometric Soc., Social Sci. Research Council. Author numerous books including: Economic Policy and Full Employment, 1947; (with Paul Samuelson) Economic Analysis of Guaranteed Wages, 1947; Monetary Theory and Fiscal Policy, 1948; Business Cycle and National Income, 1951; A Guide to Keynes, 1953; The American Economy, 1957; Economic Issues of the 1960's, 1960; The Dollar and the International Monetary System, 1965. Asso. editor Econometrics, 1933-38; bd. editors Quar. Jour. Econs., 1937-48, Review Econ. Statistics, 1938-75, Inter-Am. Econ. Affairs, 1947; Kylos, 1947-75. Home: Belmont, Mass. Died June 6, 1975.

HANSEN, CARL LUDWIG, JR., physician; b. Springfield, Mass., Jan. 23, 1920; s. Carl L. and Hazel (Wood) H.; B.A., Am. Internat. Coll., 1943; M.D., Tufts U., 1946; Ph.D., U. Rochester, 1960; m. Ruth Louise Baker, Mar. 2, 1946; children—Karen L., Leslie R., Carl L. III, Robert T. Intern, Springfield (Mass.) Hosp., 1946-47; resident Fitzsimons Army Hosp., Denver, Letterman Army Hosp., San Francisco, 1949-50; cons. extramural activities Nat. Cancer Inst., Bethesda, Md., 1965-66, program dir., 1966-68, dep. asso. dir. extramural activities, 1967-68; asso. dean Jefferson Med. Coll., Phila., also prof. radiation therapy and nuclear medicine, 1969-72. Cons., Gen. Atomic, Pacific N.W. Research Found. Trustee Am., Internat. Coll. Served to col., M.C., USAF, 1947-65. Decorated Air medal. Mem. Royal Soc. Medicine (U.K.), Am. Physiol. Soc., Radiation Research Soc., A.M.A., Sigma Xi. Presbyn. (elder). Home: Bethesda Md. Died Aug. 10, 1973; buried Arlington Nat. Cemetery, Arlington, Va.

HANSEN, JOHN ROBERT, retired state ofcl.; b. Manning, Ia., Aug. 24, 1901; s. Herman P. and Laura (Karstens) H.; student State U. Ia.; m. Mary Louise Osthoff, June 21, 1929 (dec. 1967); children—Robert, Jack; m. 2d, Dorothy Meyer, May 19, 1969. Majority owner, operator Dultmeier Mfg. Co., Manning, 1932-62; gen. mgr. Dultmeier Sales Co., Omaha, 1934-57, prin. owner, 1934-64; Western Ia. area mgr., savs. bond div. Treasury Dept., 1962-64; mem. 89th Congress, 7th Dist. Ia.; commr. Ia. Hwy. Commn., 1967-69. Mem. Ia. Bd. Control State Instns., 1957-60; mem. exec. council Gov. Ia. Commn. Alcoholism, 1958-60; mem. Ia. Commn. Interstate Coop., 1958, Ia. div. Nat. Council on Crime and Delinquency. Mem. S.W. Ia. council Boy Scouts Am., 1944-50; mem. Carroll County com. A.R.C., 1942-48, Ia. Mental Health Assn., 1958-62. Mem. Carroll County Democratic Central Com., 1932-52, chmn., 1944-52; chmn. 6th Dist. Ia., Dem. Party, also mem. Ia. Central Dem. Com., 1952-57; alternate del. Dem. Nat. Conv., 1944, 64, del., 1948, 68; Dem. nominee lt. gov. Ia., 1960. Mem. bd., past pres. Manning Gen. Hosp.; trustee Osteopathic Coll. Medicine and Surgery, Des Moines. Mem. Nat. Farm Equipment Mfrs. Assn., Former Members of Congress, Izaak Walton League. Presbyn. (elder). Rotarian (past pres. Manning). Mason (Shriner), Lion (past pres. Manning); mem. Order Eastern Star. Address: Winterset, Ia. Died Sept. 23, 1974.

HANSON, LORING OUTBIER, educator, engr.; b. Hamilton, Ill., Oct. 5, 1906; s. E. L. and Elsie A. (Outhier) H.;B.S. in Civil Engring., U. Kan., 1928; M.S., U. Wis., 1932; m. Lois Laptad, Sept. 3, 1930; children—David F., Susan E. Misc. teaching engring. postitions, 1928-42; asso. prof. applied mechanics U. Kan., 1946-55; prof., head dept. mechanics and materials, asst. dean sch. Wichita State U., 1955-71; part-time structural engr. Boeing Airplane Co. from 1952. Asso. civilian engr., then engr., U.S. Army Corps Engrs., 1942-44; served as lt., ordnance, USNR, 1944-46. Mem. Am. Soc. C.E., Am. Soc. Engring. Edn., Am. Assn. U. Profs., Nat. Soc. Profl. Engrs., Kansas Engring. Soc., Sigma Xi, Tau Beta Pi, Theta Tau. Mason. Home: Wichita, Kan., Died Jan. 7, 1975; interred Municipal Cemetery, Eudora, Kan.

HANSON, PAUL M., clergyman; b. Council Bluffs, Ia., Jan. 8, 1878; s. Frederick and Christina (Christensen) H.; m. Sadie Leeks, June 7, 1911. Pres. Council of Twelve Apostles; reorganizer Ch. of Jesus Christ of Latter day Saints. Author: Jesus Christ Among the Ancient Americans; In the Land of the Feathered Serpent.†

HARBER, WINFORD ELMER, banker; b. Pineville, Ark., July 3, 1892; s. Thomas W. and Cynthia (Franks) H.; ed. pub. schs., Seminole, Okla.; m. Maude Stroud, Feb. 1, 1936 (dec. Feb. 1957); m. 2d, Lisbeth Patton, Oct. 1965. With First Nat. Bank, Seminole, 1911, pres., 1921-70, chmn. bd., 1970-74; pres. Am. Nat. Bank & Trust Co., 1935-70, chmn. bd., 1970; dir., chmn. bd. R.F.C., Washington, 1950; dir. Liberty Nat. Bank, Oklahoma City. Bd. regents Okla. A. and M. Coll., 1945-64; mem. sch. bd., Shawnee, Okla., 1944. Served with U.S. Army, World War I. Mem. Shawnee C. of C. (bd. dirs.), Okla. C. of C. Democrat (nat. committeeman from Okla. 1948). Presbyn. Mason. Clubs: Oklahoma (Oklahoma City); Country (Shawnee). Home: Shawnee, Okla. Died Dec. 28, 1974; buried Fairview Cemetery, Shawnee, Okla.

HARBOTTLE, JOHN, author; b. Abilene, Kan., May 23, 1880; s. John and Emma (Buckingham) H.; Ped.B., Colo. State Teachers Coll., Greeley, Colo., 1902, Pd.M., 1912, A.B., 1913; m. Florence Rockwell, May 24, 1905. Teacher. Republican. Conglist. Author: The Luck of Laramie Ranch, 1913; Finding His Stride, 1915. Contbr. short stories to mags. Home: Greeley, Colo.†

HARDEN, KOMURIA ALBERT, physician, former coll. dean; b. Bessemer, Ala., Aug. 20, 1905; s. Albert and Lilly (Taylor) M.; student Wayne State U., 1923-26; B.A., U. Mich., 1927, M.D., 1931; m. Julia Woodhouse, Dec. 27, 1934; 1 dau., Katharine Judith. Intern, Freedmen's Hosp., Washington, 1931-32, chief div. chronic pulmonary diseases, 1958-65; practice medicine, specializing in internal medicine, Detroit, 1933-34, Catonsville, Md., 1935-40; asso. physician Henryton (Md.) Sanatorium, 1939-40; instr. medicine Coll. Medicine, Howard U., 1941, asst. prof. medicine, 1945-47, asso. prof., 1947-58, prof., 1958-74, vice dean Coll. Medicine, 1960-65, acting dean, 1965-66, dean, 1966-70; research fellow chest service Bellevue Hosp. Columbia div., N.Y.C., 1944-45. Diplomate Am. Bd. Internal Medicine. Fellow A.C.P., Am. Acad. Tb Physicians, Am. Pub. Health Assn.; mem. A.M.A., Nat. Med. Assn., A.A.A.S., Am., D.C. (past pres.) thoracic socs., D.C. Lung Assn. (past pres., dir.), Medico-Chirurgical Soc. D.C., Am. Cancer Soc. (trustee), Am. Heart Assn., Sigma Xi, Alpha Omega Alpha. Contbr. profl. jours. Home: Washington, D.C. Died Dec. 24, 1974; interred at Baltimore, Md.

HARDER, HOWARD CHARLES, food products mfg. co. exec.; b. Mart, Tex. May 15, 1916; s. Henry Charles and Eula Wilkinson (Leonidas) H.; student U. Tex., 1933-36; grad. Advanced Mgmt. Program, Harvard, 1947; m. Linda Bauer, Dec. 2, 1972; children—Nancy Johns, Beverly Ann. With Corn Products Refining Co. (name changed to Corn Products Co. 1958), N.Y.C., 1937-72, successively accountant, asst. treas., asst. comptroller, exec. asst. to exec. v.p., 1937-57, treas., 1957-58, comptroller, 1958-59, v.p. finance, 1959-61, sr. v.p., 1961-64, exec. v.p. adminstrn., 1964-65, pres., 1965-68, pres., chief exec. officer, 1968-69, co. name changed to CPC Internat. Inc., 1969, chmn. bd., chief exec. officer, 1969-72, also dir.; dir. Carrier Corp., Peoples Trust N.J., Otis Elevator Co., Lord & Taylor, Asso. Dry Goods Corp., Chem. Bank, United Jersey Banks, Western Electric. Trustee Tex. Christian U., Nat. 4-H Club Found. Served to capt. Ordn. Dept., AUS, 1942-46. Mem. Kappa Alpha. Mason (32 deg.). Club: Metropolitan (N.Y.C.). Home: Franklin Lakes, N.J. Died Dec. 2, 1974.

HARDESTY, MARSHALL GLADE, elec. co. exec.; b. nr. Norris úCity, Ill., Sept. 24, 1910; s. Jesse Cleveland and Cora Vale (Johnson) H.; student Northwestern U., 1929; m. Anna Margaret Stansell, June 26, 1941; children—Marshall Glade, Jr., Carol, Margaret Ann. Accountant, Commonwealth Edison Co. and Sales, Chgo., 1928-45; supr. Frazer & Torbet, C.P.A.'s, Chgo., 1945-48; with Ia. Electric Light & Power Co., Cedar Rapids, 1948, v.p. finance, 1968-72. Pres. bd. dirs. St. Lukes Meth. Hosp., Cedar Rapids, 1971-72; pres. United Community Services, Cedar Rapids, 1963-64, June Boyd Community House, Cedar Rapids, 1950-62. C.P.A., Ill. Mem. Am. Inst. C.P.A.'s, Nat. Assn. Accountants (pres. 1960), Financial Execs. Inst. (chpt. pres. 1962), Cedar Rapids C. of C. (pres. 1971). Elk, Rotarian (pres. 1961). Clubs: Mid Am. (Chgo.); Pickwick (Cedar Rapids). Home: Cedar Rapids, Ia. Died Apr. 30, 1972; buried Cedar Rapids, Ia.

HARDIE, JAMES FINLEY, clergyman; b. Selma, Ala., Jan. 29, 1880; s. Thomas Chalmers and Hannah Jane (Welch) H.; A.B., Austin Coll., Sherman, Tex., 1908, D.D., 1921; A.M., U. of Tex., 1911; B.D., Austin (Tex.) Theol. Sem., 1911; m. Martha Dickson Roe, August 14, 1913 (died April 18, 1943); children—Maybelle, James Finley; married 2d, Louisa Stuart Roe, January 15, 1946. Ordained into the ministry of the Presbytn. Ch. in United States, 1911; pastor Clifton, Tex., 1911-16, Taylor, 1916-20, 2d Ch., Houston, 1920-29, 2d Ch., Charlotte, N.C., 1929-36, Broadway Church, Fort Worth, Texas, 1936-49, First Presbyn. Ch., San Saba, Tex., from 1949. Vice chmn. Home Mission Council, General Assembly Presbyterian Church in U.S.; chmn. Home Mission Com., Synod of Texas; member home mission com., Mecklenburg Presbytery; charter mem. Assembly's work com., Presbyn. Ch. in U.S.; mem. Synod's Work Com. of N.C.; chmn. Home Mission Com. Ft. Worth Presbytery; mem. Permanent Committee on Co-operation and Union, Gen. Assembly. Trustee Austin Coll., Union Theol. Sem., Richmond, Va. Mason (32°, Shriner). Clubs: Good Fellows, River Crest Country. Home: San Saba, Tex.†

HARDIE, WILLIAM VINCENT, r.r. official; b. Hudson, N.Y., July 20, 1881; s. George and Ella Cornelia (Colton) H.; student U. of Tex., 1898-1900; m. Mayme E. Phillips, Dec. 23, 1914 (died June 23, 1927); m. 2d, Estelle Charlotte Berger, Mar. 6, 1929; 1 son, William Richardson. Tariff clerk, Santa Fe, 1900-03, traffic mgr. Okla. Traffic Assn. and Oklahoma City Chamber of Commerce, 1907-18; traffic asst., Dir. of Pub. Service, U.S. R.R. Adminstrn., 1919-20; asst. gen. freight agt. Mo.-Kan.-Tex. Ry., 1920; dir. bureau of traffic, Interstate Commerce Commn., 1920-45; traffic cons., St.L. S.F. Ry. Mason (32°, Shriner). Home: Springfield, MO.†

HARDING, EDWIN TYLER, meteorologist; b. Newman, Cal., Jan. 17, 1911; s. Winfield Tyler and Freda Elizabeth (Walden) H.; A.B., U. Cal. at Berkeley, 1932; postgrad. U.S. Naval Postgrad. Sch., 1942-43; m. Alice Isabella Currie, June 17, 1934; children—Margaret Katherine (Mrs. William Marcy Gratiot), Alice Walden (Mrs. David Ray Hammel). Tchr., prin. Cal. schs., 1933-41; commd. ensign USN, 1932, advanced through grades to capt., 1957; staff meteorologist 2d Fleet, Fleet Air Wing 17, Naval Air Tng. Unit Lakehurst, 1952-53; comdg. officer Fleet Weather Centrals, Miami, Guam, Norfolk, Port Lyautey Manus, 1944-59; comdr. Naval Weather Service Command, Washington, 1965-70; tech. editor Meteorology Internat., Monterey, Cal., 1970-73. Author: (with Capt. Kotsch) Heavy Weather Guide, 1965. Contbr. articles to profl. jours. Home: Monterey, Cal. Died Dec. 25, 1973.

HARDING, JOHN FRANCIS, lawyer, pub. co. exec.; b. Pittsfield, Mass., Apr. 25, 1908; s. Clark J. and Clara (Decker) H.; A.B. magna cum laude, Harvard, 1930; LL.B., 1934; m. Anita M. Hutchinson, Sept. 2, 1934; 1 dau., Deborah Ann. Admitted to Mass. bar, 1934, N.Y. bar, 1935, also U.S. Supreme Ct.; asso. atty. firm Cravath de Gersdorff, Swaine & Wood, 1934-44; gen. counsel, dir. Cowles Communications, Inc., broadcasting and publishing, 1944-74, sec., 1947-74, v.p., 1953-65, exec. v.p., 1965-74; v.p., sec. Cowles Fla. Broadcasting, Inc., Travelventures, Inc.; v.p., sec., dir. Cowles Tenn. Radio Properties, Inc.; counsel Macleay, Lynch, Berhard & Gregg, Washington, 1974-75. Mem. Am., Fed. (N.Y., N.J., Conn.) bar assns., Assn. Bar City N.Y., Phi Beta Kappa, Delta Sigma Rho. Clubs: Harvard, University (N.Y.C.). Home: New Fairfield, Conn. Died June 21, 1975.

HARDISON, ALLEN CROSBY, engr., agriculturist; b. Caribou, Me., Apr. 22, 1869; s. Jacob and Elizabeth Adeline(Smiley) H.; B.C.E., Me. State Coll. (now University of Maine), 1890, Civil Engr., 1894, LL.D., 1930; married to Cora L. Crane, December 13, 1892; children—Helen (dec.), Warren E., Ernest D., Ruth (dec.), Louise (Mrs. Lafe T. Browne), Robert A., Coralynn (Mrs. E. Perry Churchill), Wallace L., Janette (Mrs. Blaine Romney). In pvt. engring. practice at Santa Paula, Calif., 1890-96; sec. Paula Water Works, 1893-96; asst. engr. and asst. mgr. Inca Mining Co., Santo Domingo, Peru, 1896-1901; mgr. Gladiator Mine, Ariz., 1901-02; in pvt. engring. practice, 1902-04; in oil business, Kan. and Indian Ty., 1904-07; v.p. Santa Paula Water Works and Thermal Belt Mutual Water Co. from 1907; exec. v.p. Hardison Ranch Co., 1912-47, pres., mgr., from 1947; pres. San Cayetano Mut. Water Co., 1913-57; president Santa Paula Citrus Fruit Assn., 1951-58, Limoneira Co., from 1950; v.p. Farmers Irrigation Co.; pres. Santa Paula Savs. & Loan Assn., from 1951; v.p. Exchange Lemon Products Co., 1936-58, President of California Farm Bureau Federal, 1922-24; mem. California State Commission on Agrl. Edn., 1923-24; mem. exec. com. Am. Farm Bur. Fed., 1924-26; pres. Calif. Taxpayer's Assn. 1926-54; vice-chmn. Calif. State Bd. Agr.,1929-39; mem. U.S. Chamber of

Commerce (dir. 1934-41; chmn. Agrl. com. 1935-36). Mem. Am. Soc. Agrl. Engrs., Am. Inst. Mining and Metall Engrs., Am. Soc. C.E. Republican. Universalist. Mason. Clubs: University (Los Angeles); Commonwealth. Home: Santa Paula, Cal.†

HARDT, WALTER KELLER, pres. Integrity Trust Co.; b. Frederick, Md., Oct. 24, 1881; s. William McCulley and Mary Ida (Keller) H.; B.S., U. of Pa., 1905; m. Elizabeth Anne Williams, Pa., June 26, 1907; children—Elizabeth Mary, Richard Walter. Began as a certified pub. accountant, 1905; assistant cashier Fourth St. National Bank, 1909-12, v.p. 1912-26; v.p. Franklin Fourth St. Nat. Bank, 1926-28; became v.p. Phila. Nat. Bank, 1928; became pres. Integrity Trust Co., 1928; dir. Commonwealth Title Ins. Co., local dir. Am. Surety Co. Dir. Presbyn. Ministers Fund for Life Ins. Mem. Phi Delta Theta. Republican. Presbyn. Clubs: Midday, Down Town, University, Union League, Harris, Penn Athletic, Bank Officers of Phila. (Phila.); Merion Cricket (Haverford, Pa.). Home: Haverford, Pa.†

HARDWICK, KATHARINE DAVIS, teacher, social worker; b. Quincy, Mass., Jan. 8, 1886; d. Charles Franklin and Annie Williams (Clapp) Hardwick; A.B., Boston U., 1907. In social service exchange, Boston Family Welfare Soc., 1907-08, case worker, 1908, district secretary, 1909-17; field worker Intercollegiate Community Service, 1917-18; field worker Am. Red Cross, New Eng. Div., 1918-19, supervisor of field workers, 1919-25, dir. of institutes, 1920-22, div. exec. sec., 1922-25; lecturer Simmons Coll. Sch. of Social Work, Boston, 1919-25, asst. dir., 1925-29, dir. since 1929; consultant Boston Pub. Welfare Assn., 1934; social service dir. and asst. adminstr. in charge social services, Emergency Relief Adminstrn. (Mass.), 1934-35. Mem. Am. Assn. Social Workers, Phi Beta Kappa, Gamma Phi Beta. Republican. Unitarian. Club: College of Boston. Home: Boston, Mass. Died July 24, 1974.

HARDY, ALEXANDER GEORGE, bus. exec., lawyer; b. Medford, Mass., Mar. 22, 1920; s. William and Grace A. (Mellen) H.; student bus. adminstrn., Boston U., 1945-46; LL.B., Suffolk U., 1941; m. Elisabeth M. Stewart, Aug. 5, 1947; children—Michael Stewart, Alexander George, Robin. Admitted to Mass. bar, 1942, D.C. bar, 1955, Fed. bar, 1945, FCC bar, 1954; atty. Evarts & Gallagher, Boston, 1945-46; exec. counsel Nuremberg War Crime Trials, 1946-49; pub. counsel CAB, 1949-51; br. counsel OPS, 1951; exec. asst. to pres. Nat. Airlines, Washington, 1951-53, asst. v.p., 1953-54, v.p., 1954-55, sr. v.p., 1955-60, sr. v.p., corporate sec., Miami Fla., 1960-63; asst. to chmn. bd. Automatic Canteen Co. Am., 1963, exec. v.p., 1963-65; dir. AVEMCO Corp., 1960-74, pres., chmn. bd., 1965-74; dir. Union Trust Co. Md. Mem. Nat. Def. Exec. Res. Served with Office Naval Intelligence, USNR, 1942-45; CBI. Recipient Horatio Alger award, 1971. Mem. Bar Assn. D.C., Air Force Assn. Clubs: Nat. Aviation (gov. 1958-60, pres. 1967-68), Congressional Country (Washington); Palm Bay (Miami, Fla.). Author: Hitler's Secret Weapon, 1968. Home: Potomac, Md. Died Dec. 14, 1973; interred Parklawn Cemetery, Rockville, Md.

HARDY, CHARLES J., JR., ret. bus. exec.; b. New York, N.Y., May 23, 1895; s. Charles J. and Virginia T. (Taylor) H.; student N.Y. Military Acad., 1910-13; A.B., Williams Coll., 1917; student Columbia Law Sch., 1917; LL.B., Fordham U. Law School, 1919; m. Helen E. Hardy, October 27, 1922 (divorced); 1 dau., Ruth (Mrs. Charles G. Miller, Jr.); m. 2d, Mattie-King Shropshire, September 24, 1948. Admitted to N.Y. bar, 1922; mem. law firm of Hardy, Peal, Rawlings, Werner & Maxwell; executive vice president of the American Car & Foundry Co. (now ACF Industries, Inc.), 1946-47, became pres., 1947, later chmn. bd., chmn. exec. com. and dir., ret. 1957; now counsel to law firm Hardy, Peal, Rawlings, Werner & Maxwell; director Fasteners, Inc., Phillips Screw Co., Pollard-Alling Co. Served as ensign USN, World War I, lt. comdr., World War II. Mem. Phi Delta Theta, Phi Delta Phi. Clubs: Army and Navy (Washington); University, Traffic, River Devon Yacht, Maidstone. Home: New York City, N.Y. Died Aug. 6, 1973.

HARDY, DAVID KEITH, educator, motion picture dir.; b. Belfast, No. Ireland, June 27, 1924; s. Brian Courtnay and Ella Rachel (Prince) H.; student Sedbergh (Eng.) Sch., 1936-40; B.A., Trinity Coll., Dublin, Ireland, 1945; m. Joan Hare, 1947 (div.); children—Sarah Charlotte, Alistair David; m. 2d, Gladys Kwa-Fong Chang, Jan. 11, 1958; children—Brian, Kathryn Lee. Dir., Radio Hongkong, also Far East corr. BBC, 1945-50; with UN Radio, N.Y.C., 1950-53; N.Am. corr. London Times, N.Y.C., 1953; asst. pub. Life Mag., N.Y.C., 1954-58; producer-dir. TV documentaries ABC's Close Up series, ABC, Brinkley Jour., NBC, 1959-64; producer-dir. films BBC, Nat. Ednl. TV. Columbia Broadcasting Co. Intertel; dir. Morse Center for Study of Communications, prof. theatre arts Brandeis U., Waltham, Mass., 1967-70; pres. Univ. Film Study Center, Cambridge, Mass., 1969-70; lectr. Stamford U., 1966. Served to capt. Brit. Royal Marine Commandos, 1942-45; CBI. Recipient awards for films including, India—Writings in the Sand, Overseas Press Club award, 1965; Cambodia—The Peaceful Paradox, Prix de Rome, 1962; Rip-Roaring Day at Ripple Rock, N.A.V.P.A., 1958; The Unique Advantage, M.P.A., 1963. Mem. Overseas Press Club, Arts Theatre Club. Hongkong Corr.'s Club. Home: Newton, Mass. Died May 30, 1970.

HARDY, H(ARRISON) CLAUDE, educator; b. Glenwood, Pa., Feb. 27, 1887; s. David Nelson and Hannah E. (Potter) H.; A.B., Wesleyan U., Middletown, Conn., 1911; A.M. in Psychology and Edn., U. of Rochester, 1921; A.M. in Edn., Syracuse U., 1923; Ph.D., New York U., 1931; spl. student U. of Grenoble, 1914; m. Lula May Green, June 26, 1912 (died Oct. 25, 1918); m. 2d, Shirley Frances Newton, Nov. 19, 1919; 1 adopted son, Carroll E. Instr. modern langs., Rock Ridge Sch., Wellesley Hills, Mass., 1911-12; head modern lang. dept., Wilbraham (Mass.) Acad., 1912-16; prin., Schenevus (N.Y.) High Sch., 1916-18; supt.-prin., pub. schs. of Sidney, N.Y., 1918-20; supt. pub. schs., Fairport, N.Y., 1920-25; supt. city schs., Oneida, N.Y., 1925-27; asso. supt. schs., White Plains, N.Y., 1927-34, supt. 1934-47; mem. faculty N.Y.U., lecturer on edn.; dir. pub. relations Hartwick Coll., Oneonta, 1949-73, cons., 1956-73, asst. to pres., 1956-73, head dept. sociology, 1956-73, also prof. emeritus, curator of Yager Museum. City historian, Oneonta, New York, 1967-73. Ordained Methodist minister. Honorary member of bd. govs. White Plains Hosp.; mem. bd. trustees White Plains Pub. Library; sec. White Plains Collegiate Center, in charge univ. extension; chmn. advisory bd. White Plains branch Salvation Army; vice-pres. World Edn. Service Council; asso. exec. dir. and v.p. Save the Children Fedn., Inc., 1947, exec. v.p., 1947-49. Awarded King's Medal (Brit.), 1946; Medallion award for meritorious service, N.Y.U., 1933. Mem. bd. trustees Wesleyan U. (Conn.), also mem. Alumni Council and Alumni Assn. Fellow Inst. Am. Genealogy of Chgo.; mem. Westchester Co. Conservation Assn., White Plains Y.M.C.A. (bd. dirs.), Chamber of Commerce, N.Y. State Teachers Assn. (pres. 1942-44); life mem. N.E.A. (vice pres.; mem. dept. superintendence; mem. bd. dirs. representing N.Y. State); mem. N.Y. Schoolmasters Club (president 1946), Upper Susquehanna Hist. Soc. (president 1961), Beta Theta Pi, Phi Delta Kappa, Pi Gamma Mu. President Hardy Family Association Am., 1937-65, pres. emeritus, 1965-73 (meritorious award 1966). Methodist. Mason (32deg.), Rotarian (pres. White Plains, 1934-35), Vice president University Club (White Plains, N.Y.). Co-author and compiler: Hardy and Hardie: Past and Present, 1935. Author: His Honor, The Mayor (story of the Life of Frank Zuber). Contbr. articles to Am. Edn. Digest, N.Y. State Edn., Am. Sch. Bd. Jour., School and Society. Home: Oneonta, N.Y. Died June 7, 1973.

HARE, T(HOMAS) TRUXTUN, lawyer, author; b. Phila., Oct. 12, 1878; s. Horace Binney and Emily Power (Beale) H.; B.S., U. of Pa., 1901; m. Katherine Sargent Smith, Dec. 6, 1906; children—Thomas Truxtun, Katharine Sargent, Martha Harford, Robert Hare. In law practice at Phila., from 1905; asst. solicitor, United Gas Improvement Co., Phila. Republican. Episcopalian. Mem. Authors' League America, Delta Psi. Clubs: Philadelphia, Penn Athletic, Franklin Inn. Author: Making the Freshman Team, 1907; A Sophomore Halfback, 1908; A Junior in the Line, 1909; A Senior Quarterback, 1910; A Graduate Coach, 1911; Phillip Kent, 1914; Philip Kent in the Lower School, 1916; Philip Kent in the Upper School, 1917; Kent of Malvern, 1919. Home: Radnor, Pa.†

HARGETT, IRA MASON, clergyman; b. Mason County, Ky., May 17, 1881; s. John B. and Ida (Meenach) H.; ed. Asbury Coll., Wilmore, Ky., and Taylor U., Upland, Ind.; D.D., Asbury Coll., 1924; m. Willa Bennett, Jan. 7, 1903; children—Mason Victor (M.D.), Mrs. Harford Field, Mrs. F. Homer Hooper, Mrs. J. Edward Hedges. Ordained to Methodist ministry, 1904; pastor several churches including Linwood Boulevard Church, Kansas City Missouri, 1932-36, First Church, Oklahoma City, 1936-39, Fourth Avenue Methodist Church, from 1939. Elected to General Conference, 1928, 32, 36, and to Meth. Uniting Conf., 1939. Elected to Gen. Conf. and to S.E. Jurisdictional Conf., 1948. Militant preacher for civic righteousness; radio preacher; evangelistic pastor; preacher at Bible conferences and preaching missions. Home: Louisville, Ky.†

HARGITT, GEORGE THOMAS, prof. zoölogy; b. Fairfield, Ind., Feb. 13, 1881; s. Charles Wesley and Susan Eliza (Wood) H.; Ph.B., Syracuse U., 1902, hon. D.Sc., 1939; A.M., U. of Neb., 1903; Ph.D., Harvard, 1909; studied at Johns Hopkins University; m. Thelma Holmes; children—Thomas George, Ann Holmes. Teacher high schools, Poughkeepsie and Syracuse, 1903-07; assistant in zoölogy, Harvard, 1907-09; instr. zoölogy, Northwestern Univ., 1910-13; asst. and asso. prof. zoölogy, Syracuse Univ., 1913-19, prof., 1919-30; prof. of zoölogy, Duke Univ., from 1930; prof. zoölogy and spl. research work, Wistar Inst., Phila., 1923-25; visiting prof. zoölogy, Duke Univ., 1929-30. Fellow Am. Assn. Advancement of Science (sec. zoöl. sect., 1924-32, vice pres. zoöl. sect., 1944); mem. Am. Soc. Zoölogists, Am. Soc. Naturalists, Am. Assn. Univ. Profs., Kappa, Sigma Xi. Methodist. Author: numerous papers on biol. and embryol. topics. Home: Durham, N.C.†

HARGRAVE, FRANK FLAVIUS, educator; economist; b. Pike County, Ind., Feb. 14, 1878; s. Flavius Addison and Mary (DeBruler) H.; grad. DePauw U. Acad., 1903; A.B., De Pauw U., 1906; S.T.B., Boston U., 1912; A.M., U. of Wis., 1920; grad. student Columbia, summer 1921; m. Zetta Warren, April 17, 1918 (died Oct. 1918); m. 2d, Hannah Stoney, Aug. 30, 1924 (died Jan. 1930). Instr. economics Purdue U., 1920-23, asst. prof., 1923-27, asso. prof., 1927-32, prof., 1932-48, prof. emeritus from 1948. Mem. Ind. Acad. Soc. Scis., Ind. Hist. Soc., Phi Beta Kappa. Methodist (ret. mem. Northwest Ind. Conf., Meth. Ch.). Author: A Pioneer Indiana Railroad, 1932. Research in early railroad history, early Ind. laws on transportation and travel. Home: Lafayette Ind.†

HARGRAVE, WILLIAM LOFTIN, clergyman; b. Wilson, N.C., Nov. 10, 1903; s. Benjamin Worthington and Frances (Daniel) H.; LL.B., Atlanta Law Sch., 1924; B.D., Va. Theol. Sem., 1932, D.D., 1962; S.T.M., U. of South, 1952, D.D., 1962; m. Minnie Frances Whittington, Feb. 13, 1939; children—Frances, Elizabeth, Sarah, William. Admitted to Ga. bar, 1925; asst. trust officer Miami Bank & Trust Co. (Fla.), 1924-26; asso. firm Shutts & Bowen, Miami, 1926-27; ordained to ministry Episcopalian Ch., 1932; rector in Cocoa, Fla., 1932-43, Ft. Pierce, Fla., 1943-45, Holy Comforter Ch., Miami, 1945-48, Holy Communion Ch., Charleston, S.C., 1948-53; exec. sec. Diocese of South Fla., Winter Park, 1953-61; consecrated bishop Diocese of South Fla., 1961-70; bishop of S.W. Fla., 1970-75; pres. Wuesthoff Hosp., Cocoa, Fla., 1941-43, Porter Mil. Acad., Charleston, 1952. Pres. Fla. Council Chs., 1957-58, Fla. Migrant Ministry, 1963-66; mem. gen. bd. Nat. Council Chs. Christ, from 1964; mem. Lambeth Conf., London, Eng., 1968. Club: St. Petersburg Yacht. Home: Cocoa, Fla., Died Oct. 15, 1975; interred St. Luke's Cemetery, Courtenay, Fla.

HARKINS, THOMAS J., lawyer; b. Buncombe County, N.C., Jan. 15, 1879; s. Herschel S. and Sarah Jane (Jones) H.; student Univ. of N.C., 1897-1901; LL.D. (hon.) Cumberland U., Lebanon, Tenn., 1945; m. Roxy Seevers, Dec. 1904; 1 son, Herschel S. Admitted to Okla. Bar, 1901, and began practice at Weatherford; practiced at Asheville, 1907-59; mem. Harkins, Van Winkle, Walton & Buck. Mem. Rep. Nat. Congl. Com., 1912-14; del. to Rep. Nat. Conv., 1916; spl. asst. U.S. atty., 1922-26; U.S. atty. Western N.C. Dist., 1927-31; became spl. asst. to atty. gen. of U.S., June 1931; mem White House Conference on Education, 1955. Permanent mem. 4th U.S. Circuit Ct. Jud. Conf. Capt. N.C. Res. Inf., 1917-18. Mem. Am., N.C., Buncombe County (ex-pres) bar assns., Am. Acad. of Polit. and Social Science. Methodist. Mason (33°, sovereign grand comdr. Supreme Council, So. Jurisdiction 1952, resigned 1955; K.T., Shriner; Grand Master of Masons in N.C., 1940-41; hon. mem. Supreme Council of No. Jurisdiction, Can., Germany, France, Eng., Scotland, Greece, Italy, Venezuela, Cuba, Argentine, Mexico (P.I.); U.S.A. Club: Biltmore Forest Country. Home: Asheville, N.C.†

HARKNESS, GEORGIA ELMA, author; b. Harkness, N.Y.; d. J. Warren and Lillie (Merrill) Harkness; A.B., Cornell U., 1912; M.A. (univ. fellow), Boston U., 1920, M.R.E., 1920, Ph.D., 1923, hon. Litt.D., 1938; student Harvard, 1926, Yale (Sterling fellow), 1928-29, Union Theol. Sem., 1936-37; Litt.D., MacMurray Coll., 1943, Elmira (N.Y.) Coll. 1962; D.D., Wilson Coll., 1943, Pacific Sch. Religion, 1961; LL.D., Mills Coll., Oakland, Cal., 1958. Tchr. Latin high sch., Schuylerville, N.Y., 1912-14, Scotia, N.Y., 1915-18; instr. English Bible, Boston U. Sch. Religious Edn., 1919-20; asst. prof. religious edn. Elmira (N.Y.) Coll., 1922, asso. prof. philosophy, 1923, prof. philosophy, 1926-37; ordained to ministry Meth. Ch., 1926; asso. prof. religion Mt. Holyoke Coll., 1937-39; prof. applied theology Garrett Theol. Sem., 1939-50, Pacific Sch. Religion at Berkeley 1950-61; prof. Christianity, Japan Internat. Christian U., 1956-57. Del. Oxford Conf. on Life and Work, 1937, Madras Conf. Internat. Missionary Council, 1938, Amsterdam Conf. of World Council Chs., 1948, Lund, 1952, Evanston, 1954. Recipient Scroll of Honor award Gen. Fedn. Women's Clubs for pioneer work in religion, 1941; $7,500 prize as co-winner Abingdon-Cokesbury award for book ms., 1947. Mem. Am. Philos. Assn., Am. Acad. Religion, Phi Beta Kappa. Author 37 books including The Dark Night of the Soul, 1945, rev. edit., 1968; Understanding the Christian Faith, 1947; Prayer and the Common Life, 1948; The Gospel and Our World, 1949; Through Christ Our Lord, 1950; The Modern Rival of Christian Faith, 1952; Toward Understanding the Bible, 1952; Be Still and Know, 1953; The Sources of Western Morality, 1954; Foundations of Christian Knowledge, 1955; Christian Ethics, 1957; The Bible Speaks to Daily Needs, 1959; The Providence of God, 1960; Beliefs That Count, 1961; The Church and Its Laity, 1962; Our Christian Hope, 1964; What Christians Believe, 1965; The Fellowship of the Holy Spirit, 1966; Disciplines of the Christian Life, 1967; A Devotional Treasury from the Early Church, 1968; Stability Amid Change, 1969; Grace Abounding, 1969; The Ministry of Reconciliation, 1971; Women in Church and Society, 1972; Mysticism: Its Meaning and Message, 1973; Understanding the Kingdom of God, 1974; Biblical

Backgrounds to the Middle East Conflict, 1976. Home: Claremont, Cal. Died Aug. 21, 1974; buried, Harkness, N.Y.

HARLAND, LEWIS E., corp. exec.; b. Chgo., Jan. 8, 1905; s. George E. and Carrie D. (Dana) H.; B.S., U. Ill., 1926; m. Isabell C. Ioas, May 14, 1927. Bond salesman for Harris Trust & Savs. Bank, Chgo., 1926-27; salesman, mgr. tabulating dept. Remington Rand Co., 1927-32; office mgr. B.N. Anderson & Co., ins. agy., 1932-43; with Wm. Wrigley Jr. Co., 1943-74, exec. v.p., until 1971, dir.; dir. Santa Catalina Island Co., Avalon, Cal. Home: Western Springs, Ill. Died Nov. 12, 1974.

HARMON, DARRELL VICTOR, city planner; b. Los Angeles, Oct. 4, 1922; s. Joe V. and Elsie (Campbell) H.; student U. Cal. at Davis, 1946-49; B.S. in Horticulture, U. Cal. at Los Angeles, 1950; B.S. in Landscape Architecture, U. Cal. at Berkeley, 1955; postgrad. U. So. Cal., 1959-71; m. Mildred S. Trudel, June 18, 1955; children—Cecelia Marie, William Hayes. Designer Porter-Urquhardt, Skidmore, Owings & Merrill, Casablanca, French Morocco, 1952-54; landscape architect Los Angeles County, engr., 1955-56; project engr. Ralph M. Parsons Co., Los Angeles, 1956-59; pvt. practice cons. landscape architect, La Mirada, Cal., 1959-61; asst. planning dir. City Buena Park, Cal., 1961-64; planning dir. City Placentia, Cal., 1964-69; asst. planning dir. Tulare County, Cal., 1969-71. Vol. host Los Angeles Center for Internat. Visitors, 1964-71; active Cub Scouts. Served with USAAF, 1942-45; CBI. Decorated Bronze Star medal; recipient award of merit Buena Park C. of C., 1964; commendation Fullerton Dist. Bd. Realtors, 1966. Mem. Am. Inst. Planners, Am. Soc. Engrs. and Architects, Phi Alpha Iota. Home: Visalia, Cal. Died Apr. 25, 1971; buried Visalia Cemetery, Visalia, Cal.

HARMON, JOHN MILLARD, health and phys. edn.; b. Louisville, Ill., May 20, 1895; s. William Albert and Sarah Catherine (McKnight) H.; A.B., Baker U., Baldwin, Kans., 1921; M.S., Indiana U., 1931; Ed.D., 1932; student U. of Ill., summer 1921, U. of Notre Dame, summer 1925; m. Hazel Marie Sweet, 1928; children—John Millard, Mary Adel, Thomas Cameron. Dir. of phys. edn. and coach, Central Wesleyan Coll., Warrenton, Mo., 1921-23; dir. health and phys. edn., Evansville (Ind.) Coll., 1923-30; part-time instr. and grad. fellow, Indiana U., 1930-32; dir. phys. edn. and athletics, also chmn. phys. edn. div. Sch. of Edn., Boston University, since 1932. Served with U.S. Army during World War I; with A.E.F., 10 mos. Mem. bd. dirs. Eastern Intercollegiate Football Assn. (chmn. nominating com.); mem. bd. mgrs. New England Assn. Amateur Athletic Union; vice pres. Nat. Collegiate Athletic Assn. (mem. hockey rules com.); pres. Assn. New England Colls. for Conf. on Athletics. Mem. Am. Assn. Univ. Profs., Am. Assn. for Health, Phys. Edn. and Recreation (v.p. recreation Eastern Dist. Soc.), Coll. Phys. Edn. Assn., Phi Delta Kappa. Democrat. Methodist. Mason. Club: University (v.p.) (Boston). Home: Rockport Mass. Died Oct. 18, 1974.

HARPER, HERBERT E., corp. exec.; b. 1901; grad. Drexel Inst. Tech.; married. With Pub. Service Coordinated Transp., 1922-71, pres., chief exec. officer, dir. until 1971. Home: Maplewood NJ. Died Oct. 17, 1974.

HARPER, WILHELMINA, editor; b. Farmington, Me.; d. William and Bertha (Tauber) Harper; spl. courses Columbia, N.Y.U., N.Y. State Library Sch. Childrens librarian, br. librarian Poppenhusen br. Queensboro (N.Y.) Pub. Library, 1908-18; first asst. Camp Library, Pelham Bay Naval Tng. Sta., N.Y., 1918-19; library organizer for YMCA, Brest, France, 1919; asst. to Edward C. Carter dir. YMCA Overseas Service, 1920; organizer, supt. childrens work Kern County Free Library, Bakersfield, Cal., 1921-28; organizer Redwood City (Cal.) Pub. Library, 1929, librarian, 1930-54; editor, compiler childrens books, 1918-73; instr. childrens lit. Sch. Librarianship U. Cal., 1929, Riverside Library Sch., summers 1929, 32, San Jose (Cal.) State Tchrs. Coll., summer 1929. Mem. A.L.A. Author: Ghosts and Goblins, 1936, 65; Merry Christmas To You, 1936, 65; The Harvest Feast, 1938, 65; Easter Chimes, 1941, 65; The Gunniwolf, 1967. Home: Palo Alto, Cal. Died Dec. 23, 1973.

HARRAR, ELLWOOD SCOTT, educator; b. Pitts., Jan. 18, 1905; s. Ellwood Scott and Lucetta Elsie (Sterner) H.; student Oberlin Coll., 1922-24; B.S., N.Y. State Coll. Forestry, 1927, M.S., 1928, Ph.D., 1936; Sc.D. (hon.), Syracuse U. 1961; m. Marion Green, Sept. 10, 1927; children—Joanne, Carolyn. Asst. dendrology and wood tech. N.Y. State Coll. Forestry, Syracuse, 1926-28; instr. forest products U. Wash., Seattle, 1928-32, asst. prof., 1933-36; research asso. West Coast Lumbermen's Assn., 1928-32; project coordinator Civilian Conservation Corps, N.J., 1933; asso. prof. wood technology Duke, Durham, N.C., 1936-45, prof. wood tech, 1945-67, dean Sch. Forestry, 1957-67, James B. Duke prof. wood sci., 1967-74, emeritus, 1975--; chief materials and process labs. airplane div. Curtiss-Wright Corp., Louisville, 1942-43, chief administrv. engr., 1943-45; veneer, plywood cons. C.E. U.S. Army, Southeastern div., Atlanta, 1952-65; cons. U.S. Army Biol. Lab., Ft. Detrick, Fredrick, Md., 1961-68. Mem. forest products task force President's Bipartisan Commn. for Increased Use Agr. Products, 1956-58; mem. Gov's Adv. Com. Forestry for N.C. Recipient Gov.'s citation for outstanding contbns. to forestry N.C., 1966. Fellow Soc. Am. Foresters (com. for standardization tree names 1945-50); mem. Soc. Wood Scientists and Technologists, Internat. Soc. Tropical Foresters, Internat. Assn. Wood Anatomists (sec.-treas. 1938-45), Forest Products Research Soc. (chmn. pro tem Carolinas-Chesapeake sect. 1948, sec.-treas. 1950-53; v.p. 1957-58, pres. 1959-60), N.C. Forestry Council (pres. 1958-59), N.C. Forestry Assn. (adv. com. furniture, plywood, veneer council 1957-67), Phi Kappa Phi, Sigma Xi, Alpha Xi Sigma, Xi Sigma Pi, Lambda Chi Alpha. Presbyn. Rotarian. Club: Torch (pres. 1974-75) (Durham). Author: (with C.J. Hogue) Douglas Fir Use Book, 1930; Forest Dendrology, 1933; (with J.G. Harrar) Guide to Southern Trees, 1946, rev. edit., 1962; (with others) Forest Products, 1950, rev. edit., 1962; (with W.M. Harlow) Textbook of Dendrology, rev. edit., 1968; Hough Ency of American Woods, Vols. I-VII, 1957-75. Contbr. Ency. Brit., Ency. Americana, also to sci. and profl. jours. Home: Durham N.C. Died Feb. 5, 1975.

HARRINGTON, DANIEL, mining engr.; b. Denver, Colo., Apr. 26, 1878; s. Daniel M. and Margaret (Gleeson) H.; E.M., Colo. Sch. of Mines, 1900; m. Lauretta E. Anderson, Aug. 19, 1903; children—Marguerite (dec.), Mary Helen, Florence, Ceile Bernice. Engr. with Utah Fuel Co., 1900-07; U.S. Smelting Co., 1907; cons. mining practice, Salt Lake City, 1908-09; mine supt. Big Horn Collieries Co., Wyo., 1910-14; mining engr. and supervising mining engr., U.S. Bur. Mines, 1914-24; cons. practice, Salt Lake City, 1924-26; chief engr. Safety Div. U.S. Bur. Mines. Washington, 1926-33, chief health and safety branch, Jan. 1933-May 1948. Awarded Distinguished Service Medal by Department Interior, 1948; Industrial Achievement Medal, Colorado Sch. Mines, 1948; Special Award Medal, Joseph A. Holmes Safety Association, 1948. Member American Institute Mining and Metall. Engrs., Mine Inspectors Inst. of America, Nat. Safety Council, Rocky Mountain Coal Mining Inst., Coal Mining Inst. of America, Washington Sch. Safety Engrs., Kentucky Mining Inst.; mem. (hon. life) Am. Assn. Safety Engrs.; mem. Nat. Mine Rescue Assn., Am. Standards Assn., Federal Fire Council, Nat. Fire Waste Council, Interdepartmental Safety Council. Catholic. Club: Cosmos (Washington). Author: Improved Methods of Mining in Oklahoma (with J. J. Rutledge), 1918; Accident Prevention in Mines of Butte, Mont., 1920; Ventilation in Metal Mines, 1921; Miners Consumption in Butte, Mont. (with A. J. Lanza), 1921; Lessons from Granite Mountain Shaft Fire, 1922; Underground Ventilation at Butte, 1923; Metal-Mine Fires (with B. O. Pickard and H. M. Wolflin), 1923; Gases that Occur in Metal Mines (with E. H. Denny), 1931; Preventing Accidents by the Proper Use of Permissible Explosives (with S. P. Howell), 1936; Review of Literature on Effects of Breathing Dusts with Special Reference to Silicosis (with S. J. Davenport), 1937; Allaying Dust in Bituminous Coal Mines with Water (with J. J. Forbes and others), 1939; The Joseph A. Holmes Safety Assn. and Its Awards (with Louis Pedlow and Anna P. Brown), 1940; Barricading as a Life-Saving Measure in Connection with Mine Fires and Explosions (with W. J. Fene), 1941; Some Essential Safety Factors in Tunnelling (with S. H. Ash), 1942. All U.S. Bur. Mines. Writer of more than 300 articles on health and safety in mining. Home: Arlington, VA.†

HARRINGTON, HOWARD DEWITT, orch. cons.; b. Andover, Mass., Dec. 19, 1907; s. Virgil DeWitt and Alice (Howard) H.; student Phillips Andover Acad., 1927, Boston U., 1928-32, New Eng. Conservatory Music, 1932-38; m. Edna Grace Merritt, Sept. 2, 1936; children—Faith (Mrs. John Frederick Jones), Jonathan Brooke. Profl. tenor to 1941; mgr. Indpls. Symphony Orch., 1941-51; gen. mgr. Detroit Symphony Orch., 1951-71; cons. Am. Symphony Orch. League, 1971—74. Bd. dirs. Am. Symphony Orch. League. Home: Thomaston Maine. Died July 25, 1974.

HARRIS, D.D., auto dealer; b. Webberville, Mich., Apr. 12, 1887; s. George H. and Carrie D. (White) H.; student Mich. State Coll., 1903-04; m. Janet L. Bush, Jan. 2, 1911; children—Mary K., George D.; m. 2d, Theresa D. Jay, 1950; stepsons Robert R. and Leonard Jay. Traveling salesman, Mich., 1910-15; retail hardware, Webberville, Mich., 1915-23; Ford Dealer, Dean & Harris, Lansing, Mich., 1915-64; v.p. and dir. Bank of Lansing, 1928-65; treas. Mich. State Office Bldgs. Corp. Chmn. bd. Ford Dealers Adv. Fund Lansing Dist. Postmaster, Lansing, 1943-53; past dist. mgr. Central Mich. O.P.A.; bd. dirs. Infantile Paralysis Fund; exec. com. Dem. State Central Com.; mem. exec. com. Lansing Safety Council, past pres.; past pres. Police and Fire Commn.; mem. Mich. Inter-Industry Hwy. Safety Com.; mem. State Bldg. Com. Trustee Sparrow Hosp. Recipient Distinguished Citizen award Lansing Centennial, 1959; Distinctive Service award Lansing Dist. Ford Dealers Advt. Fund Corp., 1963. Mem. C. of C., Lansing Hist. Soc. (trustee). Democrat. Conglist. Clubs: Kiwanis, Executives of Lansing, Detroit Bankers, Shrine, Northside Commercial, City, Economic, National Auto Dealers 30 yr. Club. Home: East Lansing, Mich. Died Jan. 25, 1974.

HARRIS, GRADY DEWITT, JR., banker; b. Alex, Okla., June 27, 1926; s. Grady DeWitt and Robena H. (Dellinger) H.; A.B., U. Okla., 1945, LL.B., 1949, postgrad. Coll. Bus. Adminstrn.; m. Alice June Hunter, Aug. 23, 1947; children—Barbara Jean, Grady Hunter. Various positions Liberty Nat. Bank & Trust Co., Oklahoma City, 1950-59, sr. v.p., chmn. loan com., dir., mem. exec. com., 1956-59; pres. Fidelity Nat. Bank & Trust Co., Oklahoma City, 1960-74; chmn. First Nat. Bank, Alex, Okla., First State Bank, Blanchard, Okla.; dir. Capitol Hill State Bank & Trust Co., Kerr-McGee Oil Industries, Inc., Am. Fidelity Assurance Co. (all Oklahoma City); adv. dir. Community Nat. Bank of Warr Acres, Okla. Past pres. Travelers Aid Soc., Oklahoma City; past co-chmn. United Fund-Red Cross campaign of Oklahoma City; pres. Downtown Action, Inc., Oklahoma City; treas. Santa Claus Commn. Okla.; dir. Sunbeam Home and Family Service, Oklahoma County chpt. A.R.C., Better Bus., Oklahoma City; past dir. Okla. Heart Assn.; trustee U. Okla. Found., Inc.; bd. regents Okla. Coll. for Women. Served as lt. USNR, World War II. Recipient Outstanding Young Man of Year award, Oklahoma City, 1959; Distinguished Service award, Okla., 1960. Mem. Young President's Orgn., Assn. Res. City Bankers, Beta Gamma Sigma, Phi Delta Theta. Presbyn. (elder). Club: Economic of Okla. (past pres.). Home: Oklahoma City, Okla. Died Aug. 22, 1974.

HARRIS, HARRY EZEKIEL, SR. indsl. consultant; b. Glenham, N.Y., Apr. 4, 1878; s. Ezekiel Anthony and Mary Frances (Jones) H. ed. Newark (N.J.) Sch. of Engring.; m. Harriet Bell Clark, Dec. 31, 1898; children—Jean Bell (Mrs. Grant Bunnell, Jr.), Elinor Frances (Mrs. Malcolmn Wales Maclay), Harriet Louise (wife of Dr. Joe T. Teece); m. 2d, Virginia Stetson, July 11, 1941; 1 son, Harry Ezekiel. Began as machine designer, C.W. Hunt Co., 1899-1900; designing engineer, S. S. White Dental Manufacturing Co., 1900-01; supt. Murray Mfg. Co., 1901-02; engr. of methods and head mech. depts., Western Electric Co., 1902-11; gen. supt. Greenfield Tap and Dir Die Corp., 1911-15; pres. and gen. mgr. H. E. Harris Engring. Co., 1915-25; indsl. consultant and pres. Hubbard, Harris & Rowell, Inc., cons. engrs., 1925-41; chief, engring. dept. W.P.B., 1941-43; indsl. consultant, Bridgeport, Conn., from 1944. Mem. War Prodn. and Engring. Council; mem. Bridgeport Housing Authority. Fellow Am. Soc. M.E. (life mem.; exec. chmn. Bridgeport sect.); mem. Conn. Soc. Professional Engrs. (pres. 1946), Nat. Soc. Professional Engrs. (dir.), Am. Soc. for Engring. Education, Am. Soc. Mil. Engrs. N.Y. State Soc. Professional Engrs., Nat. Aeronautic Assn., S.A.R., Army Ordnance Assn. Epsicopalain. Mason (Shriner). Clubs: Engineers (Bridgeport and N.Y. City). Licensed professional engr., N.Y. State; registered professional engr., Conn.; certified professional engr. Nat. Bureau Engring. Registration. Inventor precision machine tools; a pioneer in accurate grinding of machine threads, which make practicable mass prodn. of airplanes and automobiles. Home: Bridgeport Conn.†

HARRIS, JULIA FILLMORE, educator; b. Detroit, Jan. 22, 1878; d. Charles A. and Ida (Fallis) Harris; B.A., U. of Minn., 1900. Founder, 1915, and prin. Miss. Harris Florida Sch., Miami, Fla. Mem. Nat. Assn. Prins. Schs. for Girls, Alpha Phi. Address: Stuart, Fla.†

HARRIS, LLOYD WEBB, mfg. co. exec.; b. Marietta, Ga., July 22, 1922; s. William Lloyd and Fannie (Webb) H.; student Ga. Tech., 1939-40, Emory U., 1940-41; m. Harriet Hanson, Aug. 16, 1947; children—Carl L., Eric W., Freya E. With Lockheed-Ga. Co., 1951-68, JetStar dist. mgr., 1964-68; pres., chief exec. officer Hawker Siddeley Internat., Inc., 1968-71; pres. Beechcraft Hawker Corp., Wichita, Kan., 1971-74. Bd. dirs. Atlanta Com. Internat. Visitors, 1967-68, Atlanta Com. Fgn. Relations, 1967-68; mem. Wichita C. of C. Internat. Visitors Council and Port of Entry Com. Served with USNR, 1944. Mem. British-Am. C. of C. (bd. dirs.). Unitarian. Clubs: Royal Aero (London Eng.); American, Wings (N.Y.C.); Cherokee Town and Country (Atlanta). Died Aug. 25, 1974; interred Marietta, Ga.

HARRIS, MAYNARD LAWRENCE, banker; b. Boston, Feb. 6, 1902; s. Edward Stephen and Pauline (Rippel) H.; student U.Utah, 1918-19; B.S. in Civil Engring., Mass. Inst. Tech., 1924; m. Edith Johnson Bushnell, Oct. 8, 1927 (dec. 1942); children—Maynard Lawrence, Christopher; m. 2d, Caroline Cutter McMillan, Jan. 26, 1945; stepchildren—Caroline Osgood McMillan, Ellen Dyar McMillan (Mrs. George M. Aman III), Andrew T. McMillan, Edith Endicott McMillan (Mrs. Dan S. Tucker). Engr., Pacific Gas & Electric Co., 1924-25; asst. sec. Nat. Surety Co., 1925-35; v.p. New Eng. Trust Co., 1936-46; treas. Franklin Savs. Bank, Boston, 1947-56, pres., 1956-57; pres. Suffolk Franklin Savs. Bank, Boston, Massachusetts, 1957-63, chairman of the board from 1963, also trustee; pres., dir. Savs. Bank Investment Fund, Boston, 1958-66; dir. New Eng. Merchants Nat. Bank. Chmn., dir. Boston Municipal Research Bur., 1959-65, vice chairman, 1965, dir., from 1965. Member of the Coordinating Com. Boston from 1959. Bd. dirs. Mass. Bay United Fund, Inc.; corporator New Eng. Deaconess Hosp., Boston; trustee Civic Found. Boston; hon. trustee Concord (Mass.) Acad. Mem. Theta Xi. Clubs: Commercial-Merchants, Union (Boston); Concord

Country. Author: For the Fun of It. Home: Carlisle, Mass. Died Jan. 12, 1974; buried Sleepy Hollow Cemetery, Concord, Mass.

HARRIS, SEYMOUR EDWIN, economist; b. N.Y.C., Sept. 8, 1897; s. Henry and Augusta (Kulick) H; A.B., Harvard, 1920, Ph.D., 1926; LL.D., U. Mass., Monmouth Coll.; Ruth Black, Sept 3, 1923 (dec.); m. 2d, Dorothy Marshall, April 27, 1968. Instr., Princeton, 1920-22; instr., Harvard, 1922, lectr., 1927, asst. prof. 1933, asso. prof., 1936, prof. 1945-64, Lucius N. Littauer prof. of polit. economy, 1957-64; chmn. dept. econs. Harvard and U. Cal., San Diego, 1964-74; vis. 1948; editor Rev. of Econ. and Statistics, 1943-64, asso. editor Quar. Jour. Econs., 1947-74; sr. cons. to sec. of treas., 1961-68. Mem. bd. Econ. Warfare Policy com., 1942; com. on postwar comml. policy, Sec. of State, 1943; advisor Latin Am. countries on econ. stabilization, 1943; economic adviser to vice chmn. W.P.B., 1944-45; mem. adv. bd. C.C.C., 1949-53; mem. Agrl. Mblzn. Policy Bd., 1951-53. Dir. office export-import price control, O.P.A., 1942-43; adviser to N.R.S.B., 1946-47; cons. to President's Council of Econ. Advs., 1950-51. Chmn., New Eng. Gov's Textile Com., 1955-60; mem. pub. adv. com. Area Redevel. Adminstrn., 1964-74. Trustee John F. Kennedy Library. Adviser, Dem. Nat. Com. Served with U.S. Army, 1918. Awarded David A. Wells Prize, Harvard, 1927; 00 1st Prize, Greater Boston Met. Contest (co-winner), 1944; Alexander Hamilton prize, sec. treasury, 1967. Mem. Am. Econ. Assn. (exec. com., v.p. 1945-48), Am. Acad. Arts and Scis. Club: Harvard (N.Y.) Author books including: How Shall We Pay for Education, 1948; Stabilization Subsidies, 1948; Foreign Economic Relations of the United States, 1948; European Recovery Program, 1948; Saving American Capitalism, 1948; Economics of Planning; Market for College Graduates, 1949; Inflation and Anti-Inflationary Policies of American States, 1950; Economics of Mobilization and Inflation, 1951; Economics of New England, 1952; Keynes' Economist and Policy Maker, 1955; Interregional and International Economics, 1958; More Resources for Education, 1960; Higher Education in the United States: The Economic Problems, 1960; The Dollar in Crisis, 1961; The Economics of the Political Parties, 1962; Higher Education: Resources and Finance, 1962; Economics of American Medicine, 1964; Economics of the Kennedy Years, 1964; Economic Aspects of Higher Education, 1964; Economics of American Medicine, 1964; The Economics of Harvard; Education and Public Policy; Challenge and Change in American Education; Statistical Portrait of Higher Education. 1972; Academic Activist, 1973. Editor publications including: Schumpeter, Social Scientist, 1951. Home: La Jolla Cal. Died Oct. 1974.

HARRISON, BRUCE MAGILL, zoölogist; b. Ottawa, Kan., Mar. 29, 1881; s. Thomas Wilson and Hester Lillias (Perkins) H.; B.S., Ottawa U., 1905, Sc.D., 1948; M.S., U. of Ill., 1908; Ph.D., State U. Ia., 1924; student Marine Biol. Lab., Woods Hole, summer 1919; grad. student U. of Chicago, summers 1909, 10, 13, 14, 16; m. Lessie May Confare, Aug. 11, 1909; children—Dwight T., Louise A. Instr. zoölogy, Iowa State Coll., 1910-12, asst. prof., 1912-25; grad. asst. in zoölogy, State U. of Iowa, 1923-24; asso. prof. zoölogy, U. of Southern Calif., 1925-28, prof. zoology, 1928-48, prof., from 1948, head dept. zoology, 1940-48; asst. to Iowa state entomologist, summers 1911, 12, 15, 17, 18, in charge Hessian fly control station, Iowa, summer 1922; exchange prof. zoölogy, U. of Oregon summer 1928, Baylor U. summer 1938. Mem. affiliated com. Y.M.C.A., City of Los Angeles, 1927-31; mem. joint state park com. of Calif., 1926-30. Fellow A.A.A.S., Iowa Acad. Science; mem. Southern Calif. Acad. Science, Western Soc. Naturalists, Entomologists Club of Southern Calif., Am. Assn. Univ. Profs., Calif. Acad. Science, Kappa Zeta, Sigma Xi, Phi Sigma. Phi Kappa Phi, Alpha Epsilon Delta. Republican. Mason. Mem. bd. elders. Presbyterian Ch., Los Angeles. Author: The Dissection of Shark; The Dissection of the Cat, 1948. Contbr. sci. articles to professional publs. Mem. bd. dirs. Westminster Foundation. Home: Los Angeles, Cal.†

HARRISON, BURR POWELL, former congressman; b. Winchester, Va., July 2, 1904; s. Thomas Walter and Nellie (Cover) H.; student Woodberry Forest Sch., 1918-20, Va. Mil. Inst., 1920-21, Hampden-Sydney Coll., 1921-22, U. Va., 1922-23, Georgetown U., 1923-26; LL.D., Hampden-Sydney Coll., 1949; m. Dorothy W. Green. Admitted to Va. bar, 1926, to practice before Supreme Ct. of Appeals of Va., 1928, Supreme Ct. of U.S., 1937; gen. law practice, Winchester, Va., 1926-42, 1946-73; mem. firm Harrison & Johnston; atty. for Commonwealth, Frederick County, Va., 1932-40; mem. Va. Senate, 1940-42; judge 17th Jud. Circuit, 1942-46; mem. 79th to 87th Congresses, 7th Dist. Va.; mem. Va. Commn. on Constl. Govt., 1963. Bd. visitors Madison Coll., Harrisonburg, Va. Home: Winchester, Va. Died Dec. 29, 1973.

HARRISON, HAROLD EVERUS, physician; b. Council Bluffs, Ia., June 1, 1904; s. Trive Joel and Anna Christine Harrison; B.S., Creighton U., 1929, M.D., 1933; m. Ann Helen King, July 6, 1929; children—Gregory Allen, Janet Claire (Mrs. Louis Henry Stahl). Rotating intern St. Joseph's Hosp., Omaha, 1933-34; comd. M.C., U.S. Army, 1934, advanced through grades to col.; retired 1964; asst. resident in obstetrics and gynecology Walter Reed Gen. Hosp., Washington, 1946-47, sr. resident, 1948-49; postgrad. tng. U. Pa., 1947-48; chief obstet. and gynecol. service Madigan Gen. Hosp., Tacoma, Wash., 1949-54, 57-64, asst. chief surg. service, 1957-59, chief profl. service, exec. officer, 1962-64; cons. obstetrics and gynecology U. Wash., Seattle, 1951-54, clin. asst. prof., 1957-64; fellow Sch. Pub. Health, U. Cal. at San Francisco, 1964; head health ins. sect. Wash. State Dept. Health, 1965-66, chief health facilities div., 1966-70. Decorated Legion of Merit. Diplomate Am. Bd. Obstetrics and Gynecology. Fellow A.C.S., Am. Coll. Obstetricians and Gynecologists (founding); mem. A.M.A., Am. Numis. Assn., Soc. Philatelic Americans, Phi Rho. Mason. Contbr. articles to profl. jours. Home: Tacoma, Wash. Died July 11, 1972; buried Council Bluffs, Ia.

HARRISON, JAMES LEFTWICH, b. Atlanta, Sept. 10, 1895; s. Thomas Perrin and Adelia (Lake) H.; B.A., U. of N.C., 1916; m. Pauline Carrington Mugge, Oct. 15, 1921; children—Mildred Carrington (Mrs. Frederick B. Dent), Pauline Leftwich (Mrs. Walter E. Winans), James Leftwich. Nat. City Bank of N.Y., N.Y.C., 1916, appointed asst. cashier, 1924, asst. vice-pres., 1929, vice-pres., 1930. Mem. The Pilgrims, Delta Kappa Epsilon. Republican. Presbyterian. Clubs: Down Town Assn., University (N.Y.C.); Bedford Golf and Tennis. Home: New York City, N.Y. Died Aug. 14, 1973; buried St. Mathews Ch., Bedford, N.Y.

HARRISON, JAY SMOLENS, music critic, educator; b. N.Y.C., Jan. 25, 1927; s. Abraham and Stella (Fleischman) Smolens; student Columbia Prep. Sch., 1940-44; A.B., N.Y. U., 1948; music student Philip James; m. Jane King Cohan, May 15, 1954 (div.); children—Paige Julie, Troy Nedda. Network radio actor, 1936-44; oboist, symphony orchs., 1940-45; instr. music N.Y. U., 1948-55, asst. prof. music, 1955-56; asso. producer Met. Opera broadcasts, 1954-56, quizmaster, 1957-58, panelist, 1958-74; TV and radio writer, 1954-74; writer, master of ceremonies History of Opera, NBC-TV; music cons. Cultural Presentation Program U.S. State Dept., 1955-74, N.Y. State Council of Arts, 1957; guest critic N.Y. Herald Tribune, 1948-52, asso. critic, 1952, music editor, 1952-60; exec. editor Music mag., 1960-61; music interviewer, NBC monitor week-end radio series; dir. Reader's Digest Music-RCA Record Club, 1961-63; with Roving Critic program, WOR radio sta., 1962-74; editor Musical Am., 1963-64; dir. editorial services Columbia Records, 1965-67; asso. prof. music Queens Coll. City U. N.Y., 1968-70; adj. prof. Fordham U., 1970-71. Mem. N.Y. Music Critics' Circle, Am. Newspaper Guild, Am. Musicological Soc., Nat. Council Govt. and Arts, Phi Beta Kappa. Contbr. to profl. publs., Book of the Month periodicals on Great Music. Home: New York City, NY. Died Sept. 12, 1974.

HARRISON, WILLIAM MOORE, co. exec.; b. Berkeley, Cal., Apr. 9, 1912; s. William and Freda (Moore) H.; m. Conchita Perelli-Minetti, Nov. 12, 1938; children—William Moore, Ann Elise. Liaison engr. Lockheed, 1940-45; officer, dir. Perelli-Minetti & Sons, Delano, Cal., 1945-55; exec. dir. Indsl. Devel. Commn., Santa Rosa, Cal., 1956-62, Oakland, Cal., 1962-67; exec. dir., pres. William M. Harrison Co., Inc., Oakland, 1967-74. Chmn., Statewide Com. for Cal. ownership of Central Valley Project, 1949-54; pres. Redwood Regional Conservation Council, 1958-59; Santa Rosa High Sch. P.T.A., 1949-54; mem. adv. com. Santa Rosa Meml. Hosp., 1961. Bd. dirs. Santa Rosa Boys Clubs, Santa Rosa Clinic, Alameda County chpt. A.R.C. Fellow Am. Indsl. Devel. Council. Clubs: Sausalito (Cal.) Yacht; Commonwealth of Cal. (San Francisco); Athenian Nile (Oakland). Home: Ventura Cal. Died July 29, 1974.

HART, CHARLES ALLAN, lawyer; b. Nova Scotia, Can., Jan. 9, 1880; s. Lauchlin J. and Jeanne (Lepper) Hart; LL.B., St. Paul College of Law, 1903; married to Katherine Stoughton, August 22, 1906 (deceased February 28, 1955); children—Katharine (Mrs. Albert E. Stephan), Charles Allan, James Stoughton. Admitted to Minn. bar, 1903, and practiced in St. Paul, 1903-07; lawyer N.P. Ry. Co., 1907-11; mem. firm Rockwood, Davies, Biggs, Strayer & Stoel and predecessor firms, Portland, Ore., 1911-64. Mem. Am., Ore. bar assns. Unitarian. Clubs: Arlington, Waverly, University. Home: Portland, Ore.†

HART, HENRY JOSEPH, r.r. counsel, exec.; b. Lynn, Mass., Jan. 25, 1880; s. Joseph Henry and Eunice Tuttle (Abbott) H.; A.B., Brown U., 1902, student Law Sch. (now Northeastern), 1903-05; m. Katherine Pauline Aldrich, Apr. 1910 (died Apr. 1915); m. 2d, Florence Merryman Bradley, Sept. 1, 1917. Admitted to Mass. bar, 1905, practiced as jr. lawyer with Choate, Hall, & Stewart, Boston, 1905-09; admitted to Conn. bar, 1909, mem. law dept. N.Y., N.H. & H. R.R. Co., New Haven, 1900-16; admitted to Me. bar, 1916, gen. counsel Bangor & Aroostook R.R. Co., Bangor, from 1916, clerk of the corp. from 1936. sec. exec. com. from 1940, v.p., from 1949. Spl. counsel Pub. Works Adminstrn., r.r. loan div., Dept. of Interior, Nov. 1933-May 1934. Mem. Am. Bar Assn., (past mem. sec. pub. utilities com.), Nat. Tax Assn. (past mem. com. on fed. corp. income taxes), Delta Kappa Epsilon. Episcopalian. Home: Bangor, Me.†

HART, JAMES HILL, lawyer; b. nr. Austin, Tex., Sept. 23, 1878; s. James Pinckney and Mary Elizabeth (Peck) H.; A.B., U. of Tex., 1899, LL.B., 1901; m. Nannie Strother Furman, Sept. 24, 1902; children—James Pinckney, Helen Furman (Mrs. Charles C. Jagou). Admitted to Tex. bar, 1902, practiced in Austin; mem. Hart, Brown & Sparks. Mem. State Bd. Law Examiners, 1930-48, chmn. 1948; mem. local Draft Bd. from 1942. Democrat. Presbyn. Mem. Kappa Sigma. Mason (33°). Clubs: St. Charles (Tex.) Bay Hunting; Town and Gown (Austin). Home: Austin Tex†

HART, SIMEON THOMPSON, prof. adminstrn. engring; b. Farmington, Conn., Feb. 3, 1878; s. John Hooker and Mary Ann (Thompson) H.; student U. of Wis.; B.S., Purdue; M.E., 1911; m. Maude Lee Clark, June 26, 1910; children—Jascah S., S. Willard, Margaret M., Nancy K., Frederick W.; m. 2d, Lenore Zerch, Dec. 26, 1938. Asst. supt., Morgan Machine Co., Rochester, N.Y., 1909-11; supt., Hartford Special Machinery Co., Hartford, Conn., 1911-15; asst. prof., W.Va. U., 1915-20; prof., adminstrn. engring., Syracuse U., head dept., from 1940. Mem. A.S.M.E. (chmn.). S.A.M., Phi Kappa Phi, Sigma Iota Epsilon, Alpha Phi Omega. Republican. Conglist. Club: Technology (pres.). Home: Syracuse, N.Y.†

HART, THOMAS, lawyer; b. Phila., Nov. 24, 1894; s. Charles Byerly and Ida Virginia (Hill) H.; A.B., U. Pa., 1916, LL.B., 1929; m. Margaret Newbold Smith, May 15, 1918 (dec. 1959); children—Margaret Newbold (Mrs. John Kapp Clark, M.D.) (dec.), Thomas (dec.); m. 2d, Virginia Dilkes Harrison, June 25, 1960. With J.B. Lippincott Co., Phila., Phila. Trust Co., Cadbury, Ellis & Haines, bankers, Phila., 1961-24; dir. Houston Hall, U. Pa., 1924-29; gen. practice law, 1929-75; sr. partner, then counsel Hart, Childs, Hepburn, Ross & Putnam; chmn. bd. dirs. Charles F. Kellom & Co. Bd. dirs. Inst. for Cancer Research, Inc.; bd. mgrs. Ludwick Inst.; trustee Young Man's Inst.; v.p., bd. mgrs. Spring Garden Coll.; past pres., bd. dirs. Athenaeum of Phila.; v.p., trustee Am. Oncologic Hosp., Lankenau Hosp.; trustee emeritus, past pres. Episcopal Acad.; pres. Magee Meml. Hosp. for Convalescents; bd. mgrs., past pres. Preston Maternity Hosp.; pres. Independence Hall Assn.; bd. dirs., past pres. Phila. Charity Ball, Inc. Served with U.S. Army, World War I; ensign to lt. (j.g.) USCGR, 1942-44. Hon. mem. 1st Troop Phila. City Cav., Pa. N.G. Mem. Swedish Colonial Soc., Am., Pa., Phila. bar assns., Juristic Soc., Colonial Soc. Pa. (council, past gov.), S.R. (past pres., hon. pres. Pa.), Soc. War of 1812 (v.p.), Mil. Order of Loyal Legion U.S. (hon.), Soc. Colonial Wars (council, past gov. Pa.), Sons of Copper Beeches, Baker Street Irregulars, Delta Psi. Republican. Episcopalian. Clubs: Sharswood Law, Socialegal, Mask and Wig (past pres.) (U. Pa.); Philadelphia, Racquet, Saint Anthony (Phila.); The Rabbit, State-In Schuylkill, Corinthian Yacht (charter) (Cape May); Rittenhouse. Author: A Record of the Hart Family of Philadelphia (1735-1920), pub. privately, 1920; Vol. 2, A History of the Schuylkill Fishing Company of the State-In-Schuylkill, 1888-1932, pub. privately, 1932. Home: Wynnewood, Pa., Died Apr. 25, 1975.

HARTMAN, JOHN DANIEL lawyer; b. Lancaster, O., Mar. 31, 1878; s. Gaylord and Louisa Jane (Brown) H.; grad. Northern Ind. Normal Sch., Valparaiso, Ind., 1900; student Ohio Normal U., Ada., O., 2 yrs.; m. Clara Kochensparger, June 1903. Admitted to Ohio bar 1906, and began practice at Lancaster; moved to San Antonio, Tex., 1906; Rep. nominee for Congress, 14th Tex. Dist., 1918; U.S. atty., Western Dist. of Tex., 1921-33. English Lutheran. Home: San Antonio, Tex.†

HARTMAN, PAUL WILLIAM, actor; b. San Francisco, Mar. 1, 1904; s. Ferris Luce and Josephine (Davies) H.; student U. Cal. at Berkeley, 1922; m. Grace Adelaide Barrett, Nov. 14, 1922 (dec. 1955); 1 son, Ferris Luce III. Dancer, actor until 1922; vaudeville headliner, 1926; dance satirist, 1932-47; comedian, 1936-56; Broadway appearances include Red, Hot and Blue, 1937, You Never Know, 1942, Top Notchers, 1942, Keep 'Em Laughing, 1942, Angel in the Wings, 1948, All For Love, 1949, Tickets Please, 1950, Of Thee I Sing, 1952, The Pajama Game, 1955, Show Boat, 1956; films include Sunny, The Man on a Tightrope, The Thrill of it All, Inherit the Wind, Soldiers in the Rain, How to Succeed in Business Without Really Trying, Luv; TV appearances, 1956-73, including Bell Telephone Hour, Ben Casey, Lucy Show, Chrysler Theatre, Andy Griffith Show, Mayberry R.F.D., Petticoat Junction, others. Recipient Stage Palm award, 1937, Tony award, 1948, Donaldson award, 1948, Page One award, 1942, Lambs award, 1957, N.Y. Daily Mirror award, 1939, Critics award, 1947, Variety Poll award, 1948. Author: Much Love, Pop, 1945. Address: Los Angeles, Cal. Died Oct. 2, 1973.

HARTMAN, ROBERT S., educator b. Berlin, Germany, Jan. 27, 1910; student U. Berlin, 1926-27, U. Paris (France), 1927-28, London Sch. Econs. and Polit. Sci., 1928-29; LL.B., U. Berlin, 1932, U. Mexico, 1941; Ph.D., Northwestern U., 1946; m. Rita Emanuel, Aug. 30, 1936; 1 son, Jan Alfred. Asst. to faculty law U. Berlin, 1932-33; referendar (asst. judge), Dist. Court Berlin, Charlottenburg, 1932-33; rep. for Walt Disney Prodns. in Scandinavia, Mexico, C.A., 1934-41; master Lake Forest (Ill.) Acad., 1942-45; instr., asst. prof. The

Coll. of Wooster (O.), 1945-48; asso. prof. Ohio State U., 1948-56; Fulbright prof. Center Philos. Studies, Nat. U. Mexico, 1957-58, research prof., 1958-73. Vis. prof. Mass. Inst. Tech., 1956-57, Yale U., 1966, U. Tenn., 1968, 69; organizing chmn. of the Council of Profit Sharing Industries, 1947, exec. sec., 1947-49; co-founder Institut fur Sozialwirtschaftliche Betriebsberatung, Dusseldorf, Germany, 1952; cons. Mexican Govt. Profit-Sharing Commn., 1963. Mem. Allgemeine Gesellschaft Für Philosophie in Deutschland, Am. Philos. Assn., Am. Assn. U. Profs., Nat. Edn. Assn., Am. Assn. Humanistic Psychology (founding sponsor), Am. Soc. Value Inquiry (pres. 1971), Delta Phi Alpha (hon.). Contbr. chpt. and articles to philos. and econ. publs. Translator publs. including: Hegel, Introduction to the Philosophy of History, 1953; Kant, Logic, 1971. Author: Profit Sharing Manual, 1948; The Partnership of Capital and Labor: Theory and Practice of a New Economic System, 1958; The Structure of Value & Foundations of Scientific Axiology, 1959, rev. 1969; The Knowledge of Good, 1965; The Hartman Value Inventory, 1966. Co-author: The Language of Value, 1957; New Knowledge In Human Values, 1958; Chronique de Philosophie, 1958. Cons. editor Kantstudien, 1952-73, Rev. Humanistic Psychology, 1963-73. Address: Cuernavaca Mexico. Died Sept. 20, 1973; buried Parque de La Paz Cemetery, Cuernavaca, Mexico.

HARTMANN, F. NORMAN, paper mfg. co. exec.; b. Toledo, July 2, 1906; s. Charles and Laura (Blanchet) H.; B.S. in Econs., U. Pa., 1928; m. Elizabeth A. Bellwoar, Apr. 7, 1928 (dec. Feb. 1972); children—Polly (Mrs. Robert Wilson), Charles B., Norene (Mrs. Jerry F. Haislip); m. 2d, Ida Rowe, Dec. 8, 1973. Salesman, sales mgr., v.p. Butler Paper Products Co., Toledo, 1928-52, pres., 1952-53; asst. to pres. Lily-Tulip Cup Corp., N.Y.C., 1953-56, v.p. planning and devel., 1956-62, pres., 1962-68; gen. mgr. Lily-Tulip div., group v.p. Owens-Ill., Inc., 1968-70, ret. Home: St. Simons Island GA. Died Feb. 5, 1974; buried Ogelthorpe Meml. Cemetery, St. Simons Island, Ga.

HARTMANN, REINA KATE GOLDSTEIN, b. Chgo., Feb. 2, 1880; d. Simon and Kate (Mayer) Goldstein; ed. in high sch., South Div.; m. Hugo Hartmann, Sept. 29, 1902; children—Dorothy (Mrs. Milton J. Klee), Hugo. Pres. Mother's Aid of Chicago Lying-In Hosp., 1917-21; pres. Nat. Fedn. of Temple Sisterhoods, 1941-46. Jewish religion. Home: Highland Park, Ill.†

HARTNETT, TIMOTHY V., corp. exec.; b. Brooklyn, N.Y., Dec. 14, 1890; s. Cornelius and Mary (O'Donnell) H.; student St. Vincent de Paul Sch., Brooklyn, 1897-1904; Sch. of Commerce, 1904-06; m. Margery Berteau, Apr. 25, 1918; 1 son, Timothy V., Jr. With British Am. Tobacco Co., New York, N.Y., 1906-14; mgr. Imperial Tobacco Co., St. John's Newfoundland, 1914-29; sales exec. Imperial Tobacco Co., Montreal, Que., 1929-30; v.p. Brown & Williamson Tobacco Corp., Louisville, Ky., 1930-36, exec. v.p., 1936-41, pres. and dir., 1941-54; chmn. Tobacco Industry Research Com., 1954-74; pres. Campbell Co., Inc., 1955-74. Served as Am. vice consul, St. John's, Newfoundland, 1919-29. Democrat. Roman Catholic. Knight of St. Gregory. Clubs: Pendennis, Louisville Country. Home: Louisville, KY. Died Jan. 25, 1974.

HARTSHORN, EDWIN SIMPSON, army officer; b. Troy, N.Y., Nov. 13, 1874; s. Edwin Alonzo and Sarah Loretta (Hovey) H.; student Hudson River Inst., Claverack, N.Y., 1889-1893; honor grad. Army Sch. of the Line, 1913; grad. Army Staff Coll., 1914, Field Artillery School, 1922, Army War College, 1923; m. Sallie Jamison Kirtland, May 16, 1908 (died June 4, 1960); children—Brigadier General Edwin Simpson, Betty Carter (Mrs. Robert Bruce Davenport). Served in Spanish-Am. War as 1st lt. 201st N.Y. Vol. Inf., later capt., 1898-99; in Philippine Insurrection as 1st lt. 27th U.S. Inf., 1899-1901; entered regular U.S. Army as 2d lt. inf., Feb. 2, 1901; advanced through grades to brig. gen., Dec. 26, 1935; served in Pulajan Insurrection, 1904; lt. col. and col. Gen. Staff, World War I; on War Dept. Gen. Staff, 1917-21, 1924-28, chief of staff, 9th Corps Area, 1930-34; exec. for Reserve Affairs, War Dept., 1935-38; retired from active service, Nov. 30, 1938. Awarded D.S.M.; Polonia Restituta (3d class); service medals Spanish-Am. War, Philippine Insurrection, WW I, State of N.Y. Cross Conspicuous Service. Mem. 7th Regt. NGNY Vets. Assn., Soc. Fgn. Wars, Mil. Order Carabao, Order Founders and Patriots Am., Soc. Colonial Wars, S.A.R. Methodist. Clubs: Army and Navy (Washington). Compiler several genealogies. Home: North Reding Beach, Fla.†

HARVEY, LAURENCE, actor; b. Yonishkis, Lithuania, Oct. 1, 1928; s. Ber Skikne and Ella Zotnickaita; studied schs. of Johannesburg, South Africa; student Royal Academy of Dramatic Art, London, England, 1946; m. Joan Perry Cohn, 1968; m. 2d, Paulene Stone; 1 dau., Domino. Came to U.S., 1952. Appeared various plays, theatre in Manchester, Eng., 1947-51; actor As You Like It, Coriolanus, MacBeth, Volpone, Stratford-on-Avon, 1952-54, Romeo and Juliet, also Troilus and Cressida, 1954; appeared in The Rivals, London, 1955, Island of Goats, N.Y.C., 1956, The Country Wife, London and N.Y.C., 1957, toured U.S. with Old Vic in Henry V, 1959, Dial "M" for Murder, 1968; television roles in England include Othello, in 1949, As You Like It, 1953, The Small Servant, 1955, Violent Years, 1959; motion picture films House of Darkness, Man From Yesterday, Cairo Road, Black Rose Scarlet Thread, Wall of Death, Gathering Storm, Innocents of Paris, Romeo and Juliet, Good Die Young, Three Men in a Boat, Silent Enemy, Room at the Top, Expresso Bongo, The Alamo, Butterfield 8, Wonderful World of Brothers Grimm, Tamiko, The Long, The Short, and The Tall, The Manchurian Candidate, The Running Man, The Ceremony, of Human Bondage, The Outrage, Darling, 1965, Life at the Top, 1965, Dandy in Aspic, 1968, Struggle for Rome, 1968, She and He, 1969, Hall of Mirrors, 1969, The Magic Christian, 1969, Child's Play, 1971, others; stage appearances Camelot, 1964, The Winters Tale, 1968; Starred in Arms And The Man at Chichester Festival Theatre; starred on TV in Arms and the Man. Dir. play entitled Simply Heavenly, 1958. Served So. African Armed Forces. Named Most Promising Actor of Yr. N.Y. Theater, 1955; nominated for performances in Room at the Top and Expresso Bongo, Brit. Film Acad., 1959-60; named best actor of year Variety Clubs of Great Britain, 1960; nominated best actor for Room at the Top, Am. Acad. award, 1960; nominated one of Filmdom's Famous 5's, 1960. Died Nov. 25, 1973.

HARVEY, LEO M., aluminum co. exec.; b. 1886; m. Lena Brody; children—Lawrence A., Homer, Mrs. Carmen Warschaw. Founder Harvey Machinery Co., 1913, Harvey Machinery Co. Inc., 1942; formerly chmn. bd. successor co. Harvey Aluminum Inc. Address: Torrance Cal. Died Jan. 18, 1974.

HARVEY, P(AUL) CASPER, profl. painter; b. Gallatin, Mo., Nov. 25, 1889; s. Rev. Wiley Wesley and Cora Frederica (Caspar) H.; parents missionaries to Africa; A.B., William Jewell Coll., Liberty, Mo., 1910; A.M., 1911; studied Kansas City Sch. of Law, 1911-12, U. Chgo., 1914; m. Victoria Adelaide Unruh, June 11, 1919. Tchr. English and journalism, high sch., Leavenworth, Kan., 1912-14; head dept. of English, 1914-20, dir. pub. service div., 1919-20, Fort Hays (Kansas) State Normal Sch.; prof. English composition, William Jewell Coll., Liberty, Mo., 1920-58, prof. emeritus, 1958, debate coach, 1920-30, and dir. publicity, 1928-35, became dir. pub. relations, 1939, dir. forensics, 1936-48; profl. painter of oil portraits and abstractions of personalities, Liberty, Mo., 1958-75; mng. editor Coll. Bull., William Jewell Coll.; dir. Living Endowment, William Jewell Coll.; tchr. pub. speaking Huff Coll., Kansas City, Mo., 1938-40. Mgr. Liberty C. of C., 1961-65. Mem. various civic committees and orgns. 1917-75; pres. Bd. Pub. Works, Liberty, 1950-59; mem. Liberty City Council, 1965-75; Mem. Clay County Home Rule Charter Commn. Mem. profl. and academic assns. Republican. Baptist Mason (K.T., Shriner). Clubs: Rotary. Claycrest, Golf. Author several books and contbr. mags., ednl. jours., newspapers; coach and judge debates and oratorical contests, 1929--, including coaching U.S. team which represented all colls. and univs. of U.S. in internat. intercollegiate debates, in Great Britain, 1939. Editorial columnist Liberty Tribune, 1963-69. Address: Liberty, Mo., Died May 28, 1975.

HARVEY, ROGER ALLEN, physician, radiologist; b. Binghamton, N.Y., Mar. 7, 1910; s. Zina Austin and Alice (Finch) H.; B.S., Hamilton Coll., 1933; M.S., U. Rochester, 1938, M.D. with honors, 1939; m. Marjorie Harding, June 20, 1940; children—Carol Eileen, Jean Emily. Intern, U. Chgo. Clinics 1939-40; resident radiology U. Rochester, 1940-42, instr. radiology, 1942-45, asst. prof., 1945-46; research asso. Manhattan Project, 1943-46; cons. AEC, Rochester project, 1946-49; prof. radiology U. Ill. Coll. Medicine, 1946-70, chmn. dept., 1946-70, acting dean med. coll., 1953-54; radiologist-in-chief, U. Ill. Hosps., 1946-70, acting med. dir., 1953-54; cons. Armed Forces Center, Chgo., USPHS, Hines (Ill.) VA Hosp.; dir. med. Betatron project U. Ill.; med. adviser to state dir. SSS, 1949-62; dir. Tb Inst. Chgo. and Cook County, 1958-71; mem. radiation protection adv. council Ill. Dept. Pub. Health, chmn., 1960-70; mem. Ill. Legislative Commn. on Atomic Energy, 1969-71. Fellow Chgo. Roentgen Soc. (pres. 1953), Assn. U. Radiologists (pres. 1957-58), Am. Cancer Soc. (nat. pres. 1967-68, dir.; pres., dir. Ill.; chmn. Region IV 1958, Distinguished Service in Cancer Control award 1964), Am. Coll. Radiology; mem. A.M.A., Chgo., Ill. med. socs. Am. Roentgen Ray Soc., Radiation Research Soc., Radiol. Soc. N.Am., Sigma Xi, A.A.A.S., Delta Upsilon, Pi Kappa Epsilon, Alpha Kappa Kappa. Mem. Hinsdale Union Ch. Contbr. articles to profl. jours. Address: Parker Colo. Died July 17, 1973; interred, Port Dickinson, N.Y.

HARVIE, ERIC LAFFERTY, barrister; b. Orillia, Ont., Can., Apr. 2, 1892; s. William McLeod and Cecile Elizabeth (Lafferty) H.; LL.B., Osgoode Hall and U. Alta., 1914; LL.D., U. Alta., 1957; Dr., U. Calgary, 1967; m. Dorothy Jean Southam, Sept. 29, 1919; children—Margaret Joy (Mrs. Donald Maclaren), Donald Southam, Frederick Nell Southam. Admitted to Alta. (Can.) bar, 1915, practiced law in Calgary; created Kings counsel, 1939; v.p., dir. Belvedere Securities Ltd.; dir. emeritus Can Imperial Bank Commerce; hon. chmn. Fathers Confedn. Bldgs. Trust; Fathers Conf. Meml. Citizens Found.; dir. Royal Can. Geog. Soc. Hon. dir. Calgary YMCA; adv. mem. nat. council Boy Scouts Can., hon. patron Calgary Regional council, Heritage Park Soc. adv. com. U. Western Ont. Sch. Bus. Adminstrn.; trustee Banff Found.; hon. gov. and fellow Glenbow-Alberta Inst.; patron Calgary Zool. Soc. Served as lt. inf., Canadian Army, 1915-17, capt. Royal Flying Corps, R.A.F., 1917-19. Decorated knight Order St. John Jerusalem, officer of Can., Order Can. Fellow Royal Soc. Arts (Eng.), Patent Inst. Can.; mem. Canadian, Calgary bar assns., Law Soc. Alta. Presbyn. Clubs: Ranchmen's, Calgary, Calgary Golf and Country. Home: Calgary Alta. Can. Died Jan. 11, 1975.

HASKELL, DUANE HEDRICK, music educator, univ. dean; b. St. Louis, Sept. 8, 1905; s. Dr. Claude D. and Mabel L. (Hedrick) H.; Mus.B., Ill. Wesleyan U., 1926; Mus.M., Eastman Sch. Music, 1945; Ph.D., Ind. U., 1951; spl. violin study with William Kritch, Louis Siegel; m. Laura A. Kerr, Dec. 21, 1932; children—James C., Ellen S. Recital appearances central Ill., 1922-26; mem. Bloomington (Ill.) Philharmonic, Rochester Philharmonic, 1926-31; faculty Rochester pub. schs., 1929-45, dir. instrumental music East High Sch., Rochester, 1930-45; head music dept. No. Mich. Coll., Marquette, 1945-49; teaching fellow, vis. prof. Ind. U., 1949-51; chmn. grad. and undergrad. music edn. dept. Chgo. Musical Coll., 1951-53, also dean summer sch.; dean Coll. Fine Arts, Ark. State U., State College, 1965-74. Founder, condr. No. Tri-City Symphony, Marquette, Mich., 1947-49. Mem. Am. String Tchrs. Assn. (founder, 1st pres. 1947-50; Distinguished Service award 1969), Music Tchrs. Nat. Assn. (pres. 1957-59), Phi Delta Kappa, Phi Mu Alpha. Mem. Christian Ch. Mason (Shriner). Home: Jonesboro, Ark. Died Mar. 29, 1974.

HASKELL, REUBEN L., lawyer; b. Bklyn., Oct. 5, 1878; s. Robert B. and Monrovia (Grayson) H.; student N.Y. Law Sch., 1896-97; LL.B., Cornell U. Coll. of Law, 1898; m. Aleda C. Baylis, Oct. 8, 1902; children—Louise C., Roger. Admitted to N.Y. bar, 1899; counsel to county clk., Kings County, 1908, 1909; borough sec., Brooklyn, 1910-13; dep. commr. pub. works, for Borough of Brooklyn, 1914; del. Rep. Nat. Convs., 1908 and 1920; former mem. Rep. State Com., N.Y.; Rep. candidate for Congress, 1912 (defeated); mem. 64th to 66th Congresses (1915-19), 10th N.Y. Dist.; judge Kings County, N.Y., 1920-25; transit commr., State of N.Y., N.Y. City, 1932-42; resumed practice of law, 1943, at 66 Court St., Brooklyn, N.Y. Former member New York National Guard; veteran of Spanish-American War. Member American, N.Y. State and Brooklyn bar assns., Arion Singing Society, Veterans Association of 13th Regiment, New York National Guard, Soc. of Old Brooklynites, Royal Arcanum and Past Regents Assn., Delta Chi. Mason (K.T.). Odd Fellow, Elk, K.P., Moose, Knights of Pythias. Home: Brooklyn, N.Y.†

HASSEL, KARL ELMER, radio exec., engr.; b. Sharon, Pa., Jan. 25, 1896; s. Charles and Mary Alice (Lunn) H.; student Westminster Coll., 1914-15, U. Pitts., 1916-18; m. Mildred Josephine Finn, Jan. 12, 1926. Organized Chgo. Radio Lab., 1919, consol. with Zenith Radio Corp., 1923, asst. v.p., dir., sec.; sec. Zenith Radio Corp. Cal. Mem. I.E.E.E. Home: Elmhurst, Ill. Died July 8, 1975.

HASSETT, WILLIAM D., ex-sec. to President; b. Northfield, Vt., Aug. 28, 1880; s. David and Mary A. (Burke) H.; student Clark University, 1902-04, honorary A.M., 1945; Litt.D., Norwich University, 1946. Reporter Burlington (Vt.) Free Press; newspaper work in Washington, 1909-21; Washington Post, 1909-11, Associated Press, 1911-15, Washington Post, 1915-21; also served during this period at different times as Washington correspondent of the Cincinnati Enquirer and the New York Telegram; in London, 1921-25; as correspondent for Philadelphia Public Ledger covered rebellion against Irish Free State and adoption of the Free State Constitution, 1921-24; for the Associated Press, covered Internat. Conference held in London to put Dawes plan into effect, 1924; with Nat. Recovery Adminstrn., Nat. Emergency Council, Washington, 1933-35; detailed to White House, 1935; sec. to the President by appointment of President Franklin D. Roosevelt, Feb. 19, 1944. At Warm Springs, Ga., on Apr. 12, 1945, announced death of President Roosevelt. Apptd. sec. to President Harry S. Truman, Apr. 16, 1945. Dir. Franklin D. Roosevelt Memorial Found., Inc.; hon. mem. F.D. Roosevelt Warm Springs (Ga.) Memorial Commn., rep. State of Vt., by apptmt. Gov. Ernest W. Gibson of Vt. Trustee Norwich U.; dir. Mayo Meml. Hosp. Northfield, Vt. Mem. Vermont Hist. Soc. Catholic. Clubs: Cosmos (bd. management), Nat. Press (Washington), Author: The President Was My Boss; contbr. nat. publs. Address: Washington, D.C.†

HATATHLI, NED, coll. pres.; b. Coalmine, Ariz., Oct. 11, 1923; s. Nez and Rena Adson (Willie) H.; B.S. with distinction, No. Ariz. U., 1951; student U. Colo., 1969, Haskell Inst., Lawrence, Kan., 1946-47; LL.D. (hon.), Eastern Mich. U., 1971; m. Florence Smiley, Oct. 23, 1947; children—Gloria Jean (Mrs. Leonard N. Begaye), Janice Carol (Mrs. Mervyn L. Hillis), Glenna Bah, Edison Kim. Mgr. Navajo Tribal Arts and Crafts Guild, Window Rock, Ariz., 1951-55; mem. council coms. Navajo Tribal Council, 1955-60, Window Rock; dir. resources div. Navajo Tribe, Window Rock, 1960-67;

edn. specialist Navajo Irrigation Project, Farmington, N.M., 1967-68; exec. v.p. Navajo Community Coll., Many Farms, Ariz., 1968-69, pres., 1969-72. Mem. spl. subcom. Indian edn. Nat. Council Indian Opportunity, 1970; mem. nat. Indian adv. com. Am. Indian Law Center, Albuquerque, 1970; rep. edn. Western States Regional Manpower Adv. Com., 1971; mem. Task Force Edn. and Tng. Minority Bus. Enterprises, 1971. Vice pres. Kit Carson council Boy Scouts Am., 1970-72. Bd. dirs. Navajo Forest Products Enterprises, Rough Rock Demonstration Sch., Chinle, Ariz. Served with USNR, 1943-45. Recipient Silver Beaver award Boy Scouts Am., 1964; Indian Achievement award, 1971; Indian Council Fire Achievement award Nat. Park Service, 1971. Mem. Nat. Indian Edn. Assn. (dir.), Dine Bi Olta Assn., Phi Kappa Phi. Author papers in field. Home: Many Farms, Ariz. Died Oct. 16, 1972; interred Coalmine Mesa, Ariz.

HATCH, ALDEN, author, journalist, historian; b. N.Y.C., Sept. 26, 1898; s. Frederic Horace and May Palmer (Daly) H.; student Horace Mann Sch., 1912-13, U. Chgo. Extension, 1918-20, Blackstone Inst., 1919-21; m. Ruth Brown, Dec. 28, 1932; 1 son, Alden Denison; m. 2d, Allene Pomeroy Gaty, Sept. 9, 1950. Author (novels): Gaming Lady, 1931; Glass Walls, 1933; Bridlewise, 1941; (biographies) Glenn Curtiss, 1942; Heroes of Annapolis, 1943; Young Willkie, 1944; General Ike, 1944, rev., enlarged edit. 1952; Franklin D. Roosevelt, 1947; Woodrow Wilson, 1948; General Patton, 1950; Red Carpet for Mamie, 1954; (histories): American Express, 1950; Full Tilt (with Foxhall P. Keene), 1938; Son of the Smoky Sea, Back to the Smoky Sea (with Nutchuck), 1941; Ambassador Extraordinary (Clara Boothe Luce), 1956; Remington Arms in American History, 1956; Crown of Glory (with Seamus Walshe), 1957; For the Life of Me (with Robert Briscoe), 1958; The Wadsworths of the Genesee, 1959; The Miracle of the Mountain, 1959; The Circus Kings (with Henry Ringling North), 1960; The DeGaul Nobody Knows, 1960; First Lady Extraordinary: Edith Bolling Wilson, 1961; Bernhard, Prince of the Netherlands, 1962; A Man Named John: Pope John XXIII, 1963; The Mountbattens, 1965; Apostle on the Move: Pope Paul VI, 1966; (with Krishna Nehru Hertheesing) We Nehrus, 1967; The Byrds of Virginia, 1969; The Lodges of Massachusetts, 1973; Buckminster Fuller at Home in the Universe, 1974. Editor: Thank You Twice, 1941. Contbr. articles polit., mil., naval and sporting events and personalities to nat. Mem. P.E.N. Republican. Episcopalian. Clubs: Rockaway Hunting (Cedarhurst, L.I.); Overseas Press. Home: Sarasota, Fla. Died Feb. 1, 1975.

HATCH, JOHN FLETCHER, naval officer; b. St. Albans, Vt., Dec. 22, 1879. Commd. ensign, U.S. Navy, 1901, and advanced through the grades to rear admiral, 1942; formerly dist. supply officer, 12th Naval Dist., San Francisco. Address: San Francisco, Cal.†

HATCHER, WIRT HARGROVE, tobacco exec.; b. Richmond, Va., Aug. 13, 1894; s. Peter Boisseau and Verbie A. (Hargrove) H.; student pub. schs., Richmond; m. Mary L. Partin, Feb. 17, 1919 (dec.); 1 son, Wirt Hargrove; m. 2d, Grace M. Trevvett, Aug. 25, 1950. With Tobacco Products Corp., 1913-24; with Philip Morris & Co., Ltd., Inc., 1924-73, v.p., 1937-57, sr. v.p., 1957-62, Sr. leaf cons., 1962-73, dir., 1962-73; dir. State-Planters Bank & Trust Co., Richmond, also Crawford Mfg. Co., Spotless Co., Benson & Hedges, Inc., N.Y. Clubs: Commonwealth, Country (Richmond). Home: Richmond, Va. Died Oct. 11, 1973.

HATHAWAY, LESTER GORDON, baking co. exec.; b. Bath, Me., Feb. 21, 1878; s. Charles F. and Carrie T. Hastings; grad. Cambridge Manual Training Sch.; married; 1 son, Kendall Gordon. With C. F. Hathaway & Sons, 1898-1925; v.p. Hathaway Baking Co. from 1926. Trustee Cambridge Y.M.C.A. Republican. Conglist. Mason (Shriner). Clubs: Reciprocity, Middlesex; Baker's (New York). Home: Cambridge, Mass.†

HATHWAY, CALVIN SUTLIFF, museum curator; b. Lockport, N.Y., July 4, 1907; s. Rev. Harry St. Clair and Jean (Groo) H.; grad. Episcopal Acad., 1925; A.B., Princeton, 1930; grad. student Harvard, 1930-31, N.Y.U., 1933-34. Asst. Phila. Mus. Art, 1930, sec. to dir., editor, 1931-32, charge dept. decorative arts and editor, 1932-33; asst. curator Cooper Union Mus., N.Y.C., 1933-34, asso. curator, 1934-42, curator, 1946-51, dir., 1951-63; R. Wistar Harvey curator decorative arts Phila. Museum of Art, 1964-73, emeritus, 1973-74; research asso. Henry Francis du Pont Winterthur Mus., 1964-68. Mem. fine arts com. for the White House, 1961-68. Served from pvt. to capt. AUS, 1942-46, mil. govt. monuments, fine arts and archives sect., 1943-46. Decorated Delaware Medal (Sweden), 1938; Bronze Star medal (U.S.), 1945; recipient traveling fellowship Am.-Scandinavian Found., 1935. Mem. Centre International d'Etude des Textiles Anciens (v.p.: Am. corr.), Internat. Inst. Conservation of Historic and Artistic Works, Inter-Soc. Color Council, Soc. Colonial Wars, S.R., Mil. Order Loyal Legion; Benjamin Franklin fellow Royal Soc. Arts (London). Club: Century Association (N.Y.C.). Home: Philadelphia, Pa. Died July 10, 1974; interred St. Thomas Episcopal Ch. Cemetery, Whitemarsh, Pa.

HAUKE, ROBERT CHARLES, lawyer; b. Detroit, Aug. 22, 1924; s. Gilbert Francis and Helen Irene (Stenner) H.; B.A., U. Mich., 1949; J.D., Wayne State U., 1960; m. Juanita V. Viau, July 10, 1948; children—David, Dennis, Dale. Tech. writer Douglas Aircraft Co., Santa Monica, Cal., 1950-55; patent agt. Hauke & Hardesty, Detroit, 1955-60; admitted to Mich. bar, 1961; patent atty., sr. partner Hauke, Gifford, Patalidis, & Dumont P.C., Lathrup Village, 1961-74; pres. Positive Transmission, Inc. Mem. Southfield Parent-Youth Guidance Commn., 1965-71, chmn., 1969-70. Bd. dirs., sec. Southfield Little League Baseball, Inc., 1961-66. Mem. State Bar Mich. (chmn. patent sect. 1967) Am., Livingston County, Southfield (dir. 1967-74) bar assns., Mich. Patent Law Assn., U.S. Trademark Assn., World Peace Through Law Center. Home: Holly, Mich. Died Sept. 27, 1975.

HAUSSERMANN, OSCAR WILLIAM, lawyer; b. Indpls., June 13, 1888; s. Christian John and Caroline (Burkhardt) H.; grad. Phillips Exeter Acad., 1908; A.B. Harvard, 1912, LL.B., 1916; J.D. (hon.), Suffolk U., 1966; D.C.L. (hon), Franklin Pierce Coll., 1967; m. Eleanor Rodman Drinker, Jan. 28, 1918; children—Oscar William, Caroline. Practiced law, Boston, 1916—; admitted to Mass. bar, 1919; partner Ropes, Gray, Boyden & Perkins, 1930-39, Haussermann, Davison & Shattuck, 1939-75; lectr. on bus. law Mass. Inst. Tech., 1921-30. Past v.p. Mass. UN Assn.; former chmn. Warrant Com. Town of Milton; gen. chmn. Greater Boston Emergency Campaign, 1935; former v.p., dir. Community Fedn. of Boston; former pres. New Eng. Alumni Assn. Phillips-Exeter Acad., Nat. Alumni Assn. Phillips-Exeter Acad., Boston C. of C.; hon. dir. Am. Research and Devel. Corp.; dir. Income and Capital Shares, Inc.; trustee Charity of Edward Hopkins (Harvard), The Chase Fund of Boston, Shareholdres' Trust of Boston. Commd. 2d lt. Plattsbury (N.Y.) Training Camp., 1917; 1st lt. 301st Machine Gun Batt., 76th Div.; personnel, later actg. adj. 1st Div. Machine Gun Regt. A.E.F., World War I Mem. Am. Mass., Boston bar Assns., Am. Bar Found., Mass. Com. Catholics, Protestants and Jews (past chmn.) Republican. Clubs: DU, Hasty Pudding (Harvard); Somerset, Harvard, Union (Boston). Contbr. legal articles. Home: Milton, Mass. Died Apr. 19, 1975.

HAUSSLER, ARTHUR GLENN, univ. adminstr.; b. Milw., Sept. 29, 1899; s. Arthur August and Mae (Reinhart) H.; LL.B., Ill. Wesleyan U., 1923, LL.D., 1954; B.E., Ill. State Normal U., 1939; M.A., N.Y. U., 1941; student U. Chgo., Northwestern U., U. Wis., So. Meth. U., U. Ill.; m. Helen Bentley, June 22, 1926. Tchr., athletic dir. Twp. High Sch., Pontiac, Ill., 1923-25, Community High Sch., Pekin, Ill., 1925-41, prin., 1941-45, West High Sch., Aurora, Ill., 1945-50; exec. v.p., sec. trustee Bradley U., Peoria, 1950-68, exec. sec. univ., 1968-74, also dir. deferred giving. Mem. Olympic Canoe Com.; mem. scholarship com. Nat. Assn. Tobacco Distbrs.; exec. sec. Estate Planners Council Central Ill., 1960. Bd. dirs. U.S. Olympic Com., 1956-65, Inst. Phys. Medicine. Named to Ill. Athletes Hall of Fame, Ill. Basketball Hall of Fame; recipient Gold Top Cane award Peoria Advt. and Selling Club; commendation Ill. Ho. of Reps., 1973. Mem. Ill. Assn. Health and Phys. Edn. (pres. 1945), No. Ill. High Sch. Conf. (pres. 1949), Am. Arbitration Assn., Estate Planners Assn., Assn. Commerce, Alpha Phi Omega, Phi Delta Kappa, Omicron Delta Kappa, Sigma Chi, Phi Delta Phi, Pi Kappa Delta. Mason. Clubs: Aurora Rotary (hon.), Pekin Rotary (pres.), Pekin Country, Town and Gown. Contbr. feature articles Chgo. Daily News, 1935-41. Home: Peoria, Ill. Died Sept. 5, 1974.

HAUTECOEUR, LOUIS, museum adminstr.; b. Paris, France, June 11, 1884; s. Albert and Jeanne (Barrault) H.; student Ecole Normale Superieure, 1905-08, Ecole Francaise de Rome, 1908-1910; Dr.esL., U. Paris, 1912; m. Marcelle Poullain Mar. 31, 1889 (dec. 1952); children—Claude, Solange; m. 2d, Marguerite Milliez, Mar. 14, 1956. Researcher on N. Africa Ministry Edn., 1909; on Tunisia, for Acad. of Inscriptions, 1909; prof. French Inst., St. Petersburg, 1912-13; head Diplomatic Information Service, Lugano, Switzerland, 1917-18; mem. com. information Peace Conf., 1919; del. League Nations Commn. for Intellectual Co-operation, 1924; prof. Faculty Arts, Caen, France, 1919-22; mus. curator, prof. Ecole du Louvre, 1920-40; prof. Ecole Nationale Superieure des Beaux Arts, 1923-40; sec.-gen. beaux arts de la France, counsellor of state, 1940-44; curator fine arts, Geneva, also prof. Geneva U., 1946-49; permanent sec. Acad. Beaux-Arts, 1955-64; dir.-gen. Fine Arts Egypt, 1927-30; curator Luxemburg Mus., 1928-40; dir. works art Paris Exhbn., 1937; dir. biennial exhbns., Venice, 1932, 34, 36, 38. Decorate comdr. Legion of Honor. Mem. Inst. France, Acad. de Saint Luc, Rome, Acad. Royale de Belgique, Acad. d'Architecture. Home: Paris, France. Died Nov. 17, 1973.

HAUXHURST, HENRY AUSTIN, lawyer; b. Bay City, Mich., May 11, 1881; s. John Walker and Mary (Fox) H.; B.S., Princeton, 1902; LL.B., Harvard, 1905; m. Vevia Sutton, Feb. 26, 1925. Admitted to Ohio bar, 1906 practiced in Cleveland. Served as civilian, Naval Intelligence, World War I; chmn. Alien Enemy Bd., No. Dist. Ohio, 1942-45; a prosecutor War Crimes Trials, Japan, 1945-46. Mem. Am. Law Inst., Am. and Cleveland (past pres.) bar assns. Clubs: Union, Tavern, Pepper Pike, University, Mayfield (Cleveland). Home: Cleveland, O.†

HAWES, AUSTIN FOSTER, forester; b. Danvers, Mass., Mar. 17, 1879; s. Frank M. and Harriet (Foster) H.; A.B., Tufts Coll., 1901; M.F., Yale, 1903; M.S., Tufts Coll., 1936; m. Alice May Clapp, June 27, 1908 (died Nov. 2, 1917); children—Elizabeth (dec.), Laura (dec.). In U.S. Forest Service, 1901-04; state forester, Conn., 1904-09; state forester, Vt. and prof. forestry, U. of Vermont, 1909-17; specialist in forestry, U.S. Dept. of Agr., 1917; in charge of wood fuel branch U.S. Fuel Adminstrn., 1918; forest economist, U.S. Forest Service, 1919-20; state forester of Conn., 1921-1944; consultant Soc. Am. Foresters, 1945. Fellow Soc. of Am. Foresters; mem. Zeta Psi; former pres. Nat. Assn. of State Foresters, 1927. Clubs: University (Hartford); Cosmos (Washington, D.C.); Appalachian. Author: (with R. C. Hawley) Forestry in New England, 1912. Home: West Hartford, Conn.†

HAWK, EUGENE BLAKE, educator; b. Blountsville, Tenn., Sept. 6, 1881; s. H. D. and Sarah Emma H.; grad. Holston Inst., Blountville, Tenn., 1900; A.B., Emory and Henry Coll., Emory, Va., 1930; B.D., Vanderbilt U., Nashville, Tenn., 1909; D.D., Asbury Coll., Wilmore, Ky., 1926, Southern Meth. U., 1928, Boston Univ., 1939; LL.D., McMurry Coll., 1935; LL.D., Emory and Henry College, Emory, Va., 1943; m. Dora Lee Patterson, Apr. 9, 1912 (died Dec. 8, 1918); children—Hiram Patterson, Richard Blake; m. 2d, Amanda B. Hawkins, July 27, 1920; 1 son, Riddell Lee. Ordained ministry Meth. Ch., 1911; pastor Polytechnic Ch., Fort Worth, 1916-20, First Ch., Temple, Tex., 1920-22; presiding elder Waxahachie dist., 1922-25; pastor First Ch., Fort Worth, 1925-31, Fourth Av. Ch., Louisville, Ky., 1931-33; dean Perkins Sch. of Theology, prof. homiletics and ministerial efficiency, Southern Meth. U., from 1933, v.p., Univ., acting pres., 1938-39, adminstrative v.p., from 1939. Mem. gen. confs., 1922, 26, 30, 34, 38, 40, 44, Uniting Conf., 1939 and South Central Jurisdictional Conf., 1940. Served as trustee Texas Woman&23s Coll., Ft. Worth. Southern Meth. U., Meth. Hosp., Fort Worth; pres. Gen. Bd. Ch. Extension, Conf. Bd. of Edn.; chmn. exec. com. United Tex. Drys. Pres. Meth. Assn. of Theol. Schs., 1943-44. Vice-pres. and mem. exec. com., Am. Assn. Theol. Schs., 1948. Mem. exec. com. from 1946. Clubs: Town and Gown, Rotary. Home: Dallas, Tex.†

HAWKES, ALBERT WAHL, former U.S. senator; b. Chgo., Nov. 20, 1878; s. Moses A. and Louise Restieaux (Starrett) H.; LL.B., Chgo. Coll. of Law (Lake Forest U.), 1900; student Lewis Inst., 1914-15; degree of Doctor of Civil Laws and Honorary Chancellor conferred by Union College, 1946; married Frances Olive Whitfield, May 15, 1901; children—Louise R. (Mrs. Morgan G. Padelford), A Whitfield (Med. Corps, U.S. Army; died in Goodenough Island, Southwest Pacific, Dec. 17, 1943). Began as office boy and clerk, 1894; director of sales General Chem. Co., 1916-18, v.p., 1918-23, exec. v.p., 1923-26; v.p. Wing & Evans, sales agents for Solvay Process Co., 1921-26—32 yrs. with Nichols Chem. Co., Gen. Chem. Co. and Allied Chem. & Dye Corp., 1894-1926; pres. Congoleum-Nairn, Inc., 1926-Dec. 1942, chmn. bd. 1937-51; past pres. Congoleum Canada, Ltd.; dir. and mem. exec., Technicolor Inc.; past dir. Michael Nairn & Greenwich, Ltd. (London); U.S. Senator from New Jersey for term expiring 1949. Formerly mem. N.J. State Labor Mediation Bd.; formerly chmn. N.J. State Com. for Sale of Defense Bonds and Stamps; formerly mem. adv. council for Nat. Defense, Trenton. Hon. chmn. British War Relief Soc., Inc., Montclair Com. Formerly pres. U.S. Chamber of Commerce; v.p., dir. and mem. exec. com. N.J. State Chamber of Commerce; mem. N.J. Sons Am. Revolution (Montclair Chapter). Dir. The Chemical Alliance, Washington, 1917-18. Episcopalian. Clubs: Union League, Economic, Kiwanis (New York); Montclair (N.J.) Golf; Essex (Newark); Metropolitan (Washington). Interested in preserving the form of govt. of U.S. and making known the truth about individual rights and the Am. Free Enterprise System. Home: Montclair, N.J.†

HAWKINS, WILLIAM BRUCE, physician; b. Springfield, Mass., July 5, 1900; s. James Alexander and Susan (Bruce) H.; M.D., Johns Hopkins, 1927; m. Doris Hawkins, June 1929 (dec. Sept. 1930); 1 son, William B.; m. 2d, Phyllis Claire Hanson, May 11, 1947; children—Susan Blair, Jean Grant. Asst. in pathology Balt. City Hosps., 1927-28, resident in pathology, 1928-29; asst. in pathology Johns Hopkins Hosp., 1928-29; instr. pathology U. Rochester (N.Y.), 1929-31, asst. prof., 1931-34, asso. prof., 1934-57, prof., 1957-71. Recipient Gold Medal award U. Rochester Alumni Assn., 1954. Dr. Henry C. and Bertha H. Buswell U. Rochester Faculty fellow, 1956-71. Diplomate Am. Bd. Pathology. Mem. Am. Assn. Pathologists and Bacteriologists, A.A.A.S., Rochester Pathol. Soc., Am. Soc. Exptl. Pathologists. Sigma Xi, Alpha Omega Alpha. Contbr. articles to profl. jours. Research in area of liver disease, effect of diet in bile fistula dogs, cause of bleeding in bile fistula dogs. Home: Rochester, N.Y. Died Feb. 4, 1971; cremated.

HAWLEY, MARGARET FOOTE, miniature painter; b. Guilford, Conn., June 12, 1880; d. Christopher Spencer and Hannah (Hubbard) Foote; after death of parents adopted by uncle, U.S. Senator Joseph R. Hawley; prep. edn., high sch., Washington, D.C.; student Corcoran Sch. of Art (gold medal for best drawings from life, 1900); pupil of Howard Helmick, Georgetown, D.C.; studied at Atelier Colarossi, Paris, 2 summers. Miniature painter and painter of small portraits. Awarded medal of honor. Pa. Soc. Minature Painters, 1918; Lea prize, Pa. Acad. Fine Arts, Phila., 1920; Charlotte Ritchie Smith Memorial prize, Baltimore Water Color Club, 1925; bronze medal, Sesquicentennial Expn., Philadelphia, 1926; Levantia White Boardman memorial prize, Am. Soc. Miniature Painters, 1931; medal, Nat. Assn. Women Painters and Sculptors, 1931; medal, Brooklyn Soc. Minature Painters, 1931. Represented in collections of Metropolitan Museum Art (N.Y. City), Brooklyn Museum and Concord (Mass.) Arts Assns., Corcoran Gallery of Art. Mem. Am. Soc. Miniature Painters, Pa. Soc. Miniature Painters, Royal Miniature Soc., London. Clubs: Cosmopolitan (New York). Address: New York City, N.Y.†

HAWLEY, RANSOM SMITH, educator; b. Ludington, Mich., Apr. 23, 1881; s. Smith and Gertrude (Shaffer) H.; B.S. in Engring., U. of Mich., 1907, M.E., 1915; m. Lois Maude Marsden, Dec. 25, 1907; children—Lelia Margaret (Mrs. Earl LeVeck), Dorothy Marian (Mrs. Albert Edward Bowles), Evelyn Winifred (Mrs. Lawrence A. Comstock), Ransom Smith Jr. Instructor Grinnell Coll., 1907-09, assistant professor, 1909-10; assistant professor mech. engring. Colo. Sch. Mines, 1910-12, prof. and head dept., 1912-17; prof. mech. engring., U. of Mich. from 1917, chmn. dept., from 1940; cons. engr. Mem. Am. Soc. Mech. Engrs., Detroit Engrs. Soc., Tau Beta Pi, Phi Kappa Phi, Triangles, Sigma Rho Tau. Clubs: Exchange, U. of Mich. Alumni. University. Methodist. Cons. editor, Heating, Piping and Air Conditioning. Home: Ann Arbor, Mich.†

HAWTREY, SIR, RALPH GEORGE, economist; b. Slough, Eng., Nov. 22, 1879; s. George Procter and Eda (Strahan) H.; student Eton and Trinity Coll., Cambridge, England, honorary fellow, 1959; Doctor of Science (hon.), London University; m. Hortense Emilia d'Aranyi, Apr. 24, 1915 (dec. 1953). Ofcl. British Treasury, 1904-44; vis. prof. Harvard, 1928-29; Henry Price prof. Royal Inst. Internat. Affairs, 1947-52. Fellow Brit. Acad.; mem. Royal Econ. Soc. (pres. 1946-48), Am. Acad. Arts and Scis. (fgn. hon.). Author: A Century of Bank Rate, 1938; Towards the Rescue of Sterling, 1954; Cross Purposes in Wage Policy, 1955; The Pound at Home and Abroad, 1963. Address: London, England.†

HAXO, HENRY EMILE, educator; b. France, Aug. 7, 1881; s. Gustave Ernest and Marie Catherine (Ruth) H.; A.B., Stanford U., 1910, A.M., 1911; summer student U. of Calif., 1908-09; Ph.D., U. of Chicago, 1913; m. Florence Josephine Shull, Aug. 1, 1916; children—Henry, Francis, Mary, John, Ruth. Came to U.S., 1902, naturalized, 1916. Teaching asst. in French and Spanish, Stanford, 1910-11; asst. prof. in French and Spanish, U. of Mont., 1913-18; asso. prof. Romance langs. U. of N.D., 1918-21, prof. and head dept. form 1921, head German dept., 1948; prof. of French, U. of Chicago, summer 1927. Mem. Am. Assn. Teachers of French, Phi Beta Kappa. Conglist. Author: Denis Piramus, La Vie Seint Edmunt, 1915; Elementary French Reader, 1936; Intermediate French Reader, 1937; Images de la France, 1946. Editor: Le Masque de Fer (Dumas), 1938; La Maison de Penarvan (Sandeau), 1940. Contbr. to lang. jours. Address: Grand Forks, N.D.†

HAYAKAWA, SESSUE, (KINTARO HAYAKAWA), Japanese film actor; b. Naaura Twp., Honshu, Japan, June 10, 1890; s. Yoichoro and Kane Hayakawa; grad. Naval Prep. Sch. (Tokyo); 1908; grad. polit. sci. U. Chgo., 1913; m. Tsura Aoki, May 1, 1914 (dec. Oct. 1961); children—Yukio, Yoshiko, Fujiko. Actor, dir. Japanese theatre; 1913; motion picture debut in Hollywood prodn. Typhoon, 1914, other roles in Wrath of Gods, 1914, Hashimura Togo, City of Dim Faces, Call of the East, Hidden Faces; formed Haworth Corp., 1918, merged with Roberts & Cole, 1920; producer motion pictures The Swamp, Vermilion Pencil, Daughter of the Dragon, 1931; actor motion pictures Yoshiwara (France), 1937, Tokyo Joe, 1949, Three Came Home, 1950, Bridge Over the River Kwai, 1957, Geisha Boy, 1958; actor on stage in the Love City, Bandit Prince (vaudeville), Honorable Mr. Wong (Tokyo), role of Claudius in Hamlet (Tokyo), 1934; prod. play Life of Buddha, Tokyo, 1949; appeared TV prodns. Judge Internat. Film Festival, Venice, 1947. Ordained Zen Buddhist priest. Recipient Golden Globe award Hollywood Fgn. Press Assn., 1957; nominated best supporting actor Acad. Award, 1957. Author: The Bandit Prince. Address: New York City, N.Y. Died 1973.

HAYDEN, CARL (TRUMBULL), former U.S. senator; b. Hayden's Ferry, now Tempe, Ariz., Oct. 2, 1877; s. Charles Trumbull and Sallie Calvert (Davis) H.; grad. Normal Sch. of Ariz., Tempe, 1896; attended Leland Stanford U., 1896-1900; LL.D., U. Ariz., 1948, Ariz. State U., 1959; m. Nan Downing, Feb. 14, 1908 (dec.). Mem. Tempe Town Council, 1902-04; treas. Maricopa County, 1904-06, sheriff, 1907-12; maj. inf., U.S.N.A., 1918; mem. Congress from riz. 1912-69; U.S. senator from Ariz. 1927-69, pres. pro tempore, 1957-69; specialized on legislation relating to irrigation of arid lands and fed. aid for hwys.; chmn. state com. on appropriations; mem. interior and insular affairs. com. Democrat. Mason. Home: Tempe, Ariz.†

HAYDEN, MERRILL A., former corp. exec., govt. ofcl.; b. New Albany, Ind., Jan. 16, 1913; s. Roy A. and Josephine (Warth) H.; B.E.E., U. Detroit, 1935; m. Evelyn M. Bradford, Oct. 10, 1936; children—Merrill A., Kathleen, Susan. With Vickers, Inc., 1935-68, successively engr., various engring., sales, mgmt. positions, 1935-55, gen. mgr. Waterbury div., 1955-57, Machinery Hydraulics div., 1957-64, v.p., 1957-64; pres. Vickers, Inc., div. Sperry Rand Corp., Detroit, 1964-68; exec. v.p. Sperry Rand Corp., N.Y.C., 1968-71; dep. postmaster gen. U.S. Postal Service, 1971-72. Mem. Soc. Automotive Engrs., Am. Soc. Naval Engrs., Soc. Naval Architects and Marine Engrs., Nat. Sales Execs., Sales Execs. Club of Waterbury (pres. 1956). Clubs: Detroit Golf. Home: Birmingham, Mich. Died Aug. 7, 1974.

HAYDN, HIRAM, editor, author; b. Cleve., Nov. 3, 1907; s. Howell Merriman and Mary (Olmstead) H.; A.B., Amherst Coll., 1928; A.M., Western Res. U., 1938, Litt. D., 1963; Ph.D., Columbia, 1942; m. Rachel Hutchinson Norris, Sept. 14, 1935; 1 dau., Mary Rachel; m. 2d, Mary Wescott Tuttle, June 5, 1945; children—Michael Wescott, Jonathan Olmstead, Miranda Merriman. Instr. Hawken Sch. Cleve., 1928-41; lectr. in English, Cleve. Coll., Western Res. U., 1939-41; asst. prof. English, Woman's Coll., U. N.C., 1942-43, asso. prof., 1943-44; exec. sec. United Chpts. Phi Beta Kappa, 1944-45; asso. editor Crown Publishers, 1945, editor-in-chief, 1948-50; N.Y. editor Bobbs-Merrill Co., 1950-54; sr. editor Random House, 1955-56, editor-in-chief, 1956-59; mem. exec. com. Atheneum Pubs., 1959-64; co-pub. Harcourt, Brace Javanovich Inc., Phila., 1964-73. With New Sch. for Social Research, 1947-60; vis. prof. communications U. Pa., 1965-66, prof. communications, Annenberg Sch. Communications, 1966. Fellow Center Advanced Studies, Wesleyan U., 1964. Lang. Assn., Am. Assn. U. Profs., Phi Beta Kappa, Alpha Delta Phi. Editor: the Am. Scholar, 1944-73; co-editor: Explorations in Living: a record of the democratic spirit, 1941; A World of Great Stories, 1947; The Makers of the American Tradition series, 1953-73; A Renaissance Treasury, 1954; The Papers of Christian Gauss, 1957; also The American Scholar Reader, 1960. Editor: The Portable Elizabethan Reader, 1946; The Twentieth Century Library series, 1946-73. Author: By Nature Free, 1943; Manhattan Furlough, 1945; The Time Is Noon, 1948; The Counter Renaissance, 1950; The Hands of Esau, 1962; Report from the Red Windmill, 1967. Home: Philadelphia, Pa. Died Dec. 2, 1973.

HAYDON, ALBERT EUSTACE, prof. history of religions, author; b. Brampton, Ont., Can., Jan. 17, 1880; s. Albert Edward and Sarah Ann (Coggins) H.; student Shurtleff Coll., Alton, Ill., 1897-98; A.B., McMaster U. of Toronto, Can., 1901, B.Th., 1903, M.A., 1907, B.D., 1906; Ph.D., University of Chicago, 1918; m. Edith Elizabeth Jones, December 28, 1904; children—Harold Emerson, Edward Morgan, Brownlee Walker. Came to U.S. to reside, 1916. Ordained to ministry of Bapt. Ch., 1903; pastor Dresden, Ont., 1903-04, Ft. William, Ont., 1904-09, First Bapt. Ch.. Saskatoon, Saskatchewan, 1911-13; gen. sec. Y.M.C.A., Saskatoon, 1913-16; pastor First Unitarian Ch., Madison, Wis., 1918-24; with dept. comparative religion U. Chgo., 1919-75, prof. since 1929, chmn. dept., 1921-45, emeritus, 1945-75. Fellow A.A.A.S.; member Am. Assn. Univ. Profs., Am. Oriental Soc., Chicago Ethical Soc. (leader). Club: Quadrangle (U. of Chicago). Author: The Quest of the Ages, 1929; Man's Search for the Good Life, 1937; Biography of the Gods, 1941. Home: Chicago, Ill. Died Apr. 1, 1975.

HAYES, EDWARD FRANCIS, investment banker; b. Cohoes, N.Y., Aug. 6, 1881; s. David and Mary Ann (Kerr) H.; student Egberts Inst., Cohoes, N.Y., 1896-99; A.B., Yale, 1905; LL.D., Fordham U., 1952. Exec. William Salomon & Co., 1905-20; v.p. Blair & Co., Inc., 1920-32; partner Glore, Forgan & Co., N.Y.C., investment bankers, from 1935; dir. Austin, Nichols & Co., Gen. Outdoor Advt. Co., North Am. Refractories Co., Petroleum Corp. Am. Fellow Morgan Library, N.Y.; lay bd. trustees Fordham U. Mem. Cardinal's Com. of Laity, N.Y.C. Adv. bd. Albertus Magnus Coll., New Haven; trustee Marymount Coll., Tarrytown, N.Y. Knight of Malta; Knight of Holy Sepulchre. Mem. Xavier Alumni Sodality (N.Y.C.), Yale Library Assos., Liturgical Arts Soc., Am. Irish, U.S. Cath. hist. socs. Clubs: Metropolitan, University, Yale, City Mid-day, Grolier (N.Y.C.). Home: New York City, N.Y.†

HAYES, HELEN HAYDEN, illustrator, designer; b. Chicago, July 3, 1881; d. Plymmon S. and Harriet (Hayden) H.; ed. pub. and pvt. schs., Chicago and Washington; Art Inst. and Art Acad., Chicago; studied under Roberto Rascovitch, Italy, and D. F. Bigelow, Chicago. Writer and illustrator Chicago Evening Post and Chicago Inter Ocean. Illustrated Cradel Songs of Many Nations, 1898; Singing Rhymes and Games, 1901; Four Piano Pieces, 1903; Ten Two-Voiced Melodies, 1902; The Song Valentines, 1907. Designer and originator of Her Memory Book, 1905 H1. Address: Champaign, Ill.†

HAYNES, CHARLES H(ENRY), banker, r.r. co. exec.; b. Ferry, N.C., Apr. 25, 1878; s. Raleigh Rutherford and Amanda Loretta (Carpenter) H.; student Baird's Mil. Sch. of Charlotte, Guilford Coll.; m. Sallie Catherine Culpepper, Apr. 4, 1945. Various positions Cliffside Mills, 1901-17, pres. 1917-45, chmn. bd., 1945-51, ret.; pres. Cliffside R.R. Co., 1917-45, chmn. bd. from 1945; v.p., dir. Haynes Bank of Cliffside, 1907-17, pres., 1917-52, chmn. bd. from 1952; dir. Cone Mills, Inc. Chmn. Cliffside Sch. Bd.; trustee Rutherford Hosp. Baptist. Mason. (Shriner). Clubs: Rutherford County (past pres.). Cleveland-Rutherford Execs.†

HAYS, ALBERT THEODORE, physician; b. St. Paul, Sept. 4, 1907; s. Albert Henry and Mary Alice (Collins) H.; M.D., U. Minn., 1933; m. Genevieve Jeanette Naylestad, Jan. 26, 1938; children—Thomas, Patricia Ann (Mrs. John Knaat), Mary (Mrs. John Schmitz). Intern, Mpls. Gen. Hosp., 1933-34; fellow in surgery U. Minn., 1934-38; practice medicine specializing in indsl. surgery, Mpls., 1937-69; active staff surgeon Northwestern Hosp., Mpls., also dir. emergency and outpatient services; cons. staff St. Mary's Hosp. Served to capt. M.C., AUS, 1943-46. Diplomate Am. Bd. Surgery. Fellow A.C.S.; mem. Hennepin County Med. Soc., Minn., Mpls. surg. socs., Mpls. Acad. Medicine, Minn. Acad. Occupational Medicine, Alpha Omega Alpha, Nu Sigma Nu. Republican. Roman Catholic. Clubs: Mpls. Athletic; Minnesota Valley Country. Home: Minneapolis, Minn. Died Nov. 6, 1972; buried Resurrection Cemetery, St. Paul, Minn.

HAYWARD, SUSAN, motion picture actress; b. Bklyn., June 30, 1919; d. Walter and Ellen (Pearson) Marrener; student pub. schs., Bklyn; m. Jesse Thomas Barker, 1944 (div.); children—Timothy and Gregory (twins); m. 2d, Floyd Eaton Chalkley, 1957. Photographer's model, 1937-38; under contract Warner Bros., 1939, Paramount Pictures, 1939-45, Walter Wangner, 1945-49, 20th Century Fox 1949; first motion picture appearance Beau Geste, 1939, other pictures include Hit Parade of 1943, Young and Willing, Fighting Seabees, 1944, And Now Tomorrow, Canyon Passage, Deadline at Dawn, 1946, The Lost Moment, 1946, Smash-Up, Tap Roots, Tulsa, 1949, House of Strangers, My Foolish Heart, David and Bathsheba, With a Song in My Heart, 1952, Snows of Kilimanjaro, 1952; I'll Cry Tomorrow, 1956; Conqueror, 1956; Top Secret Affair, 1957, I Want to Live, 1958; Thunder in the Sun, Women Obsessed, 1959; Marriage-Go-Around, 1961, Demetrius and the Gladiators, Garden of Evil, Untamed, Soldier of Fortune, The Conquered, Ada, Back Street, I Thank a Fool, Honey Pot, Where Love Has Gone, Valley of the Dolls. Named as one of two most popular motion picture stars, Foreign Press Assn. of Hollywood, 1952; Cannes Film Festival award, 1956; New York Film Critics award, best actress of year, 1958; Motion Picture Acad. award for best actress of 1959 for picture I Want to Live. Home: Los Angeles, Cal. Died Mar. 14, 1975.

HAZARD, ELMER CLARKE; b. New York, N.Y., Dec. 17, 1879; s. Edward Clarke and Florence A. (Frothingham) H.; Ph.G., New York Coll. Pharmacy, 1899; Ph.D., Columbia, 1900; M.D., U. of Md., 1903, Md. Med. Coll., 1904, U. of Algiers, 1905; Sc.D., Providence U., 1907; also "Dr. of Medicine," Persian Govt. and Soudan Govt.; m. Pearl A. White, June 25, 1907. Inherited wholesale grocery and mfg. business of C. E. Hazard & Co., New York, at one time the largest food products concern in the country; established The Dr. E. C. Hazard Diagnostic Lab., 1902, Hazard Chem. Co., 1907; mem. Elmer C. Hazard & Co., bankers, 1906-14; pres. E. C. Hazard & Co., Little Silver Sauce Co., Mercantile Trust Co., Hazard Mfg. Co., Dr. E. C. Hazard Lab.; owner Royal Sauce Co., Hazard Chem. Co.; trustee E. C. Hazard Hosp. (Long Branch, N.J.), Franklin Sq. Hosp. (Baltimore, Md.). Mem. A.M.A. Med. and Chirurg. Faculty of Md., Baltimore City Med. Soc., Am. Pharm. Assn. Soc. Chem. Industry, A.A.A.S., Kappa Psi. Democrat. Episcopalian. Home: Long Branch, N.J.†

HAZLET, STEWART E(MERSON), organic chemist, educator; b. Freeport, Ill., Feb. 4, 1910; s. Luther A. and Veretta M. (Voorhees) H.; A.B., U. Dubuque, 1931; M.S., U. Ia., 1933, Ph.D., 1935; m. Ann Louise Crow, Dec. 26, 1936 (dec.); children—Ruth (Mrs. William Kirk), Stewart (dec.), William. Instr. math. U. Dubuque, summer 1931; grad. asst. chem., U. Ia., 1931-35; instr. chemistry, George Washington U., 1935-36; instr. organic chemistry U. Ill., summer 1936; instr. chemistry Wash. State U., 1936-41, asst. prof., 1941-45, asso. prof., 1945-47, prof. chemistry, dean grad. sch., 1947-60, prof. organic chemistry, 1960-74; vis. asso. chemistry Cal. Inst. Tech., 1960-61; vis. scholar U. Cal. at Los Angeles, 1960-61; guest Mass. Inst. Tech., summer 1961. Bd. dirs. Wash. Div. Am. Cancer Soc., 1948-71, v.p., 1958, mem. exec. com., 1961-70, chmn. pub. edn. com., 1961-68. Fellow Ia. Acad. Sci., Am. Inst. Chemists, A.A.A.S.; mem. Am. Chem. Soc. (past chmn. and councilor, Wash.-Ida. border sect.), N.W. Sci. Assn. (past chmn. math.-physics-chem. sect.), N.Y. Acad. Sci., Internat. Platform Assn., Sigma Xi, Alpha

Chi Sigma, Phi Lambda Upsilon, Pi Kappa Delta. Contbr. articles in sci. and chem. jours. Specializes in organic chem. with spl. reference to aromatic compounds. Home: Riverside, Cal. Died Aug. 24, 1974.

HEAD, JEROME REED, physician, surgeon; b. Madison, Wis., May 9, 1893; s. Louis R. and Esther (Reed) H.; B.A., U. of Wis., 1914; M.A., U. of Ill., 1915; M.D., Harvard, 1922; m. Jean Milne, Dec. 16, 1922; children—Louis, Jerome, James, Charles, Stephen, Henry. Engaged in practice of medicine since 1926; interne Peter Bent Brigham Hosp., Boston, Mass., 1922-24; resident in surgery State of Wis. Gen. Hosp., 1924-26; vol. asst. surg. pathology Mayo Clinic, 1924; specialist diseases of thorax since 1927; med. dir. Edward Sanatorium, Naperville, Ill.; asso. prof. surgery, Northwestern U. Served as lt., F.A., A.E.F., 1917-19. Mem. A.M.A., Chgo. Surg. Soc., Am. Assn. Thoracic Surgery, Nat. Tuberculosis Assn., Chicago Tuberculosis Soc., Chi Psi, Nu Sigma Nu. Clubs: Tavern, University (Chgo.). Author: Politia Medici, 1953; Sonnets on Exegesis of Heraclitus and Empedocles, 1955; Lincoln-A Dramatic Poem, 1963; The History of The History of Philosophy. Home: Evanston, Ill. Died June 11, 1974; buried Albion, Wis.

HEALD, HENRY TOWNLEY, consultant; b. Lincoln, Neb., Nov. 8, 1904; s. Frederick De Forest and Nellie (Townley) H.; B.S., State Coll., Wash., 1923; M.S., U. Ill., 1925; D.Eng., Rose Poly. Inst., 1942, Clarkson Coll. Tech., 1948; LL.D., Northwestern U., 1942, Rutgers U., 1952, Columbia, 1954, Hofstra Coll., 1955, Fairleigh Dickinson Coll., 1955, Princeton, U. Pitts., 1956, U. N.Y., 1962, U. Ill., 1963, Ill. Inst. Tech., 1966; D.C.L., N.Y. U., 1956, Case Western Res. U., 1968; L.H.D., Rollins Coll., 1953, Pacific Luth. U., 1966, Brandeis U., 1966, Coll. Wooster, 1966; D.Sc. (hon.) Pratt Inst., 1954, Newark Coll. Engring., 1954, Union Coll., 1956; D.H.L., Cornell Coll., 1967; m. Muriel Starcher, Aug. 4, 1928, Asst. prof. to pres. Armour Inst. Tech., 1927-40; pres. Ill. Inst. Tech., Armour Research Found., Inst. Gas Tech., 1940-52; chancellor N.Y. U., 1952-56; pres., trustee The Ford Found., N.Y.C., 1956-65; partner Heald, Hobson & Assoss., N.Y.C., 1965-67; chmn. Heald, Hobson & Assos., Inc., 1967-71; Bd. trustees Rollins Coll., Winter Park, Fla. Recipient distinguished service awards Chgo. Jr. Assn. Commerce, 1940, Ill. Jr. C. of C., 1940; Navy award for distinguished civilian service, 1945; Washington award, 1952; Nat. Inst. Social Sci. medal, 1956; Hoover medal 1959; Distinguished Alumni Award Wash. State U., 1962; Alumni Honor award Coll. Engring. U. Ill., 1966; Albert Gallatin award N.Y. U., 1969. Chmn. Mayor's Com. (to reform) Chgo. Bd. Edn., 1946; trustee John Crerar Library, 1945-52; commr., vice chmn. Chgo. Land Clearance Commn., 1947-52; chmn. South Side Planning Bd., Chgo., 1946-52; trustee Town Hall, Inc., 1952-56; vice chmn. Mayor's Comm. for Better Housing, N.Y.C., 1954-56; commr. Nat. Commn. on Accrediting, 1950-56; chmn. N.Y. State Com. on Higher Edn., 1960. Mem. Am. Soc. Engring. End. (pres. 1942-43), A.A.A.S. (v.p. 1946-47), Am. Pub. Works Assn., Am. Soc. C.E., Am. Soc. M.E., Western Soc. Engrs. (pres. 1945-46), Nat. Acad. Engring., Tau Beta Pi. Sigma Tau, Phi Kappa Phi, Chi Epsilon, Theta Xi; also several hon. affiliations. Rotarian. Clubs: University (N.Y.C. and Winter Park); Commercial. Home: Winter Park, Fla., Died Nov. 23, 1975.

HEALY, DANIEL JOSEPH, sales exec.; b. West Chester, Pa., Sept. 3, 1896; s. John Henry and Mary Elizabeth (Corcoran) H.; student West Chester (Pa.) Bus. Coll., 1912-13, Drexel Inst., 1915-16; m. Margaret M. Marsh, May 25, 1957. With Spencer Kellogg & Sons, Inc., Phila., from 1916, v.p. charge Eastern div., from 1950; dir. Spencer, Kellogg and Sons, Incorporated, Buffalo, N.Y. Bd. dirs. Chester County Hosp., 1929-34; trustee Immaculata Coll. Mem. Oil Trades Assn., Nat. N.Y. paint, varnish and lacquer assns., Internat. Castor Oil Association (vice pres.), Linseed-Castorseed Assn. N.Y. (pres.), Newcomen Soc. N.A., Pa. Soc., Sales Execs. Club, N.Y. Clubs: Penn Athletic (Phila.); Aronimink Golf (Newton Sq., Pa.); West Chester (Pa.) Golf and Country; Uptown (N.Y.). Home: West Chester, Pa. Died Dec. 22, 1974; buried St. Agnes Cemetery, West Chester.

HEBBERD, JOHN BAILEY, educator; b. Lowell, Mass., Oct. 19, 1878; s. De Witt Clinton and Laura E. (Collins) H.; grad. English High Sch., Boston, 1898, Bridgewater (Mass.) State Normal Sch., 1906; A.B., Harvard, 1909, A.M., 1914; m. Ella Seaver Bagot, Dec. 31, 1910; 1 dau., Margaret. Prin. country sch., Hanover, Mass., 1900-02, grammar sch., Medford, Mass., 1909-10; teacher, high sch., Newton, Mass., 1910-13, head dept. mathematics, 1912-13; prin. evening high sch., Medford, 1910-11, Newton, 1911-12; asst. headmaster Dummer Acad., South Byfield, Mass., 1919-20; headmaster De Witt Clinton Hebberd Sch., Newton, from 1920. War camp community service, Montgomery, Ala., and Portsmouth, N.H., World War; dep. prison commr. and mem. Bd. of Parole and Advisory Bd. of Pardons 1913-16. Mem. N.E.A., Alumnus Harvard Grad. Sch. Edn. Assn. Republican. Episcopalian. Clubs: Charles River Country (Newton); University, Boston Art (Boston). Investigated probation system in Suffolk Co., Mass., for judges of Superior Court, 1913. Home: Newton, Mass.†

HECHT, WILBUR HUDSON, lawyer; b. N.Y.C., Apr. 25, 1905; s. Adolph and Charlotte (Tressel) H.; A.B., Colgate U., 1927; LL.B., Fordham U., 1930; m. Helen Willis, June 5, 1933; 1 dau., Barbara (Mrs. Arthur Hirst). Admitted N.Y. bar, 1930, since practiced in N.Y.C.; partner firm Mendes & Mount, and predecessor, 1945. Titular mem. Comite Maritime Inernacional; mem. council Hofstra U. Mem. Maritime Law Assn. U.S. (sec. 1954-56, v.p. 1958-60, pres. 1962-64), Am. Bar Assn. (ho. dels. 1962-64, chmn. standing com. admiralty and maritime law 1964-67), Internat. Assn. Ins. Counsel, Lambda Chi Alpha. Clubs: Down Town Assn. (N.Y.C.); Garden City Country. Home: Garden City, N.Y. Died Apr. 3, 1974; interred Greenwood Cemetery, Bklyn., N.Y.

HECKEL, ALBERT KERR, univ. prof.; b. Allegheny City, Pa., Nov. 18, 1880; s. Caspar C. and Elizabeth (Beiler) H.; A.B., Roanoke Coll., Salem, Va., 1903, A.M., 1906; student Johns Hopkins, 1903-04, Harvard Summer 1907, Ph.D., U. of Pa., 1913; m. Pearl Bash, June 29, 1907. Instr. high sch., Swissvale, Pa., 1904-07; head dept. of history, Pa. State Normal Sch., Indiana, Pa., 1907-11; asst. in history, 1911-12, Harrison fellow in history, 1912-13, U. of Pa.; instr. history Northwestern U., 1913-15; asst. prof. history and asst. dean, 1915-16, prof.and dean of the Coll., 1916-24, Lafayette Coll.; dean of men and prof. citizenship, U. of Mo., 1924-40, prof. citizenship from 1940; dean and prof. history, first college cruise around the World, 1926-27. Member Association History Teachers of Middle States and Maryland (pres., 1920-21). Am. Assn. U. Profs. Alpha Tau Omega, Alpha Pi Zeta, Phi Eta Sigma, Tau Kappa Alpha, Phi Beta Kappa. Republican. Mason. Author: On the Road to Civilization (with James G. Sigman), 1936. Contbr. to jours. Home: Columbia, Mo.†

HEDRICK, LAWRENCE E., elec. mfg. co. exec.; b. 1916; student La. State U.; married. With Westinghouse Electric Corp., after 1941, gen. mgr. subsidiary Sunnyvale Mfg. Co., 1960-63, v.p. steam div., 1963-68, v.p., gen. mgr. large turbine div., 1968-71, exec. v.p. Westinghouse Electric Europe NV, pres. power systems-Europe, after 1971. Address: Pittsburgh, Pa. Deceased* NY

HEFFERLINE, RALPH FRANKLIN, psychologist; b. Muncie, Ind., Feb. 15, 1910; s. Samuel Thomas and Blanche (Cecil) H.; B.S., Columbia, 1941, M.A., 1942, Ph.D., 1947; m. Dorothy Halliday, Aug. 25, 1939. Faculty, Columbia, N.Y.C., 1948-74, prof., 1967-74, pre-med. adviser, 1949-54, chmn. dept. psychology, 1965-68. Fellow Am. Psychol. Assn., A.A.A.S., N.Y. Acad. Scis.; mem. Psychonomic Soc., Eastern Psychol. Assn., Soc. for Gen. Systems Research, Soc. Psychophysiol. Research, Bio-Feedback Soc., Soc. Neuroscis. Sigma Xi; affiliate mem. Royal Soc. Medicine (London). Author: (with F.S. Peris and P. Goodman) Gestalt Therapy, 1950. Research on significance of patterns of muscular tension for psychoneurosis and anxiety, electromyographic study of very small responses as behavioral counterpart of mental processes. Home: New York City, N.Y. Died Mar. 16, 1974.

HEFLIN, AUBREY NEWBILL, banker; b. Fredericksburg, Va., Sept. 21, 1912; s. Joseph Granville and Addie Garnett (Newbill) H.; B.A., U. Richmond, 1933; LL.B., U. Va., 1936; grad. Stonier Grad. Sch. of Banking, Rutgers U., 1951; m. Ellen Virginia Simmerman, May 28, 1939; children—Ellen H. (Mrs. George W. Ramsey), Joseph Granville. Admitted to Va. bar, 1936; asso. atty. Parrish, Butcher & Parrish, Richmond, Va., 1936-40; with Fed. Res. Bank of Richmond, 1941-73, pres., 1968-73. Mem. exec. com. Region 3, Boy Scouts Am. Bd. dirs. Met. YMCA; trustee U. Richmond, Richmond Eye Hosp., Union Theol. Sem. Va. Served to lt. (j.g.) USNR, 1942-45. Mem. Am., Va., Richmond City bar assns., Phi Delta Phi. Lambda Chi Alpha. Presbyn. (trustee Ch., elder). Clubs: Forum, Country of Va. (Richmond), Richmond Rotary (trustee). Home: Richmond, Va. Died Jan. 16, 1973; buried Shiloh, Westmoreland County, Va.

HEFLING, ARTHUR WILLIAM, cons. engr.; b. nr. Burrton, Kan., Jan. 26, 1899; s. Robert Jackson and Alemeda M. (Shinkle) H.; B.S., U. Kan., 1924, C.E., 1932; diploma Robert H. Taft San. Engring. Center, Cin., 1960; m. Dorothy Pennock, Apr. 4, 1926; children—Barbara Jean (Mrs. Hayden F. Jones), Dorothy Ruth (Mrs. William D. Paul, Jr.). Chief field party and resident engr. F.E. Devlin, civil engr., Amarillo, 1925-26; supt. constrn. Willmering and Mullin Contractors, 1926-29; supt. constrn. Carl Pleasant, Inc., Phoenix, 1929-30; city engr. Hutchinson, Kan., 1930-33; county engr. Reno County, Kan., 1935-36; chief engr. Hefling & Hughes Engring. Co., Hutchinson, 1936-40; asso. Freese and Nichols Architects and Engrs., Ft. Worth, 1940-41; gen. practice, 1941-42, 46-48; municipal cons. engr., 1948-74. Served with USNR, 1942-46. Registered profl. engr., Kan., Okla., Tex., Colo., N.M., Ariz. Mem. Am. Legion, 40 and 8, Res. Officers Assn. U.S., Am. Soc. C.E. (life), Kan. Engring. Soc., Nat. Engring. Soc. Profl. Engrs., Kan. Water Pollution Control Assn., Kan. Sewage Works Assn., Kan. Water Well Assn. Mason (32 deg.). Home: Hutchinson, Kan. Died Nov. 30, 1974; interred Valley Township Cemetery, Burrton, Kan.

HEIDEGGER, MARTIN, philosopher; b. 1889. Prof. philosophy, Marburg U., 1923-28; prof. Freiburg i. Br. U., 1928, rector, 1933, emeritus, 1951-76. Author numerous publs., among latest being: Holzwege, 1950; Der Feldweg, 1953; Was heisst Denken, 1954; Was ist Philosophie, 1956; Zur Seinsfrage, 1956; Der Sata vom Grund, 1957; J.P. Hebel, 1957; Umterwegs zur Sprache, 1959; Nietzsche, 1961; Die Frage nach dem Ding, 1962; Kants These über das Sein, 1963: Die Technik und die Kehre, 1963; What is Philosophy, 1964; What is a Thing, 1966; Discourse on Thinking, 1966. Home: Messkirch, Federal Republic Germany. Died May 26, 1976.†

HEIDEN, KONRAD, author; b. Munich, Germany, Aug. 7, 1901; s. Johannes Hermann Rudolf and Lea (Deutschmann) H.; ed. gymnasium, Frankfurt am. Main, 1911-18, U. of Munich (law and economics), 1919-23; unmarried. On staff of Frankfurter Zeitung, 1923-30; free lance writer since 1930. Left Germany, 1933; lived in Saar Territory, 1933-35, in Paris, France, 1935-40, in U.S. after Oct. 1940. Author: History of National Socialism, 1934; Hilter, 1938; Fuehrer: Hitler's Rise to Power, 1944. Home: East Orleans, Mass. Died Sept. 1975.

HEIFETZ, BENAR, cellist; b. Moghilew, Russia, Dec. 11, 1899; s. Efim Heifetz; studied with pvt. tchrs.; student Conservatory of Music, Leningrad; m. Olga Band, July 7, 1937; 1 dau., Susanne Florence. First concert, Petersburg, Leningrad, 1915; other concerts Russia, Poland, Germany, Austria, France, Holland, Belgium, Egypt, N. Am., S. Am., Honolulu, Hawaii and P.R.: mem. Kolisch String Quartet, 1927-39; solo cellist Phila. Orch., 1939-43; cellist NBC Symphony, also mem. Albeneri Trio, 1944-74; mem. faculty Manhattan Sch. Music, 1960-74; internat. concert tours, 1957-58; nomination vis. prof. cello and chamber music U. Ind., 1957-58. Address: Great Neck, N.Y. Died Apr. 6, 1974.

HEINISCH, DON, truck mfg. co. exec.; b. Chgo., Aug. 23, 1923; s. Gustav O. and Marie (Hausdorf) H.; B.S., Washington U., St. Louis, 1942; C.P.A., LaSalle Extension U., Chgo., 1948; m. Alyce N. Lovell, Jan. 23, 1946; 1 son, Kelby G. Gen. mgr. Darling Co., 1946-50; sec.-treas. Crescent Industries div. Sears-Roebuck, 1950-56; treas. AMI div. Automatic Canteen Corp., 1956-57; pres. Recordio Corp., 1957-63; pres. Diamond-Reo div. White Motors Corp., 1963-68; pres. FWD Corp., Clintonville, Wis., from 1968. Bd. dirs. Clintonville Community Hosp.; mem. exec. com. Valley council Boy Scouts Am. Served with USAAF 1943-46; CBI. Mem. Soc. Automotive Engrs. Mason, Rotarian. Home: Clintonville, Wis., Died Oct. 29, 1974; buried Mears (Mich.) Cemetery.

HEINITSH, GEORGE W., JR., otolaryngologist; b. Spartanburg, S.C., July 6, 1903; s. George W. and Mary Adelaide (Fogartie) H.; B.S., U. N.C., 1928; M.D., Duke, 1932; m. Nellie Hamilton Graves, July 29, 1932. Intern, N.C. Tb Sanitarium, 1932; intern Duke Hosp., 1932-33, fellow, 1933-34, resident, 1934-37; practice medicine specializing in otolaryngology and ophtalmology, Southern Pines, N.C., 1946-74; mem. staff Moore Meml. Hosp., 1946-74; mem. cons. staffs local hosps. Bd. dirs. Weymouth Woods Nature Preserve. Served with M.C., AUS, 1940-46; comdr. 312th Gen. Hosp., South Pacific. Diplomate Am. Bd. Otolaryngology. Fellow Am. Acad. Ophthalmology and Otolaryngology; mem. A.M.A., Aerospace Med. Assn., N.C., Moore County med. socs., N.C. Eye, Ear, Nose and Throat Soc., Nat., N.C. (pres. 1961, dir. 1958-73) wildlife fedns., Alpha Omega Alpha, Delta Tau Delta, Phi Chi. Democrat. Presbyn. Home: Southern Pines, N.C. Died June 2, 1974; buried Old Bethesda Cemetery, Aberdeen, N.C.

HEISENBERG, WERNER, physicist; b. Wurzburg, Germany, Dec. 5, 1901; s. August and Annie (Wecklein) H.; Dr. phil., U. Munich, 1923; Dr. phil. habil., U. Gottingen, 1924; hon. doctorates U. Brussel, 1961, Techn. Hochschule Karlsruhe, 1961, U. Budapest, 1964, U. Kopenhagen, 1965, Techn U. Athen, 1966, U. Zagreb, 1969; m. Elisabeth Schumacher, Apr. 29, 1937; children—Wolfgang, Maria, Jochen, Martin, Barbara, Christine, Verena. Prof. theoretical physics U. Leipzig, 1927-41; dir. Kaiser-Wilhelm Inst. for Physics, prof. U. Berlin, 1941-45; dir. Max-Planck-Inst. for Physics, prof. U. Gottingen, 1946-58; dir. Max-Planck-Inst. for Physics and Astrophysics, prof. U. Munich, 1958-70. Pres. Alexander-von-Humboldt-Stiftung. Decorated Gro Bkreuzdes Zivilordens Alfons X (Spain); Komturkreuz des Ordens Georg I (Greece); Bayer, Verdienstorden des Freistaates Bayern; Grobes Verdienst Kreuz mit Stern U. Schulterband des Verdienstordens der Bundesrepublik Deutschland; Zweite Klasse des Ordens der aufgehenden Sonne (Japan); recipient Barnard medal Columbia, 1929; Matteucci medaille, 1929; Max-Planck medaille, 1933; Nobel prize for physics, 1932; Pour le mérite fur Wissenschaften und Kunste, 1957; Kultur-Ehrenpreis der Stadt München, 1958; Bronze medal Nat. Acad. Scis., 1964; Niels-Bohr Gold medal, Copenhagen, 1970; Sigmund-Freud Preis, Deutsche Akad. für Sprache u. Dichtung, 1970. Mem. Am. Philos. Soc. Home: , Norwegische Akademie der Wissenschaften, Göttinger Akademie der Wissenschaften, Deutsche Akademie der Wissenschaften, Rum ämische Akademie der Wissenschaften, Société Philomatique, Accademia

Nazionale dei Lincei, Spanische Akademie der Wissenschaften, Nat. Inst. Scis. India, Royal Soc. London, Phys. Soc. London, Am. Acad. Arts and Scis., Rajasthan Acad. Scis., Royal Inst. Gt. Britain, Nat. Acad. Scis., Institut Internat. de Physique Solvay, N.Y. Acad. Scis., Royal Irish Acad. in Sect. of Sci., Japan Acad. Author: Die physikalischen Prinzipien der Quantentheorie, 1930; Wandlungen in den Grundlagen der Naturwissenschaft, 1935; Die Physik der Atomkerne, 1943; Vorträge über die kosmische Strahlung, 1955; Physics and Philosophy, 1959; Introduction to the Unified Field Theory of Elementary Particles, 1966; Natural Law and the Structure of Matter, 1966; Der Teil und das Ganze, 1969 (transl. Physics and Beyond, 1971); Schritte uber Grenzen, 1971 (transl. Across the Frontiers, 1974). Munich, Germany., Died Feb. 1, 1976.

HEISERMAN, ARTHUR RAY, educator; b. Evansville, Ind., Jan. 10, 1929; s. Arthur Ray and Anne (Weisman) H.; A.B., U. Chgo., 1948, A.M., 1951, Ph.D., 1959; m. Virginia Ruth Martin, Oct. 17, 1950; children—Regan, Lisa, Gina, Alison, Arthur Martin. Writer, Sta. KTAR, Phoenix, 1951-52; instr. English, U. Neb., 1952-54; instr. English, U. Ill., Chgo., 1954-56, dir. acad. programs Univ. Coll., 1956-59, dir. Summer Sch., 1959-61, asso. dean Univ. Coll., 1961-63, master Humanities Coll., 1965-67, prof. English, 1965-75. Guggenheim Found. fellow, 1963-64. Mem. Medieval Acad. Am., Internat. Arthurian Soc., Modern Lang. Assn. Author: Skelton and Satire, 1961. Contbr. articles to profl. jours. Home: Chicago, Ill., Died Dec. 9, 1975.

HELLER, ROBERT, management engr.; b. Newcastle, Ind., Jan. 14, 1899; s. Myron and Elizabeth (Endeman) H.; student U. of Mich., 1916; B.Sc., Harvard, 1920; m. Lois Hortense Mouch, Dec. 28, 1920; children—Charles Robert, Frederick. Before leaving Harvard was associated with Prof. William Z. Ripley in govt. return of railroads to pvt. ownership and operation; began business career, Boston, 1920; established a business, working with various industries, 1923; moved to Cleveland, O., 1932; incorporated as Robert Heller & Associates, Inc., engrs. and consultants, 1935, firm served numerous large corps., also dept. fed. govt.; dir. Lincoln Electric Co.; ret., 1963. Past chmn. Nat. Com. Strengthening Congress; headed task force Post Office Dept. for Hoover Commn.; former chairman Wendell Willkie Nat. Indsl. Com. Trustee, mem. research and policy committee for Com. Econ. Devel.; director, mem. exec. com. Nat. Planning Assn.; former dir. Citizens Com. Hoover Report; Cuyhoga Co. Rep. Finance Com., Acad. Polit. Sci., Am. Polit. Sci. Assn.; dir. Hampden Fund; trustee Cleveland Development Foundation, Cleve. Soc. Blind; trustee Lake Erie Coll. Recipient Nat. Planning Assn., Certificate of Extraordinary achievement, in furthering the cause of better govt. 1949. Fellow Royal Soc. Eng.; mem. Newcomen Soc. Eng., Cleveland Mus. Natural History, United States. Cleve. chambers commerce, Cleveland Musical Arts, also Phi Delta Theta. Presbyn. Republican. Mason. Clubs: Pepper Pike, Mayfield, Hermit, Mid-Day, Harvard (Cleve.); Metropolitan (Washington); Harvard (N.Y.C., Boston). Author: Strengthening The Congress, 1945; A Proposal for Financing Tax Supported Education, 1958, Home: Bratenahl, O. Died Jan. 22, 1973; interred New Castle, Ind.

HELLMAN, C(LARISSE) DORIS (MRS. MORTON PEPPER), educator; b. N.Y.C., Aug. 28, 1910; d. Alfred M. and Clarisse (Bloom) Hellman; B.A., Vassar Coll., 1930; M.A. (Vassar Coll. Fellow 1930-31), Radcliffe Coll., 1931; Ph.D. (Scholar 1931-32, Fellow 1932-33), Columbia, 1943; m. Morton Pepper, Aug. 10, 1933; children—Alice (Mrs. Robert L. Cooper), Carol (Mrs. Paul R. Cooper). Instr., lectr., professorial lectr. Pratt Inst., 1951-64, adj. prof. history of sci., 1964-66; adj. prof. history sci. N.Y. U., 1964, adj. prof. history, 1965-66; vis. prof. history Queens Coll. of City U. N.Y., 1966-67, prof. history, 1967-73, mem. grad. faculty, 1966-73; asso. Univ. Seminar on Renaissance, Columbia, 1956-73. Sec. U.S. nat. com. Internat. Union of the History and Philosophy of Sci., 1958-60; del. Nat. Acad. Scis. to IXth Internat. Congress History Sci., 1959, sec., del. Xth Congress, 1962. Active Jewish Found., for Edn. of Girls, 1942-73. NSF sr. postdoctoral fellow, 1959-60. Fellow Royal Astron. Soc., A.A.A.S. (acting sec. sect. L 1957); mem. History of Sci. Soc. (council mem. 1949-59, 64-66, exec. com. N.Y. 1954-63, 67-73, chmn. Met. N.Y. sect. 1958-59, 65-67), Academie Internationale d'Histoire des Sciences, Am. Hist. Assn., Internat. Astron. Union (organizing com. commn. 41, 1967-72), Am. Astron Soc., Renaissance Soc. Am. (adv. council 1954), Phi Beta Kappa. Author: The Comet of 1577: Its Place in the History of Astronomy, 1944, 71; also articles and book reviews in profl. jours. Translator, editor: Kepler (by Max Caspar), 1959, 62. Home: New York City, N.Y. Died Mar. 28, 1973; cremated.

HELLMAN, HUGO EDWARD, educator, parliamentarian; b. Muenste, Tex., Aug. 18, 1908; s. August and Anna (Fette) H.; Ph.B., Marquette U., 1931, M.A., 1933, Ph.D., 1940; m. Margaret Shuengel, July 18, 1934; children—John, Robert. Tchr., Messmer High Sch., Milw., 1931-33; prof. Marquette U., 1936-40, dir. Sch. Speech, 1940-68, dean, 1968-73, dean emeritus, 1973-75, lectr. parliamentary law Sch. Law, 1970-75. Parliamentary cons. Am. Dental Hygiene Assn. others; parliamentarian Am. Bowling Congress. Mem. Speech Assn. Am., Forensic Assn., Am. Inst. Parliamentarians. Author ann. background books for high sch. debaters, 1949-75; Parliamentary Procedure, 1965; Speaking in Groups, 1965. Home: Wauwatosa, Wis. Died June 12, 1975.

HELLMAN, MARCO H., banker; b. Los Angeles, Sept. 4, 1878; s. Herman W. and Ida (Heimann) H.; ed. pub. schs. and Stanford U.; m. Reta Levis, 1908. Began as clk. Farmers and Mechanics Bank, Los Angeles, 1901; apptd. asst. cashier, Merchants Nat. Bank, 1903, elected v.p. 1909, pres. Hellman Commercial Trust & Savings Bank, 1918, chmn. bd. from 1925 until merged into Bank of America of Calif. of which was v.p.; then became chmn. exec. com. (southern div.) of Bank of America Nat. Trust & Savings Assn. until leaving that instn. Active in Calif. financial and civic orgns. Home: Los Angeles, Cal.*†

HELLWEG, J. F., naval officer; b. Balt., Mar. 16, 1879; s. Julius and Elizabeth (Singley) H.; B.S., U.S. Naval Acad., 1900; grad. Naval War Coll., 1924; m. Paule Denise Vincent, July 3, 1907; 1 son, Vincent. Commd. ensign, U.S. Navy, 1902, and advanced through the grades to commodore, 1944; served as midshipman during Spanish-Am. War, 1898; served in Boxer Uprising, China, 1900. Philippine Insurrection, 1901-02, Santo Domingo Insurrection, 1903-04; comd. U.S.S. Macdonough, 1906, U.S.S. Stewart, 1907-08, Burrows, 1910-13, Wilkes, 1916-17, Prinzess Irene (Pochontas), 1917-18, Marietta, 1918, Columbia, 1920-21, Oklahoma 1928-30; served as supervisor naval overseas transportation service, Norfolk, 1919; capt. of port, Bordeaux, France, and sr. naval officer in France, 1919-20; in charge fitting out and bringing to U.S., 5 former warships of Germany, 1920; comd. 14th Destroyer Squadron, 1924-26; supt. Naval Observator. Washington, D.C., 1930; retired. Decorated Navy Cross, Spanish War, China, Philippine, Santiago and World War I medals (U.S.), Legion of Honor (France), Medaille Militaire (Belgium). Mem. Nat. Research Council, Am. Geophysical Union, Internat. Astron. Union, Franklin Inst. (medalist), U.S. Power Squadrons, Nat. Geographic Soc., Am. Horol. Soc. (hon.). Clubs: Army-Navy (Manila); Army-Navy Country (Washington); New York Yacht; Poor Richard's (hon.) (Phila.). Author of pamphlets on navigational subjects, organization, astronomy and ordnance. Home: Washington, D.C.†

HELM, NATHAN WILBUR, prin. acad.; b. Marion, Ind., Aug. 7, 1879; s. Benjamin Abbott and Mellicent (Coggeshall) H; A.B., DePauw U., 1899, M.A., 1900; Princeton, 1900-03, M.A., 1901; m. Margaret Stevenson Nutt, of Greencastle, Ind., Nov. 7, 1903. Tutor in Latin and asst. librarian, DePauw U., 1899-1900; prof. Latin, Pennington (N.J.) Sem., 1900-01; instr. Latin, Princeton, 1901-04; tour of ednl. investigation, Japan, 1904; instr. Latin, Phillips Exeter Acad., N.H., 1904-09; prin. Evanston Acad. of Northwestern U., from 1909. Methodist. Mem. Am. Philol. Assn., Classical Assn. of Middle West and South, Classical Assn. of N.E., N. Central Acad. Assn. (ex-pres.), Ednl. Assn. N.E. Ch. (ex-sec.), Phi Kappa Psi, Phi Beta Kappa, Alpha Delta Tau. Mason. Editor: Cicero, Ten Orations and Letters, 1912. Contbr. on ednl. and classical topics; lecturer. Home: Evanston, Ill†

HENCH, ATCHESON LAUGHLIN, coll. prof.; b. Orange, N.J., Dec. 31, 1891; s. Jacob Bixler and Clara John (Showalter) H.; ed. Shady Side Acad., Pittsburgh, Pa., 1902-08; A.B., Lafayette Coll., 1912; M.A., Harvard, 1917, Ph.D., 1921; m. Virginia Bedinger Michie, Aug. 27, 1925; children—Margaret, Clare Showalter. Instr. English, Lafayette Coll., 1912-14, Pa. Mil. Coll., Chester, 1914-16; asst. prof., Wesleyan U., Middletown, Conn., 1920-22; asso. prof., U. of Va., 1922-26, prof., from 1926, Linden Kent Meml. prof. English, 1940-62, chmn. English Dept, 1951-54. Mem. Charlottesville (Va.) Sch. Bd., 1939-48; pres, Albemarle County Hist. Soc., 1943-44. with A.E.F., 1918-19. Mem. Modern Lang. Assn., Mediaeval Acad., Southeastern Folklore Soc., Am. Dialect Soc. (v.p. 1946, pres. 1947-48, Ravens (U. of Va.); Am. Name Soc., S. Atlantic Modern Humanities Research Assn., Phi Beta Kappa, Sigma Alpha Epsilon. Presbyn. Democrat. Clubs: Colonnade, University of Virginia. Contbr. Dictionary of American English, 1928-37, Middle English Dictionary, 1933-34; H. L. Mencken's American Language, Supplement I, 1945, Supplement II, 1948; articles on American Speech. Adv. editor: American Speech, 1940-41, Funk and Wagnall's College Standard Dictionary, 1942-45. Mem. editorial adv. staff World Book Ency. Dictionary, 1960-62; proofreader Vol. I, Oxford English Dictionary Supplement, 1970-74. Address: Charlottesville, Va. Died Aug. 8, 1974; interred U. Va. Cemetery.

HENDELSON, WILLIAM H., editor; b. Berlin, Germany, July 26, 1904; s. Gabriel and Martha (Sandberg) H.; ed. pvt. tutor, also Gymnasium, Berlin-Grunewald; 1 dau., Marion. Came to U.S., 1938, naturalized, 1944. Partner Knauer Machfolger Pubs., Berlin, 1922-34; editor-in-chief World Scope Ency., 1944-63, Standard Internat. Ency., N.Y.C., 1953-63, Ency. Yearbook, 1946-69, Editorial Guild, 1964-68, Funk & Wagnalls New Engy., 1971—; editorial dir. Funk & Wagnalls Standard Reference Ency., 1968-71, Funk & Wagnalls, Inc., 1971-74. Mem. Am. Hist. Assn., Acad. Polit. Sci. Club: Overseas Press (N.Y.C.). Editor: Doubleday's Ency., 1940-41; Modern Concise Ency., 1940-42; Facts, New Concise Pictorial Ency., 1941; co-editor Practical English for Germans, 1940; Greystone Panorama Books, 1941; Music Lovers' Almanac, 1943. Home: New York City, N.Y., Died May 28, 1975; interred Ferncliff Cemetery.

HENDERSON, DAVID E., lawyer; b. Onslow County, N.C., Sept. 3, 1879; s. Joseph Franklin and Mary (Shepard) H.; student U. of N.C.; m. Mattie Jenkins, Aug. 29, 1912; children—David H., Charles J., John Wesley, Martha Jane. Admitted to N.C. bar, 1905; practiced law, New Bern, N.C., 1905-18, Charlotte, N.C., from 1918; mem. firm. Henderson & Henderson; U.S. Atty. for Western Dist. of N.C., 1945-48; U.S. dist. judge for Western dist. N.C., from 1948. Mem. Mechlenburg County, N.C. State and Am. bar assns. Methodist. Mason, Junior Order, Redman, Woodman of World (mem. sovereign judiciary com.). Home: Charlotte, N.C.*†

HENDERSON, HAROLD GOULD, educator, author; b. N.Y.C., July 25, 1889; s. Harold Gould and Agnes (Roudebush) H.; B.A., Columbia, 1910, M.A., 1915, Chem. E., 1915; m. Mary Avezzana Benjamin, June 20, 1946. Research asst. to E.R. Hewitt, 1919-20; sales engr. U.S. Cast Iron Pipe & Foundry Co., Cin., 1920-24; asst. to curator Far East dept. Met. Mus., N.Y.C., 1927-29; asst. prof. Japanese Columbia, 1934-56. Served to capt. U.S. Army, 1917-19; to lt. col. AUS, 1944-46. Decorated Bronze Star medal; Order Sacred Treasure (Japanese). Mem. Japan Soc. Am. (past pres., dir.), Soc. Japanese Studies (past pres.). Roman Catholic. Clubs: Century, Union, Saint Anthony. Author: The Bamboo Broom, 1933; (with L.V. Ledoux) The Surviving Works of Sharaku, 1939; A Handbook of Japanese Grammar, 1943; An Introduction to Haiku, 1958; Haiku in English, 1965. Editor: Tales From Japanese Storytellers, 1964. Translator: Illustrated History of Japanese Art (H. Minamoto), 1934. Contbr. articles profl. jours. Home: New York City, N.Y. Died July 11, 1974; interred Elka Park Cemetery, Tannersville N.Y.

HENDERSON, HARRY PETERS, mining engr.; b. Peabody, Mass., Dec. 10, 1879; s. Joseph and Mary Read Rosworth; A.B., Harvard, 1901, S.M., 1902; m. Mabel Cummings Harrington, Sept. 17, 1913. Instr. in mining. Harvard, 1902-03; employed by mining companies, 1902-07; supt. Tonopah Development Co., and gen. supt. Goldfield Consol. Mines, 1907-10; cons. mining engr., N.Y. City, from 1910; pres., Tex. Mining & Smelting Co., Laredo, Tex., 1930-39, and several antimony mining companies in Mexico, 1927-39. Engr. with U.S. Shipping Bd., 1918. Section chief of antimony and beryllium, War Production Board, 1942-43. Mem. Am. Inst. of Mining and Metall. Engrs., Mining and Metall. Soc. of America. Clubs: Harvard (New York). Home: Concord, Mass.†

HENDERSON, JOHN O., judge; b. Buffalo, Nov. 13, 1909; LL.B., U. Buffalo, 1933; m. Clara May Reddicliffe; 1 dau., Jane (Mrs. Foli). Admitted to N.Y. State Bar, 1934; mem. Cohen, Fleishman, Augspurger, Henderson & Campbell, Buffalo; clk. Surrogate Ct. of Erie County, 1947-48; apptd. U.S. atty., Western Dist. N.Y., 1953, now chief judge. Served as lt. col. AUS, 1942-46, Mem. adv. council Practicing Law Inst., 1949-74. Mem. Erie County Bar Assn. (pres. 1949-50). Home: Eggertsville, N.Y. Died Feb. 19, 1974.

HENDERSON, VIVIAN WILSON, coll. pres.; b. Bristol, Tenn., Feb. 10, 1923; s. William Thomas and Sallie (Richmond) H.; B.S., N.C. Central U., 1947; M.A., U. Ia., 1948, Ph.D., 1952; m. Anna Powell, Sept. 8, 1949; children—Wyonella Marie, Dwight Cedric, David Wayne, Kimberly Ann. Instr. econs. Prairie View Coll. (Tex.), 1948-49; prof., chmn. dept. econs. Fisk U., Nashville, 1952-65; vis. prof. econs. N.C. State U., 1962-64; pres. Clark Coll., Atlanta, 1965-76. Dir. Citizens and Soc. Bank, 1972-76. Mem. U.S. Nat. Commn. to UNESCO, 1968-73, So. Regional Council, 1960—, Nat. Urban Coalition, 1969-71. Trustee Nat. Bur. Econ. Research, Ford Found., Tchrs. Ins. and Annuity Assn. Am. Served with AUS, 1943-46. Recipient Distinguished Service award Tchrs., Coll., Columbia, 1970. Mem. Am. Econ. Assn., Am. Acad. Arts and Scis., Black Acad. Arts and Letters, Alpha Kappa Mu. Omicron Delta Epsilon, Kappa Alpha Psi. United Methodist. Author: The Economic Imbalance, 1961; Economic Dimensions in Race Relations, 1961; Economic Opportunity and Negro Education, 1962; The Economic Status of Negroes, 1963; The Advancing South, 1967; Employment, Race and Poverty, 1967; Negro Colleges Face in the Future. Home: Atlanta, Ga., Died Jan. 28, 1976.

HENDREN, LINVILLE LAURENTINE, coll. dean; b. Carey, N.C., Mar. 3, 1880; s. Linville Laurentine and Elizabeth (Mayhew) H.; A.B., Trinity Coll., Durham, N.C., 1900, A.M., 1901; Ph.D., Columbia, 1905; m. Virginia Bryan, Dec. 27, 1911. Asst. in physics, Columbia, 1902-05; asso. prof. applied mathematics, Trinity Coll., 1905-08; prof. physics, U. of Ga., from 1908, dean Coll. of Arts and Sciences, 1932-40, dean of adminstration, 1932-40, dean of faculties, 1940-45, acting dean, College of Arts and Sciences, 1941-46. President Ga. Assn. of Colleges, 1934. Fellow A.A.A.S., Ga. State Acad. Science (pres. 1925); mem. Am. Physical Soc., Phi Beta Kappa. Democrat. Methodist. Home: Athens, Ga.†

HENIGAN, GEORGE FRANCIS, educator; B.A., Kearney State Coll., 1936; Ph.M., U. Wis., 1940; m. Palma Lucente; children—Dennis A., Cathleen (Mrs. Habeger). Prof., chmn. dept. speech George Washington U. Home: Springfield, Va. Died Dec. 8, 1973.

HENLEY, WALTER ERVIN, banker; b. Birmingham, Ala., Jan. 30, 1877; s. John Charles and Annie (Linn) H.; ed. Ala. Poly. Inst.; m. Marie Smith Whitaker (died 1938). In banking business at Birmingham, from 1897; became pres. Birmingham Trust National Bank, 1925, past chmn. bd. Past pres. Community Chest, Birmingham; past chmn. Birmingham City Planning Bd. Mem. Ala. Bankers' Assn. (past pres.); past dir. Birmingham Realty Co. Past trustee So. Research Inst. Mem. Ala. Nat. Guard, 1896-98; mem. Nat. Coal Commn., 1918. Mem. Birmingham C. of C. (past pres.), Sigma Alpha Epsilon, Omicron Delta Kappa, Blue Key. Presbyn. (trustee). Clubs: Kiwanis (past pres.), Mountain Brook. Home: Birmingham, Ala.†

HENNEMUTH, ROBERT GEORGE, diversified co. exec.; b. Scranton, Pa., Oct. 25, 1921; s. George Henry and Kathryn (Conway) H.; A.B., Syracuse U., 1943; LL.B., Harvard, 1949; m. Mary Elizabeth Tonner, June 1, 1946; children—Anne Maureen, Susan Elizabeth, Robert George. Engaged in pub. relations Syracuse U., 1946-47; instr. journalism Boston U., 1947-49; instr. law Northeastern U., 1949-61; admitted to Mass. bar, 1950, also U.S. Dist. Ct.; asso. atty. firm Nutter, McClennen & Fish, Boston, 1949-50; with Raytheon Co., 1950-75, v.p. indsl. relations, 1964-75. Chmn. Mass. Adv. Bd. Legislative Compensation; mem. Mass. Gov.'s Labor-Mgmt. Adv. Council, Mass. Gov.'s Spl. Commn. for Conversion Fed. Mil. Bases for Civilian Use; mem. New Eng. regional manpower adv. com. U.S. Dept. Labor; mem. corp. adv. council Syracuse U. Bd. dirs. Mass. Blue Cross; bd. dirs., pres. YMCA, Newton, Mass. Served to lt. (s.g.) USNR, 1943-46. Home: Wellesley, Mass. Died Apr. 22, 1975, buried at Brookline, Mass.

HENNESSEY, THOMAS MICHAEL, business exec.; b. Lawrence, Mass., Nov. 12, 1901; s. James Francis and Margaret (Thornton) H.; A.B., Harvard, 1923; m. Esther G. Dwyer, June 30, 1931; children—James T., Ann, Thomas M. Asst. to operating ofcls. N.E. Tel. & Tel. Co., 1923-25, acting dist. mgr., dist. traffic mgr., 1925-26, local toll traffic supr., 1926-27, toll traffic supt., 1927-35, gen. traffic employment supr., 1935-40, div. traffic supt., Providence, 1940-44, Boston, 1944, asst. v.p., 1944-45, dir. pub. relations, 1945-46, v.p., 1946-74; dir. New Eng. Tel. & Tel. Co.; trustee Charlestown Savs. Bank, 1956-74. Bd. dirs. N.E. Council, 1946-53, 56-60. chmn. recreational devel., 1947-48; bd. dirs. YMCA, Boston, 1948-58; chmn. Greater Boston U.S.O. campaign, 1947; bd. dirs. Winchester Hosp., 1953-57, v.p., 1954-57; bd. dirs. Greater Boston C. of C., 1953-74, chmn. bus. and indsl. com., 1954-74; bd. dirs. United Fund Greater Boston, 1957-74, v.p., 1957-60; bd. dirs. United Community Services Met. Boston, 1960-74. Clubs: Harvard (Boston); Union; Down Town, Winchester Country. Home: Winchester, Mass. Died July 25, 1974.

HENNESSY, FRANK J., lawyer; b. Omaha, Nov. 19, 1880; s. William Pope and Rose A. Hennessy; A.B., U. of Santa Clara, 1898; LL.B., U. of Calif., 1901; m. Maude R. Hennessy. Admitted to Calif. bar; U.S. dist. atty., Northern Dist. of Calif. Democrat. Roman Catholic. Address: San Francisco, Cal.*†

HENNINGS, THOMAS CAREY, SR., lawyer; b. St. Louis, Mo., Sept. 11, 1874; s. John P. and Margaret (Carey) H.; LL.B., Washington U., 1899; m. Sarah P. Wilson, May 7, 1902; children—Thomas (dec.), Ruth (Mrs. David G. Teasdale). Admitted to Mo. bar, also U.S. Cts. and Supreme Ct. of U.S.; practiced in St. Louis, 1899-1913; judge Circuit Court, St. Louis, 1913-18; v.p. Merc Trust Co., 1918-39, dir., from 1918; of counsel Green, Hennings, Kenny, Evans & Arnold. Pres. Mo. Assn. Criminal Justice, 1925-26 (a founder); pres. Community Council, St. Louis, 1925-26; chmn. Community Fund, 1924; former pres. (now hon. pres.) Big Brother Organization; pres. Thomas Dunn Meml., 1931-61, chmn. bd., from 1961; trustee Sch. of Ozarks, 1939-48; trustee, adminstrv. bd. City Art Mus., 1936-52; trustee Jefferson Memorial Project, 1961. Member Mo. Constitutional Conv., 1943. Mem. Am., Mo. State and St. Louis bar assns., Am. Bankers Assn. (pres. trust div. 1931. mem. exec. council and administrative com. 1929-31), Am. Soc. Internat. Law, Am. Judicature Soc., Mo. Hist. Soc., Phi Delta Phi. Democrat. Mason. Clubs: Racquet, Noonday (ex-pres.). Home: St. Louis, Mo.†

HENRICHS, HENRY FREDERICK, writer, publisher; b. Asendorf, Germany, Oct. 17, 1876; s. John William and Amelia (Borchers) H.; brought to U.S., 1880, naturalized, 1887; grad. Bunker Hill Mil. Acad., 1896; L.H.D., Capitol Coll. Music and Ortary, 1962; m. Ethel Winifred Masters, Apr. 15, 1900; children—Harold Garth, Carol Isabel (dec.), Monta Mildred (Mrs. Richard T. Crane). Owner, operator The Henrichs Newspaper Brokerage, Chgo., N.Y.C., Los Angeles, 1904-34; organized Sunshine Press, Litchfield, Ill., 1924; established Sunshine Mag., brs. in Gt. Britain, India, Japan, Singapore, Belguim, 1942; now pres., gen. mgr. The House of Sunshine, Litchfield, also editorial dir. Sunshine Mag., Good Reading Mag.; organized Henry F. Henrichs Publs., 1924, now internat. editorial dir., pres., gen. mgr.; also Sunshine Graphic Arts, Inc., 1965, Sunshine Sanctuary, 1966. Editor, compiler Book of Sunshine. Founder, Golden Dawn Endowment 1968. Recipient Freedoms Found. award, 1947, Certificate of Merit, City of Litchfield, 1962, Citation and Certificate Independence Hall Chgo.; named Man of Year C. of C.; Henrichs St., Litchfield named in his honor. Author: Newspaper Evaluations, 1935. Compiler: Charles M. Sheldon, In His Steps Today; editor: St. Charles of Topeka Memorial. Designer books including Antoinette in Illinois (Edward Davis), State Flowers, State Birds (Robert Walker), Light Across the Valley, He Who Seeks Gold (Everett Wentworth Hill). Erected House of Sunshine, semi-public instn., 1940, Hansel und Gretel House, 1967; owner Sunshine Park. Mem. Disciples of Christ Ch. Mason. Home: Litchfield Ill. Died 1970; buried Elmwood Cemetery, Litchfield, Ill.

HENRY, EDWARD ATWOOD, librarian; b. Naples, N.Y., May 11, 1881; s. Cyrus Dryer and Ermina Finch (Crumb) H.; A.B., Hiram (O.) Coll., 1900; B.D., U. of Chicago, 1907; studied Am. Sch. of Archaeology, Jerusalem, 1908-09, U. of Chicago, 1909-11; Litt.D., Lincoln Memorial U., 1939; m. Grace Edith Hartman, June 1, 1914; 1 son, John Gordon. With U. of Chicago, 1906-28, librarian Divinity Sch. until 1913, head of Durrett Library, 1913-18, head of readers dept. U. of Chicago Library, 1918-27, acting director Jan.-June 1928; librarian, U. of Cincinnati, 1928-1951; cataloger in the Joint U. Library, Vanderbilt Univ., and visiting lecturer in University Library Adminstration in George Peabody College Library Sch., 1951. Lecturer in New Testament lit., from 1945. Asst. prof. O.T. extension division, U. Chicago, 1912-24, and asst. prof. Semetic langs., Univ. Coll., Chicago, 1922-28. Mem. bd. dirs., and recording sec. Y.M.C.A. of Cincinnati and Hamilton County. President bd. trustees City Gospel Mission, Cincinnati, Mem. A.L.A., Bibliog. Soc. America, Ohio Library Assn. (pres. 1937-38), Campbell Inst., Kappa Delta Pi. Ind. Republican. Mem. Church of Disciples of Christ. Clubs: Torch, Clerical. Editor of College and Reference Year Book No. 2, 1930, No. 3, 1931 (both A.L.A.); Doctoral Dissertations accepted by American Universities Nos. 7-11, 1940-44. Contbr. on library topics. Address: Nashville, Tenn.†

HENRY, JERRY MAURICE, clergyman, educator; b. Poages Mill, nr. Roanoke City, Va., Aug. 7, 1880; s. John T. and Jane Frances (Grisso) H.; prep. edn., Daleville (Va.) Acad. and Coll.; A.B., Bridgewater (Va.) Coll., 1909; teacher Daleville Coll., 1909-13, 1914-17; studied U. of Va., 1913-14; A.M., George Washington U., 1919, Ph.D., 1924; m. Virginia Wickline, Aug. 9, 1909; children—Hortense May (dec.), Maurice Kent, Margaret Sangster. Prohibition speaker in Va., 1914-17; ordained ministry Ch. of the Brethren, 1906; evangelistic work, W.Va., Pa., Ohio, Ind. and Md.; pastor Washington, D.C., 1917-22; pres. Blue Ridge Coll., New Windsor, Md., from 1922. Delivered ednl. addresses at Internat. Conf. of Ch. of the Brethren, Calgary, Can., June 1923; del. World Conf. on Faith and Order, Lausanne, Switzerland, 1927. Lecturer on "World Peace." Home: New Windsor, Md.†

HENRY, JOHN ROBERT, JR., lawyer; b. Bklyn., Oct. 30, 1913; s. John Robertson and Louise Mildred (TSchetter) H.; student Andover; B.A., Yale, 1935, LL.B., 1938; m. Evelyn Earle, Mar. 29, 1947; children—Peter Robert, Susan Earle, Douglas Dyer. Admitted to N.Y. bar, 1939; asso. Sherman & Sterling & Wright, 1938-46; atty. Am. Can Co., N.Y.C., 1946-50, gen. atty., 1950-55, sec., gen. counsel, 1955-74, also v. p. Served as comdr. USNR, 1941-45. Decorated Bronze Star medal. Mem. Assn. Bar City N.Y., Alpha Delta Phi, Elihu. Republican. Methodist. Clubs: Apawamis, Manursing Island (Rye); Yale (N.Y.C.). Home: Rye, N.Y. Died Feb. 17, 1974.

HENRY, MATTHEW GEORGE, clergyman; b. Chapel Hill, N.C., Oct. 25, 1910; s. George Kenneth Grant and Mary Elizabeth (Harding) H.; A.B., U. N.C., 1931; B.D., Va. Theol. Sem., 1935, D.D., 1949; D.D., U. South, 1948; m. Cornelia Catharine Sprinkle, June 30, 1937; children—Anna Catharine, George K., Matthew G., Elizabeth H. Ordained to ministry Protestant Episcopal Ch., 1935; temporarily in charge St. Phillip's Ch., Durham, and St. Paul's Ch., Winston-Salem, N.C., 1935; in charge Christ Ch., Walnut Grove, St. Philip's Ch., Germanton, Messiah Ch., Mayodan, and Emmanual Ch., Stoneville, N.C., 1936; rector Calvary Parish, Tarboro, N.C., 1936-43, Christ Ch., Charlotte, N.C., 1943-48; bishop Diocese of Western N.C., Ashville, 1948-75. Teaching fellow in chimistry U. N.C., 1931-32. Trustee St. Augustine's Coll., Raleigh, N.C., Patterson Sch., U. South. Pres., N.C. Council Chs., 1965-67. Mem. Alpha Chi Sigma, Phi Beta Kappa, Delta Upsilon. Home: Ashville, N.C. Died Apr. 1975.

HENRY, ROBERT PATTERSON, mfg. co. exec.; b. Norristown, Pa., Sept. 22, 1911; s. Robert John and Ruth Elizabeth (Williams) H.; student U. Pa., 1930-32; grad. Charles Morris Price Sch. Advt. and Journalism, 1934; m. Marie Covington Elliott, Apr. 24, 1943. Free-lance copywriter, Phila., 1930-34; prodn. mgr. Oswald Advt. Agy., Phila., 1939-42; asst. advt. mgr. Wilkening Mfg. Co., Phila., 1946-49; mgr. advt. and sales promotion Sunroc Co., Glen Riddle, Pa., 1949-51; advt. mgr. Willson Products, Reading, Pa., 1951-57; mgr. advt. and sales promotion Schramm, Inc., West Chester, Pa., 1957-73. Bd. suprs. West Goshen Twp., West Chester, 1956-63, chmn., 1959-62. Served with AUS, 1942-45; ETO. Decorated Bronze Star. Mem. Assn. Indsl. Advertisers, Constrn. Equipment Advertisers (gen. chmn. 1970-71), Franklin Inst. Rotarian. Home: West Chester Pa. Died June 21, 1973; buried Whitemarsh Meml. Park, Ambler, Pa.

HENSON, ELMER D., ret. sem. dean; b. Colony, Okla., Aug. 7, 1901; s. Robert Alexander and Florence Belle (Bond) H.; B.A., Tex. Christian U., 1927, B.D., 1940, D.D., 1945; grad. study Union Theol. Sem., 1955; m. Eva May Kemp, Aug. 7, 1926; children—Edna Lucile (Mrs. Roy Tomlinson), Mary Lois (Mrs. Richard Wilkie). Ordained to ministry Christian Ch., 1927; pastor First Christian Ch., Van Alstyne, Tex., 1927-29, Garland, Tex., 1929-32, Commerce, Tex., 1932-37, San Angelo, Tex., 1937-45, Bethany Christian Ch., Houston, 1945-55; dean Brite Div. Sch., Tex. Christian U., Ft. Worth, 1955-71, dean emeritus, 1971-74. Pres. Tex. Conv., Disciples of Christ, 1947, dean Young Peoples Summer Conf., 1934-50, sec. com. on recommendations Internat. Conv., 1935-47; chmn. commn. on theol. edn., bd. higher edn. Christian Ch. (Disciples of Christ), 1968-69. Trustee Brite Coll., 1943-55, pres. trustees, 1944-55; trustee Tex. Christian U., 1948-55. Mem. Nat. (preaching team to Armed Forces 1942-53), Tex. (dir. 1946-49), Houston (v.p. 1955), councils chs., United Christian Missionary Soc. (bd. mgrs., trustee 1950-55), Ministerial Alliance San Angelo (pres. (pres. 1943-44), Council Southwestern Theol. Schs. (pres. 1960-61, 68-69). Theta Phi, Phi Delta Kappa. Lion (dep. dist. gov. Tex. 1934). Club: Knife and Fork (dir. San Angelo 1943-45). Home: Fort Worth Tex. Died Aug. 26, 1974; interred Greenwood Cemetery, Fort Worth, Tex.

HENZE, HENRY RUDOLF, chemist, educator; b. New Haven, Jan. 11, 1896; s. Henry Frederick and Wilhelmina Christina (Tamm) H.; Ph.B. magna cum laude, Sheffield Sci. Sch., Yale, 1918; Ph.D., Yale, 1921; m. Elizabeth Sledge, Aug. 24, 1933; 1 son, Henry Rudolf. Head dept. pharm. chemistry, med. br. U. Tex., 1921-37, prof. pharm. chemistry, 1929-49, grad. prof. chemistry, 1949-70, chmn. dept. chemistry and chem. engring., 1929-39, Univ. research prof., 1945-46, also dir. premed. and predental program. Served as officer candidate Chem. Warfare Service, AUS, 1918; maj. Chem. Warfare Res. Recipient L.E. Scarbrough Found. award, 1956, Excellence in Teaching award U. Tex., 1965. Fellow A.A.A.S., Tex. Acad. Sci.; mem. Am. Chem. Soc. (Southwestern Region award 1953), Am. Assn. U. Profs., Alpha Epsilon Delta, Phi Lambda Upsilon, Alpha Chi Sigma, Kappa Psi (nat. hon.), Sigma Pi. Episcopalian. Mason. Mem. bd. editors Jour. Organic Chemistry, 1948-55. Contbr. numerous articles in field to sci. jours. Home: Austin, Tex. Died Sept. 21, 1974; interred Austin, Tex.

HEPBURN, SAMUEL, ret. Salvation Army exec.; b. Manchester, Eng., Apr. 21, 1901; s. James Marshall and Elizabeth (Cain) H.; brought to U.S., 1915, naturalized, 1932; student Salvation Army Coll., 1919; m. Rose Evangeline Hughes, Jan. 6, 1926 (dec. Oct. 1974); children—Samuel Brengle, Joseph and Elizabeth (Mrs. George Hansen) (twins), David, Rose (Mrs. Albert Hager). Commd. lt. Salvation Army, 1919; served in field, Toledo, Sandusky, O., Cleve., Cin., 1919-36; divisional comdr., Buffalo, 1936-39, Phila., 1939-47; field sec. Eastern states, N.Y.C., 1947-52; chief exec. sec. western ty., Hawaii, Alaska, San Francisco, 1952-57, territorial comdr., 1957-62, comdr. central ty., 1962-65, nat. comdr., 1966, sr. commr., 1970. Recipient Award Merit for 50 yrs. unbroken service as Salvation Army officer, 1970; Holiness Proponent Year award Nat. Holiness Assn., 1971. Home: San Jose, Cal. Died Aug. 1974.

HEPNER, WALTER RAY, educator; b. Covina, Calif., Oct. 30, 1891; s. William Henry and Mary Minerva (Jones) H.; student La Verne (Calif.) Coll., 1909-10; A.B., U. of Southern Calif., 1913, A.M., 1916, Ed.D., 1937; also student U. of Chicago, and U. of Calif.; m. Frances Parnell Keating, July 1, 1919; 1 son, Walter Ray. Secondary sch. science teacher, Ill. and Calif., 1913-19; prin. evening high sch. Long Beach, Calif., 1919-20; vice prin. high sch., Fresno, Calif., 1920-23, asst. supt. and dir. research pub. schs., same, 1923-25, asst. supt. and prin. high sch., 1925-26, supt. 1926-28; supt. pub. schs., San Diego, Calif., 1928-34; chief Div. of Secondary Schs., State Dept. of Edn., 1934, 35; pres. San Diego (Calif) State Coll. from 1935; instr. in edn., San Jose State Teachers Coll., summer 1923; acting asst. prof. edn., Stanford, summer 1926; extension course lecturer dept. edn., Fresno State Teachers Coll., 1928-28; instr. edn., San Diego State Teachers Coll., summer 1928. Claremont Coll., summer 1930; acting prof. edn., Stanford U., summers 1927 and 1934, lecturer on edn., U. of Calif. at Los Angeles, summers 1935, 42 and 44; lecturer U. of So. Calif., summers 1938, 40, 41, 48; ednl. cons. office Mil. Govt. in Ger. of U.S., Feb.-June 1947.

Mem. N.E.A., Calif. State Teachers Assn., Calif. Soc. for Study Secondary Edn., Pacific S.W. Acad., Phi Delta Kappa, Kappa Delta Pi. Republican. Conglist. Mason. Author: (all with Mrs. Frances Keating Hepner) The Good Citizen, 1924; Junior Citizens in Action, 1927; Laboratory Textbook in Civics, 1931. Home: Baltimore Md., Died Jan. 13, 1976.

HEPWORTH, BARBARA, sculptor; b. Wakefield, Yorkshire, Eng., Jan. 10, 1903; d. Herbert Raikes and Gertrude Allison (Johnson) Hepworth; student Wakefield Girls High Sch., 1910-19, Leeds Sch. Art, 1919-20, Royal Coll. Art, London, 1920-23; traveling fellowship, Florence, Siena, Rome, 1923-25; D.Litt., U. Birmingham, 1960, U. Leeds, 1961, U. Exeter, 1966, U. Oxford, 1968, U. London, 1970; m. John Skeaping (div. 1931); 1 son, Paul (dec.); m. 2d, Ben Nicholson (div. 1951); children—Simon, Rachel and Sarah (triplets). Represented in permanent collections Mus. Modern Art (N.Y.C.), Smith Coll. Art, Detroit Mus. Art. Walker Art Center, Mpls., Tate Gallery, London, Yale U. Mus., Nat. Gallery of Victoria, Melbourne, Nat. Gallery of New South Wales, Sydney, Middelheimpark, Antwerp, Belgium, Museu de Arte Moderna de Sao Paulo, Brazil, Nat. Gallery to Can., Ottawa, Vancouver (B.C., Can.) Art Gallery, Victoria and Albert Mus., London, Riijksmuseum Kröller-Müller, Otterlo, Holland, museums of Leeds, Manchester, Birmingham, Bristol, Wakefield, Nat. Gallery of New Zealand, Washington U., St. Louis, Carlsberg Found., Copenhagen, Marie-Louise and Gunnar Didrichsen Art Found., Helsinki, Dag Hammarskjold Mus., Backakra, Sweden, UN, N.Y.C.; one-man exhbn. in Lefevre Gallery (London), 1933-52, Gimpel Fils, 1952-71, Marlborough Fine Art Ltd., 1966-70. Retrospective exhbn. XXV Venice Biennale, 1950, Whitechapel Art Gallery London, Eng., 1954, 62, Sao Paulo 5th Biennial, 1959, Tate Gallery, London, 1968, Marlborough Gallery, N.Y.C., 1974; retrospective exhbn. touring Scandinavia 1964-65, HaKone Open-Air Mus., Japan, 1970. Exhibited outdoor sculpture in Battersea Park (London), Phila., Varese (Italy), Middleheim Park (Antwerp), Holland Park (London). Twentieth century sculpture exhbn. at Phila., Chgo., Mus. Modern Art (N.Y.C.), 1952-53. A 2d prize winner in Internat. Sculpture Competition for The Unknown Political Prisoner, 1953; Grandprize, Sao Paulo Biennal, 1959; Fgn. Minister's award at Mainichi Exhbn., 1963. Author monograph. Created dame comdr. Order British Empire; hon. freeman Borough St. Ives, 1968; bard of Cornwall, 1968. Address: St. Ives, Cornwall England. Died May 20, 1975; buried Longstone Cemetery, Carbis-Bay, St. Ives, Cornwall, England.

HERBERT, ADDIE HIBLER, librarian; b. Eufaula, Okla., May 19, 1921; d. Lamar George and Jessie Beatrice (Green) Hibler; B.S. in Home Econs., Langston U., 1938-42; M.S. in Home Econs., Okla. State U., 1952; postgrad. Wichita U., 1947, U. So. Cal., summers, 1948, 50, 62, Atlanta U., 1960-61, Northeastern State Coll., summers 1965, 66; m. children—Adam William, Jr., Tamashia Yvonne, Marcell Buckner. Librarian, Moton High Sch., Taft, Okla., 1946-47; tchr., registrar Manual Tng. High Sch., Muskogee, 1947-59; counselor, librarian Sadler Jr. High Sch., 1959-64; librarian Manual Tng. High Sch., 1964-66; dir. Muskogee Schs. Media Center, 1966-72. Speaker on creation and maintenance media centers. Mem. Okla. Health Planning Council, 1968-72; sec. Muskogee PTA Council, 1966-68, 2d v.p., 1971-72; mem. Mayor's Council Youth Opportunity, 1969-70; mem. adv. com. Consultative Center Sch. Desegregation, 1967-69. Mem. Am., Okla. Eastern Dist. (chmn. 1971-72) library assns., Am. Assn. Sch. Librarians, Nat., Okla., Muskogee edn. assns., Delta Sigma Theta. Clubs: Literary Physical Social, Coterie (Muskogee). Home: Norman, Okla. Died Sept. 7, 1972.

HERBERT, THOMAS J(OHN), judge; b. Cleveland, Oct. 28, 1894; s. John T. and Jane A. (Jones) H.; A.B., Adelbert Coll. Western Res. U., 1915, LL.B., 1920; m. Jeanette Judson, Apr. 30, 1919 (dec. Dec. 1945); children—Metta Jane (Mrs. Lewis C. Stevers), Daniel Judson, John David; m. 2d, Mildred Helen Stevenson, Jan. 3, 1948; 1 dau., Rosemary Jane. Asst law dir., Cleve., 1920-21; asst. co. prosecutor, Cuyahoga County, O., 1922-23; gen. practice law, Cleve., 1924-28, 49-53; asst. atty, gen. Pub. Utilities Commn. of Ohio, 1929-33; spl. counsel to atty. gen. in liquidation of Union Trust Co., Cleve., 1933-37; atty. gen. Ohio, 1939-44; gov. Ohio, 1947-48; chmn. subversive Activities Control Bd., Washington, 1953-56; judge Ohio State Supreme Court, 1956-74. Served as 1st lt. USAAF, 1917-18, 56th Squadron R.A.F., B.E.F., France, 1918-20; comdr. 37th Div. Aviation, Ohio N.G., 1927-31, 37th Air Officer, 1931-33. Decorated Distinguished Flying Cross (Britain); D.S.C., Purple Heart (U.S.). Mem. Am., Ohio State, Cleve. bar assns., Am. Legion, Vets. Fgn. Wars, Disabled Am. Vets., Mil. Order World Wars, Army and Navy Legion of Valor, Disabled Officers Assn., Quiet Birdmen, Air Force Assn., Delta Tau Delta, Phi Delta Phi. Republican. Methodist. Mason, Moose. Clubs: Union, City (Cleve.): University, Columbus (Columbus); Burning Tree, Army and Navy (Washington). Home: Columbus, O. Died Oct. 26, 1974.

HERBERT, WALTER, opera dir.; b. Frankfurt am Main, Germany, Feb. 18, 1902; s. Milton Chase and Marie (Gans) Seligman; studied with Arnold Schoenberg, Vienna, Austria, 1920-24; student law U. Frankfurt, 1919-20; m. Madeleine Ballon, Apr. 20, 1951 (div. July 1964); 1 dau., Bettina. Came to U.S., 1938, naturalized, 1944. Guest condr. operas, symphonies, Berlin, Vienna, Budapest, Paris, Warsaw, Russia, Italy, Egypt, Japan, Can., Mexico, 1930-75; condr. opera, Bern, Switzerland, 1925-31; mus. dir. Volksopera, Vienna, Austria, 1931-38; various positions, San Francisco, 1938-43; gen. dir., condr. New Orleans Opera House Assn., 1943-54, Houston Grand Opera Assn., 1955-72, San Diego Opera, 1964-75. Mem. San Francisco, San Diego, Houston musicians unions. Home: San Diego, Cal. Died Sept. 14, 1975; buried El Camino Meml. Park, San Diego, Cal.

HERBST, STANISLAW, educator; b. Rakwere, Estonia, July 12, 1907; s. Waclaw and Maria (Nowohonska) H.; M. Philosophy, U. Warsaw, 1929, Ph.D., 1931; m. Irene Korotynska, July 6, 1936; children—Marcin, Maria. Mem. faculty U. Warsaw, 1946—, prof., 1954—, dean hist. scis., 1965-69, editor Warsaw Year Book. Mem. Municipal Council, Warsaw, 1957-62. Recipient Cross of Merit with Swords (2d class), Polonia Restituta (4th class), Labor Flag (2d class). Mem. Polish Hist. Soc. (pres. 1956-73. Author: Torun's Corporations, 1933; Livonian Wars 1938; Warsaw from the 18th to the 20th Century, 1949; Zamosc, 1955; Polish Revolutionary War 1794, 1967; Polish-Swedish War 1656; Battle of Warsaw 28-30, VII, 1656, 1973. Home: Warsaw, Poland. Died June 24, 1973; buried Powazki Cemetery, Warsaw, Poland.

HERMAN, ALEXANDER C., container mfg. exec.; b. N.Y.C., 1897; grad. Columbia, 1918; m. Florence Rogatz; children—Pat, John A. Vice pres., dir. Nat. Container Corp. Home: New York City, NY. Died Oct. 8, 1974.

HERMAN, STEWART WINFIELD, clergyman; b. York, Pa., Nov. 17, 1878; s. Simon Henry and Mary Lydia (Rupp) H.; prep. edn., York County (Pa.) Acad., A.B., Gettysburg (Pa.) Coll., 1899, M.A., 1902, D.D., 1919; B.D., Gettysburg Sem., 1902; D.D., Carthage (Ill.) Coll., 1917; m. Mary O'Neal Benner, Oct. 21, 1908; children—Stewart Winfield, Mary Elizabeth, Martha Jane, Janice Benner (dec.). Ordained ministry Luth. Ch., 1902; pastor Wrightsville, Pa., 1902-03, Zion Luth. Ch., Harrisburg, Pa., from 1904. Pres. E. Pa. Synod, 1914-15; pres. Foreign Mission Bd. United Luth. Ch., 1930-38; pres. publ. bd. United Luth. Ch., 1934-42; mem. investment commn. United Luth. Ch., 1931-38; sec. Pa. Council of Chs. from 1926; pres. Gettysburg Luth. Summer Assembly, 1912; mem. Synodical Mission Bd. and examining com., E. Pa. Synod, Synodical dir. Luth. World Action for Central Pa. Synod, Dir. Irving Coll. (Mechanicsburg, Pa.), Grace Coll. (Washington, D.C.). Trustee Gettysburg Coll. Mem. Luth. Hist. Soc. (pres.), Ministerial Assn. Harrisburg and Dauphin County, Phi Sigma Kappa (grand chaplain), Phi Beta Kappa. Republican. Mason (33°; grand chaplain Grand Lodge of Pa.); mem. Lions Internat. Clubs: University, Torch. Executive. Home: Harrisburg, Pa.†

HEROD, WILLIAM ROGERS, bus cons.; b. Indpls., Feb. 13, 1898; s. William P. and Mary Beaty (Applegate) H.; Ph.B. in Mech. Engring. magna cum laude, Sheffield Sci. Sch., Yale, 1918; m. Caroline K. Fries, Aug. 10, 1949. Student engr., test course Gen. Electric Co., Schenectady, 1919, spl. asst. constrn. engring. dept., 1919-29; asst. to pres. Internat. Gen. Electric Co., N.Y.C., 1929-34; asst. to mng. dir. Assoc. Elec. Industries, Ltd., London, 1934-37, dir., 1945-51; v.p. Internat. Gen. Electric Co., 1937-42, exec. v.p., July-Sept. 1945, pres., 1945-60, ret., 1960, dir., 1945-52; v.p. Gen. Electric Co., 1952-60, ret., 1960; dir. numerous fgn. companies, 1945-60; cons. on internat. bus., 1960-74; dir. Transatlantic Fund, Inc., 580 Park Av., Inc., others. Apptd. coordinator def. prodn. NATO, 1951, with personal rank of minister. Mem. City Planning Commn., Schenectady, 1923; mem. Mayor's Com. Golden Jubilee, N.Y.C., 1948. Served as pvt. 10th Regt., Conn. N.G., 1916; mem. R.O.T.C., Yale, 1917-18; from pvt. to 1st lt. U.S. Army, 1918; 1st lt. F.A., O.R.C., 1919-24; commd. lt. col. USAAF, 1942, col., 1943; inactive status, 1945. Mem. univ. council Yale and chmn. com. div. engring., 1948-51; ex-officio mem. Yale Alumni Bd., 1952-74; asso. fellow Pierson Coll., Yale, 1948-51. Mem. Latin-Am. Subcom. Bus. Adv. Council, Washington, 1948-51, 56-58, chmn., 1950; dir. emeritus Internat. House, N.Y.C.; dir. Spanish Inst., Inc. Profl. engr., N.Y. Decorated Commenda dell' Ordine al Merito della Repubica Italiana; Order of Sacred Treasure, 3d Class (Japan), 1957; oficial Ordem Nacional do Cruzeiro do Sul (Brazil), 1958; caballero Gran Cruz de la Orden del Merita Civil (Spain), 1958; Capt. Robert Dollar Meml. Award for distinguished contbn. to advancement fgn. trade Nat. Fgn. Trade Council, 1958. Mem. Council Fgn. Relations; dir. Nat. Fgn. Trade Council, 1946-67, N.Y. Philharmonic-Symphony Soc., 1950-74, mem. China Med. Bd., 1947-68. Mem. I.E.E.E. (life), Am. Soc. M.E. (life), Inst. Internat. Edn. (hon. trustee), Atlantic Council U.S. (dir.), Nat. Inst. Social Scis., Acad. Polit. Sci., Internat. C. of C. (U.S. council), Archaeol. Inst. Am., Assn. Yale Alumni (assembly 1972-74), Japan Soc., Asia Soc., Council on Fgn. Relations, Sigma Xi. Republican. Clubs: Explorers, Pilgrims, University, Union, Yale, Metropolitan Opera (N.Y.C.); Graduates, Lawn (New Haven); American (London); Mohawk (Schenectady). Patentee elec. discharge due change humidity atmosphere. Home: New York City N.Y. Died July 19, 1974; interred The Washington Cathedral, Washington, D.C.

HERR, JOHN KNOWLES, army officer; b. White House, N.J., Oct. 1, 1878; s. Henry Burdette and Virginia Buford (Large) H.; student Reading Acad., Flemington, N.J., 1890-95; Lafayette Coll., 1895-98; B.S., U.S. Mil. Acad., 1902, hon. Dr. of Science. Lafayette College, May 1942; m. Helen Maxwell Hoyle. Sept. 15, 1903; children—Helen Hoyle (wife of Willard A. Holbrook, Jr., U.S. Army), Fanny DeRussy. Commd. 2d lt., U.S. Army, 1902, and advanced through the grades to maj. gen., 1938; with 7th U.S. Cav., 1902-11; instr. in English and equitation, U.S. Mil. Acad., 1911-13; with 11th Cav., 1913-16; 4gh Cav., 1916-17; chief of staff 30th Div., 1918-19; Gen. Staff War Dept., 1920; asst. chief of staff, Am. Forces in Germany, 1921-22; Gen. Staff, War Dept., 1923-24; grad. field officers' course, Cav. Sch., Ft. Riley, 1925, Command and Gen. Staff Sch., Ft. 1926. Army War Coll., Washington. D.C., 1927; with 2d Cav., 1928; instr. Army War Coll., 1929-31; dir. G-2, Army War Coll., 1932; with 3d Cav., 1932; Insp. Gen. Dept. Governors Island, 1933-34; comdg. 7th Cav., Ft. Bliss, Tex., 1935-38; chief of cavalry, Washington, D.C., 1938-42, retired Feb. 28, 1942. Awarded Distinguished Service Medal. Pres. Army Mut. Aid Association. Clubs: Army and Navy (Washington, D.C.); Army and Navy Country (Arlington). Home: Washington, D.C.†

HERRICK, SAMUEL, JR., astronomer; b. Madison County, Va., May 29, 1911; s. Samuel and Fanny (Field) H.; A.B., Williams Coll., 1932, D.Sc., 1962; Ph.D., U. Cal., Berkeley, 1936; m. Betulia Toro, June 15, 1934; children—Henry Toro (killed in action in Vietnam, 1965), Nike Toro, Samuel Rufus. A.F. Morrison fellow Lick Obs., 1936-37; acting asst. prof. astronomy U. Wash., 1937; instr. U. Cal., Los Angeles, 1937-42, asst. prof., 1942-47, asso. prof., 1947-52, prof. astronomy, 1959-62, prof. astronomy and engring., 1962, chmn. dept. astronomy, 1943-45, 46-51; Hunsaker prof. Mass. Inst. Tech., 1961-62. Mathematician Nat. Bur. Standards, 1948-49; orbit determination cons. govt., industry, 1947. Guggenheim fellow, 1945-46, 52-53. Fellow Brit. Inst. Nav. (hon. mem.), Royal Astron. Soc., Am. Astronautical Soc., Brit. Interplanetary Soc., Am. Inst. Aeros. and Astronautics (dir. 1963-65); hon. mem. Inst. Nav. (exec. sec. 1945-52, pres. 1952-53, chmn. space nav. com. 1957-60); mem. Internat. Astron. Union, Am. Astron. Soc., Internat. Acad. Astronautics, Astron. Soc. Pacific, Phi Beta Kappa. Author: Tables for Rocket and Comet Orbits, 1953; Astrodynamics, Vol. I, 1971, Vol. II, 1972. Home: Beverly Hills, Cal. Died Mar. 20, 1974; interred Holy Cross Cemetery and Mausoleum, Los Angeles, Cal.

HERRINGTON, LEWIS BUTLER, pub. utilities exec.; b. Albany, Ga., Apr. 8, 1880; s. Alexander Polk and Camilla (Ogletree) H.; B.S., Centre Coll., Danville, Ky., 1901; LL.B., Mercer U., 1902; m. Susan Hume, Oct. 8, 1902; children—Lewis Butler, Eugenia Burnam (Mrs. Richard Vernon Green), Alexander Polk, Hume Chenault, Susan Hume, Mary Chenault; m. 2d, Florence Allyn Tate, 1931. Admitted to Ky. bar, 1902, and practiced at Richmond until 1915; engaged in business for self under name of L.B. Herrington & Co., pub. utility properties. Mem. advisory bd. Ky. State Geological Survey, 1912-17; member Ky. House of Representatives, 1910-12; presidential elector, 8th Congl. Dist., 1917. Mem. Nat. Electric Light Assn. (ex-pres. East Central Div.), Ky. Assn. Pub. Utilities (ex-pres.), Phi Delta Theta. Democrat. Methodist. Clubs: Pendennis, Kentucky, Louisville Country (Louisville); Atlanta Athletic Club. Home: Atlanta, Ga.†

HERRIOTT, MAXWELL HAINES, lawyer; b. Des Moines, Apr. 21, 1899; s. Frank Irving and Mary (Haines) H.; A.B., Grinnell Coll., 1920; B.A. Juris., Oxford (Eng.) U., 1922, M.A., B.C.L., 1923; LL.B., U. Wis., 1924; m. Ruth G. Hewitt, Sept. 11, 1926; 1 dau., Mary Joan (Mrs. C.A. Wright). Admitted to Wis. bar, 1925; secr to Justice Supreme Ct. Wis., 1924-26; faculty U. Wis. Law Sch., 1924-27; asso. with firm Quarles, Herriott, Clemons, Teschner & Noelke, and predecessor, Milw., partner, 1934-73; lectr. law suretyship Marquette U. Law Sch. Dir. Allis Chalmers Corp., Robertson, Inc., Milw. Pres. Whitefish Bay Library Bd., 1957-73; vice chmn. met. problems com. Greater Milw. Com.; organizer Civil War Round Table Milw., 1946; speaker on life of Lincoln. Trustee Grinnell Coll., 1945-73; bd. dirs. Childrens Aid Soc., Wis., 1934-41, pres., 1938-41. Fellow Am. Bar Found., Am. Coll. Trial Lawyers; mem. Am., Milw. (pres. 1938-39) bar assns., State Bar Wis. (bd. govs.), Am. Law Inst., Phi Alpha Delta. Clubs: Milwaukee, Milwaukee Country, Milwaukee Athletic, University (Milw.); Madison (Wis.). Home: Milwaukee Wis. Died July 13, 1973.

HERRMANN, BERNARD, composer; b. N.Y.C., June 29, 1911; ed. N.Y. U., Juilliard Sch. Founder, condr. New Chamber Orch., 1931-32; conducting appearances with N.Y. Philharmonic, BBC Symphony; staff condr. CBS. Composer scores for films including Citizen Kane, Magnificient Ambersons, Jane Eyre, Anna and the King of Siam, Snows of Kilimanjaro,

Beneath the 12-Mile Reef, King of the Khyber Rifles, Garden of Evil, The Egyptian, Prince of Players, The Trouble with Harry, The Kentuckian, Man in the Gray Flannel Suit, The Man Who Knew Too Much, The Devil and Daniel Webster, Fahrenheit 451; other works include Mobe Dick, Welles Raises Kane (ballet), Wuthering Heights (opera); also composer works for orch., chorus, chamber music, theatre. Recipient Acad. award for best score All That Money Can Buy, 1941. Home: London, England., Died Dec. 24, 1975.

HERSHEY, ROBERT LANDIS, mfg. exec., chem. engr.; b. Anderson, Ind., Dec. 11, 1901; s. Chauncey Bachmann and Elizabeth (Landis) H.; S.B., Mass. Inst. Tech., 1923, S.M., 1924, Sc.D., 1935; m. Mildred Norris Cooper, June 30, 1928 (dec. 1971); children—Elizabeth Cooper (Mrs. Ben W. Melvin, Jr.). Robert Landis, MIchael L., Stephen L.; m. 2d, Florence Elizabeth Prickett Warren, Dec. 1972. Teaching. research, dept. chem. engring. Mass. Inst. Tech., 1924-36: with E. I. duPont de Nemours & Co., 1936-66, beginning as research engr. ammonia dept., successively lab. dir., asst. dir. research, asst. gen. mgr. ammonia dept., asst. gen. mgr. polychemicals dept., gen. mgr. polychemicals dept., 1936-58, v.p. dir., mem. exec. com., 1958-66; dir. DuPont of Canada, Ltd., 1955-66. Fellow Am. Association for Advancement of Sci.; mem. American Chem. Soc., Am. Inst. Chem. Engrs. Episcopalian. Clubs: Wilmington, Wilmington Country: Vicmead Hunt; Metropolitan (N.Y.C.). Home: Kennett Square, Pa. Died June 20, 1973.

HERTZKA, WAYNE SOLOMON, architect; b. Spokane, Wash., July 13, 1907; m. Arch., Mass. Inst. Tech., 1931. With Hertzka & Knowles, San Francisco, 1933—, Hertzka & Knowles, Inc., 1958—, prin. works include Anza Elementary Sch., San Francisco, 1953, Holiday Lodge, San Francisco, 1955, Am. Fore-Loyalty Group office bldg., San Francisco, 1957, Crown Zellerbach office bldg., San Francisco, 1959, State Bar of Cal. hdgrs. bldg., San Francisco, 1960, Pacific Tel. Co. hdqrs. bldg., Sacramento, 1961, Standard Oil Co. of Cal. bldg., 1964—. Served to lt. col. AUS, 1942-46. Decorated Legion of Merit. Recipient award of merit A.I.A. for Crown Zellerbach bldg., 1961. Fellow A.I.A. (pres. No. Cal. chpt. 1955-56, pres. Cal. council 1960; nat. pres. 1961; 2d v.p. 1964). Address: San Francisco, Cal. Died Nov. 18, 1973.

HERTZOG, WALTER SYLVESTER, educator, historian; b. Shamokin, Pa., March 20, 1881; s. Theodore Burr and Fayetta (Van Schminkey) H.; student Lafayette Coll., 1900-02, hon. Litt.M., 1926; A.B., Harvard, 1905; Columbia, Grad. Sch. Polit. Science, 1907-09. Columbia Law Sch., 1909-10; Gen. Theol. Sem. and Union Theol. Sem., N.Y. City, 2 yrs.; grad. student in edn., U. of Calif., 1925-26, U. of Southern Calif., 1926-28; LL.D., Calif. Coll. of Law, 1932; m. Sadie Roselle Dinger, Apr. 21, 1906; children—Walter Sylvester (A.B., U. of Calif., A.M., U. of Southern Calif.), Mrs. Dorothy Beatrice Wyatt (A.B., U. of Calif., A.M., U. of Southern Calif.), Catherine Fayette (A.B. and A.M., Univ of Calif.). Served as instr. Mt. Pleasant Mil. Acad. (N.Y.), head of English dept. Cutler Sch. (N.Y. City), and of modern langs dept. Mercersburg (Pa.) Acad.; sociol. expert, Com. of 100 in investigation of Tammany Hall, New York; investigated Dept. of Commr. of Accounts, N.Y. City, under Mayor Mitchel; associated with Dr. Peter Roberts of Yale U. in drafting plans for first Americanization work in N.Y. City; buyer of rare books and mss. for Am. Art Galleries, N.Y. City, 6 yrs; associated with George D. Smith, buyer of rare books for Henry E. Huntington Library; hon. curator Harvard Library; with dept. of history Hollywood (Calif.) High Sch., 1912-27; dir. Am. hist., research div. Los Angeles City Schs. from 1927; dean of Student-Authors Guild of America. Dir. Mexican Expdn. of Internat. Deserts Conservation League, 1931; economic adviser to Mexican government; dir. archaeol. expdns. to Mexico, 1931-33 and 1936. Hist. research in Nat. Archives of Mexico City, 1937. Proposer of Death Valley, Calif., as a nat. park and also of Boulder Dam National Park. A pioneer in edn. over radio, Los Angeles, for ten years, delivering over 1,250 radio lectures, including 540 on American history; in charge radio programs Los Angeles public schools, 4 yrs.; research dir. Continental Educational and Religious Films, Hollywood, from 1933. Investigator in Vol. Intelligence Corps (U.S. Army) and in Nat. Intelligence Bur., World War. Presented collection of rare books to Harvard, known as the "Walter Sylvester Hertzog Memorial Collection." Mem. Calif. Soc. Colonial Wars, S.R., Mayan Soc. America (sec.), Nat. Inst. Social Science, Nat. Indian War Vets (hon.), Internat. Deserts Conservation League (trustee), Pacific Geographic Soc. (regent), Pacific Coast Scholarship Com. of Lafayette Coll. (chmn.), Columbia U. Law Sch. Assn., Alpha Sigma Phi (nat. treas.); fellow Am. Geog. Soc. Republican. Episcopalian. Mason (32°, K.T., Shriner). Clubs: Harvard of Southern Calif., Lafayette College Alumni Club of Southern Calif. (v.p.); Harvard (New York). Author of a history of Los Angeles Public Schools, 1855-1930. Autobiography of a Harvard Graduate, 1936, and writer on geneal. and ednl. subjects; editor English edit. of "Government of Mexico," 1937; contbd. chapters on "American Money" for "Bankers Guide Book," 1937. Editor Pacific Mag. Mem. advisory bd. Yenching U., Peiping, China, and Calif. advisory bd. Nat. Economic League. Home: Los Angeles Cal.†

HERVEY, DONALD FRANKLIN, educator; b. Longmont, Colo., Oct. 9, 1917; s. Edgar S. and Edna (Slee) H.; B.S., Colo. State U., 1939; M.S., U. Cal. at Berkeley, 1948; Ph.D., A. and M. Coll. Tex., 1955; m. Bettie E. Culbertson, Dec. 23, 1940; children—Vesta Dianne, Timothy Donald, Elizabeth Ellen. Range examiner U.S. Forest Service, 1939; staff Bur. Land Mgmt. (formerly Dept. Interior Agys.), 1940-43; faculty Colo. State U., 1946-74, successively instr., asst. prof., asso. prof., 1946-57, prof. range mgmt., head dept. range mgmt., 1957-63; chief forestry and range mgmt. sect. Colo. Agrl. Expt. Sta., 1952-63, asso. dir., 1963-69, dir., 1969-72, prof. range sci., 1972-74. Served from 1st lt. to capt. F.A., AUS, 1943-46. Mem. Am. Soc. Range Mgmt. (dir. 1955-58, pres. 1959), Sigma Xi, Phi Kappa Phi, Xi Sigma Pi, Beta Beta Beta. Mem. Christian Ch. (elder.) Home: Fort Collins Colo. Died May 19, 1974.

HESS, WALTER J., banker; b. N.Y.C., Dec. 28, 1901; s. Jacob H. and Ida R. (Gute) H.; A.B., Columbia, 1922, LL.B., 1924; m. Anne C. Roeding, Nov. 10, 1927. Admitted to N.Y. bar, 1925; mem. firm Christman, McKeon & Hess, N.Y.C., 1926-48; pres. Ridgewood Savs. Bank, N.Y.C., from 1948; mem. Queens adv. council Chase Manhattan Bank; pres. Instl. Investors Mut. Fund, Inc., 1955-58, now dir. Chmn. trustees Fund for Savs. Banks, 1965-68. Trustee Wyckoff Heights Hosp. Mem. Savs. Banks Assn. N.Y. (group chmn., pres. 1953-54), Queens County Bar Assn. (pres. 1941). Mason, Elk. Club: Wheatley Hills Golf (East Williston, N.Y.). Home: Holliswood, N.Y. Deceased.

HESS, WALTER RUDOLF, physiologist; b. Mar. 17, 1881; s. Dr. Clemenz and Gertrud (Fischer Saxon) H.; student medicine univs. Lausanne, Berne, Berlin, Kiel and Zurich, 1900-05; M.D., U. Zurich, 1906; Dr. honoris causa in philosophy, U. Berne, 1933, in medicine U. Geneva, 1944, in science, McGill U., Montreal, Can., 1953, in medicine, Freiburg, Germany, 1960; m. Luise Sandmeyer, 1909; children—Gertrud, Rudolf. Asst. Physician and ophthalmologist, 1905-08; oculist, 1906-12; asst. physiology, Zurich. Switzerland and Bonn, Germany, 1913-17; prof. physiology, dir. Physiol. Inst., U. Zurich, 1917-51, ret., 1951; prof. emeritus, med. faculty U. Zurich. Awarded Marcel Benoist prize (Swiss), 1933; Ludwig Medal, German Soc. for Circulation Research, 1938; Nobel prize for medicine and physiology (with Prof. Egas Moniz), 1949. Mem. or hon. mem. numerous Swiss and fgn. learned socs. Author Books, including: Die Regulierung von Blutkreislauf und Atmung, 1932; Beiträge zur Physiologie des Hirnstammes, I, II, 1932, 1938; Die funktionelle Organisation des vegetativen Nervensystemes, 1948; Das Zwichenhirn, 1949, 2d edit., 1953; Diencephalon, 1954; The Functional Organization of the Diencephalon Hypothalamus and Thalamus, 1956; The Biologie of Mind, 1964. Home: Ascona Switzerland. Died Aug. 1973.

HESSE, HERMAN CARL, educator; b. N.Y.C., Mar. 27, 1900; s. Henry Ludwig Stephen and Anna Margareta (Petersen) H.; student Newark Tech. Sch., 1916-21; B.S., Newark Coll. Engring., 1925; M.E., 1927, Doctor Engring., (hon.), 1961; m.: Helen Frances Grafe, June 12, 1926. Prodn. engr., Singer Mfg. Co., Elizabethport, N.J., 1925-28; asst. prof. mech. engring., Newark Coll. Engring., 1928-31; prof. engring. drawing and design, U. of Va., 1931-44; chief engr., Mixing Equipment Co., Rochester, N.Y., 1945-47; prof. mech. engring. Ill. Inst. Tech., Chicago, 1947-49; dean, coll. engring. Valparaiso U. (Ind.), from 1949; design engr., cons. various corps. Cons. Armour Reserach Found., Chgo., 1948-50, NDRC Project, U. of Pa., 1943-44, Chgo. Midway labs. U. Chgo. 1951-54. Licensed profl. engr., State of Indiana, Commonwealth of Va. Am. Soc. M.E., mem. Am. Gear Mfrs. Assn. (academic mem.), Am. Soc. Engring. Edn., Pi Kappa Phi, Rho Lambda Tau, Tau Beta Pi, Pi Tau Sigma. Presbyn. Author: Engineering Tools and Processes, 1941; A Manual in Engineering Drawing, published 1942; Process Equipment Design, 1945; Contbr. editor Van Nostrands Sci. Ency., 1947. Contbr. articles in engring. publs. columnist (under pseudonym Carroll Lewis) Valparaiso-Vidette Messenger. Home: Valparaiso, Ind. Died Nov. 24, 1972; interred Graceland Cemetery, Valparaiso.

HESSE, RICHARD, hardware corp. exec.; b. Chgo., 1895; m. Geraldine. Pres. Ace Hardware Corp., Chgo., 1924-74; dir. Mich. Av. Bank, Chgo. Trustee Henrotin Hosp., Chgo. Home: Chicago, Ill., Died Oct. 20, 1975.*

HESSELLUND-JENSEN, AAGE, Danish diplomat; b. Aarhus, Denmark, Apr. 22, 1911; s. Jens Anton Jensen and Dagny Hessellund (Pederson); J.D., Copenhagen U., 1936; m. Jullette Matthlassen, Apr. 4, 1936; children—Alice Yvonne (Marquesa Cesars Bisognl), Peter Pykke, Paul. With Danish Fgn. Service, 1937-74; lectr. law Copenhagen U., 1940-42, 46-48; sec. Danish legation, Stockholm, Sweden, 1942-46; sect. head Ministry Fgn. Affairs, 1946-49; counsellor, Washington, 1949-54; attached NATO Def. Coll., Paris, France, 1954-55; dir. polit. dept. Ministry Fgn. Affairs, 1956-58, permanent rep. to UN, 1958-64; ambassador to Sweden, 1964-71, to Norway, 1971-74. Decorated comdr. Order of Dannebrog; Finnish Order of White Rose; Crown Order of Thalland; grand cross Swedish Order of the Polar Star; Danish Red Cross medal; Swedish Red Cross medal. Died Apr. 1974.

HESSON, SAMUEL MOODIE, legal educator; b. Watervliet, N.Y., Oct 2, 1906; s. Neil and Elizabeth (Moodie) H.; A.B., Union Coll., Schenectady, 1927, LL.D., 1965; LL.B., Albany Law Sch., 1931; LL.M., Columbia, 1939; m. Dorothy Miller Betts, Jan. 25, 1933; 1 dau., Milda E. (Mrs. Nelson Enos). Admitted to N.Y. bar, 1931; practice in Schenectady, 1931-35; prof. law Albany Law Sch., 1935-64, dean, 1964; cons. N.Y. State Jud. Council, 1940-55, N.Y. State Law Revision Commn., 1940; v.p., dir. Schenectady Savs. and Loan Assn. Del. N.Y. Constl. Conv., 1967. Mem. Phi Beta Kappa. Presbyn. (trustee). Home: Schenectady N.Y. Died May 19, 1975.

HESTER, JOHN HUTCHISON, army officer; b. Albany, Ga., Sept. 11, 1886; s. John Temple and Lily Dale (Hutchison) H.; student U. of Ga., 1903-04; B.S., U.S. Mil. Acad., 1904-08; attended Field Officers Course, Fort Benning, Ga., 1920-21, Command and Gen. Staff Sch., 1921-23, Army War Coll., 1926-27; s. Leila Richardson, Mar. 30, 1910; children—Henry Richardson, John Hutchison. Commd. 2d lt., U.S. Army, 1908, and rose through grades to brig. gen., 1940, major gen., Feb. 1942; exec. for reserve affairs to chief of staff, Washington, D.C., 1940-41; comdg. gen., Camp Wheeler, Ga., 1941; comdg. 43d Inf. Div., 1941-43; comdg. gen. Tank Destroyer Center, Camp Hood, Tex., 1943-44, Camp Croft, S.C. from 1944. Mem. Alpha Tau Omega. Episcopalian. Home: Atlanta, Ga., Died Feb. 11, 1976.

HETHERINGTON, JOHN AIKMAN, author, journalist; b. Sandringham, Victoria, Australia, Oct. 3, 1907; s. Hector and Agnes (Bowman) H.; student Sandringham State Sch., 1931-17, All Saints Grammar Sch., St. Kilda, Victoria, 1917-23; m. Olive Meagher, Mar. 15, 1943; m. 2d, Mollie Roger Maginnis, July 26, 1967. Reporter, feature writer Melbourne Herald group, 1925-35; journalist, London and N.Y.C., 1935-38; feature editor Melbourne Herald, 1938-39; war corr. Middle East and Europe, 1940-45; editor-in-chief Adelaide News, 1945-49; dep. editor Melbourne Argus, 1952-54; feature writer Melbourne Age, 1954-67; author, freelance journalist, 1967-74. Decorated officer Order Brit. Empire; officer Royal Order Phoenix (Greece); recipient Sydney Morning Herald war novel prize, 1947, Walkley award for best mag. story, 1960, Sir Thomas White Meml. prize, 1968; Matthew Flinders prize for best biography of an Australian, 1974. Commonwealth of Australia Lit. fellow, 1967, 72. Clubs: Savage, Melbourne. Author: Airborne Invasion, 1943; Australian Soldier, 1943; The Winds Are Still, 1948; Blamey, 1954; Australians: Nine Profiles, 1960; Norman Lindsay (monograph), 1961; Forty-two Faces, 1962; Australian Painters, 1963; Witness to Things Past, 1964; Uncommon Men, 1965; Pillars of the Faith, 1966; Melba, 1967; The Morning Was Shining, 1971; Blamey: Controversial Soldier, 1973; Norman Lindsay: The Embattled Olympian, 1973. Home: Malvern Victoria, Australia. Died Sept. 17, 1974; cremated.

HETTINGER, HERMAN STRECKER, financial cons.; b. Reading, Pa., Jan. 13, 1902; s. Edwin L. and Eloise (Strecker) H.; B.S., U. Pa., 1923, M.A., 1929, Ph.D., 1933; m. Helen E. Wessells, Apr. 9, 1952. Faculty, Wharton Sch. U. Pa., 1929-42, chmn. marketing dept., 1940-42; dep. dir. domestic br. Office War Information 1942-44; devel. pub. service program Crowell-Collier Pub. Co., 1944-48; econ. cons. to broadcasting industry, 1930-55; econ. and marketing cons. Overseas Consultants, Inc., Tehran, Iran, 1949; asso. dir. research McCann-Erickson Inc., 1949-50; with D.M.S. Hegarty & Assos., Inc., N.Y.C., 1951-72, v.p., 1952-60, pres., 1960-72; dir. Wing Prodns., Inc., Bedford, Mass. Dir. research Nat. Assn. Broadcasters, Washington, 1934-35; dir. Nat. Orchestral Survey, N.Y.C., 1938-39. Various offices Nat. Pub. Relations Council for Health and Welfare Services, N.Y.C., 1946-66; mem. Books-Across-the-Sea book selection panel English-Speaking Union, 1956-72. Mem. Am. Marketing Assn., N.Y. Soc. Security Analysts, English-Speaking Union; Beta Gamma Sigma. Club: Lawyers (N.Y.C.); Dacor (Washington). Author: Decade of Radio Advertising, 1933; America's Symphony Orchestras, 1940; Financial Public Relations, 1954, others. Home: New York City NY. Died Oct. 2, 1972.

HEYER, GEORGETTE, author; b. London, Eng., Aug. 16, 1902; d. George and Sylvia (Watkins) Heyer; ed. privately; m. G.R. Rougier, Aug. 18, 1925; 1 son, Richard George. Author hist. and detective novels, 1921-73, including The Black Moth, 1921, An Infamous Army, 1937, The Spanish Bride, 1940, The Corinthian, 1941, Friday's Child, 1944, Cotillion, 1953, Sylvester, 1957, A Civil Contract, 1961, The Nonesuch, 1962, False Colours, 1964; Frederica, 1965; Black Sheep, 1966; Cousin Kate, 1968; Charity Girl, 1970; My Lord John, pub. posthumously, 1975. Address: London England. Died July 4, 1974; cremated.

HEYKE, JOHN ERICSON, JR., corp. exec.; b. New Haven, Sept. 29, 1910; s. John Ericson and Marie C. (Miller) H.; B.S., Yale, 1933; m. Gertrude B. Mack, Dec. 11, 1936; 1 son, John Ericson. Began as cadet engr.

Bklyn. Union Gas Co., 1933, chmn., dir.; dir. Bklyn. Savs. Bank, Mfrs. Hanover Trust Co. Bd. dirs. Bklyn. Inst. Arts and Sci. Served as lt. comdr. USNR, 1942-45. Mem. Am. Gas Assn. (past pres.; dir.), Soc. Gas Lighting. Clubs: Brooklyn, Yale. Home: Locust Valley, N.Y. Died Oct. 1974.

HEYL, HENRY LIVINGSTON, surgeon; b. Chgo, Oct. 2, 1906; s. Ernst Oscar and Charlotte (Taylor) H.; A.B., Hamilton Coll., 1928; M.D., Harvard, 1933; m. Katharine Agate Grove, 1944; children—Nicholas, Michael. Intern, Johns Hopkins, Boston Children's hosps., 1933-35; asst. resident surgery and neurosurgery New Haven Hosp., Lahey Clinic, Boston, 1935-38; resident neurosurgery Children's, Mass. Gen. hosps., Boston, 1938-40; asst. surgery Harvard Med. Sch., 1940; registered cons. neurosurgery Brit. Emergency Med. Service, Midland Area, Birmingham, Eng., 1940-41; neurosurgeon Am. Hosp. in Britain, 1940-41, Hitchcock Clinic, Hanover, N.H., 1942-75; asst. prof. surgery Dartmouth Med. Sch., 1946, asst. dir. med. scis., 1957-60, asso. dean, 1960-65, asso. prof. anatomy, 1962-68, prof., 1968-71, emeritus, 1971-75; sr. cons. neurosurgery VA Hosp., White River Junction, Vt., 1942-52. Exec. dir. Hitchcock Found., 1953-63. Served as neurosurgeon, capt. AUS, 1942-43. Diplomate Am. Bd. Neurol. Surgery. Mem. Am. Acad. Neurol. Surgery, Soc. Neurol. Surgeons, Assn. Research Nervous and Mental Diseases, Boston Soc. Neurology and Psychiatry, Harvey Cushing Soc., Phi Beta Kappa, Alpha Delta Phi. Conglist. Editor: Jour. Neuro-surgery, 1965-75. Contbr. articles to med. jours. Home: Norwich Vt. Died Mar. 1, 1975; interred, Norwich, Vt.

HIBBARD, CLAUDE WILLIAM, educator, paleontologist; b. Toronto, Kan., Mar. 21, 1905; s. Charles E. and Evie (Johnson) H.; B.A., U. Kan., 1933, M.A., 1934; Ph.D., U. Mich., 1941; m. Faye Louise Ganfield, Sept. 8, 1934; 1 dau., Katherine (Mrs. John P. Mull). Wildlife technician Nat. Park Service, 1934-35; mem. faculty U. Kan., 1935, 37, 38-46, curator, asst. prof., 1941-46; mem. faculty U. Mich., Ann Arbor, 1946-73, prof. geology, 1953-73, curator fossil vertebrates, 1953-73. Fellow Geol. Soc. Am.; mem. Kan. (past pres.), Mich. (past pres.) acads. sci., Mich. Geol. Soc. (past pres.), Soc. Vertebrate Paleontology (past pres.), Soc. Mammalogists, Soc. Ichthyologists and Herpetologists, Am. Assn. Petroleum Geologists, Paleontol. Soc. Discoverer of nearly complete Late Cenzoic faunal sequence. Home: Ann Arbor Mich. Died Oct. 9, 1973; interred Toronto, Kan.

HIBBS, BEN, editor, writer; b. Fontana, Kan., July 23, 1901; s. Russell and Elizabeth (Smith) H.; A.B., U. Kan., 1923; D.Litt., Northwestern U., 1947, Temple U., 1948, Southwestern Coll., Winfield, Kan., 1964; m. Edith Kathleen Doty, June 3, 1930; 1 son, Stephen Doty. News editor Fort Morgan (Colo.) Times, 1923, Pratt (Kan.) Tribune, 1924; prof. journalism Hays (Kan.) State Coll., 1924-26; editor, mgr. Goodland (Kan.) News-Republic, 1926-27; mng. editor Arkansas City (Kan.) Traveler, 1927-29; asso. editor Country Gentleman, Phila., 1929-40; editor, 1940-42; editor Sat. Eve. Post, 1942-61, sr. editor, 1962; sr. editor The Reader's Digest, 1963-72; mem. exec. com. Curtis Pub. Co., 1940-61. Mem. U.S. Adv. Commn. on Information, 1951-54. Recipient U. Pa. Journalism award, 1947; U. Kan. Distinguished Alumni citation, 1942; nat. award journalistic merit William Allen White Found., 1959; Freedoms Found. George Washington medal award, 1963; School Bell award N.E.A., 1964. Mem. Phi Beta Kappa, Sigma Delta Chi, Sigma Phi Epsilon. Republican. Methodist. Club: Merion Cricket. Contbr. articles Country Gentleman, Saturday Evening Post, Readers Digest. Home: Narberth Pa. Died Mar. 1975; interred Pioneer Meml. Cemetery U. Kan., Lawrence, Kan.

HICKS, ARCHIE RAY, JR., lawyer; b. Levanna, O., Oct. 13, 1915; s. Archie Ray and Nellie (Pangburn) H.; LL.B., Ohio State U., 1937; m. Monica Brown, Nov. 17, 1937; children—Carol J. (Mrs. John L. Cooper), Linda Kay (Mrs. Gary DeFfosse). Admitted to Ohio bar, 1937, practiced in Ripley; solicitor villages of Ripley, Aberdeen and Russellville, O., 1939-74; pros. atty. Brown County, O., 1941-49; dir. Citizens Nat. Bank, Ripley. Pres. Ripley Pub. Library. Mayor Ripley, 1940; alternate del. Republican Nat. Conv., 1948, 52, 60; sec., mem. Brown County Rep. Central Com. Trustee Brown County Gen. Hosp., 1961-70. Mem. Am., Ohio, Brown Coutny bar assns., Ohio bar Assn. Found. Kiwanian (past pres.). Home: Ripley O. Died Dec. 5, 1974.

HICKS, LEWIS WENMAN, steel exec.; b. Indiana Co., Pa., 1871; s. Alfred and Martha U.; m. Anna A. Hicks. Vice pres. Allegheny Ludlum Steel Corp., Pitts., 1900-63, dir., from 1900; pres. First Nat. Bank, Leechburg, Pa., dir. Park Coal Co., Pine Run Co., Bowman Coal Co. Mason. Home: Pittsburgh, Pa.†

HICKS, WILLIAM NORWOOD, educator; b. Durham, N.C., June 18, 1901; s. James Thomas and Ora (Holloway) H.; B.Mech. Engring., N.C. State Coll., 1922, M.S., 1929; A.B., Duke, 1924; M.A., Oberlin Coll., 1928; m. Ann Pitts, June 30, 1930; m. 2d, Mabel Lewis, Sept. 9, 1941; children—William Norwood III, Brona Frances. Mem. faculty N.C. State U., Raleigh, 1924-66, head dept. philosophy and religion, 1935-66, prof. philosophy and religion, 1949-66, prof. emeritus, 1966-73, mem. adminstrv. bd. Sch. Liberal Arts, 1961-66. Active Inter-Racial Commn. South, local United Fund, Travelers Aid Soc., Family Service Soc., Danforth Asso., 1938-43, hon. Danforth asso., 1943-63. Mem. Am. Soc. Engring. Edn., Am. Metaphys. Soc., Nat. Council Family Relations, So. Soc. Philosophy and Psychology, N.C. Philos. Soc., Blue Key, Golden Chain, Phi Kappa Phi, Tau Beta Pi, Sigma Chi. Home: Raleigh N.C. Died Dec. 17, 1973.

HIGBEE, FREDERIC GOODSON, educator; b. Fremont, O., Nov. 29, 1881; s. Jay Alvin and Cora Lavina (Goodson) H.; grad. Kenyon Mil. Acad., Gambler, O., 1898; B.S. in Mech. Engring., Case Sch. Applied Science, 1903, M.E., 1908; m. Beth Mather, June 10, 1912; children—Frederick Goodson, Jay Anders. Asst. engr. with Osborn Engring. Co., and J. B. Davis & Sons, 1903-04; instr. Case Sch. Applied Science, 1904-05; asst. prof. descriptive geometry and drawing, State U. of Ia., 1905-08, prof. and head of dept. engring. drawing, from 1908, dir. of convocations. Chmn. Iowa City Zoning Commn., 1924-25; chmn. Bd. of Adjustment, Iowa City. Fellow Iowa Academy of Science; member A.S.E.E., Sigma Xi, Tau Beta Pi, Pi Tau Sigma, Zeta Psi, Triangle (honorary); secretary Univ. of Iowa Alumni Association, 1930-35. Republican. Quaker. Clubs: Engineers', Triangle. Author: Essentials of Descriptive Geometry, 1915, 4th edit., 1930; Descriptive Geometry Problems, 1921; Engineering Drawing Problems (with Henry C. Thompson, Jr.), 1927; Drawing Board Geometry, 1937; 101 Problems in Drawing Board Geometry, 1938; Engineering Drawing Problems (with John M. Russ), 1940. Contbr. to ednl. and tech. jours. Editor T. Square Page, Jour. Engring. Edn., 1930-36; editor Jour. Engring. Drawing, 1936-37; editor Drawing and Drafting Room Practice, ASA-Z14.1, 1946. Home: Iowa City, Ia.†

HIGGINBOTHAM, JAY CEE, musician; b. Atlanta, May 11, 1906; s. Charlie and Tenpie (Lewis) H.; student Morris Brown Coll., Cin. Indsl. Sch. for Tailoring; m. Margaret Stratton, Dec. 27, 1957. Played with Chick Webb, Fletcher Henderson, Lucky Millinder, 1931-32; with Louis Armstrong, 1932-40, Red Allen sextet, 1940-49; composer Give Me Your Telephone Number, Higginbotham Blues, Swing Out. Recipient gold award Esquire mag., Metronome award winner poll Down Beat. Elk. Home: New York City, N.Y. Died May 1973.

HIGGINS, JAMES HENRY, JR., lawyer; b. Pawtucket, R.I., Feb. 11, 1910; s. James Henry and Ellen Frances (Maguire) H.; student Phillips Exeter Acad., 1927-28; A.B., Brown U., 1932; LL.B., Harvard, 1935; m. Betty Hall, May 26, 1939; children—James Henry III, Barbara Hall (Mrs. Thomas M. Rhine), Louis Hall. Admitted to R.I. bar, 1937; practiced in Pawtucket, 1937-43, Providence, 1943-75; asso. firm Greenough, Lyman & Cross, 1943-45, James L. Taft, 1945-52; partner Higgins, Kingsley & Williamson, 1952-55, Higgins, Cavanagh & Cooney, 1955-75; dir. Leonard Valve Co., Cranston, R.I., Mays Mfg. Co., Warwick, R.I. Mem. devel. com. Gov. Dummer Acad., South Byfield, Mass.; trustee U. R.I. Found.; life mem. scholarship com. Harvard Law Sch. Fellow Am. Bar Found.; mem. Am. (ho. of dels.; bd. govs.), R.I. (pres., past sec.) bar assns., Am. Judicature Soc. (dir.), Delta Upsilon. Clubs: Turks Head (pres.), Hope (Providence); Agawan Hunt (East Providence); Union League (N.Y.C.); Mid-Ocean (Bermuda); Lake Placid (N.Y.). Home: North Smithfield R.I. Died Feb. 15, 1975; interred, Lake Placid, N.Y.

HIGGINS, JOHN MARTIN, naval officer; b. Aug. 13, 1899. Entered U.S. Navy, June 1922; advanced through grades to rear adm., 1950-61, ret. Recipient numerous decorations. Home: Libertyville, Ill. Died Dec. 7, 1973.

HIGGINS, MONTGOMERY EARLE, physician; b. Sir Johns Run, W. Va., Oct. 29, 1879; s. James Leopard and Alice (Cross) H.; M.D., George Washington U., 1904, Naval Med. Sch., 1908; grad. student Allgemeines Krankenhaus, Vienna, N.Y. Post Grad. Sch., London Sch. of Tropical Medicine, Harvard Med. Sch.; m. Grace Young, July 16, 1924; 1 son, Montgomery. Physician, Panama Canal, 1905-07; apptd. asst. surgeon, U.S. Navy, 1907; advanced through grades to capt., 1929; surgeon Naval Hdqrs., Paris, 1918-19; force surgeon, Turkish waters, 1919-21; med. dir. Gendarmerie d'Haiti, Port au Prince, 1925-28; prof. tropical medicine George Washington U., 1930-31; fleet surgeon Asiatic Fleet, 1931-34; comdg. officer Naval Hosp., Portsmouth, N.H., 1936-39; med. officer, Pearl Harbor, T.H., 1941-42; on inactive list, U.S. Navy, from 1946; engaged in practice medicine, Washington. Fellow Am. Coll. Surgeons, Am. Acad. Tropical Medicine; mem. Med. Soc. D.C., A.M.A., Phi Chi, Phi Sigma Kappa. Clubs: Army-Navy (Washington); Chevy Chase (Md.). Home: Washington, D.C.†

HILBERT, GEORGE H(ENRY), publisher; b. Dresden, Germany, Jan. 10, 1881; s. Emil and Clara H.; ed. pub. schs.; m. Dorothea Bornboeft, Sept. 11, 1907. Pres. Music Periodicals, Inc., pubs. of Musical Courier (semi-monthly). Home: Bronxville, N.Y.*†

HILBUN, WILLIAM BRYAN, physician; b. Louisville, Jan. 30, 1931; s. B.B. and Genevieve E. Hilbun; M.D., U. Louisville, 1956; m. Charlotte Graham, Feb. 28, 1942; children—William Bryan, Susan Elaine. Rotating intern Baptist Meml. Hosp., Memphis, 1945-47, resident in pediatrics, 1962-63; resident City of Memphis Hosps., 1963-64; chief nursery sect. Jefferson Hosp., Pine Bluff, 1964-65, mem. infections com., 1964-65; resident in gen. psychiatry City of Louisville Hosps., 1965-67, asst. instr. psychiatry, 1965; fellow in child psychiatry Louisville Child Guidance Clinic, 1967-68, U. Fla., 1968-69; child psychiatrist, mem. pediatric staff William S. Hall Psychiat. Inst., Columbia, S.C.; chief sect. child psychiatry, asso. prof. child psychiatry and pediatrics Med. Coll. Ga., Augusta, 1970-71. Served to capt. M.C., USAF, 1958-60. Diplomate Am. Bd. Pediatrics. Fellow Am. Acad. Pediatrics; mem. A.M.A., Am. Psychiat. Assn. Home: Augusta, Ga. Died May 1, 1971; buried Louisville, Ky.

HILL, ARTHUR B., ins. co. exec.; b. Hillsboro, Ark., September 17, 1879; s. Warren J. and Louanna (Alphin) H.; A.B., Ouchita Coll., 1904; studied summer, U. of Chicago, A.M., Teachers Coll. (Columbia), 1922; m. Mary B. Lakenan, July 6, 1910; children—Martha Winifred, Billy Jean. Teacher, rural schs., Ark., 1899-1903, pub. schs., El Dorado, 1905-07; prin. high sch., Texarkana, 1907-09, Hot Springs, 1909-11, Little Rock, 1910-17; state high sch. insp., Ark., 1917-23; state dir. vocational edn., 1917-27; state supt. of schs., 1923-27; commr. Dept. of Public Utilities, State of Ark., 1941-45; was pres. Ouchita Coll.; exec. sec. Ark. Taxpayers Assn.; with Union Central Life Ins. Co. Democrat. Baptist. Home: Little Rock, Ark.†

HILL, DONALD MACKAY, lawyer; b. Brookline, Mass., Nov. 1, 1877; s. William Henry and Sarah Ellen (May) H.; A.B., Harvard, 1898, LL.B., 1901; m. Annie N. Turner, June 11, 1902 (dec.); children—Donald MacKay, Malcolm Turner, Calvin Austin. Admitted to Mass. bar, 1901, since practiced in Boston; with Carver & Blodgett, 1901-04; partner Bingham, Smith & Hill, 1904-13, Blodgett, Jones, Burnham & Bingham (became Burnham, Bingham, Gould & Murphy), 1913-33; with Donald MacKay Hill, Jr., firm now Hill & Hill, from 1933; pres. Foster's Wharf Co., North Rivers Securities Co., from 1930; treas. Laconia Car Co.; dir. Boston Ins. Co., Old Colony Ins. Co., from 1913. Candidate for Congress, 1928. Mem. Am., Mass., Boston bar assns., Royalston Improvement Soc. (pres.), U.S. Lawn Tennis Assn. (past treas.), N.E. Lawn Tennis Assn. (past v.p.), N.E. Tennis Patrons (past treas.). Clubs: University, Harvard (Boston); Longwood Cricket (Brookline, Mass.); Waban (Mass.) Neighborhood. Home: Waban, Mass.†

HILL, EDMUND WALTON, army officer; b. New London, Conn., April 26, 1896; s. Rowland D. and Angeline (Walton) H.; student, Norwich Free Acad., 1909-14, Case Sch. of Applied Science, 1914-15, Mass. Inst. of Tech., 1916-17; grad. Air Corps Tactical Sch., Command and Gen. Staff Sch., Army War Coll.; m. Mary Elizabeth Wilson, Sept. 1, 1926; m. 2d, Mildred Cary Eaton, Oct. 21, 1962; 1 stepdau., Mrs. John A. Maynard. Commd. 2d lt. Inf., U.S. Army, Aug. 9, 1917, transferred to air service, 1920, and advanced through the grades to brig. gen., 1942; air insp., U.S. Army Air Forces, July 1941 to July 1942; comdg. gen., U.S. Army Forces, Northern Ireland. Coordinator Inter-Am. Def. Bd. Mem. Kappa Sigma. Home: Belgrade Lakes Me. Died May 1, 1973; buried Veteran's Cemetery, Augusta, Me.

HILL, EDWARD LEE, educator, physicist; b. Hartford, Ark., Nov. 3, 1904; s. Robert Lee and Louise (McKnight) H.; B.S. in Elec. Engring., U. Minn., 1925, Ph.D., 1928; m. Irene Ellison, June 8, 1928. Fellow NRC, Harvard, 1928-30; mem. faculty physics U. Minn., Mpls., 1930-37, asso. prof., 1937-46, prof., 1946-62, prof. physics and math., 1962-70, emeritus, 1970-74; research physicist Physics-Tech. Inst. Leningrad, USSR, 1934-35; cons. physicist USN, 1941-45. Mem. Am. Phys. Soc., Am. Math. Soc., Am. Geophys. Union, I.E.E.E., A.A.A.S., Math. Assn. Am., Minn., N.Y. acads. scis., Sigma Xi, Tau Beta Pi. Editor: Phys. Rev., 1950. Research on quantum mechanics, theory of relativity, atmospheric physics. Home: Santa Barbara Cal. Died Jan. 7, 1974.

HILL, EUGENE LOTT, clergyman; b. Montgomery, Ala., Aug. 2, 1878; s. Rev. Luther Leonidas and Laura (Croom) H.; A.B., Southwestern U., Memphis, Tenn., 1897, B.D., 1900, D.D., 1915; A.M., U. of Ga., 1915; m. Annie Graham, June 25, 1904; children—Eugene Lott (dec.), Annie Laurie, Sarah Graham. Ordained ministry Presbyn. Ch. in U.S., 1900; pastor West Point Ga., 1900-01, Eufaula, Ala., 1901-07, First. Ch., Athens, Ga., from 1907; served as preacher at Ga. State Teachers Coll., Lucy Cobb Inst., Agnes Scott Coll. and U. of Ga. Lecturer on "Stewardship" at Presbyn. confs. Montreat, N.C., 1917, Kerrville, Tex., 1919, Union, Columbia and Louisville seminaries, 1920; toured Palestine, Egypt and Europe, 1904. Mem. exec. com. Home Missions of Presbyn. Ch. in U.S., 1912-27; mem. exec. com. on synod's work, 1922-36. Member Board of Education, Athens, 1929-43. Trustee Columbia Theological Seminary, Presbyterian College, Clinton, South Carolina, Athens General Hospital, Clarke County Tuberculosis Hospital. Director Southern Mutual Ins. Co. Moderator Synod of Ga., 1912. Mem. Alpha Tau Omega. Mason, Odd Fellow K.P. Democrat.

Clubs: Athens Country, Cloverhurst Country. Author: Studies in Christian Stewardship, 1917. Editor: Sermons, Addresses and Papers of Luther Leonidas Hill, 1919. Home: Athens, Ga.*†

HILL, GEORGE ROBERT, aircraft exec.; b. Vienna, N.J., Dec. 4, 1913; s. John Lewis and Sarah Elizabeth (Huff) H.; A.B., Rider College, 1932, also Doctor of Laws (honorary), 1956; married to Henriette C. Eigersma, July 6, 1935; children—George Robert II, Carol Ann, John Berrell. Accountant Lybrand, Ross Bors. & Montgomery, Phila., Dallas, N.Y., 1933-49; controller Curtiss-Wright Corp., 1949-52, v.p., 1952-53, v.p. for finance, 1953-57, exec. v.p., 1957-61; mem. bd. dirs. Curtiss-Wright Corp., Curtiss-Wright Can. Ltd., Curtiss-Wright Europa, N.V. (Leiden), Caldwell (N.J.) Wright Airport, Inc. Chmn. bd. trustees Rider Coll., until 1970, trustee emeritus, 1971—. Mem. Nat. Indsl. Conf. Bd., Navy League, U.S., Controllers Inst. Am., Am. Ordnance Assn. Clubs: Economic, Metropolitan, Wings (N.Y.C.); Pennington (Passaic, N.J.); Nat. Aviation (Washington); Hidden Valley Country (Reno, Nev.). Home: Mantoloking, N.J., Died Aug. 22, 1975.

HILL, JOHN CALVIN, fgn. service officer; Ft. Smith, Ark., Aug. 1, 1921; s. John Calvin and Isabel P. (Hill) H.; A.B., Princeton U.; 1943; M.A., George Washington U., 1967; m. McCoy Youmans Metts, Apr. 19, 1947; children—Katherine W., John Calvin, Isabel M. With Dept. State, 1946, fgn. service officer, 1947; 3d sec. Am. legation, Bucharest, 1947-50; asst. U.S. polit. adviser, Trieste, 1950-52; 2d sec. Am. embassy, Guatemala City, 1952-55; 2d sec. Am. embassy, Bangkok, 1955, 1st sec., 1956-58; alt. U.S. council rep. S.E. Asia Treaty Orgn., 1956-58; spl. asst. to asst. sec. state for inter-Am. affairs, 1958-60; Nat. War Coll., 1960-61; consul gen. Dominican Republic, 1961, charge d'affaires, 1962; minister-counselor, Am. Embassy, Caracas, 1962-65, charge d'affaires, 1964-65; dir. Office of North Coast Affairs, Bur. Inter-Am. Affairs, Dept. State, 1965-69; fgn. service inspr., 1969-73. Served as captain, F.A., AUS, 1943-46. Decorated Silver Star. Mem. Am. Fgn. Service Assn. Home: Washington D.C. Died Dec. 27, 1973.

HILL, JOHN LEONARD, editor, educator, lecturer; b. Owen County, Ky., Sept. 15, 1978; s. Rev. George William and Elizabeth (Haydon) H.; A.M., Georgetown (Ky.) Coll., 1899, Litt.D., 1931; A.M., Columbia, 1912; LL.D., Union U., 1935; grad. student, Harvard, U. of Cincinnati, Columbia, U.; L.H.D., Hardin-Simmons U., 1940; m. Emma Eilson, Aug. 21, 1907. Teacher Bardstown (Ky.) Coëducational Coll., 1900-01, high sch., Mt. Sterling, Ky., 1901-04, Covington, 1904-06, University Sch., Louisville, 1906-09; prof. history and polit. science, Georgetown Coll., 1909-22, dean, 1913-22; editor book and other publs. Bapt. S.S. Bd. of Southern Bapt. Conv. from 1922; editor of Home and Foreign Fields, 1932-37; lecturer on hist., lit. and inspirational topics. Sec. Gen. Assn. Baptists in Ky., 1909-22; state dir., Ky., 0,000,000 campaign, Bapt. Ch., 1919-20. Mem. bd. Nashville Y.M.C.A.; chmn., Juvenile and Humane Commn. of Davidson Co., 1938-43, Boy Scout Council, Trustee Tenn. Bapt. Orphanage; pres. Good Will Industries of Nashville; pres. Tenn. Bapt. Foundation; pres. bd. trustees Tenn. Coll. Govt. of Dist. 52, Rotary Internat., 1931-32. Democrat. Clubs: Rotary (past. pres.), Round Table. Author: Blackboard Outlines in the Life of Jesus, 1925; Some Learning Processes (with L. P. Leavell), 1934; From Joshua to David, 1934; Purely Personal, 1937; Outline Studies in Luke, 1937; Outline Studies in Mark, 1945. Compiler and editor: The Chapel Book, 1923. Home: Nashville, Tenn.†

HILL, LAWRENCE, educator; b. N.Y.C., May 14, 1879; s. Jerome L. and Anne-Amelia (Yard) H.; student McGill U., Montreal Que., 1895; B.Sc., Columbia, 1901; grad. student Harvard, 1904-05; m. Rose Seignon, July 1, 1911; children—Yvonne (Mrs. Vincent M. Jacobs), Lucienne (Mrs. Niel Wald), John L. Master mathematics Morristown (N.J.) Sch., 1905-09, Univ. Sch., Avondale, O., 1909; faculty sch. architecture Washington U., St. Louis, from 1911, asst. prof., 1914-19, asso. prof., 1919-25, prof., 1925-48, prof. emeritus, chmn. sch. architecture, 1935-48. Chmn. architects and engrs. Met. Planning Com., 1943. Fellow A.I.A. (pres. St. Louis chpt. 1943-45) Am. Assn. U. Profs., Assn. Archtl. Historians. Contbr. articles Ency. Arts, 1946. Address: Ramsey, N.J.†

HILL, LEE H., mgmt. cons.; b. Toms River, N.J., Mar. 8, 1899; s. David and Anna (Applegate) H.; E.E., Cornell U., 1921; m. Helen Wolfram, Dec. 25, 1922; 1 son, Lee. Instr. elec. engring., Cornell U., 1920-22, design and devel. engr. Westinghouse Electric & Mfg. Co., 1922-28; mgr. transformer div. Am. Brown Boveri Co., 1928-30; mgr. transformer div. Allis-Chalmers Mfg. Co., 1931-40, asst. mgr. elec. dept., 1940-41, v.p. in charge indsl. relations, 1941-45, pub. and gen. mgr. Elec. World, Elec. Constn. and Maintenance, Elec. Wholesaling, McGraw-Hill Pub. Co., 1945-47; partner Rogers, Slade & Hill, mgmt. cons., 1947-62, chmn. bd., 1962-65; pres. Burdett Mfg., 1959-66, Lee H. Hill Cons.'s, 1965-74, Hill-Donnelly Corp., Inc., 1965-74, also Pan Am. Devel. Corp., 1965-74, Fla. Airlines, Inc., 1969-74, Hill-Leasing Corp., 1969-74. Industry mem. Nat. War Labor Bd., World War II; del. Pres's Labor Mgmt. Conf., 1945. Fellow I.E.E.E. Republican. Methodist. Mason. Author: Transformers, 1940. Co-author: Management at the Bargaining Table, 1942; Pattern for Good Labor Relations, 1944; Business Management for More Profits, 1951; Business Management Handbook, 1952; Handbook of Business Administration, 1968; Upward in the Black, 1969. Contbr. to tech. mags. Home: West Palm Beach Fla. Died Jan. 27, 1974; interred Maple Grove Cemetery, Kew Gardens, N.Y.

HILL, THOMAS RUSSELL, bus. exec., lectr., writer; b. Williamstown, Ky., Dec. 15, 1894; s. George William and Mary Elizabeth (Hayden) H.; A.B., Georgetown Coll., 1915, LL.D., 1940; Dr. Humanities, Lincoln Meml. U., 1949; m. Iris Francis, Nov. 19, 1921 (dec.). Coach football, high sch. prin. and supt. schs., 1915-18; lectr. Redpath Chautauqua, summers 1915-18; pres. Hill-Lawson Co., Corbin, Harlan and Middlesboro, Ky., 1920-29; with RKO Lyceum Bur., 1927-31; state mgr. advancing to v.p. and dir. Air-Way Electric Appliance Corp., Toledo, 1929-35; chmn. Rexair, Inc., Detroit; former pres. Martin-Parry Corp., Martin-Parry, Ltd., Ward Industries Corp., Ward Industries, Ltd. Former trustee Lincoln Meml. U., Harrogate, Tenn., Kalamazoo Coll. Past pres. Middleboro (Ky.) C. of C.; past nat. councillor U.S. C. of C. Mem. Nat. Soc. Marine Architects, Kappa Alpha. Baptist (chmn. trustees). Mason (Shriner), Rotarian (hon.). Elk, Kiwanian (past pres.). Author: Press On; Out Front; How Big; Producers; Gimme; 16 to 1; Dig, Ships, Bata. Home: Detroit Mich. Died Mar. 4, 1975.

HILLEBOE, HERMAN ERTRESVAAG, physician; b. Westhope, N.D., Jan. 8, 1906; s. Peter S. and Inga (Jacobson) H.; B.S., U. Minn., 1927, M.B., 1929, M.D., 1931; grad. tng. pediatrics, U. Minn. Hosp., Mpls. 1932-34; M.P.H., Johns Hopkins Sch. Hygiene and Pub. Health, 1935; D.Sc. (hon.), U. Rochester, 1954; m. Alica Claire Champeau, Sept. 28, 1929; children—Joyce (Mrs. Josef Vana), Theresa (Mrs. Richard McUmber), Herman Ertesvaag. Began career in rural gen. practice of medicine, Swanville, Minn., 1929-31; commd. officer USPHS, sr. asst. surgeon, June 1939; in charge Tb control activities Pub. Health Service, Washington, 1942-46; Tb control officer USCG, 1942-45; apptd. chief of Tb control div. with rank of med. dir., 1944; apptd. asso. chief Bur. of State Services with rank of asst. surgeon gen., 1946; N.Y. State commr. of health, 1947-63; prof. pub. health and preventive medicine Albany Med. Sch., 1948-62; DeLamar prof. pub. health practice Columbia Sch. Pub. Health and Adminstrv. Medicine, 1963-70, prof. emeritus, 1971; vis. prof. U. Fla., U. N.C., 1972-74; med. cons. Cancer Control Adv. Bd., Nat. Cancer Inst., 1973-74. Panel experts WHO, 1948-74. Diplomate Am. Bd. Preventive Med. and Pub. Health. Mem. Am. Coll. Chest Physicians, Am. Epidemiological Soc., Am. Pub. Health Assn. (pres. 1954-55), Assn. Tchrs. of Preventive Medicine, Assn. State and Terr. Health Officers (past pres.). Presbyn. Author: (with R.H. Morgan) Mass Radiography of the Chest, 1944: (with G. W. Larimore) Preventive Medicine, 1965; (with A. Barkhuus and William Thomas) National Health Planning, 1972. Home: Tampa, Fla. Died Apr. 11, 1974.

HILLES, FREDERICK WHILEY, educator; b. Lancaster, O., June 1, 1900; s. Charles Dewey and Sarah Bell (Whiley) H.; student Taft Sch., 1915-18; Cambridge, Eng., 1922-23; A.B., Yale, 1922, Ph.D., 1926; L.H.D., St. Lawrence U., 1959; m. Susan Toy Morse, June 14, 1930; children—Susan E. (Mrs. Geoffrey Bush), Frederick W. Instr. English, Yale, 1926-30, asst. prof., 1931-40, asso. prof., 1940-48, prof., 1948-65, Bodman prof. emeritus, 1965-75, dir. humanities, 1956-59; bd. govs. Yale U. Press. Served from capt. to lt. col. U.S. Army, 1942-46. Decorated Order Brit. Empire; Legion of Merit (U.S.). Mem. Modern Lang. Assn. (N.Y.C.), Alpha Delta Phi. Republican. Episcopalian. Clubs: Century Assn., Grolier (N.Y.C.); Somerset (Boston). Author: Literary Career of Sir Joshua Reynolds, 1936. Editor: Portraits by Sir Joshua Reynolds, 1952; The Age of Johnson, 1949; New Light on Dr. Johnson, 1959; mem. editorial bd. Yale edits. Private Papers of James Boswell; co-editor From Sensibility to Romanticism, 1965. Home: Old Lyme, Conn., Deceased.

HILLIARD, EDMUND BAYFIELD, educator; b. Washington, Pa., Feb. 5, 1878; s. Samuel Haven and Alice Ann (Johnstone) H.; prep. edn. Roxbury (Mass.) Latin Sch.; A.B., Harvard, 1900; m. Edith Lockyer Freeland, Apr. 30, 1913. Master Trinity Sch., N.Y. City, 1901-02, Morristown (N.J.) Sch., 1903-08, Groton (Mass.) Sch., 1908-11; perceived needs of boys drifting into crime and served as supt. Berkshire Industrial Farm, Oct. 1, 1911-21; instead of using repressive measures, supplied new interests and activities suited to tastes of individual boys (the instn. averaged 100 on its rolls); with Kent (Conn.) Sch., 1921-25; headmaster Newcastle Sch., Mount Kisco, N.Y., 1925. Republican. Episcopalian. Mem. Theta Delta Chi. Address: Mount Kisco, N.Y.†

HILLMAN, CHRISTINE HUFF (MRS. HOWARD S. HILLMAN), educator, assn. exec.; b. Danville, Ky., Aug. 30, 1908; d. Philip T. and Margaret (Hungate) Huff; B.S., Flora Stone Mather Coll., 1940; M.S., Western Res. U., 1942, Ph.D., 1951; m. Howard S. Hillman, Jan. 31, 1940; 1 son, Colby. Dist. home mgmt. supr. Farm Security Adminstrn., 1940-42; prof. Western Res. U., 1942-45; prof. Ohio State U. and Ohio Agrl. Expt. Sta., 1952-58, Nat. Agrl. Extension Center Advanced Study, U. Wis., 1958-59, Sch. Home Econs. Ohio State U., 1965; then asst. dean U. Mass. Active Cub Scouts, YWCA. Mem. Am. Home Econs. Assn., Am. Assn. U. Profs., Am. Sociol. Soc., Soc. Research Child Devel., Phi Upsilon Omicron. Author articles and bulls. Home: Framingham, Mass. Died July 14, 1975.

HILLS, THOMAS MCDOUGALL, educator; b. Pitts., Feb. 19, 1881; s. Oscar Armstrong and Louise (Freer) H.; Ph.B., Coll. of Wooster (O.), 1902; student U. of Chicago, 1903-07, U. of Berlin, Germany, 1907-08; m. Mary Wolfhegel, Sept. 7, 1907; 1 dau., Claudia (wife of Dr. Maxwell Gosse). Prof. of geology, Toledo U., 1909-10; asst. prof., Ohio State U., 1910-20; prof. of geology. Vassar Coll., 1920-48. emeritus. chmn. dept.; prof., U.S. Sch. Mil. Aeronautics, Columbus, O., 1917-18. Pres. Vassar Bros. Hosp., Poughkeepsie, 1942-45, v.p., 1948-49; chmn. Red Cross of Dutchess County, N.Y. 1942-45. Fellow A.A.A.S., Geol. Soc. of America. Home: Poughkeepsie, N.Y.†

HILPERT, ELMER ERNEST, educator; b. Bertha, Minn., Dec. 30, 1905; s. Theodore and Emma (Paschke) H.; A.B., U. Minn., 1929, A.M., 1931; LL.B., Western Res. U.,1936; J.S.D., Yale (Sterling fellow, grad. sch. law 1936-37), 1939; m. Brunette Powers, Aug. 1, 1938; children—Margaret Ray, Elmer Ernest. Thcr., elementary schs., Verndale, Minn., 1922-23, Elk River, Minn., 1923-24, Hewitt, Minn., 1924-25; principal, Vergas, Minn., 1925-26; teaching fellow in polit. sci. U. Minn., 1930; instr. in polit. sci. Western Res. U., 1930-37, asst. prof. law, 1938-39; asst. prof. law La. State U., 1937-38; asso. prof. law Washington U., St. Louis, 1939-41, prof. law, 1941-73, prof. emeritus, 1973-75; admitted to Ohio bar 1936, Mo. bar, 1944; practiced law in St. Louis, 1944-46 (part-time) with Thomas F. McDonald and McDonald, Bartlett & Muldoon, arbitrator in various indsl. disputes, 1941-75; panel mem. Am. Arbitration Assn., Fed. Mediation and Conciliation Service, Nat. Acad. Arbitrators; compliance commr. Wage Stabilization Bd., 1952-52; staff mem. Bur. for Research in Govt., U. Minn., part time, 1928-30; staff mem. Nat. Inst. Pub. Adminstrn., N.Y.C., summer, fall, 1929; dir. research Regional Govt. Com. of Greater Cleve., summer, fall, 1934. Participator in civic campaigns. Specialist in adminstrv. and constl. law, labor law, labor relations; impartial referee Allis-Chalmers Mfg. Co.-UAW, AFL-CIO, 1953-58, 60-64. Mem. Am., Mo. (various coms.), St. Louis (various com.) bar assns., Indsl. Relations Research Assn., Am. Assn. U. Profs., Mo. Welfare League (mem. bd.), Order of the Coif, Phi Beta Kappa. Club: University Co-author: Missouri Practice Methods, 1953, rev. edit., 2 vols., 1969. Opinions as arbitrator in Am. Labor Arbitration Awards and Labor Arbitration Reports; contbr. articles in law jours. Home: St. Louis, Mo., Died Apr. 4, 1975.

HILTON, WILLIAM ATWOOD, zoölogist; b. Vannetten, N.Y., June 27, 1878; s. Willard M. and Mary Alice (Atwood) H.; B.S., Cornell U., 1899, Ph.D., 1902; studied Summer Sch. (Cornell), Wood's Hole (Mass.) and Bermuda Biol. Sta.; spent 2 summers visiting European univs., museums and biol. stations; m. Emily Stella Boardman, Sept. 3, 1912; children—Dorothea Atwood, Eleanor Boardman. Grad. scholar Cornell U., 1899-1900, grad. fellow, 1900-01; asst. in histology, same univ., 1901-03; instr., asst. prof. and asso. prof., Pomona Coll., Claremont, Calif., 1905-08; instr. histology, Cornell U., 1908-11; instr. and asst. prof. anatomy, U. of Minn., 1911-12; prof. zoology, Pomona Coll., from 1912, also editor Jour. Entomology and Zoölogy and dir. Laguna Marine Lab., now prof. of zoology emeritus; director of the Claremont College Museum. Fellow A.A.A.S., So. Calif. Acad. Sci., Entomol. Soc. Am., Herpitology League; member American Society Zoölogists, Am. Assn. Anatomists, Am. Micros. Soc., Chi. Psi. Sigma Xi (pres. Sigma Xi Club of Southern Calif., 1931-33), Phi Beta Kappa, etc. Republican. Conglist. Author: Cajal's Rules for the Scientific Investigation, 1950. Contbr. about 300 articles on gen. biology, animal distribution, nervous system and sense organs and 30 papers on Amphibia from 1946. Traveled, Alaska to Yucatan, Cape Town to Cairo and across Australia, collecting and studying animals in the field. Home: Claremont, Cal.†

HIMEBAUGH, KEITH, consultant; b. Grand Rapids, Mich., Aug. 20, 1901; s. Clyde and Blanche (Goldsmith) H.; A.B., Mich. State Coll., 1928; m. Mildred Westrate, Aug. 7, 1926; children—Keith Westrate, Rodric John. Newspaper corr., feature writer, sports corr., Lansing Capitol News (Lansing, Mich.), Detroit Free Press, Detroit News, Detroit Times (Detroit, Mich.), 1924-34; program dir. radio sta. WKAR, Mich. State Coll., East Lansing, Mich., 1927-34; joined U.S. Dept. of Agr. field information service, Washington, D.C., June 1934; apptd. asst. dir. U.S. Dept. Agr. Office of Information, July 1941, asso. dir., 1943, dir. Apr. 1944-51; agr. cons. Point IV program, Latin Am. 1951-53; Latin Am. area agr. adviser Internat. Coop. Adminstrn., 1953-56; dep. dir. U.S. Operations Mission to Guatemala, 1956-59, dir., 1959-62; sec. bd., project dir. Internat. Devel. Services, Inc., 1962-65; cons. Dept. State, from 1966;

real estate developer, 1970-74. Mem. U.S. delegation UN Food and Agr. Conf., Copenhagen, Denmark, 1946. Home: Isabella, Mo. Died Apr. 12, 1974.

HINCHEE, FRED LEE, hosp. adminstr.; b. Haileyville, Okla., Nov. 11, 1919; s. Jonah and Augusta Henry (Wiggs) H.; student U. Cal. at Santa Barbara, summer 1944; B.S. in Bus., U. Okla., 1948; M.S. in Hosp. Adminstrn., Northwestern U., 1958; m. Yvonne Dee Lindsay, June 15, 1958; 1 dau., Ellen Rachel. Registrar asst. Houston VA Hosp., 1945-55; credit asst. Chgo. Wesley Meml. Hosp., 1956-57; adminstrv. resident Hillcrest Med. Center, Tulsa, 1957-58; adminstr. Shawnee (Okla.) Municipal Hosp., 1958-63, Mission Hill Meml. Hosp., Shawnee, 1963-73. Bd. dirs., past v.p., past pres. Pottawatomie County Mental Health Assn. Served to 1st lt. USAAF, 1943-44. Mem. Am. Mgmt. Assn., Am., Okla. (chmn. central dist. 1970) hosp. assns., Am. Coll. Hosp. Administrs. Democrat. Methodist. Kiwanian (chmn. vocational guidance Shawnee 1961). Contbr. articles to profl. jours. Home: Shawnee, Okla. Died May 7, 1973.

HINCHMAN, WALTER SWAIN educator; b. Burlington, N.J., Sept. 13, 1879; s. Charles Shoemaker and Lydia Swain (Mitchell) H.; A.B., Haverford Coll., Pa., 1900, A.M., 1903; A.B., Harvard, 1901; studied U. of Berlin, 1903-04; m. Julia Henderson, June 27, 1911; children—Richard, Hildegarde, John, Mary, Dorothea, Margaret. Master of English, Groton (Mass.) Sch., 1901-20; prof. English, Haverford, 1920-22, Milton Acad., 1923-45. Mem. N.E. Assn. Teachers English, Triangle Soc., Phi Beta Kappa. Quaker. Clubs: Milton (Milton, Mass.); Union (Boston); Harvard (N.Y.); Marylebone Cricket (London). Author: Lives of Great English Writers, 1908; Tintagel and Other Poems, 1910; William of Normandy, 1910; Holmes Hinckley, 1912; History of English Literature, 1915; the American School, 1916; American Literature, 1917; Pedestrian Papers, 1928; England; Its Life and Culture, 1941. Compiler: Selections from Arnold, 1910. Editor: Macbeth, 1931. Contbg. editor Forum, 1924-28. Home: Milton, Mass.†

HINDS, JULIAN, civil engr.; b. Warrenton, Ala., Dec. 22, 1881; s. James Monroe and Sarah Elizabeth (Ferguson) H.; C.E., U. of Texas, 1908; LL.D., University of California, 1957; married to Nella Foster Ellison, July 24, 1912; 1 dau., Harriet Sarah (Mrs. John H. Waldron, Jr.); m. 2d, Drusilla Rutherford, Apr. 8, 1933. Instr. of civil engring. and drawing, U. of Tex., 1908-09; insp. and chief survey party Gulf, Tex., & Western Ry., 1909; designer C.M.&St.P. Ry., Chicago, 1909-10; with U.S. Bureau Reclamation successively as surveyman, jr. engr., asst. engr., engr., asst. designing engr., 1910-26; engr. J.G. White Engring. Co. at Pabellon, Mexico, in charge design and construction Calles Irrigation Project and Dam, 1926-29; engr. hydraulic design Dept. Water and Power, City of Los Angeles, 1929-30; chief designing engr. Met. Water Dist. of Southern Calif. on Colo. River Aqueduct, 1930-33, asst. chief engr., 1933-41, gen. mgr., chief engr., 1941-51, ret.; gen. mgr., chief engr. United Water Conservation Dist. 1952-55; cons. Bechtel Corp. Mem. Water Resources & Power Taskforce, Hoover Commission. Awarded Norman medal of Am. Soc. C.E., 1926, and Rickey medal, 1954. Mem. Am. Water Works Assn., Am. Soc. C.E. (hon.; nat. dir. 1948-50), Am. Concrete Inst., Inter-Am. Assn. San Engrs., Sigma Xi, Tau Beta Pi, Chi Epsilon (national hon. mem.). Democrat. Club: University of Los Angeles. Co-author "Engineering for Dams" (Creager, Justin, Hinds). Contbr. tech. articles to engring. jours. Contbg. author: Handbook of Hydraulics (edited by Calvin V. Davis). Home: Santa Paula, Cal.†

HINRICHS, CARL GUSTAV, chemist; b. Iowa City, Ia., Feb. 14, 1878; s. Gustavus Detlef and Anna C. M. (Springer) H.; ed. St. Louis High Sch., St. Louis Coll. Pharmacy and St. Louis U.; grad. pharm. chemist, 1899; M.S., St. Louis Univ., 1907; m. Rose Weber, May 1913; children—Carl George (dec.), Hans Carl. Instructor in chemistry, St. Louis Coll. of Pharmacy, 1897; same, med. dept. St. Louis U., 1903-07; prof. chemistry. Marion Sims Dental Coll., 1904-06; chemist for Agrl. Bd. of Mo., 1899-1903; chemist Nat. Health Soc., 1902-03; asso. prof. chemistry, St. Louis Coll. of Pharmacy, from 1920; mng. chemist Basic Chemical Co., St. Louis, 1943. Serves as expert chemist before state and federal courts; originated centrifugal analysis of powders; devised course in micro-chem. analysis. Life mem. Chem. Soc. of Paris, 1904; mem. Am. Chem. Soc. Author: Micro-chemical Analysis, with Atlas of 64 plates, 1904; Pharmacy and Chemistry at the World's Fair. 1904. Home: St. Louis, Mo.†

HINSHAW, MELVIN TALIAFERRO, college pres.; b. Yodkin Co., N.C., Jan. 9, 1878; s. Isaac Martin and Emily France (Winters) H.; student Guilford (N.C.) Coll. 3 yrs. to 1906; A.B., Central U., 1909, A.M., 1912; B.D., Temple U., Phila., Pa., 1922; m. Mildred America Caudle, 1909. Began as teacher Rutherford Coll., N.C., 1909, pres., from 1911; moved and reconstructed the plant and increased its value ten-fold. Mem. M.E. Ch. S. Address: Rucherford College, N.C.†

HINTON, L. W., state ofcl.; b. Pana, Ill., Jan. 31, 1907; s. Aaron Scott and Anne (Combest) H.; student James Milikin U., 1925-26; B.S., U. Ill., M.S. in Ednl. Adminstrn., 1930; m. Florence Louise Ostermeier, Feb. 12, 1932; children—Carolyn Sue (Mrs. Clay A. Donner), Linda Lou (Mrs. Edgar M. Huesing). Tchr. Springfield (Ill.) Pub. Schs., 1930-39; Ill. asst. supt. pub. instrn., 1943-51; asst. county supt. schs., Sangamon County, 1939-42, county supt., Springfield, 1951-67; staff Ill. Ho. of Reps., 1967-72. Mem. Ill. Edn. Assn., Ill. Assn. Sch. Adminstrs., Ill. Assn. County Supts. of Schs. (pres. 1960-72), Tchrs. Fedn., County and Rural Supts. Assn., Ill. Assn. County Ofcls. (pres. 1965-72). Mason (Shriner, Jester). Clubs: Elks, Am. Business (chmn. Easter Seal campaign 1961-72). Home: Springfield, Ill. Died Apr. 17, 1972; buried Oak Ridge Cemetery, Springfield, Ill.

HIRSCH, I(SAAC) SETH, X-ray expert; b. N.Y. City, Dec. 3, 1880; s. Abram and Ida H. student Coll. City of New York, 1894-98; M.D., Coll. Phys. and Surg. (Columbia), 1902 (Hersen prize); diploma in radiology, Cambridge U., Eng., 1920; m. Lela Calhoun Hindsman, 1924. Practiced in N.Y. City from 1902; prof. Roentgenology, New York Post-Grad. Med. Sch., 1914-17; X-ray depts. Bellevue and Allied Hosps., 1910-26; X-ray expert N.Y. State Compensation Commn.; now prof. radiology, Coll. of Medicine, New York U. Maj. Med. Corps Reserve, U.S. Army. Mem. A.M.A., Acad. Medicine New York, Radiol. Soc. N. America (v.p.), Am. Med. Editors Assn., Roentgen Soc. (Eng.), fellow Am. Coll. Physicians; hon. mem. Alpha Omega Alpha Fraternity. Author: Principles and Practice of Roentgenological Technique, 1920; Principles and Practice of Roentgen Therapy, 1923.*†

HIRSCHMAN, LOUIS JACOB, surgeon; b. Republic, Mich., Aug. 15, 1878; s. Frederick L. and Hannah (Labold) H.; M.D., Detroit Coll. Medicine, 1899; m. Lulu Frances Carstens, June 22, 1904 (died 1930); children—Ruth Carstens (Mrs. Harry F. Chapin), Alice Carstens (Mrs. John Smith Hammond), Elaine Carstens (Mrs. Ferdinand Nordstrom); married 2d, Hanna Christine Kellogg, Aug. 15, 1936. House physician, Harper Hosp., 1899-1900; dir. Harper Hosp. clinic, 1904-06; prof. and head dept. of protology, Detroit Coll. of Medicine (now known as Wayne U.), 1909-46; proctologist and head dept. of proctology, Harper Hosp., 1906-40; proctologist Women's Hosp., from 1922, Charles Godwin Jennings Hosp., from 1928; cons. proctol., Detroit Receiving Hospital, Evang. Deaconess Hospital, Harper Hosp., St. Joseph's Hosp., Mercy Hospital, Children's Hospital of Michigan, Cranbrook School, Detroit Tuberculosis Sanitarium; extramural lecturer in post-graduate medicine, University of Mich. Mem. Mich. State Bd. of Health, 1927-38 (pres. 1937-38). Maj. Med. Corps., A.E.F., July 13, 1917-Dec. 2, 1918, with Base Hosp. 17, in France; maj. Med. R.C., 1922; lt. col., 1924. Editor Harper Hosp. Bull., 1906-10. Mem. Detroit Bd. of Commerce. Fellow Am. Coll. Surgeons (a founder); mem. Am. Med. Assn. (vice pres., 1930-31), Mich. State Med. Soc. (pres. 1928-29), Wayne County Med. Soc. (ex-pres.), Northern Tri-State Med. Soc., Am. Proctologic Society (ex-pres.), Detroit Proctol. (pres., 1946-47), Detroit Medical Club (ex-president), Detroit Academy of Surgery, Detroit Academy Medicine (pres. 1944-45), Am. Legion, Am. Mil. Order of Great War, Assn. Military Surgeons of U.S., Alpha Omega Alpha, Phi Beta Pi; ex-pres. Alumni Assn. Detroit Coll. Medicine (hon. pres., 1925-26); chairman Central Certifying Com. of Am. Bd. of Surg., 1940-45; ex-chmn. certifying committee in proctology; member American Board of Proctology from 1948. Republican. Clubs: Army-Navy (Washington); Automobile, Economic, Board of Commerce (Detroit); Torch (v.p. 1934, pres. 1935-37) and Detroit Boat. Author: Handbook of Diseases of the Rectum, 1909, 13, 20, 25. Co-Author: American Year Book of Anesthesia, 1915, 18; Synopsis of Ano-Rectal Diseases, 1937-42. Asso. editor Am. Jour. Surgery, Am. Jour. Digestive Diseases. Retired. Home: Traverse City, Mich.†

HIRSHBERG, ALBERT SIMON, author; b. Boston, May 10, 1909; s. David Walter and Alice (Lilienthal) H.; B.S., Boston U., 1931; m. Marjorie Littauer, Aug. 21, 1939 (dec. 1970); children—Judy (Mrs. Paul Marandett), Albert S.; m. 2d, Bert M. Cohen, Nov. 12, 1971. In charge of writing seminar Boston U., 1963-64; part-time spl. lectr. U. So. Fla., Tampa, 1962-67. Chmn. bd. Nat. Found. for Eye Research, 1950-69; corp. mem. Perkins Sch. for Blind. Served to lt. USNR, 1943-45. Recipient Dutton prize for best sports feature, 1953, Distinguished Alumni award Boston U., 1966. Mem. Soc. Mag. Writers, Authors Guild, Authors League, Baseball Writers Am., Fernald League for Retarded Children, Sigma Delta Chi. Author 36 books including: Fear Strikes Out, 1955; Prodigal Shepherd, 1958; Basketball is My Life, 1958; 88 Men and 2 Women, 1962; Sex and Crime, 1965; He Is In Heaven, 1965; Vietnam Doctor, 1966; Backstage at the Mets, 1966; Yaz, 1968; Hawk, 1969; A Faraway Country, 1970; Addict, 1972. Author 400 mag. stories; columnist Boston Post, 1930-52, Boston Herald-Traveler, 1964-68. Home: Pocasset, Mass. Died Apr. 11, 1973.

HIXSON, ARTHUR WARREN, chem. engring.; b. Mifflinburg, Pa., July 17, 1880; s. William E. and Anna E. (Shiffer) H.; A.B., U. of Kan., 1907, M.S., 1915; Ph.D., Columbia, 1918; m. Edetha M. Washburn, June 17, 1907; chlildren—Arthur Norman, Rachel Marjorie (Mrs. R. H. Wilhelm). Began as assayer and metallurgist Detroit Copper Mining Co., Morenci, Ariz., 1906-08; chemist Illinois State Agricultural Experimental Station, 1908-09; instr. and asst. prof. metallurgy and industrial chemistry, Ia. State U., 1909-17; chem. engr. Ia. State Geol. Survey, 1909-14; asso. prof. chem. engring., Columbia, 1919-27, prof., 1927-49, head dept., 1940-48; asso. Tech. Advisory Corp., 1921-26; cons. chem. engr. Fleischmann Co., 1922-27. Chem. engr. in charge production, High Explosives Div., Ordnance Bur., U.S. Army, 1918-19; tech. adviser to Claims Board, U.S. Army, 1919-21. Inventor processes for prodn. baker's yeast, titanium pigments, alumnium from clay, chlosolvent refining of oils, food-grade phosphates, sulphur dioxide form from waste fuel gases; specializes in process development and chem. plant design. Chmn. American Chemical Industries Tercentenary, 1935; chmn. Town Planning Commn., Leonia, N.J. Fellow A.A.A.S.; mem. Am. Chem. Soc. (chmn. N.Y. sect. 1934-35), A.M. Electrochem. Soc., Am. Inst. Chem. Engrs., Soc. for Promotion Engring. Edn., Soc. Chem. Industry of Gt. Britain, Sigma Xi, Tau Beta Pi, Phi Lambda Upsilon. Republican. Presbyn. Clubs: Chemists, Faculty, Columbia Univ. (New York). Home: Leonia, N.J.†

HIXSON, WILLIAM AASE, educator; b. Gettysburg, S.D., Oct. 21, 1922; s. Harry and Lisa (Aase) H.; B.S., Ia. State Coll., 1945; Ph.D., Stanford, 1949; m. Phyllis Jane Mauritson, Aug. 25, 1946; children—Donald, Susan, Steven, Cynthia. Research engr. Gen. Electric Co., 1949-52; mem. faculty S.D. Sch. Mines and Tech., Rapid City, 1952-75, prof. elec. engring., head dept., 1955-75; examiner, cons. N. Central Assn. Colls. and Univs., 1963-75. Clk., Dist. 85 Sch. Bd., 1966-68. Served with USNR, 1943-46. Registered profl. engr., S.D. Mem. I.E.E.E. (pres. Black Hills sub-sect. 1957, 66), Am. Soc. Engring. Edn., Sigma Xi, Eta Kappa Nu, Phi Kappa Phi, Sigma Tau. Elk. Home: Rapid City, S.D. Died June 30, 1975.

HOADLEY, LEIGH, educator; b. Northampton, Mass., Aug. 14, 1895; s. Alfred Henry and Grace Bell (Leigh) H.; A.B., U. of Mich., 1921; Ph.D., U. of Chicago, 1923; m. Harriet L. Warner, Sept. 12, 1923; children—Alfred Warner, Nancy Leigh (now Mrs. Richard Norton Fryberger). Assistant in zoölogy University of Mich., 1916-17, 1919-21, U. of Chicago, 1921-23; instr. St. Xavier, 1923; Nat. Research council fellow, 1923-25, foreign fellow, 1925-26; asst. prof. zoölogy, Brown U., 1926-27; asst. prof. zoölogy, Harvard, 1927-29, asso. prof., 1929-30, professor of zoology, 1930-62, emeritus professor of zoology, 1960-75, chmn. department of zoölogy, Harvard, 1930-34; master of Leverett House, Harvard, 1941-57; exchange prof. Sorbonne (Paris). 1939; associate dean of Graduate School of Arts and Sciences, Harvard University, 1943-46. Served in U.S. Army, Ambulance Service with French Army, 1917-18; Central Medical Department, laboratory assistant in pathology, 1918; asst. pathologist laboratory Evacuation Hosp. 1, 1918-19. Trustee Radcliffe Coll., 1937-41. Benjamin Franklin fellow Royal Society Arts; mem. A.A.A.S., Am. Soc. of Zoölogists, American Assn. of Anatomists, Soc. of Naturalists, Corp. Marine Biol. Lab. (Woods Hole, Mass.), Corp. Bermudda Biol. Station, Boston Soc. of Biologists, Am. Acad. of Arts and Sciences (corr. sec., 1937-40), Soc. Study Devel. and Growth council; treas. 1938-41, Institut Internat. d'Embryologie (fellow), Phi Sigma. Sigma Xi, Phi Mu Alpha. Clubs: Club de la Fondation Universitaire (Brussels, Belgium); Harvard Faculty, Asso. Editor Biol. Bull., 1931-51, Jour. Morphology, 1937-40, Growth, 1939-62. Home: Cambridge, Mass., Died Nov. 7, 1975.

HOAG, CLARENCE GILBERT, civic sec.; b. Lynn, Mass., Feb. 15, 1873; s. Gilbert Congdon and Louisa Phoebe (Oliver) H.; A.B., Haverford (Pa.) Coll., 1893, Harvard, 1894; post-grad. work, univs. of Berlin and Zürich, 1894-95; A.M., Harvard, 1898; m. Anna Scattergood; children—Mary (Mrs. C. A. P. Lawrence) (dec.), Gilbert T. (deceased), Garrett Scattergood, John Hacker. Instr. English, Bates Coll., 1898-1900, U. of Pa., 1901-08. General sec.-treas. Proportional Representation League, 1912-26; trustee C. F. Taylor Trust. Mem. Nat. Municipal League, Am. Econ. Assn., Soc. of Friends. Author: A Theory of Interest, 1914; (with G. H. Hallett, Junior) Proportional Representation, 1926. One of the originators and first promoters (with Wm. Hoag) of the "Cincinnati Plan" of city government (applied in Cincinnati, Hamilton, Worcester, etc.). Home: Haverford, Pa.†

HOAGLAND, HENRY E., economist; b. Prairie City, Ill., May 10, 1886; s. Okey M. and Adeline (Foster) H.; grad. Western Ill. State Normal, Macomb, 1906; A.B., U. of Ill., 1909; A.M., 1910; Ph.D., Columbia, 1912; grad. study U. of Wis., 1911; m. Edna F. Hardie, Sept. 2, 1916; children—Mary Adeline, John Hardie, Teacher high sch., 1906-09; statistician and economist N.Y. State Industrial Commn., 1912-16; instr. economics, U. of Ill., 1916-18; chief of div. statistics N.Y. State Pub. Serv. Commn., 1918-20; prof. business finance, Coll. of Commerce, Ohio State University, Columbus, 1920-56, professor emeritus, after 1956; economic adviser; former dir. Home Owners' Loan Corp. and former trustee Federal Savings and Loan Insurance Corp. (resigned Oct. 1937); former chmn. Twentieth Century Fund Com. on Housing; consultant Nat. Savings and Loan League, since 1944. Mem. Am. Econ. Assn., Phi

Kappa Tau, Alpha Kappa Psi, Beta Gamma Sigma. Republican. Club: Faculty. Author: Corporation Finance, 1933, rev. 1938, rev. 1947; Work Book in Corporation Finance, 1933; Real Estate Principles, 1940, rev. 1949, 55; Real Estate Finance, 1954, rev. 1965. Contbg. editor Nat. Savs. and Loan Jour., 1945-75. Home: Columbus, Ohio. Died Sept. 17, 1975.

HOBBS, ROSCOE CONKLIN, mem. Republican Nat. Com.; b. Bentonville, Ark., July 31, 1880; s. Benjamin F. and Lydia M. (Walker) H.; LL.D. (hon.), U. Ark., 1955; m. Frances Warren, Aug. 9, 1905 (dec.); children—Sarah (Mrs. Chester Cordell), Warrene (Mrs. Henry Schlapp). Vice pres. Hobbs Western Co., St. Louis from 1930; dir. Bank of St. Louis, Gen. Contract Corp., Miss River Fuel Corp., R. E., Funsten Co., Fleishel Lumber Co., St. Joseph Belt Ry. Co., Lennox Hotel. Mem. Republican Nat. Com. for Mo., from 1958; Trustee St. Louis Pub. Library. Clubs: Noonday, Racquet, Bogey, Missouri Athletic (St. Louis). Home: St. Louis, Mo.†

HOBGOOD, CHARLES GOYNE, educator; b. Jackson, La., Sept. 7, 1911; s. James B. and Mary (Hubbs) H.; B.S., La. State U., 1936, M.S., 1938; m. Norma Benton Holden, July 14, 1937; 1 dau., Elizabeth Joy. Soil scientist Soil Conservation Service Flood Control Surveys, Ft. Worth, 1938-41; prof., head dept. agronomy and hort. La. Poly, Inst., Ruston, 1941-72; cons. Humble Oil Refining Co., summer 1963. Judge, La. Flower Show, 1952-54, 57, 60, 65, N. La. State Fair, 1950-53, 58, 61, 63. Served with AUS, 1942-46. Recipient Community Service award La. Garden Club Fedn., 1952; Outstanding Service award to soil and water conservation in La., 1971; named Educator of Year, 1972. Hon. state farmer, 1959. Mem. La. Assn. Agronomists (pres.), La. Turf and Grass Assn., Farm Bur., Am. Legion, Am. Soc. Agronomy, La. Coll. Conf., Nat. Assn. Colls. and Tchrs. Agr., Omicron Delta Kappa, Phi Kappa Phi, Lambda Chi Alpha. Contbr. articles profl. jours. Home: Ruston, La. Died Dec. 31, 1972.

HOBLER, ATHERTON W., advt. exec.; b. Chgo., Sept. 2, 1890; s. Edward and Harriet (Wells) H.; A.B., University of Illinois, 1911; married Ruth Windsor, March 30, 1914; children—Edward Windsor, Wells Atherton, Virginia (dec.), Herbert Windsor. With Appleton Mfg. Co., Batavia, Ill., successively as credit mgr., advt. mgr. and sales mgr., 1911-17; account exec. and v.p. Gardner Advt. Co., St. Louis, 1917-25; v.p. and partner Erwin, Wasey & Co., advt., N.Y. City, 1925-32; pres. Benton & Bowles, Inc., advt., New York City, 1932-42, chairman bd., 1942-52, chmn. exec. com., 1952-62, founder chmn., 1962-74. Chmn. bd. Am. Assn. Advt. Agys., 1940. Republican. Clubs: Union League, University (N.Y.C.); Bedens Brook (Princeton, N.J.); Everglades, Bath and Tennis (Palm Beach, Fla.). Address: New York City, N.Y. Died Jan. 6, 1974.

HOCKING, BRIAN, educator; b. London, Eng., Sept. 22, 1914; s. Sydney Blake and Alice (Fisher) H.; B.Sc., U. London, 1937; Ph.D., 1953; M.Sc., U. Alta. (Can.), 1948; m. Jocelyn May Hicks, Jan. 17, 1938; children—Martin Blake, Drake, Linnet Elizabeth (Mrs. Duncan MacGregor Murray). Asst. prof. entomology U. Alta., 1946-51, asso. prof., 1951-54, prof., chmn. dept., 1954-74; cons. WHO (com. on filariasis 1964-69). Served to maj. Indian Army, 1942-45. Mem. Entomol. Soc. Royal Coll. Sci. (pres. 1937), Entomol. Soc. Alta. (pres. 1967), Entomol. Soc. Can. (pres. 1960), Entomol Soc. Am., Royal Soc. Can., Royal Entomol. Soc. London, Am. Mosquito Control Assn., Inst. Biology, Entomol. Soc. Ontario, Bee Research Assn., Arctic Inst. North Am., Amateur Entomol. Soc., Filariasis Assn. Editor: Quaestiones Entomologicae, 1965-74; Six-Legged Science, 2d edit., 1971; Biology or Oblivion, 2d edit., 1972. Mem. editorial com. Annual Review Entomology, 1971-74. Home: Edmonton AB T6G 0H9, Canada. Died May 23, 1974.

HODGE, WALTER HARTMAN, U.S. dist. judge; b. Auburn, Ind., Aug. 29, 1896; s. David A. and Mabel C. (Hartman) H.; LL.B., U. Washington, 1919; m. Alice Moberg, 1923 (dec. 1929); 1 dau., Alice (Mrs. LaVern Johnson); m. 2d. Mary Hay, 1933 (dec. 1942); 1 dau., Margaret Loraine; m. 3d, Elizabeth Little, December 19, 1946. Admitted to Wash. State bar, 1919, Alaska bar, 1935; dep. pros. atty. Skagit Co., Wash., 1921-24; asst. U.S. atty. Third Div., Alaska, 1926-29; pvt. practice law, Seattle, 1929-34, Cordova. Alaska, 1935-54; judge U.S. Dist. Ct., second div., Nome, Alaska, 1954-59; asso. justice Alaska State Supreme Ct., Juneau, 1959-60; judge U.S. Dist. Ct., Dist. of Alaska, Anchorage, 1960-66; sir. U.S. dist. judge for Dist. Alaska, from 1966. Mem. Pioneers Alaska, Am., Fed., Alaska bar assns., Delta Chi. Presbyn. Mason, Elk. Home: Santa Rosa, Cal., Died July 12, 1975.

HODGE, WILLIAM VALLANCE DOUGLAS, mathematician; b. Edinburgh, June 17, 1903; s. Archibald James and Janet (Vallance) H.; student George Watson's Coll., Edinburgh, 1909-20; M.A., Edinburgh U., 1923, LL.D., 1958; B.A., Cambridge U., 1925, M.A., 1930, Sc.D., 1950; D.Sc., Bristol U., 1958, Leicester U., 1959, Sheffield U., 1960, Exeter U., Liverpool U., U. Wales, 1961; m. Kathleen Cameron, 1929; children—Michael Robert, Gillian Janet. Lectr. U. Bristol, 1926-31; univ. lectr. Cambridge U., 1933-36, Lowndean prof. astronomy and geometry Cambridge, 1936-70; fellow St. John's Coll., Cambridge, 1930-33, Pembroke Coll., Cambridge, 1935-58, master Pembroke Coll., 1958-70. Knighted, 1959. Recipient Berwick prize London Math. Soc., 1952, de Morgan medal, 1959; Royal medal Royal Soc., 1957; Copley medal Royal Soc., 1974. Fellow Royal Soc. (sec. 1957-65), Royal Soc. Edinburgh (Gunning Victoria Jubilee medal 1968); mem. Royal Danish Acad., Am. Philos. Soc. (fgn. mem.), Am. Acad. Arts and Scis., U.S. Acad. Scis. Author: Harmonic Integrals, 1941. Co-author: Methods of Algebraic Geometry, 1947-56. Home: Cambridge, England., Died July 4, 1975.

HODGES, LUTHER HARTWELL, former sec. commerce; b. Pittsylvania County, Va., Mar. 9, 1898; s. John J. and Lovicia (Gammon) H.; A.B., U. N.C., 1919; several hon. degrees from other univs.; m. Louise B. Finlayson, 1970; children by previous marriage—Betsy, Nancy, Luther. Sec. to gen. mgr. of eight mills, Spray, N.C., 1919, mgr., 1933; prodn. mng. all mills of Marshall Field & Co., 1936, gen. mgr., 1938, v.p. charge of mills and sales, 1943-50, ret. officer, dir. local corps.; head textile div. OPA, 1944; cons. to sec. of agr., 1945; head industry div. ECA, W. Germany, 1950; lt. gov. N.C., 1952-54, gov., 1954-60; sec. of commerce, 1961-65; hon. chmn. bd. Research Triangle Found. N.C. Dir. Servomation Corp., Speizman Industries, Charlotte, N.C., Fidelity Mortgage Investors, Gulf And Western Industries, Inc. Former dir. So. Regional Edn. Bd. Democrat. Methodist. Clubs: University, Rotary (Internat. pres. 1967-68). Author: Businessman in the State House; The Business Conscience. Home: Chapel Hill, N.C. Died Oct. 6, 1974; interred, Eden, N.C.

HODGES, RICHARD GILBERT, physician; b. Cambridge, Mass., Jan. 8, 1909; M.D., Harvard, 1926; children—Peter, Richard, Elizabeth. Intern, Boston Children's Hosp., 1936-38; resident Babies Hosp., N.Y.C., 1938-41, research fellow, 1941-42; chief pediatrics St. Luke's Hosp., Cleve.; asso. pediatrician Babies and Childrens Hosp., Cleve.; asso. clin. prof. preventive medicine, asst. clin. prof. pediatrics Case-Western Res. U. Mem. Pres. Johnson's Council on Epidemiology. Served to capt. M.C., USAAF, 1942-46. Decorated Legion of Merit. Mem. Am. Epidemol. soc., Soc. Pediatric Reserach, No. Ohio Pediatric Soc., Aesculapian Soc. Cleve., Cleve. Acad. Medicine. Contbr. to Practice of Pediatric (Breneman), The Standard Text of Pediatrics (Hold and McIntosh). Home: Cleveland Heights, O. Died Aug. 16, 1966.

HODGKIN, WILFRED REGINALD HAUGHTON, clergyman; b. Tunbridge Wells, Eng., Nov. 6, 1879; s. Wilfred Haughton and Leonora Irene (Smith) H.; came with parents to U.S., 1890; B. Litt., U. of Calif., 1900; grad. Church Div. Sch. of the Pacific, 1904; B.D., Pacific Sch. of Religion, 1912, D.D., 1923; m. Mary Hewitt Parsons, Sept. 10, 1906; children—Anita Marselis (dec.), Elizabeth, Mary Lambert, Wilfred Haughton. Deacon, 1904, priest, 1905; vicar All Souls' Ch., Berkeley, Calif., 1906-19; rector St. Mark's Ch., Berkeley, 1919-33; archdeacon Episcopal Diocese of Calif., 1933-39; vicar of East Contra Costa County, 1939; chaplain St. Luke's Hosp., San Francisco and Episcopal City Mission Soc., 1940; acting rector Trinity Parish, Oakland, from 1948. Dean of Convocation of San Francisco, 1910-16; deputy Gen. Conv. P.E. Ch., 1931, 34, 37, 40; mem. Forward Movement Commn. of Gen. Conv. Served with Army Y.M.C.A., World War. Chmn. Alameda County Welfare Council. Trustee Church Div. Sch. of the Pacific, Pacific Sch. of Religion, Deaconess Training Sch. of the Pacific. Mem. Nat. Tuberculosis Assn. (dir. 1927-29), Calif. Tuberculosis Assn. (pres. 1929), Theta Delta Chi. Home: Berkeley, Cal.†

HOEKENDIJK, JOHANNES CHRISTIAAN, theologian; b. Garut, Indonesia, May 3, 1912; s. Cornelis Johannes and Suzanne (van der Kris) H.; Th.D., U. Utrecht, 1948; m. 2d, Letty Mandeville Russell, Jan. 3, 1970. Sec., Student Christian Movement Netherlands, 1939-42; missions consul, Indonesia, 1945-47; sec. Netherlands Missionary Council, 1947-49; sec. Evangelism World Council Chs., Geneva, 1949-52; prof. theology Utrecht U., Netherlands, 1953-65; prof. missions Union Theol. Sem., N.Y.C., 1965-75. Served as maj. Dutch Army, 1945-47. Mem. German Soc. Missiology, Utrecht Acad. Scis. Author: Evangelism in France, 1950; The Church Inside Out, 1966; Kirche und Volk in der deutschen Missionswissenschaft, 1967; Horizons of Hope, 1970. Contbr. articles to profl. jours. Address: New York City, N.Y. Died June 25, 1975.

HOEPPEL, JOHN HENRY, congressman; b. Tell City, Ind., Feb. 10, 1881; s. John Michael and Barbara (Zoll) H.; ed. parochial and pub. schs., Evansville, Ind.; m. Annie Seitz, of Evansville, Ind., Nov. 11, 1907; children—Raymond Winfield, Mildred Victoria (Mrs. James Maitland Ruddick), Charles Jerome. Served in U.S.A. as enlisted man (except 18 mos. as officer during World War.), July 25, 1898-Aug. 16, 1921; served in Alaska, as lineman, telegraph operator and submarine cable operator, about 10 yrs.; served 27 months in France, World War; postmaster of Arcadia, Calif., 1923-31; editor Army and Navy Advocate, (monthly mag.) from 1928. Mem. 73d and 74th Congresses (1933-37), 12th Calif. Dist. Democrat. Catholic. Pub. Directory of Retired Enlisted Men of the Army. Directory of Retired Enlisted Men of the Navy and Marine Corps., 1929. Home: Arcadia, Cal.†

HOERTER, CHARLES RICHARD, sports editor; b. Bklyn., Dec. 11, 1904; s. Philip and Edith Cassler (May) H.; ed. high sch.; Bernice Langille, June 2, 1930. With N.Y. Daily News, N.Y.C., 1920-74, beginning as office boy, successively sports writer, night sports editor, asst. sports editor, asso. sports editor, 1920-57, sports editor, 1957-74. Dir. Lake Carmel Property Owners Assn. Home: Long Island City, N.Y. Died Mar. 18, 1974.

HOFFMAN, ARTHUR SULLIVANT, editor; b. Columbus, O., Sept. 28, 1876; s. Ripley Christian and Mary Eliza (Sullivant) H.; B.A., Ohio State U., 1897; post-grad. work in English, U. of Chicago, 1902-03; m. Mary Denver James, Oct. 14, 1905 (died Aug. 17, 1910); 1 child, Lyne Starling Sullivant; m. 2d, Mary Emily Curtis, Aug. 5, 1915. Teacher; editor country weekly; editorial positions, 1902-10; Chautauquan, Smart Set, Watson's, Transatlantic Tales, Delineator, Adventure; editor, Adventure, 1911-27, Romance, 1919-20; editor McClure's Magazine, 1927-28; professional critic and teacher of fiction from 1929. Mem. Beta Theta Pi. Fraternity, Phi Beta Kappa; founder first Am. Legion, 1915. Author: Fundamentals of Fiction Writing, 1922; Fiction Writers on Fiction Writing, 1923; Writing of Fiction, 1934; Fiction Writing Sefl-Taught, 1939; also magazine fiction and articles. Editor, contbr. various anthologies. Contbr. to Profl. Writers' Library, Nelson's Eng. series. Home: Carmel, N.Y.†

HOFFMAN, DORETTA SCHLAPHOFF, univ. dean; b. Wabash, Neb., Dec. 16, 1912; d. Carl and Emma (Luetchens) Schiaphoff; B.S., U. Neb., 1941, D.Sc., 1966; M.S. Mich. State Coll., 1943; Ph.D. Cornell U., 1949; D.Sc.(hon.) U. of Neb., 1966; m. Wendell Hoffman, Feb. 6, 1956; children—Roe Lowell, Roger Lester. Instr. home econs. U. Ariz., 1943-44; instr. home econs. U. Neb., 1944-49, asso. prof., 1949-50, prof., chmn. dept., 1950-54; prof., dean Coll. Home Econs., Kan. State U., 1954-75. Recipient Distinguished Alumni award Mich. State U., 1964. Fellow A.A.A.S., mem. Am. Home Econs. Assn. (past. chmn. research dept.), Am. Dietetics Assn. (past pres. Neb.), Assn. Land Grant Colls. and Univs. (past chmn., sec. resident instrn. home econs. div.) Mortar Bd., Sigma Xi, Omicron Nu Sigma Delta Epsilon. Phi Kappa Phi, Alpha Lambda Delta, Delta Kappa Gamma, Iota Sigma Pi, Phi Upsilon Omicron (nat. pres. 1970-72). Contbr. articles to profl. jours. Home: Manhattan, Kan. Died July 12, 1975.

HOFFMAN, JOSEPH GILBERT, scientist, educator; b. Buffalo, Aug. 19, 1909; s. Joseph and Helene (Seyler) H.; A.B. with honors, Cornell U., 1935, Ph.D., 1939; m. Ruth A. Buckland, Aug. 17, 1940; children—Joseph H., Paul G. Research asst. physics Cornell U., 1935-39; staff Roswell Park Meml. Inst., 1939-46, dir. cancer research, 1946-54, cons. cancer research, 1954-74; physicist Carnegie Inst. Washington, 1940-42, Nat. Bur. Standards, 1942-44; sci. staff Los Alamos Sci. Labs., 1944-46, cons., 1946-74, research prof. U. Buffalo Sch. Medicine, 1947-74, prof. biophysics, 1954-74, prof. physics 1957-74. Recipient awards Naval Ordnance, 1943, Manhattan Dist., 1945, OSRD, 1945. Fellow Am. Phys. Soc.; mem. Am. Assn. Cancer Research, A.A.A.S., Soc. Exptl. Biology and Medicine, Soc. Exptl. Biology and Medicine Western N.Y., Austin Flint Soc. Med. Research, N.Y. Acad. Scis., Sigma Xi, Phi Kappa Phi. Unitarian. Author: Size and Growth of Tissue Cells, 1953; Life and Death of Cells, 1957. Contbg. author Acute Radiation Syndrome, Ann. Internal Medicine, vol. 36, 1952. Home: Buffalo N.Y. Died Dec. 8, 1974;buried, Perry, N.Y.

HOFFMAN, MARK, musician, educator; b. Merrill, Wis., Jan. 24, 1904; s. Martin George and Margaretha (Fritsch) H.; Sr. Diploma (gold medalist) Chgo. Mus. Coll., 1921; B.M. cum laude, Eastman Sch. Music, 1929, Ph.D., 1953; (Hutcheson scholar) Juilliard Grad. Sch. Music, 1929-31; A.M., N.Y.U., 1934; study and concertizing in Germany, 1932; m. Elaine Marie Faulkner, May 31, 1925; children—Margaret Elaine (Mrs. Isaac A. Scott, Jr.), Mark. Head piano dept. Kan. State Coll., Hays, 1924-26, James Millikin U., Decatur, Ill., 1926-28; dean music Greensboro (N.C.) Coll. Music, 1934-47; chmn. dept. music U. Miss., 1947-69, prof. piano and theory, 1966-69, prof. emeritus, 1969-75. Concert appearances Town Hall, N.Y.C., Kimball Hall, Chgo.; with Rochester Philharmonic, N.Y. Civic, N.C. Symphony, Brandenburg (German) Orch.; staff pianist radio sta. WINS, N.Y.C., also WOR, 1930-34; appearances Duke U., U. N.C., French Embassy, Washington; accompanist Isaac Stern (violinist), 1948, and others. Fellow Internat. Inst. Arts and Letters; mem. Music Tchrs. Nat. Assn., Music Educators Nat. Assn., N.C. Music Tchrs. Assn. (past pres.), Nat. Assn. Schs. Music (v.p. Region 8), Miss. Music Tchrs. Assn. (founder, pres. 1954-56), Phi Mu Alpha. Contbr. to Grove's Dictionary Music and Musicians. Home: Little Rock, Ark. Died June 12, 1975.

HOFFMAN, MILTON J., theologian; b. Overisel, Mich., Jan. 31, 1886; s. Johannes and Jennie (Timmerman) H.; B.A., Hope Coll., Holland, Mich., 1909, M.A., 1912, D.D., 1918; winner Rhodes scholarship from Mich.; B.A., Oxford U., Eng., 1912; m. Anna Viola MacWhinnie, July 15, 1914; children—Lydia Viola, Mildred Patricia. Head of Latin dept., Hope Coll., 1913-17; pres. Central Coll., Pella, Ia., 1917-25; prof. ch. history, New Brunswick Theol. Sem., 1925-56. Ordained ministry Reformed Ch. in America, Dec. 1917. Mem. Holland-Am. Foundation, Assn. Am. Rhodes Scholars, Am. Ch. History Soc., Order Orange-Nassau, Phi Beta Kappa. Pres. Raritan Valley Netherlands Assn. Home: Somerset, N.J. Died July 27, 1973.

HOFFMAN, PAUL GRAY, business exec.; b. Chgo., Apr. 26, 1891; s. George Delos and Eleanor (Lott) H.; student U. Chgo., 1908-09; hon. degrees from numerous univs., including U. Cal., Columbia, Harvard, Yale; m. Dorothy Brown, Dec. 18, 1915 (dec.); children—Hallock Brown, Peter Brown, Donald Gray, Robert Chesboro, Lathrop Gray, Barbara, Kiriki; m. 2d, Anna M. Rosenberg, July 19, 1962. Began as auto salesman Studebaker Corp., Los Angeles, 1911, sales mgr. Los Angeles br., 1915, dist. br. mgr., 1917, purchased Los Angeles retail br., 1919, v.p., 1925-33, pres., 1935-48, chmn. bd., 1953; chmn. bd. Studebaker-Packard Corp., 1954-56, Hoffman Spity. Mfg. Co.; adminstr. ECA (Marshall Plan), 1948-50; pres. trustee Ford Found., 1951-53. Mem. U.S. Delegation to UN, 1956-57; mng. dir. UN Spl. Fund, 1959-66; adminstr. of UN Devel. Programme, 1966-72, UN Vols., 1970-72, UN Fund for Pupuiation Activites, 1969-72. Trustee Com. Econ. Devel., chmn., 1942-48; chmn. pub. policy com. Advt. Council; mem. bus. adv. council Dept. Commerce, 1941-61, hon. mem. bus. council, 1962-74. Trustee U. Chgo., 1937-50, Kenyon Coll., 1940-60. Trustee Automotive Safety Found., pres., 1937-41, chmn., 1941-48; dir. N.Y. Life Ins. Co., Time, Inc., Ency. Brit. Inc., Ency. Brit. Films, Inc. Hon. chmn. Fund for Republic; dir. Inst. for Internat. Order; mem. exec. com. UN Assn. U.S.A. Served with U.S. Army, 1917-19. Recipient Freedom House award, 1951, numerous other awards and medals. Mem. Am. Soc. French Legion Honor, Delta Tau Delta, Republican. Mason. Clubs: Stanwich (Greenwich, Conn.); Metropolitan (Washington); Century (N.Y.C.); Thunderbird, California. Author: Seven Roads to Safety, 1939; Peace Can Be Won, 1951; 100 Countries-One and a Half Billion People, 1960; World Without Want, 1962. Home: New York City, N.Y. Died Oct. 8, 1974.

HOFFMAN, RICHARD W., congressman; b. Chicago, Dec. 23, 1893. Owner and operator radio station WHFC and WEHS-FM, Chicago. Served as pres. bd. of edn., J. Sterling Morton High Sch. and Jr. Coll., 1933-36 and 1939-48. Served with U.S. Army, World War I. Mem. 81st and 83d Congresses, 10th Ill. Dist. Republican. Home: Riverside, Ill. Died July 1975.

HOGAN, DANIEL WISE, banker; b. Modesto, Ill., Oct. 24, 1867; s. Daniel Wise and Arminda Jane (Turner) H.; grad. Northwestern Normal Sch., and Business Inst., Stanberry, Mo., 1889; m. Anna S. Harvey, Dec. 25, 1891 (died Oct. 14, 1939); children—Clark Harvey, Daniel Wise; m. 2d, Faye B. Locker, April 20, 1946. Bank clerk, 1890-92, organized First Nat. Bank of Yukon, Yukon, Okla., 1892; organized City Nat. Bank, Muskogee, Okla., 1904, cashier Am. Nat. Bank, Oklahoma City, 1907-11; pres. City Nat. Bank & Trust Co., Oklahoma City, Oklahoma, from 1911; v.p., dir. City Nat. Bank, Sayre, Okla.; past pres. Oklahoma City Clearing House Assn. Chmn. nat. board field advisers for Okla., of Small Bus., Adminstrn., Washington. Mem. Taxpayers Research Inst. (past. pres.), C. of C. (life dir.), Okla. Bankers Assn. (charter mem., past pres., 1st treas.), Oklahoma State Fair Assn. (exec. council), Motion Picture Panel of Arbitrators, Okla. Future Farmers of Am. and 4-H Club (hon.), Collegiate Engrs., Knights of St. Patrick Assn., Newcomen Soc. Eng., Beta Gamma Sigma (hon. mem.). Methodist. Clubs: Capitol City Gun (pres.), Men's Dinner (charter mem.); Sirloin. Lotus (Oklahoma City); Beacon of Okla. City Golf and Country. Home: Oklahoma City, Okla.†

HOGAN, FRANK SMITHWICK, lawyer; b. Waterbury, Conn., Jan. 17, 1902; s. Michael F. and Anne (Smithwick) H., B.A., Columbia, 1924, LL.B., 1928, LL.D, 1952; LL.D., Suffolk Law Sch., 1955; m. Mary Egan, Nov. 11, 1936. Admitted to N.Y. bar, 1929; with Gleason, McLanahan, Merritt & Ingraham, 1928-30; partner ins. and real estate law Anthony J. Liebler, 1930-35; asst. to spl. pros. New York County, 1935-37, adminstrv. asst. to dist. atty., 1937-41, dist. atty., 1942-74. Trustee Columbia, Knickerbocker Hospital, St. Luke's Hospital. Democratic candidate for U.S. Senate, 1958. Recipient Columbia U. medal for exceptional pub. service, 1942, Columbia Alumni medal for conspicuous alumni service, 1946, Medal of Merit, New York County Grand Jury Assn., 1947, gold medal Am. Irish Hist. Soc., 1952, Medal of Merit of St. Nicholas Soc., 1951, Alexander Hamilton Medal of Alumni of Columbia Coll., 1954; Futherance of Justice award Nat. Dist. Attys. Assn., 1959. Mem. Columbia Coll. Council (chmn. 1961-62), Assn. Alumni Columbia Coll. (pres. 1946-49), Alumni Fedn. Columbia U. (pres. 1949-51), Dist. Attys. Assn. State N.Y. (pres. 1947), N.Y. State Bar Assn., Assn. Bar City N.Y. (mem. exec. com. 1959-63), Friendly Sons St. Patrick. Democrat. Roman Catholic. Club: Columbia University (N.Y.C.). Home: New York City, N.Y. Died Apr. 2, 1974.

HOGBEN, LANCELOT, author, univ. prof.; b. Southsea, Hampshire, Eng., Dec. 9, 1895; s. Thomas and Margaret (Prescott) H.; ed. Trinity Coll. (Senior scholar, Frank Smart prizeman); M.A., Cambridge U., Eng., D.Sc., London U.; LL.D. (hon.) Birmingham U.; Fellow Royal Soc.; m. Enid Charles, 1918 (div. 1957); children—Ennyd Syvia, Charles Adrian Michael, Clare Estelle, David Julian Lancelot; m. 2d, Sarah Jane Evans, 1957. Prof. emeritus med. statistics U. Birmingham, hon. sr. fellow linguistics, 1961; vice chancellor U. Guyana, 1963-75. Awarded Keith prize and gold medal by Royal Soc. of Edinburgh, 1936. Croonian Lecture, Royal Soc., 1943. Author: Comparative Physiology of Internal Secretions, 1927; Genetic Principles in Medicine, 1931; Nature and Nurture 1933; Mathematics for the Million, 1936; Science for the Citizen, 1938; Chance and Choice, 1950; Statistical Theory, 1957; Mathematics in the Making, 1960; The Mother Tongue, 1964; The Vocabulary of Science, 1970; also sci. articles in Proc. Royal Soc. Jour. of Genetics, others. Address: Glyn-Ceiriog, Llangollen, Wales. Died Aug. 22, 1975.

HOGNESS, THORFIN RUSTEN, educator; b. Mpls., Dec. 9, 1894; s. Peter Gunerius and Amanda (Rusten) H.; B.S., U. Minn., 1918, Chem. E., 1919; Ph.D., U. Cal., 1921; postgrad. (research fellow) U. Göttingen (Germany), 1926-27; m. Phoebe Dorothy Swenson, July 31, 1920; children—John Rusten, David Swenson. Instr. chemistry U. Cal., 1921, asst. prof., 1925-28, asso. prof., 1928-30; asso. prof. chemistry U. Chgo., 1930-38, prof., from 1938, later prof. emeritus, dir. phys. sci. devel., 1947-48, dir. Inst. Radiobiology and Biophysics, 1948-51, Labs. Applied Scis., from 1962, Chgo. Midway Labs., 1951. Mem. OSRD, 1941; sci. liason officer Am. embassy, London, Eng., 1942-43; dir. Med. Research Lab., OSS, 1943; dir. chem. div. on atomic energy work U. Chgo., 1943-45, cons. War Dept. and OSRD with E.T.O.U.S.A., 1945. Served with U.S. Army, 1918. Recipient Outstanding Achievement award U. Minn., 1950. Mem. A.A.A.S., Am. Chem. Soc., Sigma Xi, Phi Lambda Upsilon, Alpha Chi Sigma. Clubs: Quadrangle. Home: San Jose, Cal., Died Feb. 14, 1976.

HOLBROOK, ARTHUR TENNEY, physician; b. Waukesha, Wis., July 12, 1870; s. Arthur and Josephine (Tenney) H.; S.B., Harvard, 1892; M.D., Rush Med. Coll., 1895; post-grad. work in hosps. of Vienna, Austria, 1902; m. Bertha Andrews (dec.), July 29, 1903; children—Arthur Andrews, Herbert Tenney, Matson. House Surgeon, Presbyterian Hosp., Chicago, 1895-97; mem. staff St. Mary's Hospital, Columbia Hospital, surgeon at Milwaukee for Soo Line R.R.; president Milwaukee County Day Sch.; trustee Plymouth Ch.; etc. Served as 1st lt. asst. surg. Wis. N.G., 1898-1903, reëntered service, 1916. Fellow Am. Coll. Surgs.; mem. A.M.A., Wis. State, Milwaukee, and Milwaukee County med. socs., Milwaukee Surg. Soc., Chi Psi, Nu Sigma Nu, Loyal Legion. Republican. Conglist. Clubs: Milwaukee, University, Milwaukee Country. Contbr. numerous papers and addresses on med. topics, conservation, big game hunting, fishing and travel. Author: From the Log of a Trout Fisherman. Home: Milwaukee, Wis.†

HOLDAWAY, CHARLES WILLIAM, educator; B. Masterton, New Zealand, May 24, 1880; s. Charles and Helen Ramage Blackall (Mair) H.; B.S., Virginia Polytechnic Institute, 1912, M.S., 1914; m. Carrie Ernestine MacTavish, Dec. 25, 1907; children—Helen Louise (Mrs. John Maury Miles), Lorne Morlock, Charles Mair, Amy Ethelwyn (Mrs. William Joseph Lipfert III), John Mathew, Ernest MacTavish. Came to U.S., 1902, naturalized, 1916. in creamery bus., 1898-1904; specist., 1904, 05; asst. dairy husbandman, 1905-08, instr. in dairying, Va. Poly. Inst., 1908-14, asso. prof., 1914-18, prof., 1918-21, prof. and head of dept. from 1921, research dairyman of Expt. Sta. from 1915. Mem. A.A.A.S., Am. Dairy Sci. Assn., Va. Acad. of Science, Am. Assn. Univ. Profs., Phi Kappa Phi, Alpha Zeta, Sigma Ci. Democrat. Presbyterian (trustee and elder, Blacksburg Ch.). Mason. Club: Science (Va. Poly. Inst.). Contbr. research bulls. of Va. Agr. Expt. Sta. and articles to Progressive Farmer, Tobacco Grower. Home: Blacksburg, Va.†

HOLDEN, WILLIS SPRAGUE, coll. prof., journalist; b. Grand Rapids, Mich., Jan. 3, 1909; s. Charles Wayne and Marie (Sprague) H.; grad. Grand Rapids Jr. Coll., 1927; A.B., U. of Mich., 1930; A.M., Columbia, 1932; m. Sheila (Edna) Richart, May 24, 1934. Sports space writer Grand Rapids Herald, 1926; coll. corr. for newspapers, 1926-29; staff writer Time, news mag., N.Y.C. 1930; theater and motion picture editor San Francisco Argonaut, 1932-36, asso. editor, 1933-34, mng. editor, 1934-36; editorial writer Akron (O.) Beacon Jour., 1936-40; editorial writer. Detroit Free Press, 1940-46, columnist, 1942-46; prof. journalism Wayne State U., 1946-73, founder and chmn. dept. journalism, 1949-73; on sabbatical leave in Australia, 1956-57, 66; 29th Arthur Norman Smith lectr. in journalism U. Melbourne, 1966. Awarded Fulbright Grant, U.S. State Department, to make study Australian daily met. newspapers, 1956-57, to study indsl. arbitration-conciliation systems in Australia, 1966. Ford Found grant, 1966. Recipient sr. class Rhetoric medal, U. Mich., 1930. Mem. Assn. for Edn. in Journalism, Internat. Press Inst., Nat. Conf. Editorial Writers, also Am. Assn. U. Profs., Am. Soc. Journalism Sch. Adminstrs., Mich. acad. Sci., Arts and Letters, Australian Polit. Sci. Assn., Friends Detroit Pub. Library, Detroit Hist. Assn., Am. Civil Liberties Union, P.E.N., Sigma Delta Chi. Clubs: Torch. Schoolmen's, Press (Detroit); Wayne State University Press (Detroit). Author: Australia Goes To Press, 1961, Australian edit., 1962; also articles mags. and newspapers. Editor, Detroit in Perspective: A Journal of Regional History, 1972-73. Address: Farmington Hills, Mich. Died Aug. 8, 1973; buried, Grand Rapids, Mich.

HOLDER, IVAN WENDELL, pharmacist; b. Farmersburg, Ind., Mar. 28, 1906; s. Edward Harrison and Maud (Lynch) H.; Ph.G., Purdue U., 1927; m. Evalyn Hastings, Aug. 6, 1933; children—David, Carolyn (Mrs. William J. McClintock). Owner, operator, pres. Holder Pharmacy, Inc., Monticello, Ind., 1943-73. Mem. Ind. Bd. Pharmacy, 1962-73, sec., 1965-67. Mem. State Pharm. Assn. (pres. 1957), C. of C. (pres. 1948-55). Democrat. Presbyn. (elder). Mason. Clubs: Kiwanis (pres. 1950). Tippecanoe Country. Home: Monticello, Ind. Died Apr. 4, 1973.

HOLLAND, CHARLES HUBERT, ins. exec.; b. London, Eng., Apr. 25, 1878; s. Hubert Charles and Mary A. (Cobb) H.; grad. City of London Sch.; m. Lois Amy Barber, 1903; children—Hubert Brian, Eunice Katharine. Came to U.S., 1910. Began as jr. clk., Howard, Howes & Walters. pub. accountants London; in London office Northern Accident Ins. Co. of Glasgow, 1896-1907; in charge Australasia casualty br. Royal Ins. Co., 1907-10, v.p. and gen. mgr. New York br., as Royal Indemnity Co., 1910-18, pres. and chmn. bd. dirs., 1918-22; pres. Independence Indemnity Co., 1922-31, chmn. bd., from 1931; pres. Independence Fire Ins. Co., Independence Realty Co.; dir. Finance Corpn. America, Globe Ins. Co., Pa. Securities Corpn., Corroon & Reynolds, Inc. Chmn. traveling banks com., Liberty Loan drives, and 4-minute orator, World War. Fellow Casualty Acturial Soc.; mem. U.S. Chamber Commerce, Chamber Commerce State of N.Y., St. George's Soc. (formerly sec., N.Y.), Pilgrims of America. Episcopalian. Mason. Clubs: Down Town, Racquet (Philadelphia); Down Town (New York); Sea View Golf (Absecon, N.J.). Home: Germantown, Pa.†

HOLLAND, JOSIAH GILBERT, lawyer; b. Denver, Nov. 16, 1900; s. Theodore and Florence (Ward) H.; student U. Colo., 1918-20, Yale, 1920-22; LL.B. cum laude, Denver U., 1925; m. Elizabeth Welborn, Aug. 10, 1927 (div. 1961); children—Diana, Lorna, Penelope; m. 2d, Meriwether Lewis Montgomery, Nov. 2, 1961. Admitted Colo. bar, 1925, practiced in Denver; asso. firm Grant, Ellis, Shafroth and Toll, 1928-34; partner firm Lewis, Bond and Holland, 1934-42, White and Holland, 1945-47, Holland & Hart, 1947-75. Dir. Joy Mfg. Co., 1968-71. Mem. Colo. Legislature, 1931. Mem. Am., Colo., Denver bar assns. Republican. Episcopalian. Clubs: Denver, Denver Country, Arapahoe Hunt. Home: Denver Colo. Died Feb. 28, 1975.

HOLLAND, SAMUEL HYMAN, lawyer; b. Lutzin, Latvia, July 1, 1892; s. Zalman I. and Chaye D. (Lev) H.; came to U.S., 1909, naturalized, 1915; LL.B., John Marshall Law Sch., 1915; postgrad. U. Chgo., 1915, Nat. Autonomous U. Mexico, 1959-62; m. Tillie Perlman, Aug. 8, 1920; children—Joshua Zalman, Miriam Filler, Ruth Waddell, Judith King. Admitted to Ill. bar, 1915; practiced in Chgo., 1915-58, Mexico City, Mexico, 1959-62, Washington, 1962-73; mem. firm Holland & Shuchter, Chgo., 1930-47. Bd. dirs. Jewish Welfare Fund Chgo., 1938-53; mem. Chgo. Com. on Human Relations, 1945-58. Mem. Am. Assn. State and Local History, Am. Jewish Hist. Soc., Chgo. Bar Assn., Jewish Hist. Soc. Greater Washington (exec. v.p. 1965-73). Home: Washington, D.C. Died Nov. 25, 1973.

HOLLAND, ST. CLAIR CECIL, corp. exec.; b. Montreal, Que., Can., Oct. 28, 1894; s. George and Amelia Holland; student Westmount Acad.; LL.D., Sir George Williams U., 1971; m. Dorothy Duckett, 1919; children—George, Joan. With Shawinigan Water & Power Co., 1910; with Robert Mitchell Co. Ltd., brass, iron founders, Montreal, 1913, now pres., mng. dir., also dir. co.; pres., mng. dir. Garth Co., Prowse Ltd., Douglas Bros. Ltd.; v.p., dir. Canadian Cutler Mail Chute Co.; dir. Albion Ins. Co. Can., Guardian Trust Co., Ltd. Bd. govs. Queen Elizabeth Hosp., Montreal Children's Hosp., Federated Appeal, St. Justine Hosp., Montreal Gen. Hosp., Royal Edward Chest Hosp.; mem. nat. adv. bd., bd. govs. and hon. pres. Que. div. Canadian Mental Health Assn.; past pres. Canadian Rugby Union, Que. Rugby Union, St. John Ambulance Assn., Montreal Boys Assn., Montreal Boy Scouts Assn.; mem. adv. council Boys Clubs Can.; hon. v.p. Que. Provincial council mem. exec. com., Canadian gen. counsel Boy Scouts Can. Served with heavy arty. C.E.F., 1914-18; lt. col. ret. Royal Canadian Arty. Decorated Canadian Forces Decoration and bar, knight Order St. John; recipient Canadian Centennial medal, Nat. Merit award Canadian Mental Health Assn., 1967. Fellow Royal Commonwealth Soc.; mem. Montreal Bd. Trade, Canadian C. of C., Que. Amateur Hockey Assn. (past pres.), Que. Rugby Football Assn. (gov.), Montreal Profl. Golfers Assn., Alumni Assn. Sir George Williams U. (hon. life), Alouette Alumni Assn. (hon. life), Newcomen Soc. Mason (Shriner). Rotarian (past pres. Montreal, past dist. gov.). Clubs: Seigniory, Royal

Montreal Golf, Mount Royal, Montreal Engineers, Canadian; Royal St. Lawrence Yacht; McGill Football (past pres.); Victoria Hockey (past pres.). Home: Montreal PQ Canada. Died Jan. 9, 1974.

HOLLANDS, EDMUND HOWARD, educator; b. Watervliet, N.Y., Jan. 11, 1879; s. Edmund Sinard and Emma Augusta (Osterhout) H.; Ph.B., Cornell U., 1899, M.A., 1901, Ph.D., 1905; m. Buena Wilson, July 24, 1907; 1 son, Edmund Wilson. Sage scholar in philosophy, 1900, Sage fellow, 1903, instr., 1905 and 1907-09, Cornell U.; instr. philosophy, Princeton, 1906; actg. prof. philosophy, Hamilton Coll., Clinton, N.Y.; prof. philosophy, Butler Coll., Irvington, Ind., 1910, U. Kan. from 1913; vis. prof. philosophy, U. of Southern Calif., 1929-30. Mem. Am. Philos. Assn., Western Philos. Assn. (pres. 1925), Sigma Alpha Epsilon. Hon. fellow Sch. of Philosophy, U. of Southern Calif. Episcopalian. Club: University. Contbr. to Philos. Rev., and other periodicals. Home: Lawrence, Kan.†

HOLLISTER, RICHARD DENNIS TEALL, educator; b. Brighton, Mich., Oct. 26, 1878; s. Edward Teall and Emily Jane (Green) H.; A.B., U. of Mich., 1902, A.M., 1903; spl. work U. of Chicago, 1919; m. Jessie Ione Holmes, June 20, 1906; children—Richard Holmes, Ruth Margaret, Marion Louise. With U. Mich., from 1904, asso. prof. pub. speaking from 1920; lectr. on lit. and ednl. topics; interpreter of poetry and the drama. Mem. Nat. Assn. Teachers of Speech. Republican. Conglist. Author: Speech-Making, 1918; Theatre Art, 1924; Literature for Oral Interpretation, 1929. Home: Ann Arbor, Mich.†

HOLLOMAN, DELMAR WINSTON, lawyer; b. Frederick, Okla., June 28, 1913; s. Andrew Harvey and Dora (Prophit) H.; A.B., U. Okla., 1935; LL.B., Harvard, 1941; m. Mary Louise Clas, Oct. 11, 1941; children—Douglas Winston, Marcia Carin. Admitted to D.C. bar, 1942, Md. bar, 1950; asso. Davies, Richberg, Tydings, Beebe & Landa, 1946-50, mem. firm, 1950-75. Dir. Baruch Foster Co., Am. Steel Rolling Mills, Inc., Union Tex. Oil Co. Legal cons. Task Force on Water Resources and Power of Hoover Commn., 1953-55. Bd. dirs. Washington Heart Fund; trustee Joseph E. Davies Found., Marquis Library Soc., Inc., Eberhard Sch. Served to col., M.I. Corps, U.S. Army, 1941-46. Mem. Am. Bar Assn., Bar Assn. D.C., Am. Legion, Sigma Nu. Methodist. Mason (Shriner). Clubs: University, Congressional Country, Harvard (Washington); Denver; Hiwan Country. Home: Chevy Chase Md. Died Jan. 4, 1975.

HOLMES, CHARLES SHIVELEY, educator; b. Oberlin, O., Jan. 13, 1916; s. Harry N. and Mary V. (Shiveley) H.; grad. Deerfield Acad., 1933; A.B., Oberlin Coll., 1938; Ph.D., Princeton, 1941; m. Marian T. Crain, Aug. 6, 1937. Mem. faculty Pomona (Cal.), Coll., 1941-76, prof. English, 1957-76; Fulbright prof. U. Graz (Austria), 1955-56, U. Vienna (Austria), 1962-63. Served to lt. USNR, 1943-46. Mem. Modern Lang. Assn. Am., Philol. Assn. Pacific Coast, Am. Studies Assn. Author: The Clocks of Columbus: The Literary Career of James Thurber, 1972; also articles. Editor: (with E. Fussell and R. Frazer) The Major Critics, 1957; Thurber, a collection of critical essays, 1974. Home: Claremont, Cal., Died Jan. 15, 1976.

HOLMES, SAMUEL FOSS, teacher; b. Portland, Me., Mar. 9, 1881; s. Wilbur Fisk and Mary Evelyn (Howe) H.; grad. Me. Wesleyan Sem., Kents Hill, 1900; Ph.B, Wesleyan University, Conn., 1904, M.A., 1910; m. Mary D. Adams, Dec. 26, 1908; m. 2d, Katherine Wheeler Clark, June 30, 1929. Assistant in English, Wesleyan University, 1904-06; master in English, Peekskill (N.Y.) Mil. Acad., 1906-07; instr. English, 1907-11, master in English, 1911-18, acting prin., 1918-19, headmaster from 1919, Worcester (Mass.) Acad. Mem. Headmasters' Assn., N.E. Assn. of Colls. and Secondary Schools, N.E. Assn. Teachers of English, Delta Kappa Epsilon, Phi Beta Kappa. Republican. Episcopalian. Clubs: Worcester, Rotary, Shakespeare, Friday; Brooklawn Country (Bridgeport). Address: Worcester, Mass.†

HOLSCLAW, CHARLES H., mfg. co. exec.; b. Louisville, Dec. 13, 1904; s. Walter E. and Mayme (O'Neal) H.; B.S., Ind. U., 1928; m. Hester W. Elfreich, Sept. 30, 1931; children—Ann (Mrs. Donald Partridge), Mary (Mrs. John Heumann). Accountant, Chrysler Corp., 1928-30; with Holsclaw Bros. Inc., Evansville, Ind., 1930-73, pres., until 1973. Elk, Rotarian. Clubs: Evansville Country; Santa Claus Country; Petroleum. Home: Evansville, Ind. Died Dec. 10, 1973.

HOLT, HOMER ADAMS, former gov., lawyer; b. Lewisburg, W.Va., Mar. 1, 1898; s. Robert Byrne and Emma (McWhorter) H.; A.B., Washington and Lee U., 1918, LL.B., 1923; LL.D., W.Va. U., 1937, Bethany Coll., W.Va., 1940; m. Isabel Hedges Wood, Mar. 22, 1924; children—Julia Kinsley (Mrs. Coyle), Isabel Drury (Mrs. Dannenberg), Robert Byrne. Instr. math. Washington and Lee U., 1920-23, asst. prof. law, 1923-24, asso. prof., 1924-25; in practice law; mem. firm Hubard, Bacon & Holt, 1925-26, Dillon, Mahan & Holt, Fayetteville, W.Va., 1927-33; atty. gen. W.Va., 1933-37; gov. W.Va., 1937-41; mem. law firm Brown, Jackson & Knight, Charleston, W.Va., 1941-46; dir. Union Carbide & Carbon Corp., N.Y., 1944-55, gen. counsel, 1947-53, v.p., 1949-53, exec. com., 1950-53; mem. Jackson, Kelly, Holt & O'Farrell, 1953-75; dir. Kanawha Valley Bank Charleston, Slab Fork Coal Co. Mem.-at-large Nat. council Boy Scouts Am., 1959; chmn. W.Va. Commn. Constle Revision, 1957-63. Trustee Charleston Area Med. Center (formerly Meml. Hosp. Assn. Charleston), 1958, pres., 1961-63; trustee, mem. exec. com. Wash. and Lee U., 1940-69, now emeritus. Served to 2d lt. C.A., U.S. Army, 1918-19. Mem. Am., W.Va. (past pres.), Fayette County, Kanawha County bar assns., Bar Assn. N.Y.C., Am. Counsel Assn., Assn. Gen. Counsel (emeritus), Am. Law Inst., Am. Judicature Soc., W.Va. C. of C. (pres. 1945-46), Am. Legion, N.Y. So. Soc., Order of Coif, Phi Beta Kappa, Phi Kappa Psi, Phi Delta Phi, Omicron Delta Kappa. Democrat. Presbyn. Mason, Elk, Rotarian. Home: Charleston, W.Va. Died Jan. 16, 1975.

HOLT, L. EMMETT, JR., physician, educator; b. N.Y.C., Mar. 20, 1895; s. L. Emmett and Linda F. (Mairs) H.; A.B., Harvard, 1916; M.D., Johns Hopkins, 1920; Sc.D., N.Y. Med. Coll., 1967; m. Olivia Cauldwell, June 17, 1921; children—Neil MacL., Arnold R., Linda H. Holz. Intern, Presbyn. Hosp., 1920-21, Babies Hosp., 1921-22 (both N.Y.C.); teaching, med. research dept. pediatrics Johns Hopkins, 1922-44; prof. pediatrics N.Y. U. Coll. Medicine, N.Y.C., 1944-74, chmn. dept. pediatrics, 1944-60, med. missions to Czechoslovakia, 1947; sec. Internat. Congress Pediatrics, N.Y.C.; cons. nutrition WHO. Decorated Order White Lion, medal of Charles U. (Czechoslovakia); Mannerheim medal (Finland), Al-Istigial of Second Order (Jordan); recipient Borden Nutrition award, Am. Acad. Pediatrics, 1955; Harlow Brooks medal, New York Acad. Medicine, 1957, Modern Medicine award, 1960; McCollum award, 1960, Osborne Mendel award Am. Inst. Nutrition, 1964, Howland award Am. Pediatric Soc. 1966, Goldberger award A.M.A., 1969. Mem. A. Middle East Rehab. (pres. 1950-60), Nutrition Soc. Gt. Britain, Assn. Am. Physicians, Am. Soc. Clin. Nutrition, Am. Soc. Clin. Investigation, Am. Pediatric Soc., Soc. Pediatric Research, Am. Acad. Pediatrics, Soc. Exptl. Biology and Medicine, Am. Inst. Nutrition, Am. Soc. Biol. Chemists, A.A.A.S., Practitioners Soc., Interurban Clin. Club, Harvey Soc.; also mem. numerous fgn. pediatric socs. Club: Century Assn. (N.Y.C.). Author: Holt's Pediatries (with R. McIntosh and H.L. Barnett); Pioneer of a Children's Century, 1939, (with R. L. Duffus) Good Housekeeping Book of Infant and Child Care, 1958; pediatrics, nutrition, biochemistry articles med. jours. Died Nov. 30, 1974; buried Vinal Haven, Me.

HOLT, ROBERT HAROLD, lawyer; b. Gardiner, Me., Sept. 25, 1889; s. John Franklin and Mary G. (Robinson) H.; A.B., Harvard, 1911, LL.B., 1914; m. Lilian S. Clapp, Oct. 28, 1916 (dec. Feb. 1959); children—Richard P., Rosamund (Mrs. Wallace F. Haley), Deborah (Mrs. James R. McIntosh); m. 2d, Margaret Bartlett Wells, Mar. 26, 1960. Admitted to Mass. bar, 1914; asso. firm Gaston, Snow, Motley & Holt, and predecessors, Boston, 1914-73, partner, 1920-40, sr. partner, 1940-73. Moderator, Lexington Town Meeting, 1924-49. Served to 2d lt. U.S. Army, World War I. Mem. Am., Boston bar assns. Clubs: Union, Harvard (Boston); Duxbury (Mass.) Yacht. Home: Duxbury Mass. Died Aug. 9, 1973; interred, Lexington, Mass.

HOLY, THOMAS CELESTINE, ednl. cons.; b. Vandalia, Ia., Oct. 21, 1887; s. John and Mary Theresa (Gulling) H.; A.B., Des Moines U., 1919; A.M., Ia. State U., 1922, Ph.D., 1924; m. Gladyce Grayce Webb, Aug. 14, 1913 (dec. Sept. 1958). Rural sch. tchr., Ia., 1909-10; supt. schs., Runnells, Ia., 1912-15, Lynnville, Ia., 1915-17, 19-21; instr. Columbia Tchrs. Coll., 1924; dir. div. housing and equipment St. Louis pub. schs., 1925-27; head survey div. Bur. Ednl. Research, Ohio State U., 1927-42, dir. Bur. Ednl. Research, 1942-51; spl. cons. in higher edn. U. Cal., 1952-61; chief cons. Bd. Higher Edn., N.Y.C., 1961-62; spl. cons. Coordinating Council for Higher Edn. in Cal., 1962-64, Ore. Dept. Edn., 1965-66, Ia. Bd. Regents, 1966-69. Chmn. Ohio commn. to erect state schs. for blind and deaf, 1944-51; cons. states bldg. programs. Served with U.S. Army, World War I. Mem. N.E.A., Am. Assn. Sch. Adminstrs., Am. Ednl. Research Assn. (pres. 1934), Ohio Edn. Assn., Nat. Council Schoolhouse Constrn. (pres. 1937), Phi Delta Kappa, Kappa Phi Kappa. Democrat. Methodist. Mason (32, Shriner). Club: Faculty (U. Cal.). Author, contbr. reports on surveys of schs., equipment, salaries, health and other related topics of ednl. systems throughout U.S., 1929-73; latest reports include: The Need for Additional Centers of Public Education in California (with others), 1957; Faculty Demand and Supply in California 1957-1970 (with others), 1958; (with others) A Master Plan for Higher Education in California 1960-75; A Long-Range Plan for The City University of New York, 1961-1975 (with others) Education in the States, Nationwide Development Since 1900, 1969. Contbr. ednl. publs. Address: Prairie City, Ia. Died Apr. 19, 1973; interred Silent City Cemetery, Monroe, Ia.

HOLZAPPLE, JOSEPH RANDALL, ret. air force officer; b. Peoria, Ill., Sept. 7, 1914; s. Nathaniel A. and Annetta (Ritchie) H.; B.S., Bradley U., 1938, LL.D., 1958; grad. Armed Forces Staff Coll., 1950, Nat. War Coll., 1955; m. Lois M. Miller, Mar. 1, 1945; children—Lynn, Nancy. Commd. 2d lt. USAAF, 1941, advanced through grades to gen. USAF, 1969; pilot 38th Bomb Group, 1941-42; group operations officer 319th Bomb Group, 1942-43, comdr., 1943-45; staff Hdqrs. USAF requirements div., 1946-49; chief devel. div. Armed Forces Spl. Weapons Project, 1950-51; staff Hdqrs. Air Research and Devel. Command, 1951-54; comdr. 47th Bomb Wing, Eng., 1955-56; dep. chief staff operations, chief staff Hdqrs. USAF Europe, comdr. AIRSPECCOME, 1956-58; dep. dir. operational forces, Hdqrs. USAF, 1958-59; asst. dep. comdr. systems Air Research and Devel. Command, Wright Field, O., 1959; dir. systems mgmt. ARDC, 1960; Wright Air Devel. Div., Wright-Patterson AFB, O., 1960-61; asst. dep. chief staff Systems and Logistics Hdqrs. USAF, 1961-64, dir. weapons systems evaluation group Office of Sec. of Def., 1964-66, dep. chief staff, research and devel. Hdgrs. USAF, 1966-69; comdr. in chief USAF, Europe, 1969-71; sr. Air Force mem. mil. staff com. UN, 1968-69. Decorated Legion of Merit, D.F.C. with cluster, Silver Star, Air medal with clusters, Distinguished Unit Citation with cluster; D.F.C. (Britain); Croix de Guerre with palm, Croix de Guerre with Etoile d'argent (France) D.S.M with two oak leaf clusters, grande ufficiale Order of Merit (Italy), Grosse Verdienstkreuz with stern and schutterband (Germany). Home: Arlington Va. Died Nov. 1973.

HOLZMAN, BENJAMIN GRAD, govt. ofcl.; b. Los Angeles, Jan. 25, 1910; s. Zeke and Esther (Holzman) H.; B.S., Cal. Inst. Tech., 1931, M.S., 1933; m. Katherine Margaret Holzman, June 12, 1941; 1 dau., Katherine Margaret. Meteorologist, Eastern Airlines, Inc., Washington, 1934; chief meteorologist Am. Airlines, N.Y.C., 1935; research meteorologist Dept. Agr., Washington, 1936; teaching fellow Cal. Inst. Tech., 1937, 38; supervising meteorologist U.S. Weather Bur., Washington, 1939-42; commd. officer U.S. Army Air Force, 1942, advanced through grades to brig. gen. U.S. Air Force, 1958; staff weather officer, adviser, cons. atomic bomb tests, 1945, 51; dep. research and devel. hdqrs. Air Force Spl. Weapons Center 1952-55; dir. air weapons Hdqrs. Air Research and Devel. Command, Balt., 1955-57, dir. research, 1957-59, comdr., 1960; comdr. Air Force Cambridge Research Labs., Bedford, Mass., 1960-64; spl. adviser Hdqrs. NASA, Washington, 1964-67; dep. dir. environmental data service Environmental Sci. Service Adminstrn., Dept. Commerce, Silver Spring, Md., 1967-71. Fellow Meteorol. Soc.; mem. Geophys. Union. Home: Upper Marlboro, Md. Died July 29, 1975.

HOMER, WILLIAM OSCAR, archbishop-metropolitan and primate American Orthodox Ch.; b. New York, N.Y., June 16, 1881; s. Henry and Virginia (Maher) H.; D.D.S., U. of Pa., 1905, med. student, 2 yrs., Class of 1908; Ph.C., Temple Coll. (now Temple U.), Phila., Pa., 1906, Ph.D., 1945; grad. Ark. Sch. of Theology (Episcopal), 1909; D.C.L., Chicago Law Sch., 1915; D.D., Campbell Coll., Holton, Kan., 1916; B.S., Lewis Inst. (now Ill. Inst. Tech.), Chicago, 1928; grad. Chicago Normal Coll., 1929; grad. work, Loyola U., Chicago, 1932-37; m. Florence Lalor, Mar. 15, 1906; children—Henry Lalor, Rosalie Ashton, Virginia Florence, Rev. William Oscar, Muriel; m. 2d, Florence Barbara Heyne, Nov. 30, 1930; children—JeanMarie, Judith Diane, James Lionel. Practicing dentist and instr. in clinical dentistry, Medico-Chirurgical Coll. (now Grad. Sch. of U. of Pa.), Phila., Pa., 1905-06; catechist, later deacon in charge, Grace Episcopal Ch., Siloam Springs, Ark., 1908-09; deacon, later priest in charge, Trinity Episcopal Ch., Independence, Mo., 1909-11; rector, Grace Episcopal Ch., Chillicothe, Mo., 1911-14, Episcopal Ch., 1916-19; prof. preventive medicine and hygiene, Chicago Coll. of Osteopathy, 1924-26; also officiated at Calvary and at St. Bartholomew's Episcopal churches, Chicago, 1919-26; resigned from Episcopal Ch. and received holy orders in Am. Cath. Ch., renamed Am. Orthodox Ch., 1945, Oct. 1926, consecrated bishop, May 1930, Archibishop, Feb. 1931, chancellor of Am. Cath. Ch., 1927-30, archibishop-metropolitan and primate, from 1944. Author of article on Care of the Teeth (Draper's Self Culture); Quiz Compend in Physiology for Medical, Dental and Pharmaceutical Students; The Ecclesiastical Law of Marriage and Divorce. Address: Tucson, Ariz.†

HONEYMAN, NAN WOOD (MRS. DAVID T. HONEYMAN), ex-congresswoman; b. West Point, N.Y., July 15, 1881; d. Charles Erskine Scott and Nanny Moale (Smith) Wood; St. Helen's Hall, Portland, Ore., 1891-98, Finch Sch., N.Y. City, 1898-1901; m. David T. Honeyman, 1907; children—Nancy (Mrs. Kent Robinson), David Erskine, Judith. Mem. Ore. Ho. of Rep., 1934-36; mem. 75th Congress (1937-39), 3d Ore. Dist. Chmn. Women's Orgn. for Nat. Prohibition Reform, 1929-33; pres. Portland League of Women Voters; overseer Whitman Coll., Walla Walla, Wash., 1928-34; dir. Doernbecher Children's Hosp., Portland. Democrat. Club: Town (Portland). Home: Portland, Ore.†

HONIG, GEORGE HONIG, sculptor; b. Rockport, Ind., 1881; s. Simon and Mary (Honig) H.; ed. high sch. and Ind. U.; studied art, Art Students' League and Nat. Acad. Design, New York, m. Alda McCoy, June 12, 1917. Awarded Suydam bronze medal, 1914. Suydam silver medal, 1915, Nat. Acad. Design. Many works, among them: display fountain, Shelbyville, Ind.; soldiers' group, Joliet, Ill.; bronze portrait of Audubon, Henderson, Ky.; group, "The Spirit of Sixty-one," etc., Evansville, Ind.; 6 heroic bronze memorials in relief, at Henderson, unveiled, 1929, depicting history of the Transylvania Company; Lincoln portrait in bronze and memorial, Boonville, Ind., 1933; John R. Sterne memorial and portrait, Evansville, Ind.; sculptured relief, Abraham Lincoln's Forest College, Rockport, Ind., High Sch.; designed and erected Lincoln Pioneer Village, Rockport; designed memorial portraits of Senator James A. Hemenway and William Fortune, Boonville, Ind. Designed nat. shrine to Abraham Lincoln. "Lincoln Pioneer Village." Rockport, Ind.; World War II Memorial First Batp Bapt. Ch., Evansville, Ind.; World War II Memorial, Elks Lodge, Evansville, Ind. Mem. Soc. of Fine Arts and Museum of Evansville (treas.), Sigma Chi. Home: Evansville, Ind.†

HONNEN, GEORGE, ret. army officer; b. Phila., Nov. 16, 1897; s. Charles Baldwin and Elizabeth (Fry) H.; B.S., U.S. Mil. Acad., 1920; grad. Inf. Sch., 1921, Command and Gen. Staff Sch., 1938, Nat. War Coll., 1946; m. Helen Van R. Stillman, Jan. 12, 1927; children—Sara Elizabeth Dessez (wife of George E. Wear, U.S. Army), Jessie Evelyn Peyton (wife of Charles F. McCarty, U.S. Army). Commd. 2d lt. U.S. Army, 1920, advanced through grades to maj. gen., 1947; chief staff 3d Army, Ft. McPherson, 1941-42, 6th Army, S.W. Pacific Theatre, 1942-43, asst. div. comdr. 89th Div., 1943; comdt. cadets U.S. Mil. Acad., 1943-46; prof. mil. sci. and tactics U. Hawaii, 1946-48; asst. comdt. Inf. Sch., 1949-51; chief budget div. OCA, Dept. of Army, 1951-52; U.S. comdr., Berlin, 1954-55; chief staff Hdqrs. U.S. European Command, 1955-57, hdqrs. 3d Army, Ft. McPherson, Ga., 1957; dean The Citadel, 1958-63. Pres. Army Relief Soc., Charleston. Trustee U.S. Military Academy, West Point, N.Y. Decorated D.S.M., Legion of Merit. Mem. Ret. Officers Assn. (pres. Charleston), Am. Legion (vice post comdr.), Preservation Soc. Charleston (dir.). Home: Charleston, S.C. Died Jan. 23, 1974.

HOOD, KENNETH OGILVIE, machinery co. exec.; b. Carstairs, Alberta, Can., Aug. 20, 1906; s. Thomas and Agnes (Robertson) H.; came to U.S., 1930, naturalized, 1938; B. Engring., Marquette U., 1934; m. Ruby Bryngison, Mar. 23, 1935; children—Theodore Thomas, Janet (Mrs. Juris Chris Pujats). With Falk Corp., Milw., from 1931, regional sales mgr., 1952-60, sales mgr., western div., 1961-63, sales mgr., from 1964, v.p., from 1968. Mem. Soc. Profl. Engrs. and Scientists of Milw., Am. Inst. Mining, Metall. and Petroleum Engrs. Home: Elm Grove, Wis. Deceased.

HOOPER, BERT LESLIE, dentist; b. Des Moines, Nov. 30, 1892; s. Josephus Henry and Ellen Elizabeth (Mathre) H.; D.D.S., U. of Neb., 1915; m. Elsie Barbara Hornung, Aug. 11, 1915; 1 dau., Jean Winifred Hooper Steinacher. Instr., Lincoln (Neb.) Dental Coll., 1915-16, Kansas City Dental Coll., 1916-17; practice of dentistry, Lincoln, from 1917, specializing in prosthodontics, from 1919; prof. prosthodontics U. Neb., 1923-39, prof. dental science, 1939-54, dean College of Dentistry, 1939-58, dean emeritus, from 1958, professor of dental science and prosthodontics, 1958-61. Consultant prosthodontics V.A. President Advisory Bd. for Dental Specialties, 1939. Mem. dental advisory com. U.S. War Manpower Commn. World War II. Fellow Internat. Licensure (chmn. 1953). Am. Dental Assn. (Chmn. full denture sect. 2 yrs.; mem. council on dental edn., 1947-56, chmn. 1953, 56), Pierre Fauchard Acad., Neb., Ore. dental assns., Cornhusker Dental Study Club (organizer and pres. 1925), American Assn. Dental Research, The Dental Forum (honorary), Academy of Denture Prosthetics (president 1937), American Full Denture Society (president 1938). American Inter-professional Inst., Lincoln Chamber of Commerce, Xi Psi Phi, Omicron Kappa Upsilon, Sigma Xi. Conglist. Mason (Shriner). Contbr. dental jours. U.S. fgn. countries. Lecturer to state dental socs., etc. Home: Lincoln, Neb. Died Jan. 1, 1975.

HOOPLE, GORDON DOUGLASS, educator, physician; b. Bklyn., Feb. 19, 1895; s. William Howard and Victoria Irene (Cranford) H.; B.S. Syracuse U., 1915, M.D., 1919, LL.D. (honoris causa), 1967; postgrad. in otolaryngology Mass. Eye and Ear Infirmary, Boston, 1925-26; m. Dorothea Brokaw, 1922. Intern, Bklyn Hosp., 1919-21, U. Hosp. Syracuse, N.Y. 1924; missionary hosp. work West China, 1922-23; prof. otolaryngology Syracuse U. Coll. Medicine, 1946-53, emeritus, 1953-73, also dir. Hearing and Speech Center Former otolaryngology cons. N.Y. State VA; chmn. Onondaga County Hosp. Conf. Com., 1968, Onondaga Pastoral Counseling Center, 1968-73. Trustee Syracuse U. chmn. emeritus; mem. bd. corporators Clarke Sch. for Deaf, Northampton, Mass., 1952-57; mem. specialist med. adv. group VA, 1958-60; med. adviser Deafness Research Found., 1960-73. Served as maj., AUS, 1942-45; Diplomate Am. Bd. Otolaryngology (pres. 1958-60). Mem. Am. Laryngogical Rhinol. and Otol. Soc. (pres. 1958-59), Am. Acoustical Soc., Am. Phys. Soc., Central N.Y. Eye, Ear, Nose and Throat Soc., A.M.A. Onondaga County Med. Soc., Syracuse Acad. Medicine. Am. Otol. Soc., Inc. (pres. 1952), Am. Laryngol. Assn., Am. Acad. Ophthalmology and Otolaryngology, Syracuse U. Alumni Assn. (p.p.), Phi Beta Kappa, Sigma Phi Epsilon, Nu Sigma Nu, Sigma Xi, Alpha Omega Alpha. Republican. Methodist. Home: Syracuse, N.Y. Died June 4, 1973; buried Morningside Cemetery, Syracuse, N.Y.

HOOVER, CALVIN BRYCE, educator, economist, B. Berwick, Ill., Apr. 14, 1897; s. John Calvin and Margaret Delilah (Roadcap) H.; A.B., (Ill.) (ILL.) Coll., 1922, L.H.D., 1935; postgrad. U. Minn., 1923-25; Ph. D., U. Wis., 1922-23, 25 Litt.D., Columbia, 1934; 1935; LL.D., Case Western Res. U., 1968, Duke, 1970; m. Faith Miriam Sprole, July 5, 1919; children—Carol Faith, Sylvia Joan. Instr., Sch. Bus. U. Minn., 1923-25; asst. prof. econs. Duke U., Durham, N.C., 1925-27, prof., 1927-74, dean Grad. Sch., 1937-47, James B. Duke prof. econs. Cons. Nat. Resources Comm., 1937; cons. adv. comm. to Council of Nat. Def., 1940; dir. Research, Com. of the South, 1947; mem. Research and Analysis Div., O.S.S., 1941-44; chief economic intelligence and economic adviser U.S. group Control Council for Germany, 1945; mem. President's Com. on Fgn. Aid, 1947: spl. adviser to U.S. rep. in Europe, E.C.A., 1948. Served as pvt. inf., U.S. Army, later in F.A., 1917-19; in battles of St. Mihiel and Meuse-Argonne. Recipient Medal of Freedom. Mem. Am. (pres. 1953), So. (pres. 1936) econ. assns., Assn. for Comparative Econs. (pres. 1964), Phi Beta Kappa. Clubs: Cosmos, Century Association. Author: Memoirs of Capitalism, Communism and Nazism (autobiography), 1965; also books on econs. Home: Durham, N.C. Died June 23, 1974.

HOPE, ELIZA MILFORD TATUM, (Mrs. Robert Hervey Hope), sch. adminstr.; b. Walhalla, S.C., Mar. 20, 1908; d. Thomas Hubert and Bess McClair (Mann) Tatum; A.B., Goucher Coll., 1928; m. Robert Hervey Hope, June 10, 1933; children—Sara McClair (Mrs. James Emmanuel Bostic), Mary Tatum (Mrs. Robert A. Smoak, Jr.). Prin. pvt. sch., Ft. Bragg, N.C., 1928-29; tchr., dir. kindergarten Erlanger Sch., Lexington, N.C., 1930-33; owner, dir. Pvt. Pre-Sch., Honea Path, S.C., 1955-69; dir. Reading Clinic for Remedial Reading, 1960-63. Bd. dirs. Jennie Ervin Library, 1969-75. Mem. Am. Assn. U. Women, D.A.R. (regent 1966-69), U.D.C. Episcopalian. Home: Honea Path, S.C., Died Aug. 21, 1975.

HOPE, ROBERT HERVEY, textile co. exec.; b. Rock Hill, S.C., Aug. 31, 1906; s. Robert Hall and Sara (Parker) H.; B.S. in Textile Engring., Clemson Coll., 1926; m. Eliza Milford Tatum, June 10, 1933; children—Sara McClair (Mrs. James Emmanuel Bostic), Mary Tatum (Mrs. Robert Adam Smoak, Jr.). Designer, Erlanger Mills, Lexington, N.C., 1926-32; supt. weaving, 1932-38; supt. Erlanger-Nokomis Mills. 1938-40; supt. Jackson Mills, Wellford, S.C., 1940-42, mgr. Iva, S.C., 1946-48; mgr. Chiquola Mfg. Co. div. M. Lowenstein & Sons, Inc., Honea Path, S.C., 1948-59, v.p., supt., 1959-64, v.p., gen. mgr., 1964-70. Chmn., dist. 2 Anderson County Sch. Bd., 1952-60; sec. Belton-Honea Path Water Authority, 1960-64. Bd. dirs. Carolinas United Fund, 1962., Jenny Erwin Library; bd. dirs. Honea Path, Community Chest, 1960-64, pres. 1964. Served from 1st lt. to lt. col., AUS, 1942-46. Recipient Wisdom Award of Honor, 1970. Mem. S.C. Cotton Mfg. Assn., S.C., Anderson chambers commerce, Honea Path Mchts. Assn. (dir. 1963-64), Am. Legion (comdr. Lyndon Moore post 1953-54). Presbyn. (deacon, elder). Mason, Lion (pres. Honea Path 1953-54, dir. 1963), Clubs: Anderson (S.C.) Country; Civitan (pres. 1940) (Lexington, N.C.). Died Nov. 29, 1970. Home: Honea Path S.C. Deceased.

HOPKINS, ANDREW WINKLE, editor; b. Leeds, Columbia County, Wis., July 19, 1880; s. Richard and Harriet (Sawyer) H.; B.A., U. of Wis., 1903; studied Ia. State Coll. Agr. and Mechnaic Arts; m. Bess C. Brewer, Nov. 12, 1912; children—Robert B., Helen. Ednl. dir. Night Sch. for Men, Racine, Wis., 1903-05; live stock editor Wis. Agriculturist, 1905-08; editor Wis. Farmer, 1908-13; editor Coll. of Agr. and Agrl. Exp. Sta., U. of Wis., 1913-1950. Member Live Stock Breeders' Assn. (sec. 1913-20, dir. 1920-25), Delta Pi Dleta, Sigma Delta Chi, Alpha Zeta, Phi Kappa Phi. Conglist. Mason (32°). Club: Kiwanis (pres.). Home: Madison, Wis.†

HOPKINS, CLARENCE VICTOR, mining engr.; b. Butte, Mont., Feb. 20, 1880; s. Robert Pollock, and Olivia Hoffman (Graeter) H.; ed. Mich. Coll. of Mines, Houghton, Mich.; m. Anna Irene Doherty, June 19, 1903. Geologist and topographer on survey of St. Louis and Itasca cos., Minn., 1901, and chief draftsman same; sampler and timberman for B.&M. Mining Co., Butte, Mont., till Nov. 1, 1902; mem. firm of Hopkins & Holley, mining engrs., Lewiston, Mont., 1902-03; then mining engr., etc., various cos.; chief engr. mining and field depts., United Verde Copper Co. Democrat. Episcopalain. Mem. Am. Inst. Mining Engrs. Mason. Address: Jerome, Ariz.†

HOPKINS, FRANKLIN, composer, editor; b. Champaign, Ill., Feb. 27, 1879; s. William Cyprian (D.D.) and Julia (Gibson) H.; A.B., Harvard, 1900; m. Mildred Mathilde Pangburn, July 28, 1904. Founder, 1913. and first editor The Musical Advance, New York. Author of many brochures and articles upon monetary science and ethics. Sec. Sound Currency League America. Clubs: Harvard, Musicians', Manhattan Chess, Composer: Great English Poets Album (30 songs), 1913; Modern Poets Album (20 songs), 1913; Keats Album (8 songs), 1913; Shakespeare Album (6 songs), 1913; also hymns, anthems, etc. Said to be first consistently to provide settings to the great English poets, dating from the Elizabethan era, including Keats, Shakespeare, Burns, Moore, Shelley, Byron, Scott, Wordsworth, Tennyson, Browning, Poe and Whitman.†

HOPKINS, STANLEY MARSHALL, can mfr.; b. Portsmouth, O., Nov. 22, 1896; s. Stanley G. and Nona (Dunn) H.; student Franklin and Marshall Coll., 1916-17; m. 2d, Genevieve Lifson, Nov. 21, 1947; 1 step dau., Patricia (Mrs. Richard Sobel). With Wheeling Steel Corp., 1919-43, West coast sales mgr., 1940-43; v.p. Pacific Can Corp., 1943-55; co. purchased by Nat. Can Corp., Chgo., 1955, pres., 1960-63, vice chmn. bd., 1963-73. Served with USNRF, World War I. Home: San Francisco, Cal. Died Aug. 1973.

HOPKINS, WILLIAM KARL, supt. schools; b. Kanosh, Utah, July 31, 1879; s. Charles Weber and Lydia Ann (Penney) H.; student Brigham Young Acad., 1900-03; A.B., U. of Utah, 1903-06; student Columbia, summer 1915; m. Lodica Seely, Mar. 2, 1909; children—Seely Karl, Georgia, John Weber, Boyd, Betty, Mary. Prin. high sch., Lehi, Utah, 1906-15; supt. schs. Alpine Dist., Utah, 1915-17; rep. Ginn & Co., 1917-19; supt. pub. schs., Ogden, Utah, from 1919; dir. Federal Bldg. and Loan Assn. Mem. City Council, Lehi, Utah, 1912-16. Mem. Ogden Chamber of Commerce. Mem. Amici Fidessimi Fraternity (ex-pres.). Republican. Mem. Ch. of Latter Day Saints. Clubs: Ogden Rotary (pres. 1936-37), Ben Lomond, Weber. Home: Ogden, Utah.†

HOPPER, BRUCE CAMPBELL, educator; b. Litchfield, Ill., Aug. 24, 1892; s. Joseph and Katherine (Turnbull) H.; student U. Mont., 1913-16, B.S., Harvard, 1918, A.M., 1925, Ph.D., 1930; student Sorbonne, 1919, 20, Oxford U., 1919-20; m. Effie Toyé, Aug. 26, 1924. Editorial writer China Press, Shanghai, 1921-22; asst. in history Harvard, 1925-26, asst. prof. govt., 1930-37. asso. prof. govt., 1937-61, asso. prof. emeritus, 1961-73; lectr. Naval War Coll., Army War Coll., Armed Forces Staff Coll.; lectr. Europe, 1954, Inst. Aero. Scis., 1956; mem. group Am. profs. vis. univs. and govtl. insts. Fed. Republic of Germany, summer 1958; observer for Inst. Current World Affairs in USSR, 1926-29. Trustee World Peace Found.; mem. Air Force Acad. Site Selection Bd., Air Force Hist. Found., Ednl. Exchange Program, Dept. State. Served with Am. Field Service, French Army, 1917, Am. A.S., 96th Sq., 1917-19, hist. sect. G.H.Q. Chaumont, 1919, Sorbonne Detachment, 1919; attached Am. legation, Stockholm, 1942-43; chief hist. sect. 8th Air Force and USSTAF, 1943-45; cons. to Comdg. Gen., Air Force, 1945-47. Decorated Silver Star, Air Force Exceptional Civilian Service award, Croix de Guerre, Aero. medal (France); officier Ouissan (Alacuite (Moroccan); chevalier Legion d'Honneur (France). Mem. Fgn. Service Assn. Episcopalian. Club: Army and Navy (Washington). Author: Pan-Sovietism, 1931; Siberia's Population Capacity, 1937; The Second World War: Why?, 1940; also series of articles in Fgn. Affairs. Editor: Let's Talk About (monthly discussion brochures), 1952-53. Home: Cambridge, Mass. Died July 6, 1973.

HOPPER, VINCENT FOSTER, educator; b. West New York, N.J., Apr. 19, 1906; s. Abram Whittaker and Isabel Jayne (Timmons) H.; student Blair Acad., 1922-23; A.B., Princeton, 1927, A.M., 1928; Ph.D., Columbia, 1938; m. Grace Brewster Murray, June 12, 1930; m. 2d, Mabel Sterling Lewis, May 6, 1945; 1 son, David Whittaker. Instr., N.Y. U. Sch. Commerce, Accounts, and Finance, 1928-32, asst. prof., 1932-41, asso. prof., 1941-48, prof. gen. lit., 1948-63; asst. to head all-univ. English dept., prof. English, Washington Sq. Coll., N.Y. U., 1963-73, prof. emeritus, 1973-76. Mem. Phi Beta Kappa. Author: Medieval Number Symbolism, 1938; Chaucer's Canterbury Tales (selected), An Interlinear Translation, 1948, 2d edit., 1970; Backgrounds of European Literature (with Rod W. Horton), 1948, 2d edit., 1975; (with Bernard D.N. Grebanier) Essentials of European Literature, 1952, Bibliography of European Literature, 1954; (with Cedric Gale) Essentials of Effective Writing, 1961, Practice for Effective Writing, 1961; Essentials of English, 1961, rev. edit., 1973. Contbg. editor Ency. of Religion, 1945. Co-editor: The School for Scandal; The Rivals; The Way of the World; She Stoops to Conquer, 1958; Volpone; The Importance of Being Earnest, 1959; Lady Windermere's Fan; The Duchess of Malfi, 1960; Medieval Mysteries, Moralities, and Interludes, 1962; The Beaux; Strategem, 1963. Editor: Classic American Short Stories, 1964; 1001 Pitfalls in English Grammar, 1969, 2d edit., 1970. Home: Tenafly, N.J., Died Jan. 19, 1976.

HORGAN, DANIEL STEPHEN, pub. works adminstr.; b. Worcester, Mass., July 25, 1909; s. Daniel P. and Ellen (Somers) H.; student Worcester Poly. Inst., 1926-29; m. Mary R. Burns, Sept. 3, 1929; children—Anne M. (Mrs. James L. Blanton), Joan E. (Mrs. John J. Rosseel), Daniel Stephen. Jr. engring. aide Mass. Dept. Pub. Works, Boston, 1929-37, jr. engr., 1937-51, sr. engr., 1951-63, waterways engr., 1963-64, chief engr., 1964-73; commr. Auburn (Mass.) Water Dist.,

1950-73. Bd. dirs. Auburn Dist. Nurses Assn. Recipient Silver Beaver award Boy Scouts Am., 1951; Auburn Booster award Auburn C. of C., 1972. Mem. Mass. Soc. Profl. Engrs. (dir.), Mass. State Engrs. Assn., N.E. Waterworks Assn., Am. Pub. Works Assn., Am. Rd. Builders Assn., Mass. Hwy. Assn., Mass. Safety Council (dir.), Am. Assn. State Hwy. Ofcls. (mem. engring. policy com.). K.C., Rotarian. Home: Auburn, Mass. Died Aug. 10, 1973.

HORKAN, GEORGE ANTHONY, army officer; b. Augusta, Ga., July 1, 1894; s. Patrick Daniel and Catherine (Maloney) H.; A.B., Georgetown U., 1915; M.B.A., Babson Inst., 1925; grad. Army Motor Transport, 1921, Army Indsl. Coll., 1932. Q.M. Sch., 1938; m. Mary Thompson, Apr. 16, 1918; children—George A., Jr., Katherine Sanford. Commd. 2d lt., U.S. Army, 1917, and advanced to maj. gen. Nov. 1944; commandant Q.M. Sch., comdg. gen., Camp Lee, Va.; dir., Memorial Div., Office of q.m. gen., Washington, chief q.m. European Command, 1948, quartermaster gen. AUS, 1951-52, ret. Chmn. Com. on Blind-Made Products; mem. bd. commrs. U.S. Soldiers' Home. Decoration D.S.M. Clubs: Army and Navy, Army and Navy Country (Washington). Home: Washington, D.C. Died Nov. 2, 1974.

HORKHEIMER, ARTHUR PHILIP, publisher; b. Wauzeka, Wis., Mar. 22, 1904; s. William J. and Katherine (Doyle) H.; Ph.B., Ripon Coll., 1932; postgrad. U. Wis., 1932; m. Mary Edmunda Foley, Aug. 17, 1927; children—Mary K. (Mrs. Thomas R. Saterstrom), Patricia A. (Mrs. Raymond H. Suttles), Foley A. Tchr. rural schs., Crawford County, Wis., 1922-24; tchr., coach Highland (Wis.) High Sch., 1925-27; prin. La Valle (Wis.) Pub. Sch., 1928-35; salesman Nat. Progress Co., Lamar, Mo., 1926-34; pub., owner Educators Progress Service, Randolph, Wis., 1934—; v.p. Bohlings Dept. Store, 1956-63; dir. Continental Manors Randolph, Inc. Village pres., Randolph, Wis., 1942-65; mem. bd. suprs., Dodge County Wis., 1950-55; mem. exec. com. League Wis. Municipalities, 1953-57; chmn. finance and taxation com., 1958, v.p., 1955-58, pres. 1959-61. Dir. Dodge County Hist. Soc., 1954-75; trustee Harter and Carlin Fund, 1957—. Mem. N.E.A., Wis. Edn., Assn., A.L.A., Nat. Sci. Tchrs. Assn. (dir. 1963—), Am. Personnel and Guidance Assn., Nat. Council for Social Studies, A.A.H.P.E.R., Nat. Audiovisual Assn., C. of C. (pres. 1939), Nat. Assn. for Industry-Education Cooperation (exec. com. 1963—, dir 1968—), Phi Delta Kappa. Elks. Clubs: Randolph Men's, (pres. 1938), Fox Lake Golf (pres. 1958), Kiwanian. Contbr. articles to profl. jours. Home: Randolph, Wis. Died Aug. 23, 1974; buried St. Gabriel's Cemetery, Randolph, Wis.

HORMELL, ORREN CHALMER, coll. prof.; b. Wingate, Ind., Dec. 4, 1879; s. Garner and Mary Elizabeth (Thomas) H.; A.B., Ind. U.,1904, A.M., 1905; A.M., Harvard, 1909. Ph.D., 1921; D.C.L., Bowdoin Coll., 1952; m. Elizabeth Spaulding, Dec. 25, 1905; children—Mary Elizabeth (Mrs. Ross McDuffie Cunningham), Robert Spaulding. Instr. in history and polit. sci., Clark Coll., Worcester, Mass., 1910-11; asst. prof. history Bowdoin Coll., 1911-13, prof. history and govt., 1913-27; De Alva Stanwood Alexander prof. govt., 1927-52, emeritus; dir. Bur. of Research in Municipal Govt., Bowdoin, emeritus from 1952; lectr. on municipal govt., Harvard, 1919-20; prof. polit. science, summer sessions, U. Ill., 1924. Sch. of Citizenship of Syracuse U., 1925, 29, 33, 39, U. Mich., 1926, 28. Mem. Army Ednl. Corps, U.S. Army, with A.E.F., faculty U. of Beaune, 1919; cons. Nat. Resoruces Planning Bd., 1941-43; cons. for drafting municipal charters. Chmn. adv. council, Me. Unemployemnt Compensation Commn., from 1939. Mem. council Nat. Civil Service League. Mem. Am. Polit. Science Assn., Nat. Municipal League Civil Service Assembly of U.S. and Canada, Am. Soc. Pub. Adminstrn., Sigma Nu. Ind. Republican. Conglist. Author: A guide to the Study of Civics, 1915; (brochures) Municipal Accounting and Reporting, 1915; Budget Making for Maine Towns, 1916; Sources of Municipal Revenue in Maine, 1918; The Direct Primary, 1922; Essentials of Government, 1925; Cost of Primaries and Elections in Maine, 1926; Maine Public Utilities, 1927; Corrupt Practices Legislation in Maine, 1929; Maine Towns, 1932; Personnel Problems in Maine, 1937; Retirement Plan for Employees of Maine Towns, 1949; The Manager Plan for Maine Municipalities (with L. L. Pelletier), 1949 (above 13 under title of Bowdoin College Municipal Research Series); Electricity in Great Britain—A Study in Adminstration, 1928; Control of Public Utilities Aborad, 1930; Town of West Hartford, Conn., Survey, 1934; Zoning Manual for Maine Towns (with Roy Owsley), 1940; City Manager Government in Portland, Maine (with E. F. Dow), 1941, Contbr. to Cyclo, of American Government, Ency. Social Sciences, Am. Year Book; also to Am. Polit. Sci. Rev., American City, Nat. Municipal Rev. and Annals of Am. Acad. Polit. and Social Sci. Home: Brunswick, Me., Died Dec. 3, 1975.

HORN, EDWARD CHARLES, educator, biologist; b. Hartford, Conn., Oct. 23, 1916; s. Gustav Ferdinand and Josephine (Kugler) H.; B.S., Trinity Coll., Hartford, 1938, Sc.D., 1965; A.M., Princeton, 1940, Ph.D., 1941; m. Edith Meline Williams, Jan. 23, 1941; children—Edward Gustav, William Charles, Kathy Meline. Instr. biology Russell Sage Coll., 1941-42, U. Ariz., 1942-46; mem. faculty Duke, 1946-69, prof. zoology, 1959-69, chmn. dept., 1960-69; cons. biology div., Oak Ridge Nat. Lab., 1955-69; research investigator, 1956-57. Mem. ad hoc tng. grant cons. NIH, 1962, pre-postdoctoral and spl. fellowship program, 1964-67; mem. undergrad. Equipment awards com. NSF, 1963-64; vis. commn. life scis. Trinity Coll., 1963-69; cons. Commn. Undergrad. Edn. in Biol. Scis., 1965-69. Served with USAAF, 1943-46. Grantee NIH, 1954-57, 57-59, 60-63, 60-64, NSF, 1964-67; spl. fellow USPHS, Distinguished vis. prof. U. New S. Wales, Syndey, Australia, 1967. Fellow A.A.A.S.; mem. Am. Soc. Cell Biology, Am. Soc. Zoologists, Acad. Scis., Soc. Developmental Biology, Sigma Xi. Contbr. profl. jours. Home: Durham, N.C. Died Nov. 18, 1969.

HORN, JOHN LOUIS, prof. education; b. N.Y. City, Aug. 2, 1881; s. Alexander J. and Rosa (Krauthammer) H.; A.B., U. of Pa., 1906; LL.B., Columbia, 1910; Ed.D., U. of Calif., 1923; m. Irmengard Montrose Charlton, Feb. 8, 1916. Prof. edn., Mills Coll., Oakland, Calif., 1920-37, Dominican Coll., San Rafael, Calif., from 1937. Author: The Education of Exceptional Children, 1924; The American Public School, 1926; Principles of Elementary Education, 1929; The Education of Children in the Primary Grades, 1935; The Education of Your Child, 1939. Retired 1949. Home: Palo Alto, Cal.†

HORN, ROY DE SAUSSURE, naval officer, retired, editor, publisher; b. Boston, Ga., Feb. 2, 1894; s. Daniel McLeod and Elizabeth (Raiford) H.; student Emory U., U. Ga.; B.S., U.S. Naval Acad., 1915; m. Margaret Kerfoot, May 27, 1925 (div. 1932); 1 dau., Patricia Anne (Mrs. Harker Collins); m. 2d Anne Catherine Eichelberger, Mar. 7, 1942, Commd. ensign, U.S. Navy, 1915, advanced through grades to comdr. (ret.), 1944; served in Haitian Revolution, 1915; aboard frigate Constellation, armoured cruisers Tennessee and Montana, Battleships Arkansas, New Mexico, Mississippi, Presdl. yacht Mayflower, during World War I; aide on staff Div. Comdr. Battleship Div. 6, 1918, ret., 1919; fiction writer, editor, pub., 1925-39; recalled to active duty U.S. Navy, Nov. 1939, instr. English, history, govt. U.S. Naval Acad., 1939-45; with Office Sec. of Navy, 1946; returned to inactive duty, 1946; asst. editor, mng. editor U.S. Naval Inst. since 1946. Mem. U.S. Naval Acad. Alumni Assn. Club: Annapolis (Md.) Yacht. Home: Annapolis Md. Died Dec. 28, 1973.

HORNADAY, CLIFFORD LEE, college pres.; b. Pittsboro, N.C., Apr. 5, 1879; s. Rev. John Albert and Ellen (McCall) H.; prep. edn., Graham's Sch., Ridgeway, N.C.; A.B., Trinity Coll. (now Duke U.), Durham, N.C., 1902, A.M., 1904; studied Columbia, summers 1912, 13, 20; m. Bessie Jones, Dec. 29, 1904. Teacher, Trinity Park Sch., Durham, N.C., 1902-16; teacher modern lang. dept., Trinity Coll., 1916-22; pres. Davenport Coll., Lenoir, N.C., 1922-26; pres. Henderson-Brown Coll., from 1926. Mem. Phi Beta Kappa. Democrat. Methodist. Kiwanian (del. Nat. Conv., 1925), Rotarian. Home: Arkadelphia, Ark.†

HORNBERGER, THEODORE, educator; b. Northville, Mich., Jan. 13, 1906; s. John Jacob and Katherine (Watson) H.; B.S., U. Mich., 1927, M.A., 1929, Ph.D., 1934; student King's Coll., London, Eng., 1927-28; m. Marian Louise Welles, Feb. 7, 1929; children—Jean Alice (Mrs. Roland Cleveland), Katharine Watson (Mrs. Allan Denenberg). Instr. English, U. Mich., 1928-36, asst. prof., 1936-37; research fellow Huntington Library, 1936-37; prof. English U. Tex., 1937-46; vis. summer lectr. Harvard, 1938, Northwestern U., 1940, Duke, 1941, 42, 50, Ohio State U., 1945, U. Colo., 1966; prof. English U. Minn., 1946-60, chmn. dept., 1950-58; prof. English, U. Pa., 1960-75, John Welsh Centennial prof. history and English lit., 1968-75, acting chmn. dept., 1968-69, chmn. grad. group English, 1965-67; vis. prof. N. Am. lit. U. Brazil, 1952. Guggenheim fellow, 1967-68; Thord-Gray Lecturing fellow Am-Scandinavian Found., Uppsala U., 1973. Mem. Modern Lang. Assn. Am. (chmn. Am. lit. group 1956, chmn. Am. Lit. I 1970), History Sci. Soc. (council 1947-50), Nat. Council Tchrs. English (chmn. coll. sect. 1951-52), Coll. English Assn., Am. Dialect Soc., Colonial Soc. Mass., Phi Beta Kappa, Phi Gamma Delta. Author: Scientific Thought in the American Colleges, 1638-1800, 1945; Os Estados Unidos através de sua literatura, 1953; Benjamin Franklin, 1961. Editor; Compendium Physiae (Charles Morton), 1940; Mark Twain's Letters to Will Bowen, 1941; Literature of the United States (with Walter Blair, Randall Stewart, James E. Miller), 3d edit., 1966; William Cullen Bryant and Isaac Henderson, 1950; others. Home: Philadelphia, Pa. Died Mar. 14, 1975; buried Ann Arbor, Mich.

HORNE, FRANK S(MITH), govt. ofcl.; b. N.Y. City, Aug. 18, 1899; s. Edwin Fletcher and Cora (Calhoun) H.; B.S., Coll. City of New York, 1921; A.M., U. of Southern Calif., 1932; Opt.D., Northern Ill. Coll. of Ophthalmology, 1922; m. Frankye Priestly, Aug. 19, 1930 (died 1940); m. 2d, Mercedes Christopher, Aug. 15, 1950. Pvt. practice of optometry, Chicago and New York, 1922-26; dean and acting pres., Fort Valley (Ga.) State Coll., 1926-36; asst. dir., div. of Negro Affairs, Nat. Youth Adminstrn., Washington, 1936-38; asst. to the administrator (dir. of Racial Relations Service), Housing and Home Finance Agency (similar title and function in U.S. Housing Authority, Fed. Pub. Housing Adminstrn., Nat. Housing Agency, and Office of Housing Expediter), 1938-55; exec. dir. N.Y.C. Commn. on Intergroup Relations, 1956-62; cons. on human relations Housing and Redevel. Bd., N.Y.C., 1962-74; bd. Phelps-Stokes Fund. Mem. Am. Civil Liberties Union (bd.), Hudson Guild (bd.), Nat. Assn. Housing Ofcls., Nat. Assn. Intergroup Relations Ofcls., Nat. Housing Conf., Omega Psi Phi. Writer poetry pub. anthologies and publs. Home: New York City, N.Y. Died Sept. 7, 1974.

HORNE, HENRY ABBOTT, accountant; b. Bklyn., Mar. 28, 1878; s. Henry Bower and Theresa Eleanor (Abbott) H.; student pub. schs. of Bklyn.; student Y.M.C.A. Eve. Inst., 1896-1900, N.Y. Sch. Accounts, 1906-09; C.P.A., 1911; m. Anna Irwin, June 3, 1902 (dec.). Asst. insp. Gold & Stock Telegraph Co., 1891; insp. Gold & Stock Telegraph Co. and Stock Quotation Telegraph Co., 1892-97; asst. bookkeeper Walsh & Floyd, brokers, mems. N.Y. Stock Exchange, 1897-1900; asst. insp. N.Y. Edison Co., 1900-01; acct. Bigelow Carpet Co., 1901-10; jr., later sr. acct. Niles & Niles, C.P.A.'s, N.Y.C., 1910-15, partner, 1916-32; partner Webster, Horne & Elsdon, pub. accountants, N.Y.C., from 1933. Mem. bd. mgrs., asst. treas. Meth. Hosp., Bklyn.; adv. bd. mgrs. Bklyn. Meth. Episcopal Ch. Home; mem. Legal Aid Soc. N.Y.; trustee Meml. Library, Decatur, Mich., Served as capt. A.S., U.S. Army, 1918-19. Mem. Am. Inst. C.P.A.'s Conn., N.Y. State (pres. 1944-45); socs. C.P.A.'s Nat. Assn. Accountants. Econ. Research Round Table, Am. Legion, Res. Ofcrs. Assn., Am. Arbitration Assn., Commerce and Industry Assn. N.Y. Rep. Meth. Clubs: Bankers, Accountants (N.Y.C.); Engineers Dayton, O.). Contbr. profl. jours. Testified in McKesson & Robbins case (for accounting profession) before U.S. Securities and Exhcange Commn. Home: Brooklyn, N.Y.†

HORNE, JOSH L., editor and publisher; b. nr. Whitakers, Nash County, N.C., Dec. 21, 1887; s. Joshua Lawrence and Lula C. (Parker) H.; student Trinity Park Sch., Durham, N.C., 1903-05, Trinity Coll. (now Duke U.), 1905-09; m. Mary A. Thorp, July 17, 1912 (div. 1945); 1 dau., Mary Louise (Mrs. Melvin Jobe Warner): m. 2d, Mildred A. Nicholson, May 3, 1958. Newspaper carrier, corr. and reporter, 1898-1910; city editor Daily Record, Rocky Mount, 1910-11; founder Morning Telegram, 1911, became Evening Telegram, Jan. 1, 1912; pub. Evening Telegram, from 1911, Sunday Telegram, from 1950; pres. Rocky Mount Pub. Co., from 1911, radio stas. WCEC and WFMA; dir. Planters Nat. Bank & Trust Com., Carolina Motor Club; pres. Rocky Mount Sanitarium. Mem. Bd. of Aldermen, 1919-20; mem. Airport Commn., 1934-74; v.p., dir. Y.M.C.A., 1921-74; pres. C. of C., 1924-25 (all of Rocky Mount). Dir. Asso. Press, 1937-50. Mem. State Rural Electrification Authority, 1933-37; chmn. State Bd. Conservation and Devel.; mem. State Advt. Campaign, 1937-50; dir. State N.C. Dept. Archives and History. Pres. N.C. Press Assn., 1930-31; trustee Duke U., High Point Coll. Mem. Am. Soc. Newspaper Editors, Inter Am. Press Assn. Methodist. Clubs: Kiwanis (pres. 1922-23); Nat. Press (Washington); University, Charter Citrus (Orlando, Fla.). Home: Rocky Mount, N.C. Died Mar. 15, 1974; interred Rocky Mount, N.C.

HORNER, HARLAN HOYT educator; b. Moravia, Ia., May 4, 1878; s. Eugene Brandon and Susan Cordelia (Sears) H.; grad. high sch., Cerro Gordo, Ill., 1897; A.B., U. of Ill., 1901; A.M., N.Y. State Coll. for Teachers, 1915, hon. Ph.D., 1918; studied Harvard, summer, 1916, U. of Chicago, summer 1926; LL.D., Alfred U., 1933; m. Gioga Dagmar Gaston, Sept. 15, 1904 (died Jan. 11, 1926); m. 2d, Henrietta Anne Calhoun, M.D., Mar. 19, 1928. Instr. rhetoric, U. of Ill., 1901-02, sec. to pres., 1902-04; sec. to commr. of edn., State of N.Y., 1904-07, chief of adminstrn. div., Dept. of Edn., N.Y., 1907-10; chief of examinations div., U. of State of N.Y., 1910-15, dir. examinations and inspections div., 1915-17; dean, also dir. summer sessions, N.Y. State Coll. for Teachers, 1917-23; exec. sec. N.Y. State Teachers' Assn., also editor New York State Education, 1923-30; dir. state college edn., 1930-31; asst. commr. for higher and professional edn., State Edn. Dept., 1931-37, asso. commr. of edn., 1937-39; sec. Council on Dental Edn. of Am. Dental Assn., 1940-48. Honorary fellow American College of Dentists, 1942. Mem. N.Y. State Commn. for Crippled Children by appointment of Gov. Alfred Smith. First vice chairman Am. Council on Edn., 1941-42. Member N.E.A. (department of superintendence), Phi Beta Kappa, Sigma Alpha Epsilon, Phi Sigma Sigma, Kappa Phi Kappa, Kappa Delta Rho (hon.). Republican. Presbyterian. Mason. Rotarian; past governor 29th District Rotary International. Author: The American Flag, 1909; The Life and Work of Andrew Sloan Draper, 1934; The Growth of Lincoln's Faith, 1939; Dental Education Today, 1946; also author of a large number of magazine articles. Editor: What makes Lincoln Great (a collection of addresses of Andrew Sloan Draper on Lincoln), 1940; Dentistry as a Professional Career, 1941; also editor of pamphlets on Hudson-Fulton Celebration, Lake

Champlain Tercentenary. Lincoln Centenary and Arbor Day annals of U. of State of N.Y. Lecturer on ednl., patriotic and fraternal themes. Home: Albany, N.Y.†

HOROWITZ, SAUL, JR., constrn. co. exec.; b. N.Y.C., May 5, 1925; s. Saul and Miriam (Ravitch) H.; grad. Phillips Andover Acad., 1942; student Yale, 1942-43; B.S., U.S. Mil. Acad., 1946; postgrad. Mass. Inst. Tech., 1950; m. Mary Elizabeth Blakeney, Mar. 11, 1950; children—Mary Elizabeth, Saul Mark, Charles James, Sarah Louise. Commd. 2d lt., C.E., U.S. Army, 1946, advanced through grades to capt., 1954; assigned 11th Airborne Div., Japan, 1947-49, 76th Engr. Constrn. Battalion Korea, 1953-54; resigned, 1954; with HRH Constrn. Corp. N.Y.C. 1954-75, exec. v.p., 1958-65, pres., 1965-72, chmn. bd., 1972-75; chmn. bd. Universal Constrn. Corp., P.R., dir. Consolidated Cigar Corp., 1959-68, Scarsdale Nat. Bank (N.Y.), 1971-75; trustee Am. Savs. Bank, N.Y.C. Chmn. campaign Fedn. Jewish Philanthropies, N.Y. C., 1963. Mem. Bd. Edn., Scarsdale, 1964-65; trustee, Scarsdale, 1965-69, mayor, 1969-71; mem. Republican Nat. Finance Com., 1969-72. Vice chmn. Mt. Sinai Hosp., N.Y.C. Named Constrn. Man of Year Engring. News Record, 1975. Decorated Bronze Star medal. Mem. Bldg. Contractors and Mason Builders Assn. N.Y. (pres. 1959-60), Met. Builders Assn. N.Y. (pres. 1963-64), Asso. Gen. Contractors Am. (nat. bd. dirs., chmn. bldg. div., nat. pres. 1974). Clubs. Yale, Harmonie (N.Y.C.); Army and Navy (Washington); Beach Point (Mamaroneck, N.Y.); Scarsdale Golf (N.Y.). Home: Scarsdale, N.Y. Died June 1975.

HORTON, ARTHUR, chmn. Chicago Bridge & Iron Co. Home: Oakbrook, Ill. Died Feb. 2, 1973.

HORTON, (CHARLES) MARCUS, author; b. N.Y.C., Aug. 22, 1879; s. Heman and Ada Dora (Springsteen) H.; ed. pub. schs., N.Y.C., and under pvt. tutors; U. of N. Mex., 1904-05; m. Anna Belle Fowler, Jan. 28, 1914; 1 dau., Bonnie Jean. Took 3 yrs.' course in mech. drafting, Crescent Shipyard and Iron Works, Elizabethport, N.J.; designer for Westinghouse Machine Co., East Pittsburgh, Pa., 1901-04. Author: Bred of the Desert, 1915; Under New Management (series of articles), 1917; Opportunities in Engineering, 1919; Tommy McTighe (serial), 1921; Mechanics of the Short Story, 1929. Contbr. stories to mags. Prize winner in play contest, Albany, N.Y., with three-act play, Cynthia, Apr. 7, 1935. Home: Averill Park, N.Y.†

HOSAFROS, WAYNE ORVILLE, supt. schs.; b. Arlington, Ohio, June 2, 1926; s. Harvey Franklin and Eva (Rettig) H.; student Findlay Coll., 1946-48; B.S., Fla. State U., 1950; M.Ed., Bowling Green State U., 1957; m. Mary Lou Taylor, Mar. 8, 1948; children—Hugh, Mary Ann, Michael. Tchr., Montgomery Schs., Wayne, O., 1951-53, prin., 1953-55, supt., 1955-59; supt. Lake Local Schs., Millbury, O., 1959-65; supt. Rossford (O.) City Schs., 1965-72. Served with USNR, 1943-46. Mem. Ohio Exempted Village Sch. Supts. (pres. 1967-68). Club: Exchange. Home: Rossford, O. Died Feb. 21, 1972.

HOSKINS, ROY GRAHAM, dir. research; b. Nevinville, Ia., Ju. July 3, 1880; s. William Henry and Sarah (Graham) H.; grad. Hiawatha (Kan.) High Sch., 1899; A.B., A.M., U. of Kan., 1905; Ph.D. Harvard, 1910; M.D., Johns Hopkins, 1920; m. Agnace Seamans, Sept. 7, 1926 (died Aug. 24, 1927; 1 son, Robert Graham; m. 2d, Gertrude Austin Pavey; 1 step dau., Barbara Pavey. Began as investigator, 1904; teaching fellow zoölogy, U. of Kan., 1906; Austin teaching fellow physiology, Harvard Med. Sch., 1908-10; prof. physiology Starling-Ohio Med. Sch., Columbus, 1910-13; asso. prof. physiology, Northwestern U., Medical School, 1913-16, prof. and head of dept., 1916-18; asso. in physiology, Johns Hopkins Med. Sch., 1920-21; prof. physiology and head of dept., Ohio State U., 1920-27; research asso. physiology Harvard Med. Sch., 1927-47; dir. research Memorial Foundation for Neuro-Endocrine Research, Boston, 1927-47; research prof. Tufts Coll., from 1950; cons. in research Boston State Hosp., from 1944; spl. lectr. on social psychiatry, Simmons College; sec. Worcester Foundation for Experimental Biology, 1944-45; cons. med. sciences. O.N.R. (Boston br.), from 1948. Captain, later maj. Sanitary Corps, U.S. Army (sec. food and nutrition), 1918-19; chief of sect., 1919. Mem. A.M.A., Assn. for Study of Internal Secretions (pres. 1926), A.A.A.S., American Academy Arts and Sciences, Assn. for Research Nervous and Mental Diseases, Society for Research Psychosom. Problems (pres. 1944), Gerontological Society (president 1946), Phi Beta Kappa, Sigma Xi. Author: The Tides of Life, 1933; Endocrinology: The Glands and Their Functions, 1941. Editor: Endocrinology and Metabolism, 2 vols. (with L. F. Barker and H. O. Mosenthal), 1922. Editor-in-chief Journal of Ednocrinology, 1917-40; mng. editor Jour. Clinical Endocrinology, 1942-45. Contbr. scientific articles; research in endocrinology and insanity. Home: Waban, Mass.†

HOTCHENER, HENRY, b. Watkins, N.Y., Oct. 13, 1881; s. Saul and Hedwig (Zeigler) H.; prep. edn. Harlem Evening High Sch., N.Y. City; student Coll. City of New York, 1895-97; m. Marie (Barnard) Russak, July 9, 1916. Secretary to Daniel Guggenheim, president American Smelting & Refining Co., 1901-04; nat. lecturer throughout U.S. for Theosophical Soc., 1905-08; in real estate and building business, New York, 1909-11; traveled in Europe, Egypt and Asia, 1912 and 1913; mgr. Am. Theosophical Book Concern, 1913-14; now dir. Krotona Inst. of Theosophy; pres. Channel Publishing Soc. Jewish religion. Mason. Address: Hollywood, Cal.†

HOTELLING, HAROLD, mathematician, statistician, economist, educator; b. Fulda, Minn., Sept. 29, 1895; s. Clair Alberta and Lucy Amelia (Rawson) H.; A.B., U. Wash., 1919, M.S., 1921; student U. Chgo., summer 1920; Ph.D., Princeton, 1924, LL.D., 1955; Sc. D. (hon.), U. Rochester, 1963; m. Floy Tracy, Dec. 27, 1920 (dec. Oct. 1932); children—Eric Bell, Muriel (Mrs. Glenn L. Burrows); m. 2d, Susanna Porter Edmondson, June 14, 1934; children—George Alfred, William Edmondson, Edward Rawson, Susanna Porter (dec.), Harold, James Maynard. Employed with newspapers, State of Wash., 1915-16, 1919; teaching asst. math. U. Wash., 1920-21; fellow in math. Princeton, 1921-22, instr., 1922-24; research asso. Food Research Inst., Stanford, 1924-27, asso. prof. mathematics, 1927-31; research Rothamsted Exptl. Sta., Eng., 1929; prof. econs. Columbia, 1931-46; prof. statistics U. N. C., 1946-61, Kenan prof. statistics, 1961-66 Kenan prof. emeritus, 1966-73; vis. prof. Indian Statis. Inst., 1939-40, U. Buenos Aires, 1964; vis. lectr. in many Am., European and Asian univs. Organizer, head statis research group, div. war research Columbia, 1942-45; cons. NRA, 1933, div. tax research U.S. Treasury Dept., 1943, div. statis. standards U.S. Bur. Budget, 1944-49, N.Y. State Pub. Service Commn., 1949-50, NSF, 1952-54, other. Recipient medal Free U. Brussels, 1951; N.C. award, 1972. Fellow Econometric Soc. (pres. 1936-37, mem. council 1941-46, 55-58), Royal Statis. Soc. (hon.), Inst. math. Statis. (pres. 1941, mem. council 1957-60), Royal Econ. Soc., Am. Statis. Assn. (v.p. 1941), Am. Econ. Assn. (distinguished fellow), A.A.A.S. (Sec. Sect. K 1931-32, chmn. sect. K 1942, chmn. sect. U 1963, mem. council 1950-61); mem. Social Sci. Research Council (bd. 1945-48), Am. Math. Soc. (mem. council 1935-37, 44-46), Am. Assn. U. Profs., Internat. Statis. Inst., Nat. Acad. Sci., Phi Beta Kappa, Sigma Xi (pres. Chapel Hill Chpt. 1957-58), Indian Statis. Congress (pres. 1940), Elisha Mitchell Sci. Soc., (pres. 1949-50), Academia dei Lincei. Club: U. N.C Faculty (pres. 1963-64). Former asso. editor Annals of Math. Statistics, Econometrica; asso. editor Am. Jour. Econs. and Sociology. Contbr. to sci. publs. Address: Chapel Hill, N.C. Died Dec. 26, 1973; buried Old Cemetery, Chapel Hill, N.C.

HOUGH, LYNN HAROLD, educator, clergyman; b. Cadiz, O., Sept. 10, 1877; s. Franklin M. and Eunice R. (Giles) H.; A.B., Scio College, 1898; B.D., Drew Theol. Sem., 1905; post-grad. work, New York U.; D.D., Mt. Union-Scio Coll., 1912, D.D., Garrett Bibl. Inst., 1918; Th.D., Drew Theol. Sem., 1919; Litt.D., Allegheny Coll., 1933, College Puget Sound, 1947; LL.D., Albion Coll., 1923, U. of Detroit, 1928; U. of Pittsburgh, 1935; L.H.D., U. of Vt., 1932; D.D., Wesleyan U., Conn., 1924; J.U.D., Boston U., 1939; m. Blanche Horton, widow of the Rev. Stephen van R. Trowbridge, Oct. 13, 1936. Entered ministry of Methodist Episcopal Church, 1898; pastor various chs. N.J., N.Y.C., Bklyn., Balt., 1898-1914; prof. theology, Garrett Bibl. Inst., 1914-19; pres. Northwestern U., 1919-20; pastor Central M.E. Ch., Detroit, Mich., 1920-28, American Presbyn. Ch., Montreal, 1928-30; prof. of homiletics and christian criticism of life, Drew Theol. Seminary, Drew Univ., 1930-47, dean, 1934-47; vis. prof. Emmanuel Coll., Victoria U., Toronto, Can., 1947; chancellor's lecturer Queen's University, 1947. Pres. Detroit Council Chs., 1926-28; v.p. Religious Education Assn., 1926-28; pres. Assn. of Methodist Theological Schools, 1942; mem. exec. com. Fed. Council of Churches of Christ in America, 1936-48; member Society Biblical Literature and Exegesis, Society Midland Authors; president Religious Education Council of Canada, 1929-30. Mason (33°, Knight Templar). Clubs: Century, University, Quill (pres. 1956). Andiron (president 1956) (New York City), The Pilgrims of the United States, National Liberal, Authors' (London). Author many books, from 1906, including spl. lectures, latest include: The Dignity of Man, 1950; Great Humanists, 1952; The Great Argument, 1953; Interpretation of Book of Revelation (Interpreter's Bible, Vol. 12), 1957; The Eternal and Redeeming Word, 1958; The Living Church, 1959. Cato lectr. Gen. Conf. Meth. Ch. of Australasia, 1941. Editor and contbr. to Whither Christianity. 1929. Home: New York City, N.Y.†

HOUGH, ROBERT LEE, JR., educator; b. Los Angeles, May 19, 1924; s. Robert Lee and Kathryn (Hindinger) H.; B.A., Pomona Coll., 1949; M.S., Columbia, 1950; Ph.D., Stanford, 1957; m. June Florence Rowley, June 29, 1952; children—Alison, Carol Timothy, John. Inst. journalism News Bur., Whittier Coll., 1950-51; instr. to prof. English, U. Neb., Lincoln, 1956—, asst., asso. and full dean Coll. Arts and Scis., 1965-70. Served with AUS, 1942-44. Mem. Am. Ass. U. Profs., Nat. Council Tchrs. English, Phi Betta Kappa. Author: The Quiet Rebel, William Dean Howells as Social Commentator, 1959. Editor: James Fenimore Cooper's Satanstoe, 1962; Literary Criticism of Edgar Allan Poe, 1965; The West of Owen Wister, 1972. Home: Lincoln, Neb. Died May 12, 975; cremated.

HOUGHTON, HENRY SPENCER, physician; b. Toledo, O., Mar. 27, 1880; s. Albert Charles and Amy (Twitchell) H.; B.Ph., Ohio State U., 1901, Sc.D., 1934; M.D., Johns Hopkins, 1905; LL.D., U. of Hongkong (China), 1925; m. Caroline Carmack, June 1906; children—Edwin Wells (dec.), Benjamin Carmack, Amy Twitchell and Mary Hildebrand (twins), Albert Charles, Hugh Fuller (dec.). Asst. Rockefeller Inst., New York, 1905-06; physician Wuhu Gen. Hosp., Wuhu, China, 1906-11; dean Harvard Med. Sch. of China, Shanghai, 1911-17; with China Med. Bd., New York, 1917; acting dir. Peking Union Med. Coll., 1918-21, dir., 1921-28; dean Medical Coll., U. of Ia., 1928-33; dir. of Univ. Clinics and asso. dean div. of biol. sciences, U. of Chicago, 1933-34; dir. for China Medical Board, Inc., 1934-37; dir. of Peking Union Medical College, 1937-46. Held as polit. prisoner by Japanese Army, Dec. 1941-Sept. 1945. Fellow royal Soc. Tropical Medicine, Am. Coll. of Physicians; mem. Am. Soc. Tropical Medicine, Far Eastern Assn. Tropical Medicine, Beta Theta Pi. Conglist. Address: Carmel, Calif. Died Mar. 1975.

HOUGHTON, LUCILE C., author; b. New Castle, Ky., Apr. 11, 1879; d. James Nelson and Amanthis (Wand) Caplinger; ed. Bellewood Sem., Anchorage, Ky.; m. Henry Houghton, June 1, 1898. Presbyn. Author: A Venture in Identity, 1912. Address: New Rochelle, N.Y.†

HOULTON, RUTH, pub. health nurse; b. Elk River, Minn., March 22, 1881; dau. William Henry and Fredrietta (Lewis) Houlton; A.B., Univ. of Minn., 1903; grad. Ancker Hosp. Sch. of Nursing, Minneapolis, 1905; unmarried. State supervising nurse, Child Hygiene div., Minn. State Dept. of Health, Minneapolis, 1921-26; dir. Vis. Nurse Assn., Minneapolis, Minn., 1927-34; acting dir. course in pub. health nursing, Univ. of Minn., sch. yr. 1930-31; asso. dir. Nat. Orgn. for Pub. Health Nursing, New York, N.Y., 1935-40, gen. dir. and sec. bd. dirs., 1940-48. Served as spl. nurse France and Italy, Am. Red Cross, 1918-20. Mem. Delta Delta Delta. Home: Croton-on-Hudson, N.Y.†

HOUSE, EDWARD JOHN, pres. Appalacha Coal Co.; b. Pittsburgh, Pa., May 8, 1879; s. Edward and Ruth (Widney) H.; student Shady Side Acad., Pittsburgh, Pa., 1893-96, Andover (Mass.) Acad., 1896-97; B.S., Yale, 1900; m. Helen Horne, Dec. 6, 1910 (died Mar. 10, 1932); children—Edward John (dec.), William Pendleton, Helen. Dir. Fidelity Trust Co.; supt. Highland Park Zoological Garden, Pittsburgh. Author: A Hunter's Camp Fires, 1909. Home: Pittsburgh, Pa.†

HOUSTON, BRYAN, ret. business exec.; b. San Antonio, Tex., Aug. 26, 1899; s. Reagan and Martha (Green) H.; student U. Tex., 1920-21; m. Ruth Hamilton, 1926; children—Ruth, Betty; m. 2d, Shirley Deal, 1936; m. 3d, Barbara Mack, 1954. Service sta. operator Magnolia Petroleum Co., San Antonio, Tex., 1916-17, Stillman, Pa., 1921-22; cost accountant Tidewater Oil Co.; asst. sales mgr., Standard Oil Co. (Ohio), Cleve., 1930-35; pres. Houston and Wishar, cons., Cleve. 1935-36; v.p. Young and Rubicam, Inc., New York City, 1936-46; exec. v.p., gen. sales mgr. Pepsi-Cola Co., Long Island City, N.Y., 1946-48, dir. information Econ. Adminstrn., Washington, 1948; became exec. v.p. Sherman and Marquette, Inc., 1950; former chmn. bd. Bryan Houston, Inc., N.Y.C.; chmn. bd. Fletcher Richards Co., Inc. until 1971; sr. v.p. Interpub. Group Cos., Inc., 1972; ret., 1972; bus. cons. Served in USN, 1917-19; served as asst. dir. purchases div. Army Service Forces, Washington, 1942-43; asst. dir. for contract terminations, 1943; asst. dir. for property disposal, readjustment div., 1944; dep. dir. for rationing OPA, Washington, 1943-44; asst. dir. Bur. Pub. Relations, War Dept., 1944-45. Republican. Episcopalian. Clubs: Sleepy Hollow Country; Army-Navy (Washington). Home: Briarcliff Manor N.Y. Died Mar. 7, 1974; buried Sleepy Hollow Cemetery, Tarrytown, N.Y.

HOUSTON, HARRY RUTHERFORD;, b. Fincastle, Botetourt County, Va., May 20, 1878; s. Rutherford Roland and Margaret (Steele) H.; A.B., Hampden-Sydney (Va.) Coll., 1899; m. Elizabeth E. Watkins, Dec. 20, 1905; children—Elizabeth Bagnall, Margaret Steele (Mrs. Charles E. Swing), Harriet Rutherford (Mrs. R. M. Donaldson), School teacher, 1899; entered printing and publishing business, 1900; mem. Ho. of Delegates Va., 1905-20, 1923-24, 1926 (speaker of House, 1916-20); gen. contracting business 1917-20; investments from 1920; apptd. commr. of fisheries of Va., 1926; brokerage business, 1930-31; owner Houston Printing and Publishing House; dir. Bank of Hampton, First Nat. Bank of Hampton; asso. dir. Federal Housing Adminstrn., State of Va., 1934-35; apptd. mem. Hampton Roads Regional Defense Council, 1941. Pres. Va. Sch. of Deaf and Blind; trustee Hampden-Sydney Coll. Pres. Greater Peninsula Assn. for Consolidation Newport News, Hampton and Environs, 1940-41. Commr. Va. Pilot Assn. Col. on staff of Gov. Trinkle, 1922. Chmn. Va. State Dem. Conv. 3 times. Presbyterian. Mason (32°, Shriner), Elk, Moose, Red Man, Eagles, Woodman of the World. Clubs: Rotary (ex-pres.), Hampton Roads Golf and Country. Author: History of the Peninsula of Virginia, 1934. Home: Hampton Va.†

HOUSTON, JAMES GARFIELD, lawyer; b. Pitts., Sept. 22, 1881; s. James Wilson and Sarah (McCutcheon) H.; A.B., U. Pitts., 1903, LL.B., 1906, M.L., 1918, LL.D., 1956; m. Grace Preston, June 30, 1926. Admitted to Pa. bar, 1906; pvt. practice law, Pitts., from 1906; partner Blaxter, O'Neill & Houston, from 1937. Asso. prof. law U. Pitts., 1912-38. Served as maj., asst. adj. 18th Inf. Div., U.S. Army, 1917-18. Mem. Allegheny County (pres. 1950-51), Am., Pa. bar assns., Phi Delta Theta, Phi Delta Phi. Presbyn. (trustee). Club: Duquesne Home: Pittsburgh, Pa.†

HOUSTON, JOHN M., govt. official; b. Formosa, Kan., Sept. 15, 1890; s. Samuel J. and Dora (Nieves) H.; ed. Fairmount Coll., Wichita, Kan., 1906; m. Charlotte Stellhorn, May 28, 1920; children—Patricia Mary Jane, Robert Allen. Appeared as actor, 1912-17; engaged in retail lumber business at Newton, Kan., since 1919; mayor of Newton, Kan., 2 terms, 1927-31; mem. 74th to 77th Congresses (1935-43), 5th Kan. Dist.; mem. Nat. Labor Relations Bd. since Mar. 1943. Served in U.S.M.C., World War. Mem. Kan. Lumbermen's Assn. (pres. since 1926), Am. Legion, Vets. Fgn. Wars. Democrat. Episcopalian. Mason. (Shriner); mem. Elks (pres. Kan. Assn.). Home: Washington, D.C. Died Apr. 29, 1975.

HOVERMAN, RUSSELL MAAS, banker; b. Bklyn., Jan. 15, 1918; s. John Henry and Caroline (Koster) H.; B.S. in Econs., U. Pa., 1938; grad. Am. Inst. Banking, 1940; M.B.A., N.Y.U., 1950; m. Mary Jean Mahan, Nov. 6, 1943; children—John R., James M., Stephen K. With Williamsburgh Savs. Bank, Bklyn., 1938-74, exec. v.p., 1968-74, trustee, 1969-74. Past pres. Savs. Banks Auditors and Comptroller Forum N.Y. State. Past pres. Sch. Bd., Seaford, N.Y. Served to lt. comdr. USNR, 1941-47. Mem. Alpha Sigma Phi (Delta Xi award 1968). Lutheran. Club: Southward Ho Country (Brightwaters, N.Y.). Home: Seaford, N.Y. Died Dec. 3, 1974.

HOWARD, A. PHILO, surgeon; b. Palestine, Tex., Oct.25, 1878; s. Alfred Ryland and Georgia (Grainger) H.; grad. Staunton (Va.) Mil. Acad., 1896; M.D., U. of Pa., 1901; m. Nancy Flewellen, Nov. 30, 1908; children—Eugenia Flewellen (Mrs. Wilmer B. Hunt), Alfred Ryland, Georgia (Mrs. Henry G. Safford, Jr.), A. Philo. Became house surgeon for the I.G.N. Railroad Hospital, 1901; demonstrator of anatomy, St. Louis University, 1903-06; chief surgeon New Orleans, Texas & Mexico Ry., 1907-32, Trinity & Brazos Valley Ry., 1910-29, Burlington, Rock Island Ry. Co. at Houston from 1929; chief cons. surgeon M.P. R.R. (Gulf Coast div.); mem. staff Hermann Hosp. from 1933; pres. Houston Clinic from 1916; clinical prof. gynecology, Bayler U., med. Dept. Fellow Am. Coll. Surgeons; mem. Nu Sigma Nu. Episcopalian. Home: Houston, Tex.†

HOWARD, BAILEY KNEIRIEM, publisher; b. Jamestown, Mo., Oct. 25, 1914; s. Moran Elmo and Anna Oliva (Kneiriem) H.; student U. Mo., 1934-35, USAF Sch. Applied Tactics, Combat Intelligence Sch., Orlando, Fla., 1943; m. Virginia Louise Enochs (div. 1946); m. 2d, Frankie Louise Canaday, Nov. 5, 1949 (div. 1972); 1 dau., Stacey Ann (Mrs. Gary E. Robinson). Reporter, Kansas City (Mo.) Jour. Post, 1935-37; sales mgr. Marshall Hughes Co., Kansas City, 1937-38, T.G. Nichols Co., 1938-40; Ia. div. mgr. Roach Fowler Co., 1940-42; asst. gen. sales mgr. Quarrie Corp., Chgo., 1946-50; gen. sales mgr. ednl. div. Field Enterprises, Inc., Chgo., 1950-53, v.p., gen. sales mgr., 1953-57, sr. v.p. Ednl. Corp., 1957, exec. v.p., 1957, pres., 1957-64, pres., chief exec. officer, 1964-66, pres. parent corp., 1966-68, pres., chief exec. officer, 1968-70, chmn. bd., chief exec. officer, 1970, also dir., chmn. exec. com.; pres., chief exec. officer newspaper div. (Chgo. Sun-Times, Chgo. Daily News), 1966-71; chmn. exec. com. Field Enterprises Inc.; dir. Field Creations, Chgo., Atlanta; dir. Field Ednl. Publs. Inc., Palo Alto, Cal. Bd. dirs. Field Enterprises Charitable Corp.; trustee Field Estate, Chgo. Sun Times/Daily News Charitable Trust; founder numerous scholarship, cultural, fellowship funds; mem. Chgo. Natural History Mus. Served as capt. Combat Intelligence Corps, USAAF, 1942-45. Mem. English-Speaking Union, Chgo. Art Inst. (life), Chgo. Hist. Soc. (life). Clubs: Private Turf (Santa Anita, Arcadia, Cal.); Turf (Hollywood, Cal.); Kona Kai (San Diego); Tavern, Racquet, Chicago (Chgo.); Lakeside Golf (North Hollywood, Cal.); Post and Paddock (Arlington Heights, Ill.); Beverly Hills (Cal.).; PIP's (Beverly Hills); many others. Home: Chicago Ill. and Beverly Hills Cal. Died Aug. 12, 1974; interred Greenwood Meml. Park, San Diego, Cal.

HOWARD, CHARLES ABNER, coll. pres.; b. Greenwood County, Kan., Feb. 17, 1881; s. Abner and Catherine Mary (Lough) H.; prep. edn., Southern Kan. Acad., Eureka; Ph.B., Baker U., 1907; grad. study, U. of Calif., 1915, Stanford U., 1924; A.M., U. of Ore., 1923; LL.D., Oregon State College, 1933, U. of Portland, 1940; m. Cora DeFontaigne Shaw, Aug. 11, 1909. Teacher rural schs. and Southern Kan. Acad., 1904-06; teacher County High Sch., Klamath Falls, Ore., 1907-11; supt. schs., Coquille, 1911-17; prin. high sch., Eugene, 1917-20; supt. schs., Marshfield, 1920-26; supt. pub. instrn., Ore., 1927-37; pres. Eastern Ore. Coll. of Edn., 1937-39; pres. Ore-Coll. Edn. 1939-47, pres. emeritus, from 1947; investment rep., Equitable Savings & Loan Assn., Portland, Ore., from 1947. Bd. dirs. Children's Farm Home Ore. Mem. N.E.A., Ore. Edn. Assn., Am. Assn. of Teachers Colls., Am. Assn. of Sch. Adminstrators. Presbyterian. Phi Delta Kappa, Theta Delta Phi. Mason, Elk; mem. O.E.S. Home: Salem, Ore.†

HOWARD, CHARLES LOWELL, patent lawyer; b. Washington, D.C., March 22, 1881; s. George Henry and Roberta Traill Brooke (Macgill) H.; LL.B., M.P.L., Georgetown U., Wash., D.C., 1914; m. Helen Frances Mack, Dec. 20, 1923; 1 dau., Roberta Brooke. Feature writer for Washington, D.C., newspapers, 1902-04; asso. with his father, patent lawyer, 1905-14; admitted to practice in numerous U.S. Courts; sec. Western R.R. Assn., Chicago, 1914-23, asst. to gen. counsel, 1924-25, asst. gen. counsel, 1926-36; asst. western counsel Patent Div., Assn. of Am. Railroads, 1937, western consel of the Patent Div., 1938-49. Mem. Am. Bar Assn., Patent Law Assn., Chicago. Home: Claremont, Cal.†

HOWARD, EDWARD D., archbishop; b. Cresco, Ia., Nov. 5, 1877; s. John and Marie (Fleming) H.; A.B., Columbia Coll., Dubuque, Ia., 1899; grad. study St. Mary's (Kan.) Coll., 1899-1900, St. Paul (Minn.) Sem., 1900-06. Ordained priest R.C. Ch., 1906; prof. Columbia Coll., 1906-21, pres., 1921-24; bishop-auxiliary of Davenport, 1924-26; archbishop of Archdiocese of Portland in Oregon, also pres. of corporation of same, ret. Home: Portland, Ore.†

HOWARD, JAMES LELAND, ins. co. exec.; b. Hartford, Conn., Mar. 21, 1878; s. Frank L. and Julia L. (Cutler) H.; Ph.B., Sheffield Scientific Sch. of Yale, 1898; m. Mabel H. Hume, Apr. 30, 1913. Entered employ of The Travelers Ins. Co., 1898, asst. sec. Life dept., 1906, asst. sec., 1911, sec., 1912, v.p., 1922-49; dir. The Travelers Ins. Co., The Travelers Indemnity Co., The Travelers Fire Ins. Co., Charter Oak Fire Ins. Co., The Travelers Bank & Trust Co., Landers, Frary & Clark. Served as private, Spanish-Am. War, 1898; major, Mexican border, 1916; lt. col. Staff 26th Div., A.E.F., later assigned to Gen. Staff, A.E.F., 1917-19. Awarded D.S.C., 1918; Croix de Guerre with Palm, 1918. Appointed Chavelier de la Legion d'Honneur, Decree of Pres. of French Republic, 1919; Order of the Purple Heart, 1932. Mem. Mil. Order of Foreign Wars, Am. Soc. of the French Legion of Honor, Am. Legion. Clubs: Hartford, Hartford Golf, Farmington Country; St. Anthony, Yale (N.Y. City); Graduates (New Haven); YD. Author: The Origin and Fortunes of Troop B.; Seth Harding. Mariner. Home: Hartford, Conn.†

HOWARD, JOHN DON, cons.; b. Estherville, Ia., June 3, 1903; s. Willis Vernon and Amelia Elizabeth (Nancolas) H.; B.S. in Elec. Engring., Ia. State U., 1925; m. Nita Knowles, Dec. 28, 1926; 1 son, Richard K. Engr., Westinghouse Electric Corp., 1925-34; with Wis. Power & Light Co., Madison, 1934-41, 43-68, exec. v.p., 1962-65, pres., 1965-68, also dir.; past pres., dir. S. Beloit Water, Gas & Electric Co., Wis. Valley Improvement Co.; v.p., dir. Wis. River Power Co., 1955-68; past dir. Atomic Power Devel. Assos. Dist. mgr. WPB, 1941-43; chmn. sponsored student com. Am. Power Conf., 1962-68; mem. Assn. Edison Illuminating Cos. Registered profl. engr., Wis. Mem. I.E.E.E., Edison Electric Inst., Nat. Soc. Profl. Engrs., Wis. Utilities Assn. (pres., dir. 1963), Am. Gas Assn., Kappa Sigma, Eta Kappa Nu. Conglist. Mason (Shriner), Kiwanian; mem. Order Eastern Star (past patron). Clubs: Madison, Nakoma Golf, Forest Lakes Country. Home: Sarasota Fla. Died May 13, 1974.

HOWARD, LAWRENCE AUGUSTUS, lawyer; b. Hartford, Conn., Oct. 15, 1881; s. Arthur Ethelbert and Mary Adelaide (Bagley) H.; A.B., Yale, 1903, LL.B., 1906; LL.D. (hon.), Trinity Coll., 1950; m. Edith Howell Bond, Aug. 24, 1908; children—Barbara (Mrs. John R. Kleinschmidt), Elisabeth (Mrs. H. Parker Jones). Admitted to Conn. bar, 1906; tchr., New Jersey, 1903-05; practicing lawyer, Hartford, from 1906; condr. 5 mergers of Conn. Light & Power Co., 1929-47; defended all doctors accused of malpractice, Conn., 1922-37; partner Day, Berry & Howard from 1921; dir. Farmington Savs. Bank, Hartford Courant Co., Netherlands Ins. Co., Charles W. House & Sons Inc., J. W. Beach, Inc. Commr. uniform laws from 1940. Dir. Watkinson Library. Served as lt., U.S. Navy, 1917-20. Clubs: 20th Century (past pres.), Hartford. Country (Farmington, Conn.). Revised Charter and Ordnances of Hartford, 1908. Home: West Hartford, Conn.†

HOWARD, MARGARET DOUGLAS, educator; b. Seattle, Oct. 27, 1944; d. Gordon E. and Anne (Coyle) Howard; B.A., Wellesley Coll., 1966; M.Sc., London Sch., 1967; M. Phil., Yale, 1969. Lectr. Dalhousie U., Halifax, N.S., Can., summer 1969; asst. prof. econs. Hampshire Coll., Amherst, Mass., 1971-72. Mem. Am. Econ. Assn. Home: Northampton Mass. Died Oct. 9, 1972.

HOWARD, MILDRED LANGFORD, educator; b. Glasgow, Ky., Dec. 1, 1916; d. Carl Clifford and Julia (Franklin) Howard; A.B., U. N.C., 1936, M.A., 1951; Ph.D., U. Ill., 1956; postgrad. U. London, summer 1951. Tchr. theatre Ward Belmont Coll., Nashville, 1942-44, U. Mo., 1951-53, Tex., 1956-64; dir. theatre Am. U., Cairo, Egypt, 1961-62; asso. prof. theatre Western Ky. U., Bowling Green, 1964-68, prof. theatre, 1968-75. Dir. dramatic prodns. including J. B., 1969, The Skin of Our Teeth, 1970, The Visit, 1971, The Glass Menagerie, 1971; cons. regional dramatic workshops; judge for state dramatic festivals, speaker, lectr. state speech and theatre convs. Mem. Carolina Playmakers, Ky. Assn. Communicative Arts, Am., Ky. Southeastern theatre assns., Speech Communications Assn., Chi Omega, Phi Theta Kappa, Phi Kappa Phi. Mem. Disciples of Christ Ch. Home: Glasgow, Ky., Died Oct. 19, 1975.

HOWE, HELEN, author, monologuist; b. Boston, Mass., Jan. 11, 1905; d. Mark Antony De Wolfe and Fanny Huntington (Quincy) Howe; grad. Milton Acad., 1922; student Radcliffe Coll., 1923-24; m. Alfred Reginald Allen, May 31, 1946. Appeared in recitals of character sketches of own authorship in 45 states, since 1936; solo appearances, New York and London theatres, and supper clubs. Episcopalian. Clubs: P.E.N., Cosmopolitan (New York). Author: (novels): The Whole Heart, 1943; We Happy Few, 1946; The Circle of the Day, 1950; The Success, 1956; The Fires of Autumn, 1959; (biography) The Gentle Americans, 1965. Address: New York City N.Y. Died Feb. 1, 1975; interred Mount Wollaston Cemetery, Quincy, Mass.

HOWE, HENRY V(AN WAGSTEN), geologist; b. Fulton, N.Y., June 15, 1896; s. Herbert Crombie and Georgia (Emeny) H.; A.B., U. of Ore., 1916; student Yale, 1916-17, U. of Ore., 1919, U. of Calif., 1919-21; Ph.D., Stanford U., 1922; m. Cecil Evelyn Jones, July 26, 1918; children—Patricia Evelyn, Herbert James and Eleanor Adrienne (twins), Robert Crombie. Asst. prof. geology, La. State U., Baton Rouge, 1922-24, associate professor, 1924, professor, 1925-65, Boyd prof. geology, 1965-66, Boyd prof. emeritus, 1966-74, dir. School Geology, 1931-66, dir. emeritus, 1966-74, dean College arts and science, 1944-49; dir. research division La. Geol. Survey, 1934-40; mem. State Mineral Bd., 1937-40; chairman State Mineral Board, 1964-66. Member committee on micropaleontology, Nat. Research Council. Recipient Sidney Powers Memorial medal American Association of Petroleum Geolgists, 1960. Fellow A.A.A.S., Geological Society America, Palaeontol. Soc.; mem. Am. Assn. Petroleum Geologists, Soc. Econ. Paleontologists and Mineralogists, sec. treas. 1937-39, pres. 1941, La. Acad. (sec. 1929), Shreveport Geol. Soc., Geol. and Mining Soc. Am. Univs., Am. Geophys. Union, Phi Beta Kappa. Sigma Xi, Phi Kappa Phi, Theta Tau, Sigma Upsilon, Sigma Alpha Epsilon, Omicron Delta Kappa. Author sci. publs. Home: Baton Rouge, La. Died Sept. 27, 1974.

HOWE, JOHN LYNN, college pres.; b. Scotch Hill, Pa., Oct. 31, 1880; s. James and Jane (Rhea) H.; Ph.B., Grove City (Pa.) Coll., 1907; grad. Western Theol. Sem., 1911; m. Lora I. Chaney, 1911. Ordained Presbyn. ministry, 1911; pastor Wessington, S. Dak., 1911-14; missionary, Prince of Wales Island, Alaska, 1914-17, 1919-20; teacher physics, South Hills High Sch., Pittsburgh, Pa., 1917-18; pres. Highland Coll. from 1920. Mason. Home: Highland, Kan.†

HOWEL, CLAYTON JAMES, soft drink co. exec.; b. Center, Ala., Apr. 13, 1878; s. James H. and Molly (Sparks) H.; ed. high sch., Gayesville, Ala.; m. Josephine W. Watkins, Nov. 19, 1902; 1 dau., Annie Joe. Began as office boy in wholesale grocery, Ft. Worth, Tex., 1895; organizer, 1907, Jersey-Creme Co.; also organizer, 1909, Southern Fruit Julep Co.; moved to Chicago, 1915; organizer, 1916, pres. Orange Crush Co. Republican. Baptist. Clubs: Hamilton, Lake Shore Athletic, Westermoreland Country. Home: Chicago, Ill.†

HOWELL, CHARLES ROBERT, former congressman, former state ofcl.; b. Trenton Apr. 23, 1904; s. Robert Wilson and Harriet Newton (Bumsted) H.; grad. Hoosac Sch., Hoosick, N.Y., 1923; student Princeton, 1923-24, U. Pa., 1936-37; m. Inez Wood Howe, Oct. 3, 1928. Ins. broker, Trenton, 1928-54; elected to N.J. Ho. Assembly, 1944, 45; mem. 81st to 83d Congresses, 4th N.J. Dist.; former N.J. commr. banking and ins. Democratic state chmn. 1953; Dem. candidate U.S. Senate, 1954; pres. Bank of Manalapan, N.J.; bd. mgrs. U.S. Savs. Bank, Newark. C.L.U., N.J. Mem. Trenton (past pres.), N.J. (past v.p.) assns. life underwriters, Nat. Assn. Suprs. State Banks (past pres.), Nat. Assn. Ins. Commrs. (past pres.). Episcopalian. Introduced original fair employment practices bill in N.J. legislature, 1945. Home: Pennington N.J. Died July 1973.

HOWELL, CORWIN, lawyer; b. Newark, N.J., Dec. 6, 1881; s. Francis K. and Emma (Corwin) H.; A.B., Princeton, 1903, valedictorian; LL.B., New York Law School, 1905; m. Elizabeth Lunn, June 14, 1910; 1 son, John Corwin. Instructor New York Law School, 1905-08; admitted to N.J. bar as atty., 1906, as counsellor, 1909; admitted to United States Supreme Court, 1925, and engaged in general practice of law at Newark, New Jersey; mem. firm Pitney, Hardin & Ward from 1914. Spl. asst. to atty. gen. as hearing officer in conscientious objector, New Jersey cases, Selective Service, 1943-47, and from 1948. Trustee Protestant Foster Home Society of Newark (now Newark Home for Foster Care), Marcus L. Ward Home for Aged Men (pres. bd. trustees), Children's Aid Society of Newark (former president board trustees). Mem. American Bar Assn., N.J. State Bar Assn. (former mem. com. on canons of ethics). Essex County Bar Assn., (former mem. ethics com. and com. on admission to bar), Phi Beta Kappa. Republican. Episcopalian (former vestryman). Mason. Clubs: Country (Maplewood); Essex (Newark). Home: Summit, N.J.†

HOWELL, JAMES ALBERT, JR., physician; b. Kansas City, Mo., May 14, 1931; s. James Albert and Orpha (Wilson) H.; student La. Tech.; M.D., La. State U.; m. Barbara Jean Dickerson, May 23, 1959; children—Virginia Antoinette, Rebecca Roline. Intern, Confederate Meml. Med. Center, Shreveport, La., resident in internal medicine; mem. vis. staff; partner Willis-Knighton Clinic, Shreveport; mem. internal medicine staff, pres. med. staff, chief dept. medicine, founder, dir. intensive care unit Willis-Knighton Meml. Hosp.; staff Shreveport Emergency Blood Bank; asst. prof. dept. medicine La. State U. Sch. Medicine, Shreveport. Mem. La. Bd. Med. Examiners. Served with USAF, 1949-50. Chapel at Willis-Knighton Meml. Hosp. named in his honor. Diplomate Am. Bd. Internal Medicine. Mem. A.C.P. (asso.), La., Shreveport med. socs. Episcopalian. Home: Shreveport, La. Died Aug. 19, 1969; buried Forest Park Cemetery, Shreveport, La.

HOWER, RALPH M., educator, business cons.; b. Salina, Kan., Aug. 25, 1903; s. Edward Charles and Etta (Kistler) H.; A.B., U. Kan., 1925; B.A., Oxford U., 1928, M.A., 1953; D.C.S., Harvard, 1935; Dr. Philosophy and Letters, U. Navarra (Spain), 1967; m. Elizabeth Niven, June 27, 1928; children—Alison Mary Steuart, Robert Kistler. Instr. econs. U. Kan., 1928-30; research asst. business history Harvard, 1930-34, instr. bus. history, 1934-35, asst. prof., 1935-46, asso. prof., 1946-49, prof. bus. adminstrn., 1949-70, prof. emeritus, 1970-73; prof. Mgmt. Devel. Inst., Lausanne, Switzerland, 1960-61. Cons. adminstrn., exec. devel. several orgns. and corps.; mem. adv. com. Instituto de Estudios Superiores de la Empresa, Barcelona, Spain. Pres. Community Council of Weston, Mass., 1947-49. Bd. Assessors, Weston, Mass., 1955-60. Trustee Bus. History Found. Served to col. Q.M.C., AUS, 1942-46; ETO. Decorated Bronze Star (U.S.); Legion of Honor, Croix de Guerre with gold star (France). Mem. Am. Assn. Rhodes Scholars, Phi Beta Kappa, Beta Theta Pi. Episcopalian. Club: Harvard (N.Y.C.). Author: The Preservation of Business Records, 1937; The History of an Advertising Agency, 1939, rev. edit., 1949; The History of Macy's of New York, 1943; The Administrator (with John Desmond Glover), 1949, rev. edit., 1973; (with Charles D. Orth 3d) Managers and Scientists, 1963. Home: Weston Mass. Died Aug. 2, 1973.

HOWES, FRANK STEWART, educator, author; b. Oxford, Eng., Apr. 2, 1891; s. George and Grace (Phipps) S.; student St. John's Coll., Oxford, 1910-14; M.A., Royal Coll. Music, 1922; m. Barbara Mildred Tidd Pratt, Sept. 18, 1929; children—Eve (Mrs. Frederick Marles), Ismene (Mrs. Douglas Durand), Hugh, Fenelia (Mrs. David Wood). Asst. music critic The Times, London, 1925-43, chief critic, 1943-60; prof. Royal Coll. Music, London, 1938-70. Chmn. central mus. adv. council BBC, 1949-55. Chmn. Musicians' Benevolent Fund, 1938-56. Decorated comdr. Order Brit. Empire. Fellow Royal Coll. Music; mem. Royal Mus. Assn. (pres. 1948-58). Author: The Borderland of Music and Psychology, 1926; Byrd, 1928; Key to the Art of Music, 1935; Key to Opera, 1939; Full Orchestra, 1942; Man, Mind, and Music, 1948; Music of R. Vaughan Williams, 1954, Am. edit., 1976; Music and Its Meanings, 1958; Music of William Walton, 1965; The English Musical Renaissance, 1966; Folk Music of Britain-and Beyond, 1970. Died Sept. 28, 1974; buried Combe, Oxfordshire, England.

HOWLAND, LEROY ALBERT, mathematician; b. Acushnet, Mass., July 6, 1879; s. Franklyn and Emma H. (Hallett) H.; B.A., Wesleyan U., Conn., 1900; M.A., Harvard Univ., 1904; Ph.D., Munich, 1908; m. Ethel M. Winward, Sept. 14, 1908; children—Leroy Albert, John Loomis. Instructor mathematics, Drexel Inst., Phila., 1900-03, Wesleyan U., 1905-06; Parker fellow, Harvard, 1906-08; asso. prof. math., 1908, prof., 1913-47, emeritus from 1947, Wesleyan U.; v.p., 1921-26, 1927-35, dean 1935-47; acting pres., 1923-25. Mem. Conn. State Bd. of Edn., 1924-33. Mem. Am. Math. Soc. (council, 1916-19), Math. Assn. America, Psi Upsilon, Phi Beta Kappa, Sigma Xi. Methodist. Asso. editor Annals of Mathematics, 1910-11. Home: Middletown, Conn.†

HOWLAND, MARGUERITE ELIZABETH SMITH (MRS. CECIL M. HOWLAND), librarian; b. Wellington, Kan., Mar. 26, 1915; d. Perry Clifford and Edna (Walters) Smith; A.A., No. Okla. Jr. Coll., 1933; B.S. in Edn., Okla. State U., 1935; postgrad. Columbia, 1936; B.S. in L.S., U. Ill, 1941; m. Cecil M. Howland, Apr. 14, 1949; 1 dau., Elizabeth Ann. Tchr., Tonkawa (Okla.) High Sch., 1937-40; jr. order librarian U. Ill., Urbana, 1941-43; asst. librarian Parks Air. Coll., East St. Louis, Ill., 1943; librarian for gas dept. Phillips Petroleum Co., Bartlesville, Okla., 1943-46; sr. documents librarian Okla. State U., Stillwater, 1946-48, head documents librarian, supr. humanities and social scis. area, 1949-72. Mem. U. Ill. Library Sch. Assn., Am., Southwestern, Okla. library assns., Bus. and Profl. Women's Club (pres. 1946), Phi Kappa Phi, Beta Phi Mu, Pi Gamma Mu, Phi Alpha Theta, Kappa Delta Pi, Chi Delta Phi. Democrat. Methodist. Home: Stillwater, Okla. Died May 17, 1972.

HOWSE, WILLIAM MASSY GODWIN, merchant; b. Liverpool, Eng., Mar. 24, 1879; s. Edward and Alice (Massy) H.; ed. Anfield Board Sch. and Anfield Coll., both of Liverpool; m. Edna Emery, May, 1906; children—Alfred Edward, Robert Kenneth, Godfrey Lyle, Edna Alice, Edith Sara, William Emery. Came to U.S., 1904, naturalized citizen, 1916. Began as mcht., Liverpool, 1893, Wichita, Kan., 1904; formerly pres., now chmn. bd. The Johnston and Larimer Dry Goods Co., Wichita; chmn. bd. The Wichita Wholesale Furniture Co.; dir. The First Nat. Bank in Wichita, The Wheeler Kelly Hagny Trust Co., The Southwest Cracker Co., The Yellow Cab Co., The Pearce Dental Supply Co. Pres. Wholesale Dry Goods Inst., 4 terms. Trustee Wesley Hosp., Wichita (ex-pres); was chmn. Citizens Com. of 100 to Save Fairmount Coll. (now Wichita Municipal Univ.). Mem. Civic League of Wichita (chmn.), Wichita Chamber Commerce (ex-pres.); former dir. Chamber Commerce of U.S. Republican. Episcopalian. Mason (Consistory, Shrine). Clubs: Rotary, Wichita, Wichita Country; Rio Grande (Creede, Colo.) Address: Wichita, Kan.†

HOY, PATRICK HENRY, corp. exec.; b. Mpls., Mar. 3, 1914; s. Patrick H. and Mary (Walsh) H.; student U. Minn., 1933-35; m. Betty Bergman, July 1, 1944; children—Patrick Devin, Christopher Peter, Timothy. Sales mgr. Commander Larabee Milling Co., Mpls., 1930-40; v.p., gen. mgr. Amber Mills, 1940-43; exec. asst. to pres. Hotel Sherman, 1946-49, became exec. v.p., gen. mgr., 1949, also dir.; exec. asst. to pres. Hotels Ambassador, Chgo., 1946-49; became v.p. Ambassador East, Inc., 1949; pres. Hotel Sherman, Inc., and Ambassador East, Inc., Chgo., 1955-60; pres. Material Service div. Gen. Dynamics Corp., 1960-69; vice chmn., exec. v.p. Penn-Dixie Cement Corp., from 1969; sr. v.p. Gen. Dynamics Corp., 1960-73. Vice pres. Mexico Hotels, Ltd., 1946-52; dir. Union Asbetos & Rubber Co. Served with USN, 1942-46. Home: Chicago, Ill. Died Aug. 21, 1973.

HOYT, ALEX CRAWFORD, banker; b. Clinton, Pa., July 26, 1881; s. Lewis Stiles and Annie Julia (Crawford) H.; Ph.B., Yale, 1902; m. June Niederlander, Feb. 25, 1911; Vice pres. Citizens Nat. Bank, New Castle, Pa., 1912-23; became pres. Safe Deposit & Trust Co., 1923, which merged with Nat. Bank of Lawrence and First Nat. Bank of New Castle into the Union Trust Co. of New Castle and the First Nat. Bank of Lawrence County, 1927; pres. Union Trust Co., New Castle, from 1927. First Nat. Bank Lawrence County from 1931, also dir. Clubs: New Castle Country; Duquesne (Pittsburgh); Yale of New York City; Youngstown. Home: New Castle, Pa.†

HOYT, ELIZABETH STONE, educator; b. Morristown, Tenn., Sept. 27, 1905; d. James Wells and Ruth (Browne) Hoyt; A.B., Maryville Coll., 1927; M.A., U. Tenn., 1931; postgrad Columbia, summers 1935, 37, U. N.C., summers 1940, 42, 45, Okla. State U., 1965. Instr. history Montreat (N.C.) Anderson Coll., 1927-30, 31-45; faculty social studies, chmn. social sci. div., 1945-72, acting dean faculty, 1948-49; instr. history U. Tenn., summer 1948. Research librarian Hist. Found. Presbyn. and Ref. Chs., Montreat, summers 1950-72. Mem. Am., So. hist. assns., N.C. State Lit. and Hist. Assn., Western N.C. Hist. Assn., Delta Kappa Gamma (chpt. 2d v.p. 1968-70). Democrat. Presbyn. Contbr. articles to profl. jours. Address: Montreat, N.C. Died Jan. 1972.

HUBBARD, CARLISLE LE COMPTE, clergyman; b. Frederica, Del, Mar. 26, 1881; s. Edward Le Compte and Linda (Carlisle) H.; grad. Baltimore Poly. Inst., 1901; LL.B., Nat. U. Sch. of Law, Washington, D.C., 1904, LL.M., 1905; grad. in theology, course given by Baltimore Conf. M.E. Ch., 1911; M.A., St. John's Coll., Annapolis, 1910; D.D., Dickinson Coll., Carlisle, Pa., 1918; m. Alice Reeves Riffel, June 27, 1906; children—Agnes Mitchell, Richard Carlisle. Began practice of law at Baltimore, 1905; ordained ministry M.E. Ch., 1910; pastor successively, Frotsburg, Md., Paw Paw, W.Va., North Baltimore Sta., St. Paul's Ch., Wilmington, Del., Trinity Ch., Newburgh, N.Y., until 1928, First Ch., Oak Park, Ill., 1928-33, First Ch., Cleveland, 1933-38; became pastor First Ch., Asbury Park, N.J., 1938; now retired from active ministerial work. Mem. Theta Phi. Mason (K.T.). Clubs: Asbury Park, Rotary, Oak Park Rotary (hon.), Cambridge, Md., Rotary (hon.). Home: Cambridge, Md.†

HUBBARD, L(EVERETT) MARSDEN, banker; b. Wallingford, Conn., Feb. 15, 1882; s. Leverett Marsden and Florence (Ives) H.; grad. Wilbraham (Mass.) Acad., 1901; student Princeton, 1901-05; m. Gladys T. Woodward, 1924; 1 son, Leverett, Jr. With N. W. Harris & Co. — Harris, Forbes & Co., New York, 1905-22; pres. and dir. Travelers Bank & Trust Co. and Conn. River Banking Co., Hartford, from 1922; dir. Travelers Ins. Co. Trustee Wilbraham (Mass.) Academy. Mem. Soc. of Colonial Wars (treas.). Club: Hartford. Home: Hartford, Conn. Died May 2, 1973.

HUBER, CARL PARKER, physician, educator; b. Ann Arbor, Apr. 8, 1903; s. Carl and Lucy Ann (Parker) H.; A.B., U. Mich., 1924, M.A., 1925, M.D., 1928, Peterson fellow, 1933-35; m. Marion Elizabeth Kubik, June 20, 1929; children—G. Carl. Mariel Stow, David Garrett. Instr. obstetrics and gynecology U. Mich., 1930-36, U. Chgo., 1936-38; attending obstetrician, gynecologist Chgo. Lying-In Hosp., 1936-38; asst. prof. obstetrics and gynecology Ind. U. Sch. Medicine, 1938-44, asso. prof., 1944-48, prof., also chmn. dept., 1948-68, Sally E. and William A. Colman prof. obstetrics and gynecology, 1967-73, Colman prof., chmn., dept. emeritus, 1973-74; cons. obstetrician Ind. State Bd. Health, 1938. Diplomate Am. Bd. Obstetrics and Gynecology (dir. 1956-74, pres. 1964-66, chmn. 1968-70). Mem. N.D. (hon.), Indpls. obstet. and gynecol. socs., Am., Chgo. gynecol. socs., Central Assn. Obstetricians and Gynecologists, Am. Assn. Obstetricians and Gynecologists, Am. Coll. Obstetrics and Gynecology (pres. 1952), Am. Com. Maternal Welfare (dir. 1946-74, Sigma Xi, Alpha Sigma Phi, Phi Rho Sigma, Phi Sigma, Alpha Omega Alpha. Contbr. articles to profl. jours. Home: Indianapolis, Ind. Died July 10, 1974; buried Crown Hill Cemetery, Indianapolis, Ind.

HUCHINGSON, JAMES EDWIN, coll. pres.; b. Hico, Tex., June 17, 1881; s. John Fields and Sarah Ellen (Chenault) H.; B.C.S., Univ. of Denver, 1914, A.M., 1916; LL.D., William Jewell College, Liberty, Mo., 1936; m. Ethel Boltwood, Feb. 19, 1908; 1 daughter, Ethel. Successively teacher, prin., supervisor, Denver pub. schs., 1907-16, 1917-22, 1924-30; supervisor spl. service Detroit (Mich.) pub. schs., 1916; pres. Central Bus. Coll., Denver, 1922-24; dean Colo. Woman's Coll., 1930-32, pres., 1932-50, trustee. Served in U.S. inf., 1902-05; commander successively lt., captain, maj., col. inf., N.G., 1908-20; comd. 3d Colo. Inf. during World War I; served P.I. 13 mos. Pres. Colo. Bapt. Conv; pres. Denver Council, Camp Fire Girls of America; exec. commr. Denver Council, Boy Scouts America. Member American Council on Education. Member Nat. Edn. Assn., American Association of School Adminstrators, member Board of Edn. and publ. Northern Baptist Conv., Colorado Schoolmasters Club, Colo. Edn. Assn. (sec. 1915-16), Denver Chamber of Commerce, Delta Tau Kappa (founder), Phi Delta Kappa, Sigma Phi Epsilon, Pi Gamma Mu. Awarded English prize, U. of Denver, 1913; diploma for eminent ednl. service by Colo. State Bd. Edn., 1914. Mason (32°). Clubs: Rotary Internat. of Denver, Mikanakawa (founder). Author of Progressive Lessons in Business Writing, Denver Method, 1910, Teachers Syllabus, 1913, etc. Contbr. to ednl. periodicals. Home: Denver, Colo.†

HUDDY, R(ICHARD) T(HOMAS), educator, lawyer; b. Emporia, Kan. Sept. 20, 1904; s. Richard Francis and Margaret (Mackin) H.; student St. Mary's Coll., Kansas, 1922-24, Saint Louis University, 1924-25, U. Kan., 1925-26; Ph.B., A.M., J.D., DePaul U., 1930; postgrad. U. Ill., Kan. State Tchrs. Coll., Loyola U., Chgo.; m. Yolanda Harriet Napolilli, June 11, 1931; 1 dau., Harriet Louise (Mrs. Ignatius M. Bienias). Admitted to Kan. bar, 1930, Ill. bar, 1930; tchr. DePaul Acad. and DePaul U., 1926-32; tchr. Calumet High Sch., Chgo., 1932-33, Lake View High Sch., Schurz High Sch., Senn High Sch., summers, 1934-59; tchr. Amundsen High Sch., Chgo., 1933-70, emeritus, 1970-71. Certificated law tchr. Mem. Am. Fedn. Tchrs., Chgo. Tchrs. Union, Chgo. Bus. Tchrs. Assn., Am., Ill., Chgo. bar assns., Chgo. Area Bus. Educators Assn., Sigma Nu, Delta Theta Phi. Democrat. Roman Catholic. Author: The Law of Public School Discipline, 1933. Home: Chicago Ill. Died Apr. 18, 1974; interred Maryhill Cemetery, Niles, Ill.

HUDGINS, MORGAN HUGHES, educator; b. Portsmouth, Va., Dec. 4, 1878; s. Henry Clay and Laucrece P. (Langhorne) H.; grad. high sch., Portsmouth, 1898; grad. Va. Mil. Inst., 1901; m. Elizabeth Milnes Austin, of Waynesboro, Va., June 3, 1913. With Fishburne Mil. Sch., from 1901; comdt. of cadets, until 1912, asso. prin., 1905-13, prin. and dir., from 1913. Chmn. war activities, Waynesboro, World War; maj. staff specialist, O.R.C. Mayor of Waynesboro 8 yrs. Mem. Kappa Alpha. Rotarian Democrat. Episcopalian. Home: Waynesboro, Va.*†

HUDSON, CEYLON E., broker, banker, industrialist; b. St. Mary's, O., Aug. 21, 1901; s. James Curtis and Grace (Yingling) H.; student Purdue U., 1919-21; children (by former marriage)—Nancy Jane, Mary Ann; m. Helen Holmes, Sept. 6, 1944 (dec. 1959); 1 son, Ceylon E., Jr., step-children—Laurence, Tommie; m. Barbara Caldwell Miller, 1964; stepchildren--William, Marilyn, James. Elec. engr. Ohio Pub. Service Co., Cleve., 1920-24; customer ownership, pub. relations H. L. Doherty & Co., N.Y.C., 1925-26; field mgr. Cities Service Co., Ohio dist., Dayton, 1926-27; dist. mgr. Studebaker Securities Co., Chgo., 1927-29; established various enterprises since 1930; pres., chmn. Ceylon E. Hudson Inc.; chmn. bd. United Steel Fabricators, Inc., Wooster, O., Wayne County Nat. Bank, Magni Power Co., Wooster; pres., dir. D. C. Curry Lumber Co.; dir. United Telephone Co., Mansfield, O., Wooster Feed Co. Trustee Wooster Cemetery Assn., Coll. of Wooster. Lutheran (trustee). Club: Elks. Home: Wooster O. Died May 6, 1973.

HUDSON, FREDERICK MITCHELL, lawyer; b. Jefferson County, Ark., Feb. 2, 1871; s. James Asbury and Mary Rhoda (Warren) H.; student Hendrix Coll., Altus (now at Conway), Ark., 1885-87; A.B., Washington and Lee U., 1890, LL.B., 1892; m. Nora Bell Andrews, Oct. 27, 1896; children—Martha (Mrs. Raleigh W. Van Brunt), James Andrews, Mary Warren (Mrs. Lewis Gaston Leary, Jr.). Admitted to Ark. bar, 1892; practiced in Pine Bluff, 1892-1900; followed horticulture in Fla., in quest of health, 1900-05; practiced law in Miami, Fla., from 1905, specializing in probate practice; sr. partner Hudson, McNutt, Campbell & Isom; city atty. Pine Bluff, Ark., 1895-98; state senator, Fla., 1905-17, pres. Fla. Senate 1909-11; spl. counsel for Fla. R.R. Commn., with litigation in all state and fed cts., 1911-14. Hon. mem. bd. dirs. Fla. Florida Children's Home. Mem. Am., Fla., Dade County (past pres.) bar assns., Am. Judicature Soc., Am. Law Inst., Fla. Soc. S.A.R., Va., Fla., Ark., So. Fla. (past pres.) hist socs., Miami Pioneers, Ancient and Hon. Arty Co. of Mass. Democrat. Methodist. Clubs: Rotary (past pres.), Biscayne Bay Yacht. Home: Miami Fla.†

HUDSON, GEORGE ELFORD, prof., museum curator; b. Spartanburg, S.C., May 6, 1907; s. J.T. and Belle (Haynsworth) H.; B.S., Clemsen Coll., 1928; M.S. U. Neb., 1930, Ph.D., 1936; m. Bessie Friedrich, Sept. 10, 1929; children—Belva D., George F. Instr. zoology, U. Neb., 1931-38; asst. prof. zoology and curator Museum, State Coll. Wash. (name later changed to Wash State U.), 1938-46, asso. prof., 1946-51, prof. 1951-74. Chmn. Inland Empire chpt. Nature Conservancy. Chem warfare, World War II. Fellow A.A.A.S., Am. Ornithol. Union; mem. Am. Soc. Mammalogists, Am. Soc. Ichthyology and Herpetology, Washington Environ. Council (charter); Sigma Xi. Author articles on bird musculature, also conservation. Address: Pullman, Wash. Died Aug. 4, 1974; cremated.

HUDSON, ROBERT LITTLETON, newspaper exec.; b. St. Petersburg, Fla., Oct. 4, 1925; s. Grover Cleveland and Winifred (Root) H.; student U. Ga.; m. Martha Russ, Jan. 10, 1949; 1 son, Robert Cleveland. Sports writer St. Petersburg Times, 1948-52; sports writer Tampa Tribune (Fla.), 1953-54, sports editor, 1954-59, state editor, 1960-65, asst. mng. editor, 1965-66, mng. editor, 1966-73; exec. editor Tampa Tribune-Times, 1974-75; chmn. U.P.I. Conf., 1968, v.p. AP, Fla., 1970, pres., 1971. Pulitzer prize juror, 1971, 72; Counselor U. Tampa; mem. publs. adv. com. U. South Fla., 1973. Mem. U.S.O. Council, Fla. Bd. dirs. U. South Fla. Found. Named Fla.'s Sports Writer of Year, Fla. Sports Writers Assn. 1958; recipient Tampa C. of C. Sports award, 1958. Mem. Fla. Sports Writers Assn. (pres. 1957), Sigma Delta Chi (pres. 1968). Democrat. Episcopalian. Clubs: Downtown Sertoma, Tower (Tampa); Ye Mystic Krewe of Gasparilla. Home: Tampa, Fla. Died Feb. 1975.

HUEBNER, HERBERT ALLOWAY, lawyer; b. Washington, Mar. 21, 1902; s. Francis C. and Anna (Alloway) H.; A.B., U. So. Cal., 1923, postgrad. law sch., 1923-25; m. Lorna C. Pierce, June 18, 1925; 1 son, Harlan Pierce. Admitted to Cal. bar, 1926, U.S. Supreme Ct. bar, 1934, N.Y. bar, 1936; patent counsel and pub. relations rep. Consol. Film Industries and affiliated cos., N.Y., 1930-37; gen. counsel Republic Pictures, Los Angeles, 1937; pvt. practice patent law, Los Angeles, 1938-74. Mem. Regional Export Expansion Council, 1963-64. Mem. Am., Cal. (chmn. patent conf. 1951-52), Los Angeles bar assns., Am. Patent Law Assn. Republican. Presbyn. Mason (33 deg., K.T., Shriner), Rotarian. Clubs: Jonathan, Lakeside, Eldorado Country (Palm Desert, Cal.). Contbr. articles on masonry and patriotism, patents to various publs. Home: Los Angeles Cal. Died Mar. 25, 1974.

HUETER, HANS HERBERT, govt. ofcl.; b. Bern, Switzerland, Mar. 21, 1906; s. Otto Carl and Katharina (Schelowsky) H.; M.E., Tech. Coll., Mittweide, Germany, 1927; D.Sc. (hon.), Adelphi Coll., 1959; m. Ruth Lieselotte Jeremias, Feb. 5, 1938; children—Eike, Uwe, Wendula. Came to U.S., 1945; naturalized, 1955. Design and test engr. various plants, Germany, 1927-32; project engr. rocket research Soc. for Space Travel, Berlin, 1932-34; project engr. aircraft guidance and control equipment Siemens, 1935-37; chief test engr., then project dir. for ground support systems German Missile Devel. Center, Peenemunde, 1937-45; tech. advisor Army Ordnance, White Sands Proving Grounds, 1945-47, chief flight test engr. Guided Missile Devel. Group, Fort Bliss, Tex. and Huntsville, Ala., 1947-51; dir. systems support equipment Army Ballistic Missile Agy., Huntsville, 1951-60; project dir. Centaur and Agena missile systems, NASA, Marshall Space Flight Center, 1960-62, dir. spl. assignments office, 1963, dep. dir. indsl. operation, 1964-69, dir. safety, 1969-70. Recipient Dept. of Army award for Exceptional Civilian Service, 1959; Exceptional Service medal NASA, 1969. Mem. Am. Inst. Aeronautics and Astronautics, Assn. U.S. Army. Lutheran. Home: Huntsville Ala. Died Sept. 6, 1970.

HUFFMAN, EUGENE HARVEY, chemist; b. Lawrenceburg, Ind., Dec. 5, 1905; s. Harvey Russell and Atta (Smashey) H.; A.B., U. Colo., 1927; M.S., U. Wash., 1929; Ph.D., U. Ill., 1937; m. Elizabeth Allampress Brecher, July 13, 1961. Instr. chemistry Ore. State Coll., 1929-33, U. Ky., 1936-37, U. Wis., 1937-38; asst. prof. chemistry Coll. Puget Sound, 1938-40, Kan. State Coll., 1940-41; chemist U.S. Bur. Mines, Berkeley, Cal., 1941-43; sr. staff mem. nuclear chemistry div. Lawrence Radiation Lab. U. Cal., Berkeley, 1943-73. Fellow A.A.A.S.; mem. Am. Chem. Soc. (steering com. pilot project for tng. chem. technicians 1968-73, treas. Ky. sect. 1937), Phi Beta Kappa, Sigma Xi, Phi Kappa Phi, Phi Lambda Upsilon, Alpha Chi Sigma. Club: Faculty (U. Cal. Berkeley). Mem. editorial bd. Analytical Chemistry of the Manhattan Project, 1945-50. Contbr. articles to profl. jours. Patentee in field. Home: Berkeley, Cal. Died July 16, 1973.

HUFNAGEL, FREDERICK BERNHARD, steel mfr.; b. Mt. Vernon, N.Y., Oct. 31, 1878; s. Conrad Bernhard and Mary (Imhof) H.; M.E., Cornell U., 1900; m. Ceora Wilson Thompson, June 18, 1910; children—Frederick Bernhard, Ceora J. (dec.). Began as draftsman Am. Steel & Wire Co., 1900; successively mill forman, asst. supt., supt. of rolling mills and gen. supt. Jones & Laughlin Steel Co., 1901-20; pres. Pittsburgh Crucible Steel Co., 1920-25; pres. Crucible Steel Co. Am., 1926-44, chmn. bd. 1937-44; dir. Excess Ins. Co. Am. Trustee Grove City (Pa.) Coll. Mem. Kappa Sigma. Republican. Presbyterian. Clubs: University, Cornell (New York); Duquesne, Rolling Rock (Pittsburgh); Allegheny Country (Sewickley, Pa.); Round Hill (Greenwich); Manursing Island (Rye, N.Y.). Home: Greenwich, Conn.†

HUGGARD, VINCENT P., govt. ofcl.; b. N.Y.C., Aug. 10, 1917; s. Joseph Michael and Kathryn (Kane) H.; ed. Am. U.; m. Dorothy Frances Travers, Sept. 3, 1938 (dec.); children—Thomas, Jacqueline (Mrs. David Wyatt), Sister Mary Dorothy, Michael, Karen Ann (Mrs. Ernest Mata), Paul. Mgr. army affairs RCA, 1961-62; with Dept. Army, 1940-60, 62-74, prin. dep. asst. sec. army for installations and logistics, 1967-74. Chmn. bd. advisers devel. fund Patton Mus. Served with AUS, 1944-45. Recipient Exceptional Service medal Dept. Army (3), also Distinguished Civilian Service award. Home: Bethesda, Md. Died Jan. 25, 1974.

HUGHES, DAPHNE, social worker; b. Roseburg, Ore., June 6, 1910; d. Washington and Ethel (Baty) Hughes; B.A., U. Ore., 1931; student St. Margaret's Sch. Christian Edn., 1931-32; postgrad. Bryn Mawr Coll., 1935-39, 1942-43, profl. certificate in community orgn. and group work, 1937. College worker Episcopal Ch., Northwestern U., Evanston, Ill., 1932-35; research asst. Bryn Mawr (Pa.) Coll., 1937-38; social caseworker Youth Consultation Service, Diocese of Newark, 1939-42, exec. dir., 1943-65; dir. bur. personnel and tng. Nat. Bd. YWCA, N.Y.C., 1965-73. Hon. trustee Youth Consultation Service, Newark, Children's Aid and Adoption Soc., Orange, N.J. Nat. Council on Religion in Higher Edn. Kent fellow. Mem. Acad. Certified Social Workers, Nat. Assn. Social Workers, Am. Assn. Social Workers (pres. N.J. chpt. 1943-45), Council on Social Work Edn., Am. Guidance and Personnel Assn., Acad. Religion and Mental Health. Episcopalian. Author: (with others) Man At Work in God's World, 1956. Home: New York City, N.Y. Died Aug. 28. 1973.

HUGHES, HOWARD ROBARD, industrialist, aviator, motion picture producer; b. Houston, Dec. 24, 1905; s. Howard Robard and Alene (Gano) H.; ed. Thacher Sch., Ojai, Cal., Fessenden Sch., West Newton, Mass., Rice Inst., Houston, Cal. Inst. Tech. Owner Summa Corp. (formerly Hughes Tool Co.). Houston; pres. Hughes Aircraft Co., Culver City, Cal. Trustee Howard Hughes Med. Inst. Pictures produced include Hell's Angels, Scarface, Front Page, The Outlaw. Clubs: Los Angeles Country, Wilshire Country, Lakeside Golf, Westchester Country, Aviation Country. In plane of own design established world's land plane speed record, 352 miles per hour, Sept. 13, 1935; transcontinental record, 7 hrs. 28 min., Jan. 19, 1937; world flight record, 91 hrs. 14 min. 28 sec., July 10-14, 1938; designed, built and flew World's largest plane, Nov. 2, 1947. Awarded Harmon Trophy, 1938; Collier trophy, 1939, Octave Chanute Award, 1940, Congressional Medal, 1941; named to Aviation Hall of Fame, 1973. Home: Houston, Tex. Died Apr. 5, 1976.

HUGHES, I. LAMONT; b. Mercer, Pa., Jan. 25, 1878; s. John and Mary Elizabeth (Ketler) H.; grad. high sch.; m. Elizabeth Little, 1902; 1 son, I. Lamont. Began in employ of Edgar Thomson Works of Carnegie Steel Co., Ltd., 1897; trans. to Donora (Pa.) Works of Am. Steel & Wire Co., 1901, then in 1905 to Youngstown dist. plants and also Greenville (Pa.) plants of Carnegie Steel Co.; apptd. asst. supt. all bar mills, Youngstown dist., 1906, later supt.; asst. gen. supt. Youngstown dist. plants, Jan. 1916; gen. supt. for Canadian Steel Corp., at Ojibway, Ont., Can., June 1916; gen. supt. for U.S. Steel Ordnance Co. at Neville Island, Pa., June 1918; pres. Lorain Steel Co., Johnstown, Pa., May 1919; apptd. gen. supt. Carnegie Steel Co.'s operations in Youngstown dist. 1920; elected v.p. Carnegie Steel Co., 1925; elected v.p. in charge operations U.S. Steel Corp., hdqrs. in N.Y. City 1928; elected pres. Carnegie Steel Co., 1930, exec. and dir., 1935; v.p. Carnegie-Ill. Steel Corp., 1935-36; retired from steel business; sec. Pa. Dept. of Highways; pres. and dir. Bessemer Electric Power Co., Carnegie Land Co., Conneaut Land Co., Sharon Coke Co., Carnegie Libraries (of Braddock, Homestead, and Duquesne, Pa.); dir. Carnegie Natural Gas Co.; Penn & Lake Erie Dock Co., Pittsburgh Limestone Corp., H. C. Friek Coke Co., Trotler Water Co., Nat. Mining Co., Pittsburg & Conneaut Dock Co., Pittsburg, Bessemer & Lake Erie R.R. Co., U.S. Steel and Carnegie Pension Fund, Chamber of Commerce of Pittsburgh. Sec. of Highways, State of Pa., 1939-43. Trustee Grove City Coll. (Pa.), Carnegie Hero Fund Commn.; mem. Pittsburgh Ordnance Dist. Mem. Am. Iron and Steel Inst., Engrs. Soc. of Western Pa., Mich. Soc. S.A.R. Presbyterian. Clubs: Duquesne, University, Bankers of America. Address: Butler, Pa.*†

HUGHES, J(OHN) W(ILLIAM), pres., ins. co. exec.; b. Omaha, Nov. 6, 1881; s. William H. S. and Margaret (Berlin) H.; student Central High Sch., Omaha, 1898-1902; m. Nan Barrett, Feb. 18, 1918 (divorced); 1 dau., Marian; m. 2d, Virginia Herdman, July 22, 1935. Teller Pacific Express Co., 1900-02, Omaha Nat. Bank, 1902-12; asst. sec. Guarantee Mutual Life Co., Omaha, 1912-15, pres., dir, from 1936; dir. U.S. Nat. Bank, Republican. Clubs: Field, Country, Athletic, Omaha (Omaha). Home: Omaha, Neb.*†

HUGHES, MACK F., chemist; b. Spanish Fork, Utah, June 6, 1923; s. Frank L. and Emma (Phillips) H.; B.S., Brigham Young U., 1949; M.S., U. Cin., 1951; Ph.D., U. Utah, 1954; m. Gloria Jean Bowen, Nov. 5, 1942; children—Vicki (Mrs. Bruce Wheeler Ellinger), Jan (Mrs. Edward B. Coleman), Jill, Jack Bowen. Asso. research chemist Chevron Research Co. subsidiary Standard Oil Co. of Cal., Richmond, Cal., 1954-56, research chemist, 1956-62, sr. research chemist, 1962-68, sr. research asso., 1968-73. Served with USAAF, 1942-45. Decorated Air medal. Mem. A.A.A.S., Am. chem. Soc., Sigma Xi, Phi Lambda Upsilon. Mem. Ch. of Jesus Christ of Latter-day Saints (bishop council 1955-60, 72-73). Contbr. articles to profl. jours. Patentee in field. Home: Albany, Cal. Died Dec. 1973; interred Spanish Fork City Cemetery.

HUGHES, REES HOPKINS, coll. pres.; b. Fort Scott, Kan., June 9, 1892; s. William and Elizabeth (Hopkins) H.; A.B., Washburn Coll. (Topeka), 1913; student Kan. State Coll., 1913-14; A.M., Columbia, 1931; LL.D., Washburn Municipal U., 1942; m. Isabel Savage, Aug. 28, 1917; children—Marian Elizabeth (Mrs. Robert Shubb), William David, Janet Isabel (Mrs. Robert Carpenter). Rural tchr. Bourbon County, Kan., 1908-09; high sch. teacher Fort Scott, Kan., 1913-17; prin. Fort Scott and Parsons, Kan., high sch., 1917-21; city supt., Parsons, Kan., 1922-41; summer school faculty, Kan. State Tchrs. Coll., 1937, 39-41, pres. 1941-57, emeritus, 1957. State Text Book Commn., 1940-41; exec. com. Am. Assn. Colls. for Tchr. Edn. Rep. U.S. to seminar on International Edn., Paris, 1948; mem. U.S. Nat. Commn. on UNESCO; mem. President's Com. on Education Beyond High School; mem. Adv. Com. on Federal Coll. Student Housing, State Bd. Vocational Edn., 1940-41; bd. dirs. Coll. Emporia; mem. commn. higher edn. N. Central Assn., chmn., 1952. Mem. Kan. Ho. of Reps., 6 terms. Named One of Ten Most Outstanding Citizens in Kan., Kan. Fedn. Labor- AFL-CIO, 1961; Kansan of Year, 1963. Mem. Am. Assn. Coll. Teacher Edn. (pres. 1956-57), Kan. State Teachers Assn. (pres. 1930), Kan. State Jr. Coll. Assn. (pres. 1926-29), N.E.A., Am. Assn. Sch. Adminstrs., Kan. Acad. Sci., Horace Mann League, C. of C. (pres. 1944, bd. dirs. 1943-54), Kan. Schoolmasters Club (pres. 1943), Kappa Sigma, Kappa Delta Pi, Sinfonia (hon.), Sagamore (hon.), Tau Delta Pi (hon.). Presbyn. (elder). (pres. 1944, bd. dirs. 1943-54), Kan. Schoolmasters Club (pres. 1943). Rotarian (past pres.), Elk. Contbr. ednl. jours. Home: Pittsburg, Kan. Died Nov. 10, 1973.

HUGHES, ROBERT HUGH, editor; b. Cambria, Columbia Co., Wis., July 19, 1880; s. William E. and Ellen (Roberts) H.; ed. U. of Puget Sound, Tacoma, Wash.; Willamette U., Salem, Ore.; m. Mary M. Rader, June 14, 1905. Mgr. 1906-11, editor, 1911-20, Pacific Christion Advocate; publishing agent, M.E. Book Concern, Chgo., from 1920. Mem. Gen. Conf. M.E. Ch., 1916, 1920. Mason. Address: Chicago, Ill.†

HUGHEY, ALLEN HARRISON, supt. of schs.; b. nr. Fayetteville, Tenn., July 14, 1881; s. Alonzo Nicholas and Elnora (Reese) H.; A.B., Vanderbilt U., 1903; LL.B., George Washington U., 1908; m. Bess Lee Caruthers, Oct. 31, 1906; 1 son, Allen Harrison. Began as rural sch. teacher, 1898; pres. Weatherford (Tex.) Coll., 1903-06; editorial work U.S. Geol. Survey, Washington, D.C., 1906-09; admitted to Tex. bar, 1909; in practice at El Paso, 1909-13; prin. High Sch., El Paso, 1914-18, supt., schs., 1919-51; pres. Consultants, Inc., from 1951; established jr. coll., 1920. Home: El Paso, Tex.†

HUHN, JOHN ERNEST, ins. co. exec.; b. Christus, Germany, May 8, 1880; s. Charles August and Christell (Koellman) H.; brought to U.S., 1882; ed. high sch. and business coll., Louisville, Ky.; m. Emma Wilhelmina Hatzfeld, May 10, 1902 (died Jan. 19, 1931); 1 dau., Artus June (Mrs. Herman A. Scheer). With Liberty Bank & Trust Co., Louisville, 1895-1935, advancing through various positions to president, 1927; v.p. and dir. Advitagraph Corpn.; now conducts gen. ins. business; v.p. Lieber-Huhn Co., Inc (ins.); mem. Louisville Bd. Fire Underwriters. Royal Arch. Mason,

Elk, Moose. Clubs: Pendennis, Audubon Country (Louisville); Wonderland Park Club (Elkmont, Tenn.). Home: Louisville, Ky.†

HUKRIEDE, THEODORE W., congressman; b. Warren Co., Mo., Nov. 9, 1878; s. F. H. and Caroline (Drunert) H.; Central Wesleyan Coll., Mo., 1901-02, U. of Mo., 1902-03; m. Edyth M. Speed, of New Truxton, Mo., May 16, 1904; children—Theodore P., Herbert S., Malcolm. Admitted to Mo. bar, 1903, and began practice at Warrenton; pros. atty. Warren Co., 3 terms, 1905-10; probate judge, 1910-20; mem. 67th Congress (1921-23), 9th Mo. Dist.; U.S. marshal, eastern dist. of Mo., from 1923. Del. Rep. Nat. Conv., 1916; chmn. Rep. State Com., 1916-18. Methodist. Home: Warrenton, Mo.†

HULL, JAMES MERIWETHER, lawyer; b. Augusta, Ga., Oct. 6, 1885; s. James Meriwether and Mary Baldwin (Lyon) H.; student U. of South, U. Ga., U. Va.; m. Marion Stewart Phinizy, Nov. 10, 1909; children—Stewart Phinizy, Mary (Mrs. Darwin H. Boyd), James Meriwether (dec.). Admitted to Ga. bar, 1907, later practiced in Augusta; sr. mem. firm. Hull, Towill, Norman, Barrett & Johnson, 1922-75. Dir. Augusta Rialto Co.; asso. dir. Central of Ga. R.R. Co. Former pres. Met. Augusta Found., Ga.-Carolina council Boy Scouts Am., YMCA; hon. pres. Jr. Achievement Augusta. Served as 1st lt. U.S. Army, World War I. Fellow Am. Bar Found., Am. Coll. Trial Lawyers; mem. Phi Delta Phi, Delta Tau Delta. Episcopalian (sr. warden). Rotarian (charter pres. Augusta). Clubs: Augusta Nat. Golf, Augusta Country, Pinnacle. Home: Augusta, Ga., Died Apr. 17, 1975.

HULL, JOHN EDWIN, army officer; b. Greenfield, O., May 26, 1895; s. Jospeh Milton and Mary Ann (Mealey) H.; A.B., Miami University, Oxford, Ohio, 1917; LL.D. (honorary), 1954; graduate Co. officers course, Inf. Sch., 1924, advanced course, 1932, Command and Gen. Staff Sch., 1936, Army War Coll., 1938; D. Mil. Sci., Pa. Mil. Coll., 1953; m. Sara Lucile Davis, Aug. 21, 1919. Commd. 2d lt., inf., U.S. Army, Aug. 15, 1917, advanced through grades to general; permanent brig. gen., October 1945, permanent maj. gen., Jan. 24, 1948, with date rank from July 7, 1942; chief Theatre Group, Operations Div., Gen. Staff, 1942-44; asst. chief staff Operations div., 1944-46, Plans and Operations Div., 1946; comdg. gen. Army Forces, Pacific and Hawaiian Dept., 1946-48, also comdr. Joint Task Force 7, (first atomic weapons test, Eniwetok), Oct. 1947-June 48; comdg. gen. U.S. Army Pacific, 1948-49; dir. Weapons Systems Evaluation Group, Office Sec. Def., Washington, 1949-51; dep. chief staff for operations and adminstrn., A.U.S., Washington, Jan.-Aug. 1951, vice chief of staff, 1951-53; comdr. in chief UN Forces Far East, also comdr. in chief Far East Command, comdg. gen. Army Forces Far East, and gov. Kyukyu Islands, 1953-55; ret., 1955. Elected pres. Mfg. Chemists Assn., 1955. Decorated D.S.M. with 3 oak leaf clusters, Silver Star, Legion of Merit, Army of Occupation of Germany (World War I), Victory Medal (World War I with 4 battle clasps, and World War II), Am. Theatre, European-N. African-Middle East, Nat. Def., Korean Service medals, (U.S.); United Nations Service medal; Hon. Comdr. Order Brit. Empire; Knight Comdr. Liberian Order of African Redemption; Grand Cordon of Yun-Hui (China); Grand Officer Order of Mil. Merit (Brazil); Comdr. Philippine Legion of Honor; comdr. Mil. Order Ayacucho (Peru); Grand Ofcl. Order of Boyaca (Colombia); Most Exalted Order of White Elephant, 1st class (Thailand); Order of Mil. Taeguk with Gold Star (Korea); Grand Cordon of Order of Rising Sun (Japan); Grand Cross of Phoenix (Greece); Legion of Honor (France); Grand Ofcl. Order al Merit. (Italy). Mem. Am. Legion Vets. Wars, Phi Delta Theta. Mason, Elk. Clubs: Metropolitan (Washington); Chevy Chase; Links, Chemists (N.Y.C.). Home: Washington D.C. Died June 10, 1975; buried Arlington Nat. Cemetery, Arlington, Va.

HULL, WILLIAM CHASE, ry. official; b. Bond Hill, Cincinnati, O., Sept. 8, 1880; s. Charles Thomas and Elizabeth (Chase) H.; ed. pub. schools of Cincinnati; m. Naomi Ellis Riley, Apr. 21, 1909; children—Kathryn (Mrs. W. E. Graves), Theo Frances (Mrs. F. M. Davis). Steongrapher B.&O. R.R., Cincinnati, 1895-97; sec. to asst. freight traffic mgr., chief clerk to v.p., asst. to v.p. in charge of traffic C.&O. Ry., and Hocking Valley Ry., 1897-1918; asst. to mgr. of inland fuel traffic, U.S. R.R. Adminstrn., 1918-20; asst. to v.p. in charge of traffic C.& O. Ry. and Hocking Valley Ry., 1920-28; asst. v.p. in charge traffic C.&O. Ry., 1928-37; v.p. in charge of traffic C.&O. Ry. and Pere Marquette Ry., 1937-47, ret., 1947; v.p. Cincinnati Inter-Terminal R.R., Covington & Cincinnati Elevated R.R. & Transfer & Bridge Co. Republican. Methodist. Clubs: Chicago Traffic; Hillandale (Corinth, Miss.). Home: Corinth, Miss.†

HULSWIT, CHARLES LOUIS, utility exec.; b. Grand Rapids, Mich., Aug. 12, 1901; s. Frank T. and Cornelia (Hobeke) H.; B.S. in Elec. Engring., U. Mich., 1925; m. Elsie Bishop, Nov. 8, 1947 (dec. 1955); 1 son, Frank T. Engr. Peoples Power Co., 1925-29; constrn. engr. Am. Commonwealth Power Co., 1929; v.p. Rockland Gas Co., 1930-37, pres., 1937-52; v.p. Orange & Rockland Utilities, Inc., Nyack, N.Y., 1953; pres., from 1953, also dir. company and subsidiaries; member board of directors Brockton-Tauton Gas Company, First Nat. Bank of Spring Valley, N.Y., Dynamics Corp. Am. Mem. exec. com. Rockland County council Boy Scouts Am.; chmn. adv. com. Good Samaritan Hosp., Suffern, N.Y. Mem. Am. Gas Assn., Sigma Xi, Tau Beta Pi. Home: West Nyack, N.Y. Died Sept. 26, 1974.

HUME, DAVID MILFORD, physician; b. Muskegon, Mich., Oct. 21, 1917; s. Wallace C. and Fay (Hill) H.; B.S., Harvard, 1940; M.D., U. Chgo., 1943; m. Martha Emily Egloff, May 2, 1943; children—Susan (Mrs. Richard Atkinson), Joan (Mrs. Scott Kammire), Martha (Mrs. Ben Saunders), Jeffrey. Surg. intern Peter Bent Brigham Hosp., Boston, 1943-44, asst. resident in surgery, 1944-45, 46-47, chief resident, 1950-51, jr. asso. in surgery, 1951-55, asso. in surgery, 1955-56; asst. in surgery Harvard Med. Sch., Boston, 1944-45, 46-48, Harvey Cushing fellow, 1948-50, instr. surgery, 1950-51, 51-55, dir. Lab. for Surg. Research, 1951-56, Henry E. Warren fellow in surgery, 1951-52; Am. Cancer Soc. cancer research scholar, 1952-53, 55-56; Stuart McGuire prof. surgery, chmn. dept. surgery Med. Coll. Va., Va. Commonwealth U., Richmond, 1956-73. Past mem. program project com. Nat. Heart Inst.; past mem. nephrology planning com. and surgery study sect. NIH; past mem. adv. bd. AEC; past mem. task force com. Nat. Kidney Found.; mem. adv. group on renal transplants VA; Harvey lect., 1969. Served to lt. (j.g.), M.C., USNR, 1945-46; to lt. comdr., 1953-54. Co-recipient Francis Amory prize Am. Acad. Arts and Scis., 1962, Valentine award N.Y. Acad. Medicine, 1970; named Outstanding Harvard Alumnus of State of Va., 1968; recipient Humanitarian award Richmond chpt. Hadassah, 1971, Distinguished service medal U. Chgo., 1971, Distinguished Achievement award Modern Medicine mag., 1972. Diplomate Am. Bd. Surgery. Fellow A.C.S.; mem. A.A.A.S., A.M.A., Am. Soc. Clin. Investigation, Am. Soc. Exptl. Pathology, Am., So. surg. assns., Pan Am., Va., Richmond, Boston surg. socs., Endocrine Soc., Halsted Soc., Internat. Congress Nephrology, Internat Transplantation Soc., N.Y. Acad. Scis., Richmond Acad. Medicine, Soc. Exptl. Biology and Medicine, Soc. Univ. Surgeons, Surg. Biology Club, Soc. for Vascular Surgery, Soc. Clin. Surgery, Va. Med. Soc., Soc. Surg. Chairmen. Author: Principles of Surgery, 1969; Harvey Lectures, Series 64, 1970. Research on renal homotransplantation, hypothalmic-pituitary-adrenal relationships. Home: Richmond, Va. Died May 19, 1973; buried Mass.

HUMMEL, ARTHUR WILLIAM, historian; b. Warrenton, Mo., Mar. 6, 1884; s. William Frederick and Caroline Wilhelmina (Wehking) H.; A.B., University of Chicago, 1909, M.A., 1911, B.D., 1914, and Doctor of Philosophy, University of Leyden, Netherlands, 1931; married Ruth Emma Bookwalter, Oct. 8, 1914; children—Carol Emily, Arthur William, Jr., Sharman Bookwalter. Teacher, Kobe University, Japan, 1912-14; teacher of English, Ming-i Middle School, Fenchow, Shansi, China, 1915-24; lecturer in Chinese history, Yenching Sch. of Chinese Studies, Peiping, China, 1924-27, Columbia, 1930-32; dir. Far Eastern Seminar, Harvard Univ., 1932, U. of Calif., Berkeley, 1934, 37; lecturer in Chinese history, Columbia U., Far Eastern Seminar, 1935, Univ. of Colo., 1940; chief of Div. of Orientalia, Library of Congress, 1927-54; Guggenheim Fellowship, 1954-56; lectr. Am. U., Washington, 1954-63; lecturer George Washington Univ., 1963; vis. prof. U. Tex., 1956, Mich. State U., 1956. Mem. Am. Philos. Soc., Am. Council Learned Socs. (chairman Committee for Promotion of Chinese Studies 1930-34), American Oriental Society (president 1940) and Royal Asiatic Society, Literary Soc. of Washington, Far Eastern Assn. (pres. 1948). Mem. Society of Friends. Club: Cosmos. Author: The Autobiography of a Chinese Historian, 1931. Editor: Eminent Chinese of the Ch'ing Period, 1943. Contributor to journals. Home: Washington, D.C. Died Mar. 10, 1975.

HUMPHREY, GEORGE DUKE, educator; b. Tippah County, Miss., Aug. 30, 1897; s. John Washington and Louis Isoble (Cheeves) H.; grad. State Tchrs. Coll., Hattiesburg, Miss., 1922; B.A., Blue Mountain (Miss.) Coll., 1929; M.A., U. Chgo., 1931; Ph.D., Ohio State U., 1939; LL.D., Ohio Wesleyan U., 1959, U. Wyo., 1964; Litt.D., U. Ariz., 1962; m. Josephine Robertson, Apr. 15, 1925 (dec. Sept. 1971); 1 son, John Julius. Began as pub. sch. tchr. in Miss.; later prin. consol. sch., 3 sessions; supt. Ripley (Miss.) Sch. Dist., 4 sessions; prin. Agrl. High Sch., Tippah County, 1923; county supt. edn., Tippah County, 1924-30; supt. city schs., Kosciuko, Miss., 1931-32; high sch. supr. State of Miss., 1932-33; pres. Miss. State Coll., 1934-45; pres. U. Wyo., 1945-64, pres. emeritus, 1964, adminstr. Sch. Am. Studies, 1964-68; instr. in edn. Furman U., Greenville, S.C., summer 1932; local dir. 4 state summer normals Blue Mountain Coll.; instr. history Miss. summer normals, 3 years. Mem. State Vocational Bd.; pres. Southeastern Athletic Conf., 1938-40, mem. exec. com., 1937-40, 43-45; cons. to adv. panel on regional materials of instrn. TVA, 1941-44; mem. Nat. Commn. on Accrediting, 1961-64, pub. mem. Regional War Labor Bd., 1943-45; pres. So. Assn. Colls. and Secondary Schools, 1942-45, chmn. postwar ednl. com., 1944-45; cons. edn. policies commn. N.E.A., 1936-48; mem. exec. com. Assn. Land Grant Colls., 1944-46, mem. com. on irrigated agr. and water resources, 1948-56, chmn., 1948-55; mem. bd. NSF, 1950-62; spl. cons. on reorgn. Bur. Entomology and Plant Quarantine, U.S. Dept. of Agr., 1951; adviser U.S. Dept. Interior on saline water program, 1952-62; cons. reorgn. saline water div., 1958; chmn. Western Interstate Commn. for Higher Edn., 1954-55; chmn. Freedom Found. Award Jury, 1954. Mem. N.E.A., Am. Assn. Sch. Adminstrs., Assn. Adult Edn., Miss. Edn. Assn. (mem. legislative com. 1928-45, dir. 1929-32, pub. relations com., 1935-40, vocations commn. 1943-45), Miss Forestry and Chemurgic Assn. (dir. 1944-45), Miss. County Supts. Assn. (past chmn.), Miss. City Sch. Supts. Assn. (dir. 1931-32), Miss. Assn. Colls., (pres. 1940-41), Am. Council on Edn. (com. on So. regional studies and edn. 1944-45), Am. Assn. for Adult Edn. (mem. exec. council 1946), Wyo. Edn. Assn. (mem. exec. com. 1945), Nat. Assn. State Univs. (chmn. mil. affairs com. 1947-48, v.p. 1959-60, pres. 1960-61), Assn. Land Grant Colls. and Univs. (chmn. council, pres. 1956-57), Assn. Am. Colls. (dir. 1954-61, v.p. 1958, pres. 1959), Scabbard and Blade, Iota Lambda, Sigma Kappa Sigma, Blue Key, Omicron Delta Kappa, Phi Delta Kappa. Methodist. Mason (K.T., Shriner). Clubs: Cosmos, Laramie Country, Denver. Address: Laramie, Wyo. Died Sept. 10, 1973.

HUMPHREY, HARRY JASPER, railroad exec.; b. Berry's Mills, New Brunswick, Can., Jan. 26, 1879; s. Isaac B. and Janet (Walker) H.; ed. pub. schs., New Brunswick, Can.; m. Maude Thibadeau, May 3, 1905 (died Apr. 1938); children—Jack B., Lyle W.; m. 2d, Lenore Lyle, Oct. 25, 1941. Telegraph operator, Intercolonial Ry., 1896-97 and 1901-02, Boston & Maine Ry., 1897-1901; with Canadian Pacific Ry. from 1902, beginning as telegraph operator and advancing through various positions being apptd. vice pres. Eastern Lines operations 1934, v.p. assigned to special duties, Oct. 1944; dir. Conn. & Passumsic Rivers R.R., Massawippi Valley Ry. Co., Brit. Northwestern Fire Ins. Co., Security Nat. Ins. Co., North Am. Life Assurance Co., Crown Trust Co., Mem. Montreal and Toronto boards of trade. Pres. nat. council Y.M.C.A. of Canada, Clubs: St. James (Montreal); Rideau (Ottawa); National, Canadian, Granite, British Empire, Rotary (Toronto); Union (Saint John, N.B.). Home: Montreal, Que., Can.†

HUMPHREY, NINA S., educator; b. Richfield, O. Nov. 18, 1880; d. Truman and Alida (Hale) Humphrey; studied Oberlin Coll., 1905. Cleveland Sch. of Art, 1908-10, Chicago Acad., 1911, U. of Chicago, 1912; S.A.E., Cleveland Sch. Art, 1930; A.M., Western Reserve, 1932; European travel, 1925. Art supervisor Cuyahoga Falls, 1905-08. Oak Park, Ill., 1911-13; head dept. art Kent State Univ., 1913-44; prof. art, from 1944. Mem. N.E.A., Western Art Assn., Ohio Art Assn. Home: Cuyahoga Falls, O.†

HUNSICKER, WILLIAM COSGROVE, JR., physician; b. Phila., Mar. 16, 1902; s. William Cosgrove and Cornelia (Higbee) H.; M.D., Hahnemann Med. Coll. and Hosp., 1927; m. Helen Mae Wilson, July 23, 1928; children—Suzanne (Mrs. Thomas Late Altshuler), Judith (Mrs. John Carpenter Burr), William Cosgrove III. Intern, Hahnemann Med. Coll. and Hosp., Phila., 1927-28, chief resident in surgery, 1928-29, asso. prof. urology, head dept. urology, prof., trustee, prof. emeritus; urol. staff Crozer Hosp., Chester, Pa., Germantown Hosp., Phila., St. Lukes Hosp., Childrens Hosp.; cons. VA Hosp., Phila.; head sect. B-urology Phila. Gen. Hosp. Diplomate Am. Bd. Urology. Fellow A.C.S., Internat. Coll. Surgeons; mem. A.M.A., Am. Urol. Assn., Pa., County med. socs. Republican. Presbyn. Club: Union League (Phila). Home: North East, Md. Died Mar. 18, 1974; buried West Laurel Hill Cemetery, Phila.

HUNT, CHARLES WESLEY, prof. education; b. North Charlestown, N.H., Oct. 20, 1880; s. Wesley Abel and Rosie Jane (Bailey) H.; A.B., Brown, 1904; A.M., Columbia, 1910, Ph.D., 1924; m. Helen Elizabeth True, Aug. 8, 1912 (died Mar. 23, 1914); 1 son, Gordon Ellsworth; m. 2d, Edna Margaret Klaer, June 5, 1915; children—Margaret Klaer, Mary Katherine, John David. Teacher Vermont Academy, Saxton's River, 1904-06, Moses Brown School, Providence, R.I., 1906-08; grade teacher, the Horace Mann School, N.Y. City, 1908-09; supervising prin. Briarcliff Manor, N.Y., 1910-13; supervisor of grades, N.Y. City, 1913-14; asst. sec. Teachers Coll., Columbia, 1914-16; vice prin. Horace Mann Sch., 1918-21; instr. in elementary edn., Teachers Coll., Columbia, 1918-21; dir. extra mural instrn., U. of Pittsburgh, 1922-24; dean of Cleveland (O.) Sch. of Edn., 1924-28; prof. edn. and dean of Sch. of Edn., Western Reserve, 1928-33; pres. State Teachers Coll., Oneonta, N.Y., 1933-51. Mem. Department Superintendence of N.E.A., Am. Assn. Colls. for Tchr. Edn. (sec.-treas.), Phi Delta Kappa, Kappa Delta Pi. Republican. Methodist. Mason. Author: Costs of Secondary Schools in New York State, 1924; Everyday Reading (3 books, with Henry Carr Pearson), 1927. Home: Oneonta N.Y. Died Sept. 3, 1973.

HUNT, HAROLDSON LAFAYETTE, oil producer; b. Vandalia, Ill.; m. Lyda Bunker (dec. May 1955); m. 2d Ruth Ray, Nov. 1957. Founder, pres. Hunt Oil Co. Established Facts Forum; sponsor Life Line, radio program. Producing radio and TV programs on nat. issues. Democrat. Baptist. Author 14 books. Address: Dallas, Tex. Died Nov. 29, 1974; buried Hillcrest Meml. Park, Dallas, Tex.

HUNT, HENRY THOMAS, lawyer; b. Cincinnati, O., Apr. 29, 1878; s. Samuel Pancoast and Martha (Trotter) H.; A.B., Yale, 1900; LL.B., Cincinnati Law Sch., 1903; m. Thomasa Haydock, Oct. 18, 1906; children—Barbara, Henry Thomas, Samuel; m. 2d, Eleanor Mix, d. Dr. Abel M. Phelps, Sept. 22, 1925; children—Phelps, James. Admitted to Ohio bar, 1903; member Ohio House of Rep., 1906, 07; active in securing elective reforms; pros. atty. Hamilton County, 1908-11; mayor of Cincinnati, 1912-14; apptd. mem. bd. trustees Cincinnati Southern Ry. (owned by city), Feb. 1915. Episcopalian. Attended R.O.T.C., Ft. Benjamin Harrison, Ind., 1917; commd. 1st lt., Inf., N.A., Aug. 15, 1917, capt., Dec. 17, 1917; maj., May 1918; A.E.F., Sept. 24, 1918-Jan. 25, 1919; mem. War Dept. Claims Bd., Mar. 28, 1917-Aug. 1919; mem. War Dept. Bd. Contract Adjustment, Washington, D.C., Aug. 26, 1919-Apr. 15, 1920; mem. R.R. Labor Board, Apr. 15, 1920-Apr. 15, 1921 asso. counsel legislative investigation, N.Y. City, 1931; apptd. gen. counsel Federal Emergency Adminstration Pub. Works, 1933; acting gen. counsel Bituminous Coal Commn., 1936; spl. legal adviser to sec. of the Interior, 1937; gen. counsel Marketing Laws Survey, Works Progress Adminstrn., 1938-39; spl. legal adviser Fed. Works Agency, 1939-40, special asst. to gen. counsel, from 1941; trial examiner Wages and Hours Div., 1940-41; retired from govt. service, Feb. 1947. As legal officer of FWA aided in drafting title V of War Mobilization and Reconversion Act of 1944 (advance planning); tried to save National Planning Board by combining it with FWA. Home: Edgewater, Md.†

HUNT, JOE BYRON, state ofcl.; b. Mammoth Spring, Ark., Jan. 23, 1907; s. John Fisher and Iuka (Woodall) H.; student Okla. U., 1927-28; m. Anna Maude Dial, Oct. 8, 1935; 1 dau., Jo Ann. Ins. agt., Edna, Tex. until 1942; mgr. rating dept. Okla. Ins. Bd., 1942-54, pres., from 1955; commr. Okla. Ins. Dept., Oklahoma City, from 1955. Chief ins. man Chickasaw Nation of Indians, from 1960. Mem. Okla. Burial Bd., from 1955; state dir. Firemens Relief and Pension Fund, Policeman's Pension and Retirement System, Motor Vehicle Assigned Risk Plan, from 1955; mem. Okla. Hwy. Safety Coordinating Com.; hon. lt. gov., Okla., from 1960. Dist. vice chmn. Last Frontier council Boy Scouts Am., asst. on exec. com. Oklahoma City United Fund, 1959. Mem. Seminole (Okla.) City Council, 1935. Bd. dirs. Jane Brooks Sch. for Deaf; trustee Okla. Fire Fighter Museum. Recipient Oscar, Iota Nu Sigma, 1957; Citation for Meritorious Service, Employment for Physically Hanidcapped, 1957; Distinguished Service award Gov.'s Com. on Employment of Handicapped, 1970; Distinguished Service award Okla. Rehab. Assn., 1970; named Boss of Yr., Galatea chpt. Am. Bus. Women's Assn., 1971-72. Mem. Nat. Assn. Ins. Commrs. (fed. liaison com., zone 5 chmn. 1960-73), Profl. Fire Ins. Soc., Internat. Assn. Fire Chiefs, Okla. Retired Firemen's Assn. (hon. life), Fedn. Ins. Council, Am. Assn. U. Tchrs. Ins., Oklahoma City C. of C. Presbyn. (past pres., trustee). Lion (charter). Home: Oklahoma City, Okla., Died Feb. 8, 1975.

HUNT, RALPH LESLIE, educator; b. East Pittston, Me., May 15, 1880; s. Henry Washburn and Emma Louise (Thompson) H.; A.B., Bates Coll., 1903; A.M., Colby College, 1930; Ed.D., Univ. of Maine, 1937; m. Sadie McCullough, June 19, 1912; 1 dau., Elizabeth Louise. Instr. in science, high sch., Calais, 1903; prin. same, 1904-06; prin. Dawson County High Sch.; Glendive, Mont., 1906-20; prof. physics, U. of Mont., summer 1917; prin. high sch., Caribou, Me., 1920-21; asst. mgr. Range Div., Edison Electric Appliance Co., Chicago, Ill., 1921-22; prin. Hebron (Me.) Acad., 1922-43; teacher mathematics, Stephens High Sch.; retired, 1948. Mem. N.E.A., Me. Teachers' Assn., Me. Prins.' Assn. Republican. Mason Club: Kiwanis. Home: Thomaston, Me.†

HUNTER, CHARLES FRANCIS, educator; b. Morely, Mo., Oct. 24, 1913; s. John Jackson and Nancy (McMullin) H.; B.S., in Edn., A.B., S.E. Mo. State Coll., Cape Girardeau, 1935; Ph.M., U. Wis., 1937; Ph.D., Cornell U., 1942; m. Virginia Ann Ricker, June 18, 1944; children—Stephen, Andrew, Timothy, Julie. Asst. prof. speech U. Mo., 1942-44; dir. radio U. Mo. at Kansas City, 1945-47; asst. prof. radio Northwestern U., 1947, prof., chmn. dept. radio-TV-film, 1958-75; edn. producer NBC, Chgo., 1952-64; area coordinator Midwest program airborne TV, Lafayette, Ind., 1961-64; joint prof. end. Sch. Edn., Northwestern U., 1964-75; scon. in field, 1960-75. Recipient 1st award (for Live and Learn) Inst. Edn. by Radio-TV, Ohio State U., 1954. Mem. Speech Assn. Am., Central States Speech Assn., Assn. Profl. Broadcast Edn., Internat. Broadcasters Soc. (adv. bd. editors). Author articles in field. Home: Northfield, Ill., Died Nov. 19, 1975.

HUNTER, FREDERICK MAURICE, educator; b. Savannah, Mo., Mar. 24, 1879; s. Theodore F. and Frances M. (Tatlock) H.; A.B., U. of Neb., 1905 (Phi Beta Kappa), LL.D., 1939; mem. Intercoll. debating teams, 1902, 03; A.M., Columbia, 1919; Ed.D., U. of Calif., 1925; LL.D., Colo. Coll., 1930, U. of Colo., 1932; m. Emma Estelle Schreiber, 1907; children—Arthur Frances, Maurice Harold. Supt. of schools, Fairmont, Ashland and Norfolk, Neb., 1905-11; prof. agrl. edn. and prin. U. of Neb. Sch. of Agr., 1911-12; supt. city schs., Lincoln, 1912-17; supt. schs., Oakland, Calif., 1917-28; chancellor University of Denver, 1928-35; chancellor Oregon State System of Higher Education, 1935-46, honorary chancellor from 1946. Lecturer summer sessions, Teachers College (Columbia), 1918-19, inter-session and summer session, U. of Calif., 1923, 24, 25. Pres. N.E.A., 1920-21; chmn. Com. of 100 of N.E.A. for investigation of teacher tenure in U.S., 1923-28; mem. Ednl. Policy Com. of N.E.A. 1935-44; v.p., mem. bd. dirs. Calif. State Teachers' Assn., 1923-28. Mem. Curriculum Commn. State Dept. of Education of California, 1927-28; trustee Foundation for Advancement of Social Sciences, Univ. of Denver, 1928-35; mem. bd. dirs. Mountain States Telephone and Telegraph Co., 1934-35; mem. State Advisory Bd. for Oregon, Nat. Youth Aminstrn., 1935-39. Mem. Phi Delta Kappa. Kappa Delta Pi. Omicron Delta Kappa, Chi Phi. Republican. Conglist. Mason (33°, Scottish Rite), Rotarian. Club: University (Portland). Author: Teacher Tenure Legislation in the United States; (with staff) Books of Standards for the Erection of School Buildings (3 vols.); "Education for Citizenship in a Reorganized World"; also numerous ednl. papers. Address: Eugene, Ore.†

HUNTER, HOWARD LOUIS, coll. dean; b. Fulton, N.Y., June 17, 1904; s. Robert Bates and Belle Madeleine (Mosher) H.; Chem. B., Cornell U., 1925, Ph.D. (Heckscher research fellow 1927-28), 1928; student Mass. Inst. Tech., 1939; m. Roxana Williams Eaton, Oct. 19, 1932; children—Nancy Roxana (Mrs. James E. Padgett), Robert Eaton. Asst. prof. chemistry Clemson Coll., 1928-31, acting prof. textile chemistry, 1931-32, asso. prof., head inorganic chemistry div., 1932-41, prof. chemistry, 1945-46, prof. chemistry, dean Sch. Chemistry and Geology, 1946-55; dean Coll. Arts and Scis., Clemson U., 1955-69; councilor Oak Ridge Inst. Nuclear Studies, 1952-69. Served with C.W.S. in Devel. lab. Mass. Inst. Tech., 1941-45; lt. col. Chem. Corps Res. Fellow A.A.A.S., Am. Inst. Chemists; mem. S.C. Acad. Sci., Am. Chem. Soc. (councilor Western Carolinas sect.), Sigma Xi, Phi Kappa Phi, Phi Kappa Psi, Alpha Chi Sigma. Presbyn. Club: Fellowship, S.C. Forum. Author: Laboratory Manual in General Chemistry, 1947. Contbr. articles in tech. mags. Researcher on rare element chemistry. Home: Clemson, S.C. Died Mar. 27, 1975; buried Cemetery Hill, Clemson.

HUNTER, JAMES JOSEPH, banker; b. Barrie, Ont., Can., Aug. 30, 1881; s. James McFie and Sarah Jane (McConkey) H.; ed. public schools of Barrie, Ont.; m. Vivian Hinson Macneill, Dec. 11, 1907; children—James Chester, Rex Alexander, Gordon Macneill, Isobel Vivian. Came to U.S., 1919, naturalized, 1929. With Canadian Bank of Commerce in various places, Can., 1898-1911; in business, Vancouver, B.C., 1911-15; with Bank of Montreal, Vancouver, 1915-19; asst. mgr. Park-Union Foreign Banking Corp., San Francisco, 1919-22; with The Bank of Calif. N.A., San Francisco, president, 1933-49; retired, director Newhall, Land & Farming Company, White Investment Company, Cypress Law Cemetery Association, E. H. Edwards Co. Clubs: Pacific-Union, Stock Exchange, (all San Francisco). Home: San Mateo, Cal.†

HUNTINGTON, ALBERT TRACY, librarian; b. College Hill, O., Mar. 8, 1878; s. William Coit and S. Louise (Monreo) H.; Mt. Holly (N.J.) Acad., 1889-90; Kimball Union Acad., N.H.; grad. Norwich (Conn.) Free Acad., 1895; took entrance examination to Yale; m. Mrs. Gertrude Westfall Childs, May 24, 1914. Assistant general mgr. The Macmillan Co., New York, 1895-96; asst. librarian, New York Acad. Medicine, 1897-99; librarian, Med. Soc. Co. of Kings, 1899-1917; in pub. business in own name, etc.; editor The AEsculapian. Mem. A.L.A., N.Y. Library Club, L.I. Library Club (ex-pres.). Clubs: City, Baltusrol Golf, Essex County Country. Author of many monographs on med. library administration, etc.; writer of songs and pianoforte music. State dir. speakers' bur. War Savings Com., N.J., 1918-19. Home: South Orange, N.J.†

HUNTINGTON, ANNA HYATT, (MRS ARCHER M. HUNTINGTON), sculptor; b. Cambridge, Mass., Mar. 10, 1876; d. Alpheus and Audella (Beebe) Hyatt; ed. pvt. sch. the Misses Smith, Cambridge, Art Students' League, N.Y.C.; pupil of H.A. McNiel and Gutzon Borglum; D.F.A., Syracuse U., 1932; m. Archer M. Huntington, 1923. Works include small bronzes, in over 200 museums and art galleries including Don Quixote, N.Y.C.; stag, Oglesby Park, Wheeling, W.Va.; Don Quixote, also Stallions, Brookgreen Gardens, S.C.; Stallions, San Marcos, Tex.; Torchbearers statue, Madrid, Spain, 1955; Torch Bearers statue, Havana, Cuba, 1956; Sybil Ludington statue, Carmel, N.Y., 1961; Lincoln statue, Worlds Fair, N.Y.C., 1964-65. Hon. mention, Paris Salon, 1910; recipient many awards and prizes 1910-40; Nat. Sculpture Soc. spl. medal of honor, 1940; Allied Artists gold medal of honor, 1952; Nat. Academician; Sorolla medal for art Hispanic Soc. Am., 1957; Humanist Rosicrucian Order, Son Jose, 1960; Chevalier Legion of Honor (France), 1922; Officer, 1933; Citizen of Blois, France, 1922. Grand Cross of Alfonso XII (Spain), 1929: Certificate of Honor for El Cid, San Diego, Cal., 1933; Grand Cross of Isabella the Catholic, 1954; Woman of the Americas, 1958; hon. citizen of Cuba, 1958. Fellow Nat. Sculpture Soc. (hon.), Internat, Inst. Arts Letters, 1957; hon. mem. Instituto de Cultura Hispanica, Accademia Culturale Adriatica, Internat. Studia Scientarium Literarumque; mem. Real Academia de Bellas Artes de San Jorge (corr.), Fedn. of Arts, Nat. Inst. Arts and Letters, Hispanic Soc. Am. (v.p., trustee) Am. Acad. Arts and Letters, Spanish Acad. San Fernando (corr.). Home: Bethel, Conn. Died Oct. 1973.

HUNTINGTON, THOMAS WATERMAN, bibliographer; b. Sacramento, Calif., May 8, 1893; s. Thomas Waterman and Harriet Olive (Pearson) H.; B.A., U. of Calif., 1916; grad. student, Calif. Sch. of Medicine, 1916-18; m. Nancy A. C. Neville Cutbill, Mar. 28, 1929. With Sinclair Refining Co., Chicago, 1919-22; sec. Com. for Nat. Morale, N.Y. City, 1940-41; asst. legislative reference service, Library of Congress, 1941-42; research concerning relief and rehabilitation, 1942-43; with War Dept., Chemical Warfare Service, 1943-44, office, Sec. of War, 1944-45; office chief of staff, 1945-49; research on history Army Medal of Honor, 1946-48; with Veterans Adminstration, 1950-51; with Tactical Air Command and Air Resupply and Communications Service, United States Air Force, 1951-52 with V.A. since 1952. Awarded exceptional Service Award by Dept. of Army, 1949, for research in gathering material, for Army's ofcl. history of Army Medal of Honor. Member Commn. to Study Orgn. of Peach (Dist. of Columbia br.), Am. Soc. Internat. Law, Phi Delta Theta, Episcopalian. Clubs: Harvard Faculty (Cambridge); Cosmos (Washington). Author: many bibliographics; War Times (asso. editor), 1943-45; The Medal of Honor of the U.S. Army (co-author), 1948; Freedom from Fatigue; A Plan for Relief from the Strain of Modern Living, 1950; Relief from Nervous Tension, 1952. Club: Cosmos. Home: Washington, D.C. Died Aug. 1973.

HUNTLEY, CHESTER ROBERT (CHET), former news commentator, advt. exec.; b. Cardwell, Mont., Dec. 10, 1911; s. P.A. and Blanche (Tatham) H.; student Mont. State Coll., 1929-32, Cornish Sch. Arts, Seattle, 1932-33; B.A., U. Wash., 1934; hon. degrees Mont. State Coll., Boston U., Franklin and Marshall Coll.; m. Ingrid Rolin, Feb. 23, 1936; children—Sharon, Leanne; m. 2d, Tipton Stringer, Mar. 7, 1959. With radio sta. KPCB, Seattle, 1934-36; news broadcaster KHQ, Spokane, Wash., 1936, KGW, Portland, Ore., 1937, KFI, Los Angeles, 1937-39, CBS, Los Angeles, 1939-51, ABC, Los Angeles, 1951-55, NBC, N.Y.C., 1955-70; commentator syndicated news commentaries Horizon Communications, 1970-74; partner Levine, Huntley, Schmidt, advt. agy., N.Y.C.; chmn. Big Sky Mont., Inc. Recipient numerous awards for radio-TV journalism. Address: Big Sky Mont. Died Mar. 20, 1974; interred Sunset Hills Cemetery, Bozeman, Mont.

HUNTLEY, WILLIAM RUSSELL, investments; b. Bradford, Pa., May 6, 1879; s. Charles Russell and Ida (Richardson) H.; student Cornell U., 1897-98; m. Janie Speer, Feb. 20, 1907; 1 son, Charles Russell II. Pres. Seear Corp.; dir. George Urban Milling Co., Robertson-Cataract Electric Co. Claude-Neon Displays, Inc. Mem. S.A.R. Republican. Episcopalian. Clubs: Buffalo, Automobile of Buffalo, Country of Buffalo. Home: Buffalo, N.Y.*†

HUNZIKER, RICHARD OVERTON, former air force officer; b. Los Angeles, July 6, 1916; s. Eugene P. and Josephine (Crutsinger) H.; B.S., U. Ariz., 1948; grad. Nat. War Coll., 1958; m. Margaret Ballard, Sept., 1945; children—John R., Russell L. Commd. 2d lt. USAAF, 1942, advanced through grades to maj. gen., 1966; fighter pilot in Africa, Italy, France, Sicily, Malta and Corsica, World War II; wing comdr. Europe, U.S., 1942-57; dir. material 2d Air Force, SAC, Barksdale AFB, La., 1958-60; comdr. 21st Strategic Aerospace Div., Forbes AFB, Kan., 1960-62; dep. comdr. 1st Strategic Aerospace Div., Vanderberg AFB, Cal., 1962-65; comdr. 821st Strategic Aerospace Div., Ellsworth AFB, S.D., 1965; dep. dir. operations SAC, Offutt AFB, Neb., 1965-66; dir. material, 1966-68; dep. insp. gen. for inspection and safety Hdqrs. USAF, Norton AFB, Cal., 1968-69, ret., 1969. Decorated D.S.M. with oak leaf cluster, Silver Star, Legion of Merit, D.F.C. with 2 oak leaf clusters, Air medal with 13 oak leaf clusters; Croix de Guerre with palm and star (France). Author: Crested Ice, The Story of the Recovery of the Atomic Weapons at Thule, Greenland, 1968. Home: Carpenteria, Cal. Died May 29, 1971.

HUPPERTZ, JOHN WILLIAM, bldg. and indsl. products co. exec.; b. Cin., Sept. 24, 1927; s. John Frederick and Catherine (Thleman) H.; PH.B., Xavier U., 1948, M.B.A., 1955; m. Anne M. Hess, Nov. 11, 1950; children—John, Thomas, Barbara, Katherine, Mark, Jeffrey, Claire, Eric. With elevator div. Westinghouse Elec. Corp., Cin., 1950-51, asst. sales engr., Pitts., 1951-54, application engr., 1954-56; sales engr. Philip Carey Corp., Cin., 1956-63, mdse. mgr., 1964-68, dist. mgr., 1969, mgr. marketing, 1969-71; dir. marketing Globe Industries, Chgo., after 1971; guest instr. Xavier U., U. Cin., U. Louisville, U. Md., Syracuse U. Mem. Kenwood Civic Assn.; pres. Cin. Youth Football Leagues, 1966—. Served to capt. AUS, 1948-50. Lion, Toastmaster. Home: Flossmoor, Ill. Deceased.

HURLEY, PEARLEY B(LISS), church official; b. Welton, Ia., Mar. 2, 1878; s. John G. and Athalia Adaline (Van Horn) H.; student Milton (Wis.) Coll., 1898-99; m. Polly Goodrich Rice, Oct. 15, 1901;

children—Lucile May (Mrs. Stillman), Dayton T., K. Duane. Owner Hurley's Auto Hosp., Riverside, Calif., 1916-46. Del. of Seventh Day Baptist Conf. to commn. on Just and Durable Peace, Cleveland, Ohio, 1945. Republican. Mem. Seventh Day Baptist Ch. (pres. gen. conf. 1945-46). Del. to Biennial Fed. Council of Chs., Seattle, Wash., Dec. 1946. Clubs: Kiwanis (charter mem. 1923, served on Kiddie Kamp com., del. to Kiwanis Internat., Memphis, Tenn., 1925). Home: Riverside, Cal.*†

HUROK, SOL, impresario of ballets and concerts; b. Pogar, Russia, Apr. 9, 1888; s. Israel and Naomi Hurok; ed. in Russian schs.; HH.D., Boston Univ., 1958, Wayne U., 1960; m. Emma Runitch, 1933; 1 dau., Ruth, by first wife. Came to U.S. in 1905, naturalized, 1914. Began as mgr. weekly concerts, Hippodrome, N.Y.C., 1915; was impresario for many famous ballets, musicians, dancers, including Anna Pavlova, Feodor Chaliapin, Isadora Duncan, Russian Ballet. Ballet Theatre, Marian Anderson, Artur Rubinstein, Jan Peerce. Mischa Elman, Gregor Piatigorsky, Isaac Stern, Blanche Thebom, Patrice Munsel, Roberta Peters, Leonard Warren, The Old Vic, Alicia Markova, Andres Segovia, Victoria de los Angeles, Fritz Reiner, William Steinberg, Jerome Hines, Mattiwilda Dobbs, Cesare Valletti, Nathan Milstein, and the Royal Ballet (Margot Fonteyn and Rudolf Nureyev); presented Emlyn Williams on the stage as Charles Dickens, 1952, Jean-Louis Barrault in French plays, 1952-53, 57, Comedie Francaise, Moiseyev Folk Ballet, Theatre National Populaire, 1958, Bolshoi Ballet, Leningrad Ballet, Ballet Folklorico of Mexico, Royal Danish Ballet, Stuttgart Ballet, Mazowsze, and also Romanian Folk Ballet, cons. NBC-TV. Decorated Chevalier and Officer of French Legion of Honor; Comdr. Order Brit. Empire, 1960; recipient other awards. Autobiography: Impresario, And S. Hurok Presents Motion Picture titled Tonight We Sing. Home: New York City N.Y. Died Mar. 5, 1974.

HURTZ, LEONARD E., bus. exec.; b. Scandia, Kan., Sept. 26, 1881; s. Theodore and Margaret (Collins) Hurtz; B.S., University of Nebraska, 1903; LL.D., Grinnell Coll., 1946; married Laura Hainer, 1915; children—Leonard E., Margaret, Sarah. Began bus. career with Lincoln (Neb.) Gas and Electric Co.; supt. Lincoln Municipal Electric Light Plant, 1905-06; gen. mgr., and later, vice pres., Lincoln Telephone and Telegraph Co., 1906-21; with Fairmont Foods Co., Omaha, from 1921, dir., from 1921, chmn. bd., from 1950; past chmn. Omaha br. Fed. Res. Bank of Kansas City; dir. Omaha Nat. Bank, Chicago & North Western Ry. Co., Lincoln Telephone & Telegraph Co. Dir. Nat. Dairy Council; mem. local advisory com. Reconstruction Finance Corp. Mem. Nat. Assn. Mfrs. (dir.) Internat. Assn. Ice Cream Mfrs. (pres.), Omaha Mfrs. Assn. (dir.; pres.), Asso. Industries of Neb. (dir., past pres.), Omaha Chamber of Commerce (dir.), Phi Gamma Delta. Republican. Episcopalian (vestryman). Mason. Home: Omaha, Neb.†

HUSE, CHARLES WELLS, ret. business exec.; b. Chgo., Aug. 24, 1905; s. Charles Gammon and Juanita (Wells) H.; student Am., Swiss, English schs.; m. Eda Sherman, Sept. 27, 1941. Editorial staff Hutchinson & Co., pubs., London, Eng., 1924-25; staff London office N.Am. Newspaper Alliance, 1925-26; editorial staff The Advertiser, Tunbridge Wells, Eng., 1926-27, Boulevardier, Paris, 1928, Chronicle, San Francisco, 1929-30, and Examiner, 1931-37; dir. pub. relations Columbia Steel Co., San Francisco, 1937-50; dir. pub. relations U.S. Steel Corp., Western Dist., San Francisco, 1950-52, adminstrv. asst., office asst. to chmn., N.Y.C., 1953-56, dir. pub. relations adminstrn., 1956-64, v.p. pub. relations, N.Y.C., 1964, v.p. West, San Francisco, 1964-70; ret., 1970. Trustee San Francisco Bay Area Council; dir., mem. exec. com. San Francisco chpt. A.R.C., 1951-52, bd. dirs. Golden Gate chpt.; bd. dirs. Cal. Anti-Litter League; adv. bd. No. Cal. Industry-Edn. Council; pres. bd. dirs. Ind. Colls. of No. Cal. Served as capt. USMC, World War II, Commd. maj. Res., 1951. Mem. Newcomen Soc. N.A., Pub. Relations Soc. Am., Am. Iron and Steel Inst., American Newspaper Guild (v.p. San Francisco-Oakland chpt. 1936-37), Downtown Assn. (dir. 1951-52); Cal., San Francisco chambers of commerce, Cal. Mfrs. Assn. (pres. 1969, mem. exec. com. 1970), Bay Area Urban League (dir.), Federated Employers Bay Area (gov.), Cal., Utah hist. socs., Pub. Relations Roundtable San Francisco, World Affairs Council No. Cal. Mason (Shriner). Clubs: Pacific Union, Press (San Francisco); Burlingame (Cal.) Country; Commonwealth of Cal. Home: San Francisco, Cal. Died Nov. 1974.

HUSSAKOF, LOUIS, zoölogist; b. Kief, Russia (Soviet Rep.), Nov. 19, 1881; s. William and Bessie (Pikrasa) H.; brought to U.S. in childhood; B.S., Coll. City of New York, 1900; Ph.D., Columbia, 1906; studied at biol. stas., Bermuda, 1903, Naples, 1909; unmarried. Teacher pub. schs., N.Y. City, 1901-02; asst. Am. Mus. Natural History, 1904-08, asst. curator dept. ichthyology, 1909-10, asso. curator, 1910-13, curator dept. ichthyology, 1914-16, research associate from 1929. Made field studies for several large exhibition groups of fishes displayed in Am. Mus. Natural History, also restorations of extinct fishes. Fellow New York Acad. Sciences, Geol. Soc. America, A.A.A.S.; mem. Am. Soc. Zoölogists, Am. Soc. Ichthyologists, Paleontol. Soc. America, Sigma, Xi. Author several books on fossil fishes. Contbr. to scientific jours. Home: Brooklyn, N.Y.†

HUSSEIN, TAHA, writer; b. Egypt, 1889; ed. U. Al Azhar (Calro), U. Paris (Sorbonne), faculty letters Montpellier (France); licentiate in history, Litt.D., D.Sociology; D.(hon.), univs. Athens, Lyon, Madrid, Montpeiller, Rome, Oxford; diploma higher studies in Ancient History. Prof., Arabic lit. Faud 1st U., Cairo, Egypt, 1920-32, dean faculty arts; under-sec. state Ministry Edn.; rector Farouk 1st U., Alexandria, Egypt; minister edn., 1950-52. Past senator, writer, journalist. Decorated grand officer Legion Honor (France); comdr. Order of Nile (Egypt); Grand Cross Phoenix (Greece); recipient Grande medaille de l'Universite de Paris. Mem. Acad. Arabic Langs. (pres.), Egypt Inst., Academie des Inscriptions et des Beiles Lettres, Academia del Linci (Rome), Acad. Maintz, acads. Damascus, Teheran, Baghdad, Royal Acad. History (Madrid). Author more than 50 books, including Adib; Alwane; Jannat al Shawk; Hadith Al Arbl'a; Al Hob Al Dayeg; Dou'a al Karawan; Chajarat al Bou'ss; Al Sheikhane; Ala Hamech Al Sirat; Ali wa Banouh; Fousoul fil Adab wal Nakd; Fil Adab Al Ghahill; Qadat al Fikr; Mir'aat al Islam; Moustakbal as Sakafa fi Misr; Maal Moutanabbi; Ma' Abil Ala' fi Sijnihi; Minal Adab Al Tamcill Al Younani; Min Hadith Al Shir'r wal Nathr; Nizam Al Athinyyins; Al Wa'd Al Hak; Tajdid Zikra Abil Ala'; Al Ayyam (trans. to 18 langs.); Othman; Mouzakkarat Taha Hussein; others. Address: Guizeh, Egypt., Died Oct. 28, 1973; interred State Mus.

HUSTED, JAMES WILLIAM, former lawyer; b. Peekskill, N.Y., May 15, 1896; s. James William and Louise W. (Spaulding) H.; B.A., Yale, 1918; post grad. Harvard Law Sch., 1919-20; LL.B., Columbia, 1924; m. Alice Dodge, Oct. 2, 1926; 1 son, James William. With New Eng. Pin Co., Winsted, Conn., 1920-22; admitted to N.Y. bar then practiced in N.Y.C.; asso. with firm Winthrop, Stimson, Putnam & Roberts, 1924-30, partner, 1930-69. Hon. trustee Mus. Modern Art, No. Westchester Hosp.; trustee Winifred Masterson Burke Relief Found. Mem. Am., N.Y. State bar assns., Assn. Bar City N.Y. Clubs: Century Assn., Knickerbocker (gov.) (N.Y.C.). Home: Bedford, N.Y. Died Feb. 20, 1975.

HUSTON, LUTHER ALLISON, author, journalist; b. Paulina, Ia., Nov. 8, 1888; s. Luther Allen and Alice (Noble) H.; student U. So. Cal., 1908-11; m. Dora Lee Carey, Feb. 15, 1929; 1 dau., Ann Noble. Reporter, Bellingham (Wash.) Herald, 1912-14, Seattle Times, 1914-17; reporter, bur. mgr., fgn. corr., news editor, sales mgr. Internat. News Service, 1917-34; city editor Washington Post, 1934-35; bur. mgr., staff corr. Washington bur. N.Y. Times, 1935-57; dir. pub. information Dept. Justice, Washington 1957-61; asst. to dir. Am. Bar Assn., Washington, 1961-63; with Ernest Wittenberg Assos., pub. relations, 1964-65; Washington corr., editor and pub., 1966-75. Recipient George Polk Meml. award, 1954. Fellow Sigma Delta Chi (Wells key 1949, nat. pres. 1947-48). Episcopalian. Club: Natl. Press (gov. 1952-57, chmn. 1957). Author: Pathway to Judgment, A Study of Earl Warren, 1966; The Department of Justice, 1967. Home: Washington, D.C., Died Nov. 26, 1975.

HUTCHINGS, GEORGE ERNEST, hosp. adminstr.; b. Griffin, Ga., Jan. 20, 1915; s. Clarence Pierce and Ruby Russell (Collins) H.; B.A., Mercer U., 1937; m. Mary Lou Joiner, May 11, 1946; 1 dau., Elizabeth Russell (Mrs. Richard Stratigos). With Coleman Meadows Pate, wholesale drug co., Macon, Ga., 1935-43; asst. adminstr. Homer D. Cobb Meml. Hosp., Phenix City, Ala., 1967-69; adminstr; Marion Meml. Hosp., Buena Vista, Ga., 1969-72; adminstr. Gilman Hosp., also St. Marys Convalescent Home, from 1972. Served to col. U.S. Army, 1943-66. Mem. Am. Acad. Med. Adminstrs., Assn. U.S. Army, Officers Assn., Am. Coll. Nursing Home Adminstrs. Methodist (music dir. from 1964, lay leader 1965). Lion. Club: Civitan. Home: Columbus, Ga. Deceased.

HUTCHINSON, MELVIN TYLER, former educator; b. nr. Renick, Mo., Nov. 12, 1902; s. Lewis Turner and Cena Alice (Reineke) H.; B.A. in Edn., Ariz. State Coll., 1945, M.A. in Edn., 1952; Dr. Journalism (hon.), No. Ariz. U., 1968; m. Frances Bishoff, Sept. 29, 1939. Editor, The Pine, student newspaper Ariz. State Coll., 1932-34; advt. mgr., reporter Coconino Sun, Flagstaff, Ariz., 1934-39, editor, 1939-43; asst. prof. journalism, dir. publicity and publs. Ariz. State Coll., 1946-66, journalistic historian No. Ariz. U. (formerly Ariz. State Coll.), 1966-73. Publicity dir. Flagstaff Community Concerts, 1947-52, Boy Scouts Am., 1939-42, Ariz. Boys State, 1947-67. Dir., co-founder Am. Indian Scholarship Found., Ariz. State Coll. Indian Scholarship Com. Recipient Gold Key award Columbia Scholastic Assn., 1959. Mem. Ariz. Newspapers Assn., Am. Assn. U. Profs., Assn. for Edn. in Journalism, C. of C., Phi Kappa Phi, Phi Delta Kappa, Kappa Delta Pi (Honor Key award 1965), Sigma Pi. Methodist. Rotarian. Author: History of Arizona State College at Flagstaff from Its Origin Through a Quarter of a Century, 1951; The Making of Northern Arizona University-A Chronicle, 1972. Editor: Pow-Wow, all-Indian celebration mag., 1939-42, Pine, alumni mag., 1968-71. Home: Flagstaff, Ariz. Died June 16, 1973.

HUTCHINSON, RAY CORYTON, novelist; b. Finchley, Middlesex, Eng., Jan. 23, 1907; s. Harry and Lucy Mabel (Coryton) H.; grad. Monkton Combe Sch.; M.A., Oriel Coll., Oxford U.; m. Margaret Owen Jones, Apr. 2, 1929; children—Ann Coryton, Jeremy Olpherts, Elspeth Owen, Piers Evelyn. Served as maj. Brit. Army, 1940-45; historian Persia and Iraq Command. Recipient Gold medal for fiction Sunday Times, 1938, W.H. Smith Lit. award, 1966. Fellow Royal Soc. Lit. Mem. Church of Eng. Author: The Answering Glory, 1932; The Unforgotten Prisoner, 1933; One Light Burning, 1935; Shining Scabbard, 1936; Testament, 1938; The Fire and the Wood, 1940; Interim, 1945; Elephant and Castie, 1949; Journey with Strangers, 1952; The Stepmother, 1955; March the Ninth, 1957; The Inheritor, 1962; A Child Possessed, 1965; Johanna At Daybreak, 1969; Origins of Cathleen, 1971; Rising, 1976. Home: Redhill, Surrey, England. Died July 3, 1975; buried St. Katharine's Ch., Merstham, Surrey, England.

HUTCHISON, HARVEY MACLEARY, judge; b. Comanche Tex., Feb. 7, 1878; s. Thomas L. and Martha Elizabeth (MacLeary) H.; student U. of Tex., 1895-98; m. Anne Roth, June 14, 1905. Admitted to Tex. bar, 1900, and practiced in Comanche; removed to Puerto Rico, 1902, and practiced till 1904; law officer, later spl. fiscal, Insular Dept. of Justice, 1904-11; judge Insular Dist. Courts, Cuayama, 1911-13; Mayaguez, 1913-14; asso. justice Supreme Court of Puerto Rico, 1914-40. Address: Puerto de Tierra, P.R.†

HUTTON, HUGH MCMILLEN, editorial cartoonist; b. Lincoln, Neb., Dec. 11, 1897; s. Elmer S. and Eugenia (McMillen) H.; student U. Minn., 1919-21; m. Dorothy Wackerman, May 24, 1924; children—Elizabeth Jean, Robert Wackerman. With St. Paul Pioneer Press, 1925, United Features, N.Y.C., 1929, Phila. Pub. Ledger, 1933, Phila. Inquirer from 1934; exhibitor etchings, lithographs, cartoons. Mem. Nat. Cartoonists Soc., Am. Assn. Editorial Cartoonists. Republican. Presbyn. Club: Phila. Sketch. Contbr. cartoons to various publs. Home: Philadelphia, Pa., Died Jan. 2, 1976; interred Longwood Cemetery, Kennett Square, Pa.

HUXLEY, SIR JULIAN SORELL, author, biologist; b. Eng., June 22, 1887; s. Leonard Huxley; scholar Eton and Balliol Coll., Oxford U. (Newdigate Prize poetry 1908); m. Marie Juliette Baillot, 1919; 2 sons. Lectr. zoölogy Balliol Coll., 1910-12; research asso. (travelling in Germany), Rice Inst., Houston, 1912-13, asst. prof., 1913-16; fellow, sr. demonstrator zoölogy New Coll., Oxford U., 1919-25; mem. Oxford expdn. to Spitsbergen, 1921; prof. zoölogy King's Coll., London, 1925-27, hon. lectr., 1927-35; Fullerian prof. physiology Royal Inst., Eng., 1926-29; gen. supr. biol. films Gaumont Brit. Instructional, Ltd., 1933-36, Zoöl. Film Prodns., Ltd., 1937-42; sec. Zoöl. Soc. London, adv. editor Zoo mag., 1935-42; Beatty lectr. McGill U., Montreal, 1956. Mem. Commn. Higher Edn. W. Africa, 1944; mem. Com. Nat. Parks U.K., 1945-46; exec. sec. UN Ednl. and Cultural Orgn. Prep. Commn., 1946; dir. gen. UNESCO, 1947-48; v.p. Commn. Sci. and Cultural History Mankind, mem. Jordan expdn., 1963. Recipient Darwin medal Royal Soc., 1956; created knight, 1958. Former officer several profl. assns. Author or editor, some with others, over 40 books 1911-75, including: The Individual in the Animal Kingdom, 1911; Religion without Revelation, rev. edit. 1957; Animal Biology (with J.B.S. Haldane), 1927; The Science of Life (with H.G. and G.P. Wells), 1929; The Elements of Experimental Embryology (with G.R. de Beer), 1934; Scientific Research and Social Needs, 1934; If I Were Dictator, 1934; T.H. Huxley's Diary on the Rattlesnake (editor), 1935; The Living Thoughts of Darwin (with J. Fisher), 1939; The Uniqueness of Man, 1941; Evolution, the Modern Synthesis, 2d edit., 1963; Evolutionary Ethics (Romanes lecture Oxford) 1943; Man In the Modern World, 1947; Evolution and Ethics, 1947; Evolution in Action (editor), 1953; The Evolutionary Process (editor), 1953; From and Antique Law rev. edit; of 1966; The Kingdom of Beasts (with W. Suschitzky), 1956; Secrets of Life, 1957; Biological Aspects of Cancer, 1957; New Wine in New Bottles (essays), 1957; The Story of Evolution, 1959; The Humanist Frame (editor), 1961; Conservation of Wild Life In Central and East Africa, 1961; Essays of a Humanist, 1964; (with H.B. Kettlewell) Darwin and His World, 1965; Aldous Huxley, 1965; Memories, Vol. I, 1970, Vol. II, 1973. Biol. editor Ency. Brit., 14th edit.; editorial bd. New Naturalist series, 1944-75; editor (with others) Doubleday Pictorial Library of World History. Home: London, England. Died Feb. 14, 1975.

HUYKE, JUAN BERNARDO, educator; b. Arroyo, P.R., July 11, 1880; s. Enrique and Carmen (Bozello) H.; graduate San Bernardo College, Arroyo, P.R., and Instituto Provincial, San Juan; m. Carmen Colòn, Mar. 20, 1906; children—Carmen Andrea, Enrique Victor (dec.), Emilio Enrique, Juan Alberto, Sara (dec.), Victor, Hector José. Teacher, prin. schs., insp., gen. supt. schs. until 1910; began practice law, 1911; mem. Ho. of Delegates, P.R., 1912-20 (speaker 1918-20); commr. edn. of P.R., by apptmt. of President Harding, 1921, reapptd. by President Coolidge, 1926; acting gov. of P.R., 1922; trustee U. of P.R. from 1914, chancellor, 1921-26; chmn. Civil Service Commn., P.R., 1935-44; retired. Advocate of Americanization of P.R. Mason;

Grand Dep. Master Grand Lodge of P.R., 1918. Club: Casino de Puerto Rico. Author of many ednl. books. Editor El Pais, 1932-33. Home: Hato Rey, P.R.*†

HYATT, FRANCIS MARION, city ofcl.; b. Marietta, Okla., Feb. 21, 1905; s. Frank W. and Gertrude (Sholly) H.; student Ia. Wesleyan Coll., 1924-25; m. Alice Louise Waterman, June 17, 1934; children—Philip W., James Robert. Owner, operator radio sales and service co., Ottumwa, Ia., 1926-40; announcer, mgr. sta. WJHO, Opelika, Ala., 1940-51; announcer sta. WAUD, Auburn, Ala., 1951-60; exec. dir. Opelika Housing Authority, 1951-74. Dir. Founder's Investment Corp. Instr. shelter mgmt. Opelika Civil Def., 1963-74. Chmn. Opelika Park and Recreation Bd., 1947-52, Lee County chpt. A.R.C., 1961-64, Opelika Library Bd., 1942-46; chmn. Lee County Welfare Bd., 1958-74, Ala. pres., 1963-64; chmn. Birmingham Regional Blood Bank, A.R.C., 1967-71; mem. adv. com. Region 6 Combined Service Territory, Birmingham Area A.R.C., 1965-71; chmn. Ala. div. adv. com. A.R.C., 1971-74. Recipient Outstanding Citizen award Opelika Jr. C. of C., 1962. Mem. Ala. Assn. Housing Authorities (pres.) C. of C. (v.p. 1952), Sigma Phi Epsilon. Methodist (chmn. ofcl. bd. 1961-63). Rotarian (pres. Opelika 1945-46). Home: Opelika, Ala. Died Oct. 10, 1974.

HYATT, JAMES PHILIP, educator, clergyman; b. Monticello, Ark., Feb. 16, 1909; s. Robert Lee and Mami (Stanley) H.; A.B., Baylor U., 1929, LL.D., 1969; A.M., Brown U., 1930; B.D., Yale, 1933, Ph.D., 1938; postgrad. Am. Sch. of Oriental Research, Jerusalem (Two Brothers fellow of Yale), 1931-32, U. Marburg (Germany), summer 1932; D.D. (hon.), Christian Theol. Sem., 1967; L.H.D., Tex. Christian U., 1969; m. Elizabeth Bard, Sept. 12, 1932; children—James Lee, (dec.), Charles Sidney, David Philip. Ordained to ministry Bapt. Ch., 1929; pastor Hull Meml. Bapt. Ch., Cheshire, Conn., 1932-35; instr. Bibl. history Wellesley Coll., 1935-38, asst. prof., 1938-41; asso. prof. O.T., Vanderbilt U., Nashville, 1941-44, prof., 1944-72, chmn. grad. dept. religion, 1944-64, acting dean Div. Sch., 1956-72, Harvie Branscomb Distinguished prof., 1969-70. Vis. prof. U. Chgo., winter 1944, Garrett Bibl. Inst. summer 1945, Union Theol. Sem., N.Y.C., summer 1950, Iliff Sch. Theology, summer 1958, Perkins Sch. Theology, summer 1961. Ford faculty fellow Hebrew Union Coll., 1952; mem. O.T. sect. Standard Bible Com. Fellow Soc. for Religion in Higher Edn.; mem. Am. Oriental Soc. (v.p. Middle West br. 1943-44), Am. Acad. Religion (v.p. 1941), Soc. Bibl. Lit. (pres. So. sect. 1949-50, pres. 1956), Brit. Soc. for O.T. Study (asso.), Phi Beta Kappa. Democrat. Mem. Disciples of Christ (minister 1946-72). Author: Prophetic Religion, 1947; Introduction and Exegesis of Jeremiah, Interpreter's Bible, vol. V, 1956; Jeremiah: Prophet of Courage d Hope, 1958; The Heritage of Biblical Faith, 1964; Commentary on Exodus, 1971. Archeol. editor Jour. Bible and Religion, 1939-48; editor Jour. Bibl. Lit., 1948-49; The Bible in Modern Scholarship, 1965. Contbr. numerous articles to profl. jours. Home: Nashville, Tenn. Died Nov. 6, 1972.

HYDE, CHARLES GILMAN, engr.; b. Yantic (town of Norwich), Conn., May 7, 1874; s. George Rodney and Kate Rhoda (Dickey) H.; B.S., Mass. Inst. Technology, 1896; LL.D., University of California, 1949; m. Margherita Isola, May 21, 1901 (dec. 1951); children—Margherita, Helen, Katharine. Asst., and asst. engr., Mass. State Bd. of Health, 1896-1900; asst. engr. and in charge, Spring Garden and Torresdale Testing stas., Bureau of Water, Phila., 1900-02; resident engr., design and constrn. of Harrisburg Filtration Works, 1902-05; asst. prof., asso. prof. and professor sanitary engring., Univ. of California, 1905-44, professor emeritus from 1944, dean of men, 1926-28. Consulting engr. on many hydraulic and sanitary engring. problems, including Calif. State Dept. of Health, 1911-44; special cons., hydraulic engr., Harriman lines in Ore. and Calif., 1906-08; mem. engring. commn. design of sanitary works, Camp Fremont, Menlo Park, Calif., 1917, capt., maj., sanitary engring. sect., Sanitary Corps U.S. Army, June 11, 1918-June 12, 1919; sanitary engr., Camp Meade, Md., Aug. 5-Nov. 22, 1918; Surgeon Gen.'s Office, War Dept., Washington, Nov. 22, 1918-June 12, 1919; in charge san. engring. sect. Sanitary Corps, Surgeon Corps, Surgeon Gen.'s Office, Feb. 15-June 12, 1919; cons. San Francisco Dept. Public Health, 1932-44; mem. and chmn. bd. of cons. engrs., San Francisco Sewerage and Sewage Disposal, 1934-35; mem. bd. cons. engrs. Los Angeles Sewerage and Sewage Disposal, 1939; chmn. bd. cons. engrs., East Bay Cities Sewage Disposal Survey, 1940-41; chmn. State Com. on Water Supply, Calif. State Council of Defense, 1941-43; cons. san. engr. USN, 12th Dist., from 1944; chmn. and/or mem. sewage survey bds. Santa Clara, Santa Cruz, Orange and San Diego counties, Cal., Greater Vancouver area, B.C., Auckland Met. Drainage Dist., New Zealand. Awarded Silver Beaver, Boy Scouts Am. Congregationalist. Hon. mem. Order of the Golden Bear, 1955; member Am. Soc. C.E. (chmn. sanitary engring. div., 1934-36, dir. 1940-43, hon. mem. 1951), Am. Public Health Assn., Am. Water Works Assn. (chmn. water purification div., 1938-39; hon. mem., 1939; George W. Fuller Award, 1942), N.E. Water Works Assn., Soc. Am. Mil. Engrs., Fedn. of Sewage Works Assn. (exec. com. and bd. of control, 1932-42; hon. mem. 1943), Rho Alpha Mu, Delta Kappa Epsilon, Sigma Xi, Tau Beta Pi, Delta Omega (nat. pres. 1934-35), etc. Clubs: Bohemian, Faculty. Home: Berkeley, Cal.†

HYDE, EDWARD PECHIN, physicist; b. Balt. Co., Md., Jan 3, 1879; s. Edward Ingle and Carolina Rebecca (Clemm) H.; grad. City Coll., Balt., 1897; A.B., Johns Hopkins, 1900, Ph.D., 1906; m. Virginia Getzendanner, May 4, 1904; children—Dorothy (Madame Daniel Masson), Elisabeth (Mrs. Walter Krell). Laboratory assistant, 1902-05; assistant and asso. physicist, Bureau of Standards, 1905-08; organizer, 1908, dir., 1908-20, Nela Research Lab.; dir. of research Nat. Lamp Works of Gen. Electric Co., 1920-23. Pres. Internat. Commn. on Illumination, 1921-27, and permanent mem. of same. Mem. Nat. Research Council (engring. and foreign relations division), American Physical Society, American Electrochem. Society, National Electric Light Assn., Illuminating Engring. Soc. (pres. 1910), Soc. for Promotion Engring. Edn., Franklin Inst. (medalist), Optical Soc. Am., Société Francaise des Electriciens, Phi Beta Kappa, Sigma Xi; corr. mem. London Illuminating Engring. Soc.; asso. mem. Am. Inst. E.E., Am. Gas Assn. Republican. Now retired. Address: Paris France†

HYDE, WALTER WOODBURN, educator; b. Ithaca, N.Y., May 14, 1870; s. Orange Percy and Eloise Flower (Davies) H.; A.B., Cornell, 1893; studied Am. Schs. Classical Studies, Athens and Rome, 1898-99, Göttingen and Halle, Germany, and Geneva, Switzerland, 1900-02; A.M., Ph.D., Halle, 1902; Litt.D., U. Pa., 1948; m. Mary Drever, Aug. 6, 1955. Submaster, 1895-98, and headmaster, 1899-1900, Northampton (Mass.) High School; instructor classics, Princeton, 1906; prof. Latin, U. of Tenn., 1908; instr. Greek, Cornell, 1909; instr. Greek, 1910-14, asst. prof., 1914-24, prof. Greek and lecturer in ancient history, 1924-30, prof. Greek and ancient history, 1930-40, emeritus from 1940, U. of Pennsylvania. Mem. Am. Philol. Assn., Soc. Founders and Patriots Am., Colonial Soc. Pa., Classical (pres. 1923-24), Oriental (pres. 1922-23, 1941-42), and Anthropological Clubs of Philadelphia; fellow Royal Soc. Arts (London), mem. Sigma Phi Sigma, Phi Beta Kappa, Philomathean, Philobiblon Society, University Club of Phila. Mason. Author: de Olympionicarum Statuis, 1903; Thessaly and the Vale of Tempe, 1912; Monasteries of Meteora and Greek Monasticism, 1913; Mountains of Greece, 1915; chapter on Greek Religion in Religions Past and Present, 1917; Olympic Victor Monuments and Greek Athletic Art (Carnegie Instn.), 1921; Greek Religion and Its Survivals, 1923; Roman Alpine Routes (Am. Philos. Soc.), 1935; Paganism to Christianity in the Roman Empire, 1946; Ancient Greek Mariners, 1947; contbr. chapters to Song of Songs, 1923; School Athletics in Modern Education, 1931; John C. Rolfe Memorial Volume, 1931; also some 160 articles in sci. jours., on Greek lit., religion, archeology, athletics, geography, history and legal antiquities. Editor: Am. Medieval History in Popular Educator, 1938-39. Extensive travel, walking trips and mountain climbing, throughout Europe and Near East. Home: Philadelphia, Pa.†

HYER, JULIEN CAPERS, lawyer; b. Greenville, S.C., Apr. 1, 1894; s. William C. and Mattie (Wagener) H.; A.B., Wofford Coll., Spartanburg, S.C., 1913; LL.B., Georgetown U., 1916; LL.D. (hon.), Baylor U., 1942; m. Agnes Barnhart, Dec. 25, 1919 (dec.); children—Agnes Ann, Martha, Jeanne; m. 2d, Norma Shoemaker, Feb. 12, 1970. Asst. in law library Supreme Ct. U. S., 1914-15; practiced law Waco and Fort Worth, Tex.; mem. Tex. Senate, 1929; civil dist. atty. Dallas County, 1950-56; judge Dallas County Ct. at Law, 1956-61, 44th dist. ct., 1961-71. Served as capt. Trench Arty., 36th Div., U.S. Army, 1918-19; AEF in France; recalled to active mil. service, Jan. 1941; served as col., Judge Adv. Gen.'s Dept., 8th Service Command; judge adv. 4th U.S. Army; overseas as army judge adv., 15th U.S. Army (Germany), also with general bd. U.S.F.E.T. Decorated European ribbon, 2 battle stars, Legion of Merit with oak leaf cluster, Commendation medal. Member Am., Tex., Ft. Worth, Dallas bar assns., Mil. Order World Wars, V.F.W., Am. Legion, Pi Kappa Phi. Democrat. Methodist. Mason (K.T., Shriner), Lion (pres. Internat. Assn. Lions Clubs 1931-32). Author: The Land of Beginning Again, 2d edit., 1970; The Shepherd (syndicated feature verse collection), vol. 1, 1955, vol. 2, 1972; Texas Lions 1917-67. Contbr. verse and articles to newspapers and mags. Home: Fort Worth Tex. Died Mar. 23, 1974; buried Restland Cemetery, Dallas, Tex.

HYMON, MARY WATSON, (Mrs. George Jerome Hymon), librarian; b. Hagerstown, Md., June 19, 1918; Ed.D., Ind. U., 1960; d. Ralph Wesley and Georgia (Reed) Watson; A.B., Ky. State Coll., 1940; B.S. in Library Sci., U. Denver, 1941, M.A., 1954; Ed.D., Ind. U., 1960; m. George Jerome Hymon, Jan. 2, 1949; 1 son, Nolan Jerome. Librarian Bishop Coll., Marshall, Tex., 1941-43, 45-47, Ky. State Coll., 1943-45, Grambling (La.) Coll., 1947-74. Staff mem. La. Library Resources Survey; mem. Library Devel. Com. La., 1970-74; mem. exec. council Trail Blazer Pilot Library System, 1970-74. Recipient leadership tng. award Fund for Adult Edn., 1957-58. Mem. A.L.A., La., Adult edn. assns., Am. Assn. U. Profs., La. Library Assn. (scholarship com., mem. priorities com. academic librarians), Pi Lambda Theta. Home: Grambling, La., Died Aug. 27, 1974.

IBAVIOSA, ALFRED CRUZ, physician; b. Malabon, Rizal, Philippines, Nov. 5, 1927; s. Manuel and Maria Ibaviosa; M.D., U. Santo Tomas, Manila, Philippines; m. Catherine Lydia Thielker, Dec. 22, 1960; children—Deborah, John, James, Linda, Mary. Intern, Lutheran Hosp., St. Louis, 1955-57, resident, 1959-61, staff obstetrician and gynecologist, 1954-73; resident St. Joseph's Hosp., Kirkwood, Mo., 1957-59, St. Louis City Hosp., 1961-64; practice medicine specializing in obstetrics and gynecology, Festus, Mo.; chief obstetrics and gynecology Jefferson Meml. Hosp., Festus, 1965-73. Diplomate Am. Bd. Obstetrics and Gynecology. Fellow Am. Coll. Obstetricians and Gynecologists; mem. A.M.A. Home: Festus, Mo. Died July 28, 1973; buried Roselawn Meml. Cemetery, Crystal City, Mo.

IDDINGS, ANDREW SHEETS, lawyer; b. Dayton, O., Oct. 18, 1880; s. Charles Dickens and Belle (Sheets) I; grad. Deaver Collegiate Inst., 1898; L.H.D. (hon.), U. of Dayton, 1957; LL.D., Miami U., Oxford, Ohio, 1964. Admitted to Ohio bar, 1903, practiced in Dayton; founder, sec.-treas., gen. counsel Fyr-Fyter Co. of Dayton, 1916-47; dep. collector U.S. Internal Revenue, Dayton, 1898-1902; dep. clk. Supreme Ct. of O., 1902-06; chief dep. clk. cts., Dayton, 1906-09; U.S. commr. So. Dist. of O., 1924-26; sec., gen. atty. Dist. Tb Hosp., Dayton, 1934-66; mem. firm Iddings, Jeffrey & Donnelly. Member Dayton City Plan Board, 1933-47; mem. chmn. Dayton Met. Housing Authority, from 1934; v.p. Civic Music Assn. Dayton. Fellow Royal Geographical Soc. of London (life), Am. Bar Foundation; mem. Ohio State Bar Found. (an incorporator, sec.-treas. 1951-63), Montgomery County (past pres.), Ohio State (pres. 1941-42), Am., Internat. (charter patron) bar assns. Mason (33°). Clubs: Lawyers, Engrs., Country (Dayton); Explorers (life) (N.Y.C.). Author: Andrew S. Iddings Explorer, 1967; also author law reports. Photographic reports of travels Am. and fgn. mags. Home: Dayton, O.†

IMBRIE, JAMES, banker; b. Bayonne, N.J., Feb. 2, 1880; s. of William Morris and Janet Thompson (Currie) I.; A.B., Princeton, 1901; m. Marie McCrea-Pritchett, Jan. 15, 1903. Active head of Imbrie & Co., bankers, N.Y. City; officer or dir. various companies. Student 2d Plattsburg T.C.; commd. capt. inf., Aug. 1917; maj. 27th F.A., July 1918. Presbyn. Home: New York City, N.Y.*†

IMMELL, RUTH, teacher; b. Chambersburg, Pa., Feb. 16, 1879; d. George W. and Ellen Mary (Glosser) I.; B.E., West Chester State Normal Sch., 1900; A.B., U. of Pa., 1917, M.A., 1919. Teacher history, pub. schs., West Chester, 1901-06, Friends Sch., Baltimore, Md., 1906-07; teacher of history and civics, C. W. Henry Sch., Phila., 1908-17; dean of women, Hamline U., from 1917. Mem. Am. Assn. Univ. Women, Nat. Child Labor Assn., Beta Chapter of Pi Lambda Theta (nat. pres.). Lutheran. Club: College (St. Paul). Home: St. Paul, Minn.†

INGERSOLL, RALPH EUGENE, co-owner lumber co.; b. Manistee, Mich., Sept. 19, 1922; s. Lewis E. and Florence E. (Mayes) I.; grad. high sch.; m. Belva Jo Keene, Aug. 10, 1947; children—Cynthia, Nancy, Debbie. Partner Mayes Roofing, LaPorte, Ind., 1946-74, pres., 1972-74; real estate broker; co-owner Wilson Lumber, LaPorte, 1967-74, also dir. Bd. dirs. EARC. Served with AUS, 1942-45. Decorated Bronze Star medal. Mem. Am. Legion. Methodist (trustee 1973). Mason (Shriner). Home: LaPorte IND. Deceased.

INGHAM, CHARLES T(ATTERSALL), architect; b. Pittsburgh, Pa., Jan. 21, 1876; s. Tattersall and Ellen (Ward) I.; student U. of Pa., 1893-96; m. Cora Martha Rogers, Sept. 7, 1904; children—Charles Seth, Albert Joseph, Roger Ward, Cora May. Began practice as architect, Pittsburgh, 1897; mem. Ingham and Boyd, 1911-46; member firm of Ingham, Boyd and Pratt, from 1946. Prin. works of firm: Chatham Village Housing Development; Buhl Planetarium and Inst. of Popular Science; Historical Society of Western Pa. Bldg.; Henry Clay Frick Training Sch. for Teachers; Adminstration Bldg. of Bd. of Pub. Edn., gymnasium and dining hall for Shady Side Academy; Waverly Presbyterian Church, Juvenile Court Building (all of Pittsburgh); also high school buildings at Edgewood, Wilkinsburg, Mt. Lebanon, all of Pa. Instr. Architectural Sch. Carnegie Inst. Tech., 1917. mem. Pa. State Bldg. Code Com., 1920, City of Pittsburgh Bldg. Code Com., 1920-24; president Pa. State Bd. Examiners of Architects; mem. Commn. on Ch. Architecture, Diocese of Pittsburgh, P.E. Ch.; mem. Pittsburgh City Planning Commission. Fellow Am. Inst. Architects (ex-dir., ex-sec.; ex-pres. Pittsburgh chapter); mem. Beta Theta Pi. Republican. Episcopalian. Mason (32°). Clubs: Duquesne, Pittsburgh Architectural (ex-pres.). Home: Pittsburgh, Pa.†

INGLE, DAVID, coal operator; born Evansville, Ind., Oct. 5, 1875; s. David and Fannie (Burbank) I.; B.S., Rose Poly Inst., 1897; m. Magdaline Deutsch; children—David, Thomas H. Pres. Ingle Coal Corp., Elberfield, Ind., from 1909, later treas.; dir. Joy Mfg.

Co., Pitts., Nat. City Bank, Evansville, Ind. Clubs: University (Chicago); Duquesne (Pittsburgh). Home: Evansville, Ind.†

INGRAM, EVERETT JEFFERSON, banker; b. Ashland, Ala., Aug. 9, 1911; s. Francis Jefferson and Evelyn (Johnson) I.; B.S., Samford U., 1935; student U. Ala., 1941; m. Kay Hammett Ingram, Oct. 28, 1936; children—Carol Kay (Mrs. William H. Matthews), Lee J. Statistician accountant, supr. Birmingham (Ala.) Bd. Edn., 1935-42; successively spl. agt., asst. personnel officer, insp., spl. agt. in charge, exec. asst. to dir. FBI, Washington, 1942-65; v.p. Hamilton Nat. Bank, Knoxville, Tenn., 1966-73. Bd. dirs. Knox County chpt. A.R.C., The Arthritis Found., Jr. Achievement, Better Bus. Bur., Downtown Knoxville Assn. Mem. Pi Kappa Phi, Pi Gamma Mu. Baptist. Rotarian. Clubs: City Club of Knoxville, Cherokee Country. Home: Knoxville, Tenn. Died Jan. 8, 1973; interred Knoxville, Tenn.

INONU, ISMET, Turkish govt. ofcl.; b. Izmir, Asia Minor, Sept. 24, 1884; s. Reshid and Djervriye; student Mil. High Sch. and Mil. Arty. Coll., Istanbul; m. Emine Mevhibe, Apr. 13, 1916; children—Omer, Erdal, Ozden. Commd. capt., 1906, advanced through grades to gen., 1926; capt. 2d Army, 1906; mem. Gen. Staff, 2d Army Edirne, Eastern Thrace; mem. Expeditionary force against Arabian revolutionists, 1910; chief Gen. Staff, Army of Yemen, Arabia, 1912; dir. 1st sect. Great Gen. Staff, Istanbul, later mil. adviser to delegations to negotiate peace with Bulgaria at end of Balkan War, 1913; chief Gen. Staff, 2d Army, Eastern Thrace, 1915; comdr. 4th Army Corps against Russians on Eastern Front, World War, 1916; Comdr 20th Army Corps, later 3d Army Corps, Syria, 1917; undersec. to Ministry of War, Istanbul, 1918; comdr. Western Front, 1920-22 (won Battles of Inönü over Greece and given surname of Ionü by Kemal Ataturk); deputy from Edirne, Great Nat. Assembly; chief Great Gen. Staff, 1920; minister fgn. affairs, 1922; signed Treaty of Lausanne, July 24, 1923; ret., 1927; served as premier of Turkey, 1923-24, 25-37, 61-64, pres., 1938-50. Hon. prof. polit. sci. Ankara, faculty of law Higher Inst. Agr.; hon. pres. Turkish Ednl. Soc. Formerly v.p., pres. Rep. Peoples Party, leader of party, 1939-65. Awarded Medal of Independence 1922. Moslem. Author numerous published speeches. Home: Ankara, Turkey. Died Dec. 25, 1973.

IPPEN, ARTHUR THOMAS, educator; b. London, Eng. July 28, 1907; s. Peter Joseph and Augusta (Hechelmann) I.; diplom-ingenieur, Tech. Univ., Aachen, Germany, 1931; S.M., Cal. Inst. Tech., 1935, Ph.D., 1936; Hon. Doctorate, U. Toulouse (France), 1962; Dr. Ing. honoris causa, Tech. U., Karisruhe (Germany), 1967; D.Sc. honoris causa, U. Manchester (Eng.), 1968; m. Elisabeth Wagenplatz, Dec. 25, 1937 (dec.); children—Erich Peter, Karin Ann; m. 2d, Ruth Bishop Calvert, April 10, 1955; 1 stepdau., Julie Jean Calvert. Came to U.S., 1932. Asst. geodesy, Aachen, 1932; research, teaching asst. hydraulics Cal. Inst. Tech., 1933-36, research engr., instr., 1936-38; instr. Lehigh U., 1938-39, asst., prof. civil engring., charge of hydraulic lab. 1939-45; asso. prof. hydraulics Mass. Inst. Tech., 1945-48, prof., 1948-65, Ford prof. engring., 1965-70, dir. hydrodynamics lab., 1950-70, Inst. prof., dir. Ralph M. Parsons Lab. for Water Resources and Hydrodynamics, 1970-73, Inst. prof. emeritus, 1973-74; cons. to U.S. govt. and industry. Registered prof. engr., Mass. Recipient Vincent Bendix Research award Am. Soc. Engring. Edn., 1963; Distinguished Alumni award Cal. Inst. Tech., 1970. Diplomate Am. Acad. Environmental Engrs. Fellow Am. Acad. Arts and Scis., Am. Soc. C.E., Am. Geophys. Union, Nat. Acad. Engring.; mem. Am. Soc. M.E., Boston Soc. Civil Engrs. (past pres., hon. mem.), Japan Soc. Civil Engrs. (hon.), Am. Water Resources Assn., Am. Soc. for Engring. Edn., Internat. Assn. Hydraulic Research (past pres., hon. mem.), Sigma Xi, Tau Beta Pi, Chi Epsilon. Conglist. Author tech. books, articles. Home: Belmont Mass. Died Apr. 5, 1974; interred Belmont Cemetery, Belmont, Mass.

IRELAND, WILLIAM DUNNING, banking; b. Bangor, Me., June 1, 1894; s. Charles Rogers and Jennie May (Dunning) I.; student Me. Central Inst., 1909-12; B.S., Bowdoin Coll., 1916, hon. A.M., 1919; LL.D., 1967; m. Mary Elliott, June 7, 1919; children—Nancy, Priscilla Anne, William Dunning, Mary Louise. With R. B. Dunning & Co., Bangor, 1919-20, Richardson, Hill & Co., 1920-24, Ireland & Co., Portland, Me., 1924-30, Fidelity Ireland Corp., 1930-33, also v.p. Fidelity Trust Co., 1932-33, v.p. Nat. Rockland Bank of Boston, 1933-42; pres. Worcester County Trust Co., 1942-50; pres. and dir. Second Nat. Bank, Boston, 1950-55; pres., dir. State Street Bank and Trust Co., Boston, 1955-74, chmn. executive com., 1961-74; trustee Provident Instn. for Savings, Boston; mem. bd. dirs. Dennison Mfg. Co.; dir., mem. finance committee State Mut. Life Ins. Co.; dir. Wyman-Gordon Co., State Mut. Life Assurance Co., Crompton & Knowles Corporation, Worcester, Mass., Dennison Manufacturing Company. Chairman of the Auditorium Commn. City of Boston. Member corporation New England Deaconess Hosp. Served as pvt., advancing through grades to maj., U.S. Army, 1917-19, with A.E.F. in France. Decorated Croix de Guerre (France); Silver Star Citation. Trustee Bowdoin Coll.; corporator Simmons Coll. Mem. Mass. Bankers Assn. (past pres.), Association of Reserve City Bankers (past dir.), Greater Boston C. of C. (v.p.), Beta Theta Pi. Republican. Mason. Clubs: Union (Boston); Worchester. Home: Brunswick Me. Died Oct. 25, 1974.

IRVINE, CLARENCE (SHORTRIDGE), air force officer, mfg. co. exec.; b. St. Paul, Neb., Dec. 16, 1898; s. James and Margaret Jane (Welch) I.; student St. Paul Coll., 1912-18, U. Neb., 1921-22, Air Corps Sch. Tech., 1933-34, Coll. Armed Forces, 1937-38, Harvard Sch. Bus. Adminstrn., 1948; D.E., Clarkson Sch. Tech.; D.Sc., Adelphi Coll.; m. Ruth Ann Saltzman, Dec. 16, 1946; children—Jane Reese, James Welch; m. 2d, Carol Pierpont Jones. Served as flying cadet U.S. Army, 1918-21; maj. gen. USAF, 1921 to lt. gen. dep. chief staff 21st Bomber Command, 1944-45, SAC, from 1947; comdr. 509th Bomber Wing, 19th Air Div., 8th Air Force, Korean War; dep. chief of staff, Materiel, USAF, 1956-59, ret.; v.p., dir. planning Avco Corp., 1959-62, asst. to pres., from 1962; cons. Rockwell Internat. Decorated D.S.M. with oak leaf cluster, Silver Star medal, legion of Merit with oak leaf cluster, D.F.C. with oak leaf cluster, Air medal with oak leaf cluster, Bronze Star medal with oak leaf cluster. K.C. (4°), Elk. Clubs: Athletic (Detroit); Rivercrest Country, Colonial Country (Ft. Worth); Army-Navy Country (Washington); Burning Tree Country (Bethesda, Md.); Moraine Country (Dayton, O.); Mt. Kenya-Safari (East Africa); Nat. Space, Army Navy; Bel Air Country (Beverly Hills, Cal.); Jonathan (Los Angeles); Bermuda Dunes Country, Canyon Country, O'Donnell Golf, Tamerisk Country (Palm Springs, Cal.). Home: Redondo Beach, Cal. Died Sept. 7, 1975; interred Arlington Nat. Cemetery, Arlington, Va.

IRWIN, EDITH ALICE, librarian; b. San Francisco; d. Raymond and Alice (Hagarty) Irwin; A.B., Stanford, 1940; M.L.S., Columbia, 1941. Librarian catalog sect. Library of Hawaii, Honolulu, 1941-49; librarian Cal. State Library, Sacramento, 1950-53, periodicals librarian, 1953-66, supervising acquisitions librarian, 1967-71. Mem. Am., Cal. library assns., Stanford Alumni Assn. Home: Sacramento, Cal. Died May 22, 1971.

IRWIN, JAMES ELLIS, lawyer; b. Memphis, May 1, 1920; s. Robert L. and Ethel (Farris) I; LL.B., U. Memphis, 1940, LL.B. (hon.), Memphis State U., 1946; postgrad. U. Tenn., 1946-47; m. Nada Saskor, Apr. 29, 1946; 1 dau., Gwyneth Anne. Admitted to Tenn. bar, 1940; partner Blount & Irwin, 1947-52, Irwin & Dunlap, 1953-65; sr. partner Irwin, Owens, Gillock, Colton & Lyne, 1965-74; gen. counsel, dir. William B. Tanner Co, Inc. Chmn., Shelby County Democratic Exec. Com., 1962-74, del. nat. conv., 1964; Dem. nominee for Congress from 9th Dist. Tenn., 1968. Appeal agt. Draft Bd. 104, 1957-74. Bd. dirs. Danny Thomas Memphis Classic. Served to lt. (j.g.) USCGR, 1941-46. Mem. Am., Tenn., Memphis and Shelby County bar assns., Memphis Trial Lawyers' Assn. (pres.), Delta Theta Phi. Clubs: Colonial Country, Holly Hills Country, Winterhaven Golf and Country, Top of 100. President's. Home: Memphis, Tenn. Died Dec. 30, 1974.

ISAAC, JOSEPH ELIAS, theatre exhibitor; b. Zahle, Lebanon, Apr. 12, 1898; s. Elias Isaac and Rose (Aziz) I.; student pub. schs.; m. Alene Thomas, June 13, 1925; children—Joseph, Alfred, Samuel, Mary Jo, Barbara Alene, Rigdon, Victoria. Pres. Cumberland Amusement Co., Inc. Theatre Chain (9) Theatres, from 1928, Guaranty Deposit Bank, Cumberland, Ky., from 1936. Chmn. City Planning and Zone Commn. Served as lt. U.S. Army, 1918-19. Mem. Ky. Assn. Theatre Owners (dir.), Am. Legion. Mason (Shriner, 32 deg.). Home: Cumberland, KY. Deceased.

ISAAK, NICHOLAS, architect; b. Dardhe, Albania, Sept. 22, 1913; s. Charles and Olympia (Stephany) I.; student Sanborn Sem., 1932, St. Anselms Coll., 1933; B.S. U. N.H., 1936; m. Barbara Pineo, July 6, 1940; children—Marcia, Nicholas, Carolyn. Draftsman, supervising architects office U. N.H., 1937-40; designer Lockwood Greene Engrs., 1941-42; practicing architect Koehler & Isaack, Manchester, N.H., 1946-75; designed St. Anselms Coll. bldgs., Pease AFB bldgs., dormitory at U. N.H., bldgs. at Keene Tchrs. Coll., cts., Post Office bldg., Concord, N.H., Chancery Bldg., Manchester, Fed. office bldgs., Post Office Concord and Portsmouth, others. Water color exhibit Currier Gallery Art, 1946. Mem. City Planning Commn., Manchester; vice chmn. So. N.H. Planning Commn. Served as lt. (j.g.) USNR, 1943-46. Mem. A.I.A. (pres. N.H. chpt., Design award N.H. chpt. 1965, 68, 70), N.H. Art Assn., Soc. Archtl. Historians. Home: Auburn, N.H. Died July 23, 1975.

ISENSTEAD, JOSEPH HERMAN, physician; b. Putzig, West Prussia, Germany, Aug. 27, 1891 (came to U.S. 1936, naturalized 1943); s. Hermann and Jenny (Eisack) Eisenstadt; student Friedrich Wilhelm U., Berlin, 1910-11, 12-14, U. Munich, 1911-12; med. license U. Berlin, 1915, M.D., 1917; m. Elly Neumann, June 5, 1916; children—Erich Wolfgang, Ruth (Mrs. Milton E. Tausend). Intern, resident in mil. service, 1914-19; med. dir. Prisoner of War Camp Hosp., Crossen/Oder, Germany, 1919-21; practice medicine, Berlin, 1924-36, N.Y.C., 1937-41, Sharon Springs, N.Y., 1941-48; practice medicine specializing in treatment liver disease, Canajoharie, N.Y., 1948-73; mem. staff Amsterdam (N.Y.) Meml. Hosp. Served to 2d lt. M.C., German Army, 1914-19. Decorated Iron Cross. Mem. A.M.A., Internat. Platform Assn., N.Y. State, Montgomery County med. socs., A.A.A.S. Research in hepatology. Address: Canajoharie N.Y. Died June 3, 1973; interred, Canajoharie, N.Y.

ISHAM, HOWARD EDWIN, steel co. exec.; b. Cleve., Nov. 18, 1894; s. Frank Durban and Anna Elizabeth (Schleicher) L.; student Fenn Coll., Cleve., 1912-15, Doctor of Commercial Science, 1955; Doctor of Laws, Birmingham-Southern Coll., 1959; m. Margaret Elizabeth Valmore, September 10, 1915; children—William Valmore, Howard Edwin (dec.), Lucy Anne (Mrs. A. C. Staley, Jr.). Acct. Sherwin Williams Co., Cleve., 1916-23; propr. retail paint, wallpaper bus., Mansfield, O., 1923-26; purchasing agt. Barnes Mfg. Co., Mansfield, 1926-27; acct. Cleve. Cliffs Iron Co., 1927-29; with Firestone Tire & Rubber Co., Akron, O., 1929-38; audit supervisor Carnegie-Ill. Steel Corp., 1938-41; asst. v.p., asst. comptroller U.S. Steel Corp. (Del.), Pittsburgh, 1941-50, asst. exec. v.p. U.S. Steel Co., 1951, v.p., treas., 1952-59. Vice pres. Salvation Army New York State Adv. Conf.; bd. mgrs. Meth. Hosp., Bklyn.; vice pres. Protestant Council of City of N.Y.; treas. bd. of trustees YMCA N.Y.C.; mem. citizens adv. com. N.Y. Pub. Library; trustee Finch Coll. Mem. U.S. C. of C., Am. Iron and Steel Inst., Am. Ordnance Assn., Nat. Inst. Social Sciences, American Society Naval Engrs., N.A.M., Navy League of U.S., Nat. Security Indsl. Assn. (trustee, exec. com. and chmn. bd.), Defense Orientation Conf. Assn. Methodist (mem. bd. trustees). Mason. Clubs: Union League, Down Town Association Metropolitan, Pinnacle, Economic, Ohio Soc. (resident v.p.) (N.Y.C.); Duquesne, Pittsburgh Athletic Assn. (Pitts.); Rolling Rock (Ligonier, Pa.). Home: Butler, N.J. Died Jan. 10, 1975.

ITTLESON, HENRY, JR., banker; b. St. Louis, Oct. 25, 1900; s. Henry and Blanche (Frank) I.; student Worcester (Mass.) Acad., 1914-17; Colgate Univ., 1919-21, U. Mich., 1921-22; m. Nancy Strauss, Jan. 4, 1936; children—Henry Anthony, Pamela Lee. Chmn. bd. C.I.T. Financial Corp., N.Y.C., 1962-68, hon. chmn. bd., 1968-73, also dir.; dir. Nat. Bank N. Am. Served as lt. col. USAAF, 1942-45. Clubs: Westchester (N.Y.) Country; Turf and Field (Belmont Park, N.Y.); Tamarisk Country, O'Donnell Golf (Palm Springs, Cal.). Home: New York City, N.Y. Died Aug. 25, 1973.

IVERSEN, LORENZ, machinery co. exec.; b. Denmark, Apr. 15, 1876; s. Andreas and Elsie Marie (Christensen) I.; M.E., Univ. of Bingen am Rhine, Germany, 1902; m. Gertrude Maria Adelsperger, 1905; children—Mary Helen (Mrs. Frank A. Dixon), Pauline (Mrs. Casper Peter Mayer), Andreas Aloysius, John Donald, Robert Francis; m. 2d, Fleda Levina Foust, Oct. 18, 1935. Came to U.S., 1897, naturalized, 1907. With Mesta Machine Co., Pittsburgh, since 1902, as draftsman, 1902-12, chief engr., 1912-27, v.p., dir. and gen. mgr., 1927-30, pres., from 1930; dir. Fidelity Trust Co., Pittsburgh. Mem. Engr. Soc. Western Pa., Am. Iron and Steel Inst. Clubs: Duquesne, University, Pittsburgh Athletic, Longue Vue, Oakmount (Pittsburgh); Woodmont Rod and Gun (Md.). Licensed private airplane pilot, 1938. Home: Pittsburgh, Pa.†

IVIE, JOHN MARK, psychiatrist; b. Memphis, Feb. 17, 1933; s. James M. and Gladys (Brooks) I.; M.D., Memphis State U., 1955-59; M.D., U. Tenn., 1962; m. Shirley Marie Gilliland, Dec. 30, 1955 (div. Feb. 1966); 1 dau., Marianne. Intern, St. Joseph Hosp., Memphis, 1962-63; resident dep. psychiatry U. Tenn., Memphis, 1963-66; staff psychiatrist Tenn. Psychiat. Hosp. and Inst., Memphis, 1966-67; practice medicine specializing in psychiatry, Memphis, 1967-75; cons. Ark. Div. Vocat. Rehab. Served with USAF, 1950-55. Mem. A.M.A., Tenn., Memphis, Shelby County med. assns., Am. Psychiat. Assn., Lambda Chi Alpha, Phi Rho Sigma, Chi Beta Phi. Home: Memphis, Tenn. Died Feb. 17, 1975.

IVY, ROBERT HENRY, physician; b. Southport, Eng., May 21, 1881; s. Robert Sutcliffe and Annie Edith (Cryer) I.; D.D.S., University of Pennsylvania, 1902, M.D., 1907; D.Sc. (honorary), 1954; married Norma C. Crossland, June 19, 1912; children—Cynthia Thompson, Robert Henry, Eleanor Anne, Peter Cryer. Practiced in Phila., 1907-15, Milwaukee, Wis., 1915-17. Capt., Med. R.C., 1917, and on duty Office of Surgeon Gen., U.S. Army, Washington, until Aug. 1918; maj. Feb. 1918, lt. col., Aug. 1919; A.E.F., France, Sept. 1918-Feb. 1919; on duty Surgeon Gen.'s Office and Walter Reed Gen. Hosp., Feb.-Oct. 1919; now col. M.R.C. Member committee on surgery and chairman subcommittee on plastic and maxillo-facial surgery of National Research Council, 1940-46. Civilian consultant plastic surgery, office Surgeon Gen., U.S. Army. Mem. bd. hon. consultants, Army Med. Library, Washington, D.C. Prof. maxillo-facial surgery, U. of Pa. from 1919, prof. plastic surgery, 1944-51, emertius, 1951-74; cons. cleft palate section Pa. State Health Department; formerly trustee of University. Received certificate of appreciation, War Dept., 1946, U. Pa. Alumni Award of Merit, 1946. Fellow Am. Coll. Surgeons; mem. Am. Soc. Plastic and Reconstructive Surgery, Am., Pennsylvania State and Philadelphia County medical socs., Am. Surg. Assn., Coll. Physicians of Phila., Phila. Pathol. Soc., Phila. Acad. Surgery, Am. and Pa. State dental socs., Soc. Consultants to the

Armed Forces, American Association Plastic Surgeons, Loyal Legion. Hon. member several fgn. professional associations. Republican. Clubs: Philadelphia Country (Philadelphia); also Army and Navy (Washington). Author: Applied Anatomy and Oral Surgery, 1911; Applied Immunology (with B.A. Thomas), 1916; Essentials of Oral Surgery (with V. P. Blair), 1923. Fractures of the Jaws (with L. Curtis), 1931; A Link With the Past (autobiography), 1962. Past editor-in-chief Plastic and Reconstructive Surgery. Home: Paoli, Pa. Died June 12, 1974.

JACKS, ALLEN, newspaperman; b. Rockford, Ill.; grad. Dartmouth, 1937; m. Michele Jacks; 2 sons. Fgn. corr. A.P., Italy, Yugoslavia, Greece, Turkey, 1952-57; bur. chief, Rome, 1957-75. Served to lt. col. AUS, World War II. Home: Rome Italy. Died July 4, 1975.

JACKS, HORACE LEONARD, banker; b. Waco, Tex., June 17, 1924; s. Thomas L. and Mollie (Gibson) J.; student So. Meth. U., 1958-60; m. Mary Louise Branch, Mar. 2, 1946; children—George Michael, Mary Lynette. Bookkeeper First Nat. Bank, Waco, 1942, First Nat. Bank. Dallas, 1946-54; asst. cashier, 1954-56, asst. v.p., 1956-62, v.p., 1962-73, pres., dir. ARM, Inc., 1966-67. Bd. dirs. Children, Inc., 1969-73. Served with USNR, 1943-46. Mem. Systems and Procedures Assn. (pres. Dallas 1964-65). Home: Dallas Tex. Died Aug. 10, 1973; interred Laurel Land Cemetery, Dallas, Tex.

JACKSON, AL, drummer, songwriter, record producer; m. Barbara Jackson. With Booker T and MG's, until 1968; drummer with Otis Redding, Wilson Pickett, Carla Thomas, Staple Singers, Sam & Dave, Eddie Floyd; drummer, writer for Al Green and Willie Mitchell. Composer: (with Green and Mitchell) Let's Stay Together, Cal! Me, I'm Still in Love with You. Home: Memphis, Tenn. Died Oct. 1, 1975.

JACKSON, ARTHUR CONARD, management engr.; b. Phila., Pa., Dec. 11, 1879; s. Milton and Caroline (Swayne) J.; B.S. in Architecture, Univ. of Pa., 1901, student engring., 1901-02 (Henley crew '01); m. Edith Wilson, April 27, 1907 (dec. Jan. 1961); m. 2d, Helen Harper, Dec. 1962; children—Ruth (Mrs. William A. Boone), Caroline (Mrs. Leon A. Rushmore, Jr.), Edith W. (Mrs. Raymond E. Nelson, Jr.), Elizabeth W. (Mrs. Robert S. Kamp). Began as apprentice with Miller Lock Co., Philadelphia, Pa., 1902; consulting engineer, specializing in management problems and sales engring., Phila., 1928-34 and from 1936; adminstr. Tenn. Valley Asso. Coops., 1934-35; chmn. bd. Jackson-Walter Co.; dir. Esmeralda Purral Mining Company. Sent to Germany by Food Adminstr. Hoover to organize child feeding, 1919. Chmn. of Friends (Quakers) Gen. Conf., 21 yrs.; mem. bd. dirs. George School, Newtown, Pa. Life mem. Am. Soc. Mech. Engrs., Am. Soc. Tool Engrs. Republican. Clubs: Union League., Rolling Green Golf; Highland Park (Lake Wales, Fla.). Home: Philadelphia, Pa.†

JACKSON, CARLTON, commercial attaché; b. Eagleville, Tenn., June 26, 1880; s. Travis Marion and Nannie (Carlton) J.; A.B., U. of Nashville, Tenn., 1898; studied Vanderbilt U. and Columbia; m. Olive Wiggins, Oct. 26, 1912; 3 children. With Equitable Life Assurance Soc., St. Louis, and Kansas City, until 1904; with Nat. Bur. of Edn., at Nashville, 1904-11; mgr. for Honduras and Tabasco (Mex.) divs. of Atlantic Fruit Co., 1911-17. Commd. 1st lt. Gas Defense Div., U.S. Army, 1918; apptd. trade commr. U.S. Dept. of Commerce, Lima, Peru, Sept. 1919; commercial attaché, Mexico City, Nov. 1920; then trade commr. to Colombia and Venezuela; commercial attaché, Bogota, 1924, Havana, Cuba, 1925, Rio de Janeiro, 1926; engaged in exporting from Brazil from Oct. 1933. Club: Exporters (New York). Address: Rio de Janeiro, Brazil.†

JACKSON, E(DWARD) FRANKLIN, clergyman, member of Democratic National Committee; born at Pennsacola, Florida, July 19, 1911; the son of Charles Wesley and Phebe Elizabeth (Hart) Jackson; student Fla. A. and M. Coll., 1932, Tuskegee Inst., 1935, U. Buffalo, 1947; D.D., Livingstone Coll.-Hood Sem., Salisbury, N.C., 1948; m. Mildred Elizabeth Dodson, Sept. 1, 1937; children—Edward Franklin II, Cameron Weslev. Gloria Jean, Darryl J. Ordained to ministry A.M.E. Zion Ch., 1934; pastor in Evergreen, Ala., 1934-36, 37, Cleveland, Tenn, 1937-40, Chattanooga, 1940-42, Johnson City, Tenn., 1942-43, Buffalo, 1943-52, John Wesley Nat. Ch., Washington, 1952-75. Vice pres. D.C. Central Dem. Com., 1960-64; mem. Nat. Dem. Speakers Bur., 1960-75; mem. Dem. Nat. Com. for D.C., 1964-68. Pres. Ministers and Laymens Assn. A.M.E. Zion Ch., 1953-75, also mem. com. 100. Pres. D.C. br. N.A.A.C.P., 1959-64; v.p. Citizens Adv. Com. Civil Rights Commn., 1962-75. Named Afro Am. Man of Year, Afro-Am. Newspaper, 1957. Mem. Omega Psi Phi. Mason (33°, Shriner), Elk. Author: The Full Grown Minister, 1949; My Church, 1952. Home: Washington, D.C. Died Jan. 1975.

JACKSON, ELIZABETH NOLAND, social agy. exec.; b. Indpls., Feb. 17, 1916; d. Stephen C. and Teresa (Murray) Noland; A.B., Radcliffe Coll., 1937; postgrad. Merrill-Palmer Inst., 1960, Ind. U., 1961-62; m. Bruce Hunt Fernald, June 5, 1936 (div. Jan. 1945); 1 son, Stephen Bruce; m. 2d, Donald Warrick Jackson, Apr. 2, 1947 (dec. June 1955); children—Anthony Hargrove, Jill Noland. Free-lance writer, editor Marion County Mail, Indpls., 1954-59, exec. dir. Social Health Assn., 1959-74. Mem. Ind. Council Family Relations (past pres.), Soc. Ind. Pioneers. Republican. Episcopalain. Club: Indpls. Press. Author (with Cloyd J. Julian), Modern Sex Education, 1967; rev., 1972. articles on sex edn. profl. mags. Home: Indianapolis, Ind. Died Dec. 3, 1974; buried Crown Hill Cemetery, Indianapolis, Ind.

JACKSON, JOHN GILLESPIE, JR., lawyer; b. N.Y.C., Nov. 1, 1909; s. John Gillespie and Grace J. (Bunce) J.; A.B., Princeton U., 1932; LL.B., Columbia, 1935; m. George-Anne Collin, Aug. 4, 1950; children—Marian Q. (Mrs. William A. Davidson), John Gillespie III. With Dept. Justice, Washington, 1935-37; admitted to N.Y. bar; practiced in N.Y.C., 1937-70; partner Jackson, Nash. Brophy, Barringer & Brooks, 1937-73. Mayor, Inc. Village Mill Neck, 1964-70. Bd. dirs. Home For Old Men and Aged Couples. Served to maj. USAAF, 1942-45. Republican. Episcopalian. Home: Locust Valley, N.Y. Died Aug. 21, 1973.

JACKSON, KATHERINE GAUSS, mag. editor; b. Bethlehem, Pa., May 20, 1904; d. Christian and Alice (Hussey) Gauss; A.B., Smith Coll., 1924; m. Andrew Jackson, May 30, 1930; children—Andrew (dec.), Stuart Agar. Asst. to publicity dir. Princeton, 1924-27; asst. editor Charm mag., 1927-32; asst. editor Scribner's mag., 1932-38; sr. editor charge fiction and book revs. Harper's mag., 1938-69; cons. Harper's Mag. Press, 1969-75. Bd. dirs. Freedom House, N.Y.C., 1940-63, asst. treas., 1963-74. Editor: (with Hiram Haydn) The Papers of Christian Gauss, 1957. Home: North Egremont Mass. Died May 28, 1975.

JACKSON, LEONORA (MRS. WILLIAM DUNCAN MCKIM), violinist; b. Boston, Mass., Feb. 20, 1878; d. Charles P. and Elizabeth (Higgins) J.; ed. pub. schs., Chicago; grad. Royal Sch. of Music, Berlin; as a student in Berlin was awarded Mendelssohn State prize; m. 2d, William Duncan McKim, Oct. 12, 1915. Soloist with symphony orchestras in Germany, France, England and Scotland, receiving decoration from Queen Victoria; made 6 tours in U.S. and appeared 8 times as soloist with Boston Symphony Orchestra, also with other orchestras in Chicago, Detroit, Cincinnati, St. Louis, etc.; made tour of world, 1926. Episcopalian. Republican. Contbr. to The Violinist.†

JACKSON, LEROY FREEMAN, educational dir.; b. London, Ont., Can., July 15, 1881; s. Robert Freeman and Lizzie (Davis) J.; brought to U.S., 1889; A.B., U. of N.Dak., 1902; M.Ph., U. of Chicago, 1909; Austin scholar in history, Harvard, 1912-13; m. Emilie Caroline Baehr, June 7, 1905; children—Robert Charles, Ruth Allene. Supt. schs., Harvey, N.Dak., 1902-05; prin. high sch., Stillwater, Minn., 1905-06; supt. schs., Larimore, N.D., 1906-08; instr. and prof. Am. history, State Coll. of Wash., 1909-20; ednl. dir. Stanley McCormick Sch. (applying principles of progressive edn. to secondary and college fields), Burnsville, N.C., 1920-27, pres., from 1927 (name changed to Carolina New Coll.). Mem. 1st O.T.C. and 1st lt. C.A.C., May 13, 1917-Feb. 4, 1918; ednl. dir. Spruce Div. under Y.M.C.A., served overseas with Y.M.C.A. and Army Ednl. Corps. Mem. Am. Hist. Assn. Conglist. Mason. Author: The Peter Patter Book, 1918; Jolly Jinks Song Book (music by Edith Lobdell Reed), 1922; Ring-Go-Round (music by same), 1925; Rimskittle's Book, 1926. Home: Brunsville, N.C.†

JACKSON, LYMAN E., coll. dean; b. Oregon, Wis., Aug. 8, 1897; s. Edson Bela and Josephine F. (Bull) J.; B.S., U. of Wis., 1921, M.S., 1925; Ph.D., U. of Minn., 1931; m. Madelon Charity Willman, Aug. 26, 1922; children—Josephine Mary, Willman Edson. High sch. teacher, 1921-23; president South Dakota State College of Agriculture and Mechanic Arts, Brookings, S.D., 1941-46; dean, College Agriculture, Pa. State University, 1946-73. Served with Coast Arty., 1918. Chmn. com. on instruction in agr., and special com. on orgn., Assn. of Land Grant Colls. and univs., mem. survey commn. Minn. Schs. Agr., 1944-45; mem. S.D. Bd. Vocational Edn. Mem. Nat. Grange, Newcomen Soc.; sec.-treas. Assn. Land-Grant Colls. and Univs., Oct. 1945-January 1947 (chmn. program com. conv., 1948; chmn. com. on ednl. purposes, 1948-49); mem. Alpha Tau Alpha, Scabbard and Blade, Gamma Sigma Delta, Phi Delta Kappa, Alpha Zeta, Alpha Gamma Rho, Phi Mu Alpha. Mason. Author books including: Design for Comprehensive Education, 1945. Home: State College, Pa. Died July 23, 1973.

JACKSON, MARGARET WEYMOUTH, writer; b. Eureka Springs, Ark., Feb. 11, 1895; d. George L. D. and Martha Stuart (Connell) Weymouth; student Hillsdale (Mich.) Coll., 1914-16, hon. D.H.L., 1940; m. Charles Carter Jackson, Jan. 10, 1920; children—Martha Florence, Elizabeth Ann, Charles Weymouth. Asst. editor Farm Life, Spencer, 1916; sec. to dean Wilson Coll., Chambersburg, Pa., 1916-17, to G. Nary, Nelson Blower & Furnace Co., munitions, Boston, Mass., 1917-18; woman's editor Farm Life, 1918; asso. editor Better Farming, Chicago, 1918-19. Lived in Manitoba, Can., 1920-24. Mem. Pi Beta Phi. Democrat. Christian Scientist. Author: Elizabeth's Tower, 1926; Beggars Can Choose, 1928; Jenny Fowler, 1930; First Fiddle, 1932; Sarah Thornton, 1933; Kindy's Crossing, 1934. Contbr. serials and short stories in Good Housekeeping, McCall's, Saturday Evening Post, Ladies' Home Journal, Country Gentleman Pictorial Review, Woman's Home Companion, etc. Home: Spencer, Ind. Died Apr. 5, 1974.

JACKSON, N. BAXTER, banker; b. Nashville, Dec. 3, 1890; s. Robert Fenner and Mannie (Baxter) J.; B.S., Vanderbilt U., 1911; m. 2d, Mrs. Judith Blank, Nov. 21, 1945. Clerk First Nat. Bank Nashville, 1911-14; cashier Cumberland Valley Nat. Bank, Nashville, 1914-17; v.p. Am. Nat. Bank, Nashville, 1919-20; with Chem. Nat. Bank, N.Y.C., Chem. Bank & Trust Company, 1920-68, chmn. bd. Chem. Corn Exchange Bank to 1956, chmn. exec. com., 1956-66, hon. chmn. internat. adv. bd. Chem. Bank, 1966-69, hon. chmn. bd., 1969-73, hon. dir., 1971-73; dir. Home Life Ins. Co., Warner-Lambert Pharm. Co. Bd. dir. Beekman-Downtown Hosp., trustee Vanderbilt U., Roosevelt Hosp. Served to maj. 114th F.A., U.S. Army, 1917-19. Decorated Medal of Merit (U.S.) given with diploma by Gen. Pershing (citations and battle stars included); Black Star, Legion of Honor. Mem. S.A.R., Phi Delta Theta. Roman Catholic. Clubs: Mount Royal (Montreal, Que., Can.; Brook Downtown Association, Recess, University, Manhattan, Merchants, Links (N.Y.C.); Rolling Rock (Ligionier, Pa.); Connequot River. Home: New York City, N.Y. Died May, 1973.

JACKSON, RICHARD SEYMOUR, editor; b. New Haven, Aug. 30, 1910; s. John Day and Rose Marie (Herrick) J.; grad. Taft Sch., 1929; B.A., Yale, 1934; m. Helene Danforth Coler, Oct. 10, 1942 (div. Mar. 1954); children—Helene Danforth (Mrs. Scott MaGill), Rosemary Herrick; m. 2d, Jean W. Washburn, Nov. 15, 1956. Reporter, legislative corr. New Haven Register, 1934-37, asst. to pub., 1937-52, asst. pub., 1953-60, asso. ed., 1953-60, editor, co-pub., 1960-72, dir., 1960-74; pres. Asso. Dailies of Conn. 1942-45; pub. New Haven Jour. Courier, 1951-52; dir. Carrington Pub. Co., New Haven, 1947-64; v.p., sec. dir. Register Pub. Co., 1956-60, sr. v.p., 1960, pres., dir., 1960-73, trustee, dir., 1973-74. Mem. Mayor's Human Rights Com., 1963-64, gov.'s Clean Air Task Force, 1966, gov.'s Clean Water Task Force, 1968, Environmental Policy Com., 1970. Trustee Hosp. St. Raphael, New Haven; bd. dirs. Gaylord Hosp., Wallingford, Conn. Fellow Pierson Coll., Yale. Fellow Am. Geog. Soc.; mem. Am. Soc. Newspaper Editors, Soc. Colonial Wars, Internat. Press Inst., Soc. Cin., Inter Am. Press Assn., Newcomen Soc., Sigma Delta Chi, Chi Psi. Episcopalian. Clubs: Laurel; Devon Yacht (bd. govs.); Maidstone (East Hampton, N.Y.); Yale (N.Y.C.); Graduates Mory's, New Haven Lawn, Faculty (New Haven). Home: North Haven Conn. Died Dec. 12, 1974.

JACKSON, ROBERT, lawyer; b. Dover, N.H., May 21, 1880; s. James Robert and Lydia (Drew) J.; A.B., Dartmouth, 1900; law student Harvard, 1901-04; m. Dorothy Witter Branch, Oct. 14, 1909 (died May 31, 1933); children—Sarah Branch (Mrs. W. Forbes Morgan), Hope. Began practice of law at Concord, N.H., 1907; organizer, 1919, pres. until 1930, Dominion Stores, Ltd. Excise commr. State of N.H., 1915-17; sec. N.H. Com. on Pub. Safety, 1917. Chmn. N.H. Dem. State Com., 1919-28; mem. Dem. Nat. Com., 1928-36, sec. same and chmn. Speakers Bur., 1932-33. Trustee Tabor Acad., N.H. Hist. Soc. Episcopalian. Clubs: Metropolitan, Burning Tree, Congressional Country, National Press (Washington); University, Harvard (Boston); Union Interalliee (Paris). Home: Concord, N.H.*†

JACKSON, ROBERT MANSON, editor; b. Alamogordo, N.M., Jan. 21, 1907; s. Robert Mallory and Margaret (Manon) J.; B.J., U. of Mo., 1928; m. Helen Dowty, Nov. 17, 1936; 1 son, Robert Manson III. Mem. staff San Angelo (Tex.) Standard-Times, 1928-31; clerk to R. E. Thomason, M.C., 1931-33; asst. librarian U.S. Senate, 1933-34; sec. to Senator Tom Connally, 1934-38; staff writer Washington bur. A.P., 1938-41; mng. editor Corpus Christi (Tex.) Times, 1941-45, editor Caller-Times, 1945-73. Recipient Honor award distinguished service in journalism U. Mo., 1966. Mem. Am. Soc. of Newspaper Editors. Presbyn. Club: National Press (Washington). Home: Corpus Christi Tex. Died Oct. 2, 1973; interred, San Angelo, Tex.

JACKSON, WILLIAM NEIL, agr. co. exec.; b. Stratford, Tex., Jan. 26, 1928; s. Harry Thomas and Effie Elizabeth (Webb) J.; B.S., W. Tex. State U., 1949; m. Theresa Keeney, Jan. 8, 1955; children—Patti, Kim. Rancher, cattle buyer, 1953-67; pres. Stratford Feedyards, Inc., 1967-72; v.p. Stratford of Tex., Inc., Houston, 1969-72; dir. 1st State Bank, Stratford. Pres. Stratford Sch. Bd., 1963-66. Served with AUS, 1951-53. Mem. Christian Ch. Home: Stratford Tex. Died Oct. 9, 1972; interred, Stratford, Tex.

JACOBS, ARTHUR P., film producer; b. Los Angeles, Mar. 7, 1922; s. Arthur P. and Natalie (Ankle) J.; student U. So. Cal., 1942; m. Natalie Trundy, June 8, 1968. Messenger MGM Studios, 1943-44, apprentice publicity dept., 1944-45; publicist Warner Bros. Studios, 1946; opened own pub. relations office, 1947; formed Arthur P. Jacobs Co., Inc., representing entertainment and indsl. accounts, Beverly Hills, Cal., 1956, pres., 1956-73; pres. APJAC Internat., 1963-73; films include

What A Way to Go!, Doctor Dolittle, Planet of the Apes, Goodbye, Mr. Chips, The Chairman, Beneath the Planet of the Apes, Escape From the Planet of the Apes, Play it Again Sam, Conquest of the Planet of the Apes, Tom Sawyer, Battle for the Planet of the Apes, Huckleberry Finn. Mem. Acad. Motion Picture Arts and Scis. Home: Beverly Hills Cal. Died June 27, 1973.

JACOBS, BERNARD, radio sta. exec.; b. Chgo., Feb. 25, 1918; s. Harry Z. and Gertrude (Fabstein) J.; one son, Noah Ben Jacobs. Manager of radio station WOAK, 1948-51; founder Chicago (Illinois) Fine Arts Sta. WFMT, now pres., gen. mgr. Recipient Alfred I. duPont A00 Radio Award, 1956, 62; Thomas Alva Edison Found, award, 1958; Ohio State U. award, 1959; Soc. Typographic Arts, Certificate of Excellence for WFMT Guide, 1960; George Foster Peabody Radio Award, 1961; Alfred I. DuPont Awards Found. award, 1962. Publisher WFMT Guide. Home: Chicago, Ill., Died Nov. 1, 1975.

JACOBS, TEVIS, lawyer; b. Alameda, Cal., Feb. 21, 1906; s. Saul Robert and Sara (Brilliant) J.; A.B., U. Cal., 1926, J.D., 1928; m. Jean Schuck, May 31, 1936; children—Diane (Mrs. Moore), Stephen, Loraine (Mrs. Horne). Admitted to Cal. bar, 1928, practiced in Oakland, 1928-33, San Francisco, 1933; now partner Jacobs, Sills, & Coblentz. Vis. lectr. law U. Cal., 1955-68; dir. Grodins of Cal. Bd. dirs. U. Art Museum Council; trustee Union Am. Hebrew Congregations. Mem. Am., Cal., San Francisco bar Assns., Order of Colf. Author articles legal jours. Home: San Francisco Cal. Died Feb. 26, 1974.

JACOBSEN, A. P., govt. agrl. counsellor; b. Lergaard pr. skibby, Denmark, Feb. 17, 1879; s. Christen and Hanne Marie (Hansen) J.; B.S., Royal Danish Agr. Coll., Copenhagen, Agrl. tchr. Dalum Agrl. Sch., 1904-09; agrl. adviser to farmers' orgns., 1910-19, to Danish Govt., Copenhagen, from 1919; agrl. attache in Berlin, 1919-45. Chmn. Danish Nat. F.A.O. Com. from 1948, mem. council, 1948-51; mem. O.E.E.C. Com. on Food and Agr. from 1947. Mem. Danish Acad. for Tech. Sci. Liberal. Lutheran. Home: Lyngby, Denmark.†

JACOBSEN, CARLYLE, psychologist, educator; b. Minneapolis, Minn., Jan. 17, 1902; s. Christian and Ane (Hanson) J.; student Hamline University, St. Paul, Minnesota, 1921-22; A.B., University of Minn., 1924, Ph.D., 1928; m. Marion Myer, Dec. 17, 1927 (dec.); 1 dau., Patricia; m. 2d, Ellen Townley Cook, August 12, 1958. Instructor in psychology U. of Minn., 1924-28; prof. of medical psychology Washington U., St. Louis, Mo., 1938-46, asst. dean Sch. of Medicine, 1942-46; dean Grad. Coll., State U. of Iowa, 1946-47, exec. dean, div. health sciences and services, 1947-50; exec. dean for med. edn. State U. of N.Y., 1955-57; pres. Med. Center, Upstate Med. Center of State U. of N.Y., 1957-67. Exec. vice chmn. Med. Sch. Grants Adv. Com., Ford Found., 1956-57; mem. USPHS Nat. Advisory Council, 1956-61. Awarded Howard Crosby Warren medal for expl. psychology, 1938. Mem. Am. Psychol. Assn., Assn. for Research in Nervous and Mental Disease, Nat. Inst. Gen. Med. Scis. Council, Sigma Xi. Home: Cazenovia, N.Y. Died Mar. 13, 1974.

JACOBSEN, NORMAN, artist; b. at Cokeville, Wyo., Sept. 15, 1884; s. Julius Christian and Josephine (Otterson) J.; student Art Inst. Chicago, 1905. Lewis Inst., Chicago, 1906-07. New York Sch. of Art, 1908; m. Ethel McClellan Plummer, Dec. 25, 1917. Clubs: Kit Kat, Whitney Studio Club. Author: (with Nina Wilcox Putnam), When the Highbrow Joined the Outfit, 1917; Esmeralda—or Every Little Bit Helps, 1918; Winkle, Winkle and Lollypop, 1918. Made Illustrations for The Fox Readers, and Mother Goose Primer, 1918. Home: New York City, N.Y.†

JACOBSON, SAMUEL, business exec.; b. N.Y.C.; s. Ferdinand and Pauline (Susser) J.; student pub. schools; m. Esme Sharp, Nov. 13, 1941 (dec. Sept. 24, 1954); one daughter, Pauline. Entire career with F. Jacobson & Sons, pres. 1936-74. Home: New York City, N.Y. Died Oct. 28, 1974.

JACOBY, J(AMES) RALPH, neuropsychiatrist; b. N.Y. City, July 9, 1871; son Samuel and Rosalie (Ralph) J.; A.B., Harvard, 1891, grad. student, 1891-92; M.D., Columbia, 1895; student U. of Heidelberg, Germany, 1897-99; m. Ray Scull, Oct. 3, 1906; 1 dau., Mary Scull (Mrs. Willard R. Brown). Attending neurologist Lenox Hill Hosp. Dispensary, 1900-10, chief, of clinic, neurologic dept., 1910-25, cons. neurologist from 1925; dir. New York & Honduras Rossairo Mining Co. Recipient Freedom of City of Bridgetown, Barbados, W.I. Fellow Am. Psychiatric Assn., A.A.A.S., N.Y. Acad. Medicine; mem. Am. Geriatric Society, American Medical Association, New York State Med. Society, Assn. Research in Nervous and Mental Diseases, Soc. Med. Jurisprudence, N.Y. Acad. Medicine, N.Y. Neurol. Soc. Harvey Soc., Am. Med. Editor's and Authors' Assn., Nu Sigma Nu. Clubs: Harvard, Metropolitan, University, Church, The Pilgrims, Authors (London); South Bay Golf (Long Island); Babylon Yacht; Royal Barbados Yacht; Saint George's Society of New York. Author: Electricity in Medicine, 1919. Writer med. monographs; contbr. articles to med. jours. Home: New York City, N.Y.†

JAEGERS, AUGUSTINE, sculptor; b. Barmen, Germany, Mar. 31, 1878; s. Albert and Elizabeth (Loser) J.; brought to U.S., 1882; ed. Art Student's League and Nat. Acad. Design (New York); Ecole des Beaux Arts, Paris; unmarried. Awarded Archtl. League collaboration prize and Avery prize, 1909; executed all the sculpture on arches in the Court of the Four Seasons, San Francisco Expn., 1915; Frey Memorial, New York, 1920; etc. Mem. Nat. Sculpture Soc. Home: Jackson Heights, N.Y.†

JAFFE, DAVID LAWRENCE, educator; b. Bklyn., July 6, 1913; s. Harry and Dora (Botwinick) J.; B.S. in Engring., Coll. City N.Y., 1935; M.S. in Elec. Engring., Columbia, 1936, Ph.D. (S.W. Bridgham fellow 1937-39), 1940; m. Sylvia Ann Finkelstein, Aug. 25, 1940; children—Robert Franklin, Peter Allen, Gilbert Roy, Donald Benton. Asst. elec. engring. Coll. City N.Y., 1935-37; research problems frequency modulation Columbia, 1937-39; with CBS, 1939-42, supr. maintenance video facilities Grand Central Terminal, 1940-42; with Raytheon Mfg. Corp., 1942-44; chief research engr. Templetone Radio Corp., New London, Conn., 1944-45; co-founder Polarad Electronics Corp., Long Island City, 1945, pres., chmn. bd. 1950-69; cons. electronics industry, 1969-71; dep. dir. Nat. Maritime Research Center, Office Research and Devel., Maritime Adminstrn., U.S. Dept. Commerce, Kings Point, N.Y., 1971-73; adj. prof. elec. engring. Fla. Atlantic U., Boca Raton, 1973-75. Mem. engring. council Columbia; mem. industry adv. council Dept. Def. Bd. dirs. Armstrong Meml. Found. Fellow Radio Club Am., I.E.E.E.; mem. Soc. Naval Architects and Marine Engrs., Sigma Xi. Clubs: Columbia (N.Y.C.); Officers. Patentee microwave components and systems, radio, locating devices, microwave instruments and electromech. advise. Home: Boca Raton, Fla., Died Dec. 29, 1975.

JAINSEN, WILSON CARL, ins. exec.; b. Hartford, Conn., May 14, 1899; s. Carl W. and Julia (Goodrich) J.; student Wesleyan U.; Ph.B., Brown U., 1922; m. Ann Morgan, Sept. 21, 1953. With Hartford Accident & Indemnity Co., 1922-74, adjuster, v.p., 1922-53, pres., dir., 1953-74; pres. Greater Hartford Corp.; dir. Conn. Gen. Life Ins. Co., United Bank & Trust, Soc. for Savs., Hartford Gas Co. Former pres. Govtl. Research Inst.; chmn. Conn. Pub. Expenditure Council. Served with USN, World War I. Mem. Conn. C. of C. (v.p.). Am. Arbitration Assn. (dir.). Home: West Hartford, Conn. Died Jan. 1974.

JAMES, ALBERT WILLIAM, lawyer; b. Cobden, Ill., June 12, 1902; s. Albert W. and Alice (Broadway) J.; LL.B., Dickinson Law Sch., 1927; m. Madalin Winthrop, July 12, 1929; children—Albert W., Hugh Winthrop, Jay Paul. Clk., du Pont Co., 1920-22; atty. Fidelity & Deposit Co. of Md., 1927-29; admitted to Del. bar, 1929; instr. law Goldey Coll., 1929-33, 52-60; asso. firm Hering & Morris, 1929-36; mem. firm Morris, James, Hitchens & Williams, 1936-75. Pres. City Council of Wilmington, 1935-40; dep. atty. gen. Del. in charge of taxes, 1939-41; mayor of Wilmington, 1941-45; atty. gen., Del., 1947-51. Mem. Wilmington Community Concert Assn., Am. Bar Assn., Phi Kappa Psi. Republican. Kiwanian. Clubs: Whist, University, Torch (pres. 1941-42), Wilmington Country. Home: Wilmington, Del. Died Apr. 22, 1975.

JAMES, ELIAS OLAN, educator; b. Mansfield, Ill., Mar. 9, 1879; s. Elias Poston and Mary Isabelle (Shepherd) J.; student Union Christian Coll., Merom, Ind., 1895-99; A.B., Stanford, 1902; A.M., U. Calif., 1906; m. Flora Louise Mitchell, Apr. 26, 1905 (dec. May 10, 1910; 1 dau. Flora Elizabeth (Mrs. Stanley Hanks); m. 2d, Rosetta E. Epperson, Aug. 9, 1911; children—Mary Louise (Mrs. James E. O'Brien), David Meeker (dec.). Tchr. English, Calif. high schs. 5 yrs.; asso. prof. English, Mills Coll., 1909-20, prof., from 1920, prof. emeritus; lectr. in English, U. Calif., various summer sessions, and in univ. sessions, and in univ extension, 1919-21. Mem. Phi Beta Kappa. Author: Thieves of Mercy (verse), 1934; Elias B. Poston and his Ancestors, with a record of his descendants, 1942; The Story of the Cyrus and Susan Mills, 1953. Home: Oakland, Cal.†

JAMES, HARLEAN, planning and civic organization exec.; b. Mattoon, Ill., July 18, 1877; d. Ira and Hannah Jane (Crow) J.; A.B., in history, Stanford, 1898; spl. work, U. of Chicago and Columbia U. Court reporter, Honolulu, T.H., 1901-02; pvt. sec. to collector of customs, Honolulu, 1903-04, to gen. mgr. Calif. & Hawaiian Sugar Refining Co., San Francisco, 1905-06; corp. sec. J. B. Castle Cos., Honolulu, 1906-08; exec. sec. Women's Civic League, Baltimore, 1911-16; exec. sec. Housing Sect. (Labor) Nat. Council of Defense, 1917; exec. sec. U.S. Housing Corp., Dept. of Labor, 1918; gen. mgr. Govt. hotels, 1919-20; exec. sec. Am. Civic Assn., 1921-35. Am. Planning and Civic Assn. from 1935, Nat. Conf. on State Parks from 1935. Mem. President's Conf. on Home Building and Home Ownership (chmn. com. on organization programs; sec. com. on edn. and service); collaborator, Nat. Park Service, Dept. of Interior, Historic Am. Buildings Survey, Branch of Plans and Designs, from 1933; cons. to def. housing coordinator, Office Emergency Management, 1941; adv. com. conservation to Sec. Interior from 1948. Mem. Women's Joint Congl. Com. (chairman 1929-30), Am. inst. of Planners from 1932 (hon. mem.) A.I.A. (hon. mem.), Am. Soc. Landscape Architects (hon. mem.), Appalachian Trail Conf. received commemorative plaque, 1948); sec.-treas. Joint Com. on Nat. Capital. Reed. bronze medal award, Am. Scenic and Hist. Preservation Society, 1943, gold medal, 1953; award for service from the American Society of Planning Officials, 1954. Clubs: Potomac Appalachian. Trail, Friends of the Land, American Foresting Association (honorary v.p.), University Women's (Washington). Author: The Building of Cities, 1916; Land Planning in the U.S. for the City, State and Nation, 1926; Romance of the National Parks, 1939; also chapter in Planning and Building the City of Washington, 1932. Editor: What About the Year 2000?, 1929; Am. Civic Annual 1929-34, Am. Planning and Civic Annual from 1935; 25th Anniversary Year Book on Park and Recreation Progress, 1946. Asso. editor Federal Affairs, in National Municipal Review, 1921-26, of the New Washington and Civic Art, in Am. Magazine of Art, 1931-33; contbr. numerous articles in Ecny. Britannica and Year Book. Home: Washington, D.C.†

JAMES, MAY HALL (MAY WINSOR HALL), educator; b. North Providence, R.I., Mar. 19, 1889; d. George Miner and Lucy (Merrill) Hall; Ph.B., Brown U., 1909, M.A., 1923, Ph.D., 1925; postgrad. Harvard U., 1926-27, U. Paris, 1928, London Sch. Econs., 1929; Ph.D., Yale, 1935; m. John William James, Sept. 22, 1909 (dec.); children—William Hall, Lucy (dec.). Asst. prof. sociology, econs. Conn. Coll., 1925-27, George Peabody Coll., 1930-31; prof. sociology, econs., Sarah Lawrence Coll., 1929-31, lectr. Yale 1942-50; with New Haven State Tchrs. Coll., 1934-56, prof. social sci. 1939-56; dean of women, prof. social scis. Quinnipiac Coll., Hamden, Conn., 1956-64, dean of women emerita, 1964-72, chmn. div. liberal arts, 1958-64; lectr. history and philosophy of edn. U. Bridgeport; instr. Conn. Edn. TV, 1962-63; broker Barrows and Wallace Co., realtors, Hamden, Conn. Mem. Can., U.S. Com. Edn., 1951-58; chmn. Conn. br. Canadian-Am. Women's Com., 1943-47, chmn. Am. Sect., 1947-72; corr. edn. supplement London Times, 1950-56; del. from Conn. to Indsl. Council, Renssalaer Poly Inst., 1954-55, Conn. Conf. on Ams., P.R., 1961, Internat. Fedn. U. Women, Mexico City, 1962; instr. This Is Conn. for Conn. Ednl. TV, 1962-63. Mem. New Haven County Rent Control Bd., 1952-55. Recipient Woman of Year award New Haven br. Quota Internat., 1950, New Haven Bus. and Profl. Women's Club, 1957. Mem. Nat. Assn. Deans Women, Nat. Council Women of U.S., Am. Acad. Social and Polit. Sci., Conn. Edn. Assn., Yale U. Alumni Assn., Am. Assn. U. Women (pres. New Haven br. 1969-71), Nat. League Women Voters, Conn., Grange, New Haven Colony Hist. Soc., Old Lyme Hist. Soc., Alumnae Assn. Pembroke Coll. in Brown U. (Pembroke Alumnae Assn. Honors award 1969), Delta Kappa Gamma (hon.). Author: Sociological Survey of the Providence Public Library, 1927; Educational History Old Lyme, Connecticut 1935; Survey-European Trends in the Higher Education of Women, 1961, editor Pageant Am. Filmstrips, 1952. Contbr. Brit. Jr. Ency. Traveled throughout N. Am., S. Am. and Europe. Home: NOrthford, Conn. Died Sept. 3, 1972; interred Union Cemetery, Norwalk, Conn.

JAMES, PHILIP (FREDERICK WRIGHT), composer, conductor; b. Jersey City, May 17, 1890; s. Philip William and Ernestine (Wildhagen) J.; A.B., Coll. City N.Y., 1910, Mus.D., N.Y. Coll. Music, 1946; m. Millicent Eady, Sept. 7, 1916 (dec. July 1945); m. 2d, Helga Boyer, Feb. 3, 1952; children—Vivien, Philip. Mus. dir. operettas for Victor Herbert and prodns. Winthrop Ames, N.Y.C., 1911-16; condr. N.J. Symphony Orch., 1922-24, Bklyn. Orchestral Soc., 1927-30; prof. music, head music dept., N.Y. U., later prof. emeritus; instr. music Columbia U.; v.p. Liangollen Internat. Mus. Eisteddfod, North Wales; condr. Bamberger Symphony Orch., Radio Sta. WOR; guest condr. Nat. Symphony Orch., Washington, N.Y. Orch., NBC Orch., Phila. Orch., CBS, N.Y. Philharmonic-Symphony Orch., Bronx Symphony Orch. Served as 2d lt., inf., U.S. Army, later bandmaster and comdg. officer A.E.F. Hdqrs. Band, World War. Recipient 1st prize (¾00) NBC for suite for orch.; hon. mention for overture Bret Harte Philharmonic Symphony Soc. N.Y., 1937; Juilliard Found. Publ. award, 1937; 1st prize Women's Symphony Orch. N.Y., 1938; Award of Merit for outstanding service to Am. music Nat. Assn. Am. Comosers and Conductors, 1970. Hon. fellow Trinity Coll., London, Eng., 1938. Mem. Nat. Inst. ofArts and Letters, Soc. Publ. Am. Music (chmn. bd.), Am. Musicol. Soc., MacDowell Allied Mems. (pres. 1953), Edw. MacDowell Assn. (v.p.), A.S.C.A.P., Phi Beta Kappa, Mu Sigma. Episcopalian. Club: Century Assn. (N.Y.C.). Composer two symphonies, five suites, seven concert overtures, secular and sacred choral works, organ works, chamber music and songs. Home: Southampton, N.Y., Died Nov. 1, 1975.

JAMES, PHILLIP, arts adminstr.; b. Oct. 31, 1901; ed. Sherborne Sch., U. Coll., London U.; m. Bertha James. Sub-librarian Middle Temple, London, 1923-25; asst. keeper Victoria and Albert Mus., 1925-35, keeper library, 1935-39; with Ministry Home Security, 1939-41; joined Council for Encouragement Music and the Arts, 1941, became art dir., 1942; art dir. Arts Council Gt. Britain, 1946-58; dir. Waddesdon Manor (Nat.

Trust), 1958-60; sec., editor Museums Assn., 1960-64, now hon. fellow; librarian Royal Acad. Arts, 1969. Decorated comdr. Order Brit. Empire, comdr. Order Aztec Eagle (Mexico), comdr. Order Leopold II, chevalier Order de la Couronne (Belgium), comdr. Order of Lion (Finland), comdr. Order Merit (Fed. Republic, Germany). Fellow Univ. Coll., London, 1961. Address: Seer Green nr. Beaconsfield, Bucks, England. Died Apr. 29, 1975.

JAMIESON, DOUGLAS JAMES, dentist; b. Detroit, Aug. 21, 1906; s. Robert Raymond and Edith (Boess) J.; student Highland Park Jr. Coll., 1924-27; D.D.S., U. Mich., 1931; M.S. in Orthodontics, 1935; m. Allana Marie Minifie, Jan. 11, 1934; children—Douglas James, II, Bruce Robert, Scott Allan. Pvt. practice orthodontics, Detroit, 1935-53, Royal Oak, Mich., 1951-73. Served as 1st. lt., Dental Corps., USAAF, 1943-44. Am., Mich. State, Oakland County dental assns., Detroit Dental Clinic Club (sec.-treas. Orthodontic sect. 1949-69), Callers Club Met. Detroit (treas. 1965-71), Am. Assn. Orthodontists, Nat. Rifle Assn. (patron). Patentee in field. Club: Lakelands Golf and Country. Home: Royal Oak Mich. Died Oct. 1, 1973; buried Holy Sepulchre Cemetery, Southfield, Mich.

JARNAGIN, MILTON PRESTON, animal husbandman; b. Farmville, Va., Sept. 17, 1881; s. Milton Preston and Agnes Venable (Watkins) J.; student U. of Tenn., 1900-03, U. of Wis., 1903-04; B.Sc. in Agr., State Coll. of Ia., 1905; D.Sc., 1921, M.Agr., 1930; m. Dorothy Greve, Sept. 16, 1908; children—Milton Preston, Janet, Agnes, Dorothy. Instr. Va. Poly. Inst., Blacksbuurg, Va., 1906; head animal husbandry div., U. of Ga., 1907-48; agrl. cons. bd. regents Univ. System, Ga., from 1948; organized and directed work of livestock extension enterprises; dir. Athens Fed. Savs. & Loan Assn.; v.p. gen. Finance & Loan Company; sec. livestock sect. Federal Food Adminstrn. for State of Ga. during World War. Mem. Ga. Tax Commn., 1927-29; chmn. Ga. State Swine Com. Fellow A.A.A.S.; mem. and past v.p. Am. Soc. Animal Production; mem. Com. of One Hundred; past pres. Southeastern Livestock Assn.; mem. Am. Jersey Cattle Club (herd classification com.); dir. Ga. Aberdeen-Angus Assn.; past sec., and chmn. animal husbandry sect., Southern Agrl. Workers; mem. Ga. Acad. Science, Am. Assn. for Advancement of Dairy Science, Ga. Dairy and Livestock Assn. (past sec.), Swine Growers' Assn.; mem. bd. dirs., Walking Horse Breeders' Assn. of America; mem. Sigma Alpha Epsilon, Phi Kappa Phi (sec.). Awarded Medallion by Assn. of Southern Agrl. Workers for distinguished service 1940, citation from Future Farmer of America, 1946, cited Man of the Year in Georgia Agriculture, 1946. Democrat. Presbyterian. Club: West Lake Country. Home: Athens, Ga.†

JARRETT, HARRY B., naval officer; b. Valley Forge, Pa., Oct. 12, 1898; s. Winfield S. and May (Rowan) J.; B.S., U.S. Naval Acad., 1922; M.S., Columbia, 1929; m. Mary Ward Dunn, May 6, 1927. Commd. ensign USN, 1922, advanced through grades to vice admiral, 1954, retired, 1954. President of Navy Relief Society. Decorated Navy Cross, Silver Star, Legion of Merit with gold star, Bronze Star. Clubs: Army and Navy, Army and Navy Country. Home: Washington, D.C. Died Apr. 1974.

JAVITS, BENJAMIN ABRAHAM, lawyer, author, economist; b. N.Y.C., Oct. 21, 1894; s. Morris and Ida (Littman) J.; student Coll. City N.Y., 1909-11; LL.B., Fordham U., 1918; m. Lily Birnbaum, Feb. 12, 1926; children—Joan Ellen, Eric M. Various positions selling, mgmt., indsl. reorgn., bus. counseling, 1911-22; admitted to N.Y. bar, 1922, practiced in N.Y.C. and Washington, 1922-69; counsel, mem. Javits & Javits, N.Y.C. and Washington, ret., 1969. Sponsored movement to amend anti-trust laws, 1926; organized nat. conf. for nat. econ. planning, Washington, 1929; filed petition in bankruptcy for Am. creditors of Kreuger and Toll affairs, 1932; assisted drafting Nat. Indsl. Recovery Act, 1933; pres., founder United Shareowners Am., Inc., 1950; co-founder Investors League, Inc. Pres. bd. Shareowners Ednl. Found., Inc., Fair Return League, Inc. Republican. Mason. Clubs: Palm Beach Country; Noyak Golf, Overseas Press, City Athletic. Author: Make Everybody Rich Industry's New Goal, 1929; Business and the Public Interest-Trade Associations, The Anti-Trust Laws and industrial Planning, 1932; The Commonwealth of Industry, The Separation of Industry and the State, 1936; Peace by Investment, 1950; How the Republicans Can Win in 1952, 1952; The Manifesto of Freedom for Mankind, 1962; Ownerism: A Better World for All Through Democratic Ownership, 1969; also pamphlets, articles. Fordham U. Sch. Law known as Benjamin A. Javits Halls of Law. Home: New York City N.Y. Died May 18, 1973.

JAYNE, HORACE HOWARD FURNESS, archeologist, curator; b. Cape May, N.J., June 9, 1898; s. Horace and Caroline Augusta (Furness)J.; A.B., Harvard, 1919; A.M., U. Pa., 1933; m. Henrietta M. E. Bache, 1928. With Pa. Mus., 1921-40, asst., 1921-23, curator Oriental art, 1923-26, chief of Eastern Div. and curator of sculpture, 1926; dir. Museum of U. Pa., 1928-40; vice dir. Met. Mus. Art, N.Y.C., 1941-49; with international broadcasting div. Dept. State, 1949-53, radio script editor, 1949, chief Chinese desk, 1950-54; vice dir. Phila. Mus. of Art, 1955-65; with Mus. Fine Arts, St. Petersburg, Fla., from 1965; curator Oriental art Norton Gallery, West Palm Beach, Fla., until 1975. Mem. 1st China expdn. Fogg Museum of Harvard, 1923-24; member 2d expdn., field agent in Asia for Harvard, 1924-25; mem. U. Pa. Mus. and Brit. Mus. expdn. to U. of Chaldees; spl. rep. American Commission for Protection and Salvage of Artistic and Historic Monuments in War Areas. Trustee, Fairmont Park Art Assn. Mem. Am. Philos. Soc. Editor: Letters of Horace Howard Furness, 1920. Home: West Palm Beach, Fla. Died Aug. 6, 1975.

JEFFERIES, EMILY BROWN, (Mrs. Richard M. Jefferies, Jr.), club woman; b. Columbia, S.C., July 18, 1921; d. Edgar Allan and Ann (Sitgreaves) Brown; student Converse Coll., 1938-39; B.S. in Commerce, U. S.C., 1942; m. Richard M. Jefferies, Jr., Aug. 22, 1942; children—Richard Allan, Emily McBurney. West Low Country dist. dir., mem. state bd. Garden Club S.C., 1955-56; v.p. S.C. Judges Club, 1961-63; treas. Barnwell County Cancer Soc., 1957-59, 61-65; sec. bd. women visitors U. S.C.; v.p. U. S.C. Alumni Assn., 1950-51; mem. D.A.R., Daus. Colonial Wars, Cherokee Garden Club (pres. 1950-51), Barnwell Art Club. Page Dem. Nat. Conv., 1960; mem. S.C. adv. bd. Palmetto Outdoor Hist. Drama Assn.; mem. S.C. Gov.'s Mansion Com., Historic Columbia Found., Inc., Gov.'s Com. to Study Feasibility of State Mus.; mem. adv. bd. Robert Mills Historic House and Park; patron Columbia Mus. Art Bd. dirs. Barnwell County Tb Assn., 1947-61. Master flower show judge. Mem. Nat. Soc. Magna Charta Dames, Ams. Royal Descent, Caroliniana Soc., Friends of Library, Ainsley Hall Restoration, Sovereign Colonial Soc., Alpha Kappa Gamma, Alpha Delta Pi (pres. S.C. Found. 1962-64). Democrat. Episcopalian (pres. woman's aux. 1953-54). Clubs: Sweetwater Country (past bd. mem.) (Barnwell, S.C.); Palmetto, Forest Lake Country (Columbia). Nationally accredited flower judge. Home: Barnwell, S.C., Deceased.

JEFFERS, CLYDE G., lawyer; b. Hampton, Ia., July 2, 1881; s. Byron and Edith (Day) J.; grad. Iowa U., 1905; m. Garnette Robinson, Aug. 18, 1935; children (by first wife)—Ruty Nye, Elizabeth (Mrs. Ward Pickard), Richard, Josephine, Donald, Virginia. Began practice, 1905; pros. atty., Grant County, Wash., 1913-17; asst. atty. gen., Wash., 1922-23, Superior Ct. judge of Grant and Douglas Counties, 1923-39; justice of Supreme Court of Wash. from 1939. Mem. Sigma Alpha Epsilon. Presbyterian. Mason. Address: Olympia, Wash.*†

JEFFERSON, FLOYD WELLMAN, textile merchant; b. Louisville, Dec. 25, 1878; s. Thomas Lewis and Katherine (Wellman) J.; grad. Abraham Flexners Prep. Sch., 1898; A.B., Yale, 1902; m. Violet Spencer Woodruff, June 14, 1904; children—Janice Townsend (Mrs. William Law Walker), Floyd W.; married 2d, Marjorie Maynard, July 23, 1941. Associated with A.D. Julliard & Co., N.Y. City, 1910, div. mgr., 1910-14; div. mgr. Tatum Pinkham & Greey, N.Y. City, 1914-17; vice pres. and later chmn. exec. and finance com. Hunter Mfg. Co., 1917-27; partner Iselin Jefferson Co., Inc., N.Y. City, 1927-46, pres., dir., 1946-50, chmn. bd. from 1950; dir., co-chmn. bd. 199 Church St. br. Chem. Bank N.Y. Trust Co. dir. Fitzgerald Mills Corp., com.; director Fitzgerald Cotton Mills; treasurer, director Wellman Operating Corp.; dir. textile br. Chemical Corn Exchange Bank; dir., mem. exec. com. Dan River Mills; dir. Iselin-Jefferson Financial Corp., Iselin-Jefferson Found. Past pres., chmn. adv. com. N.Y. Board Trade. Vice pres., mem. exec. com., chmn. endowment com. Met. Oepra Assn. Mem. Am. Arbitration Assn. (vice chmn. bd., dir.), English Speaking Union, Society Colonial Wars, S.R., S.A.R., Soc. Am. Historians, Newcomen Soc. Eng. (Trustee), Alpha Delta Phi, C. of C. Clubs: Univ., Merchants, Racquet and Tennis, Union (N.Y.C.); Round Hill Golf (Greenwich); New York Southern Society (N.Y.C.); Filson (Louisville); Royal Bermuda Yacht, Mid Ocean, Coral Beach (Bermuda). Author: Arcadian Sunset; Iambic and Dactylic; There Were Giants in the Earth. Contbr. to textile publs. Home: New York City, N.Y.†

JEFFORDS, JOE SAM, state ofcl.; b. Lamar, S.C., Sept. 2, 1912; s. Samuel Joseph and Bessie Irene (Boykin) J.; B.S. in Civil Engring., Clemson U., 1936; m. Mary Emma Colclough, June 18, 1938; children—Samuel Joseph II, Ben Colough. With S.C. Hwy. Dept., 1936-42, W.C. Olsen Cons. Engrs., Raleigh, N.C., 1942-43, McClean Contracting Co., Balt., 1943-45; with S.C. Hwy Dept., 1945-74, dist. engr., 1967-74. Mem. design and drafting adv. com. Orangeburg-Calhoun Tech. Ednl. Center, 1968-74. Mem. S.C. Soc. Engrs. Methodist (ofcl. bd. 1960-66; trustee 1969-74). Lion (v.p. 1st Orangeburg 1969) Home: Orangeburg, S.C. Died Sept. 4, 1974.

JEFFORDS, LAWRENCE SUGGS, r.r. exec.; b. Florence, S.C., July 2, 1892; s. William Quinn and Sarah Margaret (Suggs) J.; ed. Clemson (S.C.) Coll.; m. Mary Howell, Sept. 27, 1922 (dec. Nov. 1962); m. 2d, Fannie Mae Weatherford Baker, July 2, 1964. With Atlantic Coast Line R.R. Co., 1910, successively rodman, transitman, resident engr., asst. div. engr., roadmaster, asst. engr. maintenance of way; transf. to Charleston and Western Carolina Ry. Co., Augusta, Ga., 1921, successively engr. maintenance of way, supt. and gen. supt.; returned to Atlantic Coast Line R.R. Co., 1944, chief of personnel, chief engr., 1945, gen. mgr., 1947, v.p. and gen. mgr., 1947, v.p. ops., 1950-62; v.p., gen. mgr., dir. C.N. & L. R.R., from 1960. Episcopalian. Club: River (Jackson, Fla.). Home: Jacksonville, Fla. Died May 10, 1974; buried New Hope Cemetery, Florence, S.C.

JEFFREY, ROBERT HUTCHINS, mfr.; b. Columbus, O., Dec. 21, 1873; s. Joseph Andrew and Celia (Harris) J.; student Real Sch., Dresden (Germany), 1888, 89; A.B., Williams Coll., 1895; grad. work in comml. law and elec. engring., Ohio State U., 1895-97; m. Alice Kilbourne, Feb. 6, 1901 (died Nov. 18, 1922); 2 children; m. 2d, Mary Allen, Mar. 26, 1924 (died September 17, 1945), With Jeffrey Manufacturing Co., 1895-1901, assistant general manager, 1901-02, v.p., 1902-09, gen. mgr., 1909-22, pres. and gen. mgr., 1922-30, chmn. bd. from 1930, chmn. exec. com., from 1951; dir. other cos. Mayor City of Columbus, O., 1901-03. Trustee Williams Coll., 1923-28. Mem. Ohio Soc. of N.Y., Chamber of Commerce (pres. 1901). Mason (32°). Clubs: Williams (New York); Columbus, Columbus Country, Rocky Fork Hunt and Country. Home: Columbus, Ohio†

JELLEMA, WILLIAM HARRY, JR., psychiat. social worker; b. Grand Rapids, Mich., Oct. 8, 1933; s. William Harry and Marie Frances (Peters) J.; A.B., Calvin Coll., 1955; A.M., U. Chgo., 1958; m. Mary Ellen Orton, Aug. 25, 1962; children—William Harry III, Jane Elizabeth Harris. Casework counselor Jewish Family and Community Service, Chgo., 1958-61; staff adviser Chgo. Jewish Community Centers, 1959-61; dir. guidance and counseling Younger Boys Camp, Am. Youth Found., 1958-61; casework supr. Family Service & Children's Aid Soc., Jackson, Mich., 1961-65; exec. dir. Family Counseling Agy., Joliet, Ill., 1965-75; pvt. practice as psychiat. social worker, 1974-75. Field work instr. U. Mich., Mich. State Schs. Social Work, 1962-64; mem. faculty Joliet Jr. Coll., 1967-68, part-time, from 1969, Coll. St. Francis, 1974-75; tech. cons. 1970 White House Conf. on Children and Youth, 1968-70; v.p. Ill. Assn. Family Agys., 1970-71; sr. high adviser 1st Presbyn. Ch., 1965-75; v.p. Chgo. Suburban Family Service Execs. Group, 1969-70; adv. bd. Will Grundy Assn. for Mental Health; aide in ednl. devel. Presbyn. Ch. U.S.A., 1968-69; lectr. St. Josephs Hosp. Sch. Nursing, 1969—; cons. Sci. Mgmt. Corp., 1974-75. Chmn. profls. and spls. sect. United Crusade Will County, 1971. Bd. dirs. Riverside Center for Sr. Citizens Will County, 1967-75, v.p., 1967-68; bd. dirs. Will County Community Action Program, 1966-67; mem. adv. council Midwest Yokefellows, 1968-69; adv. bd. Joliet Drama Guild, 1972-75, Parents Without Partners, 1973-75. Mem. Nat. Assn. Social Workers, Ill. Welfare Assn., Acad. Certified Social Workers, Assn. Marriage and Family Counselors, U. Chgo. Alumni Assn. Presbyn. (ruling elder). Rotarian. Home: Joliet, Ill., Died Aug. 24, 1975.

JEMISON, ROBERT, JR., real estate and investment banker; b. Tuscaloosa, Ala., Feb. 28, 1878; s. Robert and Eugenia Rebecca (Sorsby) J.; ed. U. of Ala., 1895-97; U. of the South, 1897-99; m. Virginia Earle Walker, Nov. 12, 1901 (dec. July 16, 1953); children—Mrs. Virginia Goodall, Robert, William W. Officer and dir. many corps. Pres. C. of C., Birmingham, 1906; vice chmn. Park Commn., Birmingham; pres. Nat. Assn. of Real Estate Bds., 1926; mem. City Planning and Zoning Com. of President's Conf. on Home Building and Home Ownership, 1931. Trustee U. of the South, Industrial Sch. of Ala.; pres. State Alumni Soc., U. of Ala., 1906; pres. Birmingham Chapter Am. Red Cross, 1917; mem. Chamber Commerce U.S.; pres. Fathers Assn. of Hill Sch., Pottstown, Pa.; dir. National Conference on City Planning. Served 11 mos. as asst. mgr. housing div., Emergency Fleet Corp., U.S. Shipping Bd., World War. Episcopalian. Mem. Phi Delta Theta, Phi Beta Kappa. Omicron Delta Kappa. Clubs: Country (pres. 1917), Mountain brook Country, Birmingham Motor and Country. Rotary (Birmingham). Home: Birmingham, Ala.†

JENCKES, VIRGINIA ELLIS, ex-congresswoman; b. Terre Haute, Ind. Nov. 6, 1882; d. James Ellis and Mary (Oliver) Somes; edited pub. schs.; m. Ray Greene Jenckes, February 22, 1912 (died 1921); 1 dau., Virginia Ray (deceased). Engaged in farming from 1912. Mem. 73d to 75th Congresses (1933-39), 6th Ind. Dist. Head of woman's work, Ind. Equality for Agriculture, 1928 Presidential Campaign. U.S. del. Inter-Parliamentary Union, Paris, 1937. Democrat. Episcopalian. Clubs: Ind. Woman's Democratic, Ind. Federated Woman's. Home: Terre Haute, Ind. Died Jan. 9, 1975.

JENKINS, DOUGLAS, foreign service officer; b. "Brick House" Plantation S.C., Feb. 6, 1880; s. James Joseph and Cecile (Swinton) J.; graduate Porter Military Acad., Charleston, S.C., 1897; read law, and admitted to S.C. bar, 1901; m. Charlotte Keith Furman, Feb. 6, 1905 (died 1915); children—Caroline Heyward (Mrs. William E. Seiffert), Douglas; m. 2d, Lucia L. Dean, Aug. 23, 1918. Reporter and city editor, Greenville (S.C.) News, until 1908; apptd. v. consul at Halifax, Can., 1908; consul, St. Pierre-Miquelon, 1908-12, Gothenburg, Sweden, 1912-13, Riga, Russia, 1913-17, Kiev, 1918, Harbin, China, 1918-22; promoted consul gen., Nov. 19, 1921. In charge German and Austro-Hungarian interests at Riga from breaking out of war until Feb. 1, 1917; in charge British and French interests at Riga, Aug. 1915-Feb. 1917; on detail in Dept. of State, Jan. 1922-July 18, 1923; counsul gen. Canton, China, 1923-30, Shanghai, 1930-31, Hongkong, 1931-34, Berlin, 1934-37, Longon, 1937-39; minister to Bolivia, 1939-41; retired with 33 yrs. service, Jan. 1, 1942. Spl. representative of the President with rank of ambassador at inauguration of President Penaranda of Bolivia on Apr. 15, 1940. Member South Carolina Hist. Society; Pan-Am. League. Home: Augusta, Ga.†

JENKINS, HARRY HIBBS, physician; b. Cookeville, Tenn., 1906; M.D., Vanderbilt U., 1930. Intern, Charity Hosp., New Orleans, 1930-32, St. Agnes Hosp., 1933; house physician in gynecology Bon Secours Hosp., Balt., 1946; mem. attending staff in obstetrics and gynecology U. Tenn. Meml. Hosp., St. Mary's Hosp., East Tenn. Baptist Hosp., Ft. Sanders Presbyn. Hosp. (all Knoxville); instr. obstetrics Tulane U., New Orleans, 1934-35. Served to col., M.C., AUS, 1941-46. Decorated Legion of Merit; Medalha de Guerra (Brazil). Diplomate Am. Bd. Obstetrics and Gynecology. Fellow A.C.S.; mem. Am. Coll. Obstetricians and Gynecologists, Central Assn. Obstetricians and Gynecologists, A.M.A. Home: Knoxville, Tenn. Died Feb. 10, 1972.

JENKINS, JOSEPH HARLEY, educator; b. Blue Ridge Ga., Mar. 3, 1890; s. Thomas Putnam and Sarah (Harris) J.; grad. Morganton (Ga.) High Sch., 1909; A.B., Mercer U., Macon, Ga., 1913, A.M., 1925; m. Belle Singletary, Dec. 23, 1912; children—Deloriss (dec.), William, Charles; m. 2d, Sallie Gilbert. Began as teacher, 1913; supt. schs., Vienna, Ga., 1922-35; president Georgia Military College, Milledgeville, Ga., from 1935; member General Assembly of Georgia, 1932-33; lt. col. Governor's staff, 1944. Democrat. Baptist (mem. exec. com. Ga. Baptist). Mason, Odd Fellow, Woodman. Clubs: Kiwanis (lt. gov. Ga. Dist., 1943), Country. Address: Vienna, Ga. Died Apr. 4, 1973.

JENKINS, WILLIAM ADRIAN, coll. pres.; b. Oxford, N.C., Feb. 11, 1879; s. Walter D. and Flora Ada (York) J.; A.B., U. of N.C., 1907; A.M. and B.D., Yale, 1912; m. Ora Lee Shepherd, Dec. 8, 1908; children—Ora Lee, William Adrian. Ordained ministry Congl. Ch. 1908; pastor in Congl. chs. successively at Chenango Forks, N.Y., Killingsworth, Conn., Sayville, N.Y., 1908-15; pastor of M.E. Ch., S., successively at Dallas, Davidson, Concord, Charlotte, Greensboro (all N.C.), 1915-26; pres. Davenport Coll., Lenoir, N.C., from 1926. Served as chaplain, U.S.A., July 1918-Sept. 1919. Mem. Alpha Chi Rho. Democrat. Mason. Home: Lenoir, N.C.†

JENKINS, WILL(IAM) F(ITZGERALD), author; born Norfolk, Va., June 16, 1896; s. George Briggs and Mary Louise (Murry) J.; student public and also private schools of Norfolk; m. Mary L. Mandola, Aug. 9, 1921; children—Mary (Mrs. Vahan Daniels), Elizabeth (Mrs. William De Hardit), Wenllian Stallings, Joan (Mrs. Adrian Evans). Fiction writer since 1915; under pseudonym Murray Leinster wrote several hundred pulp stories, also sci. fiction stories; resumed own name for stories pub. in nat. magazines; author pub. books including: (under name Will F. Jenkins) The Man Who Feared, 1942, Guns for Achin, 1943, Murder of the U.S.A., 1947; (under psuedonym Leinster) Sidewise in Time and Other Stories, 1949; The Last Space-Ship, 1951; Great Stories of Science Fiction, 1951; Space Platform, 1953; Space Tug, 1953; Quadratic, 1953; Forgotten Planet. 1954, Operation Outer Space, 1954; Gateway to Elsewhere, 1955; The Other Side of Here, 1955; Colonial Survey, 1957; War with the Gizmos, 1958; Out of This World, 1958; Thing from World's End, 1959; Twists in Time, 1960; Monsters and Such, 1960; The Aliens; Pirates of Zan, 1960; Men Into Space, 1961; Creatures of The Abyss, 1961; Wailing Asteroid, 1961; This World is Taboo, 1961; Talents, Inc., Operation Terror, 1962; The Other Side of Nowhere, Doctor to the Stars, 1964; Time Tunnel, published in 1964; author of other works in anthologies; author 12 motion pictures including Owner of the Aztec and Murder Will Out. Served with Committee on Public Information, World War I; with 98th Div., U.S. Army, 1918 and sr. publs. editor O.W.I., overseas div., N.Y. City, World War II. Awarded A00 prize by Liberty for short short story A Very Nice Family, 1937; recipient Hugo award World Sci. Fiction Assn. Roman Catholic. Inventor front projection. Home: Gloucester, Va. Died June 8, 1975.

JENKS, CLARENCE WILFRED, internat. labour ofcl.; b. Bootle, Liverpool, Eng., Mar. 7, 1909; s. Richard and Alice Sophia (Craig) J.; scholar Gonville and Caius Coll., Cambridge U., 1927-31, B.A., 1931, M.A., 1936, LL.D., 1953; LL.D., Edinburgh, 1967, Delhi U., 1970; m. Jane Louise Broverman, Oct. 19, 1949; children—Craig B., Bruce F. E. Mem. legal sect. Internat. Labour Office, Geneva, Switzerland, 1931-40, legal adviser, 1940-48, asst. dir.-gen., 1948-64, deputy dir. gen., 1964-67, prin. dep. dir. gen., 1967-70, dir. gen., 1970-73; prof. The Hague Acad. Internat. Law, 1939, 50, 55, 66; Storrs lectr. jurisprudence Yale Law Sch., 1965; adviser Venezuelan Govt. on labour legislation, 1938. Mem. Internat. Labour Office dels. at U.N. Conf. on Internat. Organization, San Francisco, 1945, U.N. Monetary and Financial Conf., Bretton Woods, 1944, The Inter-Am. War and Peace Conf., Chapultupec, Mexico City, 1945, Intergovtl. Copyright Conf., 1952, Internat. Conf. on Peaceful Uses of Atomic Energy, 1955, 58, Conf. on Statute of Internat. Atomic Energy Agy., 1956, U.N. Conf. on Law of the Sea, 1958, 60, Gen. Assembly and Econ. and Social Council of U.N., other internat. confs. and coms.; adviser to Constitutional Com. of U.N. Interim Commn. on Food and Agr., 1944, to Am. Law Inst. on essential human rights project, 1942-44; mem. Inst. of Internat. Law. Called to Bar by Gray's Inn, in 1936. Awarded Cecil Peace prize, 1928; Ann. award Am. Soc. Internat. Law, 1959; World Legal Scholarship award, World Peace Through Law Center, 1967; UN Human Rights award, 1973. Pres. Cambridge Union Soc., 1930. Mem. Internat. Acad. of Astronautics (corr.), Internat. Acad. Comparative Law. Clubs: Cosmos (Washington); Athenaeum, Reform (London). Author: The Headquarters of International Institutions, 1945; The International Protection of Trade Union Freedom, 1957; The Common Law of Mankind, 1958; Human Rights and International Labour Standards, 1960; International Immunities, 1961; The Proper Law of International Organizations, 1962; Law, Freedom and Welfare, 1963; The Prospects of International Adjudication, 1964; Space Law 1965; Law in the World Community, 1967; The World Beyond the Charter, 1969; A New World of Law?, 1969. Editor of: The International Labour Code, 1939, 52; Constitutional Provisions concerning Social and Economic Policy, 1944. Contributor legal journals. Home: Geneva, Switzerland. Died Oct. 9, 1973; buried St. George Cemetery, Geneva, Switzerland.

JENKS, STEPHEN MOORE, steel exec.; b. Port Huron, Mich., Feb. 18, 1901; s. Sidney Grant and Grace (Moore) J.; M.E., Cornell, 1923; m. Eleanore Griffiths, June 11, 1928; children—Stephen William, Nancy Kay. Engr. Am. Sheet & Tin Plate Co., 1925-29, fuel and power engr., 1929-35, asst. chief engr., 1935-36; chief engr. constrn. div. Carnegie-Ill. Steel Corp., 1936-37, Gary (Ind.) Works, 1937, asst. gen. supt., 1937-40, gen supt., 1940-49, mgr. operations Chicago district, 1949-50, v.p. operations, 1950; v.p. mfg. U.S. Steel Corp., 1951-53 asst. executive v.p. operations, 1953-58, adminstrv. v.p.-central operations, 1958-59, exec. v.p. engring. and research, 1959-66. Trustee Carnegie Institute of Technology; member of Cornell University Council. Recipient Benjamin F. Fairless award, American Inst. Mech. Engrs., 1956. Mem. Am. Soc. M.E., Am. Iron and Steel Inst., Assn. Iron and Steel Engrs., Engrs. Soc. Western Pa. (president 1963). Episcopalian. Clubs: Duquesne, University, Pittsburgh Athletic Assn. (Pitts). Home: Sewickley, Pa. Died Apr. 1974.

JENNEY, CHESTER EZEKIEL, clergyman; b. Meriden, N.H., Feb. 16, 1881; s. Frank E. and Lois A. (Cutting) J.; grad. Kimball Union Acad., Meriden, 1902; S.T.B., Boston U., 1906; studied Harvard, and Columbia; grad. Union Theol. Sem., 1911; D.D., James Millikin U., Decatur, Ill., 1920; m. Gertrude Elinor Harris, Jan. 1, 1906; 1 dau., Mary Ruth. Was pastor South Middleboro, Mass., 1 yr.; pastor M.E. Ch., Mountain Top, Pa., 1906-07, Moosic, Pa., 1907-10, Grace Presbyn. Ch., St. Louis, 1911-13, First Ch., Decatur, Ill., 1913-22, First Presbyn. Ch., St. Louis, 1922-27; exec. sec. Yenching U., China, 1927-29; pastor First Presbyterian Church, Lockport, N.Y., 1929-35. Served in World War, Jan. 28, 1918-Feb. 20, 1919; chaplain Base Hosp., Camp Grant, Ill., 6 mos.; went to France with 342d Inf., 86th Div.; trans. to 1st Div.; wounded at the Argonne, Nov. 2, 1918. Republican. Mason (32°). Club: University, Active in financial campaigns for ednl. instns., Y.M.C.A.'s, etc.; especially interested in religious development of young people. Breeder of pure-blood Jersey cattle and thoroughbred Belgian horses. Home: Garrattsville, N.Y.†

JENNINGS, JOHN EDWARD, JR., author; b. Bklyn., Dec. 30, 1906; s. John Edward (M.D.) and Florence (Thistle) J.: ed. Brown Sch., N.Y.C., 1924, Colo. Sch. of Mines, 1925, Columbia, 1925-26; m. Virginia Lee Storey, June 20, 1931 (div. 1959); m. 2d, Elise Durrin Dunlap, Jan. 9, 1960; 1 son, John Edward, III. Writer, 1932-73; books include: Out American Tropics, 1938; Next to Valour, 1939; Call the New World, 1941; Gentleman Ranker, 1942; Wheel of Fortune (serialized in Liberty Mag., July-Aug.), 1943; The Shadow and the Glory, 1943; The Salem Frigate, 1946; Boston, Cradle of Liberty, 1630-1776, 1947; River To the West, 1948; The Sea Eagles, 1950; The Pepper Tree, 1950; The Strange Brigade, 1952; Clipper Ship Days, 1953; Rogue's Yarn, 1953; Banners Against the Wind, 1954; Chronicle of the Calypso, Clipper, 1955; The Wind in His Fists, 1956; Blood on the Moon, 1957; The Tall Ships, 1958; The Golden Eagle, 1959; The Raider, 1963; Tattered Ensign, 1966. Contbr. short stories to Sat. Eve. Post, Cosmopolitan, others. Served from lt. (j.g.) to lt. USNR, 1942-44; officer in charge Naval Aviation History Unit, 1944; lt. comdr., 1948. Democrat. Episcopalian. Address: Miller Place, N.Y. Died Dec. 4, 1973.

JENNINGS, PERCY HALL, glass mfr., b. N.Y. City, May 16, 1881; s. Frederic B. and Laura Hall (Park) J.; A.B., Yale, 1904; m. Elizabeth Auchincloss, Jan. 12, 1907; children—Percy Hall, Joanna R. Elizabeth A. Frederic B. III, Laura H. With Am. Trading Co., 1904-25, chmn. bd., 1923-25; pres. Vita Glass Corp., from 1926. Maj., chief of disbursing and legal div., Air Service, U.S.A., World War. Decorated Chevalier Legion of Honor (France). Republican, Presbyn. Clubs: Yale, Huntington Country, Garden City Golf. Home: Harbor, L.I., N.Y.†

JENSEN, CHRISTEN, educator; b. Salt Lake City, Utah, Feb. 4, 1881; s. Christen, Sr. and Nel Sina (Johansen) J.; B.A., U. of Utah, 1907; M.A., Harvard, 1908; studied U. of Calif., summer, 1915; Ph.D., U. of Chicago, 1921; m. Julia Bateman, Aug. 17, 1904; children—Ardis (dec.), Lorna. Professor history and polit. sci. Brigham Young U., from 1908; dean Grad. Sch., acting pres., 1939-40, 1949-50. Mem. Am. Polit. Science Assn., Am. Soc. Internat. Law, Tau Kappa Alpha. Democrat. Mormon. Author: The Pardoning Power in the American States, 1922. Home: Porvo, Utah.†

JENSEN, CHRISTIAN NEPHI, educator; b. Ephraim, Utah, June 18, 1880; s. Jens Peter and Dorothea (Gregerson) J.; B.S.A., U.A.C., M.S.A. Ph.D., Cornell; fellow U. of Calif., 1909, Cornell, 1910-12; m. Marian Lee Choate, Dec. 21, 1909. Teacher and prin. pub. schs., 1897-1905; asst. in botany 1907-08, prof. botany and plant pathology, 1912-13, Utah Agrl. Coll.; pres. Brigham Young Coll., Logan, Utah, 1913-20; instr. Cornell U., 1920-21; supt. of pub. instrn., State of Utah, 1921-33; supt. Jordan Sch. Dist. Mem. N.E.A., Department of School Adminstrators, Sigma Xi, Delta Theta Sigma, Phi Kappa Iota. Republican. Mem. Ch. of Jesus Christ of Latter Day Saints. Address: Sandy, Utah.†

JENTZSCH, RICHARD ALVIN, orthodontist; b. Chgo., Dec. 4, 1892; s. Richard and Ella (Zuerkel) J.; D.D.S., U. Ill., 1926, M.S., 1931; m. Adeline M. Hayek, Nov. 8, 1934 (dec. 1958); m. 2d, Pauline R. Jones, Mar. 9, 1964. Faculty, U. Ill., 1926-36; practice dentistry specializing in orthodontics, from 1926. Mayor, Village of Wood Dale (Ill.), 1943-47. Served with U.S. Army, 1918-19. Mem. Ill., Chgo. (past v.p.) dental socs., Am. Dental Assn., Chgo. Assn. Orthodontists, USCG Aux., Navy League U.S., Omicron Kappa Upsilon, Tau Kappa Epsilon. Home: Fort Myers, Fla. Died Oct. 2, 1974; interred Mt. Emblem Cemetery, Elmhurst, Ill.

JEPSEN, GLENN LOWELL, geologist; b. Lead, S.D., Mar. 4, 1903; s. Victor Theodore and Kittie Elizabeth (Gallup) J.; student U. Mich., 1922-23, S.D. State Sch. Mines, Rapid City, 1923-25; B.S., Princeton, 1927, Ph.D., 1930; m. Janet E. Mayo, June 14, 1934 (div. Dec. 1953); 1 dau., Katherine Alice. Instr., English, S.D. State Sch. Mines, 1924-25; instr. geology Princeton, 1930-34, asst. prof. geology, 1934-40, asso. prof., 1940-46, Sinclair prof. vertebrate paleontology, 1946-74; dir. Princeton U. Scott Fund Expdns.; curator vertebrate paleontology Princeton Natural History Mus., 1935-74, also dir. Recipient Addison Emery Verrill medal Yale, 1962. Mem. A.A.A.S., Am. Soc. Mammologists, Geol. Soc. Am. (councilor 1951-54), Paleontol. Soc. Am. (v.p. 1955-56), Soc. Vertebrate Paleontol. (pres. 1944-45), Am. Philos. Soc., Am. Assn. U. Profs., Geol. Soc. N.J. pres. 1959-61, dir. 1961-63), Phi Beta Kappa, Sigma Xi. Home: Princeton N.J. Died Oct. 15, 1974; cremated.

JERMAN, THOMAS PALMER, banker; b. Raleigh, N.C., Nov. 30, 1906; s. Thomas Palmer and Cornelia (Petty) J.; student Augusta Mil. Acad., 1921-24; A.B., U. of N.C., 1928; m. Martha Litchford, Oct. 11, 1938 (dec.); children—Virginia, Thomas Palmer IV (dec.); m. 2d, Ruth Lanford, Dec. 28, 1966. Exec. v.p. Guaranty Trust Co. of N.Y.; partner Bache & Co.; dir. W. T. Grant Co. Union Pacific. Served with USNR, 1942-48. Episcopalian. Clubs: University (N.Y.C.); Pinehurst Country. Home: Pinehurst N.C. Died Nov. 14, 1974; interred Oakwood Cemetery, Raleigh, N.C.

JERTBERG, GILBERT H., judge; b. Springfield, Mo.; s. Henry and Augusta (Swanson) J.; A.B., Stanford, 1920, J.D., 1922; m. Henrietta Burns; 1 dau., Joan (Mrs. T. N. Russell). Gen. practice law, Fresno, Cal., 1922-55; U.S. dist. Judge So. Dist. Cal., 1955-58; judge U.S. Ct. of Appeals, 9th Circuit, Fresno, from 1958. Mem. Cal. Bd. Edn., 1943-54. Bd. govs. Fresno State Coll. Found. Mem. Fresno County C. of C. (pres. 1939), Fresno County (pres. 1940), Am. bar assns., Stanford Alumni Assn. (pres. 1941), Am. Legion, Phi Beta Kappa, Theta Chi, Phi Alpha Delta. Elk. Home: Fresno, Cal. Deceased.

JERVEY, HAROLD EDWARD, ret. govt. ofcl.; b. Charleston, S.C., Sept. 22, 1894; s. Joseph Edward and Jessie (Balentine) J.; student, Coll. Charleston, 1910-14, Med. Coll. State of S.C., 1914-16; m. Stella White, Oct. 16, 1916; children—Harold Edward, Herbert V., William T. Tchr., High Sch. Charleston, 1916-25; pub. accountant, Jacksonville, Fla., 1926-30; internal auditor S.C. Hwy. Dept., 1930-42, dir. Motor Vehicle Div., 1935-36; asst. state auditor, Columbia, S.C., 1942-69. Treas. Heathwood Hall Episcopal Sch. Trustee Protestant Episcopal Diocese of Upper S.C. Bd. dirs. Columbia Art Assn., Columbia Mus. Art, treas., 1953-

58. Recipient Silver Beaver award, Boy Scouts Am., 1944. Mem Soc. of the Cincinnati. Episcopalian (vestryman, warden). Home: Columbia, S.C. Deceased.

JEWELL, BERT MARK, labor official; b. Brock, Nemaha County, Neb., Feb. 5, 1881; s. Charles James and Ella Elizabeth (Adams) J.; educated pub. schs. Apprentice boilermaker's trade, 1900-05; with S.A.L. Ry., Jacksonville, Fla., 1907-16; apptd., May 1916, gen. organizer Internat. Brotherhood of Boilermakers, Iron Ship Builders and Helpers of America; organized crews of ship yards and war activity plants and assigned to Washington, D.C., spring of 1918, as nat. rep. of same orgn. to handle all war business of the brotherhood; pres. Ry. Employers' Dept., A.F. of L., Aug. 16, 1918-June 30, 1946; retired, July 1946-Jan. 1948. Internat. rep. Ry. Labor Execs. Assn., Jan.-June 1948; labor adviser to adminstr., Econ. Cooperation Adminstrn., from 1948.†

JEWELL, JAMES RALPH, educator; b. Athens, Tenn., Mar. 2, 1878; s. James Erastus and Mary Rebecca (Coe) J; student Highland (Kan.) U., 1898-99; A.B., Coe Coll., Cedar Rapids, Ia., 1903; A.M., Clark Univ., 1904, Ph.D., 1906; LL.D., Univ. of Ark., Fayetteville, 1927; m. Edna Lucena Keith, Aug. 21, 1907; children—Margaret Elaine, James Ralph, Keith Coe (dec.). Fellow in psychology, Clark U., 1903-06; dir. of training, Southwestern La. Industrial Inst., 1906-07; prof. history of edn., Kan. State Teachers' Coll., Emporia, 1907-09; high sch. visitor, Kan., 1909-11; prof. secondary edn. and prin. State Normal Secondary Sch., Kan. State Teachers' Coll., 1911-13; prof. edn., 1913, dean Sch. of Edn., 1914, dean Coll. of Edn., 1916-27, U. of Ark., also dir. Univ. Summer Sch.; dean Sch. of Vocational Edn., Ore. State Coll., 1927-32; dean Schs. of Edn., U. of Ore. and Ore. State Coll., dir. teacher training, Oregon State System of Higher Education, 1932-47; dean emeritus, from July 1, 1947; head, counseling and guidance div., prof. psychol., Trinity U., San Antonio, Tex., from Sept. 1, 1948. Trustee, Highland College. Member A.A.A.S., N.E.A., Am. Acad. Political and Social Science, Nat. Soc. Study Edn., Coll. Teachers of Edn., State Teachers' Assn., Phi Kappa Phi, Tau Kappa Alpha, Kappa Delta Pi, Phi Delta Kappa. Presbyterian. Author: Agricultural Education; Character Education. Contbr. to Pedagogical Seminary, School and Society, Am. Jour. of Psychology, etc. Address: San Antonio, Tex.†

JEWELL, JESSE DALE, physician, naval officer; b. Leon, W. Va., July 24, 1891; s. John Sherman and Mayme (Spiller) J.; M.D., U. Ore., 1918; m. Lola Belle Beckner, June 7, 1918. Commd. Lt. (j.g.) U.S. Navy 1918, advanced through grades to rear adm., 1944; served Mare Island (Cal.), Hosp. and Navy Yard, 1918-21, destroyer div. 36, 1921-23, Bremerton (Wash.) Navy Yard, 1923-26, mine force, Pearl Harbor, T.H., 1926-29, U.S. Naval Hosp., San Diego, 1929-32, U.S.S. Neches, 1932-34; U.S. Naval Hosp., Newport (R.I.), 1934-37, U.S. Naval Sta. Guantanamo Bay, Cuba, 1937-39, torpedo sta., Keyport (Wash.), 1939-41, U.S.S. Calif., Pearl Harbor, 1941, Navy Yard, Bremerton, 1942-43, U.S. Naval Hosp., Corona (Calif.), 1943-44, hdqrs. 13th Naval Dist., Seattle, 1944-45; released from active duty, Feb. 1, 1945. Decorated Navy Cross for service at Pearl Harbor, Dec. 7, 1941. Fellow, A.C.S.; mem. A.M.A., Nat. Sojourners. Mason. Home: Portland, Ore. Died July 11, 1975.

JEWETT, HUGH, business exec.; b. Austin, Tex., Aug. 9, 1907; s. Frank Leonard and Catherine Margaret (Caughey) J.; B.B.A., U. Tex., 1928, M.B.A., 1929; m. Sylvia Rohwer, Aug. 10, 1935; children—William Hugh, Robert Allen. With Colgate-Palmolive-Peet Co. 1930-63, comptroller, 1951, comptroller sec., 1952, v.p., comptroller, sec., 1953-63; ret., 1963. Mem. Beta Gamma Sigma, Alpha Kappa, Psi, Beta Alpha Psi. Clubs: Bankers (N.Y.C.); Canoe Brook Country (Summit, N.J.). Home: Phoenix, Ariz. Died Mar. 19, 1975.

JLLEK, LUBOR, physiologist; b. Prague, Czechoslovakia, Jan. 8, 1926; s. Frant. and Ludmila (Hemerova) J.; M.D., Charles U., Prague, 1951, Ph.D., 1958, D.Sc., 1965; m. Helena Civinova, Apr. 17, 1951; 1 son, Ondrej. Med. Faculty Charles U., Prague, 1951-75, prof. med. physiology, 1966-75, became vice dir. Inst., 1959, later dir. Inst.; also vice dean Med. Faculty, 1961-75; vis. scientist Galesburg (Ill.) State Research Hosp., 1964. Mem. Czechoslovac Physiol. Soc. (pres.), Internat. Brain Research Orgn./UNESCO, Internat. Soc. Developmental Psychobiology. Author: Stagnatn Hypoxia and Anoxia of the Brain, 1966; also numerous articles. Editor: Ontogenesis of the Brain, 1968, Vol. II, 1975. Research on metabolical functional and structural devel. of nervous system during ontogeny, reaction and adaptation of nervous tissue to hypoxia and anoxia in course of post-natal life, reversibility and prognosis of anoxic changes of brain, influence of different agts. on anoxia. Home: Prague, Czechoslovakia. Died Feb. 6, 1975.

JOBIN, RAOUL, opera singer; b. Quebec City, Canada, Apr. 8, 1906; s. Raoul and Amanda (Bedard) J.; ed. in Canada; m. Therese Drouin, Apr. 22, 1930; children—Claudette, Andre, France. Debut with Paris Grand Opera, 1930; mem. Paris Grand Opera, 1930-40, 47-55; Paris Opéra Comique, 1936-40, 1947-55; sang in concerts and opera, Belgium, Holland, Switzerland, Spain, France, Canada, U.S., Italy, Egypt; debut with Met. Opera, N.Y. City, in Manon, Feb. 19, 1940; mem. Met. Opera, 1940-50, 56, Buenos Aires (Teatro Colon), 1941-43, 45, 48, 54; Rio de Janeiro (Municipal) 1939, 41-43; Mexico (Opera Nacional), 1944-48; tchr. Conservatoire de Musique et D'Art Dramatique, Que., 1948-61, dir. Conservatoire, 1961-70; cultural adviser Delegation Générale du Quebec in Paris, 1970. Address: Quebec Can. Died Jan. 13, 1974.

JOBST, NORBERT RAYMOND, banker; b. St. Louis, Dec. 19, 1920; s. Francis Joseph and Catherine Mary (Stevens) J.; ed. Washington U., St. Louis; grad. Grad. Sch. Banking, U. Wis., 1961. Asst. cashier First Nat. Bank in St. Louis, 1956-58, asst. v.p., 1958-64, v.p., 1964-75. Bd. dirs. Nat. Found. March of Dimes. Served with Air Transport Command, AUS, 1942-46. Mem. Robert Morris Assos. Roman Catholic. Club: Mo. Athletic (St. Louis). Home: St Louis Mo. Died Feb. 8, 1975; buried Resurrection Cemetery.

JOCHEM, ANITA M., educator; b. Quincy, Ill., Feb. 12, 1912; d. Lawrence Joseph and Anna (Menke) Jochem; A.B., Coll. St. Francis, 1936; M.A., Loyola U. (Chgo.), 1941; student Chgo. Musical Coll., 1941-42, Catholic U. Am., 1958-59, U. Minn., 1960-61, Inst. U.S. Studies London, 1969-70. Tchr., St. Francis Acad., Joliet, Ill., 1936-42, St. Clement's High Sch., Chgo., 1942-44; tchr. Sacred Heart Sch., Winnetka, Ill., 1945-57, prin., 1952-57; instr. Coll. St. Francis, Joliet, Ill., 1957-62, pres., 1962-69; research, student Inst. U.S. Studies, London, Eng., 1969-70; v.p. Nazareth (Ky.) Campus, Spalding Coll., 1970-71, v.p. adminstrv. affairs Spalding Coll., Louisville, 1971-72; gen. councillor Congregation Sisters of St. Francis of Mary Immaculate, Joliet, Ill., 1972-75. Mem. nonpublic coll. adv. com. Ill. Bd. Higher Edn., 1968-69. Bd. dirs. adult edn. div. Coll. St. Francis, 1958-62; trustee (hon.) Lincoln Acad. Ill., 1965-69. Contbr. articles in field to profl. jours. Home: Joliet, Ill., Died July 29, 1975; buried Resurrection Cemetery, Lockport, Ill.

JOEHR, ADOLF, banker; b. Berne, Switzerland, 1878; s. Jakob and Elise (Bucher) Joehr; ed. Grammar School; Universities of Berne, Berlin, Paris; m. Martha Schuithess, 1909; children—Walter Adolf, Marianne. Employed as sec. to gen. mgr. Swiss Fed. Rys., 1901. Became gen. sec. Swiss Nat. Bank, 1907; joint gen. mgr., 1915-18. Joint gen. mgr. Credit Suisse, 1918, dir., 1939, chmn., from 1940. Chmn. Kraftwerk Laufenburg, Centralschweizeische Kraftwerke. Chmn. Elektro-Watt Enterprises elec. industr., S.A. Hon. mem. Assn. Suisse des Banquiers; mem. Chambre de Commerce Internationale, Chambre de Commerce de Zurich. Author: Die Volkswirtschaft der Schweiz im Kriegsfall, 1912; Die Schweizerischen Notenbanken 1826 bis 1913, 1914, 2 volumes, 1915; Die Valutaentwertung und die Schweiz, 1920; Die Zukunft der Valuten, 1922, Staatswirtschaft & Privatwirtschaft in der Schweiz, 1927; Zurich als Bank- and Börsenplatz, 1928; Die schweizerischen Grossbanken und Privatbankiers. Home: Zurich, Switzerland†

JOHNSON, ALICE FREIN, news corr.; b. Palo Alto, Cal., Oct. 4, 1900; d. Pierre Joseph and Emma Blanche (Macleod) Frein; A.B. in French, U.Wash., 1922, A.B. in Journalism, 1923; m. Jesse Charles Johnson, Nov. 14, 1925; 1 dau., Mary Virginia (Mrs. Joseph B. Jeffers, Jr.). Asso. editor Washington Newspaper, publ. for newsmen of Pacific N.W., 1924; free lance, newspapers and mags., 1926-34; advt. mgr., asst. editor Little Gardens mag., 1935-41; news staff, women's news editor Seattle Times, 1942-43. Washington correspondent, from 1943. Mem. Def. Adv. Com. on Women in Services, 1963-66. Mem. board of trustees Seattle Art Mus., 1938-43; founder, 1st chmn. Seattle Art Mus. Study Child, 1935-36. Recipient first place, distinguished reporting among daily papers, State of Washington, 1957. Mem. Kappa Alpha Theta, Theta Sigma Phi (named woman of achievement Seattle alumnae chpt. 1953). Clubs: Women's Nat. Press (pres. 1956-57); Am. Newspaper Womens. Contbr. N.A. Newspaper Alliance. Home: Bethesda, Md. Died Jan. 1973.

JOHNSON, AMOS NEILL, physician; b. Garland, N.C., June 5, 1908; s. Jefferson Deems and Mary Lily (Wright) J.; A.B., Duke, 1929; postgrad. U. N.C. Med. Sch., 1929-31; M.D., U. Pa., 1933: m. Mary Porter Allan, Mar. 16, 1934; children—Mary llan (Mrs. William R. Watts III), Amos Neill. Intern, Jackson Meml. Hosp., Miami, Fal.; gen. med. practice, Garland, 1934-75; mem. and chief staff Sampson County Meml. Hosp.; mem. staff Bladen County Meml. hosp.; instr. gen. practice Duke Med. Sch., 1944-75. Mem. N.C. Bd. Med. Examiners, 1950-56, pres., 1955; adviser Sears Roebuck Med. Found., 1962-75; mem. N.C. Bd. Hosp. Controls, 1948-52; med. adviser HEW, 1963-75, mem. med. assistance adv. com.; mem. Gov.'s Commn. To Study Pub. Sch. System N.C., Gov.'s Commn. on Econ. Devel.; med. adviser N.C. Bd. Mental Health, 1964-75; exec. com. Am. Bd. Med. Spltys., 1973-75. Dir. Lundy Packing Co., Universal Edn. Corp., Inc., Media Medica, Cape Fear Bank & Trust Co. Mem. Sampson County Bd. Edn. 1950-62; mem. Gov. N.C. Com. Court Reform, 1956. Trustee Greater Univs. of N.C., Family Health Found. Recipient N.C. Distinguished Citizen's award, 1966, posthumously, 1975; John G. Walsh award Am. Acad. Family Physicians, posthumously, 1975. Am. Diplomate Am. Bd. Family Practice (bd. dirs. 1970-75, pres. 1972-74, treas. 1974-75). Mem. Am. Acad. Gen. Practice (pres. N.C. 1952-53, chmn. edn. con. N.C. 1953-60; nat. chmn. com. edn. 1961-62, com. sci. assembly 1960-61, nat. bd. dirs. 1961-64, chmn. bd. dirs. 1962-64, pres. 1965-66, chmn. family health care services), A.M.A. (commn. accreditation hosps. 1960-70), Med. Soc. N.C. (pres. 1960-61), Sampson County (pres. 1947), 3d Dist. (pres. 1948) med. socs., Sigma Chi, Omicron Delta Kappa. Democrat. Presbyn. Address: Garland N.C. Died Apr. 23, 1975; buried Clinton, N.C.

JOHNSON, ANTON J., congressman; b. Peoria, Ill., Oct. 20, 1878; s. late Rev. C. W. and Mary Johnson; pub. sch. edn.; m. Mayme McMurray, 1905. Mem. 76th to 80th Congresses (1939-49), 14th Ill. Dist. Republican. Home: Macomb, Ill.*†

JOHNSON, BUFORD JEANETTE, psychologist; b. Thomson, Ga., Aug. 23, 1880; d. Preston Brooks and Ella (Morris) Johnson; A.B., LaGrange (Ga.) Coll., 1895; A.M., Johns Hopkins, 1915, Ph.D., 1916. Asso. psychologist, Lab. of Social Hygiene, Bedford Hills, N.Y., 1916-17; with Bureau Ednl. Expts., N.Y. City, 1917-20; psychologist and chmn. research com., 1920-22; asso. prof. psychology, Johns Hopkins, 1920-24, prof., 1924-38; prof. U. of Calif. at Los Angeles, summers, 1939, 40. Fellow A.A.A.S.; mem. Am. Psychol. Assn., Southern Soc. Philosophy and Psychology, Nat. Inst. Psychology, Soc. for Research in Child Development, Phi Beta Kappa, Sigma Xi. Club: College, Hamilton (Baltimore). Author: Mental Growth of Children, 1925; Habits of the Child, 1929; Child Psychology, 1932. Home: Baltimore, Md.*†

JOHNSON, CLARENCE HAZELTON, utility exec.; b. Topsham, Me., Nov. 25, 1906; s. Arthur Berry and Angela (Hazelton) J.; A.B. magna cum laude, Bowdoin Coll., 1928; m. Mary Gibson Chamberlayne, Apr. 3, 1937 (dec.); children—Arthur Berry, Elizabeth Lewis (Mrs. Kellenberger), Angela Hazelton, Lewis Chamberlayne, Paul Tebbetts. With Chesapeake & Potomac Telephone Cos., Washington, D.C., 1928-67, student accountant, Balt., 1928-35, auditor disbursements, Richmond, 1936-45, auditor, Washington, 1945-49, v.p., gen. mgr., 1949-52, v.p. W.Va. operations, 1952-60, dir., 1952-60, v.p. revenue requirements of 4 Chesapeake & Potomac Telephone cos., 1960-67. Mem. U.S., C. of C., Newcomen Soc. Eng., Telephone Pioneers Am., Am. Polit. Sci. Assn., Met. Washington Bd. Trade, Va. Srs. Golf Assn., Phi Beta Kappa, Delta Kappa Epsilon. Republican. Episcopalian. Clubs: Metropolitan, Columbia Country. Home: Topsham, Me. Died Nov. 28, 1973.

JOHNSON, CLINTON CHARLES, banker; b. N.Y.C., Dec. 10, 1897; s. Charles F. and Josephine (Ericson) J.; student Dartmouth, 1916-17; grad. School Banking, Rutgers U., 1940; m. Annabel Morris Hatfield, June 7, 1922; 1 dau., Dorothy (Mrs. William Tipper). With Chem. Bank, 1919-63, exec. v.p. charge internat. div. Chem. Bank N.Y. Trust Co., 1955-63, mem. adv. bd. on internat. bus.; dir. Chem. Internat. Finance, Ltd., Chem. Internat. Banking Corp. Member bd. mgrs. Am. Baptist Conv. Served with AEF, 1917-19. Decorated Order of Oranj-Nassau (Netherlands); Royal Order Vasa (Sweden); Royal Order of St. Olav (Norway). Mem. Nat. Fgn. Trade Council (dir.), Bankers Assn. Fgn. Trade (past pres.). Club: University. Home: Montclair, N.J. Died Feb. 22, 1974; interred Ocean View Cemetery, Staten Island, N.Y.

JOHNSON, CONSTANCE FULLER WHEELER (MRS. BURGES JOHNSON), author; b. Staten Island, N.Y., Sept. 16, 1879; d. Everett Pepperell and Lydia Lorraine (Hodges) Wheeler; grad. Brearley Sch., N.Y. City, 1899; m. Burges Johnson, June 14, 1904. Author: When Mother Lets Us Cook, 1908; When Mother Lets Us Help, 1909; When Mother Lets Us Keep Pets, 1911; When Mother Lets Us Travel, 1912; Private Code and Post Card Cypher (with Burges Johnson), 1914; Parodies for Housekeepers (with Burges Johnson), 1921; Mary in New Mexico, 1921; Mary in California, 1922; Carter Children in France, 1927; also poems in mags. Editor: (with husband) Year Book of Humor, 1910. Address: Schenectady, N.Y.†

JOHNSON, CROCKETT (DAVID JOHNSON LEISK), cartoonist; b. N.Y.C., Oct. 20, 1906; s. David and Mary (Burg) Leisk; student N.Y.U., Cooper Union; m. Ruth Krauss, 1940. Profl. football player; art editor several mags.; cartoonist The Little Man with the Eyes, Collier's mag.; cartoonist daily cartoon strip Barnaby, syndicated 1943-52, from 1960. One-man show Glezer Gallery, N.Y.C., 1967, IBM Gallery, Yorktown Heights, N.Y., 1975; Gen. Electric Gallery, Fairfield, Conn., 1975; mathematical paintings in collection at Smithsonian Instn. Author: Barnaby, 1943; Barnaby and Mr. O'Malley, 1944; Harold and the Purple Crayon; Harold's Fairy Tale; 6 Harold books; also illustrator other children's books. Patentee adjustable matress. Home: Westport, Conn. Died July 11, 1975.

JOHNSON, ELIZABETH FORREST, educator; b. Frederick, Md., Sept. 21, 1881; d. Chapman Love and Mary Margaret (Shriver) J.; A.B., Vassar, 1902, and graduate work same; hon. A.M., Univ. of Pennsylvania. Headmistress of The Baldwin School, Bryn Mawr, Pa., from 1915. Mem. Head Mistresses' Assn., Phi Beta Kappa. Democrat. Episcopalian. Clubs: Cosmopolitan, College, Contemporary (Phila.), Address: Bryn Mawr, Pa.†

JOHNSON, ELLIS ADOLPH, physicist; b. Quincy, Mass., Sept. 2, 1906; s. Peter George and Elizabeth (Teklo) J.; B.S., Mass. Inst. Tech., 1928, M.S., 1929, D.Sc., 1947; m. Alice Gertrude Lagasse, Aug. 4, 1934; children—Betsy W., Peter B. Trainee Bell Telephone Labs. and N.Y. Telephone Co., 1926-29; asst. elec. engr. Mass. Inst. Tech., 1929-34; asso. elec. engr. U.S. Coast and Geod. Survey, 1934-35; asst. physicist Carnegie Instn., 1935-36, asso. physicist, 1936-37, math. physicist, 1937-40, chmn. geophys. crust, 1946-48; prin. physicist Naval Ordnance Lab., 1940-42; tech. dir. spl. weapons U.S. Air Force, 1948; dir. Operations Research Office, Johns Hopkins (operating under contract with Dept. of Army), 1948-61; dir. Systems Research Center, Case Inst. Tech., 1961-65; coordinator sci. affairs Dept. Health, Edn., and Welfare, 1965-67. Served as comdr., U.S.N., 1942-46, mining officer. Decorated: Distinguished Civilian Service Citation (Navy); Legion of Merit (Navy and Air Force); Commendation Ribbon (2 Navy); Commendation (Air Force). Fellow Am. Phys. Soc.; mem. Nat. Research Council (mem. geophys. com., operations research com.). Office Naval Research (com. Arctic research), Am. Geophys. Soc., Washington Philos. Soc., Am. Optical Soc. Club: Cosmes (Washington). Author sci. publs. Holder patents. Home: Somerset, Mass. Died Dec. 16, 1973.

JOHNSON, ELVERA CROSBY (MRS. JOHN ALEX JOHNSON), librarian; b. nr. Pavo, Ga., June 24, 1912; d. Guy Ross and Emma Clower (Hardee) Crosby; student Ga. State Coll., 1930-31; B.S., Fla. State U., 1950; postgrad. U. Ga., 1968; m. John Alex Johnson, July 14, 1951. Tchr. Colquitt County, Autreyville, Ga., 1931-32, Pavo High Sch., 1944-49, Little River Sch., Miami, Fla., 1950-52, Millen (Ga.) Elementary Sch., 1952-54, Emanual County Inst., Twin City, Ga., 1954-59, Thomasville (Ga.) Jr. High Sch., 1960-63, Joseph Lamar Sch., Augusta, Ga., 1963-65, Sunset Sch., Moultrie, Ga., 1965-66; librarian Balfour Elementary Sch., Thomasville, Ga., 1966-70; dir. Thomasville Pub. Library, 1970-73, condr. summer reading program for children and young adults, 1970-72. Dir. Summer Recreational program Little River Sch. Library, 1951-52. Mem. D.A.R. Methodist. Mason; mem. Order Eastern Star (chpt. worthy matron 1954-55). Clubs: Womans (pres. 1937-38) (Pavo, Ga.); Garden, Killarney Queen (Thomasville). Home: Pavo, Ga. Died Sept. 13, 1973.

JOHNSON, GLOVER, lawyer, corp. dir.; b. Perth Amboy, N.J., Dec. 1, 1900; s. Arthur Glover and Lillian M. (Miller) J.; student Trinity Sch., N.Y.C., 1919; A.B. (Lemuel Curtis scholar), Trinity Coll., 1922, LL.D., 1960; LL.B. (Kent scholar), N.Y. Law Sch., 1925; m. Dorothy Murray Algeo, Nov. 27, 1926; children—Margaret Murray (Mrs. Charles J. Werber), Patricia Hinckley. With Morgan Guaranty Trust Co., N.Y.C., 1922-26; admitted to N.Y. bar, 1926, since practiced in N.Y.C.; with White & Case, 1926-73, partner, 1936-73, chmn. bd. Internat. Minerals & Chem. Corp., Chgo., 1967-70, vice chmn., 1970-73, also dir.; chmn. exec. com., dir. F&M Schaefer Corp.; dir. Agfa-Gevaert, Inc., F. & M Schaefer Brewing Co., Fed. Paper Board Co., Inc., N.Y.C., Rumson Merchandising Corp. Chmn. lawyers div. A.R.C., N.Y.C., 1958. Bd. govs. New Rochelle Hosp. Med. Center, 1955-73, pres., 1963-68, chmn., 1968; pres. N.Y. Sch. for Deaf, 1949-63, chmn., 1963-73; trustee Trinity Schs., N.Y.C., Pawling, N.Y., pres., 1967-68, chmn., 1968; also life trustee Trinity Coll., Hartford, Conn., 1962, also chmn. admissions com., mem. exec. com., sr. fellow, 1956-62. Mem. S.R. (bd. mgrs. 1959, 69-73), Am. (chmn. com. fed. regulation of securities 1953-54), N.Y. State, Westche N.Y.C. bar assns., Nat. Legal Aid Assn., Alumni Assn. Trinity Coll. (pres. 1947-49, 60-62), Delta Kappa Epsilon, Phi Delta Theta. Epsicopalian (sr. warden 1944-47). Clubs: Yale, Down Town Assn., Wall Street, The Brook, Board Room (N.Y.C.); Larchmont (N.Y.) Yacht (trustee 1939-62, sec. 1939-54), Siwanoy (Bronxville, N.Y.); Blind Brook (Rye, N.Y.); Old Guard Soc. (Palm Beach, Fla.). Home: New Rochelle, N.Y. Died Oct. 28, 1973; buried Woodlawn Cemetery, Bronx, N.Y.

JOHNSON, HELGI, geologist; b. Akureyri, Iceland, Feb. 3, 1904; s. Gisli and Gudrun Helga (Finnsdottir) J.; B.S., U. of Manitoba, 1926, A.M., U. of Toronto, 1929, Ph.D., 1934; m. Helen Mary Eliza Hunter, Sept. 12, 1933. Came to U.S., 1929, naturalized, 1948. Research asst. Royal Ont. Mus. of Paleontology, Toronto, 1926-29; instr. geology Rutgers U., 1929-33, asst. prof., 1933-40, asso. prof., 1940-44, prof. geology, 1944-74, dir. Mus. Geology and Paleontology, 1944-70, dir. Bur. Mineral Research, chmn. dept. geology, 1945-74; field asst. to asst. geologist Geol. Survey Can., 1925-32; geologist and regional geol. field officer Geol. Survey, Newfoundland, 1936-45; geologist Mil. Geol. br. U.S. Geol. Survey, Dept. Interior. U.S. Dept. Nat. Def., other govt. bureaus. Mem. Joint Research Committee, N.J. State Highway-Rutgers, 1947-74; executive dir. Yellowstone-Bighorn Research Assn., Inc., Red Lodge, Mont. Fellow Geol. Society, Am., Paleontol. Soc.; mem. Am. Assn. Petroleum Geologists. Am. Inst. Mining and Metall. Engrs. Am. Geophys. Union, Icelandic Nat. League, New Brunswick Sci. Soc., Sigma Xi. Rep. Unitarian. Clubs: Rutgers, University Outing. Contbr. articles on splty. in scientific pubs. Home: Somerset, N.J. Died Nov. 3, 1974.

JOHNSON, HOWARD ALBERT, clergyman, b. Atlantic, Ia., Oct. 8, 1915; s. Mark Peter and Jessie (Howard) J.; B.A., U. Cal. at Los Angeles, 1936; B.D., P.E. Theol. Sem. in Va., 1939, D.D., 1965; postgrad. Princeton, 1942, (fellow Am.-Scandinavian Found.), U. Copenhagen, 1946-48; S.T.M., Union Theol. Sem., N.Y.C., 1949; D.D., Upsala Coll., 1956, Episcopal Theol. Sem. in Ky., 1964. Ordained priest P.E. Ch., 1940; served parishes in Cal., Washington, 1940-45; asso. prof. sch. theology U. of South, 1949-53; lectr. Kierkegaard, Japanese colls. and univs., 1952; fellow St. Augustine's, Central Coll. of Anglican Communion, Canterbury, 1953-54; adj. prof. religion Columbia, 1954-58; ednl. cons. Diocese of Hong Kong and Macao, 1970; editorial asst. Soren Kierkegaard Inst., Copenhagen, 1971-74. Canon theologian Cathedral of St. John the Divine, 1954-64. Mem. Soc. Theol. Discussion; corr. mem. Soren Kierkegaard Soc. Copenhagen. Author: Kierkegaard Rikaino Kagi, 1953; (with James A. Pike) Man in the Middle, 1956; Global Odyssey, 1963. Contbr. to Sons of the Prophets, 1963, Modern Canterbury Pilgrims. Editor: Preaching the Christian Year; This Church of Ours; Either/Or (Soren Kierkegaard), rev. translation 1959; co-editor: A Kierkegaard Critique, 1962. Contbr. articles to profl. jours. Home: New York City N.Y. Died June 12, 1974.

JOHNSON, JOHN BEAUREGARD, physician; b. Bessemer, Ala., Apr. 29, 1908; s. John Beauregard and Leona (Duff) J.; A.B., Oberlin Coll., 1931; M.D., Western Res. U., 1935; D.Sc. (hon.), Tuskegee Inst., Ala.; m. Audrey Amelia Ingram, Jan. 5, 1964; 1 dau., Linda Elaine; 1 step dau., Adrienne Renee Fairley. Intern, Cleve. City Hosp., 1935-36; dir. cardiovascular research lab. Freedman's Hosp., Washington, 1949-72, also staff div. cardiovascular disease; research fellow in cardiology Columbia, 1948-49; cons. NIH Clin. Center, Bethesda, Md.; Rockefeller Found. fellow U. Rochester, 1939-41; asst. in physiology Howard U., Washington, 1936-37, asst. prof. medicine, 1941-44, asso. prof. medicine, 1944-49, acting head dept., 1944, chmn. dept. medicine, 1949-62. Mem. steering com. Met. Wash. Health and Welfare Council; mem. nat. adv. council for hypertension HEW, 1972. Recipient Susan B. and Theodore Cummings Humanitarian award Am. Coll. Cardiology, 1964, 65. Diplomate Am. Bd. Internal Medicine. Fellow Am. Coll. Cardiology (treas. 1967, gov. D.C. 1972), A.C.P.; mem. Am. (v.p. 1972), Washington (sec. 1966-68, pres. 1972) heart assns., Am. Fedn. Clin. Research, Nat. Med. Assn., (chmn. council sci. assembly 1954-63, 66-72), Am. Gynec. Soc., Sigma Xi, Alpha Omega Alpha (charter mem. Gamma chpt.). Unitarian. Democrat. Contbr. numerous articles to profl. jours. Home: Washington, D.C., Died Dec. 16, 1972; buried Lincoln Meml. Cemetery, Suitland, Md.

JOHNSON, JOHN DAVID, indsl. exec.; b. Malagash, N.S., Can., Oct. 29, 1881; s. William and Jennie (McIntosh) J.; student pub. schs., N.S.; m. Gladys Percy, Nov. 19, 1911; children—Robert, Ralph, Elizabeth. Gen. mgr. Canada Cement Co., Ltd., Montreal, from 1927, pres., 1931-48, chmn., from 1948; dir. Bldg. Products, Price Bros. & Co., Ltd., Belding-Corticelli, Ltd., Montreal, London, Gen. Investors, Ltd., Liverpool and London, Globe Ins. Co., Ltd. (Canadian com.), Webb & Knapp (Can.), Ltd. Gov. McGill U. Clubs: Mount Royal, St. James's Mount Bruno Golf (Montreal); Rideau (Ottawa). Home: Montreal, Que., Can.†

JOHNSON, KATE BURR (MRS. CLARENCE A. JOHNSON), social worker; b. Morganton, N.C., Feb. 14, 1881; d. Frederick Hill and Lillian (Walton) Burr; student Queen's College, Charlotte, N.C.; New York School Social Work, Univ. of N.C.; m. Clarence A. Johnson, Apr. 14, 1903 (died Sept. 9, 1922); children—Clarence A., Frederick Burr. Dir. Bur. Child Welfare of N.C. State Bd. Charities and Pub. Welfare, 1919-21; commr. pub. welfare, N.C., 1921-30; supt. N.J. State Home for Girls, Trenton, from 1930. Vice-pres. N.C. Conf. for Social Service, 1915-16; pres. N.C. Fedn. Women's Club, 1917-19. Chmn. com. on state and local orgns. for handicapped, White House Conf. on Child Health and Protection. Mem. Am. Assn. Social Workers, Nat. Conf. of Juvenile Agencies, N.J. Conf. of Social Work, Am. Prison Assn., League of Women Voters. Democrat. Episcopalian. Address: Trenton, N.J.†

JOHNSON, LESTER, farmer, lawyer, congressman; b. Brandon, Wis., 1901; s. John E. Johnson; student Lawrence Coll., 2 yrs.; degree in commerce U. Wis., 1921, LL.B., 1941, m. Violet Graunke (dec. Aug. 10, 1953); children—Mary Jane and Jone (twins); m. 2d, Marjorie Gray, Nov. 9, 1954. Assisted father in business, 1924-34; chief clk. of assembly, 1935-39; practiced in Black River Falls, Wis.; with state bank commn., 1942; elected dist. atty., Jackson County, 1942 and 1944 (as Progressive), and 1952 (as Democrat); mem. 83d Congress, 9th Wis. Dist., elected to fill vacancy caused by death of Merlin Hull, also mem. 83d-88th congresses, chmn. dairy subcom., agr. com., 1959; commr. U.S. Bur. Customs. Democrat. Lutheran. Home: Augusta, Wis. Died July 24, 1975.

JOHNSON, LINDSAY FRANKLIN, mining cons.; b. Greensboro, N.C., Oct. 28, 1907; s. Lindsay F. and Flora McA. (Long) J.; student Elan Coll. (N.C.), Columbia; m. Elsie M. Taverna, Apr. 9, 1934; 1 dau., E. Kerala. Resident-mcht., Malabar Coast, S. India, 1928-41; with N.J. Zinc Co., N.Y.C., 1942-70, successively adminstrv. asst., asst. to v.p., asst. gen. mgr. Palmerton (Pa.) plants, asst. to pres., 1942-55, v.p., 1955-66, pres., 1966-70, also treas., dir.; mining cons., 1970-74. Mem. Am. Inst. Mining Metall. and Petroleum Engrs. Presbyn. (elder). Clubs: Saucon Valley Country (Bethlehem, Pa.); Union, Mining (N.Y.C.); Country of North Carolina (Pinehurst). Home: Southern Pines, N.C. Died Nov. 30, 1974.

JOHNSON, MARGARET LOUISE, librarian; b. Washington, Apr. 12, 1902; d. Hosmer Melancthon and Florence Edith (Bowman) Johnson; A.B., Goucher Coll., 1924; B.S., Columbia, 1942; grad. study George Washington U., Yale. Staff, accessions dept., Library Congress, 1924-28; mem. catalogue dept., Yale U. Library, 1928-36; reference dept., 1936-43; reference librarian Smith Coll. Library, 1943-47; asst. librarian, reference librarian, 1947-48, acting librarian, 1948-49, librarian, 1949-68, librarian emeritus, 1968-73. Mem. A.L.A. Club: Zonta International. Home: Northampton, Mass. Died Apr. 20. 1973; cremated, inurned Washington, D.C.

JOHNSON, PAUL EMANUEL, former educator; b. Niantic, Conn., Feb. 19, 1898; s. John Edward and Martha (Cadwallader) J.; A.B., Cornell Coll., 1920, D.D., 1939; A.M., U. Chgo., 1921; S.T.B., Boston U., 1923, Ph.D., 1928; m. Evelyn Grant, June 2, 1922; children—Lois Kathay (Mrs. George A. Cummings), Mona Margaret (Mrs. William Valentine). Asst. in philosophy Brown U., 1924-25; instr. ethics West China Union U., 1926-27; asso. prof. philosophy Hamline U., 1928-36; dean, prof. philosophy and religion Morningside Coll., 1936-41; prof. psychology of religion Boston U. Sch. Theology, 1941-57, Danielsen prof. psychology and pastoral counseling, 1957-63, prof. emeritus, 1963-74, dir. pastoral counseling service, 1952-63. Vis. prof. Kwansei Gakuin, Aoyama Gakuin, Toyko Union Theol. Sem., Doshisha U. (all Japan), 1963-64, Christian Theol. Sem., Indpls., 1966-71; dir. Indpls. Pastoral Counseling Center, 1965-68; lectr. Duke, Garrett Theol. Sem., U. So. Cal. Sch. Religion, Pacific Sch. Religion, Sch. Theology at Claremont (Cal.), Union Coll. of B.C., Vancouver. Diplomate Am. Assn. Pastoral Counselors. Fellow Am. Psychol. Assn.; mem. Am. Philos. Assn., Am. Acad. Religion, Insts. of Religion and Mental Health, Assn. Clin. Pastoral Edn., Soc. Group Psychotherapy and Psychodrama, Am. Protestant Hosp. Assn., Phi Beta Kappa. Author: Who Are You, 1937; Psychology of Religion, 1945, rev. 1959; Psychology of Pastoral Care, 1953; Personality and Religion, 1957; Person and Counselor, 1967; The Middle Years, 1971; (with Lowell Calston) Personality and Christian Faith, 1972; Christian Love. Editor: Healer of the Mind, 1972. Contbg. editor Community Mental Health. Contbr. articles to religious publs., philos. and psychol. jours. Home: Centerville Mass. Died Sept. 1, 1974; interred Mosswood Cemetery, Cotuit, Mass.

JOHNSON, PAUL LUTHER, surgeon; b. Taylor, N.D., Aug. 5, 1917; s. Carl August and Constance (Larsen) J.; student St. Olaf Coll., 1934-35; B.A., U. N.D., 1940; B.S. in Medicine, 1941; M.D., Temple U., 1943; postgrad. State U., Ia., 1948; m. Penelope Bailey, Sept. 1, 1945; children—Paula, Dawn, Gregory, Jill. Intern, St. Joseph's Hosp., Phila., 1943, resident, 1944-45; orthopedic fellow Cleve. Clinic, 1949-51; asso. staff mem. Cleve. Clinic Found., 1951; orthopedic surgeon Quain and Ramstad Clinic, Bismarck, N.D., 1951-72; mem. staff Bismarck Hosp., St. Alexius Hosp., Bismarck, Mandan (N.D.) Hosp.; med. dir. N.D. Crippled Children's Services, 1952-72; mem. N.D. bd. examining com. for phys. therapists, 1967-72; dir. Bismarck Clinic, 1964-72. Mem. Bismarck Bd. Edn., 1957-72, pres., 1961-62, 65-66. Served with M.C., AUS, 1945-47. Diplomate Am. Bd. Orthopedic Surgery. Mem. 6th Dist. (pres. 1960), N.D. and med. socs., A.M.A. A.C.S., Am. Acad. Orthopedic Surgery (N.D. rep. 1969). Clin., Minn-Da-Man orthopedic socs. Republican. Lutheran. Mason (Shriner) Rotarian. Home: West Bismarck, N.D. Died Feb. 27, 1972.

JOHNSON, RANDALL EDWARD, radiologist; b. Williamson, W.Va., July 4, 1938; s. P.H. Johnson; M.D., W.Va. U., 1963; m. Vera A. Johnson; children—Deborah L., Melissa A. Intern, USAF Hosp., Wright-Patterson AFB, O., 1963-64; resident Wilford Hall USAF Hosp., San Antonio, Tex., 1965-68; pvt. practice medicine specializing in radiology; fellow in neuroradiology Mass. Gen. Hosp., Boston, 1971-72; asst. prof. radiology U. Neb. Sch. Medicine, 1972-73. Served to maj., M.C., USAF, 1962-71. Diplomate Am. Bd. Radiology. Mem. Radiol. Soc. N.Am., New Eng. Roentgen Ray Soc., Mass. Med. Soc., Am. Coll. Radiology, A.M.A., Mass. Radiol. Soc., Boston Neuroradiol. Soc., Am. Soc. Neuroradiology. Home: Omaha, Neb. Deceased.

JOHNSON, RICHARD ELLIS, r.r. exec.; b. Osawatomie, Kan., Nov. 10, 1909; s. Lewis M. and Cordie Alice (Beck) J.; grad. Inst. Mgmt., Northwestern U., 1955; m. Julia Ward, Sept. 16, 1931; children—

Judith (Mrs. Jock Garden), Janet. Various positions M.P. R.R., 1925-36; with C., R.I. & P. R.R., 1936-74, asst. v.p. operations, 1953-54, v.p. operations, Chgo., 1954-61, exec. v.p. and dir., 1961, president, director, 1961-74, vice chmn. bd., 1965-74; mem. bond holders protective com. Central R.R. of N.J., dir. Railway Express Agy., Inc., Kansas City Terminal Ry. Co., Waterloo R.R. Co. Pres. Royale Gardens Home Owners Assn. Mem. Assn. Am. R.R.'s (dir.), Western Ry. Club, Am. R.R. Engring. Assn., Miss. Valley Maintenance of Way Club. Mason: mem. DeMolay Legion of Honor. Clubs: Executive, Chicago, Union League (Chgo.); LaGrange (Ill.) Country. Home: La Grange Park, Ill. Died June 12, 1974.

JOHNSON, ROBERT V., editor editorial page Houston Post. Address: Houston, Tex. Deceased.

JOHNSON, ROY MELISANDER, oil producer; b. Cashton, Wis., July 11, 1881; s. Oley Andrew and Sarah Melissa (Skinner) J.; student Milton (Wis.) Coll., 1894-97; A.B., Union Coll., Lincoln, Neb., 1899; m. Odessa Otey, Apr. 27, 1913 (died Jan. 15, 1923); children—Otey, June Odessa; m. 2d, Elizabeth Thomason, June 17, 1926. Printer, 1900-07; editor and pub. Ardmore (Okla.) Statesman. 1907-13; pioneer in opening oil field in Southern Okla., 1913, and associated with C.R. Smith in discovery of Graham Oil Field, 1919; pres. Healdton Petroleum Co.; also officer or dir. other companies. Mem. Okla. State Highway Commn., 1924-27; pres. Okla. State Good Roads Assn., Southwest Highway Club; del. Rep. National Conv., 1928. Seventh Day Adventist. Mason (33°, Shriner). Address: Ardmore, Okla.†

JOHNSON, WALTER RICHARD, judge; born Omaha, Neb., Oct. 30, 1897; s. Richard and Hulda (Johnson) J.; student U. Neb., 1919, Creighton U., 1919-22; m. Mary Violet Burt, June 17, 1924; children—Janice Mary, Marcia Lou, Douglas Richard, Rady Alan. Admitted to Neb. bar, 1922; in pvt. practice, Omaha, 1922-39; mem. Neb. State Legislature, 1925, 31, 33, 37; atty. gen. of Neb., 1939-49; spl. counsel Nat. Assn. Attys. Gen., Washington, 1949-55; judge FTC, 1959-73. Served as pilot and 2d lt., Air Service, World War I. Pres. Nat. Assn. of Attorneys General, 1946-47. Mem. Am. Bar Assn., Sigma Phi Epsilon, Delta Theta Phi. Republican. Lutheran. Odd Fellow. Home: Arlington Va. Died Aug. 12, 1974; interred National Memorial Cemetery, Falls Church, Va.

JOHNSTON, HARRY RAYMOND, electric co. exec.; b. Pitts., Dec. 17, 1922; s. Harry Wright and Myrtle Estelle (Bryant) J. With Westinghouse Co., Pitts., also Raleigh, N.C., 1940-43, 45-75, traffic mgr., Raleigh, 1956-75. Pres., chmn. bd. Wake County Soc. for Prevention of Cruelty to Animals, Raleigh, 1968-75; pres. N.C. Humane Fedn., 1972-75. Served with AUS, 1943-45. Mem. Triangle Traffic Assn. (dir.). Home: Raleigh, N.C. Died Mar. 16, 1975.

JOHNSTON, MYRTLE ALICE DEAN (MRS. CARL EDWARD JOHNSTON), land devel. co. exec.; b. Sacramento; d. Herbert Lathrop and Theodora (Hastings) Dean; grad. high sch.; m. Carl Edward Johnston, Mar. 20, 1926 (dec. Dec. 1953); children—Nancy Patricia (Mrs. James), Carolyn Dean (Mrs. Robert John Slobe). With North Sacramento Land Co., Sacramento, 1937-71, pres., 1953-71. Founding asso. Nat. Hist. Soc., 1969—; chmn. A.R.C. Hosp. and Recreation Corps., 1942-47; Century Club mem. Sacramento Opera Guild; endowing mem. Sacramento Symphony Assn. Named Hon. Mayor North Sacramento, 1962. Mem. Jr. League. Democrat. Christian Scientist. Club: Del Paso Country. Home: Sacramento, Cal. Died Oct. 17, 1971.

JOINER, OTIS WILLIAM, grain co. exec.; b. Maquoketa, Ia., Jan. 10, 1919; s. Melvin William and Mary (von Schrader) J.; student Maquoketa Jr. Coll., 1936-38; B.A. in Econ., U. Ia., 1940; m. Josephine Jennette McElhinney, June 8, 1941; children—Cherie (Mrs. David Hartley Root), Mary (Mrs. John Jauchen), Thekla, Amy. Business trainee Gen. Electric Co., Schenectady, N.Y., 1940-44; with Kent Feeds Inc., Muscatine, Ia., 1946-75, v.p., gen. mgr., 1966-74, pres. 1974-75, also dir.; pres. L. Teweles Seed Co. Inc., 1972-75, chmn. bd., 1974-75; dir. Grain Processing Co., Muscatine, Muscatine Corp. Mem. adv. bd. Muscatine Community Coll. Feed Technology, 1966-75. Served with USNR, 1944-46. Mem. Am. Feed Mfrs. Assn. (dir., mem. exec. com.). Presbyn. (elder). Rotarian. Home: Muscatine, Ia. Died Apr. 6, 1975, interred Greenwood Cemetery, Muscatine, Ia.

JOLIVET, ANDRE, composer; b. Paris, France, Aug. 8, 1905; s. Victor Ernest and Madeleine (Perault) J.; ed. Lycee Colbert, Paris, also Ecole Normale de Paris; m. Hilda Gulgue, Sept. 26, 1933; children—Pierre-Alain, Christine, Merri, Dir. music Comedie Francmise, Paris, 1945-59; tech. adviser Gen. Adminstrn. Arts and Letters, Paris, 1959-62; pres. Lamoureux Concerts, Paris, 1963-68; prof. composition Conservatoire Nat. Superieur de Musique, Paris, 1966-74 mus. expert UNESCO, 1958-74. Served with French Army, 1939-40. Decorated officer Legion of Honor, comdr. Arts and Letters, Croix de Guerre; recipient Arts and Letters award. Mem. Syndicate Artists and Musicians France (hon. pres.). Composer: (piano) Mana, 2 sonatas; (chamber music) Quatuor, Suite Delphique, Rhapsodie a 7, Pastorales de Noël, Suite Rhapsodique pour Violon soul, Suite an Concert pour Violoncelle soul, Heptade pour Trompette et Percussion, Cinq Incantations, Asceses pour Flute; (vocales) Trois complaintes du Soldat, Deux Messes, Poemes intimes, Epithalame, Madrigal Songe á Nouveau reve (symphonies) Cina Danses rituelles, Trois Symphonies, Suite Transocéeane, 12 concertos, Deux Oratorios, 15 musiques de scene. Address: Paris, France. Died Dec. 20, 1974.

JONAS, FRANZ, fed. pres. of Austria; b. Vienna, Oct. 4, 1899; s. Josef and Katharine (Rokos) J.; ed. Workers' High Sch., univ. extension; m. Margarethe Towarek, Dec. 23, 1922. Type-setter, proof-reader, 1919-32; sec. Social Democratic Dist. Orgn. Vienna XXI, 1932-35; arrested for polit. reasons, accused of high treason, 1935; clk. in factory, 1938-45; chmn. local council Vienna XXI, 1946-48; city councillor for food supplies and agr., 1948, for housing, 1950; gov., mayor Vienna, 1951-65; mem. Austrian Fed. Council, 1951-53, Austrian Nat. Council, 1953-65; fed. pres. Republic Austria, 1965-74. Chmn., Fedn. Austrian Citires, 1951-65; mem. exec. com., also chmn. European com. Internat. Fedn. Communities, 1955-65; mem. presdl. council Council European Communities, 1963-65; Austrian del. local govt. conf. Council of Europe, 1956-65. Decorated Grand Golden Order Merit with star, Grand Silver Order of Merit with ribbon, grand star Order of Merit (Austria); grand cross Order Ethiopian Star; grand cross of merit with star and ribbon Order Merit Fed. Republic Germany, grand cross with ribbon Persian Homayoun Order 1st class; comdr. cross with star Greek Order King George I; Bavarian Order Merit; grand cross Finland Order Lion; grand cross Dutch-Oranien-Nassau Order; grand cross Danish Danebrog Order; grand cross Thailand Crown Order; named hon. citizen Vienna, hon. senator Vienna U. and Vienna U. Tech.; dr. hon. causa Thammasat U., Bangkok, Thailand; Thai Rajamitraphorn Order; Most Honourable Order Bath, spl. degree; grand cross Norwegian Order St. Olav with Collane Grand Cross; Iranian Pahlavi Order Collane; Grand Star of Yugoslavia; Grand Star Liechtenstein Order of Merit; others. Address: Vienna, Austria. Died Apr. 24, 1974.

JONES, ARTHUR WOODRUFF, business exec.; b. Phila., Pa., Oct. 22, 1879; s. Thomas Firth and Cornelia (Erringer) J.; ed. U. of Pa., 1900; m. Dorothea Rehn (died Dec. 5, 1926); children—Dorothea Jones Wilkie, Josephine J. Hitschier, Frances J. Adams, Anita J. Parker, Carol J. Matheson; m. 2d, Louisa Mather Wallis, Sept. 7, 1932; children—Arthur Woodruff, Thomas Firth, 2d Louisa Wallis. With William Simpson Sons & Co., from 1900, mem. firm, 1909, treas., 1911, v.p., from 1927; pres. Saving Fund Soc. of Germantown and Its Vicinity, from 1927; dir., mem. exec. com. Joseph Bancroft Sons & Co., Wilmington, Del.; dir. Market Street Nat. Bank, William Simpson Sons & Co. Pres., mem. bd. mgrs. Germantown Hosp. Phila.; bd. trustees Gen. Assembly Presbyn. Church of U.S., dir. Pa. Sch. Hort., Ambler, Pa. Clubs: University, Sunnybrook Golf, Seven Island Duck (Phila.). Home: Philadelphia, Pa.†

JONES, CHARLES HODGE educator; b. West Chester, Pa., Aug. 24, 1878; s. Benjamin Townsend and Mary Redell (Canfield) J.; prep. edn., Lawrenceville Sch., 1893-96; A.B., Princeton, 1900; studied U. of Halle, Germany, 1907-09; m. Margaret M. Shaw, June 24, 1915; children—Mary Arnot (dec.), Margaret Murdock. Teacher classics, Tome Sch., Port Deposit, Md., 1900-05; instr. classics, Princeton, 1905-09, asst. prof., 1909-18, registrar, 1910-18; asso. headmaster Princeton Prep. School, 1918-29, Silver Bay (N.Y.) Sch., 1929-31; headmaster Lebanon School (boys' Preparatory) from 1931. Democrat. Presbyn. Home: New Lebanon, N.Y.†

JONES, CHARLES PAUL, clergyman; b. Hamilton, Mo., Jan. 9, 1878; s. William Robert and Mary Jane (McNeill) J.; A.B., William Jewell Coll., 1908; hon. D.D., William Jewell Coll., 1941; m. Myrtle Jessie Moling, Feb. 2, 1898; children—Venetta Muriel (Mrs. Ian O. Hodges), Charles Trueman, Paul Dwight. Pastor of country chs., in Missouri, 1896-1904; minister Baptist Ch., Harris, Mo., 1904-08, Centropolis Baptist Ch., Kansas City, Mo., 1908-13; gen. supt. Kansas City Baptist Union, from 1914; dir. Sentinel Federal Savings & Loan Assn. Mem. exec. com. Kansas City Council of Chs., Anti-Saloon League of Mo.; dir. Social Improvement Aid of Kansas City. Democrat. Mason. Home: Kansas City, Mo.*†

JONES, DAVID, artist; b. Brockley, Kent, Eng., Nov. 1, 1895; s. James and Alice Ann (Bradshaw) J.; student Cambernell Sch. Art, 1909-14, Westminster Art Sch., 1919-21; D.Litt. honris causa, University of Wales, 1960. Worked in workshops Eric Gill, sculptor and engraver, 1922-26; engraved wood and copper various illustrated books, 1925-29; watercolor paintings, mainly still-life, landscape and seascape, 1926-56; exhibited Venice Biennial Exhbn., 1934, N.Y. World's Fair, Internat. Biennial Exhbn., Bklqn., Arts Council of Gt. Britain, Tate Gallery (London), 1954-55; works represented various pub. galleries, Britain, Europe. Served on West Front with Royal Welch Fusiliers, 1915-18. Decorated Comdr. Order Brit. Empire, 1955; recipient Hawthornden prize, 1938, Russell Loines award for poetry Nat. Institute Arts and Letters, 1954; Harriet Munro Memorial prize for poem, 1956. Fellow Royal Society of Literature; member of the Honorable Society Cymmrodorion (v.p.), Soc. Nautical Research, Soc. Wood Engravers. Mem. Roman Ch. Author: In Parenthesis, 1937; The Anathemata, 1952; Epoch & Artist (prize Arts Council Great Britain), 1959. Home: Harrow-on-the-Hill, England. Died Oct. 1974.

JONES, EDWIN LESLIE, physician; b. Elizabeth, N.J., July 18, 1920; s. Hiram Thomas and Alice (Snyder) J.; M.D., Western Res. U., 1952; m. Shirley Ann Johnson, Sept. 4, 1947; children—Leslie Regina (Mrs. Steven Haskins), Richard Edwin, Carol Lewis, Nancy Alice. Intern Univ. Hosps., Cleve., 1952-53; resident in surgery VA Hosp., Cleve., 1953-57; asso. chief surgery McDowell Meml. Hosp, 1957-58; staff Mt. Sterling (Ky.) Clinic, 1958-73. Chmn. Mt. Sterling-Montgomery County Airport Bd. Served with Armed Forces, 1942-45. Decorated Bronze Star, numerous theater and battle medals. Fellow A.C.S. Home: Mount Sterling, Ky. Died July 25, 1973.

JONES, FRANK PIERCE, educator; b. Appleton, Wis., Apr. 10, 1905; s. George W. and Maud F. (Sackett) J.; student Lawrence Coll., 1922-23, U. Wis., 1923-24; B.A., Stanford, 1926, M.A., 1928; postgrad., U. Chgo., 1929-30; Ph.D., U. Wis., 1937; studied kinesthetic perception with F.M. and A.R. Alexander, 1938-45; m. Helen Bartlett Rumsey, Aug. 10, 1931; children—Thomas R., Emlen V. (Mrs. Michael A. 23Keeffe), John Evan. Asst. in gen. lit. Reed Coll., 1927-29; instr. Greek, Latin classics Brown U., 1937-41, asst. prof., 1941-44; asst. prof. Pa. Mil. Coll., 1944-45; pvt. teaching, research in kinesthetic perception, Boston, N.Y.C., 1945-54; research asso. Inst. for Psychol. Research, Tufts U., 1954-68, lectr. classics, 1955-64, prof., classics, 1964-70, lectr. psychology, 1968-70, prof. emeritus classics, 1970-75, prof. psychology, summers 1972-74, faculty mentor Coll. Within, 1972-73. Carnegie grantee, 1954-56; USPHS grantee, 1956-64, 66-67. Mem. Am. Philol. Assn., Am., New Eng. psychol. assns., A.A.A.S., Phi Beta Kappa, Sigma Xi. Contbr. articles on classical subjects, kinesthetic perception of postural reflex patterns to profl. jours. Home: Cambridge, Mass. Died Oct. 15, 1975; buried Mt. Auburn Cemetery, Cambridge, Mass.

JONES, FREDERIC RANDOLPH, b. Scranton, Pa., 1878; s. of Randolph Postyn and L. Ludo (Phinney-Thompson) J. Editor and pub. The Youth's Mag., 1893; editorial writer New York Press, New York World and New York Evening Journal, 1898-1903; pub. The American Household, 1904-07; editor The Financial Review from 1908. President of the Jefferson Society. Author: Celtica; Commercial Mysteries, Writer on metal statistics under nom de plume of "Cadmus." Address: Valhalla, N.Y.†

JONES, FREDERICK E., dir. Continental Ins. Cos.; chmn. Buckeye Union Ins. Co., Columbus, O. Trustee Ohio State U. Home: Columbus, O. Died Dec. 8, 1974.

JONES, HENRY N(EELY), bacteriologist; b. Ashland, Me., Oct. 25, 1881; s. Rev. Henry and Manetta Rowena (Fifield) J.; A.B., Colby Coll., 1905; student Harvard, 1908-10; m. Cora Crommett, June 24, 1907; children—Henry Crommett, Arthur Fifield, State bacteriologist, Mass., 1910-14; prof. bacteriology Syracuse U., 1914-17, prof. emeritus, from 1947; city bacteriologist, City of Syracuse, N.Y., 1922-25; dir. N.Y. State Consevation Council, 1942-46. Served as 1st lt., N.Y. State Guard, World War I. Fellow A.A.A.S.; mem. Soc. Am. Bacteriologists, Sigma Xi. Episcopalian. Home: Cloyne, Ont., Can.†

JONES, HERBERT COFFIN, lawyer; b. Oskaloosa, Ia., Sept. 20, 1880; s. Stephen Alfred and Louise (Coffin) J.; A.B., Stanford, 1902, LL.B., 1904; m. Elizabeth Anne MacSwain, Dec. 24, 1918; children—Barbara MacSwain, Elizabeth MacSwain; m. 2d, Pauline Wells, November 28, 1940. Admitted to California bar, 1903; deputy county clerk. Santa Clara County, 1904; practice at San Jose, from 1905. Mem. Calif. State Senate, 1913-34; chmn. Senate Judiciary Com., 1921-29, com. on Calif. School System, of Com. on Corporation Election Expenditures, of spl. com. on Price Fixing in Cemennt Industry, mem. Legislative Tax Com. Chairman Governor's Central Valley Project Commn.; mem. Governor's Commn. on Reemployment; mem. bd. trustees, Agnews State Hosp. Mem. Am., California State (mem. bd. govs., 1935-38), Santa Clara County bar assns. (pres. 1915-17), Adult Edn. Assn. (dir.); pres. Calif. State League of Building and Loan Assns., 1927. Republican. Quaker. Clubs: Commonwealth, Lions, Semperverens (pres.). Home: San Jose, Cal.†

JONES, HOWARD PALFREY, journalist, educator, diplomat; b. Chgo., Jan. 2, 1899; s. William Cadwallader and Ida May (Noble) J.; student U. Wis., 1917-20; Litt.B., Columbia, 1921; postgrad. U. Mich., 1925-27, Columbia, 1929-30; LL.D., Fairleigh-Dickinson U., 1962, U. Wis., 1971; L.H.D., Juniata Coll., 1970; D.Hum., Monterey Inst. Fgn. Studies, 1973; m. Mary Rendall, Oct. 22, 1921; 1 dau., Patricia Ann (dec.). Newspaper work, 1921-39, including instr. Journalism U. Mich., 1925-27; lectr., prof. Columbia Grad. Sch.

Journalism, 1934-39; pub. relations sec. Nat. Municipal League, 1929-33, sec. league, editor Nat. Municipal Rev., 1933-39; civil service commr. N.Y. State, 1939-43, dep. comptroller, 1943; fgn. service officer Dept. State, 1948-65; chief U.S. Element Finance Br., Bioartite Control Office, Germany, 1947-48; dep. dir. Berlin office U.S. High Commr. for Germany, Berlin rep. ECA spl. mission to Germany, 1949-51, dir. Berlin element, 1951; counselor embassy Am. embassy China, 1952, charge d'affaires, 1952; chief of mission U.S. Fgn. Operations mission to Indonesia, 1954-55; dep. asst. sec. state for Far Eastern Affairs, 1955-58; ambassador to Indonesia, 1958-65; dean diplomatic corps, Djakarta, 1962-65; chancellor East-West Center, U. Hawaii, 1965-68; research fellow Hoover Inst. on War, Revolution and Peace, Stanford, 1968-69, sr. research fellow, 1972-73; trustee Christian Sci. Pub. Soc., Boston, 1969-72, chmn., 1970-71; cons. Stanford Research Inst., 1972-73. Cons. Va. Commn. on County Govt., 1931; dir. N.Y. State Commn. on Revision of Tax Laws, 1936-38; cons. Gov.'s Commn. on N.Y. State Constl. Conv., 1938; mem. gov. bd. U.S. Pub. Adminstrn. Service 1933-40; del. representing U.S. State Dept., Internat. Union of Cities, Lyons, France, 1934; U.S. delegation Colombo Plan Conf., Singapore, 1955; chmn. U.S. delegation on Econ. Commn. for Asia and Far East, Bangolore, India, 1956; Sladen lectr. Colby Jr. Coll., 1970. Served from maj. to col. AUS, 1943-47. Fellow Oberleencer Trust of Carl Schurz Meml. Found. to study pub. adminstrn. in Germany, 1934. Recipient 50th Anniversary award Columbia U. Grad. Sch. Journalism, 1963; Distinguished Honor award Dept. State, 1964. Mem. Indonesian Soc. U.S., Sigma Nu, Sigma Delta Chi. Mason. Clubs: University (N.Y.C.); Stanford Faculty; Cosmos (Washington); Algonguin (Boston). Author: Indonesia-The Possible Dream, 1971. Home: Atherton Cal. Died Sept. 18, 1973.

JONES, LAURENCE CLIFTON, educator; b. St. Joseph, Mo., Nov. 21, 1884; s. John Q. and Lydia (Foster) J.; Marshalltown (Ia.) High Sch., 1903; Ph.B., State U. Ia., 1907; certificate of accomplishment State U. Ia., 1947; D.H.L., Cornell Coll., 1947; M.A. (hon.), Tuskegee Inst.; H.H.D., Bucknell U., Clarke Coll., 1963, Otterbein Coll., 1965, Dubuque U., 1969; m. Grace Morris Allen, June 29, 1912 (dec.); children—Turner Harris, Laurence C. Founded, 1909, and pres. The Piney Woods (Miss.) Country Life Sch., for edn. of boys and girls in Black Belt; stated without funds, in open air; pub., editor of The Pine Torch, Piney Woods. In charge thrift stamp campaign among colored people, Miss., during World War I. Asst. dir. Armenian Relief campaign in Miss.; Negro sec. First United War Work Drive, in Miss. Recipient awards Freedom's Found., Founder's Soc. Am., citation U. Ia., 1967, Silver Buffalo award Boy Scouts Am., 1970. Mem. Miss. Assn. Tchrs. in Colored Schs., Kappa Alpha Pis; mem. Negro YMCA; mem. adv. com. Miss. Fedn. Colored Women's Clubs. Episcopalian. Author: Up Thru Difficulties, 1910; Piney Woods and Its Story, 1923; The Spirit of Piney Woods, 1931; The Bottom Rail, 1933; numerous articles regarding race problem. Chautauqua lectr. Home: Piney Woods, Miss., Died July 13, 1975.

JONES, LEWIS WEBSTER, assn. exec.; b. Emerson, Neb., June 11, 1899; s. Jerry and Estelle (Webster) J.; A.B., Reed Coll., Portland, Ore., 1922; postgrad. Columbia, 1923-24; Ph.D., Brookings Inst., 1927; spl. student Cambridge U. and London Sch. Econs., 1927-28; LL.D., Reed Coll., 1946, N.Y.U., 1952, Princeton, 1952, Columbia, 1954, U. Ark., 1957, Rutgers U., 1959, U. Mass., 1959; L.H.D., Lafayette Coll., 1952; m. Barbara Slatter, 1928; children—Barbara Ann, Peter Lewis Webster. Economist, Inst. Am. Bus., N.Y.C., 1924-26; economist Foreign Policy Assn., 1926-27, economist and editor, 1928-30; economist, Com. on Costs of Med. Care, 1930-32; mem. faculty Bennington Coll., 1932-41, acting pres., 1939, pres., 1941-47; pres. Ark. U., 1947-51; pres. Rutgers U., 1951-58; pres. Nat. Conf. Christians and Jews, Inc., from 1958. Trustee Brookings Instn.; pres. Assn. Land Grant Colls. and Univs., 1955, chmn. exec. com., 1956; cons., spl. com. to study foreign aid program U.S. Senate, 1956-57. Econ. adviser Def. Commn., 1941. Pub. mem. Nat. War Labor Bd. for N.E. region, 1943-44; President's Commn. on Higher Edn. 1946-48; chmn. bd. trustees Ednl. Testing Service, 1954-56. Mem. Am. Econ. Assn., Am. Statis Assn., Nat. Indsl. Conf. Bd. (econ. adv. council). Episcopalian. Rotarian (hon.). Clubs: University, Century (N.Y.C.). Author: (with Roger I. Lee and Barbara Jones) Fundamentals of Good Medical Care Home: Sarasota, Fla. Died Sept. 1975.

JONES, OLLIE E., banker, mfg. co. exec.; b. Wellington, Ill., Mar. 27, 1892; s. Jefferson Davis and Arminta (Thomas) J.; student Greer Coll., Hoopeston, Ill., 1906-07, U. Ill., 1908-09; m. Neva Mitchell, July 2, 1912 (dec. 1944); 1 dau., Esther (Mrs. Richard T. Doughtie); m. 2d, Mary Frances Maple, Aug. 15, 1946. With Swift & Co., 1912-57, exec. v.p., 1952-57, dir., 1941-75; chmn. bd. Wellington State Bank, 1940-75, Norton McMurray Mfg. Co., 1954-75; chmn. bd. First Fed. Savs. and Loan Assn., 1961-66, dir., 1955-75. Mem. Task Force of Hoover Commn., 1941-45; mem. War Food Com., 1942-45. Mem. Grocery Mfrs. Am., Shortening and Oil Inst. Am., Nat. Cottonseed Products Assn., Am. Soap Assn. Rotarian. Club: Executives (Chgo.). Home: Hoopeston, Ill. Died Sept. 24, 1975; interred Floral Hill Cemetery, Hoopeston, Ill.

JONES, PAUL, bishop; b. at Wilkes-Barre, Pa., Nov. 24, 1880; s. Rev. Henry Lawrence (S.T.D.) and Sarah Eastman (Coffin) J.; B.A., Yale, 1902; B.D., Episcopal Theol. Sch., Cambridge, Mass., 1906; m. Mary Elizabeth Balch, June 14, 1913. Deacon and priest, 1906. P.E. Ch.; associated with Rev. D. K. Johnston in charge St. John's Mission, Logan, Utah, 1906-11, in sole charge, 1911-14; apptd. archdeacon of Utah, Sept., 1914; consecrated bishop of Utah, Dec. 16, 1914. Sec. Missionary Dist. of Utah, 1908-14. Pres. bd. trustees St. Mark's Hosp., Salt Lake City; rector Rowland Hall Sch. for Girls. Socialist. Address: Salt Lake City, Utah.†

JONES, RICHARD LEE, ins. co. exec.; b. Albany, Ga., Dec. 21, 1893; s. Richard C. and Eliza B. (Brown) J.; student University of Cincinnati, 1912-15, University of Illinois, 1917; married Elgetha Ore Huffman, September 17, 1943; 1 son, Richard Lee III. Cashier First Standard Bank, Louisville, 1920-22; bus. mgr. Robert S. Abbott Publishing Co., 1922-27; gen. mgr. Chgo. Bee Pub. Co., 1927-28; v.p., gen. supt., personnel dir. South Center Dept. Store, Chgo., 1928-42; v.p. Nat. Investors Corp., 1946-49; v.p., pub. relations dir. South Center Dept. Store, 1949-54, v.p., 1959-60; dir. U.S. Operations Mission to Liberia, Fgn. Operations Adminstrn., 1954-55; U.S. ambassador to Liberia, 1955-60; exec. v.p. Victory Mutual Life Ins. Co., 1960-75. U.S. alternate del. 11th General Assembly of the United Nations. Served as maj. in inf. in the AUS, 1942-46; activated 178th Regtl. Combat Team, Ill. N.G., and served as comdg. officer, 1947-53; ret. with rank brig. gen., 1953. Decorated Legion of Merit. Mem. Kappa Alpha Psi. Home: Chicago, Ill., Died Oct. 13, 1975.

JONES, ROBERT HAYDON, found. exec.; b. N.Y.C., July 15, 1910; s. Haydon and Emma (Voos) J.; B.A. cum laude, Harvard, 1930; m. Florence Joan Shaw, May 15, 1937; children—Robert Haydon, Christopher Shaw, Jeffrey Owen, Jeremy Mary, Jude Anne, Pamela Cathlyn. Advt. and pub. relations exec. R.H. Macy & Co., N.Y.C., 1932-34; dir. advt. and pub. relations Doubleday, Doran & Co., 1934-37; asst. to pres. Condé Nast Publns., 1937-40; dir. advt. and pub. relations John Wanamaker, N.Y.C. and Phila., 1940-41; account exec. Batten, Barton, Durstine & Osborn, 1941-45; dir. Alley & Richards Co., Boston, 1945-47; sales mgr. Glenwood Range Co., Taunton, Mass., 1947-49; pres. Robert Haydon Jones Assos., Westport, Conn., 1949-51, 73-74; partner, v.p. Marschalk & Pratt Co., N.Y.C., 1951-54; v.p. McCann-Erickson, Inc., N.Y.C., 1954-60; sr. v.p. McCann-Erickson Internat., N.Y.C., 1960-70; v.p. Interpublic Group of cos., 1971-72; dep. dir. Epilepsy Found. Am., Washington, 1973-74; dir. Westport Co., London Co., Ltd. Mem. Staples tuition grants com., Westport, 1955-70. Mem. Westport Republican Town Com., 1948-56. Served with N.Y. State N.G., 1942-46. Mem. Assn. Ex-Mems. Squadron A. K.C. Club: Harvard (N.Y.C.). Home: Westport, Conn. Died Dec. 26, 1974.

JONES, ROBERT MARTIN, hosp. pres.; b. Albany, N.Y., July 23, 1925; s. Everet Ward and Jennie (Martin) J.; B.B.A., U. Wis., 1949; M.S. in Hosp. Adminstrn., Columbia, 1951. Asst. adminstr. Columbia Hosp., Milw., 1951-53; adminstr. Waukesha (Wis.) Meml. Hosp., 1954-69, pres., 1970-74. Dir. Rexford Paper Co., Milw., 1964-69. Bd. dirs. Waukesha YMCA, 1956-61; bd. dirs. Greater Waukesha United Fund, 1957-63, pres., 1962. Served to 2d lt. AUS, 1943-46. Recipient Man of Year award Waukesha Jr. C. of C., 1959, outstanding service award Waukesha YMCA, 1962. Fellow Am. Coll. Hosp. Adminstrs. (regent for Wis.); mem. Hosp. Council Greater Milw. Area (pres. 1960), Am., Wis. (pres. 1964, recipient excellence award 1971) hosp. assns., Tri-State Hosp. Assembly (pres. 1970-71). Home: Waukesha, Wis. Died July 6, 1974.

JONES, RODNEY WILCOX, mfr.; b. Pittston, Pa., Sept. 19, 1876; s. Enoch and Mary Rozilla (Davis) J.; student pub. schs., Utica, N.Y.; m. Charlotte Constantine, Apr. 14, 1921; children—Rodney Wilcox, Curtis Constantine, Wilbur Ward, Eleanor Rozilla. Financial dept. Quinn & O'Hara, Utica, 1893-95; mfr. W. A. Fish, mfr., 1896-1900; in knitting industry, from 1901; asso. with Robishon & Peckham Co., 1901; organizer, part owner Am. Knit Goods Co., 1902, treas., gen. mgr., 1904; established (with others) Augusta Knitting Corp., 1903, pres., from 1912; organizer Sherbourne and Bath knitting cos., Asso. Warehouse Co., 1918, which cos. merged with Augusta Knitting Corp., 1920; Genesee Knitting Mills and Alliance Knitting Co. were absorbed by Augusta, 1925; president of Utica Looms, 1926-31; director of Duofold Co. Pres. Nat. Hosp. for Speech Disorders, 1937-38; dir. Grand Central Art Sch., 1932-40. Treas. Art Alliance, 1921-33; pres. Nat. Alliance of Art and Industry, 1937-45. Mem. Am. Orchid Soc. (pres. 1942-45), Westchester Hort Soc. (pres. 1938-40), Eastern Long Island Yachting Assn. (treas. 1946-50). Clubs: Union League, National Arts (v.p. 1946-55) (N.Y.C.); Devon Yacht (chmn. racing com. 1950-53; Amagansett, N.Y.); Maidstone (Easthampton, N.Y.); Fort Schuyler (Utica, N.Y.); New Rochelle Garden (pres. 1933-34). Contbr. hort. subjects to American Orchid Soc. Bull. Home: New Rochelle, N.Y.†

JONES, THOMAS ELSA, administrative consultant; born Fairmount, Indiana, March 22, 1888; son of David and Sarah J.; graduate of Fairmont Academy, 1906; A.B., Earlham College, 1912; B.D., Hartford Theol. Sem., 1915; M.A., Columbia, 1917, Ph.D., 1926; LL.D., Berea College, 1928, Wabash, 1946, Valparaiso U., 1953, Indiana U., 1956; L.H.D., Wilmington College, 1957; m. Esther Alsop Balderston, Sept. 29, 1917; children—David Lloyd, Thomas Canby, Catharine Balderston. Teacher pub. schs., Ind., 1906-09; traveled abroad and studied in Birmingham, Eng., 1913; nat. sec. Young Friends' Movement, 1914-17; instr. Earlham Coll., 1915-16; with Friends' Mission, Tokyo, Japan, 1917-24; dir. Y.M.C.A., Vladivostock, Siberia, 1918-19; prof. economics, Keio U., Tokyo, 1920-24; Friends' reconstruction work, Tokyo, 1923-24; pres. Fisk Univ., Nashville, Tenn., 1926-46; pres. Earlham Coll., Richmond, Ind., 1946-58, ret.; adminstrv. cons. Assn. of American Colleges. President Asso. Colls. Indiana, Ind. Conf. Higher Edn. Mem. Coll. Program, Com. of Am. Friends Service Committee; mem. Internat. Commission studying conditions in South Africa, 1938. Bd. dirs. YMCA. Mem. Nat. Probation and Parole Assns. (Ind. bd.), Am. Sociol. Soc. Author: Mountain Folk in Japan — a Method of Study; Testimony by Work (report of Friends' Civilian Public Service). Address: Richmond, Ind. Died Aug. 5, 1973.

JONES, WALTER PARKER, newspaper editor; b. Sacramento, July 4, 1894; s. William Edmund and Phoebe (Parker) J.; ed. pub. schs., Sacramento; m. Kathleen Adelle Jones, Aug. 12, 1916; children—Mary Elizabeth, Walter Parker. Reporter, Sacramento Star, 1912-16, Marysville (Cal.) Democrat and Appeal. 1916-17; state capital corr. Scripps papers Cal., 1917-18, San Francisco and Los Angeles Examiners, 1918-19; polit. reporter Sacramento Bee, 1919-33, McClatchy Newspapers Cal., 1922-33; news editor, mng. editor Sacramento Bee, 1933-34; editorial dir. McClatchy Newspapers Cal., 1934-36, editor, 1936-74. Mem. C. of C., Am. Soc. Newspaper Editors. Presbyn. Rotarian. Clubs: Sutter, Del Paso Country (Sacramento). Home: Sacramento Cal. Died Sept. 8, 1974; interred East Lawn Cemetery, Sacramento, Cal.

JONES, WILLIAM JACKSON, educator; b. Gates, N.C., Aug. 2, 1879; s. Joseph and Sarah Elizabeth (Fanney) J.; A.B., Wake Forest (N.C.) Coll., 1908; student University of Chicago, 1909; m. Mollie Roberts Edwards, Nov. 24, 1908; children—Alice Freeman (Mrs. George Norman Ashley), Emma Smith (dec.). Began as lumber mfr., 1893; ordained ministry Bapt. Ch., 1904; organizer of Bapt. chs., from 1908; pastor, Salemburg, N.C., from 1908, Roseboro, N.C., from 1910; prin. Salemburg Acad., 1908-12; founder (with wife) Pineland Sch. for Girls (now Pineland Jr. Coll.), 1912, co-pres., from 1912 founder (with wife) Edwards Memorial Sch. for Boys, 1932, co-pres., from 1932; chmn. South River Assn., 1912-25, New South River Assn., 1925-30. Mem. Order of Jr. Am. Mechanics. Democrat. Baptist. Home: Salemburg, N.C.†

JONES, WILLIAM JAMES, clergyman, editor; b. Liverpool, Eng., Sept. 28, 1901; s. Evan Thomas and Margaret Ann (Davies) J.; brought to U.S., 1903, naturalized, 1917; A.B., Wheaton Coll., 1925, Litt.D., 1960; B.Th., Princeton Theol. Sem., 1928; A.M., Princeton, 1928; student U.S.C., 1934; postgrad., U. of Pa. since 1940; m. Helen Paton Lindsay, July 4, 1929; children—David Timothy, Margaret Wyllys, Gwyneth Ellen, Helen Elisabeth, Laurel Gresham. Ordained to ministry of Baptist Church, 1928; prof. English, Des Moines U., 1928-29, Huntington (Ind.) Coll., 1932-33; professor of English and history, Columbia Bible Coll., S.C., 1933-34; pastor Cassadaga (N.Y.) Bapt. Ch., 1934-39; instr., King's Coll., 1939-42; sec. Phila. Coll. Bible, 1941-42; editor Am. Sunday Sch. Union publs. from 1942. Mem. bd. of trustees Phila. Coll. Bible; secretary board dirs. American Scripture Gift Mission; gen. sec. League Evang. students, 1929-34. Mem. Modern Lang. Assn Am., Am. Assn. U. Profs. Club: Wheaton (Phila.). Home: Wayne, Pa. Died Jan. 23, 1973; buried Valley Forge Gardens, King of Prussia, Pa.

JONES, WILLIAM RALPH, stock broker; b. Streator, Ill., Jan. 21, 1880; s. John Samuel R. and Nora (Sullivan) J.; ed. high sch., Batavia, Ill., 1 yr.; m. Ruth Nellie Gregg, 1899; m. 2d, Nellie Fern Thayer, June 20, 1914. Organizer, 1912, and managing partner firm of Jones & Baker. Republican. Spirtual Scientist. Clubs: Bankers', Lawyers', Lotos Advertising, (New York); Wykagyl Country (New Rochelle, N.Y.); Seaview Golf (Absecon, N.J.); Deal (N.J.) Golf Congressional Country (Washington, D.C.); Pelham (N.Y.) Country; Sleepy Holly Country; Scarborough. Home: Deal, N.J.†

JONSON, LIBBY ANNE, charitable orgn. exec.; b. Los Angeles, Aug. 6, 1944; d. Leonard William and Maureen Kay (White) Fisher; B.A. in Sociology, Whittier Coll., 1966; postgrad. Cal. State U., Long Beach, 1966-70; M.P.A. in Health Services Adminstrn. (Dept. Health Edn. and Welfare fellow), U. So. Cal., 1973. Dir. edn. Intercommunity Exceptional Childrens Home, Long Beach, 1966-68, adminstr., 1969-74; tchr. mentally retarded Magnolia Sch. Dist., Anaheim, Cal., 1968-69; sec. bd. dirs. Intercommunity Care Centers, Inc.; adj. prof. Shaw U. Bd. dirs. Florence Nightengale P.T.A., mem. adv. bd. Work-Study Program, Long Beach Unified Sch. Dist. Recipient Diana award Eta

Kappa Sorority, 1970, 73. Mem. Am. Assn. Mental Deficiency (com. chmn.), Cal. Assn. Residencies for Retarded (com. chmn.), Cal. Tchrs. Assn., Council for Exceptional Children, Cal. Assn. for Retarded, Am. Pub. Health Assn. Comprehensive Health Assn. Home: Santa Ana, Cal. Deceased.

JORDAN, ARTHUR WHEELER, banker; b. Portland, Me., Oct. 24, 1878; s. Walter Major and Martha B. (Harding) J.; ed. pub. schs.; m. Elizabeth Mae Allen, Feb. 21, 1910. Began with Caseo Nat. Bank, Portland, 1899, name changed, 1916, to Casco Mercantile Trust Co., v.p., dir. and sec.; treas. Falmouth Securities Co., Inc., Falmouth Co., Inc. (both of Portland), Huntington Co. (real estate), Boston. Councilman, 1909-12, alderman, 1912-14, city councilor, term 1928-33 (all of Portland); chmn. State Pier Commn. and Vaughan's Bridge Commn., 1931-32. Mem. bd. dirs. Opportunity Sch. for Boys. Republican. Universalist, Mason, Elk. Clubs: Portland, Portland Athletic, Kiwanis, Economic. Home: Portland, Me.†

JORDAN, BENJAMIN EVERETT, former U.S. senator, textile co. exec.; b. Ramseur, N.C., Sept. 8, 1896; s. Henry Harrison and Annie Elizabeth (Sellers) J.; student Rutherford (N.C.) Coll. Prep. Sch., 1912-13, Trinity Coll. (now Duke), 1914-15; hon. degree, Duke, 1940; LL.D., Elon (N.C.) Coll., 1960; m. Katherine McLean, Nov. 29, 1924; children—Benjamin Everett, Rose Ann, John McLean. Worked in jewelry store, with various textile mfrs., 1915-27; organized Sellers Mfg. Co., 1927, gen. mgr. sec.-treas., dir., 1927-74; gen. mgr., sec.-treas., dir. Jordan Spinning Co., 1939, pres., treas., gen. mgr., dir. Royal Cotton Mill Co., Wake Forest, N.C., 1945-74; sec.-treas. Nat. Processing Co., Burlington, N.C., 1945-74; dir. various cos.; U.S. senator from N.C., 1958-73; chmn. Senate Com. on Rules and Adminstrn., also chmn., mem. various other Senate coms. Chmn. N.C. Democratic Exec. Com., 1949-54. Mem. N.C. Med. Care Commn., 1945-51, N.C. Peace Officers Benefit and Retirement Commn.; pres., dir., Alamance County Tb Assn. Bd. dirs. Alamance County chpt. A.R.C., Cherokee council Boy Scouts Am., Cotton Textile Inst.; chmn. trustees Alamance County Gen. Hosp. and Tb Sanitoriums; trustee Duke, Am. U., Elon Coll.; v.p. Am. group Interparliamentary Union; trustee U.S. Capitol Hist. Soc. Served with Tank Corps, U.S. Army, 1918-19; with Army of Occupation, Germany, 1919. Recipient Silver Beaver award Boy Scouts Am., 1965. Mem. N.C. Cotton Mfrs. Assn. (dir.), Durene Assn. Am. (v.p.), S.A.R., Omicron Delta Kappa. Methodist. Mason, Rotarian (dir., past pres.). Address: Saxapahaw, N.C. Died Mar. 15, 1974; interred Pine Hill Cemetery, Burlington, N.C.

JORDAN, CHARLES EDWARD, ednl. adminstr.; b. Henietta, N.C., Apr. 13, 1901; s. Henry Harrison and Annie Elizabeth (Sellers) J.; A.B., Trinity Coll., 1923; grad. Duke Univ. Law Sch., 1925; LL.D., Elon (N.C.) Coll., 1945; m. Elizabeth Davis Tyree, Dec. 12, 1932; children—Charles Edward, Elizabeth Leigh. Asst. sec. Duke, 1925-41, sec., 1941-58, became 2d v.p., 1946, became dir. div. pub. relations, 1947, also v.p. of div., emeritus v.p., 1966-74; admitted to N.C. bar, 1926; dir. Home Savs. and Loan Assn., Wachovia Bank, Occidental Life Ins. Co., Raleigh, N.C. Mem. N.C. Bd. Edn., 1957-74. Past pres. N.C. Symphony Soc., Inc. Chmn. Durham Co. Bd. Edn; past pres. N.C. State Sch. Bd. Assn.; trustee N.C. State Library. Mem. C. of C. (dir.), Pub. Relations Soc. Am., Am. Coll. Pub. Relations Assn., Community Fund, Salvation Army, YMCA (Durham), S.A.R., Delta Theta Phi, Tau Kappa Alpha, Omicron Delta Kappa. Democrat. Methodist (mem. bd. missions and ch. extension S.E. jurisdiction, Meth. Ch. in U.S. 1944-74; former trustee Lake Junaluske (N.C.) Meth. Assemby; treas. N.C. Conf. Trustees Meth. Ch. 1947-56, chmn. 1956-66; mem. gen. bd. edn., chmn. dept. of coll. and univ. religious life 1956-60; trustee N.C. Conf. Bd. Hosp. and Homes 1943-74, treas. bd. finance, 1933-46, chmn. bd. finance, pres., dir. Durham Meth. Soc., chmn. trustees, past chmn. bd. stewards Duke Meml. Ch.). Rotarian (past pres.; del. Internat. Conv., Havana, Cuba 1940). Club: Hope Valley Country (Durham). Home: Durham, N.C. Died Feb. 4, 1974.

JORDAN, HARVEY ERNEST, anatomist; b. Coopersburg, Pa., Aug. 14, 1878; s. Genaah and Emma (Harwick) J.; grad. Keystone State Normal Sch., Kutztown, Pa., 1897; A.B., Lehigh U., 1903, A.M., 1904, Sc.D., 1941; student Columbia University, 1905-06; Marine Biological Laboratory, Woods Hole, Massachusetts, summers, 1905, 1906; Ph.D., Princeton, 1907; m. Ilda May Voorhees, June 17, 1908; children—Mary Kathryn (Mrs. Frank Hague, Jr.), Harvey Ernest. Asst. in biology, Lehigh U., 1903-04; asst. in histology and embryology, Cornell U. Med. Coll., New York, 1904-06; on embryol. staff, Brooklyn Acad. Arts and Sciences, Cold Springs Harbor, L.I., summer, 1907, Woods Hole, summer, 1908; investigator at Carnegie Instn. Biol. Sta., Dry Tortugas, Fla., spring, 1907, and summer, 1914; investigator at Carnegie Instn. Biol. Sta., Montego Bay, Jamaica, spring, 1912; adjunct prof. anatomy, 1907-09, asso. prof., 1909-11, prof. histology and embryology, 1911-38, prof. anatomy and dir. of the anatomical labs., 1938-49, Med. Dept. Univ. of Va., also dean Dept. Medicine, 1939-49, ret. Democrat. Mem. German Reformed Ch. Fellow A.A.A.S.; mem. Soc. Am. Naturalists, Am. Soc. Zoölogists, Am. Assn. Anatomists (1st v.p. 1936-38), Am. Genetic Assn. Anatomists (1st v.p. 1936-38), Am. Genetic Assn. Am. Assn. Phys. Anathropologists, Am. Micros. Soc. (pres. 1940), Soc. for Exptl. Biology and Medicine, Am. Eugenics Soc., A.M.A., Va. State Med. Soc., Va. Acad. Science (pres. 1937), Phi Beta Kappa, Phi Sigma Kappa, Phi Beta Pi, Alpha Omega Alpha. Raven Soc., Sigma Xi (exec. com., 1940-45), Iota Sigma. Mem. Nat. Research Council, 1927-33. Club: Colonnade. Author: War's Aftermath (in collaboration with David Starr Jordan) 1914; A Textbook of Histology (with Dr. Jeremiah S. Ferguson), 1916; A Textbook of Embryology (with Dr. James Ernest Kindred), 1926; also various monographs and articles giving results of original investigations in cytology, anatomy, embrology, heredity, Haematology, etc. Home: Charlottesville, Va.†

JORDAN, HENRY DONALDSON, educator; b. Chgo., June 5, 1897; s. Edwin Oakes and Elsie Fay (Pratt) J.; student U. Geneva, Switzerland, 1913-14, U. Chgo., 1919-20; A.B., Harvard, 1918, A.M., 1922, Ph.D., 1925; m. Lucretia Mott Churchill, June 2, 1923; children—Barbara (Mrs. Paul I. Grinberg, Jr.), Edwin C., Winthrop D. Asst. history, Chgo., 1919-20; teaching fellow Harvard, 1921-22, Bayard Cutting traveling fellow, Eng., 1922-23, instr., tutor, 1923-25; asst. prof. Dartmouth Coll., 1925-31, Guggenheim fellow, 1930-31; asso. prof. Clark U., 1931-38, professor, from 1938, chairman of the college bd., 1954-59, dean of college, 1959-60. Trustee Bancroft Sch., Worcester, Mass., 1943-44. Ambulance driver A.R.C., France, 1917; served as 2d lt. inf., U.S. Army, 1918; analyst and adminstr. OSS, Dept. State, 1944-46. Decorated Croix de Guerre. Recipient Tappan prize Harvard, 1925. Mem. Am. Hist. Assn., Bohemians, Dickens Fellowship, Conf. on Brit. Studies, Econ. History Assn., Newcomen Soc., Phi Beta Kappa. Unitarian. Author: Europe and the American Civil War, 1931. Contbr. Dictionary of Am. Biography, Ency. Social Scis., profl. periodicals. Home: Worcester, Mass. Died Dec. 20, 1972; interred Friends' Cemetery, South Yarmouth, Mass.

JORGENSON, RALPH ENOCH, physician; b. Ephraim, Utah, Feb. 2, 1908; s. Enoch and Elvira (Nielsen) J.; M.D., U. Neb., 1932; m. Thelma Turpin, Dec. 23, 1930; children—Thelma Jean (Mrs. Kent A. Pedersen), Ralph Enoch. Intern, St. Mark's Hosp., Salt Lake City, 1932-33; resident in ophthalmology Colo. Gen. Hosp., Denver, 1945-47; pvt. practice gen. medicine, Ephraim, 1935-45; pvt. practice medicine specializing in ophthalmology, Provo, Utah, 1947-72; Lancaster course in ophthalmology, 1953; mem. active staff Utah Valley Hosp., Provo. Dir., Utah Blue Shield, 1961-62. Pres., Utah State Med. Assn. Found., 1969-72. Recipient certificate of merit Utah Med. Assn., 1970; certificate of appreciation Gov.'s Adv. Council Comprehensive Health Planning, 1972. Diplomate Am. Bd. Ophthalmology. Fellow Am. Acad. Ophthalmology and Otolaryngology, Pacific Coast Oto-Ophthalmol. Soc.; mem. Central Utah Med. Soc. (sec. 1938, pres. 1940, 44), Utah Oto-Ophthalmol. Soc. (v.p. 1952, pres. 1960-61), Utah County Med. Soc. (councilor 1955-60), Utah State Med. Assn. (pres. 1961-62), A.M.A. (del. 1968-70), Contact Lens Assn. Ophthalmologists, Alpha Kappa Kappa. Republican. Mem. Ch. of Jesus Christ of Latter-day Saints. Home: Provo, Utah. Died June 20, 1972; buried Provo City Cemetery.

JORGENSON, THEODORE, educator; b. Narvestad, Norway, Nov. 2, 1894; s. Jorgen and Tori (Ryggesaas) Narvestad; student Waldorf Luth. Coll., Forest City, Ia., 1915-18; B.A., St. Olf Coll., Northfield, Minn., 1923; Ph.D., U. Minn., 1935; post grad. work U. Oslo, Norway, 1923-24, 33-34; m. Nora Fjelde, July 14, 1933. Came to U.S., 1911, naturalized 1918. Instr. Norwegian history and lit., St. Olaf Coll., 1925-29, asso. prof., 1929-34, prof. and head of dept. of Norwegian, from 1934, chmn. lang. and lit. div., from 1950; vis. prof. U. So. Cal., 1949, 51; dir. St. Olaf Coll. Norwegian Inst.; faculty summers U. Oslo, 1963, U. Minn., 1964. Democratic-Farmer-Labor nominee for U.S. Senate (Minn.), 1946. Served in A.E.F., Gen. Pershing's hdqrs., Chaumont, France, World War, 1918-19. Created knight 1st class Royal Order of St. Olav. Mem. Minn. Ednl. Assn., Norwegian-American Cultural League, Norwegian Lang. Tchrs. Assn., Norwegian-Am. Hist. Assn., Fraternal Order of Sons of Norway, Internat. League of Norsemen, Lutheran Brotherhood, A.A.U.P., Phi Beta Kappa (past pres.), Pi Kappa Delta. Author: The Cultural Development of the Norweign People, 1930; An Outline of Norwegian Literature, 1931; History of Norwegian Literature, 1933; Norway's Relation to Scandinavian Unionism (1815-1871), 1936; Ole Edvart Rolvaag: A Biography (with Prof. Nora O. Solum), 1939; Henrik Ibsen: A Study in Art and Personality, 1945; Norwegian-English School Dictionary, 1943; Norwegian Section in Shipley's Encyclopedia of World Literature Grassroots Reports from Europe, 1947; An Ibsen Journal, 1953; The Trumpet of Nordland by Petter Dass, 1954; In the Mountain Wilderness, and other Works by Henrik Ibsen, 1956. Translated, edited Henrik Ibsen's Epic Brand and Other Poems, 1950; Norwegian Literature in Medieval and Early Modern Times, 1952: Brand, 1957; Tr. Arne Garborg, The Teacher of Righteousness, 1960. Contbg. editor Groliers Ency., Internat. Year Book; editor The Frontier Banner, 1942-46, Christian Liberty, from 1952. Contbr. articles and fiction to various periodicals. Home: Northfield, Minn. Died Feb. 14, 1971.

JORN, ASGER, artist; b. Mar. 3, 1914. Studied with Leger; collaborator with Le Corbusier on Temps Nouveaux Pavailion, Paris Universal Exhbn., 1937; co-founder Cobra internat, group; exhibited paintings, engravings, sculpture, ceramics at First Exhbn. Exptl. Art, Amsterdam, Netherlands, 1949, Brussels (Belgium) Internat. Exhbn., 1958, Dunn Internat. Exhbn., London, Eng., 1963. numerous others. Address: Paris, France. Died May 2, 1973.

JORPES, J. ERIK, biochemist; b. Kokar, Aland, Finland, July 15, 1894; s. Johan Emil and Julina (Oberg) Pettersson; M.D., Karolinska Inst., Stockholm, Sweden; m. Ida Elvira Stahl, Oct. 18, 1930; children—Birgltta (Mrs. Staffan Magnusson), Per Erik. Asso. prof. biochemistry Karolinska Inst., 1929-47, prof., 1947-63. Address: Stockholm, Sweden. Died 1973.

JOURARD, SIDNEY MARSHALL, educator; b. Toronto, Ont., Can., Jan. 21, 1926; s. Albert Louis and Anna (Rubinoff) J.; B.A., U. Toronto, 1947, M.A., 1948; Ph.D., U. Buffalo, 1953; m. Antoinette Ruth Hertz, June 20, 1948; children—Jeffrey, Martin, Leonard. Faculty dept. psychology U. Fla., Gainesville, 1958-74, prof., 1964-74; practice psychotherapy, Gainesville, 1958-74. Author: Personal Adjustment, 1958, 63; Transparent Self, 1964, rev. edit., 1971; Self-Disclosure, 1971; Disclosing Man to Himself, 1968; Healthy Personality, 1974. Home: Gainesville, Fla. Died Dec. 2, 1974.

JOYCE, NEDRA NORTON newspaper reporter; b. Reno, Oct. 11, 1937; d. Henry Eugene and Naomi (Millis) Norton; B.A. in Journalism, U. Nev., 1959; m. James A. Joyce, June 7, 1959; children—Robin, Marilee. Asst. press sec. Senator Edmund Muskie of Me., Washington, 1963-64; reporter Silver Spring (Md.) Record, 1965; reporter-columnist Rev. Jour., Las Vegas, Nev., 1967-75. Mem. Clark County Probation Com., 1971-75. Chmn. resolutions com. Nev. Young Democrats, 1971, bd. dirs. Clark County; mem. Clark County Dem. Central Com., 1972-75; del. county, state Dem. convs., 1972. Bd. dirs. Nat. Conf. Christians and Jews. Recipient Henry C. Albert award citizenship U. Nev., 1959; several journalism awards from profl. orgns., 1969-75. Mem. Edn. Writers Assn., Press Club (dir.), Delta Delta Delta. Dem. Home: Las Vegas, Nev. Deceased.

JUDSON, ALEXANDER CORBIN, univ. prof., author; b. Troy, N.Y., Dec. 21, 1883; s. Edward and Alicia Blatchford (Corbin) J.; A.B., Pomona, 1907; A.M., Yale, 1908, Ph.D., 1911; studied in Europe, 1908, 10, 1920-21, 26; m. Helen McPherson Ward, Feb. 2, 1926 (died Sept. 26, 1938); m. 2d, Margaret Davidson, Dec. 26, 1944. Instr. in English, adjunct prof., asso. prof., U. Tex., 1911-23; prof. Ind. U., 1923-50, emeritus, 1950-74; vis. prof. Claremont Coll., 1950-51. Mem. Modern Lang. Assn. Am., Am. Assn. U. Profs., Phi Beta Kappa. Republican. Presbyn. Author: The Life of Edmund Spenser, 1945; Notes on the Life of Edmund Spenser, 1949; others. Editor several books, 1912-27. Home: Claremont, Cal. Died June 30, 1973; buried Todd Meml. Chapel, Claremont, Cal.

JUDSON, ARTHUR, mgr. Philharmonic Symphony Soc.; b. Dayton, O., Feb. 17, 1881; s. Francis H. and Mary M. (Myers) J.; student Denison U., Granville, O., Dr. of Music, 1931; m. Edna H. Bench, Nov. 24, 1904; 1 son, Francis Edward; m. 2d, Daphne Duquette of Montreal, Can., June 1941. Mgr. Phila. Orchestra, 1915-35, New York Stadium Concerts, 1920-43, N.Y. Philharmonic Orchestra, 1921; organizer and dir. Columbia Broadcasting System, 1928-30; pres. Columbia Artists Management, Inc. (formerly Columbia Concerts, Inc.), 1930-48; active head Judson, O'Neill & Judd (a div. of Columbia); sec. and mgr. Phila. Summer Concerts, 1930-35. Elected Officer of French Acad., 1920. Dir. Philharmonic-Symphony Soc. (New York). Episcopalian. Club: Lotos (New York). Home: Rye, N.Y. Died Jan. 30, 1975.

JUDY, CLINTON KELLY educator; b. Vancouver, Wash., Dec. 2, 1879; s. Martin and Frederika (Kelly) J.; A.B., Univ. of Calif. at Berkeley, 1903, A.M., 1907; A.B., Oxford Univ., Eng., 1909, A.M., 1913; A.M., Harvard, 1917; unmarried. Prof. of English lang. and lit., Calif. Inst. of Tech., 1909-49, chmn. div. of humanities, 1923-49. Served as captain Coast Art. Officers Res. Corps, 1918. Member Phi Beta Kappa, Psi Upsilon. Republican. Club: Athenaeum of Pasadena. Home: San Marino, Cal.†

JULIAN, PERCY LAVON, chemist; b. Montgomery, Ala., Apr. 11, 1899; s. James S. and Elizabeth Lena (Adams) J.; A.B., DePauw U., 1920, D.Sc., 1947; A.M., Harvard, 1923; Ph.D., U. Vienna, 1951; D.Sc., Fisk U., 1947, W.Va. State Coll., 1948, Northeastern U., 1948, Morgan Coll., 1950, Northwestern U., 1951, Howard U., 1951, Lincoln U., 1954, Roosevelt U., 1961, Va. State Coll., 1962, Morehouse Coll., 1963, Oberlin Coll., 1964, Mich. State U., 1972; LL.D., Lafayette Coll., 1969, Atlanta U., 1973; L.H.D., MacMurray Coll., Jacksonville, Ill., 1969, Ind. U., 1969; D.Sc., Lincoln U.

of Mo., 1975; m. Anna Johnson, Dec. 24, 1935; children—Percy Lavon, Faith Roselle. Instr. chemistry Fisk U., 1920-22; Austin fellow chemistry Harvard, 1922-23, research fellow biophysics, 1923-24, George and Martha Derby scholar chemistry, 1924-25, univ. scholar, 1925-26; prof. chemistry W.Va. State Coll., 1926-27; asso. prof. chemistry, acting head dept. Howard U., 1927-29, prof., head dept. chemistry, 1931-32; Gen. Edn. Bd. fellow U. Vienna, 1929-31; research fellow, tchr. organic chemistry DePauw U., 1932-36; dir. research Soya Products div. Glidden Co., 1936-45, dir. research, mgr. fine chems., 1945-53; pres. Julian Labs., Inc., Laboratories Julian de Mexico, S.A., 1953-64, Julian Research Inst., Julian Assos., Inc., 1964-75. Exec. bd. Chgo. chpt. Nat. Conf. Christians and Jews, v.p. bus. adv. council Chgo. Urban League; chmn. Commonwealth Edison Environmental Adv. Council. Trustee DePauw U., Greencastle Ind., Fisk U., Nashville (emeritus), Howard U., Washington (emeritus), So. Union Coll., Wadley, Ala., Roosevelt U., Chgo.; bd. dirs. Chgo. Theol. Sem. Recipient Spingarn medal, 1947; Distinguished Service award Phi Beta Kappa Assn., Chgo., 1949; Chicagoan of Year award Chgo, Sun-Times, 1950; Chem. Pioneer award, 1968; Merit award Chgo.Tech. Socs. Council 1967; others. Fellow Chem. Soc. London, N.Y. Acad. Sci., Am. Inst. Chemists (Honor Scroll award 1964); mem. Nat. Acad. Sci., Am. Acad. Arts and Scis., Phi Beta Kappa Assos., Phi Beta Kappa, Sigma Xi. Contbr. articles to profl. jours. Holder patents. Home: Oak Park, Ill. Died Apr. 19, 1975; buried Elm Lawn Cemetery, Elmhurst, Ill.

JUNOD, HENRI PELL, coal and shipping exec.; b. N.Y.C., Dec. 20, 1900; s. Louis and Laura Duane (Ireland) J.; Salisbury Sch., 1917; B.S., Mass. Inst. Tech., 1923; m. Gertrude Madeline Busch, Jan. 21, 1939; 1 son, Henri Pell. With Pickands Mather & Co., 1923-66, office boy, with blast furnaces and coke ovens, foreman, pig iron and coke salesman, mgr. Toledo Coke, Inc., mgr. coke sales Chgo., coal dept., Cleve., mgr. coal dept., partner, 1951-60, inc., 1960, v.p., 1960-62, exec. v.p., 1963-64, vice chmn., 1964-65, chmn. exec. com., 1965-67, dir., 1960-69, pres., dir. Hamilton Supply Co., Marquette Dock Co., Portage Coal & Dock Co., P. & E. Coal Dock, Detour Dock Co., Ashtabula & Buffalo Dock Co., Erie Dock Co., Toledo Lakefront Dock Co.; Jas. Pickands & Co.; asso. mng. partner PM Assos.; exec. v.p. Inter Lake S.S. Co.; v.p. Olga Coal Co.; dir. Enos Coal Mining Co., Lubrizol Corp., Interlake Steel, Enoco Colleries. Mem. coal com. Lake Vessel Com.; mem. industry and govt. relations subcom. Nat. Bituminous Coal Policy Com. to Sec. of Interior; lake coal dock industry adv. com. OPS. Team capt., group chmn., trustee, mem. exec. com. Community Fund; vice chmn. 1959 campaign United Appeal, trustee, v.p., 1960; trustee, mem. exec. com., v.p. Community Chest, 1962; bd. dirs., exec. com. Cleve. chpt. A.R.C., 1962-71; trustee YMCA, 1961-71, Shaker Heights Nature Center; trustee, exec. com. Garden Center Greater Cleve.; devel. com. Mass. Inst. Tech. Served as lt. Royal Flying Corps, World War I. Mem. Am. Coal Sales Assn. (dir., mem. exec. com., pres.), Nat. Coal Assn. (exec. com., dir., chmn marketing com. 1962-64, vice chmn. 1964-65, chmn. 1965-66), Bituminous Coal Operators Assn. (dir.), Am. Iron and Steel Inst., Bituminous Coal Inst. (dir.), Am. Coke and Coal Chems. Inst., Lake Carriers Assn. (exec. com., dir.), Order Colonial Lords of the Manor, Newcomen Soc. N.Am., Theta Tau, Theta Delta Chi. Episcopalian. Clubs: Union, Tavern Chagrin Valley Hunt, Kirtland Country, Mid-Day, Hangar Recreation Assn. (Cleve.); River (N.Y.C.); Naples Yacht, Hole-in-the-Wall Golf, Royal Poinciana Golf (Naples, Fla.). Home: Shaker Heights, O. Died Oct. 6, 1971.

KAHN, GILBERT W(OLFF), banker; b. Morristown, N.J., July 18, 1903; s. Otto H. (banker) and Addie (Wolff) K.; prep. edn., Groton (Mass.) Sch.; student Princeton, 1923-24; studied foreign banking in England, France and Germany; m. Anne Elizabeth Whelan, Nov. 19, 1924; 1 daughter, Claire Anne; m. 2d, Sara Jane Heliker, February 1, 1933; 1 son, Gilbert Sherburne married 3d, Polly Stover, June 30, 1948. With Equitable Trust Co., 1925, Kuhn, Loeb & Co. bankers, New York, 1927-75, partner, 1931-75. Member of C. of C. State of New York. Clubs: Princeton, Piping Rock, Recess. Home: Old Brookville, L. I., N.Y., Died Dec. 15, 1975.

KAHN, HERMAN, archivist; b. Rochester, N.Y., Aug. 13, 1907; s. Isadore and Dora (Schoenberg) K.; A.B. summa cum laude, U. Minn., 1928, A.M., 1931; Univ. fellow in history Harvard, 1933-34; m. Anne Elizabeth Suess, Sept. 13, 1936; children—Michael Frederick, Melinda Deborah (Mrs. Kenneth Devens). Teaching asst. history U. Minn., 1928-31; asst. prof. history (Peru) Neb. State Tchrs. Coll., 1931-33; historian Nat. Park Service, 1934-36; archivist Nat. Archives, 1936-41; chief div. interior dept. archives, Nat. Archives, 1942-46, dir. nat. resources records office, 1947-48; dir. Franklin D. Roosevelt Library Hyde Park, 1948-61; asst. archivist for civil archives Nat. Archives, 1961-63, asst. archivist for presdl. libraries, 1964-68; asso. librarian for manuscripts and archives, also lectr. in history Yale U., 1968-75; fellow Timothy Dwight Coll., 1969-75; lectr. history Bard Coll., 1957; lectr. history Columbia, 1960-61. Pres. Dutchess County Council Social Agys., 1957. Mem. Nat. Archives Adv. Council, 1971-75; mem. adv. com. John Fitzgerald Kennedy Library. Recipient Gen. Services Adminstrn. Distinguished Service award, 1960. Fellow Soc. Am. Archivists (v.p. 1968-69, pres. 1969-70, mem. council); mem. Am., Miss. Valley hist. assns., Conn. Acad. Arts and Scis. Contbr. articles to hist., archival jours. Home: New Haven Conn. Died June 5, 1975

KAHN, LOUIS I., architect; b. Island of Osel, Russia. Feb. 20, 1901; s. Leopold and Bertha (Mendelsohn) K.; brought to U.S., 1905, naturalized, 1915; grad. Pub. Indsl. Art Sch., 1917; student Graphic Sketch Club, 1916-20; B.Arch., U. Pa., 1924; D.Arch., Poly. Inst. Milan (Italy), 1964; H.H.D., U. N.C., 1964; A.F.D., Yale, 1965; LL.D., LaSalle Coll., Phila., 1967; L.H.D., Columbia, 1974; D. Fine Arts, U. Pa., 1971; m. Esther Virginia Israeli, Aug. 9, 1930; 1 dau., Sue Ann. Designer, Office City Architect, 1924-25; chief of design Sesqui-Centennial Expn., 1925-26; study and travel in Europe, 1928-29; designer in offices of Paul P. Cret, 1929-30, Zantzinger, Borie and Medary, 1930-31; organized Archtl. Research Group, 1931-33; planned problems for Phila. City Planning Commn. under WPA, 1933-35; asst. prin. architect co-designer Jersey Homsteads Coop. Devel., Highstown, N.J. Resettlement Adminstrn., 1935-36; cons. architect for Phila. Housing Authority. 1937, for U.S. Housing Authority, 1939; designed Rational City Plan as part of Houses and Housing exhibit at Mus. Modern Art, N.Y.C., 1939; asso. with George Howe, 1941-42, prin. George Howe, Oscar Stonorov, 1942-43, Oscar Stonorov, 1943-47; pvt. practice architecture, 1953-74; asso. with Douglas Orr, 1953; prof. architecture U. Pa., 1957-74, named 1st to Paul Philippe Cret chair in architecture, 1966-71, emeritus, 1971-74; prof. architecture Yale, 1952-57; Albert Farwell Bemis vis. prof. Mass. Inst. Tech., 1956; chief critic advanced archtl. design Yale; resident architect Am. Acad. in Rome, 1950-51. Mem. Phila. Art (Commn. Recipient Centennial gold medal Phila. chpt. A.I.A., 1969, gold medal of honor N.Y. chpt., 1970; bronze plaque Home Builders Assn., 1950, Arnold Brunner prize Nat. Inst. Arts and Letters, 1960; lecture fellowship Princeton U., 1961: Graham Found. for Advanced Studies in Fine Arts fellow, 1961; medal Phila. Art Alliance, 1962; gold medal Phila. Dir.'s Club, 1964; Frank P. Brown medal Franklin Inst., 1964; medal of honor Danish Archtl. Assn., 1965; ann. award Phila. Sketch Club, 1966; Internat. silver medal for distinguished contbns. to arts U. Conn., 1969; Phila. Book award for outstanding pub. service, 1971; Royal gold medal for architecture Royal Inst. Brit. Architects, 1972. Fellow World Acad. Arts and Sci., A.I.A. (gold medal 1971, regional urban planning com., Am. Acad. Arts and Scis., Royal Soc. Arts (London), Franklin Inst., Soc. for Arts, Religion and Contemporary Culture; mem. Royal Swedish Acad. Fine Arts, Am. Soc. Planners and Architects (pres.), Fed. Phila. Housing Assn. (archtl. adv. com., regional chmn.), Art Alliance, Nat. Inst. Arts and Letters, Royal Inst. Architects of Ireland, Coll. Architects of Peru, Citizens Council on City Planning, Acad. Arts and Letters. Jewish religion. Clubs: T Square (pres. Phila.), Print. Author: (with Oscar Stonorov) Why City Planning Is Your Responsibility, 1943, You and Your Neighborhood, 1944; contbr. articles on architecture to jours. and mags. Prin. works include: Pine Ford Area Housing Devel., Middletown, Pa., Stanton Road Housing Devel. Project, Washington, 1941-42, Carver Court Housing Devel., Coatesville, Pa., Lincoln Road Housing Devel., Coatesville, Pennypack Woods Housing Devel., Phila., 1942-43, Lily Ponds Housing Devel., Washington, Willow Run War Town Devel. Project, Detroit, 1943-47, Art Gallery, Yale U., Richards Med. Research Bldg. and biol. labs. U. Pa., 1st Unitarian Ch., Rochester, N.Y., Salk Inst. for Biol. Studies, La Jolla, Cal., dormitory Bryn Mawr Coll., 2d capital of Pakistan, Dacca, Bangladesh, Indian Inst. Mgmt., Ahmedabad, Theatre Performing Arts, Ft. Wayne (Ind.) Fine Arts Found., Kimbell Mus. Art, Ft. Worth, library and dining hall Phillips Exeter Acad., factory and office bldg. Olivetti-Underwood Corp., Harrisburg, Pa., Temple Beth-El Synagogue, Chappaqua, N.Y., Paul Mellon Center for Brit. Art and Brit. Studies, Yale, office bldg., Kansas City, Mo., Middle Sch. of New Haven Pub. Schs., Hurva Synagogue, Jerusalem, Israel, New Engring. Campus, U. Tel-Aviv (Israel), Palazzo di Congressi, Venice, Italy, Inner Harbor Redevel. Bldgs., Balt. Home: Philadelphia Pa. Died Mar. 17, 1974.

KAHN, MILTON, business exec.; b. Latvia, Russia, Jan. 25, 1890; s. Harry and Etta (Levin) K.; came to U.S., 1904, naturalized, 1916; B.S., Mass. Inst. Tech., 1912; m. Edith Miller, June 7, 1921; children—Betty E. (Mrs. Lesner White), Lila R. (Mrs. Melvin Musinsky), Martin H. Apprentice Am. Writing Paper Co., Holyoke, Mass., 1912-14, supt. prodn., 1914-18; owner Kahn Paper Co., Boston, from 1919. Served as lt., Chem. Warfare Service, U.S. Army, 1918-19. Hon. life trustee Beth Israel Hosp.; dir. Children's Hosp., American Joint Distbn. Com. United Service to New Americans, United Com. Services of Boston, United Fund of Boston, from 1959; member executive committee Greater Boston Medical Foundation. Vice chmn. Boston Community Fund campaigns, 1936-48. Pres. Asso. Jewish Philanthropies, Boston, 1947-50, chmn. philanthropic campaigns, 1936, 37, 40, 41, chmn. businessmen's council. Pres. New Eng. region Council of Jewish Fedn. and Welfare Funds, 1949, 50, also nat. sec.; mem. nat. Cabinet United Jewish Appeal, nat. chmn. speaker's bur.; mem. fund raising com. Boston Coll.; hon. trustee Brandeis U. Chmn. United Jewish Appeal Resolutions Com., Atlantic City Assembly, 1947, 48, 49. National Chairman Brandeis University Associates. Member Mass. Exec. committee U.S.O., 1945-47. Milton Kahn chair in community orgn. Florence Heller Sch., Brandeis U. named in his honor, 1960; recipient Distinguished Service medal Brandeis U., 1966. Hon. mem. Tau Delta Phi. Hon. trustee Temple Adath Israel. Mason. Clubs: Kernwood Country (Salem), Belmont Country (Boston; gov.). Home: Brookline Mass. Died June 24, 1974; buried Temple Israel Cemetery, Wakefield, Mass.

KAISER, JOHN BOYNTON, assn. dir.; b. Cleveland, O., Jan. 1, 1887; s. Peter Henry and Beza N. (Boynton) K.; B.A., Western Reserve U., 1908; B.L.S., N.Y. State Library Sch., 1910, M.L.S., 1917; grad. student U. of Ill. 1 semester, 1912-13; L.H.D. (hon.), Rutgers University, 1960; married Gertrude I. Swift, November 14, 1910 (died April 2, 1940); 1 son, Boynton Swift; m. 2d, Mary K. Cooper, Dec. 31, 1942 (div. June 15, 1961); m. 3d, Margaret G. Whaley, Sept. 30, 1961 (dec. Sept. 1964); m. 4th, Gladys S. Henderson, May 1, 1972. Asst. librarian Western Res. Hist. Soc., Cleve., 1907-08; reference dept. Cleve. Pub. Library, 1908; with law div. N.Y. State Library, 1909-10; asst. state librarian in charge legislative reference work, Tex. State Library, Austin, Tex., 1910-11; lecturer U. of Ill., Library Sch., and dept. librarian economics and sociology, same, 1911-14; librarian Tacoma Pub. Library, Mar. 18, 1914-Jan. 27, 1924; dir. of libraries and Library Sch., Ia. State Univ., 1924-27; librarian Oakland Free Library and sec. Oakland Pub. Mus., Snow Mus., Oakland Art Gallery, Feb. 2, 1927-Apr. 15, 1943; director Newark (N.J.) Pub. Library, 1943-58; instructor Grad. Library School, Columbia, summers 1945, 58; executive dir. Am. Documentation Institute, 1961-73; president N.Y. State Library School Assn., Inc., 1947-73; sometime lectr. several library schs.; participated in several surveys of library facilities; cons. and advisor several schs. and socs. in field. A.L.A. del. NGO group at United Nations, 1959-62. Librarian (war service), Camp Knox, Ky., Nov. 1918-Jan. 1919, Camp Upton, N.Y., Jan.-May 1919. Am. Library Assn. asst. liaison librarian Northern Calif., 9th Service Command, U.S.A., 1942-43. Supervisor U.S. Treasury reps., Newark War Finance Commn., 1944-46. Mem. trustees adv. com. Columbia Grad. Library Sch., 1959-73. Received Edna M. Sanderson award, Columbia 1958. Mem. A.L.A. (mem. or chmn. various coms. 1929-73, mem. council 1940-45, 1949-50; 2nd vice president 1949-50), Pacific Northwest (pres. 1917-18), Cal. (pres. 1932-33), N.J. (pres. 1948-49), library assns., Pub. Personnel Assn. (pres. N.J. chpt., 1957-58), Phi Beta Kappa (pres. No. N.J. alumni 1951-53), Beta Theta Phi, Phi Delta Phi. Clubs: Rotary; faculty University California (Berkeley); Men's Faculty, California Writers (v. pres. 1940); Columbia U. (N.Y.C.). Author a number of items regarding libraries and their administration, including reports of surveys, lectures and spl. chpts. in books, articles in mags. Editor Legal Aspects of Library Administration, 1958. Contbr. to profl. and philatelic mags. Home: Winter Park, Fla. Died Sept. 30, 1973.

KALEKO, MASCHA (MRS. CHEMJO VINAVER), author, poet; b. Poland, June 7, 1912; d. Efraim F. and Shoshana (Aufen) Engel; B.A., German Schs.; m. Chemjo Vinaver, 1935; 1 son, Steven. Celebrated author poetry in German lang.; highly praised by Thomas Mann, Herman Hesse. Mem. Writers Assn. In German Lang., Pen Club London, Internat. Schutzverband deutschsprachiger Schriftsteller, Zurich. Author: Des Lyrische Stenogrammheft, Verse vom Alltag, 1933; Kleines Lesebuch Fuer Grosse, 1934; Verse fur Zeitgenossen, 1945; Der Papagei, Die Mamagei und andere Komische Tiere, 1961; Verse in Dur und Moll, 1967; Twentieth Century German Verse; Penguin Anthology, 1916; Verse in Dur Und Moll, 1967; Das Himmelgraue Poesi-Album Der Mascha Kaleko, 1968; Wie's auf dem Mond zugeht: Verse für Kinder und ihre Eitern, 1971; also many anthologies and textbooks. Readings recorded on LP Telefunken-Decca; Mascha Kaleko spricht Mascha Kaleko, 1960; LP Grammophon: Jugendilebe a.D-Hanne Wieder Singt Chansons von Mascha Kaleko, 1965. Readings on radio. Radio plays Abschied, Ein Solo fur Frauenstime, Karneval der Tiere. Home: Jerusalem, Israel. Died Jan. 21, 1975.

KALISKI, SIDNEY RICHARD, pediatrician; b. San Antonio, July 3, 1895; s. Max and Pauline (Kronthal) K.; student U. Tex., U. Chgo.; M.D., Rush Med. Coll., Chgo.; m. Sophie Faverman, Dec. 4, 1942; 1 son, Michael Paul. Intern, Cook County Hosp., Chgo., 1919-21, resident in contagious disease, 1921; resident Cook County Children's Hosp., Chgo., 1920-21; past pres. staff Santa Rosa Hosp., San Antonio; clin. prof. U. Tex. Med. Sch., Galveston, 1945-50, Baylor U. Med. Sch., Houston, U. Tex. Health Sci. Center, San Antonio; civilian cons. to surgeon gen. Dept. Army, Brook Army Hosp., Ft. Sam Houston, San Antonio, 1946-72; civilian cons. to surgeon gen. in Europe, 1955-56; civilian cons. Wilford Hall Hosp., Lackland AFB, San Antonio, 1957-69, William Beaumont Gen. Hosp., El Paso, Tex., 1957-58; pediatric cons. State Tb Hosp., San Antonio, 1957-70. Chmn., Fire and Police Civil Service Bd., San Antonio, 1931-34, 39-44. Served to maj., M.C., USAAF, 1942-45. Recipient Outstanding Civilian Service medal Dept. Army, U.S. Air Force. Diplomate

Am. Bd. Pediatrics. Fellow Am. Acad. Pediatrics; mem. A.M.A., Tex. Med. Assn., Bexar County Med. Soc., Tex. (past pres.), San Antonio (past pres.) pediatric socs., Am. Med. Soc. of Vienna (life). Contbr. numerous articles to med. jours. Home: San Antonio, Tex. Died July 20, 1974; buried Ft. Sam Houston Mil. Cemetery, San Antonio, Tex.

KALLEN, HORACE MEYER, educator; b. Berenstadt, Silesia, Germany, Aug. 11, 1882; s. Jacob David and Esther Rebecca (Glazier) K.; came to U.S., 1887; A.B. magna cum laude, Harvard, 1903, Ph.D., 1908 L.H.D., 1948; post-grad. Princeton, Oxford U. and Paris; Litt.D., Hebrew Union Coll., Jewish Inst. Religion, 1953, L.H.D., 1965; m. Rachel Oatman Van Arsdale, 1926; children—Harriet S., David J. Asst., lectr. philosophy Harvard, 1908-11; instr. logic Clark Coll., Worcester, Mass., 1910; instr. philosophy and psychology U. Wis., 1911-18; prof. New School for Social Research, N.Y.C., 1952, research prof. social philosophy, 1952-69, emeritus, 1969-74, dean grad. faculty polit. and social sci. 1944-46; Distinguished Seminar prof. L.I.U., 1964-68. Mem. labor com. Adv. Commn. Council Nat. Def.; mem. Commn. Inquiry on Terms of Peace, N.Y.C. Mayor's Com. on City Planning; chmn. commn. on edn. Am. Labor Conf. on Internat. Relations, Presdl. Commn. on Higher Edn.; cons. N.Y.C. Commn. on Intergroup Relations, 1961. Named by Wm. James editor of unfinished book, 1910; lit. executor Benjamin Paul Blood, 1920. Trustee Rochdale Inst., N.Y.C., Found. Study Modern Sci., Found. Oceanic Edn. Recipient Bernard Semel award, Mark Eisner Edn. medal, Frank Weill award, Acad. Div. United Jewish Appeal award. Fellow Jewish Acad. Arts and Scis., Internat. Inst. Arts and Letters; mem. Am. Jewish Congress (hon. v.p.), World Jewish Congress (exec. com.), Internat. League for Rights Man, Am. Philos. Soc., Soc. Sci. Study Religion (pres.), Am. Assn. Jewish Edn. (v.p.). Translator: Criminal Psychology (Hans Gross), 1910. Author: Decline and Rise of the Consumer, 1936; Art and Freedom, 2 vols., 1942; Modernity and Liberty, 1947; The Liberal Spirit, 1948; Ideals and Experience 1948; The Education of Free Men, 1949, (translated in Italian), 1964; Patterns of Progress, 1950; Democracy's True Religion, 1951; Secularism is the Will of God, 1954; Cultural Pluralism and the American Idea, 1956; Utopians at Bay, 1958; The Book of Job as Greek Tragedy, 1959; A Study of Liberty, 1959; Philosophical Issues in Adult Education, 1962; Freedom, Tragedy and Comedy, 1963; Liberty, Laughter and Tears, 1968; What I Believe and Why-Maybe, 1971. Editor: The Bertrand Russell Case (with John Dewey), 1941. Contbr. to periodicals. Died Feb. 1974.

KALMENSON, BENJAMIN, retired pictures exec.; b. Pitts., Jan. 3, 1899; s. Charles and Gail K.; m. Norma Goldman, Dec. 28, 1926; children—Mrs. Burton Levine, Howard. Began career with Crucible Steel Co. of Am.; in motion picture industry, 1927-69; with First Nat. Exchange, 1934; joined Warner Bros., 1934; pres. Warner Bros. Distbg. Corp., 1941; exec. v.p. Warner Bros. Pictures, Inc., 1956-66, pres., chief exec. officer, 1966-67; pres., dir. Warner Bros-Seven Arts, Ltd., 1967-69. Died Jan. 18, 1974.

KALVEN, HARRY, JR., educator, lawyer; b. Chgo., Sept. 11, 1914; A.B., U. Chgo., 1935, J.D., 1938; m. Betty Rymer, Nov. 6, 1945; children—James, Michael, Peter, Katherine. Admitted to Ill. bar, 1939; with Frantz & Johnson, 1939-42; instr. Law. Sch., U. Chgo., 1945, asst prof., 1946-49, asso. prof., 1949-53, prof., 1953-74, Harry A. Bigelow prof. law, 1973-74, also leader U. Chgo. Jury Project, interdisciplinary study basic issues of modern jurisprudence. Mem. com. for standard jury instrns. Ill. Supreme Ct., 1957-61. Served with Armed Forces, 1942-45. Guggenheim fellow, 1970-71. Mem. Am. Acad. Arts and Scis. Author: (with Walter J. Blum) The Uneasy Case for Progressive Taxation, 1953; (with Hans Zeisel, Bernard Buchholz) Delay in the Court, 1959; (with Charles O. Gregory) Cases and Materials in Torts, 1959, 69; (with Walter J. Blum) Public Law Perspective on a Private Law Problem: Auto Compensation Plans, 1964; The Negro and the First Amendment, 1965; (with Hans Zeisel) The American Jury, 1966. Home: Chicago Ill. Died Oct. 1974.

KAMIENSKI, BOGDAN chemist; b. Oswiecim, Poland, Mar. 14, 1897; s. Wladislaw and Jadwiga (Kuhn) K.; D.Sc., Cracow (Poland) U., 1924; m. Julia Natanson, Aug. 26, 1924; children—Elzbleta Markowska, Maria Kamienska-Zyla. Asst. chair inorganic chemistry Cracow U., 1920-24, sr. asst. phys. chemistry, 1926-29; prof. phys. chemistry, 1932-67, dean dept. physics, math. and chemistry, 1947-52; with chem. Industry and metallurgy, 1924-26; prof. chemistry Politech. High Sch., Lwow, Poland, 1929-32. Decorated officer's and comdr.'s cross Polonia Restituta; scholar Sir William Ramsay's Lab., U. London (Eng.), 1928-29. Mem. Internat. Union Pure and Applied Chemistry (mem. internat. com.), Polish Acad. Scis. (pres. 1966-69), Polish Chem. Soc. (A. Sniadecki's medal). Author: Elements of Physical Chemistry, 1947; also numerous articles on phys. chemistry. Editor: Physical Chemistry, 1963. Inventor instrument; research on physico-chem. model of sense of smell applied to air pollution investigation. Home: Krakow, Poland. Died Aug. 9, 1973.

KAMMER, EDWARD JOSEPH, clergyman; b. New Orleans, Apr. 23, 1908; s. Edward William and Mary Catherine (Kane) K.; B.A., St. Mary's Sem., 1933; M.A., Cath. U. Am., 1939, Ph.D., 1941. Joined Congregation of the Mission (Vincentian Fathers), 1927; ordained priest Roman Cath. Ch., 1933; prof. history and sociology St. Mary's Sem., Perryville, Mo., 1933-37; prof. history Kenrick Sem., Webster Groves, Mo., 1937-38; prof. sociology De Paul U., Chgo., 1941-60, dean Downtown Coll. Liberal Arts and Scis., 1943-46, Coll. Commerce, 1946-50, faculties, 1950-60, v.p., 1944-55, exec. v.p., 1955-60, trustee, 1944-60; prof. social scis. St. Mary's Sem., Houston, 1960-63; rector Assumption Sem., San Antonio, 1963-67; asso. v.p. space planning DePaul U., 1967-73; asso. pastor St. Thomas Ch., Long Beach, Miss., 1973-75. Mem. Higher Edn. Commn. Ill. Mem. Assn. Instl. Research, Soc. Coll. and U. Planning, Marquis Biographical Soc., Blue Key (Hon.), Delta Epsilon Sigma, Pl Gamma Mu, Phi Kappa Alpha. Author: A Socio-economic Survey of the Marsh Dwellers of Four South Eastern Louisiana Parishes, 1941. Home: Long Beach, Miss. Died Apr. 26, 1975.

KANE, RICHMOND KEITH, lawyer; b. San Francisco, July 3, 1900; s. Daniel H. and Beryl (Keith) K.; grad. St. George's Sch., 1918; A.B., Harvard, 1922, LL.B., 1926, LL.D., 1971; student Balliol Coll., Oxford (Eng.) U., 1922-23; m. Amanda Bryan, May 21, 1930; children—Shelah Keith Scott, Anne Tennant McGuire, Hope Stewart Childs, Constance Henley Tucker. Admitted to N.Y. bar, 1926; with firm Cadwalader, Wickersham & Taft, 1926-32, mem., 1932-40, 46-73; spl. asst. to atty. gen. U.S., 1940-42; spl. asst. to sec. navy, 1943-45. Trustee U.S. Trust Co. N.Y., 1956-72, hon. trustee, 1973-74; dir. Amerada Hess Corp., 1962-73, Crowell- Collier & Macmillan, Inc., 1957-72. Served with USNRF, 1918, U.S. Marine Corps, 1918; lt. comdr. USNR, 1937-40. Fellow Am. Bar Found.; mem. Assn. Bar City N.Y., N.Y. State, New York County, Am., D.C. bar assns., Am. Law Inst. Democrat. Episcopalian. Clubs: Somerset, Tavern, Harvard (Boston); Union, Harvard, Century, Downtown Assn., Knickerbocker, River (N.Y.C.); Metropolitan (Washington); Commonwealth, Country of Va. (Richmond, Va.). Home: Charlottesville, Va. Died May 30, 1974; buried Brook Hill Cemetery, Va.

KANNER, IRVING F., educator; b. N.Y.C., Feb. 18, 1913; s. Samuel and Rosalind (Rosenbaum) K.; student U. So. Cal., 1929-30; A.B., magna cum laude, Syracuse U., 1933; M.D., Case Western Res. U., 1937; m. Esther Levy, Oct. 17, 1938; children—Linda Jean (Mrs. David Turner Phillips), Mary Helen. Intern Cleve. Met. Hosp., 1937-38; resident USPHS Hosp., Lexington, Ky., 1938; practice medicine, specializing in internal medicine Lexington, 1938-69; prof. medicine, dir. ambulant sect. U. Ky., Lexington, 1969-74. Sec., Fayette County Med. Soc. Found., Inc., 1967-74; cons. com. office practice and mgmt. Am. Soc. Internal Medicine, 1971-74; chmn. health subcom. Mayor's Com. Improvement Greater Lexington, 1966-69; sec. Ky. Diabetes Assn., 1970-72, 2d v.p., 1972-73. Bd. dirs. Hunter Found., 1970-74. Served to lt. col. AUS, 1940-46; ETO. Decorated Bronze Star. Am. Soc. Internal Medicine grantee, 1970-71. Diplomate Am. Bd. Internal Medicine. Fellow A.C.P.; mem. Ky. (pres. 1973-74), Am. socs. internal medicine, Internat. Soc. Internal Medicine, Am. Heart Assn., Ky. Thoracic Soc., Fayette County Med. Soc. (pres. 1966), Ky. Med. Assn., A.M.A. Club: Torch. Home: Lexington, Ky. Died June 30, 1974.

KANTOR, MORRIS, artist, painter; b. Russia, Apr. 15, 1896; s. Benjamin and Rebecca (Margolin) K.; student Ind. Sch. of Art, N.Y.C.; m. Martha Ryther, Mar. 7, 1928. Exhibited, 1928-74; at Brummer Gallery, Rehn Gallery (N.Y.C.), Bertha Schaefer Gallery, also in nat. shows in U.S., 1929-74; one-man shows, 1930, 32, 35, 38, 40, 43, 45, 47, 49, 53; rep. permanent collections Smithsonian Instn., Met. Mus. Art, Modern Mus. Art, Whitney Mus. Am. Art, Art Inst. Chgo., Pa. Acad. Fine Arts, Phillips Meml. Gallery (Washington), other museums throughout U.S. Recipient 1st prize and Logan medal Art Inst. Chgo., 1931; 3d Clark prize Corcoran Gallery, 1939; Temple medal Phila. Acad., 1940; Purchase prize U. Ill., 1951. Died Jan. 31, 1974.

KAPLAN, ABRAHAM DAVID HANNATH, economist; b. N.Y. City, Apr. 26, 1893; s. Simon Eliezer and Anna (Hannath-Shapiro) K.; B.S., N.Y. University, 1913; A.M., U. of Denver, 1923, also Doctor of Political Science, 1957; Ph.D., Johns Hopkins, 1929; m. Bella Cauman, Dec. 27, 1919; children—Stephen Isaac, Nancy Sara. Taught secondary schs., N.Y.C. 1913-17 and 1919-20; mem. faculty U. of Denver, dir. social studies, graduate division government management, 1921-44; with Com. for Econ. Development, 1943-45, economist, Ho. of Reps. Spl. Com. on Post-War Econ. Policy, 1944-46; sr. staff mem. Brookings Instn., Washington, since January 1945; research professor George Washington U., 1960-74; vis prof. econ. Rollins College, 1958-59; lectr. on Am. economy, auspices U.S. Embassy India, 1958; visiting prof. U. of Del. Grad. Sch., 1962-63. Dir. Urban Study of Family Income and Expenditures (on leave), United States Bur. Labor Statistics and cooperating federal agencies, 1936-38; reporter World Monetary and Econ. Conf., London, 1933; lecturer Inst. of World Affairs, Mondsee, Austria, 1933; exec. dir. Citizens Conf. on Govt. Management, 1939-42. Cons. economist Social Security Bd., 1938-42. Served with U.S. Army, 1917-19. Hon. life mem. Denver C. of C. Fellow Am. Statis. Assn.; mem. Am. Econ. Assn., Phi Beta Kappa, Beta Gamma Sigma, Phi Delta Kappa. Club: Cosmos (Washington). Author books including: Liquidation of War Production, 1944; Guarantee of Annual Wages, 1947; Small Business: Its Place and Problems, 1948; Big Enterprize in a Competitive System, 1954; Pricing in Big Business (with assos.), 1958. Contbr. Ency. Social Scis. and Britannica, also profl. jours. Home: Chevy Chase, Md. Died June 1, 1974.

KAPLAN, KIVIE, orgn. ofcl.; b. Boston, Apr. 1, 1904; s. Benajmin J. and Celia (Solomont) K.; ed. pub. schs.; D.H.L., Portia Law Sch., Boston, Central State U., Wilberforce, O.; LL.D., Wilberforce U.; H.H.D., Lincoln (Pa.) U., Saints Jr. Coll., Jackson, Miss., Edward Waters Coll., Jacksonville, Fla.; m. Emily Rogers, June 3, 1925; children—Sylvia (Mrs. Morton S. Grossman), Jean (Mrs. Albert I. Green), Edward Kivie. Ret. pres., gen. mgr. Colonial Tanning Co., Inc., Boston; nat. pres. N.A.A.C.P., 1966-75, mem. exec. com., mem. budget com., former nat. chmn. life membership com., former mem. exec. com. Legal Defense and Edn. Fund, also mem. nat. bd. Hon. treas. Jewish Meml. Hosp., also dir. for life and chmn. endowment fund coms.; mem. bd. Newton (Mass.) Community Chest, also fund co-chmn.; mem. social action commn., vice chmn. Union Am. Hebrew Congreattions; mem. nat. health planning com. Council Jewish Fedns. and Welfare Funds; life trustee Combined Jewish Phalanthropies; treas. Combined Jewish Appeal; pres. 210 Assos., Inc.; trustee Emily R. and Kivie Kaplan Family Charitable Trust, Lincoln U., Tougaloo (Miss.) Coll.; bd. dirs. Hebrew Free Loan Soc.; treas. Roxbury Cemetery Assn.; life mem. bd. Brandeis U. Assos.; fellow Brandeis U.; donor numerous facilities to hosps., univs., congregations. Recipient Brotherhood Man-of-Year award Temple Reyim; Men of Vision award Bonds for Israel Com.; Human Rights award Pitts.; Man of Year award Temple Emmanuel Brotherhood, Newton, Mass., 1966, Brotherhood award Temple Israel, Boston, 1966, 1st ann. Averell Harriman Equal Housing Opportunity award Modern Community Developers, T. Kenyon Holly award for outstanding humanitarian Service, Amistad award Am. Missionary Assn. Jewish religion (co-founder, life trustee temple). Mem. B'nai B'rith (dir. New Eng. region Anti Defamation League, treas. nat. vocational commn.), Mason (hon.) Home: Chestnut Hill, Mass. Died May 5, 1975.

KAPLAN, MORDECAI MENAHEM, educator; b. Swenziany, Lithuania, June 11, 1881; s. Israel and Anna (Kowarsky) K.; brought to U.S., 1889; A.B., Coll. City New York, 1900; M.A., Columbia, 1902; Rabbi, Jewish Tehol. Sem. America, 1902, D.H.L., 1929; m. Lena Rubin, June 2, 1908 (dec. 1958); children—Judith, Hadassah, Naomi, Selma; m. 2d, Rivkah Rieger, June 21, 1959. Rabbi Congregation Kehilath Jeshurum, 1903-09; prin. Teachers Inst. of Jewish Theol. Sem. America, 1909-31, dean, 1931-46; prof. homiletics Rabbinical School of Jewish Theological Sem. America, 1910-47; prof. philosophies of religion from 1947; editor of The Reconstructionist, from 1935; also rabbi Jewish Center, N.Y., 1918-22; leader of Soc. for Advancement of Judaism, 1922-44; leader emeritus, from 1945. Author books inc.; The Future of The American Jew, 1948; A New Zionism, 1955; Questions Jews Ask, 1956; Judaism without Supernaturalism, 1958; The Greater Judaism in the Making, 1960; also of Daily Prayerbook, 1962. The translator and editor of the Text of Mesillat Yesharim by S. D. Luzzatto, 1937. Editor: Jewish Reconstructionist Papers, 1936. Co-editor: The New Haggadah, 1941; Sabbath Paper Book, 1945; High Holiday Prayer Book, 1948; Festival Prayer Book, 1958. Address: New York City, N.Y.†

KARR, ROBERT MCNARY, theologian; b. Bloomington, Ind., Sept. 1878; s. John and Mary Elizabeth (Alexander) K.; A.B., Monmouth (Ill.) Coll., 1907, A.M., 1909, D.D., 1922; grad. Pittsburgh Theol. Sem., 1909; m. Annis Bertha Marshall, Aug. 6, 1909; children—Margaret Elizabeth, Robert Livingstone, Katharine Louise, Frances Mary. Ordained ministry U.P. Ch., 1909; pastor successively Tacoma, Wash., Kansas City, Mo., and Oakmont, Pa., until 1922; prof. systematic theology and homiletics, Xenia Theol. Sem., St. Louis, Mo., 1922-39, also v.p., 1923-30; prof. systematic and bibl. theology, Pittsburgh-Xenia Theol. Sem., Pittsburgh, Pa., 1930-49, also registrar, 1930-49, ret. 1949. Editor and author (with others) Children of the Covenant, 1921. Home: Pittsburgh, Pa.†

KARRER, SEBASTIAN, physicist; b. Rich Hill, Mo., Apr. 10, 1889; s. Frank Xavier and Theresa (Braun) K.; A.B., A.M., U. Wash., 1913; Ph.D., U. Ill., 1918; m. Annie May Hurd, Aug. 3, 1923. Instr. physics U. Ill., 1918-19; chief physics div. Fixed Nitrogen Research Lab., Dept. of Agr., 1919-26; dir. research Consol. Gas, Electric Light & Power Co., Balt., 1926-46; cons. Nat. Def. Research Com.; chief cons., research and devel. div. N.M. Sch. Mines, 1946-48; dir. research Baso, Inc., 1948-58, v.p., 1955-58; asso. dir. central research Minn. Mining and Mfg. Co., 1960-61; research asso. Georgetown Univ. Obs., 1964-68. Recipient Modern Pioneer award Am. Mfrs. Assn.; Merit award Navy Ordnance Dept. Mem. A.A.A.S., Am. Phys. Soc., Am.

Chem. Soc., Am. Optical Soc., Md. Acad. Scis. (past pres.), Philos. Soc. Washington, Washington Acad. Scis., Newcomen Soc., Phi Beta Kappa, Sigma Xi, Gamma Alpha. Patentee thermoelectric materials and devices. Home: Port Republic, Md. Died Dec. 7, 1973.

KARTHEISER, FRANK L., r.r. exec.; b. Aurora, Ill., Apr. 19, 1893; s. Laurance and Margaret (Johns) K.; student engring. courses, Internat. Corr. Schs., 1912-14; m. Mary Louise Fieg, 1954. Timekeeper track dept. C. B. & Q. R.R., Aurora, Ill., 1909-10. mech. dept., 1910-17, 19-28, operating dept., 1928-42; asst. to v.p., Burlington Lines, 1942-49, asst. to pres., 1949-52, v.p., exec. dept., 1952-73; dir. Burlington Refrigerator Express Co. Served as ensign USNRF, 1917-19, Mem. Car Foreman's Assn. Chgo. (v.p., pres. 1932-34), Car Dept. Officers Assn. (sec.-treas. 1937-42). Clubs: Western Railway, Traffic, Executives, Serra, Union League (Chgo.). Home: LaGrange, Ill. Died Aug. 6, 1973.

KASE, MAX, journalist; b. N.Y.C., July 21, 1898. With Internat. News Service, 1917-23, 25-34; sports editor Havana Telegram, 1923-25, Boston Am., 1934-38, N.Y. Jour. Am., 1938-66. Active B'nai B'rith Sports Lodge. Died Mar. 21, 1974.

KASSAY, ALLAN ATTILA, abrasives mfg. co. exec.; b. Pecs, Hungary, Nov. 28, 1928; s. Dezso and Elizabeth (Genersich) K.; came to U.S., 1950, naturalized, 1960; B.S. cum laude, Northeastern U., 1955; M.B.A., Harvard, 1957; m. Sylvia Allen Coutts, Jan. 3, 1959; children—David Alexander, Elizabeth Allen, Stephen Anthony. With Norton Co., Newton, Mass., 1957-73, v.p., 1968-73, with Nat. Research Corp. (subsidiary Norton Co., name later changed to Vacuum Equipment and Metal div.), 1966-73, gen. mgr., 1968-71, v.p. abrasive operations Europe and Africa, 1971-73; dir. H.A. Johnson Co., Brighton, Mass., Named Outstanding Young Man, Jr. C. of C. Worcester. Club: Harvard Business School (Worcester, pres. 1964-65). Home: Southboro, Mass. Died Dec. 9, 1973.

KASTNER, ERHART, librarian; b. Augsburg, Germany, 1904; s. Heinrich Friedrich and Elisabeth Kastner; student U. Freiburg, 1924-25, U. Kiel, 1925-26; Dr. Phil., U. Leipzig, 1927. State librarian Dresden (Germany) State Library, 1928-45; dir. Herzog August Library, Wolfenbuttel Germany, 1950-68; sec. Gerhart Hauptmann, 1936-38. Served with German Army, 1940-47. Recipient Immermann prize, 1955, Lit. prize, Cologne, 1957. Author: Zeitbuch von Tumilad, 1949; Olberge, Weinberge, 1953; Stundentrommel vom heiligen Berg Athos, 1956; Die Lerchenschule, 1964; Aufstand der Dinge, 1973; Byzantinische Autzeichnungen, 1973; Krete, 1975; Griechische Inseln, 1975; Der Hund in der Sonne, 1975. Home: Oberbotzen Federal Republic of Germany. Died Feb. 3, 1974.

KÄSTNER, ERICH, author; b. Dresden, Germany, Feb. 23, 1899; s. Emil Richard and Ida Amalie (Augustin) K.; student U. Rostock, Berlin, 1921; Dr., U. Leipzig, 1925; m. Luiselotte Enderle. Author: Herz auf Taille, 1928; Lärm in Spiegel, 1929; Ein Mann gibt Auskunft, 1930; Fabian, 1931; Gesang zwischen den Stühlen, 1932; Dr. Erich Käastners Lyrische Hausapotheke, 1936; Der Kleine Grenzverkehr, 1938; Bei Durchsicht meiner Bücher, 1946; Die 13 Monate, 1955; Notabene, 1945, 1961; Let's Face It, 1963; children's books: Emil und die Detektive, 1928; Pünktchen und Anton, 1931; Der 35 Mai, 1931; Arthur mit dem langen Arm, 1932; Des verhexte Telefon, 1932; Das fliegende Klassenzimmer, 1933; Emil und die drei Zwillinge, 1934; Konferenz der Tiert, 1949; Das Doppelte Lottchen, 1949; Gullivers Reisen, 1964; Das Schwein beim Friseur, 1962; Der Kleine Mann, 1963; Der Kleine Mann und die Kleine Miss, 1967; others; (essays) Der Taegliche Kram, 1948, Die Kleine Freiheit, 1952; also radio and stage plays, songs, poetry; Als Ich ein kleiner Junge war (autobiography), 1957; Gesammelte Schriften für Erwachsene, 8 Bd., 1969. Pres. German Pen Club, 1951. Home: Munich, Federal Republic of Germany. Died July 29, 1974.

KATCHER, ARCHIE, lawyer; b. nr. Leipsic, N.D., Nov. 21, 1914; s. Lewis and Rebecca (Katcher) K.; student Lawrence Inst. Tech., 1933; B.A., Detroit Inst. Tech., 1937; J.D. cum laude, Detroit Coll. Law, 1940; m. Molly Efrusy, July 10, 1938; children—Marianne (Mrs. Aaron Lifchez), Louise S. (Mrs Gerald McCoy), Brian G., Jonathon A. Admitted to Mich. bar, 1940; printer, research clk., briefer Bankruptcy Ct. Detroit, 1934-43; referee in bankruptcy Eastern Dist. Mich., 1946, 48-56; practice law, Detroit, 1943-74; with law firm Miller, Des Roches & Stern, 1943-45; individual practice, 1945-46; with firm Freud, Markus, Gilbert & Lubbers, 1946-48; partner Katcher, Feldman & Wienner, and predecessor firm, 1956-74. Former v.p., dir. Guardian Savs. & Loan Assn.; adv. bd. Met. Fed. Savs. & Loan Assn., Detroit. Mem. Wayne-Detroit Legal Services Co-ordinating Council, 1967-74. Mem. State Bar Mich. (chmn. ethics com.), Fed., Am., Detroit (dir. 1964-70, dir. found. 1964-70, pres. 1969-70, bd. dirs. Legal Aid and Defender) bar assns., Am. Judicature Soc., Nat. Assn. Referees in Bankruptcy, Nat. Bankruptcy Conf., Detroit Coll. Law Alumni Assn. (pres. 1957-58), Am. Orgn. Rehab. through Tng. Fedn., N.A.A.C.P. (life), Union Am. Hebrew Congregations (dir., treas. Great Lakes region 1968-69), Met. Detroit Fedn. Reform Synagogues (pres. 1971-74), Gt. Lakes Council (dir. 1972-74), Anti-Defamation League B'nai B'rith (chmn. Mich. 1962-64, bd. dirs. 1954-74, mem. cabinet, legal com. 1956-74, asst. spl. counsel New Detroit com. 1968-74). Jewish religion (pres. temple 1968-69). Mem. B'nai B'rith (lodge pres. 1951-52). Author revision dist. rules bankruptcy U.S. Dist. Ct., Eastern Dist. Mich., 1954. Contbr. articles profl. jours.; lectr. seminars, bar assns. Home: Huntington Woods Mich. Died Nov. 28, 1974.

KATZ, LABEL ABRAHAM, investment co. exec., orgn. ofcl.; b. New Orleans, Sept. 22, 1918; s. Ralph and Matilda (Conterman) K.; B.A., Tulane U., 1938, LL.B., 1941; m. Alice Mayer, July 15, 1940; children—William, Robert, Walda. Admitted to La. bar, 1941, and practiced law in New Orleans until 1951; engaged in real estate investments, New Orleans, 1941-75. Mem. B'nai B'rith, 1939-75, internat. pres., 1959-75; nat. cabinet United Jewish Appeal, 1955-75; exec. com. Nat. Council Jewish Fedns. and Welfare Funds, 1957-65; bd. dirs. New Orleans United Fund. Mem. Mayor New Orleans Citizens Adv. Com. Housing Improvement, 1954-65. Home: New Orleans, La. Died Apr. 1975.

KATZENBACH, EDWARD LAWRENCE, JR., univ. ofcl.; b. Trenton, N.J., Feb. 24, 1919; s. Edward Lawrence and Marie (Hilson) K.; grad. Lawrenceville (N.J.) Sch., 1936; A.B., Princeton 1940, Ph.D., 1953; LL.D., L.I.U., 1963; m. Maude Thomas, Apr. 26, 1942 (div. 1963); children—Edward L., Matilda, Eldridge Thomas; m. 2d, Dolores Fiala, Apr. 11, 1963; children—Hadley Hadley Stephenson, Karen Ann, William Hunt. Instr. Princeton, 1946-48, 50; dep. dir. hist. sect. Dept. Def., 1951; research asso. Inst. War and Peace Studies, Columbia, 1952-55; dir. def. studies program Harvard, 1955-59; dir. acad. devel. Brandeis U., 1958-60; dep. asst. sec. def. edn. and manpower resources, 1961-64; dir. commn. on adminstrv. affairs Am. Council Edn., 1964-66; v.p. edn. Raytheon Corp., Lexington, Mass., 1966-68; v.p. for research and pub. service U. Okla., 1968-71; v.p. charge program devel. N.Y. Inst. Tech., 1971-74. Served with USMCR, 1942-45, 50-52; col. Res. Mem. Am. Hist. Assn., Acad. Polit. Sci., Council Fgn. Relations, Conf. on Pub. Service. Episcopalian. Club: Federal City. Contbr. articles profl. jours. Died Apr., 1974.

KAUFFMAN, TREVA ERDINE, home economist; b. Osborne, O., Sept. 23, 1889; d. Theodore and Anna Laura (Hershey) Kauffman; B.S., Ohio State U., 1911; M.A., Columbia Univ., 1931; graduate study at Chicago U., 1916; study of dietetics and nutrition at U. of Montreal, 1946; unmarried. Began as teacher Hamilton (O.) pub. schs., 1911; instr. Ohio State Univ. Extension Service, 1913-15; organizer of sch. lunch program in rural and centralized schs. of Ohio, 1915-16; state leader 4-H Girls Work, 1916-17; asst. prof. home economics, O. State U., 1917-20; state supervisor home economics edn., Ohio 1918-20, for N.Y. State Edn. Dept., 1920-59; acting chief, Bur. of Home Economics Edn., 1944-47; exec. sec. N.Y. State Sch. Food Service Assn., 1962-64; sometime mem. faculties Syracuse Univ., Cornell University, Columbia, New York University and others; mem. grad. faculty Russell Sage Coll. Evening div., Albany, 1959-60; cons. home econs. edn. Mem. White House Conf. on Child Health and Protection 1930, President's Conf. on Home Building and Ownership, Washington, D.C., 1931; mem. nat. com. Household Employment, New York, 1933-35; dir. and organizer, N.Y. fed. and State Temporary Emergency Relief Adminstrn. Adult Program Homemaking Edn., 1932-35; mem. adv. bd. Forecast mag., 1936-62; lectr. and adviser on home econs. edn. Am. Women's Volunteer Services, N.Y.C., 1941; mem. N.Y. state Coll. Home Econ. Council Cornell, 1944-47. Mem. N.E.A., World Assn. for Adult Edn., Am. Home Economic Association, Phi Upsilon Omicron, Kappa Delta Pi, and many other nat., state and local assns. and socs. in fields of edn., home econs., and related items, has served as mem. of chmn. coms. of many. Republican. Clubs: National Travel (New York); Woman's City (dir. from 1961), Civic Music Assn., Mendelssohn Club (Albany); Lake Placid (founder Am. Home Econs. Assn. 1964). Author several books and other items on home econs. Home: Albany, N.Y. Died Feb. 28, 1975.

KAUPER, PAUL GERHARDT, educator; b. Richmond, Ind., Nov. 9, 1907; s. Frederick J. and Mary (Tubesing) K.; A.B., Earlham Coll., 1929, LL.D., 1958; J.D., U. Mich., 1932; LL.D., Capital U., 1956, Valparaiso (Ind.) U., 1959, Tex. Luth. Coll., 1965; J.D., honoris causa, Heidelberg U., 1970; m. Anna Marie Nicklas, Sept. 22, 1934; children—Thomas Eugene, Carolyn Ann. Admitted to N.Y. bar, 1936; practice with firm White & Case, N.Y.C., 1934-36; legal research asst. U. Mich. Law Sch., Ann Arbor, 1932-34, asst. prof. law, 1936-39, asso. prof., 1939-46, prof., 1946-65, Henry M. Butzel prof. law, 1965-74, Henry Russell lectr., 1971; guest prof. Max Planck Inst., Heidelberg, 1959, 66; Rosenstiel Distinguished vis. prof. law U. Ariz., 1971; mem. legal dept. Pan Am. Petroleum & Transport Co., N.Y.C., 1942-45. Chmn. Gov.'s Transp. Study Commn., 1950; mem. Ann Arbor Charter Revision Commn., 1953, Ann Arbor Planning Commn., 1956-59. Recipient Distinguished Faculty Achievement award U. Mich., 1959. Mem. Am., Mich. bar assns., Order of Coif (pres. 1965-67, exec. com. 1968-70), Tau Kappa Alpha. Lutheran (mem. bd. coll. edn. Am. Luth. Ch. 1960-66, trustee Luth. Student Found. Ann Arbor, mem. commn. on ch.-state relations Luth. Ch. Am.). Author: Cases on Constitutional Law, 1954; Frontiers of Constitutional Liberty, 1957; (with E. Blythe Stason) Cases on Municipal Corporations, 1959; Civil Liberties and the Constitution, 1961; Religion and the Constitution, 1964; also articles. Home: Ann Arbor Mich. Died May 22, 1974.

KAVANAGH, THOMAS MATTHEW, state justice; b. Carson City, Mich., Aug. 4, 1909; s. Thomas and Margaret (Barrett) K.; J.D., U. Detroit, 1932; m. Agnes C. Miller, Oct. 27, 1930 dec. June 1974); children—Doris Jeanne (Mrs. Donald Closser), Donna Joan (Mrs. Thomas Baker), Patricia (Mrs. Owen Kean), Kathleen (Mrs. Harry Zipperer). Admitted Mich. bar, 1932; practice in Detroit, 1932-35, Carson City, 1935-55; city atty., Carson City and Perrington, Mich., 1943-54; village clk. Carson City, 1943-54; atty. gen. Mich., 1954-57; justice Mich. Supreme Ct., 1957-75, chief justice, 1964-67, 71-75. Chmn. Gt. Lakes Commn., 1955-57. Candidate for Mich. Legislature, 1938. Mem. Am., Ionia-Montcalm (pres.), Ingham County bar assns., State Bar Mich. Roman Catholic. K.C. (state dep. 1952-54; mem. supreme bd. dirs.). Lion (pres. 1941-42). Home: Lansing, Mich. Died Apr. 19, 1975.

KAY, (GEORGE) MARSHALL, geologist, educator; b. Paisley, Ont., Can., Nov. 10, 1904; s. George Frederick and Bethea (Hopper) K.; B.A., U. Ia., 1924, M.S., 1925; student U. Chgo., 1924; Ph.D., Columbia, 1929; D.Sc., Middlebury Coll., 1974; m. Inez Margaret Clark, June 8, 1935; children—Elizabeth (Mrs. R.A. Berner), Katherine (Mrs. D.B. Vielmetti), Robert, Richard. Lectr. Barnard Coll., 1929-30, instr., 1930-31; instr. Columbia, 1931-37; asst. prof., 1937-42, asso. prof., 1942-44, prof. geology, 1944-67, exec. officer dept., 1953-56, Newberry prof. geology, 1967-73, prof. emeritus, 1973-75, chmn. dept., 1971-73; adminstrn. com. war research, 1944-46. Geologist, U.S. Geol. Survey, 1943-46; organizer, dir. Gander Conf. Continental Drift, Nfld., 1967; vis. prof. Rutgers U., 1974-75. Mem. bd. mgrs. N.Y. Bot. Garden, 1961-75. Recipient George F. Kunz prize, N.Y. Acad. Sci., 1941; Distinguished Service medal U. Ia., 1971. Del. Internat. Geol. Congress, Moscow, USSR, 1937, London, Eng., 1948, Copenhagen, Denmark, 1960, Montreal, Que., 1972. Fellow Geol. Soc. Am. (Penrose medal 1971), A.A.A.S., Paleontol. Soc. (v.p. 1945), N.Y. Acad., Sci. (v.p. 1944-45), Ia. Acad. Sci., Am. Assn. Petroleum Geologists (distinguished lectr. 1943), Palaeontol. Assn., Paleontol. Soc. Japan, Soc. Econ. Paleontologists and Mineralogists, Geol. Assn. Can., Am. Geophys. Union, Geol. Soc. London (hon. fgn.), Geol. Soc. Stockholm (hon. corr.), Phi Beta Kappa, Sigma Xi (nat. bd. 1968-72). Presbyn. Author: North American Geosynclines, 1951; (with E.H. Colbert) Stratigraphy and Life History, 1965. Editor: North Atlantic-Geology and Continental Drift, 1969. Contbr. articles on stratigraphy and tectonics to profl. jours. Home: Leonia, N.J., Died Sept. 3, 1975.

KAY-SCOTT, CYRIL (FREDERIC CREIGHTON), artist; b. nr. Richmond, Va., Jan. 3, 1879; s. Wheeler Montgomery and Nellie Jane (Blake) S.; ed. U. of London; art edn., Academie Colorossi, Paris; pupil of Robert Fleury, Bonnat, Moreau and Quelvee; m. Evelyn Scott, Dec. 26, 1913 (divorced); 1 son, Creighton. Founder and former dir. El Paso (Tex.) Art Sch.; founder, dir. and head of dept. of painting in summer session, Santa Fe (N.M.) Art Sch.; prof. drawing and painting, Chappell Sch. of Art, Denver, Colo.; dean of Sch. of Art, U. of Denver. Has exhibited at Paris, London, Munich, Berlin, Brussels, New York, etc. Rep. in Denver Art Mus. and pvt. collections. Dir. Denver Art Mus. Democrat. Mem. Anglican Ch. Club: Cactus. Author: Blind Mice, 1921; Sinbad, 1923; Siren, 1925; In the Endless Sands (with Evelyn Scott), 1925. Contbr. criticism, verse and short stories to mags. Home: Denver, Colo.*†

KAZANJIAN, VARAZTAD HOVHANNES, oral and plastic surgeon; b. Armenia, Mar. 18, 1879; s. Hovhannes and Anna K.; prep. edn., Jesuit Coll., Sivas, Armenia; came to U.S. at 16; D.M.D., Harvard, 1905. M.D., 1921; D.Sc. (hon.), Bowdoin Coll., 1952; m. Sophie Cuendet, 1912 (dec. 1919); m. Marion V. Hanford, Aug. 1923; children—Helene, Sophie, Joan, Victor. Practiced dental surgery, 1905-15; prof. clin. oral surgery Harvard, 1919-41, prof. plastic surgery, 1941-47, prof. emeritus from 1947. Mem. bd. of consultation Mass. Gen. Hosp.; cons. surgeon for plastic operations Mass. Eye and Ear Infirmary; surgeon Mt. Auburn Hosp.; also mem. cons. staff several other hosps. Served as mem. Harvard Unit, B.E.F., 1915-16; maj. and surg. specialist for wounds of face and jaw until 1919. Decorated Companion St. Michael and St. George. Diplomate Am. Bd. Plastic Surgery. Fellow Am. Coll. Surgeons, Am. Coll. Dentists, Am. Acad. Ophthalmology and Otolaryngology; mem. Am. and Mass. med. assns. Am. and Mass. dental assns., Am. Assn. Plastic Surgeons, Am. Soc. Maxillofacial Surgeons, New Eng. Soc. Plastic and Reconstructive Surgery, Internat. Soc. Plastic Surgeons, Am. Assn. Plastic and Reconstructive Surgery, New Eng. Soc. Oral Surgeons; hon. fellow Brit. Assn. Plastic Surgeons, Royal Acad. Physicians, and Surgeons, Am. Acad.

Dental Sci. Club: Harvard (Boston). Author: (with Dr. John Marquis Converse) The Surgical Treatment of Facial Injuries 1949. 59, 74. Author of numerous articles on plastic and reconstructive restoration of face and jaws. Home: Belmont, Mass. Died Oct. 19, 1974; interred Mt. Auburn Cemetery, Cambridge, Mass.

KEARL, CHASE DELMAR, educator, assn. exec.; b. Provo, Utah, July 26, 1917; s. Chase and Hazel (Loveless) K.; student U. Ida., 1935-37; B.S., Utah State U., 1941; M.S., Cornell U., 1947, Ph.D., 1949; m. Marjorie Lee Lail, Feb. 1, 1943; children—Sandra, Steven, Gail, Kenneth, Rodney, Debra Ann, Shari Lynn. Missionary, Latter-day Saints Ch., Eng., 1937-39; with Adel Precision Products, 1941-42; from asst. to prof. Cornell U., 1949-73; vis. asso. prof. U. Philippines, 1954-56; farm planning adv. Dept. Agr., Uganda, 1960. Served to 1st lt. AUS, 1942-46. Mem. Am. Farm Econ. Assn. (sec.-treas.), Internat. Conf. Agrl. Economists, Alpha Zeta, Phi Kappa Phi, Pi Gamma Mu, Sigma Alpha Epsilon. Mem. Ch. of Jesus Christ of Latter-day Saints. Author articles agrl. econs. Home: Freville, N.Y. Died June 27, 1973.

KEARNEY, FRANCIS WILLIAM, educator; b. Stoneboro, Pa., Feb. 16, 1912; s. William F. and Julia (Tobin) K.; B.A., St. Bonaventure (N.Y.) U., 1934; M.A., Columbia, 1942; Ph.L., Laval (Qua.) U., 1944, Ph.D., 1945. Joined Order of Friars Minor, ordained priest Roman Cath. Ch., 1938; prof. philosphy St. Bonaventure U., 1939-41, dean dept., 1949-53, pres. univ., 1961-67; prof. philosophy St. Stephen's Coll., Croghan, N.Y., 1949-53; rector St. Francis Coll., Rye Beach, N.H., 1953-61; prof. philosophy Siena Coll., Loudonville, N.Y., 1967-70, St. Bonaventure U., 1969-76. Address: Loudonville, N.Y., Died Jan. 30, 1976.

KEATING, KENNETH B., lawyer, former ambassador; b. Lima, N.Y., May 18, 1900; s. Thomas Mosgrove and Louise (Barnard) K.; student Genesee Wesleyan Sem., 1911-15, A.B., U. Rochester, 1919, LL.D., 1954; LL.B., Harvard, 1923; LL.D., LeMoyne U., Hobart Coll., L.I. U., Hamilton Coll., Union Coll., Adelphi Coll., R.I. U., Franklin Pierce Coll., Bklyn. Coll. Law.; D.C.L., Pace Coll.; L.H.D., Yeshiva U., Alfred U., N.Y. Med. Coll., Clarkson Coll., Dowling Coll.; Litt.D., Elmire Coll.; m. Louise Depuy, Apr. 11, 1928 (dec.); 1 dau., Judith; m. Mary P. Davis, June 7, 1974. Practice law, Rochester, N.Y., 1923-48; mem. firm Harris, Beach, Keating, Wilcox, Dale & Linowitz; mem. 80th-82d congresses 40th N.Y. Dist.; 83d-85th congresses 38th N.Y. Dist.; U.S. senator from N.Y., 1958-65; asso. justice N.Y. Ct. Appeals, 1966-69; ambassador to India, 1969-72; ambassador to Israel, 1973-1975. Mem. Congl. delegation Council of Europe, Interparliamentary Union, Washington, 1953, Vienna, 1954, Helsinki, 1955, Bangkok, 1956, London, 1957; del. intergovtl. com. European Migration Confs., 1956, 57. Served with U.S. Army, World War I, from maj. to brig. gen., World War II. Decorated Legion of Merit with oak leaf cluster, Order of Brit. Empire. Mem. Am. Legion, V.F.W., Res. Officers Assn., Am., N.Y. State, N.Y.C., New York County, Rochester bar assns., U. Rochester Alumni, S.A.R., Phi Beta Kappa, Delta Upsilon. Republican. Presbyn. Mason (33 deg., Shriner), Moose, Eagle, Elk. Clubs: Brook, Sky (N.Y.C.); Genesee Valley, University (Rochester); Alfalfa, F Street (Washington). Home: Princeton, N.J. Died May 5, 1975.

KECK, HERBERT ALLEN, clergyman; b. Cawker City, Kan., Feb. 13, 1879; s. Emanuel and Marie (Schumacher) K.; A.B., Morningside Coll., Sioux City, Ia., 1901, D.D., 1917; S.T.B., Boston U., 1908; m. Harriet M. McCutchen Sept. 19, 1905; children—Richard McCutchen, Robert Clifton, Carleton Allen, Herbert Allen (dec.). Ordained to the ministry M.E. Ch., 1901; pastor Ute, Ia., 1901-02, Danbury, 1902-04, Holstein, 1904-05, Garner, 1908-12, Sioux City, 1912-18, Champaign, Ill., 1918-28, Trinity Ch., Evansville, Ind., 1928-41, First Methodist Ch., Ottumwa, Ia., 1941, pastor Kenwood Methodist Ch., Milwaukee, Wis. Mem. Wis. Conf., Meth. Ch. Mem. City Club (Milwaukee, Wis.). Republican. Mason. Kiwanian. Contbr. articles to church publs. Lecturer. Home: Evanston, Ill.†

KEEDY, EDWIN ROULETTE, educator; b. Boonsboro, Md., Jan. 19, 1880; s. Reuben Miller and Anne Elizabeth (Roulette) K.; A.B., Franklin and Marshall Coll., 1899; LL.B., Harvard Univ., 1906; LL.D., Franklin and Marshall, 1927, U. Pa., 1950. Asso. prof. law, Ind. U., 1906-09; prof. law, Northwestern U., 1909-15, U. of Pa., 1915-50, dean 1940-45. Spl. Commr. Am. Inst. Crim. Law and Criminology to investigate adminstration of criminal law in England, 1909, Scotland, 1911. Investigated administration of criminal law in France, 1931-32. Pres. Am. br. Internat. Law Assn., 1929; co-reporter (with W. E. Mikell) for criminal procedure, Am. Law Inst.; mem. Am. Bar Assn., Am. Inst. Criminal Law and Criminology (pres. 1924), Am. Law Inst., Phi Beta Kappa, Phi Kappa Psi, Phi Delta Phi. Democrat. Mem. Reformed Ch. in U.S. Commd. maj. judge advocate, Mar. 15, 1918, lt. col., Oct. 29, 1918, col., July 10, 1919; mem. Bd. of Rev. Judge Advocate Gen.'s Dept., Aug. 1918-Aug. 1919; chmn. Selective Service Board of Appeal, Phila., 1941; compliance commr. War Prodn. Bd., 1943. Clubs: University, Franklin Inn, Art Alliance, Harvard (New York); Authors' (London). Author: Cases on Agency; Cases on Adminstration of Criminal Law; also articles in legal periodicals. Home: Philadelphia, Pa.†

KEEGAN, JANE CLAUDIA, educator; b. Ft. Lyon, Colo., July 20, 30, 1922; d. John William and Mae Elizabeth (Cahill) Keegan; B.S., St. Mary Coll., 1954; M.A., U. Portland, 1966. Asso. librarian, St. Mary Coll., Leavenworth, Kan., 1958-65; asst. dean women U. Portland (Ore.), 1965-66; prof. library adminstrn. Lewis-Clark Satte Coll., Lewiston, Ida, 1966-75, mem. advminstrv. council, dean's div. chmn. com., library adv. com., faculty rank and salary com. Mem. World Book Evaluation Com., 1964; cons. library service Regional Med. Task Force, 1968-75. Mem. Ida. Gov.'s Commn. Libraries, 1969-71. Charter mem. Ida. Vote Rockers, 1969. Mem. Am., Catholic (chmn. Book Week 1962-65), Pacific N.W. (chmn. nominating com. 1970), Ida. (chmn. coll.-univ. div. 1968-69) library assns., Luna House Hist. Assn., Am. Assn. U. Profs., United Native Americans. Club: Soroptimist (rec. sec. 1968-70) (Lewiston, Clarkston, Wash.). Home: Lewiston, Ida., Died Dec. 18, 1975.

KEELER, ELLEN COUGHLIN (MRS. RALPH WELLES KEELER), b. Kingston, Pa., Dec. 13, 1880; d. James M. and Mary E. Welter; B.A., Wellesley, 1902; post-grad. work Teachers Coll. (Columbia); m. Rev. Ralph Welles Keeler, July 11, 1906; children—Eleanor Elizabeth, Ralph Welles. Teacher high sch., Wilkes-Barre, Pa., 1903-06, active in ch. work, tchr. of religious edn., First M.E. Ch., Germantown, Phila., 1918-20; nat. chmn. of exhibits, Woman's Home Missionary Soc. M.E. Ch., 1919-24; dir. religious edn., Crawford Memorial M.E. Ch., N.Y., City, 1924-29, dir. religious edn., Goodsell Memorial M.E. Ch., Brooklyn. Democrat. Mem. Federation of Women's Clubs, N.Y. City. Clubs: College, Wellesley (Phila.). Author: The Christian Conquest of America (brochure), 1919, The Balance Wheel, 1920. Writer and lecturer on the immigrant, home economics, the church, religious education, missions, Camp Fire work, etc. Home: Brooklyn, N.Y.†

KEENA, LEO JOHN, consular service; b. Detroit, Mich., Apr. 12, 1878; s. James T. and Henrietta (Boyle) K.; student Detroit Coll., 1890-96; U. of Mich., 1897-1900; m. Eleanor Clarke, Aug. 18, 1906; children—Joan Eleanor, David Pierrepont W., Peter James Trafton. Seaman U.S.S. Yosemite, Spanish-Am. War, 1898. In mining, lumbering and office equipment business. Consul at Chihuahua, Mex., 1909-10, Florence, Italy, 1910-14; consul-gen., Buenos Aires, Argentina, 1914-15, Valparaiso, Chile, 1915-19, Zurich, Switzerland, 1919-20, Warsaw, Poland, 1920-24, Liverpool, England, 1924-27, Havana, Cuba, 1927-29, Paris, France, 1929-34; counselor of Embassy, Paris, 1934; minister at Tegueigalpa, Honduras, 1935-37; minister to South Africa, 1937-43; retired. Club: University (Detroit). Address: Washington, D.C.†

KEENE, CHARLES HERBERT, med. educator; b. Palmyra, Me., Feb. 8, 1875; s. Herbert Norris and Mary Florence (Pratt) K.; A.B., Harvard, 1898, M.D., 1902, grad. study, summers 1908, 09; m. Louise Josephine McLaughlin, Nov. 30, 1904; children—Charles Russell, Marjorie Louise, Mary Elizabeth, Donald Herbert. In practice of medicine at Lowell and Boston, Mass., 1902-09; dir. hygiene and physical edn., pub. schs., Minneapolis, Minn., 1909-19; exec. sec. Del. State Tuberculosis Commn., 1919; dir. health service, N.E. div. Am. Red Cross, 1920; dir. Bur. Health Edn., Dept. Pub. Instrn., Pa., 1921-25; professor hygiene and dir. of health and physical edn., U. Buffalo, from 1925; instr., lectr. summer schs. several colls. and univs., from 1917. Served as pvt. U.S. Vols., Spanish-Am. War; mem. Mass. N.G., advancing to lt. col., 1898-1910; capt., later maj. Med. Corps, A.U.S., World War I. Medal Award of Ling Found.; William A. Howe Honor Award of Am. Sch. Health Assn.; Honor Award Am. Phys. Ednl. Assn. Fellow Am. Pub. Health Assn.; mem. A.M.A., other nat., state and local med. assns., ednl. socs., phys. edn. socs. and related assns. Mason. Clubs: Harvard (Buffalo); Harvard (Boston). Author several books in field, 1914-48; also many special articles on physical education and pub. health. Editor: Jour. of School Health, from 1937. Home: Kenmore, N.Y.†

KEITH, NATHANIEL S., urban planner; b. Cin., Dec. 30, 1906; s. Nathaniel S. and Alice (Munhall) K.; A.B. magna cum laude, Brown U., 1929; m. Marjorie MacDonald, May 21, 1932; children—Anthony (dec.), Penelope (Mrs. K. Trickett). Staff writer covering automobile, aviation, r.r. and rubber industries Wall St. Jour., N.Y.C., 1929-38, specializing in govt. finance, Washington, 1938-40; bus. editor PM, N.Y.C., 1940; editor Insured Mortgage Portfolio (pub. Fed. Housing Adminstrn.), 1941, asst. dir. pub. relations FHA, 1942; asst. dir. information Nat. Housing Agy., 1943-44, spl. asst. to adminstr. responsible for liaison with Congress, 1944-47; asst. to Housing and Home Finance Adminstr., responsible for liaison with Congress and with nat. orgns. active in housing, 1947-49, dir. slum clearance and urban devel., 1949-53; housing and redevel. cons., 1953-72, (Washington, Buffalo, San Juan, P.R., V.I., other cities). Mem. adv. com. on housing and urban devel. AID. Mem. Nat. Capital Democratic Club, Washington. Trustee Found. Coop. Housing. Mem. Nat. Assn. Housing and Redevel. Ofcls., Nat. Housing Conf. (chmn.), Phi Beta Kappa, Phi Kappa Psi. Clubs: Cosmos, Potomac Appalachian Trail. Author: (with Charles C. Colt) 28 Days, A History of Banking Crisis, 1933; (with James W. Rouse) No Slums in 10 Years, 1955; (with Carl Feiss) A Report on the Renewal Possibilities of the Historic Triangle of the City of San Juan; (with C. Feiss) The Future of Buffalo, 1958, The Community Renewal Program for Rochester, N.Y., 1963, Community Renewal Program for the Virgin Islands, 1966; The Future of Downtown Rochester, 1965; Housing America's Low and Moderate Income Families, 1968; Buffalo Community Renewal Progeam, 1971; Politics and the Housing Crisis Since 1930, 1973. Home: Washington, D.C. Died Nov. 24, 1973.

KEITH, ROBERT J., flour co. exec.; b. Eau Claire, Wis., Mar. 23, 1914; s. Alexander J. and Katharine (Kennedy) K.; student pub. schs.; m. Freda Christensen, Mar. 29, 1937; children—Katharine K. (Mrs. Jackson), Robert J. With No. States Power Co., 1931-33, Nat. Pressure Cooker Co., 1934-35; joined Pillsbury Co. (formerly Pillsbury Mills, Inc.), 1935, v.p., 1950-56, exec. v.p., 1956-65, pres., 1965-67, chmn., chief exec. officer, 1967-73, also dir., dir. First Bank System, Inc., McQuay, Inc., Dayton Hudson Corp. Clubs: Woodhill, Minneapolis. Home: Wayzata Minn. Died May 27, 1973.

KEITT, WILLIAM LAWRENCE, law librarian; b. Hubbard, Tex., Oct. 11, 1905; s. William Edward and Ernestine (Shelton) K.; A.B., U. Tex., 1926; LL.B., George Washington U., 1931; S.J.D., Harvard, 1934. Instr. Staunton (Va.) Mil. Acad., 1927-28; asst., asst.-in-charge law library in capitol Library Congress, Washington, 1928-31; law librarian and general counsel, Library of Congress, Washington, 1949-63, ret.; research fellow at Harvard Law Sch., 1931-34; admitted to D.C. bar, 1931, N.Y. bar, 1942; atty. U.S. Dept. Agr., 1934-37; legal dept. Nat. Dairy Products Corp., N.Y.C., 1937-43; asso. law firm Cummings, Stanley, Truitt & Cross, Washington, 1945-48. Mem. Am. Bar Assn., Am. Assn. Law Libraries, Sigma Phi Epsilon, Phi Delta Phi. Baptist. Author: Annotated Bibliography of Bibliographies Statutory Materials of The United States, 1934. Home: Washinngton, D.C. Died Apr. 27, 1974.

KELCEY, GUY, cons. engr.; b. Dunchurch, Ont., Can., June 1, 1889; s. George Henry and Jane (Tully) K.; brought to U.S., 1899; B.S., Carnegie Inst. Tech., 1914; D. Engring., Newark Coll. Engring., 1958; m. Grace Elizabeth Saxe, Oct. 2, 1918 (dec. May 1965); children—Theodosia (Mrs. Raymond Moyer Dean), Virginia (Mrs. George Havens Leland); m. 2d, Jane Townsend Dowell, June 1966. With City Engr.'s Office, Lackawanna, N.Y., 1907-08, Peoples Savs. & Trust Co., also E.W. Clark & Co., Pitts., 1914-17, Rush Machinery Co., Pitts., 1919-20; mgr. traffic engring. div. Am. Gas Accumulator Co., Elizabeth, N.J., 1920-41; pres. Vehicular Parking, Ltd., Newark, 1941-42; regional dir. So. states, div. local transport U.S. Office Def. Transp., Atlanta, 1942-44; hwy. transp. analyst Port of N.Y. Authority, 1944-45; partner Edwards & Kelcey, engrs., 1945-58; chmn. Edwards & Kelcey, Inc., Newark, 1957-73; participated as cons. engr. N.J. Turnpike, N.Y. Thruway, N.J. Garden State Pkwy., urban expressways in Conn., Mass., also Spain and other countries; traffic and transp. studies N.Y., other met. areas. Charge mission Am. Engrs., hwy. program in Iraq; adv. com. dept. civil engring., Newark Coll. Engring.; mem. nat. coms. on engring. and econ. problems of transp. traffic, hwys.; vis. lectr. transp. and hwy. traffic Yale, Harvard, other univs. Pilot officer AC, U.S. Army, 1917-19. Life fellow Am. Soc. C.E.; mem. Inst. Traffic Engrs. (hon. life; Motson award 1966; Burton W. Marsh award for distinguished service to traffic engring. 1972), Am. Inst. Cons. Engrs., Hwy. Research Bd., Am. Road Builders Assn. (dir. and pres. engring. div.), Internat. Rd. Fedn., Legion Aviators Post, Delta Upsilon, Chi Epsilon. Episcopalian. Clubs: Quiet Birdmen, Adventurers, Engineers (N.Y.C.); Essex (Newark). Author tech. publs. Home: Westfield, N.J., Died Aug. 9, 1973.

KELEHER, WILLIAM L., coll. prof.; b. Woburn, Mass., Jan. 27, 1906; s. William Henry (M.D.) and Elizabeth A. (Lane) K.; ed., St. Charles Parochial Sch., Woburn, 1910-18; Boston Coll. High Sch., 1918-22; A.B., Holy Cross Coll., 1922-26, M.S., 1933; A.M., Weston Coll., Mass., 1929-32, S.T.L., 1934-38. Mem. Society of Jesus, from 1926, student classics and ascetical theol., 1926-29; instr. chem., Holy Cross Coll., 1933-34; asst. provincial, Jesuits, New England, 1939-42; superior of Jesuit novices, Lenox, Mass., 1942-45; pres. Boston Coll., 1945-51; prof. psychology Holy Cross Coll., Worcester, Mass., from 1951. Home: Worcester, Mass., Died 1975.

KELKER, JAMES JOSEPH ARTHUR, civil engr.; b. Fort Wayne, Ind., May 20, 1906; s. Arthur Dennis and Clara (Kukuk) K.; B.S. in Civil Engring., Purdue U., 1929, P.C.E., 1933; m. Elizabeth McGaughey, June 17, 1932 (dec. May 1954); children—Francis James, Nancy Lee; m. 2d, Elizabeth Houston, Nov. 3, 1961. Engr. to v.p. Ohio Oil Co., Marshall, Ill., 1929-31, engr. Shreveport (La.) div., 1931-41, 46-61; pvt. practice cons. civil engr., Shreveport, 1961-73. Scoutmaster, Norweia council Boy Scouts Am., 1951-73. Served to col. Arty., AUS, 1941-46; PTO. Recipient Order of

Arrow, 1951, Silver Beaver award Boy Scouts Am., 1960. Mem. Am. Legion, Contour, Delta Chi, Chi Epsilon. Rotarian (hon.). Died Nov. 7, 1973

KELLEMS, VIVIEN, mfr., engr.; b. Des Moines, Ia., June 7, 1896; d. Rev. David Clinton and Louisa (Flint) Kellems; A.B., U. of Ore., 1918, A.M., 1920; grad. study Columbia, 1921-22; unmarried. Began in 1928 to manufacture a cable grip invented by her brother, Edgar E.; founder, pres. Kellems Co. Mem. Am. Inst. E.E. Author: Toil, Taxes and Trouble. Home: East Haddam, Conn. Died Jan. 25, 1975.

KELLENBERGER, HUNTER, educator; b. Newark O., Feb. 14, 1904; s. Charles William and Helen (Hunter) K.; A.B., Kenyon Coll., 1925; A.M., Princeton, 1928, Ph.D., 1931; m. Esther Rodman Stone, May 3, 1941; children—Gordon Hunter, Judith Rodman (Mrs. John J. Stella, Jr.). Latin master DeVeaux Sch., 1925-27; French master Northwood Sch., Lake Placid Club, N.Y., 1931-33; traveling fellow Am. Council Learned Socs., 1933-34; instr. French, Princeton, 1934-35, 37-38; asst. prof. Brown U., 1938-46, asso. prof., 1946-47, prof. French, 1947-71, emeritus, 1971-75, chmn. div. modern langs., 1946-60, chmn. dept. French, 1960-64. Chmn. Northeastern Conf. Teaching Fgn. Langs., 1954. Mem. Modern Lang. Assn. Am., Am. Assn. Tchrs. French, New Eng. Fgn. (pres. 1961-62), R.I. (pres. 1968-69) fgn lang. assns., Providence Athenaeum. Episcopalian. Author: The Influence of Accentuation on French Word Order, 1932; contbg. author The Case for Basic Education 1959. Editor com. reports. Home: Providence R.I. Died Apr. 12, 1975.

KELLER, HENRY, JR., textile co. exec.; b. Harrisburg, Pa., May 9, 1922; s. Henry and Susanna (Safnauer) K.; student U. Ga., 1947-51; LL.B., Woodrow Wilson Coll. Law, 1953; m. Jane Palmer, Apr. 9, 1944; children—Julia Louise, Jan Elaine. With U.S. Treasury Dept., Atlanta, 1948-53; spl. assignments West Point Mfg. Co. (Ga.), 1953-57, asst. treas., 1957-62, sec., 1962-65; sec. West Point-Pepperell, Inc., 1965-70, asst. treas., from 1970. Sec. Community Service Assn., Shawmut, Ala., 1962-70, W. Point Pepperell Found., 1962-70. Served with AUS, 1942-45; ETO. Mem. Ga. Bar Assn., Ga. Soc. C.P.A.'s. Baptist (deacon). Home: West Point, Ga. Deseased.

KELLEY, BETHEL BOWLES, lawyer; b. Bardstown, Ky., Dec. 6, 1912; s. John S. and Myrtle (Troutman) K.; A.B., U. Mich., 1934, J.D., 1937; m. Jane Hamilton, Dec. 21, 1940; children—Patricia, Nancy, Mary Beth. Admitted to Ky. bar, 1936, Mich. bar, 1937; asso. firm Harold R. Smith, Detroit, 1937-40, Grafton & Grafton, Louisville, 1940-41; mem. firm Cross, Wrock, Miller, Vieson & Kelley, Detroit, 1941-67, Dykema, Gossett, Spencer, Goodnow & Trigg, Detroit, 1967-74. Lawyer in residence Wake Forest U., Winston-Salem, N.C., 1974. Dir. Mich.-Ohio Pipeline Corp., Mt. Pleasant, Mich. Trustee Alma Coll. Served to lt. USNR, 1943-46. Mem. Am., Detroit bar assns., State Bar Mich., Delta Kappa Epsilon. Republican. Clubs: Detroit Athletic, Pere Marquette Rod and Gun, Secord; Orchard Lake Country. Home: Birmingham, Mich. Died June 15, 1974.

KELLOGG, ANGEL IVEY (MRS. KARL BRITTAN KELLOGG), club woman; b. Seattle, Nov. 30, 1922; d. Joseph Nettles and Margaret (Armstrong) Ivey; B.S., U. Wash., 1948; m. Karl Brittan Kellogg, Aug. 12, 1955. Dietetic intern N.Y. Hosp., 1949; dietitian Providence Hosp., Seattle, 1953-55. Chmn. local affairs Baton Rouge chpt. League Women Voters, 1955-56, chmn. state affairs, 1956-57, chmn. finance, 1956-57, 1st v.p., 1958-59, bd. dir. La., 1957-60; bd. dirs. Baton Rouge YWCA, 1957-60, sec. bd. dirs., 1958-59, chmn. pub. relations, 1957-59, chmn. nominating com., 1959-60; capt. United Givers, Baton Rouge, 1962-63, vice chmn., 1964; editor newsletter Baton Rouge Civic Symphony Women's Auxiliary, 1958-59, 1st v.p., 1958-59, pres., 1959-60; bd. dirs. Baton Rouge Civic Symphony Assn., 1957-60; family investigator Goodfellows, 1962-62; vol. Am. Cancer Soc., Baton Rouge, 1963-64, sect. leader; mem. edn. com. La. Commn. Status of Women, 1965-68; chmn. Equal Rights Amendments Com. of Baton Rouge, 1970-71. Precinct committeewoman 45th dist. Seattle Dem. Party, 1954-55. Mem. Baton Rouge Chamber Music Soc., La. Ornithol. Soc., Internat. Platform Assn., La. State Women's Polit. Caucus, Nat. Orgn. Women. Democrat. Methodist. Clubs: Bocage Racquet, Baton Rouge Country (Baton Rouge). Contbr. story mag. Home: Baton Rouge, La. Died Dec. 31, 1974.

KELLOGG, HOWARD, mfr.; b. Buffalo, N.Y., Mar. 26, 1881; s. Spencer and Jane Vrooman (Morris) K.; grad. Heathcote Sch. (pvt.), Buffalo, 1898, Phillips Acad., Exeter, N.H., 1899; A.B., Harvard, 1903; m. Cyrena A. Case, Mar. 27, 1906 (died 1931); children—Martha, Howard, Spencer; m. 2d, Mrs. Lily Ann May Bowen, July 21, 1933. Began with Spencer Kellogg, mfr. and refiner vegetable oils, Buffalo, 1903, made v.p. and gen. mgr., 1912; pres. Spencer Kellogg & Sons, Inc., 1922-47, chmn. bd., from 1947. Mem. bd. dirs. Buffalo Soc. Nat. Sciences. Republican. Presbyterian. Clubs: Buffalo Athletic, Buffalo Club, Wanakah Country, Country. Home: Derby, N.Y.†

KELLSTADT, CHARLES H., merchant; b. Columbus, O., Oct. 9, 1896; s. Charles Henry and Mary Cecilia (Lynch) K.; student Ohio State U., 1915; LL.D., Mundelein Coll., Chgo., 1959, Rockhurst (Ill.) Coll., 1960, Loyola U., Chgo., 1962; B.C.S., Duquesne U., 1960, Suffolk U., Boston, 1961; B.A., Biscayne Coll., 1973; m. Marquerite Elizabeth Stewart, Nov. 30, 1916 (dec. 1975). Asst. display mgr. Union Co., Columbus, 1913-17; advt. mgr. Frankenberger & Co., Charleston, W.Va., 1917-19; mgr. Kramer's, Akron, O., 1919-20; v.p., gen. mgr. Kinney and Levan Co., Cleve., 1921-32; with Sears, Roebuck & Co., 1932-62, pres., 1958-60, chmn. bd., chief exec. officer, 1960-62; chmn. trustee Sears Savs. and Profit Sharing Pension Fund, 1962-67, chmn. investment com., 1967-70; chmn. bd., chief exec. officer Gen. Devel. Corp., 1963-75; dir. Delta Air Lines, Jack Eckerd Corp., Stewart-Warner Corp., Gen. Devel. Corp., Affiliate Artists, Inc. City Investing Mortgage Group, Simpsons-Sears Ltd., Allstate Ins. Co., Ford Motor Co., Whirlpool Corp., Gen. Industries Co., Eastern Airlines, Mosler Safe Co., Scott Paper Co., numerous others; pub. gov. N.Y. Stock Exchange. Chmn. Logistics Mgmt. Inst.; bd. dirs. Council Better Bus. Burs., Inc.; sr. mem. Conf. Bd.; mem. industry adv. com. Advt. Council; Com. 100-Miami Beach, Fla.; mem. Hundred Club Broward County, Fla. Vice chmn. Eisenhower Exchange Fellowships; asso. mem. So. Fla. council Boy Scouts Am. Hon. dir. Rockhurst Coll., So. Research Inst., Holy Cross Hosp., Ft. Lauderdale, Fla.; bd. dirs. Henrietta Egleston Hosp. for children; active A.R.C. lay trustee Loyola U., hgo., mem. Med. Center com.; bd. advisers Cath. Charities; adv. bd. Sch. Bus., I. Miami. Knight of Malt. Clubs: Capital City, Commerce (Atlanta); Union, Advertising (Cleve.); Chicago, Commercial, Old Elm (Chgo.); Miami, Indian Creek (Miami). Home: Lauderdale-by-the-Sea, Fla. Died Oct. 1, 1975; interred Chicago, Ill.

KELLY, ALFRED HINSEY, educator, historian; b. Pekin, Ill., June 23, 1907; s. Raymond Ransom and Bessie Mae (Case) K.; Ph.B., U. Chgo., 1931, A.M., 1934, Ph.D., 1938; m. Emily May Peterson, Sept. 22, 1935; children—Elizabeth Marie (Mrs. Donald Breneau), Virginia Jayne, Alfred Herbert. Mem. faculty Wayne State U., Detroit, 1935-76, prof. history, chmn. dept., 1952-74 acting dean grad. studies, to 1976. Tech. advisor preparation Supreme Ct. brief Brown vs. Board, N.A.A.C.P., 1953; apptd. to Oliver Wendell Holmes Devise, 1970. Mich. co-chmn. Vols. for Stevenson, 1952, Detroit chmn., 1956. Served to lt. USNR, 1944-46. Mem. Am., So. hist. assns., Orgn. Am. Historians. Club: Orpheus (Detroit). Author: (with W. A. Harbison) The American Constitution: Its Origins and Development, 4th edit., 1970. Editor, author: American Foreign Policy and American Democracy, 1954, 5th edit., 1976; Foundations of Freedom, 1958. Contbr. articles profl. jours. Home: Grosse Pointe Park, Mich., Died Feb. 16, 1976.

KELLY, EDWARD WENDELL, JR., physician; b. Kosse, Tex., Apr. 28, 1907; s. Edward Wendell and Oma Ann Kelly; M.D., Howard U., 1933; m. Eula Stephens, Dec. 24, 1938; children—Edward Wendell III, Burnett Stephens. Intern, St. Mary's Infirmary, St. Louis, 1933-35; fellow in dermatology Wayne State U., 1949-52, from instr. to asso. prof., 1952-71; fellow in dermatology Detroit Receiving Hosp., 1949-52, attending in dermatology, 1952-71; dermatologist Mich. Children's Hosp.; asso. dermatologist Hutzel Hosp.; instr., cons. Detroit Gen. Hosp. Active YMCA, N.A.A.C.P. Trustee, Philander Smith Coll., Little Rock. Diplomate Am. Bd. Dermatology. Mem. A.M.A., Central States Dermatol. Assn., Nat. Med. Assn., Wayne County Med. Soc., Soc. Investigative Dermatology, Howard U. Alumni Assn., Sigma Xi, Alpha Phi Alpha. Contbr. articles to profl. jours. Home: Detroit, Mich. Died Sept. 18, 1971; buried Detroit Meml. Park Cemetery.

KELLY, GENEVIEVE RUTH, librarian; b. West Hollywood, Cal., Apr. 12, 1927; d. James John and Bertha (Gilligan) Kelly; A.B., Westmont Coll., 1948; M.A., U. So. Cal., 1951, M.S. in L.S., 1953, Ph.D. (Am. Theol. Library Assn. research grant), 1965; B.D. (Hons.), U. London, 1966. Asst. librarian Am. Baptist Sem. of West, Covina, Cal., 1951-54, librarian, 1954-75. Organist Holliston Av. United Meth. Ch. Mem. Am. (pres. 1971-72), Western (pres. 1962-63) theol. library assns., Am., Cal. library assns., Am. Baptist Hist. Soc. (bd. mgrs. 1970—), Mediaeval Acad. Am., Mediaeval Assn. Pacific, Am. Guild Organists. Baptist. Contbr. articles to profl. jours. Address: Covina, Cal., Died Oct. 15, 1975.

KELLY, GEORGE, dramatist; b. Phila., Pa., Jan. 16, 1887; s. John Henry and Mary (Costello) K.; ed. privately; A.F.D. (hon.), LaSalle Coll. of Pa., 1962; unmarried. Début in juvenile roles, N.Y.C., 1912, later with touring companies; author of a succession of one-act plays, of which Finders Keepers was the first; among full length plays are The Torchbearers (a satire on the little theatre movement in America); The Show-Off; Craig's Wife (Pulitzer prize 1925); Daisy Mayme, 1926; Behold the Bridegroom, 1927; Maggie the Magnificant, 1929; Philip Goes Forth, 1931; Reflected Glory, 1936; The Deep Mrs. Sykes, 1945; The Fatal Weakness, 1946. Recipient medal of Achievement and Creative Arts award Brandeis U., 1959; Phila. Creative Arts Theatre award, 1962; Gold medal Women's Theatre Club, N.Y.C.; Drama Award of Distinction, Cal. Alpha chpt. Theta Alpha Phi, 1968. Home: Villanova, Pa. Died June, 1974.

KELLY, JOHN CLARENCE, physician, banker; b. Slippery Rock, Pa., Dec. 27, 1881; s. John and Rebecca (Hilgar) K.; certificate engring, B.A. degree, Slippery Rock State Normal Sch., 1904; M.D., U. Pitts., 1910; LL.D., Westminster Coll., 1953; m. Agnes Elvira Carlson, Feb. 4, 1914 (dec. July 1961); children—Frank J., Crawford T. Intern McKeesport (Pa.) Hosp., 1910-11, mem. staff surgery and gynecology, from 1917; vis. surgeon Presbyn. Hosp., Pitts. Hosp., also Columbia Hosp., Wilkinsburg, Pa., 1911-17. Chmn. bd. Peoples Union Bank and Trust Co., McKeesport, from 1956; v.p. Potter-McCune Co., McKeesport, from 1952; dir. G. C. Murphy Co. Pres. McKeesport Community Fund, 1938, Daily News Baseball League, from 1957; v.p. McKeesport Boys Club, from 1957. Trustee McKeesport YMCA. Recipient Outstanding Citizen award McKeesport Optimist Club, 1949, Civic Service award McKeesport Eagles Club, 1953, Man of Year award McKeesport Jr. C. of C., 1962; hon. award Tall Cedar at Sight. McKeesport, 1951. Mason, Elk, Rotarian. Clubs: Youghiogeny Country (pres. 1964) (McKeesport); Century (hon.); (U. Pitts.). Home: McKeesport, Pa.†

KELLY, LAWRENCE VINCENT, opera producer; b. Chgo., May 30, 1928; s. Patrick James and Thelma (Seabott) K.; student Chgo. Music Coll., 1942-45, Georgetown U., 1950, DePaul U. Law Sch., 1950-51. Office mgr. Kelly Bros. Realty Inc., Chgo., 1950, sec.-treas., 1951-74, also dir.; v.p. Dearborn Supply Co., 1951-52, also dir.; ins. broker, 1953-74. Co-founder Lyric Theatre of Chgo., 1953, sec.-treas., 1953-56, mng. dir., 1954-56; founder Dallas Civic Opera, 1957, gen. mgr., 1957-74; co-founder, producer Performing Arts Found. of Kansas City, 1965-74. Republican. Roman Catholic. Home: Dallas, Tex. Died Sept. 16, 1974; buried Calvary Cemetery, Evanston, Ill.

KELLY, WALT, cartoonist; b. Phila., Aug. 25, 1913; s. Walter Crawford and Genevieve (MacAnnulla) K.; student pub. schs., Bridgeport, Conn.; m. Selby Kelly; six children. Newspaper work, Bridgeport, 1928-35; animator Walt Disney Studio, 1935-41; comml. artist N.Y.C., 1941-48; polit. cartoonist N.Y. Star, 1948-49; author Pogo comic strip, also Pogo books; East of Berlin and Short of the Moon, 1961; Ten Ever-Lovin' Blue-Eyed Years With Pogo, 1959. Home: New York City, N.Y. Died Oct. 19, 1973.

KELSER, DAVID M., sugar co. exec.; b. Milw., Feb. 13, 1906; s. George Edward and Mary (Camp) K.; A.B., Harvard, 1927; student George Proctor, Ernest Hutcheson, Carl Friedberg; LL.D. (hon.) U. Bridgeport, Fairfield U.; m. Sylvia Kodjbanoff Aug. 11, 1938; children—Basil Edward, David Spencer, Florence (Mrs. Romanov), Peter Camp. With Cuban Am. Sugar Co., 1930-59, pres., 1939-59 chmn. bd., to 1959; pres. N. Am. Sugar Industries, 1959-71. Trustee Am. Farm Sch., Salonica, Greece, Juilliard Mus. Found., Wooster Sch.; hon. chmn., bd. dirs. N.Y. Philharmonic Symphony Soc., pres., 1956; chmn. bd. dirs. Juilliard Sch. Music; bd. dirs. Lincoln Center for Performing Arts, Vitam Center, Inc., Norwalk, Conn.; trustee, treas. Naumberg Found., N.Y.C.; mem. music com. Harvard. Mem. Squadron A N.Y. N.G. (cav.), 1932-36. Mem. N.Y. State Arts Council, Soc. Mayflower Descs., Soc. Colonial Wars. Clubs: University, Harvard, Century Assn., Knickerbocker (N.Y.C.); Riding Club (Wilton). Home: Wilton, Conn., Died Nov. 26, 1975.

KELSEY, HAROLD, newspaper exec. Business mgr. Seattle-Post-Intelligence. Home: Seattle, Wash. Died Aug. 10, 1975.

KELSO, ROBERT WILSON, educator; born Washington, Illinois, Aug. 27, 1880; s. Clark and Mary Jennie (Wall) K.; A.B., Harvard, 1904, LL.B., 1907; m. Susie Belle Starr, June 19, 1909; children—Jean, Marjorie, Bertha, Shirley, Robert Starr. Began law practice in Boston, Mass., 1907; sec. Mass. State Bd. Charity, and commr. pub. welfare, 1910-20; exec. sec. Boston Council Social Agencies, 1921-29; dir. St. Louis Community Fund and Council, 1929-32; field rep. Federal Emergency Relief Adminstration, 1932-35; prof. emeritus U. of Mich. and dir. Michigan Univ. Graduate Institute of Social Work, Detroit from 1935. Coach, Harvard debating teams, 1905-12, instr. argumentation and debating, Harvard, 1909, 10; hon. lecturer on sociology, Harvard, also mem. advisory com. on debating; mem. advisory com. Washington U. Dept. of Social Work. Pres. Nat. Conf. Special Work, 1922; pres. Social Service Council of Unitarian Chs. in America, 1924; pres. Citizens Housing and Planning Council, Detroit, from 1938; chairman Michigan State Housing Commn., 1938. Author: History of Public Poor Relief in Massachusetts, 1922; The Science of Public Welfare, 1928; Poverty, 1929. Compiler of Manual of Laws Relating to the State Board of Charity of Massachusetts (with digest of Cases), 1915. Home: Pleasant Ridge, Mich.†

KENDALL, ARTHUR ISAAC, bacteriologist; b. Somerville, Mass., May 7, 1877; s. Isaac Brooks and Alice Rebecca (Fitz) K.; B.S. in Biology, Mass. Inst. Tech., 1900; Ph.D., Johns Hopkins, 1904; Dr. P.H.,

Harvard U., 1911; Sc.D., U. of Southern Calif., 1932; m. Gertrude Mary Woods, Dec. 21, 1904. Dir. Hygienic Lab., Panama Canal Commn., Ancon, C.Z., 1904-06; fellow, Rockefeller Inst. for Medical Research, and bacteriologist, Research Lab., New York City Bd. of Health, 1906-09; instr. dept. preventive medicine and hygiene, Harvard Med. Sch., 1909-12; professor bacteriology, 1912-24, dean 1916-24, Northwestern U. Med. Sch., Chicago; prof. bacteriology and public health, Washington U. Sch. of Medicine, St. Louis 1924-27; prof. research bacteriology, Northwestern U. Sch. of Medicine, 1927-42, emeritus, from 1942. Trustee Wesley Meml. Hosp., Chgo., Northwestern U., 1916-24. Chairman yellow fever commission of Internat. Health Bd., 1917. Awarded Service Medal by Panama Canal Commn., 1906. Fellow American Academy of Pediatrics. Chicago Pathol. Soc. (pres. 1917). Inst. of Medicine of Chicago (gov. 1920-24), Soc. Experimental Biology and Medicine, Phi Rho Sigma, Shen Noong, Pi Kappa Epsilon, Alpha Omega Alpha, Sigma Xi, Phi Beta Kappa, Phi Sigma. Club: Adventures. Author: Bacteriology—General, Pathological and Intestinal, 3d edit., 1928; Civilization and the Microbe, 1923; also numerous contbns. to bacteriology and hygiene. Home: Oracle, Ariz.†

KENDIG, BESS HORTON (MRS. ANDREW LEROY KENDIG), civic worker; b. Salisbury, Mo.; d. Thomas Isaac and Celia Jane (Gribble) Horton; A.A., Stephens Coll., 1915; student State Tchrs. Coll., Warrensburg, Mo., 1918; m. Andrew LeRoy Kendig, May 27, 1920; 1 son, Andrew Edward. Tchr. English, Urich (Mo.) High Sch., 1915-18; prin. Burns (Wyo.) High Sch., 1918-22; with Farmers State Bank, Burns, 1922-35. Chmn. Platte County Nat. Found. Infantile Paralysis, 1955-60; mem. gov.'s com. Safety and Physically Handicapped, 1960-62; mem. State Women's Adv. Council Civil Def., 1960; mem. adv. council A.R.C. Wyo., 1960-62, Adult Edn. and Community Service, U. Wyo., 1960-62; mem. Gov.'s Com. on Edn., 1963-73. Dir. S.E. Wyo. Mental Health Center, 1960-73; dir. Wheatland Community Scholastic Fund, Inc., 1963-73, v.p., 1965-73; bd. dirs. Wyo. Safety Found.; member nat. bd. Woman's Medical College of Pa. Mem. Wyo. Hist. Soc., Gen. (mem. elections com. 1962-64), Wyo. (treas. 1956-58, pres. 1960-62, chmn. scholarships 1962-64, leadership devel. chmn 1964-66) fedns. women's clubs, Stephens Coll. Alumni, Katie-Dids (pres. 1964-66). Democrat. Baptist. Mem. Order Eastern Star. Club: WTK (pres. 1949-50, pub. relations dir. 1962-64, edn. chmn. 1966-73). Editor: Wyo. Clubwoman, 1958-60. Home: Wheatland, Wyo. Died Mar. 9, 1973.

KENDRICK, PHILIP EUGENE, govt. ofcl.; b. Boston, May 2, 1899; s. Patrick Joseph and Ellen (Kinnaly) K.; student Boston Latin Sch.; Suffolk Law Sch.; m. Geraldine C. Fitzgerald, June 10, 1923; 1 son, Philip Eugene. With Bright, Sears & Co., mems. N.Y. Stock Exchange, 1916-35; with SEC, from 1935, regional adminstr. for N.E. from 1948; state coordinator Interdepartmental Savs. Bond Com. for Mass., from 1953. Adv. Bd. Willett Inst. Finance, Boston. K.C. (4°). Home: Peabody, Mass. Died Mar. 18, 1975.

KENEALY, WILLIAM JAMES, clergyman; b. Boston, July 30, 1904; s. William Edward and Mary Ann (Fay) K.; ascetical studies in novitiate, Yonkers, N.Y., 1922-23, Shadowbrook, Lenox, Mass., 1923-24; A.B., Boston Coll., 1928, A.M., 1929; Ph.D., Gregorian U., 1932; S.T.L., Weston Coll., 1935; LL.B., Georgetown U., 1939. Joined Soc. of Jesus, 1922, ordained priest Roman Catholic Ch., 1934; asst. prof. philosophy Boston Coll., 1929-31; admitted to D.C., Mass. bars; dean, prof. law Boston Coll. Law Sch., 1939-56, prof., 1963-68; prof. law Loyola U., New Orleans, 1956-58; prof. law Loyola U., Chgo., 1958-63; dir. nat. office Jesuit Social Apostlate, Washington, 1968-71; mem. U.S. Bishop's Campaign for Human Devel., 1970-74. Trustee Boston Coll., 1946-56, trustee, dir., 1970-74; trustee Wheeling (W.Va.) Coll., 1970-74. Served as lt. comdr., Chaplain Corps, USNR, 1943-46. Fellow Am. Acad. Arts Scis.; mem. Am., Mass. Bar Assns., Am. Law Inst., Am. Assn. U. Profs., Am. Judicature Soc., Am. Jesuit Ednl. Assn., Conf. Jesuit Law Schs. (chmn. 1959). Contbr. articles to profl. jours. Home: Chestnut Hill, Mass. Died Feb. 3, 1974.

KENERSON, EDWARD HIBBARD, publisher; b. Nahant, Mass., Oct. 31, 1880; s. Austin H. and Martha Moulton (Hibbard) K.; A.B., Dartmouth Coll., 1903; m. Margaret S. Ryder, June 19, 1905 (died June 21, 1909); 1 son, John Bodge; m. 2nd. Charlotte D. Ryder, July 10, 1914; children—David Ryder, Margaret (Mrs. Cleveland Dodge Rea), Ellen. Ednl. sales rep., Ginn & Co., 1903, became New England mgr., 1917, partner, 1920, treas., 1935-37; dir., mem. exec. com. Ginn & Co., Inc., 1939-51; vice pres. and mem. bd. of investment Winchester Savings Bank. Dir. Am. Textbook Pubs. Inst. (mem. exec. com. as sec., 1930-43, pres. 1944-45). Pres. Winchester (Mass.) Hospital. Mem. N.E.A. (dept. of superintendence), New England Hist. and Geneal Soc. (life), Am. Council of Edn. (del.), Phi Gamma Delta. Mason (K.T., Shriner). Unitarian. Club: University (Boston). Home: Winchester, Mass.†

KENERSON, WILLIAM HERBERT, educator; b. Fall River, Mass., Dec. 9, 1873; s. William Moore and Abbie Ann (Brown) K.; M.E., Brown, 1896; M.A., Harvard, 1906; Sc.D., R.I. State Coll. Agr. and Mech. Arts, 1919; m. Ellen Williams Hooper, 1897. Asso. prof. mech. engring., Brown U., 1901-13, prof. from 1913. chmn. (exec. head) div. of engring., 1916-40, prof. emeritus, from 1941; also cons. practice, supervising engr. for various enterprises; also consultant in patent causes. Chmn. Building Ordinance, Bd. of Review, Providence. Served during 1st World War as dir. conservation in R.I. for Federal Fuel Adminstration and spent 6 months with A.E.F. in France as mem. ednl. corps., organizing instrn. in engring.; exec. sec. Nat. Acad. Sciences and Nat. Research Council, 1942-45; mem. exec. com. Highway Research Bd., Washington, D.C. Mem. Governor's Adv. Commn. on Pub. Health; mem. Hoover Medal Bd. Award; trustee Providence YWCA. Named R.I. Engr. of Yr., Nat. Soc. Profl. Engrs. Fellow American Soc. M.E. A.A.A.S.; member Am. Engring. Council, Am. Soc. Mech. Engrs. (chmn. com. local sects; v.p. and chmn. com. on relations with colls.), Soc. for Promotion Engring. Edn., Providence Engring. Soc. (pres.), Newcomen Soc., Phi Delta Theta, Sigma Xi. Conglist. Clubs: University, Providence Athenaeum, Providence Art, Faculty (pres.), A.E. (Providence), Cosmos (Washington). Home: Providence, R.I.†

KENNA, HOWARD JAMES, ch. adminstr.; b. Clontarf, Minn., Oct. 16, 1901; s. John Edward and Ursula Mary (McShane) K.; A.B., U. Notre Dame, 1926, M.S., 1932, Litt.D., 1953; S.T.B., Cath. U. Am., 1929; Sc.D., Cath. U. Chile, 1956; LL.D., (hon.) U. Portland, 1963. Joined Congregation of Holy Cross, 1922; ordained priest Roman Cath. Ch., 1930; rector Moreau Sem., Notre Dame, Ind., 1937-43; dir. studies U. Notre Dame, 1944-49, v.p. acad. affairs, 1949-50; asst. gen., gen. sec. congregation Holy Cross, N.Y.C., 1950-53; rector Holy Cross Coll., Washington, 1952-55; pres. U. Portland, 1955-62; provincial superior Ind. Province of Priests of Holy Cross, 1962-73. Bd. regents U. Portland; trustee U. Notre Dame. Mem. Assn. Symbolic Logic. K.C. (4), Elk. Home: South Bend, Ind. Died Sept. 13, 1973; buried Holy Cross Community Cemetery, Notre Dame, Ind.

KENNAMER, FRANKLIN ELMORE, judge; b. Kennamer Cove, Ala., Jan. 12, 1879; s. Seaborn F. and Nancy E. (Mitchell) K.; ed. pub. schs., Marshall County, Ala., and normal sch., Scottsboro, Ala.; m. Lillie Florence, Apr. 8, 1903 (died 1939); children—Opal, Juanita, Franklin Elmore, Phillip Millholland (dec.); m. 2d, Pauline Fox, Feb. 1940. Admitted to Okla. bar, 1905; city atty., Madill, Okla., 1915-16; mayor of Madill, 1919-20; mem. Supreme Court of Okla., 1920-24; apptd. by President Coolidge, judge dist. court, eastern dist. of Okla., Mar. 1, 1924; assigned to northern dist. of Okla., Apr. 1, 1925; retired June 1, 1940. Mem. Co. I, 2d Ala. Regt., Spanish-Am. War. Mem. Okla. Bar Assn., Tulsa Bar Assn. (hon.). Republican. Mem. Ch. of Christ. Address: Chelsea, Okla.†

KENNARD, WILLIAM JEFFERS, physician, assn. cons.; b. Havana, Cuba, Sept. 26, 1906; s. Wm. Jeffers and Mary Elizabeth (Rutherford) K.; B.S., U. Pitts., 1928, M.D., 1930; grad. Med. Field Service Sch., 1933, Sch. Aviation Medicine, 1934, Nat. War Coll., 1947; m. Marian Robinson Brown, June 20, 1930; children—Ann Eloise (Mrs. David D. Johnson), Beverly Jeffers (Mrs. John C. Wren), Marian Elizabeth (Mrs. Jack G. Sarver). Commd. 1st lt., M.C., U.S. Army, 1930, advanced through grades to brig. gen., USAF, 1952; intern Walter Reed Gen. Hosp., Washington, 1930-31, resident internal medicine, 1931-32; student Army Med. Sch., 1932-33; surg. and med. insp. Air Forces and Army troops, Philippines, 1940-42; command surgeon Far East Air Force, 1941-42, N.E. Australia, 1942, 2d Bomber Command, 1943-44; comdg. officer Regional and Convalescent Hosp., Ft. George Wright, Spokane, Wash., 1944-46; chief aviation medicine and care of flyer div. Office Air Surgeon Hdqrs. USAF, Washington, 1947-49, dir. plans and hospitalization Office Surgeon Gen., 1949-51; sr. med. officer SHAPE, NATO, 1951-54; air surgeon Mil. Air Transport Service, 1954-55; ret., 1955; asso. dir., later dir. Washington office A.M.A., 1955-58; exec. v.p. Aerospace Med. Assn., Washington, 1959-67, cons., 1967-73. Decorated D.S.M., Silver Star, Legion Merit with oak leaf cluster, Purple Heart, Presdl. Distinguished unit citation with 3 oak leaf clusters, Army Commendation ribbon with 3 oak leaf clusters (U.S.); Philippine Presdl. distinguished citation; Medaille d'Honneur du Service de Sante de L'Air (France); recipient Theodore C. Lyster award, 1965. Diplomate Am. Rd. Preventive Medicine (dir., vice chmn. aerospace medicine 1959-68). Fellow Internat. Acad. Aviation and Space Medicine; mem. Soc. Med. Cons. to Armed Forces, A.M.A., D.C. Med. Soc., Am. Pub. Health Assn., Civil Aviation Med. Assn., Am. Med. Execs. Assn., Am. Coll. Preventive Medicine, Air Force Assn., Aerospace Med. Assn., Flying Physicians Assn. Baptist. Home: Arlington Va. Died Oct. 23, 1973; buried Arlington National Cemetery.

KENNEDY, ALBERT JOSEPH, settlement worker; b. Rosenhayn, N.J., Jan. 20, 1879; s. Thomas and Molly (Barnhardt) K.; grad. Marion (N.Y. Collegiate Inst.; A.B., U. of Rochester, N.Y., 1901; grad. Rochester Theol. Sem., 1904; S.T.B., Harvard, 1907; m. Edith Forbes Knowles, June 27, 1908 (divorced 1929); children—Robert Woods, Fitzroy, Edmond; m. 2d, Marjorie Patten, May 15, 1930; 1 son, Michael. Director of investigations, South End House, Boston, 1908-14; asst. sec. National Federation of Settlements, 1911-14, sec. 1914-34; associate head worker South End House, 1914-26, head worker, 1926-28; head worker University Settlement, New York, 1929-43. Lecturer on social instns., Boston School Social Work, 1914-20; dir. studies of settlement work in Minneapolis, Jersey City, New York and Pittsburgh; lecturer Boston Sch., Social Work, Harvard University, Simmons Coll., New York Sch. of Social Work, etc. Mem. Am. Assn. Social Workers. Unitarian. Author: Handbook of Settlements, 1911; Young Working Girls, 1913; The Settlement Horizon, 1922; Visual Arts in New York Settlements, 1931; Social Settlements in New York City, 1935. Conttributor to American Review, Social Forces, Social Work Year Book, Survey and Engy. Britannica. Editor of "Neighborhood" (settlement quarterly), Settlement Monographs, etc. Home: Peekskill, N.Y.†

KENNEDY, ELIZABETH SMITH, physician; b. Buchanan County, Ia., Apr. 16, 1879; d. Montrovelle Valancort and Mary (Whitney) Smith; student Upper Iowa U., 1893-95; M.D., State U. of Iowa, 1901; m. Leslie Wayne Kennedy, Dec. 24, 1906 (died 1928); children—Wayne Francis, Ruth Helen (Mrs. George F. Knuth). Began practice, Oelwein, Ia., 1901; pub. health officer and city physician, 1921-25; mem. Mercy Hosp. staff; active in civic affairs, from 1920; city physician, pub. health officer, 1945-46. Republican committeewoman, from 1934, co-vice chmn., 1942-46; chmn. 1943-46; del. Nat. Rep. Conv. 1944; pres. Fayette Med. Assn., 1938-42; active leader in Camp Fire activities, 1930-42. Mem. D.A.R., Fayette Co. 4-H (hon.), Nu Sigma Phi. Presbyterian. Republican. Home: Oelwein, Ia.†

KENNEDY, FRANK J., accountant; b. N.Y.C., Feb. 19, 1903; s. James J. and Katherine (Horgan) K.; student Fordham U.; m. Ethel Clark, Apr. 6, 1931; children—Jeanne, Kathleen, Patricia, Mary, John. Accountant, then auditor The Moto Meter Co., Inc. and Moto Meter Gauge & Equipment Corp., Long Island City, N.Y., 1921-34; with The Electric Autolite Co., Toledo, from 1934, successively auditor, asst. sec., sec., 1943-53, v.p. from 1953, adminstrv. asst. to pres., from 1954, dir., 1955-59; dir., officer several affiliated cos. Mem. Ohio, Toledo Chambers Commerce, Holy Name Soc. Roman Catholic. Home: Toledo, Ohio. Died Feb. 5, 1974; interred Calvary Cemetery, Toledo.

KENNEDY, JAMES ALOYSIUS CHARLES, lawyer; b. Omaha, Oct. 31, 1875; s. Thomas and Anna M. (Kennedy) K.; student Creighton Prep. Sch., 1888; night sch. Omaha U., 1896-97; law sch. U. Ia., 1898; LL.B., Neb. U., 1900; m. Caroline Purvis, June 1, 1905; children—Ann Marie (Mrs. James S. Hauck), Jean (Mrs. John George Jones), James Aloysius Charles. Messenger boy, bookkeeper First Nat. Bank of Omaha, 1891-98; admitted to Neb. bar, 1900; elected mem. Neb. Legislature, 1903; dep. co. atty. Douglas Co., Neb., 1903-04; apptd. U.S. referee bankruptcy, 1908-18; sr. mem. Kennedy, Holland, DeLacy & Svoboda, 1917-75; dir. Mut. Benefit Health & Accident Assn., Kennedy Co., Inc. Mem. Draft Bd. Appeals, Omaha, World War I. Served with 2d Neb. Vol. Inf., AUS, Spanish War; pvt. to 1st lt. judge adv., ordnance officer regt. Co. G. Mem. Phi Delta Phi, Phi Delta Theta. Clubs: Omaha, Country (Omaha). Home: Omaha, Neb. Died June 8, 1975; buried Holy Sepulchre Cemetery, Omaha, Neb.

KENNEDY, JAMES FRANCIS, JR., lawyer; b. Pitts., June 21, 1924; s. James Francis and Marie (Hardiman) K.; B.A., U. Pitts., 1947, J.D., 1949; m. Anne K. Griffin, June 10, 1950; children—Brian Eileen, Jane Frances, Mary, Stephen, Claire. Admitted to Pa. bar, 1950, Ohio bar, 1956; practiced in Scranton, 1950-51, Toledo, 1956; instr. Bus. Adminstrn. Sch., U. Scranton, 1949-51; trial atty. Chief Counsel's Office, Internal Revenue Service, 1951-56; partner Marshall, Melhorn, Bloch & Belt, 1956) lectr. Cleve. Bar Assn. Tax Insts., 1964-68. Dir. Entelco Corp. Served to lt. (j.g.) USNR, 1943-46. Mem. Am., Ohio, Toledo bar assns., Order of Coif, Beta Gamma Sigma. Home: Toledo O. Died Nov. 25, 1973.

KENNEDY, MARGARET, writer; b. London, Apr. 23, 1896; d. Charles and Elinor (Marwood) Kennedy; student Cheltenham Coll., 1912-15; M.A., Somerville Coll., 1919; m. David Davies, June 20, 1925 (dec.); children—Julia (Mrs. James Birley), Sarah (Mrs. Piers MacKesy), James B. Mem. Author's Soc., P.E.N., English-Speaking Union. Author: The Ladies of Lyndon; The Constant Nymph; Red Sky at Morning, 1927; Return I Dare not: the Fool of the Family, 1930; A Long Time Ago, 1934; Together and Apart, 1936; The Midas Touch, 1938; The Feast, 1947; Jane Austen, 1948; Lucy Carmichael, 1950; Troy Chimneys (James Tall Black Meml. award Edinburgh U., 1954), 1953; Act of God, 1955; Oracles, 1957; Wild Swan, 1957; Outlaws on Parnassus, 1958; A Night in Cold Harbor, 1960; Not in the Calendar, 1964; (plays) The Constant Nymph, 1926, Escape Me Never, 1934, Autumn, 1937, Happy with Either, 1948. Died 1967.

KENNERLEY, MITCHELL, publisher; b. Burslem, Eng., Aug. 14, 1878; ed. pub. schs. in Eng.; came to America, 1896. Mgr. New York branch of John Lane, pub., London, 1896-1900; bus. mgr. The Smart Set, 1900-1901; founder, 1901, and till 1904, editor and propr., The Reader Magazine; in publishing business, from 1905; published The Forum, 1910-16, The Papyrus, 1910-12; pres. The Anderson Galleries, 1916-29; managing dir. Printing House of William Edwin Rudge, from 1931. Clubs: Lotos, Am. Yacht, Manursing Island, Grolier (New York); New Oxford, Cambridge (London). Home: New York City, N.Y.*†

KENNEY, JAMES FRANCIS, found. exec.; b. Memphis, N.Y., Aug. 2, 1898; s. James Lawrence and Bridget Agnes (Clark) K.; B.C.S., N.Y.U., 1927; m. Ann McLaughlin, June 26, 1929; children—Phyllis Mary, James Lawrence. Accountant, Dunning & Boschert Press Co., Syracuse, N.Y., 1918-23, Paul B. Warner & Co., pub. accountants. 1923-28, Hurdman & Cranston, 1928-35; own office as pub. accountant, 1935-37; treas. Onondaga Silk Co., Inc., 1937-38; sec., treas. Alfred P. Sloan Found., Inc., N.Y.C., 1938-66, v.p. Finance, 1962-66, ret., 1966; v.p., dir. New Castle Corp., 1940-66; dir. Jaxon Corp. C.P.A., N.Y., 1934. Home: Ridgefield Park N.J. Died Jan. 16, 1974.

KENNY, JOHN EDWARD, business exec., engr.; b. Havre De Grace, Md., Apr. 27, 1900; s. Daniel Cyril and Catherine (Brown) K.; student U. Notre Dame, 1917-19; B.S., Carnegie Inst. Tech., 1922; m. Caroline Green, June 16, 1926; 1 dau., Katherine. Engring., sales work Foster Wheeler Corp., Chgo., 1945-58, exec. v.p., dir., 1958-59, pres., chief exec. officer, 1960-65, chmn. bd., chief exec. officer, 1965-68, chmn. bd., 1968-71; dir. Liberty Mut. Ins. Co., Foster Wheeler Corp., Manhattan Refrigerating Co., Peoples Bank of W. Pa., New Castle, Oxy-Dry Sprayer Corp., Chgo., Electrographic Corp. Served in SATC, 1918. Decorated knight of Holy Sepulchre. Registered profl. engr., Ill., N.Y., Fla. Mem. Am. Soc. M.E., Am. Petroleum Inst., Am. Inst. Chem. Engrs., Newcomen Soc., Tau Beta Pi, Phi Kappa Psi. Roman Catholic. Clubs: University, Canadian, Economic (N.Y.C.); Baltusrol Golf (Springfield, N.J.); Royal and Ancient Golf of St. Andrews (Fife, Scotland). Home: New York City N.Y. Died Dec. 29, 1974; buried St. Joseph's Cemetery, New Castle, Pa.

KENNY, JOHN V., ex-mayor; b. Jersey City, N.J., Apr. 6, 1893; s. Edward and Katherine (Ward) R.; student St. Michaels, Parochial Sch., St. Peter's Prep. Sch., Jersey City; m. Margaret Smith, Apr. 8, 1918; 1 dau., Cathrine (Mrs. Paul Hanly). Began as bookkeeper Erie R.R. Co.; formed Industrial Utilities Corp., Jersey City, and served as pres., 14 years; has served as sec. to treas., Hudson County, Jersey City tax commnr., Hudson County Freeholder; mayor, Jersey City, New Jersey, 1949-53. Democrat (committeeman, 1916; leader 2d ward, Jersey City, 1931; active in Freedom Movement, May 1949). Home: Jersey City N.J. Died June, 1975.

KENNY, NICHOLAS NAPOLEON, (Nich Kenny), newspaper columnist; b. Astoria, L.I. City, N.Y., Feb. 3, 1895; s. Richard Joseph and Josephine (Duval) K.; student short story and scenairo writing Columbia, 1922; m. Kathryn Judge, Oct. 2, 1927; children—Patricia Patricia (Mrs. Pat Goebel), Joy (Mrs. Tom Kelly). Sports writer, writer column Getting an Earful, and rewrite man Bayonne (N.J.) Times, 1920-23; sports editor, rewriteman Boston Am., 1923-24; rewrite mem. N.Y. Jour., 1924-27, N.Y. Daily News, 1927-30; radio columnist N.Y. Daily Mirror, 1930-63; writer syndicated column Nick Kenny Speaking (poetry, news about radio TV, stage and screen personalities), 1930-63, pres. Goldmine Music, Inc., music pubs., 1946-75; columnist Sarasota (Fla.) Herald Tribune, 1963-75. Served with USN, 1911-18; Mcht. Marine, 1918-20. Decorated by Cardinal Spellman for canteen work, entertaining servicemen, World War II; received awards from Army and Navy depts. for similar work. Mem. Songwriters Protective Assn., Newspaper Guild, Am. Fedn. Radio Artists, Am. Guild Variety Artists, Profl. Music Men's Contact Assn., Am. Soc. Composers, Authors and Pubs. Roman Catholic. Elk. Club: Winged Food Golf. Writer lyrics of songs including: There's a Gold-mine in the Sky, Love Letters in the Sand, Carelessly, In My Cabin of Dreams, Little Old Cathedral in the Pines, Makebelieve Island, While a Cigarette Was Burning, Beyond the Purple Hills, Scattered Toys, Gone Fishin', It's Funny But It's True, Undertow. Author: Collected Poems of Nick Kenny; Poems To Inspire; others. Lectr. newspaper bus., poetry. Home: Sarasota, Fla., Died Dec. 1, 1975.

KENT, HOLLISTER, regional planner; b. Brookline, Mass., Mar. 1, 1916; s. Ira Rich and Louise (Andrews) K.; grad. Milton Acad., 1935; S.B., Harvard, 1939; M. Regional Planning, Cornell U., 1952, Ph.D., 1956; m. Edith Rairden Rudd, June 7, 1947; children—Margaret Ann (Mrs. Alvin Patscheck, Jr.), Bruce Rairden, Polly Curtiss (Mrs. James W. Campion IV), Timothy Rich, Nicholas Coburn. Instr., Fountain Valley Sch., Colorado Springs, Colo., 1939-42; asst. dean admissions, instr. fine arts Hofstra Coll., 1947-50; gen. mgr. charge site selection for Brasilia, Brazil, 1954-56, cons., 1956; dir. town planning, Kitimat, B.C., Can., 1956-58; dir. regional planning Sargent-Webster-Crenshaw & Folley, Syracuse, N.Y., 1958-61; sr. partner Planners Collaborative, Syracuse and Norwich, Vt., 1962-75; pres. Western Australia and Overseas Devel. Corp., Appleyard Corp.; dir. Intergroup, Planning and Devel. Collaborative Internat.; vis. prof. schs. architecture Columbia, Cornell U.; adj. prof. Dartmouth, Syracuse U. Mem. diocesan council Episcopal Diocese Central N.Y., 1965-69; v.p. Old West Ch. Assn.; chmn. Kent Museum Com; v.p. Hanover Consumer Coop. Soc.; chmn. Champlain Corridor Com. Trustee Lakco, Vt. Hist. Soc., Norwich Arts Assn. Served with AUS, 1942-47. Decorated Bronze Star, Purple Heart. Mem. Am. Inst. Planners (pres. N.Y. State chpt. 1960, nat. bd. examiners 1970-75), Phi Kappa Phi, Gargoyle (pres. 1956). Democrat. Episcopalian. Clubs: D.U., Hasty Pudding (Harvard); Harvard (N.Y.C. and Vt.); St. Botolph (Boston). Author articles. Home: Norwich, Vt. Died July 9, 1974; interred Robinson Cemetery, Kents Corner, Calais, Vt.

KENT, W(ILLIAM) WALLACE, U.S. circuit judge; b. Galesburg, Mich., May 1, 1916; s. Harold S. and Alice W. (Budd) K.; B.A., Western Mich. U., 1937; J.D., U. Mich., 1940; m. LaVerne Fredlund, July 7, 1940; children—W. Wallace, Virginia Louise, Eric H., Robert J., E. Anne, Martha. Admitted to Mich. bar, 1940; asst. pros. atty., friend of ct. Kalamazoo County, Mich., 1941-44, pros. atty., 1945-46; practiced law in Kalamazoo, 1944-54; U.S. dist. judge, 1954-71; judge U.S. Ct. Appeals, 6th circuit, 1971-73. Trustee Episcopal Diocese Western Mich. Mem. Am., Kalamazoo County bar assns., State Bar Mich., Am. Judicature Soc. Mason (grand master Mich. 1960-61, grand treas. 1961-71). Clubs: Optimist, Kalamazoo (past pres.), Torch: University (Cin.). Home: Kalamazoo Mich. Died May 28, 1973; interred Mount Everest Memorial Park, Kalamazoo, Mich.

KENWAY, HERBERT WINTHROP, lawyer; b. Boston, Dec. 1, 1881; s. Herbert Phipps and Alice (kimball) K.; student Mass. Inst. Tech.; m. Elose V. Tucker, Oct. 10, 1906 (dec.); children—Herbert P., Margaret K. (Mrs. Haydon); m. 2d, Helen M. Marcy, Jan. 29, 1959. With U.S. Patent Office, 1906-08, U.S. Shoe Machinery Co., 1908-27; sr. partner firm Kenway, Jenney & Hildieth, Boston, from 1948. Mem. Boston Patent Law Assn. (pres. 1952-54). Home: Newton, Mass.†

KENYON, CHARLES (ARTHUR), playwright, screen dramatist; b. San Francisco, Nov. 2, 1880; s. Curtis George and Alice Cook (Palmer) K.; grad. Trinity Sch., San Francisco, 1899; student University of Calif. and Stanford University; m. Beverly Ransome, 1931. Mem. Authors' League America, Phi Kappa Psi. Author: The Operator (prod. under title of The Flag Station, by Arnold Daly, Berkeley Lyceum, 1906); Kindling (prod. with Margaret Illington, at Daly's Theatre, New York, 1911); Husband and Wife (prod. by Arthur Hopkins, at 48th St. Theatre, New York, 1915); The Claim (with Frank Dare, prod. by Henry B. Harris Estate, Fulton Theatre, New York, 1917); Top O' The Hill (3-act play, prod. Mayan Theatre, Los Angeles, 1929, later Eltinge Theatre, N.Y.); also photoplays and screen adaptations, The Iron Horse, The Penalty, Show Boat, The Office Wife, Millie, Night Nurse, Bought, The Working Man, I Loved a Woman, A Midsummer-Night's Dream (with Mary McCall, Jr.), The Petrified Forest (with Delmer Daves), One Hundred Men and a Girl (in collaboration), The Road Back (with E. R. Sheriff). Home: North Hollywood, Cal.†

KERMATH, JAMES EDWARD, physician; b. Detroit, July 29, 1931; s. John Leslie and Bernice (Waters) K.; M.D., U. Mich., 1957; m. Carol Ann Martin, June 22, 1957; children—Joan Leslie, Jeffry Martin, Linda Katherine. Intern, Oakwood Hosp., Dearborn Mich., 1957-58, staff surgeon, vice chief staff; resident Henry Ford Hosp., Detroit, 1958-62; staff Outer Drive Hosp., Lincoln Park, Mich., 1963. Pres., Grosse Ile Community and Youth Center. Diplomate Am. Bd. Surgery. Fellow A.C.S.; mem. A.M.A. Home: Grosse Ile, Mich. Died Feb. 15, 1972; buried Oakridge Cemetery, Flat Rock, Mich.

KERN, ALFRED ALLAN, educator; b. Salem, Va., Nov. 29, 1879; s. John Adam and Margaret Virginia (Eskridge) K.; A.B., Randolph-Macon Coll., Va., 1898, A.M., 1899; Vanderbilt U., 1899-1900; Ph.D., Johns Hopkins, 1907; Litt.D., Millsaps Coll., 1934; m. Marguerite Wightman, Sept. 4, 1917; 1 dau., Mrs. Gertrude K. Ross. Prof. English, Millisaps Coll., Jackson, Miss., 1904-20. Randolph-Macon Woman's Coll., Lynchburg, Va., 1920-48; emeritus 1948. Teacher English, summer, Johns Hopkins, 1915, 16, U. of Tex., 1918, Tulane U., 1919, U. of Va., 1922, U. of Ala., 1925. Mem. Modern Lang. Assn. America, Kappa Alpha (Southern), Sigma Upsilon (nat. pres. 1910-15), Phi Beta Kappa. Author: The Ancestry of Caucer, 1907; A First Book in English (with S. G. Noble), 1916; High School English (with S. G. Noble), 1922; The Practice of Teaching, 1944; Editor Kappa Alpha Journal, 1917-19. Editor Macbeth, 1924. Home: Lynchburg, Va.†

KERN, FRANK DUNN, botanist; b. Reinbeck, Ia., June 29, 1883; s. William Sloane and Emma (Dunn) K.; B.S., U. of Ia., 1904; M.S., Purdue, 1907; Ph.D., Columbia, 1911; D.Sc., U. of Puerto Rico, 1926; m. Jessie Rhoda Adair, Aug. 21, 1907; children—Sue Emma (Mrs. H. C. Musser), Frances Louise (Mrs. H.J. Miller). Special agent Bureau of Plant Industry, United States Dept. of Agriculture, 1904-05; asst., later asso. botanist Purdue U. Agrl, Expt. Sta., 1905-13; instr. cryptogamic botany, Purdue U., 1910-11; research scholar, N.Y. Bot. Garden, Jan. each yr. for 4 yrs.; univ. fellow in botany, Columbia, 1910-11; prof., head dept. botany. Pa. State Coll., 1913-50, dean Grad. Sch., 1922-50, emeritus; dean Colls. Agr. and Engring., U. of Puerto Rico (while on leave absence from Pa. State College, 1925-26 and 1933-34). Conducted mycol. explorations in Puerto Rico, Dominican Republic and Venezuela. Del. to Internat. Bot. Congress, Cambridge, 1930. Awarded medal for pub. instruction, Venezuela, 1934. Certificate of Accomplishment, Iowa Centennial Commencement, 1947. Fellow A.A.A.S. (vice-pres., chmn. section on botanical sciences, 1945), Ind. Acad. Science; mem. Bot. Soc. America, Am. Phytopathol. Soc., Pa. Acad. Science, American Institute Biol. Science (bd. govs.) mem. at-large, Div. Biol. and Agr. National Research Council, Torrey Botanical Club, Mycol. Soc. America, (pres. 1945), National Research Council (div. biol. and mgr.), Alpha Zeta, Phi Kappa Phi (nat. president since 1947), Sigma Xi, Gamma Sigma Delta, Phi Eta Sigma. Has specialized in researches in plant rusts and other fungous diseases in plants. Author of text on plant biology; contbr. of numerous papers to scientific jours. Home: State College Pa. Died Sept. 28, 1973.

KERN, HAROLD G., publisher; m. Elizabeth Conlon. With Hearst Corp., 1925-75; resident v.p., director, publisher of Boston American Boston Record and Boston Sunday Advertiser. Trustee Hearst Estate, Hearst Found., William Randolph Hearts Found. Home: Boston, Mass., Died Feb. 19, 1976.*

KERNAN, WALTER AVERY, lawyer; b. Utica, N.Y., Dec. 1, 1913; s. Francis K. and Mary (Spratt) K.; grad. Milton Acad., 1932; A.B., Harvard, 1936, LL.B., 1939; m. Leslie Hadden, May 10, 1942; children—Anita (Mrs. Denis Halton), Mary (Mrs. Winthrop Rutherfurd, Jr.), Emily, Nancy, Beatrice, Charles. Admitted to N.Y. bar, 1940, practiced in N.Y.C.; asso. firm Carter, Ledyard & Milburn, 1939-41, 46-51, mem. firm, 1951-75; dir. N.Y. Herald Tribune. Trustee Helen Huntington Hull Fund; hon. trustee Fordham U.; bd. govs., v.p. ops. N.Y. Hosp.; bd. govs. Real Estate Bd. N.Y.; bd. dirs. Fresh Air Fund. Served from pvt. to capt., AUS, 1941-46, PTO. Mem. Am., N.Y. State bar assns., Assn. Bar City N.Y. (mem. com. grievances, ethics com.). Clubs: Piping Rock (Long Island, N.Y.); Links, Harvard, Down Town (N.Y.C.). Home: New York City, N.Y., Died Oct. 21, 1975.

KERNAN, WARNICK J., lawyer; b. Utica, N.Y., July 24, 1880; s. William and Frances (Warnick) K.; A.B., Georgetown U., 1901; special course Cornell Law Sch., 1902-04; LL.D., Hamilton Coll., 1934; unmarried. Admitted to N.Y. bar, 1904, and practiced in Utica; mem. Kernan and Kernan; spl. dist. atty., Oneida Co., 1915-16; trustee Savs. Bank of Utica, 1916-55. Mem. Bd. Sch. Commrs., Utica, 1907-14; mem. Law Revision Commn. of State of N.Y., 1934-47, chairman, 1940-47; referee in railroad reorganization proceedings by appointment of U.S. Circuit Court of Appeals, 2d Circuit, 1935; chmn. Alien Enemy Hearing Bd. Northern Dist. of N.Y., 1941-45. by appointment U.S. atty. general. Chmn. Spl. Com. of N.Y. State Bar Assn. to investigate jud. conditions in Albany Co., 1944-45. Counsel to Temp. Commn. on Need for a State U., 1947-48. Pres. bd. of trustees Utica Pub. Library, 1929-62. Temporary chmn. Dem. State Conv., 1927. Pres. N.Y. State Bar Assn., 1940. Charter mem. Am. Law Inst.; mem. Am. Judicature Soc., Am., N.Y. and Oneida County bar associations. Roman Catholic. Clubs: University (N.Y. City); Fort Schuyler, Sadaquada Golf (Utica). Home: Utica, N.Y.†

KERNER, OTTO, judge; b. Chgo., Aug. 15, 1908; s. Otto and Rose Barbara (Chmelik) K.; A.B., Brown U., 1930; postgrad. Trinity Coll., Cambridge U., Eng., 1930-31; J.D., Northwestern U., 1934; hon. degrees Brown U., Northwestern U., St. Procopius Coll., Lincoln Coll., Quincy Coll., McKendree Coll., Culver-Stockton Coll., So. Ill. U., Ill. Inst. Tech., Bradley U., Chgo.-Kent Coll. Law, Mundelein Coll., Drake U., Ill. State Coll.; m. Helena I. Cermak, Oct. 20, 1934 (dec. 1973); children—Anton J.C., Helena C. Admitted to Ill. bar, 1934; asso. with Cooke, Sullivan, & Ricks, 1934; became partner Kerner, Jaros & Tittle, law firm, 1935; U.S. dist atty. No. Dist Ill., 1947-54; county judge Cook County, 1954-61; gov. Ill., 1961-68; judge U.S. Ct. Appeals, Chgo., 1968-74. Vice pres. Chgo. council, mem. 7th regional exec. council Boy Scouts Am., hon. commr. Chgo. council; dir. Bohemian Charitable Assn., Glenview United Fund Cancer and Red Cross funds; mem. Chgo. Crime Prevention Council 1950-53; chmn. Pres.'s Commn. on Civil Disorders, 1968. Trustee Brown U. Mem. Ill. N.G., 106th Cav., 1934-36; trans. to F.A., 1936, advancing from pvt. to capt., 1941, served to maj. gen., inf., 1941-46; PTO. Decorated Soldier's medal, Bronze Star. Recipient Silver Beaver, Silver Antelope, Silver Buffalo awards Boy Scouts Am. Mem. Am. (alternate del. 1948), Fed., Ill., Chgo., West Suburban bar assns., Bohemian Lawyers, Am. Judicature Soc., Mil. Order World Wars (1st vice comdr. 1946-47), Alpha Delta Phi, Phi Delta Phi. Democrat. Mason (33 deg.), Nat. Soujourner, Red Cross of Constantine, Moose, Odd Fellow, Royal Arcanum, Clubs: Commonwealth, Brown, Wayfarers,

Legal, Law, Economic, Commercial, (Chgo.). Home: Chicago, Ill. Died May 9, 1976; buried Arlington Nat. Cemetery.†

KERPER, HAZEL BOWMAN, (Mrs. W. G. Kerper), lawyer, educator; b. Laramie, Wyo.; d. Elmer E. and Claribel (Colby) Bowman; B.A. with honor, U. Wyo., 1926, J.D. with honor, 1928; postgrad. Stanford Law Sch., 1926-27, Spanish Lang. Sch., San Jose, Costa Rica, 1960-63; certificate in corrections Fla. State U., 1964, M.S. in Criminology, 1965; m. W. G. Kerper June 17, 1927; children—Minabelle, Loujen, Janeen, Jill (Mrs. Johne M. Lennon). Admitted to Wyo. bar, 1928, Cal. bar, 1942, Fed. Ct. bar, 1944, Tex. bar, 1971; partner firm Kerper & Kerper, Cody, Wyo., 1928-40, 43-54; practiced in Los Angeles, 1940-43; ct. commr. Park County, Wyo., 5th Jud. Dist., 1930-59, asst. atty., 1928-30; mem. pub. relations and publicity staff Children's Orthopedic Hosp., Los Angeles, 1940-43; sec., mgr. Title Ins. and Trust Co., Cody, 1954-59; exec. sec. Avanza Industria, S.A., San Jose, 1959-64, also cons. Kativo, S.A. (Costa Rica, El Salvador, Nicaragua, Panama, Guatemala); asst. prof. sociology Sam Houston State Coll., Huntsville, Tex., 1966-67, asso. prof. sociology and criminal law, 1967-68, prof. criminal justice, from 1968. Mem. (Wyo.) Dist. 6 Sch. Bd., 1930-38, clk., 1932-38. Sec., Wyo. Republican Com., 1934-36. Recipient Distinguished Prof. award Sam Houston State Coll., 1967. Mem. Cody C. of C. (sec. 1928-55), P.E.O., Mortar Bd., Delta Delta Delta (finance dir., contbr. nat. publ. 1954-59), Phi Kappa Phi, Delta Sigma Rho, Phi Gamma Mu, Delta Tau Kappa Alpha Kappa Delta. Club: Quill. Author: Introduction To The Criminal Justice System, 1972; (with Janeen Kerper) Legal Rights of The Convicted, 1974; (with George G. Killinger and Paul F. Cromwell, Jr.) Probation and Parole in the Criminal Justice System, pub. posthumously, 1976. Editorial adv. bd. West Pub. Co. Home: Cody, Wyo., Died Jan. 17, 1975; cremated.

KERR, ANDREW, football coach; b. Cheyenne, Wyoming, Oct. 7, 1878; s. Andrew and Mary Elizabeth (Fagan) K.; graduate Carlisle, Pa., High School; Dickinson Preparatory Sch.; Ph.B., Dickinson Coll., 1960; LL.D., Colgate U., 1964; m. Mary Marchand Keister, Aug. 7, 1913; children—Andrew, William Keister. Began as teacher and football coach, Johnstown (Pa.) High Sch.; teacher and athletic coach, Pittsburgh (Pa.) Central High School, 1906-16; teacher Schenley High School, Pittsburgh, Pa., 1916-22; athletic coach, University of Pittsburgh, 1914-22, Stanford University, 1922-26, Washington and Jefferson Coll., 1926-29, Colgate U., 1929-47, emeritus prof. 1947; Lebanon Valley Coll., 1947-50. Coach, East team, East-West Shrine charity game, San Francisco, from 1927. Awards, Touchdown Club of N.Y., Dickinson Coll. and Colgate U. alumni. Hon. mem. Am. Football Coaches Assn. Football Hall of Fame, 1951; Helms Foundation College Football Hall of Fame, 1953; Stagg Award, Football Coaches of America, 1963. Member of Football Coaches Association, Phi Beta Kappa (honorary), Phi Kappa Sigma. Republican. Baptist. Mason (32°, Shriner). Contbr. to mags. and newspapers. Andy Kerr stadium dedicated Colgate U., 1966. Home: Hamilton, N.Y.†

KERR, EDGAR DAVIS, clergyman, educator; b. Mecklenburg County, N.C., Nov. 17, 1881; s. John Brown and Sarah (Misenheimer) K.; A.B., Davidson (N.C.) Coll., 1904; B.D., Columbia (S.C.) Theol. Sem., 1907; B.D., Princeton Theol. Sem., 1912; studied Semitic langs., U. of Chicago; D.D. Presbyn. Coll. of S.C., Clinton, S.C., 1921; m. Helen O'Neall White, Dec. 31, 1913 (died Oct. 11, 1914); m. 2d, Lucile Wilson, Nov. 28, 1923. Ordained ministry Presbyn. Ch. of U.S., 1907; pastor Highland Park Ch., Montgomery, Ala., 1907-10, Waynesville (N.C.) Ch., 1910-11, Aveleigh Ch., Newberry, S.C., 1912-27; instr. Hebrew lang., Columbia Theol. Sem., 1915-21, prof. Hebrew and cognate langs. from 1921. Mem. Co. M. 1st N.C. Vol. Inf. Spanish-Am. War. 1898. Mem. Phi Beta Kappa Mason (K.T.). Home: Decatur, Ga.†

KERR, GEORGE HOWARD, railway official; b. Homer City, Pa., Dec. 4, 1878; s. John Aden and Mary Bell (Diven) K.; ed. public schools of Pennsylvania; m. Irene Cooper, 1908; children—Don Howard, Gladys R. Clerk Pennsylvania Railroad, Bessemer, Pa., 1900-04, rate clerk, Pittsburgh, 1905-07; traveling freight agent Eastern & Southern Despatch (Southern Ry. System), Pittsburgh, 1908-09; commercial agent Southern Ry. System, Pittsburgh, 1909-14, Atlanta, Ga., 1915-16, asst. gen. freight agt., Atlanta, 1917-20; traffic mgr. Southeastern Express Co., Atlanta, 1921; assistant freight traffic mgr. Southern Ry. System, Atlanta, 1922-24, freight traffic mgr., Cincinnati, 1925-34, asst. v.p., Washington, D.C., 1935-40, v.p., Cincinnati, from Feb. 1, 1940; dir. and v.p. Cincinnati. New Orleans & Tex. Pacific Ry. Co., Harriman & Northeastern R.R. Co.; vice president Ala. Great Southern R.R. Co.; dir. Cincinnati Union Terminal Co., Ky. & Ind. Terminal R.R. Co., Terminal R.R. Assn. of St. Louis. Republican. Methodist. Mason. Clubs: Queen City, Cincinnati Country, Commercial and Optomist, (Cincinnati). Home: Cincinnati, O.†

KERR, HAROLD DABNEY, radiology; b. Catonville Md., Oct. 16, 1892; s. William Hall and Alice M. (Getchell) K.; B.S., U. of Wis., 1916; M.D., Johns Hopkins, 1919; m. Eleanor Frances Smith, 1920; children—Margaret Sewall, Agnes Spencer. Asso. roentgenologist, Peking Union Med. Coll., China, 1927-28; instr. in radiology, U. of Mich., 1928-29; asso. prof. radiology, U. of Ia., 1930-33, prof., head dept., 1933-55, emeritus. Area cons. radiology V.A.; com. radiology Nat. Research Council; cons. radiology Anne Arundel Gen. Hosp., Annapolis, Md., Memorial Hosp., Easton, Maryland. Diplomate Am. Bd. Radiology (pres. 1954). Fellow Am. Coll. Radiology (v.p. 1948); mem. Radiation Research Soc., A.M.A., Am. Radium Soc. (Janeway lectr. 1951), Radiol. Soc. N.A., Am. Roentgen Ray Soc. (pres. 1951), Ia. Radiol. Soc.; hon. mem. Minn. Radiol. Soc., Pacific N.W. Radiol. Soc., Rocky Mountain Radiol. Soc., Md. Radiol. Soc., Am. bd. Radiology (sec. 1957-73), Dallas So. Clin. Soc., Detroit Roentgen and Radium Soc., Phi Beta Kappa, Alpha Omega Alpha, Sigma Chi, Nu Sigma Nu, Sigma Xi, Sigma Sigma. Research in radiotherapy, radiobiology. Home: St. Michaels, Md. Died July 3, 1973.

KERR, HARRY HYLAND, surgeon; b. Winnipeg, Man., Can., Apr. 30, 1881; s. James and Laurie Jane (Bell) K.; brought to U.S., 1888; M.D., C.M., McGill U., Montreal, Can., 1904; m. Dorothy Beatrice Glass, Jan. 1, 1910; 1 son, Peter. Practiced at Washington, from 1905; clin. prof. surgery, George Washington U. Med. Sch., attdg. and cons. surgeon various hosps. Commd. 1st lt. M.C., U.S. Army, July 1917; hon. discharged as lt. col., Oct. 1919. Diplomate Am. Bd. Surgery (founders group). Fellow American Coll. Surgeons; mem. Am. Surg. Assn., A.M.A., Southern Surg. Assn., Med. Soc. of D.C., Alpha Delta Phi, Sigma Xi. Presbyterian. Clubs: Metropolitan, Chevy Chase. Home: Washington, D.C.†

KERR, HOWARD ICKIS, clergyman; b. Decatur, O., Jan. 5, 1881; s. Rev. Samuel Carrick and Elizabeth (Rowley) K.; A.B., Coll. Emporia (Kan.), 1901, D.D., 1917; A.M., Princeton, 1904; grad. Princeton Theol. Sem., 1905; m. Blanche M. Miller, June 27, 1906; children—Elizabeth Miller (Mrs. William A. Buchanan), Agnes Kathryn (Mrs. H. Craige De Moss). Ordained ministry Presbyn. Ch. in U.S.A., 1905; pastor at Ottawa, Kan., 1905-09, chaplain and prof. English Bible, Park College, Parkville, Mo., 1909-16; pastor Brooklyn Ch., Oakland, Calif., 1916-21; exec. sec. Ch. Extension Bd., Presbytery of Denver (Colo.), 1921-27; pastor Hillsboro Ch., Nashville, Tenn., 1928-1944. Minister ad interim Central Presbyterian Church, Huntsville, Ala., 1944. Pastor Central Ch., 1946-50; minister Old Hermitage Ch., Hermitage, from 1950. Mem. Bd. Natl. Missions Presbyterian Church U.S.A., 1940-46. Nat. Commn. on Evangelism, 1942-46. Board of Hanchow Christian College, China. Mason, Kiwanian. Mem. Chi Alpha, Pi Gamma Mu. Clubs: Palaver, Kiwanis, Golf and Country (Huntsville). Home: Hermitage, Tenn.†

KERR, WILLIS HOLMES, librarian; b. Jamestown, Pa., June 26, 1880; s. David Ramsey and Martha Sharon (Hill) K.; A.B., Bellevue (Neb.) Coll., 1900; A.M., Columbia U., 1902; studied U. of Edinburgh, 1907-08; seminar on Far Eastern Studies, International House, University of California (Berkeley), 1934; m. Mary Wylie Nicholl, June 14, 1904 (died Jan. 30, 1936); m. 2d, Virginia Dearborn Mertzke, June 12, 1938. Registrar and instr. economics, Bellevue Coll., 1900-04; prof. English and librarian, Westminster Coll., Fulton, Mo., 1904-11; librarian. Kellogg Library Kan. State Teachers Coll., Emporia, 1911-25; librarian, Pomona Coll., Claremont, Calif., 1925-31, and librarian. Claremont Colls., 1927-48; librarian emeritus and bibliog. cons., from 1948 instr. Grad. Library Sch., U. of Chicago, June-Aug. 1938. Life mem. A.L.A. (council, 1913-18, chmn. com. on edn., 1915-18, chmn. publicity com., 1915-17, 1920-23, com. on library revenues, 1923-27, com. on fiftieth anniversary of American Library Assn., 1923-26; mem. Coll. Library Advisory Board, 1936-38; mem. bd. on resources of Am. libraries, 1943-48); mem. of Kansas Library Association (pres. 1922), Calif. Library Assn. (pres. 1931-32), Nat. Edn. Assn. (pres. library dept., 1914-24, chmn. com. on normal school libraries, 1919-25); dir. Asso. College and Reference Libraries, 1943-48. Chmn. City Planning Commn. Mem. Phi Beta Kappa, Am. Philatelic Soc., Calif. Library Assn. (com. on co-operative projects, from 1948), Bibliography Society America. Bibliography Society (London), Zamorano Club (Los Angeles); sec. Claremont Rotary Club. Camp librarian, Camp Funston, Kan., Oct. 1917-June 1918; field rep. A.L.A. Library War Service, Washington, D.C., June-Dec. 1918; A.L.A. overseas war service, Paris, Dec. 1918-Sept. 1919. Home: Claremont, Cal.†

KESSEL, REUBEN A., educator, economist; b. Chgo., Apr. 2, 1923; s. A.J. and Blossom (Naiman) K.; M.B.A., U. Chgo., 1948, Ph.D., 1954; m. Shirley Kerner, Sept. 16, 1952; 1 dau., Catherine B. Instr. econs. U. Mo., 1948-49; economist RAND Corp., Santa Monica, Cal., 1952-56; asst. prof. Sch. Bus., U. Cal. at Los Angeles, 1956-57; asst. prof. econs. dept. econs. U. Chgo., 1957-61, asso. prof. bus. econs. Grad. Sch. Bus., 1962-64, prof., 1964-75, dir. doctoral programs, 1963-65, dir. research, 1969-72; research asso. Nat. Bur. Econ. Research, N.Y.C., 1961-62; cons., dir. Bell Fed. Savs. & Loan Assn., Chgo., 1956-75; impartial econ. expert Judge Robeson, Fed. Ct. Chgo., 1966. Served with AUS, 1943-46. Recipient awards Merrill Found. for Advancement Financial Knowledge, Volker Found., Commn. on Money and Credit, NSF. Mem. Am. Econ. Assn. Author: Cyclical Behavior of the Term Structure of Interest Rates, 1965; also articles. Home: Flossmoor, Ill. Died June 20, 1975.

KESSELMAN, LOUIS COLERIDGE, educator; b. Columbus, O., Nov. 12, 1919; s. Max and Pearl (Miller) K.; A.B., Ohio State U., 1940, M.A., 1941, Ph.D., 1947; m. Jennie Stregevsky, Jan. 3, 1942; children—Penny Lou, Jonathan Rhys. Instr. polit. sci. Ohio State U., 1941-47; asst. prof. U. Louisville, 1947-51, asso. prof., 1951-53, prof., 1953-74, chmn. dept. polit sci., 1953-70; Fulbright lectr. U. Oslo, 1953-54, U. Helsinki, Finnish Sch. Social Scis., 1960-61. Economist regional War Labor Bd., Cleve., 1943; pub. panel mem., hearing officer and arbitrator Nat. War Labor Bd., 1943-45; mem. enforcement commn. regional WSB, Cleve., 1951-53; labor arbitrator Fed. Mediation and Conciliation Service, Am. Arbitration Assn., Louisville Labor-Mgmt. Commn.; TVA referee. Dir. Scandinavian Inst. on Am. Trade Unionism, 1954; cons. Ky. Com. Human Relations, 1954-57, So. Regional Council, 1957; mem. Ky. Personnel Merit System Council, 1955-57. Mem. Nat. Acad. Arbitrators, Am., Ky. (exec. bd.) civil liberties unions, Am. Assn. U. Profs., Midwest Polit. Sci. Conf., Ky. Conf. Polit. Scientists (pres. 1963-64), Am., Finnish polit. sci. assns., Pi Sigma Alpha, Phi Kappa Phi. Author: The Social Politics of F.E.P.C., 1948. Mem. editorial bd. Midwest Jour. Polit. Sci., 1957-60. Contbr. articles to profl. jours. Home: Louisville Ky. Died Aug. 20, 1974.

KESSLER, BORDON BOWNE, theologian; b. Warrenton, Mo., Oct. 15, 1879; s. John Louis and Anna (Albers) K.; B.A., Central Wesleyan Coll., Warrenton, 1900; S.T.B., Boston U., 1904, Ph.D., 1919; U. of Berlin, 1904-05, U. of Grenoble, France, 1905-06; m. Lydia Caroline Marks, July 25, 1914; 1 dau., Alice Ann. Ordained M.E. ministry, 1906; pastor Waynetown, Ind., 1906-08, Veedersburg, 1908-10, St. Paul's Ch., Lafayette, 1910-13; prof. systematic theology, Iliff Sch. of Theology, Denver, Colo., 1913-24; research in King's Coll. and British Museum, London, 1924-26. Mason. Home: Chicago, Ill.†

KETCHUM, ROBYNA NEILSON, actress; b. Winona, Minn.; d. Charlie and Christina (Nilsson) Neilson; student Chgo. Musical Coll., 1926-27, Northwestern U., 1928, LeticiaBarnum Sch. Art, 1929-30; m. Alton H. Ketchum, Apr. 27, 1940; 1 dau., Deborah. Artist's model Tree Studio Bldg., Chgo., 1926; appeared in Morris Gest's prodn. The Miracle, Vicky Baum's Grand Hotel, N.Y.C. and road tour, 1931-33, Unto the Third, N.Y.C., 1935; model John Powers, 1934-35; appeared in Shawnee on the Delaware, summer 1936; Dreams Come True, radio serial, 1936, Attorney Que, 1938-39; radio shows include There's A Law Against It, 1939-40, The Aldrich Family, 1940. Mem. Greenwich Hist. Soc., India Am. League, Am. Bell Assn., Ikebana Internat. of Tokyo, Assn. Research and Enlightenment, Internat. Platform Assn., Audubon Soc., UN Assn. U.S.A. Author articles on bells for antiques publns. Originator, designer Freedom Bells for Am. Revolution Bicentennial Commn. Home: Cos Cob Conn. Died Nov. 9, 1972; buried Putnam Cemetery, Greenwich, Conn.

KETOLA, HELEN, librarian; b. Lima, O., Mar. 9, 1915; d. Carl and Anna (Lindquist) Ketola; student Chgo. Tchrs. Coll., 1935-38; B.S., U. N.M., 1949; M.A., U. Denver, 1962. Spl. edn. techr. Chgo. Pub. Schs., 1939-43; physics group sec. Los Alamos Sci. Lab., 1949-54, tech. processes librarian, 1970-74; elementary tchr. Los Alamos Sch., 1954-59, jr. high sch. librarian, 1959-70; cons. Jr. High Sch. Library Catalog, H. W. Wilson Co., 1965-68. Served with WAC, 1943-48. Mem. A.L.A., N.M. Library Assn., (treas. 1967, v.p. 1968, pres. 1969, chmn. intellectual freedom com. 1965). Home: Los Alamos, N.M., Died Aug. 1974.

KETTEN, MAURICE (PROSPER FIORINO), cartoonist; b. Mar. 2, 1875; s. Henry and Beatrice (Pellegrini) K.; ed. Ecole Nationale des Beaux Arts and University of Paris; married Margaret Zoe Haselwood, July 5, 1902 (died January 16, 1952). Came to United States, 1898, naturalized citizen, 1920. Portrait and poster work in Paris; cartoonist Denver Post, 1899; with Evening World, New York, 1906-31. Creator of series, The Day of Rest, Can You Beat It?, Such Is Life, Little Income, Catty Club—syndicated throughout United States. Awarded medal, Beaux Arts Sch., 1892. Exhibited in Paris Salon. Mem. Soc. Illustrators. Address: New York City, N.Y.†

KEUFFEL, JACK WARREN, educator, physicist; b. Montclair, N.J., May 10, 1919; s. Adolf W. and Alice (Jaeggli) K.; A.B., Princeton, 1941; Ph.D., Cal. Inst. Tech., 1948; m. Elizabeth M. Higgins, July 6, 1946; 1 son, Warren P. OSRD Liaison officer, Admiralty Signals Establishment for Mass. Inst. Tech., Eng., 1942-43; with Radar Countermeasures Field Lab. of Harvard, Malvern, Eng., 1943-45; instr. Princeton, 1948-53; asso. prof. physics U. Utah, 1953-60, prof., 1960-74, prin. investigator Cosmic Ray Research Project, 1954-74. Recipient Willard Gardner prize, Utah Acad. Scis., 1969. Mem. Phi Beta Kappa, Sigma Xi. Research on muon capture ultra-high-energy cosmic ray muons, cosmic ray neutrino studies. Home: Salt Lake City, Utah. Died May 23, 1974; interred Big Cottonwood Canyon, Utah.

KEYES, HAROLD FRANCIS, JR., mfg. co. exec.; b. Leominster, Mass., July 19, 1912; s. Harold Francis and Evelyn (Canning) K.; student Northeastern U., 1931-37; m. Helen Bowker, Dec. 11, 1937; 1 dau., Judith (Mrs. Richard K. Jette). Staff mem. pub. accountant Hitchcock & Co., C.P.A.'s, 1938-42; treas. Flax Processing & Linen Co., 1942-43, 45-50; sec., asst. treas. Brown & Sharpe Mfg. Co., N. Kingstown, R.I., from 1951. Mem. Navy-Civilian Council, Naval Air Sta., Quonset Point, R.I., from 1963. Trustee Eastern States Exposition. Served with USNR, 1943-45. Fellow Mass., R.I. socs. C.P.A.'s; mem. Am. Inst. C.P.A's, North Kingstown C. of C. (dir. 1968). Home: Harmony R.I. Deceased.

KEYSER, CHARLES PHILIP, newspaper corr.; b. Mt. Sterling, Ill., Nov. 5, 1869; s. Francis and Mary (O'Neil) K.; ed. high sch., Mt. Sterling; m. Edna E. Huges, May 4, 1903; children—Charles Francis, Mary Catherine (Mrs. Lloyd H. Rea). Began in newspaper work, 1890; became city editor Evening Peorian, Peoria, Ill., 1894, later Evening Times, Peoria, then Peoria Transcript to 1898; with St. Louis Globe-Democrat, from 1898; corr. Ill. legislature, 1901, Mo., 1903; reported nat. polit. convs., from 1900. Washington corr., from 1903. Methodist. Clubs: National Press, Gridiron, White House Correspondents' Association. Home: Washington, D.C.†

KEYSER, STANLEY SAMUEL, cigar mfr.; b. N.Y.C., June 15, 1900; s. Benno and Tekla (Adler) K.; student pub. schs.; m. Mildred Goodstein, Nov. 6, 1926; 1 dau., Corinne Geffin. With Consol. Cigar Corp., 1919-66, exec. v.p., dir., 1950-59, pres., chief operating officer, 1959-66. Trustee Polyclinic Med. Sch. and Hosp. Elk. Home: New York City N.Y. Died Sept. 6, 1974; buried King David Cemetery Putnam Valley, N.Y.

KHAN, MIRZA ALI KULI, diplomat; b. Kashan, Persia, 1879; s. Abdul Rabim Khan and Kadijah Khanom; grad. Imperial U. of Teheran, at 16; later studied philosophy; m. Florence Breed, 1904. Came to America, 1900; Persian consul, and sec. legation, Washington, several yrs., chargé d'affaires of Persia in U. S., from 1910. Mason (32°). Translator Persian and Arabic works into English, writer on art, philosophy, edn., etc.; public speaker and lecturer. Commr. gen. of Persia to Panama Expn., 1915. Decorated with Order Nabil-ed-Dovieh, Persia, 1914. Address: Washington, D.C.†

KIEFFER, JOHN SPANGLER, ret. coll. dean; b. Hagerstown, Md., Aug. 6, 1904; s. John Brainerd and Alice Venable Bourne (Hays) K.; A.B., Harvard, 1926, A.M., 1929; Ph.D., Johns Hopkins, 1962; m. Roxana Byrd White, Nov. 26, 1929. Master in French and English, Litchfield (Conn.) Sch., 1927-28; instr. classical langs. St. John's Coll. Annapolis, Md., 1929-34, asst. prof., 1934-39, tutor, 1939-75, mem. bd. visitors and govs., 1943-51, pres., 1947-49, dir. adult edn., 1951-57, dean, 1962-69. Mem. Am. Philol. Assn., Classical Assn. Atlantic States. Democrat. Episcopalian. Clubs: Harvard Club of Maryland; -4 W. Hamilton St. (Balt.). Author: Galen's introduction to Logic: Translation and commentary, 1964. Home: Annapolis, Md. Died Mar. 29, 1975; buried Hagerstown, Md.

KIELER, CHARLES BENEDICT, physician; b. Dubuque, Ia., May 11, 1908; m. Elizabeth M. Caruthers, Dec. 30, 1938; children—Elizabeth, Ann, Catherine, Charles. Intern, Madison (Wis.) Gen. Hosp., 1936-37; resident dept. otolaryngology and oral surgery U. Hosp., Iowa City, 1937-39; mem. staff Mary Imogene Bassett Hosp., Cooperstown, N.Y., 1940-71. Diplomate Am. Bd. Otolaryngology. Home: Springfield Center, N.Y. Died Sept. 13, 1971; buried Lakewood Cemetery, Cooperstown, N.Y.

KIELSTRA, JOHANNES COENRAAD, govt. official; b. Zwartsluis, The Netherlands, Nov. 13, 1878; s. Tepke and Henriette Charlotte (Ger) K.; student Gymnasium Middelburg, Netherlands, 1890-96; LL.D., Univ. Leiden, Netherlands, 1901; exam. Netherland Indian Civil Service, 1902; m. G.H. Buys, Nov. 5, 1903; children—Johannes Coenraad, Hanna Hermanna (Mrs. Frits Hendrik Beyerinck); m. 2d, Marie Francoise Picnot, Mar. 29, 1920, Civil official Netherlands Indies, Batavia, May 1903-Sept. 1915; univ. prof. Agrl. High Sch., Wageningen (lecturer on colonial rural economics and agrarian laws) and Univ. of Utrecht (lecturer on colonial economics), 1918-33; gov. Netherlands Guyana, Paramaribol., 1933-44; Netherlands minister to Mexico, 1944-48, resigned. Chmn. Netherlands section Caribbean Commn.†

KIERAN, WILLIAM A., ins. Mgr., economist; b. Decatur, Ill., Aug. 29, 1897; s. William Henry and Mary L. (Maroney) K.; A.B., U. Ill., 1923; m. Adele Hixon, Oct. 16, 1924; children—William Hixon, Robert Edmund. Ins. rep. from 1924; So. mgr. Am. Credit Indemnity Co. of N.Y., 1937-62, credit ins. broker, from 1962. Served Combat Engrs. A.E.F., W.W.I. Mem. V.F.W. Clubs: Downtown. The Club. Home: Birmingham, Ala. Deceased.

KIESLINGER, ALOIS, geologist; b. Vienna, Austria, Feb. 1, 1900; s. Franz and Emilie (Herrschmann) K.; Ph.D., U. Vienna, 1923; m. Eugenie Spitzer, May 9, 1931; 1 son, Christoph. Asst., Paleontol. Inst., Vienna U., 1923-30; lectr. Vienna Tech. U., 1930, prof., 1937, dir. Geol. Inst., 1949-71, emeritus, 1971-75; dir. Deutsche Steinbruchkartei, 1938-42. Bauleiter, Todt Orgn. Narvik, 1942-45. Decorated Hon. Cross 1st class for art and scis. recipient Cultural prize Vienna Municipality, 1961. Mem. Austrian Acad. Sci., German Acad. Natural Scientists Leopoldina, Austrian Geol. and Mineral Soc. (hon.). Authro: Stones of Carinthia; Stones of Saltzburg; Stones of St. Stephan; Petrolgraphy for building and sculpture; Decay of stone buildings—Its origin and prevention; The Stones of Ringstrasse—Vienna. Contbr. articles to profl. jours. Home: Vienna, Austria. Died June 1, 1975; buried Vienna, Austria.

KIEV, ISAAC EDWARD, clergyman; b. N.Y.C., Mar. 21, 1905; s. Nathan and Anna (Radin) K.; student Columbia, 1924-26; M.H.L., Rabbi, Jewish Inst. Religion, 1927; D.D., Hebrew Union Coll., 1956; m. Mary B. Nover, Dec. 20, 1930 (dec. June 1964); children—Ari, Aviva (Mrs. Avigdor Warsha). Research asst. Jewish Inst. Religion, 1927-28; asst. librarian Hebrew Bibliographer, 1928-43; librarian Hebrew Union Coll. Jewish Inst. Religion, 1943-75; chaplain Dept. Hosps., N.Y.C., 1927-75, Sea View Hosp. Synagogue, 1930-75; acting rabbi Free Synagogue Westchester, 1957; asso. rabbi Congregation Habonim, N.Y.C., 1968-75. Sec. Jewish Cultural Reconstrn. N.Y., 1949-51, Jewish Book Council Am., 1970. Trustee Alexander Kohut Found., Nissan Touroff Found.; chmn. bd. trustees Israel Matz Found. Mem. Am. Acad. Religion Soc. Bibl. Lit., Hebrew Lang. Acad., Am. Acad. Jewish Research, Am. Jewish Hist. Soc., Am. Oriental Soc., Israel Exploration Soc., Soc. Jewish Bibliophies, Mekize Nirdamin Soc. Asso. editor Jewish Book Ann., 1952-75, Studies in Bibliography and Booklore, 1953-75. Translation Kafra Haggadah, 1949. Contbr. articles mags., anns. Home: New York City, N.Y., Died Nov. 3, 1975.

KIKER, HENRY A., state supreme ct. justice; b. Tallapoosa, Ga., Apr. 25, 1881; s. Dr. Henry Addison and Jeannette (McBride) K.; student Mercer U. Kathleen Garrott Pollard, Mar. 9, 1927; 1 son, Henry A. Admitted to N.M. bar, gen. practice law, Raton, N.M., 1914-25, 33-34, Santa Fe, N.M., 1933-54; dist. atty. 8th Jud. Dist. N.M., 1917-20; dist. judge 8th Jud. Dist. N.M., 1925-33; asso. justice N.M. Supreme Ct., from 1954. Mem. Am. Bar Assn. (ho. of dels, 1939-40), State Bar N.M. (pres. 1938-39). Baptist. Home: Santa Fe, N.M.†

KIKUCHI, SEISHI, educator; b. Tokyo, 1902; grad. Tokyo U., 1926. Research work in atomic physics, 1926-31; prof. Osaka U., 1931-74, Tokyo U., 1950-74; pres. Sci. U. Tokyo, 1966-70. Recipient Acad. prize, 1932, Medal of Culture, 1951. Author: Outline of Atomic Physics; Atomic Physics; Composition of the Atom. Home: Tokyo, Japan. Died 1974.

KILBOURN, WILLIAM DOUGLAS, metallurgist; b. Middletown, Conn., Feb. 3, 1880; s. Jonathan Burwell and Mary Adeline (Douglas) K.; E.M., Colo, School of Mines, 1904; m. Clara Howe, Sept. 14, 1917; children—Charlotte Lee, William Douglas. Chemist, Ill. Steel Co., Chicago, 1904-05; chemist and draftsman, Colo. Fuel & Iron Co., at Pueblo, Colo., 1905-06; engr., W. & B. Douglas, Middletown, Conn., 1907-08; night supt. Murray (Utah) Smelter, 1908-10; supt. blast furnaces, Internat. Smelting & Refining Co., Tooele, Utah, 1913-14; research metallurgist, U.S. Refining & Mining Co., 1916-17; asst. and acting supt. East Chicago Lead Refinery, 1917-20; mine operator, Colo., 1921; pres. White Iron Ores and Products Co. (mines at Madera, Colo). Inventor Kilbourn's construction strips, Arsenor, methods of handling blast furnace matte, process for reduction of metals from their ores by carbon from solid fuel, and blast furnace and sublimation processes; disclosed large bodies of arsenic ore in Colo. Mem. Sigma Nu. Presbyn. Mason (K.T.), Address: Grand Junction, Colo.†

KILBURN, CLARENCE EVANS, congressman; b. Malone, N.Y., Apr. 13, 1893; s. Frederick D. and Clara (Barry) K.; graduate Cornell U., 1916; LL.D., St. Lawrence Univ., Canton, N.Y., 1960; m. Anne Crooks, Aug. 16, 1917; children—James C., Katherine, William B. Began with Kirk-Maher Co., N.Y., 1919, v.p. 1920, pres. 1921; mng. dir. Gen. Ice Cream Corp., N.Y., successor, 1921-30; became pres. People's Trust Co., Malone, 1930; dir. Northern N.Y. Trust Co. Member 76th to 78th Congresses, 31st New York District, 79th to 82d Congresses, 34th New York Dist. 83d-87th Congresses, 33d N.Y. District, 88th Congress, 31st District New York. Served from 1st lt. to capt. inf. 1st Div., U.S. Army, 1917-19. Mem. C. of C. (past pres.), Psi Upsilon. Republican. Methodist. Elk, Mason. Home: Malone N.Y. Died May 20, 1975; buried Morningside Cemetery, Malone, N.Y.

KILBURN, ROBERT WILLIAM, dir. research; b. Great Falls, Mont., Mar. 26, 1914; s. Percy Gordon and Myrtle (Ritz) K.; B.A., U. Cal. at Los Angeles, 1938; m. Thelma Taylor, Dec. 20, 1969; children by previous marriage—Robert G., Sherry Rae. Chemist Treesweet Corp., Santa Ana, Cal., 1937-45; research chemist FMC, Santa Jose, Cal., 1945-50; dir. research Citrus World, Inc., Lake Wales Fla., 1950-74; pres. Aqua Klear Corp. Chmn. A.R.C., 1970; active Boy Scouts Am., 1951-69. Fellow A.A.A.S.; mem. Inst. Food Technologists (Chmn. Fla. chpt. 1956), Am. Chem. Soc., Pollution Control Fedn., Assn. Food Drug Ofcls. U.S., Lake Wales C. of C. (dir. 1957). Presbyn. (deacon). Club: Lake Wales Rotary (pres. 1955). Contbr. articles to profl. jours. Patentee in field. Home Lake Wales, Fla. Died Feb. 2, 1974; interred Lake Wales.

KILEY, ROGER JOSEPH, judge; b. Chgo., Oct. 23, 1900; s. Roger and Maria (Quinlan K.; LL.B., U. Notre Dame, 1923; m. Helen Burke, June 20, 1933; children—Kathleen, Deirdre (Mrs LeFevour) and Roger Joseph, Maura, Gillian (Mrs. Carey), John. Asst. football coach U. Notre Dame, 1922, Loyola U., 1923-27, Auburn U., 1930-32; admitted to Ill. bar, 1924; judge Superior Ct. of Cook County, 1940, Appellate Ct. of Ill., 1st Dist., 1941-61; judge U.S. Ct. Appeals for 7th Circuit, 1961-73, sr. judge, 1973-74. Alderman 37th Ward, Chgo., 1933-40. Adv. council U. Notre Dame Law Sch.; dir. Great books Found., Inc., St. Thomas More Assn., Inc., Catholic Charities. Mem. Am., Ill., Chgo. bar assns., Cath. Lawyers Guild. Clubs: Univeristy (Chgo.); Butterfield Country (Hinsdale, Ill.). Home: Oak Park, Ill. Died Sept. 6, 1974.

KILGOUR, DAVID ECKFORD, bus. cons.; b. Brandon, Man., Can., Dec. 26, 1912; s. Justice J.F. and Geills (McCrae) K.; student St. Andrew's Coll., Aurora, Ont., Can.; B.A., U. Man., 1933; m. Mary Sophia Russell, 1936; children—Geills McCrae (Mrs. John N. Turner), David William, Donald Alexander. With Great-West Life Assurance Co. of Winnipeg, Can., 1933-71, beginning as mem. agy. dept., sec., supt. agys., asst. gen. mgr. and supt. agys., asst. gen. mgr. and dir. agys., gen. mgr., dir., 1933-58, v.p., mng. dir., 1958-59, pres., 1959-71. Past mem. exec. com. Am. Life Conv. Past chmn. Canadian council Net Indsl. Conf. Bd.; dir. Nat. Indsl. Conf. Bd. U.S. Deceased.

KILLORAN, CLAIR JOHN, lawyer; b. Weiser, Ida., Apr. 12. 1905; s. Charles J. and Ada (Percifield) K.; A.B., U. Ida. 1928; J.D., Georgetown U., 1932; m. Anne Regina Biggs, Nov. 30, 1935; 1 dau., Claire Joanne. Admitted to D.C. bar, 1933, Del. bar, 1934; mem. firm Borton, Melson & Killoran, Wilmington, Del., 1934, Melson & Killoran, 1935-41, Clair John Killoran, 1941-45, Killoran and Van Brunt, 1946-75; dep. atty. gen. State of Del., 1937-39, chief dep. atty.-gen., 1940-43, atty.-gen., 1943-47; gen. counsel Del. Mut. Life Ins. Co., Ernest Di Sobatino & Sons, Inc., Cantera Constrn. Co., Carpenters Motor Freight, Inc.; dir. Rollins Internat., Inc., Wilmington, Del., Registrar & Transfer Co., N.Y.C. Mem. Del. State Bd. Accountants 1947-51. Keynoter Rep. State Conv., 1944-46; Rep. state chmn., 1950-56; chmn. Del. delegation Nat. Rep. Conv., 1952, del., 1956. Fellow Am. Coll. Trial Lawyers; mem. Am., Del. (pres. 1959-61) bar assns., Georgetown U. Alumni Assn. (gov., mem. senate). Kappa Sigma. Elk. Clubs: Wilmington, Biderman Golf, Wilmington Country (dir. 1959-75) (Wilmington); Lambs (N.Y.C.); Seaview Country (Absecon, N.J.). Home: Wilmington, Del., Died Oct. 29, 1975.

KIMBALL, CLAUDE D., editor, pub; b. Minneapolis, Minn., Apr. 18, 1879; s. Leonard and Mary Jane (Pierce) K.; student U. of Minn., 1898, 99; m. Eleanor Skinner, Feb. 10, 1904; children—Leonard Skinner, Claude Pierce, Eleanor. Sec. Kimball-Storer Co., printers, Minneapolis, 1907-15, pres., 1915-20; apptd. receiver Aberdeen (S.D.) American, 1922; purchased same, 1923, pub. and editor, from 1923; also pub. Aberdeen News and Aberdeen American-News Mem. Theta Delta Chi. Republican. Episcopalian. Mason. Clubs: Aberdeen Commercial, Aberdeen Country; Minneapolis Athletic. Home: Aberdeen, S.D.† N:M:1884:1973:W38

KINCAID, JAMES LESLIE, hotel corp. exec. b. Syracuse, N.Y., Nov. 28, 1884; s. James and Carrie (Dennis) K.; LL.B., Syracuse U., 1908; Ph.D. (hon.) U. Santo Domingo, 1946; m. Ada C. Shinaman, Nov. 23, 1914 (div. 1927); children—Jane (Mrs. Frederic Taylor, Jr.) (dec.), Dorothy (Mrs. William O. Kopel) (dec.); m. 2d, Mary Grant, May 23, 1940. Admitted to N.Y. bar, 1909; practice in Syracuse; asst. to pres. United Hotels Co. Am., 1919-20, v.p., 1921-26; chmn. bd. Am. Hotels Corp, (co. directing operation of 70 hotels in U.S.); now retired. Mem. Assembly N.Y. State, 1915-16. Served from pvt. to maj., N.Y. N.G. Cav., 1904-16; maj. judge adv., N.Y.G. Div. U.S. Army, Mexican border service; dir. Fed. Registration Bur., N.Y., 1917; maj. and lt. col. judge adv. AEF, 1917-19; adj. gen. N.Y., 1921-22; apptd. maj. gen. N.Y. Nat. Guard by Gov. Smith, 1923; res. brig. gen. N.Y. N.G.; called to U.S. Army, May 1943, served in Sch. Mil. Govt., U. Va.; Algiers, Africa., Aug. 1943; landed Salerno beach, D-plus-5, Sept. 1943; sr. civil affairs officer, Province Naples, Italy (Mil. Govt.) Sept. 1943-July 1944; comdr. Vesuvius Emergency Operation, Mar. 1944; staff So. line of communications supplying 7th Army, July 1944-Jan.

1945; inactive status Apr. 1945; brig. gen. AUS ret. Decorated D.S.C. (U.S.); Distinguished Service Order (Brit.); chevalier Legion of Honor (French); officer of the Crown (Belgium); officer Order Knights of Malta; Order of St. Maurice and St. Lazarus (Italy): hon. citizen of Naples, Italy; comdr. Order of Crown (Italian). Republican. Roman Catholic. Home: Captiva Island Fla. Died Apr. 10, 1973.

KINDERMAN, ROBERT HENRY, pharm. co. exec.; b. Chgo., Jan. 9, 1913; s. Fred and Laura (Zuehr) K.; B.S., U. Ill., 1935, LL.B., 1937; m. Loraine E. Loewe, Apr. 5, 1941; children—Robert Henry, Nancy, Carol. Admitted to Ill. bar, 1937; with firm Hinshaw & Culbertson, Chgo., 1937-44; trial atty. Office Chief Counsel, Bur. Internal Revenue, 1944-51; with firm Sidley, Austin, Burgess & Smith, Chgo., 1951-55; with Mead Johnson & Co., Evansville, Ind., 1955-68, sec., 1955-59, v.p. finance, 1959-61, v.p., treas., 1961-63, v.p. adminstrn., 1963-65, exec. v.p., 1965-68, also dir.; v.p. operations control div. Allied Chem. Corp., 1968-71. Trustee Mead Johnson & Co. Found., 1961-68. Mem. Am., Ind., Ill., Cal. bar assns., Beta Gamma Sigma, Phi Delta Phi, Phi Kappa Phi, Delta Phi. Home: Sun City, Ariz. Died Feb. 2, 1974.

KING, CECIL, congressman; b. Fort Niagara, N.Y., Jan. 13, 1898; ed. pub. schools, Los Angeles; married; 1 child. Businessman. Mem. Calif. Legislature, 1932-42; elected to 77th Congress, 17th Calif. Dist., to fill vacancy, 1942; mem. 78th to 90th Congresses, 17th Cal. Dist. Home: Los Angeles, Cal. Died Mar. 17, 1974.

KING, DOUGLASS STONE, otolaryngologist; b. Alliance, O., Sept. 9, 1907; s. George Lincoln and Myra (Stone) K.; M.D., Western Res. U., 1939; m. Kathryn Elizabeth Middleton, June 16, 1932; 1 son, Christopher M. Rotating intern Cleve. City Hosp., 1939-40; fellow in otolaryngology Cleve. Clinic Corp., 1940-41; basic course in otolaryngology Cleve. Clinic Corp., 1940-41; basic course in otolaryngology U. Ill. Sch. Medicine, 1946-47; practice medicine, specializing in otolaryngology, Alliance, 1947-71; mem. staff Alliance City Hosp. Served to maj., M.C., AUS, 1942-46. Diplomate Am. Bd. Otolaryngology. Mem. A.M.A., Am. Acad. Ophthalmology and Otolaryngology, Nat. Bonai Soc., Alpha Tau Omega, Phi Rho Sigma, Methodist. Kiwanian. Home: Alliance, O. Died June 24, 1971; buried Fairmound Meml. Park, Alliance, O.

KING, EDWARD DUNCAN, real estate co. exec.; b. Ga., Feb. 12, 1896; s. Alfred Fawcett and Leila (Sweat) K.; grad. Savannah High Sch.; m. Ruth Holmer, July 12, 1922; 1 son, Carl Duncan. Clk., Nat. Bank of Savannah, 1916-17, Furse & Lawton, cotton brokers, Savannah, 1917; asst. cashier Exchange Bank Savannah, 1919-22; with A.F. King & Son, realtors, Savannah, 1922-75, pres., 1941-75. Pres., Tax Payers Assn. Chatham County, Savannah, 1959-75; treas. Pure Water Council, Savannah, 1962-75; mem. Bd. Policy Liberty Lobby, Washington, Nat. Com. Against Fluoridation, Washington. Bd. dirs. Savannah Vol. Guards. Served with CAC, U.S. Army, 1917-19; AEF in France. Mem. Savannah Real Estate Bd., Ga. Assn. Real Estate Bds., Nat. Assn. Mut. Ins. Agts., Am. Legion, Vets. World War 1 U.S.A., Sons Confederate Vets., Cinema Ednl. Guild, Hist. Savannah Found., Conservatives. Baptist. Home: Savannah Ga. Died Jan. 23, 1975.

KING, EDWARD JASPER, educator; b. Iowa City, June 4, 1916; s. Irving and Alta (Burke) K.; B.A., State U. Ia., 1937; Ph.D., Yale, 1942; m. Grace E. Wentworth, Feb. 23, 1946; 1 son, Andrew W. Analyst, Dow Chem. Co., 1937-39; instr. chemistry Yale, 1942-46; mem. faculty Barnard Coll., 1946-73, prof. chemistry, 1959-73; vis. reader phys. chemistry U. New Eng., Armidale, N.S. W., Australia, 1966-67. NSF Faculty fellow, 1959-60. Fellow A.A.A.S.; mem. Am. Chem. Soc. (vis. asso. com. profl. tng.), Am. Phys. Soc., Faraday Soc. Author: Qualitative Analysis and Electrolytic Solutions, 1959; Acid-Base Equilibria, 1965; (with Paul and Farinholt) General Chemistry, 1967; Ionic Reactions and Separations, 1973. Home: New York City N.Y. Died Nov. 24 1973; interred Bothal, Northumberland, England.

KING, HAROLD DAVIS, govt. ofcl.; b. Portland, Me., Dec. 20, 1879; s. William Severy and Julia Butterfield (Davis) K.; student Farmington State Normal Sch., 1897-99; B.S., Dartmouth Coll., 1905; m. Edith Etta Thompson, Oct. 7, 1908; children—Roger Thompson (dec.), Edith Elinor, John Harold. Aid and asst. U.S. Coast and Geodetic Survey, 1902-11; in U.S. Lighthouse Service, from 1911, supt. 7th Dist., Key West, Fla., 1911-12, 6th Dist., Charleston, S.C., 1912-14, 5th Dist., Baltimore, 1914-29, dep. commr., Washington, 1929-35, commr., 1935-39, retired. Designated comdr. Squadron 11, 5th Naval Dist., World War. Fellow A.A.A.S.; mem. Am. Soc. Civil Engrs., Thayer Soc. Engrs., Washington Soc. Engrs., Phi Beta Kappa. Unitarian. Club: Cosmos. Home: Washington, D.C.†

KING, HARRY ALBERT, coll. dean; b. Washington, Aug. 26, 1901; s. Frank Arlington and Nellie Agatha (Werres) K.; Mus. B., U. Rochester, 1927; M.A., N.Y.U., 1928, Ph.D., 1939; m. Marjorie Francis Topliffe, Aug. 15, 1932; children—Kathryn Johnston, Francis A. Profl. musician Washington, Rochester symphony orchs., 1920-25, Erie (Pa.) Philharmonic Orch., 1950-58; faculty State Normal Sch., Fredonia, N.Y., 1928-74, asso. dir. Tchrs. Coll., 1948-58, dean, 1958-74; acad. dean State U. Coll. End., Fredonia, 1960-66, dean emeritus, 1966-74. Bd. dirs. Fredonia Coll. Recipient Fredonia Coll. Alumni award of merit, 1965. Mem. Am. Fedn. Musicians (v.p. Local 108), Am. String Tchrs. Assn. (past sec.), N.Y. State Music Assn. (v.p., exec. com. 1950-56), Music Tchrs. Nat. Assn., Music Educators Nat. Conf., Phi Delta Kappa, Phi Mu Alpha Sinfonia. K.C., Kiwanian. Home: Ripley, N.Y. Died June 23, 1974.

KING, JOHN JOSEPH, oil co. exec.; b. Tulsa, Feb. 28, 1922; s. Hugh, Jr. and Carolina (Dickey) K.; student Yale, 1940-41; B.S., U.S. Naval Acad., 1944; m. Dorothy Warren, July 11, 1944; children—John Joseph, Christopher W., Judith E., Margaret K., Constance E., Timothy K. Commd. ensign USN, 1944, advanced through grades to lt., 1953; served in U.S.S. Alaska, 1944-45; naval aviator, 1945-53; resigned, 1953; pres. Cortez Oil Co., Denver, 1953, Alaska Co., Denver. Mem. Denver, London petroleum clubs. Clubs: Army-Navay (Washington); Denver Cherry Hills Country (Denver). Home: Englewood, Colo. Died Apr. 1975.

KING, MARGARET ISADORA, librarian; b. Lexington, Ky., Sept. 1, 1879; d. Gilbert Hinds and Elizabeth (King) K.; ed. private schs., Lexington, Ky.; A.B., U. of Ky., 1898; B.S., Columbia U. Sch. of Library, Service, 1929. Sec. law firm, Lexington, 1899-1905; sec. to pres., and registrar U. of Ky., 1905-12, librarian from 1912. Trustee Lexington Pub. Library, 1936-42. Mem. A.L.A., Southeastern Library Assn., Ky. Library Assn. (pres. 1926-27, mem. library survey commn. 1933-35), Bradford Hist. Assn., Phi Beta Kappa. Democrat. Episcopalian. Club: Altrusa (Lexington). Home: Lexington, Ky.†

KING, MORLAND, educator; b. Bklyn., Nov. 22, 1881; s. Samuel Warner and Mary Ellen (Jeffrey) K.; B.S. in E.E. (commencement honors and Blatchford oratorical prize), Union Coll., Schenectady, N.Y., 1905, M.E.E., 1906, hon. Sc.D., 1930; m. Angelica Van Vranken Olmstead, Sept. 2, 1913; children—Margaret Leslie, Sherwood, Angelica Van Vranken. Instr. in elec. engring., Union Coll., 1906-14, asst. prof., 1914-20; asso. prof. Lafayette Coll., Easton, Pa., 1920-21; prof. and head of dept. elec. engring, from 1921; with testing dept. Gen. Electric Co., Schenectady, summer 1905, transformer engring. Office, summer 1907, standardizing lab., summer 1916, radio engring. dept. summers 1917, 18, 19; with motor power dept. Interborough Rapid Transit Co., summer 1915; supervisor student training, Internat. Motor Co., summers 1928, 29; research engineer, U.S. Army Ordance Dept., 1944-45. Fellow Am. Inst. E.E.; mem. Am. Soc. for Engring. Edn., Am. Assn. Univ. Profs., Alpha Delta Phi, Sigma Xi, Tau Beta Pi. Republican. Unitarian. Home: Easton, Pa.†

KING, RUFUS (FREDERICK), author; b. N.Y.C., Jan. 3, 1893; s. Thomas Armstrong (M.D.) and Amelia Sarony (Lambert) K.; grad. Cutler Sch., N.Y. City, 1910; B.A., Yale, 1914; unmarried. Served with Squadron A, N.Y. Cav., on Mexican border, 1916, and with 105th F.A., in France, 1916-18. Awarded Conspicuous Service Cross (U.S.) Mem. Alpha Delta Phi, Elihu Club (Yale). Republican. Clubs: Pundits, Elizabethan (New Haven); Yale (New York). Author: North Star, 1925; Whelp of the Winds, 1926; Mystery de Luxe, 1927; Murder by the Clock, 1929; A Woman Is Dead, 1930; Murder by Latitude, 1931; Murder in the Willett Family, 1931; The Case of the Constant God, 1935; Crime of Violence, 1936; Valcour Meets Murder; The Secret Agent, 1932; also motion pictures, The Silent Command, North Star, Murder by the Clock, Love Letters of a Star, Invitation to a Murder; Murder at the Vanities (mystery revue with Earl Carroll), 1933; Profile of a Murder, 1934; (play) Invitation to a Murder, 1934; (play with Milton Lazarus) I Want a Policeman, 1936; Murder Masks Miami (book), 1939; The Victoria Docks at 8 (motion picture), 1939; Holiday Homicide, 1940; Diagnosis: Murder, 1941; Design in Evil, 1942; The Case of the Rich Recluse, 1943; A Variety of Weapons; The Case of the Dowager's Etchings, 1943; The Deadly Dove, 1945; Name of Deceased, 4 Minutes 5 Seconds, etc. (magazine series), 1939; mag. serials and books, 1946-50. Secret Behind the Door (motion picture), 1948; syndicated serial An Elopement is Arranged, 1951; Duenna to a Murder, 1952; Miami Papers Please Copy, 1955; The Body in the Rockpit, 1956; Malice in Wonderland, 1958; Steps to Murder, 1960; The Faces of Danger, 1964. Home: West Hollywood, Fla. Deceased

KING, SCOTT, Motel exec.; m. Jewell King; 1 son, Richard Scott. Co—founder, owner TraveLodge Corp., 1946—68; pres., chmn. bd. Trailerancho, 1971—75. Home: La Mesa,, Cal. Died July 18, 1975.

KING, WILLIAM BULLUCK, fgn. service officer; b. Florence, S.C., Aug. 3, 1911; s. Richard Casey and Margaret (Rives) K.; student U. S.C., 1930-34; m. Fay Ball, Sept. 20, 1946. Practicing journalist, Columbia, S.C., 1935-40; fgn. and war corr. in Europe, Africa and Midle East, Asso. Press, 1940-47; dir. pub. relations in Europe, UN Children's Fund, 1949-50; officer fgn. information service U.S., 1951-73 successively in Yugoslavia, India, Iraq, Washington, 1951-59, inspection corps U.S., Information Agy., 1959-60, asst. dir. for Middle East and South Asia, 1960-63; counselor of embassy for public affairs, Karachi, Pakistan, 1963-73. Recipient service award from the United States Information Agency, 1959. Mem. Fgn. Service Assn., Sigma Delta Chi. Club: Overseas Press (N.Y.C.). Author: (with Frank O'Brien) The Balkans: Frontier of Two Worlds, 1947. Home: Washington, D.C. Died Oct 1, 1973.

KINGMAN, EUGENE, museum ofcl.; b. Providence, Nov. 10, 1909; s. Eugene Allerton and Celia Arnold (Spicer) K.; B.A., Yale, 1932, B.F.A., 1935; D.F.A. (hon.), Creighton U., 1968; m. Mary Elizabeth Yelm, June 10, 1939; children—Mary Martha, Elizabeth Anne. Instr. mural painting R.I. Sch. Design, 1935-39; dir. Philbrook Art Center, Tulsa 1939-42; asst. dir. Joslyn Art Mus., Omaha, Neb., 1946-47, dir., 1947-69, also trustee; dir. exhibits, curator art Tex. Tech. U. Mus., Lubbock, 1969-75; works exhibited Nat. Park Service Exhibit, Paris Expn., 1931; executed mural Post Office, Hyattsville, Md., 1937, Kemmerer, Wyo., 1938, East Providence, R.I., 1939, N.Y. Times Bldg., N.Y.C., 1948; lithograph in permanent collection Library of Congress. U.S. del. Conf. Regional Museums, Schaffhausen, Switzerland, 1954; cons. on exhbns. Smithsonian Instn., 1957-58, 60-61. Mem. Neb. Arts Council, v.p., 1966-75; mem. Gov's Mural Commn. 1949-69; mem. Gov. Neb. Hall of Fame Commn., Omaha, 1968-75; bd. regents Coll. of St. Mary, Omaha, 1968-69. Recipient 1st prize graphic art Okla. Artists Ann., 1940; 1st purchase prize in painting Mulvane Art Mus. Ann. Exhbn., Topeka, Kan., 1951; 1st prize; mems. exhbn., Providence Art Club, 1956; Myrtle award Hadassah, 1965; KMTV television, 1968; Best of Show and Purchase award Tex. Fine Arts Assn., 1973; many others. Mem. Am. Assn. Museums, A. Assn. Art Mus. Dirs. (v.p. 1967-68), Audubon Artists Group N.Y., Tex. Fine Arts Assn., Lubbock Art Assn. Clubs: Professional men's of Omaha (pres. 1951); Providence Art. Home: Lubbock Tex. Died Feb. 20, 1975

KINLEY, JOHN JAMES, Canadian senator; b. Lunenburg, N.S., Oct. 15, 1881; s. James Francis and Louisa Annetta (Loye) K.; student Lunenburg Acad., Royal Sch. of Inf.; m. Lila E. D. Young, Jan. 7, 1920; children—Mary Louisa (Mrs. James Ferguson Russell), John James. Apprentice and tech. tng. in pharmacy; pres. Lunenburg Foundry Co., Ltd., Lunenburg Foundry Garage Co., Ltd., Progress-Enterprise Co., Ltd. (weekly newspaper). Mayor, Town of Lunenburg, 1911-13; mem. N.S. Legislature, 1916, mem. N.S. Govt., 1924-25, 1928-29; elected to House of Commons, 1935, re-elected 1940; senator Canadian Parliament, from 1945. Served with Canadian Militia, ret. as maj.; pres. Neptune Sea Cadet Corps, St. John Ambulance Assn.; mem. nat. ambulance com. Ottawa. Decorated King Haakon's Cross of Liberty for distinguished service to Norway, World War II, Knight of Grace Order St. John of Jerusalem, King's Jubilee Medal, King's Coronation Medal, Colonial Auxiliary Services medal, Long Services medal. Liberal Presby. Freemason. Odd Fellow. Clubs: Lunenburg Yacht, Bluenose Golf, Lunenburg Curling. Home: Lunenburg, N.S., Can.†

KINNANE, RAPHAEL IGNATIUS, clergyman; b. Lima, O., June 7, 1881; s. John and Dusabelle (Rinehart) K.; grad. cum summa laude, St. Charles Coll., Ellicott City, Md., 1902; student, St. Mary's Sem., Cleve., 1905; S.T.D., Propaganda U., Rome (Italy), 1908. Ordained priest Roman Cath. Ch., 1908; chancellor Diocese of Toledo, 1911-12, vicar gen., from 1941; pastor, Port Clinton, O., 1912-27, Maumee, O., 1927-40, St. Mary's Ch., Tiffin, O., from 1940; domestic prelate, 1925, protonotary apostolic, 1946. Mem. Toledo Rationing Bd., World War II. Served as chaplain U.S. Army World War II. Address: Tiffin, O.†

KINNEY, CHARLES NOYES, chemist; b. Iowa City, Ia., 1879; s. George W. and Elizabeth Noyes Kinney; prep. ed'n in acad. of Drake Univ.; grad. Drake Univ. (studied at Mass. Inst. Technology, Yale, Chicago Univ.); m. Golda Jameson, July, 1896. Furnished expert evidence as a chemist for the State in a number of murder cases, illegal selling of liquors, food adulterations, etc. Mem. of a number of chem. socs. Home: Moines, Ia.†

KINNEY, EDMUND J., educator; b. Yellow Springs, O., Dec. 26, 1879; s. Mathias and Sara Ellen (Applegate) K.; student Antioch Coll., Yellow Springs, 1897-98; B.S., Ohio State, 1908; m. Kathryn Petrey, Dec. 28, 1908; children—Frances Ware (Mrs. Wm. A. Schell), Sara Kathryn (Mrs. James Edmundson). Research in entomology, Ky. Expt, Sta., 1908-11, asst. prof. agronomy and asst. agronomist, 1912-16, asso. prof., 1916-19, prof. agronomy 1919-50, agronomist 1919-50; head agronomy dept. and prof. agronomy U. of Kentucky, 1943-50. Fellow A.A.A.S.; mem. Am. Soc. Agronomy, Ky. Acad. Sci., Alpha Zeta, Alpha Gamma Rho. Democrat. Presbyterian. Club: University. Contbr. articles to encys., textbooks and bulls. also prof. pubs. on tobacco prodn. Home: Lexington, Ky.†

KINNEY, WILLIAM ALOYSIUS, mag. editor; b. Newark, Mar. 25, 1907; s. John Francis and Frances (Young) K.; A.B. magna cum laude, Holy Cross Coll.,

1928; m. Roseanna McQuesten, Dec. 18, 1943. News corr. United Press Assn., N.Y.C. Bur., 1929-30; staff reporter Newark Star Eagle, 1930-31; asst. night news editor Newark Bur. Asso. Press, 1931-32, night news editor, 1932-33, day news editor, 1933-34, state news editor, 1934-37, spl. assignment N.Y.C. Bur., 1937-40, asst, news editor (night), Washington, 1940-41, night news editor, 1941-42, 46; mem. bd. internat. editors World Report, 1946-47; dir. news service Nat. Geographic Soc., 1948-51, editorial staff Nat. Geographic Mag., 1951-54; self-employed as lit., research, pub. relations cons., 1954-57; publs. cons. Office of Sec. of USAF, 1957, editorial cons. and publ. specialist, 1957-58, contbg. editor, 1958, space sciences editor, The Airman Mag., Washington, 1958-73. Served with M.I., USAAF, 1942-46. Fellow Brit. Interplanetary Soc.; mem. Am. Inst. Aeros. and Astronautics, Am. Geophys. Union, A.A.A.S., Md. Hist. Soc., Nat. Geographic Soc. Roman Catholic. Club: Cosmos (Washington). Author: Medical Science and Space Travel, 1959; also short stories in mags. Co-editor, contbr.; Dateline: Washington, 1949; contbr. to Rocket and Missile Technology, 1964. Home: Washington D.C. Died Aug. 20, 1973; buried Gate of Heaven Cemetery, Washington, D.C.

KINSLOE, CHARLES LAMBERT, elec. engr.; b. Lock Haven, Pa., Oct. 15, 1881; s. Frank and Ida (Lambert) K.; grad. Central State Normal Sch., Lock Haven, 1899; B.S., Pa. State Coll., 1903, M.S. in E.E., 1907; m. Margaret White Buckhout (died 1937), July 14, 1909; children—Helen Lambert, Margaret K. (Madison), Elizabeth K. (Henning). Student engineer Westinghouse Electric and Manufacturing Company, Pittsburgh, Pennsylvania, 1903; engr. Phila. Electric Co., 1904-05, United Gas Improvement Co., Phila., 1905-06; instr. elec. engring., U. of Pittsburgh, 1906-07; with Pa. State Coll. from 1907, actg. head dept. elec. engring., 1907-09, head of dept. 1909-44; prof. emeritus, from 1944; consulting practice. Trustee, Pa. State Coll. Mem. Am. Inst. Elec. Engrs., American Society for Engring. Edn., Sigma Chi, Eta Kappa Nu, Sigma Tau, Sigma Xi, Phi Kappa Phi, Triangle. Republican. Mason. Home: State College, Pa.†

KINTNER, ROBERT CHESTER, chem. engr.; b. Milford Center, O., Mar. 3, 1900; s. John Christian and Frances Elizabeth (Campbell) K.; B.Chem. Engring., Ohio State U., 1923, M.S., 1929, Ph.D., 1931; m. LeEvelyn Gillam, Mar. 2, 1929. Chem. engr. Drackett Chem. Co., 1923-24, Crystal Carbonic Labs., 1925, Swift & Co., 1926-27; asst. dept. chem. engring. Ohio State U., 1928-29; asst. prof. Rose Poly. Inst., 1929-30, Bucknell U., 1933-37; asso. prof. Ill. Inst. Tech., 1937-42, prof., 1942-69, emeritus, 1969, asst. dean Grad. Sch., 1944-50; sr. vis. fellow U. Aston, Birmingham, Eng., 1969. Recipient Distinguished Alumnus award Ohio State U. Coll. Engring., 1971. Fellow Am. Inst. Chem. Engrs. (chmn. chem. engring. edn. project com. 1954-58; Mem. Am. Chem. Soc., Scabbard and Blade, Sigma Xi, Alpha Chi Sigma, Phi Lamdba Upsilon, Pi Mu Epsilon. Author articles bubble and drop phenomena. Home: South Holland Ill. Died Oct. 15, 1974; interred Mt. Hope Cemetery, Chicago, Ill.

KIRBY, LAVERNE HOWE, architect, engr.; b. Sherman, Tex., Aug. 19, 1912; s. Robert E. and Mabel (Howe) K.; B.S., Tex. Tech, Coll., 1945; m. Lellessee Marcella Hays, Nov. 25, 1936; children—Laverne, Nancy. Partner, Haynes, Strange & Kirby, 1946-47, Haynes & Kirby, 1947-65; gen. practice Laverne H. Kirby, architect and engr., 1965-72. Mem. A.I.A., Nat. Soc. Profl. Engrs., Am. Soc. Heating, Refrigeration and Airconditioning Engrs. Presbyn. Clubs: Lions, Lubbock. Home: Lubbock Tex. Died Oct. 26, 1972.

KIRCHWEY, FREDA, editor, writer; d. George W. and Dora (Wendell) Kirchwey; grad. Horace Mann Sch., N.Y.C., 1911; A.B., Barnard Coll. (Columbia), 1915; LH.D., Rollins Coll., 1944; m. Evans Clark, Nov. 9, 1915; children—Brewster (dec.), Michael Kirchwey, Jeffrey (dec.). Reporter, Morning Telegraph, N.Y.C., 1915-16; editorial staff Every Week, N.Y.C., 1917-18; staff Sunday Tribune, 1918; with The Nation, 1918-55; mng. editor, 1922-28, became v.p., 1922, literary editor, 1928-29, editor, 1932-55, editor and pub., 1937-55. Decorated chevalier French Legion of Honor, 1946. Mem. Commn. World Devel. and World Disarmament, Womens Internat. League Peace and Freedom, Am. Civil Liberties Union, Internat. League Rights Man, N.A.A.C.P., Com. Democratic Spain (vice chmn.), League Women Voters, Mus. Modern Art. Club: Cosmopolitan (N.Y.C.). Home: St. Petersburg Fla., Died an. 3, 1976.

KIRK, ALBERT E., clergyman; b. Halstead, Harvey County, Kan., Apr. 23, 1880; s. George and Jane (Cooper) K.; A.B., Baker U., 1902, A.M., 1903, D.D., 1917; S.T.B., Boston U. Sch. of Theology, 1907; Ph.D., Boston U. Grad. Sch., 1915; LL.D. Southwestern Coll., 1928; m. Lulah Barricklow, Aug. 17, 1904; children—Phyllis Elizabeth (Mrs. Harold C. Case), Robert Van Dyke. Entered M.E. ministry, 1903; postorates, 1903-18; executive secretary Wichita (Kansas) area M.E. Church, 1918-19; pres. Southwestern Coll., Winfield, Kan., 1919-28; sec. Div. of Ednl. Instns. of M.E. Ch., 1928-32; pastor Sterling, Kan., 1932-35; supt. Hutchinson Dist., 1935-37, Wichita Dist., 1937-41; pastor Meth. Ch., Manhattan, Kan., 1941-44; supt., Independence dist., 1944-50; religion editor Wichita Eagle. Member General Conference, 7 times to 1940; del. Methodist Ecumenical Conf., London, 1921; mem. Uniting Conf., 1939. Mason. Rotarian. Author of "Our Economic Sickness," "Vital Religion,", "It Can Happen in the Church," 1951; "A Consciousness of God," 1952, and various vocational and religions monographs Home: Wichita, Kan.†

KIRK, JOHN ESBEN, physician; b. Kallundborg, Denmark, Nov. 8, 1905; s. Ole Christian Mathias and Augusta Dorthea (Bang) K.; M.D., U. Copenhagen, 1929, Ph.D., 1936; m. Irma Muser, May 28, 1934; children—Ermalynn, Peter, Lillian, Thomas Esben, Paul Albert. Came to U.S., 1947, naturalized, 1949. Asst. Rockefeller Inst. Med. Research, N.Y.C., 1931-34; asst. resident physician Bispebjerg Municipal Hosp., Copenhagen, 1934-36; resident med. dept. U. Hosp., U. Copenhagen, 1936-39; dir. City Health Labs., Copenhagen, 1936-39; chief physician med. dept. Holstebro Co. Hosp. Denmark, 1939-47; dir. research div. gerontology sch. medicine Washington U., St. Louis, 1947-73, asst. prof. medicine, 1947-50, asso. prof. medicine, 1950-64, prof. medicine, 1964-73. Recipient Wisdom Award of Honor, 1970. Fellow A.C.P., mem. Internat. Acad. Pathology. Am. Soc. Study of Premortal Condition (pres. 1960-65), Am. Soc. Biol. Chemists, Gerontological Soc., Central So. Clin. Research, Am. Soc. Study Arteriosclerosis, Harvey Soc., Royal Soc. Medicine (London), Alpha Omega Alpha (hon.). Author: Enzymes of the Arterial Wall, 1969. Editor Jour. of Gerontology, 1948-62. Home: St. Louis, Mo. Died Apr. 7, 1975; cremated.

KIRK, RALPH G., author; b. Harrisburg, Pa., Mar. 19, 1881; s. Jacob and Alice (Kutz) K.; grad. high sch., Harrisburg, 1899; Met. E., Lehigh U., 1905; m. Helen Weidman, Mar. 26, 1913; children—Robert Weidman, Barbara. Began with Lackawanna Steel Co., Buffalo, N.Y., 1905, and continued as steel mill engr., constrn. supt. and contractor; began writing stories for mags., 1916. Mem. Tau Beta Pi. Republican. Methodist. Clubs: Santa Monica Athletic, Los Angeles Athletic, Hollywood Athletic, Pacific Coast (Long Beach). Author: White Monarch and the Gas House Pup, 1917; Zanoza, 1918; Six Breeds, 1923. Home: Harrisburg, Pa.†

KIRK, WILLIAM TALBOT, assn. exec.; b. Columbus, O., Mar. 24, 1918; s. Emmet Lyle and Katherine (Talbot) K.; B.S., Ohio State U., 1932; grad. N.Y. Sch. Social Work, Columbia, 1936, Harvard U. Sch. for Overseas Adminstrn., 1943; m. Ruth Van Voorhis, Sept. 15, 1934; 1 son, David G. Exec. sec. Protestant Family Welfare, Inc., Albany, N.Y., 1938-41; exec. dir. Provident Family & Children's Service, Kansas City, Mo., 1941-43; dir. spl. services div. Community Service Soc. of N.Y.; 1945-50; dir. Am. br., Internat. Social Service, N.Y.C., 1950-62, internat. dir., Geneva, Switzerland, 1950-62; exec. dir. Motion Picture and TV Fund, Inc., Los Angeles, until 1971, cons., 1971-74. Past pres. sch. bd., Hartsdale, N.Y. Served capt. to maj., AUS, 1943-45. Decorated Bronze Star medal. Mem. Alumni Assn. N.Y. Sch. Social Work (past pres.), Nat. Assn. Social Workers, Nat. Conf. Social Work (exec. com.), U.S. Com for Refugees, Internat. Inst. Los Angeles (past pres.), Pres., Acad. Motion Picture Arts and Scis., Beta Theta Pi. Home: Los Angeles, Cal. Died Jan. 7, 1974

KIRKBRIDE, WALTER GEORGE, bus. exec., lawyer; b. Parker's Landing, Pa., Jan. 13, 1881; s. Joseph A. and Anna Bertha (Loftus) K.; LL.B., U. of Mich., 1900; m. Alice Harrop, June 21, 1904; children—Alice (Mrs. Glen Meridith Davis), Esther (Mrs. Charles John Cole), Mabel (Mrs. Theodore Grant Patterson). Admitted to Ohio bar, 1902, practiced at Toledo; mem. Kirkbride, Cole, Freese & Mittendorf; gen. counsel Hickok Oil Corp., Toledo, from 1915, v.p., 1932-45, pres., 1945-52; chmn. bd., dir. Pure Oil Products Co. (Ohio); pres. and dir. Hickok Oil Corp., Wilson Oil Corp. (Detroit), Hickok Prodn. and Development, Hickok Pipe Lines Co., Consol. Gasoline Co.; v.p. and dir. Pocahontas Corp. (Cleveland), Highland Oil Corp. (Detroit); dir. Jacox Oil Corp., Buckeye Brewing Co., Butcher & Hart Mfg. Co. Mem. Toledo, Ohio State, Am. bar assns., Am. Law Inst. Alumni Assn. U. of Mich. (nat. pres., 1944-46, dir.; granted distinguished Alumni Award, 1951), Republican. Presbyn. Clubs: Toledo Country, Toledo (Toledo); Detroit Athletic. Home: Toledo, O.†

KIRKLAND, EDWARD CHASE, educator; b. Bellows Falls, Vt., May 24, 1894; s. Edward and Mary (Chase) K.; A.B., Dartmouth, 1916, Litt.D., 1949; A.M. Harvard, 1921, Ph.D., 1924; M.A., Cambridge U., 1956; Litt. D., Princeton, 1957, Bowdon Coll., 1961; m. Ruth Stevens Babson, Sept. 4, 1924; 1 son, Edward. Instr. in citizenship, Dartmouth Coll., 1920-21, instr. in history Mass. Inst. Tech., 1922-24; asst. prof. Am. history Brown U., 1924-30; asso. prof. Bowdoin Coll., 1930-31, prof., 1931-55, prof. emeritus, 1955-75; Pitt prof. Am. history, Cambridge U., 1956-57; Commonwealth lectr. U. Coll., London, 1952. Served as pvt. 1st class Ambulance Service, U.S. Army, with the French Army, 1917-19. Decorated Croix de Guerre (France). Guggenheim fellow, 1955-56. Mem. Am. Hist. Assn., Orgn. of Am. Historians (pres. 1955-56); Econ. History Assn. (pres. 1953-54), Am. Newcomen Soc., Mass. Hist. Soc., Colonial Soc. Mass., Am. Antiquarian Soc., Am. Friends of Lafayette, Am. Assn. U. Profs. (pres. 1946-48), Am. Acad. Arts and Scis. Phi Beta Kappa (senator 1951-70). Author: Peacemakers of 1864, 1927; A History of American Economic Life, 1932, 39, 52, 69; Brunswick's Golden Age, 1942; Men, Cities and Transportation, a Study in New England History 1820-1900, 1948; Business in the Gilded Age: The Conservatives' Balance Sheet, 1952; Dream and Thought in the Business Community, 1860-1900, 1956; Industry Comes of Age: Business, Labor and Public Policy 1860-1897, 1961. Editor: Andrew Carnegie, Gospel of Wealth, 1962; Charles Francis Adams, Jr., 1835-1915; The Patrician at Bay, 1965; A Bibliography of American Economic History since 1861, 1971. Home Thetford Center, Vt. Died May 24, 1975.

KISTLER, SAMUEL STEPHENS, educator; b. Cedarville, Cal., Mar. 26, 1900; s. Amandus Christian and Stella Elizabeth (Stephens) K.; A.B., Stanford, 1921. Chem. Engr., 1922, Ph.D., 1929; grad. Advanced Mgmt. Program, Harvard, 1951; postgrad. (internat. fellow) U. Berlin (Germany), 1929. U. Goettingen (Germany), 1930; m. Margaret Coburn, June 28, 1924; children—Walter A., Elizabeth J. (Mrs. R. E. Wallace). Prof. chemistry Coll. of Pacific, 1923-31; prof. chem. engring. U. Ill., 1931-35; group leader to dir. research Norton Abrasive Co., 1935-52; dean Coll. Engring., U. Utah, Salt Lake City, 1952-64, prof. chem. engring., 1964-68, research prof., 1968-70, ret., 1970; cons. E. I. duPone de Nemours & Co., Inc., 1931-35, Avco Research & Advanced Devel. Corp., 1959-66; dir. research Sterling Grinding Wheel Co., 1952-67; cons. Nippon Toki Kaisha, Japan, 1957-64, Minn, Mining and Mfg. Co., France, 1961, Durrschmidt Co., Lyons, France, 1958, Corning Glass Works, 1965-71. Recipient Ross Coffin Purdy award Am. Ceramic Soc., 1963, awards Am. Chem. Soc., 1966,69, award Sigma Xi, 1968. Fellow Am. Ceramic Soc.; mem. Inst. Physics, Am. Inst. Chem. Engrs., Am. Soc. Profl. Engrs., A.A.A.S., Am. Chem. Soc., Sigma Xi. Rotarian. Author chpts. in books, sci. papers. Patentee in field; developed 1st unbreakable lens; pioneer synthesizing diamonds. Home: Salt Lake City, Utah., Died Nov. 6, 1975.

KITCHEN, JOSEPH AMBROSE, b. Wyanet, Ill., Dec. 5, 1878; s. Joseph Low and Mary Adelia (Mosher) K.; LL.B., Northern Ind. Law Sch., Valparaiso, 1903; A.B., Valparaiso Coll., 1903, A.M., 1913, LL.D., 1925; B.O., Ralston U. of Expression, Washington, D.C., 1904; m. Pearl S. Smith, Aug. 25, 1904. Moved to Sentinel Butte, N.D., 1904; county supt. of schs., Billings County, N.D., 1906-14; mem. N.D. Ho. of Rep., 1920, elected State Commn. of Agr. and Labor, N.D., Oct. 28, 1921, to take place of official recalled under first recall election in N.D., reelected 5 times, 1923-31. Served in Cuba; pvt. Co. A, 161st Ind. Vol. Inf., Spanish-Am. War, 1898; commd. capt., N.D. State Home Guards, 1918; served World War in Central Officers' Training Camp, 1st Co., 3rd Bn., Camp Pike, Ark. Past dept. comdr. Vets. of Foreign Wars for N.Dak.; chaplain Vets. Foreign Wars Post and adj. Spanish War Vets., Ft. Myers. Presbyn. Home: Fort Myers, Fla.†

KITSON, GEOFFREY HERBERT, univ. adminstr.; b. June 22, 1896; s. Henry Herbert Kitson; student Charterhouse; LL.D., Leeds U., 1963; m. Kathleen Mary Alexandra Paul, 1923; 3 sons, 1 dau. Mem. Leeds (Eng.) City Council, 1930-38; chmn. Leeds Corp. Gas Com.; pres. Brit. Comml. Gas Assn., 1931; dir. Leeds Permanent Bldg. Soc., 1934; pres. Leeds C. of C., 1935-36; pro-chancellor U. Leeds. Chmn. bd. Theatre and Opera House (Leeds) Ltd. D.L. W. Riding of Yorks, 1963. Hon. col. 249 Regt., Royal Army, 1957-63. Decorated Order Brit. Empire. Club: Leeds. Home: Leeds, Eng. Died Nov. 7, 1974.

KIVETTE, FREDERICK NORMAN, naval ofcr.; b. Boise, Ida., July 7, 1902; s. Walter Raleigh and Dulcie (Fleming) K.; grad. U.S. Naval Acad., 1925, U.S. Naval War Coll., 1950; m. Elizabeth Earl Clapp, Dec. 26, 1927; 1 son, Frederick Norman. Commd. ensign U.S.N., 1925, advanced through grades to vice adm.; naval avaitor from 1928; served as comdg. officer Seaplane Tender U.S.S. Williamson, aircraft carriers U.S.S. Hoggatt Bay, and U.S.S. Midway, and Carrier Div. 16; served with Pacific Fleet in Alaska-Aleutian water and in South Pacific, also chief staff Naval Air Res. Tng. Command, and chief of staff Air Force, Atlantic Fleet; asst. chief of naval operations (air) Dept. of Navy; comdr. 7th fleet, ret. 1961. Decorated Bronze Star Medal. Died May 18, 1975.

KIXMILLER, EDGAR BYRON, lawyer; b. Bicknell, Ind., Dec. 19, 1885; s. Frederick and Ellen (Mason) K.; student DePauw U., 1904-07, U. Chgo., 1908-09; LL.B., Yale, 1913; m. Claire Willis, Dec. 24, 1913; 1 dau., Betty (Mrs. John S. Russell, Jr.). Admitted to Ind. bar, 1912, Ill. bar, 1913, asst. pros. atty. Ind., 1913-14; atty. Swift & Co. 1914-74, gen. atty. 1931-42, gen. counsel, 1942-52. Mem. Civic Fedn. (Chgo. adv. com.), Am., N.Y. State, Ill., Chgo. bar assns., Law Inst. Chgo., Judicature Soc., Phi Gamma Delta, Chi Tau Kappa. Clubs: Chicago Tax, South Shore Country, Mid-Day, Yale, Law, University (Chgo.). Author: Treatise on Federal Food Control Law, 1918; contbr. articles to jours.; former editor Yale Law Jour. Home: Chicago, Ill. Died Dec. 12, 1974

KIZER, BENJAMIN HAMILTON, lawyer; b. Champaign County, O., Oct. 29, 1878; s. Benjamin Franklin and Mary Louise (Hamilton) K.; LL.B., U. of Mich., 1902; LL.D., Linfield College, McMinville, Ore., Reed College, Portland, Ore.; m. Helen Bullis, May 19, 1915 (died Sept. 21, 1919); m. 2d, Mabel Ashley, Mar. 12, 1921; 1 dau., Carolyn Ashley (Mrs. Stimson Bulliet). Admitted to Mich. bar, 1902, Wash., 1902, practiced in Spokane; partner Kizer, Gaiser, Stoeve, Layman & Powell. Pres. Spokane City Plan Commission, 1928-44; former chairman of the Washington State Planning Council, 1933-44; chmn. Pacific Northwest Regional Planning Commn.; former pres. Am. Soc. Planning Officials; mem. bd. regents, Reed Coll., Portland, Ore., chmn. World Affairs Council of Inland Empire. Asso. Nat. War Labor Bd. (chmn. West Coast Lumber Commn.). Spl. Master, U.S. Circuit Ct. Appeals, 9th Circuit, 1942-44; director China Office, U.N.R.R.A., 1944-46. Walker-Ames professor of internat. relations, U. of Wash., 1946-47, Washington State chairman Crusade for Freedom, 1950; chairman Rhodes Scholars Exam. Com. for 6 Pacific Northwest States from 1932. Awarded Auspicious Star. Grand Cordon (China). Member Am., Wash. State (past pres.), Spokane County (past pres.) bar assns.; Order of the Coif, Phi Beta Kappa. Author: The U.S. Canadian Northwest. Home: Spokane, Wash.†

KJERSTAD, CONRAD LUND, b. Dakota Territory, July 11, 1883; s. Peter Nelson and Maria (Jonson) K.; student Augustana Coll., Sioux Falls, S.D., 1902-05; A.B., U. of S.D., 1911; M.A., U. of Chicago, 1916, Ph.D. cum laude, 1917; m. Alma Nelson,eNelson, June 30, 1916; children—Muriel Adele, Ruth Elaine, Phyllis Clare. Began as rural sch. teacher, S.D., 1905; dir. normal dept., Augustana Coll., 1911-15; fellow Dept. of Psychology, U. of Chicago, 1915-16; instr. State Teachers College, Winona, Minn., 1911-17; asst. in psychology, State Teachers Coll., Valley City, N.D., 1917-18, head dept. edn., 1919-20, head dept. edn. and psychology, 1920-24, dean faculty, 1924-29; pres. State Teachrs Colls. Dickinson, N.D., 1929-36; prof. philosophy and education and head dept., of philosophy, U. of North Dakota, from 1936; president State Normal Sch. Holding Assn., 1931-36, Dir. U.N., Center for N. Dak. Served as 1st lt. U.S. Army, World War. Fellow A.A.A.S., Am. Psychol. Assn.; mem. Am. Philso. Assn. N.E.A., Am. Assn. Teachers Colleges (chmn. com. standards and surveys), Am. Assn. Univ. Profs., N.D., Ednl. Assn., Greater N.D. Assn., Phi Sigma Pi, Phi Delta Kappa, Sigma Xi. Lutheran. Kiwanian (ex-lt. gov. Minn., S.D. and N.D. dist.), Rotarian. Home: Grand Forks, N.D., Died Dec. 23, 1967; interred Forest Hill Cemetery, Canton, S.D.

KLARMANN, ADOLF D., educator; b. Austria, Sept. 18, 1904; s. Oscar and Regina (Trompeter) K.; came to U.S., 1923, naturalized, 1929; student Berlin U., 1922-23; A.B., N.Y. U., 1926, M.A., 1927; postgrad. Munich U., 1927-28; Ph.D., U. Pa., 1930; Litt.D., Lebanon Valley Coll., 1967; L.H.D., LaSalle Coll., 1974; m. Isolde Doernenburg, Aug. 12, 1939. Instr., N.Y. U., 1926-28, U. Rochester, 1928-29, 30-31; mem. faculty U. Pa., 1929—, prof. German and gen. lit., 1955-75; vis. prof. U. Cal. at Los Angeles, U. Cal. at Berkeley, U. Colo., Johns Hopkins. Jusserand fellow, 1936, 52; Fulbright research fellow to Vienna, 1952-53; Guggenheim fellow, 1966-67; hon. mem. Phi Beta Kappa, 1967; recipient Austrian Cross of Honor for Letters and Arts I class. Mem. Internat. Assn. Germanists, Internat. Fedn. Modern Langs. and Lits., Modern Humanities Assn., Modern Lang. Assn., A.A.U.P., Am. Assn. Tchrs. German, Am. Council Study Austrian Lit. (pres. 1969-71), Acad. Lit. Studies. Contbr. articles profl. jours. Editor lit. estate of Franz Werfel, 1945-75; editor German Quar., 1963-65. Home: Philadelphia, Pa., Died Aug. 27, 1975.

KLAWANS, ARTHUR HERMAN, medical educator; b. Chgo., Aug. 14, 1902; s. Israel and Fannie Klawans; B.S., U. Chgo., 1924; M.D., Rush Med. Sch., Chgo., 1928; m. Hannah M. Stein, Mar. 14, 1927; children—Dorothy (Mrs. Hubert Rosenblum), Arthur Herman. Mem. faculty U. Ill. Med. Sch., 1941-71, clin. prof. obstetrics and gynecology, 1961-71; prof. obstetrics and gynecology Rush Med. Coll., 1970-73; cons. obstetrics and gynecologist Presbyn.-St. Luke's Hosp., Chgo., 1970-73. Diplomate Am. Bd. Obstetricians and Gynecologists, Central Assn. Obstetricians and Gyncologists, Chgo. Gynecol. Soc. Home: Chicago Ill. Died Sept. 28, 1973

KLEBENOV, LOUIS H., b. 1901; ed. Harvard, Clark U.; m. Natalie Garson; 1 son, Heywood. First v.p. Ogden Food Service, 1950-71. Home: Newton, Mass. Died Feb. 25, 1974.

KLEBERG, ROBERT JUSTUS, Jr., ranchman; b. Corpus Christi, Tex., Mar. 29, 1896; s. Robert Justus and Alice Gertrudis (King) K.; ed. pub. schs. and U. of Wis.; hon. Dr. Agrl. Sci., Tex. A. and M.U., 1941; D. Sc., U. Wis., 1967 m. Helen Campbell, Mar. 2, 1926 (dec. 1963); 1 dau., Helen King (Mrs. Lloyd L. Groves). Engaged in ranching, 1916-74; pres., chief exec. officer King Ranch, Inc.; served as trustee Henrietta King Estate, holding large investment in land and cattle; responsible for the devel. of the Santa Gertrudis breed of cattle, and The King Ranch Family Quarter Horses; pres. John B. Ragland Merc. Co.; dir. King Ranch (Australia) Pty. Ltd., King Ranch Pastoral Co., Pty., Ltd. (Australia) King Ranch Argentina, S.A., King Ranch do Brazil, Ranch darouch, Morocco, King Ranch Espana, Spain; pres. Buck & Doe Run Valley Farms Co., Coatesville, Pa., King Ranch Farm, Lexington, Ky. Mem. Tex. and Southwestern Cattle Raisers Assn. (exec. com.), Com. Econ. Devel., Thoroughbred Club Am., Sigma Chi. Clubs: Country; Truf and Field, Jockey, River, Racquet and Tennis (N.Y.C.). Home: Kingsville Tex. Died Oct. 13, 1974; interred King Ranch, Tex.

KLECKI, PAUL, condr.; b. Poland, Mar. 21, 1900; ed. Warsaw Conservatorie (Poland), Berlin Acad. Music (Germany). Tchr. composition Scuola Superiora di Musica, Milan, Italy, 1935; prin. condr. Kharkov Philharmonic Orch., 1937; with Red Cross, Geneva, Switzerland, World War II; dir. Lucerne Festival, Lausanne Compositon classes, 1944-45; guest condr. Vienna Festival, Salsburg Festival; guest condr. U.S., Israel, Australia, S. Am., Japan, USSR, various European countries, 1945—73; participant Montreux Festival, 1945-67; condr. La Scala Inaugural concerts, 1946; Condr. Israel Philharmonic for Pope Pius XII, 1949; mus. dir. Dallas Symphony Orch., 1958—67, Suisse Romande Orch., 1967—73; toured North and South Am. with London Philharmonic, 1967; hon. prof. Lausanne Conservatoire; named burgess Montreux, 1958; hon. citizen Dallas, 1965. Composer: 3 symphonies, Sinfonietta for Strings, Violin Concerto, Piano Concerto, other pieces. Address: Muri—Bern, Switzerland. Died Mar. 5, 1973.

KLEIN, ARTHUR WARNER, educator; b. New Haven, Conn., Nov. 17, 1880; s. Joseph Frederic and Ada Louise (Warner) K.; M.E., Lehigh Univ., 1899; m. Josephine Russell Brock, July 10, 1907; 1 dau., Dorothy Brock (Mrs. David Perry Nichols). Began career as cadet engineer Essex and Hudson Gas Co., Newark, N.J., 1900-01; asst. to supt. Atlanta Gas Light Co., 1901-03; prof. of mech. engineering and physics Grove City (Pa.) Coll., 1903-04; instructor Lehigh U., asst. prof., asso. prof., prof. mech. engring. from 1904. Mem. Am. Soc. Mech. Engrs., Soc. Promotion Engring. Edn., Soc. Advancement Sci. Mem. Bach Choir. Author: Kinematics of Machinery, 1917. Home: Bethlehem, Pa.†

KLEIN, GEORGE H., lawyer; b. Carlinville, Ill., Dec. 16, 1880; B.S., Blackburn U., 1899; LL.B., U. Mich., 1902. Admitted to Mich. bar, 1902, Cal. bar, 1903; sr. mem. Clark, Klein, Brucker & Waples, Detroit.†

KLEIN, JOSEPH J(EROME), author, accountant, lawyer; b. N.Y.C.; s. Pinkus and Esther (Eichler) K.; B.S., Coll. City of New York, 1906; M.A., New York U., 1909, Ph.D., 1910, C.P.A., 1911; LL.B., Fordham U., 1923; m. Janet R. Frisch, 1918; children—David Charles, Paul Lincoln. Formerly spl. lecturer and organizer municipal accounting lectures, New York U. Sch. of Commerce, Accounts and Finance; lecturer on commercial edn., Coll. City of New York, 1914-15, on auditing and accounting systems, 1916-18, on federal and state taxation, 1919-33, associated prof. taxation 1928-68. Expert Council Nat. Defense War Industries Bd., 1917-18; expert consultant, War Dept., also chmn. price adjustment section North Atlantic Div., U.S. Engrs., War Dept., 1942-44; ex-editor fed. and state taxes department of New York Globe and Associated Newspapers; sr. partner Klein, Hinds & Finke, certified public accountants; Klein, Finke & Austin, attorneys. Trustee-at-large N.Y. Fedn. Jewish Philanthropies; ex-director Y.M.H.A. (v.p.). Ex-mem. Bd. of Higher Edn., City of New York, chmn. finance com. Mem. Am. Inst. Accountants. N.Y. State Soc. of C.P.A.'s (ex-pres.), Am. Econ. Assn., Nat. Assn. Cost Accountants, Am. Accounting Assn., N.Y. Adult Edn. Council (dir.), Nat. Tax Assn., Tax Inst., Acad. Polit. Science, Commerce and Industry Assn., Am. and N.Y. State bar assns., New York County Lawyers' Assn., Trade and Commercial Bar Assn., Coll. City of New York Asso. Alumni (v.p.), Civil Legion, Phi Beta Kappa, Phi Beta Kappa Assos., Beta Gamma Sigma. Mason (32 deg., past master). Clubs: City College (v.p.), Accountants Club of America, Metropolis Country, Lawyers, Harmonie. Author: Elements of Accounting, 1914; Principlés and Methods in Commercial Education (with Dr. Jos. Kahn), 1915; Student's Handbook fo Accounting of Accounting, 1915; Bookkeeping and Accounting, 1917; Federal Income Taxation, 1929, cumulative supplements, 1930, 31, 33. Contbr. tech. publs. Home: New York City, N.Y. Died Aug. 16, 1975.

KLEINSCHMIDT, EDWARD ERNST, business exec.; b. Bremen, Germany, Sept. 9, 1875; s. John Frederick and Elise Albertine (Langwisch) K.; brought to U.S., 1884; student Cooper Inst., N.Y. City, 1894-98; D.Eng., Brooklyn Polytechnic Institute, 1958; m. Virginia Mutterer, Apr. 13, 1903 (dec. 1932); children—Virginia Ida, Edward Frederick, Bernard Louise, Doris Eleanor. Owner elec. shop, N.Y.C., 1898-1913; pres. Kleinschmidt Electric Co., N.Y. City, 1913-25; v.p. Morkrum-Kleinschmidt Co., Chicago, 1925-28; v.p. Teletype Corp., Chicago, 1928-30; v.p. Internat. Inventions Corp., Chicago, 1930-40; pres. Teletypesetter Corp., Chicago, 1928-30; pres. Kleinschmidt div. SCM Corp., from 1931. Mem. Am. Inst. Elec. Engrs. Republican. Lutheran. Mason. Clubs: Union League (Chicago); Exmoor Country (Highland Park, Ill.). Developed the picture telegraph, ry. signalling apparatus, the printing telegraph apparatus which later became known as teletype and high speed teletypwriter now made standard for U.S. Armed Services. Awarded John Price Weatherill medal for invention of Teletype, by Franklin Inst., 1940.†

KLEMME, RANDALL TELFORD, utilities exec., economist; b. Belmond, Ia., Mar. 17, 1911; s. Raymond H. and Lucy (Randall) K.; B.A., Grinnell Coll., 1932; postgrad. (Rockefeller Found. fellow), U. Chgo., 1941; Ph.D., Ia. State U., 1947; m. Margaret H. Osgood, Aug. 7, 1937. Pub., Belmond Advertiser, 1932-33; instr. Grinnell Coll., 1933-34; with Ia. Extension Service, Ames, 1935-36; instr. Platteville (Wis.) State Coll., 1936; faculty Okla. A. and M. Coll., 1937-48, v.p., 1949-52; economist Fed. Res. Bank Kansas City (Mo.), 1948-49; acting county dir. tech. coop. adminstrn. U.S. Dept. State, Pakistan, 1952-53; rep. Ford. Found., Karachi, Pakistan, 1953-55; dir. Okla. Dept. Commerce and Industry, Oklahoma City, 1955-58; commr. Internat. Congress Regional Economies, 1958; with No. Natural Gas Co., Omaha, from 1958, v.p., corporate economist, 1964; adj. prof. econs. U. Neb., Omaha, 1966. Bd. dirs., chmn. Neb. Council Econ. Edn., 1964; bd. dirs. Luth. Med. Center, Omaha, United Community Services, Omaha; trustee Midwest Research Inst.; bd. overseers Grinnell Coll. Fellow Am. Indsl. Devel. Council; mem. A.A.A.S., Am. Assn. Regional Sci., Am. Econs. Assns., Fgn. Policy Assn., Urban League, Blue Key, Sigma Xi, others. Rotarian. Contbr. articles on indsl. devel. and econs. to profl. jours. Home: Omaha, Neb. Deceased.

KLENDSHOJ, NIELS CHRISTIAN, physician, biochemist; b. Denmark, Feb. 1, 1902; s. Niels Christian and Ane Marie (Jensen) K.; B.A., Borgerdydskolen, Copenhagen, 1921; postgrad., Royal Polytech. Inst., U. Copenhagen, 1926; M.D., U. Buffalo, 1937; m. Annette Roberts Heinz, Feb. 24, 1933; children—Ole, John, Arne; m. 2d, June Esther Davis, Feb. 4, 1963. Came to U.S., 1927, naturalized, 1935. With Arner Co., Inc., Buffalo, 1927—75, successively control chemist, prodn. engr., med. and tech. dir., exec. v.p., 1927—52, pres., 1952—59; chmn. bd. Strong Cobb Arner, Inc. (merger Arner Co. and Strong Cobb and Co.), 1959—67, pres., chief exec. officer, 1963—65; biochemist Buffalo Gen. Hosp., 1937—75, cons. biochemist and physician, clin. prof. toxicology. Past mem. joint legislative com. on narcotics State of N.Y. Republican. Clubs: Buffalo, Country of Buffalo. Author: Fundamentals of Biochemsitry in Clinical Medicine, 1953; also numerous articles on medicine, toxicology. Co—discoverer blood sustances B and D.; practical application of specific blood factors in transfusions. Home: Buffalo, N.Y. Died May 12, 1975.

KLIMAS, JOHN EDWARD, educator; b. Ansonia, Conn., Mar. 10, 1927; s. John Edward and Ann (Zemaitus) K.; B.S., Fairfield U., 1953; M.S., Boston Coll., 1956; Ph.D. (USPHS fellow), State U. Ia., 1958; m. Antonia Comcowich, Aug. 7, 1954; children—John Anthony, Ann Christine, Rose Marie. Mem. faculty Fairfield (Conn.) U., 1958-68, 69-75, asso. prof. biology, 1961-67, prof., 1969-75; asst. program dir. NSF, Washington, 1968-69; cons. NSF, Interior Dept., Human Life Found., Tchr. mag., Ednl. Directions, Inc. Vice chmn. Conservation Commn. Fairfield, 1965-68. Served with USAAF, 1945-49. Mem. Nat. Assn. Biology Tchrs., Nat. Sci. Tchrs. Assn., A.A.A.S., Sigma Xi. Roman Catholic. Author: Wildflowers of Connecticut, 1968; Life-A Question of Survival, 1972; Wildflowers of Eastern America, 1974. Home: Fairfield, Conn., Died Oct. 28, 1975.

KLINE, ALLEN MARSHALL, educator; b. Ovid, Clinton Co., Mich., Jan. 24, 1881; s. Charles H. and Melissa (Ousterhout) K.; A.B., U. of Mich., 1904, A.M., 1905, Ph.D., 1907; m. Florence Reamer, July 18, 1906 (died July 6, 1925); children—Reamer, Marshall; m. 2d, Dorothy E. Brainerd, Dec. 20, 1927; 1 son Lawrence Brainerd. Asst. in history, U. of Mich., 1904-05, fellow in history, 1906-07; teacher history and civics, high sch., Springfield, O., 1907-09; lecturer in Am. history, Stanford, spring terms, 1914 and 1919; prof. history and polit. science, Coll. of the Pacific, 1909-20, dean 1918-20; prof. history Middlebury Coll, from 1920. Mem. Am. Hist. Assn., Nat. Council Geog. Teachers, Tau Kappa Alpha. Republican. Conglist. Mason. Contbr. to leading reviews on polit. and social subjects and Dictionary Am. Biography. Home: Middlebury, Vt.†

KLINE, BARTON LEEORIE, educator; b. Whitehall, Mont., Dec. 27, 1901; s. Benjamine Luther and Esther Myrtle (Coppernoll) K.; B.Sc., Cotner Coll., Lincoln, Neb., 1929; M.A., U. Neb., 1934; Ed.D., Colo. State Coll., 1948; m. Beth Doris Eaton, Oct. 31, 1920; children—Barton Leon, Donald F. Supt schs., Pleasant Dale, Neb., 1925-29, Rosalie, Neb., 1929-34, Bridgeport, Neb., 1934-38, Gothenburg, Neb., 1938-46, Beatrice, Neb., 1946-54; pres. Neb. State Tchrs. Coll., 1954-61; dir. Inst. Edn. and Research, U. Dacca; prof. edn. U. Neb. summers 1950, 51; lectr. Sch. Finance, Colo. State Coll., summer 1953; rancher Western Neb., from 1919; dir. East Pakistan project USAID, Dacca, 1962-65; adminstr. ednl. service Unit 10, Kearney, Neb., 1966-71. Liaison officer to Am. Assn. Colls. for Tchr. Edn., from 1958. Chmn. Wyo.-Neb. council Boy Scouts Am., 1935. Named Outstanding Young Man of Year, Kiwanis, 1938; Boss of Year award Jr. C. of C.,

1956. Life mem. N.E.A.; mem. Nat. Council Improvement Tchr. Edn., Neb. Schoolmasters Club, Horace Mann League, Am. Hygiene Assn., Neb. Edn. Assn., Pi Kappa Delta, Phi Delta Kappa. Methodist. Rotarian. Author research articles. Home: Lexington, Neb. Died Feb. 22, 1975.

KLINE, IRA M., educator; b. Meadway, N.Y., Aug. 1, 1880; s. Stephen and Susan (Dean) K.; B.S. in Edn., New York U., 1928, M.A., 1932; m. Saida A. McCarty, June 23, 1906; children—Dorothy Frances (Mrs. Carl F. Holtz), Ruth Elizabeth (Mrs. Arthur F. Wilks), Evelyn Marian (Mrs. Ernest Critzer). Pub. sch. teacher, N.Y. State, 1899-1911; supervising prin., Greensburg and Elmsford, N.Y., 1911-37; dir. Bur. of Appointments, Sch. of Edn., New York University, 1937-47, also professor of education, 1943-47, retired; director White Plains Fed. Savings & Loan Assn. Served with Home Guard, 1917-18. Mem. N.E.A. (v.p. and mem. exec. com. Dept. of Elementary Sch. Prins. from 1930), N.Y. State Teachers Assn., Horace Mann League (dir. 1940). Received Meritorious Service Award, New York U., 1933. Mem. Phi Delta Kappa (nat. v.p., 1934-36, pres. 1936-40). Baptist. Mason. Club: Westchester County Schoolmen's (life). Home: White Plains, N.Y.†

KLINE, QUENTIN MCKAY, savs. and loan exec.; b. Rochester, Mont., Sept. 6, 1900; s. William and Anna Marie (Kern) K.; J.D., U. Mich., 1926; m. Janella L. Greer, May 26, 1948; 1 dau., Audrey Jean. Admitted to Mich. bar, 1926; partner Kline & Langlors, 1932; pres. First Fed. Savs. and Loan Assn. of Dearborn (Mich.), 1937; Quentin M. Kline, Inc., from 1960. Municipal judge, 1928-32, grand jury prosecutor, 1933. Pres., Dearborn Taxpayers League, 1939-43; mem. Civil Def. Council, 1942-46, USCG Aux., 1942-45, Zoning Bd. Appeals, 1947-53; chmn. fund raising drive Boys Club, 1946; mem. fathers' club Pine Crest Prep Sch., mem. forward fund com. Recipient citation U.S. Treasury Dept., 1945. Mem. Mich. Bar Assn., Gamma Eta Gamma, Alpha Epsilon Mu. Mason. Club: University of Mich.; Magellan. Home: Dearborn, Mich. Deceased.

KLINE, WALTER WINTER, dentist; b. Lucasville, O., Aug. 19, 1899; s. John Rouse and Neilie (Winter) K.; D.D.S., Cin. Coll. Dental Surgery, 1923; m. Helen Louise Millar, July 18, 1927; l dau., Patricia Ann (Mrs. John Shuster). Practice dentistry, Portsmouth, O., 1923—75; owner cattle farm, Lucasville. Pres., bd. dirs. Scioto County Fair, 1972—75; v.p. Ohio Fair Mgrs. Assn., 1972—73, pres. elect., 1974. Republican. Methodist. Mason (32 deg.), Elk. Home: Portsmouth, O. Died May 16, 1975.

KLING, CHARLES FERGUS, realtor, investment banking co. exec.; b. Cleve., Nov. 27, 1913; s. John Adam and Esther Emma (Beck) K.; B.A., Yale, 1936; m. Peggy Bradley, Feb. 4, 1936; children—John Bradley, Caroline Beck (Mrs. Myron Aras). Sec.-treas. Kling Realty Co., Cleve., 1936-72, also dir.: v.p. Prescott-Merrill-Turben Co., investment bankers, Cleve., 1946-72; dir., chmn. exec. com. Van Dorn Co., Cleve., 1960-72; dir. Mem. Univ. Sch. Alumni Counsel, 1936-72. Mem. Republican Finance Highes Co., Cleve. Com., Cleve., 1936-55. Trustee Cleve. Zool. Soc. Served with AUS, 1940-46. Mem. Am. Ordnance Assn. (life); Nat. Audubon Soc. (life), Zeta Psi, Presbyn. Clubs: Kirtland Country, Pepper Pike Country, Union, Tavern (Cleve.); Hole in Wall Golf, Naples Yacht (Naples, Fla.). Home: Cleveland, O. Died May 24, 1972.

KLINGMAN, WILLIAM (WASHINGTON), bus. exec.; b. Washington, July 2, 1880; s. William and Sophia (Martin) K.; ed. pub. schs. of Eustis, Neb.; m. Julia Elizabeth Altensee, Aug. 14, 1902; children—Lloyd W., Chester W. With Equitable Life Assurance Soc. of U.S. from 1913, mgr. for Minn., N.D. and S.D., 1913-28, 2d v.p., 1928-30, v.p., 1930-38, gen. mgr. for Tex., 1938-47, retired 1947, dir., from 1949; dir. Nat. City Bank, Dallas; chmn. of bd. Citizens State Bank, Redwood Falls, Minn. Republican. Mason (Shriner). Clubs: Country, Atheltic (Dallas). Home: Dallas, Tex.†

KLOEFFLER, ROYCE GERALD, educator, engr., author; b. Armada, Mich., June 18, 1890; s. Galenus W. and Dora (Powell) K.; student Mich. State Coll., 1908-09; B.S., U. Mich., 1913; student Columbia, summer 1927; M.S., Mass. Inst. Tech., 1930; m. Hazel Marguerite Davis, Oct. 14, 1915; children—Doris May (Mrs. William Braden), Gale Davis. Engring trainee Gen. Elec. Co., 1913-15; instr. elec. engring. U. Ida., 1915-16; asst. prof. elec. engring. Kan. State U., 1916-22, asso. prof., 1922-25, prof., 1925-60, emeirtus, 1960-75, head dept. elec. engring., 1927-55; prof. Mass. Inst. Tech., summers 1933, 35; br. chief and engr. Nat. Security Agy., 1955-62. Fellow I.E.E.E.; mem. Am. Soc. Engring. Edn., Nat. Soc. Profl. Engrs., Sigma Xi, Phi Kappa Phi, Eta Kappa Nu, Sigma Tau. Author: Telephone Communication Systems, 1925; Direct Current Machinery (with Kerchner and Brenneman), 1934; Principles of Electronics, 1942; Industrial Electronics and Control, 1949; Basic Electronics (with Horrell), 1949; Electric Engeering Economics and Practice, 1952; Basic Theory in Electrical Engineering (with Sitz), 1955; Basic Electronics (with Hargrave), 1963; Election Tubes, 1966; Americanism versus International Communism, 1967; Memoirs, 1975. Home: Clearwater, Fla., Died July 29, 1975.

KLOPMAN, WILLIAM, textile mgr.; b. N.Y.C., June 26, 1900; s. William and Elizabeth (Allen) K.; m. Hazel Alice Wolfe, Dec. 4, 1920 (div. 1948); children—William Allen, Robert Bruce; m. 2d, Eunice Warn Colley, May 12, 1948. Started career with James H. Dunham & Co., 1915; Am. Rayon Products Corp. 1925; Hillcrest Silk Mills, 1930; sr. v.p., dir. Burlington Mills Corp., 1930-47; pres. William Klopman & Sons, 1947-51, Klopman Mills, Inc. 1951-74. Clubs: Union League (N.Y.C.); Arcola Country, Deal Golf. Pine Valley (N.J.); Everglades (Palm Beach). Home: Lloyd Neck, N.Y. Died Oct. 13, 1974.

KLUCZYNSKI, JOHN C., congressman; b. Chgo., Feb. 15, 1896; s. Thomas and May (Sulaski) K.; student pub. and parochial schs.; m. Mary Zapart, Apr. 15, 1936 (dec.); m. 2d, Estelle Plowy, Nov. 15, 1939. Caterer 1920, partner Syrena Restaurants, Chgo. Elected to Ill. Ho. of Reps., 1932, and re-elected for 7 terms. Mem. 82d to 93d congresses, 5th Ill. Dist., mem. Pub. Works Com., House Select Com. Small Bus. Served with 8th F.A., AEF, 1918-19. Mem. Polish Nat. Alliance, Polish Roman Catholic Union. Democrat. Roman Catholic. Club: Travelers (Chgo.). Home: Chicago Ill. Died Jan. 26, 1975.

KLUTTZ, WHITEHEAD, lawyer; b. Salisbury, N.C., Sept. 27, 1881; s. Theodore Franklin and Sallie (Caldwell) K.; Church High Sch., Salisbury; LL.B., U. of N.C., 1902; m. Margaret Linn, Apr. 22, 1911 (died Feb. 4, 1914). Admitted to N.C. bar 1902; practiced Salisbury; mem. N.C. Senate, 1906-10 (pres. 1909, 10); sec. Internat. Joint Commn. of U.S. and Can., by appmt. of Pres. Wilson, from Jan. 1914. Speaker on patriotic, religious and ednl. topics. Redpath-Horner Chautauqua, 1916. Elected trustee U. of N.C., 1909. Democrat. Presbyn. Home: Washington, D.C.†

KNAPP, ROBERT HAMPDEN, educator, psychologist; b. Portland, Ore., Apr. 16, 1915; s. Joseph Burke and Cornelia (Pinkham) K.; B.A., U. Ore., 1938, M.A., 1939; M.A., Harvard, 1940, Ph.D., 1948; M.A. (hon.), Wesleyan U., Middletown, Conn., 1956; m. Johnsia Nelson, Mar. 19, 1945 (div. 1972); children—Robert Hampden, Abigail Pinkham, Hiatt Jefferson, Sarah Elizabeth. Mem. faculty Wesleyan U., 1946-74, now prof. psychology, also chmn. dept. Dep. dir., Ford Found., 1953-54; dir. sci. faculty fellowship panel NSF, 1957-74; mem. Gov. Conn. Bd. Certification Psychologists, 1959. Chmn. Planning and Zoning Commn., Haddam, Conn., 1957-59. Democratic candidate for Conn. Legislature, 1956. Served with OSS, AUS, 1942-45. Mem. Am. Psychol. Assn. (pres. div. psychology and the arts 1967-68, exec. council 1971-74), Am. Orthopsychiat. Assn., Am. Soc. Aesthetics, Am. Assn. Humanistic Psychology, Phi Beta Kappa, Sigma Xi, Sigma Nu. Club: Harvard (N.Y.C.). Author: (with H.B. Goodrich) The Origins of American Scientists, 1954; (with J.J. Greenbaum) The Younger American Scholar, 1954; Origins of the American Humanistic Scholar, 1964; also numerous papers. Home: Cromwell, Conn. Died Aug. 7, 1974.

KNECHT, ANDREW WILSON, cons. engr.; b. Phila., May 4, 1907; s. George G. and Sylvia (Organ) K.; M.E., Stevens Inst. Tech., 1928; m. Hilda M. Birch, Sept. 6, 1930; children—Andrew Wilson (dec.), Brian B. Engr., Clyde R. Place, cons. engr., 1929-35, asso., 1937-46; office mgr. Tag Mfrs. Inst., 1935-37; chief mech., elec. engr., asst. chief engr. Walter Kidde Constructors, 1946-51; mng. partner Seelye, Stevenson, Value & Knecht, N.Y.C., 1951-72; pres. dir. STV, Inc. 1972-73. Mem. War Manpower Bd., 1945-46; cons. on fuels and conservation program Dept. Commerce, 1946. Mem. Bd. Edn., Yonkers, N.Y., 1946-51. Trustee Yonkers Gen. Hosp. Registered profl. engr., 16 states and D.C. Fellow Am. Soc. M.E. (exec. com. of com. profl. practice cons. engrs. 1956-59), Am. Soc. C.E.; mem. Am. Soc. Heating, Refrigerating and Air Conditioning Engrs., I.E.E.E., Am. Inst. Cons. Engrs. (past mem. council), N.Y. Assn. Cons. Engrs., Soc. Am. Mil. Engrs. (dir., past pres. N.Y. post), N.Y. Bldg. Congress (pres., dir.), Nat. Soc. Profl. Engrs., Cons. Engrs. Council Am. Mgmt. Assn., Am. Soc. Testing Materials, N.Y. Soc. Profl. Engrs. Clubs: Ardsley Country; Seaview Country, Union League (N.Y.C.); Ponte Vedra Country (Jacksonville, Fla.). Home: Dobbs Ferry N.Y. Died Oct. 6, 1973

KNIGHT, ALFRED, exec.; b. San Francisco, Mar. 29, 1874; s. William Henry and Ella Jeanna (Waters) K.; ed. Hugh High Sch. and Nelson's Business Coll., Cin.; LL.D., Arizona State College (Tempe), 1956; married Harriet Hieatt Black, June 4, 1896; one son, Vernon. Assistant secretary-treasurer Cincinnati Edison Electric Company, 1891-1901, general auditor The Fleischmann Co., Cincinnati, 1901-18; v.p., dir. Fleischmann Co., N.Y., 1918-29, and of its successor, Standard Brands, Inc. (and subsidiary cos.), 1929-33; retired Dec. 31, 1933; pres. Orangewood Realty Co., Phoenix, 1938-49; pres. Eureka Realty Co., 1942-50; pres. Camelback Lands, Inc., 1945-51; former vice pres., director American Dismalt Co., Fleischmann Transportation Co., Fleischmann Malting Co., Royal Baking Co.; pres., dir. Rust-Proofing, Inc., 1947-50, chmn. bd.; pres., dir. O'Connor Rust-Proofing Co., Los Angeles, from 1949, Permanizing, Inc.; owner, operator Patrick Hotel, Phoenix; dir. Good Will Industries of Arizona, Inc. Served in First Regiment, Ohio National Guard, 1890-93, battalion adjutant, 1892-93. Active in several civic groups, including Western adv. bd. Nat. Probation and Parole Assn., from 1948. Fellow Royal Astron. Soc. Royal Soc. of Arts (both London), Am. Geog. Soc., Inst. Am. Geneal.; mem. Am. Inst. Fgn. Trade (v.p., dir., chmn. bd.), many profl. and tech. assns. and orgns., including geneal, and astronomical. Republican. Conglist. Mason (K.T., 32°, R.A.M., Scottish Rite, Shriner). Clubs: Bankers of America, Town Hall (New York); Optimist, Phoenix Country, Arizona. Executives, Hiram (Phoenix); Royal Socs. Club (London). Lectr. on astronomy, art and travel. Home: Phoenix, Ariz.†

KNIGHT, ARTHUR MERRILL, JR., physician; b. Waycross, Ga., Sept. 20, 1914; s. Arthur Merrill and Agnes (Scarborough) K.; M.D.; U. Ga., 1943; m. Nina Belle Hopkins, July 11, 1936; children—Nina June (dec.), Susanne Jaquelin (Mrs. Gordon Richard Hostetter), Constance Evalyn (Mrs. William Berry Dial), Arthur Merrill III. Served with M.C., USNR, 1943—47. Diplomate Am. Bd. Internal Medicine. Fellow A.C.P., Am. Coll. Cardiology; mem. A.M.A., Am. Heart Assn., Am. Diabetes Assn. Home: Waycross, Ga. Died Oct. 18, 1971; buriend Oakland Cemetery, Waycross, Ga.

KNIGHT, FELIX HARRISON, labor union ofcl.; b. Montgomery County, Mo., Dec. 10, 1878; s. John R. and Mollie (Moore) K.; ed. public and high schs.; m. Rose M. Michal, 1904. Officer Assn. Ry. Carmen, 1902, asst. gen. pres., 1913-35, gen. pres., from 1935; dir. Union Labor Life Ins. Co. from 1935; v.p. A.F. of L., from 1936. Mem. exec. council Ry. Employees Dept. of A.F. of L. Presbyterian. Mason (32°), Odd Fellow. Home: Kansas City, Mo.*†

KNIGHT, HOWARD LAWTON, writer; b. Gardner, Mass., Sept. 20, 1881; s. Willis Eben and Lyra Sophronia (Brigham) K.; B.S., Massachusetts U., 1902, Boston U., 1902; grad. student Wesleyan U., Middletown, Conn., 1904-06; D. Agr. (honorary), Massachusetts University, 1952; m. Cora Isabelle Stickney, Aug. 29, 1906. Instr. University of Mass., 1902-04; asst. in chemistry, Wesleyan U., 1904-05; asst. nutrition investigations, U.S. Dept. Agr., 1904-06; asst. editor Experiment Station Record (U.S. Dept. Agr.), 1906-18, asso. editor, 1918-23, editor, 1923-46; asst. editor jour. of Home Econs., 1908-12; editor Proc. Conv. Am. Assn. Land Grant Colls. and State Univs., 1928, 1946-55. Fellow A.A.A.S.; mem. Phi Kappa Phi, Alpha Sigma Phi. Unitarian. Contbr. agrl. articles to reference books and other publs.; spl. editor for agriculture, 1934 edit. Webster's New Internat. Dictionary. Club: Cosmos (Washington). Home: Westminster, Md.†

KNOLLENBERG, BERNHARD, writer; b. Richmond, Ind., Nov. 26, 1892; s. George H. and Agnes (Steen) K.; A.B., Earlham Coll., 1912, LL.D., 1944; A.M., Harvard, 1914, LL.B., 1916; A.M. (hon.), Yale, 1938; m. Mary McClennen, 1920; 1 son, Walter; m. 2d Mary Lightfoot Tarleton, 1934. Admitted to bar, 1916; practiced law, 1916-38; mem. firm Lord, Day & Lord, N.Y.C., 1929-38; librarian Yale, 1938-44; cons. expert U.S. Treasury, 1939-40; sr. dep. adminstr. Lend Lease Adminstrn., 1943-44; div. dep. OSS, 1944- 45; U.S. commr. Internat. Commn. for N.W. Atlantic Fisheries, 1950-58. Mem. Conn. Hist. Commn. Served with Naval Intelligence USN., 1917-18. Hon trustee, Conn. Coll; asso. fellow Saybrook Coll., Yale. Mem. Am. Antiquarian Soc., Colonial Soc. Mass., Mass. Hist. Soc., Soc. Cin Clubs: Century Assn. (N.Y.C.); Elizabethan (New Haven). Author: Washington and the Revolution: A Re-Appraisal, 1940; Whitewater Valley, 1946; Samuel Ward, 1952; Origin of the American Revolution, 1960; George Washington: The Virginia Period, 1964; Growth of the American Revolution, 1766-1775, 1975. Contbr. Atlantic Monthly, Harpers, law and hist. jours. Home: Chester, Conn. Died July 6, 1973.

KNORR, WALTER HERBERT, metals co. exec.; b. Newark, Dec. 29, 1908; s. Fred and Marie (Rebman) K.; grad. Am. Inst. Banking; m. Bernice I. Steiert, Sept. 24, 1936; children—Roger B., Richard B., Robert J. With Continental Copper & Steel Industries, Inc., N.Y.C., 1940-74, treas., 1948-74, v.p., 1962-74; mem. finance com., pres. Condominion Insurgentes, S.A.-Mexico City, Mexico, 1950-74; treas. Continental Rubber Works, Erie, 1962-74; dir. Asceras Anglo S.A. de C.V., Mexico City. Mem. N.Y. Commodity Exchange, Nat. Assn. Accountants. Club: Colonia (N.J.) Country (dir.). Home: Clark, N.J. Died Dec. 14, 1973

KNOTT, J(OSEPH) C(ARLTON), agrl. educator; b. Tipton, Ia., May 26, 1893; s. Carlton Joseph and Ida McKee (Lupton) K.; B.S., State Coll. of Wash., 1920; M.S., 1930; Ph.D., U. of Minn., 1941; m. Bess E. Sleater, June 21, 1922 (dec.); 1 son, Robert Joseph; m. 2d, Rae Russell, July 26, 1947. Herdsman, State Coll. of Wash., 1920-26, instr. dairy husbandry, 1926-30, asst. prof., 1930-36, asso. prof., 1936-40. prof., 1940-42, dir. of agrl. extension service, 1942-46, dir. Inst. Agrl.

Scis., 1946-55, prof. dairy science, 1955-58; technical consultant to Foreign Agricultural Service in several Latin American countries, 1958-75. Mem. dairy research and marketing adv. com. U.S. Dept. Agriculture. Served with U.S. Army, 1917-19. Mem. Am. Dairy Sci. Assn., Soc. of Animal Prodn., Am. Farm Econ. Assn., A.A.A.S., Am. Legion, Sigma Xi, Phi Kappa Phi, Phi Sigma, Phi Eta Sigma, Alpha Gamma Rho. Mason. Methodist. Club: Kiwanis. Contbr. to bulletins, sci. and popular jours. Home: Pullman, Wash., Died Nov. 19, 1975.

KNOWLAND, WILLIAM FIFE, publisher; b. Alameda, Cal., June 26, 1908; s. Joseph Russell and Ellie (Fife) K.; A.B., U. Cal., 1929; m. Helen Davis Herrick, Dec. 31, 1926; children—Emelyn Jewett, Joseph William, Helen Estelle. Pres. Franklin Investment Co.; pub., editor Oakland Tribune; pres. pub. Tribune Pub. Co. Mem. Cal. Assembly, 1933-35, Senate, 1935-39. Mem. Republican Nat. Com., 1938, chmn. Rep. Exec. Com., 1941-42. Served in AUS, 1942-45; in service overseas when apptd. U.S. senator to fill the unexpired term of Hiram W. Johnson, dec., elected full term, 1946, re-elected 1952, majority leader, 1953-54, minority leader, 1955-58; mem. U.S. delegation to 11th session UN Gen. Assembly. Mem. U.S., Cal. State (dir.), Oakland (dir.) chambers commerce, Zeta Psi, Sigma Delta Chi. Republican. Methodist. Mason (33, Shriner), Native Sons of the Golden West, Eagles, Moose, Elk. Clubs: Bohemian (San Francisco); Athenian-Nile (Oakland). Home Oakland, Cal. Died Feb. 23, 1974

KNOX, WILLIAM RUSSELL, church exec.; b. Boston, Oct. 23, 1879; s. Albert Leonard and Ellen Hurlbert (Souther) K.; student Cambridge (Mass.) Manual Tng. Sch., 1899; m. Madie Rimbach, Sept. 14, 1909. Engaged in structural steel and iron engring. bus., 1899-1901; left bus. to study and practice Christian Science healing, served in most exec. offices Second Ch. of Christ, Scientist, Boston; pres. The First Ch. of Christ, Scientist, Boston, 1954-55, also mem. finance com.; trustee Church Realty Trust. Home: Boston, Mass.†

KNUDSEN, VERN O., physicist, univ. chancellor emeritus; b. Provo, Utah, Dec. 27, 1893; s. Andrew and Chesty (Sward) K.; A.B., Brigham Young U., 1915; Ph.D., U. Chgo., 1922; LL.D., U. Cal. at Los Angeles, 1960; m. Florence Telford, Dec. 19, 1919; children—Marilyn (dec.), Robert Telford Andrew, Vern Oliver Morris, Margaret Constance. Research engr., 1918-19; instr. physics U. Cal. at Los Angeles, 1922-23, asst. prof., 1923-27, asso. prof., 1927-34, prof., 1934-60, dean grad. Div., 1934-58, vice chancellor, 1956-59, chancellor, 1959-60, chancellor emeritus, 1960-74, chmn. dept. physics, 1932-38; cons. acoustics to univs., colls., music bldgs., civic auditoriums, theaters, chs. Vice pres. Los Angeles Bldg. and Safety Commn., 1940-41; pres. Hollywood Bowl, Los Angeles, 1960-61, chmn., 1961-62; pres. Cal. Inst. Cancer Research, 1963-65; war research Nat. Def. Research Com., 1941-44, NRC, 1942-45; invented instruments for measuring and correcting impaired hearing, 1924-25, ear defenders, 1938-39. Bd. dirs. Chamber Symphony Soc. Cal., v.p. 1965-74; bd. dirs. So. Cal. Choral Music Assn. Recipient A.A.A.S. prize, 1934; Wallace C. Sabine medal for original contbns. to archtl. acoustics, 1958; John H. Potts Meml. award Audio-Engring. Soc., 1964; gold medal Acoustical Soc. Am., 1967; physics bldg, U. Cal. at Los Angeles named Knudsen Hall, 1964; Tchr. of Yr., Cal Tchr. Remembrance Day Found., 1970; Distinguished Alumnus award U. Chgo. Club Greater Los Angeles, 1971. Fellow A.A.A.S., Am. Phys. Soc., Acoustical Soc. Am. (pres. 1933-35). Mem. Ch. of Jesus Christ of Latter Day Saints. Author: Architectural Acoustics, 1932; Audiometry, 1937; Acoustical Designing in Architecture (with Cyril Harris), 1950. Contbr. Sci. articles. Home: Los Angeles, Cal. Died May 13, 1974

KOBAK, ALFRED JULIAN, physician; b. Chgo., Sept. 23, 1898; s. William and Clara (Beck) K.; M.D., U. Ill., 1924, M.Sc. in Pathology and Bacteriology, 1929; m. Rose Baron, Apr. 18, 1930; children—Alfred Julian, Claire (Mrs. James D. Meyers). Research fellow in bacteriology Nelson Morris Inst., lMichael Reese Hosp., Chgo., 1925—26; resident in obstetrics Cook County Hosp., Chgo., 1925—26; resident in obstetrics Cook County Hosp., Chgo., 1927—28, attending in obstetrics, 1928—72; attending in obstetrics and gynecology Edgewater Hosp.; attending in obstetrics Mt. Sinai Hosp.; clin. asso. prof. obstetrics and gynecology U. Ill.; prof., chmn. dept. obstetrics Cook County Postgrad. Sch. Served with U.S. Army, 1917—18. Diplomate Am. Bd. Obstetrics and Gynecology. Fellow Am. Coll. Obstetricians and Gynecologists, Internat. Coll. Surgeons; mem. A.ll.A., Central Assn. Obstetricians and Gynecologists, Chgo. Med. Soc., Chgo. Gynecol. Soc., Sigma Xi, Phi Delta Epsilon (sec.-treas., v.p.). Jewish religion. Contbr. articles to profl. jours. Inverntor Kobak needle. Home: Glencoe, Ill. Died Dec. 27, 1972.

KOBER, ARTHUR, writer; b. Austria-Hungary, Aug. 25, 1900; s. Adolph Mayer and Tillie (Ballison) K.; brought to U.S. 1904; ed. Pub. high schools, N.Y.C.; m. Lillian Hellman, Dec. 25, 1925 (div. 1932); m. 2d, Margaret Frohnknecht, Jan. 11, 1941 (dec. 1951); 1 dau., Cathy. Theatrical press agt. Lee & J. J. Shubert, Edgar Selwyn, Jed Harris, Herman Shumlin, Ruth Draper, 1923-30; produced Me by Henry Myers, Princess Theatre, 1925; contbr. to N.Y. World, Evening Sun: wrote N.Y. and Hollywood columns on Morning Telegraph, 1930; screen writer (30 motion pictures), 1930-37 and 1941-46, including work on The Little Foxes, Wintertime, In the Meantime, Darling, Don Jaun Quilligan, My Own True Love. Mem. Dramatists Guild (N.Y.), P.E.N. Author: Thunder Over the Bronx, 1935; Having Wonderful Time, 1937; Pardon Me for Pointing, 1939; My Dear Bella, 1941; That Man Is Here Again, 1946; Bella, Bella Kissed a Fella, 1951; Wish You Were Here (with Joshua Logan and Harold Rome), 1952; Ooh, What You Said, 1958; A Mighty Man Is He (with George Oppenheimer), 1959. Mem. faculty New Sch. Social Research, N.Y., 1953. Authors Guild. Contbr. to The New Yorker. Home: New York City, N.Y. Died June 12, 1975.

KOCSIS, ANN, artist; b. N.Y.C.; d. John and Katie (Svidro) K.; student Art Inst. Pitts. (scholarship), N.A.D.; studied piano at Wickersham Sch. Music, Pitts. Taught piano; millinery designer, later beauty shop operator; free-lance comml. artist and fashion designer; painting accepted by Allied Artists Am.; one-man shows at Montross Gallery, N.Y.C.; group shows Mint Mus. Art, Hickory Mus. Art, Columbus Mus. Art, Morton Gallery, Contemporary Arts, Vendome, Allied Artists of Am., Carnegie Mus., Arthur Newton Gallery, Creative Art Gallery, Peter Kolean Gallery; exhibited Argent Gallery, 1947-49, Audubon Artists, 1948, Asso. Artists of Pitts., Nat. Assn. Women Artists, 1947; Am. Artist Profl. League, 1945-46, Garden of Art Westchester Fair, N.Y., 1949, Am. Artists Profl. League, 1951, Nat. Assn. Women Artists, 1952, Grand Nat. Art Exhbn., N.Y.C., 1955-56, Fla. Internat. Art Exhbn., Galerie Internationale, Internat. Art Gallery, Knickerbocker Artists Traveling Group Show throughout U.S., European tour exchange exhbn. to Athens, Greece, Salonika, Brussels, Belgium, Japan-Am. Women Artists Exchange Exhbn., and many others in galleries and colls. throughout U.S.; traveling group exhibit at Knickerbocker Artists. Represented permanent collections of Fla. So. Coll., Sq. & Compass Crippled Children's Clinic, Sonora Desert Mus., Burr Gallery, Alexander Art Gallery, Riverside Mus., IBM Gallery of Art and Scis. San Manuel Library. Tucson, Seton Hall U., Am.-Hungarian Inst., Rutgers U. Recipient hon. mention for Sahuaro, Fla. Internat. Art Exhbn., 1952; citation of merit Fla. So. Coll.; hon. mention, gold key Grumbacher blue ribbon Seton Hall U. Exhbn., 1958 hon. mention Am. Artists Profl. League, 1962. Life fellow Internat. Inst. Arts and Letters Switzerland, Royal Soc. Arts London; mem. Nat. Arts Club (life mem.); position chmn. arts com., Nat. Assn. Women Artists (nominating com.), Am. Artists Profl. League, Knickerbocker Artists (2d v.p. 1966), Tucson Fine Arts Assn. Died Nov. 10, 1972.

KOEGEL, OTTO ERWIN, lawyer; b. Boonville, Ind., Nov. 23, 1891; s. Henry and Laura Carolyn (Coe) K.; J.D., George Washington U., 1915, LL.M., 1916 (first honors highest average during course); D.C.L., Am. U., 1921; m. Rae Fisher, Sept. 30, 1916; children—James Erwin, Ruth Ann, William Fisher. Practiced in Washington, 1916-31, also Chgo., 1924-31; mem. Matthews & Koegel, Chgo., 1926-31; mem. Hughes, Schurman & Dwight, 1931-37; mem. Royall, Koegel and Wells, N.Y.C., 1937-73; counsel Rogers & Wells, 1973-75; chief counsel Twentieth Century-Fox Film Corp., asso. counsel Bur. War Risk Ins., Treasury Dept., 1918-23; asst. gen. counsel U.S. Vets.' Bur. 1923; asst. U.S. atty. for D.C., 1924; prof. law domestic relations, torts and criminal law Nat U., 1920-24; dir., counsel several corps. associated with motion picture and ins.; propr. Kaywood Farm. Active in civic affairs of Westchester County; former chmn. Citizens Com. for Fusion, Bronxville, and for Twp. of Somers; chmn. War Meat Com., World War II; legal mem. of Com on Hereditary Defectives in U.S. of 2d Internat. Congress Eugenics, N.Y., 1922; mem. com. on marriage laws Am. Assn. for Family Social Work (allied with Russell Sage Found.); mem. N.Y. State Am. Revolution Bicentennial Commn. Trustee Am. U., Washington. Recipient 1st Bishop's medal N.Y. Episcopal Diocese, 1957, citation and gold medal Republic of Korea, 1971. Mem. Am., N.Y., Chgo. bar assns., Am. Judicature Soc., Am. Scenic and Hist. Preservation Soc. (exec. com.), John Jay Homestead Assn. (pres.), Sigma Nu Phi, Pi Gamma Mu (hon.). Methodist. Mason (32 deg.). Clubs: University (Washington); Siwanoy Country (Mt. Vernon, N.Y.). Author: Common Law Marriage and Its Development in the United States, 1922; Walter S. Carter, Collector of Young Masters, 1952; articles in legal periodicals. Home: Granite Springs N.Y. Died Apr. 1975; buried Anawalk Cemetery, Anawalk, N.Y. 1975.

KOENIG, EGMONT FRANCIS, army officer; b. New York, N.Y., Apr. 23, 1892; s. Dr. Herman and Louise Alice (Bopp) K.; A.B., Columbia, 1912; grad. Command and Gen. Staff Sch., 1933; m. Eleanor Carroll Hill, June 19, 1923; children—Eleanor Carroll, Richard Hill, Alice Morgan. Private in British Army, 1914-15; asst. mgr. the Whitehouse Co., Spokane, Wash., 1915-16; commd. 2d lt., inf., U.S. Army, 1916, advancing through the grades to brigadier general, 1944; served as lt., advancing to captain and major, 21st Infantry, during World War I; commanded United States troops in Alaska, 1919-20; office asst. to sec. of war, 1921-24; instr. Army Industrial Coll., 1923-24, Cav. Sch., Ft. Riley, 1928-29, Command and Gen. Staff Sch., 1935-40; comdt. Army Air Force Intelligence Sch. Army Air Forces, 1942; U.S. mem. Bulgarian Armistice Commn., 1944; commanded all North African Base Sects., 1944; United Kingdom Base, Normandy Base and Channel Base Sects., 1945; mil. attache to Czechoslovakia, 1946-47; retired as brig. gen., May 1948. Decorations: D.S.M., Legion of Merit (twice), Bronze Star Medal; Comdr. British Empire; Office of the French Legion of Honor; etc. Mem. Zeta Psi. Clubs: Army-Navy; Valley of Montecito. Home: Santa Barbara, Cal. Died Mar. 29, 1974; interred Arlington Nat. Cemetery.

KOENIG, M(ARSHALL) GLENN, physician; b. N.Y.C., Sept. 20, 1931; s. Mortimer and Stella Koenig; M.D., Cornell U., 1957; m. Constance Rogers; children—Mark A., Scott R. Intern. N.Y. Hosp., 1957—58, asst. resident in internal medicine, 1958—59, asst. resident in internal medicine, 1959—60; USPHS postdoctoral fellow in infectious diseases Vanderbilt U., Nashville, 1960—63, instr. internal medicine, 1960—62, asst. prof., 1962—66, asso. prof., 1966—71, prof., 1971—72, also chief div. infectious diseases; vis. staff Vanderbilt Hosp., 1961—72; attending physician VA Hosp., Nashville, 1961—72, cons. infectious diseases, 1968—72. Asso. mem. commn. stretococcal and staphylococcal disease Armed Forces Epidemiol. Bd., 1964—72; mem. panel on anti—infectives drug efficacy rev. study Nat. Acad. Scis.-NRC, 1966—68; research career devel. grantee Nat. Inst. Allergy and Infectious Diseases, 1963—72. Diplomate Am. Bd. Internal Medicine. Fellow A.C.P.; mem. Am. Fedn. Clin. Research (councilor So. sect. 1965—68, pres. 1970—71), N.Y. Acad. Scis., So. Soc. Clin. Investigation, Infactious Diseases Soc. Am., Reticuloendothelial Soc., Am. Soc. Clin. Investigation, Soc. Exptl. Biology and Medicine, Am. Soc. Microbiology, Assn. Am. Physicians, A.A.A.S., Phi Beta Kappa, Alpha Omega Alpha. Asst. editor infectious deseases sect. Yearbook of Medicine, 1969—72; mem. editorial bd. Antibiotics and Chemotherapy, 1971—72. Home: Nashville, Tenn. Died Nov. 13, 1972; buried Nashville, Tenn.

KOERBLE, CHARLES EDWARD, educator; b. Milw., Dec. 18, 1914; s. Edward Ludwig and Georgia Alberta (Wilhelm) K.; B.A., Lawrence Coll., 1941; M.A., U. Wis., 1951, Ph.D., 1954; m. Betty Jean Bevis, June 15, 1951; children—Brian Edward, Barbara Lee. Machinist apprentice, 1934-37; high sch. tchr., 1941-43; social service worker, 1946-48; dir. counseling, guidance N.W. Mo. State U., 1954-56, dean faculty, 1956-60, dean students, 1960-70, prof. guidance, counseling, 1970-75. City councilman, Maryville, 1957-65, mayor, 1960-65. Served with AUS, 1943-46. Mem. A.A.A.S., N.E.A., Am. Personnel and Guidance Assn., Internat. Council Exceptional Children, Nat. Assn. Student Personnel Adminstrs., Phi Delta Kappa, Delta Tau Delta. Mason, Rotarian (pres. 1959-60). Home: Maryville, Mo., Died Sept. 18, 1975.

KOESTER, GEORGE ARTHUR, educator; b. Allen, Neb., Oct. 15, 1912; s. Gerhardt F. and Mathilda (Wessel) K.; B.A., Midland Coll., 1937; M.S., U. Colo., 1941; Ph.D., U. Minn., 1951; M. Alice M. Ringstrom, June 6, 1943; 1 son, George Thomas. Tchr. high schs., 1937-42; with San Diego State Coll., 1950-74, prof. edn., adminstrv. chmn. div. of edn., 1958-74, exec. dean, 1964-74. Bd. dirs. Luth. Assn. for Retarded Children. Served to capt. AUS, 1942-46; group leader Crossroads A-bomb Project, Marshall Islands, 1946. Mem. Am. Psychol. Assn., Phi Delta Kappa. Home: San Diego, Cal. Died Jan. 21, 1974; interred Greenwood Meml. Park, San Diego.

KOHLER, ERIC LOUIS, accountant; b. Owosso, Mich., July 9, 1892; s. F. Edwin and Kate Evelyn (Bentley) K.; A.B., U. Mich., 1914; M.A., Northwestern U., 1915; C.P.A., Ill., 1916. With Arthur Andersen & Co., C.P.A.'s Chgo., 1915-17, 19-20, 33-37, Kohler, Pettengill & Co. (later E.L. Kohler & Co.), 1922-33; prof. accounting Northwestern U. Sch. Commerce, 1922-28; mem. State Bd. C.P.A. Examiners, 1928-31; controller TVA, 1938-41; with Office of Emergency Mgmt. and WPB, 1941-42; exec. officer Petroleum Adminstrn. War, 1942-44; cons. accountant, 1945-48, 1949-76; controller ECA, 1948-49; financial adviser sec. agr., 1946; vis. prof. Ohio State U., 1955-60, U. Minn., 1955, U. Chgo., 1958, U. Ill., 1966; controller Auditorium Theatre Council, Chgo., 1960-76. Mem. adv. panel U.S. comptroller gen., 1967-76; mem. Excess-Profits Tax Council, U.S. Treasury, 1946-47. Served as capt. Q.M.C., U.S. Army, 1917-18. Recipient Alpha Kappa Psi award, 1958; elected to Accounting Hall of Fame, 1962. Mem. Ill. Soc. C.P.A.'s Am. Inst. C.P.A.'s Am. Accounting Assn. (pres. 1936, 46), Nat. Assn. Accountants, Phi Mu Alpha, Beta Gamma Sigma, Beta Alpha Psi. Club: City (pres. 1934-35) (Chgo.). Author: Accounting Principles Underlying Federal Income Taxes, 3d edit., 1927; Accounting for Business Executives, 1927; Advanced Accounting Problems, 3d edit., 1959; Principles of Auditing, 3d edit., 1963; A Dictionary for Accountants, 5th edit., 1973; Accounting for Management, 1965; co-author: Principles of Auditing, 4th edit., 1937; Principles of Accounting, 1927-31; Accounting in the Federal

Government, 1956. Contbr. to mags. on accounting and mgmt. Editor The Accounting Rev. 1928-44. Home: Chicago, Ill., Feb. 20, 1976.

KOHN, GABRIEL, sculptor; b. Phila., June 12, 1910; s. Asher and Minnie (Hoffman) K.; student Cooper Union, N.Y.C., 1929, Beaux Art Inst., N.Y.C., 1930-39, Atelier Zadkine, Paris, France, 1946. Rep. permanent collections Mus. Modern Art, Ringling Mus. Art, Sarasota, Fla, Whitney Mus., N.Y.C., Albright-Knox Gallery, Cranbrook Mus., also pvt. collections; tchr. Bklyn. Mus. Art Sch., La Jolla (Cal.) Art Center, 1962, San Francisco Art Inst., 1963, U. Wash., 1964, U. Cal. at Santa Barbara, 1967, Cal. Inst. Fine Arts, 1968; participant Internat. Sculpture Symposium, Cal. State Coll. at Long Beach. Served with USAAF, 1942-45; ETO. Decorated French Medal Liberation; recipient Ford Found. fellowship, 1960; Tamarind Litho Workshop fellowship, 1963; Guggenheim Found. fellowship, 1967-68. Died May 21, 1975.

KOHN, LOUIS A, lawyer; b. Hayti, Mo., Mar. 8, 1907; s. Israel and Rachel (Falk) K.; A.B., U. Mo., 1927; LL.B., Harvard, 1930; m. Mary Jane Bunn, Oct. 30, 1947. Admitted to Ill. bar, 1931, since practiced in Chgo.; partner Mayer, Brown & Platt, and predecessors, 1946—71. Commr. Nat. Conf. Uniform State Laws, 1953—71; mem. council U. Ill. Law Forum. 1956—58; vice—chrmn. joint com. jud. article Ill. and Chgo. bar assns., 1951-57; gen. counsel Com. Modern Cts. Ill., 1958, vice chrmn.; vice chmn. Citizens Com. Jud. Amendment, Ill., 1953—55. Mem. nominating com. Chgo. Sch. Bd., 1950-52. Organizer Stevenson for Gov. Com., Ill., 1947; adminstrv. asst. Gov. Stevenson, 1949; incorporator Volunteers for Stevenson, 1952; del. Democratic Nat. Conv., 1952; chmn. Ill. Lawyers for Kennedy, 1960. Served as officer AUS, World War II; S.W. Pacific. Decorated Bronze Star; named Chicagoan of the Year for 1962. Fellow Am. Bar Found.; mem. Am. (chmn. spl. com. adminstrv. agy. appointments), Ill., Chgo. (Bd. mgrs. 1950—52) bar assns., Am. Judicature Soc., Assn. Bar City N.Y., Am. Law Inst., Inst. of judicial Adminstrn., Phi Beta Kappa. Clubs: Law, Tavern, Harvard (Chigao, Illinois). Author articles ct. reform, trusts uniform commnl. code, Home: Chicago, Ill. Died Oct. 9, 1971.

KOKES, RICHARD JOSEPH, educator; b. Cape May, N.J., Mar. 2, 1927; s. Carl Victor and Margaret Elizabeth (Krutsch) K.; B.S., Villanova Coll., 1948; Ph.D., Cornell U., 1951; m. Marian Martin Tickel, Aug. 18, 1951; children—Susan Reid, Lisa Martin. Fellow Mellon Inst., Pitts., 1952-55; asst. prof. Loyola Coll. at Balt., 1955-58; asst. prof. Johns Hopkins U., Balt., 1958-67, prof. chemistry, 1967-70, W.R. Grace prof., 1970-73, chmn. dept., 1972-73. Cons. W.R. Grace Chem. Co. Served with USNR, 1944-46. Recipient P.H. Emmett award, 1971. Mem. Am. Chem. Soc., Catalysis Soc., Sigma Xi, Alpha Chi Sigma, Omicron Delta Chi, Phi Lambda Upsilon. Democrat. Roman Catholic. Author: (with D.H. Andrews) Fundamental Chemistry, 1962, 65; Laboratory Manual for Fundamental Chemistry. Contbr. profl. jours. Home: Towson Md. Died July 27, 1973; interred St. Mary's Cemetery, Cold Spring, N.J.

KOLB, JAMES MONROE, physician; b. Clarksville, Ark., Dec. 14, 1904; s. James Silas and Mollie Virginia (Clark) K.; A.B., Coll. of Ozarks, 1925; M.D., U. Ark., 1930; m. Reba Lois Garner, Apr. 17, 1930; children—James Monroe, Martha Jane (Mrs. James R. Callaway). Intern Mo. Pacific Hosp., Little Rock, 1930—31; practice in Clarksville, 1931—35, 39—42, 46—62; founder, 1962, since propr. Kolb Clinic, Clarksville, Ark.; mem. staff Clarksville Hosp.; mem. vis. staff Sparks lMeml. Hosp., Ft. Smith, Ark.; adv. com. Yell County Health Clinic; raiser registered Hereford cattle and Shetland ponies, 1946—69. Organizer, founder Clarksville Airport Commn., 1960—69, chmn., 1963—69. Corner, Johnson County, Ark., 1933—35; chmn. Johnson County Democratic Central Com., 1946—69; sec. Johnson County Election Commn., 1950—69; del. Dem. Nat. Conv., 1964. Trustee Coll. of Ozarks, .1935—56. Served to capt. U.S. Army Res., 1935—38; to maj. USAAF, 1942—45. Mem. Am. (ho. of dels. 1955—69, chmn. com. med. practices, 1958—65, mem. council constirutions and and bylaws 1966—69), Ark. (chmn. council 1956—57, pres. 1959—60), Johnson County (pres. 1954) med. assns., Am. Acad. Gen. Practic (pres. Ark. 1953—54, dels. 1954—64), Am. Soc. Abdominal Surgeons, Alumni Assn. Coll. Ozarks (pres. 1933—34), U. Ark. Alumni Assn. (chmn. Johnson County chpt. 1960—69), Johnson County C. of C. (past bd. dir.), Ark. Valley Hereford Assn., Ft. Smith Liverstock Exposition, Phi Rhoe Sigma. Presbyn. (elder). Mason (Shriner), Lion. Club: Clarksville Country. Contbr. med. jours. Home: Clarksville, Ark. Died Nov. 16, 1969; interred Oakland Cemetery, Clarksville Ark.

KOLKEY, EUGENE LOUIS, advt. exec.; b. Chgo., Nov. 27, 1927; s. Samuel and Florence (Bernstein) K.; B.A. in Advt. Design, U. Ill., 1949; m. Gilda Cowan, Sept. 3, 1950; children—Daniel, Sandor, Eric. Art dir. Earle Ludgin, Chgo., 1949-51, Young & Rubicam, Chgo., 1951—53; exec. v.p., exec. creative dir. Leo Burnett, Chgo., 1953—75, also dir., dir, Canadian Co. Recipient Clio TV award for best comml., 1967, 68; numerous awards from N.Y.C., Chgo. and Los Angeles Advt. and Art Directors Club, also Cannes Film Festival. Jewish religion. Clubs: Art Directors (pres. 1964), Mid—Am. Arts (chgo.). Created Tony the Tiger, 1953. Home: Highland Park, Ill. Died Oct. 11, 1975; interred Memorial Park Cemetery, Skokie, Ill.

KOMROFF, MANUEL, writer; b. N.Y.C., Sept. 7, 1890; s. Samuel and Belle (Borkes) K.; m. Elinor M. Barnard, Dec. 23, 1918 (dec.); m. 2d, Odette Steele, Oct. 19, 1938. Corr. in Petrograd, N.Y. World, Oct. 1917 Russian Revolution; v.p. Authors' Guild, 1941-43; mem. Council Authors League, 1937-47; gov. Overseas Press Club, 1942-44; adv. Council Writers' War Bd.; v.p. P.E.N. World Writers, Am. Center, 1945-47, sec., 1947-52. Author: The Grace of Lambs, 1925; Juggler's Kiss, 1927; The Voice of Fire, 1927; Coronet (2 vols.), 1929; The Fool and Death, 1930; Two Thieves, 1931; A New York Tempest, 1932; I, The Tiger, 1933; Waterloo, 1936; The March of the Hundred, 1939; The Magic Bow; A Romance of Paganini, 1940; What is a Miracle?, 1941; A Christmas Letter, 1941; In the Years of Our Lord, 1942; Don Quixote and Sancho (a play), 1942; All In Our Day, 1942; The Book of Tom Smith, A Biblio-Epitaph, 1942; The One Story; The Life of Christ, 1943; Feast of the Jesters, 1947; Echo of Evil, 1948; How to Write a Novel, 1950; Jade Star, 1951; Marco Polo, 1952; Jesus Through the Centuries, 1953; His Great Journey, 1953; Every Man's Bible, 1953; Napoleon, 1954; Gods and Demons, 1954; True Adventures of Spys, 1954; The Story of Jesus, 1955; Julius Caesar, 1955; Mozart, 1956; The Loves of Omar Khayyam, 1956; Abraham Lincoln, 1959; Men, Women and Children of the Bible, 1960; Thomas Jefferson, 1961; Beethoven and His Music, 1961;? Mathew Brady, 1962; The Third Eye, 1962; Disraeli, 1963; Waterloo, 1963; Life in the Middle Ages, 1963; Charlemagne, 1964; Talleyrand, 1965; Marie Antoinette, 1967; The Hudson River, 1967; The Whole World is Outside, 1968. Editor: Dostoyevsky's The Brothers Karamazov; Tolstoy's War and Peace, Travels of Marco Polo; Contemporaries of Marco Polo; The History of Herodotus; Tales of the Monks (Gesta Romanorum); The Romances of Voltaire; The Great Fables; Nietzsche's Zarathustra; The Apocrypha; Montesquieu's Persian Letters; Oriental Romances; Introductions to Balzac's Physiology of Marriage and Lafcadio Hearn's Some Chinese Ghosts, Reader's Digest Story of the Bible World. Editor of the Modern Library, 1921-26; The Library of Living Classics, 1928. Editor and founder of Black and Gold Library, 1926, Library of True Adventure, 1954. Del. UN for P.E.N. Internat. Writers, 1947. Spl. lectr. univs. on technique of novel. Contbr. to leading mags. Home: Woodstock, N.Y. Died Dec. 10, 1974.

KOOS, LEONARD VINCENT, educator; b. Chicago, Ill., Mar. 9, 1881; s. Adam and Mary (Zimmerman) K; B.A., Oberlin Coll., 1907, hon. Litt.D., 1937; M.A., U. of Chicago, 1915, Ph.D., 1916; m. Hazel Byrd Smith, June 14, 1916; children—Mary Cornelia, Karl Kenyon, Lenora Katherine. Teacher and supt. schs., Ill. and Minn., until 1914; asso. prof. edn. U. of Wash., 1916-18, prof., 1918-19; prof. secondary edn., U. of Minn., 1919-29, U. of Chicago, 1929-46; dir. Research Am. Assn. of Junior Colls., 1946-49; lecturer summer sessions Ohio State U., 1916, 1917, U. of Chicago, 1918, 21, Harvard, 1922, U. of Calif., 1925, Colo State Teachers Coll., 1927, Columbia U., 1929, University of Michigan, 1946, 47; vis. prof. So. Ill. U., 1958; vis. lectr. U. of Fla., 1963-65. Asst. ednl. dir. S.A.T.C., collegiate sect., District No. 12, 1918-19. Member Nat. Com. on Research in Secondary Edn. Fellow A.A.A.S.; mem. N.E.A., Nat. Soc. for Study of Edn., Ednl. Research Assn., Nat. Assn. Secondary Sch. Prins., Minn. Edn. Assn. (pres. 1927-28), Am. Assn. Univ. Profs., Phi Delta Kappa. Conglist. Coub: Quadrangle. Author: Adminstration of Secondary School Units, 1917; The Junior High School, 1920; The Junior College, 1924; The High School Principal, 1924; Junior College Movement, 1925; American Secondary School, 1927; The Questionnaire in Education, 1928; Secondary Education in California, 1929; Private and Public Secondary Education, 1931; Guidance in Secondary Schools (with G. N. Kefauver), 1932; Administering the Secondary School (with others), 1940; Integrating High School and College, 1946; Junior High School Trends, published, 1955; government bulletins. Editor: Yearbook on Extra-Curricular Activities of Nat. Soc. for Study of Edn., 1926. Editor Sch. Review, 1930-40; editor Junior College Journal, 1946-49. Member staff of Survey of Higher Edn., Cleveland, 1924; dir. Survey of Secondary Edn. in Calif., 1928; asso. dir. Nat. Survey of Secondary Edn. Compiler of Farmers' Law (Minn. edit.), 1913; Inglis Memorial Lecture, Harvard, 1925. Home: Newaygo, Mich.†

KOPPERUD, ANDREW, lawyer; b. Webster, S.D., July 4, 1924; s. Andrew and L. Mabel (Matthews) K.; B.S., U. Cal. at Berkeley, 1947; LL.B., U. Cal. at Hastings, 1950; m. Barbara Bugbee, Apr. 19, 1952; children—David M., Linda W., H. Scott. Admitted to Cal. bar, 1951; practiced in San Francisco, 1951-53; trial atty. Office Regional Counsel, Internal Revenue Service, Chgo., 1953-57; partner firm Cooley, Crowley & Gaither, San Francisco, 1957-73. Dir. Star Glass Co., San Francisco; lectr. Cal. Continuing Edn. Bar Program, 1960, 62, 65. Mem. State Bar Cal., Am., Fed., San Francisco bar assns., Phi Beta Kappa, Theta Delta Chi. Presbyn. (elder). Home: Belvedere, Cal. Died Feb. 19, 1973.

KOSOLAPOFF, GENNADY MICHAEL, educator, chemist; b. Viatka, Russia, Sept. 2, 1909; s. Michael Paul and Alexandra Vasily (Shikhova) K.; came to U.S., 1924, naturalized, 1942; B.S. in Chem. Engring., Cooper Union, 1932; M.S. in Biochemistry, U. Mich., 1933, Sc.D. in Chemistry, 1936; m. Dorothea W. Bouton, July 20, 1934; children—Alexandra, Michael, Patricia. Research chemist Libby-Owens-Ford Glass Co., 1936-38, Monsanto Chem. Co., 1938-48; asso. prof. Auburn U., 1948-53, research prof., 1953-76; research cons. indsl. and govtl. agys., 1943-76; dir. chem. research F.J. Seiler Research Lab. Office of Aerospace Research, Colo., 1963-64; cons. AEC; lectr. chemistry of phosphorus, 1949-76. Mem. Chem. Soc. London. Author: Organophosphorus Compounds, 1950, co-author 2d edit., 1972; also sects. books and encys. Abstractor, sect. co-editor Chem. Abstracts. Contbr. profl. jours. Home: Auburn, Ala., Died Jan. 1, 1976.

KOSTER, WILLEM, economist, banker; b. Utrecht, Netherlands, Sept. 24, 1911; Dr. Econs., Netherlands Sch. Econs.; m. Henriette C.J. van Mastrigt, 1937; 3 children. Civil servant Netherlands and Netherlands E. Indies Govts., The Hague and Batavia, 1936—46; alternate exec. dir. Internat. Bank for Reconstrn. and Devel., IMF for Netherlands, Norway and Union S. Africa, 1946—49; treas.—gen. Netherlands, The Hague, 1949—51; with Internat. Bank for Reconstrn. and Devel., 1951—53; gen. mgr. Netherlands Bank of S. Africa Ltd., 1953—65; lectr. econs. U. Natal, Durban, 1966—67; econ. adviser Inst. Econ. Research Small and Medium—Sized Enterprizes in Netherlands, The Hague. Decorated knight Order Netherlands Lion. Author: Aspects of Banking and Monetary Control in South Africa, 1965. Home: The Hague Netherlands. Died Apr. 28, 1975; cremated.

KOSTKA, WILLIAM JAMES, pub. relations, advt. exec.; b. Chgo., May 18, 1905; s. Matthew and Anna (Papacek) K.; B.A., Knox Coll., 1927; m. Dorothy Parmenter, June 15, 1928; children—Stefan, William. Formerly telegraph editor Chgo. Daily Drovers Jour.; central div. mgr. Internat. News Service; mng. editor Fawcett Publ.; editor Frank A. Munsey Publ., N.Y.C.: publicity dir. NBC; mng. editor Look mag.; v.p. Inst. Pub. Relations; pub. relations, advt. dir. U.S. Brewers Found., 1949; chmn. Wm. Kostka & Assos., Inc., 1949. Mem. Pub. Relations Soc. Am., Phi Beta Kappa, Sigma Delta Chi, Tau Kappa Epsilon. Clubs: Nat. Press; Denver Press. Author: The Pre-Prohibition History of Adolph Coors Company, 1873-1933, 1973. Home: Denver, Colo. Died Sept. 8, 1974.

KOSTRZEWSKI, JOZEF WIADYSLAW, archaeologist; b. Weglewo, Poznan, Poland, Feb. 25, 1885; s. Stanislaw and Elizieta (Bronkanska) K.; ed. U. Wroclaw (Poland), 1907—09; ed. U. Cracow, 1909—10, also dr. honoris causa; Dr. phil., U. Berlin, 1915; privat docent U. Lwow (Poland), 1918; dr. honoris causa U. Poznan, U. Berlin; m. Jadwiga Wroblewska, Oct. 30, 1911; children-Zbigniew, Bogdan, Przemyslaw, Maria. Docent, Lwow U., 1918; prof. prehistory Poznan U., 1919—60; asst. Archaeol. Mus., Poznan, 1914—24, dir., 1924—58. Decorated officer, comdr. Order Polonia Restituta; Order Banner of Labor; comdr. Papal Order of St. Gregory; officer Legion of Honor Mem. Polish Acad. Sci., Finnish Archaeol. Soc.; corr. and hon. mem. various sci. socs. Numerous excavations including Biskupin, Poznan. Address: Poznan, Poland. Died Oct. 19, 1969.

KOUWENHOVEN, WILLIAM BENNETT, elec. engr.; b. Bklyn., Jan. 13, 1886; s. Tunis Gerrit Bergen and Phebe Florence (Bennett) K.; E.E., Bklyn. Poly. Inst., 1906, M.E., 1907; Diplom Ingenieur, Karlsruhe Technische Hochschule, Baden, Germany, 1912, Doktor Ingenieur, 1913; LL.D., Johns Hopkins, 1962, M.D. (hon.), 1969; D.Sc. (hon.), Syracuse U., 1970; m. Abigail Baxter Remsen, June 22, 1910; 1 son, William Gerrit. Asst. in physics Bklyn. Poly Inst., 1906-07, instr. in physics and elec. engring., 1907-10; instr. in elec. engring. Washington U., 1913-14; instr. Johns Hopkins, 1914-17, asso. in elec. engring., 1917-19; engring. supt. Winchester Repeating Arms Co. (leave of absence from Johns Hopkins), 1919-20; asso. prof. elec. engring. Johns Hopkins, 1919-30, prof., asst. dean Sch. Engring., 1930-38, prof., dean Sch. Engring., 1938-54, prof. emeritus, 1954-75; lectr. in surgery Johns Hopkins Sch. Medicine, 1956-75; cons. engr. U.S. Bureau of Mines, U.S. Bureau Standards; arbitrator Nat. Assn. Arbitration. Instr., rank of capt., R.O.T.C., World War I. Recipient Ludwig Hekton Gold medal A.M.A., 1961; Edison medalist Am. Inst. E.E., 1962; Distinguished Contbn. in Sci. award A.C.P., 1969; Distinguished Service award Underwriter Labs., 1969; Helen Taussig award, 1970; Power Life award Power Groups of I.E.E.E., 1970; Sci. Achievement award A.M.A., 1972; Lasker award, 1973; named hon. mem. faculty Med. and Chir Soc., 1970. Fellow A.A.A.S., Am. Inst. E.E. (v.p. 1931-33; dir. 1935-39; chmn. Balt. sect. 1922-31); mem. Am. Soc. Testing Materials, Edison Electric Inst., Am. Welding Soc. (exec. com. research council), Nat. Acad. Sci., Am. Heart Assn. (award of merit 1969), Eta Kappa Nu. Tau Beta Pi, Sigma Xi, Pi Kappa Phi. Democrat. Presbyn. Clubs: Johns Hopkins, Baltimore Engineers; Gibson Island. Contbr. numerous articles and papers on elec. measurements, also on electric shock, magnetic analysis, electric welding, effect of electricity on heart, elec. defibrillation, closed chest cardiac massage, effects of high voltage electric fields on human beings, treatment of atrial fibrillation. Trans. American Inst. Elec. Engring., Elec. World, proc. Am. Soc. Testing Materials Welding Journal, med. and surg. jours. Home: Baltimore, Md., Died Nov. 11, 1975.

KOVARIK, ALOIS FRANCIS, educator; b. Spillville, Ia., Mar. 8, 1880; s. Wenzel J. and Barbara (Milkesh) K.; B.A., U. Minn., 1904, M.A., 1907, Ph.D., 1909; John Harling research fellow in physics and research in radioactivity, Victoria University, England, 1909-11; D.Sc., 1916; hon. M.A., Yale, 1925; hon. degree Doktor Rerum Naturalium, Karlova University, Prague, 1932; unmarried. Instructor at Decorah Inst., 1896-1900; scholar in physics, 1902-04, instr., 1904-12, asst. prof., 1912-15, asso. prof., 1915, 16, U. of Minn.; asst. prof. physics, Yale, 1916-21, asso. prof., 1921-25, prof., 1925-48, physcis, emeritus, from 1948. Mem. Radioactivity Congress, Burssels, 1910; foreign mem. Société Royale des Lettres et des Sciences de Boheme, 1934. Recipient medal of Karlova University Prague, 1925; also medal from Comenius University, Bratislava, 1932. Mem. Committee Nat. Research Council. Fellow A.A.A.S., Am. Phys. Soc., Natural History Museum; mem. Am. Mat. Soc., Math. Assn. America, Conn. Acad. of Arts and Sciences, New York Acad. of Sciences, Am. Meteorol. Soc. Société des Mathématiciens et des Physiciens of Czechoslovakia (hon.) Société Francaise de Physique, Soc. for Promotion Engring. Edn., Phi Beta Kappa, Sigma Xi, Pi Gamma Mu, Alpha Tau Omega, Acacia. Mason (32°). Clubs: Graduate, New Haven Country, N.H. Figure Skaing. Researches in radioactivity, and ionization of gases, statis. methods in studying Alpha, Beta Gamma and X rays and first automatic registration of rays, problem of age of the earth, nuclear physics, pub. in Philosophical Mag., Le Radium, Phys. Rev., Bull. Nat. Research Council, Procs. Royal Soc., etc. Active with Com. on Public Information; the submarine problem; instruction of radio engrs., U.S. Army World War. Address: New Haven, Conn.†

KOWALSKI, FRANK, govt. ofcl.; b. Meriden, Conn., Oct. 18, 1907: s. Frank and Mary (Miller) K; B.S., U.S. Mil. Acad., 1930; M.S., Mass. Inst. Tech., 1936; student Columbia, 1945; m. Helen Amelia Bober, Oct. 20, 1931; children—Carol Helene, Barry Frank. Commd. 2d lt., inf., U.S. Army, 1930, advanced through grades to col., 1944; various co., bn., regt. assignments, 1930-44; chief tng. G-3 sect. Hdqrs. European Theater, 1944; dir. Disarmament Sch., London, Eng., 1944-45; dep. chief information and edn. div. Hdqrs. European Theater, 1945; chief mil. govt. of Kyoto, Osaka prefectures, Japan, 1948-49; dep. chief civil affairs, Japan, 1949-50; chief staff Mil. Adv. Group, Japan, 1950-52; comdt. U.S. Army Command Mgmt. Sch., 1954-58; ret., 1958; mem. 86th-87th Congresses, Conn.-at-Large; mem. Armed Service, Manpower Utilization coms.; mem. Subversive Activities Control Bd., 1963-66. Decorated Legion of Merit with cluster, Bronze Star. Author 2 books also articles on mil. mgmt. Holder patents for mil. items. Home: Alexandria Va. Died Oct. 11, 1974; buried Arlington National Cemetery.

KRAFT, LOUIS, social worker; b. Moscow, Russia, Jan. 2, 1891; s. Abraham and Etta (Gellis) K.; came to U.S., 1895, naturalized, 1902; B.A., Coll. of City of N.Y.; spl. courses Sch. of Architecture, Columbia; Dr. Humane Letters, Jewish Theol. Sem., 1964; m. Pauline Roman; children—Stephen, Barbara. Exec. dir. Bronx Y.M.H.A., 1914—17; dir. Welfare activities Jewish Welfare Board, 1917—20; dir. Jewish Center Work, Jewish Welfare Bd., 1921—39; exec. dir., 1939—47, became gen. sec. nat. council 1947; sec. World Federation of YMHAs; cons. to Am. Joint Distbn. com., Geneva, Switzerland. Former pres. Nat. Conf. Jewish Social Welfare; hon. pres., past pres. Nat. Assn. Jewish Center Workers, exec. sec.; chmn. Intnerat. Conf. Jewish Social Work. Recipient Townsend Harris medal Alumni Assn. City Coll. N.Y., 1972. Author: Jewish Community Center. Home: New York City, NY. Died July 1975; interred Westchester Hills Cemetery.

KRAFVE, RICHARD ERNEST, indsl. cons.; b. Mpls. Sept. 22, 1907; s. John and Marie (Cafarella) K.; student Minn. Coll. Law, 1927, U. Minn., 1929; D.Sc., Lowell Inst. Tech., 1962; m. Virginia Frances Horton, June 8, 1935; children—Allen Horton, Richard Neil, Sales engr., sales mgr. pub. utilities, 1925—41; cons. sales and rate to utility industry Ebasco Services, Inc., N.Y.C., 1941-42; mgr. Chgo. office Cresap, McCormick & Paget, mgmt. cons., 1946-47; various exec. positons pubrchasing, mfg. and def. prodn. Ford Motor Co., 1947—52, asst. gen. mgr. Lincoln—Mercury div., 1952—55, gen. mgr. Edsel div., 1955—58, v.p. Ford Motor Co., 1956—58, v.p. Canadian activities, 1958—59; group v.p. component and comml. divs. Raytheon Co., 1958—59, exec. v.p. co., 1959—60, pres., 1960—62, dir., 1959—62; mgmt. cons., from 1962; dir. Precision Instrument Co., Palo Alto, Cal., Whittaker Corp., Stellar Industries, Inc. (both Los Angeles), Petroleum Exploration & Devel. Funds, Inc., Abilene, Tex., Containerfreight Corp., Systems Assos., Inc. (all Long Beach, Cal.), E—H Research Labs., Oakland, Cal., Los Angeles, Informatics, Inc., Canoga Park, Cal., Sci. Advances, Inc., Columbus, O., Electronic Memories & Magnetics Corp., Los Angeles, Dynasciences Corp., Los Angeles, Yardney Electric Corp., Los Angeles, Electrospin Corp., Columbus, O., Jeffery Galion, Inc., Columbus, Airtronics Corp., Washington, Served as officer AUS, 1942—46, Mem. Am. Soc. M.E., Soc. Automobile Engrs. Republican, Roman Catholic, Home: Los Angeles, Cal. Died Dec. 29, 1974; buried VA Cemetery, Los Angeles.

KRAMER, BENJAMIN, physician; b. Chatin, Russia, Aug. 15, 1888; s. Aaron and Clara Kramer; M.D., N.Y.U., 1909; m. Sarah Farber, Sept. 18, 1949; children—David, Berenice (Mrs. Edward L. Kaplan). Intern, Jewish Hosp., 1910-12; asst. attending in pediatrics Harriet Lane Home for Invalid Children, Johns Hopkins Hosp., 1921-25; cons. pediatrician Kingston Av. Hosp.; chmn. emeritus Jewish Hosp. and Med. Center Bklyn.; dir. pediatric services emeritus Maimonides Hosp.; asst. prof. physiology Ia. Med. Sch., 1913-17; instr. to asso. prof. pediatrics Johns Hopkins, 1917-25; prof. clin. pediatrics emeritus State U. N.Y., Bklyn. Diplomate Am. Bd. Pediatrics. Mem. A.M.A., Am. Pediatric Soc., Soc. Expetl. Biology and Medicine. Home: New York City, N.Y., Died Sept. 29, 1972.

KRAMER, STEPHANIE SHAMBAUGH (MRS. FERD KRAMER), landscape architect; b. Chgo., Dec. 22, 1908; d. George E. and Edith (Capps) Shambaugh; B.A., Vassar Coll., 1930; m. Ferd Kramer, Dec. 22, 1932; children—Barbara S. (Mrs. Forrest Ridgeway Bailey), Douglas, Anthony S. Engaged in practice as landscaper architect Chgo., from 1955. Mem. League Women Voters (pres. Highland Park 1954-56, state dir. 1957-68), Hull House Assn. (bd. dirs.). Home: Chicago Ill. Died Feb. 20, 1973.

KREBS, WALTER WINSTON, newspaper pub.; b. Johnstown, Pa., Mar. 8, 1894; s. Frederick and Margaret Winfred (Walters) K.; student Cornell U., 1913-17; LL.D., U. Pitts.; H.H.D., St. Francis Coll., Loretto, Pa., 1970; m. Cornelia Rogers, Jan. 18, 1939. Admitted to Pa. bar, 1920, and began practice in Johnstown; with Johnstown Tribune and Democrat, 1925, pub., 1927-63, now pres.; pres. Johnstown Tribune Pub. Co., WJAC, Inc. Served to ensign U.S. Navy Flying Corps, 1918. Recipient Pa. awards for excellence for human relations and community service, 1969. Mem. Chi Phi, Phi Delta Phi, Sigma Delta Chi. Republican. Lutheran. Died Mar. 26, 1974.

KRECKER, FREDERICK H(ARTZLER), zoologist, educator; b. Tokyo, Japan, Dec. 21, 1881; s. Frederick and Elizabeth (Overholser) K.; A.B., Princeton, 1904, fellow in biology, 1908-09, Ph.D., 1909; M.A., Cornell, 1906; student, Freiburg, Munich, 1906-08; grad. scholar U. of Chicago, 1907-08; m. Margaret E. Brown, Aug. 22, 1916; children—Frederic Merrihew, Margaret Elizabeth (Mrs. Landis D. Baker). Prof. biology Marietta Coll., 1909-14; asst. prof. zoology Ohio State U., 1914-23, prof., 1923-29; acting dir. Lake Lab., Sandusky and Put-in Bay, O., 1916-24; asst. dir. Stone Lab., Put-in Bay, 1925-36; prof., head dept. biology Ohio U., 1929-36, zoology, 1936-49, prof., from 1949. Mem. Ohio Biol. Survey Bd. from 1929. Fellow A.A.A.S.; mem. Soc. Zoologists, Ecol. Soc., Micros. Soc., Soc. Limnology and Oceanography, Sigma Xi, Gamma Alpha. Presbyn. Author: General Zoology, 1934. Contbr. to sci. jours. Home: Athens, O.†

KREEGER, MORRIS HAROLD, hosp. cons.; b. N.Y., Aug. 17, 1910; s. Barnet and Laura (Betensky) K.; A.B., Rutgers U., 1931; M.D., Jefferson Med. Coll., 1935; postgrad., U. Pa., 1936-37; m. Naomi Mayor, 1935 (div. 1963); children—Charles, Lora; m. 2d, Reneé L. Gelman, Dec. 1964; 1 dau., Anne. Intern Altoona (Pa.) Gen. Hosp., 1935-36; practice of medicine, 1937-39; med. resident Mt. Sinai Hosp., N.Y.C., 1940, asst. dir., 1941-46; exec. dir. Michael Reese Hosp., Chgo., 1946-60, hosp. cons., 1960-75, mem. bd. Chgo. Hosp. Council 1950-59, pres., 1954. Bd. dirs. Blue Cross Plan for Hosp. Care, Francis W. Parker Sch. Recipient Chgo. Com. 100 Award Honor for outstanding civic and community service, 1957. Mem. A.M.A., Ill. Chgo. med. socs., Ill. Hosp. Assn., Am. Coll. Hosp. Adminstrs., Am. Hosp. Assn., Am. Assn. Hosp. Cons., alumni assns. Rutgers U., Jefferson Med. Coll., U. Pa. Postgrad. Sch. Medicine, Sigma Alpha Mu, Phi Lambda Kappa. Home: Chicago, Ill., Died Nov. 3, 1975.

KRESS, ALBERT LELAND, mfg. executive; born Watkins Glen, N.Y., June 25, 1894; s. Grant M. and Mary Louise (Smith) K.; M.B.A., Harvard, 1933; m. Marie Alicia Celestine Loubert, Dec. 20, 1947. Engring., constrn. of waterworks, power plants, sewers, land drainage projects; engr. U.S. Rubber Co., 1918-31, chief indsl. engr., 1928-31; dep. adminstr. rubber industry codes of fair prodn. NRA, Washington, 1933-34; dir. NRA code adminstrn. Nat. Electric Mfrs. Assn., 1935-39, also dir. indsl. relations; cons. job evaluation Nat. Metal Trades Assn., 1939-41; mgmt. cons. Aeronautical C. of C., Boeing Aircraft Co., Beech Aircraft Co., 1941-42; mgmt. cons. Republic Aviation Corp., 1941-42, asst. to pres. charge indsl. relations, 1942-43; cons. labor arbitration, organizational planning, salary evaluation, 1944-51; v.p., tech. dir. John Wood Co., N.Y.C., 1951-52; mgmt. cons., 1952-55; v.p. ACF Industries, Inc., N.Y.C., 1955-73; lectr. N.Y. State Sch. Indsl. and Labor Relations Cornell U., Mem. Am. Mgmt. Assn., Am. Arbitration Assn. (nat. panel). Mason. Club: Nassau (Princeton, N.J.). Author: Foremanship Fundamentals, 1942: (with T. O. Armstrong) Foreman's Production Job, 1950; Salary and Wage Adminstrn., 1952, others. Contbr. articles profl. jours. Home: Princeton, N.J. Died Aug. 5, 1973.

KRETZMANN, M(ARTIN) F(REDERICK), pastor; b. Dudleytown, Ind., Dec. 30, 1878; s. Carl Henry and Elizabeth (Polack) K.; Concordia Coll., Ft. Wayne, Ind., 1893-97; student Concordia Sem., St. Louis, Mo., 1897-1901, D.D., 1939; m. Elizabeth Wessel, Aug. 20, 1902; children—Martin Carl Christian, Alfred Theodore, Elizabeth, Erna Elizabeth (Mrs. Arthur M. Fenker), Gerhard Robert, Elfrieda Marie. Asst. pastor St. John's Luth. Ch., Vincennes, Ind., 1901-04; pastor, Trinity, E. St. Louis, Ill., 1904-09, St. John's Kendallville, Ind., from 1909. Gen. sec. Lutheran Church (Mo. Synod), and other states, from 1920, sec. bd. dirs. from 1920. Dir. and pres. Noble County Tuberculosis Assn., from 1913. Mem. Concorida Hist. Inst. Contbr. to ch. jours. Home: Kendallville, Ind.†

KRETZMANN, OTTO PAUL, univ. ofcl.; b. Stamford, Conn., May 7, 1901; s. Karl and Thekla (Hueschen) K.; S.T.M., Concordia Sem., St. Louis, 1924; postgrad., Johns Hopkins, 1933; Litt.D. Concordia Sem., St. Louis, 1941; D.D., Thiel Coll., Greenville, Pa., 1947; LL.D., Capital U., 1950, Ind. U., 1959, Wabash Coll., 1962, Ind. State U., 1968; L.H.D., Pacific Luth. U., 1962, Cal. Luth. Coll., 1970; D.D., St. Joseph's Coll., 1967; m. Flora Ellen Rosenthal, Aug. 15, 1942 (dec. Aug. 26, 1970); children—John Paul, Mark John, Stephen Paul; m. 2d, Elizabeth Margaret Brohm, June 24, 1973. Instr., Concordia Sem., Springfield, Ill., 1924—34; exec. sec. Luth. Internat. Walther League, 1934—40; pres. Valparaiso (Ind.) U., 1940—68, chancellor, 1968—74, pres. emeritus, 1974—75. Bd. dirs. Wheat—Ridge Sanatorium, Luth. Chgo. Med. Sch. Sec. Bd. Edn. Mo. Synod.; pres. Hardt Found.; pres. Ind. Assn. Ind. and Ch. Related Colls.; bd. dirs. Ind. Conf. Higher Edn., Mus. Youth of Am.; chmn. com. on pre—prefl. edn. Assn. Am. Colls.; mem. Arbitration Bd. apptd. by Gov. Ind.; mem. Naval Res. adv. council th Naval Dist. Recipient Great Living Hoosier award, 1963. Fellow Royal Soc. Arts; mem. Ind. Hist. Commn. Acad. Polit. Sci., Tudor and Stuart Soc., Modern Lang. Assn., Am. Soc. Ch. History, Midwest Conf. Atomic Scientists and Religious Leaders, Ind. Acad. Author: The Road Back to God, 1934; Pilgrim, 1944; Sign of the Corss, 1959; Hosanna in the Whirlwind, 1969; co—author: Voices of the Passion, 1944; also articles. Editor emeritus, contrbr. The Cresset (a rev. of lit., the arts and pub. affairs). Address: Valparaiso, Ind. Died Sept. 14, 1975; buried Graceland Cemetery, Valparaiso, Ind.

KREUDER, ERNST, author; b. Aug. 29, 1903; m. Franfort U. Recipient Georg Buchner prize, 1953; Literaturpreis des Bundesverbandes der Deutschen Industrie, 1971. Mem. Acad. Sci. and Lit. Mainz, German Acad. Lang. and Poetry, PEN Club. Author: Die Gesellschaft vom Dachboden, 1946; Schwebender Weg, 1947; Die Unauffinbaren, 1948; Herein ohne anzukiopfen, 1954; Agimos oder die Weltgehilfen, 1959; Spur Unterm Wasser, 1963; Tunnel zu Vermieten, 1966; Hörensagen, 1969; Diesseits des Todes, 1972; also poems, Sommers Einsiedelei, 1956. Address: Mühital, Federal Republic of Germany., Died Dec. 24, 1972.

KREYCHE, ROBERT JOSEPH, author, educator; b. Racine, Wis., Aug. 26, 1920; s. Harold Joseph and Henrietta (Oteman) K.; B.A., M.A., Cath. U. Am.; Ph.D., U. Ottawa (Can.), 1952; m. Julianne Mangold, May 8, 1948 (dec. May 1969); children—Michael R., Thomas H., John A., Catharine A., Andrew J.; m. Ann Pritchard, Jan. 16, 1971. Mem. faculty Loyola U., Chgo., 1945-57, St. Joseph's Coll., Rensselaer, Ind., 1957-62, Rockhurst Coll., Kansas City, Mo., 1962-65; prof. philosophy U. Ariz., 1965-74. Mem. Am. Cath. Philos. Assn. (pres. 1967-68), Delta Epsilon Sigma (hon.) Author: First Philosophy, 1959; God and Reality, 1965; God and Contemporary Man, 1965; Logic for Undergraduates, 1970; The Betrayal of Wisdom, 1972; The Making of A Saint, 1973; Love Is A Therapy, 1973. Home: Tucson Ariz. Died Aug. 13, 1974.

KRIEG, LAUREL LEE, librarian; b. Burton, O., Mar. 12, 1907; d. John and Josephine Lee (Brainard) Krieg; A.B., Western Res. U., 1928; B.S., 1929; A.M., U. Chgo., 1942. Branch librarian Cuyahoga County, South Euclid, O., 1924—28, children's librarian, Alliance, O., 1929—36; county librarian, Ocean County, N.J., 1937—48; librarian, Martins Ferry, O., from 1948. Mem. Am., Ohio library assns., Cancer Soc., Oglebay Inst., Business and Profl. Women. Methodist. Club: Brooks Bird (Wheeling, W. Va.). Contbr. articles to library periodicals. Home: Martins Ferry, O. Deceased.

KRIEGER, KNUT AXEL, educatior; b. Phila., Feb. 1, 1911; s. Bengt Eric Ansheim and Julia Maud (Popple) K.; B.S. in Chemsitry, U. Pa., 1933, M.S., 1935, Ph.D., 1937; m. Miriam Rutherford Mick, Feb. 22, 1936; l son, Knut Rutherford. Mem. faculty U. Pa., 1933—75, successively asst. instr., instr., asst. prof., asso. prof., prof., 1952—75, asst. chmn. dept. chemistyr, 1969—75, acting dir. chemistry dept., 1952—54, supr. research contracts; cons. various corp. Mem. Nat. Def. Research Com., 1953—75. Mem. Am. Chem. Soc. (dir. Phila. sect. 1953—56), Catalysis Club Phila. (chmn. 1953), A.A.A.S., N.Y. Acad. Sci., Sigma Xi, Alpha Chi Sigma,

Tau Beta Pi, Pi Mu Epsilon, Phi Lambda Upsilon. Contbr. articles sci. jours. Home: Philadelphia, Pa. Died July 19, 1975.

KRIENDLER, MAXWELL ARNOLD, beverage co. exec.; b. N.Y.C., Feb. 16, 1908; s. Karl and Sadie Miller (Brenner) K.; LL.B., St. John's U., 1929; m. Charlotte Campbell, Feb. 1967; children by previous marriage—John, Christopher, Jessica P., Maxwell C.C. With 21 Club, N.Y.C., 1946-57; v.p. 21 Brands, Inc., N.Y.C., 1955-70, cons., 1970-73; dir. Iron Gate Products Co., Inc. Bd. dirs. Boys Town Italy, Joint Def. Appeal, Freedom House, George Jr. Republic, Aerospace Edn. Found., Air Force Museum, Found., Air Force Acad. Found., Air Force Assn. Fund; bd. govs. Long Island U.; regional fund chmn. Albert Einstein Coll. Medicine, Yeshiva U.; pres., dir. Jack Kriender Meml. Found. Served to col. USAAF, 1942-46; ETO; col. Res. ret. Decorated Legion of Merit, Commendation medal; recipient Exceptional Service award USAF, 1964, Man of Year award Air Force Assn., 1964, People to People Sports Com. award, 1964. Mem. Am. Legion (past post comdr.), Nat. Sojourners, Iota Theta. Mason. Club: Adventurers (N.Y.C.). Home: New York City, N.Y. Died Aug. 7, 1973.

KRINER, HARRY L(UTHER), educator; b. DuBois, Pa., Jan. 1, 1894; s. Lewis Milton and Mary Elizabeth (Harman) K.; student Lock Haven Normal Sch., 1913, Columbia, summer 1913; A.B., U. of Pittsburgh, 1920, A.M., 1927; Ed.D., Pa. State Coll., 1931; m. DeRose Hull, June 7, 1-21; children—Doris (Mrs. J.D. Rohr), Jean (Mrs. Albert Overton). Teacher-prin. elementary school, Clearfield, Pennsylvania, 1913-14; elementary sch. prin., Du Bois, 1914-16; night sch. teacher, Pitts., 1916; instr. and athletic coach, Clarion Normal Sch., 1920-23; prin. Warren High Sch., 1923-24; vis. instr. Edinboro Normal Sch., summer 1024; mem. faculty California (Pa.) State Teachers Coll., 1924-37 as dir. social science dept., 1924-37, dir. of extension, 1926-28, dir. summer sessions, 1926-37, acting pres., summer 1928, dean of instrn., 1927-37; asst. dir. of tchr. edn. and certification, Pa. Dept. Public Instrn., 1937-43; vis. instr., Pa. State Coll., summers, 1938, 39; supt. public schs., Altoona, Pa., 1943-48; pres. Shippensburg State Teachers Coll., 1948-57; dir. pub. relations, Sico Found., Mt. Joy, Pa., from 1957; vis. prof. sch. adminstrn. Grad Sch., U. Pitts., 1958-59; dir. Sico Oil Co. Mayor of Shippensburg, Pa., 1961-65. Mem., gen. chmn. Shippensburgh Sesquicentennial Celebration, 1970. Served as sgt., U.S. Army, Signal Corp., 1916-18, research div., Europe, 1918; lt. U.S. Army Reserve, Adjutant 304 Mt. Rep. Bn. Q.M., 1920-34. Bd. dirs. Red Cross, Community Chest, Tuberculosis and Cancer orgns., Heart Assn., Home Service, War Bond Sales, Vets. Employment, etc., Altoona, 1943-48. Awarded Am. Motor medal, transcontinental economy trip, 1915; recipient Certificate of Appreciation, Commonwealth of Pa., 1970, plaque Shippensburg, 1971. Mem. Am. Assn. Sch. Adminstrs., N.E.A. (mem. resolutions com. 1938-44, internat. relations com. 1936-38), Am. Legion Liaison League (1st pres.), Am. Legion, Pa. State Edn. Assn. (chmn. resolutions com., 1938-44; mem. exec. council, 1946-48), Pa. Council on Teacher Edn. (pres., 1948-50), Kappa Sigma, Phi Kappa Phi, Phi Delta Kappa, Pi Omega Pi, Kappa Delta Pi, Phi Sigma Pi. Republican. Presbyn. (elder). Mason (32°, Shriner). Clubs: Washington Co. Mt. (dir., 1926-39). Rotarian. Author: Pre-Training Factors Predictive of Teacher Success, 1931. Contbr. articles in profl. mags. Home: Shippensburg, Pa. Died Nov. 17, 1973; interred Spring Hill Cemetery, Shippensburg.

KRIPS, HENRY JOSEF, conductor; b. Vienna, Austria, Apr. 8, 1902; s. Joseph and Luise (Seitz) K.; ed. Academy of Music, Vienna, Austria; pupil of Felix Weingartner, Prof. Mandyczewski; m. Mitzi Wilheim, 1947; m. 3d, Baroness Harrietta Prochazka, Oct. 9, 1960. Music Coach, choirmaster; condr. Volsoper, Vienna, 1921-24; opera chief condr. Aussig/Elbe, 1924, Dortmund, 1925; gen. music dir. Karlsruhe, 1926-33; 1st condr. State Opera Vienna, 1933-38; prof. Acad. Music and Dramatic Art, 1935-38; guest condr. Opera, also Philharmonic Orch., Belgrade, 1938-39; reorganized Vienna State Opera, Hofmusikkapelle, Vienna, 1945; guest performances Salzburg Festival, 1946-48, Leningrad, Moscow, Nice, Paris, Marseille, Basle, London, Brussels, 1947; dir. Sch. for Conductors, Acad. Music and Dramatic Art, Vienna, 1949; chief condr. London Symphony Orch., 1950, Buffalo Philharmonic, 1954-63; condr., music dir. San Francisco Symphony Orch., 1963-64. Recipient Mozart Ring, Austria, 1965. Home: Montreux, Switzerland. Died Oct. 13, 1974.

KRISHNA, MENON VENGALIL KRISHMAN, govt. ofcl. India; b. Kozhikode, Malabar, India, May 3, 1897; s. Komath Krishna Kurup and Lakshmi Kutty Amma; student Zamorin's Coll., Kozhikode, Malabar; B.A., Presidency Coll., Madras, India, 1917; student Law Coll., Madras, 1917; B.Sc. (hon.), London Sch. Economics, 1927, M.Sc., 1934; M.A., Univ. Coll., London, 1930; tchrs. diploma Inst. Edn. External, London, 1925; Barrister-at-Law, Middle Temple, London, 1934, also Kings Inn, Dublin; LL.D., Glasgow U. (Scotland), Sagar U. (India). Faculty Nat. U., Adyar, 1920-22, St. Christopher Sch., Letchworth, Eng., 1924-25; hon. sec. India League, London, 1929-47; municipal councilor Met. Borough of St. Pancras, London, 1934-47; rep. Indian Nat.-Congress at internat. confs., 1935-39; chmn. governors St. Pancras Group Schs., London County Council; parliamentary candidate for Div. of Dunde, Scotland, 1938-40; personal rep. Jawaharal Nehru; vice pres. Exec. Council India, 1946-47; del. Gen. Assembly UN, 1946 and 1954-60; spl. rep. Govt. India, 1947; Indian High Commr. to U.K., 1947-52; Indian ambassador to Ireland, 1949-52; practiced at English bar, also Privy Council, returned to bar, 1952; became sr. counsel Supreme Ct. of India, 1953; elected member Council of States (upper house Indian parliament), 1953; minister without portfolio Central Government, 1956; elected to Lok Sabha from Bombay City, 1957; minister for defense (cabinet of Jawaharlal Nehru), 1957-62. Vis. prof. Osmania U., Hyderabad, India, 1953. Decorated Padma Vibhushan (India), 1954; Honorary Freeman of Borough of St. Pancras (London). Co-author: Conditions of India, 1933. Editor: Pelican Books, Twentieth Century Library, 1934. Died Oct. 6, 1974.

KRIZA, JOHN, dancer; b. Berwyn, Ill., Jan. 15, 1919; s. John J. and Marie (Bily) K.; student Morton Jr. Coll., 1937—38. With WPA Ballet, chgo., 1938—39, Chgo. Civic Opera Ballet, 1939—40, Am. Ballet Caravan, 1940, Am. Ballet Theatre, N.Y.C., from 1940, 1st dancer, 1955—75; created original roles in Billy the Kid, Fancy Free, Interplay, Fall River Legend, Winter's Eve; danced classical roles in Giselle, Swan Lake, Les Sylphides; Broadway musicals include Folies Bergeres, 1940, Panama Hattie, 1941, Concert Varieties, 1944; summer stock singing dancing roles include Kiss Me Kate, Brigadoon, Song of Norway; also has appeared in night clubs and on TV. Home: Berwyn, Ill. Died Aug. 18, 1975; buried Woodlawn Cemetery.

KROCK, ARTHUR, newspaperman; b. Glasgow, Ky., Nov. 16, 1887; s. Joseph and Caroline (Morris) K.; A.A., Lewis Inst., Chgo.; A.M., Princeton; Litt.D., U. Louisville, U. Ky. (hon.), 1956, Centre Coll. Ky.; m. Marguerite Polleys, Apr. 22, 1911 (dec. 1938); 1 son, Thomas Polleys; m. 2d, Martha Granger Blair, 1939. Reporter, Louisville, 1907; became Washington corr. Louisville Times, 1910, also Louisville Courier-Journal, 1911; returned to Louisville, 1915, as editorial mgr. both papers; editor-in-chief Times, 1919-23; asst. to pres. N.Y. World, 1923-27; joined N.Y. Times Bd. Editors, 1927, Washington corr., 1932-53, Washington commentator, 1953-67. Mem. Pulitzer Prize Bd., Sch. Journalism, Columbia, 1940-53. Contbr. syndicated articles from Peace Conf., Paris, France, 1918-19; one of 3 Am. members of Inter-Allied Press Com. of Fourteen which induced open sessions of the Peace Conf.; asst. to chmn. Democratic Nat. Com., New York, campaign of 1920. Decorated comdr. Legion d'Honneur (France); Officer's Cross, Polonia Restituta; Knights' Cross in Order of St. Olav (Norway); recipient Pulitzer Prize for Washington Corrs., 1935, 38, nat. correspondence 1951 (declined); Presdl. Medal of Freedom, 1970; Freedom Found. at Valley Forge award, 1971. Democrat. Clubs: Metropolitan, Gridiron, 1925 F St. (Washington). Author: The Editorials of Henry Watterson, 1923; In The Nation, 1966; Memoirs: Sixty Years On The Firing Line, 1968; The Consent of the Governed and Other Deceits, 1971. Home: Washington, D.C. Died Apr. 12, 1974.

KROHA, JIRI, architect, painter, sculptor; b. Prague, Czechoslovakia, June 5, 1893; ed. Czech Tech. U., Prague, 1911-16; Dr.h.c., Tech. U. Brno, 1970. Prof., Tech. U. Brno, 1926-52, rector, 1948-50; imprisoned in concentration camps in Dachau and Buchenwald, 1939-40; own atelier, 1948-58; prof. Czech Tech. U., Prague, 1953-58; expert adviser Ministry Edn. and Culture/J. Kroha's Cabinet Architecture, Man and his environment, 1958-74. Recipient Order of 25th Feb. 1948 award, 1949, Meml. medal 2d Nat. Resistance Movement, 1948, Nat. Artist award, 1948, Order of Labour award, 1957, Order of Republic award, 1963, Order of Victorious Feb. award, 1973. Mem. Union Czechoslovak Architects, Congress Internat. pour la Réalisation de l'Architecture Contemporaine. Author: Sociologic Fragment of Habitation, Economic Fragment of Habitation, (with K. Teige) Architecture of Vanguard, (with J. Hruza) Soviet Architecture Vanguard. Important works include Kralupy Bridge, Tech. sch. and Ins. inst. Mladá Boleslav, pavillions of U. Olomouc. Home: Brno, Czechoslovakia., Died June 7, 1974.

KROLL, LEON, artist; b. N.Y.C., Dec. 6, 1884; s. Marcus Nathaniel and Henrietta (Moss) K.; student Art Student's League, Nat. Acad. Design, N.Y.C.; with Jean Paul Laurens, Paris, France; m. Genevieve Domec, Oct. 18, 1923; 1 dau., Marie-Claude. Portrait, landscape, genre, still-life and mural artist; represented in permanent collections Met. Mus. Art, Detroit Mus., Los Angeles Mus., Art Inst. Chgo., Whitney Mus. Am. Art, Mus. Modern Art, and numerous other pub. and pvt. collections. Recipient over twenty four nat. and internat. awards including First Prize, Carnegie Internat., Pitts., 1936, several gold medals, 5 thousand dollar prizes, Benjamin Altman award landscape painting, 1965. Pres. U.S. Commn., Internat. Assn. Plastic Arts, 1954-74. Executed murals in New Justice Bldg., Washington, and other major works in govt. bldgs. and monuments. A.N.A., 1920, N.A., 1927. Mem. several profl. assns., including, Nat. Inst. Arts and Letters, Am. Acad. Arts and Letters (dir. and chmn., art com.), Chevalier Legion of Honor (France). Clubs: Nat. Arts (life) (N.Y.C.); Boston Art (hon.); Friends of Art (hon.) (Balt.). Died Oct. 25, 1974; interred Locust Grove Cemetery, Rockport, Mass.

KRON, JOSEPH, food co. exec.; b. 1912; married. With Tom Borman interests, 1944; treas. Lucky Stores, Inc., 1948-56; with subsidiaries Borman's Inc., 1953-56, with parent co., from 1956, v.p., exec. v.p., mgr. store operations, also chmn. bd.; pres. subsidiary Yankee Distbrs., Inc. Deceased.

KROOSS, HERMAN EDWARD, educator; b. N.Y.C., July 12, 1912; s. Albert William Frederick and Wilhelmina (Hinck) K.; Ph.B., Muhlenberg Coll., 1934, LL.D., 1970; M.A., U. Pa., 1935; Ph.D., N.Y.U., 1947; M. Helen Bausher, June 16, 1939. Ednl. supr. Penn Mut. Life Ins. Co., N.Y.C., 1935—40; Charles B. Knight Agy., Union Central Life, N.Y.C., 1940-41; mem. faculty N.Y.U., N.Y.C., 1947—75, prof. econs., 1953—75, chmn. dept. 1959—65. Trustee MONY Mortgage Investors. Named Man of Year N.Y.U. Grad. Sch. Bus., 1966. Mem. Econ. History Assn. (sec.—treas., 1948—75), Bus. History Conf. (pres., 1973), Phi Beta Kappa, Beta Gamma Sigma Author: American Economic Development, 1955, 66, 73; Financial History of the United States, 1953, 63; Executive Opinion, 1970; American Business History, 1972. Editor: Documentary: History of Banking and Currency, 1968. Home: Allentown, Pa. Died Mar. 21, 1975; interred Cedar Hill Meml. Park, Allentown, Pa.

KRUESI, WALTER EDISON, humanitarian; b. Menlo Park, N.J., Sept. 3, 1881; s. John and Emily (Zwinger) K.; Union Coll., Schenectady, N.Y., 1898-99, 1900-02; took tech. training in shops of Gen. Elec. Co., Schenectady, 1899-1900, and became journeyman machinist, iron moulder and electrician; B.S., U. of Pa., 1903; instr. and grad. student economics, same 1903-05; m. Charlotte Kimball, Oct. 9, 1909. Asst. gen. sec. New York Charity Orgn. Soc., 1905-07; local sec., 1907, exec. sec., 1908, 1909, N.Y. State Conf. Chartities and Correction; sec. Boston Assn. for Relief and Control of Tuberculosis, 1907-09, establishing winter day camp sanatorium and out door sch., municipalizing both; organizer Milk and Baby Hygiene Assn., Boston, 1909, and dir. until Oct., 1911; del. State of Mass, to 3d Internat. Congress on Infant Mortality, Berlin, 1911, and Internat. Hygiene Expn., Dresden, 1911; commr. of charities, Schenectady, 1912-14; asst. to mayor's com. on unemployment (New York), 1915; supt. Pub. Employment Bureaus of N.Y. City, 1916-17; commd. capt. O.R.C., 1916; on active duty on staff of Q.M. Gen. U.S.A., from 1917; Advisory mem. U.S. Employees Compensation Commn. for War Dept., from 1917; rep. of War Dept. Nat. Com. on Prisons and Prison Labor; mem. War Dept. Bd. of Control for Labor Standards in army clothing. Socialist. Unitarian. Mem. Nat. Conf. City Planning, Sigma Phi, etc. Writer on topics pertaining to pub. health, unemployment and municipal affairs. Home: New York City, N.Y.†

KRUGER, MINNA NICOLA KRUGER, physician; b. Jelgava, Latvia; d. Nicholas N. and Taube (Fridlenders) Kruger; M.D., U. Kharkov, Russia, 1915. Came to U.S., 1938, naturalized 1944. Instnl. govt. physician, Russia, Latvia, med. adminstr. Kaunatas Hosp., Latvia, 1923-36; intern. St. James Hosp., Newark, 1943-44; geriatric instnl. practice medicine, Bronx, N.Y., 1945-75; mem. staffs Beth Abraham Hosp. Chronic Diseases, 1945-58, Hebrew Home and Hosp., Bronz, N.Y., 1958-75. Recipient Citation in recognition of 50 years devotion to service of public and practice of medicine, The Med. Soc. State N.Y., 1965. Fellow Royal Soc. Promotion Health; mem. A.M.A., N.Y. State, Bronx County med. socs. Home: Long Beach, N.Y., Died May 16, 1975.

KRUGER, OTTO, actor, b. Toledo, Sept. 6, 1885; ed. Mich. U., Columbia U.; m. Sue M. MacManamy; one dau., Ottilie. Engaged as dramatic actor on stage in Royal Family, Private Lives, Counsellor-at-law, others; screen debut in The Intruder, others include Beauty for Sale, Prizefighter and the Lady, Gallant Lady, Treasure Island, Chained, Men in White, Springtime for Henry, They Won't Forget, 711 Ocean Drive, Payment on Demand, High Noon, Magnificent Obsession, Black Widow, Last Command, many other plays, TV, motion pictures. Vice pres. Motion Picture Relief Fund. Mason. Club: The Lambs (N.Y.C.). Home: Los Angeles, Cal. Died Sept. 6, 1974; interred Forest Lawn Memorial Park, Hollywood Hills, Cal.

KRULISH, EMIL, physician; b. N.Y.C., Mar. 9, 1878; s. William J. and Antonette (Cervin) K.; B.S., Southern Minn. Normal Coll., Austin, Minn., 1901; M.D., George Washington U., 1905; m. Sarah B. Sydnor Aug. 30, 1915 (d. Oct. 8, 1933); children—Emily May, Marjorie Belle, Robert Charles; m. 2d, Ruth Fletcher, July 6, 1942. Served as physician in Indian Service, 1905-07; in United States Public Health Service from 1907; duty at Ellis Island Immigration Station, New York, 1907-11; in charge of immigration activities at Galveston, Texas, 1911; detailed to Bureau of Education, with headquarters in Juneau, Alaska, in charge of medical and sanitary relief of Indians and Eskimo, 1912-15; in connection with this detail visited all points in Alaska, including Point Barrow; also acted in an advisory capacity to the Governor of Alaska in matters pertaining to pub. health and at his request drafted and had passed by the Territorial legislature the first complete sanitary code for that Territory; at Seattle, Wash., in connection with quarantine, immigration, medical relief and suppressive measures against plague, 1915-18; in charge of U.S. Marine Hospital No. 17, Port Townsend, Wash., 1918-23; exec. officer of Marine Hosp. No. 43, Ellis Island, New York (600 beds), 1923-26; detailed to Bureau of Indian Affairs, Dept. of Interior, with headquarters in Minneapolis, as med. dir. of Dist. No. 1, 1926-30; supervised the medical, dental, health and sanitary activities among Indian population of 64,000; commd. by Governor of Minnesota member on Advisory Council of Indian Affairs; detailed to Am. Consulate in Prague, Czechoslovakia, in connection with the medical inspection of aliens applying for visas, 1930-31, Am. Consulate in Copenhagen, Denmark, 1931-32; in charge of Public Health Service activities, Portland, Ore., 1932-34, Los Angeles, Calif., 1934-38; detailed to Bureau of Indian Affairs as medical officer in charge of the new million-dollar Indian Hosp. at Talihina, Okla. (largest instn. in the Indian Service), 1938; retired from service, Apr. 1, 1942. Mem. A.M.A., Assn. Mil. Surgeons of U.S. Retired Officers Assn. Presbyterian. Home: Altaden, Calif.†

KRUPA, GENE, musician; b. Chgo., Jan. 15, 1909; s. Bartley and Ann (Oslowska) K.; student St. Joseph's Coll. (Ind.), 1926-27; m. Ethel Fawcett (dec.); m. 2d, Patricia Bowler, Apr. 22, 1959 (div. 1968). Profl. drummer, 1927; drummer Chgo. night clubs, later with Joe Kayser's band, dance orchs. of Red Nichols, Russ Columbo, Mal Hallett, Benny Goodman; formed dance orch., Gene Krupa and his orch., 1938-51; jazz player Philharmonic concert tours, recordings, TV; club appearances jazz trio and quartet, 1952-73. Mem. Am. Fedn. Musicians. Home: Yonkers, N.Y. Died Oct. 16, 1973.

KRUSEN, FRANK HAMMOND, physician; b. Phila., June 26, 1898; s. Wilmer and Elizabeth Pearson (Gilbert) K.; grad. Wm. Penn Charter Prep. Sch., 1915; premed. student Jefferson Med. Coll. 1915-17, M.D., 1921, LL.D., (hon.) 1966; M.D. (hon.), Justus Liebig U., Giessen, Germany, 1962; m. Margaret Louise Borland, May 28, 1921; children—Joanne Elizabeth (Mrs. Robert M. Hart), Janice Alison. Intern, Jefferson Hosp., Phila., 1921-24, asst. surgeon, 1925-26; asst. surgeon Phila. Gen. Hosp., 1925-28; asso. in medicine and dir. dept. phys. medicine Temple U., 1929-35; asso. dean Temple Med. Sch., 1925-35; head, sect. on phys. medicine and rehab. Mayo Clinic, 1935-58, sr. cons., 1958-63; v.p. staff Mayo Clinic, 1957-58; asso. prof. phys. medicine and rehab. Mayo Found. U. Minn., 1935-41A, prof., 1941-63, prof., emeritus, 1963-73; pres. Sister Elizabeth Kenny Found., Inc.; dir. Kenny Rehab. Inst., 1960-63, prof., coordinator phys. medicine and rehab. Temple U. Sch. Medicine and Hosp., Phila., 1963-68, prof. emeritus, 1968-73, dir. rehab. planning, 1965-68, project dir. research and tng. center phys. medicine and rehab., 1964-68; sr. cons. phys. medicine and rehab. Moss Rehab. Hosp., 1964-68; project dir. research and tng. center phys. medicine and rehab., prof. phys. medicine and rehab. Tufts U. Sch. Medicine, 1968-70; chief cons. phys. medicine Army surgeon gen., 1946-49, 51-68, VA, 1946-49. Served with S.A.T.C., World War I. Dir., mem. adminstrv. bd., chmn. sci. adv. com. of Baruch Com. on Phys. Medicine, 1944-51, chmn. Baruch Com. on War and Post War Phys. Rehab., 1944-51; counselor Nat. Soc. for Crippled Children, 1947-59; chmn. Am. Bd. Phys. Medicine and Rehab., 1947-49; pres. Minn. Bd. Health, 1955-63; pres. Internat. Congress Phys. Medicine, 1960; mem. com. on rehab. Am. Heart Assn., 1957-58; chmn. Am. Rehab. Found.; chmn. Gov's. Com. Vocational Rehab., 1955-60; co-chmn. ad hoc com. Pres.'s Com. on Employment of Handicapped, 1966; mem. exec. com., bd. dirs. Goodwill Industries, Inc., 1967-73, v.p. bd. dirs., 1968-69. Trustee, Nat. Inst. on Rehab. and Health Services; bd. dirs. Elizabeth Kenny Inst. Recipient 1944 Ann. Gold Key award Am. Congress of Phys. Medicine and Rehab.; Physicians Award for services to handicapped Pres. U.S., 1953; award of Merit, State Pa., 1954; Modern Medicine Distinguished Service award, 1956; Distinguished Service award A.M.A., 1958; citation Minn. Gov., 1958; Gold medal award Conn. Soc. Phys. Medicine, 1960; Goodwill Industries award, 1961; Dignity of Man award Kessler Inst. Rehab., 1966; George G. Deaver award Inst. for Crippled and Disabled, N.Y.C., 1968; Dwight Eisenhower award, 1969; Speedy award Paralyzed Vets. Am., 1970; citation Nat. Industries for Blind, 1970. Fellow A.C.P., Royal Soc. Medicine (hon.); asso. fellow Am. Acad. Phys. Edn.; mem. Am. Acad. Phys. Medicine and Rehab. (past pres.), Am. Congress of Phys. Medicine and Rehab. (past pres.; treas. 1950-70), Soc. Phys. Medicine (past pres.), A.A.A.S., A.M.A. (chmn. council on med. physics, chmn. com. on rehab., del. from sect. on phys. medicine), World Med. Assn., Am. Assn. U. Profs., Internat. Fedn. Phys. Medicine (founder, 1st pres. 1952), Am. Med. Writers Assn., Minn. Med. Assn., Minn. Physiat. Soc (hon.), Brit. Assn. Phys. Medicine (hon.), Danish Soc. Phys. Medicine (hon.), Am. Rheumatism Assn., Liga Argentina contra el Rhumatisme (hon.), All-India Occupational Therapists Assn. (hon.), Brazilian Soc. Phys. Medicine (hon.), Pa. Soc. of S.R., Sigma Xi (pres. Mayo Found. chpt. 1958-59), Blue Key, Phi Alpha Sigma, Theta Nu Epsilon. Republican. Episcopalian. Mason. Club: University (Rochester, Minn.). Author: Light Therapy, 1933; Physical Therapy in Arthritis, 1937; Physical Medicine, 1941; Concepts in Rehabilitation of the Handicapped, 1964. Editor: Yearbook of Physical Medicine and Rehabilitation, 1949-51; Physical Medicine and Rehabilitation for the Clinican, 1951; Handbook of Physical Medicine and Rehabilitation, 1965; Iberia Jour. Editorial bd. Internat. Rev. of Phys. Medicine, Geriatrics, Geriatric Rev., Exerpta Medica. Contbr. articles to med. jours. Home: Orleans, Mass. Died Sept. 16, 1973.

KRUSEN, URSULA LEDEN, physician, educator; b. Breslau, Germany, Mar. 13, 1921; d. Peter Paul and Elizabeth (Freter) Leden; came to U.S., 1938, naturalized, 1944; B.A., Coll. New Rochelle, 1941; M.D., Loyola U., Chgo., 1944; M.S. in Phys. Medicine, U. Minn., 1949; m. Edward M. Krusen, Nov. 13, 1948; children—Richard M., Nancy E. Intern Henrotin Hosp., Chgo., 1944-45; fellow in phys. medicine Mayo Clinic, Rochester, Minn., 1946-48, first asst. in phys. medicine, 1948-50; asso. prof. phys. medicine and rehab. Southwestern Med. Sch., 1960-71, prof., 1971-73, chmn. dept. phys. medicine and rehab., 1959-66; chief dept. phys. medicine and rehab. Parkland Meml. Hosp., Dallas, 1959-66, cons. phys. medicine, rehab. Baylor U. Med. Center, 1951-73. Mem. Am. Acad Phys. Medicine and Rehab., Am. Congress Phys. Medicine and Rehab., A.M.A., So., Tex. med. assns., Tex. Soc. Phys. Medicine and Rehab., Sigma Xi. Author profl. publs. Home: Dallas, Tex. Died July 11, 1973.

KUBERT, JOSEPH MANDEL, educator; b. Chgo., June 14, 1917; s. Nathan and Rose (Kohn) K.; B.S., Ill. Inst. Tech., 1937, M.S., 1940; m. Judith Korngold, July 7, 1951; children—David Emanuel, Anne Susan, Charles Nathan. Head, survey dept. Pullman Standard Car Mfg. Co., Chgo., 1937-40; with Booz, Allen & Hamilton, Inc., Chgo., 1940-70, partner, 1948-61, v.p., 1962-70; vis. prof. bus. policy Grad. Sch. Bus., U. Chgo., 1970-74; dir. Unarco Industries, Inc., Mattel, Inc. Bd. dirs. Scholarship and Guidance Assn. Registered profl. engr., Ill. Mem. Inst. Mgmt. Consultants (charter), Chgo. Assn. Commerce and Industry (mgmt. devel. adv. council), Newcomen Soc. Clubs: Economic, Standard (Chgo.); Briawood Country (Deerfield, Ill.). Home: Glencoe, Ill. Died Sept. 1, 1974.

KUBIE, LAWRENCE S(CHLESINGER), neurologist, psychiatrist, psychoanalyst; b. New York, N.Y., Mar. 17, 1896; s. Samuel and Leah (Schlesinger) K.; A.B., Harvard, 1916: student Columbia, 1916-17; M.D., Johns Hopkins University, 1921; D.Sc. (hon.), University of Chicago, 1967; m. Susan Hoch, July 3, 1921 (divorced 1935); children—Robert Hoch, Ann Hoch, Thomas (dec.); m. 2d, Eleanor Gottheil Benjamin, Aug. 25, 1939 (div.); 1 stepson, John B. (dec.). Interne, asst. resident Henry Phipps Psychiat. Clinic, Johns Hopkins Hosp., 1921-24; instr. in physiology, Johns Hopkins Med. Sch., 1924-26; traveling fellow, Rockefeller Foundation, Apr.-Nov., 1926; Rockefeller Inst. for Med. Research, New York, 1926-28; Nat. Research Council fellowship in neurology, London, Eng., 1928-29; study in psychoanalysis, London, 1928-30; asso. in neurology, Coll. of Physicians and Surgeons, Columbia, 1930-47; adjunct attending neurologist, Neurol. Inst. of New York, 1930-39; asso. in psychiatry, Mt. Sinai Hospital, New York, 1939-43; former clin. prof. psychiatry Sch. Medicine, Yale. subcom. of psychiatry, Nat. Research Council, 1939-51; dir. training Sheppard and Enoch Pratt Hospital, Towson, Md., 1959-64, cons. in research and tng., 1964-73; vis. prof. psychiatry Jefferson Med. Coll., Phila.; clinical professor psychiatry Univ. Md. Med. Sch., 1961-73. Mem. faculty New York Psychoanalytic Inst.; lecturer psychiatry Johns Hopkins Univ. Med. Sch.; consultant to Air Surgeon's Office; sci. cons. E.T.O., 1945. Member board of trustees of George Junior Republic. Mem. A.M.A., Am. Soc. Exptl. Pathology, A.A.A.S., Am. Psychiat. Assn., Am. Neurol. Assn., Am. Psychoanalytic Assn. (sec. 1938-40), American Academy Arts and Sciences, New York County Med. Soc., N.Y. Psychoanalytic Society (president 1939), N.Y. Neurol. Soc., N.Y. Acad. Medicine, N.Y. Soc. Clin. Psychiatry, Assn. for Research in Nervous and Mental Disease, Am. Psychosomatic Soc. (pres. 1954-55), Sigma Xi, Phi Beta Kappa (hon.), Alpha Omega Alpha (hon.). Clubs: Century Association (New York City, New York); Harvard (N.Y.); Pithotomy (Johns Hopkins Med. Sch.). Author: Practical Aspects of Psychoanalysis, 1936; Practical and Theoretical Aspects of Psychoanalysis, 1950; Neurotic Distortion of Creative Process, 1958. Editor in chief: Jour. Nervous and Mental Disorders. Contbr. numerous articles technical and profl. jours. Died Oct. 26, 1973.

KUEBLER, CLARK GEORGE, provost; b. Chicago, Ill., Mar. 24, 1908; s. George Michael and Pearl Marie (Clark) K.; A.B., Northwestern U., 1930; Princeton, 1932-33; Munich U., summers, 1935-36; Ph.D., University of Chicago, 1940; LL.D. (honorary), Lawrence College, 1943, Nashotah Seminary, 1944; Olivet College, 1950; L.H.D. Yankton College, D.C.L., Atlanta Law Sch., 1948; unmarried. Instructor in classics Northwestern University, 1930-40, assistant professor, 1940-43; pres. Ripon College, 1943-54; provost Santa Barbara College, U. Cal., 1954-74. Mem. board dirs. Edn. for Freedom 1943-47; dir. Investors Syndicate, 1947-49; member Nat. Commn. on Social Reconstruction since 1940; member National Commission on Strategy and Policy (Episcopal Church), 1940-43; member bd. trustees, Northwestern Mil. and Naval Acad., 1945-53, Nashotah (Wis.) Seminary, 1948-74; trustee Pestalozzi Foundation of America 1949; member National Council of Episcopal Church, 1946. Mem. Association American Colleges (mem. bd. dirs.), Am. Philol. Assn., Classical Assn. of Middle West and South, Am. Assn. Univ. Profs., Sigma Chi, Phi Beta Kappa. Episcopalian. Club: University (Milw. and Chgo.). Home: Santa Barbara, Cal. Died Mar. 28, 1974.

KUEHNER, QUINCY ADAMS, prof. edn.; b. Little Gap, Pa., June 22, 1879; s. Augustus and Christiana (Eckhart) K.; grad. Fairview Acad., Brodheadsville, Pa., 1898; A.B., Muhlenberg Coll., Allentown, Pa., 1902, A.M., 1905; univ. scholar and Harrison fellow, Univ. of Pennsylvania, 1902-04, Ph.D., 1912; LL.D., Lenoir-Rhyne College, 1937; m. Katherine E. Follweiler, of Tamaqua, Pa., Aug. 18, 1915. Teacher, high schs., Pa., 1905-20; prof. edn. and dean of summer sch., Lenoir-Rhyne Coll., Hickory, N.C., 1920-22; prof. philosophy of edn., Temple University, from 1922. High sch. insp. Burke and Catawba counties, N.C., 1920-22. Mem. A.A.A.S., Am. Acad. Polit. and Social Science, American Assn. of Univ. Profs., Religious Edn. Assn., Nat. Education Assn., Pennsylvania State Educational Assn., Phi Delta Kappa, Pi Gamma Mu; charter asso. Federal Council Chs. of Christ in America. Democrat. Lutheran. Clubs: Social Science, Acacia, Religious Book Club, Cedar Brook Country. Wrote: The Evolution of the Modern Concept of School Discipline, 1913; A Philosophy of Education, 1935. Lecturer on ednl. and religious subjects. Home: Glenside, Pa.†

KUHL, ERNEST PETER, educator; b. Milan, O., Oct. 10, 1881; s. Henry P. and Elizabeth (Weichel) K.; A.B., Ind. U., 1907; A.m., Harvard, 1908, Ph.D., 1913; m. Lucy Van Dyke Leech, Sept. 9, 1909; children—Robert Wolfe, Lucy Elizabeth. Instr. English and rhetoric, U. of Mich., 1908-12, Dartmouth Coll., 1914-16, U. of Minn., 1916-18; prof. of English at Goucher Coll., 1918-26; extension dept. Johns Hopkins U., 1919-26; prof. of English, U. of Iowa, from 1926. Taught in Radcliffe Coll., 1914-15, summer schs., Dartmouth Coll., 1915, U. of Minn., 1917, 18, U. of Me., 1925, U. of Wash., 1929, Stanford University, 1940. Mem. Modern Lang. Assn. America, Coll. Cong. on English in Middle Atlantic States and Md. (v. chmn. 1919-20, chmn. 1920-21, sec.-treas. 1923-26). Elected pres. Poe Soc. of Baltimore, 1926. Conglist. Clubs: Tudor and Stuart (Johns Hopkins). Author: The Authorship of Shakespeare's The Taming of the Shrew, 1926. Discovered valuable Lanier letters in 1924. Has lectured on same at various colls. and univs. Contbr. to philol. jours. on Chaucer, Shakespeare and allied subjects. Home: Iowa City, Ia.†

KUHLMAN, KATHRYN, minister; b. Concordia, Mo., 1910; d. Joe and Emma (Walkenhorst) Kuhlman. Ordained to ministry Evang. Ch. Alliance, now mem. Am. Baptist Conv.; Pentecostal faith-healing, preaching tours throughout U.S.; condr. daily radio programs and weekly TV programs; pres. Kathryn Kuhlman Found. Author: I Believe in Miracles; God Can Do It Again; Captain LeVrier Believes in Miracles, 1973; Nothing is Impossible with God, 1974. Record album I Believe in Miracles. Address: Pittsburgh, Pa., Died Feb. 20, 1976.

KUIPER, GERARD PETER, astronomer; b. Harencarspel, The Netherlands, Dec. 7, 1905; s. Gerard and Anna (de Vries) K.; B.Sc., U. of Leyden, The Netherlands, 1927, Ph.D., 1933; m. Sarah Parker Fuller, June 20, 1936; children—Paul, Lucy. Came to U.S., 1933, naturalized, 1937. Research asst. astronomy, U. of Leyden, 1928-33; mem. Dutch Eclipse Expdn. to Sumatra, 1929; research fellow Lick Observatory, U. of Calif., 1933-35, research asso., 1935, lectr. Harvard, 1935-36; asst. prof. astronomy, U. of Chicago, 1936-37, asso. prof., 1937-43, prof. 1943-60, located at McDonald Observatory, Fort Davis, Tex., 1939-60, dir. of Yerkes and McDonald Obs., 1947-49, 57-60; head Lunar and Planetary Lab., U. Ariz., 1960-73. Research asso. Radio Research Lab., Harvard, 1943-45; cons., operational analysis sect., Eighth Air Force, Eng., 1944; mem. Alsos mission, 1945; Dryden research lectr. Am. Inst. Aero. and Astronautics, 1969; prin. investigator Ranger Program; mem. panel Mariner Venus-Mercury Mission. Decorated Comdr. Order Orange Nassau (Netherlands); recipient Janssen Medal, Rittenhouse medal French Astron. Soc. Mem. Nat. Acad. Scis., Am. Acad. Arts and Scis., Internat. Astron. Union. Am. Astron. Soc., Astron. Soc. Pacific, Royal Astron. Soc. London (asso.), Netherlands Soc. Scis. (fgn mem.), Royal Netherlands Acad. Scis (fgn. mem.). Author articles in Astrophys. Jour.; also 4 atlases. Editor: (book) The Atmospheres of the Earth and Planets, 1949, 52; The Solar System, 4 vols., 1953-61; Stars and Stellar Systems, 9 vols., from 1960. Home: Tuscon Ariz. Died Dec. 24, 1973.

KUJOTH, JEAN SPEALMAN, (Mrs. Richard K. Kujoth), author; b. Champaign, Ill., Apr. 20, 1935; d. Max Lang and Dorothy Ruth (Flickinger) Spealman; B.A., U. Cal. at Berkeley, 1957; M.S.W., U. Mich., 1959; M.A. in L.S., U. Wis., 1966; m. Richard K. Kujoth, Feb. 22, 1964 (div. 1973). Mem. Phi Beta

Kappa. Author: Readings in Nonbook Librarianship, 1968; Subject Guide to Periodical Indexes and Review Indexes, 1969; Libraries, Readers and Book Selection, 1969; Reading Interests of Children and Young Adults, 1970; The Teacher and School Discipline, 1970; Book Publishing: Inside Views, 1971; The Recreation Program Guide, 1972; Best Selling Children's Books, 1973; the Boys' and Girls' Book of Clubs and Organizations, 1975; Sugject Guide to Humor, 1976. Home: Milwaukee, Wis., Died Sept. 27, 1975.

KULDELL, RUDOLPH CHARLES, b. Pittsburgh, Pa., Feb. 20, 1889; s. Rev. Alexander R. and Louise (Emmord) K.; grad. U.S. Mil. Acad., 1912, Army Engr. Sch., 1915; m. Ethelyn Cramer, Aug. 20, 1912; children— Ethelyn May, Robert Cramer, Elizabeth Ann. Commd. 2d lt. Corps of Engrs., U.S. Army, 1912; advanced through grades to lt. col., 1918; dept. engr., Southern Dept., 1916-17; asst. to chief of engrs., 1918; assigned to Gen. Staff; asst. to asst. sec. of war, specializing in demobilization, 1919; resigned Apr. 20, 1920; asst. to pres. Hughes Tool Co., Houston, Tex., 1920-21, prodn. mgr., 1921-24, gen. mgr., 1924-25, v.p., 1925-31, pres., 1931-39; now pres. Mount Rose Land Corp. Volunteered for duty in U.S. Army, Dec. 1941; recommissioned lt. col., Corps of Engrs., Feb. 1942, asst. to div. engr. Southwest Div.; promoted col., Aug. 1942; assigned to duty in office Chief of Engrs., Washington, D.C., Mar. 1943, as chief of repairs and utilities branch; chief mil. construction div. and War Dept. power procurement officer, Dec. 1943-June 1944. Originated grid system progressive military maps of U.S. Asst. chief of engrs. for Military Supply; promoted to brig. gen., Army, U.S., Dec. 7, 1944; Comdg. gen. 406th Engr. Special Brigade since 1947, retired as brigadier general-honorary, 1949. Awarded Distinguished Service Medal, Oct. 1945. Mem. nat. panel of arbitrators; past dir. N.A.M., Am. Soc. Mil. Engrs. (dir.), So. States Indus. Council. Mem. Am. Soc. Mech. Engrs., Am. Management Assn., Houston Chamber Commerce (ex-pres.; ex-treas.). Republican. Methodist. Clubs: Engineers, Houston Country. Bayou, Eagle Lake Rod and Gun. Home: Houston Tex. Died Aug. 30, 1973.

KULJIAN, HARRY A., cons. engr.; b. Armenia, Dec. 21, 1893; s. Asdour and Hosanna (Hakolan) K.; brought to U.S., 1911, naturalized, 1923; S.B., Mass. Inst. Tech., 1919; Dr. Engring. (hon.), Drexel Inst. Tech., 1953; m. Alice Levonian, Sept. 22, 1922; children—Arthur, Florence (Mrs. Hrair Levonian), Edward. Turbine design dept. Westinghouse Co., East Pittsburgh, Pa., 1920; design engr. Stone & Webster, Boston, 1920-24; asst. to chief engr. Am. Viscose Corp., 1924-30; established H.A. Kuljian & Co., cons. engrs., Phila., 1931; organizer, pres., chmn. Kiljian Corp., engrs. and constructors, 1941-65, also chmn. exec. com.; designer, constructor 100 power plants U.S. and fgn. countries, numerous chem., textile, petroleum and other indsl. plants, also projects U.S. govt. Awarded Army and Navy E for outstanding engring. service to Chem. Warfare Dept.; Meritorious award (Navy); cited Engineer of the Year, Pa. Soc. Profl. Engrs., 1955; recipient Kabakjian Sci. Award, 1955. Fellow Am. Soc. M.E., Am. Soc. Elec. Engrs., Franklin Inst.; mem. Tech. Assn. Pulp and Paper Industry. Author: Man and the World of Science, 1964; Nuclear Power Plant Design, 1968. Holds over 30 patents on new machine for continuous rayon spinning and processing, boiler feed level recorder and controller, density recorder and indicator; designer numerous time-saving devices and equipment for rayon, chem. textile plants and pub. utilities. Home: Merion, Pa. Died Nov. 2, 1974.

KULLMAN, HAROLD JOHN FREDERICK, physician; b. Detroit, Dec. 24, 1901; s. Michael G. and Julia (Hansz) K.; M.D., Wayne State U., Detroit, 1927; m. Edna Mary Warner, July 13, 1935. Intern, Detroit Receiving Hosp., 1926—27; fellow in internal medicine Mayo Found., Rochester, Minn., 1928—32; practice medicine specializing in internal medicine, Detroit, 1932—42; chief medicine VA Hosp., Allen Park, Mich., 1946—54; emeritus affiliate Detroit Gen. Hosp.; emeritus prof. clin. medicine Wayne State U. Served to capt. M.C., USNR, 1942—46. Diplomate Am. Bd. Internal Medicine. Fellow A.C.P.; mem. Am. Soc. Gastrointestinal Endoscopy, A.M.A., Detroit Acad. Medicine (sec.—treas. 1953-54), Mich., Wayne County med. socs., Detroit Med. Club, Alpha Omega Alpha. Home: Dearborn, Mich. Died July 20, 1972; buried Forest Lawn Cemetery, Detroit, Mich.

KUNSMILLER, ADOLPH, banker. Chmn. Bd. Am. Nat. Bank Denver. Home: Denver, Colo. Deceased.

KUNTZ, WERNER HINRICH, clergyman; b. Lewiston, Minn., Apr. 23, 1898; s. Arnold Hilarius and Minna (Koenig) K.; student Concordia Coll., Concordia Sem.; M.A. in Social Adminstrn., Wayne State U., 1953; Litt.D. (hon.), Concordia Coll., 1968; m. Litana Messerll, Apr. 14, 1926; children—Richard A., Oralyn (Mrs. J.L. Dennison), Joanna, Susan, Judith. Ordained to ministry Lutheran Ch., 1922; pastor St. John's Ch., Grey Eagle, Minn., 1922-25, Grace Ch., Indpls., 1925-37, Baden Meml. Ch., Winfield, Kan., 1937-45; exec. sec. Social Welfare, Mich. Dist., 1945-53; exec. dir. Resettlement for European Refugees, 1951-53, Bd. World Relief for Luth. Ch., Mo. Synod, 1953-70; v.p. Asso. Luth. Charities; mem. nat. com. United Community Services Met. Detroit. Recipient Gold medal Red Cross of Yugoslavia; Christus Vivit, Concordia Sem., 1968. Mem. Am. Assn. for UN, Nat. Conf. on Social Welfare, Internat. Council on Social Welfare, Soc. for Internat. Devel., Luth. Human Relations Assn. Am. Clubs: Circumnavigators, Clipper. Home: Hot Springs, Ark., Died Nov. 28, 1973.

KURLAND, NANCY JAMIE (MRS. HENRY HANS-HEINZ SCHMIDEK), educator; b. Boston, May 3, 1938; d. James R. and Patricia (Bockser) Kurland; A.B., Vassar Coll., 1959; S.M., Simmons Coll., 1961; m. Henry Hans-Heinz Schmidek, June 30, 1966. Head psychiat. social worker South Shore Mental Health Center, Quincy, Mass., 1961-69, cons.; asst. prof. social work, faculty field adviser Simmons Coll. Sch. Social Work, Boston, 1969-72. Mem. Acad. Certified Social Workers. Home: Weston, Mass. Died 1972.

KURTZ, DANIEL WEBSTER, clergyman, educator; b. Hartville, Stark County, O., Oct. 9, 1879; s. Bishop John and Mary (Bollinger) K.; student Ohio Northern U., 1897, Mt. Union Coll., Alliance, O., 1897-98, 1900-03; A.B., Juniata Coll., Huntingdon, Pa., 1905, D.D., 1911; B.D., A.M., Yale Div. Sch., 1908; studied univs. of Leipzig, Berlin, Marburg, and University of Pa.; LL.D., La. Verne (Calif.) Coll., 1931; m. Ethel Wheeler, Sept. 7, 1909; children—Albert Wheeler, Royce Emerson, Bernard Roberson. Teacher Greek, Juniata Coll., 1909-10; licensed ministry Ch. of the Brethren, 1904, pastor 1st Ch., Phila., Pa., 1910-14; ordained bishop, 1914; pres. McPherson (Kan.) Coll., 1914-27; pastor 1st Ch. of Brethren, Long Beach, Calif., 1927-32; pres. Bethany Biblical Sem., Chicago, 1932-37; pastor Ch. of the Brethren, La Verne, Calif., from 1937. Pres. Gen. Edn. Bd. Ch. of Brethren, 1915-28 (mem.); pres. S.S. Assn. of Kan., 1918-19; moderator Gen. Conf. Ch. of Brethren, 1926-27, 1932-33, 1936-37, 1939-40; co-worker in Nat. Preaching Mission, 1936-37. Mem. Am. Acad. Polit. and Social Scis., Kan. Hist. Soc. Republican. Clubs: The Forum, Rotary, Kansas Authors. Author: Fundamental Doctrines of the Faith, 1911; Nineteen Centuries of the Christian Church, 1914; The Human Problem: Symphony of Life; The Message of the Church, 1936; The Gospel of Jesus, 1936. Collaborator: Studies in Doctrine and Devotion, 1919. Widely known as lecturer. Home: La Verne, Cal.†

KUSHNER, DANIEL STEPHEN, hosp. adminstr.; b. Phila., July 24, 1922; s. Louis A. and Anna (Valin) K.; A.B., U. Pa., 1943, M.D., 1946; m. Gail A. Robbins, July 20, 1951; children—Deborah June, Lewis Arthur, Daniel Stephen, David Edward, Sara Lynn. From intern to chief resident medicine Mt. Sinai Hosp., N.Y.C., 1946-47, 49-52; mem. staff Cook County Hosp., Chgo., 1952-65, dir. med. edn., 1961-62, attending physician medicine, 1959-65; mem. faculty Cook County Grad. Sch. Medicine, 1954-62, prof. medicine, asso. dean, 1959-62; mem. Hektoen Inst. Med. Research, Chgo., 1953-65; mem. faculty Northwestern U. Med. Sch., 1953-66, asso. prof. medicine, 1962, prof., 1965-66; prof. medicine, dean Chgo. Med. Sch., 1962-65; prof. medicine U. Miami Sch. Medicine, 1966; attending physician VA Hosp., Chgo., 1955-62; cons. medicine Oak Forest (Ill.) Hosp., 1955-65; dir. med. services Mt. Sinai Hosp. of Greater Miami, Miami Beach, Fla., 1966-74. Rep., Council med. edn., residency rev. com. on internal medicine A.M.A., 1960-67, chmn., 1967; mem. med. adv. bd. Kidney Disease Found. Ill., 1962-74. Served with AUS, 1947-49. Diplomate Am. Bd. Internal Medicine. Fellow N.Y. Acad. Medicine, A.C.P.; mem. N.Y. Acad. Scis., A.M.A., Am. Thoracic Soc., Am. Fedn. Clin. Research, Central Soc. Clin. Research, A.A.A.S., Am., Ill., Chgo. socs. internal medicine, Am., Chgo. heart assns., Assn. Study Liver Disease, Sigma Xi, Alpha Omega Alpha. Contbr. papers, revs., chpts. in books Editor: (with Dr. Hans Popper) Clinical Pathologic Conferences of Cook County Hospital, vol. 1, 1954. Home: Miami Beach, Fla. Died Jan. 6, 1974.

KYNETT, HAROLD HAVELOCK, advt. agt.; b. Phila., Sept. 13, 1889; s. Harry Havelock and Emeline Goodsell (Westcott) K.; B.S., U. Pa., 1912; m. Edna Isabel Gallager, Jan. 21, 1915; 1 dau., Mary Elizabeth; m. 2d, Starr Camp Lawrence, July 14, 1954; m. 3d, Doris Maria Grey, Jan. 19, 1966. Reporter Phila. Press, Phila, North American, 1908-13; copy writer, N.W. Ayer & Son., advt., 1913-14, Richard A. Foley, 1914-18; exec. Dippy & Aitkin, advt., 1918-20; sr. partner Aitkin-Kynett Co., advt., 1920-73, also chmn. bd.; lectr. marketing Wharton Sch., U. Pa., 1915-50; formerly 1st v.p., dir. Audit Bur. Circulations, later pres. and chmn.; dir. P.R. Mallory & Co., Inc., Indpls. Bd. dirs. Nantucket Boys Club, Nantucket Life Sav. Museum. Neem. Mystic (Conn.) Marine Hist. Assn. (dir.), Nantucket Atheneum (trustee), Phi Gamma Delta. Republican. Methodist. Clubs: N.Y. Yacht, Grolier (N.Y.C.); Merion Crickett, Racquet, Poor Richard, Midday, Union League (Phila.); Corinthian Yacht. Author: Amiable Vice, Illusion, Nostalgia, Harbor Lights, How Odd the Habit, Maine Harbor, Pried into Prejudice, Deskbound, The Folly of Abuse, Without an Idea, What Nonsense, All the Forms are Fugitive, We Crawl Before We Walk, Treasure Trove, For Better or For Worse, Fireside Admiral, The Mavic's Log, The Age of the Income Tax, Adventure Past Sixty, The Past is Prologue, Travels with Trivia, Thank You, Britain, Sunny Intervals, Pilgrim Pathways, The Peace of Retirement, The Face of Change, Spend A Penny, It Pays to Repeat, Four Generations After, Backlook and Outlook, Unforgettable Intimacies, Nantucket Brevities, The Quaker Heritage, The Pervasive Spirit, Holiday Memories, Why Nantucket? Home: Philadelphia, Pa. Died Sept. 20 1973.

LABUNSKI, WIKTOR, musician, educator; b. St. Petersburg, Russia, Apr. 14, 1895; s. Stanislaw and Lydia (Rogowski) L.; student St. Petersburg Imperial Conservatory, University of St. Petersburg, 1912-16, pupil of Felix Blumenfeld, 1912-16, Wassili Safonoff, 1917, (Piano), Joseph Vitols, 1914-16, (composition), Emil Mlynarski (conducting), 1934-35; Mus.D., Curtis Inst., 1935; m. Wanda Mlynarski, July 1, 1920; children—Stanislaw, Stephen B. Came to U.S., 192O, naturalized, 1939. Concert tours of Poland, France, Eng., Scotland, Austria, Rumania, Russia, U.S. and Can.; with Krakow (Poland) Conservatory of Music, 1919-28, Nashville Conservatory of Music, 1928-31; tchr., dir. Memphis Coll. Music, 1934-58; tchr. Conservatory Music of Kansas City, 1937-59, dir. conservatory, 1941-58; prof. music Conservatory Music U. Kansas City, 1959-63, pianist in residence, 1960-74; prof. music, artist in residence Conservatory Music, University Missouri at Kansas City, 1963-74; soloist with Mpls. Symphony, Cleve, Kansas City Philharmonic, St. Louis, Toronto symphonies, Knoxville and Chgo., Grant Park, others. Compositions: Symphony G minor, 1936, Concerto C Major for piano and orchestra, 1937. Concerto for Two Pianos and Orchestra, 1951, piano pieces, songs, transcriptions. Served as lt. Polish Army, War against Russia, 1920. Fellow Internat. Inst. Arts and Letters; mem. Music Tchrs. Nat. Association, Mo. Music Tchrs. Assn., Polish Nat. Alliance, Am. Fedn. Musicians, Alpha Psi chpt. Phi Mu Alpha-Sinfonia (hon.), Pi Kappa Lambda. Club: Kan. City Musical (hon.). Home: Kansas City, Mo. Died 1974.

LACEY, DOUGLAS RAYMOND, educator; b. Easton, Pa., Apr. 29, 1913; s. Raymond Henry and Rosalind (Runyon) L.; A.B., Ill. Coll., Jacksonville, 1935; M.A., Rutgers U., 1937; Ph.D., Columbia, 1959; Rockefeller Found. post war fellow in humanities, Inst. Hist. Research, U. London, 1946-47; m. Mary Millington Moore, Jan. 3, 1946; children—Jack Cobb, Mary (Mrs. Ronald Gates), Raymond, Pamela. Instr. history Rutgers U., 1937-38, Coll. City N.Y., 1938-40, Sarah Lawrence Coll., 1939; mem. faculty U.S. Naval Acad., Annapolis, Md., 1941-42, from 1947, prof. history, from 1955, chmn. dept., from 1970; vis. prof. U. Alta. (Can.), summer 1960. Bd. dirs. Anne Arundel County Citizens Com., 1950-53, Annapolis Citizens Com., 1953-55. Served to lt. comdr. USNR, 1942-46. Folger Library Sr. Research fellow, 1971-72. Mem. Internat. Commn. History of Representative and Parliamentary Instns., Am. Hist. Assn., Conf. Brit. Studies (chmn. nominating com. 1968-70). Author: Dissent and Parliamentary Politics in England 1661-1689, 1969. Home: Chevy Chase Md. Died July 28, 1973; buried St. Anne's Cemetery, Annapolis, Md.

LACEY, ROBERT ALEXANDER, b. in Bolton, Mississippi, Feb. 13, 1878; s. William Robert and Frances (Alexander) L.; ed. pub. schs., Bolton, Miss.; m. Maud Daughdrill, July 12, 1913. Began as clerk in country store, becoming successively bookkeeper, hotel mgr., railway accountant; assisted in construction of Panama Canal, 1906-08; with Interstate Commerce Commn., 1914-45, serving successively as accountant, dist. accountant, chief report writer and head auditor of property changes, dir. of valuation and chmn. tentative valuation com., bureau of valuation, 1943-45; valuation consultant. Awarded bronze medal by President Theodore Roosevelt for Panama Canal service, Mason. Club: Columbia Country (Chevy Chase, Md.). Home: Washington, D.C.†

LACHMAN, HARRY, landscape painter; b. La Salle, Ill., June 29, 1886; s. Benjamin and Augusta (Neustadt) L.; student U. of Mich.; m. Quon Tai. Settled in Paris, 1912; four paintings bought by French Govt. for the Musée du Luxembourg and one for the Petit Palais; represented in Art Inst. Chicago, Delgado Mus. (New Orleans), etc. Connected with Am. Red Cross, World War, with A.E.F. Engr. Corps, chief instr. landscape painting at A.E.F. art training centre, Bellevue, after the Armistice, later with Am. Com. for Devastated France; production mgr. Rex Ingram Productions, Nice, 3 yrs.; now dir. and producer at own studios in Nice. Chevalier Legion of Honor (France). Address: Nice, France. Died Mar. 19, 1975.

LACY, ARTHUR JAY, lawyer; b. Nirvana, Lake County, Mich., Sept. 30, 1876; s. Francis Daniel and Eunice Amelia (Stevens) L.; LL.B., Valparaiso (Ind.) U., 1896, U. of Mich., 1898; hon. LL.D., Milligan College, 1940; m. Beth Garwick, Nov. 1, 1898. Admitted to Mich. bar, 1899, began practice at Clare; mayor of Clare (4 terms), 1903-07; settled in Detroit, 1909; mem. Millis, Griffin and Lacy, 1912-13; judge Domestic Relations Circuit Court of Wayne County, Mich., 1913-14; mem. Anderson, Wilcox, Lacy & Lawson, 1914-47, and Wilcox, Lacy, Lawson, Kirby & Hunt, 1947-52, of counsel, 1952-59; of counsel Lacy, Lawson, Kirkby, Bolton & Hoffman, from 1959; faculty Detroit Coll. Law, 1913-28; an authority on philanthropic trusts, taxation and wills; counsel for taxpayers in Ford Stock

Valuation Income Tax Case; counsel for donors in creating Children's Fund of Mich. and Rackham Fund; counsel in reorganization of Detroit Trust Co. under Mich. Emergency Banking Act, of which, subject was co-author. Dir. Boys' Club (past pres.); adv. bd. Salvation Army, Detroit; pres. Detroit Civil Service Commn. 1917-21; pres. Lawyers Club of Detroit, 1918-20. Dem. candidate for governor of Mich., 1934. Hon. trustee Children's Hosp. of Mich.; trustee National Sanitation Found., Detroit Community Trust, Detroit Hist. Soc. Mem. S.A.R., Am., Mich., Detroit bar assns., Newcomen Soc. N.A., Delta Theta Pi, other civic, and social socs. Republican. Conglist. Mason. Clubs: U. Mich., Detroit Athletic, Detroit Golf (dir., past pres.). Home: Detroit, Mich.†

LADDON, ISAAC MACHLIN, aviation exec.; b. Garfield N.J., Dec. 25, 1894; s. M. A. and Esther (mACHLIN) l.; b.s. IN Civil Engring., McGill U., 1915, D.Sc., 1957; m. Anne MacGregor, July 12, 1920; children—Machlin Bower, Marcella Anne, Robert Leslie. Served as aero. engr. U.S. Army Air Corps, 1917-27; aero. engr. Cons. Vultee Aircraft, San Diego, Calif., 1927-41, exec. v.p., gen. manager and director; designer of boats and bombers; pres., chmn. Langley Corp., San Diego, 1956-58, chairman bd., 1958-76; dir. Servel, Incorporated, General Dynamics Corporation, Rohr Aircraft Corporation, First Nat. Bank, (all San Diego), Menasco Mfg. Co., Los Angeles. Original fellow Institute of Aero Scis.; mem. Soc. Automotive Engrs. Republican. Clubs: San Diego Yacht, San Diego Country, Cuyamaca; La Jolla Country, Kona Kai. Address: San Diego, Cal., Died Jan. 14, 1976.

LAGER, ERIC W., corp. exec.; b. Chgo., 1900; grad. U. Ill., 1921; m. Ruby Lager; 1 son, E. Willard. Chmn., pres. Indiana-Mich. Corp. Home: Palos Park Ill. Died Feb. 4, 1974.

LAGERKVIST, PAR, (FABIAN), author; b. Växjö, Sweden, May 23, 1891; s. Anders Johan and Johanna (Blad) L.; student U. Uppsala, 1911-12; Ph.D. (hon.), U. Gothenburg, 1941; m. Karen Sorensen, 1918 (div.); m. 2d, Elaine Luella Hallberg, 1925. Author of numerous books, poems, plays; first book (novel) published Människor, 1912; books pub. in U.S.: The Dwarf, 1945 (pub. in Sweden under title Dvärgen 1944); Barabbas, 1951 (pub. in Sweden 1950); The Eternal Smile and other stories, 1954; The Sibyl, 1958; The Death Of Ahasuerus, 1962; Pilgrim at Sea, 1964; The Holy Land, 1966; Herod and Mariamne, 1968; The Man Without a Soul, Let Man Live (in Scandinavian Plays), 1944; Modern Theatre, Seven Plays and an Essay, 1966; The Difficult Hour (Scandinavian Theatre), 1967. Recipient Nobel prize for lit., 1951. Mem. (an Immortal) Swedish Acad. Home: Lidingo, Sweden. Died July 1974.

LAHR, RAYMOND MERRILL, newspaperman; b. Kokomo, Ind., June 27, 1914; s. Clifford V. and Leone Fern (Groves) L.; A.B., U. Chgo., 1936; m. Sarah Louise Meyer, Oct. 2, 1941. With United Press (now United Press Internat.), 1937-73, beginning as staff Midwestern burs., successively labor reporter, Washington, congl. reporter, chief senate staff, 1947-58, chief polit. corr., 1958-73. Club: Nat. Press (Washington). Author: (with J. William Theis) Congress: Power and Purpose on Capitol Hill, 1967. Home: Falls Church, Va. Died June 14, 1973.

LAIDLAW, JOHN BLAKE, physician; b. Sioux St. lMarie, Can., Aug. 14, 1901; s. Walter and Maude (Sweeney) L.; came to U.S., 1927, naturalized; M.D., U. Toronto, 1927; m. Priscilla Lees Cummings, Sept. 13, 1947. Intern, Strong Meml. Hosp., Rochester, N.Y., 1927-28, asst. resident and resident, cons. in syphilology, 1928-32; practice medicine specializing in internal medicine, Rochester, 1930-74. Served to comdr. M.C., USNR, 1942-45. Diplomate Am. Bd. Internal Medicine. mem. A.M.A., Am., N.Y., Rochester (past pres.) socs. internal medicine, U. Toronto Alumni Assn., Rochester Acad. Med. (past dir.). Home: Rochester, N.Y. Died Oct. 27, 1974; buried Whitehaven Meml. Park, Rochester, N.Y.

LAIRD, JOHN KENNETH, JR., advt. exec.; b. Chgo., Oct. 7, 1903; s. John K. and Ida Gertrude (Mitchell) L.; A.B., U. Chgo., 1925; m. Agnes Siljan, Nov. 15, 1941; children—Nancy Lee, John Lindsay. Mem. editorial staff Chgo. Herald-Examiner, 1925-27, merchandising mgr., 1927-29; advt. mgr. Dr. West Co., 1929-32, v.p., 1932-39; contact staff Young & Rubicam Advt. Agy., 1939-41, mdsg. mgr., 1941-44; contact staff Dancer-Fitzgerald-Sample Advt. Agy., 1945; co-founder Tatham-Laird Advt. Agy., Chgo., 1946, pres., 1955-64; chmn. bd. Tatham-Laird Kudner, Inc., 1965-69. Bd. dirs. Nat. Conf. Christians and Jews. Mem. Audit Bur. Circulations (chmn. 1963-65), Am. Advt. Fedn. (chmn. 1967-68), Phi Beta Kappa, Psi Upsilon. Clubs: University (Chgo.); Skokie (Ill.) Country. Home: Wilmette, Ill. Died Dec. 27, 1973; cremated Willmette, Ill.

LAIRD, WILLIAM RAMSEY, III, lawyer; b. Keswick, Cal., June 2, 1916; s. Paul MacNeil and Rose (Roy) L.; A.B., Kings Coll., Bristol, Tenn.; LL.B., W. Va. U., 1944; m. Clara Cook, Dec. 23, 1937; children—Mary Ella, Elizabeth McNeil, William Ramsey IV. Admitted to W. Va. bar, 1944; Dir. Mchts. Nat. Bank (Montgomery, W. Va.), Upper Kanawha Valley Development Assn. Apptd. senator from W. Va. to succeed Sen. Harley M. Kilgore, 1956; mem. W. Va. Bd. Edn., 1955-56; tax commr. State of W. Va., 1955-56. Trustee Laird Found. Served with USNR, World War II. Mem. W. Va., Fayette County bar assns., Am. Legion. Democrat. Presbyn. Mason, Lion. Home: Fayetteville W. Va. Died Jan. 7, 1974; interred Huse Meml. Park, Fayetteville.

LALUMIER, EDWARD LOUIS, financial v.p. and sec. Armour & Co.; b. Centerville, Ill., Aug. 15, 1887; s. Louis Sylvester and Mary Elizabeth (Estes) L.; ed. St. Louis U.; m. Clara Jean Corbett, Nov. 26, 1921. Began with the First Nat. Bank of East St. Louis and later made connection with Armour & Co., moving to Chicago in 1916; from 1918 to 1921 was head of the accounting dept., Armour & Co., asst. comptroller, 1921-23, asst. treas., 1924 to May 1927, comptroller, May 1927, to Sept. 1928; treas. Studebaker Corp., South Bend, Ind., 1928. Returned to Armour & Co. in May 1929, and was elected vice-pres., sec. and comptroller, later financial v.p. and sec. Clubs: Union League, Chicago (Chicago); South Bend Country, Chain O'Lakes (South Bend, Ind.). Home: Chicago, Ill.†

LAMBERSON, RAY GUERNSEY, pres. Quarrie Corp.; b. Lyons, Kan., May 6, 1886; s. Frank H. and Alice May (Guernsey) L.; grad. Sterling (Kan.) High Sch., 1903; student Washburn Coll., 1904-07, LL.D., 1949; m. Myrtle Irene Whiteker, May 24, 1910; children—Virginia Rae (Mrs. John E. Looze), George W. Salesman King Richardson Co., Springfield, Mass., 1907-10; sales mgr. Midland Press, Chicago, 1910-17, pres., 1917-24; sales mgr. W. F. Quarrie & Co., 1924-29, v.p., 1929-40; pres. The Quarrie Corp., 1940-48; dir. Field Enterprises, Inc., v.p. edn. div.; pres. W.F. Quarrie & Co. Ltd. of Toronto, Canada; dir. Great Northern Life Insurance Company, 1922-38. Mem. Kappa Sigma. Mem. Christian Ch. Mason (32 °., Shriner). Clubs: Chicago Athletic; Oak Park Country. Home: Oak Park, Ill. Died May 29, 1974.

LAMBERT, HUBERT COTTRELL, govt. ofcl.; b. Farmington, Utah, Jan. 21, 1916; s. Isaac G. and Flora (Cottrell) L.; B.S., U. Utah, 1940, M.S., 1941, postgrad., 1946-49; m. Lucy Elizabeth Asay, Oct. 3, 1969; children—Hubert I., Barbara (Mrs. Joseph Lawson), Mary (Mrs. Fred Miller), John David, Carol Eunice (Mrs. Gary Townsend), Roberta Joan, Donovan Cottrell, Franklin Wayne, Frederick Hugh. Tchr. geology and geography Weber State Coll., Ogden, Utah, 1948-51; tchr. geology U. Utah, Salt Lake City, 1946-48; tchr. geology extension services Brigham Young U., Salt Lake City, 1955-70; area engr. State of Utah, Salt Lake City, 1940-45, dep. state engr., 1957-65., state engr., 1965-73. Served with USAAF, 1945-46. Mem. Nat. Forestry Assn., Utah Geol. Soc., Utah Acad. Arts, Sci. and Letters, Sigma Xi. Home: Ogden, Utah. Died Mar. 5, 1973.

LAMBERT, WALTER DAVIS, geodesist; born at West New Brighton, N.Y., Jan. 12, 1879; s. Walter and Elizabeth Bigelow (Davis) L.; A.B., Harvard, 1900, A.M., 1901; studied U. of Pa.; Sc.D. (honorary), Ohio State University, 1957; married Bertha Brown, June 18, 1917 (deceased October 1959). Instructor of mathematics, Purdue University, 1901-02; instructor mathematics and astronomy, University of Me., 1902-04; computer Coast and Geodetic Survey, 1904-07; Harrison fellow in mathematics, U. of Pa., 1907-08; instr. mathematics, same univ., 1908-11; computer, later senior and principal mathematician, and chief, section of gravity and astronomy, U.S. Coast and Geodetic Survey, retired 1949; cons. Ins. of Geodesy, Photogrammetry and Cartography, at Ohio State University. Served as first lieutenant engrs., U.S. Army, Sept. 1917-May 1919; with 101st Engr. Regt., A.E.F., and with Engr. Purchasing Office, in France, 15 mos. Decorated D.S.M., U.S. Dept. of Commerce. Fellow A.A.A.S.; member of Mathematical Assn. of America, Am. Geophys. Scis., Institut de France (corr.), Am. Astron. Soc., Seismological Soc. of America, Philos. Soc. Washington (pres.) Washington Acad. Sciences (v.p.), Internat. Astron. Union, Internat. Assn. Geodesy (hon. pres.). Phi Beta Kappa, Sigma Xi. Unitarian. Club: Cosmos. Author of various ofcl. publs. U.S. Coast and Geodetic Survey. Contbr. to Ency. Britannica, handbooks on geodesy and geophysics and sci. jours. Home: Canaan, Conn.†

LAMBERT, W(ILLIAM) V(INCENT), univ. adminstr.; b. Stella, Neb., Sept. 13, 1897; s. George W. and Addie L. (Kiester) L.; B.S. (agr.), U. of Neb., 1921; M.S., Kan. State Coll., 1923; Ph.D., U. of Cal., 1931 (Rosenberg scholar 1929-30); Sc.D. (hon.), Purdue University, 1959; m. Esther W. Posson, Sept. 15, 1923; children—Marilyn, Anne. Instr., asst. prof. genetics, Ia. State Coll., 1923-29, 1930-36, sr. animal husbandman in charge genetics investigations, bur. animal industry, U.S. Dept. Agr., 1936-40; asso. dir., Purdue U. Agrl. Expt. Sta., 1940-45; asst. research adminstr., U.S. Dept. of Agr., 1945-46, research adminstr., 1946-48; dean and dir., Coll. Agr., U. Neb., 1948-73; group leader U. Ill. team and adviser to vice chancellor in orgn. Utter Pradesh Agrl. U., Dist. Nainital, India, 1960-61. Mem. U.S. delegation Food and Agrl. Orgn. U.N., Copenhagen, 1946, Geneva, 1947; mem. bd. of alternates, President's sci. research bd., 1947, govt. inter-dept. com. on sci., 1948; mem. sci. mission to Brit. Colonies in Africa, for Brit. gov., 1949; mem. sci. mission to Iraq for Food and Agrl. Orgn., 1952; mission to Turkey for establishment new univ., 1954; chmn. Agricultural Delegation Soviet Union, 1955. Mem. agrl. adv. bd. W. K. Kellogg Found., 1954-60; trustee Farm Found., Chgo., 1952-60. Fellow A.A.A.S.; mem. Am. Soc. Naturalists, Am. Soc. Zoologists, Poultry Sci. Assn., Genetics Soc. Am., Am. Genetics Assn., Am. Soc. Animal Production (sec.-treas., 1943-45), Sigma Xi, Phi Kappa Phi. Author of many bulletins; contbr. numerous sci. papers to professional periodicals. Home: Lincoln, Neb. Died May 31, 1973.

LAMPORT, HAROLD, research physician, investment mgmt. exec.; b. N.Y.C., Feb. 16, 1908; s. Arthur Matthew and Sadie (Payson) L.; B.S. cum laude, Harvard, 1929; postgrad. U. Gottingen (Germany), 1928-29; M.D., Columbia, 1934; m. Golden R. Siwek, Mar. 27, 1933; children—Anthony Matthew, Stephanie Payson (Mrs. James C. Nohnberg). Intern, resident physician Beth Israel Hosp., N.Y.C., 1935-37; dir. Koster Research Lab., N.Y.C., 1937-39; research asst., then asso. neurology Columbia, 1939-42; mem. faculty Yale Sch. Medicine, 1942-67, research asst., 1942-44, research asso., asso. prof. physiology, 1944-65, pathology, 1965-66, lectr., 1966-67, research prof. physiology Mt. Sinai Sch. Medicine of City U. N.Y., 1966-75, designated Distinguished Service prof., 1976; research asso., then med. dir. mil. research projects Pierce Found., New Haven, 1942-45. Cons. Rand Corp., 1959-63; mem. asst. sec. com. missile casualties NRC, 1943-47; responsible investigator OSRD, 1942-45. ir. Consol. Gas Utilities Corp., Oklahoma City, 1940-60, chmn. bd., 1942-60; dir. Ark. La. Gas Co., Shreveport, 1960-75. Bd. dirs. Child Guidance Clinic Greater Bridgeport, Conn., 1960-75; pres. Sadie and Arthur Lamport Found., 1939-75, Lamport Found., 1960-75. Recipient Ultrasonic med. research prize Birtcher Found., 1955. Fellow A.A.A.S., N.Y. Acad. Medicine, N.Y. Acad. Sci.; mem. Am. Physiol. Soc., Biophysics Soc., Microcirculation Soc., Am. Heart Assn. (basic sci. council), Biomed. Engring. Soc., Internatl Soc. Biorheology, Phi Beta Kappa (pres. Western Conn. 1958-59), Sigma Xi. Clubs: Haromine, Bankers (N.Y.C.). Author articles on biophysics, physiology, blood circulation. Inventor pneumatic lever suit for altitude and blackout protection aviators, finance. Home: Westport, Conn., Died Dec. 27, 1975.

LAMPRECHT, STERLING POWER, educator; b. Cleve., Jan. 8, 1890; s. George O. and Emma Sterling (Power) L.; A.B., Williams Coll., 1911; A.M., Harvard, 1912; B.D., Union Theol. Sem., 1915; Ph.D., Columbia, 1918; studied Universite de Poitiers, France, 1919, A.M., Amherst, 1934; married Edith Taber, August 19, 1922. Began teaching at Columbia University, 1919, became asst. prof. philosophy U. Ill., 1921; prof. philosophy, Amherst Coll.; Howison lectr. U. Cal., 1938. Woodbridge lectr. Columbia University, 1949. Served as corpl., Co. K, 51st Pioneer Inf., U.S. Army, with A.E.F., May 1918-July 1919. Awarded Butler medal in philos., Columbia U., 1933. Member Am. Philos. Assn., Phi Beta Kappa, Delta Sigma Rho. Presbyn. Author: Moral and Political Philosophy of John Locke, 1918; Our Religious Traditions, 1950; Nature and History, 1950. Editor: Selections from Writings of John Locke, 1928; Henry More's An Account of Virtue, 1930; Hobbes' The Citizen, 1949. Editor Philosophy Series of Appleton-Century-Crofts. Contbr. on philos. subjects. Home: Amherst, Mass. Died Oct. 8, 1973.

LANAHAN, FRANCIS H., JR., army officer, ret.; b. Trenton, N.J., Oct. 28, 1897; s. Francis Henry and Mary Elizabeth (Rogers) L.; B.S., U.S. Mil. Acad., 1920; grad. Field Arty. Sch., 1921, Signal Corps Sch., 1928, Inf. Sch., 1934, Command and Gen. Staff Sch., 1936; m. Dorothy Carey, Feb. 18, 1928; children—Anne Clarke, Frank (dec.), Michael Carey. Private, Nat. Guard, 1917; commd. 2d lt. Coast Arty., 1920; transferred Field Arty., Sept. 1920; 1st lt., July 1920, transferred to Signal Corps, Sept. 1926; capt., Aug. 1935, and advanced to maj. gen., Mar. 1945; staff officer Signal Sch., 1928-30; instr. Command Gen. Staff Sch., 1936-40; War Dept., 1940-43; overseas, 1943-47; comdg. gen., Fort Monmouth, 1947-51; became chief signal officer SHAPE, 1951; asst. dept. chief of staff for Logistics, U.S. Army, ret.: v.p., gen. mgr. Fed. Electric Corp., Clifton, N.J., 1955-75. Mem. Assn. Grads. U.S. Mil. Acad. K.C. Club: Army and Navy Country (Washington). Address: Washington, D.C., Died Dec. 4, 1975.

LANCASTER, DABNEY STEWART, educator; b. Richmond, Va., Oct. 11, 1889; s. Robert Alexander and Williamine Cabell (Carrington) L.; B.A., U. of Va., 1911; M.S., Va. Poly. Inst., 1915; postgrad. U. Mo., 1916-17; LL.D., U. Richmond, 1943, Coll. William and Mary, 1958; m. Mary Tabb Crump, June 12, 1915; children—Mary Tabb (Mrs. G. Burke Johnston), Williamine Carrington (Mrs. H. Merrill Pasco), Elizabeth Tayloe (Mrs. William C. Washburn), Alice Dabney (Mrs. Pierpont Blair Buck). Associate master Chamberlayne School for Boys (now St. Christopher's School), Richmond, Virginia, 1911-12; with Virginia Polytechnic Institute, 1914-23 advancing to professor agricultural education; state supervisor agricultural edn. Va. State Bd. of Edn., 1923-25, sec., 1925-29; dean of men, U. of Ala., 1929-37; exec. sec. Bd. of Overseers, Sweet Briar Coll., 1937-41, bd. dirs., from 1942; Va. State supt. pub. instruction, 1941-46, pres. Longwood Coll., Farmville, Va., 1946-55, pres. emeritus, 1955-75. Pres. State Association Y.M.C.A.'s of Alabama, 1932-34; pres. Assn. Va. Colls., 1938-39; chmn. Va. Council Higher Edn., 1956-64. Trustee, Episcopal High Sch., 1945-75, Va. Theol Sem., 1948 (both Alexandria, Va.), Madison Coll., 1964-75. Mem. Nat. Assn. Deans and Advisors of Men (pres. 1936-37), A.A.U.P., Delta Tau Delta (pres. So. Div., 1941-43), Phi Beta Kappa, Phi Kappa Phi, Omicron Delta Kappa, Phi Eta Sigma. Democrat. Episcopalian. Home: Millboro Springs, Va. Died Mar. 11, 1975; interred Hollywood Cemetery, Richmond, Va.

LANDEGGER, KARL FRANCIS, industrialist; b. Vienna, Austria, Jan. 16, 1905; s. Dr. Robert Maurice and Agnes (von Domeny) L.; m. Helene Berger, Sept. 4, 1928 (div.); children—Carl Clement, George; m. 2d, Mon Ling Yu, May 5, 1962 (div.); 1 dau., MonLing. Came U.S., 1940, naturalized, 1946. Dir. Parsons & Whittemore Lyddon, Ltd., London, Eng., 1938-76, chmn., 1950-75; chmn. Cia Fed. De Fundicao, Brazil, 1955, Prince Albert Pulp Co., Ltd.; pres. Parsons & Whittemore, Inc., N.Y.C. 1944-75; dir. Black Clawson Co., Hamilton, O., 1952-75, chmn. 1955-67, chmn. exec. com., 1967-75; chmn. bd. Prinece Albert Pulp Co., Ltd., St. Anne-Nackawic Pulp & Paper Co., Ltd. Club: Metropolitan (N.Y.C.). Home: Ridgefield, Conn., Died Jan. 2, 1976.

LANDIS, MARY GREEN (MRS. JUDSON TAYLOR LANDIS), author; b. Los Angeles, Dec. 23, 1906; d. Orville John and Evaline (Dryer) Green; A.B., Greenville Coll., 1929; m. Judson Taylor Landis, June 10, 1930; children—Judson Richard, Janet Faith (Mrs. Worth Cary Summers). Tchr. social sci. high schs., Tyrone, Okla., 1929-30, Gibsonburg, O., 1930-33; cons. family life edn. to high schs., various univ. campuses, 1950. Mem. Am., Pacific sociol. assns., Nat. Council on Family Relations, Soc. for Study Social Problems, Am. Social Health Assn., No. Cal. Council on Family Relations, Population Assn. Am. Author: Teenagers Guide for Living, 1957; Youth and Marriage, 1957; Building Your Life, 1964; Readings in Marriage and the Family, 1962; Personal Adjustment Marriage and Family Living, 1970; Building a Successful Marriage, 1973; also articles various mags. Home: El Cerrito Cal. Died 1973.

LANDRETH, SYMINGTON PHILLIPS, lawyer; b. Bristol, Pa., Feb. 15, 1908; s. S. Phillips and Anna (Swain) L.; A.B., U. Pa., 1929; LL.B., Temple U., 1936; m. Polly Horan, Oct. 21, 1943; children—Symington Phillips, Mary Swain. Salesman John Wanamaker, Phila., 1929-36, Swain & Co., investment bankers, 1936-39; admitted to Pa. bar, 1939, since practiced Phila.; partner Rambo, Knox & Landreth, 1944-73; dir. Union Paving Co.; asst. city solicitor Phila., 1944-52. Mem. Am., Phila. bar assns., Lawyers Club, Am. Dialect Soc., Pa. Soc. Colonial Wars (treas.), S.R. (registrar), Colonial Soc. Pa. (pres. 1953-55), Welcome Soc. (v.p.), Loyal Legion, Huguenot Soc., Numismatic and Antiquarian Soc. Phila. (librarian), Phila. Soc. Preservation Landmarks (sec.), Bridge Whist Assn. Phila. Clubs (pres. 1960-62), Coll. Alumni Soc. U. Pa. (pres. 1963-65), Zeta Psi (pres. 1961-62). Episcopalian. Republican. Clubs: Hamilton, Church, Racquet, Meridian, Clinkers, Right Angle, Penn Athletic. Home: Philadelphia Pa. Died May 12, 1973.

LANE, EDWARD HUDSON, furniture co. exec.; b. Newcastle, Va., July 4, 1891; s. John Edward and Ella Florence (Wisely) L.; student Fork Union Mil. Acad., 1901-13, Va. Poly. Inst., 1906-10; m. Myrtle Clyde Bell, Oct. 7, 1914 (dec. Mar. 1960); children—Edward Hudson, Landon Bell, Bernard Bell, John Haden; m. 2d, Helen Hughes Brooks, Jan. 1961. Established Standard Red Cedar Chest Co. (now Lane Co., Inc.), Altavista, Va., 1912, pres., 1922-56, chmn. bd., 1956-73. Mem. bd. govs. Am. Furniture Mart, Chgo. Spl. asst. to adminstr. Nat. Prodn. Authority, 1950-51; mem. bus. adv. council Dept. Commerce, 1941-73; mem. steering com. Grad. Sch. Bus., U. Va. Dir. Ferrum Jr. Coll.; mem. bd. visitors Va. Poly. Inst. Elected Man of the Year in Furniture Mfg. Industry, 1951. Mem. N.A.M. (past v.p., dir.), Va. Mfrs. Assn., So. Furniture Mfrs. Assn., Furniture Club Am. (founder), Newcomen Soc. Clubs: Commonwealth (Richmond, Va.); Bath and Tennis (Palm Beach, Fla.). Methodist. Mason. Home: Altavista, Va. Died May 19, 1973.

LANE, EVERETT HALE, life ins. co. exec.; b. Boston, June 4, 1904; s. Patrick James and Catherine Agnes (Pomfret) L.; A.B. cum laude, Harvard, 1924, LL.B., 1927; m. Sara E. Wirt, Oct. 3, 1933; 1 dau., Sally (Mrs. Richard T. Marlette). Admitted to Mass. bar, 1927; mem. firm Lane & Lane, Boston, 1927-37; with Boston Mut. Life Ins. Co., 1937-74, exec. v.p., 1948-53, pres., 1953-74, chmn. bd., 1966-74; pres., dir. Boston Mut. Equity Growth Fund, Inc., Boston Mut. Mgmt. Corp. Chmn. Winthrop (Mass.) Sch. Com., 1931-41. Bd. dirs. Boston Met. chpt. A.R.C.; adv. bd. Suffolk U. Sch. Bus. Mem. Life Office Mgmt. Assn. (dir., past pres.), Mass., Fed. bar assns., Newcomen Soc. Clubs: Harvard (Boston); Varsity (Harvard). Home: Dover, Mass. Died Mar. 12, 1974.

LANE, HENRY HIGGINS, univ. prof.; b. Bainbridge, Putnam County, Ind., Feb. 17, 1878; s. Rev. Edwin Thornton and Jessie Fremont (Darnall) L.; Ph.B., DePauw U., 1899; A.M., Ind. U., Bloomington, 1903; studied Cornell, 1903-04, U. of Chicago, 1904-05; Ph.D., Princeton, 1915; m. Mary Juno Harper, Dec. 25, 1905; children—Edwin Harper, Henry Wallace, Eleanor Hope, Prof. biology, Hiram (O.) Coll., 1905-06; instr. zoölogy and embryology, 1906-08, prof. zoölogy, 1908-20, U. of Okla.; prof. zoölogy and embryology Phillips U. East Enid, Okla., 1920-22; prof. and head dept. zoölogy, U. of Kan., 1922-48, curator Museum of Vertebrate Paleontology, 1931-41; dir. of Dyche Museum of Natural History, 1941-44. Instr. zoülogy summers, U. of Chicago, 1905, 11, Ind. Univ., 1906, 08, U. of Southern Calif, 1924. Chief line of research, mammalogy and vertebrate paleontology. Fellow A.A.A.S., Okla. Acad. Science (1st pres.); mem. Am. Soc. Naturalists, Am. Soc. Zoölogists, Am. Micros. Soc., Sigma Chi, Phi Beta Kappa (both at DePauw), Gamma Alpha (Cornell), Sigma Xi (U. of Chicago), Biol. Soc. Washington, Am. Mus. Natural History, Am. Soc. Mammalogists (charter mem and sec.), Am. Assn. Univ. Profs., Am. Soc. Eugenics (charter mem.), Am. Soc. of Vertebrate Paleontologists. Clubs: University, Old and New, Cosmopolitan, Knife and Fork. Mem. Disciples of Christ. Contbr. to sci. jours. and to the publs. of Carnegi Instn. Author: Evolution and Christian Faith, 1923; Animal Biology, 1929; Survey of the Fossil Vertebrates of Kansas, 1947. Home: Lawrence, Kan.†

LANE, RAYMOND A., bishop; born Lawrence, Mass., Jan. 2, 1894; s. Michael and Anastasia (Doyle) L.; grad. St. John's Prep. Sch., Danvers, Mass., 1911; student Venard Coll., Clarks Summit, Pa., 1913-14; Maryknoll Sem., Maryknoll, N.Y., 1914-20. Entered Cath. Fgn. Mission Soc. of Am., 1913; ordained priest Roman Cath. Ch., 1920; missionary S. China, 1923-25, Manchuria, 1925-29: asst. to superior gen. and rector, Maryknoll (N.Y) Sem., 1929-32; apptd. Prefect Apostolic of Fushun, Manchuria, 1932, consecrated titular bishop of Hypaepa and Vicar Apostolic of Fushun, Manchuria, 1940; superior gen., Cath. Fgn. Mission Soc. of Am., 1946-56. Founded Congregation of Sisters of the Sacred Heart (native) of Fushun, Manchuria, 1931. Recipient Christopher Columbus Award, 1953, Cath. Assn. Internat. Peace Ann. Award, 1953. Author: The Early Days of Maryknoll, 1951; Stone in the King's Highway, 1953; Ambassador in Chains, 1955. Home: Maryknoll N.Y. Died July 31, 1974; interred Maryknoll, N.Y.

LANE, THOMAS ALPHONSUS, journalist, author; b. Revere, Mass., Nov. 19, 1906; s. Thomas Andrew and Julia (Fitzpatrick) L.; B.S., U.S. Mil. Acad., 1928; B.S. in C.E., Mass. Inst. Tech., 1932; grad. Nat. War Coll., 1953; m. Jean Margaret Gee, June 3, 1933; children—Jean, Michael Stuart, Julia Ann (Mrs. Donald Rasmussen), Thomas C. Commd. 2d lt. U.S. Army, 1928, advanced through grades to maj. gen., 1957; exec. officer to Air Engr., Hdqrs., USAAF, 1942; exec. officer, operations officer Engr. sect. Gen. Hdqrs., S.W. Pacific area, 1943-45; joint operations Rev. Bd., 1946; dist. engr., Little Rock, 1948-50; dist. engr. Okinawa, 1950-52; engr. commr. D.C., 1954-57; comdg. gen. Ft. Leonard Wood, Mo., 1957-60; pres. Mississippi River Commn., 1960-62; ret., 1962; syndicated columnist, author, lectr., editor, 1962-75. Instr. civil engring. and mil. history U.S. Mil. Acad., 1935-39; engring. instr. and chief logistics div. Air Command and Staff Sch., 1946-48; exec. dir. Inst. for Human Progress, 1962-63. Pres. Ams. for Constitutional Action, 1965-69, Am. Council for World Freedom, 1972-74, Decorated D.S.M. with oak leaf cluster; recipient Liberty award Congress of Freedom, 1968, 72, 73, 74, Wanderer Forum award, 1968, Freedom award Order of Lafayette, 1969, Gold Good Citizenship medal Nat. Soc. S.A.R., 1970. Fellow Am. Soc. C.E.; mem. Wash. Soc. Engrs. (hon.), Newcomen Soc. (hon.). Clubs: Army-Navy (Washington); Army Navy Country (Arlington, Va.); National Press (Washington). Author: The Leadership of President Kennedy, 1964; The War for the World, 1968; Cry Peace: The Kennedy Years, 1969; American on Trial: The War for Vietnam, 1971; The Breakdown of the Old Politics, 1974. Editor-in-chief Strategic Rev., 1972-75. Home: McLean, Va. Died Apr. 20, 1975; buried U.S. Mil. Acad. Cemetery, West Point, N.Y.

LANG, GEORGE, coll. prof.; b. Wellwood, Scotland, Feb. 22, 1879; s. George McCraken and Mary (James) L.; brought to U.S., 1883; A.B., Southwestern Presbyn, U., Clarksille, Tenn., 1905, B.D., 1906, Litt.D., 1937; post-grad. work in philosophy, U. of Edinburgh, 1908-09, in German lang., U. of Berlin, 1912-13; D.D., Ala. Presbyn. Coll., 1916; LL.D., U. of Ala., 1925; A.M., Columbia U., 1925; unmarried. Prof. philosophy, Ala. Presbyn. Coll., Anniston, Ala., 1910-15; prof. ecclesiastical history, Southwestern Presbyn. U., 1915-16; pres. Ala. Presbyn. Coll., 1916-18; pro. philosophy, U. of Ala., from 1918. Mem. Acad. Polit. Science, Royal Soc. Arts, Nat. Council of The Bible Foundation, A.A.A.S., Soc. of Biblical Literature and Exegesis, Nat. Assn. of Biblical Instrs., Ala. Acad. Science, Internat. Council of Religious Edn., Alpha Tau Omega, Phi Beta Kappa, Pi Gamma Mu, Alpha Mu Rho, Omicron Delta Kappa, Epsilon Pi. Democrat, Contbg. editor: The Presbyterian Outlook; joint editor: The Alabama Bible Journal. Home: Tuscaloosa, Ala.*†

LANG, HERBERT (OTTO HENRY), naturalist; b. Oehringen, Württemberg, Germany, Mar. 24, 1879; s. Heinrich Ludwig and Luise (Grassauer) L.; grad. Royal Lyceum, Oehringen, 1894; attended courses U. of Zürich, Sorbonne, Paris, Columbia U.; unmarried. Practical study of taxidermy in Oehringen, 1894-96; naturalist, Federal Mus., Zürich, 1896-1900, Maison Fasse, Paris, 1900-03; with Am. Mus. Natural History, from 1930; represented the museum in Tjader E.African Expdn., 1906-07; in charge of Congo expdn. in Belgian Congo, 1909-15; asst. dept. of mammalogy, 1915-19, asst. curator same, 1919-23, asso. cu, from 1924; expdn. to British Guiana, 1922-23; gen. mgr. Vernay Angola Expdn., 1925. Fellow Am. Geog. Soc., N.Y. Zoöl. Soc., N.Y. Acad. Sciences; mem. Am. Assn. Museums, Am. Soc. Mammalogists, Ecol. Soc. America, A.A.A.S.; life mem. Am. Mus. Natural History; asso. mem. Am Ornithologists' Union. Club: Explorers'. Address: New York City, N.Y.†

LANG, JOHN ALBERT, JR., govt. ofcl., educator; b. Carthage, N.C., Nov. 15, 1910; s. John Albert and Laura (Kelly) L.; B.A., U. N.C., 1930, M.A., 1931; postgrad. Mercer U., 1931-32; m. Catherine Gibson, Nov. 20, 1947; children—John Albert III, Richard Gibson, Laura Catherine, Martha Elizabeth. Head English dept. Ga. Mil. Acad., 1931-33; pres. Nat. Student Govt. Fedn., N.Y.C., 1933-35; asst. to dir., edn. program Civilian Conservation Corps, 1935-38; adminstr. for N.C., NYA, 1938-42; staff asst. Better Health Assn., N.C., 1946-47; adminstrv. asst. to Congressman C. B. Deane, 1947-56; staff specialist govt. operations com. Ho. of Reps., 1956-57; adminstrv. asst. to Congressman R.E. Jones, 1957-61; dep. for Res. and ROTC affairs Office Sec. Air Force, 1961-64; acting spl. asst. to sec. air force for manpower, personnel and res. forces, 1965-66; adminstrv. asst. to sec. air force, 1964-74; air force secretarial continuity rept., 1969-74; lectr. profl. and ednl. groups, 1933-74; professorial lectr. George Washington U., 1960-71. Vice chmn. N.C. Democratic Conv., 1946. Bd. dirs. Washington Community Chest. Served to maj. USAAF, 1942-46. Decorated Legion of Merit, Meritorious Service medal, Air Force Commendation medal, Army Commendation medal; recipient Algernon Sullivan award, 1931, Mangum Oratorial award U. N.C., 1931; citation NYA, 1938-42; scroll appreciation N.C. State Bd. Health, 1946; service citation Congl. Secs. Club, 1956; Exceptional Civilian Service award Dept. Air Force, 1961-64, 65-66, 66-69, citation N.G. Bur., 1944, Air Force Assn., 1964. Am. Legion, 1962; certificate of recognition Md. Jr. C. of C. 1961; Distinguished Service citation Res. Officers Assn., 1963. Mem. Am. Acad. Polit. and Social Sci., Am. Soc. Pub. Adminstrn., Res. Officers Assn., Am. Legion, V.F.W., U. N.C. Alumni Assn., Nat. Vocational Guidance Assn., Air Force Assn., Acad. mgmt. (exec. mem.), Phi Beta Kappa. Elk. Author articles, bulls., studies surveys, reports in field. Home: Washington, D.C. Died June 27, 1974.

LANG, LOUIS LACOURSE, life ins. co. exec.; b. Kitchener, Ont., Can., 1880; s. George C.H. and Minnie (LaCourse) L.; ed. Kitchener schs., also De La Salle Inst., Chgo.; m. Gertrude Dietrich, Aug. 19, 1901; children—Howard J., Esther G. (Mrs. Hubert A. Saunders). Chmn. bd. Mut. Life Assurance Co. Can., from 1958, also Sunshine Office Equipment Ltd., and Waterloo Trust & Savs. Co.; v.p., dir. Lang Tanning Co. Ltd., C.P. Ry., Franki of Can. Ltd., Canadian Pacific Electric Lines, Shurly-Dietrich-Atkins Ltd., Steel Co. Can., Supertest Petroleum Corp. Ltd. Chmn. bd. Freeport Sanatorium; mem. Galt Separate Sch. Bd. Vice pres., dir. Ont. div. Canadian Cancer Soc., Waterloo County Health Assn.; bd. govs. Ont. Research Found., U. Western Ont.; bd. dir. Dominion div. Boy Scouts Assn. Mem. Canadian Mfrs. Assn. (exec. com.). Clubs: Mount Royal (Montreal); Toronto, Home: Galt, Ont., Can.†

LANGE, FREDERICK EDWARD, orgn. exec.; b. Pitts., Dec. 2, 1920; s. Frederick G. and Olive (Bieber) L.; A.B., U. Pitts., 1943, M.Ed., 1951, Ed.D., 1958; m. Jean Louise Huebner, Jan. 1, 1942; children—Frederick Edward, Anita Louise, Cynthia Jean, Juliet Marie. Newsman United Press Assn., Pitts., 1939-45; asst. to dir. extension div. Johnstown (Pa.) Coll., 1946-48; asst. dir. extension U. Pitts., 1949-56, dir. community relations, 1957-58, dir. continuing edn., 1958-61; dir. corporate programs Case Western Res. U., 1961-71; dir. devel. Cleve. Zool. Soc., 1972-73; mem. faculty Cuyahoga Community Coll., 1964-73; dir. devel. Akron YMCA, 1973-74. Bd. mgmt. Pitts. YMCA; exec. local council Boy Scouts Am. Served with AUS, 1943-45, ETO. Mem. Nat. U. Extension Assn., Pa. Music Educators Assn. (exec. council 1955-58), Am. Coll. Pub. Relations Assn., Am. Alumni Council, Music Educators Nat. Conf., Speech Assn. Am., Pa. Forensic and Music League (exec. sec. 1950-59), C. of C. (dir.), Phi Delta Kappa. Home: Cleveland Ohio. Died May 12, 1974.

LANGTON, CLAIR VAN NORMAN, ednl. adminstr.; b. Millgrove, Ont., Can., Nov. 1, 1895; s. Robert and Margaret (Van Norman) L.; student Mich. State Normal Coll., 1914-16; B.S., U. of Mich., 1923, M.S., 1925, Dr. P.H., 1928; Ed.D., Univ. of Ore., 1938; LL.D., Eastern Michigan University, 1961; m. Hazel Edwards, Dec. 28, 1923; children—Margaret Marie, Robert Edwards. Came to U.S., 1900, naturalized by

Act of Congress. Dir. Midland Mich. Community Center, 1920-22; faculty div. of pub. health, U. of Mich., 1923-28; dean and dir. health and phys. edn., Ore. State U., 1928-73, prof. of physical education and hygiene from 1928, dir. institutional research, 1964-73, tech. counselor in sanitary engring., Expt. Sta. from 1928; planned and directed Wiliamette River Sanitary Survey, 1929; supt. of camps, Indian Emergency Conservation work, 1933 consultant to U. of Hawaii Territorial Bd. of Health, Dept. of Pub. Instr., summer 1946; state joint staff com., 1941-64, chmn. 1951-52. Program dir. Williamette Valley Chest X-Ray Survey, 1952; dir. State Tb and Health Assn., 1952-73, mem. exec. bd., 1953-64; Served in U.S. Army, Mexican Border, 1916; World War I, 1917-19. Recipient Gold Key with Diamond award Ore. Tb Respiratory Disease Assn., 1972. Fellow Am. Coll. Sports Medicine, Am. Pub. Health Assn., Am. Assn. for Health, Phys. Edn. and Recreation (Anderson Award 1954, Gulick Award, 1957), Am. Sch. Health Assn., Am. Acad. Phys. Edn. mem. Ore. Assn. Health, Phys. Edn. and Recreation, Basic Sci. Examining Bd., Ore., Am. Student Health Assn., Sigma Delta Psi, Phi Kappa Sigma, Delta Omega, Phi Delta Kappa, Phi Epsilon Kappa. Republican. Episcopalian. Mason (Consistory, Shriner). Club: Rotary. Author: The Practice of Personal Hygiene (with M. P. Isaminger), 1933; Orientation and School Health, 1941; Hygeine Guide Books, I, II, III, 1934, 35, 36; Health Principles and Practices (with C. L. Anderson), 1953; School Health (with R. L. Allen and P. Wexler), 1961; Principles of Health, Physical Education and Recreation (with R. O. Duncan and C. K. Brightbill), 1962. Home: Corvallis, Ore., Died Aug. 19, 1973.

LANIEL, JOSEPH, govt. ofcl. France; born Vimontiers, Normandy, France, Oct. 12, 1889. Textile mfr.; deputy from Lisieux, 1932-40; under-secretary of state for finance, 1940; dep. from Calvados to 1st and 2d Constituent Assemblies (elected 1945 and 1946), to Nat. Assembly (elected 1946 and 1951); sec. of state for finance and economic affairs (Andre Marie cabinet), July-Sept. 1948; minister of communications (Reneé Pleven cabinet), Aug.-Sept. 1951; minister of state (Rene Pleven and Edgar Faure cabinets), Sept. 1951-Feb. 1952; premier of France, 1953-55. Active in establishment and services of Resistance Movement. Mem. Rightist Independent Party. Died Apr. 1975.

LANIER, EDMOND RAOUL HENRI, nav. co. exec.; b. Paris, France Mar. 1, 1906; s. Andre and Louise (Suerus) L.; student U. Paris, Pvt. Sch. Polit. Sci.; B. Humanities, LL.B., diploma Advanced Studies in Econs.; m. France Rist, Feb. 17, 1938; children—Isabelle (Mrs. Phillippe Essig), Henri, Francois, Jean. With Gen. Transatlantic Co., 1932-74, dir., 1949, gen. mgr., 1958-64 chmn., 1964-74; chmn. Gen. Co. Tourism and Hotel Trade, 1966-74; dir. Air Force Corp., Indsl. and Maritime Union, Compagnie Mixte, Indst. and Maritime Co., Radiotechnique Co. Bd. dirs. Autonomous Ports of Le Havre and Nantes-St. Nazaire; mem. Superior Council Mcht. Marine; mem. Naval Acad., 1972. Decorated comdr. Legion of Honor, Mil. medal, Croix de Guerre, comdr. Order Merit (Germany). Mem. Sci. and Tech. Assn. for Exploitation of Oceans (pres.), Interallied Union. Clubs: Flying of France, Automobile of France. Author: From Cod Fishing to the Liner France, 1963; (play) One Decree Among So Many Others. Contbr. articles to profl. jours. Home: Paris, France. Died Oct. 27, 1974.

LANKFORD, WOODROW WILSON, banker; b. Pocomoke City, Md., Oct. 7, 1912; s. Thomas A. and Mamie (Shaw) L.; student Md. Inst., 1930-34, Balt. Coll. Commerce, 1939-41, U. Wis., 1954-56; m. Rosalie M. Schackert, Mar. 4, 1967; 1 son, Barre D. Accountant, Tongue, Brooks Co., Balt., 1935-41; with Union Trust Co. Balt., 1941-75, v.p., 1962-75, v.p., comptroller, 1958-75, ret., 1975. Mem. Bank Adminstrn. Inst. (past pres.), Financial Execs. Inst. Home: Baltimore, Md. Died Apr. 14, 1975; interred Gulf Pines Meml. Park, Venice, Fla.

LANZA, CONRAD HAMMOND, army officer, author; b. New York, N.Y., Feb. 15, 1878; s. Manfred and Clara (Hammond) L.; ed. Columbian (now George Washington) U.; grad. Arty. Sch., 1903, Army Staff Coll., 1916; m. Renée Nazareth, Sept. 27, 1923; 1 dau., Francoise M. (Mrs. Lawrence D. Burkinshaw). Entered United States Army as 2d lieutenant, arty., 1898; 1st lt., arty. corps, 1901, advancing through the grades to col., 1929; retired, 1942; served in Spanish-Am. War. Philippine Insurrection, Mexico Border Campaign, World War I and World War II. Now engaged in writing on mil. and hist. subjects. Decorated Distinguished Service Medal, Silver Star with oak leaf cluster, Purple Heart. Fellow American Geographical Society. Member American Historical Assn. Republican. Roman Catholic. Rotarian. Club: New York Athletic. Author of histories on Napoleonic campaigns; War of 1870; World War I and II. Commentator on internat. relations for mags. Lecturer. Home: Manchester, N.H.†

LAPORTE, CLOYD, lawyer; b. Springfield, Mo., July 25, 1892; s. Alphonse Adolph and Nina Agnes (Mitchell) L.; A.B. summa cum laude in duabus, Harvard, 1916, LL.B., 1920; m. Marguerite Elva Raeder, Oct. 17, 1916; children—Rita, Cloyd, Lowell. Admitted to N.Y. bar, 1921; asso. Root, Clark, Buckner and Howland, N.Y.C., 1920-25; mem. Root, Ballantine, Harlan, Bushby & Palmer and predecessor firms, 1925-54, opened Paris office, 1929-30; mem. Dewey, Ballantine, Bushby, Palmer & Wood, N.Y.C., 1955-74. Trustee, mem. exec. mortgage coms. Tchrs. Ins. and Annuity Assn. Am., 1948-62; trustee, mem. exec. com. Coll. Retirement Equities Fund, 1952-62. Chmn. Bd. Ethics City N.Y., 1960-72, chmn. N.Y. State Joint Legislative Com. on Ethics, 1964-65; past chmn. planning and program com. Jud. Conf. 2d Circuit. Bd. dirs., treas. Hosp. Rev. and Planning Council of So. N.Y., 1948-64. Life fellow Am. Bar Found. (50-year award 1972); mem. Am. Judicature Soc., Assn. Bar City N.Y., Internat., Am. (ho. dels. 1954-70, N.Y. del. 1962-70), N.Y. (chmn. exec. com. 1954-56, pres. 1956-57) bar assns., Practising Law Inst. (trustee), N.Y. County Lawyers Assn. (dir. 1952-58), Am. Soc. Internat. Law, Am. Law Inst., Harvard Law Sch. Assn. N.Y.C. (pres. 1963-64), Phi Beta Kappa (pres. N.Y. alumni 1966-67), Phi Beta Kappa Assos. (pres. 1962-69, dir. 1962-74). Clubs: Century, Down Town, Harvard, University (N.Y.C.). Pres. Harvard Law Rev., 1919-20. Home: New York N.Y. Died July 24, 1974; buried Kensico Cemetery, Valhalla, N.Y.

LAPP, CLAUDE JEROME, educator; b. Smiths Creek, Mich., June 24, 1892; s. Charles Wesley and Cora Belle (Conrad) L.; A.B., Albion Coll., 1917; M.A., U. Ill., 1920, Ph.D., 1922; m. Blanche M. Harrison, Aug. 17, 1920; children—Roger Harrison, Eloise Mae (Mrs. Philip Ruby). Faculty physics dept. U. Ia., 1922-47: dir. research, engring., sci. and mgmt. def. tng. Pa. State Coll., 1941; dir. mathematics and physics Naval Aviation Induction Center, Iowa City, Ia., 1942-43; Army ednl. insp. 7th Corps area, 1944; bus. mgr. Mil. Research Project, 1944-45; dep. dir. office sci. personnel Nat. Acad. Scis.-NRC, 1947-65, dir. spl. programs, 1965-73, also dir. fellowship office. Mem. Am. Assn. Physics Tchrs. (chmn. com. on testing 1936-45), Am. Phys. Soc., Washington Philos. Soc., Phi Beta Kappa, Sigma Xi, Eta Kappa Nu. Methodist. Clubs: Cosmos, Potomac Archers (Washington). Asso. editor Am. Physics Tchr., 1933-36. Ia. archery champion, 1936-37. Home: Alexandria, Va. Died July 27, 1973.

LAPPIN, WARREN CURTIS, educator; b. Eureka, Ill., Dec. 26, 1900; s. William Otis and Cora Anna (Dahl) L.; student Atlantic Christian Coll., 1917-19; A.B., Transylvania Coll., 1920; A.M., U. Chgo., 1929; Ed.D., Ind. U., 1941; m. Ruth Anglin, Sept. 2, 1923; 1 dau., Mary Ella (Mrs. James M. Wells). Tchr. edn., athletic coach Morehead (Ky.) Normal Sch., 1920-22; prin. Morehead High Sch., 1922-26; dir. tng. sch. Morehead State Univ., 1926-40, dean coll., 1940-66, v.p. acad. affairs, dean faculty, 1966-71. Chmn. Ky. Adv. Com. Tchr. Edn., 1965-67. Mem. Morehead City Council, 1932-36, mayor, 1936-39. Mem. Nat., Ky. edn. assns., Phi Delta Kappa. Democrat. Club: Morehead Men's. Address: Morehead, Ky. Died Aug. 7, 1975; interred Lee Cemetery, Morehead, Ky.

LAPRADE, WILLIAM THOMAS, educator; b. Franklin County, Va., Dec. 27, 1883; s. George Washington and Mary Elizabeth (Muse) L.; A.B., Washington (D.C.) Christian Coll., 1906; Ph.D., Johns Hopkins, 1909; m. Nancy Hamilton Calfee, June 11, 1913; 1 dau., Nancy Elizabeth (Mrs. J.D.T. Hamilton). Prof. history Trinity Coll. (now Duke), 1909-53, emeritus, 1953-75; prof. history U. Ill., summers 1916, 30; lectr. history and politics, tng. sch. secs. YMCA, Blue Ridge, N.C., 1918-19; prof. history U. Pa., summer 1925, U. Mich., summer 1929 Mem. exec. bd. N.C. Dept. Archives and History, 1941-75. Mem. Am. Hist. Assn., Royal Hist. Soc., Am. Polit. Sci. Assn., Am. Assn. U. Profs. (pres. 1942-43), N.C. Lit. and Hist. Assn. (pres. 1937), Phi Beta Kappa. Mem. Christian (Disciples) Ch. Author: England and the French Revolution, 1909; British History for American Students, 1926; Public Opinion and Politics in Eighteenth Century England, 1936; also articles Am. Hist. Rev., English Hist. Rev., Am. Polit. Sci. Rev., and series 18 articles on The Teaching of History and Civics, in N.C. Edn., 1921-23. Editor, Parliamentary Papers of John Robinson (for Royal Hist. Soc.), 1922; editor S. Atlantic Quar., 1944-56. Home: Durham, N.C. Died May 14, 1975; buried Durham, N.C.

LARABEE, LOTTIE B(ERTHA), coll. cons., lectr.; b. Sprague, Neb.; d. Arthur Henry and Anna (Bartels) Larabee; Mus.B., U. Sch. Music, Lincoln, Neb.; Mus.M., Am. Conservatory Music; M.A., Ph. D., N.Y. U., 1955. Prin. elementary sch., Beatrice, Neb.; music instr. Albion State Normal Sch.; music instr., dir. extension U. South Dakota, Springfield; music instr., acting head music dept. Lock Haven State Coll.; dir. Own Sch., Chgo.; research coll. and univ. adminstrn., also coll. cons., 1957-67; prof. higher edn. Ft. Lauderdale (Fla.) U., 1967-69, from asst. to the pres. to v.p. for acad. affairs, 1967-69; coll. cons., 1969-75; exec. dir. Am. Assn. Pres.'s Ind. Colls. and Univs., 1967-68. Recipient Distinguished Service award Am. Assn. Pres.'s Ind. Colls. and Univs. Pres., 1968. Mem. Am. Assn. Higher Edn., A.A.A.S., New Eng. Historic Geneal. Soc., Internat. Platform Assn., Kappa Delta Pi, Sigma Alpha Iota (past. nat. editor). Author: Adminstrators Who Subvert Learning, Their Residence and Education, 1957; A Parent's Guide to Colleges and Universities, 1963. Home: Fort Lauderdale, Fla., Died Sept. 5, 1975.

LARGE, GEORGE ELWYN, engring. educator; b. Whigville, O., July 20, 1899; s. George Edward and Helena Emma Augusta (Cleary) L.; student Ohio State U., 1918-20; B.S. magna cum laude in Civil Engring., U. Wash., 1922, C.E., 1929; m. Helen Florence Spickard, June 28, 1926; children—Mary Ellen (Mrs. James O. Mahoy), Patricia Ann (Mrs. William A. Dale). Engr. fieldman The Pacific Tel. & Tel. Co., Seattle, 1922-23; instr. dept. engring. drawing Ohio State U., Columbus, 1923-24; asst. prodn. engr. Buckeye Steel Castings Co., Columbus O., 1924-29; structures engr. Curtiss-Wright Corp., 1943; research engr. Engring. Expt. Sta., Ohio State U., 1929-38, asst. prof. civil engring., 1929, asso. prof., 1934, prof. structural engring.; 1942-73, structural engr. Univ. Architect's Office, 1945-46; chmn. civil engring. dept., 1947-53; also cons. structural engr. Honors examiner in civil engring. Swarthmore Coll., 1936, 37. Registered profl. civil and structural engr., Ohio. Mem. Am. Soc. for Engring. Edn., Am. Concrete Inst., Am. Soc. C.E. (past pres. Central Ohio sect.), Sigma Xi, Tau Beta Pi, Chi Epsilon, Triangle, Texnikoi frats. Methodist. Club: Faculty. Co-Author: Basic Reinforced Concrete Design: USD and WSD, 3d edit., 1969) (with T.Y. Chen) Reinforced Concrete Design, 1969; also Engring. Expt. Sta. bulls. Patentee. Home: Columbus, O. Died June 28, 1973.

LARKIN, ROSEMARY RITA, physician; b. Prairie du Rocher, Ill., Mar. 31, 1922; d. Ralph Robert and Marjorie Louise (Allard) Larkin; B.S., U. Ill., 1946, M.D., 1950. Intern Deaconess Hosp., St. Louis, 1950-51; gen. practice medicine, St. Louis, 1953-57, from 1958; dist. health officer Mo. Dept. Health, 1957-58; chief medicine Incarnate Word Hosp., St. Louis, 1965-66, pres. med. staff, 1966-68; condr. radio program Ask Your Doctor, Sta. KMOX, 1966-70. Active pub. edn. Am. Cancer Soc., 1961, sch. health programs Mo. Dept. Pub. Health, from 1957. Served to lt. (s.g.) USNR, 1951-53; Korea. Mem. Am., So. med. assns., Am., St. Louis (bd. dirs. 1968-69, v.p. 1969-70) acads. gen. practice, St. Louis County Med. Soc., Am. Assn. Physicians and Surgeons. Republican. Catholic. Contbr. med. jours. Home: St Louis Mo. Died July 1, 1972; interred Mt. Hope Mausoleum, St. Louis, Mo.

LARRIMORE, FRANCINE, actress; b. Verdun, France; d. J. Lewis and Sarah P. (Adler) La Remée; ed. normal sch. (now Hunter Coll.), N.Y. City; m. Con Conrad, 1922 (divorced 1924). Played leading parts in Overnight, Here Comes the Bride, Parlor, Bedroom and Bath, Fair and Warmer, Sometime (musical comedy); starred in Scandal, Nice People, Nobody's Business Nancy Ann, Parasites, This Was a Man, Let Us Be Gay, Brief Moments, Chicago, 1926-27, Shooting Star, 1933, John Meade's Woman, 1937; and others. Deceased.

LARSEN, JENS WILLARD, physician; b. Odell, Ill., July 21, 1901; s. Jens Peter and Robina (Henry) L.; M.D., Loyola U., 1928; M.Sc., U. Pa., 1941; m. Beatrice Catherine Wesby, June 8, 1927. Intern, San Francisco City and County Hosp., 1927-28; resident Woodland (Cal.) Clinic Hosp., 1928-29; resident in trauma surgery Morrisania City Hosp., N.Y.C., 1939-40; resident in surgery Riker's Island Hosp., N.Y.C., 1940, Flower and Fifth Av. Hosp., N.Y.C., 1940-41; asst. surgeon Ashland (Pa.) State Hosp., 1942-43; chief surgery U.S. VA Hosp., Amarillo, Tex., 1946-47, VA Hosp., Alexandria, La., 1947-48; postgrad. in surgery U. Edinburgh (Scotland), 1951; mem. surg. staff VA Hosp., Fort Wayne, Ind., 1956-66; med. cons. dept. indsl. relations State of Cal., Los Angeles, 1966-72. Served to capt. M.C., USNR, 1943-56. Diplomate Am. Bd. Surgery. Mem. A.M.A. Home: Reno, Nev., Died May 8, 1972; buried Greenwood Meml. Park Mausoleum, San Diego, Cal.

LARSON, ALGOT J. E., mfr.; b. June 30, 1881; student high sch., Alexander Hamilton Inst.; m. Lillian K. Karlson, Sept. 15, 1923; children—Dorothy, Donald, Millburn, Marshall. Vice pres., then pres. and gen. mgr. Art Metal Constrn. Co.; dir. First Nat. Bank Jamestown Clubs: Masonic; Union League (N.Y.C.). Address: Jamestown, N.Y.†

LARSON, FRANK OSCAR, business exec.; b. Aita, Ia., July 31, 1880; s. Olaf and Katherine (Danielson) L.; student Bethany Coll., Linsborg, Kan., 1901, 02, 03; m. Beulah Everett Rummell, Oct. 31, 1923; 1 son, Jack Everett. Vice pres. and bus. mgr. World Pub. Co., (pub. Tulsa World, Tulsa, Okla.) from 1915; pres. and gen. mgr. Newspaper Printing Corp., agt. Tulsa World and Tulsa Tribune, from 1941. Dir. Fourth Nat. Bank, Dir. Chamber of Commerce. Democrat. Christian Scientist. Clubs: Southern Hills Country, Rotary, Tulsa. Home: Tulsa, Okla.†

LARSON, LEONARD W., physician; b. Clarkfield, Minn., May 22, 1898; s. John and Ida (Anderson) L.; B.S., U. Minn., 1918, M.D., 1922; LL.D., U. N.D.; Sc.D., Jamestown Coll.; m. Ordelia Miller, Oct. 23, 1923 (dec.); children—Margery Doris (Mrs. George Mitchell), Dorothy Lenore (Mrs. John Collett); m. 2d, Esther D. Knudtson, June 27, 1969. Pathologist, Bismarck (N.D.) Hosp., 1924-70, St. Alexis Hosp., 1935-70, Quain & Ramstod Clinic, Bismarck, 1924-70, partner, 1939-63. Bd. dirs. Am. Cancer Soc., 1945-74, pres. 1966; dir. Blood Services Bd. Recipient Gold medal Am. Cancer Soc., 1953; certificate highest merit

Am. Soc. Clin. Pathologists; Outstanding Achievement award U. Minn.; N.D. Nat. Leadership award excellence. Mem. A.M.A. (pres. 1961, past trustee), N.D. Med. Assn. (pres. 1950-51), Coll. Am. Pathologists, Am. Soc. Clin. Pathologists, Sigma Xi, Alpha Omega Alpha, Phi Beta Pi. Presbyn. Rotarian. Home: Bismarck, N.D. Died Sept. 30, 1974; interred Sunset Meml. Park, Minneapolis, Minn.

LARSON, RALPH NORMAN, banker; b. Northampton, Mass., June 8, 1904; Ph.B., U. Chgo., 1925; m. Kay Meineke, 1944. With Chgo. Trust Co., 1926-30, Upper Av. Nat. Bank, Chgo., 1930-42, pres., dir., 1942; chmn., dir. Morris Plan Co. of Cal., 1947-71, hon. chmn., 1971-73; dir. Union Bank, Los Angeles, Credit Thrift Financial Corp., Evansville, Ind., Merit Life Ins. Co., Yosemite Ins. Co., Gt. Falls Ins. Co., San Francisco; Mem. exec. bd. Cal. Job Devel. Corp. Bd. dirs. San Francisco Bay Area Council, San Francisco chpt. A.R.C., Lesley Found.; bd. regents St. Mary's Coll.; trustee Nat. Found. Consumer Credit, Pacific Sch. Religion; citizens bd. U. Chgo.; trustee United Bay area Crusade. Served from lt. (s.g.) to comdr. USNR, 1942-47. Mem. Nat. Arbitration Assn., Am. Indsl. Bankers Assn. (hon. dir., past pres.), Am. Fedn. Musicians (hon.), Newcomen Soc. Conglist. Rotarian. Clubs: World Trade, Bohemian (San Francisco); California (Los Angeles). Home: Hillsborough, Cal., Died May 22, 1973.

LARSON, ROY FRANK, architect; b. Mpls., Mar. 31, 1893; s. Par Leander and Anna Amelia (Peterson) L.; B.Arch., U. Pa., 1923; D.F.A. (hon.), Moore Coll. Art, Phila.; m. Olive Hathaway Alden, Nov. 1, 1924; children—Peter Alden, David Hathaway, John Hyde. With archtl. firm Harbeson, Hough, Livinston & Larson (formerly Paul P. Cret, Architect), Phila., 1926-70, ret. sr. partner, now cons.; prin. works firm include pub., ednl., hosp., bank bldgs., city planning historic area Phila.; supervising architect Pa. State U., Jefferson U. Med. Coll. and Hosp.; cons. U.S. C.E., USAF, U.S. Navy. Past pres. Art Commn., Phila.; pres. Am. Swedish Hist. Found. and Mus.; v.p. Citizens Council on Planning; mem. archtl. panel Office Fgn. Bldgs., Dept. State, Gen. Service Adminstrn. Served as 1st lt. inf. Machine Gun Service, 1917-19. Recipient Medal Societé des Architectes Diplomés par le Gouvernement Français, 1922; Chgo. Archtl. Club traveling scholar, 1917; medal for distinguished achievement Art Alliance; decorated knight Royal Order Vasa (Sweden), 1962. Fellow A.I.A. (past chancellor coll. fellows); mem. Nat. Sculpture Soc., Pa. Assn. Architects, N.A.D., Independence Hall Assn. (v.p.), Sigma Xi, Tau Sigma Delta, Delta Upsilon. Clubs: Franklin Inn, Art Alliance, T-Square (Phila.); Century Assn. (N.Y.C.). Home: Radnor, Pa. Died June 30, 1973; interred West Laurel Hill.

LASSINGER, LARRY WAYNE, pediatrician; b. Saxonburg, Pa., Jan. 21, 1937; s. John William and Leona Lassinger; grad. Mass. Inst. Tech., 1958; M.D., U. Pitts., 1962; m. Rona Schondelmeyer, June 24, 1961; children—Brian, Kent, Kelly, Brett. Intern, Shadyside Hosp., Pitts., 1962-63; with Indian Health Service, USPHS, Santa Rosa, Ariz., 1963-65; resident in gen. practice USPHS Hosp., Norfolk, Va., 1965-66; resident in pediatrics Babies Hosp., Columbia-Presbyn. Med. Center, N.Y.C., 1966-68; chief of pediatrics USPHS Hosp., S.I., 1968-71; practice medicine, specializing in pediatrics, 1970-73; attending staff Bozeman (Mont.) Deaconess Hosp., 1971-73; cons. Bozeman chpt. Council Exception Learners. Faculty Mont. State U. Served to sr. surgeon USPHS, 1963-71. Diplomate Am. Bd. Pediatrics. Mem. A.M.A., Am. Acad. Allergy, Am. Acad. Pediatrics, Christian Med. Soc. (pres. U. Pitts. chpt. 1960-61), Mont. Med. Assn. (sec.-treas. Bozeman 1971-72). Home: Bozeman, Mont., Died Aug. 12, 1973; buried Sunset Hills Cemetery.

LATHAM, DANA, lawyer; b. Galesburg, Ill. July 7, 1898; s. Harry S. and Margaret (Dobyns) L.; A.B., Ohio Wesleyan U., 1920, LL.D., 1960; LL.B., Harvard, 1922; LL.D., Occidental Coll., Los Angeles, 1965; m. Olive Eames, June 16, 1923; children—Jeanne (Mrs. Richard Alden), Corlinne (Mrs. Kenneth W. Cooper), Polly (Mrs. Robert A. Barley). Admitted to Ill. bar, 1922, asso. Hopkins, Starr & Hopkins (now Hopkins, Sutter, Halls, DeWolfe & Owen), Chgo. and Washington, 1922-26; spl. atty. Bur. Internal Revenue, Washington and San Francisco, 1926-27; mem. firm Miller, Chevalier & Latham, 1927-29; v.p., dir. Pacific Finance Corp., 1929-34; partner Latham & Watkins, 1934-58, 61-74. Commr. of Internal Revenue, Washington, 1958-61; spl. adviser to under sec. state, 1954-55; dir., mem. exec. com. Seaboard Finance Co., 1961-69. Trustee Occidental Coll., Ohio Wesleyan U., John Tracy Clinic, Eisenhower Med. Center, Palm Desert, Cal. Mem. Am. (council sect. taxation), Internat., Los Angeles (past pres.) bar assns., Am. Law Inst., Los Angeles Traffic Assn. (past pres.), Harvard Law Sch. Assn., So. Cal. Bar (past pres.). Clubs: California, Los Angeles Country; Eldorado Country (Palm Desert, Cal.); Chevy Chase Country, Metropolitan (Washington); Newport Harbor Yacht (Newport Beach, Cal.). Contbr. articles law revs., jours. Home: Newport Beach, Cal. Died Feb. 6, 1974.

LATHROP, WALTER W., constrn. co. exec.; b. Toledo, Oct. 25, 1903; s. George and Caroline (Giesel) L.; student U. Pa., 1920-23; m. Cornelia Coley, Sept. 1, 1928; children—Cornelia (Mrs. Clinton A. Mauk), Walter W. With sales Stacy & Braum Investments, 1924-26, Felton United Co., 1926-28; organizer Lathrop Co., Toledo, 1928, chmn. bd., from 1968; dir. Toledo Trust Co., Service Products Bldg. Co. Bd. dirs. Boys' Club Toledo, Florence Crittenton Home, Lathrop Found. Mem. Toledo C. of C. (bd. dirs.). Rotarian. Clubs: Toledo Country, Toledo, Belmont Country (Toledo); Erie (Mich.) Shooting; Leland (Mich.) Country; Country of Fla. (Delray Beach). Home: Toledo O. Died Sept. 19, 1973; interred Woodlawn Cemetery, Toledo, O.

LATIMER, JOHN AUSTIN, lawyer, former govt. ofcl.; b. Greenville Co., S.C., Apr. 19, 1891; s. James Hewlett and Mary (Ramsay) L.; ed. Coll. of City of N.Y. and bus. coll., Greenville, S.C.; LL.B., Washington Coll. of Law, 1937; LL.M., 1940; m. Ruth Kennedy, Dec. 30, 1913; children—Agnes Louise (Mrs. Perry H. Taft), John Austin, James Kennedy, Ruth Marie, Elizabeth Ramsay. Sec. to L. W. & T. F. Parker of Parker Cotton Mills, Greenville, S.C., 1908-13; asst. to sec. of industrial dept. Internat. Com. of Y.M.C.A., N.Y. City, 1913-14; mem. firm W. H. Kennedy & Son, Williston, S.C., 1915-29; founder and pub. The Williston Way and 2 weekly country newspapers, 1921-36; sec. to Gov. John G. Richards, of S.C., and lt. col. on his staff, 1929-31; sec. to Senator James F. Byrnes, of S.C., 1931-32; sec. to Postmaster Gen. Farley, 1933-34, special asst., 1934-38, exec. asst., 1938-41; gen. practice of law, Washington, D.C., since 1941; counsel to U.S. Senate Com. on Post Office and Civil Service from 1949. Admitted to S.C. bar, U.S. Supreme Ct. bar. Mem. Bd. of Trade, Washington, D.C.; life mem. Alumni Assn. of Washington Coll. of Law. Democrat. Presbyterian. Mason. Home: Washington, D.C. Died Nov. 19, 1973.

LATIMER, SAMUEL LOWRY, JR., editor; b. Yorkville (now York), S.C., Nov. 14, 1891; s. Samuel Lowry and Sallie (Witherspoon) L.; student U. of S.C., 1908-11, 1912-13 and 1913-15, LL.B., 1915, Litt.D., 1948. With The State Co. from 1907, as office boy, worked part-time while attending univ., from graduation served successively as reporter, sports editor, state news editor, city editor and mng. eidtor to 1941, became editor, 1941, also publisher, 1943-60, later publisher emeritus, also director; director of S. & R. Building Company. Mem. bd. Columbia Art Museum; chairman Woodrow Wilson Centennial Celebration for South Carolina and Columbia. Chairman South Carolina Highway Safety Com., 1961. Grad. 1st O.T.C., Ft. Ogelthorpe, Ga., Aug. 1917, and served as 2d lt., 316th F.A., 81st Div., World War. Vice chmn. Columbia Housing Authority, 1934-57, chmn., from 1957; trustee U. S.C. Ednl. Foundation; mem. Nat. Commn. on Chronic Illness, chmn. editorial com. on report of The Long Term Patient; mem. Pulitzer Prize Jury (Journalism), 1949-59; mem. bd. Columbia Stage Soc.; pres. Columbia Stage Co.; mem. adv. bd. Presbyn. Coll. S.C.; mem. devel. bd. U. S.C.; counselor Erskine Coll.; past chmn. bd. Salvation Army, Columbia; trustee S.C. Crippled Children Soc. Civilian aide to sec. of Army for Third Army. Recipient Assn. U.S. Army nat. certificate, 1960; distinguished civilian service medal U.S. Army, 1963; Distinguished Alumni award U. S.C., 1964-65. Member of South Carolina Press Assn. (president 1941-42), Am. Soc. Newspaper Editors, Am. Legion (nat. exec. com. 1941-45, nat. vice comdr., 1945-46; nat. public relations commission; department commander for S.C. 1956), Nat. Assn. Nat. Vice Comdrs. of Am. Legion (president), Forty and Eight, Mil. Order World Wars (nat. gen. staff, 1947-48), Newcomen Soc. North America (past chmn. S.C.), Sigma Alpha Epsilon, Sigma Delta Chi, Blue Key. Democrat. Presbyn. Elk. Clubs: Springdale, Kiwanis, Columbia Drama, Forum, Forest Lake. Author: That's What Happened (play), 1940; An Editor's Visit to Germany; A History of The State (newspaper). Co-author inscriptions World War Meml. for S.C. Home: Columbia, S.C., Died Sept. 29, 1975.

LATTIN, LEROY EMORY, ret. mfg. co. exec.; b. Hartwick, N.Y., Aug. 21, 1896; s. Albert John and Flora Adelle (Phillips) L.; student Valparaiso (Ind.) U., 1915; m. Grace Fern Van Beek, July 27, 1917 (div. May 1952); children—Elaine Adelle (Mrs. Robert Cecil Hansen), Leonard Edgar, Robert Allen; m. 2d, Angeline Kaegel Kamp, Oct. 4, 1952; stepchildren—Leilani C., Kenneth A. Ledger clk. N.W. Bell Telephone Co., Omaha, 1920-27; engr., div. mgr. Ohio Bell Telephone Co., Cleve., 1927-35, div. mgr., Akron, 1935-39, staff, dept. head, 1939-45, v.p. 1945-48, also dir.; v.p. S.W. Bell Telephone Co., St. Louis, 1948-57; v.p., cons. to pres. Gen. Telephone Corp., N.Y.C., 1957; pres. Gen. Telephone of Cal., 1958-62, chmn. bd., 1962; pres. Universal Products Corp., San Fernando, Cal., 1960-73; dir. Packard-Bell, 1961-68; pres. Mut. 47, Rossmoor Leisure World, Laguna Hills, Cal. Art work exhibited Butler Art Tri-State shows, Akron Art Inst., Ohio Water Color Soc.; one-man show Noonan-Koclan Galleries, St. Louis. Pres., Midcontinent Devel. Council, Kansas City, Mo., 1957; pres., dir. Laymen's Movement, Wainwright House, Rye, N.Y., 1960-63, mem. bd. govs. Midwest Research Inst., Kansas City, Mo., 1960-67; chmn. 1963 Awards Jury to select Cal. Industrialist and Scientist of Year. Trustee Denison U., Granville, O.; mem. adv. council Grad. Sch. Bus. Administrn. U. So. Cal. Served as sgt. Mexican Expeditionary Forces, 1916-17; 2d lt., F.A., U.S. Army, 1917-19. Home: Laguna Hills Cal. Died Sept. 23, 1974; cremated.

LAUGEL, RAYMOND WILLIAM, fgn. service officer; b. Cleve., Nov. 12, 1922; s. Gerald Joseph and Florence Evangeline (Crowe) L.; B.A., Baldwin-Wallace Coll., 1947; M.A., U. Mich., 1949; m. Pilar Catinchi, June 14, 1969. Joined U.S. Fgn. Service, 1949; officer Am. embassy, Rome, Italy, 1949-54, Cairo, Egypt, 1955-56, Ankara, Turkey, 1956-57, New Delhi, India, 1957-60; chief fgn. operations (security) Dept. State, 1960-63; acting dep. asst. sec. state for security affairs, 1963-64; adviser U.S. Army Spl. Warfare Center, Ft. Bragg, N.C., 1964-65; assigned Nat. War Coll., 1965-66; fgn. service insp., 1966-69; dep. dir. Office Refugee and Migration Affairs, 1969-70, dir., 1971-73; counselor Am. embassy, Addis Ababa, Ethiopia, 1970-71. Bd. govs. Am. Community Sch., Addis Ababa, 1970-71; bd. govs., mem. exec. com. Ethiopian-Am. Inst., Addis Ababa, 1970-71. Served to lt. (j.g.) USNR, 1943-46. Recipient Superior Honor award Dept. State, 1964, Outstanding Civilian Service medal U.S. Army, 1966, Posthumous Presdl. certificate of appreciation, 1973. Home: Washington D.C. Died Oct. 14, 1973; interred Cleveland, O.

LAUGHLIN, HUGH C., lawyer; b. N.Y.C., June 10, 1904; s. Hugh C. and Adah Frances (Smith) L.; A.B., Ohio State U., 1924; LL.B., Harvard, 1927; m. Isabel Long, Dec. 21, 1928; children—Hugh Collins, John Long. Admitted to Ohio bar, 1927; mem. Williams, Eversman & Morgan, Toledo, 1927-32, partner, 1932-39; asso. Lazard Freres & Co., N.Y.C., 1946-49; sec., gen. counsel Anchor Hocking Glass Corp., Lancaster, O., 1939-43; v.p. Owens-Ill. Glass Co., Toledo, 1949-52, exec. v.p., 1952-71, now ret., still dir. Mem. nat. council, chmn. gen. div. laymen's work Episcopal Ch., 1961-73. Served to lt. col. AC, AUS, 1942-46. Mem. Ohio, Toledo bar assns., Chi Phi. Episcopalian. Clubs: Toledo; Metropolitan (N.Y.C.). Home: Maumee, O. Died July 15, 1973.

LAURIE, WILFRID RHODES, lawyer; b. Chatham, Ont., Can., Oct. 5, 1898; s. George E. and Annie (Rhodes) L.; J.D., U. Mich., 1922; m. Margaret Baird Thomas, Mar. 31, 1934. Admitted to Mich. bar, 1922; practiced in Detroit, 1922-25; house atty. Grinnell Bros. and Grinnell Realty Co., 1926-36, v.p., sec., 1933-36; Mich. mgr. charge property mgmt. HOLC, 1937-39; chief legal office Detroit ordnance dist. U.S. Army, 1943-63. Served with U.S. Army, World War I. Recipient Meritorious Civilian Service award War Dept., 1945; Exceptional Civilian Service and Ofcl. Commendation for exceptional performance duty, Sec. of Army, 1963. Mem. Fed. Bar Assn. (v.p. Detroit 1959), Land Contract Dealers Assn. Detroit (pres. 1935), First Protestant Soc. Detroit (trustee). Presbyn. Club: Exchange (pres. Detroit 1936). Home: Fort Lauderdale, Fla. Died Mar. 22, 1973.

LAURITZEN, IVAR, steamship co. exec.; b. Esbjerg, Denmark, Mar. 25, 1900; s. Ditiev and Maren (Breinholt) L.; student Coll. Commerce; m. Lilian Kirkebye; 1 son, Joint propr. J. Lauritzen Steamship Co., Copenhagen, Denmark, 1932-74; chmn. Esbjerg Reopeworks Ltd.; dir. Rederiet Ocean A/S, A/S D/S Vesterhavet, Copenhagen, Aalborg Shipyard, Scandinavian Canning Co., Esbjerg, Atlas Engring. Works, Baltica Ins. Co., Baltica Life Co. Bd. dirs. Baltic and Internat. Maritime Conf.; chmn. bd. Fano Nautical Sch. Jubilee Fund, Esbjerg Old Seamen's Fund; bd. dirs. J.-L. Fund, Copenhagen. Home: Copenhagen, Denmark. Died May 13, 1974.

LAVAKE, RAE THORNTON, physician; b. N.Y.C., Feb. 26, 1883; s. Charles Stebbins and Lilian Emma (Williams) LaV.; M.D., Columbia, 1910; m. Elizabeth Benita Conlin, June 1, 1914; 1 son, James Gifford. Intern, N.Y. Hosp., N.Y.C., 1909-11, St. Mary's Hosp. for Children, N.Y.C., 1911, Sloane Hosp. for Women, N.Y.C., 1911-12; pvt. practice medicine specializing in obstetrics and gynecology, Mpls.; chief of staff Abbott Hosp., 1932-39; co-founder Abbott Hosp., Mpls.; cons. obstetrics and gynecology Mpls. Gen. Hosp.; med. dir. Minn. Birth Control League, 1930-50. Served to maj., M.C., USA, World War I. Diplomate Am. Bd. Obstetrics and Gynecology. Fellow A.C.S.; mem. Am. Coll. Obstetricians and Gynecologists, Am. Assn. Obstetricians and Gynecologists, Am. Legion, Mayflower Soc. Episcopalian. Clubs: Minneapolis, 5:55, University (Mpls.). Home: Minneapolis, Minn. Died Mar. 4, 1975; buried Bloomington Cemetery, Bloomington, Minn.

LAWRENCE, CHARLES DRUMMOND, judge; b. North Yarmouth, Me., Aug. 5, 1878; s. James and Ellen Maria (Marston) L.; grad. North Yarmouth Acad., 1897, Shaw's Bus. Coll., Portland, Me., 1899; LL.B., N.Y. Law Sch., 1902; LL.M., N.Y. U., 1905, 46; m. Gertrude Borst, June 14, 1905; m. 2d Zdena Strecha, April 2, 1959. Clk., Bd. U.S. Gen. Appraisers (now U.S. Customs Ct.), 1899-1903; admitted to N.Y. bar, 1902; asst. counsel for Treasury dept. before Bd. U.S. Gen. Appraisers, 1904-07; asst. to solicitor of customs, 1907-11; spl. atty. customs div. U.S. Dept. Justice, 1911-25; asst. atty. gen. U.S., 1925-34; spl. asst. to atty. gen., 1934; judge U.S. Customs Ct., 1943-75, sr. judge, 1965-75. Mem. Met. Mus. of Art, Washington Sq. Assn.,

Greenwich Village Assn. Mem. Am., Customs bar assns., Assn. Bar City New York. Clubs: National Lawyers (Washington); Lawyers (N.Y.C.); N.Y. U. Faculty. Home: New York City, N.Y. Died Feb. 12, 1975.

LAWRENCE, E. GEORGE, educator; b. Terre Haute, Ind., Mar. 16, 1908; s. Ellsworth Lyman and Mary Catherine (Holmes) L.; student U. Detroit, 1926-28, U. Ind., 1928-30; Litt.D., Indiana Technical College, 1952; married Dorotha Louise Howe, June 25, 1930. Power plant engring. with Gen. Motors Corp., 1930-34; co-founder Lawrence Inst. Tech., Detroit, 1932, pres. and chmn. bd., 1934-64, pres. emeritus, 1964-74. Mem. Am. Soc. Engring. Edn., Engring. Soc. Detroit, Detroit Bd. Commerce, Gamma Eta Gamma. Presbyn. Kiwanian. Club: Venice Yacht. Patentee mech. device. Home: Venice, Fla., Died Aug. 9, 1974; interred Sarasota Meml. Park, Sarasota, Fla.

LAWRENCE, EDWIN WINSHIP, lawyer; b. Rutland, Vt., Mar. 27, 1881; s. George Edwin and Katherine C. (Phalen) L.; grad. high sch., Rutland, 1897; A.B., U. of Vt., 1901 (Phi Beta Kappa); m. Florence Roby, Oct. 10, 1904. Admitted to Vt. bar, 1902, and practiced at Rutland; gen. atty. Rutland R.R., from 1908; practiced with father and B. L. Stafford until former died, 1922; v.p. Killington Bank & Trust Co., from 1951; dir. Central Vt. Public Service Killington National Bank; pres. Palm-Techtler & Co., 1925-29. Assistant attorney Post Office Department, 1903, Department of Justice, U.S., 1905; spl. asst. to atty. gen. of U.S., 1908; mem. State Senate, Vt., 1923-25. Trustee U. of Vt., 1919-41. Pres. Vermont Bar Association, 1923; mem. Am. Bar Assn. Republican. Episcopalian. Home: Rutland, Vt.†

LAWRENCE, GEORGE ANDREW, beverage co. exec.; b. Hammondsport, N.Y., Nov. 10, 1914; s. Ray Gifford and Fredericka Christine (Michelfelder) L.; A.B., Cornell U., Ithaca, N.Y., 1936; m. Mary Lucy Keeler, Aug. 12, 1939; children—John Keeler, James Taylor. Trainee, Edward L. Bernays, pub. relations, N.Y.C., 1936-38; with Taylor Wine Co., Inc., Hammondsport, N.Y., 1938-75, sec.-treas., 1955-64, exec. v.p., 1962-64, pres. 1964-75, chmn. bd., chief exec. officer, 1975, also dir.; dir. Lincoln First Banks, Inc., Rochester, N.Y.; mem. N.Y. adv. bd. Liberty Mut. Ins. Co. Mem. Cornell U. Council; chmn. finance com., bd. dirs. Ira. Davenport Meml. Hosp., Bath, N.Y.; trustee Alfred (N.Y.) U., 1969-75. Mem. Finger Lakes Wine Growers Assn. (sec.-treas. 1947-75), A.I.M. (president's council 1965-75), Newcomen Soc., Nat. Planning Assn. (mem. nat. council 1972-75), Sigma Delta Chi, Kappa Delta Rho. Home: Hammondsport, N.Y., Died Aug. 28, 1975.

LAWRENCE, JOHN BENJAMIN, clergyman; b. Florence, Rankin County, Miss., July 10, 1873; s. Isaac Bass and Exer Elizah (Williamson) L.; A.B., Miss. Coll., Clinton, 1899, M.A., 1902; D.D., La. College, Alexandria, 1910; LL.D., Okla. Bapt. U., 1926; m. Helen Alford, Nov. 15, 1900 (deceased 1944); children—John Hewitt (dec.), Miriam Hoy, Katherine Alford, Elizabeth M., John Benjamin (dec.), Helen Rebecca; married 2d Miss Helen Huston, 1947. Ordained Bapt. ministry, 1900; pastor Greenwood, Miss., 1900-03, Humboldt, Tenn., 1903-07, 1st Ch., New Orleans, 1907-13, also editor Bapt. Chronicle; corr. sec. Bapt. State Conv. Bd. of Miss., 1913-21; supt. Bapt. Edn. Com. on Miss., 1913-21; pastor First Bapt. Ch., Shawnee, Okla., 1921-26. Pres. Okla. Bapt. U., 1922-26; gen. supt. of missions of Baptist Gen. Assn., Kansas City, Mo., 1926-29; exec. sec. and treas. Home Mission Bd. of Southern Baptist Convention, 1929-54, sec. emeritus, 1954; v.p. Southern Bapt. Conv., 1916-17; mem. Pub. Relations Com., hdqrs., Washington, D.C.; trustee State Industrial and Tr. Sch. of Miss., 1916-21; trustee Okla. Bapt. U. Democrat. Mason, K. of P., Odd Fellow, Shriner. Author: Power for Service, 1909; The Biology of the Cross, 1913; Church Organization and Methods (co-author), 1917; State Mission Manual for Mississippi, 1917; Paul's Bible School on Baptism; Outline Studies in the Book of Revelation, 1922; Outline Study of the Bible, 1925; Stewardship Applied in Church Finance, 1928; Missions in The Bible, 1931; The Bible, a Missionary Book, 1935; Taking Jesus Christ Seriously, 1935; Missions and The Divine Plan for Support, 1936; Preaching The Doctrine of Grace (with others), 1939; Stewardship Applied in Missions, 1940; Home Missions in the New World, 1943; The Peril of Bread, 1943; The Religion of Power, 1944; The Holy Spirit in Missions, 1946; Cooperative Southern Baptists, 1948; Kindling for Revival Fires, 1950; The Holy Spirit in Evangelism; Me and My Church, 1954; History of the Home Mission Board of the Southern Baptist Convention, 1956; A New Heaven and a New Earth, 1960. Home: Atlanta, Ga.†

LAWRENCE, JOHN MARSHALL, lawyer; b. Oklahoma City, Nov. 6, 1895; s. John Thomas and Jane (Sawyers) L.; grad. high sch., Oklahoma City; m. Ernestine Grace Bucklin, Nov. 1, 1919; children—Mary Violet (Mrs. William Lee Stubbs), John Marshall Lawrence (killed in action), Donna Jane (Mrs. Rex D. Duhon). Admitted to Okla. bar, 1927, practiced in Oklahoma City; asst. city atty., Oklahoma City, 1942-46. Served with USN, 1917-18. K.P. (supreme tribune 1954-72), Knight of Khorassan (imperial prince 1953-55). Home: Oklahoma City, Okla. Died July 19, 1972.

LAWRENCE, JOHN SILSBEE, trustee; b. Nahant, Mass., Sept. 6, 1878; s. Amory Appleton and Emily Fairfax (Silsbee) L.; A.B., Harvard, 1901; m. Emma Atherton, Apr. 29, 1907 (died Oct. 23, 1937); children—Eloise (Mrs. Harrison Gardner), Amory A., Isabel (Mrs. James Parker); m. 2d, Héléne P. Kelloy, Nov. 11, 1940. Dir. Second Nat. Bank of Boston, Mass. Hosp. Life Ins. Co. Home: Topsfield, Mass.†

LAWRENCE, RAY ELLSWORTH, civil engr.; b. Neodesha, Kan., Jan. 9, 1903; s. Franklin M. and Bessie (Bussert) L.; B.S., U. Kan., 1925, postgrad. san. engring., 1928; spl. course USPHS, Cin., 1931; m. Catherine Helia Crissman, Dec. 20, 1926; children—Ray Crissman, Mary Catherine Engle. Jr. engr. Black & Veatch, Kansas City, Mo., 1925-26, prin. engr., 1937-56, partner, 1956-70; engr. Kan. Bd. Health, 1926-33, acting chief engr., 1933; civil engring. staff U. Kan., 1926-33; engr. examiner to dir. Kan. PWA, 1933-37; engring. water supply improvements, sewers and sewage treatment facilities, Wichita, Kan.; series of projects for Dept. Def., AEC, also sewers and sewage treatment facilities for Kansas City, St. Joseph, Mo., St. Louis Met. Sewer Dist., Rochester, N.Y. Vice pres. Kansas City area council Boy Scouts Am. Served to col. C.E., AUS, World War II; chief water supply and sewage sect., engring. div. Office Chief Engrs., OQMG, 1941-44; logistical planning, restoration utilities services France and Germany, 1944-45. Decorated Legion of Merit. Registered profl. engr., Ill., Kan., Mo., Neb., N.M., N.J., N.Y. Mem. Am. Soc. C.E. (past chmn. san engring. div.), Am. Inst. Cons. Engrs., Am. Acad. Enviromental Engrs., Am. Water Works Assn. (mem. com. san. engring. environment NRC Adv. Com. Med. Sci.), Water Pollution Control Fedn. (pres. 1961), Nat. Soc. Profl. Engrs., Tau Beta Pi, Sigma Tau, Theta Tau. Methodist (past chmn. ofcl. bd.). Club: Kansas City. Author tech. papers. Home: Shawnee Mission, Kan. Died Aug. 13, 1970.

LAWSON, DAVID A., lawyer; b. Vancouver, B.C., Can., July 10, 1923; B.Comm., U. B.C., 1944; postgrad. Vancouver Law Sch. Admitted to B.C. bar, 1947; partner Lawson, Lundell, Lawson & McIntosh, Vancouver. Died Apr. 13, 1975.

LAWSON, JOSEPH WARREN, r.r. ofcl.; b. Phila., Feb. 13, 1900; s. Joseph Jones and Emily (Weaver) L.; student U. Pa.; m. Thelma Brooks, Aug. 8, 1931; 1 dau., Barbara A. Successively asst. agt. Reading Co., Corsons, Pa., freight traffic rep., Phila., traveling freight agt., Phila., traveling freight agt., Rochester, N.Y., city freight agt., Reading, Pa., indsl. agt., Phila., 1917-39, freight traffic mgr., 1945-51, gen. freight traffic mgr., 1951-58, v.p. freight traffic, 1958-60, director of market research, 1960-74; general freight and passenger agent Pennsylvania-Reading Seashore Lines, 1939-45; dir. East Pa. R.R. Co., Phila. Perishable Products Terminal, Reading & Pottsville Telegraph Co., Port Reading R.R., Reading Transportation Co., Washington & Franklin Ry., Wilmington & Northern R.R. Served with USMC, 1918-19. Mem. Am. Soc. Traffic and Transportation. Clubs: Union League, University, Traffic (Phila.); Traffic (N.Y.C.). Home: Haddonfield, N.J., Died Feb. 17, 1974; buried Harleigh Cemetery, Camden, N.J.

LAWSON, WALTER CARSON, mining engr.; b. Whittaker, Mich., Jan. 27, 1901; s. John and Mary Jane (Colf) L.; B.S., Mich. Coll. Mines, 1923, E.M., 1923, D. Engring., 1961; m. Alice Celia Trim, Apr. 20, 1923; children—Thomas A., Philip W. Instr. engring. U. Minn., 1924-25; various positions engring., prodn., mgmt. Phelps Dodge Corp., 1926-59, gen. mgr., 1955-68, v.p., dir., 1958-68; pres., dir. Tucson, Cornelia & Gila Bend R.R. Co., Apache Power Co., Valley Nat. Bank of Ariz. Mem. Am. Inst. Mining, Metall. and Petroleum Engrs. (dir. Ariz.), Am. Mining Congress (dir. Ariz, Williams Lawrence Saunders trophy for achievement in mining 1964); Mining and Metall. Soc. Am., Tau Beta Pi. Home: Phoenix, Ariz. Died Mar. 18, 1975.

LAWTON, FREDERICK JOSEPH, govt. ofcl.; b. Washington, D.C., Nov. 11, 1900; s. Richard and Brigid (O'Connell) L.; A.B., Georgetown U., Washington, 1920, LL.B., 1934; m. Cecilia Alice Walsh, June 27, 1931 (dec.); children—Richard, Mary, Kathleen. Began fed. govt. service with Treas. Dept., 1921; exec. asst., acting asst. dir., Bur. of the Budget, 1935; served as adminsistrative asst. to the Pres., 1948; appointed asst. dir. Bur. of Budget, 1949, dir. 1950-53, member Civil Service Commission, from 1953; cons. and adviser to Senate's Select Com. on Govt. Orgn., 1937-39; mem. com. on pub. works of the Nat. Resources Planning Bd., 1938-40; adviser to the fiscal, budgeting and accounting project of Commn. on Orgn. Exec. Branch of the Govt., 1948. Recipient 1961 President's award, Distinguished Fed. Civilian Ser. Catholic. Home: Kensington, Md., Died Nov. 16, 1975; buried Gate of Heaven Cemetery, Wheaton, Md.

LAY, CHESTER FREDERIC, educator, mgmt. cons., accountant, publisher; b. Pope County, Ill., Feb. 8, 1895; s. Joseph Lay and Rilda (Chester) L.; B.Ed., Ill. State U., 1917; M.A., U. Chgo., 1923, Ph.D., 1931; m. Harriet Lewis, Sept. 29, 1917; children—Lewis Chester, Coy Lafayette, Lois Jo Harriet Lackore. Instr. grad. sch. social service, also grad. sch. commerce and adminstrn. U. Chgo., 1919-22, prof., 1929-31; head dept. commerce Robert Coll., Istanbul, Turkey, 1922-23; asst. prof. econs. U. Ariz., 1923-24; head div. accounting and mgmt. Ore. State U., 1924-25; prof. mgmt. and accounting U. Tex., 1925-44; pres. So. Ill. U., 1944-48; prof. chmn., dir. grad. studies, mgmt. dept. So. Methodist U., Dallas, 1948-59; sr. prof. mgmt., accounting, grad. studies bus. adminstrn. Trinity U., San Antonio, 1959-63; prof. econs. and bus. adminstrn. Fla. So. Coll., 1963-66, chmn., 1965-66. Vice pres., dir. OBGYN Letters, Inc.; bus. editor Collected Letters Internat. Soc. Obstetricians and Gynecologists. Mem. adv. council Ill. Dept. Pub. Health; mem. Govs. Com. on Edn.; mem. Crab Orchard Lake Com., 1946-48; commr. Fla.-Polk Hist. Commn. C.P.A. Tex., Fla. Served with USN, 1918. C.P.A., Fla. Fellow Acad. Mgmt.; mem. Fla. Acad. Sci., Am., So. (chmn. mgmt. div.) econ. assns., Am. Accounting Assn., Am. Assn. U. Profs., Soc. Advancement Mgmt., S.W., So. mgmt. assns. Nat. Assn. Accountants, Financial Execs. Inst., Newcomen Soc. Eng., Southwestern Social Sci. Assn. (gen. program chmn.), Tex. Soc. C.P.A.'s. Am., Fla. insts. C.P.A.'s. Tenn., N.C., Fla., Ky., S.C., Tex., Mo., Conn., New Eng., Va. hist. socs., Am.-Assn. State and Local History, Beta Alpha Psi, Alpha Kappa Psi, Kappa Phi Kappa, Tau Kappa Epsilon. Beta Gamma Sigma, Sigma Delta Pi, Sigma Iota Epsilon (co-founder, pres.). Baptist. Rotarian. Joint author: An Executive Operations Technique, Cost Accounting, Budgeting and Control, 1955; American College Dictionary, 1964, 69; Random House Unabridged Dictionary, 1966; author: Historical Florida Rotary Lakeland, 1968. Contbr. articles to profl. jours. Address: Lakeland, Fla. Died Oct. 2, 1973.

LAYBOURNE, LAWRENCE EUGENE, journalist; b. Springfield, O., Mar. 15, 1913; s. Lawrence Everett and Jean (Broadstone) L.; A.B., Ohio State U., 1934; m. Dorothy Nesbit, May 30, 1936; children—Lucinda, Lawrence Christopher Nesbit, Anne Nesbit. News staff St. Louis Post-Dispatch, 1934-44; staff Time Inc., 1944-76, news bur. chief, Ottawa, Can., 1944-46, dep. bur. chief, Washington, 1946-49, chief Life Mag. news bur., 1949-50, chief corr. U.S.-Canadian News Service, 1950-57; mng. dir. Time Internat. of Can., Ltd., 1957-62; asst. pub. Time mag., 1962-67, Asia mng. dir., 1967-69; internat. editor Time-Life Books, 1969-70, v.p., dir. corporate affairs, Washington, 1970-76. Chmn. bd. trustees Washington Journalism Center. Mem. Council Fgn. Relations, Ohio State U. Assn. (pres. 1965-67), Phi Beta Kappa, Beta Theta Pi. Episcopalian. Home: Washington, D.C., Died Feb. 12, 1976; buried Ferncliffe Cemetery, Springfield, O.

LAYDEN, ELMER FRANCIS, football commr.; b. Davenport, Ia., May 4, 1903; s. Thomas J. and Rose (Bartemeyer) L.; LL.B., U. of Notre Dame, 1925; m. Edythe Davis, Oct. 25, 1926 (dec.); children—Joan Frances, Elmer Francis, Michael Thomas, Patrick Davis. Athletic dir. and football coach, Columbia Coll., Dubuque, Ia., 1925-27; admitted to Ia. bar, 1926, and practiced in Dubuque, 1926-27; dir. of athletics and head football coach, Duquesne U., Pittsburgh, 1927-33; dir. of athletics and head football coach, U. of Notre Dame, 1934-41; commr. of professional football, Nat. Football League, 1941-46. Mem. Am. Assn. Football Coaches (v.p. 1939). Roman Catholic. K.C., Elk. Clubs: Rotary, Country. Contbr. to newspapers and jours. Home: Evanston, Ill. Died June 30, 1973.

LAYTON, OLIVIA HIGGINS, (Mrs. Roy F. Layton), scout exec.; b. Buffalo, May 1, 1897; d. William J. and Gertrude (Cameron) Higgins; B.S., Columbia, 1919; m. Roy F. Layton, Oct. 15, 1927. Active Girl Scouts from 1939, commr. Millburn (N.J.) Twp. council, 1941-43, treas., 1943-45, chmn. membership-nominating com., 1945-47, mem. nat. personnel com., 1943-47, chmn. personnel dept. com., 1947-51, nat. president, 1951-57, member national board of directors, 1948-75, mem. Western Hemisphere Com. Girl Guides, 1957-75. Vice pres., chmn. Nursing Neighborhood House, Millburn, 1944-48; chmn. Red Cross Canteen, 1943-45. Home: Arlington, Va., Died Oct. 8, 1975.

LAZARO, HIPOLITO, tenor; b. Barcelona, Spain, 1889. Sang in Spain, Austria, Italy, S. America, Cuba and Mexico; came to U.S., 1918, and appeared in Denver, Colorado Springs, Colo., Wichita, Kan., at the Maine Festival and at cities of the East and Middle West; joined Metropolitan Opera Co.; sang as Faust, as Danielo in "La Reine Fiamette," in Rigoletto, I Puritani, etc. Address: Madrid, Spain., Died May 14, 1974.

LAZAROW, ARNOLD, educator; b. Detroit, Aug. 3, 1916; s. George and Rose (Brown) L.; B.S., U. Chgo., 1937, M.D., 1941, Ph.D., 1941; m. Jane Klein, Dec. 15, 1940; children—Paul B., Normand H. Teaching asst. anatomy U. Chgo., 1940-41; intern Woodlawn Hosp., Chgo., 1942; research asso. U. So. Cal., 1943; sr. instr. anatomy Case-Western U., 1943-46, asst. prof., 1946-48, asso. prof., 1948-54; prof., head dept. anatomy U. Minn., 1954-75; spl. cons. NIH, USPHS, 1957-61, Nat. Adv. Council Arthritis and Metabolic Diseases, 1961-65, Nat. Library Medicine, 1965-70; mem. COSATI Panel 6, Office of Sci. and Tech., White House, 1967-69.

Participant Exptl. Diabetes Symposium, Leiden, Holland, 1952; mem. adv. com. on research pathogenesis of cancer Am. Cancer Soc., 1956-59. Trustee Minn. Med. Found., 1957-64, pres., 1960-62; trustee Marine Biol. Lab. Recipient Joseph A. Capps prize in medicine, 1942. Fellow N.Y. Diabetes Assn. (hon.); mem. Am. (council 1956-62, Banting medal 1973), Twin City (pres. 1955-56) diabetes assns., Histochem. Soc. (council 1952-56, pres. 1965-66), Cleve. Diabetes Soc. (trustee 1953-54), Am. Assn. Anatomist (mem. exec. com. 1964-68), A.A.A.S., Am. Chem. Soc., Internat. Soc. Cell Biology, Soc. Exptl. Biology and Medicine, Phi Beta Kappa, Sigma Xi, Alpha Omega Alpha, Omicron Kappa Upsilon. Editor; Diabetes Literature Index, 1965-75. Co-editor: Gluthathione Symposium. Adv. editor Jour. Nat. Cancer Inst., 1950-52; mem. editorial bd. Diabetes, 1952-58. Contbr. articles profl. jours. Home: St. Paul, Minn. Died June 25, 1975; interred St. Paul, Minn.

LAZARUS, FRED, JR., mcht.; b. Columbus, O., Oct. 29, 1884; s. Fred and Rose (Eichberg) L.; ed. Columbus pub. schs.; LL.D., Ohio State U., 1951; D.C.S. (hon.), U. Cin., 1956; H.H.D., Wilberforce U., 1969; m. Meta Marx, Feb. 22, 1911 (dec. 1931); children—Fred III, Ralph, Maurice, Ann (Mrs. Stuart Schloss); m. 2d, Celia Kahn Rosenthal, Sept. 17, 1935. With F. & R. Lazarus & Co., 1903, pres., chief exec. officer, 1945-57, chmn. bd., chief exec. officer parent co. Federated Dept. Stores, Inc., 1957-67, chmn. exec. and finance com., 1967-71, chmn. exec. com., 1971-73; hon. dir. Asso. Mdsg. Corp. Hon. mem. Bus. Council, Dept. Commerce; hon. mem. research and policy com., trustee Com. Econ. Devel., N.Y.C.; mem. exec. com. Ohio Citizens Hwy. Com.; mem. nat. adv. policy com. United Shareholders Am.; mem. Commn. Money and Credit, 1958-61; mem. Pres.'s Com. Govt. Contracts, 1953-61; mem. Pres.'s Com. Equal Employment Opportunity, 1961; mem. exec. com. Ohio Research and Devel. Com., 1962-65. Hon. chmn. bd. Bellefaire Home Children, Cleve.; hon. bd. govs. Hebrew Union Coll., Cin.; hon. trustee Eisenhower Exchange Fellowships; bd. govs. A.R.C., 1953-59; hon. v.p., mem. exec. com. Am. Jewish Com. Recipient 7th ann. Tobe award for distinguished contbr. to Am. retailing, 1949; Gold award Nat. Conf. Christians and Jews, 1951; Human Rights award Joint Def. Appeal, 1955; Gold Medal award Nat. Retail Mchts. Assn., 1959; Distinguished Service award Ohio State Council Retail Merchants, 1961. Mem. Ohio Council Retail Merchants (organizer, past pres.), American Jewish Com. (hon. v.p.). Clubs: Fifth Ave. (N.Y.C.); Losantiville Country, Bankers, Queen City, Commercial, Cincinnati (Cin.). Home: Cincinnati, O. Died May 27, 1973.

LEACH, JOHN ENFIELD, lawyer; b. Jamestown, N.Y., July 25, 1907; s. John Buel and Catherine (Davies) L.; B.A., Alfred U., 1929; LL.B. (J.D.), U. Buffalo, 1932; m. Elizabeth Dayton Smith, Nov. 23, 1935; children—Sara Catherine (Mrs. Michael F. Colligan), John Enfield. Admitted to N.Y. bar, 1933; asso. firm Rann, Vaughan, Brown & Sturtevant, Buffalo, 1933-42; spl. agt. FBI, 1942-45; asso. firm Brown, Kelly, Turner, Hassett & Leach, and predecessors, Buffalo, 1945-74, partner, 1950-74. Fellow Am. Coll. Trial Lawyers; mem. Am., N.Y. bar assns., Bar Assn. Erie County (pres. 1950). Mason. Home: Orchard Park, N.Y. Died July 10, 1974.

LEACH, MARGARET KERNOCHAN (MRS. RALPH PULITZER), author; b. Newburgh, N.Y., Nov. 7, 1893; d. William Kernochan and Rebecca (Taggart) Leech; B.A., Vassar Coll., 1915; m. Ralph Pulitzer, Aug. 1, 1928 (dec. June 1939). Author: The Back of the Book, 1924; Tin Wedding, 1926; (with Heywood Broun) Anthony Comstock, 1927; The Feathered Nest, 1928; Reveille in Washington (Pulitzer prize in history), 1941; In The Days of McKinley, 1959 (1960 Bancroft prize, 1960 Pulitzer History prize); also short stories in mags. Home: New York City, N.Y. Died Feb. 24, 1974.

LEADBETTER, WYLAND F., surgeon; b. Livermore Falls, Me., Jan. 9, 1907; s. Charles K. and Maude E. (Randall) L.; B.S., Bates Coll, 1928; M.D., Johns Hopkins, 1932; m. Lois A. Billings, June 13, 1934; children—Emily, Charles, Wyland. Intern surgery Johns Hopkins Hosp., 1932-33, asst. pathology, 1933-34, asst. resident urology, 1934-36, resident urology, 1937-38; resident urology Ancker Hosp., St. Paul, 1936-37; urologist Lahey Clinic, Boston, 1938-39; pvt. practice urology, Boston, 1939-42, 45; cons. urologist VA Hosp., Boston; vis. urologist Mass. Gen. Hosp., Boston; cons. urologist Monadnock Community Hosp., Peterboro, N.H., New Eng. Deaconess Hosp., Boston Dispensary, N.E. Center Hosp., Boston; former prof. urology Tufts U. Med. Sch.; now clin. prof. surgery Harvard Med. Sch. Trustee Bates Coll. Served from maj. to lt. col. M.C., AUS, 1942-45. Diplomate Am. Bd. Urology. Fellow A.C.S., Am. Acad. Arts and Scis.; mem. A.M.A., Am. Assn. Genito-Urinary Surgeons, Internat. Soc. Urology, Am. Urol. Assn., N.E. Surg. Soc., Clin. Soc. Genito-Urinary Surgeons, Phi Beta Kappa, Alpha Omega Alpha. Home: Millinocket Me. Died Aug. 28, 1974; buried Mount Hope Cemetery, Auburn, Me.

LEAKE, JAMES MILLER, univ. prof.; b. Ashland, Hanover County, Va., Oct. 1, 1879; s. John Marion and Lizzie (Miller) L.; A.B., Randolph-Macon Coll., Va., 1902; Ph.D., Johns Hopkins, 1914; LL.D. (hon.), Randolph-Macon Coll., 1951; m. Elizabeth Ellicott Thruston, Dec. 23, 1914. Instr. French, Randolph-Macon Coll., 1901-03; ins. and newspaper work, 1903-09; prin. Ashland (Va.) High Sch., 1909-11; fellow in history, Johns Hopkins, 1913-14; asso. in history, Bryn Mawr Coll., 1914-17; prof. and head dept. history and economics, Allegheny Coll., 1917-19; prof. and head dept. history and polit. sci., U. of Fla., 1919-50, emertius; member Gainesville City Charter Commn., 1927. Awarded Henrico medallion by Johns Hopkins U., 1918, for work in Colonial history. Mem. Am. Hist. Assn., Am. Polit. Science Assn., Am. Econ. Assn., Am. Soc. Internat. Law, Am. Acad. Polit. and Social Science, Fla. Hist. Soc. (dir.), Va. Hist. Soc., Southern Hist. Soc., Southern Polit. Science Assn., Florida Acad. of Science, Sons of the Revolution in the State of Va. (life mem.), Sons of the Am. Revolution, Kappa Sigma, Sigma Upsilon, Phi Beta Kappa, Phi Kappa Phi, Pi Gamma Mu, Phi Alpha Theta, Blue Key. Democrat. Presbyterian. Mason (K.T.). Government appeal agent for the Selective Service System, 1940-45. Clubs: Kiwanis (past pres.), Gainesville Golf and Country. Author: (thesis) The Virginia Committee System and the American Revolution, 1917; History of Florida; mag. articles, book reviews, etc. Contbr. to Ency. Britannica, also Ency. Britannica Yearbooks. Home: Gainesville, Fla.†

LEAMAN, WILLIAM GILMORE, JR., physician; b. Phila., Sept. 3, 1898; s. William Gilmore and Eleanor (Pelly) L.; M.D., U. Pa., 1922; m. Eleanor May Lowe, Nov. 6, 1948; 1 dau., Nancy (Mrs. William A. Tucker). Intern. U. Pa. Hosp., 1922-24, resident in pathology, 1924-25; postgrad. studies in internal medicine Harvard, 1929; vis. physician Blockley div. Phila. Gen. Hosp., 1941-63; cardiologist Women's Med. Coll. Hosp., 1932-63; cons. in cardiology VA Hosp., Misericordia Hosp., Northestern Hosp., Nazareth Hosp. (all Phila.); prof., chmn. dept. medicine Women's Med. Coll., 1942-63, prof. medicine emeritus, 1963-73. Diplomate Am. Bd. Internal Medicine. Fellow A.C.P. (mem. com. course dirs.); mem. A.M.A., Am. Heart Assn. (dir. 1954-55, Distinguished Achievement award 1960, Distinguished Service award, 1966), Am. Assn. History of Medicine (treas. 1944-45), Am. Soc. Internal Medicine, A.A.U.P. Author: Management of the Cardiac Patient, 1940. Contbr. articles to med. jours. Home: Unionville, Pa. Died Apr. 11, 1973; buried Arlington Cemetery, Drexel Hill, Pa.

LEARY, JOHN DIGNEY, corp. ofcl.; b. White Plains, N.Y., July 6, 1911; s. Timothy A. and Sarah (Digney) L.; B.A., Yale, 1933, LL.B., 1936. Admitted to N.Y. bar, 1936; with firm Larkin Rathbone & Perry (now Kelley, Drye, Warren, Clark, Carr & Ellis), N.Y.C., 1936-41; dir. labor relations Chrysler Corp., 1951-57, dir. indsl. relations, 1957, v.p. personnel, 1958-63, v.p. adminstrn., 1963-74, dir., 1959-74. Bd. dirs. United Found. Detroit. Clubs: Economic, University (Detroit); Yale (N.Y.C.); Essex Golf and Country (Windsor, Ont.). Home: Detroit, Mich. Died Apr. 13, 1974.

LEAVELL, JAMES READER, banker; b. Montgomery City, Mo., Oct. 12, 1884; s. James A. and America (Davis) L.; ed. Westminster Coll., Fulton, Mo., and Randolph-Macon College, Ashland, Va.; m. Lorna Doone Carr, May 19, 1917. Began with Mechanics Am. Nat. Bank, St. Louis, 1905, asst. cashier, 1913-19; v.p. First Nat. Bank, St. Louis, 1919-20; became v.p. Continental & Commerical Nat. Bank of Chicago, 1920; v.p. Continental Nat. Bank and Trust Co., Dec. 1927; exec. v.p. Continental Nat. Co., 1928, exec. v.p. Continental Ill. Co., 1929; asst. to chmn. bd. Continental Ill. Bank and Trust Co., Jan. 1930, pres. Continental Ill. Bank and Trust Co. (now Continental Ill. Nat. Bank and Trust Co.), 1930-48, dir., 1931-50, ret.; dir. Gulf Life Ins. Co., Jacksonville, Fla., Ingalls Shipbldg. Corp., Pascagoula, Miss., Armour & Co., I.C.R.R. Trustee Piney Woods (Miss.) Country Life Sch., Northwestern Univ.; mem. bd. govs. U. Miss. Mem. Phi Delta Theta. Democrat. Methodist. Clubs: Chicago, Commercial; Red Creek Hunting and Fishing (Ocean Springs, Miss.). Home: Ocean Springs, Miss. Died June 1974.

LEAVENS, ROBERT FRENCH, clergyman; b. Arlington, Mass., Dec. 20, 1878; s. Albert and Emily (French) L.; grad. Boston Latin Sch., 1897; A.B., Dartmouth, 1901; S.T.B., Harvard Div. Sch., 1906; grad. study U. of Calif.; L.H.D., Mills Coll., 1937; m. Anna Whitney Cushing, Feb. 20, 1912; 1 dau., Eleanor (Mrs. David P. Smith). Master Holderness School, Plymouth, N.H., 1901-03; ordained ministry Unitarian Church, 1907; asst. minister Arlington Street Ch., Boston, Mass., 1906-08; minister First Parish Ch., Fitchburg, 1908-16; First Unitarian Ch. Omaha, Nebraska, 1916-21, First Unitarian Church, Berkeley, Calif., 1922-25, Minister Emeritus, 1947; lecturer in philosophy, Williams Inst., Berkeley, Calif., 1926-31; lecturer in religion, Mills College, Oakland, Calif., 1926-28; chaplain Mills Coll., 1932-37. Pres. Fitchburg Federation of Chs., 1915; pres. Berkeley Community Chest, 1925. Mem. Dartmouth College Alumni Council, 1918-21; member of the Fellowship of Reconciliation, War Registers League, Phi Beta Kappa. Chairman Northern California Service Board for Conscientious Objectives, 1940-46. Compiler: Great Companions, 1927. Author: Let Us Pray 1939. Home: Berkeley, Cal.†

LE BOEUF, RANDALL JAMES, JR., lawyer; b. Albany, N.Y., July 22, 1897; s. Randall James and Katharine (Washburn) LeB.; LL.B., Cornell U., 1920; m. Harriet F. Ross, June 11, 1921; children—Joan Ross, Elizabeth, Suzanne. Admitted to N.Y. bar, 1921; with Randall J. LeBoeuf, 1920-25; asst. atty. gen. State N.Y., 1925-27, spl. counsel, 1927, 1928, commr. census investigation, 1927-28; founder, counsel to LeBoeuf, Lamb, Leiby & MacRae. Am. Bar Assn. rep. on panel to pass on fed. trial examiners. Trustee Village Old Westbury. Served from pvt. to 2d lt. U.S. Army, World War I. Recipient Medal for Merit. Fellow Am. Bar Found.; mem. Am., N.Y. State bar assns., N.Y. County Lawyers Assn., Assn. Bar City N.Y., Fed. Power Bar Assn., Cornell Law Assn. (council), Am. Legion, Delta Chi, Sigma Delta Chi. Republican. Episcopalian. Clubs: Pilgrims, Piping Rock Country, University, India House, Down Town Association (N.Y.C.); Fort Orange (Albany); Grolier. Contbr. articles to law, pub. utility, hist. jours. Home: Old Westbury, N.Y. Died Aug. 16, 1975; interred Albany Rural Cemetery, N.Y.

LECKWIJCK, WILLIAM PETER EDWARD VAN, geologist; b. Antwerp, Belgium, Nov. 16, 1902; s. Edward Joseph and Rolanda (Luneman) L.; Civil Mining Engr., U. Liege, 1926; D.Sc., U. Witwatersrand (S. Africa), U. Southampton (Eng.). Field geologist Ougree-Marihaye Co. and affiliates, Morocco, Tunisia, Greece, Bulgaria, Finland, Italy, France, Luxembourg, Belgium, 1930-55, Tunisian Govt., 1938-40, Geol. Survey Morocco, 1950-52; dir. Belgian Nat. Centre for Geology Coal-Bearing Strata, 1946-67; prof. U. Louvain (Belgium), 1964-75. Leader gen. geol. execursions through Morocco, 19th Internat. Geol. Congress, 1952; pres. Internat. Subcommn. on Carboniferous Stratigraphy, 1954-65; v.p. Internat. Commn. on Stratigraphy, 1956-66; mem. council Permanent Com. Internat. Carboniferous Congresses, 1961-67; pres. Belgian Nat. Com. for Geol. Scis., 1968-75; mem. Geol. Council Belgium, 1961-75. Decorated officer Order of Crown, Order of Leopold, Commemorative medal War, Resistance medal, officer Wissam Alawait Order (Morocco). Recipient various medals Royal Acad. Belgium, Van Watershoot van der Gracht medal Royal Geol. and Mining Soc. Netherlands, 1964, Leopold von Buch plaque German Geol. Soc., 1968, Centenary plaque Hungarian Geol. Inst., 1969. Mem. Internat. Assn. (sec.-gen. 1964-70), Geol. Soc. London (hon. fgn.), Royal Flemish Acad. Belgium (dir. sci. class 1970), France (hon.), Netherlands geol. socs., past pres. 3 geol. socs. Belgium, Acad. Sci. Lorraine. Research includes detailed stratigraphy, palaeontology, sedimentology of Namurian in Belgium and other regions. Home: Antwerp, Belgium. Died June 19, 1975.

LEE, ALEXANDER EDMUND, physician, surgeon; b. Honolulu, Nov. 16, 1913; s. Charles Y. and Ivy A. (Awa) L.; A.B., U. So. Cal., 1936; student Marquette U. Sch. Medicine, 1937-39; M.D., Kan. U., 1942; m. Vivia Balfour Chang, Nov. 9, 1946; children—Terrence Irving, Debra Jean. Intern, St. Francis Hosp., N.Y.C., 1942, resident surgery, 1943-45; chief resident St. Francis Hosp., Honolulu, 1948-74, pres. dept. gen. practice, 1964-66. Mem. A.M.A., Hawaii Med. Assn., Honolulu Med. Soc., Pan Pacific Surg. Soc., Hawaiian Acad. Sci., Honolulu Surg. Soc., Am. Geriatrics Soc. Mason (K.T., Shriner). Home: Honolulu, Hawaii. Died Aug. 5, 1974; interred Diamond Head Meml. Park.

LEE, ALONZO HESTER, investment banker; b. Camp Hill, Ala., Sept. 23, 1903; s. Alonzo Braxton and Nina (Hester) L.; B.S., U. Ala., 1926; m. Allie Meagher, June 7, 1930; children—Alonzo Hester, Mary Nina (Mrs. B. Sheldon Marriott). With Ward Sterne & Co. (name changed to Sterne, Agee & Leach, 1944), Birmingham, 1926-74, successively clk., salesman trader, 1926-63, partner, 1944-74, sr. v.p., 1963-66, pres., 1966-68, chmn., 1968-74. Allied mem. N.Y. Stock Exchange; asso. mem. Am. Stock Exchange. Mem. Ala. Securities Dealers Assn., Nat. Secutiry Traders Assn., Ala., Birmingham hist. assns., Birmingham C. of C., Ala. C. of C. Baptist. Clubs: Vestavia Country, The Club, Relay House. Home: Birmingham, Ala., Died June 11, 1974.

LEE, DAVID AARON, physician; b. Boston, July 19, 1932; s. Victor and Gertrude (Pollack) L.; M.D., Boston U., 1957; m. Sara Schwartz, June 13, 1954; children—Aviva, Joseph Avram, Joshua. Intern. Univ. Hosps. of Cleve., 1957-58; resident VA Hosp., Boston, 1961-62, U. Cal. at Los Angeles, 1962-66; chief surgery Granada Hills (Cal.) Hosp.; mem. staff Northridge (Cal.) Hosp., Valley Presbyn. Hosp., Van Nuys, Cal.; clin. instr. U. Cal. at Los Angeles. Bd. dirs. Los Angeles Hebrew High Sch., 1971-74, United Jewish Welfare Fund, Los Angeles, 1971-74. Served as capt., M.C., USAF, 1957-61. Recipient Posthumous Distinguished Leadership award U. Judaism, Los Angeles. Diplomate Am. Bd. Urology. Fellow A.C.S.; mem. Alpha Omega Alpha. Jewish religion (pres. temple 1974). Home: Northridge, Cal. Died Oct. 12, 1974; buried Los Angeles, Cal.

LEE, EDGAR DESMOND, coll. pres.; b. Laddonia, Audrain Co., Mo., Jan. 26, 1880; s. Richard Henry and Mary Alice (Cele) L.; A.B. and B.S. in Edn., U. of Mo., 1908, A.M., 1909; m. Bennetta Maude Barkley, of Mexico, Mo., June 2, 1910; children—Hazel Virginia, Edgar Desmond. Teacher rural schs., 1900-04; prin. high sch., Clarksville, Mo., 1907; supt. schs., New London, Mo., 1909-12, Sikeston, 1912-18; prof. psychology and sociology, Christian Coll., 1918, v.p., 1919, pres., from 1920. Mem. Am. Assn. Jr. Colleges (pres.), N.E.A., Mo. State Hist. Soc, Phi Delta Kappa, Phi Beta Kappa. Democrat. Mason (K.T.), Knight of Constantine. Clubs: Rotary, Columbia Country. Address: Columbia, Mo.†

LEE, FREDERICK CROSBY, clergyman; b. Utica, N.Y., Feb. 5, 1878; s. Rev. Charles Follen and Cordelia (Moore) L.; A.B., Bowdoin Coll., 1900; S.T.B., Gen. Theol. Sem., 1903; m. Grace Emma Dean, June 30, 1908. Ordained to ministry of Episcopalian Ch., June 11, 1903; house chaplain to Boston Codman of Me., 1903-04; curate St. Saviour's Ch., Bar Harbor, Me., 1904-05; chaplain and instr., St. Mary's Sch., Knoxville, Ill., 1906-08; missionary, Rumford, Me., 1908-15; asst. to sec. of Diocese of Maine, 1902-06, 1913-14; rector St. Andrew's Church, Rochester, New York, 1915-47; ret., 1947. Trustee Church Home, Rochester, N.Y.; exec. sec. dept. of missions, Diocese of Western N.Y., 1921-32; sec. and registrar of Rochester diocese, 1931-44, member standing com., 1934-47, Dep. to Gen. Conv. of Episcopal Ch., 1934, 37. Club: University (Rochester). Diocesan corr. to The Living Church, 1931-40. Contbr. to religious jours. Address: Damariscotta, Me.†

LEE, HALFDAN, corp. official; b. Stavanger, Norway, Jan. 6, 1888; s. Johan and Mathea (Nyman) Lie; M.E., Ilmenau Politechnicum, Germay, 1908; m. Nina Vivian Smith, Apr. 20, 1915 (dec. Aug. 28, 1953); children—John Philip, Alice Mathea (Mrs. Albert Pratt), Richard Ward; m. 2d, Katharine Mitchell Jackson, Sept. 17, 1955 (dec. 1962); m. 3d, Florence Parker Mather, Oct. 24, 1964. Employed successively as engr. by Rust Boiler Co., Pittsburgh, Pa., Carnegie Steel Com., Braddock, Pa., Republic Iron and Steel Co., Youngstown, O., Otis Steel Co., Cleveland, O., Mesta Machine Co., Homestead, Pa., 1908-16; asst. chief engr. The Koppers Co., Pittsburgh, 1916; engr. in charge sales and vice-pres. The Koppers Construction Co., 1916-29; president of Eastern Gas & Fuel Associates, 1934-55. chmn. bd., 1955-72; chmn. bd., chmn. exec. com. Boston Gas Co.; U.S. Smelting, Refining & Mining Co.; member board directors Ludlow Corporation. Mem. Am. Gas Assn., New England Gas Assn., Eastern States Blast Furnace and Coke Oven Association, American Iron and Steel Institute. Lutheran. Clubs: Somerset (Boston); Country (Brookline). Home: Greenfield, N.H., Died Mar. 27, 1975; interred Mt. Auburn Cemetery, Cambridge, Mass.

LEE, HAROLD B., church ofcl.; b. Clifton, Ida., Mar. 28, 1899; s. Samuel Marion and Louisa Emeline (Bingham) L.; student Ida. State Normal, 1916-17, U. Utah, 1922-24, H.H.D., 1964, Utah State Agrl. Coll., 1951; Dr. Christian Service (hon.), Brigham Young U., 1955; m. Fern L. Tanner, Nov. 14, 1923 (dec.); children—Maurine (Mrs. Ernest J. Wilkins) (dec.), Helen (Mrs. L. Brent Goates); m. 2d, Freda Joan Jensen, June 17, 1963. Sch. adminstr. Salt Lake County, 1923-29; intermountain mgr. Found. Press, Inc., 1929-33; commr. Salt Lake City, 1933-37; adviser Mormon Ch. welfare plan, mem. council twelve apostles, 1941-73, mem. exec. com. ch. bd. edn. Vice chmn. Bonneville Internat. Corp., Hotel Utah; vice chmn., dir. Utah-Ida. Sugar Co.; v.p. KSL, Deseret Mgmt. Corp., Zions Securities Corp., Zions Coop. Mercantile Instn. dir. Beneficial Life Ins. Co., Union Pacific R.R., Equitable Life Assurance Soc. U.S., O.S.L. R.R., Los Angeles & Salt Lake R.R., Ore.-Wash. R.R. & Nav. Co.; mem. exec. com., dir. Zions 1st Nat. Bank. Mem. nat. bd. govs. A.R.C., 1963-70; exec. com., trustee Brigham Young U. Author: Youth and the Church. 1945. Home: Salt Lake City, Utah. Died Dec. 26, 1973.

LEE, SAMUEL HUNT, JR., educator; b. Hutchinson, Kan., Sept. 2, 1918; s. Samuel Hunt and Laura Louise (Grant) L.; B.S. U. Tex. at Austin, 1939; Ph.D., Ohio State U., 1944; m. Evalyn Madden, Aug. 25, 1949; children—Gordon Thomas, Gregroy Hunt. Chemist Morton Salt Co., Manistee, Mich., Grand Saline, Tex., 1939-40; sr. research chemist Shell Oil Co., Deer Park, Tex., 1944-46; asst. prof. chemistry U. Tex. at Austin, 1946-49; asso. prof. chemistry Okla. A. and M. Coll., Stillwater, 1949-51; chemist U.S. Naval Ordnance Testing Sta., China Lake, Cal., summer 1951; asst. prof. chemistry Tex. Tech., U., Lubbock, 1951-53, asso. prof., 1953-61, prof., 1961-75; vis. prof. Birmingham (Ala.)-So. Coll., summer 1961; sr. chemist Amoco Chem. Corp., Brownsville, Tex., summer 1957; instr. NSF Summer Inst., Tex. Tech. U., 1959, Mont. State U., 1963. Cons., instr. U.S. AID Summer Inst. Chemistry, Sardor Patel U., Vallabh Vidyanagar, Gujarat, India, summer 1966; reader, table leader in chemistry Advanced Placement Exams., Coll. Entrance Exam. Bd., Ednl. Testing Service, Princeton, N.J., 1968-75. Bd. dirs. Wesley Found. Tex. Tech. U., 1964-70. Fellow Am. Inst. Chemists, A.A.A.S., Tex. Acad. Sci. (vis. scientist 1955-63, chmn. bd. sci. edn.); mem. Am. Chem. Soc. (sec., chmn. South Plains sect. 1970-72), Tex. Interscholastic League (dir. regional sci. contest 1961-75), Sigma Xi, Phi Kappa Phi Tau Beta Pi, Phi Lambda Upsilon, Phi Gamma Delta. Democrat. Methodist. Club: Lubbock Knife and Fork (dir.). Author: An Approach to Physicial Science, 1968. Home: Lubbock, Tex. Died Apr. 3, 1975; cremated.

LEE, VOYD FRANK, educator; b. Neuville, Tex., Mar. 26, 1911; d. Ernest Christian and Doltie Willie (Willard) Frank; A.A., Lamar State Coll. Tech., 1928; student Mary Hardin-Baylor Coll., 1928-29, Sam Houston State Tchrs. Coll., summers 1929, 32-34; B.S. in Edn., U. Houston, 1953; m. Benjamin Franklin Lee, Mar. 27, 1934; 1 son, Ben Frank. Tchr. Port Bolivar Rural Sch., Tex., 1929, prin., 1930-32, prin. elementary sch., 1935-36; tchr. High Island High Sch., Tex., 1932-35; owner, dir. Kiddie Kollege Nursery Sch., Beaumont, Tex., 1949-52; tchr. Pennsylvania Elementary Sch., Beaumont Ind. Sch. Dist., 1952-53, tchr. French Elementary Sch., 1953-73. Mem. adv. com. div. instructional media Tex. Edn. Agy., 1961-73. Mem. Lamar Area Reading Council, Internat. Reading Assn., Beaumont Assn. Mental Health, N.E.A., Tex. Congress Parents and Tchrs., Tex. Tchrs. Assn., Tex., Beaumont classroom tchrs. assns., Tex. (pres. 1960-61, mem. workshop planning bd. 1958-62, adviser 1962-63; life mem.), Beaumont (pres. 1955-57) assns. childhood edn., Sabine Area Council Tchrs. Math., Internat. Platform Assn., Alpha Delta Kappa. Home: Beaumont, Tex. Died Sept. 19, 1973.

LEE, WALLACE RODGERS, mech. engr.; b. Philadelphia, Pa., Sept. 12, 1879; s. Lewis Shinnick and Margaret Ann (Rodgers) L.; B.S., U. of Pa., 1899, M.S., 1900, M.E., 1911; m. Helen Elizabeth Hall, of West Chester, Pa., Sept. 29, 1911; children—Margaret Elizabeth, Wallace Rodgers. With Baldwin Locomotive Works, Phila., from 1900, mgr. Buenos Aires br., from 1919. Mem. Am. Soc. M.E., Am. Soc. of the River Plate. Home: Spring Garden, Vicente Lopez, F.C.C.A. Address: Buenos Aires, Argentina.†

LEE, WALTER ESTELL, surgeon; b. Phila., Pa. July 22, 1879; s. William Estell and Nellie Florence (Dickerson) L.; M.D., U. of Pa., 1902; m. Margaret Gordon, June 14, 1911; 1 dau., Jean Gordon. Res. pathologist Pa. Hosp., 1902-03, resident anesthetist and chief resident phys., 1904-08; interne Germantown Hosp., 1903-04; cons. surgeon to Pennsylvania, Graduate, Germantown, Bryn Mawr and Burlington County hospitals; professor emeritus surgery, Graduate School of Medicine, University of Pennsylvania. Director of research Jeanes Foundation. Res. officer Med. Corps, U.S. Army, 1911-14; Med. Corps, French Army, 1915-16; Med. Corps, U.S. Army, 1917-19; officer Med. Res. Corps, U.S. Army from 1919 (maj. 1919, later lt. col.). Fellow Am. Surg. Assn., Am. Coll. Surgeons; mem. Internat. Surg. Soc., Am. Assn. Thoracic Surgeons, A.M.A., Pa. State Med. Soc., Am. Soc. Clin. Surgery, Phila. Acad. Surgery, Coll. of Phys. of Phila., Phila. Pediatric Soc., Phila. Co. Med. Soc., Phila. Pathological Soc., Kappa Sigma, Alpha Mu Pi Omega. Republican. Presbyterian. Mason. Clubs: University, Rittenhouse (Phila.). Author: Textbook of Surgery (with F. T. Stewart), 1931; Manual of Surgery (with F. T. Stewart), 1928. Co-editor of Progressive Medicine, 1919-33; chmn. editorial bd. Annals of Surgery, 1935-47. Contbr. to surg. jours. Address: Philadelphia, Pa.†

LEET, LEWIS DON, seismologist; b. Alliance, O., July 1, 1901; s. Kline Fetterman and Lela Grace (Caskey) L.; student Columbia, 1919-20; B.S., Denison U., 1923, D.Sc. (hon.), 1948; M.A., Ph.D., Havard, 1930; m. Frances Adeline Brokaw, Feb. 7, 1925 (div.); children—Nancy Anne, Robert Kline; m. 2d, Florence Jane Anderson Blanchard, July 2, 1956; children—Brenda Elizabeth, Darrell R. Pvt. sec., Tokyo, Japan, 1923-25; with Cleve. br. Ford Motor Co., 1925-26; tchr. Cleveland Heights (O.) High Sch., 1926-27; seismologist, 1928-74; with Harvard Grad. Sch., 1927-29, Dominion Obs., Ottawa, Can., 1929-30, Geophys. Research Corp., 1930-31; charge seismograph sta. Harvard, 1931-68, faculty, 1931-74, asso. prof., 1942-46, prof., 1946-68, emeritus, 1968-74, chmn. div. geol. scis., 1951-55. Propr., Leet Assos., 1945-74. Mem. Geol. Soc. Am., Seismol. Soc. Am., Sigma Xi, Delta Upsilon, Phi Mu Alpha. Author: Practical Seismology and Seismic Prospecting, 1938; Earth Motion from the Atomic Bomb Test, 1946; Causes of Catastrophe, 1947; Earth Waves, 1950; Physical Geology (with Sheldon Judson), 1954; Vibrations From Blasting Rock, 1960; The World of Geology (with Florence J. Leet), 1961; Earthquake-Discoveries in Seismology, 1964; Detection of Underground Nuclear Explosions, 1962. Home: Bolton, Mass. Died Jan. 2, 1974; interred Bellevue Cemetery, Harvard, Mass.

LEFEVRE, THEODORE-JOSEPH ALBERIC-MARIE, Belgian lawyer, politician; b. Ghent, Belgium, Jan. 17, 1914; s. Etienne and Marie (Rogman) L.; Humanities anciennes, Institut St.-Liévin, Ghent; doctor inris, State U. (Ghent), 1937; m. Marie-Josée Billiaert, Aug. 26, 1944; children—Marie-Caroline, Etienne, Pascal. Barrister, Ct. of Appeal, Ghent, 1940-73; mem. Chamber Representants, 1946-73; pres. Christian Social Party, 1950-61; mem. Consultative Assembly Council of Europe, 1950-59, Coal and Steel Assembly, 1952-58, European Constl. Assembly, 1952, West European Union Assembly, 1954; minister state, Belgium, 1958-73; pres. Internat. Union Social Democrats, 1959; prime minister charge econ. coordination and sci. policy, Belgium, 1961-65; minister charge politics and sci. program, 1968. Mem. armed resistance, resistance press, World War II. Decorated Legion of Honor. Author articles on politics. Home: Ghent, Belgium. Died Sept. 18, 1973.

LEHMANN, TIMOTHY, college pres.; b. Ostheim, Russia, Oct. 11, 1881; s. Carl D. and Emilie (Rosenthal) L.; brought to U.S., 1893; Elmhurst (Ill.) Coll., 1896-99, Eden Theol. Sem., St. Louis, Mo, 1899-1902, Richmond (Va.) Coll., 1902-03; D.D., Eden Theol. Sem., 1932; LL.D., Catawba Coll., 1933; m. Martha E. Menzel, June 28, 1905; children—Paul Louis, Timothy, Jr., Lillie Emma (Mrs. Lowell R. Hanon). Ordained ministry Evangelical and Reformed Church, 1902; assistant pastor St. John's Evangelical Church, Richmond, 1902-03; pastor St. John's Luth. Ch., Baltimore, Md., 1903-11, St. John's Evang. Protestant Ch., Columbus, O., 1911-28; pres. Elmhurst Coll., 1928. Lt. governor Kiwanis International District Div. 6; chmn. board dirs. Family Service Assn. of Du Page County. Home: Edinburg, Va.†

LEHOCZKY, PAUL NICHOLAS, educator, indsl. engr.; b. Pitts., Apr. 17, 1905; s. Paul and Helen von Lehoczky; B.S. in Mech. Engring, Case Inst. Tech., 1927; M.Sc., Ohio State U., 1928, Ph.D., 1931; m. Thelma M. Heisterkamp, June 22, 1934; children—Marcia Helen (Mrs. Robert K. Gillette), John Paul. With Indsl. Fibre Co., 1923-26, Dow Chem. Co., 1927; mem. dept. indsl. engring. Ohio State U., 1928-74, chmn. dept., 1944-65, prof. emeritus, 1965-74; profl. arbitrator labor mgmt. disputes, 1943-74. Fgn. editor Automotive Abstracts, 1928-31. Research engr. Ohio Indsl. Commn., 1940-41, adviser, 1941-57; chmn. wage stblzn. panel NWLB, 1943, pub. mem. dispute panels, 1943-46; commnr. conciliation, tech. div. U.S. Counciliation Service 1946-47; pub. mem. Gov. Ohio Apprenticeship Council, 1947-51; mem. Pres.'s Conf. Indsl. Safety, 1948-58. Registered profl. engr. (M.E. and I.E.), Ohio. Fellow Am. Soc. M.E.; mem. Nat. Acad. Arbitrators, Sigma Xi, Tau Beta Pi, Alpha Pi Mu (nat. pres. 1950-52, council 1952-58). Address: Columbus O. Died Feb. 25, 1974.

LEHOTSKY, KOLOMAN, educator; b. Spisská Nová Ves, Czechoslovakia, Feb. 18, 1906; s. Martin Suzanne (Yurchová) L.; Ing., Bohemian Tech. U., Prague, 1928; Ph.D., U. Mich., 1934; m. Josephine M. Beals, Aug. 26, 1941; children—Paul, Suzanne. Came to U.S., 1929, naturalized, 1934. Asst., U. Mich., 1930-34; jr. to asso. forester U.S. Soil Conservation Service, 1934-37, 38-47, forestry specialist, 1944-47; prof. forestry Escola Superior de Agriculture e Veterinaria, Vicosa, Brazil, 1937-38; asso. prof. forestry Clemson (S.C.) U., 1947-55, prof. forestry, 1955-71, established dept. forestry, 1957, Clemson Arboretum, 1951, head dept., 1956-69, prof. silviculture emeritus, head emeritus dept. forestry, 1971-75. Dir.-at-large Czechoslovak Soc. Arts and Scis. in Am., 1968-72; chmn. Foresters Council S.C., 1962-64. Served with AUS, 1942-44. Recipient 1st Charles H. Flory Distinguished Service award S.C. Forestry Assn., 1970. Mem. Soc. Am. Foresters (sec.-treas. Appalachian sect. 1973—), Sigma Xi, Gamma Alpha, Alpha Zeta, Xi Sigma Pi, Phi Sigma, Phi Kappa Phi, Gamma Sigma Delta. Home: Clemson, S.C., Died Aug. 20, 1975; buried Cemetery Hill, Clemson, S.C.

LEHRMAN, JACOB, corp. exec.; b. 1911; married. With Giant Pure Food Market, Inc., Hazleton, Pa., 1931-47; an organizer Giant Food Inc., 1935, exec. v.p., sec., dir.; dir. Giant Food Properties, Inc. Address: Landover, Md. Died Dec. 21, 1974.

LEIB, GEORGE CARR, investment banker; b. Louisville, Feb. 8, 1890; s. Louis and May (Carr) L.; m. Isabel Haldeman, Feb. 23, 1923; children—Gordon B., John H., G. Bruce. With Crocker Nat. Bank, San Francisco, 1909-10, Louis Scholls & Co., San Francisco, 1909-10; a founder Blvth Witter & Co., 1914; v.p. Blyth & Co., Inc., until 1955, vice chmn. bd., 1955-59, chmn. bd., 1959-66, hon. chmn., 1966-72. Served as capt., F.A., U.S. Army, World War I; A.E.F. in France. Mem. The Pilgrims of U.S., English Speaking Union, Fedn. des Alliances Francaises, France-Am. Soc. Clubs: Travellers (Paris); Links, Links Golf, Recess (N.Y.C.); Racquet; Piping Rock. Home: New York City, N.Y. Died June 20, 1974.

LEIBY, ADRIAN COULTER, lawyer; b. Bergenfield, N.J., Dec. 16, 1904; s. Elias B. and Mamie (Coulter) L.; B.S., Middlebury Coll., 1925; LL.B., Columbia, 1929; m. Emorie M. Atkins, July 8, 1932; 1 dau., Adrian A. Scott. Law clk. to Justice Harlan F. Stone, 1929-30; admitted to N.Y. bar, 1930, since practiced in N.Y.C.; sr. partner firm LeBoeuf, Lamb, Leiby & MacRae, 1952—. Dir. sec. Hackensack Water Co.; dir. St. Regis Paper Co., Sentinel Income Fund, Sentinel Growth Fund. Fellow N.J. Hist. Soc. (trustee); mem. Am. Bar Assn. Republican. Presbyn. Author: Revolutionary War in the Hackensack Valley, 1962; The Early Dutch and Swedish Settlers of New Jersey, 1963. Home: Bergenfield, N.J., Died Feb. 16, 1976.

LEICHTMAN, JACOB, banker; b. Poland, 1896; m. Esther Evans; 1 dau., Francine Tancer. Vice chmn. Nat. Bank of N.Am., N.Y.C. Home: New York City, N.Y. Died May 1975.

LEIDIGH, ARTHUR HENRY prof. of agr.; b. Hutchinson, Kan., Aug. 14, 1880; s. Theodore F. and Elizabeth (Reed) L.; B.S. in Agr., Kan. State Coll., 1902; M.S., Agr. and Mech. Coll. of Tex., 1923; m. Mary Josephine Edwards, June 28, 1911; children—Mary Elizabeth, Katherine Lucy (Mrs. Henry Hitt Meredith, Jr.), Edward Theodore. Agronomist with exptl. station, U.S. Dept. of Agr., Channing, Tex., 1903-05, asso. agronomist, Amarillo, Tex., 1905-08; farmer, Hutchinson, Kan., 1908-11; asst. prof. corps, dept. agronomy, Kan. State Coll., 1911-13; agronomist Tex. Agr. Exptl. Station, 1913-23, asst. dir. and agronomist Tex. Agr. Experimental Station, 1923-25; prof. of agronomy, Tex. Tech. Coll., from 1925, dean of agr. 1925-45, dean emeritus, from 1945. Mem. Governor's Cotton Com. (Tex.) Tex. State Planning Bd. Member Am. Society of Agronomy, Phi Kappa Phi Mason. Club: Lubbock Kiwanis (past pres.). Author of agrl. bulletins and pamphlets. Home: Lubbock, Tex.†

LEIGHTON, MARGARET, actress; b. Worcestershire, Eng., Feb. 26, 1922; d. A. George and Doris Isabel (Evans) Leighton; ed. Ch. of Eng. Coll., Birmingham; m. Max Reinhardt, Aug. 1947 (dissolved 1954); m. 2d, Laurence Harvey, Aug. 8, 1957 (dissolved 1961); m. 3d, Michael Wilding, 1964. Mem. Birmingham Repertory Theatre, 1938, Old Vic Co., 1944-47; plays in London inculde A Sleeping Clergyman, 1947, Philadelphia Story, 1949, The Cocktail Party 1950, The Three Sisters, 1950, Confidential Clerk, 1953, The Applecart, 1953, Separate Tables, 1954, Variation on a Theme, 1958, The Wrong Side of the Park, 1960, The Lady From the Sea, 1961; plays in N.Y.C. include Did Vic Performances, 1946, Separate Tables, 1956, Much Ado About Nothing, 1959, The Night of the Iguana, 1962, Tchin-Tchin, 1962-63, The Chinese Prime Minister, 1964, Slapstick Tragedies, 1965; appeared Meml. Theatre, Stratford-on-Avon, Eng., 1952; numerous film and TV appearances. Home: Chichester, England., Died Jan. 14, 1976.

LEIGHTY, GEORGE EARLE, labor union ofcl.; b. Phillips, Wis., Aug. 16, 1897, s. George W. and Anna B. (Klein) L.; ed. pub. schs., Phillips, Wis.; m. Marie E. McDonald, June 15, 1917 (divorced 1923); children—Lyle Freeman, Carleton Edgar; m. 3d, Florence L. Gates, Aug. 8, 1953; 1 son, George Earle. Various positions C.M.St.P.&P. R.R., 1915-37; local chmn. Order Railroad Telegraphers, 1917-42, dep. pres., 1937-39, gen. chmn., C.M.St.P.R.R., 1939-42, vice pres., 1942-46, pres. from 1946. Chmn. Nat. Employes Negotiating Com., 16 Non-operating ry. labor orgns., 1947-73; del. AFL, 1934-36, 46-73; co-chmn. United Labor Policy Com., 1950-51. Mem. Ry. Labor Execs. Assn. (chmn. 1950-73), Modern Woodmem. Am. Democrat. Editor: Trans-Communicator. Home: St Louis, Mo. Died July 17, 1973.

LEINBACH, GARY EARL, physician; b. New Haven, 1933; M.D., Cornell U., 1959. Straight intern in internal medicine Cornell U.-N.Y. Hosp., N.Y.C., 1959-60, asst. resident in internal medicine, 1960-61; asst. resident in internal medicine U. Wash. Affiliated Hosps., Seattle, 1961-62, chief resident, 1962-63; sr. fell in gastroenterology U. Wash., 1965-67, instr., sr. fellow Radioisotope Lab., 1967-69, sr. fellow, instr. nuclear medicine, 1967-68, sr. fellow, instr. research unit, 1968-69, asst. prof. medicine, 1970-73; chief div. gastroenterology, instr. medicine King County Hosp., Seattle, 1969-73. Served to capt. M.C., AUS, 1963-65. Diplomate Am. Bd. Internal Medicine. Home: Seattle, Wash. Died 1973.

LEIPER, HENRY SMITH, ch. ofcl.; b. Belmar, N.J., Sept. 17, 1891; s. Joseph McCarrell and Fanny Heywood (Smith) L.; grad. Blair Acad., Blairstown, N.J., 1909; B.A., Amherst, 1913, D.D. from same, 1935; grad. Union Sem., N.Y. City, 1917; M.A., Columbia 1917; studied Chinese at N. China Union Lang. Sch., Peking, 1919; m. Eleanor Lansing Cory, May 15, 1915 (died Jan. 30, 1935); children—Juliet McCarrell (Mrs. Homer J. Hall), Rev. Henry Welling; m. 2d, Elizabeth Glover Olyphant, July 1935. Ordained ministry Presbyn. Ch., 1915, transferred to Congl. Ch., 1920; traveling sec. Student Vol. Movement, 1913-14; acting pastor N.Y.C., 1914-16; served with Army Y.M.C.A., Siberia, 1918; missionary, A.B.C.F.M., Tientsin, China, 1918-22; asst. sec., A.B.C.F.M., N.Y.C., 1922-23; editor Congl. Nat. Council's Commn. on Missions, 1923-29; asso. editor The Congregationalist, 1927-30; speaker for Am. chs. at 400th anniversary of Augsburg Confession, Augsburg, 1930; in charge Am. Ch., Paris, 1932; exec. sec. Am. Sect. Universal Christian Council for Life and Work, also of Dept. of Relations with Chs. Abroad, Fed. Council Chs. of Christ in Am., 1930-45; Ecumenical secretary Federal Council of Churches, 1945-48; associate general secretary World Council of Churches, 1938-52, exec. sec. Congl. Missions Council, 1952-59; dir. dept. religion Chautauqua (N.Y.) Instn., 1959-75; spl. sec. Am. Bible Soc., 1959-75. Trustee Am. Coll. (Madura, India); chmn. bd. Vellore Christian Med. Coll., India; Mem. Am. Acad. of Polit. and Social Science, Beta Theta Pi, Delta Sigma Rho. Member of United Church of Christ. Clubs: Authors' (London); National Arts, Clergy, Quill (New York); Shanghai Tiffin. Author several books, 1929-37; co-author: Protestant Thought in the Twentieth Century; We Believe in Prayer, and others. Contbr. to Ency. Brit. Yearbooks, also mags. Editor: Christianity Today, 1946; Ecumenical Courier, 1948-52. Home: Leonia, N.J. Died Jan. 22, 1975.

LEIPHEIMER, EDWIN GEORGE, newspaper editor; b. of Am. parents, Heilbronne, Germany, Apr. 18, 1880; s. Eugene R. and Mary (Matthes) L.; LL.B., U. of Mich., 1901; m. Laura Armbruster, June 28, 1900; children—Marielouise, Edwin George. Began as reporter Denver, Colo., 1901; settled in Butte, Mont., 1904; editor Anaconda Standard, 1924-28; editor Mont. Standard, from 1928; pres. Standard Pub. Co. Mem. Mont. State Press Assn. (pres. 1927). Republican. Presbyterian. Mason. Clubs: Butte Town, Butte Country. Home: Butte, Mont.*†

LEITH, DOROTHY LOUISE, physician; b. Canal Fulton, O., Apr. 20, 1910; d. Thomas Stephen and Ethel Mary (Duncan) Leith; B.S. in Phys. Edn., Mich. State U., 1931; M.A. in Edn., Wayne State U., 1940, M.D., 1947. Tchr. phys. edn. Detroit pub. schs., 1932-44; tchr. summer sessions phys. edn. Mich. State U., 1937, 39; intern Grace Hosp., Detroit, 1947-48; pvt. practice medicine, Detroit, 1948-52, Imlay City Mich., 1952-73; staff Community Hosp., Almont, Mich., 1959-73. Mem. Community Fund Bd., Imlay City, Mich.; mem. motor corps A.R.C., 1939-40, first aid instr. trainer, 1941; air raid instr. Office Civilian Def., 1942. Elected coroner Lapeer County, Mich., 1951-59. Fellow Am. Acad. Family Physicians; mem. A.M.A., Mich., Lapeer, Wayne med. socs., Am. Rifleman Assn., Chi Omega, Nu Sigma Phi. Home: Imlay City, Mich. Died Aug. 8, 1973.

LEITHEAD, BARRY T., business exec.; b. Lovell, Wyo., 1907; student Drake U. Dir. Cluett, Peabody & Co., Inc., N.Y.C., Clupak, Inc., B.F. Goodrich Co., Westvaco Corp., Travelers Ins. Co., Kraftco Corp., Trans World Airlines, Inc. Trustee St. Lawrence U., Eisenhower Coll. Home: Aiken S.C. Died July 15, 1974.

LEIVA, CARLOS, del. to U.N. gen. assembly, physician; b. El Salvador, C.A., April 17, 1879; s. Carlos and Concepcion (Sifontes) L.; grad. U. of El Salvador,1907;;Salvador, 1907; grad. Inst. of Colonial Medicine, Paris U., 1909; m. Adelina Batres, Jan. 31, 1914. Licensed to practice medicine, Calif., 1919. Prof. anatomy, U. of El Salvador, 1912-18, prof. pathology, 1911, prof. surgery, 1915-18; minister for El Salvador to Washington, D.C., 1913; del. U.N., San Francisco, 1945; del. gen. assembly, U.N., N.Y., 1946. Mem. Pan-American Med. Assn. Roman Catholic. Home: San Francisco, Cal.*†

LE MAIRE, AMY DANDROW (MRS. LAMBERT D. LE MAIRE), conservationist; b. Plattsburgh, N.Y., Jan. 15, 1907; d. Nelson O. and Edwidge E. (Chalmers) Dandrow; grad. high sch.; m. Lambert D. LeMaire, June 3, 1929. Sec., No. N.Y. Telephone Corp., also N.Y. Telephone Co., 1924-40; instr., lectr., demonstrator in gardening, landscaping, flower arranging, 1949-72, conservation lectr. to garden clubs, other orgns., 1952-72; flower arrangements pub. in N.Y. state calendar, 1958-72; exhibited Internat. Flower Show, N.Y.C., 1949, 50, Syracuse (N.Y.) State Fair, 1952-56, Unitarian Ch., Schenectady, 1965-72, Schenectady Hist. Soc., 1956-59, Nat. Conv. State Garden Clubs, 1964; accredited hort. judge, N.Y., 1965-72; landscape design critic Nat. Council State Garden Clubs, 1970-72; master nat. accredited flower show judge, 1962-72; instr. adult edn. Columbia, Schenectady counties, 1949-56; instr. YMCA, YWCA ednl. programs, 1957-72; leader tng. courses Albany County Extension Service, 1961-63; conservation rep. on action for clean air com. Schenectady County Health Assn., Tb and Respiratory Disease Assn., Eastern Mohawk Area, Inc. Exec. bd. 3d dist. Federated Garden Clubs, 1949-72, treas., 1953-54, dir., 1955-56, conservation chmn., 1957-72; exec. bd. N.Y. Federated Garden Clubs, 1954-72, advt. chmn., 1957-60, chmn. conservation council, 1961-63, state legislative and conservation chmn., 1963-72, dept. head conservation and natural resources N.Y. State Fedn. Women's Clubs, 1960-62. Recipient Audubon Camp scholarship Federated Garden Clubs, 1959; citation for conservation articles Nat. Wildlife Fedn., 1963; dist. citation, also state bronze medal for inspirational leadership Federated Garden Clubs N.Y. State, Inc., 1953, Marion B. Darrow Conservation award for exceptional work in leadership in conservation, 1966. Mem. Am. Forestry Assn., Nat. Audubon Soc., Wilderness Soc., Joselyn Bot. Soc. Me., Forest Preserve Assn. (sec. 1964-67), Schenectady Hist. Soc. Aux., Scenic Hudson Preservation Soc., Schenectady Rose Soc., Hugh Plat Garden Club (past pres.). Republican. Organized and federated 24 garden clubs, 1948-72; federated 8 others. Contbr. articles on conservation to The News (Federated Garden Club publ.). Home: Scotia N.Y. Died Aug. 17, 1972; interred Scotia, N.Y.

LEMAITRE, GEORGES EDOUARD ETIENNE, educator; b. Algiers, Algeria, Nov. 26, 1898; s. George Emile and Clemence (Vadam) L.; Bachelier ès-Lettres, U. Algiers, 1916; student Ecole Normale Supèrieure, Paris, 1918-21, Agrégé de l'Université, 1921; Docteur ès-Lettres, Sorbonne, 1931; m. Wynifred Eaves, 1937 (divorced 1946). Came to U.S., 1938, naturalized, 1944. Lecturer, French Inst., London, Eng., 1925-27, Dalhousie U., Halifax, N.S., 1927-28, U. Wis., 1928-29; asst. prof., McGill U. Montreal, 1929-31, asso. prof., 1931-38; prof. Romanic langs., Stanford U., from 1939. Mem. A.A.A.S., Am. Acad. Polit. and Social Sci. Club: Authors (London, Eng.). Author: Four French Novelists, 1938; From Cubism to Surrealism, 1941; Beaumarchais, 1949; Maurois: The Writer and His Work, 1968; Jean Giraudoux: The Writer and His Work, 1971. Home: Palo Alto, Cal., Aug. 11, 1972; buried Palo Alto.

LEMKAU, HUDSON BARDON, investment banker; b. Montclair, N.J., Dec. 27, 1910; s. J.H. Walter and Edith (Hudson) L.; grad. Montclair Acad., 1928; B.A., Princeton, 1932; m. Janet Loasby, June 2, 1936; children—Arthur L., Alison (Mrs. Alex B. Vaughn), Hudson B. With Bonbright & Co., Inc., 1932-42; with Morgan Stanley & Co., N.Y.C., 1942-44, 46-74, partner, 1956; mng. dir. Morgan Stanley & Co., Inc. 1970-74; mgr. Morgan & Cie Internat. S.A., Paris, France, 1971-74. Exec. bd. Greater N.Y. council Boy Scouts Am. Served to lt. USNR, 1944-46. Mem. Investment Bankers Assn. Am. (gov. 1957-59), Nat. Assn. Securities Dealers (gov. 1961-63, vice chmn. 1963). Clubs: Lunch, Bond (gov. 1954-56, 67-69), N.Y. Yacht, Princeton, City Mid-day (N.Y.C.); Manhasset Bay Yacht (Port Washington, N.Y.); The Creek (Locust Valley, N.Y.); Princeton (N.J.) Charter (gov. 1959-69); Nantucket (Mass.) Yacht; Travellers (Paris). Home: Plandome N.Y. Died Sept. 15, 1974.

LENDALL, HARRY N(ELSON), sanitary engr.; b. Essex, Mass., July 13, 1878; s. Frank Nelson and Elizabeth Anna (Poole) L.; B.S., Coll. of Engring., Tufts Coll., Mass., 1906, C.E., 1926; m. Helen Lydia Runyon, July 26, 1922. Testing dept., Gen. Electric Co., Lynn, Mass., 1897-1902; asst. engr. preliminary surveys for sewage disposal plant, Morris Dam, Conn.; B. & M. R.R., grade crossing elimination, Lawrence, Mass., 1906-09, 1909-12. Instr. dept. civil engring., U. of Pa., 1912-14, instr., 1914-18, assistant professor, 1918-24, associate professor, 1924-49, professor, from 1949; professor emeritus municipal and sanitary engring., Rutgers Univ.; dean of men, 1923-24, chmn. athletic council, 1923-24, chmn. dept. civil engring., 1928-49; cons. for various communities in N.J. on valuation, sewage and water plant design. Recipient George W. Fuller Award, 1947. Mem. N.J. State Bd. Health, Pub. Health Council, N.J. State Dept. Econ. Development, Interstate Sanitation Commn. (commr. from N.J.), State Bldg. Code, (civilian com. mem.), Am. Soc. Civil Engrs., Am. Water Works Assn. (dir. N.J. sect., 1941-44, sec. 1938-39, trustee 1940-44), Fedn. Sewage Works Assn., Am. Soc. Engring Edn., New England WaterWorks, Am. Soc. Professional Egnrs., Zeta Psi, Sigma Xi, Tau Beta Pi, Phi Betta Kappa. Republican. Universalist. Contbr. various articles to tech. jours. Home: New Brunswick, N.J.†

LENNEBERG, ERIC HEINZ, educator; b. Duesseldorf, Germany, Sept. 19, 1921; s. Robert and Gertrud (Stern) L.; came to U.S., 1945, naturalized, 1948; B.A., U. Chgo., 1949, M.A., 1951; Ph.D., Harvard, 1956, postgrad. div. med. scis., 1956-59; m. 2d, Elizabeth Smith, May 17, 1969; children by previous marriage — Miriam, Roger. Research asso. Mass. Inst. Tech., 1952-55; asst. prof. psychology Harvard Med. Sch., Boston, 1959-67; prof. U. Mich., Ann Arbor, 1967-68; prof. psychology and neurobiology Cornell U., Ithaca, N.Y., 1968-75, vis. prof. neurology U. Rochester (N.Y.) Sch. Medicine, 1970-75. USPHS career investigator, 1960-64. Served with AUS, 1946-47. Recipient Career Devel. award, 1965-67; Guggenheim fellow, 1968-69; Boston Med. Found. fellow, 1959; Social Sci. Research Council fellow, 1955-56; Am. Council Learned Socs. fellow, 1951-52. Psychol., biol. and med. research on speech and lang. Home: Ithaca, N.Y. Died June 2, 1975.

LENSKI, LOIS (MRS. ARTHUR S. COVEY), artist, author; b. Springfield, O., Oct. 14, 1893; d. Richard Charles and Marietta (Young) Lenski; B.S. in Edn., Ohio State U., 1915; art edn. at Art Students' League, N.Y.C., also Westminster Sch. Art, London; Litt.D., Wartburg Coll., 1959, Capital U., Southwestern Coll., Winfield, Kan., 1968; 1966; L.H.D., U. N.C., 1962; m. Arthur S. Covey, June 1921 (dec. 1960); children—Stephen, Laird. Author, illustrator books for children; painter; author juvenile books under pen name Lois Lenski, 1927; latest being: Boom Town Boy, 1948; Now It's Fall, 1948; Mr. and Mrs. Noah, 1948; Cowboy Small, 1949; Cotton in My Sack, 1949; I Like Winter, 1950; Texas Tomboy, 1950; Prairie School, 1951; Papa Small, 1951; On a Summer Day, 1953; Mama Hattie's Girl, 1953; Project Boy and We Live in the City, 1954; Corn-Farm Boy and Songs of Mr. Small, 1954; San Francisco Boy and A Dog Came to School, 1955; We Live by the River, Berries in the Scoop, Big Little Davy Flood Friday, 1956; Houseboat Girl, 1957; Davy and His Dog, 1957; Little Sioux Girl, 1958; Coal Camp Girl, 1959; At Our House, 1959; We Live in the Country, 1960; When I Grow Up, 1960; Davy Goes Places, 1961; We Live in the Southwest, 1962; Policeman Small, 1962; Shoo-Fly Girl, 1963; We Live in the North, 1965; The Life I Live: Collected Poems, 1965; High-Rise Secret, 1966; Debbie Books, 1970-71; To Be A Logger,

1967; Deer Valley Girl, 1968; Christmas Stories, 1968; Adventure in Understanding, 1968; Journey Into Childhood: Autobiography, 1972. Recipient 1946 Newberry medal for Strawberry Girl, 1947; Child Study Assn. award for Judy's Journey; Children's Book Collection medallion U. So. Miss., 1969; Regina medal Cath. Library Assn., 1969. Home: Tarpon Springs, Fla. Died Sept. 11, 1974.

LENTZ, ARTHUR GEORGE, exec. dir. U.S. Olympic Com.; b. Milw., Nov. 27; s. Arthur A. and Amelia (Lee) L.; B.A., U. Ia., 1930; m. Alta H. Miller, July 31, 1931; children—Sue B. (Mrs. Arthur L. Casebeer), Judith L. (Mrs. John C. Leissring), Deborah J. (Mrs. Michael L. Brown), Mark S., Derek J.; m. 2d, Florence Mae Kyler, July 15, 1965. Engaged in newspaper work, 1930-46; asst. sports editor Capital Times, Madison, Wis., 1953-56; athletic publicity dir. U. Wis., 1946-56; pub. relations dir. U.S. Olympic Com., 1956-59, asst. exec. dir., 1959-65, exec. dir., 1965-74. Named one of five all-Am. sports publicists Helms Athletic Found., 1951; recipient award for nat. sports publicity projects, 1951, 52. Mem. Sigma Delta Chi. Clubs: N.Y. Athletic, Woodstock Country. Author Olympic books, 1956, 60, 64, 68, 72. Home: New York City, N.Y. Died Jan. 25, 1974; buried Forest Hill Cemetery, Madison, Wis.

LENZ, MAURICE, physician, educator; b. Kovno, Russia, Mar. 23, 1890; s. Dr. Benjamin and Minna (Idelson) L.; student Sch. of St. Peter and Paul, 1900-06; M.D., Columbia, 1913; m. Anna M. Malmberg, Mar. 10, 1917; children—Robert M., Benjamin N. Intern Lebanon Hosp., N.Y.C., 1913-15; gen. practice medicine, N.Y.C., 1915-17; asst. dermatology Vanderbilt Clinic and Mt. Sinai Hosp., 1919-21; study radiotherapy, Europe, 1921-23, including 1 yr. at Curie Inst., Paris, France; asst. radiotherapist Mt. Sinai Hosp., N.Y.C., 1923-26; attending radiotherapist in charge Montifiore Hosp., 1926-42, cons. radiotherapist since 1942; radiotherapist Presbyn. Hosp., 1930-46, chief radiotherapy, 1934-46; became prof. clin. radiology Coll. Phys. and Surg., Columbia, 1942, now prof. emeritus radiology; consulting radiotherapist Presbyterian, Delafield, Montefiore, and Manhattan Eye, Ear and Throat hospitals, N.Y.C. Dir. N.Y. Cancer Soc., 1940-42. Served as lt. M.C., U.S. Army, 1917-19. Recipient hon. fellowship Nat. Acad. Medicine of Columbia, 1946. Diplomate Am. Bd. Radiology. Fellow sect. radiology Royal Society Med. (hon.), Soc. Radiology Terrarum Septentrienalium (honorary); mem. N.Y. Acad. Medicine, Med. Soc. Co. N.Y., N.Y. Roentgen Ray Soc., A.M.A., Radiol. Soc. N.A., Am. Radium Soc. (pres.), Am. Coll. Radiology, Am. Roentgen Ray Soc., Am. Assn. Cancer Research, N.Y.C. Cancer Commn., Harvey Soc., St. Louis Med. Soc. (hon.), Sociedad Venezelana de Radiologia (fgn. corr. mem.). Died Jan. 4, 1974.

LEO, BROTHER, Z(ACHARY), secular name Francis Joseph Meehan, educator; b. San Francisco, Calif., Oct. 8, 1881; s. James and Mary Ellen (Gallagher) Meehan; grad. De La Salle Inst., Martinez, Calif., 1899; A.B., St. Mary's Coll., Oakland, Calif., 1903, A.M., 1908; L.H.D., Catholic U. of America, 1915, LL.D., U. of Santa Clara, Calif., 1926. Joined Brothers of the Christian Schs., 1897; instr. in English, Sacred Heart Coll., San Francisco, 1903-08; instr. English, St. Mary's Coll., Calif., 1908-14, prof. lit., from 1915, dean, 1929-30, chancellor, 1930-33, also a trustee; lecturer University of California, 1933-1940. Author: Contrast in Shakespeare's Historical Plays, 1915; Saint John Baptist de la Salle, 1921; Teaching the Drama and the Essay, 1921; Religion and the Study of Literature, 1923; English Literature, 1928. Plays; Dante the Wing-Bearer, 1921; Ecce Homo, 1923; The Tree of Kerioth, 1926. Contbr. to mags. Lecturer. Extensive research in Shakespeare and Dante. Address: St. Mary's Coll., Cal.†

LEONARD, HERBERT HENRY, mfr.; b. Orono, Me., Nov. 1, 1880; s. George W. and Harriet E. (Snow) L.; B.S., University of Maine, 1901; m. Bertha L. Clark, July 18, 1908; children—Clark H., Leta A. Merrow. Works manager Turner & Seymour Manufacturing Company, 1908-18; assistant general mgr. Stamford Rolling Mills, 1918-19; partner Indsl. Planning Corp., 1919-24; pres. Consolidated Packaging Machinery Corp., 1924-43; pres. American Machine & Foundry Corp., 1943-48; past. dir. Bagpak Inc., Am. Machine & Foundry Co., Internat. Cigar Machinery Co., American Machine Export Co., Marine Midland Trust Company. Chmn. bd. trustees Keep Vermont Beautiful, Inc. Bd. dirs. treas. Black Rock Mfrs. Assn., Packaging Machinery Mfrs. Inst. Mem. Am. Management Assn., Packaging Inst. N.Y. State Chamber of Commerce, Econ. Club of N.Y., Phi Kappa Phi, Tau Beta Pi. Republican. Methodist. Clubs: Buffalo Athletic. Rotary, Auto, Advertising of N.Y., Uptown. Home: South Shaftsbury, Vt.†

LEONARD, JONATHAN NORTON, author; b. Someville, Mass., May 25, 1903; s. Jonathan and Melanie Elisabeth (Norton) L.; A.B., Harvard, 1925; m. Maria Aizamora, Dec. 30, 1933; 1 son, Jonathan Alzamora. Free lance writer until 1943; Latin Am. editor Time mag., N.Y.C., 1943-45, sci. editor, 1945-65, staff writer Time-Life Books, 1965-68. Mem. Unitarian Ch. Author: Loki: The Life of Charles Proteus Steinmetz; Crusaders of Chemistry; Men of Maracaibo; The Tragedy of Henry Ford; Three Years Down; Tools of Tomorrow; Enjoyment of Science; Flight into Space, 1953; Time Book of Science, 1955; Exploring Science, 1959; Planets, 1966; Ancient America, 1967; Early Japan, 1968; Foods of Latin America, 1968; The World of Thomas Gainsborough, 1969; American Cooking: New England, 1970; American Cooking: The Great West, 1971; Atlantic Beaches, 1972. Home: Hastings-on-Hudson N.Y. Died May 15, 1975; interred Sandwich, Mass.

LEONARD, ROBERT BRUCE, physician; b. Cleburne, Tex., July 11, 1910; s. Andy and Mary (Martin) L.; B.S., East Tex. State U., 1947; M.D., Baylor U., 1947; m. Fredleen Power, Feb. 5, 1941; children—Betty Jo (Mrs. G.R. Singleton), Bonnie (Mrs. W.J. Hyson), Robert F., Theodore W. Intern Methodist Hosp., Houston, 1947-48; gen. practice medicine, Houston, 1946-63; staff psychiatrist Terrell (Tex.) State Hosp., 1964-73. Tchr. adult bible class First Meth. Ch., Terrell, lesson broadcast over KTER each Sunday, 1968-73. Mem. A.M.A., Tex. Med. Assn., Kaufman County Med. Soc., Theta Kappa Psi. Contbr. articles to med. jours. Home: Terrell, Tex. Died Dec. 4, 1973.

LEONARD, WALTER ANDERSON, consul; b. Essex, Ia., Aug. 3, 1880; s. Levin Anderson and Ida (Hultman) L.; B.A., U. of Neb., 1903; post-grad. work, Northwestern U., univs. of Chicago and Wis., Freiburg U. Taught school in Kankakee and Kenilworth, Ill., 1904-07; vice consul, Freiburg, Germany, 1907-08, Kehl, Feb.-July 1908; in charge commercial dept., New Trier Tp High Sch., 1908-12; consul at Stavanger, Norway, 1912-14, Colombo, Ceylon, 1914-19; assigned to Dept. of State, 1919-22; consul at Stockholm, Sweden, 1922-25, Warsaw, Poland, 1925-29, at Bremen, Germany, 1929-36; became consul gen., Stockholm Sweden, Jan. 1936; became consul gen. and 1st sec. of Legation, Tallinn, Estonia, Feb. 1, 1937; retired from the U.S. Foreign Service after more than 30 years of service; appointed consultant in the Office of Economic Warfare, Washington, D.C., 1943, Office of Internat. Trade, Dept. of Commerce, from 1945. Mason. Mem. Am. Soc. Internat. Law, etc. Home: Evanston, Ill.†

LESCOT, ELLE, Haitian diplomat, former pres. of Haiti; b. Saint Louis du Nord, 1883, ed. Cap-Haitian. Mem. legislative assembly, 1900-03, Court of First Instance, Port-au-Prince; judge of same, sec. public edn. and agriculture, during adminstrn. of Pres. Borno; sec. of justice and interior during adminstrn. Pres. Stenio Vincent; minister plenipotentiary to Dominican Republic; minister to U.S., 1937-41; President of Haiti, 1941-46. Honors: Grand Officer of Order of Honor and Merit of Haiti, and of the Order of Merit Juan Pablo Duarte of Dominican Republic; Grand Cross of same orders. Mem. governing bd. of Pan.-Am. Union. Address: Port-au-Prince, Haiti Died Oct. 1974.

LESLIE, HARRY BRAHAM, physician; b. Dayton, O., Mar. 15, 1904; s. David and Sophia (Braham) Lefkowitz; M.D., Johns Hopkins, 1928; m. Alma Ruth Koch, June 16, 1927; children—Harry Braham, Lynn (Mrs. Edward Levine). Intern, Univ. Hosp., Cleve., 1928-29, asst. resident, 1929, resident, 1930, fellow, 1931-32, later affiliate staff; asst. in pediatrics Kinderklinik, Freiburg, Germany, 1933, Kinderklinik Hosp., Vienna, Austria, 1933; asso. pediatrician Babies and Children's Hosp., Cleve., Rainbow Hosp., Cleve; affiliate staff Suburban Community Hosp., Mt. Sinai Hosp.; asso. prof. Case-Western Res. U. 1927-72. Served to maj., M.C., AUS, 1942-45. Diplomate Am. Bd. Pediatrics. Mem. A.M.A., Am. Acad. Pediatrics, Phi Beta Kappa. Jewish religion. Home: Cleveland, O. Died Jan. 3, 1973; buried Mayfield Cemetery, Cleveland, O.

LESTER, BERNADOTTE PERRIN, investment banker; b. Saratoga Springs, N.Y., May 19, 1896; s. Charles Cooke and Mary Lane (Tuck) L.; B.S., Union Coll., Schenectady, 1918, LL.D., 1958; student Columbia Law Sch., 1919-21; m. Margaret Curtiss Burton, Sept. 21, 1921; children—James Burton, Bernadotte Perrin. With legal firm Simpson, Thacher & Bartlett, N.Y.C., 1920-23; mem. firm Knight, Stetson & Lester, investment bankers, Los Angeles, 1923-28; v.p. Banks, Huntley & Co., investment bankers, 1928-32; pres., dir. Lester & Co., Los Angeles, 1932-51; sr. partner Lester, Ryons & Co., 1951-69; partner Hornblower & Weeks-Hemphill, Noyes, 1969-71; chmn. bd. City Coach Lines, Inc., Jacksonville, Fla., 1948-74, also dir. subsidiaries; dir. Baker Oil Tools, Inc., Los Angeles. Mem. Pacific Coast Stock Exchange (formerly Los Angeles Stock Exchange), 1936-51, N.Y. Stock Exchange, 1951-69, Am. Stock Exchange. Mem. Cal., N.Y. state bars, Alpha Delta Phi. Mason. Clubs: California (Los Angeles); Annandale Golf (Pasadena). Home: Pasadena Cal. Died Jan. 14, 1974.

LEV, SAUL NATHAN, ret. electronics co. exec.; b. Phila., May 7, 1910; s. Joseph and Minnie (Casel) L.; B.S. in Elec. Engring., U. Pa., 1931, M.S. in Elec. Engring., 1932; m. Freda R. Steinberg, Mar. 29, 1934; children—Joseph Allen, Marion Lea. With RCA, 1934-74, mgr. first mass prodn. TV receiver plant in U.S., 1946-51, gen. mgr. Moorestown (N.J.) missile and surface radar div., 1959-62, v.p., 1960-62, div. v.p. def. mfg. and program mgmt., 1962-65, div. d.p., gen. mgr. West Coast div., 1965-67, div. v.p., gen mgr. communications systems div., def. electronic products, 1967-69, div. v.p. mfg., 1969-73. Chmn. Newton dist. Boy Scouts Am., 1956-59, v.p. Camden County council, 1968-73, pres., 1973-74. Mem. I.E.E.E., Am. Forces Communications and Electronics Assn., Am. Soc. Naval Engrs., S. Jersey C. of C. (pres. 1971-72), Eta Kappa Nu. Jewish religion (past pres. temple). Home: Cherry Hill N.J. Died Nov. 13, 1974; interred Crescent Cemetery, Camden, N.J.

LEVENGOOD, CLAUDE ANDERSON, educator; b. Boyertown, Pa., Mar. 5, 1910; s. James Y. and Mary M. (Anderson) L.; B.S., Franklin and Marshall Coll., 1931; M.S., Northwestern U., 1934, Ph.D., 1937; m. Ruth M. Landis, Mar. 15, 1930; children—James, Peter, Julieanne. Grad. asst., part-time instr. zoology Northwestern U., 1931-37; successively instr., asst. prof., asso. prof. U. Tulsa, 1937-53, prof., chmn. dept. zoology, 1953-57, chmn. dept. life scis., 1957-75. Served as lt. USNR, World War II. Mem. A.A.A.S., Am. Inst. Biol. Scis., Sigma Xi, Delta Sigma Phi. Author: (with H.D. Chase) Laboratory Manual for General Zoology, 1939. Home: Tulsa, Okla. Died Jan. 15, 1975; interred Memorial Park, Tulsa, Okla.

LEVENTHAL, ALBERT RICE, publisher; b. N.Y.C., Oct. 30, 1907; s. Philip and Ida F. (Rice) L.; A.B., U. Mich., 1928; m. Janis H. Hilpp, Mar. 14, 1934; children—Barbara, Jane, John Philip. Reporter Bklyn. Times-Union, 1928-30, Sunday editor, 1930-32; promotion mgr. Simon & Schuster, Inc., N.Y.C., 1933-38, sales mgr., 1938-44, v.p., 1945-52, exec. v.p., 1952-57; pres. Artists & Writers Press div. Western Printing & Lithographing Co., 1958-68; pres. Golden Press, Inc., 1958-68, Am. Heritage Press, 1968-70; group v.p. McGraw-Hill Co., Inc., 1970-72, sr. cons., 1973; pres. Vineyard Books, Inc., 1973-76; partner Sandpiper Press, 1945. Mem. Am. Book Pubs. Council (bd. dirs.), Phi Beta Kappa, Phi Kappa Phi, Zeta Beta Tau. Club: Regency (N.Y.C.). Author: I Wish I'd Said That (pen name Albert Rice), 1934; False Colors, 1941; War: A Photographic History, 1973; Book Publishing in America, 1973. Contbr. articles nat. mags. Home: New York City, N.Y., Died Jan. 6, 1976.

LEVI, CARLO, writer, artist; b. 1902; studied medicine. Banished to So. Italy during Fascist regime; dir. L'Italia Libera, daily, Rome, Italy, 1945-46; contbr. articles and drawings to L'Italia Socialista, 1947-48, La Stampa, 1949-75. Author: Chirst Stopped at Eholi, 1945; Paura della liberta, 1946; Le Parole sono Piele, 1955; Il Futuro Ha Un Cuore Antico, 1956; others. Address: Rome, Italy. Died Jan. 4, 1975.

LEVIN, JACK, financial indsl. adviser, community planner; b. Portland, Ore., June 23, 1898; s. Rev. Max and Anina (Cohen) L.; A.B., Reed Coll., 1920, LL.B., Northwestern 1923, Ph.D., Am. U. Washington, 1931; post-grad. work U. of Ore., U. of Wash., Columbia; m. Lillian S. Shapiro, June 26, 1932; children—Anina Levin Weinreb, Lucille Levin Abramson, Exec., partner Levin Hardward Co., Levin Heating & Engring. Co., Portland, Ore., 1923-26; western mgr. Nat. Brass Co., Portland, 1926-29; professor interstate law Columbus U., Washington, 1938; prof. internat. law and politics George Washington U., 1946; former v.p. Balogh & Co., stock and investment brokers; former syndicate mgr. Sandkuhia Co., underwriters-brokers, Cal., N.Y., N.J., Pa., and D.C.; pres. Dr. Jack Levin & Associates, Inc., Washington; expert community planning, housing and pub. utilities. Asst. corp. counsel valuation expert counsel Pub. Utility Commn., Washington; cons. to mems. U.S. Senate and Ho. of Reps. 1930-46; chief of legal research and cons. on constnl. anti-trust laws, N.R.A., 1933-34; asst. counsel, rate expert, cons. to adminstr. Rural Electrification Adminstrn., Washington, 1935-44; cons. to expediter-adminstr., Nat. Housing Agency, 1946; lectr. on econs., law Community Center, Washington; cons. for U.S. Congress in housing and pub. utilities, Legislative Reference Service, Library of Congress, 1946-56; cons. to Congress and industry on community planning, housing and pub. utilities; dir. Inter-American Engring. Program for Latin American Republics, 1936-41; dir. U.S. Senate staff for high cost of housing, 1948. Senate Fed. housing programs, 1948-50. Trainee officer U.S. Army, World War I. Registered mem. Nat. Assn. of Security Dealers; licensed broker Washington Real Estate Commn. Mem. State and Fed. bars, A.A.A.S., Author: Power Ethics, 1931; Valuation and Regulation of Pub. Utilities (with Dr. John H. Gray), 1933; Indsl. Planning Under the Codes (with Dr. G. B. Galloway), 1935; The General Housing Bill, 1947; A 20th Century Congress (with U.S. Senate Estes Kefauver), 1947. Contbr.; Great Plains Drought (by F.D. Roosevelt), 1940; Rural America Lights Up (by Harry Slattery), 1941; Your Congress and American Housing, 1952; also various tech. publications and reports. Address: Hallandale, Fla., Died June 14, 1974.

LEVINSON, DAVID, lawyer; b. Chgo., July 24, 1889; s. Abraham and Sarah (Rubin) L.; Ph.B., U. Chgo., 1910, J.D. cum laude, 1912; m. Sara Neumann, Dec. 20, 1918 (dec. Oct. 1937); children—John (dec.), William, David; m. 2d, Minnie Buzard, June 20, 1940 (dec. Dec. 2, 1966). Admitted to Ill. bar, 1912, with Felsenthal & Wilson, Chgo., 1912-17, Sonnenschein, Berkson & Lautmann, Chgo., 1917-18; partner Sonnenschein, Berkson, Lautmann & Levinson, Chgo., 1918-31, successor firm Sonnenschein, Berkson, Lautmann, Levinson & Morse, 1931-57, Sonnenschein, Lautmann, Levinson, Rieser, Carlin & Nath, 1957-68, Sonnenschein, Levinson, Carlin, Nath & Rosenthal, 1963-68; dir. John Plain & Co. Mem. com. character and fitness Ill. Supreme Ct., 1937-41. Mem. citizens bd. U. Chgo., 1940-73. Mem. Am., Ill., Chgo. bar assns., Art Inst. Chgo., Order of Coif. Republican. Club: Standard (Chgo.). Contbr. to Basic Principles of Real Estate Leases, 1952; Law Forum (U. Ill.). Home: Highland Park, Ill. Died June 27, 1973.

LEVINSON, NORMAN, mathematician, educator; b. Lynn, Mass., Aug. 11, 1912; s. Max and Gussie (Green) L.; M.S., B.S., Mass. Inst. Tech., 1934, Sc.D., 1935; m. Zipporah A. Wallman, Feb. 11, 1938; children—Sylvia Ciel, Joan Ellen. Redfield Proctor travelling fellow Cambridge (Eng.) U., 1934-35; Nat. Research Council fellow mathematics Princeton, Inst. for Advanced Study, 1935-37; John Simon Guggenheim Meml. Found. fellow U. Copenhagen, 1948-49; faculty mem. Mass. Inst. Tech., Cambridge from 1937, acting chmn. mathematics dept., 1951-52. Fellow Am. Acad. Arts and Scis.; mem. Am. Math. Soc. Mem. editorial bd. Annals of Mathematics, Transactions Am. Math. Soc., Jour. Rational Mechanics and Analysis. Home: Concord, Mass., Died Oct. 10, 1975.

LEVIS, J. PRESTON, corp. exec. b. Alton, Ill., July 30, 1901; s. Frank and Harriet (Keiser) L.; student U. Mo., 1919-20; M.E., Cornell U., 1924; m. Charlotte Rodgers, Sept. 8, 1927; children—Harriet Levis McFarlane, Annette Levis Boice, John Preston. Began with Ill. Glass Co., 1924, co. acquired by Owens-Ill. Glass Co., 1929 (name changed to Owens-Ill. Inc. 1965), various positions, 1929-45, pres., 1941-50. chmn. bd. 1950-68, chmn. exec. com., 1968-72, chmn. finance com., 1972-73, also dir.; dir. Toledo Edison Co., Libbey-Owens-Ford Co. Trustee A.R.C., Nutrition Found., Cornell U., Toledo U. Mem. Kappa Sigma. Republican. Baptist. Elk. Clubs: Toledo, Country, Inverness (Toledo); Bohemian (San Francisco); Jupiter Island (Hobe Sound, Fla.); Seminole Golf (Riviera Beach, Fla.); Cloud, Links, Fifth Avenue (N.Y.C.). Home: Toledo O. Died Apr. 17, 1973.

LEVITSKY, LOUIS MOSES, rabbi; b. Russia, Jan. 4, 1897; s. Samuel and Freda (Wolowick) L.; came to Montreal, Can., Sept. 1904; to U.S., 1916, naturalized 1924; A.B., Coll. City N.Y., 1929; rabbi Jewish Theol. Sem. Am., 1923, D.H.L., 1933, D.D., 1949, M.H.L.; spl. courses, Columbia and Harvard; m. Anna Lillian Levy, Nov. 27, 1929; 1 dau., Barbara. Rabbi, Temple Israel, Wilkes-Barre, Pa., 1922-40, Oheb Sholom Temple, Newark, 1940; mem. faculty humanities dept. Rutgers U., 1955-65; pub. mem. Labor-Mgmt. Inst.; spl. lectr. Newark Coll. Engring.; spl. lectr. on religion Douglas Coll. for Women, 1960-61; adj. asso. prof. theology St. Elizabeth Coll., Convent Station, N.J. maj. N.J. State Guard, serving as chaplain. Founder, Inst. on Religion, Wilkes-Barre, Pa.; pres. Rabbinical Assembly Am., 1942-44; dir. Sem. Sch. Jewish Studies, 1941-67; chmn. exec. com. Com. Army and Navy Religious Activities, Jewish Welfare Bd., 1942-45; bd. dirs. Jewish Women's Inst., Newark Community and War Chest; chmn. Welfare Council of Newark, 1942-43; trustee Welfare Fedn.; mem. panel and chmn. 3 mem. panel, Nat. War Labor Bd., Region 2, 1941-46; panel mem. N.J. Labor Mediation Bd.; mem. Am. Arbitration Assn.; chmn. survey commn. Essex County Council Jewish Agys., 1940-48; mem. nat. exec. com. Am. Jewish Conf.; dir. United Synagogue of Am., (Essex County) YM and YWHA, Council of Jewish Agys., Jewish Edn. Assn. Bd. trustees, Jewish Theol. Sem. Am., 1940-46, recipient Distinguished Service medal, 1963; Rutgers U. medal, 1963; chmn. Placement Commn., Rabbinical Assembly of Am. Chmn. Jewish War Records Com. Essex County, 1940-46; vice chmn. Jewish Arbitration Commn. Essex County; mem. Essex County Round Table, Nat. Conf. Christians and Jews, Nat. Acad. Adult Jewish Edn. (chmn. bd. govs.), Nat. Clergymen's Council (Fedn. Planned Parenthood), Am. Assn. Polit. and Social Sci., Bibl. Lit. and Exegesis, N.Y. Bd. Jewish Ministers, co-chmn. Bd. Jewish Ministers of Essex County, Com. of Theologians Internat. Office of Edn., Commn. on Jewish Law, Prayer Book Commn. of Conservation Judaism in Am., Liaison Com. of Jewish Theol. Sem., United Synagogue Rabbinical Assembly; Nat. Exec. Com. Rabbinical Assembly of Am. Democrat. Mason, Rotarian. Author: A Jew Looks at America, 1939 (brochure) Freedom Under Law; What's On My Mind, 1960. Mem. bd. editors, Reconstructionist, 1941-48; Conservative Judaism. Contbr. articles in religious Jours. and Universal Jewish Ency. Address: South Orange, N.J. Died June 14, 1975.

LEVY, ISAAC D(AVID), business exec.; b. Phila., Aug. 26, 1892; s. David and Fannie L.; LL.B., U. Pa., 1913; m. Rita Kaplan, Dec. 6, 1924; children—David Richard, Ann Frances Siegel. Dir, Atlantic City Racing Assn.; directing mgr. Motor Inns, Phila. Commr. Fairmount Park. Yeoman 1st class USN, 1917. Mem. Am., Phila. bar assns. Republican. Jewish religion. Mason. Clubs: Locust, Midday (Phila.); Rockefeller Luncheon (N.Y.C.). Home: Philadelphia, Pa., Died Nov. 29, 1975.

LEVY, NATHAN, lawyer; b. S. Bend, Ind., Oct. 25, 1909; s. Louis and Bessie (Margolis) L.; A.B., U. Mich., 1931, J.D., 1934; m. Norma Jean Fuchs, Oct. 3, 1936 (dec. Jan. 29, 1973); children—Gail (Mrs. Michael S. Perlman), Paul. Admitted to Ind. bar, 1934, since practiced in S. Bend; partner firm Crumpacker, May, Levy & Searer, from 1944; city atty., S. Bend, 1941-47; adj. prof. law U. Notre Dame, 1954-63. Active local Community Chest, United Fund. Bd. dirs. United Way, from 1964, chmn. budget and consultation com., from 1964. Mem Order of Coif. Home: Mishawaka, Ind. Deceased.

LEVY, ROBERT J., bus. exec.; b. New Orleans, Aug. 31, 1902; s. Sylvan and Helen (Newburger) L.; student Tulane U., 1919-20; A.B. cum laude, Harvard, 1923; m. Patricia Shwartz, Mar. 8, 1927; 1 dau., Ann P. Clk., Samuel Newburger & Co., N.Y.C., 1923-25, partner, 1925-29; Hano Wasserman & Co., N.Y.C., 1930-32, Robert J. Levy & Co. (named changed to R.J. Levy, Harris, Inc. 1967), N.Y.C., 1932-67, chmn. bd., 1967-74; chmn. bd. Standard Shares, Inc.; sr. v.p. A.G. Becker & Co., Inc., N.Y.C., 1972-74. Hon. bd. dirs. Altro Health and Rehab. Services, Inc. Head adminstrv. officer Bd. Econ. Warfare, Washington, 1942; head liaison officer OPA, Washington, 1943. Trustee Hebrew Tech. Inst.; trustee-at-large Jewish Philanthropies. Served from maj. to lt. col., AUS, 1943-46: ETO, part time as Gen. Eisenhower's liaison officer to Gen. DeGaulle. Decorated chevalier Legion of Honor, Croix de Guerre with palm; officer Order Brit. Empire. Club: Wall Street, Home: New York City, N.Y. Died Mar. 11, 1974.

LEVY, ROBERT LOUIS, physician; b. N.Y.C., Oct. 14, 1888; s. Louis and Harriet (Strouse) L.; A.B., Yale, 1909; M.D., Johns Hopkins, 1913; m. Beatrice N. Straus, June 29, 1920 (dec. Aug. 1967); children—Barbara, Gerald Dun, Jessica. Resident house officer Johns Hopkins Hosp., 1913-14, asst. resident physician, instr. medicine Hosp. and Univ., 1914-16, 16-17; instr. physiology Harvard Med. Sch., 1916; resident physician Rockefeller Inst. Hosp., 1919-20; asso. medicine Rockefeller Inst., 1919-22; asso. attending, attending physician Presbyn. Hosp., N.Y.C., 1922-54, cons. physician, 1954-74, dir. dept. cardiology, 1925-54; cons. cardiologist Roosevelt, French, Englewood hosps.; mem. med. adv. bd. Am. Hosp., Paris; asso. Coll. Phys. and Surg., Columbia, 1922-26, asst. prof. clin. medicine, 1926-30, asso. prof., 1930-36, prof., 1936-54, emeritus 1954-74. Past chmn. subcom. cardiovascular diseases, mem. com. medicine and surgery NRC; cons. cardiology sec. war, World War II; mem. N.Y. Commn. Med. Care, 1944-46; mem. overseers com. to visit Harvard Med. Sch., 1934-44. Served to capt., M.C., U.S. Army, 1917-19. Recipient Bicentennial medal Coll. Phys. and Surg., Columbia, 1968. Fellow A.C.P., N.Y. Acad. Medicine (pres. 1957-60, trustee 1960); mem. A.M.A. (chmn. sect. pharmacology and therapeutics 1932), Am., N.Y. (pres. 1948-49) heart assns., Assn. Am. Physicians, Am. Clin. and Climatol. Assn. (pres. 1953-54), Am. Soc. Clin. Investigation, Am. Soc. Pharmacology and Therapeutics, N.Y. Med. Soc. (chmn. sec. on medicine 1925), Société Francaise de Cardiologie (corr. mem.), Soc. Exptl. Biology and Medicine, Harvey Soc., Soc. Brasileira de Cardiologia (hon.), Phi Beta Kappa, Alpha Omega Alpha. Clubs: Grolier, Century (N.Y.C.). co-author: Nomenclature and Criteria for Diagnosis of Diseases of the Heart, 1928. Editor: Diseases of the Coronary Arteries and Cardiac Pain, 1936; Disorders of the Heart and Circulation, 1951. Editorial bd. Am. Heart Jour. Contbr. papers med. jours. Home: New York City, N.Y. Died Nov. 23, 1974; buried Woodlawn Cemetery.

LEVY, ROBERT MICHAEL, paper co. exec.; b. Chgo., Mar. 1, 1916; s. Jacob J. and Mae (Wolf) L.; B.S., Armour Inst., 1937, M.S., 1939; Ph.D., Ill. Inst. Tech., 1940; m. Helen Lowenson, Sept. 1, 1940; children—Jack M., Thea M. (Mrs. Barry A. Fish), Leonard M. Research ass. Ill. Inst. Tech. Research Found., 1936-40; asst. mgr. research and devel. Olin Corp., Pisgah Forest, N.C., 1940-58; v.p. SCM-Allied Paper, Inc., Kalamazoo, 1958-74. Chmn. com. on research and edn. Western Mich. U., 1965-68; vol. exec. Internat. Exec. Service Corps, N.Y.C. Served with AUS, 1937. Recipient award Smith Corona Marchant Co., 1968. Mem. Am. Chem. Soc., Am. Inst. Chem. Engrs., I.E.E.E., Am. Inst. Physics, U.S. and Can. Tech. Assn. Paper Industry, Soc. Photog. Scientists and Engrs., Sigma Xi, Phi Lambda Upsilon. Elk. Contbr. to profl. pubs. Patentee in field. Home: Kalamazoo Mich. Died Feb. 14, 1974.

LEWIS, AUSTIN WARREN, lawyer; b. Sulphur, La., Sept. 23, 1910; s. William Warren and Lula (Vaughan) L.; student Southwestern La. Inst., 1926-29; LL.B., Tulane U., 1932; m. Natalie Scott, July 30, 1935; children—Jerry S., Sallye L. (Mrs. John E. Hammett). Admitted to La. bar, 1932; practice in Lake Charles, 1932-35; mem. Liskow & Lewis, Lake Charles, 1935-64, New Orleans, 1964-74. Mem. jud. council La. Supreme Ct., 1960-64. Served with USMCR, 1942-45. Fellow Am. Coll. Trial Lawyers (pres. until 1974); mem. Am. (mineral law and adminstrv. law sects.), La., Southwestern La. (past pres.) bar assns., Order of Coif, Home: New Orleans La. Died Nov. 18, 1974.

LEWIS, EDWIN OWEN, judge; b. Richmond, Va., July 12, 1879; s. Louis and Elizabeth (Owen) L.; student Virginia Institute, Richmond College; LL.B., U. of Pennsylvania, 1902; H.H.D. (hon.), Moore Institute of Art; m. Eleanor Anna Lord, April 26, 1905 (died Dec. 7, 1935); children—Carolyn Montague (Mrs. W. Wycliff Walton), Eleanor Lord (Mrs. Adkins Lowell); m. 2d, Agnes Almy Morris, May 4, 1943. Admitted to Pa. bar, 1902; practiced in Philadelphia, 1902-23; mem. City Council, 1907-09; permanent sec. and counsel, City Party and other independent polit. movements, 1905-12; apptd. Bd. Recreation, Phila., 1911; elected Judge, Court of Common Pleas, from 1923; president Philadelphia School of Design for Women, 1918-32; president Moore Institute Art, 1932-46; dir. Athenaneum Library (p.p.), Pa. Acad. Fine Arts (1933-45), Hist. Soc. of Pa. (v.p. 1938-53); pres. Independence Hall Assn. founded in 1942; chmn. com. to bring U.N. headquarters to Phila., 1945; chmn. adv. commn., Independence Nat. Hist. Park, from 1948. Mem. Am. Philos. Soc., Colonial Soc. Pa. (pres. 1945-46), Pa. State and Am. bar assns., Soc. of Colonial Wars (honorary gov. gen.), Pa. Soc. (historian), Gen. Soc. of Sons of the Revolution (hon. gen. pres. for life), Pa. Soc. (hon. pres. for life), Va. Soc. the Cincinnati Clubs: Rittenhouse, Pot and Kettle (Bar Harbor, Maine); The Wistar Assn. Republican. Episcopalian. Author: Street Ry. Situation in Philadelphia, 1907; Recreation of the Colonial Background in America, 1936. Home: Philadelphia, Pa.†

LEWIS, FRED B(RADLEY), business exec.; b. Anaheim, Calif., Mar. 13, 1878; s. Lafayette and Ellen (Potter) L.; B.S., Rose Poly. Inst., 1905, E.E., 1917; m. Florence Warth, Nov. 15, 1906. Elec. engr. Southern Calif. Edison Co., Los Angeles, 1905-21, mgr. operation, 1921-31, vice pres. and gen. mgr., 1931-42, also dir. Asso. Calif. Inst. Tech. from 1925. Mem. Pacific Coast Elec. Assn. (pres. 1939). Republican. Episcopalian. Clubs: California, Los Angeles Country; Union (Victoria, B.C.). Home: Los Angeles, Cal.†

LEWIS, HAROLD M(ACLEAN), cons. engr., city planner; b. Red Hook, N.Y., Aug. 8, 1889; s. Nelson Peter and Minnie Rose (MacLean) L.; A.B., Williams Coll., 1909; C.E., Rensselaer Poly. Inst., 1912; m. Harriett M. Goodin, Nov. 5, 1919; children—Oliver Nelson, Russell MacLean. Asst. engr. on design and constrn. water supply and sewerage systems in offices George W. Fuller and James C. Harding (N.Y. City), Emschergenossenschaft (Essen, Germany), and Frank L. Wilcox (St. Louis), 1912-15; asst. engr. Charles W. Leavitt, N.Y. City, also resident engr. Chas. M. Schwab estate, Loretto, Pa., 1915-17; resident engr. Charles W. Leavitt, on estate in Birmingham, Ala., 1919-20; exec. engr. Com. on Regional Plan of N.Y. and its environs, 1921-32; chief engr. and planning officer Regional Plan Assn., N.Y. City, 1932-42, sec. 1938-40; consultant Nat. Resources Planning Bd. and its predecessors, 1935-39; cons. engr. Office of Pres., Borough of Manhattan, N.Y.C., 1942-45; cons. on rezoning District of Columbia, 1954-56; gen. practice as cons. engr. and city planner to municipalities on preparation of comprehensive plans, zoning and rezoning, since 1929; lectr. Columbia U., 1938; mem. faculty, grad. div. of tng. in pub. service N.Y. U., 1939-41; lectr. Mass. Inst. Tech., 1949; spl. lecturer various other universities. Trustee of Engineering Index. Served as 2d lt. to captain Engrs. Corps. AUS, AEF, 1917-19. Licensed profl. engr., N.Y., New Jersey and Delaware. Member Am. Soc. C.E. (dir. 1939-41), Am. Inst. Planners (pres. 1944-46, distinguished service award 1957), Am. Inst. Cons. Engrs. (v.p. 1960-61), Municipal Engineers of City of New York, American Planning and Civic Association (director 1954-63), Am. Soc. Planning Ofcls., Rensselaer Soc. Engrs., Am. Legion, Phi Beta Kappa, Sigma Xi, Tau Beta Pi, Phi Delta Theta. Presbyn. (elder). Club: Williams. Author: City Planning — Why and How, 1939; Planning the Modern City (2 vols.), 1949; also articles and papers on city planning problems in tech. press and other periodicals. Address: Troy N.Y. Died Oct. 1973.

LEWIS, JOHN MILLIGAN, clergyman; b. Chattanooga, Tenn., Mar. 25, 1889; s. Wilber Mason and Jennie May (Lee) L.; A.B., Austin Coll., 1911, D.D., 1928; B.D., Austin Presbyn. Theol. Sem., 1914; m. Verda Perry, Oct. 29, 1914; children—Ruth Elaine (Mrs. R. C. Douglas), Jacque (Mrs. Robert R. Click). Ordained to the ministry of the Presbyterian Ch. U.S., 1914; pastorates Somerville, Barlett and Freeport, Tex., 1914-22; pastor 1st Presbyn. Ch., Lubbock, Tex., from 1922; moderator of the Synod of Tex., 1936-37. Trustee Austin Coll., Westminster Encampment, Kerrville, Tex. Democrat. Mason (33°), K.T. Club: Kiwanis. Home: Lubbock, Tex., Died May 15, 1972; interred Resthaven Mausoleum, Lubbock, Tex.

LEWIS, WARREN KENDALL, chem. engr.; b. Laurel, Del., Aug. 21, 1882; s. Henry Clay and Martha Ellen (Kinder) L.; S.B., Mass. Inst. Tech., 1905; Ph.D. in Chemistry, U. Breslau, Germany, 1908; D.Sc. (hon.), U. Del., 1937, Harvard, 1951, Bowdoin Coll., 1952; D.Eng. (hon.), Princeton, 1947; m. Rosalind Denny Kenway, Oct. 1909. With Mass. Inst. Tech., 1910-75, prof. chem. engring., 1915-48; ret. Mem. Am. Chem. Soc., Am. Acad. Arts and Scis., Am. Inst. Chem. Engrs., Nat. Acad. Scis., Instn. Chem. Engrs. Great Britain (hon.), Am. Inst. Mining, Metall. and Petroleum Engrs. Conglist. Club: Chemists' (N.Y.C.). Contbr. tech. jours. on chem. engring. Died Mar. 9, 1975.

LEWIS, WILLIAM BENNETT, advt. exec.; b. Lakewood, O., Aug. 12, 1904; s. Norman and Lucille (Eggert) L.; student U. of Mo., 1922-24; m. Sarah Johnson, Jan. 1, 1935; children—Lawrence Johnson, Sarah Ragan, Lucille Grigware. Began as advt. apprentice J. Walter Thompson Co., 1924; advt. copy writer, varous agys., 1925-35; dir. of programs CBS, 1936-37, v.p. in charge of programs, 1937-41; coordinator of govt. radio, Office of Facts and Figures, Washington, Jan. 1941, June 1942; chief, Domestic Radio Bur., Office of War Information, July 1942-Jan. 1943; asst. dir. Domestic Br., Office of War Information, Jan. 1943, July 1943; cons. CBS, Aug. 1943, Aug. 1944; v.p. Kenyon & Eckhardt Inc., 1944-51, pres., 1951-60, bd. chmn. 1960-67. Chmn. bd. dirs. Am. Cancer Soc. Died Feb. 24, 1975.

LICHT, GEORGE AUGUSTUS, architect; b. New York, N.Y., Nov. 4, 1878; s. Lawrence and Anna (Becket) L.; student Atelier Freedlander, New York, 1900-03, Ecole des Beaux Arts, Paris, under Jean Louis Pascol, 1904-06; m. Clara Belle Tibbits, Sept. 8, 1903; children—George Tibbits, Richard Homer, Organized and conducted Atelier Licht, New York, 1908-38; pvt. practice of architecture, New York, 1906-08; became associated with Delano and Aldrich, architects, New York, 1908, partner, 1914; vis. critic of design, Princeton, 1923-26, of advanced design, Columbia, 1926-30, New York Univ., 1930-32. Awarded Paris prize (1st holder) by Soc. of Beaux Arts Architects, 1904, Grande Medaille by Societe Centrale des Architectes Francais, 1906, Gold Medal of Archtl. League of N.Y., 1906. Fellow Am. Inst. of Architects. Mem. Archtl. League of New York, New York Soc. of Architects, Beaux Arts Inst. of Design, New Rochelle Art Assn. Republican. Episcopalian. Home: New Rochelle, N.Y.†

LICHTEN, ROBERT LYON, aero engr.; b. Phila., July 3, 1921; s. Harold and Goldie (Rosenbaum) L.; S.B. in Aero, Engring., Mass. Inst. Tech., 1943; m. Susan Rogers, June 4, 1943; children—Thomas Rogers, John Harold, David Alan. Research asst., flutter lab. Mass. Inst. Tech., 1942-43; chief aerodynamics, aircraft div. Budd Co., 1943-44; aerodynamicist Platt LePage & Kellett Aircraft Cos., 1944-46; v.p., chief engr. Transcendental Aircraft Co., 1946-47; project engr., chief exptl. project engr., dir. advanced engring. Bell Helicopter Co., 1948-71; spl. work on XV-3 convertiplane, UH-1 and Jet Ranger series helicopters. Member com. aircraft aerodynamics NASA, 1960-63. Mem. ednl. council Mass. Inst. Tech., 1958-71. Pres. Dallas Civil Liberties Union, 1967-69, v.p. Tex. Civil Liberties Union, 1968-71. Trustee Vertical Flight Found., 1967-71; bd. dirs. League for Ednl. Advancement in Dallas. Asso. fellow Am. Inst. Aero. and Astronautics, Royal Aero. Soc.; mem. Am. Helicopter Soc. (pres. 1965, chmn. bd. 1966; Klemin award 1959; mem. editorial bd. jour. 1956-64, Haveter award 1972), Assn. U.S. Army, Army Aviation Assn., Dallas UN Assn. (pres. 1968-69), Sigma Xi, Tau Beta Pi. Clubs: MIT (pres. 1966-68), Brookhaven Country (Dallas). Contbr. profl. jours. Home: Dallas, Tex. Died Sept. 18, 1971.

LIDBURY, FRANK AUSTIN, chemist; b. Middlewich, Eng., Mar. 14, 1879; s. Frank Albert and Emily (Harding) L.; B.Sc., Owens Coll. (Victoria U.), Manchester, 1898, M.Sc., 1899; studied U. of London, 1899-1900, U. of Leipzig, 1900-01; m. Bessie Dixon, June 20, 1905. Came to U.S., 1903, naturalized citizen, 1913. Chief chemist Oldbury Electrochem. Co., Niagara Falls, N.Y., 1903-05, works mgr. same, 1905-22, pres. and gen. mgr. 1922-47. Home: Niagara Falls, N.Y.†

LIEB, JOSEPH PATRICK, judge; b. Faribault, Minn., Sept. 4, 1901; s. George Francis and Mary Jane (McManus) L.; student St. Thomas Coll., St. Paul, 1919-21; LL.B., Georgetown U., 1924; postgrad. Nat. U., 1924-25; m. Helen Bowman, June 15, 1933; 1 son, Joseph Patrick. Admitted to D.C. bar, 1924, Fla. bar, 1927; spl. agt. FBI, 1925-31; asst. U.S. atty. So. Dist. Fla., 1931-34; practice law, Tampa, Fla., 1934-55; judge U.S. Dist. Ct. So. Dist. Fla., 1955-62; judge U.S. Dist. Ct. Middle Dist. Fla., 1962-71; pres. judge, 1962-67, chief judge, 1967-71. Mem. Am., Fla., Tampa, Hillsborough County bar assns., Soc. Former Spl. Agts. FBI, Delta Theta Phi. Republican. Catholic. Elk, Rotarian. Home: Tampa, Fla. Died Nov. 2, 1971; interred Myrtle Hill Meml. Park, Tampa, Fla.

LIEN, ROBERT COWLES, physician; b. Hillsboro, N.D., Sept. 24, 1926; s. Frederick Charles and Josephine (Cowles) L.; student N.D. State Coll., U. N.D.; M.D., Northwestern U., 1953; m. Rachelen Jones, Sept. 1954; children—Robert Cowles, Virginia Wade, James Frederick. Intern, Charity Hosp. of La., New Orleans, 1953-54, resident in surgery, 1955-57, chief resident, 1957-58, later vis. surgeon; resident in surgery Wesley Meml. Hosp., Chgo., 1954-55; asso. staff surgeon So. Baptist Hosp.; active staff surgeon Sara Mayo Hosp., Touro Infirmary, West Jefferson Hosp. (all New Orleans); courtesy staff Flint-Goodridge Hosp.; cons. in surgery Lallie Kemp Charity Hosp., Independence, La.; asst. prof. surgery Tulane U. Served with USAF, World War II. Diplomate Am. Bd. Surgery. Fellow A.C.S.: mem. A.M.A., La., Orleans Parish med. socs., Am. Soc. Clin. Oncology, Oscar Creech, James Rives surg. socs., Assn. Acad. Surgeons, Southwestern Surg. Congress, Sigma Xi, Rho Chi, Phi Beta Pi, Sigma Chi. Democrat. Presbyn. Contbr. articles to sci. jours. Designer radio-controlled model airplane. Home: New Orleans, La. Died Feb. 1, 1969.

LIGHT, ISRAEL, univ. dean; b. N.Y.C., Mar. 8, 1915; s. Jacob and Zelda (Herskovitz) L.; A.B., U. Cin., 1937, Ed. B., 1938, Ed.M., 1942; Ed.D., Columbia, 1949; m. Hilda Siegel, Dec. 25, 1943. Instr., Cin. Pub. Schs., 1937-41; research asso. U.S. Office Edn., 1948-49, Fed. Civil Def. Adminstrn., 1949, Am. Polit. Sci. Assn., 1949-50, Am. Council Learned Socs., 1950; editor U.S. Bur. Lab. Statistics, 1951-53; editor, grants analyst, manpower specialist, editorial adviser, chief Ednl. Program Devel. in Allied Health Professions, Pub. Health Service, Dept. Health, Edn. and Welfare, 1956-69; dean Sch. Related Health Scis., U. Health Sci., Chgo. Med. Sch., 1969-75. Mem. adv. com. Nat. Commn. for Study of Nursing and Nursing Edn.; adv. council Ill. Comprehensive Health Planning Agy.; mem. tech. rev. com. Ill. Regional Med. Program; allied health com. Chgo. Bd. Edn. Bd. dirs. Profl. Examination Service, N.Y. Served with AUS, 1941-45; ETO. Fellow Soc. for Tech. Communication, A.A.A.S., Inst. Medicine of Chgo.; mem. Am. Med. Writers Assn., D.A.V., Royal Soc. Health, Assn. Schs. Allied Health Professions, Am. Soc. Hosp. Edn. and Tng., Am. Dietetic Assn. (dir.; nat. adv. bd.). Contbr. articles profl. jours. Home: Chicago Ill. Died Feb. 20, 1975; interred Washington, D.C.

LIGON, ELVIN SETH, educator; b. Appomatox County, Va., June 4, 1878; s. Willis Hopkins and Nannie Maria (Cunningham) L.; B.A., U. of Richmond, 1898, M.A., 1899; post-grad. work, U. of Chicago, 1902; m. Virginia Dickey, Aug. 21, 1907; children—William Arthur, Elvin Seth, John Dickey. Instr. mathematics, U. of Richmond, 1898-99; asst. prin., Dothan (Ala.) High Sch., 1899-1900; prin. schs., Houston, Va., 1900-01; prin. Blakely Inst., Ga., 1901-02; pres. Newport News (Va.) Acad., 1902-07; instr. Richmond Acad., 1907-09; instr. mathematics, U. of Richmond, 1908-09; headmaster Fork Union Mil. Acad., 1909-12; pres. and propr. Blackstone (Va.) Mil. Acad., 1912-30; dean Georgia Mil. Acad., 1930-35; dean Fla. Mil. Acad., St. Petersburg, 1935-40; prin. and dir. of Guidance, Bolles Sch., Jacksonville, from 1940. Democrat. Baptist. Address: Jacksonville, Fla.†

LIGON, ELVIN SETH, JR., air force officer; b. Fork Union, Va., Jan. 9, 1911; s. Elvin Seth and Virginia (Dickey) L.; student U. Richmond, 1927-30; B.S., U.S. Mil. Acad., 1934; grad. Air Force Flying Sch., 1934. Command and General Staff Sch., 1946, Air War Coll., 1947, Nat. War Coll., 1953; m. Margaretta Flanigan; children—Elvin Seth III, John M. (dec.) Commd. 2d lt. Army, 1934, advanced through grades to maj. gen., USAF, 1958; various assignment tech. tng. installations, U.S., 1938-45; comdr. 466th Bomb Group, 8th Air Force, 1945; ovserver Baker test, Operation Crossroads, Bikini, 1946; instr. Air War Coll., 1947; asst. dir. intelligence Alaskan Command, also Alaskan Air Command Staff, 1947-49; spl. projects officer, dir. acad. staff Air War Coll., 1949-52; with Nat. Security Agy., 1953-54; dir. plans, then dir. personnel planning Hdqrs. USAF, 1954-57; comdr. recruiting service, 1957-59, dir. personnnel planning, 1959-61; mil. planning staff CENTO, 1961-63; with Allied Air Forces So. Europe NATO, Naples, Italy, 1963-65; Hdqrs. Pacific Air Forces Hickam AFB, Hawaii, 1965-75. Decorated Legion of Merit with oak leaf cluster, Distinguished Fluing Cross, Air medal with oak leaf cluster, Bronze Star medal, Meritorious Service unit insignia; Croix de Guerre with palm (France). Mem. Air Force Assn., Phi Gamma Delta, Club: Army-Navy Country (Washington). Home: Arlington, Va., Died Nov. 19, 1975; buried Arlington Nat. Cemetery.

LIM, PILAR HIDALGO (MRS. VICENTE LIM), univ. pres.; b. Boac, Marinduque, Philippines, May 24, 1893; d. Luis Alino and Eulalia (Larbizabal) Hidalgo; B.A. cum laude, U. Philippines (Manila), 1913; Dr. Pedagogy, De La Salle Coll., 1964, Philippine Women's U., Manila, 1966; Dr. Edn., U. Manila (Philippines), 1970; m. Vicente P. Lim, Aug. 12, 1917; children—Luis, Roberto, Vicente H., Patricio, Eulalia, Maria Pilar (Mrs. Conrado Ayuyao). Pres., Centro Escolar U., Manila. Pres. Nat. Fedn. Women's Clubs, 1931-41; pres. Girl Scouts Philippines, Found. for Rehab. of Handicapped. Bd. dirs. Philippine Red Cross. Recipient meritorious service award Nat. Fedn. Women's Clubs, 1952, Presdl. award for social service, 1954, Torch Bearer award Feminist Movement, 1955, Most Outstanding Alumna of U. Philippines award, 1955, Aurora Aragon Quezon medal, 1959, Most Outstanding Mother award, 1960, Gold Vision Triangle award, 1966, Presdl. award, 1966, Dakilang Guro award, 1968. Club: Zonta. Built 6 Girl Scout camps and hdqrs. P.R. Girl Scouts. Home: Manila, Philippines. Died Dec. 10, 1973; buried Manila Meml. Cemetery.

LIMOGES, JOSEPH EUGENE, bishop; b. Ste. Scholastique, Nov. 16, 1879; s. Joseph and Denise (Dumouchel) L.; ed. at Laurent Coll., and Grand Seminary of Montreal. Curate in Alfred, Ontario, 1902-03; in St. Cecile, Quebec, 1903-06; parish priest at Montcerf, Quebec, 1906-13, at Cathedral of Mont-Laurier, Quebec, 1913-18, at St. Jonte, 1918-22; bishop of Mont Laurier, from 1922; created asst. at the Pontifical Throne, Roman Count, 1947. Home: Mont-Laurier, Que., Can.*†

LINCOLN, ASA LIGGETT, physician; b. Lacey Springs, Va., May 10, 1891; s. John Edward and Alice (Cline) L.; M.D., Johns Hopkins, 1916; m. Edith Helen Maas, Jan. 31, 1918; children—Anne Hadden, John Edward. Asso. vis. physician N.Y. Hosp.; cons. physician Hackensack (N.J.) Hosp., Bellevue Hosp., N.Y.C., Greenwich (Conn.) Hosp.; prof. clin. med. Cornell U., 1940-65. Served to capt. M.C., U.S. Army, 1917-19. Recipient Acad. plaque N.Y. Acad. Medicine, 1963. Diplomate Am. Bd. Internal Medicine. Fellow A.C.P. (gov. Eastern sect. 1942-51, regent 1951-57); mem. N.Y. Acad. Medicine (v.p. 1949-51, trustee 1950-65), Nu Sigma Nu. Home: North Salem, N.Y. Died Sept. 13, 1974; buried June Cemetery, North Salem, N.Y.

LINCOLN, GEORGE ARTHUR, educator, army officer; b. Harbor Beach, Mich., July 20, 1907; s. Burr B. and Esther (Hoare) L.; student U. Wichita, 1924-25; B.S., U.S. Mil. Acad., 1929; B.A., M.A., Oxford (Eng.) U., 1932; LL.D., U. Pitts., 1968; D. Engring., Drexel U., 1972; m. Frederica Bellamy, Aug. 19, 1936; children—Frederica Esther, Daniel Bellamy, Joyce LeFevre, Lorna Harriet. Commd. 2d lt. C.E., U.S. Army, 1929, advanced through grades to brig. gen., 1945; instr. U.S. Mil. Acad., 1937-41; duty ETO, 1942-43; with Gen. Staff, War Dept., 1943-47; prof. social sci. U.S. Mil. Acad., 1947-69, head dept., 1954-69; ret., 1969; dir. Office Emergency Preparedness, Washington, 1969-73; prof. econs. and internat. studies Denver U., 1972-75. Mil. adviser to sec. state Paris Peace Conf., 1946; dep. to undersec. U.S. Army, 1948-49; spl. asst. to sec. def., 1951-53; mem. U.S. delegation NATO, 1951-52; mem. Rockefeller and Gaither coms., 1957; staff Pres. Com. Study Mil. Assistance Program, 1958; spl. adviser to adminstr. AID, 1964-65. Decorated D.S.M. with oak leaf cluster, Legion of Merit with oak leaf cluster (U.S.); hon. comdr. Order Brit. Empire. Mem. Council Fgn. Relations. Soc. Am. Mil. Engrs., Assn. Am. Rhodes Scholars. Clubs: Army-Navy (Washington); Denver Country. Co-author: Background for Our War, 1942; Economics of National Security, 1954; International Politics, 1954; Dynamics of International Politics, rev. edit., 1967. Author: Strategy of Minerals, International Realities, 1948. Home: Evergreen, Colo. Died May 24, 1975; interred Fairmount Cemetery, Denver, Colo.

LINCOLN, GEORGE GOULD, newspaper corr.; b. Washington, D.C., July 26, 1880; s. Nathan Smith and Jeanie Thomas (Gould) L.; prep. edn., Friends' Sch., Washington; A.B., Yale, 1902; m. Mary Hester Shepard, 1909 (died 1926); children—Hester Shepard (deceased), Nathan Shepard, Marjorie Gould; m. 2d, Elizabeth Wilder, 1927 (divorced 1945); m. 3d, Delia Hazeltine Pynchon, 1946. Began as reporter Wash. Times, 1902; rptr. Wash. Post. 1905-08; with Evening Star, Washington, from 1909, also Washington corr. Mem. O.T.C., Fort Myer, Va., 1917. Chmn. standing com. in charge Congl. Press Galleries, 1930-31. Mem. Delta Kappa Epsilon, Wolf's Head Soc. Republican. Episcopalian. Clubs: Nat. Press. Chevy Chase, Gridiron (pres. 1937). Home: Chevy Chase, Md. Died Dec. 1, 1974.

LINDABURY, IRVIN L., educator; b. Califon, N.J., Aug. 31, 1880; s. H.R. and Amanda (Hoffman) L.; Califon High Sch.; grad. Rider Coll., Trenton, N.J., 1900; spl. work Harvard, 1915; m. May G. Moran of Malden, Mass., June 1904; children—Grace B., Eleanor, Elizabeth M. Head of Commercial Dept. Bird's Inst., N.Y. City, 1900-04; in business, New York and Boston, 3 yrs.; later v.p. and sec. Burdett Coll., Boston. Mem. Nat. Assn. of Accredited Commercial Schs. (gov.), Eastern Commercial Teachers' Assn. (pres.), Reciprocity Club of America (pres. Boston sect.), Boston Chamber of Commerce. Republican. Episcopalian. Mason. Clubs: Boston City, 20th Century, Kernwood. Colonial Country (v.p. and dir.); Meadow Brook Golf, University Club of Malden (pres.). Home: Malden, Mass.†

LINDABURY, RICHARD VLIET, editor, educator; b. Brernardsville, N.J., Sept. 5, 1900; s. Richard Vliet and Lillie (Van Saun) L.; grad. Hill Sch., 1917; A.B., Princeton, 1921, M.A., 1923, Ph.D., 1930; m. Alice Ballantine Young, May 20, 1927; children—Alice Van Saun (Mrs. Alan Peter Carter), Margaret Boyd (Mrs. Philip Cooper, Jr.), Peter Vliet. Instr. English dept. Princeton, 1922-25, 27-29, lectr., 1945-46; research, 1930-41; with fgn. nationalities br. OSS, 1942-45; asso. editor Colliers Ency., 1946-50; editorial writer N.Y. Herald Tribune, 1952-56, poetry editor, 1956-57; editor Proc. N.J. Hist. Soc., 1959-74; asso. prof. English, Fairleigh Dickinson Coll., 1961-62. Sec. N.J. Roadside Council, 1938-42, pres., 1946-47; exec. bd. Princeton Community Players, 1934-42, 45-49, pres., 1940-41. Decorated chevalier de l'ordre de la Couronne (Belgium). Mem. Poetry Soc. Am. (exec. bd. 1959-63, pres. 1963), N.J. Hist. Soc. (2d v.p. 1959-74), Archaeol. Soc. Princeton (pres. 1959-62), Hist. Soc. Princeton (v.p. 1960-74), Soc. Colonial Wars N.J. (lt. gov. 1965-74), Shakespeare Soc. Phila., St. Nicholas Soc., Phi Beta Kappa. Author: A Study of Patriotism in the Elizabethan Drama, 1930. Home: Princeton, N.J. Died Feb. 4, 1975.

LINDBERG, CARL OTTO, mining engr.; b. Stockholm, Sweden, Oct. 8, 1879; s. student Royal Swedish War Acad.; Heidelberg U., B.S., Mich. Coll. of Mines, 1904, E.M., 1906; m. Marie Helen Boulsom, of Marquette, Mich., Feb. 19, 1902. With Cleveland Cliffs Iron Co., Ishpeming, Mich., 1905-06; gen. supt. mines and mill, Benito Juarez Mines Co., Salinas, Mex., 1907-08; asst. examining engr. with F. W. Royer, Mexico City, 1908-09; with John Hays Hammond's syndicate in Mexico, 1909-10; with Spurr & Cox, Inc., New York, 1910-11; examining mining engr. with W. Rowland Cox, New York, 1911-15; cons. mining engr. from 1915. Mem. Mining and Metall. Soc. America, Am. Inst. Mining Engrs. Inst. Mining and Metallurgy (London), Tau Beta Phi Sigma Rho. Mason (32°)*†

LINDBERGH, CHARLES AUGUSTUS, aviator; b. Detroit, Feb. 4, 1902; s. Charles Augustus (mem. Congress from 6th Minn. Dist., 1907-17) and Evangeline Lodge (Land) L.; grad. high sch., Little Falls, Minn., 1918; marticulated in mech. engring., U. Wis., 1920; left univ. to enroll in Flying Sch., Lincoln, Neb., Feb. 1922; M. Aero., N.Y. U., 1928; LL.D., Northwestern U. and U. Wis., 1928; hon. M.S., Princeton, 1931; m. Anne Spencer Morrow, May 27, 1929; children—Charles A. (dec.), Jon Morrow, Land Morrow, Anne, Reeve, Scott. Started flying 1922; airmail pilot St. Louis-Chgo., 1926; purchased The Spirit of St. Louis, Feb. 1927; flew The Spirit of St. Louis San Diego to N.Y.C., May 1927, flying time 21 hours, 20 minutes; flew non-stop N.Y.C. to Paris, May 20, 1927, 33 / house; receptions by French govt., Brussels, London, Washington, N.Y.C. and some 75 other cities in U.S.; non-stop flight Washington-Mexico City, 27 hrs. 10 minutes, 1927. Flying cadet U.S. Air Service Res., 1924, later advanced to col. 1st lt. Mo. N.G., 1925, later col. Dir. Pan Am. World Airways. Made survey of U.S. airplane prodn. for U.S. Army, 1939; toured U.S. making radio speeches urging U.S. to keep out of war, 1941. Trustee Panamin Found., Inc., Carnegie Instn., 1934. Recipient Congl. Medal of Honor (U.S.), D.F.C., D.S.C., Woodrow Wilson medal and ½,000 for good will flight to Mexico, Central Am. and West Indies, Langley medal (Smithsonian Instn.), many others; decorated chevalier Legion of Honor (French); Royal Air Cross (Brit.); Order of Leopold (Belgian) and others; Winner Orteig ½,000 prize for 1st N.Y. to Paris non-stop flight, also various other tokens of recognition; recipient Wright Bros. Meml. Trophy, 1949; Pulitzer award, Distinguished Am. biography, 1954. Author: Of Flight and Life, 1948; The Spirit of St. Louis, 1953. Died Aug. 26, 1974.

LINDBLOOM, PAULINE FUNK, librarian; b. Hazen, Ark., Dec. 31, 1911; d. Ebbert Arl and Emma (Selby) Funk; B.A., U. Kan., 1933; M.A., U. Denver, 1959; postgrad. U. Colo., 1961-75; m. Harold Seth Lindbloom, Dec. 31, 1935; children—Elise Anne Emmamuel, Betty Rae Petersen. Librarian Boulder High Sch. (Colo.), 1959-62, head librarian, dir. instructional materials center, 1962-75; Instr. U. Sask. at Regina, summer 1969. Chmn. met. area residential Mile-Hi United Fund Drive, 1955, 56; mem. Common Cause, 1970-76; mem. tchrs. adv. council to supt. Boulder Valley Schs., 1970-72. Bd. dirs. United Fund Agys., Denver, 1956-57. Mem. A.L.A., N.E.A., Assn. Communication and Technology, Colo. Assn. Librarians (bd. dirs. 1968-70), Pi Lambda Theta, P.E.O., Alpha Delta Pi. Democrat. Unitarian. Home: Boulder, Colo., Died July 26, 1975.

LINDEMANN, ERICH, psychiatrist; b. Witten, Germany, May 2, 1900; s. Erich and Anna (Raeker) L.; Ph.D., U. Marburg and Giessen, Germany, 1922, M.D., 1926; m. Elizabeth Brainerd, Sept. 30, 1939; children—Jeffrey, Brenda. Rotating intern U. Cologne Med. Coll., 1925; resident physician dept. neurology U. Heidelberg, Germany, 1926-27; research asso. psychiatry U. Ia., 1927-28, research asso. exptl. psychology, speech pathology, 1928-29, instr. psychology, 1929-31, asst. prof., 1931-35; asst. physician U. Ia. Psychopathic Hosp., 1929-35, psychiatrist outpatient dept., 1932-34; Rockefeller fellow psychiatry, physiology Harvard, 1935-36, instr. psychiatry Harvard Med. Sch., 1937-41, asso. psychiatry, 1941-48, prof. psychiatry, 1954-74, also instr. psychiatry, asso. prof. mental health Harvard Sch. Pub. Health; psychiatrist outpatient dept. Mass. Gen. Hosp., 1935-37, successively asso. psychiatrist, physician charge psychol. outpatient dept., chief psychiatrist; now vis. professor Stanford U. Medical Center; vis. professor at U. Tübingen, Germany, summer 1966; cons. psychiatrist Mass. Eye and Ear Infirmary. Mem. expert panel mental health WHO since 1957. Mem. Boston Psychoanalytic Soc. (pres. 1943-46), Am. Psychiat. Assn. (chmn. com preventive psychiatry 1952), Group for Advancement Psychiatry (chmn. com. preventive psychiatry 1950-53), NRC, Boston Soc. Psychiatry and Neurology, Mass. Assn. Mental Health, Social Sci. Research Council, Am. Psychosomatic Soc. (exec. council 1954), Am. Assn. U. Profs., A.M.A., Am. Neurol. Assn., Am. Orthopsychiat. Assn., Am. Psychoanalytic Assn., Am. Psychol. Assn., Nat. Assn. Mental Health, Am. Anthrop. Assn., Am. Assn. Applied Anthropology, Am. Psychosomatic Assn., Assn. Research Nervous and Mental Diseases, Mass. Med. Assn., Mass. Soc. Mental Hygiene, Mass. Soc. Research Psychiatry. Home: Palo Alto, Cal. Died Nov. 16, 1974.

LINDLEY, JOHN FRANKLIN, lawyer; born Reliance, S.D., Aug. 29, 1918; s. William and Ozitte (King) L.; A.B., Dakota Wesleyan U., 1938; LL.B., U. S.D., 1948; m. Carina Kragt Smeets, Apr. 4, 1952; children—Robin (foster son), Philip, James, Marianne, Suzanne, Paul. With Gen. Accounting office, Wash., 1939-41; admitted to S.D. bar, 1948; practice of laws with M.A. Brown, Chamberlain, 1948-62, Brown and Lindley, 1962-71; states attorney, Brule County, 1953, 57, 65-67; lt. gov. South Dakota, 1958-60; clk., Chamberlain Ind. Sch. Dist., 1952-60; S.D. rep. Interstate Oil Compact Commn.; civilian aide Sec. Army U.S. for S.D., 1962-64. Member S.D. Ho. of Reps., 1951-52; del. Dem. Nat. Conv., 1956; candidate for governor, S.D., 1964. Served as 1st lt., cav., AUS, 1941-46. Mem. Am. Legion, Vets. Fgn. Wars. Am., S.D. (pres. jr. sect. 1951-52), 4th Jud. Circuit (pres. 1958-59, state bar commissioner 1966-68) bar associations, South Dakota Young Democrats (state pres. 1948, nat. committeeman 1949-50, regional dir. 1951). Episcopalian. Mason (Shriner), Elk; mem. Order Eastern Star. Home: Chamberlain, S.D. Died Apr. 23, 1971; buried Chamberlain, S.D.

LINDSEY, MALCOLM F., army officer; b. Waco, Tex., July 22, 1891; s. Henry Clay and Mary Eliza (Edmond) L.; student U. of Tex., 1916, Columbia Univ., 1924; grad. Inf. Sch., 1922, Command and Gen. Staff Sch., 1932, Army War Coll.; 1935, Chem. Warfare Sch., 1935, Air Corps Tactical Sch., 1936; m. Sally Guthrie Bond, May 25, 1926; children—Marie Evans, Sally Guthrie (twins). Commd. 2d lt. Inf., Apr. 1917, and advanced through the grades to brig. gen., Nov. 1943; assigned Gen. Staff Corps, 1937-40; command garrison at Kodiak, Alaska, 1941; dep. chief of staff, 4th Army and Western Defense, Apr.-Oct. 1942; comd. regt. in 83d Div., India, Nov. 1942; G-3, of Y Force, Chinese Armies, under Lt. Gen. Stilwell, Nov. 1942; comdr. Z Force, second 30 Divs. Chinese Army to Dec. 1944; comdr. Indiantown Gap Training and Personnel Center. Home: Washington, D.C., Died Dec. 10, 1975.

LINFIELD, ADOLPHUS, clergyman, educator, ins. exec.; b. Twillingate, Newfoundland, Apr. 13, 1880; s. Josiah and Sarah Ann (Rowsell) L.; B. Religious Edn., Boston U., 1921, S.T.B., 1924, D.D., 1938; m. Bessie May Willard, Sept. 7, 1907; children—Willard Adolphus, Ruth May, Paul Robert. Came to U.S., 1895, naturalized, 1914. Ordained to ministry of Meth. Ch., 1902; pastor N.H. and Mass. schs., 1902-20; prof. practical theology Boston U. from 1920; sec. and mgr. Ministers Mut. Life Ins. Co., Boston, from 1940. Mem. N.H. Legislature, 1913-14. Chmn. bd. trustees Tilton Sch and Jr. Coll. Mem. Mass. Housing Assn. (dir. and v.p. from 1940). Home: Watertown, Mass.†

LINFORTH, IVAN MORTIMER, prof. Greek; b. San Francisco, Calif., Sept. 15, 1879; s. Edward William and Emma Amanda (French) L.; A.B., U. of Calif., 1900, A.M., 1901, Ph.D., 1905; Harvard Club (San Francisco) scholar, Harvard, 1902-03; m. Katherine Frances Storie, June 20, 1906; children—Katharine Gordon (Mrs. Malcolm Colby Henderson), Edward Mortimer, Margaret (Mrs. John Youngs Beach), Barbara (Mrs. Craig Hugh Smyth). Instr. in Greek, U. of Calif., 1905-10, asst. prof., 1910-16, asso. prof., 1916-19, prof., 1919-49, emeritus. Annual prof. Am. Sch. Classical Studies, Athens, 1934-35. Vis. prof. Classics, Andrew Fleming West Foundation, Princeton Univ., 1939-40. Fellow Kahn Foundation for Foreign Travel of Am. Teachers, 1912-13. Fellow Am. Acad. of Arts and Sciences; mem. Am. Philol. Assn. (ex-pres.), Philol. Assn. Pacific Coast (pres.), Am. Assn. Univ. Profs., Phi Beta Kappa, Phi Kappa Sigma. Club: Faculty. Author: Solon the Athenian, 1919; The Arts of Orpheus, 1941. Contbr. to philol. jours. Home: Berkeley, Cal.†

LINGLE, ELMORE YOKUM, meat packing co. exec.; b. Bethany, Mo., July 18, 1910; s. Walter Thomas and Emma (Jennings) L.; B.S., U. Mo., 1932; m. Florence Ann McIninch, Oct. 12, 1938; children—Anne (Mrs. James Douglas Esson), Susan (Mrs. Dirk Van Loon). A founder Seitz Packing Co., Inc., St. Joseph, Mo., 1936, pres., 1955-65, chmn. bd. 1965-74; dir. St. Joseph Light & Power Co., Gray Mgr. Co.; a founder Sterling Colo. Beef Co., 1966, also dir.; pres., founder Packers Adv. Co., St. Joseph, 1966-74. Mem. Nat. Cattle Industry Adv. Com. Agr. Dept., 1968. Chmn. United Fund. Bd. dirs. YMCA; trustee St. Joseph Hosp. Named Boss of Year, St Joseph Jr. C. of C., 1962; recipient for Service to Youth award YMCA, 1961, Distinguished Industry award Nat. Ind. Meat Packers Assn., 1965. Mem. C. of C. (past bd. dirs.), Nat. Ind. Meat Packers Assn. (pres. 1965-66, hon. bd. dirs. 1966-71), Am. Meat Inst. (bd. dirs.), Alpha Tau Omega. Home: St. Joseph, Mo. Died Feb. 17, 1974.

LININGER, FREDERICK FOUSE, agricultural economist; b. Martinsburg, Pa., July 29, 1892; s. Levi and Mary (Fouse) L.; studied Huston Twp. Sch., Blair County, 1898-1910, Lock Haven (Pa.) State Teachers Coll., 1910-12; B.S., Pa. State Coll., 1917; M.S., Cornell U., 1926, Ph.D., 1928; m. Mildred Tobias, Apr. 9, 1917; children—Fred Tobias, Jean Lois (Mrs. Charles Taylor). Teacher, pub. sch., 1912-13; engaged in agrl. extension serv. as county agent, Mercer County, Pa., 1917-18; farmer, 1918-20; supervisor of agr., Morrison Cove Vocational Sch., 1920-23, dir. 1923-25; asst. prof. agrl. economics, Pa. State Coll., 1926-28, asso. prof., 1928-29, prof., 1929-41 head dept., 1938-41, v. dean, Sch. of Agr., v. dir. Pa. Agr. Expt. Sta., 1940, v. dean div. since 1942; while on leave of absence engaged in research at Brookings Instn., 1933-34; advisor in China on agrl. development, food and agr. orgn. of U.N., 1948; chmn. Phila. Milk Price Com., 1948-49; now dep. dir., agr. div. FAO, U. N., Rome, Italy. Mem. N.E.A. American Academy of Political and Social Science, Pennsylvania State Education Assn., Am. Farm Economist Association, International Conf. of Agrl. Economists, Alpha Gamma Rho, Alpha Zeta, Delta Sigma Rho, Gamma Sigma Delta (pres. nat. soc. 1949). Phi Delta Kappa, Phi Kappa Phi, Sigma Xi. Democrat. Presbyn. Mason (32°). Author: Dairy Products Under the Agricultural Adjustment, Act; Consumer Cooperation Here and Abroad; also various bulls. on marketing and farm mngmt. in Pa. Home: State College, Pa. Died July 1974.

LINK, MARGARET C. SCHOTT (MRS. JOSEPH LINK, JR.), investment and lumber exec.; b. Cin., Sept. 17, 1910; d. Charles J. and Florence Closterman; student pvt. sch.; m. Loseph Link, Jr., Dec. 17, 1960; children—Walter E. Schott, Margo S. Homan. Pres., Swan Creek Lumber Co., Toledo, 1956-72, Vernon Manor Hotel, Cin., 1945-72, Investment Co. Queen City, Cin., 1956-72. Chmn. Charity Ball, Cin.; pres. W. E. Schott Family Found., St. Margaret Hall. Decorated knight Order Lady Holy Sepulere. Clubs: Surf (Miami Beach, Fla.); Bal Harbour (Fla.); Queen City, Hyde Park Country (Cin.). Home: Cincinnati, C. Died Oct. 5, 1972.

LINKLATER, ERIC, author; b. Mar. 8, 1899; s. Robert Baikie and Mary Elizabeth (Young) L.; student Aberdeen (Scotland) Sch.; M.A., LL.D., Aberdeen U.; m. Marjorie MacIntyre, June 1, 1933; children—Alison Sarah, Kristin, Magnus Duncan, Andro. Asst. editor The Times of India, Bombay, 1925-27; asst. to prof. English lit. Aberdeen U., 1927-28; Commonwealth fellow, U.S., 1928-30. Served as pvt., Black Watch, France, 1917-18; became capt. Royal Engrs., 1938, advancing to maj. 1939; mobilized comdg. Orkney Fortress Royal Engrs., 1939; assigned duty under dir. pub. relations, War Office, 1941; spl. service Iceland, 1941, Italy, 1944-45; temp. lt. col., Korea, 1951; rector Aberdeen U., 1945-48. Decorated Comdr. Order Brit. Empire. Mem. Ch. of Eng. Clubs: Savile (London): New (Edinburgh). Author: White-man's Saga, 1929; Poet's Pub. 1930; A Dragon Laughed, 1930; Juan in America, 1931; Ben Jonson and King James, 1931; The Men of Ness, 1933; Mary Queen of Scots, 1933; The Devil's in the News, 1934; Magnus Merriman, 1934; Robert The Bruce, 1934; Ripeness Is All, 1935; God Likes Them Plain, 1935; The Lion and The Unicorn, 1935; Juan in China, 1937; The Sailor's Holiday, 1938; The Impregnable Women, 1938; Judas, 1939; The Man on My Back, 1941; The Northern Garrisons, 1941; The Defense of Calais, 1941; The Highland Division, 1942; The Cornerstones, 1942; Socrates Asks Why, 1943; The Great Ship, 1943; The Wind on the Moon, 1944; Crisis in Heaven (a play), 1944; Private Angelo, 1946; The Art of Adventure, 1947; Sealskin Trousers, 1947; Love in Albania (play), 1948; A Spell for Old Bones, 1949; Mr. Byculla, 1950; Laxdale Hall, 1951; The Campaign in Italy, 1951; The House of Gair, 1953; A Year of Space, 1953; The Faithful Ally, 1954; The Ultimate Viking, 1955; The Dark of Summer, 1956; Breakspear in Gascony (play), 1958; Position at Noon, 1958; The Merry Muse, 1959; Edinburgh, 1960; Roll of Honour, 1961; Husband of Delilah, 1962; A Man Over Forty, 1963; The Prince in the Heather, 1965; Orkney and Shetland, 1965; The Conquest of England, 1966; A Terrible Freedom, 1966; The Survival of Scotland, 1968; The Stories of Eric Linklater, 1968; (with Edwin Smith) Scotland, 1968; The Royal House of Scotland, 1970; John Moore's England, 1970; Fanfare for a Tin Hat, 1970; The Corpse on Clapham Common, 1971; The Voyage of the Challenger, 1972. Home: Ross Shire, Scotland. Died Nov. 7, 1974; interred Kirkyard, Orkney, Scotland.

LINNES, LOWELL CLAUDE, devel. adminstr.; b. Hoffman, Minn., June 30, 1931; s. Claude L. and Viola (Auslund) L.; B.A., Gustavus Adolphus Coll., St. Peter, Minn., 1953; M.A., U. Minn., 1957; m. Joanne Carol Anderson, Aug. 22, 1953; children—Laurie, Steven, Jeffrey, Sarah. Dir. placement inquiries clearance office U. Minn., 1956-57; personnel dir. IBM, Rochester, 1957-67; sec. bd. devel. Mayo Found., Rochester, 1967-74; dir. Rochester Savs. and Loan Assn.; dir., asst. sec.-treas. Quarve & Anderson Constrn. Co. Pres. Rochester YMCA, 1966-68; v.p. Rochester City Charter Commn., 1968; mem. Rochester Community Relations Commn., 1968; chmn. bd. dirs. North Central Area YMCA, 1968-70, chmn. bd. dirs. Mid Am. region, 1970-74; bd. dirs. Nat. Council YMCA's, 1970-74, mem. exec. com., 1971-74; bd. dirs. Minn. Dept. Human Rights, 1968-74, vice chmn., 1970-74; mem. Minn. com. U.S. Commn. Civil Rights, 1973-74; bd. dirs. YMCA of Rockies, Estes Park, Colo., 1971-74; trustee Greater Gustavus Fund. Served with AUS, 1953-55. Named Rochester's Outstanding Young Man of the Year, 1966; recipient Outstanding Contbn. award N.A.A.C.P., 1970. Mem. Minn. Psychol. Assn., Internat. Platform Assn. Republican. Lutheran. Home: 1248 20th Rochester Minn. Died Mar. 25, 1974.

LINNIK, IURIL VLADIMIROVICH, mathematician; b. Jan. 21, 1915; s. Vladimir P. Linnik; grad. Leningrad U., 1938, D.Phys.-Math. Scis., 1940. With Leningrad br. Math. Inst., USSR Acad. Scis., 1940-72; prof. Leningrad U., 1944-72. Recipient Stalin prize, 1947, Lenin prize, 1969. Mem. USSR Acad. Scis. Research on theory of numbers; gave estimation of smallest prime number in arithmetical progression with a large difference; work in calculus of probability, heterogeneous Markov chains, math. statistics. Address: Leningrad, USSR., Died June 30, 1975.

LINVILLE, CLARENCE PHILANDER, metallurgical engr.; b. Urbana, O., Mar. 29, 1879; s. Philander Edwin and Marie Cecilia (McClellan) L.; B.Sc., Ohio State U., 1900, M.A., 1902; m. Jane Alice Evans, of Jackson, O., June 29, 1904; children—C. Edwin, Philip. Fellow in chemistry, Ohio State U., 1900-02; asst. chemist, with iron and steel companies, 1902-03; instr. metallurgy, 1903-06, asst. prof., 1906-07, asso. prof., metall. engring., 1907-12, Sch. of Mines, Pa. State Coll.; blast furnaces supt. with Joseph E. Thropp, 1912-13; asst. supt. Am. Smelting & Refining Co., Maurer, N.J., 1913-16; research metallurgist, 1916-23; instr. dental metallurgy, Columbia U. Sch. of Dental and Oral Surgery, 1921-24; metallurgist Calco Chem. Co. Bound Brook, N.J., from 1923; splty. research and process development work. Mem. Am. Inst. Mining Engrs., Am. Chem. Soc., Am. Inst. Chemists, Am. Electrochem. Soc., N.J. Chem. Soc., Sigma Xi, Chi Phi. Home: Elizabeth, N.J.†

LINZ, PAUL FRANCIS, merchant; b. N.Y.C., Aug. 21, 1899; s. Isaac and Fanny (Mayer) L.; ed. pub. schs., N.Y.C., and extension courses Columbia; m. Katherine Blaisdell. With Am. Metal Co., 1915-32; partner C. M. Loeb, Rhoads & Co., N.Y.C., 1932-49; personal asst. to Dr. Mauricio Hochschild, 1949-74; chmn. bd. S. Am. Minerals & Mdse. Corp. until 1953; chmn. bd. Merc. Metal & Ore Corp., 1953-59; dir., cons. Brandeis Goldschmidt & Co., 1960-61; pres. Primary Metal & Mineral Corp., 1961-74, Primexin, Inc. Served to lt. comdr. USNR, and with Dept. State, 1941-44. Mem. Am. Inst. Mining and Metall. Engrs., Pan Am. Soc, Clubs: Bankers (N.Y.C.); Army and Navy (Washington). Home: South Kent, Conn. Died Jan. 16, 1974.

LIPPINCOTT, ELLIS RIDGEWAY, JR., chemist, educator: b. Phila., July 6, 1920; s. Ellis Ridgeway and Florence Kirk (Stapler) L.; B.A., Earlham Coll., 1943; M.A., Johns Hopkins, 1944, Ph.D., 1947; postgrad. Mass. Inst. Tech., 1947-48; m. Rita Clifton, Aug. 14, 1948; children—Melanie, Jennifer, Wendy, Robin, Holly. Instr., Loyola Coll., Balt., 1947; instr. U. Conn., 1948-51; asso. prof. chemistry Kan. State Coll., 1951-55; prof. chemistry U. Md., College Park, 1955-74, dir. Center Materials Research, 1967-74; lectr. Mass. Inst. Tech., 1953-74; cons. Nat. Bur. Standards, Office Sec. Def., NIH; vis. scientist div. chem. edn. Am. Chem. Soc., 1963-67. Mem. adv. bd. XIII Colloquium Spectroscopicum Internationale. Recipient Hillebrand award, 1964, award Spectroscopy Soc. Pitts., 1970, Tallman prof. chemistry Bowdoin Coll., Me., 1970. Mem. Am. Chem. Soc., Am. Phys. Soc., Faraday Soc., Coblentz Soc., Washington Acad. Sci., Soc. for Applied Spectroscopy, Am. Soc. Testing Materials, Chem. Soc. London, Philos. Soc. Washington, Phi Beta Kappa, Sigma Xi, Alpha Chi Sigma, Gamma Alpha, Pi Mu Epsilon, Editor: Proceedings of the Xth Colloquium Spectroscopicum Internationale, 1962. Adv. editor sci. jour. Spect. Acta. Contbr. articles to profl. jours. Home: Vienna Va. Died Dec. 24, 1974.

LIPPMAN, HYMAN SHALIT, physician; b. Mpls., Jan. 15, 1896; s. Harry Shalit and Anna Lippmann; M.D., U. Minn., 1920, M.A. in Biology, 1920, Ph.D. in Pediatrics, 1923; m. Adelaide Jonas Hirsch, June 17, 1945; children—Henry, Arlene (Mrs. Richard Campion). Sr. intern Minn. Gen. Hosp., Mpls., 1919-20; fellow in pediatrics U. Minn., 1920-23, prof. pediatrics and psychiatry emeritus, also mem. faculty Sch. Social Work; trainee Psychoanalytic Inst., Vienna, Austria, 1927-31; student Anna Freud's Seminar in child analysis; cons. psychiatrist Children's Hosp., St. Paul, St. Paul Ramsey Hosp.; dir. Amherst Wilder Child Guidance Clinic, 1931-67; lectr. Smith Coll. Social Work, summers, 1936-44. Del., White House Conf. on Children, 1940, 50, 60; tchr. social work Unitarian Com., Germany, summer 1951; cons. Hennepin County Welfare Bd., 1970-72; mem. Minn. Gov.'s Adv. Council on Children and Youth. Bd. dirs. St. John's U., Children's Home Soc., Mpls. Diplomate Am. Bd. Psychiatry. Mem. A.M.A., Am. Orthopsychiat. Assn. (pres. 1953-54), Am. Psychiat. Assn., Am. Assn. Psychiat. Clinics for Children (pres. 1963-65), Am. Psychoanalytic Assn., Group for Advancement Psychiatry, Minn. Mental Health Assn. Jewish religion. Contbr. articles to med. jours. Pioneer pastoral counseling and psychotherapy fields. Home: St. Paul, Minn. Died Apr 17, 1972; buried Mt. Zion Cemetery, St. Paul, Minn.

LIPPMAN, LEONARD BING, transp. co. exec.; b. South Bend, Ind., Oct. 22, 1907; s. Samuel W. and Stella (Bing) L.; A.B., Harvard, 1929; J.D., DePaul U., 1940; m. Claire Mayer, July 23, 1954. With Gen. Am. Transp. Corp., Chgo., 1930-73, tax agt., ins. mgr., 1951-73, corp. sec., 1961-73; exec. dir. N.W. Suburban Mass Transit Dist., Bartlett, 1973-74. Admitted to Ill. bar, 1940. Bd. dirs. Bur. Jewish Employment Problems, Chgo. Served to capt. AUS, 1941-45; ETO. Mem. Chgo. Bar Assn., Am. Soc. Corporate Secs. (asso.). Club: Harvard (Chgo.). Home: Chicago, Ill. Died June 9, 1974.

LIPPMANN, WALTER, editor, author; b. N.Y.C., Sept. 23, 1889; s. Jacob and Daisy (Baum) L.; A.B., Harvard, 1909, grad. student philosophy, 1909-10; m. Faye Albertson, May 24, 1917; m. 2d, Helen Byrne Armstrong, Mar. 26, 1938. Formerly asso. editor New Republic; editor N.Y. World 1931; spl. writer N.Y. Herald-Tribune and other newspapers; asst. to sec. of war, 1917; sec. of orgn. directed by E.M. House to prepare data for Peace Conf. Bd. overseers Harvard, 1933-39. Capt. U.S. Army Mil. Intelligence, attached to 2d sect. Gen. Staff, Gen. Hdqrs. A.E.F. and Am. Commn. to Negotiate Peace. Mem. Nat. Inst. Arts and Letters, Am. Acad. Arts and Letters, Phi Beta Kappa (senator 1934-40). Decorated commander Legion of Honor; officer Order of Leopold (Belgium); recipient knight's cross Order of St. Olav (Norway); comdr. Order Orange Nassau (Netherlands); Pultizer prize spl. citation, 1957; Pulitzer prize, 1962; gold medal for essays and criticism Nat. Inst. Arts and Letters, 1965; Medal of Freedom, 1964. Clubs: Century, Harvard, Coffee House, River (N.Y.C.); Metropolitan, Cosmos, Nat. Press (Washington); Harvard, Tavern (Boston); Faculty (Cambridge, Mass.). Author: A Preface to Politics, 1913; Drift and Mastery, 1914; The Stakes of Diplomacy, 1915; The Political Scene, 1919; Liberty and the News, 1920; Public Opinion, 1922; The Phantom Public, 1925; Men of Destiny, 1927; American Inquisitors, 1928; A Preface to Morals, 1929; The United States in World Affairs (with William O. Scroggs), 3d edit., 1933; Interpretations, 1932; Interpretations, 1933-35; The Method of Freedom, 1934; The New Imperative, 1935; The Good Society, 1937; Some Notes on War and Peace, 1940; U.S. Foreign Policy: Shield of the Republic, 1943; U.S. War Aims, 1944; The Cold War, 1947; Isolation and Alliances, 1952; The Public Philosophy, 1955; The Communist World and Ours, 1959; The Coming Test with Russia, 1961; Western Unity and the Common Market, 1962; The Essential Lippmann, 1963. Contbr. mags. including Atlantic, Yale Rev., Harper's, Life. Editor: The Poems of Paul Mariett, 1913. Address: New York City, NY. Died Dec. 14, 1974.

LIPTON, BARBARA, physician; b. N.Y.C., Sept. 6, 1928; d. William and Sophie (Furman) L.; A.B. summa cum laude, Bernard Coll., Columbia, 1947; M.D., Yale, 1951. Intern in surgery Yale-New Haven Med. Center, New Haven, 1951-52; resident in anesthesiology Columbia-Presbyn. Med. Center, N.Y.C., 1952-54; adj. anesthesiologist Beth Israel Hosp., N.Y.C., 1954-56, asso. attending anesthesiologist, 1956-64; asso. attending anesthesiologist Mt. Sinai Hosp., N.Y.C., 1964-72, attending anesthesiologist, 1972-74; asst. clin. prof. anesthesiology N.Y.U. Sch. Medicine, N.Y.C., 1960-61; asso. clin. prof. anesthesiology Mt. Sinai Sch. Medicine, N.Y.C., 1966-72, clin. prof., 1972-74. Guest lectr. U. Rome (Italy), 1965, 70, Kyoto (Japan) U., 1966, Queen Mary Hosp., Hong Kong, 1966, Am. Hosp., Paris, France, 1967, 69, Karolinska Inst., Stockholm, Sweden, 1968, Rigshospitalet, Copenhagen, Denmark, 1968, Albert Einstein Coll. Medicine, N.Y.C., 1970, L.I. Jewish Hosp., Bklyn., 1971, Red Cross Hosp., Athens, Greece, 1971, Norwalk (Conn.) Hosp., 1972, St. Barnabus Med. Center, Livingston, N.J., 1972, Rigshospitalet, Oslo, Norway, 1972, Rio de Janeiro, Brazil, 1973. Diplomate Am. Bd. Anesthesiology. Fellow Am. Coll. Anesthesiologists, N.Y. Acad. Medicine (sec. com. on admissions 1967-69, chmn. sect. anesthesiology and resuscitation 1971-72, mem. com. on med. edn. 1972-74), N.Y. Acad. Scis.; mem. A.M.A., Internat. Anesthesia Research Soc., Assn. U. Anesthetists, Am. (com. on sci. exhibits 1972-74), N.Y. State (1st asst. sec. 1972) socs. anesthesiologists, chmn. com. on pub. relations 1974. Med. Soc. County N.Y. (com. on pub. relations 1956-74), N.Y. Soc. for Acute Med. Care (pres. 1970-74), Soc. Critical Care Medicine. Contbr. articles to med. jours. Home: New York City, N.Y. Died July 20, 1974; buried Cedar Park, Beth-l Cemetery, Paramus, N.J.

LITIN, EDWARD MORTIMER, psychiatrist; b. Mpls., Jan. 22, 1921; s. Abraham Harry and Ann Allison (Weisberg) Litinsky; B.S., U. Minn., 1943, M.B., 1945, M.D., 1946; m. Lorraine Kozberg, July 1945; children—Nancy Jo, Scott Charles. Intern U. Utah Hosps., Salt Lake City, 1945-46; resident Mayo Clinic, Rochester, Minn., 1948-51, mem. clin. staff, 1952-69, chmn. dept. psychiatry, 1963-68; practice medicine specializing in psychiatry, Rochester, 1951-69; cons. psychiatry, Hopkins, Minn., 1969-72, Peace Corps. Served to capt., M.C., AUS, 1946-48. Diplomate (Am. Bd. Psychiatry and Neurology. Mem. Am. Psychiatry Assn. (chmn. com. on mental hosps. 1963), A.M.A., Minn. Psychiat. Soc. (pres. 1967-68), Am. Orthopsychiat. Assn., Am. Acad. Pediatrics, N.Y. Acad. Scis. Home: Rochester, Minn. Died Apr. 28, 1972.

LITTLE, E(DWARD) H(ERMAN), chairman Colgate Palmolive Co.; b. Mecklenburg County, N.C., Apr. 10, 1881; s. George W. and Ella Elizabeth (Howie) L.; ed. pub. schs., Mecklenburg County, N.C., and Greys Acad., Huntersville, N.C.; m. Suzanne Heyward Trezevant, November 24, 1910. Began as salesman Colgate & Company, in North Carolina and South Carolina, 1906, dist. manager, Memphis, Tenn., 1906-10; resigned on account of health and went to Denver, Colo., for recuperation; became salesman Palmolive Co., 1915; dist. mgr. foreign business, 1926-33, dir. from 1927, v.p., 1933-38, pres. and dir. Colgate-Palmolive-Peet Co. (now Colgate-Palmolive Co.), 1938-53, chmn. bd. from 1953, also chmn. exec. com., pres., from 1957. Pres. Assn. Am. Soap & Glycerine Producers Inc., 1943, 1944, 1945. Presbyterian. Home: New York City, N.Y.†

LITTLE, ERNEST, coll. prof.; b. Johnstown, N.Y., June 9, 1888; s. John and Martha Jane (Snook) L.; B.S., U. of Rochester, 1911, M.S., 1913; A.M., Columbia, 1918, Ph.D., 1924; D.Sc., Philadelphia Coll. of Pharmacy and Science, 1939; LL.D., Temple University, 1945; graduate student, University of Graz, Austria, 1931; Phar.D., Rutgers Univ., 1947; married Margaret Lucy Weaver, July 1, 1913; children—John Ernest, Robert Weaver. Instructor, University of Rochester, 1911-14; instructor in leather chem., Pratt Inst., Brooklyn, 1914-18; asst. prof. of chemistry, Rutgers U., 1918-20, asso. prof., 1920-24, prof. of analytical chemistry, 1924-28; prof. chemistry, New Jersey Coll. of Pharmacy (now Rutgers University Coll. Pharmacy), 1918-54, emeritus; dean, 1926-46, emeritus; part time teacher Upsala College, East Orange, N.J., 1955-57. Member Com. Revision Pharmacopoeia of U.S., 1930-40 (mem. exec. com.). Member of the board trustees U.S. Pharmacopoeia, 1940-60. Past president Board of Education of Highland Park, New Jersey, past treasurer of "The Indicator," pub. of N.Y. and North N.J. Sects. Am. Chem. Soc. Rutger's Medalist; Remington Medalist. Pres. Am. Found. for Pharm. Edn., 1942-43, now chmn. bd. grants. Bd. trustees St. Johnsbury Acad.; bd. dirs. Fairbank's Museum, St. Johnsbury, Vermont. Member of Am. Chem. Soc., N.J. Pharm. Assn., Am. Pharm. Assn. (chmn. council 1952-53; pres. 1947-48), N.B. Sci. Soc. (ex-pres.), American Council on Pharmaceutical Education, American Association of Colleges of Pharmacy (ex-pres., chmn., exec. com. 1936-41), Kappa Psi, Phi Lambda Upsilon, Sigma Xi, Phi Beta Kappa, Alpha Zeta Omega, Rho Chi, Delta Sigma Theta. Conglist. Rotarian (past pres. Newark). Home: Danville, Vt. Died Oct. 30, 1973; interred Johnstown, N.Y.

LITTLE, GEORGE E., savs. and loan exec.; b. Somerville, Mass., 1880. Pres., dir. Burlington Fed. Savs. & Loan Assn. Mason. Home: Burlington Vt.†

LITTLE, HENRY G., advt. agency exec.; b. 1901. Office boy Lord & Thomas, Los Angeles, 1919, transferred to San Francisco, 1926, opened Dayton, O., office, 1935; advt. exec. Nash-Kelvinator Corp., Detroit, 1941-44; gen. mgr. Campbell-Ewald, 1944, formerly pres., chmn., dir. Died Apr. 16, 1974.

LITTLE, JOHN PAT, lawyer; b. Clyde, Miss., Oct. 17, 1909; s. Albert G. and Ida (Brittingham) L.; LL.B., Tulane U., 1932; m. Claire H. Dolph, Dec. 6, 1938; children—John Pat, Michael Frederick. Admitted to La. bar, 1932, since practiced in New Orleans; mem. firm Guste, Barnett & Little, 1957-69, Little, Schwartz & Dussom, 1970-74. Dir. Pabst Brewing Co. Mem. Judiciary Commn. La., 1973-74; spl. asst. to atty. gen. La. Trustee YMCA Greater New Orleans. Served to maj. USAAF, 1942-46. Fellow Am. Bar Found.; mem. Am., La. (chmn. com. profl. ethics and grievances 1958-64, gov. 1966-69, pres. 1967-68), New Orleans (1st v.p. 1965-66) bar assns., Sigma Alpha Epsilon, Phi Delta Phi. Clubs: Southern Yacht (New Orleans); Chicago. Home: New Orleans, La. Died June 13, 1974; interred New Orleans, La.

LITTLE, S. GEORGE, newspaper exec.; b. Marshville, N.C., Apr. 10, 1903; s. George Melton and Serena (Brooks) L.; B.A., E. Central State Coll., Okla., 1922; postgrad. Journalism student, Columbia, 1922-24; Litt.D. (hon.), Hartwick Coll., Oneonta, N.Y., 1960; m. Hazel English, June 22, 1935; 1 dau., Carolyn Virginia. Reporter, Ada (Okla.) Daily News, 1919-21, with bus. and advt. dept., 1921-22; N.Y. rep. Chgo. Jour. and Cloverleaf Newspapers, 1923-24; feature writer Newark Ledger, 1925; financial writer Daily Oklahoman, Oklahoma City, 1925-26; with Asheville (N.C.) Daily and Sunday Citizen, 1927-29; v.p. charge press and newspaper contracts Home Econs. Syndicate, N.Y.C., 1930-40; organizer, founder Gen. Features Corp., 1941, chmn. bd., 1967-74; president Litmor Pub. Corp., Center Island News Printing Corp. Spl. cons. sec. treasury, Nat. War Bond program charge newspaper dept., Washington, 1944; organizer, dir. spl. press div. for U.S. Treasury; dir. pub. relations U.S. Treasury Bond Program, 1945-46. Mem. Nat. Newspaper Promotion Assn., So. Newspaper Pubs. Assn., Sales Execs. N.Y. (elective sec. 1938-43, treas. 1943-45, dir.), Nat. Fed. Sales Execs. Baptist. Clubs: Shenorock Shore (Rye, N.Y.); Union League, Dutch Treat, Players, Quill (N.Y.C.); Nat. Press (Washington); Siwanoy Country (Bronxville, N.Y.); Mid-Ocean (Bermuda); Old Guard Soc. Breakers Golf, Beach, Everglades (Palm Beach); Bristol (Va.) Country. Author: Production of Petroleum, 1924; Biggest Financing Job Ever Known, 1945. All-time basketball center E. Central State Coll. Home: Palm Beach, Fla. Died June 20, 1974.

LITTLETON, ARTHUR, lawyer; b. Rutledge, Pa., Oct. 26, 1895; s. William Graham and Anna Newby (Kugler) L.; A.B., Central High Sch., Phila., 1912; A.B., U. Pa., 1916, LL.B., 1920; LL.D., Dickinson Sch. Law, 1961; m. Jean Russell Newbourg, June 28, 1922; children—John Ely, Frederick Charles Newbourg, Arthur Richard, Mary Anne. Admitted to Pa. bar, 1920; asso. firm Morgan, Lewis & Bockius, Phila., 1920-26, partner, 1926-73. Dir. Fidelity & Deposit Co. Md. Trustee Bull. Contributionship. Chmn. Phila. County Bd. Law Examiners, 1941-49; mem. Pa. Bd. Law Examiners, 1948-56. Served as lt. (j.g.), USN, 1917-19; with U.S. Army Interceptor Command, 1942-44. Fellow Am. Coll. Trial Lawyers, Am. Bar Assn.; mem. Pa. (past pres.), Phila. (past chancellor) bar assns., Mil. Order Loyal Legion, Phi Beta Kappa, Sigma Phi Epsilon, Phi Delta Phi. Republican. Clubs: Union League, Merion Cricket (Phila.). Home: Wynnewood, Pa. Died Dec. 19, 1973.

LIU, SHAO-CHI, former pres. Red China: b. Hunan, China, 1905; studied in Russia. Joined Socialist Youth Group (predecessor of Communist Party), 1921; mem. secretariat China Labor Union (later All-China Fedn. Labor), 1922; leader Revolutionary Trade Union Movement in China, 1927-74; leader Students Patriotic Movement against aggression by Japan, 1935; mem. polit. bur. Communist Central Com., 1932-74; sec. North China bur., Central China bur., 1936-42; mem. secretariat Central Com., 1943; now vice chmn. Chinese Peoples Revolutionary Mil. Council; vice chmn. Communist Central People's Govt., 1949; vice chmn. People's Polit. Consultative Council; chairman Chinese People's Republic, 1959; President of the Peiping regime, 1959. Member of the Sino-Soviet Friendship Association (chmn.), Internat. Labor Fedn. (chmn. 1951-74). Author: On the Party; On Inner Party Struggle; How to Be a Good Communist; Internationalism and Nationalism, Died Oct. 1974.

LIU, TA-CHUNG, educator, economist; b. Peiping, China, Oct. 27, 1914; s. Cheng-Chih and Ching-Haing (Chang) L.; B.S., Nat. Chiao-Tung U., 1936; M. Civil Engring., Cornell U., 1937, Ph.D. in Econs., 1940; m. Ya-Chao Chi, May 27, 1940; children—Ernest, Frank. Asst. comml. counselor Chinese embassy, Washington, 1941-46; prof. econs. Nat. Tsing-Hua U., Peiping, 1946-48; economist IMF, Washington, 1948-58; vis. lectr. Johns Hopkins, 1949-58; prof. Econs. Cornell U., Ithaca, N.Y., 1958-64, Goldwin Smith prof. Econs., 1964-75, dir. program comparative econ. devel., 1966-69, chmn. dept. econs., 1970-75. Cons. RAND Corp., 1955-63; dir. Ford Found. faculty summer research seminar Middle Atlantic region, 1964; Jacob Ziskind vis. prof. econs. Brandeis U. 1966-67; chmn. commn. taxation reform of Exec. Yuan Republic of China, 1968-70; cons. Inst. for Def. Analysis, 1970-75. Research fellow Brookings Instn., 1940; Ford Found. faculty research fellow, 1960-61. Fellow Econometric Soc.; mem. Academia Sinica, Am. Econ. Assn., Am. Statis. Assn. Author: (with G.H. Hildebrand) Manufacturing Production Functions in the United States, 1965; (with K.C. Yeh) The Economy of the Chinese Mainland: National Income and Economic Development, 1933-59, 1965; (with Alexander Eckstein, Walter Galenson) Economic Trends in Communist China, 1968. Home: Ithaca, N.Y. Died Aug. 14, 1975.

LIVELY, ROBERT ALEXANDER, educator, historian; b. Birmingham, Ala., July 8, 1922; s. Matthew S. and Noncie (Cook) L.; A.B., Birmingham-So. Coll., 1943; M.A. (Rosenwald fellow), U. N.C., 1947, Ph.D., 1950; m. Mary Cornelia Banks, May 20, 1944; children—Frazer, Sara, Cornelia, Instr. history Princeton, 1949-50, asst. prof., Bicentennial preceptor to prof., 1955-68, dir. Center for Studies in 20th Century Am. Statecraft and Pub. Policy, 1964-68; asst. prof. Vaanderbilt U., 1950-51; asst. prof. U. Wis., 1952-55; prof., chmn. dept. history State U. N.Y., Buffalo, 1968-73. Mem. Sch. Bd., Princeton, N.J., 1964-68. Served with USNR, 1943-46, 51-52. Guggenheim fellow, 1957-58; Distinguished vis. prof. Birmingham-So. Coll., 1963. Mem. Am. Hist. Assn., Orgn. Am. Historians, Econ. History Assn. Author: The South in Action, 1949; Fiction Fights The Civil War, 1957; This Glorious Cause, 1958; also articles. Home: Buffalo, NY. Died Aug. 6, 1973.

LLEWELLYN, FRED WARDE, lawyer, army officer; b. Hillsboro, Ore., May 8, 1878; s. Alfred William and Marian (McLeod) L.; student Pacific U., Forest Grove, Ore., 1892-97, hon. M.A., 1911; grad. Inf. Sch., 1922, Command and Gen. Staff Sch., 1926, Army War Coll., 1930; m. Maude Flesher, Jan. 4, 1905 (divorced 1914); children—Fred Warde, James Glenn; m. 2d, Mildred Shrewsbury, June 24, 1917. Began as abstractor of land titles, 1897; studied law, 1898-1902; admitted to Wash. bar, 1902; practiced law in Washington State, 1905-19; served in Washington Nat. Guard, 1898-1917; adjutant gen., Wash. State, 1911-13; mustered into Federal service for World War I, Mar. 1917; disch. as lt. col., inf., May 1919; commd. Regular Army, 1920; promoted through grades to brig. gen., 1942; asst. judge advocate gen. of Army, 1941-43; ret. 1943, as brig. gen.; practice of law with Rigby, Leon & Weill, later Leon, Weill & Mahony, 1943-50. Decorated D.S.M., service in Argonne offensive, and L.M. for service as asst. J.A.G. Mem. Wash. State, D.C. and Am. Bar Assns. Mem. Seattle, U.S. Supreme Court bars, Wash. State Supreme Court bar, U.S. Circuit Corut of Appeals (1st Circuit) bar, U.S. Dist. Court for Western Washington bar, U.S. Dist. Court for D.C. bar, and U.S. Court of Appeals for D.C. bar. Mem. Am. Legion, Seattle Post No. l, Mil. Order World Wars. Elk. Congregationalist. Republican. Home: Bethesda, Md.†

LLEWELLYN, MAXWELL BOWLER, physician; b. Oak Park, Ill., 1914; M.D., U. Minn., 1940; m. Gertrude Llewellyn. Intern, Milwaukee County Hosp., Wauwatosa, Wis., 1939-40; fellow in pathology Wayne State U., Detroit, 1940-43; resident physician Oakland County Tb San., Pontiac, Mich., 1944-45; sr. resident in pathology Henry Ford Hosp., Detroit, 1945-47; dir. pathology lab. Asbury Hosp., Mpls., 1947-49; pathologist, dir. lab. Mercy Hosp., Janesville, Wis., 1949-72. Ft.Atkinson (Wis.) Meml. Hosp., Meml. Community Hosp., Edgerton, Wis. Diplomate Am. Bd. Pathology. Fellow Am. Coll. Pathologists, Am. Soc. Clin. Pathologists, Am. Acad. Forensic Sci.; mem. Pan Am. Soc. Med. Practioners, Wis. Soc. Pathologists (past pres.), Wis. Assn. Blood Banks (past pres.), Internat. Acad. Pathologists and Bacteriologists, A.M.A., Rock County Med. Soc., Med. Soc. Wis. Home: Janesville, Wis., Died Oct. 14, 1972.

LLOYD, GLEN ALFRED, lawyer; b. Knoxville, July 26, 1895; s. Henry Baldwin and Maude (Jones) L.; A.B., Maryville Coll., 1918; J.D., U. Chgo., 1923, LL.D., 1968; LL.D., Westminster Coll., Lake Forest Coll., 1969; m. Marion Musser, 1940; children—Margaret (Mrs. James K. Hill), Mary Jones (Mrs. Robert L. Estrin), John Musser. Admitted to Ill. bar, 1924, since practiced Chgo.; partner Bell, Boyd, Lloyd, Haddad & Burns, 1931-75; dir. Am. Bus. Shares, Inc., N.Y.C., Affiliated Fund Inc., N.Y.C., Action, Inc., N.Y.C.; pres. T-Bone Ranch Co. Dep. dir. FOA, Washington, 1954. Legal advocate to dist. chief and chief price adjustment sect. Chgo. Ordnance Dist., 1942; dir. pricing hdqrs. A.S.F., War Dept., Washington, 1943-44. Mem. Exec. bd. Chgo. council Boy Scouts Am.; mem. Citizens Assn. Chgo., Met. Housing and Planning Council Chgo. Trustee Lake Forest Acad.; hon. trustee Maryville (Tenn.) Coll., Aspen Inst. for Humanistic Studies; life trustee chmn. bd. U. Chgo.; dir. Gen. Service Found.; former gen. chmn. of campaign chmn. Crusade of Mercy, Chgo. Served as Seaman USN, World War I. Mem. Am., Ill., Chgo bar assns., U. Chgo Law Sch. Alumni Assn., Phi Delta Phi. Republican. Presbyn. Clubs: Commonwealth Commercial Racquet, Chicago, Wayferers' Legal, Law (Chgo). Home: Libertyville, Ill. Died Sept. 13, 1975.

LOBINGIER, ELIZABETH MILLER, (Mrs. John Leslie Lobingier), educator, artist, author; b. Washington, Apr. 17, 1889; d. Thomas Fayette and Annie Elizabeth (Wade) Miller; grad. Ga. State Normal Sch., Athens, 1908; Ph.B., U. Chgo., 1915; m. John Leslie Lobingier, Aug. 7, 1918; 1 son, John Leslie. Instr., critic tchr. Ga. State Normal Sch., 1908-10; instr., critic tchr. U. Chgo. Elementary Sch., 1910-13, supr. art, 1913-18; supr. art Oberlin Kindergarten Tng. Sch., 1923-26, Oberlin pub. schs., 1924-26; instr. religious edn. Andover-Newton Theol. Sch., 1929-32, 34-40; instr. oil painting, div. edn. Boston Mus. Fine Arts, 1952-63; represented by landscapes in exhbns. at Boston Art Club, So. States Art League ann. exhbns., Assn. Ga. Artists circuit exhbns., Boston Arts Festival, Jordan Marsh Ann., others; one-man shows Rockport Art Assn., Copley Soc., Tufts U., Oberlin Coll., Marblehead Art Assn., Winchester Art Assn., others. Recipient Purchase Prize award Mint Mus. Fine Art, 1945, prizes Rockport Art Assn., 1947, 48, 53, 60, 63; 1st prize Boston Open Art, 1955, jury awards Rockport Art Assn., 1961, 63, 65; jury award Ogunquit Art Center, 1961, Bronze medal, 1962, 65; 1st prize Mass., Nat. League Am. Pen Women, 1963-65; others. Mem. Am. Assn. U. Women, Nat. League Am. Pen. Women, Cambridge Art Assn., Copley Soc., Boston, Winchester, Rockport art assns., Boston Inst. Contemporary Arts, Boston Soc. Ind. Artists, Oguequit Art Center, Conglist. Club: College (Winchester). Author: The Dramatization of Bible Stories, 1918; Dramatization in the Church School, 1923; Stories of Shepherd Life, 1924; Hebrew Home Life, Teachers Manual, 1926; Hebrew Home Life, Children's Reader, 1926; Informal Dramatization in Missionary Education, 1930; Ship East-Ship West, 1937; Activities in Child Education, 1950; (with Walter Sargent) How Children Learn to Draw, 1916; (with John Leslie Lobingier) Educating for Peace, 1930. Contbr. to mags. Home: Winchester, Mass., Deceased.

LOCHNER, LOUIS PAUL, newspaper corr., lectr., radio commentator; b. Springfield, Ill., Feb. 22, 1887; s. Rev. Frederick and Maria (von Haugwitz) L.; grad. Wis. conservatory Music, 1905; A.B., U. Wis., 1909; Litt.D. (hon.), Muhlenberg Coll., 1942, U. Wis., 1961; m. Emmy Hoyer, Sept. 7, 1910 (dec. 1920); children—Elsbeth, Robert; m. 2d, Hilde De Terra, nee Steinberger, Apr. 4, 1922; 1 dau., Rosemarie (dec.). Editor student and alumni mags., assn. dir., news service editor, 1909-1919; fgn. corr., 1919-46; chief Berlin Bur., A.P. Am., 1928-42; first fgn. corr. to follow German Army into Poland, Sept. 1939; war corr. on German western front (Holland, Belgium, France), and witness to French capitulation at Compiegne, 1940; with German army in Yugoslavia, Greece, Finland and Russia, 1941; news analyst, commentator NBC, 1942-44; A.P. war corr. with 9th, 1st, 3d, and 7th U.S. Armies, 1944-46. Served on several govtl. missions abroad. Bd. dirs. Am. Council on Germany, 1959; v.p. Corrs. Fund, mem. commn. for ofcl. publs. Luth. Ch., Mo. Synod, 1965. Mem. study and corr. assns., Luth. Acad for Scholarship, Luth. Human Relations Assn., Am. Acad. Polit. and Social Sci., Phi Beta Kappa, Sigma Delta Chi. Rotarian. Clubs: P.E.N. (N.Y.C.); Overseas Rotary Fellowship (N.Y.); Milwaukee Press; Lansing (Mich.) Press; Overseas Press (v.p. 1949, pres. 1950, 55; trustee Found., chmn. Edward R. Murrow Meml. Library 1967). Author seven books, latest: Herbert Hoover and Germany, 1960. Translator several fgn. books. Mem. editorial bd. The Lutheran Witness, 1951; columnist The Lutheran Layman, Lutheran Witness Reporter. Contbr. mags. Recipient 1939 Pulitzer prize for distinguished serv. as fgn. corr. Home: Wiesbaden West Germany. Died Jan. 1975.

LOCKE, ALFRED HAMILTON, elec. engr.; b. McCurtain, Okla., Feb. 9, 1922; s. Blackshear Hamilton and Ethel (Maloney) L.; B.S., U. Okla., 1950; m. Patsy Ruth Kraft, June 5, 1943; children—Linda Kathleen (Mrs. Richard Massey), Jean Louise, Allen Patrick. With Okla. Gas and Electric Co., Oklahoma City, 1950-72, now supr. sub-stas. Served to 1st lt. USAAF, 1942-45. Decorated D.F.C., Air medal with 2 oak leaf clusters. Mem. I.E.E.E. (sr., chmn. power group Central Okla. sect.), Am. Soc. Testing and Materials, Oklahoma City Engrs. Club, Nat., Okla. socs. profl. engrs. Baptist (deacon). Kiwanian (dir. 1965-70, pres. 1970-71). Contbr. articles to tech. jours. Home: Oklahoma City, Okla. Died Nov. 25, 1972.

LOCKHART, EARL GRANGER, psychologist; b. Benton Co., Ia., Jan. 25, 1879; s. Greere and Elvira (Wheeler) L.; grad. Tilford Acad., Vinton, Ia., 1897; B.S., Drake U., 1913; A.M., State U. of Ia., 1927, Ph.D., 1929; m. Mary Etta Taylor, of Linn Co., Ia., June 29, 1903; children—Harold Asa, Marshall Lee, Horace Percival, Phyllis Helene. Teacher rural schs., 1898-1902; prin. village schs., 1903-11; ordained ministry Christian (Disciples) Ch., 1904; supt. city schs., Ia. and Minn., 1912-16, 1919-20; pres. Southern Ia. Normal Coll., 1916-28; prof. psychology, Drake U., from 1929. Fellow A.A.A.S.; mem. Am. Psychol. Assn., Ia. Acad. of Science. Club: University. Author: Vocational Adjustments, 1931; The Psychology of Personality, 1931; The Psychology of Child Training, 1934; My Vocation, 1938; Improving Your Personality, 1939; Principles and Methods of Child Training, 1939; also numerous research studies in social science. Lecturer on character education, vocational guidance and child training. Home: Des Moines, Ia.†

LOCKHART, OLIVER CARY, economist; b. Albany, Ind., Jan. 9, 1879; s. Benjamin and Martha Read (Jones) L.; A.B., Indiana U., 1903, A.M., 1905; Ph.D., Cornell U., 1908; m. Joanna Kenyon Mix, of Munice, Ind., July 15, 1908; children—Elizabeth Cary (Mrs. F. Russell Engdahl), Charles Melvin, Joanna Margaret (Mrs. Edward Roberson, Jr.). Instr. economics, Cornell U., 1907-08; asst. prof. and prof. economics and sociology, Ohio State U., 1908-18; spl. asst. Tax Commn. of Ohio, 1913-15; economist Nat. Bk. of Commerce, N.Y.C., 1918-24; prof. and head of dept. of economics and dir. Bur. of Business and Social Research, U. of Buffalo, 1924-34 (on leave, 1926-27 and 1929-34); mem. Kemmerer Commn. of financial experts to Ecuador and Bolivia, 1926-27, to China, 1929; adviser to Ministry of Finance of Nat. Govt. of Republic of China, 1929-41; also asso. chief inspector Salt Revenue, Chinese Government, 1935-41 (title changed to asso. dir.-gen. Salt Adminstrn., 1937); Section head, Non-Ferrous Metals Branch, O.P.A., 1942-44; asst. chief and adviser on Far East, Div. of Investment and Econ. Development, Dept. of State, 1944-46; econ. adviser on Far East, Export-Import Bank of Washington, from 1946. Awarded Orden por Merito, first class (Ecudaor); cravat rouge aux bordures bleues blanches de l'Ordre de Jade, China. Mem. American Econ. Assn., Phi Beta Kappa, Beta Theta Pi, Delta Sigma Pi, Independent in politics. Conglist. Clubs: American, Columbia Country, Cercle Sportif Francais, Shanghai Golf (Shanghai); Cosmos (Wash., D.C.). Contbr. to econ. jours. Home: Exeter, N.H., Died Oct. 28, 1975.

LOCKWOOD, LUKE BURNELL, lawyer; b. Bklyn., Oct. 31, 1901; s. Luke V. and Alice G. (Burnell) L.; grad. Middlesex Sch., 1920; diploma magna cum laude, Harvard, 1924; A.B. cum laude, Oxford U., 1925; J.D., Harvard, 1928; m. Dorcas Washburn, June 28, 1928; children—Dorcas W., Luke Vincent II; m. 2d, Marion M. Adams, Oct. 30, 1948. Admitted to N.Y. bar, 1929, from practiced in N.Y.C.; with firm Cadwalader, Wickersham & Taft, 1928-31; partner Hill, Lockwood & Redfield, 1931-36; partner Carter, Ledyard and Milburn, 1936-40, 45-61, gen. counsel, 1962-75; civilian spl. asst. to under sec. navy, 1940; civilian spl. asst. sec. navy, 1944-45. Dir. Bartram Bros. Corp.; mem. exec. com., dir. State Nat. Bank of Conn. Sec., dir. N.Y. Met. Baseball Club. Trustee Middlesex Sch., Vincent Astor Found., 1958—; trustee, mem. mgmt. bd. Am. Mus. Natural History; trustee Helen Hay Whitney Found.; past bd. dirs. Greenwich Hosp. Assn. Served from lt. (j.g.) to lt. comdr. USNR, 1941-44; ETO, PTO. Decorated Legion of Merit. Mem. N.Y. State Bar Assn., Assn. Bar City N.Y. Clubs: N.Y. Yacht (rear commodore 1955-56, dir. 1956-62), Down Town Assn.

(pres., trustee) (N.Y.C.); Indian Harbor Yacht (Greenwich, Conn.); Crusing of America. Home: Greenwich, Conn., Died Oct. 29, 1975.

LODGE, EDMUND ANDERSON, physician; b. Erie, Kan., Feb. 6, 1889; s. Arthur and Julia Catherine (Vallette) L.; M.D., U. Kan., 1915; m. Gertrude Ethel Reed, Sept. 12, 1923; children—Edwina (Mrs. Donald Preston Andrews), Anne (Mrs. Stuart Wilson MacLaggan), Edmund Reed, Carolyn (Mrs. James Fisher Eldredge), John Vallette. Gen. intern Bell Meml. Hosp., Kansas City, Kan., 1914-15, St. Margaret's Hosp., Kansas City, 1914-15; aural intern Mass. Eye and Ear Infirmary, Boston, 1924; postgrad. in otolaryngology Grad. Sch. of U. Pa., 1921-22, N.Y. Eye and Ear Infirmary Sch. Ophthalmology, N.Y.C., 1921, 26; chief eye and ear nose and throat VA Hosp., 1942-43, Jones Eye and Ear Hosp., Johnson City, Tenn., 1942-43; mem. staff Addison Gilbert Hosp., Gloucester, Mass.; asst. instr. otolaryngology U. Kan. Served as capt. M.C. U.S. Army, 1917-21. Diplomate Am. Bd. Otolaryngology, Am. Bd. Ophthalmology. Mem. A.M.A., New Eng. Opthalmal. Soc., New Eng. Otol. and Laryngol. Soc. Home: Gloucester, Mass., Died Jan. 18, 1972; buried Beechmont Cemetery, Gloucester, Mass.

LOEB, G(ERALD) M(ARTIN), stockbroker; b. San Francisco, July 24, 1899; s. Sol and Dahlia (Levy) L.; student pub. schs.: m. Rose L. Benjamin. Apr. 11, 1947. Formerly vice chmn., dir. E. F. Hutton & Co., sr. cons.; pres. RLL-GML, Inc. Gen. chmn. N.Y. March of Dimes, 1960. Lectr. finance Harvard, U. Vt., Cornell U., Stanford, Wharton Sch. Mem. vis. com. Harvard Grad. Sch. Bus., 3 years; mem. v.s. com. Ohio finance com. Danbury Hosp. Former dir. N.Y. chpt. Am. Nat. Theater and Acad. Clubs: Explorers, Wall Street, Harvard (Boston); Knickerbocker Yacht; Olympic (San Francisco); City Athletic (N.Y.C.). Author; The Battle for Investment Survival, 1956; Checklist For Buying Stocks; one of the stories in The Sale That Did The Most For Me, 1951; also book chpt. Contbr. weekly investment column to N.Am. Newspaper Alliance Syndicate. Home: San Francisco Cal. Died Apr. 12, 1974; buried Cypress, Lawn Cemetery.

LOEB, ROBERT FREDERICK, physician, scientist, educator; b. Chgo., March 14, 1895; s. Jacques and Anne (Leonard) L.; ed. Horace Mann Sch. (N.Y.C.) 1910-13, U. Chgo., 1913-15, Sc.D., 1951; M.D. magna cum laude, Harvard, 1919, Sc.D., 1969; Dr. hon. causa, U. Strasbourg, 1951, U. Paris, 1952; LL.D. U. Wales, 1953, Amherst Coll., 1961; Sc.D., N.Y. U., 1955, Kenyon Coll., 1957, Columbia, 1961, U. Oxford, 1961, Dartmouth, 1962, Trinity Coll., Dublin, 1962, Rockefeller U., 1971; m. Emily Guild Nichols, Feb. 12, 1935; children—John Nichols, Elizabeth Guild. Intern, Mass. Gen. Hosp., 1919-20, Means vis. physician, 1959; asst. resident Johns Hopkins Hosp., 1920-21; asst. in medicine Johns Hopkins U., 1920-21; asst. resident Presbyn. Hosp., N.Y.C., 1921-23, resident, 1923-24, asst. vis. physician, 1924-30, asso. attending physician, 1930-45, attending physician, 1945-47, dir. med. service, 1947-60, cons. in medicine, 1960-73; instr. Columbia Coll. Pysicians and Surgeons, 1921-23, asso. in medicine, 1924-27, asst. prof., 1927-30, asso. prof., 1930-38; visited German Med. Clinics on Gen. Edn. Bd. grant, 1927-28; asso. med. dir. Neurol. Inst., 1938-41, prof. medicine, 1938-42, Lambert prof., 1942-47, Bard prof., 1947-60, emeritus, 1960-73; physician-in-chief pro tem Peter Bent Brigham Hosp., Boston, 1941; acting Regius prof. medicine Oxford, U. 1961. Eastman Meml. lectr. U. Rochester, 1939; Leo Loeb lectr. Washington U., 1944; mem. Nat. Sci. Bd.; U.S. cons. AEC adv. com. biology and medicine; mem. adv. bd. A.R.C., 1946; chmn. com. on blood and blood substitutes NRC, 1941; chmn. bd. sci. counsellors Nat. Heart Inst.; chmn. med. bd. rev. U.S. AEC, 1947; mem. USPHS Nat. Adv. Health Council; vice chmn. div. med. scis. NRC, 1943-44; chmn. Bd. for Coordination for Malarial Study, Washington, 1943-46; mem. Pres.'s Sci. Adv. Com., 1951-53, 59-62; cons. OSRD, 1944. Trustee Rockefeller Found., 1947-60, Rockefeller U., 1954-70; mem. bd. WHO, 1959; overseer Harvard, 1961-67; mem. bd. NSF, 1950-64. Recipient Stevens Triennial prize Columbia, 1936; Treadway award Mass. Gen. Hosp., 1958, 150th Anniversary award, 1961; John and Samuel Bard award Bard Coll., 1962; order Brilliant Star, Republic China, 1965. Fellow Royal Australasian Coll. Physicians (hon.), Royal Coll. Physicians (hon. London), Royal Soc. Medicine (hon., London), A.C.P. (master, Distinguished Tchr. award 1973); mem. Am. Acad. Arts and Scis., Assn. Am. Physicians (Kober medal 1959, pres. 1954-55), Assn. Physicians Gt. Britian and Ireland, Nat. Acad. Sci., Assn. for Study Internal Secretions, A.M.A., Harvey Soc. (lectr. 1941, pres. 1950-51), Am. Philos. Soc., Soc. for Exptl. Biology and Medicine, A.A.A.S., Interurban Clin. Club, Practitioners Soc. N.Y., Am. Soc. for Clin. Investigation (pres. 1936), N.Y. Acad. Medicine (v.p. 1941-44), Brit. Med. Assn. (corr.), Century Assn., Royal Belgian Acad. Medicine, Norwegian Med. Soc., Danish Soc. Internal Medicine, Sigma Xi, Alpha Omega Alpha, Nu Sigma Nu. Co-editor; Martini's Principles and Practice of Physical Diagnosis; Cecil-Loeb Textbook of Medicine. Asso:editor: Jour. Clin. Investigation, 1937-46. Home: New York City, N.Y. Died Oct. 21, 1973.

LOESSER, FRANK, song writer; b. N.Y.C., June 29, 1910; s. Henry and Julie (Ehrlich) L.; ed. Manhattan pub. sch. and Townsend-Harris High Sch.; student Coll. City N.Y.; m. Lynn Garland, Oct. 19, 1936; 1 dau., Susan; m. 2d, Elizabeth Josephine Jacobs (Jo Sullivan, actress-singer), June, 1959. Formerly newspaper reporter, N.Y.C., city editor small daily publ., 1929; exploitation rep. Tiffany Pictures, Inc., 1930; co-writer original Paramount screen play, Priorities on Parade; writer play How to Succed in Business Without Really Trying. Writer songs: Moon of Manakoora (from Goldwyn's Hurriciane); Says My Heart; Two Sleepy People; Small Fry; Dolores; Kiss the Boys Goodbye; I Said No; I Don't Want to Walk Without You; Jingle Jangle Jingle; Bloop Bleep; In My Arms A Touch of Texas. Served with AUS, World War II; composed war songs: Praise the Lord and Pass the Ammunition, First Class Private Mary Brown; Ballad of Rodger Young; What Do They Do in the Infantry. Co-recipient Pulitzer prize for drama, 1962. Member ASCAP. Wrote picture scores for Perils of Pauline, Variety Girl. Composer: The Most Happy Fella. Died July 28, 1969.

LOEWENBERG, BERT JAMES, historian, educator; b. Boston, Dec. 24, 1905; s. Herman and Sarah M. (Kelson) L.; A.B., Clark U., 1926, M.A., 1927, LL.D., 1970; M.A., Harvard, 1930, Ph.D., 1934; Social Sci. Research Council fellow, Oxford U., U. London, U. Edinburgh, U. Cambridge, 1934-35; m. Anne Cinamon, Oct. 9, 1932; children—Robert James, Judith Anne, Sarah Miriam. Asst. state dir. Mass. Fed. Writers Project, 1935-37; asst. prof. U. S.D., 1937-42; prof. Sarah Lawrence Coll., Bronxville, N.Y., 1942-71, prof. emeritus, 1971-74, dir. Center Continuing Edn. and Community Studies, 1965-69, dir. emeritus, 1972-74, dir. grad. program preparation for coll. teaching, 1966-71, also holder Esther Rauchenbush chair; vis. prof. U. Mo., 1939-40, U. Rochester, 1941-42, Mexican univs., 1944, Cornell U., 1946, Northwestern U., 1947, New Sch. Social Research, 1947, Ruskin Coll., Oxford, 1952, Salzburg Seminar Am. Studies, 1953, Hebrew U., 1953, N.Y.U. Grad. Sch., 1958, Exptl. Coll. V.I., 1955; Fulbright prof. U. Leeds, U. Cambridge, 1960-61; chmn. Darwin Anniversary Com., 1957-59. Trustee Sarah Lawrence Coll., 1959-61. Social Sci. Research Council fellow, 1934-35, 62-63, Newberry Library fellow, 1960, Am. Council Learned Socs. fellow, 1963. Fellow Soc. Am. Studies, Royal Hist. Soc. (Eng.); mem. Am. Studies Assn., Hist. Sci. Soc., Phi Beta Kappa, Tau Kappa Alpha, Alpha Pi Zeta. Author: Bibliography of Horace Mann, 1937; U.S.: American Democracy World Prespective, 1947; Essays in Teaching, 1950; Darwin, Wallace Natural Selection, 1958; Religion in Public Schools, 1958; Charles Darwin, Evolution and Nature Selection, 1958; Making America Democracy, 2d edit., 1960; American History in American Thought, 1972. Mem. editorial bd. Revista de Historia de America, 1940-50; American Studies, 1960-64, Sarah Lawrence Jour., 1966-71. Home: Orange, Conn. Died Aug. 13, 1974.

LOEWENSTEIN, KARL, ret. educator; b. Munich, Germany, Nov. 9, 1891; s. Otto and Mathilde (Oppenheimer) L.; student Gymnasium, Munich, 1901-07, 1910; law sch., U. Paris, Heidelberg, Berlin, Munich, 1910-14; LL.B., U. Munich, 1914, Dr. Civil and Ecclesiatic Law, 1919; A.M. (hon.), Amherst Coll., 1940; m. Piroska Rona, Nov. 23, 1933. Came to U.S., 1933, naturalized, 1939. In banking and merchandising bus., Munich,, London, N.Y.C., 1907-09; chief of sect. Bavarian O.P.A., 1917-19; passed bar exam. (assessor), Munich, 1917; admitted Bavarian bar, 1918, practiced in Munich, 1919-33; asst. prof. (Privatdozent) for constl. law, polit. theory and internat. law U. Munich Law Sch., 1929-33, prof. polit. and legal sci., 1956-57, prof. emeritus, 1957-73; asso. prof. govt. Yale, 1934-36; prof. polit. sci. and jurisprudence Amherst Coll., 1936-61, William Nelson Cromwell prof. jurisprudence and polit sci., 1949-61, emeritus, 1961; vis. prof. U. Colo., 1936, U. Cal., 1939, New Sch. Social Research, 1949, U. Mass., 1952; lectr. univs. Montevideo (Uruguay), Cordoba (Argentina), 1941, Marburg, 1954, Congress of Comparative Law, The Hague, 1937, London, 1950, Paris, 1954, Brussels, 1958, Basel, 1963, Berlin, 1965, Freiburg B., 1966; vis. lectr. Harvard, 1943, Yale Law sch., 1956-61, U. Colo., 1968, U. Nacional, Mexico City, 1969; Guggenheim fellow, 1941; Fulbright prof. U. Kyoto, Japan, 1961-62. Corr. mem. Brazilian Goethe Acad., 1949; spl. asst. to atty. gen., Washington, 1942-44; legal adviser Emergency Com. for Polit. Def., Montevideo, 1944-45; legal adviser Office Mil. Govt. for Germany (U.S.), 1945-46, cons. Civil Adminstrn. Div., 1948, 1949, 1950. Mem. Mass. Bar, Internat. Law Assn., Am. Polit. Sci. Assn., Am., Hampshire County bar assns. Club: Cosmos (Washington). Author: Volk and Parlament nach der Staatstheorie der französischen Nationalversammlung von 1789, 1922; Minderheitsregierung in Grossbritannien, 1925; Verfassungsleben in Grossbritannien, 1932; Erscheinungsformen der Verfassungsänderung, 1932; Contrôle Législatif de l'extrémisme politique dans les deémorvraties Européennes, 1938; Hitlers Germany 1939; Brazil under Vargas, 1942; Political Reconstruction, 1946; Germany and Central Europe in James T. Shotwell, Governments of Continental Europe, 1940, rev., 1951; Die Monarchie in moderner Staat, 1952; Political Power and the Governmental Process, 1957; Verfassungslehre, 1959; Verfassungsrecht and Verfassungspraxis der Vereinigten Staaten, 1959; Beiträge zur Staatssoziologie, 1961; Staatsrecht and Staatsprakes von ross britan. nien, 1967; British Cabinet Government, 1967; also several books on govt. in German. Dir. and contbr. 2 vol. treatise, La defensa politica en las Republicas Americanas, pub. by Emergency Com. for Polit. Def., Montevideo, 1948. Contbr. articles in prof. periodicals. Home: Amherst, Mass. Died July 10, 1973.

LOINES, HILDA, trustee; b. Bklyn., June 25, 1878; d. Stephen and Mary (Hillard) Loines; student Friends Sch., 1887-92, Bodman Sch. for Girls, 1895-96, Bryn Mawr Coll., 1896-99, Briarcliff Sch. Agr. and Horticulture, 1902, Barnard Coll., 1901. Chmn. sch. garden com. Bolton Assos., 1910-53; mem. council Woman's Nat. Farm and Garden Assn., 1914-63, recording sec., 1914-16, gen. sec., 1916-17; capt. 1st A.D., Bklyn. League Women Voters, 1928-32. Chmn. governing com. Bklyn. Bot. Garden, 1926-44, vice chmn., from 1944; trustee Bklyn. Inst. Arts and Scis., from 1921. Assisted orgn. Woman's Land Army, 1917. Fellow Royal Hort. Soc.; mem. N.Y. League Women Voters, Nat. Woman's Suffrage Assn. (chmn. food prodn. 1918-19), Fla. Hispanic Soc., Garden Club Am. (mem.-at-large). Home: Lake George, N.Y.†

LOKKEN, ROSCOE LEONARD, educator; b. Westby, Wis., Aug. 10, 1904; s. Theodore and Millie (Brown) L.; B.S., U. N.D., 1929, A.M., 1932; Ph.D., U. Ia., 1939; m. Madeline Berg, Aug. 10, 1929; children—Marlys A., Ronald A. Tchr. rural schs., N.D., 1922-29; tchr. social studies, high schs., N.D., 1930-36; instr. history, dean of men State Tchrs. Coll. Mayville, N.D., 1936-40; head history dept. State Tchrs. Coll., Dickinson, N.D., 1940-46; pres. Valley City (N.D.) State Coll., 1946-70, pres. emeritus, 1973-74, prof. history, 1970-71. Lokken Field, Valley City State Coll. named for him, 1971. Mem. C. of C. Assn. Valley City (dir. 1946-70), N.E.A., N.D. Ednl. Assn., N.D., Am. hist. assns., Phi Delta Kappa. Author: Iowa; Public Land Disposal, 1942; North Dakota: A Syllabus, 1945; North Dakota History and Government; North Dakota: Our State, 1974. Home: Valley City, N.D. Died May 16, 1974; interred Valley City, N.D.

LOMAX, PAUL SANFORD, educator; b. Laclede, Mo., May 3, 1890; s. James Wesley and Alsina Arabella (Artlip) L.; B.S., U. of Mo., 1917; student U. of Dijon (France), 1919, Harvard, summers 1922, 23; Ph.D., New York U., 1927; D.S. in C.Ed. (hon.), Bryant Coll., 1943; LL.D., Rider Coll., 1966; m. Emily Bertha Tschann, Dec. 25, 1919 (dec.); 1 dau., Lucille (Mrs. Donald A. Moore); m. 2d, Beatrice Marie Loyer, Aug. 15, 1929; children—Jeanne Marie (Mrs. John C. Bausmith), Donald Loyer. Was teacher in the pub. schs. of Mo., 1908-13, Univ, of Mo, High Sch., 1914-16; prof. commerce N.M. Normal U., 1916-18; specialist commercial edn., 1920-21; edn. Fed. Bd. Vocational Edn., 1919-20, N.Y. State Dept. Edn., 1920-21; Was teacher in the pub. schs. of Mo., 1908-13, Univ. of Mo. High Sch., dir. business edn. pub. schs., Trenton, N.J., 1921-24; prof. edn., N.Y.U., 1924-56 chmn. Dept. Bus. Edn., 1926-55, prof. emeritus, 1956-75. Trustee Bryant Coll., 1949-68. Served in U.S. Army. World War 1. Paul S. Lomax Bus. Edn. Center named in his honor, 1973. Mem. N.E.A., United Bus. Edn. Assn. (past pres.), Nat. Society for Study Education, Nat. Assn. Bus. Teachers Edn. (past pres.), Nat. Soc. Coll. Teachers Edn., Eastern Business Teachers Assn. (past pres.), Bus. Edn. Assn. City of N.Y. and Vicinity (past pres.), Natl. Assn. Secondary Sch. Prins., New York Schoolmasters' Club, N.Y. Acad. Pub. Edn., Alumni Fedn. N.Y.U. (dir. emeritus), Am. Legion, S.A.R., Phi Theta Pi, Delta Pi Epsilon (past pres.); Phi Delta Kappa, Pi Omega Pi. Presbyn. Author and co-author of business teaching series of eight volumes. Former editor yearbooks of Eastern Business Teachers Assn., and Journal of Business Education. Home: Maplewood, N.J., Died Feb. 6, 1975.

LONDON, DANIEL EDWIN, hotel exec.; b. Seattle, Sept. 22, 1905; s. Edwin and Anna Mary (Johnson) L.; student U. Wash. 1926; LL.D., Chapman Coll., 1955; Diploma of Honor, U. Philippines, 1968; m. Claire Chester, Mar. 15, 1928; children—Ann, Mimi. Real estate and property mgmt., Seattle, 1927-28; mgr. Exeter Apt. Hotel, Seattle, 1929-31; established, mgr. Edmond Meany Hotel, 1931-33; asso. mgr. Multnomah Hotel, Portland, Ore., 1933-35; mgr. Sir Francis Drake Hotel, San Francisco, 1935-38; gen. mgr. St. Francis Hotel, 1938-51, mng. dir., treas. corp., 1951-70; sr. v.p. Western Internat. Hotels Co., 1956-70, dir., 1952-74; v.p., dir. Eureka Financial Co., San Francisco; v.p. Western Internat. Mgmt. Co.; partner Transocean Radio; dir., mem. exec. com. Eureka Fed. Savs. & Loan Assn.; adviser to pres. United Airlines, 1971. Hon. consul gen. of Ceylon to Cal. until 1970; hon. consul gen. of Austria for No. Cal. and No. Nev., 1971-74; chmn. exec. com. Nat. Rev. Bd., State Dept., 1970-74. Commr. parks City and County San Francisco, 1944-48; dir. San Francisco Conv. and Tourist Bur., 1936; pres. Expn., Inc., 1940; v.p., dir. Golden Gate Bridge and Hwy. Dist., 1955, pres., 1959-60; mem. Goldsmiths' Co., London. Bd. dirs. San Francisco chpt. A.R.C.; nat. adv. council Thomas A Dolley Found.; cons. food to sec. war, 1943-45; commr. San Francisco Port Authority; dep. chief of protocol for State of Cal., 1970-71, chief protocol, 1971-74. Bd. govs. San Francisco

Heart Assn.; nat. bd. trustees People-to-People. Decorated Golden Order of Merit, grand officer Order of St. Hubert (Austria); comdr. Order of St. John (Eng.); Royal Order of the Crown of Thailand; Order of Merit (Germany); knight Mil. Order of St. Brigitte; chevalier l'Ordre National du Merite (France); comdr. Order of Isabella the Catholic (Spain); Royal Order Phoenix (Greece); Knight Nat. Order Merit (Italy); recipient meritorious pub. service citation U.S. Navy. Mem. Cal. (past pres.), Cal. No. (past pres.), Ore. hotel assns., C. of C. (pres. 1960; commodore Gt. Golden Fleet 1951), Navy League U.S., Brit. Am. C. of C. and Trade Center (dir. 1961, pres. 1970), U.S. Coast Guard Aux., Photog. Soc. Am. Clubs: Press, Rotary, Bohemian, Marin Yacht, Pacific Union, St. Francis Yacht (San Francisco); Royal Victoria Yacht (Victoria, B.C.); Buck's (London, Eng.). Address: San Francisco, Cal. Died May 19, 1974.

LONG, LOIS, writer; b. Stamford, Conn., Dec. 15, 1901; d. William J. and Frances Marsh (Brancroft) Long; B.A., Vassar Coll., 1922; m. Peter Arno, Aug. 13, 1927 (div. 1932); 1 dau., Pat. (Mrs. Robert W. Maxwell); m. 2d, Harold A. Fox, Nov. 26, 1953. Copy writer Vogue mag., 1922-24; dramatic editor Vanity Fair, 1924-25; writer night club column (signed Lipstick) New Yorker mag., 1925-28, fashion editor, 1925-70; toured with Richard Bennett in play The Dancers, 1923; occasional freelance writer. Mem. Fashion Group, Lucy Stone League. Club: Country Northampton County (Easton, Pa.). Republican. Home: Easton, Pa. Died July 29, 1974.

LONG, THOMAS GEORGE, lawyer; b. Dearborn, Mich., Jan. 24, 1883; s. Samuel B. and Annie E. (Brainard) L.; LL.B., U. Mich., 1901, LL.D., 1971; D.C.L., Olivet Coll., 1950; D.Hum, Lawrence Inst. Tech., 1969; m. Mabel A. Somers Aug. 13, 1912 (dec. 1956); 1 dau., Elizabeth Ann. Admitted to Mich. bar, 1904; in practice, 1904-73; mem. Butzel, Long, Gust Klein & Van Zile. Commr., Detroit Library 1944-70. moderator Mich. Conference Congl. Christian Chs., 1955-56; mem. prodential com. A.B.C.F.M., 1952-56. Trustee Oilvet Coll. Mem. Am. Bar Assn., Am. Polit. Sci. Assn., Am. Econ. Assn., Am. Acad. Polit. and Social Sci. Republican. Conglist. Clubs: Detroit, University Michigan Presidents, Emeritus. Home: Detroit, Mich. Died June 6, 1973; buried Northview Cemetery, Dearborn, Mich.

LONG, VELDON OSCAR, educator; b. Ft. Morgan, Colo., May 23, 1907; s. Franklin Oscar and Mary Agnes (Floyd) L.; student Colo. Coll., 1925-26; B.S., U.S. Naval Acad., 1930; M.S., U. Colo., 1938; grad. student U. Ill., U. Wyo.; m. Wilburta Velma Gilbert, Oct. 10, 1930 (dec. Feb. 1971); children—Gilbert Veldon, Terrill Hagler, Sharon Anne (Mrs. Donn Thomson), Diane Elayne (Mrs. Mark Mather); m. 2d, Thora Wilma Oswald Long, May 22, 1971; stepchildren—Raymond Floyd, Lawrence Edwin, Karen Elaine (Mrs. Aldon Woolley). Commd. ensign U.S. Navy, 1930, advanced through grades to lt. comdr., 1944; tchr. math., elec. engring., naval sci. U. Colo., 1938-44; mem. faculty U.S. Naval Acad., 1944-46; mem. faculty U. Wyo., 1946, prof., head dept. elec. engring. and bioengring., 1947-72, prof. emeritus on ltd. service, 1972-73; cons. transmission lines Pacific Power & Light Co., summer 1956, 60-63; adviser to Faculty Agr., Engring. and Vet. Medicine, Kabul U., also chief of party Wyo. team in Afghanistan, AID. Registered profl. engr., Wyo. Life mem. I.E.E.E., Am. Assn. Engring. Edn.; mem. Nat. Soc. Profl. Engrs., Wyo. Engring. Soc., C. of C., Nat. Rifle Assn., Asso. Students Afghanistan, Ret. Officers Assn., Naval Res. Assn., Nat. Assn. Uniformed Services, Am. Assn. Ret. Persons, Disabled Officers Assn., Navy League U.S., Pi Kappa Alpha, Alpha Phi Omega, Eta Kappa Nu, Sigma Tau. Presbyn. Mason (Shriner, 32 deg.). Address: Laramie, Wyo. Died Dec. 31, 1973.

LONGLEY, FRANCIS FIELDING, civil engr.; b. Chicago, Ill., Oct. 23, 1879; s. Wm. Hey and Isabelle (Smoot) L.; B.S., U.S., Mil. Acad., West Point, 1902; student Mass. Inst. Tech., 1903-04; m. Dorothy Loud, Sept. 25, 1907; children—John Fielding, William Loud. With Hazen & Whipple, cons. engrs., 1904-17; with U.S. Army post war ednl. program at British univs., dir. div. of san. engring., League of Red Cross Socs., Geneva, Switzerland, aiding health problems eastern and central Europe, 1919-21; dir. div. san. engring., Federal Dept. of Health, Australia, in conjunction with Internat. Health Bd. of Rockefeller Foundation, 1921-24; v.p., chief engr. and dir., Lock Joint Pipe Co., Ampere, N.J., from 1924. Maj., lt. col., col., Engrs., U.S. Army, A.E.F., 1917-18. Awarded Distinguished Service medal, U.S., Honorary Commander of the Order of the British Empire, Etoile Noire, France. Mem. Am. Soc. Civil Engrs., Engring. Inst. of Can., Am. Water Works Assn., New England Water Works Assn., Delta Upsilon. Republican. Unitarian. Clubs: Maplewood (N.J.); Country; Army and Navy (Washington, D.C.). Contbr. articles tech. socs. and press. Home: Maplewood, N.J.†

LONGLEY, WILLIAM RAYMOND, prof. mathematics; b. Nobelesville, Ind., Oct. 28, 1880; s. William Edward and Clara Vail (Wright) L.; A.B., Butler Coll., 1902; B.S., U. of Chicago, 1903, M.S., 1905, Ph.D., 1906; m. Clara Estelle Hunter, Aug. 29, 1906; 1 dau., Janet Hunter; m. 2d, Alice Joiner Bryant, May 29, 1941. Acting prof. mathematics Butler Coll., 1903-04; instr. mathematics Yale, 1906-09, asst. prof., 1909-20, prof., from 1920, dean of freshmen, 1937-38. Mem. Am. Math. Soc. (asso. editor Bulletin, 1926-37; trustee, from 1935), Math. Assn. America, Am. Assn. Univ., Profs., Teachers of Math. in New England, Sigma Xi, Phi Delta Theta. Mem. Nat. Research Council, 1935-38. Mem. Ch. of the Disciples. Club: Faculty. Author: Theoretical Mechanics (with W. A. Wilson), 1923; Algebra (with H. B. Marsh), 1926; Mathematical Tables and Formulas (with P. F. Smith), 1929; Differential and Integral Calculus (with W. A. Granville and P. F. Smith), 1929; Descriptive Geometry (Ency. Brit.), 1930; Analytic Geometry and Calculus, 1951. Home: New Haven, Conn.†

LONGSTRETH, CLYDE MARION, physician, surgeon; b. Afton, Ia., Sept. 21, 1898; s. L. B. and Morah Glenn (Young) L.; B.S., U. Ia., 1924, M.D., 1926; m. Elizabeth Leila Rudolph, Sept. 5, 1928; children—Charles Rudolph, Helen Elizabeth. Intern. U.S. Naval Hosp., Chelsea, Mass., 1926-27; flight surgeon U.S. Navy, 1927-32; intern Bellevue Hosp., N.Y. City, 1932; asst. resident Manhattan Maternity Hosp. and Dispensary, N.Y.C., 1932; asst. resident and resident N.Y. Nursery and Childs Hosp., N.Y.C., 1933-34; practice medicine specializing in Obstetrics and Gynecology, N.Y.C., 1932-72; med. dir. Clin. Research Lab., N.Y.C., 1944-66; asst. vis. staff Flower and Fifth Av., Hosp., N.Y.C., 1936-46, Met. Hosp., 1936-47; courtesy staff N.Y. Polyolinic Hosp., 1938-42, Doctors Hosp., 1938-42; instr. gynecology and obstetrics N.Y. Med. Coll., 1936-46; cons. St. Cecilia's Hosp., Bklyn. 1938-41; practice of medicine and surgery Atlantic, Ia., 1942-59; cons. Nishna Valley Med. Center, Carson, Ia., 1959-72; asso. with son. med. clinic; surg. dir. Prairie County Med. and Dental Centre. Terry, Mont., 1960-61; dep. dir. obstretics and gynecology, mem. staff Poplar (Mont.) Community Hosp., 1961-62. Served as lt. comdr. M.C., USNR, 1942-44, World War II. Fellow A.C.S. (charter mem. Ia. chpt.); mem. N.Y. State (life), N.Y. County (life) med. cocs., A.M.A. (life), N.Y. Acad. Medicine, Am. Soc. Abdominal Surgeons, Ret. Officers Assn., Am. Legion, Nat. Assn. for Uniformed Services (life), Am. Vets (past nat. 2d vice comdr.), Am. Med. Edn. Found., N.Y. Acad. Scis., Phi Chi. Author articles profl. jour. Home: Carson, Ia. Died Feb. 22, 1972.

LONGUA, PAUL J., railway exec.; b. Orange, N.J., Nov. 5, 1881; s. Paul and Lorraine (Lajoie) L.; ed. in pub. and bus. schs.; m. Anne Frances Morrissey, June 5, 1902; children—Paul J., John E., Hubert I., William A., Elaine. Connected with railroad work from 1898; with St. Louis Southwestern Ry. from 1900, sec., dir. from 1920, v.p. from 1945. Home: Montclair, N.J.*†

LONGWELL, CHESTER RAY, geologist; b. Spalding, Mo., Oct. 15, 1887; s. John Kilgore and Julia (Megown) L.; B.B., Univ. of Mo., 1915, A.M., 1916, hon. LL.D., 1940; Ph.D., Yale, 1920; m. 2d, Irene M. Moffat, June 18, 1935; children—Mari Louise, Flora May, Ray Megown. Asst. prof. geology, Yale, 1920-26, associate professor, 1926-29, professor, 1929-56, emeritus, 1956, chairman of the department, 1938-46; on staff U.S. Geol. Survey 1920-45, 1948-75; research associate Stanford University, 1955-75. Chairman, Division Geol. and Geography, Nat. Research Council, 1937-40. Served as capt., F.A., A.E.F., World War I. Fellow A.A.A.S. (v.p., chmn. sec. E 1942), Geol. Soc. America (councilor 1937-39, v.p. 1942, 48, pres. 1949); mem. American Philosophical Soc., Nat. Academy of Sciences (chairman section of geol., 1942-45), Seismological Soc. America, Am. Academy of Arts and Sciences, Am. Geol. Inst. (pres. 1954), Phi Beta Kappa, Sigma Xi, Delta Sigma Rho. Author: Geology from Original Sources (with W. M. Agar and R. F. Flint), 1929; Physical Geology (with A. Knopf and R. F. Flint), 1932, 39, 48; Walks and Rides in Central Connecticut (with E. S. Dana), 1932; Outlines of Physical Geology (with A. Knopf and R. F. Flint) 1934, 41; Introduction to Physical Geology (with R. F. Flint), 1955, 1962; author monographs and articles in field. Home: Palo Alto, Cal., Died Dec. 15, 1975.

LONGWORTH, RAYMOND A., business exec. Chmn. bd., chief exec. officer Szabo Food Service Inc., until 1970. Deceased.

LONN, ELLA, prof. history; b. La Porte, Ind., Nov. 21, 1878; d. John and Nellie (Palmbia) Lonn; Ph.B., U. of Chicago, 1900; A.M., U. of Pa., 1909, Ph.D., 1911; grad. work U. of Berlin, 1913, Sorbonne, 1913-14; unmarried. Teacher high sch., North Manchester, Ind., 1902-04, Elwood, Ind., 1904-08; instr. Fargo (N.D.) Coll., 1911-12, Grinnell (Ia.) Coll., 1914-18; instructor Goucher Coll., 1918-19, assistant professor, 1919-20, associate professor, 1920-24, emeritus, 1924-45. Fellow University of Penn., 1909-11. Awarded grant on book, Foreigners in the Union Army, by Social Sci. Research Council, 1943-44. Mem. Women's Civic League of Baltimore (chmn. Am. citizenship com.), Md. Com. for Rep. Govt. (pres. 1942-44, mem. exec. bd., 1939-47), Am. Hist. Assn. (chmn. com. on nominations, 1941-42), Southern Hist. Assn. (pres. 1945-46), Middle States Council Social Studies (pres. 1935-36), Am. Assn. Univ. Women (chmn. com. on membership, 1924-28), Am. Assn. Univ. Profs. (chmn. spl. com. on nat. headquarters, 1929, chmn. com. on membership, 1938-48), Md. History Teachers Assn. Lecturer, Baltimore and Md. (about 40 lectures per yr.). Member bd. editors. Journal Southern History, 1941-44, Author: Reconstruction in Louisiana after 1868 (Am. Hist.), 1918; Desertion During the Civil War (Am. Hist.), 1928; Salt as a Factor in the Confederacy, 1933, Foreigners in the Confederacy, 1940; The Colonial Agent in the Southern Colonies, 1945; Foreigners in the Union Army and Navy, 1949. Home: Baltimore, Md.†

LOOMIS, ALFRED LEE, physicist; b. New York City, Nov. 4, 1887; s. Henry Patterson and Julia (Stimson) L.; grad. Phillips Acad. Andover, Mass., 1905; A.B., Yale, 1909; LL.B., Harvard, 1912; D.Sc., Wesleyan U., 1932; M.Sc., Yale U., 1933; LL.D., U. of Calif., 1941; children—Alfred Lee, William Farnsworth, Henry. Admitted to New York bar; member Winthrop & Stimson, 1916-20; vice president Bonbright & Co., 1919-33; director (physicist) Loomis Laboratories, Tuxedo Park, New York 1928-41; pres. Loomis Inst. for Scientific Research, Inc., 1928-65; chief div. 14 NDRC, 1940-47. Adviser Lawrence Radiation Lab., Berkeley, Cal., founder trustee Rand Corp. Trustee Mass. Gen Hosp., Woods Hole Oceanographic Instn., Carnegie Instn. Wash. Gov., New York Hosp.; trustee Mass. Inst. Tech., 1931-62, trustee emeritus, 1962-75. Served to maj U.S. Army, World War I. Decorated Medal of Merit, 1948; King's Medal for Service, 1948. Mem. Am. Physical Soc., Am. Chem. Soc., Am. Astron. Soc., Royal Astron. Soc., Am. Philos. Soc. of Phila., Nat. Acad. Science, Inst. Radio Engrs. Clubs: Century, Union, University, Links. Home: East Hampton, N.Y. Died Aug. 11, 1975.

LOOMIS, FRANCIS WHEELER, physicist; b. Parkersburg, W.Va., Aug. 4, 1889; s. Charles Wheeler and Miriam Linnell (Nye) L.; A.B., Harvard, 1910, A.M., 1913, Ph.D., 1917; m. Edith Livingston Smith, July 24, 1922; children—Margaret, Ann Livingston, Miriam Nye. Instr., Harvard, 1913-15; research physicist Westinghouse Lamp Co., 1917, 1919-20; asst. prof. physics, New York U., 1920-22, asso. prof., 1922-29; prof. physics and head of dept. U. of Ill., 1929-57, also dir., Control Systems Lab., 1952-59; asso. dir. Radiation Lab., Mass. Inst. Tech., 1941-45, director project Charles and Lincoln Lab., 1951-52. Bd. of Governors, Argonne National Laboratory, 1946-48. First lt., later capt., Ordnance Dept., U.S. Army, 1917-19. Awarded Guggenheim fellowship for study in Gottingen and Zurich, 1928-29. Fellow Am. Phys. Soc., (pres. 1949), Am. Optical Soc., A.A.A.S. (v.p. Sect, B., 1948); mem. Am. Assn. Physics Teachers, Am. Assn. University Professors, Nat. Acad. Science, Am. Inst. Physics, Ill. Acad. Science, Phi Beta Kappa, Sigma Xi. Clubs: Chaos (Chgo.); Cosmos (Washington). Author: Molecular Spectra in Cases (with others), 1926. Contbr. to Physical Review. Home: Urbana, Ill., Died Feb. 9, 1976.

LOOMIS, JAMES LEE, insurance pres.; b. Granby, Conn., Nov. 3, 1878; s. Chester Peck and Eliza L. (Harger) L.; student N.Y. Mil. Acad., Cornwall-on-Hudson, N.Y.; B.A., Yale, 1901; student law dept., same univ., 1901-03; LL.D., Union Coll.; m. Helen Bruce, June 27, 1906; children—Jane Bruce (Mrs. S. Donald Livingston), James Lee, Chester Harger, Bruce. Admitted to the Connecticut bar, 1905, and began practice at Hartford; asst. sec. Conn. Mutual Life Ins. Co., 1909-18, v.p., 1918-26, pres., 1926-45, chmn. bd., 1945-49, ret.; dir. Phoenix Ins. Co., First Nat. Bank, Hartford County Mutual Fire Ins. Co.; trustee Soc. for Savings, Simsbury Bank & Trust Co.; trustee, N.H., New Haven & Hartford R.R., 1935-47. Fellow Yale Corp., 1935-47. Pres. Loomis Sch., Windsor; pres. Hartford Community Chest, 1935. Mem. Corbey Court (Yale). Republican. Conglist. Clubs: Graduate (New Haven); Hartford Golf, Hartford, Farmington Country (life). Home: Granby, Conn.†

LOOMIS, KENNETH BRADLEY, educator and artist; b. Steubenville, O., Aug. 25, 1900; s. Eddy John and Rosamond Crawford (Ferguson) L.; Ph.B., U. Toledo, 1940; M.A., U. Ia., 1941; stdent Art Inst. Chgo., 1919-21, Nat. Acad. Design, 1925-28, Columbia, 1928, Art Students League, 1928-30, Beaux Arts Inst. Design, 1930-33; m. Eleanor Diane Parker, Sept. 15, 1927; 1 dau., Sue Rosamond (Mrs. Joseph Bloxsom). Faculty U. Ia., 1941-44; dir. art Ill. Wesleyan U., 1944-48; dean Coll. Fine Arts, Tex. Womans U., 1948-64, emeritus; vis. prof. U. Ga., 1953-54; murals rep. Chgo. Worlds Fair, 1932, N.Y. Worlds Fair, 1939; brick mural Tex. Womans U.; rep. permanent collections Ill. Wesleyan U., State Mus. Art, Athens, Ga., Tarrytown (N.Y.) High Sch., Peddy Sch., Hightstown N.J. Mem. Denton Forum. Recipient Key to City, Paduach, Ky., 1959. Mem. Nat. Soc. Mural Painters, Delta Phi Delta. Democrat. Unitarian. Home: Denton, Tex., Died June 9, 1974.

LOOMIS, MILTON EARLY, b. Cleve., July 18, 1887; s. Leslie Rood and Mary Warwick (Early) L.; A.B., Western Reserve U., 1909; studied U. of Chicago; A.M., U. of Wis., 1912; hon. LL.D., Elmira Coll., 1939; m. Ara Pearl Scothan, June 18, 1912; children—Eleanor Louise, Robert Milton, Ralph Wilson. Instr. polit. science, U. Wis., 1912-13, U., Cin., 1913; instr. municipal govt., 1913-16, sec. in charge courses for pub. service, 1914-15, registrar, 1915-25, asst. prof., 1916-22, asso. prof., 1922-24, prof. edn., 1924-34, prof. of govt., 1934-39, dir. Inst. of Edn., 1924-26, dir. Summer

Sch., 1925-34, asst. dean Sch. of Edn., 1926-34, dean Washington Square Coll., 1934-37 — all New York U.; mem. bd. trustees, Elmira Coll., 1941-47; mem. bd. dirs. Rochester Museum Assn., since 1943; Rochester Civic Music Assn., 1943-46. Asso. commr. edn., State of N.Y., 1939-41, exec. v.p. Chamber Commerce, Rochester, N.Y. Mem. Inst. Pub. Adminstrn. (London), Newcomen Soc., Phi Beta Kappa. Clubs: Rotary. Torch (Rochester). Home: Rochester, N.Y. Died Sept. 2, 1973.

LOOMIS, WILLIAM FARNSWORTH, educator, biochemist; b. Tuxedo, N.Y., Aug. 11, 1914; s. Alfred Lee and Ellen (Farnsworth) L.; grad. St. Paul's Sch., 1932; S.B., Harvard, 1936, M.D., 1941; m. Frances Whitman, Oct. 1, 1965; 1 son, Jefferson Whitman; children by previous marriage—Joan, William, Jacqueline, Barton, Rhonda, Deanna, Cynthia. Intern medicine N.Y. Hosp., 1941-42; NRC fellow med. sci. Columbia Coll. Phys. & Surg., 1945-46; sr. fellow Am. Cancer Soc., Mass. Gen. Hosp., 1946-47; asst. prof. biology Mass. Inst. Tech., 1948-49; asst. dir. div. natural scis. Rockefeller Found., 1949-52; exec. sec. com. to reorganize Rockefeller Inst., 1952; dir. Loomis Lab., Greenwich, Conn., 1952-64; Rosenfield prof. biochemistry Brandeis U., 1964-71. Civilian OSRD, 1942-43. Served to maj. AUS, 1943-45; CBI. Hon. fellow A.A.A.S., N.Y. Acad. Scis.; mem. Am. Soc. Biol. Chemists, Harvey Soc., Am. Soc. Zoologists, Soc. Study Devel. and Growth, Royal Soc. Medicine. Clubs: Am. Alpine; Himalayan. Co-leader Nanda Devi Expdn., 1936. Author: The God Within, 1967; also research publs. Editor: (with H. M. Lenhoff) 7he Biology of Hydra, 1961. Address: LaJolla, Cal., Died Nov. 1973.

LORANCE, GEORGE TOEL, engring. cons.; b. Maryville, Mo., May 31, 1898; s. George Franklin and Minnie Eugenia (Toel) L.; B.S., Drake U., 1921; M.S. U. of Ill., 1923; m. Elizabeth Frances Richardson, Nov. 11, 1928 (dec. Oct. 1963); 1 dau., Elizabeth Louise (Mrs. Salvatore J. Matarazzo). Began as mem. of tech. staff, Bell Tele. Labs., N.Y., 1923-28; engr. and supervisor, Elec. Research Products, Inc., N.Y. and Hollywood, Calif., 1928-42; with various subsidiaries, Gen. Precision Equipment Corp., Bloomfield, N.J., from 1942; vice pres. for engring., Internat. Projector Corp., 1948-50; head radio development br. USN Electronics Laboratory, San Diego, Cal., 1950-52, asso. superintending scientist 1952-56, dep. tech. dir., 1956-58, head, electromagnetics div., 1958-62; practice as cons. radio communications, from 1962. Fellow, Soc. Motion Picture Engineers (past secretary and mem. bd. govs.). Republican. Episcopalain. Club: University (San Diego). Patentee in fields of electronics and optics. Home: Chula Vista, Cal., Died June 9, 1973.

LORD, JAMES REVELL, economist; b. Leeds, Eng., Jan. 30, 1878; s. Samuel and Martha Jane (Wood) L.; ed. pub. schs. in Eng. and U.S.; m. Mary MacKenzie, Mar. 29, 1915; children—Robert Cameron, Helen MacKenzie. Came to U.S., 1888; engaged in mining for many yrs.; became active in cause of unionism and the Rochdale Plan of cooperative stores; elected mem. exec. bd. United Mine Workers of America, Dist. 12, Ill., 1909, and elected vice-pres. of this union, 1912; pres. mining dept. Am. Federation of Labor (representing 7 internat. unions), 1913-23. Rep. A. F. of L. at British Trade Union Congress, Blackpool, Eng., 1917, and at Inter-Allied Congress, London, 1917; chmn. labor missions to Mexico, 1918 and 20; represented Pan-Am. Federation treas. Pan-Am. Federation of Labor and Chief of mining div. U.S. Employment Service. Mem. labor com. Council of Nat. Defense; mem. Nat. Com. on Coal Production, Housing Com., and War Minerals Board during war period, also mem. conciliation staff U.S. Dept. Labor, war period. Mem. Nat. Geog. Soc.; hon. mem. Western Federation of Miners, Transport Workers Union of Great Britain and Ireland. Episcopalian, K. of P., Elk. Address: Fayette, Colo.†

LORD, PHILLIPS H., (pseud. Seth Parker), radio and television dramatist and consultant; b. Hartford, Vermont, July 13, 1902; the son of Dr. Albert J. and Maude (Phillips) L.; prep. edn. Phillips Andover Acad.; A.B., Bowdoin College, 1925; (divorced); children—Patricia, Jeanne. Began career as principal Plainville (Conn.) High Sch., 1925-27; creator of Seth Parker, Uncle Abe and David, Country Doctor, The Stebbins Boys, Cruise of the Schooner Seth Parker, G-Men, Gang Busters, We the People, Mr. District Attorney, Sky Blazers, Counterspy, Policewoman, Treasury Agent; The Black Robe; starred in motion picture, Way Back Home; composer of hymns, writer books and fiction. Mem. Delta Kappa Epsilon. Conglist. Author: Seth Parker's Hymnal; Seth Parker's Album; Sunday at Seth Parker's; Uncle Hosie; Way Back Home: Scrap Book. Address: Ellsworth, Me., Died Oct. 19, 1975.

LOTZ, JOHN, linguist; b. Milw., Mar. 23, 1913; s. Martin and Catherine (May) L.; mem. Eötvös Collegium, U. Budapest, 1931-35; Doctor Philosophiae sub auspiciis Gubernatoris, Hungary, 1937; m. Ann Margaret Norsworthy, July 6, 1957; children—John M., C. Peter. Dir. Hungarian Inst., U. Stockholm (Sweden), 1936-47, asso. prof., 1942; vis. asso. prof. Hungarian studies Columbia, 1947-49, asso. prof. gen. and comparative linguistics, 1949-56, prof. linguistics, 1956-67, exec. officer dept. Uralic and Altaic langs., 1954-60, 61-65; dir. research Am. Council Learned Socs., 1959-65; guest prof. gen. linguistics U. Stockholm, 1962-63; Fulbright-Hayes guest prof. U. Budapest, 1966; dir., pres. Center for Applied Linguistics, Washington, 1967-71. Recipient Eötvös prize, 1936. Mem. Linguistic Soc. Am., Assn. Symbolic Logic, Finnougric Soc. (Helsinki, Finland). Club: Cosmos (Washington). Author articles and books on linguistics, metrics, Hungarian lang. and lit. Home: Chevy Chase, Md. Died Aug. 25, 1973.

LOUGEE, FRANCIS EATON, financial consulting co. exec.; b. Willimantic, Conn., Dec. 6, 1923; s. Louis L. and Grace (Henderson) L.; A.B., Lafayette Coll., 1948; postgrad. U. Pa., 1949-51; m. Loraine Granicher, Dec. 22, 1948; children—Wayne Henderson, Donald Eaton, Robert Bradford. Partner, Wank, Lougee, McDonald & Lee, 1951-55; advt. exec. personnel dir. Foote, Cone & Belding, San Francisco, 1955-62; v.p. advt., pub. relations Wells Fargo Bank, San Francisco, 1962-68; pres. Communications in Finance, Inc., San Francisco, 1969-72. Chmn. radio-TV com. United Bay Area Crusade, 1966-68. Served to 2d lt. AUS, 1943-45, 48-49. Mem. San Francisco Advt. Club (Advt. Man of Year 1968), Bank Marketing Assn., Am. Marketing Assn., Delta Kappa Epsilon, Pi Delta Epsilon, Kappa Phi Kappa. Republican. Episcopalian. Home: Tiburon, Cal. Died Dec. 25, 1972.

LOUGH, WILLIAM HENRY, economist; b. Dayton, O., May 11, 1881; s. William H. Sr., and Esther G. (Stubbs) L.; grad. Oshkosh (Wis.) State Normal Sch., 1899; A.B., Harvard, 1901, A.M., 1902; m. Elizabeth Howe Shepard, Aug. 24, 1907. In traffic dept. B.&O. R.R., 1902-04; editorial staff Wall St. Journal, 1904-05; instr., asst. prof. and prof. finance and transportation, New York U. Sch. of Commerce, Accounts and Finance, 1905-10; a founder, and v.p., 1910-15, Alexander Hamilton Inst.; investigated financial conditions in S. America for United States Dept. of Commerce, 1915; pres. Trade-Ways, Inc., and affiliated companies, from 1916. Exec. sec. War Dept. Com. on Education and Spl. Training, 1918; mem. Ednl. Corps U.S. Army, and dir. instrn. in business, throughout A.E.F., 1918-19. Mem. Am. Econ. Assn., American Statistical Association. Republican. Club: Harvard. Author: Lectures on Panics and Depressions, 1907; Corporation Finance, 1909; Financial Developments in South American Countries, 1915; Banking Opportunities in South America, 1915; Business Finance, 1917; High-Level Consumption, 1935. Home: New Rochelle, N.Y.†

LOUGHAN, MRS. KATHERINE O'NEIL, educator; b. Moira, N.Y., Aug. 10, 1881; d. Thomas and Margaret (Willson) O'Neil; m. J. T. Loughan (M.D.), of Los Angeles, Calif., Mar. 2, 1910 (dec.); children—Thomas O'Neill, Helen Katherine, Ruth Elizabeth. Mng. dir. Pacific Mil. Acad., from 1922. Republican. Episcopalian. Clubs: Friday Morning (Los Angeles); Hollywood Women's, Culver City Women's. Home: Los Angeles, Cal.†

LOUNSBURY, JAMES BRECKINRIDGE, physician; b. Wilmette, Ill., June 29, 1909; s. Ralph Reed and Helen (Beeks) L.; B.A., Yale, 1931, M.D., 1935; M.S., U. Mich., 1940; m. Vivian Beatrice Thomen, July 11, 1936; children—Barbara (Mrs. William Bonner Dunn), Jean (Mrs. Jerome Garie Pittman). Intern U. Mich. Hosp., Ann Arbor, 1935-36, asst. resident in surgery, 1936-37; asst. resident in obstetrics Western Res. Hosp., 1937-38; asst. resident obstetrics and gynecology, also pathology Woman's Hosp., Detroit, 1940-41; practice medicine specializing in obstetrics and gynecology, Wilmington, N.C., 1941-69; hon. staff New Hanover Meml. Hosp., Cape Fear Meml. Hosp., Wilmington; dir. Maternity and Contraceptive Clinic, Dept. Pub. Health, Wilmington, 1942-66. Lectr. pub. health and hygiene U. Mich., 1938-40. Served to lt. (j.g.) M.C., USNR, 1945-46. Diplomate Am. Bd. Obstetrics and Gynecology. Fellow A.C.S.; mem. A.M.A., Am. Coll. Obstetrics and Gynecology, Med. Soc. N.C., N.C. Obstetric and Gynecol. Soc., New Hanover County Med. Soc. Contbr. numerous articles to profl. publs. Developer Lounsbury uterine curette, 1956. Home: Wilmington, N.C., Died June 20, 1974; buried Nat. Cemetery, Wilmington, N.C.

LOVE, EDGAR AMOS, bishop; b. Harrisonburg, Va., Sept. 10, 1891; s. Julius C. and Susie (Carr) L.; student Morgan Acad., 1905-09; A.B., Howard U., 1913, B.D., 1916; S.T.B., Boston U., 1918; D.D., Morgan Coll., 1935, Gammon Theol. Sem., 1946; D.D. (honorary), Boston University, 1956; married Virginia Louise Ross, June 16, 1923; 1 son, Jon Edgar. Ordained to ministry Meth. Ch., 1915; prin acad. Morgan Coll., Balt., 1920-21, coll. prof., 1919-21; pastor, Washington, Pa., 1921-26, Annapolis, Md., 1926-29, Wheeling, W.Va., 1929-31, Balt., 1931-33; dist. supt. Washington dist. Washington Conf. Meth. Ch., 1933-40; supt. dept. Negro work Bd. Missions, Meth. Ch., 1940-52; bishop since 1952, assigned Balt. area. Sometime lectr., numerous Colls. and Univs. Trustee Morgan Coll. Corp., Balt.; mem. bd. govs. Wesley Theol. Sem., Washington; trustee Gammon Theol. Sem., Atlanta, Morristown Jr. Coll. Mem. Bd. Missions, v.p. Bd. Evangelism, Coordinating Council of Methodist Church, also Meth. Commn. on Chaplains, Gen. Commn. on Chaplains, Nat. Council Chs. of Christ in U.S.A., Omega Psi Phi. Elk, Mason (33°, So. Jurisdiction). Club: Frontiers of America (Balt.). Home: Baltimore, Md. Died May 1, 1974.

LOVEJOY, CLARENCE EARLE, newspaperman, author, ednl. cons.; b. Waterville, Me., June 26, 1894; s. Arthur Evans and Florence Mary (Early) L.; A.B., Columbia, 1917; student Sorbonne, Paris, 1919; A.M. (hon.), Colby Coll., 1937; LL.D. (hon.), Parsons Coll., 1959; m. Madelyn Genevieve Dunphy, July 9, 1935; children—Barbara Sue (Mrs. Charles T. Straugn II), Joan Anita (Mrs. Howard G. Seeley). Reporter, Pittsfield (Mass.) Jour., 1910-12, Berkshire Eve. Eagle, Pittsfield, 1912-13, Meriden (Conn.) Morning Record, 1914; with N.Y. Times 1915-20, 34-62, boating editor; founder Bronxville (N.Y.) Press, 1925, editor, publisher, 1925-27; alumni exec. and editor Columbia Alumni News, 1927-47; ednl. cons., coll. counselor to students; dir. Coll. Admissions Counseling Service, 1947-74. Served to 1st lt., 38th Inf., 3d Div., U.S. Army, 1917-19; with AEF, 16 month; capt. with 22d, 16th and 26th Inf. Regts., U.S. Army, 1920-25; detailed as capt., asso. prof. mil. sci. and tactics, R.O.T.C., Rutgers U., 1921-25; resigned Regular Army, 1925; col. Mil. Intelligence Res.; active duty to col., U.S. Army, 1942-46; dir. security and intelligence div. Mil. District No. 1, N.Y.C. and environs., later overseas as dir. pub. relations div. ETO under appointment by Gen. Eisenhower and continued by Gen. McNarney. Decorated Silver Star, Legion of Merit, Bronze Star. Mem. Am. Legion, V.F.W., Soc. Colonial Wars, S.R., Phi Kappa Sigma. Episcopalian. Mason, Club: Columbia U. (N.Y.C.). Author: The Story of the Thirty-eighth, 1919; The Lovejoy Genealogy, 1930; So You're Going to College, 1940; Lovejoy's Complete Guide to American Colleges and Universities, 1948; Lovejoy's College Guide, 1952; Lovejoy's Vocational School Guide, 1955; Lovejoy's Scholarship Guide, 1957; Lovejoy's Prep. School Guide, 1958. Editor, pub. Lovejoy's Guidance Digest (monthly). Contbr. mags., newspapers, mil., ednl. jours. Home: Little Silver, N.J. Died Jan. 16, 1974.

LOVEJOY, HATTON, lawyer; b. White Plains, Ga., Mar. 19, 1877; s. William Presley (D.D.) and Anna (Lowe) L.; B.S., U. of Ga., 1896, LL.B., 1897; m. Lora Edmundson, Aug. 27, 1904 (dec. Oct. 1944); children—Hatton (dec.), Annie (dec.), Mary, Clyde, John (dec.). Admitted to Ga. bar, 1897; began practice at La Grange; mem. firm Lovejoy & Mayer. Supt. schs., Troup Co., Ga., 1901-07; mem. Ga. Ho. of Rep., 1909-12; mem. Ga. Sch. Bldg. Authority. Past president of the board of trustees La Grange Coll.; trustee U. Ga. Found.; chmn. Callaway Foundation, Inc.; trustee and pres. Walter F. George Sch. of Law Found., Inc., president of University Georgia Press, Incorporated. Award from the Alumni Society and president University of Georgia for services to Univ. and State. Mem. Coweta Circuit (pres.), Ga. State (pres.) American bar assns., S.A.R. (pres. Ga. Society), Sigma Nu, Alumni Society U. of Georgia (pres.), Blue Key, Phi Beta Kappa Associates. Member Commn. to revise Constitution of Georgia. Democrat. Mason. Club: Rotary. Major, Ga. State Guard (retired). Home: La Grange, Ga.†

LOVELL, ERNEST JAMES, JR., educator, author; b. Roanoke, Va., Aug. 28, 1918; s. Ernest James and Virgie (Figgatt) L.; A.B., Duke, 1939; A.M., Cornell U., 1940; Ph.D., Princeton, 1946; m. Calista Belle Biles, Aug. 5, 1943; children—Anne Figgatt (Mrs. Frederick Albert Matsen III), James Lloyd. Faculty, U. Tex., 1947-75, prof. English, 1962-75. Vis. Carnegie prof. English, Columbia, 1955-56; vis. prof. U. N.C., 1957. Served with AUS, 1942-44. Recipient 3 awards lit. research and writing U. Tex. Research Inst. Mem. Modern Lang. Assn., Keats-Shelley Assn., Byron Soc. Eng. (Am. com.), Author: Byron: The Record of a Quest, 2d edit., 1966; His Very Self and Voice: Collected Conservations of Lord Byron, 1954; Captain Medwin: Friend of Byron and Shelley, 2d edit., 1963; (with Willis Pratt) Modern Drama: An Anthology of Nine Plays, 1963; Thomas Medwin's Conversations of Lord Byron, 1966. Exec. editor Tex. Studies in Lit. and Lang., a Jour. of Humanities, 1966-75. Editor: Lady Blessington's Conversations of Lord Byron, 1969. Home: Austin, Tex. Died June 22, 1975; interred Austin Meml. Park, Austin, Tex.

LOVELL, GEORGE BLAKEMAN, educator; b. New Haven, Conn., Oct. 4, 1878; s. John Epy and Adela Jane (Blakeman) L; B.A., Yale, 1901. M.A., 1903, Ph.D., 1909; m. Alice Modena Eldredge, June 17, 1902; m. 2d, Miss Rachel Anne Fuller, Feb. 21, 1945. Instr. in German. Sheffield Scientific School (Yale), 1904-14; asst. rector Hopkins Grammar Sch., 1914-16, rector, from 1916, also trustee, from 1933. Mem. N.E.A. Headmasters Assn., Country Day Sch. Headmasters Assn., New Haven Colony Hist. Soc. Conglist. Clubs: Graduate, Quinnipiack, Rotary (New Haven); Yale (New York). Editor: Arnold's Einstein Mai, 1942. Home: New Haven, Conn.†

LOVELL, MALCOLM R., b. Fall River, Mass.; s. William Buffum and Sara (Buffum) L.; A.M., University of Pa., 1914; m. Emily Monihan; 1 son, Malcolm; m. 2d, Juanita West; 1 son, Arnold Buffum. Pres. M.R. Lovell & Co., N.Y.C., 1922-33; asst. to under-sec. of agr., Washington, D.C., 1933-34; financial adviser Federal Housing Adminstrn., 1934-35; dir. of sales Title Guarantee and Trust Co., New York City, 1935-39;

mem. bd. dirs. Jacksonville Properties, Inc. (Florida) subsidiary Alfred I. du Pont Estate. Chief Mission of CARE, for United Kingdom. Dir. Internat. Service Council, Inc., from 1939; mem. exec. com. Interdenominational Com. for Religious Edn.; mem. religious edn. com. N.Y. Fedn. of Churches; v.p. of Sarah Delano Roosevelt House of Hunzer Coll. Social, Community and Religious Clubs Assn. Mem. Soc. of Descendants of Mayflower, S.A.R., Soc. Colonial Wars, Delta Kappa Epsilon. Democrat. Mem. Soc. of Friends. Club: Bond (N.Y.C.). Author: Two Quaker Sisters, 1937. Home: Columbia, S.C. Died June 27, 1975.

LOVITT, WILLIAM VERNON, educator; b. Whiting, Kan., Feb. 7, 1881; s. Perry Thomas and La Rena Phoebe (Beach) L.; A.B., U. of Neb., 1903, teaching fellow, 1904-06; Ph.M., U. of Chicago, 1907, Ph.D., 1914; grad. study, Harvard, 1912-13; m. Caroline D. Mosher, Aug. 26, 1912; children—Mary Elizabeth. Mildred Caroline (dec.), William Vernon, John Leonard. Supt. sch., Arcadia, Neb., 1903-04; instr. in mathematics, U. of Wash., 1907-12; instr. in mathematics, Harvard, 1912-13; instr. in mathematics, Purdue, 1913-16, asst. prof., 1916-18; asso. prof. mathematics, Colo. Coll., 1918-21, prof. 1921-50, also dean of men, 1928-1938. Mem. Am. Math. Assn., Am. Mathematical Soc., Sigma Xi, Delta Epsilon. Republican. Conglist. Author: Mathematics for Students of Agriculture and General Science (with A. M. Kenyon), 1917; Linear Integral Equations, 1924; The Mathematics of Business, 1926, 32; Statistics, 1929; Elementary Theory of Equations, 1939. Contbr. to math. publs. Home: Colorado Springs, Colo.†

LOWDERMILK, WALTER CLAY, soil conservationist; b. Liberty, N.C., July 1, 1888; s. Henry Clay and Helen Vashti (Lawrence) L.; grad. Park Coll., Parkville, Mo., 1909, U. Ariz., 1912; B.A., U. Oxford, Eng. (Rhodes scholar), 1914, Diploma Forestry, 1915, M.A., 1922; Ph.D., U. Cal., 1929; D. Tech. Soc. (hon.), Israel Inst. Technology; m. Inez Mary Marks, Aug. 15, 1922; children—William Francis Theodore, Winifred Esther. Asst. forest ranger, 1915; timber acquisition officer Am. Peace and Liquidation commns., 1917-19; research officer region I, U.S. Forest Service, 1919-22; research prof. forestry U. Nanking, China, 1922-27; project leader Erosion stream flow research Cal. Forest Expt. Sta., 1927-33, founder San Dimas Exptl. Forest in Hydrology; asso. chief Soil Conservation Service, U.S. Dept. Agr., Washington, 1933-47, also chief research, 1937-47, asst. chief conservation service, 1939-47, ret. 1947; cons. on conservation various fgn. govts., 1943-74; cons. Pres.' Water Resources Policy Commn., 1950, Supreme Allied Command of Japan, 1951; cons. on soil conservation and land development FAO, Israel, 1951-53; cons. water matters Econ. Development UN, 1954-55; Cons. Save the Redwoods League, 1960-69; FAO vis. prof. agrl. engrng. Technion, Haifa, 1955-57. Volunteer A.E.F., 1917; commd. Engrs. Corps, France, 1918. Chmn. com. land erosion Internat. Union Geodosy and Geophysics, 1941-44. Fellow Am. Geog. Soc., Am. Soc. Foresters; mem. Internat. Soc. Soil Sci., Pacific Sci. Assn., Washington Acad. Sci., Soc. Am. Mil. Engrs., Am. Geophys. Union (pres. 1941-44), Sigma Xi. Methodist. Club: Cosmos. Author: Tracing Land Use Across Ancient Boundaries; Palestine — Land of Promise; Eleventh Commandment; Contour Farming for the Bible Lands; also 2 vols. of memoirs, tech. reports, abstracts, articles. Home: Berkeley Cal. Died May 1974.

LOWE, CLOWNEY OSWALD, banker; b. Hinton W. Va., Oct. 14, 1906; s. Clowney Edgar and Willie J. (Brown) L.; student U. Mo., 1923-26; m. Myrtle E. Harris, July 6, 1935; children—Charles O., C. Eugene, Judith Lynn (Mrs. Montague F. Wells), Katherine S. Chmn. bd. Union Trust Nat. Bank, St. Petersburg, Fla., 1953-72. Chmn. So. Pinellas County disaster com., St. Petersburg, Fla. Home: St. Petersburg, Fla. Died Oct. 20, 1972.

LOWE, WILLIAM HERMAN, chmn. Pabco Products, Inc.; b. Evansville, Ind., Nov. 6, 1881; s. Herman and Ella (Lowenthal) L.; student Philips Exeter Acad., 1898-1901, Cornell U., 1901-04; m. Saidee Kauffman, Jan. 29, 1911 (dec.); children—Elinore (dec.), William Leon; married 2d Helen Jackson Martin, Sept. 26, 1948. With Pabco Products, Inc., from 1904, beginning as research engr., now chmn. bd. dirs.; chmn. bd. Fibreboard Paper Products Corp., from 1957; dir. Calif. Ink Co. Republican. Jewish religion. Clubs: Stock Exchange, Commonwealth. Home: San Francisco, Cal.†

LOWMAN, ARTHUR AMES; b. Toulon, Ill., Aug. 19, 1878; s. James M. and Anna Eliza (Brockway) L.; ed. grade and high sch., Toulon; m. Bessie Canoyer, 1905; children—Eleanor (Mrs. Morse C. Palmer), James M. With Ia. Telephone Co., and Neb. Telephone Co., 1909-13; Northwestern Telephone Exchange Co., 1913-14; gen. supt. of plant, Northwestern Group of Telephone Cos., 1914-19; vice-pres. Northwestern Bell Telephone Co., 1919-35, pres., 1935-42, chmn. board, 1942-43; dir. U.S. Nat. Bank of Omaha, Central Life Assurance Society, Omaha Bldg. & Loan Assn. Mem. adv. bd. Salvation Army; mem. bd. of lay regents, Creighton Univ.; mem. exec. bd. Covered Wagon Council, Boy Scouts of Am. Republican. Episcopalian. Mason (Shriner), Elk. Clubs: Omaha; Des Moines; Omaha Athletic, Home: Omaha, Neb.†

LOWMAN, CHARLES LE ROY, orthopedic surgeon; b. Park Ridge, Ill., Dec. 25, 1879; s. Charles Oscar and Ida May (Hutchins) L.; M.D., U. of Southern Calif., 1907; D.Sc., Knox Coll., 1937; m. Elizabeth Arnold, Dec. 28, 1909; children—Arnold, Elizabeth. Began as orthopedic surgeon, Los Angeles, Calif., 1910; founded Orthopedic Hosp., 1913, Los Angeles Orthopedic Foundation, 1917; attending orthopedic surgeon, Good Samaritan Hosp., 1912-20, Meth. Hosp., 1923-33, dir. education, Orthopedic Hosp., from 1917; attending surgeon, Calif. Hosp., from 1933; lecturer Pomona Coll., 1920-22; dir. sch. physical theraphy U. of So. Calif. Capt. Med. Corps, U.S. Army, World War I. Trustee Orthopedic Hosp., Nat. Foundation Infantile Paralysis Com. on After Effects, Fellow Am. Acad. Orthopedic Surgeons, Am. Acad. Physical Education, Acad. Arts and Sciences (Mexico City), A.M.A., Western Orthopedic Assn., Los Angeles Orthopedic Soc., Calif. State Med. Soc., Los Angeles Co. Med. Soc., Phi Chi. Congregationalist, Mason. Club: University. Edited book Corrective Physical Education for Groups, 1928; Technic of Under Water Gymnastics, 1937; supplement, Fundamental Exercises for Physical Fitness, 1943. Contbr. to orthopedic and phys. edn. publs. Home: Los Angeles, Cal.†

LOWRIA, REBECCA LAWRENCE, civic worker; b. Galesburg, Ill., Dec. 14, 1891; d. George Appleton and Ella (Park) L.; A.B., Vassar Coll., 1913; A.M., Radcliffe Coll., 1915; m. John Marshall Lowrie, Dec. 19, 1916. Advt. copy writer Macmillan Co., 1917, later editorial reader; editorial reader Harper and Brothers, 1918-31; caption writer Yale Picture Chronicles of America; book Reviewer New Yorker mag., 1928-29; reader for Book of Month Club, 1931-43. Editor, Vassar Alumnae Quar., 2 yrs. Trustee Vassar Coll., 2 yrs. Mem. Chgo. Orchestral Assn. Clubs: Cosmopolitan (N.Y.C.); Arts (Chgo.) Friday, Casino, Fortnightly. Author: Cambric Tea, 1928. Editor: Children's Vol., Harper's History of the World War, 1919. Contbr. revs. to Saturday Rev. Lit. Home: Chicago, Ill., Died Dec. 30, 1975.

LOZNER, JOSEPH, physician; b. N.Y.C., Dec. 5, 1905; s. Louis and Rose (Remis) L.; B.S., Coll. City N.Y., 1926; M.A., Columbia, 1927; M.D., U. Louisville, 1931; m. Etta Bring, July 14, 1946; 1 son, Jerrold Stanley. Intern, Fordham Hosp., N.Y.C., 1931-32; practice medicine specializing in internal medicine, N.Y.C., 1931-59, Phila., 1959-73; vis. physician Fordham Hosp., 1931-52, cons. and cons. emeritus, 1952-73; vis. physician, dir medicine Cancer Inst., N.Y.C., 1935-52; adj. physician Hosp. for Joint Diseases, N.Y.C., 1935-52; chief medicine VA Regional Office, Phila., 1959-64. Served with M.C., AUS, 1942-46. Diplomate Am. Bd. Internal Medicine. Fellow A.C.P.; mem. Am. Coll. Cardiology, Am. Coll. Chest Physicians, Am. Soc. Geriatrics, Assn. Mil. Surgeons U.S., A.M.A. Contbr. articles to profl. jours. Home: Philadelphia, Pa. Died Jan. 30, 1973.

LOZOWICK, LOUIS, artist; b. Russia, Dec., 1892; s. Abraham and Miriam L.; A.B., Ohio State U., 1918; student Nat. Acad. Design, 1912-15; married. Represented in permanent collection Metropolitan Mus., also many other large galleries and museums, U.S. and Paris; exhibited one man and group shows numerous cities U.S. and abroad, including one man show Whitney Mus., N.Y.C., 1972-73; circulating retrospective under auspices Am. Soc. Graphic Artists; participant in Glimpses of the Twenties, Gallery Modern Art, N.Y. Recipient numerous prizes including award Soc. Am. Graphic Artists, N.Y., 1957, awards Acad. Artists Assn., 1964, 67, Trenton Mus., 1966. Mem. Nat. Soc. Painters in Casein, Print Club of Albany, Nat. Acad. Design, Am. Soc. Painters, Sculptors and Engravers, Audubon Artists, Acad. Artists Assn., Am. Color Print Assn., Phila. Water Color Club, Am. Artists Congress, Am. Print Makers, An Am. Group, Boston Printmakers, Asso. Artists of N.J. Author: Voices of October (with J. Freeman), 1930; Treasury of Drawings, 1948; Modern Russian Art, 1925; One Hundred Am.-Jewish Artists, 1948. Contbr. critical essays on art and the theatre to various mags. World War veteran. Home: South Orange N.J. Died Sept. 9, 1973.

LUBEROFF, GEORGE, army officer; b. New York, N.Y., Dec. 14, 1879. Began as pvt., Inf., U.S. Army, 1898; advanced through ranks to col., Aug. 15, 1939; temp. rank of brig. gen. 1941; served in Spanish-American War. Philippine Insurrection, Pershing's Mexican campaign; chief Q.M., 1st Army, 1st World War; comdr. Quartermaster Depot, Jeffersonville, Ind., to May 1942; retired; recalled to active duty June 1942 to Jan. 1944. Awarded Distinguished Service medal, Legion of Honor (France). Address: Washington, D.C.†

LUBSCHEZ, BEN JUDAH, architect; b. Odessa, Russia, May 10, 1881; s. David and Fannie (Berkowitz) L.; brought to America, 1884; grad. Central High School, Kansas City, Mo., 1898; m. Bessie R. Wilson, July 18, 1916; children—Rose Fay, Davida May. Began archtl. study under Ardiance Van Brunt, Kansas City, 1895, becoming chief draftsman, 1905; partner, A. Van Brunt & Co., 1909-13; succeeded to business in own name, 1913. Mem. Soc. of Ethical Culture, New York. Author: Perspective, 1913; Over the Drawing Board, 1918; The Story of the Motion Picture, 1920; Manhattan—The Magical Island, 1927. Contbr. on architectural and photographic topics. Home: Long Island City, N.Y.†

LUCAS, ALBERT HAWLEY, clergyman and dean; b. Gibbsboro, N.J., July 25, 1894; s. Albert and Elizabeth C. (Oat) L.; grad. Episcopal Acad., Phila., Pa., 1912; B.S., U. of Pa., 1916; grad. Berkeley Div. Sch., New Haven, Conn., 1920; hon. M.A., U. of Pa., 1933; D.C.L., U. of South, 1936; D.D., St. John's Coll., 1937; D.D., Lafayette Coll., 1943; m. Frances Wharton Scott, June 29, 1921; children—Frances Wharton (Mrs. James H.M. Quinn), Albert, George Rodman, Elizabeth Oat (Mrs. C. J. Wisniewski); m. 2d, Lelia Gordon Noyes. Deacon, 1919, priest, 1920, Protestant Episcopal Church; curate St. James' Church, Phila., 1919-29; asst. headmaster and chaplain Episcopal Acad., 1921-29; headmaster St. Albans School, Washington, D.C., 1929-49; Archdeacon of Diocese of Md., 1949-73; rector St. John's Episcopal Church, Hagerstown, Md. to 1958; acting dean The Divinity School, Protestant Episcopal Ch., Phila., 1958-59, dean, 1959-73. Trustee St. James School and Hannah More Acad., 1950-73; P.E. Cathedral Found., 1932-73; exec. council Diocese of Maryland since 1949; sec. bd. examining chaplains since 1949. Canon of Washington Cathedral; clerical dep. Gen. Convention P.E. Church, 1958. Served as pvt. U.S. Marine Corps, World War. Mem. Delta Psi, Phi Beta Kappa. Address: Philadelphia, Pa. Died Nov. 10, 1973.

LUCAS, DOUGLAS P., govt. official; b. Chanderville, Ill., Apr. 6, 1881; s. William D. and Sarah (Underbrink) L.; grad. Eastern Ill. State Normal Sch., 1908; student Univ. of Chicago, summer 1913; law student, Wesleyan Univ., Bloomington, Ill., 1913-14; A.B., Univ. of Southern Calif., 1929, A.M., 1931; 1 dau., Kay; m. 2d, Dorothea Lynd, Dec. 18, 1944. Supt. schs., Westville, Ill., 1908-10; prin. schs., Missoula, Mont., 1910-13, 1915-25; supt. schs., Ajo, Ariz., 1925-26; asst. supt. schs., Hermosa Beach, Calif., 1926-28; supt. schs., Puente, Calif., 1928-45; head, New Juvenile Delinquency Unit, Dept. of Justice, Washington, D.C., from 1946; mem. U.S. Bd. of Parole. Mem. Calif. Teachers' Assn., Los Angeles County Adminstrs. Assn. (pres. 1940). Democrat. Mem. Community Ch. Mason. Club: Rotary (pres. 1941). Address: Santa Monica, Cal.†

LUCAS, J. LYNN, lawyer; b. Luray, Va., Dec. 27, 1898; s. Edwin L. and Minnie C. (Strickler) L.; A.B., Roanoke Coll., 1925; grad. law U. Va., 1928; m. Vivian D. Shenk, July 21, 1931 (dec. Feb. 1975). Admitted to Va. bar, 1928, later practiced in Luray. Past chmn. Democratic Com. of Page County, Va. Mem. Am., Va. (v.p. 1937, mem. council 1972-74), Page County (pres. 1957-60), Luray bar assns., Columbia Hist. Soc., S.A.R. (past pres. Shenandoah Valley chpt.), Internat. Assn. Ins. Counsel, Va. Trial Lawyers Assn., Am. Judicature Soc., Sigma Chi, Phi Alpha Delta. Lutheran. Mason (Scottish Rite, York Rite, Shriner), Lion (past pres. Luray). Home: Luray, Va. Died Apr. 29, 1974.

LUCAS, JAMES CLARENCE MERRYMAN, pub. utility exec.; b. Baltimore, Md., Mar. 24, 1873; s. Hary P. and Annabelle (Merryman) L.; student Baltimore City Coll., 1890-92; m. Emma Findlay Brogden, of Baltimore, Jan. 14, 1920. Began in elec. contracting business, Baltimore, 1894; organizer, pres. Gen. Utilities & Operating Co. from 1914; dir. Mercantile Trust Co., Eutaw Savings Bank. Episcopalian. Home: Baltimore, Md.*†

LUCCHESI, PASCAL FRANCIS, physician, educator; b. Sicily, Italy, 1903; M.D., Jefferson Med. Coll., Phila., 1926. Intern Phila. Gen. Hosp., 1926-28; asst. resident Phila. Hosp. Contagious Diseases, 1928, chief resident, 1928-31, acting supt., 1931-33, supt., 1931-46, supt., med. dir., 1946-51; chief bur. hosps., med. dir. Phila. Gen. Hosp., 1951; exec. v.p., med. director Albert Einstein Med. Center, Phila., 1952-70, cons. to pres., 1971-73. Mem. Pa. Bd. Pardons. Served as officer, M.C., AUS, World War II. Recipient citation meritorious service Office Inter Am. Specialists Pub. Health and Preventive Medicine. Diplomate Am. Bd. Preventive Medicine, Am. Bd. Pediatrics. Mem. Am. Acad. Pediatrics, A.M.A., Am. Pub. Health Assn., Pa. Hosp. Assn. (past pres.), Phila. County Med. Soc. Died Nov. 16, 1973.

LUCKENBACH, EDGAR FREDERICK, JR., shipping co. exec.; b. N.Y.C., May 17, 1925; s. Edgar Frederick and Andrea (Fenwick) L.; ed. pvt. schs.; grad. Advanced Mgmt. Program, Harvard, 1962; m. Audrey Jean Yost, Apr. 28, 1956; children—Edgar Frederick III, Jason Ainslie. Marine underwriter Marine Office Am., 1952-55; asst. marine supt. States Marine Lines, 1955-59; chmn. Luckenbach Steamship Co., Inc., N.Y.C., 1959, pres., 1960-74; pres. Luckenbach Terminals Co., 1961; trustee Met. Savs. Bank; dir. Tampa Ship Repair & Dry Dock Co., Inc. Chmn. shipping div. Radio Free Europe Fund, 1963; chmn. Maritime Transp. Research Bd., NRC-Nat. Acad. Scis.; mem. U.S. Oceanographic Adv. Com., chmn. Center Maritime Studies; mem. adv. bd. Grad. Sch. Bus. Adminstrn. L.I. U.; mem. adv. com. N.Y.-N.J. Port Preparedness Planning Com.; trustee Webb Inst. Naval Architecture. Dir. Nassau County Grand Juror's Assn. Served with USNR, 1943-46, to capt. 1950-52.

Decorated knight of Malta, Order St. John, Maltese Cross; recipient Third Naval Intelligence Annual award, 1956, U.S. Navy Meritorious Pub. Service citation, 1959. Mem. Am. Bur. Shipping, Nat. Cargo Bur., U.S., N.Y.C., Greater Tampa chambers commerce, Navy League U.S., U.S. Naval Inst., Naval Res. Assn., Naval Order U.S., Am. Ordnance Assn., Harvard Bus. Sch. Assn., Mil. Order World Wars. Mem. Ref. Protestant Dutch Ch. (deacon). Clubs: Alaska Big Game Trophy (Anchorage), Creek, Explorers, India House (gov.), Circumnavigators, Metropolitan (v.p., gov.), Whitehall (N.Y.C.); Camp Fire; University (Tampa, Fla.). Died Aug. 1974.

LUCKEY, ROBERT BURNESTON, marine corps officer; b. Hyattsville, Md., July 9, 1905; s. George B. and Alice C. (Owens) L.; B.A., U. Md., 1927; m. Cary D. Walker, July 15, 1933; children—Laura Thomas W., William C. Commnd. 2d lt. U.S. Marine Corps., 1927, advanced through grades to lt. gen., 1960; participated in Nicaragua campaign , 1929, S.W. Pacific campaigns, World War II; comdg. gen. 3d Marine Div., Fleet Marine Force, Pacific. Decorated Legion of Merit, Bronze Star medal (twice). Home: Vineyard Haven, Mass. Died Sept. 9, 1974.

LUDLOW, JAMES MINOR, fgn. service officer; b. Wareham, Mass., May 26, 1917; s. Theodore Russell and Helen Roosevelt (Lincoln) L.; B.A. with honors cum laude, Williams Coll., 1939; A.M., Columbia, 1940, postgrad., 1940-42; m. Jane Knight, May 31, 1946; children—James Minor, Anne Lincoln (Mrs. Wallace McLendon), Elizabeth Knight. Div. asst. State Dept., 1942-46, asst. internat. security affairs, 1946-65; acting UN adviser to asst. sec. state Near Eastern and S. Asian affairs, 1956-58; UN adviser, 1958-63; assigned 6th sr. seminar Fgn. Service Inst., 1963-64; faculty adviser Nat. Indeptl. Seminar, 1964-71, historian, 1971-74. Ad hoc adviser, U.S. rep. UN Security Council, 1950-56, U.S. delegations UN Gen. Assembly, 1950, 53-60; adviser President U.S. personal rep. Near East, 1953-55. Del. Va. Episcopal Diocesan Council, 1963-65, 73-74. Author: Negotiation: A Handbook for Beginners, 1964; A Primer of Diplomatic Persuasion, 1966. Home: Arlington Va. Died Aug. 8, 1974.

LUEBKE, MELVIN WILLIAM, educator; b. Watertown, Wis., May 3, 1924; s. William A. and Leona (Behling) L.; B.A., Concordia Tchrs. Coll., River Forest, Ill., 1945; M.Ed., Wayne State U., Detroit, 1948; m. Lucille E. Peterson, Aug. 5, 1946; children—Lean Ann, Patricia Ellen, Mary Elizabeth, Melvin W. Tchr., Lutheran Inst. for Deaf, Detroit, 1945-51; headmaster Mill Neck, (N.Y.) Manor Luth. Sch. For Deaf, 1951-72; dir. L.I. Luth. High Sch., L.I. Luth. Newspaper. Recipient Martin Luther medallion, 1966. Rotarian. Editor: (series) John of Beverley Books, 1960. Home: Mill Neck, N.Y. Died Oct. 27, 1972.

LUKAS, EDWIN JAY, lawyer; b. Jersey City, Jan. 25, 1902; s. Samuel William and Anna (Jacobs) L.; LL.B., St. Lawrence U., 1923; m. Elizabeth Schamberg, Mar. 30, 1931; children—Jay Anthony, Christopher William. Admitted to N.Y. bar, 1924; practice in N.Y.C., 1924-41; exec. dir., gen. counsel Soc. Prevention Crime, 1942-50; gen. counsel, dir. civil rights and social action dept. Am. Jewish Com., 1950-68; lectr. criminology Coll. City N.Y., 1948-50, N.Y.U., 1948-50; lectr. criminology and social legislation Columbia Sch. Social Work, 1949-58; instr. social sci. San Francisco State Coll., 1968-69; lectr. Golden Gate Law Sch., San Francisco, 1969. Home: Tiburon, Cal. Died Aug. 22, 1973.

LUM, RALPH EMERSON, JR., lawyer; b. Chatham, N.J., Feb. 22, 1905; s. Ralph Emerson and Sylvia A. (Swinnerton) L.; A.B., Williams Coll., 1927; J.D., N.Y.U., 1930; m. Phyllis Van Lear, June 21, 1932 (dec. 1963); m. 2d, Patricia Chapman Gray, Jan. 29, 1964. Admitted to N.J. bar, 1930, practiced in Newark; sr. partner firm Lum, Biunno & Tompkins, and predecessors; chmn. bd., counsel Chatham Trust Co. Mem. N.J. Assembly from Morris County, 1939-40. Trustee Newark Museum, N.J. Hist. Soc., United Hosps. Newark, Newark Safety Council; chmn. bd. Newark chpt. A.R.C.; trustee, exec. com. N.J. Safety Council; pres., trustee Chatham Free Pub. Library. Served to lt. comdr. USNR, World War II. Mem. Am., N.J., Essex County bar assns., Am. Judicature Soc., Beta Theta Pi, Phi Delta Phi. Mason. Clubs: Canoe Brook County (pres.) (Summit, N.J.); Naples Yacht, Royal Poinciana Golf, Port Royal Beach (Naples, Fla.). Home: Naples, Fla. Died Nov. 13, 1974.

LUND, FRANZE EDWARD, educator; b. Wuhu, Anhui, China, Oct. 19, 1909 (parents Am. citizens); s. Frans Edward and Augusta Elizabeth (Munn) L.; grad. Deveaux Acad., Niagara Falls, N.Y., 1928; student Trinity Coll., U. Toronto, 1928-30; A.B., Washington and Lee U., 1933, M.A., 1934; Ph.D., U. Wis., 1944; LL.D., Birmingham So. Coll., 1955; L.H.D., Hobart Coll., 1961; LL.D., Trinity Coll., 1965, Kenyon Coll., 1968; m. Martha Louise Gray, Feb. 9, 1935; 1 dau., Sigrid Gray (Mrs. R. Hutchins Hodgson, Jr.). Tchr. So. Jr. High Sch., Louisville, 1934; Howard Houston teaching fellow Washington and Lee U., 1933-34, instr., 1935-38; fellow European history U. Wis., 1938-39, 43-44; research fellow Yale, 1944-45; prof. hist. Wis. State Coll., 1939-46; chmn. dept. history and social sci. Ala. State Coll., Florence, 1946, dean of coll., 1947-52; pres. Ala. Coll., Montevallo, 1952-57, Kenyon Coll., Gambier, O., 1957-68; prof. chmn. dept. history Va. Commonwealth U., Richmond, 1969-73; dir. Peoples Bank, 1958-68, v.p., 1961-68. Chmn. Ohio Found. Ind. Colls., 1964-65; pres. Assn. Episcopal Coll., 1964-65. Mem. N. Central Assn. (com. colls.), Internat. Movement Atlantic Union (mem. adv. council), Council for Basic Edn., Ala. Assn. Coll. Adminstrs. (pres. 1951-52), So. Assn. Colls. (commn. on colls.), Assn. Am. Colls. (commn. on religion in higher edn.), So. Univ. Conf. (exec. com. 1955-56), Newcomen Soc., Am. Hist. Assn., Va. Hist. Assn., English Speaking Union, Phi Beta Kappa, Delta Upsilon. Episcopalian (pres. Tenn. Valley convocation of laymen 1950-52, exec. com. Diocese Ala. 1951-52; dep. gen. conv., 1955, 58, 61, 64; mem. diocesan council, Ohio, 1961-68; mem. gen. div. laymen nat. council, lay del. Anglican conf. 1963). Address: Richmond, Va. Died May 29, 1973; buried Lexington, Va.

LUNDERMAN, CHARLES JOHNSON, JR., lawyer; b. Paducah, Ky., Dec. 26, 1922; s. Charles Johnson and Loretta Corine (Bacon) L.; student Ky. State Coll., 1940-43; LL.B., Lincoln U., 1949; m. Belma Delores Pleasant, July 16, 1950; Admitted to Ky. bar, 1949; since practiced in Louisville. Instr. bus. law Foust-Obannon Sch., 1951-52; judge Quar. Ct., 1965-66; mem. Air Pollution Hearing Bd., 1968-73. Vice pres. Jefferson County Republican Exec. Com., 1964-73. Bd. dirs., mem. legal redress com. Louisville br. N.A.A.C.P. Served with USAAF, 1943-46. Mem. Nat. (dir. 1967-73), Louisville bar assns., Nat. Assn. Claimants Counsel Am., Nat. Inst. Municipal Law Officers, Urban League. Club: Epicurean (Louisville). Home: Louisville, Ky. Died Sept. 24, 1973; interred Cave Hill Cemetery, Louisville.

LUNDIGAN, WILLIAM, actor, TV master ceremonies; b. Syracuse, N.Y., June 12, 1914; s. Michael F. and Martha Lunidgan; student Syracuse U.; m. Rena Morgan, Aug. 2, 1945. Announcer radio sta. WFBL, Syracuse, also prodn. mgr.; motion picture actor, 1937-53; pictures include: The Fabulous Dorseys, 1946, End of the Rainbow, 1948, Pinky, 1949, House on Telegraph Hill, 1950, Love Nest, 1951, Inferno, 1953; appearing on TV, from 1953; master of ceremonies, Climax and Shower of Stars, CBS, 1955-59; mem. cast Men into Space series, from 1959. Served with USMCR, 1943-45; PTO. Mem. Screen Actors Guild (past dir.). Address: Los Angeles, Cal., Died Dec. 21, 1975.

LUNDY, FRANK ARTHUR, librarian; b. Decatur, Ill., July 16, 1905; s. William I. and Josephine (Nientker) L; student U. So. Cal., 1923-25; A.B., Stanford 1928; certificate in librarianship U. Cal., 1930, student, 1941-42, M.A.., 1948; fellow U. Chgo., 1942-44; m. Virginia MacIntosh, July 19, 1930 (div. Oct. 1965); children—Anne, Paul Robert; m. 2d, Kathryn Refro, Nov. 12, 1971. Acting reference librarian U. Ariz., 1930-31; bibliographer for library survey U. Cal., 1931-33, asst. accessions dept., 1933-36; head cataloger William Andrews Clark Meml. Library, U. Cal. at Los Angeles, 1936-39; acting head, accessions dept U. Cal. Library, 1939-40, head, 1940-42; dir, univ. libraries U. Neb., 1944-71, dir univ. press, 1955-58. Vis. lectr. U. Ill. Library Sch., summer 1943. Mem. Cal. Scholarship Fedn., 1923; cons. Library of Congress Conf. on Descriptive Cataloging, 1945; mem. Nat. Agrl. Library Adv. Com., 1962-65. Bd. dirs. Center for Research Libraries, Chgo., 1966-69. Mem. Am. (chmn. library orgn. and mgmt. sect., library administrn. div. and div. bd. dirs. 1959-61, mem. council 1959-63), Neb. (chmn. legislative com. 1948-49, chmn. fed. relations com. 1949-50, pres. 1949-50; Centennial Library award, 1967), Mt. Plains (pres. 1950-51, chmn. planning com. 1957-58) library assns., Assn. Coll. and Research Libraries (chmn. com. on financial needs 1947-49, chmn. univ. libraries sect. 1950-51, state rep. for Neb. 1952-57), Am. Assn. U. Profs. (v.p. U. Neb. chpt. 1963), U. Chgo. Grad. Library Sch. Alumni Assn. (pres. 1958-59), Beta Phi Mu, Phi Kappa Tau. Unitarian (pres. Laymen's League of Lincoln 1955-56). Rotarian. Club: Faculty. Co-author: A Survey of the Library of the University of Notre Dame (with Louis Round Wilson), 1952. Contbr. Ency. Library and Information Sci., also profl. periodicals. Home: Lincoln, Neb. Died May 17, 1975.

LUNDY, JAMES ANDREW, state and city ofcl.; b. Manhattan, N.Y., July 5, 1905; m. Margaret Ann Burns, Sept. 22, 1930; one daughter, Margaret Linda. Vice president and treasurer of R. J. Brown Corp., N.Y.C., 1930-38; pres. Lunco, Inc., Long Island City, N.Y., 1938-52; trustee Ridgewood Savs. Bank-pres. Borough of Queens, N.Y.C., 1952-57; chmn. N.Y. State Pub. Service Commn., 1959-73. Mem.-at-large Queens council Boy Scouts Am. Adminstr. OPA, Queens, 1941-43; mem., temporary sec. N.Y. State Electoral Coll., 1948. Republican candidate for comptroller State N.Y., 1958. Mem. Queens Grand Jurors Assn. Episcopalian (warden, mem. Diocesan council L.I.). Elk. Clubs: New York Athletic; Fort Orange (Albany, N.Y.). Home: Douglaston, N.Y. Died May 22, 1973.

LUNING, HENRY HERMAN, packing house exec.; b. Bklyn., Sept. 20, 1898; s. Henry John and Mary (Sheele) L.; B.S., Cornell U., 1919; m. Elizabeth Bruns, Feb. 9, 1929; 1 dau., Anne. With Swift & Co., Chgo., 1919-25; continental sales Swift & Co., Ltd., London, 1925-32; v.p., dir. Internat. Packers, Ltd., 1941-53, pres., 1953-62; v.p. Compania Swift Internacional, S.A.C., 1938-62. Clubs: Executives, Chicago, University (Chgo.). Home: Hinsdale, Ill. Died Sept. 4, 1975.

LURIE, HARRY LAWRENCE, social worker; b. Latvia, Russia (now Republic of Latvia), Feb. 28, 1892; s. Herz and Lina (Blumenthal) L.; A.B., University of Michigan, 1922, A.M., 1923; married Bernice Stewart, June 20, 1922; children—Alison (Mrs. Jonathan Peale Bishop), Jennifer (Mrs. Alvin Cooke). With Federated Jewish Charities, Buffalo, N.Y., 1913-14; with Asso. Charities, Community Fund, later Dept. of Pub. Welfare, City of Detroit, 1915-22; mem. of faculty U. of Mich., 1922-24; supt. Chicago Jewish Social Serivce Bur., 1925-30; exec. dir. N.Y. Bur. of Jewish Social Research, 1930-35; exec. dir. Council of Jewish Fedns. and Welfare Funds, Inc., 1935-54, cons., 1954-73; mem. faculty U. Cal., 1927, 39, N. Y. Sch. of Social Work, 1931, 55; spl. lectr. U. Chgo. Sch. of Social Service Adminstrn., 1926-30. Dir. survey of programs for family and child welfare N.Y. Federation of Jewish Philanthropies. Mem. Am. Assn. of Social Workers, Am. Sociol. Soc. Author section Jewish Ency. Handbook, 1954; A Heritage Affirmed, 1961. Editor Social Work Ency., 1965. Contbr. articles to profl. publs. Home: New York City, N.Y. Died June 25, 1973.

LURIE, TED R., newspaper editor; b. N.Y.C., Dec. 10, 1909; B.A., Cornell U., Ithaca, N.Y., 1930; m. Tzila Lippman; 3 daus. Immigrated to Israel, 1930. Sometime Jerusalem corr. Central News Agy., London, New Chronicle, London, CBS, and A.P.; 1st accreditated Palestine war corr. with Jewish units Middle East, World War II; dir. English broadcasts of Haganah secret transmitter, pub. relations officer Haganah, 1948; editor, mng. dir. Jerusalem Post, 1955-74. Rep. Israel 1st Asian conf. Internat. Press Inst., Tokyo, 1956, mem. assembly, Washington, 1958, mem. exec. bd., 1974; del. Press Found. Asia, 1971. Mem. Journalists Assn. (a founder, mem. presidium editors com. 1957-59, 68-69), Israel-Japan Soc. (chmn. Jerusalem br. 1958). Rotarian (pres. Jerusalem 1958-59). Address: Jerusalem, Israel. Died June 1, 1974; buried Jerusalem, Israel.

LUTTERBECK, EUGENE FEISTMANN, radiologist; b. Fuerth, Germany, Sept. 21, 1909; s. Wilhelm and Luise (Merzbacher) F.; M.D., U. Berne (Switzerland), 1936; m. Ann Mary Goggin, Sept. 6, 1952; children—Peter Michael, Karen Maura, Steven Eugene, Deborah Ann. Came to U.S., 1939. Intern, Englewood Hosp., Chgo., 1940-41; resident U. Berne, 1935-36; pvt. practice medicine specializing in radiology, Chgo.; cons. radiologist Elgin (Ill.) State Hosp., 1942-47; attending radiologist Cook County Hosp., 1948-73; cons. radiologist Mary Thompson Hosp., 1948-73, Little Company of Mary Hosp., 1961-73, South Shore Hosp., 1961-73, Cancer Prevention Center, 1958-73, Henrotin Hosp., 1962-73, Edgewater Hosp., 1965-73, others; prof. radiology Cook County Grad. Sch. Medicine, 1948-73; asst. prof. radiology Northwestern U. Med. Sch., 1964-73; vis. prof. radiology Chgo. Med. Sch., 1972-73. Recipient numerous awards. Diplomate Am. Bd. Radiology. Fellow Inst. Medicine, Internat. Coll. Surgeons, Am. Coll. Radiology, Chgo. Roentgen Soc.; mem. Soc. Nuclear Medicine (charter), Central Soc. Nuclear Medicine, German, Swiss Roentgen socs., Am. Roentgen Ray Soc., Radiol. Soc. N.Am., A.M.A., Am. Leprosy Found., German Med. Soc. Chgo., World Med. Assn., Chgo. Med. Soc., others. Mason. Club: Germania (Chgo.). Home: Chicago, Ill. Died July 30, 1973; buried Oakwoods Cemetery, Chicago, Ill.

LUTZ, ALMA, author; b. Jamestown, N.D., Mar. 2, 1890; d. George and Mathilde (Bauer) Lutz; student Emma Willard Sch., Troy, N.Y.; A.B., Vassar Coll., 1912; Boston U. Sch. Bus. Adminstrn. Litt.D., Russell Sage Coll., 1959. Active woman suffrage in N.D., 1913-18; writer for newspapers, mags., leaflets for Nat. Woman's Party, booklets for Longyear Found., Boston; researcher women's role in Am. history, woman's rights movement. Mem. adv. com. Schlesinger Library on Women in Am., 1951-73; sec. Mass. Com. for Equal Rights Amendment. Pres. bd. trustees Zion Research Library, Boston U. Mem. Nat. Woman's Party (nat. council 1930-46, 59-73, cons. Notable Am. Women), Fedn. Bus. and Profl. Women's Clubs, A.A.U.W., Assn. Alumnae Vassar Coll., Am. Hist. Assn. Democrat. Christian Scientist. Clubs: College Women's City (Boston). Author: Emma Willard, Daughter of Democracy, 1929; Created Equal, A Biography of Elizabeth Cady Stanton, 1940; With Love, Jane: Letters from American Women on the War Fronts, 1945; Susan B. Anthony, 1959; (with Mrs. Blatch) Challenging Years, The Memoirs of Harriot Stanton Blatch, 1940; Emma Willard, Pioneer Educator of American Women, 1964 (paperback edit. 1970); Crusade for Freedom, Women of the Antislavery Movement, 1968. Home: Boston, Mass. Died Aug. 31, 1973.

LUTZ, HARLEY LEIST, economist; b. near Chillicothe, O., July 30, 1882; s. Ira and Minnie (Leist) L.; A.B., Oberlin Coll., 1907, LL.D., 1932; A.M., Harvard, 1908, Ph.D., 1914; m. Rachel A. Young, Dec. 31, 1909; children—Robert Gordon, Martha Jane,

Barbara. With Oberlin Coll., 1909-23, prof. economics, 1909-23; head of dept., 1914-23; prof. economics, Stanford, 1923-28; prof. of public finance, Princeton, 1928-47. Economic adviser Joint Taxation Com. 83d Ohio General Assembly, 1919; spl. adviser Washington Tax Investigating Com., 1922; mem. Commn. of Financial Advisers to Chile, 1925, to Poland, 1926; adviser Tax Investigation Commn. of Utah, 1929; dir. N.J. Tax Survey Commn., 1930-31; dir. N.Y. Temporary Economy Commission, 1942-43; chief economist for The Tax Foundation, 1944; chief of staff, com. on Postwar Tax Policy, 1944-47. Cons. economist, Nat. Assn. of Manufacturers, 1947. Decorated Comdr. Order of Polonia Restituta. Mem. Nat. Tax Assn. (pres. 1927-28), Am. Econ. Assn., Academia de Sciencia Economica (Chile). Phi Beta Kappa. Conglist. Author: The State Tax Commission, 1918, A Handbook of Classification of Property for Taxation, 1919; Report of Joint Special Committee on Taxation, 1919; Public Finance, 1924, 29, 36, 47; The Georgia System of Revenue, 1930; The System of Taxation in Maine, 1934; The Fiscal and Economic Aspects of the Taxation of Public Securities, 1939; The Business Man's Stake in Government Finance, 1939; The Taxation of Railroads in New Jersey, 1940; Guideposts to a Free Economy, 1945. Co-author: An Introduction to Economics, 1923 (New Introduction to Economics, 1933); Getting a Living, 1940 (rev. edit. 1949). Home: Princeton, N.J. Died Jan. 3, 1975.

LUTZ, PARKE HENRY, book publisher; b. Denver, Pa., July 9, 1896; s. Henry Regar and Kate (Getz) L.; B.S., Pa. State Coll., 1918; grad. student Susquehanna U., 1922, Franklin and Marshall Coll., 1924, U. Pa., 1925; m. Cecil Biddle Ritchey. With John C. Winston Co., 1926-61, beginning as ednl. rep., successively sec., asst. to pres., v.p., gen. mgr. ednl. dept., 1926-52, exec. v.p., dir., 1952-61, now changed to Holt, Rinehart and Winston, Inc., v.p., 1961-75. Chmn. Bd. Textbook Pubs.; mem. Pa. Bd. Edn., Lancaster County (Pa.) Park Bd. Bd. dirs. Ephrata Community Hosp.; trustee Thadeus Stevens Trade Sch., Lebanon Valley Coll. Served as 2d lt. U.S. Army, 1918-19; comdr. USNR, 1942-45. Mem. Profl. Bookmen Am., Council Basic Edn., Am. Textbook Pubs. Institute, Am. Legion, Phi Sigma Kappa. Mem. Evang. United Brethren Ch. Mason. Home: Denver, Pa., Died Mar. 16, 1975.

LUXFORD, G(EORGE) A(LFRED), lawyer; b. LaSalle, Ill., Nov. 16, 1880; s. James T. and Mary (Renfro) L.; A.B., Ia. State U., 1908, LL.B., 1909; m. Maude Robinson, Nov. 4, 1901; children—Rachel (Mrs. K. C. Brauns), Richard George. Admitted to Colo. bar, 1910, and practiced in Denver; asst. city atty., Denver, 1912-14; county judge, Denver, 1921-37; dist. judge, Denver, 1942-26; judge of Supreme Ct., State of Colo., 1946-49; later in pvt. practice of law. Republican. Methodist. Mason (33°). Home: Denver, Colo.†

LUZ, KADISH, Israeli legislator; b. Bobruisk, Russia, Jan. 10, 1895; s. Zvi-Hirzsh and Esther (Zeldovich) L.; D.Phil., Hebrew U., Jerusalem; m. Rachel Kantorovich, 1924; children—Esther, Zvi, Ehud, Hana. Mem. central supervising com. Gen. Fedn. Jewish Labor, Jerusalem, 1935-40; labor council, Tel-Aviv, 1941-42; sec. Hever Haqvoutzot, 1949-51; mem. Knesset, 1951-72, speaker, 1959-69; minister agr., 1955-59. Author: (in Hebrew) Milestones in the Kibbutz; One of Twelve; Ensign and Miracle, 1972. Contbr. profl. jours. Address: Jordan Valley, Israel., Died Dec. 4, 1972.

LYBRAND, WALTER ARCHIBALD, lawyer; b. Noblesville, Ind., Aug. 30, 1879; s. Lucius and Margaret Susan (Evans) L.; student Butler Coll., Indianapolis, 1898-1901; Ph.B., U. of Chicago, 1902; student U. of Chicago Law Sch., 1902-03, Denver Law Sch., 1904-05; J.D., U. of Chicago Law Sch., 1906; m. Edna Josephine Regan, Oct. 17, 1911 (died 1926); children—Walter A. (dec.); m. 2d, Grace P. McCoy. Practiced in Chicago, 1906, in Oklahoma City, from 1907; prof. law, Epworth U., 1908-11; prof. med. jurisprudence, Okla. State Med. Sch., from 1920. Commr, for Okla. on Uniformity of State Laws. Mem. American and Okla State Bar Assn. (pres. 1924), Okla. Hist. Soc., Phi Delta Theta, Phi Delta Phi. Republican. Episcopalian. Mason (K.T., 32°, Shriner); mem. Red Cross of Constantine. Clubs: Oklahoma, Lions (hon.), Men's Dinner. Home: Oklahoma City, Okla.*†

LYMAN, EDWARD BRANDON, church exec.; b. N.Y.C., Mar. 9, 1904; s. Edward Atwater and Genevieve (Tynan) L.; A.B., Fordham U., 1925; student advertising, Columbia; m. Dorothy Murray, Jan. 26, 1939; children—Mary, Donald, Robert, John, Nancy, Richard, Christopher, David, Stephen, Brian. Asst. dir. pub. relations Standard Oil Co. (N.J.), 1925-44, also editor The Lamp, co. publ.; with Petroleum Adminstrn. for War, 1944; asso. dir. bus. development Cities Service Co., 1944-47; asst. to pres. Fordham U., 1947-51; dir. spl. projects Office Civil and Def. Moblzn. (formerly Fed. Civil Def. Administrn.), 1951, gen. mgr. Alert Am. Convoys, 1951, 52, dep. dir. pub. affairs, 1952-54, dir. pub. affairs, 1954-57, asst. adminstr., 1957-58, dep. asst. dir. for nat. orgn. and civic affairs, 1958-61; director emergency information, Department of Defense, Office of Civil Defense, 1961-63; dir. pub. affairs Archdiocese of Washington, 1963-73. Chmn. Fordham U. Centenary Com., 1941. Mem. Cardinal's Com. of Laity, 1942-51; dir. coordinating com. Cath. Lay Orgns., N.Y.C., 1946-50, pres., 1950-51; mem. exec. com. Commn. on Race Relations, Wash. Recipient citation for services, USNR, 1947, award for outstanding performance in pub. relations Am. Pub. Relations Assn., 1946, 57. Mem. Am. Pub. Relations Assn. (dir. 1945-51, pres. 1949-50). Home: Rockville, N.Y. Died May 24, 1973.

LYMAN, EVELYN MAY, educator; b. Springfield, Mass., June 18, 1910; d. Frederick Clinton and Lillie Royce (Sykes) Lyman; B.S., Mass. State Coll. (now U. Mass.), 1931; M.Ed., Boston U., 1965. Dir. homemaking YWCA, Pawtucket, R.I., 1931-37; home demonstration agt. Kennebec County, Me., Coop. Extension Service, 1937-38; dir. home econs. Mt. Silinda Inst., Mt. Silinda, Rhodesia, S. Africa, 1938-44; home demonstration agt. Oxford County, Me., 1945-47, Worcester County, Mass., 1947-55; asso. extension prof. home mgmt. U. R.I., Kingston, from 1955. Mem. Am. R.I. (v.p. 1958-60) home econs. assns., Nutrition Council R.I. (v.p. 1962-64, pres. 1964), Epsilon Sigma Phi (annalist 1963, sec. 1967-68, pres. 1969-70). Conglist. Home: Cranston, R.I., Died Mar. 23, 1973.

LYMAN, MARY ELY, retired coll. dean; b. St. Johnsbury, Vt., Nov. 24, 1887; d. Henry Guy and Adelaide (Newell) Ely; B.A., Mount Holyoke Coll., 1911; B.D., Union Theol. Sem., 1919; Ph.D., U. of Chicago, 1924; student Cambridge (Eng.) U., 1919-20; Litt.D. (hon.), Mount Holyoke College, 1937; Litt.D. (hon.), Roanoke College, 1942; LL.D., Hood Coll., 1955; Litt. D., Western College for Women, 1957; D.D. (honorary), Colby College, 1958; m. Eugene W. Lyman, Feb. 13, 1926 (died 1948); children (adopted): Laura (Mrs. Frederick K. Hackett), Charles Eugene. Teacher, Rockville (Connecticut) High Sch., 1911-13; Y.W.C.A. gen. sec., Mount Holyoke Coll., 1913-16; Frederick Weyerhaeuser prof. of religion, Vassar Coll., 1921-26; lecturer in English Bible, Union Theol. Sem. and asso. in religion, Barnard Coll., Columbia U., 1928-40; dean and prof. religion, Sweet Briar (Va.) College, 1940-50; Morris K. Jesup prof. English Bible, Union Theol. Sem., N.Y.C., 1950-55, ret.; vis. lectr. Am. Sch. Oriental Research, Jerusalem, Palestine, spring 1934; vis. prof. Vassar Coll., 1956-57. Trustee Mt. Holyoke College. Awarded Phila. traveling fellowship of Union Theol. Sem., 1919-21. Trustee, The Cummington (Mass.) School. Mem. Nat. Assn. of Biblical Instrs. (pres. 1945), Soc. Biblical Lt. and Exegesis, Am. Theol. Soc., Phi Beta Kappa Frat. Club: Mount Holyoke, Cosmopolitan (N.Y.C.). Author: Knowledge of God in Johannine Thought, 1924; Paul the Conqueror, 1919; The Fourth Gospel and the Life of Today, 1931; The Christian Epic, 1936; Jesus (Hazen Series), 1937; In Him was Life, A Study-Guide to the Gospel of John, 1961. Contbr. to Symposium: Liberal Theology, 1942; Into all the World, 1956. Also book revs. and articles. Address: Claremont, Cal. Died Jan. 9, 1975.

LYMAN, RONALD THEODORE, ins. dir.; b. Waltham, Mass., July 8, 1879; s. Arthur Theodore and Ella (Lowell) L.; A.B. cum laude, Harvard, 1902; m. Elizabeth Van Cortlandt Parker, Oct. 26, 1904; children—Ronald T., Elizabeth L. (Mrs. Frederick Frelinghuysen), Charlotte L. (Mrs. Benjamin Clark), John Lowell. Asst. treas. Waltham Bleachery & Dye Works, 1904-06, treas., 1906-25; past treas., dir. Boston Mfg. Co., Whittenton Mfg. Co., Salmon Falls Mfg. Co.; v.p., trustee Provident Inst. Savs.; past dir. State Street Trust Co., Nat. Shawmut Bank; dir. Liberty Mut. Ins. Cos., Boston Mfrs. Mut. Ins. Co. Served as maj. U.S. Army, World War I; adv. com. Council Nat. Def., World War I. Club: Somerset (Boston). Home: Waltham, Mass.†

LYNCH, KENNETH MERRILL, med. coll. ofcl.; b. Hamilton County, Tex., Nov. 27, 1887; s. William Warner and Martha Isabel (Miller) L.; M.D., U. Tex., 1910; LL.D., U. S.C., 1930; Charleston Coll., 1945; D.Sc. (hon.), Clemson Coll., 1954; m. Lyall Wannamaker; children—Kenneth Me[Merrill, Martha Juanita, Merrill, William. Resident pathologist Phila. Gen. Hosp., 1911; instr. in pathology U. Pa., 1911-13; prof. pathology Med. Coll. S.C., 1913-21, 26-60, chancellor, 1960-74, vice dean, 1935-43, dean, 1943-49, pres., dean of faculty, 1949-60; pvt. practice, Dallas, 1921-26; pathologist Roper Hosp., Charleston, 1913-21, 27-60; also pathologist other S.C. hosps. Mem. S.C. State Bd. Health, 1935-44, chmn. 1940-44; mem. Nat. Bd. Med. Examiners (regional) 1935-42; . chmn. S.C. Cancer Commn., 1939-44; chmn. sci. adv. bd. Council for Tobacco Research-U.S.A., 1957-70. Served as capt., M.C., AUS and med. aide to gov. of S.C., 1918. Recipient 1st award Scientific Exhbn. of So. Med. Assn., 1920; research medal So. Med. Assn., 1921; gold medal Scientific Exhbn. of A.M.A., 1921, hon. mention, 1922; Distinguished Service award So. Med. Assn., 1957; Distinguished Service citation and medal Am. Cancer Soc., 1958; Distinguished Service to Medicine award and medal U. Tex., 1967; Citation Scroll of Honor, Med. Coll. S.C., 1968. Mem. Nat. Adv. Neurol. Diseases and Blindness Council, USPHS, 1957-61. Fellow A.C.P. (bd. govs. 1925-27, 36-43), A.A.A.S., A.M.A. (chmn. sect. on pathology 1924, v.p. 1935-36); mem. Am. Assn. Pathologists and Bacteriologists, Am. Soc. for Cancer Research, Am. Soc. of Tropical Medicine (pres. 1930-31), Am. Soc. Clin. Pathologists (pres. 1930-31), Am. Soc. Parasitologists, S.C. Med. Assn. (pres. 1930-31), So. Med. Assn. (chmn. pathology sect. 1924, chmn. med. edn. sect. 1923, mem. council 1935-40), Soc. for Control of Cancer (bd. dirs. 1939-44), Phi Beta Kappa, Alpha Omega Alpha, Alpha Mu Pi Omega, Omicron Delta Kappa, others. Democrat. Episcopalian. Club: University (New York). Collaborator: Approved Laboratory Technique, 1931. Revisor: (H. W. C. Vines) Green's Manual of Pathology, 1934. Author: Protozoan Parasitism of the Alimentary Tract, 1930; Medical Schooling in South Carolina, 1970. Former mem. editorial bds. Am. Jour. of Tropical Medicine, Am. Jour. Clin. Pathology, Am. Jour. of Digestive Diseases and Nutrition. Contbr. numerous articles to med. jours. Home: Summerville, S.C., Died Nov. 29, 1974.

LYNN, THOMAS EDWARD, physician; b. Dubuque, Ia., Oct. 8, 1925; s. Clarence Edward and Florence (Jaeggi) L.; M.D., Northwestern U., 1950; M.Sc. in Surgery, U. Minn., 1956; m. Joan Marie Van Drisse, July 28, 1956; children—Thomas, Diane, Mary, Robert, Julie, Kathy. Intern, Mary Hitchcock Hosp., Hanover, N.H., 1949-50; resident in gen. surgery Passavant Meml. Hosp., Chgo., 1950, Mayo Found., Rochester, Minn., 1951, 53-57, Evanston (Ill.) Hosp., 1957-58; resident in thoracic surgery VA Research Hosp., Chgo., 1957; active staff St. Vincent's Hosp., Bellin Hosp., St. Mary's Hosp. (all Green Bay, Wis.). Served with M.C., USNR, 1951-53. Diplomate Am. Bd. Surgery. Fellow A.C.S.; mem. A.M.A., Central Surg. Assn., Am. Assn. Ry. Surgeons. Home: Green Bay, Wis. Died Feb. 3, 1971; buried Allouez Cemetery, Green Bay, Wis.

LYON, B. B. VINCENT, physician; b. Erie, Pa., Mar. 29, 1880; s. George Armstrong and Rose (Vincent) L.; A.B., Williams Coll., 1903; M.D., Johns Hopkins University Medical School, 1907; Sc.D., Williams Coll., 1931; graduate study in Europe, 1914, 23, 27, 37; married Clara Armstrong, Jan. 11, 1910 (div. October 25, 1944); children—Rose Vincent (Mrs. Laurence Price Sharples), B. B. Vincent Jr., Armstrong. Interne German (Lankenau) Hosp., 1907-09; clin. asst. out-patient med. dispensary, U. of Pa., German, Presbyn. and Jefferson hosps., Phila., 1910-13; asst. phys. Jefferson Hosp., from 1929, founder and chief of clinic, out-patient gastro-intestinal dept., from 1912; demonstrator in med., Jefferson Med. Coll., 1910-20, asso. in medicine, 1920-28, asst. prof., 1929-37, asso. prof. in medicine, 1937-42, clin. prof. medicine 1942-46. Served as lieutenant (s.g.) Med. Corps U.S.N.R.F., 1917-19, Naval Base Hosp., Brest, France, also with Marine Corps and U.S. Army in France. Mem. Am. Enterology, Brussels, Belgium, 1935; apptd. editor for America, Internat. Gastroenterologia, Basel, Switzerland; hon. mem. Soc. Gastro-Enterology, Brussels. Fellow Am. Med. Assn., Am. Coll. Physicians, Phila. Coll. Physicians; member Am. Gastroenterol. Assn. (pres. 1934-35). Member Pithotomy Club of Johns Hopkins, Sigma Phi. Republican. Presbyterian. Clubs: Medical (Philadelphia); Williams (New York), University (Winter Park, Fla.). Author of monograph, Non-Surgical Drainage of the Gall Tract, 1923; Atlas on Biliary Drainage Microscopy, 1935. Contbr. to medical books and encys. and many articles to med. mags. Office: Philadelphia, Pa.†

LYON, BERTRAND, teacher pub. speaking; b. Creston, Ia., Sept. 28, 1880; s. Joseph Ogden and Ella (Swett) L; grad. Corning (Ia.) Acad., 1900, Soper Coll. of Oratory, Chicago, 1903; grad. study, U. of Chicago; m. Orphena McAllister, of Kalamazoo, Mich., Apr. 16, 1903; children—Audrey L., Benjamin McAllister; m. 2d, Helen Backett, of Denver, Colo., June 4, 1927; children—Earl Emerson, and Virginia H. Instr. in argumentation and debate, Sch. of Commerce, U. of Denver, 1920-25; instr. in pub. speaking, Denver Inst. Technology, 1915-22; became pres. Lyon Sch. of Expression, Denver, 1904; lyceum and Chautauqua lecturer. Mem. Pi Gamma Mu, Internat. Lyceum Assn. Author: Taking It on High, 1921; Practical Public Speaking, 1925; Concentration the Key to Mental Mastery; Practical Memory Training, 1930. Home: Seattle, Wash.†

LYON, CHARLES GERSHOM, lawyer; b. Los Angeles, Dec. 27, 1912; s. Frederick Saxton and Grace (Road) L.; student Cal. Inst. Tech., 1929-31; B.S., Loyola U., Los Angeles, 1934; J.D., Stanford, 1937; m. Frances Featherly Freer, June 18, 1940. Admitted to Cal. bar, 1937, practiced in Los Angeles; mem. firm Lyon & Lyon, 1937-73, partner, 1948-73. Served as capt. AUS, 1944-46. Mem. Am. Bar Assn., Los Angeles Patent Law Assn., Order of Coif. Home: Pasadena, Cal. Died Sept. 28, 1973.

LYON, CLYDE LATEN, college pres.; b. Toulon, Ill., Aug. 1, 1880; s. Eugene Burr and Hattie (Newcomer) L.; A.B., Eureka Coll., 1905; student U. of Chicago, 1909-10; m. Jessie Louise Bradley, of Toulon, Ill., Dec. 30, 1901; children—Clair Morene (Mrs. Kenneth Morton), Virgil Eugene, Robert Bradley, Ione Lorene (Mrs. Forest Mossholder), Lois Harriet. Instr. Eureka Coll., 1905-09, prof., 1910-12; prof. Northern Ill. State Teachers Coll., De Kalb, 1912-30; pres. Eureka Coll., from 1930. Mem. Christian Ch. Kiwanian. Address: Eureka, Ill.†

LYON, HOMER LEGRAND, congressman; b. Elizabethtown, N.C., Mar. 1, 1879; s. C. C. and Margaret R. L.; pre. edn., Davis Mil. Sch.; U. of N.C., 1897-1900; m. Kate M. Burkhead, of Whiteville, N.C.,

1904. Admitted to N.C. bar, 1900; solicitor 8th Jud. Dist., N.C., 1913-20; mem. 67th to 70th Congresses (1921-29), 6th N.C. Dist. Democrat. Methodist. Home: Whiteville, N.C.†

LYON, WILLIAM ALEXANDER, bank exec.; b. Colt, Nov. Ark., Nov. 1, 1902; s. Ben Arnold and Roberta (Taylor) L.; student Webb Sch., Bell Buckie, Tenn., 1917-19; A.B., U. Ark., 1923; m. Martha Kay, Sept. 2, 1933; children—Jack, Ann. Tchr. Fort Smith (Ark.) High Sch., 1923-24; mem. staff N.Y. Herald Tribune, 1924-28, financial writer, 1928-43; exec. asst. to supt. banks of New York, 1943-47, 1st dep. supt., 1947-50, supt. banks, 1950-54; chmn. exec. com. Dry Dock Savs. Bank, 1955-58, pres. and trustee, 1958-66, chmn. bd., 1966-69; dir. Accumulation Fund, Inc., Allegheny Power System, Inc., Am. Distilling Co., Discount Corp. of N.Y., Monongahela Power Co., West Penn Power Co., The Potomac Edison Co., Gen. Devel. Corp. Mem. N.Y.C. Rent Guidelines Bd. Trustee City Investing Mortgage Group. C.I. Realty Investors. Mem. Nat. Assn. Suprs. State Banks (past pres.), Nat. Assn. Mut. Savs. Banks (pres. 1958), N.Y. Financial Writers Assn. (asso.). Clubs: University, (N.Y.C.); Sleepy Hollow Country. Address: North Tarrytown, N.Y., Died July 21, 1975.

LYONS, CHARLTON HAVARD, petroleum producer; b. Abbeville, La., Sept. 3, 1894; s. Ernest John and Joyce Bentley (Harvard) L.; student La State U.; B.A., Tulane U., 1915, LL.B., 1916; m. Marjorie Hall, Aug. 28, 1917; children—Charlton Havard, Hall McCord. Admitted to La. bar, 1916; practiced in Winnfield, 1918-21, Shreveport, 1921-30; petroleum producer, as C. H. Lyons, Shreveport, now partnership. Former mem. bd. visitors Tulane U. Recipient Humanitarian of Year award Abbeville Dairy Festival, 1969. Mem. Ind. Petroleum Assn. Am. (dir.), La.-Ark., Mid Continent Oil and Gas assns., Gen. Mid Continent Oil and Gas Assn. (past pres., dir.); Am. Petroleum Inst. (dir.), Shreveport Bar Assn., Am. Legion, Kappa Alpha, Phi Delta Phi. Episcopalian. Home: Shreveport, La. Died 1973.

LYONS, JOHN FREDERICK, librarian; b. near Chandlersville, O., Sept. 13, 1878; s. Andrew and Isabel (Stewart) L.; A.B. Coll. of Wooster, O., 1901; McCormick Theol. Sem., 1901-04; studied New College (Edinburgh, Scotland), Marburg (Germany), Hartford Theol. Sem., 1904-07; B.D., McCormick Theol. Sem., 1913; M.A., U. of Chicago, 1920; D.D., Wooster, 1929; m. Julia Bechtel, Sept. 14, 1904 (died July 29, 1940). Ordained Presbyn. ministry, 1904; winner of lackstone fellowship, McCormick Theol. Sem., 1904, Jacobus fellowship, McCormick Theol. 1906; pastor in Ore., 1907-12; librarian and instructor bibliography, McCormick Theological Seminary, 1912-30, librarian and professor bibliography, 1930-49, emeritus, 1949. alumni sec., from 1949. Member American Library Association, Chicago Library Club, Pi Gamma Mu, Theta Phi. Republican. Club: Prairie. Author of "The Evolution of the Book" in From the Pyramids to Paul; Centennial History of the Presbytery of Chicago, 1947. Editor of Alumni Book-List, continued by Alumni Review of Presbyterian Theological Seminary. Contributor to Journal of the Dept. of History of Presbyn. Ch., U.S.A., McCormick Speaking, and other Periodicals. Home: Chicago, Ill.†

LYONS, JOSEPH HENRY, lawyer; b. Pollard, Ala., Oct. 31, 1874; s. Mark and Amelia (Horstler) L.; A.B., U. of Ala., 1894; LL.B., Harvard, 1899; m. Olive Houston, Nov. 8, 1911; children—Champ, Margaret Wiley. Admitted to Ala. bar, 1900, and began practice at Mobile; member of law firms successively Stevens & Lyons, Lyons, Chamberlain & Courtney and Lyons, Thomas & Pipes, 1912-52, later Lyons, Piper & Cook, U.S. collector of customs, District 19, 1918-22 and from 1933. Adminstr. for Alabama of War Savings Staff. Trustee Department of Archives and Histroy of State of Ala. Democrat. Home: Mobile, Ala.†

MABLEY, JACKIE MOMS, actress, comedienne; b. Brevard, N.C., Mar.; d. James P. and Mary M. (Smith) Mabley; hon. degree in performing arts, Case Western Reserve University; married; children—Yevonne, Aiken, Christine Aikens, Bonnie, Charles. Broadway performances include Fasta and Fouioos, Swinging the Dream, Blackbirds; radio appearance on Swingtime at the Savoy; film appearance in Emperor Jones; TV appearances on shows of Smothers Brothers, Harry Belafonte, Merv Griffin, others. Guest at White House Conf. to Fullfill These Rights, 1966. Named Comedienne of the Year, 1967, 68. Mem. N.A.A.C.P., Am. Guild Variety Artists, Actors Equity, A.F.T.R.A., Screen Actors Guild. Democrat. Home: White Plains, N.Y. Died May 24, 1975.

MACAGY, DOUGLAS GUERNSEY, arts adminstr.; b. Winnipeg, Man., Can., July 8, 1913; s. Douglas Drillio and Elisabeth (Guernsey) MacA.; student U. Toronto, 1933-35, Barnes Found., Merion, Pa., 1936-39; U. Pa., 1938-39; A.B., Western Res. U., 1940; m. Jermayne Smart, Mar. 24, 1941 (div. Dec. 1954); m. 2d, Elizabeth Tillett, Feb. 19, 1955; children—Ian Douglas, Caitlin Elisabeth. Came to U.S., 1936. Asst. ednl. dept. Cleve. Museum Art, 1939, asst. painting dept., 1940-41; curator San Francisco Museum Art, 1941-43; chief Japan sect. Propaganda div. Far East Bur. Office War Information, 1943-45; dir. Cal. Sch. Fine Arts, 1945-50; v.p. Orbit Films, Seattle, 1950-51; exec. sec. N.Y. Museums Commn. UNESCO, 1951-52; spl. cons. to dir. Museum Modern Art, N.Y.C., 1953-56; dir. research Wildenstein & Co. Inc., N.Y.C., 1956-59; dir. Dallas Museum Contemporary Arts, 1959-63; cons., 1963-68; dep. chmn. Nat. Endowment Arts, Nat. Council Arts, Washington, 1968-73, acting chmn., 1969; dir. exhbns. Joseph H. Hirshhorn Mus., Washington, 1972-73. Mem. Am. Soc. Aesthetics (trustee 1946-48), Coll. Art Assn., Am. Assn. Museums. Club: Players (N.Y.C.). Author: The Museum Looks in on TV, 1956; (with Elizabeth MacAgy) Going for a Walk with a Line, 1959; Art that Broke the Looking Glass, 1961. Contbr. articles to art jours. Home: Washington, D.C. Died Sept. 6, 1973.

MACARTHUR, HARRY, theatrical editor Washington Star. Address: Silver Spring, Md. Died Sept. 12, 1973.

MACARTHUR, RUTH ALBERTA BROWN, author; b. Searsmont, Me., Nov. 14, 1881; d. William Matthew and Vesta Ella (Frost) Brown; student U. of Minn., 1901-02; business coll. course; m. William Austin MacArthur, May 3, 1911; children—Ruth Marion, William Charles and Walter Austin (twins), Meredith Jeanne, Merle Elladice. Methodist. Author: Tabitha at Ivy Hall, 1911; Tabitha's Glory, 1912; Tabitha's Vacation and At the Little Brown House, 1913; The Lilac Lady, 1914; Heart of Gold, 1915; Little Mother, 1916 (pub. in London, 1917; transl. into the Danish, 1924); Daisy, 1919; The Gingerbread House, 1920; Story of Harriet Beecher Stowe, 1922. Contbr. to American Women Poets, 1937; Caravan of Verse, 1938. Contbr. to Listen, My Children, 1940; Hear Us, America, 1941; United Song of America, 1943. Poetry Digest, 1945. Contbr. Poetry Broadcast, 1945. Home: Long Beach, Cal.†

MACAULAY, MALCOLM GEORGE, physician; b. East Angus, Que., Can., June 7, 1926; s. Thomas Gordon and Evelyn May (Sherman) MacA.; came to U.S., 1949; M.D., McGill U., 1949; m. Marion V. Johnson, June 24, 1950; children—Jeffrey, Marilyn, Thomas, Brian, Jacqueline, Gerald. Intern. St. Luke's Hosp., Newburgh, N.Y., 1949-50, resident in gen. practice, 1950-52; resident in gen. practice N.Y.U.-Bellevue Postgrad. Med. Sch., N.Y.C., 1950-52; resident in neuropsychiatry Walter Reed Army Hosp., Washington, 1953-56; asst. clin. dir. St. Albans Hosp., Radford, Va., 1968-69; pvt. practice medicine specializing in psychiatry, Beckley, W.Va. Served to maj., M.C., AUS, 1953-59. Diplomate Am. Bd. Psychiatry and Neurology. Mem. A.M.A., Am. Psychiat. Assn. Home: Beckley, W.Va. Died Mar. 3, 1974; buried Sunset Meml. Park, Beckley, W.Va.

MACCARTHY, GERALD R(ALEIGH), geologist, geophysicist; b. Ithaca, N.Y., Nov. 15, 1897; s. Gerald and Adeline (Dixon) MacC.; student Colby Coll., Waterville, Me., 1915-17; A.B., Cornell, 1919-21; A.M., U. of North Carolina, 1924, Ph.D., 1926; married Elizabeth Enloe, Dec. 25, 1924; children—Elizabeth Dixon, Margaret Fitz-Gerald (Mrs. R. L. Whitmire Jr.). Instructor Williams Coll., Williamstown, Mass., 1921-22; Instr. U. of N.C., 1922-26; asst. prof., 1926-30, asso. prof., 1930-40, prof. from 1946; geophysicist, U.S. Geol. Survey, 1937-40. U.S. Bur. Mines, Baltimore, 1942-46, U.S. Geol. Survey from 1949, summer work, 1946-48. Served with 26th div., 103rd Inf., U.S.A., 1917-19; overseas. Fellow A.A.A.S., Geol. Soc. of Am.; mem. Am. Geophysical Union, Phi Beta Kappa, Sigma Xi. Contbr. articles to sci. pubs. Home: Chapel Hill, N.C. Died Oct. 31, 1974.

MACDONALD, EDWINA LEVIN, author; b. Campti, Louisiana, May 10, 1878; d. Andrew Jackson and Minerva (Dupree) Dickerson; educated Louisiana State Normal School, Sophie Newcomb Girls' Sch., New Orleans; m. Jackson Robert MacDonald; 1 son, J. Clifford. Teacher Indianola Coll., Tecumseh, Okla., 1905-07; took up theatrical career, appearing in New York and on tours with Thomas A. Wise and others until 1914. Mem. Authors' League America, O.E.S., Daughters of Confederacy. Christian Scientist. Author: A Lady of New Orleans, 1925; Blind Windows, 1927; Heart Strings, 1930; Star Jasmine, 1933. Contbr. short stories and serials to internat. mags.; wrote under names of Edwina Le Vin, Kay Johnson and Edwina L. MacDonald. Editor of Damon and Pythias (a nat. mag. for Pythians). Author various motion pictures. Home: Tampa, Fla.†

MACDONALD, KATHERINE CUNNINGHAM (MRS.GEORGE FIELD MACDONALD), club woman; b. Pitts.; d. S. Woodward and Kate (Crawford) Cunningham; B.A., Wellesley Coll., 1924; m. George Field MacDonald, Jr., Feb. 21, 1928 (dec. Jan. 1962); children—Katherine Crawford (Mrs. Don Balman Blenko), Lois Eleanor (Mrs. B. Mark Antinucci). Chpt. regent D.A.R., 1962-65, state chmn. jr. Am. citizens com., 1965-68; pres., bd. chmn. Pitts. Hearing Soc., 1948-50; chmn. womens' ednl. com. Community Chest, Pitts., 1951, 52; mem. met. bd. YWCA, Pitts., 1951-62, chmn. vol. personnel com., 1952-55, chmn. bldg. standards com., 1955-62. Clubs: College (Pitts.) (pres. 1948-50), Longue Vue Country, Twentieth Century (dir. chmn. card com. 1959-61). Home: Pittsburgh, Pa. Died Aug. 30, 1973.

MACDONALD, MILTON THEODORE, surgeon; b. New Bedford, Mass., June 24, 1905; s. Murdock and Fannie (MacLeod) MacD.; M.D., Yale, 1930; m. Elizabeth Lydia Haskins, June 24, 1938; children—Milton Murdock, Donald Duncan, Betsey Douglas (Mrs. Everett Beaumont Mills III). Intern, St. Lukes Hosp., New Bedford, 1930-31; resident Kings County Hosp.-L.I. Coll., 1935-36; pvt. practice medicine specializing in surgery; mem. staff, surgeon-in-chief, pres. med. staff, chmn. blood bank St. Luke's Hosp., New Bedford; surg. cons. Tobey Hosp., Wareham, Mass., St. Luke's Hosp., Middleboro, Mass. Active Am. Cancer Soc., 1952-56. Served to maj., M.C., AUS, 1942-46. Diplomate Am. Bd. Surgery. Fellow A.C.S., Internat. Acad. Proctology; mem. A.M.A., New Eng. Surg. Soc. Home: New Bedford, Mass. Died Oct. 25, 1973; buried Rural Cemetery, New Bedford, Mass.

MACDONALD-WRIGHT, STANTON, artist; b. Charlottesville, Va., July 8, 1890; s. Archibald Devonporte and Annie (Van Vranken) Wright; studied with pvt. tutors, Paris; student Sorbonne, Academie Colorossi, Ecole des Beaux Arts (all Paris); m. Jean Louise Sutton, Apr. 30, 1953. One of founders Synchromism art movement, 1913; dir. Art Student's League, Los Angeles, 1922-30; study Chinese and Japanese calligraphy and aesthetics, 1933-35; dir. Works Progress Administrn. project in art So. Cal., 1935-42; study Oriental art Tokyo and Kyoto, Japan, 1937-38; asso. prof. Oriental art U. Cal., Los Angeles, 1942-50, prof., 1950-54; Fulbright exchange prof. to Japan, 1952-53; exhbns. Salon d' Automne, Paris, 1910, Salon des Independents, Paris, 1912, others in Munich, Milan, London, Warsaw, N.Y.C., 1913, Palace Legion d'Honneur, San Francisco, Stendahl Gallery, Los Angeles, Mus. Sci., History and Art, Los Angeles, Duveen-Graham Gallery, Rose Fried Gallery, N.Y.C., Galerie Arnaud, Paris; retrospective exhibition Smithsonian Instn., 1967; painter murals Santa Monica Pub. Library, petrachrome murals Santa Monica City Hall, mosaics mural Santa Monica High Sch., 1935-37; tchr. Oriental art history Scripps Coll., summer 1946; lectr. U. Hawaii, summer 1949, also Kyoiku Dai Goku and Gendai Bijutsukan, Tokyo, 1952-53; retrospective exhbn., U. Cal., Los Angeles, 1970; works in permanent collections Mus. Modern Art, N.Y.C., Bklyn. Mus. Art, Phila. Mus. Art, U. Chgo., Whitney Mus., Met. Mus., N.Y.C., others. Address: Pacific Palisades, Cal. Died Aug. 22, 1973.

MACDONNELL, JAMES FRANCIS CARLIN; b. Bay Shore, N.Y., Apr. 7, 1881; s. Mark and Margaret (Carlin) MacD.; ed. parish sch., Norwalk, Conn.; unmarried. Floor supt. R. H. Macy & Co., dept. store, N.Y. City. Anti-Wilson Democrat. Roman Catholic. Author: My Ireland, 1917; The Cairn of Stars, 1920. Contbr. poems to newspapers and mags. Home: New York City, N.Y.†

MACDONNELL, RONALD MACALISTER, Canadian govt. official; b. Vernon, B.C., Can., May 11, 1909; s. Logie and Ursilla (Macalister) M.; B.A., U. of Manitoba, 1930; B.A., Oxford, 1932; m. Margaret E. Jackman, Aug. 17, 1935; children—Logie Macalister, Mary Geddes, Margaret Kirk, Norman Cameron. Was teacher and in radio until 1934; became external affairs officer of Can., 1934; 3d and 2d sec., Washington, D.C., 1935-42; 1st sec., Moscow, 1943; 1st sec., Ottawa, 1944, counsellor, 1945; also secretary Can. sect. Permanent Joint Bd. on Def. for Canada and U.S.A.; Canadian Charge d'Affaires, Prague, Czechoslovakia, 1947-50; Canadian minister to France, 1950-52; asst. under-sec. of state for external affairs, 1952; Can. mem. Internat. Supvry. Commn. for Viet Nam and Cambodia, 1954; dep. under-sec. of state for external affairs, 1955-57, 58-59; sec.-gen. Internat. Civil Aviation Orgn., 1959-70; Canadian ambassador to Egypt (subsequently the United Arab Republic) and minister to Lebanon, 1957-58. Address: Montreal, Que., Canada. Died May 19, 1973.

MACDOUGALL, FRANK HENRY, physical chemist; b. Maxville, Ont., Can., Oct. 24, 1883; s. Duncan Peter and Janet (MacEwin) MacD.; B.A., M.A., Queen's U., Kingston, Ont., 1905; Ph.D., Leipzig U., 1907; m. Frances Aborn, 1908; children—Duncan Peck, Janet Aborn (Mrs. S. A. Granthan, Jr.), Mary Fisher (deceased); m. 2d, Anne Reichmann, 1932; 1 dau., Anne Vanderlip. Came to U.S., 1907, naturalized, 1922. Inst. in chemistry, Tex. A. and M. Coll., 1907-12; asso. prof., Calgary Coll., Can., 1912-15; instr. of chemistry, U. of Minn., 1915-17, asst. prof., 1917-19, asso. prof., 1919-24; prof. phys. chemistry 1924-75, head div., 1937-52, emeritus prof. phys. chemistry. Fellow A.A.A.S.; mem. Am. Chem. Soc. (councilor), Sigma Xi, Phi Lambda Upsilon, Alpha Chi Sigma. Clubs: Campus, Minn. Automobile (Mpls.); Pittsburgh Automobile (Pitts.). Author: Thermodynamics and Chemistry, 1921; Physical Chemistry 1936. Contbr. profl. jours. Home: Pittsburgh, Pa. Died Nov. 21, 1974.

MACDOUGALL, RANALD, writer, producer, dir.; b. Schenectady, Mar. 10, 1915; m. Nanette Fabray, 1957. Early works include numerous radio and one-act plays as This is War, Great Plays, Man Behind the Gun

(Peabody award 1942); motion pictures include Objective Burma, Mildred Pierce, Possessed, Decision of Christopher Blake, Unsuspected, June Bride, Hasty Heart, The Breaking Point, Bright Leaf, Mr. Belvedere Rings the Bell, I'll Never Forget You, Naked Jungle, Secret of the Incas, We're No Angels, The Mountain, Queen Bee, Man on Fire, The World, The Flesh and the Devil, Go Naked in the World, The Subterraneans, Quentin Werty Jigsaw, Dark of the Sun, Cleopatra, Fame is the Name of the Game, Jigsaw, The Cockeyed Cowboys of Calico County; also numerous TV shows, including Name of the Game. Recipient Laurel award, 1957. Address: Pacific Palisades, Cal. Died Dec. 11, 1973.

MACELWANE, GERALDINE FRANCES, judge; b. Detroit, July 9, 1909; d. Jeremiah Joseph and Mary Elizabeth (Hannett) Connell; LL.B., U. Toledo, 1938, J.D., 1968; A.B., DeSales Coll., 1942; m. John Patrick Macelwane, July 23, 1938; children—Mary Frances (Mrs. Stephen Pero), Kathleen Anne (Mrs. Anthony Wernert). Admitted to Ohio bar, 1932; pvt. practice, Toledo, 1932-37; asst. prosecutor, Lucas County, 1937-42; judge municipal Ct., Toledo, 1952-56, Lucas County Common Pleas Ct., 1956-74. Cons. Women's Traffic Council; del. White Ho. Conf. on Traffic Safety, Pres.'s Mid-West Conf. on Traffic Safety; dir. Toledo Council Social Agys., Maumee Valley council Girl Scouts U.S.A.; mem. exec. com., dir. Toledo-Lucas County Safety Council; chmn. jud. adminstrn. com. Ohio Jud. Conf., 1966; nat. chmn. safety on sts. com. women's conf. Nat. Safety Council. Fellow Ohio Bar. Found.; mem. Am., Ohio, Lucas County, Toledo bar assns., Nat. Safety Council (program chmn. 1965, v.p., exec. com. Women's Conf.), League Women Voters, Ohio Assn. Common Pleas Judges (v.p. exec. com., chmn. rules of superintendency com.), Nat. Conf. State Trial Judges, Nat. Assn. Women Lawyers, Toledo Bus. and Profl. Women's Club, Kappa Beta Pi, Phi Kappa Phi (hon. mem. U. Toledo chpt.), Delta Kappa Gamma (state hon. mem.). Democrat. Home: Toledo, O. Died Dec. 9, 1974.

MACENULTY, JOHN FORREST, business exec.; b. Pittsburgh, 1880; was vice-pres. and dir. Pressed Steel Car Co., until Dec. 1937, when elected pres.; vice chmn. bd. dirs. April 1945-June 1946, chmn. bd. dirs., June 1946-47, cons., from 1947. Dir. Huntingdon and Broad Top Mt. R.R. Coal Co. Address: New York City, N.Y.†

MACFARLAND, HAYS, advt. and sales exec.; b. Republican City, Neb., Apr. 12, 1890; s. David Fullerton and Ida (Hays) MacF.; Ph.B., U. Chgo., 1915; m. Faye Millard, Feb. 1, 1930; children—Elizabeth (Mrs. John A. Ruffin III), Hays, Jr. Advt. salesman, 1915-17; asst. bus. mgr. Chgo. Herald-Examiner, 1919, v.p. asst. pub. advt. dir., 1924-29; Chgo. rep. Sat. Eve. Post, 1920; sales mgr. Alemite Corp., later v.p., gen. sales mgr., 1920-23; partner Blackett, Sample, MacFarland, 1923-24; organizer advt. agy. MacFarland, Aveyard & Co., 1929, chmn. bd.; chmn. exec. com., dir. Earle Ludgin & Co.; dir. Fil-Tip Corp. Mem. exec. com. Citizens Finance Com. Ill. Served from capt. to lt. col. AEF, 1917-19. Republican. Presbyn. Clubs: Chicago, Glenview, Racquet, University, Saddle and Cycle, Tavern. Home: Chicago, Ill. Died Jan. 2, 1975.

MACFARLANE, JAMES, b. Bankfoot, Perthshire, Scotland, Feb. 18, 1873; s. Peter . and Louise (Marshall) M.; m. Janet Stewart, Aug. 21, 1900; m. 2d, Jessie Edna Daniels, July 19, 1917. Marine engr. Indra and Atlas Line, 1896-1901; supt. machinist Panama R.R., Panama, 1901-05; rebuilt and operated dredges and maintained channel for seagoing ships from French dock at La Boca, deep water terminal for the transisthmian railroad, 1905-18; supt. floating equipment and dredging, Panama Canal; also mem. Bd. of Local Inspectors. Had entire charge of dredging operations in Culebra Cut during the first trying years when slides so frequently blocked the Canal. Supt. Havana Marine Railways, Inc., 1918, gen. mgr., 1922; pres. MacFarlane Foundry and Honolulu Iron Works S.A., Sagua la Grande, Cuba, Mem. Am. Soc. M.E. Mason (Shriner). Clubs: American Country (Havana, Cuba). Address: Havana, Cuba.†

MACFARLANE, WILLIAM, insurance exec. Vice pres. and chief actuary New York Life Ins. Co. Home: New York City, N.Y. Died Jan. 22, 1974.

MACGLASHAN, DAVID POLLOCK, bookstore exec.; b. McKeesport, Pa., Jan. 7, 1914; s. Hugh and Agnes (Donaldson) MacG.; B.S., Pa. State U., 1935; m. Helen Shea, Sept. 9, 1944; 1 dau., Laurie Elizabeth. Prodn. engr. Nat. Tube Co., McKeesport, Pa., 1935-39; maintenance, modification engr. Curtiss-Wright Co., Buffalo, 1939-42, Bell Aircraft Co., Niagara Falls, N.Y., 1942-43; cons. mgmt. engr. Stevenson, Jordan & Harrison Co., Chgo., 1943-44; mgmt. engr. La France Corp., Elmira, N.Y., 1944-47; pres. Corning Drug Co. (N.Y.), 1947-61, MacGlashan's, Inc., Corning, 1961-68, Eisenhower Coll. Campus Store, Seneca Falls, N.Y., from 1968. Mem. Nat. Assn. Cost Accountants (charter mem. Elmira sect.). Rotarian. Originator computerized labor, materials control and cost system, now employed throughout automobile industry. Home: Penn Yan, N.Y. Deceased.

MACGREGOR, THEODORE DOUGLAS, author: b. Liverpool, N.S., Can., Mar. 15, 1879; s. Rev. Duncan and Elizabeth Bryden (McKeen) M.; came to U.S., 1889. Ph.B., Syracuse U., 1902; m. Lillian A. Wood, of Antwerp, N.Y., Aug. 25, 1909; children—Theodora D., Mary Frances. Began as reporter on Syracuse Herald; mem. editorial staff The Bankers' Magazine, New York, 1907-16; v.p. Edwin Bird Wilson, Inc., advertising, N.Y. City. Mem. Phi Gamma Delta. Republican. Conglist. Author: Pushing Your Business, 1908; Two Thousand Points for Financial Advertising, 1912; Bank Advertising Plans, 1913; Talks on Thrift, 1913; The Book of Thrift, 1915; Bank and Trust Company Advertising, 1917; The New Business Department, 1917; Bank Advertising Experience, 1919; MacGregor's Book of Bank Advertising, 1928. Home: White Plains, N.Y.†

MACHOLD, EARLE JOHN, lawyer; b. Ellisburg, New York, Nov. 27, 1903; s. H. Edmund and Ella J. (Ward) M.; LL.B., Syracuse U., 1927; D.Sc., Clarkson College of Technology, 1960; L.H.D., Le Moyne Coll., 1964; m. Alice Coonley, June 9, 1928; children—Anne C., John W. Admitted to N.Y. bar, 1928; asso. with Charles A. Phelps, 1928-29, Sullivan & Cromwell, 1929-30. LeBoeuf & Winston, 1930-34; partner LeBoeuf, Winston, Machold & Lamb, 1934-37. LeBoeuf, Machold & Lamb, 1937-42; pres. Niagara Mohawk Power Corp., 1942-69, chmn., chief exec. officer, 1969-73, chmn. exec. com. bd. dirs.; member board directors Marine Midland Corp., Midland Capital Corp. Mem. bd. of trustees Syracuse U., nat. plan chmn. Mem. Am., N.Y. State, Onondaga County bar assns., Republican. Methodist. Clubs: Century (Syracuse); Black River Valley (Watertown); Links. Home: Syracuse, N.Y. Died June 17, 1973.

MACIVOR, JOHN WILLIAM, clergyman; b. South Cove, Nova Scotia, Mar. 20, 1878; s. Malcolm and Margaret (Mac Ivor) Mac I.; M.A., Franklin Coll., New Athens, O., 1902; student McCormick Theol. Sem., Chicago, 1902-04, Western Theol. Sem., Pittsburgh, 1904-05; D.D., Westminster Coll., Fulton, Mo., and Grove City (Pa.) Coll., 1916; m. Blanche Elizabeth Eisenheis, June 2, 1909; 1 dau., Elizabeth. Came to U.S., 1898, naturalized citizen, 1915. Minister Watson Memorial Presbyn. Ch., Pittsburgh, 1905-16, Second Presbyn. Ch., St. Louis, from 1916. Trustee Lindenwood Coll. Mem. Gen. Council Presbyn. Church U.S.A. Mason (Shriner). Clubs: University, Glen Echo, Bellerive Country, Noonday, Home: St. Louis, Mo.*†

MACK, PAULINE BEERY, coll. dean, research dir.; b. Norborne, Mo., Dec. 19, 1891; d. John Perry and Dora (Woodford) Beery; A.B., Mo. State U., 1913; A.M., Columbia, 1919; Ph.D., Pa. State U., 1932; Sc.D., Moravian Coll. for Women, 1952, Western Coll. for Women, Oxford, O., 1952; m. Warren B. Mack, Dec. 27, 1923. Sci. tchr. Norborne High Sch., 1913-15, Webb City (Mo.) High Sch., 1915-18, Springfield (Mo.) High Sch., 1918-19; mem. faculty Pa. State U., 1919-52, Coll. Chemistry and Physics, 1940-52; dean, dir. research Coll. Household Arts and Scis., Tex. Women's U., Denton, 1952-62, dir. Research Inst., 1962-74, dir. Phila. Mass Studies in Human Nutrition, 1940-45, Pa. Mass Studies, 1935-52. Recipient Distinguished Dau. Pa. medal, 1949. Fellow Am. Pub. Health Assn., Am. Inst. Chemists, A.A.A.S., Soc. for Research in Child Devel., Am. Sch. Health Assn.; mem. Am. Assn. Textile Tech., Royal Soc. Health (Great Britain), Soc. Chem. Industry (Great Britain), Am. Council Edn., Am. Ordnance Assn., Am. Chem. Soc. (Garvan medal 1950), Am. Soc. for Testing Materials, Am. Assn. Textile Chemists and Colorists, Am. Home Econ. Assn., Tex. Pub. Health Assn., Textile Research Inst., Tex. Acad. Sci. Am. Dietetic Assn., D.A.R., Daus. Am. Colonists, Phi Beta Kappa Assos., Phi Beta Kappa, Sigma Xi, Phi Kappa Phi, Iota Sigma Pi (nat. pres. 1945-48), Omicron Nu, Sigma Delta Epsilon, Beta Sigma Phi (internat. hon. mem.), Delta Kappa Gamma. Episcopalian. Author: Chemistry Applied to Home and Community, 1926; Stuff, 1936. Cons. editor of Chemistry. Contbr. articles on research in nutrition and textile chemistry to jours. Home: Denton, Tex. Died Oct. 23, 1974.

MACKAYE, BENTON, forestry; b. Stamford, Conn., Mar. 6, 1879; s. Steele and Mary (Medbery) M.; A.B., Harvard U., 1900; A.M., Harvard Forest Sch., 1905; unmarried. Research forester, U.S. Forest Service, 1905-18; specialist in colonization, U.S. Dept. Labor, 1918-19; spl. projects in regional planning, 1920-22. Formulated project, 1921, for the Appalachian Trail (mountain footpath from Me. to Ga., now completed); orginator of plan of the "townless highway," 1930; consultant in planning study for U.S. Indian Service on Indian reservations in S.Dak., N.M. and Ariz., 1933; on regional planning staff of (U.S.) Tenn. Valley Authority, 1934-36; formulated procedure for carrying out the regional planning features of the Tenn. Valley Authority Act of 1933; cons. on flood control policies of U.S. Forest Service, Washington, D.C., 1938, 39. Formulated proposal for an Alaska-Siberia "Burma Road," 1942. On staff on (U.S.) Rural Electrification Adminstrn., 1942-45, ret. 1945. Mem. Soc. Am. Foresters, Wilderness Soc. (pres. 1945). Author: The New Exploration, 1928. Co-author (with Lewis Mumford) Regional Planning, article in Ency. Britannica, 14th edit. Home: Shirley Center, Mass.†

MACKENZIE, JOHN DOUGLAS, mining engr.; b. N.D., Aug. 16, 1897; s. John M. and Anna (Hawkinson) MacK.; B.S., U. N.D., 1918; M.S., U. Utah, 1910; M. Grace Moulton, Aug. 15, 1929; 1 son, John Douglas, Jr. Chemist, supt., asst. to mgr. Garfield plant Am. Smelting & Refining Co., 1920-27, mgr. East Helena plant, 1928-39, gen. mgr. Southwest dept., 1939-41, v.p., metall. dir., mgr. Selby (Cal.) plant, 1941-46, gen. mgr. plants Western dept., 1946-48, v.p., dir. charge smelting, refining operations 1948-58, chmn. bd., pres., 1958-62, dir.; chmn. exec. com., dir. Gen. Cable Corp., 1958-73; Revere Copper & Brass, Inc., 1958-73; dir. No. Peru Mining Corp., Ormet Corp., Southern Peru Copper Corp. Trustee Com. Econ. Devel. Recipient Distinguished Achievement award U. N.D. Mem. Am. Inst. Mining Metall. and Petroleum Engrs., Mining and Metall. Soc. Clubs: University, Mining, Bankers of Am., Pinnacle (N.Y.C.); Royal Poinciana Golf (Naples, Fla.). Home: Naples, Fla., Died Mar. 16, 1973.

MACKEY, DAVID RAY, broadcaster; b. Pensacola, Fla., Dec. 16, 1917; s. Henry Jerome and Alta Theodore (Haynes) M.; B.S., Northwestern U., 1946, M.A., 1947, Ph.D., 1956; m. Eleanor Ely, July 3, 1943; children—Douglas Alan, Marilyn, Martha Louise, Robert Jerome. Profl. broadcaster, 1935-41; prodn. mgr. Radio House, Instr. drama U. Tex., 1947-49; asst. prof. speech Pa. State U., 1951-56; prof. communications, chmn. div. communication arts Boston U., 1957-61; pres. gen. mgr. KWHK Broadcasting Co., Inc., Hutchinson, Kn., 1961-75, KTRC, Santa Fe, N.M., KBHS, Hot Springs, Ark. Mayor of Hutchinson, 1971-72; mem. Hutchinson Arts Cocunil, Burgess, State Coll., Pa., 1954-57. Served with A.C., USNR, 1942-45. Author: Drama on the Air, 1951; Nat. Assn. of Broadcasters: Its First Twenty Years, 1956. Edn. editor Jour. Broadcasting, 1956-58. Author profl. articles, speeches, scripts. Home: Hutchinson, Kan., Died Sept. 26, 1975.

MACKINNON, JOHN C., footwear co. exec.; b. Boston, 1907. Pres., B.F. Goodrich Footwear Co., Watertown, Mass.; v.p., dir. Sun Mfg., Inc. P.R., West Mfg. Co., Cabo Rojo Mfg. Co.; dir. Union Market Nat. Bank. Mem. N.E. Footwear Assn. (dir., treas.), Asso. Industries Mass. (treas., dir.), Rubber Mfrs. Assn. (exec. com. footwear div.), Nat. Footwear Mfrs. Assn. (dir.). Home: Wellesley Hills, Mass. Died July 29, 1973; buried Woodlawn Cemetery, Wellesley, Mass.

MACKINTOSH, HUGH, army officer; b. Boston, Oct. 7, 1907; s. Hugh and Elizabeth (Flynn) M.; B.S., U.S. Mil. Acad., 1929; student Indsl. Coll. Armed Forces, 1947-48; m. Bonniebell Alice O'Donnell, July 30, 1930; children—Robert Hugh, Eloise Gayle (Mrs. Omer C. Ostensoe), Richard. Commd. 2d lt., inf., U.S. Army, 1929, advanced through grades to maj. gen., 1953; assigned First U.S. Army, Europe, 1943-45, transferred Q.M.C., 1945; Q.M., 1st Army, 1946-47; assigned Office Q.M. Gen., 1948-51, Eighth U.S. Army, Korea, 1951-52; exec. dir. Mil. Subsistence Supply Agy., Hdqrs., Chgo., 1958-62; comdg. general Fort Lee, Virginia, 1962-66, ret., 1966. Decorated Legion of Merit with 2 clusters; Croix de Guerre with silver gilt star (France); Cross of Brigadeers of Royal Bn. of King George I (Greece); Ulchi Distinguished Mil. Service Medal with silver star (Korea); Comdr. Order Brit. Empire. Home: Colonial Heights, Va. Died May 8, 1974.

MACLEAN, MALCOLM SHAW, JR., educator; b. St. Paul, June 28, 1920; s. Malcolm Shaw and Marion (Brown) MacL.; B.A. cum laude, U. Minn., 1947, M.A., 1949; Ph.D., U. Wis., 1954; m. Eleonora Monti, May 22, 1948; children—Alessandra Manca, Lester Monti. Instr. U. Minn., 1949-50; instr., then asst. prof. U. Wis., 1950-56; asso. prof., then prof. Mich. State U., 1956-64; George H. Gallup prof. U. Ia., 1964-68, dir. Sch. Journalism, 1967-74. Pres. Internat. Communication Assn. Served with AUS, 1942-46. Fulbright fellow, 1956-57. Fellow Am. Sociol. Assn.; mem. Assn. Edn. in Journalism, Sigma Delta Chi, Kappa Tau Alpha. Contbg. author: Due Anni Col Pubblico Cinematografico, 1958; Research Planning, Introduction to Mass Communication Research, 1958; Dimensions of Communication, 1965; Communication and Culture, 1966; Communication: Theory and Research, 1967. Contbr. to jours. in field. Home: Solon, Ia. Died Feb. 20, 1974.

MACLEARY, BONNIE, sculptor; b. San Antonio, Tex.; d. James Harvey and Mary (Kings) McLeary (as spelled by father); art edn., Julian Acad., Paris, Art Students' League, N.Y.C., under James Earle Frazer, also Gleb Dersjensky; m. James McGahan. Received first prize, Women's Arts and Industries, N.Y.C., 1928, 29; Honorable Mention, The Offering, Nat. Arts Club, 1955. Rep. by bronze "Aspiration," Met. Mus., N.Y.C.; bronze fountain "Ouch!" Bklyn. Children's Museum; "Victory," World War meml., San Juan, P.R.; monument to Don Luis Munoz Rivera, U. of Porto Rico; Gifford Meml., Bklyn.; A. Joseph Armstrong bust, Baylor U., Waco, Tex.; Rotan Meml., Waco, My Lady Sleeps, Wesleyan Coll., Ga.; Ben Milam monument, San Antonio, Tex., "Blessed Damozel," Witte Museum, San Antonio, Tex., Meml. Relief to the "Women of the Confederacy," Montgomery, Ala.; bronze, Felicia; ceramic sculpture, Laurel; relief Happy Days; woodcarving Origin of Sound; bronze figure entitled Young Amazon; The Flame. Became an Associate

National Academican, 1930. Mem. Nat. Sculpture Soc., Nat. Assn. Women Artists and Allied Artists Am., Am. Artists Profl. League, New Orleans Art Assn., Southern States Art League, Archtl. League. Club: Texas (hon. mem.) Home: Zephryhills, Fla. Deceased.

MACLEISH, BRUCE, retail mcht.; b. Chgo., Feb. 22, 1882; s. Andrew and Marie Louise (Little) MacL.; prep. edn. Rugby Sch. and Morgan Park Acad., Chgo., A.B., U. Chgo., 1903; m. Elizabeth Jane Moore, Oct. 26, 1907; children—Jean, Hugh. With John Wanamaker, 1903-06; with Carson Pirie, Scott & Co., Chgo., 1906-71, chmn. exec. com., 1958-71, chmn. emeritus, dir., 1971-73; pres., treas. Shopping News, Inc.; dir. Asso. Merchandising Corp. Retailers adv. coms. Consumer Mem. Pres.'s Def. Commn., Dir. Office Price Adminstrn.; mem., treas. Retail Code Authority, Nat. Recovery Adminstrn., industry mem. Cook County Compliance Bd. Mem. Area Improvement Com., Chgo. Com. 15. Mem. Glencoe Plan Commn. Bd. dirs., pres. Chgo. Better Bus. Bur.; bd. dirs., pres. Chgo. Better Bus. Bur.; bd. dirs., exec. com. State St. Council; bd. dirs. Civic Fedn. Chgo.; trustee Village of Glencoa. Mem. Chgo. Assn. Commerce (dir.), State Street Lighting Assn. (dir.), Wabash Av. Assn. (dir.), Nat. Retail Dry Goods Assn. (dir.), Am. Retail Fedn. (trustee, exec. com.), Phi Delta Theta. Republican. Clubs: Commonwealth Indian Hill, Wausaukee. Home: Glencoe, Ill. Died Oct. 7, 1973.

MACMILLAN, DONALD BAXTER, explorer; b. Provincetown, Mass., Nov. 10, 1874; s. Neil and Sarah Rebecca (Gardner) MacM.; A.B., Bowdoin Coll., 1898, A.M., 1910, Sc.D., 1918; post-grad. work, Harvard Univ.; hon. D.Sc., Boston Univ., 1937; m. Miriam Look, 1935. Prin. Levi Hall Sch. N. Gorham, Me., 1898-1900; head of classical dept., Swarthmore (Pa.) Prep. Sch., 1900-03; instr. Worcester Acad., 1903-08; asst. in Peary Arctic Club North Polar Expdn., 1908-09; mem. Cabot Labrador party, 1910; ethnol. work among Esquimaux of Labrador, 1911 and 1912; leader of Crocker Land Expedition, 1913-17. Tallman Foundation prof., Bowdoin Coll., 1932-33. Ensign U.S.N.R., in aviation service, 1918-19; lt. commander USNRF, 1925; rear admiral U.S. Naval Reserves, retired, 1954. Commander of exploring expeditions to Arctic regions almost annually, 1910-58, including Bowdoin-Harvard Arctic expedition, Greenland, 1950. Recalled to service, May 1941; apptd. commdr. U.S.N.R., June 1942. Trustee Worcester Acadmey, Emerson College; director Bowdoin College Kent's Island Scientific Station; mem. of Nat. advisory bd. of Nat. Gallery of the Am. Indian. Awarded Elisha Kane Gold Medal, 1927; special Congressional medal for work on Peary North Pole Expdn., 1944; Hubbard Gold medal, Nat. Geog. Soc., 1953; Explorers Club medal, 1953. and others. Lectr. on Labrador, Iceland, Greenland and Far North. Republican. Fellow Am. Geog. Society, Royal Geog. Soc. (London); mem. several profl. socs. and orgns. Clubs: dventures, Explorers (New York); Harvard Travelers (fellow). Boston City Merchant Marine, Boston Yacht; Portland Yacht; Ill. Athletic (Chicago); Cruising Club of America, Am. Alpine, Nat. Sojourners, Propeller, Los Angeles Yacht. Author several books, 1918-43. Contbr. to mags. Home: Provincetown, Mass.†

MACMILLAN, HARVEY REGINALD, business exec.; b. Newmarket, Ont., Can., Sept. 9, 1885; s. John Alfred and Joanne (Willson) M.; B.Sc.A., U. Toronto, LL.D., 1957; M.F., Yale; D.Sc., U. British Columbia, 1950; m. Edna Mulloy, Aug. 2, 1911; children—Mrs. John Lecky, Mrs. Gordon T. Southam. Asst. dir., forestry branch, Dept. Interior, Ottawa, 1911; went to British Columbia, 1912, chief forester, 1912-15; timber trade commr., Dept. Trade and Commerce, Ottawa, 1915-16; asst. mgr., Victoria Lumber & Shingle Mfg. Co., 1916-17; asst. dir., Imperial Munitions Bd., 1917-19; organized the H. R. MacMillan Export Company, Limited, 1919, and in private business; appointed to position of timber controller, Dept. Munitions & Supply, June 1940; chmn., Wartime Requirements Bd., Nov. 1940; pres. Wartime Merchant Shipping, Ltd., 1941-43; director MacMillan, Bloedel and Powell River, Ltd., Internat. Nickel Co. Can., Ltd., MacMillan Jardine, Ltd., Hong Kong and Japan, B.C. Packers, Ltd.; mem. adv. bd. B.C. of Can. Trust. Bd. governors Atlantic Institute. Member Canadian C. of C. (past pres.). Mem. United Church. Clubs: University, Terminal City, Royal Vancouver Yacht, Vancouver (Vancouver, B.C.); The Union (Victoria, B.C.); Canadian (N.Y.C.). Home: Vancouver, B.C. Canada.

MACMILLAN, RICHARD F., pub. relations dir.; b. Mason City, Ia., Oct. 24, 1912; s. Harry L. and Helen S. (Gonser) M.; B.A., U. Minn., 1935; m. Inez Kehoe, Aug. 8, 1936; children—Douglas M., Richard G., Stephen H. Dir. athletic pub. relations U. Minn., 1936-41; sports writer Chgo. Sun, 1941-45; mng. editor Honolulu Advertiser, 1945-55, Santa Barbara News Press, 1955-56; dir. pub. relations Hawaii Visitors Bur., Honolulu, 1956-72; time-life corr. in Pacific, N.Y. Times, 1945-54, dir. pub. relations Time, Inc., Honolulu, 1955-73. Mem. Soc. Am. Travel Writers, Honolulu Press Club. Home: Honolulu Hawaii. Died July 12, 1973; interred Hawaii Meml. Park, Kaneohe, Oahu, Hawaii.

MACMILLAN, (WILLIAM) DOUGALD, III, univ. prof.; b. Washington, N.C., Nov. 2, 1897; s. William Dougald and Katharine Gaston (deRosset) MacM. Jr.; A.B., honors in English, U. of N.C., 1918, A.M., 1920, Ph.D., 1925; student U. of Chicago, 1920, Sch. of the Theatre, N.Y. City, 1921; internat. research fellow, Huntington Library, San Marino, Calif., 1934-35, vis. scholar, 1935-36; m. Laura Love Thompson, Dec. 20, 1922; children—William Dougald, Robert Thompson. Teaching fellow in English, U. of N.C., 1919-20, instr., 1920-25, asst. prof., 1925-28, asso. prof., 1928-37, prof. English from 1937, Kenan professor from 1951, chairman of the department of English, 1952-58; lectr. University of Wis., summer 1950; Guggenheim Fellowship, 1951; with Carolina Playmakers, Chapel Hill, N.C., 1919-23, asst. dir., 1922-23; vis. prof. Winthrop Coll., summer 1931, Northwestern, summer 1939, 46, U. of Tex., summer 1940, Univ. Calif., Los Angeles, summer 1948; lecturer (under Am. Univ. Union, London), Univ. Coll., Exeter, and Univ. Coll., Southampton, 1934; humanities lectr., U. N.C., winter 1949; hon. vis. prof. Sheffield, Eng., 1954-55. Served as 2d lt., Inf., U.S. Army, 1918: capt. C.W.S., U.S. Army, 1942; chem. Warfare Sch., Edgewood Arsenal, Md.; with Military Intelligence Service. War Dept. Gen. Staff, Washington, 1943-45; promoted to rank of major, 1944. Mem. Modern Lang. Assn. Am. (officer of discussion groups), Alpha Tau Omega. Democrat. Episcopalian, Editor: Plays of the Restoration and Eighteenth Century (with Howard Mumford Jones), 1931; Drury Lane Calendar. (1747-1776), 1938: Catalogue of the Larpent Plays in the Huntington Library, 1939; co-editor: The Works of John Dryden, vol. 8, plays, 1962. Asst. editor: Studies in Philology, 1931-34, 1936-50, editorial bd., 1942-50, editor, 1950-65. Contbr. articles to philol. jours. Home: Chapel Hill, N.C. Died Jan. 10, 1975; interred Chapel Hill, N.C.

MACNEIL, VIRGINIA ALLEN BAGBY, civic worker; b. Coblenz, Germany, Aug. 5, 1920 (parents Am. citizens); d. Philip Haxall and Mary Clarkson (Allen) Bagby; grad. St. Margaret's Sch., Tappahannock, Va., 1937; A.B., Sweet Briar Coll., 1941; m. Hugh Livingstone MacNeil, Nov. 25, 1943; children—Mary Allen (Mrs. Charles Edmund Gessert), Maria Antonia Wilcox, Lucy Parke (Mrs. Carolus Petrus Warmenhaven), Daphne Drake, Sayre II, Philip Bagby. Circulation dept. Pour LaVictoire, N.Y.C., 1942; sec. to ships service officer Naval Officers Tng. Sch., Ft. Schuyler, Bronx, N.Y., 1943. Vol. solicitor A.R.C., United Way, Muscular Dystrophy, Multiple Sclerosis; chmn. Panel of Eight Eastern Women's Liberal Arts Colls., from 1967. Mem. Sweet Briar Alumnae Assn. (chmn. region X, 1962-68, exec. bd.). Episcopalian (pres. women of the church 1966-68). Clubs: Sweet Briar of Southern California (pres.), Valley Hunt (Pasadena, Cal.). Home: Pasadena Cal. Deceased.

MACNEILLE, HOLBROOK MANN, educator; b. N.Y.C., May 11, 1907; s. Perry Robinson and Clausine (Mann) MacN.; A.B., Swarthmore Coll., 1928; A.B. (Rhodes scholar from N.J., 1928-30) Oxford (Eng.) U., 1930, A.M., 1947; Ph.D., Harvard, 1935; Sterling research fellow, Yale, 1935-36; m. Marjorie J. Wyllie, Mar. 27, 1953; children—Perry Robinson, Jeanette Clausine, John Holbrook. Asst. engr. Western Electric Co., 1930-31; instr. math. Swarthmore Coll., 1931-33; Benjamin Pierce instr. math. Harvard, 1936-38; asso. prof. math. Kenyon Coll., 1938-41, prof. math., 1941-47, chmn. dept., 1945-47; sci. liaison officer London mission OSRD, Am. embassy, 1944-46, head of mission, 1945-46; sci. dir. London br. office, U.S. Office Naval Research, 1946-48; chief, fundamental research br., div. of research AEC, Washington, 1948-49; exec. dir. Am. Math. Soc. 1949-54; part time research asso. Brown U. 1951-54; prof. math., chmn. dept. Washington U., St. Louis, 1954-61; prof. math. Case Inst. Tech., Cleve., 1961-74, chmn. dept., 1961-63. Recipient President's Certificate of Merit, 1948. Fellow A.A.A.S. (council 1964); mem. Math. Assn. Am. (mem. com. on ednl. media 1962-66, chmn. 1962-63, gov. 1966-69, vis. lectr. 1958-74), Soc. for Indsl. and Applied Math. (council 1961-64), London, Indian math. socs., Société Mathématique de France, Phi Beta Kappa, Sigma Xi. Asso. editor Math. mag., 1962-63. Contbr. sci. articles to research jours. Home: Cleveland O. Died Sept. 30, 1973; interred Bailey Island, Me.

MACNEILLE, STEPHEN MANN, physicist; b. Newark, Jan. 26, 1912; s. Perry R. and Clausine (Mann) MacN.; A.B., Swarthmore Coll., 1933; Ph.D., Mass. Inst. Tech., 1937; m. Patricia O'Connell, Sept. 22, 1934 (dec. Feb. 1965); children—Stephanie, Patricia, Christine, Elizabeth, Robert; m. Bess Kraly, Jan. 7, 1967. Physicist, Eastman Kodak Co., 1937-43, chief engr., 1948-53; sr. physicist Tenn. Eastman Co., Oak Ridge, 1943-46; profl. trainee Monsanto Chem. Co., Oak Ridge, 1946-47; asso. dir. research Am. Optical Co., 1953-57, dir. research, 1958-74, v.p., 1963-74, also dir. Civilian Physicist OSRD, 1944. Fellow Optical Soc. Am. (dir.); mem. Am. Phys. Soc. Home: Southboro Mass. Died Mar. 23, 1972.

MACPHAIL, LELAND STANFORD (LARRY), investment banker, sportsman; b. Cass City, Mich., Feb. 3, 1890; s. Curtis W. and Katherine (McMurtrie) MacP.; student Beloit Coll., U. Mich.; LL.B., George Washington U., 1910; m. Inez Thompson, Oct. 19, 1910; children—Marian (Mrs. Walsh McDermott), Leland Stanford, William C.; m. 2d, Jean Wanamaker, May 16, 1945; 1 dau., Jean Duncan. Admitted to D.C. bar, 1910, Ill. bar, 1911, Mich. bar, 1911; partner Fowler, McDonald & MacPhail, Chgo., 1910-15; pres. Columbus (O.) Baseball Club, 1930-32, Cin. Reds, 1933-37, Bklyn. Dodgers, 1938-42, N.Y. Yankees, 1945-48; partner MacPhail Investment Co., Grand Rapids, Mich., 1933-45; pres. Harford Co., Glenangus Farms, Inc., 1948-74, Atlantic Charter Corp., 1964-74, Traffic Control Materials & Machines Corp. Served to capt. U.S. Army, World War I; AEF; col. Gen. Staff Corps, AUS, World War II; asst. to Under-Sec. War. Mem. Beta Theta Pi, Phi Delta Phi. Founder night baseball, baseball pension plan. Home: Belair, Md. Died Oct. 1, 1975; buried Cass City, Mich.

MACPHERSON, LESLIE COOMBS, JR., editor; b. Washington, Feb. 28, 1886; s. Leslie Coombs and Martha (Gill) M.; student Park Inst. Prep. Sch.; m. Wilma E. Stone, Oct. 16, 1904; 1 dau., Dorothy M. (Mrs. Louis O. Chidester). With Post Gazette (formerly Pittsburgh Post) 1906-57, sporting editor, 1910, news editor, 1917-49, mng. editor, 1949-57; later emeritus. Mem. Pa. Asso. Press Mng. Editors Assn. (pres. emeritus), Sigma Delta Chi (mem. Pitts. chpt. Hall of Fame) Home: Pittsburgh, Pa., Died Nov. 23, 1975.

MACSHERRY, CHARLES WHITMAN, educator; b. Chgo., Mar. 5, 1911; s. Matthew Blakely and Bessie (Macdougall) MacS., B.S., Georgetown U. Sch. Fgn. Ser., 1948; M.A., U. Cal. at Berkeley, 1949, Ph.D., 1956. Statistician, State Dept., 1946-48; instr. U. Chgo., 1951-52; mem. faculty Smith Coll., 1952-73; prof. E. Asian history and art, 1956-73, chmn. dept. history, 1970-73. Am. Council Learned Socs. fellow, Harvard, summer 1950. Mem. Am. Hist. Assn., Assn. Asian Studies, Am. Oriental Soc., Coll. Art Assn., Phi Beta Kappa. Home: Northampton, Mass. Died Nov. 1973.

MACVANE, EDITH, author; b. Boston, 1880; d. Silas Marcus and Emily Grace (de Mille) MacVane; ed. Radcliffe Coll. Contbr. to Harper's, Ainslie's, Smart Set, etc. Author: Adventures of Joujou, 1906; Duchess of Dreams, 1908; The Thoroughbred, 1909; The Black Flier, 1909; Tarantella, 1911; Her Word of Honor, 1912. Contbr. to Cosmopolitan, Saturday Evening Post. Wrote Story, The Golden Voice, on which James Forbes' new play "The Golden Voice" is founded. Address: Rome, Italy†

MADDEN, LILLIAN GERTRUDE, brewery exec.; b. Louisville, Apr. 23, 1898; d. Michael Joseph and Mary Frances (Fangmann) Madden; grad. Ursuline Acad., 1916. With Falls City Brewing Co., Louisville, from 1916, successively sec. to pres., asst. sec., sec.-treas., 1916-50, pres., dir., from 1950. Mem. bd. Better Bus. Bur., Louisville. Mem. Louisville and Jefferson County Planning and Zoning Commn. Adv. bd. Ursuline Coll.; mem. bd. counselors Nazareth Coll. Recipient Pro Eclesia et Pontifice medal Pope Pius XII, 1955. Mem. Louisville Credit Women. Clubs: Altrusa, Audubon Country. Pendennis. Home: Louisville, Ky., Deceased.

MADDOX, JAMES GRAY, economist; b. Rison, Ark., Feb. 4, 1907; s. Ernest Ray and Eve (Gray) M.; B.S.A., U. Ark., 1927; M.S., U. Wis., 1930; M.P.A., Harvard, 1948, Ph.D., 1950; m. Alice Batten, June 15, 1934; children—Susanna, Jeannie (Mrs. Walter P. Sy), Melinda (Mrs. Albert S. Boyer), Swanee (Mrs. John H. Austin). Economist, FCA, 1933-36, A.A.A., 1936-37, Resettlement Adminstrn., 1937-39; div. dir. Farm Security Adminstrn., 1939-43; asst. to chief Bur. Agrl. Econs., Dept. Agr., 1943-47; asst. dir. Am. Internat. Assn., 1949-52; v.p. Internat. Devel. Services, N.Y.C., 1953; mem. staff Am. U. Field Staff, 1953-58; prof. agrl. econs. N.C. State Coll., Raleigh, 1958-73, asst. dir. Agrl. Policy Inst., 1960-67, dir., 1967-70; dir. research study Econ. Devel. and Manpower Requirements in South, 20th Century Fund, 1962-67. Mem. Am. Econ. Assn., Am. Farm Econ. Assn. Author: Technical Assistance by Religious Agencies in Latin America, 1956; The Advancing South: Manpower Prospects and Problems, 1967. Home: Raleigh, N.C. Died Dec. 15, 1973.

MADDOX, ROBERT CHARLES, physician; b. Vicksburg, Miss., Sept. 26, 1930; s. Robert Virgil and Erma (Bradshaw) M.; M.D., U. Cal. at Los Angeles; m. Carla Jo Anders, Jan. 20, 1973; children—Linda Sue M. Reece, Diane Kathryn. Intern, Colo. Gen. Hosp., Denver; resident in obstetrics and gynecology U. Cal. at Los Angeles; med. dir. Am. Potash & Chem. Corp., Stauffer Chem. Co.; flight examiner FAA; asso. prof. U. So. Cal. Med. Center, Los Angeles. Served to comdr., M.C., USNR. Diplomate Am. Bd. Obstetrics and Gynecology. Fellow A.C.S., Am. Coll. Obstetricians and Gynecologists, Internat. Coll. Surgeons; mem. Los Angeles County Obstet. and Gynecol. Soc., Los Angeles County Med. Assn. Episcopalian. Home: Palmdale, Cal. Died Jan. 3, 1974; buried Joshua Meml. Cemetery, Lancaster, Cal.

MADERNA, BRUNO, composer, conductor; b. Venice, Italy, 1920; student of Bustini, Maliapiero and Scherchen, also at Conservatorio di Musica Santa Cecilia. Composer, and conductor specializing in electronic music, 1955-73. Composer; Studi per il Processo di Kafka (for orch.), 1949; Composizione in tre tempi (for orch.), 1954; Dark Rapture Crawl (for orch.), 1957; Syntaxis, 1957. Continuum, 1958. Home: Darmstadt West Germany. Died 1973.

MAEDER, LEROY M.A., physician; b. Mpls., May 30, 1898; s. Carl and Lucinda (Weishaar) M.; M.D., U. Minn., 1922; m. Albertine Reichle, Nov. 10, 1945; children—Susan (Mrs. Anthony Robertson), Thomas, John. Rotating intern Phila. Gen. Hosp., 1922-23, asst. vis. chief psychopathologist, 1927-30; clin. tng. Phila. Hosp. for Mental Disease, 1924-25, Pa. Hosp. Mental and Nervous Disease, Phila., 1925-27; supt., med. dir. Fairmount Farm, Phila., 1927-29; psychiat. clinician Pa. Hosp., Phila., 1927-29; neurologist U. Pa. Hosp., 1927-30; neurol. clinician U. Pa. Grad. Hosp., 1927-30, psychiat. clinician, 1933-35; instr. neurology U. Pa., 1927-35; tng. psychoanalyst Phila. Psychoanalytic Inst., 1941-68. Served with U.S. Army, 1918; as 1st lt., M.C., 1922-26. Diplomate Am. Bd. Psychiatry and Neurology. Fellow Am. Psychiat. Assn., Am. Orthopaedic Assn.; mem. Am. Psychoanalytic Assn. (v.p. 1941, sec. 1949-53), A.M.A., A.A.A.S. Home: Philadelphia, Pa. Died Apr. 15, 1968; buried Minneapolis, Minn.

MAEGLI, HALLO, former graphoanalyst, airline exec.; b. Hamburg, Germany, Jan. 25, 1924; d. Juan and Gertrud M. (de Maegli) Maegli; pvt. tutoring Germany and Guatemala, Central Am., 1936-42; m. George Nesbit Urice, Sept. 18, 1947 (div. June 1953); 1 dau., J. Melanie. Came to U.S. 1945, naturalized, 1953. Passenger service agt., ticket agt. Delta Airlines, Miami, Fla., 1945-49; passenger service agt. internat. documentation agt., ticket dept. Braniff Internat., Miami, 1952-72. Tchr. graphoanalysis and interpretation fgn. langs. for various airlines, 1952-72; chmn. Internat. Congress Graphoanalysts, Chgo., 1963. Recipient Presdl. Merit award, 1965. Mem. Internat. Graphoanalysis Soc., (study group chmn. Fla. chpt.; chmn. 1963-69, asst. coordinator Congress-Seminars 1964-72), Am. Horse Show Assn., Opera Guild Miami (asso.), Internat. Platform Assn. Democrat. Presbyn. Fla. corr. B-Liner, Braniff House Organ, 1952-71. Home: Miami Springs, Fla. Died Apr. 3, 1972.

MAES, URBAN, surgeon; b. New Orleans, La., Oct. 12, 1878; s. William A. and Julia (Urban) M.; M.D., Tulane, 1900; m. Gertrude Adamson, Dec. 26, 1906; 1 son, Robert A. Practiced at New Orleans from 1900; formerly prof. clin. surgery, Sch. of Medicine, Tulane, formerly prof. of surgery, dir. of dept., La. State U. Med. Center, later emeritus; consulting surgeon Charity Hosp.; consultant in surgery, Touro Infirmary; cons. surg., Vets. Adminstrn. Hosp., New Orleans. Served as capt., maj. and lt. col. M.C., U.S. Army, World War; col. M.R.C. Fellow Am. Coll. Surgeons (bd. govs., 1929-33); mem. A.M.A. (sec. surg. sect., 1921-23, chmn. same, 1924), Am. Surg. Assn., Southern Surg. Assn. (1st v.p. 1930), Am. Assn. Mil. Surgeons, Clin. Surg. Soc. (1st vice-pres. 1931), Louisiana State Medical Soc., Orleans Parish Med. Soc. (pres. 1925), Stars and Bars, Soc. Internationale de Chirurgic, Alpha Omega Alpha. Democrat. Episcopalian. Home: New Orleans, La.†

MAESTRI, ROBERT S(IDNEY), mayor; b. New Orleans, La., Dec. 11, 1889; s. Francis and Angele (Lacabe) M.; ed. in parochial and pub. schs. and business coll., New Orleans; unmarried. Began as clk. in father's furniture store; in real estate and investment business for himself; commr. La. State Dept. of Conservation, 1929-36; mayor of New Orleans, 1936-46; dir. Am. Bank of New Orleans. Served in U.S. Army, during World War. Col. on staffs of Gov. Huey P. Long, Gov. Oscar K. Allen, Gov. Richard W. Leche. Catholic. Club: New Orleans Athletic (dir.). Home: New Orleans, La. Died May 1974.

MAGEE, JAMES CARRE, former surg. gen. U.S.A.; b. Jan. 23, 1883; s. Edward Carre and Elizabeth (Armstrong) M.; M.D., Jefferson Med. Coll., 1905; hon. Sc.D., Jefferson Medical College, 1940; m. Irene Mackay, July 22, 1908 (dec.); children—Mervyn Mackay, James Carre, Jr. Contract surgeon, U.S. Army, 1907-08; commd. 1st lt. Med. Corps, U.S. Army, 1909, advancing through the grades to col.; appointed major gen. surgeon gen., June 1939; tour expired May 31, 1943. Retired maj. gen., U.S. Army, 1943. Served in San Francisco, Philippine Islands, Kan., and Mexican border; with A.E.F. in France, 1917-19; Walter Reed Gen. Hosp., Washington, D.C., 1935-39. Mem. various boards and medical societies. Military decorations; Distinguished Service Medal; Purple Heart, Protestant. Address: Washington, D.C., Died Oct. 15, 1975.

MAGEE, RENA TUCKER, (Mrs. Franklin Rand Magee), publicity manager; b. at Indianapolis, Ind., Nov. 29, 1880; d. Hannibal and Robina (Sharpe) Tucker; student Art Students' League, New York, under De Camp, Mowbray and Barnard; m. Albert R. Kohlman, 1906 (died 1919); m. 2d, Franklin Rand Magee, Mar. 1, 1925. Head of art dept. Teachers' Coll., Indianapolis, 1903-06; art critic Indianapolis News, 1913-18, also lecturer on art, John Herron Art Inst.; associated with Milch Art Galleries, N.Y. City, 1919-29; dir. of the 6 E. 56th Street Galleries, New York, 1929-30; associated with the Marie Harriman Gallery, 1930; dir. Argent Galleries, 1935-41; asso. with antiques and art dept., Lord & Taylor, 1942-48. Mem. Nat. Sculpture Society. Contbr. to mags. on art topics. Republican. Clubs: Indianapolis Woman's, Woman's Press of Indiana. Address: New York City, N.Y.†

MAGEE, WAYLAND WELLS, mem. Federal Reserve Board; b. Chicago, Ill., Sept. 24, 1881; s. Henry Wells and Hattie Belle (Pratt) M.; S.B., U. of Chicago, 1905; studied law, Harvard, 1907, Northwestern U., 1908; studied agr., U. of Bonn., Germany, 1904, U. of Neb., 1909, Iowa State Coll. of Agr. and Mech. Arts, 1910; m. Marion Edith Thomas, October 24, 1916 (died 1920); m. 2d, Harriet Gage, May 20, 1922; children—Marion, Louise, Wayland, Kimball. Gave up law practice, Chicago, 1910, and settled on a two-section corn farm in Neb.; mgr. Summer Hill Farm, Neb., and P.F. Ranch, Wyoming from 1910; member board Omaha br. of Federal Reserve Bank of Kansas City, 1927-30; dir. Fed. Res. Bank of Kansas City, 1930-31; became mem. Fed. Reserve Bd., Washington, D.C., May 18, 1931. Formerly pres. Neb. Crop Growers Assn.; dir. and mem. exec. com. Neb. Dairy Development Soc., 1921-31; dir. Ak-Sar-Ben Live Stock Show, 1929-31. Mem. Alpha Delta Phi. Republican. Mason (32°), Elk. Club: Cosmos (Washington); Union League (Chicago); Harvard, University; Omaha, Omaha Country (Omaha). Home: Bennington, Neb.†

MAGILL, JAMES PHINEAS, investment banker; b. Phila., Oct. 31, 1885; s. Andrew and Mary Eleanor (Ash) M.; grad. Westtown Boarding Sch., 1903; B.S., Haverford Coll., 1907; LL.D., 1967; m. Ruth Marshall, June 18, 1920. Partner Eastman Dillon & Co., 1926-57, ltd. partner Eastman Dillon, Union Securities & Co.; overseer, treas. William Penn Charter Sch., 1929-59. Bd. mgrs. Haverford Coll., 1959-68, vice chmn., 1968-69; past bd. dirs. U. Pa. Mus., Pa. Acad. Fine Arts. Republican. Mem. Soc. Friends, Royal Soc. Arts (dir.), London, Eng. Clubs: Racquet (Phila.); Franklin Inn. Home: Philadelphia, Pa. Died July 13, 1974.

MAGNANI, ANNA, Italian actress; b. Rome, Mar. 7, 1918; ed. Acad. Dramatic Art, Rome. Actress on legitimate stage; motion pictures include: Open City, 1945; Quartetto Pazzo, Campo de Fiori, L'Ultima Carrozzello, Abbasso la Mieria (Down with Misery), Un Uomo Ritorna, 1945; Abbasso Ricchezza, Lo Sconosciuto de San Marino (Unknown Man of San Marino). Avanti a Lui Tremara Tutta Roma, 1946; L'Onorevole Angeline, 1947; also Dreams in the Streets, Woman Trouble, The Miracle, Volcano Extremely Beautiful, Anita Garibaldi, Golden Coach, Bellissima, The Rose Tatoo, 1955; We Women, Wild as Wind, 1957; Awakening, 1958; The Fugitive Kind, 1960; Mamma Roma, 1962; Secret of Santa Vittoria, 1968. Recipient Motion Picture Acad. award for role in Rose Tattoo, 1955. Died 1973.

MAGUIRE, PHILIP FRANCIS, JR., lawyer; b. Plainfield, N.J., Apr. 27, 1905; s. Philip Francis and Helen Jane (Powers) M.; LL.B., Stetson U., 1927; m. Frances Gaskins Darby, July 26, 1928; children—Sue Darby (Mrs. John Keely Clifford), Sheila Darby (Mrs. William Patterson Doughten). Mem. Fla., D.C. bar, U.S. Dist. Ct. So. Dist. of Fla., U.S. Supreme Ct., U.S. Ct. Appeals D.C., U.S. Ct. Claims; asso. counsel Hull, Landis & Whitehair, DeLand, Fla., 1927-28; asst. gen. counsel Fla. Real Estate Commn., Orlando, 1929-34; asst. counsel Nat. Recovery Adminstrn., Washington, 1934-35; asst. gen. counsel Resettlement Adminstrn., 1935-37; dir. Rural Rehab., Farm Security Adminstrn., 1937-39; exec. v.p. Fed. Surplus Commodities Corp., also asst. adminstr. Surplus Marketing Adminstrn., 1939-41; exec. officer Purchase Div. Office Prodn. Mgmt., 1941; asst. to chmn. War Prodn. Bd., 1942; dep. adminstr. Civilian Prodn. Adminstrn., Washington, D.C., 1946; asst. to pres. Maxson Food Systems, Inc., N.Y.C., 1947; dir. trade div. E.C.A. Mission to Greece, 1947-49; mem. White House staff, 1949-50; pvt. practice law, 1950-73. Served as maj. to col. AUS, 1942-45; N. Africa, MTO, ETO. Decorated Legion of Merit, Bronze Star (U.S.); Reconnizance Francaise, Chevalier de Merit Agricole (France); comdr. Order Ouissam Alaouite (Morocco). Mem. Sigma Nu, Phi Alpha Delta. Clubs: Army and Navy (N.Y.C.); Army and Navy, Congressional Country (Washington). Home: Washington, D.C. Died May 14, 1973.

MAHANEY, C. R., business exec.; b. Cumberland, Md., Aug. 3, 1898; s. John T. and Gennetta (Owens) M.; B.S., Chem. and Metall. E., U. of W.Va., 1923, M.S., Chem. E., 1924; m. Berte F. Zierick, Jan. 2, 1925; 1 son, Donald Russell, Mechanic, B&O. R.R., 1916-17; process engr. Westinghouse Electric & Mfg. Co., East Pittsburgh, Pa., 1924-28, studied insulation materials, laminated plastics mfg., etc., Europe, 1928-29; engr. in charge Trafford Micarta Plastics Plant, 1929-34; gen. mgr. Gatke Corp., Winona Lake, Ind., and Chicago, 1934-37; indsl. sales mgr. Panleyte Corp., N.Y. City, 1937-38; vice pres. in charge sales, 1938-39, gen. mgr. N.Y. City and Trenton, N.J., 1939, gen. mgr. Panelyte (plastics) division Saint Regis Paper Company, 1943-61; dir. St. Regis Paper Company, 1943-58, v.p., 1943-73; v.p., dir. St. Regis Sales Corp., 1946-55, St. Regis Paper Co. (Can.), Ltd., 1951-58; pres., dir. Cambridge-Panelyte Molded Plastics Co., 1955-57; v.p., dir. Mich.-Panelyte Molded Plastics, Inc., 1955-57, Chester Packaging Products Corp., Yonkers, N.Y., 1956-59. Mem. adv. council Fla. Atlantic U., Boca Raton. Dir. Jr. Achievement, Inc. Chmn. U.S. Plastic Delegation U.S.S.R., 1958; chmn. Pres.'s adv. com. Nat. Am. Exhbn., Moscow, 1959. Pvt., U.S. Army, 1917-18. Mem. Soc. Automotive Engrs., Soc. Plastic Industry (dir., chmn. bd., 1960-61), Plastic Pioneers Assn., Newcomen Soc. N.Am., Phi Lambda Upsilon. Republican. Methodist. Mason (Shriner). Clubs: Union League, Chemists; Scarsdale Golf, Town (Scarsdale, N.Y.). Home: Boca Raton, Fla., Died July 6, 1973.

MAHEU, RENE GABRIEL EUGENE, UNESCO ofcl.; b. Saint-Gaudens, France, Mar. 28, 1905; s. Joseph and Marie Madeleine (Roucoule) M.; student Lycee de Toulouse, Lycee Louis le Grand, Ecole Normale Superieure, Sorbonne; m. Ines Allafort du Verger, July 31, 1928; children—Jean, Francois. Tchr. philosophy Lycee de Coutances, France, 1930; lectr. French lit. U. Cologne, Germany, 1931-33; lectr. philosophy French Inst., London, 1933-39; dep. head French Liaison Mission attacher to Brit. Ministry of Information, London, 1939-40; tchr. philosophy Franco-Moslem Coll. at Moulay-Idriss Fez, Morocco, 1940-42; dep. head French news agy., France-Afrique, Algiers, 1943-44; attached to civil cabinet of Resident Gen. in French Morocco, Rabat and Paris, 1944-46; with UNESCO, 1946-75, successively prep. commn., London, head div. free flow of information, Paris, dir. office of dir.-gen., 1946-54, asst. dir. gen., 1954-56; UNESCO rep. to UN, N.Y.C., 1956-58; asst. dir. gen. External Relations, Paris, 1959, dep. dir. gen. 1960-61, acting dir. gen., 1961-62, dir. gen. 1962-75. Recipient Montaigne prize F.V.S. Found of Hamburg, 1973. Author: La Civilisation de l'Universel, 1966; also articles philosophy, internat. affairs. Home: Paris, France., Died Dec. 19, 1975.

MAHLER, FRITZ, condr. symphony orchestras; b. Vienna, Austria, July 16, 1901; s. Ludwig and Agnes (Schuschny) M.; studied composition with Alban Berg and Arnold Schoenberg and history of music with Guido Adler, U. of Vienna; student Conservatory of Music, Vienna; m. Pauline Koner, May 23, 1939. Came to U.S., 1935, naturalized, 1939. Condr. of symphony orchestras since 1920; with Danish Broadcasting Co., Copenhagen, 1931-35; in U.S. has conducted Denver, Newark, Boston, C.B.S. and M.B.S. symphony orchestras, and Phila. La Scala Opera Co.; dir. of music, Nat. Youth Administration in New York, 1941-42; teacher of advanced conducting, Juilliard Summer Sch., 1938-53; Fulbright sr. lectr. Tokyo U., 1967; musical dir. Erie Philharmonic Orch.; guest condr. Toronto Philharmonic Orch., Orch. Lamoureux and Orchestre Symphonique, Paris, Oslo Philharmonic Orchestra, Venice, Florence, Poland, 1961, S. Am., 1962, Japan, 1963, Rumania, Yugoslavia, Greece, 1966, Naples, Rome, Zurich, Hamburg, Seoul, 1967, Manila, 1967, radio orchs. in Stockholm, Copenhagen, Helsinki and Zurich, B.B.C., 1967; mus. dir. Hartford (Conn.) Symphony, 1953-64; Home: New York City N.Y. Died June 18, 1973; cremated.

MAIN, MARJORIE, actress; b. Acton, Ind., Feb. 24, 1890; d. Rev. Samuel Joseph and Jennie (McGaughey) Tomlinson; student Franklin (Ind.) Coll.; grad. Sch. Expression, Hamilton Coll., Lexington, Ky.; student dramatic art Carnegie Hall, N.Y.C., Fine Arts Bldg., Chgo.; m. Dr. Stanley LeFevre Krebs, Dec. 2, 1921 (dec.). Reader, player Shakespearian companies in Chautauqua; radio appearances as guest star with top stars of era; played in stock, vaudeville, road shows, N.Y. prodns.; moved to Hollywood, 1937; co-starred in series with Wallace Berry at M.G.M.; has appeared in 80 motions pictures among with were Dead End, The Egg and I (acad. nomination for role), The Women, Johnny Come Lately, Murder He Says, Meet Me in St. Louis, Friendly Persuasion, Heaven Can Wait, Shepherd of the Hills, The Harvey Girls, Barnacle Bill, Test Pilot, Honky Tonk, Jackass Mail, Belle of New York; role of Ma in Ma and Pa Kettle series; under contract Metro Goldwyn Mayer, 1941-54. Mem. D.A.R., Delta Delta Delta. Clubs: Friday Morning (Los Angeles). Home: Los Angeles, Cal. Died Apr. 10, 1975; buried Forest Lawn Meml. Park.

MALAND, TALFOURD ABBOT, mfg. co. exec.; b. Morris, Ill., June 24, 1909; s. Benjamin T. and Emma E. (Osmon) M.; student Pleasant View Coll., Ottawa, Ill., 1929, LaSalle Extension U., Chgo., 1940; m. Iola L. Hunter, June 19, 1937; 1 son, David Workman. Clk.-trust Continental Ill. Nat. Bank, Chgo., 1929-33; controller The Northwestern Corp., Morris, 1934-52; comptroller Diebel Mfg. Co., Morton Grove, 1953-60, treas., 1960-74, v.p. finance and adminstrn., 1967-74; also dir.; sec. 6505 Oakton Corp. Active Boy Scouts, Cub Scouts, Field Mus. Natural History. Mem. A.I.M. Presbyn. (ruling elder). Home: Glenview, Ill. Died Jan. 31, 1974.

MALCOLM, ROBERT BRUCE, surgeon; b. Bklyn., Sept. 18, 1934; s. Donald and Esther E. Malcolm; M.D., N.Y.U., 1960; m. Sophia Stroumbos, Apr. 15, 1972. Intern, Bellevue Hosp., N.Y.C., 1960-61, resident in surgery, 1961-62, 63-64; resident in surgery Bklyn. VA Hosp., 1964-66, attending surgeon, 1966-68; asst. chief surg. services Coney Island Hosp., Bklyn., 1966-72; teaching asst. in surgery N.Y.U., 1961-64. Served to capt., M.C., AUS, 1962-63. Diplomate Am. Bd.

Surgery. Fellow A.C.S. Home: Brooklyn, N.Y. Died May 26, 1972; buried Green-Wood Cemetery, Brooklyn, N.Y.

MALIPIERO, G. FRANCESCO, composer; b. Venice, Italy, Mar. 18, 1882; s. Luigi and Emma (Balbi) M.; m. Giulietta Olivieri. Mem. Nat. Inst. Arts and Letters (hon.), Academie Flamand Brussells, Institut de France, Royal Acad. Music (London). Composer 11 symphonies, 8 quartets, sonatas for 3, 4, 5 instruments, 10 works for orch., 4 oratorios, 14 operas. Address: Treviso Italy. Died Aug. 1973.

MALLINCKRODT, LAURENCE EDWARD, business cons., b. St. Louis, Mar. 13, 1909; s. Emil and Marie L. (Armstrong) M.; A.B., Harvard, 1930, M.B.A., 1932; m. Eleanor C. Scott, Oct. 25, 1952; children—Laurence Edward, Catherine Scott. With Scruggs-Vandervoort-Barney, Inc., 1932-67, divisional mdse. mgr., asst. gen. mdse. mgr., 1932-43, treas., 1946-54, dir., 1948-67, v.p., gen. mdse. mgr., 1952-54, pres., 1954-66, v.p. Mermod-Jaccard-King Jewelry Co., 1952-66, vice chmn., 1966-67, dir., 1948-67; engaged in practice business cons., 1967—; dir. Laclede Steel Co. Mallinckrodt Chem. Works. Bd. dirs. St. Louis Conv. Bd. (past pres.), Met. YMCA of St. Louis, Bethesda Gen. Hosp., Social Planning Council St. Louis, 1952-55, St. Louis council Boy Scouts Am., Mary Inst., 1960-70; chmn. trustee Blue Cross Hosp. Assn.; trustee George Peabody Coll., KETC St. Louis Ednl. TV Commn.; overseer Harvard Coll., 1957-63; adv. council Girl Scouts, 1963-72; past chmn. Higher Edn. Coordinating Council Met. St. Louis; mem. Mo. Commn. Higher Edn., 1963-74; pres., dir. Goodwill Industries, Govt. Research Inst.; mem. pres.'s council St. Louis U., 1954-63; past pres. Mary Inst.; bd. dirs. St. Louis Symphony Soc., Community Music Sch. Served to capt. AUS, 1943-46. Mem. Harvard Alumni Assn. (dir. 1951-54), St. Louis C. of C. (dir. 1958-60, 62-64), Nat. Retail Mchts. Assn. (past dir.). Presbyn. Clubs: Harvard of St. Louis (pres. 1953-54); Harvard (N.Y.C.); St. Louis Country, Noonday, Bogey, University (St. Louis). Home: St. Louis, Mo., Died Oct. 17, 1975.

MALLORY, KATHLEEN MOORE, missionary sec.; b. Summerfield, Ala., Jan. 24, 1879; d. Hugh Shepherd Darby and Jacqueline Louisa (Moore) Mallory; A.B., Goucher Coll., Baltimore, Md., 1902; LL.D., Selma (Ala.) U., 1946, La. Coll., Pineville, La., 1948. Began in missionary work at Montgomery, Ala., 1910; exec. sec. Woman's Missionary Union of Southern Bapt. Conv., May 1912-48. Mem. Pi Beta Phi. Home: Birmingham, Ala.†

MALLORY, PHILIP ROGERS, mfg. exec.; b. Bklyn., Nov. 11, 1885; s. Henry Rogers and Cora (Pynchon) M.; student Hill Sch., Pottstown, Pa.; B.A., Yale, 1908; student law sch. Columbia, 1908-10; m. Dortothea Barron, 1912; children—Henry Rogers, Dorothea (Mrs. Ward Grantham), George Barron; m. 2d, Mildred Courtney, June 24, 1930 (dec. Mar. 1961); m. 3d, Louise Sobotka Steffe, Nov. 1, 1961. Admitted to N.Y. bar, 1910; engaged inbond and security bus., 1910-14; gen. mgr., treas. Comml. Research Co.; organizer P.R. Mallory & Co., Inc., 1916, with plants throughout U.S. and abroad, chmn. bd., 1946-65, hon. chmn. bd., 1965-75; chmn. P.R. Mallory Internat. Inc., 1959-66, hon. chmn. bd. 1966-75; officer, dir. subsidiaries. Mem. Marine Hist. Assn. (chmn. emeritus, trustee). Clubs: New York Yacht, American Yacht (Rye, N.Y.); Yale, Metropolitan, Links (N.Y.C.); Fishers Island (N.Y.) Country, Fishers Island Yacht; N.Am. Yacht Racing; Cruising of Am.; Windermere Island (Eleuthra, Bahamas); Palm Bay (Miami, Fla.). Home: Fishers Island, N.Y., Died Nov. 16, 1975.

MALONE, JOHN LEE, lawyer, author; b. Phila., June 5, 1923; s. John L. and Anne (McDermott) M.; B.S.C., Loyola U., 1947; J.D., DePaul U., 1954; m. Ann R. Carroll, June 28, 1947; children—Suann T., Mary Ann, Michael, Nancy, Ann. Tax staff Murphy, Lanier & Quinn, C.P.A's, Chgo., 1947-55; partner Mitchell & Conway, 1955-61; mng. partner, Mitchell, Russell & Malone, 1962-64; sr. partner firm Riordan, Malone & Kelly, 1964-75; editor-in-chief Mertens Law of Fed. Income Taxation, Callaghan & Co., 1966-75. Mem. estate planning council DePaul U., 1961-75, vice chmn. exec. council, 1968; mem. pres.'s council St. Xavier's Coll., 1964-75, chmn., 1968; trustee Mundelein Coll., Chgo.; bd. dirs. Chgo. Bar Assn. Found., 1967-75, pres., 1972-75. Served to lt. (j.g.) USNR, 1943-46. Mem. Am., Ill., Chgo. (mem. exec. council com. on fed. taxation 1960; chmn. 1970-71) bar assns., Am. Judicature Soc. Clubs: Legal of Chicago, Law. Home: Chicago Ill. Died May 20, 1975; interred St. Mary's Cemetery, Evergreen Park, Ill.

MALONE, ROSSER LYNN, mfg. co. exec., lawyer; b. Roswell, N.M., Sept. 9, 1910; s. Rosser Lynn and Edna (Littlefield) M.; LL.B., Washington and Lee U., 1932, LL.D., 1958; LL.D., Cumberland U., 1958, Coll. William and Mary, Mo. Valley Coll., Oklahoma City U., U. B.C., 1959, U. N.M., 1960; m. Elizabeth L. Amis, Oct. 10, 1934. Admitted to N.M. bar, 1932, N.Y. bar, 1968; practiced in Roswell, 1932-37; city atty., Roswell, 1936-42; partner firm Atwood & Malone, 1937-67; dep. atty. gen. U.S., 1952-53; v.p., gen. counsel Gen. Motors Corp., 1967-74; dir. Security Nat. Bank of Roswell, chmn., 1960-67. Mem. Bd. Bar Examiners N.M., 1949-62; legal com. Interstate Oil Compact Commn. 1946-51; chmn. N.M. Alien Enemy Hearing Bd., 1941-42; mem. Pres. Commn. Law Enforcement, 1965-67; mem. Am. Revolution Bicentennial Commn., 1967-70; mem. Adminstrv. Conf. U.S., 1968-72. Trustee Southwestern Legal Found., Dallas, 1948-74, Law Center Found. of N.Y.U., So. Meth. U., 1961-73; trustee Washington and Lee U., rector, 1974; pres. N.M. Bar Found., 1962-66, Am. Bar Found., 1966-69; bd. dirs. Am. Bar Endowment, 1973-74. Recipient Hatton W. Sumners award Southwestern Legal Found., 1956. Served lt. comdr. USNR, 1942-46. Fellow Am. Coll. Trial Lawyers (regent 1963-67), Am. Bar Found.; mem. Inst. Jud. Adminstrn. (pres.-elect 1973-74), Roswell C. of C. (pres. 1940-41), Am. (ho. dels. 1946-74, gov. 1951-54, pres., 1958-59), Chaves County (pres., 1939-40) bar assns., Am. Law Inst. (council 1959), Nat. Council Legal Clinics (dir. 1959-65), State Bar N.M., Am. Judicature Soc., N.Y. State, Fed. (hon.), Canadian (hon.) bar assns., Assn. Bar City N.Y., Bara Mexicana (hon.), Order of Coif (hon.), Sigma Nu, Omicron Delta Kappa, Phi Delta Phi. Methodist. Clubs: Metropolitan, Century Assn. (N.Y.C.): Meadow Brook (N.Y.): Roswell Country; Country Of Fla. (Delray Beach); Chaparral (Dallas); Recess (Detroit). Contbr. chpts. to profl. pubs., articles legal jour. Home: Roswell N.M. Died Aug. 13, 1974; interred South Park Cemetery, Roswell, N.M.

MALONEY, RICHARD CLOGHER, educator; b. Chelsea, Mass., Oct. 7, 1904; s. David Joseph and Rebecca (Clogher) M.; A.B., Dartmouth, 1926; M.S., Kan. State U., 1948; m. Marguerite E. McHugh, Aug. 21, 1935; children—Thomas C., Mary R., Richard Clogher, Tchr., Nantucket (Mass.) High Sch., 1926-28, Central High Sch., Manchester, N.H., 1929-30; prin. Cyrus Peirce Sch., Nantucket, also supr. art Nantucket sch. dept., 1930-42; staff English dept. Kan. State U., 1946-50, asst. dean Coll. Arts and Scis., 1946-48, registrar, 1948-50; adminstrv. asst. Office of Pres., Pa. State U., 1950-53, asst. dean Coll. Liberal Arts, 1953-58, asso. dean, 1958-65, asso. prof. social scis., lectr. history, 1965-75. Served from lt. (s.g.) to lt. comdr., USNR, 1942-46. Mem. Marine Hist. Assn., Phi Kappa Phi, Beta Theta Pi. Author: Fifty Notable Ship Portraits at Mystic Seaport. Home: Nantucket, Mass.

MALONEY, ROBERT S., congressman; b. Lawrence, Mass., Feb. 3, 1881; s. John T. and Mary A. (Bower) M.; ed. pub. schs.; m. Marie J. Belanger; m. 2d, Ella E. Bellisle, of Lawrence. Printer; N.E. orgainzer Internat. Typographical Union, 1908-12; fraternal del. from Am. Fed. of Labor to Canadian Trade and Labor Congress, 1907. Alderman and dir. Pub. Health and Charities, Lawrence, 1912 and 1915-29; pres. City Council, 1916-20; mem. 67th Congress (1921-23), 7th Mass. Dist. (not a candidate for reelection); again dir. Pub. Health and Charities, Lawrence, term 1925-29. Republican. Home: Lawrence, Mass.†

MALZBERG, BENJAMIN, statistician; b. N.Y.C., Dec. 2, 1893; s. Nathan and Anna (Elson) M.; B.S., Coll. City N.Y., 1915; A.M., Columbia, 1917, Ph.D., 1934; fellow U. Paris, College de France, 1919-21, Ecole d'Anthropologie, Paris, 1920, Univ. Coll., London, 1921; m. Rose Hershberg, Aug. 25, 1935; children—Judith Ann, Ruth Ellen and Amy Susan (twins). Spl. investigator U.S. Interdeptl. Social Hygiene Bd., 1919; statistician N.Y. State Dept. Social Welfare, Albany, 1923-28, N.Y. State Temp. Commn. on State Hosp. Problems, 1940-44; asst. dir. statis bur. N.Y. State Dept. Mental Hygiene, 1928-44, dir., 1944-56, cons., 1956-75; dir. sect. demography Research Found. for Mental Hygiene, Albany, N.Y., 1956-64. Spl. statis cons. sect. on mentally handicapped White House Conf. Child Health and Protection, 1930; cons. mental hygiene statistics Hosp. Survey for N.Y., 1936, Study Negro in Am., 1939-40; cons. Nat. Inst. Mental Health, 1949-54; lectr. Summer Sch. Alcohol Studies, Yale, Conn. Postgrad. Seminar in Neurology and Psychiatry, Yale, also Inst. Am. Psychiat. Assn.; mem. com. migration differentials Social Sci. Research Council. Recipient Am. Field Service fellowship in sociology, U. Paris, 1919-21; grantee Nat. Inst. Mental Health, Asso. fellow N.Y. Acad. Medicine; fellow Am. Psychiat. Assn. (hon.), A.A.A.S., Am. Assn. Mental Deficiency, N.Y. Acad. Scis., Am. Sociol. Soc.; mem. Inst. Math. Statistics, Am. Statis. Assn. (com. on instn. statistics 1928-30), Population Assn. Am. Psychometric Soc., Am. Psychopathol. Assn. (life), Am. Soc. Human Genetics, Biometric Soc., Sigma Xi. Jewish religion. Author: Mortality Among Patients with Mental Diseases, 1934; Hereditary and Environmental Factors in Dementia Praecox and Manic-Depressive Psychoses (with H.M. Pollock and R. G. Fuller), 1938; Social and Biological Aspects of Mental Disease, 1940; Expectation of Mental Disease, 1968; Migration and Mental Disease (with E. S. Lee and D. S. Thomas), 1956; Cohort Studies of Mental Disease in N.Y. State, 1956; Mental Disease Among Jews in New York State, 1959; The Alcoholic Psychoses at Mid-Century, 1959; Mental Health of the Negro, 1963; Mental Health of Jews in New York State, 1963; Mental Disease Among Jews in Canada, 1963; Internal Migration and Mental Disease in Canada, 1964; Mental Disease Among Puerto Rican Population of New York State, 1965; Ethnic Variations in Mental Disease in New York State, 1966; Mental Illness in New York State—A Study of Incidence, 1967; Statistical Studies of Mental Disease in New York State, 1967; Migration in Relation to Mental Disease, 1968; Rates of Mortality Among Patients with Mental Disease, 1968; Distribution of Mental Disease in New York State, 1969; Epidemiologic Aspects of Mental Disease in New York State, 1970; Studies of Mental Disease Among Jews, 1971; Studies of Mental Retardation in N.Y. State, 1971; also articles. Home: Albany, N.Y. Died Apr. 12, 1975.

MANDEL, LEON, financier; b. Chgo., Feb. 16, 1902; s. Frederick Leon and Blanche (Rosenbaum) M.; grad. Lake Forest Acad., 1919; A.B., Cornell U., 1923; m. Edna Horn, Apr. 30, 1924 (div. 1932); children—Noel (Mrs. Horace Ried) (dec.), Leon III; m. 2d, Carola Panerai, Apr. 9, 1938. Mem. adv. bd. Lorreto Hosp., Chgo.; dir. St. Marys Hosp., Palm Beach, Fla.; mem. citizens bd. U. Chgo.; trustee Carola and Leon Mandel Fund, Loyola U.; mem. nat. adv. council Jules Stein Eye Inst., U. Cal.; cons. mem. clay target com. Internat. Shooting Union; patron Internat. Oceanographic Found. Sponsored and accompanied Field Mus. expdns. to Orinoco River, Venezuela, 1932, to Guatemala, 1934, Central Am. and Caribbean Island, 1940, Galapagos Islands, 1941. Lt. col. USAAF (inactive). Decorated Army Commendation ribbon, Navy Commendation; Cuban Distinguished Service medal; caballero Peruvian Order of Sun; grand officer Confrerie des Chevaliers du Tastevin. Mem. Mil. Order World Wars (life Chgo. chpt.), U.S. Pigeon Shooting Fedn. (past pres., dir.), Chgo. Zool. Soc. (trustee), Am. Legion, Sons Union Vets. of Civil War, Greater N. Michigan Av. Assn. (dir.), Chgo. Hist. Soc. (life), Smithsonian Soc. of Assos. (life), Am. Mus. Natural History (life), Palm Beach Art Inst., Palm Beach Civic Assn. Clubs: Tavern, Chicago Yacht, Wine and Food Society, Mid-Am. (Chgo.); Coral Reef Yacht (life) (Miami); Bucks (London, Eng.); Explorers (N.Y.C.); Society of the Four Arts, Poinciana, Palm Beach (Fla.) Gun; Travellers (Paris, France); Country (Enzesfeld, Austria). Author: Robert Herrick - The Last Elizabethan, 1927. Home: Palm Beach Fla. Died Feb. 22, 1974; buried Rosehill Cemetery, Chicago, Ill.

MANHOFF, BILL, author; b. Newark, June 25, 1919; s. Albert R. and Bertha (Magod) M.; student City Coll. N.Y., 1941; 1 dau. by previous marriage, Arlie; m. Peggy McLaughlin, July 12, 1969. Writer for radio program Duffys Tavern, 1944-46, then Danny Thomas TV program, Real McCoys TV program, others; created, produced pilots for new TV programs, also supr. prodn. comedy shows for CBS. Mem. Dramatists Guild, Writers Guild Am. Author: (play) The Owl and the Pussycat, 1964. Address: Encino, Cal. Died June 19, 1974.

MANKINS, ELVIN ORLAND, county ofcl.; b. Visalia, Cal., July 13, 1911; s. Arthur William and Mae Emma (Pardue) M.; student Porterville Coll., 1953-54, Coll. Sequoias, 1955; m. Winnie Gaynell Vowell, Nov. 22, 1942; children—Elvin Ray, Curtis Warren, James Arthur. Self-employed in auto garage, Visalia, 1928-29; food market worker, Visalia, 1930-35; market mgr. Justesen's Food Stores, Shafter, Cal., 1935-39, Frank Meat Co., Bakersfield, Cal., 1940-41; owner, mgr. Woodville Ice Business, 1941-48; agrl. insp. Tulare County, Visalia, 1948-54, dep. agrl. commr., 1954-56, agrl. commr., 1956-73. Mem. Entomol. Soc. Am., Cal. Assn. County Agrl. Commrs., San Joaquin Valley Agrl. Commrs. Assn. (pres. 1956-58), Tulare County Hist. Soc. Club: Tulare County Executive (Visalia). Home: Porterville, Cal. Died Nov. 16, 1974; interred Hillcrest-Porterville Cemeteries, Porterville, Cal.

MANLEY, FREDERICK WILLIS, army officer; b. Minneapolis, Minn., May 2, 1881; s. Willis Henry and Mary Ellen (Follett) M.; B.S., U.S. Mil. Acad., 1905; m. Lucia Bayne Grady, June 1, 1909; 1 dau., Helen Pendleton (Mrs. Max S. Johnson). Commd. 2d lt., U.S. Army, 1905, and advanced through the grades to brig. general, Oct. 1942; commanding general, Camp Rucker, Ala., 1942-44; retired from active service, Jan. 1, 1944. Decorated Purple Heart; World War Medal with 3 stars; Occupation Mexico (Vera Cruz); Legion of Honor (France); Officer Order of the Crown (Belgium); Officer Order of the Crown (Italy); D.S.M.; Philippine Commonwealth; Peace of Morocco (Spain). Clubs: Army and Navy, Chevy Chase (Washington, D.C.); Puerto de Hierro (hon. mem., Madrid, Spain). Home: St. Augustine, Fla.†

MANN, JOHN JOSEPH, stock broker; b. Hoboken, N.J., Oct. 13, 1907; s. John and Stella (Kearns) M.; student St. Peter's Prep., 1920-24; A.B., Fordham U., 1928; m. Irene McGowan, Aug. 12, 1931; children—John Jay, Monica Vicentia. Pageboy N.Y. Curb Exchange (name changed to American Stock Exchange), 1925-28, specialist clk., 1928-33, mem. from 1933, gov., 1948-51, vice chmn. 1950-51, chmn., chmn. finance com., gov.; now senior partner John J. Mann & Company, N.Y.C. Pres. adv. bd. St. Vincents Hosp., Harrison, N.Y.; mem. lay adv. bd., pres. assn. St. Agnes Hosp.; exec. bd. N.Y. chpt. United Cerebral Palsy, pres. Westchester chpt.; pres. Pryor Manor Assn. K.C. Clubs: Lawyers, Montauk, Larchmont Shore (pres.), Republican of Larchmont and Mamaroneck, Inc. (pres.), Westchester Country, Horseshoe Harbor Yacht. Home: Larchmont, N.Y., Died Dec. 24, 1975.

MANNHEIM, HERMANN, lawyer, criminologist; b. Libau, Baltic States, Oct. 26, 1889 (parents German citizens); came to Eng. 1934, naturalized 1940; s. Wilhelm and Clara (Marcuse) M.; ed. U. Munich, U. Freiburg, U. Strasbourg; J.D., U. Königsberg, 1912; LL.D., U. Utrecht (Netherlands) 1957; D.Sc. in Econs., U. Wales, 1970; m. Mona Mark, July 10, 1919. Adminstr., Königsberg, 1919-23; judge, Berlin, Germany, 1933; named ret. pres. Div. Ct. Appeal 1953; lectr. Berlin U., 1924-29, prof., 1929-33; lectr. criminology London U., 1934-46, reader, 1946-55; hon. dir. criminological research unit London Sch. Econs., 1955-57. Hon. dir. Research Inst. for Study and Treatment Delinquency. Decorated Order Brit. Empire, Order of Merit German Fed. Republic; recipient Golden Beccaria medal German Criminological Soc., 1965. Mem. Sci. Commn. Internat. Soc. Criminology (past pres.), Brit. Soc. Criminology (v.p.). Author: (with others) Prediction Methods in Borstal Training, 1955; Der Massstab der Fahrlässigkeit, 1912; Die Revision im Strafverfahren, 1925; Pressrecht, 1927; The Dilemma of Penal Reform, 1939; Social Aspects of Crime in England, 1940; War and Crime, 1941; Juvenile Delinquency in an English Middletown, 1948; Young Offenders, 1944; Criminal Justice and Social Reconstruction, 1946; Group Problems in Crime and Punishment, 1955; Comparative Criminology, 2 vols., 1965. Co-founder, co-editor Brit. Jour. Criminology, 1950, Internat. Library of Criminology, 1966. Home: London, England. Died Jan. 20, 1974.

MANNING, ESTELLE HEMPSTEAD author; b. Frankfort, Ky., Apr. 27, 1879; d. William Thompson and Clarissa (Campbell) M.; ed. in Ky. and Washington, Contbr. and reporter Washington Post. Mem. D.A.R. Author: Hafiz, 1902 N3. Address: Washington, D.C.†

MANNING, HARRY, commodore S.S. U.S.; b. N.Y. City, Feb. 3, 1897; s. William Edward and Anna (Von Luelke) M.; grad. N.Y. Maritime Coll., 1914; m. Florence Heaton, Feb. 1939 (div. 1942); 1 dau., Florence. Seaman Am. barque, Dirigo, 1914, advanced to rear adm.; comdr. S.S. America, S.S. Washington, S.S. Manhattan, 1929-41; navigator, radio operator Amelia Earhart's first world flight; commodore U.S. Lines since 1946, S.S. U.S. since 1952. Served as capt. U.S.N.R., World War II, supt. U.S. Maritime Service Radio Tng. Station, Hoffman Island, 1944-46. Decorated Navy and Marine Corps medal, Chevalier Order of Maritime Merit (France), Medal of Maritime Valor (Italy). Awarded U.S. Gold Medal of Life Saving, Benevolent Assn., N.Y. State conspicuous service cross, 2 N.Y.C. medals of heroism, U.S. Lines distinguished service medal. Mem. U.S. Naval Inst., Mil. Order World Wars, Am. Legion. Club: N.Y. Athletic. Licensed pilot, radio operator. Established new records for Trans Atlantic ship passage, July 1952; 3 days, 10 hours, 40 minutes Eastbound; 3 days, 12 hours 12 minutes Westbound. Home: Saddle River, N.J. Died Aug. 1, 1974.

MANNING, JEWEL EVANGELINE BERGER (MRS. HAROLD E. MANNING), retail exec.; b. Copenhagen, Ill., Jan. 4, 1910; d. Frank and Cora (Kemmerer) Berger; grad. high sch.; m. Harold E. Manning, Oct. 10, 1927. Bookkeeper, Cromer Ford, Naperville, Ill., 1929-37; with Maurice J. Sopp & Son Chevrolets, Huntington Park, Cal., 1937-72, sec.-treas., 1946-72, office mgr., 1951-72, bus. mgr., 1962-72. Home: Garden Grove, Cal. Died Dec. 6, 1973.

MANSKE, WALTER EARL, banker; b. Waco, Tex., Sept. 2, 1928; s. Walter Louis and Lillie Emily (Witte) M.; A.A., Tex. Lutheran Coll., 1947; B.B.A., Baylor U., 1950; m. Phyllis Mae Reichle, Mar. 26, 1955; children—Sharon, Diane. New bus. supr. Tex. Power & Light Co., Waco, 1955-59; mgr. farmers br. Carrollton, 1959-69; v.p., loan officer Central Bank & Trust Co., Farmers Branch, Tex., 1969-73. Pres. Dallas area adv. council Dallas area Chambers Commerce, 1971. Served with USAF, 1950-54. Recipient Outstanding Citizen award Farmers Branch Community Red Cross, 1966. Chmn. United Fund, 1964-65, Cancer Soc., 1968-69. Mem. Greater N.W. (pres. 1970), Farmers Branch (pres. 1962) chambers commerce. Rotarian, Mason. Club: Brookhaven Country. Home: Dallas Tex. Died Sept. 3, 1973; interred McGregor, Tex.

MANTEUFFEL, TADEUSZ, historian, educator; b. Rzezyca, Latvia, Mar. 5, 1902; s. Leon and Aniela (Zielinska) M.; Ph.D., U. Warsaw, 1924; postgrad. Ecole Pratique des Hautes Etudes, Paris, 1924-26; m. Maria Heurich, Apr. 8, 1932; children—Anna (Mrs. Szarota), Malgorzata (Mrs. Cymborowska). Archives, 1926-39; chmn. hist. div. Warsaw Underground U., 1940-44; prof. U. Warsaw, 1945-68; dir. Hist. Inst., Polish Acad. Scis., 1953-70. Decorated Order of Labour's Banner II and I class, Polonia Restituta V and III class. Mem. Polish Acad. Scis. Author: Papacy and Cistercian Order Especially in Poland, 1955; The Origin of One Heresy, 1963; Middle Ages, 1966. Home: Warsaw, Poland. Died Sept. 22, 1970; buried Powazki Cemetery, Warsaw, Poland.

MAO TSE-TUNG, govt. ofcl.; b. Shaoshan, Hsiangtan, Dec. 26, 1893; s. Mao Jen-sheng; student Hsianghsiang Middle Sch., 1910, Hunan Provincial No. 1 Middle Sch., 1913-18; m. Yang K'ai-hui (dec. 1930) m. 2d, Ho Tze-cheng (div.); m. 3d, Chiang Chi'ing; children—Mao An-ying (dec. 1950), Mao Anch'ing, Li Na. Promoter, organizer New People's Study Soc., 1917; editor, pub. Hsiang River Review, 1918; founder Hunan Reconstrn. Alliance, 1919, Hunan Students Fedn., 1919; prin. elementary sch. Hunan Province, 1920-22; founding mem. Chinese Communist Party, 1921, sec. Hunan br., 1921, sec. provincial com., 1922, mem. central com., 1923; alternate mem. KMT Central Com., 1924; dir. planned orgn. dept. Chinese Communist Party, 1924; organizer peasants assns., 1924-25; head Chinese Communist Party Peasants' Dept., 1926; pres. All-China Peasants' Assn., 1927; organizer Workers and Peasants Red Army, 1927, comdr.-in-chief, 1927; polit. commissar Red 4th Army, 1928; established local parties, Kiangsi Provincial Soviet, 1930; organized army and led attacks, 1930; chmn. China Workers and Revolutionary Com., 1930; chmn. Central Peasants and Workers Govt., 1933; led forces in Long March, 1934; polit. commissar Red 1st Front Army, 1935; chmn. mil. com. N.W. Revolutionary Army, 1936; polit. commissar Chinese Workers-Peasant Red Army Coll., 1936; chmn. coll. affairs com. Anti-Japan Mil. and Polit. Coll., 1937; chmn. Yenan People's Congress Condemning Wang Ching-wei and Supporting Chiang Kai-shek, 1940; chmn. politburo Chinese Communist Party 7th Central Com., 1945; chmn. People's Revolutionary Mil. Council, 1945-56; led forces in war against Nationalists, 1945-49; dep. Peking NPC, 1954, 58, 64; chmn. and Nat. Def. Council, 1954-59; hon. chmn. nat. com. CPPCC, 1954; mem. CCP 8th Central Com. and Standing Com. Politburo, 1956-69; chmn. Chinese Communist Party central com., 1967-76; chmn. presidium Chinese Communist Party 9th Congress, 1969, chmn. central com., mem. standing com., 1969-76; supreme comdr. Whole Nation and Whole Army, 1970-76. Author: Analysis Classes Chinese Society; Class Status and Our Present Task, 1925; Survey Human Peasants Movement, 1927; On Coalition Govt., 1945; Outlines Agrarian Law, 1947; many papers and speeches. Address: Peking, People's Republic of China. Died Sept. 9, 1976.

MAPOW, ABRAHAM B., physician; b. Phila., Sept. 21, 1907; s. Benjamin and Sarah (Rosengarten) M.; M.D., Temple U., 1933; m. Claire Nemirow, Nov. 23, 1939; children—Sheryl (Mrs. Sheldon Reisman), Marc Kevin, Lawrence Steven. Intern, Mt. Sinai Hosp., Phila., 1933-34; asso. staff Grad. Hosp. of U. Pa.; chief otolaryngology Community Hosp. of Phila.; surgeon Phila. Police and Fireman Dept., Phila. Gen. Hosp.; mem. faculty Jefferson U., Phila. Diplomate Am. Bd. Otolaryngology. Mem. A.M.A., Philadelphia County Med. Soc., Am. Soc. Otolaryngology. Jewish religion. Home: Philadelphia, Pa. Died May 4, 1969; buried Mt. Lebanon Cemetery, Springfield, Pa.

MARBY, GIDDINGS EDLON, lawyer; b. Tupelo, Miss., Oct. 8, 1877; s. Milton Harvey and Ella Dale (Bramlitt) M.; student W. Fla. Sem., Tallahassee, 1894-96, Richmond (Va.) Coll., 1896-98; LL.B., Cumberland U., Lebanon, Tenn., 1901; m. Mabel Robey, Nov. 1, 1906; 1 dau., Mabel. Admitted to Florida bar, 1901; senior partner, Mabry, Reaves, Carlton, Fields & Ward; city attorney, 1910-13, county attorney, 1917-23. Member board trustees Old Peoples Home (Tampa), Fla. Bapt. Children's Home (Lakeland), Y.M.C.A., Tampa. Mem. American. Fla. State, Hillsborough County and Tampa bar assns., Phi Gamma Delta. Democrat. Mason. Home: Tampa, Fla.†

MARCEL, GABRIEL HONORE, philosopher, writer; b. 1889; ed. U. Paris (France). Tchr., 1912-41. Recipient Grand Prix de Litterature, French Acad., 1948; Goethe prize Hamburg (Germany) U., 1956; Grand Prix Nat. des Lettres, 1958; German Booksellers Peace prize, 1964; Grand Prix Littéraire de la Ville de Paris, 1968; Erasmus prize, 1969; decorated officer Legion of Honor, comdr. des Arts et des Lettres, comdr. des Palmes Academiques (France). Mem. Acad. Moral and Polit. Scis. Author: (plays) Le Seuil Invisible, 1914, L'Iconoclaste, 1923, Un Homme de Dieu, 1925, Le Chemin de Crete, 1936, Le Fanal, 1936, La Soif, 1938, L'Horizon, 1945, Vers un autre Royaume, 1949, Rome n'est plus dans Rome, 1951; (philosophy) Journal Metaphysique, 1928, Etre et Avoir, 1935, Du Refus d l'Inovacation, 1940, Homo Viator, 1945, Le Mystere de l'etre, 1951-52, Theatre de Religion, 1959, L'Heure Theatrale, de Giraudoux a Sartre, 1959, Fragments philosphiques, 1909-1914, 1963; Regards sur le Théâtre de Claudel, 1964. Contbr. Nouvelles Litteraires. Address: Paris, France. Died Oct. 8, 1973.

MARCH, ANTHONY, editor, writer; b. N.Y.C., July 8, 1912; s. Peter Joseph and Mary Kathryn (Reimer) McCauley; student Columbia; m. Mary Marjorie Walker, Sept. 29, 1941; children—Anthony William (dec.), Stephen Walker. Reporter. Bklyn. Eagle. Portland Oregonian; asso. editor Happy Days, 1936-41; mng. editor Army Times, 1941, editor 1946-73. Served to 1st lt., cav., AUS, 1943-46. Club: Nat. Press (Washington). Author: (novel) Quit for the Next, 1945. Editor: Darkness over Europe: First-Person Accounts of Life in Europe During the War Years, 1939-45, 1969. Contbr. articles, short stories to mags. Home: Bethesda, Md. Died Dec. 7, 1973; interred Arlington (Va.) Nat. Cemetery.

MARCH, FREDRIC, actor; b. Frederick McIntyre Bickel, Racine, Wis., Aug. 31, 1897; s. John F. and Cora (Brown Marcher) Bickel; A.B., U. Wis., 1920; m. Florence Eldridge, May 30, 1927; children—Penelope, Anthony. Debut in Deburau, produced by David Belasco, 1920; appeared in Shavings, The Law Breaker, The Melody Man, Tarnish, The Half Caste, achieved spl. commendation in The Royal Family, Los Angeles; screen debut in The Dummy, one of first all talking pictures; leading man with Clara Bow, Claudette Colbert, Ruth Chatterton and Nancy Carroll; played in The Wild Party, Sarah and Son, Manslaughter, Laughter, The Royal Family of Broadway, Honor Among Lovers, My Sin, Dr. Jekyll and Mr. Hyde, Smilin' Through, Sign of the Cross, Eagle and the Hawk, Design of Living, Death Takes a Holiday, Affairs of Cellini, The Barretts of Wimpole Street, Resurrection, Les Miserables, Anna Karenina, The Dark Angel, Anthony Adverse, Mary of Scotland, A Star Is Born, Nothing Sacred, The Buccaneer, There Goes My Heart, Trade Winds, Susan and God, Victory, So Ends Our Night, One Foot in Heaven, To-morrow the World, The American Way (play), Rockefeller Center Theater, N.Y.C., 1939; Hope for a Harvest (play), 1941; Bedtime Story (screen play), 1941; I Married a Witch; The Adventures of Mark Twain; also in Thornton Wilder play, The Skin of Our Teeth, A Bell for Adano, The Best Years of Our Lives (film), Years Ago (play), Another Part of the Forest (film), 1947; An Act of Murder (film), 1948; recent plays include Autumn Garden, 1951; Long Days Journey into Night, 1956; Gideon, 1961-62; recent films include It's a Big Country, Death of a Salesman, Man on a Tightrope, Executive Suite, Bridges at Toko Ri, The Desperate Hours, Alexander the Great, The Man in the Grey Flannel Suit; The Middle of the Night, 1959; Inherit the Wind, 1960; The Young Doctors, 1961, Condemned of Altona, 1962, Seven Days in May, 1963, Hombre, 1966, Tick . . . Tick . . . Tick, 1969, The Iceman Cometh, 1973. Mem. Beta Gamma Sigma, Alpha Delta Phi. Recipient acting award Acad. of Motion Picture Arts and Sci., 1932, 47; Antoinette Perry award, 1956. Address: Los Angeles, Cal. Died Apr. 14, 1975.

MARCH, H(ERMAN) W(ILLIAM), mathematician; b. Scheyedan, Ia., Dec. 14, 1878; s. Albert Henry and Elizabeth (Pell) M.; A.B., Univ. Mich., 1904, A.M., 1905; Ph.D., Univ. Munich, 1911; m. Margaret Odell McGowan, Sept. 8, 1914; children—Robert William, Elizabeth Jean (Mrs. Charles H. Lange, Jr.). Asst. in astronomy, Univ. Mich., 1902-05; instr. in physics. Princeton, 1905-06; instr. in math. Univ. Wis., 1906-09, asst. prof., 1911-20, asso. prof., 1920-29, prof. of math., 1929-49; chmn., course in applied math. and mechanics, 1946-49, consulting math. Forest Products Lab., U.S. Forest Service at Madison, 1941-46. Fellow A.A.A.S. Mem. Am. Math. Soc., Math. Assn. of Am., Wis. Acad. Scis., Wis. Hist. Soc.; Sigma Xi. Phi Beta Kappa. Conglist. Clubs: Univ., Blackhawk Country. Contbr. articles in applied math. and physics in math. physical jours. Numerous reports on design criteria for laminates, in particular, plywood and sandwich, in aircraft constrn. issued by U.S. Forest Products Lab. in cooperation with the Army-Navy Civil Com. on Aircraft Design Criteria. Home: Madison, Wis.†

MARCHBANKS, TOM EARL, air force officer; b. San Benito, Tex., June 27, 1922; s. Tom Earl and Josie (Moody) M., student Tex. A. and M. Coll., 1939-42; m. Peggy Jean Richter, Dec. 19, 1969; children—Tom Earl III, Nancy. Commd. 2d lt. USAAF, 1943, advanced through grades to maj. gen. USAF; served in World War II, Korea, Vietnam; comdr. 433d Tactical Airlift Wing, Kelly AFB, Tex., 1962; chief Air Force Res., Washington 1968-75. Decorated D.F.C. with oak leaf cluster, D.S.M., Legion of Merit, Air medal with seven oak leaf clusters. Mem. Order Daedalians, Air Force Assn., Res. Officers Assn. Mason (Shriner), Elk. Reviser flight tng. manuals for USAF. Home: Brightwood, Va. Died Mar. 2, 1975.

MARCIN, MAX, playwright, producer; b. Province of Posen, Germany, May 6, 1879; s. Herman and Johanna (Feibel) M.; brought to U.S. in early childhood; ed. pub. schs., N.Y. City; m. Clara May Mings, of Buffalo, N.Y., Nov. 29, 1915. Mem. editorial staff, New York World, New York Press, later contbr. fiction to mags. Jewish religion. Author: Are You My Wife? 1910; The Substitute Prisoner, 1911; Britz of Headquarters, 1909; (plays) The House of Glass (with Goerge M. Cohan), 1915; See My Lawyer, 1915; Cheating Cheaters, 1916; Eyes of Youth, 1916; Here Comes the Bride, 1916; The Woman in Room 13, 1917; Silence, 1925; (with Donald Ogden Stewart) Los Angeles, 1927. Producer and author (with Frederick Isham) of "Three Live Ghosts," 1920. Producer and author (with Guy Bolton), "The Night-Cap," 1921; (with Samuel Shipman), "One A.M.," 1928; "The Humbug," 1929. Producer, "Give and Take," 1923. Home: Los Angeles, Cal.†

MARCKWARDT, ALBERT HENRY, educator; b. Grand Rapids, Mich., Dec. 1, 1903; s. Albert Martin and Anna (Miller) M.; A.B., U. Mich., 1925, A.M.; 1928, Ph.D., 1933; Litt.D., No. Mich. U., 1973; m. Grace A. McCarroll, June 19, 1934 (dec. Jan. 1972); children—Albert McCarroll, Judith (Mrs. Arthur Getis), Elizabeth (Mrs. John Oliver); m. 2d, Maybelle D. Cox, Aug. 9, 1973. Sch. tchr., Wakefield, Mich., 1925—26, Grand Rapids, 1926—27; mem. faculty U.

Mich., 1928—63, prof. English, 1947—63, 73—75, acting dir. English Lang. Inst., 1960, dir., 1961—63; prof. English and linguistics Princeton, 1963—72, prof. emeritus, 1972—75, acting dir. Center for Applied Linguistics, 1971; dir. English Lang. Inst. in Mexico, 1943—45; Fulbright lectr. univs. Vienna and Graz, Austria, 1953—54, Japan, 1968. Mem. adv. com. cultural information, chmn. adv. panel English, teaching div. USIA: cons. lang. devel. sect. U.S. Office Edn., mem. research adv. council bur. ednl. research; mem. Nat. Adv. Council on Teaching English as Fgn. Lang.; adv. com. Fgn. Service Inst. Dept. State, 1961—64. Mem. Bd. En., Ann Arbor, 1955—61, Washtenaw County, 1961—63. Recipient Distinguished Faculty Achievement award U. Mich., 1961. Mem. Am. Dialect Soc. (pres. 1962—64), Am. Studies Assn., Linguistic Soc. Am. (pres. 1962), Modern Lang. Assn. (exec. council 1955—59), Am. Name Soc. (bd. mgrs. 1957—68), Nat. Counccil Tchrs. English (pres. 1967, Distinguished Research award 1970, Distinguished Service award 1972), Am. Assn. U. Profs., Mich. Assn. Sch. Bds. (dir. 1959—63), Am. Council Learned Socs. (vice chmn. bd. dirs. 1961—64), Phi Beta Kappa. Clubs: Nassau (Princeton); Princeton of New York, Cosmos (Washington); University (Ann Arbor). Author: (with F. Walcott) Facts about Current English Usage, 1938; Scribner Handbook of English, 1940; Introduction to the English Language, 1942; American English, 1958; (with R. Quirk) A Common Language, 1964; Linguistics and the Teaching of English, 1967; Modern English, 1969; (with J. Rosier) Old English, 1972. Editor: Historical Outline of English Sounds and Inflections, 1951; Laurence Nowell's Vocabularium Saxonicum, 1952; Language and Language Learning, 1968; Modern English: Its Growth and Present Use, 1969; Linguistics and School Programs, 1970. Contbr. articles to philol. and edn. jours. Dir. Linguistic Atlas of the North Central States, 1940—75. Home: Chevy Chase, Md. Died Aug. 20, 1975.

MARCO, SALVATORE MICHAEL, educator, engr.; b. Cleve., Dec. 19, 1907; s. Michael and Angela (Lauria) Marcoguisseppe; B.S., Ohio State U., 1930, M. Sc., 1932; m. Vivian Morris, Apr. 3, 1934; children—Christopher Alan, Linda Beth. Asst. instr. dept. mech. engring., Ohio State U., 1930-33, instr., 1935-40, asst. prof., 1940-44, asso. prof., 1944-47, prof., 1947-73, chmn. dept., 1952-68; engr. Dayton Rubber Mfg. Co., 1933-35; cons. engr. machine design, heat transfer Assn. Am. R.R.'s, 1936, United Engring. & Foundry Co., Cleve. Worm Gear Co., Cone Worm Gear Co., 1936-40; research heat transfer, metal fatigue U.S.A.A.F. from 1940; cons. engr. Gear Grinding Machine Co., 1945-46, Diamond Power specialty Corp. from 1950, Battelle Meml. Inst. from 1952. Mem. Am. Soc. Engring. Edn. (past chmn. Ohio sect.), A.S.M.E. (past chmn. Columbus sect.), Soc. Exptl. Stress Analysis, Nat., Ohio (past chmn. Franklin Co. chpt.) socs. profl. engrs., A.A.U.P., Sigma Xi, Tau Beta Pi, Pi Tau Sigma. Author: Introduction to Heat Transfer (with A. I. Brown), 1942. Contbr. articles in field to tech. Jours., course developer Problems in Acoustics, 1968-73. Holder patent on variable speed transmission, electronic weighing device, electronic computing circuit, turbine driven cleaner head. Home: Columbus, O. Died Dec. 15, 1973; interred Walnut Grove Cemetery, Columbus.

MARCOUX, VANNI (VANNI-MARCOUX), baritone; b. Turin, Italy, June 12, 1879; s. M. Giovanni and Giuseppina (Jourdan) M.; studied law and passed examination for admission to the bar, but never practiced; studied voice under Collino, in Turin, and Boyer, in Paris; twice married; m. 2d, Madeleine Morlay. Debut as "Marcello" in 1st presentation of "La Boheme," Nice, 1899; Am. début as "Golaud" in "Pelleas et Melisande," Boston Opera House, Jan. 10, 1911. Had nearly 100 operatic rôles at his command.*†

MARDEN, ORISON SWETT, lawyer; b. Sea Cliff, N.Y., May 22, 1906; s. Orison Swett and Clare (Evans) M.; B.S., N.Y.U., 1928, LL.B., 1929; LL.D., Syracuse U., 1967, N.Y. Law Sch., 1967, N.Y.U., 1968; m. Virginia McAvoy, Mar. 1, 1930, children—Orison Swett, John Newcomb. Asso. White & Case, 1926—75, partner, 1946—75; admitted to N.Y. bar, 1930. Chmn. Jud. Commn. to Reapportion N.Y. State, 1966; dir. Lawyers' Com. for Civil Rights, 1963—; chmn. Nat. Deferder Project, 1963—70; nat. adv. com. Legal Scis. Program, Office Econ. Opportunity, 1966—68; chmn. adv. com. on health care A.M.A., 1969—72. Trustee N.Y.U., 1962—66, 69—75, Vera Inst. Justice 1966—75, William Nelson Cromwell Found., 1963—75, Found. for Overseas Libraries Am. Law, 1969—75; trustee Law Center Found., N.Y.U., 1960—75; pres. 1969—73. Fellow Inst. Jud. Administrn. (chrm. exec. com. 1969—71, pres 1973), Am. Coll. Trial Lawyers, Am. Bar Found. (dir. 1966—67); mem. Internat. (council 1968—75), Inter—Am., Am. (chmn. com. on legal aid work 1948—53, ho. dels. 1956—75, pres. 9166—67), N.Y. State (mem. exec. com. 1958—75, v.p. 1962—64, pres. 1964—65) bar assns., Internat. Legal Aid Assn. (pres. 1960—64), Nat. Council Legal Clinics (chrmn. 1960—66), Nat. Legal Aid and Defender Assn. (v.p. 1948—55, pres. 1955—59, Arthur von Briesen award 1961), Practicing Law Inst. (trustee 1965—68), Legal Aid Soc. N.Y.C. (dir. 1946—75, chmn. 1969—75), Am. Law Inst., Assn. Bar City N.Y. (exec. com. 1956—60, pres. 1960—62, medal 1968), N.Y. County Lawyers Assn. (dir. 1959—65, Cromwell medal 1969), Am. Judicature Soc. (dir. exec. com. 1962—65), N.Y.U. Law Alumni Assn. (dir. 1946—75, pres. 1961—62), Nat. Conf. Jud. Councils (chmn. 1963—68), Nat. Conf. Bar Pres. (chmn. 1964—65), Nat. Assn. Community Counsel (dir. 1967—70), Nat. Council Edn. for Profl. Responsibility (dir. 1966—75, chmn. 1971—75), Fed. Bar Council (Emory Buckner medal 1971), Nat. Center, for State Cts. (chmn. adv. council 1971—73), Internat. Legal Center, Delta Phi, Phi Delta Phi. Clubs: Century Assn., Downtown Assn., Lawyers (N.Y.C.); Scarsdale (N.Y.) Gold; Nat. Lawyers (Washington). editors N.Y. Law Jour., 1969—75. Home: Scarsdale, N.Y. Died Aug., 1975.

MARESCA, VIRGINIA KELLER clin. psychologist; b. Dobbs Ferry, N.Y., Nov. 7, 1923; d. Vann D. and Louetta P. (Getsinger) Keller; R.N., Diploma Sch. Nursing, 1944; B.S., Ariz. State ., 1948, M.A., 1960, Ph.D., 1963; 1 dau., Karen K. Instr., dir. Student Health Service Meml. Hosp., Phoenix, 1947-48, also instr. Union U., Albany, N.Y., 1947-48; dir. nursing New Eng. Hosp. Women and Children, Boston, 1949-50; individual practice psychology Phoenix, 1965-75. Chmn. Ariz. State Bd. Psychol. Examiners, 1973-74. Mem. Am. Western, Ariz. State psychol. assns. Home: Scottsdale, Ariz., Died Aug. 25, 1975.

MARIETTA, SHELLEY URIAH, army med. officer; b. Palmyra, Ia., Jan. 5, 1881; s. John Cramer and Harriet (Lutz) M.; D.D.S., Drake U. (Dental Dept.), 1902; M.D., U. of Ill., 1909; m. Emma Alderson, Aug. 18, 1909. Dental practice, Des Moines, Ia., 1902-05; interne, St. Annes Hosp., Chicago, 1908-09; med. practice, Des Moines, 1909-10; entered Med. Corps, U.S. Army, 1910, progressing through various grades to brigadier general, 1939, major general from Sept. 1943; specialist in internal medicine, Army Hospital, Fort Bayard, N.M., 1912-14, Fitzsimons General Hospital, Denver, Colorado, 1920-23, Station Hosp., Ft. Sam Houston, Tex., 1923-28 and 1937-38, Letterman Gen. Hosp., San Francisco, 1928-31. Walter Reed Gen. Hosp., 1931-35 and 1939, Tripler General Hospital, Honolulu, 1935-37; comdg. officer Walter Reed Gen. Hosp., Washington, from 1939 and of Army Medical Center from March 1940. Retired from active duty, August 1946. Served as organization surgeon, United States Army, Mexican Border Service, 1912; various administrative positions during World War (in France 14 months). Decorated Hon. Comdr. O.B.E.; D.S.M. Officer of French Acad. Fellow A. M.A.; mem. Assn. of Mil. Surgeons, Am. College Physicians, Am. Bd. of Internal Medicine (diplomate), Am. Coll. of Chest Physicians (pres. since 1947), Alpha Kappa Kappa (Eta chapter), Sigma Xi (U. of Ill. chapt.). Republican. Methodist. Mason (32deg., K.C.C.H.). Author several articles on professional subjects. Home: Washington, D.C. Died Nov. 22, 1974.

MARION, FRANCES, author, scenario writer; b. San Francisco, Calif., Nov. 18, 1890; d. Len D. and Minnie (Hall) Owens; ed. St. Margaret's Hall, San Mateo, Calif.; m. Fred Thomson (now dec.); children—Fred Clifton, Richard Gordon. Writer of many motion picture scenarios including "The Rogues Song," "The Big House," "The Champ," "Min and Bill," "The Prize Fighter and the Lady," "Blondie of the Follies," "Secret Six," "Riffraff." Apptd. govt. war correspondent for women's activities during World War. Awarded Acad. Motion Picture Arts and Sciences Award for "The Big House," 1930, for "The Champ," 1932. Mem. Authors League of America, The Writers, Inc., Am. Dramatists, Am. Museum of Natural History (hon.). Author: Minnie Flynn, 1925; Valley People, 1935; Molly, Bless Her, 1937; How to Write and Sell Film Stories, 1937. Contbr. fiction to various mags. Home: Hollywood, Cal. Died May 12, 1973.

MARK, MARY LOUISE, sociologist, ret. educator; b. Scioto County, O., Jan. 6, 1878; d. Peter Lewis and Mary Priscilla (Humphrey) Mark; prep. edn. Ohio U., 1898; A.B., Ohio State U., 1903; A.M., Columbia, 1907. Spl. agt. U.S. Immigration Commn., 1907-10, U.S. Bur. Census, 1911, U.S., Bur. Labor, 1912; statistician Ohio Bd. Health, 1913; asst. in econs., sociology Ohio State U., 1914, instr., 1915-18, asst. prof., 1918-23, prof. sociology, from 1923, prof. social adminstrn., 1923-43, emeritus, 1943-75. Mem. staff Survey of Indian Affairs, Inst. for Govt. Research, Washington, 1927, co-author of report to Sec. of Interior, 1928. Hon. life mem. bd. Gladden Community House. Fellow Royal Statis. Soc. London, Am. Sociol. Assn.; mem. Am. Statis. Assn., Am. Assn. U. Profs., Population Assn. Am., Am. Acad. Polit. and Social Sci., Am. Soc. for Pub. Administrn., Nat. Conf. on Social Welfare, Ohio Citizens' Council for Health and Welfare, Assn. on Am. Indian Affairs, Phi Beta Kappa, Kappa Delta, Alpha Kappa Delta. Methodist. Author: Ten Years of Birth Statistics in Ohio, 1915-24, 1928; Negroes in Columbus, 1928; Statistics in the Making, 1958 (with others) Immigrants in Cities (vols. 26, 27 of Report of Immigration Commn.), 1911; Law and Order on Indian Reservations of the Northwest, 1932, Population Characteristics by Census Tracts, Columbus, Ohio, 1930, 1933, Leisure in the Lives of Our Neighbors, 1941. Home: Columbus, 0. Died Mar. 18, 1975.

MARKLEY, KLARE S(TEPHEN), chemist; b. Phila., Dec. 16, 1895; s. Jonah Jacob and Mabel (Montague) M.; B.S. in Chem. Engring., George Washington U., 1924, M.S., 1925; Ph.D., Johns Hopkins, 1929; m. Calla Inez Lepper, Dec. 24, 1921 (dec. Dec. 1954); m. 2d, Carmen Nogueira de Mello, Mar. 14, 1955. Asst., asso. biochemist U.S. Dept. Agr., 1927-37, chief oil sect. Regional Soybean Lab., Urbana, Ill., 1937-39, chief oil and oilseed div. So. Regional Lab., New Orleans, 1939-52, with ICA, 12-60, successively assigned to Paraguay, Brazil, Nicaragua, FAO in Venzuela, Guatemala, mem. staff U.S. operations Mission, Brazil, 1954-60; industrial con., Rio de Janeiro, Brazil, 1960-73. Sci. cons. tch. intelligence com., Joint Chiefs Staff, 1945. Recipient superior service award U.S. Dept. Agr., 1950, group superior service award, 1952; Southwest regional award Am. Chem. Soc., 1951. Fellow A.A.A.S.; mem. Am. Chem. Soc. (past sec. Washington sect.), Am. Oil Chemist Soc. (past pres.), Am. Soybean Assn., Palm Soc., Fgn. Services Assn., Sigma Xi, Phi Lambda Upsilon, Alpha Chi Sigma. Club: Cosmos (Washington). Author: (with W. H. Goss) Soybean Chemistry and Technology, 1944; Fatty Acids, 1947; Soybeans and Soybean Products, 2 vols., 1950, 51; Fatty Acids and Derivatives, 4 vols.; also numerous sci. publs. Home: Rio de Janeiro, Brazil. Died July 2, 1973.

MARLIO, LOUIS, consulting engr. and economist; b. Paris, France, Feb. 3, 1878; s. Albert and Jeanne (Bossuat) M.; student Ecole Polytechnique, Paris, 1898; LL.D., U. of Paris; m. Rachel Mosseri, 1936. Came to U.S., 1940. Ingenieur en chef des Ponts ct Chaussees; Maitre des Requetes au Conseil d'Etat, France, 1910-17; asst. to minister of pub. works and transp., 1909-13; teacher, economics, Sch. of Polit. Science, 1920-28; staff of Brookings, Instn., from 1941. Former chmn. French Aluminum Co., Internat. Aluminum Cartel, French Eastern R.R. Co., Railroad Com. of Internat. Chamber of Commerce, Assn. of Electrical Power Producers. Served as Col., French Army. Commdr. Legion of Honor. Mem. French Acad. Polit. and Moral Science. Author: German Policy and Internal Waterways, 1907; International Economic Agreements; True Story of the Panama Canal, 1932; Versailles Armistice, 1934; The Future of Capitalism, 1937; Dictatorship or Liberty, 1940; La Revolution d'Hier, d'Aujourd'hui et de Demain (Brentzno's). 1943; Problémes d'Aujourd'hui (Parizeau, Montreal), 1944; The Control of Germany and Japan (with Dr. Harold G. Moulton), Brooklings Inst., 1944; Can Democracy Recover? 1945; also pamphlets pub. by Brooklings Inst., 1941, 42. Address: Washington, D.C.*†

MARMIER, PIERRE EDOUARD, physicist; b. Neuhausen, Switzerland, Jan. 8, 1922; s. Edouard and Bethe (Gottrau) M.; diploma Fed. Inst. Tech., Zurich, Switzerland, 1946, Ph.D., 1951. Faculty, Fed. Inst. Tech., Zurich, 1946-51, 55-73, prof. nuclear physics, 1958-73, dir. nuclear physics lab., 1960-73, chmn. dept. math. and physics, 1964-66, rector, 1969-73. Sr. research fellow Cal. Inst. Tech., 1952-55. Mem. Swiss, Am. phys. socs. Author: (with Eric Sheldon) Physics of Nuclei and Particles, 1968; also articles. Research in nuclear spectroscopy and nuclear reactions, use of nuclear methods on biol. research. Home: Zurich, Switzerland. Died Sept. 3, 1973; interred Fribourg, Switzerland.

MARON, SAMUEL HERBERT, educator; b. Warsaw, Poland, May 28, 1908; s. Harry and Bertha (Zellin) M.; came to U.S., 1922, naturalized, 1932; B.S., Case Inst. Tech., 1931, M.S., 1933; student Western Res. U., 1931-35; Ph.D. (scholar 1937-38), Columbia, 1938; m. Pearl Weinstein, June 28, 1936; 1 dau., Linda Anne (Mrs. Ronald E. Posner). Mem. faculty Case Inst. Tech., Cleve., 1931-75, prof. phys. chemistry, 1945-65, prof. phys. chemistry and macromolecular sci., 1965-75. Dir. research project U.S. Office Synthetic Rubber, 1943-55, mem. latex adv. com., 1946-50; cons. to industry, 1946-75. Pres. Cleve. Zionist Dist., 1939-40; mem. nat. adminstrv. com. Zionist Orgn. Am., 1939-40. Recipient certificiate certificate merit Chem. Profession Cleve., 1960; Sigma Xi research award Case Inst. Tech., 1962. Fellow A.A.A.S., Am. Inst. Chemists; mem. Am. Chem. Soc., Am. Inst. Chem. Engrs., Soc. Rheology, Am. Assn. U. Profs., Sigma Xi, Tau Beta Pi, Phi Lambda Upsilon, Alpha Chi Sigma, Sigma Alpha Mu. Author: (with J. B. Lando) Fundamentals of Physical Chemistry, 1974; also articles, chpts. in books. Home: University Heights, O., Died Jan. 13, 1975.

MARQUARDT, WALTER WILLIAM, educator; b. Dayton, O., Sept. 8, 1878; s. William Frederick and Elizabeth (Rumpf) M.; A.B., Ohio Wesleyan U., 1900, Ped.D., 1917; m. Alice M. Hollister, of Lake Linden, Mich., Dec. 24, 1902. Supt. schs., Bethel Tp., Clark Co., O., 1898; went to Philippines as teacher, 1901, became prin. high sch., Leyte; division supt. of schs., Province of Lyte; supt. Philippine Sch. of Arts and Trades, Manila; supt. of schs., City of Manila; 2d asst. dir. of edn., P.I.; dir. edn., P.I., June 20, 1916-July 1, 1919; Philippine ednl. agt., from 1919. Mng. editor The Philippine Craftsman, 1913-14; editor Vacation Assembly Herald, 1914. Regent and professional lecturer on sch. adminstration, U. of Philippines, 1916-19. Sec.-treas. Philippine Amateur Athletic Federation; contest sec., Far Eastern Athletic Assn., 1917-18; chmn. Junior Philippine Red Cross, 1918-19. Mem. Phi Beta Kappa. Republican. Methodist. Mason (32°, Shriner). Elk. Home: Dayton, O.†

MARSCH, WOLF DIETER, theologian; b. Beeskow, Oct. 2, 1928; s. Wolfgang and Ursula (Winter) M.; Th.D., U. Gottingen, 1956; M.A., U. Nashville, 1957; m. Elisabeth Hoppe, Oct. 2, 1954; children—Cornelius, Daniel. Staff, Evang. Acad., Berlin, Germany, 1958-62; prof. systematic theology Theol. Sch., Wuppertal, 1962-69; prof. theology, social ethics U. Munster, 1969-72. Mem. Paul Tillich Assn., others. Rotarian. Author: Christlicher Glaube und demokratisches Ethos, 1958; Hoffen Worauf?, 1963; Gegenwart Christi in der Gesellschaft, 1965; Die Freiheit erlernen, 1968; Zukunft, 1969; Institution im Ubergang. Ev. Kirche Zwischen Tradition und Reform, 1970. Editor periodical Wissenschaft und Praxis in Kirche and Gesellschaft. Contbr. articles to religious jours. Home: Munster, Federal Republic of Germany. Died Nov. 22, 1972.

MARSH, CLETA MCGINN (MRS. MYRON G. MARSH), hosp. adminstr.; b. Stent, Cal., July 15, 1906; d. John L. and Melissa (Shoup) McGinn; grad. French Hosp. Sch. Nursing, San Francisco, 1939; student Modesto Jr. Coll., 1964; m. Myron G. Marsh, June 7, 1923; 1 dau., Helen L. (Mrs. Robert O. Lewis). Indsl. emergency nurse Pickering Lumber Co., 1939-42; area supr. Agr. Workers Health and Med. Assn., 1942-47; owner, adminstr. Columbia Way Hosp., Sonora, Cal., 1947-58; adminstr. Sierra Hosp., pres. hosp. corp., Sonora, 1958-73. Sec., Sonora Regional Hosp. Planning Com., 1965-66. Chmn. Tri-County Mental Health Com., 1967; chmn. Yosemite Jr. Coll. health adv. com. Mem. Am. Coll. Hosp. Adminstrs., North San Joaquin Valley Hosp. Conf., Am., Cal. nurses assns. Clubs: Soroptimist (past pres. Sonora). Address: Sonora Cal. Died Apr. 29, 1973.

MARSH, ERNEST STERLING, transp. exec.; b. Lynchburg, Va., Jan. 10, 1903; s. John Sterling and Hattie (Leftwich) M.; student high sch., Clovis, N.M.; advanced Mgmt. Program, Harvard Bus. Sch., 1953; LL.D., U. So. Cal., 1963, N.M. State U., 1964; m. Agnes LaLonde, Jan. 14, 1922; children—Neva Jo (Mrs. John F. Schiltz, Jr.), Peggy Anne (Mrs. Thomas E. Lambert), Jack, Colleen (Mrs. John T. McCarthy), Larry. Clk., Atchison, Topeka & Santa Fe Ry. Co., 1918, various positions in operating dept., div. office, Clovis, div. accounts bur. Amarillo, Tex., 1932, accounting dept., Topeka, 1937, auditor of disbursements, Topeka, 1940, chief clk. to pres., Chgo., 1942, asst. to pres., 1944, exec. asst. to pres., 1945, v.p. finance, 1948, pres. Santa Fe System, 1957—66, chmn. bd., 1967—73, chief exec. officer, 1958—68, chmn. exec. com., 1959—73; chmn. bd., chief exec. officer, chmn. ex. exec. com. Santa Fe Industries, Inc., 1968—73; dir. A.I. &S.F. Ry., Harris Trust & Savs. Ban, 1958—73. Mem. industries adv. com. Advt. Council, 1959—72. Mem. Ill. Racing Bd., 1961—69. Bd. dirs. Jr. Achievement, Chgo., 1959—69, nat. bd., 1960—69; bd. dirs. Found. for Am. Agr.; mem. Nat. 4—H Service Com., Inc., 1959—73; trustee Am. Heritage Found., 1961—69, Farm Found., 1962—72, Ill. Inst. Tech. Mem. Assn. Am. Railroad (dir. 1952—68, exec. com. 1962—72 1962—68), Assn. Western Rys. (exec. com. 1957—68), Am. Royal Assn. (gov. 1960), Am. Soc. Traffic and Transp., Nat. Def. Transp. Assn. (mil. airlife com. 1967—72), Newcomen Soc., S.A.R., Def. Orientation Conf. Assn. (dir. 1963—64), Nat. Assn. State Racing Commrs., Assos. of Northwestern U., Crerar, Assos. Methodist. Clubs: Chicago Athletic Assn., Commerical, Executives (exec. com.), Traffic, Chicago, Economic (dir. 1959—68), Western Railway, Harvard Business School, Mid—Am. (Chgo.). Home: Chicago, Ill. Died Oct. 9, 1975; buried All Saints Cemetery, Des Plaines, Ill.

MARSH, GEORGE HAVENS, paper co. exec.; b. Van Wert, O., Sept. 25, 1918; s. John Robert and Florence Sprague (Havens) M.; B. Chem. Engring., Ohio State U., 1940; m. Helene Frances Cash, Oct. 5, 1947; children—George Havens, Stephen Allen. With W.Va. Pulp and Paper Co., 1940-55, Union Bag-Camp Paper Corp., 1955-59; with Champion Papers, Inc., Hamilton, O., 1959-75, v.p. mfg., 1962-75; dir. Case Brothers, Inc., Manchester, Conn. Pres., chmn. exec. com. Miami Pulp and Paper Found., Miami U., Oxford, O.; bd. dirs. Syracuse Pulp and Paper Found., State U. Coll. Forestry, Syracuse., N.Y. Elk. Mason. Methodist. Home: Hamilton, O., Died Oct. 21, 1975.

MARSH, GERALD E(LMIR), educatro; b. Albert Lea, Minn., Feb. 12, 1900; s. Joseph and Ella Rae (Dillon) M.; A.B., Carleton Coll., Northfield, Minn., 1921; M.A., Northwestern, 1928; m. Estelle Westcott, June 21, 1924; 1 dau., Sally J. (Mrs. Joseph Bertino Jr.). Tchr. Carleton Coll., Northfield, Minnesota, 1922-29; head ranger naturalist Yellowstone Park, 1927-29; tchr. U. Cal. at Berkeley, from 1929, asst. prof., 1934-38, asso. prof., 1938-48, prof., 1948-67, chmn. dept. speech, 1939-54, asst. dean coll. letters, 1942-54, asso. dean, 1954-67, dir. summer sessions, U. Cal. at Berkeley, 1954-67, emeritus, 1967-75. Mem. Cal. Commn. on Scholarships and Loans. Mem. Am. Assn. Deans and Dirs. Summer Sessions (pres. 1966), U. Cal. Alumni Assn. (hon. life), Pi Sigma Alpha, Delta Sigma Rho. Clubs: Commonwealth, Bohemian (San Francisco); City Commons, Breakfast (Berkeley). Home: Berkeley, Cal., Died Feb. 11, 1975.

MARSH, WILLIAM JOHN, composer, musician; b. Woolton, Liverpool, Eng., June 24, 1880; s. James and Mary Cecilia (McCormick) M.; Ampleforth Coll., Yorkshire; student harmony and composition under J. Clement Standish and R. W. Oberhoffer, organ under B. Sandberg Lee; unmarried. Came to U.S., 1904, naturalized citizen, 1917. Organist and choir dir. St. Patrick's R.C. Ch.; teacher piano and organ; professor of organ, composition and theory Our Lady of Victory College (Fort Worth); dir. Music Study Club Chorus. Men's Glee and Women's Choral clubs (Texas Christian U.). Mem. Am. Guild Organists. Hon. life mem. Tex. Music Teachers Assn., Texas Guild of Composers (dean), Federated Music Clubs (life), Texas Federated Music Clubs (life). Roman Catholic. Clubs: Harmony, Euterpean (asso.). Composer: Praise and Thanksgiving (cantata), 1925; Sherwood, cantata (women's voices); The Flower Fair at Peking (one-act Chinese opera, first opera to be composed and produced in state of Texas); "Texas Our Texas," officially adopted state song of Texas; The Innkeeper of Bethlehem (pageant); official mass for Texas Centennial; Queen Esther (dramatic cantata); also ten masses, motels, anthems, etc. Winner first prize, San Antonio, for best song by Texas composer, 1921 and 1922; winner double first, Dallas, 1929 (vocal and piano); winner Tex. Federation choral prize, 1929. Home: Ft. Worth, Tex.†

MARSHALL, FRANK ANTON, physician; b. Pressburg, Austria—Hungary, Dec. 17, 1905; s. Frank and Emelia (Kostelec) M.; M.D., N.Y.U., 1930; m. Irma Rocker, June 11, 1937; 1 dau., Irma Caroline (Mrs. Joseph Austin). Intern, Passaic Gen. Hosp., 1930—31; postgrad. studies in aviation medicine USAAF, 1931; postgrad. studies in cardiology VA, 1935, N.Y.U. Postgrad. Sch., 1946; X—ray interpretation tng. Mayo Found., 1938; cons. in internal medicine North Hudson Hosp., Weehawken, N.J., Christ Hosp., jersey City; lectr. N.Y. Polyclinic. Pres., Hudson County Council Social Agys., 1953; chmn. North Hudson chpt. A.R.C., 1947—48. Served to col., M.C., AUS, World War II. Diplomate Am. Bd. Internal Medicine. Fellow Am. Coll. Gastroenterology, A.C.P., Am. Coll. Cardiology; mem. A.M.A., Aerospace Med. Assn., Am. Heart Assn., Phil Beta Kappa Alumni of N.Y. (pres. 1956—57), North Hudson Physicians Soc. (pres. 1947), Hudson County Heart Assn. (pres. 1954), Hudson County Med. Soc., Med. Soc. N.J., N.J. Gastronenterology Soc., Phi Beta Kappa Assos. (life), Phi Beta Kappa, Phi Alpha, Beta Lambda Sigma. Lutheran. Kiwanian. Contbr. articles to med. jours. Home: Weehawken, N.J. Died Oct. 3, 1972; buried Fairview (N.J.) Cemetery.

MARSHALL, MARVIN GENE, lawyer; b. St. Louis, Sept. 20, 1927; s. David and Pearl (Brauner) M.; B.S. in Bus. Adminstrn., Washington U., 1948, LL.B., 1951; m. Betty Tofle, Dec. 3, 1949 (div. Jan., 1956); 1 dau., Barbara Sue; m. 2d, Alice Ann Zink, Jan. 31, 1959 (div. Aug. 1962); children—Emilie Jill, Mary Jane; m. 3d, Jeanette Kennedy Ayers, June 20, 1963; step-children—Shelly and Holly Ayers. Admitted to Mo. bar, 1951; practiced in St. Louis, 1951-73; asst. circuit atty. city of St. Louis, 1952-53; mem. firm Bartley, Goffstein, Marshall & Bollato. Bd. dirs. Ferrier Harris Home for Aged. Served with USNR, 1945-46. Mem. Mo. Bar, Am., St. Louis bar assns., Am. Trial Lawyers Assn., Lawyers Assn. Home: St. Louis, Mo. Died Oct. 28, 1972.

MARSHALL, RICHARD JACQUELIN, educator, army officer; b. Markham, Va., June 16, 1895; s. Marion L. and Rebecca (Marshall) M.; student Norfolk Acad., 1907-11; B.S., Va. Mil. Inst., 1915; U.S. Army Q.M. Sch., 1926-27, Command and Gen. Staff Sch., 1932-34, Army Indsl. Coll., 1934-35, Army War Coll., 1935-36; LL.D., Washington and Lee U., 1949; m. Nell Mutter, June 15, 1921; children—Dorothy Lummus, stepdaughter, (Mrs. W. D. Strong), Harriette (Mrs. John E. Olson); m. 2d, Isabel Crum, Dec. 28, 1935. Commd. 2d lt., U.S. Army, Nov. 28, 1916, and advanced through grades to major gen., Aug. 8, 1942; served in 1st U.S. Army Div., World War I; deputy chief of staff U.S.A.F.F.E., July 29, 1941; deputy chief of staff, S.W.P.A., 1942; comdg. gen., U.S. Army Services of Supply S.W.P.A., 1942; chief of staff U.S.A.F.F.E., 1944; deputy chief of staff U.S. Army Forces in the Pacific, June 1945, chief of staff, 1945, ret. 1946. Supt. Va. Mil. Inst. 1946-1952. Decorated: D.S.C., D.S.M., with 2 oak leaf clusters, Silver Star, Legion of Merit, Distinguished Service Star of the Philippines with oak leaf cluster, Officer of Legion of Honor (France), Grand Officer of the Orange Nassau with Crossed Swords (Netherlands). Mem. ODK, Kappa Alpha. Home: Fort Lauderdale, Fla. Died Aug. 3, 1973; buried Arlington Nat. Cemetery.

MARSHALL, WILLIAM WORTON, farmer, govt. ofcl.; b. nr. Marshall, Mo., Sept. 24, 1911; s. William Benjamin and Mary (Keys) M.; student pub. schs.; m. Evelyn Maxine Roach, Dec. 28, 1938; children—Judith Ann (Mrs. John Ray Streu), William James. Gen. livestock and grain farmer, 1929-38; Mo. Wildlife Conservation agt. and U.S. dep. Dept. Interior, 1938-43; grain, livestock farmer, Nelson, Mo., 1946; chmn. of Mo. Agrl. Stabilization Conservation Service Com., 1961-68. Served with AUS, 1943-46. Mem. Saline County Farm Bur. (past pres.). Mem. Christian Ch. Democrat. Mason (Shriner). Home: Nelson, Mo. Died Nov. 30, 1971.

MARSHBURN, JOSEPH HANCOCK, educator; b. Josselyn, Ga., Jan. 11, 1890; s. M. Thomas and Alice Verina (Hendricks) M.; A.B., U. Ga., 1911, A.M., 1912; A.M., Harvard, 1919; 1 son, Joseph Hancock. Instr. English, U. Ga., 1912—14; head dept. English, Ga. Mil. Coll., 1914—16, v.p., 1916—17, pres., 1917—20; prof. English, U. Okla., 1920—75, ret. chmn. dept. Reader, Folger Shakespeare Library, 1936, Brit. Mus., 1948—49; David Ross Boyd prof. English lit., 1949. Mem. Royal Soc. Lit., Modern Lang. Assn., Am. Assn. U. Profs., Sigma Chi, Phi Beta Kappa, Democrat, Episcopalian. Mason (K.T., Shriner), Lion. Author: lfurder and Witchcraft in England, 1550—1640, 1972; (with Alan Velie) Blood and Knavery, 1973. Home: Norman, Okla. Died Apr. 13, 1975.

MARTIN, DAVID GRIER, coll. pres.; b. Covington, Ga., Nov. 11, 1910; s. Edward Gary and Susie Eugenia (Ramsey) M.; B.S., Davidson Coll., 1932; graduate student Emory U., 1932-33; LL.D., King Coll., 1959, Wake Forest Coll., 1959, Duke University, 1960, University of North Carolina, 1963, Erskine Coll., 1964; m. Louise McMichael, July 14, 1935; children—Jack McMichael, David Grier, Susan Embry (Mrs. Joseph Howell III). Alumni sec. Davidson Coll., 1933-36, treas., bus. mgr., 1951-58, pres., from 1958. Mgr. equipment dept. Campbell Coal Co., Atlanta, 1936-40; partner, sales mgr. Grey Hosiery Mills, Bristol, Va., 1940-51; dir. Piedmont Bank & Trust Co., 1957-74. Sec. planning commn., Bristol, 1946-49, mem. bd. edn., 1947-50; mem. Charlotte-Mecklenburg Planning Commn., 1951-58, chairman, 1957-58; chmn. of Southeastern Regional Rhodes Scholarship Com., 1960-74; dir. Piedmont U. Center, 1962-74, So. U. Conference, 1963-74; treas., dir. Assn. Am. Colls., 1966-74; v. chmn. N.C. Legislature Com. on University of N.C. Trustees. Board of trustees Mary Baldwin Coll., 1957-74. Served as lt. (s.g.) USNR, 1944-45. Mem. Charlotte C. of C. (dir., chmn. govt. study com.), Phi Beta Kappa, Scabbard and Blade, Sigma Alpha Epsilon, Omicron Delta Kappa, Sigma Upsilon. Presbyn. (elder). Clubs: Charlotte (N.C.) Country; Lions (pres.) (Bristol). Address: Davidson, N.C. Died Apr. 5, 1974.

MARTIN, ELSIE STARK (MRS. WILLIAM H. MARTIN), food cons.; b. Glen Ullin, N.D.; d. George A. and Anna Jane (Knox) Stark; B.S., N.D. State U., 1915; m. William H. Martin, Dec. 17, 1959 (dec. Jan. 1962). Supr. home econs. So. Minn. Schs., Minn., 1915-17; state relations service U.S. Dept. Agr., Fargo, N.D., Mpls., 1917-26; dir. home econs. R.B. Davis Co., Hoboken, N.J. 1926-36; nat. hdqrs. dir. consumer edn., pub. relations Best Foods, Inc., N.Y.C., 1936-58; food cons., New Brunswick, N.J., from 1958; dir., sec. Womens Mdse. Counseling Service, Inc., N.Y.C., 1966. Div. chmn. met. area, A.R.C., 1940-48; nat. judge to select mother of yr. Am. Mothers Com., Inc., 1970, 71, to select doctor of yr. Med. Coll. Pa., 1973; charter mem. nat. bd. womens Med. Coll. Pa., Phila., from 1952, mem. exec. council 1966-69. Bd. dirs. N.D. State U. Found. Recipient Alumni award N.D. State U., 1965; award 23 Pan Am. countries for good will and peace work, 1939. Mem. Med. Exhibitors Assn. (dir. 1936-57), Am., N.J., N.Y. State dietetic assns., Am. Assn. U. Women, Am., N.J. (pres. 1930-32) home econs. assns., N.Y.C. Fedn. Womens Clubs (dir. from 1938), Advt. Women of N.Y. (life; pres. 1940-41, mem. pres.'s cabinet from 1967), Nat., N.Y. State, N.Y.C. (pres. 1950-52) leagues bus. and profl. women, Womans Press Club (life), Internat. Platform Assn. Mem. Order Eastern Star. Clubs: Womans University (life mem.) (Chgo.); Zonta (pres. 1940-42) (N.Y.C.). Contbr. articles profl. jours. Home: New Brunswick, N.J. Deceased.

MARTIN, FRANK, composer, Pianist, condr.; b. Geneva, Switzerland, 1890. Former prof. rhymics Jacques Dalcroze, Geneva; former prof. composition, Cologne, Germany. Compositions include 5 oratorios, operas based on Shakespeare's Tempest and Moliére's Monsieur de Pourceaugnac, 6 ballades for saxophone, trombone, flute, piano, violincello, viola; Le Vin Herbeé; Der Cornet (Bilke); 6 Monologue aus Jedermann (Hofmannsthal); Concerto for 7 winds, strings and percussion; Petite Symphonie Concertante for harp, harpsichord, piano and strings; 8 preludes for piano; etudes for string orch.; violin concerto; harpsichord concerto; cello concerto; 2 piano concertos; Trois danses for oboe, harp and string orch.; 4 cantatas; chamber music, a capella mass. Address: Naarden Holland. Died Nov. 21, 1974; interred Geneva, Switzerland.

MARTIN, FRED JAMES, editor; b. Butte, Mont., Jan. 30, 1904; s. Fred and Nellie J. (Peterson) M.; B.A., U. Mont., 1925; m. Dorothy Alkire, Nov. 6, 1930; children—Fred James, Patricia M. (Mrs. Fred Okimoto). Reporter, Mont. daily papers, 1923-30; campaign sec. U.S. Senator T. J. Walsh, 1930; sec. Mont. State Fair, 1931-32; reporter Great Falls Daily Leader, 1933-39; asso. editor Mont. Farmer, 1939-41; exec. dir. Mont., U.S. Savs. Bond div. Treasury Dept., 1941-43, 45-46; editor-pub. Park County News, Livingston, Mont., 1946-70; editor Livingston (Mont.) Enterprise (daily) Park County News (weekly), 1970-

72; campaign mgr., exec. sec. Gov. J. Hugo Aronson, Mont., 1952-55. Sec., Great Falls Airport Com., 1937-41; vice chmn. Great Falls Housing Authority, 1937-41; chmn., Mont. del. White House Conf. on Children, 1960; mem. U. Mont. Council of 50, 1964-65; pres. Livingston Community Hosp; del. Mont. Served to 1st lt. USMCR, 1944-45. Fellow Internat. Conf. Weekly Newspaper Editors, Carbondale, Ill. Mem. Mont. Press Assn. (past pres.), Livingston C. of C. (past pres.). Episcopalian. Rotarian. Home: Livingston, Mont. Died Oct. 7, 1972.

MARTIN, GEORGE R(EAD), business exec., lawyer; b. Norfolk, Va., Dec. 21, 1897; s. William Bruce and Elizabeth Marchant (Starke) M.; grad. Norfolk Acad., 1915; A.B., Univ. Va., 1918, LL.B., 1921; m. Katherine Mott, June 14, 1921; children—George Read, William Mott. Admitted to Va. bar, 1921, N.Y. bar, 1928; practiced in Norfolk, Va., 1921-26; asst. city atty., City of Norfolk, 1926-27; organized legal dept. Am. Cyanamid Co., 1927, head legal dept., 1928-51, counsel, 1951-63, v.p., 1945-58, exec. v.p., 1958-63, chmn. exec. com. 1961-63, director, 1928-63; counsel Donovan, Leisure, Newton & Irvine, N.Y.C. Enlisted U.S. Army, 1918; disch. rank of 2d lt., Coast (Heavy) Arty., Dec. 1918. Mem. Am., N.Y. bar assns., Assn. Bar City N.Y., Am. Arbitration Assn. (dir.), Newcomen Soc., Phi Beta Kappa, Phi Delta Phi, Delta Phi (past mem. bd. govs. and pres. nat. orgn.). Episcopalian. Clubs: Economic, University, Recess (N.Y.C.). Home. N.Y.C., N.Y. Died Mar. 2, 1975.

MARTIN, HUGH KREPPS, lawyer; b. Chattangoooga, Mar. 15, 1889; s. Wallace W. and Mary B. (Krepps) M.; student Ohio State U., 1911-14; m. Eleanor Ewing Harding, Aug. 18, 1947. Admitted to Ohio bar, 1914, practiced in Columbus, until ret., 1967; U.S. commr., 1926—27; asst. U.S. atty. So. dist. Ohio, 1927—32, U.S. atty., 1953—61; instr. law Franklin U., 1933—34; chief counsel, law dept. city Columbus, 1953; spl. counsel to atty. gen. Ohio, 1963-67. Mem. state bar exam. com., 1934—38, chmn. 1938—39; Rep. chmn. state jud. campaign, 1932, 34, 48, 50. Mem. spl. com. John Marshall Papers project Am. Bar Found., 1958—59. Served to maj U.S. Army, 1917—19. Mem. Internat. Platform Assn., Am. Law Inst., Am., Ohio (mem. jud. adminstrn. and legal reform com.), Columbus, Cinc. bar assns., Am. Legion (state adj. Ohio 1919—24, state comdr. 1925—26, chmn. nat. legislative com. 1926), Nat. Heart Com., Delta Chi. Republican. Conglist. Mason (32). Clubs: University. Home: Columbus, O. Died Apr. 21, 1974; buried Arlington Nat. Cemetery, Washington, D.C.

MARTIN, JAMES ROYAL, ret. educator; b. Mankato, Minn., Feb. 8, 1881; s. John Wesley and Mary Esther (Bullard) M.; Ph.B., Hamlin U., 1902; A.M., Harvard, 1920; m. Mabel Wood, Sept. 6, 1906 (died July 4, 1946); children—Shirley Lucile (Mrs. Robert E. Scofield), Gertrude Esther, James Roy. Tchr. geology and geography Boston U., 1918-50. Home: Cochitnat, Mass.†

MARTIN, LAWRENCE, geographer; b. Stockbridge, Mass., Feb. 14, 1880; s. William Proctor and Fannie Maria (Hare) M.; A.B., Cornell U.,1904, Ph.D., 1913; A.M., Harvard, 1906. Asst. geology, Cornell U., 1903-05; asst., instr. and asst. prof., U. of Wis., 1906-13, asso. prof. physiography and geography, 1913-19; special lecturer in geography, Johns Hopkins U., 1920-21, Georgetown U., 1922-23, Clark U., 1922-23, Foreign Service Sch. of State Dept., 1925, U. of Calif. at Los Angeles, 1928; drafting officer in Department of State, 1920-24; chief Div. of Maps, Library of Congress, 1924-46, also incumbent of the Chair of Geography, of the Library of Congress, 1933-46; on furlough in Map Div., Office of Strategic Services, Joint Chiefs of Staff, 1944-45; in Department of State, 1946; honorary consultant in geography, Library of Congress, 1946. Jr. geologist United States Geological Survey, 1903-24, field work in N.Y., 1903, Alaska, 1904, Pa., 1906, Lake Superior region, 1907; geologist, Wis. Geol. Survey, 1908-17; Alaska, 1905, in American Geog. Soc. party; leader Alaskan expns. of Nat. Geog. Soc., 1909, 10, 11, 13; mem. U.S. Geog. Bd., 1921-34, U.S. Bd. on Geog. Names from 1934, and Bd. of Surveys and Maps from 1927; geographical advisory committee, United States Office of Strategic Services, 1941-43; geographer Institute of Politics, Williamstown, Massachusetts, 1921-27, Nat. Research Council, 1917-18, 1923-28. Expert witness in Minn.-Wis. boundary case, 1917, in Wis.-Mich. boundary case, 1923-25, in Palmas Island arbitration, 1925-27, in Great Lakes level case, 1927-28, in Delaware-New Jersey boundary case, 1932, Guatemala-Honduras boundary arbitration, 1932. Wis.-Mich. boundary case, 1933, Virginia-D.C. boundary case, 1935, Arkansas-Tennessee boundary case, 1938. Chief del. of U.S. to 1st General Assembly of Pan-Am. Inst. of Geography and History, Mexico City, Sept. 29, and del. to 2d Assembly, Washington, D.C., 1935. Pvt., lt., U.S. Army, 1917; capt., maj., g.s., 1918; lt. col. mil. intelligence, O.R.C., 1921-36. On duty Gen. H.Q., A.E.F., and Am. Commn. to Negotiate Peace, 1918-19. Decorated Officer Order of Crown of Italy, 1922; Malte-Brun prize and gold medal Geog. Soc. of Paris, 1918. Mem. Commn. Internat. des Glaciers; corr. mem. Geog. Soc. of Hungary, Royal Geog. Soc. Vienna, Appalachian Mountain Club, Geog. Soc. of Phila., Am. Geog. Soc.; fellow Geol. Soc. America, Association American Geographers (pres. 1928-29); American Society Professional Geographers; mem. Explorers Club, Sigma Xi, Sigma Alpha Epsilon. Republican. Episcopalian. Author: Laboratory Manual of College Geography, 1913; Manual of Physical Geography Excursions, 1913; Alaskan Glacier Studies, 1914; Physical Geography of Wisconsin, 1916, 31; Earthquakes at Yakutat Bay, Alaska, in 1899; Antarctica Discovered by a Connecticut Yankee, 1940; also various reports, etc. Editor: Tarr's College Physiography, 1914; George Washington Atlas, 1932, 33; Catalogue of Hispanic-American Maps., 1935; U.S. Constitution Sequicentennial Maps, 1937-39; asso. editor Bulletin of American Geographical Soc., 1910-15, Jour. of Georgraphy, 1909-16; councillor Econ. Geography, 1925-45; contbg. editor Geog. Rev. from 1922. Address: Washington, D.C.†

MARTIN, MILWARD WYATT, lawyer; b. Eatonton, Ga., Jan. 27, 1895; s. Thomas Wyatt and Kate Creigh (McComb) M.; A.B., U. Ga., 1915; LL.B., Harvard, 1920; m. Mary Lee Thurman, Aug. 20, 1938; foster children—Mary Lee Fletcher, Dugald Angus Fletcher. Admitted to N.Y. bar, 1921; atty. Cravath, deGersdorff, Swaine & Wood, N.Y.C., 1928-31; head law dept. Allied Chem. & Dye Corp., N.Y.C., 1931-34; sr. v.p., head law dept. Pepsi-Cola Company, 1939-74, also dir. Mem. Am. Bar Assn., Assn. Bar City N.Y., Bar Assn. State N.Y. Home: Locust Valley L.I., N.Y. Died July 28, 1974; interred Locust Valley Cemetery.

MARTIN, PAUL SIDNEY, anthropologist; b. Chgo., Nov. 20, 1899; s. Ellsworth Crandall and Adelaide (Sackett) M.; Ph.B., U. Chgo., 1923, Ph.D., 1929; foster children—Carl, Marshall, Roland, Paul. Asst. in anthropology Pub. Mus., Milw., 1925; archeologist in Yucatan, Carnegie Instn., Washington, 1926-28; curator archeology State Museum, Denver, 1928-29; with Field Mus. Natural History Chgo., 1929-74, asst. curator N. Am. Archeology, 1929-34, acting curator dept. anthropology, 1934-35, head curator, 1935-64, chmn. emeritus dept. anthropology, 1964-74; lectr. anthropology U. Chgo., 1942-74. Archeol. field work, Wis., Ill., Yucatan, Colo., N.M., Ariz.; dir. Field Mus. Natural History expdns. in Am. Southwest, 1930, 31, 1933-39, 41, 46-66. Mem. Am. Anthrop. Assn., Soc. Am. Archeology, Sigma Xi. Author: Handbook of North American Archeology, 1933; Lowry Ruin in Southwestern Colorado, 1936; Archeological Work in Ackmen-Lowry Area, Southwestern Colorado, 1938; Modified Basket Maker Sites, Ackmen-Lowry Area, Southwestern Colorado, 1939; The SU SiteExcavations at a Mogollon Village, New Mexico, 1940; Anasazi Painted Pottery, 1940; Excavations at a Mogollon Village, N.M., 1943, rev. 1947; Indians Before Columbus (with G. Quimby and D. Collier), 1947; Cochise and Mogollon Sites (with J. Rinaldo and E. Antevs), 1949; Turkey Foot Ridge Site (with J. Rinaldo), 1950; Sites of the Reserve Phase (with J. Rinaldo), 1950; Tularosa and Cordova Caves (with others), 1952; Caves of the Reserve Area (with J. Rinaldo and E. Bluhm), 1954; Higgins Flat Pueblo (with others), 1956; Digging Into History, 1959; Late Mogolion Communities (with Rinaldo and Barter), 1957; Excavations in the Upper Little Colorado Drainage, Eastern Arizona (with Rinaldo), 1960; Table Rock Pueblo, Arizona (with Rinaldo), 1960; (with Rinaldo and Longacre) Mineral Creek Site and Hooper Ranch Pueblo, Eastern Arizona, 1961; also articles on exhibiting techniques and applied anthropology. Asst. editor Field Mus. Natural History Bull., 1935-64. Contbr. chpts. to books in field. Home: Tucson, Ariz. Died Jan. 20, 1974.

MARTIN, RAYMOND GEORGE, physician; b. Walla Walla, Wash., Apr. 25, 1927; s. George Thomas and Anna Mae Martin; M.D., U. Ore., 1951; m. Norma Hamilton, Sept. 29, 1956; children—Claire, Jennifer, Michael. Intern. Madigan Army Hosp., Tacoma, 1951—52; tng. U. Ore. Hosps. and Clinics, Portland, 1953—55; cons. on indsl. accidents and welfare State of Ore. Active Boy Scouts Am. Served to 1st lt., M.C., AUS, 1951—53. Diplomate Am. Bd. Anesthesiology, Mem. A.M.A., Am. Soc. Anesthesiologists, Mensa, Alpha Omega Alpha. Roman Catholic. Home: Salem, Ore. Died Oct. 10, 1970; buried Walla Walla, Wash.

MARTIN, ROBERT WILLIAM, elec. co. exec.; b. Colfax, Ia., Sept. 25, 1915; s. Lester Adelbert and Hazel (Brink) M.; student Ia. State Tchrs. Coll., Cedar Falls, 1933—35; B.S. in Commerce, State U. Ia., 1937; postgrad. Northwestern U., 1944—45; m. Evelyn Elaine Helbig; children—Robert Allan, Patricia Ann. Operating mgr. B.F. Goodrich Co., Des Moines; Ia., also Moline, Ill., 1937—40; asst. chief factory accountant Gen. Electric X—Ray Corp., Chgo., 1940—46; auditor Arthur Anderson & Co., 1946—47; controller Clark div. McGraw Electric Co., 1947—49; asst. controller parent co., 1949—56, controller, 1956, treas., 1967-73, v.p., 1971-73, exec. v.p., 1973-75, dir., 1971-75. Active Boy Scouts Am. Republican committeeman DuPage County (Ill.). C.P.A., Ill. Mem. Ill. Soc. C.P.A.'s, Financial Execs. Inst. Methodist. Mason, Elk. Home: Villa Park, Ill. Died Apr. 26, 1975.

MARTIN, WARREN FREDERIC, lawyer; b. Phila., Pa., Mar.26, 1878; s. Daniel and Henrietta M. (Weaver) M.; LL.B., U. of Pa.,1902; unmarried. Admitted to Pa. bar, 1902, and began practice at Phila.; asso. in practice with Philander C. Knox, 1917 until his death, 1921; spl. asst. to atty. gen. of U.S., Oct. 1921-June 1925. Sec. Congressional Inaugural Conn., 1921. Member bd. trustees Nat. Training Sch. for Boys. Mem. Am. and Pa. bar assns. Republican. Clubs: University, Racquet, Pickering Hunt (Phila.); Metropolitan, Chevy Chase, Burning Tree (Washington, D.C.). Address: Washington, D.C.*†

MARTIN, WILLIAM H(ENNICK), govt. ofcl.; b. Balt., Sept. 27, 1889; s. Howard Wells and Sallie E. (Hennick) M.; A.B., Johns Hopkins, 1909; S.B., Mass. Inst. Tech., 1911; D.Sc., Bethany College, 1956, Johns Hopkins, 1957; m. Margaret Grier, Oct. 1, 1914; children—William G., Isabel (wife of Dr. Robert W. Williams). With engring. dept. Am. Tel. & Tel. Co., 1911-19, dept. development and research, 1919-34; with Bell Telephone Labs., 1934-54, dir. switching research, 1938-40, dir. apparatus development, 1940-49, v.p., 1949-54; ret., 1954; dep. asst. sec. of def. for applications engring., 1954-55; dir. research and development U.S. Army, Washington, 1955. Mem. undersea warfare com. NRC, 1950-54. Recipient Presdl. Certificate of Merit, World War II. Fellow Am. Inst. E.E., Acoustical Soc. Am.; mem. Inst. Radio Engrs. (sr.), Phi Beta Kappa, Theta Xi. Clubs: Cosmos, Army and Navy (Washinton). Home: Washington, D.C. Died Apr. 1974.

MARTIN, WILLIAM OLIVER, educator; b. Columbus, O., Sept. 15, 1903; s. Oscar Cemantha D. (Dillingham) M.; A.B., Wittenberg Coll., 1925; M.A., Ohio State U., 1929; Ph.D., Harvard, 1934; m. Grace I. Dean, July 6, 1930; children—Richard, Thomas, Carol. Mgr., Redpath Chautauqua, summer 1927; from instr. to prof. philosophy and math. Ohio U., 1936-49; prof. U. R.I., Kingston, 1949-75, chmn. dept. philosophy, 1949-66. Aquinas lectr. Marquette U., 1959; lectr. many univs. Ford fellow Found. Advancement Edn., 1952-53. Nat. bd. dirs. Young Americans for Freedom. Mem. Religious Edn. Assn. U.S. and Can. (dir.), Metaphys. Soc. Am. (sec. 1952-53), Am. Philos. Assn., Philosophy Edn. Soc., Am. Cath. Philos. Assn. (mem. exec. com. 1966-69), Am. Cath. Commn. Intellectual and Cultural Affairs, U. Profs. for Acad. Order. Roman Catholic. Author: The Order and Integration of Knowledge, 1957; Metaphysics and Ideology, 1959; Realism in Education, 1969. Contbr. articles to profl. publs. Home: Narragansett, R.I., Died Aug. 3, 1975; buried St. Francis Cemetery, Peace Dale, R.I.

MARTINEAU, ROLAND GUY, physician; b. Hartford, Conn., Nov. 11, 1932; s. Herve A. and Albertine (Blaine) M.; M.D., Yale, 1958; m. Joan Marie Powell, Aug. 11, 1956; children—Marie Suzanne, David Edward. Intern, Madigan Army Hosp., Tacoma, 1958-59; resident Hosp. of St. Raphael, New Haven, 1963-66; attending radiologist Waterbury (Conn.) Hosp., 1971-74. Served to capt. M.C., USAF, 1959-63. Diplomate Am. Bd. Radiology. Mem. A.M.A. Roman Catholic. Contbr. articles to med. jours. Home: Waterbury, Conn. Died Apr. 22, 1974; buried Hartford, Conn.

MARTINON, JEAN, condr., composer; b. Lyon, France, Jan. 10, 1910; s. Pierre and Jeanne (Bidal) M.; student Lycee du Parc, Lyon, 1918-25, Nat. Music Conservatory of Lyon, 1924-25, Nat. Music Conservatory of Paris, 1926-29; 1 son by previous marriage, Francois; m. 2d, Nery Perez, 1956; children—Daniel, Jean Paul. Violin virtuoso, 1934-39, condr., 1946-76; asso. condr. London Philharmonic Orch., 1949-51; pres., artistic dir. Lamoureux Concerts, Paris, 1951-58; artistic dir. Philharmonic Orch. Israel, 1958-60; gen. music dir. City of Düsseldorf, Germany, 1960-65; artistic dir. Chgo. Symphony Orch., 1963-68; dir. Orchestre National of Paris, 1968-74, Residentie Orrest, The Hague, Netherlands, 1974-76. Decorated rosette Legion of Honor (France); Grand prize City Paris, 1943; Bela Bartok prize, Budapest, Hungary, 1948; Arts and Lit. award Ministere Beaux-Arts, 1960; Mahler medal, 1967. Lion. Club: Alpin Francais Paris-Chamonix. Composer numerous works among them Symphony No. 2 (Hymne a la Vie), 1944; Psaume 136 for soloists, chorus and large orch.; Symphony No. 3 (Irish Symphony), 1948; Due for Violin and Piano, 1953; Sonatines No. 5 and 6 for Solo Violin; Opera Hecube, 1949 (first performed Theatre de Strasbourg 1956); Violin Concerto No. 2 for Violin and Orch., Op. 51; Oratorio, Song of Songs, 1952; Concerto for Violoncello and Orch., 1964; Symphony No. 4 Altitudes, 1965; Concerto for Flute and Orch., 1971; Virgintuor, Octuor, Rhapsody for viola and piano. Address: Paris, France., Died Mar. 1, 1976.

MARTZ, VELORUS, univ. prof.; b. Urbana, Ohio, Jan. 25, 1880; s. Benjamin Franklin and Carlilia Estelle (Hall) M.; A.B., Ohio State, 1901, A.M., 1905, Ph.D., 1927; m. Amy Lee Kidwell, June 22, 1911; children—Karl, Martha (Mrs. Otto E. Grant Jr.), Robert. High sch. teacher, Mt. Sterling, Ohio, 1901-03, Eaton, 1903-04. Columbus, 1905-17, jr. high sch. prin., 1917-25; asst. prof. edn., Ind. Univ., 1925-27, asso. prof., 1927-29, prof., 1929-50; visiting prof., Ohio State Univ., summer 1931; visiting prof. edn., Higher Inst. of Edn., Cairo, Egypt, 1946-47. Mem. N.E.A., Nat. Philosophy of Edn. Soc., Philos. Soc., Hist. Soc., State Teachers Assn., Ind., Phi Beta Kappa, Phi Delta Kappa. Author: Introduction to Education (with H. L. Smith), 1941; Source Materials relating to the Development of Education in Indiana, Ind. Univ. Sch. Edn. Bull., 1945. Collaborator: Philosophical terms. Dictionary of Education, 1945. Contbr. Ency. Ednl. Research, 1941. Home: Unionville, Ind.†

MARUSZEWSKI, MARIUSZ, educator, neuropsychologist; b. Warsaw, Poland, May 17, 1932; s. Wladyslaw and Janina (Wozniak) M.; M.A., U. Moscow (USSR), 1955; Ph.D., U. Warsaw, 1960, Habilit, Faculty Psychology and Pedagogics, 1966; m. Wieslawa Wysocka, June 11, 1963; 1 dau., Agnieszka. Faculty psychology and pedagogics U. Warsaw, 1955—73, prof. neuropsychology, 1972—73, dean faculty, 1969—73; head dept. clin. psychology Warsaw Acad. Medicine, 1967—73. Mem. Polish Psychology Assn., Acad. Aphasia, World Fedn. Neurology. Author monographs. Editor: Psychologia Wychowawcza, 1958—73. Home: Warsaw, Poland. Died June 10, 1973.

MARVEL, ROBERT WILEY, coll. dean, composer; b. Webster City, Ia., Aug. 3, 1918; s. Ralph Loren and Lela (McNee) M.; B.A., U. San Antonio, 1939; M.A., Eastman Sch. Music of U. Rochester, 1940, Ph.D., 1948; m. Kay Marguerite Mason, Sept. 3, 1940; 1 son, Kenneth R. Tchr. Tex. pub. schs., 1940-42; instr. music Trinity U., 1943-44; teaching fellow Eastman Sch. Music, 1947-48; prof. music, chmn. music theory and lit. State U. N.Y. at Fredonia, 1948-59, asso. dir. dept. music, 1959-63, dir., 1963-69, dean fine and performing arts, 1969-74; composer orchestral pieces performed by Buffalo Philharmonic, Erie Philharmonic, Eastman Rochester Symphony, Montreal Symphony orchs.; cons. Nat. Assn. Schs. of Music, Nat. Music Council-Ford Found., Young Composers Project, N.Y. State Council on the Arts. Served with USAAF, 1943-46, Robert W. Marvel theatre, State U. N.Y. at Fredonia, named in his honor; Bronze bust dedicated by Lake Shore Art Assn. in his honor. Mem. Music Tchrs. Nat. Assn., Music Educators Nat. Conf. (pres. Eastern div. 1961-63), Music Library Assn., Internat. Council Fine Arts Deans, Nat. Assn. Schs. of Music. Rotarian. Club: Torch (Fredonia). Home: Fredonia N.Y. Died Apr. 17, 1974; interred Blairsburg, Ia.

MASON, ALVIN HUGHLETT, cons. scientist and engr.; b. Harborton, Va., Feb. 3, 1905; s. Alvin T. and Elizabeth (Hughlett) M.; B.S. with honor in Civil Engring., U. S.C., 1929; M.S., U. Pa., 1931, Ph.D., 1953; m. Mary R. Crow, Sept. 3, 1937. Physicist Nat. Bur. Standards, Washington, 1937-39; stress analyst, torsional vibration analyst U.S. Navy and U.S. Maritime Commn., 1939-48; physicist Office of Chief of Staff, U.S. Army, 1953-63. Registered profl. engr., Washington. Fellow A.A.A.S.; mem. Am. Geophys. Union, Va. Acad. Sci., Philos. Soc. Washington, Washington Soc. Engrs. Democrat. Methodist. Author: The Journal of Charles Mason and Jeremiah Dixon, 1969; History of Steam Navigation to the Eastern Shore of Virginia, 1973. Contbr. articles to profl. jours. Home: Arlington Va. Died Jan. 31, 1974; buried St. George's Cemetery, Accomack County, Va.

MASON, EDITH (BARNES), opera singer; b. St. Louis, Mo., Mar. 22, 1893; d. Baron Steuben and Eva (Salisbury) Barnes; ed. Miss. Wright's Sch., Bryn Mawr, Pa.; grad. H. Thane Miller Sch., Cincinnati, O., 1909; studied singing at New York, Boston, Paris and Milan; m. Giorgio Polacco, conductor, June 29, 1919; 1 dau., Grace Edith; m. 2d, Maurice A. Bernstein, Oct. 6, 1929; remarried Giorgio Polacco, May 1931; m. 4th, William Ragland, July 2, 1938. Was mem. Boston Opera Co., 1912; sang in Mexico, Havana, Venezuela, and Monte Carlo. In Paris sang at the Théâtre Lyrique, Opéra Comique and Grand Opera, 1918-21; with Met. Opera Co., New York, 1915-17; Chicago Opera Association, 1921-22, Chicago Civic Opera Co., 1923-30 and 1941-42; sang at La Scala, Milan, under Toscanini, also chosen by him to sing in Falstaff at Salzburg, 1935; sang at Teatro Reale in Rome and at Reggio Turin, and several years at Florence in May Festival. Home: San Diego Cal. Died Nov. 26, 1973.

MASON, MIRIAM EVANGELINE (MRS. MIRIAM MASON SWAIN), author; b. Goshen, Ind., Jan. 23, 1900; d. Benjamin Franklin and Laura L. (Gesaman) Mason; student Ind. Univ., 1916-17, U. Mo., 1922-23; m. M. M. Swain, Oct. 25, 1924 (div.); 1 dau., Kathleen Mason (Mrs. Allen M. Beck). Tchr. rural schs. Monroe County, 1918-19, Morgantown, Ind., 1919-20; copy writer Wm. H. Block Co., Indpls., 1920-21; editorial dept. Hall McCreary Co., Chgo., 1925-26; circulation dept. Farm Life Mag., Spencer, Ind., 1922-23, 1928-29; sold first story to Meth. Book Co., 1922 and since has pub. stories in 400 nat. mags. Author numerous books since 1935; latest publs.: Mary Mapes Dodge (biography), 1949; The Brave Pig Herman, 1949; Three Ships Came Sailing, 1949; The Gray Nosed Kitten, 1950; Homin & His Arrow, 1950; Caroline and Her Kettle, 1951; Yours With Love, Kate, 1952; Broomtail, 1952; Dan Beard, 1953; The Major and His Camels, 1953; The Sugarbush Family, 1954; Miss Posy Longlegs, 1955; Benjamin Lucky, 1956; Freddy, 1957; Katie Kittenheart 1957; Kate D. Wiggin, Little Sch. Tchr., 1957; John Smith: Man of Adventure, 1958; Small Farm for Andy, 1958; Mr. Meadowlark, 1959; Herman, the Brave Pig, 1959; Baby Jesus, 1959; The Sugarbush Family, 1959; Becky and Her Brave Cat, 1960; Trailblazers of American History, 1961; Hoppity, 1962; Miney and the Blessing, 1961; Daniel Boone, Trailblazer; Frances Willard; Girl Crusader; (with W. H. Cartwright) Trailblazers of American History, 1966; Caroline and the Seven Little Words, 1967; Sara and the Winter Gift, 1968. Republican. Lutheran. Home: Batesville Ind. Died Feb. 20, 1973.

MASSEY, LUTHER M., dentist; b. Wakefield, N.C., July 4, 1895; s. Daniel D. and Eldora Frances (Hood) M.; student Wake Forest Coll., 1913-16; D.D.S., Med. Coll. Va., 1918; grad implant dentistry Inst. Grad. Dentists, N.Y.C., 1969; m. Vivian Dawson, June 24, 1927; 1 dau., Carolyn Vivian. Practicing dentist, Zebulon, N.C., 1919-74; farmer; dir. N.C. Farm Bur. Service Co.; mem. exec. com., dir. N.C. Farm Bur. Mut. Ins. Co. Mem. N.C. Bd. Edn., 1939-44; chmn. Wake County Bd. Elections, 1939-41. Chmn. bd. trustees Meredith Coll., 1952-68, trustee, 1968-74; bd. dirs. Wake County Opportunities, Inc., State N.C. Tchrs. and State Employees Retirement System; trustee agrl. found. State Coll., N.C., chmn. research fund; trustee dental found. U.N.C. Served with Dental Co. No. I, World War I; 1st lt. Dental Res., until 1936. Mem. Am., 4th Dist. (pres.) dental assns., D.C. Dental Soc., N.C. (pres. local county unit, dir.), Four County (past pres.) heart assns., Internat. Soc. Implant Dentistry, N.C. Farm Bur. Fedn. (exec. com.), Am. Legion. Baptist (chmn. finance com.). Mason (32 deg.), Rotarian (pres.). Club: Carolina Country. Home: Zebulon, N.C. Died Sept. 19, 1974.

MASSEY, MARY ELIZABETH, educator, historian; b. Morrilton, Ark., Dec. 25, 1915; d. Charles L. and Mary (McClung) Massey; B.A., Hendrix Coll., 1937; M.A., U. N.C., 1940, Ph.D., 1947. Supr. social studies Hendrix Coll. Practice Sch., 1940-42; prof. history Flora Macdonald Coll., 1942-44; teaching fellow U. N.C., 1944-46; asst. prof. Washington Coll., Chestertown, Md., 1947-50; mem. faculty Winthrop Coll., Rock Hill, S.C., from 1950, prof. history, from 1954, chmn. dept., 1960-64; lectr. Inst. So. Culture, Longwood Coll., 1959. So. Fellowship Research grantee, summer 1958; Henry E. Hutington Research grantee, 1963; Guggenheim fellow, 1963-64; Winthrop Coll. Distinguished Prof. award, 1965; Distinghished Alumna award Hendrix Coll., 1967. Mem. Am., So. (pres. 1972) hist. assns., Orgn. Am. Historians, Nat. Hist. Soc. (bd. advisers), Am. Assn. U. Profs., Am. Assn. U. Women, Phi Alpha Theta, Phi Gamma Mu. Democrat. Author: Ersatz in the Confederacy, 1952; Refugees in the Confederacy, 1964; Bonnet Brigades: American Women and the Civil War, 1966; also numerous articles. Home: Rock Hill, S.C. Deceased.

MASSON, HENRY JAMES, univ. dean; b. New York, N.Y., Dec. 24, 1891; s. Henry James and Sarah (Pancoast) M.; Chem.E., Columbia, 1914, A.M., 1917; M.S., New York U., 1915, Ph.D., 1918; m. Edith Virginia Hewitt, Nov. 28, 1917; children—Robert Hewitt, Helen Virginia. Instr. chem. engring., Columbia, 1917-18; asst. prof. of chem. engring., New York U., 1918-28; asso. prof. 1928-32, prof. since 1932, chmn. dept. since 1935, dir. grad. div., Coll. of Engring., since 1940, director evening div. since 1941, assistant dean, coll. of engring. since 1942. Served in Chemical Warfare Service, U.S. Army, 1917-18. Mem. Am. Chem. Soc., Am. Inst. Chem. Engrs., Phi Lambda Upsilon, Tau Beta Pi, Sigma Xi. Republican. Mason. Episcopalian. Club: Faculty (New York U.). Contbr. Jour. Industrial and Engring. Chemistry. Home: Delaware, O. Died Aug. 3, 1973

MASTER, ARTHUR MATTHEW, physician; b. N.Y.C., Dec. 1, 1895; s. Isaac and Anna (Kirschner) M.; B.S., Coll. City N.Y., 1916; M.D. Cornell U., 1921; m. Hilda Altschul, May 21, 1930 (dec., Jan. 1967); children—Arthur Matthew, Edith L., Camilla (Mrs. Isadore Rosenfeld). Intern Mt. Sinai Hosp., N.Y.C., 1921-23, admitting physician, 1923-24, vol. cardiographic dept., 1926-31, adj. physician, 1928-34, asst. cardiographer, 1931-33, cardiographer, 1933, asso. in medicine, 1934, chief Cardiographic Lab., 1934-41, chief Cardiac Clinic, 1934-41, cardiologist, 1941-57, cons. cardiologist, 1957-73; Cornell U. Med. Coll. traveling fellow at U. Coll. Hosp. Med. Sch., London, Eng., 1924-25; practice medicine, specializing in internal medicine, cardiovascular diseases, N.Y.C., 1925-73; electrocardiographer Cornell Clinic, 1927-32; instr. medicine Cornell U. Med. Coll., 1932-35; cardiologist Joint Disease Hosp., 1927-30; asst. electrocardiographer N.Y. Hosp., 1927-32; chief Cardiac Clinic, 1928, asst. physician Out Patient Dept., 1932-33; cardiac cons. U.S. VA Hosp., Bronx, 1927-28; asso. in medicine Coll. Phys. and Surg. Columbia, 1936-41, asst. clin. prof. medicine, 1941-47, asso. clin. prof., 1947-56; emeritus prof. clin. medicine Mt. Sinai Sch. Medicine, N.Y.; cardiologist Gouverneur Hosp., 1937; cons. cardiologist Rockaway Beach Hosp., 1937-60, Beth-El Hosp., Bklyn., 1946-73, Peninsula Gen. Hosp., 1960-73; spl. lectr. cardiology Georgetown U. Sch. Medicine, 1942, Seton Hall Coll. Medicine, 1957-73; cons. cardiovascular disease U.S. Marine Hosp., S.I., N.Y., 1948-73; cons. medicine Englewood (N.J.) Hosp., 1952-54, cons. cardiology, 1954-73. Served with USNRF, 1917-18; from comdr. to capt., USNR, 1942-46. Recipient Jacobi Gold medal Mt. Sinai Hosp., 1952, Townsend Harris Hall award Coll. City N.Y., 1957, medal of honor Am. Coll. Chest Physicians, 1960, citation for cardiology Am. Bill Rights Assn., 1964, N.Y. Acad. Medicine plaque, 1965, N.Y. County Med. Soc. Gold medal, 1965, Drake award Me. Heart Assn., 1967 also Modern Medicine award, 1968. Diplomate Am. Bd. Internatl. Medicine. Fellow N.Y. Acad. Medicine (past chmn.), A.C.P., Am. Pub. Health Assn., Am. Coll. Chest Physicians (pres. elect), N.Y. Cardiology Soc. (hon.); mem. Israel Med. Soc. (hon.), A.M.A., N.Y. Path. Soc., Harvey Soc., A.A.A.S., Am., N.Y. (dir.) heart assns., Soc. Exptl. Biology and Medicine, N.Y. State, N.Y. County (past v.p., pres., chmn.) med. socs., World Med. Assn., Indsl. Medicine Assn., Am. Fedn. Clin. Research, Am. Geriatrics Soc., Am. Soc. for Study Arteriosclerosis, Assn. Mil. Surgeons U.S., Fedn. Am. Scientists, Gerontol. Soc., N.Y. Acad. Scis., Am. Coll. Cardiology, Cardiological Soc. India, Phi Beta Kappa. Author: The Electrocardiogram and X-ray Configuration of the Heart, 1939; Normal Blood Pressure and Hypertension: New Definitions, 1952; Cardiac Emergencies and Heart Failure, Prevention and Treatment, 1952; Visual Aids in Cardiologic Diagnosis and Treatment, 1960; The Electrocardiogram and X-ray Configuration of the Heart, 1961; The Electrocardiogram and Chest X-ray in Disease of the Heart, 1963. Mem. editorial bd. Diseases of Chest, 1951; N.Y. State Jour. of Medicine, 1952-73; Excerpta Medica, Sect. on Diseases of Chest, 1955-73; Sect. on Cardiovascular Diseases, 1958-73; Gen. Practice, 1957; The New Physician, 1958-73. Contbr. articles profl. jours. Home: New York City, N.Y. Died Sept. 4, 1973.

MATHEWS, DAVID OSCAR, r.r. exec.; b. Blair, Neb. May 13, 1903; s. Oscar Mathew and Bertha Elizabeth (Johnson) M.; LL.B., U. Neb., 1925; m. Lucile Lawrence Gillette, June 23, 1926 (div. 1965); children—Shirley (Mrs. James Lester Kaasch), Lawrence; m. 2d, Mary Ann Hurley, December 1, 1967. Admitted Neb. bar, 1925; admitted to U.S. Supreme Court, 1945, Ill. State Supreme Court, 1949, Interstate Commerce Commn., 1938; practiced law in Omaha, 1925-41; law and enforcement sect. Interstate Commerce Commn., Omaha, 1941-42; Office Gen. Counsel, Office Def. Transportation, Washington, 1942-44; spl. asst. to Atty. Gen., Dept. Justice, 1944-49; gen. counsel C. & E.I.R.R., 1949, v.p. 1950-57, pres., 1957-67, dir., 1954, chmn. exec. com., 1963; pres., dir. Chgo. Heights Terminal Transfer R.R. Co., 1957; pres., dir. C. & W.I.R.R., 1962-65; director of the Belt Ry. Co. of Chgo., Fruit Growers Express, 1957; partner Pope, Ballard, Uriell, Kennedy, Shepard and Fowle, Chicago, Illinois, 1967. Mem. Am., Nebraska State, Chicago bar assns., Assn. Interstate Commerce Practitioners, Phi Alpha Delta, Republican. Presbyn. Mason (Shriner). Clubs: Westmoreland Country (Wilmette, Ill.); Chicago, Union League, Chicago Traffic (Chgo.); Coral Ridge Country (Ft. Lauderdale, Fla.). Home: Evanston, Ill. Died Sept. 3, 1973.

MATHEWSON, CHAMPION HERBERT, metallurgist; b. Essex, Conn., Oct. 7, 1881; s. Herbert Israel and Nettie Susan (Bulkeley) M.; Ph.B., Yale University, 1902, D.Sc. (honorary), 1951; Ph.D., University of Gottingen, 1906; married Irene Hazen Young, June 19, 1912; children—Janet Irene, Hazen Young. Instr. metallurgy, Mass. Inst. Tech., 1906-07; with Yale U., from 1907, prof. metallurgy, 1919-50, emeritus, from 1950, cons. practice, ann. lectr. Am. Institute Metals, 1928; Campbell lecturer, Am. Society for Metals, 1943. Hon. mem. Australian Institute of Mining and Metallurgy. Fellow A.A.A.S.; mem. Am. Soc. Metals, Am. Chem. Soc., Am. Inst. Mining Metall. and Petroleum Engrs. (pres. 1943; Mathewson medal for metals research 1950), Am. Soc. Engring. Edn., Inst. of Metals (London), Conn. Academy Arts and Sciences, Am. Assn. Univ. Profs., Pan-Am. Inst. of Mining Engring. and Geology, Yale Engineering Assn., Sigma Xi, Tau Beta Pi, Alpha Chi Sigma. Republican. Congregationalist. Clubs: Graduate, Faculty and Chemists (New York City). Author: First Principles of Chemical Theory, 1909. Translation: The Elements of Metallography (from Ruer), 1909. Editor: Modern Uses of Nonferrous Metals, American Inst. Mining and Metall. Engrs., 1935. Specialized in studies on constitution of alloys, crystallography and recrystallization of metals. Awarded James Douglas gold medal, Am. Inst. Mining and Metall. Engrs., 1932; gold medal Am. Soc. for Metals, 1947. Home: New Haven, Conn.†

MATHISON, JOHN KELLY, educator; b. Chgo., May 1, 1916; s. John Herbert and Sarah (Kelly) M.; B.A., Northwestern U., 1938; M.A., Princeton, 1941, Ph.D. English, 1943; m. Margaret Bushnell, June 10, 1943; children—Nell John, Eleanore Sarah. Instr. English Stanford, 1941-43, 46-48; asst. prof. U. Wyo., 1948-53, asso. prof., 1953-58, prof., 1958, head English dept., 1966-73; vis. fellow (hon.) Princeton, 1957; vis. prof. U. Hawaii, summer 1966. Precinct committeeman Democratic party, 1954-62. Served with AUS 1943-46; PTO. Mem. Modern Lang. Assn., Am. Assn. U. Profs. (pres. Wyo. chpt. 1959-60), Phi Beta Kappa (pres.) Wyo 1954-55). Democrat. Roman Catholic. Contbr. book revs., articles to anthologies, profl. jours. Home: Laramie Wyo. Died Mar. 17, 1974; interred Greenhill Cemetery, Laramie, Wyo.

MATRONE, GENNARD, biochemist, educator; b. Batavia, N.Y., Jan. 22, 1914; s. Joseph and Margaret (Sogia) M.; B.S. in Dairy Chemistry, Cornell U., 1938, M.S. in Nutrition and Biochemistry, 1944; Ph.D., N.C.

State Coll., 1950, m. Alma Cox, Nov. 14, 1939; children—Margaret, Kenneth. Chemist, U.S. Plant, Soil and Nutrition Lab., 1941—52; mem. faculty N. C. State U., Raleigh, 1952—75, Reynolds distinguished prof. animal sci., 1962—75, William Neal Reynolds prof. biochemistry, 1962—75, acting chmn. biochemistry faculty; 1963—65, acting head biochemistry dept., 1965—67, head biochemsirty dept., 1967—75; cons. dept. animal industry P.R. Agrl. Expt. Sta., 1955; agrl cons. in Peru, 1962. Mem. nutrition study sect. NIH, 1966-70; mem. subcom. trace elements Nat. Acad. Sci., 1966-69. Recipient Nutrition Research award Am. Feed Mfrs. Assn., 1964; Moorman Travel Research award, 1966. Fellow A.A.A.S.; mem. Am. Soc. Biol. Chemists, N.Y. Acad. Scis., Am. Inst. Nutrition, Biometrics Soc., Am. Chem. Soc., Soc. Exptl. Biology and Medicine, Am. Soc. Biol. Chemists, Sigma Xi, Gamma Sigma Delta (research award merit N.C. State Chpt. 1963), Phi Kappa Phi. Editorial bd. Jour. Nutrition, 1964—68. Contbr. numerous articles to profl. publs. Research metabolism micronutrients, rumen metabolism, , metabolism neo-natal pig, metabolism of volatile fatty acids, metalloenzymes. Home: Raleigh N.C. Died Apr. 2, 1975.

MATSCH, FRANZ, Austrian diplomat; b. Vienna, Austria, Jan. 24, 1899; s. Franz and Therese (Kattus) M.; LL.D., U. Vienna, 1923; m. Lillian Hendrick, Dec. 5, 1928 (div.); 1 son, Thilman Matsch; m. 2d, Betti Richard, 1953. Ofcl. of Austrian Dept. for Fgn. Affairs, 1921, charge of League of Nations questions; mem. Austrian delegations to Assembly League of Nations, 1923-37; sec. expert, 1927, substitute del., 1936; mem. Austrian delegation Disarmament Conf. Geneva, 1932-35, Internat. Conf. on Obscene Publs., 1923; del. Internat. Refugees Conf., 1933, UN Trade Conf., Havana, 1947-48; sec. legation, 1927-38, counselor, 1945-47; consul general in N.Y., 1947-53; chmn. polit. com. 14th Gen. Assembly UN, 1959; Austrian liaison officer UN, 1947-73; mem. Austrian Com. for Internat. Intellectual Cooperation, 1924-38, Austrian com. UNESCO, 1946-48; E.E. and M.P. in charge internat. orgns. sect. Dept. for Fgn. Affairs, 1953-56; ambassador to UN, 1956-64, chmn. UN outer space com., 1961-65; mem. Austrian delegation to UN Gen. Assembly, 1956-71. Mem. bd. Austrian League for UN (Vienna). Roman Catholic. Home: Vienna, Austria. Died July 25, 1973.

MATTHEW, ROBERT HOGG, architect; b. Dec. 12, 1906; M.A., Melville Coll., Edinburgh; LL.D. (hon.), Sheffield U. Chief architect, planning officer Dept. Health for Scotland, 1945; architect London County Council, 1946-53; prof. architecture U. Edinburgh, 1953-68, chmn. Sch. Built Environment, 1968-75. Decorated comdr. Order Brit. Empire; created knight. Fellow Royal Soc. Edinburgh; mem. Internat. Union Architects (pres. 1961-65), Royal Inst. Brit. Architects (pres. 1962-64; Royal gold medal architecture 1970), Commonwealth Assn. Architects (pres. 1965-68), Town Planning Inst., Royal Fine Art Commn. for Scotland, Scottish Civic Trust; asso. Royal Scottish Acad. Home: East Lothian, Scotland., Died June 21, 1975.

MATTHEW, ROBERT JOHN, educator; b. Easton, N.H., Feb. 14, 1907; s. William and Stella Ada (Little) M.; A.B., U. N.H., 1928; Diplome d'Etudes Francaises, Institut Franco-American de Vichy, France, 1931; student U. Geneva, 1931-32; Doctorat d'Universite, Mention Lettres, 1932, U. de Clermont, Clermont-Ferrand, France, 1932; m. Helen Margaret Gunder, July 29, 1939; 1 son, John Little. Master in French and Spanish schools in Va., N.H., N.Y.C., 1928-34; instr. Ecole Internationale, Gland, Switzerland, 1931; Hunter Coll., N.Y.C., 1936; lectr. Am. U., Washington, 1944-45; instr. Coll. City of N.Y., evening sessions, 1933-36, mem. grad. adv. com. and supr. fgn. lang. tchr. tng., 1936-38, intstr. Romance langs., 1938-42, 1946-47, asst. prof., 1947-57; prof. French, Sweet Briar (Va.) Coll., 1957 , dir. Jr. Year in France, 1952-53, gen. dir., 1957-72. Pres., v.p. Books Across the Sea, 1941-43; mem. regional com. interchange of tchrs. under Fulbright Exchange Program. Served as 2d lt., Army Specialist Corps, U.S. Army, 1942; 1st lt., G2, Gen. Staff, Washington, 1942-44; capt. air intelligence div. AAF, Washington, 1944-45; chief counter-intelligence div. Hdqrs. Continental Air Forces, Bolling Field, 1945-46. Decorated Chevalier Palmes Academiques; Chevalier Ordre National du Merite; gold medal City of Paris, 1972. Member Mutual Aid Soc. of City Coll., English-Speaking Union, (founder and editor 1st number News), Fedn. French Alliances in U.S. Can. (mem. bd. dirs.), Am. Assn. Tchrs. French, Am. Assn. Tchrs. Spanish, Am. Assn. U. Profs., Modern Lang. Assn. Am., Fgn. Policy Assn., France-America Soc. Republican. Episcopalian. Author books, 1932 , including: Language and Area Studies in the Armed Services, 1948; Universities of the World Outside the U.S.A., 1950. Contbr. to profl. jours. and reviews. Address: Sweet Briar, Va. Died Jan. 29, 1975.

MATTHEWS, ERNEST CRAWFORD, III, lawyer; b. Nashville, Nov. 29, 1927; s. Ernest Crawford and Ozella (Young) M.; B.A., Vanderbilt U., 1949, J.D., 1952; m. Jo Ann Hammack, Dec. 23, 1950; children—Ernest Crawford IV, David M., Craig M., Charles C. Admitted to Tenn. bar, 1952, since practiced in Nashville; mem. firm Tyne, Sugg & West, 1952-56, Murray & Matthews, 1956-68, Matthews, Proctor & Gray, 1968-73. Lectr. law U. Tenn., Nashville, 1953, 54, 56-57. Mem. Nashville Estate Planning Council. Served with AUS, 1946-48. Fellow Am. Coll. Probate Counsel; mem. Am., Tenn. (gov. 1954-55, 58-59, chmn. real estate, probate and trust law sect. 1967-68), Nashville (sec., treas. 1961, dir. 1969-72) bar assns., Jr. Bar Conf. (pres. 1958-59), Order of Coif, Phi Beta Kappa, Phi Delta Phi, Sigma Chi. Baptist. Mason (33 deg.). Club: Hillwood Country. Home: Nashville Tenn. Died Aug. 15, 1973.

MATTHEWS, H(ARRY) ALEXANDER organist, composer; b. Cheltenham, Eng., Mar. 26, 1879; s. John A. and Clara (Woods) M.; studied music with father; Mus. D., Muhlenberg Coll., 1920, University of Pa., 1924; m. May Gwendolyn Davis, Aug. 1906; 1 dau., Phyllis Mary. Came to United States, 1899; teacher, Philadelphia, from 1900; organist and choirmaster St. Stephen's Church, Phila. Conductor of Phila. Music Club Chorus; head theoretical dept. Clarke Conservatory of Music. Asso. Am. Guild Organist. Mem. Am. Soc. Composers. Authors and Publishers. Wrote over 200 compositions in music, including sacred and secular cantatas, anthems, duets, solos, secular songs, piano and organ pieces, etc. Print works: (cantatas) Life Everlasting; The Conversion; The Story of Christmas; The Triumph of the Cross; The City of God (in commemoration of of Quadri-Centennial Celebration of Luth. Ch. in America); (hist. pageant) The Song of America; Easter Pageant; (opera) Hades, Inc. Home: Philadelphia, Pa.†

MATTHEWS, WALTER ROBERT, clergyman; b. London, 1881; student King's Coll.; B.D., U. of London, 1907, M.A., 1912, D.D., 1922 D.Litt., 1934; hon. D.D., St. Andrews, 1932; hon. D.D., Glasgow, 1936; hon. D.D. Trinity Coll., Dublin, 1939; S.T.D., Columbia, 1938; honorary D.D., Trinity College, Toronto, also John's College, Winnipeg, 1952; D.D., Cantabrigiensis, Cambridge, 1958; m. Margaret Bryan, 1912 (dec. 1963); children—Michael (killed in action), Barbara Hebb, Bryan. Vicar Christ Church, Hornsey, 1916-18; Boyle lectr., 1920-22; Noble lectr., 1918; Wilde lectr., 1929-32; lectr. King's College, London, 1908; prof. philosophy of religion, U. of London, 1918-31; dean King's Coll., London, 1918-31; chaplain and preacher, Gray's Inn, 1920-31; chaplain to His Majesty the King, 1923-31; dean of Exeter, 1931-34; dean of St. Paul's, 1934-67. Decorated Knight Comdr. of the Royal Victorian Order, 1935, Companion of Honor, 1962; Freedom Cross of Haakon VII (hon.), 1947; Order of the White Lion. 3d Class (Czech.), 1947. Author: God in Christian Though and Experience, 1931; The Purpose of God, 1936, revised as The Hope of Immortality, 1966; Strangers and Pilgrims, 1946; St. Paul's in War Time, 1947; The Problem of Christ in the 20th Century, 1950. Editor: A History of St. Paul's Cathedral, 1958. Address: London, Eng.†

MATTHEWS, WILLIAM, educator, author; b. London, Eng., June 25, 1905; s. William and Annie Louisa (Rodwell) M.; B.A. with Honors, U. London (Eng.), 1929, M.A. with Distinction, 1931, Ph.D., 1934; D.Lett., Claremont Grad. Sch., 1967; m. Lois Emery, Dec. 18, 1948. Instr., U. Wis., 1938; asst. prof. U. Cal. at Los Angeles, 1939-41, asso. prof., 1941-48, prof., 1948-72, dir. Center for Medieval and Renaissance Studies, 1970-72; vis. prof. U. Manchester (Eng.), 1950-51, King's Coll., London, 1955; Mellon Distinguished prof. U. Pitts., 1966-67, vis. prof., 1972-75. Mem. Philo. Assn. Pacific Coast (pres. 1966), Modern Lang. Assn. Am. (council 1966), Internat. Assn. U. Profs. English, (pres. 1971-73), Modern Lang. Assn. Am. Linguistic Soc. Am., Am. Dialect Soc., Medieval Acad. Am. Author books including: Cockney, Past and Present, 1938; Diary of Dudley Ryder, 1939; Our Soldiers Speak, 1943; American Diaries, 1945; British Diaries, 1950; British Autobiographies, 1955; The Tragedy of Arthur, 1960; Later Medieval English Prose, 1963; The Ill-Framed Knight, 1966; Charles II's Escape from Worcester, 1966; Old and Middle English Literature, 1968; The Diary of Samuel Pepys, Vols. I-IX, 1970-76; American Diaries in Manuscript, 1973. Founder Pacific Coast Philology, 1966. Home: Los Angeles Cal. Died June 10, 1975.

MATTHIESSEN, RALPH H., chmn. bd. and dir. General Time Instruments Corp., Stromberg Times Corp.; dir. Motor Haulage Co. Home: Marshall, Va. Died July 23, 1975.

MATTIMORE, JOHN CLARKE, marketing exec., writer; b. Albany, N.Y., Aug. 20, 1916; s. Horatio Seymour and Grace (Stevens) M.; A.B., Dartmouth, 1938; m. Jean Meyer, Feb. 16, 1946; children—Patrick S., Brian and Karen (twins). Eastern advt. mgr. Glamour mag., 1948-52; mng. dir. Ind. Adv. Com. to Trucking Industry, 1953-55; account exec. Kenyon & Eckhardt Advt. Agy., 1955, became v.p. 1957; pres. Robert Mullen, Inc., pub. relations, 1960-62; cons., 1962-65; pres. Selling Areas Marketing, Inc. subsidiary Time Inc., 1965-72, vice chmn., 1972-75, v.p. parent co., 1971-75; exec.-in-residence U. New Haven, 1972-75. Exec. com. bd. dirs. Muscular Dystrophy Assns. Am. Nat. dir. Orgn. Citizens for Eisenhower 1952. Served as lt., USNR, 1942-46. Mem. Authors Guild. Mem. Dutch Reformed Ch. Clubs: Stamford Yacht (dir.); Hempshere, Dartmouth (N.Y.C.). Author: (with Jean Mattimore) Cooking by the Clock, 1948. Home: Stamford, Conn. Died Nov. 16, 1975.

MATTISON, DONALD MAGNUS, artist; b. Beloit, Wis., Apr. 24, 1905; s. Magnus Wilhelm and Florence May (Knickerbocker) M.; B.F.A., Yale U. Sch. of Fine Arts, 1928; fellow Am. Acad. in Rome, 1928—31; m. Catherine Lucille Morrison, July 17, 1928 (dec. May 31, 1961); 1 dau., Georgia (Mrs. Weld Coxe); m. 2d, Mary Gebhardt Wheeler, July 7, 1962. Engaged as instr. Columbia U. Sch. of Architecture and New York Sch. of Design, 1931—32, New York U., 1931—33; dir. John Herron Art Sch., (div. of Ind. U. 1967—75), Indianapolis, 1933—67, dean, 1967-75, dean emeritus, 1975. Works: "Ignis Fatuus" (Oil painting), Yale U. Art Gallery; "American Nativity," Alexander Kirk Collection, Rome; mural decoration, Albert H. Frank Company, Cities Service Building, New York; mural Standard Life Insurance Bldg., Indianapolis; "Riverboat" (oil), "Good—by" (lithograph), Herron Art Inst., also in Booth Tarkington collection; also portraits bus. execs. and ladies. Awarded fellowship in painting Lake Forest (Ill.) Found. for Architecture and Landscape Architecture; Indianapolis Art Assn. prize on oil painting, "Negro Baptism," 1935. Prizes: Indianapolis Art Assn., Dirs.' Prize, 1945, Indianapolis Art Assn. Holcomb Prize, 1946; also recipient of Prix de Rome. Fellow of the Am. Acad. Rome; mem. Midwestern Coll. Art Conf. (past dir.), Citizens' Com. for the Army and Navy, Mural Painters of Am., North Carolina Profl. Artists, College Art Assn. of America, Nat. Assn. Schs. Design (past dir.), Indiana Artists Club. Clubs: Woodstock; Players; Dramatic; University. Home: Indianapolis, Ind. Died July 28, 1975; buried Crown Hill Cemetery, Indianapolis, Ind.

MATZ, MYRON HAROLD, physician; b. Boston, Feb. 27, 1913; s. Louis and Lena (Rosenthal) M.; M.D., U. Minn., 1939; m. Ruth G. Weinfield, July 15, 1951; children—Laura, Elliot, Andrew. Intern. Mpls. Gen. Hosp., 1939—40, Boston City Hosp., 1940—41, Carney Hosp., 1942—43; postgrad. asst., clin. fellow in dermatology Mass. Gen. Hosp., 1952-55, asst. dermatology staff, 1955-73; physician Mt. Auburn Hosp., Cambridge, lMass.; sr. dermatologist Cambridge Hosp.; dermatologist VA Hosp., Boston; asst. in dermatology Harvard, 1957—73; asso. in dermatology Mass. Inst. Tech., 1963—73. Served from 1st lt. to capt., M.C., USAAF, 1943—46. Diplomate Am. Bd. Dermatology. Mem. A.M.A., Am. Acad. Dermatology, New Eng. Dermatol. Soc., Boston Dermatology Assn. (pres. 1972—73). Jewish religion. Home: Belmont, Mass. Died Dec. 2, 1973; buried Sharon, Mass.

MAUCK, WILFRED OTTO, educator; b. Highland Park, Ill., Oct. 21, 1899; s. Joseph William and Frances (Ball) M.; A.B., Hillsdale (Mich.) Coll., 1921; M.A., Columbia U., 1926; student Univ. of London (London Sch. of Economics and Political Science), 1924—25, U. of Geneva (Switzerland), autumn 1925, Columbia U., 1926—27, Johns Hopkins, 1927—28; LL.D., Bates College, 1939, Hillsdale Coll., 1952; L.H.D., Bates College, 1939, Hillsdale Coll., 1952; L.H.D., Keuka Coll., 1949; m. Wilhelmena Robinson, September 4, 1924; children—Mary Lee, Roger. Assistant secretary New York chapter, American Institute Banking, 1922—23; assistant professor and acting head dept. history, Hillsdale Coll., 1923—24; pres. 1933—42; asso. prof. European history, Ohio U., 1928—33; adviser on student exchanges, Office of Coordinator of Inter-American Affairs, 1942—43; co-adminstr. Washington Bureau Inst. of Inst. of Internat. Edn. 1943—44; ednl. program officer, Inter-Am. Ednl. Fdn. 1944, v.p. 1945—47; v.p. Inst. Inter-Am. Affairs, dir. ednl. div. 1947—53, chief East Coast Div., 1953—56; pres. Bur. U. Travel, 1956—58; chief edn. officer Near East-South Asia, AID, 1959—75, former bd. mem. Iran Found. Elector Hall of Fame. Mem. Delta Tau Delta (nat. supr. scholarship 1931—33, 41—42). Home Washington DC Died Apr. 22, 1975.

MAUK, CHARLOTTE E., tech. editor, conservationist; b. San Francisco, Mar. 4, 1907; d. Edwin Henry and Charlotte Anna (Jones) Mauk; B.S., Coll. Chemistry U. Cal. at Berkeley, 1928. Chem. technician, U. Cal. at Davis, 1928-32, personnel technician U. Cal. at Berkeley, 1947-48; tchr. chemistry and physics high schs. Cal., 1933-42; chemist Cal. Research Corp., Richmond, 1942-44; nat. asst. sec. conservation Sierra Club, 1948-53; tech. editor Lawrence Berkeley Lab., Berkeley, Cal., 1953-71. Bd. dirs. Sierra Club Found., 1968-73. Mem. Wilderness Soc., Nature Conservancy, Nat. Audubon Soc., Sierra Club (hon. v.p. 1968, bd. dirs. 1943-68), Point Reyes Bird Obs., Save the Redwoods League. Editor: Yosemite and the Sierra Nevada (Ansel Adams, John Muir), 1948. Contbr. articles to conservation bulls. Address: Berkeley, Cal. Died Aug. 11, 1973; cremated.

MAULE, TALLIE BURTON, architect; b. Sand Springs, Okla., July 7, 1917; s. Ernest Tallie and Julia Wilhemenia (Langenkamp) M.; B.Arch., Okla. State U., 1940; M.F.A. (Lowell Palmer fellow), Princeton, 1948; diploma, (fellow Am. Acad. in Rome), Universitair Italiana, 1951; m. Vivienne Daubek, Dec. 25, 1942; m. 2d, Sara Heath, June 27, 1951. Asso., Skidmore, Owings & Merrill, N.Y.C., Chgo., Oak Ridge, Tokyo, San Francisco, 1947-55; pres. Tallie Maule Architect/Planner, San Francisco, 1955-74, chief architect San Francisco Bay Area Rapid Transit, 1966-73. Cons. architect Met. Atlanta Rapid Transit, Sao Paolo (Brazil) Metro. Mem. Planning Commn., Oak Ridge, 1950. Served with USNR, 1943-46. Fulbright grantee to Europe, 1951. Fellow Am. Acad. in Rome; mem. A.I.A., Greater San Francisco C. of C. Important works include Palo Alto Office Center, Embarcadero Transit Terminal, West Portal Transit Sta. Home: San Francisco, Cal. Died June 17, 1974.

MAURER, ROBERT ADAM, prof. law; b. Glenbeulah, Wis., Oct. 12, 1879; s. Albert G. and Mary (Sinz) M.; B.L., U. of Wis., 1901; LL.B., Georgetown U., 1906, LL.M., 1910; LL.D. (honorary), Georgetown University, 1943; married Mary Roberta Howard, June 24, 1909; children—Robert A., John H., Richard, Howard. Instr. in history, high schs., Madison and Kenosha, Wis.; head dept. of history, high schs., Washington, 1907-17; acting prin. and prin. Central High Sch., Washington, 1918-23; instr. and asst. prof. law, Georgetown U., 1913-23, prof., from 1923. Exec. sec. to food administrator of D.C., 1917-18; mem. of the D.C. Bd. of Edn., 1935-48; chmn. U.S. Regional Loyalty Bd. 4th region. Mem. of Am. Bar Assn., Phi Kappa Sigma, Delta Chi. Sec. com. of D.C. Bar Assn. on survey of the adminstration of justice in the District, and mem. Court Commn. for study of court organization and procedure, 1930, 31, Club: Cosmos, Co-author: The Constitution of the United States (Manrer and Jones), 1925; Cases on Constitutional Law; Cases and Materials on Adminstrative Law. Contbr. articles in law jours. Address: Washington, D.C.†

MAURILLO, DOMINICK FRANCIS, physician, univ. regent; b. N.Y.C., May 28, 1898; s. Alexander and Gabriella (Licardi) M.; A.B., Cornell U., 1920; M.D., U. Md., 1924; M.D. (hon.), U. Bologna (Italy), 1959; LL.D., St. Francis Coll., 1949, L.I.U., 1958; D.Sc., St. John's U., 1958; m. Anna Hefferman, children-Alexander, Lois Ann. Resident in urology Bayonne (N.J.) Hosp., 1932; pvt. practice genito-urinary surgery, Bklyn., 1932—; Postgrad. Hosp., 1929-33; mem. staff Beekman Hosp., 1934, French Hosp., 1936-45; dir. surgery St. Mary's Hosp., 1956-57, attending genito-urinary surgeon, 1942-75. Mem. bd. regents U. State N.Y., 1948-62, chmn. com. to evaluate med. edn. in Italy and Switzerland, 1950, France, 1951, Ireland, 1959, Belgium, 1959. Trustee Prudential Savs. Bank, Bklyn. Served with U.S. Army, 1918. Decorated Order Star Solidarity (Italy); officer Crown Belgium. Diplomate Am. Bd. Urology. Fellow A.C.S., N.Y. Acad. Medicine; mem. A.M.A., Kings County Med. Soc., Am., N.Y. urol. assns., Bklyn. Urol. Sco. Phi Chi. Club: Montauk (Bklyn.). Address: Brooklyn, N.Y., Died June 30, 1975; interred St. Johns Cemetery, Queens, N.Y.

MAUZÉ, JEAN, banker; b. St. Louis, Jan. 15, 1903; s. J. Layton and Eleanor (Harman) M.; A.B., Davidson College, 1923; married Abby R. Pardee, Apr. 23, 1953. With U.S. Trust Co., N.Y.C., 1941-73, sr. v.p., 1961-73; mem. investment adv. group Comml. Union Ins. Co. N.Y.; dir. Freeport Sulphur Company, Bklyn. Savs. Bank. Gov., v.p. finance, chairman finance committee New York Hospital. Served with USNR, World War II; comdr. Res. Clubs: University, River, Recess (N.Y.C.); Piping Rock. Home: New York City, N.Y. Died Nov. 1973.

MAXWELL, ARTHUR STANLEY, author, editor; b. London, Eng., Jan. 14, 1896; s. George Thomas and Alice Maud (Crowder) M.; student Stanborough Coll. (Eng.), 1912—15; Litt.D., Andrews U., Mich., 1970; m. Rachel Elizabeth Joyce, May 3, 1917; children—Maureen, Graham, Mervyn, Lawrence, Malcolm, Deirdre. Came to U.S. 1936. Editor, Present Truth, Stanborough Press, Ltd., Eng., 1920—36, gen. mgr., 1925—32; dir. Pacific Press Pub. Assn., Mountain View, Cal., also editor Signs of the Times, 1937—70. Author: Christ's Glorious Return, 1924; Protestantism Imperilled, 1926; Great Issues of the Age, 1927; Our Wonderful Bible, 1935; Discovering London, 1935; History's Crowded Climax, 1940; War of the Worlds, 1941; So Little Time, 1946; God and the Future, 1952; The Coming King, 1953; Your Bible and You, 1959; You and Your Future, 1959; Courage for the Crisis, 1961; Time Running Out, 1963; Under The Southern Cross, 1966; Good News for You, 1967; This is the End, 1967; Man the World Needs Most, 1970, 15 others; (juveniles) The Bible Story, 10 vols., 1953-57; Uncle Arthur's Bedtime Stories, 48 vols., 1924-71; The Children's Hour, 5 vols., 1945-49, 16 others. Home: Los Altos Hills, Cal. Died Nov. 13, 1970; interred Palo Alto, Cal.

MAXWELL, WILLIAM DONALD, journalist; b. Greencastle, Ind., Aug. 12, 1900; s. Harry Lincoln and Grace (Beck) M.; student De Pauw U., 1917-20. D.Litt (hon.), 1952; U. Chgo., 1920; m. Marjorie Thomas, Dec. 20, 1920; 1 son, David Beck. Reporter Chicago Tribune, 1920-22, copy reader, 1922-25, sports editor, 1925-30, news editor, 1930-38, city editor and assistant managing editor, 1939-51, managing editor and editor, 1955-69; 1st vice president Tribune Company, 1961-75; director Asso. Press, Ontario Paper Co., Ltd. Trustee McCormick-Patterson Trust; mem. bd. trustees Robert R. McCormick Charitable Trust, Northwestern U. Mem. Phi Kappa Psi, Sigma Delta Chi. Republican. Methodist. Clubs: Commercial, Mid-Am., Tavern, Skokie Country, Chicago, Lake Zurich. Home: Evanston, Ill. Died May 22, 1975.

MAY, JACQUES MEYER, physician, writer; b. Paris, France, Jan. 27, 1896; s. Paul M. and Yvonne D. (Gardoso) M.; M.D., U. Paris, 1925; professorship Med. Coll. (Agregation), 1936; m. Marie Anne Legrand, Jan. 26, 1946; children—Martine (Mrs. Messert) Michael, Francis, Bella (by previous marriage), James P., Xavier P. Came to U.S., 1947, naturalized, 1954. Prof. medicine Hanoi (Vietnam) Med. Sch., 1936-40; head dept. med. geography Am. Geog. Soc., 1948-60; lectr. Harvard Sch. Pub. Health, 1953-59, N.Y. U., 1952-61, Columbia Sch. Pub. Health, 1955-59; chief med. edn. program USOM/Saigon, 1960-64; acting chief pub. health adviser Latin Am. AID, 1964-65; cons. Office Tech. Coop. and Research Health Service; chief internat. unit nutrition program USPHS, Bethesda, Md., 1966-70: cons. AID, 1971-75. Author: An Atlas of Disease, 1950-55; The Ecology of Human Disease, 2 vols., 1958-59; A Physician Looks at Psychiatry, 1958; The Ecology of Malnutrition, 12 vols., 1960-73; numerous others. Home: Chatham, Mass. Died June 30, 1975.

MAY, MORTIMER, hosiery mfr.; b. Laconia, N.H., Dec. 20, 1892; s. Jacob and Rebecca (Weingarten) M.; B.S., Columbia, 1914; m. Gertrude Bloch, Dec. 26, 1917; children—Reba (Mrs. Robert Blum), Leon. Sec., May Hosiery Mills, Nashville, 1914, pres., 1946-58, chmn., 1958-63, hon. chmn. bd., 1963-74. Bd. govs. Devel. Corp. for Israel; mem. nat. council Am. Friends of Hebrew U.; past pres. Zionist Orgn. Am.; mem. bd. United Israel Appeal, Jewish Nat. Fund, Am. Com. for Weizman Inst., Nashville chpt. Protestants and other Ams. United; mem. Nashville Com. Fgn. Relations. Mem. Union of Am. Hebrew Congregations, World Zionist Orgn. (gen. council), World Jewish Congress (bd.), United Tenn. League (bd.), Phi Beta Kappa. Home: Miami Beach, Fla. Died May 8, 1974.

MAYER, EDGAR, physician; b. N.Y.C., Sept. 28, 1889; s. Max and Rosa (Edheimer) M.; B.A., Coll. City of N.Y., 1909; M.D., Coll. Phys. and Surg., Columbia, 1913; Trudeau Sch. of Tuberculosis, 1916. Resident physician Mt. Sinai Hosp., N.Y.C., 1914—15, Trudeau Sanatorium, Saranac Lake, N.Y., 1916—17; tuberculosis specialist Saranac Lake, from 1916; mem. faculty Trudeau Sch. of Tuberculosis since 1922, Columbia Post—Grad. Tuberculosis Sch., 1931—32; med. Dir. Will Rogers Meml. Sanatorium, Northwoods Sanatorium for Tuberculosis; med. cons. Monmouth (N.J.) Meml. Hosp., Gen. Hosp., Saranac Lake; asst. attending physician N.Y. Hosp.; trustee Nat. Jewish Hosp., Denver; chmn. Med. Adv. Bd.; dir. Farmingdale Preventorium, Otisville (N.J.) Sanatorium; clin. prof. medicine New York U. Post Grad. Center; chmn. bd. chest consultants to N.Y. State Compensation Dept.; cons. in pulmonary diseases to Govt. of India. Decorated Order of Carlos Finlay and Migule des Cespedes (Cuba), also French Legion of Honor, 1954. Member National Committee of Internat. Light Congress. Fellow Am. Coll. Chest Phys.; mem. A.M.A., Acad. of Medicine (N.Y.C.), N.Y. County Med. Soc., Harvey Soc., Nat. Tuberculosis Assn., Am. Clin. and Cimatol. Assn., Acad. of Sciences (Havana), Acad. of Medicine (Havana), Phi Delta Epsilon. Jewish religion. Author: Clinical Application of Sunlight, 1926; The Curative Value of Light, 1932, Radiation and Climatic Therapy of Chronic Pulmonary Diseases, 1944. Editor: Pulmonary Cancer, 1955, Contbr. to Jour. A.M.A., Am. Rev. of Tuberculosis, State Jour. of Medicine. Home: Tarrytown, N.Y. Died May 8, 1975.

MAYER, JOHN IGNATIUS, govt. ofcl.; b. Chgo., Sept. 8, 1907; s. Alexander and Anna (Ponic) M.; A.B., Loyola U., Chgo., 1929, J.D. cum laude, 1933; m. Annamarie McLaughlin, July 2, 1938; 1 dau., Mary Alice. Admitted to Ill. bar, 1933; pvt. practice, Chgo., 1933-43; mem. firm Ponic & Mayer, Chgo., 1936-43; with SEC, 1943-74, regional adminstr., Chgo., 1969-74; lectr. Loyola U. Law Sch., 1961-74. Bd. dirs. Chgo. Fed. Exec. Bd. Recipient medal of excellence Loyola U. Law Alumni Assn., 1966, Distinguished Service citation, 1968. Mem. Fed. Bar. Assn. (exec. council Chgo. chpt.). Blue Key. K.C. Home: Forest Park, Ill. Died Nov. 15, 1974.

MAYER, JOSEPH, educator, economist; b. San Antonio, Feb. 17, 1887; s. Henry and Aurelia (Huyer) M.; student engring. U. Tex., 1907-10; B.A. with highest honors, Southwestern U., 1911, LL.D., 1929; Jackson scholar, Perkins fellow Harvard, 1911-13, M.A., 1914; Ph.D., Columbia, 1922; m. Helen J. O'Neill. Engaged in machine bldg. and other industries, 1899-1908; asst. in math. and physics U. Tex., 1908-10; instr. math. and physics Southwestern U., 1910-11; instr. social ethics, Meeting House Hill, Dorchester, Mass., 1912-13; instr. math. U. Tex. 1913-14; instr. mechanics Elm Vocational Sch., Buffalo, 1914-16; instr. bus. Eng. and history, asst. comdt. Baylor U. and Hardin Mil. Sch., Dallas, 1918-19; lectr. bus. orgn. and mgmt. Bus. Tng. Corp., N.Y.C., 1919-20; prof. econs., sociology, and head dept. Tufts Coll. and Grad. Sch., 1924-31; exec. sec., treas. Am. Assn. U. Profs., 1929-37; cons. in sociology Library of Congress, 1930-37; prof., head dept. econs. Miami U., 1948-58; prof. math., head dept. Western Coll., 1958-61; vis. prof. sci. and tech. So. Ill. U., 1961-62; cons. price stablzn. and nat. income, 1972. Lectr., World Peace Found., Council Nat. Def., League to Enforce Peace; ednl. dir. Niagara Falls Motion Picture Co., 1914-16; sec. investigation of prostitution in Am., Bur. Social Hygiene, Inc., Rockefeller Found., N.Y.C., 1916-18; dir. W.C.C.S. activities, 1918; dir. indsl. econ. research Nat. Indsl. Conf. Bd., N.Y.C., 1920-23; cons. engr. and economist, N.Y.C., 1919-24; head consumer income and demand unit OPA, also cons. specialist Postwar Reconstrn., Bur. Labor Statistics, 1941-42; sr. staff mem. Postwar Reconstrn. Problems Brookings Instn., Washington, 1942-48; organized The Laysers, 1969. Mem. Am. Soc. M.E., Am. Econs. Assn., Am. Sociol. Soc., Eastern Sociol. Conf., Econometric Soc., Royal Econ. Soc. (Eng.), Inter-Am. Bibilog. Assn., Am. Acad. Polit. and Social Sci., Am. Soc. Internat. Law, Am. Assn. Labor Legislation, Fgn. Policy Assn., Soc. Indsl. Engrs. (pres. N.Y. chpt. 1920-22), Am. Hist. Assn., Acad. Polit. Sci., History Sci. Soc. (rec. sec.), Southwestern Scholarship Soc. (hon.), A.A.A.S. (chmn. Sec. L., v.p. 1941), Pi Gamma Mu. Clubs: Engineers' (N.Y.C.); Cosmos (Washington). Author numerous books and articles, 1920-75, including: The Seven Seals of Science, 1927, rev. edit. 1937; Social Science Principles, 1941; The Making of a Rebel, 1973; others; articles in Social Sci., Annals Am. Acad. Polit. and Social Sci. Sch. Sci. and Math., Rev. Gen. Semantics, Harvard Rev. Econs. and Statistics. Home: Winchester, Mass., Died Apr. 20, 1975.

MAYER, ROBERT B., art collector; B.A., in English, U. Chgo.; m. Beatrice Cummings, Dec. 11, 1947; children—Robert, Ruth. With Maurice L. Rothschild Co., Chgo., pres., 1957-61 (became div. Botany Ltd. 1961), ret. 1961. Served to lt. col. AUS, 1941-45; ETO, PTO. Decorated Bronze Star; named Brand Name Retailer of Year, 1959. Mem. Phi Beta Kappa. Owner largest pvt. collection contemporary art in U.S. Home: Winnetka, Ill. Died Jan. 14, 1974.

MAYERS, LEWIS, lawyer; b. N.Y.C., June 20, 1890; s. James and Rosa (Meyrowtiz) M.; A.B., Coll City N.Y., 1910; A.M., U. Wis., 1912; Ph.D., Columbia, 1914; LL.B., George Washington U., 1920; m. May E. Rivkin, Apr. 8, 1914; 1 son, Daniel E. Examiner, N.Y.C. Civil Service Commn., 1914-17; editor Inst. for Govt. Research, Washington, 1917-20; admitted to D.C. bar, 1920, N.Y. bar, 1921; pvt. practice, N.Y.C., 1920-48, 56-72; charge instrn. in law City Coll., City U. N.Y., 1928-58, prof. law, 1936-58, vis. prof. polit. sci., 1967-68. Counsel, N.Y. State Commn. on Colored Population, 1936-38; research cons. N.Y. State Law Revision Commn., 1942-44; legal cons. N.Y.C. Mayor's Com. on Permanent Home for UN, 1946; cons. Inst. Jud. Adminstrn., 1959-64. Mem. Bus. Law Assn. (pres. 1950), New York County Lawyers Assn. (dir. 1934-36), Assn. Bar City N.Y., Inst. Jud. Adminstrn. Author: The Federal Service, 1922; Law of Business Contracts, 1932; Handbook of N.R.A., 1934; Law of Business Corporations, 1939; The American Legal System, 1955, rev., 1964; Shall We Amend the Fifth Amendment?, 1959; The Machinery of Justice, 1963. Home: New York City, N.Y., Died Dec. 31, 1975.

MAYO, CHESTER GARST, st chmn. Fed. Traffic Bd.; b. Burlington, Vt., Dec. 11, 1881; s. Adm. Henry Thomas (U.S. Navy) and Mary Caroline (Wing) M.; U. of California, 1904; m. Aida Monderson McLean, 1908; 1 dau., Amanda. Appointed to Supply Corps, U.S. Navy, July 15, 1903; promoted through grades to captain, Oct. 4, 1925. Served at navy yards, Norfolk, New York, Portsmouth, N.H., Boston, and Phila., as district supply officer, 4th Naval Dist., and as navy disbursing officer, Washington, D.C., graduate Naval War College, senior course; served at sea on U.S.S. Alliance, 2d Torpedo Flotilla, U.S.S. Annapolis, U.S.S. Wyoming, also as mem. staff of Train Squadron One., U.S. Fleet; in Philippines, Samoa and Panama Canal; selected by Gen. Charles G. Dawes, 1st dir. Bur. of the Budget, and apptd. by President Harding, Nov. 1921, as 1st coordinator for traffic, and chmn. Federal Traffic Board. Retired 1946. President Jessop Products, Inc., N.Y.; President Mayo Associates, Incorporated, New York; Mem. Gamma Eta Kappa, Pi Gamma Mu. Republican. Baptist. Mason Clubs: New York Athletic, New York Yacht; St. Botolph (Boston). Home: New Rochelle, N.Y.†

MAYS, PERCY JOSEPH, banker; b. Ashland, Neb., June 10, 1909; s. Charles Percy and Leora (Tracy) M.; student Lincoln Sch. Commerce, 1926, U. Neb., 1926-27; m. Helaine Irene Heller, Feb. 21, 1932; children—Charles E., Mary Jo. With Citizens State Bank, Lincoln, Neb., 1930-74, chmn. bd., 1968-74; pres. Lincoln Credit Men's Assn., 1953-54. Bd. dirs. YMCA, 1949-50, Lincoln Found. Mem. Am. Inst. Banking (div. pres. 1952-53), Lincoln C. of C. (pres. 1968). Methodist (pres. state conf. soc. 1962-68, pres. bd. pensions 1962-68). Mason (Shriner), Elk. Clubs; Hillcrest Country, Sertoma (pres. 1956-57). Home: Lincoln, Neb. Died Nov. 6, 1974; interred Ashland, Neb.

MAZZILLI, RANIERI, pres. of Brazil; b. Caconde, Brazil Apr. 27, 1910; s. Domingos Mazzilli Sorbinho and Angela Liuzzi Mazzilli; student Law Sch., State U. Sao Paulo, 1931—32, Law Sch., State U., Rio de Janeiro, 1938—40; student Sch. Advanced Mil. Studies, 1953; m. Sylvia Serra Pitaguary, June 27, 1933; children—Maria Lucia (Mrs. Francisco C. Filho), Luiz G.S.P., Luiz H.S.P. Admitted to Brazil bar, 1940; fed. tax collector, 1931—75; dir. Treasurer's Office, Fed. Dist., 1940—45; dir. Income Tax Dept., 1945—46; sec. gen. finances Fed. Dist. City Hall, 1946—47; dir. Fed. Savs. Bank Rio de Janeiro, 1947—48; head Finance Minister's Office, 1948—50; fed. dep. from Sao Paulo,

1951—75; pres. Chamber of Deputies, 1958—75; pres. of Brazil, 1960, 61, 62—63, 64—75; dir. Bank of Ghanabara State, 1948,. Pres. elect Inter—Parliamentary Council, 1962—65; mem. world com. World Constl. Conv., 1962—75. Founder, pres. Caconde Scholarship Assn., 1954—75; mem. Joaozinho Gomes Student Home, 1954—75. Decorated insignia cavaliere di gran croce Order Merit (Italy); insignia 1st class Order Rising Sun (Japan); gran cruz extraordinaria Order Nacional del Merito (Paraguay); comdr. Legion of Honor (France); great officer Order Mil. Merit, great officer Aero. Order Mil. Merit, gran cross Nat. Order Merit (Brazil). Mem. Lawyers Order, Inst. Fiscal Law, World Parliament Assn., Social Pioneers Assn. (mem. council Caconde). Mem. Social Democratic Party. Roman Cath. Author: Problems in Tax Collection, 1942; The Reorganization of the Federal Treasurers Office, 1940; The National Treasury During the New State, 1942. Home: Sao Paulo, Brazil. Died Apr. 21, 1975.

MCADAMS, JOSEPH EDWARD, business exec.; b. Worthington, Ind., Nov. 11, 1880; s. Joseph and Sarah Melissa (Brown) McA.; student pub. schs., Worthington; m. Lulu M. Noble, Aug. 24, 1809; 1 dau., Pauline (Mrs. Jordan). Instr. high sch. Dayton (O.) YMCA, 1905-12; organizer Gem City Machine Co., 1908, pres., 1908-22, pres., treas. successor firm, Steel Products Engring. Co., Springfield; treas., dir. City Engring. Co., pres., treas. Springfield Bldg. Investment, Inc. Mem. A.S.M.E., C. of C., Dayton Horse Show Assn. (dir.), Mason. Clubs: Dayton Engineers; Springfield Golf; Pueblo (Tucson). Home: New Carlisle, O.†

MCAFEE, ROBERT WILLIAM, banker; b. Collinsville, Ill., Feb. 12, 1881; s. Robert William and Grace L. (Deane) McA.; A.B., Wabash Coll., 1903; m. Lula Hasam, June 15, 1912; 1 son, Robert William. Mgr. O.T. Bassett & Co., El Paso, Tex., 1906-17; asst. cashier State Nat. Bank, 1917-21; cashier 1922-23, v.p., 1923-43, pres., 1944-48, chmn. bd. from 1949; dir. El Paso Union Passenger Depot. El Paso Electric Co., Lea County Gas Co. Mem. C. of C. Presbyn. Club: El Paso Country. Home: El Paso, Tex.†

MCALLISTER, HARRY LEE, investment banker; b. Gaffney, S.C., Aug. 6, 1899; s. Thomas Jackson and Mattie (Cooper) McA.; student Ga. Sch. Tech., 1917-18, Furman U., 1918-19; m. Rose Sease Hoke, Dec. 30, 1924; children—Barbara H. (Mrs. Norman R. Boehmer), Thomas Alexander. With R.S. Dickson & Co., Charlotte, N.C., 1921-72, successively field rep., asst. v.p., v.p., 1921-45, chmn. exec. com., 1946-72, vice chmn. bd. dirs., 1963-72, dir., 1947-72; v.p. Ruddick Corp., Charlotte; dir. Perfecting Service Co., Henry V. Dick Co. (Charlotte), Southern Webbing Mills (Greensboro, N.C.), Carolina Fleets, Inc. (Anderson, S.C.), E.B. Stone Finance Co. Mem. exec. bd. Jr. Achievement; commr. Mecklenburg County council Boy Scouts Am., 1945-48, pres., 1948-52, mem. nat. exec. bd. and council commr., nat. council rep., adviser Sea Explorer Ship 55, awarded Silver Beaver, 1948; chmn. Red Shield council Salvation Army, Charlotte, mem. exec. bd., Charlotte; mem. exec. bd. Red Shield Boys Club, 1954-56; life mem. Boys Clubs Am. Recipient Hon. Optimist plaque for youth work, 1956. Mem. Kappa Sigma. Presbyn. Clubs: Lions, Island Point, Myers Park, Commodore Yacht (chmn. bd. govs.) (Charlotte). Home: Charlotte, N.C., Died Aug. 22, 1975.

MCARTHUR, CHARLES MORTIMER, dairy products mfr.; b. Miami, Fla., Mar. 10, 1937; s. Bivian Burrage and Frances Marie (Heffernan) McA.; B.S., U. Fla., 1959; m. Nadean Ann Orr, June 12, 1959; 1 dau., La Nae. Pres., Charles McArthur Dairies, Inc., Okeechobee, Fla., 1959-73, chmn. bd., 1964-73; chmn. bd. Americable, Inc., 1969-73; dir. 1st Nat. Bank of Miami, Worth Av. Nat. Bank, Palm Beach, Fla., Okeechobee County Bank, Charter Co., Jacksonville, Fla., Nat. Life of Fla. Corp. Bd. dirs. West Palm Beach Goodwill Industries; chmn. bd. trustees Eckerd Coll., St. Petersburg, Fla., 1971-73, Charles McArthur Found., 1968-73. Mem. Com. of 100 of Miami Beach; White House fellow, spl. asst. to Postmaster Gen., 1969-70. Mem. Young Pres.'s Orgn. (v.p., dir.). Republican. Episcopalian (lay reader, vestryman). Clubs: Surf, Miami (Miami); Everglades (Palm Beach); Metropolitan (N.Y.C.). Home: Okeechobee, Fla. Died June 1973.

MCAULIFFE, ANTHONY C., army officer, chem. mfg. exec.; b. Washington, July 2, 1898; s. John Joseph and Alice Katharine (Gannon) McA.; student W. Va. U., 1916—17; B.S., U.S. Mil. Acad., 1919; grad. F.A. Sch., 1920, m. Command and Gen. Staff Sch., 1937, Army War Coll., 1940; m. Helen Willet Whitman, Aug. 23, 1920; children—Patricia Ann, John Hilary. Commd. 2d lt., F.A., U.S. Army, 1918, advanced through grades to maj. gen., 1944, comdr. 103 Inf. Div. Comdr. 101st Airborne and other troops during siege of Bastogne (Belgian), 1944; led div. which made junction with the 5th Army in Italian Alps, 1945; comdg. gen. 24th Inf. Div., Japan, 1949; chief chem. corps. Dept. of Army, 1949, chief personnel, 1951, lt. gen., 1951, dep. chief staff for operations and adminstrn., 1953; comdg. gen. 7th Army, Germany, 1953, gen. 1955; comdr. in chief U.S. Army Europe, 1955—56, ret. 1956; gen. mgr. engrng. and constrn. div. Am. Cyanamid Co., 1956—57, v.p. 1957—63, dir., 1960—63. Chmn. State Civil Def. Commn., 1959—63. Home: Chevy Chase, Md. Died Aug. 11, 1975; buried Arlington Nat. Cemetery.

MCBEAN, ATHOLL, mfr. clay products; b. San Francisco, Calif., Feb. 11, 1879; s. Peter McGill and Agnes (Perkins) M.; grad. Hotchkiss Sch., Lakeville, Conn., 1898; m. Margaret Anita Newhall, May 12, 1909; 1 son, Peter. Chmn. bd. Newhall Land & Farming Company; president White Investment Company. Consulting prof. indsl. management Graducate Sch. Bus., Stanford U., 1935-49. Founder and dir. of Stanford Research Institute. Deputy commr. A.R.C. in Switzerland during World War. Chmn. bd. Golden Gate Internat. Expn., 1939. Pres. San Francisco Chamber Commerce, 1919-21, Industrial Assn. of San Francisco, 1921-22. Republican. Episcopalian. Clubs: Pacific-Union, Bohemian. Home: San Francisco, Cal.†

MCBRIDE, WILBERT GEORGE, mining engr.; b. Inglewood, Ont., Can., Feb. 8, 1879; s. William and Mary (McComb) M.; B.Sc., McGill U., 1902; m. Ethel Douglas, of Toronto, Ont., Aug. 16, 1904; children—Wilbert (dec.), Jean Douglas (dec.), Mary Patricia. Chief engr. Copper Queen Consolidated Mining Co., Bisbee, Ariz., 1903-07; supt. Ind. & Sonora Mine, Cananea, Sonora, Mex., 1907-09; gen. supt. Great Western Copper Co., Courtland, Ariz., 1909-16; asst. gen. mgr. Phelps Dodge Corpn., Morenci (Ariz.) branch, Aug. 1916-Oct. 1917; gen. mgr. Old Dominion Co., Globe, Ariz., from 1917. Mem. Am. Inst. Mining Engrs. Clubs: Cobre Valle Country; Rocky Mountain (New York); Arizona (Phoenix). Home: Globe, Ariz.†

MCCABE, DAVID ALOYSIUS, economist; b. Providence, R.I., Mar. 8, 1883; s. James and Anna Rebecca (Bradley) M.; A.B., Harvard, 1904; Ph.D., Johns Hopkins U., 1909; m. Irene Louise Duntlin, June 21, 1929; children—Anne Lucie, Patricia Alice. Special agent of Dept. of Agr. and Tech. Instrn. for Ireland, 1904-05; instr. economics, Catholic U. of America, 1905-08; fellow in polit. economy, Johns Hopkins, 1908-09; instr. economics, Princeton U., 1909-10, asst. prof., 1910-19, prof. from 1919; Joseph Douglas Green, 1895, professor of economics, 1938-52, professor emeritus from 1952. Special agent United States Commn. on Industrial Relations, 1914, 15; chmn. Newark Regional Labor Board, 1933-34; econ. consultant to Nat. Defense Advisory Commn., 1941. Office of Price Administration, 1942; investigator and arbitrator National War Labor Board, 1942-44; consultant, War Shipping Administration, 1945-46. First lt. Signal R.C., Aviation Sect., Oct. 12, 1917; capt., A.S.A., Oct. 9-Dec. 16, 1918. Catholic. Author: The Standard Rate in American Trade Unions, 1912; (with G. E. Barnett) Mediation, Investigation and Arbitration in Industrial Disputes, 1916; National Collective Bargaining in the Pottery Industry, 1932; Labor and Social Organization (with R. A. Lester), 1948. Home: Princeton, N.J. Died Jan. 8, 1974; interred St. Paul's Cemetery, Princeton, N.J.

MCCAFFERTY, DON, profl. football coach; b. Cleve., Mar. 12, 1921; B.S. in Edn., Ohio State U., 1947; M.Ed., Kent State U., 1952; m. June McCafferty; children—Jaclyn, Lisa, Donald, Bill. Asst. coach Kent State U., 1949-59; receivers coach Balt. Colts, 1959-62, offensive backfield coach, 1963-69, head coach, 1970-72; coach Detroit Lions, 1973-74. Served with AUS, 3 years. Address: Detroit, Mich. Died July 28, 1974.

MCCAHEY, JAMES B., corp. exec.; b. Chicago, Apr. 19, 1890; student De LaSalle Inst.; m. Claire Miller, 1917; children—James B., Claire M., Anita R., Fred M., Carol Ann. Began in coal bus., 1907; trustee and executor Dunn Estate, 1910; pres. Dunn Coal Co. from 1920; pres. Morrison Hotel Corp.; dir. Nickel Plate R.R. Clubs: St. Charles (Ill.) Country; Chicago Golf, South Shore Country, Chicago Athletic, Country, Sky Line, Mid-Day (Chicago). Home: Chicago, Ill., Died Jan. 14, 1976.

MCCAIN, WILLIAM ALEXANDER, army officer; b. Carroll County, Miss., Aug. 25, 1878; s. John Sidney and Elizabeth Ann (Young) McC.; Student Univ of Miss., 1895-96; grad. U.S. Mil. Acad., 1902, Sch. of Application for Cav. and F.A., 1905, Army Industrial Coll., 1924, Army War Coll., 1928; m. Mary Louise Earle, Mar. 17, 1905; 1 dau., Elizabeth Earle. Commd. 2d lt., Cav., U.S. Army, 1902; promoted through grades to brig. gen., 1940. Awarded D.S.M. (World War I); Oak Leaf Cluster (World War II). Medal Gold by Daughters of Confederacy, Phila. chpt. Director Army Industrail College, 1930-34. Member Soc. of the Cincinnati (Va.), Phi Delta Theta, Presbyterian. Club: Army and Navy (Washington). Home: Carrollton, Miss. Address: Doylestown, Pa.†

MCCAIN, WILLIAM DWIGHT, zinc co. exec.; lawyer; b. Dayton, O., May 23, 1913; s. William Howard and Almy Florence (King) McC.; A.B., Coll Wooster, 1935; LL.B., Cornell U., 1938; m. Marien Leona Roedel, Aug. 27, 1938; children—Frederic R., Marien L., William Dwight, Nancy A. (Mrs. Peter S. Dillingham). Admitted to N.Y. bar, 1939; asso. Cadwalader, Wickersham & Taft, N.Y.C., 1938-42, Wickes, Riddell, Bloomer, Jacobi & McGuire, N.Y.C., 1942-48; with N.J. Zinc Co., 1948-74, asso. counsel, 1951-61, counsel, 1961-74, sec., 1966-74, dir. Palmer Water Co., Palmerton Pa., Alrac Corp., Stamford, Conn. Trustee Coll. of Wooster, 1965-68. Mem. Delta Theta Phi. Republican. Presbyn. (elder, clk. session 1955-58). Home: Bethlehem Pa. Died Jan. 9, 1974; interred Bethlehem, Pa.

MCCAIN, WILLIAM ROSS, insurance; b. Monticello, Ark., Oct. 15, 1878; s. William Simonton and Eliza Catherine (Chestnutt) McC.; student Washington and Lee U., 1894-95; A.B., A.M., U. of Arkansas, 1898; LL.D. (hon.), University of Arkansas, 1944; student U. of Bonn. Germany, Sorbonne, Paris, also traveling in Europe, 1898-1900; m. Dorothy May Foster, Apr. 11, 1917; children—Elisabeth, William Ross. Admitted to Ark. bar, 1903; with A. B. Banks & Co., insurance, Fordyce, Ark., 1907-09; spl. agt. Phoenix Ins. Co., 1909-11; spl. agt. with Aetna Ins. Co., 1911-19, asst. sec. at Hartford, Conn., 1919, sec., 1923; v.p. and sec. Aetna Ins. Co., World Fire and Marine Ins. Co., Century Indemnity Co., 1927, pres. same cos., 1933-50, chmn. bd. Aetna Insurance Group from 1950. pres. South-Eastern Underwriters Association, 1927-29. Eastern Underwriters Assn., 1937-39; pres. national bd. Fire Underwriters, 1949-50; pres. Standard Insurance Co. of N.Y.; dir. Reins. Corp.; dir. Hartford Nat. Bank & Trust Company, Chemical Bank and Trust Company (New York), Connecticut Mutual Life Ins. Co.; trustee Mechanics Savings Bk. Mem. Hartford Flood Commn.; member Hartford Bridge Commn. 1939-50, chmn. 1944-50. Mem. Hartford Better Business Bureau (president). Member St. Andrews Society of N.Y., Phi Beta Kappa. Democrat. Conglist. Clubs: Hartford, Hartford Golf. Home: West Hartford, Conn.†

MCCALL, JOHN OPPIE, dental educator; b. Geneva, N.Y., Oct. 4, 1879; s. John and Caroline (McCall) Oppie (took name of McCall when adopted by Charles W. McCall); B.A., Yale, 1901; D.D.S., U. of Buffalo, 1904; m. Irene M. Tingler, Dec. 6, 1911; children—Elizabeth Raymond, Patricia Willis (dec.), John Oppie, Helen Irene, Nancy. Began practice at Binghamton, N.Y., 1904; moved to Buffalo, 1909, to Specialize in periodontia and teach in U. of Buffalo; resigned from faculty, 1919; instr. in periodontia, Columbia, 1916-23; moved to New York, 1924; specialist in peridontia; prof. periodontia, New York U. Coll. Dentistry, until 1931 (chmn. curriculum com. 1925-31); dir. Murry and Leonie Guggenheim Dental Clinic, 1931-46; resumed practice as specialist in periodontia and oral diagnosis, 1947; asso. dir. New Orgn. Sch. Grad. Dentist 1951-52, dir., 1952-55; asso. public health and preventive medicine, Cornell U. Medical Coll.; cons. to dental service of N.Y. Hosp. Com. Industrial Edn. of New York City Bd. of Edn.; former chmn. Com. on Community Dental Service of N.Y. Tuberculosis and Health Assn. Diplomate of American Board of Periodontology; Founder, fellow, and ex-pres. Am. Acad. Periodontology fellow Am. Coll. of Dentists; mem. Am. Dental Assn., Internat. Assn. for Dental Research, N.Y. Acad. of Dentistry, N.Y. State Dental Soc. (1st chmn. oral hygiene com.), A.A.A.S., American Society of Dentistry for Children, American Pub. Health Assn., First Dist. Dental Soc., Am. Academy Dental Medicine (honorary member), Delta Upsilon, Xi Psi Phi. Republican. Presbyn. Club: Delta Upsilon. Co-author of Textbook of Clinical Periodontia, Clinical Dental Roentgenology; Movable-Removable Bridgework. Author: Fundamentals of Denistry in Medicine and Public Health. Home: Jericho, N.Y.†

MCCANDLESS, BOYD BOWDEN, psychologist; b. St. John, Kan., Aug. 18, 1915; s. Homer H. and Ada (Rowden) McC.; A.B., Ft. Hays Kan. State Coll., 1936; A.M., State U., Ia., 1938, Ph.D., 1941; m. Elinore Olson, June 14, 1941; children—Beth, Mark, Christine. Research asst. Ia. Child Welfare Research Sta., 1936-39, 1940-41, research prof., dir. 1951-62; research fellow Rockefeller Found. Office Radio Research, 1939-40; mental hygienist Wayne County Tng. Sch., Northville, Mich., 1941-42; selection, classification officer U.S. Maritime Service, Alameda, Cal., 1942-46; asst. and asso. prof. psychology, chmn. gen. edn. com. San Francisco State Coll., 1946-48; asso. prof. clin. psychology Ohio State U., 1948-51; Carnegie vis. prof. of psychology, U. Hawaii, 1957; on leave as prof., head psychology Inst. Edn. and Research, U. Punjab, Lahore, West Pakistan, 1960-62; prof. edn. and psychology, div. univ. sch. clinic complex, chmn. dept. spl. edn. Ind. U., 1962-66; prof., dir. developmental psychology Emory U., Atlanta, 1966-75. Mem. Nat. Council on Research and Evaluation, Project Head Start. Mem. Soc. Research Child Devel., Am. Psychol. Assn. (mem. bd. profl. affairs, past pres. divs. devel. psychology and sch. psychology), Sigma Xi. Author: Children and Adolescents, 1961; Children: Behavior and Development, 1967; Adolescents: Behavior and Development, 1970; (with Evans) Children and Adolescents: A Psychosocial View, 1973. also articles in field. Editor: Developmental Psychology, 1968-73. Home: Atlanta, Ga., Died Dec. 5, 1975.

MCCANDLESS, BYRON, naval officer; b. Sept. 5, 1881; 1 son, Bruce (comdr. U.S. Navy); entered U.S. Navy, 1901, and advanced through the grades to commodore, 1943; retired, 1940; recalled to active duty.

Decorated Navy Cross, Legion of Merit. Address: Reseda, Cal.†

MCCANDLISH, BENJAMIN VAUGHAN, naval officer; b. Petersburg, Va., June 3, 1886; s. James Gray and Lelia (Vaughan) Mc.C.; B.S., U.S. Naval Acad., 1909; grad. U.S. Naval War Coll., 1932; m. Margherita Wilson Wood, June 12, 1914. Commd. ensign, U.S. Navy, 1909, and advanced through the grades to commodore; served in Atlantic and Asiatic waters, 1909-15; in radio and communication matters, Navy Dept., Washington, D.C., 1915-17, 1926-29, 1932-34; in destroyers and battleships, 1917-21, cruisers, 1923-26, 1934-36, 1938-40; gov. and comdt., Guam, 1936-38; capt. of yard, Norfolk Navy Yard, 1940-43; comdr. Moroccah Sea Frontier Forces, 1943-45. Decorated Navy Cross, Legion of Merit, Victory, Expeditionary, European-African and Am. Defense Service medals; officer Legion of Honneur (French); Croix de Guerre (with Bronze Palm), Cross of Grand Officer with the Order of the Crown of Italy, Grand Officer of the Order Ouessan Alouite Chenfien. Clubs: Army-Navy Country (Washington). Home: Darlington County, S.C.†

MCCANNA, HENRY ANTHONY, clergyman, church assn. exec.; b. Oak Park, Ill., Nov. 2, 1923; s. Henry Anthony and Agatha Cecelia (Flaherty) McC.; A.A., Hannibal LaGrange Coll., 1948; B.A., William Jewell Coll., 1950; B.D., M.R.E., Central Bapt. Theol. Sem., 1953, D.R.E., 1958; m. Eulita Pearl Love, Jan. 31, 1942; children—Henry Anthony III, Richard Leo, Marcus Love. Ordained to ministry Baptist Ch., 1944; pastorates So. Bapt. chs., Mo., 1946-53; prof. social ethics Central Bapt. Theol. Sem., 1953-60, also dean night sch., interim pastor Immanuel, Argentine and Oakland Park Am. Bapt. chs., Kansas City, Kan., 1953-60, 1st Bapt. chs., Newark, Union City and Paterson, N.J., 1963-65; asso. for adminstr. div. Christian life and mission Nat. Council Chs. of Christ in U.S.A., 1960-70; Northeastern regional field dir. Dick Ross & Assos., Paramus, N.J., 1970-74; minister Ramapo Valley Bapt. Ch., Oakland, N.J., 1972-74 Protestant rep. to Freedom from Hunger Found., FAO; U.S. del. to UN Hunger Conf., 1967; mem. rural relationships, nat. com. Boy Scouts Am. Trustee Bd. Edn., Teaneck, N.J. Served with AUS, 1943-46. Mem. Nat. Assn. Soil Conservation Dists., Am. Soc. Christian Ethics, Rural Sociol. Soc., Am. Country Life Assn., P.T.A., Pi Kappa Delta. Home: Teaneck, N.J. Died July 10, 1974.

MCCARTEN, JOHN, writer; b. Phila., Sept. 10, 1916; s. Bernard and Anne (McArdie) McC.; ed. Shippen Sch., Phila.; m. Nancy Wheeler. Writer for New Yorker, Fortune, Time, Am. Mercury, others; now on assignment for New Yorker mag. in Ireland. Home: Ireland. Died Sept. 26, 1974.

MCCARTER, RICHARD FARRELL, dentist; b. Tulsa, Nov. 10, 1935; s. Richard L. and Marie (Weir) McC.; B.A., Westminister Coll., 1957; D.D.S., U. Mo. at Kansas City, 1961; m. Carol Ann Olmsted, Sept. 15, 1956; children—Michael Alan, Richard Mark, Kerry Lyn, John Milton. Pvt. practice dentistry, Blue Spring, Mo., 1961-73; sec. Blue Spring Dental Lab., 1969; pres. Eastern Jackson County (Mo.) Dental Health Group, 1964-65; cons. Cramer Products, Inc. Treas. bd. edn., Blue Springs, 1967-69, pres., 1971-74. Mem. Am. Equilibration Soc., Soc. Preservation Oral Health, Kansas City Dental Clinic Club (sec. 1968-70, pres. 1971-72), Am. Dental Assn., Blue Spring Jr. C. of C., Psi Omega, Phi Gamma Delta. Home: Blue Springs, Mo. Died Sept. 12, 1974.

MCCARTHY, J. A., business exec.; b. 1879. Pres., chmn. exec. com. and dir. Pacific Portland Cement Co. Home: San Francisco, Cal.*†

MCCARTY, CHARLES PASCHAL, mayor; b. Mpls., Aug. 10, 1920; s. Charles Paschal and Irene Mary (Mullin) McC.; student St. Thomas Coll., St. Paul, 1945-48; m. Margaret Rosemary Nelson, July 10, 1945; children—Charles, Michael, Margaret, Peter, Mary, Stephen, John. Realtor, St. Paul, 1947-70; justice of peace, St. Paul, 1958-60; mayor, St. Paul, 1970-72. Served with USAAF, 1940-45. Decorated Purple Heart. Mem. V.F.W. (comdr. 1947-48). Vets. Republican League (chmn. 1947-48). Mem. Democratic Farm-Labor Party. Home: St Paul, Minn. Died Feb. 9, 1974.

MCCARTY, DWIGHT GAYLORD, lawyer; b. Sioux City, Ia., Apr. 1, 1878; s. George Buchanan and Maria (Blair) McC.; Ph.B., Grinnell (Ia.) Coll., 1901, A.M., 1904; LL.B., Harvard, 1904; m. Guinevere Craven, June 16, 1904; children—Gaylord Craven, Stanton Eliot (dec.), Dwight Gordon. Admitted to Ia. bar, 1904, and practiced at Emmetsburg; admitted to practice in Federal Courts, 1907; associated with his father, 1904-28, later practiced alone; sec. Emmetsburg Hotel Co., 1917-46. Chmn. City Plan Commn, from 1914; mem. Public Library Bd., Iowa Town Planning Assn. (v.p. 1928-29); chmn. Iowa Conf. on Planning, 1936; mem. Palo Alto County Planning Council, 1936-38; mem. Judicial Advisory Commn. for Iowa 1936-44; sec. Rep. Central Com., Palo Alto County, Ia., 1910-12; alternate del. to Nat. Rep. Conv., 1916. Trustee of Emmetsburg Cemetery Association. Mem. Am. Bar Assn., Ia. State Bar Assn. 14th Judicial Dist. Bar Assn. (pres. 1934), Palo Alto County Bar Assn. (pres. 1932), State Hist. Soc. of Iowa, Phi Beta Kappa. Republican. Conglist. Mason (K.T.), chief adviser Emmetsburg Chapter, De Molay, 1923-48 (awarded De Molay Cross of Honor 1928); K.P., Woodman. Alumni distinguished service award, Grinnel Coll., 1951. Club: Commercial. Author of several books from 1910. Home: Emmetsburg, Ia.†

MCCARTY, FRANKLIN BENNETT, physician; b. Lynn, Mass., Sept. 5, 1888; s. John Francis and Joanna (Donovan) McC.; B.S., Notre Dame U., 1907; M.D., Harvard, 1911; m. Marie Evelyn Bryan, Oct. 31, 1914; children—Mary Louise, John Bryan (dec.), Franklin Bennett. Surg. house officer Boston City Hosp., 1911-13; resident in gynecology Free Hosp. for Women, Brookline, Mass., 1913-14; fellow in surgery Rush Med. Coll., Chgo., 1918; instr. anatomy, 1915-26; asst. attending surgeon Presbyn. Hosp., Chgo., 1918-19; attending surgeon St. Joseph Hosp., also chief 2d surg. service, chmn. dept. surgery, pres. staff, cons. surgeon. Dir., Boynton Wool Co. Diplomate Am. Bd. Surgery. Fellow A.C.S. (founding); mem. A.M.A., Ill., Mass., Boylston med. socs., Alpha Omega Alpha, Nu Sigma Nu. Contbr. numerous articles to med. jours. Research on time and motion in hosps. Home: Chicago, Ill. Died May 5, 1972.

MCCASKILL, JAMES LANE, educator; b. Athens, Tenn., Sept. 13, 1901; s. James and Lucy Quintina (Moss) McC.; B.S., Miss. State Coll., 1924; M.A., George Peabody Coll., 1938; grad. study U. Chicago, 1943-44; LL.D., Shurtleff Coll., 1950; m. Anna Kathryn Brannin, Sept. 1, 1925: 1 dau., Jeanne Lane (Mrs. George Stakeman). Instr. geology Miss. State Coll., 1922-24; asst. prin. Meridian (Miss.) Sr. High Sch., 1924-29, prin., 1929-37; dir. Municipal Jr. Coll., Meridian, 1937-43; prof. edn. Miss. State Coll. for Women, 1944-45; dir. pub. relations Fla. State U., 1947-48; asst. dir. legislative-fed. relations div. N.E.A., Washington, 1945-47, asso. sec. dept. higher edn., 1948-51, dir. div. legislation and fed. relations from 1951. Coordinator Nat. Conf. Moblzn. Edn. from 1950; staff survey pub. schs., Battle Creek, Mich., 1944; coordinator Miss. Study Higher Edn., 1945; ednl. cons. Fed. Civil Def. Adminstrn., 1951. Mem. N.E.A. (asst. exec. sec. for state and fed. relations 1956-67, exec. sec. legislative commn. 1951-67, director division legislation and federal relations 1951-62), Nat. Association Secs. State Teachers Association (adminstrv. dir. 1956-74), Phi Delta Kappa. Episcopalian. Author: Procedure for Determining the Curricula of a Public Junior College, 1938; One Hundred and Sixty Years of Federal Aid to Education, 1946; articles ednl. jours. Editor: Current Trends in Higher Education, 1948; College and University Bulletin, 1948-51; Washington Outlook on Education, 1953-74. Home: Bennettsville, S.C. Died Feb. 6, 1974.

MCCASLAND, S(ELBY) VERNON, educator; religion; b. Comanche, Tex., Sept. 27, 1896; s. Thomas Pike and Laura Ann (Zachary) McC.; grad. Abilene Christian Coll., 1917; A.B., Simmons Coll., 1918; Th.B., Southern Baptist Theological Seminary, 1922; A.M., U. of Chicago, 1924, Ph.D., 1926; German—Am. exchange student in univs. of Berlin, Munster and Marburg, 1926—27; m. Louise Gaston, May 26, 1928; children—George Pike, Mary Ann. Teacher Texas pub. schs., 1914—15; instr. science Abilene Christian Coll., 1918—20; instr. languages, Ranger (Tex.) High Sch., 1922—23; fellow in New Testament, U. of Chicago, 1925—26; research fellow, Disciple; Divinity House, U. of Chicago, 1927—28; prof. and chmn. dept. religion, Goucher Coll., 1928—39; annual prof. Am. Sch. of Oriental Research, Jerusalem, Palestine, 1937—38; prof. of religion U. of Va., 1939—67; vis. prof. N.T., Lexington (Ky.) Theol. Sem., 1967—68. Chmn. Interracial Com. of Md. and Del. Council of Chs. and Christian Edn., 1936—39; mem. commn. on week day religious edn., Va. Council of Churches, from 1940; dir. Univ. of Va. Y.M.C.A., from 1942, chmn. 1944—49; member Charlottesville Interracial Commn. from 1941, chmn. 1949. Del. So. Humanities Conf., from 1950. Member American Oriental Soc., American Assn. Univ. Profs., Society Bibl. Lit. and Exegesis (pres. 1953), Nat. Assn. Bibl. Instrs. (pres. 1949), Studiorum Novi Testamenti Societas, Virginia Chess Federation (pres. 1951), Campbell Instr.; pres. Alumni of Am. Schs. Oriental Research, 1941. Democrat. Mem. Disciples of Christ (elder of Christian Temple 1938—39). Clubs: Colonnade. Author: Resurrection of Jesus, 1932; The Bible in Our American Life, 1942; By The Finger of God, published 1951; The Religion of the Bible published in 1960; The Pioneer of Our Faith, A New Life of Jesus, 1964; gen. article on The Greco-Roman World in Interpreter's Bible, Vol. vii, 1951, also articles and book reviews. Co—author: Environmental Factors in Christian History, 1939; Faith of the Free, 1940; Early Christian Origins, 1961; Religions of the World, 1969. Contbr. Interpreter's Dictionary of Bible and The Bible Companion. Home: Charlottesville, Va. Died Nov. 15, 1970.

MCCASLIN, FRANK ERWIN, cement co. exec.; b. Lake Wilson, Minn., Nov. 2, 1897; s. Archibald L. and Persis Lucinda (Hickok) McC.; student Cal. Comml. Coll., San Diego, 1915-16, George Washington U., 1917, 18; m. Lillian Sneed, Dec. 30, 1925; 1 son, Frank E. With U.S. Civil Service, Dept. of Agr., Washington, 1917; with Ore. Portland Cement Co., Portland, 1923, pres., chmn. bd., 1942, dir., 1932; dir. Equitable Savs. & Loan Assn. Hon. life dir. Lewis and Clark Coll.; dir. emeritus Good Samaritan Hosp.; past pres. Portland Community Chest; past pres. President's Council of Civic Clubs, Portland. Served in U.S. Army, 1918-20; Europe. Mem. U.S. C. of C. (past dir.), Portland C. of C. (past pres.), Pacific Northwest Trade Assn. (past pres.), Asso. Gen. Contractors Am., Western Govs. Mining Adv. Council, Am. Mining Congress (Western bd. govs.; cement adv. com.), Portland Cement Assn. (bd. dirs.). Episcopalian (past vestryman). Mason (Shriner). Rotarian (dir.; v.p., past pres.). Home: Portland, Ore. Died Oct. 19, 1973.

MCCLEARY, JESSE EARL, wholesale automotive parts distbn. co. exec.; b. Spencer, Ia., Jan. 18, 1905; s. Jesse Sylvester and Adeline (Burrell) McC.; m. Beatrice E. Wilken, Mar. 3, 1936; children—William R., Patricia R. (Mrs. Roger Van Der Vorste), Thomas M., Julianne (Mrs. Eugene A. Roth). Founder, gen. mgr., pres. McCleary Auto Parts, Inc., New Ulm and Tracy, Minn., 1944-72. Mem. New Ulm Bus. Dist., Inc., New Ulm Industries, Inc. Mem. Automotive Service Industries Assn., No. Automotive Wholesalers Assn., New Ulm C. of C. Mem. United Ch. of Christ (trustee). Mason (32 deg., Shriner). Clubs: New Ulm Country, Turner (New Ulm). Home: New Ulm, Minn. Died Apr. 29, 1972.

MCCLENDON, JAMES WOOTEN, jurist; b. West Point, Ga., Nov. 1, 1873; s. James Wooton and Annie Eliza (Thompson) McC.; B.L., U. of Tex., 1895, LL.B., 1897; m. Anne Hale Watt, December 14, 1904 (deceased on April 8, 1964); children—Mary Anne McClendon, and Elizabeth (Mrs. Frank Knight). Admitted to Texas bar, 1897, and began practice at Austin. Associated justice of Tex. Supreme Court Commn. of Appeals, 1918-20, presiding justice, 1920-23; chief justice Court of Civil Appeals, 3d Supreme Jud. Dist., 1923-49. Mem. legal advisory bd. Travis County Selective Draft, 1917-19; vol. field sec. Am. Red Cross, 1918. Dir. Scottish Rite Hosp. for Crippled Children, Tex. Masonic Home and School. Mem. Am. Bar (mem. ho. of dels., chmn. sec. adminstrn.), Tex. Bar Assn., Travis County Bar Assn. (pres.), Assn. of Judges of Courts of Civil Appeal of Tex. (pres.), Nat. Conf. Judicial Councils (chmn.), Am. Assn. Legal Authors, Tex. Supreme Court Adv. Com. on Civil Procedural Rules, Tex. Judicial Council, Am. Judicature Soc. (dir.), Scottish Rite Ednl. Assn. of Tex. (president) Tex. Fine Arts Assn. (pres.), Sigma Alpha Epsilon Chapter House Assn. (sec.-treas.), S.A.R., Inst. Judicial Adminstrn., The Philosophical Soc. of Tex., Sigma Alpha Epsilon, Order of the Phoenix, Order of Coif (hon.), Pi Sigma Alpha (hon.), Tex. State Hist. Soc., Heritage Soc. Democrat. Methodist. Mason. (33°, K.T., Shriner); grand master Masons of Tex.; mem. Knights of Malta, Red Cross of Constantine, Royal Order of Scotland, Eastern Star. Dir. and mem. bd. editors, Texas Law Review. Club: Town and Gown. Home: Austin, Tex.†

MCCLINTOCK, FRANKLIN TRUNKEY, investment banker; b. Spokane, Wash., Feb. 9, 1904; s. Robert Oliver and Gertrude Gay (Trunkey) McC.; B.S., Princeton, 1925; m. Margot deBruyn Kops, Oct. 19, 1935; son, Robert Oliver II. With Brown Bros. Harriman & Co., 1928—34; with Harriman, Ripley & Co., Inc., N.Y.C., 1934—66, v.p., 1943—72, chmn. exec. com., 1963—66, also director; consultant to Drexel Harriman Ripley, Incorporated, 1966—72. Mem. exec. com. grad. Council Princeton, 1951—53, chairman annual giving, 1951—53, president class 1925, 1957—65; trustee Princeton, 1965—67. Clubs: university, Princeton (N.Y.C.). Home: Solebury, Pa. Died Nov. 6, 1972; interred Trinity Cemetery, Solebury, Pa.

MCCLOSKEY, AUGUSTUS, ex-congressman; b. San Antonio, Tex., Sept. 23, 1878; educated in public schools and at St. Mary's College; m. Kathryn Salter, June 17, 1907; children—James A., Anthony, Mary Catherine, Thomas Q. Admitted to Tex. bar; county judge, Bexar County, Tex., 1920-28; mem. 71st Congress (1929-31), 14th Tex. Dist.; engaged in practice at San Antonio. Advocate of better pub. schs. and better roads. Democrat. Home: San Antonio, Tex.†

MCCLURE, ABBOT, b. Milwaukee, Wis., Jan. 8, 1879; s. Johnson and Ellen Louisa (Abbot) M.; student Harvard U., and Sch. of Industrial Art, Phila.; unmarried. Designer of furnishings and decorations. Republican. Episcopalian. Club: Art Club of Phila. Author: House Furnishing and Decoration (with Harold Donaldson Eberlein), 1913; Practical Book of Period Furniture (with same), 1914; Practical Book of Early American Arts and Crafts (with same), 1916. In Y.M.C.A. service in Italy, 1919-20. Address: Rome, Italy†

MCCLURE, GRACE LATIMER JONES, (Mrs. Charles F. W. McClure) educator; b. Columbus, O., Apr. 3, 1879; d. George Dudley and Eva Jane (Lattimer) Jones; A.B., Bryn Mawr, 1900, A.M., 1902; studied Ohio State U., Harvard, Dartmouth; m. Charles Freeman Williams McClure, Aug. 25, 1921. Head mistress Columbus School for Girls, 1904-38, also sec. of board; organizer and ednl. adviser to bd. of Old Trail School, Akron, O., 1920-22. Originator of Head-Mistresses Assn. Middle West, sec., 1912-14, pres., 1922-24, 1930-33, and rep. on Coll. Entrance Examination Bd., 1922-24, 1929-33; orginator, pres., Ohio Bryn Mawr Club, 1916-21; pres. Columbus Br. Assn. Collegiate Alumane, 1911-14, and state rep., 1918-21; mem. com. of revision of Coll. Entrance Examination Bd., 1924-34, Mem. N.J. Soc. Colonial

Dames of America, Am. Order of the Crown, Princeton Chapter Garden Club of America. Author: The Columbus School for Girls Grammars, 1910, 4th edit., 1925; What Makes Christmas Christmas, and other plays for children; also pamphlets and articles. Home: Princeton, N.J.†

MCCLURE, HARRY BELL, chem. mfr.; b. Phila., Apr. 6, 1903; s. Joseph and Maria (Roulston) McC.; B.S. in Chem. Engring., U. Pa., 1924, M.S. in Chemistry, 1928; D.Sc. (hon.) Morris Harvey Coll., 1948; m. Olive W. Wahl, July 3, 1929; children—Miriam Cherry, James Roulston. With Carbide and Carbon Chemicals Co., 1928-63; successively research fellow Mellon Inst. of Indsl. Research, Pitts., tech. rep. Phila. area, sales work N.Y., mgr. fine-chems. div., v.p., exec. v.p., pres., 1954-56; v.p. Union Carbide Corporation, 1956-63. Member of chemical plant facilities indsl. adv. com. WPB; cons. Nat. Def. Research Com. Mem. Armed Forces Chem. Assn. (dir.), Am. Chem. Soc., Am. Assn. Textile Colorists and Chemists, Am. Inst. Chem. Engrs., Manufacturing Chem. Assn. (chmn. bd. 1958-59), Am. Inst. Chemists, Soc. Chem. Industry, A.A.A.S., Alpha Chi Sigma, Sigma Phi Epsilon. Clubs: Chemists, University, Pinnacle (N.Y.C.). Home: Port Washington, N.Y., Died Oct. 15, 1975.

MCCLURE, RUSSELL EVERETT, city mgr.; b. Wichita, Kan., Aug. 4, 1906; s. Everett Clarence and Mable (Callender) McC.; student Fairmount Coll., Wichita, 1923-25, Inst. Tng. Municipal Adminstrn., Chgo., 1942-48; m. Joyce Thomas, Jan. 10, 1929; children—Thomas Russell, Joyce Ann. City mgr., Wichita, 1941-48, 62-72, emeritus, 1972-74, Dayton, O., 1948-53, Corpus Christi, Tex., 1953-58; gen. mgr. Khuzestan Devel. Service, Ahwaz, Iran, 1958-60; exec. v.p. Greater Downtown Wichita, 1960-62. Pres., Ohio City Mgrs. Assn., 1950-52; cons. police services USAF, Dayton, 1953. Mem. Internat. City Mgrs. Assn. (pres. 1956-57), Kan. Assn. City Mgrs. (pres. 1943-46), Nat. Municipal League, Am. Soc. Pub. Adminstrn. Mason (33 deg.). Home: Wichita, Kan. Died May 10, 1974; interred Mission Chapel Mausoleum, Wichita, Kan.

MCCONNELL, HENRY, lawyer; b. Coshoeton, O., Sept. 17, 1879; s. James Francis and Josephine (Hammel) M.; Leland Stanford Jr. U., 1899-1901; LL.B., Willamette U., Salem, Ore., 1904; m. Rachael J. King, of Danville, Ind., Sept. 28, 1910. Sec. to chief justice of Ore., 1902-07; mem. law firm of Saxton & McConnell, Baker, Ore., 1907-08; practiced with William G. Hale. Portland, 1908-09; mem. firm of Gilber & McConnell, 1909-11; associated wtih Will R. King, 1911-13; asst. to U.S. atty., Ore., 1913-14; spl. examiner, Dept. of Justice, Washington, from 1914. First lt. Inf. Ore., N.G. Asst. chmn. for Pacific and intermountain states of Dem. Nat. Com., 1912. Methodist. Mem. Ore. State Bar Assn. Commd. capt., Q.M.R.C., May 21, 1917; in active service, July 19, 1917, in cantonment div., Q.M. Gen.'s office, Washington. Home: Portland, Ore.†

MCCONNELL, JOHN GRIFFITH, business exec.; b. Montreal, Que., Can., Dec. 6, 1911; s. John W. and Lily May (Griffith) McC.; student Lower Can. Coll., McGill U., Cambridge U.; LL.D., Mt. Allison U., 1964; m. Margaret Henderson, Feb. 20, 1931 (div. 1964); 1 son, John Royden m. 2d, Elspeth Bagg, May 6, 1970. Pres. Montreal Standard Pub. Co., 1938-67, Montreal Star Ltd., 1953-70; chmn. bd., chief exec. officer Montreal Standard, Ltd., 1967-68, also dir. chmn. Comml. Trust Co., Ltd., 1964-74; dir. St. Lawrence Sugar Refineries, Ltd. Bd. dirs. YMCA. Decorated comdr. Order Brit. Empire; comdr. Order St. John. Mem. Newcomen Soc. Eng., Canadian Cancer Soc. (hon., life). Clubs: Mt. Royal, Mt. Bruno Country; Montreal. Home: Montreal Que., Canada. Died July 12, 1974; buried Mt. Royal Cemetery, Montreal.

MCCORD, ANDREW KING, corp. official; b. Blue Island, Ill., Feb. 11, 1904; s. Andrew L. and Adelaide (Krueger) McC.; A.B., Beloit Coll., 1924; law student Harvard, 1925, U. Chgo., 1926-27; m. George Lial Mickelberry, July 8, 1933; children—Colin Wallace, Leslie Jane, Andrew King. Admitted to Ill. bar, 1929; asso. with Defrees, Buckingham, Jones & Hoffman, 1929-30; atty. Oliver Farm Equipment Co., 1931-34, Farm Equipment Inst., 1933-34; asst. to pres. J. I. Case Co., 1935; asst. to pres. Oliver Corp., 1935-37, v.p., 1937-40, exec. v.p., 1941-44, 1st v.p., 1948-50, pres., 1950-56; pres., dir. Westinghouse Air Brake Co., 1956-65, chmn., pres., 1965-66, chmn., 1966-69; cons., dir. Am. Standard Inc., 1969; dir. Pitts. Forgings Co. Republican. Clubs: Rolling Rock; Duquesne, Fox Chapel, Pittsburgh Golf (Pitts.). Home: Pittsburgh, Pa. Died Dec. 1974.

MCCORD, MAY KENNEDY, columnist, folklorist; b. Carthage, Mo., Dec. 1, 1880; d. Jesse Thomas and Delia Melisa (Fike) Kennedy; educated Galena (Mo.) High School and Selden's Private College, Aurora, Missouri; married Charles Calvin McCord, January 3, 1903 (died Sept. 19, 1943); children—Charles Calvin, Maudeva (Mrs. Herman Henry Janss), Frank Leslie. Collector of ballads, customs, superstitions, language and traditions of the Ozarks; writer of column "Hill Billy Heartbeats" in Springfield (Mo.) Daily News; lectured in New York, Los Angeles, Washington and many other cities as well as to colls. and hist. soc. groups. Dir. All-Ozarks Folk Festivals; mem. Nat. Bd. Folklore, Mo. State Writers Guild, Ozarks Creative Writers' Guild, Ozark Press Assn., Mo. Fedn. of Women's Clubs, Springfield Musical Club. Home: Springfield, Mo.†

MCCORMACK, JAMES, industry exec., ret. air force officer; b. Chatham, La., Nov. 8, 1910; s. James and Mary E. (Garner) McC.; Riverside Mil. Acad., 1928; U.S. Mil. Acad., 1932; Oxford U., 1935; Mass. Inst. Tech., 1937; m. Eleanor Morrow, May 15, 1936; children—Ann Martha (Mrs. James Stanton), James Rudolph. Served in army engrs. and air force in successive grades from 2d lt. to maj. gen., 1932-55. Decorated D.S.M., other U.S. and fgn. medals. Dir., former chmn., chief exec. officer Communications Satellite Corp., now chmn. Aerospace Corp.; dir. Bulova Watch Co., Eastern Air Lines, Draper Labs., GCA Corp., Mitre Corp., Steadman Funds. Former chmn. Mass. Bay Transp. Authority; former v.p. Mass. Inst. Tech. Baptist. Home: Arlington Va. Died Jan. 3, 1975; interred Arlington Nat. Cemetery, Arlington, Va.

MCCORMICK, EDWARD JAMES, surgeon; b. Alger, Mich., Sept. 25, 1891; s. Michael James and Mary (Daily) McC.; B.A., St. John's U., Toledo, O., 1911, M.A., 1913; M.D., St. Louis U., 1915; grad. study in Chicago, New York City and Europe; LL.D. (hon.), Xavier University, 1953; D.C.L., Toledo U., 1954; L.H.D., Hahnemann Med. Coll., 1954; D.Litt., Seton Hall University, 1955; married to Josephine Beck, June 5, 1920; children—Edward James, Richard Arthur, Carol Jeanne (Mrs. William E. Sala), Kathleen Ann (Mrs. Robert H. Brooks), Mary Josephine (Mrs. Robert J. Anderson), Michael James (deceased). Intern at St. Vincent's Hospital, Toledo, O., 1915-16, house surgeon, 1916-17, surgeon since 1920, chief of staff, 1939-49, pres. adv. bd. 1947-1960; att. surg. Mercy Hosp., 1919-20; surgeon Maumee Valley Hospital, 1924, director of surgery and member exec. com., 1934-50, also member board trustees, 1940-57; visiting surgeon Toledo Hospital, 1933, Flower Hospital and Saint Charles Hospital; surgeon W. & L.E. Railway from 1919, now Nickle Plate R.R. Lt. Med. Corps, U.S. Army, 1917; attached to B.E.F., France, advancing to major, 1917-19; surg. service Walter Reed Hosp., Washington, D.C., 1919; lt. comdr. Vol. Naval Res., 1923-30; awarded Military Cross (Eng.); senior surgeon, USPHS, 1944-54, resigned; member board directors Lucas County State Bank. Mem. or past mem., frequently officer or trustee numerous civic and community coms. and commns.; also community health and welfare assns. Trustee Ohio Elks Scholarship Foundation, 1930-75, also Elks National Foundation; member board trustees Boys Club (Toledo), 1934-53. Diplomate Am. Bd. Surgery. Fellow A.C.S., Internat. Coll. Surgery; mem. A.M.A. (pres. 1953-54), and other nat., state and local med. professional and sci. assns., orgns., Phi Beta Pi, Alpha Omega Alpha, Alpha Epsilon Delta. Democrat. K.C., Elk (grand exalted ruler 1938-39; past sec. nat. vets. service commn.). Clubs: Toledo, Lions, Wabe McQuaw (Quebec). Contbr. to med. jours. Home: Toledo O. Died Jan. 7, 1975.

MCCORMICK, GEORGE WINFORD, physician; b. Clayton, N.Y., Jan. 28, 1903; s. Michael and Sophia McCormick; M.D., McGill U., 1935; m. Mary Ramsden, July 17, 1943; 1 son, George Winford. Intern. Childrens Meml. Hosp., Montreal, Que., Can., 1934—36, St. Marys Hosp., lMontreal, 1936—37; asst. resident Babies Hosp., N.Y.C., 1945—46; physician Richmond Boro Contagious Hosp., S.I., N.Y.; cons. pediatrician Richmond Meml. Hosp., S.I., S.I. Hosp.; dir. pediatrics emeritus St. Vincent's Hosp., S.I.; instr. pediatrics Columbia-Presbyn. Med. Center, N.Y.C., until 1968. Served to comdr., M.C., USNR, 1941—46. Diplomate Am. Bd. Pediatrics. Fellow Am. Acad. Pediatrics; mem. Richmond County Med. Soc. (pres. 1959—60). Roman Catholic. Home: Delray Beach, Fla. Died Dec. 24, 1973; buried Moravian Cemetery, Staten Island, N.Y.

MCCORMICK, ROBERT LOUIS LAING, govt. ofcl.; b. Wilkes-Barre, Pa., Dec. 24, 1917; s. Frank T. and Rose Marie (Lynch) McC.; A.B., Yale, 1940; student Harvard, 1941; m. Dorothy Mary Bragdon, Nov. 11, 1948; children—Robert, Josephine, Peter, John, Brigid, Anthony. With Chemical Bank and Trust Co., 1941-42; asst. to chief, finance div. Navy Dept., 1942-44, chief contract financing sect., indsl. readjustment br., 1944-45; personal aide to Brig. Gen. William H. Draper, Jr., SHAEF and Office Mil. Govt. for Germany, 1945-46; alternate U.S. mem. Directorate of Reparations, Control Council for Germany, 1945-46; asso. White, Weld & Co., investment bankers, 1946-47; asst. to chmn. 1st Hoover Commn., 1947-49, dir. research Citizens Com. for Hoover Report, 1949-54, research cons., 1954-61; cons. 2d Hoover Commn., 1953-55; v.p. Coates & McCormick, Inc., 1952-56; partner McCormick Assos., 1956-57; pres. McCormick Assos., Inc., 1957-65; dir. research Republican Nat. Com., 1965-69; staff coordinator Rep. Coordinating Com.; dep. asst. sec. for water quality and research U.S. Dept. Interior, 1969-70; cons. VA, 1971-75. Served as lt. USNR, 1942-46. Named one of the Ten Outstanding Young Men of U.S., 1952. Republican. Roman Catholic. Author articles in field. Home: McLean, Va. Died Feb. 14, 1975.

MCCOY, PHILBRICK, judge; b. South Orange, N.J., Nov. 14, 1897; s. Walter Irving and Kate Philbrick (Baldwin) McC.; student N.C. State Coll., 1915-16; LL. B., George Washington U., 1922, LL.M., 1923, LL.D., 1957; m. Kathrine Sargent Olds, Jan. 25, 1921; children—Kathleen Philbrick (Mrs. Howard L. Bryan), Marietta Meigs (Mrs. John W. Ingham). Admitted to D.C. bar, 1922, Cal. bar, 1926; practice of law, Washington, 1922-26, Los Angeles, 1926-47; judge Municipal Ct., Los Angeles, 1947-50, Superior Ct. Los Angeles County, 1950-66; justice pro-tempore Dist. Ct. Appeal, 2d Appellate Dist., from 1966. Mem. Plan Commn. City Los Angeles, 1946-47. Fellow Institute Jud. Administrator (president 1959-62); member American (chairman jud. adminstrn. 1960-61), Cal. (counsel 1930-40), Los Angeles bar assns., Am. Judicature Soc., Am. Law Inst., Phi Delta Phi, Order Coif. Episcopalian. Home: San Clemente, Cal. Died Sept. 1973.

MCCREEDY, JO ANN, educator; b. Enid, Okla., July 3, 1924; d. Thomas James and Cornelia Kathryn (Roth) McCreedy; B.A., Our Lady of the Lake Coll., 1946, B.L.S., 1949; M.L.S., Columbia U., 1958, D.L.S., 1963. Librarian Providence Central High Sch., Alexandria, La., 1948-51, Providence High Sch., San Antonio, 1951-58; instr. L.S., Our Lady of the Lake Coll., San Antonio, 1958-60, asso. prof., 1963-70, prof., chmn. dept., 1970-72. Teaching asst. Columbia, 1961-62. Mem. library adv com. Compton's Ency., 1917. Mem. Am., Tex. (pres. 1969-70), Cath. (council mem. 1970); library assns., Am. Assn. U. Profs., Am. Assn. Library Schs., Beta Phi Mu, Delta Kappa Gamma. Roman Catholic. Editor: Books for Young Adults, Catholic Library World, 1964-72. Contbr. articles to profl. jours. Home: San Antonio, Tex., Died Sept. 8, 1972.

MCCREERY, HUGH PETE, ins. agy. exec.; b. Gaston, Ind., Feb. 21, 1900; s. John Wesley and Martha (Woodring) McC.; student pub. schs.; m. Ruth Leach, Aug. 11, 1922; children—Robert L., Mary A. (Mrs. James Compton). Foreman, Pa. R.R. locomotive shops, 1923-27; mgr. Ford Sales Agy., Dugger, Ind., 1927-30, sales mgr., Sullivan, Ind., 1930-36; owner farm, Sullivan County, Ind., 1936; gen. mgr. Wabash Valley Prodn. Credit Assn., 1944-65; owner Sullivan County Ins. Agy., 1945-74; farm loan mgr. Sullivan State Bank-Farm Loans, 1965-74. Mem. Ind. State Fire Commn. Bd., 1966-74, Sullivan County Extension Com., 1957-70, Sullivan County Park and Recreation Bd., 1964-74; pres. Sullivan County Indsl. Bd., 1964-74; bd. dirs. Vigo County Adult and Child Guidance Clinic, 1964-74; pres. Sullivan County Wabash Valley Assn., 1963-74; mem. Tech. Action Panel, 1967-74; dist. mem. Sullivan, Vigo & Knox County Tourism Bd., 1965-74; pres. Ind. Dixie Bee Fedn., 1967-74; v.p. West Central Ind. Econ. Devel., 1968-74; pres. Resource, Conservation & Devel., 1971-74; mem. Sullivan County Civil Def. Adv. Com., 1964-74. County auditor Sullivan County, 1936-44; pres. county council Sullivan County, 1944-70. Bd. dirs. Ind. Tech. Coll., Terre Haute, Ind., 1967-74; mem. program adv. com. Vincennes U., 1968-74; bd. dirs., asst. sec.-treas. Katherine Hamilton Mental Health Assn., 1968-74; bd. dirs. Rehab. Alcoholics in U.S. Penitentiary, Terre Haute, Sullivan County Assn. Retarded Children, West Central Ind. Community Found., Inc., Community 71 Assn. Recipient Outstanding Community Service award Jaycees, 1968. Mem. V.F.W., Am. Legion (life). Elk. Home: Sullivan, Ind. Died Jan. 15, 1974.

MCCRUMB, FRED RODGERS, JR., physician, educator; b. Havre de Grace, Md., Dec. 23, 1925; s. Fred Rodgers and Phebe (Riley) McC.; student Loyola Coll., Balt., 1942-44; M.D., U. Md., 1948; m. Gloria Elaine Frizzell, Aug. 18, 1950; children—Sharon Elizabeth, Fred Rodgers III, Mariet Francesca. Resident internal medicine U. Md. Hosp., 1948-50, mem. faculty, 1956-76, prof. internal medicine 1963-76, dir. Inst. Internal Medicine, 1963-65; spl. asst. to dir. Fogarty Internat. Center, NIH, Bethesda, Md. Asso. mem. commn. epidemiological survey Armed Forces Epidemiol. Bd., 1959-76; cons. NIH, 1960-65. Served to capt., M.C., AUS, 1951-56, Recipient certificate of honor U. Md., 1948; La medaille d'Honneur des Epidemics, 1954. Mem. Am. Acad. Microbiology, Am. Epidemiological Soc., Am. Pub. Health Assn., Am. Soc. Tropical Medicine and Hygeine, Infectious Diseases Soc. Am., N.Y. Acad. Scis., Royal Soc. Tropical Medicine and Hygiene, Acad. Nationale de Medicine. Research on ecology and treatment of plaque; invetigation diseases mil. importance in S.E. Asia; devel. and application measles vaccination techniques. Home: New Market, Md., Died Jan. 5, 1976.

MCCUEN, CHARLES LEROY, automobile exec.; b. Stockton, Calif., May 22, 1892; s. Charles Pooler and Elizabeth S. (Pidgeon) McC.; student Poly. Coll. of Engring., Oakland, Calif., 1911-12, hon. B.S., 1934; m. Adele M. Chamberlain, May 22, 1916; children—Marshall D., Newell H., Eleanor A., Charles E. Structural engr. Panama Pacific Expn., San Francisco, 1914; design engr. Packard Motor Car Co., 1916-17; pres. Isko Co. (house refrigerators), 1918-22; exptl. engr. Rickenbacker Motor Car Co., 1922-26; engr. Olds Motor Works, 1926-29, chief engr., 1929-32; tech. asst. to pres. of Buick and Olds Motor Works, 1932-33; gen. mgr. Olds Motor Works, Oct. 1933-Aug. 1940; v.p. Gen. Motors Corp. in charge engineering 1940-47, now general manager research labs., Gen. Motors Corp. Dir. Ethyl Corp., Gen. Motors Inst. Tech. Mem. Soc. Automotive Engrs., Engring. Soc. of Detroit. Republican. Presbyterian, Mason (32°, K.T., Shriner). Clubs: Detroit Athletic, Bloomfield Hills Country (Mich.). Home: Bloomfield Hills, Mich., Died Oct. 28, 1975

MCCULLOCH, HUGH, physician; b. Marianna, Ark., Aug. 20, 1888 s. Edgar Allen and Harriett Louise (Hassell) McC.; A.B., U. of Ark., Harriett Louise (Hassell) McC.; A.B., U. Ark., 1908; M.D., Johns

Hopkins, 1912; m. Ida Louise Haardt; 1 son, Hugh. Asst. to asso. prof. clin. pediatrics Washington University, St. Louis, 1915-47; formerly chief staff, dir. med. service now hon. life trustee La Rabida Sanitarium, Chgo.; prof. emeritus, lectr. pediatrics U. Ill. Coll. Medicine. Served as capt. M.C., AUS, 1917-19; with Base Hosp. No. 21 (B.E.F. No. 12 General), Rouen, France. Recipient Distinguished Alumnus award U. Ark., 1959; Grulee award Am. Acad. Pediatrics, 1954. Diplomate American Bd. Pediatrics (founder 1934), Am. Bd. Internal Medicine. Fellow Am. Acad. Pediatrics; mem. A.M.A., Am. Pediatric Soc. (sec. 1931-46, pres. 1951-52), Am. Heart Assn. (co-founder 1925; recipient founder's award 1964). Soc. Med. Friends Wine, Phi Beta Kappa. Editor-in-chief Pediatrics, 1948-54. Home: Montgomery, Ala. Died July 25, 1974.

MCCULLOUGH, MATTHEW PEARCE, lumber and pulpwood products; b. Elkton, Md., Oct. 13, 1878; s. Clinton and Jeanette (Pearce) McC.; grad. Elkton (Md.) High Sch., 1895; m. Louise Ross, June 22, 1904 (deceased July 2, 1953); one daughter, Ruth (Mrs. Keenan Morrow). Vice president Brooks & Ross Lumber Co., Wausau, Wis., 1904-36, pres., 1936-45; v.p., dir. D. J. Murray Mfg. Co., Wausau, from 1930; pres. B. C. Spruce Mills, Ltd., Lumberton, B.C., 1926-43, Alexander-Yawkey Lumber Co., Prineville, Ore., 1940-51. Alexander-Stewart Lumber Co., Prineville, 1951-59; treas., dir. Masonite Corp., Laurel, Miss., 1926-44; pres., 1944-46, chmn. exec. committee, from 1946; president Employers Mutual Liability Ins. Co. Wausau, Wis., 1928-35, later chmn. bd.; dir. Winton Lumber Co. Mpls. Clubs: Chicago, Midday (Chgo); Glenview Country (Golf, Ill.); Everglades (Palm Beach, Fla.). Home: Chicago, Ill.†

MCCURDY, ROBERT MORRILL, librarian; b. Andover, Mass., July 7, 1878; s. Matthew S. and Lydia (Morrill) McC.; grad. Phillips Acad., Andover, Mass., 1896; A.B., Harvard, 1900; B.L.S., Albany (N.Y.) Library Sch., 1903; unmarried. Asst. librarian Gardner A. Sage Library, New Brunswick, N.J., 1903-07; order librarian U. of Ill., 1908-11; librarian Mercantile Library, Cincinnati, O., 1911-15; spl. library work, N.Y. City, 1916-17; A.L.A. library service, Charlotte, N.C., and Washington, D.C., 1917-19; lit. work, 1920-24; state librarian, also clk. Supreme Court of N.H., from 1924. Republican. Author: Garden Flowers and Wild Animals (2 vols. in The Nature Library), 1926; also articles in mags. and short stories. Address: Concord, N.H.†

MCCURDY, WESLEY, newspaper publisher; b. Winnipeg, Manitoba, Can., Apr. 2, 1881; s. Alexander Steele and Isabella (Downey) McC.; student Wesley Coll., Winnipeg, Manitoba, 1897-1900; A.B., Manitoba Univ., 1900; LL.D. (hon.), Manitoba Univ., 1946; m. Mabel Hortense Blake, Aug. 3, 1912; children—Isabel Jean (Mrs. R. L. Sanburn), Evelyn (Mrs. G. D. McKinney), Florence (Mrs. G. McL. Steele), Helen; m. 2d, Lottie Kathleen Salberg, Aug. 31, 1946. Advt. clerk, Winnipeg Free Press Co., Winnipeg, 1900-04; advt. mgr., and dir., sec.-treas., asst. to gen. mgr., 1913; pub. The Winnipeg Tribune, 1936-48; dir. The Southam Co., Ltd., Montreal, Quebec, Mem. Canadian sec. Can.-Am. Comml. Abritration Commn. Mem. Winnipeg Bd. of Trade (pres. 1933-35), Can Camber of Commerce (vice pres. for Manitoba 1934, 43, 44), Aviation League of Manitoba (pres. 1932-33), Can. Daily Newspapers Assn. (vice pres. 1941-42, pres. 1942-43, 1943-44); A founder, Manitoba Tourist and Conv. Bur., 1925, pres. 1935. Mem. Anglican Ch. Clubs: Manitoba, St. Charles Country. Home: Winnipeg, Man. Can.*†

MCCUTCHEON, STANLEY JAMES, lawyer; b. Anchorage, Alaska, Dec. 21, 1917; s. Herbert Hazard and Clara Johana (Krueger) McC.; ed. pub. schs. of Anchorage; m. Evelyn Ella Bockoven, June 14, 1942; children—Scotte, Shelle. Admitted to Alaska bar, Nov. 7, 1939, since practiced in Anchorage: now engaged in individual practice of law. Past president Alaska Airlines; v.p. Union Bank, Anchorage, 1946. Served as mem. House of Reps., Alaska Leg. 1943, 45, 46, 49, special session, 1949, 51, 55, speaker of House, regular 1949 session. Mem. econ. advisory bd. Rampart Dam. Mem. Alaska Bar Assn. (bd. govs.). Elk. Author Statehood Memorial to Congress asking statehood for Alaska, 1945. Home: Anchorage, Alaska. Died May 1975.

MCDANIEL, AGNES M. MCLAUGHLIN, (Mrs. John W. McDaniel), cattle rancher; b. nr. Clewiston, Fla., Feb. 6, 1907; d. Robert Elonzo and Susie (Brewer) McLaughlin; student Fla. State U., 1924-27; m. John W. McDaniel, June 7, 1928 (dec. Sept. 1957); 1 son, Robert E. Cattle rancher, Clewsiton, Fla. Mem. So. Bapt. Annuity Bd., 1966-75. Mem. Internat. Platform Assn., Phi Sigma Alpha. Baptist. Home: Ft. Myers, Fla., Died May 23, 1975.

MCDAVID, CHARLES WILLIAM, steel co. exec., mayor; b. Waxahachie, Tex., Sept. 21, 1914; s. William Allen and Alice (Gibson) MD.; B.S. in Archtl. Engring., Tex. Tech. U., 1938; m. Katrina Louise Brewer, Jan. 30, 1938; children—William Terry, Martha Jane (Mrs. David Earl Barber). With Central Tex. Iron Works, Waco, 1938-72, asst. mgr. sales, 1959-66, mgr. prodn. control, 1966-72; mayor pro tem City of Waco, 1971, mayor, 1972. Instr. engring. Tex. Agrl. and M U., 1942-43. Chmn., Waco Tornado Cleanup Task Force, 1953; loaned exec. United Fund Drive, Waco, 1966; chmn. Plumbing Bd. Waco, 1968: mem. Planning Commn. Waco, 1969, Waco City Council, 1969-72; sec.-treas. Heart of Tex. Council of Govts. Recipient 20 Year commendation Tex. Tech. Loyalty Fund, 1968; named Central Tex. Engr. of Year, 1970. Registered profl. engr., Tex. Mem. Tex., Nat. socs. profl. engrs., Cen-Tech Exes (past pres.), Central Tex. Geneal. Soc., S.A.R. (Tex. v.p. 1971-72), Tau Beta Pi. Methodist (adminstrv. bd.). Rotarian. Club: Ridgewood Country (Waco). Home: Waco, Tex. Died Nov. 15, 1972; buried Oakwood Cemetery, Waco, Tex.

MCDAVID, CONSTANCE LOUISE WEBB (MRS. HOMER GEORGE MCDAVID), county ofcl.; b. Covington, Ky., Aug. 27, 1896; d. Joseph F. and Josephine H. (Herrington) Webb; grad. Houston pub. schs.; m. Homer George McDavid, Apr. 27, 1924; children—Raymond H.; Donald G. With treas.'s office, Harris County, Tex., 1935, county treas., 1948. Worker, United Fund, Salvation Army. Named Outstanding Treas. in Tex., 1970; recipient civic award River Oaks Bus. and Profl. Women's Club woman of year, 1958, 65. Mem. County Treas.' Assn. Tex., Nat. Assn. County Ofcls., Nat. Assn. County Treasurers and Finance Officers (dir. 1959), Methodist. Home: Houston, Tex. Died, Feb. 12, 1973; buried Forest Park West Cemetery, Houston, Tex.

MCDERMOTT, EUGENE, instrument co. exec.; b. Bklyn., Feb. 12, 1899; s. Owen and Emma (Cahill) MCD.; M.E., Stevens Inst. Tech., 1919, D.Sc. (hon.), 1960; A.M., Columbia 1925; m. Margaret Milam, Dec. 1, 1954; 1 dau., Mary. With Geophys. Research Corp., Houston, 1925-30; v.p. Tex. Instruments Inc. (formerly Geophys. Service Inc.), Dallas, 1930-39, pres., 1939-49, chmn., 1949-58, chmn. exec. com., 1958-64, dir., 1930-73; mem. MIT Corp., Cambridge, Mass., 1960-73; chmn. vis. com. dept. psychology Mass. Inst. Tech., Cambridge, mem. vis. com. arts. Trustee, bd. govs. So. Methodist U.; trustee, chmn. exec. com. Excellence in Edn. Found.; trustee St. Mark's Sch. of Tex., Area Ednl. TV Found., Southwestern Med. Found., Presbyn. Hosp.-Children's Med. Center, So. Methodist U. Found. for Sci. and Engring., McDermott Found., Biol. Humanics Found.; past mem. coordinating bd. Tex. Colls. and U's. Civilian cons. OSRD, 1941-46. Recipient Bene Merenti medal; Santa Rita Gold medal from U. Tex. Mem. Am. Assn. Petroleum Geologists, Soc. Exploration Geophysicists (pres. 1933-34, hon. mem. 1971), Seismol. Soc. Am., Am. Phys. Soc., I.E.E.E., Am. Math. Soc., Dallas, Houston petroleum clubs. Author: (with William H. Sheldon) Atlas of Men, 1954. Contbr. articles to tech. jours. Clubs: Brookhollow Golf, Dallas Country. Home: Dallas, Tex. Died Aug. 1973.

MCDONALD, ARCHIBALD LEETE, surgeon; b. Grand Forks, N.D., Dec. 26, 1879; s. Donald and Pamelia Adeline (Leete) M.; desc. on mother's side of Gov. Leete of Conn. Colony, 1676-1683; A.B., U. of N.D., 1901; M.D., Johns Hopkins, 1905; studied Harvard Summer Sch., 1911, post-grad. work Johns Hopkins Hosp., 1919; m. Grace E. Morehous, Apr. 25, 1907. Organized depts. of anatomy and physiology, med. dept. U. of N.D., 1905-06, and in charge dept. of anatomy, 1905-11; practiced in Duluth, Minn., from 1911; obstetrician, Bethel Home for Women, 1911-15; attending surgeon and former chief of staff, St. Luke's Hosp.; attending surgeon for St. Mary's Hosp; examining surgeon for British Recruiting Mission, 1917-18; dir. Duluth Free Dispensary, 1923-28; med. dir. Miller Memorial Hosp., 1932-33; chmn. Friends of the Library, Duluth Pub. Library. Mem. Am., Minn. State and St. Louis County and assns., Interurban Acad. Medicine (pres. 1921), County Health Assn. (pres. 1920-24), Western Surg. Assn., Am. Bd. of Surgery (founder mem.); fellow Am. Coll. Surgeons. Republican. Episcopalian. Mason. Author: Essentials of Surgery, 1919. Translated from French "Aphorisms of Corvisart," Archive Medical History 1939. Home: Duluth, Minn.†

MCDONALD, CARLOS JOHN, railroad exec.; b. Monterey, Cal., Dec. 29, 1880; s. Angus and Isabelle (McEachern) McD.; student pub. schs. Houston; m. Ada Louise Buck, Sept. 12, 1906. Stenographer, then train master, S.P. Co., Houston, 1913-14, asst. supt. transportation, San Francisco, 1915-17, mgr. perishable freight traffic, also mail and express traffic mgr., 1919-29, asst. to pres., 1943-50, ret. 1950. In charge all U.S. troop movements all railroads 8 western states, then asst. dist. dir. U.S. R.R. Adminstrn., 1917-19; mem. exec. com. San Francisco Def. Council, 1944-45. Club: California Golf (past pres., past mem. bd. dirs.) (San Francisco). Address: San Francisco, Cal.†

MCDONALD, JAMES ERIC, commr. of agr. for Tex.; b. Mexia, Tex., June 4, 1881; s. James Edward and Thula (Adams) McD.; ed. pub. schs., Mexia, Tex.; m. Anita Moulis, Oct. 12, 1935; children—Audette (Mrs. Marvin D. Chapman), Inez (Mrs. Steve Hazlip), James Eric, Roy H., Harold. Engaged in farming at an early age; owner ranch in Bosque County, Tex., also citrus fruit orchards, Rio Grande Valley, Tex.; mem. Tex. House of Representatives, as rep. from Ellis County, 1929-31; Tex. commr. of agriculture, from 1931. Mem. Southern and Nat. assns. of Commrs. of Agr. Home: Austin, Tex.†

MCDONALD, ROBERT A(LEXANDER) F(YFE), educator; b. Winnipeg, Man., Oct. 4, 1878; s. Rev. Alexander and Lucinda Elma (Yorke) M.; grad. Ontario Normal Coll., Hamilton, 1905; A.B., McMaster U., 1904, A.M., 1908; student, Columbia, 1912, 1913-15, research scholar, 1914-15, Ph.D., 1915; engaged in travels and studies in England and on the European continent, 1930; married Mabel Elida Culver (A.B.), July 3, 1907. Teacher Greek and Latin, Woodstock (Ont.) Coll., 1905-13; asso. examiner Greek and Latin, Edn. Dept. of Ont., and U. of Toronto, 1907-09; head edn. dept., Bates Coll., Lewiston, 1915-48; director summer session, 1919-22; director teacher placement, 1930-48; prof. emeritus, 1948. Mem. advisory education committee Maine Public School Finance Commn., 1934; rep. of coll. faculties on exec. com. Me. Teachers Assn., 1941-43. Mem. Commn. on Professional Ethics of Me. Teachers Assn., 1943-46. Rep. Me. Teachers Assn. on Nat. Council of Edn., 1944-50. Mem. N.E.A., Nat. Society for Study of Education, Religious Education Association Phi Delta Kappa; pres. New Eng. Assn. Coll. Teachers of Edn., 1931-32. Baptist. Mason. Author: Adjustment of School Organization to Various Population Groups, 1915. Lecturer on ednl. topics. Home: Lewiston, Me.†

MCDONALD, ROBERT C., army officer; b. Crockett County, Tenn., Feb. 18, 1881; s. James Robert and Sara (Moore) McD.; M.D., Tulane U., 1909; grad. Army Med. Sch., 1911, Command and Gen. Staff Sch., 1926, Army War Coll., 1930; m. Olive Elizabeth Berry, Apr. 27, 1913; children—Robert C., Lucien B., James Gordon, Henry S., Olive Elizabeth (dec.). Commd. lt., Med. Corps, U.S. Army, 1910, advancing through the ranks to brig. gen., 1945; served with 1st Div., with Army schools and on staff of Gen. John J. Pershing, 1917-19; in surgeon general's office, Washington, D.C., 1921-25 and 1931-35; instr., Command and Gen. Staff Sch., 1930-31; surgeon, 3d Army, 1940-42; surg., 3d Service Command, 1942; comdg. officer Army Gen. Hosp., 1943; surg., 4th Command, Atlanta, Ga., 1944-45; retired from active mil. service, 1946; chief surgeon, U.S. Soldiers' Home, Washington, D.C., from 1945. Decorated Legion of Merit, Mexican Border, Victory and pre-Pearl Harbor medals. Fellow Am. Coll. Surgeons; mem. A.M.A. Mason. Sojourner. Club: Army-Navy Country (Washington). Address: Washington, D.C.†

MCDOWELL, CAROLINE DENT;, b. Eufaula, Ala., Sept. 23, 1879; d. Stouton Hubert and Anna (Young) Dent; A.B., and Mus.B., Union Female Coll., Eufaula, 1897; m. Charles S. McDowell, Jr., Oct. 15, 1902; children—Annie Dent (dec.), Carolina Joy (Mrs. J. A. Crook). Formerly teacher public schools Ala.; registrar of voters Barhour County, Ala., term 1931-47; secretary judiciary committee Alabama State Senate, 1931-35, V.p. and superintendent young people of Woman's Missionary Soc. of Ala. Conf. M.E. Chs., 1916-24; v.p. Woman's Soc. Christian Service, Ala. Conf. Methodist Ch., 1933-43; pres. Ala. div. U.D.C., 1923-25; past president Barbour County chapter, U.C.D.; dir. Ala. of Jefferson Davis Highway for 8 years; regent for Ala. of Confederate Museum, Richmond, Va.; chmn. various coms. Ala. Federation Music Clubs, and Ala. Fedn. Women's Clubs; ex-chmn. Conservation, Fed. of Ala. Garden Clubs. Democrat. Clubs: Music (pres.), Garden (pres.), Lanier (pres.). Home: Eufaula, Ala.†

MCDOWELL, JOHN, assn. ofcl.; b. Grove City, Pa., Feb. 7, 1909; s. Ezra A. and Rebecca (Johnston) McD.; A.B., Grove City Coll., 1929; B.D., McCormick Theol. Sem., 1934; m. Margaret Ray, May 31, 1935; children—Nancy L., Janet M., Evelyn R. Prin. Jamestown (Pa.) High Sch., 1929-31; ordained to ministry Presbyn. Ch., 1934; pastor Iron County, Mich., 1934-36; resident dir. Neighborhood House, Erie, Pa., 1936-40; exec. dir. Soho Community House, Pitts., 1940-44; asst. exec. sec. Nat. Fedn. Settlements, N.Y.C., 1944-47, exec. dir., 1947-58; dean Sch. Social Work, Boston U., 1958-67; dir. social welfare Nat. Council Chs., 1967-73. Mem. borough council, Waldwick, N.J., 1955-56. Mem. Am. Assn. Group Workers (pres. 1950-52), Nat. Assn. Social Workers (pres. 1957-59). Home: Bergenfield, N.J. Died 1974.

MCDOWELL, PIERCE HUBERT, real estate and ins. broker; b. nr. Sioux Falls, S.D., Aug. 12, 1902; s. John Hubert and Olive May (Pierce) McD.; LL.B., U. S.D., 1926; m. Alice Jackson, Dec. 20, 1923 (dec.); children—Elizabeth Jane, Pierce Hubert, Ann Jackson; m. 2d, Lois Hammond Tabor, Oct. 8, 1961; stepchildren—Joan Tabor Gold (dec.), Leonard G. Tabor II. Admitted to S.D. bar, 1926; pvt. practice law, 1926-27; v.p. Northwestern Nat. Bank, Sioux Falls, 1927-46, later dir., chmn. McDowell Assos., Inc., Sioux Falls, 1972-75; dir. NW Bancorp. of Mpls., Raven Industries, Sioux Falls, No. States Power Co. Pres., Municipal Airport Bd., Sioux Falls; past pres. Sioux Falls Ind. Sch. Dist. Bd. Edn. Bd. dirs., past pres. Crippled Children's Hosp. and Sch. Mem. Sioux Falls C. of C. (past pres.). Republican. Conglist. Elk (past exalted ruler), Mason (Shriner), Rotarian (past pres.). Clubs: Knife and Fork (past pres.); Minnehaha Country (past pres.). Home: Sioux Falls, S.D. Died Feb. 14, 1975; buried Woodlawn Cemetery, Sioux Falls, S.D.

MCELROY, FRANK D., coll. pres.; b. Putnam County, Ind., Feb. 28, 1878; s. Welcome R. and Mary M. (Barnett) McE.; student State Teachers Coll., Ind., 1901-04; A.B., Wabash Coll., 1906; A.M., Western Reserve U., 1925; Ph.D., Ohio State U., 1939; m. Nora Ann Lacey, Aug. 2, 1911; children—David Francis, Mary Jane. Rural school teacher, Ind., 4 years; prin. elementary school, Crawfordsville, Ind., 1904-08; prin. Hammond (Ind.) High Sch., 1909-19; asst. supt.,

Rockford, Ill. 1919-20, Akron, O., 1920-25; dir. of personnel, Cleveland Pub. Schs., 1925-29; instr. and grad. student, Ohio State U., 1929-30; pres. State Teachers Coll., Mankato, 1930-46, pres. emeritus, 1946. Mem. N.E.A., Minn. Edn. Assn., Am. Assn. Teachers Colls (v.p. 1939), Delta Epsilon, Phi Delta Kappa. Presbyterian. Mason. Club: Kiwanis. Home: Mankato, Minn.†

MCENIRY, WILLIAM HUGH, JR., univ. ofcl.; b. Bessmer, Ala., Jan. 21, 1916; s. William Hugh and Dora Elizabeth (Winters) McE.; A.B., Birmingham So. Coll., 1937; A.M., Vanderbilt U., 1938, Ph.D., 1942; LL.D., Stetson U., 1967, Bishop Coll., 1968; m. Mary McFarland Brown, Dec. 26, 1940; children—Mary Winters (Mrs. David H. Johnson), Kathryn Lee (Mrs. Tom B. Hyde). Asst. prof. and acting head, dept. English, John B. Stetson U., 1940-41, chmn. div. humanities, 1941, prof. English, head dept. English, 1942, acting dean of univ., 1947-48, prof. English, chmn. grad. council, 1948-59, dean Coll. Liberal Arts, 1952-67, univ. dean, 1958-67; vice chancellor acad. affairs, prof. English, U. N.C. at Charlotte, 1967; on loan (from U.N.C.) as acting chancellor Western Carolina U., 1973; cons. Ford Found., 1963-74. Mem. adminstrv. council So. Fellowships Fund, 1960-63, bd. dirs., 1963-74; mem. Woodrow Wilson Regional Selection Com., 1962-67; mem. Nat. Council Accreditation Tchr. Edn., 1959-61; mem. adv. council Danforth Found., 1956-63. Trustee Gualala Found., Johnson C. Smith U., Knox Coll., Galesburg, Ill. Served with AUS, 1943-45; overseas as classification specialist with 167th Gen. Hosp. in France, 1944-45. Mem. So. Assn. Colls. and Schs. (pres. 1962), N.C. Assn. Colls. and Univs. (pres.-elect 1973), Sigma Alpha Epsilon, Omicron Delta Kappa, Tau Kappa Alpha, Phi Beta Kappa. Democrat. Baptist. Home: Charlotte, N.C. Died Mar. 15, 1974.

MCEVOY, REGINALD, editor; b. Birmingham, Eng., Mar. 28, 1881; s. Bernard and Isbell (Holmden) McE.; student U. Toronto, 1898; m. Miriam Brookes, Sept. 1, 1908; children—Bernard, Winifred (Mrs. W. C. Kennedy). Reporter Toronto World, 1902-03; supreme ct. reporter, The Evening Telegram, Toronto, 1905-29, resident corr., London and France, 1918-19, editorial writer, 1929-48, editor, from 1949. Enlisted in 48th Highlanders, Toronto, 1898, 1914. Address: Toronto, Ont., Can.†

MCFADDEN, JOSEPH A., banker; m. Florence B. McFadden; children—David Breen, J. Hugh. Exec. v.p. Chem. Bank N.Y. Trust Co. Home: Ridgewood, N.J. Died Sept. 13, 1971.

MCFALL, MERRILL BORDEN, clergyman; b. Borden, Ind., Aug. 31, 1906; s. John Wesley and Iva M. (Payne) McF.; A.B., DePauw U., 1927, D.D. (hon.), 1943; B.D., Garrett Theol. Sem., 1935; m. Mary Elizabeth Glossbrenner, July 9, 1930; children—David Merrill, Jonathan Thomas, Richard Malcolm, Charles Herbert. With J.C. Penney Co., 1927-30; sales mgr. Crowder-Cooper Wholesale Shoes, Indpls., 1930-31; with Brown Shoe Co., St. Louis, 1931-32; ordained to ministry Methodist Ch., 1935; pastor in Crown Point, Ind., 1935-39, Bloomington, Ind., 1939-58, Irvington, 1958-61, First Meth. Ch., Columbus, Ind., 1961-67; exec. sec. Ministers Pension Fund, S. Ind. Conf. United Meth. Ch., Bloomington, 1967-72; chaplain Beck Chapel, Ind. U., 1967—; pastor Cross Roads United Meth. Ch., 1972—; guest preacher Nat. Radio Pulpit, 1954; goodwill ambassador to Meth. Chs. in Germany, 1949, in Korea, 1958. Mem. exec. com. gen. bd. edn. Meth. Ch., 1960-72, mem. gen. bd. Christian social concerns, 1960-72; mem. exec. com., bd. dirs. John Wesley Corp., 1970—. Pres. Am. Council Alcohol Problems, 1964-72. Trustee DePauw U., 1946-72. Recipient Indiana YMCA State Inter-racial award, 1953; named Ky. Col., 1960. Mem. Phi Gamma Delta. Mason (33deg., Shriner, chaplain grand lodge Ind. 1968-69). Home: Bloomington, Ind., Died Aug. 6, 1975.

MCFEE, INEZ N., (Mrs. M. M. McFee) author; b. Quasqueton, Ia., Feb. 14, 1879; d. Jonathan Russell and Ella M. (Mowrer) Canfield; diploma Des Moines Coll. Corr. Course; spl. student Ia. State Teachers' Coll., Cedar Falls, Ia.; m. M. M. McFee, of Winthrop, Ia., Oct. 27, 1897; children—Max Russell, Doris Genevieve. Author: Story of Idylls of the King (adopted), 1912; American Heroes from History, 1913; Boys and Girls of Many Lands, 1917; Little Tales of Common Things, 1918; The Teacher, The School and The Community, 1918; A Peep at the Front, 1919; The Tree Book, 1919; Boy Heroes in Fiction, 1920; Girl Heroines in Fiction, 1920; Stories of American Inventions, 1920; A Treasury of Myths, 1921; A Treasury of Flower Stories, 1921; Little Friends in Feathers, 1921; Story of Robt. Fulton, 1922; Story of Edison, 1922; Secrets of the Stars, 1922; Nature's Craftsmen, 1923; Lives of Busy Neighbors, 1923; Food and Health, 1924; The Young People's Cook Book, 1925; Friends and Neighbors in Fur, 1926; The Wonderful Story of Science, 1929; The World About Us, 1930; Famous Events of American History, 1930; How Our Government Is Run, 1931; also many numbers of "The Little Classics" (supplementary reading for schs.). Home: Stanley, Ia.†

MCFEELY, WILBUR MORRIS, paper and textile exec.: b. Marion, Ind., Apr. 16, 1908; s. Maynard B. and Bertha (Firth) McF.; A.B., Swarthmore Coll., 1929; D. Humanics, Springfield Coll., 1967; m. Vanetta E. Rickards, Sept. 17, 1932; children—Vanetta E. William T. Dir. ednl. work Pub. Service Corp. N.J., 1939-43; asst. to gen. comml. mgr. Pub. Service Electric & Gas Co., 1943-45; with Riegel Paper Corp., Riegel Textile Corp., 1945-74, asst. dir. indsl. relations, dir. Indsl. relations, 1951-59, v.p., 1953-59, dir., 1952-70, v.p. orgn., 1959-70, sr. specialist-conf. bd., 1970-74; dir. C.M. Masland & Sons. Mem. nat. bd. Nat. bd. Nat. Council YMCA's, past chmn. nat. bd. YMCA; v.p., mem. exec. com. World Alliance YMCA; past pres. Silver Bay Assn. Mem. Am. Mgmt. Assn. Club: University (N.Y.C.). Author: On Being the Boss, 1959, Organization Change: Perceptions and Realities, 1972; co-author: Techniques of Conference Leadership, 1946. Editor: Bull. Internat. Mgmt. Council. Contbr. articles to profl. jours. Home: Jamesburg, N.J. Died Jan. 21, 1974.

MCGAFFIN, WILLIAM, newspaperman; b. David City, Neb., Oct. 2, 1910; s. Hugh M. and Nellie M. (Derby) McG.; A.B., U. Neb., 1932; B.Sc. (Hitchcock scholar), Columbia, 1935; m. Jean Fuller, July 22, 1949; children—Christopher M., Nicholas P. Reporter, Neb. State Jour., Lincoln (Neb.) Star, Omaha World Herald, 1931—34; telegraph editor Columbus (Neb.) Telegram, 1934; wirter, editor A.P., N.Y.C., 1935—37, corr., London, Paris, French N. Africa, Egypt, Libya, India, China, Russia, 1937—44; corr. Chgo. Daily News in PTO, Japan, China, Manchuria, Czechoslovakia, Russia, London, 1944—53, UN, 1953—56, Washington, 1956—75. Covered fall of France, Battle of Britain, 1940, Battle of Malta, 1942; war corr. U.S. forces in India, China, 1942—43, battles of Saipan, Guam, Iwo Jima, Okinawa, 1944—45. Mem. Sigma Nu, Sigma Delta Chi. Episcopalian, Clubs: Nat. Press, Overseas Writers (Washington). Co—author: Anything But the Truth; Scandal in the Pentagon. Contbr. to numerous mags. Home: Falls Church, Va. Died Apr. 14, 1975.

MCGARRAGHY, JOSEPH C., judge; b. Washington, Nov. 6, 1897; s. Andrew and Mary Imogene McCarraghy; LL.B., Georgetown U., 1921; m. Marian Boyd Cameron, Feb. 24, 1939 (dec.). Asst. corp. counsel, 1924-25; mem. law firm Colladay, McGarraghy, Colladay & Wallace, 1925-40, Wilkes, McGarraghy & Artis, 1940-54; judge U.S. Dist. Ct., Washington, 1954-75. Pres., Washington Bd. Trade, 1946-47. Chmn. Greater Nat. Capital Com., 1947-50. Chmn., Republican State Com., D.C., 1949-54; del. Rep. Nat. Conv., 1952; chmn. Eisenhower-Nixon Inaugural Com., 1953. Served with C.E., U.S. Army, 1917-20. Mem. Barristers (pres. 1937-38), Am., D.C. (1st v.p. 1941-42) bar assns., Gamma Eta Gamma. Clubs: Metropolitan, Columbia Country (Washington). Home: Washington, D.C., Died Nov. 29, 1975.

MCGARRY, EDMUND DANIELS, educator, economist; b. Shenandoah Junction, W.Va., June 7, 1891; s. John Daniels and Sarah Emma (Burr) McG.; student Shepherd Coll., 1906-11; A.B., W.Va. U., 1914; M.B.A., Harvard, 1921; Ph.D., Columbia, 1931; m. Bertha Louise Reading, 1916; 1 son, Alan Reading; m. 2d, Hazel Mary Goodard, Sept. 5, 1927. Tchr. Hillsboro (W.Va.) High Sch., 1914-15; officer mgr. Morris Beef Co., London, Eng., 1917-18; traveling accountant U.S., Bur. Internal Revenue, 1919-20; asst. prof., later asso. prof. W.Va. U., 1921-27; asst. prof. economics U. Buffalo, 1927-32, prof. head dept. marketing, 1932-61; Fulbright lectr., dept. commerce U. Edinburgh, 1955-56; vis. prof. of marketing Univ. of Ariz., 1958-59; vis. prof. marketing I.P.S.O.A., Turin, Italy, 1961; cons. marketing problems numerous cos. Served as 2d lt., F.A., A.U.S., 1918. Mem. Am. Marketing Assn., Am. Econ. Assn., Beta Gamma Sigma. Clubs: Rotary, Torch. Author marketing articles. Home: Snyder, N.Y., Died Nov. 2, 1973.

MCGAVACK, THOMAS HODGE, physician; b. Waterford, Va., Apr. 7, 1898; s. John Thomas and Esther Hodge (Clapham) McG.; A.B., Hampden-Sydney Coll., 1917; M.D., Hahnemann Med. Coll., 1923; m. Freda Nichols Wicks, May 2, 1930; 1 step-dau., Daphne Cather Durant. Instr. physics, math. St. Christophers Sch., Richmond, 1917-19; intern Hahnemann Hosp., Phila., 1923-24; resident pathology Hahnemann Med. Coll. and Hosp., 1924-25; instr. medicine U. Cal. Med. Sch., 1925-27, asst. clin. prof., 1927-35: vis. physician Infant's Shelter, San Francisco, 1926-30; asst. vis. physician U. Cal., San Francisco hosps., 1925-36; asso. prof. medicine N.Y. Med. Coll., 1936-46, prof. clin. medicine, 1946-57; dir. N.Y. Med. Coll., Met. Hosp. Research Unit, 1943-57; vis. physician Flower and Fifth Av., Met. hosps., 1936-57, Bird S. Coler Hosp., cons. in endocrinology and metabolism Prospect Heights Hosp., Bklyn., 1944-57, U.S. Marine Hosp., USPHS, S.I., 1945-57, Monmouth (N.J.) Meml. Hosp., 1948-57; chief intermediate service VA Center, Martinsburg, W.Va., 1957-65, asso. chief staff, 1961-70; cons. endocrinology Kings Daus. Hosp., Martinsburg, 1957-73; profl. lectr. medicine George Wash. U. Sch. Med., 1957; Edward Henderson Lectr. gerontology Am. Geriatrics Soc., 1962-63. Dir. Harlem Valley Investment Co. Mem. W.Va. Gov.'s Commn. on Aging, 1967. Diplomate Bd. Internal Medicine. Fellow A.C.P.; mem. A.M.A., Am. Geriatrics Soc. (pres. 1956-57, dir.). Assn. Study Internal Secretions (council mem.), Soc. Exptl. Biology and Medicine, Harvey Soc., A.A.A.S. (council), Gerontology Soc. (council 1965-73). Am., N.Y. diabetes assns., Am. Goitre Assn., W.Va. County med. socs., N.Y. Acad. Medicine, W.Va. Diabetes Assn. (past pres.), Phi Beta Kappa, Alpha Omega Alpha, Theta Chi, Sigma Upsilon, Alpha Kappa Kappa. Mason (32 deg., Shriner). Author: Book on the Thyroid, 1951; co-author book on obesity, 1957, book on cerebral ischemia, 1964. Cons. editor Tice's Practice of Medicine (Endocrinology), Davis's Cyclopedia of Medicine (Endocrinology). Contbr. chpts. to med. books, articles to sectional, nat. med. jours. Address: Martinsburg, W. Va. Died May 1973.

MCGAVIN, PETER MURPHY, labor union ofcl.; b. Grand Rapids, Mich., Aug. 14, 1908; s. Frank and Mary (Murphy) McG.; ed. high sch.; m. Dorothea Giesen, Feb. 14, 1942; 1 son, Stephen Peter. Mem. organizing staff AFL, Detroit, 1940-42, Peoria, Ill., 1946-48, assigned territories Mich., Ill., Ohio, 1948-49, regional dir., Pa. and W.Va., 1949-53, asst. dir. orgn. hdqrs. AFL, 1953-55, asst. to pres. AFL, 1955; merged AFL-CIO, 1955-60, exec. sec-treas. Maritime Trades department, 1961-75. Served with AUS, 1942-46. Home: Bethesda, Md. Died July 6, 1975.

MCGEE, FRANK, news commentator; b. Monroe, La., Sept. 12, 1921; s. Robert Albert and Calla (Brown) McG.; student U. Cal., 1945-46, U. Okla., 1947-48; m. Nialta Sue Beaird, Feb. 25, 1940; children—Sharon Dian (Mrs. Peter Churchill Labovitz), Michael. Radio-TV news reporter WKY-TV, Oklahoma City, 1950-55; news dir. WSFA-TV, Montgomery, Ala., 1955-57; news commentator NBC-TV, 1957-74. Served with AUS, 1940-45. Recipient Headliners award, 1958, Robert E. Sherwood award, 1959, George Foster Peabody award, 1966; Emmy for spl. events coverage, 1967-68. Home: Scarsdale, N.Y. Died Apr. 17, 1974.

MCGEE, REGINALD EVERETT, multi-industry co. exec.; b. Timpson, Tex., Sept. 30, 1916; s. Milton Butler and Mary Lela (Humphries) McG.; B.S., Stephen F. Austin State Coll., 1940; grad. Advanced Mgmt. Program, Harvard, 1958, m. Virginia Dare Roberts, Oct. 26, 1940; children—Allen Roberts, Jane Ann, John Butler. Asst. cashier Cotton Belt State Bank, Timpson, 1937-38; tchr. accounting Kilgore (Tex.) Ind. Sch. Dist., 1940-42; accountant Arthur Andersen & Co., C.P.A.'s, Houston, 1943-45; with Tenneco Inc. (formerly Tenn. Gas Transmission Co.), Houston, 1945, treas., 1959-61, v.p., treas., 1961-63, sr. v.p., 1963-67, chief financial officer, 1963-74, exec. v.p., later pres., also dir.; v.p., treas. Tenneco Corp., Houston, 1961-63, dir., 1970-74, also treas. all affilates, 1959-63; dir. Newport News Shipbldg. & Dry Dock Co., J. I. Case Co., Phila. Life Ins. Co. Mem. pres.'s council Houston Bapt. Coll.; mem. adv. com. Mgmt. Devel. Center, U. Houston; chmn. bd. regents Stephen F. Austin State U., Necogdoches, Served with Tex.; mem. council instl. devel. Baylor U., Waco, Tex.; trustee Houston Bapt. Coll.; mem. bd. Visual Research Found. Served with AUS, 1942-43. C.P.A., Tex. Mem. Am. Inst. C.P.A.'s, Tex. Soc. C.P.A.'s, Financial Execs. Inst., Conf. Bd. Clubs: Recess, Board Room (N.Y.C.); Petroleum, River Oaks Country (Houston). Home: Houston, Tex. Died Mar. 23, 1974; interred Forest Oaks Cemetery West, Houston, Tex.

MCGETTIGAN, MARGARET MARY, (Mrs. Norbert Joseph McGettigan), travel bur. exec.; b. Phila., Oct. 30, 1929; d. Charles Andrew and Anne Bennet (McAvoy) Maloney; student Georgetown Visitation Jr. Coll., 1948-50, Chestnut Hill Coll., 1950-51; m. Norbert Joseph McGettigan, Nov. 21, 1953; children—Marianne, Maureen, Mary Alice, Suzanne, Margaret M. and Norbert (twins). With statis dept. Atlantic Refinery Co., Phila. 1951-53; treas. McGettigan's Travel Bur., Inc., Phila., 1965-74, also mgr. Motorcoach div. Community affairs chmn. Jr. Club Women of Drexel Hill, 1957-60; leader Girl Scouts Am., 1962-64. Mem. Nat. Tour Brokers Assn., Am. Soc. Travel Agts., Georgetown Vistiation Jr. Coll. Alumni Assn. Republican. Roman Catholic. Home: Bala Cynwyd, Pa., Died Dec. 21, 1974; buried St. Denis Cemtery, Havertown, Pa.

MCGINNIS, EDWARD FRANCIS, govt. ofcl.; b. Chgo., Apr. 10, 1897; s. Frank Patrick and Nellie (Sutton) McG.; student Chgo. Coll. Commerce, 1913-16; m. Wilma Fay Hargrove, May 30, 1931. Chief clk., disbursing officer 9th dist. Fed. Bd. Vocational Edn., 1919-21; supt. Nat. Subsistence Assn., 1921-24; sales mgr. Hamler Boiler & Tank Co., 1924-28; investment banker, 1928-47; sgt.-at-arms U.S. Senate, 1947-49; nat. dir. pub. relations Am. Legion, 1949-54; v.p. Joseph E. Seagram & Sons, N.Y.C., 1954-66; v.p., dir. Montgomery Fed. Savs. & Loan Assn., Underwater Storage Co., Washington; minority counsel U.S. Senate com. on Vets. Affairs, 1971-73. Mem. Am. Battle Monuments Commn. Chief sgt.-at-arms Republican Nat. Conv. 1960; nat. chmn. vets. div. Nixon-Agnew, 1968; chmn. vets. div. Presdl. Inaugural, 1969. Served with U.S. Army, 1917-19; to comdr. USNR, 1942-46. Decorated knight Holy Sepulchre, knight Malta. Mem. Am. Legion, V.F.W., AmVets., Mil. Order World Wars, Res. Officers Assn., Pub. Relations Soc. Am., Capital Hill Assos., Def. Orientation Conf. Assn., Army Navy and Air Force Vets Can. (hon.). Roman Catholic. Clubs: Army-Navy Country (Arlington, Va.); National Press, Capitol Hill (bd. govs.), Washington Country (bd. govs.), Army-Navy (Washington); Circumnavigators; Georgetown. Address: Washington, D.C. Died June 20, 1973.

MCGLINN, JOHN ALEXANDER, JR., food co. exec.; b. Phila., Apr. 19, 1911; s. John Alexander and Emma (Potts) McG.; student U. N.C., 1934; m. Ann Johnson, July 21, 1951; children—Lee, John Alexander

III, Lorin, Evan. With Campbell Soup Co., Camden, N.J., 1934-74, sales mgr. central div., 1941-53, asst. gen. sales mgr., 1953-55, product marketing mgr., 1955-56, v.p. marketing, 1956-66, sr. v.p., 1966-69, exec. v.p., 1969-74, also dir.; dir. Campbell Sales Co., Pepperidge Farm, Inc., Champion Valley Farms, Inc., Provident Mut. Life Ins. Co. Phila., Godiva Chocolatier, Inc., Lexington Gardens, Inc. Pepperidge Farm Mail Order Co., Inc. Served from ensign to lt. comdr., USNR, 1941-46; comdr. carrier based torpedo plane squadron. Decorated D.F.C., Air medal, Naval Individual Citation. Mem. Am. Radio Relay League, Grocery Mfrs. Am., Am. Soc. Corporate Execs., Newcomen Soc. N. Am., Navy League U.S., Pa. Soc., World Affairs Council Phila., Delta Kappa Epsilon. Republican. Roman Catholic. Clubs: The Courts, Merion Golf, Philadelphia Racquet, Merion Cricket, Sunday Breakfast, Vesper Club. Home: Gladwyne, Pa. Died Feb. 2, 1974.

MCGLYNN, JAMES VINCENT, educator; b. Cleve., July 20, 1919; s. Joseph Laughlin and Mary Ellen (Rowley) McG.; student John Carroll U., 1937-38; Litt.B., Xavier U., Cin., 1942; Ph.L., West Baden (Ind.) Coll., 1945, S.T.L., 1952; M.A., Loyola U., Chgo., 1946; Ph.D., Louvain (Belgium) U., 1955; postgrad. U. Freiburg (Germany), 1955-56, U. Cologne (Germany), 1955-56. Joined Soc. of Jesus, 1938, ordained priest Roman Cath. Ch., 1951; instr. St. Xavier High Sch., Cin., 1945-48; faculty U. Detroit, 1956-73, prof. philosophy, 1966-73, chmn. dept., 1959-62, 66-68, dean Grad. Sch. and research, 1962-69, acad. v.p., 1969-70, v.p., dean faculties, 1970-71. Trustee, sec.-treas. Am. Acad. Transp. Mem. Am. Cath. Philos. Assn., Internat. Phenomenological Soc., Delta Sigma Phi, Phi Delta Kappa, Phi Sigma Tau. Author: Truth II, 1953; Modern Ethical Theories, 1962; (with M. Farley) A Metaphysics of Being and God, 1966; (with D. Brezine) Future of Ethics and Moral Theology, 1968. Contbr. articles to profl. jours. Home: Detroit, Mich. Died Aug. 13, 1973; interred Colombiere Center, Clarkston, Mich.

MCGOODWIN, PRESTON, diplomate service; b. Princeton, Ky., Aug. 12, 1880; s. James Kerr and Nettie (Spratt) McG.; ed. pub. and pvt. schs., Ky. and Okla.; m. Jean Curtice, of Neosho, Mo, 1905. Reporter, city, sporting and mng. editor, staff corr., Washington corr. and editor, Owensboro, Ky., Joplin, Mo., Washington, D.C., Columbus, Cleveland and Cincinnati, Pittsburgh, St. Louis and Oklahoma City, 1900-13; E.E., and M.P. to Venezuela, 1913-21. Presbyterian. Author of various brochures on municipal government. Clubs: National Press (Washington); Venezuela and Caracas. Mem. Am. Soc. Internat. Law, Am. Acad. Polit. and Social Science, Pan Am. Soc. of U.S., Am. Asiatic Assn., Société Académique d'Historie Internationale (Paris); hon. pres. Am. Chamber Commerce of Venezuela. Specialized in tariffs and the industrial and commercial codes of Latin Am. republics. Home: Oklahoma City, Okla.†

MCGOVERN, J. RAYMOND, state ofcl.; b. New Rochelle, N.Y., Dec. 22, 1898; s. John and Mary Frances (Sheehan) McG.; student Georgetown U., 1917; B.S., Fordham U., 1921, LL.B., 1923; m. Elsie Schork, Feb. 12, 1936; children—Barbara Ann, Mary Frances, Joan, Elizabeth Gertrude. Admitted to N.Y. bar, 1925, since practiced in New Rochelle, mem. Dunlap, Otto & McGovern; state comptroller from 1951; dir., counsel First Westchester Nat. Bank, New Rochelle; dir. United Cigar-Whelan Corp., D.M. Read Co. State senator 30th senatorial dist. N.Y., 1945-50. Mem. Am., N.Y. State, Westchester Co. bar assns. Home: New Rochelle, N.Y. Died Mar. 13, 1974.

MCGOVERN, JOHN W., rubber mfg. exec.; b. Phila.; student accounting. With U.S. Rubber Co., from 1920, exec. v.p. until 1957, pres., Oct. 1957—60, mem. exec. com., dir., from 1960. Died 1975.

MCGOVERN, PHILIP PATRICK, physician; b. Cambridge, Mass., Feb. 20, 1901; s. Arthur and Catherine (Galligan) McG.; A.B., Boston Coll., 1923; M.D., Tufts U., 1927; m. Mary Blanche Hurley, Nov. 7, 1931; children—Philip Patrick, Arthur L., Sheila E. Intern, St. Elizabeth's Hosp., Boston, 1927-29, later vis. obstetrician and gynecologist; resident in obstetrics and gynecology Boston City Hosp., 1929-30, mem. staff, 1933-71; chief dept. obstetrics and gynecology Cambridge (Mass.) Hosp., 1954-65, trustee, from 1966, also cons.; practice medicine specializing in obstetrics and gynecology, Cambridge, 1930-71; vis. obstetrician and gynecologist Mt. Auburn (Mass. Hosp.; instr. obstetrics and gynecology Harvard Med. Sch., 10 yrs., Tufts U. Med. Sch., 20 yrs.; acting pub. health surgeon U.S. Immigration Service, Boston, 1942-44. Founder McGovern-Hurley Scholarship Fund, Boston Coll. High Sch., 1950. Diplomate Am. Bd. Obstetrics and Gynecology. Fellow Am. Coll. Obstetricians and Gynecologists (founding), Internat. Coll. Surgeons; mem. A.M.A., Mass. Med. Sos., New Eng. Obstet. and Gynecol. Soc., Cambridge Med. Improvement Soc., 400 Club of N.Y. Med. Coll. Democrat. Roman Catholic. K.C. Home: Cambridge, Mass. Died Sept. 10, 1971; buried Holy Cross Cemetery, Malden, Mass.

MCGRAW, DONALD C., publisher; b. Madison, N.J., May 21, 1897; s. James H. and Mildred (Whittlesey) McG.; Elizabeth Bidgood, July 9, 1921; children—Helen June (Mrs. J. Tate McBroom), Donald C., John L. Formerly v.p., dir. McGraw-Hill Pub. Co., Inc. (now McGraw-Hill, Inc.), N.Y.C., pres., 1953-66, chmn., chief exec. officer, 1966-68, chmn. exec. com., 1968-74. Home: Summit, N.J. Died Feb. 7, 1974.

MCGRAW, FRANK H., constrn. co. exec.; b. Holliday, Pa., July 25, 1871; s. John G. and Henrietta (Hart) McG.; ed. public schs.; m. May A.; 1 son, John Metz. Constrn. mgr., Westinghouse, Church, Kerr & Co., N.Y. City, 1904-20, Dwight P. Robinson & Co., Inc., 1920-29; pres. F. H. McGraw & Co., Inc., 1929-41, chmn., 1941-49; pres. McGraw Constrn. Co., Inc., Middletown, O., 1941-50, chmn. from 1950. Clubs: Engineers (N.Y. City); Forest Hill, Midday (Middletown, O.). Home: Middletown, O.†

MCGREW, DALLAS DAYTON LORE, b. of Am. parentage, Cawnpore, India, Aug. 20, 1881; s. George Harrison (D.D.) and Anna Julia (Lore) McG.; A.B., Harvard, 1903; m. Dorothea deKay Gilder, May 19, 1916 (died Mar. 10, 1920); m. 2d, Elizabeth Wright Barber, Sept. 27, 1921; children—Helena D., John R., Sarah E. Asst. to cons. architect to Philippine Commn., 1905-06; asst. supt. St. Joseph Lead Co., 1906-11; financial editor and asst. to pub. Boston Journal, 1913-16; with International Banking Corp. in China, Japan, France, 1916-21; Am. counsellor to ministry of foreign affairs, Japan, 1921-29; asso. architect, Nat. Park Service from 1939, structural engineer, U.S. Navy Yard, Wash., D.C., from 1940. In France with Am. Field Service, attached to 2d and 7th French armies, Jan.-July 1915. Club: Chevy Chase, (Washington, D.C.). Address: Chevy Chase, Md.†

MCGUIGAN, JAMES CHARLES, cardinal; b. Hunter River, Prince Edward Island, Nov. 26, 1894; s. George Hugh and Anna (Monaghan) McG.; student Prince of Wales Coll., 1908-11, St. Dunstan's U. (awarded Gov. Gen. medal), 1912-14; B.A., Laval U., Quebec, 1914; S.T.D., Grand Sem., Quebec, 1918; student Cath. U. of Am., Washington, 1927; D.D., Ph.D., J.C.D., LL.D. Ordained to Roman Cath. priesthood, 1918; prof., St. Dunstan's Coll., 1918-19; chancellor, Edmonton diocese, 1922, vicar-gen., 1923; rector Edmonton Cathedral, 1925, St. Joseph's Sem., Edmonton, 1927; dean, Edmonton Dist., 1927; apptd. Prothonotory Apostolic with title of monsignor, 1927; consultor, diocese of Edmonton, 1927. Consecrated archbishop of Regina, at Edmonton, 1930; Archbishop of Regina, Saskatchewan, 1930, Toronto, 1934; appt. asst. at Pontifical Throne and Roman Count, Oct. 1943; created Cardinal with title of Santa Maria del Popolo, Feb. 1946; Cardinal Archbishop of Toronto, from 1946; chancellor, Cath. Ch. Extension Society of Can., Pontifical Inst. Medieval Studies, Toronto; pres. bd. dirs. St. Augustine's Sem., Toronto. Papal Legate a latere, Marian Congress, Ottawa, 1947. Author: Published Sermons. Home: Willowdale, Ont., Canada. Died 1974.

MCGUIRE, ALICE BROOKS, (Mrs. J. Carson McGuire), educator; b. Phila., Aug. 9, 1902; d. John David and Anna Rebecca (Foster) Brooks; A.B., Smith Coll., 1923; B.S., Drexel U., 1926; M.S. (Carnegie fellow), Columbia, 1932; Ph.D. (Univ. fellow), U. Chgo., 1958; m. J. Carson McGuire, May 8, 1947. Librarian Slippery Rock (Pa.) State Coll., 1923-28; asst. prof. library sci. Drexel U., Phila., 1928-44; instr. library sci. U. Chgo., 1945-49, dir. children's book center, 1945-49; librarian Casis Sch., Austin, Tex., 1951-68; asso. prof. Grad. Sch. Library Sci., U. Tex. at Austin, 1968-72; tchr. workshops and summer U. Ore., U. So. Cal., U. Ariz., Columbia, U. Wash.; cons. Compton's Ency., Chgo., 1969-75, Scott Foreman Co., Chgo., 1963-68. Recipient Grolier award, 1962. Mem. A.L.A., Tex. Library Assn. (librarian of year 1969), Am. Assn. Sch. Librarians (pres. 1954), Internat. Reading Assn., Am. Assn. U. Profs., Assn. Ednl. Communication and Tech. Editor children's lit. The Reading Tchr., 1969-71. Home: Austin, Tex., Died July 9, 1975.

MCGUIRE, ANDREW THOMAS, lawyer, govt. ofcl.; b. New London, Conn., Nov. 30, 1911; s. Henry Laurence and Clara Agnes (Maher) McG.; A.B., Holy Cross Coll., 1935; LL.B., U. Conn., 1938; m. Josephine Frances McDermott, Nov. 9, 1940. Adminstrv. asst. div. airports C.A.A.; legal adviser to judges Municipal Ct., D.C., 1940-50; chief opinions and reports War Claims Commn., 1950-53; gen. counsel, 1953-54; gen. counsel Fgn. Claims Settlement Commn., Washington, 1954-75. Presdl. nominee U.S. dist. judge Div. 2, Dist. of Alaska, 1953. Lt., USNR. Recipient merit citation Nat. Civil Service League, 1955. Mem. Bar Assn. D.C., Am., Fed., Internat. bar assns., Am. Judicature Soc., Conn. State Soc., Mil. Order Carabao. Clubs: Capitol Hill, Holy Cross (Washington). Home: McLean, Va., Died Oct. 17, 1975.

MCHALE, FRANK MARTIN, lawyer; b. Logansport, Ind., Mar. 4, 1891; s. Martin and Margaret (Farrell) McH.; LL.B., U. Mich., 1916, LL.D., St. Joseph's Coll., 1963; Marion Coll., 1970; m. Mabel Elizabeth Corriden, June 25, 1924 (dec. Apr. 1968). Admitted to Ind. bar, 1915; mem. Kistler, Kistler & McHale, 1919-32, Fansler, McHale & Douglass, 1932-33, McHale, Douglass & Myers, 1933-35, McHale Arthur, Myers & Patrick, 1935-46, McHale, Patrick, Cook & Welch, 1946-60, later with McHale, Cook & Welch. Chmn. bd. So. Ind. Ry., Inc., Nat. Bank of Logansport; exec. com. dir. Am. Fletcher Corp.; former chmn. Nickel Plate Road; v.p., dir., mem. exec. com. U.S. Freight. Mem. Nat. Democratic Com., 1937-52. Served as pvt. Signal Corps and later lt. Air Service, World War I. Recipient Significant Sig award Sigma Chi. Mem. Am., Ind., Indpls. bar assns., Cass County Bar Association (pres. 1927-31), Am. Judicature Soc., Am. Legion (1st comdr. Cass County post 1919, 20, 21; Ind. dept. comdr. 1928; nat. exec. committeeman 1928-29), Sigma Chi. Gamma Eta Gamma. Decorated Knight of St. Gregory. Mem. bd. lay trustees St. Joseph's Coll. Roman Catholic. Democrat, Club: Indianapolis Athletic. Home: Indianapolis, Ind. Died Jan. 26, 1975.

MCHUGH, KEITH STRATTON, State Ofcl. b. Fort Collins, Colo., Feb. 22, 1895; s. Peter J.and Lerah (Stratton) McHugh; B.S., U. Wisconsin, 1917, LL.D., 1957: LL.D., Syracuse University, 1955, Polytech. Institute Brooklyn, 1961; L.H.D., Siena College, 1960; D. Engring., Manhattan College, 1955; married Frances Brown, August 16, 1917 (deceased June 1956); married 2d, Dorothy Barbree Miller, Dec. 14, 1957. With Am. Tel. & Tel. Co., and Bell System, 1919—59, beginning as asst, engr., comml. engr., 1929—34, asst. v.p., 1934—38, v.p., 1938—49; comml. engr. Chesapeake & Potomac Telephone Co., 1921—25; gen. comml. mgr., upstate area, N.Y. Telephone Co., Albany, 1925—27, L.I. area, 1927—29, v.p., 1929, pres., 1949—59; commr. of commerce N.Y. State Dept. Commerce, 1959—75. Dir., mem. exec. com. Air Reductn Co., Dun & Bradstreet, Inc. Chmn. N.Y. Job Devel. Authority. Trustee Carnegie Instn.; bd. dirs. N.Y. State Sci. and Tech. Found. Decorated knight Order of Crown (Belgium); recipient certificates of appreciation War Dept. and Nat. Mil. Establishment, World War 11 William Randolph Hearst Gold Medal, Downtown Lower Manhattan Assn., 1961; named Man of Year, Hundred Year Assn., 1957, Served as capt. U.S. Army, AEF, 1918—19. Mem. (life) Am. Mgmt. Assn., Chi Psi, Tau Beta Pi, Tau Pi Sigma. Clubs: Univ. (N.Y.); Ekwanok Country (Manchester, Vt.); Blind Brook (Port Chester, N.Y.); Clove Valley Rod and Gun (North Clove, N.Y.); Fort Orange (Albany, N.Y.). Home: New York City, N.Y. Died June 7, 1975; buried Gate of Heaven, Mt. Pleasant, N.Y.

MCILWAIN, CHARLES HOWARD, educator; b. Saltsburg, Pa., Mar. 15, 1871; s. William R. and Anne Elizabeth (Galbraith) M.; A.B., Coll. of N.J. (now Princeton U.), 1894, A.M., 1989; A.M., Harvard, 1903, Ph.D., 1911, LL.D., 1938; LL.D., Coll. of Wooster, 1927, U. Chgo., 1941, Rutgers U., 1941; L.H.D., Williams Coll., 1937; Litt. D., Princeton, 1946, Yale, 1952; M.A., Oxford, 1944; D.C.L., Colgate U., 1949; m. Mary B. Irwin, Aug. 10, 1899 (died 1906); children—George Irwin, Martha; m. 2d, Kathleen Thompson, Apr. 4, 1916 (died 1948); children—Olive Elizabeth (Mrs. Walter S. Kerr), Robert William (dec.), Charles Howard. Admitted to bar of Allegheny Co., Pa., 1897; teacher Latin and history Kiskiminetas Sch., 1898-1901; prof. history Miami U., Oxford, O., 1930-05; preceptor Princeton; 1905-10; Thomas Brackett Reed prof. history and polit. science Bowdoin Coll., 1910-11; asst. prof. history Harvard, 1911-16, prof. history and govt., 1916-26. Eaton prof. science of govt., 1926-46; George Eastman vis. prof. Oxford 1944; lectr. history Princeton, 1948-49. Hon. fellow Balliol Coll., Oxford. Trustee emeritus Princeton U. Fellow Am. Acad. Arts and Sciences, Medieval Acad. Am.; corr. fellow British Acad.; mem. Am. Hist. Assn. (pres. 1935-36), Am. Polit. Sci. Assn., Royal Hist. Society (corr.), Am. Philos. Soc., Mass. Hist. Soc., Colonial Soc. of N.E., Phi Beta Kappa, Phi Alpha Theta. Club: Harvard Faculty, Author: The High Court of Parliament and Its Supremacy, 1910; The Am. Revolution, 1923 (Pulitzer prize); The Growth of Political Thought in the West, from the Greeks to the End of the Middle Ages, 1932; Constitutionalism and the Changing World, 1939; Constitutionalism, Ancient and Modern, 1940. Editor: Wraxall's Abridgement of the New York Indian Records (1678-1751), 1915; The Political Works of James I, 1918; Lombarde's Archeion (with Paul L. Ward), 1956. Address: Milton, Mass.†

MCINNIS, EDGAR WARDWELL, educator; b. Charlottetown, Prince Edward Island, July 26, 1899; s. David and Eliza (Aitken) McI.; student Prince of Wales Coll., 1913-16; B.A., U. Toronto, 1923; B.A., Oxford U., 1926, M.A., 1930; LL.D., Dartmouth, 1957; D.Litt., York U., 1972; m. Lorene Hull, 1930. Asst. prof. history Oberlin Coll., 1926-28; mem. dept. history staff U. Toronto, 1928-52, prof., 1949-52; pres. Canadian Inst. Internat. Affairs, 1952-60; prof. history York U., 1960-69, prof. emeritus, 1969-73, univ. orator, 1968-70, dean faculty of grad. studies, 1963-65. Mem. Canadian delegation 7th UN Assembly, 1952; vis. prof. Bowdoin Coll., on Tallman Found., 1941-42; book reviewer and commentator on current affairs Canadian Broadcasting Corp. several years. Served with Canadian Garrison Arty., 1916-19. Rhodes Scholar attending Christ Church, Oxford, 1923; received Newdigate prize for English verse, 1925; Governor-General's Award, 1942, 1944; Tyrrell Hist. medal, 1966. Author several books, 1940-73, latest being: The Atlantic Triangle and the Cold War, 1959. Home: Toronto, Canada. Died Sept. 27, 1973.

MCINTIRE, CLIFFORD (GUY), farmer, orgn. exec.; b. Perham, Me., May 4, 1908; s. Frank Charles and Velma (Smith) McI.; B.S., U. Me., 1930; hon. degrees U. Me., Bowdoin Coll., Me. Maritime Acad.; m. Wilda Autice Holts, Sept. 11, 1931; children—Patrice Velma (Mrs. Malcolm Andrews), Blynn Clifford. Farmer, Perham, since 1930; appraiser, regional mgr. Fed. Land Bank of Springfield (Mass.), 1933-47; asst. gen. mgr. Me. Potato Growers, Inc., Presque Isle, Me., 1947-51; mem. 82d-87th Congresses from 3d Me. Dist., 88th Congress from 2d Me. Dist.; dir. natural resources dept. Am. Farm Bur. Fedn., 1965-74. Mem. Nat. Ry. Assn. Named outstanding farmer, U. Me., 1949. Mem. Alpha Gamma Rho, Alpha Zeta, Phi Kappa Phi. Baptist. Mason (Shriner), Elk, Rotarian. Home: Perham, Me. Died Oct. 1, 1974; buried Perham, Me.

MCINTOSH, BENJAMIN HARRISON, commr. of edn.; b. Ramona, Kan., Feb. 28, 1881; s. Joshua Gregg and Anna Matilda (Andrews) McI.; B.S., Kan. State Teachers Coll., Emporia, 1917; Kan. Agrl. Coll., 1914; Colo. State Teachers Coll., Greeley, 1921, 25; m. Gladys Eichenour, of Durham, Kan., May 29, 1919; children—Harold Elwood, Marilyn, Lora Mae, Norma Jean, Arlene Louise, Walter Donald. Teacher, Marion Co., Kan., 1906-08, 1910-11; supt. schs., Durham, Kan., 1913-15; teacher high sch., Leavenworth, Kan., Mar.-June 1919; prin. high sch., Telluride, Colo., 1919-20, Cheyenne, Wyo., 1920-30; state commr. of edn., Wyo., 1930-35; asst. dir. Nat. Youth Adminstrn. from 1935. Served as 2d, later 1st lt. C.A.C., U.S.A., 1917-19; capt. C.A. Res. from 1925. Mem. N.E.A. and Dept. Superintendence same, Wyo. Edn. Assn., Kappa Delta Pi, Sigma Tau Gamma, Pi Gamma Mu. Republican. Presbyn. Mason (32°). Clubs: Lions, Forum. Writer or editor course of study for Wyo. State Dept. Edn. Home: Cheyenne, Wyo.†

MCINTOSH, LOY N., lawyer; b. Bridgeport, Ill., 1890; grad. Northwestern U., 1915. Mem. firm Gann, McIntosh; Stead & O'Shaughnessy, Chgo.; chmn. Ludlow Typograph Co., Merc. Nat. Bank Chgo.; dir. Fred A. Snow Co., Finance Res. Co., Sunway Fruit Products Co., Sunway Vitamin, Inc., Wells Petroleum Co., Refiners Distbg. Corp., Sager Metal Strip Co. Home: Chicago, Ill. Died Sept. 17, 1973.

MCIVER, ANGUS VAUGHN, architect; b. Great Falls, Mont., Apr. 29, 1892; s. Kenneth B. and Viola Jane (Vaughn) McI.; B.C.E., U. Mich., 1915; m. Loneta Eileen Kuhn, Mar. 19, 1915 (dec.); 1 dau., Margo (Mrs. James Thomas Shorney); m. 2d, Valborg H. Graham, Nov. 10, 1966. Archtl. practice as prin., Great Falls, from 1915, later engaged in cons. work. Mem. Bd. Archtl. Examiners, Mont., 1953-61. Served as lt. U.S. Army, 34th Div., 1918-19. Licensed architect, Mont., civil engr., 1948. Fellow A.I.A. (dir. 1945-47, past pres. Mont. chpt.), Am. Soc. C.E.; mem. Am. Legion (past post comdr.), Chi Phi. Mason (Shriner), Rotarian. Home: Great Falls, Mont. Died July 24, 1974; interred Hillcrest Lawn Mausoleum.

MCKAY, LLEWELYN R., educator; b. Ogden, Utah, June 5, 1904; s. David O. and Emma Reay (Riggs) McK.; A.B., U. Utah, 1928, M.A., 1930; Ph.D., Stanford U., 1940; certificate from Heidelberg, 1931; postgrad. U. Mexico, 1943; m. Alice Kimball Smith, 1928; children—Richard, Douglas, Bonnie. Asst. in instrn. modern lang. dept. U. Utah, 1928-29, instr., 1929-39, asst. prof., 1939-40, asso. prof., 1940-45, prof. head dept., 1945-70; U.S. Strategic Bombing Survey, Germany, 1945; teaching adv. Army Lang. Sch., Monterey, Cal., 1950; exchange prof. German Fed. Govt., 1955; lang. cons. US Army, Pacific. Mem. Utah Acad. Sci. and Art, Am. Assn. U. Profs., Phi Delta Kappa, Sigma Kappa Phi, Tau Kappa Alpha, Pi Kappa Alpha, Phi Eta Sigma, Theta Alpha Phi. Club: Aztec. Author: Home Memories of President David O. McKay; Christmas Silhouettes; Deutsche Ubungen; several articles. Compiler: Pathways to Happiness; Secrets of a Happy Life, 1960; German Phonetics Manual; True to the Faith; Stepping Stones to an Abundant Life. Home: Salt Lake City, Utah Died Jan. 2, 1975.

MCKEE, ANDREW IRWIN, naval officer; b. Larenceburg, Ky., Feb. 17, 1896; s. Lewis Witherspoon and Eliza Schenck (Irwin) McK.; B.S. with distinction, U.S. Naval Acad., 1917; M.S., Mass. Inst. Tech., 1921; m. Katherine Brown, Oct. 4, 1919 (div. 1947); children—Andrew Irwin, Katherine (Mrs. Walter Miller Ousey), Lewis Witherspoon, Francis Brown; m. 2d, Baroness Ingeborg von Finckh, July 12, 1947. Commd. ensign USN, 1917, advanced through grades to rear adm., 1947; served in U.S.S. Huntington, engaged in troop transport to Europe, 1917-18; tranferred to Naval Construction Corps, 1918; submarine asst. to supt. constrn., Bethlehem Shipbuilding Corp., Fore Fiver plant, 1919-20; asst. repair supt. Navy Yard, Portsmouth, N.H., 1922-24; constrn. officer; submarine base, New London, Conn., 1924-26; charge submarine design desk Bur. Constrn. and Repair, Navy Dept., 1926-30; supt. new constrn. Navy Yard, Phila., 1930-34; hull supt. Mare Island Navy Yard, 1934-37; planning officer and design supt. Navy Yard, Portsmouth, N.H., 1938-44; fleet maintenance officer, service force, Pacific Fleet, 1945, in charge emergency repairs, Okinawa; comdr. Naval Shipyard, Phila., 1945-47; ret. as rear adm., 1947; v.p. Gen. Dynamics, Corp., dir. research and design Electric Boat div., 1952-61. Decorated Legion of Merit, Bronze Star Medal (twice); recipient David W. Taylor medal Soc. Naval Architects and Marine Engrs., 1956. Mem. U.S. Naval Inst., Soc. Naval Architects and Marine Engrs., Am. Soc. Naval Engrs., Sigma Xi, Pi Tau Sigma. Episcopalian. Home: New London, Conn., Died Jan. 24, 1976; buried Arlington Nat. Cemetery.

MCKEE, JESSE LYNNE, railraod exec.; b. Constantine, Mich., June 8, 1881; s. William and Bell (Cox) McK.; ed. grade schs. and high sch., Constantine; m. Ella Freeman, Dec. 31, 1909; 1 dau., Ruth Maxine. In railway service from 1907; gen. yardmaster, asst. gen. supt. and gen. supt. Michigan Central R.R., Detroit, Mich., until 1932; became asst. vice pres. N.Y. Central System, Chicago, Ill., 1932; then vice pres., Detroit then vice pres. and asst. to pres., Chicago. Home: Chicago, Ill.*†

MCKEE, PAUL GORDON, coll. prof., author; b. Sharon, Pa., Oct. 14, 1897; s. George Brady and Louella Edith (Wickey) McK.; A.B., Monmouth (Ill.) Coll. 1920, Litt.D., 1950; A.M., State U. of Ia., 1921, Ph.D., 1924; m. Sarah Grace McCullough, Dec. 27, 1921; 1 dau., Beverly Anne (Mrs. Eaton). Scholar, State U. of Ia., 1920-21, fellow, 1923-24. Supt. schs., Hanover, Ill., 1921-23; grad. supvr., Hibbing, Minnesota, 1924-26; prof. of elementary edn., Colo. State Coll., Greeley, Colo., 1926-62, dir. Ernest Horn Elementary Sch., same coll., 1932-42. dir. of elementary edn. coll., 1942-59; instructional cons. Denver Pub. Schs., 1961-74; course of study cons. to state depts. of edn.; consultant Scholastic Magazines, Incorporated; consultant Orthol. Inst., Harvard, 1941, U.S. Armed Forces Inst., Washington, 1943; vis. prof. State Univ. of Ia., 1929; editor Riverside Textbooks in Education (dealing with elementary edn.), Houghton Miffin, from 1942. Pres. Nat. Conf. on Research in English, 1939. Mem. nat. coms. for 36th, 38th, 43d, 48th yearbooks, Nat. Soc. Study of Edn. Mem. Phi Sigma Alpha, Tau Kappa Alpha, Phi Delta Kappa, Kappa Delta Pi. Episcopalian. Mason. Clubs: Greeley Country; Denver, Denver Country. Author: numerous books relating to field; also editor or contbr. various profl. publs. Home: Greeley, Colo., Died Nov. 26, 1974; buried Trinity Episcopal Ch. Meml. Garden, Greeley.

MCKEE, CAPTAIN WILLIAM, economist, author; b. Freeport, Ken., Apr. 29, 1895; s. Benjamin Prentice and Nettie (Cooper) McK.; student Southwestern Coll., 1914-15, Ottawa U., 1915-16, Central YMCA Sch. Phys. Edn., Chgo., spring 1917, U. Colo., summer 1919, Harvard Grad. Sch. Bus. Adminstrn., summers 1928, 29; A.B., Ottawa U., 1920; A.M., U. Chgo., 1924; m. Florence C. Pollard, June 18, 1929; children—William Pollard, Robert Cooper, Thomas Benjamin. Chmn. dept. econs. and bus. adminstrn. Westminster Coll., 1924-59, chmn. div. social sci., 1945-48; lectr. edn. U. Pitts., 1963-74; tchr. Youngstown Coll. Night Sch., 1927-33; bd. dirs. McDowell Nat. Bank, Sharon, Pa.; pres., bd. trustees Am. Inst. Econs.; dir. indsl. survey New Castle, Pa., 1939, Sharon, Pa., 1941; dir. econ. forums. Candidate O.T.S., 1918. Mem. Am. Econ. Assn., Am. Polit. Sci. Assn., Am. Sociol. Soc. Mason. Clubs: Youngstown (O.) Country; New Castle (Pa.) Country; Sharon (Pa.) Country. Author: Economic and Business Activities in the Shenango and Mahoning Valleys, 1940; Uses and Users of Bank Loans in Industrial Communities, 1941; Size, Security, Interest Rates, Maturities, Renewals, and Turnover of Bank Loans in Industrial Communities, 1941; (with Dr. Harold G. Moulton) A Survey of Economic Education, 1951; (with Dr. Asher Isaacs, Dr. R.E. Slesinger, Mr. W.C. Bradford) Workbook in Economics, Teacher's Manual in Economics, 1952. Editor: Lectures for Bankers and Business Executives, 1940; The What, Why and How of American Free Enterprise, 1941; American Economic Policies, 1945; American Business Policies, 1944-47; (with Dr. Asher Isaacs, Dr. R.E. Slesinger) Readings in Economics, 1951; (with Dr. Asher Isaacs, Dr. William Bradford) Working and Living in America; also sectional editor, contbr. An Introduction to Modern Economics, 1950; editorial bd. Economic Series, Polit. Sci. Series, Sociol. Series, An Introduction to Social Sci. History of Civilization. Address: New Wilmington, Pa. Died Feb. 11, 1974.

MCKEEFRY, PETER CARDINAL, Clergyman; b. Greymouth, New Zealand, July 3, 1899. Ordained priest Roman Catholic Ch., 1926; titular archbishop of Dercos, 1947; coadjutor-archbishop of Wellington (New Zealand), 1947-54, archbishop, 1954-73; elevated to cardinal, 1969. Home: Wellington, New Zealand. Died Nov. 18, 1973.

MCKEEHAN, LOUIS WILLIAMS, physicist; b. l)inneapolis, Minn., Mar. 31, 1887; s. Alfred Espy and Katherine Elliot (Williams) McK.; student U.S. Naval Acad., 1903—05; B.S. in Engring., U. of Minn., 1908, M.S., 1909, Ph.D., 1911; grad. study Cambridge, Eng., 1911—12; M.A., Yale, 1927; m. Grace Rose Badger, Aug. 14, 1912; children—John Badger, Mary Katherine (Mrs. Arthur Ronchie). Asst. in physics, U. of lMinn., 1906—09, instr., 1909—15, asst. prof. physics, 1915—18, asso. prof., 1918—19; asst. physicist U.S. Bur. Standards (on leave of absence from U. of Minn.), 1917—18; technicist Bureau of Ordnance, Navy Dept., 1919—21; mem. tech. staff, research dept., Western Electric Co., 1921—25, Bell Telephone Labs., 1925—27; prof. physics and dir. Sloane Physics Laboratory, Yale, 1927—55, emeritus. Served as lt. USNRF, 1918—19; lt. commander U.S.N.R., 1924—40; commander U.S. Naval Reserve (active duty) Bureau of Ordnance, Washington, 1940—42; capt., U.S. Naval Reserve, 1942—46 (on leave from Yale) Yale—Navy research program, 1951—75. Twice awarded Legion of Merit (USAAF) (U.S.N.). Fellow Am. Phsical Society, A.A.A.S., American Academy Arts and Sciences; member of the American Assn. University Professors, Sigma Xi. Clubs: Army and Navy, Cosmos (Washington, D.C.); Yale (New York); Graduate (New Haven). Author: (with A. F. Kovarik) Rev., Jour. Optical Soc. America, Jour. Franklin Inst., etc. Home: Jamestown, R.I. Died Mar. 28, 1975; buried Jamestown, R.I.

MCKELDIN, THEODORE ROOSEVELT, mayor of Balt.; b. Balt., Nov. 20, 1900; s. James A. and Dora (Grief) McK.; LL.B., U. Md., 1925, Ithaca Coll., 1953, Anderson Coll., 1953, Lincoln Coll., 1954; Litt.D., Ind. Central Coll., 1952, Westminster Coll., Utah, 1952; D. Polit. Sci., Steed Coll. Tech., 1954; L.H.D., Loyola Coll., Md., 1953; student econs. Johns Hopkins; LL.D., Rider Coll., Washington Coll., U. Md., Morgan Coll., Beaver Coll., Hanover Coll.; m. Honolulu Claire Manzer, Oct. 17, 1924; children—Theodore Roosevelt, Clara Whitney. Admitted to Md. bar, 1926; exec. sec. to mayor, Balt., 1927-31; pvt. practice law, 1931-43, 1947-51; mayor Balt., 1943-47, 64-67; gov. of Md., 1951-59. Mem. Md., Am. bar assns., German Soc. Md. Mason (32deg., K.T., Shriner). Clubs: Kiwanis. Home: Baltimore, Md. Died Aug. 1974.

MCKELVY, WILLIAM RUSH, lawyer; b. Corydon, Ia., Oct. 16, 1904; s. John F. and Martha J. (Shipley) McK.; B.A., U. Ia., 1927, LL.B., 1929; m. Jane Wiley, July 6, 1945; children—Marcia, Susan, Janis, William Rush. Admitted to Ia. bar, 1929, Wash. bar, 1930; asso. Skeel, McKelvy, Henke, Evenson & Betts and predecessor firms, Seattle, 1930-72, sr. partner, 1938-72. Fellow Am. Coll. Trial Lawyers: mem. Fedn. Ins. Counsel, Nat. Assn. R.R. Trial Counsel, Internat. Assn. Ins. Counsel, Am. Wash. State Seattle-King County bar assns. Contbg. author symposium; Successful Jury Trials, 1952. Home: Seattle, Wash., Died Jan. 16, 1972.

MCKENDRY, JOHN JOSEPH, museum exec.; b. Calgary, Alta., Can., Jan. 5, 1933; came to U.S., 1958; s. John Joseph and Mary (Mullan) McK.; B.A. in English Lit., U. Alta., 1958; postgrad. Inst. Fine Arts, N.Y. U., 1958-60; m. Maxime de la Falaise, July 6, 1967. With Met. Mus. Art, N.Y.C., 1960-75, curator dept. prints and photographs, 1967-75. Club: Grolier. Author: Aesop: Five Centuries of Illustrated Fables, 1964; Robert Motherwells A La Pintura: The Genesis of a Book, 1972. Home: New York City, N.Y. Died June 23, 1975.

MCKENNA, BROTHER JOSEPH G., coll. pres.; b. N.Y.C., May 20, 1922; s. John and Jennie (McAllister) McK.; B.Sc., Fordham U., 1941; M.A., Columbia, 1947, Ph.D., 1954. Joined Order Christian Bros., Roman Cath. Ch., 1936, tchr. Iona Prep. Sch. New Rochelle, N.Y., 1943-47, Rice High Sch., N.Y.C., 1942-43; dir. guidance Power Meml. Acad., N.Y.C., 1947-50; dean Iona Coll., New Rochelle, N.Y., 1950-55, v.p., 1963-65 pres., 1965-71; tchr. All Hallows High Sch., N.Y.C., 1955-57; founder, prin. Cath. Meml. High Sch., Boston, 1957-63. Founder, 1st pres. Boston Archdiocesan Guidance Council, 1961; consultor Eastern Am. province Christian Bros., 1965-73. Bd. dirs. United Cerebral Palsy Assn. Westchester County. Mem. Nat. Cath. Edn. Assn. (exec. com.), Am. Personnel and Guidance Assn. Home: New Rochelle, N.Y. Died July 28, 1973.

MCKIM, ROBERT JAMES, merchant; b. Kansas City, Mo., August 21, 1895; s. William Morton and Mary (Andes) McK.; student Tulane U.; m. Thelma M. Riley, May 17, 1922; 1 son, Robert James (dec.). Pres. Stewart Dry Goods Co., Louisville, 1930-43; pres., dir. Asso. Dry Goods Corp., N.Y.C., 1943-59, chmn. bd., 1959-67, chmn. exec. com., chmn. finance com., 1967-73; dir. Trust Co. of Fla., Orlando; adv. com. Chem. Bank N.Y. Trust Co. Served as 1st lt. inf., World War I. Clubs: The Links (N.Y.C.); Connetquot (Oakdale, L.I.); Blind Brook (Port Chester, N.Y.); Ristiguoche Salmon (Matapedia, Que.). Home: Lake Wales, Fla. Died Nov. 27, 1973.

MCKINIRY, RICHARD F congressman; b. N.Y. City, Mar. 23, 1878; s. John and Ellen (Predergast) McK.; A.B., Coll. St. Francis Xavier, New York, 1896, A.M., 1897; LL.B., New York Law Sch., 1898; unmarried. With law firm of Sheehan & Collin, New York, 1900-04; pvt. practice, 1904-14; mem. Fallon, Glennon & McKiniry, 1918-21, Mork, McKiniry & Baum, 1921; asst. dist. atty., Bronx Co., N.Y., 1914-17; sec. Supreme Court of N.Y., 1st Dist., 1917-19; mem. 66th Congress (1919-21), 23d N.Y. Dist.; apptd. city magistrate, New York, 1923. Democrat. Catholic. Mem. Assn. Bar County of Bronx, Friendly Sons of St. Patrick. Clubs: North End Democratic, Pastime Athletic, New York Athletic. Home: Bronx, N.Y.†

MCKINNEY, CORVELL, orgn. exec., trustee; b. New Orleans, Mar. 3, 1890; s. Edward Byron and Georgie (Hardel) McK.; student Soule Coll., night courses Tulane Coll. of Commerce, various extension universities, also night sch. New Orleans Inst. Banking; m. Katherine Elizabeth Turner, Jan. 11, 1930. Exec. and financial sec. to Samuel Zemurray, 1921-61, executor of estate, 1961-73; sec.-treas. Tangipahoa Tung Oil Co., 1944-59, Tung Ridge Ranch, 1950-61; sec. Zemurray Found., 1953-73. Bd. dirs. Inst. Mental Hygiene New Orleans, 1952-60, pres., 1960-62; bd. dirs. La. Assn. Mental Health, 1946-63, pres., 1955-57; bd. dirs. Nat. Assn. Mental Health, 1955-57, 59-64, sec., 1963-64; bd. dirs. Community Chest New Orleans, 1955-60, United Fund New Orleans, 1959-60; adv. com. New Orleans Salvation Army, 1962-73. Served to 1st lt., A.C., U.S. Army, 1917-18. Recipient Mental Health award La. Assn. Mental Health, 1959; Half-way House for discharged mental patients dedicated as McKinney House, 1964. Clubs: Metairie Country, Southern Yacht (life) (New Orleans). Home: New Orleans, La. Died June 6, 1973; interred Hope Mausoleum, New Orleans, La.

MCKINNEY, FRANK E., chmn. Democratic nat. com.; b. Indianapolis, June 16, 1904; s. Roscoe A. and Anna (Moss) McK.; ed. Ind. U. Extension Div.; La Salle Inst. of Accounting; Am. Inst. of Banking; LL.D., St. Francis Coll., Loretta, Pa.; m. Margaret K. Warner, Nov. 24, 1932; children—Claire, Robert, Frank E., Jr., Margaret Kathleen. Asst. cashier Peoples State Bank, 1921; pres. Fidelity Bank & Trust Co., 1935-59; chmn. bd. Am. Fletcher Nat. Bank and Trust Co., 1959; pres., dir. III Realty Corp.; dir. Indpls. Power & Light Co., Phila. Suburban Water Co. Ind. Bell Telephone Co., Indland Steel Co., Nat. Homes Corp., U.S. Corrugated Fibre Box Co. Pres. Greater Indpls. Progress Com. Dir. Indpls. Hosp. Devel. Assn., chmn. bd. Indians, Inc.; pres. bd. trustees Ind. U.; chmn. bd. Winona Meml. Found.; trustee St. Joesph's Coll. Elected treas. Marion Co., 1934, re-elected, 1936; sub-treas. Ind. Nat. Com., 1936; v.p. Dem. Nat. Finance Com., 1940; del. to Dem. National Convention, 1948, 52, 56; chmn. Democratic National Com., 1951-53. Served as colonel, U.S. Army, 1942-45; asst. dir. of Contract Settlement, Washington, 1945. Knight of Sovereign Order Knights of Malta. Mem. Ind. C. of C. (dir.), Am. Legion, K.C. Clubs: Indianapolis Athletic (dir.), Columbia, Meridian Hills Country. Highland Golf and Country. Home: Indianapolis, Ind. Died Jan. 9, 1974.

MCKINNON, NEIL JOHN, banker; b. Cobalt, Ont., Can., Jan. 17, 1911; s. Malcolm and Selina F. (McCauley) McK.; m. Phyllis A. Cowie, May 3, 1941; 2 children. Joined Canadian Bank of Commerce, Cobalt, 1925, asst. gen. mgr., head office, 1945-52, gen. mgr., 1952-54, v.p., 1954-56, pres., 1956-61, chmn., 1959-61; pres., chief exec. officer Canadian Imperial Bank of Commerce (merger Canadian Bank of Commerce and Imperial Bank of Can.), 1961-63, chmn. chief exec. officer, 1963-65, chmn., 1965-73, dir.; dir. Continental Oil Co., Campbell Soup Co., Can Life Assurance Co., Falconbridge Nickel Mines Ltd., TransCan. PipeLines Ltd., Allied Chem. Can. Ltd., MacMillian Bloedel Ltd., Honeywell, Inc., Ford Motor Co. Can., Ltd. Presbyn. Clubs: Toronto, Rosedale Golf, York (Toronto); Rideau (Ottawa); The Links (N.Y.C.); Mt. Royal (Montreal). Home: Toronto, Ont., Canada., Died Aug. 4, 1975.

MCKNIGHT, DOUGLAS, civil engr.; b. Phila., July 20, 1895; s. James and Marianna (Smith) McK.; B.S., U. Pa., 1920; m. Annesta Glynn Pierce, Jan. 16, 1923; children—Charlotte (Mrs. Harold D. Thompson), Hugh, Diana. Resident engr. Burlington R.R., 1921-25; field engr. Portland Cement Assn., Lincoln, Neb., 1925-37; chief engr. Municipal Service & Supply Co., Omaha, 1937-39; cons. engring. Douglas McKnight, Lincoln, 1939-74; pres. M.O.R.E. Service, Inc., 1954-74, founder Highroad div., 1969. Served to 2d lt. U.S. Army, 1917-18, lt. USNR, 1943-45, comdr., 1952-55. Mem. Nat. Soc. Profl. Engrs., Ret. Officers Assn. (past chpt. pres.), Profl. Engrs. Neb., Am. Interprofl. Inst. (past pres. Lincoln chpt.). Democrat. Presbyn. Home: Lincoln, Neb. Died June 22, 1974.

MCKNIGHT, ROBERT JAMES GEORGE, clergyman, educator; b. Slippery Rock, Pa., July 9, 1878; s. Robert and Elizabeth (Campbell) McK.; A.B., Geneva Coll., Beaver Falls, Pa., 1896 (D.D., 1918); grad. Reformed Presbyn. Theol. Sem., Pittsburgh, Pa., 1899; B.D., Princeton Theol. Sem., 1900; studied Johns Hopkins, 1901-02, Columbia, 1903, U. of Leipzig, 1904-05; Ph.D., U. of Chicago, 1907; m. Grace Patterson, Sept. 20, 1905; children—Robert James George, Hugh Patterson. Ordained Reformed Presbyn. ministry, 1903; pastor Middletown, Pa., 1903-04; instr. Morgan Park (Ill.) Mill. Acad., 1907-08; pastor Wilkinsburg, Pa., 1909-16; prof. Bibl. lit., Reformed Presbyn. Sem., from 1916, pres., from 1929. Pres. Keystone Driller Co., from 1935; president Kaydee Land Co. (both Beaver Falls, Pa.). Moderator Reformed Presbyterian Synod, 1934. Chautauqua Assembly lecturer and Bible teacher, summers. Home: Wilkinsburg, Pa.†

MCKNIGHT, WILLIAM HODGES, physician; b. Springtown, Tex., Jan. 4, 1894; s. William Burney and Sallie (Hodges) McK.; M.D., Harvard, 1920. Intern, Boston City Hosp., 1920-21. Diplomate Am. Bd. Preventive Medicine. Mem. A.M.A., Aerospace Med. Assn., Airline Med. Dirs. Assn., Kappa Sigma. Democrat. Methodist. Mason. Home: Mansfield, Tex. Died Sept. 18, 1969; buried Mansfield, Tex.

MCKOWN, EDGAR M., coll. dean; b. Greenville, Ind., Mar. 10, 1896; s. Derastus William and Adelia (Mettling) McK.; student DePauw U., 1918-19; A.B., Evansville Coll., 1922; S.T.B., Boston U., 1927, Ph.D., 1932; m. Mary Elizabeth Eicholz, Aug. 16, 1923; children—Dorothy Matilda (dec.), Leslie Henry. Teacher pub. schs., New Albany (Ind.) Twp., 1916-18; pastor Meth. Ch., Evansville, Ind., 1918-21; teacher, Evansville (Ind.) Pub. Schs., 1922-24; dir. young people's work, Ch. of All Nations, Boston, Mass., 1924-28; pastor Meth. Ch., Mass. and Ind., 1928-36; prof. philosophy and religion, head of dept., Evansville Coll., since 1936, dean coll. since 1941. President and one of founders Evansville Council of Week Day Religious Edn. (pres., 1943-46, treas., 1946). Chairman Evansville Council of Churches Commission on Week Day Religious Edn. 1941-52, 1941; chmn. week day religious edn. sect. Nat. Council Churches, 1954-55; asso. dean Rivervale Epworth League Inst., 1934-36; dir. religious edn. Methodist Church, Bloomington (Ind.) Dist., 1934-36; dean, Vanderburgh (Ind.) County Leadership Training Sch., 1937-40. Mem. Am. Philos. Assn., Am. Conference of Academic Deans, National Association Biblical Instrs., Nat. Assn. for Advancement of Colored People, Ministerial Assn. (Evansville), mem. Am. Assn. for The Advancement of Science, Phi Gamma Mu. Club: Schoolmen's (Evansville, Ind.). Co-author: Understanding Christianity, 1949. Contbr. articles to religious and ednl. periodicals. Home: Evansville, Ind. Died June 19, 1973.

MCLAIN, BOBBY MAURICE, physician; b. Nacogdoches, Tex., 1925; M.D., U. Tex., 1954; m. Merline Plunkett, Feb. 5, 1949; children—Rebecca Ann (Mrs. John Michael Pettet), Elizabeth Gardner. Intern, U.S. Naval Hosp., Jacksonville, Fla., 1954-55; postgrad. New Orleans Postgrad. Assembly; staff Lucy Lee Hosp., Popular Bluff, Mo.; clin. dir. McPheeters Clinic, Poplar Bluff. Served to lt. (j.g.) USNR, 1943-47; with M.C., USNR, 1954-55. Diplomate Am. Bd. Family Practice. Fellow Am. Acad. Family Physicians (charter); mem. A.M.A., Royal Soc. Health. Home: Poplar Bluff, MO., Died Nov. 20, 1973; buried Poplar Bluff, Mo.

MCLANE, CHARLES KEITH, educator; b. LaGrange, Ill., Oct. 12, 1921; s. Charles Frederick and Helen Maurine (Anderson) McL.; B.S., U. Wis., 1943, M.S., 1944; Ph.D. (NRC fellow), Harvard, 1949; m. Susan Dorothy Ammann, June 1, 1946; children—Stanley Keith (dec.), Daniel Louis. With Manhattan Dist. Engrs., U. S. Army, U. Chgo., 1944-45, Columbia U., N.Y.C., 1945-46; asst. prof. physics U. Wis. at Madison 1948-52; physicist Nat. Bur. Standards, Washington, 1952-53, 61-65; physicist Linde Co. div. Union Carbide Corp., Tonawanda, N.Y. and Speedway, Ind., 1953-60; physicist Environmental Sci. Services Adminstrn., Boulder, Colo., 1965-68; prof. aerospace engring. scis. U. Colo., Boulder, 1968-74, chmn. faculty council, 1972-73. Guggenheim fellow, 1953; AEC research grantee, 1950-52, 63-68, Def. Atomic Support Agy. research grantee, 1967-68, Air Force Office Sci. Research grantee, 1970-74. Fellow A.A.A.S.; mem. Am. Phys. Soc., Am. Inst. Aeros. and Astronautics, Am. Geophys. Union, Am. Nuclear Soc., A.A.U.P. (pres. Colo. chpt. 1974), Am. Soc. Engring. Edn. (program chmn. Rocky Mt. sect. 1972-73), Sigma Xi, Phi Beta Kappa. Contbr. articles to profl. jours. Home: Boulder, Colo. Died June 14, 1974.

MCLANE, RUBY ROACH, mem. Rep. Nat. Com.; b. Fayette County, Tenn., 1880; d. George Manly and Will-Ella (Henley) Roach; student Miss Anna Holdin's Seminary, Colliersville, Tenn.; Howard Coll., Gallatin, Tenn.; Hamilton Coll., Lexington, Ky.; m. A. V. McLane, June 1904; 1 dau., Elizabeth (Mrs. Howard Wester). Republican. Methodist. Home: Nashville, Tenn.†

MCLAREN, RICHARD WELLINGTON, judge; b. Chgo., Apr. 21, 1918; s. Grover C. and Nita (Waqgoner) McL.; B.A., Yale, 1939, LL.B., 1942; m. Edith Gillett, Sept. 20, 1941; children Patricia (Mrs. MacDonald), Richard Wellington, Sandra (Mrs. Foote), James Gillett. Admitted to N.Y. bar, 1944, Ill. bar, 1950; with firm Hodges, Reavis, Pantaleoni & Downey, N.Y.C., 1946-49; mem. firm Chadwell, Keck, Kayser, Ruggles & McLaren, Chgo., 1950-69, asst. atty. gen. anti-trust div. Justice Dept., 1969-72; judge U.S. Dist. Ct., No. Dist. Ill., Eastern Div., Chgo., 1972-76. Served to capt. USAAF, 1942-46. Mem. Am. (ho. of dels. 1963-66, vice chmn. antitrust sect. 1966-67, chmn. 1967-68), Fed., Ill., Chgo. bar assns., Am. Coll. Trial Lawyers. Clubs: Law Legal, Union League, Yale (Chgo.). Home: Winnetka, Il., Died Feb. 25, 1976; interred Christ Ch. Meml. Garden, Winnetka, Ill.

MCLAUGHLIN, CHARLES F., judge; b. Lincoln, Neb., June 19, 1887; s. William and Mary Ann (Cavanaugh) McL.; A.B., U. of Neb., 1908; LL.B., Columbia, 1910; m. Margaret Bruce, June 19, 1920; children—Edward Bruce, Mary Elizabeth (Mrs. Edmund Wellington, Jr.). Began practice of law in Omaha, Neb., 1910; master in chancery, Federal Court, 1916-17; del. Neb. State Constl. Conv., 1919-20; mem. 74th to 77th Congresses (1935-43), 2d Nebraska District; appointed judge United States District Court for Dist. of Columbia, Oct., 1949. Served in U.S. Army A.E.F., 1917-19, capt. field arty., maj. F.A. Res. Mem. Am.-Mexican Claims Commission, 1943-47. Mem. Am. and Neb. bar assns., Omaha Bar Assn. (past pres.), Phi Delta Theta, Phi Delta Phi. Democrat. Roman Catholic. Club: Metropolitan (Washington). Home: Washington, D.C., Died Feb. 5, 1976.

MCLAUGHLIN, EDWARD ALOYSIUS, physician; b. Providence, Aug. 1, 1893; s. James Henry and Mary J. (Connolly) McL.; M.D., Harvard, 1918; m. Mary F. Moriarty, Sept. 12, 1925; children—Thomas, Mary Frances (dec.), Edward Aloysisu, William. Intern, R.I. Hosp., Porvidence, 1918—20, later cons., vis. children's physician; intern Providence Lying—In Hosp., 1918—20; vis. children's physician St. Joseph's Hosp., Charles V. Chapin Hosp., Pawtucket (R.I.) Mem. Hosp.; med. dir. Providence Floating Hosp. Assn.; dir. R.I. Dept. Health, 1935—39, 41—59; surgeon Providence Police Dept., 1926—35; sch. physician, Providence, 1922—35. Pres., R.I. Infantile Paralysis Found., 1935. Decorated Knight of St. Gregory. Diplomate Am. Bd. Preventive Medicine. Mem. Friendly Sons of St. Patrick (pres. 1935). Sons of Irish Kings (chief steward 1945). Roman Catholic (trustee). K.C. (4°). Clubs: Harvard, Brown U. Home: Providence, R.I. Died July 30, 1972; buried St. Francis Cemetery, Pawtucket, R.I.

MCLEAN, DAVID J., newspaper pub.; b. Brooklyn, N.Y., July 23, 1879; s. Andrew and Ida McL; ed. Adelphia Acad., Brooklyn; m. Helen L. Douty, 1909; children—Helen D., Andrew, David J. Pub. Brooklyn (N.Y.) Citizen from 1915. Trustee Caledonian Hosp., Brooklyn Pub. Library. Mem. Brooklyn C. of C. (dir.). Democrat. Presbyterian. Club: Crescent Athletic. Address: Brooklyn, N.Y.*†

MCLEAN, FRED, v.p. and mgr. Bethlehem Alameda Shipyard, Inc.; b. Blackburn, Lancashire, Eng., Nov. 8, 1878; s. Anthony and Amelia (Davies) McL.; grad. Tech. Sch., Blackburn, 1902; m. Mabel Theresa Smith, July 27, 1905; children—Basil Anthony, Margaret Ann (Mrs. John A. Caulkin). Came to U.S., 1907, naturalized citizen, 1924. Began as mech. engr., 1902; with Stockton (Calif.) Iron Works, Stockton, 1907-08, Bucyrus Co., South Milwaukee, Wis., 1908-11, Globe Iron Works, Sacramento, Calif., 1911-13, Yuba Mfg. Co., Marysville, Calif., 1913-17, Bethlehem Steel Co., San Francisco and Alameda, Calif., from 1917; v.p. and mgr. Bethlehem Alameda Shipyard, Inc.; dir. Eureka Federal Bldg. and Loan Assn. Mem. Am. Welding Soc., Am. Metall. Assn., Alameda Chamber of Commerce, Club: Athlens Athletic (Oakland). Home: Piedmont, Calif.†

MCLEAN, JOHN GODFREY, oil co. exec., educator; b. Portland, Ore., June 29, 1917; s. Robert Norris and Clara Fredricka (Blohm) McL.; B.S., Cal. Inst. Tech., 1938; M.B.A., Harvard, 1940, D.C.S., 1948; m. Patricia Jean Smith, Aug. 30, 1940; children—Deborah Carol, John, Jeffrey. Research asst. Harvard Bus. Sch., 1940-41, instr., 1941-43; asst. prof., 1943-49, asso. prof., 1949-54, prof., 1954-56; asst. to pres. Continental Oil Co., Houston 1954-56, v.p. coordinating and planning, 1959-61, v.p. financial and transp., 1959-61, financial v.p., 1961, v.p. internat. and financial, 1961-63, v.p., gen. mgr. European operations, 1963-64, sr. v.p., 1964-68, exec. v.p., 1968-69, pres., chief exec. officer, 1969-74, also dir.; dir. Gen. Reins. Corp., Boston Co., Inc., Bank of Am., N.Y.C. Mem. Council Fgn. Relations. Author: (with Robert William Haigh) The Growth of Integrated Oil Companies, 1954. Contbr. articles to bus. publs. Home: Darien, Conn. Died May 1974.

MCLEAN, WALLACE DONALD, bank executive; b. Brentwood, New Hampshire, December 12, 1873; s. Harry Clay and Clara Adelaide (Norris) McL.; A.B., Princeton U., 1896; LL.B., Columbian U. (now George Washington), 1898; m. Ada Rorick McConnell, Oct. 2, 1915. Began as clerk, office loans and currency, Treasury Dept., Washington, D.C., 1898-1900. Practiced law in Washington, 1900-13. Asst. to pres. United States Express Co., N.Y. City, 1913. Assisted in orgn. and became gen. mgr. Morris Plan Indsl. Bank of New York (became Indsl. Bank of Commerce); later elected executive vice president, chmn. bd., chmn. exec. com. and dir. hon. life chairman Consumers Bankers Assn., Washington. Dir., Morris Plan Ins. Soc. (now Bankers Secur. Life Ins. Soc.); dir. Gen. Contract Purchase Corp. Served as consul, Marshal Chpt., Phi Delta Phi, Wash., 1898. Sec. D.C. chpt., S.A.R. Mem. bd. managers, vice president of Am. Bible Soc.; mem. board managers Seamen's House. Mem. Chamber of Commerce New York City. Clubs: Uptown, Princeton (N.Y.C.); Cap and Gown (Princeton, N.J.); Town (Scarsdale, N.Y.); Univ. (Washington, D.C.). Author of several papers on industrial banking. Home: Scarsdale, N.Y.†

MCLEARN, FRANK CECIL, newspaper exec.; b. Buffalo, July 24, 1901; s. Ernest M. and Ethel W. (Baylis) McL.; A.B., U. Mich., 1925; m. Mildred McM. Adams, Feb. 25, 1933; children—Laura A. (Mrs. John A. Stichter), Michael B. Reporter, Niagara Falls (N.Y.) Gazette, 1925-26; asso. editor Central Press Assn., Cleve., 1927, N.Y.C. corr., 1928-29, mng. editor, Cleve., 1929-34; successively feature writer, Sunday editor, mng. editor King Features Syndicate, N.Y.C., 1935-45, exec. editor, 1945-56, gen. mgr., 1957-69; pres. King Features Syndicate, Inc.; v.p. Hearst Corp., King Features Syndicate Div.; dir. Hearst Corp.; trustee Hearst Found., Inc., Wm. Randolph Hearst Estate. Mem. N.Y. State Soc. Newspaper Editors, Silurians. Episcopalian. Clubs: Metropolitan Opera, Dutch Treat (N.Y.C.); Siwanoy Country (Bronxville, N.Y.); American Yacht (Rye, N.Y.). Home: Bronxville, N.Y. Died May 24, 1969.

MCLEISTER, IRA FORD, clergyman; b. Taylorsville, Pa., Apr. 22, 1879; s. James and Elizabeth (Campbell) McL.; ed. Purchase Line Acad., Pa., 1896-98, Houghton (N.Y.) Sem. (became Houghton Coll.) 1899-1900, D.D., 1936; m. Clara Orrell, 1906; 1 dau., Mary Elizabeth (dec.). Began as school teacher 1897; taught 7 years; apptd. pastor Wesleyan Meth. Ch. of America, 1903; Sunday School sec. and editor, 1919-27; connectional editor, 1927-43; president The Book Com. of Wesleyan Meth. Connection of America; pres. bd. of trustees of Houghton, Central, Miltonvale and Marion colleges, 1935-43; dir. Grace Mission Assn., Canadaigua, N.Y. Rep. Author: History of the Wesleyan Methodist Church, 1934. Editor of Wesleyan Methodist (weekly), 1927-43; Wesleyan Young People's Journal (monthly), 1936-43; gen. evangelist, 1943. Home: Syracuse, N.Y.†

MCLENDON, ROBERT BURNS, lawyer; b. Frankston, Tex., Apr. 19, 1937; s. Robert Blakely and Mary (Moss) McL.; B.A., Baylor U., 1959, J.D., 1961; m. Margery Hamilton, Feb. 16, 1963; children—Blake, Steven. Admitted to Tex. bar, 1961; spl. agt. FBI, Justice Dept., various locations, 1961-66; atty. Gen. Telephone and Electronics, Tampa, Fla., 1966-67; partner firm Fisher, Roch, McLendon & Gallagher, Houston, 1967. Pres. Tex. Gulf Coast chpt. Leukemia Soc. Am., 1973. Fellow Tex. Bar Found.; mem. Am., Fla. bar assns., State Bar Tex. (profl. efficiency and econ. research com., grievance com.), Am., Tex., Houston, Tenn. (hon.), Neb. (hon.), Wash. (hon.), Utah, (hon.), Ida. (hon.), trial lawyers assns., Delta Theta Phi (vice dean). Mason. Home: Houston, Tex. Died Mar. 4, 1974.

MCLEOD, DUNCAN ALLEN, motor freight ofcl.; b. London, Eng., June 21, 1907; s. Duncan and Lucy (Allen) M.; student pub. schs., Spokane; m. Beulah Ruth Winnington, Mar. 8, 1928; children—Duncan Kent, Don Wynn. Clk. G.N. Ry., 1923-30; office mgr. Cater Motor Freight, Seattle, 1930-31; mgr. Nat. Carloading Corp., Butte, Mont., Spokane, Wash. and Albuquerque, N.M., 1933-39; pres. Navajo Freight Lines, Inc., Los Angeles, 1939-41; gen. mgr. Navajo Freight Lines, Albuquerque, 1946-48; pres. Albuquerque Phoenix Express, Inc., 1951-75, Trailmac, Inc., 1954-75; owner Mac Co., 1953-75, APEX Warehouse Co., 1954-75. Served from 2d lt. to capt. U.S. Army, 1941-46. Mason (Shriner), Rotarian. Home: Albuquerque, N.M., Died May 11, 1975.

MCMANUS, HOWARD NORBERT, JR., educator; b. N.Y.C., June 20, 1921; s. Howard Norbert and Mary F. (Stevens) McM.; student Queens Coll., 1939-40; B.S., U. Ia., 1951, M.S., 1952; Ph.D., U. Minn., 1956; m. Lois Barbara Kuehn, Dec. 26, 1953; children—M. Elleen, Howard J., Patricia Ann, Keith R., Donald D. Asst. prof. mech. engring. Northwestern U., 1956-57; asst. prof. mech. engring. Cornell U., 1957-61, asso. prof., 1961-67, prof., 1967-74, head dept. mech. systems and design, 1968-74; prin. mech. engr. Cornell Aero. Lab., Buffalo, 1963-64; vis. prof. U. Nottingham (Eng.), 1970-71; cons. to industry. Served with AUS, 1946-47. Charles Coffin fellow, 1951-52; Westinghouse fellow, 1952-53. Mem. Am. Soc. M.E., Am. Soc. Engring. Edn., Am. assn. Univ. Profs., Sigma Xi, Pi Tau Sigma, Tau Beta Pi, Phi Kappa Phi, Pi Kappa Alpha, Theta Tau. Roman Catholic. Research and publs. on fluid flow, heat-transfer, edn. Home: Ithaca, N.Y. Died Feb. 6, 1974.

MCMASTER, FLORENCE R., librarian; b. Chgo., July 6, 1916; d. Max and Rose (Nathanson) Riman; Ph.B., U. Toledo, 1937; B.S. in L.S., U. Ill., 1944; LL.B., Ind. U., 1961. Asst. U. Toledo Library, 1937-43, U. Ill. Library, 1943-46; librarian Indpls. Law Sch., Ind. U., from 1946, law librarian, prof. law. Admitted to Ind. bar, Fed. bar, 1961, U.S. Supreme Ct. bar, 1969. Adv. com. Ind. Legislative Adv. Commn.'s Com. to Study Library Needs of the State, 1965-66. Mem. Council on World Affairs, Am., Ind. bar assns., Ind. Women Lawyers Assn., Spl. Libraries Assn. (pres. Ind. chpt. 1957-58), Am. Assn. Law Libraries, Am. Judicature Soc., Am. Trial Lawyers Assn., Am. Assn. U. Women. Club: Altrusa. Contbr. to various collected works. Home: Los Angeles, Cal. Died July 16, 1973.

MCMORAN, GEORGE ANDREW, accountant, advt. exec.; b. Newark, Jan. 20, 1909; s. George Andrew and Lydia Bell (Cain) McM.; student Columbia, 1928—29; m. Edith M. Winebrake, Sept. 23, 1933, children—George A., Judith Ann, Bruce Parker. With Archie F. Reeve & Co., pub. accounting, N.Y.C., 1927—30; partner Reeve, Brown & Atkins, 1930—41; asst. controller Newell—Emmett Co., Inc., 1941—52; treas. Cunningham & Walsh, Inc., 1952-71, sr. v.p., dir., 1956-71, trustee employees profitsharing fund, also treas. C.P.A., 1933, Mem. N.J. Soc. C.P.A.s. Clubs: Spring Lake Golf (N.J.); J.D.M. Country (Palm Beach Gardens, Fla.). Author: (with Archie F. Reeve) Hospital Accounting, 1937, Club Accounting, 1938. Home: Sea Girt N.J. Died Sept. 12, 1975; interred Brielle, N.J.

MCNAIR, FRANK, banker; b. in Greenvillage, Pa., Jan. 28, 1881; s. of Washington and Catherine (Stouffer) McN.; student Chambersburg (Pa.) Acad.; Ph.B., U. of Chicago, 1903; m. Julia E. Wilkins, Feb. 2, 1907 (dec.); children—Catherine (dec.), Elizabeth (Mrs. Frank S. Sims), Caroline (Mrs. Glendon T. Gerlach); m. 2d, Mrs. Marvin B. Pool, June 27, 1951. Identified with the Harris Orgn. (N. W. Harris & Co., 1882, incorporated as Harris Trust & Savings Bank, 1907), from 1903, successively as bond buyer, bond salesman, asst. mgr., mgr. bond dept.; v.p., dir., 1920; exec. v.p., 1943, chmn. directors trust com. Chmn. bd. dirs. Children's Memorial Hospital; member adv. com. visiting Nurses Association. Honorary trustee University of Chicago, County Home for Convalescent Children, Home for Destitute Crippled Children, Chgo. Clubs: Chicago, University, Commercial, Onwentsia, Old Elm, Casino. Home: Lake Forest, Ill.†

MCNALLY, GEORGE FREDERICK, ednl. adminstr.; b. Queensbury, N.B., June 29, 1878; s. Moses Byron and Annie M. (Perley) McN.; B.A., U. of N.B., 1900, LL.D. (hon.), 1937; M.A., U. of Alberta, 1911, LL.D. (hon.), 1946; grad. student Columbia, 1914, 16, 18, 20; m. Charlotte Elizabeth Bleakney, July 18, 1912; children—John Frederick. Margaret Jean (Mrs. F. M. Dawson), Helen Kathleen (Mrs. M. R. Hannah), Elizabeth Anne (Mrs. J. H. Manning). Instr., Stanstead Coll., 1900-01; classical master High Sch., Moncton, N.B., 1901-06; teacher Strathona High Sch., Edmonton, Alberta, 1906-09; insp. schs., Wetaskiwin and Calgary, Alberta, 1910-13; prin. Normal Sch., Camrose, Alberta, 1914-18; supervisor schs. Province of Alberta, 1918-35; dir. summer sch. for teachers U. of Alberta, 1918-34, chmn. senate, mem. bd. govs. from 1912, chandellor 1946-52. Dep. minister edn. Alberta, 1935-46. vice chmn. Canadian delegation 1st gen. conf. UNESCO, Paris, 1946. Mem. Can. Edn. Assn. (pres. 1938-41), Can. Inst. Internat. Affairs, Nat. Adv. Council Vocational Edn. (chmn.), nat. adv. committee Rehab. Handicapped Persons (chmn.), U.N. Assn. Baptist (pres. Bapt. Union Western Can. 1919-20; pres. Bapt. Fedn. Can. 1950). Clubs: Can. (Edmonton); Rotary International Editor; Introduction to Literature, 1919; Silas Mariner, 1929; A Book of Good Stories, 1934. Home: Edmonton, Alberta, Can.†

MCNEAL, WILLIAM HORTON, gen. mgr. Home Owners Loan Corpn.; b. Marion Co., O., Oct. 8, 1878; s. William Howard and Mary Magdalene (Boyd) McN.; grad. Emporia (Kan.) Business Coll., 1900; LL.B., Kansas City Sch. of Law, 1908; m. Grace Anabel Lamb, Apr. 11, 1908; children—William Horton, Marilyn Elizabeth. Admitted to Mo. and Okla. bar, 1908; title atty. Deming Investment Co. at Oklahoma City, 1910-15; rep. Commerce Trust Co., 1915-16; mgr. for Okla. of U.S. Bond & Mortgage Co., Dallas, Tex., 1916-17; title atty. Am. Investment Co., 1919; title atty. Waddell Investment Co., Kansas City, and v.p. in charge field orgn., 1920-23; mgr. Nat. Title Ins. Div. of N.Y. Title & Mortgage Co., N.Y. City, 1923-25, v.p., 1925-33; v.p. Nat. Mortgage Corpn., 1925-32; with Home Owners Loan corp., from 1933, gen. mgr. from 1934. Christian Scientist. Mason (32°, Shriner). Clubs: Country (Rye, N.Y.); Men's (Larchmont, N.Y.). Home: Washington, D.C.†

MCNEELY, EUGENE J(OHNSON), telephone exec.; b. Jackson, Mo., Nov. 1, 1900; s. T. E. and Mattie (Johnson) McN.; B.S., U. Mo., 1922, LL.D.; H.H. D., Ind. Central Coll.; LL.D., Grinnell Coll.; m. Eunice Miller, Feb. 19, 1927 (dec. 1967); m. 2d, Alma R. Kithcart, 1968. With Southwest Bell Tel. Co., St. Louis, 1922-48, gen. paint manager, 1947-48; asst. v.p. charge personnel relations Am. Tel. & Tel. Co., N.Y.C., 1948, v.p., 1952-55, exec. v.p., 1955-61, dir., mem. exec. com., 1955-67, pres. 1961-65; dir. Travelers Insurance Company, Illinois Bell Telephone Co., Continental Oil Company, Mfrs. Hanover Trust Co., Travelers Ins. Co., So. N. Eng. Tel. Co., v.p. charge operations Northwestern Bell Telephone Co., Omaha, 1949, pres., 1949-52; trustee East River Savs. Bank; dir. Downtown-Lower Manhattan Assn., Inc. Trustee Tchrs. Coll. Columbia U. Mem. Armed Forces Communications and Electronics Assn., N.Y. C. of C., Acad. Polit. Scis., Eta Kappa Nu, Tau Beta Pi. Club: University. Home: New York City, N.Y. Died Dec. 27, 1973.

MCNEIL, ELTON BURBANK, educator, psychologist; b. Royal Oak, Mich., Jan. 1, 1924; s. Elton B. and Grace (Hueston) McN.; A.B. cum laude, Harvard, 1948; Ph.D., U. Mich., 1952; m. Marjorie Snider, Sept. 14, 1946; children—Douglas, Timothy, Laurie. Mem. faculty U. Mich., 1952-74, prof. psychology, 1964-74; field selection officer Peace Corps, 1965-74. County supr. Washtenaw County, 1956; pres. East Ann Arbor Sch. Bd., 1959. Served with USAAF, 1943-45. Decorated Croix de Guerre. Mem. Am., Mich. (pres. 1966) psychol. assns., Mich. Assn. Sch. Psychologists (pres. 1964). Sigma Xi. Author: The Nature of Human Conflict, 1965; The Concept of Human Development, 1966; The Quiet Furies, 1967; Human Socialization, 1969; The Psychoses, 1971; The Neuroses, 1971; Being Human, 1973; The Psychology of Being Human, 1974. Home: Ann Arbor Mich. Died Mar. 27, 1974.

MCNEILL, JOHN THOMAS, church historian; b. Elmsdale, P.E.I., Can., July 28, 1885; s. William Cavendish and Emily Lavinia (MacNeill) McN.; ed. Prince of Wales Coll., 1902-05; B.A., McGill U., 1909, M.A., 1910; B.D., Westminster Hall, Vancouver, 1912; studied New College, Edinburgh, 1912-13, Halle U., summer 1913; Ph.D., U. of Chicago, 1920; D.D., Westminster Hall, 1925; LL.D., Queen's U., Kingston, Can., 1947; D.D., Edinburgh U., 1950; m. Netta Hardy, Jan. 10, 1917; children—William Hardy, Leonora Isabel, Emily Elizabeth. Ordained in Presbyn. Ch., Can., 1913; pastor Chipman, N.B., 1913-14; lectr. in church history, Westminster Hall, 1914-20; instr. in ch. history, U. of Chicago, 1919; asst. prof. history, Queen's U., Kingston, Ont., 1920; prof. ch. history, Knox Coll., Toronto, 1922; prof. history of European Christianity, Divinity Sch., U. of Chicago, 1927-44; Auburn prof. of church History, Union Theological Seminary, New York, 1944-53. Mem. Am. Soc. Ch. History (ex-pres.), Am. Hist. Assn. Mem. Conference on Science, Philosophy and Religion, Mem. Presbytery of New York. Shared award, Adams prize for history, 1923. Author or co-author several books relating to field; latest publication: History of the Cure of Souls, 1951. Home: East Middlebury, Vt. Died Feb. 6, 1975; buried Middlebury, VT.

MCNEILL, ROBERT HAYES, lawyer; b. Wilkes County, N.C., Apr. 25, 1877; s. Milton and Martha (Charlotte) McN.; A.B., Wake Forest (N.C.) Coll., 1897; LL.B., 1897; LL.D., 1934; m. Cora B. Brown, Dec. 17, 1902; children—George Hamilton, Frances Olivia (Mrs.Joseph D. Easley). Admitted to N.C. bar, 1898; in practice at Jefferson, N.C., 1898-1903, Washington, D.C., from 1903; secretary United States Senate Com. on Patents, 1902-03; became mem. firm McNeill & McNeill, 1933; mem. firm McNeill & Edwards, 1939; practicing individually, 1940-48; later partner in law firm with R. A. Ricketts; practiced before committees of U.S. Senate and House of Reps., U.S. Supreme Court and all important Commns. and Bds. of the U.S. Govt. and all Washington Courts and U.S. Courts in adjoining States; special counsel for N.C.; counsel spl. com. of Congress; counsel in senatorial contest; attorney Nat. Defense Com., U.S. Senate, 1942. Washington counsel Western Tax Council, Inc.; trustee, pres. Bapt. Found., Washington. President Royla Royal Village Corp.; clk., U.S. Senate Com. on Patents, 1903-05; sec. N.C. Rep. State Exec. Com., 1904-05; pvt. sec. for U.S. Senator J. C. Pritchard, N.C.; candidate Supr. Ct. judge, N.C., 1901; Rep. candidate for gov. of N.C., 1940, for asso. justice Supereme Ct. of N.C., 1946, 50, 52. Mem. Am. Federal, North Carolina and D.C. bar assns., S.A.R. (pres. Dist. of Columbia, 1944-45; mem. national exec. committee 1948, gen. 1952, nat. treas-gen. 1951-55), N.C. Soc. (pres.), So. Soc. (pres. emeritus), McNeill Clan Assn. of Am. (pres.), Gen. Counsel Nat. Soc. Daus. Am. Revoln., 1945-50. Republican. Baptist. Clubs: St. Andrew's Society, Lincoln (Washington); National Republican (N.Y.C.). Home: Home: Washington, D.C.†

MCNUTT, WILLIAM ROY, clergyman; b. nr. Amsterdam, Bates County, Mo., April 6, 1879; s. Andrew and Adrienne (Påhud) McN.; A.B., Ottawa (Kan.) U., 1908, D.D., 1923; A.M., U. of Pa., 1909; B.D., Crozer Theol. Sem., Chester, Pa., 1912; m. Minnie E. Willard Turner, June 27, 1911; 1 daughter Frances Athena (wife of Reverend W. Clinton Powers). Teacher in Missouri public schools, 1899-1902; student pastor in Kan., 1902-08; ordained Baptist ministry, 1912; minister Angora Ch., Phila., 1909-12, Prospect Hill Ch., Prospect Park, Pa., 1912-16, First Ch., Worcester, Mass., 1916-28; prof. practical theology, Crozer Theol. Sem., 1928-44, emeritus, 1944; minister Central Baptist Church, Woodbury, N.J., from 1944. Acting pastor Am. Church, Munich, part of 1935-36. Y.M.C.A. divisional sec., Biols. France, 1918. Trustee Worcester (Mass.) Poly, Inst., 1916-28; member board directors, Mass. Bapt. Conv., 1917-23, Northern Bapt. Edn. Soc., 1920-28. Winner Kan. State Oratorical Contest, 1907, represented Kan. in interstate contest; awarded gold P by U. of Pa., 1911, as mem. winning team in Penn.-Princeton-Columbia triangular annual debate. Mem. Delta Sigma Rho; mem. "T.C." (Theological Club), Boston, Photozetetics and Heilikrenites (theol. circles), Phila. Baptist. Kiwanian. Author: Policy and Practice in Baptist Churchs, 1935; Worship in the Churches, 1941. Editor of the Bulletin of Crozer Theol. Sem., 1928-38. Home: Woodbury, N.J.†

MCPHEE, EUGENE RODERICK, univ. system dir.; b. Chippewa Falls, Wis., May 2, 1902; s. Roderick and Mary (McElroy) McP.; B.S., Eau Claire (Wis.) State Tchrs. Coll., 1923; M.A., U. Minn., 1932; L.H.D., Northland Coll., 1963; m. Frances Fulton, June 12, 1924 (dec. Mar. 1965); children—Jeanne (Mrs. Jerome Berndt), Roderick F., Michael Putnam; m. 2d, Helen Laird Matson, Mar. 5, 1966. Adminstr., Wis. Pub. Schs., 1923-30; dir. tchr. tng. Eau Claire State Tchrs. Coll., 1932-41, 46-48; dir. Wis. State Tchrs. Colls., 1948-51; dir. Wis. State Colls., 1951-64; exec. dir. Wis. Univ. System, Madison, 1964-75. Bd. dirs. Eau Claire Community Chest, 1946-48. Served to col. AUS, 1941-46. Decorated Bronze Star, Legion of Merit; Mil. Order

Italy; hon. citizen Cagliari, Sardina and Genoa, Italy. Mem. Nat., Wis. edn. assns., V.F.W., Am. Legion, Mil. Govt. Assn., Phi Delta Kappa. Elk. Contbr. articles to ednl. jours. Home: Madison, Wis. Died May 10, 1975.

MCPHERRIN, JOHN WEITZ, publishing consultant; born Des Moines, Iowa, October 15, 1897; s. John M. and Amelia (Weitz) McP.; A. B., U. Wis., 1920; m. Katherine Scheidenhelm, Sept. 16, 1922; children—Joy, Kay. Newspaper reporter Madison and Des Moines, 1919-20; asst. mgr. Cincinnati office of J. Walter Thompson, 1921-25; v.p. Chamberlain Medicine Co., Des Moines, 1926-31; products sales mgr. Bauer & Black, Chicago, 1933-39; account exec., Lord & Thomas, 1940-41; editor America Druggist (pub. by Hearst mags.), N.Y. City, 1942-51; v.p., Crowell-Collier Publishing Company, pub. American Magazine, 1951-54, asst. to pres., 1954-55; gen. program executive National Broadcasting Company, 1956-57, editorial consultant, 1958-74; pub. cons. Internat. Exec. Services Corp., Colombia, 1967. Pres. Nat. Lyric Arts Theatre Found., N.Y.C., 1968-69; Bd. dirs. Tucson Symphony Soc., 1971-72. Recipient Freedom Found. Mag. Editorial award, 1952. Member St. Andrews Soc. of New York, Soc. of Bus. Mag. Editors (pres. 1950), Am. Legion, Sigma Phi, Sigma Delta Chi, Pi Epsilon Delta. Mason. Clubs: University (Chicago and N.Y. City); Skyline Country (bd. govs. 1970-72) (Tucson); National Press (Washington); Players (N.Y.C.). Home: Tuscon, Ariz. Died Oct. 3, 1974.

MCQUEEN, ELIZABETH LIPPINCOTT, (Mrs. Ulysses Grant McQueen), author; b. Pennington, N.J., Sept. 26, 1879; d. Rev. Benjamin Crispin (D.D.), and Deborah Hand (Diverty) Lippincott; grad. Pennington Sem., 1898; m. Ulysses Grant McQueen, Mar. 14, 1900. War relief work in Palestine; founder Jerusalem News (newspaper). Founder and dir. Angelo-Am. Soc. of America; mem. Authors' League America, D.A.R. Author: Three Brothers Plotted to Own the World, 1918. Contbr. articles and poems to newspapers. Toured world in behalf of Anglo-Am. friendship, 1922-23. Address: New York City, N.Y.†

MCRAE, WILLIAM ALLAN, JR., U.S. judge; b. Marianna, Fla., Sept. 25, 1909; s. William Allan and Mary (Parker) McR.; A.B. U. Fla., 1932, J.D., 1933; Rhodes scholar Christ Ch., Oxford U. (Eng.), 1933, B.A. in Jurisprudence, 1935, B.Litt., 1936, M.A. in absentia, 1946; m. Aline Virginia Dearing, Aug. 29, 1942; children—Aline Virginia, William Allan III, Dearing. Admitted to Fla. bar, 1933; practiced with firm Knight, Adair, Cooper & Osborne, Jacksonville, 1936-38, Giles J. Patterson, 1938-40; mem. firm Holland, Bevis, McRae & Smith, Bartow 1946-61 judge U.S. Dist. Ct., Middle Dist. Fla., 1961-73, chief judge, 1971-73. Prof. law U. Fla., 1940-41; mem. Fla. constn. adv. com. Sr. cons. AEC, Washington, 1946. Trustee U. Fla., U. Fla. Law Center Assn. Endowment Corp.; chmn. bd. trustees Jacksonville U.; bd. govs. Fed. Jud. Center, 1968-70. Served from 1st lt. to col. USAAF, 1942-45. Decorated Legion of Merit. Fellow Am. Coll. Trial Lawyers; mem. Am. (chmn. Fla. com. sect. jud. adminstrn.), Fed. bar assns., Am. Law Inst., Selden Soc., Jud. Council Fla. Bar, Am. Judicature Soc. (past dir.), U. Fla. Alumni Assn. (pres. 1949-50), Order of Coif, Blue Key, Phi Beta Kappa, Phi Kappa Phi, Phi Delta Phi, Omicron Delta Kappa, Alpha Tau Omega (pres. Fla. 1931). Rotarian (pres. Bartow 1947-49.). Club: Florida Yacht. Home: Jacksonville Fla. Died Jan. 27, 1973; interred Evergreen Cemetery, Jacksonville, Fla.

MEAD, ARTHUR RAYMOND, prof. edn.; b. Grelton, O., Mar. 12, 1880; s. William and Juliaette Nash (Mead) M.; B.A., Miami U., 1909; M.A., Teachers Coll. (Columbia), 1910, Ph.D., 1917; D.Ed. (honoris Causa), Miami University, 1934; married Ethel Grace Johnson, June 15, 1911; children—Jessie Elizabeth, Lydia Anne. Instr. education, De Pauw U., 1910; scholar and research scholar in edn., Teachers Coll., 1910 and 1913-14; prof. edn., Ohio Wesleyan U., 1914-31; temp. prof. edn. various times, summers, at U. of Minn., U. of Tenn., Ohio State U., George Peabody Coll. for Teachers, Ohio U. and Pa. State Coll.; visiting prof. of edn., Teachers Coll. (Columbia), 1925-26, summer 1939; visiting prof. secondary edn. U. of Fla., 1931-32; dir. Lab. Sch., U. of Fla., 1933-35, dir. ednl. research, 1935-50; dean of instruction Athens (Ala.) College, 1951-52. President Nat. Assn. Directors of Student Teaching, Nat. Soc. College Teachers of Education, 1941-42; chmn. Nat. Com. on Practice Training, Regional chmn. Assn. for Supervision and Curriculum Development, from 1944. Member Nat. Education Assn. Soc. College Teachers Edn. (v.p. 1942-49), Soc. for Study of Edn., Ohio Coll. Assn. (sec.), Am. Ednl. Research Assn., Southern Commn. Research and Curricular Problems, Delta Upsilon, Phi Beta Kappa, Phi Delta Kappa, Tau Kappa Alpha, Kappa Delta Pi, Kappa Phi Kappa, Phi Kappa Phi. Methodist. Author: The Development of Free Schools in the United States, 1917; Learning and Teaching, 1923; Supervised Student-Teaching, 1929; Economic Status of Teachers in Florida. Home: Gainesville, Fla.†

MEAD, WILLIAM HENRY, clergyman; b. Detroit, Jan. 11, 1921; student U. Mich., 1939-40, Lake Forest Coll., 1941-42; B.D., Va. Theol. Sem., 1950, D.D. (hon.), 1966; m. Katherine B. Lloyd, July 1, 1950; children—William L., Katherine B. Ordained deacon Protestant Episcopal Ch., 1950, priest, 1951; asst. minister Christ Ch., Cranbrook, Bloomfield Hills, Mich., 1950-52; rector St. Paul's Ch., Alexandria, Va., 1952-57, St. John the Evangelist Ch., St. Paul, 1959-64; asso. dir. Parishfield Community, Brighton, Mich., 1957-59; dean Christ Ch. Cathedral, St. Louis, 1964-68; bishop Diocese of Del., 1968-74. Home: Wilmington Del. Died Feb. 25, 1974; interred Old St Anne's Cemetery, Middletown, Del.

MEADE, GEORGE PETERKIN, sugar refiner; b. Cumberland, Md., Dec. 26, 1883; s. Rev. Philip N. and Sarah (Rannells) M.; B.S., N.Y. U., 1905, Chem. E., 1921, D.Eng., 1955; postgrad. U. Mich., summer 1914; D.Sc. (hon.), La. State U., 1954, Tulane U., 1970; m. Eleanore Felicia Hussey, Aug. 7, 1912 (dec. Dec. 1969). Asst. chemist Nat. Sugar Refinery, Yonkers, N.Y., summers 1901-05, full time, 1905-07; same, Fajardo (P.R.) Sugar Co., 1908; chemist and asst. supt. Colonial Sugars Co., Gramercy, La., 1909-13; supt. and mgr. Cuban Sugar Refining Co., Cardenas, also dir. Central Control Lab. Cuban-Am. Sugar Co., 1913-23; gen. supt. Colonial Sugars Co., 1923-28, mgr. 1928-56, bd. dirs., 1950-59; bd. dirs. Cuban-Am. Sugar Co., 1950-59; pres. Bone Char Research Project, 1950. Mem. sugar com. 8th Internat. Congress of Applied Chemistry, N.Y., 1912; del. Internat. Commn. Uniform Methods of Sugar Analysis, London, 1936, Brussels, Belgium, 1949, chmn. U.S. delegation, Paris, 1954, Washington, 1958, v.p. Internat. Commn., 1954, hon. life v.p. Hamburg, 1962. Mem. tech. adv. com. Sugar Research Found.; mem. bd. trustees La. Pub. Affairs Research Council. Pres. St. James Parish Sch. Bd., 1932-56. Fellow A.A.A.S., Am. Inst. Chemists, Herpetologists League, N.Y. Acad. Scis.; mem. Am. Chem. Soc., La. Engring. Soc., Am. Inst. Chem. Engrs., Internat. Soc. Sugar Cane Technologists, Am. Soc. Ichthyologists and Herpetologists (v.p. 1953), N.Y. Zool. Soc., Phi Beta Kappa, Tau Beta Pi, Alpha Chi Sigma. Democrat. Episcopalian. Clubs: Chemists (N.Y.); Louisiana, Round Table (New Orleans). Author: Cane Sugar Handbook, 9th edit., 1963; Athletic Records: The Whys and Wherefores, 1966. Asso. editor: Sugar Jour. (New Orleans), 1956—. Contbr. tech. articles Indus. and Engring. Chemistry, Internat. Sugar Jour., Ency. Brit., etc.; also articles on Habits of Louisiana Harmless Snakes. Home: New Orleans, La., Died Oct. 22, 1975.

MEADE, ROBERT DOUTHAT, educator, author; b. Danville, Va., Aug. 16, 1903; s. Edmund Baylies and Helen (Douthat) M.; B.A., Va. Mil. Inst., 1924; M.A., U. Va., 1926; Ph.D. in History, U. Chgo., 1936; m. Lucy Boyd, Dec. 29, 1934; 1 dau., Lucy Boyd Meade Middleton. Instr., Va. Episcopal Sch., Lynchburg, 1926-27, U. Ill., 1927-28, Vanderbilt U., 1928-29, U. N.C., 1929-31, 35-36; history asst. Nat. Park Service, 1932-34; faculty Randolph-Macon Woman's Coll., Lynchburg, Va., 1936-71, prof. history, chmn. dept., 1939-71. Vis. prof. U. Va. Mem. adv. council Nat. Civil Service League, 1951-63. Recipient Distinguished Service award Va. Social Sci. Assn., 1969. Guggenheim fellow, 1953-54, 60-61; grantee Library of Congress, 1945, Carnegie Found., 1948, Rosenwald Found., 1939, Am. Council Learned Socs., 1962, Am. Philos. Soc., 1944-46, 57, Patrick Henry Meml. Found., 1946. Mem. Am., So. hist. assns., Zeta Psi. Democrat. Episcopalian. Author: Judah P. Benjamin, Confederate Statesman (So. Author's award), 1943, reprinted, 1975; Patrick Henry, Statesman in the Making, 1957; Patrick Henry, Practical Revolutionary, 1969; also articles, revs., mag. and syndicated newspaper articles. Contbr.: Lincoln for the Ages, 1960. Home: Lynchburg Va. Died Apr. 27, 1974; buried Fairview Cemetery, Warrenton, N.C.

MEARS, BRAINERD, prof. chemistry; b. Amherst, Mass., Jan. 17, 1881; s. Leverett and Mary Virginia (Brainerd) M.; B.A., Williams Coll., 1903, M.A., 1905; Ph.D., Johns Hopkins, 1908; m. Margaret Whitney, Aug. 23, 1911 (died Sept. 30, 1914); children—Whitney Harris, Margaret Brainerd; m. 2d Sally Worthington Bliss, Aug. 12, 1920; children—Brainerd, Mary Louise, Professor Chemistry, Williams College, to 1946. President Williamstown Savings Bank. Town moderator for 19 years. Capt. Chem. Warfare Service, O.R.C. Fellow A.A.A.S., Am. Inst. Chemists; member Am. Chem. Soc., Phi Beta Kappa, Sigma Xi, Phi Lambda Upsilon, Theta Delta Chi, Alpha Chi Sigma. Mason (K.T.). Club: Williams Coll. (New York). Contbr. to chem. jours. Home: Williamstown, Mass.†

MEEK, THEOPHILE JAMES, educator, author; b. Port Stanley, Ont., Can., Nov. 17, 1881; s. James and Sarah (Freele) M.; B.A., U. Toronto, 1903; student U. Marburg, 1906. U. Berlin, 1906-08, Am. Sch. Oriental Research, Jerusalem, 1908; B.D., McCormick Theol. Sem. (Nettie F. McCormick traveling fellow, 1906-08), 1909; Ph.D., U. Chgo. (fellow in Semitics, 1914), 1915; D.D. (hon.), Queen's U., 1947; m. Susan Dorothea Carrier, Dec. 17, 1909; children—Anne Dorothea (Mrs. John L. Pocock), Theophile James. Matthew Robb prof. Bibl. history, lit. James Millikin U., 1909-18; prof. O.T., history religions Meadville (Pa.) Theol. Sch., 1918-22; prof. Semitic langs., history religions Bryn Mawr Coll., 1922-23; prof. Oriental langs. U. Toronto, from 1923; vis. prof. U. Chgo., summers 1921, 22, 24, 26, spring 1942; ann. prof. Am. Sch. Orinetal Research in Baghdad, 1930-31, 39-40; Haskell lectr. Oberlin Coll., 1934, 50. Mem. mng. com. Am. Schs. Oriental Research, 1918-33, Can., exec. com., 1933-35, asso. trustee, 1935-46; mem. Humanities Research Council of Can., exec. com., 1943-50, chmn. pubs. com., 1948-51; mem. com. Near Eastern studies Am. Council Learned Socs., 1935-47. Fellow Royal Soc. Arts, Royal Soc. Can.; mem. Am. Oriental Soc. (pres. Middle West br. 1933-34; pres. 1942-43), Soc. Bibl. Lit. and Exegesis (pres. Midwest sect. 1937-38; pres. 1943-44), Can. Soc. Bibl. Studies (pres. 1950), Nat. Assn. Authors and Journalists (hon.), Pi Gamma Mu. Club: Oriental (pres. 1952-53). Author: Bilingual Hymns, Prayers, and Penitential Psalms, 1913; Old Babylonian Business and Legal Documents, 1917; Some Explanatory Lists and Grammatical Texts, 1920; The Song of Songs; An American Translation, 1927; Old Akkadian, Sumerian, and Cappadocian Texts from Nuzi, 1935; Hebrew Origins, 1936. Co-author: The Songs of Songs: A Symposium, 1924; The Religion of the Bible, 1925; The Old Testament; An American Translation (editor, from 1935), 1927; The Bible; An American Translation, 1931; From the Pyramids to Paul, 1935; The Haverford Symposium on Archaeology and the Bible, 1938; The Complete Bible: An American Translation, 1939; Ancient Near Eastern Texts, 1950; Symbolae Hrozny, 1950. Contbr. various books, encys., learned jours. Home: Toronto, Ont., Can.†

MEEK, WALTER JOSEPH, coll. prof.; b. Dillon, Kan., Aug. 15, 1878; s. William E. A. and Mary Hester (White) M.; A.B., U. of Kan., 1902; Ph.D., U. of Chicago, 1909; D.Sc., U. of Wis., 1949; citation U. of Kan., 1950; m. Crescence Eberle, Dec. 26, 1906; children—Joseph Walter, Mary Crescence, John Sawyers. Instr. physiology, U. of Wis., 1908-10, asst. prof., 1910-13, asso. prof., 1913-18, prof., from 1918, asst. dean med. sch., 1920, acting dean, 1942-45; asso. dean, 1946-49, professor and dean emeritus, from 1949. Lectr. U. Texas Medical Branch, 1951-58. Served as major, Chemical Warfare Service, U.S. Army, 1918-19. Republican. Presbyterian. Mem. Am. Physiol. Soc. (council, sec., 1924-29; pres., 1929; chmn. publ. trustees, 1932-45), Nat. Acad. Sciences, Alpha Tau Omega, Sigma Xi, Phi Beta Kappa, Gamma Alpha, Phi Kappa Phi. Mason. Club: University. Contbr. to physiol. and med. jours. on problems relating to the nervous system and the heart and history of medicine. Address: Madison, Wis.†

MEEKER, RALPH INMAN, irrigation engr.; b. Wichita, Kan., Feb. 14, 1878; s. George H. and Florence J. (Wilhelm) M.; grad. Central High Sch., Pueblo, Colo., 1899; student Sch. of Mines, Golden, Colo., 1901, 02; m. Zoe A. Stoll, Sept. 1916; 1 son, Ralph I. Practiced mining engring., Colo., 2 yrs., Hydraulic engring, 5 yrs., irrigation engring., 17 yrs.; engaged in interstate water investigations and litigation, covering Laramie, North Platte, La. Plata, Colorado, Arkansas and Rio Grande rivers; was employed by State of Colo. on investigations concerning water compact between N.M., Tex., Colo. and the federal govt. on the Rio Grance River; also proposed water compact on Arkansas River, between Colo. and Kan., on N. Platte River between Neb., Wyo., Colo., and the federal govt., and 7-state compact on Colorado River; consultant to State of Wyo. on interstate river controversies concerning Laramie, North Platte and Green Rivers until 1933 later consulting engr. to Nebraska on N. Platte River interstate suit; cons. engr. to Federal Land Bank, Wichita, Kan., 1934-35; also consultant to army engineers (Memphis office) on irrigation possibilities of Arkansas River and tributaries west of the 99th meridian, in connection with Mississippi River Flood Control; consultant to State of Kansas on Arkansas River interstate river controversy, in U.S. Supreme Court, 1930-31; pvt. practice as cons. irrigation engr. Student 2d O.T.C., Ft. Sheridan, Ill., 1917. Mem. Colo. Soc. Engrs., Am. Soc. C.E. Republican. Methodist. Home: Denver, Colo.†

MEEKS, BENJAMIN WILTSHIRE, clergyman; b. Chase, Md., Apr. 2, 1879; s. William Andrew and Mary Anne (Earl) M.; A.B., Johns Hopkins, 1903, grad. student, 1903-04; D.D., St. Johns Coll., Annapolis, Md., 1923; m. Lillian Eva Beall, Mar. 15, 1905; children—Miriam Gertrude (Mrs. Paul T. Frisch), Benjamin Wiltshire, Elinor Virginia (dec.). Ordained to ministry M.E. Ch., 1906; pastor at Epworth Ch., Baltimore, 1902-05, Solomons, 1906-07, Grace-Hampden Ch., Baltimore, 1907-09, Ryland Ch., Washington, D.C., 1909-12, 1st Ch., Martinsburg, W.Va., 1912-16, St. Mark's Ch., Baltimore, 1916-21, Centre St. Ch., Cumberland, Md., 1921-25, Grace Ch., Roland Park, Baltimore (united with Grace Ch., Baltimore, 1928), 1925-30; supt. Washington Dist., 1930-36; pastor Calvary Ch., Frederick, Md., 1936-44; Howard Park Ch., Baltimore, 1944-48. Mem. gen. confs., 1924, 32, 36, 40, 44; mem. Uniting Conf., 1939; mem. Book Com., 1932-40 and Board of Publication 1940-48; mem. of the Bd. Temperance Prohibition and Pub. Morals (exec. com.), 1931-40; sec.-treas. Commn. on Conf. Claimants Endowment Fund, Baltimore Annual Conf., from 1928; edited Epworth League page to Baltimore Meth., 1921-26, Mem. Washington Fed. Chs. (dir. and v.p. 1931-35, pres. 1935); dir. Lucy Webb Hayes Nat. Training Sch., Sibley Memorial Hosp., 1930-39; trustee American U., from 1931; mem. bd. govs. Westminster (Md.) Theol. Sem., from 1932. Republican. Home: Baltimore, Md.†

MEENES, MAX, educator, psychologist; b. May 24, 1901; s. Lewis and Ester (Sadowski) M.; B.A., Clark U., 1921, Ph.D., 1926; M.A., Princeton, 1924; student Cornell U., 1924-25; m. Goldie Martin, June 23, 1933. Instr., then asst. prof. psychology Lehigh U., 1926-30; mem. faculty Howard U., from 1930, prof. psychology, from 1936. Fellow Am. Psychol. Assn. (sec., pres. div. 1); mem. D.C. Psychol. Assn., Psi Chi (pres.). Author: Studying and Learning, 1954. Home: Washington, D.C. Died Jan. 5, 1974.

MEHAN, MONA CATHARINE, physician; b. Lowell, Mass., Oct. 28, 1909; d. Joseph Aloysius and Rosemary (Lennon) Mehan; M.D., Women's Med. Coll. Pa., 1936. Intern New Eng. Hosp., Boston, 1938—39; roentgenologist St. Johns Hosp., Lowell; cons. Beaconcrest Chronic Hosp., Lowell. Diplomate Am. Bd. Radiology. Mem. Am. Coll. Radiologists, A.M.A., Radiol. soc. N. Am., New Eng. Roentgen Ray Soc. Home: Lowell, Mass. Died Nov. 2, 1973; buried St. Patrick's Cemetery, Lowell, Mass.

MEHL, ROBERT FRANKLIN, research metallurgist, educator; b. Lancaster, Pa., Mar. 30, 1898; s. George H. and Sarah W. (Ward) M.; B.S., Franklin and Marshall Coll., 1919, D.Sc., 1938; Ph.D., Princeton, 1924; D. honoris causa, U.S. Sao Paulo, Brazil, 1944; Eng.D., Stevens Inst. Tech., 1944, Colo. Sch. Mines, 1952, Case Inst. of Tech., 1959, Carnegie-Mellon U., 1973; D.Sc., U. Pa., 1959; m. Helen M. Charles, Dec.27, Dec. 27, 1923; children—Robert F., Marjorie Ward, Gretchen. Prof. chemistry, Juniata Coll., 1923-25; nat. research fellow Harvard, 1925-27; supt. div. phys. metallurgy, Naval Research Lab., 1927-31; asst. dir. research Am. Rolling Mill Co., 1931-32; dir. Metals Research Lab., Carnegie Inst. Tech., 1932-59, head dept. metallurgy, 1935-59, dean grad. studies, 1953-60; cons. U.S. Steel Corp., Zurich, 1960-65; prof. Coll. Engring., Syracuse U., 1967-76; chmn. Inst. of Metals Div., Am. Inst. Mining and Metall. Engrs., 1938; tech. cons. Am. embassy, London, Eng. 1945; cons. Inst. for Tech. Research, Sao Paulo, 1949; chmn. met. adv. bd. NRC, 1951; cons. State Dept. Point 4 Program, Brazil, 1952; spl. lectr. Royal Sch. Mines, London, 1955; Priestly lectr. Penn State Coll., 1938; Ann Inst. of Metals lectr. Am. Inst. Mining and Metall. Engrs., 1936; Campbell Meml. lectr. Am. Soc. Metals, 1941. Lectr., Escola Politecnica, U. Sao Paulo. Brazil, 1944; 1st ann. lectr. Assocaicao Brasileira de Metals, 1944, 20th, 1964, 25th, 1969, other lectures. Recipient John Scott medal, 1934; Howe medal Am. Soc. Metals, 1939; prize award Am. Inst. Mining and Metall Engrs., 1934, 39, 44, 47; medalist Am. Ind. Radium and X-ray Soc., 1943; Associacao Brasileiro de Metais, 1944, 45; James Douglas gold medal Am. Inst. Mining and Metall. Engrs., 1945; Sauveur Achievement award, 1951; Gold medal, 1952; Clamer medal Franklin Inst., 1953; LeChatelier medal Societe Francaise de Metallurgie, 1956; Vincent Bendix award Am. Soc. Engring. Edn., 1959; Platinum medal Inst. of Medals, London, 1960; Albert E. White Distinguished Tchr. award Am. Soc. Metals, 1967. Fellow Am. Inst. Mining and Metall Engrs.; mem. Am. Chem. Soc., Nat. Scis., Am. Soc. Metals, Brit. Iron and Steel Inst. (hon.), Brit. Inst. Metals, Associacao Brasileria de Betais, A.A.A.S., Sigma Xi, Phi Lambda Upsilon, Delta Sigma Phi, Phi Kappa Phi, Tau Beta Pi, Phi Beta Kappa. Clubs: University (Pitts.); Cosmos (Washington); Athenaeum (London, Eng.). Translator: Tammann's The States of Aggregation (Aggregatzustande). Author: Metallurgia de Aco; History of Physical Mettalurgy. Contbr. numerous research articles to tech. jours. Address: Pittsburgh, Pa., Died Jan. 29, 1976.

MEHTA, GAGANVIHARI L., Indian ambassador to U.S.A. and Mexico; b. Ahmedabad, Apr. 15, 1900; s. Lallubhai Samaldas and Shrimati (Satyavati) M.; student Elphinstone Coll., Bombay, also London Sch. Econs. and Polit. Science; LL.D., Rollins College, 1953, Simpson Coll., 1956; m. Saudamini Nikanth, Dec. 3, 1924; children—Nilanjana (Mrs. Dhar), Uma (Mrs. Randeria), Aparna. Asst. editor Bombay Chronicle, 1923-25; mgr. Scindia Steam Nav. Co., Ltd., Calcutta, 1928-47; commr. Port of Calcutta, 1930-34, 40-42, 46-47; post-war policy com. industry and civil aviation, 1943-45; governing body Council Sci. and Indsl. Research, 1947-52; pres. Indian Tariff Bd., Bombay, 1947-50; mem. planning commn., New Delhi, 1950-52; mem. All-India Council Tech. Edn., Calcutta, 1950-52; chmn. Indian adv. com. Nuffield Found., 1950-52; chmn. tariff commn., Bombay, 1952; Indian ambassador to U.S.A. and Mexico, 1952-58. Adviser Indian employers' delegation Internat. Labor. Conf., 1937; del. Internat. C. of C., Berlin, 1937, Internat. Bus. Conf., N.Y. C., 1944; mem. Indian delegation Internat. Trade Conf., mem. Indian C. of C. (pres. 1939-40), Fedn. Indian Chambers Commerce and Industry (pres. 1942-43), Indian Inst. Sci. (mem. council Bangalore 1951). Author: Conscience of a Nation, 1933; From Wrong Angles, 1934; Perversities, 1942. Died Apr. 1974.

MEIGS, CORNELIA LYNDE, author; b. Rock Island, Ill., Dec. 6, 1884; d. Montgomery and Grace Cornelia (Lynde) Meigs; A.B., Bryn Mawr, 1907. Prof. English, Bryn Mawr Coll. Employee of War Dept., Washington, D.C., 1942-45. Republican. Episcopalian. Author since 1915; latest publ.: The Violent Men, 1949; The Dutch Colt, 1952. Part author and editor: A Critical History of Children's Literature, 1953; Fair Wind to Virginia, 1955; What Makes A College: A History of Bryn Mawr, 1956; Wild Geese Flying, 1957; Mystery at the Red House, 1961; The Great Design-Men and Events in the United Nations, 1945-61, 1964. Home: Havre de Grace, Md. Died September 10, 1973.

MEIGS, GRACE LYNDE, physician; b. Keokuk, Ia., Aug. 28, 1881; d. Montgomery and Grace Cornelia (Lynde) M.; A.B., Bryn Mawr Coll., 1903; M.D., Rush Med. Coll. U. (U. of Chicago), 1908, interne Cook Co. Hosp., Chicago, 1908-09; practiced in Chicago, 1909-14; dir. Div. of Hygiene of Children's Bur., U.S. Dept. of Labor, Washington, D.C., from 1914; mem. Com. on Infant Welfare of Gen. Med. Bd. of Council Nat. Defense. Club: Bryn Mawr (New York). Home: Washington, D.C.†

MEINHOLD, H. E., chmn. bd. dirs. Duffy—Mott Co. Home: New York City, N.Y. Died 1971.

MEISENHELTER, L. R., mech. engr.; b. York, Pa., Apr. 10, 1880; s. Samuel H. and Amanda (Ruppert) M.; ed. high sch., York; M.E., Pa. State Coll., 1900; m. Sarah B. MacFarland, of Phila., Pa., Nov. 20, 1913; children—Lewis R., Dorothea. Began in employ of York Mfg. Co., 1900, later with Pa. R.R., at Harrisburg; chief mech. engr. and gen. mgr. Harrisburg Engring. Co.; with Lodge & Shipley Machine Tool Co., Cincinnati, O., also spl. engr. to pres., William C. Lodge; v.p. in charge engring., Houston, Stanwood & Gamble Co., mfrs. heavy machinery, Cincinnati, and in charge of co.'s exhibit at San Francisco Expn., and dir. of exhibits; chief of transportation, machinery, mines and metallurgy, and bldgs., Sesquicentennial Exposition, Philadelphia, 1925. Mem. advisory board to War Dept. for consultation of design of machinery for making heavy ordnance and munitions, World War, also v.p. in charge engring. and sales of Houston, Stanwood & Gamble Co.; later engr. Dept. of Highways, Commonwealth of Pa. Lutheran. Mason (K.T., 32°). Designer spl. machinery for steel plants, railroad shops and Govt. ordnance and munitions factories. Home: Philadelphia, Pa.†

MEISS, MILLARD, art historian; b. Cin., Mar. 25, 1904; s. Leon and Clara (Loewenstein) M.; B.A., Princeton, 1926; postgrad. Harvard, 1928; M.A., N.Y. U., 1931, Ph.D., 1933; Litt.D. U. Florence, Princeton, Columbia; m. Margaret Louchheim, Mar. 15, 1928; children—Michael (dec.), Elinor (Mrs. Joel L. Siner). Asst. supt. bldg. constrn. Shroder & Koppel, 1926-28; lectr. history of art N.Y.U., 1931-33; lectr., asst. prof., asso. prof., prof. fine arts and archaeology Columbia, 1934-53; prof. fine arts, curator paintings Fogg Mus., Harvard, 1954-58; prof. history of art Inst. Advanced Study, 1958-74; editor in chief Art Bull., 1940-42, mem. editorial bd., from 1943; editorial bd. Mag. of Art, 1948-52. Chmn. Am. Com. Restoration Italian Monuments, Inc., 1946-51. Recipient John Wanamaker English prize Princeton, 1925, Haskins medal Medieval Acad., 1953, Morey award Coll. Art Assn., 1969; decorated Stella della Solidarieta (Italy), 1949, grande ufficiale, 1968. Fellow Am. Acad. Arts and Scis., Am. Philos. Soc. (Lewis prize), Medieval Acad. Am., Morgan Library (hon.); mem. Comite International d'Histoire de l'Art (pres. 1961-64, v.p. from 1964), Coll. Art Assn. Am. (dir., exec. com. 1940-47, 52-57, sec. 1943, v.p. 1954-56), Met. Mus. Art (hon. trustee), Accademia dei Lincei (Corr.), Accademia Senese degli Intronati (corr.), Societe des antiquaires de France (corr.), Accademia delle Arti del Disegno, Florence (corr.), Accademia Toscana Colombaria, Florence (corr.), Accademia Clementina, Bologna (corr.), Brit. Acad. (corr.). Phi Beta Kappa. Author: Painting in Florence and Siena After the Black Death, 1951; Andrea Mantegna as Illuminator, 1957; Giotto and Assisi, 1960; Giovanni Bellini's St. Francis in the Frick Collection, 1964; (with L. Tintori) The Painting of the Life of St. Francis in Assisi, 1962; French Painting in the Time of Jean de Berry: The Late XIV Century and the Patronage of the Duke, 1967; The Boucicaut Master, 1968; (with P. Brieger and C. Singleton) Illuminated Manuscripts of The Divine Comedy, 1969; The Great Age of Fresco: Discoveries, Recoveries and Survivals, 1970; The Limbourgs and their Contempories, 1974; Facsimiles of Several Illuminated Manuscripts; The Painter's Choice-Problems in the Interpretation of Renaissance Art, 1976. Contbr. articles to Am. and European jours. Home: Princeton NJ. Died June 12, 1975.

MEISTER, JOHN WILLIAM, clergyman; b. Marietta, O., Dec. 30, 1916; s. Earl Peter and Eleanor Jane (Wigginton) M.; A.B., Ohio U., 1938; B.Th., Princeton, 1941; D.D. (hon.), Hanover (Ind.) Coll. 1952; m. Miriam George, Sept. 15, 1942; children—Gretchen (Mrs. Gilbert Horn), Gregory, Peter. Ordained to ministry Presbyn. Ch., 1941; pastor, Steubenville, O., 1941-45, Sidney, O., 1941-50, First Presbyn. Ch., Ft. Wayne, Inc., 1950-67; exec. sec. Council Theol. Edn., U.P. Ch., N.Y.C., 1967-72; dir. Council Theol. Sems., 1972-74. Mem. bd. Christian edn. U.P. Ch. 1952-74, mem. radio and television commn., 1966, chmn. com. higher edn. Synod Ind., 1957-74. Mem. Gov. Ind. Adv. Com. Mental Health, 1961-74. Trustee Princeton Theol. Sem. Mem. Ft. Wayne Urban League, Ft. Wayne C. of C., Phi Beta Kappa, Kappa Delta Pi, Tau Kappa Alpha, Phi Eta Sigma, Delta Tau Delta. Mason, Rotarian. Club: Ft. Wayne Press. Author: What Baptism Means, 1960. Editor: (W. Law) A Serious Call to a Devout and Holy Life, 1955. Editorial council Theology Today, 1960-74. Contbr. articles to profl. jours. Home: Titusville, N.J., Died May 1974.

MELANDER, GEORGE HAROLD, savs. and loan exec.; b. San Francisco, Jan. 1, 1906; s. George and Maria (Berglund) M.; student Am. In Inst. Banking, 1924—45; m. Gail Garnet Gregg, Aug. 10, 1940; children—Martin Geroge, Linda (Mrs. Richard Heinz Frank), Philip. Clk. Wells Fargo Bank, San Francisco, 1924—45; treas. Fed. Home Loan Bank San Francisco, 1946—48; sec. First Savs. & Loan Assn., Berkeley, 1949—51; pres. Franklin Savs. & Loan Assn., San Francisco, 1953—74; pres., dir. Franklin Assos., San Francisco, 1958—74. Bd. dirs. Convention & Visitors Bur., Central San Francisco Assn., Market St. Devel. Project. Republican. Methodist. Rotarian, lMason. Home: El Cerrito, Cal. Died June 3, 1974; cremated.

MELCHERS, LEO EDWARD, educator, botanist; born Toledo, O., Aug. 1, 1887; s. Dr. Edward and Florentine (Laurer) M.; B.S., Ohio State U., 1912, M.S., 1913; m. Helen Stephenson, 1933. Asst. botanist, Ohio Expt. Sta., 1912-13, Kan. State Coll., 1913-15, instr. in plant pathology, 1915-16; collaborator in cereal disease investigations U.S. Dept. Agr., 1916; asst. prof. of botany Kan. State Coll., 1916-18, associate professor, 1918-19, acting head of department and plant pathologist, 1917-18, prof., head of dept. and plant pathologist, 1919-52, prof. botany from 1952; botanist Kan. State Board of Agr. from 1920; chief mycologist, Egyptian Ministry of Agr., Cairo, 1927-29; chmn. Egyption plant quarantine bd., 1928-29; explorations in Nile Valley and oases of Libyan Desert; specialist in plant pathology, breeding for disease resistance in cereal and forage crops. Mem. War Emergency Bd., Am. Plant Pathologists, 1917-18, Kan. Council of Defense, 1918; chmn. cereal disease control War Service Com., Upper Miss. Valley Plant Pathologists, 1942-48. Fellow A.A.A.S.; mem. Bot. Soc. Am., Phytopathol. Soc., Kan. Acad. Science, Sigma Xi, Gamma Sigma Delta, Phi Kappa Phi, Alpha Zeta. Conglist. Mason. Club: Country (Manhattan). Contbr. to bulls., also articles in sci. jours. on plant pathology. Home: Manhattan, Kan. Died Dec. 29, 1974.

MELCHETT, JULIAN EDWARD ALFRED, steel co. exec.; b. Eng., Jan. 9, 1925; s. 2d Baron Melchett and Amy Gwen (Wilson); ed. Eton; m. Sonia Elizabeth Graham, 1947; 1 son, 2 daus. Mem. adv. council, export credits quarantee dept. Brit. Transport Docks Bd., mem. adminstrv. council Malta Drydocks, Ltd.; chmn. Brit. Steel Corp., London, 1967-73; chmn. Brit. Field Products Ltd.; dir. Orion Bank Ltd., Guardian Assurance Co. Ltd. Mem. Nat. Econ. Devel. Council. Served to lt. Royal Naval Vol. Res. Home: London, England. Died June 15, 1973.

MELHORN, DONALD FRANKLIN, lawyer; b. Kenton, O., Apr. 28, 1889; s. Charles M. and Laura (Churchill) M.; A.B., U. Mich., 1911, J.D., 1914; m. Catharine Zettler, Oct. 22, 1930; children—Donald Franklin, David K., Catharine Rose. Admitted to Mich., Ohio bars, 1914; pros. atty. Hardin County, 1915-19; asst. atty. gen. Ohio, 1919-23; practice of law, Toledo, from 1923; mem. Marshall, Melborn, Bloch & Belt. Mem. Am., Ohio, Toledo bar assns., Lawyers Club U. Mich. Home: Toledo, O. Died Mar. 17, 1974.

MELHUS, IRVING E., plant pathologist; b. Creston, Ill., Apr. 2, 1881; s. Ole and Enger (Risting) M.; B.S., Ia. State Coll., Ames, Ia., 1906; Ph.D., U. of Wis., 1912; m. Elizabeth Williamson, Dec. 26, 1906; children—Sarah (Mrs. William Gregg Hoyman), Janet Mary (Mrs. Jack Robb Wallin). Teacher, high school, Ia., 1907-08; asst. in botany, U. of Wis., 1908-09, plant pathology, 1909-10, instr., 1910-11; plant pathologist, bureau plant industry, Dept. of Agr., 1912-16; associate prof. plant pathology, Ia. State Coll., 1916-17, prof. from 1917, chief of plant pathology, 1916-30, head of dept. of botany, 1930-46; head of sect. botany and plant pathology, 1930-46; state botanist of Ia., 1937-46. Dir. Iowa State Coll., Guatemala, Tropical Research Center, 1946. Mem. bd. dirs. Ames (Ia) Bldg. & Loan Assn., 1920-43; v.p. and pres., 1939-43. Chmn. war service com. Upper Miss. Valley Plant Pathologists, 1941-44; chmn. central com. War Service Com., 1944. Mem. Am. Soc. Naturalists, Bot. Soc. America, Am. Phytopath. Soc. (asso. editor Phytopath, 1918-20; vice pres. 1919; councillor 1922-27; pres. 1926), Crop Protection Inst. (mem. bd. govs. 1926-28, 1933-35), Torrey Bot. Club, Sigma Xi, Phi Kappa Phi, Gamma Sigma Delta, Alpha Zeta. Republican. Presbyterian. Clubs: Osborne (Ia. State Coll). Author: Elements of Plant Pathology (with Dr. G. C. Kent), 1939. Home: Ames, Ia.†

MELLEN, IDA M., biologist, author; b. N.Y. City, Jan. 9, 1877; d. Andrew Jackson and Mary Davis (Sprague) M.; grad. Lockwood Acad., Brooklyn, N.Y., 1893, Normal Kindergarten Training Sch., Brockton, Mass., 1895, Browne' Business Coll., Brooklyn, 1900. Nurses' Training Sch., Y.W.C.A., Brooklyn, 1902; student Marine Biol. Lab., Woods Hole, Mass., 1908-10, Eugenics Research Assn., Cold Spring Harbor, N.Y., 1912. Hon. D.Sc. Law reporter of N.Y. City, 1901-16; aquarist, N.Y. Aquarium, engaged in care and feeding aquatic animals in captivity, 1916-29; toured Europe, 1929, studying pub. aquarium methods; later engaged in authorship and independent research. Member

Thomas Paine Memorial Com. Member Alden Kindred of N.Y. City and Vicinity, Internat. Humane Edn. Foundation, The World Calendar Assn. Republican. Rationalist. Author: (monographs) The Whitefishes (with J. Van Oosten), 1923; A Table of Information Regarding Aquariums of the World, 1925 (revised, 1928); The Natural and Artificial Foods of Fishes, 1927; Treatment of Fish Diseases, 1928. Books; Fishes in the Home, 1927, rev. 1954; Young Folks' Book of Fishes, 1927; Roof Gardening, 1929; 1001 Questions Answered About Your Aquarium (with Robert J. Lanier), 1935, rev., 1953; A Practical Cat Book, 1939; The Science and the Mystery of the Cat, 1940; Outstanding Members of the Mellen Tribe in America, 1941; Twenty Little Fishes (juvenile), 1942; Thw Wonder World of Fishes, 1952; The Natural History of the Pig, 1952; contbr. encys.; author articles and lectures on zoölogy and eugenics. Radio speaker in field. A pioneer in quatic-animal Therapy. Home: New York City, N.Y.†

MELTON, WILLIAM WALTER, clergyman; b. Navarro County, Tex., Jan. 19, 1879; s. Amos W. and Minnie (Summers) M.; A.B., Baylor U., 1919; Th.G., Southwestern Sem., 1912; m. Orah Shipp, Sept. 14, 1905; children—John Wade, Margaret, Walter Truett, Robert, Gladys, Joe Allen. Pastor University Ch., Waco, Tex., 1912-41, sec. Bapt. Gen. Conv. of Texas, 1941-46; pastor Columbus Av. Bapt. Ch., Waco, Tex., from 1946. Author: Five Books of sermons and autobiography. Home: Waco Tex.†

MELVILLE, K(ENNETH) I(VAN), educator; b. Jamaica, B.W.I., July 5, 1902; s. Nathan Josiah and Rose (Smith) M.; B.S., McGill U., Montreal, Que., Can., 1926, M.D., C.M., 1926, M.Sc., 1931; m. Gladys Vivian Brother, Apr. 14, 1933; children—Enid Lorraine (Mrs. Virgil Wright), David Louis. Mem. faculty McGill U., from 1930, prof., chmn. dept. pharmacology, from 1953. Cons., Royal Victoria, Montreal, Gen., Montreal Children's hosps. Recipient for research in anesthesia Internat. Coll. Anesthesists, 1952. Mem. Pharmacol. Soc., Can. (pres.), Am. Soc. Pharmacology and Exptl. Therapeutics. Contbg. author: Pharmacology in Medicine, 1965; also author numerous articles. Research on action of drugs on coronary circulation, drugs affecting blood pressure and heart function. Home: Montreal, Que., Can. Died Jan. 29, 1975.

MEMMINGER, LUCIEN, consular service; b. Tampa, Fla., Aug. 11, 1879; s. Rev. Robert Withers and Susan (Mazyck) M.; U. of the South, 1896-1900; m. Mabel Dibell, May 25, 1921; children—Lucien Dibell (died in military service, Aug. 24, 1944), Charles Gustavus, Elisabeth Anne. Began as newspaper man; apptd. vice and deputy consul gen., Boma, Africa, 1907, Naples, 1908-10. Beirut, 1910-11, Smyrna, 1911, Paris, 1911-13; consul at Rouen, 1913-15, Madras, 1915-19. Leghorn, Italy, 1919-23, Bordeaux, France, 1923-31; consul gen., Belfast, Ireland, 1931-37, Copenhagen, 1937-41, Pretoria, 1941-43, Paramaribo, Surinam, 1943, ret., 1944. Mem. Alpha Tau Omega. Episcopalian. Address: Asheville, N.C.†

MENAGH, LOUIS RANDOLPH, JR., ins. exec.; b. Brooklyn, Sept. 2, 1892; s. Louis R. and Cora D. (Britten) M.; Litt.B., Rutgers U., 1914; LL.D., Bryant College, 1961; m. Myra F. Herder, May 16, 1931. With Prudential Ins. Co., Newark, N.J., 1914-62, v.p. and comptroller, 1947-57, exec., v.p., 1957-61, pres., 1961-62. Adviser N.J. Legislature on various pension matters, 1946; treas. Newark U. and trustee, 1942-48; chmn. council Rutgers U., Newark br., from 1949. Fellow Soc. Actuaries; mem. Ins. Accounting and Statistical Assn., Lambda Chi Alpha. Club' New York Accountants. Home: Maplewood N.J. Died June 20, 1973.

MENCONI, RALPH JOSEPH, sculptor, medal designer; b. Union City, N.J., June 17, 1915; s. Raffaello E. and Josephine (Zampieri) M.; grad. Scarborough Prep. Sch., 1932; student Hamilton Coll., 1932-33, D.F.A. (hon.), 1971; student N.A.D., 1933-36; B.F.A., Yale, 1939; m. Marjorie Livingston Ewen, Oct. 12, 1946; children—Ralph Joseph, II, Susan Ewen. Commd. works for AFL-CIO Hdqrs., Washington, Spear Library. Princeton, N.J., Pace Coll., Koppers Co., South Bend (Ind.) Pub. Library, Reredos Emanuel Luth. Ch., Pleasantville, N.Y., 1965, Project Mercury Pad 14, Cape Kennedy, Fla., MacArthur Meml., Norfolk, Va., U.S. Capitol medal Capitol Hist. Soc., Sigma Delta Chi monument DePauw U., busts and fountain Pace U., others; portrait busts include Gen. Sommervel, F. Ecker, Samuel Gompers, Conrad Hilton, Levi Esckol, Lyndon B. Johnson, Roy and Lila Cullen, Robert F. Kennedy, Gov. Melvin Evans, Judson B. Branch, others; three historic medals series, Gt. Religions of the World series, spl. medals, Pres. Kennedy Campaign medal, 1963, Winston Churchill medal, 1965, Pres. Nixon Inaugural medal, Man's 1st Lunar Landing medal, Apollo XII, XIII, XIV and XV Flights medal. Del., Fine Arts Fedn., N.Y.C., 1966. Village trustee, Pleasantville, 1959-64, police commr., 1960-64; mem. panel for U.S. coin and medals Am. Bicentennial Commn., from 1970. Served to maj. C.E., AUS. Decorated Bronze Star; recipient award N.A.D., 1940, Michelangelo award Sons Columbus of Am., 1970, Sculptor of Year award Am. Numis. Assn., 1971, Speer Meml. prize. Mem. Century Assn., Nat. Sculpture Society (council from 1965, 1st v.p. from 1967. Municipal Soc. N.Y.C. (dir. 1954-60), Delta Upsilon. Home: Pleasantville N.Y. Died Nov. 18, 1972; buried Carmel, N.Y.

MENDENHALL, GEORGE NEWTON, clergyman, educator; b. nr. Jerico Springs, Mo., Sept. 1, 1878; s. Jasper Newton and Margaret Ellen (Rickey) M.; prep. edn., Warrensburg (Mo.) State Normal Sch. and Midland Acad., Atchison, Kan.; A.B., Midland Coll., 1905; B.D., Western Theol. Sem., Atchison, Kan., 1908; A.M., State U. of Ia., 1921, Ph.D., 1922; m. Mamie C. Johnson, of Ericson, Neb., June 15, 1910; children—Newell Newton, Alfred Louis, George Emery, Olney Wendell, Mildred Christine, Helen Elizabeth. Ordained Luth. ministry, 1908; pastor McCool Jct., Neb., 1908; prin. Midland Acad., 1909-10; pastor Pueblo, Colo., 1911-14, Muscatine, Ia., 1914-18, North Liberty, Ia., 1919-22; head dept. of edn. and psychology, Midland Coll., 1922-27; head dept. of psychology and philosophy, from 1927. Mem. N.E.A. and Dept. of Superintendence same. Neb. State Teachers' Assn., Neb. Assn. Ch. Colleges. Republican. Author: Wells By The Wayside, 1913. Assisted in preparation of Ia. plan for moral instrn. in pub. schs. Home: Fremont, Neb.†

MENDENHALL, WILLIAM ORVILLE, coll. pres.; b. Ridge Farm, Ill., May 10, 1879; s. Albert W. and Almeda (Ress) M.; A.B., Penn Coll., Ia., 1900, A.M., 1901; A.B., Haverford (Pa.) Coll., 1901; studied Clark Univ.; Ph.D., U. of Mich., 1911; LL.D., Univ. of Wichita, 1929; L.H.D., College of Osteopathic Physicians and Surgeons, 1941; D.D., Whittier College, 1946; married Lucy Osgood, June 22, 1907; 1 son, William Rees. Instructor in mathematics, Stanford, 1906-07; prof. mathematics, Earlham Coll., 1907-18, also dean of men; pres. Friends U., Wichita, Kan., 1918-34; pres. Whittier (Calif.) Coll., 1934-43; later minister at large, Soc. of Friends, with special assignment to Am. Friends Service Com. Chmn. nat. student div., Y.M.C.A., 1933-37. Mem. Sigma Xi. Member Society of Friends; presiding clerk Five Years Meeting of the Society of Friends, 1927-35. Club: Lions (past dist. gov.). Address: Whittier, Cal.†

MENDES, MURILO MONTEIRO, author, educator; b. Juiz de Fora, Brazil, May 13, 1901; s. Onofre and Elisa (Monteiro Barros) Mendes; ed. Instituto de Alta Cultura (Brazil); m. Saudade Cortesao, July 7, 1947. Prof. Brazilian lit. U. Rome (Italy), 1957—; formerly in charge confs. of the Univs. Brussels (Belgium), Louvain (Belgium), Amsterdam (Netherlands), Paris (France). Recipient Internat. prize poetry Etna-Taormina, 1972. Mem. Internat. Assn. Art Critics, European Soc. Culture, European Community of Writers. Author: Poemas, 1930; A Poesia em Panico, 1938; O Visionario, 1941; As Metamorfoses, 1944; Mundo Enigma, 1945; Poesia Liberdade, 1947; Tempo Espanhol, 1959; A Idade do Serrote, 1968; Convergencia, 1970; Podiedro, 1972. Home: Rome, Italy., Died Aug. 13, 1975.

MENZIES, PERCIVAL KEITH, physician; b. Ailsa Craig, Ont., Can., June 16, 1886; s. John E. and Margaret McL. Menzies; M.D., U. Toronto, 1910; m. Olive M. Campbell, June 6, 1918; children—John K., Gordon C. Intern, Sick Children's Hosp., Toronto, Ont., 1911-12, Hosp. for Ruptured and Crippled, N.Y.C., 1912-13; fellow in pathology U. Toronto, 1910-11; fellow in surgery Mayo Clinic, Rochester, Minn., 1913-14; sr. attending surgeon Syracuse (N.Y.) Community Gen. Hosp., Syracuse Meml. Hosp., Crouse-Irving Meml. Hosp., Syracuse; prof. emeritus clin. surgery State U. N.Y., Syracuse. Served with M.C., Can. Army, 1914-20. Diplomate Am. Bd. Surgery. Fellow A.C.S.; mem. A.M.A. Home: Syracuse, N.Y. Died Feb. 25, 1971; buried Syracuse, N.Y.

MERCER, BEVERLY HOWARD, corp. exec.; b. Ellicott City, Md., Feb. 23, 1894; s. Eugene Peyton and Isabelle (Saffell) M.; LL.B., U. of Md., 1924; m. Hannah Wheatley, Nov. 1, 1919; 1 dau., Elizabeth (Mrs. Grady R. Funk). Pres., Fidelity & Deposit Co. Md., Balt., 1911-33, v.p., 1933-44, 2d v.p., 1944-48, 1st v.p., 1948-50, pres., 1950-64, dir., 1946-75; dir., mem. exec. com. Monumental Life Ins. Co.; mem. trust and exec. coms. Md. Nat. Bank; mem. exec. com. Surety Assn. Am., Assn. Casualty and Surety Cos.; dir. Savs. Bank Balt., Arundel Corp. Trustee Johns Hopkins Hosp.; mem. bus. adminstrn. dept. P.E. Ch. Diocese of Md.; pres. bd. Loyola Coll.; mem. Greater Balt. com. and Downtown Com.; chmn. Community Chest Campaign; Mem. Nat. Assn. Casualty and Surety Execs. (past pres.), Balt. Assn. Commerce (dir.), Newcomen Soc., Beavers, Gamma Eta Gamma. Clubs: Country, Maryland, Center (Balt.); Metropolitan (N.Y.C.). Home: Howard County, Md., Died Mar. 8, 1975.

MERCER, SAMUEL ALFRED BROWNE, coll. prof.; b. Bristol, Eng., May 10, 1880; s. Samuel and Elizabeth (Browne) M.; B.Sc., Bishop Field Coll. and Central Training Sch., St. John's, Newfoundland, 1900; B.D., Nashotah House Wis., 1904; studied Semitic langs. and lits., U. of Wis., 1905; B.A., Harvard, 1908; continued Semitic studies at Göttingen, Heidelberg, the Sorbonne (Paris), and Munich, Ph.D., U. of Munich, 1910; D.D., Nashotah House, 1917; LL.D from same, 1932; Th.D., Paris, 1938; D.S.Litt., Kenyon College, 1939; Doctor of Divinity, Trinity Coll. (Toronto), 1950; m. Genevieve Magee, August 15, 1910; 1 dau., Harriet Martha. Ordained deacon and priest, P.E. Ch., 1904; prof. of Hebrew and O.T. lit., Western Theol. Sem., Chicago, 1910-22; dean of Bexley Hall, Gambler, O., 1922-23; prof. Semitic langs. and Egyptology, Trinity Coll., Toronto, 1923-46; prof. emeritus, 1946. Mem. many tech., profl. and scientific, assns. and orgns. Decorated Lauréat de l'Academie Francaise; Officer de l'Instruction Publique francaise; Order of the Trinity (Abyssinia). Author many books, including, Pyramid Texts, Translation and Commentary, 1952; Earliest Intellectual Man's Idea of the Cosmos, 1956; also published many articles on Semitic law and religion and on Egyptology. Home: Worcester, Mass.†

MEREDITH, EDNA ELLIOTT, publisher; b. Des Moines, Ia., Apr. 25, 1879; d. Samuel Mathew and Adeline Mary (Jones) Elliott; student Ia. State Coll.; m. Edwin Thomas Meredith (ex-sec. of Agr.); children—Mildred Marie (Mrs. F. O. Bohen). Edwin Thomas, Jr. Formerly bus. mgr., pres. Meredith Pub. Co., Better Homes and Gardens and Successful Farming, now dir. Clubs: Women's (Des Moines); Sulgrave (Washington). Home: Des Moines, Ia.*†

MEREDITH, ERNEST SIDNEY, clergyman; b. Canton, O., May 26, 1879; s. William Davis and Sarah (Kee) M.; grad. Mt. Union Prep. Sch., 1897; B.Sc., Mt. Union Coll., 1900, Ph.B., 1902; M.A., Harvard, 1904; LL.B., Northeastern U. Law Sch., 1921; student Oxford U., England, 1911, Harvard Law Sch., 1922; m. Florence Lyndon, June 27, 1905. City editor Canton (Ohio) News, 1902; asst. pastor Harvard Ch., Brookline, Mass., 1902-05; ordained Unitarian ministry, 1905; minister First Parish, W. Roxbury, Boston, 1905-12, Third Religious Soc. of Dorchester, Boston, Mass., 1912-16. First Parish, Watertown, 1916-47. Chaplain Ancient and Hon. Arty. Co., 1906-07; president Mass. Conv. Congl. Ministers, 1923-25; pres. Unitarian Sunday Sch. Soc., 1931-34; v.p. Harvard Divinity Sch. Alumni Assn., 1929-31, pres. 1931-34; pres. S. Middlesex Conf. of Unitarian and Other Liberal. Chs., 1928-37; pres. Ministerial Union of Unitarian Denomination, 1930-37; mem. Harvard U. Visitation Com. of Divinity Sch., 1931-39; became mem. fellowship com. Am. Unitarian Assn., 1938. Lt. chaplain Camp Zachary Taylor, 1918-19; capt., chaplain, U.S.A.R., 1919; became attached to Div. Hdqrs., Boston, 1937. Chaplain Sons of Vets, of Civil War (Mass, div.), 1930-31. Mason Clubs: Sigma Alpha Epsilon. Harvard Faculty, Oakley Country. Home: Watertown, Mass.†

MERILLAT, LOUIS ADOLPH, veterinarian, editor; b. Wooster O., Mar. 22, 1868; s. David A. and Cecil (Guerne) M.; ed. high sch. Mt. Eaton, O.; D.V.S., Ontario Vet. Coll. (U. of Toronto), 1888; m. Mary Smith, Mar. 16, 1891; 1 son, Louis Adolph. Sec. McKillip Vet. Coll., 1892-1900; prof. surgery, Chicago Vet. Coll., 1901-16; mem. Wright & Merillat (vet. hosp), 1901-17; asso. editor Veterinary Medicine (monthly), 1913-21, managing editor, 1921-23; editor North American Veterinarian, 1924-29; executive secretary American Veterinarian Med. Assn.; president board veterinary examiners, Illinois Department Registration and Edn., 1926-43. Commd. maj. Vet. Corps, U.S. Army, Oct. 15, 1917; lt. col., June 1919; lt. col. Vet. O.R.C., served as div. vet. 41st Div., U.S. Army; comdg. officer advance sect. Vet. Hosp., Neuchâteau, Vosges, France; exec. officer Franco-Am. Vet. Liaison Mission, Paris; chief vet. 1st Army, A.E.F. Chevalier Legion of Honor (French), 1919. Mem. Am. Vet. Med. Assn. (sec., pres.), Illinois Vet. Assn. (pres.), Chicago Vet. Soc. (pres.). Democrat. Presbyterian. Mason (K.T., Shriner). Author: Animal Dentistry, 1901; Principles of Veterinary Surgery, 1906; Veterinary Surgical Operations, 1907; Treatment of Wounds, 1913; Surgical Treatment of Colics of the Horse, 1914; Veterinary Military History of the United States (vols. I and II), 1935. Editor of Jour. of Am. Veterinary Assn. and Am. Jour. of Veterinary Research. Home: Chicago, Ill.†

MERMEY, MAURICE, pub. relations counsel; b. Hungary, Sept. 21, 1901; s. Israel Joseph and Hannah (Goldman) M.: brought to U.S., 1902, naturalized, 1909; student N.Y. State Coll. Forestry, Syracuse U.; m. Augusta Miriam Rosenthal, October 30, 1926 (div. 1943); 1 dau., Mrs. Nina Klippel; m. 2d, Fayvelle Schulman, Feb. 25, 1944; children—Michael Victor, Constance Sara (Mrs. David C. Yates). Newspaper reporter, 1922-26; staff corr., Chgo. mgr., cable editor United Press, 1926-28) pub. relations cons. from 1928; exec. sec. Retail Code Authority, N.Y.C., 1933-34; dir. exhibits and concessions N.Y. World's Fair, 1936-39; vice chmn. Edward Gottlieb and Assos., Ltd., lectr. pub. relations N.Y. U., 1948-51; dir. Bur. Edn. on Fair Trade, from 1949; exec. sec. mayor's com. airport devel., comptroller's adv. council emergency taxes, N.Y.C., 1935-36; dir. Bur. Advancement Ind. Retailing. Exec. com., dir. Nat. Jewish Welfare Bd., 1942-64, hon. dir., from 1964; bd. dirs. YM and YWHA, 1948-53. Mem. Soc. Silurians, Pub. Relations Soc. Am., Tau Delta Phi. Editor: (with E. B. Weiss) The Shopping Guide. Home. Larchmont N.Y. Died Oct. 10, 1974.

MEROLA, GAETANO, conductor; b. Naples, Italy, Jan. 4, 1881; s. Giuseppe and Louise (Iaccarino) M.; prep. edn., Coll. of Jesuits, Naples; musical edn., Coll. Music, S. Pietro a Yajella, Naples; m. Rose Cudek, Jan. 12, 1907. Came to U.S. 1899, naturalized citizen, 1907. Became asst. condr. Metropolitan Opera Co., N.Y. City,

1900; became condr. Henry Savage s English Opera, 1903, Manhattan Opera House, N.Y. City, 1906, London (Eng.) Opera House, 1911; became gen. dir. San Francisco and Los Angeles Opera Assn., 1923*†

MERRILL, JOHN OGDEN, architect; b. St. Paul, Aug. 10, 1896; s. Henry Alexander and Mabel Elizabeth (Baldwin) M.; student U. Wis., 1914-16; B. Arch., Mass. Inst. Tech., 1921; m. Ross MacKenzie, June 1, 1918; children—Elizabeth Ross (Mrs. John H. C. Reid), John Ogden, Jean MacKenzie (Mrs. William S. Norton); m. 2d, Viola Berg, Apr. 27, 1946. Chief architect Mid-West states Fed. Housing Adminstrn., 1939; partner Skidmore, Owings & Merrill, architects-engrs., N.Y.C., Chgo. and San Francisco, 1939-58, partner (ret.) from 1958; charge design and constrn. City Oak Ridge, 1943-49, post-war master plan for Oak Ridge, 1948, devel. permanent facilities for U.S. Army and Air Force, Okinawa, 1950-54, Ft. Hamilton VA Hosp., Bklyn., 1946. Dir. revision Chgo. Bldg. Code, 1947-49. Served as capt. C.A.C., U.S. Army, 1917-19. Recipient Honor award (for Chgo. Civic Center) A.I.A., 1968. Fellow A.I.A. Home: Colorado Springs, Colo. Died June 10, 1975.

MERRILL, JULIA WRIGHT, librarian; b. Chillicothe, O., Sept. 11, 1881; d. Chester Wright and Mary (Franklin) Merrill; student U. of Cincinnati, 1898-1900; B.L.S., U. of Ill., 1903; studied U. of Wis., summer, 1905. Apprentice and asst. Public Library, Cincinnati, 1900-02; instr., field agt. and asst., Legislative reference dept. Wis. Free Library Commn., Madison, 1903-06; acting librarian Public Library, Cedar Rapids, Ia., 1906; head of city and county extension Public Library, Cincinnati, 1907-17; field visitor for state and instr. University Library Sch., Wis. Free Library Commn., 1917-22; chief of organization div. Ohio State Library, Columbus, 1922-25; instr. at different periods (on leave of absence) various univs., 1917-30; exec. asst. in library extension, A.L.A., 1925-32, chief of pub. library div. and dept. of information and advisory service, A.L.A., 1933-46; instr. Columbia U., summer, 1947. Mem. Am. Assn. Univ. Women, Fgn. Policy Assn., Nat. Municipal League, City Charter Com., United Nations Com. League of Women Voters. Episcopalian. Contributor to professional magazines. Home: Cincinnati, O.†

MERRILL, RICHARD NYE, clergyman; b. Philadelphia, Pa., May 24, 1881; s. Philip Shull and Mary Matilda (Coburn) M.; A.B., Allegheny Coll., Meadville, Pa., 1904, D.D., 1928; D.D., U. of Chattanooga, 1922, m. Agnes Espy, Oct. 13, 1904; children—Richard Nye, Major John Espy. Ordained ministry M.E. Ch., 1904; pastor Phila., 1904-07, Newcastle, Pa., 1907-12, Grove City, Pa., 1912-13, Westfield, N.Y., 1913-16, Miami, Fla., 1916-29, Long Beach, Calif., 1929-38. First Ch., Phoenix, Ariz., 1938-47, ret. 1947. Mem. bd. Fgn. Missions of M.E. Church, 1924-29; mem. Gen. Conference of M.E. Ch., 1924, 28, 32; mem. Commn. on Relation to Other Churches, 1928-32. Pres. bd. Community Plaza, Los Angeles; v.p. bd., Cook Sch. Christian Training for Indians; trustee Mt. Zion (Ga.) Inst., Latin-Am. Mission of M.E. Ch.; mem. nat. cons. Modern Missions Movement; dir. Phoenix Chapter Amer. Red Cross, Good Samaritan Hospital, Phoenix, Citizens Good Govt. Council, Phoenix, Ariz. Council of Chs. Pres. Phoenix Ministerial Assn., 1940-41 and 1946-47, Salt River Valley Meth. Ministers' Assn. Dir. San Diego Meth. Home. Mem. Phi Delta Theta (Golden Legion). Mason Kiwanian. Developer of "larger parish plan" for administration of suburban chs.; contbr. to The Upper Room; speaker at the Meth. Council of Cities. Home: San Diego, Cal.†

MERRITT, JAMES WHITE, ch. ofcl.; b. Monroe County, Ga., Dec. 29, 1886; s. George Bozeman and Martha (White) M.; ed. Gainesville (Ga.) Pub. Sch., 1898—1901; LL.D., Mercer U., 1934; m. Zillah Johnson, Oct. 3, 1916; children—James White, Zillah Johnson. In U.S. Postal Service, Gainesville, 1901—09; asst. cashier and cashier 1st Nat. Bank, 1909—20; field sec. S.S. dept. of Ga. Bapt. Conv., 1920—25, exec. sec., treas. exec. com. Ga. Bapt. Conv., 1930—55, pres., 1954—55, treas., 1956—72, also bus. mgr. Christian Index (ofcl. jour.), 1925—30, treas. dir., 1930-55; v.p. Bapt. Young People's Union Ga., 1913-16, pres., 1917-20, mem. exec. com., 1918-55; pres. Ga. Bapt. Assembly, 1930—31; mem. exec. com., sr. sec. So. Bapt. Conv., 1954—64; mem. exec. com. Ga. Bapt. Conv., 1954—72; treas. Ga. Bapt. Hosp. and sec. Ga. Bapt. Hosp. Com., 1930—55, mem. Ga. Bapt. Hosp. Commn., 1930—72, acting supt., 1945—46; dir. United Hosps. Service Assn. of Atlanta, 1937—55; mem. planning div. Met. Atlanta Community Services, Inc., 1930—55; sec. States Secs.' Assn. So. Bapt. Conv., 1939—43, v.p., 1943, pres., 1944—46; mem. endowment com. Ga. Bapt. Conv., 1943—55. Recipient Algernon Sydney Sullivan award N.Y. So. Soc., through Mercer U., 1932. Democrat. Mason. Contbr. to Christian Index, So. Bapt. Ency., and ch. jours. Home: Gainesville, Ga. Died June 16, 1972.

MERRITT, LEROY CHARLES, educator; b. Milw., Sept. 10, 1912; s. Arthur F. and Amanda (Polze) Schimmelpfeunig; B.A., U. Wis., 1935; Ph.D., U. Chgo., 1942; m. Mary Averill Liebenberg, Sept. 14, 1935; children—James LeRoy, Lauren Vail, Jeannette Averill. Cons. Am. Library Assn. Bd. on Resources, 1940—41; editorial asso. Cooperative Com. on Library Bldg. Plans, 1946; librarian, asso. prof. library sci. Longwood Coll., Farmville, Va., 1942—46; prof. librarianship U. Cal., Berkeley, 1946—66, asso. dean Sch. Librarianship, 1964—66; dean Sch. Librarianship U. Ore., Eugene, 1966—70. Served with AUS, 1944—45; ETO. Mem. Am. (editor Newsletter on Intellectural Freedom 1962-70), Cal. (past com. chmn.), Ore., Spl., Pacific Northwest library assns., Assn. Coll. and Reference Libraries, Assn. Am. Library Schs. (past pres.), Soc. Am. Archivists, Am. Documentation Inst., Ore. Assn. Sch. Libraries. Club: Commonwealth (San Francisco). Home: Eugene, Ore. Died May 22, 1970.

MERROW, CHESTER EARL, congressman; b. Center Ossipee, N.H., Nov. 15, 1906; s. Llewellyn and Florence (Nichols) M.; student Brewster Academy, 1921-25; B.S., Colby Coll., 1929; A.M., Teachers Coll., Columbia U., 1937; m. Nellie Margaret Sands, June 12, 1933; 1 son, Daniel S. Instr. science Kents Hill (Me.) Sch., 1929-30; instr. Montpelier Sem., 1930-37, asst. headmaster, 1935-38; instr. polit. science and history Vt. Jr. Coll., Montpelier, also dean, 1937-38. Mem. N.H. Ho. of Reps., 1939-40, chmn. House Ways and Means Com., mem. Com. on Banks, 1939-40; mem. 78th to 87th congresses, 1st N.H. Dist., mem. Com. Fgn. Affairs, chmn. subcom. on internat. orgns. and movements, 1953-55, mem. U.S. delegation from Ho. Reps. to Canada-U.S. Interparliamentary Group, 1959-60. Member Republican Congressional Campaign Com.; mem. U.S. Nat. Commn. UNESCO, 46-49, 53-56; 59-60. Delegate internat. conf. edn., cultural relations UN, London, Nov. 1945; congressional adv. to first conf. UNESCO, Paris, Nov. 1946; rep. U.S.A. at 10th session Gen. Assembly UN. Trustee Brewster Free Acad. Mem. Grange, Ahepa, Phi Beta Kappa. Mason., Elk. Lectr. nat. and internat. affairs. Home: Center Ossipee N.H. Died Feb. 11, 1974.

MERRY, ROBERT WATSON, educator; b. Iowa City, Oct. 29, 1913; s. Glenn Newton and Luella Helen (Eakins) M.; A.B., Harvard, 1935, M.B.A., 1939, D.C.S., 1943; m. Kay Marguerite Bingold, Apr. 15, 1936; children—Marilyn Jo, Glenn Woodruff; m. 2d, Margaret Habein, Aug. 28, 1961. With Lit. Guild Am., 1931-32, Ednl. Pub. Corp., 1935-36, Bklyn. Trust Co., 1936-38; research Harvard Grad. Sch. Bus. Adminstrn., 1939-43, asst. prof., 1943-48, asso. prof., 1948-53, prof., from 1953, dir. doctoral program, 1958-62, chmn. doctoral program, 1962-67, chmn. M.B.A. program, 1967-69, dir. course devel., 1970-72, dir. course devel. and ednl. services, from 1972. Vis. prof. bus. adminstrn. U. Wichita, 1960-61; mgmt. cons. various corps., univs., ednl. founds., 1941; dir. Inst. Coll. and U. Adminstrs., 1954-65; adv. bd. Atlanta U. Grad. Sch. Bus. Adminstrn., 1966-69; adv. com. Dept. Bus. Adminstrn. Simmons Coll., 1966-69; bd. visitors Boston U. Coll. Bus. Adminstrn., 1966-69; mem. Advanced Mgmt. Program faculty Inst. Centroamericana de Administracion de Expresas, Managua, Nicaragua, 1967-71, project adviser, 1970-72, adv. com., from 1972; ednl. chmn. European Profs. Case Workshop, 1973. Trustee Sarah Lawrence Coll., 1967-69. Mem. Am. Assn. Higher Edn., Am. Assn. U. Profs., Acad. Mgmt. Home: Lexington, Mass. Died Nov. 14, 1973.

MERRYFIELD, MARY AINSWORTH, journalist; b. Ft. Doge, Ia., Oct. 11, 1911; d. William Leroy and Nellie (Sunderland) Ainsworth; B.A., U. Ia., 1930; m. Maurice Richard Merryfield, Sept. 7, 1940. Tchr. high sch., Ottumwa, 2 years; stylist, corporate personality (Jane Alden), Alden's Mail Order Co., 7 years; became writer Crowell-Collier Mags., then promotion dir. State Street Council, Chgo.; conducted 1 hour weekday radio show Mary Merryfield's Radio Jour., NBC, Chgo., 7 years; writer weekly feature, including Talkbacks, Chgo. Tribune, also 6-days-a-week human relations column; also emcee weekly Talkback show WTTW-TV, Chgo. Recipient award Council Fgn. Relations; Alumni Gold Key award Nat. 4-H Club. Mem. Pi Beta Phi. Home: Dixon Ill. Died Mar. 1, 1974; buried Grand Detour, Ill.

MERTENS, GEORGE WILLIAM, corp. exec.; b. Lenzen on the Elbe, Germany, Nov. 22, 1878; s. Wilhelm and Wilhelmina (Mertens) M.; ed. schs., Oak Park, Ill., and Seattle, Wash.; m. Grace Chester Lear, Sept. 25, 1912; 1 son, Peter Lear. Came to U.S., 1884, naturalized citizen, 1896. Began with The Pacific Coast Co., 1895, successively office boy, clk., telegraph operator, train dispatcher, supt., asst. v.p., v.p., 1895-1940, pres. and dir. 1940-52, dir. and v.p., from 1952; pres. Pacific Coast Coal Co., Pacific Coast Lumber Co. of Cal., Pacific Coast Heating & Appliances Co. Clubs: Rainier, Seattle Tennis (Seattle). Home: Seattle, Wash.†

MERTINS, (MARSHALL) LOUIS, author; b. Jackson County, Mo., Dec. 7, 1885; s. Carl Henry and Mary E. (Koger) M.; student Kansas City Sem., 1906-07; student William Jewell Coll., 1905-10, LL.D., 1939; m. Lena Lee Holman, Sept. 28, 1907; children—Blanche (Mrs. Louis Garcia), Virginia Lee (Mrs. Lee McIntosh), Sara (Mrs. Malcolm Dewees), Louis II; m. 2d, Mrs. Esther Pedersen Erickson, May 12, 1939. Ordained minsitry Baptist Ch., 1906; orgainzer, pastor Swope Park Ch., Kansas City, Mo., 1911-15; pastor 1st Ch., Nevada, Mo., 1915-16; Chautauqua and lyceum lectr., 1916-26; radio broadcaster of The Poet Dreams; lectr., world lit. Valley College, San Bernardino, Cal. Member California Writers Guild (founder 1932; mem. exec. bd.; v.p. 1959), Internat. Mark Twain Society (hon.), Sigma Tau Delta, Pi Gamma Mu, Lambda Chi Alpha. Director Progressive-Commonwealth Fedn.; v.p. (nat.) I Am an American movement. Mem. Mystic Order Pyramids, Supreme Council, Clubs: E. Clampus Vitus, P.E.N. (exec. bd.), Beloved Vagabonds; Fortnightly (past pres.). Author books, from 1917; latest publ.; The Intervals of Robert Frost (with Esther Mertins), 1947; also feature (syndicated) in fgn. newspapers; radio commentator. Donor collection holograph mss. of famed authors to William Jewell Coll., comprehensive annotated Robert Frost collection to U. Cal. Home: Redlands, Cal., Deceased.

MERWIN, FREDERIC EATON, educator; b. East Palestine, O., Apr. 27, 1907; s. Charles Lewis and Estella Dora (Meek) M.; B.A., Ohio Wesleyan U., 1929; M.A., U. Wis., 1935, Ph.D., 1937; m. Jacqueline Olver Schmitt, Aug. 12, 1939; children—Miles Michael, Frederic Eaton. With East Palestine (O.) Daily Leader, 1922-29; reporter Indpls. Times, 1929; night bur. mgr. United Press, Cleve., 1930; telegraph editor Canton (O.) Repository, 1930-33; grad. asst. lectr. Sch. Journalism, U. Wis., 1933-37, asst. prof. Syracuse Sch. Journalism, 1937-40; mgr. N.Y. Press Assn., 1940; prof., dir. Sch. Journalism, Rutgers U., 1940-69. Pres. Am. Assn. Tchrs. Journalism, 1944-46; asst. chief div. information channel Office Facts and Figures, Washington, 1942. Recipient Nat. Merit award Am. Legion Press Assn., 1958. Mem. N.J. Press Assn., Assn. Edn. Journalism, Sigma Delta Chi, Phi Gamma Delta, Kappa Tau Alpha (nat. pres. 1952-54). Republican. Methodist. Editor bibliography Journalism Quar., 1935-45; editor annual Research in Progress for Nat. Council on Journalism Research, 1940-49, Journalism Series of Rinehart & Co.; mem. editorial bd. Journalism Quar., Jersey Publisher, 1958; co-editor: The Newspaper and Society, 1942; The Press and Society, 1951. Home: Metuchen, N.J., Died Oct. 28, 1975; interred St. Luke's Meml. Garden, Metuchen.

MESEROLE, CLINTON V., JR., consultant; b. Englewood, N.J., Sept. 3, 1918; s. Clinton V. and Ida Lewis (Brooke) M.; grad. Lawrenceville (N.J.) Sch., 1938; student Princeton, 1942; m. Barbara Thompson, June 20, 1942; children—Clinton V. III, William B., Michael R., Barbara A., Hilary M. Pres., dir. Phoenix Assurance Co. N.Y.; chmn. bd. Pacific Ins. Co. N.Y., Jersey Ins. Co. N.Y., Bankers and Shippers Ins. Co. N.Y.; v.p. Continental Ins. Co.; cons. in field, from 1971. Served with AUS, 1942-46. Clubs: Knickerbocker Country (Tenafly, N.J.); Downtown Assn. (N.Y.C.); Englewood Field. Home: Englewood, N.J. Died Oct. 20, 1974.

MESTA, PERLE, former govt. ofcl., hostess; b. Sturgis, Mich.; d. William B. Skirvin; ed. pvt. sch., Galveston, Tex.; m. George Mesta (dec. 1925). E.E. and M.P. from U.S. to Grand Duchy of Luxembourg, 1949-53. Active participant in Am. politics, from 1935; chmn. pub. relations com., mem. council Nat. Woman's Party; co-chmn. Pres. Truman's inaugural ball, 1949. Decorated grand cross Couronne de Chene, Croix de Guerre (Luxembourg). Democrat. Clubs: Sulgrave, Chevy Chase (Washington); Spouting Rock (Newport, R.I.). Home: Washington, D.C. Died Mar. 16, 1975.

METCALF, CLARENCE SHERIDAN, librarian; b. McConnelsville, O., Sept. 17, 1878; s. Frank Forrest and Ada (Winn) M.; student Ohio Med. U., 1896; m. Alice Bottman, Oct. 26, 1899; children—Margaret Ada (Mrs. Francis Sykora), Frances Forrest (Mrs. Thomas J. McDowell), Alice Elizabeth (Mrs. David C. Spaulding, Jr.). Clerk Hocking Valley R.R. Co., 1897-1904; auditor the Bruce Electric Constrn. Co., 1904-08; state examiner of pub. utilities, O., 1908-16; auditor City of Cleveland, 1916-20, finance dir., 1920-21; sec. Lee Rd. Savings & Loan Co., 1922-23; sec.-treas. Cleveland Pub. Library, 1924-41, librarian Dec. 1941-1950; mem. faculty, Library Sch., Western Res. U. Trustee Cleveland Soc. for the Blind. Mason. Executive vice-president, Great Lakes Historical Socity. Clubs: Chamber of Commerce, Midday, Cleveland City, Cleveland Advertising, Rowfant. Home: Lakewood, O.†

METCALF, MARTIN KELLOGG, naval officer; b. Calif., Feb. 28, 1881; entered U.S. Navy, Sept. 1899; advanced to capt., June 1926; retired, Jan. 1938; recalled to active duty and advanced to rear admiral, Mar. 1942. Home: Bethesda, Md.*†

METZ, CHARLES WILLIAM, biologist; b. Sundance, Wyo., Feb. 17, 1889; s. William Summerfield and Jennie (Gammon) M.; B.S., Pomona Coll., 1911; student Stanford, 1911—12; Ph.D., Columbia, 1916; m. Blanche E. Stafford, Aug. 20, 1913; children—Charles Baker, William Stafford, Jane Gammon, Alburn Stafford. Mem. staff dept. genetics Carnegie Instn., 1914—30, dept. embryology, 1930—40; vis. prof. zoology Johns Hopkins, 1930—37; prof., head dept. zoology U. Pa., 1940—55, prof., 1955—59, emeritus, 1959—75; investigator Woods Hole Marine Biol. Lab., 1959—75. Anti—malaria research USPHS, 1917—19. Fellow A.A.A.S.; mem. Am. Acad. Arts and Scis.; Am. Philos. Soc., Genetics Soc. Am., Am. Soc. Naturalists, Am. Soc. Zoologists, Nat. Acad. Scis., Sigma Xi, Phi Beta Kappa. Home: Woods Hole, Mass. Died June 5, 1975.

METZDORF, ROBERT FREDERICK, appraiser, bibliographer; b. Springfield, Mass., July 2, 1912; s. August Edward and Alvina (Darmstatter) M.; A.B., U. Rochester, 1933, M.A., 1935, Ph.D., 1939. Asst. to librarian U. Rochester, 1933—34, curator R.B. Adam collection, 1938—48, curator rare books, 1948—49, asst., then insr. English, 1939—49; cataloguer Houghton Library, Harvard, 1949—52, resident fellow Adams House, 1949—52; curator manuscripts Yale, 1952—58, univ. archivist, 1958—61, sec. Boswell Papers Editorial Com., 1952—61, research fellow library, 1952—61, fellow Davenport Coll., 1953, exec. fellow, 1955—58, asst. master, 1959—61, asst. v.p. charge lit. property Parke—Bernet Galleries, N.Y.C. 1961—62, v.p., 1962—64, dir. 1963—64. Co—founder, partner Shoe String Press, Hamden, Conn., 1952—55; editor Papers Bibliog. Soc. Am., 1959—67, councillor, 1967—75; sec. Yale edit. works Samuel Johnson, 1958—75. Trustee U. Rochester, 1967—73, hon. trustee, 1973—75; trustee Four Oaks Found. Mem. Antiquarian Booksellers Assn. Am. (chmn. Mid—Atlantic chpt. 1966—67), bibliog. socs. Am., London, Oxford, Cambridge, U. Va., Johnsonians, Manuscript Soc., Phi Beta Kappa, Theta Chi, Delta Phi Alpha. Clubs: Rowfant (Cleve.); Grolier, Century Association (N.Y.C.); Elizabethan (New Haven). Author or compiler: Catalogue Autograph Collection of University Rochester, 1940; Check List of Literary MSS in Library of Arthur A. Houghton, 1953, new edit., 1969; MSS. at Yale, 1954; The Tinker Library, 1959; also articles profl. jours. Editor: R.H. Dana Autobiographical Sketch, 1953. Home: Colebrook, Conn. Died Mar. 16, 1975.

METZGER, HERMAN ARTHUR, petroleum exec.; b. N.Y.C., July 1, 1900; s. Sylvain and Tillie (Block) M.; M.E., Cornell U., 1921; m. Evelyn Borchard, June 28, 1934; children—James B., Edward A., Eva B. Constrn. mgr. Barrancabermeja Refinery, Tropical Oil Co., 1924, asst. gen. mgr. Tropical Oil Co., 1925-28, exec. rep. in Bogota, Tropical Oil Co. and Andian Nat. Corp., 1928-36; pres., gen. mgr. Standard Oil Co. (N.J.) Argentine affiliate, 1944-54; v.p., dir. Creole Petroleum Corp., N.Y.C., 1954-62; N.Y. rep. Brown & Root, Inc., from 1963. Mem. Council Fgn. Relations, Pan Am. Soc., Fgn. Policy Assn. Clubs: Jockey (Buenos Aires); Economic, Cornell (N.Y.C.). Home: New York City, N.Y. Died Oct. 18, 1974.

MEYER, GEORGE A., dir. Bur. Motor Carrier Safety, ICC. Home: Arlington Va. Died Jan. 22, 1974.

MEYER, JOHN CHARLES, air force officer; b. Bklyn., Apr. 3, 1919; s. August H. and F. Dorothy (Gatehouse) M.; B.A., Dartmouth, 1947; grad. Air War Coll., 1959; m. Mary Moore, Apr. 4, 1945; children—Peter (dec.), M. Christine, John Charles, Michael A., Margaret D., Martha K. Commd. 2d lt. USAAF, 1940, advanced through grades to maj. gen. USAF, 1967; flew 200 combat missions, ETO, World War II, 31 missions in Korea; mem. faculty Air War Coll., 1956-59; comdr. 57th and 45th Air Div., SAC, 1959-62; dep. dir. plans SAC, 1962-63; comdr. 12th Air Force, TAC, 1963-66; dep. dir. of joint staff Joint Chiefs Staff, 1966-67, dir. operations, 1967-70. Chmn. pub. employees div. Waco (Tex.) Community Chest, 1965. Decorated D.F.C. with 6 oak leaf clusters. Silver Star with oak leaf cluster, Legion of Merit, D.S.C. with 2 oak leaf clusters, Air medal with 4 oak leaf clusters, Army Commendation medal, Purple Heart; Croix de Guerre with palm (France and Belgium). Mem. Am. Legion (past post comdr.). Clubs: Wings, Lotus (hon.) (N.Y.C.). Home: Bethesda, Md., Died Dec. 2, 1975.

MEYER, JOHN DA COSTA, lawyer; b. Pardoe, Pa., Jan. 26, 1878; s. L. George (M.D.) and Maria Jane (Albin) M.; grad. Poland (O.) Union Sem., 1895; A.B., Grove City Coll., 1900; LL.B., U. of Pittsburgh, 1908; m. Sarah L. Trowbridge, Oct. 5, 1910 (died 1926); children—Elisabeth Trowbridge, Lucile Albin, Jean Da Costa; m. 2d, Margaret Spraggon, June 30, 1928 (died 1932); children—John Da Costa, George William; m. 3d, Marie McGinley, May 25, 1936. Admitted to Pa. bar, 1908, and began practice at Pittsburgh; asst. dist. atty. Allegheny County, 1919-24; U.S. atty., Western Dist. of Pa., 1925-29; spl. dep. atty. gen. State of Pa., 1933-35. Mem. Pa. Nat. Guard 15 yrs., capt. 5 yrs. Mem. Am., Pa. State and Allegheny County bar assns. Republican. Presbyterian. Mason (32°), Odd Fellow, K.P. Club: Breckenridge Heights Country. Home: Terentum, Pa.†

MEYER, KARL FRIEDRICH, pathologist, bacteriologist; b. Basel, Switzerland, May 19, 1884; s. Theodor and Sophie (Lichtenhahn) M.; D.V.M., U. Zurich, 1909, Ph.D., 1924; postgrad., univs. Munich, Paris, Zurich, Bern; M.D. (hon.), Coll. Med. Evangelists, 1936, U. Basel, 1952; M.D. (hon.), U. Zurich, 1937, D.V.M., 1949; LL.D., U. So. Calif., 1946, U. Cal., 1958; D.Sc., Ohio U., 1958, U. Pa., 1959; m. Mary Elizabeth Lindsay, July 16, 1913 (dec. 1958); 1 dau., Charlotte; m. 2d, Marion Lewis, Feb. 26, 1960. Came to U.S., 1910, naturalized, 1922. Pathologist dept. agr., Transvaal, 1908-10; asst. prof. pathology and bacteriology U. Pa., 1910-11, prof., 1911-13; dir. lab. and expt. farm Pa. Livestock San. Bd., Phila., 1912-13; prof. bacteriology and protozoology U. Cal., 1914-15; asso. prof. tropical medicine Hooper Found. Med. Research, U. Cal., 1915-21, prof. research medicine and acting dir., 1921-24, dir., 1924-54, then emeritus; cons. Cal. Dept. Pub. Health, S.P. Ry., from 1920; prof. bacteriology No. U. Cal., 1924-48, prof. exptl. pathology, 1948-54, then emeritus; lectr. large univs., other orgns., from 1931. Mem. nat. adv. health council NIH; mem. nat. med. and health adv. com. A.R.C.; cons. to sec. war; mem. U.S. Army Epidemiol. Bd. Recipient many honors and awards. Fellow Nat., N.Y. acads. sci., A.A.A.S., Am. Acad. Arts and Scis., Am. Pub. Health Assn.; mem. Am. Assn. Pathologists and Bacteriologists, Am. Soc. Microbiology, Am. Assn. Immunologists, Soc. Exptl. Biology, Am. Soc. Tropical Medicine, Am. Vet. Med. Assn., Inst. Food Technologists, Inter-Am. Soc. Microbiology, Nat. Acad. Scis., Sigma Xi. Clubs: Commonwealth, The Family (San Francisco). Author: Practical Bacteriology, 1923; Disinfected Mail, 1962. Home: San Francisco, Cal. Died Apr. 27, 1974; buried San Francisco.

MEYER, PAUL D., physician; b. Butler, Pa., 1908; M.D., Ohio State U., 1935. Intern, Childrens Hosp., Columbus, O., 1935-36, St. Francis Hosp., Columbus, 1935-36; resident in radiology Cin. Gen. Hosp., 1946, chief resident, 1946-47; radiologist Grant Hosp., Columbus, 1947-66; instr. dept. radiology Ohio State U., Columbus, 1948-53, asst. prof., 1954-66. Diplomate Am. Bd. Radiology. Fellow Am. Coll. Radiology; mem. A.M.A., Radiol. Soc. N.Am. Home: Columbus, O. Died 1966

MEYER, THEODORE ROBERT, lawyer; b. San Diego, Sept. 25, 1902; s. George P. and Annie B. (Lemon) M.; A.B., U. Cal. at Berkeley, 1922, J.D., 1924; LL.D., U.Cal. at Santa Cruz, 1971; m. Virginia Organ, July 31, 1931; children—Priscilla (Mrs. John Cole), (Mrs. G. William Sheldon). Admitted to Cal. bar, 1924, practiced in San Francisco; with firm Brobeck, Phieger & Harrison, from 1927, partner, from 1936. Dir. Grant Co., Newhall Land & Farming Co. Trustee Mechanics Inst. San Francisco, 1952—, pres., 1962-68; regent U. Cal., 1962-68, chmn. bd. 1966-68. Mem. Am. Bar Assn., Bar Assn. San Francisco (pres. 1957), State Bar Cal. (bd. govs. 1959-62, pres. 1961-62), Am. Law Inst. Clubs: Bohemian, Pacific-Union (San Francisco). Home: Oakland, Cal., Died Mar. 31, 1973.

MEYER, WILSON, business exec.; b. San Francisco, Jan. 23, 1896; s. George Henry Christian Meyer; A.B., U. Cal., 1918; m. Mabel Wilson, Dec. 21, 1920; children—Jeffery Wilson, Harriet (Mrs. Charles M. Querre). With Wilson & Geo. Meyer & Co., San Francisco, from 1919, pres., 1928-59, chmn. bd., from 1959; dir. Wells Fargo Bank; hon. dir. Broadway-Hale Stores, Inc. Pres. bd. trustees San Francisco War Meml., 1964-66, later trustee; dir. San Francisco Opera Assn. Served as capt. U.S. Army, 1917-18. Decorated knight cross 1st class Royal Order St. Olav (Norway). Fellow Royal Hort. Soc. London, Cal. Acad. Scis. (trustee); mem. Soc. Cal. Pioneers (dir.), Am. Legion. Clubs: Cercle de l'Union, Pacific Union, Bohemian (San Francisco). Home: San Francisco, Cal. Died Oct. 26, 1973.

MEYNELL, SIR, FRANCIS, book designer, publisher, poet; b. May 12, 1981; ed. Downside and Trinity Colls., Dublin, Ireland; (D.Litt. (hon.), Reading U., 1964. Dir. Daily Herald, 1918—20; founder, dir. Nonesuch Press, England, 1923-36, 51-75; dir. Mather & Crowther Ltd., 1937—61. Adv. on consumer needs Bd. of Trade, during World War II; typographic adv. H.M. Stationery Officer, 1945—66; adv. council Victoria and Albert Mus., 1946-58; mem. Royal Mint adv. com., 1954—70. Bd. dirs. The Bodley Head. Created knight, 1946; named Royal Designer for Industry, 1945. Mem. Cement and Concrete Assn. (dir.-gen. 1946—58). Author: The Weekend Book, 1923; The Typography of Newspaper Advertisements, 1929; The Nonesuch Century, 1936; Seventeen Poems, 1945; English Printed Books, 1946; Poems and Pieces, 1961; By Heart, 1965; My Lives, 1971. Contbr. articles to Encyclopaedia Britannica, Manchester Guardian, News Chronicle and other publs. Designer all Nonesuch Press books. Home: Lavenham, Suffolk, England. Died July 10, 1975.

MICHALEK, ANTHONY, congressman; b. Bohemia, Jan. 16, 1878; s. James and Theresa Marie (Zellinger) M.; attended pub. schs. short time; unmarried. Bookkeeper by occupation. First man of Slavonic blood to sit in Am. Congress; mem. Congress, 5th Ill. Dist., 1905-07. Republican. Address: Chicago, Ill.†

MICHELS, WALTER CHRISTIAN, educator, physicist; b. Utica, N.Y., June 14, 1906; s. Christian A. and Anna (Haigis) M., E.E., Rensselaer Poly. Inst., 1927; Ph.D., Cal. Inst. Tech., 1930; m. Lorraine Elder, June 21, 1930; 1 dau., Leslyn Jane; m. 2d, Agnes K. Lake, June 4, 1941. Test engr. Utica Gas & Electric Co., 1926-27; teaching asst. Cal. Inst. Tech., 1927-29, teaching fellow, 1929-30; fellow NRC, Princeton, 1930-32; asso. physics Bryn Mawr Coll., 1932-34, asso. prof., 1934-46, Marion Reilly prof., 1946-72, head dept., 1936-70, prof. emeritus, from 1972, lectr., 1972-73. Chmn., Commn. on Coll. Physics, 1960-64; physicist Bur. Ordnance, USN, 1941-43. Served as comdr. USNR, 1943-46. Decorated Legion of Merit. Mem. Am. Phys. Soc., Am. Assn. Physics Tchrs. (pres. 1956-57, Oersted medal 1964), A.A.U.P., A.A.A.S., Franklin Inst., Am. Inst. Physics (governing bd. 1957-60), Sigma Xi. Mem. Soc. of Friends. Author: Advanced Electrical Measurements, 1941; Electrical Measurements and Their Applications, 1957; co-author: Elements of Modern Physics, 1951; Foundations of Physics, 1968; Physics: Its Origins and its Applications, 1973; also articles. Sr. editor Internat. Dictionary of Physics and Electronics, 1956, editor in chief 2d edit., 1961; editor U. Physics series, 1957-64, Am. Jour. Physics, 1959-66, Momentum Books, 1964-70. Home: Wayne Pa. Died Feb. 27, 1975; buried Radnor Meeting, Villanova, Pa.

MICHELSON, ALBERT SIDNEY, mfg. co. exec.; b. Akron, O., Oct. 14, 1895; s. Frederick William and Josephine (Munson) M.; ed. pub. schs.; m. Velora Getz, Oct. 24, 1925; 1 son, Richard Albert, Sr. v.p., dir. McNeil Machine & Engring. Co., Akron; sec.-treas., dir. Cleve. Crane & Engring. Co.; dir. J.E. Myers & Co. Died July 16, 1974.

MIDDLEBROOK, WILLIAM THEOPHILUS, univ. adminstr.; b. Vergennes, Vt., Apr. 9, 1891; s. Theophilus Carter and Annie Maria (Clark) M.; A.B., Dartmouth, 1912, M.C.S., 1913; m. Margaret Mary Bull, Sept. 16, 1920; children—William Theophilus, John Edward, Anne Clark (Mrs. Kurt Moedritzer), Margaret Woods (Mrs. Richard Strate). Traveling auditor, traveling freight agt., spl. rep. exec. dept. Gt. No. Ry., 1913-17, 19-20; asso. Griffenhagen & Assos., indsl. engrs., 1920-22; controller Purdue U., 1922-25; comptroller, sec. bd. regents U. Minn., 1925-43, v.p. bus. adminstrn., sec. bd. regents, 1943-59; dir. Survey Higher Edn. South Korea, 1959-60; adminstrv. cons. Nicollet Clinic, Mpls., from 1962. Mem. Survey U. Philippines; U.S. Army cons. U. Ryukus, Okinawa, 1962; Ford Found. cons. U. Cordoba, Argentina, U. Calcutta, India, U. South Argentina, Cath. U. Chile. Pres., Otter Creek Coal Co.; dir. Parents Mag. Chmn., Nat. Fedn. Com. Coll. and Univ. Bus. Officers, 1951-54; mem. Nat. Com. for Preparation of Manual Coll. and Univ. Bus. Adminstrn., 1952-55; chmn. Cal. and Western Conf. Univ. Cost and Statis. Study, 1958. Chmn. bd., mem. exec. com. Midwest Inter Library Corp., Chgo., 1951-54. Served to 1st lt. Q.M.C., U.S. Army, 1917-19. Recipient Hon. Alumnus U. Minn. Hon. Athletic M, 1959, Regents medal U. Minn., 1965, Nicollet scroll, 1966. Mem. Nat. (past pres.), Minn. (past pres.), Central (past pres.) assns. univ. and coll. bus. officers, Grey Friars, Phi Beta Kappa, Phi Sigma Kappa. Kiwanian. Clubs: Campus, Gown in Town (Mpls.). Author: How to Estimate the Building Needs of a College or University, 1958. Contbr. articles to profl. jours. Home: Wayzata, Minn. Died Feb. 16, 1974.

MIDDLETON, JOHN ALBERT, coll. pres.; b. Foreston, S.C., Jan. 2, 1914; s. Brewington and Lula (Hayes) M.; A.B., Allen U., 1939, LL.D., 1966; B.D., Howard U., 1942; Th.M., Iliff Sch. Theology, 1956; LL.D., Payne Coll., 1966, Bethune-Cookman Coll., 1967, Payne Theol. Sem-Wilberforce U., 1970; m. Merlissie Tyson, Dec. 24, 1943; children—Ann Fay (Mrs. Ronald Reed), Johnsy Althea, Phillip Brewington. Ordained minister A.M.E. Ch., 1938; pastor chs., Va., Md., 1942-47; prof. Morris Brown Coll. and Turner Theol. Sem., Atlanta, 1947-56; pastor Allen Temple A.M.E. Ch., Atlanta, 1956-65; pres. Morris Brown Coll., 1965-75. Altanta campaign dir. United Negro Coll. Fund; mem. Ga. Council on Human Relations; mem. Atlanta Bd. Edn., 1969-75. Bd. dirs. Interdenominational Theol. Center, Atlanta, Carrie Steel Pitts Home, Atlanta, Atlanta U. Center Corp., Atlanta council Boy Scouts Am. Mem. Frontiers Internat., Sigma Phi Pi, Alpha Phi. Home: Atlanta, Ga. Died June 21, 1975.

MIDDLETON, WILLIAM SHAINLINE, physician; b. Norritown, Pa., Jan. 7, 1890; s. Daniel Shepherd and Ann Sophia Holstein (Shainline) M.; M.D., U. Pa., 1911, Sc.D., 1946; sc.D., Cambridge, 1950, U. Wis., 1971; LL.D., Temple U., 1956; L.H.D., Franklin and Marshall Col., 1957; Litt.D., Marquette U., 1958; m. Maude H. Webster, Sept. 30, 1921 (dec. June 1968); m. 2d, Ruth Addams, June 14, 1973. Intern Phila. Gen. Hosp., 1911—12; Instr. clin. medicine U. Wis. Med. Sch., Madison, 1912—15, asst. prof., 1915—25, asso. prof. medicine, 1925—33, prof., 1933—60, dean Med. Sch., 1935—55, dean, prof. medicine emeritus, 1960—75. Galens vis. prof. medicine U. Mich. Med. Sch., 1940; Enrest A. Sommer Meml. lectr. medicine U. Ore. Med. Sch., 1941; David J. Davis lectr. U. Ill., 1947; Walter Estell Lee lectr. U. Pa. Sch. Medicine, 1951; vis. prof. medicine U. Okla., 1964—64; chief med. dir. VA, Washington, 1955—63; cons. research, edn. VA Hosp., Madison, 1964—70, distinguished physician, 1970—75. Served to capt. M.O.R.C., U.S. Army, World War 1; BEF and AEF in France; from lt. col. to col. M.C., AUS, 1942;45; ETO. Decorated D.S.M., Legion of Merit with oak leaf cluster (U.S.); Croix de Guerre with palm (France); Hon. officer Order Brit. Empire; recipient Council award Wis. State Med. Soc., 1938; U. Pa. Alumni Awardof Merit; Centennial award Northwestern Univ., 1951; exceptional service award VA, 1958; Erwin R. Schmidt Interstate Teaching award Interstate Postgrad. Med. Assn., 1966; Distinghished Teaching award U. Wis., 1969, 72. Diplomate Pan Am. Med. Assn. Master A.C.P. (Alfred Stengel Meml. medalist 1962 pres. 1950); fellow Coll. Physicians Phila. (hon.), Royal Coll. Physicians (London), Am. Coll. Hosp. Administrs. (hon.), Royal Soc. Medicine (hon.), Charles B. Puestow Surg. Soc. (life); mem. A.A.A.S.,

Soc. Med. Consultants to Armed Forces, Constantinian Soc. (hon.), Soc. Cin., A.M.A., Assn. Am. Physicians, Am. Soc. Clin. Investigation, Central Soc. Clin. Research (pres. 1933), Am. Clin. and Climatol. Assn., Montgomery County Med. Soc., Am. Assn. History Medicine (pres. 1934), Wis. Acad. Scis., Arts and Letters, Am. Legion; hon. fgn. mem. Assn. Physicians Gt. Britain and Ireland; fgn. corr. Sociedad de Medicina Internade Buenos Aires; hon. mem. IMed. Library Assn., Milw. Acad. Medicine, Honolulu County Med. Soc., Spokane, Minn. socs. internal medicine, Kings Own Old Comrades Assn., Associón Medica de Puerto Rico, Am. Thoracic Soc., Med. Soc. D.C.; mem. Wis. Soc. Internal Medicine, Phi Beta Kappa, Sigma Xi, Alpha Omega Alpha, Alpha Tau Omega, Phi Beta Pi, Beta Pi, Phi Kappa Phi, Sigma Sigma. Clubs: Army and Navy (Washington); Madison. Contbr. articles to profl. jours. Home: Madison, Wis. Died Sept. 1975.

MIDGLEY, ALBERT LEONARD, dental and oral surgeon; b. Worcester, Mass., Apr. 8, 1878; s. James and Mary Amelia (Keefe) M.; student Brown U., 1897-98; D.M.D., cum laude, Harvard, 1901; hon. Sc.D., Marquette U., 1922, Temple U., 1934; m. Jennie Frances Corliss, July 17, 1906; children—Mary Alberta, Catherine Louise, Helen Jane. Practiced dentistry in Providence, R.I., from 1901; dental surgeon Rhode Island Hosp. and St. Joseph's Hosp., 1901-38; later consulting dental surgeon; oral surgeon John W. Keefe Surgery, 1912-33, Forsyth Dental Infirmary, 1945-20; dental surgeon St. Vincent's Infant Asylum, 1902-11; consulting dental surgeon Memorial Hospital and Joseph Samuels Dental Clinic for Children; clinical instructor at Harvard University Dental School, 1906-16, lecturer on exodontia and anesthesia, 1917-19; also lecturer on oral surgery, Forsyth Dental infirmary, 1916-20. Served on Med. Advisory Bd., No. 2, R.I., World War; dental surgeon, same, from Feb. 1941; former lt. comdr. Dental Corps, U.S.N.R., Mem. R.I. Bd. of Registration in Dentistry, 1907-41 (pres. 1913-19; sec. 1920-35); sec. bd. trustees John W. Keefe Surgery, 1925-34; mem. Dental Ednl. Council of America, 1910-35, pres., 1916-20, sec., 1921-35; mem. bd. dirs. Providence Dist. Nursing Assn. Fellow Am. Coll. Dentists (a founder; sec. 1922-25; pres. 1936; regent 1937-43), Am. Acad. Dental Surgery of N.J.; hon. fellow Am. Acad. Dental Science. Fellow A.A.A.S.; member International Assn. Dental Research, National Assn. Dental Examiners (pres. 1911), Am. Dental Assn., R.I. State Dental Society (pres. 1915), Harvard Dental Alumni Assn., Guild of St. Apollonia, Providence Dental Guild (organizer), Delta Sigma Delta, Kappa Upsilon, Phi Sigma Tau. Roman Catholic. Clubs: Turks Head, Harvard Club of R.I., Catholic Club of R.I. Author: Studies in Dental and Oral Science, 1911; contbr. chapter, "Surgical Treatment of Maxillary Fractures," to Army Dentistry. Contbg. editor Jour. of the Am. Coll. of Dentists and The Apollonian. Mem. Thomistic Guild. Home: Providence, R.I.†

MIELZINER, JO, stage designer; b. Paris, France, Mar. 19, 1901; s. Leo and Ella (Friend) M.; student N.A.D., Art Students League, Pa. Acad. Fine Arts, also in Paris, Vienna; D.F.A., Fordham U., 1947, U. Mich., 1971; H.H.D., Otterbein Coll., 1967, U. Utah, 1972; m. Jean Macintyre, May 26, 1938; children—Michael, Neil, Jennifer Ann. Designer stage settings for operas, ballets, mus. comedies, 1924-76; works include settings for The Guardsman, Strange Interlude, Street Scene, Barretts of Wimpole Street, Winterset, I Married an Angel, Boys from Syracuse, Two on an Island, Pal Joey, Glass Menagerie, Carousel, Dream Girl, Annie Get Your Gun, Finian's Rainbow, Another Part of the Forest, Happy Birthday, Allegro, Streetcar Named Desire, Mister Roberts, Summer and Smoke, Death of a Salesman, South Pacific, Guys and Dolls, A Tree Grows in Brooklyn, The King and I, Picnic (winner Oscar for color art direction 1955), Me and Juliet, Can-Can; scenic designer for: Tea and Sympathy, By the Beautiful Sea, All Summer Long, Fanny, Silk Stockings, Cat on a Hot Tin Roof, Pipe Dream, The Lark, Middle of the Night, The Most Happy Fella, Happy Hunting, Oh Captain, Look Homeward Angel, The World of Susie Wong, Gypsy, Mr. President, All American, Period of Adjustment, But for Whom, Charlie, After the Fall, The Owl and the Pussycat, The Crucible, (opera) Don Giovanni, (ballets) PAMTGG, Who Cares?; designer Broadway prodns. including The Playroom, 1965, Venus Is, 1966, My Sweet Charlie, 1966, Mata Hari, 1967, I Never Sang for My Father, 1968, 1776, The Others, Out Cry, 1973, Child's Play, 1973, Miss Moffat, In Praise of Love, 1974; others; producer mus. Happy Hunting; designer setting, lighting UN Conf., San Francisco, 1945, Michelangelo Pieta, Vatican Exhibit, N.Y.C. World's Fair; collaborating designer Repertory Theatre for Lincoln Center for Performing Arts; producer, designer A.T.& T. Show, N.Y. World's Fair; cons. designer The Forum, Los Angeles Music Center, So. Ill. U. Theatre, Edwardsville, Loretto-Hilton Theater, Webster Coll., Webster Groves, Mo., Lincoln Square Theatres; co-designer U. Mich. Theater, Ann Arbor, Wake Forest U. Theaters, Winston-Salem, N.C.; spl. cons. Skidmore, Owings & Merrill, Millman and Sturges; lectr. stage design Fordham U., summer 1946; exhibited designs in one-man shows Library and Mus. Performing Arts at Lincoln Center, 1966, Brandeis U., 1966, Coffee House Club, N.Y.C., 1966, Va. Mus. Fine Arts, Richmond, 1967, Internat. Exhbns. Found., 1968. Chmn., Am. Theatre Planning Bd. Served with USMC, 1918-19; maj. USAAF, 1942-44. Recipient Antoinette Perry awards (5) and Donaldson awards (5) for set design. Maharam awards (2), Drama Desk award, 1970; Ford Found. award in Program for Theatre Design, 1960, Creative Arts award Brandeis U. Benjamin Franklin fellow Royal Soc. Arts. Mem. S.A.R. Soc. Brit. Theatre Lighting Designers. Roman Catholic. Clubs: Coffee House, Century Assn. (N.Y.C.). Author: Designing for the Theatre, 1965; Shapes of Our Theatre, 1970. Home: New York City, N.Y. Died Mar. 15, 1976.

MIESSNER, W(ILLIAM) OTTO, prof. music. composer, author; b. in Huntingburg, Ind., May 26, 1880; s. Charles and Mary (Reutepohler) M.; grad. high school, Huntingburg, Ind., 1898, ed. in music, Cincinnati Coll. of Music, and under pvt. tutors in piano, voice, composition, Chicago, New York, and Berlin; hon. Dr. Ped., Cincinnati Conservatory of Music; Dr. Mus., Chicago Musical Coll.; m. Emma Elizabeth Snider, June 20, 1911; children—Wilda Louise, Wilfred Charles. Supervisor music pub. schs., Boonville, Ind., 1900-04, Connersville, 1904-09, Oak Park, 1910-14; director School of Music, Milwaukee State Teachers Coll., 1914-22, Chicago Mus. Coll., summer master school, 1922, 32; dir. Miessner Inst. of Music, Chicago, 1924-48, chmn. Dept. of Music Edn., U. of Kansas, 1936-45; educational director Operadio Mfg. Co. 1949-52; pres. Music Educators Nat. Conf., 1923-24 (member Research council 15 years); president of Miessner Piano Company, 1922-28. Member Phi Mu Alpha Sinfonia, Phi Delta Kappa, Pi Kappa Lambda. Composer numerous works for instruments and voice; co-author, co-composer numerous-instructional items Young America Sings, 1953. Contributor to yearbooks of Music Educations Nat. Conf. and Music Teachers Nat. Assn. Club: Cliff Dwellers (Chgo.). Address: Connersville, Ind.†

MIGATZ, MARSHALL, producer. Founder Academy Playhouse, Lake Forest, Ill., 1963. Home: Lake Forest Ill. Died May 25, 1973; buried Meml. Park Cemetery Skokie, Ill.

MIGEL, JULIUS A., orgn. ofcl.; b. Santiago, Chile, 1878; s. Solomon and Hannah Migel; student Colgate Acad.; A.B., Colgate U., 1905; m. Margarget Dauchy, Nov. 1910; children—Hamilton, Dauchy (M.D.), Marguite (Mrs. Clayton Y. Goss), Robert, Kim (Mrs. Richard Aycrigg), Partner, M.C. Migel and Co., broad silk mfrs., also H.R. Mallinson Silk Mfrs.; pres. J.A. Migel, Inc., silk mfr.; v.p. Am. Silk Spinning Co.; pioneer wide, roller-bearing, individually motor-driven looms; pioneer mfr. rayon dress fabric, application of trade names to textiles, Exec. council, treas. Clarence Streit's Atlantic Union, 1938-43; founder Wendell Wilkie's Americans United for World Orgn.; founder Americans United for World Govt., 1945; founder World Movement for World Govt., Luxemburg, 1945; sec. corp., mem. exec. council United World Federalists, Inc., also mem. internat. council of World assn.; v.p. Inst. for Internat. Order. Recipient alumni award for distinguished service Colgate U., Man. of Year award United World Federalists. Mem. Delta Kappa Epsilon (pres. 1905). Club: Yale (N.Y.C.). Home: Charleston, R.I., Died Feb. 16, 1976.

MIHALYFI, ERNO, Hungarian govt. ofcl.; b. Hungary, Sept. 3, 1898. Editor Fuggetien Magyarorszag, 1939; founding mem. Smallholder's Party; chmn. Hungarian—Soviet Friendship Soc., 1966—71; minister information, 1947; fgn. minister, 1947; chmn. Inst. Cultural Relations, 1949—50, Assn. Hungarian Journalists, 1946—56; dep. minister edn., 1951—58; now mem. Nat. Pesidium, Patriotic People's Front and Presdl. Council; editor Magyar Nemzet. Decorated banner order 1st degree Hungarian People's Republic, 1970. Address: Budapest, Hungary. Died 1972.

MIKULES, T(HOMAS) LEONARD, educator, editor; b. Washington, Mar. 6, 1909; s. Alexander Leon and Cordelia Leonard (Kelly) M.; A.B., Harvard, 1930, A.M., 1932; Ph.D., U. Cal. at Los Angeles, 1958; m. Roberta Macky Whitehead, June 9, 1951. Instr. English, Fesseden Sch., West Newton, Mass., 1930-31, Metairie Park Country Day Sch., New Orleans, 1932-35, Harvard and Radcliffe Colls., 1936-39, Naval Acad., 1941-42, U. Cal. at Los Angeles, 1950; editing pub. information Rural Electrification Adminstrn., 1936-41, VA, 1946; asst. regional pub. relations mgr. Western states, Ford Motor Co., 1947-49; past editor and pub., mgn. editor U.S. Naval Inst., Annapolis, Md.; asst. prof. English Sch. Fgn. Service, Georgetown U., Washington, 1960-66; asso. prof. English, Anne Arundel Community Coll., Arnold, Md., 1966-69; prof. catedratico Inst. N.Am. Studies U. Coimbra (Portugal), 1967-68; sr. editor Westinghouse Learning Corp., Annapolis, 1969-72. Served to comdr. USNR, 1941-46. Decorated Bronze Star World War II. Member Modern Lang. Assn. Am., Am. Inst. Graphic Arts, Naval Inst., Am. Assn. U. Profs., Columbia Hist. Soc., Capitol Hill Restoration Soc., Citizens Progressive Housing Assn., Delta Phi Epsilon. Democrat. Roman Catholic. Clubs: Harvard (Md.); Army and Navy . (Washington); Annapolitan, Harvard (past sec.-treas.) (Annapolis); Players (N.Y.C.). Author: A Manual of Style, 1972. Home: Annapolis, Md., Died Aug. 31, 1972.

MILBANK, THOMAS POWELL FOWLER, corp. dir.; b. N.Y.C., Nov. 21, 1913; s. Dunlevy and Katharine Sebning (Fowler) M.; student Sorbonne, 1934-36; m. Loyce Stinson. Estate mgr.; dir. Bank of N.Y., N.Y.C. Trustee, sec. Teachers Coll., Columbia: dir., treas. Tolstoy Found.; trustee Presbyn. Hosp., N.Y.C. Served to lt. comdr. USNR, 1941-46; with office Chief Naval Operations, 1941-45; asst. naval attache, Cairo, Egypt, 1945-46. Republican. Presbyn. Clubs: Metropolitan (Washington); L'union Interallie (Paris, France); Century Assn., Downtown Assn., Union, Racquet and Tennis, N.Y. Yacht (N.Y.C.); Circolo del Golf di Roma (Italy). Home New York City N.Y. Died Oct. 31, 1974.

MILES, GEORGE CARPENTER, mus. cons., author; b. St. Davids, Pa., Sept. 30, 1904; s. John Blanchard and Marian (Carpenter) M.; grad. Gilman Sch., 1922; B.A., Princeton, 1926, M.A., 1930, Ph.D., 1937; m. Lucy Eleanor Briggs, Apr. 1, 1937; 1 dau., Marian (Mrs. James R. McCredie). Tchr., Robert Coll., Istanbul, Turkey, 1926—29, 31—33; archaeologist, Iran, 1934—37; researcher Inst. Advanced Study, Princeton, N.J., 1938; instr. Princeton, 1939—40; with Am. Numismatic Soc., N.Y.C., 1946—75, curator Islamic Coins, chief curator, 1952—68, exec. dir., 1966—72, cons., 1972—75; vis. prof. Islamic archaeology U. Alexandria, UAR, 1953—54; mem. Inst. Advanced Study, 1961. Mem. mng. com. Am. Sch. Classical Studies, Athens, Greece, 1960—75, chmn. Gennadius Library Com., 1972—75; bd. scholars Dumbarton Oaks, Washington, 1968—75; mem. exec. com. Ency. Islam, Leiden, 1951—75. Served to comdr. USNR, 1941—46. Guggenheim fellow, 1960; hon. fellow Royal Numismatic Soc. London (medalist). Mem. Am. Philos. Soc., Hispanic Soc. Am. (medallist), Am. Oriental Soc. (v.p., 1961), Archeol. Inst. Am. (pres. N.Y. 1966—67), Ordre des Palmes Academiques; corr. mem. Inst. d'Egypte, Real Academia de Cordoba, Royal Academia de la Historia Madrid; hon. mem. Soc. Francaise de Numismatique, Soc. Belge de Numismatiaque. Clubs: Century, University. Am. Alpine (N.Y.C.); Alpine (London). Author: Numismatic History of Rayy, 1938; Umayyads of Spain, 1950; Arabic Glass Weights, 1951; Contributions to Arabic Metrology, 1963; Visigoths of Spain, 1952; Arab Amirs of Crete, 1970; also articles. Exploration and excavation in Greece, 1956, 60—61, 65, 67. Home: Ardsley—on—Hudson, N.Y. Died Oct. 15, 1975; interred Kensico Cemetery, Greenburgh, N.Y.

MILES, WALDO GARLAND, lawyer; b. Wise, Va., June 12, 1911; s. Wade M. and Mollie S. (White) M.; student U. Richmond, 1930-33; A.B., Washington and Lee U., 1934, LL.B., 1938; m. Christine Junchen, Feb. 9, 1944; children—LaRue Carter Dakin, Christine Mollie Feazell. Admitted to Va. bar, 1937; asso. firm Carter & Williams, Danville, 1938-41; partner firm Williams, Miles & Williams, Danville, 1941-48, Woodward, Miles & Flannaghan and predecessor firms, Bristol, Va. from 1948. Mem. Va. Mental Health Study Commn., 1963-65, Va. Mental Retardation Planning Council, 1964-70, Va. Adv. Legislative Council Sub-com. Studying Grants-in-aid, 1965, Va. Adv. Council on Econ. Edn., from 1965; pub. mem. Va. Tax Study Commn., 1956-57, 62-63; mem. Bristol Sch. Bd., 1958-63, chmn., 1962; mem. Va. Bd. Edn., 1963-71, chmn., 1970-71; chmn. Gov.'s Regional Conf. on Edn., 1967; vice chmn. Va. Pub. Defender Commn., from 1972. Mem. Va. exec. com. Democratic State Central Com., 1960-68. Pres. Bristol Mental Health Clinic, 1957, Bristol Meml. Hosp., 1958-60, bd. dirs., 1956-65; bd. dirs. Bristol chpt. A.R.C., 1954-60; bd. visitors Va. Poly. Inst., 1966-70, Sullins Coll., trustee Va. Council Health and Med. Care. Served as lt. comdr. USNR, 1942-45; lt. comdr. Res. Fellow Am. Coll. Probate Counsel; mem. Bristol C. of C. (dir. 1952-54, 56-58, 68-72, exec. com. 1960-64). Am., Fed., Va. pres. 1962-63), Bristol (pres.) bar assns., Am. Judicature Soc., Am. Law Inst., Va. C. of C. (dir.), Washington and Lee U. Law Sch. Alumni Assn. (mem. council 1963-65, pres. 1964-65), Omicron Delta Kappa, Pi Delta Epsilon, Phi Delta Phi, Phi Gamma Delta. Methodist. Clubs: Bristol (Va.) Country; Commonwealth (Richmond, Va.). Home: Bristol Va. Died Sept. 18, 1973; interred Mountain View Cemetery, Bristol, Va.

MILHAUD, DARIUS, composer, condr.; b. Aix-en-Provence, France, Sept. 4, 1892; s. Gabriel and Sophie (Allatini) M.; student Conservatory of Music, Paris, 1910-15; m. Madeleine Milhaud, May 4, 1925; 1 son, Daniel. Composer from 1912; mem. Superior Council of French State Radio, 1935-40; mem. cons. com. French Opera Comique, 1936-39; mem. Superior Council Conservatory of Music, Paris, 1937-40; prof. of composition, Mills Coll., Calif., 1940-71; prof. Conservatory of Music, Paris, 1947. Decorated grand officer Legion of Honor (France); grand croix l'Ordre du Mérite. Mem. Academia Royale des Sciences et Lettres des Beaux Art de Belgique, Institut (Paris). Compositions include 18 string quartets, 8 sonatas, 3 symphonic suites, 12 symphonies, 6 chamber orchestra symphonies, 14 operas, 15 ballets, music for films, theaters. Home: Geneva Switzerland. Died June 22, 1974.

MILLAR, BRANFORD PRICE, educator; b. Monroe, Conn., Mar. 20, 1914; s. Morgan and Harriet Agnes (Hogg) M.; A.B. magna cum laude, Harvard, 1935, A.M., 1938, Ph.D., 1936; m. Teresa Calamara, June 20,

1939; children—Andrew Craig, Constance Irene. Instr. English, Harvard, 1935—41, Md. State Tchrs. Coll., 1941—43; from asst. prof. to prof. English, Mich. State U., 1946—58, asst. dean Sch. Grad. Studies, 1950—55; pres. Portland (Ore.) State U., 1959—68, Distinghished Service prof. English, 1969—75, spl. asst. to pres., 1974—75; Distinguished Research prof. Ore. State System Higher Edn., 1968—69, cons., panelist, Nat. Endowment for the Humanities, 1969—75. Bd. dirs. Portland Art Mus., 1971—73. Mem. Modern Lang. Assn., Phi Beta Kappa. Club: University (Portland). Author articles profl. and ednl. jours. Editor: Centennial Review Arts and Sciences, 1956—58. Address: Portland, Ore. Died 1975.

MILLER, ALBERT FULLERTON, paper co. exec.; b. Columbus, O., Apr. 19, 1910; s. Albert M. and Fanny (Fullerton) M.; A.B., Williams Coll., 1932; m. Mary Dixon Sayre, June 21, 1947; children—Dixon F., Phebe C., Lisa Hayes, Blythe Frances Sayre. With Central Ohio Paper Co., Columbus, 1932-66, v.p., sec., 1951-66; chmn., treas. CO-CO Del., Inc.; pres. Fullerton Miller Investments, Gay St. Realty Co., Central Realty Co.; dir. Ohio Nat. Bank. Treas., Charity Assistance Found., Franklin County; sec. Columbus Children's Hosp.; Mem. Ohio Rep. Finance Com., 1956-62. Fiscal trustee Columbus YWCA, 1956-61, later treas.; trustee Columbus Symphony Orch., pres., 1963-66; bd. dirs. Devel. Com. Greater Columbus, from 1958. Served as maj. Office Chief of Engrs., U.S. Army, Far East Forces, Manila, 1945. Mem. Nat. Paper Trade Assn. (dir.). Conglist. (chmn. trustees). Clubs: Rotary, University, Rocky Fork Hunt; New Century (London, Eng.). Home: Bexley, O. Died Jan. 5, 1973.

MILLER, CARL WALLACE, physicist; b. Somerville, Mass., Mar. 28, 1893; s. Charles Naham and Lula (Lombard) M.; student Somerville Latin Sch., 1907-11; A.B., Harvard, 1915, A.M., 1921, Ph.D., 1923; student U. Zurich, 1915-16; m. Edna Louise Savary, Jan. 1, 1920; children—Virginia (Mrs. Travis J. Covington), Carlton S. Instr. physics N.Y.U., 1922-24; asst. prof. physics Brown U., 1924-29, asso. prof., 1929-45, prof., 1945-55, prof. emeritus, 1955-75; research asso. Office Naval Research Beavertail project, Yale, 1952-54. Participant Nat. Geog. Soc. eclipse expdn. to Siam, 1948. Inspection supvr. Army Ordnance, 1918-19. Recipient Franklin L. Burr prize for expdn. Nat. Geog. Soc. Fellow A.A.A.S., Am. Phys. Soc., Royal Photog. Soc., Photog. Soc. Am. (asso.); mem. Am. Assn. U. Profs., Providence Engring. Soc., Phi Beta Kappa, Sigma Xi. Baptist. Club: Appalachian Mountain (Boston). Author: Introduction to Physical Science, 2d edit., 1935; Principles of Photographic Reproduction, 1942; A Scientist's Approach to Religion, 1947. Home: Laconia, N.H., Died Jan. 8, 1975.

MILLER, CHARLES MOSHER, banker; b. Balt., Feb. 8, 1906; s. Roland L. and Ethel (Mosher) M.; student U. Md.; m. Alma Stephens Wagner, Oct. 26, 1971. With Provident Savs. Bank Balt., from 1946, pres., 1960-66, chmn. bd., from 1966; dir. Union Trust Co. Md., Noxell Corp., Strayer's Bus. Coll., Inc. Pres. Com. Downtown Balt., 1964-66. Club: Maryland Elkridge (Balt.). Home: Towson Md. Died July 6, 1974.

MILLER, EDWARD WHITNEY, gear mfg. exec.; b. Torrington, Conn., May 26, 1880; s. Edward Trapple and Mary Elizabeth (Whitney) M.; M.E. (hon.), Stevens Inst. Tech., 1942; D.Engring. (hon.), Norwich U., Northfield, Vt., 1954; m. Grace Agnes Spencer, June 20, 1907; children—Edward Spencer, Adrianne, Marilynn, Margery. With Fellows Gear Sharper Co., Springfield Vt., from 1898, successively machine apprentice, mech. draftsman, chief draftsman, chief engineer, general manager, vice pres., pres., chmn., from 1967; director Springfield Terminal R.R., Cine Automatic Machine Co., Windsor, Vt. Director Conn. River Watershed Council; chmn. anti-stream pollution com. Vt. Dist. No. 5. Member board trustees Norwich University, Northfield, Vermont, also Lyndon College, Springfield, Coll. Mem. Am. Gear Mfrs. Assn. (past pres.), Am. Ordnance Assn. (dir. Yankee post, councilman-at-large), Newcomen Soc. Clubs: Century, Engineers (N.Y.C.). Author articles machinery publs., editorials pub. pres. Patentee. Home: Perkinsville, Vt.†

MILLER, EDWIN MORTON, physician; b. Ida Grove, Ia., June 10, 1888; s. J.D. and Mary (Jacobs) M.; M.D., Rush Med. Coll., 1913; m. Blanche Guthrie, Sept. 8, 1917; children—Mary (Mrs. Naquin), Edwin M., Dean D., Nancy (Mrs. Wynn). Intern, Presbyn. Hosp., Chgo., 1913—14, mem. staff, 1915—72, chmn. dept. surgery, 1949—54, v.p. med. staff, 1947—53; clin. prof. surgery Rush. Med. Coll. Served as capt. M.C., U.S. Army, 1917—19, lt. col. M.C., AUS, 1943—45. Diplomate Am. Bd. Surgery (founding mem.). Mem. A.M.A., Chgo. Med. Soc., Chgo. Surg. Soc. (past treas., v.p., pres.), Am. Surg. Assn., Inst. Medicine Chro., Internat. Surg. Soc. Med. Alumni Assn. U. Chgo. (Distinghuished Service award 1963, pres. 1967—68). Contbr. articles to profl. jours. Home: Chicago, Ill. Died Feb. 4, 1972; buried Ida Grove, Ia.

MILLER, FREDERIC K(ELPER), coll. pres.; b. Lebanon, Pa., Nov. 28, 1908; s. Harry E. and Laura E. (Kelper) M.; A.B., Lebanon Valley Coll., 1929; M.A., U. Pa., 1931, Ph.D., 1948; Litt.D. (honorary), Munenberg Coll., 1954, numerous other hon. degrees, m. Marion E. Stover, June 27, 1936; 1 dau., Janet Louise. Tchr., coach Lebanon (Pa.) Sr. High Sch., 1934-39; prof., chmn. dept. history Lebanon Valley Coll., Annville, 1939-51, asst. to pres., 1948-50, acting pres., 1950-51, pres., 1951-67. Mem. exec. com. Found. for Ind. Colleges 1962-75; dep. sec. edn., commr. higher edn. Commonwealth of Pa., 1967-71; pres. Commn. for Ind. Colls. and Univs., 1971-75. Pres. bd. of dirs. Lebanon YMCA, 1954-67; bd. dirs. Good Samaritan Hosp., 1956-75, pres., 1964-66; chmn. bd. dirs. Univ. Center at Harrisburg, 1961-63. Served in U.S. Army, 1943-45; ETO. Mem. Am. and Pa. hist. assns., Am. Assn. U. Profs., Am. Assn. Sch. Adminstrs., N.E.A., Middle States Assn. Colls. and Secondary Schs. (mem. commn. on instns. of higher edn.), Am. Legion, Pa. Assn. Colls. and Universities, and Pi Gamma Mu. Republican. Mem. United Methodist Ch. Author: The Rise of An Iron Community; Life of William Rank. Contbr. Pa. History, Pa. Bibliography, Basic Am. Documents. Home: Annville, Pa., Died Mar. 7, 1975.

MILLER, FRIEDA SEGELKE, govt. official; b. LaCrosse, Wis., Apr. 16, 1889; d. James Gordon and Erna (Segelke) Miller; A.B., Milwaukee-Downer Coll., Milwaukee, Wis., 1911; postgrad. U. of Chicago, 1911-15; D.H.L., Russell Sage Coll., Troy, N.Y., 1941; unmarried; 1 adopted dau., Elisabeth. Research asst., dept. social economics, Bryn Mawr Coll., 1916-17; sec. Phila. Women's Trade Union League, 1918-23; inspector, joint bd. of sanitary control Women's Garment Industry, New York, 1924-26; mem. research staff, N.Y.C. Welfare Council, 1927-29; dir. div. of women in industry and minimum wage, N.Y. State Dept. of Labor, 1929-38; indsl. commr. N.Y. State, 1938-43; spl. asst. to U.S. Ambassador John G. Winant, London, 1943-44; dir. women's bureau U.S. Dept. of Labor, 1944-53. Student of labor conditions, Eng., Germany, Austria, 1923; attended Internat. Congress of Working Women, Vienna, 1923, Inter-Am. Regional Conf., Internat. Labor Orgn., Santiago, Chile, 1936, internat. labor confs., Geneva, 1936, 1938; alternate del. Internat. Labor Conf., New York City, 1941, adviser, Philadelphia, 1944; govt. rep. Conf. Delegation on Constitutional Questions, Internat. Labor Orgn., London, 1946; adviser U.S. delegation Gen. Assembly of United Nations, London, 1946; govt. mem., 98th session of governing body, and substitute govt., rep., 99th session, Internat. Labor Office, Montreal, 1946; substitute govt. del., 101st session, Geneva, 1947; substitute govt. del. and adviser Internat. Labor Conf., Montreal, 1946; mem. U.S. del., Internat. Labor Conf., Geneva, 1950-51, adv. 1952; adv. to U.S. Rep., 7th session Econ. and Social Council, U.N., Switzerland, 1948; member committee of experts on women's work International Labor Office. Committee member (formerly bd. mem.) Pub. Affairs Com., Inc. Consultant nat. bd. Y.W.C.A. Club: Cosmopolitan (New York). Died July 1973.

MILLER, G. F., glass co. exec.; b. 1911. With Anchor Hocking Corp. and predecessors, from 1931, plant mgr., Lancaster, O., 1944-50, factories mgr. tableware div., 1950-58, v.p., 1958-63, corporate v.p., gen. mgr. tableware div., 1963-67, exec. v.p., from 1967, also dir. Deceased.

MILLER, GEORGE HENRY, physician; b. Beallsville, O., 1887; M.D., U. Pa., 1917; m. Martha Hall Gordon, July 20, 1918; children—Martha (Mrs. Graham A. Vance), George Henry. Intern, Bryn Mawr Hosp., 1917—18; research fellow Nelson Morris Inst. Med. Research, U. Ia., 1920, asso. prof. pharmacology 1922—25, asso. prof. internal medicine, 1925—32; dean medicine Am. U. Beirut, Lebanon, 1932—44; dir. edn. A.C.S., 1944—58. Served with U.S. Army, 1918—19; AEF. Decorated officier Order Academie Republique Francaise; Order of Merit (Lebanon). Diplomate Am. Bd. Internal Medicine. Mem. A.M.A. (field rep. council on med. edn. and hosp. 1959—63), Am. Soc. Pharmacology and Exptl. Therapeutics, Soc. for Exptl. Biology and Medicine. Home: Gainesville, Fla. Died Dec. 17, 1972; interred Beallsville, O.

MILLER, HAZEL BELLE, (Mrs. Esmond A. Van Name), physician; b. Bklyn., Sept. 17, 1912; d. Frank W. and Florence (Brodie) Miller; B.S., N.Y. U., 1929; M.D. cum laude, Woman's Med. Coll. Pa., 1934; m. Esmond A. Van Name, June 7, 1934; children—Barry Allen, Kerry Everett. Intern, Jersey Med. Center and Margaret Hague Maternity Hosp., 1934-35; gen. practice Hollis, L.I., 1935-60, Garden City, N.Y., 1960-75; physician in clinics N.Y. Skin and Cancer Hosp., 1935-41; mem. obstet. staff Mary Immaculate Hosp., 1936-75, obstet. clinic, 1936-63. Active Boy Scouts Am. Fellow Am. Acad. Family Physicians (charter, past chpt. pres.), Nassau Acad. Medicine; mem. Am. Geriatrics Soc., Am. Soc. Clin. Hypnosis, Women's Med. Soc. N.Y. State (hon., pres. 1966-68, Woman of Year 1975), Am. Med. Womens Assn. (del. to Med. Womens Internat. Assn., rep. to UN), Soroptomists, Alpha Omicron Pi, Zeta Phi, Alpha Omega Alpha. Address: Garden City, N.Y., Died Feb. 25, 1975.

MILLER, HOWARD SHULTZ, congressman; b. Somerset, Pa., Feb. 27, 1879; s. Mahlon and Jennie (Shultz) M.; LL.B., Neb. State U., 1901; m. Fluta Roberts, Sept. 30, 1908; children—Russell Roberts, Howard Wendell, Isabel (Mrs. Hohnbaum). Admitted to Neb. bar, 1901; farmer, 1901-29 and after 1940; v.p. Sabetha Coop. Elevator Co.; mem. 83d Congress 1st Kan. Dist. Pres. Walnut Creek Watershed Assn.; bd. dirs. Hiawatha Community Hosp. Assn., N.E. Kan. Agrl. Research Assn. Received Good Year award for distinguished service in soil conservation, 1952. Mem. Grange, Farm Bur., Farm Union. Conglist. Mason (past member). Kiwanian. Home: Hiawatha, Kan.†

MILLER, HUGH engr.; b. Roselle, N.J., Feb. 1, 1881; s. Charles Dexter and Julia (Hope) M.; C.E., Princeton, 1901; post-grad. work, Harvard, summers 1910, 12; m. Clara Fay, Nov. 2, 1904; children—Donald Hope, Francis Fay; m. 2d, Izetta Jewel Brown, Apr. 16, 1927. With H. de B. Parsons; cons. engr., New York, 1901-02; instr. engring., Princeton, 1902, pvt. tutor, 1902-03; with Centennial Copper Mining Co., 1903-09; prof. civ. engring., Clarkson Coll. of Technology, Potsdam, N.Y., 1909-15; lecturer on civ. engring., Rice Inst., Houston, Tex., 1915-17; prof. civ. engring., George Washington U., 1921-26; dean Coll. of Engring. same univ., 1922-26; prof. civil engring., Union Coll., 1926-33; state engr. for Mo. of Federal Emergency Adminstrn. of Public Works, 1933-35; chief engr. Pub. Works Adminstrn. for W.Va., 1935-Aug. 1937; president Hugh Miller Associates, Inc., Charleston, West Virginia, 1937-40; renegotiator, War Dept., Price Adjustment Board, Washington, 1940-48. Capt. engrs., U.S.A., 1917-21; lt. col. U.S. Res., from 1926. Mem. Am. Soc. C.E. (life), Princeton Engring Assn., Princeton Club of Wash., D.C. (bd. dir., 1943-46), Sigma Xi, Sigma Tau; fellow A.A.A.S. Presbyterian. Clubs: Colonial (Princeton); Army-Navy Country, Arlington, Va.; La Jolla Beach and Tennis. Home: La Jolla, Cal.†

MILLER, HUGO EUGENE, physician; b. Colomer, Ind., Dec. 23, 1903; s. Wilford Stanton and Eva Ora (Obenchain) M.; M.D., U. Minn., 1928; m. Kathryn Harriet Howser, June 1, 1935; children—Susan (Mrs. Herbert Zinschlag), Hugo Eugene. Intern, Mpls. Gen. Hosp., 1928-29, resident in surgery, 1929-30, resident in urology, 1930-31, attending in urology, 1931-73; attending in urology St. Mary's Hosp., Asbury Meth. Hosp., Eitel Hosp.; asso. Mt. Sinai Hosp. (all Mpls.); clin. asst. prof. urology U. Minn. Served with USNR, 1943-46. Diplomate Am. Bd. Urology. Mem. A.M.A., Hennepin County Med. Soc., Am. Urol. Assn., Twin City Urol. Soc., Alpha Omega Alpha, Alpha Sigma Phi. Republican. Contbr. articles to profl. jours. Inventor modification of Nesbit resectoscope; also inventor other resectoscope, method of resecting through perineal urethrotomy. Home: Minneapolis, Minn. Died Dec. 11, 1973; cremated.

MILLER, JOHN KING, physician; b. Sierre Leone, Africa, June 9, 1906; s. Harland Travey and Jane Miller); M.D., U. Neb., 1933; m. Lenore May Sportsman, Aug. 6, 1935; children—Robert M., Harland, Penelope Helene. Teaching fellow in pathology U. Neb., 1931-32; intern Meml. Hosp., N.Y.C., 1933, Methodist Hosp., Omaha, 1934; resident in pathology U. Louisville Hosp., 1936; dir. clin. research N.Y. Dept. Health, Albany; attending pathologist and physician Albany Med. Coll., Union U.; emeritus prof. medicine; cons. clin. pathologist VA Hosp., Albany. Served to col. M.C., AUS, 1942-46. Diplomate Am. Bd. Pathology. Fellow Am. Pub. Health Assn.; mem. A.C.P., Am. Soc. Hematology, Royal Soc. Health. Episcopalian. Contbr. numerous articles to med. jours. Research in microbiology and clin. application to infectious dis. Home: Albany, N.Y. Died Oct. 20, 1972; buried All Saints Cathedral, Albany, N.Y.

MILLER, KENNETH S., banker; b. Victoria, B.C., Can., Sept. 2, 1906; s. Nathaniel Scott and Annie (Scott) M.; student Pacific N.W. Sch. Banking, U. Wash., 1941; m. Carrie L. Boultinghouse, Dec. 3, 1938; children—Elsie (Mrs. James M. Lasher), Kenneth S. Asst. cashier Am. Nat. Bank, Aberdeen, Wash., 1923-31; cashier 1st Nat. Bank Madras, Ore., 1931-35; asst. mgr. various brs. U.S. Nat. Bank, Portland, Ore., 1935-45, v.p., First Bank Ore., Portland, from 1945. Rotarian, Elk. Club: Aero of Ore. (pres.). Home: Portland, Ore. Died Sept. 17, 1974.

MILLER, MARY BRITTON, writer; b. New London, Conn., Aug. 1883; d. Charles Philip and Grace (Rumrill) Miller; ed. pvt. schs., student Gilman Sch., Cambridge, Mass. Author (under own name) Songs of Infancy and Other Poems, 1928; Menagerie, 1928; Without Sanctuary, 1932; Intrepid Bird, 1934; The Crucificion (long poem), 1944; Give a Guess, 1957; All Aboard, 1958; A Handful of Flowers, 1959; Listen—The Birds, 1961; (under pen name of Isabel Bolton) Do I Wake or Sleep, 1946; The Christmas Tree, 1949; Many Mansions, 1952; Jungle Journey, 1959; Under Gemini, 1966; The Whirligig of Time, 1971; contbr. short stories to New Yorker, Harper's Bazaar, Botteghe Oscure, Discovery. Recipient Nat. Acad. Arts and Letters award, 1953; Nat. Found. Arts and Humanities grant, 1961; grant Philip M. Stern Found., 1965; Chapelbrook Found. grant, 1969. Home: New York City, N.Y. Died Apr. 1975.

MILLER, PARK HAYS, editor; b. Allegheny, Pa., Dec. 21, 1879; s. Oliver Laid (M.D.) and Mary Jane (Cunningham) M.; A.B., Western University of Pa. (now U. of Pittsburgh), 1899, M.A., 1926; grad. Western Theol. Sem., 1902; D.D., Centre Coll., 1930; m. Bessie P. Crider, Aug. 7, 1907; children—Grace,

Park Hays. Instr. mathematics, Stewart's Prep. Sch., Sewickley, Pa.,* 1902-03; ordained Presbyn. ministry, 1904; supply, First Ch., Uniontown, Pa., 1903-04; pastor Compton Hill Chapel, St. Louis, 1904-08, Ch. of the Evangel, Phila., 1908-14; asst. editor Presbyn. Bd. of Publ. and Sabbath Sch. Work, May 15, 1914-23; asso. editor dept. editorial work, Bd. of Christian Education of the Presbyn. Ch., U.S.A., 1923-30, asso. editor, supervisor ednl. materials, 1930-37, editor, 1937-42; asso. sec. Div. Edn. in Home, Church and Community, and editor-in-chief, 1942, ret., 1949. Mem. Ednl. Commn. and chmn. Com. on Uniform Series, Internat. Council Religious Education. Republican. Writer church literature, from 1914. Home: Drexel Hill, Pa.†

MILLER, RAY HAGGARD, state ofcl., pharmacist; b. Pittsville, Mo., May 2, 1912; s. Fred and Fern (Haggard) M.; grad. Kansas City (Mo.) Coll. Pharmacy, 1933; m. Rosemary Heiler, June 6, 1936. Clk. Katz Drug Co., Kansas City, Mo. 1931-34; pharmacist Hall Pharmacy, Kansas City, 1935-37; sales rep. Upjohn Co., Marshallton, Ia., Denver, Topeka, Kansas City, Kan., 1937-49; owner Miller Drug, Inc., Leavenworth, Kan., 1949-68, pres., 1961-68; dir. Mid-Continent Chem. Co., Leavenworth. Mem. Kan. Bd. Pharmacy, from 1967, pres., from 1969. Charter mem. St. Mary Coll. Pres.'s Council, from 1969; mem. adv. bd. St. John's Hosp., from 1971, Leavenworth United Fund, from 1971. Mayor, Leavenworth, from 1969. Bd. dirs. Community Hotel. Mem. Kan. Pharm. Assn. (pres. 1966). Roman Catholic. K.C., Rotarian. Home: Leavenworth, Kan. Died Jan. 3, 1973.

MILLER, ROBERT WARREN, photog. equipment mfr.; b. Brackenridge, Pa., Dec. 4, 1917; s. Albert Earl and Emily (Galbreath) M.; B.Sc., B.A., Ohio State U., 1939; M.Sc., Mass. Inst. Tech., 1952; m. Anna Lou Stevenson, Dec. 16, 1938; children—Ann (Mrs John Snider), Lynne (Mrs. Robert Kuhn), R. Stevenson. With Eastman Kodak Co., 1939-74, successively trainee Eastman Kodak Stores, Atlantic City, accounting dept., mgmt. staff, 1939-59, v.p., Rochester, N.Y., 1959-74, also dir.; dir. Marine Midland Trust Co., Kodak-Pathé, Can. Kodak; pres.-elect Blue Cross-Blue Shield. Mem. exec. com. Region 2, Boy Scouts Am., mem. devel. com. Mass. Inst. Tech. Bd. dirs. Genessee Valley Group Health Assn., Gen. Hosp., Rochester Hosp. Service; trustee Rochester Inst. Tech., U. Rochester, George Eastman Mus., Rochester Art Gallery. Mem. Indsl. Mgmt. Council (dir.), N.A.M. (dir.), Rochester C. of C. (trustee), Ohio State U. Alumni Assn. (dir.), Beta Gamma Sigma, Beta Alpha Psi, Kappa Sigma. Presbyn. Clubs: University, Genesee Valley, Country of Rochester. Home: Brighton N.Y. Died Jan. 13, 1974; interred Meml. Mausoleum, St. Petersburg, Fla.

MILLER, RUSSELL COOPER, educator; b. Tower City, Pa., Feb. 2, 1901; s. Samuel Cooper and Mildred (Mandaville) M.; B.S., Pa. State U., 1922; Ph.D., Cornell U., 1925; m. Helen E. Weed, Aug. 25, 1925; children—David W., Carolyn F. Asst., Ohio Agrl. Expt. Sta., Wooster, 1922-23; with dept. animal husbandry Cornell U., 1923-26; mem. faculty Pa. State U., University Park, from 1926, prof. agrl. and biol. chemistry, from 1944, head dept. animal husbandry, 1959, head dept. animal industry and nutrition, from 1960, chmn. div. animal sci. and industry, from 1961. Cons. Pa. Dept. Agr., from 1955. Mem. Am. Chem. Soc. (chmn. Central Pa. sect. 1940), Fedn. Am. Socs. Exptl. Biology, Am. Inst. Nutrition Am. Soc. Animal Prodn., Sigma Xi, Phi Lambda Upsilon, Gamma Sigma Delta, Alpha Zeta, Republican. Presbyn. Mason (32., Shriner). Author tech. papers on biochemistry, nutrition. Home: State College, Pa. Died May 31, 1974.

MILLER, SETON INGERSOLL, motion picture producer-writer; b. Chehalis, Wash., May 3, 1902; s. Harry John and Mabel (Ingersoll) M.; student Phillips Exeter Acad., 1920-21; Ph.B., Yale, 1925; m. Bonita-Jessie Nichols, June 16, 1927; children—Keith Sanford, Bonita Ann; m. 2d, Ann Marie White, Jan. 26, 1944; 1 dau., Catherine Frances. Partner and asso. prof. Robert Stillman Productions. Acted in play Brown of Harvard; wrote High School Hero, Paid to Love, Crowd Roars, The Last Male, Once in a Lifetime, If I had a Million, Eagle and the Hawk, Frisco Kid, Two in the Dark, The Leathernecks Have Landed, Kid Galahad, The Adventures of Robin Hood, Dawn Fatro, Sea Hawk, Here Comes Mr. Jordan, My Gal Sal, The Black Swan, Singapore, Mississippi Gambler, Fighter Squadron and others; wrote and produced Ministry of Fear, Two Years Before the Mast, California, Calcutta, Rogue for Hire (television series); associate producer The Sound of Fury, Acad. award for best screen play, 1941, Here Comes Mr. Jordan. Mem. Screen Writers Guild, Acad. Motion Picture Arts and Scis. Club: Pacific Writer Yacht. Home: Beverly Hills, Cal. Died Mar. 29, 1974.

MILLER, WALTER JOHN, clergyman, astronomer; b. Rochester, N.Y., May 6, 1904; s. Andrew John and Agnes Frances (Burns) M.; B.A., Woodstock Coll., 1930, M.A., Ph.L., 1931, S.T.L., 1937, S.T.D., 1938; A.M., Harvard, 1941; Ph.D., 1943. Joined Soc. of Jesus, 1924; ordained priest Roman Cath. Ch., 1937 asst. prof. physics Georgetown U., Washington, 1931-32; mem. Fryeburg (Me.) solar eclipse expdn. Georgetown Coll. Obs., 1932, asst. astronomer. 1932-34; prof. math. Woodstock Coll., 1933-34, prof. math. and statis. analysis, 1944-45; asst. chaplain Kings County Hosp., Bklyn., 1939; prof. math. Canisius Coll., Buffalo, 1943-44; asst. papal astronomer Vatican Obs., Castel Gandolfo, Italy, 1945-55; founder, dir. Fordham U. Astron. Lab., N.Y.C., 1955-73. Recipient research grants NSF 1956, 58, 59, 67, Am. Acad. Arts and Scis., 1960. Mem. N.Y. Acad. Scis., A.A.A.S., Am. Assn. Jesuit Scientists, Am. Astron. Soc. Astron. Soc. Pacific Royal Astron. Soc., Royal Astron. Soc. Can., Astronomische Goesellschaft, Societa Astronomica Italiana, Internat. Astron. Union (mem. variable stars commn. 27). Founder, author series sci. papers Vatican Variables, from 1948. Contbr. numerous articles on the faint variable stars of the Cygnus Cloud to profl. jours. Home: New York City, N.Y. Died Nov. 30, 1973; buried Shrine of the N.Am. Martyrs, Auriesville, N.Y.

MILLER, WILBUR K., judge; b. Owensboro, Ky., Oct. 9, 1892; s. Reuben A. and Margaret (Morehead) M.; ed. U. Mich.; m. Marie Louise Hager, June 2, 1917. Admitted to Ky. bar, 1916, and practiced in Owensboro; county atty., Daviess County, Ky., 1922-30; chmn. Pub. Service Commn. of Ky., 1934-35; judge Spl. Ct. Appeals of Ky., 1940-41; judge U.S. Ct. of Appeals for D.C., 1945-64, sr. judge, 1964-73. Served in field arty. U.S. Army, World War I. Mem. Phi Delta Phi, Phi Kappa Sigma. Home: Alexandria, Va., Died Jan. 24, 1976; buried Owensboro, Ky.

MILLET, JOHN ALFRED PARSONS, pyschiatrist; b. Broadway, Worcestershire, Eng., July 8, 1888; s. Francis Davis and Elizabeth Greeley (Merrill) M.; student Marlborough Coll., Eng., 1902-06; A.B., Harvard U., 1910, M.D., 1914; m. Alice Murrell, May 21, 1913 (div.); children—Jeanne Alice (Mrs. William T. King), John Bradford, Elizabeth (Mrs. Henry Sanford); m. 2d, Carmen deGonzalo Manice, Aug. 7, 1941. Began practice medicine, 1914; gen. practice later specialist in Psychiatry hosps., clinics and univs., N.Y., asst. clin. prof. Psychiatry College Phys. and Surgery, 1952; clinical research on allergic disturbances; organized neuropsychiatric clinic Lake George Found., Glens Falls, N.Y., 1940, asso. attending psychoanalyst Columbia Dept. Psychiatry, 1947-54; chmn. Mental Health Bd. Rockland County, 1955-58; pres. Assn. Psychoanalytic Medicine, 1954-57; chief of psychiatric service, Am. Rehab. Com., 1946-70; lectr. psychiatry Columbia, 1956-59; attending psychiatrist N.Y. State Psychiatric Inst., 1957-60; prof. psychiatry, asst. dean N.Y. Sch. Psychiatry, 1959-64; prof. emeritus, 1965-76; pvt. practice supervising advanced students Columbia Psychoanalytic Clinic for Tng. and Research; hon. Cons. Columbia Clinic, 1962-76, Dir. Ruth M. Knight Counseling Service Manhattan Sch. Music, 1965-76. Served from 1st lt. to capt., MC AUS, 1917-19; A.E.F. Decorated Office d'Academie with Silver Palms. Trustee Manhattan Sch. of Music, N.Y.C. Diplomate Am. Bd. of Neurology and Psychiatry. Fellow A.M.A., Am. Psychiatric Assn., N.Y. Acad. Medicine; mem. nat., state and local profl. and med. assns. in gen. and spl. fields, Acad. Psychoanalysis (pres. 1959), World Fedn. Mental Health (chmn. U.S. Com., Inc., 1965-68). Episcopalian. Clubs: Hasty Pudding, Delphic (Cambridge, Mass.); Harvard, Century Assn. (N.Y.). Author book, chpts. in books and numerous articles. Address: New York City, N.Y., Died Feb. 18, 1976.

MILLETT, FRED BENJAMIN, coll. prof., author; b. Brockton, Mass., Feb. 19, 1890; s. Daniel Edwin and Mary Avalina (Churchill Porter) M.; A.B., Amherst Coll., 1912, L.H.D., 1957; student Harvard, summer 1913, U. Chicago, 1916-18 (Ph.D., 1931); hon. A. M., Wesleyan U., 1939. Lecturer in English, Queen's U., 1912-16; fellow in English, U. of Chicago, 1916-18; asst. prof., Carnegie Inst. Tech., 1919-26, asso. prof., 1926-27; asst. prof., U. of Chicago, 1927-33, asso. prof., 1933-37; visiting prof. of English, Wesleyan U., 1937-39, prof., from 1939, acting dir. Honors Coll., 1943-46, dir. from 1946; consultant humanities div. Rockefeller Foundation, 1942-43; consultant, information and education div., War Dept., 1945. Founder of the Washington Street Press, 1945; advisor in College English, 1948-50. Served as private United States Army, May-December 1918; 2d lt., Q.M.C. Reserve, 1918-23. Mem. Modern Lang. Assn. America, Modern Humanities Research Assn., Am. Assn. U. Profs. (mem. council 1946-49, 54, pres. 1952-54), Coll. English Assn. (pres. New Eng. sect. 1956), Phi Beta Kappa. Democrat. Author or co-author several books relating to field; latest publs.; Reading Fiction; Reading Poetry; Reading Drama (all 1950). Mem. editorial bd. American Literature, 1952-56. Address: Whitman, Mass., Died Jan. 1, 1976.

MILLIKEN, WILLIAM THOMAS, clergyman, educator; b. Cargill, Ont., Can., Jan. 4, 1871; s. John Wesley and Matilda (Kidd) M.; B.S., Chicago Sem. of Science (now defunct), 1901; M.A., Ewing (Ill.) Coll., 1904, D.D., 1911; student extra mural, Crozer Theol. Sem. 4 yrs., also Southwestern Baptist Theological Seminary; m. Emily Frances Mosher, May 4, 1896 (died Feb. 4, 1942); children—Wesley Daniel, Frank William Pansy Louise (Mrs. Henry Douglas Turner); one step-son, Sidney A. Mosher. Came to U.S., 1896 naturalized, 1918. Teacher, Maple Hill, Ontario, Can., 1891-93; student missionary in Saskatchewan, Manitoba and New Ontario, 1893-96; ordained Bapt. ministry, 1898; pastor successively Mapleton, Minn., Hebron Ch., St. Paul, Park Rapids, Minn., Ft. Collins, Colo., Detroit, Minn., Oregon City, Ore., until 1920, Salem, 1920-23; dir. religious edn., Ore. Bapt. Conv., 1922-29; dean, acting head, Western Bapt. Theol. Sem., 1927-34, president May 1934-44, dean and acting president, 1944, became prof. of Greek and New Testament, 1945, later president emeritus; instructor Greek; pastor Grace Church, Portland, Oregon, 1931-46. Member of fraternity Pi Gamma Mu. Republican. Mason. With others wrote Church School Improvement, 1925; wrote courses in homiletics, and in ch. history, for corr. schs. Baptist denom. Author of numerous poems in various journals, also Natural System of Teaching Greek; author: Rhymes of a Sky Pilot. Address: Portland, Ore.†

MILLS, CHARLES WINFRED, elec. engr.; b. Newport, Tenn., Aug. 10, 1923; s. William Mitchel and Nora Mae (Holt) M.; B.S., Tri State Coll., Angola, Ind., 1948; m. Elizabeth Parker, Jan. 31, 1945; children—Connie (Mrs. Larry Tew), Larry Mitchel, Samuel Parker, Wendy Elizabeth. Engr., Jefferson Standard Broadcasting Co. WBTV, Charlotte, N.C., 1948-59; project engr. Cryovac div. W.R. Grace & Co., Duncan, S.C., 1959-66; pres., gen. mgr. Control Systems, Inc., Greenville, S.C., 1967-75. Served with USAAF, 1942-45. Mem. I.E.E.E., Instrument Soc. Am. Club: Sertoma Sunrisers. Patentee electronic devices: Home: Greenville S.C. Died Feb. 22, 1975.

MILLS, GEORGE HENRY, naval officer; b. Rutherfordton, N.C., Aug. 5, 1895; s. John Craton and Lenora Warford (Poole) M.; student Bingham Mil. Sch., 1911-13; B.S., U.S. Naval Acad., 1918; m. Leonore Eliza Wickersham, Dec. 28, 1923; 1 dau., Georgia Lee. Comd. ensign, U.S. Navy, 1918, and advanced through the grades to commodore, 1939. Decorated Victory Medal with Atlantic Fleet clasp. Club: Toms River (N.J.) Yacht. Home: Wheaton, Md., Died Oct. 14, 1975.

MILLS, JAMES THEODORE, physician; b. Austin, Minn., Nov. 14, 1900; s. James Bishop and Lena (Erickson) M.; student St. Thomas Coll., St. Paul, 1914—19; B.S., U. Minn., 1921; M.D., 1925; m. Rosemary Zonne, Oct. 20, 1925; children—Hildegarde (Mrs. Chester Fullinwider, Jr.), James, Diana (Mrs. David T. Blackburn), Rosemary (Mrs. John Coats). Intern Washington Boulevard Hosp., plastic Chgo., 1915; trainee surgery with Dr. Ferris Smith, Grand Rapids, Mich., 1925—32; pvt. practice plastic surgery, Dallas, 1932—74; prof. emeritus clin. surgery, div. plastic surgery S. W. Med. Sch., U. Tex., Dallas. Chmn. emeritus adv. bd. Crippled Children's Div. State of Tex. Served capt. M.C., USNR, World War 11. Vice chmn. Am. Bd. Plastic Surgery, 1953, chmn., 1954. Mem. Am. Assn. Plastic Surgeons (pres. 1948), Am. Soc. Plastic and Reconstructive Surgery (pres. 1953), Beta Theta Phi, Nu Sigma Nu. Episcopalian. Clubs: Brooks Hollow Golf, Dallas (Dallas). Home: Dallas, Tex. Died Jan. 15, 1974.

MILLS, WILLIAM O., congressman; b. 1925. Adminstrv. asst. to Congressman Rogers C.B. Morton; mem. 92d Congress from 1st Md. Dist. filling vacancy left by Sec. Interior Rogers C.B. Morton. Republican. Died 1973.

MILROY, ROBERT ARTHUR, physician; b. Batavia, Ill., Apr. 24, 1915; s. Robert Arthur and Evelyn (Feldott) M.; M.D., U. Ill., 1941; m. Helen Virginia Keifer, Sept. 22, 1945; 1 son, Robert Dennis. Rotating intern St. Louis City Hosp., 1941—42; resident in radiology VA Hosp., Hines Ill., 1946—49; asso. radiologist, 1966—67; sr. staff St. Joseph' Hosp., Aurora, Ill., St. Charles Hosp., Aurora, Copley Hosp., Aurora; radiologist Porter Meml. Hosp., Valparaiso, Ind., Jasper County Hosp., Rensselaer, Ind., 1953—57, Caylor Nickel Clinic, Bluffton, Ind. Served as capt., M.C., AUS, 1942—46. Diplomate Am. Bd. Radiology. Mem. A.M.A., Am. Coll. Radiology. Home: LaGrange Park, Ill. Died Mar. 29, 1967; buried Mt. Olivet Cemtery, Aurora, Ill.

MINARD, DUANE ELMER, lawyer; b. Rockaway Valley, N.J., Apr. 27, 1880; s. George Wesley and Mary Ella (Hayes) M.; ed. intermittent schooling; m. Sara Trego Bennett, June 22, 1903; children—Dorothy Bennett, Sara Frances (wife of Dr. Arthur Lawton Bennett), Duane Elmer, Jr. Clk. in market, Boonton, N.J., 1897-99, law office, Newark, 1899-1903. Admitted to N.J. bar, U.S. Dist. Ct., Dist. of N.J., U.S. Circuit Ct., 3d Circuit, 1903, Interstate Commerce Commn., 1915, U.S. Supreme Ct., 1928; practiced, Newark, from 1903; partner law firm Cortlandt & Wayne Parker, 1906-12, Hobart & Minard, 1925-37, Hobart, Minard & Cooper, 1937-49, Minard, Cooper, Gaffey & Webb from 1949. Clk. to U.S. dist. atty. N.J., 1903-04; asst. gen. solicitor Erie R.R. Co., N.Y.C., 1912-20, gen. atty., 1920-25, local atty. N.J., also legal officer N.Y., from 1902; dir. N.Y., Susquehanna Western R.R. Co. from 1923; atty. U.S. R.R. Adminstrn., 1917-20. Asst. atty. gen. N.J., 1929-34, spl. asst. atty. gen., 1934-42; spl. counsel to gov. N.J., 1938 (Del. & Raritan Canal water rights); atty. N.J. State Planning Bd., 1938; v.p. N.J. Taxpayers Assn., 1934-37, mem. legislative com., 1936-37, bd. dirs., 1938-48, chmn. com. on fed. matters, 1941, mem. exec. com., 1945-46; gen. counsel N.J. Assn. Real Estate Bds. from 1940. Counsel (state water law) Natural Resources Planning Bd., Dept. Interior, Washington, 1938-40; spl.

counsel N.J. and N.Y. Joint Bridge and Tunnel Commn., 1924-27 (relating to Jersey City entrance and exit Holland Tunnel); spl. prosecutor Cumberland County, N.J., 1932-33 (Vineland Trust Co. frauds); counsel Union Oil Co. of Calif., 1905 (securing War Dept. license for constrn. oil pipeline across Isthmus of Panama to supply fuel oil for Panama Canal Constrn.); counsel of dirs. Morris & Essex R.R. Co., 1942 (negotiations and litigation with D., L. & W. R.R. Co. on terms of acquisition of M. & E. R.R.); counsel Interstate Commn. on Del. River Basin, 1942-43 (drafting and promoting enactment of concurrent legislation by N.Y., N.J., Pa., Del., establishing uniform standard of steam waters purity in Del. watershed; handling litigation contesting validity and enforcement of legislation). Atty. Boonton Twp., Morris Co., N.J., 1914-27, Boonton Twp. Sch. Dist., 1946-51; mem. Boonton Twp. Bd. Edn.; counsel Boonton Twp. Mil. Service Com., from 1944; legal cons. Boonton Twp. Zoning Commn. and Planning Bd., 1948-50; pres. Boonton C. of C., 1940. Mem. House of Assembly, N.J., 1910. Served with 1st Regt., N.J.N.G., 1902, disch. for phys. disability, 1903, Judge Adv. Gen.'s Dept., 1909, capt. Co. M. 1912. Fellow Am. Geog. Soc.; mem. Am. Mus. Natural History, Methodist. Clubs: Explorers (N.Y.C.); Downtown (Newark); Skytop (Pa.). Author: Centennial Book (History) Rockaway Valley Methodist Church, 1942. Compiler: American Colonial History (2 vols.), 1931. Home: Boonton, N.J.†

MINDSZENTY, H. E. CARDINAL JOZSEF, cardinal; b. Csehmindszent, Hungary, Mar. 29, 1892; s. Janos Pehm and Borbala Kovacs. Ordained priest Roman Cath. Ch., 1915; bishop of Veszprem, 1944; imprisoned, 1944-45; archbishop of Esztergom and primate of Hungary, 1945-75; cardinal, 1946; sentenced to life imprisonment, 1949; released, 1956; granted asylum U.S. legation, Budapest, 1956-71. Mem. Sacred Congregations of Sacraments, of Ceremonies, of Sems. and Univs. Study. Author: My Mother (3 vols.); pastoral letters. Address: Vatican, Italy. Died May 1975.

MINEO, SAL, actor; b. Bronx, N.Y., Jan. 10, 1939; ed. Lodge Sch. Appearances on Broadway include Rose Tattoo, The King and I, Something About a Soldier; motion picture appearances include Six Bridges to Cross, The Private War of Major Benson, Rebel Without a Cause, Giant, Crime in the Streets, Somebody Up There Likes Me, Rock Pretty Baby, The Young Don't Cry, Dino, Tonka, Private's Affair, The Gene Krupa Story, Exodus, Escape to Zahrian, Greatest Story Ever Told, Cheyenne Autumn; TV appearances on Comedy Hour, Omnibus, Goodyear Playhouse, Studio One, others. Nominated for Oscar award. Home: West Hollwyood, Cal., Died Feb. 12, 1976.

MINER, CARL SHELLEY, cons. chemist; b. State Center, Ia., Aug. 5, 1878; s. Marvin E. and Flora B. (Shelley) M.; student Coe Coll., Cedar Rapids, 1 yr.; B.S., U. of Chicago, 1903; D.Sc. (hon.) Coe College, Cedar Rapids, Ia., 1948; m. Alice Reed Dunshee, Jan. 11, 1912; children—Barbara Dunshee Parker, Carl Shelley; married 2d Elizabeth Muther Kohlsaat, Oct. 6, 1949. Research, Corn Products Co., Chicago, 1903-06; cons. chemist, from 1906, operating under title of Miner Labs., 1908-56. Editor Chicago Chem. Bull., 1918-19. Developer of mfr. of furfural from oat hulls. Consultant Baruch Rubber Com. Member chemical referee board, Office Production Research and Development, War Production Board, Member of the board Universal Oil Products Co., Modern Pioneer award, 1940; Perkin medal Am. sect. Society Chem. Industry, 1949; Honor Scroll, American Inst. Chemists, 1950. Mem. Am. Chem. Soc. (chmn. Chicago sect. 1922), A.A.A.S., Am. Assn. Cereal Chemists, Alpha Chi Sigma, Sigma Xi, Phi Delta Theta. Club: Chemists; University, Chicago Golf. (Chgo.). Home: Chicago, Ill.†

MING, WILLIAM ROBERT, JR., educator, lawyer; b. Chicago, May 7, 1911; s. William Robert and Annie Elizabeth (Johnson) M.; Ph.B., U. of Chicago, 1931, J.D. cum laude, 1933; m. Irvena Elizabeth Harvey, June 18, 1941. Admitted to Ill. bar, 1933, U.S. Supreme Ct. bar, 1937; asst. atty. Ill. Commerce Commn., 1933-37, counsel, 1949-50, cons. from 1950; pvt. practice law Dickerson & King, Chicago, 1933-37; asst. prof. law Howard U., 1937-39, asso. prof., 1939-40, prof., 1940-46; asst. gen. counsel O.P.A., Washington, 1942-43, asso. gen. counsel, 1946-47; asso. prof. U. of Chicago, 1947-50, prof. law, 1950-53; practicing as member law firm of Moore, Ming & Leighton, Chgo., 1953-61, then mem. law firm of McCroy, Ming and Black; special asst. attorney gen. of Ill., 1949-53; sec. Practical Trades Inst., Inc., Chgo., from 1947; sec., gen. counsel Practical Electronics Mfg. Co., Chgo.; co-counsel Chicago division Am. Civil Liberties Union, 1947-53. Mem. exec. com. Juvenile Protective Assn., Pub. Housing Assn.; mem. exec. bd. Met. Housing Council. Served as pvt. and capt. J.A.G.D., AUS, 1943-46. Mem. Am. Vets. Com. (nat. chmn. 1957-59), Joint Com. on Ill. Civil Procedure, Nat. Assn. for Advancement Colored People (nat. legal com., mem. nat. bd. dirs. 1958), Illinois, Chicago and Cook Co. bar assns., Order of Coif, Kappa Alpha Psi. Elk. Club: Quadrangle (Chicago). Contbr. articles to legal jours. Home: Chicago Ill. Died June 30, 1973; buried Holy Sepulchre Cemetery, Chicago, Ill.

MINIHAN, JEREMIAH FRANCIS, bishop; b. Haverhill, Mass., July 21, 1903; s. Timothy and Nora A. (Duggan) M.; A.B., Georgetown U., 1925, L.H.D., 1954; S.T.D., Propaganda U., Rome, 1930; LL.D., Boston Coll., 1948; Litt.D., Merrimack Coll., 1954. Ordained priest Roman Catholic Ch., 1929; sec. to Cardinal O'Connell, Boston, 1933-43; chancellor Archdiocese Boston, 1943-46; pastor St. Catherine's Parish, Norwood, 1946; titular bishop Paphos, aux. bishop Boston, 1954-73. Home: West Roxbury, Mass. Died Aug. 14, 1973.

MINKOWSKI, RUDOLPH LEO B., astronomer; b. Strasbourg, France, May 28, 1895; s. Oscar and Marie (Siegel) M.; Ph.D. in Physics, U. Breslau, Germany, 1921; LL.D., U. Cal., 1968; m. Luise Amalie David, Aug. 23, 1926; children—Eva (Mrs. Thomas), Herman. Came to U.S., 1935, naturalized, 1940. Asst. Physikalisches Staatsinstitut, Hamburg, Germany, 1922, privat-dozent, Hamburg, 1926-31, A.O. prof., Hamburg 1931-35; staff Mt. Wilson Obs., Carnegie Inst., 1935-48, Mt. Wilson and Palomar Obs., Pasadena, Cal., 1948-60, U. Cal. at Berkeley, 1961-65; vis. prof. U. Wis., 1960-61. Recipient Catherine Wolfe Bruce medal, 1961. Mem. Am., Royalastron. socs., Nat. Acad. Sci., Astron. Soc. Pacific. Home: Berkeley, Cal., Died Jan. 4, 1976.

MINOR, MILTON CARLISLE, banker; b. Gordon, Kan., July 14, 1892; s. Milton Taylor and Anna Jane (Snodgrass) M.; A.B., U. Kan., 1913; LL.B., Harvard, 1916; m. Mary Louise Durham, Aug. 7, 1937; children—Mona Louise, Milton Carlisle, Marion Taylor, Marilyn Ann. Admitted to Ky. bar, 1917; practiced law, Danville, 1917-37; instr. Centre Coll., Danville, 1921, asso. prof., 1922-32, prof. econs., 1933-37; pres. Farmers Nat. Bank of Danville, 1937-74, also chmn. bd., dir.; partner M. T. Minor & Son, 1947-74; dir. Old Bank of Perryville, Louisville br. Fed. Res. Bank of St. Louis. Dir. Danville Library. Mem. Ky. Bar Assn., Ky. Tax Research Assn. (pres.), Alpha Tau Omega, Delta Sigma Rho, Omicron Delta Kappa. Democrat. Mem. Christian Ch. Mason. Home: Danville, Ky., Died May 29, 1974; buried Bellevue Cemetery, Danville, Ky.

MINOT, GEORGE EVANS, mng. editor; b. Belgrade, Me., Dec. 18, 1898; s. George Linville and Elnora (Farnham) M.; A.B., Bowdoin Coll., 1919; Litt.D., Suffolk Unieristy, 1955; married Ruth Elizabeth Woodend, September 24, 1921; children—Olive, John Granville, George Evans, Jr. Reporter, writer spl. articles, editorials, book reviews, Boston Herald, 1919-28; night city editor, 1928-30, city editor, 1930-33, news editor, 1933-40, mng. editor, from 1940-67. In U.S. Army, Plattsburg, N.Y., 1918; mem. Draft Bd. No. 5, Arlington, Mass., 1940-47. Mem. Delta Kappa Epsilon. Republican. Congregationalist. Mason. Author: Murder Will Out, 1928; Recreation in New England, 1929. Home: Cambridge, Mass., Died Feb. 3, 1976.

MINTON, OLLIE FRANCIS, postmaster; b. Nashville, Tenn., Oct. 15, 1879; s. Peter Perkins and Sarah Frances (Hope) M.; ed. Howard Sch., Hume-Fogg High Sch., and Watkins Night Sch., until 1897; m. Sue Bessie Worsham, June 2, 1909; children—Ollie Francis, Henry Perkins, Henry Bell (dec.), James Samuel (dec.), Ann Liza, Robert Douglas. Began as a tinner, 1896; clothing salesman, 1897-1902; apptd. temporary clk. Nashville Post Office, 1902, regular apptmt., 1903, continuing through various grades to asst. postmaster, 1926, acting postmaster, 1928, postmaster, 1929-33. Mem. Nashville Chamber Commerce (bd. govs.). Republican. Methodist. Mason (32°), K.P. Club: Nashville, Exchange (pres.). Home: Nashville, Tenn.†

MIRACLE, JOHN HERBERT, utilities exec.; b. Harmony, Ark., Dec. 20, 1901; s. William Frye and Alice Saphronia (Payne) M.; student Draughons Coll., 1919-20, LaSalle Extension U., 1937-39; m. Berniece Viva Elza, Mar. 30, 1923; children—Herbert Garon and Berniece Sharon (Mrs. James M. Hamilton) (twins). Accounting, adminstrv. positions oil and utilities, 1920-31; with United Gas Corp., 1931-66, successively accountant, chief statistician, sec. and asst. treas., 1931-51, v.p., 1951-66, v.p., treas., 1957-66, v.p., dir., treas. United Gas Pipe Line Co., Union Producing Co.; dir. Duval Corporation. Member of Shreveport and Bossier City C. of C. Methodist (steward, trustee). Club: Shreveport (sec.-treas., dir.), Petroleum (Shreveport). Home: Shreveport, La., Died May 6, 1974.

MIRANDA, HEBER ISAAC, corp. exec.; b. Ashland, Ky., Nov. 26, 1906; s. David M. and Carlie (Commense) M.; student U. Ky., 1944; Indsl. Safety Engring. degree N.Y. U., 1945; m. Josephine Helen Dailey, June 25, 1923; children—William Jouett, Doris Kathryn (Mrs. Thomas C. Clyburn), Karra Esther (Mrs. David Frank Beam). Exec. dir. Ky. Sesquicentennial Commn., Lexington, 1941-42; pres. Fowler Skylight Corp., Lexington, from 1948, Land Investment Corp., from 1965; pres. New Burley Tobacco Warehouse. Asst. Ky. finance chmn. Truman-Barkely Campaign, 1947. Mem. A.S.C.A.P., Broadcast Music, Inc. Democrat. Methodist. Mason (32°, Shriner). Club: Optimist (v.p. 1964-65). Author, composer mus. compositions: Shine, Miss Liberty, Shine, 1960; Patch Up the Crack in the Liberty Bell, 1963; Let Freedom Ring, 1963; Roses in December, 1965. Home: Lexington, Ky. Died Oct. 9, 1973; buried Lexington (Ky.) Cemetery.

MIRSKY, ALFRED EZRA, biochemist; b. Flushing, L.I., N.Y., Oct. 17, 1900; s. Michael David and Frieda (Ittelson) M.; grad. Ethical Culture Sch.; A.B., Harvard, 1922; Ph.D., U. Cambridge, 1926; M.D. (hon.), U. Gothenburg, 1954; m. Reba Paeff, May 25, 1926 (dec. Nov. 1966); children—Reba II (Mrs. Robert Goodman), Jonathan; m. 2d, Sonya Wohl, Aug. 24, 1967. Prof. and librarian Rockefeller U. Mem. Am. Philos. Soc., Nat. Acad. Sci., Am. Chem. Soc., Soc. Biol. Chemists, Soc. Gen. Physiologists, Genetics Soc., Am. Naturalists Soc., Deutsche Akad. der Naturforscher, Am. Acad. Arts and Scis., Phi Beta Kappa. Editor: The Cell. Research on proteins and properties of cell nucleus. Home: New York City, N.Y. Died June 19, 1974.

MIRSKY, I. ARTHUR, physician; b. Montreal, Que., Can., Mar. 28, 1907; s. Solomon and Esther (Shapiro) M., B.Sc., McGill U., 1927, M.Sc., 1929, M.D., C.M., 1931; fellow U. Chgo., 1933-35; grad. Chgo. Psychoanalytic Inst., 1951; m. Eleanor Annette Fels, Aug. 25, 1931; children—Elisabeth Monica, Lynn Ellen. Came to U.S., 1931, naturalized, 1940. Extern, fellow exptl. medicine N.Y. Postgrad. Hosp., 1931-33; asst. dir. dept. metabolic research Michael Reese Hosp., Chgo., 1933-35; staff, dir. May Inst. Med. Research, Jewish Hosp., Cin., 1935-51; instr. dept. biol. chemistry U. Cin., 1938-40, asst. prof., 1940-46, asso. prof. psychiatry, asso. prof. exptl. medicine, 1946-51; cons. Hosp., 1946-51; cons. surgeon gen. USPHS, 1946-51, 56-58; cons. clin. research VA, Dayton, O., 1948-51; prof. chmn. dept. clin. sci. U. Pitts., 1951-66, Univ. prof.-at-large, dir. lab. clin. sci., 1966-72; distinguished physician VA Hosp. Brentwood, Los Angeles, from 1972; prof. medicine, prof. psychiatry U. Cal. Los Angeles, from 1973; cons. in metabolic disorder Montefiore Hosp., Pitts., 1953-57; mem. adv. com. research VA, Washington, 1961. Mem. mental health study sect. Nat. Inst. Mental Health. Served from maj. to lt. col. M.C., USAAF, 1942-46. Fellow A.A.A.S., A.C.P., Am. Diabetes Assn. (editor Diabetes Abstracts, Proc. Am. Diabetes Assn. 1941-47, mem. council 1941-49), Am. Geriatrics Soc., Am. Soc. Clin. Pathology, Pitts. Diabetes Assn., Clin. Soc. N.Y. Diabetes Assn., N.Y. Acad. Sci.; mem. A.M.A., Am. Physiol. Soc., Am. Psychiat. Assn., Assn. Am. Physicians, Am. Psychosomatic Soc. (pres. 1956-57; asso. editor Psychosomatic Medicine 1948-60, mem. council 1948-50), Am. Soc. Clin. Investigation (asso. editor Am. Jour. Clin. Investigation 1947-51), Am. Soc. Study Arteriosclerosis, Assn. Study Internal Secretions, Assn. Research Nervous and Mental Diseases, Central Soc. Clin. Research, Council on Diabetes Cin. (pres. 1948-50), Fedn. Clin. Research, Ohio State Med. Soc., Phila. Psychonalytic Soc., Pitts. Neuropsychiat. Soc., Soc. Biol. Research, Soc. Exptl. Biology and Medicine, Gerontological Soc., Am. Psychoanalytic Assn., Sigma Xi. Contbr. articles to profl. jours. Home: Malibu, Cal. Died Sept. 16, 1974.

MITCHELL, C. LIONEL, business exec.; b. 1917; student Ga. Inst. Tech.; married. Founder, pres. Mitchell Engring. Co., 1947-61; with Ceco Corp., Chgo., from 1961, v.p. corporate planning, 1966-69, sr. v.p. corporate devel., from 1969, also dir.; dir. 1st Columbus Nat. Bank, Miss Industries Inc. Deceased.

MITCHELL, DAVID FARRAR, dental educator; b. Arkansas City, Kan., Dec. 15, 1918; s. Lester David and Lucille (Farrar) M.; student U. Tex., 1937-38; B.S., U. Ill., 1940, D.D.S., 1942; Ph.D., U. Rochester Sch. Medicine and Dentistry, 1948; m. Trone Hawkes, Feb. 6, 1943; children—Dana S., Lindsay T., David F. Asso. prof., chmn. div. oral histopathology U. Minn., Mpls., 1948-55; prof., chmn. dept. oral diagnosis, oral medicine Ind. U. Sch. Dentistry, Indpls., 1955-75; cons. VA, Mpls. 1950-55. Mem. USPHS clin. research fellowship rev. com., 1963-66; cons. Ind. Tng. SCh., Indpls., 1955-73, 5th Army Hdqrs., Indpls., 1957-60; editorial dental cons. Saunders Co., Phila. Served from 1st lt. to maj. Dental Corps, AUS, 1942-46. NIH fellow; USPHS Sr. Research fellow U. Rochester, 1946-48; recipient Ann. award for meritorious teaching Ind. U., 1959; Diplomate Am. Acad. Oral Pathology (fellow 1951, pres. 1961, pres. bd. 1969); Fellow A.A.A.S.; mem. Am. Dental Assn. (chmn. research sect. 1955), Indpls. Dist. Dental Soc. (editor 1960-66), Soc. Exptl. Biology and Medicine, Internat. Assn. Dental Research (v.p. No. Am. div. 1973, pres. 1975), Sigma Xi, Omicron Kappa Upsilon, Delta Sigma Delta, Beta Theta Pi. Editor: Jour. Dental Research, 1969-75. Contbr. articles to profl. books; sr. contbr. Oral Diagnosis/Oral Medicine, 2d edit., 1971. Contbr. numerous articles to profl. jours. Home: Indianapolis, Ind., Died July 17, 1975; buried Crown Hill Cemetery, Indpls.

MITCHELL, GEORGE FREDERICK, tea expert; b. Mt. Pleasant, S.C., Dec. 13, 1881; s. John Magill and Etta Julia (von Kolnitz) M.; B.S., Clemson (S.C.) Coll., 1902; m. Nell Rose Baggett, Mar. 28, 1917 (dec. Oct. 1929); 1 dau., Neil Rose (Mrs. John W. Heiss, (dec.); m. 2d, Lily Braxton Wallace, Nov. 3, 1934, 1 son, George Braxton. Grad. asst. agr. Clemson Coll., 1902; agrl. asst. U. Fla., 1903; sci. asst., experiments in growing and mfg. tea in America, Dept. Agr., 1903-12;

supervising tea examiner to adminstr. Tea Act, 1912-29; studied in Far East, cultivation, mfr. and comml. handling of tea, for U.S. Govt., 1917-18; plant mgr. Maxwell House Tea div. Gen Foods Corp., 1929-48; independent tea cons. from 1948. Past. pres. Merchants & Mfrs. Assn. of Bush Terminal; tea cons. General Foods Corp., Anthhony Gibbs, United Coffee and Tea Instant; mem. U.S. Bd. Tea Experts, 1917-47; past pres. Tea Assn. U.S.A. Mem. N.Y. So. Soc., S.C. Soc. N.Y.C., Clemson Coll. Alumni (past pres. N.Y. chpt.). Democrat. Episcopalian. Clubs: Tea Club (pres. N.Y.C.); Cosmos (Washington); Rockaway Hunting (Lawrence); Lawrence Beach (Atlantic Beach, N.Y.). Author of departmental bulls. and pamphlets on tea and cassina; contbr. encys. Patentee machine for pruning tea; processes for manufacture of beverages from cassina (an American plant containing caffeine); radio-tel. device; processes for preparing tea and resultant products. Home: Washington D.C. Died July 21, 1973; buried Confederate Cemetery, Fredericksburg, Va.

MITCHELL, J. MURRAY, govt. ofcl.; b. Washington, Mar. 20, 1898; s. John Murray and Lillian (Talmage) M.; grad. St. Marks Sch., 1917; student Harvard, 1921; m. Lanier Comly, June 28, 1919 (dec. Apr. 1950); children—Lillian Talmage (Mrs. David Blair Hamilton), J. Murray, Jr.; m. 2d Phyllis Brewster Burke, June 22, 1951. Joined N.Y. Trust Co., N.Y. City, and predecessors, 1919, v.p., 1928-38; sec. N.Y. Clearing House Assn., 1937; dir. several corps., ednl., charitable, med. organs.; exec. officer, spl. adv. to chief E.C.A. Mission, Am. Embassy, Brussels, Belgium, 1948-49; asst. to C.E. Wilson, dir. Office Def. Moblzn., Washington, since 1950; by appointment of Pres. Truman, represents Mr. Wilson on sr. staff Nat. Security Council. Served as 2d lt., U.S. Army, World War I; Am. adv. to Civilian Tech. Corps. (British), 1941; spl. asst. to chief Naval Air Transport Service, and spl. asst. dir. Army Specialist Corps, 1942; asst. exec. officer, Officer Procurement Service Army Service Forces, 1942, spl. service div., 1943-44; dep. chief plans and operations div. G-5 (mil. govt.) sect. Allied Force Hdqrs., Mediterranean Theatre of Operations, 1944-45; advanced through grades from lt. col. to col. Decorated Legion of Merit; officer Order of British Empire; Order of Crown of Italy; Bronze Battle stars; Croix de Guerre with Palm (France). Mem. Huguenot Soc. Episcopalian. Mason. Clubs: Tuxedo, Links, Racquet and Tennis, Colony (N.Y. City); Metropolitan, Chevy Chase (Washington). Home: Washington, D.C. Died Sept. 21, 1973.

MITCHELL, JOHN GORDON, educator; b. Tenn., Sept. 14, 1878; s. Spencer and Mary (Young) M.; ed. Central Normal Coll., Waddy, Ky., Viola. (Tenn.) Coll., Dibrell Normal Sch., Sparta, Tenn.; A.B., George Peabody Coll. for Teachers, Nashville, Tenn., 1897; A.M., U. of Okla., 1919; m. Elsie Judson Gold, of Gordonsville, Tenn., Sept. 3, 1907; 1 dau., Mary Gordon. County supt. schs., Smith Co., Tenn., 1904-05; prin. high sch., Gordonsville, Tenn., 1902-04; supt. city schs., Checotah, Okla., 1905-11, Pryor, Okla., 1911-19; pres. Central State Teachers Coll., Edmond, Okla., from 1919. Democrat. Methodist. Mason (32°, K.T., Shriner). Kiwanian. Home: Edmond, Okla.†

MITCHELL, JOHN HARRINGTON, physician; b. Columbus, O., Jan. 14, 1904; s. Albert D. and Margaret A. (Harrington) M.; student Fordham, 1921-22; A.B., Ohio State U., 1928, M.D., 1928; m. Norma Prasuhn, June 4, 1932; children—Suzanne, James. Intern Grant Hosp., Columbus, 1928-29; resident physician St. Francis Hosp., Columbus, 1929-31; resident pathologist White Cross Hosp., Columbus, 1931-33; resident psychiatry Columbus State Hosp., 1958, 59, Ohio State U., 1960, 61; instr. pathology coll. medicine Ohio State U., 1931-33, asso. clin. prof. medicine, 1949-52, clin. prof. medicine, 1952-75; engaged in pvt. practice psychiatry and allergy; staff Mt. Carmel Hosp. Pres. Met. Health Council, 1946. Fellow Am. Coll. Allergists (pres. 1950-51), A.C.P.; mem. A.M.A. (chmn. sect. allergy 1970-71), Beta Theta Pi, Alpha Kappa Kappa. Roman Catholic. Club: Scioto Country. Author tech. treatises psychosomatic factors in allergic disorders. Home: Columbus, O. Died Feb. 11, 1972.

MITCHELL, LEBBEUS (HORATIO), author; b. Judsonia, Ark., Dec. 13, 1879; s. Alpheus B. and Martha (Freeman) M.; student State University of Iowa, 1899-1903; m. Muriel Jane Moscrip, June 21, 1916; children—Barbara Ruth (Mrs. Kenneth Louis Walter), Robert Moscrip. Began career as reporter on Republican, Cedar Rapids, Iowa, 1903; dramatic editor and critic, Kansas City Post, 1908-12; later with New York Evening Telegram, New York Globe, asst. dramatic editor and critic, New York World, and press editor The Film Daily; was theatrical advance agent and pres. rep. Wintrhop Ames and Guthrie McClintic; publicity rep. Goldwyn Pictures Corp., First National Pictures, Inc., Warner Bros. Pictures, etc, Republican. Author: Bobby in Search of a Birthday, 1916; The Circus Comes to Town, 1921; Here, Tricks, Here! 1923; One Boy Too Many, 1926; The Parachute Murder, 1933; The Murder of the Resurrected Man, 1936. Home: Bayside, L.I., N.Y.†

MITCHELL, LYNN BOAL, educator; b. Piqua, O., June 14, 1881; s. Thomas E. and Nan B. (McClay) M.; B.A., Ohio State U., 1903; M.A., Cornell U., 1904, Ph.D., 1906; student Stanford, 2 quarters, 1919, summer 1929; m. Grace Louise Taylor, July 2, 1907; children—David Boal, Thomas Jerome. Fellow Cornell U., 1905-06; instr. Latin and Greek, Winona Acad., Winona Lake, Ind., 1906-08; prof. Latin and Greek, William and Vashti Coll., Aledo, Ill., 1908-12; became prof. Latin and Greek, U. of N.M., 1912, also dean Coll. Arts and Sciences, 1917-29, dir. summer session, 1922-25, became chmn. Div. of Honors, 1939; liaison agent for Army and Navy, 1942; now retired; prof. Latin, U. of Okla., summer 1917, Ohio State U., summer 1920. Mem. N.E.A., Classical Assn. Middle West and South (v.p. for N.M.), Am. Assn. Univ. Profs., Medieval Acad. America, State Schoolmasters' Club of N.M. (pres. 1926), Phi Beta Kappa, Phi Kappa Phi, Pi Gamma Mu, Theta Alpha Phi, Phi Alpha Theta. Episcopalian (lay reader). Mason (33°, K.T., Red Cross of Constantine, grand master, 1944-45). Wrote the Latinity of Trokelowe and Blaneford. Contbr. Dictionary British Mediaeval Latin, also to ednl. publs. Home: Albuquerque, N.M.†

MITCHELL, MARTHA ELIZABETH BEALL JENNINGS;, b. Pine Bluff, Ark., Sept. 2, 1918; student Stephens Coll., U. Ark.; B.A., U. Miami; m. Clyde W. Jennings (div.); 1 son, Jay; m. 2d, John Mitchell, 1957 (separated 1973); 1 dau., Martha. Address: New York City, N.Y. Died May 31, 1976.

MITCHELL, REXFORD SAMUEL, univ. pres.; b. Manawa, Wis., Jan. 5, 1896; s. Leonard and Winifred (Bard) M.; A.B., Lawrence Coll., 1920; A.M., U. of Chicago, 1925; Ph.D., U. of Wis., 1937; m. Muriel Larson, June 9, 1921; children—Muriel Elizabeth, Jane Kevill. Instr. social science and speech State Teachers Coll., River Falls, Wis., 1920-28, dean of men, 1923-28; prof. of speech, asst. to pres., asso. dean, alumni sec., Lawrence Coll., Appleton, Wis., 1928-39; pres. Wis. State U. (now U. Wis. at La Crosse), 1939-65. Served with A.E.F., World War, 1917-19. Mem. Am. Legion, Phi Beta Kappa, Tau Kappa Alpha, Sigma Phi Epsilon. Club: Rotary (La Crosse). Home: La Crosse, Wis. Died July 4, 1973.

MITCHELL, ROLAND BURNELL, med. scientist; b. Denton, Tex., Mar. 24, 1910; s. Robert Marion and Robbie (Hawkins) M.; B.S., N. Tex. State Coll., 1932; M.A., U. Tex., 1937, Ph.D., 1939; m. Julianne Still, Sept. 6, 1938; children—Bonnie Ann, Susan. Sci. tchr. Tex. pub. schs., 1928-34; supr. sci. tchr. S.W. Tex. Tchrs. Coll., 1935-37; bacteriologist Bur. Plant Industry, Dept. Agr., 1937-42, Tex. Pub. Health Labs., 1942; asst. dir. bur. labs. Fla. Bd. Health, 1946-48; prof. pub. health bacteriology U. Fla., 1947-48; chief dept. aerobiology Sch. Aviation Medicine, USAF, 1948-51, chief dept. microbiology, 1951-57, acting dir. med. sci. div., 1954-57, dir., 1957-59; chief med. scis. dept. Sch. Aerospace Medicine, Aerospace Med. Div., Brooks AFB, Tex., 1959-61, chief biosystems research div. USAF Sch. Aerospace Medicine, Aerospace Med. Div., 1961-63; dir. biol. scis. Office Dep. for Research and Development, Hdqrs. Aerospace Med. Div., 1963-71; dir. research Fla. Div. Health, Jacksonville, from 1971. Served from 1st lt. to maj. USAAF, 1942-46. Mem. Soc. Am. Bacteriology, Soc. Exptl. Biology and Medicine, Aeromed. Assn., Assn. Mil. Surgeons, Sigma Xi. Methodist. Home: Jacksonville, Fla. Died May 15, 1974; interred Denton, Tex.

MITCHELL, STEPHEN ARNOLD, lawyer; b. Rock Valley, Ia., Mar. 3, 1903; s. Stephen Arnold and Dorothy Norton (Higgins) M.; student Ia. and Ore. parochial and pub. schs.; student Creighton U., 1922-23, hon. degree, 1958; LL.B., Georgetown U., 1928; hon. degree De Paul U., 1957, St. Bernards Coll., 1958; m. Evelyn Josephine Miller, Feb. 16, 1931; children—Stephen Arnold, Michael (dec.), John Anthony. Dairy farmer, Waterloo, Ia., 1920-21; credit mgr. Gen. Motor Acceptance Corp., Washington, 1924-28, legal and exec. positions N.Y. office, 1928-32; asso. Taylor, Miller, Busch & Boyden, Chgo., 1932-36, partner, 1936-42; chief French div. Lend Lease Adminstrn., Washington, 1942-44; adviser on French econ. affairs Dept. of State, Washington and Paris, France, 1944-45; partner Bishop, Mitchell & Burdett, 1945-50, Mitchell, Conway and Bane, 1950-53, Mitchell and Conway, 1953-62, Mitchell & Russell, from 1962, Mitchell, Mitchell & Alley, Santa Fe and Taos, N.M., from 1964. Chmn. 1st No. Savs. & Loan Assn., Taos. Counsel, Commn. to Investigate Dept. of Justice, 1952; mem. Chgo. Med. Center Com., 1951-52; dir. Fair Campaign Practices, Inc. Chmn. Dem. Nat. Com. 1952-55; del. and chmn. adv. com. rules Dem. Nat. Conv., 1956, counsel rules com., 1960; del. nat. conv., 1956, 64, 68; chmn. McCarthy for Pres. conv. com.; vice chmn. Humphrey-Muskie Citizens com., 1968. Trustee Ft. Burgwin Center, De Paul U.; regent, v.p. Museum N.M. Roman Catholic. Clubs: Tavern, University (Chgo.): Federal City (Washington). Author: Elm Street Politics, 1959. Co-Author: As We Knew Adlai, 1966. Home: Rancho de Taos N.M. Died Apr. 23, 1974.

MITCHELL, THOMPSON HAMPTON, communications exec.; b. New Boston, Tex., May 7, 1901; s. Reuben Malin and Minnie F. (Cooper) M.; grad. Severn Sch., 1921; B.S., U.S. Naval Acad., 1925; m. Eugenie Quist Stanley, 1948; 1 son, Thompson Hampton. Mem. engring. dept. RCA, San Francisco, 1927-28, dist. mgr., Los Angeles, 1928-30. Honolulu, T.H., 1930-35; mgr. RCA Communications, Los Angeles, 1935-42. exec. v.p., 1944-53, dir., from 1944, pres. 1953-66, chmn. exec. com., 1966-70; pres., dir. Radio Corp. of Philippines, Manila, from 1944; adv. com. Bankers Trust Co. N.Y. Served to col. Signal Corps, AUS, 1942-44. Decorated Legion of Merit; recipient Marconi Medal for Achievement in Radio. Mem. Am. Ordnance Assn., I.E.E.E., Newcomen Soc. Am., Mil. Order World Wars, Navy League U.S. Episcopalian. Clubs: Rotary, Propeller, N.Y. Yacht, Am. Yacht. Harvor View, India House, Overseas Press. Patentee for communications system. Home: Bronxville, N.Y. Died Nov. 11, 1973.

MITFORD, NANCY, writer; b. London, Eng., Nov. 28, 1904; d. Lord Redesdale and Sydney Bowles. Author: Pursuit of Love, 1945; Love in a Cold Climate, 1947; The Blessing, 1950; Madame De Pompadour, 1954; Noblesse Oblige, 1957; Voltaire in Love, 1958; Don't Tell Alfred, 1961; Pursuit of Love, 1963; Water Beetle, 1963; The Sun King, 1966; Ladies of Alderly; Letters During The Years 1841-1850; 1967; Frederick the Great, 1970. Home: Versailles, France. Died June 30, 1973.

MOBLEY, ERNEST CRAMER, clergyman; b. Monroe, Ga., Oct. 31, 1878; s. William Thomas and Elizabeth E. (Guthrie) M.; ed. U. of Ky. and Coll. of the Bible, Lexington, Ky.; grad. study, Columbia and Oxford, Eng.; m. Elizabeth Irby, Oct. 31, 1905; children—Wilfred Irby, Ernest Cramer Alfred Wallace, Benjamin Irby. Ordained ministry Christian (Disciples) Ch., 1900; pastor successively Rome, Ga., Southampton, Eng., Winnipeg, Can., Gainesville, Tex., Amarillo, Tex., until 1920; lyceum lecturer, 1920-21; pastor Central Ch., Huntington, Ind., 1921-22, First Church, Oklahoma City, 1923-32, became pastor First Ch., Little Rock, 1932. Served with Y.M.C.A. in France, World War. Del. to World's Missionary Conf., Washington, D.C., 1925; mem. Commn. Evangelism, World Peace and Christian Citizenship, Internat. Soc. Christian Endeavor. Served as mem. or officer Okla. State Church Board, Okla. Christian Missionary Board, Okla. Sunday School Assn., Nat. Commission on Ministers of Christian Ch., Oklahoma City Chamber Commerce, Okla. Ednl. Council; dir. Anti-Saloon League of America; pres. Ark. Christian Endeavor Union, and Ministerial Alliance Greater Little Rock; active mem. Chamber Commerce, Y.M.C.A. and Y.W.C.A.; mem. bd. Ark. Christian Missions. Democrat. Mason (K.T., Shriner); mem. O.E.S., Clubs: Rotary (dir.), Men's Dinner (v.p.). Contbr. Christian Evangelist, Dallas News, Atlanta Constitution, Kansas City Star. Home: Enid, Okla.

MOBLEY, LAWRENCE EUGENE, educator; b. Holly, Mich., July 8, 1925; s. Albert Earl and Naomi Irene (Marvin) M.; B.A. with honors, Andrews U., 1950; M.A., U. Mich., 1952; Ph.D., Mich. State U., 1961; m. Ila Jane Morefield, June 10, 1951; children—James Irving, Lari Elizabeth. Instr. English, librarian Adelphian Acad., Holly, 1950-52; instr. English, Loma Linda U., Riverside, Cal., 1952-56, asst. prof., 1956-61, asso. prof., 1961-65, prof., chmn., 1965-70, prof., from 1972; prof., chmn. dept. English, San Bernardine Valley Coll., San Bernardino, Cal., 1965-68; prof., chmn. English dept. Saniku Gakuin Coll., Japan, 1970-72. Served with AUS, 1943-46; ETO. Mem. Modern Lang. Assn., Nat. Council Tchrs. English, Western Lit. Assn., Tchrs. English as a Second Lang. Democrat. Seventh-day Adventist. Contbr. articles on Mark Twain to profl. jours. Home: Loma Linda, Cal. Died May 15, 1974; interred Monticeto Meml. Cemetery, Loma Linda, Cal.

MÓD, ALADÁR, author; b. Karakó, Hungary, 1908; s. Sandor and Rosalia (Major) Oszkó; Secondary sch. tchr. degree, U. Budapest, 1934, Dr. Hist. Scis. 1954; m. Margaret Spira, June 21, 1938; children—Anna (Mrs. János Valkó), Gábor. Underground polit. activity; co-worker of leftist periodical Gondolat 1934-37; editor communistic sci. periodical Tarsadalmi Szemle, 1945-54; prof. Marxist dept. Roland Eotvos U., Budapest, Hungary, 1954-73. Decorated major state and party medals. Mem. Soc. for Disseminating Sci. Knowledge (v.p.), Acad. Scis. (hist. com.). Mem. Communist party. Author: Materialistic Ontology, 1934; 400 years Struggle for an Independent Hungary, 1943; Revolution and Independence-War 1848-49, 1948; Marxism and Patriotism, 1965; Dispute of our age 1965; Fate and Responsibility, 1967; Alternatives, 1970; Nation—Socialist Nation, 1974. Mem. editorial bd. Valóság. Home: Budapest, Hungary. Died Nov. 1973.

MOE, HENRY ALLEN, found. exec.; b. Monticello, Minn., July 2, 1894; s. Christian and Sophia Martha (Gaustad) M.; B.S., Hamline U., 1916, L.H.D., 1929; Rhodes Scholar from U.S. at large to Oxford U., England, 1920-23; B.A. in Jurisprudence, first class honors, Brasenose Coll., Oxford, 1922, B.C.L., 1923, M.A., 1933; L.H.D., Kenyon Coll., 1941; LL.D., Johns Hopkins, Yale, Columbia, Wesleyan U.; Litt.D., New Sch. for Social Research; D.Litt., Princeton, 1955, Emory U.; M.D., Cath. U. Chile, 1957; LL.D., U. Cal., 1958, Brown U., Swarthmore Coll., Rockefeller U., LL.D., Dartmouth Coll., 1966; D.C.L., University Oxford (Eng.), 1960; L.H.D., So.Ill. U.; m. Edith Louise Monroe, Dec. 18, 1924; 1 son, Christian Hollis. Admitted to New York bar; barrister at law of the Inner Temple, London. Editorial staff St. Paul Dispatch and

Pioneer Press, 1916-17; Hulme lecturer in law, Oxford U., 1923-24; lecturer in law, Columbia U. Law Sch., 1927-29; regents prof. U. Cal., Berkeley, 1965. Dir. Leatherstocking Corp., Cooperstown, N.Y. Hon. vice chmn. N.Y. State Council on Arts; chmn. Nat. Endowment for the Humanities, 1965-66. Trustee, v.p. Maude E. Warwick Fund; pres. emeritus John Simon Guggenheim Meml. Found.; trustee emeritus Wesleyan U.; trustee Scriven Found. (cons.); trustee, cons. Clark Found.; vice chmn. trustees Mus. Modern Art, N.Y.; chmn. trustees Inst. Modern Art N.Y.; trustee Am. Acad. in Rome; pres., chmn. trustees Mary Imogene Bassett Hosp.; pres., trustee Farmers' Mus., Cooperstown, N.Y.; trustee Louis Comfort Tiffany Found., Harry Frank Guggenheim Found. Recipient Award for Distinguished Service to the Arts, Nat. Inst. Arts and Letters, 1955, Public Service medal Nat. Acad. Scis., 1958; award of merit, Phila. Mus. Coll. Art; Cosmos Club award, 1965; Laurel Leaf award Am. Composers Alliance, 1966. Hon. fellow Brasenose Coll., U. Oxford, England, 1955; Benjamin Franklin fellow Royal Soc. Arts, London. Fellow Am. Acad. Arts and Scis.; mem. Am. Philos. Soc. (pres. 1959-70), N.Y. State Hist. Assn. (chmn. bd. trustees, pres.), Assn. Am. Rhodes Scholars (asst. treas., dir.), Phi Beta Kappa. Served to lt. (j.g.) USNRF, active duty 3 yrs., World War I. Club: Century (hon) (N.Y.C.). Home: Sherman, Conn. Died Oct. 2, 1975; buried churchyard Congl. Ch., Sherman, Conn.

MOEHLMAN, CONRAD HENRY, church history; b. Meriden, Conn., May 26, 1879; s. Rev. John Henry and Helen (Coords) M.; U. of Rochester, 1898-1901, M.A., 1917, D.D., 1929; B.A., U. of Mich., 1902; B.D., Rochester Theol. Sem., 1905; post-grad. work, U. of Chicago, 1908-09; Ph.D., U. of Mich., 1918; D.D., Hillsdale (Mich.) Coll., 1929; m. Bertha Young, Jan. 30, 1906 (died Apr. 15, 1949), children—Arthur, Robert, Frederick (dec.), Grace Anna (Mrs. Gilbert B. Forbes); married second, Carol R. Webster, May 21, 1954. Ordained to the ministry of the Bapt. Ch., 1905; pastor Central City, Neb., 1905-06; instr. ch. history, Rochester Theol. Sem., 1907-08, Hebrew lang. and lit., 1909-10, asso. prof., 1910-12, Trevor prof. N.T. interpretation, 1913. Pettingill prof. ch. history, 1919-28; lecturer on religion, U. of Rochester, 1922-28, 1942-46; Michigan School of Religion, 1927; James B. Colgate prof. history Christianity, Colgate-Rochester Div. School, 1928-44; emeritus professor 1944; vis. prof., sch. of religion U. So. Cal., 1952-55, Oberlin, 1956. Mem. Soc. Bibl. Literature and Exegesis, American Church Hist. Soc. (pres. 1933), Archeol. Soc., Am. Geog. Soc., Conf. on Science, Philosophy and Religion (a founder), Phi Beta Kappa, Theta Phi, Pi Gamma Mu, Theta Chi. Clubs: City (pres. 1936-37), Torch, Alpha Chi. Author: Theos. Soter as Title and Name of Jesus; Topics in Church History; Getting Acquainted with the Bible; Outline of the History of Christianity; The Unknown Bible; The Story of the Ten Commandments; What is Protestantism?; Sayings of Jesus; The Catholic-Protestant Mind; When All Drank and Thereafter; The Story of Christianity; The Christian-Jewish Tragedy; History of Christianity—Methodology; The American Constitutions and Religion; The First Christians and Jesus; In Defense of the American Way of Life; Protestantism's Challenge; Christianty and War; Understanding the Contemporary World Crisis; School-Church: The American Way; The Church as Educator; The Wall of Separation between Church and State, 1951; Ordeal by Concordance, 1955. Editor of the Record of Rochester Theological Seminary, 1913-19, 1921-23; editor Colgate-Rochester Bulletin, 1930-38. Gave address upon "The College Man and Religion in the Future" at centennial celebration of the founding of U. of Mich., 1937. Address: Rochester, N.Y.†

MOELLER, EDITH, condr.; b. Gelsenkirchen, Germany, Oct. 7, 1916; d. Friedrich Wilhelm and Anna Karoline (Wehling) Moeller; student Tochterschule Gelsenkirchen, 1931-38, seminar fur Fursorgerinnen, 1939-42. Choir leader, dir. Children's Home for Homeless Children, 1956-75; condr. Obernkirchen Children's Choir. Address: Buckeburg, Germany., Died July 10, 1975.

MOELMANN, JOHN MATTHEW, lawyer; b. Chgo., Nov. 20, 1911; s. Clarence E. and Mabel (Buckelmueller) M.; student Northwestern U., 1928-30; A.B. with honors, U. Ill., 1932, J.D., 1934; m. Harriet Bannatyne, Sept. 9, 1939; children—John B., Lynda J. (Mrs. Charles Vonesh), Lawrence R. Admitted to Ill. bar, 1934, practiced in Chgo.; sr. partner Hinshaw, Culbertson, Moelmann, Hoban & Fuller, from 1949. Bd. dirs., sec. Oak Park YMCA; bd. dirs., Def. Research Inst., pres., 1966-69, chmn. bd., from 1970; trustee Union League Found. for Boys; trustee Seabury-Western Theol. Sem., 1963-69, Northwestern Mil. and Naval Acad., 1959-70; gov. Ins. Hall of Fame, chmn., 1971-73. Served to lt. USNR, World War II. Fellow Am. Coll. Trial Lawyers; mem. Soc. Trial Lawyers (past pres.). Am., Ill., Chgo. (bd. mgrs. 1963-65) bar assns., Internat. Assn. Ins. Counsel. Episcopalian. Clubs: Union League (Chgo.); Lake Geneva (Wis.) Country. Home: Oak Park, Ill. Died Aug. 8, 1974; interred Forest Home Cemetery, Forest Park, Ill.

MOFFETT, ROSS E, artist; b. Clearfield, Ia., Feb. 18, 1888; s. James Warren and Margaret (Gelvin) M.; student Art Inst. Chgo., 4 yrs., Art Students' League, N.Y.C., with Charles W. Hawthorne; m. Dorothy Lake Gregory, 1920 (dec. Oct. 1975); children—Elizabeth Gregory, Alan Whitney. Landscape and figure painter, and etcher; series mural paintings Eisenhower Mus., Abilene, Kan.; exhibited ann. shows at large gallaries adeand mus. U.S., including Worcester Art Mus., 1975, Provincetown Art Assn., 1975; represented in various pub. collections. Asst. prof. Sch. Fine Arts, Miami U., Oxford O., 1932-33, 1945-46. Recipient numerous prized and awards. Mem. Audubon Artists, Nat. Acad., Mass. Archaeol. Soc., Delta Phi Delta (hon.). Served in U.S. Army, 1918. Author: Art in Narrow Streets, 1964. Home: Provincetown, Mass., Died Mar. 13, 1971.

MOHR, WESLEY GEORGE, devel. co. exec.; b. Douglas, Wyo., May 3, 1925; s. Carroll Shonerd and Julia (Loser) M.; student U. Colo., 1942-45; m. Elizabeth C. Klick, Apr. 7, 1946; children—Wesley G., Larry D. Constrn. mgr. Deal Lumber & Constrn. Co., Laramie, Wyo., 1946-50; project mgr. M. H. Golden Constrn. Co., San Diego, 1951-56; pres. Mohr Adams Plourde Co., 1956-60; v.p. Del E. Webb Corp., 1960-66; pres. Del E. Webb Internat., 1966-67; pres. Embarcadero Plaza Inc., 1967-68; exec. v.p. Daley Corp., 1968-69, Caster Mobilhomes Corp., 1969; sr. v.p., dir. new communities div. AVCO Community Developers Inc., 1969-73; sr. v.p. Western region U.S. Home Corp., 1973-75; dir. Met. Investment Co., Rancho Presidio Hotel, Inc., Lamorada Internat. Dir. San Diego County Planning Congress, 1952-54; chmn. Chula Vista Planning Commn., 1953-54; mem. Am. Indsl. Devel. Council, 1956-75; chmn., South Bay Coordinating Com., 1952-54. Served from ensign to lt. (j.g.) USNR, 1942-46, PTO; lt. comdr., 1950-51, Korea; comdr. Res. ret. Mem. A.I.A. (asso.), Sigma Chi. Home: San Diego, Cal. Died 1975.

MOJICA, JOSE, tenor; b. San Gabriel, Jalisco, Mexico, Sept. 14, 1899; s. Jose and Virginia M. (de Mojica) M.; grad. Escuela de Argicultura y Veterinaria, Mexico City, 1915; studied music with Alejandro Cuevas; unmarried. Début in Mexico City, Oct. 5, 1916; sang with Rosa Raisa, Mexico City, 1917, with Titta Ruffo and Raisa, also with Caruso, 1919; joined Chicago Opera Assn., Nov. 1919. Principal roles; Dinorah, leading with Galli Curci, 1919-20; leading roles in Thais, with Mary Garden, 1920-21; creator of the leading tenor role in the Russian opera The Love of Three Oranges; in Salome, 1921-22, Pelleas and Melisande, 1925, with Garden. Made 12 Spanish feature productions for Fox Film Corp., from 1929; later making Spanish pictures in Mexico and touring in concerts in South America. Address: Lima, Peru., Died Sept. 21, 1974.

MOLEY, RAYMOND, journalist; b. Berea, O., Sept. 27, 1886; s. Felix James and Agnes (Fairchild) M.; Ph.D., Baldwin-Wallace Coll., 1906, LL.D., 1933; A.M., Oberlin Coll., 1913; Ph.D., Columbia, 1918; LL.D., Washington and Jefferson Coll., 1933, Claremont Men's Coll., 1966, U. Hartford, 1970; Litt.D., Miami U.; D.C.L., Whitman Coll., 1950; m. Eva Dall, Aug. 14, 1916; children—Malcolm, Raymond (twins); m. 2d, Mrs. Frances S. Hebard, Jan. 15, 1949. Supt. schs., Olmsted Falls, Ohio, 1907-10; tchr. West High Sch., Cleve., 1912-14; instr. and asst. prof. politics Western Res. U., 1916-19; dir. Cleve. Found., 1919-23; asso. prof. govt. Columbia, 1923-28, prof. pub. law, 1928-54; asst. sec. state, 1933; editor Today mag., 1933-37; contbg. editor Newsweek mag., 1937-68. Dir. Americanization, Ohio State Council Def., 1918-19; research dir. N.Y. State Crime Commn., 1926-27; cons. crime surveys of Mo., Ill., Pa. and Va.; mem., research dir. N.Y. State Commn. Adminstrn. of Justice, 1931-33. Trustee Clarement Men's Coll., Baldwin-Wallace Coll., Vt. Coll.; adviser Lincoln Found. Author: Lessons in American Citizenship, 10 edits., 1917-30; The State Movement for Efficiency and Economy, 1918; Lessons in Democracy, 1919; Commercial Recreation, 1919; Parties, Politcs and People, 1921; The Cleveland Crime Survey (a summary), 1922; Politics and Criminal Prosecution, 1929; Our Criminal Courts, 1930; Tribunes of the People, 1932; After Seven Years, 1939; The Hays Office, 1945; Twenty Seven Masters of Politics, 1949: How to Keep Our Liberty, 1952; What Price Federal Reclamation, 1955; Political Responsibility, 1958; The American Century of John C. Lincoln, 1962; The Republican Opportunity, 1962; The First New Deal, 1966; Daniel O'Connell: Nationalism Without Violence, 1974; also articles on politics and nat. affairs. Editor, part author Mo. Crime Survey, 1926; part author Ill. Crime Survey, 1929. Home: Phoenix, Ariz. Died Feb. 18, 1975.

MOLINA, EDWARD CHARLES DIXON, engr.; b. N.Y.C., Dec. 13, 1877; s. Antonio Mariano and Therese (St. Remy) M.; student pub. schs.; D.Sc. (hon.), Newark Coll. Engring., 1952; m. Virginia Costales, Nov. 29, 1900; children—Antonio Edward, Virginia Teresa. With engring. dept. Am. Tel. & Tel. Co., 1901-18, dept. development and research, 1919-33; switching theory engr. Bell Telephone Labs., N.Y.C., 1934-42; spl. lectr. mathematics Newark Coll. Engring., 1946-58, adjunct professor, from 1958. Alternate on John Fritz Medal Board of Award, 1958. Division war research Columbia, 1943-45. Awarded Elliott Cresson medal Franklin Inst., 1952. Fellow Inst. Math. Statictics, A.A.A.S., Royal Econ. Soc. London, Am. Statis Assn., Am. Inst. E.E. (bd. examination from 1952), Am. Soc. Quality Control; mem. Am. Math. Soc., Math. Assn. Am., Am. Astron. Soc., Econometric Soc., Met. Mus. Art, Telephone Pioneers of Am., Acoustical Soc. Am., Am. Soc. Engring. Edn., Omicron Delta Kappa, Eta Kappa Nu (eminent mem.). Democrat. Clubs: Railroad Machinery (N.Y.C.); Essex County Torch (East Orange, N.J.). Invented translator in dial telephone systems, 1905. Home: East Orange, N.J.†

MOLINARE, ANTHONY WILLIAM, lawyer; b. Custer Park, Ill., Oct. 19, 1901; s. Antonio and Maria (Russo) M.; student Crane Jr. Coll., 1926; LL.B., Chgo. Kent Coll. Law, 1924; m. Marie Thresa Girard, Aug. 24, 1925; 1 dau., Lois Marie (Mrs. Roland A. Abrahamson). Engr., sales engr. Link Belt Co., 1919-25; admitted to Ill. bar, 1924; patent lawyer Goodman Mining Machine Co., 1926-27; asso. firm Burton & Burton, 1927-34; pvt. practice in Chgo., 1934-39; mem. firm Bair, Freeman & Molinare, 1939-69, sr. partner, 1965-69; sr. partner Molinare, Allegretti, Newitt & Witcoff, Chgo., 1970-72. Mem. Am., 7th Circuit Fed. bar assns., Am., Chgo. patent law assns. Roman Catholic. Club: North Shore Country (Glenview, Ill.). Patentee trailers, locks, laundry appliances fields. Home: Wilmette, Ill. Died June 5, 1974; buried All Saints Cemetery, Des Plaines, Ill.

MOLLENKOPF, JACK KENNETH WEBSTER, coll. football coach; b. Convoy, O., Nov. 24, 1903; s. Albert Edison and Rose Altha (Webster) M.; B.S., Bowling Green U., 1931; m. Gladys Ruddock, Aug. 18, 1928; 1 son, Jack Phillip. Football coach, tchr., Rossford, O., 1930-34, Waite High Sch., Toledo, 1934-47, football line coach Purdue U., 1947-55, head football coach, from 1956. Home: West Lafayette, Ind., Died Dec. 4, 1975.

MOLLER, KNUD OVE, pharmacologist; b. June 21, 1896; Ph.D., M.D., U. Copenhagen. Prof. pharmacology, 1937-66; chmn. Danish Pharmacopoeia Commn., 1938-67; chmn. Danish Com. of Fgn. Scientists in Danish Labs., 1946-51; mem. Nordic Pharmacopoeia Council, 1948-67; co-founder, editor Acta Pharmacologica et Toxicologica, 1945-64; co-founder, chmn. Nordic Soc. for Pharmacology; co-founder, mem. Internat. Council for Pharmacologists, 1953-62; mem. WHO expert adv. panel internat. pharmacopoeia, 1951-71, WHO sub-com. on internat. proprietary drug names, 1959-71. Mem. Royal Danish Acad. Scis. and Letters. Author: Pharmakologie fur Zahnarzte, 1934; Stimulants, 1945; Manual in Pharmacology, 1966. Address: Helsingor, Denmark. Died Aug. 1973.

MOLLET, GUY, govt. ofcl., mem. French parliament; b. Flers, Orne, France, Dec. 31, 1905; s. Pierre and Marie (Lelievre) M.; Licencie eslettres and langs., Diplome d'Etudes Superieures, 1932; m. Odette Fraigneau, Apr. 23, 1930; children—Jacqueline, Dolly. Maitre d'internat., 1923-25; prof. Arras Lycee de Garcons, 1925-48; pres. du Conseil General du Pas-de-Calais, Maire d'Arras, 1945; mem. Commission de la Constitution, 1941-46; v.p. Conseil du Gouvernement Leon Blum, 1947; sec. gen. Socialist Party, Paris, from 1946; French rep. Consultative Assembly of Council of Europe at Strasbourg since 1948; president of that Assembly, member of the Permanent Commission of that Assembly, pres. of Commn. for gen. affairs; minister of state for Council of Europe, in govt. Pleven, July 1950-Mar. 1951, v.p. Council in govt. of Queuille, Mar. to Aug. 1951; mem. Assembly of European common property of coal and steel, pres. Socialist group. Vice pres. Socialist International; pres. Socialist Intergroup of Assembly of Council of Europe. Decorated Legion of Honor, Medaille de la Resistance, Croix de Guerre, Palmes Academiques (France); several foreign decorations. Home: Arras France. Died Oct. 3, 1975.

MONROE, VAUGHN, orchestra leader; b. Akron, O., Oct. 7, 1911; s. Ira C. and Mabel Monroe; ed. pub. schs., 2 yrs. coll.; m. Marian Baughman; children—Candace, Christina. Trumpeter, choir dir., singer until 1940; leader of own orchestra, records for R.C.A. Victor; own radio show; restaurant owner, Boston. Mem. Police Athletic League, N.Y.C. Methodist. Club: N.Y. Athletic. Composer: Racing with the Moon, Something Sentimental, and others. Home: Stuart, Fla. Died May 21, 1973.

MONTAGUE, JOSEPH FRANKLIN, surgeon; b. N.Y.C., Aug. 6, 1895; s. Joseph and Mary Frances (LeDieu) M.; M.D., N.Y. U., 1917. Began practice medicine, specializing in intestinal diseases, 1917; mem., lectr. rectal clinic Bellevue Med. Coll. Served with USN and USMC, World War; surgeon N.Y. State Nautical Sch., 1919, N.Y. State Indsl. Commn., 1920; founder Med. Writers' Inst.; cons. Instrument Research Inst., from 1958; prof. affiliate in communications Colo. State U. Fellow Soc. Nuclear Medicine, Internat. College Surgeons, Am. Geog. Soc., Am. Pub. Health Assn., Am. Geriatric Soc., Am. Med. Writers Assn. (pres. N.Y. chpt.), Am. Coll. Nutrition, Am. Coll. Gastroenterology (asso.); mem. A.M.A., Am. Med. Authors Assn. (pres.), Soc. Tech. Writers and Editors, N.Y., N.Y. County med. socs., World Med. Assn., N.Y.

Path. Soc., N.Y. Acad. Sci., A.A.A.S. Order Mil. Surgeons, Health Guild Am. (pres.), Am. Anthrop. Assn., Am. Soc. Tropical Medicine, Am. Assn. History Medicine, Pub. Health Assn. N.Y., Am. Chem. Soc., Instrument Soc. Am., Am. Astron. Soc., Authors Guild Am., Soc. Tech. Writers, Gourmet Soc. (pres.), N.Y. Soc. Med. Research, Am. Legion, Am. Polar Soc., Royal Soc. Health, Eng., Am. Physicians Art Assn. (pres.), Friends Albert Schweitzer (pres.), Nat. Assn. Sci. Writers, N.Y. Physicians Art Assn., Internat. Soc. Study Diseases of Colon (pres. 1968-71), Nu Sigma Nu. Clubs: N.Y. Athletic, Lambs, Chemist, Princeton Explorers (N.Y.C.); National Press (Washington), Circumnavigators, Overseas Press. Author: Pruritus of the Perineum, 1923; Treatment of Hemorrhoids, 1926; Troubles We Don't Talk About, 1927; Enfermedades que no se habla; 1927; Maux dont On Ne Parle Pas, 1927; Taking the Doctor's Pulse, 1928; Psyllium Seed The Latest Laxative, 1932; I Know Just the Thing for That, 1934; Why Bring That Up, 1935; How to Conquer Constipation, 1938, Broadway Stomach, 1940; Nervous Stomach Trouble, 1941; How to Overcome Nervous Stomach Trouble, 1943; Desordenes Nerviosos del Estomago, 1948; Mali Chi Si Taccioni, 1956; Leiden Von Denen Man Nicht Spricht, 1956; Disturbi Nervosi dello Stomaco, 1957; How to Overcome Colitis, 1957; How to Conquer Nervous Stomach Trouble, 1964; The Why of Albert Schweitzer, 1966; Your Heart, 1969. Editor in chief Health Digest mag.; cons. editor Surg. Digest, Clinical Medicine, Medical Digest. Editor: Interviews with Cardiologists on Heart Ailments, 1968. Contbr. Jour. Am. Med. Assn., Internat. Clinics, Internat. Record Medicine. Pioneer in writing popular health books and in application of motion pictures to surg. edn.; inventor sigmoidoscopes and proctologic instruments. Home: Garrison, N.Y. Died Feb. 6, 1974.

MONTANA, BOB, cartoonist; b. Stockton, Cal., Oct. 23, 1920; s. Ray and Roberta (Pandolfini) M.; student Boston Mus. Fine Arts, 1932-33, Phoenix Art Inst., 1943, Art Student's League, N.Y.C., 1946; m. Helen W. Wherett, Apr. 13, 1946; children—Paige, Lynn, Raymond, Donald. Creator syndicated comic strip Archie, 1942; v.p. Village Gallery, Inc., 1966-75, Archie Comic Publs., Inc., 1965-75. Served with AUS, 1942-46. Mem. Nat. Cartoonist Soc. Home: Meredith, N.H. Died Jan. 4, 1975.

MONTGOMERY, EDWARD GERRARD, agricultural specialist; b. Milan, Mo., May 10, 1878; s. Richard Shadow and Elizabeth (Mooney) M.; B.S., U. of Neb., 1906, M.A., 1909; m. Ruth Bell, June 18, 1908; 1 dau., Nancy C. Prof. agronomy, U. of Neb., 1906-11; prof. farm crops, Cornell U., 1912-20; chief of foreign marketing, U.S. Dept., Agr., 1920-21; chief of food stuffs div., U.S. Dept. Commerce, 1921-34; exec. sec. Canning Code, 1935; research work on agrl. economics, Nat. Industries Conf. Bd. and Brookings Instn., 1936-37; research, Commodity Exchange Adminstrn., U.S. Dept. Agr., 1937; economist, Social Security Board, 1938-41, Bd. of Economic Warfare from 1941, Bureau of Foreign and Domestic Commerce, 1944-48, ret., 1948. Mem. Alpha Zeta, Sigma Xi fraternities. Unitarian. Club: Cosmos, Author: Examining and Grading Grains (with T. L. Lyon), 1908; The Corn Crops, 1912; Productive Farm Crops, 1914; also numerous bulletins and mag. articles. Home: Chevy Chase, Md.†

MONTGOMERY, GEORGE GRANVILLE, corp. exec.; b. Hollister, Calif., Oct. 4, 1894; s. Edward B. and Mary Lyman (Swan) M.; student U. Cal. at Berkeley, 1912-13; LL.D., St. Mary's College, 1958; m. Claudine Spreckels, Apr. 17, 1929; children—Anne (Mrs. Putney Westerfield), George Granville, Claudine (Mrs. Stephen C. Brown). Admitted to Calif. bar, 1916; engaged in practice of law, Oakland, Calif., 1916-20; asst. mgr. Am. Factors, Ltd., San Francisco, 1921-28; gen. partner Anderson & Fox, San Francisco, 1928-33; vice pres. Castle & Cooke, Ltd., sugar factors and shipping agents, San Francisco, 1934-54, chmn. finance com., 1950-54; chmn., dir. Kern County Land Co.; dir. Wells Fargo Bank, Castle & Cook, Inc., Stockdale Devel. Corp., Pacific Nat. Life Assurance Co., Watkins-Johnson Co., Pacific Lumber Co. Mem. Bus. Council. Adv. council Stanford U. Grad. Sch. Bus.; regent U. San Francisco; trustee St. Luke's Hosp.; bd. advisers Nat. Fund Med. Edn. Served as capt. 144th F.A., AEF, 1917-19. Republican. Episcopalian. Clubs: Bohemian, Pacific-Union, San Francisco Golf, Burlingame Country; The Links (N.Y.C.); Eldorado Country (Palm Springs); Cotton Bay (Eleuthera). Home: Hillsborough Cal. Died Jan. 1, 1974.

MONTGOMERY, JOHN RHEA, inst. exec.; b. Trenton, N.J., Nov. 6, 1892; s. John A. and Helen B. (Stryker) M.; student Rand Collegiate Sch., 1905-09; A.B., Princeton, 1913; m. Mary Carroll Frick, Apr. 14, 1917; children—Mary Carroll (Mrs. P. M. Beecheno), Helen B. (Mrs. J. H. Jarratt, Jr.). Bank runner, 1913; with William Salomon & Company (merged with Blair & Co., Inc.), 1913-20; with Blair & Co., Inc., 1920, pres., 1939-45, ret.; pres. Overlook Hosp., Summit, N.J., 1947-51, Peabody Inst., Balt., 1956-61. Chmn. adv. council Md. Employment Security Bd., 1956-57. Trustee Peabody Inst.; trustee, mem. exec. com. Church Home and Hosp., Balt. Served as lt. (j.g.) USN, World War I. Episcopalian. Mason. Clubs: Princeton, Anglers (N.Y.C.); Short Hills (N.J., past pres.); Colonial (Princeton); Maryland, Elkridge (Balt.). Home: Baltimore, Md. Died Sept. 8, 1973.

MONTGOMERY OF ALAMEIN, 1ST VISCOUNT OF HINDHEAD, (Field Marshal Bernard Law Montgomery); b. Nov. 17, 1887; s. Rt. Rev. H. H. Montgomery; m. Elizabeth Carver (dec. 1937); 1 son, David. Comdr.-in-chief Brit. Occupation Forces in Germany, 1945-46; chief Imperial Gen. Staff, 1946-48; chmn. Western Europe Comdrs.-in-chief Com. 1948-51; dep. supreme allied comdr., Europe, 1951-58. Decorated knight of Garter, knight Grand Cross of Bath, companion Distinguished Service Order. Author: The Memoirs of Field-Marshal Montgomery, 1958; The Path to Leadership, 1961. Home: Isington Mill nr Alton, Hampshire, England. Died Mar. 24, 1976.

MOODY, ERNEST ADDISON, educator; b. Cranford, N.J., Sept. 27, 1903; s. John and Anna Mulford (Addison) M.; A.B., Williams Coll., 1924; M.A., Columbia, 1933, Ph.D., 1936; m. Josephine Lane, Oct. 11, 1928; children—Anne Elizabeth (Mrs. Walter J. Frank), Jean Farrington (Mrs. Halford Maninger) Mem. faculty Columbia, 1939-51; operator ranch in Tex., 1951-58; prof. philosophy U. Cal. at Los Angeles, 1958-70, chmn. dept. 1961-64; spl. research history logic, history mechanics, medieval philosophy. Recipient Nicholas Murray Butler Silver medal in philosophy Columbia, 1956. Fellow Mediaeval Acad. Am. (Haskins medal 1956); mem. Am. Philosophical Association (president Pacific div. 1963), History Sci. Soc. Author: The Logic of William of Ockham, 1935; Truth and Consequence in Medieval Logic, 1952. Co-author The Medieval Science of Weights, 1952. Contbr. articles profl. jours. Home: Camarillo, Cal., Died Dec. 21, 1975.

MOODY, SIDNEY CLARKE, business exec.; b. Evanston, Ill., Nov. 13, 1895; s. Francis Kempton and Emma (Bridges) M.; A.B., Williams Coll., 1917; m. Frances Trent Glenn, May 7, 1924; children—Mary Aileen, Sidney Clarke, Jr. Began with Calco Chem. Co., 1919; asst. gen. mgr. Calco Chem. div. Am. Cyanamid Co., 1943-45, gen. mgr. from 1945, dir. from 1944, v.p., 1946-60, ret. Served as 2d lt. F.A., U.S. Army, 1918. Mem. Phi Beta Kappa, Zeta Psi. Republican. Presbyterian. Clubs: Williams' Chemists, Maidstone. Home: Plainfield, N.J. Died Nov. 20, 1974.

MOON, HENRY DUKSO, educator, physician; b. San Francisco, Sept. 28, 1914; s. Yang M. and Chan S. (Lee) M.; A.B., U. Cal. at Berkeley, 1935, M.A., 1937, M.D., 1940; m. Lona A. Lowe, Nov 22, 1941; children—Nancy L., Henry B., Thomas L. Intern U. Cal. Hosp., 1941, Franklin Hosp., San Francisco, 1942; resident U. Cal. Hosp., 1943-44; instr. pathology U. Cal. at San Francisco, 1943-44, asst. clin. prof. pathology, 1947-52, lectr. pathology and oncology, 1952-53, acting chmn. dept. legal medicine, 1953, asso. prof. pathology, 1953-58, prof. pathology, from 1958; chmn. dept. pathology U. Cal. Med. Sch., from 1956; pathologist U. Cal. Hosp., 1953-56, pathologist in chief, from 1956; vis. pathologist San Francisco Gen. Hosp., from 1952; chief pathology service VA Hosp., San Francisco, 1947-51, later cons. pathologist; cons. surg. gen. USPHS, NIH, 1954-65; sci. adv. bd. Armed Forces Inst. Pathology, 1965-70. Served from 1st lt. to maj. M.C., AUS, 1944-47. Diplomate Am. Bd. Pathology. Mem. A.A.A.S., A.M.A., Cal. Soc. Pathologists, Cal. Med. Assn., San Francisco Med. Soc., Am. Coll. Pathologists, Am. Assn. Pathologists and Bacteriologists, Am. Soc. Exptl. Pathology, Internat. Acad. Pathology, Exptl. Biology and Medicine, N.Y. Acad. Sci. Died Aug. 2, 1974.

MOON, VIRGIL HOLLAND, pathologist; b. Craig, Ind., July 31, 1879; s. William Louis and Lida Ann (Stanley) M.; A.B., U. of Kan., 1910; M.Sc., 1911; M.D., Rush Med. Coll., 1913; m. Beryl Kelly, Dec. 20, 1916; 1 dau., Gladys W. (Mrs. Harold C. Colborn); m. 2d, Magdalena Altmann, May 8, 1955. Began as research pathologist, McCormick Inst., Chicago, Ill., 1911-14; fellow in pathology, Rush. Med. Coll., 1913; prof. pathology and bacteriology, Ind. Univ., Indianapolis, Ind., 1914-27; prof. pathology, Jefferson Med. Coll., Philadelphia, Pa., 1927-48; emeritus, 1948; prof. of pathology University of Miami from 1950; vis. prof. athology, Bowman Gray Sch. Medicine, Winston-Salem, N.C., 1948; chief visiting pathologist Phila. Gen. Hosp.; dir. of laboratories Jefferson Hosp., 1927-48; civilian cons., Surgeon Gen. office, 1945. Mem. Am. chpt. Internat. Soc. Geographic Pathology (chmn. 1931-53), A.A.A.S., Am. Acad. Polit. and Soc. Sci., Am. Assn. Pathol. and Bacteriol., Soc. Exptl. Biol., Soc. Exptl. Pathol., Coll. Am. Pathologists, Am. Human Serum Assn., Coll. Physicians (Phila.), Pathol. Soc. Phila. (pres. 1932-33), Physiol. Soc. Phila., A.M.A. (chmn. sect. on pathology and physiology, 1946), Pa. State and Philadelphia County med. socs., Sigma Xi, Alpha Omega Alpha, Phi Chi. Author: Shock and Related Capillary Phenomena, 1938; Shock; Dynamics, Occurence and Management, 1942; chapt. on dynamics of shock in Blood Substitutes and Blood Transfusion, 1942; Chapt. on physiologic and chemical factors in shock, Medical Physics, 1944; sect. on disturbances of circulation, Anderson's Text Book of Pathology, 1948; chap. on Shock, Ferris Reconstructive and Plastic Surgery, 1949; articles on anti-vivesection in mags.; numerous reports of experimental studies on shock, inflammation, edema, pneumonia, cirrhosis, etc. in various med. and other sci. jours. Home: Coral Gables, Fla.†

MOORE, ARTHUR JAMES, bishop; b. Waycross, Ga., Dec. 26, 1888; s. John Spencer and Emma Victoria (Cason) M.; student Emory U., 1909-11; D.D., Asbury Coll., Wilmore, Ky., 1922, Central Coll., Fayette, Mo., 1924, Emory U., 1934; LL.D., Asbury, 1930, Southwestern U., 1935, Randolph-Macon Coll., 1939, Fla. Southern Coll., 1941; m. Mattie T. McDonald, Apr. 26, 1906; children—William Harry, Wilbur Wardlaw, Alice Evelyn, Dorothy Emma, Arthur James. Entered ministry M.E. Ch., S., 1909, ordained, 1914; pastor various chs. until 1920, Travis Park Ch., San Antonio, Tex., 1920-26, First Ch., Birmingham, Ala., 1926-30; elected bishop May 20, 1930; bishop in charge missionary activities Meth. Church in China, Japan, Czechoslovakia, Belgium, Belgian Congo, Poland, Korea, 1934-40; president Wesleyan College, Macon, Ga., 1941. Mem. Commn. Inter-Denominational Relations and Church Union, 1934-39; pres. bd. of Missions and Church Extension, Meth. Ch. Mason (32°, K.T.). Mem. Phi Beta Kappa. Author: The Sound of Trumpets, 1934: Central Certainties, 1942. Christ After Chaos, 1944; Christ and Our Country, 1945; The Mighty Saviour, 1952; Immortal Tidings in Mortal Hands, 1953. Home: Atlanta, Ga. Died June 1974.

MOORE, CARL ALLPHIN, educator; b. Doniphan, Mo., May. 23, 1911; s. Charles Burton and Janey (Allphin) M.; B.S. in Petroleum Engring., U. Tulsa, 1936; M.S. in Geology, State U. Ia., 1938, Ph.D. in Geology, 1940; m. Mary Catherine Moody, Aug. 27, 1937; children—Willis Henry, Caroline Kahoe. Research geologist Standard Oil Devel. Co., 1939-42; field subsurface geologist Carter Oil Co., 1942-46; prof. geology, chmn. Sch. Geol. Engring., U. Okla., 1946-62, prof. petroleum and geol. engring., from 1964; adminstr. Peace Corps in Bolivia, 1962-64. Recipient outstanding teaching award Okla. U. Found., 1953, Standard Oil Ind. Found., 1970, Brandon Griffith award as outstanding engring. prof., 1972. Mem. Am. Assn. Petroleum Geologists, Oklahoma City Geol. Soc., Sigma Xi, Gamma Tau Kappa, Pi Epsilon Tau, Sigma Gamma Epsilon. Baptist (deacon, Sunday Sch. tchr.). Author: Handbook of Subsurface Geology, 1963. Editor Biennial Geological Symposia, Univ. Okla, 1948-62; asso. editor Shale Shaker, 1953-54. Home: Norman, Okla. Died Apr. 14, 1973; interred Norman, Okla.

MOORE, CLYDE B., educator; b. Albion, Neb., Jan. 13, 1886; s. John W. and Altha L. (Book) M.; grad. Neb. State Tchrs. Coll., 1909, B. Ed., 1913; A.B., Neb. Wesleyan U., 1912; A.M. Clark U, 1916; Ph.D., Columbia, 1920; m. Leila M. Admire, Oct. 24, 1912 (dec. Mar. 1967) 1 dau., Maxine (Mrs. Milo J. Peterson). Tchr. rural schs., 1903-04; prin. village schs., 1907-08; supt. schs., 1909-15; prof. edn. Wis. State Normal Sch., La Crosse, 1917-19; psychologist U.S. Army, 1918-19; asst. prof. edn. U. Pitts., 1920-23, asso. prof., 1923-24, prof. charge extension div. chmn. Sch. Edn., 1924-25; prof. edn. Cornell U., from 1925. Spl. lectr. U. Ky., 1926; vis. prof. Columbia, summer 1930; lectr. tchrs. assns., ednl. cons.: dir. study 15 sch. systems Fund Advancement End., Ford Found., 1960; mem. Mid-Century White House Conf., 1950; mem. bd. of edn., Ithaca, New York; studied ednl. systems in Europe, 1932-33, 39, 52, Mexico, 1946, Japan, 1955-56; editorial consultant Inter-Am. Inst. Agrl. Scis., 1959; mem. Nat. Council for Accreditation Tchr. Edn., 1952-58. Recipient Alfred E. Smith award and gold medal, 1950. Fellow A.A.A.S.; mem. Am., N.Y. State ednl. research assns., Nat. Soc. Study Edn., N.E.A., Nat. Soc. Coll. Tchrs. of Edn., Nat. Council Social Studies, Dept. Supervisors and Dirs. Instrn., Am. Assn. Sch. Adminstrs., N.Y. State Sch. Bds. Assn. (Distinguished Service award 1954; pres.), N.Y. State Ednl. Conf. Bd. (chmn.), A.A.U.P., Phi Delta Kappa, Kappa Phi Kappa, Alpha Kappa Delta, Phi Kappa Phi. Rotarian. Author books, from 1916, latest being: (with L. A. Wilcox) The Teaching of Geography, 1932; Our American Citizenship, 1936; (with Arville Wheeler Spelling to Write: (with W. E. Cole) Sociology in Educational Practice, 1952; J. Sterling Morton; Arbor Day Boy, 1962; Robert H. Goddard: Rocket Boy, 1966; Frederic Remington: Young Artist, 1971. Sr. author of Scribner Social Studies Series, 8 vols., 1948-60. Contbr. to ednl. jours. Home: Ithaca N.Y. Died Nov. 4, 1973; cremated.

MOORE, ESCUM LIONEL, physician; b. Mattie, Ky., Dec. 17, 1907; s. Columbus Botner and Gypsie Leonora (McComas) M.; grad. Berea Coll. Acad., 1927; B.A., Berea Coll., 1930; B.M., U. Con., 1936, M.D., 1937; m. Edna Carolyn Rinck, June 20, 1936; children—Carolyn Ann, Escum Lionel. Intern, Good Samaritan Hosp., Lexington, Ky., 1936-37, resident, 1937-38; practice of medicine, Lexington, 1938-73, specializing internal medicine; staff Good Samaritan, Central Baptist hosps. Trustee Berea Coll. Served from 1st lt. to maj., M.C., AUS, 1942-46. Mem. A.M.A., So., Ky. med. assns., Am. Assn. Railroad Surgeons, Fayette County Med. Soc., Berea Coll. Alumni Assn. (exec. com.), Tau Kappa Alpha, Phi Rho Sigma. Presbyn. Mason. (Shriner). Home: Lexington, Ky., Died June 29, 1973; buried Lexington (Ky.) Cemetery.

MOORE, GEORGE GORDON, railway ofcl.; b. Cin., O., Aug. 4, 1878; s. Gideon Moore and Rose (Brignole) M.; grad. Woodward High Sch., Cincinnati, 1895; m. Sallie Maud McCay, Dec. 24, 1899 (died May 8, 1918); children—Charlotte Eugenia (wife of Brig. Gen. Paul Hyde Prentiss, U.S. Army, ret.), George Gordon; m. 2d, Alvina Hollenberg, Oct. 18, 1919 (died Apr. 17, 1951). Clk. C.&O. Ry., Cin., 1897; employed as clerk, stenographer, freight agt., for various railroads, 1897-1912; supt. Galveston, Houston & Henderson R.R. Co., Galveston, 1912-18, v.p. gen. mgr., sec. and treas., 1920-43, president, 1943-55; dir. chairman operating com. and terminal supt., Galveston Terminal Assn., 1918-20; dir. First Hutchings-Sealy National Bank. Pres. Galveston C. of C., 1934-36. Trustee Rosenberg Library (v.p. bd. mgrs.), Galveston County Meml. Hosp. Rep. Epis. Mason. Club: Country. Home: Galveston, Tex.†

MOORE, HAROLD EMERSON, educator; b. Vigo County, Ind., Feb. 28, 1903; s. Charles Henry and Rosa (Jones) M.; A.B., Ind. State Teachers Coll., 1924; M.A., Ind. U., 1929, Ed.D., 1945; m. Mary M. Parish, Aug, 2, 1925 (dec.); children—Shirley, Charles, Harold; m. 2d, Allis Haren, Aug. 1959. Rural school teacher, Sullivan County, Ind., 1921-22, high schs., 1924-25; high sch. principal, Vigo County, Prairie Creek, 1925-26, Vigo County, Otter Creek, 1926-31; summer instr. State Teachers Coll., 1926-31, 1935-36; asst. dir., elementary and high sch. inspection, State Dept. of Edn., 1931-33; county supt. of schs., Vigo County, Ind., 1933-36; principal U. Sch., dir. Bur. Teacher Recommendations, asst. prof. edn. Ind. U., 1936-46, prof. edn., 1950-51; supt. schs., Mishawaka, Ind., 1946-48; supt. schs., Kansas City, Mo., 1948-50 specialist U.S. Office Edn., locating bldg. and needs of schs. war affected areas, 1941-43; asst. reg. dir. Def. Health and Welfare, 1942-43; prof. edn., dir. ednl. research Sch. Edn., U. Denver, 1951-61; supt. schs., Littleton, Colo., 1961-64; prof. edn. Coll. Edn., Ariz. State U., Tempe, 1964-73, emeritus, from 1973, also chmn. dept. ednl. adminstrn. Chmn. Nat. Conf. Profs. Ednl. Administrn., 1954-55. Mem. Council Ednl. Facilities Planners, Am. Assn. Sch. Administrn., Am. Edn. Research Assn., Ariz. Edn. Assn., N.E.A. (life), Nat. Soc. Study Edn., Terre Haute Literary Club, Phi Delta Kappa. Author: Indiana Elementary and High School Attendance Register (with R. W. Holmstedt), 1933; Twentieth Century Woodbook in Government (with Gale Smith), 1935; The Government of Indiana (with O. G. Jamison), 1936; Current Practices in Institutional Teacher Placement (with others) 1941; Columbus, Indiana, School Building Survey, 1945; Rushville, Bedford, Hagerstown, Crown Point and school bldg., surveys, 1945-46; The Modern Secondary School Plant, 1948; The Big City School Superintendency; Staff Participation in Policy Making and Planning in Large City School Systems, 1951; Personnel Administration in Education, 1955; A Research and Development Activity Related to 1965 High Priority Areas in School Personnel Administration; The Administration of Public School Personnel, 1966. Editor: High Priority Areas in School Personnel Administration 1965; Planning for Education in 2000 A.D., 1967; Design for Lifetime Learning in a Dynamic Social Structure: Education 1980, 68. Home: Scottsdale, Ariz. Died June 1, 1974.

MOORE, HARRY WILLIAM, tool co. exec.; b. Freeport, Ill., Mar. 1, 1891; s. David and Mary (Bender) M.; student U. Ill., 1910, Internat. Corr. Schs.; m. Margaret Bickenback, 1912; 1 son, K. Alden. Tool maker Nat. Sewing Machine Co., Belvidere, Ill., 1910-12; instr. advanced manual tng. East High Sch., Des Moines, 1913; instr. algebra and geometry West High Sch., Waterloo, Ia., 1914; tool and die maker Nat. Cash Register, Dayton, O., 1915, 21-24; supt. design dept. Legler Eilerman Die Casting, Dayton, 1917; with armament design dept. Wright Field, Dayton, 1927-28; chief mech. engr. Master Electric Co., Dayton, 1928-30; with Globe Tool & Engring. Co., Dayton, from 1930, chmn. bd., from 1948. Mem. bd. Harry and Margaret Found. Home: Sarasota, Fla. Deceased.

MOORE, HENRY TRUMBULL, lawyer; b. El Paso, Tex., May 22, 1903; s. Henry Walter and Leila (Trumbull) M.; A.B., U. Tex., 1924, LL.B., 1926; m. Bonnie Platt, Oct. 10, 1928 (div. 1941); children—Robert H., Henry Trumbull; m. 2d, Jeanette Amos, Nov. 5, 1941 (div. June 1954); m. 3d, Jean L. Higginbotham, July 18, 1955 (div. 1966); 1 dau., Maureen A.; m. 4th, Ruth Ebert, 1966; stepchildren—Susan Wheat, William B. Wheat. Admitted to Tex. bar, 1926, Cal. bar, 1939; practiced in El Paso, Tex., 1926-39, Los Angeles, 1939-74; mem. firm Moore & Welker, 1939-41, Moore, Howarth & Trinkaus, 1947-52, Moore, Trinkaus & Binns, 1953-55, Moore, Trinkaus & Currer, 1956-58, Moore & Trinkaus, 1958-62, Moore & Moore, 1962-74; spl. asst. atty. gen. State Tex., 1931; judge corp. ct., El Paso, 1927-31. Elector for Tex. in Presdl. election, 1936. Mem. Am., Tex., Los Angeles County, Beverly Hills (gov. 1962, 69-71), Westwood, Inter-Am. bar assns. State Bar Cal. (del. 1964-74, 69-74), Am. Judicature Soc., Acad. Polit. Sci., Internat. Acad. Law and Sci. (v.p.), Am. Trial Lawyers Assn., Soc. Internat. Law, Los Angeles World Affairs Council, Am. Trial Lawyers Assn., Tex. Bar Found. (charter), Phi Delta Phi, Alpha Phi Epsilon. Presbyn. Home: Malibu, Cal. Died May 27, 1974.

MOORE, JOHN PEABODY, electrical engr.; b. Columbus, Ga., Nov. 6, 1879; s. Montague Montgomery and Sarah Elizabeth (Peabody) M.; ed. high sch., Columbus, and Ala. Poly. Inst.; m. Nellie Gertrude Williams of Indianapolis, Ind., Oct. 28, 1908. With Gen. Electric Co., Schenectady, N.Y., 1898-1904; Nat. Ry. Constrn. Co., Indianapolis, Ind., 1905-08; instr. elec. ry. engring, Pa. State Coll., 1909-10; elec. engr. Wyandotte Constrn. Co., Kansas City, Mo., 1911-13; engring. dept. Westinghouse Electric & Mfg. Co., 1914-15; sr. elec. engr. Interstate Commerce Commn., Bur. of Valuation, Washington, 1916-21; appraisal engr. U.S. Treas. Dept., Washington, D.C., 1922-23; elec. and appraisal engr., 1924-26, Mem. Am. Inst. E.E., Am. Electric Ry. Assn., Am. Assn. Engrs., Washington Soc. Engrs., Am. Soc. Engrs., Sigma Alpha Epsilon, Nat. League Masonic Clubs. Mason (32°, Shriner). Republican. Methodist. Home: Washington, D.C.†

MOORE, JOSEPH WALDRON; b. Cohoes, N.Y., Nov. 4, 1879; s. Joseph William and Jane Elizabeth (Younglove) M.; M.D., Albany Med. Coll. (Union U.), 1901; m. Mabel G. Trafton, Oct. 1906 (died Oct. 2, 1937); m. 2d, Susan D. Harper, Jan. 10, 1942 (died July 27, 1944). In hosp. service N.Y. State, 1906-30; acting supt. Matteawan State Hosp., 1927-30; chmn. N.Y. State Parole Bd., 1930-38, and 1940-42. Capt. later maj. Med. Corps, U.S. Army, Jan. 1918-July 1919. Mem. Am. Psychiatric Assn. Presbyterian. Mason (K.T.). Club: Ft. Orange. Home: Albany, N.Y.†

MOORE, PHILIP WYATT, business exec.; b. Brookline, Mass., Oct. 18, 1880; s. Emery Beals and Sarah Montelius (Tompson) M.; prep. edn., pub. schs., Brookline; B.S., Mass. Inst. Tech., 1901; m. Caroline Seymour Daniels, Jan. 28, 1909; children—Philip Wyatt, Harriet Lucy, Francis Daniels. With engring. dept. Pennsylvania Steel Co., Steelton, Pa., 1901-03, sales dept., Chicago, 1903-06; joined Poor & Co. 1906, became pres., also dir. of company and subsidiaries. Mem. Delta Upsilon. Clubs: University, Chicago, Commercial, Indian Hill, Tavern, Laurentian. Home: Hubbard Woods, Ill.†

MOORE, RAYMOND CECIL, geologist; b. Roslyn, Wash., Feb. 20, 1892; s. Bernard Harding and Winnifred (Denney) M.; A.B., Denison University, 1913, Sc.D., 1935; Ph.D., U. of Chicago, 1916; m. Georgine Watters, 1917; 1 dau., Marjorie Ann; m. 2d, Lilian Boggs, 1936. Instructor in geology Denison Univ., 1912-13; mem. U.S. Geological Survey, 1913-49; instr. geology U. of Chicago, 1916; asst. prof., 1917; asst. prof. geology U. Kan., 1916-18, asso. prof., 1918-19, prof. from 1919, Solon E. Summerfield distinguished prof. geology, from 1958, also head dept., 1920-39, 40-41, 52-54. State geologist of Kan., 1916-54; principal geologist Kan. Geol. Survey, from 1954; geologist govt. boat expdn. through Grand Canyon of Colorado, Ariz., 1923; research asso. in petroleum geology, auspices Am. Petroleum Inst., 1926-27; geologist Gen. MacArthur's staff, Tokyo, Japan, 1949; Fulbright prof. Rijks Universiteit Utrecht, 1951-52; Walker-Ames prof. U. Wash., 1957; cons. Humble Oil and Refining Co., Ariz. Power Authority on Colo. River Devel. Served as U.S. Army, fuels and lubricants div. Office Quartermaster Gen., Washington. Recipient Hayden Meml. Geol. medal Phila. Acad. Natural Sci., 1956, medal Paleontological Soc., 1963, Prix Paul Fourmarier from Royal Acad. Belgium 1966, Mary Clark Thompson medal Nat. Acad. Sci., 1970, Distinguished Service citation U. Kan., 1970. Fellow Geol. Soc. Am. (v.p. 1956-57, pres. 1957-58), Paleontological Soc. (pres. 1947), mem. Am. Assn. Petroleum Geologists (Powers medal 1959), Soc. Systematic Zoology (pres.), Kan. Geol. Soc., Soc. Econ. Paleontology and Mineralogy (hon. mem., pres. 1928), Am. Acad. Arts and Scis., geol. socs. of London (Wollaston medal 1968), Belgium, France, Holland, Switzerland, Germany, Argentina, Japan, Accademia Nazionale di Scienze Lettere e Artidi Modena (hon.), Norske Videnskaps-Akademi i Oslo, Internat. Geological Congress (pres. commn. on stratigraphy, 1952-60), Am. Commn. on Stratigraphic Nomenclature (chmn. 1947-49), Sigma Xi, Phi Beta Kappa, Lambda Chi Alpha, Gamma Alpha, Sigma Gamma Epsilon. Baptist. Mason. Club: University. Author: Historical Geology, 1949; Invertebrate Fossils, 1952. Organizer, dir. Treatise on Invertebrate Paleontology (over 250 world's leading specialists as authors), 27 vols., 1948; various other books and technical articles on petroleum, regional and structural geology, physiography, stratigraphy, and invertebrate paleontology (especially Paleozoic crinoids, bryozoans, and corals). Editor Bull. of Am. Assn. Petroleum Geologist, 1920-26, Jour. Paleontology, 1930-39, Jour. Sedimentary Petrology, 1931-39; Univ. Kansas Paleontological Contributions, from 1946. Home: Lawrence, Kan. Died Apr. 16, 1974; buried Pioneer Cemetery, Lawrence, Kan.

MOORE, ROBERT LEE, mathematician; b. Dallas, Nov. 14, 1882; s. Charles Jonathan and Louisa Ann (Moore) M.; B.S. and A.M., U. Tex., 1901, fellow, 1901-02; Ph.D. (fellow 1903-05), U. Chgo., 1905; m. Margaret MacLellan Key, Aug. 19, 1910. Asst. prof. math. U. Tenn., 1905-06; instr. math. Princeton, 1906-08, Northwestern U., 1908-11; instr. math. U. Pa., 1911-16, asst. prof., 1916-20; asso. prof. U. Tex., 1920-23, prof., 1923-37, distinguished prof., 1937-53, prof. math. and astronomy, from 1953. Vis. lectr. Am. Math. Soc., 1931-32. Fellow A.A.A.S. (v.p. 1947); mem. Nat. Acad. Scis., Am. Math. Soc. (v.p. 1923, pres. 1937-39), Societe Polanaise de Mathematique, Tex. Acad. Sci. Author: Fundamental Theorems Concerning Point Sets, 1936; Foundation of Point Set Theory, 1932, rev. edit., 1962. Asso. editor Trans. Am. Math. Soc., 1913-26; editor Colloquium publs., 1928-36, also colloquium lectr., 1929. Home: Austin, Tex. Died Oct. 4, 1974; buried Austin, Tex.

MOORE, WILLIAM F., oil co. exec.; b. Richwood, Ga., June 12, 1899; s. Fleming Jordan Moore and Ruth (Lester) M.; student pub. schs. of Birmingham, Ala.; m. Mary M. Manley, Jan. 6, 1925; children—Robert William, Virginia Carole. Power plant operator The Texas Co., Port Arthur, Tex., 1920-22, power engr. refining dept., Lockport, Ill., 1922-25, asst. to mgr. exec. dept., 1925-29, asst. to v.p. exec. dept., 1929-30, chief operating officer Gasoline Products Co., Process Management Co., Gray Processes Corp., N.Y. City, 1930-38, asst. mgr. purchasing dept. The Texas Co., N.Y. City, 1938-39, mgr. purchasing dept., 1939-43, asst. to v.p. fgn. operations dept., 1943-45, gen. mgr. fgn. operations dept., 1945-47; pres. Arabian Am. Oil Co., San Francisco and N.Y. City, 1947-53; indsl. cons. to dir. Fed. Bank of Lebanon and to chmn., dir. Middle East Export Press, Beirut, Lebanon, 1952-58. Served in U.S. Navy, 1916-20, overseas. Mem. Am. Petroleum Inst. Home: Bethesda, Md. Died May 3, 1975; interred Gate of Heaven Cemetery, Silver Spring, Md.

MOOREHEAD, AGNES ROBERTSON, actress; b. Clinton, Mass., Dec. 6, 1900; d. John Henderson and Mary Mildred (McCauley) Moorehead; B.A. hon. doctorate Muskingum Coll., 1947; M.A., U. Wis.; Ph.D., Bradley U.; student Am. Acad. Dramatic Art; m. John Griffith Lee, June 5, 1930; m. 2d, Robert Gist, 1953. Began as teacher of public speaking and English, Centralized High Sch., Soldiers Grove, Wis. then teacher of dramatics at Dalton Sch., N.Y.C.; first stage appearance at Municipal Opera, St. Louis, then appeared with Coll. Dramatic Club and Am. Acad. Stock Co., N.Y.C.; founded Mercury Theatre; appeared in Marco's Millions, Scarlet Pages, All the King's Men, Courage, Soldiers and Women, The Pink Judge, Lord Pengo, Rivalry, Subscription Murder, 6161; appeared as an actress in motion pictures. Citizen Kane, 1941, Magnificent Ambersons, The Left Hand of God, 1955, The Big Street, Jane Eyre, Since You Went Away, Mrs. Parkington, Dark Passage, Johnny Belinda, Magnificent Obession, All That Heaven Allows, The Opposite Sex, The Swan, The Stratton Story, Show Boat, Untamed, Journey into Fear, Dragon Seed, Caged, Meet Me In Las Vegas, Raintree County, The True Story of Jesse James, Mainstreet to Broadway, The Blue Veil, The Conqueror, Pollyanna, Who's Minding The Store, The Jeanne Eagles Story, The Tempest, 20 and 2, Jessica, How The West Was Won, Hush, Hush, Sweet Charlotte, The Singing Nun, others. During 4 yrs. toured with Drama Quartette's prodn. Don Juan in Hell, 5 tours G. B. Shaws prodn.; toured with show Fabulous Redhead; toured with Paul Gregory's prodn. The Rivalry. First radio appearance as singer on KSO and KMOX, St. Louis, 1923-24, actor on Seth Parker Family Hour with Phillip Lord, radio program, 20 weeks; appeared on radio programs from 1929, including March of Time, Cavalcade; TV appearances including series Bewitched, Orson Welles Mercury Theatre of the Air, Shirley Temple Theatre, Hitchcock, Twilight Zone, Channing, Have Gun Will Travel, The Rebel, Night Gallery, The Virginian, Terror By Night, Suddenly Single, Dr. Frankenstein; seminar drama and speech University of Southern Cal. Records: Sorry Wrong Number, Our Common Heritage, Don Juan in Hell, The Psalms. Recipient N.Y. Film Critics award for best actress of 1942 for role as spinster in The Magnificent Ambersons; nominated for Academy Award for Mrs. Parkington and Magnificent Ambersons; recipient Radio Life award, Hollywood Fgn. Corrs. award for best supporting role in Mrs. Parkington; nominated for Acad. Award for Johnny Belinda, 1948; Emmy award Wild, Wild West, 1967, 6 Emmy nominations for Bewitched. Mem. Phi Beta (hon.), Lambda Alpha Lambda, Dalta Gamma. Presbyterian. Mem. O.E.S.; Rebeccas. Clubs: Twelfth Night, Town Hall (N.Y.C.); Episcopal Actors Guild. Home: Died Apr. 30, 1974; interred Dayton Meml. Park and Cemetery, Dayton. O.

MOORMAN, HENRY DEHAVEN, congressman; b. nr. Glen Dean, Ky., June 9, 1880; s. William Robert and Bettie (DeHaven) M.; ed. pub. schs.; unmarried. Admitted to Ky. bar, 1900, and began practice at Hardinsburg; pres. Hardinsburg Nat. Farm Loan Assn.; v.p. Bank of Hardinsburg & Trust Co.; County judge, Breckenridge Co., Ky., 1905-09; commonwealth atty., 9th Ky. Jud. Dist., 1914-27; mem. 70th Congress (1927-29), 4th Ky. Dist. Served in U.S. Vols., Spanish-Am. War; with Field Arty., U.S.A., France, World War. Pres. Breckenridge Memorial Assn. Mem. Commonwealth Attorney's Assn. of Ky. (pres.), Am. Legion (constl. com.). Democrat. Baptist. Mason (Shriner). Elk. Club: Pendennis (Louisville). Has developed Memorial Farms nr. Hardinsburg, in memory of brother, Lt. Roy E. Moorman. Home: Hardinsburg, Ky.†

MOORMAN, ROBERT BURRUS BUCKNER, educator, civil engr.; b. St. Louis, Nov. 12, 1904; s. Robert Buckner and Alice Patee (Burrus) M.; B.S. with honors, U. Ill., 1929, M.S., 1931; Ph.D., Ia. State Coll.,

1937; m. Josephine Margaret Nelson, Sept. 9, 1931. Grad. research asst. civil engring. U. Ill., 1929-31, spl. research asst. theoretical and applied mechanics, 1931; asst. prof. civil engring. U. Miss., 1932-35; from asst. to prof. civil engring. U. Mo., 1935-52; prof., chmn. civil engring. dept. Syracuse U., 1952-57; prof. civil engring. Poly. Inst. Bklyn., from 1957, head dept., 1957-67. Tchr. evening course structural frames U. Akron, 1943-44, grad. courses in structures U. Tex., summer 1950; structural engr. Svedrup & Parcel, summers 1939, 40, cons. applied mechanics, 1942-43, 46-48; structural designer, bur. yards and docks Navy Dept., summer 1940; engr. Boeing Aircraft Co., Seattle, summer 1941; structures cons. Goodyear Aircraft Corp., 1943-44; bridge engr. R. Stuart Royal & Consoer Townsend & Assos., 1944-45; engr. guided missiles Johns Hopkins Applied Physics Lab., 1945; cons. stress and analysis St. Louis Car Co., 1946, Tech. Appliance Corp., 1955-58; cons. structures Erdman & Hosley, engrs., 1954-57; cons. Syracuse (N.Y.) City Planning Commn., 1955-56; structural cons. Aluminum Assn., from 1963, John Graham & Co., 1970-71. Registered profl. engr., N.Y., Mo., Ky. Fellow Am. Soc. C.E. (pres. mid-Mo., Syracuse sects.; chmn. structures group Met. sect. 1965-66); mem. Am. Concrete Inst., Am. Soc. Engring. Edn., Internat. Assn. Bridge and Structural Engring., Sigma Xi, Tau Beta Pi, Sigma Tau, Chi Epsilon (nat. pres.), Phi Mu Alpha. Author: (with John I. Parcel) Analysis of Statically Indeterminate Structures, 1955. Contbr. articles to profl. publs. Home: Brooklyn, N.Y. Died Feb. 2, 1974.

MOORMAN, ROBERT WARDLAW, educator; b. Berwyn, Ill., Sept. 16, 1919; s. Thomas S. and Amanda (Clawson) M.; B.C.E., Clemson U., 1940; M.S., U. Ia., 1947, Ph.D., 1955. Naval architect Charleston (S.C.) Navy Yard, 1940-41; asst. prof. dept. engring. mechanics Clemson (S.C.) U., 1947-57, prof., head dept., from 1957. Served to maj. C.E., AUS, 1941-46; ETO; col. U.S. Army Res. Decorated Bronze Star medal. Registered profl. engr., S.C. Fellow Am. Soc. C.E.; mem. Am. Soc. Engring. Edn., Am. Acad. Mechanics, S.C. Soc. Engrs., Sigma Xi, Tau Beta Pi, Phi Kappa Phi. Episcopalian. Rotarian. Club: Clemson Fellowship. Home: Clemson, S.C. Died Feb. 17, 1974.

MOOS, CHARLES J.; b. St. Cloud, Minn., June 24, 1880; s. John C. and Mary (Henneman) Moos; M.A., St. John's U.; Ph.G., Minnesota School of Pharmacy, 1900; LL.B., St. Paul Coll. of Law, 1918; m. Katherine Grant, of Faribault, Minn., May 23, 1906; children—Gretchen, Malcolm. Exec. sec. to Gov. Van Sant, 1902-05; sec. State Bd. of Pharmacy, 1905-10; adv. mgr. Riverside Press, 1912-17; gen. industrial N.P.R.R., 1917-19; organizer, 1919, and v.p. McCree-Moos Co., gen. contractors; pres. Ben Franklin Building & Loan Assn.; vice pres. Joyce Insurance, Inc. Postmaster of St. Paul, 1921-33. Republican presidential elector, 1916; del. Rep. Nat. Conv., 1920; mem. Rep. State Central Com.; mgr. various polit. campaigns; dir. Roosevelt Memorial Assn., 1919. Mem. Minn. Pharm. Assn., Minn. Bar Assn., Northwestern Gen. Contractors' Assn., Minn. State Editorial Assn. Club: Minnesota. Home: St. Paul, Minn.†

MOOSBRUGGER, FREDERICK, naval officer; b. Oct. 9, 1900. Commd. ensign USN, 1923, advanced through grades to rear adm., 1953; head Pacific Fleet Tng. Command. Decorated Navy Cross. Died 1974.

MORA, JOSE ANTONIO, diplomat; b. Montevideo, Uruguay, Nov. 22, 1897; s. Jose Antonio and Emma (Otero) M.; LL.B., U. of Montevideo, 1923, LL.D. and Social Sciences, 1925; D.H.L., Rollins Coll., 1958; D.C.L., U. Pitts., 1959; LL.D., Colgate U., 1959; Dr.h.c., U. Salamanca, 1964, U. Ceará, 1964; m. Susana Nery, Oct. 14, 1943; children—Gladys, Susana, Juan A. Joined the civil service in Uruguay; sec. of legation, Madrid, Spain, 1926-28, Rio de Janeiro, 1928-30, Washington, D.C., 1929-30; dir, internat. orgn. in Ministry Fgn. Affairs, Montevideo, 1933-41, minister, 1971-72; minister plenipotentiary, Bolivia, 1942-45; del. of Uruguay to internat. confs.; adv. del. Conf. of San Francisco, 1945; dir. Bur. Internat. Orgn., 1945; rep. Uruguay on governing bd. of Pan Am. Union 1946-56; minister plenipotentiary, Washington, 1946-51, ambassador, 1951-56; vice chmn. Council of OAS, 1948-49, chmn., 1954-55; sec. gen. OAS, 1956-1968. Mem. Am. Soc. Internat. Law, Am. Soc. Polit. and Social Scis. Author: Sentido internacional del Uruguay, 1938; La organización judicial en la Conferencia de San Francisco, 1946. Home: Uruguay. Died Jan. 26, 1975.

MORAN, ALFRED E., physician; b. Chgo., Nov. 3, 1928; s. Edward and Sarah Moran; M.D., Loyola U., Chgo., 1955; m. Jeannette Sikler. Intern, Cook County Hosp., Chgo., 1955-56; resident in obstetrics and gynecology Little Company of Mary Hosp., Evergreen Park, Ill., 1958-61, later sr. staff; sr. staff St. Bernard's Hosp., Chgo.; active asso. staff Palos Community Hosp., Palos Heights, Ill., Christ Community Hosp., Oak Lawn, Ill. Served to capt. M.C., USAF, 1956-58. Diplomate Am. Bd. Obstetrics and Gynecology. Fellow Am. Coll. Obstetrics and Gynecology; mem. A.M.A. Home: Evergreen Park, Ill. Died Oct. 19, 1973; buried St. Mary's Cemetery, Evergreen Park, Ill.

MORAN, JULIA PORCELLI, sculptor; b. N.Y.C., Apr. 18, 1917; d. Francis Paul and Maria (Franchina) Porcelli; pvt. study art; student Art Students League; m. Philip R. Moran, Apr. 8, 1953; children—Terese, Angela J., Joseph P., Lauren F. Profl. sculptor, exhibited numerous group shows; chmn. Arts and Culture Com., Town of Greenburgh, N.Y.; initiator monthly cultural programs; lectr. in field; judge art shows, N.Y.C. and Westchester County. Executed life-size statue St. Thomas Aquinas, Buffalo. Dir. pub. relations White Plains (N.Y.) bd. Girl Scouts U.S.; co-chmn. cultural arts dist. P.T.A. exec. bd. Chmn. Elmsford (N.Y.) Democratic party. Recipient 1st prize sculpture Art in the Park, Tarrytown, N.Y., 1970, 2d prize Village Art Center, 1953, numerous others. Mem. Art Students League (life), Westchester Art Soc., Marmaroneck Artists Guild. Roman Catholic. Address: Elmsford, N.Y., Died Dec. 14, 1974; buried Gate of Heaven Cemetery, Valhalla, N.Y.

MORAN, W(ALTER) H(ARRISON), educator; b. Fairmont, W.Va., Feb. 4, 1889; s. Henderson Milroy and Sarah Ellen (Rogers) M.; A.B., W.Va., U., 1920; M.S., Ohio State U., 1921, Ph.D., 1923; m. Edna Florence Solomon, Dec. 24, 1925; 1 son, Walter Harrison. Asst. in chemistry, Ohio State U., 1920-23; assistant prof. chem., Kan. Agrl. Coll., 1923-24; asst. prof. physiol. chem., Baylor U. Sch. of Medicine, 1924-26, asso. prof., 1926-30; lecturer W.Va. U., summers 1928, 46; asso. prof. chem., U. of N.D., 1930-40, prof. in charge organic chem. and med. biochemistry 1940-51, prof. from 1951. Served with F.A., U.S. Army, 1917-19. Mem. Am. Chem. Soc., N.D. Ednl. Assn., N.D. Acad. Sci. (pres. 1945), Phi Beta Kappa, Sigma, Gamma Alpha, Phi Beta Pi (hon.). Home: Grand Forks, N.D., Died Apr. 17, 1975; interred Meml. Park Cemetery, Grand Forks, N.D.

MORDVINOFF, NICOLAS, artist; b. St. Petersburg, Russia, Sept. 27, 1911; student Lycée Janson de Sailly, Paris Ecole des Roches, France, U. Paris; m. Barbara Ellis, 1956; children—Michael, Alexandra, Peter. Came U.S., 1946, naturalized, 1952. Books illustrated: Thunder Island (W.S. Stone), 1942; Pépé Was the Saddest Bird (Stone), 1944; The Ship of Flame (Stone), 1945; Tahiti Landfall (Stone), 1946; Rainbow in Tahiti (C. Guild), 1948; Cezar and the Music Maker (E. and M. Schwalze), 1950; The Two Reds (W. Lipkind), 1950; Finders Keepers (W. Lipkind), 1951; Just So Stories (Rudyard Kipling), 1952; Big Steve (Marie H. Block), 1952; The Magic Feather Duster, 1858; The Four Leaf Clover, 1959; The Little Tiny Rooster, 1960; Billy The Kid, 1961; Russet and the Two Reds, 1962; The Boy and The Forest, in 1964; many others; paintings exhibited, Paris, Tahiti, Honolulu, New Zealand, San Francisco, L.A., Phila.; exhibited one-man shows, N.Y.C., 1949, Wickersham Gallery, 1970, Galerie 9, Paris, 1970; prints included in permanent collections Met. Mus. Arts, N.Y. Central Pub. Library. Recipient A.L.A. Caldecott medal for illustration most distinguished book, 1952; Herald Tribune award, 1954; N.Y. Times 100 best books, 1951, 10 best books, 1953, 54, 59; A.L.A. distinguished books of year 1952, 54, 58. Author, illustrator: Bearsland; Coral Island, 1957. Home: Hampton, N.J. Died May 5, 1973.

MOREL, JEAN, opera and concert condr.; b. Abbeville, Somme, France, Jan. 10, 1903; s. Charles Victor Léon and Marie Clémence Eugénie (Cellier) M.; studied piano with Isidore Philipp, counterpoint, composition with Noel Gallon, Gabriel Pierné. Came to the U.S., 1939. Debut as conductor with principle Paris orchestras, Lamoureux, Pasdeloup, Société des Concerts du Conservatorie, 1933; conductor Paris Opera Comique, 1936; permanent condr., musical dir. Orchestre Symphonique de Paris, 1937; guest concerts France and European countries; condr. French and Italian Repertoire, Municipal Theatre, Rio de Janeiro, 1939; appeared as condr. Mexico City Nat. Opera and Orchestra, 1943; guest condr. other South Am. Republics, Cin. Symphony, 1952, NBC, 1951, 54, Santa Cecilia, Rome, 1952, 53, 55, 56, Boston Symphony, 1954, San Francisco Opera, 1955, Chgo. Symphony, 1956, N.Y. Philharmonic, 1959; concerts Carnegie Hall, N.Y.C., St. Louis Symphony, Montreal; condr. N.Y.C., Center Opera Co., 1944-52, Met. Opera, 1956-71, Convent Garden, London, 1960, Louisville, 1970; tchr. conducting Julliard Sch. Music, 1949-71, mus. dir. Opera Theater, 1964-65. Chevalier Légion d'Honneur. Home: New York City, N.Y. Died Apr. 14, 1975.

MORELL, ROSA BLANCA ORTIZ (MRS. RAMON B. MORELL), educator; b. Ponce, P.R., Apr. 5, 1902; d. Obdulio and Eusebia (Amengual) Ortiz A.B., B.S., Inst. Santiago de Cuba (Cuba), 1921; Ph.D., U. Havana (Cuba), 1941; m. Ramon B. Morell, June 28, 1924; children—Ida Rosa (Mrs. Silvio Grave de Peralta), Aldo R., Ilia E. (Mrs. Edwin Rojas), Ilma T. (Mrs. Edilberto Manduley), Guido O. Prof. Spanish and history Friends Jr. Coll., Holguin, Cuba, 1921-24; prof. Spanish, head dept. Spanish, 1941-61; prof. lLatin, dean Sch. Philosophy, U. Holguin, Cuba, 1957-60; asst. prof. Spanish, Guilford Coll., Greensboro, N.C., 1962-70. Mem. Am. Assn. Tchrs. Spanish and Portuguese, S. Atlantic Modern Lang. Assn. Mem. Soc. of Friends. Home: Greensboro, N.C. Died Mar. 4, 1972.

MORELOCK, GEORGE LESLIE, church official; b. Franklin, Tenn., Jan. 8, 1880; s. William Lowry and Tennessee Adeline (Jackson) M.; grad. Mooney Sch., Murfreesboro, Tenn., 1903; A.B., U. of the South, 1913; grad. study, Stanford, 1913-14; LL.D., Millsaps Coll. Jackson, Miss., 1937; m. Ruth Murphy, June 7, 1906; children—Mary Louise (Mrs. W. A. Jenkins), Elizabeth Ruth (Mrs. Robert Just), George Leslie, Jr. Principal of high school, Carthage, Tex., 1903-04; superintendent high school, Friendship, Arkansas, 1904-06; v.p. Columbia Jr. College, Milton, Ore., 1906-07; v.p. McFerrin Sch., Martin, Tenn., 1907-09, co.-pres., 1909-11, pres. 1914-22; gen. sec. Gen. Bd. of Lay Activities M.E. Church, South, 1922-40; exec. sec. Gen. Bd. of Lay Activities of the Meth. Ch. 1940-48, emeritus, 1948. Mem. Bd. of Evangelism of Meth. Ch. Interdenominational Council on Men's Work. Mem. United Stewardship Council. Mem. Fed. Council of Chs. of Christ in America. Member Methodist General Conference, 1922, 1939, 1940, 1948, Oxford Conference on Life and Work, 1937. Mem. Phi Beta Kappa, Kappa Sigma, Phi Beta Kappa, Kappa Sigma, Phi Delta Kappa. Author: A Steward in the Methodist Church; The Official Board of the Methodist Church; The Board of Stewards, The Way to Spirtual Power, The Ideal Layman, The Stewardship Interpretation of Life, Laymen and Evangelism, We Are in the Fight, Spiritualizing Church Finance, A Fellowship Church, Why Go to Church, Adequate Support of the Ministry, Christian Stewardship, World Reconstruction; Methodist Men. Builders of the Kingdom. Editor: The Meth. Layman. Home: Miami, Fla.†

MORENCY, PAUL WILFRID, broadcasting cons.; b. Oak Park, Ill., Oct. 19, 1899; s. Ludger and Alvina C. (Bedard) M.; Ph.B., U. Chgo., 1923; LL.D., Trinity Coll., Hartford, Conn.; m. Dorothy W. Marshall, Dec. 7, 1967. Engaged in newspaper advt., 1924-27; mgr. field service Nat. Assn. Broadcasters, 1927-29; pres. Broadcast-Plaza, Inc., operating stas. WTIC AM-FM and TV, Hartford, 1929-68; dir. Bedard-Morency Mill Co. Mem. Conn. Commn. Arts; pres. Hartford C. of C.; chmn. exec. com., dir. Broadcast Music, Inc. Corporator Hartford Hosp., Inst. Living, Mt. Sinai Hosp. Served in 149th F.A., 42d Div., U.S. Army, AEF, 1917-20; AEF. Recipient Conn. medal for extraordinary civilian service in war by Gov. Baldwin, 1946. Mem. Am. Legion, V.F.W., Alpha Delta Phi. Clubs: Golf, Gun (chmn. bd.), University (pres. Hartford 1942-43). Home: Avon, Conn. Died Oct. 15, 1974; interred Cedar Hills Cemetery, Hartford, Conn.

MORENO, JACOB L., psychodramatist, sociometrist, group psychotherapist; b. Bucharest, Rumania, May 20, 1889; s. Nissim and Pauline (Wolf) M.; student, faculty philosophy U. Vienna (Austria), 1910-12, med. sch., 1912-17; M.D., 1917; Dr. honoris causa, Med. Faculty U. Barcelona (Spain), 1968; hon. degree U. Vienna, 1969; m. Zerka Toeman, Dec. 8, 1949; children—Regina, Jonathan. Came to U.S., 1925, naturalized, 1935. Supt. Mitterndorf State Hosp., nr. Vienna, 1918; officer of health, Voslau, Austria, 1918-25; engaged in pvt. psychiat. practice Voslau and Vienna, 1918-25; pub. Daimon, monthly mag. of philosophy and lit., 1918; founded Das Stegreiftheater (The Spontaneity Theatre), 1921-25; inventor of stage especially adapted to spontaneity work, 1922; originated first living newspaper and idea of psychodrama, 1923; inventor and patentee of radio film, for electromagnetic recording of sound on discs for radio transmission and reception, 1924; licensed physician, N.Y. State, 1927; engaged in pvt. psychiat. work, N.Y.C., 1928; began psychodramatic work with children Plymouth Inst., Bklyn., and introduced spontaneity test at mental hygiene clinic, Mt. Sinai Hosp., N.Y. City, 1928; did psychodramatic work at Grosvenor Neighborhood House and Hunter Coll., 1929; founded Impromptu Theatre, Carnegie Hall, 1929-31; pub. Impromptu Mag., 1931; gave public demonstration of first living newspaper in U.S. at Guild Theatre, 1931; made sociometric studies, Sing Sing Prison, 1931-32; responsible for first group psychotherapy conf. in U.S. at Phila., arranged by Am. Psychiat. Assn., 1931; did first long-term sociometric community work at N.Y. State Training Sch. for Girls, Hudson, N.Y., 1932-38; adviser, subsistence homestead div. U.S. Department of Interior, 1934; founder and physician in charge Beacon Hill Sanitorium, then Moreno Sanitorium, 1936-68; adj. prof. sociology Grad. Sch. Arts, and Scis., N.Y. U., 1951-66; founded Therapeutic Theatre, first theatre for psychodroma, 1936; founded Sociometry, A Jour. of Interpersonal Relations, 1937; spl. lectr. New School of Social Research, 1937-38, Teachers Coll., Columbia U., 1939-40; founded Psychodramatic Inst., Beacon, N.Y., 1940; assisted in foundation of theater for Psychodrama, St. Elizabeths Hosp., Washington; founder Sociometric and Psychodromatic Insts., now Moreno Inst., 1942; pres. Moreno Acad. Hon. pres. First through 7th Internat. Congresses Psychodrama, 1st through 6th Internat. Congresses Group Psychotherapy. Recipient Golden Doctor Diploma U. Vienna, Austria, 1969; plaque at house in Voslau, nr. Vienna for work as pub. health officer 1918-1925, 1969. Fellow Am. Psychiat. Assn. (life), Am. Sociometric Assn. (pres. 1945), Am. Soc. Group Psychotherapy and Psychodrama, Med. Soc. of N.Y. State (citation for 50 yrs. med. practice 1967; life); life mem. A.M.A. Am. Sociol. Soc. Author of several books, including: The Words of the Father, 1941; Group Psychotherapy, A

Symposium, 1945; The Theater of Spontaneity, 1947, 2d rev. edit., 1973; Sociometry, Experimental Method and the Science of Society, 1951; Who Shall Survive?, 1934, 2d rev. edit. 1953; Sociometry and the Science of Man, 1956; Psychodrama, Vol. I, 1946, 4th rev. edit., 1972, Vol. II, 1959, 2d rev. edit., 1975, Vol. III, 1969, 2d rev. edit., 1975. Editor: Internat. Handbook of Group Psychotherapy, 1966; Progress in Psychotherapy, Vols. I-V, 1956-60; founder, editor Sociometry, Jour. Interpersonal Relations, 1937-56, Group Psychotherapy, 1947-74, Internat. Jour. Sociometry and Sociatry, 1956-74. Home: Beacon N.Y. Died May 14, 1974.

MORENO-LACALLE, JULIAN, author, educator; b. Manila, P.I., Oct. 18, 1881; s. José and Florencia Victoria (Pérez) M.; A.B., U. of St. Thomas, Manila, 1895; A.M., U. of Md., 1918; post. grad. work, U. of St. Thomas, also in Spain and Zurich, Switzerland; m. Carmen Martel, of Madrid, 1903; children—Elvira, Julian, José, Antonio, Carmen, Florencia. Translator Exec. Bur. P.I., 1900-05, Pan. Am. Union, Washington, D.C., 1906-12; instr., asso. prof. U.S. Naval Acad., 1914-20; prof. and dean of Spanish Sch., Middlebury Coll., 1920-29; prof. Rutgers U., New Brunswick, N.J., 1929—; dir. Iberia News Service. Decorated Order of Liberator (Venezuelan), 1911; Knight Comdr. Spanish Order Isabella, 1926. Mem. Phi Beta Kappa, Alpha Sigma Phi. Author: Elementos de Espanol, 1918; Elements of Spanish Pronunication, 1918; Spanish Composition, 1921; Advanced Spanish Composition, 1928; also transls., etc., various other publs. in Spanish. Home: New York City, N.Y.†

MORESI, HARRY JAMES, JR., physician; b. Jeanerette, La., Oct. 15, 1932; s. Harry James and Rosemary (Killeen) M.; M.D., Tulane U., 1957; m. Genevieve Ruth Wilson, Aug. 17, 1957; children—Anne Michele, J. Michael, Mary Elise, Jean Margaret, Harry James III. Intern, Confederate Meml. Med. Center, Shreveport, La., 1957-58; resident in radiology Oschsner Found. Hosp., 1961-64; radiologist Iberia Parish Hosp., 1964-71, Dauterive Hosp., New Iberia, La., 1966-71; cons. radiologist Abbeville (La.) Gen. Hosp., 1966-71. Dir. A. Moresi Co., Ltd. Served as capt. M.C., USAF, 1958-61. Diplomate Am. Bd. Radiology. Mem. A.M.A., So. Med. Assn., La. Med. Soc., Iberia Parish Med. Soc., Am. Coll. Radiology, Radiol. Soc. La., Beta Theta Pi, Nu Sigma Nu. Republican. Roman Catholic. Home: New Iberia, La., Died Sept. 10, 1971; buried Jeanerette, La.

MOREY, LEE B., lawyer; b. Clinton, Ind., Jan. 20, 1894; A.B., Wabash Coll.; LL.B., Harvard. Admitted to N.Y. bar, 1921; practice of law, N.Y.C.; mem. firm Chadbourne, Parke, Whiteside & Wolff. Mem. Assn. Bar City N.Y. Home: Tucson, Ariz. Died Nov. 28, 1973.

MOREY, SYLVESTER MARVIN, advt. exec.; b. Greenwich, N.Y., Apr. 22, 1896; s. Clayton L. and Lillian H. (Phelps) M.; graduate Phillips Andover Academy, 1914; B.S., Dartmouth College, 1918; married Minetta E. Meyer, Oct. 11, 1923; 1 son, Clayton Phelps. Copywriter George L. Dyer Co., 1920-24, Blackman Co., 1924-28, Gardner Advt.Co., 1929; advt. mgr. Sinclair Refining Co., 1930-41; pres. Hixson-O'Donnell Advt., Inc., 1941-48, Morey, Humm & Johnstone, Inc., 1949-56, Morey, Humm & Warwick, Inc., 1956-59; chmn. bd. Geyer, Morey, Ballard, Inc., from 1959. Dir., chmn. board, sec., treas. Myrin Institute; member bd. Rudolf Steiner Found., N.Y.C., Waldorf Ednl. Found., Found. Am., Wash.; dir., mem. exec. com. Nat. Outdoor Advt. Bur.; dir. Rudolf Steiner, Sch., 1938-50. Mem. Inst. Creative Research, Chi. Phi. Clubs: Dartmouth, University (N.Y.C.). Author: American Indians and Our Way of Life, 1961; Can The Red Man Help the White Man, 1970; Respect for Life, 1974. Home: Great Barrington, Mass., Died Oct. 26, 1975.

MORGAN, ARTHUR ERNEST, civil engr., educator; b. Cincinnati, O., June 20, 1878; s. John D. and Anna Frances (Wiley) M.; ed. high sch.; hon. D.Sc., U. of Colo., 1923; hon. Dr. Engring., Case School of Applied Sciences, 1932; hon. D.Sc., University of N.C., 1937; hon. LL.D., Antioch College, 1943, Brandeis U., 1972; D. Humanities, Ohio State U., 1973; married Urania T. Jones, Sept. 1904 (died 1905); 1 son, Ernest; m. 2d, Lucy Middleton Griscom, July 6, 1911; children—Griscom, Frances (Mrs. Landrum Bolling), Lucy (deceased). Practiced in St. Cloud, Minn., 1902-07; supervising engr., U.S. Govt. Drainage Investigations, 1907-09, in charge design of reclamation works in Southern States; pres. Morgan Engring. Co., 1909-15; pres. Dayton-Morgan Engring. Co. from 1915; apptd. chief engr., 1913, Miami Conservancy Dist., designed to prevent recurrence of Dayton flood; chief engr. Pueblo Conservancy Dist., to protect Pueblo, Colo., from floods, 1921; has planned and superintended construction 75 water control projects. Drafted revised drainage codes adopted by Minn. legislature, 1905, Ark. legislature, 1909, and assisted in drafting those adopted by Miss., 1911, Ohio, 1914, Colo., 1922, New Mexico, 1927; pres. Antioch Coll., 1920-36; chmn. Tenn. Valley Authority, 1933-38; pres. Community Service, Inc., from 1941, pres. Yellow Springs Housing Corporation; temp. chmn. Conciliation and Arbitration Bd. U.S. Steel and C.I.O., 1950. Member University Commission appointed by govt. of India, 1948-49; Am. dir. Mitraniketan, South India ednl. project. Recipient Distinguished Alumni award, 1974. Fellow A.A.A.S.; member Am. Sociol. Soc., Am. Soc. C.E. (hon.), Am. Eugenics Soc., Rural Sociol. Soc. Author: The Drainage of the Saint Francis Valley in Arkansas (U.S. Govt.), 1909; The Miami Valley and the 19 Flood, 1918; My World, 1927; A Compendium of Antioch Notes, 1930; The Seedman, 1933; The Long Road, 1936; The Small Community, 1942; Small Community Economics, 1943; Edward Bellamy, a Biography, 1944; The Philosophy of Edward Bellamy, 1945; Nowhere was Somewhere, 1946; A Business of My Own, 1946; History of the Miami Conservancy District, 1951; Industries for Small Communities, 1953; Search for Purpose, 1955; The Community of the Future, 1956; It Can be Done in Education, 1962; Observations, 1968; Dams and Other Disasters: A Century of the Army Corps Engineers in Civil Work, 1971; The Making of the TVA, 1974. Contbr. leading mags. Address: Yellow Springs, O., Died Nov. 12, 1975; ashes interred Yellow Springs.

MORGAN, CLIFFORD THOMAS, psychologist; b. Minnetola, N.J., July 21, 1915; s. Samuel and Ethel Josephine (Dixon) M.; A.B., Maryville Coll., Maryville, Tenn., 1936; A.M., U. Rochester, 1937, Ph.D., 1939; m. Jean Chase Snow, Nov. 28, 1946; children—Peter Charles, Patricia Ann, Michael Thomas. Asst. psychology U. Rochester, 1936-38, research fellow, 1938-39; research asso. Psychol. Corp. New York, 1937-39; instr. in psychology, Harvard and Radcliffe Coll., 1939-42, faculty instr., 1942-43; tchr. aid div. of physics, Nat. Defense Research Com. Washington, D.C., 1943-46; asso. in psychology, Johns Hopkins Univ., 1943-45, asst. prof., 1945-46, asso. prof., 1946-48, chmn. dept. psychology, 1946-54, chmn. biol. sci. group, 1951-53, dir. Systems Research Lab., 1946-49, prof. 1948-57, fellow, 1957-60; lectr. dept. psychology U. Wis., Madison, 1959-62, U. Cal., Santa Barbara, 1962-65; faculty Univ. of Tex., Austin, Tex., 1968-76; consulting editor McGraw-Hill Book Co., 1950-59. Mem. NRC, 1950-53. Fellow A.A.A.S. (v.p. 1960), Am. Psychol. Assn. (div. physiol. and comparative psychology (pres. 1946-48, chmn. publs. bd. 1960-61); mem. Am. Physiol Soc., Soc. Exptl. Psychologists. Methodist. Author: Physiological Psychology, 1943; textbooks in field. Co-author: Applied Experimental Psychology, 1949; How to Study, 1957. Cons. editor Journal of Comparative and Physiological Psychology, 1947-54, Ann. Rev. of Psychology, 1953-59, Contemporary Psychology, 1955-60; editor Psychol. Abstracts, 1960-63; Psychonomic Sci., 1964-76. Contbr. psychol. jours. Home: Austin, Tex., Died Feb. 12, 1976.

MORGAN, DAVID PERCY, chem. consultant; b. Lenox, Mass., Sept. 4, 1894; s. David Percy and Edith (Parsons) M.; A.B., Harvard, 1916; Ph.D., Columbia U., 1923; m. Alma de Gersdorff, June 7, 1919; 1 dau., Helen Suzette (Mrs. Robert C. Alsop). NRC fellow Harvard Med. Sch., 1923-24; partner, firm of Loomis, Stump & Banks, cons. chem. engrs., N.Y.C., 1924-28; chem. consultant Scudder, Stevens & Clark, investment counsel, N.Y.C., 1929-40; with chem. div. adv. com. to Nat. Defense Council, 1940; with Office Prodn. Management, 1941; with Supply, Priorities and Allocations Bd., 1942; dir. chem. div. War Prodn. Bd., 1942-43; dir. Chemicals Bureau, W.P.B., 1943-45; in charge chem. market research and development W. R. Grace & Co., N.Y., 1946; adminstr. research and development Mathieson Chem. Corp., 1948, v.p. and treas., 1949-50, v.p. and dir. of development, 1950-52, v.p., sec. exec. com., 1953, asst. to pres., 1954-56; cons., from 1956. Served as lt. (s.g.), Flying Corps, U.S. Naval Reserve, 1917-19. Decorated Navy Cross, 1919. Fellow A.A.A.S., Am. Inst. of Chemists; mem. Am. Chem. Soc., Am. Inst. Chem. Engrs. (asso.), Soc. of Chem. Industry, Sigma Xi, Phi Lambda Upsilon. Clubs: Chemists, Cosmos (Washington): Stockbridge (Mass.) Golf; Harvard, Century Association (N.Y.C.). Author tech. papers and articles on chem. industry, econs. investments. Home: New York City, N.Y. Died Apr. 21, 1974.

MORGAN, FRED BRUCE, JR., educator; b. Charleston, W.Va., Mar. 12, 1919; s. Fred Bruce and Helen (Pidcock) M.; A.B., Maryville (Tenn.) Coll., 1939; Th.B., Princeton Theol. Sem., 1942, Ph.D., 1958; postgrad. Far East Inst., Yale, 1946-47, Coll. Chinese Studies, Peking, 1948; M.A. (hon.) Amherst Coll., 1963; m. Ruth Marian McNamee, May 27, 1942; children—Dorothy Jill (Mrs. G. Ian Marshall), Timothy Bruce, Rebecca Anne. Ordained to ministry Presbyn. Chg., 1942; minister in W.Va., Pa., Tsingtao, China, Hong Kong, also cons. agrl. co-operatives to Brit. Colonial Adminstrn., 1949-50; prof. N.T., Chiengmai, Thailand, 1950-51; univ. pastor Princeton, 1952-54; mem. faculty Wilson Coll., Chambersburg, Pa., 1954-59, Syracuse U., 1959-60; mem. faculty Amherst Coll., 1960-72, prof. religion and Am. studies, 1963-72, acting dean faculty, 1970-71; prof. Am. studies and religion, dean coll. Carleton Coll., Northfield, Minn., 1972-75. Mem. gen. council U.P. Ch. in U.S.A., 1968-71. Grantee Danforth Found., 1957-58; postdoctoral fellow Lilly Endowment, 1965-66. Mem. Am. Assn. U. Profs., Assn. Asian Studies, Soc. Sci. Study Religion, Am. Soc. Christian Ethics. Democrat. Author: Called in Revolution, 1956; Christians The Church and Property, 1963; Thai Buddhism and American Protestantism, 1966. Home: Northfield, Minn. Died Oct. 2, 1975; interred Bloomsbury, N.J.

MORGAN, HENRY WILLIAMS, SR., (Harry Morgan), coal producer; b. Cumberland, Md., Feb. 7, 1881; s. Thomas P. and Edith (Johnson) M.; ed. pub. schs. and bus. coll.; m. Louise Herr, of Georgetown, N.D., dau. later Austin Herr, Washington banker, Sept. 20, 1902; children—Henry W., Thomas P., Austin Herr, Calvert Brent. Actively identified with coal mng. from 1920; a leader in development, financing and operation of anthracite field in southwest Va.; also in reopening, financing, developing and operation of coal mines in Old Richmond coal basin closed at end of Civil War; chmn. bd. John R. McLean Mining Corp.; pres. Great Valley Morgan Coal Corp., Merrimac Morgan Coal Corp., Great Southern Morgan Coal & Coke Mining Corp. (Richmond, Virginia); v.p. Va. Central Ry.; dir. Delva Corp. (Wilmington, Del.). Pres. Anthracite Coal Operators Assn. of Va.; hon. mem. Alumni Assn. Va. Mil. Inst. Served as intermediary in textile strike, Danville, Va., 1931. Episcopalian. Was instrumental in settlement of students' strike at Va. Mil. Inst., where his four sons were in attendance, 1927, Mem. finance com. Fed. of Am. Scientists. Home: Washington, D.C.†

MORGAN, JESSE ROBERT, educator; b. Fayette Mo., Aug. 17, 1880; s. Douglas Jasper and Henrietta (Stanley) M.; student U. of Colo., 1898-1900; Pd.M., Colo. State Teachers Coll., Greeley, 1911. A.B., 1912. A.M., 1915; D.Sc., Colo. State College of Edn., 1948; unmarried. Assistant principal high school, Saguache, Colo., 1900-04; instr. and prin. high sch., Trinidad, Colo., 1905-09, supt. schs., 1909-18; also mem. faculty summer sch., Colo. State Teachers Coll., 1910-17; asst. in charge and supervisor professional training for Colo., Wyo., N.M., Utah, U.S. Vets. Bur., Rehabilitation Div., 1918-23; field sec. Colo. Sch. Mines, 1923, also head of dept. English and economics, 1923-26, dean of faculty and head of dept. langs. 1926-46, emeritus, 1946, dir. summer sch., 1926-42. Spl. lecturer in Eng., and Spanish. Regis Coll., Denver, from 1948. Mem. Am. Inst. Mining and Metall. Engrs., Am. Soc. Engring. Edn., Colo. Ednl. Assn., Am. Assn. of Univ. Profs., Phi Delta Kappa. Sigma Alpha Epsilon, Sigma Tau Delta, Pi Gamma Mu. Square and Compass, Blue Key. Republican. Episcopalian. Mason (32°). Clubs: Kiwanis, Colorado Schoolmasters, Teknik, Press, Scholia, Colordo Colorado Poetry Society. Author: Sentiments of Yours, Engineering Spanish. Home: Golden, Colo.†

MORGAN, MARSHALL SHAPLEIGH, banker; b. Phila., Pa., June 2, 1881; s. Randal and Anna (Shapleigh) M.; ed. Germantown Acad., DeLancey Sch.; A.B., U. of Pa., 1904; m. Louise Johnson, June 6, 1906; children—Grace Price (Mrs. Henry S. Jeanes, Jr.), Anna S. (Mrs. Edward M. Greene, Jr.), Randal, 3d, Marcella L. (Mrs. William Lang Day). With United Gas Improvement Co., one year; served as officer and dir. various st. ry. and interurban cos. in Ind. and O., 1905-20; asst. to chmn. of bd., Fidelity-Phila. Trust Co., 1920-37, pres., 1937-47; dir. North Pa. R.R. Co., Phila. Saving Fund Soc., Ins. Co. of North America, Supplee-Biddle Hardware Co., Am. Briquet, Stonega Coke & Coal Co., Virginia Coal & Iron Co., Whitehall Cement Mfg. Co., Phila. Transportation Co., Lehigh Coal & Navigation Co., Cranberry Improvement Co. Westmoreland Coal, and Westmoreland, Inc. Dir. Franklin Inst., Pa. Acad. Fine Arts, Southeastern Pa. Chapter Am. Red Cross, Sheltering Arms of P.E. Ch., Merchants Fund (v.p. and dir.). Mem. Sons of the Revolution. Republican. Episcopalian. Clubs: Rittenhouse, Midday, Philadelphia, Radnor Hunt. Home: Malvern, Pa.†

MORGENSTERN, JULIAN, rabbi, educator; b. St. Francisville, Ill., Mar. 18, 1881; s. Samuel and Hannah (Ochs) M.; B.A., U. of Cincinnati, 1901; rabbi, Hebrew Union College, 1902; U. of Berlin, 1902-03, U. of Heidelberg, 1903-04, Ph.D., 1904, D.H.L., 1937, L.H.D., 1937, D.D., 1947; m. Helen Thorner, Apr. 18, 1906; 1 dau., Jean Hannah (Mrs. William A. Greenebaum). Rabbi at synagogue, Lafayette, Ind., 1904-07; prof., Bible and Semitic langs., Hebrew Union Coll., from 1907, acting pres., 1921, pres. 1922-47, pres. emeritus, 1947. Member Central Conference American Rabbis (secretary, 1907-13), American Oriental Soc. (pres. Western br. 1919-20, and of gen. soc. 1927-28), Soc. Biblical Literature and Exegesis (president Midwest branch, 1938-39, and of general society, 1940-41), Alumni Assn., Hebrew Union College (pres. 1916-18), World Union for Progressive Judaism (Am. v.p.), Jewish Agency for Palestine; hon. fellow Soc. Oriental Research, Am. Acad. for Jewish Research; mem. B'nai B'rith, Theta Phi. Author: The Doctrine of Sin in the Babylonian Religion, 1905; A Jewish Interpretation of the Book of Genesis, 1920; Studies in the Calendars of Ancient Israel, 1924, 37; The Oldest Document of the Hexatench, 1927; The Book of the Covenant, 1928-32; Amos Studies, Volume 1, 1941; The Ark, The Ephod and The Tent of Meeting, 1945. Contbr. to mags. Home: Cincinnati, O.†

MORIN, RELMAN, journalist; b. Freeport, Ill., Sept. 11, 1907; s. Frederick Upton and Wilhelmina Louise (Relman) M.; A.B., Pomona Coll., 1929, Litt.D. (hon.) 1963; spl. Student Lingham U., Canton, China, Shanghai Coll., Yen-Ching Univ., Peiping, China; m. Florence Pine, 1936 (div. 1946); 1 dau., Mary; m. 2d,

Dorothy Wright Liebes, Apr. 21, 1948. Reporter, Los Angeles Times, 1923-39, Shanghai Evening Post, 1930, Los Angeles Record, 1931-34; joined Asso. Press, 1934, fgn. corr. Tokyo, Japan, 1937-40, roving corr., Far East, 1940-41 (interned by Japanese in Saigon, Indo-China, 1941-42); war corr. for Asso. Press, Eng., North Africa, Italy, India, Middle East, France, 1942-45; chief, Asso. Press Paris bur., 1945-47, chief Washington bur., 1947-48, N.Y.C. from 1948. Recipient Pulitzer prize in journalism, 1951, 58; George Polk award, 1957. Guggenheim fellow, 1961, Benjamin Franklin fellow Royal Soc. Arts. Mem. Archaeol. Inst. Clubs: Writers, Nat. Press (Washington), Athletic (Los Angeles); Century, Coffee House, University, Dutch Treat (N.Y.C.). Author: Circuit of Conquest, 1943; East Wind Rising, 1960; Churchill: Portrait of Greatness, 1965; Assassination: The Death of President Kennedy, 1968; Dwight D. Eisenhower; A Gauge of Greatness, 1969. Co-author: The Newsman Speaks; Southern Schools: Progress and Problems. Home: New York City, N.Y. Died July 16, 1973.

MORISON, SAMUEL ELIOT, historian, author; b. Boston, July 9, 1887; s. John Holmes and Emily Marshall (Eliot) M.; ed. Noble's Sch., Boston, St. Paul's Sch., Concord; A.B., Harvard, 1908, Ph.D., 1912, Litt.D., 1936; M.A., Oxford (Eng.) U, 1922; student Ecole des Sciences Politiques, Paris, 1908-09; L.H.D., Trinity Coll., 1935, Amherst Coll., 1936; Williams Coll., 1950, Bucknell U., 1960; LL.D. (hon.), Union Coll., 1939, U. Me., 1968; Boston Coll., 1960; Litt.D., Yale, 1949, Oxford U., 1951, Notre Dame, 1954, Holy Cross, 1962; m. Elizabeth S. Greene, May 28, 1910 (dec. Aug. 1945); children—Elizabeth Gray (Mrs. Edward Spingarn), Emily Marshall (Mrs. H. Brooks Beck), Peter Greene (dec.), Catharine (Mrs. Cooper); m. 2d, Priscilla Barton, Dec. 29, 1949 (dec. Feb. 1973). Instr. history U. Cal., 1914; instr., lectr., prof. history Harvard, 1915-55; Harold V. Harmsworth prof. Am. history Oxford U., 1922-25. Served as pvt., inf., U.S. Army, 1918-19; attached Russian div. Am. Commn. to Negotiate Peace, Paris, 1919; Am. del. Baltic Commn. of Peace Com., 1919; historian U.S. naval ops. World War II; from lt. comdr. to rear adm. USNR, 1942-51. Decorated Legion of Merit; recipient Bancroft prize Columbia, 1949, 72, Theodore Roosevelt medal, 1956, Edison award, 1957, Alfred Thayer Mahan award Navy League, 1961, Emerson-Thoreau medal Am. Acad. Arts and Scis., 1961, Gold medal history Nat. Inst. Arts and Letters, 1962, Balzan Found. award history, 1963; Presdl. medal Freedom, 1964. Fellow Soc. Antiquaries, Am. Philos. Soc., Am. Acad. Arts and Scis., Brit. Acad.; mem. Am. Antiquarian Soc. (past pres.), Colonial Soc. Mass., Mass. Hist. Soc., Soc. Cincinnati, Charitable Irish Soc., Real Academia de la Historia (Madrid), Am. Acad. Arts and Letters. Democrat. Episcopalian. Clubs: St. Botolph, Cruising Club, Somerset, Tavern (Boston). Author: Life of Harrison Gray Otis, 1913; Maritime History of Massachusetts, 1921; Oxford History of the United States, 1927; Builders of Bay Colony, 1930; Tercentennial History of Harvard University (Juserand medal and Loubat prize), 5 vols., 1930-36; Puritan Pronaos, 1936; Growth of the American Republic (with Henry Steele Commager), 1950; Admiral of Ocean Sea (Pulitzer Prize), 1942; History U.S. Naval Operations World War II, 15 vols. 1947-62; By Land and by Sea, 1953; Christopher Columbus, Mariner, 1955; Freedom in Contemporary Society, 1956; The Story of Old Colony of New Plymouth, 1956; Strategy and Compromise, 1958; John Paul Jones (Pulitzer Prize 1960), 1959; The Story of Mound Desert Island, 1960; One Boy's Boston, 1962; The Two-Ocean War, 1963; Journals and other Documents of Columbus, 1963; Vistas of History, 1964; (with Mauricio Obregon) The Caribbean as Columbus Saw It, 1964; Spring Tides, 1965; The Oxford History of the American People, 1965; The Life of Commodore Matthew C. Perry, 1967; H.G. Otis, Urbane Federalist, 1969; The European Discovery of America, The Northern Voyages, 1971; Samuel de Champlain, Father of New France, 1972, The European Discovery of America, The Southern Voyages, 1974. Home: Northeast Harbor, Me. Died May 15, 1976.

MORREL, WILLIAM GRIFFIN, mfg. exec.; b. Sherman, Tex., Oct. 21, 1908: s. William deKalb and Inez (Griffin) M.; B.S., Va. Mil. Inst., 1928; m. Virginia Louise Baldwin, Oct. 8, 1932; children—William Griffin, Bernard Baldwin. Inst. elec. engring. Va. Mil. Inst., 1928-30; various positions Chesapeake & Potomac Tel. Co. Va., 1930-46; traffic employment Am. Tel. & Tel. Co., N.Y.C., 1946-48; v.p., gen. mgr. Chesapeake & Potamac Tel. Co. Md., 1948-52, v.p., 1952-60, also dir.; dir., mem. adv. bd. Davison Chem. Co. div. W.R. Grace & Co., 1954-56; exec. v.p., dir. Black & Decker Mfg. Co., 1960-65; pres., dir. Rowan Controller Co., Westminster, Md., 1965-68; chmn. bd. Md. Industries, Inc., from 1968; dir. First Nat. Bank, Provident Savs. Bank, Peterson, Howell & Heather, Monumental Corp.; corporator Savs. Bank Balt. Vice pres. Balt. Area council Boy Scouts Am.; vice chmn., dir. Balt. chpt. A.R.C. Trustee Goucher Coll. Mem. Balt. Assn. Commerce (dir.), Md. Hist. Soc. Presbyn. (elder). Clubs: Elkridge (Md.); Princess Anne Country (Virginia Beach, Va.). Home: Baltimore, Md. Died Mar. 4, 1975; interred Lynchburg, Va.

MORRELL, FRED, forester; b. Palmyre, Neb., March 20, 1880; s. Elijah and Elizabeth (Cocshedge) M.; B.S.C., U. of Neb., 1902, grad. work, 1904-06; M.F., Ia. State Coll., 1920; m. May Grace Edholm, Sept. 22, 1906; children—Fred Rowe, Mary (dec.). High sch. teacher, 1903-05; jr. forester, 1906; forest insp., 1907-08; asst. regional forester, 1909-19; regional forester, 1920-29; asst. chief, Forest Service, 1930-33; chief Office of Civilian Conservation Corps Activities, U.S. Dept. of Agr., 1934-43; later Wash. rep. Am. Paper and Pulp Assn. Sr. mem. Soc. of Am. Foresters; hon. mem. Rotary Internat. Home: Alexandria, Va.†

MORRIS, ALPHEUS KASPAR, vice pres. Miami Univ.; b. nr. Rushville, Ind., May 15, 1878; s. White Brown and Mary (Payne) M.; grad. Vories Bus. Coll., Indianapolis, Ind., 1900; A.B., Miami U., Oxford, O., 1908; LL.D., Miami Univ., 1946; m. Mary Arminta Baughman, July 26, 1911; children—Genevieve Hellene (Mrs. Clifford Ellsworth Scott), Wilford Ernest, Esther Jeanne. Farmer, 1878-99; in employment of Hibben Hollweg & Co. (Indianapolis, Ind.) and Marshall Field & Co. (Chicago, Ill.), 1900-04; supt. of schools, Clark County, O., 1908-09; sec. Y.M.C.A., Hamilton, O., N.Y. City, State of Ohio, 1909-19; gen. sec., Metropolitan Y.M.C.A., Cincinnati, 1919-22; asst. pres. and v.p. Miami U., Oxford, O., 1922-45, acting pres., 1945, 46; pres. and dir. Oxford (O.) Nat. Bank, from 1934; owner, mgr. farm, from 1937. Trustee and vice pres. Fort Hamilton Hosp. Mem. exec. bd. Coll. Y.M.C.A. and Westminster Foundation. Mem. Miami Valley Chautauqua Assn., Phi Eta Sigma, Phi Beta Kappa, Omicron Delta Kappa, Delta Kappa Epsilon, Elder or trustee Presbyn. Ch., Oxford O., 1925-43. Mem. Grange, Kiwanis Club, Oxford Men's Club, Oxford Forum. Home: Oxford, O.†

MORRIS, ARTHUR J., banker, lawyer; b. Tarboro, N.C., Aug. 5, 1881; s. Joseph and Dora Livingston (Jacobs) M.; grad. U. Va., 1899, LL.B., 1901; LL.D., U. Miami, Fla., 1957; m. Bertha Myers, Apr. 5, 1905; children—Mrs. Earle H. Kincaid, Mrs. E.C. Walton, Mrs. C.R. Hall, Mrs. E.G. Childers. Began practice of law, Norfolk, 1901; originator Morris Plan system indsl. banking represented by Morris Plan banks in various cities of U.S., beginning at Norfolk, Va., 1910; hon. chmn. Morris Plan Corp. Am., through which the system is organized; hon. chmn. Financial Gen. Bankshares, Inc.; chmn. emeritus Bank Commerce (Morris Plan) N.Y.; hon. chmn. Bankers Security Life Ins. Soc. (formerly Morris Plan Ins. Soc.); adv. dir. Nat. Bank Ga. (Atlanta), Valley Fidelity Bank and Trust Co. (Knoxville); hon. dir. Bank Va. (Richmond). Mem. Am. Bankers Assn., Am. Bar Assn., Va. State Bar Assn., Bar City N.Y., Consumers Bankers Assn., Phi Beta Kappa Assos. Republican. Presbyn. Clubs: Republican, Bankers, Canadian (New York); Westchester Country (Rye, N.Y.); University (Washington); Princess Anne Country (Virginia Beach, Va.); Farmington Country (Charlottesville, Va.); Keswick (Keswick, Va.). Home: Ossinging, N.Y. Died Nov. 18, 1973; interred Sleepy Hollow Cemetery, North Tarrytown, N.Y.

MORRIS, BERT MILLER, chemist, educator; b. San Jose, Cal., Mar. 24, 1916; s. Bert Jasper and Della P. (Miller) M.; B.S., U. Cal. at Berkeley, 1937; M.A., Harvard, 1939, Ph.D., 1941; m. Elizabeth Leigh Ferry, July 5, 1941 (dec. Oct. 1966); children—Douglass Bert, David John; m. 2d, Pearl Eloise Lyman Simkin, July 1, 1967. Research chemist Hercules Experimental Station, Wilmington, Del., 1941-46; asst. prof. chemistry San Jose State Coll., 1946-50, asso. prof., 1950-54, prof., 1954-75, chmn. dept., 1961-69, chmn. faculty council, 1956-58. Active Boy Scouts Am. Mem. Am. Chem. Soc. (chmn. Santa Clara Valley 1958), A.A.A.S., Am. Assn. U. Profs., Cal. Assn. Chemistry Tchrs., Assn. Cal. State Coll., Profs., Lambda Chi Alpha, Alpha Chi Sigma. Club: Commonwealth of Cal. Home: San Jose, Cal. Died July 25, 1975.

MORRIS, DAVE HENNEN, JR., banker; b. New York, N.Y., June 14, 1900; s. Dave Hennen and Alice V. (Shepard) Morris; A.B., Harvard, 1921, M.B.A. with distinction, 1923; m. Alice Gifford Agnew, January 4, 1926; (divorced May 24, 1945); children—Susan Bliss, Marian, D. Hennen 3d; m. 2d, (Mrs.) Mary Hebard Sise, July 20, 1946; (div. Nov. 1956); married 3d, (Mrs.) Marylee D. Shrady, Dec. 20, 1957; 1 stepson, Henry M. Shrady. Clerk, Merrill Trust Co., Bangor, Me., summer 1922; with Bank of New York and Fifth Avenue Bank, now The Bank of New York, 1923-75, v.p., comptroller, 1931-32, v.p., 1932-75; chmn. and director Constellation Insurance Company; trustee Am. Irving Savs. Bank; dir. Internat. Boiler Works, Sterling Offices Limited, Trustee, sec., trustees property nat. bd. YWCA; dir., treas. Sheltering Arms Childrens Service; pres., trustee The Browning Sch.; trustee, treas. Russell Sage Foundation. On leave of absence, served on spl. bd. to consider and advise on certificates, tax amortization, War Dept., Mar.-Aug. 1941, and as asst. to sec. of treas., Sept. 1941-Feb. 1942. Served as 2d lt., Inf., AUS, 1918, Inf. Res., 1924-34; 1st lt., later capt., Co. B, 17th Regt., N.Y. Guard, Dec. 1940-Jan. 1942; capt. Army of U.S., 1942; promoted col.; served in Asiatic-Pacific Theater, 3 yrs.; assigned Office of Fgn. Liquidation Commr., State Dept.; inactive status since July 1946. Decorated Legion of Merit. Republican. Episcopalian. Clubs: Union (New York); New York Yacht. Home: New York City, N.Y. Died Apr. 2, 1975.

MORRIS, DON HEATH, coll. chancellor; b. DeSoto, Tex., Aug. 13, 1902; s. Byrom Palmer and Annie Laura (Nance) M.; A.B., Abilene Christian Coll., 1924; M.A., U. Tex., 1930, student summers, 1925, 28, 29, 30; LL.D., McMurry Coll., 1956, Pepperdine Coll., 1963; Litt.D., Okla. Christian Coll., 1968; m. Alberta Allen, Nov. 1, 1924; children—Jacquelin, Patricia, Thomas Asbury. Tchr., Red Oak (Tex.) High Sch., 1920-22, Abilene High Sch., 1924-28; instr. speech Abilene Christian Coll., 1928-32, v.p.; head dept. speech, 1932-40, pres., 1940-69, chancellor, 1969-74. Mem. Tex. Tchrs. Assn. (life), Phi Delta Kappa, Alpha Chi. Mem. Ch. Christ. Club: Rotary Internat. Home: Abilene Tex. Died Jan 9, 1974.

MORRIS, EMORY WILLIAM, found. exec.; b. Nashville, Mich., May 14, 1905; s. Edgar Thurber and Elizabeth Jane (Hand) M.; D.D.S., U. Mich., 1928; D.Sc. (hon.), Tufts Coll., 1943, Loyola U., 1958, U. Mich., 1963; LL.D., Mich. State U., 1955; m. Mary Virginia Cavanaugh, Mar. 17, 1934. Engaged in private practice oral surgery, Battle Creek, Mich., 1928-33; dir. dental edn. W. K. Kellogg Found., Battle Creek, 1933-34, asso dir., treas., 1934-40, gen. dir., 1940-65, pres., 1943-67, chmn. bd., from 1967, trustee, from 1936. Dir. Kellogg Co., Security Nat. Bank Battle Creek. Mem. citizens bd. U. Chgo., adv. com. ednl. relations with Latin Am. Inst. Internat. Relations; trustee Lane-Thomas Found., Battle Creek Area Hosp. Funds. Decorated officer Cross Merit (Fed. Republic Germany), Order Agrl. Merit (Columbia); recipient Gold Key award Tri-State Hosp. Assembly, 1958, William John Gies award Am. Coll. Dentists, 1964, Med. Service Mich. State Med. Soc., Wolverine Frontiersman award, 1965, Outstanding Service award Mich. Assn. Professions, 1966, Presdl. citation Am. Pub. Health Assn., 1966, Sesquicentennial award U. Mich., 1967, award honor Am. Hosp. Assn., 1967; named to Hall Fame, Mich. Health Council, 1967; commd. Ky. Col. Fellow Am. Pub. Health Assn., Am. Coll. Dentists, Am. Coll. Hosp. Adminstrs. (hon.); mem. Am. Assn. Dental Schs. (hon.), Am. Hosp. Assn. (hon.), Am. Dental Assn. (hon.), Mich. Pub. Health Assn. (hon.), Costa Rican Dental Soc. (hon.), Delta Sigma Phi, Delta Sigma Delta, Omicron Kappa Upsilon. Mason. Home: Battle Creek, Mich. Died July 6, 1974.

MORRIS, GEORGE L. K., painter, sculptor; b. N.Y.C., Nov. 14, 1905; s. Newbold and Helen S. (Kingsland) M.; graduate Groton Sch., 1924; A.B., Yale, 1928; m. Estelle C. Frelinghuysen. Student painter in Paris with Fernand Leger, also N.Y.C., 1928-30; editor Yale Lit. Rev., also Miscellany mag., N.Y.C., 1929-31, Plastique mag., Paris, 1937-39, World of Abstract Art, 1957; founder, art editor Partisan Rev., 1937-43; Am. editor art d'Aujourd dui; instr. painting Art Students League, 1945-46; artist-in-residence St. John's Coll., 1960-61, 66; dir. N.Y.C. Center Music and Drama, from 1966; exhibited in Valentine Gallery, N.Y.C., 1933, Berkshire Mus. Pittsfield, Mass., 1933, Mus. Living Art, N.Y.C., Saybrooke Coll., Yale, 1935, Reinhardt Gallery, 1936, Pierre Gallery, Paris, 1936-38, Mayor Gallery, London, 1936, Passeloit Gallery, Seligmann Galleries, 1938, Downtown Gallery, N.Y.C., 1943, 44, 47, 50, 64, 66, Galerie Allendy, Paris, 1946, Alan Gallery, N.Y.C., 1955, 57, Inst. Contemporary Art, Washington, 1958, Corcoran Gallery, Washington, 1965, Berkshire Mus., 1966, Hirschl and Adler galleries, N.Y.C., 1971, 74, Lenox (Mass.) Library, 1974, Cin. Art Mus., 1975, Nat. Inst. Arts and Letters, 1975, Am. Acad. Arts and Letters 1976; rep. collections U. Ill. Hessischer Landesmuseum, Darmstadt, Germany, Pa. Academy, Met. Mus. Art, Wichita, Whitney, Phila. Berkshire museums, Yale Gallery, Phillips Meml. Gallery, U. Ga., Munson-Proctor-Williams Mus., Utica, N.Y., N.C. Mus., Montclair (N.J.) Art Mus., Dallas Mus., Chattanooga Mus., High Mus., Atlanta, Honolulu Mus. Bd. dirs. Lenox Library. U.S. del. UNESCO Conf., Venice, 1952. Recieient Pepsi-Cola Achievement award, 1948, Temple gold medal Pa. Acad. 1966, Saltus Gold medal Nat. Acad. 1973. Mem. Am. Abstract Artists, 1936 (founder, exhibitor; pres. 1948-49), Nat. Inst. Arts and Letters, Fedn. Modern Painters and Sculptors, Artists Equity (dir.), Zeta Psi. Clubs: Elizabethan, Lenox (Mass.); Stockbridge (Mass.) Golf; River, Century (N.Y.C.); Polo (Paris, France). Adv. bd. Partisan Rev. Home: New York City, N.Y. Died June 26, 1975.

MORRIS, JACK SIDNEY, lawyer; b. Chgo., May 26, 1906; s. Louis M. and Hattie (Gordon) M.; Ph.B., U. Chgo., 1927, J.D., 1928; m. Melba Lea Hakan, June 8, 1941; 1 dau., Marilyn Ann. Admitted to Ill. bar, 1928, practiced in Chgo.; partner Schuyler, Stough & Morris. Lectr. real estate law. Mem. Am. (chmn. tax aspects of real estate transactions com. real property, probate and trust law div. 1961-64, real estate contracts com. 1964-67, liaison com. 1970-72), Ill. (chmn. real estate law sect. 1957-59), Chgo. (chmn. com. real property law 1958-60), 7th Fed. Circuit bar assns., Am. Judicature Soc. Club: Standard (Chgo.). Author several legal articles, chpt. in book. Home: Chicago, Ill. Died Apr. 26, 1974; buried Shalom Meml. Park, Palatine, Ill.

MORRIS, VICTOR PIERPONT, coll. dean; b. Sioux City, Ia., Nov. 24, 1891; s. James Madison and True Augusta (Pierpont) M.; A.B., U. of Ore., 1915, A.M., 1920; Ph.D., Columbia, 1930; m. Grace Parker, June 15, 1925. Began as teacher in high sch., 1915; asst. prof.

economics, Grinnell Coll., 1922-24; instr. Ore. State Coll., Corvallis, Ore., 1924-26; prof. U. of Ore. from 1926, dean Sch. of Business Adminstrn., after 1936, acting pres., 1953-54, Miner prof. bus. adminstrn., 1957-59. Chief party Econ. Devel. Adv. Group, Korea, ICA, 1959-60, Fgn. Policy Forum; mem. Bd. of Education, City Planning Commn. (Eugene, Ore.); chmn. Ore. Ednl. Commn., 1933-35, chmn. Commn. on Study of Workman's Compensation Law, 1939-45; chmn. trustees Northwest Christian Coll. (Eugene, Ore.); mem. merit system council, State Bd. of Health chmn. State Committee on Postwar Readjustment and Development apptd. by Gov., 1943-49; mem. adv. com. Bonneville Adminstrn.; dist. adv. bd. Ore. and Cal. lands and resources Bur. Land Mgmt. Mem. Am. Assn. Collegiate Schs. Bus. (exec. com.), American Economic Assn., Acad. of Polit. Science, Delta Upsilon, Beta Gamma Sigma, Phi Delta Kappa. Republican. Mem. Disciples of Christ. Club: City (Portland). Author: Oregon's Experience with Minimum Wage Legislation, 1930. Editor: Proceedings of the Columbia Basin Session of Inst. of World Affairs, 1932; Proceedings of Conference on Higher Education, U. of Ore., 1934; Report of Education Commission to 1935 Legislature, U. of Ore., 1935. Contbr. to jours. Home: Eugene, Ore. Died June 21, 1974; buried Rest Haven Meml. Park, Eugene, Ore.

MORRISON, HARRY STEELE, author; b. Mattoon, Ill., Nov. 26, 1880; s. Thomas J. and Angeline (Cunningham) M.; attended Mattoon High Sch. 1 yr., and pvt. schs., New York and Chicago, office boy, real estate office, Chicago, at 15; at 16 took 7 months' trip in Europe, starting with only ½ and working his way from place to place; interviewed various monarchs and notables; on his return entered the literary and lecture fields, and lectured in large cities of the East; made second European trip, 1900, visiting Paris Expn. In 1901 made trip around the world; attended corenation of King Edward, 1902; editor of Railroad Men, 1902-05. Author: A Yankee Boy's Success, 1898; The Adventure of a Boy Reporter, 1900; How I Worked My Way Around the World, 1903. Home: Princeton, N.J.†

MORRISON, HARVEY ARCH, educator; b. Milo, Ia., Dec. 2, 1879; s. James Harvey and Jennie (Mitchell) M.; grad. Lincoln (Neb.) Normal Sch., 1894; B.S., Union Coll., College View, Neb., 1900, A.M., 1906; m. Vera Estell Thompson, June 6, 1906; children—Hilden Lucien (dec.), Alethea D., Cleo E. Prof. mathematics, Union Coll., 1900-09; same, South Lancaster (Mass.) Coll., 1909-10; prof. mathematics and treas., 1911-14; pres. Union Coll., 1914-22; pres. Washington Missionary Coll., 1922-27, and 1935-36; gen. sec. Dept. of Edn. of Gen. Conf. Seventh-Day Adventists, 1936-46; gen. mgr. Review and Herald Pub. Assn., from 1946. Republican. Seventh Day Adventist. Home: Washington, D.C.†

MORRISON, JAMES B(ROWN), communications exec.; b. Virginia City, Nev., Dec. 21, 1901; s. Chancellor D. and Alice (Brown) M.; grad. U.S. Naval Acad., 1923; m. Mathilde C. Prescott, Mar. 4, 1924 (dec. 1970); 1 son, James Brown. Commd. ensign, U.S. Navy, 1923, resigned, Feb. 1925; engineer Chesapeake & Potomac Tel. Co., Washington, 1925, gen. plant mgr., 1942-46; vice pres., gen. mgr., 1946-48; v.p. operations Wis. Tel. Co., Milw., 1948, pres., 1948-53; pres. Chesapeake & Potomac Tel. Co. (D.C.), Chesapeake & Potomac Tel. Co. of Md., Va. and W.Va., 1954-65, chmn. bd., 1965-67; dir. Riggs Nat. Bank (Washington), Northwestern Mut. Life Ins. Co. (Milw.). Episcopalian. Clubs: Columbia Country, Chevy Chase Metropolitan, Army and Navy, Burning Tree (Washington); Commonwealth (Richmond, Va.). Home: Washington, D.C. Died Mar. 18, 1975.

MORRISSEY, BERNARD DELBERT, educator; b. Farmersville, Ill., Mar. 20, 1907; s. Dennis and Anna (Haley) M.; A.B., St. Louis U., 1928, A.M., 1930; Ph.D., Northwestern U. 1957. Teaching fellow in Latin, St. Louis U., 1928-30; instr. St. Louis U. High Sch., 1930-42; lectr. English, St. Louis U., 1936-42, instr., 1945-50; asst. prof. to prof. English, Beloit (Wis.) Coll., 1955-72, chmn. dept., 1969-72, chmn. div. humanities, 1960-64, 66-70, prof. emeritus from 1972; vis. lectr. U. Wis., Rock County, Janesville, from 1972. Asso., cons.-examiner Commn. Instns. Higher Edn. of North Central Assn. Colls. and Secondary Schs., from 1970. Served with USCG, 1942-45. Mem. Modern Lang. Assn. Home: Beloit, Wis. Died Apr. 2, 1975; buried St. Maurice Cemetery, Morrisonville, Ill.

MORSE, CHARLES FREDERIC, musician; b. Mishawaka, Ind., Mar. 26, 1881; s. George and Augusta (Loring) M.; prep. edn., high sch., Mishawaka; student U. of Mich. and Univ. Sch. of Music, Ann Arbor; grad. Mich. Conservatory of Music, 1901; pupil of Alexandre Guilmant and Lucien Wurmser, Paris, 1906-07; m. Mary Christie Walsh, of Detroit, Mich., June 29, 1921. In Detroit from 1900, except 4 yrs. as head of music dept. State Normal Sch., California, Pa., and periods of study in U.S. and abroad; co-founder and sec. Detroit Inst. Musical Art until 1919; organist and choir-master Grosse Pointe Memorial Ch.; also concert organist, pianist and lecturer. Condr. Orpheus Club (male voices), Madrigal Club (women's voices), Music Study Club Chorus; choral instr. Ford Hosp. Nurses' Training Sch. Former dean Mich. chapter Am. Guild of Organists; pres. Fine Arts Soc., Mich. Music Teachers' Assn. Episcopalian. Club: Bohemians. Address: Detroit, Mich.†

MORSE, ROBERT HOSMER, (JR.), business exec.; b. N.Y.C., Mar 10, 1899; s. Robert Hosmer and Bernice (Jones) M.; educated Interlaken School, Kentucky Mil. Inst., Culver Mil. Acad., Notre Dame, Harvard; m. Helen Susannah Bech, Sept. 23, 1920; children—Robert Hosmer III, Marilynn and William Beck. Employee Fairbanks, Morse & Co., Indianapolis, 1916-28, asst. mgr. Indianapolis works; assistant to president Central & Southwest Utilities Company, Dallas, Tex., 1928-30; vice pres., treas. Inland Utilities Co., Kansas City, Mo., 1930-32; br. mgr. Fairbanks, Morse & Co., Cincinnati, O., 1932-34, Dallas, Tex., 1934-38, mgr. stoker div., 1938-39; br. mgr. Boston, Mass., 1939-42; asst. gen. sales mgr., Chicago, 1942-43; v.p., gen. sales mgr. 1943-48; v.p. in charge all co. operations, 1948-50, pres., 1950-59; pres. Canadian Locomotive Co., Ltd., Kingston, Ont., 1950-73; dir. Fairbanks, Morse & Co., Municipal Acceptance Corp., U.S. Gypsum Co. Continental Ill. Nat. Bank & Trust Co. of Chgo.; mem. gen. adv. bd., Lumbermens Casualty Co. Served in A.U.S., 1917-19; with A.E.F., 18 months. Trustee Fairbanks, Morse and Company Pension Fund. Member A.S.M.E. Mason (Shriner). Clubs: Chicago, Racquet, Chicago Athletic Association, Casino, Glen View (Chgo.); Question; Bath & Tennis, Everglades (Palm Beach, Florida); Bohemian (San Francisco). Home: Lake Forest, Ill. Died Aug. 10, 1973.

MORSE, WAYNE LYMAN, U. S. senator; b. Madison, Wis., Oct. 20, 1900; s. Wilbur F. and Jessie (White) M.; Ph.B., U. Wis., 1923, M.A., 1924; LL.B., U. Minn., 1928; J.D., Columbia, 1932; LL.D., Cornell Coll., 1946, Drake U., 1947, Coll. So. Jersey, 1947, Centre Coll., 1952; Pd.D., Salem Coll., 1965; D.C.L., Parsons Coll., 1965; LL.D., Wilberforce U., 1966, Pacific U., 1969; m. Mildred Downie, June 18, 1924; children—Nancy Faye (Mrs. Hugh Campbell, Jr.), Judith Mary Wade Eaton, Amy Ann (Mrs. John Bilich). Instr. U. Wis., 1924; asst. prof. U. Minn., 1924-29; teaching fellow Columbia, 1928-29; asst. prof. law U. Ore., 1929-30, asso. prof., 1930-31, dean, prof. law, 1931-44; adminstrv. dir. U.S. atty. general's survey release procedures; spl. asst. to atty. gen. U.S., 1936-39; Pacific Coast arbitrator Dept. Labor (maritime industry), 1938-42; chmn. President's Emergency Bd., 1941; alternate pub. mem. Nat. Def. Mediation Bd., 1941; mem. NWLB, pub. rep., 1942-44; U.S. senator, 1945-69, mem. coms. on fgn. relations labor and publ. welfare, small business, D.C., spl. com. aging; distinguished vis. scholar State U. N.Y., 1969-70; labor arbitrator, from 1969. U.S. rep. 15th session UN Gen. Assembly, 1960; mem. Ore. Crime Commn.; mem. Gov.'s Commn. to Consider Jud. Reforms (chmn. subcom. on criminal procedure reform); chmn. Gov.'s Comm. Improvement of Sentencing, Probation and Parole; mem. Nat. Conf. Family Relations; chmn. Pres.'s Spl. Bd. Atlantic and Gulf Coast Maritime Industry Dispute, 1963; chmn. Pres.'s Emergency Bd. Airlines Dispute, 1966, President's Spl. Bd. Railroad Dispute, 1967. Mem. Am., Ore., Lane County, Fed., D.C. bar assns., Am. Law Inst., Order of Coif, Delta Sigma Rho, Gamma Eta Gamma, Scabbard and Blade, Pi Kappa Alpha, Democrat. Conglist. Mason (Shriner), K.P., Rotarian. Author: A Survey of Grand Jury System, 1931; (with Ronald Beattie) The Administration of Criminal Justice in Oregon, 1932; Attorney General's Survey of Release Procedures, 1939. Contbr. to law revs., periodicals. Home: Eugene Ore. Died July 22, 1974.

MORSELL, JOHN ALBERT, assn. exec.; b. Pitts., Apr. 14, 1912; s. Samuel Richard and Maud Lydia (Wright) M.; B.S.S., City Coll., N.Y., 1934; M.A., Columbia, 1938, Ph.D., 1951; m. Marjorie Ellen Poole, Aug. 21, 1937; 1 son, Frederick Albert. Dir. Inst. Community Relations, Sydenham Hosp., N.Y.C., 1946-49; study dir. Bur. Applied Social Research, Columbia, 1949-51, Internat. Research Asso., Inc., N.Y.C., 1951-56; with N.A.A.C.P., from 1956, asst. to exec. sec., 1956-64, asst. exec. dir., from 1964. Mem. Bd. Higher Edn. N.Y.C., from 1970. Recipient UN Service medal for field research Korea, 1951. Fellow Am. Social. Assn.; mem. Am. Assn. Pub. Opinion Research, Phi Beta Kappa. Home: Brooklyn, N.Y. Deceased.

MORTENSEN, SOREN HANSEN elec. engr.; b. Eskelund-Jylland, Denmark, Nov. 4, 1879; s. Hans Madsen and Maren (Sorensen) M.; B.A., Ribe Latin Sch., Denmark, 1897; E.E., M.E. Polytechnicum Mittwida, Germany, 1902; D.Eng., Ill. Inst. Tech., 1944; m. May Kingsly Seaman, Oct. 2, 1907 (dec. Oct. 1937); children—Mary Jane (Mrs. N. C. Munson), Dan Seaman; m. 2d, Helen Tearse, June 20, 1939 (dec. Jan. 1955). Came to U.S., 1902, naturalized, 1910. With mech. engring. dept. Westinghouse Electric Mfg. Co., Pitts., 1902-05; with Allis Chalmers Mfg. Co., Milw., 1905-52, successively designer motors and generators, elec. engr. Norwood works and West Allis plants, engr. charge design, 1905-42, chief elec. engr., 1942-52. Commd. officer Danish Army; cons. Oakridge and Manhattan projects, World War II. Recipient Lamme medal Am. Inst. E.E., 1944. Registered profl. engr. Fellow Am. Inst. E.E. (nat. dir. 1944-48); mem. Engrs. Soc. Milw. (dir. 1931), Nat. Electric Mfrs. Assn., Art Inst., Am. Standards Assn., Internat. Conf. Large Electric High-Tension Systems (U.S. nat. com.), Eta Kappa Nu. Republican, Presbyn. (elder). Clubs: City, Milwaukee (Milw.). Author: (textbook) Electric Machine Design, 1949. Patentee self-starting synchronous motors, hydraulic driven alternators, high speed turbo generators, others. Home: Wauwatosa, Wis.†

MORTHLAND, DAVID VERNON, lawyer; b. Warren, Mo., Feb. 6, 1880; s. Joseph Morrison and Mary Elizabeth (Frederick) M.; LL.B. cum laude, Univ. of Mo., 1907; m. Nelle Lane, June 30, 1909 (died Dec. 2, 1930); children—Joseph Lane, Mary Frances, Mildred Elizabeth, David Vernon (deceased), Francis William; m. 2d, Olga C. Anderson, June 16, 1932. Admitted to Mo. bar, 1907, Wash. bar, 1908; in practice at St. Joseph, Mo., 1907-08, Yakima, Wash., from 1908; member Washington State Senate, 1917-29, 1933-34; chmn. Charter Com., Yakima, 1929. With Y.M.C.A., Camp Lewis, Wash., 1918. Mem. Am. Bar Assn., Wash. State Bar Assn., Order of the Coif, Phi Delta Phi, Delta Tau Delta. Republican. Baptist, Modern Woodman. Club: Rotary (past pres.). Home: Yakima, Wash.†

MORTON, ALFRED HAMMOND, govt. ofcl.; b. Chicago, Oct. 5, 1897; s. Edward C. and Mary (Hammond) M.; B.S., U. Ill., 1919; M.S., Columbia, 1923; m. Helen Mills, Feb. 3, 1925; 1 dau., Mary (Mrs. Benjamin H. Torrey). European mgr. Radio Corp. of Am., 1929-34; mgr. program dept. N.B.C., 1934-36, v.p. in charge stas., 1936-38, v.p. in charge television, 1938-42; pres. Nat. Concert & Artists Corp., 1942-48; dir. TV 20th Century Fox Film Corp., 1948-50; TV cons., 1950-52; became dep. adminstr. Internat. Information Adminstrn., Oct. 1952; also dir. Internat. Broadcasting, Voice of Am. Served as capt. F.A., A.U.S., 1928-19. Decorated Chevalier Legion of Honor (France). Mem. Am. Inst. E.E., Inst. Radio Engrs., Psi Upsilon. Home: Southbury, Conn. Died Apr. 9, 1974.

MORTON, LOUIS, educator, historian; b. N.Y.C., Dec. 30, 1913; s. Nathan and Celia (Edelstein) M.; B.S., N.Y. U., 1935, M.A., 1936, Ph.D., Duke, 1938; M.A. (hon.), Dartmouth, 1962; m. Ruth Goldstein, Dec. 28, 1941; children—David K., Rachel L., Nathaniel B. Instr. history Coll. City N.Y., 1939-41; research asso. Colonial Williamsburg, 1941-42; historian, dep. chief historian, chief Pacific br. Office Mil. History, U.S. Army, 1946-59; prof. history Dartmouth, 1960-76, chmn. history dept., Daniel Webster prof., 1968-76, provost, 1971-72. Lectr., cons. service colls., 1 1955-76; Harmon Meml. lectr. USAF Acad., 1961; lectr. Rice U., 1962-64, U. Cal., San Diego, 1965. chmn. bd. Hist. Evaluation and Research Orgn., 1962-66; mem. Nat. Council Accreditation Tchrs., 1967-70, USAF Hist. Adv. Group, 1968-71; chmn. adv. com. NASA Hist. Office, 1968-76; hist. adv. coms. Sec. Army, Sec. Air Force; chmn. history jury Pulitzer prize. Served to capt. AUS, 1942-46; lt. col. Res. Decorated Bronze Star. Recipient Superior Performance and Outstanding Employee awards U.S. Civil Service, 1957-58; Rockefeller Pub. Service award, 1959. Research grantee Carnegie Corp. N.Y., 1960-62, 63-76. Fellow Soc. Am. Historians; mem. Council Fgn. Relations, Am. Hist. Assn. (chmn. program com. 1967), Orgn. Am. Historians U.S. Naval Inst., Inst. Strategic Studies Am. Assn. U. Profs., New Eng. Hist. Assn. (pres. 1968-69), Internat. Studies Assn., Phi Beta Kappa. Author: Robert Carter of Nomini Hall: A Virginia Tobacco Planter of the 18th Century, 1941; The Fall of the Philippines, 1953; War in the Pacific: Strategy and Command, 1963; Writings on World War II, 1967. Co-author: Command Decisions, 1960; Total War and Cold War, 1962; Theory and Practice in American Politics, 1964; Schools for Strategy, 1965; The Historian and the Diplomat, 1967. Editor: War in the Pacific, U.S. Army in World War II, 11 vols., 1949-63; gen. editor Wars and Military Instructions of the United States, 17 vols., 1963-76; bd. editors Mil. Affairs, 1948-51, 68-76, Jour. Modern History, 1960-63. Home: Hanover, N.H., Died Feb. 12, 1976.

MORTON, RICHARD LEE, educator; b. "Falkland," Prince Edward County, Va., Sept. 20, 1889; s. John Robert and Mildred Henry (Watkins) M.; B.A., Hampden-Sydney (Va.) Coll., 1910, Litt.D., 1926; M.A., U. of Va., 1915, Phelps-Stokes fellow, 1917-18, Ph.D., 1918; M.A., Harvard, 1917; m. Estelle Dinwiddie, December 20, 1919; children—Mary Louise (Mrs. William J. Murtagh), Nancy Dinwiddie (Mrs. Arthur W. Gardiner). Asso prof history and government Coll. of William and Mary, Williamsburg, Va., 1919-21, prof. and head of history dept., 1921-58, Chancellor prof. history, 1958, emeritus, 1959, chairman division of social sciences, 1944-47. Mem. advisory com. of historians, Colonial Williamsburg, Inc., 1939-44; grant-in-aid from Social Science Research Council, 1931; grant from Gen. Edn. Bd., 1942-43; mng. editor William and Mary Quar., 1943-46, later member bd. editors. Served in U.S. Army, 1918. Mem. council, Inst. Early Am. History and Culture, 1944-45, 47-50, 52-55, from 1956. Mem. American Hist. Assn., Soc. of Am. Historians, So. Hist. Assn., Va. Hist. Soc., Va. Social Science Assn. (pres. 1931), Assn. for Preservation Virginia Antiquities, Raven, Phi Beta Kappa, Omicron Delta Kappa, Sigma Upsilon, Tau Kappa Alpha, Sigma Pi. Democrat. Episcopalian (warden). Rotarian. Author: The Negro in Virginia Politics, 1919; History of Virginia since 1861 (Vol. 3 of History of Virginia, Vol. 1 by P. A. Bruce and Vol. 2 by L. G. Tyler), 1924;

Virginia and Her Builders (with M. F. Altstetter), 1932. Contbr. to Dictionary of Am. Biography and Richmond, Capital of Virginia 1937. Editor: Present State of Virginia (by Hugh Jones), 1956; Struggle Against Tyranny — Virginia, 1677-1699, 1957; Colonial Virginia, 2 vols., 1960. Home: Williamsburg Va. Died Sept. 8, 1974.

MORWITZ, SAMUEL MORDECAI, physician; b. Russia, 1886; M.D., Rush Med. Coll., 1911. Intern, Milwaukee County Hosp., Wauwatosa, Wis., 1911-12; postgrad. in otolaryngology U. Vienna, 1921; asso. otolarygnologist Mt. Sinai Hosp., from 1923; asso. prof. dept. otolaryngology emeritus U. Ill. Diplomate Am. Bd. Otolaryngology. Fellow A.C.S.; mem. A.M.A., Am. Acad. Ophthalmology and Otolaryngology. Home: Chicago, Ill. Died Feb. 22, 1972.

MORY, E. LAWRENCE, business exec.; b. Boyertown, Pa., 1880. Pres. and dir. Boyertown Burial Casket Co.; vice pres. Mory-Buckwater, Inc., Phila., Pa.; dir. National Bank of Boyertown, Mem. bd. mgrs. Reading (Pa.) Hosp. Home: Boyertown, Pa.†

MOSCONA, NICOLA, bass-baritone; b. Athens, Greece, Sept. 23, 1907; s. Michael and Maria M.; hon. deg. for singing Nat. Conservatory of Athens, 1930; m. Antigone, Feb. 3, 1945. Came to U.S., naturalized, 1946. Debut, Nat. Opera of Greece, 1930, Italian debut, Cremona, 1937. Am. debut with Met. Opera Assn., 1937, leading bass-baritone, 1937-75; sang at Teatro Della Scalla, Milan, 1938, also London Music Festival and Luzerne Festival; frequent soloist under Arturo Toscanini. Decorated Golden Cross Order of Phoenix, Golden Medal from Vets. of War, Silver Plaque Nat. Opera (Greece). Mem. Am. Guild Mus. Artists, Fedn. Radio Artists, Athenian Soc., Am. Hellenic Progressive Assn. Home: New York City, N.Y. Died Sept. 17, 1975.

MOSCRIP, WILLIAM SMITH, cattle breeder; b. Maiden Rock, Wis., Sept. 22, 1878; s. Daniel Henderson and Laura Arabel (Smith) M.; ed. high sch., St. Paul, Minn., St. Paul Coll., and St. Paul Sch. Law; m. May Martin Lee, June 27, 1908. Began in boyhood as dairyman and breeder of milk cattle, specializing in pure-bred Holstein-Friesians since 1904; proprietor of North Star Farm; pres. Twin City Milk Producers Assn. Mem. bd. dirs. St. Paul Assn. of Commerce; dir. and mem. exec. com. Nat. Coop. Milk Producers Assn.; v.p. Minn. Live Stock Breeders Assn.; dir. Nat. Dairy Assn., Nat. Dairy Council, Minn. Live Stock Sanitary Bd., Minn. State Fair Bd.; dir. Minn. Holstein Breeders Assn., Northern States Power Co.; pres. Holstein Friesian Assn. of Am. Republican. Methodist. Club: St. Paul Athletic, Chosen "Master Farmer," 1931; received University of Wisconsin Recognition for Service Rendered Agriculture, 1937. Home: Lake Elmo, Minn.†

MOSES, ALFRED GEIGER, rabbi; b. Livingston, Ala., Sept. 23, 1878; s. Rabbi Adolph and Emma (Isaacs) M.; B.A., U. of Cincinnati, 1900; grad. Hebrew Union Coll., Cincinnati, 1901; (Litt.D., U. of Ala., 1911); m. Birdie Feld, June 2, 1915; 1 dau., Shirley E. Rabbi Temple Shaarai Shomayim, Mobile, Ala., from June 1, 1901. Member Department of Public Welfare, Mobile City and County; field rep. Jewish Welfare Board, U.S. Army and Navy. Pres. Iberville Hist. Soc., Mobile; member Soc. for Internat. Peace and Arbitration, Central Conf. Am. Rabbis, Phi Beta Kappa. Clubs: Elks, Shrine. Author: Jewish Science, Divine Healing in Judaism, 1916; A Peace Anthology—The Bible Message on Peace, 1916; Jewish Science, 1920. Address: Mobile, Ala.*†

MOSES, ELBERT RAYMOND, lecturer, educator; b. Sterling, Minn., June 3, 1879; s. Abram and Minerva (Dunbar) M.; grad. Cummock Sch. of Oratory, Evanston, Ill., 1900; student Coll. of Wooster (O.), 1903-05; grad. Muskingum Coll., New Concord, O., 1907; D.Litt., Westminster College, New Wilmington, Pa., 1929; m. Martha Miller, June 15, 1907 (dec.); children—Elbert R., Lowell M., Jane (Mrs. John MacAllister); m. 2d, Anna Throp Welbourn, Mar. 27, 1920; 1 dau. Annette D. (Mrs. Martin Godfrey) Instr. in pub. speaking, Huron (S.D.) Coll., 1900-02, Muskingum Coll., 1905-10; prof. pub. speaking, Westminster Coll., 1910-17, 1919-23; instr. Bible reading and pulpit oratory, Pittsburgh-Xenia Theol. Sem., 1924-29, Western Theol. Sem., 1926-33, Gettysburg Theol. Sem., 1931-34; instr. pub. speaking Westinghouse Electric and Mfg. Co., 1929-42, Am. Inst. Banking, 1931-44, Robert Morris Sch. of Business, 1934-35; v.p. Nat. Lincoln Chantauqua, 1917-19; founder, 1924, pres. emeritus Pittsburgh Sch. of Speech; mem. speakers bureau National Defense Council, Pittsburgh, 1942. Member International Platform (vice p. 1942), S.A.R., Delta Sigma Rho, Tau Kappa Alpha. Republican. Alumni Award, Northwestern U. (field of speech), 1942. Mem. United Presbyn. Ch. Mason (32°). Lectures: Abraham Lincoln; James Whitcomb Riley; Born Without a Chance; Master Builders of Am. Pioneer broadcaster Gems of American Literature, KDKA. Club: Lions. Writer of When I Was a Country Boy; My Kind of a Boy; Friendly Traveler; The Torch of Freedom. Winner Ohio state oratorical contest, 1904; author: Cabin to Capitol (recorded for class room use), 1949; owner and sales mgr., Cabin to Capitol Records. Home: Lake Worth, Fla.†

MOSES, EMILE PHILLIPS, marine corps officer; b. Sumter, S.C., May 1880; s. Altamont and Octavia (Cohen) M.; student U. of S.C., 1897-99, LL.D., 1943; student Ga. Sch. Tech., 1901-02; grad. Advanced Class, Army F.A. Sch., 1926, Army War Coll., 1930, Naval War Coll., 1931, Naval War Coll., Advanced Course, 1939; m. Carolyn Iver Angier, Oct. 22, 1914; children—Elizabeth (Mrs. E.A. M. Banks), Emile Phillips, Jr. Apptd. 2d lt., U.S. Marine Corps, 1904, and advanced through the grade to maj. gen., 1942; comdr. Marine Barracks, Paris Island, S.C., 1941-44; retired for phys. disability incident to service, 1944. As pres. of Marine Corps Equipment Bd. contributed largely to development and adaptation to mil. use of the amphibian tractor, and to design and use of ramp on Higgins landing boats. Mem. Omicron Delta Kappa. Home: La Jolla, Cal.†

MOSES, SIEGFRIED, Israeli ofcl.; b. Lautenburg, Germany, May 3, 1887; s. Julius and Hedwig (Graetz) M.; student U. Berlin, 1904-07; J.D., U. Heidelberg, 1908; Dr.phil.h.c., U. Jerusalem, 1972; m. Margarete Orthal, Dec. 13, 1921; children—Eli, Rafael. Practice law, 1912-36; organized food control, Danzig, World War I; dep. mng. dir. Organ. German Towns, 1919; controller footwear supply, 1920-22; pub. auditor, 1932-36 dir. Schocken chain stores, Germany, 1923-29, mem. bd., 1930-34, chmn. 1935; emigrated to Palestine, 1936; mng. dir. Haavara (orgn. for transfer Jewish property from Germany to Palestine), 1937-38; pub. auditor, 1938-49; state comptroller Israel, 1949-61. Dir. Bank Leumi le Israel, ATA Textile Co. Ltd. Pres. Zionist Orgn. Germany, 1933-37, Council Jews from Germany, 1957-74, Leo Baeck Inst., 1955-74, Orgn. Central European Immigrants in Israel, 1953-74. Bd. dirs. Van Leer Jerusalem Found. Author: Deutsches Kohlen-Wirtschaftsgesetz, 1920; Reform des Obligationen-Wesens, 1933; The Income Tax Ordinance Palestine, 1942, 2d edit., 1946; Jewish Postwar Claims, 1944. Address: Jerusalem, Israel. Died Jan. 14, 1974; buried Jerusalem, Israel.

MOSES, WALTER H., lawyer; b. New Orleans, Aug. 25, 1898; s. Joseph W. and Irma (Moses) M.; B.A., Harvard, 1918, LL.B. cum laude, 1921; m. Helen Watson, Nov. 1921; 1 son, John Watson; m. 2d, Eleanor Plummer, Dec. 1930; 1 son, Walter Harper. Admitted to Ill. bar, 1921, U.S. Supreme Ct., 1927, Cal. bar, 1930; mem. firm Moses, Bachrach & Kennedy, and predecessors, Chgo., 1925-30, 39-59, Beilenson & Moses, Los Angeles, 1930-31; sr. mem. firm Moses, Gibbons, Abramson, Becco & Fox, and predecessor firms, Chgo., 1960-70; mem. Abrahamson, Becco & Fox, Chgo., from 1970. Pub. mem. regional WLB, World War II; Ill. Supreme Ct. mem. character and fitness com. 1st Appellate Dist., 1957-60; mem. citizens com. Family Ct. Cook County, 1963-70, Sch. Bd. Nominating Com. Chgo., 1963-66; mem. Chgo. Crime Commn., 1964-70. Bd. dirs. Ill. Humane Soc. Fellow Am. Bar Found.; mem. Am. (ho. of dels. 1966-69), Ill., Cal., Chgo. (bd. mgrs. 1958-64, 2d v.p. 1960, 1st v.p. 1961, pres. 1962) bar assns., Bar Assn. 7th Circuit, Chgo. Law Inst., Harvard Law Sch. Assn. Clubs: Harvard Downtown, Law (Chgo.). Author: Stock Brokerage Law for Stockholders and Their Employees, 1937. Bd. editors Harvard Law Rev., 1920-21. Home: Winnetka, Ill. Died July 20, 1973.

MOSS, CHASE, banker; b. Lewisburg, Tenn., Aug. 16, 1912; s. James Lee and Ruth (Adams) M.; student U. Tenn., 1931-32, Stonier Grad. Sch. Banking, 1948-50; m. Dorothy Muse, June 2, 1947; children—Joseph Chase, Lee Muse, John Adams. Mgr. J.C. Adams Co., 1933-37; with 3d Nat. Bank of Nashville, 1937-73, exec. v.p., 1970-72, chmn., 1972-73; chmn. 3d Nat. Corp., 1972-73. Bd. dirs. Nashville Mental Health Assn., 1966-74; mem. budget com. United Givers Fund, 1965-69. Mem. U. Tenn. Devel. Council, 1970—. Served with AUS, 1943-46. Mem. Am. (regional v.p. 1966-68), Tenn. (pres. 1969-70, exec. council) bankers assns., Lewisburg C. of C., Phi Gamma Delta. Presbyn. (elder). Home: Nashville, Tenn., Died Jan. 30, 1974.

MOTCHAN, LOUIS A., physician; b. Cairo, Ill., 1908; M.D., Washington U., St. Louis, 1933. Intern, St. Louis City Hosp., 1933-34, asst. resident in medicine, 1934-35, resident, 1935-36; clin. tng. Washington U. Clinics, 1936-37; asso. attending physician in-patient dept., clin. attending physician out-patient staff Cedars of Lebanon Hosp., Los Angeles. Served to maj. M.C., AUS, 1942-46. Diplomate Am. Bd. Internal Medicine. Mem. A.M.A., Am. Diabetes Assn., Am. Heart Assn. Home: Los Angeles, Cal. Died Feb. 24, 1973; buried Memphis, Tenn.

MOTT, FRANCIS EDWARD, telephone co. exec.; b. Shelby, O., Mar. 3, 1904; s. Alonzo and Mary (Klees) M.; student U. Cin., 1922-23; B.S., Ohio State U., 1927; m. Hermogene Kennedy, Sept. 3, 1929; children—John Kennedy, Thomas Edward, Constance Anne (Mrs. James G. Marrie). With Ohio Bell Telephone Co., 1927-69, sec., treas., 1966-69. Dir., treas. St. Johns Hosp. Employees of Cleve. Fed. Credit Union, Kirby Manor Home for Sr. Citizens; trustee Consumer Credit Counseling Service. Home: Lakewood, O. Died 1973.

MOUDY, ALFRED L., lecturer; b. Jackson Twp., Dekalb Co., Ind., Apr. 30, 1879; s. William and Ellen Jane (Carnahan) M.; grad. Tri-State Coll., Angola, Ind., 1910; spl. study Columbia, 1912; grad. Arty. Sch. of Fire, Fort Sill, Okla., 1917; spl. study Colo. State U., 1920; grad. Command and Staff Sch., Fort Leavenworth, Kan., 1925; m. Nora May Ginder, of Butler, Ind., Sept. 7, 1904 (she died March 14, 1938). Served as teacher in country schools, Ind., 1899-1906; teacher and superintendent schs., Waterloo, Ind., 1906-17, 1920-23; lecturer and field rep. Flying Squadron Foundation, from 1923. V.p. Deubener Shopping Bag, Inc., Indianapolis. Pvt., inf., Ind. N.G., 1903-06, 2d lt., 1906-09, 1st lt., 1909-12, capt., 1912-17; maj., F.A., U.S.A., 1917-19; lt. col. F.A., U.S.R., and Ind. N.G., from 1920. Pres. Nat. Better Govt. Assn., Inc. Mem. Mil. Order Foreign Wars, Am. Legion. Republican. Mason (Shriner), Odd Fellow, K.P. Lecturer on ednl. subjects. Constitution of U.S., etc. Home: Waterloo, Ind.†

MOULDS, GEORGE HENRY, educator; b. Buck Creek, Ia., Mar. 30, 1915; s. George Thomas and Laura Myrtle (Henry) M.; B.A., Wheaton (Ill.) Coll., 1938; M.A., State U. Ia., 1940; Ph.D., U. Chgo., 1959; m. Blanche Mildred Kilbourn, June 8, 1943; children—Kathleen Ann, Janice Irene. Tchr. social studies, prin. Mystic (Ia.) High Sch., 1940-42; mem. faculty Kent State U., from 1948, prof. philosophy, from 1962, chmn. dept., from 1970. Cons., Nat. Interscholastic Acad. Games, 1967. Served to 2d lt. AUS, 1943-45; ETO. Decorated Bronze Star. Mem. Am. Assn. U. Profs., Am. Philos. Assn., Philosophy Edn. Soc., Am. Soc. Polit. and Legal Philosophy. Author: Thinking Straighter, 1965; (with Greene and Allen) The Propaganda Game, 1966. Home: Kent, O. Died Dec. 5, 1973; interred Harlington Cemetery, Waverly, Ia.

MOULTON, DUDLEY, agriculture; b. San Jose, Calif., Dec. 29, 1879; s. Stillman Agustus and Lydia Frances (Dudley) M.; grad. Acad., U. of Pacific, 1897; A.B., Stanford, 1903, M.A., 1906; m. Maude Neosho Chidester, Aug. 15, 1914; children—Robert Chidester, Kenneth Stillman. Entomologist, Santa Clara County, Calif., 1904-06; spl. agt. Bur. Entomology, U.S. Dept. Agr., Walnut Creek, 1906-09; dep. state commr. of horticulture, Calif., 1909-12; agrl. commr. San Francisco and San Francisco County, 1915-31; dir. Dept. of Agr., State of Calif., 1931-1933. Mem. Am. Entomol. Soc., Am. Assn. Econ. Entomologists, Pacific Coast Entomol. Soc., A.A.A.S., Sigma Xi. Republican. Conglist. Contbr. many bulls. to U.S. Dept. Agr. and papers to scientific mags. Spl. research in Thysanoptera (made one of world's largest collections of this group). Home: Redwood City, Cal.†

MOULTON, GERTRUDE EVELYN; b. Rio Grande, Gallia County, O., June 5, 1880; d. Albanus Avery and Laura Lillian (Allen) Moulton; A.B., Oberlin Coll., 1903; A.B., Rio Grande (O.) Coll., 1905; studied Western Reserve U., Harvard, Columbia, New York U.; B.S., U. of Ill., 1917, M.D., 1919; A.M., New York U., 1936. Teacher physical training, pub. schs., Cleveland, O., 1904-07; instr. physical training of women, 1907-09, acting dir., 1909-11, dir., 1911-15, med. adviser to women, 1919-23, Univ. of Ill.; prof. hygiene and physical edn., dir. women's gymnasium, Oberlin Coll., 1923-45; asso. supervisor in phys. edn. for women, U. of Mich., 1945-46; prof. phys. edn. Rio Grande Coll., Rio Grande, O., from 1946. Pres. Midwest Assn. Health, Phys. Edn. and Recreation, 1944-47. Fellow Am. Phys. Edn. Assn., A.M.A., Mem. Am. Acad. of Physical Education. Mem. Alpha Epsilon Iota, Alpha Omega Alpha. Conglist. Contbr. to Jour. of Health, Physical Education, The Physical Educator, etc. Address: Rio Grande, O.†

MOULTON, MARY KENNINGTON, librarian; b. Wuhu, Anhwei, China, Sept. 26, 1913; d. Thomas Wilfred and Olive Dell (Ward) Kennington; brought to U.S., 1927, naturalized, 1946; student Aurora Coll., 1932-33, U. Mass., 1936-40, U. Chgo., 1942-43. Record librarian Mass. Meml. Hosp., Boston, 1936-40; reference librarian research div. N.E.A., Washington, 1940-41; children's librarian, St. Charles, Ill., 1944-45; self employed landscape architect, St. Charles, 1947-63; librarian, curator spl. collections Morton Arboretum, Lisle, Ill., from 1963. Trustee Pub. Library, St. Charles, 1951-63. Recipient design award A.I.A., 1963. Mem. Am. Bookworkers Guild, Am. Hort. Soc., Am. Soc. Landscape Architects. Home: Downers Grove, Ill. Died Apr. 7, 1972; interred Little Woods Cemetery, nr. St. Charles, Ill.

MOULTON, ROBERT HURT, journalist, author; b. Nashville, Tenn., June 8, 1880; s. Frank and Mildred Thetis (Hurt) M.; B.S., Sch. of Mines (Columbia), 1900; m. Agnes Ruth Lively, Sept. 8, 1914; children—Robert Hurt, Suzanne Ruth and David Harmon (twins). Reporter, Chicago American, 1908-09; free lance writer, from 1909; contbr. to all important mags. and newspapers, U.S. and England; articles illustrated by photographs taken by himself; special writer on economics of grain marketing for Chicago Bd. of Trade from 1914. Author: The Story of Wheat, Trading in Grain, etc.; librettist of the musical plays "A Modern Miracle" and "The Girl of Tomorrow." Mem. Alpha Delta Phi. Home: Glencoe, Ill.†

MOUNT, GEORGE HAINES, psychologist; b. Fairfield, Ia., May 1, 1879; s. Jededigh and Margaret Ann (Dey) M.; A.B., Parsons Coll., Fairfield, 1903;

M.Di., Ia. State Teachers Coll., Cedar Falls, 1905; A.M., State U. of Ia., 1908, Ph.D. from same, 1940; m. Margaret Ann Lyon, Aug. 18, 1903 (dec.); children—John William, George Edwin; m. 2d, Frances Earl Hill, Jan. 13, 1932; 1 dau., Mary Ann. Instructor in science, high sch., Algona, Ia., 1903-05, prin. schools, Kanawha, Ia., 1905-07; asst. in psychology and education, State U. of Iowa, 1908-10; prof. psychology and edn., Northern State Normal, Marquette, Mich., 1910-11; same, Ia. State Teachers Coll., 1911-21; prof. philosophy and psychology, Dubuque (Ia.) U., 1921-24; prof. psychology, Duke U., 1924-25; prof. same, University of Southern California, 1925-33, head of dept., 1927-30; consultant psychologist, from 1933. Civilian psycholigist Santa Ana (California) Army Air Base, 1942-44. Staff psychologist and dir. Personnel Institute, Los Angeles, 1944-46; later personnel director Alpha Beta Food Markets, Inc., Los Angeles. Consultant in psychology, Los Angeles Diagnostic Clinic, 1929. Member Iowa War Work Council and secretary Y.M.C.A. for S.A.T.C., Iowa State Teachers College, 1917. Fellow A.A.A.S.; mem. American Psychol. Assn., Western Psychol. Assn., Calif. Psychopathic Assn., N.E.A., Am. Assn. Univ. Profs., Southern Soc. for Philosophy and Psychology, Ia. Acad. Science, Sigma Xi, Phi Delta Kappa, Pi Gamma Mu, Phi Kappa Phi, Psi Chi. Republican. Methodist. Home: Los Angeles, Cal.†

MOUNT, RUSSELL THEODORE, lawyer; b. N.Y.C., Apr. 18, 1881; s. James Theodore and Louise (Inslee) M.; student Lawrenceville (N.J.) Sch., 1896-98; A.B. magna cum laude, Princeton, 1902; LL.B., Columbia, 1906; m. Nora Alice Shenstone, Apr. 25, 1911; 1 dau., Hester (Mrs. Mills M. Fries). Admitted to N.Y. bar, 1906; law clk. Convers & Kirlin, N.Y.C., 1906-13; pvt. practice, 1913-16; partner Duncan & Mount, 1916-47, Mendes & Mount, from 1947. Mem. Maritime Law Assn. U.S., Am. Soc. Internat. Law, Bar Assn. City, N.Y., Phi Beta Kappa. Clubs: University, Down Town Assn. (N.Y.C.); Colonial (Princeton); Montclair (N.J.) Golf. Home: Montclair, N.J.†

MOUNTAIN, HARRY MONTGOMERY, ins. exec.; b. Monett, Mo., Jan. 20, 1901. Began career with Aetna Ins. Group, 1921, asst. manager, 1944-49, mgr., 1949-50, v.p., Western dept. mgr., 1950-52, exec. v.p., 1955-59, pres., 1959-66, also dir. Home: West Hartford, Conn. Died June 1973.

MOUZON, JAMES CARLISLE, educator; b. San Antonio, Jan. 8, 1907; s. Edwin DuBose and Mary (Mike) M.; A.B., So. Meth. U., 1927; Ph.D., Cal. Inst. Tech., 1932; Sc.D. (hon.), So. Methodist Univ., 1966; m. Elizabeth Walker, Sept. 10, 1932; children—Elizabeth (Mrs. James R. Butterfield), Margaret (Mrs. Glenn A. Prag). Head sci. dept. Wesley Jr. Coll., 1927-28; grad. asst. and fellow Cal. Inst. Tech., 1929-32; instr. physics Duke, 1932-35, asst. prof., 1935-42, asso. prof., 1942-44; physicist Naval Ordnance Lab., 1942-43; sr. physicist, head elec. sect. Brown instrument div. Mpls. Honeywell, 1944-47, dir. research, 1947-49; mem. planning div. Research and Devel. Bd., 1949-50; chief atomic warfare div. Office Asst. Operations Analysis, USAF, 1950-53; chief intelligence div. Johns Hopkins Operations Research Office, 1953-57; research planning staff Engring. Research Inst., U. Mich., 1957, prof. elec. engring., 1957-72, prof. emeritus, 1972-75; cons. Willow Run Labs., 1957-60, asso. dean Coll. Engring., 1960-66, dir. Coll. Engring. Brazilian Program, 1961-67, Ford Found. Engring. Faculty Devel. Program, 1960-75. Mem. com. internat. exchange persons Conf. Bd. Asso. Research Councils, 1967-70; cons. Asso. Research Councils, 1967-75, chmn. engring. selection com., 1968-69; cons. Indsl. Nucleonics Corp., 1965-75. Fellow Am. Phys. Soc., A.A.A.S.; mem. I.E.E.E., Am. Soc. Engring. Edn. (chmn. Mich. sect. 1964-65, exec. bd. council sects. and brs. East 1964-66), Am. Assn. Physics Tchrs., Sigma Xi, Tau Beta Pi, Sigma Alpha Epsilon, Eta Kappa Nu. Club: Cosmos (Washington). Author articles in field. Patentee in field. Home: Ann Arbor, Mich. Died Aug. 13, 1975; cremated.

MUDD, EUGENE J., banker; b. St. Charles County, near St. Charles, Mo., Mar. 16, 1879; s. Dr. James R. and Mary Caroline (Boschert) M.; A.B., St. Louis U., 1901; m. Helen Rechtern, Sept. 4, 1907. Started with Nat. Bank of Commerce in St. Louis as collector, 1902, became discount clerk, cashier; v.p. and dir. Mercantile Commerce Bank & Trust Co., St. Louis, from 1929, exec. v.p., from 1944; pres. Bank of Commerce Liquidating Co., St. Louis. Mem. St. Louis C. of C. K.C. Clubs: Missouri Athletic, Noonday. Home: St. Louis, Mo.†

MUDD, STUART, microbiologist; b. St. Louis, Sept. 23, 1893; s. Harvey Gilmer and Margaret de la Plaux (Clark) M.; B.S., Princeton, 1916; A.M., Washington U., St. Louis, 1918; M.D., Harvard, 1920; m. Emily Borie Hartshorne, Sept. 12, 1922; children—Emily Borie, Stuart Harvey, Margaret Clark, John Hodgen. Research fellow Harvard, 1920-23; asso. Rockefeller Inst., 1923-25; asso. in pathology Henry Phipps Inst., U. Pa., 1925-31, asst. prof. exptl. pathology 1925-31; asso. prof. bacteriology U. Pa., 1931-34; prof., 1934-51, prof. microbiology, 1951-59, prof. emeritus, 1959-75; dir. microbiologic research VA Hosp., Phila., 1959-70. Recipient John Fleming medal Am. Inst. Geonomy and Natural Resources, 1967. Fellow A.A.A.S., Am. Pub. Health Assn., Coll. Physicians Phila., N.Y. Acad. Scis.; mem. World Acad. Art and Sci. (v.p. 1962, charter mem), Am. Human Serum Assn. (pres. 1940-41), Physiol. Soc., Am. Assn. Pathologists and Bacteriologists, Am. Assn. Immologists, Royal Soc. Medicine Gt. Britain (affiliate), Societe d'Encouragement au Progres France (comdr.), Consejo Superior de Investigaciones Scientificas Madrid (hon.), Soc. Exptl. Pathology, Soc. Exptl. Biology and Medicine, Harvey Soc., Soc. Am. Bacteriologists (pres. 1945), Histochem. Soc. (pres. 1952), Internat. Assn. Microbiol. Socs. (v.p. 1953-58, pres. 1958-62), Phi Beta Kappa, Sigma Xi, Alpha Omega Alpha. Democrat. Episcopalian. Clubs: Princeton, Cosmos (Washington); Merion Cricket. Editor: Blood Substitutes and Blood Transfusion, 1942; The Population Crisis and the Use of World Resources, 1964; Conflict Resolution and World Education, 1966; Infectious Agents and Host Reactions, 1970; formerly asso. editor Jour. Immunology, Jour. Histochemistry and Cytochemistry, Jour. Bacteriology. Home: Haverford, Pa. Died May 6, 1975; buried Church of the Redeemer, Bryn Mawr, Pa.

MUEHLEISEN, EUGENE FREDERICK, dentist; b. St. Louis, Sept. 15, 1903; s. Fred and Mary Minnie (Michel) M.; D.D.S., U. So. Cal. Sch. Dentistry, 1927; m. Omega Kenley, June 9, 1929; children—Eugene Fred. Dentist, San Diego, from 1959. Asso. State Bd. Examiners Dental Assts. So. Cal., 1958-65. Chmn. bd. N.W. San Diego YMCA, 1942-55, later adviser to bd.; mem. San Diego Recreation Dept. Park, Lakes and Recreation Bd., 1958-71, chmn., 1960; mem. adv. com. San Diego County Sch. Com. Redistricting of Schs., 1955-67. Mem. San Diego County Dental Soc. (life mem., certificate of merit), U. So. Cal. Sch. Dentistry, Am. Dental Assn. (life mem.). Baptist (pres. Am. Bapt. Men 1966-67; mem. State Bd. Bapt. Laymen 1967-71). Kiwanian (pres. East S.D. chpt. 1940-41). Home: San Diego, Cal. Died Mar. 17, 1973; buried El Camino Park, Sorrento Valley, Cal.

MUENCH, HUGO, JR., physician; b. St. Louis, Oct. 17, 1894; s. Hugo and Eugenia (Thamer) M.; A.B., Cornell, 1915; M.D., Washington U., 1918; Dr.P.H., Johns Hopkins, 1932; A.M. (hon.), Harvard, 1946; m. Helen Ruth Harrison, Dec. 28, 1920; 1 son, James Frederick. Intern mil. hosps., 1917-20; county health officer Bertie County, Windsor, N.C., 1920-21; mem. field staff, internat. health div., Rockefeller Found., 1921-46, charge statis. work, 1932-37, fellowship adviser, 1937-46; prof. biostatistics Harvard Sch. Pub. Health, 1946-72, asst. dean, 1946-54. Mem. commn. on evaluation Poliomyelitis vacinne. Diplomate (founders group) Am. Bd. Preventive Medicine and Pub. Health. Fellow A.A.A.S., Am. Statis. Assn., Am. Pub. Health Assn.; mem. Institute of Math. Statistics, American Epidemiological Society, Delta Omega (past national pres.). Author: Catalytic Models in Epidemiology, 1959. Contbr. papers, book chapters, articles in gen. field of statistics applied to pub. health, med. and lab. problems. Home: Cambridge, Mass., Died Nov. 16, 1972.

MUHAMMED, ELIJAH (ELIJAH POOLE), clergyman; b. Sandersville, Ga., Oct. 10, 1897; m. Clara Evans; 6 sons. Mem. Black Muslims, 1923-75, leader, 1934-75. Home: Chicago, Ill. Died Feb. 25, 1975.

MUILENBURG, JAMES, educator; b. Orange City, Ia., June 1, 1896; s. John William and Gertrude (van Rooyen) M.; A.B., Hope Coll., 1920, D.D., 1955; A.M., U. Neb., 1923; Ph.D., Yale, 1926; L.H.D., U. Me., 1936; D.D., Pacific Sch. Religion, 1945; S.T.D., Ch. Div. Sch. of Pacific, 1960; m. Mary Kloote, June 30, 1921; children—James Edward, Laurence Edgar, Janet Gertrude. Instr. in English, U. Neb., 1920-23, Yale, 1925-26; asst. prof. bibl. lit. Mt. Holyoke Coll., 1926-28, asso. prof. bibl. lit., 1928-32; dean Coll. Arts and Science, U. Me., 1932-36; prof. O.T. lit. and Semitic langs., Pacific Sch. of Religion, 1936-45; prof. Hebrew and Cognate Langs., Union Theol. Sem., N.Y.C.; vis. prof. U. Chgo., summer, 1940, Columbia, 1941, 42, 44. Served from pvt. to 1st lt. U.S. Army, 1917-19; with A.E.F. 10 months. Mem. Am. Schools of Oriental Research (resident dir. 1953-54), Soc. Bibl. Lit. and Exegesis, Am. Oriental Soc., Nat. Assn. Biblical Instrs., Theol. Discussion Group, National Council Religion Higher Edn., Phi Beta Kappa, Phi Kappa Phi. Conglist. Editor and compiler: Specimens of Biblical Literature, 1923. Author: The Literary Relations of the Teaching of the Twelve Apostles and the Epistle of Barnabas (monograph); History of Religion of Israel, Interpreter's Bible, Vol. I, Commentary on Isaiah, Vol. V; also monograph on beginning of Revolution of 1688. Contbr. to Excavations of Tell-en-Nasbeh, 1947, Peake's Commentary on the Bible. Home: New York City, N.Y. Died May 10, 1974.

MUIR, ROY CUMMINGS, elec. engr.; b. Arcadia, Wis., Dec. 30, 1881; s. John Cherry and Ann (Michie) M.; B.S. in E.E., U. of Wis., 1905; hon. Dr. Engring., U. of Wis., 1939; Manhattan Coll., 1942; m. Marian Page Bedford, Jan. 24, 1920; children—Elizabeth, Robert C., John Morley. With Gen. Electric Co. from 1905, v.p. in charge engring., 1934-44, v.p. and gen. mgr. apparatus dept.; 1945-48; v.p., gen. mgr. nucleonics dept., 1948-49; cons., from 1949. Presdl. Certificate of Merit, 1948. Mem. bd. mgrs. Ellis Hospital; trustee Union College Fellow American Society Mech. Engineers, Am. Inst. Elec. Engrs.; mem. Am. Soc. for Engineering Edn., Newcomen Soc. of England, Tau Beta Pi, Eta Kappa Nu. Republican. Unitarian. Clubs: Mohawk, Mohawk Golf, Edison (Schenectady) University (New York); Field (Sarasota, Fla.). Contbr. to tech., ednl. publs. Home: Schenectady, N.Y., Died May 19, 1973.

MULCAHY, FRANCIS PATRICK, marine corps officer; b. Rochester, N.Y., Mar. 9, 1894; s. Thomas Joseph and Nellie (McEligott) M.; Ph.B., U. Notre Dame, 1914; m. Elinor Wolf, July 23, 1919 (dec. Mar. 26, 1922); m. 2d, Elizabeth Bertrand, Nov. 14, 1934; children—Thomas, Patricia. Commd. 2d lt. USMC, June 26, 1917, transferred to Marine Corps aviation, Oct. 17, 1917, and advanced through grades to lt. gen., 1946; combat pilot, France, 1918; aviation duty Haiti, 1920-21, 23-25, Nicaragua, 1927, 31-33, Virgin Islands, 1938-40, South Pacific, 1942-44, Central Pacific, 1944-45; ret. from active duty, Apr. 1946. Decorated Navy D.S.M. with gold star, Army D.S.M., Legion of Merit. Democrat. Roman Catholic. Home: Coronado, Cal. Died Dec. 11, 1973.

MULHAUSER, FREDERICK LUDWIG, educator; b. Cleve., June 21, 1911; s. Frederick L. and Helen E. (Fletcher) M.; B.A., Coll. Wooster, 1932; M.A., Yale, 1934, Ph.D., 1937; postgrad. Kenyon Sch. English, 1949, Wadham Coll., Oxford (Eng.) U., 1949-50; m. Margaret M. Lehman, Aug. 28, 1937; 1 son, Frederick Van Norden. Instr. English, Hiram Coll., 1936, Northwestern U., 1937-41; mem. faculty Pomona Coll., from 1941, prof. English, from 1952, Phebe Estelle Spalding prof. English, from 1962. Tchr. G.I. Univ., Florence, Italy, 1945, prof. U. Pisa (Italy), 1963-64. Served with inf. AUS, 1944-45. Guggenheim fellow, 1956-57; recipient Wig Distinguished Prof. award Pomona Coll., 1960, (posthumously), 1974. Fulbright fellow, 1963-64; Rockefeller Found. scholar, 1971. Mem. Modern Lang. Assn., Phi Beta Kappa. Editor: (with A.L.P. Norrington and H. L. Lowry) The Poems of Arthur Hugh Clough, 1951, 2d edit. rev. and enlarged, 1974; Correspondence of Arthur Hugh Clough, 1957. Home: Claremont, Cal. Died Feb. 25, 1974.

MULHOLLAND, JOHN HUGH, surgeon; b. N.Y.C., June 28, 1900; s. John and Annastasia (O'Brien) M.; A.B., N.Y. U. Coll. Arts, 1922, M.D., Med. Coll., 1925; m. Claire Shoemaker, July 31, 1930; children—Lucie (Mrs. Joseph F. Perez) and Claire (Mrs. Warren Skinner (twins). Surg. interne res., 3d Div., Bellevue Hosp., N.Y.C., 1926-28, asst. surgery N.Y. U. Coll. Medicine, 1928-31, instr., 1931-36, asst. clin. prof., 1936-41, prof. clin. surg., asst. dean, 1938-46, George David Stuart prof. surg., dir. surgery Bellevue, Univ. hosps., 1946-66, also later prof. surgery; cons. surgeon Beth Israel Hosp., N.Y., Booth Meml. Hosp., N.Y. Infirmary, Fitkin Meml. Hosp., Neptune, N.J., Monmouth Memorial Hosp., United Hosp., Portchester, First Army; vis. prof. surgery Harvard, 1957, Marquette U., 1961. Mem. Am. Bd. of Surgery, 1949. Commd. lt. col. M.C., U.S. Army, 1942, col., 1945; dir. and chief of surgical services, 1st Gen. Hosp. (Bellevue Affiliated Unit). Decorated Bronze Star; Croix de Guerre avec Etoile Vermeila (France); Commonwealth Fund fellow, 1940; recipient Achievement award N.Y.U., 1961, 62, Alumni Distinguished Service award, 1959, Presdl. citation, 1966. Diplomate Am. Bd. Surgery. Fellow Am. Sur. Assn. (pres., 1957-58); Am. Coll. Surgeons (bd. govs. 1947-50), Am. Assn. for Surgery of Trauma, N.Y. Acad. Medicine (chmn. sect. on surgery, 1949-50); mem. Soc. for Exptl. Biology and Medicine, Soc. Med. Consultants, World War II, Buffalo (hon.), N.Y. surg. socs., N.Y. State (chmn. sect. on surgery 1949-50), and County med. societies, A.M.A., So. Surg. Assn., Harvey Soc., Halsted Soc., N.Y. Acad. Scis., A.A.A.S., Com. on Surg., Nat. Research Council, Soc. Clin. Surgery, Soc. University Surgeons USPHS (mem. surgery study sect. Research Grants Div.), Soc. Grad. Surgeons, Korean Med. Assn. (hon.), Soc. Internationale de Chirurgie, Royal Soc. Med. (England), Sigma Xi, Pi Kappa Alpha, Alpha Omega Alpha. Clubs: Ardsley Country; University (N.Y.). Consulting author: Cole and Elman's Textbook of Surgery; author (with Edward Ellison and Stanley R. Friesen) Current Surgical Management III, 1965. Contbr. to Surgical Literature. Editor in chief Annals of Surgery, 1957-70. Home: Southbury, Conn. Died May 16, 1974; buried New North Cemetery, Woodbury, Conn.

MULLAN, EUGENE HAGAN, U.S. Pub. Health Service; b. Oakland, Calif., July 18, 1879; s. Dennis W. and Ada R. (Pettit) M.; prep. edn. Georgetown (D.C.) Prep. Sch.; B.S., St. Johns Coll., Annapolis, Md., 1899; M.D., U. of Md., 1903; m. Eleanor V. Gildea, Nov. 4, 1905; children—Eleanor (Mrs. Karl Johanboeke), Mary (Mrs. J. J. Kobes), Virginia (Mrs. James D. Sams), Hugh, Barbara. Commd. asst. surgeon U.S.P.H.S., 1905, passed asst. surgeon, 1909, med. dir., 1931; served in immigration duty at Ellis Island, N.Y., 20 yrs., at Montreal, Can., 8 yrs.; hosp. duty Marine Hosp., Louisville, Ky., 5 yrs., Cape May, N.J., 1 yr., Perryville, Md., 1 yr.; served in the yellow fever epidemic, New Orleans, 1905; med. dir. Am. Embassy, Paris, and Consulate, Bordeaux, 1939-40. Member A.M.A.

Catholic. Author of several pamphlets, results of studies on mental condition of immigrants, pub. by U.S. P.H.S. Address: Montreal, Que., Can.†

MULLANEY, EUGENE L(IGURI), business exec.; b. N.Y.C., June 12, 1890; s. James A. and Catherine (McCrane) M.; LL.B., N.Y. U., 1912; m. Kathryn Lorrayne Romanoff, Oct. 28, 1921; 1 dau., Eugenie Katherine. Partner Tanzer-Mullaney, N.Y.C., from 1927; pres., dir. Ace Investment Co.; dir. E. Z. Mills, Inc., N.Y.C., Gillette Safety Razor Co., Boston, Energy Control Co., Inc., H. Reeve Angel and Co., Inc. Served with 7th Regt., National Guard, Mexican Border, 1916; 107 U.S. Inf., A.E.F., 1918-19. Recipient N.Y. State Medal of Honor. Mem. American, N.Y. State bar assns., American Judicature Society, New York County Lawyers Association, Am. Legion, Vets. 7th Regt., Delta Chi. Clubs: Union League, Metropolitan Opera (N.Y.C.); Garden City (N.Y.) Golf. Home: Wilmington, Del. Died Sept. 10, 1973.

MULLEN, JOSEPH, pres. Southern Acid & Sulphur Co., Inc.; b. Norfolk, Va., 1875; B.E., Johns Hopkins U., 1895; m. Elizabeth Welsh Cocke, Oct. 22, 1902; children—Elizabeth W., Emily Nash, Janet C., Joseph, Jr. Sec., v.p. and dir., later pres., Southern Acid and Sulphur Co., Inc., St. Louis; dir. Jefferson Lake Sulphur Co., New Orleans, Ohio Sulphur & Fertilizer Co. (formerly Ohio Sugar Co.). Clubs: Noonday, Missouri Athletic (St. Louis). Home: St. Louis, Mo.*†

MULLER, HENRY NICHOLAS, JR., elec. engr., assn. exec.; b. Pitts., June 27, 1914; s. Henry Nicholas and Mary Elizabeth (Harmer) Muller; grad. St. John's Mil. Acad., 1931; B.A. in Physics, Dartmouth, 1935; m. Harriet Motter Kerschner, May 16, 1936; children—Henry Nicholas III, Edward Kerschner. With Westinghouse Electric Corp., 1935-67, exec. asst. to v.p. engring., 1952-56, exec. asst. to v.p. apparatus products, 1955-56; chief engr. Canadian Westinghouse Co. Ltd., 1956-57, v.p., 1957-61, v.p. light apparatus, 1961-62, v.p. engring., 1962-67, engring. adminstr., Pitts., 1967, dir., 1961-67; v.p., tech. dir. Nat. Elec. Mfrs. Assn., N.Y.C., 1967-71; exec. sec. Westinghouse Ednl. Found., 1948-55; mgr. Westinghouse Ednl. Center, 1948-55. Exec. com. Engring. Manpower Commn., 1951-55; mem. adv. coms. SSS, 1951-53. Overseer, Thayer Sch. Engring., Dartmouth, 1953-61; chmn. engring. adv. com. Hamilton Inst. Tech., 1958-67; mem. bd. govs., mem. senate, also planning and bldg. com. McMaster U., Hamilton, Ont., Can. Fellow I.E.E.E., Am. Soc. M.E. (pres., treas., chmn. nat. membership devel., edn. com., chmn. mgmt. div., regional v.p., chmn. organizational com. and finance com.); mem. Engring. Inst. Can., Council Internat. Progress Mgmt. (dir.), Assn. Profl. Engrs. Ont. (chmn. Hamilton chpt.), C. of C., Newcomen Soc. N.Am., Delta Tau Delta. Clubs: Pittsburgh Field; Hamilton Golf and Country, Hamilton, Rotary (Hamilton, Ont., Can.); Talbot Country (Easton, Md.); Engineer's (N.Y.C.). Author: Electrical Transmission and Distribution Reference Book (with others), 1942. Home: Easton, Md. Died Aug. 29, 1974; buried Pine Knoll Cemetery, Hanover, N.H.

MULLGARDT, WILLIAM OSCAR, architect; b. Washington, Mo., June 5, 1878; s. John Christian and Wilhelmina (Hausgen) M.; ed. pub. sch. and high sch., Washington, Mo., St. Louis (Mo.) Coll. of Pharmacy, St. Louis Sch. of Fine Arts, and Atelier Washington U.; m. Adele Bartlett Haynes, Oct. 7, 1907 (died 1916); 1 son, William Haynes; m. 2d, Josephine Meredith Moore, Sept. 1, 1921; 1 son, William Oscar II (died 1923). Began as student and draughtsman, 1900; associate, Mauran, Russell & Crowell, 1920-30, partner in firm Mauran, Russell, Crowell & Mullgardt from 1930. Firm's architectural works in St. Louis include: U.S. Court House and Custom House, office bldg., Monsanto Chem. Co., Globe Democrat. Pub. Plant, Daily Record Plant, Post Dispatch Pub. Plant (Pulitzer Pub. Co.), Soldiers Memorial; also architects for Exchange Nat. Bank, Jefferson City, Mo.; State Hosp., Farmington, Mo.; State Clinic Bldg., Farmington, Mo.; government work; Clinton Peabody Terrace, housing project, U.S. Housing Adminstrn., St. Louis Ordnance Plant. McQuay-Norris Armor Piercing Core Plant, McQuay-Norris Mfg. Co. and Chevrolet Shell Div., (Gen. Motors Corp.) Engring Plant (all in St. Louis). Allegheny Ordnance Plant, Cumberland, Md. Pres. St. Louis Archtl. Club, 1913-15, 1920-21; exec. U.S. Housing Emergency Fleet Corp., 1918; chmn. St. Louis Building Congress, 1932-34; mem. dist. adv. council Historic Am. Bldg. Survey, 1934; mem. architects' jury Fed. Housing Adminstrn. Housing Program, 1935; mem. bd. dirs. St. Louis Regional Planning Commn., 1938; chmn. Gen. Council Civic Needs, 1939-41; chmn. steering com. to revise St. Louis Bldg. Code, 1937-43; chmn. survey com., survey and mass evacuation, St. Louis Am. Red Cross; mem. advancement com. St. Louis council Boy Scouts America; vice pres. St. Louis, St. Charles, Alton, Lakeway Assn., from 1940; dir. Mo. Welfare League, 1937; mem. bd. govs. St. Louis Automobile Club of Mo., from 1941; dir. St. Louis Chamber of Commerce, chmn. archtl. div., also chmn. civic development com., 1939-41. Chmn. archtl. div. State Bd. of Registration for Architects and Professional Engrs., 1945. Given Meritorious Civilian Award by Bur. of Yards and Docks, Navy Dept., Jan. 1911. Mem. St. Louis Bd. Bldg. Appeals, from 1946. Presbyterian. Fellow A.I.A. (sec. St. Louis chapter, 1921-23, pres. 1933-35), Club: Missouri Athletic (St. Louis). Home: St. Louis, Mo.*†

MULLIGAN, WILLIAM JOSEPH, lawyer; b. Thompsonville, Conn., June 2, 1881; s. William and Frances (Browne) M.; student Phillips Exeter Acad., 1900, Williston Acad., 1901, Yale Law Sch., 1904; LL.D., Holy Cross 1919, Fordham U., 1919; m. Kathleen Byron Keefe, June 15, 1905; children—William Joseph, Jr., Jean (Mrs. Lee S. Johnson), Kathleen (Mrs. Harrison Dunning). Admitted to bar, 1904, engaged in practice of law at Thompsonville and Hartford Dir. Riverside Trust Co., Hartford; chmn. bd. dirs. Hartford Fed. Savs. & Loan Assn. Decorated Knight of St. Gregor by Pope Benedict XV, 1919. Knight of Malta by Pope Pius XII, 1950; Knight of the Holy Sepulchre, Pope Pius, 1951; awarded Medaille de la Reconnaissance Francaise, 1920. Mem. Am. and Hartford County bar asso ciations. Knight of Colubmus. (supreme master 4th°). Clubs: Hartford, Yale (Hartford, Conn.); Yale (N.Y.). Home: Hartford, Conn.†

MULLINS, D. FRANK, JR., physician; b. Canton, Ga., 1915; M.D., Emory U., 1942. Intern, Grady Meml. Hosp., Atlanta, 1942-43, asst. resident in pathology, 1942-43; pathologist Foster Gen. Hosp., Jackson, Miss., 1943-44; cons. pathologist Milledgeville State Hosp.; instr. pathology Emory U., 1942-43; asst. prof. pathology and bacteriology La. State U., 1946-47; prof. bacteriology and vet. hygiene U. Ga. Sch. Vet. Med., Athens, 1947-73; vis. prof. pathology Med. Coll. Ga., 1969. Served from capt. to maj. M.C., AUS, 1944-46. Diplomate Am. Bd. Pathology. Mem. A.M.A., So. Med. Assn., Am. Soc. Clin. Pathologists, Coll. Am. Pathologists. Home: Evans Ga. Died Feb. 2, 1973.

MULVANIA, MAURICE, college prof.; b. Princeton, Mo., Oct. 4, 1878; s. John and Ursula (Harper) M.; S.B., Western Normal Coll., Shenandoah, Ia., 1906; S.M., U. of Tenn., 1912; Ph.D., U. of Wis., 1925; m. Eunice V. Colwell, Aug. 7, 1904; children—Cyril H., Walton M., Robin C. Instr. biology, Western Normal Coll., 1906-09; asst. bacteriology, U. of Tenn., 1911-13, bacteriologist Agrl. Expt. Sta., 1913-15, asst. prof. bacteriology, 1915-18; asso. prof., 1918-23, dean pre-med. sch., 1920-23; instr. horticulture, U. of Wis., 1923-25; head dept. biology, Florida Southern Coll., Lakeland, from 1926; in charge ecol. research for Mediterranean fruit fly eradication work, U.S. Dept. Agr., 1930; dir. lab. Civic Health Center, Knoxville, Tenn., 1921-22. Mem. A.A.A.S., Sigma Xi. Contbr. Jour. of Bacteriology, etc. Address: Lakeland, Fla.†

MUNCE, ROBERT J(OHN), chancellor; b. Washington, Pa., Jan. 25, 1895; s. Robert J. and Elizabeth M. (Donley) M.; A.B., Washington and Jefferson Coll., 1918; A.M., U. Mich., 1926; grad. study U. Mich. and U. Pittsburgh; LL.D., Emerson Coll., 1956; m. Elizabeth M. Young, June 11, 1925 (dec.); 1 dau., Ferna Charity (Mrs. D. B. Kirk) (dec.); m. 2d, Mary Ann Curtis, Oct. 8, 1960. Instr. physics U. Pittsburgh, 1920-22, lectr. sociology, 1934-46, asst. registrar, 1942-46; asst. prof. physics Washington and Jefferson Coll., 1922-34; asst. registrar Washington U., St. Louis, 1946-47; registrar Washington Univ.-Coll., St. Louis, 1947-48; dir. eve. div. Suffolk U., Boston, 1948-49, dean coll. liberal arts, 1949-54, pres. Univ., 1954-60, chancellor, 1960-75. Trustee, clerk Bd. of Endicott Jr. Coll., Beverly, Mass. Mem. Newcomen Soc. North America, Bostonian Society. Republican. Presbyn. Mason. Clubs: State, Incorporated; Rotary. Home: Boca Raton, Fla. Died Apr. 30, 1975; buried Village Cemetery, Surry, N.H.

MUNDEN, KENNETH WHITE, archivist, editor; b. Elizabeth City, N.C., Feb. 16, 1912; s. Joshua Warren and Elizabeth Jane (White) M.; student Duke, 1929-31; A.B., George Washington U., 1943; m. Lia Ghezzi, Aug. 24, 1946; children—Robin Ghezzi, Gordon Ghezzi. Statistician, War Dept., 1934-39; archivist Nat. Archives, 1939-43, 58-68; archivist Dept. Army, 1948-50, 52-57; archivist Fed. Civil Def. Adminstrn., 1958; editor Am. Film Inst., 1968-72; archival cons. Dept. Army, 1972-74; historian Office Econ. Opportunity, 1972-73. Lectr. archival methodology Temple U., Am. U., 1951-68. Served with AUS, 1942-48, 51-52; lt. col. Res. ret. Recipient Waldo G. Leland prize Soc. Am. Archivists, 1963, Meritorious Achievement award Gen. Services Adminstrn., 1963; Meritorious Service award Civil War Centennial Commn., 1966; decorated Bronze Star. Mem. Internat. Council Archives. Soc. Am. Archivists, Am. Hist. Assn., Theater Library Assn., Am. Assn. State and Local History, Soc. Cinema Studies. Author: Combined British-American Records of Mediterranean Theater of Operations in World War II, 1948; Preservation of Records Essential to Continuity of State and Local Government, 1958; (with H.P. Beers) Guide to Federal Archives Relating to the Civil War, 1967. Editor: Archives & The Public Interest; Selected Essays by Ernst Posner, 1967; The American Film Institute Catalog of Motion Pictures Produced in the United States: Feature Films, 1921-30, 1971. Editor, The American Archivist, 1960-68. Home: Arlington, Va. Died Sept. 17, 1974; interred Arlington Nat. Cemetery.

MUNDT, KARL EARL, U.S. senator; b. Humboldt, S.D., June 3, 1900; s. Fedinand J. and Rose E. (Schneider) M.; A.B., Carleton Coll., Northfield, Minn., 1923; A.M., Columbia, 1927; LL.D., Rider Coll., 1952, St. Johns U., Huron (S.D.) Coll., 1961, Dakota Wesleyan U., 1966; m. Mary E. Moses, June 24, 1927. Tchr. high sch. speech and social science, Bryant, S.D., 1923-24, supt. of schs., 1924-27; chmn. speech dept. and instr. in social sci. Gen. Beadle State Teachers Coll., Madison, S.D., also part time devoted to insurance and loan business, Madison, 1927-36; sec.-treas. Mundt Loan & Investment Co., Inc., Madison, 1936-48; mem. 76th to 80th Congresses (1939-49), 1st S.D. Dist.; mem. House Fgn. Affairs, Com., House Com. on UnAm. Activities, Senate Com. Appropriations, Fgn. Relations, Investigations; mem. U.S. Senate, 1948-73. Author Voice of Am. act passed by 80th Congress; author Congl. resolution leading to creation UNESCO Div. of U.N.; co-author of Mundt-Nixon Anti-Communist Bill. Mem. S.D. Game and Fish Commn., 1931-37; chmn. Alexander Hamilton Bicentennial Commn., 1955-57; sec. Bryant Commercial Club, 1 yr. Cofounder Nat. Forensic League (held membership certificate No. 1), nat. pres. from 1933. Co-chmn. Nat. Rep. Campaign Speakers Bur., 1952. Recipient Good Govt. award Good Govt. Soc., 1957; 3 Freedoms Found. awards; Distinguished Service award. All Am. Conf. to Combat Communism; Distinguished Service award Ams. Constl. Action, 1963. Mem. S.D. State Poetry Soc. (v.p.), Pi Kappa Delta, Delta Sigma Rho, Tau Kappa Alpha. Republican. Methodist. Mason (32 deg., Shriner), Elk, Odd Fellow, Woodman; mem. Order Eastern Star. Clubs: Madison (S.D.); Kiwanis (former dist. gov. Minn. Dakota Dist.), Izaak Walton League (former nat. v.p.; former State pres.); National Press and University (Washington, D.C.). Contbr. to mags.; editor The Rostrum (Nat. Forensic League mag.); staff writer Republican Magazine, Chicago. Home: Madison, S.D. Died Aug. 1974.

MUNN, RALPH, librarian; b. Aurora, Ill., Sept. 19, 1894; s. Walter Ferguson and Jennie (Wood) M.; LL.B., U. Denver, 1916, A.B., 1917; B.L.S., N.Y. State Library Sch., 1921; Litt.D., U. Pitts., 1940; LL.D., Waynesburg, 1960; m. Anne Shepard, June 6, 1922; children—Robert Ferguson, Margaret Jean (Mrs. Emory S. Lowry). Reference librarian Seattle (Washington) Public Library, 1921-25, assistant librarian, 1925-26; librarian Flint (Mich.) Pub. Library, 1926-28; dir. Carnegie Library, 1928-64; dean Carnegie Library Sch., Pitts., 1928-62. U.S. del. UNESCO Library Seminar, Sweden, 1950. Served with U.S. Army, Apr. 1917-July 1919. Mem. A.L.A. (pres. 1939-40), Pa. Library Assn. (pres. 1930-31). Sigma Pi, Phi Delta Phi. Republican. Presbyterian. Rotarian. Surveyed libraries of Australia and New Zealand for Carnegie Corp., 1934, library needs of New York City for City Planning Commission, 1943. Home: Pittsburgh, Pa. Died Jan. 22, 1975.

MUNRO, LESLIE KNOX, diplomat; b. Auckland, New Zealand, Feb. 26, 1901; s. Colin Robert and Marie Caroline (Knox) M.; LL.B., Sr. Scholar Roman Law, Auckland U. Coll. (U. Entrance scholarship), 1922, M.L., 1923; m. Christine Mary Priestley, Oct. 1927 (dec. 1929); 1 dau., Ann Christine; m. 2d, Muriel Olga Sturt, Oct. 1931; 1 dau., Esme Sturt. Commenced law practice, Auckland, 1924; lectr. jurisprudence, Roman law, constl. law, history Auckland U. Coll., 1924-38, dean faculty law, 1938; reporter New Zealand Law Reports, 1936; speaker internat. affairs New Zealand Broadcasting System, 1936-39; asso. editor New Zealand Herald, 1941-42, editor, 1942-51; New Zealand ambassador to U.S., 1952-58; pres. of the UN 12th Gen. Assembly, 1957; New Zealand rep. on Security Council, 1954-55. New Zealand del. Imperial Press Conf., 1946; guest War Office on tour battlefields from Normandy to Berlin, 1946; guest French govt., 1946, State Dept., 1951. Council mem. Auckland U. Coll., 1939-52; mem. senate U. New Zealand, 1948-52, Auckland Grammar Sch. Bd., 1945-52, chmn. 1951-52. Decorated Knight Commander Royal Victorian Order, 1957. Mem. Auckland Law Soc. (pres. 1936-38), New Zealand Law Soc. (council mem. 1936-39). Clubs: Northern, Auckland, Rotary (Auckland, New Zealand). Home: Hamilton, New Zealand. Died Feb. 13, 1974.

MUNRO, THOMAS, educator; b. Omaha, Feb. 15, 1897; s. Alexander A. and Mary (Spaudling) M.; student Amherst Coll., 1912-15: A.B., Columbia, 1916, A.M., 1917, Ph.D., 1920; L.H.D., Coe Coll., 1955; m. Lucile Nadler, May 18, 1925; children—Eleanor, Donald, Cynthia, Elisabeth. Instr. philosophy, econs. Columbia, 1918-24; asso. ednl. dir. Barnes Found., vis. prof. modern art. U. Pa., 1924-27; asso. prof. philosophy L.I. U., 1927-28; prof. philosophy Rutgers U., 1928-31; lectr. fine arts N.Y. U., 1927-30; lectr. People's Inst. N.Y.C., 1928, 29; prof. art Western Res. U., 1931-67, prof. emeritus, from 1967, chmn. div. art, 1933-51; curator edn. Cleve. Mus. Art, 1931-67; vis. prof. aesthetics Sorbonne, Paris, 1950. Mem. Internat. Com. 3d to 6th Congresses Aesthetics, 1956-68; mem. UNESCO adv. com. arts gen. edn., 1948, 50; fine arts com. Cleve. City Planning Commn., 1946-60. Served with psychol. div. Med. Dept., U.S. Army, 1918. Decorated officer Legion of Honor (France). Fellow Am. Acad. Arts and Scis., A.A.A.S., Royal Soc. Arts (London); mem. French Soc. for Aesthetics (Paris), Am. Philos. Assn., Coll. Art Assn. (dir. 1957-60), Am. Assn. U. Profs., Am. Assn. Mus., Interallied Union (Paris),

Am. Soc. for Aesthetics (pres. 1942-44, hon. pres. from 1962), Chi Psi. Author: Scientific Method in Aesthetics, 1928; Great Pictures of Europe, 1930; The Arts and their Interrelations, 1949; Toward Science in Aesthetics, 1956; Art Education, 1956; Evolution in the Arts, 1963; Oriental Aesthetics, 1965; Form and Style in the Arts, 1970. Co-author: An Introduction to Reflective Thinking, 1923; American Economic Life, 1925; Primitive Negro Sculpture, 1926; Art and Education, 1929; Methods of Teaching the Fine Arts, 1935; Art in American Life and Education, 1941; The Future of Aesthetics, 1942. Editor Jour. Aesthetics and Art Criticism, 1945-64, contbg. editor. Contbr. numerous articles on art, philosophy, edn. to various mags., Ency. Brit. Home: Sarasota, Fla. Died Apr. 14, 1974.

MUNSELL, WILLIAM OLIVER, wholesaling exec.; b. Bloomfield, Ind., Sept. 25, 1870; s. Dr. Levi S. and Jane (Young) M.; ed. pub. schs. of Mo.; m. Joey B. Souie, Oct. 5, 1893; 1 dau., Dorothy (Mrs. L. S. Pendergrass). Mgr. Partin & Orendorff Plow Co., Portland, Ore., 1912-19, Oliver Chilled Plow Works, 1919-21; pres. Mitchell, Lewis & Staver Co., agrl. machinery wholesalers, 1921-42, chmn. 1942-59; director United States National Bank. Mem. Portland C. of C. Club: Rotary (pres. 1924). Home: Portland, Ore.†

MUNTER, EVELYN LAVON (MRS. ROBERT DUANE MUNTER), bus. exec.; b. Vinton, Ia., Apr. 15, 1928; d. Leo Glenn and Covie Ellen (Petro) Liebsch; student Upper Ia. Coll., 1967; m. Robert Duane Munter, Aug. 25, 1946; children—Ronald, Kathleen (Mrs. Dennis Truckenbrod), Jack, Susan, Nancy. Payroll supr. State Farm Mut. Ins. Co., Lincoln, Neb., 1947-48; dir. Union Bank & Trust Co., Strawberry Point, Ia., from 1962, sec. to pres. 1968-71; sec., dir. Munter Agy., Inc., Strawberry Point, from 1971, N.E. Ia. Realty, Inc., Strawberry Point, from 1966; dir. Rodas Chevrolet, Inc., Strawberry Point, from 1967. Pres. Clayton County Republican Women, 1964-67; v.p. Rep. Women of 2d Congl. Dist. of Ia., 1967-68. Mem. P.E.O. Methodist. Mem. Order Eastern Star (grand marshal Ia. 1972). Home: Strawberry Point Ia. Died Sept. 12, 1973.

MUNTER, RICHARD STROBACH, lawyer; b. Spokane, Wash., Aug. 27, 1893; s. Adolph and Rosalia (Strobach) M.; LL.B., U. Mich., 1916; m. Helen H. Highhouse, June 28, 1923. Admitted to Wash. bar, 1916, in gen. practice, Spokane. Served to 2d lt. U.S. Army, 1917-19. Fellow Am. Coll. Trial Lawyers; mem. Spokane (pres. 1926-27), Washington (pres. 1947-48), Am. (ho. of dels. 1951-63) bar assns. Republican. Clubs: Spokane (pres. 1947-48), Spokane Country. Home: Spokane, Wash., Died Sept. 27, 1973; buried Greenwood Meml. Cemetery, Spokane.

MUNZ, PHILIP ALEXANDER, botanist; b. Saratoga, Wyo., Apr. 1, 1892; s. Alexander and Caroline (Wolf) M.; A.B., U. Denver, 1913, A.M., 1914; Ph.D., Cornell U., 1917; m. Alice Virginia McCully, June 10, 1925; children—Robert Alexander, Frederick Wolf. Grad. assistant in biology Cornell University, 1914-15, in botany, 1916-17; asst. prof. botany Pomona Coll., Claremont, 1917-23, asso. prof., 1923-26, prof., 1926-44, dean of faculty, 1941-42; prof. botany and horticulture Bailey Hortorium, Cornell U., 1944-46; dir. Rancho Santa Ana Botanic Garden, 1947-60. Guggenheim fellow, S.Am., 1938-39. Fellow A.A.A.S., California Acad. Sci.; mem. Bot. Soc. Am., Torrey Botany Club, N.E. Botany Club, Am. Soc. Plant Taxonomists, Phi Beta Kappa, Sigma Xi. Author: Manual of Southern California Botany; A California Flora, 1959; Contributor to many papers and bulletins. Home: Claremont, Cal. Died Apr. 13, 1974.

MURCH, JAMES DEFOREST, editor, author; b. New Vienna, O., Oct. 23, 1892; s. Everett Delonzo and Ella (Savage) M.; A.B., Ohio U., 1915; spl. course U. Cin., 1918; D.D., N.W. Christian Coll., 1929; Litt.D., Milligan Coll., 1959; L.H.D., Pacific Christian Coll., 1968; m. Olive Cameron, Aug. 25, 1915; 1 son, James. Ordained ministry Disciples of Christ, 1915; pastor Obersvatory Hill Ch., Pitts., 1915-16; asst. editor Christian Standard, 1916-18; editor Lookout, 1918-25; prof. Christian edn. Cin. Bible Sem., 1925-37; editor Restoration Herald, 1925-34; lit. editor Standard Pub. Co., 1934-43, mng. editor, 1943-45; founder, editor Standard Bible Tchr. and Leader, 1944-45; editor, mgr. United Evang. Action, 1945-58; mng. editor Christianity Today, 1958-61; editor Christian Unity Quar., 1941-46. Pres., Ohio Christian Endeavor Union, v.p. World Christian Endeavor Union, 1920-21; co-founder, trustee Christian Restoration Assn. 1925-37 (pres. assn. 1925-34), Cin. Bible Sem., 1925-38 (pres. 1925-28); mem. bd. Minn. Bible U., 1936-39; chmn. bd. Clarke Estate 1922-58; del. World Conv. Chs. of Christ, Eng., 1935, Edinburgh, 1960; commn. restudy Internat. Conv. Disciples of Christ, 1943-48; mem. cont. com. N. Am. Christian Conv., 1934-73; bd. dirs. Nat. Religious Broadcasters, 1942-68, pres., 1956-57; publs. dir. Nat. Assn. Evangelists, 1945-58, bd. adminstrn., 1958-71; pres. Nat. Press Radio Bible Service. Bd. dirs. Disciples of Christ Hist. Soc., 1941-68; mem. exec. com., past pres. Nat. Sunday Sch. Assn. Trustee Internat. Soc. Christian Endeavor, 1958—. Recipient Distinguished Service award Ohio U., 1964. Fellow Internat. Inst. Arts and Letters; mem. Am. Soc. Ch. History, S.A.R., Phi Kappa Tau, Tau Kappa Alpha, Omicron Delta Kappa, Sigma Delta Chi. Republican. Author: Successful Prayer Meetings, 1930; Studies in Christian Living, 1937; Christian Ministers Manual, 1937; Sunday School Handbook, 1939; Victorious Christian Living; God Still Lives, 600 Doctrinal Illustrations, 1941; Christian Education and the Local Church, 1943; Cooperation Without Compromise, 1956; Teach Me to Pray, 1958; Christians Only: A History of Christian Churches and Churches of Christ, 1961; Teach or Perish, 1962; Church State Relations: The American Way, 1963; The Free Church, 1966; The Protestant Revolt, 1968; B.D. Phillips—Life and Letters, 1970; Adventuring for Christ, 1973; also brochures pamphlets and hymns. Home: Cincinnati, O., Died June 16, 1973.

MURDOCH, JAMES VESEY, banker; b. Pembroke, Bermuda, Nov. 29, 1906; s. Robert Vesey and Ellen (Rothwell) M.; ed. Saltus Grammar Sch. Bermuda; m. Pamela Indoe, 1933; 1 son, 1 dau. With Bank Bermuda Ltd., various locations, 1921-72, sec. and asst. trust officer, Hamilton, 1947-59, sr. trust officer, 1959-72; dir. Frith's Liquors Ltd., Bermuda Radio & TV Co. Ltd., others. Chmn. entertainment com. Trade Devel. Bd. Trustee Saltus Grammar Sch. Address: Hamilton, Bermuda. Died Feb. 28, 1974; buried St. John's Ch., Pembroke, Bermuda.

MURDOCK, KENNETH BALLARD, educator; b. Boston, June 22, 1895; s. Harold and Mary (Lawson) M.; A.B., Harvard, 1916, A.M., 1921, Ph.D., 1923; Litt.D. Middlebury Coll. 1930; L.H.D. Trinity Coll., 1932, U. Vt., 1938; LL.D., Bucknell U., 1933; Ph.D., U. Uppsala (Sweden), 1950; m. Laurette Eustis Potts, June 24, 1922; children—Mary Laurette, Sara; m. 2d, Eleanor Eckhart McLaughlin, Jan. 1, 1942; 2 stepsons, Charles C., Donald H. McLaughlin, Jr. Asst. in English, Harvard, 1916-17, 1919-20, asst. dean, 1919-24, instr. English, 1923-26, sec. dept., 1924-28, asst. prof. English, 1926-30, asso. prof., 1930-32, prof., 1932-64, Francis Lee Higginson prof. English lit. emeritus, 1964-75, 1st dir. Villa Itatti 1961-64, dean faculty arts and scis., 1931-36, master Leverett House, 1931-41. Trustee Am. Scandinavian Found. Officer, A.R.C., Boston, 1917-18. Served as ensign USN, 1918-19. Decorated Knight Order of North Star (Sweden), 1950. Mem. Am. Acad. Arts and Scis., Am. Antiquarian Soc., Colonial Soc. Mass. (editor publs. 1925-30, pres. 1938-45), Mass. Hist. Soc., Societas Scientiarum Finnica, Modern Lang. Assn. Am., Modern Humanities Research Assn., Am. Hist. Assn., Soc. Mayflower Descs., Am. Philos. Soc. Episcopalian. Clubs: Century (N.Y.C.); Somerset, Harvard (Boston); Odd Volumes, Tavern. Editor: publs. New Eng. Quar., 1928-38, 39-62; Am. Lit., 1929-38, 39-49; Univ. editor Harvard Brads. Mag., 1929-31. Author: of Increase Mather, 1924; The Sun at Noon, 1939; Literature and Theology in Colonial New England, 1949; part I The Literature of the American People, 1951. Editor: Selections from Cotton Mather, 1926; Handkerchiefs from Paul, 1927; A Leaf of Grass from Shady Hill, 1928; The Day of Doom, 1929; Manuductio ad Ministerium, 1938; (with F. O. Matthiessen). The Notebooks of Henry James 1947; (completed by Elizabeth Williams Miller) Magnalia Christi Emericana (Cotton Mather), annotated edit. Contbr. to Commonwealth History of Mass., Dictionary of Am. Biography, Ency. Brit., others. Home: Boston, Mass., Died Nov. 15, 1975.

MURPHY, FRANCIS P., editor; b. Marlborough, Mass., July 1, 1896; s. Peter B. and Ellen (Dacey) M.; student Boston U., 1914; m. Callie M. Clifford, Sept. 15, 1928; children—Eleanor Jean (Mrs. Paul J. Dennehy), Frances Patricia (Mrs. Richard T. Shea), Callie Mary (Mrs. David W. Murphy), Peter Benedict, Sarah Ann (Mrs. James H. Healy), Philip, Charles Michael. Member staff of Worcester Telegram, 1917-66, mng. editor, 1945-1966; asst. editor Cath. Free Press, Worcester, 1966-73. Served with 33d Engrs. U.S. Army, World War I. Mem. Am. Soc. Newspaper Editors. Roman Catholic. Author: By-Liners, 1947. Home: Worcester, Mass., Died July 4, 1973.

MURPHY, ROBERT F., state ofcl.; b. Somerville, Mass., Jan. 24, 1899; s. Frank E. and Alice J. (McCarthy) M.; student Dean Acad., Franklin, Mass., 1919-20, Trinity Coll., Hartford, Conn., 1920-24; m. Loretta Noonan, Oct. 12, 1933. Profl. baseball, football player; various positions, editorial, circulation depts. newspapers, Malden, Mass., 1928-54; indsl. relations counselor, 1955-56; lt. gov., Mass., 1956-61; commissioner Met. District Commission, from 1961. Del. Democratic Nat. Conv., 1940, 44, 52; mem. Mass. Ho. of Reps., 1943-54, majority leader, 1949-52; Dem. nominee for gov. of Mass., 1954. Served with USN, World War I. Recipient award Malden Infantile Paralysis Com., 1938. Mem. Am. Legion, Vets Fgn. Wars. Elk, K.C. Home: Malden, Mass., Died Jan. 9, 1976.

MURPHY, VINCENT R., naval officer; b. Norfolk, Va., May 20, 1896; s. Michael J. and Margaret A. (McDermin) M.; B.S., U.S. Naval Acad., 1917; m. Elizabeth Dudley Watson, May 6, 1922; children—Vincent R., Robert D. Commd. ensign USN, 1917, advanced through grades to rear adm., 1945; sea and shore service, 1917-46; comdr. U.S.S. Alabama, 1944-45; ret. from active service, Nov. 1, 1946; exec. v.p., Navy Relief Soc., Nov. 1946-52. Decorated Legion of Merit, Bronze star, Victory medals (both World Wars), Am. Defense, Am. Theatre, Pacific Theatre campaign ribbons. Home: Washington, D.C. Died July 9, 1974.

MURRAH, ALFRED PAUL, judge; b. Johnston County, Okla., Oct. 27, 1904; s. George Washington and Nora (Simmons) M.; LL.B., U. of Okla., 1927; LL.D., Oklahoma City U., 1954; m. Agnes Milam, June 29, 1930; children—Ann, Alfred Paul, Sue. Admitted to Okla. bar, 1928; judge U.S. Dist. Court, 1937-40, U.S. Circuit Court of Appeals 10th Jud. Circuit, 1940-70. Recipient Distinguished Service citation U. Okla., 1954; Hattom W. Sumners award, 1954. Mem. Am., Okla. bar assns., Order of Coif, Lambda Chi, Phi Alpha Delta. Democrat. Methodist. Mason (32). Address: Oklahoma City, Okla., Died Oct. 30, 1975.

MURRAY, DWIGHT HARRISON, physician; b. Springville, Ind., May 16, 1888; s. Albin Winfield and Anna (Ferguson) M.; B.S., Ind. U., 1914, M.D., 1917; postgrad. Naval Med. Sch., Washington, 1919-20, U. Pa., 1920; m. Genevieve Cecelia Collins, Oct. 5, 1921; children—Anna Jean (Mrs. Robert Daniel Huber), Dwight Harrison. Intern Navy Base Hosp., Brest, France, 1919; asst. chief medicine U.S. Naval Hosp., Mare Island, Cal., 1920-22; practice of medicine, Napa, Cal., from 1922; chief med. service Parks Victory Hosp., Napa; med. cons., trustee Napa State Hosp. Hon. civilian cons. Surg. Gen. USN; physician for Napa County. Served as lt. (j.g.) USN, 1918, lt. (s.g.) M.C., USN, 1919-22. Mem. A.M.A. (bd. trustees 1945-55, chmn. 1951-55, pres. 1956-57, del. World Med. Assn., alternate del. 1952, 53, 55, mem. liaison coms. for ofcls. fed. govt., labor ofcls., officers Am. Hosp. Assn.), Cal. Med. Assn. (chmn. legislative com. 1940-55), Napa County Med. Soc. (pres.), Am., Cal. acads. gen. practice, Am. Legion, Vets. Fgn. Wars, C. of C., Sigma Alpha Epsilon, Alpha Omega Alpha, Nu Sigma Nu, Golden Key Soc. Republican. Mem. Christian Ch. Mason (32°), Elk. Home: Napa, Cal. Died Oct. 1974.

MURRAY, FRANK HURON, physician; b. Blairsville, Pa., Dec. 25, 1889; s. Thomas and Ida May (Shaw) M.; M.D., Hahnemann Med. Coll. and Hosp., Phila., 1915; m. Julia Ralston Young, Sept. 4, 1935. Intern, Children's Hosp., Phila., 1915-16; resident in surgery Crozer Hosp., 1916-17, mem. active surg. staff, 1919-28, proctologist, 1929-74; postgrad. gastro-intestinal studies U. Pa. Hosp., 1923-24, postgrad. in gen. surgery, 1926-27, proctologist, 1928-29, asso. proctologist Grad. Sch., 1929-41; asso. prof. proctology Women's Med. Coll. Pa., Phila., 1941-61. Served as capt. M.C., U.S. Army, 1917-19. Diplomate Am. Bd. Colon and Rectal Surgery. Fellow A.C.S., Internat. Coll. Surgeons, Soc. Colon and Rectal Surgeons; mem. A.M.A. Home: Swarthmore, Pa. Died Mar. 28, 1974; buried Woodlands Cemetery, Philadelphia, Pa.

MURRAY, JOHNSTON, gov. Okla.; b. Emet, Indian Ter., Okla., July 21, 1902; s. William Henry and Mary Alice (Hearell) M.; LL.B., Oklahoma City Coll. Law, 1946; LL.D., Okla. City U., 1951; m. Willie Roberta Emerson, May 1, 1933; 1 son, Johnston. In newspaper work, 1918-24; with Standard Oil Co., S.A., 1924-30; later with Consol. Gas Co.; personnel dir. Douglas Aircraft Co., Oklahoma City, 1942-44; mem. Crouch, Rhodes & Crowe, Tulsa and Okla. City; sec. State Sch. Land Commn., 1946-50; gov. Okla., 1950-55. Mason. (32°), K.P., Odd Fellow. Clubs: India-Oklahoma, Oklahoma, Sequoyah Dinner, Johnston County. Home: Oklahoma City, Okla. Died Apr. 1974.

MURTAGH, JOHN MARTIN, judge; b. N.Y.C., Feb. 26, 1911; s. Thomas P. and Mary (Mee) M.; A.B. cum laude, Coll. City N.Y., 1931; J.D., Harvard, 1934; LL.D., Le Moyne Coll., 1956; m. Mary B. Maguire, Oct. 25, 1947; children—Joan, Thomas, Maeve, John Martin. Admitted to N.Y. bar, 1935; asst. atty. gen. State N.Y., 1938-41; spl. asst. to atty. gen. U.S., 1941-42; commr. investigation City N.Y., 1946-50, chief city magistrate, 1950-60; chief justice Ct. Spl. Sessions, N.Y.C., 1960-62; adminstrv. judge Criminal Ct., City N.Y., 1962-66; justice Supreme Ct. N.Y. State, 1966-72; designated to preside over extraordinary spl. and trial term parts Supreme Ct. State N.Y. in 5 counties City N.Y., 1972-76. Prof. law Fordham U Law Sch. Mem. Jud. Conf. State N.Y., 1962-66. Adv. council Pres.'s Assos. of Pace Coll.; adv. group narcotics research unit Rockefeller Inst. Chmn. bd. dirs. Nat. Council on Alcholism, 1967-69. Served from lt. to lt. col. USAAF, World War II. Recipient Silver Key award Nat. Council on Alcholism, 1917. Mem. Am., N.Y. State bar assns., Assn. Bar City N.Y., N.Y. County Lawyers Assn., Am. Judicature Soc., Alumni Assn. Coll. City N.Y. (dir., pres. 1967-69), Phi Beta Kappa. Author: (with Sara Harris) Cast the First Stone, 1957, Who Live in Shadow, 1959. Home: New York City, N.Y., Died Jan. 13, 1976.

MURTAUGH, JOSEPH STUART, orgn. exec.; b. Weston, Mass., July 15, 1912; s. Joseph Paul and Anna (Stuart) M.; student S.D. Sch. Mines and Tech., 1929-30; B.A., Coll. St. Thomas, St. Paul, 1933; postgrad. Georgetown U., 1944-45; m. Dorothy Helen Steinmetz, May 22, 1937; children—Michael Stuart, Patricia Joan, James Alan, Paul Evan. Tchr., Internat. Inst., St. Paul, 1934-35; statistician area office WPA, St. Paul, 1935-37, asst. statistician Minn. WPA, 1938-40; chief statistics sect. NYA, 1941-42; sr. indsl. analyst WPB, 1942-44; chief facilities analysis br. Office Surgeon Gen. U.S.

Army, 1944-45; program analyst UN Relief and Rehab. Adminstrn., 1946; med. economist hosp. div. USPHS, 1947-50, chief reports and analysis br. Bur. Med. Services, 1951-53, asst. exec. officer bur., 1953-55; asst. chief Office Research Planning, NIH, 1956-59, chief Office Program Planning, 1960-68; exec. sec. Bd. Medicine, Nat. Acad. Scis., Washington, 1968-70; dir. dept. planning and policy devel. Assn. Am. Med. Colls., from 1970. Recipient Superior Service award Dept. Health, Edn. and Welfare, 1965, Distinguished Service award, 1967. Mem. Am. Acad. Polit. and Social Sci., Am. Pub. Health Assn., Am. Statis. Assn. Home: Garrett Park, Md. Died Dec. 3, 1973.

MUSCAT, VICTOR, metal mfr.; b. N.Y.C., Jan. 29, 1919; s. Lazarus and Beatrice A. (Hiller) M.; student U. Ariz., 1936-40; m. Doris R. Bock, May 8, 1949; children—Laura Lynn, Lawrence Bock, Victor Hiller, Stephen Hoyt. Organized Victor Metal Products Corp., Newport, Ark., aluminum tube and can mfrs., 1946, chmn. bd., mem. bd. dirs.; pres. Victor Industries, Inc., U.S. Can Corp.; chmn. Aluminum & Chem. Corp. Ark. chmn. UN Com. Served to capt. USAAF, World War II. Recipient ann. governor's indsl. award, Ark., 1957. Mem. Young President's Orgn. Clubs: Racquet; Burning Tree Country. Home: Greenwich, Conn. Died Oct. 5, 1975.

MUSTON, RONALD C. G., architect; b. Leicester, Eng., June 2, 1905; s. Colin Joseph and Clara (Cartwright) M.; student Auckland U., New Zealand Inst. Architects, 1922-26; m. Grace Emily Cable, Feb. 3, 1937 (dec.); children—Patricia Ann (Mrs. Kerry George Ansell), Jennifer Frances; m. 2d, Joan Hunter Murray-Orr, 1973; children—David, Craig, Elizabeth (Mrs. R. Pike). With Edw. Mahoney and Sons, Gummer and Ford, Bohringer, Taylor and Johnson, 1922-31; partner L. Walker, 1937-41; prin. Structon Group Architects, from 1944. Mem. New Zealand Bldg. Research Bur.; convener of judges Nat. Bank of New Zealand art awards, from 1959. Mem. Emergency Precaution Service, 1939-42. Chmn. Mary Percy Dowse Cultural Found.; chmn. bd. trustees Nat. Art Gallery, Nat. Mus., Nat. War Meml. Served to capt. New Zealand Army, 1942-44. Decorated officer Order Brit. Empire, 1959; recipient Gold medal New Zealand Inst. Architects, 1954. Fellow Royal Inst. Brit. Architects, A.I.A. (hon.), Royal Soc. Arts (London), New Zealand Inst. Architects (pres.): mem. Assn. New Zealand Art Socs. (pres.). Important works include Hotel Franz Joseph, Ch. of St. James, War Meml. Cultural Centre Lower Hutt, Nat. Bank New Zealand Head Office Bldg., Wellington, St. Mary's Convent, Wellington, Student Union U. Wellington, Nelson Cathedral Extensions, Dowse Art Gallery. Home: Lower Hutt, New Zealand. Died May 30, 1974.

MUSULIN, BORIS, educator; b. Chgo., Sept. 6, 1929; s. Milan and Mary (Palaska) M.; certificate Chgo. City Jr. Coll., 1947; student Loyola U., Chgo., 1947, U. Ill. Med. Sch., 1949-50; Ph.B., Northwestern U., 1949, Ph.D., 1954; m. Shelba Jean Choate, Aug. 1961. Teaching asst. Northwestern U., 1951; DuPont research instr. U. Minn., Mpls., 1953-54; asst. prof. chemistry Mich. State U., East Lansing, 1954-56; asst. prof. chemistry So. Ill. U., Carbondale, 1956-61, asso. prof., 1961-69, prof., from 1969. Vis. asso. prof. Theoretical Chemistry Inst., Madison, Wis., 1963-64. Fellow A.A.A.S., Am. Inst. Chemists; mem. Am. Chem. Soc., Am. Phys. Soc., Ill. Acad. Sci. (treas. from 1967), Sigma Xi, Phi Lambda Upsilon, Alpha Sigma Lambda, Alpha Chi Sigma. Contbr. articles to profl. jours. Home: Carbondale, Ill. Died June 30, 1973.

MUSURILLO, HERBERT, author, educator; b. N.Y.C., June 13, 1917; s. Henry and Rose (Capece) M.; B.A., Georgetown U., 1939; M.A., Catholic U., 1941; D.Phil., Oxford (Eng.) U., 1951; Ph.D., Fordham U., 1954. Tutor, Facultés de Namur (Belgium), 1948-49; prof. classics St. Andrew-on-Hudson, Poughkeepsie, N.Y., 1951-55, Bellarmine Coll., Plattsburgh, N.Y., 1955-62; prof. classics Fordham U., 1963-74, chmn. dept., 1966-69. Mem. N.Y. Classical Soc. (pres. 1969-71), Am. Philol. Assn. (dir.), Internat. Papyrology Assn. Author: Acts of the Pagan Martyrs, 1954; Methodius of Olympus: The Symposium, 1958; Symbol and Myth in Ancient Poetry, 1961; Acta Alexandrinorum, 1961; (with J. Daniélou) From Glory to Glory, 1961; Methode d'Olympe: Le Banquet, 1963; Jean Chrysostome: La Virginité, 1966; Gregorii Nysseni De vita Moysis, 1964; Symbolism and the Christian Imagination, 1964; The Fathers of the Primitive Church, 1966; The Light and The Darkness: Studies in the Dramatic Poetry of Sophocles, 1967; Acts of the Christian Martyrs, 1971. Cons. editor: Thought, The Way, Classical Folia. Contbr. articles to profl. jours. Home: Bronx, N.Y. Died May 27, 1974; buried Jesuit Martyrs Shrine, Auriesville, N.Y.

MYERBERG, MICHAEL, theatrical producer; b. Balt., Aug. 5, 1906; s. Nathan Jacob and Anna (deBoskey) M.; student Balt. Prep. Sch., Balt. City Coll., Johns Hopkins, 1924-26; m. Adrienne Matzenauer, Mar. 9, 1935; children—Edward Antoni, Paul Henry. Prodn. vaudeville, band acts, 1925-30; producer legitimate theatre, 1930-36; mgr. Leopold Stokowski, Phila. Ballet, other artists, assisted prodn. 100 Men and a Girl, mgr. stereophonic sound track for Fantasia, 1938; organized All Am. Youth Orchestra, auspices U.S. State Dept., 1940, (with Leopold Stokowski), toured S.Am., 1940, U.S. tour, 1941; prod. Skin of Our Teeth, 1942, Stardust, 1943, Lute Song, 1945, The Barrier, 1948, Hansel and Gretel (motion picture), 1954, Patterns (motion picture), 1955, Waiting for Godot, 1956, Compulsion, 1958. Recipient Pulitzer prize for prodn. Skin of Our Teeth, Christopher's award for Patterns, D.A.R. award for Hansel and Gretel. Home: Queens, N.Y. Died Jan. 6, 1974.

MYERS, ALBERT G, banking executive; b. Chesterfield Co., S.C., Jan. 15, 1880; s. Stephen H. and Minnie (Crump) M.; ed. pub. schs.; Dr. Textile Sci. (honorary), N.C. State College; LL.D., Belmont Abbey College, N.C., 1957; married Elfreida Nail, Jan. 26, 1916; children—Albert G., Freida M. Shelton. Chmn. bd. Citizens Nat. Bank; director, chmn. exec. com. Textiles-Inc., Gastonia, Jefferson Standard Life Ins. Co., Greensboro; dir. Piedmont and Northern Ry. Co.; mem. N.C. adv. bd. Liberty Mut. Ins. Co., Boston. Mem. W.P.B., 1942. Chmn. N.C. State Ports Authority, dir. N.C. Textile Found.; trustee Greater U. N.C., 1931-33. Mem. Am. Cotton Mfrs. Inst., Inc. So. Combed Yarn Spinners Assn., N.C. Cotton Mfrs. Assn., C. of C., Newcomen Soc., N.A.M. (so. adv. council, N.Y. So. Soc., Omicron Delta Kappa. Mason. (Shriner), Clubs: Biltmore Forest Country (Ashville); Gaston Country (Gastonia). Home: Gastonia, N.C.†

MYERS, EDWARD CHARLES, steel corp. exec.; b. York, Pa., Jan. 3, 1912; s. Edward Charles and Matilda M. (Benfer) M.; A.B., Bucknell U., 1934; grad. Advanced Mgmt. Program, Harvard, 1949; m. Edna Ruth Cleckner, June 19, 1936; children—Wendy Ann, Sandra Sue. Observer, Homestead plant Carnegie Steel Co., 1934; plant dir. personnel, welfare and tng. Carnegie-Ill. Steel Corp., 1936; staff asst. pub. relations dept. U.S. Steel Corp. of Del., 1938, staff asst. pub. relations, also coordinator law, indsl. relations and pub. relations depts., 1940-42, asst. dir. pub. relations, 1942-43, asst. to v.p. indsl. relations dept. U.S. Steel Corp. of Del., 1943-51, U.S. Steel Co., 1951-53, asst. v.p. indsl. relations 1953-58, v.p. personnel U.S. Steel Corp., 1958-62, v.p., asst. to pres., 1962-69, v.p., asst. to vice chmn., from 1969. Mem. President's Com. on Employment of Physically Handicapped; exec. com., dir. Nat. Safety Council; mem. Nat. Council Crime and Delinquency; vice chmn. Greater Pitts. Airport Adv. Com.; mem. organizational services com. Community Chest Pitts.; mem. United Fund Allegheny County. Bd. dirs. Duquesne U., West Pa. Hosp., Pitts. Pirates Found.; v.p. Civic Light Opera Assn. Greater Pitts.; bd. dirs., chmn. exec. com. Comprehensive Health Planning Assn. Western Pa., Pitts. Blind Assn.; trustee Community Services Pa., Bucknell U.; regional bd. dirs. Nat. Conf. Christians and Jews; v.p., bd. dirs. Pitts. chpt. Nat. Football Found. and Hall of Fame; mem. men's adv. bd. Home for Crippled Children. Named Pitts. Man of Year in human relations, 1968; recipient Silver Anniversary award Sports Illustrated, 1958. Mem. Greater Pitts. C. of C., Nat. Urban League (mem. commerce and industry council), Am. Iron and Steel Inst., Pub. Affairs Council (dir., exec. com., pres., chmn.), N.A.M. (mem. pub. affairs com.), The Conf. Bd. (pub. affairs research council), Hwy. Users Fedn. (mem. program evaluation subcom.). Sigma Chi, Kappa Phi Kappa. Presbyn. (elder). Clubs: University, Longue Vue, Duquesne (Pitts.); Rolling Rock (Ligonier, Pa.). Home: Ligonier, Pa. Died Mar. 17, 1975; buried St. Michael's of the Valley, Rector, Pa.

MYERS, FRED EDWARD, JR., petroleum co. exec.; b. DuBois, Pa., Dec. 21, 1921; s. Fred Edward and Frances Irene (Frederick) M.; B.A., Drake Coll.; m. Ruth E. Halma, Aug. 3, 1946; children—Jan, Nancie, Dale. With Frederick A. Dewey Co., 1948-51, Williams Oil Co., 1952-61; with La. Land & Exploration Co., N.Y.C., from 1962, asst. sec., 1963-65, sec., from 1965. Served to sgt. maj. AUS, 1942-45; ETO, PTO. Mem. Am. Soc. Corp. Secs. Mem. Reformed Ch. of Am. (elder). Club: Hemisphere (N.Y.C.). Home: Middleton, N.J. Died Dec. 24, 1973; buried Fair View Cemetery, Middletown, N.J.

MYERS, GEORGE BOGGAN, clergyman, educator; b. Holly Springs, Miss., Oct. 13, 1881; s. George Clifton and Ida Greer (Bracken) M; grad. St. Thomas Hall, Holly Springs, Miss., 1899; LL.B., U. of Miss., 1903; B.D., University of the South, Sewanee, Tennessee; D.D., Divinity School of P.E. Church in Philadelphia, 1943; m. Verna Payne Henderson, Jan. 18, 1911 (died 1919); children—Alice Alexander (Mrs. Olin Gordon Beall), Alexander Henderson; m. 2d, Margaret Jefferys Hobart, Oct. 2, 1920; children—Rosamond Hobart (Mrs. Peter E. Thornton), George Clifton (dec.), Marie Elizabeth (Mrs. C. Winter), Henry Lee, Elvis Lucas, Hobart Jefferys. Deacon, 1907, priest, 1908, P.E. Ch.; rector of Trinity Cathedral, Little Rock, 1912-14; dean Holy Trinity Cathedral, Havana, Cuba, 1914-22; prof. religious philosophy and practical theology, U. of the South, from 1922. Acting chaplain, U. of the South, 1945-46; priest-in-charge Otey Memorial Parish, Sewanee, from 1947. Delegate Gen. Conv. P.E. Church, 1919. Civilian chaplain 7th Regt., U.S. Marines, Cuba, 1918; mil. aide on staff comdr. Miss. Nat. Guard, 1899-1900; comdr. Army of Tenn. Dept., U.S.C.V., 1900-01. Mem. Internat. Congress of Philosophy, A.A.A.S., Am. Classical League, English-Speaking Union (pres. Hudson Stuck Chapter, 1936-46), Victoria Inst. (London), Delta Tau Delta, Pi Gamma Mu. Democrat. (Clubs: E.Q.R., Sewanee Civic Assn. (pres. 1946-48) (Sewanee). Contbr. to Dictionary of Am. Biography. Retired. Home: Sewanee, Tenn.†

MYERS, HAROLD B., mfg. exec.; b. Decatur, Ill., Apr. 26, 1896; s. Joseph C. and Harriett M. (Nicholson) M.; B.S., U. Ill., 1922; m. Evely Gooch, Mar. 19, 1927; children—James L., Carol A. With Internat. Harvester Co., 1922-61, gen. auditor, Argentina, 1928-36, gen. auditor, Chgo., 1936-44, asst. comptroller, 1944-52, comptroller, 1952-57, v.p., comptroller, 1957-61; dir. Fed. Life Ins. Co. Mem. Controllers Inst. Am., Am. Inst. Accountants, Beta Gamma Sigma, Beta Alpha Psi. Home: Wilmette, Ill. Died Oct. 4, 1973; interred Meml. Park Cemetery Mausoleum, Skokie, Ill.

MYERS, WELDON THOMAS, college prof.; b. Rockingham County, Va., Oct. 25, 1879; s. Benjamin Allen and Sallie (Garber) M.; B.A., Bridgewater (Va.) College, 1901; M.A., U. of Va., 1907; Ph.D., 1912; studied London University, England, 1922; m. Mande Kennedy, 1912 (died July 8, 1938); 1 daughter, Josephine Florence (Mrs. Marshall H. Kearney); m. 2d, Lucia Giddens, June 2, 1944, Professor of Latin and Greek, Bridgewater (Va.) College, 1901-05; instructor in Latin, 1906-07, in English, 1909-12, adj. professor English, 1912-14, prof. English Summer Sch., 1912-18, U. of Va.; prof. English and head of dept., Converse Coll., Spartanburg, S.C., 1914-48; prof. Eng. Wofford Coll., summers, 1927-32. Asst. camp librarian, Camp Greene, N.C., Aug.-Sept. 1918. World War; camp librarian, Camp Wadsworth, S.C., Dec. 1918-Apr. 1919. Mem. Phi Beta Kappa, Delta Sigma Rho. Democrat. Methodist. Author: Relations of Latin and English as Living Languages in England during the Age of Milton, 1913. Home: Letohatchee, Ala†

MYLER, JOSEPH LARKIN, news editor; b. Iola, Kan., Jan. 22, 1905; s. Emberson William and Laura Kate (Bacon) M.; student Iola Jr. Coll.; B.A., U. Kan., 1930; m. Helen Elizabeth Austin, Oct. 24, 1934. News editor Herington (Kan.) Times, 1926-27; mng. editor Iola (Kan.) Register, 1928-29, 30-32; newswriter, editor United Press Assns. (now U.P.I.) 1933-72, successively in Kansas City, Mo., Jefferson City, Mo., Dallas, N.Y.C., Washington bureaus; covered atomic bomb tests, Bikini, 1946, also first airdrop U.S. hydrogen bomb, Bikini, 1956. Recipient award for outstanding achievement domestic news class Nat. Headliners Club, 1955. Mem. Nuclear Energy Writers Assn., White House Corr. Assn. Author articles on atomic energy. Contbr. Brit. Book of the Year, 1957. Home: Arlington, Va. Died July 5, 1973.

MYLKS, GORDON WRIGHT, physician; b. Kingston, Ont., Can., 1904; s. Gordon Wright and Lucy (Rowe) M.; M.D., C.M., Queen's U., 1929; m. Clara B. Kingston, May 12, 1932; children—Nancy Jane (Mrs. William John Bethume), Barbara Helen (Mrs. Nichols Diamant), Herbert Gordon. Intern, Englewood (N.J.) Hosp., 2 yrs. French Hosp., N.Y.C., 1 yr.; resident in obstetrics and gynecology Rotunda Hosp., Dublin, Ireland; resident in gen. surgery Royal Infirmary, Edinburg, Scotland; hon. staff Kingston Gen. Hosp., Hotel Dieu Hosp., Kingston; past asso. prof. obstetrics and gynecology Queen's U., Kingston. Mem. adv. bd. Kingston br. Royal Trust Co. Recipient award for meritorious service Queen's U., 1971. Diplomate Am. Bd. Obstetrics and Gynecology. Fellow A.C.S., Am. Coll. Obstetrics and Gynecology (life fellow); mem. Royal Coll. Surgeons Can., Can. Soc. Obstetricians and Gynecologists, Can., Ont. (life, chmn. sect. obstetrics and gynecology 1957-60, dir. dist. 7, pres. 1965-66) med. assns., Kingston Acad. Med. (life, past pres.), N.Y. Acad. Scis., Pan Pacific Surg. Assn. Mem. United Ch. (mem. session, chmn. choir). Home: Kingston, Ont., Can. Died Feb. 22, 1973; buried Kingston, Ont., Can.

NABERS, JANE PORTER (MRS. DRAYTON NABERS), civic worker; b. Birmingham, Ala., Nov. 16, 1913; d. James Devereux and Jennie (Pollard) Porter; A.B., Goucher Coll., 1934; m. Drayton Nabers, Sept. 22, 1936; children—Jane Porter (Mrs. Frank H. McFadden), Drayton, Susan Porter (Mrs. Wyatt R. Haskell). Mem. Jr. League of Birmingham (Ala.), 1935-73, treas., 1941-42, chmn. sustaining group, 1966-67; mem. citizens com. adv. bd. Juvenile and Domestic Relations Ct. Jefferson County, 1966-73; mem. bd. Linly Keflin Unit, 1962-73, treas., 1964-67, v.p., 1967-68, pres., 1968-69; rec. sec. Opera Guild Bd., 1964-66; trustee Birmingham Hist. Soc., 1947-70; bd. dirs. Bapt. Hosps. Found., Birmingham, 1967-71; mem. com. 100 Women Birmingham, 1964-67. Bd. dirs. Ala. Boys Indsl. Sch., 1952-73, pres., 1960-68, v.p., 1968-73; bd. dirs. Jefferson County chpt. A.R.C., 1969-72; trustee Children's Hosp., 1947-73, 3rd v.p., 1961-63, 2d v.p., 1970-73. Presbyn. (elder). Co-editor: Sketches of Alabama, 1970. Home: Birmingham, Ala. Died Jan. 26, 1973.

NABESHIME, ISUNATOSHI, utility exec.; b. Apr. 14, 1910; ed. U. Tokyo (Japan). With Sumitomo Electric Industries, Ltd., Osaka, Japan, 1933, dir., 1956, mng. dir., 1958-61, pres., 1966-69. Dir. Tokai Rubber Industries, Meldensha Electric Mfg. Mem. Kansal Econ. Fedn., Japan Fedn. Employers, Fedn. Econ. Orgns. Rotarian. Home: Osaka, Japan. Died 1969.

NACHT, OSIAS, real estate exec.; b. Rumania, Sept. 23, 1895; s. Jonas and Regina (Birkental) N.; M.B.A., U. Bucarest, 1915; m. Fedora Tenenhaus, Jan. 1, 1920; children—Charlotte (Mrs. Pierre Coblence), John. Founder, organizer Farola and Laromet, rolling mills, Rumania, 1925; owner Freeport Machine Works, 1942-52; pres. Southametco, Inc., N.Y.C., 1940-65, Steemet, Inc., N.Y.C., 1950-74, Felomer, Inc., N.Y.C., 1950-74, C.M.U.F., Paris, France, 1930-74, Societe Immobiliere de la Peyriere, Paris, 1950-74, Rancho Del Ciervo Estates, Inc., Santa Barbara, Cal., 1960-69. Served as lt. Rumanian Army, 1916-18. Home: New York City, N.Y. Died 1974.

NAFZIGER, RALPH OTTO, educator; b. Chgo., Apr. 18, 1896; s. Albert and Emmy (Brennemann) N.; B.A., U. Wis., 1921, M.A., 1930, Ph.D., 1936; m. C. Monona Hamilton, June 18, 1932; children—Ralph Hamilton, James Albert Richmond. Asst. editor N.D. State Coll., Fargo, 1921-22; editor Enderlin (N.D.) Ind., 1922; editorial writer Fargo Daily Tribune, 1923-24; reporter Fargo Forum, 1924-25; mem. news staff Omaha World-Herald, 1925-28; editor Univ. Press Bur., U. Wis., 1928-30; asst. prof. journalism U. Wis., 1930-35, dir. Sch. of Journalism, 1949-66, emeritus prof. journalism, 1966-73; asso. prof. journalism U. Minn., 1935-37, prof., 1937-49, dir. research div. Sch. Journalism, 1944-49; Asia Found. adviser and cons. Indian Inst. Mass. Communication, New Delhi, 1966-67; cons. Office Coordinator of Information, Washington, summer 1941; chief Media Div., Office of Facts and Figures (Office of War Information), 1942; press specialist State Dept. program, Germany, 1952; lectr. UNESCO seminar journalism research, U. Strasbourg, fall 1957, bd. trustees Internat. Center of Journalism, 1958-73; chmn. internat. seminar journalism edn., Manila, P.I., 1961; dir. studies Berlin Inst. Mass Communications in Developing Countries, 1964; dir. UNESCO seminar on journalism edn., Nagpur, India, 1964; lectr., cons., 1966-67; lectr. East-West Center, Honolulu, summer 1971. Recipient Sigma Delta Chi research award, 1937; citation meritorious service to edn. journalism So. Ill. U., 1970; Paul J. Deutschmann award Assn. for Educators in Journalism, 1972. Served with inf. U.S. Army, 1918-19; AEF. Mem. Am. Assn. Tchrs. Journalism (pres. 1941), Am. Assn. Schs. and Depts. of Journalism (chmn. council on research, 1942-46; mem. accrediting com. 1946-50; pres. 1958), Assn. for Edn. in Journalism (exec. sec. 1967-73), 1967), Delta Sigma Phi, Phi Kappa Phi, Alpha Zeta, Sigma Delta Chi (Distinguished Teaching in Journalism award 1971). Author, compiler: International News and the Press, 1940. Editor: Introduction to Mass Communications Research, 1963. Editorial bd. Journalism Quar., 1935-55. Home: Madison, Wis. Died Sept. 25, 1973; buried Madison, Wis.

NAGLEY, FRANK ALVIN, b. Watseka, Ill., Aug. 29, 1880; s. Josiah and Sarah Catherine (Wright) N.; grad. high sch., Sheldon, Ill., 1903; A.B., Northwestern U., 1907; fellowship, same univ., 1908; studied U. of Chicago, 1910, U. of Calif., summer 1924; A.M., U. So. Cal., 1926; m. Mildred Mary Leach, June 29, 1915; 1 son, Winfield Eugene. State College sec. Y.M.C.A., in N.Dak., 1909; dir. Sherman Park, Chicago, under South Park Commrs., 1909-12; with employment dept. Sears, Roebuck & Co., Chicago, 1912-15; asst. sales mgr., jr. sales div. The N. K. Fairbank Co., Chicago, 1915-16; with adv. dept. Elgin Motor Corpn., Chicago, 1916-17; dir. business research dept. Farm Journal, Phila., Pa., 1918; adv. work, Portland, Ore., 1919-22; asst. prof. marketing, U. of Ore. Sch. of Business, 1922-25; same U. of Southern Calif. Coll. of Commerce, 1925. Mem. Nat. Assn. Teachers of Marketing and Advertising, Nat. Assn. Univ. and Coll. Profs., Square and Compass, Pi Kappa Alpha, Alpha Kappa Psi, Alpha Delta Sigma. Republican. Methodist. Mason. Club: Los Angeles Advertising. Author: Brains in Business, 1924. Home: Los Angeles, Cal.†

NALLY, FRANCIS IGNATIUS, newspaperman; b. Toledo, Feb. 15, 1908; s. Martin J. and Julia Flora (Scanlon) N.; A.B., St. John Coll., Toledo, 1929; student Laval U., Que., 1946-47; m. Catherine F. Held, Aug. 19, 1939; children—Patrick J., Mary Frances, Michael J., Anne M., Theresa M., Catherine M., Daniel J., Brigid M., Martin J., Nora M., Julia M. Reporter Toledo Blade, 1929-34; news editor Catholic Chronicle, 1934-73, ret., 1973. First pres. Toledo Cath. Interracial Council, 1958; co-organizer, pres. Toledo Council Cath. Men, 1944, pres. Nat. Council Cath. Men, 1952-53. Home: Maumee, O. Died Apr. 15, 1975; buried Calvary Cemetery, Toledo, O.

NAMARA, MARGUERITE, soprano; b. Cleveland, O., Nov. 19, 1893; d. William Arthur and Marguerite (McNamara) Banks; student Ursuline Acad., Cleveland, O., 1901-03; Girls Collegiate Inst., Los Angeles, 1905-08; studied singing under Jean de Reszke; coached with Melba, deBussy, Julia Culp; married Frederick H. Toye, January 10, 1910; 1 son, Frederick N.; m. 2d, Guy Bolton, June 1917; 1 dau., Peggy; m. 3d, George Hoy, Feb. 22, 1936. Debut in Faust, Genoa, Italy, 1909; in concerts with Caruso, Amato, Godowsky, many others; with John Charles Thomas in Alone At Last, 1917; soloist with leading symphony orchestras of Europe and U.S.; toured with London Symphony under Sir Landon Ronald, 1921-22; with St. Louis Symphony under Rudolph Ganz, 1922; with Minneapolis Symphony under Dr. Emile Oberhoeffer; with Chicago Opera Assn., 1919-22; with Opera Comique, Paris, 1923-25 (prin. roles, Thais, Manon, Traviata, La Boheme, Tosca, Carmen); in Mikado and Pinafore, N.Y. City, 1925-26; concertized Paris, England and U.S., 1926-29; on London stage in Ivor Novello's "Party," 1932; starred in film based on life of Carmen, British International Pictures, 1932; first British musical film; concerts, guest opera performances, legitimate stage (Enter Madame and Lo and Behold) and Am. films (Thirty Day Princess and Peter Ibbetson), 1933-36; concerts Los Angeles, San Francisco, Washington, N.Y. City, 1936-39; featured in Night of Love, musical play, season 1940-41; prima donna in Claudia, 1941-43. Boston, N.Y. concerts, 1943-44; also benefits, war-time concerts in South and East; concerts in Boston, New York, Los Angeles, 1946, 1947; concerts and exhbns. paintings in Paris and London, spring 1947; exhibition paintings, Nov. 1945, Art League, N.Y.; concerts in N.Y. and Pacific Coast. London, Paris; teaching voice placement and interpretation. Address: Marbella, Spain., Died Nov. 3, 1975.

NAPIER, J. PATTON, research co. exec.; b. 1908; married. With A.C. Nielsen Co., Chgo., 1938-74, exec. v.p., dir.; mng. dir. A.C. Nielsen Co. Ltd., Oxford, Eng. Home: Died Dec. 29, 1974.

NAPIER, WALTER PHARO, banker; b. Karnes County, Tex., Feb. 21, 1881; s. Walter Terry Colquitt and Virginia (Maley) N.; prep. edn. pub. schs., San Antonio, Tex.; student Law Sch., U. of Tex., 1900; m. Estelle Trolinger, Dec. 10, 1900; 1 daughter, Estelle Trolinger (Mrs. Estelle N. Corrigan). Admitted to Tex. bar, 1903, and began practice in Kaufman County; practiced at San Antonio, 1904-29; pres. Alamo Nat. Bank of San Antonio, May 1929-Jan. 1947; director Taft (Tex.) Cotton Oil Co. Served as colonel 2d Texas Cav., U.S. Army, World War I. Mem. Am., Tex. State bar assns., Am. Bankers Assn., Texas Bankers Assn., Sigma Chi. Methodist. Mason (32°, Shriner). Clubs: San Antonio Petroleum, San Antonio Country. Home: San Antonio, Tex.†

NARDIN, FRANCES LOUISE, educator; b. Vandalia, Mo., Feb. 6, 1878; d. James Frederick and Sarah Ellen (Thompson) N.; B.S., U. of Mo., 1907, A.M., 1913, Ph.D., 1914; unmarried. Mem. faculty of English, U. of Mo., 1914; dean of Women, U. of Wis., from 1918. Chmn. patriotic edn., Mo. div. of Woman's Com., Council of Nat. Defense, 1917-18. Mem. Am. Assn. Univ. Women, League of Women Voters, Business and Professional Women's League, Modern Lang. Assn. America, Pi Lambda Theta, Phi Kappa Phi. Episcopalian. Clubs: Civics, Womans (Madison, Wis.), Altrusa. Author: The Progress of Liberty (patriotic pageant), 1917; Notebook for English Composition, 1917; The Bugle Calls the Children (pageant), 1918; Makers of America—A Civic Ritual, 1920; The Freshman and Social Life (in the Freshman Girl and Her College), 1925. Home: Madison, Wis.†

NARRIN, ELGIN EDWIN, investment co. exec., b. Grayling, Mich., May 19, 1903; s. Fred and Jessie (Downey) N.; B.S. in Commerce, Northwestern U., 1929; m. Harriet Dawson Gorby, Oct. 31, 1929; children—Carol Elizabeth (Mrs. David Bruce Wendt), Richard Elgin. Asst. financial editor Chgo. Jour. Commerce, 1929-36; investment counselor Moody's Investors Service, Chgo., 1936-40; mgr. Marietta Research and Investment Co., Milw., 1940-48, gen. mgr., 1948-69, sec.-treas., 1945-66, pres., 1966-69, also dir.; v.p. Kyle Co., Wilmington, Del., 1961-72, dir., 1953-72; sec. Greenhope Co., Milw., 1949-69, dir., 1949-69; v.p., gen. mgr., chief officer ACK Co., Milw., 1967-73; cons. investments for individuals and banks. Chartered financial analyst. Mem. Investment Analysts Soc. Chgo., Investment Analysts Soc. Milw. (pres. 1957-58), Acacia, Deru Soc., Alpha Kappa Psi, Beta Alpha Psi. Republican. Methodist. Mason. (K.T. Shriner, 33). Home: Brookfield, Wis. Died Apr. 14, 1973.

NASH, ETHEL MILLER HUGHES (MRS. ARNOLD SAMUEL NASH), educator; b. Liverpool, Eng., June 20, 1909; d. Edmund Miller and Lillian (Ellery) Hughes; B.A. with honours, U. Liverpool, 1931; spl. student Yale, 1939; M.A., U. N.C., 1949; m. Arnold Samuel Nash, July 1, 1933; children—A. E. Keir, David Charles. Came to U.S., 1939, naturalized, 1956. Psychologist, Toronto (Ont., Can.) City Schs., 1941-42; lectr. Assn. for Family Living, Chgo., 1946; lectr. dept. sociology, marriage counselor, U. N.C., Chapel Hill, 1949-53; asst. prof. preventive medicine, asso. in obstetrics and gynecology Bowman Gray Sch. Medicine, Winston-Salem, N.C., 1956-66; clin. asso. prof. obstetrics and gynecology U. N.C., 1966-73, faculty U. N.C. Population Center; clin. asso. Psychiat. Assos. of Chapel Hill, Mem. Am. Sociol. Assn., Soc. for Study Social Problems, Soc. for Sci. Study Sex, Am. Orthopsychiat. Assn., Am. Assn. Marriage Counselors (dir. 1963-64 pres. 1965-66), Nat. Council on Family Relations (bd. dirs.). Author: With This Ring, 1942. Editor: Marriage Counseling in Medical Practice, 1964. Contbr. articles to profl. publs. Home: Chapel Hill, N.C. Died Feb. 28, 1973; interred Blundellsands, England.

NASON, HARRY BAXTER, JR., newspaper editor; b. Phila., Pa., July 20, 1895; s. Harry Baxter and Anna Rose (Hennessy) N.; ed. pub. schs.; m. Letty Emma Bradin, June 25, 1919 (div. 1931); children—Jane Baxter, Harry Baxter, III; m. 2d, Elizabeth Malcolm Durham (Vivian Shirley), Oct. 7, 1933 (div. 1944); 1 dau., Virginia Malcolm; m. 3d, Helen Stockley Albertson, Aug. 5, 1944 (dec. 1956); m. 4th, Marion Bainbridge, Jan. 16, 1957 (div. 1962); m. 5th, Ruth Reynolds Rhodes, 1962. Reporter, copy reader, make-up editor Philadelphia newspapers, 1912-24; city editor Evening Public Ledger, 1924; managing editor The Illustrated Sun, 1925-27; mng. editor Evening Public Ledger, 1927-31; asst. editor Public Ledger, 1931-33; editor New York Post, 1933-41; exec. editor Evening Public Ledger, Phila., 1941; pub. dir. War Emergency (Big Inch) Pipelines, Inc., 1942; asst. mng. editor Phila. Record, 1943-46; pub. dir. City of Norfolk, Va.; promotion dir. Phila. City Planning Exhbn., 1947; pub. relations counsel, Phila. Com. of 15, 1948; editor Adirondack Daily Enterprise, Saranac Lake, N.Y., 1951; editor Daily Citizen-Times, Honesdale, Pa., 1955-57; city editor Phila. Daily News, 1957-59; radio news editor WPEN Broadcasting Co., Phila., 1959-61. Served U.S. Navy, 1917-19. Home: Fort Myers Beach, Fla. Died June 28, 1974; cremated, Saranac Lake, N.Y.

NATHAN, EDWARD ISAAC, consular service; b. Phila., Pa., July 10, 1878; s. Marcus N.; A.B., U. of Pa., 1902, LL.B., 1905; m. Anne Nefsky, of Lincoln, Neb., 1907. Practiced law, Phila., 1905-07; consul at Patras, Greece, 1907-09, Mersina, Turkey, 1909-17, Vigo, Spain, 1917-21, Palermo, Italy, 1921-28, Santiago de Cuba, 1928-31, Monterrey, Mexico, from 1931. Served as v.p. Internat. Relief Com. at Adana, Turkey, 1909. Mem. Am. Oriental Soc. Republican. Jewish religion. Rotarian. Address: Monterrey, Mexico†

NATZLER, GERTRUD AMON (MRS. OTTO NATZLER), potter; b. Vienna, Austria, July 7, 1908; d. Adolf and Helene (Gruenwald) Amon; ed. in Europe; m. Otto Natzler, June 7, 1937. Came to U.S., 1938, naturalized, 1944. Exhibited in one-man shows at Fine Art Gallery, San Diego, 1940, 42, San Francisco Mus. Art, 1943, 63, Los Angeles County Mus., 1944, 66, Art Inst. Chgo., 1946, 63 La Jolla (Cal.) Art Center 1953, Cin. Art Mus., 1954, 60, Joslyn Art Mus., Omaha, 1955, Springfield (Mo.) Art Mus., 1955, Jewish Mus., N.Y.C., 1958, Bezalel Nat. Mus., Jerusalem, Israel, 1959, Mus. Modern Art, Haifa, Israel, 1959, Kunstgewerbemuseum, Zurich, Switzerland, 1959, Stedelijk Mus., Amsterdam, Netherlands, 1959, Tulane U., 1961, St. Paul Art Center, 1963, Mus. Contemporary Crafts, N.Y.C., 1963, Birger Sandzen Meml. Gallery, Lindsborg, Kan., 1964, Palm Springs (Cal.) Mus., 1968, Pacific Luth. U., Tacoma, 1968, Carleton Coll., Northfield, Minn., 1970, George Walter Vincent Smith Art Mus., Springfield, Mass., DeYoung Meml. Mus., San Francisco, 1971; retrospective exhbn. Renwick gallery Smithsonian Instn.; represented in permanent collections numerous Am. and fgn. museums, including Met. Mus. Art, N.Y.C., Everson Mus. Art, Syracuse, N.Y., Cin. Art Mus., Los Angeles County Mus. Art, Mus. Modern Art, N.Y.C., Art Inst. Chgo., Phila. Mus. Art Joslyn Art Mus., Omaha, Phoenix Art Mus., Balt. Mus. Art, Newark Mus., Walker Art Center, Mpls., Smithsonian Instn., Washington, E.B. Crocker Art Gallery, Sacramento, Oakland (Cal.) Art Mus., Minn. Mus. Art, Kunstgewerbemuseum, Zurich, Victoria and Albert Museum, London, Mus. Fine Arts, Dallas, Des Moines Art Center, Santa Barbara Mus. Art, George Walter Vincent Smith Art Mus; Seattle Art Mus., Detroit Inst. Art, San Francisco Mus. Art, Portland (Ore.) Mus. Art, Nat. Mus. History and Tech., also Colls. and univs. Documentary film The Ceramic Art of the Natzlers (Christopher award); subject of book Natzler Ceramics in the L. M. Sperry Collection, The Ceramic Work of Gertrud and Otto Natzler, 1971, Form and Fire - Natzler Ceramics, 1939-72, 1973. Home: Los Angeles, Cal. Died June 3, 1971. N:M:1888:1973:W37

NAWN, HUGH, constrn. exec.; b. Boston, May 28, 1888; s. Henry Pickering and Elizabeth (Burns) N.; grad. Rosbury Latin Sch., 1907; B.S., Harvard, 1910; m. Mildred Brennan, Sept. 29, 1917; children—Henry Pickering II, Jane, Hugh. With Hugh Nawn, Inc., Boston, 1910-73, beginning as foreman, successively gen. mgr., 1910-22, pres., 1922-73; dir., exec. com. Liberty Mut. Ins. Co.; incorporator Roxbury Instn. for Savs., Morgan Meml. Inc. Club: Harvard (Boston). Home: Brookline, Mass. Died Aug. 1973.

NEAL, GEORGE FRANKLIN, naval officer; Rhea Springs, Tenn., May 2, 1879; s. John Randolph and Mary Elizabeth Caroline (Brown) N.; student, Univ. of Tenn., 1895-97; B.S., U.S. Naval Acad., 1901; grad. Naval War Coll., 1932; hon. LL.D., John R. Neal Sch. of Law, 1910; m. Mattie Steele Milton, Jan. 5, 1910; children—Harriet Katharine, Mattie Lindsay (Mrs. James Treadwell). Commd. ensign U.S. Navy, 1903, and advanced through grades to rear adm., 1934; served in U.S.S. Monongahela, Chesapeake, Kearsarge, Leyden, Yankton, Castine, Cincinnati, Wyoming, Navajo, South Carolina, North Carolina, Cummings, Dorsey, Mississippi, Ramapo, New York; mem. staff of comdr. battle force, U.S.S. Pennsylvania and California, 1925-26; mem. staff of comdr.-in-chief, U.S. Fleet, aboard U.S.S. Seattle and Texas, 1926-28; head, dept.

of elec. engring., U. S. Naval Acad., 1923-25; comdr. receiving ship, Boston, 1919-21; at Naval Training Sta., San Diego, Calif., 1933-35; aide to Sec. of Navy, 1927-31; comdr., mine force, Pacific Fleet, 1935-37; pres. of Gen. Ct. Martial Bd. and acting comdr., 12th Naval Dist., 1939-41; ret. from active service, 1941. Awarded Navy Cross, Distinguished Service Order (Britian). Mem. Sigma Alpha Epsilon. Democrat, Methodist. Mason. Clubs: Army Navy Country (Washington), Rotary (Coronado). Home: Coronado, Cal.†

NEALE, JOHN ERNEST, Brit. Historian; b. Liverpool, Eng., Dec. 7, 1890; M.A., Liverpool U., 1915, D.Litt (hon.); student Univ. Coll., London, 1914-19; D.Litt. (hon.) Birmingham, Cambridge, Leeds, Wales, London universities; Dr. Letters of Humanity (hon.), Amherst Coll.; married to Elfreda Skelton, Oct. 10, 1932; 1 dau., Stella. Asst. history dept. Univ. Coll., 1919-25. Astor Prof. English history, 1927-56, prof. emeritus, 1956-75, Creighton lectr., 1950; prof. modern history Manchester U., 1925-27; Ford's lectr. English history Oxford, 1941-42; Raleigh lectr. Brit. Acad., 1948. Mem. treasury com. House of Commons Records Brit. Govt., 1929. Trustee London Mus., from 1945. Created knight, 1955. Fellow Brit. Acad., 1949; mem. Royal Hist. Soc. (hon. v.p. 1955); fgn. hon. mem. Am. Acad. Arts and Scis. Author: Queen Elizabeth I, 1934; The Age of Catherine de Medici, 1943; The Elizabethan House of Commons, 1949; Elizabeth I and Her Parliaments, 1559-1581, 1953; Elizabeth I and Her Parliaments, 1584-1601, 1957; Essays in Elizabethan History, 1958. Member of the editorial board History of Parliament Trust, from 1951. Contbr. papers hist. jours. Home: Becansfield, Buckshire, England., Died Sept. 2, 1975; ashes interred Stonefall, Harrogate, Eng.

NEARY, WILLIAM HERRMANN, retired lawyer; b. Louisville, May 21, 1905; s. George William and Elizabeth (Herrmann) N.; B.A., So. Meth. U., 1925; LL.B., Harvard, 1928; m. Peggy McLarry, Apr. 18, 1929; children—William Denny, Frederick Richard, George McLarry. Admitted to Tex. bar, 1929, las; asso., then partner firm Thompson, Knight, Simmons & Bullion, and predecessors, 1938-70. Mem. Am., Dallas bar assns., State Bar Tex., Southwestern Legal Found., Sigma Alpha Epsilon. Presbyn. (elder). Club: Dallas Athletic. Home: Richardson, Tex., Died Oct. 11, 1975; buried Hillcrest Gardens, Dallas.

NEEDHAM, FLORIAN BERLE, railroad ofcl.; b. Mountain Grove, Mo., Aug. 17, 1900; s. Marcus Edwin and Effie (Blanchard) N.; grad. Kansas City (Mo.) Bus. Coll., 1919; m. Gladys Hildreth, Oct. 2, 1920; children-Berle Hildreth, William Richard, James Edwin. With C., R.I. & P. R.R., 1919-73, gen. auditor, chief accounting officer, 1962-73; v.p. gen. auditor Rock Island Motor Transit Co.; gen. auditor, dir. Pullman R.R. Co., Peoria Terminal Co., Peoria & Bureau Valley R.R. Co.; v.p., gen. auditor, dir. Rock Island Improvement Co., bus. mgr. Joliet (Ill.) Jr. Coll., from 1967. Mem. Mokena (Ill.) Planning Commn.; mem. Will County (Ill.) Bd. Suprs., 1965; county auditor, Will County, 1968. Treas. Mokena Republican Mens Club. Mem. Ill. C. of C., Chgo. Assn. Commerce and Industry. Methodist (chmn. finance com., trustee). Mason (Shriner), Lion (pres. Mokena). Home: Mokena, Ill., Died July 23, 1973.

NEFF, FRANK AMANDUS, educator; b. Slatington, Pa., June 11, 1879; s. Amandus Peter and Clara Ann Rebecca (Kern) N.; A.B., Lafayette Coll., Easton, Pa., 1906; M.A., Harvard U., 1910; student U. of Kan., summers, 1923-24; U. of Tex., 1917-18, U. of Neb., summers, 1928-31, 1934-37; Ph.D., U. of Neb., 1938; dau. by 1st marriage, Aline Louise (Mrs. Theodore Arms); m. 2d, Iona Keeler Wagner, Aug. 18, 1911; children—John Keeler, Mary Vaughan, Ann Abbott. Teacher Slatington (Pa.) High Sch., 1906-07, New Castle (Pa.) High Sch., 1907-09; acting asst. prof., history and Am. Govt., Beloit (Wis.) Coll., 1910-11; prof. social sciences, Fairmount Coll., Wichita, Kan., 1911-26, registrar, 1912-26, v.p. 1915-26, dir. extension dept., 1912-26, faculty mgr., athletics, 1913-26, acting pres., Mar.-Sept., 1922; dean Coll. of Business Adminstrn., U. of Wichita, from 1926, acting pres., 1927; sr. dean, from 1927; faculty rep. Central Intercollegiate Athletic Conf., 1926-41; univ. rep. to the North Central Assn. of Colls. and Secondary Schs., 1923-41; chmn. bd. of deans in charge adminstrn., U. of Wichita, 1933-34. In O.T.C., artillery branch, U.S. Army, 1918. Area dir. in Kansas, War Manpower Commn., 1942-45. Mem. City of Wichita Bd. of Edn., 1923-41 (pres. 1926-27). Mem. Am. Economic Assn.; Soc. for Advancement of Management. Republican. Conglist. Mason. Clubs: Crestview Country, Hammer and Tongs (Wichita). Author: Municipal Finance, 1939; Steps in Economic Progress, 1939; Economic Doctrines, 1946. Home: Wichita, Kan.†

NEHRLING, ARNO HERBERT, horticulturist; b. Freistadt, Mo., July 25, 1886; s. Henry and Sophia (Schoff) N.; student Shaw Sch. Botany, Washington U., 1905-09; m. Irene Dahlberg, Sept, 18, 1923; children—Arno Herbert, Dorothy Irene (Mrs. Warren P. Higgins). Asst. floriculture U. Ill., 1910-13; prof., head dept. Mass. Agrl. Coll., 1914-17; pres. McDonald Floral Co., Crawfordsville, Ind., 1917-21; prof. floriculture Cornell U., 1921-27; sales mgr. Hill Floral Products Co., Richmond, Ind., 1927-33; dir. exhbns. Mass. Hort. Soc., Boston, 1933-65, exec. sec., also dir. publs., 1947-63. Recipient Tessie K. Scharps Meml. membership award for outstanding service to horticulture Hort. Soc. N.Y., 1954; distinguished achievement citation and plaque for outstanding service to cause of home beauty Asso. Bulb Growers of Holland, 1954; gold medal Men's Garden Clubs Am., 1956; Arthur Hoyt Scott garden and horticulture award Swarthmore Coll., 1957; citation Am. Hort. Council, 1958; named horticulturist of the year U. Mass., 1958; large gold medal Mass. Hort. Soc., 1958; gold medal Hort. Soc. of New York, 1963. Chmn. Nat. Flower Show Com., Soc. Am. Florists (pres. 1937-38, member of the Floricultural Hall of Fame 1964); mem. Chrysanthemum Soc. America (secretary 1930-37, president 1942), Massachusetts Agricultural Club (secretary 1943-45), North America Lily Soc. (president 1954-55); Am. Hort. Council (v.p. 1954-56, dir.), Hort. Club of Boston (pres. 1955-58), Northeastern Florists Assn. (regional dir.), Am. Rose Soc. (registration com.), Am. Tulip Soc. (dir.), Am. Carnation Soc. (hon.), Kappa Sigma, Alpha Gamma Rho, Pi Alpha Xi (1st nat. pres.). Author: (with Mrs. Nehrling) An Easy Guide to House Plants, 1958, Gardening, Forcing, Conditioning and Drying for Flower Arrangements, 1958, Peonies Outdoors and In, 1960, Propagating House Plants, 1962, The Picture Book of Perennials, 1964, The Picture Book of Annuals, 1966, Easy Gardening with Drought Resistant Plants, 1968. Home: Needham Heights, Mass. Died Nov. 23, 1974.

NEIHARDT, JOHN GNELSENAU, author; b. nr. Sharpsburg, Ill., Jan. 8, 1881; s. Nicholas N. and Alice May (Culler) N.; completed scientific course, Neb. Normal Coll., 1897; Litt.D., U. of Neb., 1917; LL.D., Creighton University, Omaha, Neb., 1928; Litt.D., University of Missouri, 1947; married Mona Martinsen, Nov. 29, 1908 (dec. 1958); children—Enid, Sigurd, Hilda, Alice. Lived among Omaha Indians, 1901-07, to study their character, hist., etc.; later asso. with the Ogalala Sioux Indians; apptd. poet laureate, Neb., by act of legislature, 1921; prof. of poetry, U. of Neb., 1923; lit. editor St. Louise Post-Dispatch, 1926-38; Honnold lecturer, Knox Coll., 1939. Dir. information, Office Indian Affairs, Chicago, 1944-46; field rep. Office of Indian Affairs, 1946-48; poet in residence and lecturer in English, U. of Missouri, 1949-66; lecturer emeritus University of Missouri. Awarded gold scroll medal of honor as foremost poet of nation for "The Song of the Messiah," by National Poetry Center, New York, N.Y., 1936; award for poetry by Friends of American Writers Foundation, Chicago, Ill., 1936, Gov.'s Centennial award as Neb. Poet of Century, 1967; Thomas Jefferson award, U. Mo., 1968; citation, named Prairie Poet Laureate Am., United Poets Laureate Internat., 1968; Golden Laurel Wreath, Pres. Republic Philippines, 1968; Ann. Statewide Neihardt Day, proclaimed by Gov. Neb., 1968. Fulbright lectr., India, 1963. Fellow International Institute of Arts and Letters; member of Sigma Tau Delta; hon. Companion Order of Indian Wars of U.S. Author: The Divine Enchantment, 1900; The Lonesome Trail, 1907; A Bundel of Bundle of Myrrh, 1908; Man-Song, 1909; The River and I, 1910; The Dawn-Builder, 1911: The Stranger at the Gate, 1912; Death of Agrippina, 1913; Life's Lure, 1914; The Song of Hugh Glass, 1915, annotated edit. for school use, 1919; The Quest (collected lyrics), 1916; The Song of Three Friends (prize as best volume verse by Poetry Soc. America), 1919; The Splendid Wayfaring, 1920; Two Mothers (drama), 1921; Laureate Address, 1921; The Song of Three Friends and The Song of Hugh Glass (annotated edition for school use), 1924; The Song of the Indian Wars, 1925 (annotated for school use 1928); Poetic Values—Their Reality and Our Need of Them, 1925; Collected Poems, 1926; Indian Tales and Others, 1926; also revised edit. of The River and I, 1927; Black Elk Speaks, 1932; The Song of the Messiah, 1935; The Song of Jed Smith, 1941; A Cycle of the West (the five epic "Songs," above listed pub. in sequence as originally planned) 1949; When the Tree Flowered, 1951; Eagle Voice, 1953; Ich Rufe Mein Volk, published in Germany, 1953; Lyric and Dramatic Poems, published in 1965. Member National Inst. Arts and Letters, The Westerners (a founder, life mem.). Acad. Am. Poets N.Y. (chancellor), Poetry Soc. Am. (v.p. Middle West). Lectures at colls., univs. Bronze bust placed in rotunda, Neb. Capitol. Home: Columbia, Mo., Died Nov. 20, 1975.

NEIL, ALBERT BRAMLETT, jurist; b. Lewisburg, Tenn., Feb. 28, 1873; s. Dr. James Benton and Talitha Jane (McCord) N.; student Terrell Coll., 1892-93, Winchester Normal Coll., 1893-94; LL.B., Cumberland U., Lebanon, Tenn., 1896, hon. LL.D., 1935; m. Josephine Pendleton, Sept. 11, 1911; children—Jane Lindsay (Mrs. George Pullen Jackson, Jr.), Josephine, Albert Bramlett. Admitted to Tenn. bar, 1896; judge criminal court, 10th Dist. of Tenn., 1910-18; circuit judge, 1918-42; dean Cumberland U. Coll. of Law, 1935-40; associate justice Supreme Court of Tenn., 1942-47, chief justice, from 1947. Chmn. Tenn. Code Commission; chmn. State Judicial Council. Member General Assembly of Tennessee, 1899; presidential elector 5th Congl. Dist. of Tenn., 1900. Chmn. Judicial Council Tenn. Mem. Am., Tenn., Nashville bar Assns., Am. Judicature Soc. Alpha Tau Omega, Elk. Mem. Disciples of Christ. Home: Nashville, Tenn.†

NEILL, ALEXANDER SUTHERLAND, author, psychologist; b. Oct. 17, 1883; s. George and Mary Sinclair (Sutherland) N; ed. Edinburgh (Scotland) U.; m. Ada Lillian Lindesay-Neustatter (dec. 1944): m. 2d, Ena May Wood, 1945; 1 dau. Office boy, then draper, tchr., journalist and educator; co-founder Internat. Sch., Hellerau, Dresden, 1921. Author: A Dominie's Log, 1915; A Dominie Dismissed, 1916; The Blooming of Bunkie, 1919; A Dominie in Doubt, 1920; Carroty Broon, 1921; A Dominie Abroad, 1922; A Dominie's Five, or Free School, 1924; The Problem Child, 1926; The Problem Parent, 1932; Is Scotland Educated?, 1936; That Dreadful School, 1937; The Last Man Alive, 2d edit., 1970; The Problem Teacher, 1939; Hearts, not Heads, 1945; The Problem Family, 1948; The Free Child, 1953; Freedom Not License, 1966. (compilation) Summerhill, 1962; Talking of Summerhill, 1967, (autobiography) Neill-Neill-Orange Peel. Home: Leiston, Suffolk, England. Died Sept. 1973.

NEISSER, HANS PHILIP, economist; b. Breslau, Germany, Sept. 3, 1895; s. Gustav and Else (Siberstein) N.; D.U.J., U. of Breslau, 1919, D.S.S., 1921; m. Charlotte Schroeter, 1923; children—Marianne H.E., Ulric R. Came to U.S., 1933, naturalized, 1939. Research ofcr. various commn. econ. German Govt., Berlin, 1922-27; editor econ. weekly Mag. Wirtschaft, 1925-26; instr. lectr. U. of Kiel, Germany, 1927-33; research prin. Inst. World Economy, Kiel, 1927-33; prof. monetary theory U. of Pa., 1933-43; prin. econ. div. research O.P.A., Washington, 1942-43; prof. econ. Grad. Faculty, Polit. and Social Sci., New Sch. for Social Research, N.Y.C., 1943-65, emeritus 1965-75; research prin. Inst. World Affairs, 1943-51; Fulbright lectr. U. of Queensland, 1954. Fellow Econometric Society; mem. Am. Econ. Assn. Author: The Exchange Value of Money, 1927; Some International Aspects of The Business Cycle, 1936; National Income and International Trade, 1954 (with Modigliani); On the Sociology of Knowledge, 1965; also articles in field economics. Home: Bronx, N.Y. Died Jan. 1, 1975.

NELL, RAYMOND BOYD, psychologist; b. Allen, Pa., Jan. 12, 1891; s. Adam and Phiana (Diller) N.; B.S., Gettysburg Coll., 1912; M.A., Thiel Coll., 1920; A.B., U. Minn., 1927; A.M., Columbia, 1927; scholarship student Augsburg Sem., U. Minn., Harvard, Columbia; m. Daisy Irene Wentz, June 16, 1916; children—Raymond Boyd II, Anna, Catherine, Irene May. Ordained to ministry, 1921; pastor, Columbia Heights, Minn., 1921-23; tchr. pub. sch., Mt. Holly, Pa., 1912-13; prof. Wartburg Coll., Clinton, Ia., 1913-16; supt. Nachusa (Ill.) Orphanage 1915; prof. edn. Augsburg Coll., 1916-23; head dept. edn. Hamline U., 1923-37, dir. ednl. research, 1924-28, dean, 1928-33, chmn. div. social studies, 1934-36; with MacPhail Sch. Music, 1924-26; dean Susquehanna U., 1937-38; psychologist Pa. State Coll., 1938-40; prof. psychology and edn. Huntington Coll., 1940-42; dir. War Manpower Tng. Center, Lancaster, Pa., 1942, transferred to Dickenson Coll.; dir. guidance Va, Md., 1947-50; head dept. psychology U. Balt., 1947-71, prof. emeritus; research for Martin Marietta, 1964-66. Fellow Royal Soc. Arts (London); mem. Am. Assn. University Prof Professors (pres. Hamline chpt. 1927-28), Nat. Housing Assn., A.A.A.S., Am. Acad. Polit. and Social Sci., Minn. Edn. Assn. (pres. higher edn. div. 1926-27, chmn. research com. 1928-31), Minn. Assn. Collegiate Registrars (founder; pres. 1932-34), Assn. Minn. Colls. (sec.-treas. 1932-36), Minn. Assn. Coll. Tchrs. Edn. and Psychology (pres. 1933-34), Md. Assn. Colls. (pres. 1957-58), Maryland Historical Society, Maryland Academy Science, Sigma Alpha Epsilon, Kappa Phi Kappa, Pi Gamma Mu, Psi Chi, Phi Delta Kappa, K.P. Clubs: Oxford, Midway. Author books in field. Home: East Berlin, Pa., Died Jan. 8, 1973.

NELSON, DOTSON MCGINNIS, college president; b. Charleston, Mississippi, Dec. 18, 1880; s. Jonathan Taylor and Sarah Isabella (Cornick) N.; B.S., Mississippi College, 1907, LL.D., 1932; A.M., Indiana University, 1919, Ph.D., 1925; m. Mary White, June 18, 1914; children—Dotson McGinnis, Mary White. Teacher and prin. pub. schs. in Miss. 6 yrs.; asst. prof. chemistry, Miss. Coll., 1911-14, prof. physics, 1914-21; exec. sec. Miss. Bapt. Edn. Commn., 1921-25; prof. physics, Miss. Coll., from 1925, pres., from 1932. Mem. A.A.A.S., Optical Soc. America, Am. Assn. Physics Teachers, Am. Assn. Univ. Profs. Democrat. Baptist (deacon). Mason. Odd Fellow, Woodman of the World. Contbr. scientific articles. Home: Clinton, Miss.†

NELSON, ERLAND NELS PETER, educator; b. Ruskin, Neb., July 28, 1897; s. Hans and Frederikke (Olsen) N.; B.A., Peru State Teachers Coll. (Neb.), 1927; M.A., U. of Neb., 1930, Ph.D., 1937; summer student, U. of Chicago, 1931, 33, U. of Minn., 1935; m. Naida Editha Randall, Aug. 6, 1924; children—Isabelle Frederikke, Erland Randall. Rural teacher, Dundy County, Neb., 1920; supt., Comstock, 1922-24, Juniata, 1924-26; professor of commerce, Dana College, Blair, Neb., 1926-29; president Dana College, 1929-36; head department psychology and education Newberry (S.C.) Coll., 1936-43; pres. Carthage (Ill.) Coll., 1943-49; prof. of psychology Univ. of South Carolina, 1949-73. Vice pres. bd. edn. United Luth. Ch. in Am., 1956-60; chmn. Lutheran Student Center, U.S.C. Bd. of dirs. Richland County Mental Board. Fellow American Psychological Association; member of Soc. for Psychol. Study Social

Issues, S.C. Soc. Philosophy, S.C. Psychological Assn. (pres. 1963-64), Southeastern Psychol. Assn., Am. Assn. Univ. Professors, Ed. Soc. Phi Delta Kappa, Gamma Sigma. Demcorat. Author: (monographs) Student Attitudes toward Religion, 1939; Conservatism-Radicalism among College Students; Persistence of Attitudes of College Students Fourteen Years Later, 1954; Patterns of Religious Attitude Shifts from College to Years Later, 1956. Contbr. to psychol. jours., etc. Home: Columbia, S.C., Died Mar. 11, 1973.

NELSON, IRVING ROBERT, physician; b. Bklyn., Nov. 21, 1921; s. Samuel and Rose (Shirvan) N.; M.D., Bowman Grey Sch. Medicine, Winston-Salem, N.C., 1943; m. Mildred Dobin, Nov. 14, 1958; children—Madeline, Jo-Ann, Shelley, Debi-Lou. Intern, Kings County Hosp., Bklyn., 1943-44; staff physician Franklin Gen. Hosp., Valley Stream, N.Y.; asst. physician St. Joseph's Hosp., Far Rockaway, N.Y. Served as capt., M.C., USAAF, 1944-49. Diplomate Am. Bd. Family Practice. Fellow Am. Geriatrics Soc. mem. Am. Acad. Family Practice, A.M.A., Nassau County Med. Soc., Rho Sigma. Home: North Woodmere, N.Y. Died Oct. 21, 1972; buried Mt. Ararat Cemetery, Pinelawn, N.Y.

NELSON, OLIVER EDWARD, composer, conductor; b. St. Louis, June 4, 1932; s. Eugene Cornelius and Lucille (Wilverton) N.; student Washington U., St. Louis, 1954-58, Lincoln U., Jefferson City, Mo., 1958-59; m. Audre N. McEwen, Dec. 30, 1958; children—Oliver Edward, Nyles Oliver, Saxophone player with Quincy Jones and Louis Bellson orchs., N.Y.C., 1960, Duke Ellington and Count Basie orchs., 1961; leader own orch. Lincoln Center Concert, 1964; CBS-TV commn. Repertorie Theatre, 1965; scored music for CBS-TV series Mr. Broadway, 1965; writer, scoring TV series Ironside for Universal Pictures, 1967-75; tchr. summer session Washington U., 1966; pub. mus. ednl. material Noslen Music Co., Hollywood, Cal., Broadcast Music, Inc. Served with USMCR, 1952-54. Recipient New Star award Jazz Critics Poll, 1962, Edison award, Holland, 1965, Best Arrangement award Nat. Acad. Recording Arts and Scis., 1966; commd. by Broadcast Music, Inc. for Jazzhattan, Suite, 1967. Mem. Am. Fedn. musicians. Author: Patterns For Saxophone, 1966. Composer: Blues and the Abstract Truth, 1960; Afro-American Sketches, 1961; Dirge for Orch., 1962; Soundpiece for Contralto, String Orch. and Piano, 1963; Soundplace for Orch., Piano Compositions, 1964; More Blues and the Abstract Truth, 1965; The Kennedy Dream Suite, 1967 (number 20 (tie) in Top 20 Jazz Albums); Concerto for Xylophone, Marimba and Vibraphone, 1967. Home: Los Angeles, Cal., Died Oct. 27, 1975.

NELSON, O(SCAR) A(LFRED), merchant; b. Galesburg, Ill., Oct. 31, 1883; s. Peter and Bertha (Gustafson) N.; student Brown's Bus. Coll., Galesburg, 1901-02; m. Margarethe Olga Thiel, Oct. 3, 1907; 1 son, Hollis H. Propr. Western Tag & Envelope Co., Berkeley, Cal., 1913-39, Nelson Paper Co., 1939-52; mgr. Vita Oil Co., Berkeley, 1921-37, pres., 1937-54, retired; sec. Gales S. Berg Co., 1968-73. Republican. Presbyterian. Mason (Shriner). Clubs: Commonwealth (San Francisco); Athens Athletic (Oakland). Home: Dunsmuir, Cal. Died Aug. 29, 1973; Cremated.

NELSON, OSWALD GEORGE (OZZIE), TV actor, dir., writer, producer; b. Jersey City, Mar. 20, 1907; s. George Waldumar and Ethel Irene (Orr) N.; Litt.B., Rutgers U., 1927, L.H.D., 1957; LL.B., Rutgers U., 1930; m. Harriet Hilliard, Oct. 8, 1935; children—David, Eric. Organized dance orch. 1930, played numerous hotels, theatres, ballrooms, to 1943; radio programs include Joe Penner, Bob Ripley, Peg Murray and Red Skelton; began own radio program, Adventures of Ozzie and Harriet, 1944, producing, directing and acting in TV Adventures-series, 1951-66; dir., actor TV series Ozzie's Girls, 1973-75; recorded for Brunswick, Vocalian, Victor and Bluebird; pub. songs: And Then Your Lips Met Mine, Baby Boy, Size 37 Suit, Swinging on the Golden Gate; motion pictures: Sweethearts of the Campus, Honeymoon Lodge, Strictly in the Groove, Big City, Take It Big, People Are Funny, Here Come the Nelsons, Impossible Years; dir. motion picture Love and Kisses, 1965. Winner N.Y. Daily Mirror Popularity Contest for orch. leaders, 1931; Nat. Family Week Radio Citation by Inter-Council Com. on Christian Family Life; Distinguished Achievement Award for Comedy Script Writing, 1947 (Radio Life mag.); voted best husband and wife team in TV by readers TV-Radio Mirror mag. 7th consecutive year; Distinguished Eagle Scout award, 1973. Republican. Clubs: Ivy (Rutgers); Los Angeles Tennis. Home: Hollywood, Cal. Died June 3, 1975.

NELSON, RICHARD ALFRED, orgn. ofcl.; b. Utica, Neb., Sept. 8, 1909; s. Claude C. and Nancy E. (Hurlburt) N.; student U. Neb., 1927-28, San Diego State Coll., 1928-30; m. Carol Woods, May 21, 1932; children—Richard Alfred, Nancy Carol (Mrs. James Horton Bell), William Woods. With Benbough Furniture Co., San Diego, 1930-46, asst. to pres., 1939-46; formed Nelson-Thomas & Co., retail office furniture, San Diego, 1946, pres., 1946-60; formed Nelson Enterprises, Inc., 1950; exec. dir. Davis Meml. Goodwill Industries, Washington, 1961-69, dir. indsl. div., Long Beach Cal., 1969-74. Active Goodwill Industries Am., 1947, nat. pres., 1953-61, dir., 1952-63; past officer San Diego Council Chs., Goodwill Industries, Community Chest, Campfire Girls, Conv. and Tourist Bur. (all San Diego). Founding mem. Exec. Furniture Guild Am., 1947, past sec., v.p. Presbyn. (deacon, elder, trustee, lay preacher). Mason (Shriner), Kiwanian. Lectr. Home: Lakewood, Cal. Died Aug. 31, 1974; interred Fairhaven Meml. Park, Santa Ana, Cal.

NELSON, VIRGINIA WINSLOW, (Mrs. Riley C. Nelson), sch. adminstrn.; b. Waterloo, Ia.; d. Fred Albert and Kate (Trenor) Winslow; student pub. schs.; m. Riley C. Nelson, June 12, 1924 (dec. Jan. 1958); children—Riley R., Beverly Jean, Carolyn (Mrs. Allen Nelson). Owner, dir. Powell Sch. for Retarded Children, Red Oak, Ia. Fellow Am. Assn. Mental Deficiency; mem. Bus. and Profl. Womens Club; Am. Legion Aux., Ia. Welfare Assn., Neb. Assn. for Retarded Children. Conglist. Mem. Order Eastern Star. Clubs: Monday, Altrusa. Home: Red Oak, Ia., Died Mar. 17, 1975.

NERI, M. PHILIP, surgeon; b. Providence, R.I., July 27, 1927; s. Paul and Theresa (Valente) N.; M.D., Harvard, 1957; m. Anne Marie Rapa, May 25, 1950; children—Susan, Karen. Intern N.Y. Upstate Med. Center, Syracuse, 1957-58; resident in surgery Boston-Mass. Meml. Hosps., Providence VA Hosp.; attending surgeon Westerly (R.I.) Hosp.; practice medicine, specializing in surgery, 1963-72; mem. staff Alexian Bros. Hosp., San Jose, Cal., chief of staff 1971-72, treas., 1917, pres., 1972, also mem. found. Mem. Santa Clara County (Cal.) Disaster Com., Cerebral Palsy Found., Retarded Children's Assn. Served with USCGR, 1945-46. Memorialized by State of Cal., 1973. Diplomate Am. Bd. Surgery. Fellow A.C.S.; mem. A.M.A., Cal., Santa Clara County med. assns., Phi Beta Kappa. Home: San Jose, Cal., Died Oct. 19, 1972; buried Santa Clara County Mission Cemetery, San Jose, Cal.

NERUDA, PABLO, poet; b. 1904; ed. U. Chile; D.Litt. (hon.), Oxford U., 1965. Consul, Rangoon, Burma, 1927, Colombo, 1929, Batavia (Djakarta), 1930, Buenos Aires, 1933, Madrid, 1936; refugee resettlement work, Paris, 1938-39; sec. Chilean embassy, Mexico, 1939, ambassador, 1940-42; mem. Chilean Senate, 1945. Mem. World Peace Council, 1950-73; pres. Chilean Writers Union, 1959-73; mem. Lenin Peace Prize Com. Recipient Internat. Peace prize, 1950, Lenin Peace Prize, 1953, Nobel prize in lit., 1971. Hon. mem. Chile and Harvard univs. Author: Crepuscularío, 1923; Veinte Poemas de Amor y una Cancion Deseperada, 1924; Residencia en la Tierra, 1925-35; Tercera Residencia, 1943; Canto General, 1950; Las Uvas y el Viento, 1954; Memorial de Isla Negra, 1954; Odas Elementales, 1934-60; Estravagrio, 1959; Piedras de Chile, 1961; Cancion de Gesta, 1961; Cantos Ceremoniales, 1962; The Heights of Macchu Picchu, 1967; (films) The Fame and Death of Joaquin Murientaz. The Life of Pablo Neruda. Address: Santiago, Chile. Died Sept. 23, 1973.

NESBIT, WALTER, ex-congressman; b. Belleville, Ill., May 1, 1878; s. Charles and Helen (Green) N.; ed. pub. and night schs., Belleville; m. Regina Marxer, of Millstadt, Ill., May 28, 1902; children—Frank Marion, Walter William (dec.), Adolph Barney, Helen Mary (Mrs. Basyl Kercheval). Coal miner, Belleville, 1892-1912; sub-dist. sec. United Mine Workers of Am., 1912-15, traveling auditor, 1915-17, state sec.-treas. Dist. 12, 1917-33. Mem. 73d Congress (1933-35), Ill. at large. Mem. Journeyman Barbers of Am.; hon. mem. Vets. Fgn. Wars, Spanish-Am. War Vets. Accorded certificate of honor and membership in U.S. Civil Legion for service to U.S. during World War and for service rendered Red Cross, and industrial sect. of the U.S. Labor Bd. Democrat. Clubs: German (Belleville); German (Chicago). Home: Belleville, Ill.†

NESLEN, C(HARLES) CLARENCE, ex-mayor; b. Salt Lake City, Utah, Apr. 17, 1879; s. Robert F. and Eliza (Saville) N.; prep. edn., Y.M.C.A. night sch.; student Latter Day Saints U., 1895-97; m. Grace Cannon, Oct. 26, 1905; children—Clarence Cannon, Robert Cannon, Gertrude Cannon, George Quayle, Charles Richard. Real estate business, 1910-17; commr. water supply and water works, Salt Lake City, 1918-20; mayor of Salt Lake City, 1920-28; mem. Utah Ho. of Rep., 1931-32; state senator, 1932-35; commr. ins. State of Utah. Chmn. Draft Board, World War I; maj. chaplain 145th F.A., Utah N.G., from 1926. Del. to Dem. Nat. Conv., 1912. Pres. Salt Lake Oratorio Society. Bishop in Latter Day Saints Ch. Club: Timpanogas. Home: Salt Lake City, Utah.†

NEUHAUS, EUGEN, artist, educator; b. Barmen, Rhine Prov., Germany, Aug. 18, 1879; s. Emil and Julie Bertha (Müser) N.; grad. Royal Art Sch., Kassel, 1899; grad. Royal Sch. for Applied Arts, Berlin, 1902; Ph.D. honoris causa, Marburg, Germany, 1933; m. Louise Anne Yoerk, Apr. 26, 1905; children—Eugene, Robert, Victor (deceased); married 2d, Leona May Fassett, October 14, 1944. Came to U.S., 1904, naturalized citizen, 1911. Exhibitor landscape paintings, San Francisco, Chicago, Phila., etc.; represented in pub. and private collections; chmn. western advisory com. Dept. of Art and mem. Internat. Jury of Awards, San Francisco Expn., 1915; lecturer on history and theory of art Mills Coll., 1918-27; mem. faculty U. Cal., from 1907, prof., 1927-49, prof. emeritus, from 1949. Mem. San Francisco Art Assn., Am. Soc. Aesthetics, Delta Epsilon, Skull and Keys, Mask and Dagger. Clubs: Faculty, Kosmos, Sierra Ski. Author: Painters, Pictures and the People; Art of the Exposition; The San Diego Garden Fair; The Appreciation of Art; The History and Ideals of American Art; World of Art; William Keith (biography); The Art of Treasure Island, 1939. Translator; Materials of the Artist (Max Doerner). Address: Orinda, Cal.†

NEUMANN, ROBERT, author; b. Vienna, Austria, May 22, 1897; s. Samuel and Josephine (Pilpel) N.; student U. Vienna; m. Stephanie Grunwald, 1920 (div. 1941); 1 son, Henry (dec. 1944); m. 2d, Lore Fraziska Becker, 1941 (div. 1952); m. 3d, Evelyn Hengerer, 1953 (dec. 1958); 1 son, Michael Robert Henry; m. 4th, Helga Heller, Sept. 9, 1960. Author: (German translated into English) Flood, 1930, Ship in the Night, 1932, Mammon, 1933, Sir Basil Zaharoff (biography), 1935, The Queen's Doctor, 1936, A Woman Screamed, 1938, 48, By the Waters of Babylon, 1939, Shooting Star, 1954, Festival, 1963, Pictorial History of the 3d Reich, 1962, others; (written in English) Scene in Passing, 1945; The Inquest, 1947, Children of Vienna, 1946, Blind Man's Buff, 1949, In the Steps of Morell, 1952, Insurrection in Poshansk, 1952, The Plague House Papers, 1959, The Dark Side of the Moon, 1961, others; (in German) Olympia, 1961, Der Tatbestand, 1965, Parodies, 3 vols., 1969, Autobiography, 2 vols., 1963, 68, German complete edit., 20 vols., 1959-75, Oktoberreise mit einer Geliebten, 1970; Ein unmöglicher Sohn, 1972; (films) Abdui the Damned, 1934, Dynamite Nobel, 1937, Those are the Men, 1941, Herrscher ohne Krone, 1956, The Life of Adolf Hitler, 1962; (screenplays) Geschichte einer Geschichte, Schiosspension Furstenhorst, Die Begnadigung, 1969, Emigration, 1970. Recipient Austrian Cross of Honour 1st class arts and scis., 1965, Vienna Gold medal honor 1967, others. Mem. P.E.N. (internat. v.p., hon. pres. Austrian sect.), Deutsche Akademie fur Sprache und Dichtung, Freie Deutsche Akademie der Kunste, Schweizerischer Schriftstellerverein, others. Home: Locarno-Monti, Switzerland. Died Jan. 3, 1975.

NEUMEYER, CARL MELVIN, educator, musician; b. Illinois City, Ill., Aug. 10, 1911; s. Frank Edward and Anna Sophia (Lotz) N.; B.Mus., Murray State U., 1934; M.Mus., Ill. Wesleyan U., 1939; D.Mus.Ed., Ind. U., 1954; m. Margaret Jeanette Lewis, Aug. 28, 1934; children—Roberta (Mrs. David R. Ewbank), Patricia (Mrs. James W. Stirling). Supr. music pub. sch., Martinsville, Ill., 1934-37, Geneseo, Ill., 1937-42; asst. dean Sch. of Music, So. Meth. U., 1942-52; dir. Sch. of Music, prof. Ill. Wesleyan U., 1952-72. Bd. dirs. Nat. Music Council, 1970-72; chmn. bd. Sinfonia Found., 1970-72, trustee, 1956-72, pres. bd., 1964-67; bd. dirs. Bloomington (Ill.) Symphony Soc., 1952-67, pres., 1955-58. Fellow Internat. Inst. Arts and Letters; mem. Nat. Assn. Schs. of Music (pres. 1969-72), Ill. Music Educators Assn., Music Educators Nat. Conf., Music Tchrs. Nat. Assn., Phi Mu Alpha (nat. pres. 1967-70), Pi Kappa Lambda, Phi Kappa Phi, Phi Delta Kappa. Methodist. Mason (32 deg.), Rotarian. Author: History of National Association of Schools of Music, 1954. Home: Normal, Ill. Died Dec. 7, 1972; buried Funks Grove, Ill.

NEVILLE, PHILIP, U.S. judge; b. Mpls., Nov. 5, 1909; s. James E. and Laura (Kelly) N.; B.A., U. Minn., 1931, LL.B., 1933; m. Maurene Morton, Feb. 6, 1934; children—Laura, James, Philip. Admitted to Minn. bar, 1933; law clk. to chief justice Minn. Supreme Ct., 1933-35; gen. law practice Mpls., 1935-67; mem. faculty Minn. Coll. Law, 1936, 37-38; spl. lectr. bus. law, mem. faculty U. Minn., 1937-67; municipal judge Village of Edina, Minn., 1948-52; regional dir. OPS, 1951-52; U.S. dist. atty. for Minn., 1952-53; U.S. dist. judge Dist. Minn., 1967-74. Sec.-mem. Minn. Bd. Law Examiners, 1941-52. Mem. Am., Minn. (pres. 1963-64), Hennepin County (pres. 1956-57) bar assns., Am. Judicature Soc., Am. Coll. Trial Lawyers, Order of Coif, Sigma Alpha Epsilon, Phi Delta Phi, Delta Sigma Pi. Episcopalian. Clubs: Athletic, Minikahda, Minneapolis (Mpls.). Author: Syllabus in Business Law (with Wells J. Wright), 1947. Home: Edina, Minn. Died Feb. 13, 1974.

NEVIN, CHARLES MERRICK, geologist; b. Helton, Pa., Sept. 12, 1892; s. William Scott and Lida (Merrick) N.; B.S., Pa. State Coll., 1916; M.S., Cornell, 1922, Ph.D., 1925; m. Ruth Coats, Sept. 6, 1924. Consultant in geology; mem. faculty, Cornell, prof. of geology. Mem. Geol. Soc. of Am., Am. Assn. Petroleum Geologists, Am. Geophys. Union, Soc. of Economic Geologists, Sigma Xi, Phi Kappa Phi, Sigma Gamma Epsilon. Home: Ithaca, N.Y. Died Mar. 24, 1975.

NEVINS, RALPH GRIFFITH, JR., environ. engr.; b. Kingsley, Kan., Nov. 15, 1925; s. Ralph Griffith and Ethel (Dykeman) N.; B.S. in Naval Tech., U. Minn., 1945. B. Mech. Engring., 1947, M.S., 1949; Ph.D., U. Ill., 1953; m. Janet Audrey Juul, Aug. 24, 1946; children—Katherine Juul, Kristine Ellen. Instr., U. Minn., 1946-48; mem. faculty Kan. State U., Manhattan, 1948-73, prof. mech. engring., 1952-73, head dept., 1957-67, dir. Inst. Environmental Research 1962-73, dean engring., 1967-73; John B. Pierce Found. fellow Yale, 1973-75; research engr. Mpls. Honeywell, Inc., summers, 1955-57; cons. in field, 1960-75. Mem. div. engring. and indsl. research NRC-Nat. Acad. Scis., 1963-66; ad. hoc. engring. study group USAF Sci. Adv. Bd., 1965-67; mem. Kan. Ednl. Authority, 1967-68. Bd.

dirs. Project Concern, 1961-72, chmn., 1965-67. Served with USNR, 1943-46. Kan. Power and Light Distinguished prof., 1963-67; recipient Distinguished Alumnus award mech. and indsl. engring. dept. U. Ill., 1970, Richards Meml. award Pi Tau Sigma 1970, Distinguished Service award U. Ill. Coll. Engring., 1971. Registered profl. engr., Kan. Fellow Instn. Heating and Ventilating Engrs. (London), Am. Soc. Heating, Refrigerating and Airconditioning Engrs. (nat. bd. dirs. 1964-66, chmn. TC 1.4 com. 1961, 55P com. 1963-66, 71-75, 62P com. 1965-75, standards com. 1968-73, program com. 1973-75; Distinguished Service award 1972, E.K. Campbell award of merit 1974); mem. Am. Soc. M.E. (chmn. Kan. 1963-64), Am. Soc. Engring. Edn. (chmn. Midwest sect. 1965-67, nat. v.p. 1968-69), Biomed. Engring. Com. (chmn. 1967-68), Environmental Engring. Div. (dir. 1968-70), Engrs. Council for Profl. Devel. (engring. edn. and accreditation com. 1967-72, chmn. region I, 1970-72), Kan. Bd. Engring. Examiners, Engrs. Found. Kan. (bd. trustees 1969-73), Kan. Engring. Soc., Nat. Soc. Profl. Engrs., N.Y. Acad. Scis., Manhattan C. of C. (bd. dirs. 1967-70), Sigma Xi, Sigma Tau, Pi Tau Sigma, Phi Gamma Delta, Phi Kappa Phi, Pi Mu Epsilon. Home: Madison, Conn. Died Oct. 30, 1974.

NEW, WILLIAM LAFAYETTE, telephone exec.; b. nr. Swainsboro, Ga., Mar. 20, 1901; s. William Madison and Daisy (Powell) N.; student Mercer U., 1921, 26; m. Minnie Lee Grant, Aug. 8, 1924; children—Elizabeth (Mrs. O. F. Loosier, Junior), Grant. Prof., Latin and algebra Lyons High Sch., 1926; auditor So. Bell Tel. & Tel. Co., Atlanta, 1927-35; bus. mgr. Thomaston Telephone Co., (Ga.), 1935-49; pres., owner Commerce Telephone Co. (Ga.), 1950-68, ret. Lt. col. Gov's. Staff, 1963-73. Adv. council Ga. Recreation Com. Bd. trustees Brewton Parker Coll. Recipient certificate for distinguished service, Am. Legion, 1945; citizenship award Vets Fgn. Wars, 1962; recreation award Am. Legion and Ruritan Club, 1962. Mem. Knight of The Garter, Commerce C. of C. Baptist. Mason (Shriner). Kiwanian. Home: Altamonte Springs, Fla. Died June 17, 1973; buried Jackson County Meml. Cemetery, Commerce, Ga.

NEWBURGER, MORRIS stockbroker; b. Phila., Feb. 26, 1906; s. Alfred Henry and Roselia (Seasongood) N.; grad. Phillips Exeter Acad., 1922; B.A., Harvard, 1926; m. May Untermeyer, Apr. 11, 1935; children—Michael, Maury. Partner Newburger Loeb & Co., investment securities, N.Y.C., 1931-68; dir. and sec. Exchange Firms Information Corp. Trustee May and Morris Newburger Found. Served as maj. USAAF, 1942-46. Mem. N.Y. Cotton Exchange, Chgo. Bd. Trade. Clubs: Harmonie, Lawyers (N.Y.C.). Home: New York City, N.Y. Died Sept. 12, 1968.

NEWBURN, HARRY KENNETH, educator; b. Cuba, Ill., Jan. 1, 1906; s. Charles R. and Alice (Bayless) N.; student Western Ill. Tchrs. Coll., 1923-25, B.E., 1928; A.M., State U. Ia., 1931, Ph.D., 1933; L.H.D., No. Mich. U., 1957, Cleve. State U., 1973; LL.D., U. Ariz., 1971; m. Wandalee Brady, June 16, 1928; children—Jacquelyn, Robert Lee, Michael K. Tchr. social scis., Astoria, Ill., 1925-27; supt. schs., Pearl City, Ill., 1928-30; prin. Twp. High Sch., Bradford, Ill., 1930-31; with State U. Ia., 1931-45, as prin. U. High Sch., 1931-38, asst. prof. edn., 1934-36, asso. prof., 1936-41, dir. U. High Sch., 1938-41, dean, prof. Coll. Liberal Arts, 1941-45; pres. U. Ore., 1945-53; pres. Ednl. Television and Radio Center, 1953-58; cons. Ednl. Mission of ICA in Brazil, 1956-57; cons. Ford Found., 1958-59; pres. Mont. State U., 1959-63; prof. edn. Ariz. State U., Tempe, 1963-74, dean Coll. Edn., 1968-69, pres., 1969-71, prof. higher edn., 1971-73; acting pres. Cleve. State U., 1965-66, interim pres., 1972-73, ednl. cons., 1965-74; cons. AID mission, Venezuela, 1962. Dir. Helena br. Fed. Res. Bank, Mpls., 1961-63, chmn., 1962-63. Mem. adv. council Pacific area A.R.C., 1962-65, chmn. Maricopa County chpt., 1972-74; commr. for Mont., Western Interstate Commn. Higher Edn., 1962-63; mem. Nat. Commn. on Accrediting, 1950-54; mem. Pres.'s Commn. on Higher Edn., 1946-47. Mem. exec. com. Am. Council Edn., 1951-53, mem. commn. adminstrn., 1963. Recipient Carnegie grant, 1938, 52. Mem. N.E.A. (pres. Assn. Higher Edn. 1946-47), Phi Delta Kappa, Kappa Delta Pi. Conglist. Mason, Rotarian. Contbr. articles to profl. jours. Home: Tempe Ariz. Died Aug. 25, 1974.

NEWELL, GEORGE T., banker; b. Troy, Pa., June 9, 1896; s. Perry George and Mary C. (Lester) N.; student Elmira Business Coll., Elmira, N.Y., 1913-14. Am. Inst. Banking, N.Y.C. With 2d Nat. Bank, Elmira, 1914-18; Industrial Bank of N.Y. (merged with Mfrs. Trust Co.), 1919-22; asst. sec. Mfrs. Trust Co., 1923-32, asst. v.p., 1932-35, v.p. from 1935; dir. Henneberry Rotogravure Co., 34th St.-Midtown Assn., Inc., Appleton-Century Crofts, Incorporated. Gov. The Am. Found. Religion and Psychiatry, Inc. Member N.Y. Credit Men's Association, Robert Morris Assos., Am. Arbitration Assn. Episcopalian. Clubs: Union League, Empire State (N.Y.C.); Waccabuc (N.Y.) Country; Racquet (Chgo.). Home: Danbury, Conn. Died July 28, 1974.

NEWHALL, NANCY, author; A.B., Smith Coll., 1930. Dir. numerous exhbns. Mus. Modern Art, George Eastman House, Smithsonian Instn., Sierra Club, USIA; acting curator photography Mus. Modern Art, N.Y.C., 1942-45; cons. on exhbns. and publs. George Eastman House; asso. curator photography collection Exchange Nat. Bank Chgo. Author, editor: This is the American Earth. Author: Ansel Adams, Vol. 1: The Eloquent Light; P.H. Emerson, The Fight for Photography, 1975. Co-author: Masters of Photography. Editor: Time in New England. Home: Albuquerque, N.M. Died July 7, 1974; cremated.

NEWHALL, RICHARD AGER, coll. prof.; b. Minneapolis, Minn., June 12, 1888; s. Harry Frank and Elizabeth (Barrett) N.; B.A., U. of Minn., 1910, M.A., 1911; M.A., Harvard University, 1914, Ph.D., 1917, Litt.D. (hon.), Williams College, 1943, Guggenheim fellow, 1930-31; m. Elizabeth Howe Bliss, June 21, 1919; children—Roger, Jane (Lyons), Daniel Lawrence. Instructor and tutor, Harvard Univ., 1915-17, 1919; instr. in history, Yale University, 1919-20, asst. prof. history, 1920-24; prof. European history, Williams College, 1924-34, William Dwight Whitney professor, 1934-48, Brown prof. history, 1948-56, emeritus. Consultant, Historical Section, Joint Chiefs of Staff. Chairman of the advisory committee Hist. Div., U.S. Air Forces. Served as 2d lieutenant infantry, O.R.C., 1917-19, attached to 1st Div. A.E.F., 1917-18; severely wounded at Cantiguy, May 28, 1918. Decorated Silver star with oak leaf cluster; Order of the Purple Heart. Fellow; Royal Hist. Soc.; mem. Am. Hist. Assn., Mediaeval Acad. Am., Phi Beta Kappa, Phi Gamma Delta. Dem. Swedenborgian. Club: Williams (N.Y.). Author: The English Conquest of Normandy, 1416-1424, 1924; The Crusades, 1927; Muster and Review, 1940; The Chronicle of Jean de Venette (with Jean Birdsall), 1953. Co-editor, 1927 — (with L. B. Packard and S. R. Packard) Berkshire Studies in European History. Editor Report of Round Table and Gen. Confs., Inst. of Politics, 7th, 8th and 9th sessions, 1927-29. Contbr. articles and reviews. Home: Williamstown, Mass. Died June 18, 1973.

NEWLAND, DONALD ELMER, urologist; b. Drakesville, Ia., Dec. 7, 1905; s. Elmer Ree and Eva Grace (Knight) N.; B.S., M.D., U. Ia., 1930; M.S. in Urology, U. Pa., 1938; m. Mary Helen Tucker, June 12, 1930; children—Jean Miriam (Mrs. Edward G. Robertson III), Nancy Lou (Mrs. Jimmy Dan Lawrence). Intern, Denver Gen. Hosp., 1930-32; gen. practice medicine, Routt County, Colo., 1932-36; resident in urology L'Hotel Dieu, Montreal, Que., Can., 1937; practice medicine, specializing in urology, Denver, 1938-73; mem. staff St. Luke's Hosp., Denver, pres., 1954; head dept. urology Denver Gen. Hosp., 1959-69; hon. med. staff Lutheran Hosp.; asso. staff Mercy, Presbyn., St. Joseph's hosps.; attending staff Children's Hosp., St. Anthony's Hosp. (all Denver). Asso. clin. prof. urology U. Colo. Sch. Medicine, 1953-59, head dept. urology, 1956-59. Served with M.C., AUS, 1942-45. Diplomate Am. Bd. Urology. Mem. A.M.A., Colo., Denver med. assns., Am. Urol. Assn. (South Central sect.), Alpha Omega Alpha, Alpha Kappa Kappa, Roundup Riders of the Rockies. Methodist. Clubs: Denver Athletic, Executive, Valley Country (Denver). Contbr. articles to profl. publs. Home: Denver, Colo., Died Feb. 20, 1973; interred Fairmount Mausoleum, Denver, Colo.

NEWMAN, ELLIOT VOSS, medical educator; b. Boston, Jan. 23, 1914; s. Leon and Ellen (Bettoney) N.; A.B., Harvard, 1935, M.D., 1939; m. Ailsa Campbell Mackay, Aug. 23, 1940; children—Elliot Campbell (dec. 1968), John Hughes. Intern, Newton (Mass.) Hosp., 1939-40, Mass. Gen. Hosp., Boston, 1940-41; fellow in medicine Johns Hopkins Med. Sch., 1941-42, Instr. medicine, 1942-46, asst. prof. medicine, 1946-49, asso. prof. medicine, 1949-52; asst. resident medicine Johns Hopkins Hosp., 1942-44, resident physician, 1944-46, vis. physician, 1946-52; prof. exptl. medicine, head clin. physiol. labs., dir. Clin. Research Center, Vanderbilt U. Hosp., Nashville, 1952-73, Joe and Morris Werthan prof. exptl. medicine. Chmn. heart program-project com. NIH; mem. nat. adv. heart council NIH, USPHS, chmn. task force on arteriosclerosis Nat. Heart and Lung Inst. Fellow A.C.P.; mem. So. Soc. Clin. Research, Fgn. Relations Council, Am. Heart Assn., Am. Physiol. Soc., Med. and Chirurg. Faculty Md., Soc. Exptl. Biology and Medicine, Am. Soc. Clin. Investigation, Assn. Am. Physicians, Tenn. Med. Assn., Am. Clin. and Climatol. Assn., N.Y. Acad. Scis., Sigma Xi, Alpha Omega Alpha. Clubs: Peripatetic Soc., Round Table, Nashville Exchange. Author articles in med., sci. books and jours. Mem. editorial bd. Circulation Research. Home: Nashville Tenn. Died Sept. 24, 1973.

NEWMARK, MARCO ROSS, retired merchant; b. Los Angeles, Calif., Oct. 8, 1878; s. Harris and Sarah (Newmark) N.; A.B., U. of Calif., 1902; studied polit. economy and philosophy, U. of Berlin, Germany, one semester; m. Constance Meyberg, June 6, 1906; children—Harris, Eleanor (Mrs. Justin Scharff). Became v.p. M. A. Newmark & Co., wholesale grocers 1930, partner, 1908, retired, 1931; pres. The Harris Newmark Co. V.p. Nat. Wholesale Grocers' Assn., 1930; mem. Los Angeles Mchts'. and Mfrs'. Assn. (treas. 1916-19; dir. 1933), Los Angeles Chamber Commerce (dir. 1931); pres. Los Angeles Produce Exchange, 1920. Chairman exec. com. Southern Calif. div., Camp Library Fund, U.S. Army, 1917. Organizer and ex-pres. Nathan Straus Palestine Soc.; pres. Fedn. of Jewish Welfare Orgns. of Los Angeles, 1933-37; pres. Hist. Soc. of Southern Calif., 1940-41; pres. Midnight Mission for Homeless Men, 1942. Mem. Native Sons of the Golden West, Zeta Beta Tau (hon.), B'nai B'rith (pres. Los Angeles Lodge 1906 and 1920). Republican. Mason (32°, K.C.C.H., Shriner). Mem. Los Angeles Athletic and Authors Clubs. Co-editor (with M. H. Newmark, dec.): Sixty Years in Southern California (by Harris Newmark), 1916, 3d edit., 1930. Co-Author (with M. H. Newmark, dec.): Census of Los Angeles City and County for 1850, 1929. Contbr. to mags. Home: Los Angeles, Cal.†

NEWMYER, ALVIN LEROY, lawyer; b. Washington, Jan. 9, 1884; s. Lewis and Mary (Bensinger) N.; LL.B., George Washington U., 1906; m. Harriet Myers, June 6, 1916; children—Alvin L., Armand, Lewis. Admitted to D.C. bar, 1906; practicing atty., trial atty. firm of Newmyer and Bress; lectr. Practicing Law Inst. of Am. Bar Assn.; prof. emeritus of law George Washington U. Recipient 1st annual alumni award for distinguished career, George Washington U., 1949. Fellow Am. College Trial Lawyers; mem. Am. Bar Assn., Bar Association D.C., Washington Bd. Trade. Mason (32°, Shriner). Home: Washington, D.C. Died May 22, 1973.

NEWSOM, EDWIN EARL, pub. relations counsel; b. Wellman, Ia., Dec. 13, 1897; s. John Edward and Emma Ellen (Day) N.; A.B., Oberlin Coll., 1921; L.H.D., Boston U., 1948; LL.D., Ia. Wesleyan Coll., 1961; m. Lois Ruth Rinehart, June 14, 1923; children—John Richard, Barbara (Mrs. John Palmer Little). Tchr., Western Res. Acad., Hudson, O., McBurney Sch. for Boys, N.Y.C., Meml. High Sch., Pelham, N.Y., 1921-25; staff mem. Literary Digest, N.Y.C., 1925-27; exec. sec. Oil Heating Inst., 1927-29; v.p. John Day Pub. Co., 1929-31; dir. pub. relations and sales Distbrs. Group, Inc., 1931-33; partner Norman Bel Geddes & Co., 1933-35; sr. partner Earl Newsom & Co., pub. relations counsel, 1935-65, cons. Earl Newsom & Co., Inc., 1966-73; cons. Office Pub. Affairs Dept. State, 1952; Mem. adv. com. Pres.'s Com. Internat. Information Activities, 1953, Commr. Internal Revenue, 1954; dir., mem. adv. council com. Modern Cts., 1959-73. Trustee Village Pelham Manor, N.Y., 1945-47. Bd. dirs. The Tibetan Found., 1969-73; bd. dirs., exec. com. Free Europe, Inc., 1955-68, hon. life mem.; trustee Boston U., 1953-60, Emma Willard Sch., 1948-56, Oberlin Coll., 1950-65. Served as pilot USN Air Corps, World War I. Mem. Acad. Polit. Sci., Nat. Inst. Social Sci. (exec. com.). Clubs: Union League, The Links (N.Y.C.); Blind Brook (Portchester, N.Y.); Pelham Country. Home: Salisbury, Conn. Died Apr. 11, 1973.

NEWTON, CHARLES HOWARD, educator; b. Plattsmouth, Neb., Nov. 4, 1930; s. Edgar Sylvester and Mildred (Clark) N.; B.A. in Sociology and Psychology, U. Neb., 1956, M.A. in Sociology, 1958; Ph.D., Fla. State U., 1961; m. Janis Lea Arnold, Dec. 18, 1954; children—Charles H., Jim Harold. Asst. prof. sociology U. Richmond, 1961-63; asso. prof. Memphis State U., 1963-64, prof., 1964-75, chmn. dept. sociology and anthropology, 1972-75, chmn. research com., coordinator Bur. Social Research dept. sociology, 1970-75. Chief cons. Memphis Juvenile Ct., 1964-72, chmn. adv. com., 1966; lectr. Memphis Police Acad., 1964-75; mem. adv. com. vocational tech. tng. program Shelby County Penal Farm, 1965-75; chmn. Tenn. Assn. Advancement Child Care, 1968-75; mem. budget com. Shelby United Neighbors, 1968-75; social service com. Family Service Memphis, 1968-75; spl. cons. commr. Tenn. Dept. Corrections, 1971-75. Served with USAF, 1948-52; Korea. Named Distinguished Educator, 1973. Mem. So., Am. sociol. assns., Alpha Kappa Delta. Author: (with Warren Chukinas, Patricia Scott) Educational Sociology; An Annotated and Cross Referenced Bibliography, 1964. Editor: Alienation in Mass Society (Paul Meadows), 1967; co-editor several pubs. proc. Law Enforcement Inst., 1967-68. Home: Memphis, Tenn., Died Nov. 12, 1975.

NEWTON, COSETTE FAUST (MRS. FRANK HAWLEY NEWTON), museum ofcl., writer; b. Kemp, Tex., July 18, 1889; d. Edwin Michael and Sue (Noble) Faust; certificate Denton Normal Coll., 1906, Sam Houston Normal Sch., 1907; B.A., B.S., Poly. Coll. Ft. Worth, 1911; M.A., U. Tex., 1912; Ph.D., Radcliffe Coll., 1916; M.S., U. Chgo., 1923, J.D., 1924; M.D., Baylor U., 1923; B.E., M.E., Columbia Coll. Expression Chgo., 1924; J.S.D., N.Y. U., 1925; certificate Sorbonne, 1927; m. Frank Hawley Newton, June 14, 1918. Tchr. pub. schs., Baird, Tex. 1907-08; head dept. English. Mexia (Tex.) High Sch., 1912-13; asst. prof. English So. Meth. U., Dallas, 1917-18, asso. prof., dean of women, 1918; pres. Miramir Mus., Dallas, 1963-75. Mem. Nat. League Am. Pen Women, Nat. Poetry Soc., Poetry Soc. Tex., Kappa Alpha Theta, Zeta Phi Eta. Mem. Order Eastern Star. Author: (with Stith Thompson) Old English Poems, 1918; Rainbow-Hued Trail Around the World, 1932; Relatives in Rhyme at Christmas Time, 1938; Around the World in Rhyme, 1939; Kinship Songs, 1939; Dark Interval, 1941; War-Blown, 1941; Songs for Singers, 1942; S.S. Miramar Verses; The Great American "Accident", 1951; Macarthur's Hour, 1951; Romance of A Rosebud; Garden Songs. Contbr. to periodicals and anthologies including: Kaleidograph Press. Expns. Press,

Southwester, Crown Publs. Poetry Digest, Corpus Christi Chronicle. Home: Dallas, Tex. Died Apr. 11, 1975.

NEWTON, EDITH, artist; b. Saginaw, Mich., June 7, 1878; d. Alfred Whittlesey and Emily (Whittlesey) Newton; studied at Corcoran Sch. of Art (Washington) and Art Students League (New York). Painter and lithographer, also writer in connection with own art work; represented in Library of Congress, Whitney Museum Am. Art, Metropolitan, Seattle (Wash.) and Newmark (N.J.) museums, N.Y. Public Library, Mem. Am. Artists Group, Inc., Am. Soc. Etchers, Engravers, Lithographers and Woodcutters. Awarded purchase prize Nat. Exhbn. of Am. Prints, Library of Congress, 1946. Address: New Milford, Conn.†

NICE, MARGARET MORSE (MRS. LEONARD BLAINE NICE), ornithologist; b. Amherst, Mass., Dec. 6, 1883; d. Anson Daniel and Margaret (Ely) Morse; A.B., Mt. Holyoke Coll., 1906, D.Sc., 1955; M.A., Clark U., 1915; D.Sc., Elmira Coll., 1962; m. Leonard Blaine Nice, Aug. 12, 1909; children—Constance, Marjorie (Mrs. Carl B. Boyer), Barbara (Mrs. Stanley Thompson), Janet. Study birds of Okla., 1919-28; specialized in ecology and behavior of song sparrow, Columbus, O., 1928-43; research devel. of behavior in precocial birds, 1951-61. Fellow Am. Ornithologists Union (Brewster medal 1942), Okla. Acad. Sci.; mem. Wilson (pres. 1937-39), Cooper ornithol. socs., Nat. Audubon Soc., Wilderness Sos., Nat. Parks Assn., Linnaean Soc. N.Y., other U.S. and fgn. ornithol. socs. Author: Birds of Oklahoma, 1924; Population Study of Song Sparrow, 1937; The Watcher at the Nest, 1939; Behavior of the Song Sparrow, 1943; Development of Behavior in Precocial Birds, 1962. Asso. editor Wilson Bull., 1939-49, Bird Banding, 1935-42, 46-74. Home: Chicago, Ill. Died June 26, 1974.

NICHOLAS, LINDSLEY VINCENT, oil exec.; b. Franklin, Pa., Jan. 10, 1879; s. William Wynes and Anzonette (Vincent) N.; ed. high sch., St. Paul, Minn.; m. Inez Wightman, of Ottawa, Kan., May 15, 1904; children—William Wynes II, Frances Steele (Mrs. Dudley W. Faust), Anzonette Vincent. Salesman Standard Oil Co. (Ind.), 1899-1909; owner Meridian Oil Co., Omaha, 1910-11; pres. L. V. Nicholas Oil Corpn., 1911-21; in oil finance and investment business, Chicago, 1928-33; pres. Warner-Quinlan Co., N.Y. City, 1933; pres. and chmn. bd. dirs. Warner-Quinlan Co. of Me. and subsidiaries, also Warner-Quinlan Co. of Tex. Mem. Nat. Petroleum Marketers Assn. (pres. 1921-28), Ind. Oil Men of America (pres. 1921-28), Am. Petroleum Inst. (dir. 1921-28). Republican. Presbyn. Mason (32°). Home: New York City, N.Y.†

NICHOLS, HENRY JOSEPH, banker; b. Groveland, Ill., May 29, 1877; s. Francis Marion and Eliza Ann (Jones) N.; student pub. schs. of Council Bluffs, Ia.; m. Nelle Hassett, May 23, 1921; 1 dau., Marjorie (Mrs. Alex H. Beard). Financial rep. Swift's N.E. interests, 1908-30; dir. Nat. Shawmut Bank of Boston, from 1930; dir. Dorchester Mut. Fire Ins. Co., Plymouth County Nat. Bank, Mchts.-Warren Nat. Bank; trustee, v.p. Warren Inst. Savs. Treas. Mass. division Am. Cancer Soc. Republican. Conglist. Clubs: Algonquin, Downtown, Beacon Society (Boston). Home: Boston, Mass.†

NICHOLS, JAMES WALTER, communications co. exec.; b. Abilene, Tex., Nov. 14, 1927; s. Elmer Lee and Gladys (Williamson) N.; B.A., Abilene Christian Coll., 1947; postgrad., U. Ia., 1947-51; m. Bettye Elrod, Apr. 25, 1953; children—Mark Lee, Jay Matthew. Preacher, Central Ch. of Christ, Cedar Rapids, Ia., 1947-51; radio speaker Herald of Truth, 1951-54; gen. mgr. Chronicle Pub. Co., 1955-57; exec. v.p. Fidelity Enterprises, Abilene, 1957-66, pres., 1966-69; pres. Hallmark Group Cas., Inc., Dallas (merger Fidelity Enterprises, Inc. and Dynamic Theatre Networks, Inc.), 1969-73; chmn. bd. dirs. Pacific Western Mobile Estates, Hallmark Film Prodns., Hallmark Assos., Hallmark Communications Marketing, HFP Corp.; dir. U.S. Capital Corp., GDL Prodns., Inc. Mem. adv. bd. Abilene Christian Coll., 1955-73. Trustee Columbia Christian Coll. Mem. Am. Inst. Mgmt. Home: Dallas, Tex. Died June 13, 1973.

NICHOLS, JOHN WESLEY, banker; b. Atlantic, Ia., Jan. 26, 1897; s. Gay E. and Emma (Shenton) N.; student Drake U., Harvard Sch. of Business; m. Myrna M. McCready; 1 son, John Jay. Began with Remington Lumber Co., Hibbing, Minn., 1919; banking and liquidation work, Ia., 1920-29; with Continental Ill. Nat. Bank & Trust Co., Chgo., 1929-61, asst. cashier, 1935-38, 2d v.p., 1938-43, vice president, 1943-53, sr. v.p., 1953-61; dir. R. C. Mahon Co. (Detroit), United of America Bank (Chgo.), J. I. Case Company (Racine, Wis.) Pioneer Tex. Co., Dallas, Am. Hoist & Derrick Co., St. Paul, Aetna State Bank, Chgo. Mem. Evanston (Ill.) City Council 1957-65. Served with U.S. Army, 1918. Mem. Ill. C. of C. (past dir.), Assn. Res. City Bankers (past dir., treas.) Am., Ill. bankers assns. Newcomen Soc. of Eng. Republican. Clubs: University (Chgo.); Westmoreland Country (Wilmette, Ill.). Home: Evanston, Ill. Died Sept. 17, 1974; buried Meml. Park Cemetery, Wilmette, Ill.

NICHOLS, MARVIN CURTIS, cons. engr.; b. Roanoke, Tex., Dec. 18, 1896; s. Joseph Marvin and Cora (Curtis) N.; B.S. in Civil Engring., U. Tex., 1918; M.S., U. Ill., 1921; m. Ethel Nichols, May 3, 1919, children—James R., Robert L. County hwy. work, Caldwell and Rockwall counties, Tex., 1919-22; asst. city engr., Amarillo, Tex., 1922-26, city engr., 1926-27; partner Hawley and Freese, cons. engrs., and successors Hawley, Freese & Nichols, Freese and Nichols, Freese, Nichols & Endress, Ft. Worth, 1927-69; partner Freese, Nichols & Turner, Houston, 1946-59; specialist hydraulic problems; architect-engr. for installations for U.S. Army and Navy, USAAF, World War II; farm operator, Chisholm and Greenville, Tex. Chairman Texas Planning Board, 1933-34; cons. administr. General Services Adminstrn., 1950-53; member Texas Water Resources Com., 1953-57; chairman Texas Water Development Board, 1957-63; director Southwest National Bank of Fort Worth. Recipient Keystone award, Boys Clubs Am. Member Am. Soc. C.E., C. of C., Nat. Soc. Profl. Engrs., Am. Inst. Cons. Engrs. S.A.R. Sigma Xi, Tau Beta Pi, Delta Kappa Epsilon, Chi Epislon. Methodist. Clubs: Colonial Country. Rotary, Fort Worth. Home: Fort Worth, Tex. Died Apr. 10, 1969; interred Greenwood Cemetery, Fort Worth, Tex.

NICHOLSON, JOHN FREDERICK, agriculturist; b. Brodhead Wis., July 9, 1878; s. Frederick William and Alice (Cronk) N.; B.S., U. of Wis., 1900, M.S., 1902; m. Hazel Isaacs, July 14, 1904; children—Ruth Alice, Esther, Elizabeth Ann. Asst. bacteriologist, Wis. Expt. Sta., 1900-02, N.Y. Expt. Sta., Geneva, N.Y., 1902-03; asst. bacteriologist, 1903-05, prof. botany and entomology, 1905-09, Okla. Agrl. Coll. and Expt. Sta.; prof. bacteriology, U. of Ida., 1909-15; vice-dir. Idaho Expt. Sta., 1913-15; supervisor farm marketing St.L.&S.F.R.R., 1915-16; prof. agronomy and agronomist of Expt. Sta., U. of Ariz., 1916-17; marketing specialist for State of Ark. and U.S. Dept. of Agr., 1917; farming, 1918-19; county agrl. agent St. Charles Co., Mo., 1920-22; state agrl. extension agent U. of Mo., from 1922, also acting dir. Agrl. Extension Service, part of 1930; on leave as state dir. rural rehabilitation, Farm Security Adminstrn., 1934-36. Methodist. Mason. Author bulls. and articles on bacteriol. and farm marketing subjects, and studies in adminstration of agrl. extension work in Mo. Home: Columbia, Mo.†

NICHOLSON, NOLLIE DAVIS, (Mrs. Jesse W. Nicholson) editor; b. Winchester, Va., Oct. 17, 1879; d. Edward Brown Davis and Florence (Ramey) Davis; ed. public schs.; m. Jesse W. Nicholson, of Frederick, Md., Oct. 24, 1900; children—Davis (dec.), Jesse Frank, Dorothy Mildred, David Brown. Owner and editor The Woman Voter (nat. newspaper) from 1926. Pres. Nat. Woman's Democratic Law Enforcement League, also pres. The National Sentinels; organizer and former pres. Chevy Chase Br. of Nat. League Am. Pen Women; mem. Teuch Tighlman Chapter, D.A.R. Mem. Dem. Nat. Com., 1923-24; nat. vice chmn. Congressional Com. Episcopalian. Club: Congressional Country. Speaker and writer against repeal of Prohibition Amendment. Home: Chevy Chase, Md.†

NICHOLSON, REX LEE, mfg. co. exec.; b. Calhoun County, Tex., Mar. 14, 1902; s. Absolom H. and Rebecca J. (Dally) N.; Structural Engr., Chgo. Tech. Coll., 1926; m. Mary Runyon, Oct. 24, 1926; children—Janice Grace, Laura Lee. With cattle ranch nr. Amarillo, Tex., 1910-24; gen. supt., partner Stabbert Constrn. Co., Tacoma, 1924-27; asst. adminstr. Fed. Works Agy., Western U.S., Alaska, Hawaii, 1937-44; mng. dir. Builders of the West, Inc., San Francisco, 1944-45; founder, 1945, later pres. Pacific Tractor & Implement Co., Richmond, Cal., 1945—, also chmn. bd.; organizer Indsl. Trucklease Co., San Francisco, 1948; prin. owner Columbia Tractor & Implement Co., Portland, Ore., 1950-74; pres. Liquid Carbonic Corp., 1956-57; pres. Liquid Carbonic div., sr. v.p., mem. bd. mgmt. Gen. Dynamics Corp., 1957-61; v.p., dir. Liquid Carbonic do Brazil, Inc., Manitou Carbonic Corp.; dir. Ariz.-Detroit Corp., Krueger Mfg. Co., Prather Tractor Co., Homecraft, Inc., Liquid Carbonic Canadian Corp., Ltd., Liquid Carbonic Venezolana, S.A., Cases and Chems., Internat., S.A., Liquido Carbonico Colombiana, S.A., Liquid Carbonic del Peru, S.A., Liquido Carbonic de Mexico, S.A., Liquid Carbonic West Indies Ltd., Kings Mfg. Co., Ariz.-Detroit Corp., Mile High Service Co., Croycraft Medicine Center; chmn. bd. Far-Horizons Mobile Home Parks Inc., Rex Broadcasting Corp., Cascade-Builders Inc., Fi Dorado Lodge and Land Properties, Golden Gate Way Bldgs. Inc., Prather Ford Tractor Co. Inc., pres. San-Larendo Indsl. Park, Inc., Amphi-Plaza Shopping Centers, Inc., Tucson, Manana Land Develop. Co.; organizer Nicholson Enterprises, Inc. 1961. Engaged in reorgn. adminstrn. pub. lands U.S. and Tys., Dept. Interior, 1946; orgn. FCDA, Washington, 1951; dir. Hoover Report on Govt. Reorgn.; cons. sec. Interior. Mem. U.S., Cal. chambers commerce, Newcomen Soc. N.Y. and London. Presbyn. Clubs: Kiwanis, Commonwealth (San Francisco); Chicago; Glenview (Golf, Ill.); Toastmasters Internat.; Claremont Country (Oakland, Cal.); Tucson Nat. Country, Skyline (Tucson). Author articles agrl., indsl. potentials western and pub. lands. Home: Pacheco, Cal., Died Nov. 21, 1974.

NICHOLSON, WILLIAM MCNEAL, physician; b. Bath, N.C., Sept. 27, 1905; s. John Thorne and Ann Catherine (McNeal) N.; A.B., Duke, 1927; M.D., Johns Hopkins, 1931; m. Eunice Stamey, Nov. 30, 1928; children—Anne Kathryn (Mrs. Fayette Perry Grose), William McNeal, Samuel Thorne. Asst. in pathology Johns Hopkins, 1931-32, asst. in medicine, 1932-35; asso. in medicine Duke Med. Center, 1935-42, asso. prof. medicine, 1946-52, prof., 1952-74, asst. dean in charge continuing med. edn., 1949-68, emeritus, 1968. Asso. physician Duke U. Hosp., 1935-52, physician, 1952-74. Mem. N.C. Air Control Council. Mem. Am. Clin. and Climatol. Assn., A.C.P., Am. Diabetes Assn., A.M.A., Am. Soc. Clin. Investigation, So., Durham-Orange County (pres. 1952-53) med. assns., N.C. Med. Soc., Sigma Xi, Phi Beta Kappa, Alpha Omega Alpha. Club: Hope Valley Country. Chmn. editorial bd. N.C. Med. Jour. Home: Durham, N.C. Died Sept. 8, 1974.

NICHOLSON, WILLIAM RAMSEY, JR.;, b. Philadelphia, Pa., Mar. 8, 1879; s. William Ramsey and Anna J. (Hopson) N.; ed. Hamilton Sch., Phila., 1893-99; m. Ethel W. Sutton, Jan. 22, 1903; children—William Ramsey III, Winifred S. Began as salesman for wholesale hay concern, later engaged in mining in Mexico, then asst. mgr. Hotel Lafayette, Phila. sec. and treas. Haney-White Co. builders supplies, from 1902; treas. Glenwood Foundry Co.; dir. Textile Nat. Bank, Phila., from 1920; organizer and sec. Law Enforcement League of Phila., from 1921. Sec. Y.M.C.A., Camp Meade, Pa., World War. Mem. Phila. Real Estate Bd. Mem. Pa. State Fish and Game Protective Assn., Lumbermen's Exchange. Republican. Presbyn. Mason (Shriner), K.T. Clubs: Union League, Penn Athletic, City, Lumbermen's Golf (Phila.); Boys Club of America (dir.); Cricket, Boys of Germantown (sec. from 1925); Cedarbrook Country, Old York Road Golf, Egypt Mills Hunting and Fishing (treas.). Home: Philadelphia, Pa.†

NIESET, ROBERT THOMAS, bio-physicist; b. Gibsonburg, O., Aug. 6, 1912; s. Henry J. and Anna (Reineck) N.; A.B., Catholic U., 1934, M.A. in Philosophy, 1935; Ph.D. in Biophysics, U. Mich., 1943; m. Mary Elizabeth Young, June 21, 1939; children—James Robert, Anne, Jane, Marjorie, Richard. Research scientist U. Mich., 1943-46; sr. fellow Am. Cancer Soc., 1946-47; asso. prof. physics Tulane U., 1947-51, prof. physics, 1951-62, dir. biophysics program, 1947-62, chmn. dept. physics, 1960-62; V.p. research and devel., dir. Kalvar Corp., New Orleans, 1956-67; dir. Delta Capital Corp., 1961-66; pvt. cons. physics and photography. Bd. dirs. New Orleans Philharmonic Symphony Soc., 1962-68. Recipient Naval Ordnance Devel. award, 1945, citation Manhattan Dist., 1945, OSRD, 1945. Fellow Am. Phys. Soc.; mem. I.R.E., A.A.A.S., Sigma Xi. Home: Mandeville, La., Died June 12, 1975; buried Metairie Cemetery, New Orleans, La.

NIGGEMAN, LOUIS WILLIAM, ins. exec.; b. N.Y.C., Nov. 21, 1915; s. Louis W. and Ida (Kohring) N.; student U. N.H., 1933-34, N.Y.U., 1934-35, Stanford, 1952; m. Winifred Rowe, June 15, 1940; children—Susan, Jon, Louis Peter. Chief underwriter, asst. dir., dir. ins. War Shipping Adminstrn., Washington, 1942-46, spl. cons. dir. gen. of UNRRA, 1945-47; asso. Fireman's Fund Ins. Co., N.Y.C., 1946, mgr. dept., 1949-51, v.p., 1953, v.p. charge Pacific Coast-Rocky Mountain operations, San Francisco, 1953-56, charge world wide Marine operations, 1956-59; exec. v.p., dir. Am. Express Co.; chmn. bd., chief exec. officer Fireman's Fund Ins. Co.; pres., dir. The Am. Ins. Co., Nat. Surety Corp., Firemen's Fund Inc. Co. Tex., Am. Automobile Ins. Co., Asso. Indemnity Corp., Nat. Surety Corp. of Cal.; vice chmn. Shaw & Begg Ltd., Can. Consol. Fire & Casualty Ins. Co., Fed. Fire Ins. Co. Can.; dir. Fireman's Fund Am.; vice chmn. Life Ins. Co., Plymouth Ins. Co.; dir. Crusader Ins. Co., Ltd., Eng., Bowmaker Leasing Ltd., London, Intercontinental Reins. Co. Hamilton, Bermuda. Mem. Pacific Coast com. Am. Bur. Shipping; mem. Com. on Classification Ins. Treas., Episcopal Diocese of Cal.; mem. Golden Gate Coll. Assos.; trustee, past pres. William Babcock Meml. Endowment; past pres., chmn. finance com. Internat. Hospitality Center. Trustee Tilton Sch., Am. Inst. for Property and Liability Underwriters; bd. govs. Ins. Inst. Am. Mem. U.S. Salvage Assn. (past dir.), Nat. Cargo Bur. (past dir.), Pacific Fire Rating Bur. (past dir.), Underwriters N.Y. (past dir.), Nat. Bd. Fire Underwriters (exec. com.), Am. Inst. Marine Underwriters (past dir.), San Francisco C. of C. (pres., dir.), Cal. State C. of C. (dir.), Cal. Ins. Fedn. (pres.), Am. Ins. Assn. (vice chmn. bd. trustees), Assn. Cal. Ins. Cos. (v.p.), Ins. Soc. N.Y., Maritime Law Assn. U.S., C. of C. of U.S. Home: Kentfield, Cal. Died Feb. 14, 1974.

NILES, HENRY CLAY, educator; b. Kosciusko, Miss., Mar. 26, 1920; s. Jason Adams and Myrtis (Gilliland) N.; B.A., Miss. Coll., 1941; B.D., Columbia Sem., 1944; S.T.M., Harvard, 1948, Ph.D., 1951; m. Jean Isabel MacKenzie, June 24, 1950; children—Henry Clay III, Naomi Lee, John MacKenzie. Ordained to ministry Presbyn. Ch., 1944; pastor Livingston (Ala.) Presbyn. Ch., 1944-47, Montevallo (Ala.) Presbyn. Ch., 1951-52; asst. prof. Bible and religion, dir. chapel Westminster Coll., Fulton, Mo., 1952-63, from asso. prof. to Daniel Shaw Gage prof., 1963-75; chmn. Joint dept. religion Westminster Coll. and William Woods Coll., 1969-73.

Study grantee Soc. for Religion in Higher Edn., 1966-67; Churchill fellow. Mem. Soc. Bibl. Lit. Home: Fulton, Mo., Died Sept. 5, 1975.

NILSSON, FRITIOF, writer; b. Dec. 4, 1895; ed. U. Lund, Sweden. Former lawyer; humorist, playwright, author numerous short stories and novels, 1931-72; authority on South Swedish folklore. Principle works include Bombi Bitt och jag, 1932; Bock i Örtagard, 1933; Smaländsk Tragedi, 1936; Bokhandlaren som slutade bada, 1937; Historier fran Färs, 1940; Tre Terminer, 1943; Bombi Bitt och Nick Carter, 1946; Vänner Emellan, 1955; Flickan med Bibelspraken, 1959; Vers Pa Växel, 1964; Millionären, 1965. Some of his works have been translated to English and have appeared in various periodicals. Address: Kivik, Sweden. Died Jan. 31, 1972; buried Ravlvnda Churchyard, Sweden.

NINNIS, FREDERICK CHARLES, mining; b. Atlantic, Mich., Sept. 11, 1880; s. William Henry and Susanna (Doidge) N.; ed. high sch., Silver City, Nev.; spl. mining course, U. of Nev., 1906-07; m. Lillian N. MacDonald, Nov. 9, 1909; 1 son, Frederick Charles. Began as miner and leaser, Nev. and Alaska; supt. Consol. Mines Corp.; pres. West End Extension Mining Co. Former mem. Rep. State Central Committee Nev. Milling Co., 1917-26; pres., treas. West End Republican. Episcopalian. Mason (Shriner), Elk. Contbr. to tech. jours. Home: Tonopah, Nev.†

NIVISON, ROBERT, paper co. exec.; b. Guardbridge, Fifeshire, Scotland, Dec. 24, 1879; s. Robert and Margaret (Boe) N.; student St. Andrews U.; m. Josephine Shepard, June 24, 1908; children—Margaret Helen, Robert. Paper maker in Scotland until 1904; supt. and mgr. paper mills, Gardiner and Waterville, Me., from 1904; v.p. and mgr. mills, Hollingsworth & Whitney Co., Waterville, Presbyn. Mason. Club: Rotary. Home: Waterville, Me.*†

NOBLE, NELLE SPARKS, physician and surgeon; b. Casey, Ia., Mar. 7, 1878; d. Andrew E. and Elizabeth (Sparks) Noble; Ph.B., Drake U., 1898, M.A., 1901, LL.B., 1900, M.D., 1905; unmarried. Admitted Ia. bar, 1900; practiced Des Moines, Ia., 1900-02; practicing med., Des Moines, from 1905; mem. staff Lutheran and Methodist hosps. Formerly dir. of Drake U. Mem. and staff Health Center Drake U. Mem. Am. Med. Women's Assn. (pres. 1940), Am. Med. Assn., Polk County Med. Soc., Professional Women's League (Des Moines), Acad. Gen. Practitioners, D.A.R., Eastern Star, P.E.O., Phi Beta Kappa. Republican. Mem. Disciples of Christ Ch. Clubs: Women's (Des Moines). Home: Des Moines, Ia.†

NOCE, DANIEL, army officer; b. Denver, Colo., Nov. 3, 1894; s. of Angelo Noce; student Colo. State Coll. of Agrl. and Mech. Arts, 1912-13; B.S., U.S. Mil. Acad., 1917; B.S. in C.E., Mass. Inst. of Tech., 1921; grad. Engr. Sch., 1923, Command and Gen. Staff School, 1933, Army War College, 1937; LL.D., Louisville University; married Mildred Newcomb Wilson, June 3, 1918; children—Robert W., Mildred W. (Mrs. Philip B. Melody), Commd. 2d lieutenant, Corps of Engrs., U.S. Army, April 20, 1917, and advanced through the grades to lt. gen., 1952; served as major commanding 602d Engineers, World War I; commanding engr. Amphibian Command since inception, May 11, 1942; appointed on Gen. Staff, European Theater of Operations, May 23, 1943, Mediteranean Theatre, 1944-45; chief Civil Affairs Div., Dept. of the Army, 1947-48; Chief of Staff. A.S.F., 1946; chief of staff European Command, 1949-52; insp. gen. Dept. of Army from 1953-54. Decorated D.S.M., Legion of Merit, numerous fgn. decorations. Mem. Am. Soc. C.E., Soc. of Am. Mil. Engrs. Home: Fort Meyer, Va. Home: Fort Meyer, Va. Address: Rappahannock County, Va.

NOE, SAMUEL VANARSDALE, supt. schs.; b. Springfield, Ky., Apr. 26, 1910; s. James Richard and Cora (VanArsdale) N.; student U. Mich., Harvard, Peabody Coll.; A.B., Centre Coll., Danville, Ky., 1922, LL.D., 1962; M.A., Columbia, 1928; m. Elizabeth McDonald, Aug. 7, 1930; 1 son, Samuel VanArsdale. Prin., Eminence (Ky.) Sch., 1922-24, supt. schs., 1924-28; prin. elementary and high schs. in Louisville, 1928-50; adminstrv. asst. to supt. Louisville schs., 1950-60, supt. schs., 1960-69; vis. prof. U. Louisville Grad. Sch., 1947-60. Bd. dirs. Louisville Met. YMCA, Louisville chpt. A.R.C. Served to maj. AUS, 1943-46; Italy. Decorated Bronze Star medal; knight officer Order Crown Italy. Mem. Am., Ky. assns. sch. adminstrs., N.E.A. (life), Ky. (past officer, bd. mem.) Edn. Assn., Nat. Sch. Pub. Relations Assn., Louisville C. of C., Beta Theta Pi. Presbyn. (elder, clk.). Kiwanian (past pres. Louisville). Home: Louisville, Ky. Died Jan. 29, 1972.

NOLAN, CHARLES PAUL, fgn. service officer; b. Chelsea, Mass., Nov. 22, 1909; s. John Joseph and Mary Caroline (Tiernan) N.; A.B., Boston Coll., 1931; M.S., Sch. Fgn. Service, Georgetown U., 1933; m. Jean Osgood Wright, May 31, 1937; 1 dau., Anne Dashiell. Economist, Bur. Labor Statistics, 1934-35; indsl. economist Dept. Labor, 1938-41; instr. econs. Columbus U., 1940-42; divisional asst. Dept. State, Washington, 1941, asst. adviser commodities div., 1945, asst. adviser shipping div., 1945, asst. chief, aviation div., 1948, officer charge transp. and communications Office Regional Am. Affairs, 1951, fgn. service officer, 1955-69; 1st sec., comml. attaché, Buenos Aires, 1956-61; spl. advisor Bur. Econ. Affairs, Dept. State, Washington, 1961-63, dep. dir. Office Telecommunications and Maritime Affairs, 1963-64; Am. consul gen., Seville, Spain, 1965-69; U.S. rep. Inter-Am. com. experts on maritime freight and ins. rates, Washington, 1952-56; U.S. del. Pan Am. Hwy. Congress, Mexico City, 1952-53, vice chmn., Caracas, 1954; mem. U.S. delegation Inter-Am. Econ. Conf., Washington, Panama, Caracas, Quintandinha, Buenos Aires; vice chmn. U.S. delegation Inter-Am. Travel Congress, San José 1956; chmn. U.S. delegation Inter-American Port and Harbor Congresses, 1956; 1963. Recipient Commendable Service award, 1956, Meritorious Service award Dept. State, 1958. Mem. Pi Gamma Mu. Club: Washington Golf and Country. Home: Arlington, Va. Died July 17, 1973.

NOLAN, JEANNETTE COVERT (MRS. VAL NOLAN), author; b. Evansville, Ind., Mar. 31, 1896; d. Charles Grant and Grace Louise (Tucker) Covert; grad. high sch., Evansville; Litt.D., Ind. U., 1967; m. Val. Nolan, Oct. 4, 1917; children—Val, Alan, Kathleen (Mrs. Alan H. Lobley). Reporter, spl. feature writer Courier Jour., Evansville, 1915-16; writer adult and juvenile fiction and biography. Mem. Woman's Press Club Ind., Nat. Fedn. Am. Presswomen, Ind. Acad., Ind. Hist. Soc., Ind. War History Commn., Ind. Lincoln Found., Women in Communications Inc. (hon. life), Psi Iota Xi (hon.). Democrat. Author: Barry Barton's Mystery, 1932; Second Best, 1933; The Young Douglas, 1934; New Days, New Ways, 1936, English edit., 1937; Red Hugh of Ireland, 1938; Hobnailed Boots, 1939; Where Secrecy Begins, 1939; The Gay Poet, 1940; Profile in Guilt, 1941; The Story of Clara Barton and the Red Cross, 1941; James Whitcomb Riley, 1941; The Little Giant, The Story of Stephen A. Douglas and Abraham Lincoln, rev. edit., 1964; Final Appearance, 1943; Hoosier City, 1943; O. Henry, 1943; Treason at the Point, 1944; Patriot in the Saddle, 1945; I Can't Die Here, 1945; Gather Ye Rosebuds, 1946; Florence Nightingale, 1946; This Same Flower, 1948; Andrew Jackson, 1949; John Brown, 1950; La Salle, 1951; Poet of the People (with Horace Gregory and James T. Farrell), 1951; The Story of Ulysses S. Grant, 1952; Abraham Lincoln, 1953; The Victory Drum, 1953; The Story of Joan of Arc, 1953; George Rogers Clark, 1954; Martha Washington, 1954; Sudden Squall, 1955; A Fearful Way to Die, 1956; Benedict Arnold, 1956; Dolly Madison, 1958; Spy for the Confederacy, 1960; John Marshall, 1962; The Shot Heard Round the World, 1963; John Hancock, Friend of Freedom, 1966; Belle Boyd, Secret Agent, 1967; Indiana, 1969; Yankee Spy, 1970; Aaron Burr, 1972; The Ohio River, 1973. Columnist, Lines with a Hoosier Accent, Indpls. Star, 1943-44. Home: Indianapolis, Ind. Died Oct. 12, 1974; buried Evansville, Ind.

NOLAN, MAE ELLA, congresswoman; b. San Francisco, Calif., Sept. 20, 1886; d. William H. Hunt; ed. St. Vincent's Convent; m. John I. Nolan, congressman, of San Francisco, Mar. 23, 1913 (died Nov. 18, 1922). Elected Jan. 23, 1923, to fill unexpired term of husband in 67th Congress, and to 68th Congress (1923-25), 5th Calif. Dist., to which he had been elected. Republican. Catholic. Home: San Francisco, Calif. Died July 12, 1973.

NOLAN, RALPH PETER, constrn. and dredging co. exec.; b. New Orleans, Oct. 29, 1892; s. John Peter and Agnes (MacPherson) M.; student Rueby Acad., New Orleans, 1904-90; m. Ruth Brownlee, June 28, 1916; children—Ralph Peter, Warren John, Thomas Howard. Asst. gen. supt. Johnson Iron Works, New Orleans, 1909-18; pres. Union Iron Works, New Orleans, 1918-40, Algiers Pub. Service Co., New Orleans, 1937-61; chmn. bd. Williams-McWilliams Industries, Inc. New Orleans, 1962-73; dir. Whitney Nat. Bank, New Orleans, 1930-73, Tideland Life Ins. Co. Sec. New Orleans Ry. Terminal Bd., 1945-55; mem. New Orleans Charter Com.; mem. New Orleans Sewerage and Water Bd., 1947-73, pres., 1967-73; pres. Bd. Port Commrs., 1955-60. Home: New Orleans, La. Died Feb. 12, 1973.

NOLAND, IVESON B., bishop; b. Baton Rouge, Sept. 10, 1916; s. Ives B. and Camille (Reynaud) N.; B.A., La. State U., 1937; B.D., Sewanee U., 1940, D.D., 1952; m. Nell Burden, Feb. 3, 1936; children—Iveson B., III, John Burden, Daniel Woodring. Ordained to ministry Episcopal Ch.; rector in Charlotte, N.C., 1946-50, Lake Charles, La., 1950-52; bishop Episcopal Diocese La., 1952-75. Mem. bd. examining chaplains Diocese N.C. Served as chaplain AUS, 1942-45; PTO. Mem. Phi Kappa Phi, Sigma Nu, Scabbard and Blade. Home: New Orleans La. Died June 25, 1975.

NOLL, CHARLES FRANKLIN, agronomist; b. Green Park, Pa., July 22, 1878; s. Jonas and Rosanna (Hostetter) N.; B.S., Pa. State Coll., 1906; M.S., Cornell U., 1911, Ph.D., 1923; m. Nora Crilly, Sept. 15, 1901; children—John Jacob, Charles Joseph, William Edward, Alice Catherine. Began as teacher in pub. schools, 1896-99, 1900-02; special field asst. in div. zoölogy, Pa. Dept. of Agr., 1906-07; mgr. Nostrand Fruit Farm, Shelter Island, N.Y., 1907-08; with dept. of agronomy, Pa. State Coll., from 1908, in charge of field experiments, 1908-37, head of dept., 1937-45; retired. Mem. Am. Soc. Agronomy, Alpha Zeta, Sigma Xi, Phi Kappa Phi, Gamma Sigma Delta. Author of numerous experiment station bulletins. Address: State College, Pa.†

NOLL, RAYMOND RUNDELL, clergyman; b. Ft. Wayne, Ind., Oct. 10, 1881; s. Frank J. and Ella (Rundell) N.; student St. Mary's (Kan.) Coll., 1897-98, St. Meiniad (Ind.) Coll., 1901; S.T.D., N.Am. Coll., Rome, Italy, 1905. Ordained priest Roman Catholic Ch.; asst. pastor St. Patrick's, Indianapolis, 1905-10; pastor St. Francis, Indianapolis, 1910-27, St. Philip's, Indianapolis, 1927-34, vicar gen. SS Peter and Paul Cathedral, Indianapolis, 1934; made Prothonotary Apostolic by Pope Pius XII, 1939. Served with U.S. Army as Chaplain 338 F.A., 88 div., 1917-18. Home: Indianapolis, Ind.†

NOOE, ROBERT SHARPE, banker; b. Statesville, N.C., Sept. 5; s. Robert Edward and Mary (Sharpe) N.; A.B. in Econs., U. N.C., 1927; m. Sarah Evelyn Little, Nov. 27, 1935. With William R. Compton Co., N.Y.C., 1927-28, CIT Corp., 1928-37, Southeastern Finance Co., Wilson, N.C., 1937-42; with Wachovia Bank and Trust Co., Winston-Salem, N.C., 1946-73, sr. v.p. Served to maj. USAAF, 1942-46. Home: Winston-Salem, N.C. Died June 1973.

NOOE, ROGER THEOPHILUS, clergyman; b. Wilmore, Ky., Sept. 25, 1881; s. Theophilus and Jemima (Holladay) N.; student Asbury Coll.; A.B., Transylvania Coll., Lexington, Ky., 1901, also D.D.; grad. College of the Bible, Lexington, 1903; student U. of Chicago; m. Nancy Mitchell, Dec. 10, 1903; children—Roger Gowen, Mary Louise, Willa Mima. Ordained minister Christian (Disciples) Ch., 1903; pastor Crestwood, Ky., 1903-07, Crescent Hill, Louisville, Ky., 1907-11, Frankfort, Ky., 1911-25, Vine St., Nashville, from 1925; prof. pastoral theology and lecturer, Vanderbilt School of Religion, 1925-33. Chaplain-col. on staff gov. of Tenn., 1933-37. Lecturer and preacher in Europe, 1918; del. to Stockholm Conf., 1925, Lausanne Conf., 1927; del. to World Sunday Sch. Conv., Rio de Janeiro, 1932, to world conv. Disciples of Christ, Leicester, Eng., 1935, to Oxford Conf., 1937; traveled in Europe and Near East, 1918, S.A., 1932. Russia, 1935, Orient, 1937, Mexico, 1941. Trustee Milligan Coll., Nashville Y.M.C.A., Assn. for Promotion of Christian Unity, Tenn. Christian Missionary Soc., Colegio Ward (Buenos Aires), Disciples of Christ Board of Edn., Ch. Peace Union; pres. Internat. Conv. of Disciples of Christ, 1939; mem. Am. section World Council of Churches; chmn. Commn. on World Order for Disciples of Christ; accredited visitor to World Council of Churches, Amsterdam, 1948. Mem. Nashville Chamber Commerce, Theta Phi. Democrat. Mason (32°). Clubs: Palaver, Richland Golf. Home: Nashville, Tenn.†

NORBERG, BARBARA DREW COLLINS (MRS. NILS GUNNAR NORBERG), actress, civic worker; b. Fresno, Cal.; d. Clinton Darwin and Gertrude Sarah (Drew) Collins; B.A., Leland Stanford U., 1933; student Fresno State Coll., 1934; m. Nils Gunnar Norberg, Sept. 5, 1936; children—Eric Gunnar, Karin Collins. Profl. actress various prodns. with Henry Duffy Players, Hollywood, Cal., San Francisco, 1934-35; leading actress Golden Bough Players, Fresno, Carmel, Cal., 1934-64, Wharf Players, Monterey, Cal., 1950-51, Barn Theatre, Carmel Valley, Cal., 1951-52, Forest Theatre Guild, Carmel, 1953-72; owner, designer Carmel Yarn Shop; dir., sec.-treas. Carmel Playhouse Corp., 1950-63. Den mother Boy Scouts Am., Carmel, 1953-56; mem. Carmel Arts Commn., 1963-67, chmn., 1965-67; sec.-treas. Carmel Bus. Assn., 1941-48; v.p. Monterey County Symphony, 1948-52. Sec., v.p. Carmel Republican Women, 1946-49. Bd. govs. Community Theatre Monterey Peninsula. Mem. Delta Gamma. Home: Carmel, Cal. Died Aug. 26, 1972.

NORCROSS, BERNARD MALLON, physician; b. Buffalo, 1915; s. Bernard Mallon and Clara Harriet (Schottke) N.; B.A., Canisius Coll., 1934; M.D., U. Buffalo, 1938; m. Jayne Eleanor Smith, June 27, 1942; children—Bernard Mallon III, Digby Ann (Mrs. Robert E. Wolfe), James Frederick. Intern, Buffalo Gen. Hosp., 1938-39, resident in medicine, 1939- physician, 1969, attending physician, 1970, sec.-treas. staff, 1973-75, also physician Arthritis Clinic; practice medicine specializing in rheumatic disease, Buffalo; asst. in medicine Edward J. Meyer Meml. Hosp., Buffalo; cons. in rheumatic diseases Chronic Disease Research Inst.; cons. physician in rheumatic diseases Brooks Meml. Hosp.; asst. clin. prof. medicine State U. N.Y. at Buffalo. Bd. dirs. United Fund Drive, Western N.Y. chpt. Arthritis Found., Nazareth Home. Served to capt. M.C., AUS, 1942-46. Diplomate Am. Bd. Internal Medicine. Fellow A.C.P.; mem. A.M.A., Am. Rheumatism Assn., N.Y. State, Erie County med. socs. Contbr. articles to med. jours. Home: Buffalo, N.Y. Died Jan. 11, 1975; buried Forest Lawn Cemetery, Buffalo, N.Y.

NORDMARK, GODFREY, lawyer; b. Birmingham, Ala., Aug. 8, 1907; s. G.G. and George (Schoolar) N.; student U. Colo., 1932-35; J.D., Westminster Law Sch., 1938; m. Berniece Decker, 1926 (div. 1940); 1 dau., Susan (Mrs. Paul Robinson); m. Edna D. McCormick, 1969. Admitted to Colo. bar, 1938; prin. engr., draftsman, supr. claims and easements Divs. Engring. and Lands, U.S. Forest Service, Denver, 1927-41; asso. Edgar McComb, lawyer, Denver, 1942-44, McComb &

Nordmark, 1944-48, McComb, Nordmark & Zariengo, 1948-51; private practice law, 1951-52, Ft. Collins, Colo., 1969-73, partner Sheldon & Nordmark, 1952-69; instr. med. jurisprudence Westminster Law Sch., 1958, U. Denver, 1959. Mem. Am., Colo., Denver bar assns., Internat. Assn. Ins. Counsel, Law Club Denver. Clubs: City, Denver Athletic. Home: Fort Collins, Colo. Died Jan. 28, 1973.

NORDSTROM, LLOYD WALTER, retail exec.; b. Seattle, June 8, 1910; s. John Wilhelm and Hilda (Carlson) N.; student U. Wash., 1928-32; m. Illsley Ball, June 3, 1933; children—Loyal (Mrs. John McMillan), Linda (Mrs. David A. Mowat), Susan (Mrs. Richard Eberhardt). With Nordstrom, Inc., Seattle, 1932—, co-pres., co-chmn., 1970—; trustee Wash. Mutual Savs. Bank, 1964—. Served to lt. USNR, 1943-46. Mem. Nat. Shoe Retailers Assn. (pres. 1958-59), Central Assn. Seattle (pres. 1969-70), Beta Theta Pi. Clubs: University, Seattle Golf, Washington Athletic (Seattle). Home: Seattle, Wash., Died Jan. 20, 1976.

NORFOLK, DUKE OF, (FitzAlan Howard, Bernard Marmaduke), earl marshall Eng.; b. June 12, s. Henry and Gwendolan (Constable-Maxwell) F.-H.; grad. Oratory Sch. Caversham; m. Lavinia Mary Strutt; children—Anne, Mary, Sarah, Jane. Mayor, Arundel, 1935-36; joint parliamentary sec. Ministry. Agr., London, 1941-45; lord lt. Sussex, 1949-75; earl marshall, hereditary marshall, chief butler Eng.; premier duke and earl; 2d lt. Royal House Guards. Pres., Council for Preservation Rural Eng., 1945-75. Served with Brit. Mil. Forces, 1939-41. Decorated knight Order of Garter, Privy Councillor, Grand Cross Royal Victorian Order, knight Order Brit. Empire, Territorial Decoration; named Elder Bro., Trinity House, 1965; recipient Distinguished Service medal U.S.N.G., 1969. Club: Marlybone Cricket (pres. 1957-58, mgr. for events in Australia, New Zealand 1962-63). Address: Sussex, England., Died Jan. 31, 1975.

NORMAN, CARL ADOLPH, educator; b. Borga, Finland, Jan. 12, 1879; s. Carl Herman and Julia Elizabeth (Norrman) N.; M.E., Royal Tech. Inst., Stockholm, Sweden, 1900; grad. study Technische Hochschule, Berlin, 1900-01; U. of Chicago, 1905-06; m. Elizabeth Holcombe, June 27, 1914; children—Elizabeth, Inez Maynard. Came to U.S., 1902, naturalized, 1917. Draftsman and designer for various firms in U.S., 1902-07; supt. oil refinery and paraffine wax works for Nobel Bros., Baku, Russia, 1908-10; in pvt. research, 1910-12; cons. engr., Gen. Electric Co., and inventor, 1912-17; prof. machine design, dept. mech. engring. Ohio State U., 1917-50, emeritus; also cons., research, or development engr., internat. Harvester Co., Dayton Rubber Mfg. Co., Goodyear Tire and Rubber Company. Consulting engineer on gas turbines, Engring. Expt. Station, Ohio State University. Member American Society M.E. American Society for Engineering Education, Columbus Consumers Cooperative, Incorporated (first president), Sigma Xi, Tau Beta Pi. Club: Faculty. Author: Children of the Plain (vol. of short stories in Swedish), 1900; Economical Utilization of Liquid Fuel, 1921; Principles of Machine Design, 1925; Fundamentsls of Machine Design (with E. S. Ault and I. F. Zarobsky), 1938 (book) Introduction to Gas Turbine and Jet-Propulsion Design (with R. H. Zimmerman), 1948; Philosophy for Men in Action (in preparation); contributor tech. articles; also articles on religious, economic and social subjects. Inventor of belt testing machine, etc. Home: Petersburg, Fla.†

NORRIS, RICHARD A., banker; b. Washington, July 6, 1904; s. William Henry and Mary Ella (Walker) N.; student Stonier Grad. Sch. Banking, Rutgers U., Nat. U. Law Sch.; m. Alma Schlosser, June 14, 1928; 1 son, Richard Alfred. With Lincoln Nat. Bank of Wash., 1921-58, pres., 1953-58; pres. Riggs Nat. Bank of Washington, 1959-69, vice chmn., 1969-71; dir. Jefferson Fed. Savs. & Loan Assn., Frank Parsons Paper Co., Inc., Drug Fair Inc., Schwartz Bros., Inc., Central Charge Service; trustee Equitable Life Ins. Co. Bd. dirs. pub. trustee Greater Washington Ednl. TV Assn.; adv. bd. dirs. YMCA Met. Washington; hon. dir. Doctors Hosp., Inc., Washington Med. Center, Inc.; bd. dirs. Arthritis and Rheumatism Assn. Met. Washington. Mem. Am. Inst. Banking (past pres. Washington chpt.), Am. (exec. council 1962-65), D.C. (treas., past pres.) bankers assns., Washington Clearing House Assn. (past chmn.) Met. Washington Bd. Trade (dir.). Episcopalian. Mason (Shriner), Kiwanian. Clubs: Columbia Country, Internat. Home: Chevy Chase Md. Died Mar. 13, 1974; interred Rock Creek Cemetery, Washington, D.C.

NORRIS, WALTER BLAKE, educator; b. Chelsea, Mass., Sept. 4, 1879; s. Edwin Somerby and Lois Florida (Clement) N.; A.B., Harvard, 1901; studied Johns Hopkins, 1908-09; m. Frances Harrison Hollyday, June 6, 1911 (died 1948); 1 dau., Elizabeth Hollyday (Mrs. J. C. Eakens). Principal Hubbardston (Mass.) High School, 1901-02; instructor Attleboro (Mass.) High School, 1902-03; professor English, Bridgewater (Va.) Coll., 1903-05; instr. Wenonah (N.J.) Mil. Acad., 1905-07; instructor English and history, 1907-19, asst. prof., 1919, asso. prof. 1919-26, prof., 1926-42, sr. prof., 1942-46, prof. emeritus, U.S. Naval Acad. Mem. Williamstown Inst. of Politics, 1924. Editor: (with M. E. Speare) World War Issues and Ideals, 1918; (with M. E. Speare) Vital Forces in Current Events, 1920. Author: (with H. F. Krafft) Sea Power in American History, 1920; Annapolis; Its Colonial and Naval Story, 1925; History of St. Anne's Parish, Annapolis, 1935; Outline of American Foreign Policy, 1943. Contbr. on ednl., lt. and naval history topics to mags. and revs. Address: Annapolis, Md.†

NORTH, STERLING, editor, author, lectr.; b. Edgerton, Wis., Nov. 4, 1906; s. David Willard and Elizabeth (Nelson) N.; student U. Chgo.; m. Gladys Delores Buchanan, June 23, 1927; children—David Sterling, Arielle. Reporter, Chgo. Daily News, 1929, lit. editor, 1933-43; lit. editor N.Y. World-Telegram and Sun, 1949-56; editor The Forge, U. Chgo., 3 yrs. Author: Plowing on Sunday, 1934; Night Outlasts the Whippoorwill, 1936; Seven Against the Years, 1939; The Pedro Gorino (with Capt. Harry Dean), 1929; Speak of the Devil (with Clip Boutell), 1945; So Dear to My Heart, 1947 (made into moving picture by Walt Disney); Reunion on the Wabash, 1952; The Birthday of Little Jesus, 1952; Abe Lincoln, Log Cabin to Whitehouse, 1956; Son of the Lampmaker, 1956; George Washington, 1957; Young Thomas Edison; Thoreau of Walden Pond; Captured by the Mohawks; Mark Twain and the River; Rascal, 1963 (Dutton Animal-Book, Aurianne, also Dorothy Canfield Fisher awards); Hurry Spring, 1966; Raccoons Are the Brightest People, 1966; The Wolfling, 1969. Gen. editor series history books, North Star Books. Contbr. to Harper's Nation, Dial, Poetry, Esquire, Atlantic Monthly, Yale Rev., Readers Digest. Home: Morristown, N.J. Died Dec. 21, 1974.

NORTHUP, DAVID WILMARTH, educator; b. The Dalles, Ore., Apr. 4, 1906; s. Harry Eaton and Virgilia Griffith (Cooper) N.; student Ore. State U., 1924-26; A.B., Reed Coll., 1930; A.M., U. Ore., 1932; Ph.D., U. Ill., 1935; m. Violet Olson, Jan. 5, 1935; children—Patricia Virgilia, Diana Eleanor. Mem. faculty U. W.Va. Med. Sch., 1935-72, prof. physiology, 1949-72, ret., 1972, chmn. dept. physiology, 1955-65. Maj. with Civil Air Patrol, 1958—. Mem. Am. Physiol. Soc., Sigma Xi, Phi Beta Pi, Phi Kappa Tau. Contbr. articles profl. jours. Home: Morgantown, W.Va., Died Mar. 13, 1973; interred Homewood Cemetery, Pittsburgh, Pa.

NORTON, JOHN NATHANIEL, ex-congressman; b. Polk Co., Neb., May 12, 1878; s. Charles O. and Mary S. (Hurtig) N.; prep. edn., pub. schs., Polk Co. and Bryant Normal U.; grad. Nebraska Wesleyan U.; A.B., U. of Neb., 1903; m. Selma Josephine Floodman; children—William Wendell, Evelyn Maurine. Actively interested in farming; clk. and recorder Polk Co., Neb., 1906-09; mayor of Osceola, Neb., 1908-09; mem. Neb., Ho. of Rep., 1911-17; mem. Neb. Constl. Conv., 1919-20; Dem. nominee for gov. of Neb., 1924; mem. 70th Congress (1927-29) and 72d Congress (1931-33), 4th Neb. Dist. Former pres. Neb. Farm Bur. Federation. Chautauqua and lyceum lecturer. Methodist. Woodman. Home: Polk, Neb.*†

NORTON, JOHN WILLIAM ROY, pub. health physician; b. Laurinburg, N.C., July 11, 1898; s. Lafayette and Iola Josephine (Reynolds) N.; A.B., Duke U., 1920; student U. of N.C. Med. Sch., 1924-26; M.D., Vanderbilt, 1928; M.P.H., Harvard, 1936; m. Jaunita Harris Ferguson, Apr. 8, 1928; children—Geraldine, Jean, Lafayette Ferguson. Prin. and athletic coach, pub. schs. of N.C., 1920-24; city health supt. Rocky Mount, N.C., 1931-35; interne Henry Ford Hosp., Detroit, 1928-29, asst. resident, 1929-30; div. dir. N.C. Bd. Health, 1936-38; prof. pub. health adminstrn., U. of N.C., 1938-40; chief health officer T.V.A., 1945-48; sec. and state health dir., N.C. State Board Health, Raleigh, 1948-65, director local health div., 1966-72, emeritus, 1972-74. Served as pvt., F.A., United States Army, 1918, disch. rank of 2d lt.; entered M.C., U.S. Army, 1940; commd. capt., 1940, advanced to col., 1945; asst. chief preventive med., E.T.O., 1942; dep. chief hygiene Allied Force Hdqrs., 1942-43; 7th Army Med. Insp., 1943; dir. epidemiology, Office Army Surgeon Gen., 1944; chief preventive med. services, Ninth Service Comd., 1944-45; disch., 1945. Awarded first prize for best scientific exhibit Annual Meeting of N.C. Med. Soc., 1947, Reynolds medal and scroll, Annual meeting N.C. Pub. Health Assn., 1948; Lasker award Planned Parenthood Federation, 1952; McCormack award, 1960; Distinguished Service award University North Carolina Medical School, 1961. Diplomate Am. Bd. of Preventive Medicine and Pub. Health. Fellow American College of Physicians, Royal Society of Health (hon.), Am. Coll. Preventive Medicine (pres. 1954-55); member A.M.A., Am. Pub. Health Assn. (pres. 1962-63), So. Med. Assn.; N.C. State Med. Soc. (sec. sect. pub. health and edn., 1934, chmn. sect., 1935), N.C. Pub. Health Assn. (sec.-treas.), 4th Dist. Med. Soc. (vice pres.), Nash-Edgecombe Counties (N.C.) Med. Soc. (sec.-treas.); southern branch Am. Public Health Assn. (pres. 1955), Assn. State & Terr. Health Officer (pres. 1955), Sigma Xi, Delta Omega, Alpha Omega Alpha. Democrat. Methodist. Mason. Co-author: History of Public Health in North Carolina, 1972. Home: Raleigh, N.C., Died Mar. 28, 1974; interred Sneads Grove, Scotland County, N.C.

NORWOOD, ELISABETH FESSENDEN GRAGG, Christian Science teacher and practitioner; b. Roxbury, Mass., Nov. 5, 1879; d. Isaac Paul and Eldora Olive (Wait) Gragg; ed. Girls' Latin Sch., Boston, and private schs.; m. Charles Augustus Norwood, March 25, 1916 (deceased). Entered practice of Christian Science healing in 1915; received a certificate as teacher of Christian Science, 1922; supt. The Mother Ch., Boston, Mass., Sunday Sch., 1926-29, second reader, 1929-32, pres. June 1942-June 1943; mem. Bible Lesson Com., June 1942-46; apptd. mem. Bd. Lectureship of the Mother Church, from 1946. Home: Brookline, Mass.†

NOTMAN, JAMES GEOFFREY, business exec.; b. Montreal, Que., May 6, 1901; s. Charles Frederick and Alice Hudson (Pyke) N.; B.Sc., McGill U., 1922; m. Grace Caroline Williamson, June 2, 1925; children—Joan Caroline (Mrs. Malcolm McDougall), Margaret Alice (Mrs. Orla Larsen) With prodn. office Dominion Engring. Works, Ltd. 1922-23, engring. dept., 1923-24, gen. mgrs. office, 1924-26, asst. to gen. mgr. charge mfg., 1926-30, mgr. mfg., 1930-49, v.p. charge mfg., 1949-50; exec. v.p. Canadair, Ltd., 1950-51, pres. 1952-65, chmn. 1965-66, dir.; v.p. Gen. Dynamics Corp., 1951-66; v.p., chmn. Montreal adv. bd., div. Crown Trust Co.; chmn. bd., dir. Fulcrum Corp., Westmount Life Ins. Co., Atlas Copco Can., Ltd., Liquid Carbonic Canadian Corp., SF Products, Ltd.; dir. Miller Constrn. Co., Canadian Marconi Ltd., Montreal Locomotive Works Ltd., Allied Chem. Corp., Allied Chem. Canadian, Ltd. Dorchester Commerce Realty, Ltd., John Inglis Co., Ltd., Chromium Mining & Smelting; emeritus dir. Canadian Imperial Bank Commerce. Asst. coordinator prodn. Dept. Munitions and Supply, 1942-45. Gov., pres., Royal Victoria Hosp., 1966-71; gov. McGill U., 1958-68. Decorated Order Brit. Empire; officer Order Hosp. St. John of Jerusalem. Hon. fellow Canadian Aero. Inst.; mem. Corp. Profl. Engrs., Montreal Bd. Trade, Engring. Inst. Can., Canadian C. of C., RCAF Assn., Phi Delta Theta. Clubs: Rideau (Ottawa); Wings (N.Y.C.); Nat. Aviation (Washington); Mount Royal. Home: Montreal, Que., Canada. Died Mar. 30, 1974; buried Mount Royal Cemetery.

NOURSE, CHARLES JOSEPH, lawyer; b. N.Y.C., Feb. 24, 1888; s. Charles Joseph and Julia Livingston (Peabody) N.; A.B., Harvard, 1909; LL.B., Columbia, 1912; m. Margaret Lawrence Strong, June 3, 1922. Admitted to N.Y. bar, 1911, practiced in N.Y.C.; mem. firm Ver Planck, Prince and Burlingame, later Burlingame, Nourse and Pettit, 1927-42; mem. firm Winthrop, Stimson, Putnam and Roberts, 1942-72, of counsel, 1972-74. Served from 1st lt. to capt., U.S. Army Air Service, 1917-18. Mem. Down Town Assn. Republican. Episcopalian. Clubs: Century Assn., Harvard (N.Y.C.); Piping Rock (Locust Valley, N.Y.); Seawanhaka Corinthian Yacht (Oyster Bay, N.Y.). Home: New York City and Oyster Bay, N.Y. Died Apr. 25, 1974.

NOURSE, EDWIN GRISWOLD, economist; b. Lockport, N.Y., May 20, 1883; s. Edwin Henry and Harriet Augusta (Beaman) N.; A.A., Lewis Inst., 1904; A.B., Cornell U., 1906; Ph.D., U. Chgo., 1915; (hon.) LL.D., Ill. Inst. Tech., 1950; D.Sc., Ia. State U., 1958; m. Ray Marie Tyler, Aug. 17, 1910; 1 son, John Tyler, Instr. finance Wharton Sch. Finance and Commerce, U. Pa., 1909-10; prof., head dept. econs. and sociology U.S.D., 1910-12, U. of Ark., 1915-18; prof. agrl. economics Ia. State Coll., and chief agrl. econs. sect. Ia. Expt. Sta., 1918-23, chief agrl. div., 1923-29, dir., 1929-42, Inst. Econs. Brookings Instn., Washington; v.p. Brookings Instn., 1942-46; chmn. Council Econ. Advisers, Exec. office Pres., 1946-49; vis. Distinguished prof. Pa. State U., 1959. League of Nations Com. Nutrition, 1935-37. Senior fellow Guggenheim Meml. Found., 1950-52. Recipient award Freedom's Found., 1950; award Am. Marketing Assn., 1955, Rosenberger medal U. Chgo., 1959. Am. del. Internat. Inst. Agr., Rome, 1924, 36. Fellow Am. Acad. Arts and Scis., Am. Econ. Assn. (pres. 1942); mem. Am. Philos. Soc., Joint Council Econ. Edn. (vice chmn.), Am. Farm Econ. Assn. (pres. 1924), Social Science Research Council (chmn. 1942-45), Alpha Zeta, Phi Kappa Phi, Pi Gamma Mu. Unitarian. Clubs: Chevy Chase (Md.); Cosmos. Author: Agrl. Economics, 1916; Chicago Produce Market (Hart, Shaffner & Marx prize series), 1918; American Agriculture and the European Market, 1924; The Legal Status of Agricultural Co-operation, 1927; The Co-operative Marketing of Livestock (with J.G. Knapp), 1931; America's Capacity to Produce (with associates), 1934; Marketing Agreements Under the Agricultural Adjustment Act, 1935; three years of the Agricultural Adjustment Administration (with J.S. Davis and J.D. Black), 1937; Industrial Price Policies and Economic Progress (with H.B. Drury), 1938; Price Making in a Democracy, 1944; The 1950's Come First, 1951; Economics in the Public Service, 1953. Contributor to revs. and econs. jours. Home: Chevy Chase, Md. Died Mar. 7, 1974.

NOVOTNY, ANTONIN, Pres. of Czechoslovakia; b. nr. Prague, Czechoslovakia, Dec. 10, 1904. Mem. Community Party, 1921-75; served as sec. at various times, 1936-68; mem. Czechoslovakia Politburo, 1951; vice premier Czechoslovakia, 6 mos., 1953; 1st party sec., 1953, party chief, 1954-68; pres. Czechoslovakia, Nov. 1957-68. Home: Prague, Czechoslovakia. Died Jan. 28, 1975.

NOYES, JANSEN, investment banker; b. Densville, N.Y., Nov. 1, 1884; s. Frederick W. and Emma Catherine (Hartman) N.; grad. Lawrenceville (N.J.) Sch., 1905; A.B., Cornell U., 1910; m. Agnes Blancke, June 6, 1914; children—Nancy (Mrs. Alfred Faris King, Jr.), Jansen, Shirley (Mrs. Shirley N. Hall), Blancke. With Imbrle & Co. and Hallgarten & Co., 1910-16; formed own firm Hemphill White & Chamberlain, 1916, name changed to Hemphill, Noyes and Co., 1921; merged to become Hornblower and Weeks-Hemphill Noyes, 1965; dir. Cuneo Press, Inc., Fishers Island Corp. Dir. Nat. Horse Show Am., Inc. Trustee, chmn. finance com. Lawrenceville Sch. Clubs: Bankers, Bond, Cornell, Links (N.Y.); Fishers Island Country, Fishers Island Yacht; Montclair Golf; Recess; Seminole Golf. Home: Fishers Island, N.Y. Died July 15, 1974.

NUCKOLLS, CLAIBORNE GEORGE, editor; b. Austin, Tex., Nov. 13, 1878; s. Samuel and Louise (Horton) N.; ed. Pearsall (Tex.) pub. schs.; m. Alma Kelly Woods, Feb. 19, 1901 (died May 31, 1946); 1 son, Claiborne LeRoy. Engaged in work successively as printer's devil, law student, court stenographer, 1896-1908; reporter, telegraph editor, city editor, New Orleans, San Antonio, Corpus Christi, 1908-25; staff reporter, Phoenix Gazette, 1925-28, city editor, 1928-29, mng. editor, 1929-30, editor 1930-47, ret. 1947. Served N.M. Nat. Guard, 1900-02. Mem. Phoenix Chamber of Commerce. Democrat. Episcopalian. Home: Phoenix, Ariz.†

NUNLIST, FRANK JOSEPH, JR., rubber products co. exec.; b. Columbus, O., Sept. 8, 1913; Chem. E., Columbia, 1940; m. Winifred Kendall, 1944; children—Ronald K., Ellen Grace. With Am. Radiator & Standard San. Corp., N.Y.C., 1931-39, Art Metal Constrn. Co., N.Y.C., 1939-41; with L. J. Mueller Furnace Co., Milw., 1941-54 (merged with Worthington Corp. 1954), gen. sales mgr., 1951-54; with Worthington Corp., 1954-69, v.p. operations, dir. 1960-62, pres., 1962-67, chief exec. officer, 1965-67, chmn. bd., 1967; pres., chief exec. officer Studebaker-Worthington, 1967-68; asst. postmaster gen. U.S., 1969-71; chmn. bd. Pantasote Co., 1972-74; dir. Herff-Jones Inc., Am. Precision Industries Inc. Chmn. N.J. Safety Triennial Campaign Fund. Trustee New Jersey Safety Council, Inc. Named Industrialist of Year, N.J., 1967. Mem. Am. Mgmt. Assn. (pres.'s assn.), Delta Upsilon. Clubs: Bethesda (Md.) Country; Union League, Board Room, Economic (N.Y.C.). Author: Management Leadership in the Year 2000. Home: Potomac, Md. Died May 12, 1974; interred Gate of Heaven Cemetery, Silver Spring, Md.

NUQUIST, ANDREW EDGERTON, educator; b. Osceola, Neb., Dec. 3, 1905; s. Andrew F. and Maude (Edgerton) N.; A.B., Doane Coll., 1927; M.A., U. Wis., 1936, Ph.D., 1940; m. Edith E. Wilson, May 21, 1933 (dec. Mar. 1970); children—Andrew S., Joyce Elizabeth; m. 2d, Isabel Jackson, 1971. Short-term missionary tchr. Lu Ho Acad., Tunghsien, Hopei, China, 1927-30; telephone solicitor, 1930-32; tchr. Oscoela (Neb.) High Sch., 1932-35; grad. asst. U. Wis., 1935-38; instr. to asso. prof. U. Vt., Burlington, 1938-51, prof. polit. sci., 1951-71, emeritus, 1971, ret., 1973, McCollough prof. polit. sci., 1956-75, chmn. dept., 1952-66, vis. prof. polit. studies and pub. adminstrn. Am. U., Beirut, 1958-59. Weekly columnist Town Govt. in Vt., Rutland Herald, 1946-48. Chmn. commn. to study occupational disease hazards in Vt., 1947-49; dir. Govt. Clearing House, U. Vt., 1950-61; mem. Vt. Gov.'s Planning Council, 1963-65; acting exec. dir. Vt. League Cities and Towns, 1967-68; mem. Vt. Legislative Apportion Bd., 1971-75; chmn. Vt. Price Control Bd., 1968-75. Pres. Vt. Assn. for Crippled Inc., 1942-46; pres. Vt. Children's Aid Soc., 1970-75. Rep. primary candidate U.S. Congress, 1946. Mem. Am., N.E. (pres. 1954-55) polit. sci. assns., Am. Assn. U. Profs., Nat. Municipal League, Am. Soc. Pub. Adminstrn., Municipal Finance Officers Assn. Mason. Author: (with others) Goals for Political Science, 1951; Town Government in Vermont, 1964; (with Edith Nuquist) Vermont State Government and Administration, 1965. Home: Burlington, Vt. Died Sept. 4, 1975.

NUSE, ROY CLEVELAND, artist; b. Springfield, O., Feb. 23, 1885; s. Charles Elias and Etta Virginia (Butts) N.; student Cincinnati Art Acad., 1905-12, John Herron Art Inst., Indianapolis, Ind., summer, 1912, Oberlin Coll., summer, 1913, home study dept., U. of Chicago, 1914-15, Pa. Acad. Fine Arts, 1915-18; m. Ellen Frances Guthrie, June 27, 1911; children—Jean Paul, Oliver William, Dorothy Virginia, Lucile Emily, Janet Frances, Robert Charles. Instr. in drawing and painting, Cincinnati Art Acad., 1910-12, Oberlin Coll., 1912-15; dir. Beechwood Sch. of Fine Arts, Jenkintown, Pa., 1915-33; instr. in drawing and painting, Pa. Acad. Fine Arts, Phila., from 1925, also head of coördinated courses between the Pa. Acad. and U. of Pa. Vice-pres. Fellowship of the Pa. Acad. of Fine Arts and winner Fellowship gold medal, 1940. Represented in permanent collections of the Pa. Acad. Fine Arts and Jefferson Medical College, Phila., Hahnemann Med. Coll., Phila. Awarded Cresson Scholarship, Pa. Acad. Fine Arts, 1917-18, Thouron prize, 1918, Toppan prize, 1918; first prize medal, Phila. Sketch Club, 1921. Home: Rushland, Pa., Died Nov. 25, 1975.

NUSSBAUM, MAX, clergyman; b. Suczava, Austria, Apr. 4, 1908; s. Joseph and Rachel (Bittkover) N.; student U. Breslau, 1928-34; Ph.D. summa cum laude, U. Wurzburg, 1934; Rabbi, Breslau Theol. Sem., 1934; D.D., Hebrew Union Coll.-Jewish Inst. Religion, 1959; Litt.D., Dropsie Coll., 1961; m. Ruth Offenstadt, July 14, 1938; children—Hannah (Mrs. Ronald Marsh), Jeremy. Came to U.S., 1940, naturalized, 1946. Rabbi, Great Jewish Congregation, Berlin, Germany, 1936-40, Beth Ahaba, Muskogee, Okla., 1940-42; dir. Hillel Council, State U. Okla., 1941-42; rabbi Temple Israel, Hollywood, Cal., 1942-74; mem. faculty Hebrew Union Coll. Jewish Inst. Religion. Mem. cabinet Jewish Welfare Fund; active Community Chest; mem. rabbinical adv. council United Jewish Appeal; nat. chmn. Am. Zionist Council, 1964-66; chmn. Am. sec. of World Jewish Congress, 1964-68, now hon. chmn. Am. sect. vice chmn. N.Am. sect.; mem. Nat. Council Joint Distbn. Com., Cal. Com. Food for Peace Program; nat. vice chmn. Reform Jewish Appeal UAHC/HUC-JIR. Bd. dirs. United Israel Appeal. Mem. Am. Jewish Congress (nat. v.p., hon. pres. Western region); mem. Zionist actions com., Central Conf. Am. Rabbis (exec. bd.), Western Assn. Reform Rabbis (past pres.), So. Cal. Assn. Liberal Rabbis (past pres. bd.), Nat. Conf. Christians and Jews, Zionist Orgn. Am. (past pres., past chmn. nat. exec. com.). Mem. B'nai B'rith. Author: Yehuda Halevi's Philosophy of Nationalism, 1933; Kantianismus and Marxismus in der Sozial-philosophie Max Adlers, 1934; Nachman Krochmal, the Philosopher of Israel's Eternity (Am. Jewish Yearbook), 1942-43; Eretz Yisrael Galut and Chutz L'Aretz in Their Historic Settings, 1952; The Temple Israel Pulpit, 1957. Contbr. other publs. Home: Hollywood, Cal. Died July 20, 1974; interred Hillside Meml. Park, Los Angeles, Cal.

OAKES, CLARENCE PERRY, inst. exec.; b. Merwin, Mo., June 17, 1900; s. Arthur Jay and Josephine (Cline) O.; student Coll. Emporia, 1918-19; A.B., U. Kan., 1922; postgrad. New Coll., Oxford U., 1931, Selwyn Coll., Cambridge U., U. Heidelberg (Germany), 1931; m. Mildred Read, Nov. 24, 1938; 1 dau., Jolene (Mrs. Jess Keith Wells). Sec.-treas. Oakes Printing Co., Independence, Kan., 1923-37, pres., 1937-49; roving columnist 42 fgn. countries Midwest News Syndicate, 1933-37; lectr. Lee Keedick Lectr. Bur., N.Y.C., 1935-41; chief polit. affairs Dept. State, Bremen, Germany, 1949-52; with CIA, 1953-61; exec. dir. Inst. Am. Strategy, Chgo., 1961-63, operating dir., 1964-65, dir., from 1965, spl. projects dir., 1965-67, sec., from 1967. Mem. Kan. Ho. of Reps., 1939-40, Kan. Senate, 1941-42, 49-50. Chmn. KaKawk com. Sea Scouts, 1939-49. Served with U.S. Army, 1918; from lt. to capt. USNR, 1941-46. Mem. Spl. Agts. Assn., Navy League, Assn. U.S. Army, Res. Officers (pres. Bremen, Germany chpt. 1950-51, Naval Armory chpt. Chgo. 1963-64). Retired Officers Assn. (v.p. from 1971), Am. Legion (naval mem. NSC 1947-49), N.E.A., Delta Upsilon, Alpha Kappa Psi, Phi Mu Alpha. Republican. Presbyn. Mason, Rotarian. Club: Lake Shore (Chgo.). Author: Strengthening and Protecting Our American Heritage Through Community Action, 1967. Editor: Education and Freedom in a World of Conflict, 1963. Co-editor: Education About Communism, 1964. Home: Wilmette, Ill. Died Nov. 15, 1973.

OAKES, ROBERT A., lawyer; b. Chgo., Feb. 3, 1909; Ph.B., U. Chgo., 1930, J.D., 1932. Admitted to Ill. bar, 1932, Cal. bar, 1947; partner firm Oakes & McDonald, San Diego. Served to maj. USMCR, 1942-45. Mem. San Diego (dir. 1954-56), Am. bar assns., State Bar Cal. (mem. com. on corps. 1957-60), Phi Delta Phi. Home: Cal. Died Sept. 12, 1973.

OAKSEY, GEOFFREY LAWRENCE, Brit. judge; b. London, Eng., Oct. 2, 1880; s. Lord Trevethin and Jessie (Lawrence); student Haileybury Coll., 1894-99; M.A., New College, Oxford, 1903, Hon. Fellow, 1944, Hon. D.C.L., 1947; m. Marjorie Robinson, Dec. 22, 1921; children—Mary Elizabeth, Enid Rosamond, Anne Jennifer, John Goeffrey Tristram. Called to Bar, Jan. 1906; counsel for Canadian Provinces and C.P.R. in Privy Council, 1907-14; counsel for Canada in N. Atlantic Fisheries arbitration, The Hague, 1910; examiner in ecclesiastical causes, 1927-32; atty. gen. to Prince of Wales and Duchy of Cornwall, 1928-32; counsel to Jockey Club, 1922-32; judge High Court, 1932-44; Lord Justice, 1944; British Judge internat. military tribunal, Nuremburg, 1945 (president); Lord of Appeal in ordinary, from 1947; vice lieutenant for Wiltshire, 1949. Joined Royal F.A., Essex Brigade, 1914; Herts Brigade, France and Palestine, 1915-18; comd. Herts Yeomanry Brigade, 1919-26, R.A. col. 1926-37. Awarded D.S.O., and T.D., mentioned in dispatches twice. King's Counsel, 1925, created Lord Oaksey Jan. 1, 1947. Chmn. Quarter Sessions Wiltshire, 1945. Mem. Ch. of Eng. Clubs: Brooks', St. James St. (London). Twice pres. English Guernsey Cattle Soc. Home: Wilthsire, Eng.†

OATES, WHITNEY J., educator; b. Evanston, Ill., Mar. 26, 1904; s. James Franklin and Henrietta May (Jennings) O.; A.B., Princeton, 1926, A.M., 1927, Ph.D., 1931; L.H.D., Rockford Coll., 1961, Brown U., 1961; D.Litt., Middlebury Coll., 1964; L.H.D., Washington and Lee U., 1967; m. Virginia Hill, Sept. 1, 1927; 1 dau., Henrietta Jennings. Instr. classics Princeton, 1927-30, asst. prof., 1931-39, asso. prof., 1940-45, prof., 1945-70, chmn., dept. classics, 1945-61, chmn. spl. program in humanities, 1945-60, chmn. council humanities, 1953-70; Rockefeller post-war fellow, 1948, Andrew Fleming West prof. classics, 1949-62, Avalon prof. humanities, 1962-70; emeritus, from 1970; broadcast Invitation to Learning Program, from 1940. Co-dir. Nat. Woodrow Wilson Fellowship program Assn. Grad. Schs. in Assn. Am. Univs., 1951-52; trustee Woodrow Wilson Nat. Fellowship Found.; mem. bd. dirs. Am. Council Learned Socs. (treas. until 1971); trustee Princeton U. Press. Sr. fellow Center Hellenic Studies Harvard, Washington. Served from 1st lt. to capt. USMCR, 1943-45. Mem. Am. Philol. Assn., Classical Assn. Atlantic States, Phi Beta Kappa (senator-at-large, pres. united chpts. from 1964), Phi Beta Kappa Assos. Democrat. Episcopalian. Club: Century Assn. (N.Y.C.) Author: The Influence of Simonides of Ceos upon Horace, 1932; Aristotle and the Problem of Value, 1963. Editor: The Complete Greek Drama (with E. G. O'Neill, Jr.), 1938; The Stoic and Epicurean Philosophers, 1940; Greek Literature in Translation (with C. T. Murphy), 1944; Greek and Roman Classics in Translation (with C. T. Murphy and K. Guinagh), 1946; Basic Writings of St. Augustine, 1948. Contbr. various articles, revs. to periodicals. Home: Sarasota, Fla. Died Oct. 14, 1973.

OBEE, CHARLES WALTER, biologist; b. Whitehouse, O., June 16, 1879; s. John and Margaret (Billing) O.; Ph.B., Adrian (Mich.) Coll., 1906, A.M., 1908; M.S., U. of Mich., 1910; m. Lillian Hallam Jennings, Sept. 7, 1910 (died May 8, 1919); children—Donald Jennings. Byron Billing; m. 2d, Mabel Bible, June 29, 1921; children—Alfred Charles, Naomi Cathleen. Teacher district schools, Lucas Co., O., 1897-1901; prin. Raisin Valley Sem., nr. Adrian, 1906-08; asst. in zoölogy, U. of Mich., 1908-10; prof. biology and geology, Adrian Coll., 1910-20; prof. biology and geology, Kansas City U., 1921-25; pastor Gordon Place M.P. Ch., Kansas City, Kan., 1925-29; prof. biology and geology, Kansas City U., from 1926. Prohibition candidate for regent of U. of Mich., 1913, and for supt. of pub. instrn., 1915. Ordained minister M.P. Ch. Mem. Sons of Vets. Mem. family of 10 children, 9 of whom taught in pub. schs., 6 were coll. grads., 4 ordained to ministry. Home: Kansas City, Kan.*†

OBERG, KALERVO, educator; b. Nanaimo, B.C., Can., Jan. 15, 1901; s. August and Hilma (Uusitale) O.; B.A., U. B.C., 1928; M.A., U. Pitts., 1930; Ph.D., U. Chgo., 1933; m. Lois P. Rimmer, June 30, 1945; 1 stepdau., Earline (Mrs. Robert B. Churbuck). Came to U.S., 1929. Internat. African Inst. fellow London Sch. Econs., 1933-34; Social Sci. Research Council fellow, Uganda, 1934-36; econ. analyst Agr. Dept., N.M., 1939-42, Coordinator's Office Inter-Am. Affairs, Ecuador and Peru, 1942-43, Fgn. Econ. Adminstrn., Washington, 1943-46; anthropologist Smithsonian Instn., Brazil, 1946-52; social sci. cons. ICA and predecessor agys., Brazil, 1953-59; social sci. cons. AID, Surinam, 1959-63; prof. anthropology Cornell U., Ithaca, N.Y., 1963-65, Stanford, 1965, U. So. Cal., 1965-67, Ore. State U., Corvallis, 1968-71. Fellow Am. Anthrop. Assn. Author: Culture Shock, 1954; Types of Social Structure among the Lowland Tribes of South and Central America, 1955; The Social Economy of The Tlingit Indians, 1973; also articles. Contbr. to Ency. Brit. Home: Corvallis, Ore. Died July 11, 1973; buried Twin Oaks Meml. Gardens, Corvallis.

O'BRIAN, JOHN LORD, lawyer; b. Buffalo, N.Y., Oct. 14, 1874; s. John and Elizabeth (Lord) O.; A.B., Harvard University, 1896; LL.B., U. of Buffalo, 1898; LL.D., Hobart College, 1916, Syracuse University, 1938, Brooklyn Polytechnic Inst., 1943, Brown U., 1945, Harvard, 1946, Yale, 1948; m. Alma E. White, Sept. 17, 1902 (dec.); children—Alma (Mrs. Kellogg Mann), Janet (Mrs. Winfield L. Butsch), Frances (Mrs. Ames B. Hettrick (dec.) Alison (Mrs. S. Davis Boylston), Esther (Mrs. Thurston T. Robinson). Adm. to New York bar and in practice at Buffalo, 1898-45; member of firm Covington and Burling, Washington, D.C.; member New York Assembly, 1907-09; United States Atty. Western District of N.Y., March 4, 1909-Dec. 2, 1914; delegate-at-large, N.Y. Constitutional Conv., 1915; chmn. draft bd. of appeals, Western N.Y., 1917; head War Emergency Div., Dept. of Justice, 1917-19; Buffalo Trustee Albright Art Gallery, 1921-30; community fund, 1923-42; Family Service Soc., 1925-42; vice chmn. N.Y. State Reorgn. Com., 1925-26; asst. to atty. gen. of U.S., 1929-33; gen. counsel Office of Prodn. Management, also Supply Priorities and Allocation Board, Washington, D.C., 1941, and War Prodn. Board until Dec. 1944; mem. Nat. Adv. Bd. on Moblizn. Policy, 1951-52. Tucker Found. lectr., The Changing Aspects of Freedom, Washington and Lee University, 1952, Godkin Foundation lectr., Harvard Univ., 1955. Decorated Officer Order of Leopold II (Belgium). Awarded Chancellor's Medal, University of Buffalo, 1940, for distinguished public service; Presidental Medal for Merit, 1946, for outstanding service in the war effort; award, Nat. Conf. Christians and Jews, for service in field of human relations, 1953; annual medal N.Y. Bar Assn., 1957; ann. award of Fellows Am. Bar Found., 1960. Fellow Am. Acad. Arts, Scis.; mem. Am. Law Inst., various bar assns., Washington Nat. Monument Soc., Washington Literary Society. Order of Coif. Republican. Regent University of State of New York, 1931-47; trustee Univ. of Buffalo,

1903-29; overseer Harvard Univ., 1939-45. Pres. Harvard Alumni Assn., 1945, nat. chmn. Endowment Harvard Divinity Sch., 1950-57. Republican candidate U.S. Senate New York, 1938. Episcopalian; chancellor P.E. Diocese of Western New York, 1932-46. Mem. Delta Upsilon, Phi Delta Phi, Phi Beta Kappa (hon.). Clubs: Century, Harvard (New York); Buffalo (president 1940); Metropolitan (pres. 1954-56), Alibi (Washington); Alfalfa (pres. 1952). Home: Washington, D.C.†

O'BRIEN, SEUMAS, sculptor, author; b. Glenbrook, County Cork, Eire, Apr. 26, 1880; s. John J. and Elizabeth Harding (Aherne) O'B.; ed. Presentation Brothers' Sch., Cork, Cork Sch. of Art, Cork Sch. of Music, Nat. Coll. of Art (Dublin), Royal Coll. of Art (London); unmarried. Instr. in art, Cork Sch. of Art, Mt. St. Joseph's Monastery, Cork, Queenstown Tech. Sch., Nat. Coll. of Art, Dublin, until 1912; exhibited at Royal Hibernian Acad.; awarded silver medal (sculpture), by Bd. of Edn., London, 1912. Came to U.S., 1913; instr. in art, Newark (N.J.) Sch. of Fine and Indsl. Arts. Am. rep. Irish Playwrights' Assn. Mem. Am. Irish Hist. Soc., Stephen Crane Assn. Author of books and plays from 1916. Address: Glen Ridge N.J.*†

O'BRIEN, WILLIAM AUGUSTINE, judge; b. San Francisco, June 26, 1903; s. William James and Margaretta Helena (Costello) O'B.; A.B., U. of San Francisco, 1924, LL.B., 1926; m. Robena King, June 24, 1933 (dec. Mar. 1952); children—William King, Sallyanne (Mrs. Gerald C. Davalos); m. 2d, Elinor M. Shaw, Sept. 12, 1959. Admitted to Cal. bar, 1926; asst. U.S. Dist. atty. No. Dist. Cal., 1927-32; pvt. practice, San Francisco, 1932-56; mem. faculty Sch. Law, U. San Francisco, 1927-34; gen. counsel Housing Authority City and County San Francisco, 1938-56; appointed judge municipal ct., 1956, 63, presiding judge, 1959-63; judge Superior Ct. State Cal., 1963-70. Mem. Cal. Code Commn., 1948-53. Mem. Am., San Francisco (bd. govs. 1938, 46) bar assns., U. San Francisco Alumni Assn., State Bar Cal. Club: Bohemian. Home: Atherton, Cal. Died June 18, 1973; interred Holy Cross Cemetery, Colma, Cal.

OCHLEWSKI, TADEUSZ, musician; b. Olszana, Ukraine, Mar. 22, 1894; s. Jozef and Jadwiga (Konarzewska) O.; ed. St. Petersburg Conservatory, 1915-17; diploma Warsaw Conservatory, 1925; m. Janina Wysocka, Dec. 18, 1923; 1 dau., Maria. Concert master Warsaw Opera Orch., 1925-35; 2d violinist Polish Quartet, 1934-39; violin tchr. Warsaw Conservatory, 1927-39; tchr. string ensembles State Music Coll., Cracow, 1948-50; mgr. Mus. Movement Orgn., 1934-39; founder, dir. State Polish Music Publs., Cracow, Poland, 1945-65, hon. pres. editorial council, 1966-75; founder, dir. old music chamber ensemble Con moto ma cantabile, Warsaw, 1965-75. Decorated Gold Cross Merit; comdr.'s cross Order Polonia Restituta; recipient prize City of Cracow, 1965; award Union Polish Composers, 1950; others. Mem. Soc. for Pub. Polish Music (dir. 1930-39), also music assns. Contbr. essays on musical life in Poland to perdiodicals. Editor, Old Polish Instrumental Music; series Florilegium Musicae Antiquae. Home: Warsaw, Poland., Died Jan. 26, 1975.

O'CONNOR, CHARLES, ex-congressman; b. Knox Co., Mo., Oct. 26, 1878; s. Charles and Catherine (McCarthy) O'C.; grad. Colo. State Teachers Coll., 1901; LL.B., U. of Colo., 1904; m. Elizabeth Buell, Aug. 7, 1905; children—Lawrence B., Donald Ransom (dec.), Buell. Admitted to Colo. bar, 1904, and began practice at Boulder; 1st asst. atty. gen., Colo., 1911-13; moved to Tulsa, Okla., 1919; mem. 71st Congress (1929-31), 1st Okla. Dist. Mem. Okla. State Bar Assn., Phi Delta Phi. Acacia. Republican. Episcopalian. Mason (32°, K.T., Shriner), Elk. Club: Tulsa, Home: Tulsa, Okla.†

O'CONNOR, GEORGE GRAY, army officer; b. Pasadena, Cal., Aug. 25, 1914; s. J. Robert and Marion (Gray) O'C.; student U. Cal. at Los Angeles, 1931-33; B.S., U.S. Mil. Acad., 1938; postgrad. Command and Gen. Staff Coll., 1950-51, Army War Coll., 1954-55; M.A., George Washington U., 1963; m. Hope Brown, Aug. 20, 1938; children—Robert G., William G. Commd. 2d lt. U.S. Army, 1938, advanced through grades to lt. gen., 1969; comdg. officer 6th Div. Arty., Asiatic-Pacific Theatre, 1945-46; S-3 and exec. officer phys. edn. dept. U.S. Mil. Acad., 1946-50; chief war history div. Office Chief Mil. History, Washington, 1951-54; chief of staff Hdqrs. BASEC, Communications Zone USAREUR, 1955-57, group comdr. 36th F.A. Group, 1957-58; chief joint war plans div., dep. dir. strategic planning, dir. plans Office Dep. Chief of Staff Operations, Washington, 1958-60; exec. officer J-5 joint staff U.S. Army Element, Office Joint Chiefs of Staff, Washington, 1960-62; dep. chief of staff U.S. Army Element, Hdqrs. UN Command/U.S. Forces in Korea, 1962-63; dep. chief of staff Hdqrs. 8th Army, Korea, 1963-64; asst. div. comdr. 4th Inf. Div., Ft. Lewis, Wash., 1964-66, asst. div. comdr., Vietnam, 1966; asst. div. comdr. 25th Inf. Div., Vietnam, 1966-67; asst. div. comdr. 9th Inf. Div., Vietnam, 1967, comdg. gen., 1967-68; dep. chief of staff for individual tng. Hdqrs. USCONARC, Ft. Monroe, Va., 1968-69; comdg. gen. VII Corps, Germany, 1969-71. Decorated D.S.M., Silver Star medal with two oak leaf clusters, Legion of Merit with oak leaf cluster, Bronze Star medal, Air medal with 18 oak leaf clusters, Republic of Vietnam Gallentry Cross with gold star, Republic of Vietnam Nat. Order 5th Class. Home: Sierra Madre, Cal. Died Mar. 24, 1971.

O'CONNOR, GERALD BROWN, physician; b. San Francisco, 1900; M.D., St. Louis U., 1925. Intern, So. Pacific Gen. Hosp., 1925-26; resident St. Francis Hosp., San Francisco, 1 year later vis. plastic surgeon; 1st asst. to Sir Harold Gillies, London, Eng., 6 months; plastic surgeon San Francisco Polyclinic, Mary's Help Hosp., French Hosp., St. Mary's Hosp., So. Pacific Hosp., U.S. Marine Hosp.; cons. Letterman Gen. Hosp., San Francisco; clin. instr. plastic surgery Stanford. Served to comdr. M.C., USNR, 1943-46. Diplomate Am. Bd. Plastic Surgery. Fellow A.C.S., Internat. Coll. Surgeons; mem. A.M.A., Am. Assn. Plastic Surgeons. Home: Belvedere, Cal. Died Oct. 30, 1972.

O'CONNOR, JOHNSON, psychometrician; b. Chgo., Jan. 22, 1891; s. John and Nelie (Johnson) O'C.; A.B., Harvard, 1913. A.M., 1914; m. Ruth David, Dec. 17, 1913 (dec. Feb. 1920); 1 son, Chadwell; m. 2d, Eleanor Manning, June 3, 1931. Astronomical mathematical research with Percival Lowell, 1911-18; metall. research Am. Steel & Wire Co., Worcester, Mass., 1918-20; elec. engring. with Gen. Electric Co., West Lynn, Mass., 1920-22; organized Human Engring. Lab. for Gen. Electric Co. to study applicants and new employees, 1922; lectr. psychology Stevens Inst. Tech., 1928-31, asso. prof., dir. psychol. studies, 1931-46; lectr. psychology Mass. Inst. Tech., 1928-31, asst. prof., 1931-34; organized Human Engring. Lab. at Stevens Inst. Tech., 1930, became Johnson O'Connor Research Found., 1942; pres., dir. Human Engring. Lab. (Boston, Chgo., Phila. Fort Worth, Tulsa, Los Angeles), Johnson O'Connor Research Found. (N.Y.C., San Diego, Washington, Atlanta, Baytown, Tex., Detroit), Fundación de Investigaciones Johnson O'Connor, A.C. Mem. Sec. of Navy Civilian Adv. Com., 1946. Wertheim fellow, 1927. Fellow Am. Acad. Arts and Scis. Author: Born That Way, 1928; Psychometrics, 1934; Johnson O'Connor English Vocabulary Builder, 1937 (Volume I, new edit. 1949, Volume II, new edit. 1951, Vol. III, part I, 1971); Unsolved Business Problems, 1940; The Too Many Aptitude Woman, 1941; Structural Visualization, 1943; Apitudes and the Languages, 1944; Ideaphoria, 1945; The Unique Individual, 1947; Johnson O'Connor Science Vocabulary Builder, 1955; co-author: Ginn Vocabulary-Building Program, 1966; contbr. to magazines. Home: Boston, Mass. Died July 1, 1973.

O'CONNOR, PAUL LYNCH, clergyman, educator; b. Joliet, Ill., Aug. 10, 1909; s. James C. and Marie (Lynch) O'C.; Litt.B., Xavier U., Cin., 1932; A.M., Phil Lic., Loyola U., Chgo., 1937; S.T.L., St. Louis U., 1942; LL.D., Loyola U., Miami U., U. Cin. 1964; L.H.D., Hebrew Union Coll., 1964, St. Thomas Inst., 1973. Joined Soc. of Jesus, 1929, consecrated priest Roman Catholic Ch., 1941; instr. English, Latin and Greek, St. John's Coll., Toledo, 1932-34, St. Ignatius High Sch., Cleve., 1937-38; asst. dean U. Detroit Coll. Liberal Arts, 1942-44; dean Xavier U. Evening Sch., 1946-48, dean Xavier U., 1948-55, trustee, 1948-74, pres., 1955-72, chancellor, 1972-74. Treas., Ohio Research and Devel. Found.; mem. Commn. on Higher Edn. Assistance for Ohio. Bd. dirs. Am. Council on Edn. Served to lt. Chaplain Corps, USNR, 1944-46. Mem. Nat. Cath. Ednl. Assn., Jesuit Ednl. Assn. (chmn. com. on liberal arts colleges), North Central Assn., Assn. Am. Colls., Ohio Coll. Assn. (pres. 1962-63), Am. Legion. Home: Cincinnati O. Died Sept. 10, 1974.

O'CONNOR, RICHARD, newspaperman, author; b. La Porte, Ind., Mar. 10, 1915; s. Richard Edward and Hilda (Waldschmidt) O'C.; ed. pub. schs., Milw.; m. Olga Derby, Dec. 28, 1939. Newspaperman in Chgo., Detroit, New Orleans, Boston, Washington, Los Angeles and N.Y.C., 1936-57; free lance, from 1957. Author: Ambrose Bierce, 1967; Bret Harte, 1966; Jack London, 1964; The Lost Revolutionary, 1967; Black Jack Pershing, 1961; Gould's Millions, 1962; Bat Masterson, 1957; Hell's Kitchen, 1958; Company Q, 1957; Pacific Destiny, 1969; The Cactus Throne, 1971; The Oil Barons, 1971. Home: Ellsworth, Me. Died Feb. 15, 1975.

O'CONOR, DANIEL JOSEPH, JR., mfg. exec.; b. Cin., June 28, 1916; s. Daniel Joseph and Ruth K. (Breuer) O'C.; grad. Georgetown Prep. Sch., Garrett Park, Md., 1933; B.S. in Elec. Engring., Mass. Inst. Tech., 1937; m. Catherine Ellen Burke, Nov. 4, 1937; children—Mary Catherine, Patricia Ann, Daniel Joseph, III, Thomas Burke. Engr. Allis Chalmers Mfg. Co., Milw., 1937-40; successively engr., asst. chief, pres., also dir. The Formica Co., Cin., 1940-61, subsidiary of Am. Cyanamid Co. from 1956, exec. v.p., dir. parent co., 1964-67. Mem. Newcomen Soc., Sigma Chi. Clubs: University (N.Y.); Queen City (Cin.); Morris County Golf (Morristown, N.J.). Home: Morristown, N.J. Died Jan. 2, 1974; buried Gate of Heaven Cemetery, Cin.

O'DANIEL, JOHN WILSON, army officer; b. Newark, Del., Feb. 15, 1894; student Delaware Coll., Newark; B.S., University of Delaware, 1917; graduate Infantry School, 1928, Command and General Staff School, 1939; m. Ruth Bowman, March 24, 1920; children—Anne (Mrs. H. P. Groesheck), John W., Jr. (killed in action as paratrooper, 1944). Served as corpl. and sergt., Del. Nat. Guard; commd. 2d lt. inf., U.S. Army, Oct. 1917, advancing to maj. gen., Oct. 1944; served with 11th Inf., A.E.F., in Meuse-Argonne and St. Mihiel (wounded); comdg. officer, Co. E., 25th Inf., Ariz., 1919-24; instr. N.J. Nat. Guard, 1924-27; comdg. officer Mil. Police, Hawaii, 1930-31; with Civilian Conservation Corps, 1933-36; prof. mil. science, Acad. of Richmond County, Ga., 1936-38; instr., O.R.C., 1939-40; comdg. officer 2d Batn., 24th Inf., 1941; asst. chief of staff, plans and training officer, 3d Army, San Antonio, 1942; received overseas assignment, 1942; participated in landings, N. Africa, 1942, Sicily and Salerno, 1943, Anzio and southern France, 1944; comdg. gen., 5th Army invasion training center, N. Africa, Jan.-June, 1943; div. comdr. 3d Inf. Div., Feb. 17, 1944-July 10, 1945; comdt. Infantry Sch. Ft. Benning, Ga., July 10, 1945-48; mil. attache, Moscow, U.S.S.R. from Sept. 4, 1948, Decorated D.S.C., D.S.M. with oak leaf cluster, Purple Heart, Legion of Merit and Oak Leaf Cluster, Silver Star and Oak Leaf Cluster, Bronze Star (U.S.); Italian Silver Medal; Croix de Guerre, Legion of Honor (France). Home: San Diego, Cal. Died Mar. 27, 1975.

ODELL, MARQUERITE TWILA, civic worker; b. St. Louis, Apr. 1, 1916; d. James R. and Grace (Loftis) Odell; B.A., Lindenwood Coll., 1969. Dir. Nursery Sch., Fairfield, Conn., 1948-55; personnel dir. Binkley Mfg., Warrenton, Mo., 1955-59; dir. student activities Lindenwood Coll., St. Charles, Mo., 1959-68; field dir. Girl Scouts U.S., Edwardsville, Ill., from 1969. Bd. dirs., sec. Community Council, 1965-69; chmn. St. Charles County Commn. Women, from 1969; mem. Planning Com. for Aged, from 1969. Mem. Bus. and Profl. Women's Club, Mo. Assn. Women Deans and Counselors, Student Personnel Workers. Democrat. Episcopalian. Club: Zonta (pres. St. Charles 1967-70). Home: St. Charles Mo. Died Nov. 28, 1973.

ODEN, JOSHUA, clergyman; b. Muskegon, Mich., June 19, 1880; s. Rev. Martin P. and Emma O.; student Augustana Coll., Rock Island, Ill., 1899, B.D., 1908; B.A., Bethany Coll., Lindsborg, Kan., 1902, D.D., 1928; grad. Bethany Normal Sch. and Bethany Sch. of Commerce, 1903; student Chgo. Theol. Sem., 1905; grad. work Northwestern U.; m. Helga Sudeberg, May 25, 1909; 1 son, Joshua. Ordained ministry of Luth. Ch., Augustana Synod, 1908; pastor Irving Park Ch., Chgo., from 1908. Mem. bd. dirs. Augustana Hosp., from 1943. Pres. Ill. Conf. Luther League of Augustana Synod, 1917-25; pres. Synodical Luther League Council of Augustana Synod, 1928-37; v.p. commn. on young peoples work Am. Luth. Conf., 1933-37, pres. 1937-40; chmn. Centennial Com. for Ill. Conf. of Augustana Luth. Ch. Celebration, 1953; v.p. Chgo. Ch. Fedn., 1930-32, pres. 1934-36, mem. bd. trustees, 1943; chmn. Chicago Protestant Com. for Religious Activities, Century of Progress Expn., Chgo., 1933-34. Served as chaplain under Nat. Luth. Council during World War I. Clubs: Svithiod, Swedish, Lake Shore (Chgo.). Editor: Luther League Manual, Daily Devotions for Luth. Youth. Student of internat. young people's problems. Decorated by King of Sweden; 300th Anniversary Medal landing of Swedes in Wilmington; Centennial Anniversary Silver Medal; Royal Order of Vasa. Originator of Protestant Novena, 1939. Home: Chicago, Ill.†

ODERMATT, GOTTHARD, banker; b. Aug. 2, 1902; m. Theodora Fuchs, 1933. Pres. Obwaldner Kantonalbank, Sarnen, Switzerland, from 1960; pres. adminstrv. council Obwaldner Electrical Works. Mem. Officers Assn. Obwaldner. Died Feb. 7, 1970.

ODLOZILIK, OTAKAR, educator; b. Kostelec, Czechoslovakia, Jan. 12, 1899; s. Florian and Genevive (Novak) O.; Ph.D., Charles U., Prague, 1923; Litt.D., Hobart and William Smith Coll., 1943; unmarried. Came to U.S., 1939. Lectr. in history Charles U., 1926-28, prof. in history, 1934-39, 1945-48; lectr. in Czechoslovakia, Sch. Slavonic Studies, U. of London, 1928-30; vis. prof. European history U. of Colo., summers 1939, 40, 48, 49, Washington and Jefferson Coll., spring 1940, Northwestern U., summer 1941, U. of Kan., spring 1949; lectr. Columbia, 1941-43, T.G. Masaryk prof. history, 1949-55; prof. of Modern European history U. Pa., from 1955; external adviser to the Czechoslovak Ministry of Fgn. Affairs, London, 1944-45. Mem. Czech. Acad. of Arts and Scis., Royal Bohemian Soc. of Arts and Scis., Slavonic Inst., Prague, (1930-48). Author: Wycliff and Bohemia, 1937; The Czechoslovak Inheritance, 1945; The Caroline University, 1948; Outline of Czechoslovak History (in Czech), 1937; Charles Elder of Zerotin (in Czech), 1936; The Hussite King, 1965. Home: Philadelphia, Pa. Died July 14, 1973.

O'DONNELL, WILLIAM EMMETT, clergyman, coll. dean; b. Ft. William, Ont., Can., July 29, 1907; s. William Kelly and Mary Elizabeth (Teevens) O'D.; student St. Thomas Mil. Acad., 1921-23, Nazareth Hall, St. Paul, 1923-27, St. Paul Sem., 1927-33, S.T.B., Cath. U. Am., 1933; U. Minn., summer 1933; D.Sc.H., U. Louvain (Belgium), 1938. Ordained priest Roman Cath. Ch., 1933: tchr. history St. Thomas Coll., St. Paul, 1938-45, dean coll. 1945-73, v.p., 1958-62, acad. v.p., dean of Coll., 1962-73. Mem. Am. Conf. Academic Deans (chmn. 1961-62), Am., Minn. hist. socs., Am. Cath. Hist. Soc., Assn. Minn. Colls. (pres. 1958-59), Minn. Pvt. Coll. Council, Delta Epsilon Sigma (nat. pres. 1958-60), Phi Alpha Theta. Author: The Chevalier de la Luzerne, 1938. Home: St. Paul, Minn. Died May 8, 1974; interred Ressurection Cemetery, St. Paul.

O'DONNELL, WILLIAM FRANCIS, coll. pres.; b. Burnet, Tex., May 1, 1890; s. William and Angeline (Beasley) O.; A.B., Transylvania Coll., Lexington, Ky., 1912; student U. of Ky., 1911; M.A., Teachers College, Columbia University, 1932; LL.D., Transylvania College, 1943; m. Madeline Riley, October 29, 1909; children—Loraine (Mrs. James A. Miller), Margaret, William Francis, James. High sch. prin., Carrollton, Ky., 1912-13; supt. schs., Carrollton, 1913-26, Richmond (Ky.) Pub. Schs., 1926-41; teacher English, Morehead (Ky.) State Teachers Coll., 1933; pres. Eastern Kentucky State Teachers College, Richmond, 1941-60, emeritus from 1960. Member of Central Kentucky Education Assn. (pres. 1934), State Athletic Assn. (pres. 1929-41), Ky. Edn. Assn., Nat. Edn. Assn., Am. Assn. Sch. Administrs. Democrat. Methodist. Mason, Elk. Club: Rotary (pres. Richmond). Home: Richmond, Ky. Died Mar. 5, 1974.

ODRIA, MANUEL A., Pres. of Rep. of Peru; b. Tarma, Peru, Nov. 26, 1897; s. Arturo Odria Alvarez and Zoila Amorette; ed. Escuela Militar de Chorrillos, Escuela de Guerra, Escuela Superior de Guerra Naval. Served as prof. Escuela de Chorrillos; sub-dir. and dir. Escuela Superior de Guerra. Staff officer in Peruvian Army, 1927; advanced to general of the army, 1946, also serving as chief of staff; participated with distinction in armed conflict with Ecuador; minister of govt. and police, 1947-48; pres. Mil. Tribunal of the govt., 1948-50; constitutional pres. of Rep. of Peru, 1950-56. Decorated Sword of Honor (Escuela de Chorrillos), Grand Cruz of Orden del Sol del Peru, Orden de Ayacucho, El Merito Policial (Peru); also numerous decorations and honors from fgn. countries. Home: Lima, Peru. Died Feb. 18, 1974.

OENSLAGER, DONALD MITCHELL, scene designer; b. Harrisburg, Pa., Mar. 7, 1902; s. John and Jane (Connely) O.; student Philips Exeter Acad., 1917-19; A.B., Harvard, 1923; A.F.D. (honorary), Colorado Coll., 1953; m. Mary Osborne Polak. Mar. 17, 1937. Awarded Sachs traveling fellowship and studied scenic prodn. and design in theaters of Europe, 1923-24; under direction of Macgowan, Jones and O'Neill worked in Provincetown Playhouse and Greenwich Village Theatre, 1924-25; first New York prodn. Sooner and Later, a ballet for Neighborhood Playhouse, 1925; prof. emeritus of scenic design Sch. of Drama, Yale; grant from State Dept. to lectr. on theatre and state design in South Am. 1950, Yugoslavia, 1953, Ireland, Iceland, Finland, 1955; Ford Found. grant theatre research 1960. U.S. State Dept. adv. com. on the arts; artist in residence, Am. Acad. Rome, 1953; mem. drama panel cultural presentations program Dept. State, 1963-66. Comdg. capt. AC Camouflage officer (maj.), May 1942, Hdqrs., 2d A.F., Fort George Wright, Spokane, Wash. and Colorado Springs, Colo. On duty overseas Mar., 1945, as combat intelligence office, 315th Bombardment Wing Hdqrs., South Pacific Area. Designed settings for plays, operas, ballets including Good News, Brand, Overture, The Winter's Tale, The Emperor Jones, Uncle Tom's Cabin, The Lady from the Sea, The Farmer Takes a Wife, First Lady, Stage Door, Johnny Johnson, You Can't Take It with You, A Doll's House, I'd Rather Be Right, Of Mice and Men, The Circle, The American Way, Candida, The Man Who Came to Dinner, Claudia, The Doctor's Dilemna, L'Histoire du Soldat (for League of Composers), Three to Make Ready, Pygmalion, Born Yesterday, Years Ago, Park Avenue, Present Laughter, Fatal Weakness, Tristan and Isolde, The Rosenkavalier (for Phila. Orch.), Salome, Amelia Goes to the Ball, Otello, The Abduction from the Seraglio (for Met. Opera), Angel in the Wings, Life with Mother, Goodbye My Fancy, The Father, Sabrina Fair, Coriolanus, Madame Will You Walk, Ballad of Baby Doe, Major Barbara; J.B.; Mary Stuart; The Pleasure of His Company; The Marriage-Go-Round; Orpheus and Eurydice; The Mikado; L'Orfeo (opera); The Prisoner (opera); A Case of Libel; The Irregular Verb To Love; The Lady from Colorado (opera); One by One (officially opened on Broadway under title Spofford); Tosca (opera); Der Rosenkavalier (opera); Antigone (drama). Designer Ft. Worth Performing Arts Center, 1963, Hemis Fair, San Antonio, 1968, also designed the fountains and lighting for N.Y. World's Fair, 1964-65; cons. in theatre architecture: Am. Pavillion Theatre, Brussels World Fair, 1958, Montreal Cultural Center, 1961, Philharmonic Hall, Lincoln Center, New York, 1962, N.Y. State Theatre, Lincoln Center, 1964, Spingold Theatre, Brandeis U., 1965, John F. Kennedy Center for Performing Arts, Washington, 1968, Meeting Center of Albany South Mall Project, 1969, Northwestern High Sch. for Performing Arts, Detroit, 1967, Vilas Communications Hall, U. Wis., 1969, Essex Community Coll., Balt., 1969; lectr. Salsburg Seminar Am. Theatre, 1968, 71. Mem. U.S. nat. commn. for UNESCO, 1963-69, exec. com., 1966-69; mem. Art Commn. of City of New York, 1965-75, pres., 1969-75. Bd. dirs. Bklyn. Inst. Arts and Scis. 1957-75; pres. bd. dirs. Neighborhood Playhouse Sch. of Theater, 1928-63; bd. dirs. MacDowell Assn. 1962-67. Parson Sch. of Design, 1958-70, ANTA (v.p. 1962-69, bd. dirs. 1964-68), Am. Theatre Wing; trustee emeritus Pratt Inst., 1948-75, sec., 1970; bd. dirs., Am. Acad. Dramatic Arts, 1964-75, Mus. City N.Y., 1964-75. Recipient Antoinette Perry award for set design for A Majority of One, 1963-68. Benjamin Franklin fellow Royal Soc. Arts (London); mem. of Municipal Art Soc. (dir. 1954-68), Drawing Soc. (nat. com.), Am. Fedn. of Arts (mem. bd. trustees 1966-75), Master Drawings Assn. (v.p., dir.). Episcopalian. Clubs: Harvard, Century Assn., Grolier, Coffee House; Salmagundi. Author: Scenery, Then and Now, 1936; The Theatre of Ball, 1940. Editor: Notes on Scene Painting, 1952. Home: New York City, N.Y. Died June 21, 1975.

OFFIK, WOLFGANG GEORGE, engr.; b. Davos, Switzerland, May 31, 1913; s. Georg Victor and Frieda (Roth) D.; B.S. in Elec. Engring., Inst. Tech., Karisruhe, Germany, 1934; M.S., Inst. Tech., Stuttgart, Germany, 1939; m. Anna Wuerthner, May 26, 1939; children—Reiner, Karin Erika, Michael Wolfgang. Came to U.S., 1953, naturalized, 1959. Chief advanced design methods Gerhard Fleseler Werke Kassel, Germany, 1938-42; exec. v.p. engring. Bachem-Work Waldsee, Germany, 1942-45; design engr. Lockheed Aircraft, Burbank, Cal., 1953-56; maj. project leader N.Am. Aviation, Inc., Columbus, O., 1956-60; chief tech. analysis sect. Martin Co., Denver 1960-63; sr. staff engr. advanced design Chrysler Corp., Huntsville, Ala., 1964-70; owner Gamco Products, Huntsville, from 1970. Registered profl. engr., Colo., Ala. Asso. fellow Am. Inst. Aeros. and Astronautics; mem. Am. Astronautical Soc. (sr.), Am. Ordnance Assn., Air Force Assn. Home: Huntsville Ala. Died Sept. 9, 1973.

OGDEN, ARTHUR E., physician; b. Boston, 1922; M.D., Boston U., 1948. Surg. intern Boston City Hosp., 1948-49, asso. anesthesiologist, 1953-60; resident in anesthesiology VA Hosp., West Roxbury, Mass., 1949-50, asst. anesthetist, 1950; dir. dept. anesthesiology Cin. Gen. Hosp., Holm's Hosp., Children's Hosp.; cons. anesthesiologist VA Hosp., Cin.; instr. anesthesiology Harvard, 1956-60, Boston U., 1956-60; asso. prof. U. Cin. Served to lt. M.C., USNR, 1950-52. Diplomate Am. Bd. Anesthesiology. Mem. A.M.A., New Eng. Soc. Anesthetists, Am. Soc. Anesthesiologists. Deceased.

OGILVIE, NOEL JOHN, Dominion geodesist, Internat. Boundary commr.; b. Hull, Quebec, Can., Oct. 13, 1880; s. John Charles and Charlotte Amelia (Holt) O.; special training in mathematics, surveying and astronomy; m. Gladys Wallace, Dec. 24, 1907; children—Charlotte (Mrs. Warren Buskard), James, Jane, Noel John, Louise. In charge of surveys of Internat. Boundary, Brit., Columbia, 1904-14; asst. dir. Geodetic Survey, Can., 1914-17, dir., from 1917; in charge of geodetic survey, Brit. Columbia coast, 1915-17; His Britannic Majesty s Internat. Boundary Commr. from 1931. Chmn. Nat. Com. of Can. Internat. Geodetic and Geophysical Union, from 1925. Mem. Engring. Inst. of Can., Royal Astronomical Soc. of Can., Canadian Inst. of Surveying, Am. Soc. of Civil Engrs. Clubs: Rideau, Canadian (Ottawa). Mason. Mem. Aglican Ch. Home: Ottawa, Ont., Can.†

OGILVIE, NORMAN JOHN, glass co. exec.; b. Omaha, Sept. 2, 1916; s. Norman Hugh and Mary (Mead) O.; B.A., Northwestern U., 1938; m. June Clawson, July 27, 1942; children—Norman John, Patricia, James, Bruce, Laurie, Andrew, Mary, Blaine, Stuart, Douglas. Prodn. scheduler Anchor Hocking Glass Corp., Lancaster, O., 1938-41, asst. plant mgr., 1945-49, plant mgr., 1949-61, dir. research and engring., 1961-63, v.p. research and engring., 1963, v.p. tableware mfg., 1963-66, v.p. operations container div., 1966-68, v.p., gen. mgr. container div., 1968-70, exec. v.p., gen. mgr. container group, 1970-72, exec. v.p., gen. mgr. tableware and indsl. products group, from 1972, also dir. Served from pvt. to maj. AUS, 1941-45. Decorated Silver Star medal, Bronze Star medal with oak leaf cluster, Purple Heart with oak leaf cluster. Mem. Newcomen Soc., Sigma Chi. Republican. Roman Catholic. Home: Lancaster, O. Died Dec. 19, 1973.

OGLE, MARBURY BLADEN, educator; b. Howard County, Md., Aug. 23, 1879; s. Richard Lowndes and Fanny D. (Knight) O.; ed. Baltimore City Coll., 1894-99; A.B., Johns Hopkins, 1902, Ph.D., 1907; m. Anetta Iona Fleming, June 14, 1904; children—Marbury Bladen, Robert Bertram, Richard Earl. Asst. prof. Latin, Vermont U., 1907-09, prof., 1909-25; prof. classical languages and chmn. dept., Ohio State U., 1925-34; prof. in charge Sch. Classical Studies, Am. Acad. in Rome, 1931-34; prof. classical langs., chmn. dept. U. Minn., 1934-47, emeritus, from 1947; visiting prof., summers, Columbia U., U. of Chicago, U. of Colo.; winter, Stanford U., 1931. Dir. Am. Philol. Assn., 1936-43, pres. 1943. Mem. Council, Am. Acad. in Rome, from 1936, Middle West and South, Phi Beta Kappa. Episcopalian. Democrat. Club: Campus (U. of Minn.). Author: English and Latin, 1926; co-author: Translation of Walter Man, de Nugis Curialium, 1924; Critical Text of the Poetical Works of Rodulphus Tortarius, 1933. Contbr. to classical mags. Address: Capistrano Beach, Cal.†

O'HARA, JOSEPH PATRICK, congressman; b. Tipton, Ia., Jan. 23, 1895; s. Patrick and Catharine (Doyle) O.; LL.B., U. Notre Dame, 1920; student Inns of Court, London Eng., 1919; m. Leila Lee White, June 18, 1921; children—Joseph Patrick, Jr., Edward, Terrence. Admitted to Minn. bar, 1921, began practice Glencoe, Minn.; county atty., McLeod County, 1934-38; member of 77th to 85th Congresses, 2d Minn. Dist., ret. 1958; practiced law, Washington. Vice chairman, Republican Congressional Committee; member of the board of visitors U.S. Naval Academy. Served in A.E.F. Mem. Am. (ho. of dels. 1941-42), Minn. (v.p. 1940), 8th Jud. Dist. bar assns., Am. Legion (state comdr. 1925-26). Republican. Roman Catholic. Clubs: Crow River Country (Hutchinson, Minn.); Columbia Country Club (Chevy Chase, Maryland). Home: Washington, D.C. Died Mar. 4, 1975.

OHLSON, ALGOTH, coll. pres.; b. Sweden, July 28, 1880; s. Olaus Nilson and Mathilda (Lind) O.; A.B., Yale, 1915; A.M., Harvard, 1916; grad. study, U. of Chicago, 1923-24; LL.D., Augustana Coll., 1942; D.D., Upsala Coll., 1942; m. Ruth Eleanor Carlson, Sept. 6, 1911; children—John Algoth, Alice Eleanor (Mrs. S. L. Cederborg), Carl Venell. Came to U.S., 1900, naturalized citizen, 1907. Ordained ministry Swedish Evang. Covenant, 1915; pastor Lowell, Mass., 1915-18, Chicago, 1918-24; also instr., Union Theol. Coll., 1918-24; pres. North Park College, Chicago, 1924-50. Decorated Knight of the North Star by King of Sweden, 1947. Mem. Nat. Assn. Secondary Sch. Principals. Club: Yale. Home: Chicago, Ill.†

OHM, ROBERT ERVIN, univ. dean; b. Sheboygan, Wis., Oct. 17, 1917; s. Frank B. and Elsie (Kaliebe) O.; B.S. cum laude, U. Wis., 1939, M.S., 1940; Ph.D., U. Chgo., 1962; m. Ruth Boettner, Mar. 19, 1948; children—Susan, Ellen. Tchr. Midlothian (Ill.) Pub. Schs., 1941-42; asso. prof. edn., dir. lab. sch. Antioch Coll., 1946-55; asst. prof. edn., prin. lab. schs. U. Chgo., 1955-60; adminstrv. coordinator MAT program, asst. prof., 1960-61; asso. dir. edn. professions div., prof. ednl. adminstrn. U. Okla., Norman, 1962-67, dean Coll. Edn., dir. edn. professions div., 1967-73. Instl. rep. Am. Assn. Colls. Tchr. Edn.; mem. commn. on edn. for teaching profession Nat. Assn. State Univs. and Land Grant Colls. Bd. dirs. S.W. Alliance for Latin Am. Served to lt. comdr. USNR; 1942-46; ret. Res. Decorated Air gold medal with two gold stars. Mem. Am. Ednl. Research Assn., Am., Okla. assns. sch. adminstrs., Assn. Deans State Univs. and Land Grant Colls., Am. Assn. Higher Edn., Am. Soc. Pub. Adminstrn., Nat. Conf. Profs. Ednl. Adminstrn., Am. Assn. Colls. for Tchr. Edn., Higher Edn. Alumni Council, Phi Delta Kappa. Author: Leadership Games: Secondary Principalship and Elementary Principalship, 1968. Editor: (with D. D. Johns) Negotiations in the Schools, 1965; (with W. G. Monahan) Educational Adminstration-Philosophy in Action, 1964. Contbr. Numerous articles to profl. pubs., chpts. to books Home: Norman, Okla. Died Oct. 14, 1973; cremated.

OISTRAKH, DAVID, violinist; b. Odessa, Russia, 1908; ed. Odessa Conservatory; married; 1 son, Igor. First public appearance as violinist at 12 yrs. of age; made concert tours in USSR and many fgn. countries; soloist with major symphony orchestras in U.S. and abroad; teacher Tschaikowsky Conservatory, Moscow, from 1937. Recipient numerous prizes USSR and fgn. countries, including 1st prize Eugene Ysaye competition (internat.), Brussels, 1937, Stalin prize, 1942. Mem. jury Queen Elizabeth violin competition, Brussels, 1955. Records with Angel, Decca, Vanguard. Home: USSR. Died Oct. 24, 1974.

OJEMANN, RALPH HENRY, psychologist, educator; b. Peoria, Ill., Aug. 30, 1901; s. Rolf Gerdes and Johanna C. (Menninga) O.; B.S., U. Ill., 1923, M.S., 1924; Ph.D., (Fellow in Edn., 1928-29), U. Chgo., 1929; m. Freda Elizabeth Metzger, Aug. 27, 1925; children—Robert Gerdes, George Alvin, Kathryn Elizabeth. Asst. in sci. and edn. U. Ill., 1925-28; asst. prof. edn. U. Kan., summer 1929; asso. prof. psychology and edn. Child Welfare Research Sta., U. Ia., 1929-50, prof., 1950-65; dir. child-ednl.-psychol. preventive div. Cleve. Ednl. Research Council, 1965—; vis. prof. Cleve. State Health Assn., Am. Psychol. Assn., A.A.A.S., Am. Ednl. Research Assn., Am. Assn. Sch. Adminstrs., Nat. Soc. for Study Edn., Soc. Research Child Devel., Midwestern Psychol. Assn., World Fedn. for Mental Health, Royal Soc. Health, Internat. Assn. for child psychiatry and Allied Professions, Nat. Conf. on Family Relations, Nat. Congress of Parents and Teachers. Author: Researches in Parent Edn. II, U. of Ia. Studies Child Welfare, Vol. VIII, 1934, Researches in Parent Edn. III, Vol. X, 1935, Researches in Parent Edn., IV, Vol. XVII, 1939; Personality Adjustments of Individual Children, 1954; Developing a Program for Education in Human Behavior, 1959. Editor: Four Basic Aspects of Preventive Psychiatry, 1957; Recent Contributions of Biological and Psychosocial Investigations to Preventive Psychiatry, 1959; Recent Research Looking Toward Preventive Interventions, 1961; Recent Research on Creative Approaches to Environmental Stress, 1963; The School and the Community Treatment Facility in Preventive Psychiatry, 1965. Editor: Giving Emphasis to Guided Learning, 1967. Mem. editorial bd. Child Development Abstracts and Bibilography, 1937-53. Contbr. articles on adolescent development, ednl. psychol., mental hygiene, and adult edn. to psychol. and ednl. jours. Adult lectr. and discussion leader; researcher in devel. and learning at adolescent and adult levels and edn. in human relations and mental health. Home: Shaker Heights, O. Died Feb. 2, 1975.

O'KEEFE, ABBIE MABEL, physician; b. Portsmouth, N.H., Oct. 31, 1881; d. Cornelius and Ellen (Dwyer) O'Keefe; M.D., Women's Med. Coll. of Pa., 1905. Interne, West Phila. Hosp. for Women, 1905-06; in practice, Boston, 1907-15; resident anesthetist, N.E. Hosp. for Women and Children, 1908-15, asst. surgeon, 1913-15; asso. physician Smith Coll., from 1915; prof. from 1929. Mem. Am. Med. Assn., Internat. Assn. Med. Women, Am. Med. Women's Assn., Inc. (1st v.p. 1937-38), Am. Student Health Assn., Am. Assn. Univ. Women, Alpha Epsilon Iota. Roman Catholic. Club: Women's City (Boston).†

O'KEEFE, RICHARD BERNARD, union ofcl.; b. Salem, Mass., May 9, 1914; s. James P. and Josephine M. (Grant) O'K; grad. high sch.; m. Helene Katherine Reddy, Sept. 3, 1939; children—Mary Louise (Mrs. Paul M. Tuttle), Katherine (Mrs. Richard A. O'Leary), Judith (Mrs. Joseph M. Lubas), Joanne (Mrs. Phillip M. Ricciardiello), Michael. Sec., Local 21 Leather Workers Internat. Union AFL-CIO, Peabody, Mass., 1938-41, pres. Local 21, 1941-42, bus. mgr. Local 21, 1942-55, internat. pres., 1955-73; sec.-treas. Mass. Indsl. Union Council AFL-CIO, 1963-73; exec. v.p. Mass. Labor Council AFL-CIO 1960-65; mem. Nat. AFL-CIO exec. bd. Chmn. Salem Democratic City Com. Dem. candidate U.S. Congress, 1946; councillor at large, Salem, 1969-70. Pres. North Shore Catholic Charities; mem. exec. com. Mass Bay United Fund, Mass. United Community Services, North Shore Mental Health Assn. Mem. Ancient Order Hibernians, New Eng., Mass, police chiefs assn. Home: Salem, Mass. Died Dec. 2, 1973.

O'KELLY, RICHARD MARY, railroad ofcl.; b. London, Eng., Apr. 7, 1915; s. Richard Mary and Margaret (Kiernan) O'K.; came to U.S., 1930, naturalized, 1937; student N.Y. U.; m. Evelyn T. McKenna, Nov. 23, 1946; children—Linda Anne Mary, Richard Mary III, James Mary. With Great No. Ry. Co., 1930-70, asst. sec.-treas., N.Y.C., 1952-57, sec., treas., St. Paul, 1957-70; sec. Burlington No., Inc., St. Paul, 1970-75. Treas. United Way St. Paul; bd. dirs., treas. St. Paul Soc. Blind; bd. dirs. Guest House, Lake Orion, Mich; treas City of Arden Hills. Clubs: St. Paul Athletic. Home: St. Paul, Minn., Died Aug. 10, 1975; interred St. John the Baptist Cemetery, New Brighton, Minn.

OKKELBERG, PETER OLAUS, zoologist; b. Goodhue, Minn., Nov. 12, 1880; s. Bersvend L. and Anne Kjerstina (Hesselberg) O.; A.B., U. of Minn., 1906, A.M., 1909; Ph.D., U. of Mich., 1918; m. Maud Zencie Hagberg, Sept. 2, 1915. Instr. in zoology, U. of Mich., 1910-18, asst. prof., 1918-27, asso. prof., 1927-29, asso. prof. and exec. sec. of dept., 1929-32, prof. and exec. sec. of dept., 1932-33, prof. and sec. Grad. Sch., 1933-36, prof. and asst. dean Grad. School, 1936-47, prof. and asso. dean Grad. School, 1936-47, prof. and asso. dean Graduate School, 1947-51; emeritus, from 1951; asso. dean emeritus Grad. School, from 1951. Mem. Am. Soc. Zoologists, A.A.A.S., Am. Soc. Mammalogists, Mich. Acad. Science, Arts and Letters (editor, 1925-33). Home: Ann Arbor, Mich.†

OLDACRE, WILLIAM ALBERT, lawyer; b. Walker County, Ala., Jan. 21, 1932; s. Daniel Lester and Dorothy (Fountain) O.; B.S. in Commerce, U. Ala., 1953, LL.B. in Law, 1958; m. Sue Alice Eskridge, Jan. 28, 1955; children—William Albert, Nancy Leah, Suzanne, Leslie Dianne. Admitted to Ala. bar, 1958, since practiced in Montgomery; partner firm Hill, Hill, Stovall, Carter & Franco, from 1961. Active Autauga County council Boy Scouts Am. Served to 1st lt. AUS, 19. Mem. Am. Judicature Soc., U. Ala. Alumni Council, Omicron Delta Kappa, Phi Delta Phi, Lambda Chi Alpha. Presbyn. Mason, Lion. Home: Prattville, Ala. Deceased.

O'LEARY, JAMES LEE, neurologist; b. Tomahawk, Wis., Dec. 8, 1904; s. James and Mary (Whalen) O'L; S.B., U. Chgo., 1925, Ph.D., 1928, M.D., 1931; D.Sc. (hon.), Washington U., 1975; m. Nancy Lucas Blair, June 5, 1939; children—Mary Blair, Nancy Lee. Instr. anatomy U. Chgo., 1927-28; asst. prof. anatomy Washington U. Sch. Medicine, St. Louis, 1928-33, asso. prof. neuroanatomy, 1934-42, asso. prof. neurology, 1946, prof. neurology, 1947-75, head dept. 1936-70. Served from maj. to lt. col., M.C., AUS, 1943-46. Recipient Distinguished Service award U. Chgo. Med. Alumni Assn., Lennox award, 1968. Mem. Am. Neurol. Assn. (pres., Jacoby award 1971), Am. Assn. Anatomists, Am. Electroencephalographic Soc., Harvey Cushing Soc. (asso.), Assn. Brit. Neurologist (hon.), Phi Beta Kappa, Alpha Omega Alpha. Author: (with Sidney Goldring) Science and Epilepsy, 1976. Home: St. Louis, Mo. Died May 25, 1975; interred Calvary Cemetery, St. Louis.

OLIVE, JOHN RITTER, sci. orgn. adminstr.; b. Richwood, O., May 26, 1916; s. Archer and Anna (Ritter) O.; B.S., Ohio State U., 1946, M.S., 1947, Ph.D., 1949; D.Sc. (hon.), Colo. State U., 1972; m. Marguerite Petty, Sept. 19, 1940; children—John Kent, Craig William, Marilyn Kay (dec. 1964). Mem. Faculty Ohio State U., 1946-49; prof. zoology, asst. dir. Colo. Research Found., Colo. State U., 1949-59; with Am. Inst. Biol. Scis., from 1959, acting dir., 1962-63, dir., from 1963. Mem. bioinstrumentation adv. council Shark Research Panel, Surtsey (Iceland) Research Soc., from 1965; liaison officer Nat. Acad. Scis.-NRC, from 1963. Served with USAAF, 1942-45. Recipient Sigma Xi Travel award Internat. Limnology Congress, 1953; Oliver P. Pennock Distinguished Service award Abell Hanger Found., 1958; Asso. Students Top Prof. award, 1958; Distinguished Service award Abell-Hanger Found., 1958. Fellow A.A.A.S.; mem. Canadian Soc. Zoologists, Assn. Island Marine Labs., Ecol. Soc. Am., Soc. Limnology and Oceanography, Freshwater Biol. Assn., Internat. Assn. Limnology, Colo.-Wyo. Acad. Sci., Sigma Xi, Xi Sigma Xi, Phi Kappa Phi, Omicron Delta Kappa. Author articles on productivity fresh water lakes. Home: Bethesda, Md. Died Mar. 30, 1974; interred Rushville Cemetery, Rushville, O.

OLIVER, GEORGE JEFFRIES, educator; b. Berryville, Va., Apr. 26, 1898; s. George Hansford and Kate (Cunningham) O.; student U. Richmond, 1916-18; B.A., Coll. William and Mary, 1931; M.A., Columbia, 1936, Ph.D., 1950; m. Clara Ellen Bell, Feb. 3, 1923; 1 son, George Jeffries, Prin. Stevensville (Va.) High Sch., 1919-20, Capeville (Va.) High Sch., 1920-27; div. supt. schs. Northampton County, Va., 1927-37, Henrico County, 1937-38; supr. secondary edn. Va. Dept. Edn., Richmond, 1938-40, dir. instrn., 1940-45; dir. summer session Coll. William and Mary, 1945-52, coordinator br. activities, 1952-59, head dept. edn., dir. extension, 1945-59; provost Richmond Professional Insti, 1959-62, pres., 1962-67. Member board of visitors U.S. Army Transportation School, Fort Eustis, Virginia. Served as officer F. A., U.S. Army, World War I. Mem. So. Assn. Colls. and Secondary Schs. (exec. com.), Nat. Soc. Study Edn., Assn. Supervision and Curriculum Development, Eastern Shore of Va. Hist. Soc., Soc. Cincinnati, Association of Virginia Colleges (pres. 1963-64), Phi Beta Kappa, Phi Delta Kappa, Kappa Delta Pi, Episcopalian. Home: Williamsburg, Va. Died June 15, 1973.

OLIVER, WILLIAM BURNS, food products mfg. exec.; b. Chateaugay, N.Y., Oct. 3, 1911; s. T. Arthur and Myrtle Viola (Burns) O.; B.S., Ind. U., 1934; m. Agnes Cluthe, Sept. 28, 1934. Auditor, Haskins & Sells, N.Y.C., also Atlanta, 1935-39; sec.-treas. H. W. Lay & Co., Inc. (co. became Frito-Lay, Inc. in 1961), Atlanta, 1939-42, v.p. sales, 1946-50, exec. v.p., 1950-61, exec. v.p., dir., Dallas, 1961-66, pres., dir., from 1966, chmn. bd., 1967-72; v.p., dir. PepsiCo, Inc. Pres., Internat. Potato Chip Inst.; dir. Atlanta Freight Bur. Budget com. United Fund, Atlanta; mem. exec. bd. Circle Ten council Boy Scouts Am.; mem. adv. bd. Salvation Army. Bd. dirs. Jr. Achievement Dallas, Jr. Achievement of Ga. Served to maj. USAAF, 1942-46. Mem. Lambda Chi Alpha. Presbyn. Mason (Shriner). Clubs: Brook Hollow Golf, Preston Trail Golf (Dallas). Home: Dallas, Tex. Died Oct. 24, 1974.

OLIVIER, CHARLES POLLARD, astronomer; b. Charlottesville, Va. Apr. 10, 1884; s. George Wythe and Katherine Roy (Pollard) O.; A.B., U. Va., 1905, A.M., 1908, Ph.D., 1911; grad. study U. Cal., 1909-10; m. Mary Frances Pender, Oct. 18, 1919 (dec. 1934); children—Alice Dorsey (Mrs. A.E. Hayes) Elise Pender (Mrs. E.O. Ferris); m. 2d, Ninuzza Seymour, Oct. 23, 1936; m. 3d, Mrs. Margaret Ferguson Austin, July 24, 1950. Prof. astronomy and physics Agnes Scott Coll., 1911-14; asst. prof. astronomy U. Va., 1914-23, asso. prof., 1923-28; prof. astronomy, dir. Flower Obs., U. Pa., 1928-54, Cook Obs., U. Pa., 1940-54, emeritus, 1954-75; founder, emeritus pres. Am. Meteor Soc.; active Internat. Geophys. Year. Served with U.S. Army, 1918-19. Mem. Am. Astron. Soc., Internat. Astron. Union (chmn. meteor commn. 1924-34), Am. Philos. Soc., Société Astronomique de France, Meteoritical Soc. (past mem. council), Va. Acad. Sci., Rittenhouse Astron. Soc. (past pres.), Raven Soc., Phi Beta Kappa, Sigma Xi, Sigma Alpha Epsilon. Constitutional. Episcopalian Colonnade (U. Va.); Faculty (U. Pa.). Author: Meteors, 1925; Comets, 1930. Contbr. to publs. of Leander McCormick Obs., Lick Obs. Bulls., Flower Obs. Publs. and reprints; also articles in jours. and encyclopedia. Home: Narberth, Pa. Died Aug. 14, 1975; interred Charlottesville, Va.

OLIVIER, STUART, newspaper pub.; b. Staunton, Va., July 2, 1880; s. Warner Lewis and Martha (Statton) O.; ed. U. of Va., 1897-99; m. Sarah Reeside, June 12, 1905; children—Stuart, Ann Fox. Began as reporter on Baltimore News and advanced to pub. and gen. mgr.; later brought chain of middle west newspapers, sold them, 1934. Clubs: Maryland, Elkridge, Harford. Contbr. to mags. and author of several successful plays. Address: Baltimore, Md.†

OLSEN, HERB, artist; b. Chgo., July 12, 1905; s. Louis M. and Ida Marie (Westeen) O.; student pub. schs.; m. Doris Anderson, May 4, 1935. Works exhibited in numerous one-man shows; exhibited in group shows in all major museums; represented in collections of Grand Central Kennedy & Co., N.Y.C., also Camelback Galleries, Phoenix, Arizona, and others. Recipient 1st prize Nat. Acad. Design, 1949, Obrig award, 1953; 1st prize Hudson Valley, 1951, Gold medal, 1953; Gold medal Swedish-Am. Exhibit, 1953, Silver medal, 1952; 1st prize laymans award Salmagundi Club, 1951, Ranger Fund purchase award, 1953; 1st prize All New Eng. for water color, 1953; Fairchild award Conn. Water Color Soc., 1954; A.N.A., 1949, Silvermine award Salmagundi Club, 1955, 1st prize for water color, 1957; 2d prize New Haven R.R. Competition, 1956; Digby Chandler award Allied Artists of America, 1956; purchase prize Grumbacher-Audubon Artists, 1957; 1st prize Balt. Water Color Soc., 1957; award Nat. Inst. Architects, 1957; 1st prize Hudson Valley, 1960, also Springville Nat. Exhbn., Utah, 1960; Ranger Fund purchase award, 1961; Gold medal Hudson Valley, 1962; Digby Chandler award Allied Artists Am., 1962; Edwin Palmer Meml. prize N.A.D.; 2d award Utah Invitational and Museum Purchase, 1964, 1st prize, 1965; Purchase award Columbus Mus. Fellow Royal Soc. Arts London; mem. Am. (Watercolor U.S.A. award 1972), Phila., Balt., Conn. water color socs., Artists and Writers, Authors Guild. Club: Salmagundi (N.Y.C.). Author: Watercolor Made Easy; Painting the Figure in Water Color, 1958; Painting Children in Water Color, 1961; Herb Olsen's Guide to Watercolor Landscape, 1965; Painting the Marine Scene in Watercolor, 1967. Home: Westport, Conn. Died Nov. 12, 1973; interred Chicago, Ill.

OLSEN, WILLIAM ANDERSON, educator; b. Copengagen, Denmark, Dec. 15, 1896; s. Thorwald Peter and Anna Louise (Anderson) O.; A.B., Cornell U., 1923; A.M., U. N.C., 1928; m. Sarah Louise Duncan; Aug. 31, 1925; children—William Anderson, Daniel Duncan. Instr. English, U. N.C. at Chapel Hill, 1923-29, asst. prof., 1929-37, asso. prof., 1937-41, became prof., 1941, later prof. emeritus, also head of speech div., 1947-56; instr. Ia. State U., 1925. Served with USNRF, 1918-19. Mem. Speech Assn. Am., Pi Kappa Phi. Democrat. Club: University North Carolina Faculty (organizer, 1st pres.). Home: Chapel Hill, N.C. Died Jan. 1, 1974.

OLSON, NORMAN O., accountant; B.A., St. Olaf Coll.; M.A., U. Minn.; m.; children—Laurel Sue, Lizbeth, Laird, Lance, Linden. With Arthur Andersen & Co., Chgo., first as accountant, later as partner. Trustee Lutheran Gen. Hosp., Chgo. C.P.A., Ill. Mem. Am. Inst. C.P.A.'s (mem. com. auditing procedure), St. Olaf Coll. Alumni Assn. (pres.), Am. Hist. Assn. (dir.). Co-author: Accounting for Goodwill; In Pursuit of Professional Goals. Home: Palatine, Ill. Died Oct. 24, 1974.

OLSON, RAYMOND, ins. co. exec.; b. Chgo., June 11, 1904; s. Edwin A. and Mae (Fitzgerald) O.; student U. Mich., 1922-26, Northwestern U. Law Sch., 1926-29; m. Virginia C. I. Ericsson, May 19, 1931; children—Raymond, Judith (Mrs. David T. Uehling), Lynn, Elisabeth. Admitted to Ill. bar, 1929, practiced in Chgo.; mem. firm Olson & Olson, from 1933; counsel Mut. Trust Life. Ins. Co., Chgo., from 1931, pres., 1943-64, chmn. bd., 1964-69. Mem. Assn. Life Insurance Counsel (hon.). Clubs: Legal, Chicago (Chgo.); Skokie (Ill.) Country. Home: Glencoe, Ill. Died Apr. 25, 1974.

OLSON, ROY HOWARD, lawyer; b. Chgo., Jan. 16, 1896; s. Andrew and Augusta Matilda (Johnson) O.; student Northwestern U., 1915-16; B.S., U. Minn., 1923; B.S. in Elec-Engring., U. Minn., 1923, postgrad., 1923-25; J.D., Chgo. Kent Coll. Law, 1927; m. Muriel Sommermeyer, Aug. 29, 1927; children—Dean McBride, Gwendolyn. Asso. with Bradbury & Caswell, patent lawyers, Mpls., 1923-25; patent dept. Western Electric Co., Chgo., 1925-28, Cheever & Cox, patent lawyers, Chgo., 1928-32, Cox, Moore & Olson, and successor firm Moore, Olson & Trexler, 1932-53; sr. partner Olson; Trexler, Wolters & Bushnell. Hon. mem., pres. bd. Presbyn. Home; trustee Kent Coll. Law. Served with II Corps Hosp. Unit 12, France, 1917-19. Mem. Am., Chgo. bar assns., Am. Patent Law Assn., U. Minn. Alumni Assn., Am. Legion, Theta Tau, Phi Alpha Delta, Eta Kappa Nu, Acacia. Presbyn. Mason. Clubs: Exmoor Country; Union League, Chicago Yacht; Sheridan Shore Yacht (commodore); Great Lakes Cruising (commodore). Home: Highland Park, Ill. Died Feb. 5, 1974.

OLYPHANT, JOHN KENSETT, JR., banker; b. N.Y.C., Oct. 2, 1895; s. John Kensett and Nannie Humphreys (Heilman) O.; A.B., Harvard, 1918; m. Adele Sloane Hammond, Feb. 5, 1927; children—Adele, David, John Vernon Bevan. Vice chmn., trustee Hanover Bank, N.Y.C.; dir. N.J. Zinc Co., Eagle Fire Co. N.Y., United Fruit Co., Greenfield Tap and Die Co. Mem. N.Y. County Rep. Com. Vice pres., trustee Boys' Club N.Y.; trustee James Found. N.Y., Inc. Commd. 1st lt. inf. O.R.C., Nov. 1916; advanced to capt. inf. O.R.C. Aug. 1917; asst. instr. and instr. 1st, 2d, third officers training schs., Plattsburg Barracks and Camp Upton, N.Y.; commanded K Co. 306th inf., 77th div., A.E.F. Episcopalian. Clubs: Harvard, River, India House. Home: Dongan Hills, S.I., N.Y. Died Oct. 5, 1973; buried Greenwood Cemetery, Bklyn.

O'MALLEY, FRANCIS JOSEPH, educator, editor; b. Clinton, Mass., Aug. 19, 1911; s. Michael Francis and Ellen (Tierney) O'M.; A.B. maxima cum laude, U. Notre Dame, 1932, A.M. maxima cum laude, 1933,

LL.D., 1971; L.H.D., St. Benedict's Coll., 1960. Successively instr., asst. prof., asso. prof., prof. English, Univ. of Notre Dame, 1933-74, also co-organizer of program in Philosophy of Lit. in dept. of English, 1938; co-founder, mng. and asso. editor. Rev. of Politics, from 1938. Recipient Ann. Faculty award for distinguished service U. Notre Dame, 1957, Charles Sheedy award for excellence in teaching Coll. Arts and Letters, 1970. Democrat. Roman Catholic. Contbr. to periodicals; author studies of William Blake, Cardinal Newman, Georges Bernanos, Leon Bloy, others. Home: Notre Dame, Ind. Died May 7, 1974.

O'MALLEY, JOSEPH EDWARD, physician; b. St. Louis, 1923; M.D., U. Md., 1950. Intern, St. Francis Hosp., Hartford, Conn., 1950-51; resident in gen. surgery VA Hosp., New Orleans, 1951-53; resident in plastic surgery Owens Clinic Plastic and Reconstructive Surgery, 1953-55; courtesy staff Touro Infirmary, Eye Ear Nose and Throat Hosp., Charity Hosp. (all New Orleans), Orange Meml. Hosp., Winter Park Hosp., Fla. Sanitarium and Hosp., Seminole Meml. Hosp., West Orange Meml. Hosp., Claremont Hosp. (all Orlando, Fla.); asst. in surgery (plastic surgery) Tulane U., 1953-55. Diplomate Am. Bd. Plastic Surgery. Fellow A.C.S.; mem. A.M.A., So. Med. Assn., Am. Soc. Plastic and Reconstructive Surgery, Am. Soc. Aesthetic Plastic Surgery. Home: Orlando, Fla. Died June 1973.

ONASSIS, ARISTOTLE SOCRATES, shipowner, business exec.; b. 1906; ed. Evangeliki Scholl, Smyrna; m. Athina Livanos, 1946 (div. 1961); children—Alexander (dec.), Christina; m. 2d, Jacqueline Lee Bouvier Kennedy, Oct. 20, 1968. With members of family who escaped sacking of Smyrna, 1922, went first to Greece, then Buenos Aires, 1923; engaged in tobacco bus. merchandising; became Greek consul, Buenos Aires; negotiated purchase of first ships, Can., 1932-33; ordered first tanker, Sweden, 1936; following end of World War II, built numerous supertankers, U.S., France, Germany, Japan; holder of interest in Société des Bains de Mer, Monte Carlo. Home: Skorpios, Greece. Died Mar. 15, 1975; buried Skorpios.

O'NEIL, JAMES JULIAN, surgeon; b. Council Bluffs, Ia., Jan. 20, 1919; s. William Joseph and Emma (Dutcher) O'N.; B.S.M., Creighton U., 1941, M.D., 1943; m. Rosemary Elizabeth O'Neil, Aug. 5, 1943; children—James J., Robert Hugh. Intern, Meml. Hosp., Wilmington, Del., 1943-44; resident U. Ill., 1946-47, Ill. Eye and Ear Infirmary, Chgo., 1947-48; pvt. practice, Omaha, 1948-74. Pres. Mid-Am. Otolaryngologic Labs., Inc., Omaha Profl. Publs., Omaha. Cons. Union Pacific Strategic Air Command; examiner FAA; mem. exec. bd. Neb. Blue Shield, from 1956. Chmn. Neb. Deafness Research Found.; founder St. Vincent's Home for Aged; trustee Drs. Hosp. Served with M.C., AUS, 1943-46. Recipient award of merit Am. Cancer Soc. Diplomate Am. Bd. Otolaryngology. Fellow A.C.S.; mem. Internat. Coll. Surgeons (regent from 1962), Royal Soc. Medicine (London), Am. Coll. Chest Physicians. Editor Neb. Med. Jour., from 1958. Contbr. articles to jours. Home: Omaha, Neb. Died Oct. 15, 1974.

O'NEIL, LEW DREW, educator; b. Boston, July 19, 1881; s. Phillip Ambrose and Mary Elizabeth (Drew) O'N.; A.B., Boston Coll., 1902, A.M., 1917, Ph.L., 1918; student Columbia, 1903-06; m. Alice Barnet Cahill, Sept. 22, 1917; children—Burton Leo, Martha. Began as engr. Gen. Electric Co., 1906; treas. Burke, Deutsch & Co., 1907, Cauto Produce Co., 1908-10, St. Louis Supply Co., 1911; mem. O'Neil, Alden & Hindenlang, investments, 1911-14; lecturer and writer Investment Bankers Bur., 1915-16; with economics dept., Boston U., 1917, head of dept. 1926-44, dir. eve. div. U., 1924-39, dir. Eve. Coll. Commerce, 1939-44 (leave absence 1943-44); prof. Newton (Mass.) Junior Coll. Chief examining and personnel utilization div. First Regional United States Civil Service Commn.; 1943-45 supervisor ferrous and non-ferrous metals sect., Reconstruction Finance Corp., Boston, Mem. U.S. Army Service Forces Survey Team, U.S. Navy Manpower Survey Command. First Naval Dist. Mem. Am. Economic Assn., Am. Assn. Univ. Teachers of Insur., Delta Phi Epsilon (past nat. pres.), Phi Chi Theta, Theta Kappa Phi (hon.). Mem. Boston C. of C., Boston Life Underwriters Assn. (hon.), Boston chapter Chartered Life Underwriters (exec. com.). Club: Executives. Home: Needham Heights, Mass.†

O'NEILL, JAMES ALBERT, utility co. exec.; b. Syracuse, N.Y., Dec. 7, 1917; s. Albert T. and Helen F. (Lynch) O'N.; B.B.A., Manhattan Coll., 1939; LL.B., U. Buffalo, 1942; m. Virginia E. Ronan, Sept. 29, 1942; children—James P., Thomas J., Peter J., Andrew R., Michael, Mary Ann, Kathleen, Monica. Admitted to N.Y. bar, 1942; spl. agt. FBI, 1942-46; atty. Buffalo Niagara Electric Corp. (now Niagara Mohawk Power Corp.), 1946-50, sr. and gen. atty. central div., Syracuse, 1956-66, adminstrv. v.p. western div., Buffalo, 1966-68, pres. corp., dir., 1968-73, chief exec. officer, 1971-73; dir., v.p. Canadian Niagara Power Co. Ltd., 1966-73; v.p., dir. Utilities Mut. Ins. Co., N.Y.C.; dir. Marine Midland Banks, Inc., Buffalo. Bd. dirs. Empire State Atomic Devel. Assos., Edison Electric Inst., Community-Gen. Hosp. Greater Syracuse; mem. exec. com. Northeast Power Coordinating Council; chmn. exec. com. N.Y. Power Pool; bd. regents Le Moyne Coll.; vice chmn. bd. trustees Niagara U. Mem. N.Y. State, Am., Onondaga County bar assns., Am. Judicature Soc., Asso. Industries N.Y. State, Nat. Alliance Businessmen, Assn. Governing Bds. Univs. and Colls. Clubs: Century, Onondaga Golf and Country (Syracuse); Buffalo; Oswelewgois, Herschel Fishing; Board Room (N.Y.C.): Fort Orange (Albany). Home: Fayetteville, N.Y. Died Apr. 28, 1973; buried St. Mary's Cemetery, DeWitt, N.Y.

OPPELT, WOLFGANG WALTER, physician; b. Bochum, Germany, Apr. 22, 1933; s. Walter Hans and Claire Oppelt; B.A., U. N.D., 1955, B.S., 1956; M.D., Harvard, 1958; m. Ursula Ruckes, Feb. 1, 1964; children—Suzanne Margaret, Peter William. Research asst., Nat. Found. fellow depts. physiology and biochemistry U. N.D., summers 1955-57, vis. prof. Sch. Medicine, 1970; med. intern Peter Bent Brigham Hosp., Boston, 1958-59, asst. resident in internal medicine, 1959-60, sr. resident, 1963-64; clin. asso. clin. pharmacology and exptl. therapeutics sect. Nat. Cancer Inst., NIH, Bethesda, Md., 1960-63; asso. in physiology George Washington U. Sch. Medicine, Washington, 1962-63; asst. in medicine Harvard Med. Sch., 1963-64; asst. prof. pharmacology and medicine U. Fla. Coll. Medicine, Gainesville, 1964-68, asso. prof., 1968-70, prof., 1970-73, chief div. clin. pharmacology, 1966-73, dir. clin. research center, 1970-73; head med. oncology program, 1973; chmn. pharmacy and therapeutics com. J. Hillis Miller Health Center, 1967-73, mem. tumor bd., 1964-73; dir. med. dept. Lakeside Labs., Milw., 1973-74. Mem. cancer task force Fla. Regional Med. Programs, 1968-70; vis. prof. Inst. for Toxicology, U. Tubingen (Germany), 1968-69. Served to surgeon USPHS, 1960-63. Recipient Burroughs-Wellcome award in clin. pharmacology, 1966-71; named Outstanding Prof. in Basic Scis., U. Fla. Coll. Medicine Class of 1969, One of 5 Outstanding Tchrs., Class of 1974. Diplomate Am. Bd. Internal Medicine. Mem. A.M.A., Wis., Milwaukee County med. socs., Am. Fedn. Clin. Research, Am. Therapeutic Soc., A.A.A.S., Soc. Gen. Physiologists, Am. Soc. Pharmacology and Exptl. Therapeutics, Am. Coll. Clin. Pharmacology (regent) So. Soc. Clin. Investigation, Phi Beta Kappa, Sigma Xi, Alpha Omega Alpha. Home: Milwaukee, Wis., Died Feb. 8, 1974; buried Cabot, Pa.

OPPENHEIM, ADOLF LEO, educator, Assyriologist; b. Vienna, Austria, June 7, 1904; s. Alfred and Johanna (Rotter) O.; Ph.D., U. Vienna, 1933; m. Elizabeth Munk, Nov. 9, 1930. Came to U.S., 1941, naturalized, 1946. Lexicographical research work Assyriology, U. Vienna, Coll. de France (Paris), 1938-39; mem. staff Oriental Inst., U. Chgo., 1947-73, prof. Assyriology, editor-in-chief Assyrian Dictionary, also dir. Assyrian Dictionary project, 1954-73, John A. Wilson Distinguished Service prof., 1969-73. Recipient Gordon Laing award U. Chgo. Press, 1966. Fellow Brit. Acad. (corr.). Author: Untersuchungen zum babylonischen Mietrecht, 1936; Catalogue of the cuneiform tablets....in N.Y. Pub. Library, 1948; The Interpretation of Dreams in the Ancient Near East, 1956 (French transl. 1959); Ancient Mesopotamia, 1964 (French transl. 1970); Letters from Mesopotamia, 1967; Glass and Glassmaking in Ancient Mesopotamia, 1970. Home: Berkeley, Cal. Died July 21, 1974.

OPPENHEIMER, FRANCIS J. (FRANCIS OPP), writer, caricaturist; b. New York, Mar. 23, 1881; s. Moses and Elizabeth Marie (Gilmore) O.; student Coll. City of N.Y. (short time); business coll.; pvt. study of philosophy; m. Beatrice Bisno, 1920. Specialized in foreign criminology; lecturer on lit. social and philos. subjects. Asso. mng. dir. Nat. Liberal Immigration League, part of 1906-07, also studied immigration in France, England, Ireland and Italy, 1925; press rep. of Bd. of Estimate and Apportionment, City of New York, 1910; lit. editor The News Letter, New York, 1911. Mgr. Municipal Expn. given by the City of N.Y. Was asso. editor of "The Modern Theatre." Organized, 1909, Dental Hygiene Exhibit for the Dental Hygiene Council of State of N.Y., in conjunction with Assn. Improving Condition of the Poor. Spl. work for New York U., 1916; dir. civic exhibit, Coll. City of N.Y., 1917; with Commn. on Training Camp Activities, War and Navy Depts., 1918; asso. dir. U.S. War Expn., 1918; spl. writer Magazine of Wall Stree, 1920; member editorial staff of New York Evening Mail, 1923; special writer for Success Magazine, 1924-25. Originator of League of Ideas. Author: History of Restriction of Immigration; The Failure of Pacifism; The New Tyranny. Spl. investigations of the Jews of Greater New York, and has written articles on their temples, philanthropies, wealth and success in the arts and professions. Contbr. to mags. and newspapers. Home: Floral Park, L.I., N.Y.†

OPPICE, HAROLD WHINERY, dentist; b. Marshalltown, Ia., Jan. 14, 1895; s. Joseph S. and Elizabeth M. (Whinery) O.; student Northwestern U. Dental Sch., 1914-17; D.D.S., Chicago Coll. of Dental Surgery, Loyola U., 1920; m. Janet Brown, Sept. 17, 1917 (died July 15, 1950); children—Robert B., Ruth Caroline (Mrs. Lawrence Miller). Gen. practice dentistry, Marshalltown, Ia., 1920-24, Chicago from 1924; mem. faculty Chicago Coll. of Dentistry, Loyola U., from 1924, prof. of crown and fixed bridge prosthesis from 1945; cons. surgeon gen., U.S. Army from 1950, dept. of medicine, U.S. Navy, from 1950. Trustee Village of Lincolnwood from 1949. Fellow Am. Coll. of Dentists (hon.); mem. Am. Dental Assn. (chmn. nat. health program com., 1939-41, mem. bd. trustees, 1944-49, pres., 1950-51), Ill. State Dental Soc. (mem. exec. counsel, 1934-37, editor, 1937-40), Chicago Dental Soc. (treas., 1940-41, sec., 1941-43, pres., 1944-45), Chicago Odontographic Soc., Ki Psi Phi (supreme sec. and treas., 1939-48), Omicron Kappa Upsilon. Mason (master 1936). Club: Lions (Lincolnwood). Home: Omaha, Neb., Died Jan. 25, 1976.

O'REILLY, EDWARD SYNNOTT, soldier, writer; b. Denison, Tex., Aug. 15, 1880; s. Daniel H. and Mary A. (Synnott) O.; pub. schs. of Tex. and Chicago; m. Sophia Blakeney, May 28, 1905; children—John Daniel, Edward B. Engaged in newspaper work at Chicago, St. Louis and San Antonio, Tex.; managing editor of the San Antonio Light, Joliet (Ill.) Herald-News; staff corr. Associated Press, Mexico and Chicago; war corr. in many countries. With U.S. Army in Cuba and Philippines, Spanish-Am. War, 1898; drill instr. Chinese Imperial Army, 1901-02; officer in Mexican Army, 1913-14; maj., Tex. N.G., from 1918. Chevalier Legion of Honor (France). Author: Roving and Fighting, 1918; The Grail-a play (with George Scarborough); Shanghai Bound (novel and motion picture. Home: New York City, N.Y.†

ORME, JAMES BOOTH LOCKWOOD, ret. lawyer; b. Washington, July 31, 1884; s. William B. and Julia (Lockwood) O.; B.S., Mass. Inst. Tech., 1906; postgrad. George Washington U., 1909-10, N.Y. Law Sch., 1912; m. Violet Dewey Young Gentry, Nov. 30, 1964. Admitted to N.Y. bar, 1925; with patent div. Allied Chem. & Dye Corp., 1926-29; mem. firm Ward, Haselton, McElhannon, Orme, Brooks & Fitzpatrick, N.Y.C., 1937-72. Served with U.S. Army, 1917-19. Mem. Am. Bar Assn. (past pres.), N.Y. Patent Law Assn. Republican. Mem. P.E. Ch. Clubs: Union, Metropolitan Opera, Amateur Comedy (past pres.); Beach, Everglades Bath and Tennis (Palm Beach). Home: Palm Beach Fla. Died Dec. 18, 1973.

ORMOND, JESSE MARVIN, clergyman, educator; b. Greene County, N.C., Jan. 20, 1878; s. John James and Nancy Jane (Cuninggim) O.; A.B., Trinity Coll. (now Duke U.), Durham, N.C., 1902; B.D., Vanderbilt, 1910; student Divinity Sch., U. of Chicago, summer, 1909; D.D., Randolph Macon Coll., Ashland, Va., 1939; m. Katrina Kern, June 23, 1910; children—John Kern, Janet, Margaret, Jessie Katrina, Elizabeth Eskridge. Ordained ministry M.E. Ch. S., 1910; various pastorates until 1921; prof. pastorial theology, Southern Meth. U., Dallas, Tex., 1921-22; prof. practical theology, School of Religion (now Div. Sch.), Duke U., 1923-48, ret.; secretary Duke Commn. from 1926, Trustee N.C. Conf. Meth. Ch. from 1912, sec.-treas. from 1925; bd. of edn., same, 1914-22, bd. of missions, from 1922, gen. bd. of missions and church extension, from 1940; mem. Gen. Conf. M.E. Ch., S., 1930, 34, 38, and chmn. N.C. delegation; mem. Uniting Conf., Meth. Ch., 1939, Gen. Conf., 1940, 44. Mem. Am. Sociol. Soc., Am. Country Life Assn., Scholarship Fraternity of Duke U., Kappa Alpha, Phi Beta Kappa, Pi Gamma Mu. Theta Phi. Mason. Author: The Country Church in North Carolina, 1931; By the Waters of Bethesda, 1936. Home: Durham, N.C.†

ORR, ROBERT MCDANIEL, librarian; b. Springfield, Ill., Aug. 21, 1913; s. James Riggs and Elizabeth (McDaniel) O.; A.B., U. Ill., 1936, B.S. in L.S., 1937; m. Helen Edith Smith, May 29, 1941; children—Susan, Robert, John, Michael. Jr. asst. Detroit Pub. Library, 1937-39; asst. extension librarian Lincoln Library, Springfield, 1939-40; dist. librarian Work Projects Adminstrn., 1940-41; dist. librarian Ill. State Library, 1945-47; librarian, Branch County, Mich., 1947-49; dir. pub. libraries Grosse Pointe (Mich.) Sch. Dist., 1949-73. Served with AUS, 1941-45. Mem. Mich. Library Assn. (pres. 1951-52), A.L.A., Grosse Pointe Businessmens Assn. Rotarian (pres. 1957-58). Episcopalian (lay reader). Contbr. articles to profl. jours. Home: Grosse Pointe, Mich. Died Aug. 1, 1973; buried at Buffalo, Ill.

ORROK, DOUGLAS HALL, educator; b. Arlington, N.J., Feb. 10, 1906; s. Robert Hall and Margaret (Paton) O.; B.A., Amherst Coll., 1928; M.A., Columbia, 1929, Ph.D., 1935. Mem. faculty Tex. Tech. Coll., 1936-38, Wilkes Coll., Wilkes-Barre, Pa., 1939-46; prof. French Bucknell U., from 1946. Home: Winfield, Pa., Died Oct. 5, 1975.

OSBORNE, ERNEST LESLIE, army officer, mgmt. cons.; b. Denver, Mo., June 15, 1889; s. Jerome Monroe and Flora (Harroun) O.; Ph.B., Yale, 1912; S.B., Mass. Inst. Tech., 1914; student Pace Inst., 1919-20; LL.B., La Salle Extension U., 1922; postgrad. Columbia, 1933-34; m. Gladys Maria Fogg, Jan. 1, 1920; 1 dau., Phyllis Marie (Mrs. Herbert Orville Whitten). Field engr. Pub. Service Commn., N.Y.C., 1914-15; engr. Gunn, Richards & Co., N.Y.C., 1915-16; partner Woodling & Osborne, N.Y.C., Newark, Boston, 1920-21; specialist charge merchandising and mgmt. research, and statistics James W. Eadie Jr., Boston, 1921-29; controller Hahn Dept. Stores, Inc., N.Y.C., 1929-30; controller, sec., treas. Dictograph Products Co., Inc., N.Y.C., 1931-33; chmn. adv. group Nat. Recovery Adminstrn., also Dept. Commerce, Washington, 1934-36; econ. and statis. analyst ICC, Washington, 1936; sr.

tech. adviser, mgmt. engr. Social Security Bd., Washington, 1936-41; mgmt. engr., col. Dept. Army, Washington, 1949-59; mgmt. counsellor, Washington, from 1959; cons. economist Research Council, Controllers Inst. Am., 1933-38. Served as lt. U.S. Army, 1912-13, major, 1916-19, col. AUS, 1941-49. Recipient Certificate Achievement, Dept. Army, 1959; Outstanding Service certificate Am. Soc. Mil. Comptrollers, 1957; decorated Imperial Cross St. Nicholas. Mem. Am. Soc. Mil. Comptrollers (sec., pres. Washington, life mem. nat. council), U.S. Capitol Hist. Soc., S.A.R., Transp. Research Forum, Royal Statistical Soc. (London), Am. Soc. Mil. Comptrollers, Am. Legion, Assn. U.S. Army, Sigma Xi, Theta Tau, Phi Gamma Delta. Republican. Mem. Christian Ch. Clubs: Mass. Institute of Technology (v.p. 1957-59), Yale (Washington). Editor: Standard Accounting Guide, 1928. The Armed Forces Comptroller, 1956-57. Home: Washington, D.C. Died Mar. 20, 1973.

OSBORNE, FRANK WELLMAN, editor; b. Lynn, Mass., Apr. 18, 1878; s. Wellman and Ellen M. (Rolfe) O.; A.B., Harvard, 1899; m. Margherite O. Cassino, Mar. 7, 1910. Editor Black Cat (mag.), from 1913. Club: Oxford (Lynn). Home: Salem, Mass.†

OSBORNE, MARGHERITA OSBORN, editor; b. Peabody, Mass., Nov. 27, 1878; d. Samuel Edson and Melvina King (Osborn) Cassino; ed. Peabody High Sch. and Radcliffe Coll.; m. Dana Lamper Forbes, Apr. 25, 1899 (died Dec. 13, 1902); children—Dana Lamper, Mrs. Margherita Cassino Redfield; m. 2d, Frank Wellman Osborne, May 7, 1910. Editor Everyday Housekeeping, 1908-11; editor Little Folks Magazine 1908-25; editor book publs. of P. F. Volland Co. Home: Lynn, Mass.†

OSGOOD, ROBERT WILLIAM, electronic component co. exec.; b. Endeavor, Pa., Feb. 9, 1920; s. James Edward and Sarah Elizabeth (Gimmel) O.; grad. high sch.; m. Marie Anne Washek, Nov. 27, 1943; 1 dau., Nancy Kathleen. Tool and mold maker Warren Plastics Corp. (Pa.), 1944-54, machine shop supt., 1954-56; plant mgr. Warren Components div. El-Tronics, Inc., 1956-59, gen. mgr., 1959-61, divisional pres., 1961-68, gen. mgr. Monarch Fuse div., 1965-67; became co-owner, v.p., gen. mgr. Warren Components Corp., 1968, pres. until 1973; dir. White Avionics Corp., L.I., N.Y., 1962-64. Recipient Vendor of Year award Gen. Electric Co., 1964. Mem. Soc. Mfg. Engrs. (chmn. constn. and by laws), Soc. Plastics Engrs. Republican. Moose. Patentee in field. Experimented in rotary plastic molding, semi-conductors, header design, glass to metal sealing techniques. Home: Warren, Pa. Died Jan. 30, 1973; interred St. Joseph's Cemetery, Warren.

OSGOOD, SAMUEL MAURICE, educator, historian; b. Middleboro, Mass., Mar. 2, 1920; s. Samuel P. and Henriette (Gufflet) O.; B.A., U. Nev., 1949; M.A., Clark U., 1951, Ph.D. in History, 1953; m. Sara Ann Gordon, May 22, 1948; children—Philip Gordon, Steven Gordon. Mem. faculty Clark U., 1952-54, Brown U., 1954-58, Drexel Inst. Tech., 1958-66; prof. history, chmn. dept. State U. Coll. at Geneseo, N.Y., 1966-68; prof. modern European history Kent (O.) State U., 1968-75. Fulbright lectr. univs. Bordeaux, Grenoble and Lyon (France), 1964-65, univ. Paris-Nanterre and Nantes (France), 1965-66. Served with USNR, 1941-45. Research grantee Am. Philos. Soc., 1956, 57, 61, 68. Mem. Am. Hist. Assn., Soc. French Hist. Studies, A.A.U.P., Ohio Acad. History, Soc. d'Histoire Moderne, Soc. des Professeurs Francais en Amerique, Compagnon du Baillot Bordelais (hon.), Phi Kappa Phi. Author: French Royalism Under the Third and Fourth Republics, 1961; Napoleon III; Buffoon, Modern Dictator of Sphinx, 1963; The Fall of France, 1940; Causes and Responsibilities, 1965; French Royalism Since 1870, 1970; Napoleon III and the Second Empire, 1973. Home: Kent, O., Died Aug. 6, 1975.

OSGOOD, WILLARD SUMNER, constrn. co. exec.; b. Iowa Falls, Ia., Oct. 20, 1913; s. Summer Jerome and Stella Joan (Thompson) O.; student Grinnell Coll., 1930-31, Ellsworth Coll., 1932-33, Drake U., 1934-35; B.A., State U. Ia., 1941; m. Wilnetta Snyder, Jan. 31, 1935 (dec. Dec. 1970); children—Willard Summer, Steven, Thomas, Richard. With Brown & Root, Inc. and subsidiaries, 1942-74, exec. v.p. Valentine Pulp & Paper Co. subsidiary, Lockport, La., 1956-64, project mgr., Call, Colombia, 1964-65, France, 1952-53, Venezuela, 1953-54, pres. Mid-Valley, Inc., Houston, 1966-74. Vice chmn. Lafourche Parish Hosp. Bd., Lockport, 1961. Mem. Houston Engring. Soc., T.A.P.P.I., USCG Aux. (comdr. 1960). Baptist. Rotarian (pres. Lockport 1960-61). Mason (Shriner). Home: Bellaire, Tex. Died Oct. 1, 1974.

O'SHAUGHNESSY, IGNATIUS ALOYSIUS, oil co. exec.; b. Stillwater, Minn., July 31, 1885; s. John and Mary (Milan) O'S.; student St. Thomas Coll., 1901-07, LL.D., 1948; LL.D., U. Notre Dame, 1946, Loyola U., De Paul U.; m. Lillian G. Smith, Oct. 7, 1908; children—John Francis, Eileen Ann (Mrs. John J. O'Shaughnessy), Marian Gertrude (Mrs. Thomas B. Burke), Lawrence Milan, Donald Eugene; m. 2d, Blanche GaNun Finn, Nov. 16, 1966. Sec. St. Thomas Coll., 1906; organized Globe Oil & Refining Co., 1917, pres., 1917-70; pres. Globe Pipe Line Co., 1934, Lario Oil & Gas Co., 1927; dir. First Nat. Bank of St. Paul. Trustee St. Paul Sem., U. Notre Dame; bd. dirs. St. Thomas Coll., Minn. Med. Found. Recipient Ignatian award Georgetown U.; Leatare medal Notre Dame U., 1953; Franciscan award; U. Minn. Regents medal; Pax Christi award St. Johns U.; Greatest St. Paulite award; named Papal count, 1967; decorated Papal chamberlain of Sword and Cape, knight of Holy Sepulchre, of Malta, knight comdr. of St. Gregory; recipient St. George medal Boy Scouts Am.; mem. 25 year Club Petroleum Industry. Mem. Am. Petroleum Inst. (dir.), St. Paul Assn. Commerce, St. Paul Inst. Gen. and Applied Sci. Roman Catholic. Clubs: Minnesota, Somerset, Town and Country, Athletic (St. Paul); Surf, Indian Creek Golf (Miami Beach, Fla); Wichita (Kan.), Chicago Athletic; Bal Harbor (Fla.); Key Largo (Fla.) Home: St. Paul, Minn. Died Nov. 21, 1973.

OSSERMAN, KERMIT EDWARD, physician; b. N.Y.C., June 21, 1909; s. Edward and Rose (Bowman) O.; A.B., Johns Hopkins, 1929; M.D. cum laude, U. Md., 1933; m. Dorothy S. Jacobs, June 2, 1935; 1 dau., Ruth Sue. Adj. physician dermatology Bronx Hosp., 1935-39; clin. asst. dermatology Mt. Sinai Hosp., 1935-40, sr. clin. asst. gynecologist, 1940-44, sr. clin. asst. medicine, 1944-51, research asst. medicine, 1945-51, asst. attending physician, 1955-61, physician in charge Myasthenia Gravis Clinic, Mt. Sinai Hosp., 1951-72, asso. attending physician, 1961-69, attending physician, 1970-72; asso. attending physician Sydenham Hosp., 1951-62; asso. in medicine Columbia, 1961-67; asso. clin. prof. medicine Mt. Sinai Sch. Medicine, City U. N.Y., 1966-69, clin. prof. medicine, 1970-72; cons. physician City Hosp. at Elmhurst and Knickerbocker Hosp. Fellow A.C.P., N.Y. Acad. Medicine, N.Y. Acad. Scis.; mem. Harvey Soc., Am. Acad. Neurology, Royal Acad. of Medicine (asso. London), Am., N.Y. diabetes assns., Am. Heart Assn., A.M.A., N.Y. State, N.Y. County med. socs., Am. Soc. Pharm. and Exptl. Therapeutics, Phi Sigma Delta, Phi Lambda Kappa, Kappa Alpha Tau. Author textbook: Myasthenia Gravis, 1958. Asso. editor: Jour. Mt. Sinai Hosp. Contbr. articles in field to profl. jours. Home: New York City, N.Y. Died Jan. 22, 1972.

OSTHAGEN, CLARENCE HILMANN, govt. ofcl.; b. North Bergen, N.J., Apr. 9, 1904; s. Hilmann Marius and Elise (Ulriksen) O.; student Cooper Inst. Tech., 1920-25; B.S. in Engring., U. Ky., 1930; postgrad. Columbia, 1930-31, George Washington U., 1934-37. Asst. to spl. rep. Allis-Chalmers Mfg. Co., 1920-25; indsl. engr. Henry L. Doherty Co., 1930-31; cons. engr., 1931-33; dep. adminstr. pub. utilities and transp., also exec. asst. div. bus. coop. NRA, 1933-36; acting dir. project control, dir. adminstrv. operations, asst. dir. personnel, dir. employee mgmt. Fed. Works Agy., 1936-42, mgmt. engr., 1946-48; dep. asst. sec. for personnel mgmt. Dept. Air Force, 1948-50; asst. sec. and acting under sec. commerce Dept. Commerce, 1950-53; prin. mgmt. cons. Rogers, Slade & Hill, N.Y.C., 1953-56; v.p., exec. dir. Tidewater, Va. Devel. Council, Norfolk, 1956-63; dir. mechanization div. Office Asst. Postmaster Gen., 1963-64; commr. Community Facilities Adminstrn., Housing and Home Finance Agy., 1964-66; dir. space and mechanization requirements Office Asst. Postmaster Gen., 1966-69; spl. asst. to asst. postmaster gen. U.S. Postal Service, 1969-71; mgmt. indsl. cons. engr., 1971-75. Served to col. USAAF, World War II; col. Res. Decorated Legions of Merit, Dept. Air Force Commendation ribbon with 2 oak leaf clusters; recipient Exceptional Civilian Service decoration Dept. Air Force, 1951, exceptional service award Dept. Commerce, 1952, Meritorious Service award P.O. Dept., 1968, Centennial medallion and named mem. Hall Distinguished Alumni U. Ky., 1967. Registered profl. engr., N.J., N.Y. Va., D.C. Mem. Soc. Advancement Mgmt., Am. Soc. Pub. Adminstrn., Soc. Am. Mil. Engrs., Am. Inst. Indsl. Engrs., Nat. Soc. Profl. Engrs., Am. Indsl. Devel. Council, Internat. Personnel Mgmt. Assn., Soc. Personnel Adminstrn., Air Force Assn., U. Ky. Alumni Assn., Nat. Sojourneers, Order DeMolay, Sigma Chi, Omicron Delta Kappa. Lutheran. Mason (Shriner). Clubs: Virginia, Norfolk Yacht and Country (Norfolk); Sphinx (Washington). Author mgmt. orgn. and indsl. engring. articles. Home: Ridgefield, Park, N.J., Died Nov. 25, 1975; interred Fairview Cemetery, Fairview, N.J.

OSTRANDER, LEE H., investment banker; b. Randolph, Neb.; s. William J. and Mina (Jacobsen) O.; student U. Chgo., 1922-23, Morningside Coll., 1923-26; m. Mary Elizabeth Lamar, June 10, 1926; children—Lee H., Susan, William L., Mary Elizabeth. Salesman, White Weld & Co., 1926, syndicate mgr., 1928-30; with Bonbright & Co., Chgo., 1930-32. Chase, Harris, Forbes & Co., 1932-33, R.W. Pressprich & Co., Chgo., 1933-40; Chgo. resident mgr. Lazard Freres & Co., 1940-42, Graham Parsons & Co., 1943-44; partner William Blair & Co., Chgo., 1944-72. Gov., N.Y. Stock Exchange, 1964-67. Trustee Highland Park Hosp.; past pres. Highland Park Community Chest. Mem. Nat. Assn. Securities Dealers (gov.), Holland Soc., Investment Bankers Assn. Am. (gov.). Clubs: Bond (pres. 1959-60), Attic (Chgo.); Exmoor Country (Highland Park). Home: Highland Park, Ill. Died Feb. 11, 1975; interred North Shore Garden of Memories, North Chicago, Ill.

OSTROWSKY, ABBO, artist; b. Elisavetgrad, Russia, Oct. 23, 1889; s. Favel and Rebecca (Boguslavsky) O.; ed. Art School, Odessa, Russia, N.A.D., N.Y.C.; unmarried. Came to U.S., 1908, naturalized, 1914. Dir. Peoples Traveling Exhibit, provinces of Poltava, Kiev and Kherson, Russia, 1906-07; founder, dir. Ednl. Alliance Art Sch., N.Y.C., 1914-55; chmn. visual arts com. Nat. Fedn. Settlements. Represented in Bibliotheque Nationale, Paris; New York Pub. Library; Tel Aviv Museum, Palestine; Gregg collection U. of Neb.; Library of Congress, Washington; Met. Museum of Art; Abraham Lincoln High Sch., Brooklyn. Home: Rego Park, Queens N.Y. Died June 19, 1975.

OTIS, ASHTON M., fruit grower; b. Poplar Ridge, N.Y., May 1, 1880; s. James J. and Julia (Taber) O.; student Alexander Hamilton Inst., 1923-25; m. Marie Barker, Oct. 25, 1906; children—Charlotte E. (Mrs. Craig), Dorothy Felice (Mrs. Brummeler). Asst. hotel mgr., 1902-07; grower citrus fruits, Whittier, from 1907; dir. La Habra Citrus Assn., Northern Orange County Citrus Exchange, Cal. Fruit Growers Exchange, Fruit Growers Supply Co., La. Habra Water Co., Murphy Ranch Mutual Water Co.; chmn. adv. bd. La Habra Br. Bank of Am. Trustee, chmn. bd. Cal. Yearly Meeting of Friends of Ch.; mem. editorial council The Am. Friend; pres. bd. trustees Whittier Coll. Republican. Mem. Friends Ch. Club: Lions (Whittier). Address: Whittier, Cal.†

OTJEN, WILLIAM JOHN, lawyer; b. La Bette County, Kan., Oct. 19, 1880; s. John Christian and Sophia (Nuhfer) O.; student prep. sch.; student Valparaiso U., Ind. U.; LL.B., Northwestern U., 1905; m. June B. Cullison, June 15, 1907; children—Mary Elizabeth, Carolyn, William John, Helen. Admitted to Olka. and Ind. bars, 1905; now sr. partner firm of Otjen and Carter of Enid, Okla.; city atty., Enid, 1912-14, spl. asst. atty. gen. of Okla., 1915; organizer, operator Otjen Gen. Agy., Ins.; pres. Southwestern Nat. Life Ins. Co., Ranola Oil Co.; v.p., dir. Banfield Bros. Packing Co.; dir. Central Nat. Bank. Mem. Okla. Ho. of Reps., 1923-25, Okla. Senate, 1925-32; candidate for Republican nomination, gov. Okla., 1926, 42; Rep. nominee U.S. Senate, 1944; mem. bd. adjustment, City of Enid, 1940-45, chmn., 1945-73. Mem. Nat. Council Boy Scouts Am., 1941-43. Served as cpl. U.S. Vols., Spanish-Am. War, P.I. Recipient Distinguished Service awards Garfield County and State bar assns. Mem. Am., Okla., Garfield County (pres. 1925) bar assns., United Spanish War Vets (sr. vice-comdr.-in-chief 1931-32, comdr.-in-chief 1932-33, chmn. nat. com. on legislation and adminstrn. 1954-59, chmn. nat. com. appeals and grievances, chmn. nat. resolutions com.). Presbyn. Mason. Elk. Rotarian. Home: Enid, Okla., Died May 22, 1973.

OTTINGER, SIMON, lumber co. exec.; b. N.Y.C., Oct. 28, 1884; s. Marx and Clara (Lightstone) O.; student Columbia Grammar Sch.; pvt. tutors, U.S. and Europe; m. Ruth Silberman, Apr. 9, 1929 (dec. 1969); 1 dau., Susan Caryl (Mrs. K. Evan Friedman). Financial v.p., sec. U.S. Plywood Corp., N.Y.C., v.p. Kalistron, Inc. Hay & Co., Ltd., Can., Kosmos Timber Co., Tekwood, Inc.; ret., 1959. Clubs: Harmonie; North Shore Country (Glen Head, L.I.). Home: New York City, N.Y. Died June 2, 1974.

OTTO, EBERHARD, egyptologist; b. Dresden, Germany, Feb. 26, 1913; s. Hermann and Dorothea (Leplow) G.; Ph.D., U. Gottingen, 1938, Ph.D. habil., 1942; m. Gudrun Stumpp, May 15, 1941; children—Bernhard, Konrad. Asst. prof. U. Gottingen, Hamburg, 1949-55; prof. U. Heidelberg, 1955-74. Hon. prof. Instituto Sudamericano de Asuntos Legales, Buenos Aires, Argentina. Mem. Akademie der Wissenschaften Heidelberg, Deutsches Archäologisches Institute, Berlin. Author: Die biographischen Inschriften der ägypt. Spätzeit, 1954, Kleines Wörterbuch der Agyptologie, 1956, Agypten, der Weg des Pharaonenreiches, 1966, Wesen und Wandel der ägyptischen Kuitur, Home: Mulben, Federal Republic of Germany. Died Oct. 11, 1974; interred Mulben, Federal Republic Germany.

OTTO, HENRY J., educator; b. Brownton, Minn., Mar. 20, 1901; s. Christoph H. and Anna (Uecker) O.; A.B., Carleton Coll., 1923; M.A., U. Minn., 1927, Ph.D., 1931; m. Mildred Alice Wagner, Aug. 18, 1931 (dec. 1958); children—Gordon Henry, Byron Leonard; m. 2d, Cecelia Henderson, Apr. 6, 1963. Tchr. sci. and math. Long Prairie (Minn) High Sch., 1923-25; supt. schs., Buffalo Lake, Minn., 1925-28; asst. prof. edn. Northwestern U., 1930-34; cons. edn. W.K. Kellogg Found., 1934-42; prof. elementary curriculum and adminstrn. U. Tex. 1942-69, emeritus, 1969—, chmn. dept. ednl. adminstrn. 1959-66. Recipient outstanding achievement award U. Minn., 1951. Mem. N.E.A., Tex. Elementary Prins. and Suprs. Assn., Nat. Dept. Elementary Sch. Prins., Phi Delta Kappa. Lutheran. Author of 40 books in field elementary edn., 1934—, also monographs. Home: Austin, Tex. Died Aug. 5, 1975; interred Austin, Tex.

OUKRAINSKY, SERGE (LEÓNIDE ORLAY DE CARVA), choreographer and ballet master; b. Odessa, Russia, Dec. 3, 1885; s. Alexis and Ludmilla (Znatchko Yovorskaia) O. de C.: student Lycée Condorcet, 1896-98, Lycée Carnot, 1898-1900, Acad. Julian (all Paris,

France). 1900-01; came to U.S., 1913, naturalized, 1928; unmarried. Began as mime in French Musical Festival, Théâtre du Châtelet, Paris, 1911: partner and solo dancer with Anna Pavlowa, Pavlowa Ballet Russe, 1913-15; guest 1913-15; guest artist Chgo. Opera Assn., 1915-16, first dancer, 1916-17; founded Pavley-Oukrainsky Ballet Sch., 1917, and directed sch., 1917-31; in charge ballet for Chgo. Opera, 1921-22; created Pavley-Oukrainsky Ballet, first Am. ballet and ofcl. ballet of Chgo. opera, 1921-22; toured U.S. and various fgn. countries 1922-25; toured U.S., 1926-27; ballet master Los Angeles and San Francisco opera cos., 1927-30; dance dir. Warner Bros., Fox studios and Tec Art. 1927-30; dir. Serge Oukrainsky Ballet, from 1931. Choreographer 20 full-length ballets, 4 motion picture sequences and 47 operatic Ballets. Mem. Am. Guild of Musical Artists (past nat. dir., hon. life mem.). Democrat. Mem. Greek Orthodox Ch. Home: Hollywood, Cal. Deceased.

OUSDAL, ASHJORN PEDERSEN, osteo. physician and surgeon; b. Flekkefjord, Siradalen, Norway, July 26, 1879; s. Peder Torjesen and Antoinette (Liland) O.; came to U.S., 1898, naturalized, 1915; grad. The Trieder Coll., Oslo, 1904; student Lakeview High Sch. (nights), Chicago, 1905; R.N., Green Gable Sanitarium, Sch. for Nurses, 1909; D.O., Coll. of Osteopathic Physicians and Surgeons, 1916; M.D., Collegium Medicinae Pacificum, Los Angeles, Calif., 1917; spl. research studies in microscopic geology, Univ. of Calif. at Los Angeles, 1936-40; grad. research in microscopic geology, Univ. of Southern Calif., 1940; m. Kittie Montgomery, Sept. 29, 1909. Worked in various stores as salesman, Chicago, 1905-07; engaged as nurse, 1909-11; practicing as osteopathic physician and surgeon, Santa Barbara, Cal., from 1917; mem. Sixth Pacific Sci. Congress of the Pacific Science Assn. Served with Vols. of America and in Red Cross Drive During World War. Trustee Coll. Osteopathic Phys. and Surgeons (resigned after 25 years) Hon. mem. Oriental Foundation; mem. A.A.A.S., Masonic Research Society, California, Santa Barbara Botanical Society, Soc. Research on Meteorites (internat.), Norwegian-American Hist. Soc. Scandinavian Foundation, Sigma Xi. Mem. (life) General Alumni Assn. U. of Southern Calif., Asso. Research, U. of Southern California. Republican. Mason (Scottish Rite, K.T.), Shriner, Clubs: Authors (Hollywood, Calif.); La Cumbre Golf and Country (Santa Barbara). Author: Vinland Saga (play), 1936; Human Advance Toward Orderly Form of Government, 1940; Teleological Visualization Chart; Medicine and Science of Living; Our Revolting Society. Contributor to osteopathic jours; for 4 years wrote daily features on osteopathy in News-Press, Santa Barbara, Calif. Noted as student of paleontology; had own fosil museum for scientific investigation. Inventor of and held patent on Solar-Ray (therapeutics). Research lab. at home on meteoric fossils. Home: Santa Barbara, Cal.†

OVERPECK, ARELI CHARLES, mining engr.; b. Naples, N.Y., Mar. 24, 1879; s. Alemeth E. and Emma A. (Tyler) O.; B.S. in M.E., S.D. Sch. of Mines, 1902, E.M., 1904; m. Helen L. McMahon, Sept. 14, 1904. Deputy oil insp. Black Hills Dist., S.D., 1901, 02; assayer and chemist, Nat. Smelting Co.'s plant, 1902-03; gen. supt. The Dakota-Calumet Co. and The Continental Copper Mining & Smelting Co., 1903-12, dir. latter. Mem. Am. Inst. Mining Engrs. Progressive. Methodist. Mason. Address: Hill City, S.D.†

OVERSTREET, ALAN BURR, educator; b. San Francisco, Aug. 18, 1915; s. Harry Allen and Elsie Lucy (Burr) O.; B.A. in Internat. Relations, U. Cal., at Berkeley, 1937, M.A., Harvard, 1940, Ph.D. (Sumner prize), 1948; m. Jeanne Marion Slate, July 31, 1944. Instr., tutor in govt. Harvard, 1939-41, vis. lectr., 1948-50; instr. govt. Wesleyan U., Middletown, Conn., 1941-46, asst. prof., 1946-47; asso. prof. govt. Smith Coll., 1950-62, prof., 1962-75, acting chmn. dept. govt., 1952-53, 71-75, dir. Jr. Year for Internat. Studies in Geneva, Switzerland, 1953-54, 55-57, 59-64, 66-68; vis. prof. Grad. Inst. Internat. Studies, Geneva, 1956-57, 59-64, 66-68. Mem. Am. Assn. U. Profs., Am. Internat. polit. sci. assns., Am. Soc. Internat. Law. Home: Bennington, Vt., Died Dec. 29, 1975.

OVERTON, EUGENE, lawyer; b. Ft. Grant, Ariz., May 11, 1880; s. Gilbert Edmund and Jane Dyson (Watkins) O.; student pub. schs. of Los Angeles; m. Georgia Alberta Caswell. Nov. 19, 1907; 1 son, Mark Deering. Admitted to Calif. bar, 1902, practiced in Los Angeles; v.p., dir. Earle C. Anthony, Inc., Calif. Packard Distbr., K.F.I. Radio Sta., The Spalding Co., Bell Petroleum Co. Mem. Bd. Harbor Commrs., Los Angeles, 1939-47, pres., 1949-47. Served as lt. comdr., U.S.N.R.F., World War I. Mem. Los Angeles C. of C. (past dir.), Pacific Coast Assn. Port Authorities (pres. 1943-44), Calif. State and Los Angeles (pres. 1926-27) bar assns. Clubs: Bohemian (San Francisco); California, Los Angeles Yacht, Bel-Air Bay, Los Angeles Tennis (Los Angeles); Catalina Island Yacht. Home: Los Angeles Cal.†

OVERTON, PAUL, lawyer; b. Willis, Tex., Mar. 18, 1879; s. James Frank and Mary (Sturgeon) O.; prep. edn., pub. schs., San Antonio, Tex.; student Columbian Coll. (now George Washington U.), 1896-97; LL.B., Cornell U., 1900; m. Angelo Bouilly, June 3, 1916; children—Theodora Angelo, Alaire, Mary Ann. Admitted to Tex. bar, 1900, and practiced at San Antonio until 1902; asst. to atty. gen. of Philippine Islands, 1903; in practice at Los Angeles, from 1904; asst. gen. counsel Los Angeles Gas & Electric Corpn., 1911-17, gen. counsel from 1917; also gen. counsel Am. States Water Service Co. of Calif. Mem. Am. and Los Angeles bar assns., State Bar of Calif. Democrat. Mason (32°, Shriner). Clubs: University, City Engineers, Brentwood Country. Home: Los Angeles Cal.†

OWEN, CLIFFORD H., lawyer; b. Lincoln, N.Y., Dec. 13, 1878; s. Harvey J. and Esther O.; student Haverling Acad.; grad. Yale, 1902, LL.B., 1905; m. Ruth M. Pepper; 1 dau., Ruth Mary. Admitted to N.Y. bar, 1905; began practice of law with Wise & Seligsberg, later joined Holm, Whitlock & Scasff, with firm for over 40 yrs.; sec. and gen. counsel for S. H. Kress & Co., Bankers Development Corp.; sec. and dir. I. Lefkowitz & Sons. Methodist. Home: New York City, N.Y.†

OWEN, GEORGE HODGES, govt. ofcl.; b. Germany, Sept. 16, 1912 (parents Am. citizens); B.A., U. Paris (France), 1932; M.A., Ecole des Sciences Politiques, 1935; LL.B., Fordham U., 1942; m. Sofia AntuNa-Zumaran, 1947; children—William, Hugo, Isabella, Georgina. Admitted to N.Y. bar; tchr. law Fordham U., 1937-42; atty. U.S. Dept. of Justice, 1942; with U.S. Dept. of State, 1945-72, dir. visa office, 1967-72, ret. Served with USMC, 1943-45. Owen Hills, Antarctica, named in his honor. Club. Union (N.Y.C.). Home: Washington, D.C. Died Sept. 3, 1974; buried Gate of Heaven Cemetery, Hawthorne, N.Y.

OWEN, WALTER EDWIN, physician; b. Clinton, Mo., July 5, 1907; s. Walter Edwin and Eugenia Salmon (Britts) O.; B.A., Westminster Coll., 1929; M.D., Washington U., St. Louis, 1937; m. Mary Margaret Reardon, Oct. 17, 1942; children—Margaret Lewis (Mrs. Robert Jobes), Walter Edwin III, John Corbett. Intern, Research Hosp., Kansas City, Mo., 1937-38; resident Tulane U. Grad. Sch. Medicine-New Orleans Hosp., 1939-41; practiced medicine, specializing in otolaryngology, Peoria, Ill., 1941-75; staff Methodist Hosp.; asso. staff St. Francis Hosp., Proctor Hosp.; cons. otolaryn, bronchoscopy Peoria Municipal Tb Hosp., Peoria State Hosp.; cons. otolaryngology Acheson Topeka & Santa Fe R.R.; instr. French K. Hansel Found., St. Louis, 1946-58. Diplomate Am. Bd. Otolaryngology. Fellow A.C.S. (gov. 1955-58); Am. Acad. Ophthalmology. and Otolaryngology; mem. Am. Thoracic Soc., Am. Coll. Allergists, A.M.A., Phi Delta Theta, Phi Beta Pi. Home: Peoria, Ill. Died Mar. 2, 1975; buried Swan Lake Cemetery, Peoria, Ill.

OWENS, LEO EDWARD, newspaper publisher; b. Eau Claire, Wis., Feb. 18, 1889; s. William Michael and Anna (Murphy) O.; M.E., U. Minn., 1911; LL.D., Whittier Coll., Cal., 1968; m. Marie Reilly, Oct. 6, 1923 (div. Nov. 1947); children—Lee E., Ellen (Mrs. Ronald J. Vincent), Owen M., Peter J.; m. 2d, Josephine Harding, Mar. 31, 1959. Mech. supt., prodn. mgr. Mpls. Tribune, 1911-17, Louisville Courier Jour., 1919-21, N.Y. World, 1922-27; pub. St. Paul Dispatch-Pioneer Press, 1927-39; pub. newspapers, Brownsville, Harlingen and McAllen, Tex., 1942-41, Richmond, Cal., 1948-72, Whittier, Cal., 1951—; chmn. bd., dir. Owens Pub. Co. Mem. Com. 25 Palm Springs. Served as 2d lt., constrn. div. AC, U.S. Army, 1917-18. Clubs: Thunderbird County; Home: Palm Springs, Cal., Died 1975.

OWSLEY, CHARLES FREDERICK, architect; b. Weathersfield, O., Jan. 10, 1880; s. Charles Henry and Mary Jane O.; B.S., U. of Pa., 1903; student Atelier Godfroy, Frenet, Paris, 1904; m. Katherine McKelvey, Sept. 7, 1905; children—Katherine, Richard, Charles, Henry, Mary Jane. With Owsley, Boucherle & Owsley, 1909-12, Owsley and Owsley, 1912-14, Charles F. Owsley, 1914-19, Owsley Co., 1920-24, Charles F. Owsley, 1924-45, from 1948, Owsley & Samuels, 1945-48. Lecturer art and archeology; exhibited paintings: Butler Ark Inst., Youngstown, O., Past pres. Ohio State Bd. Examiners of Architects; chmn. com., master plan commn., Greater Youngstown Area Foundation; chmn. com. Ohio Gen. Improvements Commn. Fellow Am. Inst. Architects; mem. Architects Soc. of Ohio, Chamber of Commerce, East Ohio Conservation Club, Friends of Am. Art, North Side Civil Assn., Elk. Clubs: Rotary (past pres.), Youngstown, Mahoning Valley Gun, Ruckeye Art, Union League (past pres.). Home: Hubbard, O.†

OXNAM, ROBERT FISHER, univ. pres.; b. Boston, May 31, 1915; s. Garfield Bromley and Ruth (Fisher) O.; A.B., DePauw U., 1937; M.A., U. So. Cal., 1942, M.S. in Pub. Adminstrn., 1947, Ph.D., 1948; LL.D., Am. U., 1959, DePauw U., 1961, W. Va. Wesleyan Coll., 1964; L.H.D., Norwich U., 1966; m. Dalys E. Houts, Oct. 14, 1939; children—Robert Bromley, Philip Linton, Mary Elizabeth. Asst. dir. pub. relations U. So. Cal., 1940-41, asst. dir. coordination office, 1941-42; asst. dean Coll. Liberal Arts, asst. prof. polit. sci. Mawxell Sch., Syracuse U., 1948-53, dean Sch. Speech and Dramatic Art, 1951-53, asst. to chancellor, 1950-53; v.p. adminstrv. affairs, asso. prof. govt. Boston U., 1953-57; pres. Pratt Inst., Bklyn., 1957-61, Drew U., 1960-74. Bd. mgrs. Meth. Hosp., 1958-66; exec. com. World Meth. Council, 1960-71; mem. Commn. Structure of Methodism Overseas, 1956-68; lay del. Gen. Conf. Meth. Ch., 1964; mem. coll. fed. agy. council N.Y. region Civil Service Commn., 1961-65, pres., 1963-65. Bd. dirs. U.S. Olympic Com., 1962-66. Served from pvt. to capt. AUS, 1942-46; ETO. Mem. Am. Assn. U. Profs., Am. Soc. Pub. Adminstrn., Am. Polit. Sci. Assn., Am. Acad. Polit. and Social Sci., Assn. Meth. Schs. Colls. Middle States (pres. 1963-64, mem. gen. commn. ecumenical affairs 1968-72), Beta Theta Pi, Pi Sigma Alpha, Phi Alpha Theta, Alpha Phi Omega, Sigma Tau Rho. Clubs: Century (N.Y.C.); Morris County Golf. Home: Madison, N.J. Died July 19, 1974.

OZBIRN, MRS. E. LEE (KATIE FREEMAN OZBIRN), club woman; b. Era, Tex.; d. Wiley Howell and Laura (Seagraves) Freeman; B.A., U. Okla., 1921; m. E. Lee Ozbirn, Nov. 24, 1921 (dec. Oct. 1954); 1 dau., Le Kathrin (Mrs. Lewis H. Bond). Bd. dirs. Gen. Fedn. Women's Clubs, 1940-59, state pres., 1940-43, gen. fed. dir., 1943-44, chmn. exetension, 1944-47, chmn. pub. affairs dept., 1952-54, 1st v.p. 1958-60, dean state presidents, 1958-60, pres., 1960-62, then hon. pres. Mem. Gov.'s Def. and War Council of World War II; mem. nat. adv. bd. for Peace Corps, from 1961; v.p. Am. Cancer Soc., 1955-57, hon. life mem. bd. dirs., from 1959, v.p. Okla. div., from 1945, mem. Okla. bd. dirs., Okla. exec. com.; bd. dirs. Vis. Nurses Assn., Okla., from 1956, Oklahoma City Health Council, from 1956, Phila. Women's Med. Coll., from 1956, exec. com. Freedom From Hunger Found.; bd. dirs. World Neighbors, Inc., from 1958. Recipient Am. Cancer award in Okla., 1951; Outstanding Community Service award Quota Club, Oklahoma City, 1952, Soroptimist Club, 1952, award Nat. Safety Found., Am. Outdoor Advt. Assn., Am. Heritage Found., bronze medal U. Panama, citation Inst. Internat. Edn., spl. award CARE Mission in Panama. Mem. Internat. Council Women's Clubs, Okla. P.T.A., P.E.O. Mem. Christian Ch. Clubs: Chautauqua (N.Y.) Women's; Red Bud, Twentieth Century (Oklahoma City). Home: Oklahoma City, Okla. Died Jan. 24, 1974.

PACEY, WILLIAM CYRIL DESMOND, univ. adminstr.; b. Dunedin, New Zealand, May 1, 1917; s. William and Mary Elizabeth (Hunt) P.; B.A., Victoria Coll., U. Toronto, 1938; Ph.D., Trinity Coll., Cambridge. 1941; m. Mary Elizabeth Carson, June 17, 1939; children—Philip, Mary Ann (Mrs. David Johnson), Patricia (Mrs. Charles Thornton), Peter, Margaret, Michael, Penelope. Prof., Brandon Coll., U. Man., 1940-44; prof., head dept. English, U. N.B., Fredericton, 1944-69, acting dean arts, 1955-56, dean grad. studies, 1960-70, acad. v.p., 1970-72, 73-75, acting prs., pres., 1972-73. Exec. officer, editor Wartime Information Bd., Ottawa, Ont., 1943. Sr. research fellow Can. Council, Cambridge U., 1962-63, mem. acad. panel, 1967-70. Fellow Royal Soc. Can. (sec. sect. II 1966-69). Author: Frederick Philip Grove, 1945; Creative Writing in Canada, 1952; The Cow with the Musical Moo, 1942; Hippity Hobo and the Bee, 1953; The Picnic and Other Stories, 1958; Ten Canadian Poets, 1958; The Cat, the Cow, and the Kangaroo, 1967; Ethel Wilson, 1968; Essays in Canadian Criticism, 1969; Frederick Philip Grove, 1970; Major Canadian Writers, 1974; Waken, Lords and Ladies Gay; The Selected Short Stories of Desmond Pacey, 1974. Editor: A Book of Canadian Stories, 1947; The Selected Poems of Sir Charles G.D. Roberts, 1955; Our Literary Heritage, 1967; Tales from the Margin, 1971; selections from Major Canadian Writers, 1974; The Collected Letters of Frederick Philip Grove, 1975; The Collected Letters of Sir Charles G.D. Roberts, co-editor New Voices, 1956; A Literary History of Canada, 1967. Contbr. to books, articles profl. jours. Home: Fredericton, NB, Canada., Died July 4, 1975.

PACHUCKI, ADOLF KASIMER, assn. exec.; b. Schenectady, July 14, 1903; s. Adolf and Josephine (Szalwinski) P.; student N.Y. U., 1923; Mgmt. Inst., Clarkson U., Potsdam, N.Y., 1955; m. Elizabeth T. Rainka, July 18, 1961. Various positions Bur. Internal Revenue, Albany, 1934-63; county clk. Children's Ct., Schenectady, 1932-33; nat. sec. Polish Nat. Alliance, Chgo., sec. Alliance Printers & Pubs., Inc., Chgo., 1963-75. Mem. Schenectady Vol. Fire Dept., 1938-63. Recipient awards for suggestions Internal Revenue Service, 1958-59, 60, 61. Mem. Chgo. Assn. Commerce and Industry, Am. Legion, Phi Kappa Tau. Home: Chicago, Ill. Died Jan. 30, 1975.

PACKARD, ARTHUR JOSEPH, hotel exec.; b. Faribault, Minn., Oct. 14, 1901; s. Daniel W. and Ida (Fieser) P.; student pub. schs.; m. Jean Chamberlin, June 10, 1926; 1 son, Arthur Joseph. Student exec. Sears, Roebuck Sch., 1924-25; mgr. hotels, Wooster and Mt. Vernon, O., 1926-28; mem. investment banking staff Briggs Investment Co., Detroit, 1928-34; pres. Packard Hotels Co., Hotel Red Book Pub. Co., also Graystone Hotels Co., Restwood Motel Co., Arthur J. Packard Co., Shawnee Hotel Co.; dir. Red Book Pub. Co., Knox County Savs. Bank, Red Roof Inns, Halmar Electronics Inc., Restwood Motel Co. Pres. Mt. Vernon Community Fund, 1936-38. Named Outstanding Hotelman of the Americas, 1958. Mem. YMCA (dir.), Ohio (pres. 1944), Am. (pres. 1952-53, dir. emeritus for life) hotel assns. Republican (dir. Ohio finance com.). Mason (Shriner), Rotarian. Clubs: Country, Old Homestead (Mt. Vernon); Tavern (N.Y.C.); Country (Columbus, O.); Burning Tree (Washington). Home: Mt Vernon, O. Died. May 17, 1974.

PACKER, (DOUGLAS) FRANK (HEWSON), newspaper exec.; b. Dec. 3, 1906; s. Robert Clyde and Ethel Maud P.; ed. Sydney Ch. of Eng. Grammar Sch., New South Wales; m. Gretel Joyce Bullmore, 1934 (dec. 1960); 2 sons; m. 2d, Florence A. Porges, 1964. Cadet reporter Daily Guardian, 1923, asst. bus. mgr., 1926; dir., gen. advt. mgr. Daily Guardian and Smith's Weekly, 1927; co-founder Australian Womens Weekly, 1933; mng. dir. Australian Consol. Press, Ltd., 1936-74; pres. Australian Newspapers Conf., 1939-40, Australian Asso. Press Pty., Ltd., 1951; dir. Reuters, Ltd., 1954-56, 62-74; chmn. TV Corp., Ltd., 1955, Gen. TV Corp. Pty., Ltd., Melbourne, 1960. Served with Australian Imperial Forces 1941-42, 44-45. Decorated comdr. Order Brit. Empire, 1951, knight, 1971; created knight, 1959. Clubs: Devonshire, Savage (London); Australian University, Australian Golf, Royal Sydney Yacht Squadron, Royal Sydney Golf (Sydney); New York Yacht. Contbr. articles to Australian Womens Weekly, 1933; Daily Telegraph, 1936; Sunday Telegraph, 1939. Home: Sydney, Australia. Died May 1, 1974.

PADGETT, DORA ADELE, (Mrs. Edward R. Padgett, Sr.), orgn. exec., editor; b. Washington, Mar. 16, 1892; d. Luther Howard and Jane (Wells) Styron-Simpkins; grad. Wash. Normal Sch., 1912; student Cornell U., 1915; m. Edward Riddel Padgett, Oct. 21, 1920 (dec. 1925); 1 son, Edward R. Feature writer Washington and Detroit newspapers, 1912-22; publicity rep. Nat. Rivers and Harbors Congress, 1925-29; editor Planning and Civic Comment, quar. Am. Planning and Civic Assn. and Nat. Conf. State Parks, Washington, from 1935; sec. Am. Planning and Civic Assn., from 1959, Com. of 100 on the Fed. City, from 1959; exec. sec. Nat. Conf. State Parks, from 1959; asso. editor Nat. Geneal. Soc. Quar., 1945-58. Mem. D.A.R. (chpt. regent 1949-51), Dau. Am. Colonists (state Regent D.C. 1946-49), Nat. Geneal. Soc. Contbr. to Nat. Geneal. Soc. Quar. Compiler genealogy Styron Family of Va. and N.C.; Howard Family of Ocracoke Island, N.C., 1755-1955. Author articles parks and planning. Home: Cincinnati, O., Died Jan. 24, 1976.

PAGE, CHARLES RANDOLPH, ins. co. exec.; b. San Francisco, May 24, 1878; s. Charles and Sally (Meyers) P.; B.A., Yale; m. Louise Hoffacker, Mar. 26, 1903; children—Charles, Edward B., John R., Stanley A., Thomas S. Started with Fireman's Fund Ins. Co., San Francisco, chmn., from 1943; chmn. Home Fire & Marine Ins. Co., San Francisco, Western Nat. Ins. Co., Fireman's Fund Indemnity Co.; dir. Cal. Pacific Title & Trust Co., Nat. Surety Co. Chevalier French Legion of Honor. Home: San Francisco, Cal.†

PAGNOL, MARCEL PAUL, film producer, playwright; b. Aubagne, Marseille, France, Feb. 25, 1895; s. Joseph and Augustine (Lansot) P.; student Lycee Theirs, Marseille; tchrs. diploma U. Montpellier; m. Simone Collin, 1916; two sons, one daughter; m. 2d, Jacqueline Bouvier, Oct. 6, 1945; 2 sons. Co-founder Fortunio (later Les Cahiers du Sud), lit. mag., 1911; tchr. English sch. in Tarascon, 1912, later Pamiers sur Ariege, Lycee St. Charles in Marseilles; prof. Lycee Condorcet, 1922; founder mag. Les Cahiers du Film, 1931; playwright Topaze, 1928, Marius, 1929, Fanny, 1931; head motion picture firm Films of Marcel Pagnol, 1931-74; films prod. include Harvest, The Bakers Wife, Well-Digger's Daughter, Manon des Sources, 1952, Letters from My Windmill, 1954, Fanny, 1961. Portuguese consul, Monaco with inf. French Army, 1914-17. Elected to French Acad., 1947; decorated officer Legion of Honor (France); recipient N.Y. Film Critics award for prodn. best fgn. film, 1939. Mem. Soc. French Dramatic Authors and Composers (pres. 1944-46). Author: la Petite Fille aux yeux sombres; Hamlet; Les temps des secrets; Lettres de mon moulin; others. Home: Paris, France. Died Apr. 1974.

PAIGE, SIDNEY, geologist; b. Washington, Nov. 2, 1880; s. Nathaniel and Rosa Elizabeth (Goldsmith) P.; student U. of Mich., 1901-03; grad. work in geology, Yale, 1908; m. Hildegard Brooks, Mar. 20, 1909; 1 son, Potter Brooks; m. 2d, Frances Hall, Mar. 1, 1924; children—Sidney Hall, Henry Hall. With engrs. Nicaragua Canal Commn., 1898-1900; U.S. Geol. Survey, 1903-07; geologist, Panama Canal Commn., 1907; with U.S. Geol. Survey, 1909-26; consulting geologist, 1926-33; adviser Bur. of Mines, Dept. of Economy. Republic of Turkey, 1933-35; prin. geologist North Atlantic Div., U.S. Army Engr., 1935-46. Visiting professor engineering geology Columbia University, 1946-58; dir. and exec. sec. Com. Geographical Exploration, Joint Research and Development Board, Washington, 1947-49; cons. geologist. Mem. Society Econ. Geologists, N.Y. Academy of Science, Am. Society of Civil Engineers, Geol. Soc. Am., Geol. Soc. Washington, Am. Inst. Mining and Metall. Engrs., Am. Assn. Petroleum Geologists, Chi Psi. Sigma Xi. Club: Cosmos (Washington). Author papers on stratigraphy structure, ore deposits, and petroleum in Alaska and United States. Home: Alpine, N.J.†

PAINE, GEORGE PORTER, assn. exec.; b. Ripon, Wis., May 3, 1909; s. George Porter and Edna (Springer) P.; student Phillips Acad., Andover, 1925-27; B.S., U. Pa. Wharton Sch., 1933; m. Enid Homersham Cox, Feb. 1, 1940; children—Robin George Porter, Christopher; m. 2d, Ruth Elizabeth Benson, June 25, 1950. Staff sec. N.A.M., N.Y.C., 1940-42; asst. sec. Am. Standards Assn., N.Y.C., 1946-56; exec. dir. Am. Assn. Textile Chemists and Colorists Research, Triangle Park, N.C., 1956-74. Am. del. Internat. Orgn. for Standardization, Zurich, Switzerland, 1947; del. Internat. Electrotech. Commn. Golden Jubilee, Phila., 1954, Congress Internat. Fedn. Assns. Textile Chemists and Colourists, London, Eng., 1959. Trustee Textile Research Inst., 1963-69. Served to capt. USNR. Mem. Council Engring. and Sci. Soc. Execs. (dir. 1967-70), Soc. Dyers and Colourists, Naval Order U.S. Delta Kappa Epsilon. Club: Chemists (N.Y.C.). Home: Chapel Hill, NC. Died Apr. 22, 1974.

PAINE, ROWLETT, ex-mayor; b. Memphis, Dec. 22, 1879; s. John J. and Elizabeth (Rowlett) P.; grad. high sch., Memphis; m. Anna Belle Hughes, 1918; children—Elizabeth Rowlett, Annabell Hughes, Janie Virginia. Wholesale grocery business, Memphis, from 1899. U.S. food adminstrator, Memphis, 1917; vice-chmn. Am. Red Cross, 1917-18; four-minute speaker; mayor of Memphis, two terms, 1920-28. Reorganized city govt. on business basis; apptd. the 1st woman judge of Juvenile Court in the South. Mem. Cotton States Merchants' Assn. (ex-pres.), Southern Wholesale Grocers Assn., Memphis Assn. Credit Men (ex-pres.), Memphis Chamber of Commerce. Democrat. Episcopalian. Rotarian. Home: Memphis, Tenn.†

PAIST, THERESA WILBUR, Mrs. Frederic M. Paist); b. Boone, Ia., June 6, 1880; d. Dwight Locke and Edna (Lyman) Wilbur; student Stanford; m. Frederic M. Paist, Jan. 31, 1912; children—Gertrude Wilbur, Frances Helen, Theresa Wilbur, Frederic Mack (dec.), Horace Curtis. Teacher of mathematics, Pasadena High Sch., 1903-04; traveling sec. State Com. Y.W.C.A. of Calif. and Nev., 1904-06; traveling sec. Nat. Bd. Y.W.C.A., most of time at state univs., 1907-11; pres. Y.W.C.A., of U.S., 1921-26; ex-pres. Nat. Bd. Y.W.C.A. Trustee Tennent Coll. Republican. Presbyn. Home: Wayne, Pa.†

PALACIOS, ALFREDO L., Socialist leader in Argentina, lawyer, professor; b. Buenos Aires, Argentina, Aug. 10, 1881; s. Aurelio and Ana (Ramon) P.; J.D., University of Buenos Aires; Dr. honoris causa of universities of San Marcos, Arequipa, Cuzco, La Paz and Rio de Janeiro; unmarried. Professor political economy, University of La Plata; professor industrial legislation, University of Buenos Aires; dean of Faculty of Juridical and Social Sciences, University of La Plata, 1922-25; dean of Faculty of Law and Social Sciences, University of Buenos Aires, 1930; dep. to Nat. Congress, 1904-08, 1912-15; nat. senator, from 1932. Responsible for passage of many Argentinian laws, chiefly humanitarian, covering the subjects of Sunday labor, suppression of white slave trade, regulation of labor of women and children, protection of salaries of laboring classes, maternity protection, labor accidents, etc. Author numerous books on political and social subjects. Hon. prof. U. of San Marcos, Lima, Peru. Address: Buenos Aires, Argentina.*†

PALENCIA, ISABEL DE, author; b. Málaga, Spain, June 12, 1881; d. Juan and Anne (Guthrie) de Oyarzábal; student Convent of the Assumption, Málaga, U. of Madrid, and London U.; m. Ceferino Palencia, July 8, 1909; children—Ceferino, Marissa. Began in journalism, serving on staff of El Sol, Madrid; Madrid corr. London Daily Herald, 6 yrs.; founder and editor mag. La Dama; also did news coverage for Laffan News Bur., London, and for Standard (London newspaper); also lectured extensively in U.S. and Europe. Plenipotentiary minister for Spain to Sweden, 1936, later also to Finland. Spanish Republican Catholic. Author: Study in Child Psychology (Spanish); Sower Sowed His Seed (novel in Spanish); Hookie (novelette in Spanish); Regional Costumes of Spain (Spanish and English), 1930; Saint Anthony's Pig (English juvenile), 1940; I Must Have Liberty, 1940, autobiography in English; author Dialogues with Sorrow (drama); Smouldering Freedom; Alexandra Kollontay (biography), 1947; Why Mexico? Home: U1Mexico City, Mexico.†

PALLETTE, EDWARD CHOATE, physician; b. Los Angeles, July 9, 1904; s. Edward Marshall and Elizabeth (Brown) P.; M.D., Harvard, 1929; m. Beulah Martel Langley, Mar. 1928; children—Edward Marshall II, Patricia P. Breen, Antonia (Mrs. Robert W. Priestley); m. 2d, Ruth Batten De Warwick, Jan. 1960. Intern, resident Roosevelt Hosp., N.Y.C., resident in gen. surgery, 1929-32; mem. surg. staff St. Vincent's Hosp., Los Angeles; surg. cons. Wadsworth Gen. VA Hosp., Sawtelle, Cal. Dir., U.S. Nat. Bank of San Diego, Los Angeles Life Ins. Co. Served to lt. col., M.C., AUS, 1942-45; CBI. Diplomate Am. Bd. Surgery. Fellow A.C.S.; mem. A.M.A., Los Angeles Surg. Soc., Nu Sigma Nu, Beta Theta Pi. Contbr. articles on gen. and vascular surgery to med. jours. Home: Los Angeles, Cal. Died Oct. 20, 1973; buried Forest Lawn Cemetery, Glendale, Cal.

PALM, FRANKLIN CHARLES, educator; b. Willmar, Minn., Aug. 16, 1890; s. Alvin and Frances L. (Branton) P.; A.B., Oberlin, 1914; A.M., U. Ill., 1915, Ph.D., 1918. Prof. history Colo. Coll., Colorado Springs, 1918-21; asst. prof. modern European history U. Cal., 1921-29, asso. prof., 1929-39, prof., 1939-57, emeritus, 1957-73; mem. summer session faculty U. Cal. at Los Angeles, 1932, 39, U. So. Cal., 1941; travel research in Europe, 1923, 36. Mem. Am. Hist. Assn., Royal Soc. Arts, Phi Sigma Kappa. Elk. Clubs: Faculty; Exchange; Claremont Country (Oakland). Author: The Economic Policies of Richelieu, 1920; Syllabus of Modern European History, 1925; A Syllabus of the History of Western Europe, 1927; Politics and Religion in Sixteenth-Century France, 1927; The Establishment of French Absolutism (1574-1610), 1928; Calvinism and the Religious Wars, 1932; Europe since Napoleon (with F. E. Graham), 1934; The Middle Classes-Then and Now, 1936; European Civilization: A Political, Social, and Cultural History (with J. W. Thompson and J. J. Van Nostrand, Jr.), 1939; England and the Establishment of the Second French Empire, 1848-1852; A Study of the Rise of a Utopian Dictator, 1948; Western Civilization, A Social and Cultural History (Vol. II, since 1660), 1949; (with C. R. Webb, Jr.) Western Civilization, 1958; also articles mags. Home: Berkeley, Cal. Died Sept. 12, 1973.

PALMER, ALDEN CLAUDE, life ins. publishing exec.; b. Dubois County, Ind., May 3, 1887; s. Bayless E. and Sarah C. (Hall) P.; LL.B., Ind. U., 1910; m. Edythe Allison, Apr. 11, 1911; children—Helen Catherine (Mrs. Mel C. Browning), Alden Claude, Mary Edythe (Mrs. Don L. Gore). Stenographer in pub. bus., farm publs., 1904-10; advt. various farm publs., 1911-19; dir. study life ins. Research & Review Service, Indpls., 1919-27, sales and tng. dir., 1936-57, v.p., 1936-72, chmn. bd. dirs., from 1952, later chmn. emeritus; mgr. Pa.-N.J. area Peoria Life Ins. Co., Phila., 1927-32; gen. agt. for Minn., Home Life Ins. Co., N.Y., Mpls., 1932-34; gen. agt. Berkshire Life of N.H., Cin., 1934-36, Atlantic Life, Cin., 1936-37. Ins. Commr. State of Ind., Indpls., 1957-60; dir. Short Course in Life Underwriting Purdue U., Lafayette, Ind., 1939-44, Kan. U., Lawrence, 1942-43; vice pres. Palmer-Gore Ranch, Inc. dir. Hawkeye Nat. Life Ins. Co., Des Moines. Republican. Mem. Soc. of Friends. Mason. Club: Columbia. Author: Opportunity in Life Underwriting, 1935; The Recruiting Process, 1936; Introduction to Life Underwriting, 1941; also educational letters designed for life underwriters, 1952-72; The Alden Palmer Letters, 1968. Home: Eugene, Mo. Died Feb. 27, 1972; interred at Spencer, Ind.

PALMER, BRUCE BARTLETT, news dir.; b. Blue Earth, Minn., Nov. 26, 1908; s. Julian Manchester and Maud Edith (Bartlett) P.; student Cornell Coll., 1925-28; B.J., U. Mo., 1930; m. Leila Glen Eckles, Sept. 5, 1936 (dec. Sept. 1973); children—Bruce Laird, Sheila Glen. Reporter Okla. Pub. Co., Oklahoma City, 1930-32, editor, 1936-46; mem. staff Asso. Press, Mpls., 1932-36; news dir. WKY Radio, Oklahoma City, 1946-50, KWTV, Oklahoma City, 1953-66, Lowe Runkle Co., Oklahoma City, 1966; information officer USIA, Colembo, Ceylon, 1951-53. Trustee Oklahoma City Gridiron Found., 1970-71. Served with AUS, 1943-45. Decorated Bronze Star. Mem. Radio TV News Dirs. Assn. (pres. 1965), Sigma Delta Chi (chpt. pres. 1957). Mason. Home: Oklahoma City, Okla. Died Sept. 13, 1973.

PALMER, CHARLES FORREST, real estate exec.; b. Grand Rapids, Mich., Dec. 29, 1892; s. Walter Millard and Jeannette Hinsdill (Seymour) P.; student Dartmouth, 1914-15; LL.D., Emory U.; m. Laura Sawtell, Oct. 30, 1918; children—Margaret (Mrs. Earl C. Moses, Jr.), Laura (Mrs. T.W. Benedict), Jeannette (Mrs. J.P. Cath). Asso. with Wm. R. Staats Co., realtors, in Pasadena, Cal., Santa Barbara, Cal., San Diego, Chgo., 1912-17; owner C. F. Palmer Co., realtors, Santa Barbara, 1919-20; pres. Palmer, Inc., bus. real estate, Atlanta, 1921-73; U.S. del., Internat. Fedn. for Housing and Town Planning, Mexico City, 1938; Hastings, Eng., 1946; economist and lectr. at numerous univs. Organizer, Techwood Homes, first United States slum clearance project, Atlanta, 1933, chmn. exec. com., 1934-38; chmn. Atlanta Housing Authority, 1938-40; def. housing coordinator Nat. Def. Commn. and Exec. Office of Pres., 1940-42; rep. of Pres. and head spl. housing mission to Gt. Britain, 1942; spl. asst. to Pres., 1943; chmn. Franklin D. Roosevelt Warm Springs (Ga.) Meml. Commn.; mem. Nat. Council, Boy Scouts Am. Chmn. adv. com. grad. sch. city planning Ga. Inst. Tech. Nat. adv. council, Urban Am., Inc. Trustee Jesse Parker Williams Hosp., 1928-40. Mem. Atlanta adv. com. to comdg. gen. Third U.S. Army. Served as lt. Cavalry, U.S. Army, 1917-19. Mem. So. Conf. of Bldg. Owners and Mgrs. (pres. 1923-24), Nat. Assn. Bldg. Owners and Mgrs. (pres. 1930-32), Housing Centre (London), Nat. Planning Assn., Atlanta Hist. Soc. (past v.p.; dir.), Council Fgn. Relations U.S.A., Am. Soc. Planning Ofcls., Nat. Housing and Town Planning Council (Eng.), Ga. World Congress Center (founder, co-chmn. exec. bd.), Internat. Fedn. Housing and Town Planning (Netherlands), Nat. Assn. Housing Ofcls. (pres. 1940), Atlanta C. of C. (pres. 1938), Am. Legion, Mil. Order of Fgn. Wars, English-Speaking Union, Ga. Writers' Assn. (trustee), Delta Kappa Epsilon. Presbyn. Rotarian (Ga. Dist. gov. 1947-48). Clubs: Capital City, Piedmont Driving, Warm Springs Golf; Burning Tree, Cosmos, (Washington); Royal and Ancient Golf; St. Andrews' (Scotland). Author: Adventures of a Slum Fighter, 1955. Contbr. articles on realty and housing to publs. Home: Atlanta, Ga. Died June 16, 1973; interred West View Cemetery, Atlanta.

PALMER, E(PHRAIM) LAURENCE, naturalist; b. McGraw, N.Y., July 8, 1888; s. Ephraim Clark and Laura Lincoln (Darrow) P.; grad. Cortland (N.Y.) State Tchr.'s Coll., 1908; B.A., Cornell U., 1911, M.A., 1913, Ph.D., 1917; m. Katherine E. H. Van Winkle, Dec. 24, 1921; children—Laurence Van Winkle (dec.), Richard Robin. Asst. in botany, Cornell U., 1910-13; instr. botany and elementary agr., 1913, asst. prof. botany, 1914, prof. natural science and extension Instr., 1915-19, Ia. State Tchrs. Coll., Goldwin Smith fellow in botany, Cornell U., 1916-17, asst. prof. rural edn., 1919-22, prof., 1922-52, emeritus prof. nature, conservation edn., 1952, editor Cornell Rural School Leaflet, 1919-52; dir. nature edn., Nature Mag., 1925-59, contbg. editor Natl. Hist. magazine, 1960-62. Enlisted in U.S. Naval Reserve, June 6, 1918. On staff summer sch., U. of Cal. at Los Angeles, 1922, 24, Ia. Agrl. Coll., 1923, 33, Utah Agrl. Coll., 1925, 26, 27, U. of Hawaii, 1931, University Washington, 1937; extension lecturer University California, Berkeley, 1926-27; University Minnesota, 1959; dir. conservation education Nat. Wildlife Fedn., 1950-57; life mem. adv. Council Lab. of Ornithology, Cornell. Fulbright fellow to New Zealand, 1949. Recipient Hornaday gold medal International Union Cons. of Natural Resources 1961; Silver Buffalo award Boy Scouts America, 1964. Member Ecological Society of America, Am. Nature Study Soc. (sec. 1925-29, pres. 1936-37), Am. Soc. Mammalogists, Nat. Council Nature Study Supervisors (pres. 1927), Dept. Science Instruction of N.E.A. (pres. 1929), Wildlife Soc., Wildlife Com. Nat. Research Council, (chmn. 1943-45), Nat. Audubon Soc. (dir. 1943-49), Nat. Assn. Biology Teachers (pres. 1947, hon.), Internat. Union Cons. of Natural Resources (hon. mem.), Nature Conservancy (bd. govs., Nash Conservation award 1954), Sigma Xi, Gamma Alpha, Phi Delta Kappa, Kappa Phi Kappa, Phi Kappa Phi; fellow A.A.A.S., Iowa Academy Sci., Rochester Mus. Sci. Club: Rotary. Author several books relating to field. Editor, McGraw-Hill Nat. Hist. series. Specializes tchg. conservation, nature study and science. Home: Ithaca, N.Y. Died Dec. 18, 1970.

PALMER, STANLEY GUSTAVUS, dean coll. engring.; b. Waterville, Me., Sept. 18, 1887; s. Gustavus Steward and Mary Elisabeth (Stanley) P.; B.S., U. of Nev., 1909; M.E., Cornell U., 1910; m. Ethel G. Prouty, June 12, 1912; children—Robert Stanley, Ruth Estella. Student engineering Telluride Power Co., Logan, Utah, 1910-11; electrician Truckee River Power Co., 1911; electrician Southern Pacific R.R. Co., 1911-15; instr. U. of Nev., 1915-17, asst. prof., 1917-18, prof. elec. engring. and head dept. 1918-46; dean, College of Engring., from 1942. In charge elec. and mech. groups S.A.T.C., U. of Nev., 1918; asst. academic dir. and student counselor, A.S.T.U., U. of Nev., 1943-44. Mem. Am. Assn. Univ. Profs., Am. Inst. of Elec. Engrs., Am. Soc. for Engring., Edn., A.A.A.S., Sigma Alpha Epsilon, Phi Kappa Phi. Republican. Methodist. Mason (33° Scottish Rite, Shriner, O.E.S.). On U. of Nev. Alumni Honor Service Roll. Home: Reno, Nev., Died Oct. 31, 1975.

PALMER, WILLISTON BIRKHIMER, army officer; b. Chicago, Ill., Nov. 11, 1899; s. Charles Day and Edith Howard (Birkhimer) P.; B.S., U.S. Mil. Acad., 1919; unmarried. Commd. 2d lt., U.S. Army, 1918, and advanced through the grades to gen., 1955; comdg. VII Corps Arty., 1944-45; comd. 82d Airborne Div., 1950, comdg. 2d Armored Div., 1951; comdg. X Corps (Korea), 1952; vice chief of staff U.S. Army, 1955; dep. comdr. in chief Europe, 1957; dir. mil. assistance Dept. Def., Washington, from 1960; later vice chief Staff U.S. Army. Clubs: Army and Navy, Chevy Chase (Washington). Home: Washington, D.C. Died Nov. 1973.

PALUMBO, LEONARD, physician; b. N.Y.C., May 18, 1921; s. Leonard and Jennie Palumbo; M.D., Duke, 1944. Intern in obstetrics and gynecology Duke Hosp., 1944-45, intern in pathology, 1948, asst. resident in gynecology, 1945-47, asst. resident in endocrinology, 1947, sr. asst. resident in obstetrics and gynecology, 1948-49, resident in obstetrics and gynecology, 1949-50, aslo vis. lectr.; mem. attending staff obstetrics and gynecology N.C. Meml. Hosp.; asso. prof. obstetrics and gynecology Duke, 1950-52; prof. obsterics and gynecology, dir. div. gynecol. oncology dept. obstetrics and gynecology U. N.C., 1952—. Diplomate Am. Bd. Obstetrics and Gynecology (asso. examiner). Mem. South Atlantic Assn. Obstetricians and Gynecologists, A.M.A., So. Med. Assn., Am. Coll. Obstetricians and Gynecologists, N.C. Med. Soc., N.C. Obstet. Soc., Southeastern Soc. Obstetricians and Gynecologists (founding mem., past pres.), Bayard Carter Soc. Obstetricians and Gynecologists (founder mem., past pres.), Robert A. Ross Obstet. and Gynecol. Soc., Soc. Gynecol. Oncology (founding mem.), Phi Beta Kappa, Sigma Xi, Alpha Omega Alpha (sec.-treas. local chpt.). Home: Chapel Hill, N.C. Died Apr. 21, 1974; buried Maplewood Cemetery, Durham, N.C.

PANASSIE, HUGHES LOUIS MARLE HENRI, jazz musicologist; b. Paris, Feb. 27, 1912; s. Louis and Jeanne (Bruvére) P.; ed. Collége de Villefranche-de-Rouergue; div., children—Louis, Henri, Therese. Founder, pres. Hot Club of France, 1932, also founder, dir. club's bulletin; organizer Jazz Festival of Nice, 1948, also various internat. jazz confs.; collaborator weekly Jazz Panorama on radio-TV, 1947-74. Author numerous books and articles on jazz. Address: Montauban France. Died Dec. 8, 1974.

PANCOAST, RUSSELL THORN, architect; b. Merchantville, N.J., Feb. 13, 1899; s. Thomas J. and Katharine Rogers (Collins) P.; student George Sch., 1915-18; B.Arch., Cornell, 1922; m. Katherine Bennett French, Sept. 29, 1923; children—Martha French, Lester Collins. Archtl. draftsman, 1922; prin. architl. firms, Pancoast & Sibert, 1926-27. Russell T. Pancaost, 1927-42, 44-47, Russell T. Pancoast & Assos., 1947-54, Pancoast, Ferendino, Skeels & Burnham, 1954-63, Pancoast, Ferendino, Grafton & Skeels, 1964-67, Pancaost, Ferendino & Grafton, 1967-72; director United National Bank. Miami Beach First National Bank. City planner City of Plantation, Florida, also member zoning board, Fellow A.I.A. (past sec., pres. Fla. S. chpt.); mem. Fla. Assn. Architects (past pres.), Fla. State Bd. Architecture (past pres.), Phi Kappa Psi. Mem. Soc. Friends. Club: Miami. Home: Miami, Fla., Died Nov. 28, 1972.

PANDOLFI, FRANK LOUIS, opera dir.; b. Mormanno, Cosenza, Italy, July 23, 1901; s. Domenico and Francesca (Rotondaro) P.; came to U.S., 1912; grad. high sch.; pvt. mus. tng.; m. Carmela M. Cavalier, July 4, 1938; 1 son, Francis. Singer in profl. theatre, 1926-36; pvt. vocal tchr., Hartford, Conn., 1936-47; head opera dept. Hartford Conservatory Music, 1936-47; exec. dir. Conn. Opera Assn., Hartford, 1942-75; lectr. U. Conn., 1958-59. Decorated commendatore dell' Ordine della Stella della Solidarieta Italiana, 1968; fellow Cesare Barbieri Center Italian Studies, Trinity Coll., Hartford, 1960. Home: West Hartford, Conn. Died Feb. 4, 1975.

PANTSIOS, ATHAN ANASTASON, adhesives products co. exec.; b. Macedonia, Greece, May 2, 1912; s. Anastas K. and Joan (Marin) P.; came to U.S., 1928, naturalized, 1944; Sc.B. with honors, U. Chgo., 1934, M.S., 1936, Ph.D. in Organic Chemistry, 1938; m. Pauline L. Engdahl, May 2, 1941; children—Paula Penelope, Joan Louise, Catherine Stacy. With Ill. Adhesive Products Co., Chgo., 1940-74, pres., tech. dir., 1968-74. Mem. exec. bd. Hyde Park Coop. Soc. Eli Lilly fellow, 1938-40. Mem. Am. Chem. Soc., A.A.A.S., Research and Engring. Council of Graphic Arts, Phi Beta Kappa, Sigma Xi. Clubs: Chicago Chemists, Chicago Mountaineering. Patentee in field. Home: Chicago, Ill. Died Oct. 7, 1974.

PANYUSHKIN, ALEXANDER S(EMYENOVICH) (PANYOOSH'KIN), Soviet ambassador to U.S.; b. Kuibyshev, Russia, 1905; received mil. edn.; married; 2 sons. Served with Russian Red Army; began diplomatic career, 1939; Soviet ambassador to China, 1939-44; retired because of ill health, 1945-47; ambassador to Washington 1947-52; official rep. of Soviet Union on Allied Far Eastern Commn. Mem. revision com. of Communist Party's Central Exec. Com. Decorated Order of Lenin, Order of the Red Banner. Home: Moscow, USSR. Died Nov. 15, 1974.

PAPANEK, ERNST, educator; b. Vienna, Austria, Aug. 20, 1900; s. Johann Alexander and Rosa (Spira) P.; student U. Vienna Med. Sch. and Faculty Philosophy, 1919-27; grad. Fed. Tchrs. Coll., Vienna, 1925; grad. Pedagogical Inst. City of Vienna, 1927; M.S., Columbia, 1943, Ed.D., 1960; m. Helene Goldstern, June 28, 1925; children—Gustav F., George O. Came to U.S., 1940, naturalized, 1949. Tchr., ednl. dir., Austria, 1919-32; editor-in-chief Internat. Pedagogical Information, London, Paris, Prague, 1936-38; organizer, gen. dir. Children's Home and Sch. for Refugee Children, Organization pour la Sante et l'Education France, 1938-40; social worker, then ednl. cons. Children's Aid Soc., N.Y.C., 1943-45; dir. child project dept. Unitarian Service Com., Boston, 1945-47. exec. dir. Am. Youth for World Youth, N.Y.C., 1946-48, Bklyn. Tng. Sch. for Girls, 1948-49, Wiltwyck Sch. for Boys, N.Y.C., 1949-58; prof. edn. City U. N.Y., Queens Coll., 1959-71. Vis. prof. Hiroshima U., Japan, 1967, New Sch. for Social Research, N.Y.C., 1968-71. Mem. bd. edn. Wiltwyck Sch. for Boys, 1968-73; mem. bd. Am. Orgn. pour Sante et Edn., 1943-73, League for Indsl. Democracy, 1941-73. Chmn. internat. affairs com. Social-Democratic Party, 1956; mem. U.S. delegation Socialist Internat., 1957-73. Recipient Distinguished Service award League for Indsl. Democracy, 1962; silver plaque Hiroshima U., 1966. Fellow Royal Soc. Health U.K.; mem. Am. Assn. U. Profs., Am. Fedn. Coll. Tchrs., Comparative Ednl. Assn., Soc. Applied Anthropology, Individual Psychology Assn. N.Y. (exec. v.p. 1946-73), Internat. Soc. Adlerian Psychology (chmn. internat. com. 1951-69), Comparative Ednl. Assn., Am. Assn. Workers for Maladjusted Children (vice chmn. 1970, permanent rep. UN 1959-73), Internat. Assn. Orthopedagogy (exec. com. 1962-73), Am. Sociol. Assn., Fedn. Internat. des Communautes d'Enfants (vice chmn. Am. br. 1966-70), Internat. Union Social Democratic Tchrs. and Profs. (chmn. Am. br. 1956-73), Am. Friends of Austrian Labor (acting vice chmn. 1941-73), Internat. Assn. Social Workers, Assn. Psychiat. Treatment of Offenders, World Fedn. for Mental Health, Am., N.Y. State psychol. assns., John Dewey Soc., Am. Group Therapy Assn., World Edn. Fellowship. Author: Jewish Youth After the Catastrophe, 1948; The Delinquent Child, 1960; Current Psychiatric Therapies, 1962; The Austrian School Reform, 1963; Acting Out, 1965; Summerhill; For and Against, 1969. Contbr. numerous articles to profl. jours. Address: New York City, N.Y. Died Aug. 5, 1973; interred Vienna, Austria.

PAPESH, ALEXANDER ANTHONY, architect; b. Cleve., July 17, 1928; m. Jerry and Mary (Flak) P.; diploma Ecole de Beaux Arts, Fontaine Bleau, France, 1954; B. Arch., Case Western U., 1955; m. Reba Lue Tucker, Jan. 3, 1958; children—Cynthia, Alexander, Rebecca, Rochelle. Chief architect Daborn Engring. Co., Cleve., 1955-63; prin. architect Osborn-Papesh Architects-Engrs., Cleve., 1963-71. Served with AUS, 1946-47. Recipient design competition award Bithorn Stadium, San Juan, Puerto Rico, 1958; Ohio Prestressed Concrete Inst. certificate merit, 1966. Mem. A.I.A., Omicron Delta Kappa, Epsilon Delta Rho. Works include stadiums, other sports facilities, research labs., office bldgs. Home: Broadview Heights, O. Died Nov. 1971.

PARCEL, JOHN IRA, cons. engr.; b. Westfield, Ill., Oct. 24, 1878; s. Samuel Newton and Helen Marshall (Rigg) P.; A.B., Westfield Coll., 1903; B.S. in C.E., U. of Ill., 1909; study and travel in Europe, 1921-22; m. Florence Mary Kirkup, Aug. 14, 1915. Draftsman with Am. Bridge Co., 1906-07; engr. bridge dept. C.M.&St.P. Ry., 1907-08; instr. instructural engring., U. of Minn., 1909-13; asst. prof. U. of Ill., 1913-14; asso. prof. structural engring., U. of Minn., 1914-19, prof. in charge of structural engring., 1919-36. Cons. engr. various projects, including Minneapolis Municipal Auditorium and bridges over Miss. and Mo. rivers; asso. with Sverdrup & Parcel from 1928, full time partner, from 1936. Mem. Am. Society Civil Engineers, American Inst. Cons. Engineers, American Concrete Institute, Sigma Xi, Zeta Psi. Author: (brochure) Secondary Stresses in Steel Bridges (with George A. Maney), 1922; Static-ally Indeterminate Stresses (with same), 1925; contbr. numerous articles to tech. jours. Home: St. Louis, Mo.†

PARDRIDGE, WILLIAM DEWEESE, pub. co. exec., economist; b. Chgo., Jan. 12, 1916; s. Clinton Edwin and Marie (DeWeese) P.; student U. Chgo., 1933-41, 64-65, U. Md., 1961-64; m. Muriel M. Morrissey, Feb. 28, 1944 (div. Aug. 1955); m. 2d; Kathleen M. Toon, June 15, 1960 (div. Oct. 1967); children—William Morrissey, Michael Morrissey. Editor, pub. Air Affairs, Washington, 1944-51; editorial dir., vice chmn. The Wealth of a Nation, Economic Inequities, Stanardsville, Va., 1965-75; econ. analyst writer in 50 daily newspapers in 50 states, 1965-75. Spl. research fellow U. Chgo., 1942-43. Served with USAAF, 1941-42, AUS, 1942-43. Mem. Am. Econ. Polit. Sci. and Sociology Assn. Republican. Home: Washington, D.C. Died May 27, 1975; interred Holly Meml. Cemetery, Albermarble County, Va.

PARHAM, JAMES A., journalist; b. Lumberton, N.C., Feb. 7, 1881; s. Eli and Zilah C. (Bullard) P.; student Campbell (N.C.) Coll., 1901-03; m. Mary Brooks, Dec. 24, 1910. Prin. pub. schools, N.C., 1903-05; employed by N. C. Baptist Pub. Co., Fayetteville, N.C., 1905-06; reporter and copyreader Raleigh (N.C.) News and Observer, 1906-09; pub. and editor Fayetteville (N.C.) Index (weekly), 1909-12; telegraph editor Raleigh News and Observer, 1912-13; news editor Wilmington (N.C.) Star, 1913-17; mng. editor Charlotte (N.C.) Observer, 1917-41, asso. editor, from 1941. Democrat. Baptist. Clubs: Rotary, Executives (charter mem.). Home: Charlotte, N.C.†

PARIS, CHARLES WESLEY, farm coop exec.; b. Atlanta, Jan. 10, 1916; s. Sam J. and Jennie (Shaw) P.; student corr. courses in accounting and bus. adminstrn.; m. Helen Elizabeth Oldham, June 16, 1935; children—Elaine (Mrs. J. A. Winkler), Anita (Mrs. S.C. Middleton), Sam W., Peggy Elizabeth. Various accounting and credit positions, 1932-34; with Cotton Producers Assn., Inc. (name changed to Gold Kist Inc., 1970), 1934-72, mgr., chief exec. officer, 1968-72; exec. v.p. G & M, 1968-72; pres. Coop. Mills, Atlanta 1955-72; vice chmn. Country Best, Washington, 1970-72, A.G. Foods Inc., Fleetwood, Pa., 1970-72; pres. United Coops., Alliance, O., 1965-68, also dir.; pres. Gold Kist, S.A., Lima, Peru; dir. Coop. Mills, Ohio, C.N.&L. R.R., Cotton States Life & Health Ins. Co., Cotton States Mut. Ins. Co. Pres. Ga. Agri-Bus. Council. Mem. Nat. Council Farmer Coops. (dir.), Nat. Broiler Council (pres. 1964-65), Am. Fedn. Poultry Producer Assns. (pres.), Farmers Chem. Assn. (dir.), Am. Poultry Hist. Soc. (com. of 50), Inst. Am. Poultry Industries (dir. 1962-66), Atlanta, Ga. chambers commerce, Ga. Poultry Fedn., Ga. Plant Food Soc., Lay Soc. Diabetic Assn. Baptist (deacon). Mason, Kiwanian. Club: Cherokee Town and Country. Home: Atlanta, Ga. Died June 10, 1972.

PARK, ISABELLE SPRINGER, (Mrs. David Eugene Park), club Woman; b. El Paso, Tex., Nov. 9, 1895; d. Thomas Hanson and Mary Louise (Rogers) Springer; certificate Ethical Culture Sch., N.Y.C., 1915; m. William J. Millard, June 9, 1917; children—William J., Mrs. Elizabeth Malley; m. 2d, David Eugene Park, Sept. 26, 1931; 1 son, David Eugene. Vice pres., sec. Am. Woman's Club, Buenos Aires, Argentina, 1932-36, v.p., Bogota, Colombia, 1937-38; charter mem. Campo Allergo Liberary, Caracas, Venezuela, 1939; pres. Am.

unit Venezuela Red Caracas, 1940-42; Cross, . mem. bd. Harris County unit Am. Cancer Soc., Houston, 1958-62, sec.; mem. bd. Pan Am. Round Table, Houston, 1959-60, asso. state dir. Tex., 1967-75; mem. Woman's com. Nat. Found. Poliomyelitis, N.Y.C., 1948-49. Mem. Am. Inst. Mining, Metall. and Petroleum Engrs. Women's Aux. (mem. bd. 1946-52, v.p.), D.A.R. (mem. bd. N.Y.C. chpt. 1955-57, bd. Houston chpt. 1961-66) Daus. Republic Tex. Home: El Paso, Tex., Died Sept. 26, 1975.

PARKER, EDWARD PICKERING, mfg. games; b. Salem, Mass., Nov. 4, 1912; s. Foster Hegeman and Anna Merrill (Pickering) P.; grad. Phillips Exeter Acad., 1930; A.B. cum laude, Harvard, 1934; m. Natalie Stevens, Apr. 9, 1938; children—Diane, Anne Pickering, Sally Sheldon. With Parker Bros., Inc., Salem, 1934-74 president, later chmn. bd.; v.p. Hawthorne Hotel; v.p., dir. Salem Coop. Bank, Pres. United Fund Salem; Treasurer Salem Tb Assn. Served with USNR, World War II; Capt. Res. ret. Decorated Bronze Star (2). Mem. Toy Mfgrs. of U.S.A. (pres.), Marine Soc. New England. Clubs: Harvard (Boston and N.Y.C.); University (Chgo.); Eastern Yacht; Manchester Yacht; Cruising of Am.; Myopia Hunt. Home: Beverly Farms, Mass. Died Jan. 1, 1974; buried Harmony Grace Cemetery, Salem, Mass.

PARKER, EILA MOORE JOHNSON (MRS. BARTON WISE PARKER), club woman; b. El Paso, Tex., Feb. 9, 1900; d. Robert Franklin and Lida (Stearns) Johnson; student U. Cal. at Berkeley, 1919-21, Armstrong's Coll. Bus. Adminstrn., 1922-23; m. Barton Wise Parker, June 27, 1933; 1 son, Bob Hugh Smith. Office sec. U. Cal., Berkeley, 1924, Berkeley Unified Sch. Dist., 1925-45. No. Cal. pres. W.C.T.U., 1965-72, Alameda County pres., 1956-62, Alameda County treas., 1969-73; pres. Frances Willard Club, Oakland, chmn. bd. trustees, 1956-68; mem. Cal. Council Alcohol Problems, 1958-73. Methodist (v.p. womans soc. Christian service 1954-55). Mem. Order Eastern Star. Home: Berkeley, Cal. Died June 13, 1973; buried Sunset View Country, Albany, Cal.

PARKER, GABE EDWARD, register of U.S. Treasury; b. Fort Towson, Ind., Ty., Sept. 29, 1878; s. John Clay and Eliza E. (Willis) P.; B.A., Henry Kendall Coll., Muskegee, Okla., 1899; m. Louise Elizabeth George, Dec. 25, 1900. Teacher and prin. Spencer Acad., Nelson, Okla., 1899-1900; prin. and supt. Armstrong Acad., Okla., 1900-13; mem. Okla. Constl. Conv., 1907; register of U.S. Treasury, 1913-15; supt. Five Civilized Tribes, Muskegee, Okla., from 1915. Democrat. Presbyn. Mason (32°). Address: Muskogee, Okla.†

PARKER, JOHN CASTIEREAGH, JR., engineer; b. Detroit, Apr. 15, 1879; s. John Castlereagh and Mary (Dimler) P.; B.S., U. Mich., 1901, A.M., 1902, E.E., 1904, D.Eng., 1940; D.Eng., Stevens Inst. of Technology, 1935; m. Elizabeth Brooks Payne, June 20, 1910; children—John Castlereagh III, Mary Elizabeth Sherwood, Brooks O'Connell. With Gen. Elec. Co., Schenectady, N.Y., 1902-03; instr. in elec. engring., Union Coll., Schenectady, 1903-04; asst. to engr. in charge Ontario Power Co., Niagara Falls, Ont.,1904-05; asst. v.p. Niagara, Lockport & Ontario Power Co., Buffalo, N.Y., 1905-06; mech. and elec. engr. Rochester Gas & Electric Co., 1906-15; prof. in charge elec. engring., U. of Mich., 1915-22; elec. engr. Brooklyn Edison Co., N.Y., 1922-26, v.p. in charge engring., 1926-32, pres., 1932-36; vice president Consolidated Edison Company, New York 1936-49; trustee Brooklyn Savings Bank, Barnard Coll., Brooklyn Inst. Arts and Sciences; mem. N.Y. State C. of C. Fellow Am. Inst. Elec. Engrs. (past. pres., dir.), Am. Soc. Mech. Engrs.; mem. Am. Soc. Civ. Engrs., Sigma Xi, Tau Beta Pi, Phi Gamma Delta. Republican. Episcopalian. Clubs: Engineers, Downtown Athletic, Phi Gamma Delta (N.Y. City); Century. Home: U1New York City, N.Y.†

PARKER, MAURICE, lawyer, corp. exec.; b. Pitts., Oct. 13, 1916; s. Israel and Mary Parker; B.A., Pa. State U., 1939; J.D., U. Pitts., 1942; m. Hilda Boreman, 1941; children—Stephen, Marilou. Admitted to Pa., U.S. Supreme Ct. bars; practice of law, 1946-52; cons., former chmn. bd. Wilson Bros. and subsidiaries; chmn. bd. Parker Levitt Corp., Howard Johnson's Motor Ldg., Coraopolis, Pa., Air Poll. Control Corp., IDC Inc., Lakeland (Fla.) Hilton. Served to lt. comdr. USNR, 1941-46. Decorated Bronze Star medal. Clubs: Town and Tennis (N.Y.C.); Westmoreland Country (Pitts.); Boca Raton (Fla.) Golf. Home: Pittsburgh, Pa. Died Feb. 11, 1974.

PARKER, ROSS ISAAC, retired exec.; b. Kansas City, Kan., Aug. 29, 1890; s. Henry Allen and Elizabeth (Jacques) P.; B.S., U. Kan., 1912; m. Lois Harger, June 2, 1915; children—Elizabeth Jean (Mrs. J. R. Ware), Ross Isaac, Lois Harger (Mrs. E.W.J. Faison). With Gen. Electric Co., 1912-55, Chicago office, 1919-55, comml. vp., 1948-55, ret. Mem. Am. Inst. E.E., Western Soc. Engrs., Newcomen Soc. Eng., Indiana Soc. Chicago, Ill. Srs. Golf Assn., Chicago Assn. Commerce and Industry (dir.). Electric Assn. of Chicago, Tau Beta Pi, Theta Tau., Beta Theta Pi. Republican. Presbyn. Clubs: Engineers, University, The Chicago (Chicago); Mohawk (Schenectady); Hinsdale (Ill.) Golf. Home: Hinsdale, Ill. Died Jan. 21, 1973.

PARKHURST, HELEN, educator; b. Durand, Wis., Mar. 8, 1892; d. James H. and Ida (Smalley) Parkhurst; B.S., Wis. State Tchrs. Coll., 1907; grad. student Columbia (summers) 1908, 09, 10, U. Rome, Italy, Jan.-June 1914; studied with Dr. Maria Montessori, 1914; U. Munich, Germany; M.A. in Edn., Yale, 1943. Teacher, 1909-11; head primary tng. dept. Central Wash. Coll. Edn., 1911-12, Central State Tchrs. Coll., Wis., 1912-14; originated lab. plan, Tacoma, Wash., 1910 (later called Dalton lab. plan); started Dalton Sch., N.Y.C., 1916, head mistress, 1916-42; vis. fellow in edn. Yale, 1942-43; head Research Assos., Inc., N.Y.C., 1943-45; edn. cons. Hoffman Sch., Columbia Grammar Sch. for Boys, 1945-47; producer of Child's World radio program, 1947-49, TV program, 1947-48, radio program Children Should be Heard, 1950, Know Your Child, from 1949; pres. Your Child, Inc., from 1942. Decorated Officer Order Orange-Nassau (Netherlands); recipient awards for Child's World: Radio-TV Critics, 1948, Nat. Com. Christians and Jews, 1949. Magazine Digest, 1949, O. Radio Inst., Spl., 1949; nat. award American Medical Association, 1958. Mem. Guild of Ind. Schs., Nat. Assn. Adminstrv. Women, Children's Found. (v.p. 1939-41), Internat. Edn. Assn. (v.p. 1939-41), Am. Women in Radio and TV, Conn. Council Chs., Kappa Delta Pi. Episcopalian. Author: Education on the Dalton Plan, 1922; Work Rhythms in Education, 1935; They Found Jimmy (novel), 1947; Know Your Child (chart), 1950; Exploring The Child's World (introduction by Aldous Huxley), 1951; (with Christine Hotchkiss) Undertow, pub. 1959. Contbr. numerous articles to jours., mags. Visited Japan by ofcl. invitation, 1924-25, 1934-35, 1937, China, 1925; Internat. New Edn. Fellowship, Denmark and Frankfurt, 1929, Nice, France, 1932, Cape Town, South Africa, 1934, Japan, 1935. Lectr., teacher edn. in U.S. and abroad. Home: New Preston, Conn. Died June 1, 1973.

PARKS, WILBUR GEORGE, educator, chemist; b. Rockwood, Pa., Dec. 20, 1904; s. George and Ruby Pearl (Gardner) P.; A.B., U. Pa., 1926; M.A., Columbia, 1928, Ph.D., 1931; m. Margaret Mather Merriman, Nov. 24, 1928; children—Ann Mather, George Merriman. Mem. faculty dept. chemistry, U. R.I., 1931-68, prof. chemistry, 1939-68, chmn. dept., 1950-68, prof. emeritus, 1968-75, dir. sci. criminal investigation labs.; exec. dir. adv. bd. Quartermaster Research and Devel. Nat. Acad. Scis.-NRC, 1943-68; dir. Gordon Research Confs. Mem. sci. adv. panel to sec. army. Trustee Colby Jr. Coll., New London, N.H., New Hampton (N.H.) Sch. Recipient medal for outstanding civilian service U.S. Army. Fellow N.Y. Acad. Scis.; mem. Am. Inst. Chemists (Gold medal 1962), Am. Inst. Chem. Engrs. A.A.A.S., Sigma Xi, Phi Lambda Epsilon. Clubs: Chemists (N.Y.C.); University (Providence); Lions. Contbr. sci. papers Phys. Chemistry. Home: Kingston, R.I. Died Oct. 9, 1975; buried New Fernwood Cemetery, Kingston, R.I.

PARMENTER, FREDERICK JAMES, surgeon; b. Buffalo, N.Y., Nov. 24, 1880; s. Will Louis and Clara (Smith) P.; student DeVeaux Coll., Hobart Coll.; M.D., U. of Buffalo, 1903; m. Ella Kimberly, Nov. 26, 1910 (died Jan. 20, 1942); 1 dau., Mary K.; m. 2d, Esther M. Punnett, April 26, 1943 (died 1948). Practiced at Buffalo, from 1903; became prof. urology, U. of Buffalo, 1918, prof. emeritus; cons. urol. Buffalo General, Meyer Memorial and Children's hospitals. Mem. Med. Advisory Bd. No. 42, World War I. Mem. A.M.A., Med. Soc. State N.Y., Erie County Med. Soc., Buffalo Acad. Medicine, American Urol. Assn., Alumni Assn. U. of Buffalo, Kappa Alpha. Republican. Episcopalian. Club: Saturn. Home: Williamsville, N.Y.† N:M:1884:-1976:W38

PARR, CHARLES MCKEW, author, historian; b. Balt., Nov. 23, 1884; s. Charles Edward and Helen B. (McKew) P.; student U.S. Mil. Acad., 1906, Columbia, 1930; LL.D., U. Bridgeport (Conn.), 1961; m. Ruth Butler, June 22, 1916; children—Charles McKew, Alexander Shipman, Dir. Thomas Y. Crowell Co., Parr Electric Co., Inc., Parr Marine & Export Corp. Spl. asst. to sec. of state, 1918; fgn. agt., War Trade Bd., Bur. Exports Washington, 1918; counsular service in Spain and Canary Islands, 1919; sr. elec. cons. WPB, 1942; chmn. Industry Adv. Com., 1952; Mem. Conn. Ho. of Reps. from Chester, 1942-49, Conn. Sentate from Middlesex County, 1950-54. Donated McKew Parr Magellan collection to Brandeis U., 1961; chmn. Middletown (Conn.) Library - Service Center, 1955-57; chmn. trustee div. Conn. Library Assn., 1953; chmn. Chester (Conn.) Pub. Library, 1955-65. Decorated comdr. Orden Militar d Cristo (Portugal), comdr. Order Orange-Nassau (Netherlands). Mem. Am. Air Force Acad. Library, Am., Conn., N.J. library assns., John Carter Brown Library Assos., Yale Library Assos., Am. Geog. Soc., Am., Deep River hist. socs., N.J. Hist. Soc., Hispanic Soc. Am., West Point Soc. N.Y., Bibliophile Soc. Brandeis U., S.A.R., Md. Soc. Colonial Wars, Nat. Assn. Elec. Distbrs. (bd. dirs.), Essex Elec. League (bd. dirs.), Newark C. of C. (bd. dirs.), Soc. De Geografia de Lisboa, Soc. Nautical Research, Hist. Assn. London, Hakluyt Soc. London, De Linschoten-Ver- eeniging, Nederlandsch Historisch Scheepvaart Museum Biblioteca Capitular Columbina Sevelle. Rotarian. Clubs: Essex (Newark); Hartford (Conn.); N.Y. Athletic, Players (N.Y.C.). Author: Over and Above Our Pacific, 1941; So Noble a Captain, 1953; Magallanes, 1955; Jan Van Linschoten, The Dutch Marco Polo, 1964; Ferdinand Magellan Circumnavigator, 1964; The Voyages of David DeVries, 1969. Home: Chester, Conn., Died Feb. 7, 1976.

PARROTT, ALONZO LESLIE, clergyman, coll., pres.; b. Monterey, Tenn., May 20, 1891; s. Thomas Carrol and Samantha (Hollaway) P.; A.B., A.M., Southwestern, Memphis, Tenn., 1922; B.D., Trevecca Coll., Nashville, Tenn., 1922; D.D., Bethany-Peniel Coll., Bethany, Okla., 1938; m. Lucile Elliott, Dec. 18, 1913; children—Lorene (Mrs. Ralph E. Perry), Alonzo Leslie, John Carrol. Ordained to ministry of Church of the Nazarene, 1917; pastor, First Ch. of Nazarene, Clarksville, Tenn., 1917-22, First Ch., Bethany, Okla., 1922-31, First Ch., Springfield, Ill., 1931-38; pres. Olivet Nazarene College, Kankakee, Ill., 1938-47; field sec. Samaritan Hosp. Sch. of Nursing from 1947. Mem. Phi Delta Lambda. Club: Rotary. Home: Bourbonnais, Ill., Died Jan. 20, 1976.

PARSONS, ANDREW CLARKSON, supt. schs.; b. Savonburg, Kan., Feb. 5, 1881; s. Leonard and Phoebe (Fausett) P.; grad. Eldorado Normal and Business Coll., 1898; student Warrensburg (Mo.) Normal Sch., 1899, U. of Okla., 1901-02; A.B., U. of Neb., 1903; grad. student U. of Colo., U. of Chicago; LL.D., Oklahoma City Coll., 1923; m. Nellie May Hunt, Aug. 27, 1913; children—Betty Nell, Andrew Clarkson, Jr., Jane. Prin. pub. schs., Ft. Calhoun and Blair, Neb., 1903-09; prof. psychology and edn. and dir. training sch., Southeastern State Normal Sch., Durant, Okla., 1909-10; asst. state supt. pub. instrn., Okla., 1911; sec. State Bd. Edn., 1912; state insp. high schs. and prof. ednl. adminstration, U. of Okla., 1912-22; chmn. Okla. High Sch. Conf., 1912-23; became supt. schs., Oklahoma City, 1922; v.p. Globe Fire Insurance Co. Established system of accredited high schs. in Okla., also Sch. for Crippled Children, Oklahoma City; mem. bd. regents Oklahoma City Coll. Mem. N.E.A. (state dir.), Okla. Edn. Assn. (ex-pres.), Nat. Soc. for Study of Edn., Phi Delta Kappa, etc. Democrat. Methodist. Mason. Kiwanian. Author of various courses of study, etc. Home: Norman, Okla.*†

PARSONS, C(HAUNCEY) LELAND, aerospace engr.; b. Washington, Feb. 3, 1919; s. Henry Spaulding and Gladys Crosby (McCarthy) P.; B.A., Am. U., 1941; postgrad. U. Md., 1946-49; m. Mabel Eleanor Wright, Jan. 10, 1942; children—Richard James, John Frederick. Physicist, ship magnetics, U.S. Navy, Norfolk, Va., 1941-45; physicist, ship model magnetics U.S. Naval Ordinance Lab., White Oakd, Md., 1945-62; aerospace engr., spacecraft magnetics NASA Goddard Space Flight Center, Greenbelt, Md., 1962-73. Pres. Burtonsville (Md.) Vol. Fire Dept., 1959-73. Mem. Am. Geophys. Union, Am. Inst. Aeros. and Astronautics, A.A.A.S., Potomac River Power Squadron (comdr. 1967, U.S. Power squadron dist. 5 edn. officer 1970). Clubs: Rose Haven Yacht (commodore 1969) (Rose Haven, Md.); Potomac Navigator (pres. 1966) (Washington). Patentee in field. Home: Burtonsville, Md. Died July 3, 1973.

PARSONS, MARION RANDALL, writer; b. San Francisco, Dec. 14, 1880; d. Charles Wells and Nancy (Garabrant) Randall; pvtly. ed.; m. Edward Taylor Parsons, Mar. 7, 1907 (died 1914). Mountain climber; first ascent of Mt. Bruce, Southern Selkirks, 1914; more than 50 ascents of major peaks in Sierra Nevada, Cascade ranges, Olympics, Selkirks and Canadian Rockies, 1903-02. Served with Civilian Relief br. of Am. Red Cross, in France, July 13, 1918-Aug. 5, 1919; in charge relief for refugees, Dept. of Landes, Aug.-Dec. 1918; dir. 3 arrondissements, Dept. of Ardennes, Jan.-July 1919. Decorated Médaille de la Reconnaissance Francaise. Club: Sierra of San Francisco (dir. 1914). Author: A Daughter of the Dawn, 1923; also articles in Travel Mag., Smart Set and Overland Monthly. Editor of Travels in Alaska, by John Muir, after his death. Home: Berkeley, Cal.†

PARSONS, RALPH MONROE, engr., constrn. co. exec.; b. Springs, L.I., N.Y., June 22, 1896; s. Frank W. and Sarah (Monroe) P.; student engring., Pratt Inst., N.Y.C., 1914-16, Engring. (hon.), 1957; m. Ruth Bennett, Oct. 17, 1917 (dec. 1961); m. 2d, Kathryn C. Persons, Dec. 28, 1969. Aero. engr. Navy Dept., 1921-24; chief engr. Interocean Oil Co., Balt., 1924-28, Leamon Process Co., Newark, O. 1928-30; pres., gen. mgr. Ralph M. Parsons Co. (Del.), 1930-41; v.p., dir. Cal. Shipbldg. Corp., 1940-44; pres., gen. mgr. Ralph M. Parsons Co. (Nev.), Los Angeles, 1944-64, chmn. bd., chief exec. officer 1964-74; chmn. bd., chief exec. officer Parsons Corp., Ralph M. Parsons Co. Asia, Ralph M. Parsons Co. (U.K.) Ltd., Ralph M. Parsons G.m.b.H., Ralph M. Parsons Constrn. Co. Can. Ltd., Parsons-Jurden Corp., also Parsons Internat. Mem. corp. vis. dept. of civil engring. Mass. Inst. Tech., 1964-74; asso. Woods Hole (Mass.) Oceanographic Instn. 1966-74; trustee Harvey Mudd Coll., Claremont, Cal.; trustee Pratt Inst., 1963-74, Webb Inst. Naval Architecture, 1966-74. Served to lt. (j.g.) USNRF, 1917-21. Recipient Golden Beavers award for engring. The Beavers, 1963, Moles award, 1974. Mem. Am. Inst. Mining, Metall. and Petroleum Engrs. Clubs: Marco Polo, Harbor View, Sky, India House (N.Y.C.); California, Jonathan, University, Petroleum, Los

Angeles Country (Los Angeles). Home: San Marino, Cal. Died Dec. 20, 1974; interred Forrest Lawn, Glendale, Cal.

PARTCH, HARRY, composer, b. 1901; recorded compositions include: Wayward, 1943, Cloud Chamber Music, 1950, Plectra and Percussion Dances, 1953, Bewitched, 1957, Windsong (filmtrack), 1958. Recipient Marjorie Peabody Waite award 1,500, 1966. Home: San Diego, Cal. Died Sept. 3, 1974.

PAS, ION, author, journalist; b. Bucharest, Oct. 6, 1895; self-educated. Publicity work, 1914-74; dir. Nat. Theatre Bucharest, 1946; minister arts, 1947-48; prime dep. minister culture, 1955-58; pres. Radio-Television, 1958-65; pres. Rumanian Inst. for Cultural Relations with Fgn. Countries, 1965-74. Mem. central com. Rumanian Communist party, 1948-69; dep. Grand. Nat. Assembly, 1946-68. Named Hero of Socialist Labour, 1971. Mem. Union Journalists of S.R.R., S.R.R. Writers Union (v.p.), Journalists Trade Union (pres. 1944-47). Author: The Days of Your Life, 1950; Chains, 1952. Address: Bucharest, Rumania. Died May 12, 1974.

PASCALL, THOMAS M., physician; b. N.Y. City, Nov. 14, 1880; s. George William and Minnie A. (Stagg) P.; ed. Newark pub. schs. and pvt. tutors; Ph.G., N.J. Coll. Pharmacy, 1900; M.D., U. of Md., 1906; D. Pharm., hon. Rutgers U., 1943; m. Jean L. Robinson, Feb. 5, 1910; 1 dau., Jean M. (Mrs. Ruel S. Dally). Intern Sparrows Point (Md.) Hosp., 1906-07; St. Michael's Hosp., Newark, 1908, assistant visiting surgeon, 1908-13; prof. pharmaceutical jurisprudence and hygiene N.J. Coll. of Pharmacy, 1908-11; chief surgeon Public Service Corporation, 1911-51; cons. Fidelity Union Trust Co., from 1916. Mem. A.M.A., Indsl. Surgeons of U.S.A.., N.J. State and Essex Co. med. socs. Author: Lethal Effects of Electricity, 1946. Address: Newark, N.J.†

PASCHALL, J(OSHUE) E(RNEST), lawyer, state legislator; b. nr. Black Creek, N.C., Aug. 9, 1896; s. Joshua Walter and Sallie (Poole) P.; student U. N.C., 1917; A.B., Atlantic Christian Coll., 1918, LL.D., 1961; LL.B., Am. U., Los Angeles, 1926; m. Claire Hodges, Dec. 18, 1919 (dec. 1973); children—Julia Daly (Mrs. Charles W. Mauze), James E. With Branch Banking & Trust Co., Wilson, N.C., 1919-74, asst. cashier, 1933-43, dir., 1943-74, cashier, 1943-52, v.p. 1942-52, pres., 1952-64; dir. Wilson Savs. & Loan Assn., pres., 1944-74; mem. N.C. Ho. of Reps., 1964-72; engaged in law practice, Wilson, 1964-74. Mem. Banking Commn. N.C., 1961-65. Vice chmn., bd. trustees, mem. exec. com., chmn. finance com. Atlantic Christian Coll.; bd. dirs. Coastal Plain Planning and Devel., assn. pres., 1965-66. Served with USNRF, 1918-19. Mem. Am., N.C., Wilson County bar assns., C. of C. (pres. 1945), Am. Legion (post comdr. 1935-36). Mem. Christian Ch. (ofcl. bd., trustee). Elk, Moose, Rotarian. Club: Wilson. Home: Wilson N.C. Died Nov. 6, 1974.

PASOLINI, PIER PAOLO, poet, writer, film dir.; b. 1922; Author: Poesie a Casarsa, 1942; I Diari, 1945; Dov'e la mia Patria, 1949; Poesia dialettale del '900, 1952; La Meglio Gioventu, 1954; Dal Diario, 1954; Pagazzi di Vita, 1955; Canzoniere Italiano, 1955; Le Ceneri di Gramsci, 1957; L'Usingnolo della Chiesa cattolica, 1958; Una· Vita violenta, 1959; Sonetto primaveril, 1960; La Poesia popolare italiana, 1960; Orestiade de Exchilo. 1960; Passione e Ideologia, 1960; Roma 1950, 1960; dir. films Accattone, 1961; Mamma Roma, 1962; Il Vangelo Second Matteo, Uccelacci e uccellini. Address: Rome, Italy., Died Nov. 2, 1975.*

PATMAN, WRIGHT, congressman; b. Patman's Switch, Tex., Aug. 6, 1893; s. John and Emma (Spurlin) P.; grad. high sch., Hughes Springs, Tex., 1912; LL.B., Cumberland U., 1916; m. Merle Connor, Feb. 14, 1919 (dec. July 1967); children—Connor Wright, James Harold, William Neff; m. 2d, Pauline Tucker, Oct. 9, 1968. Cotton farmer, Tex., 1913-14; admitted to Tex. bar, 1916, began practice at Hughes Springs; asst. county atty. Cass County, Tex., 1916-17; dist. atty. 5th Jud. Dist., Tex., 1924-29. Mem. Tex. Ho. of Reps., 1921-24; mem. 71st-94th Congresses from 1st Tex. Dist. Served as pvt., machine gun officer, World War I, 1917-19. Mem. Am. Legion, D.A.V. Democrat. Baptist. Mason (33 deg.). Home: Texarkana, Tex. Died Mar. 8, 1976.

PATMOS, MARTIN, physician; b. Hudsonville, Mich., Nov. 11, 1901; s. Joseph and Lucy Patmos; M.D., U. Mich., 1928; M.S. in Medicine, U. Minn., 1934; m. Alice Eleanor Brown, June 7, 1935; children—William M., Jean (Mrs. A. Bertrand Segur). Intern, Blodgett Meml. Hosp., Grand Rapids, Mich., 1928-29; fellow in medicine Mayo Found., 1929-32; practice medicine specializing in internal medicine, Kalamazoo; mem. staff Bronson Meth. Hosp., Borgess Hosp.; chief sect. on upper respiratory disease Gardiner Gen. Hosp., 1944-71. Served wtih M.C., AUS, 1942-46. Diplomate Am. Bd. Internal Medicine. Fellow A.C.P.; mem. A.M.A., Am. Hosp. Assn., Kalamazoo Rose Soc., Presbyn. (elder). Home: Kalamazoo, Mich. Died Sept. 2, 1971; buried Riverside Cemetery, Kalamazoo, Mich.

PATRICK, GEORGE NEILL, banker; b. Bklyn., Mar. 17, 1880; s. John and Janet (Law) P.; A.B., Amherst Coll., 1903; m. Ida Poole Brown, Apr. 17, 1907; children—Catherine Poole (Mrs. Alfred Mass), Janet Law (Mrs. Kirkwood A. Tischler). Clk. S. F. Johnson & Co., N.Y. City, 1903-04; cashier Chisholm & Chapman, N.Y. City, 1904-06; mgr. Troy (N.Y.) office Graham, Taylor & Co., 1906-09; mgr. J. L. Graham & Co., 1909-16; resident partner (Troy) J. L. Graham & Co., 1916-18, Auchincloss, Joost & Patrick, 1918-22, Joost, Patrick & Co., 1922-37, H. T. Carey, Joost & Patrick, from 1937, all mems. N.Y. Stock Exchange; instr. Am. Inst. of Banking, 1932-33. Pres. Troy C. of C. 1937; honorary president Troy Area Boy Scouts America; dir. Leonard Hosp., Troy; former dir. Y.M.C.A., Troy; dir. Troy Pub. Library. Awarded Silver Beaver, Boy Scouts of America. Member Psi Upsilon. Republican. Presbyterian. Mason; trustee King Solomon Lodge F.&A.M., Troy, N.Y. Clubs: Troy, Troy Country; Amherst, Psi Upsilon (New York). Home: Troy, N.Y.*†

PATRICK, REMBERT WALLACE, educator, author; b. Columbia, S.C., June 9, 1909; s. Joel Edward and Lucile (Williams) P.; A.B., Guilford Coll., 1930; A.M., U. N.C., 1934, Ph.D., 1940; m. Eleanor Grace Bangs, Dec. 22, 1933; children—Rembert Wallace, Sharon Lee, John Robinson Gangs. Instr. and coach North (S.C.) Consol. Schs., 1931-33, prin., 1934-36; asst. prof. history Meredith Coll., Raleigh, N.C., 1939-40; asst. prof. social sci. U. Fla., 1940-43, asso. prof., 1943-45, prof., 1945-47, prof. Am. history, social sci., 1947-59, Julien C. Yonge grad. research prof., 1959-66, chmn. dept. history, 1950-55; grad. research prof. U. Ga., 1966-69; vis. prof. Columbia, summer 1956; Young lectr. Memphis State U., 1957; Fleming lectr. La. State U., 1959. Chmn. Fla. Library Bd., 1953-54; clk. Southeastern Friends Conf., 1958-60. Recipient ¾0 award Ph.D. dissertation (U.D.C.) 1940; Bohenberger award for best first book by So. writer, 1946; Merit Award Fla. Jr. C. of C., 1946. Faculty fellow Am. Security Business, 1952; Ford faculty fellow Yale, 1954-55. Mem. Am., Miss Valley hist. assns., So. Hist. Soc. (pres. 1962), Am. Assn. State and Local History (council 1956-60, v.p. 1960-66, exec. council 1966—), Fla. Hist. Soc. (past. (past dir., rec. sec.), Fla. Library Assn. (v.p. 1953-54), So. Polit. Sci. Assn. (sec.-treas. 1942-44), Sigma Alpha Epsilon (chpt. adviser). Democrat. Mem. Soc. Friends. Author: Jefferson Davis and His Cabinet, 1944; Florida Under Five Flags, rev. 4th edit., 1967; Florida Fiasco, 1953; Fall of Richmond, 1960; Aristocrat in Uniform, 1963 (with others) The American People (2 vols.); New Land, New Lives, 1966; The Reconstruction of the Nation, 1967; also articles in magazines and newspapers. Editor: Rambler (Guide to Florida), 1964. Mng. editor Jour. Politics, 1942-44; editorial bd. Jour. So. History, 1950-54; editor Fla. Hist. Quar. 1952-62, The Opinions of the Confederate Attorneys General, 1950; gen. editor Florida Reprint series, 22 vols. Home: Athens, Ga., Died Nov. 16, 1967.

PATTEN, DAVID, newspaper editor; b. Boston, Mass., Apr. 12, 1888; s. Frederick Marcy and Dora Josephine (Wilbour) P.; grad. high sch., Brookline, Mass., 1906; student Wesleyan University, Middletown, Conn.; m. Martha Louise Fuller, May 1, 1912; children—Dora (Mrs. George C. Vaughan), Henrietta (dec.), Davice (dec.). Reporter Fall River (Mass.) News, 1917; reporter Providence (R.I.) Journal, 1918-20, night city editor, 1920; city editor Providence Bulletin, 1924, mng. editor, 1925-46; mng. editor Providence Evening . Journal-Bulletin, 1946-53. Mem. American Society of Newspaper Editors, Associated Press Managing Editors' Association, Beta Theta Pi. Clubs: R.I. Country, Providence Art. Home: Barrington, R.I., Died Dec. 23, 1975; buried Wilbour Cemetery, Little Compton, R.I.

PATTERSON, CALEB PERRY, educator; b. Saltillo, Tenn., Jan. 23, 1880; s. Robert Henry and Mary Ann (Creasy) P.; B.A., Vanderbilt U., 1911, M.A., 1911; grad. study, U. of Chicago, 1911-12; M.A., Harvard, 1916; LL.B., U. of Tex., 1921; Ph.D., Columbia, 1923; m. Tommie Cochran, Aug. 8, 1907. Instr. in literature, Vanderbilt U., 1910-11; prof. history and govt., W. Tenn. Teachers Coll., Memphis, 1912-17; instr. history, Columbia, 1918-19; instr. in govt., U. of Tex., 1919-20, adjunct prof., 1920, asso. prof., 1920-25; prof., 1925-28, graduate professor, 1928-57, professor emeritus, from 1957. Carnegie research prof. in Europe, 1926, Rockefeller Spellman research prof., England, 1931-32. Mem. Am. Polit. Science Assn., Southwestern Social Science Assn.; founder Hon. Scholarship Soc. in Polit. Science (pres. 10 yrs., now hon. pres.); hon. mem. Eugene Field Society of National Authors: hon. mem. Internat. Mark Twain Soc. S.A.R., Am. Bar Assn., Pi Sigma Alpha, Phi Kappa Psi. Town and Gown. Author or co-author of books relating to field; latest publication: Presidential Government in the United States, 1947; the Constitutional Principles of Thomas Jefferson, 1953. Co-author of The American Presidency in Transition, 1949; Oil in Texas, 1951; Introduction to Jurisprudence, 1952. Asso. editor of Education; editor Southwestern Social Science Quarterly for 10 years. D.C. Health's Political Science Series. Contbr. to Brooklyn, Boston U., Georgetown, Cal., U. of Wash., Texas Law Revs., Minn. Law Rev. Am. Bar Journal. Home: Austin, Tex.*†

PATTERSON, HANNAH JANE; b. Smithton, Pa., Nov. 5, 1879; d. John Gilfallen and Harriet (McCune) P.; A.B., Wilson Coll., Chambersburg, Pa., 1901. Mem. Woman's Suffrage Party of Pa. (state chmn., 1912-15); sec. Nat. Am. Woman's Suffage Assn., 1916; mem. res. dir. Woman's Com. Council Nat. Defense, Sept. 1917-19, asso. dir. field div., 1919; asst. to sec. of war, 1919. Received D.S.M., 1919. Mem. bd. trustees Wilson Coll. Clubs: College, Woman's City, Twentieth Century. Consultant for women, J. H. Holmes & Co., investment brokers. Home: Pittsburgh, Pa.†

PATTERSON, MARY KING, editor; b. Chgo., 1885; d. William and Mary (McMahon) King; student Sacred Heart, St. Mary's High Sch., bus. coll.; m. Joseph Medill Patterson (dec.); 1 son, James Sunday editor Chicago Tribune, 1914-26; woman's editor Liberty Mag., 1926-30; woman's editor N.Y. News, fiction editor Chicago Tribune, N.Y. News Syndicate, from 1930; dir. Tribune Co., Chgo., Chicago Tribune Bldg. Corp., Chicago Tribune-New York News Syndicate, Inc., News Welfare Assn., Inc.; trustee McCormick-Patterson Trust. Roman Catholic. Clubs: Women's Nat. Press (Washington); Newspaper Women's, Cosmopolitan (N.Y.C.). Home: New York City, N.Y., Died Dec. 27, 1975.

PATTERSON, ROBERT DEMPSTER, ins. co. exec.; b. Glasgow, Scotland, July 10, 1896; s. William and Mary (Dempster) P.; came to U.S., 1911, naturalized, 1918; S.B., Mass. Inst. Tech., 1920; m. Laura Cornell-Dobbs, Apr. 17, 1968. Engr., E.L. Phillips & Co., Inc., N.Y.C., 1920-22; sales engr. Fireproof Products Co., Inc., N.Y.C., 1922-27; mgr. Albany (N.Y.) office Rogers Caldwell & Co., 1927-31; v.p., treas. Prescott Grover & Co., N.Y.C., 1931-34; financial v.p. John Hancock Mut. Life Ins. Co., Boston, 1934-61; v.p., treas., dir. Foursquare Corp., Foursquare Fund, Inc.; dir. Garden City Trust Co., High Voltage Engring Corp., Curtis Pub. Co. Ivy Fund, Trusteed Funds; trustee Union Savs. Warren Bank, Boston, Curtis Estate. Mem. bd. commrs. sinking fund City of Boston. Mem. Boston Mus. Fine Arts, Cambridge Sch. Design, Copley Soc., Sigma Alpha Epsilon, Theta Tau. Home: Boston, Mass. Died Oct. 5, 1972; interred Mt. Auburn Cemetery, Cambridge, Mass.

PATTERSON, SAMUEL WHITE, educator; b. N.Y. City, Dec. 25, 1883; s. Matthew and Mary (Maxwell) P.; A.B., Coll. City N.Y., 1903; A.M., Columbia, 1910, Masters Diploma in History of Edn., 1910; A.M., N.Y. U., 1906, Ph.D., 1913; m. May Blauvelt, Feb. 28, 1919 (dec.). Instr. English, Columbia, 1914-17; lectr. on Am. instns. Bd. Edn., N.Y. City, 1909-26; head English dept. N.Y. Tchrs. Tng. Coll., 1920-30; mem. faculty Hunter Coll. from 1930, professor of education, 1948-52, professor emeritus, 1952-75, lecturer Am. history, 1944-45, acting dir. eve. and extension sessions, 1941-42. Mem. bd. dirs. Internat. Assn. Daily Vacation Bible schs. from 1946. Mem. Surgeon Gen. Staff, U.S. Army, 1918. Recipient medal and citation from Treasury Dept., 1946; certificate of merit Rice Leaders of World Assn., 1956; medal Freedoms Found. of Valley Forge, 1963; named in his honor Alcove in Colburn Library of Bexler Hall. Mem. Ch. Hist. Soc. Am., Am. Acad. Polit. and Social Sci., Acad. Polit. Am. Christian Palestine Com. (mem. of the auxiliary council), Met. Mus. Art. Am. Friends Bodley's Oxford U., St. Andreed Soc., Municipal Art Soc. N.Y., Pilgrims of U.S., Am. Revolution Roundtable (founder mem.), Phi Beta Kappa. Episcopalian. Clubs: Schoolmasters (past pres.), Columbia Alumni. Author: Spriit of the American Revolution as Revealed in Poetry of the Period, 1915; Famous Men and Places in the History of N.Y. City, 1923; Geography of New York and Far Away Lands, 1929; Teaching the Child to Read, 1930; Old Chelsea and St. Peter's Church, 1935; Etchings in Verse, 1939; Horatio Gates-Defender of American Liberties, 1941; History of Hunter College, 1955; Poet of Christmas Eve, A Life of Clement Clarke Moore, 1956; Knight Errant of Liberty, 1958; When Saint Nicholas Got Back, 1958; Occasions Glimpsed from the Mount, 1961; The Good Samaritan and His Friends, 1968; My Beloved Hudson Valley, 1968. Editor: Adam Bede, 1923; Jr. High Sch. Literature Series, 1928; Autobiograph of Olin Scott Roche, 1930; Thirty-Sixth Yearbook of Nat. Soc. for Study of Education, Part 1 (with W. S. Gray and others), 1937. Contbr. to edn. and hist. periodicals. Home: New York City, N.Y., Died Nov. 20, 1975.

PATTERSON, WILLIAM HARVEY, funeral director; b. Cynthiana, O., Dec. 28, 1918; s. James Harvey and Blanche Elizabeth (Little) P.; grad. Cin. Coll. Embalming, 1940; grad. Realtors Inst. Ohio State U., 1968; m. Kathleen F. Wilson, July 7, 1942; children—Kay Elizabeth (Mrs. John V. Rittenhouse), Michael. Owner, Patterson Funeral Home, Leesburg, O., 1947-74; owner Patterson Auction Service, 1966-74, Patterson Realty, 1968-74; partner Harfer Homes, constrn. co., 1971-74. Mem. Highland County Bd. Health, 1968-74. Served with AUS, 1941-45. Decorated 4 Bronze Stars. Mem. Ohio Auctioneer Assn. (dir. 1970-73), Highland County Bd. Realtors (dir. 1973-74, pres. 1971), Nat. Auctioneers Assn., Am. Legion. Mason (Shriner), Elk. Home: Leesburg, O. Died Feb. 24, 1974; interred Pleasant Hill Cemetery, Leesburg.

PATTERSON, WILLIAM MORRISON, author, educator; b. of Am. parents, at Mexico City, Mexico, Mar. 11, 1880; s. Rev. William McKendree and Delia (Morrison) P.; B.A., Vanderbilt, 1899; studied U. of

Chicago and Harvard; Ph.D., Columbia, 1916; European research and study. Spl. fellow, U. of Chicago, 1899-1900; head of English dept. Neb. Wesleyan U., 1903-06; head of modern lang. dept., Morristown (N.J.) Sch., 1909-13; Cutting traveling fellow, Columbia, 1915-16; instr. in English, Columbia, 1916-17; in charge (temp.) Slater Mil. Corps, Columbia, 1917; spl. agt. Dept. of Commerce (Latin Am. div.), 1917-18; pres. Jute Products, Inc., New York, 1920-22; chmn. modern lang. dept. U. of Del., 1923-26; investigator at Marine Biol. Lab., Wood's Hole, Mass., summer 1927; guest of Columbia U., for research in Psychol. Lab. (spl. phonetics), 1927-28. Mem. Modern Lang. Assn. America, Am. Assn. Univ. Profs., Poetry Soc. America, N.Y. Soc. Colonial Wars, Phi Beta Kappa. Delta Kappa Epsilon. Chevalier Legion of Honor (France), 1927. Mem. M.E. Ch., S. Club: University (New York). Author: The Rhythm of Prose, 1916, 17; also articles in mags. Lecturer on Phonetics and Origin of Language. Address: New York City, N.Y.†

PATTON, JAMES WELCH, educator; b. Murfreesboro, Tenn., Sept. 28, 1900; s. James Wesley and Elizabeth (Welch) P.; A.B., Vanderbilt U., 1924; A.M., U. N.C., 1925, Ph.D., 1929; m. Carlotta Dorothea Petersen, June 25, 1930; 1 dau., Emily Frances (Mrs. Deluca). Faculty history Ga. State Woman's Coll., 1925-27; asso. prof. hist. The Citadel, 1929-30; asst. prof. hist. Wittenberg Coll., 1930-31; prof. history Converse Coll., 1931-42; prof. history and polit sci., head dept. N.C. State Coll., 1942-48; prof. history U. N.C., Chapel Hill, 1948-73, dir. So. Hist. collection, 1948-67. Mem. adv. council Civil War Centennial Commn., 1958-73. Pres., S.C. Hist. Assn., 1938-39. Fellow Soc. Am. Archivists; mem. Am., So. (pres. 1956) hist. assns. Orgn. Am. Historians, Hist. Soc. N.C. (pres. 1966), English-Speaking Union (br. pres. 1966), Soc. Am. Archivists, N.C. Lit. and Hist. Assn. (pres. 1964), Phi Beta Kappa, Phi Kappa Phi, Sigma Chi. Democrat. Episcopalian. Author: Unionism and Reconstruction in Tennessee, 1934; The Women of the Confederacy (with Francis B. Simkins), 1936; editor: Minutes of the Greenville Ladies' Association in Aid of the Confederate Army, 1937; contbr. to Dictionary Am. Biography, Dictionary Am. History. Editor: Messages, Addresses, and Public Papers of Luther H. Hodges, Governor N.C., 1954-61, 3 vols., 1960, 62, 63. Home: Chapel Hill, N.C. Died May 17, 1973; interred Chapel Hill Cemetery.

PATTULLO, GEORGE, author; b. Woodstock, Ont., Can., Oct. 9, 1879; s. George Robson and Mary (Rounds) P.; ed. Woodstock Collegiate Inst.; m. Lucile, d. J.B. Wilson, Nov. 5, 1913. In newspaper work, Montreal, London, Eng., and Boston until 1908. Mem. Zeta Psi. Clubs: Brook Hollow (Dallas; The Players; Union (New York); Old Guard (Palm Beach, Fla.). Author: The Untamed, 1911; The Sheriff of Badger, 1912; Horrors of Moonlight, 1939; A Good Rooster Crows Everywhere, 1939; All Our Yesterdays, 1948; Always New Frontiers, 1951; Era of Infamy, 1952; Morning After Cometh, 1954; How Silly Can We Get?, 1956; Some Men In Their Time, 1959; also numerous short stories in Saturday Evening Post, McClure's, American, Popular, etc. Spl. corr. Sta. Evening Post with AEF in France, 1917-18, Germany, 1919. Home: New York City, V1N.Y.†

PAUL, ARTHUR, econ. cons.; b. Chestnut Hill, Pa., Aug. 28, 1898; s. Henry N. and Margaret C. (Butler) P.; Chestnut Hill Acad., St. George's Sch.; A.B., Princeton U., 1920; m. 2d, Adeline V. N. Hitch, Apr. 25, 1932; children—Leslie Paul (Mrs. Donald L. Symington), Adeline (Mrs. Myron A. Hofer), John R. V.p. Dexdale Hosiery Mills, Lansdale, Pa., 1921-42, dir.; dir. Eectronized Chemical Corp., U.S. Commercial Co., 1943-45, Chief, Office of Imports, Bd. Econ. Warfare, 1942-43; dep. exec. dir. Bur. Areas, Fgn. Econ. Adminstrn., 1943-45; exec. dir., 1945; dir. Office Inernat. Trade, and asst. to sec. Dept. Commerce, 1945-47; pres. Overseas Corp. 1947-59, Indevco, Inc., 1951-58, Carbon Heater Corp., 1955-59; econ. advisor Royal Govt. Afghanistan, from 1960; dir. Turbo Machine Co. Decorated Chevalier Legion of Honor, 1947. Mem. U.S. del. to Internat. Labor Office, Geneva, 1937, New York City, 1941. Mem. advisory council, Dept. Econ. and Social Instn. of Princeton, Academy Polit. Science, Am. Acad. Polit. and Social Science, Nat. Planning Assn. Democrat. Clubs: Princeton (New York and Philadelphia); Nassau (Princeton, N.J.); Athenaeum (Phila.). Home: North Egremont, Mass., Died Jan. 9, 1976.

PAUL, GEORGE PHILIP, physician; b. Troy, N.Y., Nov. 11, 1879; s. Philip and Catharine (Hart) P.; ed. Round Lake Mil. Acad.; M.D., Univ. and Bellevue Hosp. Med. Coll. (New York U.), 1902; studied in Europe, 1906-07; C.P.H., Sch. for Health Officers, Harvard U., 1915-16; unmarried. Practiced at Troy, N.Y., and Round Lake, N.Y.; was with Internat. Health Bd. of Rockefeller Foundation, in British W.I., Fiji Islands, Australia, and India; also asso. med. dir. Aetna Life Ins. Co., Hartford, Conn.; has served with N.Y. State Dept. of Health. Capt. Med. Corps, U.S. Army, World War. Mem. emeritus, Assn. of Life Ins. Med. Dirs. of America. Methodist. Author: Nursing in the Acute Infectious Fevers, 1906; Materia Medica for Nurses, 1907. Home: Round Lake, N.Y.†

PAUL, JOHN BENJAMIN, musician, educator; b. Moran, Kan., May 19, 1915; s. John J. and Olive (Magee) P.; B.M.E., U. Kan., 1937; M.M., U. So. Cal., 1942; D.Mus. (hon.), St. John's U.; m. Martha Paul, Apr. 22, 1944; children—John, Michael, Dennis, Patrick, Christina, Mary Catherine. Tchr. music Mulvane (Kan.) Pub. Schs., 1937-41; mem. faculty Occidental Coll., Los Angeles, 1941-42, Coll. William and Mary, Va. Poly. Inst., Norfolk, Va., 1945-50; mem. faculty Catholic U. Am., Washington, 1950-74, dean Sch. of Music, 1965-70. Served with USNR. Mem. Phi Kappa Lambda, Sigma Alpha Epsilon. Co-editor Werder-Paul Piano Series. Home: Silver Spring, Md. Died Aug. 27, 1974.

PAUL, JOHN HARLAND, physician; b. Tracy, Minn., Apr. 16, 1900; s. Alexander and Jane (Davis) P.; grad. Shanghai-Am. High Sch., 1917; student Columbia, 1919; Ph.B., Yale, 1923; M.D., Harvard, 1927, C.P.H., 1927; M.P.H., Johns Hopkins, 1950; postgrad. Oxford (Eng.) U., 1921, Heidelberg U., 1925, 26; m. Jane-Ellen Norman, Dec. 19, 1936; 1 dau., Heather. Intern USPHS Hosp., N.Y.C., 1927-28; surgeon Carnegie Inst., Washington, 1928-30; surgeon, sci. researcher in meteorology and oceanography in research vessel Carnegie, 1929; mem. staff, spl. research mem., field rep. Internat. Health div. Rockefeller Found., N.Y. C., 1930-50; dir. bur. entomology Fla. State Bd. Health, Jacksonville, 1943-46; sr. surgeon, med. dir. res. USPHS, 1950-55; chief of party health, welfare and housing. Inst. Inter-Am. Affairs, Peru and Washington, 1950-54; dir. Health Center, Basra, Iraq, 1954-55; epidemiologist and dep. dir. Hillsborough County (Fla.) Health Dept., 1956-58; dir. Orange County (Fla.) Health Dept., 1958-60; dir. Suwannee, Lafayette and Dixie counties health depts., 1960-64; med. cons. adjudication VA Regional Office, St. Petersburg, Fla., 1965-71. Diplomate Am. Bd. Preventive Medicine. Fellow Am. Coll. Preventive Medicine, Am. Pub. Health Assn., Fla. Acad. Preventive Medicine; mem. Am. Acad. Preventive Medicine, Boylston Soc., Aesculapian Soc. Rotarian. Research in acute respiratory diseases, Norway, N.Y.C., Harvard, 1930-32; research in virus, spl. studies Yellow Fever Commn., Lagos, Nigeria, 1932; study mission for control yellow fever and malaria, established labs. for virus research, Brazil and Colombia, 1933-36; established yellow fever research labs., Uganda, Africa, 1937-39; studies in malaria control, established central lab. and tng. program for malaria control and epidemiol. studies, Haiti, 1940-43, spl. studies imported strains of malaria parasites from vets. Fla. State Hosp., Tallahassee, 1946-47; studies of immunity in malaria and application of malaria therapy to patients with gen. paresis in Fla. State Hosp., Chattahoochie, 1946-47; field studies in ecology, epidemiology, trials of new techniques for malaria control, established tng. centers for malaria control personnel, mainland China and Taiwan, 1947-49. Author: The Last Cruise of the Carneige, 1932. Contbr. articles to U.S., fgn. med. jours. Home: Windermere, Fla., Died May 4, 1971; interred Woodlawn Meml. Park, Orlando, Fla.

PAUL, JOSEPH EDWARD, physician; b. Balt., July 28, 1917; M.D., U. Pa., 1953. Intern Bryn Mawr (Pa.) Hosp., 1953-54, resident in radiology, 1954-57; NIH fellow in cardiovascular research, 1956-57; asso. radiologist Hurley Hosp., Flint, Mich. Diplomate Am. Bd. Radiology. Mem. Am. Coll. Radiology. Died Oct. 5, 1969.

PAUL, WILLIAM EDWARD, clergyman; b. near Brooklyn, Ia., June 30, 1880; s. James L. and Ellen (Parker) P.; A.B., Grinnell Coll., 1905, D.D., 1925; B.D., Chicago Theol. Sem., 1907; m. Frieda W. Conrad, Nov. 25, 1907; children—Horace J., Gordon A., Miriam C. (dec.), Virginia (Mrs. Virgil Hill). Ordained to ministry Presbyn. Ch., 1908; minister Riverside Chapel, Minneapolis, 1907-19; supt. Union City Mission, Mpls., from 1919; pioneered nationally in church camping, and in organizing standards of Bible conf. camps; organized 8 dists. of the Internat. Union of Gospel Missions. Pres. bd. of dirs. of the Children's Gospel Mission of Minneapolis. Civic Award for most distinguished service to Minneapolis, 1940. Mem. Am. Camping Assn. (exec. dir.), Phi Kappa Delta. Address: Minneapolis, Minn.†

PAWLOWSKI, BOGUMIL, educator, botanist; b. Cracow, Poland, Nov. 25, 1898; s. Witold and Zofia (Pazdanowska) P.; Dr. Phil., Jagellonian U., Cracow, 1922, Docent of Plant Systematics and Plant Geography, 1930; m. Stanislawa Bulanda, July 29, 1931. Asst., Bot. Inst., Jagellonian U., Cracow, 1922-25, adj., 1925-38, titular prof., 1938-51, prof. botany, 1951—, dir. chair of plant systematics and geography, 1960-65; dir. Bot. Inst., Polish Acad. Scis., 1961-68. Mem. Polish Acad. Scis. Warsaw, Polish Bot. Soc., Société Botanique de France, Zoologisch-Botanische Gesellschaft (Vienna), Internat. Assn. for Plant Taxonomy, Assn. Internationale de Phytosociologie, Bayerische Botanische Gesellschaft, Czechoslovakian Bot. Soc., Bulgarian Bot. Soc., Poznanskie Towarzystwo Nauk. Author: (with W. Szafer, S. Kulczynski) Rosliny, Polskie, 1924; (with others) Die Pflanzenassoziationen des Tatra-Gebirges, 1923-28; Studien über mitteleuropäische Delphinien aus der sogennanten sektion Elatopsis, 1933; Uber die Klimaxassoziation in der alpinen Stufe der Tatra, 1935; Flora Tatr-Flora Tatrorum, Vol. 1, 1956; Les associations végetales des praires fauchables de la partie septentionale des Tatras et de la Région Subtatrique (with S. Pawlowska, K. Zarzycki), 1960; Dispositio systematica specierum europearum generis Delphinium L., 1963; Remarques sur l endemism dans la Flore des Alpes et des Carpates, 1970. Editor: (with W. Szafer) Flora Poiska, Vol. VII, VIII, IX, 1955-60; Flora Polska, Vol. X, XI, 1963-67, (with A. Jasiewicz) Flora Polska, Vol. XII, XIII, 1971-72. Home: Cracow, Poland. Died July 27, 1971; buried Rakowice Cemetery, Cracow.

PAXSON, HENRY DOUGLAS, lawyer; b. Bryn Mawr, Pa., June 30, 1904; s. Henry Douglas and Hannameel (Canby) P.; B.A., U. Pa., 1926, LL.B., 1929; m. Adele Warden, Jan. 3, 1936; children—Mary-Helen (Mrs. Alain le Menestrel), Sally Canby (Mrs. Robert L. Davis). Admitted to Pa. bar, 1929, since practiced in Phila.; partner firm Dilworth, Paxson, Kalish, Levy & Coleman, 1933. Past mem. Phila. County Bd. Law Examiners. Trustee emeritus Abington Meml. Hosp.; pres. Phila. Lyric Opera Co., 1962-66, chmn. bd., 1966-75; pres. Acad. Vocal Arts, 1960-75; adv. bd. New Sch. Music. Decorated Al Merito della Repubblica Italiana. Mem. Am., Pa., Phila., bar assns., Masters of Foxhounds Assn. Am., Delta Psi. Republican. Episcopalian (rector's warden, vestryman). Clubs: Union League, Racquet, St. Anthony (Phila.); Saucon Valley Country (Bethlehem, Pa.); Huntingdon Valley Hunt (master 1946-57) (Bucks County). Home: Bucks County, Pa. Died May 30, 1975.

PAXTON, ALEXANDER GALLATIN, cotton mcht.; b. Vicksburg, Miss., Oct. 4, 1896; grad. Washington and Lee University, 1917; m. Ruth Chapman, 1923; children—Robert Gallatin and Mary Burton (Glasco) (dec.). Commd. 1st lt. F.A. Res., Nov. 1917, capt. F.A. Sec., O.R.C., Jan. 1920, Maj. Miss. N. G., 1926, advanced through grades to maj. gen., 1944; ret. as lt. gen.; ordered to fed. duty, 1940, as comdg. officer 114th F.A., Camp Blanding, Fla.; chief of staff 31st Inf. Div., Camp Blanding, later Camp Bowie, Tex., July 1942; comdg. arty. 33d Div., during re-occupation of Luzon, 1945; comdg. gen. 31st Inf. Dixie Div., Korean Emergency, 1951. Owner, operator A.G. Paxton Co., cotton shippers, domestic-export, Greenville, Miss.; also pres. A.G. Paxton Co., cotton mchts.; chmn. bd. A.G. Paxton Co., Inc., 1963-74, Paxton Bonded Warehouse, 1963-74. Mem. N.Y., Greenville cotton exchanges. Mem. adv. commn. Civil War Centennial; pres. Miss. Heart Assn. Mem. Greenville Sch. Bd., 1946-49, Greenville City Council, 1949-51. Bd. dirs. Am. Heart Assn., 1960-69. Decorated Air medal, Legion of Merit, Bronze Star; named Cotton Man of Year, 1961; recipient Distinguished Service award Am. Legion, 1967. Mem. Am. (pres. 1960-61), So. (pres. 1948-49) cotton shippers assns. Methodist. Rotarian. Author: The Vicksburg Campaign — A Story of Perseverance; The Atlanta Campaign, The Retrograde of the Confederacy; The Peninsular Campaign; Three Wars and a Flood, 1971. Home: Greenville, Miss. Died Aug. 9, 1974.

PAXTON, WILLIAM FRANCIS, II, business cons.; b. Paducah, Ky., Apr. 30, 1907; s. William Percy and Flora (Dickie) P.; student Tulane U.; m. India Lang Watkins, Feb. 3, 1934 (dec. Jan. 1970); children—Barbaranelle (Mrs. Russell S. Shelton), William Francis III; m. 2d, Martha Louise Wurth, July 24, 1971. With Claussner Hosiery Co. div. Indian Head Mills, Inc., 1927-65, pres., 1957-65; v.p., dir. So. Textile Machinery Co., Paducah, 1952-74, Watkins, Inc., Paducah, 1937-67; sec., dir. Marvei Splty. Co., Paducah, 1937-74; pres., dir. Forest Hills Pub. Project Corp., 1968-74; dir. Rubel Dry Goods Co., Paducah Newspapers, Inc.; business cons., 1965-74. City commr., Paducah, Ky. until 1967. Mem. Paducah Bd. Edn., 1944-52; pres., dir. Paducah Community Chest, 1950; pres. Four Rivers council Boy Scouts Am., 1946-52, chmn. 1940-46. Del., Republican Nat. Conv., 1952, 64. Trustee W.P. Paxton Trust. Recipient Silver Beaver award Boy Scouts Am. Mem. Delta Tau Delta. Elk. Club: Paducah Country (pres. 1945-47, 51-52, dir. 1961-64). Home: Paducah, Ky. Died Aug. 9, 1974; buried Mt. Carmel Cemetery, Paducah, Ky.

PAYSON, JOAN WHITNEY, civic worker; b. N.Y.C., Feb. 5, 1903; d. Payne and Helen (Hay) Whitney; grad. Miss Chapin's Sch., 1921; student Barnard Coll.; hon. degrees Hofstra Coll.; m. Charles S. Payson, July 5, 1924; children—Sandra (Lady Weidenfeld), Payne (Mrs. Henry B. Middleton), Lorinda (Mrs. V. de Roulet), John Whitney, Daniel Carroll (killed WWII). Partner Payson & Trask, N.Y.C., 1947-75, Country Art Gall., 1953-75; co-owner Greentree Stable, 1945-75, Greentree Stud, Inc., 1945. Gov. Soc. N.Y. Hosp.; trustee N. Shore Hosp., Manhasset, L.I. (past pres.) United Hosp. Fund. Asso. Hosps. Museum Modern Art, The Met. Mus. Art, N.Y.C., Lighthouse, St. Mary's Hosp., Palm Beach, Fla.; pres. Helen Hay Whitney Found.; pres. New York Metropolitan Baseball club, Inc. Mem. Jr. League N.Y. Clubs: Coloney, Women's City, Women's Nat. Republican (N.Y.C.). Home: Manhasset, N.Y. Died Oct. 4, 1975; buried Falmouth Foreside, Me.

PEABODY, MALCOLM ENDICOTT, clergyman; b. Danvers, Mass., June 12, 1888; s. Endicott and Fannie (Peabody) P.; ed. Groton Sch., 1900-07; Harvard, 1907-

10 (A.B.); Trinity Coll., Cambridge, Eng., 1910-11; Episcopal Theol. Sch., Cambridge, Mass., 1913-16 (B.D.); D.D., Hamilton Coll., 1939; D.D., Hobart Coll., 1942; S.T.D., Syracuse U., 1943; m. Mary Elizabeth Parkman, June 19, 1916; children—Mary Endicott (Mrs. Ronald Tree), Endicott, George Lee, Samuel Parkman, Malcolm Endicott. Master, Boys School, Baguio, Philippine Islands, 1911-13; ordained deacon P.E. Ch., June 10, 1916, priest, May 3, 1917; curate Grace Ch., Lawrence, Mass., 1916-17, 1919-20; rector, same, 1920-25; rector St. Paul's Ch., Chestnut Hill, Pa., 1925-38; bishop coadjutor, Diocese of Central N.Y., 1938-42, bishop, from 1942. Pres. Synod of II Province P.E. Church, 1948. Member bd. of overseers of Harvard College, from 1955. Served as chaplain, Am. Red Cross, with Base Hosp. 5, 1917-18; chaplain, 102d Field Arty., 26th Div., U.S. Army, with A.E.F., 1918-19. Member National Council P.E. Ch., 1938-48; chmn. dept. religious liberty Nat. Council Chs. of Christ in Am., from 1952. Home: Boston, Mass. Died June 1974.

PEALE, MUNDY INGALLS, aviation exec.; b. Joliet, Ill., June 15, 1906; s. George and Myra (Ingalls) P.; Ph.B., U. Chgo., 1929; Eng. D. (hon.), Clarkson Coll. Tech., 1954; hon. doctorate in law, Hofstra Coll., 1959; m. Betsey Farwell, June 3, 1931; children—Georgia, Mundy Ingalls, Sandra, Betsey. Factory rep. Sikorsky div. United Aircraft Corp., 1931, service rep. Hamilton Standard div., 1934, sales and export mgr. Skorsky div., 1936, quality mgr. Sikorsky div., 1938; with Republic Aviation Corp., Farmingdale, N.Y., 1939-64, successively asst. dir. exports, asst. dir. mil. contracts, gen. mgr. Evansville (Ind.) div., v.p., gen. sales mgr., dir., 1944-64, pres., 1947-64; pres. Bull Mountain Cattle Co., Laramie, Wyo.; dir. Am. Can Co., ACF Industries Mem. Hoover Commn. Task Force on Procurement, 1954; mem. procurement and prodn. adv. com. Def. Dept., 1954. Mem. N.Y. State Adv. Council Advancement Indsl. Research and Devel. Chmn. bd. trustees Clarkson Coll. of Tech., Potsdam, N.Y. Decorated officer French Legion of Honor: commendatore Al Merito della Republica. Citation as outstanding alumnus U. Chgo., 1954. Mem. Aircraft Industries Assn. (chmn. bd. govs. 1953), Inst. Aero. Scis. (pres. 1957), Phi Kappa Psi. Home: Laramie, Wyo. Died Nov. 1, 1972; cremated.

PEALE, RICHARD P., utility exec.; b. Norwich, Conn., 1903; ed. Norwich U., 1925. Treas. Conn. Light & Power Co., Research Park, Inc., Rocky River Realty Co., Shelton Canal Co., Windsor Locks Canal Co., Conn Gas Co. Home: West Hartford, Conn. Died Dec. 28, 1972; buried Maplewood Cemetery, Norwich, Conn.

PEARCE, JAMES WILLIAM, educator; b. High River, Alta., Can., Oct. 28, 1924; s. William Maddock and Kathleen (Williams) P.; M.D., C.M., Queen's U. (Can.), 1947; D.Phil. Oxford (Eng.) U., 1951; m. Isabelle Elizabeth Young, July 18, 1956; children—Gwyneth Rowena, Andrew David. Lectr., asst. prof. physiology U. Western Ont. (Can.), London, 1952-55; prof. physiology U. Alta., 1955-67, U. Toronto (Ont.), 1967-75. Chmn. panel on aviation medicine Def. Research Bd., 1961-65. Mem. Physiol. Soc. (Gt. Britain), Canadian (pres. 1967-68), Am. physiol. socs. Contbr. articles to profl. jours. Home: Bolton, Ont., Can. Canada. Died July 10, 1975.

PEARCY, FRANK, physician; b. Kelso, Wash., Aug. 24, 1895; s. Joel Nathaniel and Mary Matilda (Pike) P.; M.D., Rush Med. Coll., 1928, Ph.D. in Physiology, 1924; m. Dorothy Kendrick, Aug. 24, 1930; children—John Kendrick, Norman Frank. Intern, Billings Hosp., Chgo., 1927-28; resident Rockefeller Inst. Med. Research, 1928-29; Freudian Analysis, 1930-32; Adlerian Analysis, 1932-34; asst. to Alfred Adler, 1932-37; asst. chief medicine Psychol. Clinic L.I. Coll. Medicine, 1932-37; clin. mem. N.Y. State Psychiat. Inst., 1936-40; mem. staff Bellevue Hosp., 1940-46; cons. VA Hosps., Dallas, 1946-49; asst. and asso. in physiology U. Chgo. Med. Sch., 1921-24; instr. physiology State U.N.Y. at Buffalo, 1922-23; asso. prof. physiology U. W.Va., 1924-27; chmn. dept. physiology N.Y.U., 1926-27, instr., 1940-46; asst. clin. prof. neuropsychiatry U. Tex. Southwestern Med. Sch., Dallas, 1948-53. Diplomate in psychiatry Am. Bd. Psychiatry and Neurology. Mem. A.M.A., Am. Psychiat. Assn., Am. Physiol. Soc., Am. Assn. for Advancement of Psychotherapy. Contbr. articles to profl. jours. Home: Dallas, Tex. Died July 23, 1974; buried Hillcrest Mausoleum, Dallas, Tex.

PEARL, JOSEPH, coll. prof.; b. Podhajce, Poland, Dec. 16, 1885; s. William and Rebecca (Halperin) P.; A.B., cum laude, Coll. City N.Y., 1906; Ph.D., New York U., 1913; student Columbia U., 1906-10; m. Anna Farb, Feb. 6, 1910; 1 dau., Florence (wife of Colonel David J. Graubard). Came to U.S., 1902, father naturalized, 1906. Fellow, Coll. City N.Y., 1906, tutor classical langs. (Townsend Harris Hall), 1910-14, instr. classics, 1914-24, supervisor, 1924-28, asst. prof., 1928-30; asso. prof., Brooklyn Coll., 1930-34, prof., from 1934, chmn., from 1941, acting dean of faculty Brooklyn Coll. from 1950. Awards: Ward medals; gold medal in Greek; University scholarship in Latin, Columbia U. Mem. Am. Philol. Assn., N.Y. Classical Club, American Assn. Univ. Profs. Phi Beta Kappa. Jewish religion. Democrat. Author: Epic Nomenclature of Vergil (privately printed), 1913; Latin, First and Second Years, 1920; Companion to Caesar, 1927; Latin Word Lists, 1929; Companion to Cicero, 1930; Companion to Vergil, 1932. Home: New York City, N.Y. Died Dec. 8, 1974.

PEARS, SIDNEY JOHN, accountant; b. London, Eng., Aug. 5, 1900; s. Sidney and Alice Ella (Grossmith) P.; grad. Rugby, 1919; m. Molly Kathleen Wallers, Sept. 14, 1927; children—Mary Ann (Mrs. William F.S. Letten), Patricia (Mrs. Richard B. Hill), Sally Karina. Gov., Cable Trust (Holding) Ltd.; partner Cooper Bros. & Co., Chartered Accountants, 1926-46, sr. partner, 1946-71; partner Coopers & Lybrand, 1957-71; chmn. bd. dirs. Cables Investment Trust Ltd., Globe Investment Trust Ltd., Electra Finance Co. Ltd., Electra Investments Ltd., Electra House Ltd., Aberdeen, Edinburgh & London Trust Ltd.; dir. Electra Investments (South Africa), Ltd., Electra Investments (Can.), Ltd., Electra Investments (Lambia) Ltd., Electra Investments (Rhodesia) Ltd., Singer, Friedlander Ltd., Telephone & Gen. Trust Ltd.; part-time mem. U.K. Atomic Energy Authority, 1960-72; dir. contracts Ministry Supply, 1941. prin. controller costs, 1942-45, vice chmn. adv. com. Royal Ordnance Factories accounting, 1946-50; mem. com. enquiry into cement industry Ministry Works, 1946, mem. bldg. working party, 1948; dep. chmn. wool working party Bd. Trade, 1946; dir. Nat. Film Finance Corp., 1948-52, Festival Gardens Ltd., 1952-53; mem. adv. com. Revolving Fund for Industry, 1953-56, export credits guarantee dept. com., 1955; bd. referees Bd. Inland Revenue, 1956-57; mem. com. milk distbrs. remuneration Ministry Agr., Fisheries and Food, 1959-61. Fellow Inst. Chartered Accounts Eng. and Wales, 1931, mem. council, 1946-67, v.p., 1959-60, pres., 1960-61. Mem. City Livery Co., Worshipful Co., Frame-Work Knitters (master 1942). Home: Sussex, England., Died Oct. 10, 1975.

PEARSON, DANIEL CECIL, supt. N.M. Mil. Inst.; b. Pearisburg, Va., June 20, 1881; s. Thomas Jefferson and Nancy Haven (Cecil) P.; student U. of Tenn., 1899-1900; grad. Va. Mil. Inst., 1904; grad. work U. of Chicago; m. Senah Elizabeth Fry, June 9, 1908; children—Daniel Cecil, Nancy Howe, Robert Hiram, Jean Vance, Mary, Thomas Lloyd. Sub. prof. Va. Mil. Inst., 1904-05; comdt. N.M. Mil. Inst., 1905-08, principal, 1909-18; engaged in business, Pearisburg, 1918-26; supt. N.M. Mil. Inst., 1926-47. Colonel N.M.N.G. on staff of gov. Mem. Kappa Alpha (Southern). Mem. Chamber of Commerce, Roswell; mem. bd. Carnegie Library; mem. council Girl Scouts. Democrat. Mason (32°, K.T., Shriner), Rotarian. Home: Roswell, N.M.†

PEARSON, HARRY A., electro-acoustic engr.; b. Sosnowiec, Poland, Aug. 8, 1910; s. Benjamin and Pauline (Gittler) P.; came to U.S., 1920, naturalized, 1921; B.S., Cooper Union, 1932; B.S. in Elect. Engring., N.Y.U., 1934; postgrad. Poly. Inst. Bklyn., 1942; m. Jeanne Lerner, Sept. 1, 1934; 1 son, Daniel Paul. Design draftsman high tension elec. equipment Burndy Engring. Co., 1927-30; lab. asst. Hearing aids and audiometers Sonotone Corp., Elmsford, N.Y., 1930-31, research engr. microphones and amplifiers, 1932-34, head lab., 1934-41, asst. dir. research, 1941-53, dir. research lab., 1953-73. Active White Plains N.Y.O. Council Community Services. Registered profl. engr., N.Y. Fellow Audio Engring. Soc.; mem. Acoustical Soc., I.E.E.E. (sr.). Patentee in field. Home: White Plains, N.Y. Died Aug. 12, 1973.

PEARSON, JAMES LARKIN, author; b. Moravian Falls, N.C., Sept. 13, 1879; s. William Thomas and Mary Louise (McNeill) P.; student N.C. country schs.; m. Cora Wallace, May 1, 1907 (died 1934); 1 dau., Agnes Vivian (adopted); m. 2d, Eleanor Louise Fox, Apr. 6, 1939. Country printer, 1900; editor, pub. The Fool-Killer (humorous monthly), 1901-29; gen. mgr. Pearson Pub. Co. Mem. McNeill Family Assn. Mem. N.C. Literary and Hist. Assn., Poetry Soc. of N.C., N.C. Folklore Soc. Author: Castle Gates, 1908; Pearson's Poems, 1924; Fifty Acres and Other Poems, 1933, revised and enlarged edit., 1937; Source Material for History of Wilkes County, N.C., 1939. Contbr. to many mags and newspapers. Home: Guildford College, N.C.†

PEARSON, NORMAN HOLMES, educator, editor; b. Gardner, Mass., Apr. 13, 1909; s. Chester Page and Fanny Holmes (Kittredge) P.; student Phillips Acad., 1927-28; A.B., Yale, 1932; B.A., Magdalen Coll., Oxford U., 1934, M.A., 1941; Ph.D., Yale, 1941; grad. study U. Berlin, 1933; m. Susan Silliman Bennett, Feb. 21, 1941; stepchildren—Susan S. Tracy (Mrs. Susan Addiss), Elizabeth B. Tracy. Faculty, Yale, 1941-75, prof. English and Am. studies, 1962-75, chmn. Am. studies, 1957-67; vis. prof. English, U. Kyoto, Doshisha U., 1970; vis. fellow Huntington Library, 1948; Guggenheim fellow, 1948-49, 55-56; pres. Bryher Found., 1949-52; chancellor Acad. Am. Poets, 1964-75; counsellor Smithsonian Instn., 1966-75. Civilian with O.S.S., 1942-46. Decorated Medal of Freedom (U.S.); Medaille de la Reconnaissance, Chevalier Legion of Hon. (France); Knight of St. Olaf. 1st class (Norway); Knight of Dannebrog 1st class (Denmark). Mem. Am. Studies Assn. (pres. 1968), Modern Lang. Assn. Am., Eng. Inst. (chmn. 1948), Coll. Eng. Assn. (nat. v.p. 1955-56, pres. N.E. assn. 1951-52), Conn. Acad., P.E.N. Conglist. Clubs: Elizabethan (Yale); Grolier, Century Assn. (N.Y.C.). Author: Four Studies, 1962; American Literature, 1964, rev. 1969; Some American Studies, 1964. Editor: Complete Novels of Hawthorne, 1937; The Oxford Anthology of Am. Literature (with W. R. Benet), 1938; Walden, 1948; Poets of English Lang. (with W. H. Auden), 1950; The Pathfinder, 1952; Decade, 1969. Contbr. to various jours. Home: Hamden, Conn., Died Nov. 1975.

PEASE, HERBERT HOYT, mfr.; b. New Britian, Conn., Aug. 10, 1881; s. L. Hoyt and Julia L. (Sawyer) P.; Ph.B., Yale U., 1902; m. Mary Curtiss. Treas. New Britain (Conn.) Machine Co., 1910, pres. 1920-51, chmn. bd.; pres. New Britain-Gridley Machine Co., 1929-36; dir. The New Britain Trust Co., A. G. Spalding & Bros., Inc., Hartford Co. Mutual Fire Ins. Co., New Brit. Gen. Hosp. Past pres. Nat. Machine Tool Builders Assn. Dir. Alumni Bd. of Yale U.; dir. Y.M.C.A. Clubs: Shuttle Meadow, New Britain; Yale (New York). Home: New Britain, Conn.†

PEASE, ROLLIN, singer; b. Cambridge, Mass., July 13, 1879; s. Daniel and Katherine (James) P.; A.B., Northwestern U., 1898; m. Lena Mason, Feb. 14, 1906; children—Margaret Ellen, Constance. Began as teacher and concert singer, 1902; bass soloist in oratorio performance with principal choral societies of America; specialist in dramatized performances of "Elijah" with Salt Lake City Tabernacle Choir; teacher of singing, U. of Minn., 1913-17, Northwestern U., 1917-24, U. Ariz., from 1931; editor The Sinfonian, 1922-32; lecturer on hymnology at confs. and theol. schs.; speaker and singer for pub. relations dept. of the U.S. Forest Service; teacher master classes, U. of Ida., summers. Member Chicago Artists Assn., Phi Mu Alpha Presbyterian. (choirmaster Trinity Ch.). Home: Tucson, Ariz.†

PECK, CASSIUS R, lawyer; b. Brookfield, Vt., July 1, 1880; s. Cassius and Luna Arnold (Sprague) P.; A.B., U. Vt., 1902; studied law office Edmund C. Mower, Burlington, Vt.; m. Lillian Louise Valentine, June 8, 1903; 1 dau., Alma Louise (wife Dr. David Mason); m. 2d, Kate Daniels Field. Nov. 27, 1930. Admitted to Vt. bar, 1903, practiced as partner Mower & Peck, Burlington, 1903-05; asst. U.S. atty., Guthrie, Okla., 1905-06; atty., mem. Osage Indian Alotting Commn., Dept. Interior, Pawhuska, Okla., 1906-09; pvt. practice law Coos Bay, Ore., 1909-17, Portland, 1919-49; sec.; gen. counsel, dir. Portland Gen. Electric Co., Portland Traction Co., 1926-47; ret. LaJolla, Cal., from 1950. Served as capt., maj., U.S. Army, World War I. Chmn. bd. trustees LaJolla Town Council, from 1950. Mem. Am. Legion (chmn. constl. com. Minneapolis conv. 1919; past comdr. Portland post), Am. Bar Assn., Phi Beta Kappa, Phi Delta Theta. Republican. Presbyn. Home: LaJolla, Cal.†

PECK, CECIL CLAY, banker, mfr.; b. Auburn, N.Y., Feb. 22, 1880; s. Linus Jones and Sophina Adelaid (Carver) P.; ed. pub. schs., St. Clair, Mich., and Albion (Mich.) Coll.; m. Luella H. Loughead, Dec. 12, 1919. Began as messenger, Commercial Bank, Port Huron, Mich., 1898; pres. U.S. Savs. Bank, Port Huron; v.p. Pressed Metals of America; treas. Port Huron Sulphite & Paper Co., Dunn Sulphite Paper Co., Canada Forwarding Co., Fort Shelby Hotel Co.; dir. Peerless Cement Co., North Shore Transit Co. Republican. Episcopalain. Mason, K.P., Elk. Home: Port Huron, Mich.†

PECK, HARVEY WHITEFIELD, educator; b. Warren, O., Oct. 30, 1879; s. Benjamin Harvey and Margaret Whitefield (Matthews) P.; A.B., Oberlin Coll., 1905; A.M., Yale, 1907, Ph.D., 1913; grad. work, Harvard, 1908-10; A.M., Columbia, 1921; m. Glenna Lucille Hughes, July 30, 1907. Asst. in English, U. of Mo., 1907-08; instr. in English, Colby Coll., 1910-12, U. of Tex., 1913-19; prof. of economics, Allegheny Coll., 1919-20; asso. prof., U. of Vt., 1921-25; prof. of economics, Syracuse U., 1925-47; prof. banking and finance, U. of Texas, 1947-51. Mem. Am. Assn. of Univ. Profs., Am. Economic Assn., Eugene Field Society, Tax Policy League, Syracuse Defense Council. Club: Faculty (Syracuse). Author: Taxation and Welfare, 1925; Economic Thought and Its Institutional Background, 1935. Home: Morovia, N.Y.†

PECK, HERBERT MASSEY, lawyer; b. Rockbridge County, Va., Nov. 5, 1879; s. Hugh A. and Anna Daggs (McCormick) P.; Ph.B., Lawrence College, Appleton, Wis., 1904; LL.B., U. of Va., 1908; m. Frances McCoy Sawyer, Oct. 26, 1910 (died Sept. 8, 1931); children—Page (Mrs. McMillan Lambert), Frances (Mrs. James E. Thompson), Margaret (Mrs. Ralph W. Latham, Jr.). Practice law at Oklahoma City, Okla., 1908; asst. county atty., Oklahoma County, 1911-13; asst. U.S. dist. atty., Western Dist. of Okla. 1915-17; spl. asst. U.S. atty., 1919-20; U.S. atty. Western Dist. of Okla., 1920-23; v.p. and trust officer, Am. First Nat. Bank, Oklahoma City, 1923-28; gen. counsel Okla. Pub. Co., 1928-50. Enlisted in U.S. Army, 1917; commd. captain F.A. 90th Division, Nov. 27, 1917; maj., Aug. 22, 1918; hon. discharged lt. col. R.C., June 30, 1919. Recipient Alumni Distinguished Service award, Lawrence Coll. Mem. Am., Okla. bar assns., Phi Delta Theta, Phi Delta Phi, Phi Beta Kappa. Mason (Shriner). Democrat. Presbyterian. V.p. Nat. Council YMCA, 1927. Home: Oklahoma, Okla.†

PEDEN, MARIE MCKINNEY (MRS. RALPH HUTCHINGS PEDEN), editor; b. Greenville, S.C., Sept. 15, 1912; d. M. Ansel and Lillie (Barton) McKinney; B.A., Brenau Coll., 1932; m. Ralph Hutchings Peden, Oct. 19, 1934 (dec. 1969); children—Patricia Elaine, Ralph Hutchings. Bookkeeper Ivey's & Cabaniss-Gardner Co., Greenville, 1934-42; substitute tchr. city schs., 1953-54; asst. women's editor Greenville Piedmont, 1955-58, woman's editor, 1958. Pres. local P.T.A., 1953-54; publicity chmn. local U.S.O. Vol. Corps, 1958-60, co-chmn. publicity, 1960-62. Recipient state awards in field, 1960-71; Greenville Bus. and Profl. Women's Career Woman of Year, 1963; Spl. award Nat. Fedn. Music Clubs, 1964, 68, spl. award of merit, 1971; Community Service award Salvation Army, 1965; Appreciation plaque from Gen. Hosp. for publicity service to community; named Newspaper Woman of Yr. S.C., 1967. Mem. S.C. Congress Parents and Tchrs. (life), Women in C. of C. (charter; community service award 1965), Delta Zeta. Presbyn. Clubs: Augusta Road Community (officer, com. chmn. 1952-58), Zonta (charter mem., v.p. 1961-62, Woman of Yr. 1972), Woman's (charter mem.) (Greenville). Home: Greenville, S.C. Died June 20, 1973.

PEDERSEN, NIELS ALVIN, coll. dean; b. Ephraim, Utah, March 3, 1879; s. Soren and Ane (Laursen) P.; student Stanford, 1903-05; A.B., U. of Utah, 1906; A.M., Harvard, 1913; Ph.D., U. of Calif., Berkeley, 1924; m. Beatrice Russell Anderson, July 23, 1906; children—Edith Faye (Mrs. Theodore MacLean Switz), Jean Russell (Mrs. Clayton Garr Loosli), Helen Holland (Mrs. Thomas O. McCraney), Beatrice Russell (Mrs. William Wallace Alsup), Elizabeth Holland. Teacher Utah State Normal Sch., 1901-03; speech instr. U. of Utah, 1906-07; instr. in dept. English, Utah Agrl. Coll., 1907-09, asst. prof., 1909-12, prof. and head dept., 1913-45, dean of the Sch. of Arts and Sciences, 1932-45, dean emeritus, Mem. Utah Ednl. Assn., Logan Home Bldg. Soc. (dir.), Phi Kappa Phi. Club: Logan Men's, Logan Knife and Fork (pres.). Home: Logan, Utah.†

PEEBLES, JOHN BRADBURY, elec. engr., educator; b. Petersburg, Va., Oct. 1, 1881; s. William Lemuel and Annie Leighton (Bradbury) P.; B.E. in E.E., Union Coll., 1906; M.S., Ga. Inst. Tech., 1926; m. Elizabeth Copeland, June 22, 1909; children—John Bradbury, Jr., Eleanor Bobo (Mrs. R. E. Bittner), Test engr. Gen. Electric Co., 1906-07, engr. Pa. Ry. Tunnels, N.Y. City, 1907-09; asst. prof. applied math. Wofford Coll., Spartanburg, S.C., 1909-12; prof. math. Emory Coll., Oxford, Ga., 1912-18; prof. elec. engring. and applied math. Emory Univ., Atlanta, 1919-27, chmn. div. engring., 1927-41, prof. elec. engring and head dept. 1945-50; v.p. Pan Electronics Corp., from 1951; design engr. Robert and Company, Atlanta, summer 1941; research engr. and v.p., Pan Electronics Labs., Inc., Atlanta, 1942-45 (war plant World War II). Served as major, engr. U.S. Army, 1918-19; maj. Engrs. Res., 1919-35. Fellow Am. Inst. Elec. Engrs.; mem. Ga. Acad. Sciences, Ga. Engring. Soc., Southeastern Soc. Physicists, Sigma Phi Soc., Omicron Delta Kappa, Sigma Pi Sigma. Methodist. Mason. Developed a method of stablising Quartz Oscillators of any reasonable frequency (responsible for Pan Electronic Labs, Inc., winning Army and Navy "E" Award). Home: Atlanta, Ga.†

PEEK, ERNEST DICHMANN, army officer; b. Oshkosh, Wis., Nov. 19, 1878; s. Herman W. and Sophie (Dichmann) P.; grad. U.S. Mil. Acad., 1901, U.S. Staff Coll., 1911, U.S. War Coll., 1920; student Babson Inst., Wellesley, Mass., 1929-30; LL.D., U. of Wyo., 1940; m. Ann F. Ryan, June 26, 1909. Commd. 2d lt. engrs., U.S. Army, 1901, and promoted through the grades to brig. gen., 1937, maj. gen., Oct. 1940; engr. officer staff Gen. Pershing, Bacolod (P.I.) expdn., building roads and wharves, 1901-03; river and harbor work, 1903-17; arrived in France, Jan. 1918, began construction of light rys., participating in St. Mihiel and Meuse-Argonne offensives; in office of asst. sec. of war, 1924-28; engr. N. Atlantic Div. in charge river and harbor work and flood control, 1936-37; comdg. 4th Brig., Ft. Warren, Wyo., Aug. 1937-Apr. 1940; chief of staff 9th Corps Area, Apr.-Nov. 1940; comdg. gen. 9th Corps Area, Presidio of San Francisco, Calif., 1940-41; retired because of physical disability, October 31, 1942. Decorated Silver Star for gallantry at battle of Bacolod, P.I. and D.S.M. (U.S.), Legion of Honor and Etoile Noire (French). Episcopalain. Club: Army and Navy (Washington, D.C.); Pacific Union (San Francisco). Home: San Francisco, Cal.†

PEERS, ROBERT ALWAY, physician; b. Woodstock, Ont., Can., Dec. 13, 1875; s. Richard and Margaret Hatch (Alway) P.; student Woodstock (Ont.) Coll. Inst., 1888-92, Albert Coll., Belleville, Ont., 1892 and 1893; fellow Trinity Med. Coll., Toronto, 1894-99; F.T.M.C., Trinity U., Toronto, Can., 1899, M.D., C.M., 1899; m. Lucy Fitzgerald Stewart, July 20, 1901; children—Robert Stewart, Francis Hamilton. Naturalized Am. citizen, 1904. Mem. first. Calif. Tuberculosis Comm., 1914; bd. dirs., Central Calif. Corp., Auburn, Calif., 1923-46, Central Bank of Calif., 1923-28, Nevada County Bank, 1925-27; mem. advisory bd. Auburn Branch Bank of America, 1929-46. Served as capt., Am. Red Cross, World War I; in foreign service, 1918. Mayor, City of Colifax, Calif., 1922-45; consultant Colfax Hosp. for Tuberculosis. Mem. Cal. Dept., Pub. Health, 1914-31. Recipient award for outstanding contbn. field thoracic diseases Am. Acad. Tb Physicians, 1959. Diplomate Am. Bd. Internal Medicine. Fellow A.C.P., Am. Coll. Chest Physicians, Am. Acad. Tuberculosis Physicians; mem. nat., state and local med. socs., several spl. med. assns., has served as pres. of other exec. officer of serveral. Republican (del. nat. convention 1936 and 1940). Mason (Shriner). Author: A Primer for the Tuberculous and other Essays on Tuberculosis, 1930. Home: Palo Alta, Cal.†

PEIRCE, FREDERIC MARSHALL, ins. co. exec.; b. Cambridge, Mass., Jan. 23, 1910; s. Edwin W. and Frances (Quick) P.; student U. Omaha. 1927-29; m. Virginia Jay, May 13, 1933; children—Barbara (Mrs. James C. Anderson III), John. Cashier, agt., supr. Neb. gen. agy. John Hancock Mut. Life Ins. Co., Omaha, 1937-40; asst. sec. Capitol Life Ins. Co. of Denver 1944-45, asst. sec., asst. treas., 1945-47; sr. mgmt. cons. Life Ins. Agy. Mgmt. Assn., Hartford, Conn., 1947, asst. dir. charge co. consultations, 1948, asso. dir. co. relations div., 1949-53, asst. to mng. dir., 1954-56, dir. instnl. relations, 1956, mng. dir., 1956-58; pres. Gen. Am. Life Ins. Co., St. Louis. 1958-69, chief exec. officer, 1965-73, chmn. bd., 1969-74, chmn. exec. com., 1973-74, also dir.; chmn. bd., fed. res. agt. Fed. Res. Bank of St. Louis, 8th Fed. Res. Dist., 1966-74; dir. Anheuser-Busch, Inc., Alton Box Board Co., McDonnell-Douglas Corp. Vice pres., mem. exec. bd. St. Louis area council Boy Scouts Am.; pres. Civic Progress, Inc., 1967-69; met. chmn. Nat. Alliance of Businessmen, 1968. Mem. pres.'s council St. Louis U.; bd. dirs. Inst. Life Ins., chmn., 1972; trustee St. Louis Law Enforcement Found., St. Luke's Hosp.; trustee, exec. com. Washington U.; trustee, 1st v.p. Mo. Pub. Expenditure Survey; treas., bd. dirs. Municipal Theater Assn.; bd. dirs. Danforth Found.; bd. dirs., exec. com. United Fund Greater St. Louis; trustee S.S. Huebner Found. Ins. Edn. Mem. Newcomen Soc. N.Am., Life Underwriters Assn. St. Louis. Republican. Clubs: Bellerive Country, Noonday, Ambassador, Missouri Athletic, Advertising, Round Table, Bogey, Racquet, Media, St. Louis, Stadium (St. Louis). Contbg. author Life and Health Insurance Handbook, 1964; Life Insurance Sales Management Handbook, 1971. Home: St. Louis Mo. Died May 13, 1974; interred Oak Grove Cemetery, St. Louis, Mo.

PEIRCE, THOMAS MAY, JR., school exec., accountant; b. Phila., Pa., Apr. 14, 1878; s. Thomas and May and Ruth (Stong) P.; ed. Central Manual Training High Sch., Phila., 1892-95, U. of Pa., 1895-99 (B.S.), Peirce Sch., Phila., 1899-1901; m. Grace A. Bennett, Sept. 9, 1905; children—Thomas May 3d (lt. U.S.N.R.), Ann Bennett. Inst. Peirce Sch. 1901-02; sec.—treas. Oscar Smith & Sons Co., 1902-16, Hercules Cement Corp., 1916-20, North Pitman Land Co., 1908-36; v.p. and dir. Honorbilt Products, Inc., from 1922; pub. accountant, from 1921, C.P.A. (Pa.), from 1931; administrative exec. and partner Peirce Sch., form 1934. Served as aide-de-camp to 1st lt. and adj., 2d Pa. Vol. Inf., 1898. Member Pennsylvania Inst. C.P.A.'s, American Institute of Accountants, Nat. Assn. Cost Accountants, Nat. Business Teachers Assn., N.E.A., Eastern Commercial Teachers Assn., Pa. Pvt. Business Schs., Pa. Approved Pvt. Business Schs. (chmn.), Pa. Museum, Pa. Hist. Soc., Pa. S.R., Delta Upsilon. Club: Overbrook Golf. Universalist. Mason. Kiwanian. Author of brochures, The Case for Guarantee of Bank Deposits, Bank Failures—Causes and Remedies. Home: Philadelphia, Pa.†

PELENYI, JOHN, diplomat; b. Budapest, Hungary, Feb. 15, 1885; s. Louis and Harriet (Daman) P.; grad. Consular Academie, Vienna, 1907; m. Sue Wade Harman, Jan. 17, 1923. Began as attaché, Austro-Hungarian Consulate, Pittsburgh, Pa., 1908, Chicago, 1909, apptd. vice consul, 1909; transferred to Cleveland, 1911, apptd. consul, 1916; consul Austro-Hungarian Fgn. Office, 1917-20; counselor of legation, 2d class, 1920, 1st class, 1929; counselor of Hungarian legation, Washington, D.C., 1922-30; permanent del. of Hungary to League of Nations and to Internat. Labor Orgn., with rank of minister resident, 1930, E.E. and M.P., 1932; del. to Disarmament Conf., and to other confs. called by League of Nations, 1930-33. E.E. and M.P., U.S., 1933-40, accredited also to Cuba and Mexico, 1934-40, resigned Nov., 1940; lecturer, Dartmouth Coll., 1941, prof. political science, from 1942. Home: Hanover, N.H. Died Apr. 19, 1974.

PELLY, THOMAS MINOR, congressman; b. Seattle, Aug. 22, 1902; s. Bernard and Elizabeth (Minor) P.; student Hoosac Sch.; m. Mary Taylor, May 24, 1927; children—Thomas Minor, Marion Elizabeth. Asst. trust officer Seattle Nat. Bank, 1927-29; v.p. Lowman & Hanford Co., 1930-35, pres., 1935-55; dir. Seattle Trust and Savs. Bank, No. Life Ins. Co., Seattle; mem. 83d-92d Congresses 1st Wash. Dist. Club: Rainier (Seattle). Home: Washington D.C. Died Nov. 21, 1973.

PELTASON, PAUL EVANS, investment banker; b. St. Louis, May 28, 1898; s. Charles and Lena (Evans) P.; A.B., U. Mo., 1919; m. Ruth Mayer, June 15, 1921; children—Ellen (Mrs. Henry Steinbaum), Paul Evans, Charles Mayer. Formerly sr. partner Peltason, Tennenbaum Co., St. Louis, from 1932; chmn. bd. dir. Signal Hill Telecasting Corp., 1952-65. Mem. Phi Beta Kappa. Club: Westwood Country (past pres.). Home: Clayton, Mo. Died Aug. 13, 1974.

PELTIER, GEORGE LEO, cons. of bacteriology; b. Merrill, Wis., May 8, 1888; s. Emile and Georgiana (Laramie) P.; A.B., U. of Wis., 1910; A.M., Wash. U., St. Louis, 1912; Ph.D., U. of Ill., 1915; m. Floy Quin, Sept. 23, 1913 (dec. 1962); children—Sally (Mrs. John W. Osborn), Leonard. Teacher of science, Wauwatosa (Wis.) High Sch., 1910-11; fellow of botany, Wash. U., 1911-12; asso. floricultural pathologist, U. of Ill., 1912-16; prof. of plant pathology, Ala. Poly. Inst., and plant pathologist, Ala. Agrl. Expt. Sta., 1916-20; same, U. of Neb. and Neb. Agrl. Expt. Sta., 1920-37; prof. of bacteriology and chairman of department University of Neb., 1937-53, prof. emeritus, 1953; cons. Cranberry Growers, Inc., 1951-59; consultant, 1959-75; asso. with U.S. Dept. Agr. as agt., plant pathologist or sr. botanist, summers 1911, 22, 24, 26, 35, 38. Fellow A.A.A.S., American Academy Microbiology (charter member); mem. Bot. Soc. America, Am. Phytopathol. Society, Society American Bacteriologists, Nebraska Academy of Science (president 1927), Sigma Xi, Gamma Alpha, Phi Kappa Phi, Gamma Sigma Delta, Phi Sigma, Theta Nu. Catholic. Author: Laboratory Manual of General Bacteriology (with C. E. Georgi, L. F. Lingren), 1939; Laboratory Manual of Microbiology (with K. H. Lewis), 3d edition, 1962. Asso. editor of Phytopathology, 1919-22, 1930-33, 1941-44. Author of many articles and bulletins. Home: Tucson, Ariz. Died Feb. 22, 1975.

PELTON, ROGER TROWBRIDGE, mining engr.; b. Poughkeepsie, N.Y., Nov. 15, 1880; s. John W. and Mary R. (Trowbridge) P.; M.E., Sch. of Mines (Columbia), New York, 1903; m. Jennie Jewell Powell, Dec. 9, 1908; children—Elizabeth, Virginia Jewell. Mining engr., with Copper Queen Consol. Mining Co., 1904-07, chief engr., 1907-19; consulting engr., from 1919; county engr., Cochise County, Ariz., 1929-32, 1935-39; state engr. Arizona Civic Works Adminstrn., 1933. Member Am. Inst. Mining and Metall. Engrs., Sigma Chi. Address: La Jolla, Cal.†

PENDLETON, RUTH JANE, librarian; b. nr. Beatyville, Ky., Aug. 10, 1910; d. Hampton and Callie (Howell) Pendelton; A.B., Union Coll., 1934; B.A., George Peabody Coll., 1940; postgrad. U. Ga., 1952, U. Fla., 1960. Librarian, Homerville (Ga.) High Sch., 1941-47, R.E. Lee High Sch., Thomaston, Ga., 1947-73; librarian George A. Harrison Meml. Library, Thomaston, Ga., 1968-73. Mem. N.E.A., Am., S.W., Ga. library assns., Ga., Upson County edn. assns., Women's Security Christian Service, Beta Sigma Phi. Home: Thomaston, Ga. Died Sept. 1973.

PENDLETON, WILLIAM GIBSON, clergyman, educator; b. Wytheville, Va., Feb. 11, 1880; s. Robert Nelson and Frances Hite (Gibson) P.; student Washington and Lee U., 2 yrs. academic and 2 yrs. law course to 1903; grad. Va. Theol. Sem., 1907; B.D., 1912; D.D., Washington and Lee, 1920; m. Maria Mason Dawson, Oct. 7, 1908 (died 1921); m. 2d, Eleanor Fletcher Hotchkiss; 1 dau., Frances Gibson. Deacon, 1907, priest, 1908, P.E. Ch.; rector Hungar Parish, Eastville, Va., 1907-13, Hamilton Parish, Warrenton, 1913-20; rector and prin. Va. Episcopal Sch., Lynchburg, Va., from 1920. Mem. Delta Tau Delta. Democrat. Mason. Club: Rotary. Home: Lynchburg, Va.†

PENFIELD, JEAN NELSON, Mrs. William W. Penfield), lawyer, parliamentarian; b. Greencastle, Ind., Nov. 4, 1872; d. Franklin Perry and Eliza Jean (Brannan) Nelson; Ph.B., DePauw U., 1893; student Metropolitan Sch. of Music and Sargent Sch. Dramatic Art, New York, 1894-96; LL.B., Brooklyn Law Sch. (St. Lawrence U.), 1916; m. Judge William Warner Penfield, Dec. 15, 1897 (died June 21, 1935); children—Jean Louise (dec.), William Warner (dec.). Winner of Interstate Coll. Oratorical Contest, at Minneapolis, 1892 (11 states contesting); one of seven Incorporators of Woman Suffrage Party and city chairman for Greater New York 1911-12. Mem. bd. dirs. Internat. Com. on Marriage and Divorce. In charge dept. of practical law for women, Brooklyn Law Sch. of St. Lawrence U., during World War I. Member National League American Pen Women, National Society Magna Charta Dames, Kappa Kappa Gamma (nat. pres. 1902-04), Phi Delta Delta (hon. nat. v.p.), Woman's Practical Law Assn. Rep. Clubs: Westchester Woman's, Bronx Woman's. Author: Mother Mine; The Sea; White Tree Tops; Hold High The Flag; and other poems; lecturer; composer of secular and sacred songs; History and Genealogy of Penfield Family in America—a Tercentenary Tribute, 1650-1950. Home: New York City, N.Y.†

PENHALLOW, DUNLAP PEARCE surgeon; b. Amherst, Mass., Aug. 9, 1880; s. David Pearce and Sarah A. (Dunlap) P.; prep. edn. private sch., Montreal, Can.; B.S., Harvard, 1903, M.D., 1906; m. Katheryn McConnel Hitchcock, Oct. 6, 1926; children—Virginia W., Sarah Dunlap, David Pearce. Intern Carney Hosp., Boston City Hosp., and 4th asst. visiting surgeon latter until 1909; practiced gen. surgery, Boston, 1909-15; resident surgeon East Boston Relief Sta., 1910-13; instr. surgery, Tufts Coll. Med. Sch., 1910-11, asst. demonstrator anatomy, 1913-15. Served as pvt., corpl.

and sergt., Mass. Nat. Guard; 1st lt. and capt. M.C., 1900-17; with Am. Red Cross overseas, 1915; dir. Unit, Am. Women's War Hosp., Paignton, Eng., chief surgeon, 1915-18; promoted maj., 1917; comdg. officer Hosp. Mil. V.R. No. 76, France, Mar.-Sept. 1918; mobile operating team, St. Mihiel and Argonne offensives; dir. Field Hosp., sanitary train, regtl. surgeon 5th F.A., and med. insp.; 1st Division, acting division surgeon, 1st Division; chief of surgical service, Camp Mead, Maryland, 1919-Vets.' Bur., N.Y. City, 1921-22; chief surgeon U.S. V.B. Hospital No. 35, St. Louis, 1922; commanding Officer United States Veterans Hospital No. 32, Washington, D.C., 1923; senior surgeon Reserve, U.S. P.H.S., 1923-25; colonel, Medical Reserve Corps, U.S. Army, comdg. 364th Med. Regiment; on active service as med. inspector and later corps surgeon, 2d Army Corps, 1941; comdg. Army station hosp. and post surgeon, Pine Camp, N.Y., 1942. Ret. as col., 1945. Prof. clin. orthopedics, Georgetown University Medical School. Visiting surgeon in orthopedics. Freedmen's Hospital; surgical staff Providence Hospital. Assoc. staff Mercy Hosp., House of the Good Samaritan, Watertown, N.Y.; ret. from all teaching and hosp. activity. Med. dir. Jefferson Co. Welfare Assn. Fellow A.C.S., International College of Surgeons; mem. Internat. Med. Soc., Jefferson Co. Med. Soc., Mass. Med. Society, Assn. Military Surgeons of U.S., Clinical Club of Washington, Descendants of Colonial Govs., Champlain Soc. Can., Vets. Foreign Wars, Mil. Order Foreign Wars, Mil. Order World War, Soc. Colonial Wars, Delta Upsilon. Member Church of England. Republican. Clubs: Harvard, Cosmos, Army and Navy Country (Washington, D.C.), Varsity (Harvard). Author: Text Book of Military Surgery, 1916-18. Contbr. on surg. subjects; contbr. to Oxford Loose-Leaf Surgery. Address: Philadelphia, N.Y.†

PENN, JOHN CORNELIUS, educator; b. The Netherlands, Nov. 26, 1881; s. Jacob and Annigje (Stobbe) P.; brought by parents to U.S., 1890; grad. Calumet High Sch., Chicago, 1901; B.S. in C.E., Armour Inst. Tech., 1905, C.E., 1910; m. Mae Van Wyngarden, June 6, 1922; 1 dau., Jane Ann. Asst. city engr., Chicago, 1905-10; instr., Armour Institute Technology (now Illinois Institute of Technology), 1910-14, asst. prof. civil engring., 1914-18, asso. prof., 1918-21, asst. to dean and examiner, 1921-27, acting dean of engring., 1927, dean, 1928-34, dir. civil engring., 1934-37, prof. civil engring., 1937-49, retired. Mem. Am. Soc. Engring. Edn., Am. Society Civil Engrs., Ill. Soc. Professional Engrs., A.A.A.S., Western Soc. Engrs., Theta Xi, Tau Beta Pi. Chi Epsilon. Republican. Mem. Dutch Ref. Ch. Mason. Club: Knickerbocker. Home: Chicago, Ill.†

PENNELL, RALPH MCT., army officer; b. Martin Twp., Anderson County, S.C., Aug. 18, 1882; s. James Robert and Nannie Malvina (Browne) P.; B.S., U.S. Mil. Acad., 1906; distinguished grad. Command and Gen. Staff Sch., 1923, Army War Coll., 1927, Naval War Coll., 1928; m. Norma Scott Bestor, Apr. 14, 1909; children—Norma Katharine (wife of Lt. Col. Richard K. Boyd), Robert (major, U.S. Army), Elizabeth (wife of Lt. Col. Osmund A. Leahy, U.S. Army), Margaret. Commd. 2d lt., U.S. Army, 1906; promoted through grades to maj. gen., Feb. 26, 1942; served as lt. col., F.A., Nat. Army, Aug. 1917-July 1918; col. F.A., U.S. Army, July 1918-June 1920; commanded 27th Div. overseas; commandant, The Field Artillery School, Ft. Sill, Okla., Oct. 28, 1944. Awarded D.S.M., 1920, Oakleaf Cluster, 1943; Legion of Merit, 1946. Home: Lawton, Okla. Died Apr. 17, 1973.

PENNOCK, GILBERT LEE, clergyman; b. Little Rock, Ark., Dec. 30, 1880; s. Edwin Thaddeus and Laura Belle (Hamma) P.; A.B., Antioch Coll., Yellow Springs, O., 1902; A.M., Ohio State U., 1904; B.D., Episcopal Theol. Sch., Cambridge, Mass., 1911; studied U. of Berlin, 1911; Ph.D., New York U., 1919; m. Grace Adelaide Troll, Oct. 18, 1915; children—Dorothy Léonie, Gilbert Lee, Stephen George. Fellow and teacher, Ohio State U., 1902-04; teacher English, high sch., Marietta, O., 1904-05, Oberlin Coll., 1905-07, Ohio State U., 1907-08; deacon, 1910, priest, 1911, P.E. Ch.; teacher Boone U., Wuchang, China, 1912; asst. minister St. John's Ch., Jersey City, N.J., 1912-14; rector Calvery Ch., Bayonne, N.J., 1914-17; canon missioner, Diocese of Newark, 1917-19; rector and archdeacon Christ Ch., Newton, N.J., 1919-23; rector Holy Trinity Ch., Oxford, O., and prof. of classics and Biblical Lit., Oxford Coll. for Women, 1923-28, acting pres., 1928; lectr. Miami U., from 1929. Author: The Consciousness of Communion with God, 1919; A College Greek Book, 1929. Home: Oxford, O.†

PEPPARD, MURRAY BISBEE, educator; b. Concord, Mass., May 23, 1917; s. Victor Edwin and Edna Caro (Bisbee) P.; A.B., Amherst Coll, 1939; M.A., Yale, 1942, Ph.D., 1948; m. Josephine Neville Smith, Oct. 25, 1941; children—Victor Edwin, Josette Marie, George Neville. Instr., Amherst Coll., 1942, Yale, 1945-46; mem. faculty Amherst Coll., 1946-74, prof. German, 1962-74. Served with USNR, 1942-45. Decorated Navy Commendation ribbon. Mem. Am. Assn. Tchrs. German. Am. Assn. U. Profs., Phi Beta Kappa, Phi Gamma Delta. Rotarian. Author biographies of N. Nekrasov, Durrenmatt, Brothers Grimm. Home: Amherst Mass. Died Sept. 3, 1974.

PEPPER, WILLIAM MULLIN, JR., lawyer, lexicographer, newspaperman; b. Sharon Hill, Pa., Aug. 25, 1903; s. William Mullin and Sarah (Thomas) P.; student U.S. Naval Acad., 1923-25; J.D., U. Fla., 1929; m. Kathryn Tucker, Nov. 16, 1925 (dec.); children—William Mullin III, Patricia Kathryn (Mrs. W.A. Gager, Jr.); m. 2d, Kathryn Angle Scarritt, Dec. 30, 1963. With Gainesville (Fla.) Daily Sun, 1917-63, successively reporter, sports editor, desk editor, editor and pub., co-pub., editor, 1945-63, newspaper cons., lexicographer; admitted to Fla. bar, 1929, practiced Miami, 1929-32, Gainesville, 1963-65; staffwriter A.P., 1935-41. Sec., gen. legal counsel Inter Am. Press Assn. Tech. Center, 1963-65. Mem. journalism jury Pulitzer prize, 1953, 54. Served as lt. comdr. USNR, 1941-45; comdr., ret., 1963. Recipient Maria Moors Cabot award, 1960, Tom Wallace award Inter Am. Press Assn., 1964. Mem. Inter Am. Press Assn. (former chmn. awards com., dir., mem. exec. com., hon. life), Phi Delta Theta. Author: English-Spanish Dictionary of Newspaper and Printing Terms, 1959; Practical Translator, Dictionary of Journalism and the Graphic Arts, 1971. Address: Crystal River, Fla. Died May 15, 1975.

PERCY, ATLEE LANE, educator; b. Doylestown, Pa., Nov. 24, 1880; s. Frank and Sara E. (Hagaman) P.; student Chicago Law Sch., 1902-03, Bennett Accountancy Inst., Phila., 1911-14, Temple U., Phila., 1914-15; B.B.A., Boston U., 1917, M.B.A., 1927; A.B., Taylor U., Upland, Ind., 1922; C.P.A., Mass. and New Hampshire; married Clara E. Pittenger, June 4, 1902 (died November 26, 1946); 1 daughter, Beatrice (Mrs. Paul Roland Whitworth); married 2d, Elsbeth Melville, September 2, 1948. Admitted to Indiana bar, 1902; in practice law and accounting, Marion, 1902-04; instr. pub. and pvt. secondary schs., comml. colls. and univs., 1904-19; mem. faculty Boston U., from 1919, prof. accounting and head dept. commercial edn., 1921-42; chairman Div. of Commercial Education, 1934-42; chmn. dept. of accounting, 1942-46; dir. Summer Session, 1934-52; dean of univ., 1946-58. Mem. profl., scientific orgns. and assns., past pres. of several. Methodist. Mason, Odd Fellow. Club: University, Co-author, editor text and work book in accounting. Home: Newtonville, Mass.†

PERKINS, DONALD, publisher; b. Tacoma, Feb. 25, 1912; s. Locke McIndoe and Ruth (Roberts) P.; A.B., U. Wis., 1932; M.B.A., Harvard, 1934; m. Helen Kramer, June 12, 1942; children—Maryann, Patricia. Vice pres., advt. dir. Cowles Mags., Inc., N.Y.C., 1951-64, exec. v.p. Cowles Mags. and Broadcasting, Inc. (name changed to Cowles Communications, Inc.), 1964-71, pres. Family Circle magazine, 1967-71. Served as lt. Bur. Ordnance, U.S.N., 1942-44; gunnery officer U.S.S. St. Louis, 1944-46. Clubs: Harvard (N.Y.C.); Racquet and Tennis. Home: New York City, N.Y. Died May 1973.

PERKINS, FREDERICK ORVILLE, advt. exec.; b. Utica, N.Y., Feb. 15, 1879; s. Horace Wm. and Mary Janet (Catlin) P.; ed. pub. schs., Utica; m. Florence Irene Goodenough, Mar. 17, 1914; 1 son, Horace Orville. Western manager, Longmans Green & Co., publishers, Chicago, Illinois, 1903-09; secretary Atkinson, Mentzer & Co., New York, 1909-11; v.p. The Prang Co., 1911-18; staff of asst. sec. of war, 1918-19; vice pres. J. Walter Thompson Co., New York, 1919-31; with Young & Rubicam, from 1931. Editor: The Blue Bird (by Maeterlinck), 1914; Peter Pan (Barrie), 1916; Life of the Bee (Maeterlinck), 1917; Insect Adventures (Fabre), 1917. Home: Greenwich, Conn.†

PERKINS, FREDERICK POWERS, ins. exec.; b. Skowhegen, Me., Aug. 18, 1904; s. DeForest H. and Jennie (Powers) P.; B.S. Bowdoin Coll., 1921-25; m. Eleanor Sturgis, July 12, 1930; 1 son, William. With Aetna Life & Caslty Co., Hartford, Conn., 1925-69, beginning in actuarial dept., successively asst. actuary, asso. actuary, actuary, 1925-54, v.p., 1954-58, sr. v.p., 1958-69, also dir.; dir. Conn. Bank & Trust Co. (hon.), State Bank for Savs. Trustee Bowdoin Coll., Open Hearth Assn. (v.p. 1972); corporator Hartford Hosp., 1952. Mem. Soc. of Actuaries, Am. Acad. Actuaries, Delta Kappa Epsilon, Phi Beta Kappa. Clubs: Hartford Golf, Bowdoin of Conn. (pres. 1953-55) (Hartford). Home: Hartford, Conn., Died Nov. 4, 1975.

PERKINS, LUCY ANN, social worker; b. Louisville; d. Emmitt and Alice (Williams) Perkins; B.A., U. Louisville, 1944; M.S.W., Atlanta U., 1946; postgrad. Western Res. U., 1948-51, Coll. William and Mary, 1956-57, Sr. caseworker Cuyahoga County Child Welfare Bd., Cleve., 1947-52; sr. worker in charge dist. office Family Service Soc., Hartford, Conn., 1952-56; casework supr. Friends Assn. for Children, Richmond, Va., 1956-57; caseworker supr. Family Service and Travelers Aid, Inc., Utica, N.Y., 1957-63; casework supr. Wiltwyck Sch. for Boys, N.Y.C., 1963-65; chief pyschiat. social worker Chgo. State Hosp., also Children and Adolescent Services Reoed Zone Center, 1965-70; Chief psychiat. Social Worker N. Central Regional Mental Health-Mental Retardation Bd., 1968-69; dir. Soundview Community Mental Health Center, Albert Einstein Coll. Medicine of Yeshiva U., dept. psychiatry, Bronx, N.Y., 1970-75. Cons., lectr., supr., project demonstrator Marcy (N.Y.) State Hosp., 1958-63. Mem. Nat. Assn. Social Work, Am. Orthopsychiat. Assn. Social Work Vocational Bur., Conf. Social Welfare, Zeta Phi Beta. Home: Riverdale, N.Y., Died Mar. 18, 1975.

PERKINS, THOMAS LEE, lawyer; b. Newport News, Va., Nov. 9, 1905; s. William R. and Mary (Bell) P.; grad. Phillips Andover Acad., 1924; LL.B., U. Va., 1940; LL.D. (hon.), Furman U., 1964; m. Dorothy L. Morgan, Nov. 18, 1931; children—Nancy Lee (Mrs. Nancy P. Horton), Parke Morgan (Mrs. Harold E. Aken, Jr.). Broker, N.Y.C., 1930-40; mem. N.Y. Stock Exchange, 1930-52. admitted to N.Y. bar, 1940, practiced in N.Y.C.; counsel firm Perkins, Daniels & McCormack. Chmn. bd. A. Cyanamid Co., 1958-61, mem. finance com., dir.; chmn. Duke Power Co.; dir. Gen. Motors Corp., Morgan Guaranty Trust Co. N.Y., J.P. Morgan & Co., Discount Corp. N.Y. Trustee N.Y. Pub. Library. Republican presdl. elector, 1952. Trustee Phillips Andover Acad.; chmn. trustee Duke Endowment; trustee, mem. exec. com. Duke. Mem. Am. Bar Assn., Assn. Bar City of N.Y., Phi Delta Phi, Phi Delta Theta. Clubs: Regency Whist, Rockefeller Center Luncheon, Madison Sq. Garden, Hemisphere, Links (N.Y.C.); Apawamis, Shenorock Shore, Am. Yacht (Rye); Blind Brook (Port Chester, N.Y.); Lyford Cay (Bahamas). Home: Rye N.Y. Died June 21, 1973; interred Greenwood Union Cemetery, Rye, N.Y.

PERLMAN, DAVID, educator; b. N.Y.C., Nov. 12, 1909; s. Herman and Rose (Kupo) P.; B.S., Coll. City N.Y., 1930; A.M., Columbia, 1932, Ph.D., 1936; m. Evelyn Rose, June 29, 1934; 1 dau., Frances (Mrs. Sanford Freedman). Faculty, Coll. City N.Y., 1930, fellow, 1930-34, tutor, 1934-37; instr., 1937-48, asst. prof. chemistry, 1948-56, asso. prof. chemistry, 1956-62, prof. chemistry, 1962-72. Cons., Refining Uninc., N.Y.C., 1946-60. Mem. Am. Chem. Soc., Am. Assn. U. Profs., A.A.A.S., Sigma Xi. Patentee in field of vegetable oils. Home: Mount Vernon N.Y. Died Apr. 5, 1972.

PERLMANN, GERTRUDE ERIKA, educator; b. Reichenberg, Czechoslovakia, Apr. 20, 1912; d. Walter and Elise (Gibian) Perlmann; D.Sc., German U. Prague, 1936. Fellow, Biol. Lab., Carlsberg Found. Copenhagen, Denmark, 1937-39; research asst. dept. phys. chemistry Harvard Med. Sch., Boston, 1939-41, research fellow medicine 1945; research fellow medicine Mass. Gen. Hosp., Boston, 1941-45; vis. investigator Rockefeller Inst., N.Y.C., 1945-47, asst., 1947-51, asso., 1951-57, asst. prof., 1957-58, asso. prof. biochemistry, 1958-72, prof., 1972-74. Mem. Am. Chem. Soc., Am. Soc. Biol. Chemists, Am. Biophys. Soc. Brit. Biochem. Soc., Harvey Soc. Home: New York City, N.Y., Died Sept. 9, 1974.

PERLMUTTER, IRVING K. physician; b. Newark, 1915; M.D., Jefferson Med. Coll., 1939. Intern, Newark Beth Israel Hosp., 1939-40, attending gynecologist, 1946-72; tng. 3d div. Bellevue Hosp., N.Y.C., 1946; asso. attending gynecologist St. Barnabas Hosp., Newark. Served with AUS, 1940-45. Diplomate Am. Bd. Obstetrics and Gynecology. Mem. A.M.A., Am. Coll. Obstetricians and Gynecologists. Home: Maplewood, N.J. Died Feb. 9, 1972.

PERLMUTTER, OSCAR WILLIAM, univ. dean; b. July 5, 1920; s. Julius B. and Hermine (Langer) P.; M.A., U. Chgo., 1949, Ph.D., 1959; m. Eila Helen Siren, Sept. 10, 1945; children—William, Charles, Francis Xavier, Josette-Marie, Gregory. Lectr., U. Chgo., 1948-51; prof., v.p. St. Xavier Coll., Chgo., 1947-59; Ford faculty fellow Yale, 1952-53; acad. dir. Inst. European Studies, Univs. Vienna, Freiburg and Paris, 1959-62; vis. prof. U. Minn., 1962-63; honors prof. U. Santa Clara (Cal.), 1963-64; prof. polit. sci., dean fine and profl. arts Kent State U., 1964-66; prof. polit. sci., dean Coll. Arts and Scis., State U. N.Y. at Albany, 1966-72; acad. v.p., dean faculties St. John's U., Collegeville, Minn., 1972-75. Ednl. cons. U.S. Office of Edn., Dept. Health, Edn. and Welfare, Washington, Office Econ. Opportunity, Exec. Office Pres., Washington, chmn. nat. standing com. on advanced placement Coll. Entrance Exam. Bd.; mem. council on continuing edn. and community service Minn. Higher Edn. Coordinating Commn.; curriculum cons. to various colls., univs. Exec. dir. N.Y. State Commn. to Rev. Legislative and Jud. Compensation, 1970; mem. Study Commn. for Campus Ministry in Higher Edn., 1970. Active Chgo. Cath. Interracial Council, 1950-57, Chgo. chpt. Nat. Council Christians and Jews, 1950-59, Episcopal Ch. Counseling, Albany, 1967-75. Served with USAAF, 1942-46; ETO, PTO. Decorated officler L'Order des Palmes Academique (France). Mem. Am. Assn. Sch. Adminstrs., Am. Pol. Sci. Assn., Assn. Fine Arts Deans, Am. Sociol. Assn., Nat., Minn. edn. assns. Author: The Endless Pavement. Contbr. articles to profl. jours., children's lit. Home: St Joseph, Minn. Died Mar. 5, 1975; buried St. John's Abbey, Collegeville, Minn.

PERON, JUAN, president Argentine Rep.; b. Lobos, Argentina, Oct. 8, 1895; s. Mario Tomás Peron and Juana Sosa de Peron; ed. Olivos Internat. Coll., Internat. Poly. Sch., Argentine Mil. Sch.; m. María Eva Duarte, Oct. 21, 1945 (died July 26, 1952); m. 2d, Isabel Peron. Commd. lt. inf., 1913, and advanced to rank of gen., 1950; apptd. a.d.c. to Col. Fasola Castaño 1930; apptd. a.d.c. to minisaer of war, 1936, also mil. attaché Argentine Embassy, Santiago, Chile, 1936; head of

Argentine mission which toured Europe, 1939-41; named chief of staff 1st Army Div., 1943, also apptd. chief of secretariat Ministry of War, 1943; sec. of labor and welfare, 1943-45; v.p. Argentine Republic, 1945; president, 1946-55, later, until 1974; lived in exile (following fall of govt.), Spain, from 1955. Prof. mil. history Superior War Sch., 1930-36; apptd. prof. mil. tech. course on mountaineering, 1941. Author: The Eastern Front in the 1914 World War, 1928; Treatise on Military History, 1932; 1870 Military Operations, 1939. Home: Buenos Aires, Argentina. Died July 1, 1974.

PERRIN, HALFORD GUY, health ofcl.; b. Kansas City, Mo., July 23, 1905; s. Guy Henry and Mary (Beebe) P.; B.S., U. Kan., 1927; m. Frances Nierman, Sept. 8, 1928 (dec. May 1933); 1 dau., Mary Dell (Mrs. Robert F. Mahood); m. 2d, Marcile Isaacson, Oct. 6, 1934; children—James H., Christina. Owner, Perrin Equipment Co., 1927-35; rep. Am. Seating Co., Grand Rapids, Mich., 1935-42; bus. mgr. Kansas City Municipal Hosps., 1942-47; exec. dir. Bishop Clarkson Meml. Hosp., Omaha, 1947-68; dir. devel. Episcopal Diocese of Neb., 1968-69; exec. dir. Greater Omaha Comprehensive Health Planning Council, since 1969-74; also hospital consultant. Board dirs. Douglas-Sarpy county chpt. A.R.C., Omaha; trustee Nebraska Epilepsy League. Chmn. of div. of laymen's work Episcopal Diocese Neb. Fellow Am. Coll. Hosp. Adminstrs. (regents council, 1965-68); member Am. (trustee), Mo. (past pres.), Neb. (past pres.), Midwest (pres. 1952-53) hosp. assns., Episcopal Hosp. Assembly (past pres.), C. of C., Hosp. Research and Devel. Inst., Beta Gamma Sigma (charter mem. U. Kan.), Alpha Kappa Psi. Rotarian. Contbr. articles to profl. jours. Home: Omaha, Neb. Died Jan. 31, 1974.

PERRY, LYMAN SPENCER, naval officer; b. Andover, O., Mar. 10, 1897; s. Furman Epaphrus and Ellen (Spencer) P.; grad. Naval Acad. Prep. Sch., 1915; B.S., U.S. Naval Acad., 1919; m. Anna Holder Abson, Aug. 9, 1919; 1 son, Lyman Spencer Abson. Commd. ensign U.S. Navy, 1919, and advanced through grades to commodore, 1946; aide to Sec. of Navy, 1943-44; comdr., Naval Training and Distribution Center, Camp Peary, Va., 1944-46; ret. from active service, 1946; dir. of athletics, Asso. Colls. of Upper N.Y., from 1946. Com. mem., Nat. Council on Phys. Fitness, 1943-44. Awarded Victory medals (both World Wars), Am. Defense medal, European-African medal, Sec. of Navy commendation ribbon, Expert Rifleman medal. Mem. U.S. Naval Inst., Am. Legion, Retired Officers' Assn. Episcopalian. Club: Yacht (New York City). Contbr. articles to N.Y. Herald-Tribune and Naval Inst. proceedings. Selected for 1st All-Am. football team from U.S. Naval Acad., 1918. Home: Cosey Point, Md. Died June 2, 1975.

PERRY, WILLIAM GRAVES, architect; b. Boston, Mass., Nov. 8, 1883; s. Charles French and Georgianna West (Graves) P.; student Noble and Greenough Sch., Boston, 1893-1900; A.B., Harvard, 1905; S.B., Mass. Inst. Tech., 1907; diploma, architect, Ecole des Beaux Arts, Paris, 1913; m. Eleanor Gray Bodine, Aug. 6, 1908 (div.); children—Eleanor Gray, Baird, William Graves, Louise Bodine Carpenter; m. 2d, Frances McElfresh Ames, July 16, 1945. Draughtsman, Shepley, Rutan & Coolidge, 1907, 1914-15; instr. archtl. design, Harvard, 1915-16; practiced independently, 1915-19; mem. Perry, Shaw & Hepburn, Boston, 1923-68, Perry, Dean & Stewart, 1968-75; firm architects of Roxbury Latin School Bldg., (Boston), Harvard Coop. Soc. Store, Radcliffe Coll. Lecture Hall, Cambridge, Mass., St. Paul's Ch. and Parish House, Newburyport, Mass., Houghton Library for Rare Books, Harvard Coll., Restoration of Colonial City of Williamsburg, Va., Aldrich and Kresge Halls, Harvard Sch. Bus. Adminstrn., Alfred P. Sloan Metals Lab., Mass. Inst. Tech., Furman U., Greenville, S.C., Student Union. Williams, Coll., Am. Embassy residence, London, restoration Gov. Tryon Palace, New Bern, N.C. Past pres. Mass. Bldg. Congress, 1933-35; mem. Nat. Commn. Fine Arts, Washington, 1945-53. Served to capt. inf. Mass. State Guard, 1916-17; capt. Air Service, U. S. Army, 1917-19; comdg. 477th Aero Squadron, 1917-18; equipment officer staff of Air Service comdr., 1st Army A.E.F., 1918-19; St. Mihiel and Argonne engagements; Army Air Service citation. Recipient Elise Willing Balch medal. Nat. Soc. of Colonial Dames Am., chapter II, Phila., 1933. Chmn. nat. adv. com. Historic Am. Bldgs. Survey, 1932. N.A. Fellow A.I.A. Past trustee Colonial Williamsburg, Va. Sec. Rotch Traveling Scholarship, 1951-62. Clubs: Episcopalian Club of Mass. (past pres.); Union, (Boston); Hasty Pudding, Owl (Harvard Univ.); Century Assn. (N.Y.C.). Home: Andover, Mass. Died Apr. 4, 1975; buried Oak Hill Cemetery, Newburyport, Mass.

PERSE, SAINT-JOHN (ALEXIS SAINT-LÉGER LÉGER), poet, diplomat; b. Guadelpupe, Fr. West Indies, May 31, 1887; license in law diploma Ecole des Hautes Etudes; Litt.D. (hon.), Yale; m. Dorothy Milburn Russell, 1958. Came to U.S., 1940. Diplomat polit. and comml. div. French Fgn. Office, 1914; sec. French embassy, Peking, China, 1916-21; various assignments Ministry Fgn. Affairs to 1940, minister's prin. sec., 1925-32; sec.-gen., 1932-40; ambassador of France 1932; cons. French lit. Library of Congress, Washington, 1941-75. Mem. Am. Acad. Arts and Letters, Am. Acad. Arts and Scis., Modern Lang. Assn., Bavarian Acad. Arts and Letters. Decorated grand officer Legion of Honor; comdr. Order of Bath, comdr. Royal Victorian Order, comdr. Order Arts and Letters, grand cross Brit. Empire; recipient Nobel prize for lit., 1960. Author: (poems) Eloges, 1910; Anabase, 1925; Exile and Other Poems, 1942; Winds, 1946; Seamarks, 1957; Chronicle, 1960; Birds, 1963; Dante, 1966; others. Home: Hyeres, France. Died Sept. 20, 1975.

PERSON, HJALMER T., civil engr.; b. Hitchcock, S.D., Feb. 7, 1903; s. John F. and Marie (Larsen) P.; B.S. in C.E., S.D. State Coll., 1925; M.S., Ia. State Coll., 1927; C.E., S.D. State Coll., 1932; m. Maurine E. Hollo, May 29, 1931; children—John Granger, Hjalma Maurine. Asst. prof. civil engring., South Dakota State College, 1927-29; asst. and associate professor, Wyoming University, 1929-34, professor and div. chmn. 1934-48, dean of engineering, 1948-64, later pres., emeritus, 1964-74; cons. J. T. Banner & Assos., 1964-74; dir. ESMWT Program, 1942-45; (part time) dir. U.S. Coast and Geodetic Survey and State surveys, 1933-34. Detailer Pitts. Des Moines Steel Co., summer 1926; bridge designer So. Dak. Hwy. Dept., summer 1928; detailer Am. Br. Co. summer 1929; bridge designer Mo. State Highway Dept., summers 1930 and 1931; spl. engr. Wyo. State Planning Bd., summers 1936, '37, '38. Soil Conservation Service, 1939; cons. engr. for W. W. Flora, summers 1940-41; pvt. engineering practice since 1935; partner Person and McGau, 1942-50; partner J. T. Banner & Associates, 1950-74; consultant to Wyoming State Engineer on Upper Colorado, Cheyenne, Bear, Yellowstone and Snake River Compact Commission since August 1946; Wyo. commr. Upper Colo. River Basin Commn.; mem. Presidents Mo. Basin Survey Commn., 1952-53; chairman Wyo. State Planning Bd., 1934-35; pres. and v.p. Wyo. Bd. Exam. Engrs. since 1935; past pres., Wyo. sect. Am. Soc. C.E.; past pres., Wyo., Engring. Soc.; mem. Wyo. Reclamation Assn. (sec. 1938-55); director Western Zone, Nat. Council, State Bds. of Examing Engrs., 1940-43, v.p., 1943-44, pres., 1944-46, chairman commission on qualifications for registration, 1947-49, representative Engrs. Council Professional Development, 1948-49, recipient Distinguished Service certificate, 1955; member Laramie Chamber of Commerce (director 1944-46). Secretary Association of Western State Engineers, 1939 and 1944. Member Am. Soc. Eng. Edn. (mem. comm. on exam. edn. div., 1944-46). Pacific Northwest Development Assn. (dir)., Am. Soc. C.E. (mem. comm. on Registration Engineers 1945-49, exec. com. irrigation and drainage div. 1954-59, chmn. 1959, chmn. Wyo. Membership Com.; dir.), National Reclamation Association, Wyo. Engrs. Soc., Sigma Xi, Phi Kappa Phi, Sigma Tau. Rotarian. Recipient Four States Irrigation Council Headgate award, 1958. Home: Laramie, Wyo. Died Dec. 13, 1974.

PERSONS, JOHN CECIL, banker; b. Atlanta, May 9, 1888; s. William Matthew and Alice Virginia (Longshore) P.; LL.B., U. Ala., 1910, LL.D., 1952; m. Elonia D. Hutchinson, June 12, 1913; children—John Cecil (dec.), Elonia Nelson (Mrs. Wm. K. McHenry, Jr.), Alice Virginia (Mrs. Bruce H. Stewart). Admitted to Ala. bar, 1910, and began practice at Tuscaloosa; treas. U. Ala., 1912-13; city atty., Tuscaloosa, 1915; pres. Persons Lumber Co., Tuscaloosa, 1916-21; began banking with Mchts. Bank & Trust Co., 1919; v.p. First Nat. Bank, Tuscaloosa, 1922-27; pres. Traders Nat. Bank, Birmingham, 1927, Am.-Traders Nat. Bank, 1928-30; pres. First Nat. Bank Birmingham, 1930-53, chmn. bd., 1953-68, also dir.; dir. Ala. Gt. So. R.R. Co., Avondale Mills. Trustee So. Research Inst. Served to maj., inf. U.S. Army, 1917-18; mem. N.G., 1918-40; div. comdr. 31st (Dixie) Div., U.S. Army, 1940-48; comdr. assault troops in capture island Morotal; ret. lt. gen. N.G., 1948. Decorated D.S.C., D.S.M. (U.S.); Fla. cross State Fla., D.S.M. State Ala., Joint citations from govs. Fla., Ala., Miss., Le. for services comdg. troops from these states during 1940-45; recipient Magnolia cross State Miss.; named Most Distinguished Alumnus, U. Ala., 1966; Ala. Acad. Honor, 1968. Mem. Phi Beta Kappa, Scabbard and Blade, Phi Kappa Sigma, Omicron Delta Kappa. Democrat. Baptist. Mason. Clubs: Birmingham Country, Mountain Brook Country, Downtown. Home: Birmingham, Ala. Died Dec. 22, 1974; interred Elmwood Cemetery.

PERTAIN, CHARLES ANDREE, mfg. co. exec.; b. Bklyn., Sept. 17, 1913; s. Charles Albright and Leah Theodora (Andree) P.; student Colgate U., 1931-34; B.S., N.Y. U., 1935, M.B.A., 1938; m. Jane Mark, Dec. 20, 1941; children—Tina (Mrs. Donald Anderson), Ellen (Mrs. Murray Chalmers), Linda. Sec., No. Paper Mills, Green Bay, Wis., 1946-54; asst. controller Marathon Corp., Menasha, Wis., 1954-55; treas. Appleton Wire Works, Wis., 1955-74, v.p. 1957-74; dir. Albany Internat. Corp., First Nat. Bank, Neenah. Commr., Neenah Joint Sch. Dist., 1965-71. Served with AUS, 1942-46. C.P.A., N.Y., Wis. Mem. Am. Inst. C.P.A.'s, Sigma Chi. Presbyn. (elder 1960-63). Mason (Shriner). Clubs: North Shore Golf (Menasha, Wis.); Riverview Country Club (Appleton, Wis.). Home: Neenah Wis. Died Sept. 4, 1974.

PETERS, CHARLES CLINTON, prof. edn.; b. Duffield, Pa., Nov. 24, 1881; s. George W. and Mary Virginia (Myers) P.; A.B., Lebanon Valley Coll., Annville, Pa., 1901-05; A.M., Harvard, 1910; Ph.D., U. of Pa., 1916; studied Columbia; m. Dixie May Stone, June 12, 1907; children—Eleanor S., G. Herbert Palmer, Max Stone. Prof. classical langs., and mathematics, Clarksburg (Mo.) Coll., 1905-07 (pres. 1906-07); prof. philosophy and edn., Westfield (Ill.) Coll., 1907-11; dean and prof. philosophy and edn., Lebanon Valley Coll., 1911-13; supt. schs. Royersford, Pa., 1913-16; instr. edn., Lehigh U., 1916-17; with Ohio Wesleyan U., 1917-27, prof. edn., 1920-27; visiting professor Univ. of Miami (Fla.), 1926-27, 1945-47; professor edn. and dir. of educational research, Pa. State Coll., 1927-45, emeritus since 1945; professor edn. summers, Ohio State U., univs. of W.Va., Kan. Calif., Wis., also Stanford and Syracuse univs.; curriculum cons., Bethlehem (Pa.) Pub. Schs., from 1948. Chief Ednl. Surveys Unit Nat. Roster, War Manpower Commn., 1944. Mem. Ednl. Research Assn., Nat. Coll. Teachers of Edn., Psychometric Soc., Am. Acad. of Polit. & Soc. Science, Phi Delta Kappa, Kappa Delta Pi, Kappa Phi Kappa, Pi Gamma Mu, Theta Chi. Democrat. Methodist. Author: Human Conduct, 1918; Foundations of Educational Sociology, 1924, 1930. Contbr. Part. III, "Measuring Merit and Standards of Text-Books" (Ind. Survey, Vol. II, 1925); Objectives and Procedures in Civic Edn., 1930; Motion Pictures and Standards of Morality, 1933; Statistical Procedures and their Mathematical Bases (with Van Voorhis), 1935, 1940; The Curriculum of Democratic Education, 1942; Teaching High School History and Social Studies for Citizenship Training, 1948. Home: Marietta, Ga. Died Oct. 26, 1973.

PETERS, HARRY ALFRED, educator; b. Mauch Chunk, Pa., Aug. 4, 1879; s. Harry Alfred and Abigail Catherine (Horn) P.; grad. Phillips Acad., Andover, Mass., 1898; A.B., Yale, 1902, hon. A.M., 1933; L.H.D., Kenyon Coll., 1933; m. 2d, Ruth Miller, Oct. 16, 1929; 1 son (by 1st marriage), Richard Dorland. Master modern langs, and Latin, 1902-08, headmaster, University Sch., Cleveland O., 1908-47, emeritus, from 1947. Visited with Am. Sch. Boys' Tour, leading schs. of Gt. Brit., Holland and Ger., 1913; traveled widely in U.S., Can., Europe, Palestine, Egypt. Served as maj. in charge Univ. Sch. Battalion, 1916-17. Chmn. of Chamber of Commerce Com. on Edn., 1923-27. Responsible for special emphases at University School on machine shop work which resulted in current co-operative jobs for .- several war plants, Mem. North Central Acad. Assn. (ex-pres.), Nat. Collegiate Athletic Assn., Ohio High School Prins. Assn., Headmasters Association (ex-president), Country Day Sch. Headmsaters Association — (ex-president), Nat. Assn. Secondary School Prins., Ednl. Records Bur. Advisory Com., Nat. Prep. Sch. Midwest Com. of Student Christian Assn., Phi Beta Kappa. Contbr. to ednl. journals, Presbyterian. Republican. Clubs: University, Country, Rotary. Home: Cleveland Heights, O.†

PETERS, RUSSELL HOLT, business exec.; b. Omaha, July 26, 1899; s. Alleyne Davis and Maude Russell (Holt) P.; B.A., Cornell, 1920; Rhodes scholar, Oxford U., 1921-23; m. Gretchen Dishong, Oct. 19, 1929. Reporter and polit. corr. Omaha Bee-News, 1923-25, Sunday editor, 1925-30, news editor, 1930-36, mng. editor, 1936-37; mng. editor Seattle Post-Intelligencer 1937-43; pres. Penobscot Publishing Co. and co-publisher, Bangor Evening and Sunday Commercial, 1946-52; asst. to pres. Bangor & Aroostook R.R. Co. 1952-59, St. Croix Paper Co., from 1959. Mem. Rhodes Scholar Selection Com. Lt. comdr., U.S.N.R., 1943-46. Mem. Chi Psi. Presbyn. Home: Bangor, Me., Died Oct. 11, 1975.

PETERSEN, CHARLES, accountant; b. nr. Lake Wilson, Minn., Mar. 6, 1906; s. Chris Nels and Anna Christina (Andersen) P.; B.S., U. Wyo., 1947, postgrad., 1947-49; postgrad. U. Mo., 1966-68; m. Alice Elizabeth Muenster, Apr. 13, 1930; 1 dau., Merrillynn Ann. Employee, U.S. Post Office Dept., Cheyenne, Wyo., 1936-57; pvt. practice as pub. accountant, Laramie, Wyo., 1948-57; auditor, auditor in charge U.S. AEC, Kansas City, Mo., 1957-62, 66-68, Miamisburg, O., 1962-63, 65-66, Los Alamos, N.M., 1963-65, Albuquerque, N.M., 1968-70; pvt. practice C.P.A., Albuquerque, N.M., 1970-74. Treas., Albuquerque AEC Employees Fed. Credit Union, 1970. C.P.A., Wyo. Mem. Am. Inst. C.P.A.'s, Alpha Kappa Psi. Mason. Address: Albuquerque, N.M. Died Sept. 18, 1974.

PETERSEN, HARRIET LEA MURRAY (MRS. EINER JALMER PETERSEN), govt. ofcl.; b. Bath, Me.; d. George Edward and Margaret Anne (Cantelo) Murray; student public schools; student U. Me., 1965-66; m. Einer Jalmer Petersen, Dec. 25, 1928; children—Philip Allan, Margaret Anne (Mrs. Laurence Francis Haley), Diane. With State Govt., 1959-73; real estate broker, 1961-73. City chmn. Me. Heart Drive, 1954-55, Me. Cancer Drive, 1957, 58; orgnl. chmn. for recognition reception for Am. Mother of the year, 1952; active drives Me. Med. Center Bldg., YWCA Bldg., March of Dimes, Community Chest, United Fund. Mem. Portland Republican City Com., 1950-61, vice chmn., 1958-59; mem. Cumberland County Rep. Com., 1954-61; hon. v.p. Me. Rep. Conv., 1958. Mem. D.A.R. (rec. sec. 1960-62), Me. Hist. Library Soc. Clubs: Portland Republican Women's, Lincoln. Home: Portland, Me. Died Apr. 15, 1973.

PETERSEN, LEROY A., corporation exec.; b. Amery, Wis., Nov. 10, 1893; s. Chris and Christina Dagmar (Larsen) P.; A.B., U. of Wis., 1917; m. Helga Elizabeth Anderson, June 25, 1921; children—Bruce Royal, Joan Lisbeth. With Otis Elevator Co., since 1921, salesman, Atlanta, Ga., 1923-24, branch office mgr., Springfield, Mass., 1924-25, gen. sales engr., N.Y. City, 1925-38, vice pres., 1938-43, exec. vice pres., 1943-45, pres. and chief executive officer, 1945-61, chmn. bd., 1961-66; past chmn. bd. Otis Elevator Co., Ltd., Can.; mem. bd. dirs., Irving Trust Co., Corn Products Company, Ruberoid Company (all of N.Y.C.), Met. Life Insurance Company. Trustee Consolidated Edison Co., New York; mem. exec. com., Employers Liability Assurance Corp. Served as 1st lt., World War I. Mem. Phi Beta Kappa, Omicron Delta Gamma. Clubs: Union League, University (New York); Augusta (Ga.) Nat. Golf; Royal and Ancient Golf (St. Andrews Scotland); Anglo-Am. Fish and Game (Que.); Round Hill (Greenwich, Conn.); Blind Brook (Portchester, N.Y.); Clove Valley Rod and Gun. Home: Greenwich, Conn. Died Jan. 29, 1974.

PETERSEN, ROBERT WARREN, lubricant mfg. co. exec.; b. Mpls., Sept. 26, 1925; s. Warren Adrian and Edna Irene (Andersen) P.; student St. Ambrose Coll., 1943-44, Ill. State Normal U., 1944-45, Columbia U., 1945; B.A., State U. Ia., 1945; m. Helen Erlene Palmer, Nov. 26, 1955; children—Dana Elizabeth, Robert Warren, Eric Palmer. With Northland Products Co., Inc., Waterloo, Ia., 1951-73, v.p., 1951-63, pres., 1963-73; dir. Nat. Bank of Waterloo. Pres. Waterloo Indsl. Devel. Corp., 1970-73; pres. Waterloo Profl. Hockey Club, 1969-73, also dir. Mem. Riverfront Commn., 1952-54, Park Cemetery, 1971-73; chmn. Waterloo Women's Profl. Golf Assn. Open, 1957; bd. dirs. Family Service League, Jr. Achievement Black Hawk. trustee First Presbyn. Found. Served with USN, 1943-46. Mem. Soc. Automotive Engrs., Soc. Lubrication Engrs., Ind. Oil Compounders Assn., Waterloo Ambassadors (pres. 1963), Jr. C. of C. (dir. 1963-55), C. of C. (dir. 1957-59), Phi Kappa Psi (v.p. 1947-48). Presbyn. (trustee 1964-68, elder 1973). Mason (32 deg., Shriner), Rotarian (pres. 1961-62). Club: Sunnyside Country (dir. 1964-66) (Waterloo). Home: Waterloo, Ia. Died Dec. 10, 1973; interred Waterloo Meml. Park Cemtery.

PETERSON, ALBERT EDMUND, lawyer; b. Chgo., Oct. 5, 1906; s. Albert and Mary (Eddis) P.; student Beloit Coll., 1923-25; LL.B., U. Ill., 1928; m. Sue Heynen, Oct. 18, 1926. Admitted to Ill. bar, 1928; asso. Cheney, Evans & Peterson, attys., Chgo., 1928-31; with Chgo. Title & Trust Co., 1931-74, atty. law div., title officer, v.p. charge title legal dept., 1931-59, gen. counsel, Sec., head law div., 1959-69, sr. v.p., 1969-70. Bd. dirs. Mary Barteime Home for Girls of Met. Chgo., 1960-74, treas., 1962-66; bd. dirs. Washington and Jane Smith Home, 1965-74. Served from lt. (j.g.) to lt. USNR, 1943-46. Mem. Am. Ill., Chgo. bar assns., Law Inst. Chgo. Clubs: Union League of Chicago, Ridge country. Home: Chicago, Ill. Died June 7, 1974; interred Mt. Hope Cemetery, Chicago, Ill.

PETERSON, DONALD BOLCH, banker; b. Woodbine, Ia., Nov. 6, 1911; s. John C. and Eva (Bolch) P.; student Chgo. Tech. Coll., 1929-30, U. Mich., 1930-31; m. Harriet C. Hoffland, July 3, 1949; children—Douglas Don. Clk., First Nat. Bank, Woodbine, Ia., 1934-36; asst. cashier Am. Nat. Bank, Idaho Falls, Ida., 1936-42; v.p. Comml. Bank of Tillamook (Ore.), 1936-48, Comml. Bank of Ore., Tillamook and Hood River, 1948-54; pres. Comml. Bank of Salem (Ore.), 1954-73, Coban, Inc. Chmn. Ore. Banking Bd., dist. adv. bd. SBA. Bd. mem., sec.-treas. Salem Meml. Hosp. Found; numerous civic orgns., including conmr. Boy Scouts Am. Served to capt. AUS, 1942-45. Decorated Bronze Star; recipient awards U. S. Treasury Dept., SBA; named Boss of Year Salem Jaycees, 1971. Mem. Salem C. of C., Am. (agrl. com.), Western Ind. (exec. council, pres.) bankers assns. Presbyn. (elder Mason (Shriner), Lion (past pres. Salem). Club: Salem Knife and Fork (past pres.). Home: Salem, Ore. Died Feb. 22, 1973; interred Belcrest Meml. Park, Salem.

PETTEGREW, JON PRICE, mfg. co. exec.; b. Columbus, O., May 6, 1937; s. C. Wilbert and Margaret E. (Wilcox) P.; A.B., Miami (O.) U., 1959; m. Jeanne Ritter, Dec. 27, 1958; children—Lisa, Peter, Jill. With C.E. Merrill Book Co. div. Prentice-Hall, Columbus, O., 1959-62; sales promotion specialist General Electric Co., Pittsfield, Mass., 1962-65, sales promotion tech. lit. specialist, Louisville, Ky., 1965-67; sales promotion and mdse. mgr. Whirlpool Corp., Benton Harbor, Mich., 1967-74. Recipient Spoke award Louisville Jr. C. of C., 1967. Clubs: Louisville Yacht; St. Joseph River Yacht (St. Joseph, Mich.); U.S. Power Squadrons. Home: St. Joseph, Mich. Died May 1, 1974.

PETTENGILL, SAMUEL BARRETT, congressman; b. Portland, Ore., Jan. 19, 1886; s. Samuel and Sue (Clagett) P.; A.B., Middlebury (Vt.) Coll., 1908; LL.B., Yale, 1911; LL.D. Harding Coll., and Franklin Coll. and Middlebury Coll., Norwich U., D.C.L., Marietta College; married Josephine H. Campbell, June 1, 1912 (died 1948); 1 dau., Susan Harry (Mrs. T. B. Douglas); m. 2d, Helen M. Charles, July 16, 1949. In practice of law, South Bend, 1911-49; mem. legal dept. Pure Oil Co., Chicago, 1949-56. Mem. 72d Congress (1931-33), 13th Ind. Dist. and 73d to 75th Congresses (1933-39), 3d Ind. Dist. Mem. Sch. Bd., South Bend, 1925-28. Gen. counsel Transp. Assn. of America, 1943-45. Recipient Am. Freedoms award, 1950, 60; Patriotic Service award S. A. R., Caleb B. Smith award Masons. Mem. Am., Ind., U.S. Supreme Ct. bar assns., Grafton Hist. Soc. (pres. 1962-72). Delta Kappa Epsilon; Chi Tau Kappa. Ind. Conglist. Mason (33°). Author: Hot Oil; Jefferson, the Forgotten Man; Smokescreen; For Americans Only; The Yankee Pioneers - A Saga of Courage. numerous mag. articles. Home: Grafton, Vt. Died Mar. 20, 1974; buried Grafton Village Cemetery.

PETTICORD, PAUL PARKER, sem. pres..; b. Lost Springs, Kan., June 22, 1907; s. E.W. and Laura A. (Parker) P.; B.A., Ohio State U., 1929; M.A., U. So. Cal., 1931; D.D., Asbury Coll., 1948; LL.D., Houghton Coll., 1957; m. Grace E. Spaulding, June 7, 1930; children—Marilyn J. (Mrs. Harold Elmer), Pauline E. (Mrs. Myron Tweed). Ordained to ministry Evang. U.B. Ch., 1951; pastor, Corvallis, Ore., 1930-34, Yakima, Wash., 1935-41, Salem, Ore., 1941-42; pres. Western Evang. Sem., 1946-75. Supt., Pacific N.W. Conf. Evang. U.B. Ch., 1942-48, dir. Christian edn., 1938-48; pres. Nat. Assn. Evangs. 1956-58; v.p. Christian Holiness Assn., 1969-75. Chmn. bd. dirs. Oriental Missionary Soc., 1950—. Named Internat. Holiness Exponent of Year, Christian Holiness Conv., 1973. Rotarian. Home: Portland, Ore., Died July 18, 1975.

PETTIJOHN, JULIA IVANS, (Mrs. Bruce A. Pettijohn), lawyer; b. Bklyn., Jan. 27, 1918; d. Peter A. and Wanda (Szwaba) Ivans; A.B., U. Ala., 1941; J.D., Fordham U., 1944; m. Bruce A. Pettijohn, May 10, 1944; 1 dau., Celeste Ann. Admitted to N.Y. bar, 1946, U.S. Supreme Ct. bar, 1961; partner Pettijohn & Pettijohn, Harrison, N.Y., 1946-58, sr. partner, 1953-58; individual practice law, Slingerlands, N.Y., 1958-75. Acting rec. clk. Westchester County Land Records Office, 1952; asst. atty. N.Y. State Bd. Equalization and Assessment, 1971. Republican dist. leader Country Club Dist., Harrison, N.Y., 1953-57. Mem. Nat. Assn. Women Lawyers, Am. Assn. U. Women. Club: Westchester Country. Address: Slingerlands, N.Y., Died Jan. 23, 1975; buried St. Mary's Cemetery, Port Chester, N.Y.

PETTIS, JERRY LYLE, congressman; b. Phoenix, July 18, 1916; s. Dwight and Clora (Zimmerman) P.; B.A., Pacific Union Coll., 1938; postgrad. U. So. Cal.; m. Shirley Neil McCumber, Mar. 2, 1947; children—Peter, Deborah. Coll. tchr., 1941-42; newscaster, 1945; asst. to pres. United Airlines, 1945-50; rancher, 1946; founder Audio-Digest Found., 1951, Magnetic Tape Duplicators, 1951; v.p. devel. Loma Linda U., 1961-64, chmn. bd. councillors, 1960-75; mem. 90th-94th congresses from 37th Dist. Cal.; mem. Ways and Means Com. Mem. Cal. Republican Central Com., 1964-75; mem. Task Force on Internat. Econ. Policy; mem. Nat. Commn. on Fire Prevention and Control. Served with Air Transp. Command, World War II; PTO. Mem. Am. Farm Bur., Airline Pilots Assn. Clubs: Capitol Hill, Army-Navy Country (Washington); Pauma Valley (Cal.) Country. Home: Loma Linda, Cal. Died Feb. 14, 1975.

PETTIT, PAUL BRUCE, educator; b. Greensburg, Ind., July 9, 1920; s. Herman Benjamin and Orpha (Moberly) P.; B.A., Alfred U., 1942; M.A., Cornell U., 1943, Ph.D., 1949; m. Bernice Minker, Nov. 27, 1946 (div.); children—Faith Caldwell, Alexander Drummond. Bus. and company mgr. Corneli U. Theatre, 1942-46; instr. Cornell U., 1946-47; mem. faculty State U. N.Y. at Albany, 1947-72, prof., 1959-72, chmn. dept. speech and dramatic art, 1963-69, chmn. dept. theatre, 1969-72; Fulbright prof. English, Athens (Greece) Coll., 1950-51; vis. Univ. fellow Empire State Coll., 1971-72; producer-dir. Greek Cypriot Nat. Theatre, Cyprus, 1963-64; pres. Plays for Living, Albany Family and Children's Service, 1967-72; State Dept. cons. Syrian Arab Republic, 1963, 64, 65. Mem. Albany Citizens Planning Com. Bd. dirs. Northeastern N.Y. Speech Center, 1966-69. Recipient spl. award Kodak Internat. Color Picture Competition, 1964; State U. N.Y. Research Found. fellow, 1959, 60, 64, 71. Mem. Am. Ednl. Theatre Assn., Early English Text Soc., N.Y. State Community Theatre Assn., Am. Community Theatre Assn., Lambda Chi Alpha, Theta Alpha Phi. Home: Albany, N.Y. Died Aug. 1972.

PETTYS, ANNA C., newspaper publisher; ad. Colo. State Coll. Edn.; m. Alonzo Petteys; 4 children. Publisher (with son) Sterling (Colo.) Jour.-Advocate. Chmn. Colo. Bd. Edn. Chmn. Asso. State Bds. Edn. Am. Author: Doctor Portia. Office: Sterling, Colo. Deceased.

PEYTON, BERNARD, mfg. exec.; b. Santa Cruz, Cal., Jan. 29, 1896; s. William C. and Anne Ridgely (duPont) P.; student Hill Sch., 1914; A.B., Princeton, 1917; Sc.D., Clarkson Coll., 1949; LL.D. (honorary), Harding College, 1963; married Kathleen B. Anderson, Dec. 10, 1919; children—Anne (Mrs. Richard Perry, Jr.), Bernard, Jr., Malcolm C.; married second, Margaret C. duPont, Oct. 20, 1956. Vice pres. Granton Chem. Co., N.Y.C., 1919-27, pres., 1927; treas. Standard Stoker Co., 1936-42; v.p., treas., dir. N.Y. Air Brake Co., 1942-49, pres., 1949-54, chmn. bd., 1954-58; dir. E. I. de Nemours & Co., Inc. Mem. Phi Beta Kappa. Clubs: Pine Valley (N.J.) Golf, Ekwanok Country (Manchester, Vt.). Home: Princeton, N.J., Died Dec. 18, 1975.

PFEFFER, DELMONT KAHLER, investment banker; b. West Valley, N.Y.; A.B., Syracuse U., 1923. Instr. econs. Emory U., 1923-24; asst. mgr. municipal bond dept. Guaranty Co. N.Y., 1924-34; asst. v.p. First Nat. City Bank N.Y., 1934-41, v.p., 1942-61, sr. v.p., 1961-67; with F.S. Smithers & Co., Inc., N.Y.C., 1968-74. Mem. Mayor's Com. Mgmt. Survey, 1950-55, Trustee Citizens Budget Commn., N.Y., 1960-69, v.p., 1968-69. Mem. Investment Bankers Assn. Am. (gov. 1945-46, v.p. 1954-56). Clubs: Municipal Bond (pres. 1940-41), Municipal Forum, Bond, Lawyers (N.Y.C.). Home: New York City, N.Y., Died Jan. 27, 1974.

PFEIFER, JOSEPH LAWRENCE, congressman, M.D.; born Brooklyn, New York, Feb. 6, 1892; son Henry and Mary (Gabriel) P.; M.D., Long Island Med. Coll., 1914; m. Adeline L. McKean, Feb. 12, 1917; children—Frances Marie, Loretta Adeline, Joseph Lawrence, Thomas Edward, Monica Anne, Ann Marie. Intern. St. Catherine's Hosp., Brooklyn, 1914-15, successively asst., asso., then chief attending surgeon; was asst. surgeon Kings County Hosp.; mem. 74th to 81st Congresses (1935-51), 3d N.Y. Dist. Mem. Med. Advisory Bd., Columbia Univ., World War. Fellow Am. Coll. Surg. Author of papers on med. subjects. Home: Brooklyn, N.Y. Died Apr. 19, 1974.

PHELAN, ANDREW J., airline co. exec.; b. N.Y.C., 1907; student N.Y. U., also Pace Inst. With Panagra, 1941-67, v.p., comptroller, 1961-67; v.p. treas. Braniff Airways, Inc. Home: Dallas, Tex. Died Aug. 8, 1973.

PHELAN, BALFOUR, corp. ofcl.; b. Vicksburg, Miss., Aug. 3, 1894; s. Sidney Marcellus and Charlotte (Willis) P.; student Smith Acad., St. Louis, 1909-13; B.A., Yale, 1917; m. 2d, Dorothy Cummins, Apr. 11, 1950; 1 dau., Patricia Maureen. (Mrs. Gordon John Beattie). Sales capacity with paper concerns, 1920-25; mgr. Chgo. sales Am. Coating Mills, Elkhart, Ind., 1925-36; with Container Corp. of Am. 1936-59, successively asst. sales mgr., sales mgr., gen. sales mgr., v.p., 1954-59. Served as pvt. 1st class U.S. Army, 1918-19; ambulance driver attached French Army. Mem. Soc. for Preservation and Encouragement Barbershop Quartet Singing in Am. Episcopalian. Mason. Club: Chicago Athletic. Home: Colorado City, Colo. Died Dec. 1, 1973; buried Elm Lawn Cemetery, Litchfield, Ill.

PHELAN, JAMES M., mgmt. cons; b. Chicago, Ill., Jan. 25, 1914; s. Charles Albert and Ellen (Moloney) P.; ed. Loyola U. Sch. Commerce; m. Mary L. Smith, June 30, 1940; children—James Michael, Thomas Warren, Robert Brian, Mary Ellen, Dennis John. With Mitchell Hutchins Co., brokers Chgo., 1928-35; A.T., Kearney & Co., Inc., and predecessor firms, mgmt. consultants, 1935-74, partner, 1944-74, pres., 1962-69, chmn. bd., 1969-74; mng. partner A.T. Kearney Personnel Services, 1962-71; chmn. bd., pres., dir. Nuclear-Chgo. Corp., Des Plaines, Ill., 1956-63, chmn. bd., dir., 1963-66; dir. Lawter Chems., Inc., Chgo., Falk Corp., Milw., Kroger Co., Cin., Istel Fund, Inc., N.Y.C., Maypro, Inc., Milw. Mem. citizens bd., council Grad. Sch. Bus., U. Chgo. Mem. Assn. Cons. Mgmt. Engrs. (pres. 1966-68), C. of C. U.S., Ill. C. of C., Inst. Mgmt. Consultants (a founder), Chgo. Assn. Commerce and Industry (dir.). Roman Catholic. Clubs: Economic, Mid-Day (trustee) (Chgo.); Milwaukee. Home: Deerfield, Ill. Died July 30, 1974.

PHELAN, WILLIAM ROWE, ins. co. exec.; b. Bklyn., Mar. 23, 1917; s. Charles Henry and Margaret H. (Junk) P.; A.B., Holy Cross Coll., 1938; certificate Harvard, 1943; M.B.A., N.Y.U., 1948; m. Ruth Antoinette Milde, July 20, 1946; children—James C., Frances Anne, William Rowe, Mary Agnes, Margaret Helen. Successively jr. accountant, sr. accountant, auditor Aetna Life & Affiliated Cos., N.Y.C., 1939-42, asst. mgr. statis. dept., 1946-49; controller U.S. Fidelity & Guaranty Co., Balt., 1949-57, v.p., treas., 1957-72, sec., 1963-72; asst. sec. Del Mar Co. subsidiary, 1953-57, v.p.-treas., dir., 1957-72, sec., 1963-72; controller, asst. sec. Fidelity & Guaranty Ins. Underwriters, Inc. subsidiary, 1955-57, treas., asst. sec., 1957-60, v.p., treas., 1960-72, sec., 1963-72, dir.; dir. Lyric Co.; treas., sec., dir. Mchts. Indemnity Co., N.Y., 1962-66, Mchts. Fire Assurance Co., 1962-66; v.p., treas., sec. Fidelity and Guaranty Life Ins. Co., 1960-72, Thomas Jefferson Life Ins. Co. of N.Y., 1971-72. Lectr. accounting, finance, mgmt. U. Balt.; vice chmn. Fire and Casualty Ins. Conf., Controllers Inst. Am., Boston, 1953, chmn. Chgo., 1954. Mem. Archdiocesan Finance Com., 1966-72. Trustee Bon Secours Hosp.; trustee, chmn. finance com. U. Balt., 1969-72; bd. dirs. Assn. Ind. Colls. in Md., Md. region Nat. Conf. Christians and Jews; treas., trustee Lyric Found., Inc. Served as lt. USNR, 1942-46; comdr. USNR (selected Reserve of Renown 1955); comdg. officer Naval Res. Supply Co., 1956-60. Decorated knight St. Gregory. Mem. Financial Execs. Inst. (sec.-treas., dir. Balt. control 1953-54, v.p., dir. 1954-55, pres., dir. 1955-56, nat. dir. 1960-63), Ins. Accountants Assn., Nat. Assn. Cost Accountants, Assn. Casualty and Surety Cos. (accounting com. 1950-72), Nat. Bd. Fire Underwriters (accounting com. 1955-58, blanks com. 1956-58, 60-63), Nat. Assn. Accountants, A.I.M., Am. Mgmt. Assn., Ins. Accounting. Statis. Assn., Accountants Guild Bklyn. Clubs: Baltimore Country, Casualty and Surety, Merchants (Balt.).

Contbr. numerous articles on accounting and mgmt. subjects to trade publs. Home: Baltimore, Md. Died Oct. 10, 1972.

PHELPS-RIDER, ALICE, poet, musician, dairy farmer; b. Oak Park, Ill.; d. Ellsworth Richard and Edith (Phelps) Rider; Mus.M., Wis. Coll. Music, 1921, B.Dramatic Art, 1921; student U. Wis., 1921-23; music student Am. Conservatory, Bush Conservatory, pvt. tchrs., Chgo. Piano, voice tchr., Markesan, Wis.; owner, mgr. dairy farms, 1951-73; dir. choral groups; programs in poetry readings, compositions of her own, also piano, vocal solos, dramatic readings from standard repertoire. Pres., Wis. Universalist Conv., 1940-46, v.p., 1937-40, trustee, 1948-51. Mem. Wis. Fellowship Poets, Nat. League Am. Pen Women (publicity chmn. Chgo. br. 1929), Am. Poetry League, Wis. Fedn. Women's Clubs (music chmn. 6th dist. 1924), Chgo. Artists Assn., Wis. Regional Writers Assn., Wis. Hist. Soc. and Women's Aux., Humane Soc. U.S., Animal Protective League, Defenders of Wild Life. Republican. Clubs: Columbian Woman's (pres. 1924-38) (Markesan, Wis.). Collection of Poems, 1936; The Enchanted Hour, 1940; Selections, 1951; Wisconsin Pioneers and Other Poems, 1958; also poems in numerous mags., newspapers, brochures, anthologies. Home: Markesan, Wis. Died June 10, 1973.

PHILIP, JOHN JAY, advt. agy. exec.; b. Chgo., May 25, 1924; s. William Henry and Eva Emma (Jarema) P.; B.A., Drake U., 1949; m. Edith Elizabeth Beeler, Mar. 4, 1950; children—Frank Gerald, Linda Lee. Merchandising mgr. Chgo. Times, Chgo., 1941-43, 46-47, Des Moines Register and Tribune, 1947-49; advt. mgr. Avildsen Tools & Machines, Inc., Chgo., 1949-52; exec. v.p., sec. Jones & Taylor, Inc., advt. agy., South Bend, Ind., 1952-74. Served with AUS, 1943-46. Mem. Am. Mktg. Assn., Sales and Advt. Execs. Club. Elk. Club: Indiana (South Bend). Home: South Bend, Ind. Died Feb. 25, 1974; buried St. Joseph Valley Meml. Park.

PHILLIP, HARDIE, architect. Mem. Am. Inst. Architects from 1925, fellow from 1936. Address: Laguna Hills, Cal. Died Oct. 1973.

PHILLIPS, BERNARD, educator; b. Mpls., Apr. 28, 1915; s. Benjamin and Rose (Kapitchnekov) P.; B.A., U. Minn., 1935, M.A., 1937; Ph.D., Yale, 1940; m. Beatrice Blondus Dec. 31, 1939; children—Charlotte Andrea (Mrs. Robert S. Glass), Bonnie Rae. Instr. philosophy U. Minn., 1940-45; asst. prof. Carleton Coll., 1946-48; asso. prof., then prof. U. Del., 1948-59, chmn. dept. philosophy, 1948-59; prof. New Sch. Social Research, 1958-61; prof. religion Temple U., Phila., 1961-74, founder dept., chmn., 1961-70. Fulbright prof., India, 1950-51, Japan, 1953-54. Mem. Am. Philos. Assn., Am. Acad. Religion, Phi Beta Kappa. Editor: The Essentials of Zen Buddhism, 1962. Contbr. articles to profl. publs. Home: Wyncote, Pa. Died Mar. 3, 1974; interred Montefiore Cemetery, Philadelphia, Pa.

PHILLIPS, CABELL BEVERLY HATCHETT, journalist, author; b. Williamsburg, Va., June 4, 1904; s. Harry Newton and Annie (Maddux) P.; student U. Richmond, 1922-26; m. Syble Ruth Keeney, June 21, 1930; 1 son, Beverly Michael. Reporter, Richmond (Va.) Times-Dispatch, 1926-28, 32-36; info. officer WPA, Washington, 1936-38; asst. dir. info. Dept. Justice, 1940-44; Washington corr. Chgo. Herald-Examiner, 1945; mem. staff Washington Bur. N.Y. Times, 1945-71. Author: Dateline Washington, 1948; The Truman Presidency, 1966; From the Crash to the Blitz, 1929-39, 1969; also articles in mags., text books, contemporary history series in N.Y. Times Home: Hilton Head Island, S.C., Died Nov. 14, 1975.

PHILLIPS, GEORGE WALLACE, clergyman; b. Jamaica, B.W.I., Feb. 18, 1879; s. George and Emma Caroline (McIntosh) P.; A.B., U. of Chicago, 1909; D.D., Berkeley Bapt. Div. Sch., 1928; m. Cora Jane Handy, Aug. 31, 1909; children—Mildred Caroline (Mrs. Fred Judson), George Wallace, Wendell Shepard, Ethel Ann (Mrs. Arnold Anderson). Came to U.S., 1902, naturalized, 1913. Ordained ministry Baptist Church, 1909; served in various pastorates, 1909-18; instr. Lebanon (O.) University, 1916-18, pastor 10th Av. Baptist Church, Oakland, California, 1918-45, pastor emeritus, from 1945; estbd. radio sta. KSFO, 1925. Mem. Nat. Poetry Soc. Republican. Clubs: Round Table (Oakland); Rotary (Hayward); Poets of the Pacific. Author: The Hour of Prayer, Vol. 1, 1928; Vol. 2, 1929; Vol. 3, 1932; Little Library, Series 1 and 2, 1933; Living Issues, Vol. 1, 1931; The Most Beautiful Saying of Jesus, 1926; Issues of the Hour, 1942; God in the Space Age, 1964; also various brochures, Instituted the Hour Prayer, daily broadcast, from 1925. Home: Los Gatos, Cal.†

PHILLIPS, HARMON, newspaper editor; b. Bellmont, Ill., Oct. 12, 1903; s. Charles R. and Minnie (Blair) P.; grad. high sch.; m. Lora Hutchinson, 1925; 1 son, Charles Robert. Reporter, Tulsa Tribune, 1927-37, city editor, 1937-44, mng. editor, 1944-75, now exec. editor. Home: Tulsa, Okla. Died Jan. 23, 1975.

PHILLIPS, HARRY CLINTON, b. Randolph, Vt., Aug. 30, 1880; s. Frank Alexander and Abbie Richardson (Chadwick) P.; ed. high sch. and business Coll.; m. Bessie E. Woodward, Mar. 18, 1903 (dec. Feb. 1937); children—Kathryn T., Hester Co., Clinton W. Secretary Lake Mohonk Conference on Internat. Arbitration, 1902-23; sec. U.S. Bd. of Indian Commrs., 1911-13; sec. Lake Mohonk Indian Conf., 1913-23 (corr. sec. 1903-10); in charge publicity humanitarian work of Lake Mohonk, N.Y., 1916-23; cons. specialist in letter writing and orgn., from 1922. Mem. exec. com. 1st and 2d Nat. Arbitration and Peace Congresses, New York, 1907, Chicago, 1909. Mem. Washington Board of Trade; former pres. Citizens Forum (Washington), Central High Sch. Parent-Teacher Assn. Democrat. Presbyterian. Mason. Club: Lions. Editor ann. reports and publs. of Lake Mohonk conference; occasional contbr. to mags. Home: Washington, D.C.†

PHILLIPS, HENRY BAYARD mathematician; b. Yadkin College, N.C., Sept. 27, 1881; s. Henry Thomas and Linnie V. (Robbins) P.; B.S., Erskine Coll. 1900, LL.D., 1939; Ph.D., Johns Hopkins, 1905; m. Charlotte T. Perry, June 29, 1929. Instr. mathematic U. Cin., 1905-07; instr. Mass. Inst. Tech., 1907-34 prof., head dept. math., 1934-47, emeritus, from 1947. Fellow Am. Acad. Arts and Scis.; mem. Am. Math. Soc., Phi Beta Kappa Sigma Xi. Home: Lincoln, Mass.†

PHILLIPS, HENRY LEE, oil and gas co. exec.; b. Manchester, O., Dec. 4, 1889; s. Dudley Bloomhuff and Fanny Spahr (Bates) P.; A.B., Ohio State U., 1912, J.D., 1915; m. Ethel Burns, Dec. 19, 1927; children—Ann (Mrs. David L. Chandler), Mary (Mrs. Lewis R. McCann). With The Charles Page interests, 1915-16; in legal dept. Sinclair Cos., 1916-19, exec. dept., 1919-21; vice-pres. Sinclair Crude Oil Purchasing Co., Feb. 1921-Dec. 1922, pres., 1922-30; pres. Sinclair Oil & Gas Co., 1930-53, chmn. bd. 1953, ret.; dir. Sinclair Oil Corp., Nat. Bank of Tulsa. Dir. Am. Petroleum Inst. Served in inf. and J.A.G. Dept., U.S. Army, 1918-19. Mem. Phi Delta Phi. Episcopalian. Clubs: Shenorock Shore (Rye, N.Y.); University (N.Y.). Home: Rye, N.Y., Died Nov. 17, 1975.

PHILLIPS, IRNA, radio writer and supervisor; b. Chicago, Ill., July 1, 1901; d. William and Betty (Buxbaum) Phillips; ed. pub. schs. and high sch., Chicago; student Northwestern U., 1918-19, U. of Ill., 1919-22; grad. work. Sch. of Journalism, U. of Wis., 1924; unmarried; 2 adopted children—Thomas Dirk, Katherine Louise. School teacher, Dayton, O., 1925-30; radio writer and actress since 1930; writer of well known radio serial programs, including Today's Children (which was first great success and broadcast 5 yrs.), then replaced by Woman in White, Road of Life, Guiding Light, Right to Happiness, Lonely Women, now re-named Today's Children; Young Doctor Malone, The Brighter Day; currently writing As The World Turns, television drama. Home: Chicago, Ill. Died Dec. 23, 1973.

PHILLIPS, JAMES FREDERICK, ret. air force officer; b. Cambridge, Ida., Feb. 25, 1900; s. Nelson George and Laura (Bender) P.; B.S., U. Ia., 1922; grad. Engr. Sch., 1924, Army Fluing Sch., 1928, Chem. Warfare Sch., 1935, Army Air Forces Tactical Sch., 1939; m. Marcelia Lindeman, June 27, 1927; children—Laura Marley, Frederica Lindeman. Commd. 2d lt. U.S. Army, 1923 and advanced through the grades to maj. gen., 1950; exptl. devel. work in aerial photography and mapping, Wright Field, Ohio, 1929-35; staff work on aero. Research, devel. and prodn. aircraft, 1940-45; chief material div. Office Asst. Chief of Staff, Material and Services; Hdqrs. AAF, 1944-45; fgn. service, 2945-46; A.F. sec. Research and Devel. Bd., 1947-50; CG Cambridge Research Center, 1951-53; staff asst. Aircraft Industries Assn.; dir. Guided Missile Council Aerospace Industries Assn.; cons. missiles and space vehicles. Distinguished marksman, and mem. 3 Internat. Internat. Rifle Teams, 1923, 24, 25. Mem. Tau Beta Pi, Sigma Xi, Theta Tau. Clubs: Cosmos, Army and Navy (Washington). Home: Washington, D.C., Died Feb. 5, 1973.

PHILLIPS, JOHN SPINNING, naval officer (ret.); b. Alexandria, Va., Feb. 28, 1895; s. Russell Traul and Elizabeth (William) P.; B.S., U.S. Naval Acad., 1917; m. Elizabeth Horn Mayberry, July 25, 1922. Commd. ensign U.S. Navy, 1917, and advanced through grades to rear adm., 1947; served aboard various types of ships in Atlantic, Pacific, European, Asiatic and Australian waters; instr. U.S. Naval Acad., 1929-31, Northwestern U., 1934-36; comdt. Naval R.O.T.C. unit, Rensselaer Polytech. Inst., 1942-43; with Office of Naval Intelligence and Commander-in-chief's hdqrs., U.S. Navy Dept., 1943-45; ret. from active duty, Jan. 1, 1947. Awarded Navy Cross (for action at Pearl Harbor), Silver Star. Mem. Naval Hist. Foundation, U.S. Naval Inst., Naval Acad. Alumni Assn. Roman Catholic. Club: Army-Navy Country (mem. bd. govs.). Home: Ft. Lauderdale, Fla., Died Dec. 17, 1975.

PHILLIPS, ROWLEY WILHELM, financial exec.; b. Bklyn., Nov. 28, 1890; s. Lewis Rowley and Elizabeth Frances Smith P.; ed. N.Y.; m. Harriette Staples Wheeler, Sept. 30, 1914; children—Harriette Wheeler (Mrs. Edgar H. Redington, Jr.), Elizabeth R. (Mrs. Silas W. Howland, Jr.), Jean K. (Mrs. Charles Anderson McLeod), Barbara (Mrs. Gilbert S. Shove). With Mackay & Co., 1909-13; Conn. mgr. Baker Young & Co., Boston, 1913-15; sec., v.p., chmn., gen. mgr. R.F. Griggs Co., 1915-40; now chmn. bd., dir. Phillips & Benjamin Co., Smith Estates Inc. (N.J.); dir., mem. exec. com. Bridgeport Brass Co.; dir. United Stock Yards Corp., Sioux City Stockyards Co., Sioux city Terminal Ry. Co., Sioux Falls Stock Yards Co., Portland Union Stock Yards Co., Bigelow Co., Yardney Electric Corp., Yardney Chem. Co. (N.Y.C.). Republican. Episcopalian. Mason. Clubs: Engineers, Union League (N.Y.C.); Lawrence Beach; Regency, Whist (N.Y.C.); Greenwich Country, Beach (Greenwich). Address: Greenwich, Conn. Died Oct. 11, 1974; interred Grove St. Cemetery, New Haven, Conn.

PHILLIPS, WALTER SARGEANT, educator; b. Lynn, Mass., Oct. 20, 1905; s. Fred A. and Mary Genevieve (Sargeant) P.; A.B., Oberlin (Ohio) Coll., 1929, student 1931—32; Ph.D., U. Chicago (fellow in botany, 1933-35), 1935; m. Kathryn I. Tankersley, Aug. 25, 1935 (dec. Dec. 29, 1936); m. 2d, Thelma F. Kinyoun, Mar. 21, 1940. Instr., Ming Shen Sch., Taiku, Shansi, China, 1929—31; instr. U. of Miami, Fla., 1935, asst. prof. of botany, 1935—38, asso. prof., 1938—40; asst. prof. botany, U. Ariz., 1940—43, asso. prof., 1943—47, prof. botany, 1947—, head dept. botany and range ecology, 1947—63; asst. botanist in Exptl. Station, 1940—47, botanist, 1947—75. Recipient Fulbright award, Australia, 1954—55. Mem. Bot. Soc. Am., Ecologial Soc. of Am., Am. Fern Soc. (treas. 1958—62), Am. Soc. Range Management, Tucson Natural History Soc. (sec., 1944—46, pres., 1946—47), Phi Kappa Phi (sec. since 1950), Sigma Xi, Kappa Sigma. Author: Ecology of Southern Florida and Arizona, 1940; Ferns of the Southwest, 1946—47; Vegetation of Northern Great Plains, 1963. Contbr. articles in bot. jours. Home: Tucson, Ariz. Died Apr. 7, 1975.

PHILLIPS, WENDELL, explorer, educator; b. Oakland, Cal., Sept. 25, 1921; s. Merley H. and Sunshine (Chrisman) P.; A.B. with honors, U. Cal., 1943; Ph.D., U. Brussels, 1972; Sc.D., Marietta Coll., 1952; Litt.D., U. Redlands, 1953; J.D. Calvin Coolidge Coll., 1954; LL.D., Coll. Emporia, 1961; L.H.D., Sterling Coll., 1961; D. Comml. Sci., Colo. State U., 1962; H.H.D., Trinity U., 1962; D.C.L., Pacific U., 1963; Pd.D., Whitworth Coll., 1964; Ed.D., Kyrung-Pook Nat. U., Taegu, Korea, 1966; D.P.S., U. Pacific, 1967; D.F.A., John Brown U., 1968; Dr. Canon Law, Eastern Coll., 1968; D.P.A., Union Coll., 1968; D.B.A., Fla. So. Coll., 1968; D.Lit., U. Miami, 1969; D.C.L., Coll. Ida., 1970; S.T.D., Grand Canyon Coll., 1971; D. Arts, Ft. Lauderdale U., 1973; D. Journalism, Cal. Baptist Coll., 1969; Ed.R.D., Emmanual Coll., 1969; D.Sc., U. Utah, 1972; D.Comparative Lit., Davis and Elkins Coll., 1973; m. Shirley Au, Sept. 14, 1968 (div. Dec. 1968). Mem. U. Cal. Mus. Paleontology Expdn., no. Ariz., 1940, Monument Valley, So. Utah, Grand Canyon, 1942, marine zool. collections, New Hebrides, Solomons, Marianas, Marshalls, 1943-44; organizer, leader African Expdn., including Egypt, Sinai, Sudan, Kenya, Belgian Congo, Union South Africa, S.W. Africa, Angola, Uganda, Tanganyika, Zanzibar, No. and So. Rhodesia, Mozambique, Madagascar, 1947-49; chief lectr. Lost World Treasure Island, San Francisco World's Fair, 1940; mem. Carnegie Inst. Paleobotanical Expdn., Ore., 1941; hon. cons. Micro-film projects Library Congress, 1949; pres. dir. Philpryor Corp., 1951-58; chmn. bd. P.T.P. Corp., Phillips Pacific; dir. gen. antiquities Sultanate Oman, 1953-70; economic adv. Sultan of Oman, 1956-70; leader of the Oman-Dhofar Expedition, 1960; pres. Am. Found. for Study Man, 1949-75, found. organizer Mt. Sinai Expdn., with Library Congress, Alexandria U., 1950; leader Arabian Expdn., I-II with Carnegie Mus., 1950-51; leader Yemen Expdn., 1951-52, Oman Expdn., I-II, 1952-53, Oman-Sohar Expdn., 1958; lectr., N.Y.U., 1958; prof. archeology U. Wyo., 1968. Trustee San Francisco Theol. Sem., Hawaii Loa Coll.; hon. chancellor Fla. So. Coll. Served with U.S. Mcht. Marine, 1943-45. Decorated Knight Order St. Catherine (Greece); recipient Brussels U. Commemorative medal, 1969; Golden Plate award Am. Soc. Achievement 1972. Wendell Phillips Centre for Intercultural Studies, Wendell Phillips Lectureship in Intercultural Studies both at U. Pacific, Stockton, Cal., founded 1968; Wendell Phillips Centre for Advanced Theol. Studies, Berkeley, Cal., 1968. Fellow Royal Geog. Soc. London, Egyptian Geog. Soc., Royal Anthrop. Inst. Gt. Britain and Ireland, Am. Geog. Soc., Royal Central Asian Soc., Royal Asiatic Soc., Am. Schs. Oriental Research Am. Mus. Natural History; mem. Am. Oriental Soc., A.A.A.S., N.Y. Acad. Sci., Royal Archeol. Inst. Gt. Britain and Ireland, Middle East, French Insts., Soc. Vertebrate Paleontology, Soc. Study Evolution, Am., Middle East anthrop. assns., Soc. Am. Archeology, Hawaiian Geog. Soc. (Distinguished Speaker 1973), Inst. Internat. Chateaux Historiques Switzerland (corr.), Honolulu Acad. Arts, Hakluyt Soc., Jr. C. of C. (hon., Outstanding Young Man, 1955), Alpha Gamma Nu (hon.). Presbyn. Clubs: Explorers, Ends of Earth, Circumnavigators (gov.), Dutch Treat; Adventures (hon.) (Honolulu). Author: Qataban and Sheba, 1955; Unknown Oman, 1966; Oman, A History, 1967; An Explorer's Life of Jesus, 1974. Contbr. articles to profl. publs. Home: Honolulu, Hawaii., Died Dec. 4, 1975.

PICKARD, ANDREW EZRA, citrus grower; b. Toronto, Ont., Can., July 6, 1878; s. James and Mary Ann (Marquis) P.; came to U.S., 1890; ed. St. Cloud

Tchrs. Coll., U. Minn., 1903; agr. and econs. courses U. Minn., 1905-10; m. Margaret Jane Armstrong, Aug. 30, 1903; children—Rowan Marquis, Jean (Mrs. Robert Scholer), Josephine (Mrs. Walt Killam), Elizabeth (Mrs. Julian Fishburne) m. 2d, Calla Marshall Shehyn, Sept. 3, 1934. Supt. city schs., Hinckley, Minn., 1903-12, Cokato, Minn., 1912-15; pres. Collegiate Bus. Inst., Mpls., 1915-26; citrus grower and processor, Orlando, Fla., from 1926; dir. Minute Maid. Pres. Citrus Sub-Exchange, 1934-44; dir. Lake Region Citrus Packing Assn., Orlando Citrus Growers, Citrus Mutual. Mem. Fla. Poultry Assn. (pres. 1936-40), Fla. Grape Growers (pres. 1940-50), Realty Bd. Orlando (pres. 1935), C. of C. (v.p. 1936). Republican. Methodist. Mason (32 deg., Shriner), Odd Fellow, Kiwanian (pres. Mpls. 1922, dist. gov. 1924). Author: Rural Education, 1915; Industrial Work for Boys; Industrial Work for Girls. Address: Orlando, Fla. Deceased.

PICKERING, ERNEST, educator; b. Cherryvale, Kan., July 15, 1893; s. Steven Arnold Douglas and Luella Mae (Cleek) P.; B.S. in A.E., Univ. of Kan., 1919; B.S. in Architecture, Univ. of Ill., 1920, M. Architecture, 1926; student Ecole des Beaux Arts, Atelier Gromort-Expert, (Plym European fellowship) 1921-22; student Harvard, 1927-28; Doctor of Fine Arts, Moore Inst. of Art, 1954; m. Elizabeth Mae Stout, Sept. 16, 1919; 1 dau., Nancy Ellen. Instr. in architecture, Univ. of Ill., 1922-25; prof. of architecture, Univ. of Cincinnati, 1925-46, dean Coll. of Applied Arts, 1946. U.S. rep. to Planning Conf., Tokyo, sponsored by UN Economic Commission on Asia and Far East, 1958. Recipient Société des Architectes Diplomés par le Gouvernement medal. Chmn. Cincinnati City Planning Commn., 1945-48, 58. Fellow Am. Inst. Architects (past pres. Cin. chpt.), Nat. Assn. Schs. Art; mem. Archaeol. Inst. Am., Nat. Assn. Schs. Design (pres.), MacDowell Soc. (past pres.), Scarab (past nat. pres.), Newcomen Soc. N. Am., Omicron Delta Kappa, Delta Upsilon. Author: Architectural Design, 1933; Shelter for Living, 1941; (with Reuben Hill and Howard Becker) Marriage and the Family, 1941; The Homes of America, 1951. Contbr. sect. on Am. homes, Colliers New Ency. Home: Cincinnati, O. Died Aug. 30, 1974; interred Oak Hill Cemetery, Glendale, Cin.

PICKETT, BETHEL STEWART, coll. prof.; b. Tillsonburg, Ont., Can., June 4, 1882; s. Samuel and Ellen Maria (Stewart) P.; B.S.A., U. of Toronto, 1904; M.S., U. of Ill., 1906; m. Bertha Gay Beamer, Dec. 11, 1907; children—Barzillai Stewart, Llewellyn Elmer, Arthur David, Ellen Gay. Came to U.S., 1905, naturalized, 1924. Sec. Ont. Agrl. Coll., 1901-05; asst. in pomology, U. of Ill., 1906-08; prof. and head dept. of horticulture and forestry, U. of N.H., 1908-12; prof. of pomology, U. of Ill., 1912-23; prof. of horticulture and head of dept. horticulture and forestry, Iowa State College, 1923-47, retired as head department, July 1947; professor of horticulture; on leave for 2 years to act as horticultural adviser to the government of Syria. President Federated Garden Clubs of Ia., 1928-29; gen. mgr. Mid-West Hort. Expn., 1930-32; pres. Am. Pomological Soc. 1932-41; dir. and supt. of pomology, International Hort. Expn., Chicago, 1936. Mem. Nat. Apple Inst. (pres. 1935-36), Iowa Hort. Soc. (pres. 1930-33, dir. since 1933), American Garden Foundation (pres. since 1945), American Soc. Hort. Science, A.A.A.S., Sigma Xi, Alpha Zeta, Phi Kappa Phi, Gamma Sigma Delta. Democrat. Methodist. Author: Elements of Fruit Growing, 1920. Contbr. many articles to professional jours.; author of numerous bulletins of agrl. expt. stations. Home: Rogers, Ark. Died Jan. 25, 1975.

PICOFF, RONALD CHESTER, physician; b. Bklyn., July 7, 1935; s. Henry and Anna Picoff; M.D., Columbia, 1960; m. Ghita Maringer, Jan. 2, 1960; 1 dau., Leah Jane. Intern, Mary Fletcher Hosp., 1960—61; resident in pathology U. Vt., Burlington, 1961—64, trainee in exptl. pathology, 1964—65, asst. prof. pathology, 1966—69, asso. prof., 1969—74, acting chmn. dept., 1974; asso. attending pathologist Med. Center Hosp. Vt., dir. Sch. Cytotech., 1969—74. Diplomate Am. Bd. Pathology, Mem. A.M.A., Am. Soc. Clin. Pathologists (council on hematology, commn. on continuing edn. 1972), Phi Beta Kappa, Alpha Omega Alpha. Jewish religion. Home: Shelburne, Vt. Died Apr. 15, 1974; buried Hebrew Holy Soc. Cemetery, South Burlington, Vt.

PIDCOCK, BRIAN MORRIS HENZELL, surgeon; b. Winchester, Eng., May 8, 1930; came to U.S., 1958; M.B., B.S. St. Bartholomews Hosp. Med. Coll., London, 1958; m. Muriel Pidcock, 1969; 1 dau., Katherine. Intern Bryn Mawr (Pa.) Hosp., 1959-60; resident Beth Israel Hosp., Boston, 1962-63, Pa. Hosp., Phila., 1963-66, Chester County (Pa.) Hosp., 1964; practice medicine, specailizing in surgery, 1968-71; asst. attending surgeon Montefiore-Morrisania Affiliation, N.Y.C.; asso. surgeon Albert Einstein Med. Center, N.Y.C. Diplomate Am. Bd. Surgery. Home. Yonkers, N.Y., Died Aug. 20, 1971.

PIERCE, BESSIE LOUISE, professor of history; born Caro, Mich., Apr. 20, 1888; d. Clifton J. and Minnie Cornelia (Pierson) Pierce; B.A., State U. of Ia., 1910, Ph.D., 1923; M.A., U. of Chicago, 1918. Instr. in history, high schs., Ia., 1910-16; instr. in history, State Univ. of Ia., 1916-19, asso., 1919-23, asst. prof., 1923-26, asso. prof., 1926-29; asso. prof. Am. history, University of Chicago, 1929-43, professor from 1943. President National Council for Social Studies, 1926; member committee on civic education by radio of Nat. Advisory Council on Radio Education; mem. advisory com., Franklin D. Roosevelt Library; division I City of Chicago Historian, World War II. Mem. Am. Hist. Assn. (mem. council exec. com. 1937-41), Mississippi Valley Historical Association, Am. Acad. Political and Social Science, American Assn. Univ. Profs., Nat. Council for Social Studies (ex-sec. treas., ex-pres., ex-mem. exec. bd.; award merit for leadership in social science), Com. on Gen. Education Armed Forces, Am. Assn. Univ. Women (mem. com. Fellowship Awards and internat. fellowships 1943-49), Am. Assn. State and Local History. P.E.N., Alpha Xi Delta, Pi Lambda Theta, Phi Beta Kappa. Episcopalian. Author several books from 1924. Home: Iowa City, Ia. Died Oct. 3, 1974.

PIERCE, CHARLES MILTON, elec. contractor; b. Detroit, Jan. 17, 1916; s. Charles Deloss and Mary Elizabeth (Brewer) P.; ed. Cranbrook High Sch., Detroit Trade Sch.; m. Jean Marie Shillady, Jan. 4, 1940; children—Carol (Mrs. Stanley Moyer), Mary (Mrs. Allan P. Cary). Charles D. (dec.), Hugh Richard, Margaret Jane, John Kelly, Patricia Karen. With John Miller Elec. Co., Troy, Mich., 1940-74, beginning as apprentice, successively journeyman, estimator, purchasing, v.p., 1940-67, pres., 1967-74, chmn. bd., 1972-74. Mem. Troy C. of C. Roman Catholic. Clubs: Bloomfield (Mich.) Open Hunt (past v.p.); Recess, Detroit Athletic (Detroit); Oakland Hills Country (Birmingham, Mich.). Home: Bloomfield Hills, Mich. Died Mar. 19, 1974.

PIERCE, CLIFFORD DAVIS, lawyer; b. Somerville, Tenn., April 7, 1898; s. John and Eula (Davis) P.; LL.B., George Washington U., 1921; m. Isabelle Curran, June 7, 1922; children—Helen Claire, Clifford Davis, Jr. Admitted to Tenn. bar, 1921, and later practiced in Memphis, specializing in insurance and estate law. Chmn. roll call A.R.C., Memphis, 1933; chmn. food com. City of Memphis, 1946; mem. President's Com. N.E.P.H., 1947-50, Mayor's Com., N.E.P.H., 1948; v.p. Automotive Electric Service Company. Served in S.A.T.C., George Washington U., 1918. Mem. Am., Tenn., Memphis and Shelby County (director 1946-48) bar assns., Am. Legion, Kappa Alpha. Meth. (mem. bd. of stewards, lecturer in Bible class). Mason (Shriner, Scottish Rite). Clubs: Lions of Memphis (past pres., sec., dist. gov.); Lions Internat. (rep. to convs. Mexico, Central and South Am., 1944, to Conf. Dumbarton-Oaks Report, State Dept., Oct. 1944; 2d v.p. 1944; pres. 1946-47; special rep. of Lions Internat. to Paris Peace Conf., 1946). Clubs: Tennessee; Lady Luck Fishing (Moon Lake, Miss.). Owner Merihil Farm, Somerville, Tenn.; breeder registered milking shorthorn cattle. Home: Memphis, Tenn., Died July 15, 1974.

PIERCE, EDWARD ALLEN, business exec.; b. Orrington, Me.; s. Arthur Allen and Anne Frances (Gerry) P.; LL.D., Bowdoin Coll., Brown U.; m. Luella Van Hoosear, Dec. 18, 1909. Dir, v.p. Merrill, Lynch, Pierce, Fenner & Smith, Inc., N.Y.; mem. bd. directors Dictaphone Corp. Clubs: Metropolitan, Wall Street (N.Y.C.); Hope (Providence); Sleepy Hollow Country. Home: New York City, N.Y. Died Dec. 16, 1974.

PIERCE, EDWARD J., chmn. bd., chief exec. officer Harlem Savings Bank of N.Y. Home: New York City, N.Y. Died June 1974.

PIERCE, GEORGE WILLIAM, lawyer; b. Muncie, Ind., June 18, 1908; s. Wesley Cullum and Cora (Bruns) P.; A.B., DePauw U., 1928, M.A., 1929; M.A., Harvard, 1930, J.D., 1933; postgrad. Northwestern U., 1934-35, N.Y. U., 1948-49; m. Virginia Haymond, June 26, 1937; children—George Kenner, Walter Haymond. Admitted to Ind. bar, 1933, Ill. bar, 1934; mem. firm Campbell Clithero & Fischer, Chgo., 1933-37, White, Pierce, Beasley & Gilkison, Muncie, 1937-75. Mem. Muncie Pub. Library Bd., 1940-55; pres. Delaware County United Fund, 1948-49; sec. Muncie Civic and Coll. Symphony Assn., 1948-73, Storer Scholarship Com., 1953-75. Mem. Am., Ind., Indpls., Muncie bar assns., Am. Coll. Probate Counsel, Am. Judicature Soc., Am. Right of Way Assn., Ind., Muncie chambers commerce, Delaware County Hist. Assn., Delta Tau Delta. Republican. Presbyn. Mason (Shriner), Elk, Rotarian. Clubs: Torch, (Muncie); Athenaeum Turners (Indpls.). Contbr. articles to profl. jours. Home: Muncie Ind. Died Mar. 18, 1975; buried Buck Grove Cemetery, Muncie, Ind.

PIERCE, RICHARD DONALD, clergyman, coll. dean; b. Manchester, N.H., Feb. 25, 1915; s. Lewis Herbert and Eliza Ann (Bradley) P.; A.B., U. of N.H., 1935; B.D., Andover Theol. Sem., 1938; S.B., Simmons Coll., 1946; Ph.D., Boston U., 1946; S.T.M., Harvard, 1948; A.M. (hon.), Emerson Coll., 1955, LL.D., 1966; Litt. D., Mercy Coll., 1972. Asst. librarian, Andover-Newton Theol. Sch., 1938-40, asso. librarian, 1940-47, lectr. in ch. history, 1944-72; lectr. history Boston U., 1948; prof. history and dean of chapel Emerson Coll., Boston, 1947-73, prof. religion, 1958-73, chmn. faculty, 1952-58, dean, 1958-73, v.p., 1969-73; lectr. in history and humanities Suffolk U., 1955-57; ordained to ministry Congl. Ch., 1939, Unitarian Ch., 1944; acting minister Bapt. and Congl. chs., Temple, Me., 1937-52, emeritus, 1952-73. Vice pres. Benevolent Frat. Unitarian Chs., Gibson House, Lend-a-Hand Soc. (also pres.); pres. Edward Everett Hale House, Inc.; sec. Evangel. Missionary Soc. in Mass.; trustee, sec. Emerson Coll., Manchester Coll. (Oxford); pres. Robbins Inst. Speech Correction. Corporator Frances Merry Barnard Home, Inc.; trustee, v.p. Soc. for Promotion Theol. Edn.; bd. trustees Mass. Charitable Soc. Mem. Colonial Soc. Mass., Me., N.H. hist socs., Unitarian Hist. Soc., Mass. Soc. Colonial Wars (chaplain), Soc. Cincinnati (chaplain gen.), Soc. for Propagating Gospel Among Indians and Others (pres.), Unitarian Service Pension Soc. (pres.). Clubs: Ministers, Union Winthrop, Harvard, Harvard Musical Association (Boston); Harvard (N.Y.C.); Union Interalliee (Paris, France); United Oxford-Cambridge (London, Eng.). Author: The Legal Aspects of the Andover Creed, 1946; The Records of the First Church in Boston, 3 vols., 1961; also articles. Home: Boston, Mass. Died Aug. 1, 1973.

PIERCE, W(ILLIS) CONWAY, educator; b. Carrollton, Ky., Dec. 2, 1895; s. Willis C. and Jennie (Peay) P.; B.S., Georgetown Coll., 1920, D.Sc., 1950; M.S., University of Chicago, 1925, Ph.D., 1928; LL.D., University of Cal., 1965; m. Kate Shewmaker, Sept. 2, 1921; 1 son, Willis Conway. Instr. chemistry U. Ky., 1921-23; instr. U. S.D., 1923-27; instr., asst. prof., asso. prof. U. Chgo., 1928-41; tech. aide, sect. chief OSRD, 1941-45; prof., chmn. chem. dept. Pomona Coll., 1945-53; prof. chemistry, chmn. div. phys. sci. U. Cal. at Riverside, 1953-61, prof. chemistry, 1960-63, prof. emeritus, 1963-75; petroleum research fellow Am. Chem. Soc., 1957-58; asst. to chancellor U. Cal. Irvine, 1963-65. Mem. Am. Chem. Soc., Sigma Xi. Author textbooks, tech. publs. Home: Medford, Ore. Died Dec. 23, 1974.

PIERIOT, LUCILLE GEORGETTE, communications cons.; b. Boston, Aug. 12, 1928; d. George Eugene and Elsa Anna (Wilberding) Pieriot; B.F.A., Carnegie-Mellon U., 1950; m. Joseph A. Taylor, Aug. 25, 1965; 1 dau., Emily. Actress Stage, films and TV, N.Y.C. and Hollywood, 1950-60; editor Overseas Press Bull., N.Y.C., 1960-64; Midwest pub. relations dir. Time, Inc., Chgo., 1964-65; partner Compass Communications Internat., communications cons., Boston and Austin, Tex., from 1965. Coordinator, Media 3 Americas Internat. communications seminars, S. Am., Mexico and Austin, from 1971. Speechwriter, researcher mayoral campaign John V. Lindsay, N.Y.C., 1965. Exec. bd. Austin Civic theatre Zachary Scott Center, 1972-75. Named Outstanding Young Actress of 1950, N.Y. Theatre Guild. Mem. Pub. Relations Soc. Am. (chpt. dir. 1972-74), Tex. Pub. Relations Assn. (Silver Spur award 1974), Nat. Acad. TV Arts and Scis., Women in Communications (nat. pub. relations dir., editor nat. mag. Metrix from 1971). Republican. Club: Chicago Press. Editor Tex. Town and City mag., from 1972. Address: Austin, Tex., Died Mar. 25, 1975.

PIGGOT, CHARLES SNOWDEN, scientific research; b. Sewanee, Tenn., June 5, 1892; s. Dr. Cameron and Anne (Cockey) P.; ed. Boys' Latin Sch., Baltimore, Md., 1907-11; B.A., U. of the South, Sewanee, Tenn., 1914, D.Sc.; grad. U. of Pa., (Phil.), 1914-16; Ph.D., Johns Hopkins, 1920; Ramsay fellow, Univ. Coll., London, Eng., 1922-23; m. Ruth Muriel Marguerite Blaine, Aug. 10, 1927; children—Deboorne, Anne Marguerite. Research chemist, U.S. Indsl. Chem. Co., Baltimore, 1920-22, 1924-25, Geophys. Lab., Carnegie Instn., Washington, 1925-47; Research and Development Bd. Nat. Mil. Establishment, 1946-49; chief sci. attaché U. S. Embassy, London, 1949-51; research associate Yale University, 1952, ret.; survey Scientific Research Insts. of India, 1955. Served as lt., U.S. Army, F.A., Poison Gas Research, 1916-19; with U.S. Navy, from 1941, capt. 1946; member of staff of Joint Task Force One, Bikini, 1946. Decorated Officer, Mil. Order of the British Empire, 1946; recipient special commendations and citations, U.S. Navy. Fellow Am. Geog. Soc., Geol. Soc. of Am.; mem. Am. Chem. Soc., Geophys. Union, Washington Acad. Sciences, Philos. Soc. of Washington, Nat. Acad. Sciences, Royal Instn. Great Britain, Sigma Xi, Phi Beta Kappa, Sigma Alpha Epsilon, Phi Eta. Clubs. Chemists (Johns Hopkins); Arts, Cosmos (pres.), (Washington); Explores (N.Y.); Athenaeum (London). Contbr. sci. jours. on catalytic chemistry, isotopes of lead, geologic time, core samples from the ocean bottom at great depths, determination of geologic time scale in ocean sediments, etc. Home: Washington, D.C. Died July 6, 1973.

PIKE, DOUGLAS HENRY, editor, educator; b. Tuhshan, China, Nov. 3, 1908; s. Douglas Fowler and Louise (Boulter) P.; B.A., U. Adelaide, 1947, M.A., 1951, D.Litt., 1957; m. Olive Hagger, Nov. 25, 1941; children—Douglas, Andrew. With Vicotrian Edn. Dept.; lectr. history U. Western Australia, 1949—50; reader history U. Adelaide, 1950—61; prof. history U. Tasmania, 1961—63; gen. editor Australian Dictionary of Biography, 1966-74; prof. history Australian Nat. U. Mem. Nat. Memls. Com. Australia. Recipient Ernest Scott Meml. prize in history U. Melbourne, 1969; Britannica Australia award in humanities, 1971. Fellow Australian Acad. Humanities (sec., treas.). Club:

University (Sydney). Author: Paradise of Dissent: Southern Australia 1829—1857, 1957; Australia: The Quiet Continent, 1962. Died May 19, 1974.

PIKE, H. HARVEY, merchant; b. New York, N.Y., Aug. 24, 1887; s. Henry Harvey and Edith (Roe) P.; A.B., Williams Coll., 1909; student New York U. Night Law Sch., 1909-10; m. Constance Wilkinson, Dec. 13, 1919; children—Patricia C. (Mrs. Harry Irgens Larsen), Nancy (Mrs. William F. Talbert), Daphne (Mrs. J. Peter Gratiot). With Brown Brothers & Co., N.Y., 1909-11; with H. H. Pike & Co., Inc., and predecessors, 1919-64, pres. and dir., 1944-64; partner H. H. Pike & Son, 1924-66. Pres. N.Y. Coffee and Sugar Exchange, Inc., 1931-33. Pres. Cuban C. of C. in U.S., 1955-57. Served to capt. F.A., 77th Div., A.E.F., 1918-19. Mem. Fgn. Policy Assn. (dir.), Council Fgn. Relations. Episcopalian. Clubs: Down Town Assn., Century Assn. (N.Y.). Home: New York City, N.Y. Died July 26, 1973.

PIKE, SUMNER TUCKER, state ofcl.; b. Lubec, Me., Aug. 30, 1891; s. Jacob Clark and Mary Susan (Tucker) Pike; B.A., Bowdoin College, 1913, LL.D., 1941; LL.D., Bates College, 1945; S.C.D., Centre Coll., 1947; LL.D., Colby Coll., 1948; unmarried. Clerk in public utility companies, Boston, Savannah, Ga., Lowell, Mass., Beaumont, Tex., 1913-19; v.p. Equipment Sales Co., Dallas, Tex., and Kansas City, Mo., 1920-22; asst. to pres. G. Amsinck & Co., N.Y. City, 1923; financial employee and sec. Continental Ins. Co., N.Y. City, 1923-28; v.p. and dir. Case Pomeroy & Co., N.Y. City, 1928-39; business adviser to U.S. Sec. of Commerce, Washington, 1939-40; mem. Temporary Nat. Econ. Committee, 1940-41; commr. of Securities and Exchange Commn., Phila., Pa., 1940-46; dir. Fuel Price Div., Office Price Adminstrn., Washington, 1942-46; mem. U.S. A.E.C., 1946-51; chmn. Me. Pub. Utilities commn., 1953-56. Mem. Me. Legislature, from 1959. Chmn. Gov.'s Com. on Passamaquoddy Tidal Power, from 1959. Served Candidate to capt., C.A.C., Army, 1917-19. Overseer Bowdoin Coll., from 1938. Mem. Am. Assn. Petroleum Geologists, Am. Geog. Soc., Delta Upsilon, Phi Beta Kappa. Republican. Mason. Clubs: Metropolitan (Washington); University, India House, Lambs, Downtown Athletic (N.Y.C.); Portland (Me.). Home: Lubec, Me., Died Feb. 21, 1976.

PINCKNEY, FRANCIS DOUGLAS, state ofcl.; b. Mt. Pleasant, S.C., Mar. 11, 1900; s. Francis Douglas and Mary (Adams) P.; student Coll. of Charleston (S.C.), 1918-20; grad. Ordnance Field Service Sch., 1938, Command and Gen. Staff War Coll., 1942; m. Mary Davie Bull, Nov. 14, 1923; children—Mary (Mrs. Allan W. Wendt), Alice (Mrs. John W. Evans). Bookkeeper, Standard Oil Co. N.J., 1920-21; asst. office mgr., salesman Wholesale Provision House, Charleston, 1921-23; partner Glover-Pinckney Tire Co., Charleston, 1923-26; owner tire co. in Orangeburg, S.C., 1926-40; joined S.C. N.G., 1919, advanced through grades to maj. gen., 1958; chief manpower sect. S.C. Hdqrs., SSS, 1940-41; comdr. 165th Ordance Battalion, ETO, 1941-46; successively col. Ordance Corps, S.C., N.G., then S.C. maintenance officer and dep. chief staff, 1946-58; adj. gen. S.C., 1958-71. Decorated service ribbons and campaign medals. Mem. Am. Legion (past post comdr.), Mil. Order World Wars, Assn. U.S. Army, N.G. Assn. S.C. (past pres.). Episcopalian. Elk, Mason, Rotarian (past pres. Orangeburg). Home: Columbia, S.C. Died June 9, 1974.

PINGREE, GEORGE ELMER, corp. official; b. Georgetown, Mass., June 26, 1876; s. Charles Hazen and Lucy Sarah Lord (Harris) P.; student Phillips Acad., Andover, Mass., 1894-97; B.A., Dartmouth, 1901; m. G. Maxine Grant, Nov. 24, 1910. With Internat. Standard Electric Corp., from 1903, pres., from 1925; v.p. Internat. Telephone and Telegraph Corp., from 1925; dir. many foreign companies. Engaged in special work, British War Office, World War. Mem. Alpha Delta Phi. Sphinx Senior Soc. Retired from business June 1, 1936. Decorated Comdr. Order of the Crown (Belgium). Clubs: University (New York); Golf (Northport, Me.). Home: Belfast, Me.†

PINK, CHARLOTTE (MRS. JOHN M. PINK), social worker, educator; b. Cassville, Wis., Feb. 6, 1896; d. Joseph J. and Leonora (Martin) Seipp; student Platteville Tchrs. Coll., U. Chgo.; m. John M. Pink, Nov. 22, 1927; 1 dau., Rita Mary (Mrs. Louis Eversoll). Tchr. elementary sch., also dramatics, various Wis. schs., 1915-18; tchr. speech and lip-reading for deaf Milw. Tchrs. Coll., 1920; tchr. charge speech and lip-reading Day Schs. for Deaf Children, Tacoma, Wash., 1920-21, St. Paul, 1921-22, Racine, Wis., 1924-27; conducted own sch. adult deaf, Racine, summers 1925-27. Mem. bd. jury commrs. Grant County, Wis., 1947-73; vice comdr. Wis. div. Am. Cancer Soc., 1940-54, state comdr., state chmn. vols., 1954-66, now hon. life mem. state bd. dirs., v.p. Wis. bd. dirs., 1954-60, hon. mem. bd. dirs. Grant County chpt.; vol. librarian Lancaster Meml. Hosp.; promoter, vol. hostess Sr. Citizens Library Exchange; mem. bd., policy adv. com. Sr. Citizens Southwestern Wis. Community Action Program S.W. Dist. Named Woman of Year by Wis. div. Am. Cancer Soc., 1955. Mem. Cath. Daus. Am. (grant regent Lancaster 1940-45; chmn. legis. com. Ct. St. Rita 1970-73), Missionary Assn. Cath. Women (nat. bd., nat. treas., pres. Lancaster unit 1945-73), Meml. Hosp. Aux., Nat. Council Cath. Women. Roman Catholic. Home: Lancaster, Wis. Died June 1973.

PINKERTON, ROY DAVID, editor; b. Crookston, Minn., June 28, 1885; s. Henry David and Hattie May (Newton) P.; A.B., U. Wash., 1911; m. Flora Hartman, Aug. 21, 1912; children—Roy Hartman, Robert Newton; m. 2d, Airdrie Kincaid, May 16, 1923; 1 dau., Airdrie Paula Martin. Reporter Tacoma Times, 1905; reporter, and later asst. city editor The Ledger, Tacoma; copy reader Los Angeles Tribune, 1911; sub-editor Los Angeles Express, 1912; city editor The Sun, Seattle, 1913, Seattle Star, 1914; editor The Times, Tacoma, 1915-21, The Star, Seattle, 1921-23; asso. editor The Press, Cleve., 1924; editor The Sun, San Diego, 1925; founded and became editor and pub. Ventura County Star-Free Press, 1925-60; editorial dir. John P. Scripps Newspapers until 1960, later pres.; accredited war corr., Korea, 1961. Pres. Ventura Concert Series Assn., 1940-47; sec. Ventura County War Chest, 1943-44, v.p., 1945; dir. Ventura C. of C., 1928-31, Ventura County C. of C., 1927-30. Mem. Cal. Newspaper Pubs. Assn. (chmn. communications com., 1933-35; chmn. edn. for journalism com., Am. Soc. Newspaper Editors, Sigma Alpha Epsilon, Sigma Delta Chi. Clubs: San Francisco Commonwealth; Ventura Rotary (pres. 1929-30); Overseas Press of Am. Author: The County Star; My Buena Ventura, 1961. Home: Ojai, Cal. Died May 5, 1974.

PINKLEY, ROY H(ENRY), transit exec.; b. Chillicothe, Mo., May 5, 1877; s. Charles O. and Laura (Belle) P.; B.S. in elec. engring., U. Mo., 1899, E.E., 1902; m. Sophie Waring, June 22, 1904 (died July 1906); 1 son, George Roger; m. 2d, Mabel Helen Duncan, Sept. 10, 1908; children—Helen (Mrs. Kelly), Margaret (Mrs. Varda). Asst. gen. mgr. Milw. Electric Ry. & Light Co., 1925-29, v.p., 1929-38; pres., dir. Milw. Electric Ry. & Transport Co., 1938-52, Milw. & Suburban Transport Corp., 1952-53; chmn. bd., 1954; hon. chmn. bd., from 1955. Former mem. Milw. Safety, Harbor comms. Served with Mo. N.G., 1895-99. Mem. Am. Transit Assn. Conglist. Mason. Club: Milwaukee Athletic. Home: Milwaukee, Wis.†

PIPER, MARGARET REBECCA, author; b. Ashby, Mass., Dec. 16, 1879; d. Henry Francis and Rebecca Emily (Boutelle) P.; B.L., Smith Coll., 1901, M.A., 1910; studied New York University; m. Isaac Chalmers, April 22, 1923. Teacher, public schools, Vt. and N.H., 1901-07; fellow in English, Smith College, 1909-10; head English dept., Washington (Pa.) Sem., 1910-13; teacher English dept., Hood Coll., Frederick, Md., 1913-15. Unitarian. Author: Sylvia 's Experiment, 1914; The Princess and The Clan, 1915; Sylvia of the Hilltop, 1916; House on the Hill, 1917; Sylvia Arden Decides, 1917; Wild Wings, 1921. Editor Boy Scouts of America, Pen and Brush Club. Address: Hong Kong.†

PIPPENGER, WAYNE GRISE, physician; b. nr. South Bend Ind., May 30, 1906; s. Charles C. and Elsie M. (Grise) P.; B.S., Ind. U., 1928, M.D., 1930; postgrad. U. Chgo., 1934; m. Gladys A. Wise, July 9, 1931; children—William W., Richard W., Charles E., Roger L. Intern, St. Elizabeth Hosp., LaFayette, Ind., 1930-31; gen. practice medicine, Camden, Ind., 1931-34, LaFayette, 1934-35, Brook, Ind., 1935-55; dir. student health Ball State U., Muncie, Ind., 1955-72; med. dir. Wesley Manor Med. Center, Frankfort, Ind., 1972-75; mem. courtesy staff Clinton County Hosp., Frankfort, 1972-75; mem. courtesy staff Ball Meml. Hosp., Muncie; mem. staff Jasper County Hosp., Rensselaer, Ind., 1935-55, pres., 1954-55. Pres., Brook's Theatre Corp., 1945-55. Fellow Am. Acad. Family Practice; mem. Am., Ind. (past mem. ho. of dels., sec. coll. health sect. 1971), Delaware-Blackford County (mem. drug com. 1971) med. assns., 10th Dist. (pres. 1955), Jasper-Newton County (past pres.) med. socs., Muncie Acad. Medicine, Am. Acad. Gen. Practice, Mid Am. Coll. Health Assn., Nat. Athletic Trainers Assn. (adv. mem.), Delaware County Tb Assn. (hon. mem., 1st v.p. 1971, pres. 1972). Fellow Am. Coll. Health Assn. Methodist. Mason, Lion (pres. Brook 1938). Home: Frankfort, Ind., Died Apr. 1, 1975.

PIPPING, HUGO EDVARD, economist; b. Helsingfors, Finland, June 12, 1895; s. Knut Hugo and Anna (Westermarck) P.; M.A., U. Helsingfors, 1917, Ph.D., 1928; Dr.rer.pol. (hon.), 1955; Ph.D., (hon.), U. Uppsala, 1965; m. Ella Geologica Tammelander, July 8, 1922; children—Jost Joachim (dec.), Helena (Mrs. Carl Fredrik Meinander), Fredrik. With Univ. Library of Helsingfors, 1916—28; prof. econs. and statistics Swedish Sch. Econs., Helsingfors, 1928—41; reader U. Helsingfors, 1935—41, prof. econs., 1941—59, dean faculty social scis., 1945—50, vice rector, 1950—58, chancellor Abo Acad., 1958—67; mem. bd. mgmt. Oy Kaukas Ab. 1932—75; mem. supervisory bd. Nordiska Foreningsbanken, 1952—72, sec. gen. planning com., 1940—42. Mem. Bd. Swedish Peoples Party in Finland, 1929—44. Vice chmn. Swedish Lit. Soc. of Finland, 1947—66. Decorated grand cross Finnish Order Lion; comdr. Finnish White Rose and Swedish Polar Star. Recipient award Lit. Soc., 1962, medal, 1965. Hon. mem. Econ. Soc. Finland (sec. 1929—44); mem. Societas Scientiarum Fennica, Hist. Soc. Finland. Author: Myntreformen ar 1865, 1928; Behov och levnadsstandard, 1935; Finlands naringsliv. 1936; Standard of Living, 1953; Finland's Bank 1811—1877 and 1878—1914, 1961, 69; Bankliv genom hundra ar, 1962. Editor: Ekonomiska Samfundets Tidskrift, 1948—67. Home: Helsingfors, Finland. Died Apr. 13, 1975.

PIRKEY, HENRY WARREN, JR., electric utility exec.; b. Annona, Tex., July 24, 1907; s. Henry Warren and Leilia (Giddens) P.; grad. Tyler (Tex.) Comml. Coll.; m. Addie Williams, July 2, 1928; children—Charles Warren (dec.), Leilia (Mrs. August C. Erickson). With Southwestern Electric Power Co., 1925-72, exec. v.p., 1966, pres. 1966-72, also dir.; dir. Central & S.W. Corp., 1st Nat. Bank Shreveport. Treas., Shreveport-Bossier City Econ. Devel. Found., 1967-69, dir., 1966-70; dir. Pub. Solicitation Rev. Council, Shreveport, 1967-70, v.p., 1971. Trustee Gulf South Research Inst., Southwest Atomic Energy Assos.; bd. dirs. Nat. Assn. Electric Cos., 1970—, Edison Electric Inst., 1971. Mem. Nat. Assn. Accountants (past pres. Shreveport chpt. past nat. v.p., dir.), Shreveport C. of C. (treas. 1958-62, bd. dirs. 1957-59, 67-72, v.p., treas. 1969, pres. (1970), Mo. Valley Electric Assn. (pres. 1969-70), S.W. Electric Conf. (chmn. 1969-70). Home: Shreveport, La., Died Nov. 3, 1972.

PISER, ALFRED LIONEL, physician; b. Chgo., Nov. 27, 1909; s. Louis and Jennie Piser; M.D., U. Ill., 1935; m. Janis Schuman, June 21, 1936. Intern, Edgewater Hosp., Chgo., 1934-35; postgrad. in ophthalmology U. Ill., 1937-38. Served wtih M.C., AUS, 1942-46. Diplomate Am. Bd. Ophthalmology. Fellow Am. Acad. Ophthalmology and Otolaryngology; mem. A.M.A. Democrat. Jewish religion. Mason, Elk, Lion. Home: Palm Springs, Cal. Died Apr. 8, 1974; buried Desert Meml. Park, Palm Springs, Cal.

PLAEHN, ERMA BELLE, educator; b. Reinbeck, Ia., Oct. 28, 1906; d. George and Anna Laura (Strohbehn) Plaehn; B.A., Cornell Coll., Mt. Vernon, Ia., 1924-28; M.A., U. Ia., 1932, Ph.D., 1936; postgrad. U. Chgo., 1930, Harvard, 1931, Oxford U. (Eng.), 1957. Tchr. secondary schs., Algona, Ia., 1928-31; demonstration tchr. Univ. High Sch. U. Ia., 1931-36; prof. polit. sci. U. No. Ia., 1946-73, chmn. dept., 1969-71; cons. in field. Del. Ia. Democratic Party convs., 1960-72. Mem. Ia. Conf. Polit. Scientists (pres. 1954, 68), Cornell Coll. Alumni Assn., Govs. Commn. Status Women, Am. Assn. U. Women, Am. Assn. U. Profs. (pres. chpt. 1954, 63), League Women Voters, Assn. UN, Am. Civil Liberties Union, Nat. Council Teaching Social Studies, Am., Midwest polit. sci. assns., Hist. Soc. Ia. Co-author filmstrips. Home: Cedar Falls, Ia. Died Sept. 11, 1974.

PLAFKER, NATHAN VICTOR, dentist; b. N.Y.C., Oct. 17, 1905; s. Jacob and Fannie (Schachner) P.; D.D.S., Temple U., 1927; grad. student Crozer Theol. Sem., 1944-52; m. Anna Pearl Fisher, July 31, 1940. Pvt. practice dentistry, Chester, Pa., 1927; pres. Chester-Crosby Corp., Chester, from 1966, New Chester Devel. Co., Chester, from 1970. Lectr. comparative religion YMCA, Chev Sholom Synagogue Center, Bapt. Inst. Dental cons. SSS, 1941-46. Chmn. Chester Housing Authority, 1958-60, Fair Employment Commn., 1958-63, Chester City Planning Commn., from 1962. Recipient Man of Honor award Kiwanis Club, Chester, 1963. Club: Philosophy (Chester). Home: Chester, Pa. Deceased.

PLAMENATZ, JOHN PETROV, educator; b. Cetinje, Montenegro, May 16, 1912; s. Peter and Ljubica (Matanovitch) P.; M.A., Oriel Coll., Oxford U., 1937; m. Marjorie Hunter, 1943. Lectr. social and polit. theory Oxford U., 1950—67, Chichele prof. social and polit. theory, 1967—75, fellow All Souls Coll., 1936—51, ofcl. fellow Nuffield Coll., 1951—67. Fellow Brit. Acad. Author: Consent, Freedom and Political Obligation, 1938; English Utilitarians, 1950; Revolutionary Movement in France, 1815—71, 1952; From Marx to Stalin, 1953; German Marxism and Russian Communism, 1954; On Allen Rule and Self—Government, 1960; Man and Society, vols. I, II, 1963; Idelology, 1970; Democracy and Illusion, 1973; Karl Marx's Philosophy of Man, 1975; also articles. Address: Oxford, England. Died Feb. 19, 1975; interred Oxford, England.

PLANJE, CHRISTIAN WILLIAM, mgmt. consultant; b. nr. The Hague, Netherlands, May 9, 1905; s. A. C. and Wilhelmina (Hartogh) P.; B.S., U. Ill., 1927; m. Alice M. Wyatt, June 27, 1928; 1 dau., Marilyn J. (Mrs. Donald A. Wolvers). Came to U.S., 1912, naturalized, 1919. Gen. supt. Northwestern Terra Cotta Corp., Chgo., 1927-34; research engr. Portland Cement Assn., 1934-36; v.p. Gladding, McBean & Co., San Francisco and Seattle, 1944-55, pres., dir., Los Angeles, 1955-62, chmn. bd. dirs., 1960-62; pres., dir. Gladding, McBeam & Co., Ltd., Vancouver, B.C., 1950-62; prin. Case & Co., Inc., 1962-63, mng. partner, dir., 1963-67, v.p., dir. 1967-73; pres., dir. R. E. Case and Co. Los Angeles, 1967-73; pres., R. E. Case and Co. San Francisco, 1968-73; chmn. Alloy Steel & Metals Co., 1963-65; sr. v.p., dir. Mosaic Tile Co., 1965-68) dir Vetco Offshore Industries Inc.; dir. emeritus Western Gear Corp. Fellow Am. Ceramic Soc.; mem. Mcht. and Mfrs. Assn. (dir.), Am. Ceramic Soc., Inst. Ceramic Engrs., Am. Inst. Mining Metall. and Petroleum Engrs. Clubs: Rainier (Seattle); California (Los Angeles);

Pacific Union (San Francisco); Annandale Golf (Pasadena). Home: Pasadena, Cal. Died Sept. 11, 1973; interred Forest Lawn Meml. Park, Glendale, Cal.

PLANK, KENNETH ROBERT, architect; b. Sumner, Mich., Aug. 1, 1907; s. Spencer R. and May (Barnes) P.; B.S. in Architecture, U. Mich., 1942, M. City Planning, 1949; m. Edna M. Renfroe, Nov. 13, 1945; children—Kim Edward, Beverly Ann. City planner, Detroit, 1949; architect, Giffels & Vallet, Inc., Detroit, 1951-52; pvt. practice architecture, Grand Ledge, Mich., 1950-51; dir. Met. Planning Commn., Savannah, Ga., 1953-55; architect firm Sargent, Webster, Crenshaw & Folley, Watertown, N.Y., 1956-58; planning urban planner Dept. Housing and Urban Devel., Chgo., 1958-70. Asso. prof. architecture U. Fla., Gainesville, 1952-53. Mem. zoning study com., planning commn., Naperville, Ill., 1968-70. Served to lt. comdr., USNR, 1943-46. Recipient pub. relations award Detroit chpt. A.I.A., 1953. Mem. Chgo. chpt. A.I.A., Ret. Officers Assn. Episcopalian. Home: Dowagiac, Mich. Died Dec. 26, 1973.

PLATT, ELEANOR, sculptor; b. Woodbridge, N.J.; d. George Gilbert and Eva (Smith) Platt; student Art Students League, N.Y., 1929-33, N.Y. Continuation Sch., 1933-34; recipient Chaloner scholarship, 1939, $1,000 grantee Am. Acad. of Arts and Letters, 1944; recipient Guggenheim scholarship, 1945; m. Victor Russo, Aug. 6, 1955 (dec.). Executed commns.; Lewis D. Brandeis for Supreme Court, Met. Mus., Boston Mus., Harvard Law Sch., N.Y. Bar Assn., U. Louisville, 1943, replica of Lewis D. Brandeis, Hebrew U., Palestine; Einstein for Met. Mus., Calif. Inst. Tech., U. Wis., U. Cin., U. Pa., 1943, Frederick P. Keppel for Carnegie Corp., N.Y., Columbia Univ., 1943, Judge Learned Hand for Harvard Law Sch. Library, 1947; Col. Henry L. Stimson; Justice Felix Frankfurter for Harvard Law Sch.; Margaret Mitchell in Ala. State Capitol; portrait bust Chief Justice Earl Warren for Nat. Lawyers Club Washington; executed medals: Manley O. Hudson James Ewing; replica of Henry L. Stimson in Godesberg Germany; plaques in Syracuse U. N.Y. State Bar Bldg., others; busts Rabbi William Rosenblum at Temple Israel, N.Y.C., Justice Bernard Botein in Supreme Ct. Appellate Div., N.Y.C., others. Past mem. Art Commn. City N.Y. Mem. Nat. Sculptural Soc. N.A.D. Address: New York City, N.Y. Died Aug. 30, 1974.

PLATT, RUTHERFORD, author; b. Columbus, O., Aug. 11, 1894; s. Rutherford Hayes and Maryette (Smith) P.; student Groton Sch., 1908—11; grad. Hotchkiss Sch., 1914; B.A., Yale, 1918; m. Eleanor Spahr; m. 2d, Jean Dana Noyes; children—Katharine, Barbara, Rutherford, Alexander, Susan. Editorial staff World's Work, 1920-22; with Doubleday Page & Co., publishing, 1922—25, Platt Forbes, Inc., advt., 1926—53; staff Macmillan North Polar Expdns., 1947, 54; biol. adviser Disney True Life Films, 1952—53; pres. Platt Prodns. Ednl. Films, N.Y.C., 1959—75. Served to 1st lt., 323d F.A., U.S. Army, 1917—19, Fellow A.A.A.S.; mem. Ecol. Soc. Am. Club: Yale. Author: This Green World; The Woods of Time; American Trees; Worlds of Nature; River of Life; Wilderness; Adventure in the Wilderness. Home: Lakeville, Conn. Died Mar. 28, 1975.

PLATZMAN, ROBERT LEROY, educator, physicist, chemist; b. Mpls., Aug. 23, 1918; s. Alfred and Rose Platzman; B.S., U. Chgo., 1937, M.S. in Physics, 1940, Ph.D. in Chemistry, 1942; postgrad. (Guggenheim fellow), U. Copenhagen (Denmark), 1946-48, (Guggenheim fellow), U. Rome (Italy), 1948; m. Eva Maria Platzman, 1947; children—Loren Kerry, Elena Maria, Kenneth Rainer. Asso. prof. physics Purdue U., 1949-58; Fulbright prof. physics and chemistry U. Paris (France), 1959-61; sr. physicist Argonne Nat. Lab., 1958-65; prof. physics and chemistry U. Chgo., 1966-73, also master phys. scis., collegiate div. and asso. dean coll.; cons. Nat. Bur. Standards, Argonne Nat. Lab., Oak Ridge Nat. Lab. Chmn. Gordon Conf. Radiation Chemistry, 1956; vice chmn. subcom. penetration charged particles, com. nuclear sci. NRC; 1950-59, chmn. subcom. effects ionizing radiation, 1958-70. Fellow Am. Phys. Soc., Phys. Soc. (London), mem. Radiation Research Soc. (councillor 1954-58). Author sci. articles. Home: Chicago, Ill. Died July 2, 1973.

PLIMPTON, RUSSELL ARTHUR, art orgn. dir.; b. Hollis, N.Y., Aug. 26, 1891; s. Arthur Salem and Sarah Isabella (Tomes) P.; A.B., Princeton, 1914; M.A. (hon.), U. Minn., 1956; student art history in Europe, 45 summers. With Met. Mus. Art, N.Y.C., 1914-21, asst. curator decorative arts dept., 1916-21; dir. Mpls. Inst. Arts, 1921-56, then trustee; dir. Soc. of the Four Arts, Palm Beach Fla., 1956-70, emeritus dir., 1970-75. Served with F.A., U.S. Army, 1918-19; overseas. Deocrated Order of Vasa (comdr.), King's Medal (Sweden). Mem. Assn. Art Mus. Dirs. (pres. 1956), Am. Assn. Museums, Am. Fedn. Arts, Soc. of the Four Arts. Republican. Clubs: Bath and Tennis, Everglades, Rotary (Palm Beach); Minneapolis, Princeton (N.Y.C.); Nassau. Lectr. on decorative arts and painting. Home: Palm Beach, Fla., Died Dec. 8, 1975.

PLOWDEN, ELDRIDGE RODGERS, educator; b. nr. Staunton, Va., Sept. 16, 1899; s. James McCallum and Margaret Louisa (Rodgers) P.; B.S., Va. Mil. Inst., 1923; A.M., Columbia, 1948, Ed.D., 1950; m. Mary Kate Roberts, Sept. 10, 1927; children—Eldridge R., Mary Katherine. Apprentice acid maker Va.-Carolina Chem. Co., Portsmouth, Va., and Birmingham, Ala., 1923-24; acid maker, 1924-27, foreman, 1927-28; vocational teacher Ensley High Sch., Birmingham, 1928-29, coordinator trade and indsl. edn., Birmingham, 1929-34; state supervisor trade and indsl. edn., 1934-47; prof. trade and indsl. edn., chmn. dept. vocational edn. U. of Ala., from 1947. Tech. dir. Am. staff Inst. of Inter-Am. Affairs, Edn. Div., Rio de Janeiro, Brazil, 1950; advisor indsl. edn. First Inter-Am. Seminar on vocational edn., 1952; associate chief edn. field party and technical dir. indsl. edn. inst. Inter-Am. Affairs Mission to Brazil, 1955; adminstrator of vocational education U.S. Operations Mission to Thailand, 1956-59; chief adviser tech. edn. U.S. Operations Mission to Greece, 1959, mem. survey and planning group tech. edn., Cambodia, 1961; mem. East African Educational Planning Group, Nairobi, Kenya, 1961-64; chief adviser tech. and vocational edn. U.S. AID Mission to Turkey, Ankara, from 1965. Official observer SEATO study group skilled manpower shortages, 1957. Mem. Nat. Assn. State Suprs. Trade and Indsl. Edn. (pres. 1945), Am. Vocational Assn. (life), Iota Lambda Sigma, Phi Delta Kappa. Dem. Presbyn. Author: Diversified Occupations Bull., 1934. Address: Washington, D.C., Died Nov. 24, 1975.

PLOWHEAD, RUTH GIPSON, (Mrs. E. H. Plowhead), author, editor; b. Greeley, Colo., Dec. 11, 1877; d. Albert E. and Lina (West) Gipson; desc. Elder Brewster of the Mayflower; grad. Coll. of Ida. Acad., Caldwell, Ida., 1896; student U. of Ida., 1900-1901; hon. M.A., Coll. of Ida., Caldwell, 1941; m. Edward Hayes Plowhead, June 20, 1906; children—Ruth (Mrs. Kenneth Wiltsie), Eleanor (Mrs. John Randolph). Flower garden editor Gem State Rural, Caldwell, Ida., 1896-1916, Ida. Farmer (Spokane), 1916-28; editor Idaho Odd Fellow. Member American Rose Soc., D.A.R. (historian Pocahontas chapter); charter mem. Beta Sigma (now Delta Gamma Sorority). Republican. Presbyterian. Author: Lucretia Ann on the Oregon Trail, 1931; Lucretia Ann in the Golden West, 1935; Lucretia Ann on the Sagebrush Plains, 1936; Josie and Joe, 1938 (Jr. Literary Guild Book); The Silver Nightingale, 1955; Belinda's Log Cabin Quilt, 1938; Holidays with Betty Sue and Sally Lou, 1939; Josie and Joe Carry on, 1942; Mile High Cabin, 1945. Contributor feature articles to Woman's Home Companion, Country Life, American Magazine, and other magazines, also to newspapers; stories to Child Life and Junior magazines, Story Parade, Child Life Story Book. Home: Caldwell, Ida.†

PLUNKERT, WILLIAM JOSEPH, agy. exec.; b. Washington, May 4, 1900; s. John Francis and Margaret Ann (Quill) P.; student Columbia U., 1923-24, N.Y. U., 1925, U. Cal., Los Angeles, 1926-29, New Sch. for Social Research, 1945-48, Yale Sch. Alcohol Studies, 1956; m. Frances Audrey Moore, Apr. 4, 1936 (dec. June 1969). Nat. dir. transient program Fed. Emergency Relief Adminstrn., Washington, 1933-35; research asso., dir. Cal. Relief Adminstrn., San Francisco, 1935-38; Eastern regional rep. United Community Def. Services, N.Y.C., 1952-55; asso. dir., dir. field service Nat. Council on Alcoholism, N.Y.C., 1955-62; asst. exec. dir. Community Council Greater N.Y., 1962-65, asst. dir., 1965-69, asst. dir., then dir. Alcoholism Programs, 1965-69; exec. dir. Alcoholism Recovery Inst., Inc., 1970-72. Bd. dirs. Lower Eastside Service Center. Mem. Acad. Certified Social Workers, Am. Pub. Health Assn., Nat. Assn. Pub. Health Ofcls., Nat. Assn. Social Workers, Nat. Conf. Social Welfare, N.Y. State Welfare Conf., Pub. Health Assn. N.Y.C., Royal Soc. Promotion Health. Contbr. articles to profl. jours. Home: New York City, N.Y. Died Oct. 28, 1972.

POAG, THOMAS E., univ. dean; A.B., Morgan State Coll.; M.A., Ohio State U.; Ph.D., Cornell U. Prof., head dept. speech and drama, also dean Sch. Arts and Scis., Tenn. State U., Nashville. Address: Nashville, Tenn. Died Apr. 3, 1974.

POINDEXTER, CLAUDE HENDRICKS, ins. co. exec.; b. Ellijay, Ga., July 24, 1901; s. John D. and Hattie (Deaver) P.; grad. Ga. Normal Coll., Douglas, 1923; m. Valdese Lott, Aug. 30, 1952; children—Betty (Mrs. Poindexter Drake), Kay (Mrs. William Gerald Cox). Founder ins. assn., 1930; pres., chief exec. officer Coastal State Life Ins. Co., Inc., Atlanta, 1947-74; dir. Fulton Nat. Bank. Mem. Atlanta Music Festival, Sherwood Forest Civic Assn.; state crusade chmn. Am. Cancer Soc., 1968-69. Chmn. bd. trustees Norman Coll., Norman Park, Ga. Mem. Nat. Assn. Life Cos. (pres. 1955, dir. 1955-73), Am. Life Conv. (state v.p.), Atlanta C. of C., Atlanta Art Assn., Baptist (deacon). Clubs: Capital City, Atlanta Athletic (Atlanta). Home: Atlanta, Ga. Died Apr. 2, 1974.

POLAKOV, WALTER NICHOLAS, engineer; b. St. Petersburg, Russia, July 1879; s. Hon. Nicholas N. and Aline A. (Khvostoff) P.; M.E., Royal Inst. of Tech., Dresden, Saxony, 1902; spl. course in psychology and industrial hygiene, University of Moscow; m. 2d, Barbara Gesinska, 1929. Came to U.S., 1906; formerly superintendent motive power N.Y., N.H.&H. R.R. Co.; expert consulting engr. Bd. of Estimates and Apportionment, City of New York, and Dept. of Docks and Ferries, 1909-10; cons. engr. Penn Central Light & Power Co., 1912-14; power expert, U.S. Shipping Bd., 1918; pres. Walter N. Polakov & Co., industrial consultants; management consultant Supreme Economic Council, U.S.S.R., 1929-31; cons. engr. Tenn. Valley Authority, 1933. Fellow Inst. Management; mem. Am. Soc. Mechanical Engineers, Am. Management Assn., Soc. Industrial Engrs., Am. Mil. Engrs., Civil Legion, Taylor Soc. to Promote Science of Management; hon. mem. Nat. Assn. Stationary Engrs. Author: Mastering Power Production, 1920; Foremanship, 1923; Man and His Affairs, 1925; Power Plant Management, 1931; The Power Age, 1933; also numerous tech. papers read before scientific socs., and articles in engring. mags. Home: Sherman, N.Y.†

POLITELLA, JOSEPH, educator; b. Roccamonfina, Sessa, Italy, Sept. 20, 1910; s. Anthony and Catherine (Ionta) P.; came to U.S., 1919, derivative citizen; B.S., Mass. State Coll., 1933; A.M., Amherst Coll., 1935; Ph.D., U. Pa., 1938; postgrad. Boston U. Sch. Theology, 1940-41; m. Ellen Sue Duke, Sept. 2, 1950. Chmn. dept. English, Northland Coll., Ashland, Wis., 1941-42; asso. prof. philosophy Kent (O.) State U., 1946-50, prof. philosophy, 1950-73, emeritus, 1973, chmn. grad. studies in philosophy, 1970-73. Tchr. bible Religious Edn. Program, St. Paul's Episcopal Ch., Akron, O., 1952-75. Served to capt. USAAF, 1942-46. Fellow Royal Asiatic Soc.; mem. Am. Acad. Religion (pres. Midwest area), Soc. for Asian and Comparative Philosophy, Ohio Philos. Assn. Author: Platonism, Aristotelianism and Cabalism in the Philosophy of Leibniz, 1938; Mysticism and the Mystical Consciousness, 1964; Seven World Religions, 2 vols., 1965; Hinduism, its Scriptures, Philosophy and Mysticism, 1965; Buddhism, A Religion of Compassion and a Way of the Spirit, 1967; Taoism and Confucianism, The Way of Heaven and the Way of Man, 1967. Home: Kent, O. Died Jan. 31, 1975.

POLLACK, ABOU DAVID, pathologist; b. N.Y.C., Feb. 26, 1908; s. Harry and Ethel Annie (Samuels) P.; A.B., Cornell U., 1929; M.D., U. Rochester, 1933; m. Leona P. Pearlstien, July 4, 1929; children—Adam E., Matthew. Intern Strong Meml. Hosp., Rochester, N.Y., 1933-34; fellow in pathology Mt. Sinai Hosp., N.Y.C., 1934-39, asst. chief pathologist, 1939-46, asso. chief pathologist, 1946-47; pathologist U.S. Army Biol. Labs., Fort Detrick, Frederick, Md., 1947-53; pathologist in chief Balt. City Hosps., 1953-71; pathologist Johns Hopkins Hosp., 1953-71. Asst. prof. pathology Sch. Medicine, Johns Hopkins, 1953-58, asso. prof., 1958-70, prof., 1970-71; cons. Dept. Army, 1955-62, Armed Forces Inst. Pathology, others. Served to col. AUS, 1942-46; ETO, NATOUSA. Diplomate Am. Bd. Pathology. Fellow N.Y. Acad. Medicine; mem. Am. Soc. Exptl. Pathology, Soc. Exptl. Biology and Medicine, Path. Soc. Gt. Brit. and Ireland, Am. Assn. Pathologists and Bacteriologists, Internat. Acad. Pathology Harvey Soc., Sigma Xi, Alpha Omega Alpha. Contbr. numerous articesl to profl. publs. Home: Baltimore, Md., Died Aug. 1, 1971; buried Baron Hirsch Cemetery, S.I. N.Y.

POLLAK, EGON, conductor; b. Prague, Bohemia, Mar.3, 1879; s. Ernst and Josefine (Reitler) P.; married, June 4, 1906; children—George Wenzel, Carl Alexander. Began as conductor opera in Prague, 1901; later conductor in opera houses, Bremen, Leipzig. Frankfort-on-Main, Hamburg, etc.; conductor Chicago Civic Opera Co. various seasons from 1915. Rotarian. Home: Hamburg, Germany. Address: Chicago, Ill.†

POLLARD, ROBERT NELSON, U.S. dist. judge; b. King and Queen County, Va., June 16, 1880; s. Henry Robinson and Jessie (Gresham) P.; LL.B., U. of Richmond (Va.), 1903; student U. of Va., 1903-04; m. Mary F. Butler, Nov. 24, 1915; children—Fred G., Robert N., Mary Butler, Arthur Butler (dec.). Admitted to Va. bar, 1904, practiced in Richmond; judge Law and Equity Court, Richmond, 1930-36; judge U.S. Dist. Court, Eastern Dist. of Va., from 1936. Trustee U. Richmond. Mem. Kappa Sigma, Phi Delta Phi. Democrat. Baptist. Home: Richmond, Va.*†

POLLITZER, ANITA, (Mrs. Elie C. Edson), writer, lectr., leader Women's movement; b. Charleston, S.C.; d. G. M. and Clara (Guinzburg) Pollitzer; B.S., Columbia, 1916, A.M., 1933; m. Elie C. Edson, Dec. 29, 1928. Active nationally as leader in woman suffrage and equal rights for women; speaker and organizer in many states in behalf of suffrage ratification, 1919-20; 1st nat. sec. Nat. Woman's Party, 1921-26; active in campaign for equality of women in 43 states, from 1926; active in securing married women's right to work in govt. service, 1937, and in securing equality for women in provisions of 1st Nat. Fair Labor Standards Act., 1938; nat. vice chairwoman Nat. Woman's Party, 1927-38, mem. nat. exec. council and vice chairwoman congl. com., 1939-45, chairwoman N.Y.C. com., 1942-45, nat. chairwoman, 1945-49, hon. chairwoman, from 1949. Instr. summer schs. U. Va. and Columbia; lectr. on art; exhibitor at Phila. Water Color Show and in Charleston, S.C. Recipient Mitchell Medal. Incorporator, and charter mem. World Woman's Party for Equal Rights, Nat. Council of Women of U.S. (mem. nat. exec. com.); mem. Am. Assn. U. Women, Alumni Assn. Columbia, Nat. Fedn. Bus. and Profl. Women's Clubs, Internat. Fedn. Bus. and Profl. Women's Clubs. Acad. Polit. Sci. Rep. State of S.C. at Internat. Feminist Conf., Sorbonne,

1926; rep. Nat. Women's Party, 1st session of U.N., San Francisco, 1945; also sessions of Econ. and Social Council and Status of Women Commn., U.N., 1946. Contbr. articles on equal rights andstatus of women to mag. and newspapers. Home: New York City, N.Y., Died July 3, 1975.

POLLOCK, CLEMENT PERRY, mining co. exec.; b. Kanarraville, Utah, Apr. 7, 1905; s. William W. and Zina (Parker) P.; B.S., U. Utah, 1930; m. Helen E. Latimer, June 12, 1935; children—Sharen Lee (Mrs. Martin L. Leymeister, Jr.), William Warren. With Internat. Smelting Co., 1926-33; with Am. Smelting & Refining Co., 1934-71, exploration mgr., 1954-62, v.p., 1962-71; pres. ASARCO Exploration Co. Can. Ltd., 1963-71; v.p., dir. Lake Asbestos Co. Que. Ltd., 1958-71. Mem. Am. Inst. Mining Engrs., Geol. Soc. Am., Mining and Metall. Soc. Am. Clubs: University, Mining (N.Y.C.); Westchester Country (Rye, N.Y.). Home: Greenwich, Conn. Died June 11, 1973.

POLSKY, BERT ALFRED, business exec.; b. Orwell, O., Nov. 1, 1881; s. Abram and Mollie (Bloch) P.; student Culver Mil. Acad., 1899, Buchtel Prep. Sch., 1899-1900, Buchtel Coll., 1900-02; LL.D., University of Akron, 1948; married Hazel May Steiner, Feb. 17, 1904; children—Thomas E., Margaret Elizabeth (Mrs. H. Cleves Dodge). With A. Polsky Co., Akron, from 1902, sec., 1912-29, v.p., mng. dir., 1929-45, pres., 1945-53, chmn. bd., 1953, hon. chmn. bd.; dir. Allied Stores Corp. (formerly Hahn Dept. Stores), 1929-36, Goodyear Tire & Rubber Co., 1947-58. Pres. bd. trustees Akron (Ohio) Community Trusts, 1956-59; trustee Akron Beacon Jour. Fund, United Found. of Summit Co., United Community Council, C. W. Seiberling Meml. Found. Former trustee U. Akron, temp. past chmn. bd. trustees. Received Lions Club award, 1951. Mem. C. of C. (pres. 1919-20). Club: Akron Rotary. Home: Akron, O.†

POMEROY, HOWARD EDWIN, clergyman; b. Worcester, Mass., Jan. 6, 1900; s. Martin Edwin and Georgia Etta (Garey) P.; A.B., Clark U., 1920; B.D., Hartford Theol. Sem., 1923; S.T.M., Newton Theol. Inst., 1930; postgrad. Clark U., 1923-24, Boston U., 1930-35, Harvard Div. Sch., 1935-36; m. Mildred May Clifford, Sept. 5, 1923; children—Russell Edwin, Eleanor May. Ordained to ministry Congl. Ch., 1923; pastor Lake View Ch., Worcester, Mass., 1923-26, Boylston Ch., Jamaica Plain, Boston, 1926-75; chaplain Boston Fire Dept., 1945-1954. Mem. Nat. council Boy Scouts Am., 1944-52, recipient Silver Antelope award, 1945. Trustee Mass. Bible Soc., rec. sec., 1956-75. Mem. Am. Congl. Assn. (dir. 1940, pres. 1962-75), Boston Area Council Chs. (pres. 1950-53). Republican. Club: Boston Congregational (pres. 1938-39.) Home: Jamaica Plain, Mass. Died Feb. 9, 1975, buried Forest Hills Cemetery, Boston.

POMPIDOU, GEORGES JEAN RAYMOND, pres. of France; b. Montboudif, Cantal, France, July 5, 1911; s. Leon and Marie-Louise (Chavagnac) P.; ed. Ecole Normale Superieure, also Ecole Libre des Sciences Politiques; m. Claude Cahour, 1939; 1 son, Alain. Prof., Lyceum of Marseille (France), also Lyceum Henri IV, Paris, 1938-44; charge de mission ministry Gen. de Gaulle, 1944-46; mem. Coneil d'Etat, 1946-54, dir. MM. de Rothschild Freres, Paris, 1956-58, 59-62; dir. in cabinet Gen. de Gaulle, Pres, du Conseil, 1958-59; mem. Conseil Constitutionnel, 1959-62; prime minister of France, 1962-68; pres. of France, 1969-74. Decorated officer of the Legion of Honor, and also many fgn. decorations. Author: Pages choisies de Taine, 1954; Pages choisies des romans de Malraux, 1955; Anthologie de la Poesie Francaise, 1961. Home: 24 Quai de Bethune Paris 4eme France. Died Apr. 1974.

PONS, LILLY, opera singer; b. Cannes, France; d. Auguste and Maria (Naso) Pons; student piano at Paris Conservatory, pupil Alberti di Gorostiaga; d. Mus. (hon.) Adelphi Coll., 1946; m. August Mesritz, Nov. 15, 1925 (div. 1933); m. 2d, Andre Kostelanetz, June 2, 1938 (div.); Am. citizen 1940. Made her début as Lakmé, Mulhouse (France) Municipal Opera, Jan. 1929; first appearance at New York as Lucia, Met. Opera Co., Jan. 1931; mem. Met. Opera Co., San Francisco Opera Co., Chgo. Opera Co., Teatro Colon, Buenos Aires, Covent Garden, London. Prin. roles: Lucia in Lucia di Lammermoor, Gilda in Rigoletto, Rosina in Barber of Seville, Lakme in Lakme, Linda in Linda di Chamonix, Anima in La Sonnambula, Shemakhan in Le Coq d'Or, Marie in Daughter of the Regiment. Appeared in motion pictures I Dream Too Much, 1935; That Girl from Paris, 1936; Hitting a New High, 1938, and numerous later pictures; yearly concert tours throughout U.S.; guest appearances radio and TV; recordings Columbia Records. During World War II, toured battle fronts North Africa and Europe, India, China and Burma. Awarded Asiatic-Pacific campaign service ribbon, India-Burma Theater. Made an hon. consul of Cannes, France, 1934; received gold medal of the city of Paris, 1937; Officer Legion of Honor, Order Cross of Lorraine, comdr. Nat. Merit (France); Order Crown of Belgium; awarded medal from Soc. of Belgian Wounded, 1938; ofcl. dau. of LeClerc Div. A town in Maryland named Lillypons in her honor. Home: Dallas, Tex., Died Feb. 13, 1976; buried Cannes, France.

POOL, GEORGE FRANKLIN, chem. co. exec.; b. Deer Lodge, Mont., Mar. 12, 1910; s. Leonard Jay and Emma (Ludford) P.; grad. Advanced Mgmt. Program, Harvard, 1954; m. Doris Grossnickle, June 4, 1938; children—Anne Elizabeth, Judith Irene (Mrs. Allen Perlman). Dist. mgr. Compressed Indsl. Gases, Phila., 1932-40, Nat. Cylinder Gas Co., 1940-43; exec. v.p., dir. Air Products & Chems., Inc., Allentown, Pa., 1943, later vice chmn. bd., dir. Trustee Sacred Heart Hosp., Allentown. Clubs: Lehigh County, Lehigh Valley (Allentown). Home: Allentown, Pa. Deceased.

POOL, JUDITH GRAHAM, research physiologist; b. N.Y.C., June 1, 1919; d. Leon Wilfred and Nellie (Baron) Graham; B.S., U. Chgo., 1939, Ph.D., 1946; m. Ithiel de S. Pool, 1938 (div. 1953); children—Jonathan R., Jeremy D., Lorna N. Graham Pool; m. 2d, Maurice Sokolow, 1972 (div. 1975). Instr. Hobart Coll., 1943—45; research asso. Stanford Research Inst., 1950—53; research asso. Stanford (Cal.) Med. Sch., 1953—60, sr. research asso., 1960—75, dir. hemophilia research, 1953—75, prof. medicine, 1972—75. Mem. adv. com. nat. blood resource br. Nat. Heart and Lung Inst., 1969-73; med. and sci. adv. com. World Found. Hemophilia; A.R.C. blood program Nat. Hemophila Found.; VA Career Devel. Adv. Com.; Paul M. Appeler Meml. lectr. U. Cal. at San Francisco, 1974. Recipient Murray Thelin award Nat. Hemophilia Found., 1968; Elizabeth Blackwell award Hobart and William Smith Colls., 1973. Fulbright grantee, 1958—59. Mem. A.A.A.S., Am. Physiol. Soc., Am. Soc. Hematology, Western Soc. Clin. Research, Soc. for Exptl. Biology and Medicine, Internat. Soc. Thrombosis and Hemostasis, Am. Heart Assn. (council on thrombosis), Assn. Women in Sci. (co—pres. 1971—72), Am. Assn. U. Profs. (exec. com. Stanford chpt. 1971—72), Profl. Women Stanford Med. Sch. (chmn. 1970—71), Phi Betta Kappa, Sigma Xi. Democrat. Mem. editorial bd. Transfusion, Am. Jour. Hematology. Home: San Francisco, Cal. Died July 13, 1975.

POOR, WHARTON, lawyer; b. Washington, Mar. 10, 1888; s. John Caldwell and Ella (Wharton) P.; A.B., Harvard, 1908, LL.B., 1911; m. Phoebe M. Manice, Oct. 3, 1913. Admitted to N.Y. bar, 1913, later practiced in N.Y.C.; mem. Haight, Deming, Gardner, Poor & Havens, specializing in shipping matters, from 1924. Mem. Maritime Law Assn. U.S., Assn. Bar City of N.Y. Author: Charter Parties and Ocean Bills of Lading, 2d edit., 1930. Home: Flushing, N.Y. Died Jan. 27, 1974.

POOR, WILLIAM BUNKER, engring. cons.; b. Weymouth, Mass., Oct. 11, 1901; s. Sumner Charles and Julia Augusta (Bunker) P.; B.S. in Mining Engring., Ohio State U., 1926; m. Pauline Neff, Sept. 5, 1925; children—William Howard, Beverly Louise (Mrs. Fred F. Lee). Constrn. engr. U.S. Smelting. Refining & Mining Co., Fairbanks, Alaska, 1926-28; gas engr. Columbia Engring. & Mgmt. Corp., Columbus, O., 1928-30; successively distbn. engr., prodn. and transmission engr., supervising engr. charge design and constrn. natural gas facilities United Gas Pipe Line Co., Shreveport, La., 1930-44; chief engr. Tennessee Gas Transmission Co., Houston, 1944-48; successively chief engr. and project mgr. Mich.-Wis. Pipe Line Co. constrn., constrn. gas engr., mgr. gas and petro-chem. dept. projects in U.S. and Can. Ford, Bacon & Davis, Inc., 1948-55, v.p., 1959-67; engring. cons., 1967-72. Registered profl. engr., N.Y. N.J., Tex., Okla., Kan. Neb., Mo., Ia., Ill., Wis., Ind., Mich., Alberta, Can. Mem. Am. Inst. Mining and Metall. Engrs., Am. Gas Assn. Nat. Constructrs Assn., Pipeline Contractor's Assn. Club: N.Y. Athletic, (N.Y.C.). Home: Sebago, Me., Died Oct. 28, 1973; interred South Bridgton (Me.) Cemetery.

POPE, ARTHUR, artist b. Cleve., Jan. 31, 1880; s. John Lang and Frances Emily (Whipple) P.; A.B., Harvard U., 1901; student Harvard U. Grad. Sch., 1901-02; m. Mysie Black Bell, June 9, 1906; children—Mary Bell (Mrs. Benjamin F. Cornwall), Hugh, Murray. Austin teaching fellow Harvard U., 1901-06, instr., 1906-09, asst. prof., 1909-19. prof. fine arts, 1919-49; acting director Fogg Museum of Art, 1945-46; dir. Fogg Museum of Art (Harvard Univ.), 1946-48; exhibited paintings occasionally in Boston and N.Y. City. Trustee Isabella Stewart Gardner Museum in Boston. Clubs: Harvard (N.Y. City); The Country (Brookline). Author: Introduction to Language of Drawing and Painting—Vol. I, The Painter's Terms, 1929, Vol. II, The Painter's Modes of Expression, 1931; Art, Artist and Layman, 1937; The Language of Drawing and Painting, 1949. Home: Brookline, Mass.†

POPE, CLIFFORD HILLHOUSE, herpetologist, writer; b. Washington, Ga., 1899; s. Mark Cooper and Harriet Alexander (Hull) P.; student U. Ga., 1916—18; B.S., U. Va., 1921. Herpetologist Chinese div. Central Asiatic Expdns., Am. Mus. Natural History, 1921—26, asst. curator dept. amphibians and reptiles, 1928—35; curator div. amphibians and reptiles Field Mus. Natural History, Chgo., 1941—53, mus. leader three expdns. to Mexico and expdns. to various parts of U.S. Hon. Boy Scout. Fellow N.Y. Zool. Soc.; mem. Am. Soc. Ichthyologists and Herpetologists (past pres.). Author: The Reptiles of China, 1935; Snakes Alive and How They Live, 1937; Turtles of the United States and Canada, 1939; China's Animal Frontier, 1940; Amphibians and Reptiles of the Chicago Area, 1944; The Reptile World, 1955; Reptiles Round The World, 1957; The Giant Snakes, 1961, also articles in field. Home: Escondido, Cal. Died June 3, 1974; cremated.

POPE, HAROLD LINDER, mechanical engr.; b. Newton, Mass., Nov. 5, 1879; s. Col. Albert A. and Abby (Linder) P.; grad. Peekskill (N.Y.) Mil. Acad., 1898; grad. Mass. Inst. Tech., 1902; m. Clara Hinckley, Mar. 17, 1901. Asst. supt. John T. Robinson & Co., Hyde Park, Mass., makers Pope-Robinson automobiles, 1902-03; designer and engr. Pope Mfg. Co., Hartford, Conn., makers Pope-Hartford automobiles, 1903-05; mgr. Pope Mfg. Co., Hagerstown, Md., makers Pope-Tribune automobiles and bicycles, 1905-07; mgr. and engr. Pope Motor Car Co., Toledo, O., makers Opoe-Toledo automobiles, 1907-09; mgr. for Willis-Overland Automobile Co., Toledo, O., June-Sept. 1909; chief engr. Matheson Automobile Co., Wilkes-Barré, Pa., 1909-10; mgr. and engr. West Works, The Pope Mfg. Co., Hartford, in direct charge of truck dept., Sept., 1910-Sept., 1914; works mgr. Ferro Machine & Foundry Co., Cleveland, 1914-16; factory mgr. and engr. Wright-Martin Aircraft Corpn., N.Y. City, Sept. 1916-Sept. 1917; v.p. and factory mgr. Wright-Martin Aircraft Corpn. of Cal., Los Angeles, from 1917. Mem. Am. Soc. M.E., Soc. Automotive Engrs., Instn. Automobile Engrs. (England). Mason. Clubs: Engineers (New York); Sachems Head Yacht. Home: Los Angeles, Cal.†

POPE, LARRY JACOB, librarian; b. Cin., Feb. 26, 1937; s. Jesse B. and Estelle M. (Moneyhon) P.; A.B., U. Ky., 1959, M.S., 1961; m. Genevieve Scott Johnston, July 10, 1965. Librarian, serials cataloger main library U. Ky., Lexington, 1961-64, head circulation librarian, 1964-66; asst. periodicals librarian Eastern Ky. U., Richmond, 1966-67, chief periodicals librarian, 1967-75. Mem. Am., Southeastern library assns., Ohio Valley Group Tech. Service Librarians, Theatre Guild Soc. Home: Richmond, Ky. Died Apr. 3, 1975; interred Brooksville, Ky.

POPE, LISTON, educator, clergyman; b. Thomasville, N.C., Sept. 6, 1909; s. Robie Lester and Dora (Younts) P.; A.B., Duke, 1929, B.D., 1932, D.D., 1951; Ph.D., Yale 1940; S.T.D., Boston U., 1950; D.D., Grinnell Coll., 1957; Th.D., U. Geneva, 1959; D.D., Bucknell U., 1960; L.H.D., Coe Coll., 1953, Bradley U., 1957, Rollins Coll., 1960; m. Bennie Purvis, Feb. 3, 1934 (dec.); children—Mary (Mrs. Clement Barbey), Liston, Alison; m. 2d, Gerd Thoresen. Asso. pastor Wesley Meml. Church, High Point, N.C., 1932-35; ordained to Congl. ministry, 1935; pastor Humphrey St. Congl. Ch., New Haven, 1935-38; lectr. social ethics Yale, 1938-39, asst. prof., 1939-44, asso. prof., 1944-47, Gilbert L. Stark prof. social ethics, 1947-73, dean Div. Sch., 1949-62; Alden Tuthill lectr. Chgo. Theol. Sem., 1945; Merrick lectr. Ohio Wesleyan U., 1950; Wallace lectr. Macalester Coll., 1950; Gray lectr. Duke, 1952; Shaffer lectr. Northwestern U., 1954; Hein lectr., 1958; Finch lectr. High Point Coll., 1960. Chmn. exec. com. Am. Assn. Theol. Schs., 1957-62. Trustee Phelps-Stokes Fund, 1946-59, Vassar Coll., 1954-60, Theol. Edn. Fund, 1959-62, Franklin and Marshall Coll.; pres. bd. dirs. Prospect Hill Sch., 1953-55, 59-60. Recipient John Addison Porter prize Yale, 1940; Julius Rosenwald fellowship for research, Africa, 1949. Fellow Saybrook Coll. Yale. Mem. Nat. Council Religion Higher Edn., World Council Chs. (exec. com. 1954-61), Phi Beta Kappa, Phi Delta Theta, Omicron Delta Kappa, Sigma Upsilon. Clubs: Morys, Faculty (New Haven). Author: Millhands and Preachers, 1942; The Kingdom Beyond Caste, 1957. Editor: Social Action mag., 1944-48; Labor's Relations to Church and Community, 1947. Contbr. articles to N.Y. Times, Sat. Rev., other jours. Home: Trondheim, Norway. Died Apr. 15, 1974.

POPE, ROY L(EON), accountant; b. Troup, Tex., Feb. 5, 1904; s. Charles Morse and Eugenia (McCuistion) P.; student U. Tex., 1923-27; m. Louise J. Roessler, Oct. 10, 1928; 1 son, Charles W. Sec. bd. dirs. Southwestern Engraving Co., Atlanta, 1927-30, San Antonio, 1930-35; pvt. accounting practice, San Antonio, 1935-73; partner Howard & Pope, 1938-50, Roy L. Pope & Co., 1950-53; sr. partner Roy L. Pope & Spillers Co., 1953-69; partner Alexander Grant & Co., 1970-73. C.P.A., Tex. Mem. Tex. Soc. C.P.A.'s, (past pres. state and local; state dir.), San Antonio C. of C. Unitarian. Mason (32 deg.), Rotarian. Home: San Antonio, Tex. Died Aug. 28, 1973.

POPEJOY, THOMAS LAFAYETTE, educator; b. Raton, New Mexico, Dec. 29, 1902; s. Fred and Ellen (Floyd) P.; B.A., Univ. of N.M., 1915; student U. Ill., summers 1925, 26; A.M., U. N.M., 1929; student U. Cal., summers 1934, 35; LL.D., U. Ariz., 1954; LL.D., U. Albuquerque, 1968; m. Bessie Kimball, June 21, 1921; children—Jeanne Kimball, Tom Lafayette. Instr. in econs. U. N.M., 1925-29, asst. prof., 1929-37, prof., 1937-48, exec. asst. to pres. 1938-48, pres., asst. . 1948-68; comptroller, 1938-48, acting registrar, . 1941-44, chmn. bd. of deans, 1944-45; research dir. N.M. Taxpayer's Assn., 1932; state dir., Nat. Youth Adminstrn., 1935-39, dep. adminstr., Washington, D.C., 1939-40; regional consumer relations rep. OPA, Denver, 1942. Mem. exec. com. Western Interstate Commn. Higher Edn., 1953—, pres. 1951-53; mem. pres.'s council Western Athletic Conf., 1961-68, chmn.

1961-62, 65-66; mem. exec. com. Asso. Rocky Mountain Univs., Inc., 1968 1961-68, pres. 1960-61; pres. Nat. Assn. State Univs., 1963-64. Pres. Albuquerque Little Theatre, 1968-69. Mem. bd. visitors Air U., USAF, 1961-64, St. John's Coll., Santa Fe; trustee Sania Sch. of Girls, Sch. Am. Research. Mem. Albuquerque C. of C. (dir.). Blue Key, Alpah-Phi Omega, Pi Gamma Mu, Sigma Chi, Phi Kappa Phi, Tau Kappa Alpha, Alpha Kappa Psi. Democrat. Episcopalian. Clubs: Albuquerque Country, Rotary (pres. 1946-47). Author: The Causes of Bank Failures in N.M., 1920-25, 1931; The University of New Mexico, A Calculated Risk. Contbr. articles to N.M. Business Rev. Home: Albuquerque, N.M., Died Oct. 24, 1975.

PORTER, DAVID RICHARD, educator; b. Oldtown, Me., Apr. 21, 1882; s. Willis M. and Esther F. P.; A.B., Bowdoin, 1906; Rhodes scholar, Oxford U., A.B., 1907, A.M., 1910; m. Alice Hinckley, 1908; children—Esther, Geo. Hinckley, Jean, Robert Gordon. With Nat. Council Y.M.C.A., New York, 1907-34; master Mount Hermon Sch., 1934, headmaster, 1935-43; War Prisoners Aid, 1943-47. Compiler of Poems of Action, 1912; The Enrichment of Prayer, 1917. Editor: Dynamic Faith, 1927; The Life Work of George Irving, 1945. President General Cum Laude Society, 1941-44. Home: Abington, Eng. Died May 21, 1973.

PORTER, EDWARD ARTHUR GRIBBON, lawyer; b. Lisburn, No. Ireland, Nov. 1, 1895; s. Thomas Johnstone and Ellen Hughes (Fawcett) P.; came to U.S. 1906, naturalized, 1922; B.S., Haverford Coll., 1918; LL.B., U. Pa., 1922; LL.D., LaSalle Coll., 1955; m. Louise Fromefield, Jan. 21, 1928; 1 dau., Anne (Mrs. William S. Butler). Admitted to Pa. bar, 1922, practiced in Phila; asso. Saul, Ewing, Remick & Saul, 1922—31, partner, 1931—74. Dir. Superior Tube Co., Electric Trachometer Corp. Served with 1st Brit. Ambulance Unit for Italy, World War 1; served to lt. comdr. USCGR, World War 11. Decorated Croce Merito de Guerra (Italy). Mem. Am., Pa., Phila. bar assns. Democrat. Episcopalian. Home: Media, Pa. Died May 3, 1974.

PORTER, FAIRFIELD, painter; b. Winnetka, Ill., June 10, 1907; s. James Foster and Ruth Wadsworth (Furness) P.; B.S., Harvard, 1928: student Art Students League, N.Y., 1928-29, 29-30; D.Fine Arts, Colby Coll., 1969, Md. Inst., 1970; L.H.D., L.I. U., 1972; m. Anne Elizabeth Channing, Sept. 22, 1932; children—John Fairfield, Laurence Minot, Jeremy, Katharine Minot, Elizabeth. Exhibited in group shows Phila. Acad., 1933. Chgo. Art Inst., 1938, U. Neb., 1955: one man shows Tibor de Naby Gallery, N.Y.C., 1952-55, 57-75; exhibited at Venice Biennale, 1968; editorial asso. Art News, 1951-59; techr. art Queens Coll., spring 1969: artist in residence Amherst Coll., 1969-70. Recipient Longview award for criticism in The Nation, 1959; Thomas R. Proctor prize N.A.D., 1971. Author: Thomas Eakins, 1959. Address: Southampton, N.Y., Died Sept. 18, 1975.

PORTER, IRVIN LOURIE, banker; b. Alexis, Ill., Nov. 18, 1881; s. John Bowen and Ella M. (Small) P.; student Knox Coll.; m. Madeline Blair, Oct. 19, 1914; children—Mrs. Blair Bacon, Joan, Mrs. Madeline Coyne. Vice pres. and dir., sec. exec. com.; vice-chmn. trust investment com., First Nat. Bank of Chicago (Ill.); dir. Ambassador East, Inc., Chicago Mill and Lumber Co., Harnischfeger Corp., Kearney & Trecker Corp. Mem. bd. and treas. Chicago Transit Authority. Treas. U. of Ill.; trustee, chmn. finance com. Knox Coll., Galesburg, Ill.; financial adviser to Arts Club of Chicago. Chairman Chicago and Cook County (Illinois) Third War Loan Drive. Member Investment Bankers Association, American Inst. of Banking, Assn. of Reserve City Bankers, Beta Theta Pi. Clubs: Chicago, Athletic, Mid-Day (Chicago); Chicago Golf (Wheaton, Ill.); Exmoor Country (Highland Park, Ill.). Home: Kenilworth, Ill.*†

PORTER, JOHN JERMAIN, mfr. cement; b. Washington, D.C., June 14, 1880; s. Jermain Gildersleeve and Emily Starrett (Snowden) P.; B.S., U. of Cincinnati, 1901; m. Edith Louise Frazer, June 10, 1908; children—Jermain Doty, Louise Snowden (Mrs. Wendell Thomas). Chemist, forman and supt. in iron and steel industry, 1901-06; asst. prof. chemistry, U. of Cincinnati, 1907-11; cons. metall. engr., 1911-12; v.p. and gen. mgr. Security Cement & Lime Co. and North American Cement Corporation, 1913-32; president North American Cement Corp., 1932-44; chmn. bd. N.Am. Cement Corp., 1944-49. hon. chmn. bd., from 1949; dir., v.p. Porter Chemical Co.; dir. and v.p. Nicodemus Nat. Bank of Hagerstown; director Insuranshares Corporation of Maryland. Cons. on potash to Bureau of Mines and War Industries, Bd., World War. Trustee Hagerstown Pub. Library, Westminster Theol. Sem. Mem. Md. Acad. Science. Republican. Methodist. Club: Engineers (New York). Home: Hagerstown, Md.†

PORTER, PAUL ALDERMANDT, lawyer; b. Joplin, Mo., Oct. 6, 1904; s. John J. and Dolly (Carpenter) P.; ed. Ky. Wesleyan Coll., 1923-26, LL.D., 1945; U. Ky. Law Coll., 1926-29; m. Bessie Edgar Benton, June 14, 1930 (div. June 1956); children—Betsy Gilman, Ann Dinsmoor; m. 2d, Kathleen Winsor, June 26, 1956. Newspaper reporter; city editor Lexington (Ky.) Herald, 1926-29; in practice of law, central Ky., 1928-29; editor Mangum (Okla.) Daily News and LaGrange (Ga.) News, 1929-32; spl. counsel Dept. Agr., 1932-37; Washington counsel, CBS, 1937-42; lectr. on adminstrv. law Law. Coll. of Catholic U., Washington, 1941-59; dep. adminstr. in charge rent div. OPA, 1942-43; asso. adminstr. War Food Adminstrn.; asso. dir. Office Econ. Stblzn., July 1943-Feb. 1944; campaign publicity dir. Dem. Nat. Com., 1944; apptd. mem. FCC and designated chmn. 1944; apptd. adminstr. OPA, 1946; apptd. chief Am. Econ. Mission to Greece with rank of ambassador, Dec. 1946; in practice law, with firm Arnold & Porter, Washington; rank of ambassador, as U.S. rep. on Palestine Conciliation commn., July 1949. Mem. President's Commn. Campaign Costs, 1961-62. Mem. Nat. Press Assn., Fed. Communications, Ky. bar assns., Sigma Alpha Epsilon, Phi Alpha Delta. Democrat. Baptist Home: Washington, D.C., Died Nov. 26, 1975.

PORTER, WILLIAM ARNOLD, lawyer; b. Chgo., Jan. 6, 1906; s. Edgar Selic and Martha (Tolleson) P.; LL.B., Nat. U., 1929; J.D., George Washington U., 1968; m. Florence Oyler, Dec. 5, 1931. Admitted to D.C. bar, 1930, practiced in Washington; partner Robb, Porter, Kistler & Parkinson, 1946-69; counsel Dempsey & Koplovitz, 1969-70. Served as lt. comdr. USNR, 1942-45; asst. dir. telecommunication ODM, as presdl. adviser on telecommunications, 1953-54. Mem. Am. (ho. of dels. 1952, chmn. standing com. on communications 1954-56), D.C., Fed. Communications (pres. 1951) bar assns., Am. Judicature Soc., Sigma Nu Phi. Methodist. Mason. Club: University (Washington). Home: Bethesda, Md., Died Jan. 10, 1976; interred Orchard Mesa Cemetery, Grand Junction, Colo.

PORTER, WILLIAM LUTHER, lawyer, financial exec.; b. Washington, May 23, 1918; s. James A. and Anna (Foster) P.; B.S., Am. U., 1949, LL.B., 1954, J.D., 1968; m. Mae C. Hill, June 27, 1942. Accountant, auditor Smith & Davis, Washington, 1945-47; sr. partner Porter, Adams & Cramer, Washington, 1947-48; agt. Internal Revenue Service, Washington, 1948-59; sr. accountant M.B. Hariton & Co., Washington, 1959-66; commr. D.C. Pub. Service Commn., Washington, 1966-70; treas. Center for Community Change, Washington, 1970-72; prof. accounting Washington Tech. Inst., 1970-71; partner Lucas, Tucker & Co. C.P.A.'s, Washington, 1971-75. Financial adviser Jamaica Pub. Utilities Commn., Kingston, Jamaica, 1971-75; cons. Potomac Electric Power Co., 1973-75; v.p., gen. counsel Marine Services Ltd., 1973-75. Chmn. Southwest Neighborhood Assembly, Washington, 1968-70; mem. D.C. Mayor's Econ. Devel. Com.; vice chmn. D.C. Bd. Higher Edn.; bd. dirs. Washington Home Rule Com. Inc., Interracial Council Bus. Opportunity; bd. dirs. D.C. chpt. A.R.C. treas. Greater Washington Ednl. Telecommunications Assn. Mem. Democratic Central Com., 1964-66. Served with AUS, 1943-44. C.P.A., D.C. Mem. Am., D.C. (sec.) insts. C.P.A.'s, Washington Bar Assn., Am. Assn. U. Profs., Assn. Practicing C.P.A.'s, Urban League, Nat. Assn. Regulatory Utility Commrs., Internat. Platform Assn., Met. Washington Bd. Trade, Nat. Assn. State Bds. Accounting, Brookings Instn., Omega Psi Phi. Clubs: Pigskin; Prince Georges Country; Constant Spring Golf (Kingston, Jamaica). Home: Washington D.C. Died Jan. 1975.

POSEY, LEROY R., educator; b. La Grange, Tex., Feb. 17, 1880; s. Leroy and Mary (Swain) P.; grad. Tillotson Coll., 1906; A.B., Fisk U., 1914; student U. of Chicago, 1925-26; M.A., O. State U., 1930; m. Maymie Ethel Scott, Aug. 27, 1914; children—Dr. Leroy r., Jr., Carrie Lee (Mrs. Jackson), Cecil Constance. Prin. Attucks High Sch., Hopkinsville, Ky., 1914-19; head biology, dir. and examiner summer normals, Prairie View Coll., 1919-23; head mathematics, So. U., Baton Rouge, La., from 1923, dir. extension sch., 1926-37. Mem. Central Assn. Sci. and Math., Assn. Am. Inventors, La. Colored Teachers, Nat. Assn. A.C.P., Am. Teachers Assn. Republican. Baptist. Author (articles): A General Formula for Magic Squares, 1946; Some Fundamental Concepts of Common Fractions, 1941; How to Transform the Unit Circle into a Visual Aid Model, 1944; How to Introduce Algebra, 1947; An Easy Method of Deriving the Elementary 'Number Facts,' 1945. Home: Baton Rouge, La.†

POSSEL, RENÉ DE, mathematician; b. Marseilles, France, Feb. 7, 1905 s. Raoul and Marthe (Seignon) P.; ed. Ecole normale suérieure, Paris, France; Ph.D. agrégé; m. Yvonne Liberati, 1938; children—Yann, Maya, Daphné. Instr., Faculty of Sci. Marseilles, Clermont—Ferrand and Besancon; prof. differential and integral calculus at Besancon, later Clermont; prof. rational mechanics and analysis in Algiers; prof. numeric analysis at Paris; lectr. Paris Poly.; dir. Blaise—Pascal Inst., also Programming Inst.; pres. orgn. com. Internat. Calculus Center, Rome, Italy. Decorated officer Legion of Honor; several times laureate of Inst.; recipient prize Internat. Union Railroads. Author: Surfaces de Riemann et polygone fondamental de Poincaré; Dérivation abstraite des fonctions d'ensemble; Principes mathématiques de la mécanique classique; Bien—ordonnance effective de l'ensemble des parties d'un ensemble bien ordonne; Principe de Huyghens pour une onde electromagnetique. Home: Bourg—la—Reine, France. Died Feb. 26, 1974.

POST, CHARLES ADDISON, banker; b. Clinton, Conn., Sept. 25, 1886; s. Ezra Edward and Abbie (Bissell) P.; Ph.B., Brown U., 1910; D.S. in Bus. Adminstrn. (hon.), Bryant Coll., 1965; m. Jenny Jensen, June 14, 1941; children—Marcia (Mrs. Marcia Cammann), Katharine. Clk., Clinton Nat. Bank, 1910-14; asst. cashier Birmingham Nat. Bank, Derby, Conn., 1914-26; asst. sec. R.I. Hosp. Trust Co., Providence, 1926-34; pres. Citizens Savs. Bank, Providence, 1934-62, chmn. bd., 1962-73, trustee 1934-73; dir. Citizens Trust Co., Providence, 1934, chmn. bd., 1948-65. Trustee R.I. Pub. Expenditure Council. Hon. bd. dirs. World Affairs Council R.I. Mem. Mut. Savs. Banks Assn. R.I. (sec.-treas.), Nat. Assn. Mut. Savs. Banks (dir. 1940-67), Zeta Psi. Clubs: Agawam Hunt, Art, University (Providence). Home: Barrington R.I. Died Oct. 26, 1973.

POST, MARJORIE MERRIWEATHER, business woman, philanthropist; b. Springfield, Ill., Mar. 15, 1887; d. Charles William and Ella Letitia (Merriweather) Post; Litt.D., L.I. U., 1955; LL.D., Hobart and William Smith Coll., 1958; L.H.D., Bucknell U., 1962; m. Edward B. Close, Dec. 3, 1905; children—Adelaide (Mrs. Augustus Riggs IV), Eleanor (Mrs. Leon Barzin); m. 2d, Edward F. Hutton, July 7, 1920; 1 dau., Nedenia (Mrs. Clifford P. Robertson, III); m. 3d, Joseph E. Davies, Dec. 15, 1935 (div. 1955); m. 4th, Herbert A. May, June 18, 1958 (div. 1964). Owner, operator Postum Cereal Co., Ltd., Battle Creek, Mich., 1914-22; dir. Gen. Foods, 1936-58, dir. emeritus, 1958-73; dir. Nat. Savs. & Trust Co., Washington, 1959-73. Vice chmn. Emergency Unemployment Drive, N.Y.C., 1929-33; first v.p., mem. exec. com., dir. Nat. Symphony Orch. Assn.; mem. bd. Washington chpt. A.R.C. Hon. mem. bd. dirs. Good Samaritan Hosp., Palm Beach, Fla.; mem. arts edn. com. Nat. Cultural Center, Wash.; hon. trustee L.I. U.; 1st life trustee, 1st alumna trustee Mt. Vernon Sem., Washington. Decorated Legion of Honor (France); Order of Leopold, Order of Crown (Belgium); Order of Adolph de Nassau (Luxembourg); Order of Juan Pablo Duarte (Dominican Republic); Order of So. Cross (Brazil); recipient Am. Symphony Orch. League award, 1956, numerous citations for philanthropic activities. Mem. Colonial Dames Am., Soc. Daus. Founders and Patriots, D.A.R., Living Descs. of Blood Royal, Colonial Dames Am., James Towne Soc., Descs. Colonial Am. Clergy, Daus. Barons of Runnemede. Clubs: Garter Membership, Windsor Castle; Field (Greenwich, Conn.); Colony (N.Y.C.); Chevy Chase, Sulgrave (Washington); Everglades, Bath and Tennis, Seminole (Palm Beach, Fla.); Gulf Stream (Delray, Fla.). Home: Washington, D.C. Died Sept. 12, 1973.

POSTON, LAWRENCE SANFORD, JR., educator; b. Louisville, Feb. 27, 1902; s. Lawrence Sanford and Lucy Muriel (Gray) P.; grad. Louisville Boys High Sch., 1919; A.B., U. Louisville, 1923; A.M., Ind. U., 1926; Ph.D., U. Chgo., 1938; m. Nancy Wyatt Greene, July 28, 1928; 1 son, Lawrence Sanford. Acting instr. Spanish, Ind. U., 1924—26; asst. prof. modern langs., Furman U., 1926—30; asso. prof., 1930—33; research asso., U. Chgo., 1935—38; asst. prof. modern langs., Knox Coll., 1938—42, asso. prof., 1942—46, prof., 1946—48; prof. modern langs., U. Okla., 1948—74, chmn. dept. modern langs., 1949—57. Head Lang. Inst. Unit, Office of Edn., Washington, 1959—62. Corporal, Ky. N.G., 1920—23. Mem. Modern Lang. Assn. Am., Am. Assn. Tchrs. of Spanish and Portuguese, Am. Assn. Tchrs. French, Linguistic Soc. Am., A.A.U.P., Nat. Assn. R.R. Passengers, Am. Council Teaching Fgn. Langs. South Central Modern Lang. Assn. Democrat. Episcopalian. Author: French Syntax List, 1943; worked on Spanish Syntax List, 1937; on Tentative Dictionary of Medieval Spanish (Boggs, et al.), 1946; author: An Etymological Vocabulary to the Celestina, A—E (essential portion lithoprinted), 1940; (with others) Modern Spanish, 1960. Coordinator, co-author: Continuing Spanish, 1967. Contbr. scholarly jours. Winner trophy Ky. State Tennis Umpires championship. Home: Norman Okla. Died Oct. 14, 1974; buried Internat. Order Odd Fellows Cemetery, Norman, Okla.

POTRATZ, HERBERT AUGUST, educator, chemist; b. Sumner, Ia., July 2, 1902; s. August and Roslein (Schumacher) P.; student Crane Jr. Coll., 1924—26; B.S., U. Ill., 1928; M.S., U. Colo., 1931; Ph.D., 1935; m. Vivian Leone Miller, Oct. 1, 1942; children—Antoinette (Mrs. David B. Mathis), George August. Instr. Blackburn Coll., Carlinville, Ill., 1928—29; instr. U. Colo., 1929—42, asst. prof., 1938—42; research asso., sect. chief Manhattan Project, Chgo., 1942—44, group leader Los Alamos, 1944—46; asso. prof. chemistry Washington U., St. Louis, 1946—57, prof., 1958—71; prof. emeritus, asso. dean grad. sch. arts and sciences, 1971—75; cons. AEC, 1953—65. Fellow A.A.A.S., Am. Inst. Chemists; mem. Am. Chem. Soc., Am. Assn. U. Profs., Sigma Xi, Alpha Chi Sigma, Omicron Delta Kappa. Author research publs. in field. Home: St. Louis, Mo. Died Mar. 28, 1975; buried Oak Grove Cemetery, St. Louis County, Mo.

POTTER, CLARKSON, broker; b. Kansas City, Mo., Sept. 19, 1880; s. Henry S. and Margaret (Lionberger) P.; ed. pvt. schs., 1887-91, Smith Acad., 1891-94, St. Paul's Sch., Concord, N.H., 1894-97; A.B., Yale, 1901; m. Amy Holland, June 21, 1902. With Mississippi Valley Trust Co., St. Louis, 1901-04, bond dept. Mercantile Trust Co., Mar.-Sept. 1904; at St. Louis, with F. S. Moseley & Co., of Boston, commercial paper, 1904-08; v.p. W.R. Compton Bond & Mortgage Co., from 1908. Chmn. liberty loan city campaign, St. Louis, 1917; apptd. asst. dir. War Loan Organization by Sec. McAdoo, Jan. 1918. Mem. Business Men's League, Civic League, Episcopalian. Clubs: Noonday, St. Louise Country, Racquet, City (St. Louis); University (Chicago); Yale (New York). Home: St. Louis, Mo.†

POTTS, ROY C., marketing cons.; b. Washington, Mich., May 21, 1881; s. John C. and Mattie (Hart) P.; B.S., Michigan. Agrl. Coll., 1906; m. Helen M. Mittendorf, Feb. 16, 1910; children—Glenna Irene, Chester Marshall, Gertrude Jean. Prof. of dairying, Okla. Agrl. and Mech. Coll., Stillwater, Okla., 1906-15; chief div. dairy and poultry products, Food Distbn. Adminstrn., U.S. Dept. Agr., 1915-43. Mng. dir. Roy C. Potts Assn.; pres. and treas., Indsl. Royalties, Inc., Universal Box Handle Corp. Mem. American Marketing Assn., National Grange, Alpha Zeta. Author various bulletins on marketing dairy products. Address: Washington, D.C.†

POULOS, RALEIGH ANEST, shopping center exec.; b. Galveston, Tex., Aug. 8, 1922; s. Anastasio Pete and Christine (Kalaboukidou) P.; student pub. sch.; m. Martha Panagos, Oct. 19, 1968. Mgr. D. Masus & Sons, Monroe La., 1945-52; gen. mgr. Palais Royal, specialty stores, Houston, 1952-67; gen. mgr., partner Town and Country Village, Houston, 1967-75; partner Moody, Moody, Poulos, 1974-75. Commr. Housing Authority, Monroe, 1950-52. Mem. bd. devel. YMCA, Houston, 1963-67. Served with AUS, 1942-45. Mem. Tex. Retail Fedn., C. of C. Mem. Greek Orthodox Ch. Home: Houston, Tex. Died Feb. 23, 1975.

POWELL, LYMAN THEODORE, JR., lawyer; b. Superior, Wis., Nov. 18, 1902; s. Lyman Theodore and Eleanor (McCord) P.; grad. Phillips Exeter Acad., 1923; B.A., Yale, 1927; LL.B., U. Wis., 1929; m. Alice Josephine Creber, Nov. 28, 1929; children—Lyman Theodore III, Frances (Mrs. William H. Perry, Jr.). Admitted to Wis. bar, 1929; asst. to U.S. atty. Western Dist. Wis., 1930-33; partner firm Powell, Sprowls & Gee, Superior, 1933—. Pres. Gitche Gummee council Boy Scouts Am., 1949-52, vice chmn. region 10, 1952-60, chmn. region 10, 1960-63, mem. nat. exec. bd., 1960-63, mem. coms. nat. exec. bd., 1960—. Dir. 1st Nat. Bank Superior, Wis. Bd. dirs. Mont du Lac Ski Area; dir. Nat. and Wis. div. Am. Automobiel Assn. Recip. Silver Beaver award, 1952, Silver Antelope award, 1956. Mem. Am., Wis., Douglas bar assns., Superior Assn. Commerce, Chi Psi, Phi Delta Phi. Republican. Conglist. (past dir.). Club: Kitchi Gammi (Duluth, Minn.). Home: Superior, Wis., Died Apr. 4, 1974.

POWELL, RALPH LORIN, educator; b. Salt Lake City, Jan. 31, 1917; s. Milton Leaver and Harriet (Richinson) P.; S.B., U. Ida., 1938; B.A. (Levi Strauss scholar 1939-40), U. Cal., 1940; certificate Cal. Coll. in China, 1944; M.A. (John Harvard fellow 1948-50), Harvard, 1950, Ph.D., 1953; m. Helena Finch, Apr. 6, 1942. Lectr., then asst. prof. Princeton, 1950-54; prof. Nat. War Coll., 1954-56, 58-61; counselor embassy for pub. affairs Am. embassy, Taipei, 1957-58; prof. Far Eastern internat. relations Sch. Internat. Service, Am. U., 1960-75, chmn. profl. programs sub-faculty, 1963-64, chmn. internat. representation program, 1965; vis. prof., Sch. Advanced Internat. Studies, 1969; mem. bd. cons., Nat. War Coll., 1966-68; cons. Dept. State, 1963-75, mem. adv. com. on China, 1966-69; cons. Inst. for Def. Analyses, 1969-75; cons. Research Analysis Corp., 1964-72, vis. prof., project dir. for Communist China; mem. research council, Center for Strategic and Internat. Studies, 1972. Trustee Princeton in Asia, 1954-60. Served to maj. USMCR, 1941-48. Decorated Order of Brilliant Star with spl. cravat (Republic of China). Ford Found. grantee, 1964-65. Mem. Internat. Inst. for Strategic Studies, Washington Inst. Fgn. Affairs, Am. Polit. Sci. Assn., Assn. Asian Studies, Ret. Officers Assn., First Marine Div. Assn., Phi Beta Kappa. Author: The Rise of Chinese Military Power, 1895-1912, 1955; Politico-Military Relationships in Communist China, 1963. Contbr. articles profl. jours. Home: McLean, Va. Died May 22, 1975; buried Arlington Nat. Cemetery, Arlington, Va.

POWELL, RAY E., business exec.; b. Tablegrove, Ill., Dec. 7, 1887; s. Joseph D. and Sarah E. (Anderson) P.; student Monmouth (Ill.) Coll.; U. Ill.; LL.D., Laval U. (Que.), 1949, McGill U., 1956; D.Sc., Monmouth (Ill.) Coll., 1955. Sr. v.p., dir. Aluminum, Ltd.; pres. Aluminum Co. of Can., Ltd., 1937-57; dir. Dominion Bridge Co., Bell Telephone Co. of Can., Bank of Montreal, Royal Trust Co. Gov. McGill U., Montreal Gen. Hosp. Served as capt., U.S. Army, 1917-19. Home: Montreal, Can. Deceased 1973.

POWELL, WILSON MARCY, educator; b. Litchfield, Conn., July 18, 1903; s. Wilson Marcy and Elsie (Knapp) P.; grad. St. George's Sch., Newport, R.I., 1922; A.B., Harvard, 1926, Ph.D., 1933; m. Fredrika Richardson, Oct. 25, 1930; children—Wilson Marcy, David Richardson, Fredrika (Mrs. James A. Spillman); m. 2d, Dorothy Gardner Powell, June 29, 1956; 1 dau., Claire (Mrs. William N. Bove). Asst. in physics Harvard, 1929-30, 34-35; instr. Conn. Coll., 1935-37; asst. prof. Kenyon Coll., 1937-46: research asso. Radiation Lab., U. Cal., Berkeley, 1942-46, asso. prof. physics, 1946-52, prof., 1952-71, emeritus, 1971-74. Mem. Swarthmore eclipse expdn., Mexico, 1923, Sumatra, 1925; dir. Kenyon Coll. cosmic ray expdn., 1940, 41. Fellow Woods Hole Oceanographic Inst., 1937; Guggenheim fellow, 1941-42. Fellow Am. Phys. Soc., N.Y. Acad. Sci. Home: Berkeley, Cal. Died Mar. 2, 1974; interred Sunset View Cemetery, El Cerrito, Cal.

POWELSON, ABRAM JAMES, lumber co. exec.; b. Fairview, Ill., Dec. 17, 1893; s. Abram Messler and Margaret Miller (Davis) P.; A.B., Knox Coll., 1915; m. Esther Grattan Mayes, Nov. 24, 1917; children—Nancy (Mrs. Frank L. McCormick), James S. Auditor J.C. Simpson Lumber Co., Galesburg, Ill., 1915-19; v.p. Simpson-Powelson Lumber Co., Galesburg, 1920-37, exec. v.p., 1938-47, pres., 1947-60, chmn. bd., 1961-68, chmn. exec. com., 1969-74; dir. First Nat. Bank, Sterling, Ill. Trustee Knox Coll., 1946-74. Served to capt. U.S. Army, 1917-19. Mem. Sterling C. of C. (treas. 1940), Beta Theta Pi, Delta Sigma Rho. Republican. Conglist. Elk, Rotarian. Clubs: Dairymen's Country (Chgo.); Soangetaha Country (Galesburg). Home: Galesburg, Ill. Died Mar. 17, 1974.

POWER, ETHEL B., writer; b. Marblehead, Mass., Apr. 23, 1881; d. Stephen W. and Jennie D. (Chinn) Power; prep. edn., Walnut Hill Sch., Natick, Mass.; grad. Cambridge Sch. of Architecture and Landscape Architecture, 1919. Editor House Beautiful (mag.), Sept. 1921-Dec. 1933. Club: Cosmopolitan (New York). Author: The Smaller American House, 1927.†

POWER, THOMAS S., air force ofcr. B. N.Y.C., June 18, 1905; s. Thomas S. and Mary (Rice) P. Entered service, 1928; grad. A. C. Primary Flying Sch., 1928. Advanced Flying Sch., 1929; LL.D., U. Akron, 1963, Creighton University, 1964, Saint Mary's College, 1964; married to Mae Ayre, Apr. 3, 1936. Commd. 2d lt. advanced through grades to gen. USAF, 1957; pilot N. Africa, Italy, 1942—43; comdr. 314th bomb wing 21st Bomb Command, 1944—45; asst. chief staff operations U.S. Strategic Air Forces, 1945; asst. dep. task force comdr. for air Operation Crossroads, Bikini Atoll, 1946; dep. asst. chief air staff operations USAF hdqrs., 1947; vice comdr. SAC, 1948—54; comdr. air reserach and devel. command, 1954—57; comdr.—in—chief SAC, Offutt AFB, Neb., 1957—64, dir. Joint Strategic Target Planning Staff, 1960—64, dir. Joint Strategic Target Planning Staff, 1960—64; retired, 1964; vice chmn. bd. Eversharp, Inc.; dir. Hedge Fund of Am., Inc., Summit Capital Fund, Inc., Bucyrus—Erie, Inc. Decorated Distinguished Service medal (2), Silver Star, Legion of lferit with oak leaf cluster, D.F.C., Bronze Star Medal, Air Medal with oak leaf cluster, Commendation Ribbon with one cluster, Croix de Guerre with palm; recipient H. H. Arnold award Air Force Assn., 1959; named Knight St. Sylvester with grand cross by Pope Paul, 1964. Author: Design for Survival, 1965. Home: Palm Desert, Cal. Died Dec. 7, 1970; interred Arlington (Va.) Nat. Cemetery.

POWERS, LEONARD STEWART, educator; b. Mayodan, N.C., Jan. 5, 1919; s. Charles Jesse, Sr., and Nanny Mae (Stewart) P.; A.B., Duke, 1940, LL.M. with distinction, 1956; J.D. with honors, U. N.C., 1950; m. Carmen Bunn, Nov. 28, 1957; children—Richard Lee, Leonard Stewart, Laurie Josephine. Admitted to N.C. bar, 1950; practiced in Reidsville, 1950-53; prof. law Wake Forest U., 1950-55; adminstrv. asst. to Chief Justice of N.C., 1955-56; prof. law U. N.C., 1956-57, U. Fla., 1957, asso. dean Coll. Law, 1966-71. Exec. sec. N.C. Commn. Higher Edn., 1954-55; chmn. Southeastern Conf. of Assn. Am. Law Schs., 1967; mem. Fla. Commn. Capital Punishment, 1963-65; reporter for Revision of Fla. Wrongful Death Laws, 1968-70. Mem. Human Relations Adv. Bd. Gainesville, 1966-68. Served with USAAF, 1942-46. Named outstanding faculty mem., U. Fla. Coll. Law, 1966. Mem. Am., N.C. bar assns., Bar Assn. 8th Jud. Circuit Fla., U. Fla. Law Center Assn. (sec.), Order of Coif, Phi Delta Phi (nat. council). Democrat. Episcopalian. Home: Gainesville, Fla. Died Mar. 25, 1972.

POWERS, SUE MCFALL, educator; b. Clarksville, Tenn., March 28, 1878; d. Samuel Barney and Mary E. (Williamson) Powers; B.S., Peabody Coll., 1921; student, U. of Va., U. of Tenn.; D. Litt. (hon.), Southwestern Coll., 1930; unmarried. Teacher, Tenn. elementary schs., 1904; principal, Whitehaven (Tenn.) High Sch., 1910-22; supt. Shelby Co. (Tenn.) schs. from 1922. Chmn. internat. relations of Tenn. Congress, Parent Teachers Assn.; chmn. Nat. Council of Adminstrative Women in Education; member State Board of Education, 1924-30. Mem. Pub. School Officers Assn., Am. Assn. Univ. Women. Delegate to Internat. Assn. of Ednl. Assns., Oxford, Eng., 1935. Democrat. Methodist. Home: Memphis, Tenn.*†

POWERS, WILLIAM T(HOMAS), clergyman, coll. dean, biologist; b. Chgo., Feb. 28, 1911; s. William Patrick and Margaret (Touhy) P.; A.B., St. Mary's Sem., Perryville, Mo., 1933, A.M., 1938; B.S., De Paul U., 1940, M.S., 1941; Ph.D., Princeton, 1947. Entered Congregation of the Mission, 1930; ordained priest Roman Catholic Ch., 1938; instr. De Paul U., 1938, Princeton U., 1943-44; chmn. biology dept. De Paul U., since 1947, dean of the Univ. Coll., 1951-55, dean liberal arts, 1955-62, mem. bd. trustees, 1948-74, mem. U. Council, 1948-74; dean of studies St. John's Coll., 1962-74. Fellow A.A.A.S., N.Y. Acad. Sci., Am. Assn. Univ. Profs., Nat. Cath. Ednl. Assn., Sigma Xi. Club: Princeton (Chgo.). Home: Perryville, Mo. Died Sept. 23, 1974.

POWNALL, CHARLES ALAN, naval officer; b. Alglen, Pa., Oct. 4, 1887; s. Howard and Louisa (Walter) P.; grad. U.S. Naval Acad., 1910, M.S., 1917; naval aviator, Naval Aviation Sch., Pensacola, Fla., 1927; post grad. student Columbia, 1917; m. Mary Chenoweth, June 1, 1912; 1 dau., Louisa. Commd. ensign, U.S. Navy, 1910, advancing through the grades to rear adm. (permanent), 1942; with rank of capt. comd. U.S.S. Enterprise, Dec. 1938—March 1941; comd. carrier task force during initial operations in Central Pacific; served as Comdr. Air Forces Pacific Fleet, Jan.—Aug. 1944. Chief of Naval Air Training, Naval Air Training Bases, Pensacola, Fla.; gov. Guam 1946—49. Decorated Navy Cross, World War 1; Distinguished Service Medal and commendations ribbon, World War 11. Mason (3°). Clubs: Army and Navy (Washington, D.C.); Army—Navy Country (Arlington, Va.). Address: San Diego, Cal. Died July 20, 1975.

POYNTER, JULIET JAMESON, educator; b. Shelbyville, Ky., Feb. 19, 1881; d. Rev. Wiley Taul and Clara (Martin) Poynter; grad. Science Hill Sch., Shelbyville, Ky., 1900; A.B., Wellesley Coll., 1905; unmarried. Teacher of math., Science Hill Sch., 1905-07, asso. prin. 1905-37, prin., 1937-39. Mem. bd. of vis. Centre Coll., Danville, Ky., 1931-58, mem. bd. trustees, 1949-58; bd. trustees Scarritt Coll. for Christian Workers, 1948-57; mem. Bd. Edn. Ky. Conf. of Meth. Ch., 1939-49, mem. bd. Christian social relations, 1956-60; mem. commn. on secondary schs. Southern Assn. Colls. and Secondary Sch., 1927-37, Ky. Assn. Colls. and Secondary Schs., 1937-40. Mem. Bd. Missions and Ch. Extension of Meth. Ch., 1948-52, mem. Woman's Div. Christian Service, 1948-52. mem. Jurisdictional Council Meth. Ch., 1944-49, 53-57; chmn. bd. King's Daus. Hosp. (Shelbyville), 1941-43. Mem. bd. trustees Lincoln Found. of Lincoln Inst., 1947-66. Mem. Am. Assn. U. Women (dir. southeast central sect. 1916-17; v.p. Kentucky div. 1938-40), Ky. Assn. Deans Women (v.p. 1938-40), Ky. Council on Human Relations (exec. com. 1954-58, vice chmn. exec. com. 1954-56, dir., 1954-60), So. Regional Council, Nat. Assn. of Prins. Schs. for Girls (v.p. S. Sec. 1927-30, 34-35), Nat. Assn. Deans of Women. Wellesley Coll. Alumnae Assn., Y.W.C.A. Omen. field com. 1907-19; mem. Ky. state com. 1921-32). Phi Sigma. Republican. Methodist. Club: Arts (Louisville). Home: Shelbyville Ky. Died Nov. 4, 1974.

PRACHT, CHARLES FREDERICK, congressman; b. Pitman, Schuylkill County, Pa., Oct. 20, 1880; ed. pub. schs.; asso. in toy novelty and notions business, 1897-14; children's agt. and investigator in county commrs. office, 1915-29; served in dept. of accounts under the clerk of Quarters Sessions, 1930-31; personal property assessor in Bd. of Revision Dept., 1932-42; mem. Republican Exec. Ward Com. for 35 yrs., chmn. 26 consecutive yrs.; v.p., Thirty-third Rep. Club. Mem. 78th Congress (1943-45), 5th dist. Pa. Republican. Mason. Home: Philadelphia, Pa.†

PRATT, HAROLD IRVING, investment mgr.; b. Bklyn., Feb. 8, 1904; s. Harold Irving and Harriet (Barnes) P.; grad. Groton Sch., 1922; A.B., Harvard, 1926, M.B.A., 1929, LL.D., 1960; posgrad. Trinity Coll., Cambridge Eng., 1926-27; LL.D., Pratt Inst., 1968; m. Ellen Rice Hallowell, June 10, 1929; children—Harriet P. (Mrs. John B. Morris), Margaret (Mrs. Richard H. Cardozo), Ellen (Mrs. George Stoia), Harold. Clk. City Bank Farmers Trust Co., N.Y.C., 1929-31; jr. exec. Charles Pratt & Co., 1931-36, partner, 1946-75; asst. sec. U.S. Trust Co. N.Y., 1936-41; chmn. bd. Wall Street Growth Fund, Inc., 1955-73, dir., 1946-73, Pres., dir. Community Hosp., Glen Cove, 1946-61; chmn. trustees Pratt Inst., 1959-66; overseer Harvard, 1960-66; trustee Groton Sch., 1957-70, trustee Marine Hist. Assn. Served to lt. comdr. USNR, 1941-45. Decorated Bronze Star medal combat V (U.S.); Croix de Guerre withbronze star (France). Republican. Episcopalian (vestry). Clubs: Down Town Assn. (trustee), Harvard, Racquet and Tennis, N.Y. Yacht, Cruising of Am. (N.Y.C.); Piping Rock, Sewanhaka Corinthian Yacht (L.I.) Home: Oyster Bay, N.Y., Died Nov. 3, 1975.

PRATT, JOHN L., senior consultant Lend-Lease Adminstrn.; formerly exec. v.p. Gen. Motors; apptd. mem. Productions Planning Bd., Feb. 1941; now senior consultant Lend-Lease Adminstrn. Home: Raleigh Hotel. Address: Washington, D.C., Died Dec. 20, 1975.*

PRATT, STEVE, educator; b. Los Angeles, Feb. 16, 1917; s. George and Grace (Haines) P.; B.A. in Psychology, U. Cal. at Los Angeles, 1940; M.A. in Edn.,

Purdue U., 1952, Ph.D. in Clin. Psychology, 1952; m. Rita Stevenage, May 1, 1953; children—Keila (Mrs. Marty Hittelman), Yvonne, Leila, Steve. Dir. Guidance Center, U.S. Civil Service, 1946-49; clin. and research fellow Purdue U., 1950-52; dir psychol. services Larned (Kan.) State Hosp., 1953-61, 64-65, supt., 1962-63; supt. (and 1st psychologist to become one) Jacksonville (Ill.) State Hosp., 1966-70; prof. community psychology U. Wichita, 1970-73; cons. lectr. in field. Mem. Gov. Kan. Council State-Wide Mental Health Planning, 1963-65. Bds. dirs. Jacksonville Area Comprehensive Health Planning Coun., Arts Council Jacksonville, Inter-Agy. Council (Jacksonville). Served with AUS, 1943-46. Mem. Jacksonville C. of C. (bd. dirs.), Am. Psychiat. Assn. (1st place achievement award 1960), Kan. (pres. 1963-64), Ill., Midwestern psychol. assns., Soc. Psychol. Study Social Issues, Sigma Xi. Author: Action Psychology, 1964; Contract-System Psychology, 1964. Contbr. profl. jours. Home: Wichita Kan. Died July 28, 1973.

PRATT, WALTER MERRIAM, b Prattville, Chelsea, Mass., July 13, 1880; s. Hermon W. and Emily Frances (Merriam) P.; student Bellingham High Sch., Chelsea; grad. Noble Sch., Boston, 1899; m. Marietta Harkness, Apr. 6, 1914 (dec. 1931); m. 2d, Irene S. Whitty, Dec. 16, 1938. With Train Smith Co., paper mfrs., Boston, 1899; founder, 1907, ofcl. until 1923, Denison—Pratt Paper Co.; organizer, 1923, since pres. Pratt Paper Co.; pres. Boston Acceptance Corp. Mem. Progressive State Committee, Mass., 1912; del. Republican Nat. Conv., 1916. Mem. corp. Adams Nervine Hosp.; trustee Theodore Roosevelt Asso. New York; dir. Soldiers and Sailors Club; v.p. Asso. Vets. Assn. Member cav., Mass. N.G., 1905—07, F.A., 1907—09, 2d lt. inf., 1909—11, later capt.; capt. mil. intelligence div., Gen. Staff, U.S. Army, 1918—19; lt. col., 1919. Fellow Royal Soc. Arts (England); mem. N.E. Historic Geneal. Soc. (pres. 1948—54), Gen. Soc. Mayflower Descs. (gov. gen. 1948—54), Soc. Colonial Wars (gov. gen. 1954—57), other geneal. and hist. socs. and assns., civic groups, community orgns. Republican. Conglist. Mason (Shriner). Clubs: Union, Boston Authors (Boston); Republican; Army and Navy (Washington); Sojourners (trustee) Badminton and Tennis. Author: The Burning of Chelsea, 1908; Tin Soldiers, 1912; Yearbook Military Order World Wars, 1923—25; Seven Generations, 1930; Adventure in Vermont, 1943; House of Edward Winslow, 1948; John Hancock and His Time, 1956. Home: Brattleboro Vt. Died Sept. 26, 1973.

PRESS, OTTO, clergyman, editor; b. Francesville, Ind., Apr. 21, 1880; s. Rev. G. and Julia (Guenther) P.; grad. Elmhurst (Ill.) Coll., 1898; grad. Eden Theol. Sem., Webster Groves, Mo., 1901; m. Laura Irion, Sept. 12, 1905; children—Minna (dec.), Ernst, Laura, Otto. Ordained ministry Evang. Synod of N.A., 1901; pastor Friedens Ch., Gay Hill, Tex., 1901-05, Immanuel Ch., Sedalia, Mo., 1905-09; asst. pastor St. Paul's Ch., St. Louis, 1909-22; editor Friedensbote from 1922. Pres. Mo. Dist., Evang. Synod of N.A., 1919-21. Home: St. Louis, Mo.†

PRESTON, ROBERT LOUIS, physician; b. Howells, Neb., Aug. 5, 1904; s. Sylvester A. and Clara Ellen (Bonine) P.; M.D., U. Neb., 1928; m. Sidney Kennedy Field, Dec. 15, 1972. Intern, L.I. Coll. Hosp., Bklyn., 1928-29; asst. to Dr. Fred Albee, 1930-35; attending orthopedic surgeon N.Y.U. Hosp., Bellevue Hosp. Manhattan VA Hosp., Doctors Hosp., Columbus Hosp.; cons. orthopedic surgeon Goldwater Meml. Hosp., Holy Name Hosp., Inst. Phys. Medicine and Rehab.; clin. prof. orthopedic surgery N.Y.U. Postgrad. Med. Sch. Served to lt. col., M.C., AUS, 1942-46. Decorated Legion of Merit. Diplomate Am. Bd. Orthopaedic Surgery. Fellow A.C.S.; mem. A.M.A., Am. Acad. Orthopaedic Surgeons, Am. Rheumatism Assn., N.Y. Rheumatic Assn. (pres. 1954-55). The Surgical Management of Rheumatoid Arthritis, 1969. Contbr. numerous articles to med. jours. Home: New York City, N.Y., Died Nov. 5, 1974; buried Woodlawn Cemetery.

PREVOST, CLIFFORD ALFRED, pub. relations counsel; b. London, Canada, Nov. 9, 1898; s. Napoleon Joseph and Mary Elizabeth (Taylor) P.; student pub. and high schs., London, Ont., Can., 1905-15; came to U.S., 1920, naturalized, 1926; m. Adelaide Harriet Forsythe, Sept. 27, 1922; children—Corinne Adelaide, Arthur Corty. Reporter, London (Ont.) Free Press, 1915-18; reporter, Border Cities Star, Windsor, Can., 1918; city editor, London (Ont.) Advertiser, 1919; with Detroit Free Press, 1920-44, Washington corr., from 1933; Washington corr., Miami Herald and Akron Beacon Journal, from 1939. Mem. Overseas Writers Assn., White House Correspondents Assn. Mason. Club: Nat. Press of Washington (pres. 1942). Home: Armonk, N.Y., Died Jan. 26, 1976.

PREWITT, ETHAN C., lawyer; b. Crawfordsville, Ind., Jan. 17, 1903; A.B., Wabash Coll., 1924; LL.B., U. Mich., 1927. Admitted to Mich. bar, 1937; mem. firm Clark, Klein, Winter, Parsons & Prewitt, Detroit. Asst. atty. gen. Mich., 1938. Mem. Am., Detroit bar assns., State Bar Mich. Address: Detroit, Mich. Died 1971.

PRICE, CHRISTOPHER HERBERT, chemist; b. Wigan Lancashire, Eng., Mar. 8, 1908; s. Frederick and Helena (Naylor) P.; Ph.C., Wigan Mining and Tech. Coll., 1931; F.P.S., F.R.I.C., Manchester U., 1956; m. Diana Blanche Jackson, July 16, 1938; children—Christopher Boyce Vernon, Peter Barry Vernon. Chemist, Parke Davis & Co., London, Eng., 1934—42; lectr. Plymouth Poly. Inst., Eng., 1942—46, Tech. Coll., Port Elizabeth, S. Africa, 1946—56; prof. Rhodes U., Grahamstown, S. Africa, 1956—72. Chmn., Albany Essential Oils Pty. Ltd. Mem. S. African Drug Control Council. Bd. dirs. S. African Pharmacy. Chmn. United party Br., Grahamstown. Mem. Internat. Acad. for History Pharmacy, Pharm. Soc. S. Africa (hon. life, pres. 1956), S. African Pharmacological Soc. Rotarian (pres. Grahamstown br. 1973-74). Sci. editor: South African Pharm. Jour. Contbr. articles to profl. Jours. Home: Grahamstown, Republic of South Africa. Died Dec. 19, 1974; interred Grahamstown, Republic of South Africa.

PRICE, FRANK WILSON, clergyman; b. Kashing, Che., China, Feb. 25, 1895 (parents Am. missionaries); s. Philip Francis and Esther Eckard (Wilson) P.; A.B., Davidson Coll., 1915, D.D., 1940; postgrad. Southeastern U., Nanking, China., 1917-18, Hartford (Conn.) Theol. Sem., 1919-20; B.D., Yale, 1922, Ph.D., 1938; M.A., Columbia, 1923; m. Essie Ott McClure, June 14, 1923; children—Mary Virginia (Mrs. Raymond Edsel Miller), Frank Wilson. prin., Hillcrest Sch., Nanking, China, 1915-17; sec. YMCA, Nanking, 1917-18; sec. Chinese Labor Corps in France, 1918-19; ordained to ministry Presbyn. Church, 1922; missionary Presbyn. Ch., China, 1923-52; prof. Nanking Theol. Sem., 1923-52, head, West China unit, 1939-45; prof. Hanchow Christian U., West China Union U.; missionary sec. Ch. of Christ in China, 1948-50; pastor New Monmouth Ch., Lexington, Va., 1953-55; dir. Missionary Research Library, N.Y.C., 1956-61, also adj. prof. missions Union Theol. Sem., and research sec. Div. Fgn. Missions, Nat. Council Chs. of Christ in U.S., 1956-61; prof. internat. studies Mary Baldwin Coll., 1961-66; moderator Gen. Assembly, Presbyn. Church in U.S., 1953-54. Mem. Chinese del. Life and Work Conf., Oxford U., 1937, Internat. Missionary Conf., Madras, India, 1938, Whitby, Can., 1947; asst. to Chinese del., Orgn. Conf. UN, San Francisco, 1945. Active war relief work West China, 1939-45, chmn. liaison group, Chungking, China, 1944-45. Decorated for wartime service Nat. govt. China, 1945. Mem. Assn. Asian Studies, Phi Beta Kappa, Sigma Upsilon. Rotarian. Author: (Chinese and English) Religion and Character in Christian Middle Schools of China, 1929, China Rediscovers Her West, 1939, We Went to West China, 1943, The Rural Church in China, 1938 and 1948, As the Lightning Flashes, 1948, China-Twilight or Dawn?, 1948, Chinese Christian Hymns (trans.), 1953, Marx Meets Christ, 1957. Translator: Sun Yat-sen's Three Principles of The People, 1927, Chiang Kai-shek's Wartime Messages, 1944. others. Home: Lexington Va. Died Jan. 9, 1974.

PRICE, GRANVILLE, educator; b. Dodge, Tex., May 25, 1906; s. Francis Monroe and Florence (Grubbs) P.; B.A., U. Tex., 1926. M.A., 1930; student New Sch. Social Research, 1935, U. Minn., 1939-40; Ph.D., U. Mo., 1954; m. Katherine A. Ramsey, Apr. 14, 1938 (dec.); 1 son, James (dec.); m. 2d, Eleanor Anglin, Aug. 9, 1968. Reporter, city editor Galveston (Tex.) News, 1925-29, Austin (Tex.) American, 1928; copyreader N.Y. Herald Tribune, 1930-33, 35, 37; asst. prof. journalism U. Tex., 1933-44, asso. prof., 1944-53; prof., chmn. dept. journalism U. Ida., 1954-62; prof. journalism No. Ill. U., DeKalb, 1962-74. Dir. Suburban Press Research Center, 1966-74. Mem. Assn. Edn. Journalism, Am. Assn. U. Profs., Sigma Delta Chi, Kappa Tau Alpha, Pi Sigma Alpha, Alpha Kappa Delta. Kiwanian. Home: DeKalb Ill. Died May 2, 1974.

PRICE, HENRY VERNON, educator; b. Keswick, Ia., Feb. 23, 1910; s. Henry Marten and Edna (Higgins) P.; B.A., U. Ia., 1931, Ph.D., 1940; M.S., Northwestern U., 1935; m. Mary Margaret Slate, Apr. 1, 1934; children—John Martin, Robert Vernon, Margaret Ann. Tchr. math. pub. schs., Calumet City, Ill., 1931-34; tchr. math. Univ. High Sch., Iowa City, 1934-40, head dept., 1940; from instr. to prof. dept. math. U. Ia., 1940. Vis. prof. U. Mich., summer 1952, U. Cal. at Los Angeles, summer 1955. Mem. Nat. (pres. 1970), Ia. (past pres.) councils tchrs. math., Central Assn. Sci. and Math. Tchrs. (pres. 1953-54), Conf. Bd. Math. Scis., Math. Assn. Am., N.E.A., Phi Beta Kappa, Sigma Xi, Phi Delta Kappa. Methodist (trustee). Rotarian. Author: (with L.A. Knowler) Basic Skills in Mathematics, 1952; (with P. Peak, P.S. Jones) Mathematics, An Intergrated Series, Books I and II, 1965, Book III, 1966, Book IV, 1967. Home: Iowa City, Ia. Died June 4, 1973.

PRICE, J. ST. CLAIR, educator; b. Barbados, B.W.I., Nov. 16, 1888; s. Jacob and Sarah Ann (Spooner) P.; brought to U.S., 1906; B.A., Lincoln U., 1912; U. Mich., 1917; Ed.M., Harvard, 1927, Ed.D., 1940; m. Maude Edeeta Jones, Nov. 25, 1916. Prin. Adams St. Sch., Ypsilanti, Mich., 1917—18; tchr. edn. W.Va. Collegiate Inst., 1920—23; head dept. edn. W.Va. State Coll., 1923—30; asso. prof. edn. Howard U., 1930—40, prof. from 1940, dir. summer sch., 1940—43, asso. dean coll. liberal arts, dir. evening school, 1942—43, dean, 1943—56, emeritus. Mem. ednl. survey com. W. Va. State Bd. Edn., 1927; pres. Ann Arbor (Mich.) br. Nat. Assn. Advancement Colored People, 1919—20. Mem. Nat. Assn. Study Negro Life and History (life), A.A.A.S., Am. Assn. Sch. Administrs., Soc. Advancement Edn., Am. Assn. U. Profs., Am. Statis. Assn., Am. Coll. Personnel Assn., N.E.A. (planning com. nat. com. vets. edn., 1946). Author articles profl. jours. Home: Bronx, N.Y. Died Apr. 10, 1975.

PRICE, JOHN ROY, govt. ofcl.; b. Mt. Hope, W.V.a, June 15, 1900; s. John Milton and Roselia (Morton) P.; B.S., W.Va. Wesleyan Coll., 1923, D.Sc., 1948; grad. student Marshall Coll., Columbia; fellow Mellon Inst. Indsl. Research, U. Pitts., 1930-31; LL.D., Parsons Coll., 1956; m. Pauline Bernice Milnes, June 30, 1931; children—John Roy, Pauline Ellen. Research chemist vinyl plastics Union Carbide Corp., 1928-31, product development, tech. sales, 1931-39, tech. liaison to govt. war def. agys., 1939-44, div. mgr., 1944-53, merchandising mgr., 1953-58; asst. dir. resources and prodn. Office Civil and Def. Moblzn., Exec. Office of the Pres., 1958-75, chmn. com. specialized personnel, emergency resources adv. com., telecommunications adv. bd.; U.S. rep. indsl. planning com. NATO; mem. Civil and Def. Moblzn. Bd.; liaison rep. Exec. Office of the Pres. to Nat. Indsl. Conf. Bd. Pres. Pine Grove Farms, Chariton, Ia., 1962-75. Pres. bd. edn., Manhasset, trustee, Mayor 1956-58; Munsey Park, 1962-70 Trustee W.Va., Wesleyan Coll., 1948-73, pres. bd. trustees, 1969-73, also chmn. long-range planning com.; trustee Chatham Coll., Study for Presidency, 1971-75. Recipient silver award Soc. Plastics Industry, 1959; adv. council Grinnell Coll. Mem. Soc. Plastics Industry, Laymen's Movement for Christian World, Nassau Council Christian Chs., Nat. Football Found. Omicron Delta Kappa. Conglist. Clubs: Port Washington (L.I.) Yacht; Chemists (N.Y.). Home: Manhasset, N.Y., Died June 15, 1975; buried Chariton, Ia.

PRICE, VIOLA MILLRON (MRS. EDMUND GLEN PRICE), church woman; b. Troutville, Pa., June 22, 1901; d. Perry and Virgie (Dunlap) Milliron; student Carion State Coll., 1919—21, Pa. State U., 1922; L.H.D., Thiel Coll., 1969; m. Edmund Glen Price, June 24, 1923; children—Jean Marie (Mrs. William Littell, Jr.), Virginia Lou (Mrs. Russell E. Morgan). Pres. central conf. Ohio, Womens Missionary Soc., 1943—44, recording sec. Pitts. synod, 1950—52, promotion sec., 1952—54, v.p., 1954—57; pres. Pitts. synod United Lutheran Ch. Women, 1958—60, life membership sec. nat. orgn., 1952—55, adminstrv. com., 1955—62, pres., 1962—68, bd. mgrs. exec. com., 1964—67; exec. council Luth. Ch. Am., 1968—72; nat. com. Luth. World Fedn.; bd. dirs. Western Pa. Luth. Student Found, Pres. Fedn. Womens Clubs, Lorain, O., 1937—39; mem. council Girl Scouts, Lorain, 1935—45, Alleghany County, Pa., 1950—53; mem. motor corps A.R.C., Lorain, 1941—45, Grey Lady, Pitts., 1951—52. Book reviewer, 1945—75. Bd. dirs McKeesport (Pa.) YMCA, 1948—49, Lorain Community Fund, 1943—44. Recipient citation for outstanding work Luth. Ch., Thiel Coll., 1956; Distinguished Service award Clarion State Coll., 1971; Role of Honor for civic achievement, Lorain, 1940. Mem. D.A.R., Huguenot Soc. Pa., League Women Voters. Mem. Order Eastern Star. Clubs: Twentieth Century (Pitts.); Woman's (Mt. Lebanon, Pa.). Home: Pittsburgh, Pa. Died Jan. 16, 1975.

PRICE, WILLIAM FRANCIS, lawyer; b. Decatur, Ill., Apr. 21, 1909; s. William Rhinehart and Frances (Browning) P.; student James Millikin U., 1926—29; Ph.B., U. Chgo., 1930, J.D., 1932; m. Margaret L. Hicks, June 23, 1934; children—Margaret W. (Mrs. William D. Trader), William S., Susan P. (Mrs. Michael Powell) (step child); m. 2d, Virginia E. Busse, Nov. 3, 1945; 1 son, Stephen B. Admitted to Ill. bar, 1932, practiced in Chgo.; partner firm Pope & Ballard, 1932—52, Vedder, Price, Kaufman & Kammholz, 1952—69, retired, 1969. Dir. Diversey Corp. Mem. Am., Chgo. bar assns. Kappa Delta Chi, Sigma Alpha Alpha Epsilon, Phi Delta Phi. Episcopalian. Home: Glencoe, Ill. Died Aug. 10, 1973.

PRICE, WILLIAM SYLVESTER, educator; b. Cin., Aug. 30, 1901; s. William C. and Florence Eunice Ott (Miller) P.; A.B., U. Cin., 1926; A.M., U. Chgo., 1934; Ph.D., O. State U., 1948; m. Marguerite Carlin, May 20, 1944. Répétiteur d'anglais, Ecole Normale d'Instituers, Macon, s. et. l., France, 1926-27; asst. prof. modern langs. The Citadel, 1928-40; teaching fellow Ohio State U., 1944-47; chmn. dept. modern langs. U. Tulsa, 1948-74. Decorated Chevalier dans l'Ordre des Palmes Académiques (France). Home: Tulsa, Okla., Died Feb. 28, 1974.

PRICHARD, THEODORE JAN, architect; b. Thief River Falls, Minn., May 28, 1902; s. William W. and Anita Rabling (Skewis) P.; A.B., U. Minn., 1925; M. Arch., Harvard, 1944, postgrad. Grad. Sch. of Design, 1945, 48-49; m. Frances Jensen Currie, Aug. 11, 1959; 1 stepson, William M. Currie. Mem. faculty U. of Ida., Moscow, 1926-74, prof., head dept. art and architecture, 1929-67, prof. architecture emeritus, 1967-74, acting dean Coll. of Letters and Sci., 1962-63; designer Whitehouse & Price, Spokane, 1942; with G.A. Pohrson, 1943; mem. Pricehard & Blanton, Architects, Moscow, 1967-74. Licensed architect, 1940. Mem. State Bd. Archtl. Examiners. Fellow A.I.A. (corp. mem.; pres. Ida. 1961); mem. Am. Assn. U. Profs., Soc. Archtl. Historians, Phi Beta Kappa (hon.), Delta Sigma Phi. Episcopalian. Kiwanian. Club: Spokane. Home: Moscow Ida. Died Dec. 7, 1974.

PRICKETT, ALVA LEROY, educator and adminstr.; b. Auburn, Ill., Jan. 30, 1890; s. Frank and Mary Elizabeth (Wood) P.; A.B., U. of Illinois, 1913, A.M., 1918; student U. of Chicago, summer 1919; m. Sarah Bonnie Stevenson, Dec. 31, 1917; children—Ruth Jessie (Mrs. John Woodburn Houghton), Ralph Stevenson. Claim adjuster, Sears Roebuck & Co., 1914-15; asst., textbook dept., Rand-McNally & Co., 1915-17; financial agent, Buena Vista Coll., Storm Lake, Ia., 1918; head of economics dept., Hibbing (Minn.) Junior Coll., 1918-19; asst. prof. econ., Indiana U., 1919-22, asso. prof. of accounting, 1922-29, prof. accounting, 1929-60, professor emeritus of accounting, 1960-73, chairman department, 1929-55, dean Sch. Business, 1943-45; engaged in independent audit work, accounting installation and as corporation consultant, 1914-17 and 1919-40. Mem. numerous profl. assns. and orgns., has been pres. or other exec. officer in several. Methodist. Author and co-author many books on statistics, bookkeeping and accounting 1927-73, many have gone through several editions, most have been of the textbook nature. Contbr. papers to tech. publs. Home: Bloomington, Ind. Died Dec. 15, 1973.

PRIDE, H(ERBERT) HAMMOND, educator; b. Framingham, Mass., Mar. 14, 1891; s. Galen Herbert and Caroline How (Hammond) P.; grad. Ambert College, 1913; M.S., N.Y.U., 1928, Ph.D., 1926; m. Virginia Videtto, Sept. 5, 1922; children—Henry Hammond, Frankie Hall. Prof. mathematics N.Y.U., 1914-56; Grand Marshall New York University, 1934-56. Served as capt. 111th Inf., United States Army, World War I. Mem. Phi Beta Kappa, Theta Xi. Methodist. Author: Advanced Algebra and Trigonometry, 1938, rev. edit., 1950. Home: Hendersonville, N.C. Died Sept. 20, 1973.

PRIDE, MAYNARD PRINCE, surgeon; b. Rockland, O., June 1, 1914; s. Eber Prince and Amy (Bradley) P.; A.B., Marietta Coll., 1935; M.D., Western Res. U., 1939; m. Frances Barnes; children—John B., Robert M., Janet (Mrs. Keith Anderson); m. 2d, Carol Sue Randall, June 15, 1958; children—Amy D., Heidi S. Intern, U. Hosps., Cleve., 1939-41, resident, 1941-43; practice medicine specializing in surgery, Morgantown, W.Va., 1946-73; instr. Western Res. U., 1946; clin. prof. surgery W.Va. U., 1970-73. Mem. W.Va. Licensing Bd., 1966-73. Dir. First Nat. Bank Morgantown. Active Community Chest. Mem. Am. Bd. Surgery, Southeastern Surg. Congress, Am., So., W.Va., (pres. 1969-70) med. assns., Fedn. Med. Licensing Bds. (dir. 1972), Morgantown C. of C. (dir.). Home: Morgantown, W.Va. Died Aug. 6, 1973.

PRIEST, IVY BAKER, state govtl. ofcl.; b. Kimberley, Utah, Sept. 7, 1905; d. Orange Decatur and Clara (Fearnley) Baker; ed. Bingham Canyon (Utah) High Sch.; m. Roy Fletcher Priest, Dec. 7, 1935 (dec.); children—Patricia Ann, Peggy Louise (dec.), Roy Baker (dec.), Nancy Ellen; m. 2d, Mr. Stevens (dec.). Rep. Nat. committeewoman for Utah, 1944-52; asst. to chmn. Republican Nat. Com., 1952; treas. U.S., 1953-60; now treas. of Cal. Pres. Women's Legislative Council of Utah, 1937-39; mem. bd. dirs. Nat. Safety Council, 1953-58, mem. Women's Activities Conf., 1955-75; mem. bd. trustees Nat. Soc. for Crippled Children and Adults, 1957-75. Mem. Church of Jesus Christ of Latter-day Saints. Author: Green Grows Ivy, 1958. Home: Sacramento, Cal. Died June 23, 1975.

PRINGLE, KENNETH RALPH, educator; b. Appleton, Wis., July 26, 1904; s. Ralph W. and Lilian (Smith) P.; A.B., U. Ill., 1926; A.M., U. Mich., 1930; student Harvard, summer 1933; Ph.D., Western Res. U., 1934. Tchr. English and Latin, Morgan Park Mil. Acad., Chgo., 1926-29; mem. faculty Kent (O.) State U., 1931-73, prof. English from 1947, chmn. dept., from 1962. Served to 1st lt. USAAF, 1942-47. Mem. Modern Lang. Assn., Am. Assn. U. Profs., Assn. Dept. English (adminstrv. com. 1966-69), N.E. Ohio Coll. English Group (pres. 1964-65), Delta Upsilon, Pi Kappa Delta, Tau Kappa Alpha. Home: Kent, O. Died Apr. 26, 1973.

PRINGLE, WILLIAM JAMES, advt. and marketing cons.; b. Chgo., Apr. 24, 1905; s. William J. and Dorothy (Sisson) P.; Ph.B., U. Chgo., 1925; m. Bertha Brown Speed, June 30, 1926; children—Thomas W., Mary H., William James, Mark Speed. Sports editor Pasadena Post, 1925; reporter Los Angeles Times, 1926—28; account exec. Lord & Thomas, advt., Los Angeles, 1928—40, v.p., 1941—42; v.p., dir. and Los Angeles mgr. Foote, Cone & Belding, 1943—56; marketing cons., 1957—75; co—founder Stuart Co.; dir. K—Latn Corp. Bd. dirs. Pasadena Found. Med. Research, Hathaway Home Children. Mem. Soc. Pub. Relations Cousellors, Chi Psi (nat. exec. council, dir. ednl. trust; Albert S. Bard award 1968), Alpha Delta Sigma (hon.). Clubs: University (Los Angeles); Annandale Golf. Co—author: Take the Air (play), 1941. Contbr. to nat. magas., bus. publs. Home: Pasadena, Cal. Died July 28, 1975.

PRIOR, HARRIS KING, mus. dir.; b. Hazardville, Conn., Mar. 10, 1911; s. Leland Jay and Flora Amanda (King) P.; B.S., Trinity Coll., 1932, M.A., 1935; student Harvard, Yale, U. Paris, U. Brussels, N.Y. U.; D.F.A. (hon.), Cal. Coll. Arts and Crafts, 1959; m. Anne Foss Hirschmann, Apr. 23, 1963. Asst. instr. English, fine arts Trinity Coll., 1932-36; head Sch. Fine Arts, Olivet Coll., 1937-39; instr. fine arts Bennett Jr. Coll., Millbrook, N.Y., 1941-42; dir. community arts program Munson-Williams-Proctor Inst., Utica, N.Y., 1947-56; exec. dir. Am. Fedn. Arts, N.Y.C., 1956-62; dir. Meml. Art Gallery, U. Rochester, 1962-75, mem. editorial bd. The Art Gallery mag., 1973-75. Served from lt. (j.g.) to capt. USNR, World War II, Korea. Mem. Coll. Art Assn., Am. Assn. Museums Rochester C. of C., Assn. Art Mus. Dirs. Phi Beta Kappa, Alpha Chi Rho. Rotarian. Club: Century Assn. (N.Y.C.). Home: Rochester, N.Y., Died Mar. 18, 1975.

PROCTOR, DAVID, lawyer, corp. dir.; b. Cuero, Tex., Aug. 5, 1893; s. V. B. and Fannie (White) P.; LL.B., U. Tex., 1915; m. Jean Blocker. Practiced law, 1915; with Gulf Oil Corp., 1919-59, v.p. and gen. counsel, 1945-54, exec. v.p. and gen. counsel, 1954-56, exec. v.p., 1956-58, chmn. bd., 1958-59, dir. Mem. Nat. Petroleum Council, Am., Tex. bar assns., Am. Petroleum Inst. (dir. 1955-60); Phi Gamma Delta. Phi Delta Phi. Clubs: Rolling Rock (Ligonier, Pa.); Boca Raton, Royal Palm Yacht and Country (Boca Raton, Fla.). Home: Boca Raton, Fla. Died Feb. 24, 1974; interred Boca Raton Cemetery.

PROFFITT, MARIS MARION, educator, writer; b. Franklin, Ind., Dec. 27, 1876; s. Francis Marion and America (Richardson) P.; Ph.B., Franklin Coll., 1905; M.A., University of Chicago, 1924; Ph.D., Am. U., 1936; m. Mary Elizabeth Higgins, Aug. 7, 1919. Began as teacher pub. schs., Ind., 1896, later prin. schs.; then teacher David Ranken Jr. Sch. of Mechanical Trades, St. Louis; became head of non-vocational dept. William Hood Dunwoody Industrial Inst., Minneapolis, Minn.; prof. psychology and industrial edn., U. of Md., 1919-25; teacher summer sessions, Municipal U., Akron, O., 1926-31; prof. edn. Ohio State U., summer 1938; adj. prof. edn., George Washington U., 1938-43; U.S. Office of Edn., Washington, D.C., 1925-46; chief, Division of Gen. Instructional Services; member of Phi Delta Kappa, Phi Delta Theta. Republican. Presbyterian. Mason. Made spl. study of government Indian schs., 1929, and assisted in educational surveys of Utah, Rutgers College, Negro colleges, universities, and Buffalo and Cincinnati public schools, etc.; coordinator for adminstrn. five official projects conducted by the U.S. Office of Edn., 1936-37, Am. Council on Education, Washington, D.C., 1947-49. Club: Cosmos (Washington, D.C.). Author various Govt. ednl. publs. in fields of indsl. arts, part-time and pvt. schs., sch. attendance, etc.; author: Book of Readings and Prayers for Young People; also articles in mags. Lectr. Home: Washington, D.C.†

PROSSWIMMER, PAUL E., banker; b. N.Y.C., 1902; student N.Y.C., 1924. Chmn. bd. Franklin Corp.; dir. Franklin N.Y. Corp., Beneficial Nat. Life Ins. Co., Beneficial Nat. Corp.; cons., dir. Franklin Nat. Bank. Home: Great Neck, N.Y. Died Oct. 27, 1973.

PROTITCH, DRAGOSLAV, diplomat; b. Cacak (Serbia), Yugoslavia, July 15, 1902; s. Mihailo and Jelena (Dimitrijevitch) P.; grad. Faculty of Law, Belgrade U., 1923; Dr. Econs. and Polit. Sci., Brussels Free U., 1926; m. Mileva Gvozditch, Sept. 15, 1938; children—Jelena, Mihailo. Financial attache Yugoslav legation, Brussels, 1923-26; attache Ministry Fgn. Affairs, Belgrade, 1926-38; sec. Yugoslav legation, Vienna, 1928-29; 2d sec. Yugoslav legation, London, 1929-33; 1st sec. Ministry Fgn. Affairs, 1933-38, counsellor, 1938-40; counsellor Yugoslav legation, Athens, 1940-41, Cairo, 1941, Yugoslav embassy, London, 1942-46; charge d'affairs of Yugoslav to Netherlands, 1942-46; dir. adminstrv. and gen. div. Dept. Security Council Affairs, Secretariat UN, 1946-48, prin. dir. dept. Polit. and Security Council Affairs, 1948-54, under-sec. in charge, 1955-58, under sec. in charge trusteeship and information from non-self governing territories, 1958-63, under-sec. for spl. polit. affairs, 1963-64; dir. UN Tng. Programme Fgn. Service Officers from newly ind. countries, 1962-70. Participated in work of Yugoslav dels. League of Nations, 1927-28, conf. of Little Entente and Balkan Entente, 1928, 33, 34, 36, 37, 38; rep. Yugoslav Govt. Allied Conf. of Ministers of Edn., 1944, 45; del. Yugoslav Govt. to UNESCO Conf., 1945. Author: External Commercial Policy of Kingdom of Serbs, Croats and Slovenes, 1926. Contbr. econ. and polit. articles to Belgrade Economist, 1924-25. Home: Wolfeboro, N.H. Died Dec. 21, 1974.

PROUTY, CHARLES TYLER, univ. prof.; b. Washington, May 30, 1909; s. Ward and Claire Eleanor (Streeter) P.; A.B., Dartmouth, 1931; A.B., Cambridge, 1933; A.M., 1938; Ph.D., 1939; A.M. (hon.) Yale, 1948; m. Ruth Belew, Aug. 29, 1936. Instr. Suffield (Conn.) Sch., 1933-34; instr. English, Lehigh Univ., 1936-38; research fellow The Folger Shakespeare Library, Washington, 1939-40; asst. prof. English, U. of Mo., 1940-42, asso. prof., 1944-46, prof. English, 1946-48; prof. English, Yale, 1948-74, dir. Yale Shakespeare Inst., 1955-62. Chmn. continuing vis. com. bd. trustees Lehigh U. Served as research analyst War Dept., 1942-45. Recipient War Dept. Commendation for Meritorious Civilian Service. Mem. Adv. council Folger Shakespeare Library. Fellow Royal Soc. of Literature, Bibliog. Soc.; mem. English Grad. Union, Modern Lang. Assn. Am., English Assn., Union Soc., Shakespeare Assn. Am., Renaissance Soc. Am., Conn. Acad. of Arts and Scis., Phi Beta Kappa. Conglist. Clubs: Graduates, Elizabethan. Author of: George Gascoigne. Editor: George Gascoigne's A Hundreth Sundrie Flowers, published 1942; The English Heritage (with others), 1945; studies in Honor of A. H. R. Fairchild, 1946; William Shakespeare's Much Ado About Nothing, 1948; The Sources of Much Ado About Nothing, 1950; Thomas Kyd's The Spanish Tragedy, 1951; An Early Elizabethan Playhouse, 1953; The First Part of the Contentions and Shakespeare's 2 Henry VI, 1953. Gen. editor: The Life and Works George Peele since 1952; The Yale Shakespeare, since 1952; editor Yale Facsimile of Shakespeare's First Folio, 1954, Shakespeare's Twelfth Night, 1958; Studies in the Elizabethan Theatre, 1961. Contbr. numerous articles to Eng. and Am. jours. Home: New Haven, Conn. Died May 1974.

PROUTY, OLIVE HIGGINS, author; b. Worcester, Mass., Jan. 7, 1882; d. Milton Prince and Katharine (Chapin) Higgins; B.L., Smith Coll.; m. Lewis I. Prouty (dec. 1951); children—Jane Chapin, Richard, Ann (dec.), Olivia (dec.). Author: Bobbie, General Manager, 1913; The Fifth Wheel, 1916; The Star in the Window, 1918; Good Sports, 1919; Stella Dallas (dramatized for stage and motion pictures), 1922; Conflict, 1927; White Fawn, 1931; Lisa Vale, 1938; Now, Voyager (dramatized for motion pictures), 1941; Home Port, 1947; Fabia, 1951; Pencil Shavings, 1961. Home: Brookline, Mass. Died Mar. 24, 1974.

PROUTY, WILLIAM FREDERICK, geologist; b. Putney, Vt., Aug. 15, 1879; s. Charles Eaton and Corintha S. (Walker) P.; B.S., Syracuse U., 1903, M.S., 1904; Ph.D., Johns Hopkins, 1906; m. Lucile W. Thorington, June 9, 1909; children—Frederick Morgan, William Walker, Chilton Eaton. Instr. geology, Syracuse U., 1903-04; asst. on Geol. Survey of Md., summers, 1904, 1905; asso. prof. geology and mineralogy, U. of Ala., 1906-12, prof., 1912-19; chief asst. Geol. Survey of Ala., 1906-19; prof. stratigraphical geology, U. of N.C., 1919-24, prof. structural and economic geology, from 1924, head dept. of geology, from 1933; geologist, N.C. Geol. Survey, 1920-24; cons. geologist, Bd. of Consultants Tenn. Valley Authority, from 1938. Paleontologist W. Va. Geol. Survey, 1922-25. Fellow Geol. Soc. America, A.A.A.S.; mem. Soc. Economic Geologists, N.C. Acad. of Science, Mitchell Soc., Am. Geophysical Union, Meteorical Soc., Phi Delta Theta, Phi Beta Kappa, Sigma Xi, Gamma Alpha, Phi Kappa Phi, Sigma Gamma Epsilon. Author of numerous scientific publications. Home: Chapel Hill, N.C.*†

PROVINE, LORING HARVEY, architect; b. Quincy, Ill., Aug. 18, 1880; s. James Harvey and Abbie Luella (Ross) P.; B.S., U. of Ill., 1903; A.E., 1909; m. Bertha Walker, Aug. 31, 1904; children—Loring Walker (dec.), Elizabeth Walker, Helen Ann. Archtl. work for architects in Chicago and St. Paul, Minn., 1903-06, and Brayton Engring. Co., St. Paul, 1906-07; structural engr. and supt. for Stone & Webster Engring Corp., Boston, Mass., 1907-14; prof. architectural engring. and in charge archtl. dept., U. Ill., 1914-48, emeritus. Cons. on bldg. code, Nat. Bd. Fire Underwriters, New York; tech advisor to Ill. fire marshal. Mem. commn. apptd. to codify the building laws of Seattle, Wash., 1911. Made preliminary estimate and design Keokuk (Ia.) Power house; had charge of buildings in connection with power development for Pacific Light & Power Corp., Los Angeles, Calif.—the highest head of water and the longest and highest power transmission in U.S. at that time. Pres. board of dirs. Champaign County Tuberculosis Sanitorium. Chmn. Examining Com. for Architects of the State of Ill. Fellow Am. Inst. Architects (mem. board of directors, 1944-47, and committee on education; former president Illinois Chapter); member American Soc. Testing Materials, Com. Fire Waste Council, Ann. Fire Coll. of Univ. of Ill. (dir.), Nat. Fire Prevention Assn. (mem. com. on fire engring.), Assn. Collegiate Schools of Architecture (pres. 1946-47), Tau Beta Pi, Sigma Xi, Alpha Rho Chi, Scarb, Zeta Psi. Presbyterian. Contbr. to mags. Rewrote building code for Nat. Bd. Fire Underwriters, New York, 1943. 1949. Registered architect, structural engineer and professional engineer. Illinois. Home: Urbana, Ill.†

PRYOR, ROGER, advt. exec.; b. N.Y.C., Aug. 27, 1901; ed. pvt. schs. Actor, dir. Broadway plays including: Saturday's Children, Royal Family, Up Pops the Devil, Front Page, Blessed Event; motion picture debut in Collegiate Model; motion pictures include: Moonlight and Pretzels, Thoroughbreds, Identity Unknown, Cisco Kid Returns, Scared Stiff; former master ceremonies Gulf Screen Guild, radio, also former narrator Theatre Guild, radio, later v.p. broadcast prodn. Foote, Cone & Belding, N.Y.C. Home: Pompano Beach, Fla. Died Jan. 31, 1974.

PUCKETT, B. EARL, chmn. bd. Allied Stores Corp.; b. Fairfield, Ill., Dec. 6, 1897; s. Theodore and Joanna (Churchwell) P.; student So. Ill. State Normal U., Eureka Coll., LL.D. (hon.); LL.D., Drury College; C.P.A.; married Agnes C. Wiedenhorn, Sept. 12, 1923 (dec.); 1 son, Bruce E. (dec.). Dept. store exec., 1927-53; pres. Frederick Loeser & Co., Bklyn., to 1933; chmn. bd. Allied Stores Corp.; officer or dir. 40 subsidiaries;

dir. Lehman Corp., Fed. Res. Bank N.Y., N.Y.C., Twentieth Century-Fox Film Corp. Club: Union League. Home: Fairfield, Ill., Died Feb. 12, 1976.

PUGSLEY, CHESTER DEWITT, lawyer; b. Peekskill, N.Y., Mar. 29, 1887; s. Cornelius Amory and Emma Catherine (Gregory) P.; A.B., Harvard, 1909, postgrad. Law Sch.; m. Lanetta Roake, July 10, 1948. Admitted to N.Y. bar, 1913, and began with Morris and Plante, N.Y.C.; mem. Rabenold and Scribner, N.Y. C., 1917-27; dir. Westchester County Nat. Bank, Peekskill, 1915-33, v.p., 1918-30, vice chmn. and counsel, 1930-33. Treas. Lake Mohonk (N.Y.) Conf. on Internat. Arbitration, 1915-16; alternate del. to Dem. Nat. Conv., 1916; chmn. membership com. League to Enforce Peace, 1916; Dem. and Progressive nominee for Congress, 25th N.Y. Dist., 1916; chmn. Peekskill Centennial Celebration, 1916. Resettled trust for internat. scholarships at Harvard Law Sch. for lectureship, 1950. Hon. trustee Rollins Coll. Served as pvt. U.A. F.A., 1918, World War. Mem. S.A.R., N.Y. State, Westchester County bar assns., Harvard Law Sch. Assn., Harvard Law Sch. Assn. of N.Y.C., N.Y. State C. of C. Home: Peekskill N.Y. Died Oct. 8, 1973.

PULESTON, WILLIAM DILWORTH, author; b. Monticello, Fla., Sept. 1, 1881; s. Samuel Richard and Lulu (Dilworth) P.; grad. U.S. Naval Acad., 1902, Naval War Coll., 1915, Army War Coll., 1925; LL.D., Stetson U., 1941; m. Marian Stanwood Emery, Aug. 12, 1911. Commd. Ensign, U.S. Navy, 1904; promoted through grades to capt., 1926; served on various ships until 1912; comdr. destroyer "Drayton," 1912; comdr. "Brooklyn," "Cushing," "Sigourney," "Stringham" and escort comdr. for troop convoys, World War; comdr. div., later squadron of destroyers and battleship "Mississippi," 1917-34; asst. chief of staff in scouting fleet in 1924 and battle fleet, 1928-29; mem. staff Naval War Coll., 1915-16, and Army War Coll., 1929-32; dir. Naval Intelligence, 1934-37, retired, 1937; recalled to active duty and served as special adviser to Sec. of the Treasury, 1939-40; returned to active duty January 1942. Served during World War II as spl. advisor to sec. of Navy on econ. warfare. Capt. U.S. Navy, retired. Received campaign medals, Spanish-American, Mexican and World War; Navy Cross for service in command of destroyers in European waters; Legion of Merit (United States) 1945; also decorations from governments of Sweden, Belgium, Mexico and Ecuador. Democrat. Presbyterian. Clubs: Metropolitan, Chevy Chase, Army-Navy (Washington); Yacht (New York); Mountain Lake (Lake Wales, Fla.). Author: The Dardanelles Expedition, 1925; High Command in the World War, 1934; The Life and Work of Captain Alfred Thayer Mahan, 1939; The Armed Forces of the Pacific, 1941; History of Naval Academy, 1942, The Influence of Sea Power in World War II, 1947. Contbg. editor Scientific American. Contbr. to Seribners, Atlantic Monthly, U.S. Naval Inst. Home: Lake Wales, Fla.†

PULLEN, WILLIAM RUSSELL, librarian; b. Lexington, Va., Nov. 10, 1919; s. James Edward and Nettie Allen (Mays) P.; B.A., U. N.C., 1942, B.S. in L.S., 1947, M.A., 1948, Ph.D. in Polit. Sci., 1951; m. Pauline Purdin Evans, July 7, 1949; children—Linda Belle, Mark Evans. Asst. to dir. State Records Microfilm project Library of Congress, 1949-50; documents librarian U. N.C Library, 1951-57, asst. librarian, 1957-58; librarian Ga. State U., Atlanta, 1959-74. Served with USAAF, 1942-45. Fellow Carnegie Project Advanced Library Adminstrn., Rutgers U., 1958. Mem. A.L.A., Southeastern, Ga. library assns., Alpha Kappa Psi, Omicron Delta Kappa. Methodist. Editor: Southeastern Librarian, 1961-64. Compiler: A Check List of Legislative Journals, 1955. Home: Atlanta, Ga. Died Oct. 23, 1974.

PULLIAM, EUGENE COLLINS, newspaper pub.; b. Grant County, Kan., May 3, 1889; s. Irvin Brown and Martha Ellen (Collins) P.; grad. prep. sch. Baker U., Baldwin, Kan., 1906; postgrad. De Pauw U., 1906-10, LL.D., 1969; LL.D., Wabash Coll., 1949, Ind. U., 1954, Ariz. State U., 1955, Baker U., 1958, Norwich U., 1964, Vincennes U., 1966; Litt.D., Ind. Tech. Coll., 1950, Huntington Coll., 1960, Franklin Coll., 1968, Butler U., 1972, Hillsdale Coll., 1974; m. 3d, Nina G. Mason, 1941, children by previous marriage—Eugene Smith, Corinne, Suzanne. Reporter, Kansas City (Mo.) Star, 1910-12; editor Atchison (Kan.) Champion, 1912-15, Franklin (Ind.) Star, 1915-23; pres. Central Newspapers, Inc., Muncie Newspapers, Inc., Pubs. Muncie Star and Muncie Press, Phoenix Newspapers, Inc., pubs. Ariz. Republic and Phoenix Gazette, Indpls. Newspapers, Inc., pubs. Indpls. Star and News; dir. Am. Grad. Sch. Internat. Mgmt.: dir. Bur. Advt., A.P., N.Y.C. R.R.; trustee Freedoms Found., Wm. Allen White Found.; former trustee DePauw U.; adv. bd. Nieman Found.; dir. Union Printers Home Assn.; elector Hall of Fame, Soc. Newspaper Editors. Decorated knight of grand cross Order of Isabel the Cath. (Spain); recipient Golden Plate award Am. Acad. of Achievement, 1968; John Peter Zenger award, 1966; W.A. White Found. 21st Ann. Nat. award journalistic merit, 1971; Ariz. Press Club Distinguished Service award, 1973. Mem. Sigma Delta Chi founder nat. journalistic frat., mem. exec. council, Wells Meml. key 1969), Delta Kappa Epsilon. Methodist. Mason, Elk, Rotarian. Clubs: Ulen Country (Lebanon); Columbia, Indianapolis Athletic, Indianapolis Country, Highland Country (Indianapolis); National Press (Washington); Blind Brook (N.Y.); Paradise Valley (Phoenix); Bohemian (San Francisco). Home: Indianapolis, Ind., also Paradise Valley, Ariz, Died June 23, 1975; buried Oak Hill Cemetery, Lebanon, Ind.

PULSIFER, LAWSON VALENTINE, chemical engr.; b. Manchester, Conn., Sept. 10, 1881; s. Nathan Trowbridge and Almira Houghton (Valentine) P.; A.B., Harvard, 1903; m. Ethel Burke, June 25, 1910. Began with Valentine & Co., 1903, chief chemist, 1910-29, also v.p. in charge of all mfg., pres., 1929-31; v.p. Congoleum-Nairn, Inc., 1931-39; dir. Valspar Corp., 1946. mem. exec. com., from 1947; v.p., 1947; cons. practice; invented first waterproof varnish, 1908. Cons. chemist Govt. depts. during World War. Mem. Soc. Chem. Industry, Am. Soc. for Testing Materials, Soc. Automotive Engrs., Delta Kappa Epsilon. Progressive Republican. Conglist. Home: Orange County, N.Y.†

PUPPEL, I. DARIN, physician; b. Venice, Italy, Apr. 5, 1909 (parents Am. Citizens); s. Oscar and Madelyn (Baldwin) P.; M.D., M.S., Ohio State U., 1936; m. Cecilia Gross Lewis, Dec. 11, 1937; children—Sandra Darin (Mrs. John Hennig Kroll), Madelyn Darin. Intern in medicine Washington U. Sch. Medicine, Barnes Hosp., St. Louis, 1938—39, intern in surgery, 1939—40; asst. resident in surgery Ohio State U., Columbus, 1940—42, chief resident, attending surgeon 1942—43; asst. prof. surgery, 1943—60; attending surgeon Grant Hosp., also St. Anthony Hosp., Columbus; staff Children's Hosp., Columbus. Diplomate Am. Bd. Surgery. Recipient award for service Grant Hosp. Fellow A.C.S.; mem. A.M.A., So. Med. Assn. (life), Am. Heart Assn., Am. Geriatrics Soc., A.A.A.S., Central Soc. Clin. Research, Central Surg. Assn., Columbus Surg. Soc., Am. Thyroid Assn., Ohio Thoracic Soc., Ohio Acad. Sci., Sigma Xi, Phi Eta Sigma. Presbyn. (elder). Contbr. articles on thyroid disease and surg. procedures to med. and surg. jours. Home: Columbus, O. Died Dec. 17, 1973; buried Glen Rest Meml. Estates, Columbus, O.

PURNELL, MAURICE EUGENE, lawyer; b. Dallas, Sept. 7, 1906; s. Charles Stewart and Ginevra (Locke) P.; A.B., So. Meth. U., 1925; LL.B., Harvard, 1928; m. Marjorie Maillot, May 29, 1934; children—Marjorie Maillot, Maurice Eugene. Admitted to Tex. bar, 1928; asso. Locke, Locke, Stroud & Randolph, 1928, mem., 1934-39, Locke, Locke, Dyer & Purnell, 1939-45; sr. partner Locke, Purnell, Boren Laney & Neely, specializing corp. matters, financial planning and administrn. estates; dir. A.H. Belo Corp., Pioneer Natural Gas Co., Lomas & Nettleton Financial Corp., Mosher Steel Co., McAlester Fuel Co. Bd. dirs. Dallas Museum of Fine Arts (pres. 1956-59), Dallas Symphony Soc., Hockaday Sch. Mem. Am., Dallas bar assns., State Bar Tex., Am. Law Inst., English Speaking Union, Phi Beta Kappa, Sigma Alpha Epsilon. Clubs: Brook Hollow Golf (pres. 1958), Critic, Dallas, Koon Kreek, City, Petroleum (Dallas); Lawyers, University (N.Y.C.); Home: Dallas Tex. Died Nov. 24, 1972.

PURYEAR, VERNON JOHN, educator, author; b. Sulphur Springs, Okla., Mar. 31, 1901; s. William Page and Martha Anna (Hawkins) P.; A.B., Baylor U., 1921; A.M., U. of Mo., 1925; Ph.D., U. of California, 1929; research fellow of Social Science Research Council, 1930-31; married Thelma M. Robinett, June 18, 1929. Instr. history, U. of Mo., 1926-28; teaching fellow in European history, U. of Calif., 1928-29; prof. history and polit. science, Albany (Ore.) Coll., 1929-33; asso. prof. Social Science, Humboldt State Coll., Arcata, Calif., 1933-34; prof., 1934-37; asst. prof. of history, University of California, 1937-42, asso. prof., 1942-48, professor 1948-52, professor of political science, 1952-70; visiting professor of history, University of Oregon, summer session, 1932, Miami University, Oxford, O., summer session, 1935, Coll. of Pacific, summer 1948, U. of Chicago, 1949. Mem. Am. Hist. Assn. (mem. exec. council Pacific Coast br. 1937, 52), Am. Polit. Sci. Assn., Acad. of Polit. Sci., American Acad. Polit. and Soc. Sci., Fgn. Policy Assn., Alpha Pi Zeta. Awarded H. B. Adams prize of Am. Hist. Assn. for essay pub. in 1931. Baptist. Clubs: Faculty (Berkeley and Davis); Rotary. Author: England, Russia and the Straits Question (1844-56), 1931; International Economics and Diplomacy in the Near East, 1935; France and the Levant, 1941; Napoleon and the Dardanelles, 1951. Contbr. to social science jours. Home: Davis, Cal. Died Nov. 10, 1970.

PUTMAN, RUSSELL LORAIN, publisher; b. Wilmot, Stark Co., O., Feb. 5, 1895; s. Walter Scott and Abigail E. (Bower) P.; student Oberlin (O.) Coll., 1913-16; A.B., U. Wis., 1917; m. Hazel Virginia Magnuson, 1935; 1 son, Richard Harry. Began as cub copy writer A.W. Shaw Co., became v.p. sales and dir.; advt. dir. Angus Pub. Co., N.Y.; dir. Hospital Year Book, Chicago; mgr. Aviation Mag., N.Y.C.: founder and pres. Putman Pub. Co., pubs. indsl. mags., Chemical Processing, Food Processing and Marketing, Plant Services, Whats New in Chemical Processing Equipment, Today's Chemical Materials, Food Ingredients and Equipment, 1938-73; pres. Nat. Bus. Publs., 1950-52. Served with U.S. Army, 1917-19; instr. in flying and pursuit pilot in France, World War I; with U.S. Army Air Corps, World War II, 1943-45, as capt., later lt. col; pub. relations ofcr. Middle East; assisted Maj. Gen. Hurley on spl. mission to India, Burma, China; asst. to chief of staff, 9th Air Force, Eng., Normandy; chief of staff 1st Tactical Air Force, Rhine Area; lt. col. Reserves. Decorated Legion of Merit. Republican. Clubs: Chicago Athletic, Lake Shore (Chgo.); New York Yacht, Lotos, Pinnacle (N.Y.C.); Anglers (Key Largo, Fla.). Series of letters from overseas while in service, published as "Sincerely, Put," 1945. Home: Pullman, Mich. Died Jan. 15, 1973.

PUTNAM, BORDEN ROGER, publishing exec.; b. Muskegon, Mich., Nov. 13, 1895; s. William Casius and Eleanor (Welch) P.; B.C.S., Washington Coll. Accounting, 1924, M.C.S., 1924; student Washington Coll. Law, 1924-26; m. Mable Ernst, June 15, 1919 (div. June 1939); children—Borden R., Donald H., Mary E.; m. 2d, France Wisenant, Apr. 6, 1940; 1 son, William C. Spl. adv. council Bur. Internal Revenue, 1919-29; treas., dir. McGraw-Hill Pub. Co., 1929-43; financial exec. Vick Chem. Co., 1940-46; bus. mgr. Newsweek, 1946-49, v.p., treas., chmn. exec. com., dir. Newsweek, Inc., from 1955, partner J. K. Lasser & Co., 1949-52; v.p., treas. Old Town Corp., 1952-55; dir. Rinehart & Co., K.F. S.D. Inc., (San Diego). Clubs: New York Athletic, Engineers (N.Y.C.). Home: Plymouth, N.H. Died June 1973.

PUTNAM, BRENDA, sculptor; b. Mpls.; ed. Boston Mus. Fine Arts, Corcoran Sch. Art, Art Students League; studied with James Earle Fraser, Charles Grafly, Archipenko, Libero Andreotti. Work permanently represented Folger Shakespeare Liberary, Washington, Acad. Arts and Letters, Hall of Fame, N.H. U., Detroit Inst. Art, Dallas Mus. Fine Art, Brookgreen Garden, S.C., Lunchburg, Va., South Orange, N.J., U.S. Post Office, Caldwell, N.J., St. Cloud, Minn., Norton Gallery Art, Washington, Ho. Reps., Washington; former tchr., ret., 1952. Recipient Gold medal Pa. Acad. Fine Arts, 1923; prize Nat. Assn. Women Artists, 1923, Avery prize Archtl. League, 1924. Mem. Nat. Inst. Arts and Letters, Nat. Acad. Design (academician, gold medal 1935, Barnett prize 1922), Nat. Sculpture Soc., Nat. Arts. Club. Author: The Sculptor's Way, 1939; Animal X-rays, 1947. Spl. collection works, relative data available Carnegie Library Syracuse U. Home: Wilton, Conn., Died Oct. 18, 1975.

PUTNAM, CLARENCE IRWIN, newspaper pub.; b. San Francisco, Calif., Mar. 23, 1879; s. Charles Sumner and Marie (Davis) P.; grad. high sch., San Francisco; student St. Vincent's Coll., Los Angeles, 1894-96; m. Mary Katherine Hanley, July 31, 1904. Began as reporter Los Angeles Herald, 1896; mgr. Calif. Asphaltum Sales Agency, 1901-05; mgr. C. E. Sherin Adv. Agency, N.Y. City, 1905-09; New York rep. for 17 U.S. newspapers, 1909-14; New York rep. Boston American, 1914-24; pub. Washington (D.C.) Times, from 1925; v.p. Washington Times Pub. Co. Served as pvt. Battery E 3d Arty., U.S.A., Spanish-Am. War. Mason. Clubs: Press, City, Racquet, Columbia Country, Indian Springs Golf (Washington); Amateur Billiard (New York). Home: Washington, D.C.†

PYE, WILLIAM SATTERLEE, naval officer; b. Mpls., June 9, 1880; s. James and Clara Almeda (Satterlee) P.; grad. U.S. Naval Acad., 1901; m. Annie Etheldra Briscoe, Oct. 20, 1904; children—William Satterlee, John Briscoe. Midshipman U.S. Navy, 1901; advanced through grades to capt., 1923, vice adm., 1940. On staff of comdr. in chief U.S. Fleet, 1917-18; head of U.S. Naval Mission to Peru, 1929-32; comdr. Destroyer Battle Force, 1939; vice-adm. comdg. Battleships, 1940; comdr. Battle Force and 2d in comd. of fleet, 1941; pres. Naval War Coll., Nov. 1942-Mar. 1947; military analyst, San Diego Union, 1947-49. Decorated with Navy Cross, Legion of Merit. Republican. Episcopalian. Address: Washington, D.C.†

QUAIN, EDWIN ALPHONSUS, clergyman, publisher; b. N.Y.C., Apr. 6, 1906; s. John and Nora (Cunneen) Q.; A.B., Woodstock Coll., 1929, A.M., 1930, S.T.L., 1937; Ph.D., Harvard, 1941; L.H.D., Georgetown U., 1972. Entered Soc. of Jesus, 1924; ordained priest Roman Catholic Ch., 1936; tchr. Greek and English, Georgetown Prep. Sch., 1930-33; instr. dept. classics Grad. Sch., Fordham U., 1941-45, asst. prof., 1945-48, asso. prof., 1948-55, prof., 1955-75, dean Grad. Sch., 1951-53, acad. v.p., 1952-56, dir. univ. press, 1947-52, 56-72; acting pres. U. Scranton, 1975. Bd. dirs. Georgetown U., 1966-72, chmn., 1968-72, acting pres., 1969. Recipient Bene Merenti, Fordham U.; Pres.'s medal Georgetown U.; Pro Deo et Universitate, U. Scranton. Mem. Am. Philol. Assn., Jesuit Ednl. Assn., Nat. Cath. Ednl. Assn., Assn. Am. U. Presses, Alpha Sigma Nu. Club: Grolier. Author (with others) A Monument to St. Jerome, 1952. Co-editor Traditio, 1950-75. Translator (with others) Works of Tertullian, 1950, 2d vol., 1959. Contbr. articles to learned jours. Home: Bronx, N.Y., Died Dec. 23, 1975; buried Auriesville, N.Y.

QUICKERT, MARVIN H., physician; b. Gilroy, Cal., 1929; M.D., U. Cal. at San Francisco, 1953. Intern, Santa Clara County Hosp., San Jose, Cal., 1953—54; resident in ophthalmology U. Cal. at San Francisco, 1957—60; Heed fellow in ophthalmic plastic surgery Manhattan Eye and Ear Infirmary—N.Y. Eye, Ear, Nose and Throat Hosp., 1960—61; staff O'Connor

Hosp., San Jose Hosp., Good Samaritan Hosp., Santa Clara County Hosp; asst. clin. prof. dept. ophthalmology U. Cal. at San Francisco. Served to lt. M.C., USNR, 1954—57. Diplomate Am. Bd. Ophthalmology. Mem. A.M.A., Am. Acad. Ophthalmology and Otolaryngology, Pacific Coast Ophthal. and Otolaryn. Soc., Assn. Research in Vision and Ophthalmology, Am. Soc. Ophthalmic Plastic and Reconstructive Surgeons. Home: Saratoga, Cal. Died Mar. 23, 1974.

QUIGLEY, JACK CLEMENT, architect; b. Miami, Fla., July 31, 1930; s. William Edward and Cyrene (Arnall) Q.; student U. Miami, 1952-55. Archtl. designer Geo. D. Moffat, Miami, 1949-52; cons. archtl., interior projects, 1952-63; prin. firm Jack Clement Quigley, A.I.A., Maimi, Fla., 1964-75. Mem. Am. Inst. Architects. Clubs: Jockey (Miami); Ocean Reef (Key Largo, Fla.). Home: Miami, Fla. Died Apr. 27, 1975.

QUIGLEY, THOMAS M., business cons.; b. Roxbury, Pa., Nov. 28, 1889; s. Robert Clark and Emma (Shoemaker) Q.; student pub. schs.; m. Margaret Brown, Nov. 23, 1912; 1 son, Jack A. With Chgo. Towel Co. from 1918, dir. from 1932, pres., mgr., 1937-50, chmn. until 1960; then cons. F. W. Means & Co. Clubs: South Shore Country, Olympia Fields Country, Coral Ridge Country. Home: Ft. Lauderdale, Fla., Died May 23, 1974.

QUINLAN, GEORGE AUSTIN, county ofcl.; b. Waco, Tex., Oct. 10, 1880; s. George Austin and Mary Kate (Saunders) Q.; B.A., Georgetown University, Washington, D.C., 1902 (valedictorian); student Massachusetts Inst. of Technology, 1908; m. Elizabeth Mai Connor, June 6, 1911; children—Elizabeth, George Austin, Louis Roberts. Practiced civ. engring., Dallas, 1908-10; civ. engr. with Great Lakes Dredge & Dock Co., 1910-12; contracting engr. in construction of highway bridges, 1912-14; county supt. highways, Cook Co., Ill., 1914-17, from 1919; sec.-treas. Consoer, Townsend/ Quinlan. Served as capt. and maj. engrs., 1917-19. Mem. Am. Soc. C.E., Am. Assn. Engrs., Western Soc. Engrs., Sigma Chi. Catholic. Club: Engineers'. Home: Wilmette, Ill.†

QUINN, BERNARD G., labor official; b. Philadelphia, Aug. 4, 1879; s. Thomas John and Katharine Margaret (Gorman) Q.; ed. Diocesan Catholic Schs.; m. Mary Frances Barry, June 28, 1905; Became mem. of Brotherhood of Leather Glazers, 1895; with Amalgamated Leather Workers A.F.L., 1901; gen. vice pres. United Leather Workers Internat. Union, 1920, gen. pres. from 1938, sec.-treas., 1941-51; internat. rep., Amalgamated Meat Cutters & Butcher Workmen of N.A., A.F.L. from 1951. Democrat. Roman Catholic. Home: Philadelphia, Pa.†

QUINN, EDWARD JAMES, physician; b. Castleton, Vt., Apr. 25, 1897; s. Patrick and Mary Quinn; M.D., U. Vt., 1921; m. Frances Katherine Wolohan, July 18, 1969. Intern, Albany (N.Y.) City Hosp., 1921, Union Hosp., Fall River, Mass., 1921—22; fellow Lahey Clinic, Boston, 1945; dir. Chelsea Naval Hosp., Boston; preceptor Deaconess Hosp., Boston, Palmer Hosp. Boston, 1947—48; mem. staff Rutland (Vt.) City Hosp., 1970—75, Hale Hosp., Haverhill, Mass., Jordan Hosp., Plymouth, Mass.; asst. dir. dept. anesthesiology Faulkner Hosp., Boston; asst. dir. dept. anesthesiology Lowell (Mass.) Gen. Hosp., 1952—55, chief and dir. dept., 1954—66, cons. staff, 1966—75. Served to lt. comdr. M.C., USN, 1942—46. Diplomate Am. Bd. Anesthesiology. Mem. A.M.A., New Eng. Soc. Anesthetists, Am. Coll. Anesthetists, Am. Soc. Anesthesiologists, Internat. Anesthesia Research Soc. Home: Castleton, Vt. Died Jan. 6, 1975; buried Fair Haven, Vt.

QUINN, (ELISABETH) VERNON, author, editor; b. Waldorf, Md., Jan. 5, 1881; d. Rev. William Thomas and Elisabeth (Peck) Q.; ed. pvtly. until 1897; Peabody Coll. (U. of Nashville), 1897-98; studied langs. in New York, 1900-05. Began, 1905 as proof-reader with Frederick A. Stokes Co., pubs., New York, and left as editor, 1918; editor half time for F. A. Stokes Co., from 1922. With Y.M.C.A. in France and Germany, 1918-22. Has traveled in all countries N. and S. America, also in Europe and Africa. Chmn. publicity Women's Overseas Service League, New York. Democrat. Methodist. Author: Beautiful America, 1923; Beautiful Mexico, 1924; Beautiful Canada, 1925; The Story of Rubber, 1928; The Exciting Adventures of Captain John Smith, 1928. Writer, editor or translator; The Kewpie Primer, 1916; Wonder Book of Fairy Tales, 1917; The Spanish Fairy Book, 1918. Big Beasts and Little Beasts, 1924; Stories for Six-Year-Old, 1924; Hands Up. (pseud. Capini Vequin); etc. Mem. D.A.R. Club: Appalachian Mountain. Home: New York City, N.Y.†

QUINN, ROBERT EMMETT, judge; b. Phoenix, R.I., April 2, 1894; s. Charles and Mary Ann (McCabe) Q.; A.B., Brown U., 1915; LL.B., Harvard, 1918; m. Mary Carter, Aug. 3, 1923; children—Norma Marie, Robert Carter, Pauline Fulton, Cameron Peter, Penelope Dorr. Admitted to R.I. bar, 1917, since practiced in Providence; mem. U.S. Diplomatic Intelligence Service in Eng. and France, 1917-19; mem. R.I. Senate, 1923-25, 1929-33; lt. gov. state of R.I., 1933-36, gov., 1937-39; judge R.I. Superior Ct., 1941-75; chief judge U.S. Ct. Mil. Appeals 1951-75. Mem. Am., R.I., Kent County (pres.) bar assns., Phi Kappa. Democrat. Roman Catholic. Clubs: Turks Head (Providence); West Warwick Country, Wannamorsett, Brown, Harvard, Army and Navy. Home: West Warwick, R.I. Died May 19, 1975.

QUIRK, FRANCIS JOSEPH, artist, educator; b. Pawtucket, R.I., June 3, 1907; s. Edward R. and Anne (O'Neill) Q.; diploma R.I. Sch. Design, 1929, postgrad., 1930; postgrad. U. Pa., 1941-42; studied in Provincetown, Mass., and Woodstock, N.Y., also France and Italy; m. Anna F. Feeley, Sept 12, 1936; children—James R., Ada-Lee A. Head art dept. Montgomery Sch., 1930-35; prof. art history, drawing and painting Ogontz Coll., 1935-40, co-head art dept., 1940-50; prof. contemporary perspective-painting Hussian Art Sch., Phila., 1948-50; chmn. dept. fine arts Lehigh U., 1950-70, prof., 1952-70, curator permanent collections, dir. exhbns., 1970-; TV programs These Our Own, sta. WFIL-TV, Phila., Art as We See It, sta. WGPA, 1955-61; Works exhibited nat. shows: represented permanent collection Lehigh U., U. Mass., Colby Coll., Wilson Coll., Allentown Coll., Kraushaar Coll., Parker Coll., Ships Mus., Savannah, Canton Inst. of Art Stroudsburg Hosp., Bethlehem City Center, Deiruff High Sch., Allentown, Pa., Ga. Mus. Art, Notre Dame U. Art Gallery, Smithsonian Instn. other pub., pvt. collections; portraits displayed City Hall, Litzenberger House, Bethlehem, Am. Consulate, Zurich, Switzerland, others. Bd. advisers Archtl. Commn., Bethlehem; chmn. fine arts, architecture coms. City Centre. Recipient Chassey Meml. Benedict award; Tiffany Found. fellow; Judges award Ocean Park, 1956; Old Orchard award, 1962; Lindback award distinguished teaching, 1965; Ossabaw Island Project grantee, 1968, fellow, 1972. Mem. Kinney Shoes Assn. (pres.), Sigma Phi Epsilon (hon. life). Roman Catholic. Bethlehem, Pa. Deceased.

RAASCH, RICHARD FREDERIC, physician; b. Boone, Ia., Jan. 19, 1921; s. Frederic A. and Adelia F. (Farnsworth) R.; M.D., U. Neb., 1945; m. Georgia Lucile Thompson, June 15, 1948; children—Rodney James, Roderic Allan, Renee Jeanette, Randall Scott, Rochelle Ann, Robbin Lea. Intern, Kings County Hosp., Bklyn. 1945—46, resident in diagnostic radiology, 1949—51; resident in pathology Lincoln Gen. Hosp., 1948—49; resident in radiology Univ. Hosp., Omaha, 1951—52, Methodist Hosp., Omaha, 1951—52; pres. med. staff St. Joseph's Hosp., Dickinson, N.D. Mem. adv. bd. St. Joseph's Sch. Practical Nursing; mem. N.D. Med. Econ. Commn. Served with AUS, 1943—45; to capt., M.C., 1946—48. Diplomate Am. Bd. Radiology. Mem. A.M.A., Am. Coll. Radiology, N.D. Radiol. Soc. (sec.—treas., pres.), 9th Dist. Med. Soc. (sec.—treas., pres.), N.D. Tb and Respiratory Disease Assn. Methodist (Sunday sch. tchr., finance com.). Home: Dickinson, N.D. Died Dec. 26, 1971; buried Dickinson, N.D.

RABE, ROBERT EMANUEL, psychiatrist; b. Canton, O., Oct. 13, 1925; s. Robert and Helen Rabe; M.D., Wayne State U., 1955; m. Charlotte Biddle, Sept. 30, 1950; children—Robert M., Paul A., Christopher D., John T., Warren. Intern, Detroit Meml. Hosp., 1955—56; resident Pontiac (Mich.) State Hosp., 1956-57, Detroit Receiving Hosp., 1957-59; pvt. practice medicine specializing in psychiatry, Detroit, 1959—69, Santa Barbara, Cal., 1969—74; mem. staff Detroit Receiving Hosp., 1959—69; Cons. Santa Barbara County, 1970-73; mem. staff Los Angeles Mental Health Dept., 1973-74; mem. teaching staff Camarillo State Hosp. Served with AUS, 1944—45. Decorated Purple Heart. Diplomate Am. Bd. Psychiatry and Neurology. Mem. Am. Psychiat. Assn. Home: Santa Barbara, Cal. Died Mar. 22, 1974.

RABINOWITCH, EUGENE, educator, phys. chemist; b. St. Petersburg (Leningrad), Russia, Apr. 27, 1901; s. Isaac and Zinaida (Weinlud) R.; Ph.D., U. Berlin, 1926; D.H.L. (hon.) Brandeis U., 1960; D.Sc. (hon.), Dartmouth, 1964, Columbia Coll., Chgo., 1967, Alma (Mich.) Coll., 1970; m. Anna Mejerson, Mar. 12, 1932; children—Alexander and Victor (twins). Research asso. U. Gottingen, 1929-33, Univ. Coll., London, 1934-38, Mass. Inst. Tech., 1939-44, Manhattan Project, 1944-46: 46: research prof. botany and biophysics U. Ill., 1947-68, mem. Center Advanced Studies, 1966-68; prof. chemistry and biology State U. N.Y., Albany, from 1968; sr. adviser Center for Science and Human Affairs, from 1968. Recipient 1965 Kalinga prize UNESCO; Kettering award Am. Soc. Plant Physiol., 1967. Mem. Am. Chem. Soc., Am. Phys. Soc., Fedn. Am. Scientists, Am. Biophys. Soc. Author: (monographs) Rare Gases (German), 1928; Periodic System (German), 1930; Photosynthesis, Vol. 1, 1945, Vol. II 1, 1950, Vol. II 2, 1956; Minutes to Midnight, 1950; Dawn of a New Age, 1964; also articles. Editor, editorial writing Bull. Atomic Scientists. Home: Albany N.Y. Died May 15, 1971.

RACKLEY, FRANK BAILEY, bus. cons.; b. East McKeesport, Pa., Sept. 30, 1916; s. Frank W. and Hazel (Bailey) R.; student U. Pitts., 1935; Carnegie Inst. Tech., 1936-38; m. Marguerite Moe Rackley; children—Margo, Frank B., Richard, Jo Ann. Office boy Carnegie Ill. Steel Co., Pitts., 1938-39, salesman, Milw., 1939-40. Chgo., 1940-48. mgr. stainless sales western div., 1948; gen. mgr. sales Jessop Steel Co. Washington, Pa., 1948; v.p. charge sales, 1948-49, exec. v.p., pres., dir., chmn. bd., chmn. exec. com., chief exec. officer, 1950-73; pres., Rackley, Inc. chmn. bd. chief exec. officer Jessop Steel Internat. Corp., N.Y., Jessop Steel of Canada Ltd. Ajax Distb. Co. Ltd., Jessup Serv. Div., Steel Warehousing Corp. Chgo., Green River Steel Corp., Owensboro, Ky., Jessop Steel of Cal., Los Angeles; dir. Washington br. Pitts. Nat. Bank, Mellon-Stuart Co., Pitts. Brewing Co., (Pitts.), Commercial Machines, Inc. (Conway, Pa.), Key Biscayne Bank (Fla.), Chmn. Washington County Indsl. Devel. Com., Washington County Cerebral Palsy Dr., Arthritis and Rheumatism Found. Dr., indsl. div. Community Chest, A.R.C. drives, Washington County Tb Assn.; state co-chmn. Nat. Found. for Infantile Paralysis Dr.; nat. asso. Boy's Clubs of Am.; bd. dirs. United Negro Coll. Fund, Am. Mental Health Found., WQED-TV, St. Paul Orphanage, Pitts., Washington (Pa.) Hosp. Mem. Am. Iron and Steel Inst., Am. Ordnance Assn., A.I.M. (pres.'s council), Pa. Soc. Profl. Engrs., Am. Rocket Soc., U.S. C. of C., Pa. Economy League R (dir.), Navy League of U.S., Young President's Orgn. Mason (Shriner, Jester), Clubs: Amen Corner, University, Duquesne (Pitts.); Lake Shore Mid-America (Chgo.); Marco Polo (New York City); Vero Beach (Fla.) Yacht; Riomar Bay (Fla.) Yacht; Eau Gallie Yacht (Eau Gallie, Fla.); Mountain (gov.) (champion, Pa.) Valley Brook Country (McMurray, Pa.). Home: Washington, Pa. Died Nov. 12, 1973; interred Washington, Pa.

RADCLIFFE, GEORGE L., lawyer; b. Lloyds, Md., Aug. 22, 1877; s. John Anthony Le Compte and Sophie D. (Travers) R.; grad. Cambridge (Md.) Sem., 1893; A.B., Johns Hopkins, 1897, Ph.D., 1900; LL.B., U. of Md., 1903; LL.D., Washington Coll., 1933, U. of Md., 1943; m. Mary McKim Marriott, June 6, 1906; 1 son, George Marriott. Prin. Cambridge Sem., 1900-01; teacher Baltimore City College, 1901-02; admitted to Md. bar, 1903; atty. for Am. Bonding Co., 1903-04, 2d v.p., 1906-14, pres., 1914-30; director and member executive committee Fidelity & Deposit Co.; dir. Fidelity-Balt. Nat. Bank and Trust Co. Mem. Baltimore Bd. Liquor License Commns., 1916-19; sec. of state of Md., 1919-20; apptd. regional adviser, 1934, of Pub. Works Adminstrn. for states of Md., Del., Va., W.Va., N.C., Tenn., Ky. and D.C.; member United States Senate, 1935-47. Member Maryland State Council of Defense, World War I; apptd. spl. commissioner to organize war work records of Md., 1919; apptd. to similar position World War II. Pres. Md. Chapter Nat. Foundation Infantile Paralysis. Trustee St. Mary's Seminary Junior College, Md.; honorary v. chmn. The Harry S. Truman Library, Inc. Mem. Archaeol. Inst. Am., Am., Md. Balt. bar assns., English Speaking Union (pres. Md. from 1956), Nat. Conf. Christians and Jews (chmn. Maryland 1953-54), UN Assn. Md., St. George's Soc. Balt., Am. Hist. Soc., Md. Hist. Soc. (pres. trustee), Kappa Alpha. Chmn. Md. Dem. Campaign Com., 1932, 36, 44. Mason (33°). Clubs: Bankers (New York City); University, Johns Hopkins, Maryland, Merchants, Bachelors Cotillon. Baltimore Country. Author: Governor Hicks of Maryland and the Civil War, 1902. Home: Baltimore Md. Died July 29, 1974.

RADFORD, ARTHUR WILLIAM, naval officer, banking cons.; b. Chgo., Feb. 27, 1896; grad. U.S. Naval Acad., 1916; commd. ensign U.S. Navy, 1916, advanced through grades to adm., 1949; duty Atlantic and Pacific Fleets, 1918-19; flight tng. Naval Air Sta., Pensacola, Fla., 1920; with Bur. Aero., Navy Dept., 1921-23; joined Aircraft Squadrons, Battle Fleet, and subsequently served in air units attached to U.S.S. Colorado and U.S.S. Pennsylvania; duty Naval Air Sta., San Diego, 1927-29; then officer charge Alaskan Aerial Survey, 6 months; assigned U.S.S. Saratoga, 1929-30; aide and flag sec. on staff, comdr. aircraft Battle Force, U.S. Fleet, 1931-32; assigned Bur. Aeron., 1932-35, then served as navigator U.S.S. Wright; assigned U.S.S. Saratoga, 1936-37; comdr. Naval Air Sta., Seattle, 1937-40; at sea in U.S.S. Yorktown, 1940-41; dir. aviation tng., Bur. Aero. 1941-43; assigned Pacific, 1943-44; asst. dept. chief naval operations for air, Navy Dept., 1944 (acting dept. June-July 1944); various commands, 1945-49; comdr. in chief Pacific and U.S. Pacific Fleet, and high comdr. Trust Ty., 1949; comdr. Philippine-Formosa Area, 1952; chmn. Joint Chiefs of Staff, 1953-57; retired, 1957; cons. devel. fgn. and domestic business Bankers Trust Co., from 1957; dir. U.S. Freight Co., Molybdenum Corp. Am., Witco Chem. Co., Decorated D.S.M. with gold star, Legion of Merit with gold star, Victory medal, Atlantic Fleet clasp, American Def. Service medal, Fleet clasp, Asiatic-Pacific area campaign medal, World War II Victory medal: companion Order of Bath (Eng.). Home: Washington D.C. Died Aug. 17, 1973.

RADFORD, GEORGE STANLEY, cons. engr.; b. Detroit, Mich., May 20, 1881; s. George W. and Laura Frances Hotchkiss (Doolittle) R.; B.S., U.S. Naval Acad., 1903; M.S., Mass. Inst. Tech., 1905; m. Clara Kerr McCormick, Dec. 26, 1906. Officer, construction corps, U.S. Navy, 1903-15; cons. engr., Remington Arms Co., 1915-17; contract mgr., U.S. Shipping Bd. Emergency Fleet Corp., 1917-18; cons. engr. to various dustries with special reference to improvement of product and economy of manufacture, from 1918. Fellow Am. Soc. of England, Army Ordnance Assn., U.S. Naval Inst. Republican. Episcopalian. Clubs: Army and Navy (Washington); Union League (New York). Author: The Control of Quality in Manufacturing, (pioneer work in this subject) 1922. Home: New Canaan, Conn.*†

RADHAKRISHNAM, SARVEPALLI, Former pres. India; b. S. India, Sept. 5, 1888; s. Veeras—wamiah and Sitamma R.; M.A., Madras (India) U., 1909, Oxford (Eng.) U., 1936; D.Litt. (hon.), Andhra, Agra, Allahabad, Patna and Lucknow unives.; LL.D. (hon.), Banaras Hindu U., Univ. Ceylon, U. London; D.L., Calcutta U., 1940; fellow All Soul's Coll., Oxford U., 1940, D.C.L., 1952; Litt. D., Cambridge U., 1953. Haskell lectr. comparative religion U. Chgo., 1926, Hibbert lectr., 1929; Upton lectr. Manchester Coll., Oxford U. 1926, prof. comparative religion, 1929; pres. postgrad. council arts Calcutta U., 1927—31; vice chancellor Banaras Hindu U., 1939—48, Sir Sayaji Rao Gaekwad prof. Indian culture and civilization, 1941—52; Nirmalendu Ghosh lectr. comparative religion U. Cal., 1937, Kamala lectr., 1942, chancellor Delhi U., 1952—62; pres. Sihitya Akademic (Nat. Acad. Letters), 1965. Chmn. exec. com. Indian Philos. Congress, Bombay, 1925—37, gen. pres. 3d session, 1927; pres. All Asia Edn. Conf., Banaras, 1930. Mem. Internat. Com. intellectural coop. League Nations Geneva, 1931—39; pres. exec. bd. UNESCO, Paris, 1949, pres., 1952; Indiana ambassador to USSR, 1949—52; v.p. Repbulic India, 1952—62, pres., 1962—67; chmn. Council of States (parliament), 1952—62. Fellow Royal Asiatic Soc., Brit. Acad. (hon.); mem. P.E.N. (pres. India 1949, now internat. v.p.) Recipient West German award pour le mérite, 1955; Order of Merit (hon.), 1963. Author: Indian Philosophy, 1923—26. Home: Madres India. Died Apr. 17, 1975; cremated.

RADZAT, GILBERT FRANCKE, banker; b. Los Angeles, June 15, 1939; s. Gerhard Francke and Olga (Steck) R.; B.S., U. So. Cal., 1962, M.B.A., 1963. With Union Bank, 1963-74, sr. v.p., San Francisco, 1970-74. Served with USMCR, 1962-68. Mem. Mortgage Bankers Assn. (chmn. urban affairs com.), Bldg. Industry Assn., Bay Area Mortgage Bankers Assn., Nat. Assn. Home Builders. Clubs: St. Francis Yacht (San Francisco); Jonathan (Los Angeles); Balboa Bay (Newport Beach, Cal.). Home: San Francisco Cal. Died Jan. 20, 1974.

RAFFMAN, HALSEY LESTER, x-ray co. exec.; b. Bloomingdale, N.J., Jan. 2, 1911; s. Louis and Rebecca (Silver) R.; B.S., N.Y. U., 1932; D.D.S., Columbia, 1936; m. Sylvia Brumberger, Apr. 14, 1938. Intern, Morrisanla City Hosp., N.Y.C., 1936-37; pvt. practice dentistry, 1937-42; organizer, pres. Halsey X-Ray Products, Inc., 1938; dir. U.S. Radium Corp., Morristown, N.J., 1969-73, v.p., 1969-73, also mng. dir. Served to maj. USAAF, 1942-46. Mem. Am. Soc. Metals, Am. Dental Assn., Alpha Omega. Mason, K.P. Inventor X-ray and photographic accessory Field. Home: Brooklyn N.Y. Died Mar. 17, 1973.

RAHI, MICHEL, govt. postal exec.; b. Cairo, UA.R., Nov. 22, 1912; student univs. Cairo, Paris (France); Bachelor Law, Paris, Dr. Law; grad. Inst. Advanced Internat. Studies, U. Paris; m. Corinne Attallah. With Egyptian Postal Adminstrn., 1934—50; with internat. bur. Universal Postal Union, Bern, Switzerland, 1950-73, 1st sec., 1950—56, counselor, 1956—63, asst. dir.—gen., 1964—66, dir.—gen., 1967-73. Died Jan. 19, 1973; interred Heliopolis, Egypt.

RAHV, PHILIP, prof. English, Brandeis U.; founding co-editor Partisan Rev. Editor: The Great Short Novels of Henry James. Author: Image and Idea; The Myth and the Powerhouse; Literature and the Sixth Sense, 1969. Home: Boston Mass. Died Dec. 22, 1973.

RAIGUEL, GEORGE EARLE, physician, lectr.; b. Phila., Oct. 26, 1880; s. Henry Reichart and Ellen Penrose (Magee) R.; M.D., Hahnemann Med. Coll., Phila., 1902; spl. studies, Harvard and Oxford U., Eng.; m. Mary Matlack, Jan. 29, 1908; children—Katherine (dec.), Eleanor (dec.). Practiced in Phila., 1902-11, specializing in ophthalmolgy; staff lecturer on internat. policies and current events, for Am. Soc. for Extension Univ. Teaching, League for Polit. Edn., Brooklyn Inst. Arts and Sciences, Inst. Arts and Sciences of Columbia Univ., and the Philadelphia Forum. Lecturer on current history and world politics. Y.M.C.A. service in Eng., Ireland, France, Italy, Siberia. Spl. rep. of P.O. Dept. in Europe, 1923; investigated econ. and polit. conditions in Russia, summer, 1924, again, 1931, 34; official del. to Pan-Pacific Conf. on Edn., Honolulu, 1927. Mem. Pa. Hist. Soc., S.R. Contbr. Ladies' Home Journal. Clubs: Contemporary, Franklin Inn (Phila); Town Hall (New York). Mason. Co-Author: (with Wm. K. Huff) This Is Russia; Scarlet Valley. Weekly news comment entitled In Other Words. Author: Wind and Fog. 1950. Address: Philadelphia, Pa.†

RAIMONDI, LUIGI, archbishop; b. Acqui-Lussito, Italy, Oct. 25, 1912; s. Giovanni and Maria (Giacchero) R.; student Acqui Sem., 1924-36, Appolinaris Inst., Lateran U., 1936-38, Pontifical Ecclesiastical Acad., 1936-38; Th.D., Dr. Canon Law, 1938. Ordained priest Roman Cath. Ch., 1936, consecrated bishop, 1954; sec. Apostolic Nunciature, Guatemala, 1938-42; auditor Apostolic delegation, Washington, 1942-49; counselor, charge d'affaires Internuntiature, New Delhi, India, 1949-53; Apostolic nuncio, Haiti, 1954-56; Apostolic del. in Mexico, 1957-67, in U.S., 1967-73; named cardinal, 1973. Decorated grand cross Honor and Merit (Haiti); Sovereign Mil. Order Malta; Order Holy Sepulchre. Home: Rome Italy. Died June 24, 1975.

RAKE, JOHN FREDERICK, clergyman; b. Washington County, O., Oct. 3, 1878; s. Elijah and Sarah (Snodgrass) R.; ed. pub. schs., Washington County, 1885-89, private normal sch., same county, 1889-1902, Moody Inst., Chicago, 1903-05; D.D., Franklin (Ind.) Coll., 1934; m. Nelle Deshler, June 21, 1905; children—Lorraine Pierson, Paul Frederick, Lois Custer (Mrs. Wendell Phillip Metzner), Eleanor Margaret (Mrs. Clude Castle). Ordained Baptist ministry, 1904; pastor Denver, Indiana, 1905-08, Crawfordsville, Ind., 1908-11, St. Louis, Mo., 1911-16. First Church, Evansville, Ind., from 1916. Trustee Northern Bapt. Theol. Sem., Chicago; mem. bd. dirs. Ind. Bapt. State Conv., 27 yrs.; teacher Agoga Bible Class 33 yrs. (average attendance 350). Pres. and mem. Evansville Bd. of Edn., 1926-31. Republican. Home: Evansville, Ind.†

RAKEMAN, CARL, painter; b. Washington, D.C., Apr. 27, 1878; s. Joseph and Eva R.; pupil of Royal Acad., Munich; also at Düsseldorf and Paris; m. Linda Heinline, Dec. 12, 1919. Mural decorations in U.S. Capitol, Washington, D.C.; paintings for U.S. Govt.; portraits in pub. bldgs., also in U.S. Soldiers' Home, Tenn.; Hayes Memorial Museum, Fremont, O.; State House, Columbus, O.; Kenyon Coll., Gambler, O.; etc. Mem. Art and Archaeology League, "X" Painters of Washington. Home: North Chevy Chase, Md.†

RALEIGH, HENRY PATRICK, illustrator; b. Portland, Ore., Nov. 23, 1880; s. John Stephen and Margaret (Mather) R.; ed. Mark Hopkins Acad. of Art, San Francisco, Calif.; m. Dorothy Scott, 1912 (divorced 1926); children—Sheila, John, Nora; m. 2d, Holly Wilcox, 1927 (divorced 1933); 1 son, Henry Patrick. Illustrator, lithographer, painter, and etcher for mags. Mem. Guild of Free Lance Artists, Soc. Illustrators, Painter-Gravers America. Clubs: Salmagundi, Coffee House. Home-Studio: New York City, N.Y.†

RALLS, ARTHUR WILLIAMS, surgeon; b. The Grove, Tex., 1881; s. Rev. Hamilton Blount and Alice (Williams) R.; M.D., Atlanta Coll. of Physicians and Surgeons (now med. dept. of Emory Univ.), 1902; post-grad. work, European clinics of London, Paris, Berlin and Vienna, 1909; finished Sch. of Mil. Surgery, U.S. Army, Camp Greenleaf, 1918; finished U.S. Army Sch. of Surgery, Mayo Clinic, 1918; m. Miss Lola Johnson, 1904. Founded Rall's Sanatorium, 1906; chief surgeon Gulf States Steel Co., 1909-32; now owner and operator of Forrest Gen. Hospital. Gadsden, Ala. Capt. in Med. Dept., U.S. Army, World War; surgical chief U.S. Hosp. No. 51, Hampton, Va., 1919; maj. Med. Dept., O.R.C., U.S. Army. Life Counsellor Ala. State Med. Assn., 1914-23; pres. Emory Univ. Medical Alumnus, 1926. Clubs: Reserve Officers Club of Gadsden (pres.), Gadsden Rotary (pres. 1925). Home: Gadsden, Ala.*†

RAMAN, CHANDRASEKHARA VENKATA, Indian physicist; b. 1888; M.A., Ph.D., LL.D., D.Sc., Presidency Coll., Madras, Prof. physics Calcutta U., 1917-33; research asso. Cal. Inst. Tech., 1924; pres. Indian Sci. Congress, 1928; prof. Indian Inst. Sci., Bangalore, 1930; dir. Raman Research Inst. Hebbal. Recipient Mateucci medal, Rome, 1929, Hughes medal Royal Soc., 1930, Franklin medal, Philadelphia Institute, 1941; Nobel Prize (physics), 1930. Hon. fellow Royal Irish Acad., Hungarian Acad. Scis., Zurich Physics Soc., Indian Mathematical and Chem. Socs., Optical Soc. Am.; mem. Indian Acad. Scis. (pres. 1934-70). Author: Theory of Bowed Strings and Violin Tone; Diffraction of X-rays; Theory of Musical Instruments; Physiology of Vision, 1968. Address: Bangalore, India., Died Nov. 21, 1970.

RAMSAY, ROBERT LEE, educator; b. Sumter, S.C., Dec. 14, 1880; s. Franklin Pierce and Mary Ellen (Mebane) R.; A.B., Fredericksburg (Va.) Coll., 1899; Ph.D., Johns Hopkins, 1905; m. Margaret Whitehead Prentis, formerly of Va., Aug. 21, 1912; children—Robert Mebane, Joseph Prentis. Instr. in English and Greek, Fredericksburg Coll., 1898-1900; fellow in English, Johns Hopkins, 1904-05, asst., 1905-07; instr. in English, U. of Mo., 1907-09; Johnston Research Scholar, Johns Hopkins, 1909-11; asst. prof. English U. of Mo., 1911-12, asso. prof., 1912-21, prof. from 1921. Staff, summers, U. of Chicago, Johns Hopkins, Columbia, U. of Va., U. of Wis. Mem. Modern Lang. Assn. America, Phi Beta Kappa. Presbyterian. Author: Principles of Modern Punctuation, 1908. Editor or co-editor and compiler various other books. Contbr. to philol. jours. Home: Columbia, Mo.*†

RAMSDELL, LEWIS STEPHEN, mineralogist; b. Clinton, Mich., June 4, 1895; s. Dwight Horace and Phebe (Voorheis) R.; A.B., U. of Mich., 1917, M.S., 1920, Ph.D., 1925; student U. of Manchester (Eng.), 1933; m. Lois Calkins, June 16, 1920; children—Elizabeth Jean (Mrs. Douglas E. Mills), Helen Winifred (Mrs. Jay W. Reeve). Petrographer, Norton Co., Worcester, Mass., 1920—21; mem. faculty U. of Mich. from 1921, prof. of mineralogy from 1945, chmn. dept. of mineralogy from 1951. Fellow Mineral. Soc. of Am., Geol. Soc. of Am.; mem. Am. Crystallographic Assn., Sigma Xi, Gamma Alpha, Sigma Gamma Epsilon. Republican. Methodist. Author: Mineraology (with E. H. Kraus and W. F. Hunt), 1959. Contbr. tech. articles on crystal structure and crystallography in scientific publs. Editor: American Mineralogist from 1957—75. Home: Ann Arbor, Mich. Died July 14, 1975.

RAMSOWER, HARRY C(LIFFORD), dir. agrl. extension; b. Granville, O., Jan. 6, 1880; s. James Napoleon and Catherine (Graves) R.; educated Doane Acad., Denison U., 1899-1902; B.S. in Agr., Ohio State U., 1906, spl. student, engring., 1906-08; Ed.M., Harvard, 1925, Ed.D., 1930; m. Helen Warden Keller, June 9, 1909; children—Harry Clifford, Isabel. Asst. prof. agronomy, Ohio State U., 1908-13, prof. agrl. engring., 1914-20, dir. agrl. extension service, 1920-48; dir., emeritus, from 1949. Member Grandview Heights Board Education (ex-president). Mem. Assn. Land Grant Colls. (Mem. com. on extension orgn. and policy, chmn. on Relations), mem. land grand coll. Postwar Agrl. Policy Com. Am. Country Life Assn., Grange, Phi Delta Kappa, Gamma Sigma Delta, Epsilon Sigma Phi, Alpha Zeta. Protestant, Mason (K.T.). Clubs: Faculty, Kiwanis. Author: Equipment for the Farm and the Farmstead, 1916. Home: Columbus, O.†

RANCE, SIR HUBERT ELVIN, British army officer; b. Plymouth, Eng., July 17, 1898; s. Frederick Hubert and Florence (Shaw) R.; student Wimbledon Coll., 1910-15, Royal Mil. Coll., Sandhurst, 1915-16; m. Mary Noel Guy, Jan. 25, 1927; children—Elizabeth, David. Commd. Worcestershire Regt., Brit. Army, 1916; served in World War I, 1916-18, in India, 1920-1923, 1936, Singapore, 1932-33, grad. Staff College, Camberly, 1935; Staff Officer War Office, 1936-38; instr. Staff Coll., 1938-39; G.H.Q. B.E.F., 1939, to evacuation of Dunkirk, 1940; staff appointments United Kingdom, 1940-45; maj. gen. in charge of civil affairs, Burma, 1945-46, dep. comdr. Southwestern Dist., Taunton, 1946; gov. of Burma, 1946-48; retired from service, 1948. Chmn. Standing Closer Assn. Com., Brit. West Indies, from 1948; Brit. co-chmn. Caribbean Commn. from 1948. Decorated Knight of Grand Cross of St. Michael and St. George, Knight of Grand Cross of Brit. Empire, Companion of the Bath. Club: Army and Navy (London). Home: Ilaro Court Barbados; also Oakhurst Camberley, Eng. Died Jan. 24, 1974.

RANCK, EDWARD CARTY, author; b. Lexington, Ky., July 18, 1879; s. George Washington and Helen (Carty) R.; student of Harvard Univ., 1910-12. Dramatic editor Cincinnati Post, 1905, St. Louis Star, 1907-08, Brooklyn Daily Eagle, 1917-18, also sent to France as spl. corr.; dramatic editor Ainslee's Mag., 1919; editorial staff New York Sun, 1921; owner and editor Kentucky Roadbuilder, 1924-25; dramatic and lit. editor Brooklyn Daily Times, 1926-27; editor Queens Co. Evening News, 1928-29; free lance writer from 1929. Author: History of Covington, Kentucky, 1903; Poems for Pale People, 1906; The Doughboys' Book, 1925; also (plays prod.) The Night Riders, 1912; We, the People, 1913; The Mountain, 1913 (played at Provincetown Theater, New York, 1933); Blind Mice, 1920; The Weakest Link (prize winning play in contest conducted by Penn Pub. Co., 1927); also short stories, poems and articles in mags. Wrote libretto for "Merrymount," grand opera in 3 acts, composed by Rossetter G. Cole of Chicago. Home: Peterborough, N.H.†

RAND, WILLIAM BLANCHARD, maritime co. exec.; b. N.Y.C., May 13, 1913; s. William Blanchard and Ellen (Emmet) R.; B.A., Yale, 1936; m. Emily Franklin, Sept. 7, 1946; children—John F., Laura M.; m. 2d, Eileen McNulty Brady, Nov. 26, 1970. With Air Reduction Sales Co., N.Y.C., 1937-40; with U.S. Lines Co., 1946-66, gen. freight traffic mgr., 1954-57, v.p., 1957-60, exec. v.p., 1960-61, pres., 1961-66, also dir.; dir. Grace Nat. Bank, Roosevelt S.S. Co., Am. S.S. Owners Protective & Indemnity Assn., One Broadway Corp., Gen. Am. Investors Co.; trustee Atlantic Mut. Insurance Company, Dollar Savs. Bank of N.Y.C. Director Community Hospital, Glen Cove, United Seamen's Service, National Foreign Trade Council; board managers Seamen's House br. YMCA. Served to lt. col. AUS, 1940-46; CBI. Mem. Nat. Def. Transportation Assn. (nat. v.p. water). Soc. Naval Architects and Marine Engrs. (asso.), Maritime Assn. Port N.Y. (dir.). Clubs: Piping Rock (Locust Valley, N.Y.); Meadowbrook (Westbury, N.Y.); Foreign Commerce (life) (N.Y.C.); American (London, Eng.); Propeller (N.Y.). Home: Glen Head, L.I. N.Y. Died June 20, 1975; interred Salisbury, Conn.

RANDALL, DAVID ANTON, librarian; b. Nanticoke, Pa., Apr. 5, 1905; s. David Virgil and Harriet (Witt) R.; B.A., Lehigh U., 1928; grad. student Harvard Law Sch., 1929; m. Margaret Rauch, July 12, 1929 (div.); children—Bruce Emerson, Ronald Rauch; m. 2d, Mary Altmiller, Nov. 23, 1956. With various bookstores, N.Y.C., 1929-34; mgr. rare books Charles Scribners Sons, N.Y.C., 1935-55; librarian Lilly Library, Ind. U., 1955-75. Mem. Phi Beta Kappa. Democrat. Lutheran. Clubs: University, Grolier (N.Y.C.); Caxton (Chgo.). Author: (with Wm. Van Winkle) Bibliography Henry Wm. Herbert, 1936; (with John T. Winterich) Primer of Book Collecting, 1946; (with Mrs. Carroll Wilson) 13 Author Collections, 1950; Dukedom Large Enough,

1970. Am. editor Bibliog. Notes and Queries, 1936. Contbr. articles mags. Home: Bloomington Ind. Died May 25, 1975.

RANDALL, GEORGE WILLIAM, accountant; b. N.Y.C., Dec. 25, 1912; s. George Dutton and Katherine Anne (Gallagher) R.; B.B.A., Coll. City N.Y., 1937; m. Jane McGarry, Aug. 8, 1942; children—Jane—Alyce (Mrs. Iverson Leonard), Margaret (Mrs. Kenneth Rosenberg), Robert, Katherine Anne. Accountant, Arthur Andersen & Co., N.Y.C., 1940—46, Peat, Marwick, Mitchell & Co., N.Y.C., 1946—47; partner Schutte & Williams, Mobile, Ala., 1947—70; partner Harris, Kerr, Forster & Co., Mobile, 1970-75. Served with AUS, 1943—45. C.P.A., Ala., N.Y., La. Mem. Am. Inst. C.P.A.'s Ala. Soc. C.P.A.'s, Am. Contract Bridge League, Beta Gamma Sigma. Co—author: Industrial Accountants Handbook, 1956. Home: Mobile, Ala. Died July 13, 1975; buried Catholic Cemetery of Mobile, Ala.

RANDALL, JOHN ARTHUR, educator; b. Durham, Me., July 25, 1881; s. Greenfield Augustus and Julia Dyer (Penley) R.; Ph.B., Wesleyan U., Conn., 1905; attended War Coll., 1929; m. Alice Gertrude Cooke, June 27, 1907; children—Jean Elizabeth, Marcia Cook, Shirley Anne; m. 2d, Georgiana W. Hathaway, July 11, 1936. Pres. Rochester Atheneaum and Mechanics' Inst., 1922-36; dir. ednl. aid Nat. Youth Adminstrn., 1936-37; ednl. consultant from 1937; also asst. chief investigator, U.S. Senate Crime Com. Attached to Gen. Staff, War Dept., Washington, D.C., 1918-22, as editor, ednl. consultant, sec. Advisory Bd., dir. instsn.; col. Organized Reserves. Mem. American Soc. Mechanical Engrs., A.A.A.S., N.E.A., Adult Edn. Assn. (dir.), Beta Theta Pi. Republican. Unitarian. Author: Heat, 1913; Elements of Industrial Heat, 2 vols., 1933; also series ednl. monographs; editor of 13 books pub. by War Dept. Address: Yarmouth, Me.†

RANDOLPH, EDGAR EUGENE, chem. engr.; b. Mecklenburg County, N.C., July 22, 1878; s. John and Eugenia (Grier) R.; A.B., U. of N.C., 1904, A.M., 1906, Ph.D., 1907; Carnegie research asst., Coll. City of N.Y., 1905; grad. student Mass. Inst. Tech., summers 1922, 23, 24; m. Ora M. Huffman, Dec. 30, 1909; 1 dau., Edith (Mrs. B. T. Williams). Prof., Lenoir-Rhyne Coll., 1907-09, Elon Coll., 1909-18, A.&M. Coll. of Tex., 1918-20; with State Coll. of Agr. and Engring., U. N.C., from 1920, head of chem. engring. dept., 1924-46; teacher summers, Appalachian State Teachers Coll., 1911, 12, 13, Tulane U., 1919, N.C. State Coll., 1921; chem. engr. N.C. Dept. Conservation and Development, summer, 1925, N.C. Budget Bureau, summer, 1931, N.C. State Corp. Commn., 1932; ranger Yellowstone Nat. Park, summer 1920; cons. chem. engr., from 1946. Delegate Chemical Engineering Congress, World Power Conference, London, 1936. Director Bank of Elon. College, 1915-18, alderman Town of Elon Coll., 1916-18; mem. Raleigh Recreation Bd., 1935-37. Registered chem. engr. in N.C. Mem. Am. Inst. Chem. Engrs., Soc. for Promotion Engring. Edn., Am. Chem. Soc., N.C. Soc. of Engrs., Raleigh Engrs. Club, N.C. Acad. Science, Am. Soc. for Testing Materials, Southeastern Gas Assn. (hon. life), Y.M.C.A., Tau Beta Pi, Phi Kappa Phi. Democrat. Lutheran (trustee). Club: Civitan. Author: Chemical Quality of the Surface Waters of N.C., 1924; Introduction to Chemical Engineering, 1934, rev., 1938. 1946. Author bulls. and articles in sci. jours. Home: Raleigh, N.C.†

RANDOLPH, FRANCIS FITZ, investment banker; b. Elmira, N.Y., Feb. 24, 1889; s. George Fitz and Annie Rogers (Dearborn) R.; graduate Philips Exeter Acad., 1907; B.A., Yale, 1911, M.A., 1914; LL.B., Harvard, 1914; m. Sarah Tod Bulkley, Nov. 3, 1923 (div.); children—Sarah (dec.), Francis, Elizabeth Anne (Mrs. Philip Cole), Peter Bulkley; m. 2d, Mary Hill Hadley, Nov. 27, 1965. Admitted to N.Y. Bar, 1914; with Cravath & Henderson, 1914-17; asst. counsel B&O R.R., 1915-16; with J. & W. Seligman & Co., from 1920, partner from 1923, sr. partner from 1940; chmn. bd. and exec. com. Glove & Rutgers Fire Ins. Co. and Am. Home Fire Ins. Co., 1940-52, now dir., mem. exec. com.; v.p. M-K-T R.R. Co., 1923-26, dir. mem. exec. com., 1932-46; chmn. bd., 1940-68, pres., 1940-60, chmn. exec. com. Tri- Continental Corp.; exec. com. Nat. Investors Corp., Broad St. Investing Co., Union Service Corp., Whitehall Fund. Inc.; dir., mem. exec. com. Am. Reinsurance Co., 1928-68. Am. Home Assurance Co., Internat. Life Assurance Co., Ins. Co. State of Pa.; chmn. bd., chmn. finance com., dir. Newport News Shipbuilding & Drydock Co., 1940-61; trustee, mem. Savs. Bank. Served with "Squadron A," N.Y. N.G., 1914-17, serving on Mexican border; 1st lt. 1917, capt. 6th F.A. and 1st Div. Staff, A.E.F., 1918-19; chief Paris Bur. for Armenia and Rumania, Am. Relief Adminstrn., 1919; mem. War Loan staff U.S. Treasury at Peace Conf., Paris, 1919-20. Cited twice Gen. Orders 1st Div., A.E.F., Silver Star Medal Battle of Soissons, Victory Medal with clasps for 5 major operations, Army of Occupation, Germany medal. Fourragere of the Croix de Guerre (France); Conspicuous Service Cross (N.Y. State)). Chmn. Met. (N.Y.) Camp and Hosp. Council, A.R.C. 1945; trustee, chmn. finance com. Vasser Coll., 1946-65, YWCA of City N.Y., 1943-61; trustee Coll. Retirement Equities Fund, 1952-58; treas. Russell Trust Assn. 1942-55, Metropolitan Opera Guild; dir. Metropolitan Opera Assn.; fellow-in-perpetuity Metropolitan Mus. Art; fellow, lifetime patron Pierpont Morgan Library. Mem. Soc. 1st Div. Am. Expeditionary Forces, Soc. Colonial Wars, Skull and Bones Soc. (Uale), N.Y. Zool. Soc. (life), Phi Beta Kappa, Delta Kappa Epsilon. Clubs: Union, Century, Downtown, University, Pilgrims, Garden City Golf (N.Y.); Mill Reef (Antiqua, W.I.); Choate, Anglers. Home: New York City N.Y. Died Oct. 12, 1973.

RANDOLPH, LEE F., art dir.; b. Ravenna, O., June 3, 1880; s. Reuben F. and Clara N. (Lee) R.; ed. Cincinnati Art Acad., Art Students' League (New York), Ecole des Beaux Arts (Paris), Atelier Léon Bonnat, Julian Acad., also at Rome and Florence 4 yrs.; m. Marion Wilson Ellis, 1910 (died 1927); m. 2d, Hilda Southwell Bunt, Sept. 21, 1933. Director of Calif. School of Fine Arts, 1917-42, also prof. drawing, painting and anatomy, hon. dean, active in war work. Figure, portrait and landscape painter, and etcher; exhibited Paris Salon, International Exhibition (Rome), Art. Inst. Chicago, Cincinnati Museum, San Francisco Museum Art; etching in collection of the Luxembourg Museum, Paris. Mem. San Francisco Art Assn., Calif. Soc. Etchers, Carmel Art Assn. (bd. dirs.). Episcopalian. Club: Bohemian. Address: San Francisco, Cal.†

RANKIN, WATSON SMITH, physician; b. Mooresville, N.C., Jan. 18, 1879; s. John Alexander and Minnie Isabella (McCorkle) R.; ed. high schs., Mooresville and Statesville, N.C.; studied medicine at N.C. Med. Coll., Davidson Coll., 2 yrs.; M.D., Univ. of Md., 1901; post-grad. Johns Hopkins Med. Sch., 1 yr.; resident in Obstet. Hosp., U. of Md., 6 mos.; resident pathologist, Univ. Hosp., Baltimore, 13 mos.; m. Elva Margaret Dickson, Aug. 14, 1906; 1 son, Jesse Dickson. Prof. pathology, med. dept., Wake Forest Coll., 1903-05, dean sch. of medicine, 1905-09; state health officer of N.C., 1909-25; trustee Duke Endowment from 1925, dir. hosp. and dependent children sections, 1925-50. Made important investigations in book-worm disease frequency in N.C., 1904 and 1905. Trustee Wake Forest Coll. 1909-25. Mem. American, N.C. and Mecklenburg County med. socs., Am. Pub. Health Assn. (chmn. sect. vital statistics; pres. 1919-20; chmn. exec. com. 1929-31; field dir. Com. on Municipal Health Practics, 1924; A.M.A. (mem. council on health and pub. instrn. and chmn. sect. preventive medicine); mem. Com. on Costs of Med. Care, 1927-32; sec., later pres. Conf. Secretaries of State and Provincial Bds. of Health; mem. N.C. Conf. for Social Service; v.p. Nat. Assn. Study and Prevention Tuberculosis, 1916-17; v.p. Nat. Assn. Study and Prevention Infant Mortality; mem. council on community relations and adminstrative practice Am. Hosp. Assn. (trustee Assn. 1935-39); mem. Omicron Delta Kappa, Alpha Omega Alpha; hon. mem. Phi Beta Kappa. Democrat. Baptist. Clubs: Rotary, Charlotte Country. Contbr. to med. jours. Home: Charlotte, N.C.†

RANSOM, JOHN CROWE, poet, educator; b. Pulaski, Tenn., Apr. 30, 1888; s. John James and Ella Ransom; scholar Oxford (Eng.) U., 1910-13, B.A., (Lit. Hum.), Christ Ch. Coll., 1913; m. Robb Reawill, Dec. 22, 1920; children—Helen Elizabeth, David Reawill, John James. Mem. faculty Vanderbilt U., 1914-37, prof. English, 1927-37; Carnegie prof. poetry Kenyan Coll., 1937-58; hon. cons. Am. letters Library of Congress; sr. fellow (summers) Kenyon Sch. English, now Sch. Letters, Ind. U.; lect. Colo. State Tchrs. Coll., Peabody Coll. Tchrs. U. N.M., U. Fla., U. Ky., U. Tex., Woman's Coll. N.C., U. Chattanooga, W. Tenn. Tchrs. Coll., Bread Loaf Sch. English, Harvard; an editor and publisher The Fugitive, Nashville. Served as 1st lt., F.A., U.S. Army, 1917-19; instr. Saumur Arty. Sch., France, 1918. Recipient Acad. Am. Poets fellowship, 1962; Guggenheim fellow creative writing, 1931-32; recipient Bollingen award in poetry Yale U. Library, 1951, Russell Loines award in lit. Nat. Acad. Arts and Letters, 1951 Fellow Acad. Am. Poets; mem. Phi Beta Kappa, Kappa Sigma. Methodist. Author Chills and Fevers, 1924; Two Gentlemen in Bonds, 1927; God Without Thunder, 1929; I'll Take My Stand, 1930; The New Criticism, 1941; also publisher Selected Poems, 1945, rev. edit. (Book of Yr. in Poetry award 1964), 1963; Beating the Bushes, 1972; contbr. groupbooks and symposia. Editor: The Kenyon Rev., 1939-59; The Kenyon Critics (with introduction), 1951; Selected Poems of Thomas Hardy, with Introduction, 1961; Collected Poems, 1963. Home: Gambier O. Died July 3, 1974.

RAPER, JOHN ROBERT, biologist; b. Davidson County, N.C., Oct. 3, 1911; s. William Franklin and Julia (Crouse) R.; A.B., U. N.C., 1933, M.A., 1936; M.A., Harvard, 1939, Ph.D., 1939; research fellow botany Cal. Inst. Tech., 1939-41; m. Ruth Scholz, Dec. 19, 1936 (div. Oct. 1948); 1 son, William Thomas; m. 2d, Carlene Marie Allen, Aug. 9, 1949; children—Jonathan Arthur, Linda Carlene. Instr. botany U. Ind., 1941-43; research biologist plutonium div. Manhattan Dist., 1943-46; asst. prof. U. Chgo., 1946-49, asso. prof., 1949-53, prof., 1953-54; prof. botany Harvard, 1954-74, chmn. dept. biology, 1970-74; guest research prof. Botanisches Inst. der Universitat Koln, Germany, 1961. Guggenheim fellow, 1960-61; Fulbright Research award, 1960-61. Mem. Am. Acad. Arts and Scis. (sec. 1962-64), Nat. Acad. Scis., Soc. for Study Devel. and Growth, Am. Soc. Naturalists, Bot. Soc. Am., Genetics Soc. Am., Mycol. Soc. Am. (v.p. 1957, pres. 1958), Sigma Xi. Author: Genetics of Sexuality in Higher Fungi, 1966. Home: Lexington Mass. Died May 21, 1974.

RAPUANO, MICHAEL, landscape architect; b. Warner, N.Y., Mar. 16, 1904; s. Louis and Mary (Fazio) R.; Bachelor Landscape Architecture, Cornell U., 1927; fellow Am. Acad. in Rome (Italy), 1927-30; m. Catherine Reid Peck, Aug. 22, 1931; children—Marge Reid, Michael Reid. Engaged in private practice, 1939-75; with firm, Gilmore D. Clark & Michael Rapuano, 1939-75. Mem. Buck's County (Pa.) Park Commn., 1954-75. Trustee Am. Acad. in Rome, 1946—, pres., 1958-68. Registered profl. engr., State of N.Y. Sec. Municipal Art Commn. of City of N.Y., 1939-47. Fellow Am. Soc. Landsacpe Architects, N.A.D.; mem. Nat. Inst. Arts and Letters, Commn. on Fine Arts. Club: Century Assn. (New York). Home: Newton, Pa., Died Sept. 13, 1975.

RASBACH, OSCAR, musician; b. Dayton, Ky., Aug. 2, 1888; s. Jacob and Clare (Ruland) R.; ed. pub. schs. Los Angeles, 1895-1906; studied piano with Theodor Leschetizky, and composition with Hans Thornton, Vienna, Austria, 1909-11; m. Ruth Marie Luke, Jan. 10, 1923; children Charlene (Mrs. Hastings), Roger Duane. Tchr. piano, composer, dir., from 1911. Composer of numerous works including: (Songs) Trees, Mountains, A Wanderer's Song, The Redwoods (with Joseph B. Strauss); (operattes) Dawn Boy, Open Song. (works for piano) Folk Song Sonatinas, Evening at Padua Hills, Etude Melodlque. Mem. A.S.C.A.P., Music and Arts Club of Pasadena. Republican. Mason. Home: Pasadena, Cal. Died Mar. 24, 1975. cremated.

RASH, FRANK DILLMAN, dir. selective service; b. St. Charles, Ky., Sept. 1, 1878; s. James Rhea and Louise Victoria (Dillman) R.; A.B., South Kentucky Coll., Hopkinsville, Ky., 1897; S.B., Mass. Inst. Tech., 1901; m. Susan Elizabeth Atkinson, Dec. 10, 1902; 1 son, Dillman Atkinson. Asst. engr. St. Bernard Mining Co., Earlington, Ky., 1901, chief engr., 1902-06, gen. mgr., 1906-11, vice pres. and gen. mgr., 1911-20, pres., 1920-24; pres. St. Bernard Coal Co., also vice pres. West Kentucky Coal Co., 1924-25; pres. Inland Waterways Co., 1926-27; mgr. Louisville agency Reconstruction Finance Corp., 1932-34; pres. Fed. Land Bank of Louisville, 1934-35; cons. engr., 1924-37; mng. dir. Louisville branch Federal Reserve Bank of St. Louis, 1938-40; state dir. of selective service, Ky., from 1940; dir. Louisville Railway Co. Served as 1st lt., advancing to col., 149th Inf., Nat. Guard, Army of U.S. and Reserve, 1904-36. Decorated Mexican Border and World War medals (U.S.), Post-World War I Hon. Cross of Valor (Poland). Curator Transylvania Coll., Lexington, Ky. Trustee Kentucky Female Orphans Sch., Midway, Ky. Dir. Old Masons Home (Shelbyville, Ky.); dir. and vice pres. Masonic Widows and Orphans Home (Louisville), Vice chmn. Louisville Red Cross. Mem. Am. Inst. Mining and Metall. Engrs., Engrs. and Architects Club, Newcomen Soc., Am. Legion (Ky. state comdr., 1924-25; nat. exec. committeeman, 1925-45). Clubs: Pendennis, Louisville Country (Louisville); Madisonville (Ky.) Country, Contbr. articles on bituminous coal mining and forestry as related to mining to tech. publs. Home: Louisville, Ky.*†

RASHEVSKY, NICOLAS, math. biologist; b. Chernigov, Russia, Sept. 20, 1899; s. Peter and Nadezhda (Konstantinovich) R.; grad. U. Kiev (Russia), 1919; m. Emily Zolotareva, Nov. 12, 1920; children—Emilie (Mrs. K. Strand), Nina (Mrs. C. O. Carlson), Nadezhda (Mrs. M. S. Pittman, Jr.). Came to U.S., 1924, naturalized, 1939. Instr. in physics U. Kiev, 1919, Robert Coll., Constantinople, Turkey, 1920-21; prof. physics Russian U. at Prague, Czechoslovakia, 1921-24; research physicist Westinghouse Research Labs, East Pittsburgh, Pa., also lectr. physics U. Pitts., 1924-34; Rockefeller fellow in math. viophysics, U. Chgo., 1934-35, asst. prof., 1935-38, asso. prof., 1938-46, prof., 1946-47, prof. math. biology, chmn. com. on math. biology, 1947-65; prof. math. biology, research math. biologist U. Mich., 1965-70, prof. emeritus, 1970-72; vis. research Prof. math. biology Central State U., Wilberforce, O.; Cons., FDA, 1953-55; guest lectr. U. Uppsala (Sweden), U. Brussles (Belgium), U. Lille (France), U. Leyden (Netherlands), 1962, Yale, 1962, Tech. Hochschule Darmstadt, Hau der Technik, Essen, U. Cologne, U. Berlin (all Germany), 1963, Moscow State U., Leningard State U., Soc. Naturalists (all USSR), 1964, Brussels, Umea (Sweden), Leipzig, Milan, 1967; vis. lectr. U. Leipzig (Germany), U. Umea (Sweden), U. Lyons (France), 1970; pres. Math. Biology, Inc., 1970; mem. Internat. Brain Research Orgn., UNESCO; dir. internat. post-doctoral course on physicomath aspects of biology, Varenna, Italy, summer 1960; research adviser U. Genoa (Italy), autumn 1960; gen. chmn. 1st Internat. Symposium on Math. Theories of Biol. Phenomena, N.Y.C., 1961. Fellow A.A.A.S.;

charter mem. Internat. Biometric Soc., mem. Biophys. Soc. Author: Mathematical Biophysics, 1938, rev., 1960, Advances and Applications of Mathematical Biology, 1940; Mathematical Theory of Human Relations, 1947; Mathematical Biology of Social Behavior, 1951, rev. edit., 1960; Mathematical Principles in Biology and their Application, 1960; Some Medical Aspects of Mathematical Biology, 1964; Looking at History through Mathematics, 1968. Founder, editor Bull. Math. Biophysics, 1939. Contbr. sci. articles to numerous publs. Soc. Math. Biology Founded in his memory. Home: Holland, Mich. Died Jan. 16, 1972.

RATHBUN, JOHN CAMPBELL, physician, educator; b. Toronto, Ont., Can., May 8, 1915; s. John Bell and Gladys (Jamieson) R.; student Upper Can. Coll., 1928—33; M.D., U. Toronto, 1939; m. Catherine Coleman Moore, Jan. 10, 1942; children—Fredericka (Mrs. Inigo Adamson), Catherine (Mrs. Roy Brown), Flora (Mrs. Roger Hoag), Elizabeth (Mrs. Carl Snyder), Mary Kate, Amy. Practice medicine specializing in pediatrics, London, Ont., Can., 1948-72; faculty U. Western Ont., 1959-72, prof., head dept. pediatrics, 1955-72; physician—in—chief War Meml. Children's Hosp., London, 1955-72; pres. med. staff Victoria Hosp., London, also trustee. Cons. Children's Psychiat. Research Inst., Beck Meml. Sanitorium; mem. univ. consultation com. Med. Research Council. Mem. med. adv. bd. Ont. Soc. Crippled Children. Served to lt. comdr. Royal Navy (Eng.) and Royal Canadian Navy, 1940—46. Fellow Royal Coll. Physicians Can., Am. Acad. Pediatrics; mem. Am. Pediatric Soc., Canadian Soc. Clin. Investigation, Am., Canadian diabetic assns., U. Western Ont. Faculty Club, London C. of C., Alpha Omega Alpha. Club: London Hunt and Country. Contbg. author: Textbook in Pediatrics, 1956. Contbr. articles to profl. jours. Home: London, Ont., Canada. Died Oct. 31, 1972.

RAVDIN, ROBERT GLENN, physician; b. Phila., Feb. 15, 1923; s. Isidor Schwaner and Elizabeth (Glenn) R.; student Harvard; M.D., U. Pa., 1945; m. Phyllis Johnson; children—Peter, Vivien, Charlotte; m. 2d, Carolyn Port; children—Harriet, William. Intern, Presbyn. Hosp., Columbia, N.Y.C., 1945—46; resident Hosp. of U. Pa., Phila., 1949—53, attending surgeon, co—dir. neoplastic Chemotherapy Clinic; cons. VA Hosp., Phila.; asst. instr. surgery, fellow Harrison dept. surg. research U. Pa., 1949—52, Am. Cancer Soc. fellow, 1952—53, instr. surgery, 1952—54, asso. in surgery, 1954, asst. prof., 1955—61, asso. prof., 1961—72, J. William White asso. prof. surg. research 1964—72. Cons. breast cancer task force Nat. Cancer Inst. Bd. dirs. Phila. div. Am. Cancer Soc. Diplomate Am. Bd. Surgery. Fellow A.C.S.; mem. A.M.A., Pa. (cancer commn.), Philadelphia County (bd. censors) med. socs., Am. Thyroid Assn., Am., So. surg. assns., Am. Soc. Clin. Oncology, Halsted Soc., John Morgan Soc., Phila. Acad. Surgery, Sigma Xi. Contbr. articles to med. jours. Home: Armore, Pa. Died Mar. 27, 1972; buried Pa.

RAVESON, SHERMAN HAROLD, artist; b. New Haven, June 11, 1907; A.B., LL.B., Cumberland U. Art editor, Vanity Fair mag., 1929-34, Life mag., 1935, Esquire mag., 1936; with Pettingell & Fenton, 1937-41; v.p., art dir. Sterling Advt. Agy., N.Y.C., 1951-55; one-man shows Assn. Am. Artists, 1941, Grand Central Art Gallery, N.Y.C., 1955, 56, Carriage House Studios, Phila., 1956; works represented in collections numerous racetracks, U.S. Pres., advt. dir. Mountain Living mag., 1970-74. Editor: Classified Boating Directory of Fla. East-West Coast, 1967-70, Palm Beach Shopping Guide to Worth Av., 1967-70. Home: Franklin N.C. Died Nov. 20, 1974.

RAWN, ARNOLD EDWARD, army officer, lawyer; b. Valley Falls, Kan., Oct. 22, 1906; s. William E. and Ruby A. (Moon) R.; student Kansas City Sch. Law, 1928-30; LL.B., LaSalle Extension U., 1941; B.S., Kan. State Coll., 1954; m. Dorothy E. Kutina, Dec. 31, 1937. Inducted as pvt. U.S. Army, 1930, advanced through grades to capt., 1947; with adj. gen. dept., 1941-43; asst. judge adv., 1944-47; ret., 1947; admitted to Neb. bar, 1941; tchr. history, bus. law, econs., Bakersfield (Mo.) High Sch., 1957; practiced law in Deshler, from 1959; atty. Housing Authority, Deshler Planning Commn., County Mental Health Bd., Deshler Am. Legion, Deshler Nursing Home; city atty., Deshler, Neb.; adv. bd. Parkview Haven Nursing Home. Mem. Am., Neb., Seventh Jud. bar assns., Deshler C. of C., Ret. Officers Assn., Kan. State Coll. Alumni Assn., Am. Legion, Am. Judicature Soc., Assn. Alumni Judge Adv. Gen.'s Sch., Phi Alpha Theta. Democrat. Methodist. Clubs: Dale Carnegie Internat. Speakers (grad. effective speaking course.), Toastmasters Internat. Home: Deshler, Neb. Died Dec. 29, 1973; interred Farrar Cemetery, Valley Falls, Kan.

RAY, JOHN ARTHUR, government service; b. Orangeville, Tex., July 14, 1879; s. Dr. Alfred Judson Ray and Matilda Caroline (Routh) R.; A.B., Baylor U., 1898; B.A., Yale, 1899, M.A., 1903; Docteur de Université de Paris, 1906; m. Mrs. Elise Provenchere Moore, June 30, 1943. Instr. Baylor U., 1901-02; same, Williams Coll., 1905-06, U.S. Naval Acad., 1906-09; consul at Maskat, Arabia, 1909-11, Maracaibo, Venezuela, 1911-13, Sheffield, England, 1913-14, Odessa, Russia, 1914-18, Bushire, Persia, 1918, Lourenco Marquez, East Africa, 1919-21 (resigned); attached to Conf. on Limitation of Armament, Washington, D.C., 1921; prof. modern langs., Vanderbilt U., 1922-23; same, U.S. Naval Acad., 1923-25; prof. Spanish and Italian, Washington U., St. Louis, Mo., 1925-38; head of French dept., Baylor U., Waco, Tex., 1938-42; spl. asst. to U.S. ambassador to Guatemala, 1942-46. Served as cpl. Tex. Volunteer Cavalry, 1898. Address: Whitewright, Tex.†

RAY, JOHN HENRY, congressman, lawyer; b. Mankato, Minn., Sept. 27, 1886; s. John Henry and Genevieve (Eldredge) R.; A.B., U. of Minn., 1908; LL.B., Harvard, 1911; m. Hama Olive Thompson, Oct. 9, 1912; children—Virginia Thompson (Mrs. James E. Potts), John Henry, III, Gordon Ray. Entered law offices of Koon, Whelan and Hempstead, Minneapolis, 1911, becoming mem. firm 1917; apptd. asst. sec. and asst. trust officer Wells-Dickey Trust Co., 1918; asst. to spl. rep. of Sec. of War in adjustment of War Dept. claims against allied govts., Feb.-Sept. 1919; mem. own law firm, Minneapolis, 1919-23; gen. atty. Am. Telephone & Telegraph Co., 1924-28, gen. solicitor, 1928-30; v.p., dir. and gen. counsel Western Electric Co., 1930-36; counsel Am. Telephone & Telegraph Co., 1936-1942, v.p. and gen. counsel, 1942-51; gen. law practice asso. as counsel with Skadden, Arps, Slate & Timbers, from 1951. First lt., Judge Advocate Gen. Dept., Washington, 1918-19. Member 83d-87th Congresses, 15th District N.Y. Member American, Fed. Communications and N.Y. State bar assns., Assn. of the Bar (N.Y.C.), N.Y. County Lawyers Assn., Beta Theta Pi. Clubs: University (N.Y.); Richmond County Country (N.Y.). Home: Staten Island N.Y. Died May 21, 1975.

RAY, WILLIAM WALLACE, lawyer; b. Deseret, Utah, Dec. 19, 1880; s. William A. and Minerva A. (Hinckley) R.; B.A., U. of Utah, 1902; m. Leda Rawlins, June 20, 1905. Practiced alone, 1904-09; member Rawlins, Ray & Rawlins, 1909-28; U.S. atty., Dist. of Utah, 1913-19; mem. law firm Ray, Rawlins, Jones & Henderson. Regent U. of Utah, 1916-20; mem. Colo. River Commn. of State of Utah; spl. master U.S. Supreme Ct. in original case, State of Wash. vs. State of Ore. Democrat. Mem. Am. Bar Assn., Utah State Bar Assn. Home: Salt Lake City, Utah.†

RAYMOND, ANAN, lawyer; b. Rapid City, S.D., Nov. 6, 1890; s. Spencer H. and Marinda (Platt) R.; student S.D. Sch. Mines, Rapid City, 1903-07; A.B., U. Neb., 1911, LL.B., 1913; m. Florence Hostetler, May 11, 1915; children—Margaret Marinda (Mrs. Robert J. Manning), David Hostetler (dec.), Sarah Elizabeth (Mrs. N. Peter Rathvon, Jr.), Spencer Henry. Admitted to Neb. bar, 1913; asso. Francis A. Brogan, Omaha, 1913-14; mem. Brogan & Raymond, 1915-17, Brogan, Ellick & Raymond, 1919-29; v.p. and gen. counsel State Bank of Chicago, 1929; v.p. Foreman State Trust Savs. Bank, Chicago, 1929-31; mem. law firm Raymond, Mayer Jenner & Block, and predecessor firms, 1931-68; dir. Selected Am. Shares, Inc., State Nat. Bank of Evanston (Ill.), 1960-75. Trustee U. Nebraska Found.; mem. Northwestern U. Assos.; trustee Kenilworth, Ill., 1937-45, pres. 1945-49. Served as capt. to maj. U.S. Army, World War I; col. Inf., U.S. Ret. Recipient Distinguished Service award U. Neb., 1962. Fellow Am. Bar. Found.; mem. Am., Ill., Fed., Internat., Chgo., Neb. (pres. 1929) bar assns., Selden Soc., Am. Legion (comdr. Omaha post 1925), Res. Officers Assn., Order of Coif, Phi Beta Kappa, Phi Kappa Kappa Psi, Phi Delta Phi, Delta Sigma Rho. Conglist. Clubs: Chicago, Glenview, Mid-Day, Chicago Literary, Chicago Law (pres. 1956-57), Kenilworth, Caxton. Contributor of various articles to legal jours. Home: Kenilworth, Ill., Died Oct. 30, 1975.

RAYMOND, ERNEST, author; b. Argentieres, Frances, Dec. 31, 1888; s. William Bell and Ida Agnes (Calder) R.; student Chichester (Eng.) Theol. Coll., 1912—14, Durham U., 1914; m. Zoe Irene Maude Doucett, June 1922 (div.); children—Lella Deirdre, Patrick Ernest; m. 2d, Diana Joan Young, May 1940; 1 son, Peter John Francis, Ordained to ministry Ch. of Eng., 1914; resigned orders, 1923; writer, lecturer, from 1923—75. Borough councillor Hampstead Boro Council, London, 1962—65. Served with Brit. Army, 1915—19. Decorated knight officer Order of Merit (Italy), officer Order Brit. Empire; recipient Brit. Book Guild Gold medal 1936. Fellow Royal Soc. Lit.; mem. Soc. Authors London (councillor, pension fund trustee), Keats—Shelley Meml. Ass., Dickens Fellowship (past pres.). Mem. Ch. Eng. Liberal. Club: Garrick (London). Author: Tell England, 1922; We, the Accused, 1935; Gentle Greaves, 1949; The Visit of Brother Ives, 1960; Paris, City of Enchantment, 1961; Mr. Olim, 1961; The Chatelaine, 1962; One of our Brethren, 1963; Late in the Day, 1964; The Tree of Heaven, 1965; The Mountain Farm, 1966; The Bethany Road, 1967; (autobiography) The Story of My Days, 1968; Please You, Draw Near, 1969; Good Morning, Good People, 1970; numerous others. Contbr. poems and articles to periodicals. Home: London, England. Died May 14, 1974; buried Hampstead Cemetery, London, England.

RAYMOND, PERCY EDWARD, paleontologist; b. New Canaan, Conn., May 30, 1879; s. George Edward and Harriet Frances (Beers) R.; Ithaca High Sch.; A.B., Cornell Univ., 1902; Ph.D., Yale Univ., 1905; A.M. (hon.), Harvard University, 1942; m. Eva Grace Mayham Goodenough, Aug. 3, 1904; 1 dau., Ruth Elspeth. Asst. in paleontology, Cornell U., 1901-02; asst. in hist. geology, Yale, 1905; asst. curator in charge invertebrate paleontology, Carnegie Mus., Pittsburgh, 1904-10; invertebrate paleontologist, Geol. Survey of Can., 1910-12; prof. invertebrate paleontology, Univ. of Pittsburgh, 1909-11; asst. prof., 1912-17, Harvard, asso. prof., 1917-29; prof. paleontology, 1929-45, prof. emeritus, from 1945; curator invertebrate paleontology, Museum Comparative Zoology, 1912-45, emeritus, from 1945. Fellow Geol. Soc. of America, Paleontol. Soc. (pres. 1934), A.A.A.S., Am. Acad. of Arts and Sciences; mem. Pewter Collectors Club of America (pres. 1946-47), Gamma Alpha, Sigma Xi. Clubs: Faculty of Cambridge (Mass.); Rushlight (pres. 1941-43). Republican. Episcopalian. Author: Prehistorie Life, 1939; numerous articles on paleontology and geology in scientific periodicals, also articles on antique pewter. Awarded Walker prize for contributions to natural history, 1928. Home: Lexington, Mass.*†

RAYNER, ERNEST ADOLPHUS, educator; b. Plymouth, Mo., July 15, 1878; s. of W. Harris and Celia (Rockwell) R.; B.S., Cornell Coll., Ia., 1901, M.A., 1912; B.D., Drew Theol. Sem., 1904, Th.D., 1915; Ph.D., New York U., 1915; m. Klara A. Bruske, Sept. 17, 1904; children—Dorothy Louise, Helen Harris. Ednl. work in Philippines, 1906-11; grad. study in U.S., 1911-15; prof. philosophy and psychology, Neb. Wesleyan U., 1915-19; pres. Union Coll. of Philippines, and prof. philosophy and psychology, 1919-23; engaged in spl. psychol. study of primitive peoples of the Philippines. Lecturer in U.S. on Oriental situation, 1923-24; dept. of psychology U. of Southern Calif., 1924-33; prof. psychology, San Diego State Coll., 1933-35; supt. research on prevention juvenile delinquency, San Diego County, and dir. Escondido Child Guidance Clinic, from 1935. Mem. Soc. for Adult Edn. (editorial staff and program dir.), Am. Psychol. Assn., Phi Beta Kappa. Author: Pangasinan Grammar and Dictionary; An Educational Survey of the Philippines; Psychological Moments. Contbr. to mags. Address: Escondido, Cal.†

RAYNOLDS, JOHN MADISON, banker; b. Central City, Colo., June 18, 1878; s. Joshua S. and Sarah (Robbins) R.; grad. Phillipe Acad., Andover, Mass., 1896; A.B., Harvard, 1900; m. Mabel Van Eaton, of Indianapolis, Ind., 1915; children—Ruth, Sarah, Kate. Settled in Albuquerqe, N.M., 1915; became pres. First Nat. Bank, 1916, later chmn. bd. and pres.; retired. Home: Albuquerque, N.M.†

RAYSOR, THOMAS MIDDLETON, prof. of English; b. Chapel Hill, Tex., Mar. 9, 1895; s. Paul Montgomery and Mary Elizabeth (Matthews) R.; student U. of Tex., 1912-13, U. of Chicago, 1914; A.B., Harvard, 1917, Ph.D., 1922; m. Ellen Devereux Koopman, July 5, 1923; children—Cecily Devereux, Joan Gilmer. Instr. in Latin, Allen Acad., Bryan, Tex., 1914-15; instr. in English, Agrl. and Mech. Coll. of Tex., 1917-18; asst. prof. English, U. of Minn., 1923-24; asso. prof. English, State Coll. of Washington, 1924-30 (leave of absence 1926-28); prof. U. of Neb. from 1930. Sheldon traveling fellow, Harvard, 1922-23; Guggenheim fellow, 1926-27; Johns Hopkins resident fellow, 1927-28. Served with A.E.F., in France, 1918-19; graduate in arty., O.T.S. (Saumur) after Armistice. Mem. Modern Lang. Assn. America, Phi Beta Kappa. Editor Coleridge's Shakespearean Criticism (2 vols.), 1930, 2d edit., 1960; Coleridge's Miscellaneous Criticism, 1936; Selected Critical Essays on Wordsworth and Coleridge, 1958; editor and part author: English Romantic Poets, 1950, rev. edit., 1956. Contbr. to philol. jours. Home: Lincoln Neb. Died Sept. 8, 1974.

RAZRAN, GREGORY, psychologist; b. nr. Slutsk, Russia, June 4, 1901; s. Solomon and Rebecca (Ongeyber) R.; came to U.S., 1920, naturalized, 1927; B.S., Columbia, 1927, A.M., 1928, Ph.D., 1933; m. Elna Bernholz, Sept. 15, 1939; 1 dau., Lydia. Univ. scholar, Columbia, 1929-30, lectr. psychology, 1930-38, research asso., 1938-40; from instr. to prof. emeritus Queens Coll., N.Y.C., 1940-73, chmn. dept., 1945-66; Distinguished prof. Eckerd Coll., St. Petersburg, Fla., 1972-73; statistical cons., O.S.S., 1941-44; co-chairman International Pavlovian Conference on Higher Nervous Activity, N.Y.C., 1961. Guggenheim fellow, 1948-49. Fellow Am. Psychol. Assn. (pres. div. gen. psychology), A.A.A.S., N.Y. Acad. Scis., (chmn. div. psychology); mem. Eastern Psychol. Assn. Author: Mind in Evolution; An East-West Synthesis, 1971; also monographs, contbr. articles on conditioning and learning theory. Home: Fresh Meadows N.Y. Died Aug. 31, 1973.

READ, CLARK PHARES, educator; b. Ft. Worth, Feb. 4, 1921; s. Clark P. and Helen (Chaudoin) R.; student Tulane U., 1943-45, U. Tex., 1945-46; B.A., M.A., Rice U., 1948, Ph.D., 1950; m. Leota A. Wolff, Oct. 24, 1944; children—Jo Hanna (Mrs. Stephen S. Tobias), Victoria Helen, Thomas Jefferson, Cathleen Eliot. AEC fellow Rice U., 1949; asst. prof. zoology U. Cal. at Los Angeles, 1950-54; asso. prof. pub. health Johns Hopkins, 1954-

59; prof. biology, chmn. dept. Rice U., 1959-73; prof. epidemiology Baylor U. Sch. Medicine, 1961-65; research prof. Tex. A. and M. U., 1963-70. Chmn. tropical medicine study sect. USPHS, 1960-65. Chmn. Houston br. Am. Civil Liberties Union, 1968-70. Mem. adv. bd. U. Tex. Sch. Pub. Health, 1967-73, Martin L. King Found., 1968-73; trustee Marine Biol. Lab. Served with USNR, 1941-45. Guggenheim fellow, 1959-60; grantee USPHS, 1954-73. Mem. Am. Soc. Parasitologists (Henry B. Ward medal 1959), Soc. Gen. Physiologists, Am. Soc. Tropical Medicine, Soc. Protozoologists, Sigma Xi, Democrat. Unitarian. Author: Introduction to Parasitology, 1961; Parasitism and Symbiology, 1970; Animal Parasitism, 1972; also sci. papers. Home: Houston, Tex. Died Dec. 24, 1973.

READ, FLORENCE MATILDA, college pres., b. Delevan, N.Y., Nov. 12, 1885; d. William Ervin and Cornelia Minerva (Waldo) R.; B.A., Mount Holyoke Coll., 1909, hon. Litt.D., 1929; LL.D., Oberlin Coll., 1939, Atlanta University, 1953, Reed Coll., 1961. Alumnae secretary Mount Holyoke Coll., 1909-11; sec. to pres., later sec., Reed Coll., Portland, Ore., 1911-20; asst. sec., later exec. sec., Internat. Health Bd. Rockefeller Found., N.Y.C., 1920-27; pres. Spelman Coll., 1927-53, emeritus, 1953; acting pres., Atlanta U., 1936-37. Served with med. section, Council of Nat. Defense, Washington, D.C., and with Y.M.C.A., in France, 1918-19. Trustee Atlanta University; mem. board trustees Morehouse College. Awarded the Royal Medal of Reward in Gold with Crown by Denmark in 1927. Mem. Am. Assn. Univ. Women, Mount Holyoke Coll. Alumae Assn., Phi Beta Kappa. Author: The Story of Spelman College, 1961. Club: Cosmopolitan (N.Y.C.). Address: Claremont Cal. Died Apr. 29, 1973; buried Delevan, N.Y.

READ, GEORGE WINDLE, JR., army officer; b. Ft. Grant, Ariz., July 29, 1900; s. George Windle and Burton (Young) R.; basic course Cavalry Sch., 1921; grad. Command and Gen. Staff Sch. 1941; m. Ernestine Renzel, Nov. 18, 1933. Commd. 2d lt., inf. res., U.S. Army, 1919, advanced through grades to lt. gen., 1955; participated in 3 major campaigns, overseas, World War I; and 5 major campaigns in Europe with 6th Armored Div., World War II; now comdg. gen. Hdqrs. 2d U.S. Army Station. Decorated D.S.M., Silver Star, Legion of Merit, Bronze Star with oak leaf cluster; Order of Merit (Chile); Legion of Honor, Croix de Guerre with palm (France); Croix de Guerre with palm (Belgium); Croix de Guerre (Luxembourg). Home: Aptos, Cal. Died Dec. 15, 1974.

READ, HELEN APPLETON, art historian; b. Bklyn., 1887; d. Ruel Ross and Mary (Schaumburg) Appleton; grad. Bklyn. Heights Sem.; A.B., Smith Coll., 1908; student Art Students League, 1909-12; m. Charles Albert Read, May 29, 1914; 1 dau., Helen (Mrs. Edmund K. Trent). Art critic Bklyn. Daily Eagle, 1912-38; contbg. art editor Vogue mag., 1925-31; dir. Portraits, Inc., 1943-57, pres., 1957-74; dir. exhbn. 400 Years of German Painting, 1939, Am. painting sent to Latin Am. capitols, 1943, under auspices coordinator cultural relations between N. Am. and S. Am. Recipient Medal of Honor, Salmagundi Club, 1967; medal Smith Coll., 1968. Lectr. Am. and German art, romantic art, Am. colls. and univs. Mem. Alumnae Assn. Smith Coll., Bklyn. Jr. League (charter). Clubs: Cosmopolitan, Smith College (N.Y.C.). Author: Robert Henri, 1931; Caspar David Friedrich, 1939. Contbr. to art publs. Home: Brooklyn, N.Y., Died 1974.

READ, HERBERT HAROLD, geologist; b. Whitstable, Kent, Eng., Dec. 17, 1889; s. Herbert and Caroline (Keam) R.; B.S., Imperial Coll., U. London (Eng.), 1912, D.Sc., 1924; D.Sc., Columbia, 1954, U. Dublin (Ireland), 1956; m. Edith Browning, June 21, 1917; 1 dau., Marguerite (Mrs. Peter Alexander Colligan). With H.M. Geol. Survey, Scotland, 1914-31; George Heidman prof. geology U. Liverpool (Eng.), 1931-38; prof. Imperial Coll., U. London, 1939-55, prof. emeritus, 1955-70, pro-rector, 1952-55, dean Royal Sch. Mines, 1943-45; Walker-Ames vis. prof. U. Wash., Seattle, 1949, Alexander du Toit Meml. lectr. Johannesburg, S.Africa, 1951. Fellow Royal Soc. (Royal medal 1963), Royal Soc. Edinburgh, Geol. Soc. London (Wollaston medal 1952, Bigsby medal 1955); fgn. mem. Geol. Soc. Portugal; corr. mem. Societe Geologique de Belgique (A. Dumont medal 1950), Geol. Soc. Am. (Penrose medal 1967), Societe geologique de France, French Acad. Scis., Associe de l'Academie Royale de Belgique (priz Fourmarier 1960); mem. Royal Coll. Sci. London (asso.), Norweigian Acad., Geol. Soc. Edinburgh (past pres.), Geol. Soc. Liverpool (past pres.), Geologists Assn. (past pres.), Geol. Soc. London, Internat. Geol. Congress. Author: Geology, 1949; The Granite Controversy, 1954; (with J. Watson) Introduction to Geology, Vol. I, 1962; Beginning Geology, 1966; also numerous articles. Office: Boulder Colo. Died Mar. 29, 1970.

READ, HORACE EMERSON, lawyer, educator; b. Port Elgin, N.B., Can., Apr. 8, 1898; s. Charles Herbert and Gertrude Nettie (Oulton) R.; B.A., Acadia U., Wolfville, N.S., 1921; D.C.L. (Hon.), 1951; LL.B., Dalhousie U., Halifax, N.S., 1924; LL.M., Harvard, 1925, S.J.D., 1934; K.C., Nova Scotia 1941; LL.D., Queen's U., 1961, Dalhousie U., 1972; m. Helena Louise Miller, Dec. 23, 1925; children—Aveleigh Ann, Robert Miller. Barrister, solicitor, partner Archibald & Read, Truro, N.S., 1924; mem. faculty Dalhousie U., 1925—72, Munro prof. law, 1931—34, dean Law Sch., 1950—64, dean emeritus, Sir James Dunn prof. law, 1964—72, univ. v.p. 1964—69; research fellow Harvard Law Sch., 1933—34; prof. law U. Minn., 1934—50; vis. prof. Hastings Coll. Law, U. Cal., summer 1962; admitted to Minn. bar, 1940. Mem. adv. com. Interstate Commn. on Crime, 1935; retained in Trail Smelter Arbitration, Can.—U.S., 1937; chmn. N.S. Labor Relations Bd., 1950—72; dir. N.S. Center for Legislative Research, 1950—65; mem. Commn. Uniformity Legislation in Can., 1950—68, pres., 1957—58; UN Observer Costa Rican election, 1958; chmn. com. ednl. standards, Conf. Governing Bodies of Legal Profession Can., 1953—64, pres., 1957—58; chmn. Royal Commn. on Automobile Ins. N.S., 1956—57. Served as flying officer R.A.F., B.E.F., 1916—19; wing comdr. Civil Air Patrol, Minn., 1941—43; comdr. Canadian Navy, 1943—45; chmn. Canadian Naval Regulations Revision Com., chmn. Naval Orders Com., 1943—45; drafted Naval Service Act of Can., 1944; directed complete revision Can. Naval Regs. (K.R.C.N.), 1943—45. Decorated Order Brit. Empire, 1946. Mem. Canadian Bar Assn. (v.p. 1951—53), Am. Soc. Internat. Law, Assn. Canadian Law, Tchrs. (pres. 1956—57), Canadian Inst. Internat. Affairs, Barrister' Soc. Nova Scotia (council 1950—64; hon. pres. 1966—67), Internat. Law Assn. (v.p. Canadian br. 1964—68), Order of Coif, Phi Delta Phi, Acacia. Bapt. 1st Mason. Clubs: Harvard. Author: Equity and Public Wrongs, 1933; Recognition and Enforcement of Foreign Judgements in Common Law Units of British Commonwealth, 1938. Editor: Cases on Personal Chattels, 1931, 2 editions, 1940; Cases on Equity, 1931; Selected Materials on Legislation, 1937; Cases and other Materials on Legislation, 1948. Asso. editor Dominion Law Reports, 1932—34; mem. editorial adv. bd. Canadian Bar Review, 1950—64. Editor: Cases and Materials on the Law of Contracts in Can., 1955. Home: Halifax Nova Scotia Canada. Died Feb. 26, 1975.

READ, JOHN ROYALL, ret. bus. exec.; b. Wytheville, Va., Oct. 24, 1881; s. John Thomas and Josephine (Withers) R.; student pub. schs. Wytheville, Va.; m. Katherine Harwood Taylor, Dec. 30, 1905; children—John Royall, Beverley. Shipper Aluminum Co. America, New Kensington, Pa., 1895-97; electrician Sterling White Lead Co., Parnassus, Pa., 1897-98; student Westinghouse Electric & Mfg. Co., East Pittsburgh, Pa., 1898-1902; elec. engr. Cherokee Gold Dredging Co., Oroville, Calif., 1902-03; elec. engr. Northern Calif. Power Co., Redding, 1903-04; dist. office elec. engr. and salesman Canadian Westinghouse Co., Ltd., Vancouver, B.C., 1904-07, dist. office mgr., 1907-37, v.p., Hamilton, Ont., 1937-39, pres., Hamilton, Ont., 1939-49, chmn. bd., from 1944; gen. mgr. Bridge River Power Co., Vancouver, B.C., 1919-25; pres. Hamilton Munitions, Ltd.; pres., dir. B.F. Sturtevant Co. of Can., Ltd.; dir. Can. Westhinghouse Co., Hamilton Munitions, Ltd., B. Greening Wire Co., Westinghouse Elec. Corp., Westinghouse Air Brake Co., Pittsburgh, Union Switch and Signal Company, Swissvale, Pa.; dir. The Bank of Toronto, Toronto Gen. Trusts Corp., Canadian Surety Co., Toronto; Canadian Radio Patents, Ltd., Thermionics, Ltd. Mem. Canadian Mfrs. Assn., Canadian Elec. Assn., Am. Inst. E. E., Assn. Professional engrs. of Province of Ontario, Hamilton C. of C. (dir.), Ont. Motor League. Anglican. Clubs: Electric, Hamilton, Golf and Country (Hamilton, Ont.); Electric, Vancouver (Vancouver, B.C.); Tamahaac, Rideau (Ottawa); Toronto; Duquesne (Pitts). Retired. Home: Richmond, Va.†

READ, MARY LILLIAN, educator; b. at Cedar Rapids, Ia., Mar. 1, 1878; d. John A. and Mary Elizabeth (Barlow) R.; spl. student U. of Chicago 3 yrs.; Clark U. 1 yr.; B.S., Columbia, 1906, also kindergarten supervisor's diploma. Teacher, girls' finishing sch., Washington, D.C., and elementary grades, Elmwood Sch., Buffalo, N.H.; resident social settlement work, Buffalo and N.Y. City, 2 yrs.; investigator, Federal Immigration Commn., 1 yr.; organizer sect. on home in relation to child welfare for New York Child Welfare Exhibit, 1911; organizer, 1911, and dir. Sch. of Mothercraft, N.Y. City; ednl. dir. Nat. Assn. for Mothercraft Edn. Visited schs. in England and Belgium, and attended Internat. Eugenics Congress, London, 1912. Methodist. Author: The Mothercraft Manual, 1916. Address: Peoria, Ill.†

READ, WALDEMER PICKETT, educator; b. Marion, Ida., July 19, 1897; s. George Franklin and Louisa (Pickett) R.; student Latter Day Saints U., 1923; B.S., U. Utah, 1928; M.A., U. Chgo., 1933, Ph.D., 1947; m. Ethel Elizabeth Olsen, Oct. 24, 1924; children—Ronald F., Waldemer Paul, Karen Louisa (Mrs. James Allen Epperson), David Wilford. Tchr. jr. high Tooele Sch. Dist., 1925-27; prin. Latter Day Saints Sem., Manti, Utah, 1928-29; instr. philosophy U. Utah, 1929-42, asst. prof., 1942-45, asso. prof., 1945-48, prof., from 1948, head dept., 1948-64. Mem. Am. Philos. Assn., Mountain-Plains Philosophy Conf., Utah Acad. Scis. Arts and Letters. Author: The Quest for Complete Living, 1934; Knowledge and Goodness, 1961. Editor, contbr.; Great Issues Concerning Freedom, 1962. Home: Salt Lake City Utah. Died Mar. 1975.

REATH, THOMAS, lawyer; b. Phila., Nov. 2, 1890; s. Thomas and Eliza Andrews (Groome) R.; student St. Paul's Sch., Concord, N.H., 1903-07; A.B., U. Pa., 1912, LL.B., 1915; m. Mary Thompson, Apr. 25, 1916; children—Thomas Jr., Henry Thompson, Robert Andrews. Admitted to Pa. bar, 1915, practiced in Phila.; mem. Drinker Biddle & Reath, 1924-68, of counsel, 1968-75. Home: Flourtown Pa. Died Feb. 5, 1975.

RECKORD, MILTON A., adj. gen. of Md.; b. Harford County, Md., Dec. 28, 1879; s. John H. and Lydia A. (Zimmerman) R.; LL.D. (hon.), U. of Md., 1944; Dr. Mil. Sci. and Tactics, Western Md. Coll., 1943; LL.D. (hon.), Pa. Mil. Coll., 1944; m. Bessie Payne Roe, Nov. 11, 1912 (died 1943); 1 dau., Gladys (Mrs. H. F. Jones, Jr.). Enlisted Md. Nat. Guard, 1901, commd. capt. inf., Dec. 1903; entered Federal Service as Maj., 1917, col., 1918; col. Inf. Officers Res. Corps, 1919; appt. col. in Adj. Gen.'s Dept. Nat. Guard of Md., Apr. 1921 and advanced through the grades to brig. gen., April 1924, Lt. gen., 1964; reentered Fed. Service, Feb. 1941 and assumed command of 29th div. in training at Ft. George G. Meade, Md., became comdg. gen. 3d corps area, Jan. 1942; provost marshal gen. European Theater, Dec-1943—June 1945; duty in office of chief of staff, Washington, D.C., June—Nov. 1945; inactive duty, May 1946; adj. gen. Md. from 1945. Decorated Distinguished Service Medal with 2 oak leaf clusters, Bronze Star. Officer Legion of Honor, Croix de Guerre with Palm World War 1, second Croix de Guerre with Palm, World War 11 (France); Order Comdr. of the Bath (England). Mem. Nat. Rifle Assn. (former exec. v.p.), N.G. Assn., Adj. Gen. Assn. Democrat. Presbyterian. Mason. Clubs: Maryland, Baltimore Country; Army—Navy (Washington). Home: Ruxton, Md. Died Sept. 8, 1975.

RECORD, JAMES ROBERT, newspaper editor; b. Paris, Tex., Oct. 3, 1885; s. Julius Polk and Katie (Cross) R.; grad. Paris High Sch., 1901; student U. of Notre Dame (Ind.), 1901-04, U. of Tex., 1904-05; m. Alabell Brown, Dec. 5, 1917. Began as reporter Paris (Texas) News, 1905; reporter Star-Telegram, Fort Worth, Tex., 1907-09, sports editor, 1909-11, city editor, 1911-17, news editor, 1917-23, mng. editor, 1923-56, associate editor, from 1956. President emeritus Texas Associated Press Mng. Editors Assn.; mem. Am. Society Newspaper Assn. Mem. Kappa Sigma. Democrat. Catholic; Knight of St. Gregory. K.C., Elk. Club: Ft. Worth. Editors, Nat. Associated Press Managing Editors. Home: Ft. Worth Tex. Died July 1, 1973.

REDDIX, JACOB L., coll. pres.; b. Vancleave, Miss., Mar. 2, 1897; s. Nathan and Frances F. (Brown) R.; B.S., Ill. Inst. Tech., 1927; m. Daisy Uvasine Shirley, Feb. 23, 1928; 1 dau., Shirley Ann. Instr. math. Roosevelt High Sch., Gary, Ind., 1927-39; Rosenwald fellow U. Chicago, 1939-40; cons. coops. Dept. Agr., 1940; pres. Jackson State Coll., 1940-67; participant Mediterranean Seminar, Inst. Man and Sci., Tunisia, 1967; study edn. Republic of Liberia, Phelps-Stokes Fund, 1949. Omega Psi Phi Achievement Award, 1937. Mem. N.E.A., Am. Legion, Phi Beta Sigma Mason (33 .). Baptist. Author: A Voice Crying in the Wilderness. Home: Jackson, Miss. Died May 9, 1973.

REDMOND, JOHN HARRIS, cons. co. exec.; b. Columbus, O., July 24, 1912; s. John Dugan and Hazel Dell (Shaver) R.; B. Mech. Engring., Ohio State U., 1933; postgrad. Sch. Bus. Adminstrn., Harvard, 1958; m. Ruth H. Leach, Apr. 14, 1932 (dec. July 1948); children—John Sidney, Ruth Hazel; m. 2d, Rose Polansky, Oct. 22, 1949; children—Philip Robert, Thomas Paul. With Westinghouse Electric Corp., 1933-37, Armstrong Cork Co., 1937-40; v.p., gen. mgr. Precisioneering, Inc., 1947-48; with Koppers Co., Inc., Pitts., 1948-64, v.p., tar div., 1961-64, gen. mgr. tar div., 1962-64; v.p., gen. mgr. engineered products group Crane Co., N.Y.C., 1964-65, v.p. research, devel. and planning, 1965-70; pres. Redmond Assos., Wyckoff, N.J., 1970-74. Cons., Pa. Dept. Labor and Industry, from 1951, U.S. Dept. Commerce, Bus. and Def. Services Adminstrn., from 1950; mgmt. cons. to mfg. industry. Pres. bd. suprs. Peters Twp., Pa., 1961-62. Served to col. Ordnance Corps., AUS, 1940-46. Mem. Am. Coke and Coal Chems. Inst. (dir. 1961-62), Nat. Fire Protection Assn. (dir. 1956-57), Nat. Planning Assn. (mem. com. on civilian applications results mil. research and devel.), Soc. Mfg. Engrs., A.I.M., Am. Mgmt. Assn., A.A.A.S., Am. Forestry Assn. (life), Am. Acad. Polit. and Social Sci., Internat. Platform Assn., Soc. for Internat. Devel., Res. Officers Assn. (life), Mem. Dutch Reformed Ch. (elder). Clubs: Duquesne (Pitts.); Harvard (Boston). Home: Wyckoff, N.J. Died Feb. 8, 1974.

REDMOND, KENNETH H, fruit marketing exec.; b. Elwood, Ind., 1895; m. Margaret Redmond; 1 son. Pres., mem. exec. com., dir. United Fruit Co., Boston. Home: Waban, Mass., Died Nov. 7, 1975.*

REECE, ERNEST JAMES, librarian; b. Cleveland, O., Nov. 4, 1881; s. James and Eva Mary (Cobbledick) B.; Ph.B., Adelbert Coll. (Western Reserve U.), 1903; post-grad. work, 1905-06; certificate Library Sch., 1905; student Oberlin Grad. Sch. of Theology, 1906-08; student U. of Ill. Grad. Sch., 1916-17; m. Sabra Elizabeth Stevens, Aug. 21, 1915; 1 son, Allan MacDonald. Reference asst. Cleveland Pub Library,

1905-06; librarian, Punahou Sch., Honolulu, T.H., 1908-11; instr. U. of Ill., Library Sch., 1912-15; asso. same, 1915-17; prin. Library Sch., N.Y. Pub. Library, 1917-26; asso. prof. of library administration, Sch. of Library Service, Columbia, 1926-35, prof. of library service, 1938-48, asso. dean, 1944-47, prof. emeritus, from 1948; vis. prof., U. of Ill. Library Sch., Mar.-May 1949, Feb.-June 1915; asst. and acting Librarian, Dayton (Ohio) Public Library and Mus., Feb.-Dec. 1950; exec. officer, U. of Ill. Library Sch., 1952. Pres. Assn. Am. Library Schs., 1922-23, chmn. com. on standards, 1930-33; mem. A.L.A. (chmn. com. on recruiting, 1932-36; mem. exec. bd. 1923-27; mem. council 1922-30, 1932-35, 1937-39; chmn. profl. training sect. 1920-21; chmn. com. on coms. 1927-30; chmn. adv. board for study of special projects 1937-39, chmn. nominating committee, 1945-46), Ohio Library Assn., N.Y. Library Club (mem. council 1923-27, 1928-32 and 1934-36; pres. 1934-35), Phi Beta Kappa. Alpha Tau Omega. Managing editor College and Research Libraries, 1944-45. Author: State Documents for Libraries, 1915; Curriculum in Library Schools, 1936; Programs for Library Schools, 1943. Contributor to professional periodicals. Home: Urbana, Ill.†

REED, FORREST FRANCIS, book co. exec.; b. Fulton, Miss., Sept. 11, 1897; s. Charles Nathaniel and Alma (Gregory) R.; LL.B., Andrew Jackson U., 1940; m. Katherine Mueller, Dec. 17, 1925; children—John Martin, Martha (Mrs. M. Thomas Collins, Jr.). Mgr., Ark. Book Co., 1930-35; organizer, pres. Tenn. Book Co., Nashville, 1935-65; owner Reed & Co., pubs., Nashville, 1965-75. Pres. Tenn. Conv. Christian Chs., 1957. Bd. dirs. Coll. of Bible, 1954-60, Disciples of Christ Hist. Soc., 1952-75, chmn. bd., 1962-66, endowed the soc.'s Forrest F. Reed Lectures, 1965. Mem. Am. Booksellers Assn., Tenn. Edn. Assn., A.L.A., Tenn. Hist. Soc., U.S. C. of C., S.A.R., Tenn. Businessmen's Assn. (pres. 1961). Club: Civitan (local pres. 1951). Home: Nashville, Tenn. Died Mar. 22, 1975; interred Woodlawn Cemetery, Nashville, Tenn.

REED, FRANCIS CABLES, lawyer; b. N.Y.C., Nov. 10, 1903; s. William Henry and Mary Robinson (West) R.; grad. Hotchkiss Sch., 1921; Ph.B., Yale, 1925; LL.B., Harvard, 1928; m. Virginia Rodman, June 25, 1927; children—Mary Caroline Reed Hopkins, Elizabeth Ann (Mrs. John P. Wilson). Admitted to N.Y. bar, 1929, D.C. bar, 1973; asso. firm Hughes, Schurman & Dwight, N.Y.C., 1928-35, partner, 1935-37, Hughes, Hubbard and Reed, 1937-74; dir. Nat. Securities & Research Corp., One William St. Fund, Inc., Collins & Aikman Corp., Hillenbrand Industries, Inc. Bd. dirs. YMCA of the Oranges, from 1947. Trustee, Practicing Law Inst., 1960-73. Served as col. M.I. div. War Dept., 1942-46. Decorated Legion of Merit (Army). Mem. Am., N.Y., D.C. bar assns., N.Y. County Lawyers Assn., Assn. Bar City N.Y., Am. Judiciary Soc., Zeta Psi. Clubs: Downtown Assn. (N.Y.C.); Essex County Country; Orange Lawn Tennis (South Orange, N.J.); Pine Valley Golf; Hyannisport. Home: West Orange, N.J. Died Mar. 4, 1974.

REED, FRANK WALKER, ret. educator; b. Wytheville, Va., June 17, 1881; s. David and Elizabeth Ann (Johnson) R.; A.B., U. Nashville, 1902; M. A., Ph.D., U. Va. (Vanderbilt fellow), 1907; m. Kate Green, Jan. 3, 1920; children—Peyton Davidson, John Waller. Instr. mathematics and astronomy U. Ill., 1907-17; instr. mathematics Cornell, 1919-23; asst. prof. Ohio U., 1923-24, asso. prof., 1924-36, prof. mathematics, 1936-51, ret. 1951. Served as capt., Ill. N.G., 1917-18. Fellow A.A.A.S.; mem. Am. Astron. Soc., Am. Math. Soc., Math. Assn. Am., Sigma Xi. Author sci. papers. Home: Athens, O.†

REED, GEORGE HENRY, educator; b. N.Y.C., Dec. 21, 1905; s. Frederick George and Emma (Ohlsen) R.; B.S., U. Rochester, 1927; M.S., State U. Ia., 1929, Ph.D., 1931; m. Phyllis Jane Lee, Feb. 1, 1936; children—Frederick Lee, Patricia Lee. Instr. chemistry U. Ill., 1931—34, asso., 1934—39; asso. prof. chemistry Knox Coll., 1939—46, Abbott Found. prof. chemistry, 1946—56; prof., chmn. chemistry dept. Union Coll., Schenectady, 1956—71, prof. emeritus, from 1971—75; on sabbatical leave, 1963—64. Served as capt. Chem. Corps, AUS, 1942—46. Mem. Am. Chem. Soc., Ill. Acad. Sci., Sigma Xi, Phi Lambda Upsilon, Alpha Chi Sigma, Delta Kappa Epsilon. Presbyn. Home: Schenectady, N.Y. Died Mar. 23, 1975.

REED, GEORGE MATTHEW, plant pathologist; b. Ingleside, Pa., May 2, 1878; s. Robert and Mary (Walkinshaw) B.; A.B., Geneva Coll., Beaver Falls, Pa., 1900; A.M., U. of Wis., 1904, Ph.D., 1907; m. Mary Agnes Lymer, June 12, 1902. Prof. natural science, Amity Coll., College Springs, Ia., 1900-03; asst. in botany, U. of Wis., 1904-07, instr., 1907; asst. prof. botany, U. of Mo., 1907-12 prof., 1912-18; pathologist in charge cereal smut investigations, U.S. Dept. of Agr., 1919-20; with Brooklyn Botan. Garden, 1921-46; curator emeritus, from 1946. Mem. A.A.A.S., Bot. Soc. America, Am. Phytopathol. Soc., Wis. Acad. Science, Arts and Letters, Am. Genetic Assn., Am. Soc. Naturalists, Sigma Xi. Author of numerous papers on plant pathology, especially on powdery mildew, smut and rust. Address: Pittsburgh, Pa.†

REED, JOSEPH VERNER, financier; b. Nice, France, Jan. 18, 1902; s. Verner Zevola and Mary Dean (Johnson) R.; came to U.S., 1912; grad. Phillips Acad., Andover, Mass., 1922; Ph.B., Yale, 1926; H.H.D., Trinity Coll., 1962; D.H.L., Fairfield U., 1964; m. Permelia Pryor, Dec. 31, 1927; children—Laurel (Mrs. Robert A. Hemmes), Adrian, Nathaniel, Samuel, Joseph Verner. With Brown Bros.-Harriman, N.Y.C., 1928-29; propr. Macgowan & Reed, theatrical producers, N.Y.C., 1929-32; with Hobe Sound Co., N.Y.C., from 1933; a developer Jupiter Island Club, Hobe Sound, 1933; exec. producer Am. Shakespeare Festival, Stratford, Conn., from 1960; pres. Triton Press, N.Y.C., 1949-69. Spl. asst. to U.S. Ambassador Houghton, Paris, France, 1957-60. Mem. Yale U. Council, 1962-68; chmn. Conn. Commn. on the Arts, until 1968. Clubs: Fifth Avenue, Union, River, Century (N.Y.C.); Round Hill, Field (Greenwich, Conn.). Author: The Curtain Falls, 1935; To the Embassy, 1964. Home: Greenwich Conn. Died Nov. 1973.

REED, M(ALCOLM) W(ILLARD), business exec., engr.; b. Lexington, Mass., Dec. 17, 1895; s. Frank Haskell and Gertrude (Fobes) R.; B.S., U.S. Naval Acad., 1916; m. Dorothy Vickery, Sept. 14, 1918; children—Richard W., Dorothy W. (Mrs. L. S. Williams), Phyllis (Mrs. J. F. Andrews), Mary W. (Mrs. J. W. Hirt), Elizabeth (Mrs. W. M. Furey), Malcolm W., Jr., David M. Foreman rope dept. Am. Steel & Wire Co., New Haven, 1919-22, asst. supt., 1922-25, supt., 1925-28; asst. mgr. operations Worcester (Mass.) Dist., 1928-32; chief engr. and asst. to v.p., 1932-36, v.p. in charge operations, 1937-39 (both at Cleveland); chief engr. Carnegie-Ill. Steel Corp., Pitts., 1939-46, v.p. engring., 1947; chief engr. U.S. Steel Corp. of Delaware, 1948, Pitts., v.p. engring., 1949; dir. mem. exec. com. U.S. Steel Corp. of Del., 1949-50; exec. v.p. engring. and raw materials U.S. Steel Co., 1951, dir., mem. exec. com., 1951-60; exec. vice pres. engring. and raw materials, mem. operations policy com. U.S. Steel Corp., 1953-58, exec. v.p.-internat. and raw materials, 1958-61. Engring. assignment. Am. Steel & Wire Co., Worcester, Mass., 1917-19, World War I. Mem. Am. Iron and Steel Inst., Am. Ordnance Assn., Pittsburgh C. of C., Engrs. Soc. of Western Pa. Clubs: Duquesne, Fox Chapel Golf; Pine Valley Golf; Rolling Rock, Laurel Valley Golf. Home: Oakland Pa. Died May 21, 1975; buried Allegheny Cemetery, Pitts.

REED, PHILLIP ALLEN, indsl. engr., educator; b. Oshkosh, Wis., Feb. 6, 1934; s. Howard Elton and Cynthia (Swallow) R.; student Wis. State U., 1951-52; B.S., U. Wis., 1956, M.S., 1956; Ph.D., Ga. Inst. Tech., 1969; m. Jeri Kathryn Risley, Jan. 19, 1955; children—Kathryn Jo, Gwendolyn Jane, Allison Joy, Elisabeth Esther. Systems analyst Rex Chainbelt Inc., Milw., 1956-62; mgmt. systems research specialist Lockheed-Ga. Co., Marietta, 1962-65; asst. prof. indsl. engring. Ga. Inst. Tech., Atlanta, 1967-68; asso. prof. indsl. engring. Purdue U., Lafayette, Ind., 1968-72. Active Boy Scouts Am., Atlanta. Registered profl. engr., Ga. Mem. Am. Inst. Indsl. Engrs., Inst. Mgmt. Scis., Operations Research Soc. Am., Am. Prodn. and Inventory Control Soc., Am. Soc. Engring. Edn., Simulation Councils, Inc., Sigma Xi, Tau Beta Pi, Pi Tau Sigma (F.M. Young award), Alpha Pi Mu, Pi Tau Sigma, Theta Tau. Author: The Effects of Side Rake Angle On Single Point Cutting Tool Pressures, 1956; Perception of Needs and Opportunities for Improvement Within An Industrial Organization: Special Emphasis on its Relation to Structure, 1968. Editor: Production and Inventory Management. Home: West Lafayette Ind. Died July 17, 1972.

REED, SAMUEL MACON, mathematics; b. Charlotte Court House, Va., July 4, 1879; s. Richard Clark and Mary Cantey (Venable) R.; prep. edn., Univ. Sch., Nashville, Tenn.; student Vanderbilt, 1897-99 1901-02; A.B., first honors, U. of S.C., 1906; A.M., Columbia, 1922; m. Louise Campbell, July 21, 1909; children—Samuel Macon, Frederick Venable. Prof. Greek and Latin, Presbyn. High Sch., Columbia, S.C., 1899-1901, 1903-04; prof. mathematics and history, high sch., Rowland, N.C., 1902-03; asst. prof. mathematics, U. of S.C., 1905-06; prof. mathematics and science, Peacock Mil. Sch., San Antonio, Tex., 1907-08; headmaster Donaldson Mil. Sch., Fayetteville, N.C., 1908-16; asso. prof. Greek, Latin and mathematics, Davidson Coll., 1916-20, head math. dept., Hampden-Sydney (Va.) Coll., from 1922, dean, 1923-36. Mem. Phi Delta Theta, Omicron Delta Kappa, Phi Beta Kappa. Presbyn. Retired. Home: Columbia, S.C.†

REED, WAYNE OTIS, ednl. cons.; b. Douglas, Neb., July 2, 1911; s. Len A. and Leola (Rogge) R.; A.B., Neb. State Teachers Coll., Peru, 1935; A.M., U. Neb., 1941, Ph.D., 1949, LL.D., 1964; H.H.D., Coll. Osteo. Med. and Surgery, 1963; m. Adele Penterman, Nov. 28, 1946. Tchr. in rural sch., Otoe County, Neb., 1930-33; prin. high sch., Palmyra, Neb., 1935-36, supt. schs., 1936-38; county supt. schs., Otoe County, Neb., 1939-43; supt. pub. instrn. State of Neb., 1943-50; pres. Neb. State Tchrs. Coll., Peru, 1950-51; asst. commr. state and local sch. systems, U.S. Office Edn., Dept. Health, Edn. and Welfare, Washington, 1951-55, asst. commr. for ednl. services, 1955-57, dep. U.S. commr. edn. 1957-65, asso. U.S. commr. edn. for fed.-state relations, 1965-73; cons. aerospace edn. council Air Force Assn. Recipient Superior and Distinguished Service awards HEW; Distinguished Service award Edn. Commn. of States; Vandenburg award, Fairchild award Air Force Assn.; Frank G. Brewer trophy Nat. Aero. Assn.; Ednl. Achievement award Nat. Council Chief State Sch. Officers; Distinguished Ednl. Service award Peru (Neb.) State Coll.; Service award Nat. Assn. State Bds. Edn.; Wheatley award Univ. Aviation Assn., Future Farmers of Am. Mem. N.E.A., Am. Assn. Sch. Adminstrs. (1952 Yearbook com.), Neb. State Edn. Assn. (past v.p., life mem.), Nat. Congress Parents and Tchrs. (life mem.), Horace Mann League, Native Sons and Daus. Neb., Neb. Hist. Soc., Kappa Delta Pi, Phi Delta Kappa. Republican. Home: Washington, D.C. Died Oct. 28, 1974; buried Rose Hill Cemetery, Otoe County, Neb.

REEMELIN, OSCAR BEN, utilities exec.; b. Cheriot, O., Aug. 29, 1881; s. Edward C. and Belle (Bradford) R.; B.S., U. Cin., 1904; m. Ella Giele, June 25, 1914; children—Benjamin G., Mary K. (Mrs. Crowel Werner), Robert. With Dayton Power & Light Co., from 1905, v.p., from 1925, also dir. Vice pres. city council, Oakwood, O., 1919-25, sch. bd., 1929-35, Dayton chpt. Boy Scouts, 1923-53; chmn. Miami Valley Conservation Com., 1952-56. Clubs: Engrs. (pres. 1935). Kiwanis (pres. 1925) (Dayton). Home: Dayton, O.†

REES, EDWIN HENRY, advt. and pub. relations exec.; b. Wilmington, Del., Dec. 3, 1922; s. Isadore and Miriam (Davis) R.; student Fordham U., 1941-42; m. Claudette Madeleine Bertrand, Oct. 23, 1968; children—Randall Lowell, Robin Irene, Danielle Ann. Staff corr. Time and Life, 1945-61; regional corporate dir. communications TRW, Inc., 1962-69; v.p. pub. relations and advt. Flying Tiger Line, Inc., Los Angeles, 1969-74. Served with USAAF, 1942-45. Decorated D.F.C. Mem. Author's Guild, Aviation Space Writer's Assn. Home: Playa del Rey, Cal. Died Mar. 14, 1974; buried Hillside Meml. Park and Mausoleum, Los Angeles.

REESE, BENJAMIN HARRISON, journalist; b. Sedalia, Mo., Aug. 31, 1888; s. Robert J. and Katherine (Morgan) R.; grad. Hobart (Okla.) High Sch., 1906; m. Estelle Ferrier, Dec. 25, 1909; 1 son, Benjamin H. Reporter Hobart Chief, 1906, Joplin (Mo.) Globe, 1906-07; copy editor St. Louis Republic, 1907-08; city editor Joplin Globe, 1908-09; mng. editor St. Louis Star, 1912-13; city editor St. Louis Post-Dispatch, 1913-38, mng. editor, 1938-51; resident co-chmn. adv. bd., Am. Press Inst. at Columbia U. from 1951. Mem. Am. Soc. of Newspaper Editors. Home: Spring Lake N.J. Died June 10, 1974.

REESE, JOHN D., physician; b. Ventura, Cal., 1907; M.D., U. Cal. at San Francisco, Intern, Marine Hosp., New Orleans, 1934-35; resident in pathology John Gaston Hosp., Memphis, 1946-47; pathologist Moore County Hosp., Pinehurst, N.C., N.C. Sanitarium McCain, 1949-50; asst. pathologist VA Hosp., Oteen, N.C., 1950; past mem. staff VA Hosp., Columbia, S.C.; prof. pathology and bacteriology U. Miss., 1947-49. Served to maj., M.C., AUS, 1941-46. Diplomate Am. Bd. Pathology. Mem. Am. Assn. Pathologists and Baceteriologists, Am. Soc. Microbiology, Am. Sco. Exptl. Pathology. Home: Philipsburg, Pa. Died May 12, 1973; buried Philipsburg, Pa.

REESE, WEBSTER PAUL, eucator; b. Floyd Knob, Ind., Feb. 20, 1879; s. Paul and Naomi (Wooldridge) R.; B.S., U. of Mo., 1917; M.S., U. of Kan., 1919; grad. study, Columbia, 1921, U. of Calif., 1929-30; m. Elma Ida Smith, Oct. 18, 1908; children—Genevieve Lenora, Vincent Iden, Ardalea Ramona. Prin. grad. sch., Lone Elm, Kan., 1905-07; prin. high sch., Welda, Kan., 1908; supt. schs., Bronson, Kan., 1911-15, Delphos, Kan., 1917-19, Peabody, Kan., 1919-23; prof. edn. and head of dept., also dean of summer sessions, Southwestern College, Winfield, Kansas, from 1923, dean of men, from 1934. Mem. N.E.A., Kan. Sch. Masters Club, Phi Delta Kappa, Pi Gamma Mu. Republican. Methodist. Mason (32°). Author: Grading Systems and Their Results, 1919; Personality and Success in Teaching, 1928; An Evaluation of the Program for Training Secondary Teachers in Kansas, 1931; History and Development of the Kansas Program for Training High School Teachers in Public Institutions, 1932. Home: Winfield, Kan.†

REEVE, ARTHUR BENJAMIN, author; b. Patchogue, N.Y., Oct. 15, 1880; s. Walter F. and Jennie (Henderson) R.; B.A., Princeton, 1903; student New York Law Sch., 1903; m. Margaret A. Wilson, Jan. 31, 1906. Asst. editor Public Opinion, 1903-06; editor Our Own Times (annual, vols. IV-X), 1906-10; on staff The Survey, 1907. Republican. Mem. Phi Beta Kappa. Clubs: Princeton (New York); University (Brooklyn); Northport Yacht. Author: The Silent Bullet, 1912; The Black Hand, 1912; The Poisoned Pen, 1913; also The Adventures of Craig Kennedy, Scientific Detective, in Cosmopolitan, 1910-18; Great Cases of William J. Burns, in McClure's, 1911-13; The Dream Doctor, 1914; Guy Garrick, 1914; The War Terror, 1915; The Exploits of Elaine, 1915; The Gold of the Gods, 1915; Constance Dunlap, 1915; The Romance of Elaine, 1916; Social Gangster, 1916; Ear in the Wall, 1916; Treasure Train, 1917; The Adventures, 1917; Love Philter, 1918; Black Menace, 1918. All books acquired by Harper & Brothers, 1917, and issued in set of 12 vols.

Collaborated with Charles W. Goddard on "The Exploits of Elaine," moving picture serial, 1914-15; with Chas. A. Logue, 1916-18, in production of moving picture serials, "The Hidden Hand" and "The House of Hate." Home: Brooklyn, N.Y.†

REEVERTS, EMMA (MARIE), coll. dean of women; b. Belmond, Ia., Aug. 28, 1898; d. Andrew (John) and Dorothea (Watermulder) Reeverts; student Bradley Polytech. Inst., Peoria, Ill., 1916-18; A.B., Hope Coll., Holland, Mich., 1920; A.M., U. of ich., Ann Arbor, 1935; student U. of Chicago, 1941, Northwestern U., Evanston, Ill., 1947. High sch. English instr., Iowa and Wis., 1920-24; prin. Annville (Ky.) Inst., 1924-29; instr. English Berea (Ky.) Coll., 1929-46, part-time, 1963-68, also condr. tours of Appalachia; asso. prof. English Hone Coll., Holland, Mich., after 1946, dean of women 1947-63. Mem. A.A.U.P., Am. Assn. Univ. Women. Nat. Assn. Deans of Women, Michigan Association of Womens Deans and Counselors (v.p. 1952-54, pres. 1955-57), Mortar Bd., Phi Kappa Phi. Reformed Church of America. Home: Holland, Mich., Died Mar. 28, 1973; interred Oregon, Ill.

REEVES, RUSSELL HENRY, editor; b. Cleve., July 17, 1905; s. Clarence Rupert and Mary Ellen (Frank) R.; B.S. in Journalism, Ohio State U., 1927; m. Dorothy Elizabeth Warner, June 29, 1928; children—Roger Alan, Bruce Warner, Thomas Clarence. With Cleve. Plain Dealer, 1927-71, reporter, 1927-28, copy editor, 1928-37, makeup editor, 1937-42, news editor, 1942-56, asst. mng. editor, 1956-62, night mng. editor, 1962, day mng. editor, 1963-71. Bd. dirs. East Cleveland (O.) Library, 1950-51, East Cleveland Sch. Bd., 1951-56, Garden Valley Neighborhood House, 1957-58. Recipient Wolfe hon. journalism medal Ohio State U., 1927. Mem. Sigma Delta Chi. Democrat. Presbyn. Clubs: 1 Cleveland, City, Mid-Day (Cleve.). Home: Euclid, O. Died Aug. 28, 1974; interred Lakeview Cemetery, Cleveland, O.

REEVES, WILLIAM HARVEY, lawyer; b. New Brunswick, N.J., July 8, 1895; s. William Henry Taylor and Anna (Van Kirk) R.; A. B., U. Pa., 1916, A.M., 1919; LL.B., Columbia, 1925; m. Caroline Laura Buck, Aug. 29, 1931; children—Aletheia Reeves Kerr, H. Van Kirk. Examiner, FTC, 1918—19; lectr. Sch. Bus., Columbia, 1920—41; admitted to New York bar, 1926; private practice, New York City, 1926—41, 1945-70; counsel for census foreign—owned property in United States and American—owned assets abroad, U.S. Treasury Dept., 1941—43, liaison U. S. Treasury, Dept. State, 1943—45. Participant at the White House on International Cooperation, November—December 1965. Served with USNRF, World War 1. Recipient Bicentennial Silver Medallion for work in internat. law, Columbia, 1954. Mem. Internat. (patron, chmn. com. on sovereignty 1958—66), Am. (com. fgn. and internat. bus. law from 1960, chmn. from 1967, chmn. com. international law in courts 1963—68). New York State bar assns., Bar Assn. City N.Y., Am. Soc. Internat. Law, Am. Fgn. Law Assn. (past pres.), Internat. Law Assn., Am. Asiatic Assn., Am. Acad. Polit. Sci., St. Nicholas Soc., Delta Sigma Rho. Clubs: University (Washington, N.Y.C.); Pequot Yacht. Bd. editors The Internat. Lawyer, 1966—68. Contbr. articles law publs., polit. sci. jours. Home: Southport, Conn. Died July 9, 1970.

REGAN, JAMES JOSEPH, lawyer; b. Bklyn., Mar. 31, 1905; s. Michael J. and Mary F. (Bergen) R.; LL.B. cum laude, Fordham U., 1927; m. Harriet Greenberg, Nov. 8, 1940; 1 dau., Micaela R. Luhr. Admitted to N.Y. bar, 1928; asso. Medina & Sherpick, N.Y.C., 1928-42, 45-47; partner Sherpick, Gilbert, Regan & Davis, N.Y.C., 1947-55, Sherpick, Regan & Davis, N.Y.C., 1955-65, Choate, Regan, Davis & Hollister, N.Y.C., 1965-74. Sec. The Self-Insurers Assn., 1948, Nat. Council State Self Insurers Assn., 1958-72. Acting police justice, Great Neck, N.Y., 1956-62. Served to lt. comdr. USNR, 1942-45. Mem. Assn. Bar City N.Y., N.Y. County Lawyers Assn., Am., N.Y. bar assns. Unitarian. Club: Lawyers (gov.). Home: Port Washington, N.Y. Died Aug. 3, 1974; buried Nassau Knolls Cemetery, Port Washington, N.Y.

REHBERGER, GEORGE EDWARD, physician, author; b. Baltimore, Md., Nov. 28, 1880; s. John Henry and Sarah Jane (Everett) R.; grad. Baltimore City Coll., 1898; A.B., Johns Hopkins, 1901, M.D., 1905; post-grad. work same univ., 1909; m. Lena Ellen Martin, Jan. 5, 1910. Asst. phys., Craig Colony for Epileptics, Sonyea, N.Y., 1906-10; gen. practice in Wash. and British Columbia, 1910-16; devoted time to study and revision of ms. for publication, 1916-18; course in surgery, Med. officers' T.C., Camp Greenleaf, Ft. Oglethrope, Ga., 1918. Served as pvt. 5th Md. Inf., U.S. Vols., Spanish-Am. War, 1898; mem. escort detachment Mil. Hdqrs'., Port of Embarkation, Hoboken, N.J., 1918, title of 1st lt. Md. Corps; ward surgeon, U.S.A. Gen. Hosp. No. 19, Oteen, N.C., 1919. Mem. A.M.A., Phi Beta Kappa. Author: Clinical Medicine, 1920. Home: Baltimore, Md.†

REHM, THEODORE A., corp. exec.; b. Meriden, Conn., Oct. 26, 1901; s. Albert F. and Wilhelmina (Ross) R.; B.S., U. Pa., 1924; m. Marianna Barnes, Feb. 8, 1939; children—Sanchia, Palmer (dec.), Joan, Beverly, Perdita, Nadine. Began career with Fed. Res. Bank Phila.; co-organizer Keystone Orgn., Boston, 1932, v.p. charge supervisory and operating phases 1932-54, ret.; established investment cons. orgn., Phoenix; pres., dir. Flagstaff Indsl. Park, Inc., Western Computing, Phoenix. Mem. Phoenix Soc. Financial Analysts, Gen. Alumni Assn. U. Pa., Scottsdale Dog Fanciers Assn., Sigma Chi. Clubs: Middlesex County Kennel, Golden Retriever Am., Paradise Valley Country, Arizona. Home: Paradise Valley Ariz. Died July 3, 1974.

REICHARDT, KONSTANTIN, educator; b. St. Petersburg, Russia, Apr. 30, 1904; s. Robert and Adelheid (Hoffmann) R.; student Sch. of Swiss Ref. Ch., St. Petersburg, Russia, 1912-14, Masimilians Gymnasium, Munich, Germany, 1914-15, Prinz Heinrichs Gymnasium, Berlin, Germany, 1915-23; Ph.D., Berlin U., 1927; A.M. (hon.), Yale, 1947; m. Patricia Lorraine Barker, Nov. 3, 1944; 1 dau., Maria Erica. Came to U.S., 1938, naturalized, 1944. Lectr., Old Norse, U. Berlin, 1926-29; asst. and lectr. U. Cologne (Germany), 1930; prof. Scandinavian and Germanic philology, head Scandinavin dept. U. Leipzig, 1931-37; lectr. German and Norse philology U. Minn., 1938-39, prof. German and Scandinavian langs., 1939-45, prof. linguistics and comparative philology, chmn. dept., 1945-47, chmn. com. Russian area studies, 1946-47; prof. Germanic philology Yale, 1947-70, Leavenworth prof. Germanic lang. and lit., 1970-72, emeritus, 1972-75, dir. grad. studies Germanics, 1961-72, acting chmn. dept. Germanic langs., 1965-66, acting chmn. dept. Medieval studies, 1967-68, adviser on Scandinavian and Icelandic lit. to Univ. Library, 1948-72, fellow Davenport Coll., Yale, 1948-75; Fulbright lectr., Marburg. Germany, 1957-58, traveling fellow Norway, 1927, 28; del. Prussia Acad. Scis. to investigate German manuscripts, Royal Library, Copenhagen, 1930; del. Rask-Orsted Found, 1938, Internat. Germanists Congress, Copenhagen, 1960. Decorated knight's cross Icelandic Order Falcons. Recipient William C. DeVane medal Yale, 1973. Bollingen Found. fellow, 1955. Mem. Icelandic Acad. Sci. Unitarian. Author: Studien zu den Skalden des 9, und 10, Jahrhunderts, 1928; Thule, 1934; Runenkunde, 1936; Germanische Welt vor tausend Jahren, 1936; etc. Editor: Altnordische Uebungstexte, 1934-75; co-editor Festschift-H.J. Weigand, 1957. Translator: Sigurd Hoel, Ein Tag in Oktober (from Norwegian), 1932; Frans G. Bengtson, Karl XII (from Swedish), 1938. Contbg. author Grimms Deutsches Worterbuch, Walde-Pokorny, Indogermanisches Worterbuch, Hessen's Irish Dictionary: also numerous articles German, Swedish and Am. periodicals. Chmn. editorial com. William Dwight Whitney Linguistic Series, 1949-72. Home: New Haven, Conn., Died Jan. 19, 1976.

REID, DUNCAN EARL, educator, physician; b. Burr Oak, Ia., Dec. 22, 1905; s. George and Emma (Ballentine) R.; B.S., Ripon Coll., 1927; M.D., Northwestern U., 1932; M.A. (hon.), Harvard, 1947; m. Clare Belle Hipp, Dec. 7, 1933; children—Duncan Earl, Janet Christine Reid (Mrs. John Keller), David Christopher. Intern gen. surgery St. Luke's Hosp., Chgo., 1931-32, resident gynecology, 1932; intern pathology Cook County Hosp., Chgo., 1933; resident obstetrics Boston Lying-in-Hosp., 1933-35, asst. obstetrician, 1936-46, sr. obstetrician, 1946, 47, obstetrician-in-chief, 1947-59, chief staff, 1959-66, Boston Hosp. for Women, from 1966; Austin teaching fellow Harvard Med. Sch., 1938-39, instr. obstetrics, 1941-47, William Lambert Richardson prof. obstetrics, from 1947, head dept. obstetrics, 1947-59, head dept. obstetrics and gynecology, from 1959, Kate Macy Ladd prof. obstetrics and gynecology, from 1964; cons. obstetrics Beth Israel, Children, Mass. gen. hosps.; clin. cons. obstetrics and gynecology Boston City Hosp. Rockefeller fellow Harvard Med. Sch., 1936-37. Diplomate Am. Bd. Obstetrics and Gynecology. Fellow A.C.S.; mem. Am. Assn. Obstetricians and Gynecologists, Am. Coll. Obstetricians and Gynecologists (past pres.), Am., Boston gynecol. socs., A.M.A., Boston Surg. Soc., Mass. Med. Soc., Gynecol. Investigation. Author: A Textbook of Obstetrics, 1962; (with others) Principles and Management of Human Reproduction, 1971. Home: Brookline Mass. Died Nov. 1973.

REID, E. EMMET, chemist; b. Fincastle, Va., June 27, 1872; s. Thomas Alfred and Virginia (Ammen) R.; M.A., Richmond (Va.) Coll., 1892, LL.D., 1917; Ph.D., Johns Hopkins, 1898; m. Margaret Kendall, Dec. 28, 1915; children—Emmet Kendall, Alfred Gray, Martha Bell, Teacher science, Mt. Lebanon (La.) Coll., 1892-94; prof. chemistry, Coll. of Charleston, S.C., 1898-1901, Baylor U., Waco, 1901-08; research asst. and Johnston scholar, Johns Hopkins, 1908-11; research chemist, Colgate & Co., 1911-14; asso. prof., later prof. organic chemistry, Johns Hopkins, 1914-37, prof. emeritus from 1937; visiting prof. U. of Chicago, summer 1930. Gas warfare investigations, Bur. of Mines, War Dept., May 1917-Jan. 1919; research adviser to U. of Richmond, U. of S.C., Furman U., U. of Ala., Ga. Poly., Howard Coll., Birmingham-Southern Coll. Consultant du Pont Co., Hercules Powder Co., Socony-Vacuum Oil Co., Thiokol Corp., Chemical Warfare Service. Awarded Herty medal, 1947. Member American Chemical Society, Phi Beta Kappa. Democrat. Baptist. Translator of Sabatier's Catalysis in Organic Chemistry, 1921. Author: Introduction to Research in Organic Chemistry, 1924; College Organic Chemistry, 1929, Contbr. numerous papers to Am. Chem. Jour., Jour. Am. Chem. Soc., etc. Awarded Herty medal, 1947. Home: Baltimore Md. Died Dec. 21, 1973.

REID, JOHN, JR., architect; b. San Francisco, Dec. 26, 1879; s. John and Ann Marshall (Cunningham) R.; A.B., U. of Calif., 1904; diploma, Ecole Des Beaux Arts, Paris, 1909; unmarried. Began practice 1909; cons. architect, construction of City Hall and Civic Center, San Francisco, 1912-17; city architect, City Planning Commn., San Francisco, 1918-30; cons. architect. Bd. Edn., Berkeley, Calif., 1937-38. Fellow (1937) A.L.A. (certificate of honor from N. Calif. Chapter, 1927; mem. Phi Delta Theta, Tau Sigma Delta. Presbyterian. Republican. Club: Bohemian (San Francisco). Home: San Francisco, Cal.†

REIDY, E. T., railroad exec.; b. Chgo., Apr. 4, 1903; s. Michael M. and Margaret (Donlan) R.; m. Fleurette M. Bentley, June 26, 1926; children—E. T., Maureen M. With C.G.W. R.R., 1926-73, beginning as clk., successively sec. to operating v.p., sec. to pres., asst. corporate sec., corporate sec., gen. mgr., v.p., 1926-57, became pres. and chmn. exec. com., 1957, chmn. bd. and pres.; dir. St. Paul Union Depot Co., Minn. Transfer Ry., Kansas City Union Depot. Home: Knasas City, Mo., Died Oct. 14, 1975.

REIFENSTEIN, EDWARD CONRAD, Med. educator; b. Syracuse, N.Y., Jan. 22, 1880; s. Henry William and Emma (Mayer) R.; M.D., Syracuse U., 1904; m. Florence M. H. Kappesser, Dec. 7, 1904; children—Edward Conrad, George Henry, Robert Warren. Asso. with Coll. of Medicine, Syracuse U., from 1904, as instr. in histology, 1904-07, in medicine, 1907-15, asst. prof., 1915-17, asso., 1917-18, prof. clin. medicine, 1918-32, prof. of medicine, 1932-46, prof. emeritus medicine, from 1946. Director of Medicine, University Hosp. of the Good Shepherd, Syracuse Free Dispensary; consultant City Hosp. (Syracuse, N.Y.). Syracuse Psychopathic Hosp., Broad St. Hosp. (Oneida, N.Y.), Lee Memorial Hosp. (Fulton, N.Y.), Potsdam Hosp. (Potsdam, N.Y.). Served as capt., Med. Corps, U.S. Army, 1918-19. Trustee Syracuse U., from 1944. Fellow A.C.P.; diplomate Am. Board of Internat. Medicine; mem. Syracuse Acad. Medicine, N.Y. Acad. Medicine, A.A.A.S., Sigma Xi, Alpha Kappa Kappa, Phi Kappa Phi. Republican. Episcopalian. Mason (32°). Clubs: Golf, Country (Syracuse). Contbr. numerous articles on internal medicine and cardiology. Home: Syracuse, N.Y.†

REIFENSTEIN, EDWARD CONRAD, JR., med. research adminstr., endocrinologist; b. Syracuse, N.Y., Dec. 7, 1908; s. Edward Conrad and Florence Marie Henrietta (Kappesser) R.; A.B., Syracuse U., 1930, M.D. magna cum laude, 1934; research fellow in medicine Harvard Med. Sch., 1940-46; m. Esther Claire Tilden, June 9, 1934; children—Edward Conrad III, Susan Tilden (Mrs. Beyers). Rotating intern Syracuse (N.Y.) U. Hosp., 1934-35, med. resident, 1935-36; psychiat. resident Syracuse (State) Psychopathic Hosp., 1936-37, cons. in medicine and psychiatry, 1937-40; med. resident (part time) Syracuse U. Free Dispensary, and practice medicine specializing in internal medicine and psychiatry with Dr. E. C. Reifenstein, Sr., Syracuse; ward asst. Syracuse U. Hosp., instr. in medicine and psychiatry, Syracuse U. Coll. Medicine, 1937-40; practice with Dr. Fuller Albright, internal medicine and endocrinology, grad. asst. in medicine Mass. Gen. Hosp., Boston, 1940-46; clin. endocrinologist and research asso. Meml. Hosp. Cancer Center, Sloan-Kettering Inst., N.Y.C., 1946-50, clin. research cons., 1946-49, exec. dir. med. and research div., 1949-50, Ayerst, McKenna & Harrison, Ltd., N.Y.C.; dir. Okla. Med. Research Inst. and Hosp., Oklahoma City, 1950-53; prof. research medicine U. Okla. Sch. Medicine, 1950-53; dir. biol. and therapeutic research div. Schering Corp., Bloomfield, N.J., 1953-54; sr. asso. clin. research dir. Squibb Inst. Med. Research, E.R. Squibb & Sons div. Squibb Corp., Princeton, N.J., 1954-74; asst. clin. prof. medicine N.Y. Med. Coll., 1954-74; asst. attending physician Flower and Fifth Av. Hosp., 1954-74; med. cons. Bone Density Research and Evaluation Center, Coll. Physics and Chemistry, Pa. State U., 1954-57. Mem. Com. on Therapeutic Nutrition, Food and Nutrition Bd., NRC, 1950-53, com. on cancer diagnosis and therapy Div. Med. Scis. NRC, 1951-54, Metabolism and Nutrition Study Sect. NIH, 1951-54. List of Sci. Personnel, War Manpower Commn., 1942-46; responsbile investigator, OSRD, 1942-46. Diplomate Nat. Bd. Fellow Am. Psychiat. Assn., A.C.P. (life); mem. A.M.A. (study group on metabolic diseases, subcom. on steroids and hormones, com. on research, council on pharmacy and chemistry, 1952-54), N.Y., N.J., Syracuse acads. medicine, N.Y. Acad. Scis., Soc. Exptl. Biol. Medicine, Gerontol. Soc., Am. Fed. Clin. Research, Am. Soc. Clin. Investigation, A.A.A.S., Endocrine Soc., Am. Geriatrics Soc., Am. Soc. Clin. Pharm. Therapeutics, Am. Assn. for Cancer Research, Am. Med. Writers Assn., So. Med. Assn., So. Soc. Clin. Investigation, Central Soc. Clin. Research, Am. Fertility Soc., Alpha Omega Alpha, Sigma Xi, Alpha Kappa Kappa, Psi Upsilon, Phi Kappa Phi, Pi Delta Epsilon. Episcopalian. Author articles in jours.; editor Transactions of Macy Conferences on Convalescence and on Metabolic Interrelations; co-author book on metabolic bone disease, 1948. Described (with others) Klinefelter Syndrome, Reifenstein's Syndrome, 1943, 47, 65. Home: Kinnelon, N.J., Died July 1975.

REILLY, JOSEPH F., stockbroker; b. Corona, N.Y., 1906. With firm Laidlaw & Co., N.Y.C.; pres. Am. Stock Exchange Clearing Corp., N.Y.C., also chmn. Vice chmn. Am. Stock Exchange. Home: Brooklyn N.Y. Died Feb. 1974.

REILLY, THOMAS DANIEL, lawyer; b. Dayton, O., Apr. 19, 1927; s. Daniel George and Mildred Louise (Boyce) R.; student U. Dayton, 1945-48; J.D., U. Cin., 1951; m. Frances Millicent Terrill, Feb. 16, 1957; children—Vivian Marie, James Daniel, Patricia Eileen, Thomas Edward. Admitted to Ohio bar, 1951; practiced in Dayton, O., 1951-74, Kettering, O., 1964-74; mem. firms Magsig, Brumbaugh, Ryan & Reilly, Dayton, 1951-58, Shea & Reilly, Dayton, 1958-72, Parkin, Reilly, Hunt & Jennings, Dayton, 1973-74, Reilly & Dodsworth, Kettering, 1964-74; asst. atty. gen Ohio, 1959-62, 71; spl. asst. to prosecutor Montgomery County (O.), 1965. Sec. South Dayton (O.) Med. Assn., 1968-74, dir., 1968-74. Mem. central, exec. coms. Montgomery County Dem. Party, 1961-74, also ward leader; parlimentarian com. Montgomery County Dem. Party, 1966-74; campaign chmn. Montgomery County atty. gen., 1966, 1970. Served with USNR, 1944-45. Recipient Comnrs. award Montgomery County, 1968. Mem. Dayton (Service award 1971), Ohio bar assns., Am. Judicature Soc., Phi Delta Phi. Home: Kettering O. Died May 26, 1974.

REINHARDT, EMMA, educator; b. Pittsfield, Ill.; d. John and Amelia (Mart) Reinhardt; A.B., U. Ill., 1924, A.M., 1925, Ph.D. 1927. Joined Eastern Ill. U., Charleston, Ill., 1927, asst. prof., 1927-29, asso. prof., 1929-34, prof. edn. and head dept., 1934-63, prof. emerita, 1963-73. Mem. N.E.A. (life), Ill. State Hist. Soc. (life), Nat. Retired Tchrs. Assn., Am. Assn. Ret. Persons, Ill. Edn. Assn. (2d v.p. 1946-47; exec. com., Eastern Div., 1954-57, sec. Eastern Div., 1935-38, pres. 1958-59), Nat. Woman's Book Assn., Nat. League Am. Pen Women, Pike County Hist. Soc., U. Ill. Alumni Assn. (life), U. Ill. Found., Nat. Fedn. Women's Clubs, Am. Assn. U. Women, Am. Assn. U. Profs., Nat. Soc. for Study of Edn., Am. Ednl. Research Assn., Nat. Soc. Coll. Tchrs. of Edn., Nat. Fedn. Press Women, Ill. Woman's Press Assn. (3rd v.p. 1956-57), Ill. State U. (pres.'s com.), Phi Beta Kappa, Pi Gamma Mu, Kappa Delta Pi (Honor Key), Delta Kappa Gamma (state pres., 1938-40; nat. pres. 1940-42; recipient nat. achievement award). Presbyn. Clubs: President's (U. Ill.); Business and Professional Women's. Author: American Education, 1959, rev. edit., 1960; articles ednl. mags. Home: Pittsfield, Ill. Died Nov. 11, 1973.

REINHARDT, GUSTAV ADOLPH, metallurgist; b. New Washington, O., Apr. 22, 1881; s. Louis and Barbara (Metzger) R.; B.S. in Chemistry, Case Sch. Applied Science, 1905; Metall. Engr., Harvard, 1913; m. Emma J. Parmater, June 20, 1917; children—Louis John, Gustav. Chemist, Dominion Iron & Steel Co., Sydney, N.S., 6 mos., 1905. Carnegie Steel Co., Ohio Works, Youngstown, 1906; chief chemist Salem Iron Co., Leetonia, O., 1906-07, Cleveland (O.) Furnace Co., 1907-09, Crowell & Murray, Cleveland, 1909-11; asst. to Dir. Albert Sauveur, prof. metallurgy, Harvard, 1912-13; metall. engr., Youngstown Sheet and Tube Co., 1913-29, dir. metallurgy and research, from 1929. Mem. Am. Iron and Steel Inst., Am. Inst. Mining and Metall. Engrs., Am. Welding Soc., Welding Research Council, Am. Soc. for Testing Materials, Am. Standards Assn., Am. Ordnance Assn., Assn. Am. Steel Mfrs. (pres. 1928-30), Iron and Steel Inst. (Eng.), Inst. of Metals (Eng.). Republican. Conglist. Mason (K.T., Shriner). Retired. Home: St. Petersburgh, Fla.†

REINHARDT, JAMES MELVIN, educator, author, handwriting identification expert; born on farm near Dalton, Ga., Oct. 5, 1894; s. Theophilus Walton and Sarah (Pelfrey) R.; A.B., Berea (Ky.) Coll., 1923; student U. of Chicago, summers 1924, 25; A.M., University of North Dakota, 1925, Ph.D., 1929; m. Cora Lee Cook, June 22, 1922; 1 dau., Madge (Mrs. Rolland Ritter). Managing editor Berea (Ky.) Citizen, 1921-23; mem. sociology faculty U. of N.D., 1924-28, Morris Harvey Coll., Barboursville, W.Va., 1928-29. U. of Ore., 1929-30, Coll. of City of Detroit, 1930-31; asso. prof. sociology, U. of Neb., 1931-37, professor sociology, 1937-54, prof. criminology, 1954-63, chairman of department sociology, 1951-54, prof. emeritus, 1963-74; vis. lectr. U. Omaha, from 1964; spl. lectr. to nurses in training, Lincoln General Hospital, 1937-46; vis. lecturer FBI Nat. Acad., Washington, 1946-60. Member Neb. bd. counselors Unemployment Compensation Division, Department of Labor; mem. Gov's. Com. to Investigate Penal Instns.; cons. Nebraska Prison Adminstrn. Elected to Nat. Police Officers Hall of Fame, 1963. Mem. Internat. Assn. for Identification, Internat. Assn. Chiefs of Police (asso. mem.), Soc. for Sci. Study of Criminology, Mid-West Sociol. Soc. (1st v.p. 1938-39; pres. 1942-44), Am. Assn. U. Profs., A.A.A.S., National Assn. for Psychiatric Treatment of Offenders, Alpha Kappa Delta, and Phi Kappa Phi. Awarded Silver Star for gallantry in action, A.E.F. (Intelligence Service), 1918. Unitarian. Author: Principles and Methods of Sociology (with G. R. Davies), 1932; Current Social Problems (with John M. Gillette), 1933, rev. ed. 1937; Social Psychology, 1938; Problems of a Changing Social Order (with J. M. Gillette), 1942; Social Problems and Social Policy (with Meadows and Gillette), 1952; Society and the Nursing Profession, 1953: Sex Perversions and Sex Crimes, 1957; Murderous Trial of Charles Starkweather, 1960; The Psychology of Strange Killers, 1962. Contbr. to sociol. and criminol. jours. Home: Lincoln Neb. Died Apr. 23, 1974.

REISER, OLIVER LESLIE, educator; b. Columbus, O., Nov. 15, 1895; s. Henry Edward and Sophie (Schwenker) R.; B.A., Ohio State U., 1921, M.A., 1922, Ph.D., 1924; m. Hyla Slifkin, Dec. 22, 1933; 1 dau., Karen Lois. Instr. philosophy Ohio State U., 1925; asst. prof. philosophy U. Pitts., 1926, asso. prof. philosophy, 1929, prof., 1943, prof. emeritus, 1966; later research asso. Inst. Philosophy, Psychology and Phys. Research, Dehradun, India; chmn. Com. on Cosmic Humanism. Bd. sponsors Internat. Center for Integrative Studies, N.Y., Conf. on Sci. and Religion; bd. advisers Council for Study Mankind, Santa Monica. Fellow A.A.A.S.; mem. Am. Philos. Assn., Phi Beta Kappa, Sigma Xi. Author: Alchemy of Light and Color, 1928; Humanistic Logic, 1930; Philosophy and the Concepts of Modern Science, 1935; The Promise of Scientific Humanism, 1940; A New Earth and a New Humanity, 1942; The World Sensorium, 1946; World Philosophy, 1948; Nature, Man, and God, 1951; The Integration of Human Knowledge, 1958; Man's New Image of Man, 1961; Cosmic Humanism, 1966; This Holyest Erthe, 1974; Cosmic Humanism and World Unity, 1975. Editorial bd. Darshana (India); cons. Internat. Logic Rev. Home: Pittsburgh, Pa. Died June 6, 1974.

RELIN, BERNARD, business exec.; b. N.Y.C., Apr. 25, 1914; s. Morris and Celia R.; LL.B., St. John's U., 1936; m. Irene Arnstein, Sept. 6, 1941; children—Neil, Margaret. Chmn. bd., pres. Rheingold Corp.; chmn. bd. Bernard Relin & Assos., Inc. Clubs: Lotos, Bankers of Am. Home: New York City N.Y. Died Mar. 7, 1974.

REMBERT, GEORGE WILLIAM FRANCIS, M.D.; b. Natchez, Miss., Mar. 25, 1879; s. George Washington and Frances Elizabeth (Stewart) R.; M.D., Tulane, 1903. Fellow Am. Coll. Phys., A.M.A.; mem. Southern Med. Assn., Miss. State Med. Assn. Am. Heart Assn., Am. Legion. Clubs: Rotary, Universit. Home: Jackson, Miss.†

REMEY, CHARLES MASON, religious leader, architect, author, lectr.; b. Burlington, Ia. May 15, 1874; s. George Collier and Mary Josephine (Mason) R.; student Cornell U., 1893-96; Ecole des Beaux Arts, Paris, 1896-1903; traveled in Europe and the Orient; Architecte Diplômé, par le Gouvernment Francais; m. Mrs. Gertrude Heim Klemm, July 11, 1931 (dec. Aug. 1932). Instr. architecture George Washington U., 1906-08, asst. prof., 1908-10; studied Oriental architecture; lecture tour around the world; architect for structures in Modern Israel; apptd. to design Baha'i temples to be built upon Mt. Carmel, Israel, Teheran, Irna; architect Baha'i temples Kampala, Africa, Sydney, Australia, Baha'i archives building at Mt. Carmel; past president of Internat. Baha'i Council. Patron in perpetuity Met. Mus. Art. Mem. Imperial Order of Dragon, Mil. Order Fgn. Wars of U.S., Mil. Order of Carabao, Mil. Order of Dragon, Naval Order of U.S., Soc. Mayflower Descs, S.R., Gen. Soc. Colonial Wars, Hugenot Soc. Am., Mil. Order Loyal Legion of U.S., S.A.R., Naval and Mil. Order Spanish-Am. War, Order Founders and Patriots of Am., Soc. Descs. Colonial Clergy, Ancient and Hon. Arty. Co., Soc. Am. Wars U.S., Am. Peace Soc. (dir.), Naval Hist. Foundation of United States, Vets, Fgn. Wars, Pilgrim John Howland Society, Clubs: Cosmos (Wash.); Chevy Chase; French Alpine; Swiss Alpine. Author various publs. on architecture and activities of Baha'i World Faith. Address: Florence, Italy.†

REMON, CANTERA ALEJANDRO, economist, Panamanian diplomat; Panama City, Panama, Feb. 20, 1912; s. Alejandro and Maria (Cantera) Remon; student finance, Georgetown U., 1936; student La Salle U., 1938; m. Ana Isabel Valdes, Sept. 16, 1943; 1 dau., Ana Isabel. Mem. Panama Nat. Assembly, 1952-56; minister of interior Govt. of Panama, 1955, minister of pub. works, 1956, comptroller gen., 1959-64; permanent rep. of Panama to UN, 1958-59; consul gen. Panama Consulte Gen., N.Y.C., 1964-73; gen. mgr. Cia. Cooperative Pesquera S.A., 1948-51, pres., 1952-60; pres. Pana Am. Seafood Corp., 1957-61. Decorated Legion of Merit (U.S.). Home: Bronx N.Y. Died June 17, 1973.

RENAUD , (ABEL) ETLENNE BERNARDEAU, educator; b. Billancourt-Boulogne, France, June 14, 1880; s. Benj. Pierre and Adelphine Elizabeth (Bernardeau) R.; grad. College St. Nicholas, Paris, 1901; student U. of Paris, 1901-06, A.B., 1905; post-grad. work in France, 1906-07, at Catholic U., Washington, D.C., 1907-08; A.M., U. of Colo., 1915; Ph.D., U. of Denver, 1920; m. Elizabeth Eudora de Cora, July 29, 1914. Came to U.S., 1907, naturalized, 1913. Teacher St. Charles Coll., Ellicott City, Md., 1908-09; in Santa Fe, N.M., 1909-10, teaching French and studying archaeology; instr. Romance langs., U. of Colo., 1914-16; prof. same, U. of Denver, 1916-20, acting prof. archeology, from 1920, prof. anthropology, 1924, prof. emeritus, from 1948; lecturer on French lang. and lit. anthropology and archeology; in Europe, 1923-24, 1928, 1937; dir. field expdn. Colo. Museum of Natural History, summer, 1929; dir. archeology survey of Eastern Colo., 1930-33, Western Neb., 1933, Eastern Wyo., 1931, N.E. New Mexico, 1934-35, S. Wyoming, 1935-39, Southern Colorado, 1940-43; dir. Army Specialized Training Program, unit, 1946; expdn. to Mexico, 1947. Lt. Inf., U.S. Army, 1918-19. Fellow A.A.A.S., Colo.-Wyo. Acad. Science (pres.); mem. Am. Anthrop. Assn., N. Mex. Archeol. Soc., Denver Archeol. Soc., Am. Acad. Political and Social Science, Colorado Hist. and Natural Science Soc., Archeol. Inst. America, Institute Internat. d'Anthropologie, Société Prehistorique de France, Société des Americanistes de Paris, Association Franeaise pour l'avancement des Sciences, Sigma Phi, Lambda Chi Alpha, Alpha Zeta Pi (nat. pres.), Pi Gamma Mu, Delta Epsilon. Club: Teknik. Contbr. to archeology, anthropology, etc. Pub. 20 repts. on archeology of Western plains. Made officer d'Acadímie, 1933, Chevalier Légion d'Honneur (both French). 1935. Consular agent for France, 1932-37. Home: Denver, Colo.†

RENDLEMAN, JOHN SAMUEL, lawyer, univ. pres.; b. Anna, Ill., June 21, 1927; s. Ford Lee and Jean (Shomaker) R.; student Coll. St. Thomas, 1945, Ia. State Coll., 1945-46; B.S., So. Ill. U., 1948; J.D., U. Ill., 1951; m. Lenora Norris, Dec. 15, 1956; children—Jean Farrin, John Samuel III, Mary Elizabeth, David Scott; 1 son by previous marriage, Charles Mathew. Admitted to Ill. bar, 1951; legal counsel So. Ill. U., 1951-61, exec. dir. bus. affairs, 1961-63, gen. counsel, 1963-64, v.p., 1964-68, chancellor Edwardsville Campus, 1968-71, pres., 1971-76. Spl. asst. atty. gen. Hodge Investigation, 1956-57; nat. chmn. Vanderbilt Traffic Survey; dir. 1st Nat. Bank, Cobden, Ill., 1st Granite City Nat. Bank; mem. com. to improve legislative processes Ill. Gen. Assembly, 1965-76. Bd. dirs. Arts and Edn. Council Greater St. Louis, St. Elizabeth's Hosp., Granite City, St. Louis Symphony, Design Sci. Inst., Washington; trustee McKendree Coll. Served with USNR, 1945-46. Mem. Am. (exec. council), Ill. (exec. com.) bar assns., St. Louis Commerce and Growth Assn. (1st v.p. 1972—), Phi Kappa Tau (pres. 1956), Chi Delta Chi, Pi Delta Rho, Sigma Alpha Epsilon. Presbyn. Elk. Club: University. Home: Edwardsville, Ill., Died Mar. 4, 1976.

RENFRO, HAROLD BELL, geologist, petroleum engr.; b. Lufkin, Tex., Jan. 16, 1915; s. P. D. and Ruby (Hines) R.; student Lamar Inst. Tech., 1930-31, U. Houston, 1931-33; B.S. in Petroleum Engring., U. Tulsa, 1939; M.S. in Geology, U. Wis., Ph.D. in Geology, 1947; m. Joan Arden Ross, Feb. 1, 1942; children—Robert Bruce, Janet Arden (Mrs. James R. Elder); m. 2d, Alma Chastain Hutchings, Sept. 28, 1963; step-children—Gertrude, Sally, William S. Prof. geology U. Tulsa, 1946-48; dir. exploration and engring. Stoddard Oil Co., Dallas, 1948-53; organized H.B. Renfro and Co., Dallas, 1953; asso. McGhee Prodn. Co., Dallas, 1954-57; organized, chmn., bd. dirs. Neches Petroleum Corp., 1963-70; dir., exec. com., prin. agt. Petroleum Reserves, Inc., N.Y.C., Houston, Dallas, 1955-58; cons. Ling-Temco-Vought, Inc., Hudson Inst., Harmon, N.Y., Lawrence Radiation Lab., Livermore, Cal., Lockheed Aircraft Corp., MITRE Corp. Bd. dirs. Dallas Council World Affairs, Southwestern Engring. Found., Dallas; bd. dirs. Community Guidance Service, Dallas, 1950-60, chmn., 1955-57. Served to lt. USNR, 1942-46. Mem. Am. Assn. Petroleum Geologist (co-compiler geol. hwy. map U.S.), Am. Inst. Mining, Metall. and Petroleum Engrs., Soc. Petroleum Engrs., Council Sci. Socs. Dallas-Ft. Worth Area (pres. 1960), Community Opera Guild (pres. 1957), Dallas Geol. Soc. (pres. 1966), Sigma Xi, Gamma Alpha, Lambda Chi Alpha, Pi Epsilon Tau. Baptist. Clubs: Engineers (pres. Dallas 1958), Petroleum Engineers (pres. Dallas 1952); Research on Lower Pennsylvania sedementary rocks Northeastern Okla., stratigraphy and structural geology of Wilmington oil field, application nuclear explosives to natural resources. Home: Dallas Tex. Died June 22, 1972.

RENNAY, LÉON, baritone singer; b. St. Louis, 1878; s. Theodore and Adelaide (Vion) Papin; present name adopted; ed. prep. schs. in U.S., and Sorbonne, Paris; unmarried. Début at Salle Erard, Paris, 1900; sang at Newport, R.I., during season of 1904, and subsequent seasons there; engaged by Renaldo Hahn to interpret his songs at his London début concert, 1906; gave numerous concerts in Rome and Florence, Italy, appearing before Queen Helena; specialty is interpretation of ancient and modern French classic songs; held chair of lyric diction, David Mannes School of Music, New York. Home: New York City, N.Y.*†

RENOUVIN, PIERRE EUGENE GEORGES, educator; b. Paris, France, Jan. 9, 1893; s. Georges and Mme. Dalican Renouvin; Univ. Teaching Degree, Dr. Letters; m. Marie—Therese Gabalda, June 10, 1918; children—Michel, Jacqueline, Anne—Marie (Mrs. Antenen). Prof. history Lycee Orleans, 1919—20; curator Library Internat. Contemporary Documentation, 1920—36; instr., then prof. Faculty Letters, Paris, 1933—64; prof. Ecole Libre des Scis. Politiques, 1938, then Inst. d'Etudes Politiques, 1938; dean Faculty Letters, Paris 1955—58, dean emeritus, 1958. Pres. Commn. Modern and Contemporary History, Nat. Center Sci. Research, 1956—60; mem.

progress bd. Inst. Polit. Studies, Paris, 1958; gov. bd. Ecole Nationale d'Adminstrn., 1959; pres. Foundation Nat. des Scis. Politiques, 1959—70; dir. Rev. Historique mag., from 1945-73. Decorated Grand Croix Légion D'Honneur, grand officer Order Nat. du Mérite, Croix de Guerre, comdr. Palmes Academiques. Mem. of the Inst. Author: Les Assemblees Provinciales de 1787; Les Origines Immediates de la Guerre de 1914; La Crise Curopeene et la Premiere Guerre Mondiale; La Question d'Extreme—Orient, 1840—1940; Les Relations Internationales de 1815 a 1870; Les Relations Internaionales de 1871; a 1914; L'Apogee de l'Euorpe; Les Crises du xxth Siecle; (with J. B. Duroselle) Introduction à l'Histoire des Relations Internationales; L'Armistice de Rethones—11 November 1918; L'Opinion publique en France en 1917. Home: Paris, France. Died Dec. 8, 1974.

RENTSCHLER, CALVIN BALTHASER, physician; b. Hamburg, Pa., Apr. 20, 1897; s. James Washington and Laura Amelia (Balthaser) R.; M.D., U. Pa., 1924; M.S. in Surgery, U. Minn.; m. Julia Catharine Pepper, June 25, 1937; children—Donald Pepper, Homer Pepper (dec.), Curtis Pepper, Betty (Mrs. Woodrow Wilson Muth), Norman Pepper, Claudia Pepper, Judith Pepper. Intern, Reading (Pa.) Hosp., 1924—25, chief gen. surgery; fellow in gen. surgery Mayo Clinic, Rochester, Minn., 1925—29. Recipient Alumni award of merit U. Pa., 1952. Diplomate Am. Bd. Surgery. Fellow A.C.S.; mem. A.M.A. Democrat. Lutheran. Home: Reading, Pa. Died May 20, 1973; buried St. Michael's Cemetery, Tilden Twp., Pa.

RETI-FORBES, JEAN, pianist, educator; b. Saltcoats, Sask., Can., 1911; d. G.W. and Clara (Boyle) Sahlmark; student U. Toronto, 1929-31; grad. Royal Acad. Music London, 1933; m. Rudolph Reti, July 3, 1943 (dec. 1957) m. 2d, W. Stanton Forbes, Nov. 15, 1963. Came to U. S., 1940, naturalized, 1964. Faculty, Sarah Lawrence Coll., 1947-48; played first performance of Reti's piano concerto with Detroit Symphony, 1948; after death of Reti prepared for publ. his Tonality-Atonality-Pantonality and Thematic Patterns in Sonatas of Beethoven; concertized and lectured throughout U.S. and Europe, 1959-72; asso. prof. U. Ga., Athens, 1964-72, also charge Olin Downes Papers U. Ga. Library. Vice pres., trustee Jay Hambidge Art Found. Rabun Gap, Ga. Can. Council grantee for work on Reti manuscripts, 1962. Mem. Am. Musicol. Soc., Kappa Lambda. Author: (poetry) To Dwell in Sound, 1972; Notes on Playing the Piano, 1974; Child of the Piano, 1976. Editor: Lucy M. Stanton, Artist (W. Stanton Forbes), 1975. Home: Athens, Ga. Died May 7, 1972.

REVSON, CHARLES HASKELL, cosmetic co. exec.; b. Boston, Oct. 11, 1906; s. Samuel and Jeanette (Weiss) R.; ed. pub. schs., Manchester, N.H.; m. Johanna C. C. de Knecht, Oct. 26, 1940; children—John Charles, Charles Haskell; m. 3d, Lynn Sheresky, 1964. Cosmetic salesman small N.J. firm with hdqrs. N.Y.C., 1930—32; formed partnership with bro. Joseph and Charles Lachmman, 1932, under name Revlon Nail Enamel Corp. (now Revlon, Inc.), pres. co., 1932—62, chmn. chief exec. officer from 1962—75; chmn. Revlon Internat. Corp., from 1938—75. Formed and served as pres. Vorset Corp. for mfg. pyrotechnics for Navy, World War 11; won Army—Navy "E" (1942—47). Overseer Albert Einstein Coll. Medicine. Recipient Horatio Alger award Am. Schs. and Colls. Assn. for outstanding achievement, 1950. Clubs: Old Oaks Country (Purchase, N.Y.); American (London). Home: Rye, N.Y. Died Aug. 24, 1975.

REX, CHARLES HENRY, elec. engr.; b. Lexington, Mo., Jan. 12, 1903; s. Cleveland Alonzo and Addie (Wilker) R.; B.S., U. Ill., 1926; m. Alice Letatia Doherty, Nov. 25, 1935; children—Diane (Mrs. Denis G. Cain), Gartland Charles, Kathleen Alice, Michael Richard. Exchange installer Western Electric Co., Kansas City, 1923-24; with Gen. Electric Co., Chgo., Lynn, Mass., Hendersonville, N.C., 1926-68, spl. rep., 1935-42, design, devel. engr., 1942-68. Mem. night visibility com., hwy. research bd., NRC, 1956. Registered profl. engr., Mass., N.C. Fellow Illuminating Engring. Soc. (bd. fellows, 1960-61); mem. Illuminating Engring. Soc., Internat. mem. Commn. on Illumination, Inst. Traffic Engring., I.E.E.E. Club: Hendersonville Country. Patentee various roadway lighting devices. Contbr. numerous articles to profl. jours. Home: Hendersonville N.C. Died Nov. 18, 1973.

REYNOLDS, CARROLL FOSTER, librarian; b. Granville, O., Oct. 14, 1910; s. Wayland Fuller and Inez (Brohard) R.; B.S. W. Va. U. 1932; B.S. in L.S., Columbia, 1935; M.A., U. Pitts., 1940, Ph.D., 1950; m. Erma Ruth Lewis, Dec. 21, 1938; children—Judith Lenore (Mrs. Gerald Hill), Marilyn Margaret (Mrs. Gordon Seybold), Beverly Ann (Mrs. John M. Poellot). Asst. librarian W. Va. U., 1935-36; curator of documents U. Pitts., 1936-37; reference librarian Okla. State U., 1937-40; mem. staff U. Pitts. Library from 1940, dir. Falk Library of Health Professions, from 1957, dir. emeritus, also asso. prof. emeritus history health scis., 1975; vis. librarian U. Ibadan (Nigeria), 1964, Mahidol U., Bangkok, 1967-68. Cons., Asia Found., Bangladesh, 1973; Rockefeller Found., Nigeria, Thailand, 1964, 67-68. Mem. A.L.A., Med. Library Assn. (treas. 1963-64), Spl. Libraries Assn. Home: Pittsburgh, Pa. Died Sept. 3, 1975; buried Jefferson Meml. Park, Pittsburgh, Pa.

REYNOLDS, CLARENCE, organist; b. Phillipsport, N.Y., June 1, 1880; s. Rev. Charles H. and Sarah Frances (Van Inwegen) R.; pupil of Landon and DeKontaski (piano), R. Huntington Woodman (organ), Vogt, of Metropolitan Conservatory of N.Y. City (composition); Mus.D., Temple U., 1918; m. Marjorie Green, Jan. 17, 1912; 1 dau., Marjorie. Organist Ocean Grove (N.J.) Auditorium, 1908-17; organist and choir dir. Baptist Temple, Phila., 1915-18; city organist of Denver, Colo., from 1918. Condr. of Temple Oratorio and orchestral concerts, Phila., 1917-18; condr. Municipal Chorus, Denver, 1919-29; has played in more than 2,000 recitals. Home: Denver, Colo.†

REYNOLDS, H. WALTER, lawyer; b. N.Y.C., Aug. 1, 1901; s. Walter S. (M.D.) and Emma B. (Euler) R.; student Columbia, 1920; LL.B., N.Y. Law Sch., 1925; m. Ivah Smith, June 26, 1926. Admitted to N.Y. bar, 1926, N.J. bar, 1940; practice of law, N.Y.C., 1926-62; atty., gen. Counsel, v.p. Colgate-Palmolive Co., 1942-62, sec., 1961—71, mem. exec. com., 1966-67, dir., 1954-67, ret. Home: White Plains, N.Y. Died Sept. 2, 1972; interred Ferncliff, Hartsdale, N.Y.

REYNOLDS, MILTON, pen mfg. exec., round-world record flyer, explorer; b. Albert Lea, Minn., July 10, 1892; s. Simon and Rose (Vehon) R.; student pub. schools Quincy, Ill.; m. Edna Loebe, Oct. 19, 1917 (dec. Apr. 1952); children—Marjorie Jeanne, James Milton; m. 2d, Manuela Salas, Apr. 15, 1953; children—Alicia, Milton. Chmn. Reynolds Pen Co., also Reynolds Printasign Co.; dir. Syntex Co. Mem. Mexican Geog. Soc. Clubs: Circumnavigators: Adventures; Mexico City Counry, Club de Golf Mex. Inventor ball pen. Explorer, adventurer, round-the-world record flights, air exploration of Chinese Tibet high mts. Author: Hasta La Vista, 1944; Rocketing Round the World, 1946. Address: Mexico City, Mexico., Died Jan. 23, 1976.

REYNOLDS, OLIVER CHARLICK, lawyer; b. N.Y.C., Jan. 13, 1884; s. William M. and Jessie (Charlick) R.; A.B., Princeton 1904; LL.B., N.Y. Law Sch., 1907; m. Mildred Ellis, Nov. 11, 1925; 1 son, David C. Admitted to N.Y. bar, 1907; law clk. Eaton, Lewis & Row, 1906—10; partner Reynolds, Richards & McCutcheon (now Reynolds, Richards, La Venture, Hadley & Davis), from 1911. Trustee nat. bd. YWCA; trustee Am. Schs. Oriental Research. Mem. Am. Bar Assn., Assn. Bar City N.Y. Presbyn. Clubs: Century, Down Town Assn., University, Grolier (N.Y.C.). Home: New York City, N.Y. Died May 27, 1970; interred Washington, Conn.

REYNOLDS, ROYAL, army med. officer; b. Elmira, N.Y., Oct. 14, 1881; s. George Gardner and Lucy (Pratt) R.; ed. Elmira Free Acad., 1898-1902; M.D., U. of Pa., 1906; m. Romietta Rucker Redman, Sept. 15, 1909; children—Royal, Betty (Mrs. Wm. H. Allen, Jr.), Lucy (Mrs. O. C. Troxel, Jr.). Med. officer, U.S. Army, from 1909; served in army posts here and in P.I.; promoted through grades to brig. gen., 1942; comdg. officer Base Hosp. No. 27, A.E.F., France, in World War I; chief eye, ear, nose and throat services several army general hosps., 1919-39; post surgeon and prof. mil. hygiene, West Point, 1939-42; comdg. officer Kennedy Gen. Hosp., Memphis, Tenn.; ret. from U.S. Army, 1945; in practice of otolaryngology, Washington, D.C., from 1945. Officer of French Academy; received French Epidemiological decoration. Fellow Am. Coll. Surgeons; mem. A.M.A., Assn. Mil. Surgeons, Psi Upsilon. Clubs: Army and Navy (Washington). Home: Washington, D.C.†

REYNOLDS, VICTOR GEORGE FASSETT, univ. publisher; b. Laceyville, Pa., Oct. 11, 1905; s. Hallock Solomon and Rubie Ann (Fassett) R.; B.S., Dartmouth, 1927; m. Lucille McCall, Sept. 5, 1936. With coll. dept. Ronald Press Co., N.Y.C., 1927-34, F. S. Crofts, N.Y.C., 1934-37; coll. dept. sales, sales promotion dir. The Macmillan Co., N.Y.C., 1937-43; univ. pub., mem. faculty Cornell U. and mgr. Cornell U. Press, 1943-63; dir. U. Press of Va., Charlottesville, 1963-69; editor, pub. U. Press New Eng., Hanover, N.H., 1970-73; dir. Franklin Publs., Inc. Dir. Am. Book Pubs. Council, 1952-54; sec.-treas. Assn. Am. U. Presses, 1951-53, pres., 1953-55. Chmn. exec. com. Friends of the Dartmouth Library, 1955-57. Life mem. Am. Hist. Assn., Hist. Soc. Pa., Pa. Hist. Assn., Va. Hist. Soc. Ind. Democrat. Home: Hanover N.H. Died Dec. 22, 1973.

REZNIKOFF, CHARLES, author; b. Bklyn., Aug. 31, 1894; s. Nathan and Sarah Yetta (Volvofski) R.; student Sch. Journalism U. Mo., 1910-11; LL.B., N.Y. U., 1915; m. Marie Syrkin, May 27, 1930. Admitted to N.Y. bar, 1916. Author: By the Waters of Manhattan: Selected Verse, 1962; Testimony: The United States, 1885-1890: Recitative, 1965; Family Chronicle, 1969; By the Well of Living and Seeing, 1975; Collected Poems, Vol. I 1918-1936, 1976. Editor: Louis Marshall: Selected Papers and Addresses, 1957. Recipient Morton Dauwen Zabel award for poetry Nat. Inst. and Arts and Letters, 1971. Home: New York City, N.Y., Died Jan. 22, 1976.

RHODES, DONALD GENE, newspaper editor; b. Sedalia, Mo., Jan. 16, 1931; s. Benjamin Franklin and Opal (Sawyer) R.; student Central Mo. State Coll., 1956-57. With Daily Star-Jour., Warrensburg, Mo., 1949-52, 54-74, city editor, 1964-66, sports editor, wire editor, 1968-74. Served with USMC, 1952-54. Mem. Am. Legion, V.F.W., Delta Lambda, Tau Kappa Epsilon (mem. pub. relations com.). Democrat. Methodist. Elk. Home: Warrensburg, Mo. Died July 24, 1974; interred Memorial Gardens, Warrensburg.

RHYS, NOEL ANDREW, broadcasting co. exec.; b. Maidstone, Eng., Dec. 24, 1899; s. Isaac and Agnes Emily (Chittenden) R.; student St. John's Sch., Leatherhead, Eng., 1909-13, King's Sch., Rochester, Eng., 1913-14; m. Annette Oldham, June 30, 1943. Came to U.S., 1934; naturalized, 1948. Reporter, Daily Mirror, London, Eng., 1916; sub-editor George Newnes Ltd., 1917, Daily Express, 1919-20; asst. editor Moving Picture News, 1920-22; dir. promotion Goldwyn Films, 1922-23; gen. mgr. Picture Playhouses Ltd., 1923-26; editor European edit. Golden Book, 1926-34; free-lance script writer, Hollywood, Cal., 1934-41; with Keystone Broadcasting System, N.Y.C., 1941-73, exec. v.p., 1956-73; business mgmt. in theatrical prodns. Vagabond King, Pomander Walk, Her Past, White Eagle, others, 1926-32. Nat. chmn. radio div. Nat. Conf. Christians and Jews, 1965; mem. Menninger Found; active Am. Red Cross, Assn. Retarded Children, United Cerebral Palsy Assn. Served as orderly British Red Cross, Serbia, 1914-15; as pilot officer RAF, 1917-19. Mem. Civil War Round Table, Am. Revolution Round Table, Broadcast Pioneers. Composer, author short stories, contbr. to trade press. Home: New York City N.Y. Died May 9, 1973.

RICARDO, HARRY RALPH, mech. engr.; b. London, Jan. 26, 1885; s. Halsey Ralph and Catherine Jane (Rendel) R.; B.A., U. Cambridge, 1906; m. Beatrice Bertha Hale, 1911; children—Cicely Kate (Mrs. Bertram), Angela Edith (Mrs. Hughesdon), Camilla Bertha (Mrs. Bosanquet). Cons. engr. Rendel Palmer & Tritton, 1907—14; cons., adviser Brit. Govt. depts., 1914—17; founder, chmn. bd. Ricardo & Co., cons. engrs., 1917—64, pres., from 1964—75. Mem. tech. com. Brit. War Cabinet. Knighted; recipient James Alfred Ewing medal for engring. research, 1940; James Watt medal, 1953; Horning medal, 1955; medal, comdr. Order of Merit, Soc. for Advancement of Research and Invention, Paris, 1964. Fellow Royal Soc., 1929 (Rumford medal 1944); mem. Instn. Mech. Engrs. (pres., Clayton medal), Instn. Civil Engrs., Soc. Automotive Engrs. Author: The Internal Combustion, 1923; Engines of High Output, 1926; The High Speed Internal Combustion Engine, 1931; Memories and Machines: The Pattern of my Life, 1968; also articles. Research on motor fuels, gasoline engines, diesel engines; inventor of internal combustion devices. Home: Sussex, England. Died May 18, 1974.

RICCIUTO, HARRY ADRIAN city ofcl. Harrisburg (Pa.); b. Harrisburg, Pa., Dec. 22, 1921; s. Antonio and Benita (Andreano) R.; student Thompson Coll., 1949—54; m. Anna Leah Kopko, June 25, 1943 (div. Jan. 1969); 1 dau., Barbara Jean. Clk., insp. Robert W. Hunt Co., engrs., Harrisburg, 1941—43, 1946—49; clk. Harrisburg Water Dept., 1949—54; chief clk. Harrisburg Dept. Pub. Safety, 1954—60; dep. dir. Harrisburg Dept. Accts. and Finance, 1960—71; city clk., Harrisburg, from 1971. Served with AUS, 1943—45. Mem. Mcpl. Finance Officers Assn., Am. Legion, Pa. Local Govtl. Secs. Assn. Home: Harrisburg Pa. Died Sept. 1974.

RICE, ARTHUR HENRY, editor, educator; b. Saginaw, Mich., Sept. 6, 1900; s. Henry Benjamin and Florence Julia (Lyon) R.; Teacher's Certif., Central Mich. U., Mt. Pleasant, 1925, A.B., 1926; M.A., U. of Mich., 1934, Ph.D., 1947; LL.D., Central Mich. U., 1950; m. Lauretta M. Bluem, Jan. 4, 1925 (dec. Sept. 15, 1956); children—Florence Alice (Mrs. G.A. Belt), Arthur Henry, Stuart Terry; m. 2d, Mary T. Tomancik, Nov. 10, 1957; one son, Thomas Ambler. Reporter, dept. editor Saginaw Daily News, 1919-23; spl. corr. various Mich. daily newspapers, 1923-29; instr. in journalism Central Mich. U., 1925-26, dir. publs. and publicity, 1926-29; dir. publs. and pub. relations Mich. Edn. Assn., 1929-47, mng. editor Mich. Edn. Jour., 1929-34, editor, 1934-47; mng. editor The Nation's Schools, 1947-50, editor, 1951-63, editorial adviser, 1963-75; prof. edn., co-ordinator Instructional Systems Teacher Edn., Ind. U., 1964-69, prof. sch. adminstrn., 1969-70, prof. edn. emeritus, 1970-75; mng. editor Mich. Edn. Bulletin, 1933-47; lectr. edn. Northwestern U., 1948-60; instr. summer sessions, U. Mich. 1947, 1948, U. Del., 1954, U. Colo., 1952, 1956, U. Houston, 1956; dir. workshops, moderator panel discussions on sch. adminstrn., sch. pub. relations. Served in S.A.T.C., Ann Arbor, 1918. Recipient Burke Aaron Hinsdale Scholar award, U. Mich., 1945-46. Asso. mem. Mich. Ednl. Planning Commn., 1935, sec. com. on information. Mem. Mich. Edn. Assn. (life), Ednl. Press Assn. Am. (v.p. 1945-47, pres. 1947-48, exec. com. 1949-50, co-dir. EdPress mag. clinic U. Wis., Summer 1946, Distinguished Service award 1956,), N.E.A., Am. Assn. Sch. Adminstrs. (author anniversary publ. From the Beginning-the A.A.S.A. Centennial Story 1964), Nat. Sch. Pub. Relations Assn. (editor Today's Techniques, 1st Yearbook, 1943; Ninety Guides to

Better Public Relations, 1946; co-editor, Public Relations for Rural and Village Teachers, 1946; author Scientific Approach to School Public Relations, 1963; editor bulletin), Southeastern Assn. Sch. Bus. Ofcls. (hon. life), Council Ednl. Facility Planners (life), Internat. Assn. Sch. Bus. Ofcls., Am. Ednl. Research Assn., Nat. Soc. Study Edn., Assn. Higher Edn., Adult Edn. Assn., Am. Acad. Polit. and Social Sci., Schoolmasters Club, Phi Delta Kappa (editorial cons. 1952-54), Phi Sigma Sigma, Phi Kappa Phi, Alpha Delta. Methodist. editor or compiler various publs. Contbr. ednl. mags. Home: Bloomington Ind. Died May 17, 1975; interred Oakwood Cemetery, Saginaw, Mich.

RICE, CHARLES ATWOOD, b. Honolulu Sept. 12, 1876; s. William Hyde and Mary (Waterhouse) R.; ed. Oahu Coll. (Honolulu), Heald's Business Coll. (San Francisco); m. Grace E. King, June 20, 1899 (dec. Mar. 4, 1940); children—Edith J. K. (Mrs. John Christopher Plews), Juliet Atwood (Mrs. Frederick Warren Wichman); m. 2d, Patricia C. Smith, Apr. 21, 1941; 1 son, Charles A., Jr. Treas. and mgr. William Hyde Rice, Ltd. (owners of Kipu Ranch); pres. Atwood Distbg. Co., Ltd., Garden Island Motors, Limited. Member House of Rep., H.T., 1905-11, Senate, 1913-38; delegate to Republican Nat. Conv., Chicago, 1912; mem. Rep. Nat. Com., 1912-16; chmn. Hawaii Legislative Commn. to Washington, 1921; del. Dem. Nat. Conv., 1944, 1952; elected to Hawaii Constitutional Conv., 1950. Conglist. Mem. Kauai Library Assn., Kauai C. of C. Clubs: Pacific; Chiefs of Hawaii, Kauai Yacht. Home: Lihue, Kauai, Hawaii.†

RICE, HENRY IZARD BACON ins. exec.; b. Coles Ferry, Va., Sept. 2, 1881; s. Henry Crenshaw and Marie Gordon (Pryor) R.; student Mt. Hermon, Mass., 1900; A.B., Yale, 1904, A.M., 1905. With Conn. Mut. Life Ins. Co., Hartford, Conn., from 1905, asst. actuary, later asso. actuary, 1911-23, acturary, 1923-31, v.p. and actuary, 1931-46, v.p., 1946-51, retired 1951. Fellow Actuarial Soc. Am.; incorporator Conn. Inst. for the Blind. Clubs: Yale Alumni Assn., Hartford Golf (Hartford); Yale (N.Y. City); Farmington Curling (Farmington, Conn.); Conn. Water Color Soc. Home: Farmington, Conn.†

RICE, JOSEPH LEE, JR., utility exec.; b. Butte, Mont., Aug. 31, 1902; s. Joseph Lee and Lulu (Evans) R.; B.S., U. of Pa., 1925; m. Frances Plunkett, July 17, 1928; children—Joseph Lee III, David, Jere Anne (Mrs. Vockins). Chmn., dir., mem. exec. com. Allegheny Power System, Inc.; chmn., dir., mem. exec. com. Potomac Edison Co., West Penn Power Co., Monongahela Power Co. Clubs: University (N.Y.C.); Treasure Cay Golf and Country (Abaco, Bahamas). Home: Great Abaco Island Bahamas. Died Sept. 19, 1974.

RICH, BENJAMIN LEROY, lawyer; b. Ogden, Utah, Oct. 18, 1878; s. Ben E. and Diana (Farr) R.; LL.B., Columbian (now George Washington) U., 1903; m. Anna Clegg, Aut. 29, 1900; 1 son, Benjamin Lund. in practice of law, St. Anthony, Ida., mem. Millsaps & Rich., 1903-05; at Salt Lake City, Utah, from 1905; mem. law firm Booth, Lee, Badger, Rich & Rich for 40 years; sr. mem. firm Rich & Strong. Chairman Rep. Co. Com., Salt Lake Co., 1914-18. Vice chmn. Utah George Washington Bicentennial Commn. Mem. Am. and Utah State bar assns., Bar Assn. of City and County of Salt Lake (pres. 1933), S.A.R. (pres. Utah Soc. 1931; v.p. general of national society, 1933), Society of Mayflower Descendants, Kappa Sigma. Home: Salt Lake City, Utah.†

RICH, EDWIN GILE, editor, author; b. Farmington, Me., Sept. 30, 1879; s. Joseph Waldo Winal and Adella Catharine (Parsons) Rich; A.B., Harvard University, 1902; m. Rosalie V. Olding, March 30, 1930. Assistant editor of School Journal, 1902-04, editor, 1914; in text-book business with The Macmillan Co., 1905-08, D.C. Heath & Co., 1908-11, Eaton & Co., 1912-13; editor Le Livre Contemporain, 1918-25; gen. mgr. Small, Maynard & Co., 1919-25, Dial Prees, 1926, Andrew Melrose, Ltd., London, 1927, Curtis Brown, Ltd., from 1927. Author: Why-So Stories, 1918. Translator: Lafond's Covered with Mud and Glory, 1918; Camile Saint-Saëns—Musical Memories, 1919; Pierre Pons, 1927; The Bullfighters, 1927. Editor: The Adventures of Don Quixote, 1921, Arabian Nights, 191921; Grimm's Fairy Tales, 1921; Gulliver's Travels, 1922; Fontaine's Fables, 1922; Perrault's Tales, 1923. Clubs: Harvard, Explorers, The Players (New York). Home: New York City, N.Y.†

RICH, JOHN FREDERICK, fund-raising cons.; b. London, Eng., June 1, 1902; s. Max Isaac and Esther Mary (Lorenzen) Reich; came to U.S., 1915, naturalized, 1928; B.A., Haverford Coll., 1924; m. Virginia Elizabeth Percy, Oct. 11, 1928; children—Edward Percy, Elizabeth Lorenzen (Mrs. F. Kent Mitchel). Reporter, Evening Pub. Ledger, Phila., 1925-29; with pub. relations dept. Bell Telephone Co. of Pa., 1929-36; relief commr. Am. Friends Service Com., Spain, 1937-39, China and India, 1943, Eng., 1944-46; pres. John F. Rich Co., fund-raising cons., Phila., 1946-69, chmn. bd., 1969-73; established John F. Rich Co., Ltd., London, Eng., 1959, cons., 1967-73; pres. Preston Drainage Co., Haverford, Pa. Mem. corp. Haverford Coll., Friends Hosp., Emlen Instn.; hon. sec. Brit. Schs. and Univs. Found.; bd. dirs. Brit. Cathedrals and Hist. Churches Found. Mem. Am. Assn. Fund-Raising Counsel, Pub. Relations Soc. Am. Mem. Soc. of Friends. Rotarian. Clubs: Penn Athletic (Phila.); British Schools and Universities (N.Y.C.). Contbr. articles to profl. jours. Home: Haverford, Pa. Died Apr. 21, 1973; interred Falls Meeting Friends Burial Ground, Fallsington, Pa.

RICH, RICHARD H., business exec.; b. Atlanta, Dec. 24, 1901; s. Herman and Rosalind (Rich) Rosenheim; B.S., Wharton Sch., U. Pa., 1923; spl. work, Harvard, 1924; LL.D., Emory U., 1965; m. Virginia Lazarus, Dec. 29, 1930 (dec. 1957); children—Sally E., (Mrs. W. H. Adolph), Virginia G. (Mrs. Robert J. Barnett), Michael P. With Rich's Inc., Atlanta from 1925, dir. from 1929, pres., 1949—61, chmn., chief exec. officer from 1961; dir. Ga. Internat. Corp., Trust Co. of Ga., Amfac, Inc., So. Bell Telephone & Telegraph Co. Former civilian aide to U.S. sec. of army. Served in USAAF, 1942—45; exec. officer tng. wing. St. Petersburg, Fla., Lincoln, Neb., 1943; service in Brazil, Fgn. Econ. Adminstrn., spl. asst. to Am. ambassador to Brazil, 1943. Life trustee, pres. Rich Found; trustee St. Josephs Infirmary, Richard B. Russell Found., Young Harris Coll.; bd. dirs. Atlanta chpt. A.R.C., Atlanta Boy Scouts; past state chmn. exec. com. Ga. Chpt. Nat. Ga. chpt. Found. Infantile Paralysis; dir. Atlanta Conv. Bur.; former chmn. Met. Atlanta Rapid Transit Authority. Formerly chmn. Atlanta Arts Alliance, now mem. exec. com. Recipient gold medal Nat. Retail Mchts. Assn., 1963; Outstanding Civilian Service medal Dept. Army; award Ga. chpt. Pub. Relations Soc. Am., 1973. Mem. Mil. Order of World Wars, C. of C. (past pres., dir.), Am. Legion, Retail Mchts. Assn. (former pres.), Atlanta Music Festival Assn. Jewish Reformed religion. Rotarian (past pres.). Clubs: Commerce (dir.), Atlanta City, Standard; Boca Raton (Fla.). Home: Atlanta, Ga. Died May 1975.

RICHARD, IRWIN, mfr.; b. New Hanover, Pa., Jan. 27, 1881; s. George Washington and Emma (Houck) R.; m. Carrie Renninger; children—Mrs. Beulah Henry, Mrs. Florence Miller, Clarence, Nelson, Claude, Alice, Beatrice, Paul, Ralph. Propr. Red Hill Broom Works; dir. Schwenkville Nat. Bank; chmn. Red Hill Water Commn. Pres. Eastern Broom Mfrs. and Supply Dealers Assn., Broom Inst., Red Hill Bd. of Trade. Trustee Perkiomen Sch. Mem. Patriotic Sons of America. Lutheran. Mason (Shriner). Rotarian. A leader in orgn. of broom industry, accomplishing standardization of brooms on nat. scale in cooperation with U.S. Dept. Agr. and U.S. Dept. Commerce. Home: Red Hill, Pa.†

RICHARDS, JAMES AUSTIN, clergyman; b. Andover, Mass., Mar. 28, 1878; s. James Forsaith and Ellen Augusta (Brown) R.; grad. Phillips Andover Acad., 1896; A.B., Harvard, 1900; post-grad. work same univ.; grad. Union Theol. Sem., 1904; D.D., Chicago Theol. Sem., also from Oberlin College; m. Hazel Temple Read, Sept. 4, 1907; children—Elizabeth Putnam (Mrs. Chalmer John Roy), Laura Ellen, James Austin. Asso. pastor Bedford Park (N.Y.) Presbyn. Ch., 1904-05; pastor United Ch., Newport, R.I., 1905-09, Mt. Vernon Ch., Boston, Mass., 1909-18, Winnetka Congl. Ch., Boston, Mass., 1909-18, Winnetka Congl. Ch., 1918-28, First Ch., Oberlin, O., 1928-42; pastor The Community Ch. (Congl.), Mount Dora, Fla., from 1942. Mem. Delta Upsilon. Club: Rotary, Author: The Sufficiency of Jesus, 1927; Windows in Matthew, 1932. Contbr. of numerous articles. Home: Mount Dora, Fla.†

RICHARDS, MARY ANNE MITCHELL, (Mrs. William Randolph Richards III), home economist; b. Atlanta, Mar. 26, 1936; d. John Henry and Margery (Davis) Mitchell; student Hollins Coll., Va.; B.S., Coll. William and Mary, 1958; m. William Randolph Richards III, July 26, 1960; children—Ashley Mitchell, William Randolph IV. Editor, Extension News Service, Lexington, Ky., 1959-61; staff home economist Favorite Recipes Press, Inc., Louisville, 1961-75, exec. editor, 1962-75, v.p., dir., 1966-75. Bd. dirs. YWCA, North Hills Planning Bd., Planned Parenthood Assn. Mem. Am. Assn. U. Women (Distinguished Service award, past pres., dir.), Bus. and Profl. Womens Club (pres.), Am., Louisville (past pres.) home econs. assns., D.A.R., U.D.C., Delta Delta Delta, Theta Sigma Phi. Republican. Home: Louisville, Ky., Died Nov. 2, 1975.

RICHARDS, RALPH WEBSTER, geologist; b. Waterville, Me., May 30, 1879; s. Albert Melville and Lydia (McIntyre) R.; A.B., Colby Coll., 1901; A.M., Tufts Coll., 1902; m. Marie de Beauvais, Dec. 25, 1906; children—Shirley (dec.), Betty, Jeanne. Instr. geology, Tufts Coll., 1902; asst. instr. geology, Harvard, 1902-03; miner, 1904-07; petrographer, 1905-07; aid U.S. Geol. Survey, 1907-08, jr., 1908-09, asst., 1910-12, asso., 1912-13; geologist fgn. dept. Pearson & Son, Ltd., 1913-15; geologist Associated Geol. Engrs., 1915-16, Petroleum Exploration, Inc., 1916-18; asst. valuation expert, U. S. Internal Revenue Bur., 1918-19; cons. geologist, 1919-24; geologist fgn. dept. Standard Oil Co. (N.J.), 1925-29; geologist U.S. Geol. Survey, from 1930; represented survey on tech. and adv. com. Federal Oil Conservation Bd., 1931-32. Mem. Geol. Soc. of America, Soc. of Econ. Geologists, Am. Assn. of Petroleum Geologists, Am. Inst. of Mining and Metall. Engrs., Geol. Soc. of Washington, Alpha Tau Omega. Republican. Methodist. Clubs: Cosmos, University. Author: Synopsis of Mineral Character, 1907; also pamphlets and bulletins issued by U.S. Geol. Survey. Home: Washington, D.C.†

RICHARDS, STEWART WATSON, lawyer; b. Bklyn., Aug. 6, 1903; s. John W. and Bertha E. (Miller) R.; A.B., Williams Coll., 1926; LL.B., Harvard, 1929; m. Helene M. Davidson, Nov. 30, 1946. Admitted to N.Y. bar, 1930, later practiced in N.Y.C.; partner Beer, Richards, Haller & O'Neill, and predecessor, 1945-73, Richard & O'Neil, 1973-75, specializing in trade-marks, unfair trade practices; with Office Gen. Counsel, WPB, Washington, 1943-45, asst. gen. counsel WPB, 1945. Bd. dirs. Bklyn. Home for Children. Mem. Am. Bar Assn., Assn. Bar City, N.Y., Harvard Law Sch. Assn. Presbyn. Clubs: Harvard, Metropolitian Brooklawn Country. Home: Fairfield, Conn., Died Jan. 22, 1975.

RICHARDSON, CHARLES TIFFANY, investment exec.; b. N.Y.C., May 12, 1880; s. William and Sarah Matilda (Anderson) R.; B.A., Harvard, 1902; m. Alice Everard Strong, Sept. 10, 1911; children—William E., Anne Schuyler (Mrs. Morris T. Hoversten), Charles Tiffany. Former dir. Pierce Oil Corp., Green Bay & Western R.R.; gen. partner Auerbach. Pollack & Richardson and predecessor firms, mem. N.Y. Stock Exchange. Past mem. bd. Herman Knapp Meml. Eye Hosp., N.Y.C. Clubs: Links, Anglers (N.Y.C.). Home: New York City, N.Y.†

RICHARDSON, FRANCIS HARRIE, electronics engr.; b. Vancouver, B.C., Can., June 27, 1898; s. Peter Frank and Florence Victoria (Heathorn) R.; M.E., U. of Edinburgh, 1919; student McGill U., 1914, 19—20 Mass. Inst. of Tech., 1941—42, Bur. of Standards, 1944—45; m. Rose Mansbridge, June 10, 1922; children—Peter Wentworth, Mary Rose (Mrs. William Wheeler Anderson). Cons. engr. Montreal and N.Y., 1922—32; engr.—economist N.Y. and Boston, writer on tech. matters, 1932—41; research asso. radiation lab., Mass. Inst. Tech., 1941—42; adminstrv. sec. Joint Research & Development Bd., 1946—47; dep. exec. sec. research and development bd. of Nat. Mil. Establishment, 1947—51. Served as capt. Royal Canadian Engrs. and RAF, 1915—19; col. USAF, 1942—46; chief electronic research for A.A.F. Hdqrs., Washington, 1942—45; dir. Cambridge Field Sta., A.A.F. (electronic research), 1945—46; col. USAF, 1951—55; tech. dir. Arnold Engring. Development Center, Tullahoma, Tenn., 1955—57; tech. dir. plans and programs Hdqrs. Air Research and Development Command, Andrews AFB, Md., 1957—60; tech. dir. Air Force Flight Test Center, Edwards AFB, 1960—62; sr. engr. RCA Missile Text Project, Patrick AFB, Fla., 1962; Dir. marketing missile div. Chrysler Corp., 1962—64; asst. dir. Tenn. Space Inst., Tullahoma from 1964. Decorated Legion of Merit (U.S.). Mem. Am. Rocket Soc., Soc. Am. Mil. Engrs., Am. Inst. Aeros. and Astonautics. Club: Army and Navy (Washington). Home: Manchester, Tenn. Died May 5, 1975.

RICHARDSON, FRANK HOWARD, physician; b. Brooklyn, N.Y., July 1, 1882; s. William James and Mary Carrington (Raymond) R.; A.B., Cornell U., 1904, M.D., 1906; grad. student Vienna U., 1909; m. Clara Louise Dixon, Sept. 8, 1915; children—Mary Faison(Mrs. Victor A. Gauthier, Jr.), Howard, Raymond Moseley, Clarence Dixon, Ruth (Mrs. T. C. Innes). House physician and surgeon Bklyn. Meth. Hosp., 1906—07; resident physician N.Y. Infant Asylum (now N.Y. Nursery and Child's Hosp.), 1908; gen. practice of medicine, Bklyn., 1909—16; specialist in diseases of children, Bklyn., Black Mountain and Asheville, N.C., from 1918; formerly regional cons. N.Y. Dept. Health. Alderman, vice mayor, Black Mountain. Served as 1st lt., later capt. M.C., U. S. Army, with A.E.F. attached successively to 102d Field Signal Batn., 106th Inf. (27th Div.), in Brit. Field Army in Belgium and France, 1918; cited in 27th Div. orders "for fearlessness and unremitting attention to the wounded of his regiment during the battle of the Le Selle River, Oct. 19—20, 1918." Former pres. Bklyn. Pediatric Soc. Fellow Am. Coll. Physicians, Am. Acad. Pediatrics; licentiate Am. Bd. Pediatrics; past pres. 10th Dist., Med. Soc. of N.C.; mem. N.C. Pediat. Soc. Baptist. Clubs: Lions, Nat. Writers Club. Author: For Boys Only, 1952; The Nursing Mother, 1953; For Girls Only, 1953; How to Get Along with Children, 1954; For Teenagers Only; Who says We're Too Young to Get Married, 1957; For Young Adults Only, 1961; For Parents Only: The Doctor Discusses Discipline, 1962; A Christian Doctor Talks with Young Parents, 1963; Grandparents and Their Families: A Guide for Three Generations, 1964. Home: Black Mountain, N.C. Deceased.

RICHARDSON, HOLDEN CHESTER, naval officer; b. Shamokin, Pa., Dec. 7, 1878; s. William Abbott and Elmira Jane (Douty) R.; grad. U.S. Naval Acad., 1901; M.S., Mass. Inst. Tech., 1907; m. Margaret Jones, of Hampton, Va., July 20, 1908; 1 dau., Margaret Jane. Ensign U.S.N., June 7, 1903; asst. naval constructor, Oct. 12, 1904; naval constructor, Oct. 12, 1912; comdr., Jan. 1, 1921. Mem. and sec. Nat. Advisory Com. for Aeronautics, 1915-Jan. 1917. Pilot's license, Aero Club of America, Sept. 25, 1919; designated naval aviator, Apr. 12, 1915; expert aviator, Aero Club of America, June 23, 1915. Constrn. officer, Pensacola, Fla., Dec. 1916-Mar. 1918; supt. constrn. of aircraft. Curtiss plant,

Buffalo, Mar. 1918-Mar. 1919. Pilot NC-3, transatlantic flight, May 1919. Chief engr., Naval Aircraft Factory, Philadelphia, 1919-23; member Bureau of Aeronautics, Navy Dept., 1922-29; retired as capt. (C.C.) May 1, 1929; dir. engring. Allied Motor Industries, Chicago, 1929-33. Mem. Soc. Naval Architects and Marine Engrs., Soc. Automotive Engrs., Sigma Chi; fellow Royal Aeronautical Soc. Episcopalian. Mason. Clubs: Army and Navy, Nat. Town and Country. Address: Washington, D.C.†

RICHARDSON, JAMES OTTO, naval officer; b. Paris, Tex., Sept. 18, 1878; s. John James and Fannie (Foster) R.; grad. U.S. Naval Acad., 1902; m. May Fenet, Sept. 20, 1911; 1 son, Joe Fenet. Commd. ensign, June 1904; promoted through grades to rear adm., Dec. 12, 1934. Asst. chief Bur. Ordnance, 1924-27, dir. officer Personnel, 1928-30; comdg. officer U.S.S. Augusta, 1931-33; budget officer, Navy Dept., 1934-35; chief of staff for comdr. in chief U.S. Fleet, 1935-36; comdr. Destroyers, Scouting Force, 1936-37; asst. to chief of naval operations, 1937-38; chief Bur. of Navigation, 1938-39; comdr. Battle Force. U.S. Fleet, 1939-40; comdr. in chief U.S. Fleet, 1940-41; mem. Gen. Bd., Navy Dept., 1941-42; retired Oct. 1, 1942 with rank of adm. Exec. vice pres. Navy Relief Soc. June 1942-May 1945; released from active duty. Jan. 1947. Clubs: Army-Navy, Army and Navy Country (Washington); Chevy Chase, Alfalfa. Home: Washington D.C. Died May 2, 1974.

RICHARDSON, RUSSELL, author; b. Malone, N.Y., Dec. 23, 1881; s. Charles Spencer and Frances (Weed) R.; A.B., Hamilton Coll., Clinton, N.Y., 1905, M.A., 1910; student, history and economics, U. of Chicago, 1909-10, modern history, U. of Berlin, 1910-12; studied French at Lyons, France, and U. of Chicago; unmarried. With Marshall Field & Co., Chicago, 1905-06, Western Electric Co., 1906-08. Mem. Alpha Delta Phi, Phi Beta Kappa. Republican. Presbyn. Author: Europe from a Motor Car, 1914. Home: Chicago, Ill.†

RICHTER, JULIUS physician; b. Allegheny, Pa., Dec. 19, 1876; s. Julius August and Julia (Meyer) R.; M.D., U. Buffalo, 1904; postgrad. in gen. surgery N.Y. Postgrad. Sch.; m. Margaret Campbell, 1905 (dec. 1958); m. 2d, Elizabeth Thompson Sinclair, Apr. 1, 1969. Cons. surgeon Millard Fillmore, Meyer Meml. hosps. (both Buffalo); bd. dirs., cons. surgeon Lafayette Gen. Hosp.; asso. mem. med. staff Buffalo Gen. Hosp.; asst. prof. surgery U. Buffalo, also asso. prof. anatomy. One-man shows Albright-Knox Art Gallery, Buffalo. Diplomate Am. Bd. Surgery (founder mem.). Fellow A.C.S.; mem. Erie County Med. Soc. (dir.), Buffalo Acad. Medicine (dir.), Buffalo Surg. Soc. (founder, past pres.), Buffalo Soc. Artists (council). Presbyn. Club: Buffalo Print. Home: Buffalo, N.Y. Died May 26, 1974; buried Forest Lawn Cemetery, Buffalo, N.Y.

RIDDER, BERNARD HERMAN, publisher; b. N.Y.C., March 20, 1883; s. Herman and Mary (Amend) R.; A.B., Columbia, 1903; post graduate study, Leipzig; m. Hilda Luytis, 1905; m. 2d, Nell Hickey, 1915; m. 3d, Agnes Kennedy, 1944; children—Herman H., Bernard Herman, Joseph, Daniel H., Rosemary (Mrs. Malcolm Sanders). Chmn., Northwest Publs., Inc.; pres., dir. St. Paul Arcade Co., Otto Bremer Co.; sec., dir. Grand Forks Herald, Inc.; v.p., dir. Boulder Publishing, Inc., Ridder Publications, Inc., Aberdeen News Co.; bd. directors Dispatch Realty Co., Mid-Continent Radio—Television, Inc., Midwest Radio—Television, Am. Nat. Bank. Decorated grand commander Order of Isabel la Catolica. Mem. Phi Sigma Kappa. Clubs: Seminole, Everglades (Palm Beach, Fla.); Somerset Country, Minnesota, St. Paul Athletic. Author: Hypenations, 1915. Home: St. Paul, Minn. Died May 1975.

RIDEAL, ERIC KEIGHTLEY, educator; b. London, Eng. Apr. 11, 1890; s. Samuel and Elizabeth (Keightley) R.; student Cambridge U., 1908—11, Bonn U., 1911—12; M. A., U. London, 1911, Ph.D., 1912, D.Sc.; D.Sc. (hon.), U. Bonn, U. Turin (Italy), U. Birmingham, U. Belfast, U. Dublin; D. Tech., U. Brunel, 1965; m. Margaret Atlee Jackson, June 21, 1921; 1 dau., Mary Chichester Oliver. Lectr., Univ. Coll. London, 1918; prof. U. Ill., Urbana, 1921; H.O. Jones lectr. Cambridge U., 1922; prof. chemistry Cambridge U., 1930—46; dir. Royal Instn., London, 1946—49; prof. King's Coll. London, 1950—55; sr. research fellow Imperial Coll. South Kensington, London, 1955-74. Served to capt. Royal Engrs., World War 1. Created knight, 1951; mem. order Brit. Empire, 1921; recipient Gold medal Soc. Engrs., 1930. Fellow Royal Soc. (Navy medal 1951), Royal Inst. Chemistry, Trinity Hall Cambridge, King's Coll. London; mem. Faraday Soc. (pres. 1938—45), Chem. Soc. Gt. Brit., Soc. Chem. Industry (pres., Messel medal 1970), Am. Chem. Soc. (hon.), Société de Chemie Physique (hon.), Real Sociedad Espanola (hon.). Author: Ozone, 1913; (with H.S. Taylor) Catalysis in Theory and Practice, 1917; Concepts in Catalysis, 1967; Surface Chemistry, 1930; (with S.J. Davies) Interfacial Phenomena, 1963; (with S. Rideal) Disinfectants and Disinfection Water Supplies, 1914. Home: London; England. Died Sept. 25, 1974; buried Cromer, Norfolk, England.

RIDGWAY, HOWARD EUGENE, food co. exec.; b. Chgo., Jan.7, 1905; s. Edmund Goforth and Louise Augusta (Goetting) R.; student Principia Jr. Coll., 1924; B.A., Wis. U., 1926; m. Mary Agusta Powars, Sept. 15, 1932; 1 son, Robert Allen. With Laclede Christy Clay Products Co., St. Louis, 1927-31, Alcorn Combustion Co., Phila., 1931-37; with Seven-Up Co., St. Louis, 1937, v.p., 1940-65, sec.-treas., 1961-65, exec. v.p., 1965-71, sr. v.p., 1971-72, chmn. bd., 1972-74, also dir.; founder, 1st pres. Dominion Seven-Up Co., Toronto, Ont., Can., 1938-65, also dir.; founder, 1st pres. Seven-Up Export Corp., N.Y.C., 1948-65, also dir.; dir. Seven-Up Research Corp., Dev-Vend Corp., Boatmen's Nat. Bank, St. Louis, Chemtech Corp., Warner Jenkinson Co. Mem. U.S. C. of C., Principia Alumni Assn. (exec. com. 1969-70), Alpha Tau Omega. Christian Scientist. Mason (Shriner). Clubs: Algonquin Golf, Bellerive Country, University, Stadium, Saint Louis, Mo. Athletic (St. Louis). Home: St Louis, Mo. Died Sept. 24, 1974; interred Valhalla Cemetery, St. Louis, Mo.

RIDLON, JOSEPH RANDALL, medical dir.; b. Gorham, Me., Apr. 18, 1882; s. Francis A. and Evelyn M. (Randall) R.; A.B., Bowdoin, 1903; M.D., Med. Sch. of Me., 1906; student, London Sch. Tropical Medicine, 1913; m. Agnes E. Pyke, July 2, 1913; 1 dau., Mary Evelyn (Mrs. John R. McGraw). Asst. surgeon, U.S. Pub. Health Service, 1908; passed through successive grades to med. dir., 1934; saw service in all parts of country, in Puerto Rico and England; was in charge U.S. Quarantine Sta., Charleston, S.C., serving in U.S. Coast Guard as Dist. Med. Officer, 6th Naval Dist.; also port med. Sigma, A.M.A., Am. Coll. Phys. (fellow), Assn. Mil. rep., War Shipping Administration. Mem. Kappa Surgeons. Presbyterian. Address: Gorham Me. Died June 2, 1973.

RIECHMANN, DONALD AUGUST, libriarian; b. Centralia, Ill., Dec. 12, 1919; s. August C. and Anna (Riechmann) R.; A.B., Elmhurst Coll., 1942; B.S. in L.S., U. Chgo., 1947; m. Ruth Elizabeth Koenig, Apr. 7, 1956. Asst. exec. sec. A.L.A., Chgo., 1947—48; exec. asst. dir. Enoch Pratt Free Library, Balt., 1948—50, gen. reference, 1950—51; dir. Hazleton (Pa.) Pub. Library, 1951—53; head merc. br. Free Library Phila., 1953—63, coordinator dist. service, 1963—66; dir. Albuquerque Pub. Library from 1966; Part-time inst. Drexel Inst. Tech. Library Sch., 1961—66. Served with AUS, 1942—46. Mem. A.L.A. (pres. elect reference services div.), Spl. Libraries Assn. Editor: Between Librarian, 1948—51; Pa. Library Assn. Bull., 1952—57. Home: Albuquerque, N.M. Died Nov. 3, 1971.

RIEFLER, WINFIELD WILLIAM, economist; b. Buffalo, N.Y., Feb. 9, 1897; s. Philip D. and Clara (Gartner) R.; A.B., Amherst Coll., 1921; Ph.D., Brookings Grad. Sch., 1927; Dr. Humane Letters (Honorary) Amherst College, 1944; m. Dorothy Miles Brown, Dec. 5, 1924; children—David Winfield, Donald Brown. Fgn. trade officer Dept. of Commerce, Buenos Aires, Argentina, 1921-23; div. research and statistics Federal Reserve Bd., 1923-33, exec. sec. com. on bank reserves, 1930-32, econ. adviser to exec. council, 1933-34; chmn. Central Statis. Bd., 1933-35; econ. adviser to Nat. Emergency Council, 1934-35; prof. Sch. Economics and Politics of Inst. for Advanced Study 1935-48; on leave of absence to act as minister to London (spl. asst. to ambassador), 1942-44; chmn. League of Nations Delegation on Econ. Depressions, 1945; director Federal Reserve Bank of Phila., 1941-42; asst. to chmn. of bd. govs. Fed. Reserve System, 1948-59, secretary federal open market com., 1952-59. Chmn. bd. Sch. of Advanced Internat. Studies 1948. With AEF, 1917-19. Awarded Croix de Guerre (France). Mem. delegation for study of econ. depression, 1937-46, mem. subcommittee on financial statistics, 1938-46, alternate mem. finance com., 1937-46, all League of Nations; dir. Fgn. Policy Assn., 1938-40. Trustee Inst. for Advanced Study, 1936-41; dir. Nat. Bur. of Economic Research, 1936-42, and 1945-48; dir. Council on Fgn. Relations, 1945-50; chairman 20th Century Fund Com. on Foreign Economic Relations, 1946; chmn. Social Science Research Council Com. on Social and Economic Aspects of Atomic Energy, 1945. Fellow of the American Statistical Association (president 1941); member Alpha Delta Phi, Phi Beta Kappa, Delta Sigma Rho. Clubs: Cosmos (Washington, D.C.); Reform (London, Eng.) Century Club, New York City. Author: Money Rates and Money Markets in the United States, 1930. Home: Sarasota Fla. Died Apr. 5, 1974.

RIEFSTAHL, RUDOLF M., educator; b. Munich, Bavaria, Aug. 9, 1880; s. Wilhelm Meyer (aus Speyer) and Pauline Riefstahl; adopted mother's surname; Ph.D., U. of Strassburg, 1904; married. Lecturer at Ecole Normale Supéricure, and at the Sorbonne, Paris, 1904-11; came to U.S., 1915; dir. Historic Exhbn. for Textiles, Nat. Silk Conv., Paterson, N.J., 1915; lecturer, U. of Calif., 1916; prof. of fine arts, New York U., from 1924; visiting prof. at Robert Coll., Constantinople, spring term, from 1927; specializes in study of Turkish Art; made expdns. during 5 yrs. in Anatolia, Syria, Transylvania, Palestine, for study of Islamic architecture; lectured at diverse museums in U.S. Naturalized citizen of U.S., 1922. Author: Parish-Watson Collection of Mohammedan Potteries, 1922; Persian and Indian Textiles of the Late 16th Century to the Early 19th Century, 1923; Turkish Architecture in Southwest Anatolia, 1929. Translator Bode and Kuenel's Antique Rugs from the Near East, 1922. Contbr. to art mags. Address: New York City, N.Y.†

RIEGEL, BYRON, educator, chemist; b. Palmyra, Mo., June 17, 1906; s. William Henry and Ellena (Beagle) R.; A.B., Central Meth. Coll., 1928, D.Sc., 1963; student Princeton, 1929-30; A.M., U. Ill., 1931, Ph.D., 1934; NRC fellow Technische Hochschule, Danzig, 1935-36, Harvard, 1936-37; D.Litt., Ohio No. U., 1969; m. Belle M. Huot, Aug. 25, 1934; 1 son, Byron William. Instr. chemistry, Central Meth. Coll., 1928-29; research asso. George Washington U., 1934-35; instr. in chemistry Northwestern U., 1937-40, asst. prof., 1940-43, asso. prof., 1943-48, prof., 1948-51, lectr., 1951-59, vis. prof., 1971-72; dir. chem. research G.D. Searle and Co., Chgo., 1951-71. Pres. abstracting bd. Internat. Council Sci. Unions, from 1969. Recipient certificate of appreciation War and Navy Depts., 1948; Honor Scroll, Chgo. chpt. Am. Inst. Chemists, 1966; Distinguished Alumni plaque Central Coll., 1949. Mem. Am. Chem. Soc. (Chgo. sect.; dir. 1948-50, chmn. 1950-51, trustee 1954-57; nat. councilor 1949; mem. and chmn. various coms. including exec. com. div. organic chemistry 1950-51, mem. editorial bd. Jour. Organic Chemistry 1953-58, regional dir. 1959-61, dir.-at-large, 1963-68, ex-officio, 1969-71, Midwest award St. Louis sect., 1968, nat. pres. 1970, chmn. bd. 1971, NRC Div. Chemistry and Chem. Tech. chmn. subcom. steroid nomenclature 1948-54, com. nomenclature 1950-57, chmn. 1954-55, mem. at large 1951-53, 58-59, Am. Chem. Soc. rep. 1954-57, 60-72, exec. com. 1960-61, Internat. Union Pure and Applied Chemistry Distinguished Service award Chgo. sect. 1975), Am. Soc. Biochemists, Am. Assn. Cancer Research, A.A.A.S., Am. Assn. U. Profs., Sigma Xi, Phi Lambda Upsilon (hon.), Alpha Chi Sigma. Clubs: Chicago Chemists, Sheridan Shore Yacht. Contbr. articles to profl. jours. Home: Evanston, Ill. Died May 20, 1975; interred Meml. Park, Skokie, Ill.

RIEGEL, CATHERINE THIRZA, librarian; b. Independence, Kan., Apr. 30, 1911; d. Augustus John and Mae Josephine (Randall) Riegel; A.B., N.Y. State Tchrs. Coll., Albany, 1932, B.S. in Library Sci., 1936, M.A., 1950; postgrad. U. Vt., State U. N.Y. at Albany. Asst. librarian Albany Pub. Library, 1932-33; tchr. English, Roessleville High Sch., Albany, 1933-34, librarian, English tchr., 1934-48; dir. library service Colonie Central Schs., Albany, 1948-54, supr. libraries, 1954—; instr. N.Y. State Coll. for Tchrs.; bibliographer N.Y. State Edn. Dept. Mem. N.Y. State Tchrs. Assn., N.E.A., N.Y. Library Assn., N.Y. State Assn. Elementary Prins., N.Y. State Edn. Assn., Delta Kappa Gamma. Independent. Mem. Ref. Ch. Home: Albany, N.Y., Died July 26, 1974.

RIESMAN, JOHN PENROSE, surgeon; b. Elkins Park, Pa., June 5, 1912; s. David and Eleanor (Fleisher) R.; A.B., Harvard, 1934; M.D., U. Pa., 1938; postgrad. Yale, 1947-48; m. Margaret Haynes Cope, Aug. 5, 1942; 1 dau., Janet Ann. Intern Phila. Gen. Hosp., 1938-40, staff resident, 1938-43; practice medicine specializing in surgery, New Haven, 1948-72; attending surgeon Yale-New Haven Hosp.; physician-in-charge dispensary U.S. Steel Corp., New Haven, 1968; cons. surgery Griffin Hosp., Derby, Conn. Vets. Home and Hosp., Rocky Hill; clin. instr. surgery Yale Med Sch., 1950-72. Trustee Assos. of Yale Med. Library. Served to lt. comdr., M.C., USNR, 1943-46. Mem. New Haven County Med. Assn. (bd. censors 1969-72), New Haven Colony, Branford hist. socs. Clubs: Beaumont Medical (sec.-treas. 1960-68, v.p. 1968-70), Branford Yacht, New Haven Yacht, Graduates, Yale Faculty (New Haven). Home: Branford, Conn. Died Sept. 8, 1972; interred Walpole Meeting House Cemetery, South Bristol, Me.

RIEVE, EMIL, labor leader; b. Zyradow, province of Poland, June 8, 1892; s. Fred and Pauline (Lange) R.; elementary school edn.; m. Laura Wosnack, July 1, 1916; 1 son, Harold; came to U.S., 1904, naturalized, 1924. Pres. Am. Fedn. of Hosiery Workers, 1929-39, Textile Workers Union of America 1939-56; chmn. exec. Council, Textile Workers Union Am., 1956-60, pres. emeritus, 1960-64; v.p. CIO, 1940-55, AFL-CIO, 1955-65; rep., Code Authority Hosiery Industry, 1933-35. Mem. Gov. Lehman's spl. com. State Def. Council; labor adv. commn. to Council of National Defense. Alternate member Nat. Mediation Bd., mem. U.S. Govt. Wage and Hour Industry Coms.; U.S. Labor rep. to Internat. Labor Office, Geneva, Switzerland, 1936; C.I.O. delegate to World Fedn. of Trade Unions, 1945-47; del. to numerous labor convs. and congresses; mem. executive council Internat. Confederation of Free Trade Unions since 1949; chmn. C.I.O. Econ. Policy Com.; mem. labor adv. com. Nat. Security Resources Bd., 1950; mem. Wage Stblzn. Bd., 1950-52; mem. C.I.O. Polit. Action Com. Alternate mem. Nat. War Labor Bd., Am. Arbitration Assn., National Planning Assn. Torch of Hope Award, 1954. Chmn. Philip Murray Meml. Found. Lutheran. Author: Free Enterprise for Whom?, 1948. Home: Lauderhill Fla. Died Jan. 24, 1975.

RIGG, GEORGE BURTON, educator; b. Woodbine, Ia., Feb. 9, 1872; s. George Franklin and Margaret Ellen (Hushaw) R.; B.S., State U. of Ia., 1896; M.A., U. of Wash., 1909; Ph.D., U. of Chicago, 1914; m. Marie Bugh McCuskey, Mar. 30, 1900; children—Margaret (Mrs. Clifford Bender), Raymond Ruel, Charlotte Marie (Mrs. David T. Williams). Began as teacher in country sch., Iowa, 1891; teacher in high sch., Rockwell City, Ia., 1893-95, asso. prin., 1896-98; teacher of science, Woodbine (Ia.) Normal Sch., 1898-1907; teacher of biology, Lincoln High Sch., Seattle, Wash., 1907-09; instr. in botany, U. of Wash., 1909-15, asst. prof. botany, 1915-22, asso. prof., 1922-28, prof. 1928-47, emeritus from 1947, head of dept., 1940-42; mem. staff of Oceanographic Labs., 1930-47; mem. university com. in charge of lignin and cellulose research, 1940-47; Scientist in charge expdns. for investigations of kelp as source of potash, United States Bureau Soils, Puget Sound region, 1911, 12, western Alaska, 1913; dir. biol. survey in Wash. for State Dept. Fisheries, 1922; field work on peat hogs Eastern U.S., 1935, 41; in charge survey of peat resources of state of Wash. for State Division of Mines and Geology, 1948-58. Named Eminent Ecologist of Year, Ecolo. Soc., 1956. Mem. Bot. Soc. of America (pres. Pacific Section, 1940), Am. Soc. Plant Physiology, Ecol. Soc. America, Western Soc. Naturalists (ex-pres.), Washington Acad. of Science, New York Acad. Science, A.A.A.S., Am. Assn. Univ. Profs., Gamma Alpha, Sigma Xi, Phi Sigma, Alpha Kappa Lambda. Methodist. Mason Odd Fellow. Clubs: Faculty, Catalysts. Author: Laboratory Exercises in Elementary Botany (with T. C. Frye), 1911; Northwest Flora (with T.C. Frye), 1912; Elementary Flora of the Northwest (with same), 1914; The Pharmacist's Botany, 1924; College Botany, 1930; Peat Resources in Washington, 1958; also articles on peat bogs, marine plants in profl. jours. Home: Seattle, Wash.†

RIGGS, ARTHUR STANLEY, editor, author; b. Cranford, N.J., April 8, 1879; s. James Forsyth and Isabella (Brittin) R.; educated at home private tutors and father; m. Elisabeth Adams Corey, Apr. 15, 1901; died Dec. 25, 1944. Clerk statistical department Standard Oil Company, N.Y. City, 1896 to 1900; reporter New York Times, New York Mail and Express, Commercial Advertiser, 1900; exchange editor Elec. Review, asst. editor Mining and Metallurgy, editor Elec. Age, 1901-52; editor Manila Daily Bulletin, The Critic, Manila Freedom, Manila Cablenews, 1902-04; mag. conbr. and staff lecturer on art, architecture and history in several colls. and univs., 1905-25; dir. and sec. Archeol. Soc. Washington and editor and sec. Art and Archeology (bimonthly mag.), 1925-35. Mem. N.Y. Naval Militia, 1896-1902; with U.S. Naval Auxiliary Force, Spanish-Am. War; lt. comdr. U.S. Naval Res., 1935, comdr., 1942, on active duty, Aug. 1941-June 1945, as librarian Office of Censorship, retired, June 1945. Awarded spl. letter of commendation by sec. of navy for outstanding performance of duty. Decorated Knight Commander, Royal Order of Isabel the Catholic (Spain); Officer Order of the Crown (Italy). Pres. Instituto de las Españas, Washington sect., 1933-35; asso. mem. Mil. Order Carabao; mem. Authors League America, Am. Professional Artists League, Veterans Assn. of the Naval Militia of New York, Chi Psi Omega. Clubs: Cosmos (Washington); Franklin Inn (Philadelphia). Author: Vistas in Sicily, 1911; France from Sea to Sea, 1913; With Three Armies, 1918; The Spanish Pageant, 1928; The Romance of Human Progress, 1938; Titian the Magnificent, 1946; Velázquez; Painter of Truth, 1947. Address: Washington, D.C.†

RIGGS, FRANCIS BEHN, educator; b. Princeton, Mass., July 24, 1881; s. Benjamin Clapp and Rebecca (Fox) R.; grad. Groton Sch., Mass., 1899; A.B., Harvard, 1903, d.M., 1923; studied Columbia, 1903-05; m. Valerie Burckhardt Hadden, N.Y. City, Oct. 6, 1910; children—Lorna Hadden, Francis Behn, Valerie Hope, Austen Fox. Marine engr., 1903-13; headmaster St. Bernard's Sch., Gladstone, N.J., 1913-15; founder, and headmaster Riggs' Agrl. Sch., Lakeville, Conn., 1915-22; founder, and headmaster Indian Mountain Sch. for Younger Boys, Lakeville, form 1922. Mem. N.E.A., of Dept. of Elementary Sch. Principals of N.E.A., Nat. Soc. for Study of Edn., War Resisters League, Fellowship of Reconciliation. Club: Century. Home: Lakeville, Conn.†

RIGGS, JOSEPH A., mfg. co. exec.; b. Toledo, July 9, 1899; s. Henry Earle and Emma (Hynes) R.; B.S., U. Mich., 1922; m. Gretchen Walser, Oct. 29, 1923; children—Ruth (Mrs. Donald N. Wendel), Joseph A., Henry E. With Goss Printing Press Co., from 1922, dir., from 1937, v.p., 1934-44, exec. v.p., gen. mgr., 1944-60; dir. Miehle-Goss-Dexter, Inc., Chgo., from 1957, exec. v.p., 1957-62, chmn. bd., 1962-63; pres. Goss Co. div. Miehle-Goss-Dexter, Inc., 1960-64; dir. Brown & Sharpe Mfg. Co., Providence. Trustee, Village Hinsdale, Ill., 1938-42; commr. Hinsdale Utilities Commn., from 1960, chmn., from 1961. Mem. Phi Gamma Delta. Clubs: University, Mid-America (Chgo.); Hinsdale Golf. Home: Hinsdale Ill. Died 1973.

RIISAGER, KNUDAGE, composer; b. Port Kunda, Mar. 6, 1897; s. Henrik Emil and Henrikke (Olufsen) H.; examen polit. sci. U. Copenhagen (Denmark), 1921; student music, 1916-24; student Paul Le Flem, Paris, 1923-24, Albert Roussel, Paris, 1923-24, Hermann Grabner, Leipzig (Germany), 1932; Mus.D. (hon.), U. Seattle (Wash.), 1972; m. Ase Klenow, July 6, 1920; children—Torben, Elsebet. With Ministry Finances Denmark, Copenhagen, 1925-47, chief, 1939-47; dir. Royal Conservatory Denmark, Copenhagen, 1956-67; composer numerous works for orch., including several overtures, 4 symphonies and various instrumental combinations; ballets include Quarrtsiluni, 1942, Etudes, 1948, Moonreindeer, 1958, Ballet royal (for wedding Princess heritier Margrethe), 1967, others; opera buffa, Susanne, 1950; unaccompanied works, especially for piano, violin. Decorated knight of Daneborg, comdr. Danebrog, comdr. 1st degree; officier Legion d'honneur (France); Verdienstkreig 1st Class (Germany); knight 7-Cross Star (Brazil). Author: essay collection Det usynileg Monster, 1950. Address: Copenhagen, Denmark., Died Dec. 26, 1974.

RILEY, WALTER JAMES, banker; b. Chgo., Dec. 9, 1875; s. Lyman and Catherine Hoester) R.; LL.B., Chicago-Kent Coll. Law, 1910; LL.D., St. Joseph Coll., East Chicago, Ind., 1965. Admitted to Ind. bar and began practice at East Chicago; entered banking business, East Chicago, 1909; founder, hon. chmn., dir. 1st Nat. Bank East Chicago; founder, hon. chmn. dir. Riley Co., Inc.; dir. Northern Indiana Public Service Co., Hammond, Ind., 1942-62, City judge East Chicago, 1910-13; mem. Bd. of Works, East Chicago, 1914-18; chmn. Interstate Harbor Commn., 1922-24; mem. Ind. state exec. council and chmn. for Lake County, Governor's Unemployment Relief Commn., 1930-32. Del. Rep. Nat. Conventions, 1928, 32, 48, 52. Honorary chmn. lay adv. bd. St. Catherine's Hospital. Col. and aide-de-camp to gov., Indiana Nat. Guard, 1917-21. Mem. adv. com. Ind. State Dept. Commerce and Pub. Relations, 1945-57. Decorated Cavelieri Magistrali, Rome Chapter, Knight of Malta (papal). Mem. East Chicago Mfrs. Assn. (founder, sec. treas. 1915-70; hon. dir.). K.C., Elk. Clubs: Chicago Athletic Assn. South Shore Country (Chicago); Indianapolis Athletic. Home: Munster, Ind. Died June 1, 1973; buried Mt. Olivet Cemetery, Chgo.

RIMINGTON, CRITCHELL, pub. cons.; b. Phila., Feb. 16, 1907; s. Hugh Henry and May (Critchell) R.; student Howe (Ind.) Mil. Sch., Westminster Sch., Simsbury, Conn.; m. Jeanette Warmuth, Dec. 30, 1939. Editorial dept. George H. Doran Co., 1928, Doubleday, Doran & Co., 1928-30; v.p. John Day Co., 1930-35; editor Robert McBride & Co., 1935-41; dir. pub. relations Norman Bel Geddes & Co., N.Y.C., 1941-42; asso. editor Yachting Mag. 1942-44, mng. editor, 1944-52, editor, 1952-66, pres., pub., 1955-71, chmn. pub., 1971-72, cons., 1972-76. Trustee Internat. Oceanographic Found., Marine Hist. Assn. Mem. Soc. Naval Architects and Marine Engrs. Clubs: Corinthians, Little Ship (London); N.Y. Yacht, City Island Yacht, Royal Danish, Cruising of Am., Royal Bermuda Yacht, Royal Cork. Author: Bon Voyage Book, 1934; Fighting Fleets, Merchant Fleets, 1944; This Is the Navy, 1945; The Sea Chest; A Yachtman's Reader, 1947. Editor The Sea Chest: The Yachtman's Digest, 1939-44. Author articles on yachting, marine and naval subjects. Home: Rowayton, Conn., Died Jan. 30, 1976.

RING, FLOYD ORVAL, physician; b. Dows, Ia., Jan. 21, 1921; s. Charles Oscar and Edna Ann Ring; M.D., U. Neb., 1948; m. Margaretta A. Brandon, Feb. 14, 1943; children—Leilani (Mrs. Tom Beach), Floyd Orval, Kathleen Mary (Mrs. Terry A. Davis). Intern, Wayne County Gen. Hosp., Eloise, Mich.; fellow Menninger Found. Sch. Psy., 1949-51; resident in psychiatry Winter VA Hosp., Topeka, 1949-51, U. Neb., 1951-52; asso. staff St. Joseph's Hosp., Luth. Hosp., Clarkson Hosp. (all Omaha); cons. Armed Forces Exam. Service; asst. prof. psychiatry Neb. Psy. Inst., Omaha, U. Neb. Served with AUS, 1940-45. Diplomate Am. Bd. Psychiatry and Neurology. Fellow Am. Psychiat. Assn.; mem. A.M.A., Am. Group Psychotherapy Assn. Home: Tucson, Ariz., Died Sept. 9, 1970; buried Lincoln, Neb.

RINGOLD, JAMES, banker; b. Clearmont, Mo., Dec. 28, 1879; s. George M. and Judy S. R.; student Dixon (Ill.) Coll.; m. Lavinia C. Craft, June 1906; children—Marjorie, Katharine, Began with Jackson Bank, Clearmont, 1895; with Nat. Bank, St. Joseph, Mo., 1899-1905; with U.S. Nat. Bank, Denver, from 1905, pres., 1923-35; dir. U.S. Nat. Bank, Denver, Colo.; mem. Liberty Loan Committee, Denver, World War; chairman for Mercer County, United States Treasury War Finance Com. Chmn. Colo. State Com. R.F.C., and Agrl. Credit Corp. Clubs: Denver, Denver Country, Trenton, Trenton Country. Address: Denver, Colo.†

RINKOFF, BARBARA JEAN, (Mrs. Herbert Rinkoff), author; b. N.Y.C., Jan. 25, 1923; d. John J. and Sophia B. (Frank) Rich; B.A., N.Y. U., 1943; m. Herbert Rinkoff, Dec. 17, 1944; children—Robert, Richard, June. Med. social worker Beekman Downtown Hosp., N.Y.C., 1943-47; author, Mt. Kisco, N.Y., 1964-75. Instr. creative writing Mt. Kisco Elementary Sch., 1966, 67. Mem. curriculum council Bedford (N.Y.) Central Sch. Dist. 2, 1960-66. Recipient Book of Year award Child Study Assn., 1968, 69, 70, 72, Top Honor Book, Chgo. Exhbn., 1971, Graphic Arts award Printing Industries Am., 1971. Mem. Alpha Kappa Delta. Author numerous books, including: Elbert, The Mind Reader, 1967; Member of the Gang, 1968; Name: Johnny Pierce, 1969; The Pretzel Hero, 1970; A Guy Can Be Wrong, 1970; Rutherford T. Finds 21 B, 1970; The Watchers, 1972; Let's Go to a Jetport, 1973; Guess What Trees Do, 1974. Home: Mount Kisco, N.Y., Died Feb. 18, 1975.

RIORDAN, LEO (THOMAS ALOYSLUS), public relations exec.; b. Scobeyville, N.J., June 2, 1903; s. Thomas and Anna Rocha (Kelly) R.; A.B., St. Joseph's Coll., Phila., 1926; m. Kathryn Mary Steed, June 11, 1937; children—John Thomas, Thomas Arthur (dec.). Sports reporter Phila. Public Ledger, 1926-36; sports editor Ledger Syndicate, 1937-39; sports editor and columnist Phila. Evening Ledger, 1939-42; asst. sports editor Phila. Inquirer, 1942-43, exec. sports editor, 1943-59; pub. info. officer Jefferson Med. Coll. and Hosp., 1959-67, dir. pub. info., 1967-69; asst. to v.p. for devel. Thomas Jefferson U., Phila., 1969-75. Recipient M. L. Annenberg award spl. merit, 1948. Mem. Hist. Soc. Pa., Am. Cath. Hist. Soc. Phila. (bd. mgrs.), Baseball Writers Assn. Am., Football Writers Assn. Am., Athenaeum of Phila., Colonial Phila. Hist. Soc., Sigma Delta Chi. Roman Catholic. Contbr. articles to nat. mags. Home: Philadelphia, Pa. Died June 6, 1975.

RIPLEY, JOSEPH PIERCE, investment banker; b. Oak Park, Ill., Mar. 29, 1889; s. Joseph Trescott and Harriet Theresa (Konantz) R.; M.E., Cornell U., 1912; m. Florence Guild Albro, June 14, 1916; children—Joseph Pierce (dec.), John Clark, Warren Albro (killed in service with U.S.M.C.). With J. G. White & Company, engineers N.Y. City, 1912-22; with W. A. Harriman & Company, Inc., investment bankers, N.Y. City, 1922-25, sec., 1923-25; with The Nat. City Co. (later The City Co. of N.Y., Inc.), 1925-34, as asst. v.p., 1925-27, v.p., 1927-33, exec. v.p., 1933-34; pres. Brown Harriman & Co., Inc. (name changed to Harriman Ripley & Co., Inc., Jan. 1, 1939), investment bankers, New York, 1934-42, chmn., 1942-58, chmn. bd., 1958-66; hon. chmn. Drexel Harriman Ripley, Inc., 1966-74; dir. Clupak, Inc.; hon. dir. McGregor-Doniger, Inc., Abitibi Power & Paper Co., Ltd. Trustee emeritus Cornell U. Decorated comdr. Royal Norwegian Order St. Olav; comdr. Order of the White Rose Finland. Member of Council Foreign Relations, Beta Theta Pi. Republican. Episcopalian. Clubs: Bohemian (San Francisco); Links, Cornell, University (N.Y.C.). Home: New York City N.Y. Died Nov. 17, 1974.

RIPLEY, WILBER FRANKLIN, Christian educator; b. nr. Canon City, Colo., Dec, 4, 1878; s. Aaron and Lucy Mariah (Lucas) R.; A.B., William Jewell Coll., 1901, D.D., 1931; student Southern Bapt. Theol. Sem. Louisville, Ky., 1904-05; B.D., Central Bapt. Theol. Seminary, Kansas City, Kan., 1918; married Sadie Jeannette Stoutemyer, Nov. 29, 1906; 1 dau., Jeannette (Mrs. Richard Creighton Palmer). Pastor Bapt. Ch., Princeton, Mo., 1901-04; exec. sec. Colo. Bapt. State Conv., 1906-11; pastor Las Animas, Colo., 1911-16, Yecker Av. (now Immanuel) Bapt. Ch., Kansas City, Kan. 1916-18, First Bapt. Church, rinidad, Colo., 1918-19; director promotion and dir. religious edn., Colo. Bapt. State Conv., 1919-43. Mem. bd. of dirs. Kan., Colo. Woman's Coll. (Denver). Mem. Sigma Nu. Republican. Mason. Home: Silver Spring, Md.†

RIPPERGER, HELMUT LOTHAR, author, lectr., librarian; b. N.Y.C., July 21, 1897; s. Albert A. and Sidonie Adeline (Faucheur) R.; student Fordham U., 1915-17. Editor Berlin (Germany) Evening News, 1923; Am. vice consul. Bremen, Germany, 1923-27; with Oxford U. Press, 1929-36; dir. Univ. Books. 1936-38; cons. Japan Reference Library, 1938-41; spl. assignment, War Dept., Washington, 1942-43; librarian M. Knoedler & Co., from 1952. Served as pvt. U.S. Med. Corps, 1917-18. Democrat. Roman Cath. Club: Grolier (N.Y.C.). Author: Stin i Svetol (poems), 1920; The Music Quiz, 1938; The Junior Music Quiz, 1940; Coffee Cookery, 1940; Mushroom Cookery, 1941; Cheese Cookery, 1941; Spice Cookery, 1942; Feast Day Cookbook, 1951; What's Cooking in France, 1952. Translator: Dialogues with Rodin, by Helen Hindenburg, 1936; The Triptych of the Three Kings by F. Timmermans, Mohammed, by Essad Bey, 1936; Mein Kampf, by A. Hitler, 1939; The Golden Legend, by Jacobus de Voragine, 1941; The World of Yesterday, by Stefan Zweig, 1943. Editor: Record Collector's Guide, 1947. Contbr. to newspapers and mags. Address: New York City N.Y. Died Aug. 4, 1974.

RISDON, FULTON, surgeon; b. St. Thomas, Ont., Can., Mar. 21, 1880; s. John Charles and Jennie Little (Fulton) R.; D.D.S., U. of Toronto, 1907, M.B., 1914; post grad. work Manhattan (N.Y.) Ear, Nose and Throat Hosp. and St. Joseph's Hosp., Chicago; m. Sylvia Margarete Bosworth, Apr. 1919; George McDonald), John L. B. Pvt. practice surgery, reconstrn., of face and jaws, from 1914; asso. prof. oral surgery, U. Toronto; cons. to Dept. of Pensions and Nat. Health and Nat. Defence; surgeon in charge of reconstructive surgery Toronto Western Hosp. and Christie St. Mil. Hosp. Served with Canadian Army Med. Corps, volunteer med. officer, The Toronto Regt., 1915-35, retired with rank of major. Decorated Long Service, Jubilee and Army Service medals. Fellow Royal Coll. of Surgeons (Can.); mem. Am. Bd. of Plastic Surgery, Nat. Research Council of Can. (chmn. sect. on plastic surgery). Clubs: Lambton Golf and Country, Badminton and Racquets, Arts and Letters (Toronto). Contbr. articles relating to reconstruction of face and jaws to professional publs. Home: Toronto, Ont., Can.†

RISEMAN, JOSEPH EPHRAIM FRANK, cardiologist, educator; b. Boston, Aug. 31, 1903; s. Joel and Rose (Berger) R.; student Tufts Coll., 1921; S.B.,

Harvard, 1924, M.D., 1929; m. Rose Cooper, Dec. 20, 1927; children—Barbara (Mrs. David Hamburg), Donna (Mrs. Robert L. Gould). House officer in medicine Beth Israel Hosp., Boston, 1929-31, resident in medicine, 1931-33, asso. in research, 1933-64, asst. in medicine, 1933-37, asst. vis. physician, 1936-37, asso. vis. physician, 1938-46, vis. physician, 1946-65, physician, 1965-71; practice medicine specializing cardiology, Boston, 1933-71; cons. in cardiology Heywood Meml. Hosp., Gardner, Mass., from 1943, Athol (Mass.) Meml. Hosp., from 1950, Groton (Mass.) Community Hosp., from 1954, Marlboro (Mass. Hosp., from 1955; teaching fellow in medicine, Harvard Med. Sch., Boston, 1931-32, asst. in medicine, 1932-37, instr., 1937-43, asso., 1943-49, clin. asso., 1949-52, asst. clin. prof. medicine, 1952-70; teaching fellow in medicine Tufts U. Med. Sch., Boston, 1932-34, asst. in medicine, 1932-38, instr., 1938-54, clin. instr., 1954-56. Spl. examiner Mass. Bd. Indsl. Accidents, 1951; monthly columnist ECG Clinic in Med. Counterpoint, 1969-74; lectr. to med. groups throughout U.S. and S.Am. Diplomate Am. Bd. Internal Medicine. Mem. A.M.A., Am. Heart Assn. (fellow council on clin. cardiology), Law-Sci. Acad. Am. (asso.), Am. Soc. Clin. Investigation, New Eng. Heart Assn., Mass. Med. Soc. Peruvian Soc. Cardiology, Phi Delta Epsilon. Republican. Jewish religion. Author: P-Q-R-S-T, 5 edits., 1944-68; (with Elliot L. Sagall) Cardiac Arrhythmias, 1963, Electrocardiogram Clinics, 1958; Directions in Cardiovascular Medicine, 1973, 74. Contbr. articles to profl. jours. Research on angina pectoris; developer Riseman oxygen analyzer, drug theosodate. Home: Needham, Mass. Died Jan. 5, 1974.

RISSBERGER, HAROLD P., banker. Sr. v.p. Nat. Comml. Bank & Trust Co., Albany, N.Y. Home: Albany, N.Y., Died Apr. 12, 1972*

RISSER, HUBERT ELIAS, educator, mineral economist; b. Kansas City, Kan., Apr. 28, 1914; s. Elmer B. and Della (Rowlen) R.; Engr. Mines. Colo. Sch. Mines, 1937; M.S. in Mining, U. Kan., 1953, Ph.D. in Econs., 1956; m. Sarah Ann Griffith, June 4, 1939; children—Nancy Arleen, Rita Ann. With Ala. By-Products Corp., Birmingham, 1937-41, 47-50, mine supt.; staff engr. Nat. Safety Council, Chgo., 1946-47; instr., then asst. prof. mining engring. U. Kan., 1950-57; mining cons. Kan. Geol. Survey, 1952-57; mineral economist Ill. Geol. Survey, 1957-60, prin. mineral economist, 1960-73, asst. chief, 1967-73; prof. mineral econs. U. Ill., 1960-73; mineral economist U.S. Geol. Survey, 1973, asst. dir., 1974; vis. Coulter prof. mineral econs. Colo. Sch. Mines, 1970; cons. to govt. and industry, 1954-74. Mem. panel mineral econs., com. earth sci. and tech. Nat. Acad. Sci., 1966. Served to maj. C.E., AUS, 1941-46. Recipient Distinguished Achievement award Colo. Sch. Mines, 1970; Mineral Econs. award, 1975. Mem. Am. Econ. Assn., Geol. Soc. Am., A.A.A.S., Ill. Acad. Sci., Soil Conservation Soc. Am., Am. Inst. Mining, Metall. and Petroleum Engrs. (chmn. St. Louis 1962, chmn. econs. com. 1966, chmn. council econs. 1968, Krumb lectr. 1972), Ill. Mining Inst. (exec. bd. 1964-74), Sigma Xi, Tau Beta Pi, Sigma Tau, Theta Tau. Republican. Methodist. Kiwanian (v.p. Champaign-Urbana 1967). Club: Cosmos. Author: The Economics of the Coal Industry, 1958; also numerous articles. Home: Reston, Va. Died Sept. 6, 1974; interred Mt. Hope Mausoleum, Urbana, Ill.

RITTERSPORN, BERNARD ANDREW, clothing mfr.; b. Galgoz, Austria, Sept. 17, 1897; s. Joseph and Marie (Bierman) R.; brought to U.S., 1909, naturalized, 1918; student pub. schs., Chgo.; m. Annabel Jacobs, June 21, 1924; children—Bernard Andrew, Richard Colt, Gail Ann. With Hart Schaffner & Marx since 1917, 2d v.p. 1937-45, v.p. in charge materials purchases, 1945-65; v.p. Wallach Bros., Newark, from 1942; pres. Smith Benson McLure, advt. agy., Chgo., from 1959. Home: Winnetka Ill. Died Feb. 2, 1974.

RIVERA CARBALLO, JULIO ADALBERTO, pres. of El Salvador; b. 1921; ed. mil. schs. in El Salvador and Italy. Various command positions in armed forces; chief Dept. Pub. Safety; dir. Manuel Enrique Araujo Mil. Sch.; mem. Civilian Mil. Directorate, 1961-62; pres. El Salvador, from 1962. Leader Party of Nat. Conciliation. Address: San Salvador El Salvador. Died July 1973.

RIVES, TOM CHRISTOPHER, U.S.A. officer; b. Montgomery, Ala., Dec. 3, 1892; William Henry and Alice Bloddworth (Taylor) R.; B.S., Ala. Poly. Inst., 1916, E.E., 1917; M.S., Yale, 1927; grad. Signal Sch. company officers course, 1922, Air Corps Tactical Sch., 1937, Army Industiral Coll., 1938; m. Annie Spann, Dec. 5, 1917; children—Annie S. (wife of Capt. John S. Lucas, Jr.), Janey L., Elizabeth E. (Mrs. Cecil Sanders). Served as officer Alabama National Guard, 1915—19; commd. capt., Signal Corps, U.S. Army, 1920, and advanced through the grades to brig. gen., 1944; transferred to U.S. Air Force, 1945; prof. of elec. engring. U. of Ill. from 1949. Decorated Legion of Merit, Distinguished Service Medal; Order British Empire. Sr. mem. of Inst. Radio Engrs. Home: St. Petersburg, Fla. Died June 17, 1975.

RIXEY, GEORGE FOREMAN, army officer; b. Jonesburg, Mo., Mar. 2, 1888; s. Thomas Pierce and Frances (Mason) R.; student Central Coll., Fayette, Mo., 1904-05. U. of Mo., 1905-07, Vanderbilt U., 1907-08; A.B., Central Wesleyan Coll., Warrenton, Mo., 1909; D.D., American U., Washington, D.C., 1943; m. Leisle Young, Oct. 21, 1910; children—George Foreman (dec.), George Young, Charles Osborn, Thomas Dyer. Admitted to Mo. Conf., Methodist Episcopal Ch., South, 1909; ordained elder, 1913; pastor, Centenary Meth. Ch., Louisiana, Mo., 1909-13, Troy (Mo.) Meth. Ch., 1913, Meth. Ch., Gallatin, Mo., 1913-16, Elm St. Meth. Ch., Chillicothe, Mo., 1916-17. Chaplain, U.S. Army, 1917-48, commd. 1st lt., C.A. section, O.R.C., on active duty 1917, advancing through the grades to brig. gen., 1944; chaplain, 64th Inf., 1917-22, at El Paso, Tex.; A.E.F., France; at camps Funston, Meade and Fort Washington; post chaplain, Fort Washington, 1922-27, chaplain, 26th Cav., Camp Statsenbergh, P.I., 1928-29, Sternberg Gen. Hosp., Manila, P.I., 1929-30; post chaplain, Presidio of San Francisco, 1930-35; chaplain, U.S. Army forces in China, Tientsin, 1935-37; post chaplain Fort Slocum 1937-40; exec. office Chief of Chaplains, Washington, D.C., 1940-42, dep. chief of chaplains, 1942-45; asst. The Inspector Gen., 1945-46; chaplain 2d Army, 1946-48; chaplain U.S. Forces in Korea, 1947-48, ret. 1948. Decorated D.S.M., Silver Star, Commendation Ribbon, Victory, Defense, European Theater, Am. Theater, World War II medals. Mason (K.T.). Home: Washington D.C. Died May 13, 1974.

ROACH, PHILIP FRANCIS, coast guard officer; b. Sedalia, Colo., Feb. 11, 1881; s. Philip and Mary (Kelly) R.; grad. Whitewater (Wis.) State Teachers Coll., 1903, U.S. Coast Guard Acad., 1907; m. Helen Agnes Bryan, Nov. 4, 1939. Commd. ensign, U.S. Coast Guard, 1907; on staff of commandant of Coast Guard, 1919-21, and 1933-41; aide to Captain of Port of New York, N.Y., 1931-32; on staff comdr. Eastern Area, 1933-34; senior officer afloat, Pacific Ocean, 1934-38; on staff comdt. 12th Naval Dist., and Coast Guard officer, 1942-45; advanced to commodore, June 1943, retired as rear adm., March 1, 1945; recalled to active duty June, 1945; assigned to U.S. Maritime Commn. as chmn., West Coast Final Guarantee Survey Bd., Scattle Area. Awarded Navy Cross, World War I. Mem. U.S. Naval Inst. Roman Catholic. Clubs: University, Army and Navy (Washington, D.C.); Commercial, Commonwealth, St. Francis Yacht, Bohemian, Burlingame Country (San Francisco); Tennis (Seattle), Address: Seattle, Wash.†

ROBB, MAX, chmn. exec. com. Bankers Securities Corp. Home: Philadelphia, Pa., Died Dec. 31, 1975.

ROBB, WALTER JOHNSON, author; b. Leon, Ia., Feb. 8, 1880; s. William Henderson and Mary (Harrab) R.; ed. schs. Kan. and Okla.; m. Dollie McKay, Feb. 27, 1902; children—John C., Marion McKay. Teacher country schs. in Garfield and Kingfisher counties, Okla., 1896-1907; teacher Philippine civil service, 1907-18; newspaper work and foreign news correspondence, Manila, 1918-41; accompanied 1st Philippine Independence Mission to U.S., 1919; public lecturing on war in Pacific, 1942-43; asst. field corr., Foreign Broadcast Intelligence Service, San Francisco, 1943-44; lecturer, O.W.I. Far East Training Course, U. of Calif., on Philippines, 1944; writer, O.W.I. overseas branch, San Francisco, Philippine Division, 1945-46; writer The Asia Foundation, San Francisco. Decorated comdr. Legion of Honor, Philippines, 1964. Author: The Khaki Cabinet and Old Manila, 1926; Romance and Adventure in Old Manila, 1928; Filipinos, 1939; and essay series, all at Manila, 1923-41; The Philippine Mission Trail, Galleon Commerce, Americans in the Philippines. Man Tracks on Luzon 10,000 Years Old. Home: San Francisco, Cal.†

ROBBINS, OMER ELLSWORTH machine tool mfr.; b. Milan, Ind., Oct. 30, 1890; s. Bennett and Elizabeth (Foster) R.; ed. pub. schs.; m. Maude Matthews, Apr. 2, 1920 (dec. 1928); children—Omer Ellsworth, James Bennett; m. 2d, Marie Dunham (dec. 1951); m. 3d, Martha Gannaway, Feb. 11, 1956. Apprentice, toolroom Marmon Co., Indpls., 1909-15; factory mgr. Mich. Machine Co., Detroit, 1920-29 pres. Robbins Engring. Co., Detroit, 1929-51, Omer E. Robbins Co., Detroit, 1948-60; dir. Ex-Cell-O Corp., Detroit. Nat. pres., chmn. bd. Am. Baptist Assembly, 1956-59; bd. mgrs. Am. Bapt. Bd. Edn. and Publs., 1956-59, pres., 1964-65. Trustee Cal. Bapt. Theological Sem.; trustee life mem. univ. fellow U. Redlands; trustee Berkeley (Cal.) Bapt. Div. Sch.; bd. dirs. Highland Park (Mich.) YMCA. Recipient citation as one of outstanding Bapt. laymen Berkeley Bapt. Div. Sch. and Am. Bapt. Conv., 1957. Served with U.S. Army, World War I. Mem. Engring. Soc. Detroit. Rotarian (past pres. hon. mem. Highland Park), Mason (32°). Home: Dearborn, Mich., Died Sept. 3, 1973.

ROBERSON, VIRGIL ODELL, JR., textile mfr.; b. Guilford County, N.C., Feb. 29, 1908; s. Virgil Odell and Carrie M. (Brown) R.; student pub. schs. Greensboro, N.C.; m. Janie E. Brame, Dec. 25, 1935; children—Virgil III, W. Earl, Foy Jane. With United Mchts. & Mfrs., Inc., 1943, successively plant mgr., group mgr., gen. mgr. all mfg. facilities, 1943-51, v.p. charge fabric prodn. div., 1951-73, also mem. exec. Com.; dir. Textile Hall Corp. Trustee Sirrine Found. of Clemson Coll. Mem. Am., S.C., N.C., Ga. textile mfg. assns., C.S. Textile Mfrs. Assn., S.C. C of C. (dir. at large), Clubs: Green Valley Country; Poinsett (Greenville). Presbyn. Home: Greensville, S.C. Died Apr. 9, 1973; interred Greensville, S.C.

ROBERTS, ALEXANDER CRIPPEN, coll. pres.; b. Plainfield, Ia., June 5, 1878; s. Jesse Miles and Cornelia Locey (Crippen) R.; grad. Ia. State Teachers Coll., Cedar Falls, Ia., 1901; A.B., U. of Wis., 1906; A.M., U. of Wash., 1917, Ph.D., 1922; m. Emily Hannah Fields, July 15, 1903; children—Margaret Marian (Mrs. Harold Thomas Condon), Cass Bentley, Bruce Joseph and Mabel Lucille (Mrs. James Russell Morris). Teacher of country schools, Butler County, Iowa, 1896-98; teacher grade school, Wisconsin Rapids, Wis., 1898-99; teacher high sch., Waverly, Ia., 1901-02; supt. schs., Marathon, Ia., 1902-04, Cresco, Ia., 1906-09, Fairfield, Ia., 1909-10; prin. high sch., Everett, Wash., 1910-18; supt. schs., Everett, 1918-20; pres. State Normal Sch., Centralia, Wash., 1920-21; associate, lecturer and prof. edn. U. of Wash., 1921-27, dir. extension service, 1924-27, dean of summer sch., 1925-27; pres. San Francisco State College, 1927-Aug. 1945; retired; lecturer, summers, Univ. of Wash., Univ. of Ore., Cheney State Normal Sch., U. of Calif., Univ. of Tex., Univ. of Southern Calif., Chico State Coll., Fresno State Coll.; lecturer in secondary edn., University of California, 1928-29. Mem. Calif. Teachers Assn. (life), Phi Beta Kappa, Phi Delta Kappa, Alpha Phi Gamma, Kappa Delta Pi. Republican. Methodist, Mason. Clubs: Commonwealth, Kiwanis (Camas, Wash.). Author: Studies in Scholarship, 1924. Co-Author: The High School Principal, 1927; Extraclass and Intramural Activities in High Schools, 1928; Principles of American Secondary Education, 1932; Study Guide in Secondary Education, 1933. Address: Camas, Wash.†

ROBERTS, (CHARLES) WES(LEY), orgn. dir. Rep. Nat. Com.; b. Oskaloosa, Kan., Dec. 14, 1903; s. Frank H. and Dailey (Needham) R.; student Kan. State Coll., 1920—24; m. Ruth Patrick, Nov. 22, 1919; 1 son, Patrick. Co—editor, co—pub. Oskaloosa (Kan.) Ind., Meriden Message, McLouth Times (weekly), 1926—36; campaign mgr. gubernatiorial candidate Will G. West, Kans., 1936; exec. sec. Kan. State Rep. Com., 1936—38, asst. state chmn., 1938, chmn., 1947—50; sec. Payne Ratner, gov. Kans., 1939—43; dir. publicity Kan. State Highway Commn., 1946—47; mgr. senatorial campaign, Frank Carlson, 1950; pub. relations and publicity bus., Holton, 1951; exec. dir. Eisenhower Nat. Hdqrs., Washington, 1952; orgn. dir. Rep. Nat. Com. from 1952, assisted coordination activities of Nat. Com. and ind. orgn. Citizens for Eisenhower, 1952. Served as maj. intelligence and operations, 4th air wing bomber squadron, U.S.M.C., 1943—46. Received distinguished service award as Man of Year, Pi Kappa Alpha, 1952. Mem. Midwest State Chmns. Assn. (vice chmn. 1947—50). Home: Holton, Kan. Died May 1975.

ROBERTS, DAVID RENSHAW, univ. dean; b. Tuckahoe, N.Y., Aug. 14, 1911; s. Harry B. and Beatrice (Renshaw) R.; B.S., Boston U., 1933; A.M., Harvard, 1940, Ph.D., 1941; m. Mary Jane Putnam, Jan. 29, 1945; 1 dau., Cynthia H. Instr. Econs. Allegheny Coll., 1941-43; economist various govt. agencies, 1943-48; asso. prof. econs. Carnegie-Mellon U., 1948-55; dean Coll. Bus. Adminstrn., Butler U., 1955-71, dean Grad. Sch., 1971—; cons. U.S. Bur. Budget, other agencies. Mem. Greater Indpls. Progress Com. Mem. Am. Econ. Assn., Ind. Acad. Social Scis. (pres. 1963). Episcopalian. Author: Executive Compensation, 1959. Contbr. articles to sci. jours. Home: Indianapolis, Ind., Deceased.

ROBERTS, DWIGHT CONKLIN, cons. petroleum engr.; b. Chgo., Aug. 7, 1898; s. Dwight Jay and Carrie (Conklin) R.; A.B., Stanford, 1923, E.M., 1925; m. Gertrude Mae Rankin, Oct. 30, 1948, Insp., petroleum engr. div. oil and gas Cal. State Mining Bur., 1925—28; petroleum engr. Graham—Loftus Oil Corp., Los Angeles, 1928—29; chief petroleum engr. Neil Anderson, Oil Umpire, Long Beach, Cal., 1929—31; cons. petroleum engr., geologist, Los Angeles, 1931—33; tech. sales engr. Alexander Anderson, Inc., Fulleton, Cal., 1933—36; petroleum engr., geologist E.A. Parkford, Los Angeles, 1936—37; tech. sales engr. to asst. gen. mgr. Sperry—Sun Well surveying Co., Long Beach, Cal., 1937—39, Houston 1939—43; petroleum engr. to lead petroleum engr. devel. Standard Oil Co. Cal., Kettleman Hills, Cal., 1944—52, lead petroleum engr. devel., Taft, 1952—54, sr. engr. devel. and reservoir, 1954—57, sr. engr., Greeley, 1957—62, dist. engr. Greeley—Kem River Dist., 1962—63; asst. to mgmt. Triangle Service, Inc., Bakersfield, Cal., 1964—73; cons. geologist and petroleum engr., from 1974. Served with CAC, U.S. Army, 1918. Mem. Am. Assn. Petroleum Geologists, Petroleum Prodn. Pioneers, Am. Inst. Profl. Geologists, Soc. Petroleum Engrs. Contbr. profl. jours. Home: Bakersfield Cal. Deceased.

ROBERTS, FRANK NEEDHAM, army officer; b. Oskaloosa, Kan., Dec. 28, 1897; s. Francis Henry and Daisy May (Needham) R.; student Baker Univ., 1915-17; B.S., U.S. Mil. Acad., 1920; grad. Inf. Sch., 1921, Command and Gen. Staff Sch., 1940; m. Clara Reeder McCoy, Oct. 7, 1920; m. 2d Esther E. Hopper, August 2, 1949; children—Frank N., Margaret E. Commissioned 2d lieutenant in the Infantry. July 1920, and advanced through the grades to major gen., 1955;

instr. Inf. Sch. 1921-23; served in Philippines, 1924-27; instr. U.S. Mil. Acad., 1927-31; served with 30th Inf., Presidio of San Francisco, 1931-34; language officer and asst. mil. attaché, China, 1934-38; commanding battalion, 20th Infantry, Ft. Warren, Wyo., 1940-41; Mil. Intelligence Div., War Dept. Gen. Staff, 1941-42; asst. chief of staff, G-2, U.S. Army Forces, China-Burma-India, 1942; Operations Div., War Dept. Gen. Staff, Aug. 1942; chief of staff, U.S. mil. mission to Moscow, 1944; mil. attaché to Am. Embassy, Moscow, Oct. 1945; Am. Embassy, Ankara, Turkey, 1946; prof. mil. science and tactics, U. of Calif., Los Angeles, 1948-50; mil. adviser to spl. asst. to the President, also to dir. M.S.A., member National Security Council Planning Board, 1950-53; chief staff, Allied Forces Southern Europe, Naples, Italy, 1954-56; comdg. gen. Ft. MacArthur, Cal., and chief Cal. Mil. Dist., 1956-58; member board national estimates CIA, 1958-60. Decorated D.S.M. with 2 Oak Leaf Clusters, Navy Cross; Hon. Comdr. Order British Empire. Mem. Sigma Phi Epsilon. Home: Claremont, Cal., Died Dec. 23, 1975.

ROBERTS, HENRY STOUTTE, educator, biologist; b. Macon, Ga., Nov. 14, 1913; s. Henry Stoutte and Annie (Baldwin) R.; A.B., Mercer U., 1934; Ph.D., Duke, 1948; m. Clotilda Anne Houle, Nov. 8, 1943; children—Henry Stoutte III, Frederick Eugene, Tchr., Ga. pub. schs., 1934-40; asso. prof. zoology Duke U., 1948-64; prof. biology, head dept. Washington and Lee U., 1964-74. Served to 1st li. AUS, 1942-46. Mem. Am. Soc. Zoologists, Am. Soc. Cell Biology, Am. Inst. Biol. Scis., Va. Acad. sci., Assn. Southeastern Biologists, Phi Beta Kappa. Home: Lexington Va. Died Feb. 21, 1974.

ROBERTS, ISAAC WARNER, banking executive; b. Phila., Apr. 30, 1881; s. George R. and Miriam P. (Williams) R.; B.S., Princeton, 1903; LL.B., U. Pa., 1906, LL.D., 1959; m. Caroline Henry, Oct. 12, 1909; children—Algernon, Bayard H., Mary (Mrs. Randal Morgan), Brooke, Howard H. Vice-pres. Phila. Saving Fund Soc., 1931-41, pres. 1941-49, ret., now director; dir. Bell Telephone Company of Pa., Philadelphia Contributionship for Insurance of Houses from Loss by Fire (chmn.), Phila. Contributionship Ins. Co. (chmn.), Food Distbn. Center Phila, Old Phila. Devel. Corp., Pa. Ins. Company. Served as capt., Ground Forces, Air Service U.S.A., 1917-18. Home: Haverford, Pa.†

ROBERTS, JOSEPH THOMAS, physician, lectr.; b. San Marcos, Tex., Oct. 21, 1909; s. Dr. Joseph Thomas and Georgia Mary (Talmadge) R.; A.B., Southwest Tex. Teachers Coll., 1929; M.D., 1936, Ph.D., 1941; M.S., Tulane, 1933; m. Mary Gertrude Goldston, June 10, 1938; children—Joseph, Alton, James, Charles. Med. resident Milne—Municipal Boys Home, New Orleans, La., 1932—33; interne Lakeside Hosp., Cleve., 1939—40; various med., acad. positions from 1932, including chief med. officer Gallinger Municipal Hosp., Washington, 1943—47; adj. clin. prof. medicine Georgetown U., George Washington U., 1943—47; dean, Sch. Medicine, prof. medicine, head dept. medicine, med. dir. Hosp. and Clinic, U. Ark., 1947—48; chief medicine Ark. State Hosp. for Nervous Diseases, 1947—48; chmn. dean's com., cons. internal medicine VA Hosp., North Little Rock, Ark., 1947—48; cons. medicine Army and Navy Gen. Hosp., Hot Springs, Ark., 1948; chief med. service, VA Hosp., Batavia, N.Y., 1949—50; chief cardiology sec., VA Hosp., Buffalo, 1950—66; lectr. medicine U. Buffalo Sch. Medicine, 1949—59, asst. prof. medicine, 1959—67; chief cardiology sec., VA Hosp., Buffalo, 1950—66; lectr. medicine U. Buffalo Sch. Medicine, 1949—59, asst. prof. medicine, 1959—67; responsible investigator, med. research com. NRC; chief med. service VA Hosp., Ft. Howard, lMd., 1966—67; assigned Physical Disability Agy., U.S. Army Central Phys. Evaluation Bd., Walter Reed Army Med. Center, also chief med. Service, chief profl. servies, dep. dir. Andrew Rader Army Clinic, chief profl. and med. services Mil. Dist. Washington. Med. mem. disability policy bd. dept. Vets benefits VA Central Office, Washington from 1970. Served as maj. M.C., United States Army Reserves, 1950—55. Diplomate Am. Bd. of Internal Medicine and Cardiovascular Diseases. Fellow A.C.P. (life), A.A.A.S.; mem. Internat. Acad. Pathology, Am. Registry Cardiovascular Pathology (founder, adv. com.), A.M.A. (hon. mention, 1949, 55, Certificate Assn. (founder, 1st pres.), Washington Heart Assn. (exec. com.), Am. Diabetes Assn., Diabetes Assn. D.C. (exec. com., sec.), Lay Diabetic Soc. D.C. (pres.), Internat. Assn. Med. Mus., New Orleans and Texas Acad. Sci., Cleve. Med. Acad., Cleve. Med. Library Assn., Am. Fedn. Clin. Research, Am. Assn. Anatomists, So. Med. Soc., Med. Soc. D.C., Med. Soc. N.Y., Sigma Xi, Theta Kappa Psi (nat. sec.—treas. 1948—50, nat. councillor 1950—52), Phi Beta Pi, Alpha Chi. Methodist Mechanisms of Disease (with W.A. Sodeman), 1950—67; Progress in Arthritis (with Talbott and Lockie), 1957; Ency. of Heart Disease (with Luisada et al.), 1959; Blood and Lymph Vessels (with Abramson), 1961; (with Luisada et al) Development and Structure of the Cardiovascular System, 1961; also articles in sci. jours. Awarded Lemmann prize in clin. medicine, Tulane U., 1936; 1st prize for sci. research med. Soc. State of N.Y., 1957; citation as most outstanding grad. S.W. Tex. Tchrs. Coll., 1959; Meritorious Service plaque and hon. faculty mem. U.S. Army Intelligence Sch., 1969; Armed Forces Res. medal for 20 yrs. service; Certificate Appreciation Pres. U.S. and Chief staff U.S. Army, 1970; others. Home: Rockville, Md. Died July 2, 1975; buried Arlington (Va.) Nat. Cemetery.

ROBERTS, KATHLEEN ELIZABETH, physician; b. Albion, Pa.; d. James and Mable (Consedine) Stelin; M.D., Syracuse U., 1949; m. Arden Roberts; children—Constance, Kathleen, William. Intern Syracuse; resident Cornell; fellow Cornell U., 1950-52; physiology asst. Sloan Kettering Inst., N.Y.C., 1952-57; pvt. practice medicine specializing in kidney disease, internal medicine, emphysema, arthritis, cardiovascular and renal disease, N.Y.C., 1957-75. Mem. Am. Soc. Clin. Investigation, Am. Physiology Soc., Western Soc. Clin. Investigation, Harvey Soc., Sigma Xi. Author: Clinical Physiology, Electrolyte Changes in Surgery, 1961; Forgotten Organ. Home: Candor, N.Y., Died May 23, 1975.

ROBERTS, MILNOR, mining engr.; b. New York, Mar. 10, 1877; s. William Milnor and Adeline (de Beelen) R.; A.B., Leland Stanford Jr. U., 1899; unmarried. Instr. mineralogy, Stanford U., 1900, 01; prof. mining engring. and metallurgy and dean Coll. Mines, University of Washington, 1901-47, dean emeritus from 1947; consultant for State of Washington to Metals Reserve Company, 1942-45; mining engineer in the West, in B.C. and Alaska, and cons. engr. various mining cos., from 1899; mem. Wash. State Geol. Survey, 1901, 02; chmn. scientific com., Lewis and Clark Expn., 1905; cons. engr. for City of Seattle, 1910, 11, for U.S. Ry. Adminstrn., 1917-18, for U.S. Post Office Dept., for U.S. Bur. of Mines, 1918-21, for Securities and Exchange Commission, 1939; president City Land Co. Mem. Seattle War Savings Com., 1917-19. Fellow A.A.A.S.; mem. Am. Inst. Mining and Metall. Soc. America (councillor, 1925-28), Am. Mining Congress, American Soc. for Engring Edn., Wash. State Planning Council (tech. advisory board, 1934-45), Engineers Council for Professional Development (b. examiners), N.W. Mining Assn., West Coast Mineral Assn. (pres. 1949, 1952-54), Ret. Staff Mems. Assn. (pres. 1956-58), Sigma Xi; pres. Pacific Northwest Soc. Engrs., 1909. Republican. Episcopalian (diocesan council 1921-24). Clubs; University, Harbor, Seattle, Gold, Faculty. Editor of various mining bulls, and contbr. to trans. engring. socs., mining jours. Jour. Geology, Nat. Geog. Mag., etc. Mem. Seattle Chamber Commerce. Home: Seattle, Wash.†

ROBERTS, ROY (ROY BARNES JONES), actor; b. Tampa, Fla., Mar. 19, 1906; s. Hilliard Mitchell and Lula Mary (Tait) Jones; m. Lillian Moore, Aug. 11, 1947. Broadway appearances include Twentieth Century, 1932, Boy Meets Girl, 1935, Hooray for What, 1937, Room Service, 1938, Ladies and Gentlemen, 1939, My Sister Eileen, 1940, Watch on the Rhine (tour), 1942; films include A Bell for Adano, 1945, Smokey, 1946, Gentlemen's Agreement, 1947, My Darling Clementine, 1947, He Walked by Night, 1948, Force of Evil, 1949, The Enforcer, 1951, Chapman Report, 1962, King and Four Queens, 1956, Hotel, 1967; TV appearances include Gale Storm Show, 1956-59, Lucy Show, 1967-70. Active Children's Charities of Masquers Club. Served with AUS, 1943-44. Recipient George Washington Honor medal Freedom Found., 1971. Clubs: Lambs (N.Y.C.); Masquers (Hollywood, Cal.). Home: Los Angeles, Cal. Died May 28, 1975; buried Greenwood Meml. Park, Fort Worth.

ROBERTSON, CARY, journalist; b. Louisville, Apr. 18, 1902; s. Archibald T. and Ella (Broadus) R.; student Wake Forest Coll., 1920—22, U. Va. 1922—25; Nieman fellow, Harvard, 1945—46; m. Priscilla Smith, May 26, 1934; children—Charlotte, Harry, Cary. With Louisville Courier—Jour., from 1925, reporter, 1925—27, day city editor, 1927, makeup editor, 1928, Sunday editor, 1930—68 book editor from 1968; Kentucky correspondent Newsweek mag. from 1950; lectr. univs. Mem. adv. com. Assn. Chamber Music Players, Vienna, Va., from 1948. Dir. George Rogers Clark Heritage, Inc. (chm. 1966); trustee Louisville Chamber Music Soc., pres., 1964, 65. Mem. Am. Assn. Sunday and Feature Editors (v.p. 1964, pres. 1965), Locally Edited Mag. Editors Assn. (chmn. 1950), Anchorage Trails (hon.; pres. 1961), Sigma Delta Chi. Club: Owl Creek Country (Anchorage, Ky.). Home: Anchorage, Ky. Died Sept. 15, 1975; interred Cave Hill, Louisville, Ky.

ROBERTSON, JAMES G., banker; b. Hartford, Conn., Sept. 29, 1878; s. William Henry and Emily (Pitcher) R.; LL.B., U. Ill., 1901; m. Helen Shaffer, Jan. 12, 1952. Admitted to Ill. bar; practiced in Chgo., 1901-04; credit mgr. Firestone Tire & Rubber Co., 1907-08, treas., 1908-22; chmn. Am. Vitrified Products Co., Cleve.; dir. Firestone Bank, Akron, O., Ohio Edison Co. Co-trustee George R. Hill Estate. Mem. Akron C. of C. (past pres.). Mason (32°, Shriner). Home: Akron, O.†

ROBERTSON, SAMUEL BROWN, rubber exec.; b. Milton, Mass., July 21, 1878; s. William Graeme and Jean (Wilkinson) R.; B.S., Mass. Inst. Tech., 1899; m. Anne Welty, 1909; 1 dau., Jane. With Pa. R.R. Co., engring. dept., advancing to div. engr., div. supt., gen. supt., 1899-1919; with B.F. Goodrich Co. from 1919, in Akron, O., dir. of engring., 1919-27, v.p. and gen. mgr. Pacific Goodrich Co., Los Angeles, 1927-31, v.p. and gen. mgr. tire div., Akron, 1931-37, exec. v.p. and dir., 1937, pres., 1937-39; dir. and pres. B. F. Goodrich Rubber Co. of Canada, Miller Rubber Co., Phila. Rubber Works; dir. Internat. B.E. Goodrich Corpn. Clubs: Akron City, Portage Country (Akron); Jonahtan (Los Angeles); Question (Chicago). Home: Akron, O.†

ROBERTSON, VIRGIL OTIS, lawyer; b. Williamsburg, Miss., Feb. 27, 1879; s. George Carson and Martha (Holcomb) R.; grad. high sch., Haticsburg, Miss., 1898; B.S., U. of Miss., 1902, LL.B., 1904; m. Florence Flournoy Fore, July 4, 1915. Prof. rhetoric and English composition, U. of Miss., 1902-04; admitted to Miss. bar, 1904; practiced at Jackson, Miss.; pres. Coca-Cola Bottling Corp. of Boston. Dir. vocational training div. of Industrial Accident Bd. of Mass. in charge of rehabilitation program for cripples, 1919-20. Mem. Am. Econ. League, Kappa Alpha (grand historian, 1905-12). Clubs: Rotary, Boston Art. Editor: Kappa Alpha Catalogue, 1913. Home: Brookline, Mass.†

ROBESON, FRANK LEIGH, college prof.; b. Farmville, Va., June 24, 1884; s. George Maxwell and Anna Martin (McConnell) R.; B.S., Va. Poly. Inst., 1904, M.E., 1905; A.M., Columbia, 1913; Ph.D., Johns Hopkins, 1923; m. Mary Anna Matthews, June 26, 1912; 5 children. Asst. in math. and mech. drawing Va. Poly. Inst., 1904-06, instr. math. and mech. engring., 1910-12, asso. prof. physics, 1913-17, prof. physics from 1917; supt. Farmville Mfg. Co., 1907-10. Fellow A.A.A.S.; mem. Am. Physical Soc., Va. Acad. Science (pres.-elect, 1937), Omicron Delta Kappa, Phi Kappa Phi, Sigma Xi, Tau Beta Pi. Democrat. Episcopalian. Mason. Author: Physics, 1942. Address: Blacksburg Va. Died Sept. 2, 1974.

ROBESON, LILA P., contralto; b. Cleveland, O., Apr. 4, 1880; grad. Western Reserve U., 1902 student voice with I. Luckstone and O. Saenger, New York. Formerly sang in church; operatic début with Aborn Opera Co., Boston, Apr 4, 1911; joined Met. Opera Co., 1912*†

ROBESON, PAUL, concert singer, actor; b. Princeton, N.J., Apr. 9, 1898; s. William Drew and Maria Louisa (Bustill) R.; A.B., Rutgers Coll., 1919; LL.B., Columbia University, 1923; hon. L.H.D., Hamilton Coll., 1940; M.A. (hon.), Rutgers U., 1932; L.H.D., Moorehouse Coll., 1943; hon. Dr. Humane Letters, Howard U., 1945; m. Eslanda Cardoza Goode, Aug. 17, 1921; 1 son, Paul. Appeared first in play Voodoo, with Margaret Wycherly, later in same play in England with Mrs. Patrick Campbell; in prin. role of Emperor Jones, 1923; appeared successively in All God's Chillun, Porgy, Black Boy; gave first concert as basso interpreter of Negro spirituals, N.Y. City, 1925; concert tour, Europe, 1926-28; Am. concert tour, 1929; appeared in London as Othello in Othello, in The Hairy Ape, 1931, Stevedore, 1933; concert tour, Europe, 1931, 1938, Russia, 1936; star or feature parts in motion pictures, Emperor Jones, Showboat, Saunders of the River, King Solomon's Mines, Jeriocho; played Othello in Othello, New York, 1943-44, coast to coast tour, 1944-45; also radio singer. Mem. Phi Beta Kappa, Alpha Phi Alpha, Sigma Tau Delta. Four-letter man, Rutgers; picked by Walter Camp as All-American end., 1917 and 1918; recipient Stalin Peace Prize, 1952. Home: Phila., Pa., Died Jan. 23, 1976.

ROBIN, TONI, new product devel. exec.; m. Martin F. Snyder. Artist fashion dept. N.Y. Times, then mem. staff The Times Mag.; fashion editor Holiday mag.; chief exec. officer Johnstone, Inc., pub. relations (merger with Marschalk Co. 1968), to 1968; vice chmn. Marschalk Co., 1968-71; exec. v.p. Bernard D. Kahn Assos., N.Y.C., 1971-74. Served with A.R.C., World War II. Address: New York City, N.Y. Died June 19, 1974.

ROBINS, THOMAS MATTHEWS, army officer; b. Snow Hill, Md., Mar. 14, 1881; s. John Littleton and Julia (Matthews) R.; student Dickinson Coll., Carlisle, Pa., 1897-99, hon. A.B., 1919; B.S., U.S. Mil. Acad., 1904; grad. Engr. Sch., 1908. Command and Gen. Staff Sch. (honor grad.), 1923, Army War Coll., 1926; m. Eleanor Foote Reifsnider, 1913; children—Thomas Matthews, Elizabeth Billingslen (Mrs. August F. Weinel). Commd. 2d lt. C.E., U.S. Army, June 15, 1904, and advanced through the grades to brig. gen., asst. chief of engrs., Sept. 1, 1939; major gen., Jan. 1942, maj. gen., retired. Engaged as cons. engr. Decorated D.S.M. Mem. Am. Soc. Engrs., Sigma Alpha Epsilon. Episcopalian. Club: Army and Navy (Washington, D.C.). Address: Portland, Ore.†

ROBINSON, ABRAHAM, mathematician, philosopher, educator; b. Waldenburg, Germany, Oct. 6, 1918; s. Abraham and Hedwig Latte (Bahr) R.; M.S.C., Hebrew U., Jerusalem, 1946; Ph.D., London U., 1949, D.Sc., 1957; M.A., Yale, 1968; m. Renee Kopel, Jan. 30, 1944. Sci. officer Royal Aircraft Establishment, Farnborough, Eng., 1942-46; sr. lectr. math., dep. head dept. aerodynamics Coll. of Aeros., Cranfield, Eng., 1946-51; asso. prof., prof. applied math. U. Toronto, Can., 1951-57; prof., chmn. dept. math. Hebrew U., Jerusalem, 1957-62; prof. math. and philosophy U. Cal. at Los Angeles, 1962-67; prof. math. Yale, 1967-74, Sterling prof., 1971; vis. prof. Princeton, 1960-61, univs. Paris, Rome and Tubingen, 1966, Cal. Inst. Tech., 1967, Heidelberg U., 1968; vis. fellow St. Catherines Coll., Oxford, 1965; cons. IBM Research Lab., 1962-64; mem. fluid motion com. Aero. Research Council Gt. Britain,

1949-51. Served with Free French Air Forces, 1940-42. Recipient Brower medal Dutch Math. Soc., 1973. Fellow Am. Acad. Arts and Scis.; mem. Nat. Acad. Scis., Am., London math. socs., Assn. for Symbolic Logic (pres. 1968-70). Author 9 books including: On The Metamathematics of Algebra, 1951; Theorie metamathematique des Ideaux, 1955; Complete Theories, 1956; (with J.A. Laurmann) Wing Theory, 1956; Introduction to Model Theory and to the Metamathematics of Algebra, 1963; Numbers and Ideals, 1965; Non-standard Analysis, 1966; Contributions to Non-Standard Analysis, 1972. Contbr. articles to profl. jour. Home: Hamden, Conn. Died Apr. 11, 1974; buried Jerusalem, Israel.

ROBINSON, BERNARD WHITFIELD, physician; b. Chgo., June 6, 1918; M.D., Harvard, 1944; m. Agnes Thorne. Intern, Freedmen's Hosp., Washington, 1945, asst. resident in radiology, 1945—46; resident in radiology Providence Hosp., Chgo., 1948—49; radiologist VA Hosp., Tuskegee, Ala., 1950—51, VA Office, Detroit, 1951—53; radiotherapist West Side VA Hosp., Chgo., 1955—63, VA Hosp., West Haven, Conn., 1963—67; dir. VA Hosp., Martinez, Cal., 1967—69, VA Hosp., Allen Park, Mich., 1969—72; clin. instr. radiology Chgo. Med. Sch., 1959—62, asso. in radiology, 1962—64; asst. clin. prof. Yale Sch. Medicine, 1964—67. Served with USNR, 1943—44; with M.C., 1953—55. Diplomate Am. Bd. Radiology. Mem. A.M.A., Nat. Med. Assn., Am. Coll. Hosp. Administrs., Radiol. Soc. N.Am., Am. Coll. Radiology, Alpha Phi Alpha. Contbr. articles to med. jours. Home: Allen Park, Mich. Died Aug. 23, 1972; buried Chicago, Ill.

ROBINSON, C. RAY, lawyer, rancher; b. Merced, Cal., 1904; s. J.A. and May (Kelley) R.; A.B. with honors in Polit. Sci. U. Cal, 1925, J.D., 1929; m. Pauline Irwin, 1932 (dec. 1960); children—C. Ray, Anthonie. Admitted to Cal. bar, 1929, U.S. Supreme Ct., 1963; practiced in Merced, 1929-74; pres. Pacific Turf Club, Inc. (Golden Gate Fields), Albany, Cal. Mem. Cal. Assembly, 1931-35, floor leader, 1933-35. Bd. govs. Cal. Maritime Acad., 1942-45. Served as lt. comdr. USNR, 1940-44; legal officer COMSOPAC, 1943-44, staff Adm. Halsey. Exec. com., nat. counsel Jockeys' Guild, Jockeys' Guild Found. Decorated bronze stars, Adm. Halsey and Sec. Navy Forestall. Mem. State Bar Cal. (gov. 1940-43, v.p. 1941-42), Am., Merced, Los Angeles, San Francisco County bar assns., Am. Arbitration Assn., Fed. Communications Bar Assn., Am. Coll. Trial Lawyers (bd. regents 1951-54, pres. 1953), Phi Beta Kappa, Phi Alpha Delta. Republican. Elk. Clubs: Commonwealth (San Francisco); California (Los Angeles); Sutter (Sacramento). Home: Merced Cal. Died Jan. 29, 1974.

ROBINSON, CLARENCE C(RAMER), educator; b. New York, N.Y., Oct. 22, 1879; s. Joseph Clark and Mary Frances (Cramer) B.; student, Pa. State Coll. (part time) 1920 1922; M. Music (hon.) Cincinnati Conservatory, 1927; m. Bessie Lillian Boles, Sept. 19, 1911. Pvt., music instrn. with noted teachers, N.Y. and Chicago; concert work, Dunbar Male Quartet, 1904-08 and 1909-12; instr. voice, theory, choral conductor, U. of Okla., 1908-09; dir. music, Pa. State Coll., 1912-22; dir. sch. music, Ohio Univ., 1922-47, prof., from 1947; composer of choral music, sacred and secular; adjudicator of Welsh eisteddvods, and sch. contests. Served as Army songleader, Camp Upton, World War I; also music adminstr. War Camp. Community Service after armistice, San Francisco. Mem. Nat. Music Teachers Assn., Phi Mu Alpha, Kappa Alpha Southern, Kappa Kappa Psi (hon.) Mason (32°, Scottish Rite). Republican. Episcopalian. Club: Rotary. Home: Athens, O.†

ROBINSON, DAVID HUNTER, engring. co. exec.; b. Blackstock, S.C., Aug. 5, 1911; s. David Walter and Beatrice (Hunter) R.; B.S. in C. E., Clemson U., 1941; M.S., U. Mo., 1952; m. Mamie Marie Osteen, Sept. 5, 1942; children—Melanie Marie, Rosalie Hunter. Asst. prof. mechanics and hydraulics dept. Clemson U. (S.C.), 1947-52; owner, chief exec. officer Robinson Engring. Service, Anderson, S.C., 1952-73; pres. Avon Devels., Inc., Seneca, S.C., 1957-67; cons. land devel., sanitation-waste treatment. Chmn. profl. div. United Fund, Anderson, 1959; treas. Anderson Community Concerts Assn., from 1958. Served to maj. AUS, 1941-46; ETO. Decorated Bronze Star. Registered profl. engr., S.C., Ga. Mem. Am. Soc. C.E., Am. Soc. Profl. Engrs., S.C. Soc. Profl. Engrs., (past bd. dirs.), Anderson C. of C. (dir. 1971-72), Am. Water Works Assn., Ind. Telephone Pioneer Assn., Assn. Communication Engrs., Water Pollution Control Fedn. Rotarian. Home: Anderson S.C. Died Sept. 13, 1973.

ROBINSON, DONALD ALLISTER, army officer; b. Chippewa Falls, Wis., Mar. 29, 1881;s. Herbert Fisk and Mary (Patton) R.; B.S., U. S. Mil. Acad., 1906; grad. Mounted Service Sch., 1912, Cav. Sch., 1924, Command and Gen. Staff Sch., 1925, Army War Coll., 1933; m. Priscilla Carleton, d, Maj. Gen. B. A. Poore, July 24, 1917; children—Donald Allister, Carleton Fisk, Priscilla Poore, Cynthia Patton. Private Troop B, 3d Cav., Spanish-Am. War, 1898; commd. 2d, lt. Inf., U.S. Army, 1906; transferred to cav., 1907, and advanced through the grades to brig. gen., Jan. 29, 1941; served with 29th Inf., 11th Cav., 15th Cav. in Cuba, Philippines and U.S., 1906-17; maj. and lt. col. Gen. Staff, with A.E.F., France, World War; mem. Haskell Mission to Armenia and with Army of Occupation, Germany, to Mar. 1921; Bureau of the Budget, Washington, D.C., 1921-23; with 4th Cav., 8th Cav., 10th Cav., 11th Cav at various stations, 1923-35; instr. Command and Gen. Staff Sch., 1928-30; asst. chief of Staff G-3, Philippine Dept., 1935-37; comd. 12th Cav., 1937-39; chief of staff, 1st Cav. Div., 1939-40; chief of staff 9th Army Corps, 1940-41; chief of staff, 2d Army, Mar.-Nov. 1914; comdg. gen., Cav. Replacement Training Center, U.S. Army, Nov. 1941-Dec. 1942; retired Mar. 31, 1943. Decorations: Distinguished Service Medal, World War I, Distinguished Service Medal Oak Leaf Cluster, World War II, Spanish-Am. War medal, Army of Cuban Pacificiation medal, World War Victory medal with 2 battle clasps, Army of Occupation (Germany) Service medal, Defense Service medal. Mem. Assn. of Grads. of U.S. Mil. Acad., U.S. Cav. Assn. Episcopalian. Home: Port Angeles, Wash.†

ROBINSON, HUBBELL, TV exec.; b. Schenectady, Oct. 16, 1905; s. Hubbell and Marcia (Johnson) R.; grad. Phillips Exeter Acad., 1923; A.B., Brown U., 1927; m. Therese Lewis, Dec. 4, 1940 (div. Nov. 29, 1948). Dramatic critic Exhibitors Herald, 1927, reporter Schenectady Union Star, Albany Knickerbocker Press, 1928; radio producer Young & Rubicam, 1928; v.p. radio dir., 1942; v.p., program dir. ABC, N.Y.C., 1944-45; v.p. Foote, Cone & Belding, advt. agv, 1946; v.p., program dir. CBS, 1947-56, exec. v.p. CBS TV, 1956-59, sr. v.p. TV programs, 1962; exec. producer Hawk; exec. in charge prodn. Stage 67; organized Hubbell Robinson Prodns., Inc., Ind. TV prodn. co., 1959. Chmn. bd. N.Y. County Multiple Sclerosis Soc.; bd. dirs. Nat. Parkinson Disease Soc., Am. Found. for Dance, Joffrey Ballet. Recipient TV Acad. award, 1956; TV Acad. medal for distinguished service, 1957, 58; award for eminent contbr. to TV, Television Producers Guild, 1962. Mem. Brown Football Assn. (dir.), Alpha Delta Phi. Democrat. Episcopalian. Club: Brown University (dir. N.Y.). Home: New York City N.Y. Died Sept. 4, 1974.

ROBINSON, JAMES MILTON, pub. co. exec.; b. Savannah, Ga., Oct. 25, 1919; s. Arthur Maurice and Bertha (Giddens) R.; grad. high sch.; m. Elsie Ruth Young, Dec. 16, 1938; children—James M., Thomas Y. With Albany Herald Pub. Co. (Ga.) 1936—, exec. editor, 1958—, v.p., 1966—; v.p., dir. Gray Communication Systems Inc., Albany. Trustee Albany Pub. Library. Recipient several profl. awards. Chmn., Easter Seal Co., 1957-58; adv. bd. Salvation Army, 1962—; mem. Bishops Council, Ga., 1961-63. Recipient several profl. awards. Mem. Am. Soc. Newspaper Editors, Ga. A.P. News Council (co-founder, past chmn., Sigma Delta Chi. Democrat. Episcopalian. Club: Doublegate Country (Albany). Home: Albany, Ga., Died May 8, 1974

ROBINSON, JOHN Q(UENTIN), realtor; b. West Newton, Pa., Mar. 19, 1898; s. John Q. and Clara (Boyd) R.; B.A., Washington-Jefferson Coll., 1921; postgrad., N.Y. U., 1928, 42; m. Marian Markle Jackson, Feb. 10, 1923; children—Claire (Mrs. William A. Salmond), John Quentin. Prin. John Q. Robinson, Ins., N.Y.C., 1921-55; prin. John Q. Robinson, Real Estate and Ins., Montclair, N.J., 1955-73; asso. Ins. DeLanoy & Kipp, 1955-73; customers rep. N.Y. Stock Exchange firms Moore, Leonard & Lynch, Hornblower & Weeks, and Edward A. Purcell, 1930-38. Real estate agt. United Ch. Homes of N.J. for sr. citizens, from 1968; Mem. Montclair Citizens Com. for Educational Planning, 1970. Republican fund dir., 1944-60. Served with U.S. Army, 1917-19. Mem. Orgn. for Trans-Atlantic Union (co-founder, treas. 1946-49), Atlantic Union Com. (dir. 1949-60, treas. 1955-57), Montclair Bd. Realtors (pres. 1971-72), Nat., N.J. (dir. 1971-73) assn. realtor bds., Essex County Grand jurors Assn. (pres. 1959-60), N.J. Assn. Grand Jurors (pres. 1961-62), Washington-Jefferson Coll. Alumni Assn. (past pres.), Optimist Club, Kappa Sigma. Mason (32 degree Shriner, K.T.). Home: Montclair N.J. Died Mar. 19, 1973.

ROBINSON, MYRON WILBER, mfr.; b. N.Y. City, Aug. 11, 1881; s. John Murdoch and Carrie Eliza (Hall) R.; grad. Phillips Exeter Acad., 1899; student Sch. of Mines (Columbia), 1900-03, Sheffield Scientific Sch. (Yale); m. Florence Lamb, July 14, 1903. Began in real estate and ins. business, 1903, later became connected with mfr. of Crex Carpets; now chmn. bd. Crex Carpet Co.; pres. Myron W. Robinson Co., Inc., Grass Furniture Co. Mem. Am. Mfrs.' Export Assn. (pres.), Am. Peat Soc. (pres.), Inter-Am. High Commn. Colonel, Chief of staff and personal aide to Gov. Walter E. Edge of N.J. Mem. S.A.R., Sigma Chi, Book and Gavel (Yale). Republican. Presbyn. Mason (32°, Shriner), Elk. Clubs: Columbia, Yale, Republican Press (New York); Union League (Hackensack). Home: Hackensack, N.J.†

ROBINSON, ROBERT, chemist; b. Sept. 13, 1886; s. W.B. Robinson; ed. U. Manchester; D.Sc., univs. Liverpool, London, Wales, Sheffield, Belfast, Delhi, Cambridge, Nottingham, Bristol, Oxford, Sydney; LL.D., univs. Birmingham, Edinburgh, St. Andrews, Glasgow, Liverpool, Manchester; hon. Dr., univs. Paris, Madrid, Zagreb; m. Gertrude Walsh, 1912 (dec. 1954), 1 son, 1 dau.; m. 2d, Stearn S. Hillstrom, 1957. Prof. organic chemistry U. Sydney (Australia), 1912-15, U. Liverpool, 1915; dir. research Brit. Dyestuffs Corp., 1920; prof. chemistry St. Andrews U., 1921; prof. organic chemistry Manchester U., 1922-28, Univ. Coll., London 1928-30; Bakerian lectr., 1929; fellow Magdalen Coll. and Waynflete prof. chemistry Oxford U.; 1930-55, prof. emeritus; hon. fellow Magdalen Coll.; dir., cons. Shell Chem. Co. U.K. Ltd.; dir. Shell Research Ltd. Pres. Chem. Soc., 1939-41, Royal Soc., 1945-50. Longstaff medalist Chem. Soc.; Davy medalist Royal Soc., 1930; medalist, medalisst, 1932; Paracelsus medalist Swiss Chem. Soc., 1939; Copley medalist, 1942; Albert gold medal Royal Soc. Arts, 1947; Franklin medal Franklin Inst., Phila., 1947; Nobel prize for chemistry, 1947; Priestley medal Am. Chem. Soc., 1952, 53; Hofmann Meml. medal German Chem. Soc.; Faraday and Flintoff medal Chem. Soc. London, Medal of Freedom (U.S.); created knight, 1939; Decorated Order of Merit, 1949, 2d Order Rising Sun with Broad Rays (Japan), 1964. Fellow Royal Soc., Royal Inst. Chemistry, Weizmann Inst. Sci. Rehovot, Israel (hon.); comdr. Legion of Honor Fgn. mem. Nat. Acad. Scis. (Washington), Am. Acad. Arts and Scis. (Boston), Am. Philos. Soc. (Phila.), Soc. Chem. Industry (pres. 1958-59), Brit. Assn. Advancement Sci. (pres. 1955); hon. mem. Chemists Club of N.Y., N.Y. Acad. Scis. Author Structural Relations of Natural Products, 1955. Home: Grimm's Hill Lodge Great Missenden, Bucks England Died Feb. 8, 1975.

ROBINSON, SIDNEY W., lawyer; b. Reno, Apr. 6, 1903; A.B., U. Nev., 1924; LL.B., Stanford, 1937. Admitted to Nev. bar, 1928, since practiced in Reno. Mem. Nat. Conf. Commrs. Uniform State Laws, 1941—59. Mem. Am., Washoe County (sec. 1933—34, pres. 1934—35) bar assns., State Bar Nev. (bd. govs. 1942—46, 49—50, 56), Am. Judicature Soc. Home: Reno, Nev. Died Dec. 9, 1974.

ROBISON, HENRY JOHN, state welfare ofcl.; b. Palmyra Twp., O., Sept. 27, 1894; s. Warren J. and Della (Davis) R.; B.S., Kent State University, 1918, LL.D., 1954; m. Vernan A. White, September 15, 1923; one daughter, Carolyn Robison (Mrs. John A. Lautzenheiser). Probate judge Portage County, Ravenna, O., 1923-36; chief div. social adminstrn. Ohio Dept. Pub. Welfare, 1936-49, asst. dir. dept., 1949-53, dir. dept., 1953-57; dir. agy. relations Columbus Hosp. Fedn., 1957-63, then asst. dir.; later asso. dir. Mid-Ohio Health Planning Fedn. Mem. pub. welfare com. United Community Council Ohio Assn. Philanthropic Homes; mem. Gov.'s Com. Comprehensive Mental Health Planning and Mental Retardation; mem. bd. Instructive District Nurses Assn.; dir. Cerebral Palsy, Columbus and Franklin County; mem. Franklin County Mental Health Assn., Columbus Council Alcoholism. Met. Health Com. United Community Council; mem. health services adv. com. Franklin County Dept. Welfare; pres. Blind Assn. Central Ohio; mem. Ohio com White Ho. Conf. Children and Youth, 1960; mem. Ohio Vocational Rehab. Services Commn., State Adv. Council Mental Health and Mental Retardation. Recipient spl. citation in field pub. welfare adminstrn., Kent State U., 1960. Mem. Nat. Soc. Prevention Blindness, Ohio Welfare Conf., Am. Pub. Welfare Assn., Nat. Conf. Social Work, Nat., Ohio leagues nursing. Phi Sigma Kappa. Mem. Community Ch. Home: Columbus O. Deceased.

ROCAP, JAMES E., lawyer; b. Kan., May 21, 1881; student Ohio State U.; LL.B., Ind. U., 1903. Admitted to Ind. bar, 1903; practice of law, Indpls.; mem. firm Rocap, Rocan & Resse. Mem. Am., Ind., Indpls. bar assns., Sigma Nu Phi.†

ROCKEFELLER, WINTHROP, former gov. Ark.; b. N.Y.C., May 1, 1912; s. John D. Jr. and Abby Greene (Aldrich) R.; ed. Lincoln Sch., N.Y.C., Loomis Sch. Windsor, Conn., 1928-31, Yale, 1931-34; LL.D., U. Ark., Hendrix Coll., Coll. William and Mary, Coll. Ozarks; L.H.D., N.Y. U.; H.H.D., U. San Francis Xavier, Sucre, Bolivia; D.C.L., Southwestern at Memphis; m. Barbara Sears, Feb. 14, 1948 (div. 1954); 1 son, Winthrop; m. 2d, Jeannette Edris, June 11, 1956 (div. 1971). With Humble Oil & Refining Co. (Tex)., 1934-37, Chase Nat. Bank, 1937-38; exec. v.p. Greater N.Y. Fund, 1938; fgn. dept. Socony-Vacuum Oil Co., 1939-51; trustee Rockefeller Brothers Fund, dir. Rockefeller Center, Inc. Chmn. bd. The Colonial Williamsburg Found. Republican Nat. Committeeman, Ark., 1961—; gov. Ark., 1967-70. Chmn. Ark. Indsl. Devel. Commn., 1955-64; mem. nat. adv. health manpower council NIH. Trustee Nat. Urban League, 1940-64, Loomis Sch., Nat. 4-H Club Found., Vanderbilt U. Served from pvt. to lt. col. U.S. Army, 1941-46; with 77th Inf., Invasion Guam, Leyte, Okinawa. Recipient Bronze Star medal with oak leaf cluster, Purple Heart. Mem. Santa Gertrudis Breeders Internat. Assn. (pres., dir.), Delta Kappa Epsilon, Kappa Delta Pi. (hon.) Baptist. Clubs: Yale, Links (N.Y.C.); Little Rock Country; Pleasant Valley Country. Home: Morrilton Ark., Died Feb. 22, 1973.

ROCKWELL, WALTER F;, bus. cons.; b. Boston, Mass., Oct. 30, 1899; s. Frederick J. Rockwell; B.S., Tufts Coll., 1920, M.S. 1945; m. Kathryn McElroy; children—Joan McE. (Mrs. Malcolm M. Barnum) (dec.), Hays H., Bruce McFarland. Vice pres., gen. mgr., dir. Timken-Detroit Axle Co., 1933-40, pres., dir. 1940-

53; chmn. bd. dir. Acro Mfg. Co., 1953-57; chmn. finance com. Rockwell Mfg. Co., 1957-62; bus. consultant, Detroit, from 1962; dir. Robertshaw Controls Company, Rockwell Standard Corporation; dir. N. Am. Rockwell Corp., to 1969. Mem. Am. Ordnance Assn. (life), Automobile Old Timers (life). Clubs: Detroit, Detroit Athletic, U. Chicago, Country of Detroit. Home: Grosse Pointe Farms, Mich., Died May 29, 1973; interred Woodlawn Cemetery, Detroit, Mich.

RODDEWIG, CLAIR M., business exec.; b. Newcastle, Neb. Apr. 18, 1903; s. Ernest Jospeh and Anna L. (Casey) R.; student Creighton U., 1923-26; J.D., John Marshall Law Sch., 1947; LL.D., DePaul U., 1963; m. Geraldine Hendrick, Oct. 25, 1937; children—Mary Joan (Mrs. John T. Geary), Geraldine Claire (Mrs. William J. McMahon), Richard. Admitted to Neb. bar, 1926, S. D. bar, 1931, Ill. bar, 1946; practice law, Omaha, 1926-31, Winner and Witten, S.D., 1931-39; atty. ICC, 1939-42; gen. counsel, atty. Office Def. Transp., 1942-45; gen. counsel C. & E. I. R.R., 1945-47, v.p., 1947, pres. 1949-57; pres. Assn. Western Rys., 1957-70; Vice chmn., dir. Mut. of Omaha, 1970-75; chmn., dir. Omaha Indemnity Co., First Nat. Bank Oak Lawn (Ill.); dir. Mut. Omaha Growth Fund, Mut. Omaha Income Fund, Inc., Mut. Omaha Fund Mgmt. Co., Mut. Omaha Interest Shares, Mut. Omaha Am. Fund, United Benefit Life Ins. Co., Companion Life Ins. Co., Concordia Savs. & Loan Assn., Constn. Ins. Co., Tele-Trip Co., Inc. Asst. atty. gen. S.D., 1933-36, atty. gen. 1936-39. Vice chmn. Chgo. Com. Urban Opportunity, from 1965; mem. exec. com. Chgo. Area council Boy Scouts Am., 1963-70, adv. bd., from 1970; mem. adv. com. Ill. Bd. Higher Edn., 1965-70; mem. citizens bd. U. Chgo., from 1965; pres. Chgo. Bd. Edn., 1962-64; mem. Public Bldgs. Commn. Chgo., 1963-75; chmn. Chgo. Plan Commn., 1957-61; mem. Commn. on High Speed Rail Transit, 1965-68; mem. Joint Youth Devel. Com., from 1962, Community Improvement Adv. Com., from 1968. Parking Adv. Council, from 1968. Bd. dirs. Catholic Charities Chgo., St. Bernard Hosp.; chmn., dir. St. George Hosp.; trustee, mem. legal bd. DePaul U., 1955-67, bd. dirs., 1967-72; bd. lay trustees St. Mary's Coll., Notre Dame, Ind., 1965-68; mem. bd. Met. Fair and Expn. Authority, from 1969, Chgo. Transit Authority, from 1970; trustee John Marshall Law Sch., 1967, St. Xavier Coll., Chgo.; chmn. bd. St. Barnabas Sch., 1967-69, mem., from 1969. Recipient Alumni Honor citation Creighton U., 1956, Silver Beaver award Boy Scouts Am., 1969, St. Vincent-DePaul medal DePaul U., 1969; named Man of Year, Chgo. Jr. Assn. Commerce, 1964. Mem. Am. Soc. Traffic and Transp. (founder mem), Nat. Freight Traffic Assn., Asso. Traffic Clubs Am., Am. Judicature Soc., Am. Ill., Chgo. bar assns., Newcomen Soc. N.Am., Clubs: Chicago, Commercial Traffic Beverly Country, Executive (Chgo.); Traffic (N.Y.); Western Railway. Home: Chicago Ill. Died Feb. 23, 1975.

RODELL, MARIE FREID, literary agt.; b. N.Y.C.; d. Isadore and Elizabeth (Serber) Freid; B.A., Vassar Coll., 1932. Asst. to editor William Morrow & Co., N.Y.C.; fiction editor Modern Age Books, N.Y.C., head mystery dept. Duell Sloan & Pearce, N.Y.C.; self-employed literary agt., N.Y.C., 1948-75. Literary trustee, Rachel Carson, 1964; bd. dirs. Rachel Carson Trust for Living Environment, 965; Mem. Soc. Authors Reps., Authors Guild. Author: 3 novels, 1 textbook, also articles, short stories. Address: New York City, N.Y. Died Nov. 9, 1975.

RODGERS, HENRY DARLING, banker; b. Albany, N.Y.. Sept. 25, 1879; s. James and Catharine E. (Burton) R.; ed. pub. sch. and Albany (N.Y.) High Sch.; m. Louise Woodward Allen, Sept. 4, 1907; children—Henry Allen, Prentice Johnson, John, Louise Allen (Mrs. William Blake Ackerman). Messenger, Albany Savings Bank, 1896, became asst. treasurer, 1905, treasurer, 1913, trustee, 1929 (resigned January 1947), executive vice president, later president, 1941, retired 1944; director Savings Banks Trust Co. of New York, 1939-45. Institutional Securities Co. of N.Y., 1939-45, Albany Ins. Co. Served with Troop B., New York Nat. Guard, 1902-08. Treas. Albany County Red Cross, 1917-19. Chmn. advisory com. Draft Bd. No. 341 during World War II. Trustee and sec. Presbytery of Albany; treas. bd. of trustees Fourth Presbyterian Ch. Clubs: Albany Country, Fort Orange (Albany). Home: Albany, N.Y.†

ROE, DUDLEY GEORGE, ex-congressman; b. Sudlersville, Md. Mar. 23, 1881; s. William Dudley and Mattie Neal (George) Roe; A.B., Washington Coll., Chestertown, Md., 1901, A.M., 1903; LL.B., Univ. of Maryland, 1905; hon. LL.B., Washington Coll., 1943; m.m. Anna J. T. Metcalfe, Apr. 17, 1906; children—Dudley George, Brown Metcalfe, William Medford Dudley; married 2d, Edith E. Welch, October 27, 1948. Dir. Sudlersville Bank, 1912-28, pres., from 1928; pub. Centreville Observer, 1924-36; dir. Queen Anne's Record and Observer, 1936-47; elected to Md. Ho. of Delegates, 1907, to Md. State Senate, 1923, 1926, 1930 and 1938; mem. 79th Congress (1945-47), 1st Md. Dist. Lay delegate Gen. Conv. Protestant Episcopal Ch. from Diocese of Easton, 1919, 222, 25, 28, 31, 37, 40, 43. Mem. bd. visitors and govs. Washington Coll., from 1920. Mem. Md. Legislative Council, 1939-43. Mem. Theta Chi. Democrat. Mason. Elk. Vestryman St. Luke's Parish, Queen Annes County, Md. Address: Sudlersville, Md.†

ROEBER, EDWARD CHARLES, educator; b. Rhinelander, Wis., Apr. 14, 1913; s. Walter Carl and Claribel (Chapman) R.; A.B., Lawrence Coll., 1935; M.A., Northwestern U., 1942, Ph.D. (All univ. fellow 1940-41), 1942; m. Grace Belle Raettig. Aug. 30, 1935; children—Bonnie Aileen, Edward Dean, Marcia Claire, Laura Janeth. Tchr. Manitowoc and Racine (Wis.) pub. schs., 1935-42; prof. ed. Hamiline U., St. Paul, 1943-45; dir. counseling Kan. State Tchrs. Coll., Pittsburgh, 1945-47; asso. prof. edn. U. Mo., 1947-53; prof. edn. U. Mich., 1953-66; R. W. Holmstedt distinguished prof. edn. Indiana State University, Terre Haute from 1966; cons. division higher edn. U.S. Office Edn., 1958, Bur. Labor Statistics, Dept. Labor, 1954, 59. Mem. Am. (pres. 1961-62), Wolverine personnel and guidance assns., Nat. Vocation Guidance Assn. (pres. 1958-59), Am. Coll. Personnel Assn., Am. Ednl. Research Assn., Assn. Counselors Edn. and Supervision, Am. Psychol. Assn., Mich. Coll. Counselor Assn. Co-author: Occupational Information, rev. edit., 1958; Casebook of Counseling, 1954; Organization and Administration of Guidance Services, 1955; Orientation to the Job of Counselor, 1962; The School Counselor, 1963; Interpreting Guidance Programs to School Personnel, 1968; A Strategy for Guidance, 1969. Home: Terre Haute, Ind. Died Feb. 8, 1969; buried Roselawn Cemetery, Vigo County, Ind.

ROEBUCK, ARTHUR WENTWORTH, Canadian senator; b. Hamilton, Ont., Feb. 28, 1878; s. Henry Simpson and Lydia (Macklem) R.; student Harbord Collegiate; Osgoode Hall Law Sch.; m. Inez Perry, 1918; 1 dau., Glenna (Mrs. A.E. Patterson). Candidate for Ont. Legislation, 1911, 1914, House of Commons, 1917; elected, Ont. Legislature, 1934, House of Commons, 1940; atty. gen., Minister Labour; mem. Ont. Hydro Electric Power Commn., 1934, re-elected, 1937; apptd. Can. Senate, 1945, chmn. special select com. human rights and fundamental freedoms; barrister, solicitor; Queen's counsel; bencher Law Soc. Upper Can. Member Toronto Men's Liberal Assn. Liberal. Clubs: Granite, Thornhill Golf (Toronto), Home: Toronto, Ont., Can.†

ROELOFS, HOWARD DYKEMA, educator; b. Grand Rapids, Mich., Apr. 7, 1893; s. Gerrit and Mary (Dykema) R.; student Amherst Coll., 1911-13; A.B., U. Mich., 1915, M.A., 1916; Ph.D., Harvard, 1925; L.H.D., Ripon (Wis.) Coll., 1949; m. Miriam Hubbard, July 26, 1917; children—Mary Moore (Mrs. Gilmore Stott), Gerrit Hubbard, Alice Dykema (Mrs. Lyman Jellema), Howard Mark, Miriam Hubbard (Mrs. William H. Ellis III), Joan Cornelia (Mrs. Woodward Garber). Asso. prof. philosophy Stanford, 1927-31; vis. prof. U. Calif., 1931, Amherst Coll., 1931-32; Obed J. Wilson prof. ethics and head dept. philosophy U. Cincinnati, from 1932. Mem. Am. Philos. Assn., Guild Scholars, Phi Beta Kapa. Episcopalian. Clubs: University (Buffalo); Literary (Cincinnati). Author: Christianity and Reason (with others), 1951. Contbr. profl. jours. Home: Glendale, East Aurora N.Y. Died Aug. 12, 1974.

ROENNE, TORBEN HENNING, Danish diplomat; b. Copehagen, Denmark, Apr. 14, 1919; s. Gerhard and Ines (Jensen) R.; Doctor's degree in Polit. and Econ. Sci., U. Copenhagen, 1945; LL.D., Doane Coll., 1966; m. Consuelo Langaard, June 23, 1949. Joined Danish Fgn. Service, 1945; attache embassy, Paris, France, 1947-49; sec. Danish Fgn. Ministry, 1949-50; pvt. sec. to minister affairs, 1950-53; dept. head econ. dept. Fgn. Ministry, 1952-54; 1st sec. embassy, Rome, Italy, 1954-57; dept. head polit. dept., also sec. fgn. policy com. Danish Parliament, 1958-59; head NATO dept. Fgn Ministry, 1959-62; A.D. and P. to Norway, 1962-65, to U.S. 1965-71; permanent undersec. state Ministry Fgn. Affairs, Copenhagen, 1971. Decorated comdr. Order Dannebrog (Denmark); Knight Order Legion of Honor (France); knight Order Icelandic Falcon (Iceland); officer Order Merit (Italy); officer Order Oranien-Nassau (The Netherlands); grand cross Order St. Olav (Norway); comdr. Order Crown Order (Thailand); officer Order Vasa (Sweden); named hon. citizen State of Tex., New Orleans, Kansas City, Mo., Mpls., other Am. cities. Home: Denmark. Died Oct. 19, 1973.

ROETHLISBERGER, FRITZ JULES, educator; b. N.Y.C., Oct. 29, 1898; s. Friedrich Carl and Lina (Richon) R.; A.B., Columbia, 1921; B.S., Mass. Inst. Tech., 1922; M.A., Harvard, 1925; hon. doctorate, St. Gall (Switzerland) Sch. Econs., Bus. and Pub. Adminstrn.; m. Margaret Dixon, Nov. 27, 1929 (dec. Nov. 1963); 1 dau., Jean. Practice of engring. in chem. industry, 1922-24; instr. indsl. research Harvard Grad. Sch. Bus. Adminstrn., 1927-30, asst. prof., 1930-38, asso. prof., 1938-46, prof. human relations, 1946, Wallace B. Donham prof. human relations, 1950-67, emeritus, 1967-74. Recipient Harvard Ledie prize, 1959; Taylor Key award Soc. Advancement Mgmt., 1956. Mem. Am. Sociol. Soc., Soc. Applied Anthropology, Am. Acad. Arts. Author: (with W.J. Dickson) Management and the Worker, 1939; Management and Morale, 1941; Training for Human relations 1954; (with A. Zaleznick and C.R. Christensen) The Motivation, Productivity and Satisfaction of Workers, 1958; (with W.J. Dickson) Counseling in an Organization; A Sequel to the Hawthorne Researches, 1966; Man-In-Organization, 1968. Home: Cambridge, Mass. Died May 17, 1974.

ROGERS, ARTHUR AMZI, supt. of banks; b. Bloomington, Ill., Dec. 22, 1881; s. Lucius and Eunice (Freeman) R.; B.S., U. of Ida., 1906; m. Florence S. Skattaboe, May 16, 1908; children—Arthur Lucius, Harry Freeman. Bank employe, Moscow, Ida., 1906-10; organized Bank of Winchester, Ida., 1910, and served as cashier until 1917; successively asst. cashier, cashier and pres. First National Bk., Eugene, Ore., 1917-33; Fed. of Land Bk., Spokane, Wash., 1933-39; supt. banks of Ore., from 1939. Mem. Nat. Assn. Supervisors of State Banks (mem. chmn. exec. com., pres.), Salem (Ore.) C. of C., Phi Delta Theta. Presbyterian. Elk. Club: Rotary (Salem). Home: Salem, Ore.†

ROGERS, BURTON R(AY), veterinarian; b. Polk City, Ia., Nov. 1, 1879; s. George W. and Elizabeth Mary (Keim) R.; D.V.M., Ia. State Coll., 1899; post-grad. study, McKillip Vet. Coll., 1900; m. Margaret Fritz, from Sept. 18, 1901. Federal meat insp., 1900-05, from 1931; anatomist, vet. div., Kan. State Coll., 1906-14; dean and sec. St. Joseph Vet. Coll., and pres. and gen. mgr. St. Joseph Vet. Labs., 1914-17; prof. anatomy, McKillip Vet. Coll., Chicago, 1918-20; veterinarian Western Weighing and Inspection Bur., 1919-30; vet. insp. U.S. Bur. Animal Industry, 1931. Mem. U.S. Live Stock Sanitary Assn., Am. Vet. med. Assn., Ill. Soc. of Bacteriologists, Ill. Assn. for the Crippled. Originated (1901) plan for automatic tracing of animal tuberculosis through a system of marking origin of hogs, and has written much on this and other subjects, including the following: Angiologist vs. Bacteriologist in Influenza and Pneumonia (also "colds" poliomyelitis, encephalitis, meningitises), 1918; Encephalic Strongylgenic Embolisa New Theory of Equine Encephalomyelitis, 1912; Story the Germs Told, 1910; Automatic Quick Economic Plan for Tuberculosis Eradication, 1908; New Visions of and Old Plague, 1918; Spare Time Dissection for Busy Practitioners, 1915; Real, but Ignored Problems of Education, 1909; Sturdy Farm Boy versus High School Kid as a Veterinary Matriculant, 1915; Inflammatology Thesis, 1934; Crymogenic Pathology, 1938. Organized (1931) open sanitary knife pouches now used in packinghouses. Mem. A.A.A.S.; Internat. Congress for Microbiology. Home: Chicago, Ill.†

ROGERS, CHARLOTTE BOARDMAN, editor; b. Bridgeton, N.J., Dec. 24, 1878; d. John Brown and Sara Chester (Jones) R.; ed. Dearborn-Morgan Sch., Orange, N.J., Wrote and edited textbooks in English branches for United Correspondence Schs. and instr. journalism, same, 1900-01; asst. editor Literary Life, 1901-02; on staff Dry Goods, Toilettes, Jr. Toilettes, 1902-03; asso. editor Bookseller, Newsdealer and Stationer, from Oct., 1903. Club: Criticism. Co-Author: Foolish Etiquete; Foolish Almanac. Translator: A Mistress of Many Moods, 1901; also novels and short stories from the French. Compiled. How to Play Chess. Address: New York City, N.Y.†

ROGERS, PLEAS BLAIR, corporation executive and army officer; b. in Alice, Texas, Nov. 14, 1895; s. John Harris and Harriette (Burwell) R.; grad. Wentworth Mil. Acad., 1915; student U. Tex., 1915-16; grad. Co. Officers Course, Inf. Sch., 1923, Troop Officers Course, Cav. Sch., 1925, Field Officers Course, Inf. School, 1930, Command and General Staff Sch., 1935, Army War Coll., 1938; m. Clara Louise Fink, July 3, 1918; children—Harriette Louella (Mrs. Charles J. Geyer, Jr.), Blair Louise (Mrs. J. Russell Major); m. 2d, Mrs. Helen Moore Williams, December 20, 1947; m. 3d, Mrs. Luther Wolf Cone, September 7, 1963. Served from private to 2d lieutenant, 2d Texas Infantry (Fed. Serv.), May 1916-Mar. 1917; 2d lieutenant to capt., Inf. (machine gun), 36th Div., World War I; 1st lieutenant Inf. Regular Army, 1920; service with 9th Inf.; instr. Inf. School; with 45th Inf. and 57th Inf. (Philippine Scouts); Hdqrs. 3d Inf. Brigade (Philippine Scouts); instr. Cav. Sch.; Q.M. Corps (Remount Service); organized and comd. Central Base Sect. (Eng.), Apr. 1942-Aug. 1944; organized and comd. Seine sect. (France), Aug. 1944-Nov. 1945; apptd. brig. gen. Mar. 1943; returned to U.S., 1945; sr. instr. O.R.C., N.Y. State, 1946-47; ret. as brig. gen., U.S. Army, 1948; mgr. H. W. Dick Co., Inc., Charles Town, W.Va. Awarded D.S.M., Legion Merit, Bronze Star Medal, Comdr. Order Brit. Empire, Ofcr. Legion Honor (France), Comdr. Order du Commericial Merite (France), Crois de Guerre with Palms (France), Mexican Border, Victory (Meuse Argonne), American Defense, European-African-Middle East medals. Mem. Masters of Foxhounds Assn., W.Va. Thoroughbred Breeders and Horsemen' Assn. (pres.), Phi Gamma Delta. Clubs: Rotary (hon., Front Royal, Va.); Army-Navy (Washington). Home: Hawthorndale, Charles Town, W.Va. Died Dec. 25, 1974; buried Oakwood Cemetery, Austin, Tex.

ROGERS, THOMAS WESLEY, economist, educator; b. Fayetteville, Tenn., Sept. 30, 1900; s. John Anderson and Lou Emma (Davis) R.; A.B. magna cum laude, Birmingham-Southern Coll., 1927; A.M., U. Chgo., 1928; student Indiana U. Law Sch., 1929-31; J.D., DePaul U. Law Sch., 1948; m. Rena Cruce, July 17, 1929; children—Nancy Lou, Rena Carolyn. Began as cost clerk, Birmingham, Ala., 1918; clk., foreman, supt. and asst. to v.p., Stockham Pipe Fittings Co., Birmingham, 1918-27; student and research fellow, U. Chgo., 1927-28; asst. prof. Sch. of Commerce, Drake U., Des Moines, Ia., 1928-29; faculty mem. Sch. of Business, Ind. U., 1929-41 (on leave 1937-41); successively dir. research gen. mgr., exec. v.p., sr. v.p., economist Am. Finance Conf., 1938-64; prof. econs. David Lipscomb Coll., 1963-70. Lectr. and cons. on credit and monetary affairs. Mem. Governor's Commn. on Unemployment Relief, Bloomington, Ind., 1933-35; active in public welfare work, Monroe County, Ind., 1930-37. Recipient Chartered Assn. Exec. award Am. Soc. Assn. Executives, 1963. Mem. Am. Econ. Assn., Nat. Arbitration Assn., Am. Finance Assn., Am. Marketing Assn. Nat. Conference Consumer Credit (chmn. 1955-58; nat. com. uniform traffic laws and ordinances), Hwy. Research Bd. (com. registration and titling practices 1961-64), Am. Acad. Polit. Sci., Am. Statis. Assn., Omicron Delta Kappa, Delta Sigma Pi, Pi Gamma Mu, Kappa Phi Kappa, Recipient of Star of Service Award, Bloomington, Ind. Kiwanis Club, 1933, for distinguished public service (member club, 1929-40). Democrat. Mem. Ch. of Christ. Author numerous articles on consumer credit including, State Installment Sales Laws, Easy Credit Can Be Tough, also research articles and brochures in field. Editor Times Sales Financing, 1945-59. Home: Nashville, Tenn. Died Feb. 4, 1973; buried Forest Hills Cemetery, Birmingham, Ala.

ROGLIANO, FRANCIS TEOBALDO, physician; b. Tuckahoe, N.Y., July 1, 1915; s. Alfred and Maria Nancy (Morrone) R.; M.D., Columbia, 1939; m. Eleanore Meda Rice, Aug. 20, 1942. Intern, Grasslands Hosp., Valhalla, N.Y., 1940-42, asst. resident in medicine, 1942, resident, 1946-47, attending cardiologist, until 1973, pres. med. bd., 1966-73; dir. medicine Mt. Vernon (N.Y.) Hosp.; vis. staff Lawrence Hosp., Bronxville, N.Y. Served to maj., M.C., AUS, 1942-46. Recipient medallion for pub. health Westchester Community Coll., 1973. Diplomate Am. Bd. Internal Medicine. Fellow A.C.S.; mem. A.M.A., Am. Heart Assn. Roman Catholic. Home: Mt. Vernon, N.Y., Died May 30, 1973; buried St. Mary's Cemetery, Yonkers, N.Y.

ROHDE, MAX SPENCER, surgeon; b. Burlington, Ia., July 16, 1884; s. Hans Fredrich and Sara (Phelps) R.; student Mass. Inst. Tech., 1903-04, Biol. Lab., Woods Hole, Mass., summer, 1907; B.S., State Insane Asylum, summer 1910; student Charité Hosp., Berlin, Germany, 1911; M.D., Johns Hopkins, 1912; m. Lucile Pierce, Jan. 9, 1916 (divorced 1919); one daughter Elizabeth Ann Puleston; married second Kom-Oie Keah. Intern house surgeon, Kansas City (Mo.) Gen. Hosp., 1912-13, Bellevue Hosp., N.Y. City, 1914-16; externe Brady Urol. Inst., Johns Hopkins, 1916-17; began practice at N.Y. City, 1917; dir. Urol. Advisory Exemption Bd., New York U. of Chicago, 1908; lab. externe, Dancers (Mass.) Hosp. Div., 1917-18; alternate med. dir. U.S. Lines, 1917; organizer, 1918, med. and surg. dir. and sec. bd. of governors of Lexington Hosp., 1919-29; organizer, 1930, med. and surg. dir. Medical Arts Sanitarium, 1930-34; physician and surgeon Huyler's Candy Factory, 1918-21; surgeon Page and Shaw Candy Factory, Tiffany Candy Factory and Grace Church Choir School, 1918-21; chief of clinic, Bellevue O.P.D. Urol. Dispensary and James Buchanan Brady Urol. Inst. New York Hospital, 1919; adj. surgeon hernia dept. Ruptured and Crippled Hospital, 1919-21; asst. visiting urol. surgeon New York Hosp., 1921-29; asst. visiting surgeon urological department, Bellevue Hosp., 1929-40, associate visiting surgeon, 1940-47; cons. surgeon Panama American Line, 1924; clin. instr. in urology, Cornell U. Med. Sch., 1924-27; sec. bd. dirs. Reid, Yeomans & Cubit, 1919-29; pres. 36 E. 76th St. and 32-34 E. 76th St. Corps. 1938-54; pres. Gotham Med. Centre, Inc., 1934-45; pres. Gotham Sanitarium, Inc. 1934-45; sec. bd. govs. Gotham Hosp., 1934-45; v.p. Assn. of Private Hospitals, Inc., 1940-48; pres. 1033 St. John Realty Corp. 1946-50, 240 Wadsworth Av. Realty Corp. 1948-51. Diplomate in urology; fellow American College Surgeons, Internat. Coll. Surgeons, Eastern Med. Soc., Gorgas Memorial Inst., Acad. Medicine N.Y. City; mem. A.M.A., Am. Urol. Assn., Osler Soc. (pres. 1939-40), Bellevue Alumni Soc., Delta Kappa Epsilon, Nu Sigma Nu. Democrat. Moose. Clubs: University, Yale Club D.K.E., New York Athletic. Contbr. on genito-urinary subjects. Address: New York City N.Y. Died May 16, 1973.

ROHRLICH, CHESTER, lawyer; b. N.Y.C., Aug. 21, 1900; s. Herman and Gussie (Raff) R.; LL.B., N.Y. U., 1921; m. Edith Wachtel, June 30, 1923; children—Adele, Elinor (Mrs. Bevin D. Koeppel). Admitted to N.Y. bar, 1922, since practiced in N.Y.C.; partner firm Goldmark and Rohrlich, and predecessors, Cook, Nathan & Lehman, 1925-74; Rohrlich adj. prof. law N.Y.U. Law Sch., 1945-74. Dir. I.T.T. Rayonier (B.C.) Can. Trustee Jewish Child Care Assn., from 1940, pres., 1946-49; v.p., bd. dirs. N.Y. Assn. New Americans, from 1949. Trustee William Wollman Found., 1955-63. Mem. Am., N.Y. State bar assns., N.Y. County Lawyers Assn. (chmn. com. on fgn. and internat. law 1955-64). Clubs: Harmonie, Lawyers (bd. govs.) (N.Y.C.); Beach Point. Author: Law and Practice in Corporate Control, 1933; Organizing Corporate and Other Business Enterprises, 1949; 4th edit. Contbr. articles to profl. jours. Chair in corp. law and finance named in his honor N.Y.U. Law Sch., 1968. Home: New York City, N.Y. Died Dec. 17, 1974.

ROISMAN, JOSEPH, violinist; b. Odessa, Russia, July 25, 1900; s. David and Maria (Schein) R.; grad. (Gold medal, Free Artist award), Odessa Conservatory, 1918; Laureat, Berlin (Germany) Conservatory Music, 1914; m. Pola Kvassay, Feb. 13, 1925. Came to U.S., 1930, naturalized, 1944. Concertmaster, Odessa Opera and Symphony, 1918-22, also toured Russia in solo recitals and chamber music concerts; 1st violinist Budapest String Quartet, 1927-68; concert tours U.S., Australia, Indonesia, N. Africa, S.A., Europe, Japan, Israel; professorial lectr. U. of N.Y. at Buffalo. Recipient Elizabeth Sprague Coolidge medal Library of Congress, 1948; medal Govt. Israel, 1959. Home: Washington, D.C. Died Oct. 9, 1974.

ROJAS PINILLA, GUSTAVO, pres. of Colombia; b. Tunja, Colombia, S.A., Mar. 12, 1900; s. Julio and Hermencia (Pinilla) R.; grad. Normal Sch., Tunja, 1915; B.L., Boyaca Coll., 1917; B.S., Tri-State Coll., Angola, Ind., 1927; Gen. Staff Degree, Superior Sch. War, Colombia, 1941; m. Carola Correa, May 10, 1930; children—Gustavo, Maria Eugenia, Carlos Julio. Commd. sub-lt. Colombian Army, 1920, advanced through grades to gen., 1949; comdg. officer Buenaventura Garrison, 1933-35; study fabriciation of rifle, machine gun ammunition, Germany, 1936; tech. engr., adv. Colombia Ammunition Factory, 1937-38; comdg. officer arty. bn., 1939, arty. sch., 1942; mem. Colombian Lend Lease Commn., Washington, 1943; vice dir. Superior Sch. War, 1944; gen. dir. comml. civil aviation, 1945-46; comdg. officer first brigade Colombian Army, 1947, third brigade, 1948, comdg. officer Colombian Army, 1949, Colombian Mil. Forces, 1950-51; Colombian rep., vice dir. staff Inter-Am. Def. Bd., Washington, 1951-52; minister communications presdl. cabinet, Colombia, 1949-50, ministerio de querra, 1952-54; president of Republic of Colombia, 1954-57. Decorated Cruz de Boyaca, Cruz Militar Antonio Nario, Medalla Militar Antonio Jose de Caldas, Medalla de Nueve de Abril Ciudad de Cali; Legion of Merit (U.S.), Orden del Libertador (Venezuela.) Mem. Colombian Soc. Engrs. Address: Bogota Colombia Died Jan. 1975.

ROLFING, R. C., business exec.; b. 1891. Chmn. bd., chief exec. The Wurlitzer Co., Chgo. Home: Wilmette Ill. Died Oct. 24, 1974; buried Charles City, Ia.

ROMANS, JOHN FRANCIS, mfg. co. exec.; b. Cleve., May 1, 1904; s. Carl and Rose (Kalfus) R.; extension student, Cleve. Coll.; m. Lucille V. Yarsh, May 20, 1935; children—Joan Louise, Linda Ann. Mfg. engr. Eaton Yale & Towne, Inc., Cleve., 1930-46, staff exec., 1959-70, v.p., 1965-70; mgr. machinery div. Motch & Merryweather Machinery Co., Cleve., 1946-53, div. gen. mgr., 1954-59. Served with cav. U.S. Army, World War I. Mem. Cleve. C. of C. Mason, Elks Club: Clevelander. Home: Cleveland, Ohio., Died Apr. 11, 1974; interred Sunset Meml. Park, North Olmsted, Ohio.

ROMER, ALFRED SHERWOOD, zoologist and paleontologist; b. White Plains, N.Y., Dec. 28, 1894; s. Harry Houston and Evalyn (Sherwood) R.; A.B., Amherst Coll., 1917, D.Sc., 1952; Ph.D., Columbia, 1921; D.Sc., Harvard, 1949, Dartmouth, 1959, U. Buffalo, 1960, Lehigh U., 1963; m. Ruth Hibbard, Sept. 12, 1924; children—Sally Hibbard (Mrs. Paul R. Evans), Robert Horton, James Henry. Instr. anatomy Bellevue Med. Coll., N.Y. U., 1921-23; asso. prof. vertebrate paleontology U. Chgo., 1923-31, prof., 1931-34; prof. zoology, curator vertebrate paleontology Harvard, 1934-65, Alexander Agassiz prof. zoology, 1947-65, emeritus, 1965-73; dir. Biol. Labs., 1945-46; dir. Museum Comparative Zool., 1946-61. Pres. XVI Internat. Zool. Congress, Washington, 1963. Served from pvt. to 2d lt. U.S. Army, France, 1917-19. Recipient Hayden medal Acad. Natural Sci. Phila. Mem. Nat. Acad. Sci. (Thompson, Elliot medals), Am. Assn. Anatomists, Paleontol. Soc. (medal, v.p. 1939), Soc. Vertebrate Paleontology (pres. 1940), Am. Soc. Zoologists (pres. 1950), A.A.A.S. (v.p. 1948, pres. 1966, chmn. 1967) Royal Soc. Edinburgh (fgn. mem.), Soc. Animal Morphologists and Physiologists (Indian, hon.), Soc. Systematic Zoology (pres. 1952), Soc. for Study Evolution (pres. 1953), Am. Philos. Soc., Geol. Soc. (London, Wollaston medal 1973), Soc. Naturalists, Geol. Soc. Am. (Penrose medal), Am. Acad. Arts and Scis., Am. Soc. Mammalogists, Am. Soc. Ichthyologists and Herpetologists, Academia Nacional de Ciencias en Cordoba (Argentina), Bayerische Akademie der Wissenschaften (corr.), Linnean Soc. (London, Zool. medal 1972), Zool. Soc. (hon. fellow) (London), Senckenberg Nat. Gessellschaft (corr.), Royal Soc. London (fgn.), Argentina Paleontol. Soc. (hon.), Sigma Xi. Author: Vertebrate Paleontology, 1933, 3d edit., 1966; Man and the Vertebrates, 1933; The Vertebrate Body, 1949, 4th edit., 1970; Osteology of the Reptiles, 1956; The Vertebrate Story, 1959; The Procession of Life, 1968; Notes and Comments on Vertebrate Paleontology, 1968; also various sci. pubs. Home: Cambridge, Mass. Died Nov. 5, 1973; interred Pelham, Mass.

ROMFH, EDWARD COLEMAN, banker; b. Camden, Ark., Feb. 8, 1880; s. George Boddie and Elvira Virginia (Jordan) R.; m. Marie deCamp, Jan. 25, 1905; children—Edward Coleman, Jr. (deceased), Laurence deCamp, Jules Modeste. Asst. cashier, Bank of Bay Biscayne, Miami, Fla., 1898; organizer, 1902, cashier until 1912, pres. 1st Nat. Bank of Miami, 1912-46; organizer, mgr., until 1920, local telephone co.; co-founder and organizer, Miami Beach First Nat. Bank, 1920, dir. until 1934; past chmn. bd. 1st Trust Co., Little River Bank & Trust Co., Miami, Coral Gables First Nat. Bank. Finance committeeman, Town Council, Miami, 1912-17; city commr. of Miami, 1921-23; mayor of Miami, 1923-27. Democrat. Clubs: Bath, Surf, Indian Creek (Committee of 100), (Miami Beach). Home: Miami, Fla.†

ROMNES, H(AAKON) I(NGOLF), corp. exec.; b. Stoughton, Wis., Mar. 2, 1907; s. Hans and Ingeborg (Fosdal) R.; B.S. in Elec. Engring., U. Wis., 1928, LL.D., 1960; D. Eng., Poly. Inst. Bklyn., 1965, Newark Coll. Engring., 1969. U. Akron, 1971; m. Aimee Champion, Dec. 26, 1930; 1 dau., Karen (Mrs. A. T. Olenzak). With Bell Telephone Labs., N.Y.C., 1928-35; toll transmission engr., radio engr., plant extension engr. Am. Tel. & Tel. Co., 1935-50, gen. mgr., dir. operations long lines dept., 1950-52, asst. chief engr., chief engr., v.p., 1952-59, vice chmn. bd., 1964-65, pres., 1965-67, chmn. bd., chief exec. officer, 1967-72, pres., 1970-72, chmn. exec. com., 1972; dir. Western Electric Co., 1959-63, Chem. Bank, Chem. N.Y. Corp., Cities Service Co., Inc., U.S. Steel Corp., Colgate-Palmolive Co.; trustee Mut. Life Ins. Co., N.Y., Seamen's Bank for Savs. Mem. Bus. Council, Mass. Inst. Tech. Corp., nat. corps. com. United Negro Coll. Fund, Urban Coalition Edn. Task Force and Steering Com., United Community Campaigns Am., N.Y., Nat. Center for Vol. Action, Nat. Citizens Com., Bus. Com. for the Arts; nat. chmn. UN Day, 1969. Trustee Edwin E. Aldrin Fund for Advancement Knowledge, Presbyn. Hosp., Inst. for Future, Com. for Econ. Devel., Nat. Safety Council; bd. dirs. Am. Cancer Soc., Downtown-Lower Manhattan Assn., United Fund of Greater N.Y., Nat. Center for Vol. Action, Council for Financial Aid to Edn.; mem. U. Wis. Found.; mem. bd. Planned Parenthood-World Population; adv. bd. Salvation Army; bd. govs. United Way; trustee, pres. Wis. Alumni Research Found., The Conf. Bd. (past vice chmn. bd.). Named Man of Year, U. Wis. Alumni Assn. N.Y., 1967; recipient Distinguished Service award Wis. Alumni Assn., 1968. Fellow I.E.E.E.; mem. U.S., N.Y., chambers commerce, Armed Forces Communications and Electronics Assn., Telephone Pioneers Am. (pres. 1964-65); UN Assn. (dir.), Eta Kappa Nu, Tau Beta Pi. Clubs: International (Washington); Blooming Grove Hunting and Fishing (Hawley, Pa.); Economic of N.Y., University, Baltusrol Golf; Links. Home: Chatham N.J. Died Nov. 19, 1973.

ROMUALDEZ, MIGUEL, Dagami, Leyte, P.I., Sept. 29, 1881; s. Daniel and Trinidad (Lopez) R.; A.B., Ateneo de Manila, 1898; LL.B., Sto. Tomas U., 1907; m. Brigida Zialcita, Aug. 1, 1900; children—Estela, Miguel, Daniel, Eduardo, Amelia, Alberto, Froilan. Admitted to P.I. bar, 1910; U.S. bar, 1927, Shanghai internat. bar, 1920; began practice at Manila, P.I.; pres. La Previsors Filipina (bldg. and loan assn.); dir. Philippine Refining Coprn., 1917-20, Bank of the P.I., 1925-27, Manila R.R. Co., 1927-29. Mem. Philippine Ho. of Rep., 1912-16; mayor of Manila, Feb. 1924-Aug. 1927. Maj. and judge advocate Philippine N.G., 1917-18. Mem. Veteranos de la Revolucion, La Solidaridad Filipina (dir.), Am. Bankers Assn. Catholic. Club: Tiro al Blanco. Home: Manila, Philippines.†

RONNE, TORBEN, Danish diplomat; b. Frederiksberg, Denmark, Apr. 14, 1919; s. Gerhard and Ines (Jensen) R.; Degree in Polit. and Econ. Sci., Copenhagen U., 1945; LL.D., Doane Coll., 1966; m. Consuelo Langaard, 1949. With fgn. service, 1945—; attache, Paris, 1947-49; with Ministry Fgn. Affairs, 1949-54; pvt. sec. Minister Fgn. Affairs, 1950-53; first sec., Rome, 1954-57; chief sec. fgn. policy com. Folketing, 1958-59; head NATO dept. Ministry Fgn. Affairs, 1959-62; ambassador to Norway, 1962-65, to U.S.A., 1965-71; permanent undersec. State Fgn. Affairs, 1971—. Numerous decorations. Home: Copenhagen, Denmark., Died Oct. 19, 1973.

ROOD, JOHN, sculptor, writer; b. Athens, O., Feb. 22, 1902; s. George D. and Frances E. (Snedden) R.; ed. pub. schs., also pvt. studies; m. Mary Lawhead, Sept. 7, 1927 (div. July 1947); m. 2d, Dorothy B. Atkinson, Mar. 15, 1948; m. 3d, Kathrine Kressman Taylor, Dec. 5, 1967. Artist in residence U. Minn., 1944-46, asso. prof. art, 1946-57, prof. art, 1957-64, prof. emeritus, 1964-74; artist in residence Ohio U., 1946-47; sculptor of Persephone at Wellesley Coll., Bridgman Ct. at Hamlin U., facade and west entrance St. Mark's Episcopal Cathedral, Mpls., facade Mt. Zion Luth. Ch., Mpls. Fountain Ct. at Mpls. Pub. Library. Mem. Am. Assn. U. Profs., Soc. Minn. Sculptors, Minn. Artists Assn., Artists Equity Assn. (pres.). Clubs: Mineapolis, Cosmos. Author: Sculpture in Wood, 1950; Sculpture With A Torch, 1963; also chpt. in book. Editor, Manuscript, lit. mag., 1933-36. Home: Washington D.C. Died Mar. 20, 1974.

ROOKS, LOWELL W(ARD), army officer; b. Colton, Wash., Apr. 11, 1893; s. Albert and Ruth Naomi (Richardson) R.; ed. State Coll. Wash., 1913-14; U. of Wash., 1914-17; Inf. Sch., 1926-27; Command and Gen. Staff Sch., 1933-35; Army War Coll., 1936-37; m. Martha Caroline Phillips, Oct. 27, 1920; children—Shirley Carolyn, Martha Jane. Commd. 2d lt. June 5, 1917; promoted through grades to maj. gen., 1943; overseas in World War I; served seven years on Mexican border at Nogales; two years in P.I.; instr. Inf. Sch., 1930-33; Command and Gen. Staff Sch., 1937-41; head Ground Forces Training Div., Army War Coll., 1941-42; in N. African campaign; also G-3 (plans and ops.) for D-Day invasion; witnessed signing of Italian armistice; attended Quebec Conference; commanded 90th Div. in Battle of the Bulge and penetration of Siegfried Line in Belgium, Luxembourg and Germany; primary role in planning campaign which resulted in the Ruhr pocket, its elimination, and the advances to the Elbe River and through Bavaria into Austria; headed Allied party which liquidated self-styled Acting German Govt. and German High Command; retired Dec. 31, 1945. Apptd. chief exec. officer UNRRA Jan. 1, 1946, dir. gen., 1947-apptd. State Dept. Fgn. Service with rank of minister, as asst. dep. for mil. affairs N. Atlantic Council Deputies, 1950. Decorated D.S.M. in North African and Italian campaigns: Companion of the Bath (British); Legion of honor, Croix de Guerre with Palm (French); Ordem do Merito Militar (Brazil); Comdr. of the Order of the Crown with Palm, Croix de Guerre with Palm (Belgium). Mem. Alpha Tau Omega. Clubs: Army and Navy Country, Army Navy Town Club (Washington, D.C.). Home: Nogales, Ariz. Died Jan. 17, 1973; buried Arlington Nat. Cemetery.

ROONEY, JOHN J., congressman; b. Bklyn., Nov. 29, 1903; s. James and Ellen (Fitzsimons) R.; student St. Francis Coll., Bklyn., 1920-22, LL.D.; LL.B., Fordham U., 1925; m. Catherine Kramm Curran; children—John James, Edward, Mary (Mrs. Michael G. Farrell), Arthur, William. Practiced law, Bklyn., 1926-40, asst. dist. atty., Kings County, 1940-44; elected to congress 4th New York dist., at spl. election, June 6, 1944; mem. 83d-93d Congresses 14th N.Y. Dist. Founder Am. Hosp., Rome, Italy. Regent Smithsonian Instn.; mem. council regents St. Francis Coll.; regent Smithsonian Inst.; bd. dirs. Haym Salomon Home Aged. Decorated Knight comdn, with star Ecclesiastic Order St. Gregory the Great; Cross grand comdr. Royal Order Phoenix (Greece); order merit (Italy); Polonia Restituta. Mem. Bklyn. Bar Assn., Dist. Attys. Assn. State N.Y., Celtic Circle, St. Patrick Soc. Bklyn., Ancient Order of Hibernians in Am. (v.p. N.Y.). Democrat. K.C., Elk. Clubs: Brooklyn-Manhattan Trial Counsel, Lawyers, Montauk. Home: Brooklyn, N.Y., Died Oct. 26, 1975.

RORER, GERALD FRANCIS, pharm. chemist; b. Wyncote, Pa., Feb. 11, 1908; s. William H. and Helen (Crawley) R.; B.S., Haverford Coll., 1929; B.S., Phila. Coll. Pharmacy and Sci., 1931, D.Sc., 1970; m. Mary Amelle Runk, Jan. 27, 1939; children—Gerald Barcroft, Edward Crawley, Herbert Taylor. Dir. William H. Rorer, Inc., Fort Washington, Pa., 1940-76; v.p., 1944-50, exec. v.p., treas., 1950-59, pres., 1959-62, chmn. bd., pres., 1962-66, chmn. bd., 1966-76; chmn. bd. merged co. Rorer-Amchem, Inc., 1968—. Pres. Pocono Lake Preserve Assn., 1974-75. Pres. bd. dirs. Chestnut Hill Acad., 1961-64; bd. mgrs. Germantown Dispensary and Hosp., Phila., 1964—; trustee Acad. Natural Scis., Phila., 1964-76; vice chmn., 1967; bd. dirs. Pa. Plan to Develop Scientists in Med. Research, U. Pa., 1962-72; bd. mgrs. Haverford Coll., 1967-73. Mem. Pharm. Mfrs. Assn. (pres. 1944-46, dir. 1964-72), Hist. Soc. Pa., Mil. Order Loyal Legion, Pa. Soc. S.R. Episcopalian. Clubs: Philadelphia Cricket (pres. 1961-64), Merion Cricket, Union League (Phila.); Royal Poinciana Golf; The Courts; Sunnybrook Golf; Merion Golf. Home: Gladwyne, Pa., Died Feb. 20, 1976; interred Ch. of Redeemer, Bryn Mawr, Pa.

RORTY JAMES, writer; b. Middletown, N.Y., Mar. 30, 1890; s. Richard McKay and Octavia (Churchill) R.; A.B., Tufts Coll., 1913; m. Maria Lambin, Sept. 20, 1920; m. 2d, Winifred Raushenbush, Mar. 29, 1928; 1 son, Richard. Advertising copy writer, 1913-17; newspaper and mag. writer, editor and author from 1920. Cons. Tenn. Valley Authority, Knoxville, 1946-49. Served as stretcher bearer, ambulance service, U.S. Army, 1917-19. Awarded D.S.C. Author: Children of the Sun, 1926; Our Master's Voice, 1934; Order on the Air, 1934; Where Life Is Better, 1936; American Medicine Mobilizes, 1939; Tomorrow's Food (With N. Phillip Norman), 1947. Selected Poems, 1930-70, 1971. Home: Flatbrookville, N.J., Died Feb. 25, 1973.

ROSAMOND, WILLIAM IRBY, architect; b. Memphis, Nov. 4, 1912; s. William Irby and Lucy May (Pope) R.; B.S., Ga. Inst. Tech., 1936; m. Lilla Pratt, Oct. 10, 1939; children—William Henry, Lilla Merrill. Asso. archtl. firms, Miss., Tenn., 1936-39; v. p. Investment Banking & Mortgage Loan Co., Memphis, 1939-41; pvt. archtl. practice, Columbus, Miss., 1939-41, 46-73; pres. Columbus Reprodn. Co., Inc., Willa corp.; v.p. 1112 Main Corp.; prin. William I. Rosamond & Assos. P. A., Columbus, Miss.; dir, First Columbus Nat. Bank, Liberty Savs. & Loan Assn. Pres. Columbus-Lowndes County Community Fund, 1963. Mem. City Planning Commn., Columbus, 1947-48. Bd. dirs., sec. bd. State YMCA. Recipient certificate of award Gulf State Regional Dist. A.I.A., 1957. Mem. A.I.A. (pres. Miss. chpt. 1957), V.F.W., Am. Legion, Newcomem Soc. N.Am., Miss. Econ. Council, Beta Theta Pi. Mason (32 deg., Shriner), Rotarian. Clubs: Columbus Country, Lowndes County Chowder and Marching, Magowah Gun and Country (Columbus). Home: Columbus Miss. Died Nov. 23, 1973.

ROSCH, JOSEPH, lawyer; b. Wurtsboro, N.Y., Dec. 9, 1879; s. Joseph and Rachel A. (Smith) R.; student Buffalo Law Sch.; LL.B., U. of Buffalo, 1900; m. Ethel B. Forsyth, June 8, 1901; children—Eugene F., Robert Earl (dec.), Ethel Winifred (Mrs. Emil Peters), Joseph Alton (dec.). Admitted to N.Y. bar, 1901, and began practice at Port Jervis; practiced at Liberty, N.Y., 1904-21; justice Supreme Court of N.Y., 1921-28; counsel D. & H. R. R. Corp. from 1928, Spl. county judge and surrogate, Sullivan County, 1906-13. Mem. Constl. Com., N.Y., 1915. Trustee Albany Savings Bank (mem. exec. com.), Albany Law Sch. (v.p.), N.Y. State Hist. Assn. Mem. Am. Bar Assn. (house of delegates), N.Y. State Bar Association (ex-pres.), Fedn. of Bar Assns. of Third Jud. Dist. (ex-pres.), Albany, Sullivan County bar assns., Am. Law Inst., Am. Judicature Soc., Republican. Mason, Odd Fellow, Elk. Clubs: Fort Orange (Albany); Mohawk Golf (Schenectady); Sportsmen's Pheasant Preserve; Sullivan County Golf and Country (Liberty). Home: Liberty, N.Y.†

ROSE, DON, lawyer; b. Grove City, Pa., Feb. 8, 1881; s. Homer Jay and Margaret Jane (Shaw) R.; A.B., Princeton U., 1902; student U. of Pittsburgh Law Sch.; m. Jean Evans, Margaret (Mrs. Wm McCune, Jr.), Anne (Mrs. John Kennedy Foster), Donald, Jr., Jean (Mrs. William Penn Snyder III). Admitted to the practice of law, 1905, engaged in gen. practice, Pitts.; partner firm Rose, Houston, Cooper and Schmidt; associate counsel Consolidation Coal Company; advisory Counsel Joy Manufacturing Company. Member American, Pa. and Allegheny County bar assns. Republican. Presbyterian. Mason. Clubs: Duquesne, Harvard-Yale-Princeton (Pittsburgh); Allegheny Country (Sewickley Heights Borough); Elm (Princeton, N.J.); Rolling Rock Club (Ligonier, Pa.). Home: Sewickley Heights Borough, Pa.†

ROSE, JOHN KERR, geographer, economist; b. Boynton Township, Ill., Sept. 25, 1905; s. John Frederick William and Mary Alice (Kerr) R.; A.B., Ind. U., 1928, A.M., 1931, Ph.D., U. Chgo., 1935; J.D., George Washington U., 1945; m. Priscilla Hollis Webster, Feb. 10, 1934; children—John K. (dec.), Priscilla Page, Susan Noyes (Mrs. John Lemp, Jr.), John Frederick William, Helen Hollis (Mrs. James Harley Jr.), Leonore Hayden (Mrs. W. Ellard Taylor), Stephen Webster. Sci. instr., tutor, lectr., instr. in Ill. and Ind., 1928-35; Soc. Sci. Research Council fellow U. Chgo., 1935-36; research asso. edn. George Washington U., 1937-43; lectr. U.S. Dept. Agr. Grad. Sch., 1938-40, Cath. U. Am., 1941; cons. Nat. Resources Planning Bd., Washington, 1940-41; from asst. to sr. econ. analyst, head econ. sect. Rural Electrification Adminstrn., 1936-42; prin. analyst Bd. Econ. Warfare, 1942-43; head analyst, chief resources div. Fgn. Econ. Adminstrn., 1944-45; with Office Internat. Trade Promotion, Dept. Commerce, 1945-46, Bunce Econ. mission to Korea and Japan, 1946; analyst (geographer) Legislative Reference Service, 1946-55; sr. specialist Natural Resources and Conservation, 1955-73; admitted to bar U.S. Dist. Ct., D.C., 1945, U.S. Ct. Appeals, 1946, Ill. bar, 1946, Korea bar, 1946; partner firm Spaulding, Reiter & Rose, from 1951. Mem. staff Select Com. Fgn. Aid (Herter Com.), U.S. House of Reps., 1947-48. Mem. Am. Soc. Profl. Geographers (pres. 1946), Assn. Am. Geographers, A.A.A.S., Phi Beta Kappa, Sigma Xi, Phi Delta Phi. Methodist. Asso. author: World Political Geography, 1948; Fascism in Action, 1947; Final Report on Foreign Aid, 1948; The Brannan Plan, 1950; Geography in the Twentieth Century, 1951; Trends in Economic Growth--A Comparison of the Western Powers and the Soviet Bloc, 1955. Contbr. Ency, Brit. Book of Year and Ency. Brit., 1949-73. Home: Washington, D.C. Died Jan. 24, 1974.

ROSE, KURT EUGENE, psychiatrist; b. Worms, Germany, Oct. 7, 1909; came to U.S., 1935, naturalized, 1941; s. Eugene and Mina (Kahn) R.; M.D., U. Zurich (Switzerland), 1935; grad. Boston Psychoanalytic Inst., 1957; m. Marguerite Avery, Aug. 2, 1952; children—Jonathan A., Judith Ann. Intern Utah State Hosp., Provo, 1936-37, asst. physician, 1938-41, later asst. staff physician; intern Holy Cross Hosp., 1937-38, resident, 1941-42; sr. physician Norwich (Conn.) State Hosp., 1946; mem. staff, fellow Judge Baker Guidance Center, Boston, 1946-47; practice medicine, specializing in psychiatry, 1948-72; research cons. Habit Clinic (now Douglas A. Thorn Clinic); psychiatrist VA Mental Hygiene Clinic, Boston, also James Putnam Children's Center, 1948-54; asso. psychiatrist Children's Med. Center, Harvard, 1954-59; tng. psychiatrist Emma Pendleton Bradley Home, 1957-68; pvt. practice, 1959-72; cons. Providence (R.I.) Child Guidance Clinic, R.I. Med. Center, St. Mary's Home, Providence, U.S. Naval Hosp., Newport, R.I., St. Aloysius Home; sch. psychiatrist, Portsmouth, R.I. Served to maj. M.C., AUS, 1942-46. Diplomate Am. Bd. Psychiatry and Neurology. Mem. Am. Psychiat. Assn., Boston Psychoanalytic Inst. Home: Barrington, R.I., Died Aug. 30, 1972; buried Temple Beth-El Cemetery.

ROSE, WILLIAM CLAYTON, army officer, real estate executive; b. Brooklyn, Alabama, July 6, 1890; s. John Edward and Mary Emma (Brooks) R.; B.S., Mississippi A. and M. College (now Mississippi State), 1910; attended Command and Gen. Staff Sch., 1928-29, Army War Coll., 1935-36, Grad. Nat. War Coll.; m. Rita Keane, Nov. 15, 1919. Commnd. 2d lt., Inf., U.S. Army, 1911, advanced through ranks to major general, 1945; assistant to the adj. general, Apr. 1941-June 1942; with War Manpower Commn., successively as chief of mil. div., chief of exec. services, and vice chmn. 1942-45. Chief of staff and mil. adviser U.S. High Commr. to Philippine Islands, 1945-46; retired from Army, 1946. Vice pres. Hawaiian Sugar Planters Assn., 1946-49; manpower consultant Office Sec. of Defense, 1950-51; pres. Chevy Chase Realty Co. Inc., 1952-55; v.p. Samuel E. Bogley Md., Inc., 1956-58. Mem. U.S. Olympic Com., 1922-40, 50, bd. dirs., from 1963; pres. U.S. Modern Pentathlon Assn., from 1963;. Awarded Legion Merit; Mex. Border Medal; Victory medals of W.W. I and II; Am. Defense Service, Pacific Theater and Am. Campaign medals; Mil. Merit Medal of Philippine Republic. Roman Catholic. Clubs: Chevy Chase (Md.), Army and Navy (Washington); Army and Navy (Manila). Home: Washington, D.C. Died Sept. 9, 1973; interred Arlington Nat. Cemetery.

ROSEKRANS, SARAH H. DIDRIKSEN (MRS. MILTON CHARLES ROSEKRANS), physician; b. Hartford, Conn., July 10, 1901; d. Sevrin Kristian and Ida (Hoff) Didriksen; B.A., U. Minn., 1924, M.B., 1927, M.D., 1928; m. Milton Charles Rosekrans, Mar. 21, 1927; children—Elizabeth Ann (Mrs. Robert Lahn), Laura Lee (Mrs. Howard Stanley). Student, Am. Conservatory Music, Chgo., 1932-36; intern, Fairview Hosp., Mpls., 1927-28, resident 1927-28; practice medicine, Houston, Minn., 1928-29, specializing in obstetrics and gynecology, Chgo., 1943-44, Neillsville, Wis., 1934-70; mem. staff Meml. Hosp., Neillsville; mem. staff U. Mich., Ann Arbor, 1944-45. Mem, Am, Assn. U. Women, Bus. and Profl. Womens Club. Home: Neillsville Wis. Died Nov. 1970.

ROSEMAN, ALVIN, univ. dean; b. Cleve., Mar. 31, 1910; s. Benjamin and Ruth (Stern) R.; A.B., Western Res. U., 1931, J.D., 1933; M.A., U. Chgo., 1935; m. Edith Freund, Apr. 20, 1935; children—Kenneth, Janet. Staff cons. Am. Pub. Welfare Assn., 1933-35; exec. officer Social Security Bd., 1935-39; asst. adminstr. FSA, 1939-42; asst. exec. dir. War Manpower Commn., 1942-43; dep. chief of mission UNRRA, Cairo, Egypt, 1944-45; chief internat. activities Bur. Budget, Exec. Office of Pres., 1945-49; U.S. rep. to UN agencies, Geneva, Switzerland, 1949-51; dir. orgn. and planning Mut. Security Adminstrn., 1951-53; dep. chief Am. Mission for Aid to Greece, 1953-54; dir. pub. services ICA, 1954-57; dir. U.S. Operations Mission to Cambodia, 1957-59; regional dir. for Far East, ICA, 1959-60; asst. dir. gen. UNESCO, 1960-63; asso. dean, prof. internat. affairs, U. Pitts. Grad. Sch. Pub. and Internat. Affairs, 1963-74; asst. dir. charge population affairs AID mission to India, 1971-72. Dir. University Science Center, Inc. Vice pres. Superior Park Devel. Co., 1910 South Taylor Corp. Mem. citizens adv. council Health and Welfare Assn. Allegheny County. Recipient citation for distinguished pub. service, 1957, Distinguished Fed. Civil Service Career award, 1959. Mem. Am. Soc. Pub. Adminstrn. (chmn. ednl. com., internat. com.), Internat. Inst. Pub. Adminstrn., World Affairs Council Pitts. (trustee), Am. Polit. Sci. Assn., UN Assn. of Pittsburgh (v.p.), Phi Beta Kappa, Order Coif. Co-author: Professional Education and World Affairs: Technical Assistance on Revenue Systems, 1969. Author: Shelter Care and the Local Homeless Man. Contbr. articles profl. publs. Home: Pittsburgh, Pa. Died Feb. 20, 1974.

ROSENAU, FREDERICK J., chmn. bd. Rosenau Bros., Inc., children's dress mfrs., Phila. Home: Rydal Pa. Died Sept. 30, 1974.

ROSENBAUM, DAVID, pathologist; b. Paterson, N.J., Sept. 14, 1910; s. Hyman and Jennie (Ruben) R.; M.D., N.Y.U., 1934; m. Della Spark, Oct. 29, 1937; children—Arthur S., Victor E., Jenny L. Intern, Barnert Meml. Hosp., Paterson, 1934-35; resident Harlem Hosp., N.Y.C., 1935-36, Montefiore Hosp., N.Y.C., 1936-38; pvt. practice medicine specializing in pathology; pathologist St. Lawrence State Hosp., Ogdensburg, N.Y., 1938-41, Norristown Pa.) State Hosp., 1941-43; chief lab. service VA Hosp., Indpls., 1946-73; clin. prof. pathology Ind. U. Sch. Medicine; cons. Marion County (Ind.) Blood Bank. Pres., Ensemble Music Soc., Indpls., 1972-73. Served to capt., M.C., AUS, 1943-46. Diplomate Am. Bd. Pathology. Mem. A.M.A., Am. Soc. Clin. Pathology, Internat. Acad. Pathology. Home: Indianapolis, Ind. Died Mar. 16, 1974.

ROSENBLOOM, BENJAMIN LOUIS, congressman; b. Braddock, W.Va., June 3, 1880; studied at W.Va. U.; unmarried. Admitted to bar, W. Va., 1904, to Supreme Court of U.S., 1911; mem. Senate of W.Va., 1914-18; mem. 67th and 68th Congresses (1921-25), 1st W.Va. Dist.; del. to W.Va. Conv., 1933, to ratify 21st Amendment to Constitution of U.S.; elected vice mayor of Wheeling, 1935, for term of 4 years. Democrat. Home: Wheeling, W.Va.*†

ROSENSTERN, IWAN, physician; b. Gehrden, Germany, June 4, 1882; s. Joseph and Ida Rosenstern; came to U.S., 1937; M.D., U. Munich, 1906; m. Gertrude May, May 2, 1938. Clin. dir. The Cradle, Evanston, Ill.; mem. staff Childrens Meml. Hosp., Chgo. Diplomate Am. Bd. Pediatrics. Home: Evanston, Ill. Died May 31, 1973; buried Rosehill Cemetery Chicago, Ill.

ROSENSTIEL, LEWIS S, founder, chmn., chief exec., exec. finance coms. Schenley Distillers Corp.; b. Cin., July 21, 1891; s. Solon M. and Eliza (Johnson) R.; student pub. schs.; m. Dorothy Heller, Oct. 31, 1917 (died Dec. 3, 1944); children—David, Louise; married 2d, Leonore Kattleman, June 1946; one daughter, Elizabeth. Founded Schenley Industries, Incorporated, 1933, chairman executive and finance com., from 1933, chmn. bd. 1934-68, pres., 1948-68, also dir. Sub-chmn. Fedn. Jewish Philanthropic Societies. Trustee, Mount Sinai Hospital. Recipient of the gold medal award from The George Washington Carver Memorial Institute, 1950. Author: Current Views on Prohibition, 1932; ABC Plan for True Temperance, 1932; Consumer Is Boss, 1941; A Conservation Plan for the Distilled Spirits Industry Under Emergency Conditions, 1941; A Capitalistic New Deal, 1943; A Plan for Sustained Prosperity, 1949. Home: Miami Beach, Fla., Died Jan. 21, 1976.

ROSENSTOCK, ARTHUR, labor union exec.; b. N.Y.C., Feb. 5, 1903; s. Abram and Ella (Ehrlich) R.; student Law N.Y.U., 1921-22; m. Eleanor Purdy, Aug. 23, 1928. With Am. Newspaper Guild from 1933, pres. N.Y., 1953-55, internat. v.p., 1956-57, internat. pres. from 1959, chmn. com. guild unity, 1948-58. Past movie and drama critic Bronx Home News; supervisory librarian N.Y. Post. Del. numerous AFL-CIO convs.; v.p. for N.A., Internat. Fedn. Journalists, 1960-61, del. conv., Berne, Switzerland, 1960. Active A.R.C., Community Chest; member executive committee Food for Peace. Home: New York, N.Y. Died Apr. 1975.

ROSENTHAL, SAM, elec. wholesalers co. exec.; b. Chgo., Sept. 15, 1891; s. Simon and Jennie (Weinstein) R.; student pub. schs. Chgo.; m. Myrtle Wolfe, Oct. 14, 1926; children—Jeanne R., Jerry. Began cereer as clerk at Joseph N. Eisendrath Co., Chgo., 1905-19, also asst. bookkeeper, purchasing agt.; partner Hyland Elec. Supply Co., 1919-73, v.p., gen. mgr., sec., 1919-56, treas., 1953-57, treas., chmn. bd., 1957-73. Served with Nat. Industry Adv. Bd., Washington, 1942-45. Trustee (nat.) Nat. Jewish Hosp. (Denver), Sinai Temple (Chgo.). Mem. Nat. Assn. Elec. Distbrs., Elec. Wholesalers Assn., Electric Assn. Chgo. Mason. Clubs: Ravisloe Country, Standard. Home: Chicago Ill. Died June 21, 1973.

ROSIN, HARRY, sculptor; b. Phila., Pa., Dec. 21, 1897; s. Aron and Bertha (Baker) R.; student Sch. Indsl. Arts, Phila., 1919-20, Pa. Acad. Fine Arts, Phila., 1923-26; m. Vilna Spitz, Sept. 19, 1936; 1 dau., Victoria. With Samuel Yellin, iron worker, Phila., 1914-17; lived in Europe, 1926-32; exhibited Modern Am. Artists of Paris, 1932; Salon DeL'Oeuvre Unique, 1932; Met. Mus. sculpture show, 1952; received commn. to execute figure of Christ in concrete for French Govt. in Guadaloupe, French West Indies, 1932; instr. figure constrn., sculpture Pa. Acad. Fine Arts, from 1939; exhibited in U.S. at Pa. Acad. Fine Arts, Art Inst., Chgo., Carnegie, Whitney and Phila. museums, Century of Progress Expn., Chgo., Golden Gate Expn., San Francisco, Tex. Centennial, N.Y. World's Fair, others; prin. works include Samuels Meml. Fairmount Park, Phila., 1941; Deerfield Boy, Deerfield Acad., 1953; heroic statue Connie Mack, City of Phila., 1956; Valley Forge Cadet, Valley Forge Mil. Acad., 1957; heroic statue John B. Kelly, Phila., 1965; facade Chester County Ct. House, West Chester, Pa., 1967; facade relief St. Luke's and Children's Hosp., Phila., 1969; did 12 medals for Nat. Wildlife Fedn., 1971. Recipient Stewardson prize, European scholarship, 1926, Widener Gold medal, 1939, Fellowship Gold medal, 1940 (all Pa. Acad. Fine Arts); Am. Acad. Arts and Letters A00 grantee, 1946; Gold medal award Regional Art Show, Phila., 1950; Bouregy Portrait prize Audubon Artists N.Y., 1956; Percy M. Owens Meml. for a Distinguished Pa. artist, 1965. Home: New Hope Bucks County Pa. Died Sept. 28, 1973.

ROSS, CLARENCE SAMUEL, geologist; b. Eldora, Ia., Sept. 20, 1880; s. James S. and Martin H. (Daniels) R.; student Kan. State Agrl. Coll., 1907-08; A.B., U. of Ill., 1913, A.M., 1915, Ph.D., 1920; m. Helen Hall Frederick, Nov. 2, 1918; children—Betsy Leota, Malcolm. Geologist U.S. Geol. Survey, from 1917. Chmn. com. for investigation of clay minerals of National Research Council, 1928-33; representative minerals of Nat. Research Council, 1928-33; rep. Mineral. Soc. of America on Nat. Research Council, 1931-33. Mem. Geol. Soc. Am. (v.p. 1936), Mineral. Soc. America (pres. 1935), Washington (D.C.) Acad. Sciences (v.p.) 1943, Geological Society of Washington (president 1942), Edward Orton, Jr. Memorial Lecturer for 1945, Am. Ceramic Soc., Washington Petrologists Club, Society Econ. Geologists, Soc. Econ. Paleontologists and Mineralogists. Conglist. Roebling Medal, Mineral Soc. of America, 1946. Author: Origin of Copper Deposits of Ducktown Type in Southern Appalachian Region; Titanium Deposits of Nelson and Amherst Counties, Virginia; also numerous govt. articles to mags. Home: Takoma Park, Md.†

ROSS, DAVID, broadcaster, poet; b. N.Y.C., July 7, 1891; s. Samuel and Fanny (Schmuller) R.; student Rutgers Coll., N.Y. U.; children (by previous marriage) David, Helen (Mrs. Banice Webber); m. 2d, Beatrice Pons, Oct.14, 1937; 1 son, Jonathan. Announcer, commentator radio, TV, CBS and NBC, 1930-58; reader poetry Poet's Gold, CBS radio, 1934-42, Word's in the Night, NBC radio, 1953-58; author Poet's Gold anthology poems, 1955; commentator, editor Illustrated Treasury of Poetry for Children, 1970; writer poems appearing in lit. mags., 1930-75; reader poetry Library of Congress, 1957, colleges in U.S., 1968-69. Recipient Gold medal Am. Acad. Arts and Letters, 1933; Lyric Poem award Poetry Soc. Am., 1957, Sam DeWitt Lyric Poetry prize, 1963, Christopher Morley prize, 1969. Fellow Poetry Soc. Am. (past. v.p., bd. dirs. 1966—, critic poetry workshop, 1970-71). Club: Players (N.Y.C.). Home: New York City, N.Y., Died Nov. 12, 1975; cremated.

ROSS, DAVID FRANCIS, educator; b. Ann Arbor, Mich., Nov. 27, 1925; s. Francis E. and Faith Clare (Mullett) R.; student Mich. State Coll., 1943, U. Mich., 1946-48; A.B. magna cum laude, Harvard, 1950, M.A., 1951, Ph.D., 1956; m. Elizabeth Ann Bloomstrom, June 25, 1949; children—Faith Elizabeth, Eric David. Instr. econs. Golegio de Agricultura y Artes Mecanicas, U. Puerto Rico, 1952-54; economist, asst. dir. econ. research Adminstrn. de Fomento Economico, P.R., 1954-57; asso. prof. econs. Fla. State U., 1957-59; prof. econs., head dept. Bethany (W.Va.) Coll., 1959-61, dean faculty, 1961-64; prof. econs. Cuttington Coll., Suacoco, Liberia, after 1964; ordained priest Episcopal Ch.; vicar St. Andrew's Ch., Lexington, Ky.; asso. prof. econs. U. Ky. Served with AUS, World War II; ETO. Fellow Royal Econ. Soc.; mem. Am. Econ. Assn., N.A.A.C.P., Phi Beta Kappa, Omicron Delta Epsilon, Protestant Episcopalian. Co-author: Honduras—A Problem in Economic Development, 1960. Author: The Long Uphill Path., 1966; also articles, book revs. Exec. editor Growth and Change: a Jour. of Regional Devel. Home: Lexington, Ky., Died July 7, 1975.

ROSS, HAROLD ELLIS, educator; b. Leadville, Colo., Oct. 23, 1881; s. John Warren and Fanny Jane (Coleman) R.; B.S.A., Cornell, 1906, M.S.A., 1909; m. Jessie F. Williams, Dec. 25, 1907; children—Jane Elizabeth, John Warren, Harold Ellis. Asst. in dairy industry, Cornell, 1906, prof. 1910-46, prof. emeritus, from 1946. Mem. Dairy Science Association, Sigma Xi, Gamma Alpha. Mason. Methodist. Author: Dairy Laboratory Guide, 1910; Laboratory Guide in Market Milk; The Care and Handling of Milk, 1927, rev., 1939; Laboratory Guide in Dairy Industry, 1928. Home: Ithaca, N.Y.†

ROSS, JOHN ALEXANDER, JR., educator; b. Belfast, Me., Sept. 19, 1878; s. John Alexander and Louise (Todd) R.; B.S., Mass. Inst. Tech., 1901; Sc.D., Clarkson College Technology, Potsdam, N.Y., 1933; LL.D., St. Lawrence University, 1942; m. Helen Webster True, Sept. 24, 1902. Ship draftsman, Bur. Constrn. and Repair, U.S. Navy, 1901-05; instr., warship design, Mass. Inst. Tech., 1905-07, naval architecture, U. of Mich., 1907-08, mech. engring., Case Sch. of Applied Science, 1908-09, machine design, Cornell U., 1909-10; prof. mech. engring., Lafayette Coll., 1910-11, in charge dept. mech. engring., Clarkson Coll. Tech., 1911-40; dean adminstrn., Clarkson Coll. Tech., 1929-40, pres., 1940-48. Mem. Am. Soc. Mech. Engrs., The Newcomen Soc. Conglist. Clubs: Torch, Rotary (Potsdam, N.Y.). Home: Potsdam, N.Y.†

ROSS, STOYTE O., air force officer; b. Jacksonville, Fla., Apr. 13, 1906; s. Frank A. and Mary A. (Bowles) R.; student U. Fla., 1926-27; m. Meta Elise Bryce, Dec. 9, 1931; children—Meta Elise, Stoyte O. Commd. lt. U.S.A.A.F., 1929. advanced through ranks to brig. gen., 1952; Maxwell AFB, Montogomery, Ala., 1929-30, attended Air Force Tech. Sch., 1930; instr. pilot, flight comdr., stage comdr. Tng. Command, Randolph Field. Tex., 1937-44; comdr. Lake Charles, La. Advanced Flying Sch., 1942, comdr. Victoria, Tex., 1943-44, Clark Field, P.I., 1947-50, commandant extension course inst. Air U., Maxwell AFB, Montgomery, 1947-51, comdr., 1951, brig. gen. U.S.A.F., 1952, comdr. Hdqrs. Command. Bolling AFB, Washington, 1952-56; assigned fgn. duty, Copenhagen, Denmark, 1957-60. Awarded Legion of Merit for outstanding work in career. Home: Jacksonville, Fla. Died Dec. 31, 1973.

ROSS, THOMAS JOSEPH, pub. relations counsel; b. Bklyn., July 27, 1893; s. Thomas J. and Mary (Egan) R.; A.B., St. Francis Xavier Coll., N.Y.C., 1913; LL.D., Georgetown U., 1949, Manhattan Coll., N.Y.C., 1950; L.H.D., Marymount Coll., Tarrytown, N.Y., 1968; m. Marion A. Byrne, Oct. 6, 1917; children—Thomas J., John B., Gerard T., Joan M. Reporter, N.Y. Sun, 1913-16; polit. reporter and legislative corr. N.Y. Tribune, 1916-17; accompanied Justice Hughes on campaign tour for presidency; became asso. with Ivy Lee, pub. relations counsel, 1919; sr. partner Ivy Lee and T.J. Ross, 1934-61; pres. T.J. Ross and Assos., Inc., 1961-65, chmn. bd., 1965-71, chmn. exec. com. bd. dirs., from 1971; pres. Harrison-Rye Realty Corp.; dir. Home Ins. Co., 1949-72; trustee Emigrant Savs. Bank, 1943-72. Mem. Cardinal's Com. of Laity; chmn. bd. Health and Hosp. Planning Council N.Y.; trustee Marymount Manhattan Coll., 1961-67, Alfred Smith Found., Marymount Coll., 1956-68; lay trustee Fordham U., 1958-66; bd. dirs. United Hosp. Fund, Greater N.Y. Fund; adv. bd. St. Vincent's Hosp.; mem. adv. com. N.Y. Foundling Hosp. Joined 1st Plattsburg Tng. Camp, 1917; 2d lt. 18th Cavalry, 76th and 4th F.A., U.S. Army, 1917; 1st lt., 1st F.A., 1918. Mem. Pub. Relations Soc. Am., Council on Fgn. Relations, Newcomen Soc., Army Ordnance Assn., Soc. Silurians. Roman Catholic. Knight of Malta, Knight Grand Cross of Holy Sepulchre. Clubs: Pacific-Union (San Francisco); Cloud (pres. 1953-55, bd. govs.) Advertising, Economic (N.Y.C.); Westchester Country (Rye, N.Y.); Detroit (Detroit). Home: Rye, N.Y. Died May 27, 1975.

ROSSDALE, ALBERT BERGER, congressman; b. N.Y.C., Oct. 23, 1878; s. Herman and Betty (Berger) R.; ed. pub. schs. and Evening High Sch., New York; unmarried. Propr. Rossdale Co., wholesale jewelry. Mem. 67th Congress (1921-23), 23d N.Y. Dist. Del. Rep. State Conv., Albany, 1922, Rochester, 1924; alternate del. Rep. Nat. Conv., Cleveland, 1924. Was postoffice clk., New York, 1900-10; ex-pres. Nat. Fedn. Post Office Clks.; active interest in postoffice affairs and effected various reforms in the postal service; long advocated the enactment of legislation establishing the present pension system for U.S. govt. employees. Mem. N.Y. State Hudson-Fulton Celebration Commn., 1907-09. Mason. Clubs: John Hay Republican (pres. 3yrs.), Nat. Republican, Post Office Square Club of New York (hon. Mem.). Home: Newtown, Conn.†

ROSSEN, RALPH, physician; b. Hibbing, Minn., Nov. 18, 1909; s. Abraham and Libby (Litman) R.; grad. Hibbing Jr. Coll., 1929; b. Medicine, U. Minn., 1933, M.D., 1934; m. Beatrice R. Cohen, July 28, 1934; children—Arlene (Mrs. Richard Cardozo), Fredrica (Mrs. David Weiss). Intern, U. Minn. Hosps., Mpls., 1934-35, fell in neuropsychiatry, 1935-36; clin. dir., dir. research program St. Peter (Minn.) State Hosp., 1936-38; dir. EEG and Research Lab., Hastings State Hosp., 1938-54, also supt., med. dir. 1938-54; commr. mental health State of Minn., 1950-52; dir. L.E. Phillips psychobiol. research Mt. Sinai Hosp., Mpls., 1954-74, also psychiat. cons.; dir. L.E. Phillips Psychobiol. research North Meml. Hosp., Mpls., 1954-74, dir. L.E. Phillips Clin. EEG and Sleep and Dream Lab., 1959-74, also psychiat. cons.; psychiat. cons. State Prison, Stillwater, Minn., 1940-54, State Tng. Sch. for Boys, Red Wing, Minn., 1940-54, Nat. Council State Govs., 1949-53, St. Mary's Hosp., Mpls., Glenwood Hills Hosp., Mpls.; clin. prof. neuropsychiatry U. Minn., until 1961. Mem. Minn. Gov.'s Adv. Com. on Mental Health, 1960-62, Com. on Health, Welfare and Rehab., 1966-71, Blue Ribbon Com. on Mental Health, 1966; cons. to Minn. gov. on mental health and retardation, 1962-66. Served to it. comdr. USNR, 1942-45. Diplomate Am. Bd. Psychiatry and Neurology. Fellow Am. Psychiat. Assn. (life, certified psychiat. hosp. adminstr. 1954, nat. examiner mental health adminstrs. 1965-71), Am. Acad. Neurology, Am. Coll. Chest Physicians, Am. Coll. Cardiology; mem. A.M.A., Hennepin County Med. Soc., Am. Med., Central EEG assns., Am. EEG Soc., Am. Heart Assn., Am. Epilepsy Soc., Eastern Psychoanalytic Assn., Minn. Neurol. Assn., Minn. Psychiat. Assn., N.Y. Acad. Scis. Contbr. articles to med. jours. Home: Minneapolis, Minn. Died June 26, 1974; buried Nat. Cemetery, Ft. Snelling, Minn.

ROSSER, JOHN ELIJAH, educator; b. Covington, Ga., May 19, 1881; s. John Elijah and Julia (Pace) R.; Ph.B., Emory Coll., Ga., 1902; work in sociology, U. of Chicago, summers, 1905, 06, 07; fellow in history and English, Vanderbilt U., 1906-07; unmarried. V.p. Sparks Collegiate Inst., Ga., 1902-04, 1905-06; supt. pub. schs., Nashville, Ga., 1904-05; prin. Nacogdoches (Tex.) High Sch., 1907-09; sec. U. of Tex., 1909-10; state registrar vital statictics, 1911; southwestern rep. of Houghton, Mifflin Co., from 1911. Mem. Internat. Lyceum Assn., Sigma Nu. Democrat. Methodist. Contbr. verse, sketches, special articles and short stories, to Life, Puck, Judge, Lippincott's Magazine, Cosmopolitan. Success, Delineator, etc. Address: Dallas, Tex.†

ROTH, GEORGE BYRON, educator; Eaton, O., May 22, 1879; s. Charles Conrad and Magdelena (Miller) R.; prep. edn., Mich. Mil. Acad., Orchard Lake; student Western Reserve U., 1902-04; A.B. Univ. of Mich., 1906, fellow in pharmacology, 1907-08, M.D., 1909; m. Dorothea Payne, Sept. 14, 1912; 1 dau., Dorothy. Instr. in pharmacology, U. of Mich., 1909-13; pharmacologist, U.S. Pub. Health Service, 1913-21; asst. prof. pharmacology, Western Reserve U., 1921-24; prof. pharmacology, George Washington U., 1924-45, emeritus, from 1945. Fellow Internat. Coll. of Anesthetists; mem. A.M.A., Am. Soc. Pharmacology and Exptl. Therapeutics, Soc. Exptl. Biology and Medicine, Am. Physiol. Soc., Med. Soc. D.C., Am. Assn. Univ. Profs., Sigma Xi, Delta Upsilon, Phi Beta Pi. Mason. Club: Cosmos. Author: Practical Pharmacology, 1929. Contbr. articles on pharmacology to many mags. Mem. Revision Com. U.S. Pharmacopoeia XI. Home: Washington, D.C.†

ROTH, STEPHEN JOHN, judge; b. Hungary, Apr. 21, 1908; s. Charles J. and Johanna (Zillai) R.; brought to U.S., 1913, naturalized, 1933; Ph.B., U. Notre Dame, 1931; LL.B., U. Mich., 1935; m. Evelyn L. Gunner; children—Diane, Susan, Kayla, Charles, Bradford. Admitted to Mich. bar, 1935; practice law, 1935-37, 39-41, 43, 45-48, 50-52; asst. pros. atty., Genesee County, Mich., 1937-38, pros. atty., 1941-42, circuit judge, 1952-62; atty. gen. Mich., 1949-50; U.S. dist. judge Eastern Dist., Mich., 1962-73. Candidate Mich. Supreme Ct., 1955. Served to 2d lt. AUS, 1943-45. Decorated Knight Order Crown Italy. Home: Grand Blanc Mich. Died July 11, 1974; interred Evergreen Cemetery, Grand Blanc.

ROTHBERG, MAURICE ophthalmologist; b. N.Y.C., Oct. 18, 1907; s. Samuel and Ada (Shayne) R.; M.D., U. Ind., 1931; m. Josephine Belle Kann, Dec. 18, 1938; children—Peter Alan, Stephen Porter, Deborah Ann. Intern Indpls. City Hosp., 1931-33, resident, 1934; resident Herman Knapp Meml. Eye Hosp., N.Y.C., Bklyn. Eye and Ear Hosp.; practice medicine, specializing in ophthalmology, 1940-72; pres. staff St. Joseph Hosp., Fort Wayne, Ind., 1964-65. Dir. Ind Bank & Trust Co. Bd. dirs. Allen County League for Blind, Fort Wayne Jewish Fedn., 1968-70, Vita B. Bolman Found. Served to lt. col. M.C., AUS, 1941-46. Diplomate Am. Bd. Ophthalmology. Fellow A.C.S.; mem. Am. Acad. Ophthalmology and Otolaryngology, A.M.A. Jewish religion (dir. temple 1970-72). Home: Fort Wayne, Ind., Died Oct. 9, 1972; buried Jewish Cemetery, Fort Wayne, Ind.

ROTHE, GUILLERMO, lawyer, Argentine minister of justice and education; b. Totoral, Province of Córdoba, Argentina, Dec. 10, 1879; s. Enrique and Lisaura (Armesto) R.; bachelor degree, Colegio National de Monserrat (Córdoba), 1897; doctor of law and social sciences, Faculty of Law and Social Sciences, U. of Córdoba, 1901; m. Matilde Molina Quintana. Prof. constitutional law, U. of Córdoba, 1905; judge of Civil Court, Province of Córdoba, 1908; atty. of Govt. of Córdoba, 1901-12; nat. dep., 1912-16, 1920-22; dep. to Constitutional Conv. of Córdoba, 1912; provincial minister of Govt. of Córdoba, 1922-24; dean of faculty of Law and Social Sciences, U. of Córdoba, 1924-28, vice-rector of the university, 1926-28; judge of Superior Tribunal of Justice of Córdoba, 1925-30, pres., 1939; federal interventor in Province of Santa Fé, 1930-31; minister of justice and pub. instrn., 1931-32; nat. senator from Córdoba 1932-41; atty for Province of Córdoba in Buenos Aires. Mem. Soc. de Droit Comparée (Paris), Acad, de Ciencias (Córdoba). Clubs: Jockey, Circulo de Armas (Buenos Aires); Social, Jockey, Rotary, Golf (Córdoba), Museo Social Argentino. Author: Antecedentes de la reforma de la Provincia de Córdoba, 1923; Proyecto de eódigo de procedimientos penal para la Provincia de Córdoba, 1924; Reforma de la ley organica del poder judicial de la Provincia de Córdoba, 1924; also numerous academic and political lectures and discourses and contributions to scientific reviews, etc. Address: Buenos Aires, Argentina.†

ROUDEBUSH, FRANCIS WILSHIRA, architect; b. Milford, O., Apr. 30, 1899; s. Frank Wallace and Stella (Carver) R.; A.B., Princeton, 1922, M.F.A., 1925; m. Elizabeth Long Summey, May 22, 1931; children—Ann Carver, Peter Wilshire. Draftsman, Delano & Aldrich, architects, 1925-34; pvt. archtl. practice, N.Y.C., 1934-75; instr. archtl. design Cooper Union, N.Y.C., 1925-35; lectr. Princeton, 1948-51, mem. adv. council dept. art and archaeology. Asso. dir. bldg. services U.S.O., 1943-46. Served as pvt. U.S. Army, 1918. Mem. A.I.A., N.Y. State Assn. Architects, S.R., Municipal Arts Soc. N.Y. (dir.). Club: Century Assn. (N.Y.C.). Archtl. works include bldgs. for Smith Coll., Princeton, Vassar Coll. Address: Salisbury Conn. Died May 1975.

ROUILLER, CHARLES, educator, physician; b. Geneva, Switzerland, Apr. 25, 1922; s. Robert and (Passerat) R.; studied medicine, Geneva; M.D.; m. Arlette Ferrarini, 1949. Asst. path. Inst., Geneva, 1949-53; asst. cancer research inst., VilleJuif, France, 1954-55; head electronic microscopy service, exptl. medicine lab. Coll. France, 1956-58; prof. histology and gen. embryology med. dept. U. Geneva, 1958-73, vice rector, 1971-72, rector 1972-73. Mem. Internat. Soc. for Cell Biology, Am. Soc. for Cell. Biology, Internat. Assn. for Study Liver, Deutisch Gesellschaft fur Elektronemikroskopie, Société suisse Biologie cellularie et molec. Contbg. author: The Biochemistry and Physiology of Bone, 1956. Editor: Treatise of the Liver, Morphology, Biochemistry and Physiology, I, 1963, II, 1964; (with A. Muller) The Kidney, Morphology, Biochemistry Physiology, I, 1969, II, 1969, III, 1971, IV, 1971. Home: Geneva, Switzerland., Died May 4, 1973.

ROUNSEVILLE, ROBERT FIELD, actor, singer; b. Attleboro, Mass., Mar. 25, 1919; s. Wilfred Ellsworth and Kathleen (Robinson) R.; student Tufts U., 1932-34, B.A. (hon.), 1952; m. Ann Duelk, June 10, 1936; 2 children. Operatic debut in Pelleas and Melisande, N.Y.C., 1948, later performed with opera companies including Chgo. Civic Opera, N.Y.C. Opera, Teatro La Fenice, Venice, Italy, Phila. La Scala, Little Orch. Soc. N.Y., Balt. Civic Opera, St. Louis Municipal Opera; Broadway debut in Babes in Arms, 1937, later appeared in stock companies throughout U.S.; appeared in Gilbert and Sullivan repertory, N.Y.C., 1952, 64; played title role in Candide, N.Y.C., 1956, Charlie Dalrymple in Brigadoon, N.Y.C., 1957, Padre in The Man of La Mancha, N.Y.C., 1966; toured in Candide, 1958, Rosalinda, 1962, Threepenny Opera, 1962-63; film performances include The Tales of Hoffman, 1951, Carousel, 1955; frequent TV appearances in programs including Your Show of Shows, Jackie Gleason Show, Voice of Firestone, Bell Telephone Hour. Mem. Actors Equity Assn., Am. Guild Variety Artists, Screen Actors Guild, A.F.T.R.A., Am. Guild Mus. Artists. Home: Katonah, N.Y. Died Aug. 1974.

ROURKE, ANTHONY J(OHN) J(OSEPH), physician; b. Prides Crossing, Mass., July 25, 1904; s. Thomas and Hanora Rose (Linehan) R.; grad. Bentley Coll. Boston, 1927; student Suffolk Law Sch., Boston, 1927-30; M.D., U. Mich., 1936; m. Genevieve Cartmill, Sept. 1, 1934 (dec. Oct. 1967); 1 son, Anthony John Joseph; m. 2d, Dorothy Kronebusch, Sept. 2, 1968. Intern U. Mich. Hosp., 1936-37, asst. dir., 1938-40; asst. supt. Columbia-Presbyn. Med. Center-Vanderbilt Clinic, N.Y.C., 1937-38; physician supt. Stanford U. Hosp., 1940-52; dir. out patient clinics, prof. hosp. adminstrn., sch. medicine Stanford U., 1940-52, lectr. sch. nursing, 1940-52; lectr. sch. pub. health U. Cal., 1948-52; lectr. adminstrv. medicine various univs.; exec. dir. Hosp. Council Greater N.Y., 1952-54; hosp. cons., from 1952; pres. Anthony J.J. Rourke, Inc., The Rourke Found., Inc. Pres. San Francisco Hosp. Conf., 1946-48; cons. hosp. adminstrn. Cal. Dept. Health, 1944-52; adv. com Fed. Hosp. Council, 1947-50, mem., 1950-53; mem. civilian adv. com. Dept. Def., 1953-61. Chmn. bd. Irwin Meml. Blood Bank; dir. Inst. Municipal Hosp. Execs., Municipal Hosp. Execs. Conf.; gov. Greater N.Y. Hosp. Assn. Corporator, Bentley Coll. Served as 1st lt. U.S. Army Res.; surgeon USPHS Res. Diplomate Am. Bd. Preventive Medicine and Pub. Health. Fellow Am. Pub. Health Assn., Am. Coll. Hosp. Adminstrs.; mem. Am. Hosp. Assn. (pres. 1951-52), Internat. Hosp. Fedn., Soc. Med. Adminstrs., Cal., N.Y., Westchester acads., medicine, World, Am. med. assns., Am. Assn. Hosp. Cons. (pres. 1963-65), Am. Dietetic Assn. (adv. bd.), Greater Hosp. Assn. N.Y., Nat. Health and Retirememt Assn., Assn. Cal. Hosps., Assn. Western Hosps., Westchester Acad. Medicine, Hosp. Soc. N.Y., Phi Rho Sigma. Clubs: University (N.Y.C.); Presidents (U. Mich.). Mem. editorial bd., columnist Modern Hospital. Address: New Rochelle N.Y. Deceased.

ROUSE, LOUIS AUSTIN, mgmt. exec.; b. Lawton, Okla., Mar. 11, 1915; s. John Louis and Betty Elizabeth (Austin) R.; Asso. in Sci., Cameron State A. and M. Coll., 1936; m. Ethel Mac McKenzie, Aug. 13, 1935; children—Ronald Louis, Tyler Van, Louise Austin. Career govt. employee Gen. Admistrn., Dept. of Interior, 1936-37, R.R. Retirement Bd., 1937-42; adminstrv. analyst WPB, 1942-44, Dept. of Army, 1944-48; methods examiner Dept. of Def., 1948-52; asst. mgmt. officer Exec. Office of the Pres., 1952-58; fgn. service officer, after 1958; dir. Latin Am. programs Exec. Mgmt. Services, Inc., Arlington, Va., 1972-75; staff U.S. Operations Mission to Manila, P.I., ICA, 1958-60; pub. adminstrn. adviser to Latin Am., Agy. for Internat. Devel., after 1960. Baptist. Mason (Shriner). Home: Arlington, Va., Died May 13, 1975.

ROUSSEAU, THEODORE, museum curator; b. Freeport, L.I., N.Y., Oct. 8, 1912; s. Theodore Duncan and Marta (Fremery) R.; student Lycee Henry IV, 1923, Eton Coll., 1924-29; A.B. cum laude, Harvard, 1934, M.A., 1937; 2 certificats d'etudes superieures, Sorbonne, 1933. Instr. dept. fine arts Harvard, 1937, Harvard Travelling fellow, 1938-39; speaker French programs C.S. Monitor Radio, 1939-40; asst. curator paintings Nat. Gallery Art Washington, 1940-41; asst. curator paingtings Met. Museum Art, 1947, curator, 1948-68, vice dir., curator in chief, 1968-74. Pres. Spanish Institute, Inc. Served to lt. comdr. USNR, 1941-46; asst. naval attache, Lisbon and Madrid; art loot investigation of France, Spain, Germany, Austria for OSS, 1945-46, also service in Japan; lt. comdr. Res. Decorated Legion of Merit; chavalier Legion of Honor, chevalier de l'Ordre des Arts et Lettres (France); officer Order of Orange-Nassau (The Netherlands); Order Alfonso X el Sabio (Spain); knight officer Order Merit Republic Italy. Mem. Hispanic Soc. Am. (corr., trustee); corr. mem. Acad. San Fernando, Madrid. Clubs: Racquet and Tennis, Century (N.Y.C.); Metropolitan (Washington); Travellers (Paris, France). Author articles profl. jours., bulls. Home: New York City N.Y. Died Dec. 31, 1973.

ROUSSELOT, LOUIS M., surgeon; b. N.Y.C., 1902; M.D., Columbia, 1927, M.Sc. in Surgery, 1933, Med. Sci.D. in Surgery, 1934. Resident pathology Presbyn. Hosp., N.Y.C., 1927-28, intern surgery, 1923-30, asst. resident, resident surgery, 1933-34; resident surgery Babies Hosp., 1935-36; dir. surgery St. Vincent's Hosp. and Med. Center, N.Y.C., 1948-67; cons. surgery VA Hosps. in Bronx and Bklyn., St. Joseph's Hosp., Westchester, N.Y., Holy Name Hosp., Bergen Pines County Hosp., N.J., Beth Israel Hosp., N.Y.C., Phelps Meml. Hosp. Am., Misericordia Hosp., N.Y.C., Greenwich (Conn.) Hosp., 1948-68; prof. clin. surgery N.Y. U. Med. Sch., 1948; dep. asst. sec. def.health affairs, 1968-70, asst. sec. def. health and environmemt, 1970-71; spl. asst. to dir. Bur. Health Manpower Edn., NIH, 1971-73. Bd. govs. Am. Nat. Red Cross. Served to col., M.C., AUS, 1944-45; ETO. Decorated Legion of Honor (French), Legion or Merit, Knight Malta, Knights Holy Sepulchre Jerusalem. Diplomate Am. Bd. Surgery. Fellow A.C.S., Am. Surg. Assn.; mem. A.M.A., Soc. Univ. Surgeons, Am. Gas-troenterol. Assn., D.C. Med. Soc., Halsted Soc., N.Y. Acad. Sci., Soc. Surgery Alimentary Tract (founder). Home: Bethesda Md. Died Mar. 28, 1974.

ROUTH, JAMES (EDWARD), educator; b. Petersburg, Va., Jan. 1, 1879; s. James Edward and Sallie Harrison (Dunlop) R.; A.B., Johns Hopkins, 1900, Ph.D., 1905; m. Florence H. Fischer, May 30, 1917; children—James Edward, Conrad Fischer, Elizabeth Dunlop (Mrs. G. L. Trimble). Instructor in English, University of Texas, 1906-07, Washington University, St. Louis, 1907-10; assistant professor English, U. of Va., 1910-11; same, Tulane U., 1912-15, asso. prof., 1915-18; Lanier prof. English, Oglethorpe U., 1918-35; dean of dept. of literature and journalism, 1928-35; prof. English, Univ. System of Georgia, Atlanta Branch, 1935-50, prof. emeritus, from 1950, part time tchr., 1950-52; mem. faculty Johns Hopkins University, 4 summers between 1921 and 1926. Mem. Modern Language Assn. America, Phi Beta Kappa, Phi Kappa Psi. Author or co-author books relating to field; contbr. to learned jours. Home: Atlanta, Ga.*†

ROVELSTAD, A(DOLPH) M(ARIUS), educator; b. Elgin, Ill., June 15, 1881; s. Andrew and Inge Marthea (Korsmo) R.; A.B., St. Olaf Coll., 1903; A.M., U. of Mich., 1906, Ph.D., 1921; Buhl Classical Fellow, 1905-06, summer, 1920; University fellow, 1914-15; m. Blanche I. Wollan, Aug. 18, 1908; children—Helen D. (Mrs. Helen R. Grande), Robert W., Homer D. Principal high sch., Glenwood, Minn., 1903-05; head Greek dept. Luther Coll., Decorah, Ia., 1907-10, head Latin dept., 1910-27; classical Mediterranean cruise (with bur. of univ. travel), summer 1912; head Latin dept. St. Olaf Coll., 1927-30; prof. Latin, U. of N.D., 1930-45; prof. classical lang. and head dept., U. of N.D., from 19445. Advisor Lutheran Student Assn., U. of N.D.; mem. Edward W. Hazen Foundation, Am. Philol. Assn., Archeol. Inst. Am., Am. Classical League, Classical Assn. of Middle West and South (exec. com. 1927-30, chmn. for state of North Dakota from 1932), Am. Assn. U. Profs., N.E.A., N.D. Education Assn. Republican. Lutheran. Club: Fortnightly, Franklin (Grand Forks, N.D.). Contbr. to classical and other ednl. periodicals. Home: Grand Forks, N.D.†

ROW, EDGAR CHARLES, motor exec.; b. St. Mary's O., Jan. 10, 1896; s. Carlton and Edith (Stephan) R.; student Valparaiso U., 1914; m. Ann M. Miller, Mar. 27, 1920; 1 dau., Marjorie Ann. With planning dept., purchasing dept., later sales and mfg. Dodge Bros., Detroit, 1916-32; gen. mgr. Anniston (Ala.) Ordnance Depot, 1943-45; joined Chrysler Corp., Detroit, 1932, dir. operations export div., 1941; asst. to pres. Chrysler Corp. Can., Ltd., Windsor, Ont., 1945-46, v.p., gen. mgr., 1946-51, president, 1951-56; pres. Chrysler Export Div., 1956; mem. bd.; adminstrv. v.p. Chrysler Corporation, 1956-58, 1st v.p., mem. bd., 1958-61. Director of Polymer Corp., Ltd. Vice President Canadian Indsl. Def. Preparedness Assn. Served as 2d lt., 329th Machine Gun Bn., U.S. Army, France, World War I. Mem. Newcomen Soc. Clubs: Windsor Yacht (Windsor); Detroit Athletic, Grosse Pointe Yacht, Recess, Economic, Beach Grove Golf; Essex Golf and Country (Windsor). Home: Detroit Mich. Died Nov. 1973.

ROWAN, HUGH WILLIAMSON, army officer; b. Newport, R.I., Mar. 16, 1894; s. Hamilton and Elizabeth Hamilton (Simpson) R.; Ph.B., Yale, 1915; student Harvard, 1915-17; grad. Chemical Corps Sch., 1921, Army Industrial Coll., 1925; m. Frances Bethel, June 28, 1928; children—Frances, Hamilton. Commd. 2d lt., U.S. Army, 1917, and advanced through the grades to brig. gen., 1944; served as div. chemical officer, 89th Div., A.E.F., 1918-19; resigned from military service, 1919; chemist, Tide Water Oil Co., Bayonne, N.J., 1919-20; with Chemical Corps, U.S. Army, since Oct. 1920; served in European Theater Operations, U.S. Army, 1942-45, chief chem. warfare officer, Hdqrs., 1942-45; reverted to grade of Col., 1946, serving as pres. The Chemical Corps Board Army Chemical Center. Maryland; became brigadier gen. and retired in 1953. Pres. Shore Owners Assn. Lake Placid, N.Y., from 1963. Decorated Legion of Merit. Bronze Star, Army Commendation Ribbon, Comdr. British Empire, Chevalier, Legion d'Honneur, Croix de Guerre (2 palms). Me. Am. Chem. Soc. Clubs: Army and Navy (Washington); Chevy Chase (Md.); Lake Placid (N.Y.). Author of several textbooks of Chem. Corps Sch., Army Chem. Center, Md. Home: Chevy Chase Md. Died May 7, 1973.

ROWE, JOHN LEROY, educator; b. Oconomowoc, Wis., May 18, 1914; s. Alfred A. and Abbie (Erickson R.; B.Ed., Wis. State U., 1935; M.A., U. Ia., 1939; Ed.D., Columbia U., 1946. Asso. prof. bus. edn., head bus. dept. Boston U., 1945-48; asso. prof. edn. Columbia U. Teacher's Coll., 1948-52; prof. bus. edn. No. Ill. U., 1952-55; prof. bus. edn. dept., chmn. U. N.D. from 1955, Chester Fritz distinguished prof. from 1973. Mem. Gov. N.D. Commn. for Crippled Children, 1967-70; apptd. N.D. Bicentennial Commn., 1968. Regent

Mary Coll. Mem. Am. Vocational Assn. (v.p. 1971), Catholic Bus. Edn. Assn. (pres. Midwest unit 1967), Nat. Assn. for Bus. Teacher Edn. (pres. 1957-58), Delta Pi Epsilon, Phi Delta Kappa, Kappa Delta Pi, Pi Omega Pi, Sigma Tau Delta. Democrat. Roman Catholic. Author (with others) Typewriting 75, Basic Typewriting 75, Advanced Typewriting 75, Expert and Typewriting 75, Profl. Coll. Series, 1970; (with Lloyd and Winger) Gregg Typing 191 Series: General Typing, Vocational Office Typing, High School, 1964, Typing 300, 1972; (with others) Typewriting Drills for Speed and Accuracy, 1966. Home: Grand Forks, N.D. Died Sept. 21, 1975; interred St. Catherine's Cemetery, Mapleton, Wis.

ROWE, THEODORE SPURLING, rubber co. exec.; b. Brewer, Me., Feb. 22, 1902; s. Herbert Warren and Blanche Eva (Spurling) R.; B.S., U. Me., 1926; m. Carolin Wilhelmina Boehm, June 30, 1931; 1 dau., Julie Ann (Mrs. Scott Thomas Schueneman). Sales engr. Atlantic Precision Instrument Co., Boston, 1926-27; product sales mgr. B.F. Goodrich Co., Akron, O., 1927-39; v.p. Samuel Moore & Co., Mantua, O., 1939-43; pres. dir. Hamilton Kent Mfg. Co., Kent, O., 1943-68, chmn. bd., 1968-73; pres., dir. Hamilton Kent of Can., Cooksville, Ont., 1954-68, chmn. bd., 1968-73; pres., dir. Hamilton Kent of Ga., Stone Mountain, 1962-68, chmn. bd., 1968-73; pres., dir. Hamilton Kent of Mo., Kansas City, 1965-68, chmn. bd., 1968-73; pres., dir. Flexlock Corp., Kent, 1952-68, chmn. bd., 1969-73; pres., dir. Freeport Rubber Co., Ltd. (Bahamas), 1959-68, chmn. bd., 1968. Mem. Franklin Bd. Edn., Kent, 1948-51, pres., 1950; chmn. Franklin Twp. Zoning Bd., 1953-62; dist. chmn. Boy Scouts Am., 1955-56. Trustee Henrietta Hamilton Found., Porthouse Found., Hattie Larlham Found., Mantua, Ohio. Mem. Am. Soc. Testing and Materials, Am. Concrete Pine Assn., Rubber Mfrs. Assn., C. of C. (dir. 1956-58), Phi Kappa Sigma (grand officer from 1961). Rotarian (pres. 1952-53). Clubs: Twin Lakes Country (dir. 1947); University (Akron). Home: Kent, O. Died July 1973.

ROWELL, HENRY THOMPSON, univ. prof.; b. Stamford, Conn., Mar. 12, 1904; s. Edward Everett and Ruth (Thompson) R.; A.B., Yale, 1926, Ph.D., 1933; Litt.D. (hon.) U. of South, 1958; m. Tanja Ramm, Feb. 21, 1931; children—Louisa (Mrs. Bruce R. Stark), Margit-Ruth. Instr. classics, Yale, 1931-35, asst. prof. Latin, 1935-40; prof. Latin, John Hopkins, from 1940, chmn., dept. classics, from 1946; dir. summer sessions, Am. Acad. Rome, 1937-39, 47-48, 50-51, prof.-in-charge Sch. Classical Studies, 1961-63; sic. asst. excavations Dura-Europos, Syria, 1929-31; vis. dept. classics Harvard, from 1965. Trustee, Am. Acad., Rome, from 1946, also 2d v.p. Served Corps Mil. Police, AUS, advancing from maj. to lt. col., Mediterranean, S.W. and Middle Pacific theaters, 1942-45; chief, edn. sub-commn., Allied Commn. for Italy; with G-3, Philippine Civil Affairs Detachment. Awarded Philippine Liberation medal, 5 battle stars; decorated Cavaliere Ufficiale della Corona d'Italia. Del. Am. Council Learned Socs., 1953-55. Mem. Archaeol. Inst. Am. (pres., 1953-56), German Archaeol. Inst. (corr.), Assn. Internat. d'Archeologie Classique (exec. com. 1961-63), Am. Philol. Assn., Soc. Promotion Roman Studies, Classical Assn. Atlantic States. Clubs: Yale (N.Y. City); 14 West Hamilton St. (Baltimore). Author: Rome in the Augustan Age, 1962. Editor American Jour. Philol., from 1940, editor-in-chief, from 1946; editor and revisor of Daily Life in Ancient Rome book, 1940. Contbr. articles on Roman army and Latin lit. to ednl. and professional periodicals. Home: Baltimore Md. Died Feb. 4, 1974.

ROWLAND, ROGER WHITTAKER, refractories mfr.; b. Springfield, Mass., Feb. 4, 1895; s. Sleigh and Celia (Mellaly) R.; B.S., Pa. State Coll., 1917, C.E., 1945; m. Atlana B. Willis, Aug. 30, 1922; children—Roger W., Natalie W. (Mrs. Harold D. Lehr). Various engring. positions steel industry, natural gas, pub. utilities, 1919-29, ceramics, 1929-69; pres. New Castle Refractories Co., Corundite Refactories, Inc.; chmn., dir. Pa. Mfrs. Assn. Casualty Ins. Co., Pa. Mfgrs. Assn. Fire Ins. Co. dir., exec. com. Joseph Dixon Co.; vice chmn., dir. First Nat. Bank, New Castle, Pa.; dir. Union Trust Co., Swindell Dressler Co. Mem. Pa. Republican State Exec. Com., del. Rep. Nat. Convs. Sec. property and supplies Commonwealth of Pa., 1939-41. Pres., dir. James Meml. Hosp.; v.p., trustee Pa. State U. 1939-63, pres. bd. of trustees, 1963-70, pres. emeritus, 1970-74. Served with the First Pursuit Group, AEF, World War I. Fellow Am. Ceramic Soc.; mem. Western Pa. Engrs. Soc., Pa. Profl. Engrs. Soc., Am. Soc. M.E., Am. Iron and Steel Inst. Presbyn. (trustee). Clubs: Union League (Phila); Duquesne (Pitts.); New Castle Country. Home: New Castle, Pa. Died Apr. 14, 1974; interred New Castle, Pa.

ROWNTREE, JENNIE, educator; b. Rochester, Wis., June 9. 1890; d. George W. and Clara (Leaxley) Rowntree; student Milw. Downer Coll., 1908-10; B.S., U. Wis., 1918; M.S., U. Chgo., 1925; Ph.D., State U. Ia., 1929. Instr. U. Toronto, 1918-19, Milw. Downer Coll., 1920-22. asst. prof. home econs., 1922-24, U. Wash., 1925-32, asso. prof., 1930-32, prof. from 1932, dir. sch. home econs. from 1945; tech. asst. FAO of United States in Cairo, Egypt, 1956. Mem. Am. Inst. Nutrition, Am. Dietetics Assn., Am. Home Econs. Assn., Sigma Xi, Conglist. Author: Handbook of Child Guidance, 1931; Nutrition Guide for Home Front, 1941. Contbr. to Jour. of Nutrition and popular publs. Home: Seattle, Wash. Died June 21, 1974.

ROY, JAMES EVANS, psychiatrist; b. Campbellton, N.B., Can.; s. Thomas Sherrard and Mary (Evans) R.; M.D., Harvard, 1939; m. Virginia Zepp, Feb. 12, 1938; children—Thomas Sherrard II, James Evans, David Truslow; m. 2d, Ruth M. Drake, Mar. 4, 1972. Intern, Newton (Mass.) Hosp., 1939-40; house officer Boston Psychopath. Hosp., 1940-41, jr. physician, 1941-42, sr. physician, 1942-45; practice medicine, specializing in psychiatry, 1949-74; clin. dir. Vt. State Hosp., 1945-57; chief neuropsychiatry Worcester Meml. Hosp., 1970-73, cons. psychiatrist, 1973-74. Asst. prof. psychiatry U. Vt., 1945-57. Diplomate Am. Bd. Psychiatry and Neurology. Mem. A.M.A., Am. Psychiat. Assn., New Eng. Soc. Psychiatry. Mason. Home: Worcester, Mass., Died Jan. 28, 1974; buried Campbellton, N.B., Canada.

ROYSTER, SALIBELLE, author; b. Smith Mills, Ky., Aug. 7, 1895; d. Levin Clarke nnd Sallie Belle (Martin) Royster; A.B., Evansville Coll., 1924, M.A., 1926; M.A., Columbia, 1938; postgrad. U. Chgo., 1930, U. Cambridge, 1936. Tchr. English Reitz High Sch., Evansville, Ind., 1924-40, head English dept., 1940-62; lectr. English U. Evansville (Ind.), 1962-69. Recipient 2d award Nat. League Am. Pen Women, 1968. Mem. Am. Assn. U. Women, D.A.R., Nat. League Am. Pen Women (v.p. elect So. Ind. br. 1972-74), Tyro Press Club (pres. 1972), Pi Lambda Theta. Club: Musicians (Evansville). Author: Skyway to Poetry, 1966; Realms of Gold, 1974. Editor: Cliffs Notes, 1962-66. Contbr. articles to profl. jours. Home: Evansville, Ind. Died May 3, 1975; interred Smith Mills, Ky.

ROZMAREK, CHARLES, hon. pres. Polish Nat. Alliance & Polish Am. Congress, Inc.; b. Wilkes-Barre, Pa., July 25, 1897; s. John and Magdalina (Chybki) R.; A.B., U. Pa., 1922; student Harvard Law School, 1925; LL.B., Boston U., 1927; m. Wanda Blinstrub, June 24, 1928; children—Elaine Regina, Marilyn Teresa. Admitted to Pa. bar, 1928; solicitor for Larksville, Pa., 1930-33, Pringle, Pa. 1933-35; dep. atty. gen. Pa., 1935-37; mercantile appraiser of Luzerne County, Pa., 1937-39; pres. Polish Nat. Alliance, 1939-67, hon. pres., 1967-73; pres. Polish Am. Congress, 1944-68, hon. pres., 1968-73; pres. Alliance Printers and Pubs., 1939-67. Del. at large from Ill. to Nat. Democratic Conv., 1944. Vice pres. bd. dirs. Alliance Coll., 1939-67. Mem. Chgo., Ill. bar assns. Home: Chicago Ill. Died Aug. 5, 1973.

RUBEY, WILLIAM WALDEN, geologist; b. Moberly, Mo., Dec. 19, 1898; s. Ambrose Burnside and Alva Beatrice (Walden) R.; A.B., U. of Mo. 1920, D.Sc., 1953; student Johns Hopkins, 1922, Yale, 1922-24, D.Sc., 1960; D.Sc., Villanova U. 1959; m. Susan Elsie Manovill, Nov. 27, 1919; children—Susie Lee Putnam (Mrs. Edwin Randolph Middleton, dec.), Jean Manovill (Mrs. Francis Joseph Eisenman, Jr.), Elizabeth Walden (Mrs. Thomas A. Dean). Asst. valuation engr., Johnson Huntley, Pittsburgh, Pa., 1920; geologic aid, United States Geol. Survey, 1920-21; asst. geologist, 1921-22; instr, in geology, Yale, 1922-24; with U.S. Geol. Survey, 1924-60, successively asso. geologist, geologist, sr. geologist, prin. geologist, geologist in charge div. area geology and basic scis., staff geologist, research geologist; guest scientist Inst. Geophysics U. Cal. Los Angeles, 1954, prof. geology and geophysics, 1960-69, then prof. emeritus geology and geophysics; vis. prof. geology Cal. Tech., 1955. Johns Hopkins, 1956; Silliman lectr. Yale, 1960. Mem. com. on geo-physics and geog. Research and Devel. Bd., 1947-50; com. math., physics, engring. sci. Nat. Sci. Found., 1951-53; dir., v.p. Am. Geol. Inst., 1950-51, 58-59; mem. Nat. Sci. Bd. from 1960. Recipient Award of Excellence, U.S. Dept. of Interior, 1943. Distinguished Service award, 1958. Mem. Nat. Acad. Scis., Am. Philos. Soc. (council 1956-59), Am. Acad. Arts and Scis., Acad. Med. Wash.; A.A.A.S. (dir), Am. Assn. Petroleum Geologists, Am. Geophys. Union, Geol. Soc. Washington (pres. 1948), Washington Acad. Sci. (pres. 1957), Geol. Soc. Am. (councilor 1941-43, v.p., 1948-49, pres., 1949-50), Seismol. Soc. Am., Geochem. Soc. (dir. 1955-57), Am. Ornithologists Union, Phi Beta Kappa, Sigme Xi, Sig,a Gamma Epsilon, Phi Gamma Delta Club: Cosmos (Washington). Author govt. reports and tech. articles in sci. jours. Home: Pacific Palisades, Cal. Died Apr. 12, 1974.

RUBIN, REUVEN, artist; b. Galatz, Rumania, Nov. 13, 1893; s. Joel and Fany (Rabinowitz) R.; student Ecole des Beaux Arts and Academie Colarossi, Paris, 1913-14; LL.D., Jewish Inst. Religion, N.Y.C., 1945; m. Esther Davis, Mar. 16, 1930; children—Daivd J., Ariella. One-man shows Anderson Galleries, N.Y.C., 1920, Studio Grivitzi, Bucharest, 1922, Tower of David, Jerusalem, 1924, Bernheim Gallery, Paris, 1925, Tel Aviv, 1927, Druet Gallery, Paris, 1928, New Gallery, N.Y.C., 1928, Arthur Tooth Gallery, London, 1930, Bezalel Mus., Jerusalem, 1936, Milch Gallery, N.Y.C., 1940, Retrospective, Wildenstein, N.Y., 1962; exhibited in group shows Artists Orgn., Jerusalem, 1926, San Antonio Mus., 1945, Mus. Modern Art, 1942, Musee Nat. d'Art Moderne, 1960, Met. Mus., N.Y.C., 1952, Inst. Contemporary Art, Boston Nashville Museum; represented in permanent collection Mus. Modern Art, N.Y.C., N.Y. Jewish Mus., N.Y.C., Los Angeles Mus., Princeton Mus., San Antonio Mus., Musee d'Art Moderne, Paris, Newark Mus., Manchester (Eng.) Mus., Melbourne Mus., Israel Mus., Tel Aviv Mus., Mus. of Vatican, Rome, others; Israeli minister to Rumania, 1949-50. Pres., Israel-Rumania Friendship League, 1967—. Recipient Plumer prize, prize City Tel Aviv for life's artistic achievement, 1964; Israel Prize Art Laureate, 1973. Rotarian (founder). Author: The Godseekers, woodcuts, 1912; Visages d'Israel, 1960; Rubin-My Life, My Art, 1969; The Story of King David (Lithographs), 1970; Visions of the Bible (introduction by D. Ben Gurion), 1972; The Prophets (introduction by Dr. Haim Gamzu), 1973. Home: Tel Aviv, Israel. Died Oct. 13, 1974; buried Tel Aviv (Israel) Old Cemetery.

RUBINOWICZ, WOJCIECH, physicist; b. Sadagóra, Bukowina, Austria, Feb. 22, 1889; s. Damian and Malgorzata (Brodowska) R.; Ph.D., Czernowitz U., 1914, venia legendi, 1918; Dr. honoris causa, Humboldt U., Berlin, 1960, Jagiellonian U., Cracow, 1964, Wroclaw U., 1970; m. Elzbieta Norst, July 21, 1921; 1 son, Jan. Asst., Czernowitz U., 1912-17, docent, 1918-20; asst. to Sommerfeld, Munich U., 1917-18; prof. Ljubljana U., 1920-22, Lwow Poly. U., 1922, Lwow U.,1937, Warsaw U., 1946-60. Recipient State Sci. prize 1st class, 1951, Marian Smoluchowski medal Polish Phys. Soc., 1968, Order of Labour 1st class, 1969, etc. Mem. Polish Acad. Scis., Internat. Union Theoretical and Applied Mechanics, Polish Phys. Soc. (pres.), Phys. Inst. Polish Acad. Scis. (chmn. sci. adv. bd.), Math. Soc. Author: Die Beugungswelle in der Kirchhoffschen Theorie der Beugung, 1957, rev. edit., 1966; Quantum Mechanics, 1968; Vectors and Tensors, 1950; (with W. Krollkowski) Theoretical Mechanics, 1955, 64, 67, 72, Quantum Theory of Atom, 1954, rev. edit., 1957. Pioneer work in selection and polarization rules for electric dipole radiation, 1918, electric quadrupole radiation theory, 1930, equivalence of Young's and Fresnel's views in Kirchhoff's diffraction theory, 1917. Home: Warsaw, Poland., Died Oct. 13, 1974.

RUBSAMEN, WALTER HOWARD, educator, musicologist; b. N.Y.C., July 21, 1911; s. Charles Adolf and Pauline (Beutenmueller) R.; A.B., Columbia, 1933; Ph.D., U. Munich (Germany), 1937; m. Gisela Roth, May 2, 1955; children—Valerie, Glen, Hope (Mrs. Rudolph Platzek), Eric. Mem. faculty U. Cal. at Los Angeles, 1938, prof. music, 1955-73, chmn. dept., 1965-73, chmn. faculty, 1968-70; vis. prof. U. Berne (Switzerland), 1957-58, U. Chgo., summer 1947, Columbia, summers 1950, 57; lectr. univs. Munich, Heidelberg (Germany), Turin, Milan, Rome and Venice (all Italy), U. Basel (Switzerland). Guggenheim fellow, 1947, 57; Ford Found. fellow, 1955; grantee Am. Council Learned Socs., 1963. Am. Philos. Soc., 1946. Mem. Am., Internat. musicol. socs., Gesellshaft für Musikforschung, Soc. Italiana di Musicologia, Dante Alighieri Soc. So. Cal. (pres. 1969-70). Author: Literary Sources of Secular Music in Italy, 1943; Music Research in Italian Libraries, 1951; (with others) Chanson and Madrigal, 1480-1530, 1964; also articles. Home: Los Angeles Ca. Died June 1973.

RUBY, HARRY, composer; b. N.Y. City, Jan. 27, 1895; s. Barnett and Tillie Rubinstein; ed. N.Y. City pub. schs. and Comml. High Sch., 1907-10; m. Dorothy Herman, 1915; 1 dau., Toby (Mrs. Gerard Oestreicher); m. 2d, Cleo Carter, 1931; m. 3d, Eileen Percy, May 2, 1936. Began as song plugger, 1913. Composer (lyrics by Bert Kalmer), My Sunny Tennessee, I Love You So Much, I Wanna Be Loved By You, Thinking of You, Up in the Clouds, Three Little Words, Nevertheless; composer (plays); The Ramblers. Five O' Clock Girl, Good Boy, Animal Crakers, Top Speed, etc.; composer music and co-author with Bert Kalmer (motion pictures): The Cuckoos, Horsefeathers, Duck Soup, Kid from Spain, Bright Lights, etc.; (Broadway show) High Kickers. Author: Kalmer & Ruby Song Book, 1936; (words and music) Songs My Mother Never Sang, 1943. Personal life partial source of movie Three Little Words, 1950. Address: Beverly Hills CA. Died Feb. 23, 1974.

RUDE, JOE CHRISTOPHER, physician; b. Granite, Okla., Oct 27, 1905; s. Joe Christopher and Ella Nancy (Lowder) R.; B.A., U. Okla., 1926, B.S., 1928, M.D., 1930; m. Eleanor Wallenfelo, May 5, 1934; children—Eleanor Jo, Franklin J., Elizabeth Carolyn, Joe Christopher II Intern, Parkland Hosp., Dallas, 1930-31; asst. resident radiology U. Mich., 1933-34; resident radiology N.Y. Hosp. and Cornell Med. Center, 1935-38; Littauer Fellow in radiology Harvard, 1938-39; also asst. roentgenologist C.P. Huntington Meml. Hosp., Boston, 1938-39; instr. radiology U. Tex., Galveston, 1940, chief dept., prof. radiology, 1949-53; instr. Duke, 1941-42; radiologist Brackenridge Hosp., Austin, Tex., from 1953; cons. radiology Bergstrom AFB; nat. cons. to Office Surgeon Gen., 1955-58, Austin State Hosp., from 1953; hon. cons. 2d Air Force Stratrgic Air Command. Mem. Teletherapy Evaluation Bd., Oak Ridge, 1950-53. Col., M.C., U.S. Army Res. Diplomate Am. Bd. Radiology. and Nuclear Medicine. Fellow Am. Coll. Radiology; mem. Aerospace Med. Assn., Radiol. Soc. N.Am., A.M.A., Tex., Travis County med. socs. Home: Austin, TX. Died Sept. 7, 1974.

RUDERMAN, JAMES, skyscraper designer. Designer numerous bldgs., including churches, sch. bldgs., apt. bldgs., theatres, hosps., factories, banks and hotels;

devel. use of existing street-level constrn. on which to erect new structures; projects include Pan-Am. bldg., Park Av., N.Y.C., Chem. N.Y. Trust, Bankers Trust, Colgate-Palmolive, Mfrs., Hanover, Internat. Tel. & Tel. bldgs., numerous others Park Av., N.Y.C., also 32-story apt. house, Glasgow, Scotland. Home: New York City, N.Y., Died Jan. 1966.

RUDOLPH, HERMAN LOUIS, physician; b. Reading, Pa., Mar. 20, 1909; s. Jacob and Jennie (Mazor) R.; U.S., magna cum laude, Albright Coll., 1931; m.D., Jefferson Med. Coll., Phila., 1935; m. Esther Soskin, May 28, 1939; children—Ross, Robert I., Lawrence L. Intern Morrisania City Hosp., N.Y.C., 1934; rotarint intern St. Joseph's Hosp., Reading, 1935-36 asso. medicine, 1936-59, chief dept. phys. medicine and rehab., 1942-59; cons. phys. medicine and rehab. Valley Forge Army Hosp., 1948-49; v.p. staff Community Gen. Hosp., Reading, 1965, pres. med. staff, 1966, chief dept. phys. medicine and rehab., 1950; med. dir. Berks County Cerebral Palsy Treatment Center, 1949-66; cons. phys. medicine and rehab. VA Hosp., Lebanon, Pa., 1947-66, Berkshelm County Hosp., 1954-56, VA Hosp., Martinsburg, W.Va., 1962-66; area cons. VA, 1960-66; cons. amputee clinic Bur. Vocational Rehab., also Reading Hosp., 1961-66; asst. prof. phys. medicine and rehab. Jefferson Hosp. and Med. Sch., 1947—. Mem. comn. phys. medicine and rehab. Pa. Med. Soc., 1947-60; mem. med. adv. com. Pa. Soc. Crippled Children and Adults, 1950-60, Berks County Arthritis and Rheumatism Found., 1950-60; pres. Berks County Med.-Dental Bur., 1960; mem. Berks County Sr. Citizens Council, 1965-75, sheltered workshop com. United Community Services, 1965-66; Jewish Community Center, Reading, 1946-75; rep. mayor Reading to President's Com. Employment Physically Handicapped, 1960. Served to maj., M.C., AUS, 1942-46. Recipient Alumni citation Albright Coll., 1953; named Pa. Physician of Year, Gov. Com. Employment Handicapped, 1965. Diplomate Am. Bd. Phys. Medicine and Rehab. Mem. Am., Pa., Berks County (chmn. com. phys. medicine and rehab. 1965, com. cerebral palsy 1949-75) med. assns., Am. (pres. 1964-65), Pa. (past pres., sec.) acads. phys. medicine and rehab., Phila. Soc. Phys. Medicine and Rehab., Am. Congress Phys. Medicine and Rehab. (past pres., sec. Eastern sect.), Am., Phila. rheumatism socs., Am. Acad. Cerebral Palsy, Berks County Heart Assn. (bd. dirs.), Nat. Rehab. Assn., Alpha Omega Alpha, Phi Delta Epsilon. Club: Berkleigh County (past bd. govs.) (Kutztown, Pa.). Author articles in field. Address: Reading, Pa., Died 1975.

RUEDEMANN, ALBERT DARWIN, ophthalmologist; b. Albany, N.Y., Sept. 26, 1897; s. Rudolph and Elizabeth (Heitmann) R.; M.D., U. Mich., 1921; m. Nancy Lindstron, Aug. 30, 1923; children—Albert Darwin, Paul, Nancy Lee (Mrs. Michael Furbush), Resident, also instr. ophthalmology U. Mich., 1921-24; practice medicine, specializing in ophthalmology, 1926-71; chief staff ophthalmology Cleve. Clinc, 1924-27, Harper Hosp., Detroit, 1947-63; chief ophthalmologist Detroit Receiving Hosp., 1947-64, cons., 1964-71; dir., pres. Kresge Eye Inst., Detroit, 1948-68; cons. ophthalmology St. Luke's Hosp., Cleve., 1927-48, Crile Gen. Hosp., Cleve., 1943-47, Herman Kiefer Hosp., Detroit, 1947-71, Detroit VA Hosp., 1947-71, Mt. Sinai Hosp., Detroit, 1952-71, Detroit Meml. Hosp., 1952-71. Prof. ophthalmology Wayne State U., 1947-68, prof. emeritus, 1968-71. Diplomate Am. Bd. Ophthalmology. Fellow Internat. Coll. Surgeons (hon.), A.C.S.; mem. Am. Acad. Ophthalmology and Otolaryngology (pres.), A.M.A. (chmn. ophthalmology sect. 1956), Am. Soc. Ophthal. and Otolary. Allergy (pres. 1956),Am. Ophthal. Soc., Assn. Research in Ophthalmology, Pan Am. Assn. Ophthalmology, Nat. Soc. Prevention Blindness, Mexican Soc. Ophthalmology, Sigma Xi, Alpha Omega Alpha. Home: Detroit, Mich., Died Dec. 30, 1971.

RUGEN, MYRTLE LOUISE, ednl. adminstr.; b. Chgo., Dec. 3, 1904; d. August H. and Louise (Huebner) Rugen; Ph.B., U. Chgo., 1934, M.A., 1938; postgrad. Northwestern U., No. Ill. U., 1925, Nat. Coll. Edn. Tchr. one room country sch., Mount Prospect, Ill., 1924-30, country sch., Northbrook, Ill., 1930-36, Glenview Pub. Schs., 1936-51; adminstr., prin. Westbrook Sch., Glenview, Ill., 1951-55; prin. Glenview (Ill.) Jr. High Sch., 1955-68. Mem. Glenview (Ill.) Health Council. Mem. Ill. Glenview edn. assns., League Women Voters, Glenview Hist. Soc., Delta Kappa Gamma. Mem. Ch. of Christ. Home: Northbrook IL. Died Sept. 4, 1971.

RUHEMANN, HELMUT, picture restorer; b. Berlin, Germany, May 8, 1891; s. Hugo and Rose (Bodlaender) R.; student Art Acad. Karlsruhe, 1908-09, Art Acad. Munich, 1910-11, Acad. Julien, Paris, 1912-13; m. Anna Berta Pfuetzner, 1926; children-Frank, Rainer. Artist, Berlin, also Madrid, Spain, 1911-20; free lance picture restorer, Berlin, 1920-29; curator, chief restorer State Galleries, Berlin, 1929-33; free lance restoring Nat. Gallery, London, others from 1934; lectr. Courtauld Inst. Art, London U., from 1935, lectr-in-charge tech. dept., 1946-51; cons. restorer Nat. Gallery, London, 1946-53, engaged in training restorers from 1946; lectr. picture restoration and masters' techniques, detection of forgeries, Europe and U.S. from 1935; one-man UNESCO mission to Guatemala, 1956. Decorated comdr. Brit. Empire. Founding fellow Internat. Inst. for Conservation Historic and Artistic Works. Author: Artist and Craftsman, 1948; (with Ellen Kemp) The Artist at Work, 1951. Co-editor: La Conservation des Peintures, 1938; The Cleaning of Paintings: Problems and Potentialities, 1968. Home: London NW 8, England. Died May 3, 1973; cremated.

RUHOFF, JOHN RICHARD, chem. co. exec.; b. DePue, Ill., June 29, 1908; s. Otto E. and Alice (Spensley) R.; B.S., U. Wis., 1929; Ph.D., Johns Hopkins, 1932; m. Mary Bridges, Aug. 25, 1934; children—Anne Bridges (Mrs. David Rippy), Mary Spensley (Mrs. George Harrington). Fellow Johns Hopkins, 1932-33; research asst. Harvard, 1933-35; research chemist U.S. Rubber Co., 1935-37; with Mallinckrodt Chem. Works, 1937-42, from 1946, v.p. from 1950, also dir. Served to lt. col. Manhattan Dist., AUS, 1942-46. Mem. Am. Inst. Chem. Engrs., Am. Chem. Soc., Sigma Xi, Phi Lambda Upsilon. Alpha Chi Sigma. Home: Webster Groves, Mo. Died Sept. 7, 1973.

RUIZ, CORTINES ADOLFO, pres. of Mexico; b. Veracruz, Mexico, Dec. 30, 1891; s. Adolfo and Maria (Cortines) R.; Received edn. as accountant; m. Maria Izaguirre; 1 son, Adolfo, Chief Bur. of Statistics, 1932-35; chief clk. Fed. Dist. Govt., 1935-37; rep. in Nat. Congress, 1937-40; gov. State of Veracruz, 1944-47; sec. of interior in cabinet of Pres. Aleman, 1947-51; candidate of the Revolutionary Instns. Party for pres. of Mexico, Oct. 1951, pres., 1952-58. Home: Mexico City Mexico. Died Dec. 3, 1973.

RUMBLE, DOUGLAS, educator; b. Forsyth, Ga., Oct. 15, 1880; s. Woodbridge and Josephine (Richardson) R.; A.B., Emory Coll., 1904, A.M., 1907; A.M., Harvard, 1908; student U. of Chicago, summers 1909, 17, 19; m. Exa Woodruff, Sept. 5, 1910; children—Exa Wylene (Mrs. Wendell Jennison Whitcher), Douglas, Jr., John Cleveland. Adjunct prof. math. Emory Coll., 1905-07, asso. prof., 1910-14; asso. prof. math. Southwestern U., Tex., 1914-15, Emory U., 1915-18; prof. math. Emory U., 1918-49, chmn. dept., 1928-48; vis. prof. John B. Stetson U. from 1949. Member Math. Assn. of Am., Ga. Acad. Sci., Gamma chapter (Ga.) Phi Beta Kappa. Methodist. Democrat. Address: DeLand, Fla.†

RUNNELS, RICHARD STITT, household products mfg. exec.; b. Wabash, Ind., Dec. 19, 1923; s. William and Miriam (Stitt) R.; B.S., Ind. U., 1947; m. Josephine Cooley, Dec. 27, 1948; children—Richard S., Miriam Ann. With Proctor & Gamble Co., Cin., 1947-74, asso. comptroller, 1955-61, comptroller, 1961-67, v.p. finance, sec., 1967-74, v.p. toilet goods div., 1968-70, v.p. food products, 1970-72, v.p. adminstrv. services, 1972-74. Home: Cincinnati, O. Died Oct. 19, 1974; interred Corolla, N.C.

RUSH, MADELON REINE FRANCIS (MRS. ALAN SYDNEY RUSH), club woman; b. Long Branch, N.J.; d. Charles Asa and Helen (Lylburn) Francis; B.S. cum laude, Syracuse U., 1927; m. Alan Sydney Rush, Aug. 14, 1929 (dec. Apr. 1946); children—Alan Francis, William Asa. Legal Sec. Applegate, Stevens, Foster, Leonard and Reusille, Lawyers, Red Bank, N.J., 1928-29; parish sec. Holy Trinity Episcopal Ch., West Palm Beach, Fla., 1947-57, dir. pub. relations Hotel George Washington, 1961-62, asst. sec. Hotel Pa., 1962-63; asst. parish sec. Ch. Bethesda-by-the-Sea, Palm Beach, Fla., 1958-60. Fla. rec. sec. Am. Assn. U. Women, 1960-64, pres. Palm Beach County, 1965-67; sec. Fla. div. Nat. Secs. Assn., 1962-63. Dir. Community Services Council, West Palm Beach, Fla., 1951-52; sec. Palm Beach County Library Adv. Bd., 1965-68. Mem. Phi Kappa Phi, Gamma Epsilon Pi, Zeta Tau Alpha. Home: Palm Beach, Fla. Deceased.

RUSSELL, HORACE, lawyer; b. Puckett, Miss., Nov. 7, 1889; s. Virgil and Eleanor (Everitt) R.; A.B., Miss. Coll., 1912; LL.B., Cumberland U., 1916, LL.D., in 1952; D.C.L., U. of the South, 1937; m. Julia Myers, June 21, 1916; children—Horace (dec.), Philip Everitt, Elsie Jean (Mrs. Rogers P. Conant). Admitted to Ga. bar, 1916; practiced in Atlanta, 1916-32; gen. counsel Fed. Home Loan Bank Bd., Washington, 1932-38, gen. law practice in Chgo., from 1938; mem. firm Russell, Bridewell & Lapperre. Mem. Gen. Council, City of Atlanta, 1921-27. Fellow Am. Bar Found; mem. C. of C. (pres. 2 years), Southeastern Fair Assn. (past pres.), Family Welfare Soc. Atlanta (past pres.), Ga. Bldg. and Loan League (past pres.), Am., Ill., Chgo., Fed. (pres. 1937) bar assns., Kappa Sigma. Democrat. Methodist. Mason. Clubs: Skokie County (Glencoe, Ill.); Cosmos (Washington). Author: Savings and Loan Associations. Contbr. law jours. and encys. Home: Glencoe IL. Died Oct. 20, 1973.

RUSSELL, KENNETH SHERMAN, hosp. adminstr.; b. Grant County, Wis., Mar. 24, 1907; s. John W. and Mae Lina (Culver) R.; student Platteville (Wis.) Normal Sch., 1927; m. Sarah Butson, Jan. 1, 1930; 1 dau., Joyce Ann (Mrs. Donald Morman). Acting supt. Grant County Hosp., 1933-35; with Wis. State Prison, 1936-42, 44-46; mgr. dairy, 1942-44; supt. Sauk County, Wis., 1946-53; adminstr. Masonic Home and Hosp. for Ill., 1953-64, Racine County (Wis.) Instns., 1964-71; adminstr. Crawford Meml. Hosp., Robinson, Ill., 1971-73, Highland Hosp., Belvidere, Ill., 1973-74. Treas., No. Ill. Hosp. Services, Inc.; mem. ad-hoc com. Comprehensive Health Council, 1968; 1st v.p. Ill. Assn. Homes for Aging, 1960-64; treas. Racine County Alcoholic Council, 1966-68. Bd. dirs. No. Ill. Lung Assn.; bd. dirs., chmn. campaign United Givers Fund, Belvidere. Mem. Internat. Platform Assn. Methodist. Kiwanian (pres. 1951, 61), Mason. Contbr. articles to profl. jours. Home: Belvidere, Ill. Died Feb. 28, 1974; interred Whig Cemetery, Grant County, Wis.

RUSSELL, MELVIN GRAY, JR., Physician; b. Peniel, Tex., Aug. 7, 1922; s. Melvin Gray and Theo Kathleen (Stewart) R.; M.D., Southwestern Med. Sch., U. Tex., 1951; m. Elizabeth Jane Kemp, June 12, 1948; children—Thomas Kemp, Melvin David. Intern, Parkland Hosp., Dallas, 1951-52, vis. staff pediatrics, 1955-75; resident in pediatrics Childrens Med. Center, Dallas, 1952, chief resident in pediatrics, 1954, active staff, 1955-75; mem. active staff Methodist Hosp., Dallas; clin. asso. prof. pediatrics Southwestern Med. Sch. Past pres. Children's Inc., sch. for retarded children; mem. med. adv. bd. Dallas Council Retarded Children. Served with USNR, 1943-46. Recipient service awards Salvation Army, Children's Inc., Boy Scouts Am., Kiwanis Club, YMCA-YWCA. Diplomate Am. Bd. Pediatrics. Fellow Am. Acad. Pediatrics; mem. A.M.A., Tex., Dallas (past pres.) pediatric socs., So., Pan Am., Tex. med. assns., Dallas County Med. Soc., Dallas So. Clin. Soc., Dallas and Oak Cliff C. of C., Ex-Students Assn. U. Tex. (life), Phi Chi Kiwanian pres. Oak Cliff club). Home: Dallas, Tex. Died Mar. 31, 1974; buried Laurel Land Cemetery, Dallas, Tex.

RUSSELL, THOMAS WRIGHT, ins. exec.; b. Hartford, Conn., Sept. 1, 1880; s. Thomas W. and Ellen (Fuller) B.; grad. Yale, 1901; m. Dorothy Mason, Jan. 16, 1913; children—Dorothy (Mrs. Wiliam A. Chapman), Thomas Wright, Judith (Mrs. William N. Driscoll). Retired 1946; dir. Conn. Fire Ins. Co., Conn. Gen. Life Ins. Co., Emhart Mfg. Co., Hartford Nat. Bank & Trust Co., Phoenix Insurance Company, Stanley Works. Connecticut State fuel adminstr., World War I; dep. adminstr. Conn. State Def. Council, World War II; chairman Republican State Finance Committee, Connecticut. President Hartford Community Chest, 1932. Dir. Hartford Hosp. Mem. Phi Beta Kappa, Soc. Colonial Wars. Clubs: Links, Yale (N.Y. City); Graduate (New Haven), Country (Fishers Island, N.Y.) Home: Hartford, Conn.†

RUSSELL, WILLARD LORANE, lawyer; b. Hallettsville, Tex., Aug. 14, 1898; s. Henry Hamilton and Annie (Hemphill) R.; B.S., U. Tex., 1924; A.M., Baylor U., 1930; LL.B., South Tex. Sch. Law, 1933; LL.D., Tex. Wesleyan Coll., 1959, Howard Payne Coll., 1965; m. Stella Wolters, Dec. 24, 1928. Supt. pub. schs., Hallettsville, 1925-29; instr. Baylor U., 1930; admitted to Tex. bar, 1933, practiced in Houston; chmn. bd. Shiner Oil Mill & Mfg. Co. (Tex.); v.p., dir. So. Warehouse Corp.; owner, operator farm and ranch enterprises. Founder, donor Russell Found., religious, edn., charitable trust, 1948. Trustee U. St. Thomas, Houston, Baylor U., Waco, Tex., Baylor Med. Coll., Houston; bd. dirs. Houston St. and Newsboys Club, Lincoln Ednl. Found., N.Y. Mem. State Bar Tex., Am., Houston bar assns., Am. Judicature Soc., Ind. Rice Growers Assn. Baptist. Mason (Shriner), Odd Fellow, Rotarian. Clubs: Farm and Ranch, Torch (Houston); Knife and Fork (dir.). Author: Peace and Power Within, 1951; Invincible Forces, 1959; Belief and Respect, 1961; Belief and Human Worth, 1967; Peace and Power within the Individual and Among Our People, 1970. Contbr. articles to mags. Home: Houston TX. Died Nov. 22, 1974.

RUST, ADLAI H., ins. exec.; b. Bloomington, Ill., Apr. 16, 1892; s. Francis M. and Julia (Hollis) R.; LL.B., Ill. Wesleyan U., 1914, LL.D., 1957; m. Florence Barry, May 4, 1917; children—Edward B., Mary Lou (Mrs. Henry R. Schaefer); m. 2d, Margaret Marquis, Jan. 10, 1932; 1 son, Adlai M. Admitted to Ill. bar, 1914, and practiced at Bloomington, 1914-29; gen. counsel State Farm Ins. Cos., 1922-35; exec. v.p., dir. State Farm Mut. Automobile Ins. Co. 1935-54, pres. 1954-58, chmn., 1958, also dir.; chmn., dir. State Farm Life Ins. Co., 1951-70, State Farm Fire and Casualty Co., 1951-70. Mem. Am. Aberdeen Angus Breeders Assn. (past pres.), Nat. Assn. Ind. Insurors (past pres.), Am. Bar Assn., Phi Gamma Delta, Phi Delta Phi. Club: Union League (Chgo.). Home: Bloomington IL. Died Feb. 22, 1974.

RUSTAD, ELMER LEWIS, govt. ofcl.; b. Wakonda, S.D., Aug. 11, 1908; s. John and Hannah (Forsethlien) R.; B.A., Sioux Falls Coll., 1929; M.A., U. Minn., 1938; postgrad. U. So. Cal., 1939; m. Berniece E. Hillery, Aug. 8, 1932; children—Patricia (Mrs. Walter J. Herrmann, Jr.), Robert L. successively coach, prin., supt. Egan (S.D.) Consol. Schs., 1929-34; guidance dir., prin. Jr. High Schs., Aberdeen, S.D., 1934-41; state dir. U.S. Savs. Bonds div., S.D., 1941-52, asst. nat. dir., nat. sales mgr. U.S. Savs. Bonds div. U.S. Dept. of Treasury, Washington, 1952-69, nat. dir. U.S. Savs. Bond div., 1969-72. Served as lt. comdr. USNR, 1943-46. Mem. Am. Legion, YMCA. Baptist. Lion, Elk. Home: McLean, Va. Died July 29, 1975; inurned Nat. Cemetery, Falls Church, Va.

RUSZNYAK, ISTVAN, physician; b. Budapest, Hungary, Jan. 22, 1889; s. Samuel and Rosalie (Beer) R.; grad. Med. U., Budapest, 1911; m. Jolan Egri, Oct. 21, 1934; children—Eva, Maria (Mrs. Gabor Pulay), Martha. Asst., U. Budapest, Inst. Pathology, 1911-12, staff, dept. internal medicine, 1912-31, prof., dir. clinic internal medicine, 1946-63; prof., dir. clinic internal medicine U. Szeged (Hungary), 1931-46; pres. Hungarian Acad. Scis., Budapest, 1949-70, dir. research inst. exptl. medicine, 1960-70, sci. adviser inst. from 1970. M.P., 1945-67. Recipient Kossuth prize Hungarian Govt., 1949, 56; Gold medal Hungarian Acad. Scis., 1961; Lomonoszov Gold medal Acad. Scis. USSR, 1968. Mem. Bulgarian (corr.), USSR (fgn.), Czechoslovakian (regular fgn.), Polish (fgn.), Rumanian (hon.) acads. scis., German Acad. Scis. Berlin (corr.), Swiss Acad. Med. Scis. (corr.), Yugoslavian Acad. Scis. and Arts (Corr.), Societe Internationale de Medicine Interne, Union Internationale d'Angiologie (found. hon.), J.E. Purkyne Czechoslovak Med Soc., Brit. Med. Assn. (fgn. corr.), Internal. Soc. Lymphology (hon.). Author: (with others) Lymphatics and Lymph Circulation, Physiology and Pathology, 1960, 2d edit., 1967. Home: Budapest II, Hungary. Died Oct. 15, 1974.

RUTHERFORD, CHARLES HENRY, JR., lawyer; b. Nashville Tenn., Nov. 15, 1906; s. Charles H. and Ella Clyde (Wheeler) R.; B.A., Vanderbilt U., 1930, J.D., 1931; m. Alice Maude Martin, Aug. 8, 1962; children—Charles H. III, Miriam Austin, Robert Wheeler, Anne C., Linda C. Admitted to Tenn. Bar, 1930, practiced Nashville, from 1931. Mem. Am. Arbitration Assn., Delta Theta Phi. Presbyn. Democrat. Mason (Shriner), Kiwanian. Club: Nashville Torch. Contbr. articles in field to profl. jours. Home: Nashville TN. Died Jan 31, 1973.

RUTLEDGE, ARCHIBALD (HAMILTON), author; b. McClellanville, S.C., Oct. 23, 1883; s. Henry Middleton and Margaret (Seabrook) R.; Porter Acad., Charleston, S.C., 1898-1900; B.S., Union Coll., N.Y., 1904, A.M., 1907; married Florence L. Hart, December 19, 1907 (died 1934); m. 2d Alice Lucas, 1936. Author numerous books from 1909, The Everlasting Light, 1949. Made poet laureate of S.C. by legislation. Home: McClellanville SC. Died Sept. 1973.

RUYL, BEATRICE BAXTER, author; b. Denver, Apr. 7, 1879; d. Joseph Nickerson and Edith (Shedd) Baxter; art studies, Boston Mus. Fine Arts, 1898-99, Colorossi Studio and atelier Eduard Steichen, paris, 1900-01; m. Louis Herman Ruyl, of New York, Dec. 24, 1901. Illustrated various books for R.H. Russell, H. M. Caldwell & Co., Little, Brown & Co., E. P. Dutton & Co., Baker & Taylor Co. Author: Little Indian Maidens at Work, 1909; Zodiac Birthday Book, 1910. Address: Hingham, Mass.†

RYAN, ARCHIE LOWELL, clergyman; b. Clay Center, Kan., Apr. 15, 1881; s. Rev. Joseph Malcolm and Clara Leanore (Lapham) R.; A.B., Baker U., Baldwin, Kan., 1906, D.D., 1926; S.T.B., Boston U. Sch. Theology, 1913; A.M., Northwestern U., 1927; m. Celia Martha Allen, June 17, 1908; children—Allen Lowell, Martha Marguerite, Lloyd Mulin. Instr. in English, Baker U., 1906-07; ordained ministry M.E. Ch., 1910; pastor successively Le Hunt, Kna., Methuen and South Braintree, Mass., until 1914; field sec. Bd. of Sunday Schs. M.E. Ch., for Philippine Islands, 1914-20; joint field sec. for same and World's S.S. Assn., for P.I., 1920-30; prof. religious edn., Union Theol. Sem., Manila, 1914-32, pres., 1925-32; editor Philippine Islands Sunday Sch. Jour., 1923-30; advisory sec. Philippine Council of Religious Edn.; business secretary World's Sunday School Association, 1932-33; pastor successively Piedmont, Shawnee, and London Heights, Kansas City, Kans., 1934-42; superintendent Kansas City District, 1942-48; pastor, Stephens Memorial Methodist Ch., Kansas City, Kan., from 1948. Delegate to World's S.S. Conv., Tokyo, 1920, Glasgow, 1924, Los Angeles, 1928. Jurisdictional Conf., Meth. Ch., Tulsa, Okla., 1944, El Paso, Tex., 1948. Mem. Kappa Sigma, Phi Delta Kappa, Pi Gamma Mu. Republican. Mason. Author: Temperance Sermons (with others), 1914; The Religion of an Intermediate Boy, 1916; When We Join the Church, 1920; Religious Education in the Philippines, 1930; A Good Minister, 1930. Winner nat. oratorical contest, Intercollegiate Prohibition Assn., 1906. Home: Kansas City, Kan.†

RYAN, CORNELIUS JOHN, author, fgn. corr.; b. Dublin, Ireland, June 5, 1920; s. John Joseph and Amelia (Clohisey) R.; ed. Christian Bros., Dublin, Irish Acad. Music; fellow econs. and social scis. U. Manchester (Eng.), 1964; Litt.D., Ohio U., 1974; m. Kathryn Ann Morgan, May 27, 1950; children—Geoffrey John, Victoria Ann. Came to U.S., 1947, naturalized, 1950. Jr. sec. to Garfield Weston, Brit. M.P., London, 1940-41; reporter Reuters's News Agy., London, 1941-42; reporter London Daily Telegraph, 1943, war corr., Europe, Pacific, 1943-47, Middle East bur. chief, Jerusalem, 1946-47; stringer Time and Life, N.Y.C., also St. Louis Post Despatch, 1946-47; contbg. editor Time, N.Y.C., 1947-49; mem. spl. projects dept., prod. TV show Newsweek, N.Y.C., 1949-50; asso. editor Coiller's, N.Y.C. 1956; staff writer Reader's Digest, Pleasantville, N.Y., 1962-65, roving editor, 1965; writer, N.Y.C., 1956; bd. dirs. Ryan Holdings Co., Ireland, Conn. State Nat. Bank. Mem. nat. bd. Boys Club of Am. Recipient awards for most distinguished mag. writing in 1956, U. Ill.; Benjamin Franklin Award, Overseas Press Club award, Christopher Lit. award for best book on fgn. affairs, 1959; Bancarelie prize for literature, Italy, 1962, Gold Medal for lit. Eire Soc. Boston, 1966; decorated the Medaille de la France Liberee, Legion of Honor (France), Mem. Nat. Press Club, Author's League Am., Writers Guild Am. Clubs: Union Interailiee (Paris, France); Dutch Treat; Silver Spring Country; Players; Mid-Ocean (Bermuda). Author: Minute to Ditch, 1957; The Longest Day, 1959; (with Frank Kelley) Star Spangled Mikado, 1948, MacArthur, 1951; (with Dr. von Braun, others) Across the Space Frontier, 1952; Conquest of the Moon, 1953; The Last Battle, 1965; A Bridge Too Far, 1974. Home: Ridgefield CT. Died Nov. 23, 1974.

RYDSTROM, ARTHUR GORDON, business exec.; b. Boston, Dec. 24, 1905; s. Alvah W. and Bessie Mae (Hooper) R.; student Roxbury Latin Sch., Boston, 1919-25; A.B., Dartmouth, 1929; student Columbia, 1929-30; m. Harriett L. Lowry, Oct. 23, 1931; children—Donald H., Carolyn C. With Bankers Trust Co., N.Y.C., 1929-48, clk., 1929-38, asst. treas., 1938-41, asst. v.p., 1941-44, v.p., 1944-48; asso. Claude K. Boettcher, investments, Denver, 1948-53; sr. v.p., dir. Webb & Knapp, Inc., 1953-57; chmn., dir. Lowry & Co., Inc., N.Y. Capt. USNR, inactive from 1945. Clubs: Denver Country, Cherry Hills Country. Home: Denver, Colo., Died Feb. 8, 1976.

RYLAND, EDWARD, business exec.; b. King and Queen County, Va., July 5, 1880; s. Josiah and Lucy O. (White) R.; grad. Va. Mil. Inst., 1901; m. Kathleen Winston, December 15, 1920; children—Josiah, Patsy Marshall, Kathleen Winston. With Va.-Carolina Chem. Corp., from 1901, as sulphuric acid maker and plant supt., 1904-17, div. mgr. of mfg., 1917-33, mgr. mfg. dept., 1933-39, v.p., 1939-50, mem. bd. dirs., 1949-50. Mem. Kappa Alpha. Club: Hermitage Country. Baptist. Mason. Home: Richmond, Va.†

RYLAND, JOHN PETER, airline exec.; b. Melbourne, Australia, July 26, 1911; s. Ernest Augustus and Flavie (Borelli) R.; student Xavier Coll., Melbourne; 1929; B.Agrl.Sci., Melbourne U., 1934: m. June Robinson, July 20, 1949; children—Jann Caroline, Paul John, Jill Melita. Mgr. Ansett Airways Ltd., Melbourne, 1946; asst. gen. mgr. Trans-Australia Airlines, Melbourne, 1946-55, gen. mgr. from 1955. Served to group capt. Royal Australian Air Force, 1939-45. Decorated D.F.C.; comdr. Order Brit. Empire; cavaliere dell'Ordine al Merito della Repubblica Italiana. Fellow Australian Inst. Mgmt. (v.p. Victoria div.), Inst. Transport. Home: Malvern, Victoria, Australia. Died Oct. 20, 1973; interred Melbourne, Australia.

SAAL, IRVING RANDOLPH, lawyer; b. Petersburg, Va., Oct. 7, 1879; s. Moses R. and Rachel (Rosenbaum) S.; LL.B., Tulane U., 1904; student U. Va.; m. Gertrude Goldsmith, May 6, 1908; children—Phyllis (Mrs. Leon E. Newman), Jane (Mrs. William F. Sigmund), Marie (Mrs. Horace I. Pack). Admitted to La. bar, 1904, practiced in New Orleans; mem. firm Milling, Saal, Saunders, Benson & Woodward, and predecessors. Mem. Am., La., New Orleans bar assns. Home: New Orleans, La†

SACHS, ALEXANDER, economist; b. Rossien, Lithuania, Aug. 1, 1893; s. Samuel and Fay (Alexander) S.; came to U.S., 1904; B.S., Columbia, 1912; postgrad. Harvard, 1915-17; m. Charlotte A. Cramer, Aug. 30, 1945. With Lee Higginson & Co., N.Y.C., 1913-14; Francis Parkman fellow, Harvard, 1916, a fellow in jurisprudence and sociology, 1917; ceonomist to Walter Eugene Meyer, 1922-29; v.p. and dir. 1936-42, econ. adviser and dir. Lehman Corp. 1942, ind. counsellor in adminstrn, econs.; mem. adv. com. Walter Kidde Nuclear Labs.; research asso. and spl. cons. Operations Research Office Johns Hopkins; econ. adviser to Petroleum Industry War Council, 1942; became spl. cons. to dir. OSS 1944; organizer and chief, div. econ. research and planning Recovery Adminstrn., 1933; founder Central Statis. Bd.; lectr. Swathmore Coll., 1933; lectr. Inst. Pub. Affairs, U. Va., 1934, 35, 36; New Sch. for Social Research, 1939, St. John's Coll., Annapolis, and Town and Gown Meetings, Annapolis, 1942-43; Inst. of World Affairs, 1946, U. Chgo., 1966, Am. Mgmt. Assn., 1937, Am. Mining and Metall. Engrs., 1938. Chmn. adv. com. on econs. to Interstate Oil Compact Commn. 1938-73, also councillor econs. com., 1945-73; dir. Electro Nucleonics. Spl. cons. to under sec. polit. affairs State Dept., 1968-73. Mem Internat. Conf. on Problems of the Pacific, 1936, 2d Assembly Conf. on Inflation, Columbia, 13th Conf. on Sci., Philosophy and Religion, 1952; mem. Nat. Policy Com. 1936-73, exec. com. Council for Democracy and Citizens for Victory; chmn. Conf. Bus. Economists, 1957-58. Decorated hon. comdr. Order of Brit. Empire. Fellow Royal Econ. Soc., Royal Statis. Soc.; mem. Am. Econ. Assn., Econometric Soc., Am. Statis Assn., Am. Polit. Sci. Assn., Conf. Bus. Economists, Royal Philos. Soc. Glasgow, Econ. History Soc. (Eng.), Am. Finance Assn. Vet. Strategic Service, Brit. Soc. History and Philosophy Sci., St. George's Soc. of N.Y., Industry and Trade Law Inst. Democrat. Clubs: Harvard Downtown, Broad Street. Contbr. or author: America's Recovery Program, 1934; Financial Dynamics of Recovery, 1938; Fortune Round Table on Taxation, 1939; Strategic Materials and Flexible Logistics Petroleum Pipeline for War Prosecution, 1942; Restoring Bases American Foreign Investment, 1950, Rights, Promises and Property, 1952, A Critique of the Cycle Theory, 1953; Production since 1900; New Perspective, 1955; On American Triple Inflation as Crisis Source and Challenge, 1958; contbr. to econ. financial and gen. periodicals; mem. bd. editors World Perspective Series, Credo Series. Originated atomic project, in confs. with pres., 1939, served as presidential rep. on organiziing com. Home: New York City, NY. Died June 23, 1973.

SACKETT, ARTHUR JOHNSON, civil engr.; b. Ft. George, Fla., May 25, 1884; s. John Warren and Louise (Johnson) S.; student U. Pa., 1905-06; m. Julia Hopkins, Nov. 5, 1922; 1 dau., Louise (Mrs. Bernard McCray). Asst. engr. constrn. East River Tunnel for Pa. R.R., 1906-11; asst. engr. on constrn. Catskill Aqueduct, Mason & Hanger Co., 1911-17, chief engr. on constrn. Camp Taylor, 1917, chief engr. co., 1919-29, pres., 1929-55, also dir.; chmn. bd., dir. Silas Mason Co., 1949-55; chairman bd., dir. Mason & Hanger-Silas Mason Co., Inc., 1955-75, breeder Aberdeen Angus Cattle. Served as maj. Q.M.C., U.S. Army, 1918-19. Mem. Am. Soc. C.E., Soc. Am. Mil. Engrs. Episcopalian. Mason. (Shriner). Clubs: Turf and Field, Engineers (N.Y.C.); Virginia Country, Commonwealth (Richmond, Va.). Home: St. Augustine, Fla., Died Oct. 30, 1975.

SACKETT, WALTER GEORGE, bacteriologist; b. Sterling, Ill., July 5, 1880; s. Walter C. G. and Emma L. (Hagey) S.; Ohio State U., 1898-99; B.S., U. of Chicago, 1902, Ph.D., 1918; m. L. Margaret Ferguson, of Reidsville, N.D., June 28, 1905; children—Mariana Wray, Elizabeth Hagey. Sanitary water analyst, Chicago Sanitary District, 1899-1900; prof. natural science, Meredith Coll., Raleigh, N.C., 1902-04; spl. agt. Bur. Plant Industry, U.S. Dept. Agr., 1904; instr. in bacteriology and hygiene and asst. bacteriologist, Expt. Sta., Mich. Agrl. Coll., 1904-06; asst. prof. bacteriology and hygiene and asst. bacteriologist, same, 1906-08; bacteriologist, Colo. Expt. Sta., from 1908. Methodist. Fellow A.A.A.S.; mem. Soc. Am. Bacteriologists, Colorado Scientific Soc., Phi Beta Kappa, Sigma Xi, Alpha Zeta, Phi Kappa Phi, Gamma Alpha; ex-sec.-treas. Mich. Acad. Science. Mason. Club: Kiwanis (ex-pres.; dist. gov. Colo.-Wyo. dist. 1932). Author: chapters I-V, "Bacterial Diseases of Plants" in Microbiology, 1911; also many bulls. on bacteriol. subjects. Home: Ft. Collins, Colo.†

SADLER, FRANK HOWARD, naval officer; b. Newbern, Ala., Nov. 28, 1880; s. William Hull and Elizabeth Cornelia (Saunders) S.; student Southern U., Greensboro, Ala., 1895-98, R. L. Werntz Prep. Sch., Annapolis, Md., 1898-99; grad. U.S. Naval Acad., 1903; U.S. Naval War Coll., 1927; m. Mary Brown, Aug. 19, 1908. Commd. ensign U.S. Navy, 1905, and advanced through grades to selection for rear adm., 1935. Served at Naval Training Sta., Newport, R.I., 1911-13, exec. officer, 1916-17; comdr. or exec. officer various ships, 1918-21; in Bur. Engring., Navy Dept. Washington, D.C., 1921; exec. officer U.S. Naval Torpedo Sta., Newport, 1921-23; capt. U.S. Navy Yard, Cavite, P.I., 1923-24; comdr. 16th Naval Dist., 1924; mem. staff U.S. Naval War Coll., Newport, 1927-28; head dept. engring., U.S. Naval Acad., 1930-31, head post grad. sch., 1931-33; mem. Advanced Class U.S. Naval War Coll., 1935-36; comdr. Cruiser Div. 6, Scouting Force, U.S. Fleet, 1937-38; mem. Gen. Bd. Navy Dept., 1938-39; comdt. 15th Naval Dist., from 1939. Decorated Navy Cross, Victory medal, Philippine Campaign medal, Cuban Pacification medal, Mexican Service medal. Democrat. Methodist. Mason. Club: Army and Navy (Washington, D.C.). Address: Washington, D.C.*†

SADOW, LEONARD BERNARD, mfg. co. exec.; b. N.Y.C., Feb. 22, 1914; s. Joseph and Rose (Patterson) S.; B.A., Bklyn. Coll., 1934; J.D., N.Y. U., 1939, postgrad., 1972; m. Jessie Brinberg, May 21, 1939; children—Stephen, Mark. Admitted to N.Y. bar, 1939; U.S. Supreme Ct. bar, 1968; mem. firm Hendon & Klein, N.Y.C., 1938-42; v.p., sales mgr. Stylecraft Box Co., Bklyn, 1945-49; with Longines-Wittanuer Watch Co., Inc., N.Y.C., 1949-73, v.p., counsel, 1970-73; exec. v.p., 1972-73; sec., counsel Longine Wittnauer Inc., 1971-73; officer, dir. LeCoultre Watch Co., N.Y.C., 1970-73; and other subsidiaries. Tchr. credit mgmt. Coll. City N.Y., 1950-51; cons. tariff questions Am. Watch Assn., 1968-73; testimony given before Tariff Commn., FTC, others. Served with USNR, 1942-45; PTO. Mem. N.Y. County Lawyers Assn., Assn. Bar City N.Y., Ordnance Assn. K.P. Club: Overseas Yacht (N.Y.C.). Patentee in mech. field. Contbr. articles to profl. jours. Deceased.

SAGAZ, ANGEL, Spanish diplomat; b. Madrid, Spain, Mar. 1, 1913; s. Luis and Francisca (Zubelzu) S.; law degree U. Vallacolld, 1932; m. Ursula, May 27, 1957; children—Jose, Gabriel, Juan Carios, Manuel, Santiago. Joined Diplomatic Service, 1942; served in Finland, Sweden, U.S., Can.; dir. gen. for Am. affairs in Ministry Fgn. Affairs, Madrid; ambassador to Cairo, U.A.R., 1966-71; accredited as ambassador to Sudan, Somalia, North Yemen, S. Yemen; now ambassador to U.S., Washington. Decorated Grand Cross of Isabel la Catolica, Great Cross of Spanish Order of Civil Merit;

Order of U.A.R. 1st Class; knight Grand Cross, Order of San Gregorio. Roman Catholic. Club: Real of Campo (Madrid). Home: Madrid Spain. Died May 1975

SAGE, CHARLES H(ENRY), business exec.; b. Denver, Colo., Jan. 7, 1891; s. Charles Henry and Helen Elizabeth (Shiells) S.; grad. Neenah (Wis.) High School; m. Lyda Pynn, Apr. 14, 1914; children—Robert Shiells, Jeanne Elinor (Mrs. Albert Turner Groves). With Kimberly-Clark Corporation, Neenah, Wisconsin, from 1907, vice president, member executive com.; dir., from 1936; vice president and dir. Kimberly-Clark Corp. of Canada, Ltd., Kapuskasing and Toronto, Ont., from 1943; pres. and dir. Spruce Falls Poer Power & Paper Co., Ltd., Kapuskasing and Toronto, from 1942; vice pres. and dir. Upper Canada Timber Co., Ltd., Toronto, from 1937, LongLac Pulp and Paper Co., Ltd., Terrance Bay and Toronto, from 1943, Pulp Wood Co., and Realties, Inc., Neenah, Wis., from 1938, North Star, Timber Co., Duluth, Minn., from 1942; sec., dir. Twin City Real Estate Corp., Neenah, Wis., from 1945. Dir. Wm. Bonifas Lumber Co., Marenisco, Mich., Reliance Land & Timber Co., Duluth, Minn., Bon-Kimlark Mineral Company, Paper Patents Company, First National Bank, Neenah, Trustee-treas. Theda Clark Memorial Hosp., Neenah; trustee Kimberly-Clark Retirement Trust Mem. Pub. Lib. Bd., Neenah, Am. Pulpwood Assn. (dir.), Canadian Pulp and Paper Assn. (mem. exec. com.), Newsprint Assn. of Can. (mem. exec. com.), Phi Delta Theta. Republican. Presbyterian. Clubs: Union League (New York); Chicago, Great Lakes Cruising (Chicago); Toronto; Business Men's (dir.), North Shore Golf, Neenah-Nodoway Yacht (Neenah); Butte des Morts Golf (Appleton). Home: Neenah, Wis., Died Sept. 1972.

SAID, MARAGHAI MOHAMMAD, premier of Iran. Address: Tehran, Iran. Died Nov. 1, 1973.

SAINT, HARRY YOUNG, lawyer; b. East Palestine, O., Mar. 9, 1873; s. William Monroe and Hannah (Young) S.; A.B., Ohio Wesleyan U., 1894; LL.B., U. of Mich., 1896; m. Myra Estella Kelsey, Dec. 14, 1904; children—Ellis Chandler, Kelsey Young. Admitted to Ohio bar, 1896, and began practice at Cincinnati; in office of gen. counsel Scripps-McRae newspaper interests, 1896-1900; in newspaper work with Scripps-McRae pubs., 1900-06; admitted to Wash. bar, 1910; registrar U.S. Land Office, Yakima, Wash., 1909-13; and engaged in business and law in Eastern Wash. and Seattle, 1913-19; mem. exec. staff, U.S. Shipping Bd. Mcht. Fleet Corp., 1919-33, dir. supplies, 1926-33. Wash. state chmn. World War Food Prodn. Bd., World War I. Mem. Central Coal Commn., 1919-20; mem. bd. created by U.S. Sec. of Interior to investigate Alaska transportation, 1920; spl. expert U.S. Maritime Commn., 1937-42, then transferred to War Shipping Adminstrn.; resigned Nov. 15, 1945; asso. with M. P. Smith & Sons Co., N.Y. Mem. Phi Delta Phi, Phi Kappa Psi. Rep. Meth. Mason (32°). Club: Nat. Press. Author: (novel) Life Story of the Old and New South. Home: Dingman's Ferry, Pa.†

ST. JOHN, FORDYCE BARKER, surgeon; b. Hackensack, N.J., Feb. 10, 1884; s. David and Jennie (Angle) St. J.; B.S., Princeton, 1905; M.D., Coll. Phys. and Surgs., Columbia, 1909; m. Jane Rignel, Aug. 30, 1919; children—Jane Faulkner (wife of Dr. Benson B. Roe), Mary Evans (Mrs. John W. Douglas). Fordyce Barker, Jr., and Elizabeth Lyman (Mrs. Justus Fennel) Intern surgery The Roosevelt Hospital, New York City, 1910-12; in private practice, N.Y.C. from 1912; member faculty Columbia since 1912, professor clinical surgery, 1929-48, emeritus prof. clin. surgery from 1948; asst. vis. surgeon Presbyn. Hosp., N.Y., 1912-15, attending surgeon, 1921-46, dir. 1st surg. div., 1919-21; cons. surgeon Presbyn., Neurol., Babies and Bronx V.A. Hosps. (N.Y.), Hackensack Hosp., Greenwich (Conn.) Hosp., Mt. Vernon (N.Y.) Hosp.; Cons. Surgeon Princeton Hosp., Princeton, N.J.; dir. Equitable Life Assurance Soc. U.S., Hackensack Trust Co., The Hackensack Cemetery Co. Charter trustee Princeton. Served as capt. and maj., M.C., U.S. Army, France, 1917-18; comdg. officer, mobile hosps., 1918-19; disch. rank lt. col. Decorated D.S. M.; Selective Service medal World War II. Charter mem. Am. Bd. Surgery. Fellow A.C.S.; mem. A.M.A., Am. Surg. Assn., Interurban Surg. Soc., Internat. Surg. Soc., Soc. Clin. Surgery. Republican. Episcopalian. Clubs: Eclat, Princeton Univ., New York Century Assn. Home: New York City, N.Y. Died Sept. 19, 1973.

ST. JOHN, GUY BASCOM, sociologist; b. at Winona, Minn., Nov. 18, 1878; s. William H. and Alice (Cole.) S.; student Art Inst., Chicago, 1897-98; grad. Pratt Inst., Brooklyn, 1900; grad. Teachers College (Columbia), 1908; grad. New York Sch. of Philanthropy, 1908; unmarried. Formerly teacher industrial edn., New York pub. schs., also Govt. schs., Philippine Islands; in charge survey and exhibit work, in various communities, in connection with Bur. Social Service, Bd. Home Missions, Presbyn. Ch. in U.S.A., 1908-15; in charge religious exhibits at Panama P.I. Expn., San Francisco, 1915; mgr. traveling exhibit of Nat. Religious Forces, from 1915. Made studies of social conditions in P.I., China, Japan, India and Alaska, also of congested and industrial centers in U.S. Writer and lecturer on sociol. subjects. Home: Roselle, N.J.†

SALA, ANTOINE, French naval officer; b. Bayonne, France, Oct. 8, 1897; s. Leon and Catherine (Detroyat) S.; ed. Naval Coll., Brest, France, 1916; m. Jacqueline Barrois, June 19, 1936; children—Catherine (Mrs. Gerard Thibaud), Pierre, Philippe, Marie Anne. Commd. in French Navy, 1915, advanced through grades to admiral, 1956, naval air pilot, 1918; naval air and naval commands including light cruiser div., 1939-45; naval attache, London, 1945-49; comdr.-in-chief French Naval Forces in Mediterranean, 1951-55; naval dep. for SACEUR, 1955-58. Decorated Croix de Guerre, grand officer Legion d'Honneur, comdr. order Brit. Empire, also other fgn. decorations. Mem. Academie de Marine (sec.). Address: Paris, France. Died June 28, 1973.

SALMAGGI, ALFREDO, impressairo; b. Aquila, Italy, Mar. 4, 1886; s. Felice and Micolina S.; ed. European Conservatories; m. Elvira Canzano, 1910; children—Lina, Felix, Guido, Dora, Alfred, Henry, Mario and (twins) Robert and Edward. Presenting grand opera in U.S., Canada and S. America, from 1915; presented popular-priced operatic productsion at N.Y. Hippodrome, 1933-38; presenting operatic performances, Brooklyn (N.Y.) Acad. of Music, from 1939; introduced more than 500 new singers to the public; instr. of voice; editor Lyric Courier; author of numerous brochures on vocalization. Founder Brooklyn Opera Guild, 1948. Home: Brooklyn, N.Y., Died Sept. 5, 1975.

SALMON, DAVID ALDEN, ex-govt. exec.; b. Westport, Conn., Jan. 30, 1879; s. David Ami and Frances A. (Morehouse) S.; student, Stamford Business Coll., 1896; m. Anna E. Marine, Aug. 16, 1904; 1 dau., Barbara A. (Mrs. Clement W. Gerson); m. 2d, Irene L. Perkins, Apr. 17, 1941. Salesman, 1896-98; clerk, War Dept., 1898-1906, Dept. of State, 1906-07; acting chief, Bur. Indexes and Archives, 1916, chief, 1916-19; directed to proceed to Am. Missions in Europe to investigate methods of handling corr., 1919-21; archivist, Conf. on Limitation of Armament, Washington, 1921, on Central Am. Affairs, 1922-23, Am. Delegation, Conf. for Limitation of Naval Armaments, Geneva, 1927, Internat. Radiotelegraph Conf., Washington, 1927; sec., London Naval Conf., 1930; chief, Div. Communications and Records, 1931; mem. Bd. of Review for Efficiency Ratins, 1931-33, Bd. of Appeals and Review, 1933-41, Com. on Archives, from 1935, Efficiency Rating Com., 1941-42. Special consultant to the asst. sec. of state, Aug. 4, 1943; adviser Div. Cryptography, Dept. of State, 1944; spl. detail to fgn. service, in Europe, 1947; ret. from govt. service, Dept. of State, Nov. 1948. Home: Washington, D.C.†

SALTER, JOHN THOMAS, educator, author; b. Three Oaks, Mich., Jan. 17, 1898; s. William Lee and Alvena Christine (Lampe) S.; A.B., Oberlin Coll., 1921; Ph.D., U. Pa., 1928; m. Katharine Shepard Hayden, Aug. 25, 1921; children—Katharine Shepard, Patricia Learned, Jean Hinds, Joel Hayden, Christopher Lord. Instr. polit. sci. U. Pa., 1921-26; prof. polit. sci. Ursinus Coll., Collegeville, Pa., 1926-27; asso. prof. polit. sci. U. Okla., 1927-30, U. Wis., from 1930; vis. prof. polit. sci. Stanford, 1942-43; historian USAAF, 1945; chief spl. studies unit, hist. br. War Assets Adminstrn., 1946-47; vis. prof. polit. sci. Am. U., summer 1947; Fulbright vis. prof. U. Philippines, 1949-50; prof. Inst. Pub. Adminstrn., U. Philippines, 1952-53; vis. prof. Rockford Coll., summers 1956, 57, 59; vis. prof. (Smith-Mundt Act), Nat. Chengchi U., Nat. Taiwan U., 1957-58; vis. prof. Long Island U., summers, 1960, 61, 62; cons. Grad. Sch. Pub. and Internat. Affairs, U. Pitts., summer 1958. Asst. editor Anns. Am. Acad. Polit. and Social Scis., 1923-26; editor Okla. Municipal Rev., sec. Okla. Municipal League, 1927-30. Served in S.A.T.C., Oberlin Coll., 1918. Fellow Social Sci. Research Council, 1930, 31-32; recipient scroll of recognition for services rendered people of Free China, Minister of Edn., Republic of China, 1958. Mem. Am. Polit. Sci. Assn., Fgn. Policy Assn., Am. Acad. Polit. and Social Sci. Author: Boss Rule: Portraits in City Politics, 1935; The Pattern of Politics: The Folkways of a Democratic People, 1940; Philadelphia's William S. Vare, 1971. Editor: The American Politican, 1938; Public Men: In and Out of Office, 1946. Contbr. articles to mags., jours., chpts. to books. Address: Oberlin, O. Died Nov. 1, 1973; buried Westwood Cemetery, Oberlin, O.

SALVATORELLI, LUIGI, historian, journalist; b. Marsciano, Italy, Mar. 11, 1886; s. Salvatore and Anna (Alessandri) S.; ed. U. Rome, 1903-07, D. es L., 1907. Sec., Ministry Edn., 1909-16; prof. U. Naples, 1916-21; polit. co-dir. La Stampa, Turin, Italy, 1921-25, polit. leader writer, 1948-74; mem. Liberation Com., also Partito d'Azione, 1942-46. Mem. Central Bd. Hist. Studies, 1945-74. Decorated officier de la Legion d'Honneur; cavaliere di Gr. Croce al merito della Republica (Italy). Author: Il significato di Nazareno, 1911; Vita di San Francesco d'Assisi, 1926; Il Pensiero politico Italiano dal 1700 al 1870, 1940; Pensiero e azione del Risorgimento, 1943; Chlesa e Stato dalla Rivoluzione francese ad oggi, 1955; Leggendae realtà di Napoleone, 1960; Spiriti e figure del Risorgimento, 1961; Miti e Storia, 1964; (with Giovanni Mira) Storia d'Italia nel periodo fascista, 1956, 64; Storia del Novecento, 1957, 64; Un cinquantennio di rivolgimenti mondiali, 1971. Address: Rome, Italy. Died Nov. 3, 1974; interred Marsciano, Perugia, Italy.

SAMFORD, FRANK PARK, ins. co. exec.; b. Troy, Ala., Nov. 1, 1893; s. William Hodges and Kate (Park) S; student State Normal Coll., Troy; B.S., Alabama Polytech. Inst., 1914; LL.D. (hon.), Howard Coll., Auburn U.; m. Hattie Mae Noland, Dec. 23, 1919; children—Frank Park Jr., Ann (Mrs. Sam E. Upchurch), Dep. ins. commr. of Ala. 1915-19; Ala. mgr. Lumbermans Mut. Casualty Co., 1919-21; sec. Liberty Nat. Life Ins. Co., 1921-32, v.p., 1932-34, pres., 1934-60, chmn. bd. 1960-73; dir. Malone Freight Line, Brown-Service Mfg. Co. Bd. dirs. Life Ins. Sales Research Bur., 1931-34; bd. dirs., exec. com. Birmingham C. of C., 1937; pres. Indsl. Insurer's Conf., 1938-40; pres. Birmingham Community Chest, 1940-42; bd. dirs. Jefferson County Community Chest, Ala. Heart Assn.; pres. Jefferson Tb Sanitorium Soc., 1942-44; bd. dirs. Asso. Industries of Ala.; state v.p. Am. Life Conv.; pres. Ala. State C. of C. 1946-49, Pres. bd. trustees Samford U.; trustee Ala. Poly. Inst., So. Research Inst. Mem. Alumni Assn. Ala. Poly. Inst. (pres. 1943-44), Alpha Tau Omega, Omicron Delta Kappa. Democrat. Baptist. Mason (Shriner). Clubs: Rotary (pres. 1936-37); dist. gov. 1940-41), Birmingham (Birmingham); Birmingham Country; Mountain Brook Country. Home: Birmingham, Ala. Died Sept. 1973.

SAMPLE, PAUL STARRETT, artist; b. Louisville, Sept. 14, 1896; s. Wilbur Stevenson and Effie Averille (Madden) S.; B.Sc., Dartmouth, 1921, A.M. (hon.), 1936, D.H.L., 1962; Dr. Fine Arts (hon.), Nasson Coll., 1964; m. Sylvia Anne Howland, Dec. 1, 1928; 1 son, Timothy. Asso. prof. fine arts, U. So. Cal., 1926-38; artist in residence Dartmouth, 1938-62; war corr. Life mag., World War II; rep. in Met. Mus. of Art, Springfield (Mass.) Mus. Fine Arts, U. Iceland, Reykjavik, Swarthmore Coll., U. Minn., U. So. Cal., War Dept., Washington, Cornell U., N.J. State Mus., Trenton, Miami (Fla.) U., San Diego Mus., U. Neb., Bklyn. Mus., Williams Coll., Addison Gallery, Andover, Mass., Butler Art Inst., Youngstown, O., Joslyn Meml., Omaha, Brooks Meml., Memphis, Boston Mus. Fine Arts, Mus. Art, Providence, Colgate U., Chgo. Art Inst., Art Mus. New Britain (Conn.), Dartmouth, Sweet Mus., Portland, Me., Pa. Acad. Fine Arts, Parrish Mus. (L.I.), High Mus. Art, Atlanta, Smithsonian Instn., Washington, numerous others. Recipient numerous awards including Halgarten prize N.A.D., 1931, Isador gold medal, 1933; Temple gold medal Pa. Acad. Fine Arts, 1936; hon. mention Carnegie Internat.; Nat. Acad. prize, 1947; John Elliot Memi. award, 1954; First Benjamin Altman prize Nat. Acad., 1962. Served from quartermaster to ensign, USNR, 1918-19. Episcopalian. N.A. Mem. Am. Water Color Soc., Cal. Art Assn. (past pres.), Delta Kappa Epsilon, Casque and Gauntlet. Clubs: Century Assn., Lotos, Anglers (N.Y.C.); St. Bernard Fish and Game (Quebec, Can.). Home: Norwich, Vt. Died Feb. 26, 1974.

SAMPLE, WILLIAM DEVORE, pub. relations exec.; b. Sharon, Pa., Feb. 18, 1929; s. Donald D. and Helen (McIntyre) S.; B.A., Westminster Coll., 1951; M.A., Pa. State Coll., 1956; m. Joan Nicholas, Aug. 6, 1957; children—Meredith, Charlotte, Donald, Scot, Laura. Pub. relations dir. Erie (Pa.) Playhouse, 1956; instr. Allegheny Coll., Meadville, Pa., 1956-57; chmn, radio-TV dept. St. Lawrence U., Canton, N.Y., 1957-60; asst. to mgr. pub. relations Lukens Steel Co., Coatesville, Pa., 1960-67; dir. corporate pub. relations Nat. Gypsum Co., Buffalo, 1968-71; v.p. pub. relations and pub. affairs Snelling and Snelling, Inc., Paoli, Pa., 1971. Bd. dirs. Amherst (N.Y.) Players. Served with AUS, 1952-55. Recipient Spoke award Pa. Jr. C. of C., 1961. Mem. Pub. Relations Soc. Am., Buffalo C. of C. Presbyn. Home: Exton, Pa. Died June 13, 1971; interred Brandywine Cemetery, Chester County, Pa.

SAMPSELL, MARSHALL GROSSCUP, lawyer; b. Chgo., Jan. 22, 1904; s. Marshall Emmett and Edna Florence (Smith) S.; grad. Hill Sch., Pottstown, Pa., 1922; Ph.B., Yale, 1926; LL.B., Harvard, 1929; m. Margaret Carr, Jan. 13, 1934; children—Mary Adams, Miranda Carr. Admitted to Ill. bar, 1929; asso. Isham, Lincoln & Beale, Chgo., 1929-38, partner, 1938-72; dir. Central and S.W. Corp., R.R. Donnelley & Sons Co. Mem. Am. Ill., Chgo. bar assns., Phi Beta Kappa, Beta Theta Pi. Republican. Episcopalian. Clubs: Attic, Casino, (Chgo.). Home: Chicago Ill. Died Jan. 19, 1973.

SAMS, HOWARD WALDEMAR, corp. exec.; b. Warrensburg, Mo., Jan. 13, 1897; s. Walter and Susan Ellen (Jacobs) s.; LL.D., DePauw U.; D.H.M., Westminster U.; m. Barbara Johnston Hereth, Mar. 19, 1941; children—Mary Penelope, Thomas Howard, Timothy Hereth, David Waldemar. Mgr., Harper, Halfield, Beach theatres, Chgo., 1916-17; salesman Goodyear Tire & Rubber Co., Chgo., 1919-22; sales mgr. Universal Battery Co., Chgo., 1922-27; Chgo. dist. mgr. E. T. Cunningham, Inc., 1927-28, N.Y. dist. mgr., 1929-30; gen. mgr. Silver Marshall, Inc., 1930-33, Howard Radio Corp., South Haven, Mich., 1933; mgr. wholesale div. P. R. Mallory & Co., Inc., Indpls., 1933-46, advt. mgr., 1934-46, gen. sales mgr., 1940-45, chmn. postwar planning com., 1942-46, cons., 1946-47; founder chmn. emeritus Howard W. Sams & Co., Inc., electronic engring. analysts, also Bobbs-Merrill Co.; chmn. bd., dir. Waldemar Farms, Inc., Terre Haute Castings, Park-loo, Inc., Waldemar Industries, Inc.; dir.

Ind. Nat. Bank of Indpls., Ransburg Electro-Coating Corp., Indpls. Bd. dirs. Indpls. Meth. Hosp., Crossroads, Inc., Vis. Nurse Assn., Indpls. Zool. Soc.; trustee Park-Tudor Sch. Recipient award Fedn. Radio Service Men's Assn., 1947, Radio Technicians Guild Am., 1948, Nat. Alliance TV Electronic Service Assns., 1953-68. Home: Indianapolis, Ind. Died May 19, 1974.

SANBORN, FREDERIC ROCKWELL, lawyer; b. Glens Falls, N.Y., Feb. 14, 1899; s. Francis N. and Bertha E. (Rockwell) S.; B.A. magna cum laude, Columbia, 1919, M.A., 1921, LL.B., 1921; D.Phil. in Law, Oxford U., Eng., 1924; m. Janet Sweet, Dec. 30, 1924 (dec. Mar. 1969); children—Frederic R. G., Victoria. Admitted to N.Y. bar, 1924; asso. John M. Woolsey, 1924-27; asso., partner Putney, Twombly, Hall & Skidmore, N.Y.C., 1927-54; prof. internat., constl., adminstrv. law Bklyn. Law Grad. Sch., 1927-38, 62; prof. internat. law St. Johns Coll. Grad. Sch., 1928-30; U.S. justice Supreme Ct. for Restituition, Berlin, Germany, 1954-59; with Internat. Finance Corp., Washington, 1962-63; legal cons. Nat. Com. on Food Marketing, Washington, 1965-66; gen. counsel emeritus, dir. Brit. Schs. and Univs. Found., N.Y.C. Mem. Mayor's Com. on Police Protection and Air Warden Service; zone comdr. Air Warden Service, N.Y.C.; chmn. Coordinating Council Juvenile Delinquency. Pres., bd. dirs. 82d Precinct Community League; v.p., sec., bd. dirs. Bklyn. Free Kindergarten Soc. Mem. N.Y. County Lawyers Assn. (life) Am., Bklyn. bar assns., Empire State Soc., S.A.R. (dir.), Am. Soc. Internat. Law, Phi Beta Kappa, Evarts Inn (hon.) of Phi Delta Phi, Delta Tau Delta. Episcopalian (trustee, treas.). Clubs: Cosmos (D.C.); Brooklyn, British Schools and Universities (past sr. pres., dir., life mem.) (N.Y.C.); Rembrandt, Ihpetonga (past pres.) (Brooklyn Heights, (N.Y.). Author: Origins of the Early English Maritime and Commercial Law, 1930; Design for War, 1951. Co-author: Perpetual War for Perpetual Peace, 1953. Contbr. articles mags., law jours., also Ency. of Social Scis. Home: Brooklyn, NY. Died Nov. 6, 1973; cremated.

SAND, INGE (MRS. HANS J. CHRISTENSEN), ballet dancer; b. Copenhagen, Denmark, July 6, 1928; d. Ernst and Else (Johannsen) Sand; student Royal Danish Ballet, 1935-45, Royal Opera, London, 1950. Mr. Wood and Mme. Egorova, Paris, 1949-50, various schs. U.S.A.; m. Hans J. Christensen; 1 dau., Liselotte Sand. With Royal Danish Ballet, Copenhagen, 1945-74, prin. dancer, 1950-72 soloist in Norway, 1951, Eng., 1952, U.S.A., 1954-57, 60-61, 64, Ireland, 1956, Portugal, 1958, S.Am., 1961, Japan, Egypt, Germany, Italy, 1962; touring mgr. Royal Danish Theater, 1972-74. Decorated knight of Dannebrog, 1960; recipient various Danish and Am. awards. Home: Copenhagen, Denmark. Died Feb. 9, 1974.

SANDER, LUDWIG, artist; b. N.Y.C. July 18, 1906; student Art Students League, N.Y.C., 1928-30; pupil of Alexandre Archipenko, also Hans Hofmann; B.A. N.Y.U., 1952. One man shows include Castelli Gallery, N.Y.C., 1959, 61, Kootz Gallery, N.Y.C., 1962, 64, 65, A.M. Sachs Gallery, N.Y.C. 1967, 69, Gimpel-Hanover Galerie, Zurich, 1969, Lawrence Rubin Gallery, N.Y.C., 1970, 72, Waddington Galleries, London, 1972, Knoedler Contemporary Art, N.Y.C., 1974; traveling shows and nat. exhbns.; represented in permanent collections Albright-Knox Art Gallery, Buffalo, Balt. Mus. Art, Brandeis U., Art Inst. Chgo., Guggenheim Mus., Mass. Inst. Tech., Whitney Mus., Walker Art Center, Mpls., N.Y. U., San Francisco Mus. Art, U. la. Mus. Art; tchr. Bard Coll., 1956-58, U. Pa. Grad. Sch. Fine Arts, 1966, Colo. Coll., 1951-53. Served with inf. AUS, 1942-45; ETO. Recipient award Longview Found., 1959, Nat. Council Arts, 1967; Guggenheim fellow, 1968; citation and award Nat. Inst. Arts and Letters, 1971; Purchase award Am. Acad. Arts and Scis., 1973. Home: New York City, NY. Died July 3, 1975.

SANDERS, JOHN OLIVER, consular service; b. Cassville, Barry Co., Mo., May 31, 1881; s. Washington Lafayette and Caroline (Vineyard) S.; grad. N. Tex. State Normal Coll., Denton, Tex., 1907; student law, arts and sciences, various periods, University of Texas, A.B., 1916. With Bureau of Education, Philippine Islands, 1912-14; supt. govt. farm at Ballesteros, P.I., 1913-14; with U.S. Land Office, Washington, D.C., 1917; consul at Bluefields, Nicaragua, 1917-20, at Ft. William, Can., 1920-21, at Maracaibo, Venezula, from 1921. Mem. Tex. N.G., 1904-07, 1916-17. Baptist. Home: Cassville, Mo.†

SANDERS, ROBERT L., educator, composer; b. Chgo., July 2, 1906; s. Frank Smith and Laurilla Theresa (Smith) S.; Mus. B., Bush Conservatory, 1924, Mus.M., 1925; fellow Am. Acad. in Rome, 1925-29; Mus.D., Chgo. Conservatory, 1939; m. Marie Hiebl. Aug. 4, 1927 (dec. Sept. 1967); children—Timothy, Barrett, Prof. Chgo. Conservatory, 1929-38; instr. Meadville Theol. Sch., 1930-38; organist, music dir. First Unitarian Ch., 1930-38; instr. U. Chgo., 1937-38; asst. condr. Chgo. Civic Orch., 1933-36; prof. music and dean Ind. U., 1938-47; prof. Bklyn. Coll., 1947-72, chmn. dept. music, 1947-54; condr. Port Singers, Port Washington, N.Y., 1952-54. Guggenheim fellow, 1954-55. Composer: Little Symphony in G; Ballet L'Ag'ya; Concerto for Violin; Trombone Sonata; Trio in C Sharp Minor; Quartet; Quintet; An American Psalm, Symphony for Band: The Hollow Men; Symphony in A; Little Symphony No. 2 in B flat; The Mystic Trumpeter; Paeans and Prayers; Celebration of Life; Horn Sonata; Brass Trio; Concerto for the Brass Trio; Concerto for the Brass Section; Little Symphony No. 3 in D; Lesson Chant Propers for the (R.C.) Mass in English; Song of Myself (Walt Whitman); Clarinet Sonata. Music co-editor of Hymns of the Spirit; contbr. Hymns for the Celebration of Life, 1964. Unitatian-Universalist. Home: Deiray Beach, FL. Died Dec. 26, 1975.

SANDERS, WILLIAM KING, gas co. exec.; b. Poteau, Okla., Apr. 28, 1905; s. Wiley L. and Martha (Miller) S.; m. Bertha B. Capper, Dec. 2, 1933; 1 son, Charles King. With Panhandle Eastern Pipe Line Co., Kansas City, Mo.; 1928-50, pres., chief exec. officer, 1965-68, chmn. bd., chief exec. officer, 1968-71, dir., cons., 1971-73; dir. Trunkline Gas Co., Houston, 1950-73, pres., 1957-73; dir. Kaiser Steel Corp., Oakland, Cal., So. Nat. Bank, Houston. Home: Houston, TX. Died Apr. 24, 1973.

SANDERSON, HENRY STEPHEN, mining engr.; b. Rochester, N.H., Aug. 25, 1878; s. Stephen Francis and Nellie (Strout) S.; degree of Metall. Engr., U. of Minn., 1901; m. Margaret Ella Jamieson, of Denver, Sept. 29, 1903. U.S. mineral surveyor, 1901, also in consulting practice, mine examinations, etc.; dir. Pingrey Mines Co. Republican. Methodist. Mason (32°). Home: U1Denver, Colo.†

SANDERSON, JULIA, actress, singer; b. Springfield, Mass., Aug. 22, 1887; d. Albert and Jeanette E. Sackett; ed. schs. of Springfield and Phila., Pa.; m. "Tod" Sloan, Sept. 1, 1907; m. 2d, Lt. Comdr. Bradford Barnette, June 6, 1917; m. 3d, Frank Crumit, July 1, 1927 (dec.). Debut with Forepaugh Stock Co., Phila., continuing there 1 year; appeared in "Winsome Winnie," at the Casino, New York, 1902, later as Mrs. Pineapple, in "A Chinese Honeymoon"; played with De Wolf Hopper as Mataya, in "Wang," at Lyric Theatre, New York, 1904; made brief tour in vaudeville, 1907; appeared in "The Honorable Phil," in London, Eng., later with J. P. Huntley in mus. comedy, at New Amsterdam Theatre, New York; as Aileen Cavanagh, in "The Arcadians," Liberty Theatre, New York, 1910; as Dora Dale, in "The Sunshine Girl," in leading cities of U.S.; appeared in "The Girl from Utah," mus. comedy, Chicago, 1915; starred with The Sybil Co., 1916-17; appeared in "Rambler Rose," 1916-18, "The Canary," 1918-20, "Hitchy Koo," 1920-21, "Tangerine," 1921-23, " Ziegfeld Follies," 1923, "Moonlight." 1923, "No, No, Nanette," 1925-26, "Queen High," 1926-27, "Oh Kay," 1927-28. Radio broadcaster since 1927. Home: Longmeadow Mass. Died Jan. 27, 1975.

SANDLIN, MARLIN ELIJAH, investment co. exec.; b. Colmesneil, Tex., July 22, 1909; s. John Mancel and Matilda E. (Mann) S., A.B.U., Tex., 1930; m. Mary Elizabeth Brown, Dec. 17, 1931; children—Carole Elizabeth Burnett, Suzanne Sparger Sefanides, Marlin Elijah. Admitted to the Texas bar, 1930; practiced in Woodville, Tex., 1931-36; asst. sec. of state Tex., 1936-39; legal adviser to commr. Gen. Land Office, 1939; mem. firm Fountain & Sandlin, Houston, 1939-41, Fountain, Cox & Sandlin, 1941-43; sec., dir. Woodley Petroleum Co., Houston, 1944-47, v.p., 1946-58, exec. v.p., 1958-60, also dir.; pres., dir. Woodley Canadian Oil Co., 1952-60, Minn. Pipe Line Co., 1953-67, Sharpstown Tower Corp., from 1962; vice chmn. bd., dir. Great No. Oil Purchasing Co., 1954-55; v.p., gen. counsel, dir. Great No. Oil Co., 1955-64, chmn. bd., 1960-64, dir., chmn. exec. com., 1964-65, dir. 1966-69; v.p., dir. Seven J. Stock Farm, Inc., 1948-60; chmn. Caribbean Sulphur Shipping Co., Ltd., Nassau, Bahamas, 1963-67. Pan. Am. Sulphur Sales Co., 1963-67, Pan. Am. Sulphur Co., Ltd., London, 1960-72; vice chmn. bd. Fertilizantes Fosfatados Mexicanos, S.A. de C.V., Mexico, 1956-72, Compania San Noe, S.A. de C.V. Mexico, 1965-72; vice chmn., chief evex. officer Azufrera Panamericana S.A., 1967-72; v.p., dir. South Saskatchewan Pipe Line Co., 1954-67; chmn. bd. Tocide Chem. Corp., 1974; dir. Bank of S.W. Nat. Assn., N.W. Houston Water Supply Corp., Pasco, Inc., Am. Gen. Mgmt. Co. Mem. adv. council, past chmn. Arts and Scis. Found., U. Tex.,Austin; exec. com. Winston Churchill Meml. Fund; adv. bd., dir. found. St. Joseph's Hosp., Houston. Mem. Fellows Tex. Bar Found., Texas, Houston bar assns., Am. Petroleum Inst., Anglo-Texan Soc. (chmn. Houston), Houston Council World Affairs (dir.), Tex. Mid-Continent Oil and Gas Assn., English-Speaking Union U.S. (past dir. nat. bd.; dir., past pres. Houston), Philos. Soc. Tex. Methodist (steward). Mason (past master); mem. Order Eastern Star (past patron). Clubs: Coronado, River Oaks Country, Petroleum (past pres.) (Houston). Home: Houston, Tex. Died May 28, 1974; interred Magnolia Cemetery, Woodville, Tex.

SANDOVAL, HILARY JOSEPH, JR., former govt. ofcl.; b. El Paso, Tex., Jan. 29, 1930; s. Hilary Joseph and Theodora (Aguirre) S.; B.A., U. Ariz.; m. Dolores B. Morales, Aug. 11, 1951; children—Mary Dolores, Irene Roberta, Hilary Joseph III, George Edward, Anthony F. Pres. Sandoval News Service, Inc., 1953-69; adminstr. Small Business Adminstrn., 1969-70. Area coordinator internat. Exec. Service Corps., 1967; mem. Lubbock (Tex.) adv. council Small Bus. Administrn. Chmn. exec. com. El Paso County Republican Party, 1962; asst. chmn. Republican Party Tex., 1966. Served with AUS, 1951-53; capt. Res. Mem. El Paso Sales and Marketing Execs. Internat., Mid-Am. Periodicals Distbrs. Assn., Bur. Ind. Pubs. and Distbrs. (co-chmn.), League United Am. Citizens (pres. council 8), El Paso C. of C. Rotarian (bd.dirs. El Paso). Home: El Paso, Tex. Died June 13, 1973.

SANDS, DIANA PATRICIA, actress; b. N.Y.C., Aug. 22, 1934; d. Rudolph and Shirley (Walker) Sands; grad. Performing Arts High Sch., N.Y.C., 1952; student New Dance Group, Internat. Dance Studio, also privately ed. in acting, speech and singing. Theatrical appearances include An Evening with Will Shakespeare, 1953. The World of Sholem Aleichem, 1953. Major Barbara, 1954. Man With the Golden Arm, 1956, A Land Beyond the River, 1957, The Egg and I, 1958, A Raisin in the Sun, 1959, Another Evening with Harry Stoones, 1961, Black Monday, 1962, Brecht on Brecht, 1962, Tiger, Tiger, Burning Bright, 1962, The Living Premise, 1963, Blues for Mr. Charlie, 1964, The Owl and the Pussycat, 1964, Two for the Seesaw, 1967, MacBeth, 1967, Caesar and Cleopatra, 1967, Phaedra, 1967, Anthony and Cleopatra, 1967, Wait Until Dark, 1967; mem. Pantomime Art Theatre Repertory Group, 1955, Compass Players, 1962; motion pictures include Carriberan Gold, 1952, Four Boys and a Gun, 1957, A Raisin in the Sun, 1960, An Affair of the Skin, 1963, Mr. Pulver and the Captain, 1963; numerous TV appearances, from 1960. Recipient Off-Broadway mag. award, 1958; Outer Circle Critics Best Supporting Actress award, 1959; Internat. Artist award, 1961; Theatre World award, 1963; Obie award, 1964; Whitbread award (Eng.), 1966; N.Y. area Emmy award, 1964; also Toni and Emmy nominations. Home: New York City, N.Y. Died Sept. 21, 1973.

SANDS, STAFFORD LOFTHOUSE, lawyer; b. Nassau, Bahamas, Sept. 23, 1913; grad. pub. high sch.; m.; 1 dau., Mercedes; m. 2d, Ulli Lillas, Dec. 1965. Pres., chmn. bd. City Meats Ltd. Mem. House Assembly Bahamas for City Constituency of New province, 1957-67; minister finance and tourism, 1962-67. Created knight, 1964; comdr. Order Bit. Empire, 1955. Home: Nassau, Bahamas, Died 1972.

SANDY, WILLIAM CHARLES, indsl. co. exec.; b. Sheldrake-on-Cayuga, N.Y., June 20, 1915; s. William Charles and Vida (Dowers) S.; A.B., Cornell U., 1937; postgrad. Stanford Exec. Program, 1966; m. Barbara F. Kennelly, May 29, 1939; children—Barbara Mae (Mrs. John J. Patton), Judith Elizabeth (Mrs. Stanley M. Coleman), Bonnie Louise, Sandy. Employed with Guaranty Trust Co., N.Y.C., 1937-51; with Tenn. Gas Transmission Co. (now Tenneco Inc., 1966), Houston, 1951-72, treas., 1963-66, v.p., 1966-72; dir. Bayshore Nat. Bank, La Porte, Tex., Pligrowth Fund, Inc., Hedburg & Gordon Fund, Inc., One Eleven Mgmt. Co. Mem. council Cornell U. Served with USNR, 1943-46. Mem. Houston Soc. Financial Analysts. Home: Houston, Tex. Died Sept. 12, 1972; inurned Meml. Oaks Cemetery, Houston, Tex.

SANFORD, THOMAS RYLAND, clergyman; b. Montross, Va., Sept. 4, 1878; s. Millard Fillmore and Eleanor Rebecca (Nevitt) S.; prep. edn., Burkeville (Va.) Acad. and Windsor (Va.) Acad.; student U. of Richmond, 1898-1903, D.D., 1922; m. Margaret E. Taylor, of Chesterfield, Va., June 17, 1903; children—Thomas Ryland, Eleanor Frances, Taylor Howe, Robert Nevitt, Fillmore Hargrave, Margaret Hilda, John Doward, Franklin Kerfoot. Ordained ministry Bpt. Ch., 1900; pastor successively chs. in Va., Chesterfield Co., Buckingham Co., Hampton, Chatham, South Boston, Fredericksburg, until 1930; served as pastor, First Bapt. Ch. Norfolk, Va., 4 yrs., Main St. Church, Luray, from 1935. Founder, 1909, pres. until 1917, trustee Hargrave Mil. Acad. (formerly Chatham Training Sch.). Mem. Bapt. Home Mission Bd., Va. Bapt. Bd. of Missions and Edn. Trustee Va. Bapt. Foundation, U. of Richmond. Mem. Sigma Phi Epsilon, Omicron Delta Kappa. Mason. Modern Woodman, Rotarian. Home: Luray, Va.†

SANG, PHILIP DAVID, ice cream co. exec.; b. Chgo., Nov. 27, 1902; s. Jacob and Etta (Grinker) S.; B.S. in Mech. Engring., Ill. Inst. Tech., 1923; D.H.L., Lincoln (Ill.) Coll., 1955, M.E. 1969; D.H.L., So. Ill. U., 1963, Rosary Coll., 1970; Litt. D., Rutgers U., 1961; LL.D., U. Ky., 1958, Knox Coll., 1968; D.Sc., Lincoln Meml. U., 1969; D. Edn., Chgo. Med. Sch., 1970; D. Bus. Adminstrn., North Central Coll., 1971; L.H.D., Hebrew Union Coll.-Jewish Inst. Religion, 1973; Ph.D., Hebrew U., Jerusalem, Israel, 1974; m. Elsie Olin, Aug. 21, 1923; children—Robert H., Donald G. Pres., Goldenrod Ice Cream Co., Chgo., 1963-75; treas. Humiston-Keeling & Co., wholesale druggists, Chgo., 1945-75. Co-sponsor Freedom Hall Oak Park, Ill.; treas Civil War Jewish Hist. Commn.; mem. Civil War Centennial Commn. of Ill. Bd. dirs. Jewish Fedn. Met. Chgo., 1955-66, Gottlieb Meml. Hosp., Chgo. Symphony Orch. Assn.; trustee Ill. Inst. Tech., Lyric Opera of Chgo.; trustee, mem. exec. com. Chgo. Med. Sch.; bd. govs. Hebrew Union Coll., 1959-71; bd. govs., hon. fellow Weizmann Inst. Sci., Israel, 1969-75; vice chmn. bd. overseers Bibl. and Archaeol. Sch., Jerusalem, 1959-71; exec. com. Friends of Rutgers

Library; adv. council U.S. Civil War Centennial Commn., 1961-65; bd. adv. Presdl. Mus, Odessa, Tex. Recipient George Washington award Freedom Found., 1963-69, Lincoln Medallion Lincoln Sesquicentennial Commn., 1960; recipient (with wife) Joshua Ben Gamala Nat. Gold medal award. Fellow Royal Soc. Arts; mem. Automatic Retailers Am. (dir., finance com.), Internat. Assn. Ice Cream Mfrs. (dirs., exec. com. 1949-68), Ill. Hist. Soc. (pres. 1967-68, merit award 1962, pres.), Am. Jewish Hist. Soc. (pres. 1967-69, Lee Max Friedman Gold Medal award 1970), Jewish Publ. Soc. Am. (v.p.), Alliance Francaise Chgo. (dir.), Ulysses S. Grant Assn. (dir.), Hist. Record Assn. (ed. adv. bd.), Sigma Alpha Mu, Phi Beta Kappa (hon.). Jewish religion (chmn. bd. temple 1964-70). Clubs: Executives, Standard (Chgo.); Caxton, Grolier. Collector, exhibitor hist. documents and rare manuscripts on human freedom and Am. history; exhibited Knox Coll., North Central Coll., Univs. Ia., Ill., Ky., No. Ill., Wyo., Rutgers, Brandeis, Rosary Coll., Hawaii, Ill. State Hist. Library, Lincoln Coll., Lincoln U. (Pa.), Ill. Inst. Tech., Newberry Library, Chgo., Ga. State Archives, Atlanta, Music Center Los Angeles, others. Home: River Forest, Ill., Died May 16, 1975.

SANGER, WILLIAM THOMAS, educator; b. Bridgewater, Va., Sept. 16, 1885; s. Samuel F. and Susan A. (Thomas) S.; B.A., Bridgewater (Va.) Coll., 1909; M.A., Ind. U., 1910; student Columbia, summer 1911; fellow in psychology, Clark U., 1912-13 and Mar.-June, 1915, Ph.D., 1915; LL.D., Hampden-Sydney Coll., 1926. Coll. William and Mary, 1953; L.H.D., Bridgewater Coll., 1939; LL.D., U. Richmond, 1939, U. of N.C., 1950, Va. Union U., 1956; D.Sc., U. Fla., 1953; D.C.L., Med. Coll. Va., 1957; m. Sylvia Gray Burns, Aug. 20, 1913; 1 son, Julian. Prof. history and philosophy, Bridgewater Coll., 1910-12, prof. philosophy and edn., 1913-16; instructor in edn., Madison College, Harrisonburg, Va., summers 1913-16, registrar and instr., 1916-17, dean, head of dept. of edn. and dir. summer session, 1917-19; asst. in high sch. inspection of Va., 1917-19; spl. collaborator and mem. field staff Va. State Sch. Survey, 1919; dean and prof. psychology and edn., Bridgewater Coll., 1919-21; instr. in psychology, U. of Utah, summer, 1920; in edn., U. of Va., summers 1921, 22; exec. sec. Va. State Teachers Assn. and editor Va. Jour. of Edn., 1921-22; sec. Va. State Bd. of Edn., 1922-25; pres. Med. Coll. of Va. 1925-56, chancellor, 1956-59, chancellor emeritus, 1959-75. Director of the Central National Bank. Dir. Meharry Medical College, Nat., Virginia societies for crippled children and adults, National Health Council, Bridgewater College, Virginia Council on Health and Med. Care, Richmond Area U. Center. Mem. N.E.A., Va. Edn. Assn., A.A.A.S., Va. Acad. Sci., Richmond Acad. Medicine, Med. Soc. Va., Am. Dental Assn. (hon.), Phi Delta Kappa, Phi Beta Kappa, Alpha Omega Alpha, Omicron Delta Kappa, Omicron Kappa Upsilon. Member Presbyn. Ch. Author numerous articles in ednl. and med. jours. Home: Richmond, Va. Died Apr. 17, 1975.

SANTELMAN, ELMAR WILLIAM, mfr.; b. Cayuga, Ill., Apr. 5, 1905; s. Fred and Dorothea (Herzog) S.; A.B. with honors, Carleton Coll., 1931; M.B.A., Stanford, 1933; m. Rjae Janice Massey, April 21, 1937; children—Kent William, Janet Massey (Mrs. Gompers). With Continental and Comml. Nat. Bank, Chgo., 1925-27; property mgmt. Progress Mortgage Co., 1934-38; mgr. Paso Robles Hot Springs Hotel, 1938-41; owner Universal Loose Leaf Co., also pres. Columbia Wholesale Stationers, Inc., 1946-50; pres. Universal Mfg. Stationers, Inc., Los Angeles, 1950-73; pub. accountant Pres. Feather River Canyon Council, 1937-38. Served with USAAF, 1942-46; lt. col. USAF ret. Mem. Wholesale Stationers Assn. (bd. controls), C. of C., So. Cal. Alumni Cerleton Coll. (pres.), Air Force Assn. (comdr. Pasadena area squadron). Club: Los Angeles Athletic. Home: Altadena, Cal. Died Feb. 22, 1973.

SANTOS, EDUARDO, ex-pres. of Colombia; b. Bogotá, Colombia, Aug. 28, 1888; student, La Salle Inst. and Sr. Coll. of Our Lady of the Rosary, Bogotá; LL.D., Nat. Univ. of Bolivia, also Dr. of Polit. and Social Sciences. Served successively as pres. of Municipal Council of Bogotá, gov. of Dept. of Santander, mem. and pres. of House of Reps., senator and pres. Senate, minister of fgn. relations; served several times as del. to League of Nations, twice chmn. Colombian delegation; rep. of Colombia to Disarmament Conf. in Geneva, 1932; chmn. nat. bd. of dirs. of Liberal party; elected President of Colombia, Aug. 1938. Awarded: Grand Cross of Boyaca (civil class). Considered leading newspaperman of Colombia; dir. of El Tiempo Bogotá, from 1912; contbr. to newspapers in Colombia and Madrid, Spain (under pseudonyms). Died Mar. 1974.

SARGEANT, GASTON, operatic basso; b. Meadville, Pa., Aug. 10, 1880; s. William Gaston and Jessie (Benson) S.; student Allegheny Coll., 1895-97; served in Mass. Heavy Arty., Spanish-Am. War, 1898; studied at Royal Conservatory, Liege, Belgium, 1905, 06, under Seguin, later with noted bassos, Fournets and Plancon, Paris; m. Mamie Franklin Jaffray, of N.Y. City, Feb. 11, 1915; début as Chiffonier, in "Louise," at Royal Opera, Covent Garden, London, and sang there for 10 seasons, in French, Italian and German repertoire; studied with Sr. Thomas Beecham, creating roles in many operas; was leading basso in first English performances of Wagner's "Ring of the Nibelung," 1911-12; with Ernest Denhof for 2 seasons, also singing in "Meistersinger," "Tristan and Isolde," "Electra," "The Flying Dutchman" etc.; with Municipal Opera, Nice, 1913-15; interpreter, in Belgium hosps. 10 mos. during first yr. of World War; concert tour with Melba in U.S., 1915; leading basso, Chicago Opera Assn., season 1916-17.*†

SARVIS, GUY WALTER, univ. prof.; b. Emmington, Ill., July 6, 1879; s. David Millard and Alice Emily (Rathbun) S.; A.B., Drake Univ., 1908; A. M., U. of Chicago, 1911; m. Pearl Maude Taylor, Sept. 6, 1908; children—David L., Mary Alice, Elizabeth Evans (Mrs. Erwin Luse), Alva Taylor, Sec. Y.M.C.A., Calcutta, India, 1901-03; dean coll. arts, prof. sociol. and economics, U. of Nanking, China, 1911-26; field agt. Internat. Famine Relief Commn., Hantan (China), 1921; mem. commn. on social research, Inst. Social and Religious Research, N.Y. City (Shangahi), 1923; mem. laymen's inquiry, 1930-31; instr. Wharton Sch. Finance, U. of Pa., 1926; dean and prof. sociol. Hiram Coll., 1927-30; prof. missions and hist. of religion, Vanderbilt, 1931-34, Southern Meth. U., 1934-35; head dept. sociol. Ohio Wesleyan U., 1935-49; head dept. sociol., Wesleyan Coll., Macon, Ga., 1949-51, retired. Member Am. Sociol. Soc., Am. Oriental Soc., Inst. Pacific Relations, Ohio Valley Sociol. Soc. (pres. 1942-44), Phi Beta Kappa, Alpha Kappa Delta. Democrat. Mem. Disciples of Christ Ch. Home: Orlando, Fla.†

SASTROAMIDJOJO, ALI, Indonesian rep. to UN, b. Grabag-Merbabu, Central Java, May 21, 1903; ed. elementary schs., Java, high sch., Jakarta (then Batavia); completed edn. in Netherlands; LL.D., U. Leyden, 1927; m. Titi Roelia, 1922; 2 sons, Kemal Mahisa and Karna Radjasa, 2 daus., Sawitri and Gayatri; m. 2d, Kurnianing, Jan. 1970. Established law practice in Jogiakarta, Java. 1928; became mem. exec. P.N.I. (Partai Nasional Indonesia-Indonesian Nationalist Party) joining edtl. staff of party organ; went to Surakarta, 1929, continuing in law practice and contributing articles to the weekly Timbul (Awakening) and newspaper Darmokando (The Monitor); with other members of Partindo (successor to P.N.I. which had been dissolved by Dutch Colonial Govt. in 1931) formed new party, Gerindo (Indonesian Movement), 1937; Ofcl. office provincial govt., 1942-45; apptd. dep. minister of Information by Pres. Soekarno in first Cabinet of Republic of Indonesia, 1945; later made sec.-gen. Nat. Def. Council ofJogjakarta; mem. Indonesian del. to Inter-Asian Relations Conf., New Delhi, India, spring 1947; apptd. minister edn. and culture, summer 1947; served as dept. chmn. Indonesian delegation which agreed to Renville Truce Agreement signed Jan. 1948; spokesman for his country at U.N. Security Council discussion of Dutch-Indonesian dispute, 1948; on return to Indonesia, dep. chmn. Republican del. for negotiations with Dutch to implement truce; interned by Dutch with other cabinet ministers on island of Bangka, off Sumatra, Dec. 1948; after release acted as dep. chmn. Indonesian delegation at Djakarta for renewed negotiations with Dutch to implement truce; Mem. Republican delegation to Round Table Conf. to settle Indonesian question, The Haque, 1949; ambassador to U.S., Mexico and Can., 1950-53; prime minister of Indonesia, 1953-55, 56-57; chmn. Indonesian delegation Colombo Conf., 1954; pres. Afro-Asian Conf., Bandung, 1955; Indonesian permanent representative to UN, 1957-60, v.p. Gen. Assembly, 13th session. Vice chmn M.P.R.S., 1960-67. Articles in English include Survey of the Indonesian Nationalist Movement (Indonesian Life, March-April, 1947); The Status of the Republic of Indonesia in International Law (with Robert Delson, Columbia Law Review, March 1949); Memoirs Milestones On My Journey, 1977. Home: Jakarta, Indonesia. Died Mar. 14, 1975; interred Taman Pahlawan, Jakarta.

SATHRE, PETER O., laywer; b. Adams, Minn., Feb. 7, 1878; s. Jacob P. and Malene (Valemar) S.; LL.B., U. of N.D., 1910; m. Mina Hilstad, Apr. 14, 1912; children—Donald. Charlotte. Admitted to N.D. bar, 1910; in practice at Finley, 1910-32; state's atty. Steele County, 1912-20; mem. State Senate, 1927-32; asst. to U.S. dist. atty., 1932-33; atty. gen. of N.D., 1933-37; apptd. asso. justice Supreme Court of N.D., Dec. 1, 1937; asst. atty. gen. of State of N.D. Mem. Am. and N.D. State bar assns., Sons of Norway. Republican. Lutheran. Mason, Shriner, Woodman. Home: Bismarck, N.D.*†

SATO, EISAKU, prime minister of Japan; b. Tabuse, Yamaguchi, Japan, Mar. 27, 1901; s. Hidesuke and Moyo (Sato) S.; LL.B., Tokyo Imperial U., 1924; m. Hiroko Sato, Feb. 25, 1926; children—Ryutaro, Shinji. With Ministry Railways, Japan, 1924-47, vice minister transp., 1947-48; chief cabinet sec. 2d Yoshida Cabinet, 1948-49; mem. Yamaguchi House Reps., 1949-51; minister postal services, minister telecommunications, 1951-52; minister constrn., minister state in charge Hokkaido Devel., 1952-53; minister finance, 1958-60; minister internat. trade and industry, 1961-62; minister of state charge Hokkaido Devel., 1963-64; minister of state charge sci. tech., minister 18th Olympic games in Tokyo, 1963-64; prime minister Japan, 1964-72. Pres. Liberal-Democrate Party, 1964-72. Recipient Nobel Peace Prize, 1974. Home: Tokyo, Japan. Died June 3, 1975.

SAUER, CARL (ORTWIN), geographer; b. Warrenton, Mo., Dec. 24, 1889; s. William Albert and Rosetta J. (Vosholl) S.; A.B., Central Wesleyan Coll., Warrenton, 1908; studied Northwestern U., 1908-09; Ph.D., U. of Chicago, 1915; D. Phil. honoris causa, U. Heidelberg, 1956; LL.D., U. Syracuse, 1958, U. Cal. at Berkeley, 1960; Ruris Uteriusque Doctorem, U. Glasgow, 1965; m. Lorena Schowengerdt, Dec. 30, 1913; children—Jonathan, Elizabeth (Mrs. Edward FitzSimmons). Map editor Rand McNally Co., Chicago, 1912-13; instructor State Normal School, Salem, Massachusetts, 1913-14; instructor geography, 1915, assistant professor, 1918, asso. prof., 1920, prof., 1922, U. of Mich.; prof. geog. and chmn. dept., U. of Calif., 1923-57. Asst. geologist Ill., Geol. Survey, 1910-12; agent in agrl. economics, U.S. Dept. Agr., 1919-20; a founder of Mich. Land Econ. Survey, 1922; John Simon Guggenheim memorial fellow, 1931; consultant Soil Conservation service; mem. com. on Latin-Am. Studies of the Am. Council of Learned Socs., 1940. Mem. adv. bd. Guggenheim Mem. Found.; co-chmn. Wenner-Gren Princeton Conf., 1955. Recipient Charles P. Daly medal, sr. medal Am. Geog. Soc., 1940; Vega medal Swedish Soc. Anthropology and Geography, 1957, Alexander von Humboldt Centennial medal West Germany, 1959, Victoria medal Royal Geog. Soc., 1975. Pres. Assn. Am. Geographers, 1940, hon. pres. 1955; corr. mem. Am. Geog. Soc. (Bowman Meml. lectures 1952), Gesellschaft für Erdkunde zu Berlin, Academia Nacional de Ciencias Antonio Alzate (Mexico), Geographische Gesellschaft in Wien; hon. mem. Royal Dutch, Royal Scottish, Finnish geog. socs.; mem. Am. Philos. Soc. Author: Agricultural Origins and Dispersals, 1952; Land and Life, 1963; The Early Spanish Main, 1966; Northern Mists, 1968; Seventeenth Century North America, 1971, also others. Editor: Univ. of Calif. Series in Geography and Ibero-Americana; contbg. editor Geographical Review. Author of studies in hist. and physical geography based on field work in Latin America, the Am. Southwest, Ozarks, Ky., Great Lakes, also land use report of Science Adv. Bd., 1934. Home: Berkeley, Cal. Died July 18, 1975; interred Warrenton, Mo.

SAUERBREI, HAROLD, profl. football exec.; b. Berea, O., Mar. 28, 1916; s. Fred and Laura Louise (Kaatz) S.; student Balwin-Wallace Coll., 1938-39; children—Harold Thomas, Preston Taylor, Bruce Taylor, Laurel Taylor; m. 2d, Virginia Schrock Taylor, June 23, 1961. Reporter-columnist Berea (O.) News, 1938-41; sports writer Cleve. Plain Dealer, 1942-53; pub. relations dir. Cleve. Browns, 1954-60, bus. mgr., 1961-62, v.p., gen. mgr., 1963-75. Served with USNR, 1943-46. Recipient Column Writing award Ohio Newspaper Pubs. Assn., 1940, Sports Writing award Cleve. Newspaper Guild, 1950. Mem. Lambda Chi Alpha. Rotarian. Club: Shaker Heights Country (bd. dirs.). Contbr., editorial asst. History of Cleveland Browns, 1965. Home: Aurora, O., Died Sept. 5, 1975.

SAUL, MAURICE BOWER, lawyer; b. Phila., Oct. 6, 1883; s. Charles G. and Eliza B. Saul; A.B., Central High Sch., Phila., 1902; student U. Pa., 1902-06, LL.B., 1905; m. E. Adele Scott, Oct. 30, 1911; children—Robert M., Barbara, Christopher Scott. Admitted to Pa. bar, 1906, since practiced in Phila.; asso. With John G. Johnson, Phila., 1906-17; mem. firm Pritchard, Saul, Bayard & Evans, Phila., 1917-21, Saul, Ewing, Remick & Saul, 1921-69. Dir. W. Va. Northern R.R., John B. Stetson Co., Phila. Trustee U. of Pa.; dir. The School in Rose Valley. Dir. Phila. Voluntary Defender Assn. Mem. Am., N.Y., Pa. and Phila. bar assns., Order of Coif, Alpha Chi Rho. Republican. Universalist. Clubs: Rittenhouse (Phila.); Lawyers, Le Coir d'Or, Univ. Pa. (N.Y.C.). Home: Moylan, Pa. Died June 10, 1974.

SAUNDERS, BENJAMIN H., lawyer; b. near Jonesboro, Ind., Feb. 22, 1894; s. Benjamin H. and Rebecca (Ice) S.; student Ind. U., 1913-16, A.B., George Washington U., 1924, J.D., 1925; m. Ruth Englesby, Dec. 12, 1933; children—David Benjamin, John Parker. Admitted to Ind. bar, 1923. D.C. bar, 1928, Ill. bar, 1954; with Bur. Internal Rev., 1922-24; spl. atty. Office Gen. Counsel, 1924-26; mem. Hamel, Morgan, Park & Saunders, and predecessor firms, Washington, 1927-73. Trustee, Fohs Found, chmn. 1965-70; trustee Strayer Jr. Coll. Served as 2d lt. to 1st lt. U.S. Army, France, and Army of Occupation in Germany, 1917-19; from maj. to lt col. A.A.F., 1942-45. Decorated Commendation Ribbon (Army). Mem. Am., Fed., D.C. bar assns., Am. Legion, Sigma Chi, Phi Alpha Delta. Republican. Presbyn. Mason (Shriner). Clubs: Chevy Chase, Metropolitan, Army and Navy (Washington); Emeritus (Ind). Home: Chevy Chase, Md. Died June 15, 1973.

SAUNDERS, CARL MAXON, newspaper cons.; born Grand Rapids, Mich., Oct. 26, 1890; s. Fred and Fanny Francisci (Sommer) S.; graduate Grand Rapids High Sch.; Litt.D. (hon.), Albion College, 1951; married Grace Strong, July 5, 1914 (died September 2, 1952); children—Dorothy (Mrs. George Reinhard), Lelia (Mrs. Robert Tuttle); m. 2d, Katherine Long Taylor, October 22, 1955. Began as reporter in Grand Rapids News, 1909; reporter Kalamazoo Telegraph-Press, 1911, mng. editor, 1912; copy editor Detroit Free Press, 1913-14; editorial writer Grand Rapids Herald, 1915-28, asso. editor, 1928-32, editor, 1932-33; editor Jackson Citizen Patriot, 1934-60; former newspaper consultant to nine newspapers; pres. Community

Foundn., Inc.; past pres. Univ. of Mich. Press, Jackson War Chest, Service Men's Center; past dir. Nat. Asso. Press Managing Editors Association; member board of directors John George House, Community Chest, Area Development Corporation. Member Michigan Crime & Delinquency Council. Monitor of Jackson Labor Management Council. Member Gov.'s Conservation Study Committee. Recipient of the Pulitzer award for editorial writing, 1949; citation Citizens Com. for Hoover Report; U. of Minn. Distinguished Service in Journalism award, 1955; recipient Headliners' award, for year 1958; citation Mich. Med. Soc.; nat. award Associated Press Managing Editors. Member of American Society of Newspaper Editors, Mich. Press Assn. Republican. Episcopalian. Mason. Clubs: Town, Country, Tippecanoe, Rotary (ex-pres.) (Jackson); Grand Rapids Advertising (hon.); Silver Lake. Author: Booth of Michigan; also articles on conservation. Home: Jackson, Mich. Died Oct. 2, 1974.

SAUNDERS, HAROLD WILLIAM, educator; b. Oskaloosa, Ia., Jan. 15, 1909; s. William John and Emma (Davis) S.; B.A., Penn Coll., 1930; M.A., State U. Ia., 1936, Ph.D., 1942; m. Lucile Pauline Rich, June 10, 1933; children—Janet, Martha, Sally. Tchr. high sch., Salem, Ia., 1930-34, Perry, Ia., 1934-35; faculty U. Ia., Iowa City, 1935-74, prof., 1949-74, inactive, 1972, chmn. dept. sociology and anthropology, 1946-59; vis. prof. sociology U. Hawaii, 1963; research asso. Inst. for Community Studies, 1966-74. Mem. tech. rev. com. Ia. Commn. for Aging, 1968-72; pres. Midwest Council for Social Research in Aging, 1967-69. Trustee William Penn. Coll. Fellow Am. Sociol. Assn. (regional rep. from Midwest to nat. council 1960-63); mem. Population Assn. Am., Soc. for Applied Anthropology, Midwest Sociol. Soc. (pres. 1955-56) Alpha Kappa Delta, Order of Artus. Author: (with C.A. Hickman, et al) World Economic Problems, 1947. Editor: (with N.C. Meier) Polls and Public Opinion, 1949. Contbr. Population Theory and Policy, Am. Peoples Ency. and Yearbook. Home: Tempe, Ariz. Died Sept. 5, 1974.

SAUNDERS, MERRELL KERBY, air conditioning engr. and contractor; b. Coeur d'Arlene, Ida., Apr. 19, 1909; s. Carleton Earl and Mabelle (Kaesemeyer) S.; grad. Ferris Coll., 1929. Founder, Kerby Saunders, Inc., N.Y.C., 1940, chmn. bd., 1946-73; co-founder, 1945, pres. Carleton-Stuart Corp., N.Y.C. Recipient citiation sec. war for essential work in prodn. atomic bomb, 1945. Clubs: Metropolitan (life), Turf and Field, Church, N.Y. Athletic, Madison Square Garden, United Steeplechase and Hunt Assn. (life) (N.Y.C.); Essex Hunt, Tewksbury Foot Bassets, Essex Fox Hounds (Far Hills, N.J.); Bath and Tennis, Everglades (Palm Beach, Fla.); Spouting Rock Beach Assn. (Bailey's Beach), Reading Room (Newport, R.I.); Saratoga (N.Y.) Reading Room. Contbr. to research engring., constrn. atomic bomb. Home: Mendham, N.J., Died Dec. 13, 1973; interred Hill Top Cemetery, Mendham, N.J.

SAUNDERS, MICHAEL GRAHAM, educator; b. London, Eng., June 11, 1920; s. Eric Graham and Rose Kathleen (Gasson) S.; student Launceston Coll., 1927-38; B.Sc., Victoria U., Manchester, England, 1941, M.B., Ch.B., 1944, M.Sc., 1944, M.D., 1964; m. Leonore M. Gladwell, Apr. 27, 1946; children—Christopher, Gail, Jennifer, Deborah, Erica. Intern Manchester (Eng.) Royal Infirmary, 1943-44, resident neurology, 1944-45; resident neurosurgery Winwick Emergency Hosp., 1945; lectr. physiology U. Manchester, 1946-49; asst. prof. physiology U. Man., Winnipeg, Can., 1949-60, asso. prof., 1960-72, prof., 1972-75, dir. computer dept. Faculty of Medicine, 1968-75; dir. electroencephalograph dept. Winnipeg Gen. Hosp., 1949-75, Children's Hosp., 1960-75. Pres., Citizenship Council Man., 1972-75; chmn. adv. council to Man. Govt. on Multiculturalism, 1972-75. Mem. Assn. Computing Machinery, I.E.E.E., Canadian (pres. 1961-63), Am. (mem. council 1962-64), Central (pres. 1962) electroencephalography socs. Editorial bd. Journal of Electroencephalography and Clinical Neurophysiology, 1964-68. Home: Winnipeg, Man., Canada. Died Apr. 4, 1975.

SAUNDERS, PAUL ROME, educator; b. Tacoma, Sept. 21, 1916; s. Rome C. and Hazel (Richardson) S.; B.S., U. Cal. at Berkeley, 1939; Ph.D., Cal. Inst. Tech., 1943; m. Esther Y. Varnes, Dec. 26, 1947; children—Vicky, Linda, Kathy. Asst. prof., then asso. prof. pharmacology U. So. Cal. Sch. Medicine, 1949-58, asso. dean, prof. pharmacology, 1958-62, prof., chmn. dept. biol. scis. at univ., 1962-68, prof. physiology, asso. dean Sch. Medicine, 1968-74, former dir. marine sci. program. Mem. Am. Soc. Pharmacology and Exptl. Therapeutics, Soc. Exptl. Biology and Medicine, Internat. Soc. Toxinology. Author sci. papers. Home: South Pasadena, Cal. Died Oct. 31, 1974.

SAUNDERS, W(ILLIAM) V(INCENT), naval ofcr.; b. Bloomfield, Ia., Sept. 8, 1898; s. William Latimer and Martha Garrison (Davis) S; B.S., U.S. Naval Acad., 1922; m. Elizabeth Louise Harwood, Feb. 29, 1940; children—Constance Elizabeth, Franklin Harwood, Susan Craig. Commd. ensign U.S. Navy, 1922, and advanced through grades to rear adm., 1947; duty in U.S.S. Pittsburgh, Simpson, Lawrence, 1922-28; flight training for naval aviation, 1928-29; sr. aviator, U.S.S. Arkansas, Milwaukee, 1929-31; hydrographic office, U.S. Navy Dept., Washington, 1931-33; officer, aircraft carrier squadron, U.S.S. Lexington, 1933-36, Canal Zone squadron, 1936-38; comdr. U.S.S. Enterprise aircraft squadron, 1938-40; comdr. Naval Air Sta., Anacostia, Va., 1940-42; duty in aircraft carrier, U.S.S. Ranger, 1942-43; comdr. U.S.S. Hogatt Bay and anti-submarine group, 1943-45; chief of staff to comdr. aircraft, U.S. Naval Air Sta., San Diego, Calif., 1945; aide to asst. sec. of Navy for air, later to under sec. of Navy, 1945-47; ret. May 1, 1947; pres. W. A. Sheaffer Pen Co. of Can., Ltd., 1947-53; president, Saunders-Cook Limited 1953-67. Decorated Legion of Merit, Bronze Star, Sec. of Navy commendation, Navy Unit citation, various campaign and area medals. Mem. U.S. Naval Inst., Bd. of Trade (Toronto). Mem. United Ch. Can. Mason. Clubs: Granite, Toronto Golf, Toronto Hunt (Toronto); Army-Navy (Washington); N.Y. Yacht. Home: Annapolis, Md. Died May 8, 1974.

SAUTHOFF, HARRY, ex-congressman; b. Madison, Wis., June 3, 1879; s. August and Hermine (Brueggemann) S.; A.B., U. of Wis., 1902, LL.B., 1909; m. Alice Thoroughgood Kimball, Aug. 10, 1918; m. 2d, Mrs. Lenore Gilmour, June 18, 1937. Served as teacher in Lake Geneva (Wis.) High School and Northern Ill. State Normal School, 1902-06; instr. in Latin, Madison high schs., 1902-07; admitted to Wis. bar, 1909; in practice at Madison, Wis.; mem. Kroncke & Murphy, 1909-30, Sauthoff, Hansen, O'Brien & Kroncke from 1931; dist. atty. Dane County, Wis., 1915-17; pvt. sec. to Gov. John J. Blaine, 1921; state seantor, Wis., 1925-29; mem. 74th and 75th Congresses (1935-39), 77th and 78th Congresses (1941-45), 2d Wis. District; Wis. representative at International Conf. between U.S. and Canada, 1921, at Miss. Valley Conference, 1921. Curator Wis. Hist. Soc. Mem. Am. and Wis. State bar assns., Madison Chamber of Commerce, Sons of Vets. of Civ. War, Phi Alpha Delta. Progressive, Mason (33°), Elk, Moose, Eagle. Home: Madison, Wis.†

SAVINO, PATRICK RONALD, physician; b. Naples, Italy, Sept. 27, 1917; s. Charles and Rose (Ranadlo) S.; B.S., St. John's U., 1940; M.S., Fordham U., 1942; D.D.S., Marquette U., 1946, M.D., 1950; m. Blanche Guerrasio, July 1944. Came to U.S., 1920, naturalized, 1927. Instr. anatomy and physiology Fordham U., 1940-42; instr. oral medicine Marquette U., 1946-47, oral-maxillofacial surgery, 1951-52, asst. prof., 1953-54, dir. dept. medicine, 1955, asso. prof., 1955-57, prof., chmn. dept. medicine Marquette U. Dental Sch., prof. medicine Med. Sch., 1957, Grad. Sch., 1962-74; surg. staff Milwaukee Hosp., 1952-74. Served to capt. USAF, 1952-55. Fellow Am. Coll. Dentists, Am. Geriatric Soc.; mem. Wis. Soc. Oral Surgeons, Royal Soc. Health (Eng.), Am. Acad. Dental Medicine, A.A.A.S., Am. Dental Assn., Wis. Acad. Dental Medicine (pres.), N.Y. Acad. Sci., Omicron Kappa Upsilon, Alpha Kappa Kappa. Author: Diagnosis and Treatment of Facial Pain, 1953; Diagnosis and Treatment of Disorders of Temporomandibular Joint. Home: Brookfield, Wis. Died Nov. 1, 1974.

SAWYER, ALAN KENNETH, lawyer; b. Auburn, N.Y., June 7, 1904; s. Charles Addison and Florence (Seeley) S.; A.B., Syracuse U., 1926; LL.B., U. Buffalo, 1930; m. Edythe P. Curran, July 6, 1931; children—Patricia (Mrs. Joseph H. Lane, Jr.), Priscilla (Mrs. James E. Gotsick), A. Blair. Admitted to N.Y. bar, 1931; asso. Falk, Phillips, Twelvetrees & Falk, Buffalo, 1930, 32-35; sec. U.S. Fed. Judge, John Knight, 1931-32; partner Williams and Sawyer, 1935-69; dir., sec. Seely Instrument Co., Inc., Henry & Henry, Inc.; v.p., sec. Aeronautical Mfg. Corp., Niagara Falls, N.Y. Mem. counsel League of Women Voters of Buffalo, Inc., 1945-73. Past bd. dirs. Niagara Frontier Vocational Rehab. Center, Inc. Mem. Am., N.Y. State, Erie County bar assns., Am. Judicature Soc., U. Buffalo Law Alumni Assn. (dir.). Republican. Presbyn. Mason (K.T., Jester). Clubs: Brookfield Country (past dir., past pres.); Buffalo. Home: Kenmore, N.Y. Died Aug. 7, 1973.

SAWYERS, MOTT RANDOLPH, clergyman; b. Unionville, Ia., July 5, 1870; s. Sylvester Heartwell and Mary Flavia (Miller) S.; A.B., Parsons Coll., Fairfield, Ia., 1890, D.D., 1914; student Princeton, 1891; grad. Princeton Theol. Sem., 1895; grad. study Union Theol. Sem., 1898-99; Ph.D., Western Union Coll., Lemars, Ia., 1913; m. Rebecca Margaret Taylor, July 17, 1907; 1 dau., Ruth LaRue. Ordained ministry Presbyn. Ch., 1903; pastor Unionville and Moulton, Ia., 1895-96, Centerville, 1897; state sec. Ia. Anti-Saloon League, 1899-1902; pastor Mt. Ida Presbyn. Ch., Davenport, Ia., 1902-11; gen. sec. Y.M.C.A., Davenport, 1911-13; pastor Avondale Presbyn. Ch., Cincinnati, O., 1914-15; lecturer Redpath Lyceum Bur., 1910-17; in Y.M.C.A. service at various army posts 1917-19; also lecturer on United States Constitution; pastor Centerville, 1920-40, pastor emeritus May 1, 1940; interim pastor, Congl. Ch., Anoka, Minn., 1941, First Presbyn. Ch., Rochester, Minn., Sept. 1942-Aug. 1943. Mem. bd. dirs. Greater Mpls. Council of Chs. Mem. Iowa Nat. Guard 3 years; served with Y.M.C.A., Spanish-Am. War. Awarded testimonial of good citizenship "for more than 20 years of useful public service," 1940; recipient Minute Man medal Nat. Soc. S.A.R., 1958. Mem. Internat. Magna Charta Assn. (v.p. Ia.), S.A.R. (pres. Minnesota, nat. chaplain 1949-54; chmn. Minn. observance 175th anniversary of formation of the U.S. Constitution 1959-1963), mem. Centerville Association of Commerce (life); hon. mem. Chapparal Society, Poets and Authors. Republican. Club: Commercial (ex-pres.). Writer Pep Talks, syndicated weekly newspaper feature, and contbr. stories and verse to mags. Author: Famous Friends of God, 1933; The Shepherd Who Abided, 1937; The Chaplain Speaks, 1951. Author of ofcl. nat. S.A.R. hymn, adopted 1956. Home: Minneapolis, Minn.†

SAX, GEORGE DAVID, banker; b. Peoria, Ill., Apr. 14, 1904; s. Louis and Nellie (Abromowitz) S.; grad. Brown's Bus. Coll., Peoria, 1923; m. Rhoda Bronstein, Sept. 12, 1932; children—Samuel William, Edward Lee, George Jay. Engaged in finance, 1921-38; chmn. bd. DuPage Trust Co., Glen Ellyn, Ill., 1939-51; owner, builder Saxony Hotel, Miami Beach, Fla., 1949-61; chmn. bd. Exchange Nat. Bank Chgo., 1953-74. Recipient of the Horatio Alger award, 1965. Mem. Am. Inst. Banking, Am., Ind. bankers assns. Com. Econ. Devel., Navy League U.S., Phi Epsilon Pi. Jewish Reform religion. Mason (Shriner). Club: Covenant (Chgo.). Home: Chicago, Ill. Died Mar. 12, 1974.

SAX, KARL, coll. prof.; b. Spokane, Wash., Nov. 2, 1892; s. William L. and Minnie (Morgan) S.; B.S., Wash. State Coll., 1916; M.S., Harvard, 1917, D.Sc., 1922; D.Sc. (hon.), University Massachusetts, 1965; married Hally Jolivette, Sept. 22, 1915; children—Karl Jolivette, William Peter, Edward Alan. Instr. in genetics, U. of Calif., 1919; plant breeder Riverbank Lab., 1919-20; biologist Me. Agrl. Expt. Sta., 1920-28; asso. prof. cytology, Arnold Arboretum, Harvard, 1928-35, dir. arboretum. 1947-54, prof. of botany, 1935-59; vis. prof. forestry U. Fla., 1959; vis. prof. botany Yale U., New Haven, 1959-60; vis. prof. genetics N.C. State Coll., 1960-61, U. Cal. at Davis, 1961-62; vis. prof. of radiation biology, U.Tenn., 1962; lectr. U. Ga., 1963, Nat. Inst. Health fellow, 1964; Guggenheim fellow Oxford (Eng.) U., 1961; professor of genetics Cornell, 1964. Served as second lt., C.A.C., U.S. Army, 1918-19. Mem. Nat. Acad. Scis., Genetics Soc. Am. (pres. 1958-59), Planned Parenthood League Mass. (pres. 1958-59), Bot. Soc. Am., Am. Hort. Soc.; fgn. mem. French Acad. Agr., Japanese Genetics Soc. Unitarian. Home: Media, Pa. Died Oct. 8, 1973.

SAXE, THOMAS EDWARD, II, bus. exec.; b. Milw., Oct. 9, 1903; s. John Edward and Elizabeth (Crosswaite) S.; A.B., U. Minn., 1925; m. Helen Duff, Feb. 6, 1940 (dec. Apr. 1950); 1 son, Thomas Brock; m. 2d, Rosalind Saindon Axton, May 5, 1962. Founder, White Tower Mgmt. Corp. 1926, pres., 1926-70, chmn. bd., 1970-75; owner T.E.S. Realty Co., Wash.; dir. State Nat. Bank Conn. Pres. Saxe Found., Inc. Bd. dirs. St. Joseph's Hosp., Stamford, Conn. Diabetes Assn., Young Women's Towne House, Stamford Boys' Club, Stamford Mus.; trustee Stamford Day Nursery; endowment trustee Stamford Cath. Library, Inc. Mem. Soc. Am. Magicians, U.S. Navy League, Nat., N.Y. State restaurant assns., Am. Inst. Mgmt. (pres.'s Council N.Y.C.), New Canaan Hort. Soc., Phi Alpha Delta. Decorated knight Sovereign Mil. Order of Malta; knight of St. Gregory the Great; Star of Solidarity (Italy). Roman Catholic. Clubs: Rotary (hon.), Nat. Exchange (hon.); Country of New Canaan, Sun and Surf, Sittin' Starin' N' Rockin' (founder, pres. 1950); (New Canaan); Skeeters, Circumnavigators (N.Y.C.); Midtown; University, Field (Sarasota, Fla.). Home: New Canaan, Conn., Died Dec. 20, 1975.

SAYLER, JOHN WILLIAM, ins. co. exec.; b. Kansas City, Mo., Dec. 13, 1908; s. William II and Bonnie K. (Riddler) S.; B.S., Kan. U., 1931; m. Roberta Nelson, Oct. 20, 1934; children—John W., Robert N. Agy. dept. Bus. Men's Assurance Co., 1932-44, asst. v.p., 1944-45, dir. sales, 1945-47, v.p., charge of sales, 1947-64, exec. v.p. sales, 1964-72, vice chmn. bd., chmn. exec. com., 1972-73, chmn. bd., 1973, also dir. C.L.U. Chmn. agy. sect. Am. Life Conv., 1966. Mem. Am. Coll. C.L.U.'s, Kan. U. Alumni, Life Ins. Agy. Mgmt. Assn., Delta Upsilon. Episcopalian. Clubs: Kansas City, Indian Hills Country, Kansas City, Mo. Home: Shawnee Mission, Kan. Deceased.

SAYLOR, HARRY TRUAX, newspaper editor; b. Oakwood, Ill., Mar. 22, 1893; s. Zarah Stanton and Frances (Truax) S.; student Oakwood High Sch., 1907-10; m. Ernestine Dinsmore, Dec. 25, 1917 (died Jan. 24, 1939); married second, Margaret Mulqueen, February 22, 1941; (deceased November 6, 1953). Reporter Danville Press, 1912-16; reporter and city editor Springfield News-Record, 1916-20; mng. editor Elgin Courier, 1919, all of Illinois; mng. editor Camden Courier, 1920-29, Phila. Record, 1929-34. editor, 1934-47; editor New York Post, 1934-39; also editor Courier-Post newspapers of Camden, N.J. dir. and v.p. Courier-Post Co.; dir. Phila. Record Co. to 1947; dir., adv. editor, New Orleans Item, 1949-56; adv. editor United Features Syndicate, Inc., 1949-56; pres. Phila. Daily News, Inc., from 1956. Pres. Record Assos., Inc., 1947-49. Served as seaman USN, World War. Home: Merion, Pa. Died Aug. 16, 1973.

SAYLOR, JOHN PHILLIPS, congressman; b. Somerest County, Pa., July 23, 1908; s. Tillman K. and Minerva (Phillips) S.; A.B., Franklin and Marshall Coll., 1929; LL.B., Dickinson Law Sch., 1933; LL.D., St. Francis Coll.; m. Grace Doerstler, 1937; children—John Phillips II, Susan Kathleen. Former partner Spence, Custer, Saylor & Wolfe; mem. 81st (spl. election Sept.

1949) and 82d Congresses from 26th Pa. Dist., 83d to 92d Congresses from 22d Pa. Dist.; mem. exec. com. Republican Congl. Com. Pres., dir. Johnstown Fed. Savs. & Loan Assn. Mem. Pub. Land Law Rev. Commn.; mem. Nat. Forest Reservation Commn. Trustee Massanutten Acad., Woodstock, Va.; bd. regents Mercersburg (Pa.) Acad.; exec. bd. Robert Peary council Boy Scouts Am. Served with USNR, World War II; capt. Res. Recipient Nat. Parks Assn. award, 1954; Nat. Conservation award, 1958; named Outstanding Conservationist of Year, Pa. Outdoor Writers' Assn., 1964; Conservationist for 1964, Nat. Wildlife Fedn.; Bernard M. Baruch Conservation award, 1967, Isaac Walton League Conservation award, 1970. Mem. Am., Pa., Cambria County bar assns., Am. Legion, V.F.W., Amvets. Mem. United Ch. Christ. Mason (33 deg.). Elk. Home: Johnstown, PA 15901 Died Oct. 28, 1973.

SAYRE, HARRISON MONELL, found. dir.; b. Newark, May 21, 1894; s. Joseph M. and Ella G. (Brown) S.; A.B., Wesleyan U., Conn. 1916; LL.D., Capital U., 1954; m. Mary E. White, Oct. 25, 1921; children—Mary Dixon, James White, Adelaide B., Jean H., Robert F. Debating coach and tchr. Central High Sch., Middletown, Con., 1914-17; asst. in philosophy Wesleyan U., 1916-17; editor World News, 1923-32; founder (with Preston Davis) and mng. editor My Weekly Reader, 1928-40, Current Events, Our Times, and Unit Study Books; pres. Am. Edn. Press, Inc., Charles E. Merrill Co., ednl. pubs., to 1949. Chmn. Franklin County War Services Bd., 1943-45. Trustee Columbus Gallery of Fine Arts, Alfred L. Willson Charitable Found., Wesleyan U., 1939-59; pres. Nat. Council on Founds., 1960-64; chmn. United Hosps. Bldg. Fund, 1948-53; pres. Columbus Hosp. Fedn., 1953-57, life trustee, 1968; life dir. Citizens Research, Inc., 1967; dir. Columbus Found., 1944-69. Mem. Phi Beta Kappa, Alpha Chi Rho. Clubs: University, Rocky Fork, Kit Kat. Home: Columbus, O. Died May 15, 1974.

SCARBOROUGH, JAMES BLAINE, ret. educator; b. Mt. Gilead, N.C., June 22, 1885; s. Isham Wilson and Jane (Haywood) S.; A.B., U. N.C., 1913, A.M., 1914; Ph.D., Johns Hopkins U., 1923; m. Lessie Neville, June 30, 1915 (dec.); children—Lucile Elizabeth, James Blaine (dec.), Ernest Neville; m. 2d, Julia Kauffman, Aug. 18, 1930; 1 son, William Kauffman. Instr. math., N.C. State Coll., Raleigh, 1914-18; instr. math., U.S. Naval Acad., Annapolis, Md., 1918-21, asst. prof., 1921-28, asso. prof., 1928-37, prof., 1937-50, prof. emeritus, from 1950. Cons. in numerical analysis Naval Ordinance Lab.; sr. cons. Trident Engring. Assn., 1961. Fellow A.A.A.S.; mem. Am. Math. Soc., Math. Assn. Am., Phi Beta Kappa. Recipient Cain Math. medal U. N.C., 1912. Presbyn. Club: Naval Academy Officers (Annapolis). Author: Numerical Mathematical Analysis, 1930, 50, 55, 58, 62, 66; The Gyroscope: Theory and Applications 1958; Differential Equations and Applications, 1965; co-author: Fundamentals of Statistics, 1948. Contbr. articles on math. subjects to profl. jours. Home: Annapolis, Md. Died Dec. 29, 1974; interred Annapolis, Md.

SCARPELLO, GAETANO, justice; b. Misilmeri, Palermo, Italy, Aug. 31, 1903; s. Angelo and Maria Francesca (Di Pisa) S.; Dr. Jurisprudence, U. Palermo, 1924; m. Antonio Maletesta, Apr. 18, 1938; children—Maria Francesca (Mrs. Andrea Di Martino), Caterina (Mrs. Antonio Munafo). Justice appeals, 1943-49; Justice Supreme Ct. Cassation, 1949; chief legislative office Ministry Justice, 1949-65; presiding Justice Supreme Ct. Cassation, Rome, 1965-69, procurator gen., 1969-70, chief justice, 1970—. Mem. exec. com. World Assn. Judges. Editor: (with G. Branca) Commentario del Codica Civile. Home: Rome, Italy, Died 1974.

SCATCHARD, GEORGE (SKATCH'ÄRD), educator, phys. chemist; b. Oneonta, N.Y., Mar. 19, 1892; s. Elmer Ellsworth and Fanny Lavinia (Harmer) S.; Oneonta Normal Sch., 1898-1909; A.B., Amherst Coll., 1913, Sc.D. (hon.), 1948; Ph.D., Columbia, 1917; m. Willian Watson Beaumont, July 28, 1928. Asst., Amherst Coll., 1911-13; lab. asst., Columbia U., 1913-14, asst., 1914-15, Goldschmidt fellow, 1915-16, research asst., 1916-17; asso. prof. chemistry, Amherst Coll., 1919-23; Nat. Research fellow, Mass. Inst. Tech., 1923-24, temp. asst. prof. physical chemistry, 1924-26, asso. prof., 1926-37, prof., 1937-57, prof. emeritus of physical chemistry, from 1957. Guggenheim fellow, 1931-32. Served as 1st lt., Sanitary Corps, U.S. Army, 1917-19. Chief Research Control Branch and Scientific Adviser to Deputy Military Gov. Office of U.S. Military Govt. in Germany, 1946. Recipient Theodore Richard Williams Medal, 1954; Kendall Co. award in Celloid Chemistry, 1962. Mem. National Academy of Sciences, A.A.A.S., Am. Acad. Arts and Sciences, Am. Assn. Univ. Profs., Am. Chem. Soc., Phi Gamma Delta, Phi Beta Kappa, Phi Lambda Upsilon, Sigma Xi, Alpha Chi Sigma. Home: Cambridge, Mass. Died Dec. 9, 1973.

SCHAAF, FERDINAND RICHARD, banker; b. Hamburg, Germany, Apr. 15, 1878; s. Richard and Catherine (Schlueter) S.; brought by parents to U.S., 1880; ed. common schs. and Bryant & Stratton Business Coll., student corr. law sch.; unmarried. Clk., Standard Oil Co., Whiting, Ind., 1898-1904; twp. trustee, Whiting, 1904-08; organizer Hammond (Ind.) Savings & Trust Co., 1906; postmaster, Hammond, 1912; reorganizer East Chicago (Ind.) State Bank, 1912; pres. Citizens Nat. Bank, Hammond, 1913; organizer Farmers & Merchants Bank, Highland, Ind., 1914; pres. First Nat. Bank, Gary, Ind., 1917-32; organizer, 1921, and pres. Bankers Trust Co., Gary; organizer, 1926, and pres. Northern Ind. Bankers Finance Co.; organizer, 1929, and pres. Gary First Nat. Corpn.; dir. Lake County Title Co. Member Japan Society New York. Republican; county chmn., 1908-12. Mason. Clubs: Gary Country; Chicago Athletic, South Shore Country (Chicago); Columbia (Indianapolis); Seaview Golf (Absecon, N.J.); Los Angeles Country Club of Beverly Hills, Calif. (res. mem.). Home: Gary, Ind.†

SCHAEFFER, HARRY BRENT, clergyman, educator; b. Newberry, S.C., Aug. 30, 1891; s. William Calhoun and Jennie (Hahn) S.; B.A., Newberry (S.C.) Coll., 1910, M.A., 1912; B.D., Lutheran Southern Seminary, Columbia, S.C., 1925; D.D. from Newberry College, 1928; m. Lora Neas, of Newport, Tennessee, Aug. 28, 1916; children—Dorothy Clare, William Brent, Margaret Elizabeth. Ordained Luth. ministry, 1915; pastor successively at Chattanooga, Tenn., Kings Mountain, N.C., and Charleston, S.C.; pres. Lenoir Rhyne Coll., Hickory, N.C., from 1926. Rotarian (gov. 58th Dist. 1931-32). Home: Hickory, N.C. Died Feb. 1, 1975.

SCHAEFFER, HENRY, theologian; b. Palatinate, Germany, Sept. 28, 1881; s. John and Margaret (Korn) S.; brought to U.S., 1891; ed. Bloomfield (N.J.) Acad. and Coll., 1901-07; U. of Chicago, 1907-08; awarded traveling scholarship, same univ., 1908; Am. Sch. for Oriental Study, Jerusalem, 1908-09; Heidelberg U., 1908; B.A., U. of Pa., 1911, Ph.D., 1912; B.D., Luth. Theol. Sem., Phila., 1917, S.T.M., 1918; Union Theol. Sem. and Columbia, 1918-19; D.D., Muhlenberg Coll., 1929; m. Elizabeth M. Kessler, June 4, 1913 (dec.); 1 son, George Kessler; m. 2d, Charlotte C. Liebbe, June 14, 1924; children—Henry Paul, Charlotte Elizabeth, Charles Luther, Prof. German and French, Episcopal Acad., Phila., 1913-15; ordained ministry, 1907; pastor Christ Luth. Ch., Chestnut Hill, Phila., 1915-19; prof. Biblical lit., Luth. Theol. Sem., Waterloo, Can., 1919-20; prof. O.T. interpretation, Luth. Theol. Sem., Maywood, Ill., 1920-42; pastor St. Paul Lutheran Church, Marion, Ohio. Mem. finance com., Chicago Church Fedn., Am. Acad. Polit. and Social Science, Am. Oriental Soc., Chicago Soc. Biblical Research, Am. Soc. Church History, Internat. Council Religious Edn. (profs. adv. sect.), Chicago United Luth. Ministerial Assn. (chmn. leadership com.), Chicago Ch. History Club; chmn. parish edn. com., Ill. Synod, U.L.C.A. Republican. Author: Social Legislation of Semites, 1915; Hebrew Tribal Economy, 1922; Call to Prophetic Service, 1926; Latest Archaeological Discoveries, 1937. Home: Marion, O.*†

SCHAEFFER, J(ACOB) PARSONS, anatomist; b. Shamokin Dam, Pa., Aug. 20, 1878; s. George Keyser and Elizabeth (Long) S.; Central Pa. Coll.; grad. U.S. Sch. of Embalming, 1900; B.E., Keystone State Normal, 1901, M.E., 1903; M.D., U. of Pa., 1907; A.M., Cornell U., 1909, Ph.D., 1910; hon. M.A., Yale, 1913; hon. Sc.D., Susquehanna U., 1925; honorary Litt.D., Jefferson Medical College, 1950; m. Mary Mabel Bobb, Aug. 5, 1903; 1 son, Bobb. Supervising prin. E. Greenville Pub. Schs., 1901-03; resident physician U. of Pa. Hosp., 1908; demonstrator med. anatomy, 1907, instr., 1908-10, asst. prof., 1910-11, Cornell U.; asst. prof. anatomy, Yale, 1911-12, prof., 1912-14; prof. gen. anatomy and dir. Daniel Baugh Inst. of Anatomy of Jefferson Med. Coll., Phila., 1914-48, prof. anatomy emeritus Jefferson Med. Coll., from 1948. Co-recipient Gold medal, A.M.A., 1931; Strittmatter award, 1944; The Clarence E. Shaffrey, S.J. Medal award, 1959. Mem. Assn. Am. Anatomists, A.A.A.S., Am. Genetic Assn., Phila. Acad. of Natural Scis., Am. Philos. Soc., Coll. of Phys. Phila., A.M.A., Med. Soc. of Pa., Sigma Xi (hon.), Alpha Omega Alpha (hon.), Omega Upsilon Phil; corr. fellow Am. Laryngol. Assn. Presbyterian. Clubs: Graduate (New Haven), University, Medical (Phila.), Cornell, Yale. Author: The Nose and the Olfactory Organ in Man; The Nose, Paranasal Sinuses, Lacrimal Passageways and Olfactory Organ in Man; The Respiratory System, in 6th to 12th editions of Morris' Human Anatomy; The Dissection of the Human Body; Waymarks in the Legalizing of Practical Anatomy in America; Outlines and Directions for the Dissection of the Human Body. Co-author: The Head and Neck in Roentgen Diagnosis. Editor: 10th, 11th edit, Morris Human Anatomy. Contbr. to Special Cytology, to The Nose, Throat and Ear and Their Diseases, Otolaryngology, also many papers and monographs on anatomy and embryology in scientific and tech. jours. and revs. Home: Philadelphia, Pa.†

SCHAFFER, LOUIS HUTZLER, physician; b. Balt., Nov. 5, 1930; s. Alexander Jonas and Ruth (Hutzler) S.; M.D., Johns Hopkins, 1956; m. Marianne Weil, Oct. 19, 1957; children—Natalie, Michael Weil, Andrew. Internal medicine intern Univ. Hosps. of Cleve., 1956-57, asst. resident in internal medicine, 1957-58; asst. resident in pvt. medicine Johns Hopkins Hosp., Balt., 1960-61, fellow in cardiology, 1961-62, physician outpatient dept., 1963-73; active staff Sinai Hosp. of Balt., 1963-73; attending physician Balt. City Hosp., 1963-73; attending staff Greater Balt. Med. Center, 1964-73; asst. in internal medicine Johns Hopkins, 1964-73. Mem. med. com. Asso. Jewish Charity and Welfare Fund, Balt. Bd. dirs. Balt. Jewish Com., Balt. Symphony Orch. Served to lt. M.C., USNR, 1958-60. Diplomate Am. Bd. Internal Medicine. Home: Baltimore, Md. Died Feb. 4, 1973; buried Balt. Hebrew Cemetery, Baltimore, Md.

SCHAIRER, OTTO SORG, v.p. Radio Corp. of America; b. Saline, Mich., Oct. 7, 1879; s. George Edward and Sophia (Sorg) S.; A.B., U. of Mich., 1901, B.S. in E.E., 1902, Doctor of Engineering (honorary), 1942; admitted to Pennsylvania bar, 1912; m. Elizabeth Blanche Swift, June 28, 1905; children—George Swift, Robert Sorg, Julia Elizabeth. Engr. apprentice, Westinghouse Electric & Mfg. Co., 1902-03, with patent dept., 1903-19, dir. patent development, 1919-26, mgr. patent dept., 1926-29; dir. patent development Radio Corp. America, 1929-39, v.p. in charge patent dept., 1930-41; v.p. in charge RCA Labs., 1941-45, staff vice president, 1945, retired, 1946; consultant, from 1945. Mem. Am. Institute E.E., Institute of Radio Engineers, American Bar Assn., American Patent Law Association, New York Patent Law Assn., A.A.A.S., Photog. Soc. of Am., Royal Photog. Soc. Gt. Britain. Republican. Presbyterian. Clubs: Miniature Camera (New York); Nassau, Springdale Golf, Old Guard, Highland Park, Fla., (Lake Wales, Fla.). Home: Princeton, N.J.†

SCHAPIRO, J. SALWYN, prof. history; b. Hudson, N.Y., Dec. 19, 1879; s. Moses and Sarah S.; B.S., Coll. City of N.Y., 1904; Ph.D., Columbia, 1909; m. Mary Katsin, Aug. 4, 1909 (divorced 1931); children—Mrs. Blanche Ethel Grant, Mrs. Anne White; m. 2d, Kathrine Kerestesy, Sept. 1, 1931. With Coll. City of New York since 1907, beginning as tutor in history, promoted instr. in history, 1909, asst. prof., 1915, asso. prof., 1916, prof., 1922-47; vis. prof. Columbia U., 1943, New School, 1943-45; prof. emeritus, 1947. Citation by War Dept., 1946; Townsend Harris Medal by Associate Alumni of City Coll. 1947. Mem. Am. Jewish Com., Council Institute Internationale d'Historie Politique Constitutionelle. Mem. bd. dirs. N.Y. Am. Adult Edn. Council, 1942-45; Hist. Service Bd., 1943-45; mem. Am. Hist. Assn. (mem. council, 1943-46), Council on Fgn. Relations, Phi Beta Kappa, Phi Alpha Theta. Club: Faculty (N.Y. U.). Author: Social Reform and the Reformation, 1909; Modern and Contemporary European History, 1918; Modern Times in Europe, 1927; Civilization in Europe, 1928; Condorcet and the Rise of Liberalism, 1934; Liberalism and the Challenge of Fascism: Social Forces in England and France (1815-1870), 1949 The World in Crisis, 1950; Liberalism: Its Meaning and History, 1958; Movements of Social Dissent in Modern Europe, 1962; Anticlericalism: Conflict between Church and State in France, Italy and Spain, 1967. Contbr. chapter to Essays in Intellectual History, 1929, also articles Cyclo. of Social Science and articles and revs. in mags. Editorial bd. of Jour. of the History of Ideas and The American Scholar. Home: New York City, N.Y. Died Dec. 30, 1973.

SCHAUFUS, CHARLES PATRICK, mfg. co. exec.; b. Waltham, Mass., Mar. 17, 1922; s. Arthur Leyson and Mary Alice (Ward) S.; student Wentworth Inst., 1952, Boston State Tchrs. Coll., 1954, Boston U. Med. Sch., 1955-56; m. Dorothy Eleanor Monahan, June 11, 1944; children—Donna (Mrs. John J. Dacey), Carole (Mrs. Donald G. Brophy), Charles Patrick, Stephen W., Lynne M. Foreman, Lovell Chem. Co., Watertown, Mass., 1945-54; with Millipore Corp. filter mfg. and equipment, Bedford, Mass., 1954-74, tech. sales staff, 1968-71, asst. to v.p. mktg., 1971-74. Cons., U.S. Pharmacopia, 1969-73. Vice pres. Pillsbury Lake Mgmt., Webster, N.H., 1967. Served with USNR, 1942-45. Mem. Soc. Cosmetic Chemists, Soc. Indsl. Microbiology, Am. Soc. Microbiology, Parenteral Drug Assn. (dir. 1968-74, pres. 1970-71). K.C. Club: Pillsbury Lake (N.H.) Boosters. Patentee in field. Contbr. articles to profl. jours. Home: Waltham, Mass. Died July 1974.

SCHEELINE, JULIA SCHOENFELD, (Mrs. Isaiah Scheeline), social worker; b. Bellaire, O., Apr. 19, 1878; s. Alexander and Rose (Hartman) Schoenfeld; A.B., Alleghany Coll., Meadville, Pa., 1897, hon. A.M., 1915; student Woman's Med. Coll., Toronto, Can., 1898; A.M., Columbia, 1909; m. Isaiah Scheeline, of Altoona, Pa., Sept. 25, 1916; 1 son, Isaiah. Head resident, Columbian Settlement, Pittsburgh, 1900-03; sec. immigrant aid com. Council of Jewish Women, 1910-11; field sec. Playground Recreation Assn. America, 1911-14; dir. western div. State of Pa. Child Labor Assn., 1913-16; head resident director of the Irene Kaufman Settlement, Pittsburgh, Pennyslvania, 1914-16; county chairman, home and war relief, Woman's Com. of Council Nat. Defense, Blair County. Made investigation of amusement resources of working girls in N.Y. City which led to first dance hall regulations; investigation of after-care for tuberculosis patients discharged from New York sanitaria, which led to marked reforms. Mem. Am. Sociol. Soc., Phi Beta Kappa. Home: Hollidaysburg, Pa.†

SCHELL, HERBERT HANNAN, corp. exec.; b. New York, N.Y., Apr. 1, 1892; s. Edward and Maria (Clohessy) S.; ed. Poly. Prep. Country Day Sch., Brooklyn, N.Y., 1905-10, Phila. Textile Inst., 1910-13; m. Abigail M. O'Leary, Jan. 8, 1919; children—Herbert H., Edward Timothy, Martha Dail, With Sidney

Blumenthal & Co., Inc., 1926-54, v.p. 1929, dir., gen. mgr. 1930, pres., gen. mgr. 1934, chmn. bd., chief exec. officer, 1953, retired 1954; pres. and dir. Shelton Looms Distributing Corp., San Francisco. Trustee, member executive committee Dollar Savings Bank of N.Y.; dir., mem. executive com. Long Island Trust Co.; mem. adv. com. Chase Nat. Bank, Dir. Am. Found. Tropical Medicine. Mem. N.A.M. (dir., mem. exec. com.), N.Y. Acad. Scis., Marine Hist. Assn. Nat. Indsl. Information Council (nat. vice chmn.), Inter-Am. Council of Commerce and Production (trustee U.S. sect.), Jr. Achievement (mem. adv. council), del. to Internat. Labor Conf. Brussels, Geneva, Lyon. Served in U.S. Army, World War. Clubs: Union League, Canadian (N.Y.C.); Recess (Detroit); Cherry Valley Golf (Garden City, N.Y.); Royal Bermuda Yacht; Lawrence Beach (Atlantic Beach, L.I.). Home: Garden City, L.I. N.Y. Died July 1, 1973.

SCHELL, SAMUEL DUVALL, lawyer; b. Frederick, Md., Nov. 20, 1896; s. John E. and Ida May (Fleming) S.; ed. public schools, Frederick, Maryland; LL.B., Georgetown University; unmarried. Asst. to county treas., Frederick, Md., 1914-15; asst. to gen. freight and passenger agent, H. & F. Ry Co., 1915-18; with U.S. Shipping Bd. and Merchant Fleet Corp., 1919-59, pres. and chmn. bd., 1936; formerly exec. dir. U.S. Maritime Commn. and exec. dep. adminstr. War Shipping Adminstrn. Admitted to Fed. Cts. and Md. bar; mem. firm Canfield, Schell, Hannan & Bastiello. Mem. industry storage adv. com. Munitions Bd., Dept. of Defense. Served with Engrs. Corps, U.S. Army, A.E.F., 1918-19. Received Presdl. Citation. Mem. Am., Fed. and D.C. bar assns., Vets. Fgn. Wars, Nat. Defense Transportation Assn. (national vice president), Veterans of World War I, Am. Legion, Frederick Co. Fish and Game Protective Assn., Delta Theta Phi. Democrat. Lutheran, Mason, Elk. Clubs: Propeller of U.S. (nat. v.p.); Congressional Country (Washington). Author numerous articles on Merchant Marine. Home: Braddock Heights, Md. Died Feb. 24, 1975.

SCHELL, WILLIAM PETER, clergyman; b. Reading, Pa., Apr. 17, 1878; s. Frank Reamer and Carolina Louise (Hickok) S.; grad. Lawrenceville (N.J.) Sch., 1896; A.B., Williams Coll., 1901; grad. Auburn Theol. Sem., 1904; D.D., Mo. Valley Coll., 1922, Williams, 1923; m. Emily Stebbins Mayo, Oct. 12, 1904 (died Jan. 5, 1925); children—(adopted) Eleanor Frances, Robert Gordon; m. 2d, Harriet A. De Hondt, Oct. 19, 1929. Ordained Presbyn. ministry, 1904; pastor Springville, N.Y., First Ch., Seneca Falls, N.Y., to 1913; Bd. of Foreign Missions Presbyn. Ch. U.S.A. 1913-48, exec. secretary, 1921-48; field rep. Biblical Sem. in N.Y., from May 1948. Has served as pres. Presbyn. Union of N.Y. City, chmn. bd. mgrs. Missionary Edn. Movement of U.S. and Can.; also preacher in colls. and prep. schs.; mem. Gen. Council Presbyn. Ch. in U.S.A.; speaker at army camps, Chaplain's Training Sch. and Camp Taylor, Louisville, Ky., World War. Mem. bd. dirs. Auburn Theol. Sem.; vice chmn. trustees Yenching U., Peking, China; chmn. Internat. Med. Missionary Soc.; mem. bd. trustees Bibl. Sem., N.Y. Mem. Presbyterian Union, English-Speaking Union, China Soc., Kappa Alpha, Gargoyle (Williams). Republican. Clubs: Clergy, Chi Alpha. Home: Bronxville, N.Y.†

SCHELLBERG, WILLIAM HENRY, b. Omaha, Neb., Dec. 14, 1881; s. John David and Hansine (Hansen) S.; ed. grade schs., Omaha; m. Miss Jelinek, Oct. 20, 1910. Began as stenographer Union Stock Yards Co. of Omaha, Ltd., 1901, and continued with the co., pres., 1929-43, was also gen. mgr. and dir. Lutheran. Home: Omaha, Neb.*†

SCHEMAN, LOUIS, physician; b. N.Y.C., Dec. 25, 1907; s. Abraham and Rebecca (Goldberg) S.; M.D., N.Y.U., 1933; m. Marjorie Rusnak, Dec. 2, 1941; children—Nancy (Mrs. Steven Johnson), Andrew. Intern, Michael Reese Hosp., Chgo., 1933-36, resident in orthopedic surgery, 1939-41; resident in surgery Mt. Sinai Hosp., N.Y.C., 1936-37; asso. attending in orthopedic surgery Cook County Hosp., Chgo., 1945-49; sr. attending in orthopedic surgery Highland Park (Ill.) Hosp.; cons. in orthopedic surgery Lake County Gen. Hosp.; clin. asso. prof. bone and joint surgery U. Chgo. Served to lt. col. M.C., AUS, 1941-45. Diplomate Am. Bd. Orthopedic Surgery. Fellow Am. Acad. Orthopedic Surgeons, A.C.S., Internat. Coll. Surgeons, Chgo. Inst. Medicine; mem. A.M.A. Contbr. articles to profl. jours. Home: Highland Park, Ill., Died Nov. 3, 1972; buried Shalom Meml. Park, Palatine, Ill.

SCHER, PHILLIP GEORGE, bishop; b. Belleville, Ill., Feb. 22, 1880; s. Phillip Joseph and Catherine (Wagern) S.; ed. St. Peter's Cathedral Sch., Belleville, Ill., 1887-93, Pontifical Coll. Josephenum, Columbus, O., 1893-96; Ph.B., Univ. dir Propaganda Fide, Rome, 1896, S.T.L., 1902. Ordained priest Roman Cath. Ch., 1903; prof. Josephenum Coll., 1903-04; asst. at St. Bibiana Cathedral, Los Angeles, 1904, successively pastor Our Lady of Sorrows Ch., Santa Barbara, Our Lady of Mt. Carmel Ch., Montecito, St. Bridget's Ch., Hanford, St. Francis Ch., Bakersfield, St. Joseph's Ch., Capitola, 1905-30; pastor Old Missions at Monterey and Carmel, 1930-32; vicar gen. and administrator of the Diocese, 1931-33, bishop from 1933. Address: Fresno, Cal.†

SCHIAPARELLI, ELSA, couturiére; b. Rome, Italy; ed. in schs. of France. Switzerland, Eng.; married and divorced; 1 dau., Marisa (Mrs. Robert Lawrence Berenson) Active designer of fashions for women since late 1920's; a leading couturiére from 1935; established own shop, Paris, 1930, and removed to present larger premises, 1935; following end of German occupation, re-opened Paris shop, 1945; established branch for design and manufacture, N.Y. City, 1949, having previously opened Schiaparelli Parfum, Inc., in that city. Was in Eng. at outbreak of World War I, and shortly went to U.S. where spent several years; returned to Paris and became French citizen; during German invasion, World War II, turned over Paris home for use of Am. Friends Service (Quakers), also for Use as meeting place for Am. ambulance personnel; while in N.Y. City in this war period served as nurses aid Bellevue Hosp. Home: Paris, France. Died Nov. 13, 1973.

SCHIFF, SYDNEY KAUFMAN, lawyer; b. Milw., Aug. 21, 1900; s. Isaac and Carrie (Marks) S.; Ph.B., U. Chgo., 1921, J.D., 1923; m. Evelyn Wilson, 1946. Admitted to Ill. bar, 1923; mem. firm Schiff Hardin & Waite, Chgo., 1927-71; counsellor at law, from 1972; dir. Equitable Gas Co., Pitts., Ill. Consol. Telephone Co., Mattoon. Cons. Northwestern Pub. Service Co., Huron, S.D. Mem. citizens bd. U. Chgo. Clubs: Tavern (Chgo.); Racquet, O'Donnell Golf (Palm Springs, Cal.); Lawyers (N.Y.C.). Home: Chicago, Ill. Died May 15, 1973.

SCHILLER, AVERY REUBENS, utility exec.; b. Spokane, May 19, 1890; s. Jacob A. and Celia (Reubens) S.; B.S., Harvard, 1911, M. Elec. Engring., 1912; LL.D., New Eng. Coll., 1953; m. Dorothy Madeline Crawford, Oct. 15, 1912 (dec. Mar. 1964); m. 2d, Anabelle Landers, Dec. 31, 1965. Statistician Stone & Webster, Boston, 1912-14; clk. to asst. gen. mgr. Conn. Power Co., New London, 1914-17; supr. distbn. Adirondack Electric Power Corp., Glens Falls, N.Y., 1917; elec. engr. John A. Stevens, Inc., Lowell, Mass., 1920-22; asst. to pres. Manchester Traction Light & Power Co. (N.H.), 1924-26; with Pub. Service Co. N.H., Manchester, from 1926, v.p. charge operations, 1926-41, v.p., gen. mgr., 1941-42, pres., 1942-65, chmn. bd., 1965-70, chmn. emeritus, hon. dir., 1970-74; hon. trustee Amoskeag Savs. Bank, Manchester. Civilian aide to sec. army, 1954-62. Served from pvt. to 1st lt. U.S. Army, 1917-19. Recipient Charles Holmes Pattee medal U. N.H., 1956; Named Man of Year, Manchester C. of C., 1958. Fellow I.E.E.E. Clubs: Abenagui Beach (Rye Beach, N.H.); Harvard (Boston and N.H.); Manchester Country. Home: Manchester, N.H. Died Jan. 19, 1974; interred Pine Grove Cemetery, Manchester, N.H.

SCHIMPFF, CHARLES HENRY, trust co. exec.; b. Peoria, Ill., Apr. 7, 1897; s. Gustave H. and Lillie M. (Cullom) S.; student Bradley Polytech. Inst., 1911-15, Cornell U.S., 1915-17; m. Jane S. Wheeler, Oct. 18, 1919; 1 son, Charles W. Engaged in mfg., 1919-21, installment finance, 1922-28, investment banking, 1929-41, bank holding, 1942-44, mutual fund mgmt., 1947-75; pres., dir. Am. Mut. Fund, Inc., Los Angles, 1960-68; chmn., dir. The Capital Group, Inc., 1967-75; dir. Conrac Corp. Pres. Investment Co. Inst., 1962. Served with USAC, 1918-19. Mem. Phi Kappa Psi. Clubs: California, Los Angeles, Valley Hunt (Los Angeles). Home: San Marino, Cal., Died May 3, 1975.

SCHIOTZ, AKSEL, educator, tenor; b. Roskilde, Sept. 1, 1906; student langs. U. Copenhagen (Denmark); m. Gerda Haugsted: 5 children. Operatic debut, 1939; recital singer, 1942—; appearances in Eng., 1946, U.S., 1948; mem. faculty Royal Conservatory Music, U. Toronto, 1958—, now prof. voice. Died Apr. 19, 1975.

SCHJELDERUP, HARALD KRABBE, educator; b. Dypvaag, Norway, May 21, 1895; s. Kristian Vilhelm Koren and Hendy (Hassel) S.; Ph.D., 1920; m. Mildrid Bordewick, 1924 (div. 1947); m. 2d, Sigfried Hanssen Brusted, 1954. Prof. philosophy U. Oslo (Norway), 1922-28, prof. psychology, 1928-65. Mem. Nat. Film Council, 1947; mem. Scandinavian Culture Commn., chmn. sect. I, 1954-57. Decorated knight Order St. Olaf; recipient Monradske Gold medal, 1916. Mem. Norwegian Psychoanalytic Assn. (chmn. 1954), Norwegian Acad. Sci. and Letters, Finnish Acad. Sci., Internat. Soc. for Clin. and Exptl. Hypnosis (dir. 1958). Author: Til Sansefornemmelsernes Psyko-fysiologl, 1919; Filosofiens historie, 1924; Psykologi, 1927; Nevrosene og den devrotiske karakter, 1940. Contbr. articles to profl. jours. Home: Oslo, Norway. Deceased.

SCHLADERMUNDT, PETER, indsl. designer, architect, painter; b. Bronxville, N.Y., Jan. 14, 1907; s. Herman Theodore and Anna R. (Gardner) S.; B.F.A., Yale, 1929; m. Jean Lichty, Aug. 8, 1934; children—Joan (Mrs. William B. Osgood III), Susan (Mrs. Donald F. Daly), Eric Peter. Designer Kenneth Franzheim, Sloan & Robertson, Raymond Hood, N.Y. City, 1929-32; indsl. designer Henry Dreyfuss, 1933-35; indsl. designer Norman Bel Geddes, N.Y.C. 1935-38, design dir., 1938-42, partner, 1943-44; partner Van Doren, Nowland & Schladermundt, N.Y.C., Phila., 1944-49, Nowland & Schladermundt, N.Y.C., 1950-54; prin. Peter Schladermundt Assos. (named changed to Peter Schladermundt Co.), 1955-75. Mem. A.I.A. Mem. Reformed Ch. Clubs: Yale (N.Y.C.); Gardiners Bay Country (Shelter Island); Yacht (Shelter Island). Contbr. profl. jours. Developer, designer products, packaging, corporate idenity grahics for indsl. clients, U.S. Dept. Commerce. Home: Bronxville, N.Y., Died July 2, 1975; buried Grove Cemetery, Eastford, Conn.

SCHLAIKJER, ERICH MAREN, cons. geologist, engineer; b. Newton, O., Nov. 22, 1905; s. Erich and Clara (Ryser) S.; B.S., Harvard, 1929, M.A., Columbia, 1931, Ph.D., 1935; m. Josephine Ayres, Apr. 28, 1951; children—Maren, Michael, Patrecia Jo. In charge, 10 geol. and paleontol. expedn., Gt. Plains Area of U.S. for Harvard U., 1925-34, Yukon Terr. Alaska Expdn. for Am. Museum of Nat. History, 1936, with Barnum Brown, Am. Museum-Sinclair Expdn., southwestern Wyo., 1937; m.e Am. Museum-Sweet Expdns., Big Bend Area, Tex., 1939-40, Comml. Petroleum and Mining Geology, Rocky Mountain Area, 1946-49, tutor of geology, Bklyn. Coll., 1932-34, instr., 1935-39, asst. prof., 1940-47, prof., 1948-50; pres. Lakota Petroleum Corp., 1950-67. Served in U.S. Air Force, 1st lt., 1942, active duty advanced to lt. col., 1945. Awarded Bronze Star Medal, Army Commendation Ribbon, seven campaign stars to the Asiatic Pacific Theatre Ribbon. Awarded (with Barnum Brown) Cressy Morrison prize, N.Y. Acad. Sci., 1939. University fellow Columbia U. Fellow Geol. Soc. Am., Paleontol. Soc. Am., A.A.A.S.; mem. Am. Assn. Petroleum Geologists, Nat. Soc. Profl. Engrs., Am. Geophys. Union, Soc. for the Study of Evolution, Am. Inst. Profl. Geologists (charter), Sigma Xi. Clubs: Explorer's (dir., 1942-43, sec., 1947-49 and various coms.), Harvard (N.Y.C.); Petroleum, Columbine Country (Denver) Contbr. articles on geology and paleontology to profl. jours. Home: Littleton, Colo., Deceased.

SCHLEE, STANLEY CURREN, judge; b. nr. Yale, Mich., July 30, 1910; s. Henry G. and Bertha (Curren) S.; A.A., Port Huron Jr. Coll., 1931; A.B., U. Mich., 1933, J.D., 1936; m. Jean Elizabeth Porter, Nov. 13, 1937; children—James, Richard, Barbara. Admitted to Mich. bar, 1936; practiced in Port Huron, Mich., 1937-67; asst. pros. atty. St. Clair County, Mich., 1951-54; judge 31st Jud. Circuit, St. Clair County, Port Huron, 1967-72. St. Clair County Republican chmn., 1954-62; del. Republican Nat. Conv., 1956. Served with AUS, 1944-46. Decorated Bronze Star medal. Mem. St. Clair County Bar Assn. (pres. 1950), V.F.W., Am. Legion. Episcopalian. Mason (Shriner), Elk. Club: Black River Country. Home: Port Huron, Mich. Died Aug. 26, 1972; interred Port Huron, Mich.

SCHLESINGER, EDWARD RALPH, physician; b. N.Y.C., July 27, 1911; s. Louis H. and Theresa (Siegel) S.; B.S., Columbia, 1931, M.D., 1934; M.P.H., Johns Hopkins, 1941; m. Sylvia Nelson, Dec. 21, 1939; children—Ann-Louise (Mrs. Stuart B. Silver), Stephen. Intern, Mt. Sinai Hosp., N.Y.C., 1934-37, Babies Hosp., N.Y.C., 1937-38; intern in contagious diseases Willard Parker Hosp., N.Y.C., 1937; L. Emmett Holt fellow in diseases of children Columbia Coll. Phys. and Surg., 1939; dir. Bur. Maternal and Children Health, N.Y. State Dept. Health, Albany, 1946-52, asso. dir. div. med. service, 1952-59, asst. commr. spl. health service, 1960-66; prof., head maternal and child health program Grad. Sch. Pub. Health, U. Pitts., 1966-74, asso. dean acad. affairs, 1969-74; prof. preventive medicine and community health Albany Med. Coll., 1959-66. Mem. steering com. Regional Pediatric Program. Bd. dirs. Hill House Assn., Terrace Village Health Center. Diplomate Am. Bd. Pediatrics. Fellow Am. Pub. Health Assn. (chmn. maternal and child health sect.), Am. Acad. Pediatrics; mem. Assn. Tchrs. Maternal and Child Health (past pres.), A.A.A.S., Am. Acad. Polit. and Social Scis., Phi Beta Kappa, Sigma Xi. Author: Health Services for the Mother and Child; Long Term Childhood Illness; The Maternal and Child Health Section: A Political & Social History. Contbr. articles to profl. jours. Home: Pittsburgh, Pa. Died Aug. 21, 1974; buried Wellwood Cemetery, Pine Lawn, N.Y.

SCHLESSER, GEORGE ERNEST, educator; b. Portland, Ore., Apr. 12, 1907; s. George Ernest and Anna Maude (Lucia) S.; B.S., U. Ore., 1930, M.A., 1931; student Stanford 1933; Ph.D., Yale, 1937; m. Lois Elizabeth Piper, Aug. 16, 1938; 1 son, Thomas Piper. Research asst. U. Ore., 1930-31; secondary sch. tchr., 1931-35; teaching fellow Yale, 1935-37; instr., asso. prof. Colgate U., 1937-49, prof., 1949-73, chmn. dept. edn., 1949-73, dir. summer Programs, 1950-73, dir. tchr. edn. Five-Coll. Coop. Study, 1965-68, acting dir. graduate studies, 1968-69, dir. grad. studies, 1969-73, dir. ednl. research measurement ednl. change, 1967-73; vis. lectr. U. Mich., summer 1938, San Diego State Coll., 1948. Dir. research Kettering-Colgate Ednl. Change Project, 1967-73; Pres. Hamilton Community Forum, 1948-50. Social Sci. Research Council grantee for measurement persistence of indsl. personnel, 1952; Coll. Entrance Exam. research grantee for measurement and analysis academic motivation, 1959-65. Mem. Am. Psychol. Assn., N.Y. State Edn. Research Assn., Am. Edn. Research Assn., Am. Assn. U. Profs., Phi Delta Kappa, Phi Beta Kappa (hon.). Author books, articles on edn. and psychology, Personal Values Inventory. Home: Hamilton, N.Y. Died May 14, 1973; interred Colgate U. Cemetery, Hamilton, N.Y.

SCHMERTZ, ROBERT J., profl. basketball team exec.; b. 1928; s. Louis Schmertz; ed. N.Y. U.; m. Phyllis Kane; children by previous marriage Ronald, Nancy, Jane. Pres., chmn. bd. Leisure Tech. Corp., Lakewood, N.J.; former part owner Portland Trailblazers Nat. Basketball Assn. team; now chmn. bd., owner Boston Celtics Nat. Basketball Assn. team. Served with USAF, until 1945. Mem. Nat. Assn. Home Builders (past pres.). Home: Lakewood, N.J. Died July 23, 1975.

SCHMICK, FRANKLIN BUSH, investment banker; b. St. Louis, Dec. 17, 1904; s. William Louis and Daisy (Leonard) S.; student Washington U., 1921-22, Lake Forest Coll., 1922-23; m. Lenore Mueller; 3 children. Pres. First Consol. Securities Co., 1936-38, Fisher Schmick & Watts, 1937-38; v.p. Straus Securities Co., 1939-45; partner Straus & Blosser, Chgo., 1945-51; v.p., dir. H. M. Byllesby & Co. to 1957, pres., 1957, also dir.; dir. Continental Connector Corp., DeJur-Amsco Corp., Advance-Ross Electronics Corp., Byllesby Energy and Shale Corp., Mueller Co. Helene Curtiss Industries, Inc., Chgo., Milw., St. Paul & Pacific R.R., Susquehanna Corp. Chmn. Ill. Bldg. Authority; dir. Lincoln Park Zool. Soc. Trustee U. Chgo. Cancer Research Found. Clubs: Attic, Chgo. Athletic Assn., Midday, Wall Street, Tavern, Bob O'Links Golf. Home: Chicago Ill. Died Nov. 3, 1973.

SCHMIDLIN, THEODOR, Swiss ambassador; b. Berne, witzerland, June 17, 1917; s. Titus and Marie S.; Dr. Law, U. Berne; m. Claire Lemke, Sept. 7, 1944. With polit. dept. Swiss Govt., 1942—; assigned to Belgrade, Prague, Moscow; Consul gen., Salgon; dep. chief of mission, Bonn, Germany; ambassador to Malaysia, Kuala, Lumpur, 1968—. Home: Switzerland, Died Apr. 1974.

SCHMIDT, LOUIS BERNARD, prof. history; b. Belle Plaine, Ia., Sept. 8, 1879; s. Otto and Louise (Mall) S.; Ph.B., Cornell Coll., Ia., 1901, A.M., 1906, Litt.D., 1934; post-grad. study, U. of Chicago, U. of Wis., U. of Ia.; m. Georgia Perle Wilson, June 16, 1903; children—Robert William Francis, Louise Bernard, H. Asst. prof. history, Ia. State Coll. Agr. and Mech. Arts, 1906-11, asso. prof., 1911-19, professor and head department history and government, 1919-45, professor history, from 1945; professor American history and internat. relations, summers, U. of Alabama, 1928-32, 1946, Univ. of Texas, 1935, 39, 1942. University of Oregon, summer 1947. Lecturer at U.S. Army Sch., Iowa State College, summer 1918; chmn. War Issues Course S.A.T.C., same coll., fall of 1918. Research Asso. State Hist. Soc. of Ia. at various intervals. Mem. advisory board Columbia U. Studies in History of Am. Agr.; mem. editorial bd. Miss. Valley Hist. Review. Mem. Am. Hist. Assn., Miss. Valley Hist. Assn., State Hist. Soc. of Ia., Iowa Society of Social Science Teachers (pres., 1916) Southern Hist. Assn., Agrl. Hist. Soc. (pres., 1933-34), Iowa Authors Club, Phi Beta Kappa, Phi Kappa Phi, Gamma Sigma Delta, Pi Gamma Mu. Methodist. Democrat. Author: The Economic Hist. of Am. Agriculture as a Field for Study, 1915; (studies) The Influence of Wheat and Cotton on Anglo-American Relations During the Civil War, 1918; The Internal Grain Trade in the United States, 1860-90, 1921-22; The Agricultural Revolution in the Prairies and the Great Plains of the United States, 1934; Whither Agrarian Economy in the United States, 1936; Internal Commerce and the Development of National Economy before 1860, 1939; The Family Farm in the Machine Age, 1941; Topical Studies and References on the History of American Agriculture, 4th edit. rev., 1940; Topical Studies and References on the United States as a World Power, 1898-1945, 2d edit. rev., 1945; Topical Studies and References on the Farmers' Movement in the United States, 1650-1948, 1948; Agricultural Organizations, in A Century of Farming in Iowa by the Iowa State College Staff, 1946; Iowa; Hawkeye State, 1950; also on many other historical and educational subjects. Editor (with E.D. Ross) of Readings in the Economic History of American Agriculture, 1925. Contbr. to hist. mags. and periodicals, the Dictionary of Am. Biography, and the Ency. of Social Sciences. Home: Tucson, Ariz.†

SCHMIDT, WALTER A., investment banker; b. Hinsdale, Ill., Aug. 8, 1895; s. Adolph G. and Jennie (Gray) S.; student pub. schs., Hinsdale; m. Eleanor M. Marshall, June 29, 1922; 1 son, Walter Marshall. Messenger White Weld & Co., Chgo., 1912; mgr. bond dept. Standard Trust & Savs. Bank, 1922-25; Cal. rep. Halsey, Stuart & Co., 1925-26, syndicate dept., Chgo., 1927-28, sales mgr., Phila., 1929-32, N.Y.C., 1932-37; organizer, chmn. Schmidt, Roberts & Parke, Inc. merged with W.H. Newbold, & Son & Co. 1974, Phila., 1937-74. Gov. Phila.-Balt. Stock Exchange, 1957-65. Past chmn. admissions com., organizer, treas. J. Wood Platt Caddy Scholarship Trust, 1958-73. Mem. finance com. Phila. YWCA. Served as 1st sgt., World War I; St. Mihiel, Argonne. Mem. Bond Club (pres. 1943, award 1972), Municipal Bond Club, Investment Bankers Assn. Am. (past gov., past chmn. fed. legis. com., past chmn. Eastern Pa.; v.p. 1952-54, pres. 1955, 60-Year award 1972). Republican. Presbyn. Mason. Clubs: Rolling Green Golf, Union League (finance com., past gov.), U.S. Srs. Golf Assn. Home: Swarthmore, Pa. Died May 9, 1975.

SCHMIDT-ISSERSTEDT, HANS PAUL ERNST, conductor; b. Berlin, Germany, May 5, 1900; s. Paul Schmidt and Therese Isserstedt; student Hochschule für Musik, Berlin, U. Berlin, U. Heidelberg; Dr. phil., U. Münster, 1932; m. Helga Swedlund, 1936; children—Peter Smith, Erik Smith. Sr. conductor opera, Rostock, Darmstadt, Hamburg, Germany; opera dir. German Opera House, Berlin; chief conductor N. German Radio, Hamburg, from 1945, Stockholm Philharmonic Orch., 1955-64; guest conductor throughout Europe and U.S. Decorated Bulgarischer Kronenorden (Bulgaria) Kommanderukruz zun Vasa-Orden (Sweden), 1964. Mem. Kongl. Svenska Musikaliska Academien. Composer: (3 act opera) Hassan gewinnt; also orch., chamber and vocal music. Home: Hamburg, Germany. Died May 28, 1973.

SCHMITZ, LEONARD STOCKWELL, office equipment mfg. exec.; b. Chgo., Aug. 28, 1908; s. Mathias Leonard and Mary (Matthews) S.; A.B., Dartmouth, 1930; J.D., John Marshall Law Sch., 1936; m. Betty Willmarth, May 22, 1937; children—Leonard W., Steven M., Deborah. Admitted to Ill. bar, 1937; practiced in Chgo.,1940-60; chmn. bd. Acme Visible Records, Inc., Crozet, Va., 1960-72. Mem. Am. Bar Assn. Clubs: Chicago Yacht; Boar's Head, Farmington Cluntry (Charlottesville, Va.); Yacht and Country (Stuart). Home: Jensen Beach, Fla., Died Feb. 8, 1974; interred Greenwood, Va.

SCHMITZ, WOODROW ADOLPH, lawyer; b. Manitowoc, Wis., Nov. 7, 1912; s. Edward S. and Clara (Mueller) S.; student U. Wis., 1939; LL.B., Marquette U., 1942; m. Marjorie Gherna, Oct. 7, 1950; 1 dau., Merry Clare. Admitted to Wis. bar, 1942; mem. firm Schmitz & Schmitz, Manitowoc, from 1942; comn. Circuit Ct., Manitowoc, from 1948; atty. City of Manitowoc, 1949-72; counsel, dir. Kingsbury Breweries Co., 1950-60. Dir. Holiday House Manitowoc; sec. Manitowoc Motor Coach Co., Inc. Bd. dirs. Meml. Hosp., Manitowoc, Retarded Children's Assn., Manitowoc. Served to lt., inf., Aus, 1942-46. Decorated Purple Heart. Mem. Am. Legion, Am. Vets., Wis., Manitowoc County (pres. 1971-73) bar assns. Mason, Elk, Odd Fellow. Home: Manitowoc, Wis. Died Jan. 21, 1973; interred Evergreen Cemetery, Manitowoc, Wis.

SCHMUTZ, CHARLES AUSTIN, publisher; b. Richmond Hill, L.I., N.Y., June 15, 1900; s. August and Anna (Young) S.; ed. pub. schs. of Long Island; married Helen Muriel Rudolph, June 3, 1930; children Roger Clayton, Charles Austin. Reporter for the New York Tribune, 1918-20; financial-business analyst Standard Statistics Co., N.Y. City, 1920-41; mng. editor, editor-in-chief Standard & Poor's Corp., 1941-57, director, from 1940, became president, 1946, vice chmn., 1958-67. Mem. Soc. Silurians. Mason (Shriner, K.T.). Clubs: The Gulf and Bay (Sarasota, Fla.); North Hempstead Country; Lakewood Country (St. Petersburg, Fla). Home: Great Neck, L.I., N. Y. Died Oct. 12, 1974.

SCHNEBLY, JOHN THOMAS, physician; b. Topeka, Nov. 14, 1910; s. Joseph Ralph and Rose Ethel (Zimmerman) S.; M.D., U. Kan., 1935; m. Vivian Andrews, Apr. 15, 1936; children—Robert Andrews (dec.), Evalyn Sue (Mrs. Leif Arne Bilen), John Thomas, Sharon Elaine. Intern, Kansas City (Mo.) Gen. Hosp., 1935-36; eye house officer Mass. Eye and Ear Infirmary, Boston, 1936-38; asst. surgeon Childrens Hosp.; surgeon Washington Hosp. Center, Holy Cross Hosp., Silver Srping, Md.; hosp. vol., St. Lucia, Honduras. Mem. Montgomery County Corrections Adv. Com., 1970; instnl. rep. Boy Scouts Am. Bd. dirs. Vols. for Visually Handicapped, Inc., EAR, Inc., Washington. Served to maj. M.C., AUS, 1941-45. Diplomate Am. Bd. Ophthalmology. Mem. A.M.A., Am. Acad. Ophthalmology and Otolaryngology. Presbyn. (trustee, elder). Lion (past dir. Silver Spring). Home: Silver Spring, Md. Died June 2, 1974.

SCHNEIDER, ALMA KITTREDGE, govt. ofcl.; b. Denver, Aug. 21, 1901; d. Charles Marble and Anna Frederica (Von Myrbach) Kittredge; student U. of Denver, 1936 and 1949; pvt. tutors in music, art and crafts; m. Daniel Jacob Schneider, June 2, 1926. Reporter on East Jefferson Sentinel and Jefferson County Republican, Lakewood, Colo., 1934-42; licensed real estate saleswoman from 1943; supt. United States Mint, Denver from 1953. Active worker Republican part from 1930; precinct committee-women Morrison, Colo., 1932-49, vice chmn. county central com., county of Jefferson, 1934-42, vice chmn. Colo. State Central Com., 1942-48; asst. dir. women's div. nat. com., 1945, mem. nat. com. for Colo., 1948, mem. nat. policy com., 1949, elected v. chmn. Rep. Nat. Com., 1952; del. to all state convs. since 1928, to nat. conv. and mem. resolutions com. for Colo., 1944. Mem. bd. control State Indsl. Sch. for Girls, 1943-53, chmn., 1950-53; mem. adv. bd. State Child Welfare Bur., 1946-48. Member A.R.C. (volunteer since 1929), chmn. Jefferson County area, 1936-49, chmn. Jefferson County Fund Drive, 1947. Named Business and Profl. Woman of the Year, 1954. Mem. Nat. (dir. from 1956), Denver Met. (dir.) safety councils, Fed. Bus. Assn. (dir. Denver 1953-75), Business and Professional Womens Club, D.A.R. Episcopalian. Clubs: Lincoln, Womens Republican (co. and state). Home: Lakewood, Colo. Died June 10, 1975; buried Crown Hill Cemetery, Colo.

SCHNEIDER, STANLEY FREDERICK, motion picture co. exec.; b. N.Y.C., Jan. 27, 1929; s. Abraham and Ida (Briskin) S.; student Syracuse U., 1946-47; m. Margaret Louise Wilson, July 14, 1955; children—Richard Alan, Beth Shari, Todd Joseph. With Columbia Pictures Corp., 1946-75, v.p., 1963-68, 1st v.p., now pres.; v.p. Colgens Records, Screen Gems-Columbia Music, Royal Internat. Films; dir. Columbia Pictures Internat. Corp. Asso. chmn. entertainment div. Fedn. Jewish Philanthropies; mem. leadership council United Jewish Appeal. Bd. dirs. Am. Jewish Com. Home: New York City, N.Y. Died Jan. 22, 1975.

SCHNEIDER, WILMAR RUFUS, supt. schs.; b. Independence, Kan., Aug. 28, 1913; s. G. E. Rufus and Concordia Wilhelmina (Lueders) S.; A.B., Washington U., 1934, M.S., 1936, postgrad. 1950, 54, 60; postgrad. U. Mo., 1938, St. Louis U., 1942, Harris Tchrs. Coll., 1952-53; m. Eleanor M.E. Pralle, Aug. 21, 1937; children—Susan (Mrs. Walter Rehwaldt), Randall, Claire (Mrs. Jere Brew), Margaret (Mrs. J. Robert Gill). Tchr., Webster Groves (Mo.) High Sch., 1935-36; asst. prof. Westminster Coll., Fulton, Mo., 1936-41; tchr. Hadley Tech. Sch., St. Louis, 1941-50; registrar Harris Tchrs. Coll., St. Louis, 1950-54; asst. prin., prin., dir., dist. supt. St. Louis Pub. Schs., 1954-74. Bd. dirs. St. Louis White House Conf. on Edn., South Side YMCA. Mem. Mo. State Tchrs. Assn. (mem. exec. com.), Nat. Assn. Secondar Sch. Prins., Phi Beta Kappa, Sigma Xi, Phi Delta Kappa. Republican. Lutheran. Home: St. Louis, Mo. Died Apr. 23, 1974; interred Concordia Cemetery, St. Louis, Mo.

SCHNURPEL, HANS KARL, realtor; b. Eisenach, Germany, June 12, 1896; s. Gustav and Bertha (Kaiser) S.; J.D., Creighton U., 1938; m. Helen Mamie Persell, May 10, 1937. Came to U.S., 1927, naturalized, 1933. Admitted to Neb. bar, 1938; owner Lynwood Realty Co. (Cal.), 1945-73, Real Estate Sch. So. Cal., 1952-73. Del. Internat. Real Estate Congress, 1961. Mem. S.E., Downey (Cal.), Compton-Lynwood (dir. 1959-64) bds. realtors, Cal. Real Estate Assn., Nat. Assn. Real Estate Bds., Internat. Real Estate Fedn., Internat. Platform Assn., Town Hall Cal. Elk, Optimist (pres. local Club 1970). Club: Lynwood (dir.). Home: Lynwood, Cal. Died Mar. 4, 1973.

SCHNUTE, WILLIAM JACOB, physician; b. Evansville, Ind., May 23, 1914; s. William G. and Fredaricka (Heinz) S.; M.D., Ind. U., 1938; m. Doris Schnute; children—Jane (Mrs. Phillip Baugher), William J., Carl, James. Intern, U. Hosp., Ann Arbor, Mich., 1938-39, asst. resident, 1939-40, resident in orthopaedic surgery, 1940-41; staff orthopaedic surgeon Chgo. Wesley Meml. Hosp.; cons. orthopaedic surgeon Hinsdale (Ill.) Sanitorium and Hosp., Community Meml. Gen. Hosp., La. Grange, Ill., U.S. Naval Hosp., Great Lakes, Ill.; instr. orthopaedic surgery U. Mich., 1941-43; asso. prof. orthopaedics Northwestern U. Med. Sch., Chgo., also lectr. Grad. Sch.; lectr. Northeastern Ill. State Coll., Law-Sci. Acad., Crested Butte, Colo. Pres., Ill. Assn. for Crippled, 1964-65, Easter Seal Soc., 1951-56. Trustee, Village of La Grange, 1956-71. Diplomate Am. Bd. Orthopaedic Surgery. Fellow A.C.S.; mem. A.M.A., Am. Acad. Orthopaedic Surgeons, Am. Orthopaedic Assn., Chgo. Med. Soc., Chgo. Inst. Medicine, Clin. (sec.-treas. 1970-72), Chgo. (pres. 1954), U. Mich. orthopaedic socs., Assn. Am. Med. Colls., Lutheran Med. Missionary Assn. (pres. 1967-71), Russell Hibbs Soc. (pres. 1969-70), Phi Beta Pi. Lutheran. Asso. editor Jour. Bone and Joint Surgery, 1962-68; mem. editorial bd. Am. orthopaedic Assn. News. Home: La Grange, Ill. Died Oct. 27, 1972; buried Bronswood Cemetery, Oakbrook, Ill.

SCHOCKEN, THEODORE, publishing co. exec.; b. Zwickau, Germany, Oct. 8, 1914 (came to U.S. 1937, naturalized 1942); s. Salman and Lilli (Ehrmann) S.; M.B.A., Harvard, 1940; m. Dora Landauer, Apr. 11, 1941; children—Miriam (Mrs. Dan N. Michael), Naomi (Mrs. John L. Landau), Eva. Dir. Schocken A.G., Germany, 1933-38; partner Schocken Veriag Geramny, 1935-38; statistician Sears, Roebuck & Co., Chgo., 1940-42; treas. Schocken Books, Inc., N.Y.C., 1946-65, pres., 1965-75; vice-chmn., dir. Merkur A.G., Germany, 1948-51; pres. Parka Corp., N.Y.C., 1944-75. Bd. overseers Jewish Theol. Sem. Am., N.Y.C.; bd. dirs. Leo Baeck Inst., N.Y.C., Schocken Inst. Jewish Research, Jerusalem, Israel. Served to 1st. lt. AUS, 1942-45. Club: Harvard (N.Y.C.) Home: Scarsdale, N.Y., Died Mar. 20, 1975; buried Sharon Gardens, Valhalla, N.Y.

SCHOEN, EDWARD, JR., lawyer, govt. ofcl.; b. Newark, Dec. 4, 1911; s. Edward and Florence (Schloss) S.; grad. Newark Acad., 1929; A.B., Brown U., 1933; LL.B., Rutgers U., 1936; m. Mary Whitaker, 1964. Admitted to N.J. bar, 1936, N.Y. bar, D.C. bar, Md. bar, U.S. Supreme Ct. bar, Ga. bar; practiced in Newark, later N.Y.C.; asst. prosecutor Essex County (N.J.), 1946-53; spl. asst. atty. gen. U.S. Washington, 1953-54; gen. counsel Small Bus. Adminstrn., Washington, 1954-56; asso. regional adminstr. SEC, N.Y.C., 1957-60; sr. trial atty. antitrust div. Dept. Justice, N.Y.C., 1963-64; asso. firm Phillips, Nizer, Benjamin, Krim and Ballon, N.Y.C., 1964-68; hearing examiner Social Security Adminstrn., Atlanta, 1968-74; U.S. adminstrv. law judge Bur. Hearings and Appeals,

HEW, 1974. Served as maj. USAAF, 1941-46; maj. res. ret. Decorated Purple Heart. Mem. Am., Fed., N.J., Essex County, Atlanta bar assns., State Bar Ga., Assn. Bar City N.Y., Fed. Trial Examiners Conf., Assn., Health, Edn. and Welfare Dept. Hearing Examiners, V.F.W., Am. Legion, Delta Kappa Epsilon. Clubs: Fort McPherson Officers (Atlanta); Army-Navy (Washington). Home: Atlanta, Ga. Died May 31, 1974; buried Hillside Cemetery, Elizabeth, N.J.

SCHOENE, WILLIAM JAY, entomologist; b. Henderson, Ky., July 27, 1879; s. William Martin and Ellen (Jay) S.; B.S., in agr. U. of Ky., 1905; student Cornell U., 1908; M.S., U. of Chicago, 1910; Ph.D., Ohio State U., 1928; m. Rena Belle Yankey, June 4, 1907; children—Charles Andrew, Sara Elizabeth (Mrs. W. Richardson), Mary Margaret (Mrs. Roger Moore), Willena Jay. Student entomologist, N.Y. exptl. Station, 1905, asst. and asso. entomologist, 1906-13; state entomologist of Va. and prof. entomology, Va. Poly Inst., 1913-26; entomologist at Expt. Sta. and prof. entomology, Va. Poly. Inst. from 1926. Mem. Am. Soc. of Economic Entomology, Entomol. Soc. of America, Grange, Sigma Xi. Presbyterian. Mason. Contbr. Bulletins of Expt. Sta. and articles on entomology to jours. Address: Blacksburg, Va.†

SCHOENEMANN, OSCAR PAUL, physician; b. Bklyn., May 26, 1899; s. Paul and Helene Schoenemann; M.D., Columbia, 1928; m. Helen Martha Hornbostel, Jan. 27, 1935; children—Paul Thomas, Robert Laurence. Intern, Methodist Hosp., Bklyn., 1928-30, asso. attending in surgery, 1931-38, asso. urologist, 1940-49, chief urologist, 1950, later cons.; asso. attending surgeon Kings County Hosp., Bklyn., 1931-38; attending thoracic surgeon Kingston Av. Hosp., 1934-38, cons. urologist, 1949-74; Courtesy staff. Bklyn. Hosp., 1936. student urology Dr. Joseph F. McCarthy Polyclinic, N.Y., 1938-39; preceptor under Dr. Stanley Woodruff, Bayonne, N.J., 1939-40; cons. urologist Halloran VA Hosp., S.I., N.Y., 1946-51; instr. anatomy L.I. Coll. Hosp., 1931-35; lectr. in field. Served with U.S. Army, 1917-18. Diplomate Am. Bd. Urology. Fellow A.C.S., Am. Urol. Assn. (pres. N.Y. sect. 1951-52); mem. A.M.A., N.Y. Acad. Medicine (chmn. sect. urology 1946-47), Kings County, N.Y. State med. socs., Bklyn. Urol. Soc. (pres. 1943), Phi Delta Theta. Clubs: Rembrandt, Omega. Author: Paper on Management of Bladder in Paraplegics, 19 Home: Harwinton, Conn. Died Aug. 27, 1974; buried Harwinton, Conn.

SCHOENSTEIN, PAUL, journalist; b. N.Y.C., June 10, 1902; s. Rudolf and Kornel (Grossman) S.; ed. City Coll. and U. Cal.; m. Miriam Laura Stahl, Oct. 27, 1929; children—Ralph S., Carole S. With Herald Tribune, N.Y.C., 1923-25, Record, Los Angeles, 1925, Bronx Home News, N.Y.C., 1926; with Jour. Am., N.Y.C., 1926-66, city editor, 1938-56, asst. mng. editor, 1956-61, mng. editor, 1961-66; mng. editor World Jour. Tribune, N.Y.C. 1966-67; with spl. projects depts. Hearst Newspapers. Recipient Pulitzer Award, 1943. Home: New York City, N.Y. Died Apr. 14, 1974.

SCHOLES, CHARLES MARCEL, aviation co. exec.; b. League City, Tex., Aug. 26, 1903; s. Robert Hamilton and Geneva (Dibrell) S.; LL.B., Houston Law Sch., 1936; m. Dora Frances Petmecky, Dec. 22, 1945. With Humble Oil & Refining Co., Houston, 1920-72, pilot, 1940-42, chief pilot, 1942-45, mgr. aviation dept., 1945-72. Mem. Nat. Pilots Assn., Air Force Assn., Airplane Owners and Pilots Assn., Tex. Aero. Assn., Tex. Pvt. Flyers, Quiet Birdman. Methodist. Mason. Home: Austin, Tex. Died Mar. 18, 1972.

SCHOLES, SAMUEL RAY, chemist; b. Marquette, Wis., Jan. 22, 1884; s. Samuel and Harriet Newell (Mozley) S.; A.B., Ripon (Wis.) Coll., 1905; Ph.D., Yale, 1911; Sc.D. (honorary), Alfred U., 1952; m. Lois Elizabeth Boren, Apr. 10, 1914; children—Samuel Ray, Lois Ann (Mrs. B. H. Colvin). Addison Boren, James Bert. Instructor Wausau (Wisconsin) High School, 1905-08; laboratory assistant, Yale, 1908-10; research fellow, U. of Pittsburgh, 1911-13; chemist, H. C. Fry Glass Co., Rochester, Pa., 1913-20; asst. dir. Mellon Inst. (U. of Pittsburgh), 1914-17; prof. chemistry, Geneva Coll., 1918-20; supt. Utility Glass Wks., Lonaconing, Md., 1920-21; chemist Federal Glass Co., Columbus, O., 1921-29; lecturer on glass technology, Ohio State University, 1926-29; technical director Fostoria Glass Co., Moundsville, W.Va., 1929-31; glass technologist New York State College of Ceramics, 1932-46 and 1948-74, dean, 1946-48, asso. dean, 1948-52; emeritus professor of Alfred University, from 1952. Fellow A.A.A.S., American Ceramic Society (Albert V. Bleininger medal 1952), Soc. Glass Tech. (British); mem. Sigma Xi, Acacia, Alpha Chi Sigma, Keramos. Republican. Unitarian. Mason, Rotarian. Inventor improved glass melting pot. Author: Modern Glass Practice, 1935; Glass Tank Furnaces (transl.), 1937; Opportunities in Ceramics, 1953; Earth and Fire, 1961. Editor: Glass Industry Handbook, 1941. Contbr. articles on glass; wrote The Community Church and other hymns. Home: Alfred, N.Y. Died Aug. 16, 1974; interred Alfred Cemetery.

SCHOOTEN, SARAH SCHILLING, pediatrician; b. Rangoon, Burma, Oct. 1, 1894; d. Gerhard John and Elizabeth (Bull) Schilling: B.S., Wayne U., 1924. M., 1925, M.D., 1926; m. Cornelius J. Schooten, June 16, 1916; 1 dau., Marjory Elizabeth (Mrs. John F. Lewan). Nurse, A.R.C., France, 1914-16; tchr. Santiago (Chile) Coll., 1917-19; intern, resident in pediatrics Providince Hosp., Detroit, 1925-28, attending pediatrics, 1929-74; pvt. practice, Detroit, 1930-74; attending in pediatrics Chrittenden Hosp., 1939-74, Highland Park (Mich.) Gen. Hosp., 1962-74; chief pediatrics Booth Meml. Hosp., 1930-58, Woodward Gen. Hosp., 1955-74; pediatrician Edwin Denby Home for Children, 1930-74, Sadie Sacksider Home for Underpriviledged Children, 1940-60, Sarah Fisher Home for Children, 1926-74; diagnostician Detroit Dept. Health, 1940-57. Mem. Brother's Bro. Found., 1970. Trustee Fund for Crippling Diseases; mem. adv. bd. Sarah Fisher Children's Home, W. D. Fryfogle Research Found., Salvation Army Children's Home. Recipient Wayne State U. Alumni award, 1962; Founders award Salvation Army, 1967; commended by Mich. State Med. Soc., 1970; named Headliner Woman of Wayne State U., 1970. Mem. Highland Park Bd. Commerce, Mich. Assn. Professions (charter), A.M.A., Mich., Wayne County, Blackwell Women's med. socs., Am. Med. Women's Assn., Pan.-Am. Med. Women's Alliance, Detroit Pediatric Soc. (citation for service to children world 1972), Rosedale Park Women's Assn., Founder Soc. of Detroit Inst. of Arts, Nu Sigma Phi. Republican. Conglist. Club: Woman's City. Home: Detroit, Mich. Died Apr. 21, 1974; interred Woodlawn Cemetery Mausoleum.

SCHRADER, ROBERT ESTES, hi-bred corn co. exec.; b. Bridgeport, Ill., Aug. 21, 1915; s. Edwin Findley and Estelle Grace (Milligan) S.; student U. Ill., 1934-37; m. Cathryn C. Ramsey, June 27, 1938; children—Alice (Mrs. Howard S. Gruber), Timothy R., Ellen (Mrs. Walter Knollenberg). Owner, Schrader Hybrid Corn Co., Bridgeport, Ill., 1935-38; insp. Ill. Crop Improvement Assn., 1937-39; prodn. mgr. Ill. and Wis., Pioneer Hi-Bred Corn Co., Champaign, Ill., 1939-74; owner-mgr. Sno Flok Tree Co., Champaign, 1950-72. Cubmaster, scoutmaster, explorer adviser Arrowhead council Boy Scouts Am., 1952-62. Bd. dirs. YMCA. Mem. Nat. (trustee), Ill. (pres.) Christmas tree growers assns., Alpha Gamma Rho. Methodist (mem. ofcl. bd.). Club: Exchange (pres.) (Champaign, Ill.). Pioneer mech. detasseling machine. Home: Champaign, Ill. Died Nov. 6, 1974.

SCHRANK, RAYMOND EDWARD, physician; b. Lomira, Wis., Oct. 20, 1912; s. Julius and Helena S.; B.A. cum laude, Ripon Coll., 1934; M.D., U. Wis., 1938; m. Bertha Schorer, June 21, 1938 (dec. 1963); children—Sondra, Helaine (Mrs. Keith Baldwin), Raymond Edward II, Donna (Mrs. Joseph Houdek), Wanda, Julie (Mrs. David Kindschuh), William m. 2d, Ruth Neumann, Aug. 7, 1965; 1 dau., Ann Lara. Intern, Akron (O.) City Hosp., 1938-39; instr. anatomy U. Wis., 1940-41; mem. staff Waupun (Wis.) Meml. Hosp., 1955, chief staff, 1955, chmn. dept. medicine, 1969-70, chmn. dept. obstetrics, 1970-71, physician-in-charge med. edn. community orientation, 1971. Dir. Wis. Blue Cross Plan, Milw., 1971-73. Bd. dirs. Luth. Home, Fond du Lac, Wis., 1969-73. Served as capt., M.C., AUS, 1944-46. Diplomate Am. Bd. Family Practice (charter). Mem. A.M.A., Am. Legion. Home: Waupun, Wis. Died Nov. 18, 1973; buried Highland Memory Gardens, Beaver Dam, Wis.

SCHREIBER, MANUEL, psychiatrist; b. London, Eng., June 13, 1907; s. Abraham and Rebecca Schreiber; M.D., U. Ill., 1940; m. Naomi Piell, Dec. 25, 1937; children—Ina Ann, Allen Fox. Intern, St. Luke's Hosp., Spokane, Wash., 1939-40; resident in psychiatry Elgin State Hosp., 1940-41, 46-47, staff psychiatrist, 1947-50; chief neuropsychiat. Mental Hygiene Clinic, VA Regional Office, Milw., 1950-51; med. dir. Dodge County Child Guidance Clinic, Juneau, Wis.; med. cons. psychiat. health care services State of Cal., Los Angeles; mem. faculty U. Cal. at Los Angeles. Served to capt. M.C., AUS, 1941-46. Diplomate Am. Bd. Psychiatry and Neurology. Fellow Am. Psychiat. Assn.; mem. A.M.A. Home: Los Angeles, Cal. Died Mar. 24, 1974; buried Hollywood, Cal.

SCHROEDER, GEORGE WILLIAM, ch. ofcl.; b. Pinckneyville, Ill., Oct. 28, 1914; s. George Henry and Adele (Walthers) S.; B.A. with honors, So. Ill. U., Carbondale, 1945, M.S. in Edn., 1946; LL.D., So. Baptist Coll., Walnut Ridge, Ark., 1953; m. Lorraine Antoinette Wilson, June 11, 1932; children—Harriet Lorraine, George Torrington, Lawson Lee. Exec. sec. brotherhood dept. Ill. Bapt. Assn., Carbondale, 1940-46; asst. sec. brotherhood commn. So. Bapt. Conv., Memphis, 1946-51, exec. sec., 1951-71; mem. exec. com. Bapt. World Alliance, 1960-71. Republican. Mason, Kiwanian (regional leader 1967, dist. leader 1968). Author: Brotherhood Guidebook, 1958; You Can Speak for God, 1960. Home: Memphis, Tenn. Died May 29, 1971; interred Mueller Hill Cemetery, Pinckneyville, Ill.

SCHROEDER, HENRY ALFRED, physician; b. Short Hills, N.J., June 18, 1906; s. Henry Alfred and Natalie (Munde) S.; A.B., Yale, 1929; M.D., Columbia, 1933; M.A. (hon.), Dartmouth, 1967; hon. degree Windham Coll., 1974; m. Janet Gregg; children—Henry Alfred, David; 1 adopted dau., Eugenie (Mrs. Marius Darrow). Intern in medicine Presbyn Hosp., N.Y.C., 1934-36; research fellow in pharmacology U. Pa. Med. Sch., Phila., 1936-37; asst. resident physician Hosp. of Rockefeller Inst., N.Y.C., 1937-39, asst. in medicine, 1939-42, asso. in medicine, 1942-46; asst. physician Barnes Hosp., St. Louis, 1946-58; asso. prof. medicine Washington U. Sch. Medicine, St. Louis, 1946-58; asso. prof. physiology Dartmouth Med. Sch., Hanover, N.H. 1958-66, prof., 1966-71, prof. emeritus, 1971-75; dir. research Brattleboro (Vt.) Retreat, 1958-65, Brattleboro Meml. Hosp., 1965-75. Mem. panel on aviation medicine, research and devel. bd. Dept. Def., 1947-53; cons. WHO, Internat. Commn. on Radiol. Protection, IAEA, President's Council on Environmental Quality, other fed agys.; vice chmn. symposium WHO, Prague, Czechoslovakia, 1960; Am. Heart Assn. George Brown Meml. lectr., 1966; founder Trace Element Lab., 1958. Trustee, Marlboro (Vt.) Coll., 1961-62. Served from lt. to comdr. M.C., USNR, 1941-46. Diplomate Am. Bd. Internal Medicine, Am. Bd. Preventive Medicine. Fellow A.C.P., Aerospace Med. Assn., Am. Coll. Preventive Medicine, Am. Heart Assn. (past mem. exec. com., dir., chmn. council on circulation 1950) N.Y. Acad. Medicine; mem. A.M.A., Am. Inst. Nutrition, A.A.A.S., Am. Gerontol. Soc., Am. Am. Physiol. Soc. (distinguished mem. circulation group), Central, So. socs. for clin. research, Harvey Soc., Soc. for Exptl. Biology and Medicine, N.Y. Acad. Scis., St. Louis Med. Soc. (hon.), Sigma Xi, Nu Sigma Nu. Episcopalian (lay reader). Author: Shirt-tail and Pigtail; Hypertensive Diseases; Mechanisms of Hypertension; A Matter of Choice; The Elements Within Us; Pollution; Profits and Progress; The Trace Elements and Man; Elements in Living Systems; co-author Personality in Arterial Hypertension. Contbr. numerous articles to sci. jours., chpts. to med. textbooks. Research on hypertension and gerontology, causes of high blood pressure trace elements; developer low sodium diet. Home: St. Thomas, V.I. also West Brattleboro, Vt. Died Apr. 20, 1975; Interred West Brattleboro.

SCHROPP, RUTLEDGE CLIFTON, physician; b. St. Cloud, Minn., Sept. 21, 1922; s. Clifton Frank and Isabel Margaret (Rutledge) S.; M.D., Washington U., St. Louis, 1946; M. Lois Louise Harnagel, June 25, 1945; children—Steven, Carol, Patricia. Intern, St. Louis City Hosp., 1946-47; pathologist Mercy Hosp., Des Moines, 1947-48, mem. staff; tng. in surgery VA Hosp., Des Moines, 1950-54, mem. surg. staff, 1954-55; mem. staff Ia. Methodist Hosp., Ia. Lutheran Hosp., Broadlawns Hosp., Mercy Hosp., N.W. Hosp., all Des Moines. Served as capt. M.C., AUS, 1948-49. Diplomate Am. Bd. Surgery, Fellow A.C.S., Ia. Acad. Surgery; mem. A.M.A. Home: Des Moines, Ia. Died May 8, 1973; buried Glendale Cemetery, Des Moines, Ia.

SCHRUNK, TERRY DOYLE, mayor; b. Stayton, Ore., Mar. 10, 1913; s. James and Pearl Margaret (Doyle) S.; student U. Portland, 1933-35; A.B., U. Ore., 1942; LL.D., U. Portland, 1972; m. Virginia Dorothy Price, May 17, 1936; children—Michael, Judy Ann, Patrick. With Fire Dept., Portland, Ore., 1935-49; sheriff Multnomah County, Ore., 1949-56; mayor of Portland, 1957-73. Past chmn. adv. bd., past pres. U.S. Conf. Mayors; past pres. League Ore. Cities; hon. life mem. Japan-Am. Conf. Mayors and C. of C. Presidents, 1973-75. Active YMCA; dir. Pal Boys Club of Portland, 1950-75, pres. Ore. chpt., 1955. Bd. dirs., chpt. mem. Town Affiliation Assn. U.S. Served as lt. USNR, 1942-45. Decorated Purple Heart, Silver Star; Order of Rising Sun, 3 class (Japan); recipient Nat. Florello La Guardia award for public adminstrn., 1969, good citizenship medal Nat. Soc. S.A.R., 1970; awards World Council, 1966, B'nai B'rith, 1968, Am. Legion, 1971, Kiwanis Internat. 1972, Salvation Army, 1972, Boys Club Am., 1967, 68, Ore. Sheriffs Assn., 1956; named hon. citizen Sapporo, Japan, 1972. Mem. Ore. Fire Fighters Assn. (past exec. dir.), V.F.W. (life), Am. Legion (life), Nat. (past gov.), Ore past pres.) sheriffs assns., Portland C. of C. (life mem.; dir. 1972). Presbyn. Eagle, Mason. Clubs: City of Portland (hon. life), Downtown and North Rotary (hon.). Home: Portland, Ore., Died Mar. 4, 1975.

SCHUETTE, CURT NICOLAUS, cons. mining and metall. engr.; b. Milw., Feb. 21, 1895; s. William Theodore and Ernestine Johanna (Mischel) S.; B.S., U. Cal. Coll. Mining, 1917; m. Lillian Harrison Brown, July 16, 1927 (dec. Aug. 8, 1937); m. 2d, Erna Hansen, Sept. 8, 1939. Metallurgist U.S. Bur. of Mines, 1917; production supt. New Idria Mines, 1917-18; research metallurgist U.S. Bur. of Mines, 1918-19, 1920-21; supt. Mariscal Mine, Tex., 1919-20; mgr. Silver Gulch Mining & Milling Co., Colo., 1921-22; research for Santa Cruz Portland Cement Co., 1922-24; cons. on design and operation of plants for gold, silver, quicksilver, etc., and mgmt. of mines from 1925; author of the primary concentration theory of the genesis of quicksilver ore bodies; gen. mgr. New Almaden Corp., 1940; spl. lecturer on strategic metals U. of Calif., 1941. Valuations and appraisals U.S. Army Corps of Engineers from 1948. In military service during World War I, assigned to research on quicksilver U.S. Bur. of Mines. Mem. Am. Inst. Mining and Metall Engrs. (mem. coms. on licensing, pyrometallurgy, econs. and statistics, Legion Honor). Author: The Metallurgy of Quicksilver (with .L. H. Duchak), 1925; Quicksilver, 1931. Contbr. to Modern Uses of Nonfarrous Metals, 1935, 53, Quicksilver in Oregon, 1938. Contbr. Ency. Brit., also profl. jours. Mineral named Schuetteite because of long-life study of mercury deposits. Home: Sebastopol, Cal., Died Feb. 6, 1975; buried Sebastopol, Cal.

SCHULER, DONALD VERN, librarian; b. Ecorse, Mich., May 13, 1927; s. Paul E. and Margaret Rose (Roeschke) S.; B.S. (Jenison scholar 1945), Mich. State U., 1949; LL.D., Cleveland-Marshall Law Sch., 1960; M.L.S., Case-Western Res. U., 1965; m. Verna Jean Smith, Apr. 20, 1950; children—Karon, Guerre, Kerry. Chief of police, Cassopolis, Mich., 1950-51; claims examiner Continental Ins. Co., Cleve., 1960-65; head cataloger Law Sch., Ohio State U., 1965-66; asst. library dir. Appellate div. Law Library, Hall of Justice, Rochester, N.Y., 1967; dir. Grove City (O.) Libraries, 1968-74. Served to maj. AUS, 1945-46, 51-54. Mem. A.L.A., Am. Assn. Law Librarians, Ohio Law Library Assn. (sec. 1966), Ohio Library Assn. Home: Columbus, O. Died Dec. 11, 1974.

SCHULTE, JOHN H., physician; b. Cin., 1923; s. Clifford Louis and Helen Ann (Hiller) S.; M.D., U. Cin., 1948, D.Sc. in Indsl. Medicine, 1962; m. Emma Kay Wessling. Intern, U.S. Naval Hosp., San Diego, 1948-49, resident in internal medicine, 1949-50; tng. Sch. Submarine Medicine, New London, Conn., 1950-51; tng. in radiobiology Reed Coll., Portland, Ore., 1957; fellow in occupational medicine U. Cin., 1961-62; prof. preventive medicine Ohio State U., 1967-72. Served to capt. M.C., USN, 1948-67. Recipient Sir Henry Wellcome Essay award, 1960, Adolph Kammer merit in authorship award, 1965. Diplomate Am. Bd. Preventive Medicine. Fellow Indsl. Medicine Assn., Am. Coll. Preventive Medicine, Am. Pub. Health Assn. Acad. Occupational Medicine; mem. A.M.A., Assn. Mil. Surgeons U.S. Home: Columbus, O. Died Apr. 18, 1972; buried Cincinnati, O.

SCHULTZ, ALFRED PAUL, physician; b. in Germany, May 14, 1878; s. Paul W. and Hedwig (Wagner) S.; A.B., Coll. City of New York, 1897; M.D., Coll. Phys. and Surg. (Columbia), 1901. Practiced in New York, 1901-06, Monticello, N.Y., from 1906. Phys. German Hosp. Dispensary, 1901, 1902. Author: Race or Mongrel, 1908; Muttersprache, Volkstrum and Menschenwert, 1910; Die Einwanderer und ihre Nachkommen in den Vereinigten Staaten, 1911; Das Aussterben der Besseren, 1911; The End of Darwinism, 1911. Address: Monticello, N.Y.†

SCHURMAN, JACOB GOULD, III, ret. investment banker; b. San Francisco, May 19, 1916; s. Robert and Berenice (Wilson) S.; student U. Besancon (France), 1933-34; A.B. magna cum laude, Stanford, 1938; postgrad. Harvard Law Sch., Columbia Law Sch.; LL.B., U. Cal., 1946; m. Juanita Hill, Aug. 20, 1940; children—Jacob Gould IV, Juana Maria. Asst. cashier Am. Trust Co., San Francisco, 1946-51; partner Schwabacher & Co., San Francisco, 1951-69; mng. trustee A.W. Wilson Trust (San Francisco real estate). Trustee San Francisco Mus. Art. Served to lt. comdr. UNSR, 1941-46. Mem. Cal. Bar Assn., Phi Beta Kappa, Phi Delta Phi. Republican. Roman Catholic. Clubs: Pacific Union, Burlingame Country. Home: San Francisco, Cal. Deceased.

SCHWARZ, FREDERICK AUGUST OTTO, lawyer; b. N.Y.C., Apr. 7, 1902; s. Henry Frederick and Irma (Hemmer) S.; student Hill Sch., Pottstown, Pa., 1917-20; A.B., Harvard, 1924, LL.B., 1927; m. Mary Delafield DuBois, Jan. 20, 1934; children—Frederick A.O., Henry Marshall, John Clausen, Robert DuBois, Mary DuBois (Mrs. Newton P.S. Merrill). Admitted to N.Y. bar, 1929; with firm Davis Polk & Wardwell, 1927-74, partner, 1935-74; dir. Chubb Corp., Gen. Mills., Inc., Fed. Ins. Co., Vigilant Ins. Co., Pullman, Inc.; trustee U.S. Trust Co. of N.Y., Provident Loan Soc. Gen. counsel U.S. high commr. Germany, 1953-54. Trustee Presbyn. Hosp. N.Y.C. Mem. Assn. Bar City N.Y., Am., N.Y. State bar assns., N.Y. County Lawyers Assn., Phi Beta Kappa. Clubs: Century Assn., Down Town Assn., Links, Wall Street, Harvard (N.Y.C.). Home: New York City, N.Y. Died Oct. 27, 1974; buried Putnam Cemetery, Greenwich, Conn.

SCHWARZ, GUENTER, educator, physicist; b. Cologne, Germany, Nov. 26, 1913; s. Heinrich and Grete (Rosenbaum) S.; engring. diploma Tech. U. Berlin, 1938; Ph.D., Johns Hopkins, 1942; m. Inge Solomon, Aug. 9, 1942; children—Eva Harriet, Judith Ann. Came to U.S., 1938, naturalized, 1944. Mem. faculty, U. Ill., 1942-46; research physicist Johns Hopkins, 1946-49; prof. physics Fla. State U., Tallahassee, 1949-74, dir. Center for Research in Coll. Instrn. of Sci. and Math., 1966-71; vis. prof. Reed Coll., So. Meth. U., Andhra U., Waltair, India. Fellow A.A.A.S., Am. Phys. Soc. Contbr. articles to profl. jours. Home: Tallahassee, Fla. Died Nov. 17, 1974; interred Tallahassee, Fla.

SCHWENGEL, FRANK RUDOLPH, corp. exec.; b. Chgo., Oct. 21, 1885; s. Theodore August and Wilhelmina (Jaenecke) S.; grad. St. Michael's Chgo., 1902; m. Jeanne Sanderson Jan. 24, 1918. Chmn. bd. Joseph E. Seagram & Sons; v.p. Distillers Corp.-Seagram's, Ltd. Montreal. Chmn., Samuel Bronfman Found. Mil. service, 1903-36, with U.S. Army, overseas, 1917-19; apptd. brig. gen. Army U.S., 1926; ret. maj.-gen., Ill. N.G., 1936. Awarded 3 citations, World War. Fellow Smithsonian Instn.; mem. Mil. Order World Wars, Am. Legion, Soc. Am. Legion Founders (past nat. pres.), V.F.W., Assn. U.S. Army, Army, Navy and Airforce Vets. Can. (v.p. U.S. unit), Acad. Natural Sci. Clubs: Army and Navy (Washington); Rancheros, Visitadores (Santa Barbara, Cal.). Home: Scarsdale, N.Y. Died May 4, 1974.

SCOFIELD, PERRY LEE, dentist; b. Virgil, S.D., Oct. 24, 1890; s. Mathias Burnett and Mary Elizabeth (Rhoades) S.; student Huron Coll., 1911-14; D.D.S., Northwestern U., 1917; m. Zella Frederica Reese, Dec. 30, 1919; children—Marvin Rolfe, Alan Eugene, Gordon Lloyd. Instr. operative dentistry Northwestern U., Chgo., 1917-18; pvt. practice dentistry, De Smet, S.D., 1919-75. Mayor, De Smet, S.D., 1933-48. Served as 1st lt. AUS, 1918-19. Mem. Am. Legion, Am. Dental Assn. (life), S.D. Dental Soc. (state pres. 1936, honored guest of yr. 1974). Mason (32°), Lion. Home: De Smet, S.D., Died Aug. 6, 1975.

SCOTT, ALFRED WITHERSPOON, educator; b. Macon, Ga., June 25, 1896; s. George Edward and Mamie Lee (Wing) S.; B.S., U. of Ga., 1918; student U. of Minn., 1919-21; Ph.D., Princeton U., 1922; m. Jane Shields Sams, Aug. 8, 1923; children—Alfred Witherspoon, Richard Sams, George Edward. Asso. prof. of chemistry, U. of Ga., 1922-27, prof., head of dept. from 1927, chmn. div. of phys. sciences after 1936; chairman chemistry section, University System of Georgia, after 1936, chairman of physical science division, after 1959; past counselor Georgia Engring. Exptl. Sta.; state entrance examiner to Ga. med. schs., from 1934; asso. dir. Dixie Camp for Boys, 1916-44, dir., 1944-53; asso. dir. Dixie Camp for Girls, 1920-53; cons. Dixie Camps for Boys and Girls, from 1953; mem. exec. com. Southeastern Conf. Univ. Athletic Assn., 1943-62; v.p. Nat. Collegiate Athletic Assn., 1960-62. Fellow AAAS, American Institute Chemists, mem. Am. Chem. Soc. (chmn. Ga. Sect. 1936), Ga. Acad. Science (pres. 1932), Am. Assn. Univ. Profs., Phi Delta Theta, Phi Lambda Upsilon, Alpha Chi Sigma, Phi Beta Kappa, Phi Kappa Phi, Sigma Xi, Presbyterian. Club: Athens Country. Author: A Laboratory Outline of General Chemistry and Qualitative Analysis, 1924; A Laboratory Outline of General Chemistry and Semi-Micro Qualitative Analysis, 1941; Elememtary Organic Chemistry, 1949. Editor: Physical Science, 1934. Contbr. to chem. jours. Home: Athens, Ga. Died May 24, 1974; interred Oconee Cemetery, Athens.

SCOTT, BUFORD, investment banker; b. Richmond, Va., Sept. 9, 1895; s. Frederic William and Elisabeth Mayo (Strother) S.; student U. of Va., 1914-16; m. Mary Lowe Nixon, Oct. 2, 1930; children—Sidney Buford, Margery Nixon, Mary Denny, Elisabeth Strother, George Ross. Sr. mem. firm of Scott & Stringfellow, investment bankers, Richmond, Va., 1939-73; dir. Richmond Terminal Ry. Co., 1939-73. Dir. Am. Internat. Corp., Atlantic Land and Improvement Co., L. & N. Railroad Co., Larus Brother Co.; bd. mgrs. Adams Express Co. Mem. N.Y. Stock Exchange, Richmond Stock Exchange; asso. mem. Am. Stock Exchange. Stockholder adv. First and Merchants Nat. Bank. Served with provisional commns. to capt. Co. C, 51st infantry, 6th div., World War I. Vice pres., dir. Sheltering Arms Hosp.; pres. Police Benevolent Assn.; dir. Meml. Found., Richmond Meml. Hosp., Atlantic Rural Expn.; mem. bd. visitors Medical Coll. Va.; chmn. bd. trustees invested funds of the Diocese of Virginia. Mem. Delta Psi. Conservative Democrat. Episcopalian. Clubs: Country, Commonwealth (Richmond); Union (N.Y.C.). Owns, operates 1200 acre beef cattle farm. Home: Richmond, Va. Died June 1973.

SCOTT, CLYDE F., paper exec.; b. Mound, Kan., May 10, 1881; s. Hiram and Jennie (Forbes) S.; student Central Bus. Coll., Sedalia, Mo.; 1901, 02; m. Clara Varnon, Dec. 30, 1902 (died 1934); 1 son Richard V.; m. 2d Elsie A. Salsbery, Apr. 17, 1943. With Bemis Bros. Bag Co., Kansas City, Mo., from 1904, mgr. Kansas City, 1918-49, dir. from 1945, then sr. counsellor. Mem. C. of C., Central Indsl. Dist. Assn. Mem. Christian Ch. Clubs: Kansas City, Mission Hills Country. Home: Kansas City, Mo.*†

SCOTT, CYRIL MEIR, mus. composer, author; b. Oxton, Cheshire, Eng., Sept. 27, 1879; s. Henry and Mary (Griffiths) S.; student Dr. Hutch's Conservatorium, Frankfurt-am-Main, Germany; m. Rose Laure Allatini; children—Vivian Mary, Desmond Cyril. Compositions include operas, cantatas, concertos, chamber works, piano pieces, a symphony, songs. Received 2 Carnegie awards; medal of Leonardo de Vinci Soc., Florence, Italy, Author: Music: Its Secret Influence Throughout the Ages, 1933; Outline of Modern Occultims, 1935; The Greater Awareness, 1936; Man Is My Theme, 1940; Doctors, Disease and Health, 1938; The Ghost of a Smile, 1940; Victory Over Cancer Without Radium or Surgery; for Laymen and Doctors, 1939; Musical Plays: Smetse Smee, The Boccaccio Touch, etc. Address: London, Eng.*†

SCOTT, EDWIN WILLIAM, govt. ofcl.; b. DuBois, Pa., Nov. 20, 1902; s. Charles DeWitt and Ruby (Palmer) S.; LL.D., Detroit Coll. Law, 1931; m. Dorothy Elsie Wetmore, Mar. 20, 1927 (dec. Jan. 1974); children—Shirley Ann (Mrs. David Frederick Byers), Edwin William. Newspaper reporter, asst. city editor Detroit Times, 1929-44; with N.W. Ayer Advt., Detroit, 1945-46; asst. pros. atty. County of Wayne, Mich., 1947-49; exec. sec. Newspaper Guild Detroit, 1947-57; with Fed. Mediation and Conciliation Service, 1958-73, beginning as commr., successively nat. office rep., Washington, missile site coordinator, Washington, asst. dep. dir., Washington, 1958-64, regional dir. Region 7, San Francisco, 1965-73. Mason. Home: San Francisco, Cal. Died Nov. 13, 1974; interred Forest Lawn Cemetery, Detroit, Mich.

SCOTT, ERNEST, retired lawyer; b. Phila., Dec. 25, 1903; s. Joseph Alison and Frances (Pepper) S.; A.B., U. Pa., 1925, LL.B., 1929; m. Lydia Wister Tunis, Nov. 29, 1930; children—Annis Lee (wife of Dr. P. Evans Adams), Barbara Markoe (Mrs. James W. Lillie, Jr.), Diana (Mrs. G. Frederick Oppenlander), Cintra Wharton (Mrs. Franklyn L. Rodgers), David Rodick. Admitted to Pa. bar, 1929, since practiced in Phila.; past partner Pepper, Hamilton & Sheetz. Past dir. Fidelity Trust Co. Past mem. Pa. Bd. Law Examiners, 1957-59; chmn. Wayne (Pa.) War Price and Rationing Bd., 1941-46. Past pres. United Fund Phila. Life trustee U. Pa., past chmn. bd. law trustees Law Sch.; past trustee Ch. Found. Episcopal Diocese Pa. Mem. Am., Pa., Phila. (chancellor 1962) bar assns., Phi Beta Kappa, Zeta Psi, Episcopalian (counsel, past vestryman). Clubs: Midday (Phila.); Merion Cricket (Haverford, Pa.). Home: Berwyn, Pa. Died Sept. 7, 1973.

SCOTT, HENRY CLAY, lawyer; b. Hemphill, W. Va., Sept. 29, 1930; s. Ellis Judson and Lilly Maud (Wood) S.; B.S., B.A., Ohio State U., 1957, LL.B., 1958; m. Mary Elizabeth Doherty, Oct. 16, 1953; children—Kathryn Ann, Michael David, Robert Adam, Barbara Ellen. Clerk, office of pros. atty., Franklin County, O., 1957-59; admitted to Ohio bar, 1959; since practiced in Columbus. Mem. Ohio Supreme Ct. Criminal Rules Adv. Com. Pres. Capital City Young Rep. Club, Columbus, 1964. Served with USAF, 1951-55. Mem. Am., O., Columbus bar assns., Am. Judicature Soc., Franklin County Trial Lawyers Assn., Am., O. trial lawyers assns. Home: Grandview Heights, O. Died Mar. 6, 1974.

SCOTT, HERMON HOSMER, elec. engr., inventor; b. Somerville, Mass., Mar. 28, 1909; s. Edward and Alice G. (Hosmer) S.; B.S., Mass. Inst. Tech., 1930, M.S., 1931; D.Sc., Lowell Technol. Inst., 1969; m. Eleanor M. Bates, Aug. 28, 1938; children—Pricilla Whitney, Jane (Mrs. Rutherford). Devel., exec. engr. Gen. Radio Co., 1931-46; pres., dir. engring. Tech. Instrument Corp., 1946-47; pres. H. H. Scott, Inc., Maynard, Mass., 1947-75. Trustee Union Savs. Bank, Powder Mill Realty Trust. Chmn., treas. Lincoln Center, Mass., 1968-75, pres., 1947-68; trustee Opera Co. Boston, New Eng. Deaconess Hosp., Joslin Diabetes Found. Recipient Potts medal Audio Engring. Soc. Fellow Acoustical Soc. Am., I.E.E.E. (audio and acoustics group achievement award), Audio Engring. Soc. (pres. 1961-62); mem. Phi Delta Theta. Inventor dynamic noise suppressor, R-C oscillator and selective circuits; holder patents on devices for radio and reproducing instruments, electronic instrumentation. Home: Lincoln, Mass. Died Apr. 13, 1975.

SCOTT, J. G., pres. Pacific Gamble Robinson Co. Address: Seattle, Wash. Died Jan. 17, 1974; interred Minneapolis, Minn.

SCOTT, LESLIE M., ret. newspaperman; b. Portland, Ore., Feb. 18, 1878; s. Harvey W. and Margaret (McChesney) S.; A.B., U. of Ore., 1899; m. Elizabeth Coleman, Mar. 28, 1906; children—Elesa (Keeney), Elizabeth (dec.), Harvey. Reporter Oregonian, 1896-1904, asso. editor, 1904-10; v.p. Oregonian Pub. Co., 1911-50; U.S. marshal for Ore., 1911-13; chairman Oregon State Indsl. Welfare Commn. for Women, 1928-29, Highway Commn., 1932-35; state treasurer, Ore., 1941-49. Mem. Portland C. of C., (pres. 1938), Riverview Cemetery Assn. (dir.), Oregon Hist. Soc. (trustee 1913-56, emeritus from 1956), Portland Lang Sync Soc., (pres. 1939), 50 Year Alumni Club (pres. 1953). Republican. Mason (33°, K.T.); Grand Master, Ore. Masonic Grand Lodge, 1933-34; member in Ore. of Supreme Council, Scottish Rite, So. jurisdn. 1943-68, insp. gen., Ore., 1943-68, grand prior, 1963-68. Author of Masonic history, also monographs on Oregon history Compiler of Religion, Theology and Morals (by Harvey W. Scott), 2 volumes, 1917; History of the Oregon Country (by same), 6 volumes, 1924; Shakespeare (by same), 1 vol., 1928; writer on Pacific Northwest history. Editor Oregon Hist. Quarterly, 1929-33. Home: Portland, Ore.†

SCOTT, LOUIS ALLEN, lawyer; b. Melissa, Tex., June 15, 1895; s. Lewis Alfred and Louise (Allen) S.; B.A., U. Tex., 1920, LL.B., 1921; m. Lillian Laffey, Aug. 1, 1923; children—Louis Allen, John David, Barbara Scott. Admitted to Tex. bar, 1921 practiced in El Paso; partner firm Scot, Hulse, Marshall & Feuille, 1957-75. Vice pres., dir. Mut. Fed. Savs & Loan Assn., El Paso, 1951-70. Rio Grande Compact commr. for Tex., 1948-69. Trustee El Paso pub. schs., 1931-33. Bd. dirs. El Paso Symphony Assn.; trustee El Paso Mus. Art. Served as 1st lt. U.S. Army, 1917-19. Mem. Am., Tex., El Paso (pres. 1934) bar assns., Beta Theta Pi, Phi Delta Phi. Clubs: El Paso (El Paso). Home: El Paso, Tex. Died Mar. 5, 1975.

SCOTT, R(OBERT) D(OUGLAS), coll. prof.; b. Bala, Kan., Nov. 12, 1878; s. Thomas and Emily Adelia (Burnell) S.; State Agrl. Coll., 1904; A.M., U. of Neb., 1910; student U. of Chicago, summers 1917-22, Nat. Univ. of Ireland, Dublin, summer 1927; Ph.D., Columbia, 1930; m. Charlotte Whedon, June 23, 1917. Instr., Lincoln (Neb.) High Sch., 1907-10; instr. dept. of English, U. of Neb., 1910-12, asst. prof., 1912-14, asso. prof., 1914-23, prof. and chmn. Freshman English, 1924-46, chmn., dept. dramatic lit., 1931-34, prof. emeritus, from 1946. Mem. Société de Linguistique de Paris, Am. Assn. Univ. Profs. Republican. Author: (with J. L. Gerig) Medieval Irish Literature (The Columbia Univ. Course in Literature, Vol. 4), 1928; James Macuherson's Ossian (The Columbia Univ. Course in Lit., Vol. 12), 1928; The Thumb of Knowledge in Legends of Finn, Sigurd, and Taliesin, 1930; A Student's Guide to English Composition, 1946. Home: Lincoln, Neb.†

SCOVILLE, HAROLD RALPH, lawyer; b. Rupert, Ida., June 7, 1910; s. Ralph Eugene and Margarthe (Nazinski) S.; student liberal arts U. Ariz., 1929-31, LL.B., 1935; m. Velma Franco, June 29, 1935 (div. Jan. 1964); children—Robert, Stanley; m. 2d, Marion Johnson, Feb. 21, 1964. Admitted to Ariz. bar, 1935, U.S. Supreme Ct., 1943, D.C. bar, 1964; gen. practice, Phoenix, 1935-40; dep. prosecutor Maricopa County, 1940-42, county atty., 1942-43, judge Superior Ct., 1943-47; practiced in Phoenix, 1947-74; mem. firm Lewis, Roca, Scoville, Beauchamp & Linton, 1949-67. Pres., Phoenix Community Council, 1949-74, Ariz. Boys Ranch, 1950-54. Chmn. central Ariz., Kennedy presdl. campaign, 1960; chmn. Maricopa County Democratic Central Com., 1965-66. Mem. Am., Maricopa County (pres. 1950) bar assns., State Bar Ariz., Internat. Soc. Barristers. Home: Phoenix, Ariz. Died Apr. 8, 1974.

SCULLY, CORNELIUS DECATUR, mayor; b. Pittsburgh, Pa., Nov. 30, 1878; s. John Sullivan and Mary E. (Negley) S.; B.S., U. of Pa., 1901; LL.B., U. of Pittsburgh, 1904; m. Rosalie Pendleton, June 10, 1905; children—Alice Pendleton (Mrs. John C. Fisher Motz), Elizabeth Negley (Mrs. William Sanders), Cornelius Decatur, John Pendleton. Admitted to Pa. bar, 1904; mem. firm Lee & Mackey, 1904-08, Mackey & Scully, 1908-10; Machard, Scully & Mehard, 1912-19; solicitor City of Pittsburgh, 1934; pres. City Council, 1935-36; mayor of Pittsburgh 1936-46; dir. Hope Engring. Co., Pittsburgh Tube Co. Mem. bd. Allegheny Sanitary Authority. Mem. Am. Bar Assn., Kappa Sigma. Democrat. Episcopalian. Mason, Eagle. Clubs: Duquesne, University, Junta Philosophical (Pittsburgh). Home: Pittsburgh, Pa.†

SEAMAN, A(LBERT) OWEN, army officer; b. Greenville, Ill., Feb. 7, 1878; s. Jonathan and Mary Elizabeth (Owen) S.; student Greenville (Ill.) Coll., 1893-97; m. Florence Thompson Look, Jan. 22, 1908; 1 son, Jonathan Owen. Enlisted with 4th Ill. Inf., May 1898, and served in U.S. Army; commd. 2d lt. inf., 1901, and advanced through the grades to brig. gen., 1936; served as col. of inf. during World War; retired from active service, July 31, 1940. Decorated D.S.M. and campaign medals. Mason (Shriner). Clubs: Army and Navy, Army and Navy Country (Washington, D.C.). Contbr. to mil. jours. Home: Washington, D.C.†

SEAMAN, IRVING, business exec.; b. Milw., Aug. 8, 1881; s. William Stewert and Kate Darling (Hibbard) S.; B.S., U. Wis., 1903; m. Anne Douglas, July 28, 1920; children—Douglas, Irving, Richard, David Page. With Electric Storage Battery Co., Phila., 1903-06, W.S. Seaman & Co., 1906-10, sec.-treas., 1910-19; sec.-treas., bd. dirs. Seaman Body Corp., 1919-36; bd. dirs. Second Wis. Nat. Bank, Bank of Commerce, 1928-33; pres. Calumet Bradley Land Co., 1930-42; chmn. examining com. Northwestern Mutual Life Ins. Co., 1934-35, bd. trustees, 1936; asso. mgr. Nash Kelvinator Corp., 1936-38; pres., treas. Merchants Towel Service Company, 1942-45. President board directors Family Welfare Assn., 1919-25; board directors Milwaukee County Community Fund, 1931-32. Trustee Village of River Hills, 1930-43. Recipient distinguished pub. service award U.S.N., 1952. Mem. Wis. Mfrs. Assn. (bd. dirs. 1918-39), Navy League U.S. (pres. Milw. council 1945-46, pres. Wis. council 1946, bd. dirs. 1947, v.p. 1953), U.S. Senior's Golf Assn., Chi Psi. Episcopalian. Clubs: Univ. Milw. (bd. dirs. 1939-44), Country (bd. dirs. 1929-31, 1934-37), Town (Milwaukee). Home: Milwaukee, Wis.†

SEARES, FREDERICK HANLEY, astronomer; b. Cassopolis, Mich., May 17, 1873; s. Isaac Newton and Ella (Swartwout) S.; B.S., U. Cal., 1895, grad. student, 1895-99, LL.D., 1930; LL.D., U. Mo., 1934; student U. Berlin, 1899-1900, U. Paris, 1900-01; m. Mabel Urmy, May 26, 1896 (dec. May 1940); 1 son, Richard Urmy; m. 2d, Mary Cross Joyner, July 11, 1942. Fellow in astronomy U. Cal., 1895-96, instr., 1896-98; prof. astronomy and dir. Laws Obs., U. Mo., 1901-09; supt. computing div. Mt. Wilson Obs. of Carnegie Instn. of Washington, and editor obs. publs., 1909-25, asst. dir., 1925-40, research asso. 1940-46. Chmn. com. on stellar photometry, Internat. Astron. Union, 1919-38. Awarded Bruce medal, 1940. Mem. Nat. Acad. Scis., Am. Philos. Soc., Am. Astron. Soc. (council 1929-32), A.A.A.S., Astronp Soc. Pacific (pres. 1929), Royal Astron. Soc. (asso.), Beta Theta Pi, Phi Beta Kappa, Sigma Xi, Tau Beta Pi. Club: Athenaeum. (Pasadena). Author: Bulletins of Laws Observatory, Vol. I. 1902-08; Practical Astronomy for Engineers, 1909; Mount Wilson Catalogue of Magnitudes, 1930; Catalogue of Magnitudes and Colors, 1941; also papers in astron. journals on comet orbits, stellar photometry, distribution of stars, sun's general magnetic field. Collaborating editor Astrophys. Jour., 1927-34, 41-45, joint editor, 1934-41. Home: Pasadena, Cal.†

SEARS, FRANCIS W(ESTON) educator; b. Plymouth, Mass., Oct. 1, 1898; s. Walter Herbert and Ella Maria (Blackmer) S.; B.S., Mass. Inst. Tech., 1921, M.S., 1924; m. Mildred Cornwall, Dec. 23, 1935. Instr. Mass. Inst. Tech., 1921-29, asst. prof., 1929-35, asso. prof., 1935-43, prof., 1943; Appleton prof. natural philosophy Dartmouth. Mem. Am. Phys. Soc., Optical Soc. Am., Am. Assn. Physics Tchrs. Author: Principles of Physics, 1945. Address: Hanover, N.H., Died Nov. 12, 1975.

SEARS, GEORGE WALLACE, prof. chemistry; b. Kidder, Mo., July 9, 1878; s. William Wallace and Angeline Augusta (Johnson) S.; B.S., with honors, Drury Coll., 1908; M.S., U. of Ill., 1911, Ph.D. in Chemistry, 1914; m. Edith Clementine Fink, June 20, 1911; children—Howard William (dec.), George Wallace, Margaret Marie. Teacher chemistry and physics, high sch., Springfield, 1909-10; asst. in chemistry, U. of Ill., 1911-14, instr., 1914-17; with U. Nev., from 1917, as instr. in chemistry until 1918, asso. prof., 1918-24, prof., 1924-49, head of dept., 1926-49; cons. chemist, U.S. Bur. Mines, 1927-29. Mem. A.A.A.S., Am. Assn. Univ. Profs., Am. Chem. Soc. Sigma Xi, Phi Lambda Upsilon, Phi Kappa Phi, Kappa Alpha. Methodist. Author: A Systematic Qualitative Chemical Analysis, 1922, 2d edit., 1926; Essentials of General Chemistry, 1938; Laboratory Manual of General Chemistry, 1940; also various research papers, chiefly on rarer metals and chem. edn. Home: Reno, Nev.†

SEARS, PHILIP MASON, former govt. ofcl.; b. Boston, Dec. 29, 1899; s. Philip Shelton and Mary Cabot (Higginson) S.; A.B., Harvard, 1922; m. Zilla MacDougall, Dec. 29, 1924; children—Philip Mason, Charlotte MacDougall (dec.). U.S. rep. Trusteeship Council UN, 1953-60, pres., 1955-56; U.S. del. Silver Jubilee, Emperor of Ethiopia, Addis Ababa, 1955, Independence Celebration of Ghana, West Africa, 1957; spl. U.S. ambassador Independence Celebration, Cameroun, West Africa, 1960; U.S. ambassador, chmn. UN Vis. Mission to East Africa, 1960; alternate U.S. rep. 13th Gen. Assembly UN. Mem. Mass. Legislature, 1935-48. Chmn., Mass. Republican State Com., 1949-50; del. Rep. Nat. convs., 1948, 52. Served as pvt. U.S. Army, World War I; served from lt. comdr. to capt. USNR, 1941-46. Mem. Am. Legion. Episcopalian. Mason. Home: Dedham, Mass. Died Dec. 1973.

SEASTONE, CHARLES VICTOR, microbiologist, educator; b. Madison, Wis., Jan. 11, 1908; s. Charles Victor and Susan (Bouton) S.; A.B., U. Wis., 1927; M.D., Harvard, 1932; m. Elise Midelfart, Sept. 8, 1934; children—Sarah Margrete, Charles Victor. Asso., Rockefeller Inst. Med. Research, Princeton, N.J., 1934-39; with dept. med. microbiology U. Wis. Med. Sch., Madison, 1939-74, prof., 1946-74, chmn. dept., 1946-70. Served to maj., M.C., AUS, 1942-45. Mem. Soc. Am. Bacteriologists, Soc. Exptl. Biology and Medicine, Am. Assn. Immunologists. Home: Madison, Wis. Died Aug. 18, 1974; interred Forest Hill Cemetery, Eau Claire, Wis.

SEATON, FREDERICK ANDREW, newspaper publisher; b. Washington, Dec. 11, 1909; s. Fay Noble and Dorothea Elizabeth (Schmidt) S.; student Kan. State U., 1927-31, LL.D., 1955, U. Alaska, 1958; H.H.D., Maryville Coll., 1956; LL.D., Miami U., 1959, Gettysburg Coll., 1959, U. Hawaii, 1959, U. Redlands, 1959, U. Md., 1960, John Carroll U., 1960, Rose Poly. Inst., 1960; D. Eng., Worcester Poly Inst., 1959, Colo. Sch. Mines, 1960; m. Gladys Dowd, Jan. 23, 1930; children—Donald Richard, Johanna Christine Epp, Monica Margaret Hansen, Alfred Noble. Pres. Neb. TV Co., Hastings, Sheridan (Wyoming) Newspapers, Inc., Seaton Pub. Co., Lead, S.D., Winfield (Kan.) Pub. Co., Inc., Seaton Pub. Co., Hastings, Neb., Alliance (Neb.) Pub. Co., Neb. Broadcasting Co., Hastings, Manhattan (Kan.) Broadcasting Co.; v.p. Seaton Pub. Co., Inc., Manhattan, Kan., Midwest Broadcasting Co., Coffeyville, Coffeyville Pub. Co.; dir. First Nat. Bank, Hastings, 1961-74. Chmn. senior advisers to Nixon campaign, 1968. Bd. visitors Freedoms Found.; state chmn. of Radio Free Europe Fund, 1965, bd. dirs.; bd. advisers Nat. Trust for Historic Preservation; mem. Presdl. Commn. to Commemorate Bi-centennial Anniversary of Revolutionary War. Hon. mem. of Nat. Council, Boy Scouts Am.; asst. sec. of def. for legislative affairs, 1953-55; adminstrv. asst. to the Pres. of U.S., Feb., 1955, dep. asst. to Pres. of U.S., June, 1955; Sec. of the Interior, 1956-61. Served two terms in Neb. Unicameral, 1945-49; mem. Neb. Judicial Council, 1948-50; chmn. Neb. Legislative Council, 1947-49. Vice chmn. Young Rep. Club of Kan., 1932-34, state chmn., 1934-36, reelected 1936, resigned 1937; Young Rep. nat. committeeman for Kan., 1935; vice chmn. Kan. Rep. State Com., 1934-37; vice chmn. Kan. Rep. delegation to Cleveland, 1936; sec. to Alfred M. Landon in nat. campaign, 1936; apptd. U.S. senator Neb., 1951, on death of Sen. Wherry; mem. personal adv. staff of Pres. Eisenhower during nat. campaign, 1952. Past pres. Asso. Press Newspapers of Neb.; past chmn. bd., pres. Inland Daily Press Assn. Trustee U. of Neb. Found., Hastings Coll. Recipient Medal of Freedom. Mem. Nat. Editorial Assn., Neb. Press Assn., Newcomen Soc. N.A., St. Andrews Soc., Beta Theta Pi (dist. chief 1936, 37), Hon. Innocents, U. Neb., Sigma Delta Chi, Pi Kappa Delta. Episcopalian. Mason (Shriner), Elk. Clubs: Lochland Country; University (Lincoln. Neb.); Rotary (Hastings) National Press, Kenwood Country. Home: Hastings, Neb. Died Jan. 17, 1974; interred Hastings, Neb.

SEAVER, HENRY LATIMER, prof. of history; b. Boston, Mass., Jan. 16, 1878; s. Latimer Small and Minnie (Church) S.; A.B., Harvard, 1900, A.M., 1914; m. Susan Russell Seaver, Sept. 14, 1908 (dec. 1964). Instr. English, Harvard, 1900-01; instr. dept. English and history, Mass. Inst. Tech., 1901-33, prof. history in dept. architecture, 1933-47; Sunday docent Boston Art Museum, 1907-33. Mem. Am. Assn. Univ. Profs., Mass. Hist. Soc., Phi Beta Kappa. Author: The Great Revolt in Castile, 1928. Home: Lexington, Mass., Died Nov. 26, 1975.

SECONDARI, JOHN HERMES, film prodn. exec.; b. Rome, Italy, Nov. 1, 1919; s. Epaminonda and Linda (Agostini) S.; B.A., Fordham U., 1939; M.S., Columbia, 1940; m. Rita Hume, Oct. 2, 1948 (dec.); 1 son, John Gerry; m. 2d, Helen Jean Rogers, July 1, 1961; 1 dau., Linda Helen. Came to U.S. 1924, naturalized, 1929. With U.P.I., 1939-40, CBS, Rome, 1946-48; dep. chief information div. ECA, Spl. Mission to Italy, 1948-51; chief Washington news bur. ABC, 1956-59, exec. producer spl. projects, 1960-68; pres. John H. Secondari Prodns., Ltd., 1968-75; producer, writer over 100 TV documentaries and spls. Served from pvt. to capt. AUS, 1941-46. Recipient awards N.E.A., Ohio State U., Page One, Overseas Press Club, Radio-TV Daily, also Emmy, Peabody, Marconi, Christopher, Western Heritage, Brotherhood awards. Mem. Nat. Acad. TV Arts and Scis. (bd. govs.), Radio and TV News Dirs. Assn., Overseas Writers, Radio TV Corrs. Assn. Club: Nat. Press (Washington). Author: Coins in the Fountain, 1952; Temptation for a King, 1954; Spinner of the Dream, 1955. Home: New York City, N.Y. Died Feb. 1975.

SECUNDA, SHOLOM, composer, condr., lectr.; b. Alexandria, Russia, Aug. 23, 1894; s. Abraham and Anna (Nedabelka) S.; came to U.S., 1908, naturalized, 1918; student Cooper Union, N.Y.C., 1912-13, Columbia, 1913-14, Inst. Mus. Art, 1914-19; m. Betty Almer, Oct. 25, 1927; children—Sheldon, Eugene. Chorus boy comedy theatre, N.Y.C., 1916-17; tchr. music, 1915-23; composer, 1916-74; arch. condr., 1917-74; lectr. mus. subjects N.Y. U., Hunter Coll., 1939-74; music dir. Bklyn. Jewish Center, 1947-61, condr. ann. summer symphony Concord Hotel; prof. music dept. Jewish Tchrs. Sem., 1966-74; music critic Jewish Daily Forward. Served with USNRF, World War I. Works include 60 oparettas, grand opera Sulemith, 1925; Bel Mir Bist du Schoen (most popular song 1939); composer, condr., producer pageants and similar shows for nat. orgns. at Madison Sq. Garden, Carnegie Hall, others; composer scores for various films; composer oratorios If Not Higher, 1964, Yizkor, 1967, Shabbat HamaikahPassover Festival Kol Nidre Service; Welcoming the Sabbath (Columbia records); Lichvod Hashabbat; String Quartet in C minor; Concerto for Violln and Orch. in C minor; chamber, symphonic music; various other recs. Mem. A.S.C.A.P. Home: New York City, N.Y. Died June 13, 1974.

SEDGWICK, PAUL J(OSEPH), univ. prof.; b. Cincinnati, Sept. 22, 1896; s. Frank Edwin and Leonora Elizabeth (Freisens) S.; S.B., U. of Chicago, 1918, Ph.D., 1922; m. Lillian Grace Reynolds, Sept. 6, 1924; 1 dau., Joanne Virginia. Fellow U. of Chicago, 1919-22; with Syracuse U. from 1922, prof. botany; curator for bot., Museum of Natural Science. Served as ensign, U.S.N.R., 1918. Mem. Bot. Soc. Am., A.A.A.S., Sigma Xi Sci Soc., Biol. Phiotog. Assn. Am., Biol. Stain Commn. Specializes in plant morphology, growth and movement of plants, visual aids in teaching. Baptist. Home: Syracuse, N.Y. Died Feb. 2, 1973.

SEDITA, FRANK ALBERT, mayor; b. New Orleans, June 20, 1907; s. Vincent and Crocifissa (Militello) S.; LL.B., U. Buffalo, 1931; m. Sara R. Vacanti, July 11, 1934; children—Frank A., Paulette. Admitted to N.Y. bar, 1932; dep. sheriff 1933-35; asst. corp. counsel, Buffalo, 1935-38, sec. div. of water, 1938-41; clk. City Ct. of Buffalo, 1941-47, 1st dept. Surrogate's Ct., 1947-49, asso. Judge City Ct., 1949-57; mayor City of Buffalo, 1958-61, 66-75; collector of customs, 1962-65. Home: Buffalo, N.Y., Died May 2, 1975.

SEDLANDER, NORMAN ROBERT, educator; b. Ludington, Mich., June 28, 1920; s. Hjalmar J. and Hilma Marie (Wigren) S.; B.S. in Civil Engring., Mich. State U., 1944, M.S., 1951; Ph.D., Cornell U., 1958; m. Miriam Carola Neidlinger, Apr. 19, 1947; children—Norman Robert, Mary Lee. Prodn. engr. Autopulse Corp., Ludington, 1947; instr. to asst. prof. engring. drawing and light constrn. Mich. State U., East Lansing,

1947-58; asso. prof. engring. graphics U. Mich., Ann Arbor, 1958-60; prof. civil engring. U. Toledo, 1960-74. Served to lt. (j.g.) USNR, 1943-47. USPHS research grantee, 1963-66. Mem. Am. Soc. C.E., Am. Soc. Engring. Edn., Water Pollution Control Fedn., Am. Water Works Assn., Royal Soc. Health, Societas Internat. Limnolgia, Sigma Xi, Chi Epsilon, Sigma Lambda Chi, Pi Kappa Phi. Research in water pollution. Home: Toledo, O. Died Jan. 3, 1974; interred Lake View Cemetery, Ludington, Mich.

SEDLAR, SASA, educator; b. Krsko, Yugoslavia, June 17, 1913; s. August and Maria (Sosa) S.; Dipl. Engr. Architect, Tech. Faculty, U. Ljubljana (Yugoslavia), 1937, D.Sc., 1970; m. Danuska Lapajnar, May 21, 1945. Research fellow, 1939-43; cons. planner, 1945-60; prof. U. Ljubljana, 1960—, dean Faculty Architecture, Civil Engring. and Geodesy, 1969-71. Mem. planning council Municipality of Ljubljana, 1966—. Mem. Architect's Assn. Yugoslvaia, Town Planning Assn. Yugoslavia, Internat. Fedn. for Housing and Planning (mem. bur.). Contbr. articles, revs. to profl. jours. Developed regional plans and devel. plants for many Yugoslavian cities. Home: Ljabljana, Yugoslavia., Died Feb. 5, 1975.

SEELE, KEITH C(EDRIC), Egyptologist, educator; b. Warsaw, Ind., Feb. 13, 1898; s. Henry D. and Ora Capitola (Dick) S.; B.A., Coll. Wooster, 1922, L.H.D., 1947; B.D., McCormick Theol. Sem., 1926; T.B. Blackstone fellow U. Berlin 1926-28; fellow Inst. Internat. Edn., Berlin, 1926-27; further study, Berlin, 1930; Ph.D., U. Chgo., 1938; m. Diederika A.H. Millard, June 29, 1929. Tchr., Assiut Coll., 1922-23; mem. epigraphic survey expdn. Oriental Inst. U. Chgo., Luxor and Sakkara, Egypt, 1929-36, faculty Egyptology, U. Chgo., 1936-64, prof., 1950-64, prof. emeritus, 1964-71; dir. Oriental Inst. Egyptian Assuan High Dam Program, 1960-71. Del., Congress Orientalists, Paris, 1948, Cambridge, 1954; Institut d'Egypte of Cairo del. UN Conf. Conservation and Utilization Resources, Lake Success, N.Y., 1949. Mem. Egypt Exploration Soc. (London), Societe Francelse d'Egyptologie (Paris), Deutsches Archaologisches Institut, Institut d'Egypte (Cairo corr. mem.), Phi Beta Kappa. Author: Medinet Habu II: Later Hist. Records of Ramses III (with H.H. Nelson, J.A. Wilson), 1932; Medinet Habu III: The Calendar, the Slaughterhouse, and Minor Records of Ramses III (with H.H. Nelson, J.A. Wilson, S. Schott), 1934; Reliefs and Inscriptions at Karnak I. Ramses III's Temple within the Great Inclosure of Amon (with H.H. Nelson, S. Schott), 1936; II. Ramses III Temple within the Great Inclosure of Amon and Ramses III's Temple in the Inclosure of Mut (with Nelson, Schott), 1936; The Mastaba of Mereruka (with P. Duell and C.F. Nims), 1938; Festival Scenses of Ramses III (with Nelson, others), 1940; When Egypt Ruled the East (with G. Steindorff) 1941, rev. 1957; Coregency of Ramses II with Seti I and the Data of the Great Hypostyle Hall at Karnak, 1940; Reliefs and Inscriptions at Karnak III; The Bubastite Portal (with S. Schott, G.R. Hughes, others), 1953; Medinet Habu V: The Temple Proper, Part I (with G.R. Hughes, others), 1957; The Tomb of Tjanefer at Thebes, 1959; The Beit el-Wal; Temple Ramesscs II (with Hughes, E.F. Wente), 1967; Ausgrabungen von Khor-Dehmit bls Bet el-Wall (with H. Riche, L. Habachi, L.Y. Zabkar), 1967., also articles in profls. jours. Editor: Blackfeet and Buffalo, Memories of Life among the Indians, 1962; Jour. Nr. Eastern Studies, 1948—; Most Ancient Egypt, 1964. Excavated in Babkalabsha area, Nubia, 1960-61, at Qustul, Ballana, Arminna, 1962-64, discovering important cemeteries, other remains of all Nubian cultures 3000 B.C. to A.D. 1000 Home: Homewood, Ill. Died July 23, 1971.

SEELER, ALBERT OTTO, physician, educator; b. Derry, N.H., Dec. 25, 1915; s. Karl Emil Felix and Clara Baylies (Cornell) S.; A.B., Harvard, 1934, M.D., 1938; m. Edwina DeWitt Dusenbery, Nov. 29, 1941; children—Alan Thayer, Joan DeWitt, Marcia Drake, Karl Albert, John Henry. Intern. Meml. Hosp., Worcester, Mass., 1938-40; pharmacologist Merck Inst. Therapeutic Research, 1940-44, asst. dir., 1944-45; asst. resident medicine, resident and research fellow medicine Thorndike Lab., Harvard med. unit Boston City Hosp., 1945-48; asst. prof. indsl. medicine Harvard Sch. Pub. Health, 1948-50, instr. Med. Sch., 1950-54, clin. asso. medicine, 1954-76, lectr. on medicine, 1963-76; practice internal medicine, 1950-56; physician Mass. Inst. Tech., 1956-59, physician-in-chief, 1959-60, prof., dir. med. dept., 1960-76; physician-in-chief II Med. Service, Harvard-Boston City Hosp., 1959-73; physician Mount Auburn Hosp., 1955-76. Diplomate Am. Bd. Internal Medicine. Fellow A.C.P.; mem. A.M.A., Mass. Med. Soc., New Eng. Grenfell Assn. (dir.). Club: St. Botolph (Boston). Home: Waban, Mass., Died Feb. 12, 1976; buried Derry, N.H.

SEELEY, WALTER JAMES, educator; born at Hazleton, Pennsylvania, Nov. 30, 1894; s. Frank Wesley and Mame (Seaborne) S.; E.E., Polytechnic Inst. of Brooklyn, 1917; M.S., Univ. of Pa., 1924; m. Emetta Susan Weed, Sept 1, 1920; children—Carolyn Ada (Mrs. H. A. Scott), Mary Elizabeth (now Mrs. J. R. Hill), and Naomi Ruth (now Mrs. B. A. Ross). Instr. elec. engring., Univ. Pa., 1919-25; asst. prof., Duke Univ. 1925-27, asso. prof., 1927-29, prof., 1929-64, prof. emeritus, 1964, chairman dept. electrical engring., 1935-64, dean of the college of engineering, 1953-64, dean emeritus, 1964; asst. to cons. engr. on street lighting, Trenton, N.J., 1920-24; consultant to mfrs. radio apparatus, 1920-24; spl. engr. Duke Power Co., summers 1926-40, cons. 1950-74; part-time employee Naval Ordnance Lab., Washington, 1941-46, full time summers 1941-46. Director Wilmore Electronics. Served as ensign United States Naval Res., spl. bd. anti-submarine devices, 1917-19; consultant Naval Ordnance Lab., 1941-46. Registered engineer. Chairman of North Carolina State Board of Registration for Engineers and Land Surveyors. Fellow Am. Inst. E.E. (vice pres. 1949-51, mem. nat. coms.), sr. mem. Inst. of Radio Engrs.; mem. Am. Soc. E.E., Professional Engrs. of N.C., N.C. Soc. Engrs., Binaural Sons of the C. National Society Professional Engineers, Sigma Xi, Tau Beta Pi, Pi Mu Epsilon, Sigma Pi Sigma, Omicron Delta Kappa. Independent Democrat. Methodist. Clubs: Charlotte Engineers, Durham Engineers. Author: Impedance Computing Tables, 1936; Mannual of Direct and Alternating Current Circuit Experiments, 1930; An Introduction to the Operational Calculus, 1941. Home: Durham, N.C. Died July 29, 1974.

SEIDEL, HARRY GEORGE, govt. ofcl.; b. Paris, France, Jan. 31, 1922; s. Harry George and Rosamond (Harris) S.; grad. Milton (Mass.) Acad., 1940; A.B., Princeton, 1944; m. Geraldine Anne Parker, Sept. 23, 1951; children—Harry George, Rosamond H., Allan K., Janice L. With Standard Oil Co. (N.J.), 1946-72, pres. Esso Standard Algeria, 1966-68, gen. mgr. Esso Standard Kenya, 1968-72; dir. AID mission to Morocco, 1972-73. Active Boy Scouts Am. Served with USNR, 1941-46. Mem. Mil. Order World War II. Rotarian. Clubs: Princeton, University (N.Y.C.). Died Dec. 1973.

SEIDEL, JOHN GEORGE, art connoisseur and appraiser; b. Milw., July 6, 1902; s. George Peter and Anna Marie (Orth) S.; ed. Milw. U. Sch., museums and galleries in Europe and Am.; m. Lena Mae Pettyes, Dec. 4, 1937; 1 son, John Frederick. Student appraiser Am. Appraisal Co., 1928-32, dir. fine arts div., 1940-55; practicing art appraiser, 1928-73, practicing connoisseur, appraiser, pres., dir. John G. Seidel Assos., Inc., Milw., 1955-73; art cons. Marquette Univ.; cons. Am. Appraisal Co.; lectr. Chmn. acquisition com. Com. for Selection of Dir. Milw. Art Center, 1955. Fellow Valuers Institution, London, Eng.; mem. Am. Soc. of Appraisers (sr.), Appraisers Association America, American Assn. Museums, Midwest Mus. Conf., Milw. Art Center, Internat., Am. insts. for conservation of historic and artistic works, State Hist. Soc. Wis., Friends of Milw. Pub. Mus., Milw. Assn. Commerce. Hon. and charter mem. So. Ill. U. Library Assn. Clubs: Milwaukee Athletic, Rotary, Milwaukee (dir.). Home: Milwaukee, Wis. Died Nov. 2, 1973.

SEIDL, FRANK J(OSEPH), SR., grain mcht.; b. Vienna, Austria, June 7, 1880; s. Frank Joseph and Margaret (Rank) S.; grad. Milw. State Tchrs. Coll., 1901; m. Lisette Reuter, July 10, 1907; children—Stuart, Frank J., Elizabeth, Virginia. Came to U.S., 1891, naturalized, 1901. With Rahr Malting Co., 1904-18; buyer Seidl Grain Co., 1918-31; mgr. barley dept. Archer-Daniels-Midland Co., from 1931, v.p., from 1947; pres. Cranberry Lake Development Co., Phillips, Wis. Clubs: Athletic. Automobile, Interlachen Golf (Mpls.). Home: Minneapolis, Minn.†

SEIDLITZ, WALTER GEORGE, business exec.; born St. Louis, May 25, 1899; s. Charles Frederick and Margaret (Fichtel) S.; B.S., Ill. Inst. Tech., 1935; m. Adelia Henry, Oct. 7, 1922; 1 son, Walter George. Apprentice draftsman, Wagner Electric Co., 1919-23; chief draftsman, Valley Electric Co., 1923-26; machine designer and development engr., Western Electric Co., Chicago, 1926-35; tech. advisor Revere Copper and Brass, Inc., Chicago, 1935-41, plant mgr., 1941-44, vice pres. from 1944. Served U.S. Navy, World War I. Mem. Am. Soc. for Metals, Chicago Assn. Commerce and Industry, Ill. State C. of C., U.S. C. of C., Ill. Mfg. Assn., Nat. Assn. Mfrs., Am. Ordnance Assn. Republican. Conglist. Holder patents for rolling mill equipment and auxiliary devices. Home: River Forest, Ill. Died June 12, 1974; cremated.

SEIME, REUBEN INGMAR, physician; b. Ferryville, Wis., Aug. 24, 1907; s. Severt and Carrie (Brudos) S.; M.D., McGill U., 1938; m. Ruth Irene Brook, May 28, 1938; children—Carolyn (Mrs. Philip M. Leech), Susan (Mrs. Russell W. Hook), John, Jane. Intern, Detroit Receiving Hosp., 1938-39; resident in radiology Univ. Hosp., Ann Arbor, Mich., 1951-53; jr. instr. radiology U. Mich., 1953-54. Diplomate Am. Bd. Radiology. Fellow Am. Coll. Radiology; mem. A.M.A. Home: Grand Rapids, Mich. Died Sept. 2, 1969; buried Cascade Cemetery, Cascade, Mich.

SEITZ, WILLIAM CHAPIN, educator; b. Buffalo, June 19, 1914; s. George William and Cora Elizabeth (Chapin) S.; student Albright Art Sch., 1932-33; B.F.A., U. Buffalo, 1946; M.F.A. (Proctor fellow 1951-52), Princeton, 1952, Ph.D., 1955; m. Irma J. Seigelman, Dec. 1, 1938. Instr. art history U. Buffalo, 1946-48, asst. prof., 1948-49; critic in residence Princeton, 1952-53, asst. prof., bi-centennial preceptor, 1956-60; asso. curator painting and sculpture exhbns. Mus. Modern Art, N.Y.C., 1960-65, curator, 1965; prof. fine arts, dir. Rose Art. Mus., Brandeis U., 1965-70; vis. prof. history art Harvard, 1969-70; William R. Kenan, Jr. prof. history art U. Va., Charlottesville, 1970-74; Kress prof. Nat. Gallery Art, Washington, 1971-72; exhibited one man shows Arista Gallery, N.Y.C., 1938, Willard Gallery, N.Y.C., 1949, 51, 53, Princeton Mus., 1949, 51; exhibited group shows Bklyn. Mus., Whitney Mus. Am. Art, Albright Art Gallery, Allen Meml. Art Mus., Oberlin Coll., Cleve. Mus., Milw. Art Inst., Columbus (O.) Gallery Fine Arts, U. Ill. Mus. Modern Art. Nat. Council Learned Socs. fellow, 1952-53; Fulbright fellow, 1957-58. Mem. Coll. Art Assn., Soc. for Aesthetics, Am. Assn. U. Profs., Assn. Mus. Dirs. Author: Claude Monet, 1960; Monet, Seasons and Moment, 1960; The Art of Assemblage, 1961; Mark Tobey, 1962; Arshile Gorky, 1962; Hans Hofmann, 1963; Art Israel, 1964; The Responsive Eye, 1965; Henri de Toulouse-Lautrec; At the Circus, 1965; San Paulo 9: Edward Hopper and Environment U.S.A., 1967; Seventh Biennial Canadian Painting, 1968; Kinetic Art, 1969; Sculpture, Its Image in the Arts, 1969; Turner, 1970; Manet, 1971; George Segal, 1972. Contbr. articles profl. jours., mus. bulls. Home: Charlottesville Va. Died Oct. 26, 1974.

SELBY, CLARENCE DAVEY, physician; b. Des Moines, Ia., July 21, 1878; s. Sanford and Lizzie Foster (Davey) S.; M.D., Western Res. U., 1902; m. Olivia Roberts, Oct. 18, 1905; 1 son, Robert Vincent. Demonstrator histology Med. Dept., Western Res. U., 1901; asst. to city bacteriologist, Cleve., 1902; intern Lakeside Hosp., Cleve., 1902-03; resident pathologist St. Alexis Hosp., 1903-04; asst. to Dr. George Crile, 1904-05; removed to Toledo, 1905; vis. surgeon St. Vincent's Hosp., 1906-34, cons. in surgery, mem. adv. com., chief of staff, 1920-26; vis. surgeon Flower Hosp., 1911-20; med. cons. Gen. Motors Corp., 1935-49; became resident lectr. Sch. Pub. Health, U. Mich., 1949; cons. Inst. Indsl. Health, from 1950. Commr. of health, 1916-18, mem. Charter Commn., 1928-29, Recreation Commn., 1932-34 (all Toledo). Cons. hygienist USPHS, 1918-19, surgeon (reserve), 1919-29, cons. div. indsl. hygiene and mem. adv. health council, 1940-46. Chmn. subcom. on indsl. health and medicine Office of Def. Health and Welfare Service, Office of Emergency Mgmt., 1940-42. Sec. health service sect, NSC, 1919; mem. conf. bd. Physicians in Industry, from 1938; chmn. com. indsl. health and medicine, NRC, 1942-46. Recipient Distinguished Service citation, A.M.A., 1953. Fellow A.C.S., A.M.A. (sec. sect. preventive medicine and pub. health and indsl. medicine, 1920, chmn. 1940-41, chmn. 1940-41, chmn. Ohio com. on hosps. 1921-23, mem. council indsl. health 1938-53), Am. Assn. Indsl. Physicians and Surgeons (dir. 1930-34, pres. 1938), Mich. Assn. Indsl. Physicians and Surgeons (pres. 1942), Am. Pub. Health Assn. (chmn. sect. indsl. hygiene 1930-40); mem. Mich., St. Clair County med. socs., Ohio Med. Assn. (sec.-treas. 1908-18, pres. 1925), Acad. Medicine Toledo and Lucas County, Toledo Hosp. Council (pres. 1932), Ohio (pres. 1923), Toledo (pres. 1922-28) pub. health assns., Nu Sigma Nu. Republican. Episcopalian. Mason (32°, K.T., Shriner). Clubs: Rotary, Elks, Lions (pres. 1922), High Twelve (Port Huron). Mng. editor Ohio State Med. Jour., 1908-18. Home: Port Huron, Mich.†

SELF, WILLIAM KING, bldg. and constrn. co. exec.; b. Marks, Miss., Dec. 23, 1918; s. Peyton M.B. and Sallie (King) S.; B.S., Washington and Lee U., 1939; m. Joan Hallett (dec.); 1 son, William King. Chief exec. officer Pacific Bldgs., Inc., Marks, Miss.; owner, pub. The Delta Rev. mag.; former dir. Fed. Res. Bank, St. Louis, S. Central Bell Tel. & Tel. Co. Chgo. Bd. Trade, N.Y. Cotton Exchange, Miss. Small Bus. Adv. Council. Mem. Miss. Council on Arts, Delta Area council Boy Scouts Am. Trustee Miss. Coll. Served with USNR, World War II. Mem. Miss. Mfrs. Assn. (past dir.), Nat. Indsl. Conf. Bd., Young Pres.'s Orgn., Pi Kappa Alpha. Baptist. Clubs: Memphis Country; Capital City (Jackson, Miss.); (Atlanta); Boston (New Orleans). Home: Marks, Miss., Died Feb. 16, 1975.

SELL, HENRY BLACKMAN, editor; b. Whitewater, Wis., Nov. 14, 1889; s. Henry Thorne and Mary (Blackman) S.; student Culver (Ind.) Mil. Acad.; m. Maud Ann O'Harrow, 1914 (dec.). Lit. editor Chgo. Daily News, 1916-20; editor Harper's Bazaar, 1920-26; pres. Blaker Advt. Agy., 1928-50, Vitamins Plus, Inc., 1937-41, Sell's Specialties, Inc., 1942-60; editor Town and Country mag., 1949-65, editor-at-large, 1965-72; editor-at-large Harper's Bazaar, 1973-74; dir. Hotel Representative, Inc., N.Y.C. Spl. cons. to sec. agr., Washington, 1940-43; mem. small bus. adv. com. Dept. Commerce. Decorated officer French Legion Honor. Author: (with Victor Weybright) Buffalo Bill and the Wild West, 1955-56. Home: New York City, N.Y. Died Oct. 23, 1974.

SELLARS, ROY WOOD, author; b. Egmondville, Ont., Can., July 9, 1880; s. Ford Willis and Mary Arabella (Stalker) S.; grad. Ferris Inst., Big Rapids, Mich., 1898; A.B., U. Mich., 1903, Ph.D., 1908; student Hartford Theol. Sem., U. Wis., U. Chgo., also 1 yr. Germany, France; m. Helen Maud Stalker, June 10, 1911; children—Wilfrid Stalker, Cecily Helen. Mem. faculty U. Mich., Ann Arbor, 1905-73 asso. prof., 1918-23, prof., 1923-56, prof. philosophy emeirtus, 1956-73. Western (pres. 1923), Eastern (v.p. 1921) philos. assns., Ph Beta Kappa. Clubs: Golf, Univeristy, Research. Author: Critical Realism, 1916; The Next Stem in

Democracy, 1916; The Essentials of Logic, 1917; The Essentials of Philosophy, 1917; The Next Step in Religion 1918; Essays in Critical Realism, 1921; Evolutionary Naturalism, 1921; Principles and Problems of Philosophy, 1926; Religion Coming of Age, 1928; The Philosophy of Physical Realism, 1932; The Humanist Manifesto, 1933; Lending a Hand to Hylas, 1968; Reflections on American Philosophy from Within, 1969; The Principles, Perspectives and Problems of Philosophy, 1969. Contbr. articles to profl. jours. m Home: Ann Arbor, Mich., Died Sept. 4, 1973.

SELLERS, JAMES CLARK, examiner of questioned documents (handwriting expert); b. Heber, Utah, Oct. 16, 1891; s. Archibald and Elizabeth (Guys) S.; student Latter Day Saints U., Salt Lake City, 1909, U. So. Cal., 1926; m. Jeannette Daniels, Oct. 25, 1922 (dec.); 1 son, David Clark; m. 2d, Frances M. Hausler, Oct. Dec. 12, 1955. Began study in field of sci. identification, 1914, established offices, Salt Lake City, 1914, Pocatello, Ida., 1915, Seattle, 1919; has maintained office in Los Angeles from 1924 and lab. equipped with up-to-date equipment devoted exclusively to examination of problems involving authenticity of handwriting, typewriting, papers and inks; has examined documents for FBI, U.S. Secret Service, Internal Revenue, Post Office, etc., has examined documents in many outstanding cases as People of Cal. vs. William Edward Hickman, 1927, State of N.J. vs. Bruno Richard Hauptmann, 1935, William Shakespeare signature problem, London, Eng., 1938, and others. Served as air machine gun instr. U.S. Army, 1917-18; AEF. Mem. Am. Acad. Forensic Scis. (past chmn. document sect.), Internat. Assn. Identification (life mem.; past v.p. So. Cal.), Am. Soc. Questioned Document Examiners (pres. 1946-50), So. Cal. Acad. Criminology (pres. 1933-40, dir. 1933-47), Service Clubs' Council (pres. Los Angeles 1932), Am. Legion (comdr. 1933-34). Republican. Mason (K.T., Shriner). Clubs: Kiwanis (lt. gov. Calif.-Nev. Dist. 1938; author Code of Ethics, 1943; pres. Los Angeles 1932), Trojan (dir. 1942-48), San Gabriel Golf and Country. Author: Handwriting Identification and Expert Testimony, 1930; Scientific Identification vs. Guesswork, 1938; Spurious Typewritten Documents, 1934. Contbr. numerous articles in nat. publs. Specialist on questions involving identity and age of paper, ink and pencil writings. Lectr. Recognized for methods originated or developed for proof of facts in courts. Home: San Marino, Cal. F1Died Apr. 10, 1973.

SELLERS, WALTON PRESTON, agriculturist; b. Iota, La., Oct. 15, 1901; s. William P. and Mamie (Fisher) S.; B.S., Southwestern La. Inst., 1925; B.S., La. State U., 1927, also grad. study; m. Lennie M. Thompson, July 2, 1931; children—Walton Preston, William Ralph, Cheryl Lynn. Tchr., Reserve High Sch., La., 1926-27, Church Point High Sch., 1927-29; county agrl. agt. Franklin Parish, Winnsboro, La., 1929-42; flight instr. Clent Breedlove Aero. Service, Lubbock, Tex., 1942-44; specialist agrl. extension service La. State U. and A. and M. Coll., Baton Rouge, 1944-48; agrl. technician Dept. Agr., later ICA, Panama, 1948-57, ICA, Guatemala City, Guatemala, 1957-59, Port Au Prince, Haiti, 1959—. Mem. Epsilon Sigma Phi. Methodist (past. sr. warden). Mason. Home: Washington, La., Died Jan. 6, 1969.

SEMBACH, J, tenor; b. Berlin, Germany, Mar. 9, 1881; s. Edward and Frederike (Becker) S.; ed. Friederich Real Gymnasium, Berlin; studied music and violin under Prof. Felix Schmidt, Gustave Walther, also Jean de Reszke, Paris, France; m. Caecilie Vogel. Appeared at Royal Opera House, Vienna, Dresden, Berlin, Covent Garden, London; came to U.S., 1914, and was long a mem, Metropolitan Opera Co. Naturalized citizen of U.S., 1921.*†

SEMBOWER, ALTA BRUNT, (Mrs. Charles J.), writer; b. Erie, Kan., Aug. 13, 1878; d. John Rich and Lois (Van Laningham) Brunt; A.B., Ind. U., 1901; m. Charles Jacob Sembower, June 26, 1901. Contbr. short stories and articles to mags. Alpha Theta, Phi Beta Kappa. Home: Indianapolis, Ind.†

SENFT, CRAIG T., publishing co. exec.; b. Phila., Feb. 16, 1915; s. Charles Myers and Hazel (Brumaghim) S.; ed. Perth Amboy Jr. Coll., 1933-34, Rutgers U., 1934-36; m. Lois Form, Oct. 5, 1957; children—Peter, Ann, Jeffrey, Michael. With Prentice-Hall, Inc., N.Y.C., 1940-58, mgr. ednl. book div., 1950-54, v.p., 1954-58; v.p., mgr. sch. dept. Holt, Rinehart & Winstoh, 1958-60, exec. v.p., 1961-63; pres., chief exec. officer, dir. Silver-Burdett Co., 1963-68; pres. Am. Book Co., 1968, Litton Ednl. Publishing, Inc., N.Y.C., 1969-75; dir. Nepeaque Co., Van Nostrand-Reinhold Ltd., London, Eng., Van Nostrand-Reinhold Ltd., Toronto, Ont., Can. Pres., Am. Textbook Pubs. Inst., 1963-64; mem., vice chmn. Govt. Adv. Com. Internat. Book Programs, 1963-64, 66-70. Mem. Ridgewood (N.J.) Bd. Edn., 1967-68. Vice chmn. bd. fellow Fairleigh Dickinson U., 1968-70; trustee Ridgewood (N.J.) Pub. Library, 1963-70, pres., 1966-69; trustee Ramapo Coll. Served with AUS, World War II. Decorated Bronze Star medal, Purple Heart. Mem. N.J. Library Trustees Assn. (exec. bd. 1965, pres. 1968-69). Clubs: Skytop (Pa.). Home: Ridgewood, N.J. Died Aug. 27, 1975.

SENIOR, CLARENCE, educator; b. Clinton, Mo., June 9, 1903; s. Joseph C. and Maggie (Ollson) S.; A.B., U. Kan., 1927; A.M., U. Mo. at Kansas City, 1941; postgrad. U. Vienna, Internationallsche Volkshochschule, Elsinore, Denmark, 1928, 31; Ph.D., Columbia, 1955; m. Ruth L. Miller, Jan. 24, 1934; 1 son, Paul Norman. Field sec. Adult Edn. Assn., Cleve., also sec. Cleve. Labor Coll., 1927-29; nat. exec. sec. Socialist party U.S., 1929-36; labor editor Milw. Leader, 1937; dir. Information Center of Ams., N.Y.C., Washington, Mexico City, 1938-41; dir. Inter-Am. Inst., U. Kansas City, 1940-42; cons. U.S.-Mexico oil commr., 1942; work on Latin Am., Bd. Econ. Warfare, 1942-43; field work, regional resources devel. project on Lat. Am., Nat. Planning Assn., 1943-44; Latin Am. research Fgn. Econ. Adminstrn., Washington, 1944-45; dir. Social Sci. Research Center, U. P.R., 1945-48; research asso. Bur. Applied Social Research, lectr. sociology Columbia, 1951-60; prof. sociology Bklyn. Coll., City U. N.Y., 1961-71, dir. Center for Migration Studies, 1965-71; cons. Dept. Labor, P.R., 1949-69. Mem. Bd. Edn. N.Y.C., 1961-68. Mem. Am., Rural sociol. socs., Internat. Union for Sci. Study Population, Am. Econ. Assn., Population Soc. Am. Author: The Puerto Rican Migrant in St. Croix, 1946; Puerto Rican Emigration, 1947; The Puerto Rican in New York City, 1948; Strangers and Neighbors, 1952, Land Reform and Democracy, 1958; The Puerto Ricans, 1965; Our Citizens from the Caribbean, 1965; Santiago Iglesias, Labor Crusader, 1972. Co-author; The Puerto Rican Journey, 1950; One America, 1951; Understanding Minority Groups, 1956; Jamaican Migration to Great Britain, 1956; The Caribbean Its Economy, 1955; In a Strange Land, 1961; The School Dropout, 1964; Imperatives in Education, 1965; The Assault on Poverty, 1966; The Status of Puerto Rico, 1966. Home: Rio Grande, P.R. Died Sept. 9, 1974.

SENOUR, CHARLES, ret. cons. civil engr.; b. St. Louis, Apr. 30, 1892; s. Harry Koch and Mary (Clase) S.; B.S. in Civil Engring., Washington U., 1915; m. Alice E. Richmond, June 10, 1916; 1 son, John Charles. With U.S. Corps Engrs., Miss. River Commn., 1915-50, surveyor, St. Louis and Vicksburg, Miss., 1915-17, jr. engr., 1917-23, asst. engr., 1923-26, asso. engr., 1926-29, engr., 1929-30, sr. engr., 1930-36, prin. engr., 1936-41, head engr., 1941-45, chief civilian engr., asst. to pres. Miss. River Commn., div. engr. Lower Miss. Valley div. Corps Engrs., 1945-50; pvt. practice as cons. civil engr., Texarkana, Tex., 1950-53, N.Y.C., 1953-55, Coral Gables and Miami, Fla., 1955-69. Fellow Am. Soc. C.E.; mem. Sigma Nu. Christian Scientist. Home: Miami, Fla. Died Sept. 28, 1972.

SENSENBRENNER, JOHN STLIP, business exec.; b. Neenah, Wis., Apr. 20, 1886; s. Frank J. and Margaret (Stilp) S.; A.B., Princeton, 1909; m. Julia Reese Smith; children—Gretchen, Frank James, Helen Mary, John Stilp. Began as apprentice Kimberlay-Clark Corp., 1907, dir., 1916 Pacific Coast sales mgr., 1921-26, gen. sales mgr. and vice pres., 1926-42, mem. exec. com., 1928-42, resigned active bus. connection to enter U.S. Army, 1942. Director Kimberly-Clark Corp., Neenah Wis. Served F.A. U.S. Army, 1918; commd. major and assigned to purchases div., War Dept. Gen. Staff, 1942; grad. U.S. Army Sch. of Mil. Govt. Va., 1943; sent to E.T.O., assigned to G-5, S.H.A.E.F., 1943-44; renegotiation div., War Dept. Gen. Staff, 1945; mem. Gen. Staff Corps and vice chmn. War Dept. Price Adjustment Bd., with rank of lt. col., 1945-46, promoted col., 1946, chmn. bd., 1947; chief of renegotiation br. and vice chmn. War Contracts Price Adjustment Bd., 1947. Decorated Legion of Merit, Army Commendation Medal. Mem. Am. Legion, Vets. Fgn. Wars, Mil. Govt. Assn. Clubs: Chicago Athletic, Chicago; Neenah, Neenah Nodaway Yacht, North Shore Golf (Neenah); University (Milwaukee); Army-Navy (Washington) Princeton (N.Y.C.); Oceanside Golf and Country (Ormond Beach, Fla.), Bath and Tennis (Palm Beach, Fla.). Home: Neenah, Wis., Died Oct. 8, 1973.

SENTNER, DAVID, journalist, poet; b. N.Y.C.; s. Joseph and Juanita (Brandon) S.; B.A., Columbia, 1923, B.Lit., 1923; m. Mary Southerland Steele; one dau., Joyce. Mem. N.Y. bureau, United Press, 1924; special writer and dramatic editor, Internat. News Service, 1924-35, fgn. corr., Internat. News Service, 1935-38; mem. editorial staff. N.Y. Journal-Am., 1938-42; Washington corr., Washington bur. chief, contbg. editor Hearst Newspapers & Hearst Headline Service, 1942-75, Washington rep. Hearst Mags. Dir Internat. Eye Found. Served with 27th Div., A.E.F., France, during World War I. Recipient Alfred A. Knopf Poetry Prize; also the Am. Legion Medal of Merit. Mem. Dramatists Guild, White House Corrs. Assn., Sigma Delta Chi, Am. Legion. Clubs: Gridiron. Columbia University (N.Y.); National Press (Washington). Author: Cobblestones: Hollywood Comet: How the FBI Gets Its Man. Home: Washington, D.C. Died Apr. 22, 1975.

SEPPELT, IAN HOWE, wine and brandy co. exec.; b. Seppeltsfield, S. Australia, Dec. 16. 1909; s. Udo Waldemar and Helen Gertrude (Howe) S.; B.Sc., U. Adelaide, 1932; student Ecole d'Agr. de Montpellier (France), 1933-34, Inst. Agronomique, Paris, 1934-35; m. Eileen May Sudholz, Feb. 25, 1936; children—Margaret (Mrs. Ian Leonard), Brian, Malcolm, Graham, Rodney. With B. Seppelt & Sons Ltd., distillers and wine makers, 1936—, gen. mgr., 1956-63, chmn. bd. dirs., 1963-73. Mem. Australian Wine Bd., 1950-73, chmn., 1958-73; mem. Australian Overseas Trade Publicity Com., 1958-73; mem. council Australian Wine Research Council, 1955-73; mem. Australian Export Devel. Council, 1965-69, Australian/Japan Bus. Corp. Com., 1963-68. Mem. council Salisbury (S. Australia) Coll. Advanced Edn. Decorated Order Brit. Empire. Mem. Australian Inst. Dirs., Royal Agr. Soc. S. Australia (council 1951-73), Australian (v.p. 1971), S. Australian (pres. 1969-71), chambers mfrs. Clubs: Adelaide, Amateur Sports, Public Schools, Commerce, Commercial Travellers. Home: Tanunda, Australia. Died Nov. 7, 1973; buried Seppelt Mausoleum, Seppeltsfield, Australia.

SERLING, ROD, writer-producer; b. Syracuse, N.Y., Dec. 25, 1924; s. Samuel L. and Esther (Cooper) S., B.A., Antioch Coll., 1950; L.H.D., Emerson Coll., 1971, Ithaca Coll., 1972, Alfred U., 1972; m. Carolyn Kramer, July 31, 1948; children—Joyce, Ann. Network radio writer, 1946-48; TV writer, 1948-75; plays produced on Kraft Theatre, Studio One, U.S. Steel Hour, Playhouse 90, Suspense, Danger, others; writer-producer of The Twilight Zone, Rod Serling's Night Gallery; narrator spl. In Search of Ancient Astronauts. Served with paratroopers AUS, World War II. Recipient Emmy for best teleplay writing, 1955, 56, 57, 59-60, 61, 63-64; recipient Sylvania award, 1955, 56; Peabody award, 1957, Christopher award, 1956, 71; Laurel award Writers Guild Am., posthumously 1975. Mem. Nat. Acad. TV Arts and Scis. (gov. N.Y.C. 1956-57, Cal. 1959, nat. pres. 1965-66). Author: Patterns, 1957; Requiem for a Heavyweight, 1962; The Season to be Wary, 1968; Rod Serling's Twilight Zone; Rod Serlings Twilight Zone Revisited; Night Gallery, Night Gallery Two; More Stories From The Twilight Zone. Home: Pacific Palisades, Cal. Died June 28, 1975; interred Interlaken, N.Y

SEROTTA, ELLIOTT CECIL, accountant; b. Savannah, Ga., July 1, 1912; s. Abram J. and Dora (Lewis) S.; student Jr. Coll. Augusta, Ga. 1929; B.S. in Commerce magna cum laude, U. Ga., 1931; m. Eve Dorothy Robinson, Feb. 18, 1940; children—Betty Jayne, Abram Jacob. Adminstrv. positions Augusta Arsenal, 1935-46; pvt. practice accounting, 1946-52; partner firm Bell and Serotta, C.P.A.'s, Augusta, 1952-55; owner accounting firm, Augusta, 1955-71; pres. Serotta, Madlocks & Serotta, C.P.A.'s, 1971; asst. sec. Stapleton Garment Inc., asst. sec., dir. Richmond Shippers, Inc., Augusta, Benson Mfg. Co.; dir. Kamo Mfg. Co. Inc., Marks Realty Co., Sales Agts., Inc. Co-founder, dir. Southeastern Research Found. Lectr. on various subjects, 1952; lectr. Minority Bus. Enterprises, 1970; moderator, participant radio-TV C.P.A. Internal Revenue Service Income Tax Information Programs, 1953-60. Head adviser Aleph Zadik Aleph, 1934-52, adviser emeritus, 1952-71, So. regional dept., 1937-42; organizer troop 18 Boy Scouts Am., 1940, committeeman, 1940, treas., troop committeeman, 1959. Bd. dirs. YMHA Augusta, 1937-42, 57; trustee Maxwell J. and Naomi P. Estroff Found., Belle S. Marks Found., Libby Fink Found., Hannah Simowitz Found. Recipient commendation certificate for 10 years service Army Service Forces, 1945. C.P.A., Ga. Mem. Am. Inst. C.P.A.'s (pub. relations com. 1954-56), Ga. Soc. C.P.A.'s (pres. Augusta chpt. 1952-54, regional v.p. bd. trustees 1952-54, trustee at large 1956-58 chmn. pub. relations com., 1953-55, chmn. history and archives com. 1959-64, chmn. profl. and trade group cooperation com., mem. bull. com., mem. com. assistance to minority bus. Enterprises 1970-71), Augusta C. of C. (chmn. adminstrv. com. 1958), Beta Gamma Sigma, Beta Alpha Psi, Phi Kappa Phi. Jewish religion (financial sec. 1950-53). Mason (32 deg., chmn. pub. relations com. 1963), Elk; mem. B'nai B'rith (pres. Augusta 1937; chmn. youth orgn. com. Augusta, vice chmn. So. region adult div.). Clubs: Toastmaster (pres. Augusta 1951), Optimist chmn. publicity com., vice-chmn. youth appreciation com. 1963-64) (Augusta). Reviewer, Auditing Handbook, 1971. Home: Augusta Ga. Died Dec. 3, 1971.

SERRIES, MAVIS MCGREW, (Mrs. George Emile Serries), educator; b. Norton, Kan., Jan. 13, 1925; d. Roy Douthett and Ruth Ellen (Fisher) McGrew; B.A., Denver U., 1947, M.A., 1949; m. George Emile Serries, Sept. 11, 1953; children—Renee (Mrs. John Swanson), Michelle, Paul. Instr.-theatre Denver U., 1947-50, established (with Dr. Campton Bell) touring Children's Theatre, 1947-51; dir. Youtheatre, First Meth. Ch., Pasadena, Cal., 1951; instr. theatre Boston U., also established Children's Touring group, 1951-53; dir. dramatics Chestnut Hill (Mass.) Sch., 1954-64; instr. children's theatre and creative drama Emerson Coll., Boston, also dir. Emerson Coll. Strolling Players, 1964-68; established, tchr. creative drama program Waltham (Mass.) elementary schs., 1969-75. Mem. Am. Ednl. Theatre Assn., New Eng. Theatre Conf. (v.p. 1968-69), Zeta Phi Eta. Home: Brookline, Mass., Died June 1, 1975.

SETZLER, FRANK MARYL, former curator; b. Fremont, O., Sept. 21, 1902; s. Henry Frank and Maria (Blaess) S.; student Ohio State U., 1924-27; Ph.B., U. Chgo., 1928; Sc.D., Ind. U., 1971; m. Susan Louise Perkins, May 17, 1930; children—Frank Perkins, Paul Elliott. Archeologist, Ind. Hist. Soc., State of Ind., 1927-

30; asst. curator archaeology U.S. Nat. Mus., Smithsonian Instn., 1930-35, head curator dept. anthropology, 1935-60; mem. adv. bd. Nat. Park Service, 1939-75. Precinct committeeman Republican Party, 1966-69; Union Twp. chmn., 1970-75. Recipient Franklin L. Burr prize Nat. Geog. Soc., 1950. Fellow A.A.A.S.; mem. Soc. Am. Archeology, Am. Anthrop. Assn., Anthrop. Soc. Wash., Ind., Washington acads. sci., Sigma Xi. Club: Cosmos (Washington). Leader numerous archeol. expdns. Smithsonian Instn. Home: Culver, Ind. Died Feb. 13, 1975; buried Culver Masonic Cemetery, Culver, Ind.

SEVERSKY, ALEXANDER P. DE, aero. engr., airplane designer; b. Tiflis, Russia, June 7, 1894; s. Nicholas and Vera (Vesilleff) deS.; grad. Imperial Naval Acad. Russia, 1914, postgrad. Mil. Sch. Aeronautics, Russia; D.Sc. (hon.), Rollins Coll., Fla., 1944, So. Ill. U., 1957; m. Evelyn Olliphant, June 23, 1925. Came to U.S., 1918, naturalized, 1927. Commd. lt. Russian Naval Air Service, 1915, assigned to bombing squadron, Baltic Sea; shot down during bombing expdn. and lost his right leg, July 1915; returned to Air Service and flying by spl. permission of Emperor Nicholas II; chief pursuit aviation on Baltic Sea; credited with shooting down 13 enemy planes, 1917; vice chmn. Russian Naval Aviation Mission to U.S.; asst. to Naval attache charge of aviation matters Russian embassy, 1918; aero. engr., test pilot, U.S. govt., 1918; cons. engr. U.S. Air Service, 1921; pres., gen. mgr., dir. and founder Seversky Aero. Corp., 1922-35, Seversky Aircraft Corp., 1931-39, dir. successor firm Republic Aviation Corp., 1939-40; cons. Chrysler Corp., 1933; founder, pres. Aircraft Ordnance Corp., 1940-72; founder, pres. Seversky Aviation Corp., N.Y.C., 1948-74; founder, pres., dir. Seversky Electronatom Corp., 1952-68, chmn. bd., 1968-74. Bd. dirs. N.Y. State Aviation Edn. Commn., 1942. Trustee N.Y. Inst. of Tech.; special cons. to sec. of war, 1945; personal rep. Sec. of War at Atom Bomb tests, Bikini, 1946; ofcl. lectr. U.S. Air U., 1946; cons. to chief staff U.S. Air Force, 1957. Trustee, v.p. Air Force Hist. Found., 1954-74. Served as maj. Air Corps, U.S. Army, 1928-33. Named to Aviation Hall of Fame, 1970; decorated Gold Sword and Knight St. George (Russia), officer Legion of Honor (France); Presdl. medal for Merit (U.S.); recipient Air Force Exceptional Service award, 1969, also numerous pvt. assn. awards. Fellow Soc. Exptl. Test Pilots, Royal Soc. Arts, N.Y. Acad. Scis., Am. Inst. Aeros. and Astronautics; mem. several U.S. and fgn. profl. aero. assns. Clubs: Circus Saints and Sinners, Engrs. Wings, Adventurers, Nat. Press. Author: Victory Through Air Power, 1942 (also Walt Disney-Seversky adaption for screen, 1943); Air Power, Key to Survival, 1950; America; Too Young to Die, 1961. Contbr. numerous articles to profl. jours. Invented 1st gyroscopically stabilized bombsight; in-flight refueling system; fuel-carrying aircraft wing; developed advanced design amphibian (world speed records 1933, 35) and all-metal monoplane; P-35 and P-47 fighters; developed Ionocraft Prototype; inventor wet-type electrostatic precipitator for air pollution control. Home: Northport, N.Y. Died Aug. 24, 1974.

SEVERSON, HAROLD CLIFFORD, veterinarian; b. Presho, S.D., July 14, 1910; s. Ole H. and Mae Rebecca (Phillips) S.; student U. S.D., 1931-32, Dakota Wesleyan U., 1932-33: D.V.M., Kan. State U., 1951; m. Lillian Helen McKesson, Oct. 31, 1943; 1 son, Orval Harold. Employed in sales, 1934-40, 43-46; practice vet. medicine, Winner, S.D., 1951-72. Served with AUS, 1940-43. Mem. Am., S.D. (Veterinarian of Year 1968, pres. 1958) vet. med. assns., C. of C., V.F.W., Am. Legion. Republican. Lutheran. Mason (Shriner), Blk, Rotarian. Home: Winner, SD. Died Feb. 6, 1972; buried Winner, S.D.

SEVIER, CLARA DRISCOLL, (Mrs. H. H. Sevier), author; b. St. Mary's, Tex., Apr. 2, 1881; d. Robert and Julia (Fox) Driscoll; ed. pvt. schs., Tex., New York and France; m. Henry Hulme Sevier, of Texas, July 31, 1906. Honored by the organization of the Daughters of the Republic of Texas by title of "Custodian of the Alamo" on account of her successful efforts to save the historic site to the state. V.chmn. exec. bd. Texas Centennial Expn.; dir.-gen. Austin Pan-Am. Round Table; pres. Daughters of the Republic of Texas, from 1925. Pres. Corpus Christi Bank & Trust Co.; dir. Corpus Christi Nat. Bank; sole owner and mgr. of the ranches, petroleum fields, farms and other properties of the R. Driscoll Estate. Democratic nat. committeewoman for Texas from 1928. Clubs: Violet Crown Garden (pres.); Teaxs of N.Y. City (hon. life pres.), Author: The Girl of La Gloria, 1905; In the Shadow of the Alamo, 1906. Wrote "Mexicana," a comic opera, 1906. Home: Corpus Christi, Tex.†

SEWALL, SYDNEY, orthopedic surgeon; b. Brockton, Mass., May 25, 1912; s. Samuel and Elizabeth Sewall; M.D., U. Md., 1937; children—Steven, Kenneth, Sydney R. Intern, Hartford (Conn.) Municipal Hosp., 1937-38, resident, 1939-40; tng. Hosp. for Joint Diseases, 1946-49; pvt. practice medicine specializing in orthopedic surgery, Hartford; attending orthopedic surgeon St. Francis Hosp.; asso. orthopedic surgeon Newington (Conn.) Hosp. for Crippled Children; chmn. orthopedic dept. Mt. Sinai Hosp. Diplomate Am. Bd. Orthopedic Surgery. Fellow A.C.S., Internat. Coll. Surgery; mem. Eastern Orthopedic Assn., A.M.A., Am. Acad. Orthopedic Surgeons, Am. Fracture Assn. Home: West Hartford, Conn. Died Feb. 27, 1974.

SEWARD, GEORGE WINN, physician, surgeon, b. Hillsboro, Ill., Dec. 27, 1906; s. George LeMar and Bernice Zoe (Winn) S.; B.S., Knox Coll., Galesburg, Ill., 1929; M.D., Creighton U., Omaha, 1933; m. Eva Ollie Taylor, July 19, 1930; children—Sandra (Mrs. John Sanford Murray), Cynthia (Mrs. Jeff Swenson), George Taylor, Steven LeMar. Intern, Ill. Eye and Ear Infirmary, 1933-35; practice medicine, specializing in ophthalmology and otolaryngology, North Manchester, Ind., 1935-75; postgrad. course Cook County Hosp., Chgo., 1946, Gill Meml. Clinic, Roanoke, Va., 1947-72. Mem. Ind. Bd. Hard of Hearing Clinic, 1948-53. Coordinator, Underprivileged Children Project, North Manchester, 1938-42. Mem. adv. bd. dirs. Gill Meml. Clinic. Served to maj. USAAF, 1942-46. Recipient Hon. Citizen of Day award C. of C., 1949. Mem. A.M.A., Ind. Med. Assn. (Wabash County del. 1947-53), Wabash County Med. Soc. (pres. 1947-48), Ind. Ophthalmology and Otolaryngology Soc., Wabash County Cancer Soc. (pres. 1945-53), Wabash County C. of C. (membership chmn. 1950-60). Lutheran. Mason (Shriner), Elk, Kiwanian, Izaak Walton League. Home: North Manchester, Ind. Died Feb. 11, 1975; interred Oak Lawn Cemetery, North Manchester, Ind.

SEWELL, DAN ROY, physician; b. Jacksboro, Tex., Feb. 21, 1904; s. Dan Roland and Elda Anne (Bryson) S.; M.D., Washington U., St. Louis, 1931; m. Margery Ardrey, July 11, 1934; children—Lois (Mrs. Philip F. Mesner), Dan A., Margaret. Rotating intern U. Okla. Hosps., Oklahoma City, 1931-32, sr. intern in surgery, 1932-33, resident in gen. surgery, 1933-34; practice medicine specializing in surgery, Oklahoma City, 1934-41; commd. U.S. Army Air Force, 1941, advanced through grades to col.; comdr. hosps., Kindley AFB, Bermuda, 1949-51, Scott AFB, 1951-55, Lowry AFB, Denver, 1955-S9; ret., 1959; dir. employees health service Denver Gen. Hosp., 1960-72; instr. gross anatomy U. Okla., 1934-35, instr. gen. surgery, Decorated Air Force Commendation medal. 1935-41. Diplomate Am. Bd. Surgery. Mem. A.M.A. Home: Aurora, Colo. Died Apr. 14, 1973; buried Fairmont Cemetery, Denver, Colo.

SEWELL, WARREN PELMER, clothing mfg. exec.; b. Graham, Ala., Oct. 29, 1888; s. Willis Columbus and Willie (Gay) S.; student pub. schs., Graham; m. Ava Lee Fowler, June 19, 1912; children—Frances (Mrs. Lamar R. Plunkett), Charlotte (Mrs. Jack W. Worley), Warren Palmer, Formerly traveling salesman for John E. Hurst, Balt.; pres. Warren Sewell Clothing Co., Bremen, Ga., from 1947; pres. Goldkist, Inc., Atlanta, Cotton Producers Assn., Inc., Atlanta; v.p. Comml. and Exchange Bank, Bremen, 1945; chmn. bd. Hubbard Pants Co., Higgins Slacks, Lineville, Ala.; dir. Comml. Bank, Bowdon, Ga., Bank of Canton. Baptist. Home: Atlanta, Ga. Deceased.

SEXSON, JOHN AMHERST, educator; b. Omaha, Neb., Nov. 6, 1881; s. Andrew Jackson and Bertha (Kyle) S.; A.B., Colo. State Teachers' Coll., 1908; A.M., U. of Denver, 1920; Ed.D., Colorado State Teachers Coll., 1934; Ed.D., U. of Southern Calif., 1938; Dr. Humanics, Los Angeles Coll. of Osteopathy, 1942; m. Margaret S. Guillet, Dec. 23, 1906; 1 son, John Amherst. Teacher rural schs., Neb., 1900-05; supt. schs., in Colo., Maneos, 1905-08, Telluride, 1908-12, Sterling, 1912-24; supt. schools, Bisbee, Ariz., 1924-28, Pasadena, Calif., 1928-48, ret. Maj. San Corps, U.S. Army, 1918-19. Mem. Colo. State Bd. Examiners, 1914-24, Ariz. State Bd. Edn., 1926-27. Mem. Pasadena Chamber of Commerce. Pres. Calif. State Teachers Assn. 1935-39; mem. N.E.A., Am. Assn. Sch. Adminstrs. (pres. 1938-39), Ednl. Policies Commission, 1935-42. Republican. Presbyterian. Mason (32°, Shriner). Clubs: University, New Century, Rotary Home: Altadena, Cal.†

SEXTON, ANNE HARVEY, educator, author; b. Newton, Mass., Nov. 9, 1928; d. Ralph C. and Mary Gray (Staples) Harvey; student pub. schs., Wellesley, Mass.; Litt.D. (hon.), Tufts U., 1970, Regis Coll., 1971, Fairfield U., 1971; m. Alfred M. Sexton, Aug. 16, 1948 (div. 1974); children—Linda Gray, Joyce Ladd. Scholar, Radcliffe Inst. Ind. Study, 1961-63, Am. Acad. Arts and Letters, 1963-64; Ford Found. grant, 1964-65; First Lit. Mag. travel award, 1965-66; tchr. Wayland High Sch., 1967-68; mem. faculty Boston U., 1970-71, prof. lit., 1972-74; Crawshaw prof. lit. Colgate U., Hamilton, N.Y., 1972. Recipient Pulitzer prize, 1967; Guggenheim award, 1969. Mem. Phi Beta Kappa (hon.). Author: To Bedlam and Part Way Back, 1960; All My Pretty Ones, 1962; Live or Die, 1966; Love Poems, 1969; Transformations, 1971; Book of Folly, 1972; The Death Notebooks, 1974; The Awful Rowing Toward God; 1975. Home: Weston, Mass. Died Oct. 4, 1974.

SEYRIG, HENRI ARNOLD, archaeologist; b. Hericourt, France, Nov. 10, 1895; student U. Paris, 1919-22. Mem. French Sch. at Athens, 1922-29; dir. antiquities for Syria and Lebanon 1929-41; dir. French Inst. Archeology, Instanbul, Turkey, 1941; cultural adviser Free French delegation U.S.A., 1942-45; dir. French Inst. Archaeology, Beirut, Lebanon 1946-60, 62-66; dir. Museums of France, 1960-62. Home: Neuchatel, Switzerland. Died Jan. 21, 1973.

SHACKELFORD, FRANCIS, lawyer; b. Albany, Ga., Sept. 21, 1909; s. Charles Mercer and Mary (Livezey) S.; student Lawrenceville (N.J.) Sch., 1927-29; A.B., Princeton, 1933; LL.B., Harvard, 1936; m. Renèe Marie Flectcher; children—R. Claire, Elizabeth C., Frank C., C. Fletcher. Admitted to Ga. bar, 1936, N.Y. bar, 1938; asso. firm Davis, Polk, Wardwell, Gardiner & Reed, N.Y.C., 1936-42; now mem. Alston, Miller & Gaines; 1st counselor Dept. Army, 1950-52; asst. sec. Army, 1952-53; dir. Magic Chef. Inc., Atlanta Motor Lodges, Inc., So. Iron & Equipment Co., Cotton States Life & Health Ins. Co., Cotton States Mutual Ins. Co.; pres. Met. Atlanta Community Services, Inc., 1963-65; chmn. Met. Atlanta Commn. on Crime and Juvenile Delinquency, 1966-68. Served as lt. (j.g.) to lt. commdr. USNR, 1942-46: Guadalcanal. Trustee, chmn. Charles Loridan Found., Vasser Wooley Found. Mem. Am., N.Y., Ga., Atlanta bar assns., Atlanta C. of C. (dir. 1968), Assn. AUS (pres. Hub of South chpt. 1960-61). Independent Democrat. Episcopalian. Clubs: Capital City, Piedmont Driving, Lawyers (president, 1957-58), Commerce (Atlanta), Shake Rag (Atlanta). Contbr. articles in field to profl. jours. Home: Atlanta, Ga. Died Nov. 30, 1973.

SHACKFORD, JOHN WALTER, clergyman, educator; b. Walkerton, Va., Jan. 10, 1878; s. Joseph Wesley and Cora (Kingsbury) S.; A.B., Randolph-Macon Coll., Ashland, Va., 1900, D.D., 1912; B.D., Vanderbilt, 1903; m. Love Branner Atkins, Feb. 14, 1907; children—John Branner, James Atkins, Joseph Temple, Ella Kingsbury, Love Branner, Margaret Jackson, Elizabeth Bland. Ordained ministry M.E. Ch., S., 1897; state student sec. Y.M.C.A., Tenn., 1902-03; sec. young people's missionary edn., Gen. Bd. Missions, M.E. Ch., S., 1903-06; pastor Rivermont Av. Ch., Lynchburg, Va., 1906-10, Colonial Av. Ch., Norfolk, 1910-13, Broad St. Ch., Richmond, 1913-15; supt. dept. leadership and teacher training, Gen. Sunday Sch. Bd., M.E. Ch., S., 1915-22, gen. sec. same, 1922-20; pastor Central Church, Albemarle, N.C., 1930-31, Hawthorne Lane Ch., Charlotte, N.C., 1931-34, St. John's Church, Rock Hill, S.C., 1934-36; Washington St. Ch., Columbia, S.C., 1936-38; dist. supt. Rock Hill District, Rock Hill, S.C., 1938-43; pastor Buncombe St. Ch., Greenville, S.C., 1943-45, Chestnut Av. Church, Newport News, Va., 1945-50; pastor Churchland and West Norfolk, Va., from 1950. Mem. Commn. on Reference and Council which drew up plan of merger of Sunday Sch. Council of Evang. Denominations and Internat. Sunday Sch. Assn., 1922; m. Bd. of Edn. Meth. Ch. Mem. Phi Beta Kappa, Alpha Tau Omega. Author: The Program of the Christian Religion, 1917; Education in the Christian Religion, 1931; Jesus and Social Redemption, 1940, also chapter on Christian Education in Religion and the Church Tomorrow, 1935. Home: Churchland, Va.†

SHAFER, DON CAMERON, author; b. at Charlotteville, N.Y., Oct. 7, 1881; s. Stillman Goss and Anna Gordon (Herron) S.; ed. pub. schs.; m. Janeth E. Mitchell, of Roxbury, N.Y., Jan. 10, 1910. Learned printer's trade; began writing as reporter on Schenectady Union, 1903, later spl. writer for New York World, Sun, Press and Times, also contbr. to popular mags.; publicity mgr. Gen. Electric Co. from Dec. 11, 1906. Author: Stories of an Old Dutch Town (verse), 1908; Beginning Electricity, 1913; Everyday Electricity, 1914. Home: Scholharie, N.Y.†

SHAFFER, BERTRAM, physician; b. Phila., May 19, 1906; s. Isadore and Blanceh Shaffer; M.D., U. Pa., 1931, D.Sc. in Dermatology and Syphilology, 1939; m. Bess Sadiker, Aug. 2, 1931; children—Judith Nan (Mrs. Donald Safir), Barbara Surell (Mrs. Michael D. Varbalow). Intern, Hosp. of U. Pa., Phila., 1931-33, fellow in dermatology and syphilology, 1935-38; chief of clinic Grad. Sch. Medicine, U. Pa., 1935-38, asso. prof., 1958-74; med. dir. Skin and Cancer Hosp., 1950-53; chief attending, then chief emeritus attending dermatologist Albert Einstein Med. Center, Phila., 1971; asso. prof. dermatology and syphilology U. Pa. Diplomate Am. Bd. Dermatology. Fellow Soc. Investigative Dermatology, Am. Acad. Dermatology, A.C.P. (life), Coll. Physicians Phila.; mem. Am. Dermatol. Assn., A.M.A., Pan. Am. (life, diplomate sect. dermatology), Philadelphia County med. socs., Phila. Dermatologic Soc. (pres. 1953-54), Alpha Omega Alpha. Contbr. numerous articles to med. jours. Home: Wyncote, Pa., Died June 18, 1974; buried Roosevelt Meml. Park, Trevose, Pa.

SHAFFER, ELMER ELLSWORTH DALE, ret. entertainment co. exec.; b. Chgo., Aug. 12, 1917; s. Charles Benjamin and Isobel (Rhodes) S.; grad. Lake Forest Acad., 1935; A.B., Kenyon Coll., 1939; m. Jane Ellen Harrison, Nov. 25, 1939; children—Charles Benjamin III, Candace Beth; m. 2d, Phyllis Coren, June 1965; m. 3d, Ruth Jones, Apr. 1966 (div.); m. 4th, Shirley Ann Ball, July 1968 (div.); m. 5th, Shelby Jean Faddis, Nov. 22, 1970. Chmn. bd., dir. Detroit Race Course, Inc., 1948-72; pres. Thoroughbred Racing Assns. U.S., Inc., 1960-61; now chmn. Haberstrol Farm Products Inc., Mt. Clemens, Mich. Vice chmn. Kentucky Racing Commn., 1947-49, chmn., 1949-51.

Trustee Kenyon Coll., 1949-53. Served as lt. (j.g.) USNR, 1943-46. Mem. Alpha Delta Phi, Clubs: Thoroughbred of America (pres. 1947-48) (Lexington, Ky.); Detroit Athletic, Standard City (Detroit); Bloomfield Hills (Mich.) Country; Crown Colony (Bahamas); Palm Bay Country (Miami); Fox Den Country. Home: Concord, Tenn. Died July 2, 1974.

SHAFFER, ROY LEE, coll. pres.; b. Greensburr, Pa., Sept. 3, 1881; s. Emanuel Edward and Elizabeth (Rowe) S.; student Central Pa. Coll., 1898-99; A.M., Dickinson Coll., 1910, hon. M.A., 1914, student law sch., 1905-10; M.A., Teachers Coll., Columbia U., 1917; Ph.D., New York U., 1933; m. Ruth Fishburn, Apr. 28, 1914; children—Mary Emma, Anna Lee. Teacher, 1899; steward Hotel Del Monte, Calif., 1903, Hotel Grace, St. Louis, 1904; supervisor, prin., Morris Twp., N.J., 1910-16, Middletown Twp., 1916-18; head dept., practice and observation, Newark State Teachers Coll., 1918-21; asst. commr. of edn., in charge of elementary edn., N.J., 1921-25; pres. State Teachers Coll., Paterson, 1925-33, State Teachers Coll., Jersey City, 1934-40, N.J. State Teachers Coll., Newark, 1940-44. Fought through Philippine campaign as corpl. under U. S. Grant III, 1902. Mem. Community Chest, Newark, N.J., 1934-40. Mem. Am. Assn. Teachers Colls., Am. Assn. Sch. Adminstrs., Council of Edn. of N.J., C. of C. (Trenton). Protestant. Mason. Mem. Cincinnatus (Morritown), Vets. Fgn. Wars. Clubs: Rotary (Newark), Schoolmasters of N.J. and Bergen County. Home: Highlands, N.J.†

SHAIKEN, JOSEPH, physician; b. Russia, Sept. 17, 1905; s. Jacob and Rachel Shaiken; M.D., Marquette U., 1930; M.Sc. in Gastroenterology, U. Pa., 1934; m. Rose Ross, July 7, 1927; children—Vida S. Eisenberg, Myra S. Steiner, Eugene. Intern, Milwaukee County Gen. Hosp., 1929-30, jr. resident physician, 1930-31, sr. resident physician, 1931-32, attending staff in gastroenterologist, until 1974, also mem. teaching staff; attending gastroenterologist, chief staff Mr. Sinai Hosp., Milw.; asso. prof. medicine Marquette U. Med. Sch., Milw. Diplomate Am. Bd. Internal Medicine. Fellow A.C.P., Am. Coll. Gastroenterology (past. pres.); mem. A.M.A., Phi Delta Epsilon, Alpha Epsilon Pi, Kappa Alpha. Home: Milwaukee, Wis. Died Feb. 3, 1974; buried Spring Hill Cemetery, Milwaukee, Wis.

SHAINMARK, ELIEZER L., editor; b. Warsaw, Poland, Sept. 13, 1900; s. David and Libby (Kahn) S.; B.S., N.Y. U., 1921; m. Edythe Witt, Jan. 31, 1925; 1 son, Norman. Reporter, Norfolk Virginian-Pilot, Richmond Times-Despatch, 1923-25; night editor, feature editor, N.Y. Graphic, 1925-29; night mng. editor, N.Y. Jour.-Am., 1929-35; asst. mng. editor, Chgo.-Am., 1936-41, mng. editor 1941-45; mng. editor, White House corr. Hearst Washington Bur., 1947; mng. editor Chgo. Herald-Am., 1948-50; editorial asst. to pub. Esquire, Coronet mags., 1950-51; asst. to adminstr. FSA, 1952-53; v.p. Guild Films, N.Y.C., 1953-58; pres., editor Gilmark Featues, 1958-63; editor N.Y.C. Commerce News, 1963-76. Pub. relations adviser N.Y.C. Econ. Devel. Adminstrn., 1963-76; lectr. New Sch. Social Research, 1970-76. Cited by treasury and army for war aid. Mem. Soc. Am. Editors, Pub. Relations Officers Soc. (pres.), Sigma Delta Chi. Club: National Press Silurians. Home: New York City, N.Y., Died Jan. 5, 1976; interred Beth David Cemetery, Elmont, N.Y.

SHALTER, IRWIN MAURER, educator; b. Tuckerton, Berks Co., Pa., Feb. 3, 1880; s. Michael Jonas and Emma R. (Sailer) S.; grad. Keystone State Normal Sch., 1897; A.B., Muhlenberg Coll., 1903, A.M., 1905; m. Ida Bittner Guest, June 10, 1911. Began teaching at Allentown, Pa., 1905; headmaster Allentown Prep. Sch. from 1917. Democrat. Lutheran. Elk. Home: Allentown, Pa.†

SHAMBORA, WILLIAM E(DWARD), army med. officer; born Hazle Brook, Pa., Sept. 5, 1900; s. Andrew and Ann (Bidal) S.; B.S., Georgetown U., 1923, M.D., 1925; student Army Med. Sch., 1926, Med. Field Service Sch., 1927; grad. Command and Gen. Staff Sch., 1935, Army War Coll., 1938; m. Margaret Idell Meyers, June 27, 1925; children—William E., Margaret Wood (wife of S. W. Selfridge, U.S.N.), Robert Andrew. Apptd. 1st lt., M.C. Res., May 1925, called to active duty, July 1925; commd. 1st lt., U.S. Army, 1926, promoted through grades to major general, 1952; intern Fitzsimmons Gen. Hosp., Denver, 1925-26, 27-28; served with Philippine Div. and Sternberg Gen. Hosp., P.I., 1928-30; regtl. exec. officer 2d Inf. Div., Ft. Sam Houston, Tex., 1935-37; chief tng. div., later chief logistics div. Med. Field Service Sch., Carlisle Barracks, Pa., 1938-41; assigned med. sect., GHQ, Washington, 1941, Army Ground Forces, 1941-42, chief surgeon, 1942-44; surgeon 9th Army, E.T.O., 1944-45; comdt. Army Med. Dept. Schs., Ft. Sam Houston, 1945-47; chief surgeon U.S. Army, P.T.O., Hawaii, 1947-50; surgeon 1st Army, Governors Island, N.Y., 1950-51; chief surgeon Far East Command 1951-53; comdg. gen. Brooke Army Medical Center, Fort Sam Houston, Tex., 1953-60. Decorated D.S.M. with oak leaf cluster, Legion of Merit. Army Commendation Ribbon; Order. of Brit. Empire; Legion of Honor, Croix de-Guerre with palm (France); Order of Freedom (U.S.S.R.); Order of Solidare (Italy); Gold Star of Elchi (Korea); Legion D'Honor de Sante (France). Member A.M.A., N.Y. Acad. Scis., Assn. Mil. Surgeons, Tex. Surg. Soc., Alpha Omega Alpha, Omega Epsilon Phi. Clubs: Torch, Rotary. Home: San Antonio, Tex. Died Jan. 5, 1975.

SHAMEL, ARCHIBALD DIXON, plant physiologist; b. nr. Taylorville, Ill., Oct. 15, 1878; s. Conrad and Caroline (Alkire) S.; B.S., U. of Ill., 1898; m. Agnes Fay Brewer, Sept. 25, 1907; children—Carol Agnes, Norman Archibald, John Dixon. In charge farm crop dept., U. of Ill., 1898-1902; of tobacco investigations, U.S. Dept. Agr., 1902-09, and of fruit improvement investigations, as prin. physiologist, Department Agriculture, 1909-44; research associate, University of California Citrus Experiment station, 1944; ret. Pioneer in hybrid corn investigations, and introduced the soybean from the Orient, 1895-1905. Inventor of tobacco seed separator, steampan soil sterlizer, humidifier for storage rooms and co-inventor tobacco stalk cutter; organized Illinois Corn Breeders' Association, 1898; developed and introduced method for protecting tobacco seed from crossing; originator of individual tree performance record method and furrow-manure method of soil fertilization. Visited Cuba to study tobacco, Brazil to study tropical fruits, Hawaii to study sugar cane and pineapple bud selection, Honduras and Guatemala to study banana improvement, Porto Rico to study citrus bud selection work, and Mexico to study avocado varieties. Pres. City Park Commn., Riverside, Calif. Fellow A.A.A.S.; mem. Sigma Alpha Epsilon, Alpha Zeta. Presbyterian. Mason (32°). Author: Manual of Corn Judging, 1900; The Improvement of Sugarcane Through Bud Selection; The Improvement of Smooth Cayenne Pineapple through Bud Selection. Contbr. to scientific, tech. and professional publs. Home: Riverside, Cal.†

SHAMROY, LEON, cameraman; b. N.Y.C., July 16, 1901; s. Elisha and Miriam (Soujon) S.; student Cooper Union, 1918, Coll. City of N.Y., 1919-20; studied mech. engring. Columbia; m. Mary Anderson, May 13, 1953. With lab. Fox Film Corp., Hollywood, 1920-24; photographed serials and stunt pictures, Charles Hutchison of Pathe, 1924-27; co-producer and photographer (with Dr. Paul Fejos) exptl. film The Last Moment (voted honor film of 1928 by Nat. Bd. of Rev.), 1927; asso. with Robert J. Flaherty in photographing a documentary film of Acoma Indians, N.M., 1928-29; cinematographer for Huntington Ethnol. Expdn., Japan, Manchurai, China, Celebes, Philippines, Bali, Malay States, Siam, Burma, India, Egypt, 1930-31; dir. photography B.P. Schulberg Prodns., 1933-37; dir. photography Selznick Internat., 1938; dir. cinematography 20th Century-Fox, 1938-74; recent pictures include 12 O'Clock High, 1949 (Look award), The Robe (introduced cinemascope), 1952, Love Is a Many Splendored Thing, The King and I, South Pacific, Porgy and Bess, Cleopatra, The Cardinal, The Agony and the Ecstacy, Planet of the Apes, Justine (Laurel award Internat. Motion Picture Exhibitors 1969). Pres., Award Winners Sch. of Photography, Inc., 1946. Recipient 18 Acad. nominations, 4 Acad. awards Acad. Motion Picture Arts and Scis.: 1st award for color photography The Black Swan, 1942; awards for color photography Wilson, 1944, Leave Her to Heaven, 1945, Cleopatra, 1963; film achievement award for creating new technique of color-photography, lighting Look Mag., 1945; Film Daily Critics award, 1949, 53, 54, 55, 63. Mem. Am. Soc. Cinematographers (past pres.), Motion Pictures Assn. Am. (chmn. photog. com., research div. 1946-50), Soc. Motion Picture Engrs. Club: Los Angeles Press. Home: Los Angeles, Cal. Died July 6, 1974.

SHANE, JOSEPH BROOKS, educator; b. Phila., Oct. 26, 1903; s. Charles and Mary Buckley (Winmill) S.; A.B., Swarthmore Coll., 1925; A.M., U. Pa., 1930; m. Theresa Cooper, Sept. 1, 1927; children—John Buckley, Joseph Lawrence. Faculty, George Sch. (Pa.), 1925-28, dean, 1938-48; headmaster Oakwood Sch., Poughkeepsie, N.Y., 1948-50, also tchr. edn. dept. Vassar Coll.; v.p. Swarthmore (Pa.) Coll., 1950-74. Past pres. Dutchess County Group on World Affairs; exec. com. Pa.-N.J.-Del. Planning Com.; adv. council Media Fellowship House; del. Friends World Conf., Oxford, Eng., 1952. Bd. dirs. Pa.-N.J.-Del. Met. Project, Inc.; bd. mgrs. Pendle Hill, Wallingford, Pa., George Sch, Friends Schs. Tchr. Tng. Program. Mem. Delawar County C. of C. (edn. com.), Friends Council on Edn., Foxhowe Assn. (pres.), Phi Delta Kappa, Kappa Sigma. Home: Swarthmore, Pa. Died Apr. 27, 1974.

SHANLEY, GEORGE PATRICK, clergyman, educator; b. Chicago, Ill., Aug. 23, 1879; s. Thomas R. and Anna (Hardyman) S.; A.M., St. Louis U., 1904. Joined Soc. of Jesus (Jesuita), 1897; instr. and prof. classics, St. Mary's (Kan.) Coll., 1904-06, St. Louis U., 1906-09, U. of Detroit, 1913-14. St. Xavier's Coll., Cincinnati, O., 1915-16, St. Ignatius Coll., Chicago, 1916-18; dean arts and science dept., Loyola U., Chicago, 1918-22: dean arts and science dept., Marquette U., Milwaukee, 1922-23, Loyola U., Chicago, from 1923. Home: Chicago, Ill.†

SHAPIRO, ARTHUR, physician; b. N.Y.C., June 24, 1910; s. Louis and Flora Shapiro; M.D., Columbia, 1937; m. Eva Posen, May 25, 1934; children—Judith Ellen (Mrs. Harry Baxter), Naomi Jo (Mrs. Michael Rosenfeld). Intern, Coney Island Hosp., Bklyn., 1937-38; dir. RMK Research Lab., 1934-37, research asso., 1937-40; research asso. pediatric research lab. Jewish Hosp., 1941-43, clin. asst. vis. physician, 1941-51; dir. Waldemar Med. Research Found., 1949-54; med. cons. psychiat. div. Kings County Hosp., Bklyn., 1949-52, 60-69, internist in charge psychosomatic service, 1953-54, 60-69, asso. vis. physician; asso. attending physician St. John's Episcopal Hosp.; med. dir. Investors Overseas Services; clin. asso. prof. medicine State U. N.Y. at Bklyn., 1953-60, asso. prof., 1960-65, prof., 1965-69, dir. psychophysiol. lab. dept. psychiatry; dir. Inst. Research Hypnosis, 1960-69, pres., 1962-64; mem. sci. faculty Sarah Lawrence Coll., 1943-46; adj. prof. chem. engring. klyn. Poly. Inst., 1968-69. Diplomate Am. Bd. Internal Medicine. Mem. A.M.A., Am. Heart Assn., Assn. for Advancement Psychotherapy, A.A.A.S., Am. Acad. Psychotherapy, Soc. Clin. and Exptl. Hypnosis, Soc. Psuchophysiol. Research, Assn. Psychophysiol. Study Sleep, Assn. for Advancement Med. Illustration. Cons. editor Psychophysiology. Home: New York City, N.Y. Died Sept. 28, 1969; buried Beth Moses Cemetery, Farmingdale, L.I., N.Y.

SHAPLEY, ALAN, marine corps officer; b. N.Y. C., Feb. 9, 1903; s. Lloyd Stowell and Elizabeth (McCormick) S.; student Peddie Sch., Hightstown, N.J., 1922; B.S., U.S. Naval Acad., 1927; m. Eleanor Oll, July 19, 1927; children—Henry Oll, Louise E. Commd. 2d lt. USMC, 1927, advanced through grades to maj. gen., 1955; comdg. officer 4th Marine Regt., Guadalcanal, Bougainville, Guam, Okinawa, 1942-45; chief staff 1st Marine Div., Korea, 1953-54; dir. Marine Corps Res., 1957; comdg. gen. Fleet Marine Force, Hawaii until 1962. Decorated D.S.M. Home: Washington, D.C. Died May 13, 1973.

SHARKEY, THOMAS CLIFFORD, physician; b. Covington, Ky., May 16, 1932; s. Clifford J. and Margaret M. Sharkey; M.D., St. Louis U., 1956; m. Ruth Heskamp, Sept. 15, 1956; children—Michael, Timothy, Matthew, Margaret Ann. Intern, St. Mary's Hosp., Cin., 1956-57, resident, 1959-62; resident Christ Hosp., Cin., 1962-63; active staff Greenfield Municipal Hosp., 1963-73; chief staff Highland Dist. Hosp., Hillsboro, O., 1965; courtesy staff Clinton Meml. Hosp., Wilmington, O. Served to capt. M.C., USAF, 1957-59. Diplomate Am. Bd. Surgery. Fellow A.C.S.; mem. A.M.A. Home: Hillsboro, O. Died Aug. 29, 1973; buried St. Mary's Catholic Cemetery, Hillsboro, O.

SHARP, ALEXANDER, naval officer; b. Washington, D.C., Aug. 13, 1885; s. Alexander and Josephine (Hand) S.; B.S., U.S. Naval Acad., 1906; grad., Naval War Coll., 1924; m. Cornelia D. Janin, May 17, 1911; children—Alexander, Edward Janin (dec.). George Hand, Lieut. U.S. Navy, 1906, and advanced through grades to vice adm., 1942; served in destroyers, cruisers, battleships; comd. 6 destroyers, cruiser Concord, battleship Idaho; comdr. U.S.S. Downes, World War I, Battleship div., Battleships, Atlantic Fleet, Service Force Atlantic and Minecraft, Pacific Fleet, World War II. Awarded D.S.M. (2) for service in World War II. Mem. U.S. Naval Inst., Nat. Geog. Soc. Republican. Roman Catholic. Clubs: Army Navy (Washington), Hawthorne County (La Plata, Md.). Home: Welcome, Md. Died June 20, 1975.

SHARP, CLARENCE BRYAN, constrn. co. exec.; b. Corning O., May 29, 1896; s. William Morris and Carrie Lew (Emma) S.; student pub. schs., Pa.; m. Mildred Cline, July 18, 1922; children—Mary Jane (Mrs. Cornelius York), Helen (Mrs. Ellis Potter), Robert Morris, Mildred (Mrs. Douglas Chapman). Supt. Streets and Water Works, Albion, 1920-22; foreman bridge constrn. G.A. Flink Constrn. Co., Harrisburg, Pa., 1922-24; demonstrator tractors and trailers Rogers Bros. Corp., Albion, 1924-30; supt. erection bridge dept. Pittsburg Des Moines Steel Co., Pitts., 1930-39, Savin Constrn. Corp., East Hartford, Conn., 1939-44; v.p., gen. mgr. Whaling City Dredge & Dock Corp., Groton, Conn., 1944-58, pres., 1958-74; pres. Transport Resource Analysis Corp. Arbitrator, Conn. Hwy Dept., 1962-68; mem. Southeastern adv. bd. Hartford Nat. Bank & Trust Co., New London, Conn., 1963-68. Mem. Nat. Council on Crime and Delinquency, 1962-68; chief, Albion Vol. Fire Co., 1916-74; life mem., 1931-74; chmn. Groton YMCA, 1962-74; mem. Nat. Right to Work Com., 1962-74. Mayor, councilman Groton, 1956-70. Pres. Eastern Conn. Symphony Orch. Bd. dirs. United Fund Southeastern Conn.; bd. incorporators Lawrence & Meml. Hosp., New London, Conn. Served with C.E., U.S. Army, 1917-19. Registered profl. engr., Conn. Mem. Conn. Rd. Builders Assn. (pres., dir. 1960-64), Conn. Soc. C.E. (dir., v.p.; recipient H. Jackson Tippett award, 1958), Groton C. of C. (pres., dir. 1956-66, Man of Year award 1964), 309th U.S. Army Engr. Assn. (pres., trustee 1965-68), V.F.W., Internat. Oceanographic Found., Conn. Chiefs of Police Assn. (hon.), Navy League. Republican. Mason (32 deg.), Mole, Elk. Clubs: Stop That Club (Wethersfield, Conn.); Shennecossett Yacht (Groton); Officer (Hartford, Conn.). Home: Groton, Conn. Died Jan. 29, 1974.

SHARP, HUGH RODNEY, b. Seaford, Del., July 30, 1880; s. Eli Richard and Sallie (Brown) S.; A.B., U. of Del., 1900; m. Isabella du Pont, June 6, 1908; children—Hugh Rodney, Bayard, Anne du Pont (dec.). Trustee U. of Delaware; dir. Wilmington Soc. Fine Arts; mem. Sigma Nu. Republican. Clubs: University, Wilmington Country. Identified with numerous civic and philanthropic activities, notably in connection with U. of Del.; donor of auditorium, Mitchell Hall, to U. of Del. Home: Wilmington, Del.*†

SHARP, JAMES H., v.p. Merck & Co. Home: Wilton, Conn. Died July 26, 1974.

SHATTUCK , (SIDNEY) FRANK, paper exec.; Neenah, Wisconsin, April 28, 1878; son of Frank Coolidge and Clara (Merriman) S.; B.S., Yale, 1899; married Ruth Harwood, Dec. 28, 1908; children—Frank C., James H., Ann, Mary P. With Kimberly-Clark Corp., paper mfr., Neenah, 1900-45, retired as vice pres., director. Trustee Carroll College, Waukesha, Wis. Mem. Delta Phi. Republican. Presbyterian. Club: University (Chicago). Home: Neenah, Wis.†

SHAVER, ROBERT EZEKIEL, educator; b. Greenville, Ky., Sept. 12, 1905; s. Robert Andrew and Maude (Rice) S.; B.S., U. of Ky., 1927, C.E., 1931; m. Frances Reid, May 31, 1937; children—Anne Prewitt, Andrew Reid, Susan Rice. Engr. Ky. Dept. Highways, Frankfort, 1927-31; instr. civil engring., U. of Ky., 1931-33, asst. prof., 1933-36, asso. prof., 1936-45, prof. civil engring., 1945-47, head dept. civil engring. 1947-57, dean of the College of Engineering, 1957-66, director of physical development, 1966-68. Member of the research com. Ky. Dept. Hwys.; chmn. edn. com. Nat. Council State Bds. Engring. Examiners, 1961-62; chmn. Ky. Bd. Registration Profl. Engrs., 1961-63. Registered profl. engr. State Ky. Mem. Am. Soc. C.E. (past president Kentucky section; regional director 1966-69), American Society Engring. Edn. (mem. exec. com. engineers college adminstrv. council), National Society Engineering Educators (president Southeastern section 1964-65), Engrs. Council Profl. Devel. (exec. com. 1961-62), Ky. Soc. Profl. Engrs. (pres. 1962-63), Newcomen Soc. Eng., Chi Epsilon, Tau Beta Pi, Omicron Delta Kappa, Sigma Phi Epsilon. Democrat. Presbyn. Clubs: Rotary, Triangle. Home: Lexington, Ky., Died July 15, 1973; interred Lexington, Ky.

SHAW, ALBERT SIDNEY JOHNSTON, state ofcl.; b. Liberty, Miss., Feb. 21, 1880; s. Richard J. and Laura (Dunn) S.; A.B., Southwestern U., Clarksville, Tenn., 1900; m. Daisy V. Aycock, Mar. 31, 1904 (dec. June 27, 1948); children—Frank, Virginia (Mrs. Whittle), Sydney M., Carol (Mrs. Barthold); m. 2d, Kathryn Spears Grant, July 5, 1950. Tchr. schs., 1900-04; abstract and loan business, 1904-19; sec. Commr. Land Office, Oklahoma City, 1919-23; treas. State of Okla., 1923-27, 43-47, 51-55, auditor, 1927-31, 47-51, from 1955, corp. commr., 35-41; v.p., dir. Home Fed. Savs & Loan Assn., Oklahoma City, from 1929. Presbyn. Odd Fellow (past grand master). Home: Oklahoma City, Okla.†

SHAW, CHARLES GREEN, artist; b. N.Y.C., May 1, 1892; s. Charles Green and Eva (Morris) S.; student Friends Sch., Berkeley Sch.; Ph.B., Yale, 1914; postgrad. Columbia, 1915. Writer 1919-74; began painting, Paris, 1932; exhibited numerous one-man shows, N.Y.C., Allen Hite Inst., U. Louisville; exhibited U.S., London, Paris, Berne, Honolulu, Rome, Copenhagen, Munich; represented San Francisco Mus. Art, Yale U. Gallery Fine Arts, Gallatin Collection, Phila. Mus. Art, Mus. Art of Tomorrow, Berkshire Mus., Balt. Mus. Art, Mus. Modern Art Lending Service, Am. Fedn. of Art travelling show, 1955-56, Met. Mus., Mus. Modern Art, N.Y.C., Whitney Mus. Am. Art, Detroit Inst. Art, Bklyn. Mus. Art, Guggenheim Mus., Museé de l Art Moderne, Paris, Cleve. Mus., Dayton Art Inst., Cin. Mus., Lawrence Mus., Nantucket Found., many others; represented permanent collections Art Inst. Chgo., Boston Mus. Fine Arts, Denver Art Mus., N.C. Mus. Art, Nat. Collection of Fine Arts, Washington, R.I. Sch. Design, IBM, Cornell U., Santa Barbara Mus. Art, St. Lawrence U., Chase Manhattan Bank, Am. embassy, Addis Ababa. Ethiopia, Bogota, Colombia, others; touring exhbn., 1956-57; designer posters and mag. covers, 1940-74; designer, maker montages, 1945-74. Served overseas, World War I. Recipient Michael Strange Poetry award, 1954; award Nantucket Art Assn., 1958, 1st prize, 1960; ann. award Cardinal Poetry Quar., 1966; 1st prize for painting Century Assn., N.Y.C.; Distinguished Service citation World Poetry Soc. Author: Heart in a Hurricane, 1927; The Low Down, 1928; Night Life, 1931; N.Y. Oddly Enough, 1938; Giant of Central Park, 1940; It wasn't Spilt Milk, 1947; Moment of the Now, 1969. Contbr. to The Connoisseur, House & Garden, Town and Country, Antiques, New Yorker, Princeton Library Chronicle. Illustrator: The Milk That Jack Drank, 1945; Dark Is Dark, 1947; Winter Noisy Book, 1949. Owner and assembler C.G. Shaw Theatrical Print Collection. Fellow Internat. Inst. Arts and Letters (life); mem. Poetry Soc. (London). Nantucket Art Assn. (Exec. com.), Mus. Modern Art N.Y. (adv. bd. 1937-41), Am. Abstract Artists, Fedn. Modern Painters, Artists Equity Assn., Am. Poets Fellowship Soc., Soc. N.Am. Poets, Delta Psi. Club: Century Assn. (N.Y.C.). Author: (poems) Into the Light, 1959, Image of Life, 1962, Time Has No Edge, 1966. Contbr. N.Y. Herald-Tribune Literary Review, Quicksilver; over 1500 poems pub. in U.S., Eng., France, Italy, Germany, Can., India. Home: New York City, NY. Died Apr. 2, 1974.

SHAW, DEXTER NICHOLS, lawyer; b. Lowell, Mass., Apr. 8, 1900; s. Edwin Tyler and Daisy Blanche (Dexter) S.; B.S., Mass. Inst. Tech., 1922, M.S., 1923; J.D., Temple, 1929; m. Edna Elizabeth Olney, Oct. 29, 1932; children—Janet (Mrs. Curtis L. Muehl), Mary Lucinda (Mrs. William Radomsky. Research chemist Goodyear Tire & Rubber Co., 1923-24; admitted to Pa. bar, 1929; asso. firm Howson & Howson, Phila., 1924-34, partner, 1934-73. Mem. Am. (bd. mgrs. 1959-61), Phila. (pres. 1947-48) patent law assns., Am., Pa., Phila. bar assns., Mayflower Soc. Mason. Clubs: Union League, Engineers (Phila.); St. David's Golf (Wayne). Home: Wayne, Pa. Died July 25, 1973; interred Lowell, Mass.

SHAW, EUGENE, retail co. exec; b. Brookline Mass., Sept. 9, 1920; s. Eugene and Tassie (Rosenblatt) S.; B.S., Johns Hopkins, 1943; postgrad. U. Md. Law Sch., 1940-41; m. Beverly Schur, Apr. 16, 1959; children—Leslie Ann, Michael, Thomas. With Lerner Stores Corp., N.Y.C., 1946-74, regional v.p., Atlanta, 1959-69, exec. v.p. operations, N.Y.C., 1969-74. Chmn. advanced gifts United Jewish Appeal, Atlanta, 1967-68. Served to lt. (j.g.) USNR, 1943-46. Home: White Plains, N.Y. Died Sept. 22, 1974.

SHAW, FREDERIC LONSDALE, educator; b. Stafford, Eng., Apr. 14, 1880; s. Henry John and Mary Cecelia (Lonsdale) S.; grad. Queen Elizabeth Coll., England, 1900; m. Nellie B. Bringgold, of West Concord, Minn., Dec. 31, 1917; children—Samuel Kenneth, Robert Lonsdale, Donald Allan and Dorothy Mary (twins), Michael H., Marjorie Anne and Maxine Alice (twins). Came to U.S., 1900, naturalized citizen, 1911; teacher and principal public schools, S.D., until 1910; co. supt. schs., Beadle Co., S.D., 1910-13; traveling rep. to W. M. Welch Scientific Co., 1913-18; state supt. pub. instrn. of S.D., Sept. 1918-25; mem. S.D. Ho. of Rep., from 1925. Mem. S.D. State Teachers' Assn., S.D. Pub. Health Assn., etc. Republican. Episcopalian. Odd Fellow, K.P. Home: Huron, S.D.†

SHAW, GEORGE BERNARD, business exec.; b. Newport, Ky., June. 7, 1905; s. George A. and Blanche (Irwin) S.; Geneva Krabach, Feb. 1, 1936; 1 dau., Georgia A. Br. mgr. Gen. Motors Acceptance Corp., 1927-43; mem. Eastern dist. price renegotiation bd. USAAF, 1943-46; dir. comml. sales Glenn L. Martin Co., Balt., 1947-52, v.p. procurement, 1952-56, pres. subsidiary Martin Internat., 1957-59; bus. cons., 1959-60; v.p. ACF Industries, Inc., N.Y.C. 1960-70; mem. bus. interests mgmt. com. Equitable Trust Co., Balt.; dir. Fecor Industries, York, Pa. Chmn., Md. Hosp. and Higher Ednl. Facilities Authority. Trustee Ch. Home and Hosp. Balt., Md. Hosp. Laundry, Balt. Mem. Air Force Assn., Nat. Aero. Assn. Home: Baltimore, Md. Died Jan. 26, 1975.

SHAW, GUY LOREN, congressman; b. Summer Hill, Ill., May 16, 1881; s. Fred and Clara Sanderson S.; ed. U. of Ill. Prep. Sch. and Coll. of Agr., U. of Ill.; m. Bessie Dillon, of Normal, Ill., Sept. 14, 1910. Farmer. Mem. Ill. Constl. Conv., 1920; m. 67th Congress (1921-23), 20th Ill. Dist. Republican. Mem. Christian (Disciples) Ch. Mason (K.T., 32°). Home: Beardstown, Ill.†

SHAW, HENRY G(EORGE), company exec.; b. Sturgis, Mich., Oct. 9, 1879; s. Rev. Robert P. and Mary C. (Thornton) S.; student U. Mich., 1904-05; m. Margaret L. Knight, Sept. 2, 1908; children—Thornton Knight, Mary Alice (dec.), Margaret S. Haley. Dept. Mgr. Gailey Supply Co., Seattle and Spokane, 1897-1904; organized own bus. under name Shaw Supply Co., Inc., surg. and hosp. supplies, Tacoma, 1906, served as pres. mgr.; trustee Tacoma Drug Co., from 1926, Northwestern Drug Co. from 1946. Pres. Westminster Found., U. Wash., 1947-48, v.p. Citizens Adv. Commn., 1944-45. Mem. Family Welfare Assn. (pres. 1924). Tacoma Council Chs. (pres. 1947-49), Am. Surg. Trade Assn. (dir. 1947-49, pres. 1950-52), Tacoma C. of C. Presbyn. Club: Rotary (Tacoma). Home: Tacoma, Wash.†

SHAW, JAMES EDWARD, educator; b. Cin., July 24, 1914; s. Chauncey and Margaret (Doogan) S.; A.B., Xavier U., 1936; LL.B., Harvard, 1942; LL.M., Boston U., 1950, M.B.A., 1952; m. Mary G. Crowley, June 23, 1942; children—Pauline, Margaret L. and Timothy J. (twins), Dorothy, Michael, Stephen, Susan, James, Stanley, Mary, Judith. Admitted Mass. bar, also U.S. Supreme Ct.; sr. mem. Shaw, Gylnn & Wittenberg, Boston and Dunstable, Mass.; gen. counsel, also monthly columnist Mass. Farm Bur. Fedn., Inc., 1958-74; gen. counsel Middlesex County Farm Bur., Inc., N. Middlesex Regional Sch. Dist., Townsend, Mass.; town counsel Dunstable; prof. law, chmn. bus. law dept. Coll. Bus. Adminstrn., Boston Coll. Chmn. Dunstable March of Dimes, 1954-60; treas. Dunstable Boy Scouts Am. troop, 1956-59; mem. gen. council New Eng. Apple Council, Inc. Auditor, Dunstable, 1958-59. Board trustee Groton (Mass.) Community Hosp., 1952-74. Served to maj. USMCR, World War II. Mem. New Eng. Regional Bus. Law Assn. (pres. 1963-74.), Am. Judicature Soc., Am. Trial Lawyers Assn., American Assn. U. Profs., Am. Bus. Law Assn., Am., Mass. bar assns., Mass. Trial Lawyers Assn., Mass. Conveyancers Assn. Recipient Insignis award Xavier U. High Sch., Cin., 1962. Club: Boston Coll. Lay Faculty (pres. 1960-61). Author: Marketing Law, 1953; Trademarks and Unfair Competition, 1954; Adminsistration of Commercial Justice, 1962; The Concept of Justice, 1965. Staff editor marketing law dept. Am. Bus. Law Jour., 1963-74. Contbr. monthly column to various farm periodicals. Home: Dunstable, Mass. Died Apr. 6, 1974.

SHAW, JOHN JACOB, physician; b. Newark, Apr. 17, 1907; s. Isaac M. and Anna (Klingman) S.; B.A., Cornell U., 1928; M.D., U. Md., 1932; m. Jane Levy, Sept. 9, 1937; children—Nancy (Mrs. Norman H. Scher), John Marx. Intern, Newark City Hosp., 1933-35, asst. physician, asso. attending physician, from 1951; matriculate and extern kin and cancer unit Postgrad. Hosp. of Columbia Coll. Physicians and Surgeons, 1941-46; chief dermatology and collagen disease Newark Presbyn. Hosp.; attending physician Hosp. for Crippled Children, Newark, from 1951. Diplomate Am. Bd. Dermatology. Fellow Acad. Med. No. N.J.; mem. A.M.A., Indsl. Med. Assn., Essex County Med. Soc., N.J. Dermatol. Assn., Soc. Investigative Dermatology, Phi Delta Epsilon. Jewish religion. Home: Orange, N.J. Died July 5, 1974; buried B'nai Jeshuroun Cemetery.

SHAW, PATRICK, Australian diplomat; b. Kew, Melbourne, Australia, Sept. 18, 1913; s. Patrick and Janet (Denholm) S.; B.A. with honours, U. Melbourne, 1935, diploma in pub. adminstrn., 1938; m. Catherine Helen Jeffree, Apr. 9, 1938; children—Janet (Mrs. Robert Mounci), Karina (Mrs. Douglas Campbell). With Australian Commonwealth Pub. Service, 1936-39; joined Dept. External Affairs, 1939; 3d sect. legation, Tokyo, Japan, 1940-42; ofcl. sec. Australian High Commn., Wellington, New Zealand, 1943-45; 1st sec., charge d'affaires legation, Chungking and Nanking, China, 1945-47; head Australian mission in Japan, also Brit. Commonwealth mem. Allied Council Japan, 1947-49; head Pacific div. Dept. External Affairs, 1950; consul-gen. in Switzerland, also permanent del. European office UN Geneva, 1951-53; asst. sec. charge UN affairs, econ. relations, also econ. and tech. assistance Dept. External Affairs, 1953-56; Australian ambassador to Fed. Republic Germany, also head Australian Mil. Mission, Berlin, 1956-59; Australian ambassador to Indonesia, 1960-62; 1st asst. sec. Dept. External Affairs, 1962-64, dep. sec., 1964-65; ambassador, head Australian Mission to UN, 1965-70; Australian high commr. to India, ambassador to Nepal, 1970-74; ambassador to U.S., 1974—. Participant del., adviser numerous internat. confs. and meetings. Decorated comdr. Order Brit. Empire. Clubs: Commonwealth, Royal Canberra Golf (Canberra). Died Dec. 27, 1975.

SHAW, ROBERT, judge; b. Jersey City, May 22, 1907; s. Andrew and Mary (Smith) S.; LL.B., Rutgers U., 1932; m. Jeannette E. Van Houten, Oct. 14, 1943. Admitted to N.J. bar, 1935; practice in Newark, 1935-62; sr. mem. firm Shaw, Pindar, McElroy, Connell & Foley, 1962; U.S. dist. judge Dist. N.J., 1962. Mem. N.J. Legislature from Essex County, 1937-38; mayor Caldwell Twp., 1955-61. Served with AUS, 1943-45, Mem. Nat. Lawyers Club, Am., N.J., Essex County bar assns. Club: Essex Fells (N.J.) Country. Home: Fairfield, N.J., Died July 9, 1972; buried Prospect Hill Cemetery, Caldwell, N.J.

SHAW, SILAS FREDERICK, cons. petrol. engr.; b. Kidder, Mo., Apr. 30, 1877; s. John Tinkham and Florence (Genung) S.; E.M., Columbia, 1903; m. Grace Chandler Diehl, Mar. 11, 1911; children—Grace Ellen Cline, Mary Elizabeth Reynolds, Constance Diehl Dove, Dorothy Shaw Bonner, Virginia Frederica Leith. Mining work in U.S. and Mexico, 1903-08; gen. mgr. of Montezuma Mines, Costa Rica, 1909-11; supt. various mines in Mexico for Am. Smelting & Refining Co., 1912-20; gen. mgr. Purcell interests in Mexico, 1920-26, also supt. Am. Metal Co., Mexico; cons. gas-lift engr. Shell Corp., Okla., 1926, Standard Oil Co., N.J. subsidiaries (trips to Colombia, Peru, Roumania, Poland, Italy, and various Mid-Continent States in connection with gas-lift operations), 1926-32, Westgate-Greenland Oil Co., 1933-52, also several smaller cos., Angelo-Canadian Oil Co., Ltd., Calgary, 1937-45, Federated Petroleums, Ltd., Calgary, 1949-52; cons. engr. Dittmar & Co., San Antonio, 1950-52, Home Oil Co., Calgary, Alt., Can., from 1955; spl. lectr. 1939; asso. prof. of petroleum engrineering, A. & M. College of Texas, 1942-43; professor petroleum engineering, 1945. Member American Association Petroleum Geologists, Am. Inst. Mining Engrs., Mining and Metallurgical Soc. Am., Am. Petroleum Inst., Tau Beta Pi. Republican. Author: Gas-Lift Principles and Practices; petroleum section Peele's Mining Engineers Handbook. Contbr. to mining and petroleum publs., also papers to tech. socs. Home: San Antonio, Tex.†

SHAW, SYDNEY DALE, artist; b. Walkley, Eng., Aug. 16, 1879; s. Benjamin and Elizabeth (Dale) S.; came to America, 1892; ed. Art Students' League, New York; Académie Colarossi, Paris, France; Ecole Nationale des Beaux Arts, Paris; m. Mary Dorothy Davis, July 7, 1923. Painter of landscapes and street scenes, principally. Exhibited at Soc. of Am. Artists; Pa. Acad. Fine Arts; Art Inst. Chicago; Internat. Exhbn., Rome, 1911; Internat. Soc. Painters and Sculptors, New York; Panama P.I. Expn., 1915. Hudnut prize, Am. Water

Color Soc., 1917. Mem. Am. Water Color Soc., Calif. Art Club, Los Angeles. Club: Salmagundi (New York). Home: Freeport, N.Y.†

SHAW, WALTER CARLYLE, business exec.; b. Stewartstown, Pa., 1881. Chairman bd. and dir. G.C. Murphy Co. Trustee McKeesport Hosp. Mem. Youghlogheny Country Club (president). Mason. Home: McKeesport, Pa.†

SHAZAR, ZALMAN, pres. Israel; b. Mir., Russia, Nov. 24, 1889; s. Judah Leib and Sarah (Ginsburg) S.; student Acad. Jewish Studies, St. Petersburg, Russia, 1907-11, univs. Freiburg and Strassbourg, 1912-14; D.H.L., Jewish Theol. Sem. Am., 1958; Ph.D., (hon.), Rio de Janeiro, 1966, Hebrew U., 1967; m. Rachel Katznelson, May 2, 1920; l dau., Rhoda. Editor, Davar, Israel labor daily, 1925-49; mem. 1st, 2d and 3d Israeli Parliaments, 1949-55; 1st minister edn., 1949-51; head dept. edn. World Zionist Movement, 1954-63; pres. State of Israel, 1963-73. Author: (autobiography) Morning Stars, 1950; (biography) Light of Personalities, 1955; also articles Jewish history, Messianic movements. Home: Jerusalem, Israel. Died Oct. 5, 1974.

SHEA, JOHN JOSEPH, banker; b. N.Y.C., Dec. 24, 1906; s. Jeremiah and Honora (Shea) S.; student Am. Inst. Banking, 1929-33, N.Y.U., 1956; m. Mary Frances Clark, Jan. 25, 1930; 1 dau., Maryann (Mrs. John J. Kinelski, Jr.). With Equitable Trust Co. (name now changed to Chase Manhattan Bank), N.Y.C., 1924-71, asst. v.p., 1951-56, v.p., 1956-68, sr. v.p., 1968-71, Mem. Bankers Assn. for Fgn. Trade, Am. Mgmt. Assn., Nat. Com. on Internat. Trade Documentation, Bank Adminstrn. Inst., Stock Transfer Assn., Am. Soc. Corp. Secs. Home: River Edge, NJ. Died July 21, 1974; buried Gate of Heavens Cemetery, Hawthorne, N.Y.

SHEARER, MAURICE EDWIN, marine corps officer (ret.); b. Indianapolis, Ind., Dec. 19, 1879; s. Samuel Henry and Mary Jane (McClellan) S.; ed. pub. schs. of Indianapolis; m. Madeline M. Brown, Dec. 28, 1908 (div. 1925); m. 2d Nancy C. Sheppard, June 6, 1928. Enlisted U.S.M.C., Aug. 5, 1901; commd. 2d lt., 1905, and advanced through grades to brig. gen., 1944; served China, Philippines, Hawaii, Nicaragua, Cuba, Porto Rico, A.E.F., Europe, Mexico; ret. from active service, 1944. Awarded D.S.M., D.S.C., Navy Cross, Silver Star, Crois de Guerre with palm and Legion of Honor (France). Episcopalian. Clubs: Army Navy (Washington), Ocean Dunes (Daytona Beach, Fla.). Home: Daytona Beach, Fla.†

SHEDD, CLARENCE PROUTY, univ. prof.; b. Worchester, Mass., June 24, 1887; s. Norman Elwyn and Caroline Crawford (Hubbard) S.; A.B., Clark U., 1909, A.M., 1914, L.H.D., 1951; B.D., Yale, 1925, Ph.D., 1932; D.D. (Clarence Prouty fellow of religion in higher edn.), Pacific Sch. Religion, 1963; m. Gladys Hadwin Van Mater, Aug. 1, 1913; children—Kathleen (Mrs. Myron Wright), Barbara Louise (dec.), Charles Van Mater. Asso. with YMCA, 1909-26, at New Bedford, Mass, 1909-11, gen. sec. at Worcester Poly. Inst., 1911-14, state student sec. Mass. and R.I., Boston, 1914-19, personnel and S.A.T.C. sec. War Work Council, N.Y.C., 1917-19, asso. nat. student sec., nat. council, N.Y.C., 1919-26; lectr. Yale Div. Sch., 1923-26, asst. prof., 1926-28, asso. prof., 1928-39, Stephen Merrell Clement prof. of Christian methods, dir. studies on religion in higher edn., 1939-55, emeritus; historian World's Com. YMCA, Geneva, 1952; vis. prof. Religion Higher Edn., Union Theol. Sem., N.Y., 1955-56, Pacific Sch. Religion, Berkeley, Cal., 1955-59; cons. editor Ronald Press N.Y., 1945-73, cons. Danforth Found. Study Campus Ministry. Dir. studies and confs. Cal. Jr. Coll. Assn., 1956-59; cons. moral and spiritual values in jr. colls.; mem. Nat. Intercollegiate Christian Council. Bd. dirs. YMCA, New Haven, mem. nat. student com.; student counseling com. Edward W. Hazen Found.; trustee Clark U. Fellow Nat. Council on Religion in Higher Edn.; mem. Assn. Student Christian Assn. Secs., Nat. Conf. Christian Workers Colls. and Univs., United Student Christian Council, Phi Mu Upsilon. Democrat. Conglist. Clubs: Rotary, Faculty (Yale); Yale (N.Y.C.). Author or co-author books relating to field, including Two Centuries of Student Christian Movements, 1934; The Church Follows Its Students, 1938; latest publs.; History of Religion In State Universities, 1949; Henry Dumant et Le Development Internationale des Y.M.C.A., 1949; Religion in State Teachers Colleges, 1952; Religion in Urban Universities, 1952; Moral and Spiritual Values in Public Higher Education, 1954; History of World's Alliance of YMCA's (with others), 1955; Religion in State Universities, 1959. Home: Jamesburg, NJ. Died Nov. 24, 1973.

SHEEAN, JAMES VINCENT, writer; b. Christian County, Ill., Dec. 5, 1899; s. William and Susan MacDermot) S.; ed. U. Chgo.; m. Diana Forbes-Robertson, Aug. 24, 1935; children—Linda, Ellen. Author: An American Among the Riffi, 1926; The Anatomy of Virtue, 1927; The New Persia, 1927; Gog and Magog, 1929; The Tide, 1933; Personal History, 1935; Sanfelice, 1936; The Pieces of a Fan, 1937; A Day of Battle, 1938; Not Peace But a Sword, 1939; Bird of the Wilderness, 1941; Between the Thunder and the Sun, 1943; This House Against This House, 1946; A Certain Rich Man, 1947; Lead Kindly Light, 1949; The Indigo Bunting, 1951; Rage of the Soul, 1952; Lily, 1954; Mahatma Gandhi, 1955; Nehru, Ten Years of Power, 1959; Dorothy and Red, 1963; Personal History, rev. edit., 1969. Home: Arolo, Italy. Died Mar. 16, 1975; interred Leggiuno, Province of Varese, Italy.

SHEEHAN, DONALD HENRY, coll. pres., historian; b. N.Y.C., Oct. 31, 1917; s. Henry John and Winifred Mildred (Atwater) S.; A.B., Duke, 1938; M.A., Columbia, 1940, Ph.D., 1950; Litt. D., Gonzaga U., 1971; m. Katherine Taft Chubb, May 16, 1941; children—Kerry Chubb (Mrs George Zack), Jeffrey Atwater, Andrew Taft. Asst. to dir. Heritage Press, 1941; comml. agt. Dept. Commerce, 1942-43; instr. history Newark Coll. Rutgers V., 1947; curator manuscripts N.Y. Hist. Soc., 1948; instr. history Columbia, 1948-52; mem. faculty Smith Coll., 1952-68, prof. history, 1961-68, chmn. dept., 1962-66, sec. faculty, 1953-56, asst. to pres., 1956-61; pres., prof. history Whitman Coll., 1968-74; vis. lectr. Bard Coll., 1952, Hartford Coll., 1955-57, Manchester (Eng.) U., 1961-62 Amherst Coll., 1962-63. Mem. Northampton Sch. Com., 1964-66; acting dir. Sch. Liberal Studies, Pierce Coll., Athens, Greece, 1966-67. Trustee Hartford Coll. Women, 1957-68; bd. overseers Williston Acad., 1959-62, chmn., 1961-62. Served to lt. (j.g.) USCGR, 1943-46; PTO. Mem. Am., Miss. Valley hist. assns., Am. Studies Assn., (pres. New Eng. 1958-59; mem. exec. council 1959-62), Phi Beta Kappa. Author: This Was Publishing, 1952; (with others) The New College Plan, 1958. Editor: The Making of American History, 2 vols., rev. edit., 1963; This is America, 2 vols., 1951; co-editor: Essays in American Historiography, 1960. Home: Walla Walla, Wash. Died Mar. 7, 1974.

SHEEP, WILLIAM L., army officer; b. Oct. 24, 1881; M.D., George Washington U., 1906; grad. Army Med. Sch., 1910. Commd. 1st lt., Med. Corps, May 25, 1910; promoted through grades to brig. gen. (temp.), Oct. 2, 1940; comdg. Lawson Gen. Hosp., Atlanta, Ga., from 1941. Address: Atlanta, Ga.*†

SHEIN, HARVEY M., psychiatrist; b. Providence, May 10, 1933; s. Stanley and Thelma Shein; M.D., Harvard, 1961; m. Elva Rodenhizer; children—David, Elizabeth, Susan. Intern, Beth Israel Hosp., Boston, 1962-63; resident McLean Hosp., Belmont, Mass., 1963-65, Mass. Gen. Hosp., Boston, 1973; pvt. practice medicine specializing in psychiatry, Belmont and Newton; asso. psychiatrist McLean Hosp., 1969-74, clin. dir., 1974; asst. prof. psychiatry Harvard, 1968-70, asso. prof., 1970-74. Served to 1st lt. AUS, 1955-57. Diplomate Am. Bd. Psychiatry and Neurology (examiner 1973-74). Fellow Am. Psychoanalytic Assn.; mem. Soc. for Neurosci., Am. Assn. Dirs. Psychiat. Residency Tng. (pres. 1974), Am. Soc. for Neurochemistry, Am. Assn. Neuropathologists, Assn. for Acad. Psychiatry, Boston Psychoanalytic Soc. and Inst. Home: Newton, Mass. Died July 18, 1974; interred Providence, R.I.

SHELBY, THOMAS HALL, univ. prof. and dean; b. Henderson County, Tex., June 22, 1881; s. John McNitt and Josephine (Jackson) S.; A.B., U. of Tex., 1907; A.M., U. of Chicago, 1921; m. Dora Ethel Beasley, Dec. 22, 1907; children—Thomas Hall, Dorothy Mae. Teacher rural sch.; elementary prin., Hillsboro, Tex., 1904-05; supt. schs., Hubbard, Tex., 1907-10; 1st asst. state supt. of pub. instrn. for Texas, 1910-13; prof. edn. Sam Houston State Teachers Coll., Huntsville, Tex., 1913-16; supt. city schs., Tyler, Tex., 1916-20; dir. extension, U. of Tex., 1920-24; prof. ednl. adminstrn. and dean of extension U. of Tex., from 1925. Mem. White House Conf., 1933; mem. at large Nat. Council of Boy Scouts of America, from 1930. Mem. N.E.A. Dept. of Superintendents, Tex. State Teachers Assn. (pres. 1919, exec. com., 1935-39), Nat. Univ. Extension Assn. (pres. 1929); Rockefeller traveling scholarship for study of Radio in Education, summers 1938-39. Phi Delta Kappa. Democrat. Methodist. Mason. Clubs: Town and Gown; Scholia, Rotary (dist. gov., 129th dist., Internat. 1946-47). Author of school survey reports pub. as U. of Tex. bulls. and contbr. to ednl. jours. Lecturer on education. Home: Austin, Tex.†

SHELDEN, MIRIAM ALDRIDGE, univ. dean; b. Washington, N.Y., Sept. 30, 1912; d. Obed Wheeler and Marita Rushmore (Vail) S.; B.S., Russell Sage Coll., Troy, N.Y., 1933; A.M., N.Y. U., Ph.D., 1958; O.D., Gymnastic Peoples Coll., Ollerup, Denmark, 1933. Instr., Berea (Ky.) Coll., 1933-38, Womans Coll., U. N.C., Greensboro, 1938-42; dean of women U. Ill., Urbana, 1947-67, dean of student personnel, asso. prof. higher edn., 1968-75; asso. chancellor for affirmative action, 1972-75. Served from ensign to lt. comdr. Womens Res., USNR, 1942-47; promoted to comdr. Res.; planned establishment of Waves on primary naval air stas. within U.S. later established program for Waves in Hawaii; ret., 1972. Mem. Nat. Assn. Women Deans and Counselors (past pres.). Home: Lake Worth, Fla. Died May 12, 1975.

SHELLEY, GUY MORRELL, engring. co. exec.; b. Wichita, Kan., Aug. 3, 1924; s. Guy M. and Erma B. (Wilson) S.; B.S., Kan. State U., 1948; m. Eddie A. Hammond, Feb. 2, 1951; children—Karen, Linda. Designer, Koch Engring. Co., Wichita, 1948-50; partner GMS & Co., Wichita, 1950-65, owner, 1965-75; partner Shelley-Wilson, Wichita, 1970-75; dir. Aerodome, Inc., 1969-75. Served with USNR, 1944-46. Registered profl. engr., Kan. Mem. Nat. Soc. Profl. Engrs. (nat. dir. 1964-65), Am. Concrete Inst., Prestressed Concrete Inst., Kan. Engring. Soc. (state dir. 1958-59, pres. 1960-61). Moose, Lion. Home: Wichita, Kan. Died Sept. 17, 1975.

SHELLEY, JOHN FRANCIS, city official; b. San Francisco, Sept. 3, 1905; grad. Law Sch., U. San Francisco; children—Joan Marie, Kathleen Patricia, Kevin Francis. Elected mem. Cal. State Senate, 1938 and 1942, serving as Dem. floor leader; pres. San Francisco Central Labor Council, AFL, 1937-48; pres. Cal. State Fedn. Labor, 1947-50; mem. 81st Congress (spl. election, 1949), 82d to 88th congresses, 5th Cal. Dist.; mem. Appropriations com.; mayor of San Francisco, 1964-67. Home: San Francisco, Cal. Died Sept. 1, 1974.

SHEPARDSON, CHARLES NOAH, cons.; b. Littleton, Colo., Jan. 7, 1896; s. Noah and Mary Margaret (Chatfield) S.; B.S., Colo. State University (formerly Colo. A.&M. Coll.), 1917, LL.D., 1959; M.S., Ia. State Coll., 1924; m. Nellie V. Trammel, Aug. 19, 1917 (died Aug. 17, 1920); m. 2d, Florence Redifer, July 31, 1923. Animal husbandman extension dept. U. of Wyo., 1919-20; asso. prof. Colo. State Univ., 1920-28; head dairy husbandry department, 1928-44, dean of agriculture, Tex. A. and M. Coll., 1944-55; mem. bd. govs. Fed. Res. System, 1955-67, cons. bd. govs., 1967-75; chmn. Resident Instrn. Sect., Assn. of Land Grant Coll. and Univ., 1947. U.S. del. World's Dairy Congress, Berlin, 1937; dir. Houston br. Fed. Res. Bank of Dallas, 1950-55. Mem. Tex. State Bd. Examiners for Tchr. Edn., 1953-55; mem. gen. adminstrn. bd. United States Department Agriculture Graduate School, 1956-64. Served as captain, infantry, U.S. Army, 1917-19; with A.E.F., 15 months. Mem. Am. Dairy Sci. Assn., N.E.A., A.A.A.S., Am. Jersey Cattle Club (dir. 1940-43), Tex. Dairy Products Assn. (pres. 1942-44), Inter-Am. Committee for Dairy Industry, Alpha Zeta, Gamma Sigma Delta, Phi Kappa Phi, Sigma Phi Epsilon. Republican. Mem. Disciples of Christ Ch. Mason. Club: Cosmos. Died Aug. 21, 1975.

SHEPHERD, FRED N., banker, b. Ottumwa, Ia., Sept. 4, 1878; son of Thomas K. and Melissa (Whitcomb) S.; grad. Hastings (Neb.) Coll., Acad., 1895; grad. Am. Inst. of Banking, N.Y. City, 1914; A.B., Park Coll., Parkville, Mo., 1900, LL.D., 1925; m. Dora Marie Hard, Feb. 8, 1910. Formerly newspaper corr., underwriter, business mgr.; cashier Empire Nat. Bank, Lewiston, Ida., 1912-17; field mgr. U.S. Chamber of Commerce, Washington. 1917-22; pub. Banking, 1922-37, editor, 1932-37; exec. mgr. Am. Bankers Assn., New York, 1922-37; mem. Los Gatos adv. bd. Bank of Am. Nat. Trust and Savings Association. Mem. Rep. State Central Com., Ida., 1916-17. Mem. agrl. commn. of American Bankers Association, 1917-21. Club: Saratoga Men's (pres. 1942-43). Home: Saratoga, Cal.†

SHEPHERD, MOZELLE MILLER, state Dem. committeewoman, educator; b. Westville, Fla.; d. Morgan C. and May (Neel) Miller; B.S., Fla. State Coll. for Women, 1940; M.A., Fla. State U., 1948, postgrad., 1948-53; m. Alex Shepherd, Jan. 5, 1950 (div. 1958). Tchr. Westville Jr. High Sch., 1930-45, prin., 1956-65; 1st supr. instrn. Holmes County (Fla.), 1945-53; grad. asst. Fla. State U., 1953; tchr. pub. schs., Chipley, Fla., 1953-54, Jinks Jr. High Sch., Panama, City Fla., 1954-56; prin. Prosperity, Westville, 1966-71; mayor, Westville, 1970-71. Chmn. Holmes County Devel. Commn., chmn. 1960-63; county chmn. various community drives. Mem. Fla. Dem. exec. com., 1944-71. Recipient achievement award, Delta Kappa Gamma, 1963, Fla. Gov.'s Industry Appreciation award, 1966. Mem. Fla. Edn. Assn. (pres. dist. 2, 1966-67), Fla. Dept. Elementary Prins., Assn. for Supervision and Curriculum Devel., Holmes County Edn. Assn., Delta Kappa Gamma, Kappa Delta Pi. Presbyn. Clubs: Bonifay Garden, Dogwood Lakes Country. Home: Westville, Fla. Died Dec. 12, 1971.

SHEPLEY, ETHAN A.H., lawyer; b. St. Louis, May 3, 1896; s. John F. and Sarah (Hitchcock) S.; student Hill Sch., Pottstown, Pa.; A.B., Yale, 1918, LL.D., 1954; LL.B., Washington U., 1922; LL.D., Westminster Coll., 1955, St. Louis U., 1955, Drury Coll., 1955, U. Mo., 1957, Northwestern U., 1958; m. Sophie S.C. Baker, July 9, 1921; children—Ethan A.H., Sarah B. (Mrs. William G. Moore, Jr.), Lewis B., Sophie S. (Mrs. Jack E. Pelissier). Admitted to Mo. bar, 1922, practiced in St. Louis; partner Nagel & Kirby and successor firms, 1930-54; dir. Mallinckrodt Chem. Works, Anheuser-Busch, Inc. Bd. dirs. Washington U. Corp., 1940-54, 61-75, pres. corp., 1951-54, chancellor univ., 1954-61. Del.-at-large Mo. Constl. Conv., 1943-44. Del. Episcopal Gen. Conv., 3 times. Pres., Community Chest, 1930, United Charities, 1940, Greater St. Louis Community Chest, 1947-48; sponsoring mem. Civic Progress, Inc.; mem. Mo. Citizens Commn. Study Edn. Chmn. Republican Finance Com. of Mo., 1947-48; Rep. candidate for gov. Mo., 1964. Mem. Am., Mo. St. Louis bar assns.; hon. mem. Phi Beta Kappa, Omicron Delta Kappa, Phi Delta Phi. Home: Clayton, Mo. Died June 21, 1975; buried Chapel Christ Ch. Cathedral, St. Louis, Mo.

SHEPPARD, JACK MURFF, physician; b. Haughton, La., May 6, 1917; s. Julius Kelly and Audrey (Murff) S.; M.D., La. State U., 1940; m. Genevieve White, Sept. 27, 1943; children—Mary Audrey S. Robbins, Jack Murff, Thomas T., Stephen W. Intern, Shreveport (La.) Charity Hosp., 1940-41, jr. resident in surgery, 1941-42; gen. practice medicine, El Dorado, Ark.; staff Union Meml. Hosp., El Dorado, Warner Brown Hosp., El Dorado. Bd. dirs. Methodist Children's Home, Little Rock. Served to capt. M.C., AUS, 1942-45; ETO. Diplomate Am. Bd. Family Practice. Mem. Union County Med. Soc. (past pres.). Methodist (bd. finance). Mason (Shriner, Jester). Home: El Dorado, Ark. Died Jan. 17, 1973; buried Arlington Cemetery, El Dorado, Ark.

SHEPS, MINDEL CHERNIACK, physician; b. Winnipeg, Man., Can., May 20, 1913; d. Joseph Arthur and Fania (Goldin) Cherniack; came to U.S., 1947, naturalized, 1956; M.D., U. Man., 1936, D.Sc. (hon.), 1971; M.P.H., U. N.C., 1950; m. Cecil George Sheps, May 29, 1937; 1 son, Samuel Barry. Intern, Saskatoon (Sask., Can.) Hosp., 1935-36; resident Children's Hosp., Winnipeg, 1937, Marie Curie Hosp., London, Eng., 1938; cons. in biostatistics Beth Israel Hosp., Boston, 1958-64; sr. cons. in internal medicine Lemuel Shattuck Hosp., Boston, 1959-60; research asso. dept. biostatistics Sch. Pub. Health, Harvard, 1954-57, asst. prof. preventive medicine, 1957-60; lectr. dept. preventive medicine Boston U., 1954-56; research prof. population statistics Grad. Sch. Pub. Health, U. Pitts., 1961-65; prof. biostatistics Sch. Pub. Health and Adminstrv. Medicine, Columbia, N.Y.C., 1965-68; prof. biostatistics dept. Sch. Pub. Health, U. N.C., Chapel Hill. Mem. Winnipeg Sch. Bd., 1942-44. Diplomate Am. Bd. Preventive Medicine. Mem. Population Assn. Am. (v.p.), Am. Statis Assn., Biometric Soc., Assn. Tchrs. Preventive Medicine, Am. Pub. Health Assn., A.A.A.S., Internal. Union for Sci. Study Population. Author: (with J.A. Menken) Mathematical Models of Conception and Birth, 1973. Editor: (with J. Ridley) Public Health and Population Change: Current Research Issues, 1965. Home: Chapel Hill, N.C. Died Jan. 15, 1973; buried Durham, N.C.

SHERBURNE, HAROLD HEWITT, investment banker; b. Pomfret, Vt., Aug. 6, 1912; s. Albert Edward and Alice Rockwell (Hewitt) S.; B.A., Dartmouth, 1930, M.C.S., Amos Tuck Sch. With buying dept. Smith, Barney & Co., N.Y.C., 1934-39, Charles W. Scranton & Co., New Haven, 1939-42; resident partner charge N.Y.C. office Bacon, Whipple & Co., 1946-75; dir. Windsor Life Ins. Co. Am., Med. Care Systems. Chmn. Inst. planning com. Wharton Sch. of U. Pa., 1961-64. Served as comdr. USNR, 1942-45; dir. aviation div. Supply Property Adminstrn., 1945-46. Mem. Investment Bankers Assn. Am. (chmn. edml. com. N.Y. group 1959-60, exec. com. 1959-62; net. bd. govs. 1960-64). Clubs: Links, Dartmouth, Wall St., Bond (N.Y.C.); Quinnipiack, Lawn (New Haven); Bond (Hartford); Pine Orchard (Conn.) Yacht and Country. Home: New York City, N.Y. Died Jan. 24, 1975.

SHERER, ALBERT W., advertising exec.; b. Chicago, Ill., Aug. 10, 1883; s. Samuel James and Clara Louise (Parker) S.; grad. Chicago Manual Training Sch., 1900; A.B., Univ. of Chicago, 1906; m. Linda Van Nostran, Sept. 26, 1911; children—Linda Jane. (Mrs. Stanley R. Morton), Albert W., Jr. Entered business as adv. mgr. McCray Refrigerator Co., Kendallville, Ind., 1907; in employ Chicago office Associated Sunday Mags. of N.Y., 1910-15; with Curtis Pub. Co. of Phila., 1915-24, mgr. Chicago office, 1924-28; vice pres. Lord & Thomas, advertising agency, Oct. 1928-Feb. 1937; adv. mgr. National Biscuit Co., May 1937-Oct. 1944; vice pres. McCann-Erickson, Inc., from Oct. 1944. Trustee, Univ. of Chicago, Baptist Theol. Union. Mem. Delta Kappa Epsilon. Baptist. Clubs: University, Quadrangle, Commercial, Commonwealth, Casino (Chicago); Yale (New York). Home: Chicago, Ill. Died Dec. 22, 1973.

SHERIDAN, EDWARD FRANCIS, bank mgmt. cons.; b. Jersey City, Feb. 9, 1907; s. Edward F. and Frances M. (Truscott) S.; grad. N.Y. U., 1947, Rutgers Grad. Sch. Banking, 1956; m. Ann M. Meyer, June 16, 1929; 1 son, Edward Francis. With Chem. Bank N.Y., 1925-45; operations officer First Nat. Bank N.J., 1946-72; bank mgmt. cons., 1972-74. Pres., trustee Bergen County Clearing Assn. Fed. Res. Bank N.Y. Annex. Mem. N.J. Bankers Assn. (chmn. mgmt. and operations com.). Club: Upper Montclair Country. Home: Clifton, NJ. Died July 19, 1974.

SHERIDAN, LEO J., real estate exec.; b. Chgo., Apr. 24, 1897; s. John J. and Mary Ellen (Guhin) S.; LL.D., DePaul U.; m. Irene Leader, June 25, 1921 (dec. June 1962); children—Donald, Irene (Mrs. George A. Martin, Jr.), Mary (Mrs. John P. Gallagher), Catherine (Mrs. William F. Walsh), Leo, John; m. 2d, Beatrice Rice Gillick, Apr. 24, 1965. Asst. to v.p. S.W. Straus & Co., real estate financing, 1919-26, chmn. bldg. com., v.p., 1927, v.p., dir. charge finance comml. and residential bldgs., 1928-29; pres. L.J. Sheridan & Co., real estate and property mgmt., 1929-51, chmn., 1951—; chmn. Sheridan Devel. Corp.; dir. Burlington Soap Co., Inland Life Ins. Co., Founders Investment Co., Carson Pirie Scott & Co., Central Cold Storage Co. U.S. ambassador to Ireland, 1968-69. Commr. of accounts and finance Highland Park (Ill.) City Council, 1943-47; chmn. Chgo. Central Area Com. past pres. Cath. Charities, archdiocese Chgo. Trustee, past chmn. bd. lay trustees DePaul U.; citizens bd. Loyola U., U. Chgo., U. Chgo. Cancer Research Found. Served in U.S. Army A.S., Signal Corps, 2d lt. Res., flying status, 1918-19. Mem. Nat. Assn. Bldg. Owners and Mgrs. (past pres.), Bldg. Owners' and Mgrs' Assn. Chgo. (past pres.), Chgo Real Estate Bd., Nat. Assn. Real Estate Bds., Chgo. Assn. Commerce and Industry (past dir.), Urban Land Ist., Am. Legion, Lambda Alpha. Clubs: Dairymen's Country (Wis.); Chicago Athletic Association, Mid-Day, Executives'. Chicago, Commercial, Economic, Builders'; Mid-America, Irish Fellowship (v.p.) (Chgo.); Knollwood Country; Duckville (Utah) Gun. Author: Sheridan-Karkow Formula for Determination of Rental Values; Trends Influencing Chicago's Central Business Districts. Contbr. reports on econ. status of office bldg. Industry. Asso. editor Brick and Clay Record, 1915-16. Home: Lake Forest, Ill., Died Nov. 10, 1975.

SHERIFF, ROBERT CEDRIC, author; b. in England, June 6, 1896; s. Herbert Hankin and Constance (Winder) S.; student Kingston Grammar School and New College, Oxford, England; unmarried. With Sun Ins. Co. of London, England, 1914-29. Served as infantry capt., 1914-19. Produced first play, "Journey's End" at Savoy Theatre, London, 1929. Fellow Soc. of Antiquaries, England. Clubs: Garrick, Leander, Author: Journey's End., 1929; Badgers Green, 1930; St. Helena (with Jeanne de Calais), 1934; (novels) Fortnight in September, 1931; Greengates, 1936; Hopkins Manuscript, 1938; Chedworth, 1945; Another Year 1947. Has written numerous screenplays, including H. G. Wells' "Invisible Man," Hilton's "Goodbye, Mr. Chips," Galsworthy's "Over the River," Remarque's "Roa Back," Mason's "Four Feathers," Knight's "This Above All," "Odd Man Out," 1947; Quartet, 1948; (novel) Another Year, 1948. Home: Surrey, England. Died 1975.

SHERMAN, ALLAN, entertainer; b. Chgo., Nov. 30, 1924; s. Percy and Rose (Sherman) Copecon; student U. Ill., 1941-45; m. Dolores Chackes, June 15, 1945; children—Robert, Nancy. Recording albums include My Son, the Folksinger, 1962, My Son, the Celebrity, 1962, My Son, the Nut, 1963, Allan in Wonderland, 1963. For Swinging Livers Only, 1964, Peter and the Commissar, 1964; records include Hello Mudduh, Hello Fadduh, 1963, Crazy Downtown, 1965. Recipient Grammy award for best comedy performance Hello Mudduh, Hello Faddah, Nat. Acad. Rec. Arts and Scis., 1963. Mem. A.F.T.R.A., Am. Guild Variety Artists. Screen Actors Guild, Writers Guild, Am. Acad. Recording Arts and Scis. Author: Instant Status, 1964; A Gift of Laughter, 1965; Hello Muddah, Hello Faddah, 1963. Home: Los Angeles, Cal. Died Nov. 20, 1973.

SHERMAN, CARL BENJAMIN, utility exec.; b. Rusk, Cherokee County, Tex., Dec. 1915; s. Clifford Carl and Birdie Louise (Babers) S.; J.D., Baylor, 1938; m. Mary Virginia Lorlgan, Nov. 16, 1940; children—Steven David, Jonathan Scott, Kirk Babers. Admitted to Tex. bar, 1938; practice in Rusk, Tex., 1938-39; with FBI, 1939-51; with Houston Lighting & Power Co., 1951-74, v.p., 1952-67, dir., 1960-74, asst. to pres., 1963-67, exec. v.p., 1967-70, pres., 1970-74; dir. Houston br. Fed. Res. Bank, Hughes Tool Co., Houston. Mem. exec. bd. Sam Houston council Boy Scouts Am.; gen. campaign chmn. United Fund Houston-Harris County, 1960. Bd. dirs. Houston Research League, Austin, Better Bus. Bur. Houston, United Fund Houston-Harris County, Jr. Achievement Houston, Houston, Livestock and Rodeo Assn.; bd. regents S. Tex. Coll.; mem. devel. bd. U. Houston. Mem. Nat. Assn. Electric Cos. (dir.), Houston C. of C. (dir.). Mason. Clubs: Headliners (Austin, Tex.); Houston, One Hundred (dir.), Plaza, Lakeside Country, River Oaks Country, Astrodome (Houston). Home: Houston, Tex. Died Nov. 22, 1974.

SHERMAN, CHARLES PHINEAS, univ. prof., lawyer; b. West Springfield, Mass., June 8, 1874; s. Phineas A. and Fanny (Lyman) S.; A.B., Yale, 1896, LL.B., 1898, D.C.L., 1899; studied in Rome and Paris; LL.D., Nat. University, 1928; m. Julia M. Rungee, Sept. 5, 1906 (died Jan. 3, 1938); 1 daughter, Valerie Frances (Mrs. Harold T. Beal); married 2d, Elsa T. Liefeld, July 1, 1944. Admitted to Conn. bar, 1898, Mass. bar and Supreme Court of United States, 1904; practiced at New Haven and Boston; instr.-elect polit. science, University of Tex., 1904; instr. law, Yale, 1905-07, asst. prof., 1907-17; spl. lecturer Georgetown U. Law Sch., 1918; prof. law, and editor-in-chief Boston U. Law Review, Boston Univ., 1920-22, lecturer Washington and Lee U., 1924, William and Mary Coll., from 1924; lecturer Boston U. Law Sch., 1935-39, prof. law from 1939; prof. law, Nat. U. Law Sch., 1926-35; librarian Yale Law Library, 1906-09; curator Yale Wheeler Library of Roman, Canon, Continental-European, and Latin-American Law, 1906-17. Charter mem. Am. Assn. Law Libraries; mem. Am. Bar Assn., Promotion Roman Studies Soc., New Eng. Historic-Geneal. Soc., Selden Soc., Classical Assn. of London, British School at Rome, New Commonwealth Soc. of London, Stair Soc. of Edinburgh, Am. Soc. Polit. and Social Science, Riccobono Seminar of Roman Law of Washington, Am. Soc. Internat. Law; Pi Gamma Mu, Acacia, Book and Gavel (Yale). Mason (32°, K.T.). Author: The Maritime Law of Rome and Some Comparisons with Modern Jurisprudence, 1899; First Year of Roman Law, 1906; Roman Law in the Modern Collaborator, Wigmore Celebration Legal Essays, 1919. Epitome of Roman Law, 1937; Roman Civilization in World (3 vols.), 1917, 2d edit., 1922, 3d edit., 1937; the Modern World, 1942; Academic Adventures, 1944. Home: Washington, D.C.†

SHERMAN, EDGAR JAY, ednl. exec.; b. Lawrence, Mass., Aug. 24, 1902; s. Roland Henry and Alma (Haerle) S.; grad. Phillips Acad. Andover, 1921; Princeton, 1925; m. Mary Whittington, May 2, 1924 (dec. Apr. 1945); children—Edgar Jay, Richard Whittington, John Alden, David Wright, William Delano; m. 2d, Anne Rooney Crow, July 6, 1946. Pres., Dixie Waste Mills, Charlotte, N.C., 1925-30; campaign dir., John Price, Jones Corp., N.Y.C., 1930-39; sr. asso. Raymond Rich Assos., N.Y.C., 1939-41; controller Welfare Council N.Y.C., 1941-43; dir. regional operations Nat. Assn. Mfrs., N.Y.C., 1943-47; sec. Brand Names Found., N.Y.C., 1947-48; financial cons. for higher edn., 1948-73. Vice pres. Ind. Colls. No. Cal. San Francisco, 1959-73. Home: San Francisco, Cal. Died Sept. 30, 1973.

SHERMAN, JOHN JAMES, physician; b. Ironton, O., July 27, 1913; s. William Tecumseh and Susan (McDevitt) S.; M.D., Rush Med. Sch., 1941; postgrad. U. Pa., 1952-53; m. Frances Elizabeth Reynolds, May 16, 1941; children—Frances Sue (Mrs. Richard Carr), William Jerome. Intern, U.S. Naval Hosp., Pensacola, Fla., 1941-42; resident in surgery Oklahoma City Gen. Hosp., 1946; resident in surgery St. Mary's Hosp., Huntington, W.Va., 1946-47, then mem. surg. staff; resident in surgery VA Hosp., Dayton, O., 1947-49; mem. surg. staff Meml. Hosp., Orthopedic Hosp. (both Huntington). Served with M.C., USNR, 1941-46. Diplomate Am. Bd. Surgery. Fellow A.C.S.; mem. A.M.A., Phi Chi. Republican. Roman Catholic. Home: Martin, Ky. Died Dec. 6, 1973; buried Calvary Cemetery, Ironton, O.

SHERMAN, LEWIS FRANK, municipal ct. judge; b. Glasgow, Mont., Feb. 10, 1917; s. Frank Laurence and Margery (Jones) S.; A.B., U. Cal., 1946, J.D., 1949; m. Mary Lois Maxwell, Dec. 27, 1944; children—Janet Margery, Frank Garth. Admitted to Cal. bar, 1949; practiced in Berkeley, 1949-67; mem. Cal. State Senate, 1967-70; judge Berkeley-Albany Municipal Ct., 1971-74. Chmn. Alameda County Republican Central Com., 1961-66. Served with USAAF, 1941-44. Decorated D.F.C., Air medal with 15 oak leaf clusters, Croix de Guerre. Mem. Berkeley-Albany, Alameda County, Am. bar assns., State Bar Cal., Alameda County Lawyers Club, Order of Coif. Home: Berkeley, Cal. Died Nov. 22, 1974.

SHERMAN, PHILIP FRANCIS, lawyer; b. Sioux Falls, S.D., May 2, 1898; s. Edwin A. and Katharine (Elwell) S.; A.B., Carleton Coll., 1919; LL.B., Harvard, 1922; m. Ruth Grosz, Dec. 16, 1939; 1 dau., Mary Katharine. Admitted to Minn. bar, 1922; practiced law, Mpls., 1922-37; asst. atty. gen. Minn., 1938-44; legal dept. Pillsbury Mills, Inc., from 1944, gen. counsel, 1954-63. Adv. bd. Jones-Harrison Home. Mem. Phi Beta Kappa. Conglist. Clubs: Minneapolis, Minneapolis Athletic. Home: Minneapolis, Minn., Died Mar. 11, 1973; interred Sioux Falls, S.D.

SHERWIN, CARL PAXSON, physician; b. Bristol, Ind., May 21, 1885; s. Richard James and Clara Adelaide (Paxson) S.; student J.B. Stetson U., De Land, Fla., 1907-08; B.S., Hanover (Ind.) Coll., 1909; M.A., Ind. U., 1910; M.S., U. of Ill., 1912; studied U. of Berlin and the Sorbonne, Paris; Dr. Sc., summa cum laude, Tübingen U., 1915; M.D., Fordham, 1920, LL.D., 1924; Dr. P.H., New York U., 1923; m. Effie Nickless, Sept. 6, 1911; children—Carl Paxson, Isabel Ann. Teaching fellow, Ind. U., 1909-10; chemistry asst., U. of Ill., 1910-12; instr. high sch., Quincy, Ill., 1912-13; research asst. in biochemistry, Tübingen U., 1913-15; asst. prof. biochemistry, Fordham Med. Sch., 1915-17; biochemist with U.S.P.H.S., at Spartanburg, S.C., summer 1916; prof. of biochemistry, Fordham U., 1917-19, prof. and head chem. dept., 1919-30, prof. biological chemistry, 1919-33; specializing in practice diseases of metabolism; dir. dept. metabolism St. Vincent's and Broad St. hosps.; asso. attending physician French Hosp.; cons. physician St. Mary's Hosp., Alice Hyde Meml. Hosp., Malone, N.Y., Miseracordia Hosp., N.Y. City. Med. Consultant to Office of Price Administration. Fellow A.M.A., Acad. of Medicine, N.Y. Acad. Science (v.p.), Am. Geog. Soc.; mem. Soc. Exptl. Biology and Medicine, Am. Soc. Biol. Chemists, Am. Physiol. Soc., Am. Chem. Soc., Am. Pub. Health Assn., A.A.A.S., Am. Pharmaceutical Assn., Harvey Soc., Sigma Chi, Chi Zeta Chi, Delta Sigma, Rho Gamma Mu. Clubs: Indiana, Illinois University. Author: (with Benjamin Harrow) Chemistry of the Endocrines, 1934, Text on Biochemistry, 1935; also sections on Putrefaction and Amino Acids In Hawks Practical Physiological Chemistry. Contbr. to Ann. Review of Biochemistry and to Bridges' Dietetics for the Clinician. Dir. of the Bureau of Good Housekeeping Magazine, 1941-44. Home: Zephyrhills, Fla. Died Dec. 18, 1974; interred Floral Memory Gardens, Dade City, Fla.

SHERWOOD, THOMAS KILGORE, educator; b. Columbus, O., July 25, 1903; s. Milton Worthington and Sadie (Tackaberry) S.; B.Sc. McGill Univ., 1923, D.Sc. (hon.) 1951; S.M. Mass. Inst. Tech., 1924. Sc.D., 1929; E.D. (hon.), Northeastern U., 1948; m. Betty Macdonald, Sept. 7, 1927 (dec. 1950); children—Thomas K. III. Richard M., Lorna Marcia; m. 2d, Virginia Howell Smith, June 17, 1953. Asst. dept. chem. engring. Mass. Inst. Tech., 1924-26, asst. prof., 1930-33, asso. prof., 1933-41, prof., 1941—, Lammot duPont prof. chem. engring., 1965-69, also dean engring., 1946-52; asst. prof. chem. engring. Worcester Poly. Inst., 1928-30; Priestley lectr. Pa. State U., 1959; vis. prof. chem. engring. U. Cal. at Berkeley, 1970-76; cons. chem. engr., 1926-76; mem. com. div. MPE Scis., Nat. Sci. Found., 1954-58; NRC council com. air quality mgmt., 1967-76. Served as tech. aide, sect. chief, div. mem. Nat. Defense Research Com. OSRD, 1940-46, as cons. to Baruch com., 1942, as expert cons. (Alsos Mission) War Dept., 1944. Recipient William H. Walker award, Am. Inst. Chem. Engrs., for publs. in chem. engring. 1941. Founders' award, 1963; U.S. Medal for Merit, 1948. Mem. Am. Acad. Arts and Scis., Nat. Acad. Engring. (founding mem.), Am. Chem. Soc., Am. Soc. M.E., Am. Inst. Chem. Engrs., Nat. Acad. Scis. (chmn. engring. sect. 1962-65), Canadian Inst. Chemistry (hon. life), Sigma Xi, Tau Beta Pi. Republican. Unitarian. Author: Absorption and Extraction, 1937, 2d edit. (with R.L. Pigford) 1952; (with C.E. Reed), Applied Mathematics in Chemical Engineering, 1939; A Course in Process Design, 1963; (with R.C. Reid) Physical Properties of Gases and Liquids, 1958, 2d edit., 1966. Contbr. articles on various chem. engring. subjects to tech. pubs. Home: Berkeley, Cal., Died Jan. 14, 1976.

SHIELDS, EDWIN JOHN, engring. co. exec.; b. Harvard, Ill., Feb. 6, 1912; s. John J. and Ida (Nolan) S.; B.S., U. Minn., 1933; m. Mary Elizabeth Martin, June 24, 1937; children—Richard J., M. Karen (Mrs. Robert Martin), Thomas M., Nancy E., Marcia M. Bridge designer Ill. Dept. Hwys., Springfield, 1934-40; project engr. Sverdrup & Parcel & Assos., Inc., St. Louis, 1940-66, mgr., Boston, asst. v.p. Fellow Am. Soc. C.E.; former adv. mem. Am. Iron and Steel Inst., Cons. Engrs. Council New Eng. (v.p. 1969-71; pres. 1972). Chmn. engring. sect. Massachusetts Bay United Fund, 1970-71. Project engr. on 1st prize award entry internat. idea contest Great Belt Crossing, Denmark, 1967. Home: Sudbury, Mass. Died July 15, 1973.

SHILLINGLAW, DAVID LEE, investment banker; b. Sioux Falls, S.D., June 6, 1889; s. Colin Melville and Emma Violet (Todd) S.; student Ia. State Tchrs. Coll., 1907-11; A.B., U. Ia., 1914, LL.B., 1915; m. Ovaga Jirkona, May 8, 1969. Admitted to Ia. bar, 1915, practiced in Waterloo, 1915-20; in charge constrn. YMCA, Europe, 1917-18, in charge liquidating properties, Europe, 1919-20; asso. Chgo. br. Liquid Carbonic Co., 1922; with Forgan, Gray & Co., Chgo., 1923-33, v.p., 1924-33; founder David L. Shillinglaw & Co. (now Shillinglaw Bolger & Co., Inc.), 1933, pres., 1933-49; v.p. Health-Mor Sanitation Systems, from 1928; with Cutler Yantis & Co. Chgo.; dir. Protectoseal Corp. Asst. to dir. Dept. Revenue, State of Ill., 1940-44. Nat. bd. dirs., v.p. Am. Assn. for the UN Dir. Central YMCA, Chgo., 1925-50, Wash. and Jane Smith Home; pres. bd. govs. Internat. House, U. Chicago; pres. Internat. House Assn., 1954. Served to lt. C.E. U.S. Army, 1918; mem. gen. sales bd. Am. Army, 1919. Mem. Nat. Assn. Tax Adminstrs. (sec. 1940-44), Soc. Am. Mil. Engrs. (past sec. pres. Chgo chpt.), Am. Legion (state comdr. Ill. 1928-39), Delta Sigma Rho, Phi Kappa Psi, Phi Delta Phi. Republican. Mason. Clubs: Quadrangle, Mid-Day, Economic, Union League (Chgo.). Home: Chicago, Ill., Died Feb. 13, 1976.

SHINKMAN, PAUL ALFRED, journalist; b. Grand Rapids, Mich., Oct. 8, 1897; s. Joseph C. and Emeline (Boxheimer) S.; A.B., U. of Mich., 1920; spl. courses, Columbia U. and Sorbonne; m. Elizabeth Benn (dau. Sir Ernest and Lady Benn), 1935; children—Paul Glanvill, Christopher Joseph, Bernard Francis III. Began as cub reporter, Grand Rapids Press; reporter, Chgo. City News Bur., 1920-21; reporter, Paris edit., Chgo., Tribune, 1924-26; Paris corr., the Italian Mail; Chicago Trib. corr. in Paris, 1927, London, 1927-29; covered Lindberg's and A Earhart's transatlantic flights, prayer book debate in the House of Commons, funeral of Thomas Hardy in Westminster Abbey, en of Cosmo Lang. Canterbury Cathedral, as Archibishop of Canterbury; returned to U.S., 1929; editorial staff, King Features Syndicate City, 1929-38; N.Y. corr., Central Press Assn.; radio commentator The Story Behind the News; roving corr. Internat. News Service, Ce Europe summer 1938; first interview with Lord Runicman in Prag (exclusive to U.S.), 1938, also exclusive interviews with Premie of Czechoslovakia and Jan Masaryk, Czech Ambassador to London; lectured throughout U.S. on European problems leading to World War 1938-42; chief, German section, Daily Report, U.S. Foreign Broadcast Intelligence Service, 1942-44; Office of War Information 1944-46; radio news commentator, Station WBCC, Washington, D.C., 1946-51; fgn. service officer, Vienna, Austria, 1951-53; editor N.E.A. News, asst. editor N.E.A. Journal, 1957-63; radio news commentator Stations WASH and WDON, also writer Central Press Assn., 1963-75. Appointed mem. Gov. of Mich's bd. visitors (1944) Nat. Naval Med. Center; Missions to Berlin, Germany, in May and October 1950 as cons. for Dept. State. Hon. trustee Baxter Sem., 1957-75. Mem. Am. Austrian Soc. (mem. bd. trustees), Acad. Polit. Sci. Clubs: National Press; Overseas Writers; Anglo-Am., Press (Paris, France); American Corr. Union (London); Sigma Dleta Chi. Episcopalian. Contbr. to U.S. and British publs. Home: Washington, D.C., Died Dec. 19, 1975.

SHINN, JOHN CALVIN, govt. ofcl.; b. Germantown, O., Nov. 26, 1918; s. Henderson L.V. and Carrie Margaret (Buehler) S.; A.B., Heidelberg (O.) Coll., 1940; student Grad. Sch. Pub. Affairs, Am. U., 1940-41; m. Martha Janette McDowell, May 17, 1947; children—Franklin McDowell, Sandra Elizabeth. Aide wage and hour div. Dept. Labor, 1941-42, field liaison officer wage and hour and pub. contracts divs., 1946-51; liaison officer, spl. asst. to exec. dir. Wage Stb!zn. Bd., 1951-53; with Dept. Labor, 1953-73, spl. asst. to asst. sec. Labor for manpower, 1957-59, asst. commr. Bur. Labor Mgmt. Reports, 1960-63, dep. dir. office labor-mgmt. and welfare pension reports, 1963-67, dep. asst. sec. labor labor-mgmt. relations, 1967-73. Council Christian social action United Ch. Christ, 1963-67, chmn., 1967-73; mem. gen. bd. Nat. Council Chs., 1967-73, v.p., 1969-73. Served to lt. AUS, 1942-45. Mem. Am. Soc. Pub. Adminstrn., Indsl. Relations Research Assn. Home:McLean, Va. Died May 28, 1973.

SHIPHERD, H(ENRY) ROBINSON, minister; b. Sag Harbor, N.Y., July 12, 1878; s. Jacob Rudd and Anna E. (Rowe) S.; A.B., Harvard, 1908, A.M., 1912, Ph.D., 1914; Litt.D., Lincoln Memorial University, 1930; m. Sarah Annis Billard, June 30, 1906. Teacher of English lang. and literature, Harvard, Radcliffe, Lowell Inst., 1906-08, 1910-12, Harvard Summer Sch., 1908-18, Francis W. Parker Sch., 1908-10, Gettysburg Coll., 1914-16, U. of Cincinnati, 1916-22, Boston U., 1922-27; sec. Business Training Corp., New York, 1927-29; pres. Lincoln Memorial U., Harrogate, Tenn., 1930-31; head English dept. U. of Kansas City, 1933-34; ordained Congl. ministry, 1937; pub. editorial consultant. Ednl. dir. 80th Div. A.E.F., 1918-19, 1st Army, A.E.F., France, 1919; mem. Army Ednl. Corps. Mem. Advisory Com. on Education by Radio, apptd. by Sec. Wilbur, 1929 (chmn. fact-finding subcom.). Mem. Phi Beta Kappa, Delta Upsilon, Pi Gamma Mu. Republican. Conglist. Author: The Fine Art of Writing—for Those Who Teach It, 1926; Manual and Models for College Composition, 1928. Home: Southold, N.Y.†

SHIPTON, CLIFFORD KENYON, librarian; b. Pittsfield, Mass., Aug. 5, 1902; s. George and Edith May (Kenyon) S.; B.S., Harvard, 1926, M.A., 1927, Ph.D., 1933, D.Litt., 1964; m. Dorothy Boyd MacKillop, June 11, 1927; children—Ann Boyd, Nathaniel Niles, George MacKay. Instr. history Brown U., 1928-30; instr. and tutor, Harvard, 1933 and 1936; editor Sibley Publs., Mass. Hist. Soc., after 1930; custodian Harvard U. Archives, 1938-74; librarian, dir. Am. Antiquarian Soc., 1940-74; dir. Past chmn. finance com., Shirley, Mass.; clerk First Parish of Shirley. Mass. Trustee Fruitlands Mus., Wayside Mus. Fellow Soc. Am. Archivists; mem. Am. Antiquarian Soc., Am. Acad. Arts and Scis., Mass. Hist. Soc., Colonial Soc. Mass. (pres.); hon. mem. Beverly Hist. Soc. Clubs: Grolier; Odd Volumes. Author: Biographical Sketches of the Graduates of Harvard College, Classes of 1960-71, 1933-74; Roger Conant 1945; Isaiah Thomas, 1948. Home: Shirley, Mass. Died Dec. 4, 1974.

SHIR, MARTIN M., physician; b. Boston, 1897; M.D., Harvard, 1921; m. Lillian Shir. Intern, New Haven Hosp., 1921-22; resident John E. Berwind Maternity Hosp., 1922, Manhattan Maternity Hosp. and Dispensary, N.Y.C., 1923-24; cons. obstetrician and gynecologist Jewish Hosp.; asso. obstetrician and gynecologist Kings County Hosp., Bklyn.; instr. L.I. Coll. Medicine, Bklyn. Diplomate Am. Bd. Obstetrics and Gynecology. Fellow A.C.S.; mem. A.M.A. Home: New York City, N.Y. Died Aug. 2, 1974.

SHIRER, JOHN WESLEY, surgeon; b. Braddock, Pa., 1899; M.D., U. Pitts., 1925. Intern, Mercy Hosp., 1925-26; resident pathology U. Toronto, 1926-27; fellow surgery Cleve. Clinic, 1927-29, chief surg. resident, 1929-31; asst. surgeon Children's Hosp., Pitts.; cons. surgeon Western State Psychiat. Hosp., Pitts.; sr. staff Magee-Woman's Hosp., Presbyn.-Univ. Hosp.; sr. cons. surgeon Eye and Ear Hosp., Pitts.; clin. asso. prof. surgery emeritus U. Pitts. Mem. Pa. Med. Soc. (past pres.). Home: Pittsburgh, Pa., Died July 6, 1974.

SHOENBERG, SYDNEY MELVILLE, corp. exec.; b. Leadville, Colo., Aug. 23, 1881; s. Moses and Dollie (Bernheimer) S.; ed. Smith Acad.; Washington U. U.; m. Stella Hays, Oct. 27, 1909. Vice pres., dir. May Dept. Stores Co., N.Y.; dir. C.I.T. Financial Corp., N.Y.C., First Nat. Bank, St. Louis, St. Louis Union Trust Co. Clubs: Westwood Country, Missouri Athletic. Home: St. Louis, Mo.†

SHOFNER, ORMAN EUGENE, radiobiologist; b. Houston, Nov. 1, 1938; s. Amos Eugene and Mary (Witcher) S.; B.S., Mid-Western U., 1964; postgrad. S.W. Found. Research and Edn., 1954-56, U. St. Thomas, Mo. Sch. Medicine, 1958, Phillips U., 1964-65; M.S., Ohio State U.; M.L.S., U. Okla.; m. Shirley Ann Ricks, June 1, 1968. Chief technologist Des Moines Gen. Hosp., 1960-61; dir. dept. radiology Sam Houston Meml. Hosp., 1963-65; computer scientist McDonnell Aircraft MACTEX, Houston, 1965-68; radiobiologist, computer scis. Computer Concepts, Inc., Houston, from 1968; former angiographic radiobiologist, Detroit cons. Am. Para-Med. Accrediting Commn., instr. coordinator, radiol. clin. asso. Grandview Hosp., Dayton, O. Decorated Order Golden Ray; recipient Internat. Radiography award, 1960, Order of Blue Cathode European Assn. Radiology Technologists. Diplomate Am. Bd. Bio-Analysts. Fellow Internat. Coll. Med. Tech. (v.p.); mem. Am. Radiography Technologists (trustee, v.p.), Nat. Coll. Radiography Technologists (pres.), A.A.A.S., Am. Med. Writers Assn., Am. Heart Assn. Radiol. Council, Ohio Soc. Med. Technologists, Internat. Soc. Radiographers and Radiologic Technologists (lectr.), Am. Inst. Documentation, Brit. Inst. Radiology, Assn. Am. Med. Personnel (pres. bd. trustees), Soc. Nuclear Medicine, Soc. Radiographer, Mensa, Am. Soc. Med. Technologists, Mich. Soc. Radiologic Technology, Aerospace Med. Assn., Am. Assn. Allied Health Personnel (pres. bd. trustees), Internat. Platform Assn., U.S. Jr. C. of C., Gamma Delta, Sigma Zeta, Beta Beta Beta, Alpha Psi Omega. Author: The Art and Science of Angiography, 1973; Angiography for the Radiologic Technologist, 1974. Editor Jour. Am. Radiography Technologists, 1964, jour. Assn. Allied Med. Personnel; contbg. editor Internat. Clin. Pathology News, 1965. Contbr. articles to profl. jours. Home: Dallas, Tex. Deceased.

SHONNARD, CHRISTY FOX, (Mrs. Ludlow Shonnard, Jr.), journalist; b. Rochester, N.Y.; b. James Franklin and Marjorie (Mossman) Fox; grad. Marlborough Sch. Girls, Los Angeles; B.A., U. So. Cal.; m. Ludlow Shonnard, Jr.; children—Ludlow Shonnard III, Christy Susan. Reporter-corr. Los Angeles Times, soc. editor, columnist 1953-75; performer, radio writer Christy Fox show, KNX, CBS, Los Angeles; numerous guest appearances as mistress of ceremonies on TV spls., Los Angles. Trustee, Webb Sch., Claremont, Cal., 1968-75; mem. Jr. Philharmonic, Pasadena Guild Childrens Hosp., Art Alliance of Pasadena Art Mus. Bd. dirs. Trojan League, Mem. Nine O'Clock Players, Women in Communications, Pi Beta Phi. Club: Valley Hunt (Pasadena). Home: Pasadena, Cal., Died Nov. 21, 1975; interred Forest Lawn Cemetery, Glendale, Cal.

SHOR, FRANC MARION LUTHER, writer, editor; b. Phila., Mar. 24, 1914; s. George Gershon and Lelah (Luther) S.; student Amherst Coll., Colo. Coll., U. Ill., Yale, U. Pa., 1931-43; m. Jean Bowie, 1948 (div.); m. 2d, Donna Hamilton, 1964 (div.); children—Lawrence, Brian Robert and Donnali (twins). Reporter and copyreader with Jefferson City Capital News, Asso. Press, Chgo. Herald-Examiner, Chgo. Daily News, N.Y. American, Denver Post, San Francisco Call-Bull., San Francisco Chronicle, 1934-41; China corr. Readers Digest, 1948; free-lance photographer, writer, lectr., 1949-52; staff Nat. Geo. Mag., 1953-74, asst. editor, 1956-58, sr. asst. editor, 1958-64, asso. editor, 1964-74. Exec. officer, acting deputy dir. China office UNRRA, 1946-47; panel chmn. Nat. Endowment for Humanities, 1967; mem. jury Phi Beta Kappa Ralph Waldo Emerson Award, 1969, 70; chmn. bd. Parks and History Assn., 1968-69; chmn. bd. Washington Community Sch. Music, 1967-69. Served with AUS, 1942-46; mng. editor Stars, Stripes. Decorated Order Brit. Empire; Order of Taj (Iran); Order Cloud Banner, Order Brilliant Star (China); recipient citation for photographic reporting Overseas Press Club, 1955. Fellow Royal Geog. Soc. Royal Central Asian Soc., Medieval Acad. Am. Club: Cosmos (Washington). Organizer, leader (with Jean Bowie Shor) expdn. to Central Asia, 1949-51; completed traverse Wakhan Corridor, Afghanistan. Home: Washington, D.C. Died July 15, 1974; buried Cascade, Colo.

SHORES, ROBERT JAMES, editor; b. Minneapolis, Mar. 14, 1881; s. Arthur J. and Ella Medora (Harvey) S.; ed. Shattuck Sch., Faribault, Minn.; Columbian (now George Washington) U., and Cornell U.; m. Marie Lowe, d. Admiral David Smith, U.S.N., September 26, 1914. Entered newspaper work, 1902, and continued in same until 1910, working in Butte, Seattle, Salt Lake City, Des Moines, Minneapolis, St. Paul, Lake City, Des Moines, Minneapolis, St. Paul, San Francisco and New York; editor Chit-Chat (Seattle), 1903; editorial writer, Newspaper Enterprise Assn., San Francisco, 1906; lit. editor, The Pittsburgh Spectator, 1912; founder, and editor, The Idler, 1910-12; mng. editor New York Editorial Service, 1914—. Staff Motion Picture Mag., Motion Picture Classic; contbr. Harper's Weekly, Illustrated Sunday Forum, etc. Mem. Authors' League America. Author: The Story of Willie Complain, 1902; At Molokai and Other Verse, 1910; Gay Gods and Merry Mortals, 1910; New Brooms, 1913. Home: New York City, N.Y.†

SHORTRIDGE, WILSON PETER, educator; b. Medora, Ind., July 28, 1880; s. William Howard and Rhoda Ann (Roberts) S.; A.B., Ind. U., 1907; A.M., U. of Wis., 1911; Ph.D., U. of Minn., 1919; m. Blanche Alter, Aug. 31, 1904; children—Milford Howard (dec.), Blanche Pauline, Wilson Poole, Rhoda Mildred. Teacher pub. schs., Elkhart, Ind., 1908-11; teacher North High Sch., Minneapolis, 1911-17; asst. in history,

U. of Minn., 1917-18; asst. prof. history, U. of Louisville, 1918-19, prof., 1919-22; prof. history, W.Va. U., from 1922, dean of Coll. of Arts and Sciences from 1929. Mem. Am. Hist. Assn., Phi Beta Kappa. Presbyterian. Mason (32°). Author: The Transition of a Typical Frontier, 1922; The Development of the United States, 1929; also articles in hist. publs. Home: Morgantown, W.Va.†

SHORTS, ROBERT PERRY, banker; b. Morris, Man., Can., Dec. 30, 1879; s. Robert and Eliza Jane (Armstrong) S.; grad. Central Mich. State Normal Coll., 1900; LL.B., U. Mich., 1906; m. Helen Hubbard Houseman, Nov. 12, 1907; children—Robert Lester (dec.), Mrs. Susan Ryan. Prin. pub. schs. Lainsbury, Mich., 1901-02; practice law, Saginaw, Mich., 1907; gen. counsel and dir. U.S. Health & Accident Ins. Co., 1907-14; 1st v.p., dir. Mass Bonding & Ins. Co., Boston, 1914-18; v.p. F.W. & F. Carlisle Co., Saginaw, 1919-20; v.p., dir. 2d Nat. Bank, Saginaw, 1921-28, pres., 1929-57, chmn. bd., 1957-65, hon. chmn., 1965-75; dir. Mich. Bell Telephone Co. Bd. dirs. Saginaw Community Chest. Recipient Horatio Alger award Am. Schs. and Colls. Assn., 1963. Mem. Saginaw Bd. Commerce (pres. 1924-25), Phi Kappa Psi. Republican. Methodist. Mason (32, Shriner), Rotarian. Clubs: Saginaw, Saginaw Country, Detroit. Speaker and writer on econ. subjects; many addresses pub. by various corps. and financial mags. Home: Saginaw, Mich. Died Aug. 12, 1975.

SHOSTAKOVICH, DMITRI, Russian composer; b. Leningrad, Sept. 26, 1906; student Leningrad Conservatory (studied piano under Nikolaiev, composition under Steinberg and Glazunow); married; 1 daughter, Galina, 1 son, Maxim. Composer (operas) The Nose, Lady Macbeth of Mtsensk; (ballets) Limpid Stream, Golden Age, The Bolt; (symphonies) Ode to October, May 1st; also 10 other symphonies, 24 preludes for piano, pieces for string octet, 3 string quartets, quintet for piano and strings, 2 piano sonatas, trio for piano, violin, and cello Op. 67, and Concerto for piano and orchestra; oratorio Song of the Forests, Op. 81; 7th Symphony performed for 1st time in Western Hemisphere by Toscanini, N.Y. City, July 19, 1942; 9th Symphony, U.S. premiere, July 1946; composer music for 28 films, 12 theatrical prodns.; wrote Khoranshchina (Russian film of Modest Moussorgsky's opera), 1960; Recipient world peace prize, World Peace Council, 1952. Address: Moscow USSR. Died Sept. 7, 1975.

SHOUDY, WILLIAM ALLEN, cons. engr.; b. Brooklyn, N.Y., Apr. 5, 1878; s. Joseph Allen and Caroline (Travis) S.; M.E., Stevens Inst. Tech., Hoboken, N.J., 1899; m. Marion Bartlett Hawkins, Oct. 24, 1906; children—Elizabeth Jaquith, Carol (Mrs. Ronald C. Lindsay), William Allen Jr. Began as craftsman, 1899-1901; asst. to eastern mgr., Am. Linseed Co., 1901-03; instr. and asst. prof. engring. practice, Stevens Inst. Tech., 1903-11; mech. engring. asst. to mgr. Baltimore Copper Smelting and Rolling Co., 1911-12; engr. of tests, Brooklyn Edison Co., 1913-16; asst. mech. engr., J.G. White Engring. Corp., 1916-19; power engr., Am. Sugar Refining Co., 1919-21; supt. steam stations and advisory engr., Adirondack Power and Light Corp., 1921-25; asso. prof. mech. engring., Columbia, 1923-37; cons. engr. from 1925; acting chief mech. engr. Chas H. Tompkins Co. 1946-48, J. G. White Engring. Co., China, 1948-49, Fellow Am. Society M.E. (vice pres., 1935-37), Sigma Xi, Tau Beta Pi, Phi Sigma Kappa. Republican. Conglist. Home: Basking Ridge, N.J.†

SHOUSE, JOUETT, lawyer; b. Woodford County, Ky., Dec. 10, 1879; s. John Samuel and Anna (Armstrong) S.; student Mexico (Mo.) High Sch.; U. of Missouri, University of Miami; married Marion Edwards, Oct. 18, 1911; children—Elizabeth, Marion; m. 2d, Catherine Filene (Dodd), Dec. 2, 1932. Engaged in newspaper work and business enterprises in Lexington, Ky., 1898-1911; removed to Kinsley, Kan., 1911, and engaged in farming and stock-raising; Member of Kansas State Senate, 1913-15; member 64th and 65th Congresses (1915-19), 7th Kansas District, asst. sec. of the Treasury, Mar. 5, 1919-Nov. 15, 1920, with jurisdiction over revenue agencies. Del. at large Dem. Nat. Conv., 1920, 24, 32; chmn. Dem. Nat. Exec. Com., August 1928-July 1932; pres. Assn. Against Prohibition Amendment, Aug. 15, 1932, until its dissolution, Dec. 31, 1933; pres. Am. Liberty League from Organization, 1934 until dissolution, 1940. Practiced law in Washington. Past chmn. bd. Kinsley Bank (Kan.); dir. MSL Industries, Incorporated; trutrustee of the National Realty Trust, Member Phi Delta Theta. Mem. Christian (Disciples) Ch. Clubs: Metropolitan, 1925 F Street (Washington); Jockey; American Boxer (del. Am. Kennel Club). Home: Washington, D.C.†

SHREVE, EARL OWEN, former v.p. Gen. Elec. Co.; b. Mapleton, Ia., Oct. 31, 1881; s. James Elmer and Addie Alma (Cone) S.; B.S. in E.E. Ia. State Coll., Ames, Ia., 1904; LL.D., Union College, Schenectady, N.Y., 1949; m. Annabelle Thomson, Sept. 9, 1908. Began as telegrapher C.M.&St.P. R.R., Charter Oak, Ia.; test course for student engrs. Gen. Electric Co., Schenectady, N.Y., 1904, salesman for Supply Dept., 1906; resident agent for State of Nevada, 1907-08, turbine sales specialist, San Francisco office, 1909-11, appratus salesman, 1911, mgr. apparatus sales, San Francisco office, 1914, asst. mgr., 1916, mgr. San Francisco office, 1917-26, mgr. indsl. dept., Schenectady, 1926-29, asst. v.p., 1929, v.p. in charge sales, 1934; former dir. Gen. Electric Supply Corp., Schenectady Trust Co.; former vice pres. in charge sales, 1934; former dir. Gen. Electric Supply Corp., Schenectady Trust Co.; former vice pres. in charge customer relations, 1945. Awarded Marston medal, Ia. State Coll., 1938. Gov. National Electrical Mfrs. Assn.; mem. N.Y. State C. of C.; pres. Chamber of Commerce of U.S., 1947-48; mem. Am. Management Assn.; nat. rep. and mem. exec. bd. Schenectady Council, Boy Scouts of America; mem. bd. Nat. Elec. Mfg. Assn.; v.p. and mem. bd. Nat. Fire Protection Assn. Hon. Mem. Tau Beta Pi, Eta Kappa Nu. Mem. U.S. Nat. Commn. for U.N.E.S.C.O. Home: New York City, N.Y.†

SHROYER, CURTIS CLINTON, assn. ofcl.; b. Portage, O., Sept. 20, 1894; s. Olen J. and Nellie E. (Stacey) S.; grad. Ottawa (O.) Bus. Coll., 1915; student Toledo U., 1928; m. Myrtle McWilliams, July 28, 1923. With Gen. Electric Co., 1926-71, exec. v.p. subsidiary Sabroske Electric Inc., elec. contractor, Fremont, O., 1954-71. Mem. Am. Numismatic Assn., 1934-73, dist. sec., 1948-49, bd. govs., 1951-60, 1st v.p., 1960-61, pres., 1961-63. Home: Toledo, O., Died Nov. 23, 1973; buried Weston, O.

SHULER, ROBERT PIERCE (BOB SHULER), clergyman, lecturer; b. Grayson County, Va., Aug. 4, 1880; s. John William Webster and Elvira (Cornett) S.; A.B., Emory and Henry Coll., Emory, Va., D.D., same, and Asbury Coll., Wilmore, Ky.; LL.D., John Bronw Univ., Siloam Springs, Ark.; Springs, Ark.; m. Nelle Reeves, Oct. 4, 1905; children—William Reeves, Dorothy, Robert Pierce, Jack Cornett, Nelle, Richard Clifton (dec.), Edward Hooper, Phil Ross. Ordained ministry M.E. Ch., S., 1904; pastor, successively Pocahontas, Norton, Cumberland Gap, Va., Elizabethtown, La. Follette, Tenn., Grandview, Temple, Austin, Paris, Tex., and Trinity Ch., Los Angeles, from 1920. Polled 564,000 votes for U.S. Senate, Prohibition ticket, 1932. Ex-pres. Ministerial Union of Los Angeles. Fundamentalist. Author: What New Doctrine Is This?; Some Dogs I Have Known; also numerous booklets and tracts. Editor and pub. The Methodist Challenge. Home: El Monte, Cal.†

SHULL, CHARLES ALBERT, plant physiologist; b. Clark County, O., Jan. 19, 1879; s. Harrison and Catharine (Ryman) S.; student Antioch Coll., Yellow Srpings, O., 1900-02; B.S., U. of Chicago, 1905, Ph.D., 1915; Marine Biol. Lab., Cold Spring Harbor, L.I., N.Y., summer 1907; m. Lena Mearle Larkin, Nov. 30, 1907; 1 son, Sherman Kingsley. Fellow in zoölogy, U. of Chicago, 1905-06; asst. prof. biology, 1906-08, prof. biology and geology, 1908-12, Transylvania U., Lexington, Ky.; asst. in botany, 1912-15, asso. prof. plant physiology and genetics, 1915-18, U. of Kan., chmn. dpet. dept. of botany, 1918; prof. plant physiology and head dept. of botany, U. of Ky., 1918-21; asso. prof. plant physiology, U. of Chicago, 1921-25, prof., 1925-44, professor emeritus, from 1944; sec. Poetry Council of N.C., Inc., 1951-60; science writer, The Asheville Citizen-Times, 1948, from 1953; guest prof. U. W.Va., 1928, Oregon State Coll., 1931, Okla. A. and M. College, 1938; Hales lecturer, St. Louis, Mo., 1935; lecturer Kress Fund, Clemson College, 1948. Fellow A.A.A.S. (life mem), Chicago Academy of Sciences; member of American Society of Naturalists, Cowles Botanical Society (president 1943), East and West Assn., Am. Society Plant Physiologists (past president; awarded Barnes life membership, 1929, Stephen Hales prize, 1934), American Association University Profs., Chicago Academy of Sciences (member board of governors 1941-44), Illinois Acad. of Science, Wilderness Soc., Save the Redwoods League, Men's Garden Club of Asheville, Am. Literary Assn., Phi Beta Kappa, Sigma Xi, Gamma Alpha, Phi Beta Kappa Asso. Presbyn. Clubs: Collegiate, Chaos, X-Club. Author: Barnes' Plant Physiology (rev. edit.), 1930; Methods in Plant Physiology (with W. E. Loomis), 1937; Experiments in Plant Physiology, 1926-44; asso. editor, Botanical Gasette, 1926-44. Contbr. scientific articles. Lecturer on popular and technical subjects. Home: North Caldwell, N.J.†

SHULLENBERGER, WILLIAM ARTHUR, clergyman; b. Shippensburg, Pa., June 10, 1881; s. John A. and Anna Christine (Artz) S.; grad. high sch., Maryville, Mo., 1899; A.B., Drake U., 1904, grad. study, 1905, D.D., 1922; m. Grace D. Tilton, Oct. 27, 1908; children—Wendell Arthur, Gale Tilton, Cleo Chilton. Ordained ministry Christian (Disciples) Ch., 1906; pastor Grant City, 1906-08, Trenton, Mo., 1908-10, Mexico, Mo., 1910-16, Central Ch. of Christ, Des Moines, Ia., 1916-26. Central Christian Ch., Indianapolis, from 1926; special lecturer on practical theology, Coll. of Bible, Drake U., 1916-26 and Coll. of Religion, Butler U., 1926-50. Mem. Bd. Edn., 1924-34, trustee, v.p., Pension Fund, chmn. Commn. on Budgets and Promotion (1931-41) and v.p., dir. Christian Bd. of Publ.; bd. mem. Assn. Colleges and Universities, Disciples of Christ, mem. Commission on World Order, all of Christian Church. Director Association for Promotion of Christian Unity, 1922-33; dir. Ind. Council International Relations, 1928-35; mem. exec. com. Indianapolis Church Fedn. 1928-49; trustee Drake U., 1917-49, Butler University (1938-44). Fraternal del. Disciples of Christ in U.S. and Can. to Brit. Chs., Leicester, Eng., 1935; pres. Internat. Conv. Disciples of Christ, 1941-42. Delegate to Delaware Conference on Basis of a Just and Durable Peace 1942, and Cleveland Conference 1945. Mem. Nat. Alumni Assn. Drake U. (pres. 1917-34), Phi Beta Kappa, Pi Gamma Mu. Democrat. Mason (32°). Clubs: Kiwanis, Indianapolis Literary (pres. 1946-47), Indianapolis Athletic, Meridian Hills Country. Contbr. to religious publs. Home: Indianapolis, Ind.†

SHUMATE, WADE HAMPTON, educator; b. Sherman, Tex., July 10, 1879; s. Wiley Huffaker and Huldah Lucretia (Cannon) S.; ed. Tex. Christian U., Waco, 1899-1902; A.B., U. of Okla., 1914; A.M., U. of Chicago, 1923; m. Maude Elizabeth Chenault, of Sherman, Tex., Apr. 15, 1906; 1 dau., Wahlelu Maude. Began career as athletic coach, Poly. Coll., Ft. Worth, Tex., 1903-05; prin. Mangum (Okla.) High Sch., 1905-07; rural prin., 1907-08; supt. schs. Granite, Okla., 1908-11, Fairview, 1911-13; head dept. edn., dir. training sch., North Eastern Teachers Coll., Tahlequah, Okla., 1914-20; supt. schs. Sallisaw, Okla., 1920-26, Mangum, 1926-33; pres. Southeastern State Teachers Coll., Durant, Okla., from 1933. Veteran Spanish-Am. War, 1898-99. Mem. Okla. Edn. Assn. (life), Phi Delta Kappa, Kappa Delta Pi. Democrat. Mem. Disciples of Christ. Mason (32°, Shriner). Clubs: Chamber of Commerce, Rotary. Home: Durant, Okla.†

SHUMWAY, ADELINA RITTER, dental mfg. exec.; b. Rochester, N.Y., Aug. 20, 1875; d. Frank and Elizabeth (Fertig) Ritter; student Rochester Free Acad., 1890-1894; m. Robert Crittenden Shumway; children—Helen Elizabeth (Mrs. John Mayer), Frank Ritter, Partner, owner Ritter Co., Inc., from 1915, pres. 1919-26, dir., from 1926, chmn. bd. 1933-53, hon. chmn., from 1953. Republican. Christian Science. Clubs: Century (Rochester); Field, Woman's (Greenwich). Home: Greenwich, Conn.†

SHURTER, ROBERT LAFEVRE, educator; b. Ellenville, N.Y., Oct. 22, 1907; s. Henry J. and Elizabeth (Ostrander) S.; A.B., Amherst Coll., 1928; A.M., Columbia, 1929; Ph.D., Western Res. U., 1936; m. Mae F. Potter, June 19, 1928; children—Peter G., Marilyn. Mem. faculty Case Western Res. U., from 1930, prof. English and head dept. lang. and lit., 1946, dir. div. humanities and social studies, 1949-59; vis. prof. Mass. Inst. Tech., 1938-39; cons. to many corps., from 1949. Chmn. adv. com. Martha Holden Jennings Found. Mem. Modern Lang. Assn., Am. Assn. U. Profs., Am. Soc. Engring. Edn., Tau Kappa Alpha Pi Delta Epsilon. Author: Argument, 1939; Effective Letters in Business, 1948; Written Communication in Business, 1957, 2d edit., 1973; Concise Grammar Reference, 1959; The Utopian Novel in America, 1865-1900, 1973; other textbooks. Editor: Looking Backward (Edward Bellamy) (Modern Library edit.), 1951. Home: Sarasota, Fla., Died Nov. 18, 1974; interred Ellenville, N.Y.

SHURTLEFF, FLAVEL, city planning; b. in Boston, Mass., Nov. 27, 1879; s. Flavel and Harriett (Bent) S.; A.B., Harvard, 1901, LL.B., 1906; m. Isabel Martha Brown, June 28, 1910; children—Flavel, Ruth Brown, Martha Isabel. Practiced law in Boston, 1906-21; an organizer, 1910, and sec. Nat. Conf. on City Planning, 1910-35; sec. Am. City Planning Inst., 1918-34; counsel Am. Planning and Civic Assn. from 1935; lecturer on city planning and zoning; asso. prof. planning legislation and adminstration, Mass. Inst. Tech., from 1940. Republican. Conglist. Mem. American City Planning Institute, American Bar Association, Delta Upsilon. Author: Carrying Out the City Plan, 1914; also various articles on same subject. Home: Marshfield Hills, V1Mass.†

SIBLEY, GEORGE H., business exec.; b. Denver, Nov. 3, 1898; s. John Baker and Josephine (McNasser) S.; A.B., Princeton, 1920; LL.B., Harvard, 1923; m. Leah M. Patt, June 12, 1925; children—John Winthrop, Ann Wickham; m. 2d, Maude W. Burke, Nov. 4, 1956; m. 3d, Dorothy Russell, July 10, 1965. Instr. at Ecole d' Auteuil, Paris, France, 1923; admitted to Colo. bar, 1963; atty. firm Murray Aldrich & Roberts (now Milbank Tweed, Hope & Hadley), N.Y., 1923-27; investment banking J. & W. Seligman & Co., N.Y., 1927-37; gen. atty. E. R. Squibb & Sons, mem. exec. and finance coms.; v.p., gen. atty. and dir. E. R. Squibb & Sons Inter-Am. Corp., E. R. Squibb & Sons de Mexico, E. R. Squibb & Sons Internat. Corp., E. R. Squibb & Sons do Brasil, Inc., Squibb Properties Corp., Jones Estate Corp., Lentherie, Inc., Lentheric S.A., Inc., E. R. Squibb & Sons of India, Ltd.; dir. E. R. Squibb & Sons, Ltd. (Eng.), E. R. Squibb & Sons, A.O. (Turkey), E. R. Squibb & Sons S.A. (France), E. R. Squibb & Sons, Argentina, S.A., E. R. Squibb & Sons of Can., Globe Collapsible Tube Corp., Lentheric Ltd. (Eng.), Lentheric (Belgium), Rubber Corporation of America; S.A. Trustee Greenwich Savings Bank, 1946-74. Former trustee American U. N.Y. State Inst. Applied Arts and Scis. Former dir. World Trade Corp. Past pres. Soc. for Prevention Crime; chmn. exec. com. Am. Arbitration Assn.; vis. lectr. Harvard Law Sch., 1946; dir. Citizens on Courts, Inc., Brazilian com. Nat. Fgn. Trade; spl. asst. atty. gen. State Colo., Denver, 1964-65; del. Rep. Nat. Conv., 1932, state conv., 1932, 36, 40;

mem. N.Y. County Rep. com. 1930-74. Mem. N.A. M. (internat. econ. relations com.), Am. Drug Mfrs. Assn. (chmn. fgn. trade sect., mem. legislative sect.), Assn. Bar City of N.Y. (chmn. com. med. jurisprudence), U.S. Navy League, Am. Legion. Episcopalian. Clubs: N.Y. Young Republican (pres., 1931-32), Assn. N.Y. State Young Republican (pres., 1933-35); University, Downtown Athletic (former gov.), Princeton, Elm (pres. bd. trustees 1932-37). Author: Biographical Sketch of John G. Wynant; Identification of Drugs by Color; Commercial Arbitration as an Economic Way to International Cooperation. Home: Jamestown, Colo. Died July 17, 1974; cremated.

SICELOFF, L(EWIS) PARKER, univ. prof.; b. Butler, Mo., Jan. 21, 1880; s. Lewis Philip and Anna Marie (Courtney) S.; A.B., Central Coll., Mo., 1900; Ph.D., Columbia U., 1912; m. Margaret McAdory, Nov. 8, 1930. Instr. mathematics Buchanan Jr. Coll., 1900-02, pres., 1902-04; instr. Coll. City of N.Y., 1905-06; instr. math., Columbia U., 1906, asst. prof. asso. prof., prof., 1939-50, prof. emeritus from 1950. Mem. Am. Math. Soc., Math. Assn. America. Home: New York City, N.Y.†

SICILIANOS, DEMETRIOS CONSTANTINE diplomat; b. Constantinople, Turkey, Apr. 9, 1880; s. Constantine and Maria Philippe (Axelos) S.; ed. univs. of Geneva, Paris and Athens; LL.D., from Athens 1900; unmarried. Began as attaché of Greek Foreign Office, 1902, and advanced through the grades of diplomatic service; E.E. and M.P. to U.S., from 1935. Awarded Great Cross of St. Sava (Jugoslavia); Great Cross of Hungary; Great Cross of Phoenix (Greene); Comdr. of Order of St. George (Greece). Author: The Greek Ikon Painters after the Conquest of Constantinople. Home: Athens, Greece†

SIEGEL, KEEVE MILTON, physicist; b. N.Y.C., Jan. 9, 1923; s. David P. and Rose (Jelin) S.; B.S., Rensselaer Poly. Inst., 1948, M.S., 1950; m. Ruth Elizabeth Boerker; 2 sons, Leigh, David. Faculty, U. Mich., 1948-67, head upper atmosphere group, 1949-50, head theory and analysis groups, 1951-52, head theory and analysis dept., 1952-56, prof. elec. engring., 1957-67, head Radiation Lab., 1957-61. Pres., Conduction Corp., 1960-67, chmn. bd., 1961-67; chmn., chief exec. KMS Industries, Inc., 1967-75. Adj. prof. Oakland U., 1967-75. Adv. bd. radio propagation Jour. Research, Nat. Bur. Standards, 1958-62; sci. adv. bd. USAF, 1958-66; cons. U.S. Army, 1958-61; editorial bd. Jour. Math. Physics, 1959-62; mem. adv. group radio expts. in space NASA, 1960-64; cons. Advanced Research Projects Agy., 1959-60; chmn. U.S. Commn. VI, URSI, 1964-67, 69-72; mem. at large nat. com., 1967-75; vice chmn. Internat. Commn. VI, 1964-67, 69-72, chmn., 1972-75. Mem. Community adv. bd. St. Joseph Mercy Hosp., Ann Arbor, Mich., 1969-74. Trustee Rensselaer Poly. Inst., 1969-74. Served with Signal Corps, AUS, 1942-45. Recipient Meritorious Civilian Service award Dept. Air Force, 1966. Fellow A.A.A.S., I.E.E.E. (chmn. administrv. com. profl. group antennas and propagation 1966-67), Sigma Xi; mem. N.Y. Acad. Scis., Am. Phys. Soc., Am. Math. Soc. Editor: (with J.W. Crispin, Jr.) Methods of Radar Cross-Section Analysis. Home: Ann Arbor, Mich. Died Mar. 14, 1975; buried Arborcrest Cemetery, Ann Arbor, Mich.

SIEGEL, WILLIAM ELY, banker; b. N.Y.C., Dec. 8, 1909; s. Herman P. F. and Eva (Ely) S.; A.B. in Econs., U. Cal. at Los Angeles, 1933; grad. Pacific Coast Banking Sch., U. Wash., 1950; m. Doris Genevieve Taylor, Dec. 31, 1932; 1 son, Richard Taylor. With Security First Nat. Bank, Los Angeles, 1933-73; (merged to form Security Pacific Nat. Bank), v.p., 1950-60, sr. v.p., 1960-61, exec. v.p., 1961-73, chmn. exec. com., 1962-73, vice chmn. bd., 1969-73, sr. vice chmn. bd., 1973; sr. vice chmn. Security Pacific Corp. Bd. dirs., trustee Huntington Hosp.; trustee U. Cal. Los Angeles Found. Lt. col. inf., AUS, 1941-46; active Attu, Kwajalein, Leyte, Okinawa, occupation Korea. Decorated Silver Star, Bronze Star with cluster, Combat Infantryman's Badge, Purple Heart. Mem. Res. City Bankers Assn., Am. Bankers Assn., Cal. Bankers Assn. (dir., past pres.), Los Angeles C. of C., Sigma Alpha Epsilon. Clubs: California, Bel Air Bay, Los Angeles Country. Home: Pacific Palisades, Cal. Died July 30, 1973.

SIGMAN, JULES ISRAEL, indsl. banker; b. Krakow, Poland, Apr. 7, 1904; s. Jacob and Fanny (Auerbach) S.; Diplome d'Etudes Modernes, Faculty of Letters, U. Strasbourg (France), 1929, Docteur es Lettres, 1934, grad. in sci. and polit. economy Faculty of Law, 1933; grad. Grad. Sch. Bus., Columbia, 1957; m. Selma S. Krieger, Dec. 17, 1935; children—Harry Claude, Felice Bette. Pres., chmn. bd., founder Isis Co., Nat. Luggage Mart, City Factors Corp., N.Y., 1941-50; pres. Western Thrift & Loan, Los Angeles, from 1957; chmn. bd. Rosemead Finance Corp., from 1957; chmn. bd., pres. First Cal. Investment & Securities Corp., First Cal. Investment Co., from 1956; dir. Western Thrift & Loan, Wiltern Ins. Co., Harfel Corp., I Sigman Corp. Trustee Jacob & Fanny Sigman Found.; dir. Hillel Hebrew Acad., Los Angeles Jr. Hebrew High Sch., Beth Jacob Congregation, Los Angeles Yeshivah High Sch., Jewish Home for the Aged, Los Angeles. Mem. Cal. Assn. Ind. Loan Cos., Am. Ind. Bankers Assn., Los Angeles Finance Assn., So. Cal. Mchts. Assn. Home: Beverly Hills, Cal. Deceased.

SILIN, CHARLES INTERVALE, educator; b. Ukraine, Feb. 15, 1897; s. Morris S. and Sarah (Perry) S.; came to U.S., 1907, naturalized, 1920; S.B., Harvard, 1918; certificate U. Lyon (France), 1919, U. Paris (France), 1924; Ph.D. in Romance Langs., Johns Hopkins, 1934; m. Phyllis Purnell, Sept. 9, 1929; children—Phyllis J. (Mrs. Philip A. Roussel), Barbara P. (Mrs. Jerome A. Ramsey). Instr. French, U. N.C., 1919-21, John Hopkins, 1921-23, 24-25; asso. prof. Romance langs. U. Md., 1925-27; mem. faculty Tulane U., 1927-61, prof. French, head dept., 1945-61; M.D. Anderson prof. French, chmn. div. fgn. langs. U. Houston, 1961-71, chmn. French sect., 1960-61. Mem. nat. selection com. Fulbright Program, 1952-54; bd. dirs. New Orleans Jr. League Lecture Series for Children, 1946-49. Trustee Metairie Park Country Day Sch., 1946-50. Decorated Chevalier Legion of Honor, Chevalier des Palmes Académiques (France). Mem. Modern Lang. Assn. Am. (pres. S. Central chpt. 1953), La. Coll. Conf., Am. Assn. U. Profs., Omicron Delta Kappa, Phi Sigma Iota. Author: Benserade and His Ballets de Cour, 1940; also articles profl. jours. Editor: Adventures of a Literary Historian (Lancaster), 1942. Bd. editors The French Rev., 1942-45; asso. editor S.-Central Modern Lang. Assn. Bull., 1941-50. Home: Houston, Tex. Died Aug. 21, 1974.

SILVER, ARTHUR ELMER, cons. engr.; b. Dexter, Me., Aug. 14, 1879; s. Charles Bradbury and Rebecca Evelyn (Dearth) S.; B.S., U. Me., 1902; Doctor of Engineering, University of Maine, 1954; m. Anna Jessie Teall, Aug. 31, 1914; children—Anna Boughton (dec.), Charles Warren, Mary (twins), Elisabeth. Student engr. Gen. Electric Co., Schenectady, N.Y., 1902-04; in charge meter dept. Raleigh Electric Co., 1904-05, operating engr., chief engr. Carolina Power & Light Co., Raleigh, N.C., 1905-10; elec. engr. design and constrn. Electric Bond & Share Co., N.Y.C., 1910-14, asst. chief engr., 1914-20, cons. elec. engr., 1920-32, cons. elec. engr. Ebasco Services, Inc. (Subsidiary rendering client services), 1932-48. Co-recipient award for best nat. paper in engring. field, Am. Inst. E.E., 1931-32, Lamme medallist, 1951. Fellow A.A.A.S., Am. Inst. Electrical Engineers; mem. National, N.Y. State socs. profl. engineers, International Conference on Large Electric Systems, Montclair Society Engineers, Maine Soc. N.Y., Phi Kappa Sigma, Phi Kappa Phi. Republican. Clubs: Green Mountain (Vt., also N.Y.C.); Commonwealth, Cosmopolitan, Deer Lake, Dunworkin (Montclair). Home: Upper Montclair, N.J., Died Mar. 26, 1975; buried Mount Hebron Cemetery, Upper Montclair, N.J.

SILVER, FRANCIS ALOYSIUS, lawyer; b. Butte, Mont., June 24, 1895; s. Joseph R. and Mary (Madeiros) S.; student Georgetown U., 1913-14; LL.B. cum laude, Creighton U., 1916; grad. F.A., Officers Tng. Sch., 1918; m. Elizabeth Lamarue Booth, Sept. 3, 1927 (dec. Nov. 19, 1961); children—Mary Lou, Robert, Elizabeth (Mrs. M. A. Barley). Admitted Mont. bar, 1916, practiced law, Butte, 1916-18, alderman 1919-21; rep. Mont. State Legislature, 1921-23; asst. U.S. atty., State Mont., 1925-27; county commr. Silver Bow County, Mont., Feb.-Sept. 1927; sec., counsel Bd. R.R. Commrs., Mont., 1927-35; sr. atty. FCC, Washington, 1935-36; prin. atty. ICC, 1936-42; asst. gen. counsel Office Def. Transp., 1942-45, gen. counsel, 1945-49; cons. transp. specialist Nat. Security Resources Bd., 1949-50; gen. counsel Def. Transport Adminstrn., 1950-55; chief, moblzn. planning, asso. gen. counsel ICC, 1955-58, asso. gen. counsel ICC 1958-65; practice law, Arlington, Va., from 1965; spl. counsel Am. Transit Assn., Washington, from 1966. Served to 2d lt. U. S. Army, 1918; F. A. Res. Corps. 1918-28. Mem. Va. Bar Assn., Delta Theta Phi. Club: Nat. Lawyers. Home: Arlington, Va. Deceased.

SILVERCRUYS, BARON, ambassador; b. Tongres, Belgium, Oct. 17, 1893; s. Baron and Flora (Cocq) S.; student U. of Louvain, 1910-12; U. of Brussels 1913-14, 1920; Dr. of Laws U. of Brussels, 1920; LL.D., McGill U., 1939, U. Toronto, 1944, Temple U., 1945, Drexel Inst., 1946, Bowdoin Coll., 1956; m. Rosemary Turner McMahon, 1953. Attaché, Belgian legation, Washington, 1918; sec. Belgian Delegation to Washington Conf., 1921-22; pvt. sec. to Belgian Minister for Fgn. Affairs, 1922-26; counselor, Belgian embassy, Washington, 1927-29, Belgian legation in China, 1929-31; Belgian embassy, London, 1931-36; minister to Canada, 1937-44, ambassador, 1944-45; Belgian del. to Conf. on Internat. Organization, San Francisco, 1945; signatory No. Atlantic Treaty, 1949; del. Japan Peace Treaty Conference, San Francisco, 1951; ambassador to U.S., 1945-59. Dir. Belgian Am. Ednl. Found. Home: Washington, D.C. Died Jan. 25, 1975; buried St. Marys Cemetery, Nantucket, Mass.

SILVERCRUYS, SUZANNE (MRS. EDWARD FORD STEVENSON), sculptor, lectr., painter; b. Maeseyck, Belgium; d. Baron and Baroness Silvercruys; student Les Filles de la Croix, Liege, Newham Coll., Cambridge, Georgetown Visitation Convent, Washington; B.F.A., Yale Sch. Fine Arts, 1928; studied in Paris and Belgium; L.H.D., Temple U., 1942; LL.D., Mount Allison U., Sackville, Can.; m. Henry Walcott Farnam, Jr., May 18, 1922 (dec.); m. 2d, Edward Ford Stevenson, June 1939 (dec. Nov. 6th, 1960). Came to U.S., 1915, naturalized, 1922. Began as sculptor, 1925; executed busts: Pres. Hoover for U. Louvain, Belgium; Cyrus H.K. Curtis for Poor Richard Club, Phila.; Statue of Padre Eusebio Francisco Kino in Statuary Hall, The Capitol; His Excellency the right honourable The Lord Tweedsmuir, Gov. Gen. Can. for Ottawa Govt.: busts of Quintuplets for sci. record of trustees; bust of Dr. Dafoe; busts Senator Barry Goldwater, Cardinal Cushing; bust Lord Tweedsmuir, Met. Mus., N.Y.C.; World War meml. Shawinigan Falls, Que.; Dr. Lewis Douglas, McGill U., Wendell L. Wilkie; heroic statue of Gen. A.N. McAulliffe at Bastogne; heads of Senator McCarthy, of gens. Chennault, Bradley, Doolittle, Spaatz, Wainwright, Honorable Joseph W. Martin; heads of Gens. Vandenberg, Twining, White, McConnell for USAF Acad.; statue of D. Mabel Heath Palmer; heroic statue Princess Noccalula, Gadsden, Ala. Awarded 1st prize and silver medal, Beaux Arts, N.Y., 1926; 1st prize Rome Alumni Competition, 1927; also Belgian decorations, Chevalier de L'Ordre de Leopold, Officer de L'ordre de la Couronne of Belgium; Medaille de la Victoire. Medaille Commemorative, and Queen Elizabeth War Medal, Ambulanciere de Guerre; Officier d'Academie de France; medal of the Coronation of Their Brit. Majesties. Del., Belgian Govt. to U.S., 1916-18; spoke for Belgian Relief throughout U.S. Raised funds in U.S. for Belgian-Am. Home for Orphans opened at Ostend, 1931. Alternate Conn. Republican Nat. Conv., 1932; founder, nat. and Conn. state chmn. Minute Women of U.S.A. Mem. Phi Mu Gamma (hon.). Catholic. Club: Poor Richard of Philadelphia (hon.). Author: Suzanne of Belgium (autobiography), 1932; There Is No Death (play), 1933; A Primer of Sculpture, 1941. Lectures on process of sculpture making with demonstration. Radio artist, NBC. Home: Tucson, Ariz. Died Mar. 31, 1973.

SILVERMAN, ROLAND E., oral surgeon; b. Cleve., Aug. 17, 1911; s. Louis and Lena (Minsky) S.; A.B., Heidelberg Coll., 1934; D.D.S., Western Res. U., 1938; m. Betty Jane Wyatt, Sept. 12, 1940; 1 dau., Susan Jean. Practice dentistry specializing in oral surgery, Tiffin, O., 1938-42, 46-74; cons. oral surgeon Tiffin State Hosp.; mem. staff Mercy Hosp., Tiffin, Willard (O.) Hosp., Fremont (O.) Meml. Hosp.; vis. oral surgeon Fostoria City Hosp. Mem. Tiffin Bd. Health, 1946-56, Tiffin Bd. Edn. Pres., bd. dirs. Betty Jane Meml. Rehab. Center, 1956-60; past trustee Heidelberg Coll. Served to lt. col. USAAF, 1942-46. Decorated Bronze Star medal. Fellow Am. Coll. Dentists; mem. Am. Soc. Oral Surgeons, Am. Acad. Oral Medicine, Internat. Acad. Dentistry, North Central Dental Soc. (past pres.), Acad. Dentistry for Handicapped. Episcopalian. Mason. Home: Tiffin, O. Died Feb. 25, 1974.

SIMES, LEWIS MALLALLEU, lawyer, educator; b. Clarence, Mo., July 17, 1889; s. Lewis Edward and Jennie (Van Gundy) S.; A.B., Southwestern Coll., 1909; Ph.B., U. Chgo., 1912, J.D., 1914; J.S.D., Yale U., 1927; LL.D., Southwestern Coll., 1937; m. Blanche Daugherty, Aug. 10, 1914; children—Paul Ritchey, Lewis Edward. Mem. law firm, Patterson, Heyfron & Simes, Missoula, Mont., 1917-19; prof. law U. Mont., 1919-22, Ohio State U., 1922-32; prof. law U. Mich., 1932-59, dir. legal research, 1942-54; Floyd Russell Mechem U. prof. law, 1947-59, prof. emeritus, 1959; prof. law U. Cal., Hastings Coll. Law, 1960-72, emeritus, 1972; adviser Restatement of Property, Am. Law Inst., 1932-43; draftsman, model probate code, Real Property, Probate and Trust Law sect. Am. Bar Assn., 1946. Mem. Am., Mich. State bar assns., Order of Coif. Republican. Presbyn. Author: Law of Future Interests (with A.F. Smith), 1956; Cases on Future Interests, 1939; Cases on Fiduciary Administration (with W.F. Fratcher), 1956; Cases on Trusts and Succession, 1942; Problems in Probate Law (with Paul E. Basye), 1946; Handbook of Future Interests, 2d edit., 1966; (with others) American Law of Property, 1952; Public Policy and the Dead Hand, 1955; A Handbook for more Efficient Conveyancing, 1961; (with C.B. Taylor) Improvement of Conveyancing by Legislation, 1960, Model Title Standards, 1960. Home: Mill Valley, Cal. Died Dec. 9, 1974.

SIMMONS, GRANT G(ILBERT), SR., business exec.; b. 1893. Hon. chmn. bd. Simmons Co. Home: Greenwich, Conn. Died June 7, 1974.

SIMON, CLARENCE JOSEPH, lawyer; b. Milw., May 12, 1911; s. Arthur and Edna Margurite (Merkel) S.; Ph.B., U. Wis., 1933, LL.B., 1935; m. Margaret Joan Perkins, Nov. 24, 1938; children—John, Catherine (Mrs. Thomas Leo Mullocly), Robert, Thomas, Marion. Admitted to Wis. bar, 1935; practiced in Medford, Wis., 1935-38, Elroy, Wos., 1938-44, Medford, 1944-51 asst. counsel Wis. Pub. Welfare Dept., Madison, 1951-53; counsel Wis. Dept. Regulation and Licensing, 1963-70; pvt. practice law, Rhinelander, Wis., 1970-74, mem. firm. O'Melia & Kaye, 1970-74. Dist. atty., Taylor County, Wis., 1944-47, Justice of the Peace, 1941-44, Social Security examiner, 1970-74. Dist. chmn. Boy Scouts Am., 1948-51; sec., dir. Elroy Fair Assn., 1940-44; treas., dir. Taylor County Fair, 1945-51; chmn. Juneau County Tax Payers Assn., 1940-44; exec. sec. Taylor County Park Bd., 1945-47; chmn. Taylor County Sch. Commn., 1947-49; chmn. OPA County Bd., 1945-46. Mem. Wis., Oneida County bar assns. Republican.

Roman Catholic. K.C. Club: Rhinelander Country. Contbr. articles to profl. publs. Home: Rhinelander, Wis. Died Dec. 10, 1974; interred Medford, Wis.

SIMON, WEBSTER GODMAN, ret. univ. dean; b. Cin., Oct. 3, 1892; s. Jacob Weber and Fanny (Godman) S.; A.B., Harvard, 1914, A.M., 1915; Ph.D., U. Chgo., 1918; student U. Cambridge (Eng.), spring 1932; LL.D., Marietta Coll., 1952; m. Agnes Warren, June 22, 1916; 1 dau., Frances Grace. Instr. in math. Harvard, 1915-16; with Western Res. U., Cleve., 1918-61; instr. in math., 1918-20, asst. prof., 1920-24, asso. prof., 1924-26, prof., 1926-61, dean faculties arts and scis., 1936-61, v.p., 1940-61, v.p., dean, prof. emeritus, 1961-74. Mem. library bd., Shaker Heights, 1945-59; trustee Shaker Heights Hist. Soc., 1948-59; treas. Cuyahoga Council League Nursing, 1962-66. Trustee Cuyahoga County Community Coll., 1962-69. Fellow A.A.A.S.; mem. Am. Math. Soc., Math. Assn. Am., Am. Assn. U. Profs., Phi Beta Kappa, Sigma Xi. Methodist (trustee). Contbr. to jours. Home: Cleveland, O. Died Aug. 17, 1974.

SIMONS, MANLEY HALE, naval officer; b. Portland, Me., May 1, 1879; s. Manley Haleand Ruth Theodora (Paine) S.; B.S., U.S. Naval Acad.; grad. U.S. Naval War Coll., 1924; m. Katherine V. Nazro, Oct. 17, 1907; children—Manley Hale, Arthur Evart. Commd. ensign, U.S. Navy, 1903, advancing through the grades to rear adm., 1934, retired 1943; comd. transport Kroonland, World War I; comd. 3d Div., U.S. Battle Fleet; served as dir. of fleet training and chief of staff to Vice Adm. Laning, cruisers, U.S. Fleet; comdt. 5th Naval Dist. and Sea Frontier, during World War II; comdt. navy yard Portsmouth, Va., 1937-41; pres. Simonsdale Corp., 1940-41. Decorated Navy Cross and citation for hazardous duty (World War I), Legion of Merit for German submarine destruction (World War II); awarded medal of valor, Vets. of Foreign Wars, 1943. Mem. Am. Legion. Club: Army and Navy (San Francisco, Calif.). Home: Pasadena, Calif.†

SIMPSON, CHARLES WILLIAM, mfg. exec.; b. Barton, Vt., May 30, 1879; s. Charles and Mary (Bradshaw) S.; student pub. schs.; m. Annie McIver, Sept. 7, 1899. Various positions Fairbanks Scale Co., St. Johnsbury, Vt., F. M. Davis Mining Co., Colo.; in charge steam whistle dept. Walworth Co., South Boston, Mass.; mfr. injectors, valves, whistles Hancock Inspirator & Injector Co., Boston; foreman automatic dept. Windsor (Vt.) Machine Co., 1909-11, European rep., 1911-27, mgr. factory, Windsor, Vt., 1927-33; gen. works mgr. charge mfg. Nat. Acme Co., Cleve., 1933-40, exec. v.p. from 1940, dir., from 1947. Mem. Cleveland C. of C., Am. Ordnance Assn. Mason (32°). Club: Mayfield Country (Cleve.). Home: Shaker Heights, O.†

SIMPSON, CLARENCE OLIVER, dentist; b. Hindsboro, Ill., Sept. 8, 1879; s. Taylor and Elizabeth (Watson) S.; grad. Chicago Coll. Dental Surgery, 1902, Barnes Med. Coll., 1906; m. Gladys Louise Cox, Feb. 16, 1916; children—Taylor Carlyle, Theodore Oliver. Practiced gen. dentistry, 1902-18, dental radiography and diagnosis only, from 1918; prof. dental anatomy, histology and operative dentistry, Barnes Dental Coll., 1903-10; professor radiodontia, Washington University School of Dentistry, 1926-36, professor of radiodontics, from 1945. Awarded Callahan Memorial medal, Ohio State Dental Soc., 1939. Member International College Dentists, American Dental Association, St. Louis Society Dental Science (president, 1910), St. Louis Dental Soc. (pres., 1918), Mo. State Dental Assn. (pres., 1923), Kappa Sigma, Xi Psi Phi, Omicron Kappa Upsilon. Lectured throughout U.S. and Canada. Author: The Technic of Oral Radiography, 1926; Advanced Radiodontic Interpretation, 1932; Toothsome Topics, 1932; Principles and Practice of Radiodontics, 1936; also articles to jours. Club: University. Home: St. Louis, Mo.†

SIMPSON, FLOYD ROBERT, educator; b. Quincy, Ill., May 26, 1906; s. Emmett A. and Ethel (Oakford) S.; A..B., U. Minn., 1933, M.A., 1938, Ph.D., 1943; m. Mildred M. Orlebeke, Aug. 31, 1941; children—Stephen Orlebeke, Robert David, John Douglas. Accounting asst. Mpls. Gas Light Co., 1928-29; revenue accountant, supr. Ill. Bell Telephone Co., 1929-32, 34-36; teaching asst. U. Minn., Mpls., 1936-38, instr., 1938-43; asst. prof. U. Wash., Seattle, 1943-46, asso. prof., 1946-48; prof. Carleton Coll., Northfield, Minn., 1948-49; prof., chmn. div. bus. and econs. Los Angeles State Coll., 1949-65, dean grad. studies, 1961-64; dean Sch. Bus. and Econs., sr. acad. dean Cal. State U., Los Angeles, 1964-72, dean emeritus, prof. econs. Active Boy Scouts Am., P.T.A. Fed. Res. Bank fellow, 1949. Mem. Am. Acad. Mgmt., Am. Econs. Assn., Am. Finance Assn., A.A.A.S., Smithsonian Assos., Los Angeles C. of C. (edn. com.), Western Econ. Assn., Western Assn. Collegiate Schs. Bus. (past pres.), Pi Sigma Epsilon, Alpha Kappa Psi, Beta Gamma Sigma, Phi Chi Theta (hon.). Episcopalian. Contbr. articles and revs. to profl. jours. Home: Glendale, Cal. Died Aug. 30, 1974; buried Little Fork, Minn.

SIMPSON, JAMES ALEXANDER, lawyer; b. McEwen, Tenn., Jan. 28, 1890; s. Alexander Day and Altie (Head) S.; student U. Ark., 1905-06, Hawkins Tng. Sch., Gallatin, Tenn., 1907-09; LL.B., Vanderbilt U., Nashville, 1912; m. Josephine W. Evins, June 8, 1920; 1 son, Joseph Woodward; m. 2d, Florence Evans, Apr. 14, 1928; children—James Evans, Henry Evans. Admitted to Ala. bar, 1912; asso. firm Tillman, Bradley and Morrow, Birmingham, 1912-19; asso. with R. L. Lange, 1919, in organizing firm now named Lange, Simpson, Robinson & Somerville; dir., mem. exec. com. Ingalls Iron Works Co., Black Diamond Coal Mining Co., Exchange Security Bank, First Ala. Bancshares Inc. Chmn. Ala. Personnel Bd., 1972-73. Chmn. judiciary com. Ala. Ho. Reps., 1927-31; chmn. judiciary com. Ala. Senate, 1935-43; chmn. finance and taxation com., Ala. Senate, 1943-47, pres. pro tem, 1943-47; conservative Dem. candidate for U.S. Senate against Lister Hill, 1944; against John Sparkman, 1946. Trustee, Birmingham Mus. Fine Arts, Lyman Ward Mil. Acad., SOS Found. of Jefferson County, Ingalls Found., Eye Found., Vanderbilt U. Served in Mex. Border Mobilization, 1916; in World War I, 1917-18. Fellow Am. Coll. Trial Lawyers, Am. Bar Found.; mem. Am., Birmingham bar assns., Ala. State Bar, Sigma Alpha Epislon, Phi Delta Phi, Omicron Delta Kappa. Omega Alpha Kappa. Presbyn. Clubs: Mountain Brook Country, Exchange, Redstone, Relay House, The Club. Home: Birmingham, Ala. Died July 8, 1973; buried Elmwood Cemetery, Birmingham, Ala.

SIMPSON, JESSE L., state ofcl.; b. Troy, Ill. Jan. 13, 1884; son of George P. and Alice (Greening) S.; grad. Ill. Wesleyan U. Sch. of Law, 1909; m. Ella M. Kriege, July 25, 1914; children—Virginia (Mrs. Gordon Burroughs), David L. Began as telegraph operator, 1902, admitted to Ill. bar, 1909, and since in gen. practice law; city atty., Edwardsville, Ill., 2 terms; master in chancery Circuit Court, 2 terms; former judge of Supreme Ct. of Ill.; mem. Ill. Commerce Commn. from 1953; pres. Edwardsville Bldg. & Loan Assn. Mem. Am., Ill. State, Madison Co. bar assns. Republican. Methodist. Mason, K.P., Modern Woodman. Home: Edwardsville, Ill. Died May 7, 1973.

SIMPSON, JOHN FREDERICK, neurologist; b. Denver, Dec. 18, 1928; s. Elmer and Frances (Hofman) S.; M.D., U. Wis., 1957; m. Harriet Karen Kirchhoff, Aug. 21, 1954; children—Alan Bradford, Douglas Michael. Intern, Boston City Hosp., 1957-58, resident, 1958-59; resident U. Mich. Hosps., Ann Arbor, 1961-64; practice medicine specializing in neurology, Ann Arbor, 1964-75; cons. neurology Wayne County Gen. Hosp., 1963-72, VA Hosp., Ann Arbor, 1964-70; instr. neurology U. Mich. Sch. Medicine, 1964-66, asst. prof., 1966-69, asso. prof., 1969-73. Served to lt., M.C., USNR, 1959-61. Diplomate Am. Bd. Psychiatry and Neurology. Fellow A.C.P.; mem. A.M.A., Am. Acad. Neurology, Soc. for Neurosics., A.A.A.S., Mich. Neurol. Assn., Nu Sigma Nu. Democrat. Episcopalian. Author: (with K.R. Magee) Clinical Evaluation of the Nervous System, 2d edit., 1972. Home: Ann Arbor, Mich. Died Jan. 25, 1973; buried Washtenong Meml. Park, Ann Arbor, Mich.

SIMPSON, JOHN WILLIAM, physician; b. Decatur, Ala., Nov. 18, 1889; A.B., Vanderbilt U., 1910, M.D., 1918; m. Emily Simpson. Intern, St. Thomas Hosp., Nashville, 1917-18; resident St. Christopher's Hosp. for Babies, Bklyn., 1920-21; pvt. practice medicine specializing in Pediatrics, Birmingham, Ala., 1922-65; clin. asso. prof. pediatrics Med. Coll. Ala., 1945-60; mem. staff Baptist Hosps., Children's Hosp., Crippled Children's Clinic, South Highlands Infirmary, St. Vincent's Hosp., Hillman Hosp., Jefferson Hosp.; asso. dir., dir. dept. child health Birmingham Pub. Schs., 1924-65; co-founder, dir. Charlanne Sch., 1936-56; chief med. cons. Cerebral Palsy Center, Spastic Aid Ala., 1948-65; cons. cerebral palsy crippled children's service Ala. Dept. Edn., 1940-73. Mem. Jefferson County Bd. Health, 1931-56, chmn. 5 yrs.; mem. Ala. Bd. Health, 1948-62. Bd. dirs. Ala. Soc. Crippled Children and Adults, United Cerebral Palsy Assns. Ala.; life mem., bd. dirs. Ala. Found. Speech and Hearing; bd. dirs., chmn. sch. com. Ala. Found. to Aid Aphasoid Children; bd. dirs. Jefferson County Children's Aid Soc.; 1st pres., bd. dirs. Jefferson County Health Council. Served as 1st lt. M.C., U.S. Army, 1918-19. Diplomate Am. Bd. Pediatrics. Mem. Am. Acad. Pediatrics (chmn. com. on handicapped children Ala. chpt. 1955-73), A.M.A., Ala. State Med. Assn. (past pres.), Jefferson County Med. Soc. (past pres.), Am. Acad. Cerebral Palsy. Editor, Jour. Jefferson County Med. Soc., 3 yrs.; asso. editor Ala. State Med. Jour., 10 yrs. Home: Birmingham, Ala. Died May 22, 1973.

SIMPSON, LOLA JEAN, author, editor; b. Woodland, Calif., July 20, 1880; d. John Lowrey and Gertrude Ann (Pendegast) S.; A.B., U. of Calif., 1899. Head of English dept., high sch., Woodland; teacher of adult classes, extension div. U. of Calif., 1919-21, editor The Spokesman, extension div. mag., 1921-26; asso. editor Parents' Mag. from 1927. Mem. advisory bd. The Independent Woman (mag. of Nat. Business and Professional Women's Club). Author: Backfire, 1927; Treadmill, 1929. Contbr. to Harper's, Century, The New Yorker, Delineator, etc. Home: New York City, N.Y.†

SIMPSON, WILLIAM ROBERT, electronics co. exec.; b. Omaha, Sept. 30, 1922; s. William L. and Marjorie L. (Baker) S.; student Kan. State U., 1942-43, Stanford, 1943-44; hon. degree, Platte Coll., Columbus, Neb.; m. Dorothy M. Allgood, Nov. 21, 1942; children—Linda (Mrs. Thomas Hennessy), Sandra Fabela, William Robert. Vice pres. Electronic Devel. Co., Omaha, 1946-49; partner K & S Instrument Co., Omaha, 1949-52; pres. J.A. Batson Corp., Omaha, 1952-53; with Dale Electronics, Inc., Columbus, 1953-75, pres., 1962-75, also dir.; pres. Dale Electronics Can. Ltd., Welwyn Can. Ltd.; dir. Lionel Corp. Bd. dirs. Behlen Community Hosp., Columbus, Columbus Conv. Center. Served with Signal Corps, AUS, 1942-45. Decorated Bronze Star medal. Mem. U.S., Columbus chambers commerce, Neb. Assn. Commerce and Industry, Young Pres.'s Orgn., Am. Mgmt. Assn., Electronic Industry Assn., Am. Def. Preparedness Assn., Am. Legion, V.F.W. Mason (Shriner). Club: Elks Country (Columbus). Home: Columbus, Neb. Died Jan. 22, 1975.

SIMS, WALTER ARTHUR, ex-mayor; b. Dawson County, Ga., Sept. 19, 1880; s. John Newton and Susan (Groover) S.; spl. course in science, Hunter's Sch., Atlanta; LL.B., U. of Ga., 1899; m. Edna Cheshire, Jan. 7, 1903; children—Lowry A., Hal. W., Evelyn. Began law practice at Atlanta, 1899; member City Council, Atlanta, 1921-22; mayor of Atlanta, 1923-26; mem. State Senate, Ga., 1933-34. Democrat. Baptist. Mason, Odd Fellow, K.P., Elk. Home: Atlanta, Ga.†

SINDELAR, PAUL JOSEPH, physician; b. Cleve., Sept. 5, 1929; s. Frank John and Rose J. (Nemecek) S.; M.D., St. Louis U., 1955; m. Nancy Reifke, June 1, 1957; children—Ann, Eileen, Mark, Mary, Ellen, John, Molly, James. Intern, St. Luke's Hosp., Cleve., 1955-56; resident Cleve. Clinic Hosp., 1956-60; chief obstetrics and gynecology St. Alexis Hosp. Cleve., 1970-71. Dir. First Fed. Savs. & Loan, Cleve. Active March of Dimes, Cancer Soc., Right ot Life. Served to capt. M.C., AUS, 1960-62. Diplomate Am. Bd. Obstetrics and Gynecology. Fellow Am. Coll. Obstetrics and Gynecology, A.C.S.; mem. A.M.A., Ohio State Med. Assn., Linacre Soc., Cleve. Acad. Medicine (dir. 1973-74). Train Collectors Soc., Nat. Wildlife Soc. Republican. Roman Catholic. K.C. Home: Shaker Heights, O. Died May 7, 1974; buried Calvary Cemetery, Cleveland. O.

SINGER, HENRY B, lawyer; b. Carbondale, Pa., Oct. 21, 1873; s. Samuel and Dorothea (Bergman) S.; Ph.B., N.Y.U., 1895, LL.B., 1896; m. Frances Moses, June 29, 1904; 1 dau., Joan (Mrs. Charles A. Weil). Admitted to N.Y. bar, 1897; mem. Stern, Singer & Barr, 1900-10; pvt. practice, 1910-20; mem. Moses & Singer, from 1920 (all N.Y. City); dir. Ivers-Lee Co. Mem. Am., N.Y. State bar assns., N.Y. Co. Lawyers Assn. Mason. Clubs: Harmonie, Lawyers, North Shore Country. Home: New York City, N.Y.†

SINGER, RUSSELL E., assn. exec.; b. Yatesville, Pa., May 29, 1897; s. Wilson L. and Mary (Fitzgerald) S.; m. Ruth S. Wilson, June 19, 1920; m. 2d, Edith Hand, Dec., 1964; m. 3d, Gladys Montgomery, June, 1975. With U.S. C. of C., 1920-24; with Am. Automobile Assn., 1924-65, exec. v.p., 1936-65; dir. Am. Security and Trust Co., Washington. Served AUS, 1918-19. Decorated Knight Royal Order of Vasa (Sweden), Knight Order of Dannebrog (Denmark). Home: Chevy Chase, Md. Died Sept. 14, 1975.

SINGH, RAJA SIR MAHARAJ, U.N. official; b. Punjab, India, May 17, 1878; s. Raja Sir Harman Singh and P. Golaknath; student Harrow Sch., England, Balliol Coll., Oxford, 1896-1900; barrister, Middle Temple, London; m. Gunwati Mayadas, Feb. 13, 1918; children—Ranbir Singh, Mahindar Singh, Premkaur. Prime Minister, Jodhpur, 1931-32; high commr. to S. Africa, 1932-35; mem. United Provinces govt., 1935-37; mem. United Provinces Legislative Assembly, 1937-45; vice chancellor, Lucknow U., 1943; mem. United Provinces Legislative Council, 1946; del. to U.N., 1946. Featherweight boxer for Oxford, Cambridge, 1899; won 50 tennis cups in All-India tournaments; capt. Balliol football XI. Anglican Ch. Home: Lucknow, India.†

SINGLEY, ALBERT HENRY, dentist, farmer; b. Moulton, Ia., Dec. 27, 1905; s. George Adam and Eva (Barnes) S.; D.D.S., State U. Ia., 1929, postgrad., 1931-32; postgrad. U. Cin., 1929-30, State U. Minn., 1951; m. Ruth Irma Zeigler, Aug. 5, 1933; children—Colleen Dolores (Mrs. Charles John Pinkerton), Nancy Kay (Mrs. John Gilbert Martin). Gen. practice dentistry, Victor, Ia., 1930-31, Fairfield, Ia., 1931-71; farm owner-mgr., 1943-67. Practitioner, U.S. Soil Conservation Commn., Washington and Jefferson County, Ia., 1947-67. Dental health chmn. Jefferson County, Ia. Dept. Health, 1935-65; dental cons. Jefferson County Hosp., Van Buren County Hosp. Mem. Am., Ia. (past pres. S.E. Dist., past program chmn. Ia. Conv.) dental assns., Am. Hereford Assn., Ia. Hist. Soc., Geneal. Soc. Des Moines. Republican. Methodist. Mason (Shriner), Elk, Lion (past pres.). Club: Walton (Fairfield). Home: Fairfield, Ia. Died Jan. 19, 1974; interred Evergreen Cemetery, Fairfield, Ia.

SIONS, HARRY, editor; b. Phila., Feb. 20, 1906; s. Simon and Rebecca (Anthony) S.; B.A., U. Pa., 1928; m. Louise Lux, Aug. 14, 1947. Editor Salute mag., 1945-46; with Holiday mag., 1946-64, sr. editor, 1949-57, editorial dir., 1957-64; sr. editor Little, Brown and Co., N.Y.C., 1965-74. Seminar lectr. various colls. and univs., also symposium participant on journalism and editor-writer relationships various univs., mem. nat. adv. bd. William E. Wiener Oral History Library of Am. Jewish Com., N.Y.C. Served with AUS, 1942-45; combat corr., mng. editor Italian edit. Yank mag. Decorated Bronze Star; Cavaliere Ufficiale dell 'Ordine al Merito della Republica Italia, 1961. Mem. Phila. Art Alliance, Rosenbach Found. Mus., Library Co. of Phila., Hist. Soc. Pa., Friends of Library of U. Pa. Clubs: Franklin Inn, Philobiblon (Phila). Home: Philadelphia, Pa. Died Mar. 26, 1974.

SIPPLE, LESLIE B, educator; b. near Mexico, Mo., Sept. 19, 1880; s. Lewis Harper and Nannie Reiley (Mildred) S.; B.Ped., State Teachers Coll., Kirksville, Mo., 1911, B.S. in Edn., 1914; student Kan. State Agrl. Coll., 1914; A.M., Columbia, 1929; student U. of Calif., summer 1937, U. of Washington, Seattle, summer 1940; LL.D., Southwestern Coll., Winfield, Kansas, 1941; m. Jessie Maxwell, Apr. 27, 1904; children—Lewis Maxwell, Anna Mary (Mrs. Lee Hunt). Rural school teacher, 1898; prin. Kirksville, Mo., 1901-07; county supt. of schs., Adair County, Mo., 1907-14; mem. faculty State Teachers Coll., Kirksville, Mo., 1914-16, State Teachers Coll., Kearney, Neb., 1916-19; prof. of edn. and dean, State Teachers Coll., Aberdeen, S.D., 1919-28; instr. in sch. adminstrn., State Agrl. Coll., Fort Collins, Colo., summers 1925, 26, 27; prof. of edn. and dean Coll. of Edn., dir. summer sessions, U. of Wichita (Kan.), 1929-1950; dir. spl. edns. Kan State Dept. Pub. Instrn. Mem. Laymen's Foreign Missions Research Staff in India and Burma, 1930-31; mem. N.E.A., Kan. State Teachers Assn., Nat. and State Vocational Guidance Assns., Kan. Assn. Coll. Deans, Am. Assn. School Adminstrs., Nat. Assn. Coll. Teacher Placement Officers, Kan. Assn. Coll. Teachers of Edn., American Association University Professors, Kappa Delta Pi. Methodist. Author: Education in India, 1931; Education in Burma, 1931. Home: Topeka, Kan.†

SIQUEIROS, DAVID ALFARO, painter, b. Mexico City, Mexico, 1896; student Escuela Nacional de Bellas Artes, also schs. in Spain, France, Italy, 1917-22, Officer Carranza's Army, 1910-16; mil. attache, Paris, 1917; editor Vida Americana, Spain; sec.-gen. Sindicato de Pentores, also editor house organ El Machte; organizer with Amado de la Cueva, Alianza de Obreros Pintores, Guadalajara, 1925; founder Federacion Minera de Jalesco; rep. various Mexican workers' orgns. to Russia, 1928, del. workers' meetings in S.A., 1929; polit. exile, 1931; prof. Chouinard Sch. Art, Los Angeles, 1932-33; developed method for use air brushes to apply paint to outdoor murals; del. Congress Mexican Artists to Congress Revolutionary Artists, N.Y.C., 1936; established art sch., N.Y.C., 1936; prin. works include fresco Chouinard Sch. Art, Plapa Art Center, Los Angeles, Mus. Modern Art, N.Y.C., Museo de Sao Paulo, Museo de Rio De Janeiro; murals in Bellas Artes, Hosp. de la Raza, Centro Medico; Museo de Historia, Castillo de Chapultepec, Escuela Nacional Preparatoria, U. Gudalajara (all Mex.) also in Argentina, Chile, Cuba. Served with Spanish Republican Army, 1937. Contbr. articles on art Mexican, European, South American periodicals. Home: Cuernavaca, Mexico. Died Jan. 6, 1972.

SISAM, CHARLES HERSCHEL, mathematician; b. Cedar Rapids, Ia., Sept. 8, 1879; s. Herschel and Alice (Lincoln) S.; B.A., U. of Mich., 1902; M.A., Cornell U., 1903, Ph.D., 1906; studied Göttingen, Germany and Turin, Italy; m. Cora Anna Hutton (A.B., U. of Ill.), June 27, 1906; 1 dau., Cora Lowell. Instr. mathematics, U.S. Naval Acad., 1904-06; instr. mathematics, 1906-07, asso., 1907-09, asst. prof., 1909-18, U. of Ill.; prof. mathematics, Colorado Coll., from 1918. Mem. Am. Math. Soc. Math. Assn. America, Colo. Ednl. Assn., Sigma Xi, Phi Beta Kappa, Delta Epsilon. Republican. Conglist. Clubs: Winter Night, Kiwanis. Author: Analytic Geometry of Space, Analytic Geometry, College Algebra, Introduction to College Mathematics, Concise Analytic Geometry. Contbr. numerous research papers in mathematics, particularly on algebraic surfaces. Asso. editor Trans. Am. Math. Soc., 1930-36; asst. editor Econometrica, 1936. Home: Hyattsville, Md.†

SJÖQVIST, ERIK, classical archaeologist; b. Ronneby, Sweden, July 15, 1903; s. John August and Maria (von Hermansson) S.; A.B., Uppsala U.., 1923, A.M., 1926, Ph.D., 1940; m. Gurli Wallbom, Aug. 10, 1941. Came to U.S., 1951. Mem. Swedish Archaeol. Expdn. to Greece, 1926, field dir. Mission to Cyprus, 1927-31; librarian Royal Library, Stockholm, 1933-39; asso. prof. classical archaeology U. Stockholm, 1940-50; dir. Swedish Archaeol. Inst. in Rome, 1940-48; pvt. sec. to H.R.H. The Crown Prince of Sweden, 1949-50, H.M. The King of Sweden, 1950-51, keeper King's book collection, 1951; vis. prof. Princeton, 1948-49, prof. classical archaeology from 1951. Decorated Comdr. North Star (Sweden); Comdr. Crown of Italy; Order British Empire. Fellow Swedish Archaeol. Soc.; mem. Internat. Assn. Classical Archaeology Rome, Italian Accademia del Lincei. Author: The Swedish Cyprus Expedition, Vol. I, II, 1934-36; Problems of the Late Cypriote Bronze Age, 1940; Roman Historical and Topographical Studies (in Italian), 1946; Rome through the Centuries (with H. Schuck), 1949. Home: Princeton, N.J. Died July 16, 1975.

SKAUG, ARNE, economist, Norwegian diplomat; b. Horten, Norway, Nov. 6, 1906; Econs. degree Oslo U., 1930, London Sch. Econ. m. Ingegerd Gimse, 1949. With Central Bur. Statistics, 1930-39; Rockefeller Found. fellow, U.S.A., 1939-41; mgr. Norwegian Govt. Service, N.Y., 1941-44; staff Norwegian Ministry Supply, London, 1943-44; comml. counsellor Norwegian embassy, Washington, 1944-46; dir. Central Bur. Statistics, Oslo, 1946-48; under-sec. state Fgn. Ministry, 1948-49; permanent del. for Norway, OEEC, Paris, 1949; permanent rep. NATO Council, Paris, 1953-55; minister commerce and shipping, 1955-62; ambassador to U.K., also Ireland, 1962-68, Denmark, 1968-74. Decorated knight Grand Cross Royal Victorian Order; knight grand cross Star Order St. Olav. Address: Copenhagen, Denmark. Died Mar. 4, 1974.

SKAUG, JULIUS, lawyer; b. Beltrami, Minn., Jan. 1, 1881; s. Richard M. and Marie (Johnson) S.; student State Tchrs. Coll., 1901-04, U. Minn., 1907-08; m. Emma T. Loe, Oct. 10, 1910; 1 dau., Norna T. (Mrs. Arthur A. Mosher). Supt. schs., Lake Park, Minn., 1904-07; admitted to bar, Minn., 1908, S.D., 1911; practiced in Mpls., 1908-11, Ipswich, St. D., 1911-18, Mobridge, S.D., from 1913; mem. Morrison & Skaug, from 1923; county judge Edmunds Co., 1914-18. President of Mobridge Board of Education, 1919-25. Member of the Greater South Dakota Assn. (dir. 1930-36), Am., S.D. State (pres. 1952-53) bar assns., State Hist. Soc. Republican. Conglist. Mason (Shriner); mem. Order Eastern Star. Club: Rotary (dist. gov. 1945-46). Home: Mobridge, S.D.†

SKINNER, CHARLES H(ENRY), univ. prof.; b. Tipton County, Ind., Apr. 9, 1889; s. Benjamin Franklin and Mary (King) S.; A.B., Ind. U., 1913, Ph.D., 1925; M.S., State U. of Ia., 1916; m. Alma Snow Boots, Sept. 1, 1915; children—Charles Henry, Frank Edward. Instr. physics, DePauw U., Greencastle, Ind., 1913-15, Wash. U., St. Louis, 1915-18; asso. prof. physics, Ohio Wesleyan U., 1918-26; prof. physics, Marquette U., 1926-43; acting prof. physics, Ind. U., 1943-46; acting prof. math. Purdue U., 1946-49. Republican Methodist. Mem. Phi Beta Kappa, Sigma Xi, Pi Mu Epsilon, Acacia. Home: Lebanon, Ind. Died May 8, 1974.

SKINNER, DAVID WILLIAM, camera co. exec.; b. Chgo., Oct. 13, 1902; s. Robert Andrew and Elizabeth-Hannah (Williams) S.; S.B., Mass. Inst. Tch., 1923; m. Isabelle Kingston Burbank, Aug. 26, 1939. Mfg. supt. Gen. Electric Co., Lynn, Mass., 1924-35, Schenectady, 1935-36, Bridgeport, Conn., 1936-40, Phila., 1940-42; gen. factory mgr. SKF Industries, Inc., Phila., 1942-44; mfg. mgr. Polaroid Corp., Cambridge, Mass., 1945-49, asst. gen. mgr., 1949-56, v.p., 1952-69, gen. mgr., 1956-69, vice chmn., 1969-74, dir., 1951-74. Mem. adv. com. Nichols Coll., Dudley, Mass.; mem. alumni council, class agt. Mass. Inst. Tech., Cambridge. Bd. dirs. Newton (Mass.) YMCA. Mem. Cambridge C. of C. (past pres., dir.). Home: Waban, Mass. Died Nov. 16, 1974.

SKINNER, JAMES M(ORTIMER), JR., Corp. exec.; b. Phila., Nov. 19, 1914; s. James M. and Florence (Sayre) S.; student Penn. Charter Sch., 1925-32, U. Pa., 1932-34; m. Eleanor Oakes, Nov. 27, 1936; children—Patricia Florence, Mary Oakes. Joined Philco Corp., Phila., 1934, v.p. distribution 1952-55, v.p. TV div., 1955, pres., 1956-61; dir. First Pa. Banking and Trust Co. Trustee U. Pa. Home: Philadelphia, Pa. Died Feb. 19 1974. buried West Laurel Hill Cemetery, Phila.

SKOGH, HARRIET MATHILDA, librarian; b. Moline, Ill., Mar. 16, 1881; d. Peter and Hulda (Munson) Skogh; grad. high sch., Moline, 1898; studied Wis. Summer Library Sch., Ia. Summer Library Sch.; LL.B., Lincoln Coll. of Law, Springfield, Ill., 1922. Asst. librarian Moline Pub. Library, 1898-1914; with Ill. State Library, from 1914, as cataloguer until 1917, reference librarian, 1917-21, supt. gen. division, 1921-40, chief of general reference, from 1940. Admitted to bar of Illinois, 1924. Member A.L.A., Illinois Library Association (pres. 1925-27), Wis. Library Sch. Assn. (asso.), Special Libraries Assn., Abraham Lincoln Assn. Ill. State Hist. Soc., Nat. Association State Libraries (pres. 1930-31), Lincoln Coll. of Law Alumni Assn., Ill. League of Women Voters, Pi Gamma Mu, Vachel Lindsay Association. Conglist. Club: Springfield Woman's. Home: Springfield, Ill.*†

SKOOG, BERTIL O., brewery exec.; b. 1914; B.B.A., U. Chgo., 1936. With Jos. Schlitz Brewing Co., Milw., 1948-75, asst. controller, 1957-64, asst. sec., 1964-69, treas., asst. sec., 1969-75. C.P.A., Ill. Died Apr. 23, 1975.

SKORNECK, ALAN BERNARD, physician; b. Morristown, N.J., Feb. 1, 1917; s. Jack and Rose (Scheier) S.; M.D., U. Minn., 1943; m. Bernice Greenberg, July 9, 1949; children—Ansel Jeffrey, Carolyn. Intern, Queens Gen. Hosp., Jamaica, N.Y., 1944; med. intern Peter Bent Brigham Hosp., Boston, 1945; asst. resident in medicine Yale, New Haven, 1945-46, Nat. Cancer Inst. trainee in radiology, 1947, asst. resident in radiology, 1948-49; asst. resident in roentgenology Montefiore Hosp., N.Y.C., 1946; chief dept. radiology VA Hosp., Newington, Conn., 1950-53, VA Hosp., West Haven, Conn., 1953-58; radiologist Imperial Hosp., Inglewood, Cal., Washington Hosp., Mar. Vista, Cal.; asst. in medicine Yale Coll. Medicine, 1945-46, clin. instr. in radiology, asst. in radiology, 1947-48, asst. clin. prof., 1951-58; asst. clin. prof. radiology U. Cal. at Los Angeles, 1958-72, asso. clin. prof., 1972-74. Served to 1st lt., M.C., AUS, 1944-45. Diplomate Am. Bd. Radiology. Mem. A.M.A., Am. Coll. Radiology, Phi Delta Epsilon. Jewish religion. Home: Rancho Palos Verdes, Cal. Died Apr. 28, 1974; buried San Pedro, Cal.

SKUCE, WALTER CHARLES, govt. cons.; b. Ottawa, Ont., Can., Dec. 1, 1904; s. Daniel and Sarah (Bickerton) S.; student Ottawa Collegiate Inst., 1918-23; m. Ruth Ann Shafer, Sept. 29, 1928; 1 son, Richard Alan. Came to U.S., 1923, naturalized 1938. Worked on mfg. methods, various divs., Gen. Electric Co., Schenectady, 1923-42,, supr. inventory control, 1937-42; mgr. transp. products div. Owens-Corning Fiberglas Corp., Toledo, 1945-52, adminstr. sales research and devel., also mgr. residential bldg. materials div., 1952-55, exec. dir. govt. services, 1965-67, cons., 1967-69; cons, exec. office Pres. U.S., 1969-73. Dir. controlled materials plan div. and dep. vice chmn. operations WPB, Washington, 1942-45; asst. to dir. of prodn. Nat. Security Resources Bd., 1948; asst. adminstrn. prodn. controls NPA, Wahsington, 1950-51; dir. Econ. Policy Assn.; v.p., hon. dir. U.S. Exposition of Sci. and Industry. Mem. Am. Ordnance Assn. (chmn. priorities and allocations sect., dep. dir. moblzn. readiness div.). Episcopalian. Clubs: Kenwood Golf and Country; Metropolitan (Washington). Author: Control of Industrial Inventory, 1945; Effective Formanship, 1941; chpt. in yearbook Nat. Assn. Cost Accountants, 1938. Home: Kenwood, Md. Died May 29, 1973.

SLATE, WILLIAM L., agronomist; b. Norwalk, O., Jan. 15, 1884; s. William L. and Orpha F. (Norris) S.; B.Sc., Ohio State U., 1909; m. Edna E. Jackson, June 16, 1915; 1 dau., Jeanne Marian. Asst. agronomist New Hampshire U., 1909-11; agronomist U. of Maine, 1911-13; agronomist Storrs Agrl. Expt. Sta., 1913-23; dir. Com. Agrl. Expt. Sta., at New Haven, 1923-48, emeritus; dir. Storrs Agrl. Expt. Sta., at U. of Conn.; lecturer soils (prof.), Yale Sch. Forestry; consultant Agr. Expt. Sta., Puerto Rio, 1948-49. Chmn. State Planning Bd., 1934-37. Fellow A.A.A.S., Am. Soc. Agronomy; mem. Sigma Xi, Alpha Gamma Rho. Congilst. Club: Graduate. Author or joint author of various bulletins and papers in fields of soil and crop science, especially pastures. Home: Hamden, Conn. Died Jan. 27, 1974.

SLATTERY, JOHN LAWRENCE, lawyer; b. Flemington, N.J., Sept. 2, 1878; s. Michael and Margaret (Purcell) S.; Ph.B., Lafayette Coll., 1901; student New York Law Sch.; m. Lear E. Humphrey, Feb. 14, 1906. Began practice in N.D., 1903; moved to Mont., 1904; co. atty., Valley County, Mont., 1907-08 and 1913-14; mem. Mont. Senate, term 1919-23; U.S. atty. Dist. of Mont., 1921-26. Republican. Mem. Delta Kappa Epsilon, K.C. Home: Great Falls, Mont.†

SLECHTA, MARY ROSE, physician; b. Liberal, Kan., Sept. 8, 1938; d. Joe F. and Rose (Slehofer) Slechta; B.A., Southwestern Coll., 1961; M.D., U. Tenn., 1965. Intern Bapt. Meml. Hosp., Memphis, 1965-66; resident psychiatry U. Tenn., 1966-69; psychiatrist Larned (Kan.) State Hosp., 1969-70, Tenn. Psychiat. Hosp. and Inst., Memphis, 1971-73. Teaching asst. in chemistry Southwestern Coll., 1959-60, Okla. U., 1960-61. Recipient Order of Mound, Southwestern Coll., 1961. Mem. Alpha Omega Alpha. Methodist. Club: International (Memphis). Home: Memphis, Tenn. Died May 1973.

SLEETER, RICHARD L., physician; b. Rockford, Ia., 1916; M.D., Washington U., St. Louis, 1943; m. Isabel Sleeter; children—Richard L., Carolyn. Intern Salt Lake County Hosp., Salt Lake City, 1944, asst. resident in pediatrics, 1944, resident, 1944-46; prof. pediatrics, asst. dean Med. Sch., dir. crippled children's div. U. Ore. Served to capt. M.C., AUS, 1946-47. Diplomate Am. Bd. Pediatrics. Mem. A.M.A., Am. Acad. Pediatrics, North Pacific Pediatrics Soc. Home: Portland, Ore. Died Aug. 22, 1972; buried Portland, Ore.

SLICHTER, ALLEN MCKINNON, steel co. exec.; b. Madison, Wis., Feb. 18, 1898; s. Charles Sumner and Mary Louise (Bryne) S.; B.S., U. Wis., 1918; LL.D., U. Wis., Milw., 1969, m. Dorothy Lillian Fritsch, July 9, 1921; children—Marjorie Ann (Mrs. John N. Dickinson), Donald Allen. With Stowell Co., South Milwaukee, Wis., 1920-25; with Pelton Steel Casting Co., Milw., 1925-74, pres., 1947-62, chmn. bd., 1962-74, also dir.; dir. Dickten Masch Mfg. Co. Bd. dirs. Mt. Mary Coll., Greater Milw. Com., U. Wis. Found., St. Francis Hosp., Milw., St. Catherine Residence, Milw., Mt. Mary Coll. Found. Served as ensign USNRF, 1918-19. Recipient Pro Urbe award Mt. Mary Coll., 1972. Mem. Am. Foundrymens Soc. (v.p. 1962, pres. 1963), Steel Founders Soc. Am. (dir. 1953, pres. 1964-65; Lorenz medal 1956), Phi Beta Kappa, Alpha Kappa Psi, Chi Phi. Clubs: Milwaukee, University, Town (Milw.); Madison (Wis.). Home: Milwaukee, Wis. Died Aug. 30, 1974.

SLINGLAND, GEORGE KUETT, lawyer; b. Peterson, N.J., Nov. 6, 1895; s. Charles and Mary Frances (Ryerson) S.; LL.B., N.Y. Law Sch., 1916; m. Charlotte

M. Whiteman, Apr. 26, 1922; children—Carolyn M. (Mrs. James W. Truitt), Nancy A. (Mrs. Fiske Field), George W. Admitted to N.J. bar, 1916, practiced in Paterson; partner Slingland, Bernstein & van Hartogh; judge Municipal Ct., Glen Rock, N.J., 1932-34; chmn. adv. bd. Pompton Lakes office of First Nat. Bank Passaic County, N.J. Chmn. bd. trustees YMCA No. Passaic Valley; trustee Ocean Grove (N.J.) Camp Meeting Assn. Mem. Passaic County Bar Assn. Methodist (trustee, pres. bd. 1939-61). Clubs: Rotary, Paterson Y's Men's. Home: Glen Rock, N.J. Died Nov. 19, 1974; buried Laurel Grove Cemetery, Totowa, N.J.

SLOAN, HUBERT JOHN, ret. educator assn. exec.; b. Nauvoo, Ill., May 28, 1903; s. William Finley and Myrtle (Cannon) S.; B.S., U. Ill., 1926, M.S., 1927; PhD., Cornell U., 1929; student U. Chgo., 1944; m. Dorothy Howe Wilson, July 30, 1931; m. 2d. Margaret Canfield, December 28, 1960. Asst. poultry husbandry U. Ill., Champaign, 1929-31, asso., 1931-36; prof. poultry husbandry U. Minn., 1936-48, prof., chief div. poultry husbandry, 1948-52, dir. agrl. exptl. sta., 1953-66, asso. dean Inst. Agr., 1966-70, acting dean Inst. Agr., 1973-74, dean Coll. Agr., 1970-71, emeritus, 1971. Mem. Poultry Sci. Assn. (dir. 1950-55, pres. 1952-53), A.A.A.S., World's Poultry Sci. Assn., Sigma Xi, Gamma Sigma Delta, Phi Sigma, Phi Zeta, Alpha Zeta, Alpha Gamma Rho. Home: St. Paul, Minn. Died May 1, 1974.

SLOAN, MARY HERRON, (Mrs. Thomas Patrick Sloan, Jr.), journalist; b. Monongahela, Pa., July 22, 1915; d. Donald James and Catherine Procia (Downer) Herron; B.S. in Journalism, Ohio U., 1937; m. Thomas Patrick Sloan, Jr., Sept. 5, 1938; children—Thomas Patrick III (dec.), Samuel Downer, Catherine Jo (Mrs. Molter). With advt. dept. Monongahela (Pa.) Daily Rep., 1937-38; news writer Radio WALR, Zanesville, O., 1938-39; feature writer, Mon Valley corr. Washington (Pa.) Observer, 1937-55; news desk Charleroi (Pa.) Mail, 1955-59; make-up editor Clairton (Pa.) Progress, 1966-67; editor Elizabeth (Pa.) Herald, 1962-67, Monongahela Key News, 1959-61. Sec., Washington (Pa.) Art Assn., 1969-72; pres. Monongahela Hist. Soc., 1966-72; mem. Monongahela Hosp. Woman's Assn. Bd. dirs., field rep. Am. Cancer Soc., Washington, 1967-71. Bd. dirs. Arts Council Washington County; sec. bd. dirs. Washington-Greene County Tourist Promotion Agy., Washington County Landmarks and Historic Sites Found. Mem. Needlework Guild Am. (br. pres. 1965-69). Episcopalian. Clubs: Valley Art (pres.), Monongahela Valley Country, Friday Conversational (1st v.p. 1969). Author: First 50 Years of Monongahela 1769-1819, 1969. Home: Monongahela, Pa., Died Apr. 2, 1974.

SLOANE, WILLIAM, (MILLIGAN, III), book publisher; b. Plymouth, Mass., Aug. 15, 1906; s. Joseph Curtis and Julia Larned (Moss) S.; grad. The Hill Sch., 1925; A.B., Princeton, 1929; m. Julia Hawkins, Sept. 8, 1930; children—William Curtis, Jessie Miranda (Mrs. John E. Steely, Jr.), Julie Ann (Mrs. Peter Polymenakos). In play dept. Longmans, Green & Co., N.Y.C., 1929-31, editor dept., 1931; mgr. Fitzgerald Pub. Co., 1932-37; asso. editor Farrar & Rinehart, 1937-38, mgr. trade dept. Henry Holt & Co., 1939-46, v.p., 1944-46; pres. William Sloane Assos., Inc. 1946-52; editorial dir. Funk & Wagnalls Co. and Wilfred Funk, Inc., 1952-55; dir. Rutgers Univ. Press, 1955-74. Dir. Council on Books in Wartime; chmn. editorial com. Armed Services Edits. Emissary Book Pub. Bur. and U.S. O.W.I. to China, 1943-44; rep. Book Pubs. Com. sent to Germany, 1948; exec. com. Assn. Am. U. Presses, 1961-62, v.p., 1966-67, pres., 1969-70; staff Bread Loaf Writers Conf., 1944-72; mem. Govt. Adv. Com. on Library Programs, 1967-70; chmn. lit. com. Commn. on Arts in N.J., 1966; chmn. pub. com. Assn. Press, 1969-73, Phi Beta Kappa. Clubs: Publishers Lunch, Princeton Charter, Players (N.Y.C.) Author: To Walk the Night, 1937: The Edge of Running Water, 1939. Editor: Space, Space, Space, 1953; Stories for Tomorrow, 1954. Home: New York City, N.Y. Died Sept. 24, 1974.

SLOBODKIN, LOUIS, sculptor, author, illustrator; b. Albany, N.Y., Feb. 19, 1903; s. Nathan and Dora (Lubin) S.; educated Beaux Arts Inst. Design, N.Y.C., 1918-23; m. Florence Gersh, Sept. 27, 1927; children—Larry, Michael. Collaborating sculptor in various studios both in U.S. and abroad, 1931-35; head of sculptor dept., Master Inst. of United Arts, Roerich Mus., 1934-37; instr. of sculpture, Sch. Art League class, 1935-36. Awarded commission for Post Office Bldg., Washington, D.C.; executed Tropical Postman in aluminum, 1935; 2 panels Madison Sq. Post Office, N.Y.C., 1936; models for stone carving, Memorial Tower, Phila. 2 granite eagles for Johnstown, Pa., 1937; awarded competition for Federal Bldg., N.Y. World's Fair, 1938; executed statue of Lincoln, Symbol of Unity, for Federal Bldg. garden, 1939; bronze statue, Young Abe Lincoln, for Interior Bldg., Washington, 1939; head of sculpture div. N.Y. City Art Project, 1941-42; 2 panels in sandstone for North Adams, Mass. Lectures at museums. Mem. exec. bd. Sculptor's Guild, An Am. Group (pres.); mem. Nat. Schulptor's Soc. Municipal Arts Soc., Am. Inst. Graphic Arts (chmn. artists com.). Has exhibited in all important museums of U.S. Recipient many awards and honors. Illustrator numerous books. Author: Sculpture Principles and Practice, 1949; Bixxy and the Secret Message, 1949; Mr. Mushroom, 1950; Our Friendly Friends, 1951; Dinny, 1951; The Space Ship Under the Apple Tree, 1952; Circus April 1st, 1953; Mr. Petersands Cats, The Horse With the High Heeled Shoes, 1954; The Amiable Giant, 1955; Millions and Millions, 1955; Little Mermaid Who Could Not Sing, 1956; One is Good, 1956; Melvin the Moose Child, 1957; The Space Ship Returns, 1958; The First Book of Drawing, 1958; Trick or Treat, 1959; Excuse Me, 1959; Up High, 1960; Gogo, 1960; Nomi and the Lovely Animals, 1960; A Good Place to Hide, 1961; Picco, 1961; The Three-Seated Spaceship, 1962; The Late Cuckoo, 1962; Luigi and the Long-Nosed Soldier, 1963; Moon Blossom and the Golden Penny, 1963; The Polka Goat, 1964; Yasu and the Strangers, 1965; Colette and the Princess, 1965; Read about the Policemen, 1966; Read about the Postman, 1966; Read about the Fireman, 1967; Read about the Busman, 1967; Round Trip Spaceship, 1968; Wilbur the Warrior, 1971; Spaceship in the Park, 1972; verse and drawings TV prodn. Carnival of the Animals (Saint-Saen), 1974. Home: Bay Harbor Islands, Fla. Died May 8, 1975; buried Lakeside Meml. Cemetery, Miami, Fla.

SMALL, FRANCIS ALOYSIUS, clergyman; b. Milford, Mass., Feb. 25, 1916; s. James Gerard and Mary (Birmingham) S.; A.B., Boston Coll., 1940. M.A., 1943; Ph.L., Weston Coll., 1941; S.T.L., 1947; M.S., Columbia, 1956. Ordained priest Roman Catholic Ch., 1946; instr. European history Fairfield (Conn.) U., 1948-51, asst. prof., 1951-53, asso. prof., 1953-63, head dept. history, govt., 1951-63, head librarian, 1952-74, coordinator div. social scis., 1953-63, mem. corp., 1963-74. Mem. research adv. com. Conn. State Library, 1965; mem. Gov's Com. on Libraries, 1961-62. Mem. Am., New Eng., Conn., Catholic library assns., Beta Phi Mu. Club: International Torch. Home: Fairfield, Conn. Died Jan. 28, 1974.

SMALL, FRANK, JR., congressman; b. Temple Hills, Md., July 15, 1896; s. Frank and Annie Amelia (Norris) S.; student pub. schs.; m. Grace Gwynn, Aug. 15, 1915; children—Anna Grace, Frank. With Clinton Bank since 1923, pres. since 1928; automobile dealer, Frank Small, Jr., Inc., Anacostia, D.C., since 1929; Frank Small, Jr., Inc., Capitol Hill, Washington, from 1938; dir. Nat. Capital Bank, Washington, Washington Petroleum Products Corp.; mem. 83d Congress, 5th Dist. Md. Mem. Washington Board Trade, Washington Automotive Trade Assn. (dir.), Nat. Assn. State Racing Commrs. (national pres. 1951-52). Republican. Club: South Gate Lions (Prince Georges Co.). Home: Clinton, Md. Died Oct. 24, 1973.

SMALL, SERGINE ANNE (MRS. DONALD DAVID SMALL), educator; b. Chgo., Jan. 28, 1949; s. Alfred Rapp and Erma Alice (King) Oliver; B.S. in Edn., Ind. U., 1969; M.Ed., U. Toledo, 1971; m. Donald David Small, June 6, 1970. Tchr. English, Crete (Ill.)-Monee High Sch., 1969-70; instr. karate Prairie State Coll., Chicago Heights, Ill., 1970; tchr. English, McCord Jr. High Sch., Sylvania, O., 1970-71, Whitmer High Sch., Toledo, 1971; dir. karate programs U. Toledo, 1970. Bd. dirs. Am. Karate System; bd. govs. Amateur Athletic Union, 1973. 1st chmn. nat. women's karate com. 1973. Recipient Women of Toledo award, 1974. Mem. Am. Karate Assn. (dir., Outstanding Instr. award 1973), Ohio Edn. Assn., Alpha Lambda Delta, Pi Lambda Theta, Phi Kappa Phi. Clubs: Basenji of Am., Greater Toledo Obedience Tng. Home: Toledo, O. Died Dec. 1, 1974; buried Arrowwoods, Indianapolis, Ind.

SMALL, SYDNEY FRENCH, ry. official; b. Norfolk, Va., Oct. 31, 1893; s. John French and Eliza Hackley (Bates) S.; ed. Norfolk Acad., 1907-10; m. Nathalie Pace. Feb. 23, 1921. With N.&W. Ry from Sept. 16, 1911, as clerk and stenographer operating dept., 1911-13, sec. to gen. mgr., 1913-20, sec. to v.p. in charge operation and traffic, 1920-24, sec. to pres., 1924-29, asst. to pres., 1929-35, v.p. in charge taxation and pub. relations from 1935, vice-pres., asst. to pres. from 1941; v.p. Va. Holding Corp.; dir. Roanoke Gas Company, National Bank of Com. (Norfolk); chmn. Va. Ry. Assn., Richmond, Mayor City of Roanoke, 1934-38. Mem. Va. Conservation and Econ. Development Commn. Trustee University of Virginia Grad. Sch. Bus. Served as 2d lt. Air Service, U.S. Army, 1917-19. Episcopalian. Clubs: Shenandoah, Rotary, Roanoke Country, Commonwealth (Richmond); Lake Placid (N.Y.). Home: Roanoke, Va., Deceased.

SMALL, W(ILLIAM) A(RDEN), business exec.; b. Chicago, Feb. 23, 1894; s. William Alexander and Margaret Priscilla (Deacon) S.; ed. in pub. schs. of Chicago; m. Elizabeth Foresman, Sept. 12, 1923; children—William Arden, Elizabeth Foresman (Mrs. John Rehm Shafer), Margaret Priscilla (Mrs. David Fellows Hart). President and treasurer Tucson (Arizona) Daily Citizen, 1939-66; v.p., treasurer Tucson Newspapers, Inc., 1940-66, pres., 1966; pres. Citizen Pub. Co., Star Pub. Co.; vice pres. Parkview Drugs, Inc., 1965-66; director Arizona Bank. Dir. Tucson Airport Authority. Served with U.S. Army, World War I with 26th Inf. Republican. Clubs: Tucson Country, Old Pueblo (Tucson); Rotary; LaJolla (Cal.) Country. Home: LaJolla, Cal., Died Sept. 5, 1975.

SMALLEY, WILLIAM CAMERON clergyman; b. Southport, England, Dec. 9, 1880; s. Rev. James and Janet (McTaggart) S.; student, Brandon Coll., Manitoba, 1905-12; D.D. (hon.), Northern Baptist Seminary, Chicago, 1946; m. Margaret Alice Cowell, Sept. 1913, one dau., Margaret Cowell (Mrs. C. Hampton Smith). Pastor of several Baptist churches, Manitoba, 1907-19; supt. Baptist Convention of Manitoba, 1919-24; pastor Fourth Av. Baptist Church, Ottawa, Can., 1924-28; gen. sec., Baptist Union of Western Canada from 1929. Odd Fellow (Grand Chaplain, Sovereign GrandLodge, 1926-34). Home: Edmonton, Alberta, Canada.†

SMALLWOOD, ROBERT BARTLY, business exec.; b. Londonderry, O., Sept. 26, 1893; s. William Joseph and Josephine (Mendenhall) S.; A.B., Ohio State U., 1917; m. Mabel Baker, 1971; 1 dau., Jane (wife of Capt. Arthur Gerould Newton, U.S. Navy). Railroad foreman, later salesman, and sales mgr., 1919-22; asst. to pres. Winslow Glass Co., Columbus, O., 1922-24; gen. sales mgr. Moores & Ross, Columbus, O., 1924-32; sales promotion and organization dir., The Borden Co., New York, N.Y., 1933-36, gen. sales mgr., 1936-38; former chmn. bd. Thomas J. Lipton, Inc., Hoboken, N.J., pres. and chief executive officer, 1938-59, ret.; past pres. and chairman of board Thomas J. Lipton, Ltd., Toronto, Can., Continental Foods, Inc.; mem. adv. bd. Unilever, London and Rotterdam, Bankers Trust Co., N.Y.C.; v.p., div. Ritz Assos., Inc., 465 Park Assn.; dir. Lever Bros. Served with U.S. Army, 1917-19; bn. comdr. 345th F.A., France, 1918; attached G.H.Q., Paris, 1919; lt. col. 134th F.A., 1932. Special adviser to adminstr. Office Price Control, Washington, D.C., 1943-45. Chmn. Tea Council of U.S.A. Mem. World Med. Assn. (dir.), Newcomen Soc., Delta Upsilon. Clubs: Links Golf, Racquet and Tennis (N.Y.C.); 1925 F Street (Washington); Royal Ashdown Forest Golf (Eng.). Home: New York City, N.Y. Died June 12, 1974.

SMART, WALTER KAY, prof. (retired); b. Payson, Ill., June 18, 1878; s. Kimball E. and Mary E. (Kay) S.; grad. Evanston Acad., 1898; Ph.B., Univ. of Chicago, 1902, Ph.D., 1911; m. Julia F. King, Aug. 31, 1905; 1 dau., Mary Elizabeth. Instr. English, 1904, prof. and head dept. of English, 1910. Armour Inst. Tech.; lecturer Sch. of Commerce, 1910-20, prof. English, Schools of Commerce and Journalism, Northwestern U., 1920-43. Member Alpha Kappa Psi, Sigma Delta Chi, Beta Gamma Sigma, Republican. Clubs: University of Evanston. Author: Handbook of Effective Writing, 1922, 31, 42 (with D. R. Lang); English Review Grammar, 1925, 30, 40; Business Letters (with L.W. McKelvey), 1933, 41. Editor: How to Write Business Letters (with others), 1916, 23. Home: Evanston, Ill.†

SMAY, JOSEPH EDGAR, prof. of architecture; b. Nevada, Ia., June 4, 1898; s. Elmer Elsworth and Hattie Estella (Crippen) S.; B.S., Ia. State Coll., 1923, M.S., 1929; student Harvard, summers 1930, 31; m. Mildred Cecilia Koontz, Nov. 1, 1923; children—Richard Edgar, Robert Joseph. Assistant professor dept. of architecture, U. of Neb., 1923-29, also archtl. draftsman Davis and Wilson, Lincoln, Neb.; dir. and founder School of Architecture, U. of Okla., 1929-47; prin. architect on Bus. Adminstrn. and Biol. Science bldgs., U. Okla. Licensed architect, Okla., certified Nat. Council Archtl. Registration Bds.; licensed engr., Okla. Mem. State Bd. Archtl. Examiners, 1936-42, 52-62, pres., 1961. Nat. council rep. Sooner dist. Boy Scouts Am., 1940-41. Served as apprentice seaman, USN, 1918, capt. engrs. O.R.C., overseas with Army Service Forces, 1941-42, capt. Hon. Res. U.S.A., ret. Mem. A.I.A. (chmn. com. on membership 1939-42, president Oklahoma chapter, 1936-38, secretary-treasurer, 1951-57, 60-66, national Council Architecual Registration Boards. (sec.-treas. 1957, 61, pres. 1958, exec. dir. 1957-58), Okla. Society Profl. Engrs. (chairman 8th dist. 1947, vice chmn. central chpt. 1951, dir.), State Soc. Registered Architects (pres. 1936-37), Okla. Edn. Assn. (pres. art sect. 1940-41), Am. Legion, Theta Xi, Tau Beta Pi, Sigma Tau. Democrat. Mason (32°). Clubs: Faculty. Home: Norman, Okla. Died June 15, 1974; buried Internat. Order Odd Fellows Cemetery, Norman, Okla.

SMELO, LEON SAMUEL, physician; b. Phila., Feb. 22, 1911; s. William and Anna (Steinberg) S.; A.B., U. Pa., 1931, M.D., 1935; m. Mary Ann Carver, Sept. 11, 1940; 1 dau., Martha (Mrs. Robert Wagoner). Intern, Phila. Gen. Hosp., 1936-37, metabolic dept. resident physician, 1938; asst. med. dir. Renziehausen Found., Children's Hosp. Pitts., U. Pitts. Med. Sch., 1939-41; practice medicine specializing in internal medicine, Birmingham, Ala., 1942-75; chief sect. on metabolism and endocrinology dept. medicine Bapt. Med. Center, 1966-75; asso. prof. medicine Med. Coll. Ala., 1971-75. Chmn. med. adv. bd. Birmingham Indsl. Health Council; asso. dir. Camp Seale Harris, 1948-74; physician Univ. Group Diabetes Program, 1960-75. Diplomate Am. Bd. Internal Medicine. Fellow A.C.P., Internat. Coll. Physicians; mem. Am. Fedn. Clin. Research, A.M.A., Am. (mem. council 1958-75). Ala. (pres. 1971-72) diabetes assns., So., Ala. med. assns., Birmingham Acad. Medicine, Birmingham Soc. Internists (v.p., dir. 1948-49), Jefferson County Med.

Soc., Birmingham Metabolic and Diabetes Assn. (pres., dir. 1948-49). N.Y. Diabetes Assn. Home: Birmingham, Ala. Died Mar. 18, 1975.

SMEMO, JOHANNES, clergyman, hymnist; b. Roros, Norway, July 31, 1898; s. John and Mali (Grytbak) S.; cand. theol. ch. Coll., Oslo, 1924; D.D., Luther Theol. Sem., St. Paul, Minn., 1957. Chaplain, Drammen, Norway, 1925-33; vicar, Sor-Fron, Norway, 1933-34; pres. Practical Theol. Sem. Church Coll., Oslo, Norway, 1934-46; bishop Agder, Norway, 1946-51, Oslo, Norway, 1951-68. Decorated Order of St. Olav. Author: Kjaerligheten hos troens apostel, 1926; Er prekenens tid forbi?, 1938; Livet ovenfra, 1940; Guds ja, 1954; Salmer fra Sosterkirker, 1964; Gamle salmer og nye, 1965; Ung Sang, 1967. Home: Oslo, Norway. Died Mar. 7, 1973; buried Var Frelsers Gravlund, Oslo.

SMIGEL, ERWIN O., educator; b. N.Y.C., Nov. 3, 1917; s. Joseph O. and Ida (Sachs) S.; A.B., U. N.C., 1939, postgrad., 1939-40; M.A. (penfield fellow), N.Y.U., 1942, Ph.D., 1949. From instr. to asso. prof. sociology Ind. U., 1948-57; sr. fellow law and behaviorial scis. U. Chgo. Law Sch., 1957-58; asso. prof. N.Y. U., 1958-59, prof. sociology, 1959-73, chmn. dept. sociology Univ. Coll., 1958-62; chmn. dept. sociology Washington Square Coll., 1962-66, head all-univ. dept. sociology, 1966-73. Sr. research asso., mem. exec. com. Center for Policy Research; condr. Sunrise Semester, CBS-TV, 1970. Served with USAAF, 1942-46. Mem. Am. Sociol. Assn., Soc. Study Social Problems, Indsl. Research Assn., N.Y. Acad. Sci., Am. Assn. U. Profs., Eastern Sociol. Soc. Co-author: Nursing Home Administration, 1962. Author: The Wall Street Lawyer, 1964. Editor: Work and Leisure, 1963; (with L. Ross) Crimes Against Bureaucracy. Contbr. to profl. jours. Editor: Social Problems, 1957-61, asso. editor, 1961-63. Home: New York City, N.Y. Died Aug. 30, 1973.

SMISSMAN, EDWARD ERVIN, educator; b. East St. Louis, Ill., July 29, 1925; s. Henry and Golda (Baron) S.; U.S. in Chemistry with highest honors, U. Ill., 1948; Ph.D., U. Wis., 1952; m. Clarine Jane Feir, Jan. 28, 1951. Asst. prof. U. Ill., 1951-55; asst. prof., asso. prof. pharm. chemistry U. Wis., 1955-60; prof. med. chemistry, chmn. dept. U. Kan., Lawrence, 1960-74, Univ. Distinguished prof., 1964-74. Research prof. U. Cal. at San Francisco, 1963. Served with USCGR, 1943-46. Mem. Am. (chmn. div. medicinal chemistry 1959-60, councilor 1961), Brit. chem. socs., Am. Pharm. Assn., Sigma Xi, Phi Lambda Upsilon, Rho Chi, Phi Kappa Phi, Phi Eta Sigma. Mason. Home: Lawrence, Kan., Died July 14, 1974.

SMITH, ALBERT C., army officer; b. Warrenton, Va., June 5, 1894; s. Eugene Albert and Blanch Baker (Cowper) S.; grad. Gordon Inst., 1907-09, Va. Polytechnic Inst., 1910-13, B.S., U. S. Military Acad., 1917; m. Mary Josephine Gorman, Apr. 14, 1920; children—Albert Cowper, Robert Alexander. Commd. 2d lt., Cav., 1917, and advanced through grades to maj. gen., 1945; served in France and Germany, 1917-19; instr. U.S. Military Acad., 1922-26, instr., asst. prof., 1929-34; Command and Gen. Staff Sch., student and instr., 1936-40; comdg. gen. 14th Armored Div.; Philippines, 1946-47, Japan, 1947-49; comdg. gen. 24th Inf. Div., 1948-49, 2d Armored Div., 1949-50; dep. comdg. gen. Fifth Army, 1950-51, acting comdg. gen., 1951-52; office, Chief of Mil. History, 1952-55, chiief of mil. history Dept. of Army 1953-55, Decorations: D.S.M., Silver Star, Bronze Star; French Legion of Honor, Croix de Guerre. Clubs: Executives, Ill. Athletic, Chgo. (Chgo.); Army-Navy. Address: Washington, D.C., Died Jan. 24, 1974; buried Arlington Cemetery, Fort Myer, Va.

SMITH, BOYD MILFORD, educator; b. Greenland W. Va., Aug. 29, 1887; s. Milford M. and Frances (Thalaker) S.; student W.Va. Prep. Sch., Davis and Elkins Coll., Harvard U.; LL.B., W.Va. Univ., 1910; A.M., Yale, 1938; m. Anne Marie Smith, June 27, 1924; Asso. editor Randolph Rev. (newspaper), 1913-15; with The Faultless Rubber Co., successively sec. to pres., prodn. mgr., promotion sales mgr., mgr. N.Y. office, 1915-17; W.Va. Coal & Coke Co., 1920-22; house mgr., dept. drama, Yale Univ., 1927-29, bus. mgr., asst. prof. dept. drama, 1929-31, bus. mgr., sch. fine arts, 1931-47; gov. bd. Yale Art Gallery, 1940-57 (prof., 1937-67); prof. of drama, Yale 1946-57, chairman of the department, 1946-54, acting dean of School of Fine Arts 1955, associate dean of School of Architecture, 1955-57; executive officer, Div. of Arts since 1947, fellow Silliman Coll. since 1948. Member of the Dramatists Guild of Authors League America. Served as 1st lieut., squadron comdr., U.S. Air Service, 2 yrs., World War I; served successively as group comdr., adminstrv. insp., Salt Lake, A.A.F., World War II; exec. officer, Dalhart A.A.F.; air insp. budget and fiscal officer, dir. Adminstrn. and Services, dir. of tech. training, Alamogordo, N.M., A.A.F.; to inactive status as lt. col., A.C., 1945, as col. 1949. Mem. Am. Ednl. Theatre Assn.; corporate mem. Am. Nat. Theatre and Acad.; mem. bd. trustees, Nat. Theatre Conf. Club: Faculty. Author. The Patriarch, 1926. Home: Sarasota, Fla. Died Apr. 26, 1973.

SMITH, C. H. ERSKINE, lawyer; b. Pittsburg, Kan., July 28, 1934; s. Percy Davis and Josephine (Fain) S.; student George Washington U.; B.A., Birmingham So. Coll., 1957; LL.B., U. Ala., 1958; m. Esther Pruitt; children—Leigh, Julie, Dana, Scott, Nicole. Sec. congressman 9th Congl. dist. Ala., 1952-55; with pub. relations dept. Gulf States Paper Co., Tuscaloosa, Ala., 1956-58; admitted to Ala. bar, 1958, practiced in Birmingham. Vis. lectr. real estate law U. Ala.; lectr. Ala. Bar Assn.; sec.-treas., dir. Ala. Title Co., Inc. Organizer, 1st chmn. Jefferson County Com. for Econ. Opportunity, 1965; pres. Ala. Civil Liberties Union, 1968, mem. nat. bd. dirs.; chmn. Ala. adv. com. U.S. Commn. on Civil Rights. Chmn., Democratic Campaign Com. Jefferson County, 1960. Mem. Am., Ala. (past chmn. jr. bar. sect.), Birmingham (past chmn. pub. relations) bar assns., Am. Judicature Soc., Phi Beta Kappa, Sigma Phi Epsilon, Sigma Delta Kappa (past nat. v.p.), Omicron Delta Kappa. Contbr. articles to profl. jours. Home: Hanceville, Ala. Died July 25, 1973; interred Cullman City Cemetery.

SMITH, CHARLES COPELAND, clergyman; b. Leicester, England, May 30, 1878; s. Thomas and Eliza (Copeland) S.; M.A., Owen's Coll., Manchester, 1901; B.D., Didsbury Theol. Coll., 1904; m. Caroline Emma Riley, of Heanor, Derbyshire, Aug. 7, 1907. Ordained Methodist ministry, 1900; asst. to Dr. Hugh Price Hughes, sociologist, London, 1903-07, to Dr. F. L. Wiseman, Birmingham, 1907-10; came to U.S., 1922; pastor Salem, S.D., and Oshkosh, Wis.; engaged in the promotion of Neighbor Guild (Chicago). also pres.; pres. Am. Inst. of Moral Hygiene. Received King's medal and thanks of Parliament, 1919, for establishment and supervision of war relief work, Isle of Man. Mem. Pi Gamma Mu. Mason. Clubs: Press, City. Author: Record and Reminiscence, 1904; Straight Answers to Life Questions; Where Are the Dead?, 1931. Home: St. Charles, Ill.†

SMITH, CHARLES GEORGE PERCY (LORD DELACOURT-SMITH), trade union ofcl.; b. Windsor, Eng., Apr. 25, 1917; s. Charles and Ethel (Ralfe) S.; M.A. (hon.), Oxford; m. Margaret Hando, Dec. 26, 1939; children—Carolyn (Mrs. Roger Pudney), Stephen, Lesley. Asst. sec. Civil Service Clerical Assn., London, 1939-53; gen. sec. Post Office Engring. Union, London, 1953—. Adviser, Prison Officers Assn., 1955-70; mem. Brit. Airports Authority, part time 1965-70; pres. Postal Telephone & Telegraph Internat., 1969. Mem. Parliament, 1945-50; minister state Ministry Technology, 1969-70. Served with Brit. Army, 1940-45. Created life peer, 1967, privy councillor, 1969. Home: London, England. Died 1972.

SMITH, CHARLES WILLIAM, lawyer, pub. utilities cons.; b. Balt., May 18, 1896; s. Thomas Little and Rebecca Frances (Chilcote) S.; B.C.S., Southeastern U., 1923; B.S., Nat. U., 1924; LL.B.; U. Balt., 1932; m. Catherine Agusta Meehan, June 23, 1928; children—Charles W., Charlotte M. (Mrs. Joseph F. Hennessy), Frances (Mrs. Justin A. Virtrano). Millworker, 1915; successively stenographer, clk. and bookkeeper, 1916-20; auditor U.S. Income Tax Unit, 1920-29; chief auditor Pub. Serv. Commn. of Md., 1929-36; chief Bur. of Accounts, Finance and Rates, Fed. Power Commn., 1936-55; then cons. pub. utilities; tchr. accounting Johns Hopkins U. Evening Sch. Econ., 1930-38; maj. role in obtaining Supreme Ct. recognition of prudent investment principle of public utility regulation; expert witness in numerous public utility cases; C.P.A. of N.C. and Md.; mem. bars of Md. and U.S. Supreme Ct. Mem. Md. Assn. of C.P.A's (ex-pres.), Am. Bar Assn. (mem. council pub. utilities sect.), Am. Inst. Accountants, Am. Accounting Assn., Am. Econ. Assn., Delta Sigma Pi, Beta Alpha Psi. Author: Practical Accounting Systems; also articles on accounting, financial and econ. subjects. Address: Baltimore, Md., Died Feb. 20, 1976.

SMITH, CYRIL JAMES, pianist, educator; b. Middlesbrough, Yorks, Eng., Aug. 11, 1909; s. Charles Ernest and Eva Mary (Harrison) S.; ed. Royal Coll. Music, London, Eng.; m. Phyllis Doreen Sellick, Oct. 16, 1937; children—Graham, Claire. prof., Royal Coll. Music, London, 1934—; concert pianist world tours, 1937-67. Mem. Brit. musical delegation to USSR, 1956; mem. Jury Munich, Germany Internat. Piano Competition, 1965, 67, Amsterdam Jury, 1967. Decorated Order Brit. Empire; works dedicated to him by Vaughan Williams, Arthur Bliss, Gordon Jacob. Address: London, England. Died Aug. 2, 1974.

SMITH, DAVID V., educator, forester; b. Lumpkin, Ga., July 12, 1921; s. David V. and Nelle (Siddall) S.; B.S.F., U. Ga., 1946; M.F., Duke U., 1950, postgrad. 1950-52; Ph.D., Coll. Forestry at Syracuse, 1968; m. Mary Frances Evans, June 8, 1947; children—Susan C., Mary Katherine. Jr. forest technician S.C. Commn Forestry, Walterboro, S.C., 1947, sr. forest technician, 1948, asst. forester, 1949; grad teaching asst. Duke U., 1950-51, instr., 1952, vis. asst. prof. summer 1953; asst. prof. forestry Va. Poly. Inst., Blacksburg, 1952-57, asso. prof., 1957-70; prof. forest engring. Stephen F. Austin State U., Nacogdoches, from 1970. Forest cons. cities Pulaski and Martinsville, Va.; Norfolk and Western Rys., Roanoke, Va., Barnes Lumber Co., Charlottesville, Va., Appalichian Power Co., Roanoke, Lester Brothers Lumber Co., Martinsville, Freeport Sulphur Co., N.Y.C., Allied Chem. Co., Morristown, N.J. Temple Industries, Diboll, Tex. Served to 1st lt. with AC, AUS, 1942-45; ETO. Mem. Am. Soc. Photogrammetry, Am. Congress on Surveying and Mapping, Photogrammetric Soc. (London), Soc. Photo-optical Instrumentation Engrs., Soc. Am. Foresters (chmn. chpt. 1958), Sigma Xi, Alpha Gamma Rho, Phi Sigma Xi. Methodist. Home: Nacogdoches, Tex. Deceased.

SMITH, DELOS OWEN, journalist; b. St. Joseph, Mo., Mar. 2, 1905; s. Edmond Wesley and Addie (Greenwood) S.; m. Jeannette Allain Reynes, Oct. 27, 1930; 1 son, Delos Reynes. Reporter, editor United Press Assn. (name changed to United Press Internat. 1958). from 1931, music critic, music editor, from 1949, sci. editor, writer daily column Science Today, from 1952; contbr. periodicals on music, sci. subjects. Mem. Nat. Assn. Sci. Writers. Author: Music in Your Life, Lives of the Great Composers, 1957. Home: New York City, N.Y. Died 1973.

SMITH, EARL BAXTER, lawyer; b. Boise, Ia., May 9, 1896; s. Cyrus and Julia B. (Baxter) S.; B.Sc., U. Ida., 1919; m. Pearl Morgan, July 22, 1920; children—William Morgan, Eugene Coleman. Admitted to Ida. bar, 1923; practice of law, 1923-54, 69-75; justice Supreme Ct. Ida., Boise, 1954-69. Mem. Ida. Constl. Revision Com., from 1969. Mem. Am. (past ho. of dels.), Ida (pres. 1945, 48) bar assns., Ida. State Bar (commr. 1942-48), Nat. Assn. Probate Counsel, Scribes, Am. Legion, Sigma Alpha Epsilon. Mason (Shriner), Elk. Home: Boise, Ida., Died Sept. 28, 1975.

SMITH, EDWARD ST. CLAIR, highway engr.; b. Harlan, Ia., July 26, 1879; C.E., State U. of Ia., 1900; m. Dorothy Cornell, of Lincoln, Neb., Apr. 24, 1913. Asst. engr. maintenance of way and double track constrn., C.,M.&St.P. Ry., 1900-04; resident engr. and acting div. engr., in constrn. Black Hills div., same rd., 1906-08; terminal engr. in constrn. tide water terminals, etc., Seattle, Wash., 1908-10; chief engr. Sacramento Valley Land & Irrigation Co., 1912-13; state highway engr. of Ida., 1913-15; organized first highway dept. in Ida.; div. engr., 1916-21; insp. gen., 1921-22, W.Va. State Road Commn.; contracting engr., 1922-23. Asso. mem. Am. Soc. C.E. Republican. Baptist. Home: Charleston, W.Va.†

SMITH, EDWARD WARREN, physician; b. Ont., Can., 1915; s. Morley Thomas and Mabel J. (Kellett) S.; M.D., Temple U., 1941; m. Charlotte Edith Remington, Apr. 25, 1942; children—Edward Morley, Geoffrey Remington, Charlotte Diana (Mrs. Bruce A. Crane). Intern, Westchester County Hosp., 1941-42; resident in ophthalmology Manhattan Eye, Ear, and Throat Hosp., N.Y.C., 1946-48, attending ophthalmologist and surgeon, 1949-65; attending ophthalmologist New Rochelle (N.Y.) Hosp., 1948-68, Roosevelt Hosp., N.Y.C., 1955-62. Served to lt. comdr., M.C., USNR, 1942-46. Diplomate Am. Bd. Ophthalmology. Home: New York City, N.Y. Died Dec. 29, 1974; buried Salisbury, Conn.

SMITH, EDWIN BERT, univ. prof.; b. Worcester, N.Y., Sept. 27, 1880; s. George and Julia (Hard S.; grad. Normal Sch., Oneonta, N.Y., 1903; student Syracuse Univ., 1905-07; Jenkins scholar. Columbia Univ., 1907-08, B.S., 1908; A.M., Univ. of Denver, 1916; Ph.D., U. of Calif., 1921; m. Mabel C. Russell, Sept. 18, 1908. Teacher public schools, N.Y., 1903-04; prin. Pacific Grove Acad., 1908-10; prof. history, Calif. Poly. School, 1910-14; prof. history, State Teachers Coll., Greeley, Colo., 1914-23; teaching fellow, U. of Calif., on leave of absence, 1920-21; prof. history and polit. science, Ohio U., 1923-36, prof. of government from 1937; prof. govt., Miami U., summer, 1939. Participated in survey of Ohio counties for Governor's Commn. on County Govt., 1934. Del. to Anglo-Am. Hist. Conf., Univ. of London, 1936. Mem. Nat. Council for Social Studies, Am. Hist. Assn., Am. Assn. Univ. Profs., Nat. Edn. Assn., Ohio Edn. Association, American Political Science Association, Acad. of Polit. Science, Ohio College Association, Sigma Phi Epsilon, Alpha Pi Zeta. Presbyterian. Author: The Teaching of Civics, 1919. Co-Author: Standardization of Subject Matter, 1923. Editor: Educational Reconstruction, 1919-21. Contbr. to professional and ednl. publs. Home: Athens, O.†

SMITH, ELBERT LUTHER, JR., indsl. traffic exec.; b. nr. Bristol, Va., Mar. 11, 1926; s. Elbert Luther and Earla (Whitaker) S.; student LaSalle U., 1954-55, U. Tenn., 1962; m. Juanita Cross, Nov. 26, 1954. Shipping and receiving clk. Universal Moulded Product Corp., Bristol, Va., 1946-52; traffic specialist Am. Thread Co., Bristol, Tenn., 1951-52; traffic supr. Sperry Farragut Co., Bristol Tenn., 1952-56; material handling, traffic mgr. Raytheon Co., Bristol, 1956-74, Mem. YMCA Indsl. Recreational Council, 1951-52; bd. govs. Eastern Star Home for Aged, Richmond, Va. Served with AUS, 1944-46. Mem. Traffic Club, V.F.W. Lion, Mason 32ffl K.T., Shriner); mem. Order Eastern Star (worthy grand patron 1965-66). Home: Bristol, Va. Died Dec. 22, 1974; interred Mountain View Cemetery, Bristol, Va.

SMITH, ERWIN FLETCHER, physician; b. Washington County, Tex., June 11, 1902; s. Oscar L. and Fannie Jane (Fletcher) S.; M.D., U. Tex., 1928; m. Dorothy Diggons, Apr. 25, 1947; children—Gail (Mrs. John Walker Payne III), Erwin Fletcher. Intern, Kansas City (Mo.) Gen. Hosp., 1928-29; asst. resident in obstetrics and gynecology N.Y. Nursery and Childs Hosp., 1929-30, resident, 1930-32; chief service

Municipal Sanitarium, Otisville, N.Y.; vis. attending University, St. Clare, French, Womens hosps.; dir. obstetrics N.Y.C. Hosp., Welfare Island; attending gynecologist, asso. attending obstetrician and gynecologist Lying-In div. N.Y. Hosp., 1943; dir. obstetrics and gynecology Manhattan Gen. Hosp.; Elmhurst (N.Y.) Gen. Hosp.; obstetrician Cabrini Meml. Hosp., N.Y.C., Rahway (N.J.) Gen. Hosp.; asst. prof. obstetrics and gynecology Cornell U.; mem. faculty Columbia-Presbyn. Med. Center. Diplomate Am. Bd. Obstetrics and Gynecology. Fellow A.C.S.; mem. A.M.A., Alpha Kappa Kappa, Sigma Nu. Mason (33°). Home: New York City, N.Y. Died Nov. 2, 1974; cremated.

SMITH, FRANCIS EDWARD, broker; b. Salem, Mass., May 16, 1878; s. Albert H. and Harriet Lane (Smith) S.; ed. Boston; m. Elsie Cora Davis, July 15, 1903; children—Lyman Bradford, Mrs. Marion Lane Willing, Mrs. Janet Winchester Barnes, Robert Moors. Engaged in brokerage bus., from 1894; partner Moors & Cabot; dir. Financial Pub. Co., Boston; director Exolon Co., mfrs. abrasives, 1923-37, sec., 1924-30. Active in Boy Scouts of America, 15 yrs. (scoutmaster, 14 yrs., scout commr., 1 yr.). Commr. of trust funds, Town of Winchester, Mass. Dir. Home for Aged, Winchester; trustee Handel and Haydn Fund, Charlesbank Homes, Winchester Pub. Library, 1923-53, permanent fund Mass. br. Sons Am. Revolution, Permanent Fund of Mass. Forest and Park Assn. Corporator of Franklin Square House of Boston. Life mem. Bostonian Soc. (treas. and dir. 1932-48), N.E. Historic Genealogical Soc. Republican. Conglist. Club: Winchester Country. Home: Winchester, Mass.†

SMITH, FRANK GERARD, sugar producer; b. N.Y. City, July 21, 1878; s. Edwin Clinton and Cornelia (Cooper) S.; grad. high sch., New Rochelle, N.Y., 1894, Drisler Prep. Sch., 1896; E.E., Columbia, 1900; m. Elsemor Currier, of New Rochelle, June 27, 1901; children—Charlotte Currier (Mrs. Miguel Muñiz, Jr.), Edwin Clinton, Frank Gerard. Draftsman, Gen. Elec. Co., 1901; engr. J. L. Mott Iron Works, 1901-06; chief accountant U.S. Metals Refining Co., 1906-08; mgr. Internat. Metals Selling Co. and L. Vogelstein & Co., 1908-12; asst. and gen. mgr. Francisco Sugar Co., 1912-24; exec. v.p. Cuban Cane Products Co., Eastern Cuba Sugar Corpn. Mem. Am. Chamber Commerce. Republican. Presbyn. Clubs: New York Athletic, Columbia Univ., Flat Rock Golf, Westport Yacht (New York); American (pres.), Sugar (dir.), Havana Country, Jockey, Midday, Union, Sevilla Biltmore (Havana). Home: Havana, Cuba.†

SMITH, FREDERIC WILLIAM, lawyer; b. Newark, N.J., Jan. 26, 1880; s. Edwin and Ella L. (Francisco) S.; B.S., Rutgers Coll., 1902, M.S., 1905; LL.B., New York U., 1904; m. Grace Harris, Nov. 12, 1913 (died Apr. 28, 1923); children—Grace Winifred, Harris Frederic. Admitted to N.J. bar, 1905; practiced alone until 1917; mem. Day, Day, Smith & Slingerland, 1917-18; mem. Smith & Slingerland, from 1918; vice pres. Pocono Hotels Corp.; also officer or dir. various other companies; dir. Maplewood Bank & Trust Co., Newark Provident Loan Assn., Fidelity Union Trust Co. Became pres. National Council Y.M.C.A.'s of U.S., 1933; pres. Newark Welfare Fed. (community chest), 1931-35. Pres. Centenary Fund and Preachers' Aid Soc.; pres. Newark Y.M.C.A.; mem. advisory council Newark Welfare Federation. Trustee Assn. to Provide Home for Friendless; trustee State Y.M.C.A. (N.J.); trustee of Rutgers Univ. Member American Bar Association, N.J., State and Essex County bar assns., Delta Upsilon. Republican. Methodist. Mason. Clubs: Essex (Newark); Shongum (N.J.); Sky Top (Pa.). Home: Maplewood, N.J.†

SMITH, GEORGE C(LINE), president C. of C. of Metropolitan St. Louis; b. Newton, Kan., July 1, 1886; s. William C. and Cora O. (Wolgamott) S.; A.B., University of Oklahoma, 1908; studied U. of Wisconsin (scholarship), 1908-09; Andrew D. White fellow, Cornell U., 1909-11; m. Eleanor Gertrude Perry. Dec 1, 1913; 1 George Cline. Organizer Criminal Justice Commn., Baltimore. 1922; mem. Md. Tax Revision Commn., 1923; chmn. Am. Industrial Development Council, 1925-33; member President Hoover's Conference on Home Building and Home Ownership; chmn. 8th Federal Reserve Dist. "Share the Work" Movement, 1932, Formerly gen. traffic manager Mo.-Kan.-Tex. Lines, St.Louis, and asst. to president same. Enrollment agent U.S. Pub. Service Res., U.S. Dept. Labor, World War; also chmn. Community Labor Board, Allegany and Garrett counties, Md.; manager War Resources Com. (Region No. 5), War Industries Board; mgr. Allegany County (Md.) War Chest; mem. indsl. coms. of Southeastern and Mo. Valley regional coms. Nat. Resource Planning Bd.; mem. advisory bd. and chmn, post-war planning com. Am. Indsl. Development Council; mem. board governors Auto Club of Mo.; Municipal Theater Association; member Citizens Com. for Post-war Improvements (St. Louis); mem. City Airport Commn. (6yrs.), St. Louis Council of Defense; Council. Com. for Econ. Development; mem. adv. council Am. Indsl. Development Council, Washington; mem. Citizen's Com. on Atomic Energy Information; trustee Jefferson Nat. Expansion Meml. Assn.; mem. bd. govs. Greater St. Louis Community Chest; alumni council U. of Okla. Research Inst.; Interstate com. Miss. Valley Parkway Commn.; com. on economic policy United States C. of C.; trustee Nat. Council for Community Improvement. Organized the St. Louis Crime Commission, 1949. Member The Round Table, Newcomen Soc., Artists Guild. Mem. Am. Marketing Soc., St. Louis Real Estate Exch. Member consulting staff Alexander Hamilton Institute, New York. Member Phi Beta Kappa, Kappa Alpha (Southern), Delta Sigma Pi, Delta Sigma Pho. Republican. Methodist. Clubs: University, Mo. Athletic, Noonday, Industrial (St. Louis), Author of brochures and articles on industrial and marketing subjects. Home: Greenwich, Conn. Died June 17, 1973.

SMITH, GEORGE FREDERICK, business exec.; b. Chgo., Mar. 16, 1897; ed. pub. schs. Chgo.; D.Sc., Phila. Coll. Pharm. & Sci.; LL.D., Rutgers; m. Estelle Taylor, Sept. 20, 1919; children—Dorothy (Mrs. Charles Hoffman Wilson), Patricia Ann (Mrs. Morley P. Thompson). Began as salesman R. H. Hollingshead Co., San Francisco br., Becoming v.p., gen. mgr., 1930; with Johnson & Johnson from 1933, pres., dir. 1943-60; dir. various subsidiary cos.; mem. board managers New Brunwick Savings Instruction. Past vice chaiman New Jersey Turnpike Authority; director American Foundation Pharm. Education; mem. bd. dirs. Regional Plan Assn.; mem. nat. council Jr. Achievement, Inc.; v.p. Health Information Found; trustee Nat. Fund for Med. Edn., Com. Econ. Development; del. to N.J. Constnl. Conv.; chmn. Middlesex Co. Planning Bd., 1945-49. Served with AUS, World War I; with A.E.F., 17 mos.; disch. as 1st lt. Member United States Chamber of Commerce (national defense com.), World Medical Assn. (member bd. of directors U.S. committee), N.J. State C. of C. (v.p. dir.), New Brunswick C. of C. (pres. 1942-44), Am. Drug Mfrs. Assn. (v.p.), N.J. Acad. Polit. Sci. Clubs: Union (board govs.) (New Brunswick); Plainfield (N.J.) Country (bd. trustees); Pine Valley (N.J.) Country: Skytop (Skytop, Pa.) Home: Metuchen, N.J. Died July 1974.

SMITH, GRETCHEN HART, (Mrs. Sidney Weber Smith), club woman; b. Omaha, July 14, 1902; d. George W. and Martha J. (Vogt) Hart; violin student, 1916-27; student U. Omaha, 1921-26; m. Sidney Weber Smith, Mar. 9, 1927. Bd. dirs. Ida. Fedn. Garden Clubs, 1953-74, rec. sec. 1955-57, pres., 1957-59, state chmn. flower show schs., 1961, state historian, 1963-74; pres. Magic Valley Iris Soc., So. Ida., 1963-64; life mem., dir. Nat. Council State Garden Clubs, 1957-59, 61-63, amateur accredited judge flower shows, 1960; Pacific region chmn. Blue Star Meml. Hwys., 1965-67, 69-74; pres. Twin Falls (Ida.) Garden Club, 1957-58, 65-67, 67-68; state chmn. Symposium Advanced Flower Show Sch., 1966, 69, 72; master flower show judge, 1969; accredited judge Am. Iris Soc., 1947-74, regional v.p. 1948-50, 72-74; regional dir. Am. Hemerocallis Soc., 1952-54, charter mem., 1946-74; life accredited flower show judge, 1968; critic Nat. Council Landscape Design, 1968; mem. nomaniting com. Nat. Council State Garden Clubs, 1967-69, area chmn. calendar com., 1969-74, dist. chmn. environmental conservation com., 1970, Pacific regional dir., 1973-75. Mem. Am. Hort. Soc., Am. Rose Soc., Am. Primrose Soc. (accredited judge 1959), Am. Daffodil Soc. (accredited judge), African Violet Soc. Am. (life, accredited judge 1961), Leaf and Petal Club (pres.), Nat. Fedn. Music Clubs (life), Nat. Tulip Soc., Nat. Chrysanthemum Soc., Am. Dahlia Soc., Twin Falls Music Club (pres. 1970). Republican. Episcopalian. Address: Twin Falls, Ida., Died Apr. 13, 1974.

SMITH, GUY CHESTER, former advertising exec.; b. Fall River, Kan., Oct. 11, 1890; s. George W. and Carrie (Finney) S.; student U. of Kan., 1908-10; m. Marion Leigh, Jan. 21, 1921; children—Barbara Leigh, Marion Leigh; m. 2d, Anna Louise Griffith, July 27, 1929; children—Anna Louise, Katharine Kiersted. Advertising writer for Chicago mail order houses, 1912-14, for Chamberlin Co., 1914-17; exec. v.p. Brooke, Smith French & Dorrance, Inc., 1917-58, chmn. bd., 1958-60; pres. Guyanna Corp., personal holding company; dir. Nat. Outdoor Advertisement Bur., Inc. Served in naval aviation ground school, 1918. Trustee Advt. Research Found., 1935-37; mem. nat. advt. com. of United Service Orgn.; mem. Jury of Awards, 12th Annual Exhbn. of Outdoor Advertising Art; mem. com. on referenda U.S. Chamber of Commerce; formerly sec., v.p., and chmn., now mem. advisory council Am. Assn. Advt. Agys.; chmn. publicity and advt. com. War Chest of Met. Detroit; mem. War Advt. Council; consultant, Office of War Information on Nat. Fuel Conservation Program; cons. War Manpower Commn. Labor Utilitization Program. Mem. Phi Gamma Delta Episcopalian. Clubs: Country of Detroit, Detroit, Bloomfield Hills Country (Bloomfield Hills, Mich.); Country of N.C., Tin Whistles (Pinehurst, N.C.). Contbr. to advertising publs. Home: Southern Pines, N.C. Died Aug. 22, 1973; interred Bethesda Cemetery, Aberdeen, N.C.

SMITH, H. ALLEN, author; b. McLeansboro, Ill., Dec. 19, 1906; s. Harry Arthur and Addie (Allen) S.; ed. in parochial schools; m. Nelle Mae Simpson, Apr. 14, 1927; children—Allen Wyatt, Nancy Jean (Mrs. Donnell Van Noppen, Jr.). Began with Huntington (Ind.) Press, at age of 15; worked on newspapers, Jeffersonville, Louisville, Ky., Sebring, Fla. (editor American, a daily at age of 19), Tampa, Tulsa, Okla., and Denver, Colo.; joined United Press as feature writer, N.Y.C., 1929; staff World-Telegram, 1936-41. Author: Robert Gair: A Study, 1939; M. Klein's Kampf, 1940; Low Man on a Totem Pole, 1941; Life in a Putty Knife Factory, 1943; Lost in the Horse Latitudes, 1944; Rhubarb, 1946; Lo, The Former Egyptian, 1947; Larks in the Popcorn, 1948; We Went Thataway, 1949; Low and Inside (with Ira L. Smith), 1949; People Named Smith, 1950; Three Men on Third (with Ira L. Smith), 1951; Mister Zip, 1952; Smith's London Journal, 1952; The Compleat Practical Joker, 1953; The World, the Flesh, and H. Allen Smith, The Rebel Yell, 1954; The Age of the Tail, 1955; Write Me a Poem, Baby, 1956; The Pig in The Barber Shop, 1958; Don't Get Perconel With a Chicken, 1959; Waiklki Beachnik, 1960; Let the Crabgrass Grow, 1960; How To Write Without Knowing Nothing, 1961; To Hell in a Handbasket (autobiography), 1962; Two-Thirds of A Coconut Tree, 1962; A Short History of Fingers and Other State Papers, 1963; Poor H. Allen Smith's Almanac, 1965; Son of Rhubarb, 1967; Buskin With H. Allen Smith, 1968; The Great Chili Confrontation, 1969; Rude Jokes, 1970; The View from Chivo, 1971; The Best of H. Allen Smith, 1972; Low Man Rides Again, 1973. Editor: Desert Island Decameron; Gene Fowler's Lady Scatterly's Lovers. Writer nat. mags. Home: Alpine, Tex., Died Feb. 24, 1976.

SMITH, H(ENRY) GORDON, business exec.; b. Winthrop, Mass., Aug. 7, 1891; s. Gershom and Margaret A. (Mann) S.; A.B., Harvard, 1913, M.B.A., 1914; m. Ruth Kent Barrington, Oct. 19, 1915; children—Muriel (Mrs. John W. Farmer), Ruth (Mrs. James E. Wilson III). Asst. to mgr. retail stores Regal Shoe Co., 1914-15; with Nat. Cash Register Co., 1915-17; asst. to vice-pres. U.S. Rubber Co., New York, 1917-23, asst. to pres., 1923-28, vice pres. and gen. mgr. Winnsboro (S.C.) Mills, 1928-31, mgr. textile div., 1931-45, v.p. and general manager textile division 1945-56, also dir. Director South Carolina Cotton Manufacturers Assn., 2 yrs.; dir. Cotton Mfrs. Assn. of Ga., 4 yrs. chmn. research com., 2 yrs.; mem. bd. dirs. Southern Indsl. Relations Conf., Blue Ridge, N.C., since 1937; dir. Textile Research Inst., New York, since 1948. Mem. Community Ch., Jackson Heights, N.Y. Mason. Clubs: Harvard (New York); Pomonok Country (Flushing, N.Y.); Highland Country (La Grange, Ga.); Jackson Heights Tennis; Farmington Country (Charlottsville, Va.) Home: Thomson, Ga. Died Feb. 11, 1975.

SMITH, HOWARD LELAND, architect; b. Avoca, N.Y., Jan. 27, 1894; s. Charles Howard and Essie (Crandall) S.; A.B., Carnegie Inst. of Tech., 1916, A.M. 1917; student under Lailcux of the Ecole des Beaux Arts, Paris, 1919; m. Martha Bodine Strong, Oct. 1. 1921; children—Adeline Birdsall Smith (Mrs. William Wescott Broom), Partricia Ann (Mrs. Maxwell Bishop Courage). Began as architectural designer for Foster Warner, Rochester, N.Y. 1913; with Cass Gilbert, N.Y. 1919; then cons. architect Hudson River Bridge Co., N.Y. practiced under own name in N.Y. City until 1935; chief architect for FHA, 1935-44, principal archtl. advisor on adminstrv. staff, underwriting div., 1944-47; cons. architect Rental Housing Div., 1947-50, chief tech. advisor Coop. Housing Div., 1950-53; with Richard Hawley Cutting & Assos., architects and engrs., 1953-58, dir. overseas operations, 1956; cons. Internat. Technologists S.A. Architect Dem. Nat. Com. for Nat. Convention, Phila., 1936 (on leave from govt. position); lectured and gave radio broadcasts on principles of planning small houses, 1937-38, Served in 307th Inf., 77th Div., U.S. Army, with A.E.F. during World War. Mem. Am. Inst. Architects, L.I. Soc. Architects, Nat. Adv. Council on Sch. Bldg. Problems. Democrat. Mem. Dutch Reformed Ch. Mason (32). Invented the Multi-Use Blackboard fixture, recognized by Nat. Edn. Assn. as the outstanding development in classroom equipment at Cleveland Conv., 1934. Contbr. articles on housing, prefabrication. Home: Canandaigua, N.Y. Died Mar. 19, 1974.

SMITH, JOEL PERRY, physician; b. Richland, Ga., Aug. 15, 1912; s. Joel Olin and Mary (Perry) S.; O.D., So. Coll. Optometry, 1937; O.D., Emory U., 1942; B.S., LaGrange Coll., 1944; M.D., U. Ga. 1947; m. June Goforth, June 5, 1933; children—Joel Perry II, Michael Gordon, Ellen Janet, Lynda Jean. Owner, LaGrange Optical & Jewelry Co. (Ga.), 1934-44; intern Norfolk (Va.) Gen. Hosp., 1947-48; resident surgery Crawford W. Long Hosp., Atlanta, 1948-49; pvt. practice medicine specializing in ophthalmology and otolaryngology Atlanta, 1949-75; staff mem. Ga. Bapt., Grady, Crawford W. Long, Henrietta Egleston hosps., Atlanta; clin. instr. otolaryngology Emory U. Med. Sch., 1956-75; founder, med. dir. Drs. Meml. Hosp., Atlanta, 1969-75. Dir. Electronic Equipment Co. Atlanta. Sec., dir. Ga. Found. Otolarnygology; mem. Deafness Research Found., N.Y.C. Served as capt. AUS, 1953-55. Fellow Soc. Mil. Ophthalmology: mem. A.M.A., So., Ga. med. assns., Alpha Kappa Kappa. Democrat. Methodist. Mason (32 deg., Shriner), Lion. Club: Atlanta Athletic. Contbr. article to profl. jours. Home: Atlanta, Ga. Died Mar. 3, 1975.

SMITH, J(OSEPH) RUSSELL, geographer; b. nr. Lincoln, Va., Feb. 3, 1874; s. Thomas R. and Ellen H. Smith; B.S., U. Pa., 1898, Ph.D., (fellow in econs. 1902-03), 1903, Doctor in Economic Science, 1957; Sc.D.,

Columbia University, 1929, University Leipzig, 1901-02; m. Henrietta Stewart, June 16, 1898; children—Newlin Russell, James Stewart, Thomas Russell. Instr. history George Sch., Newton, Pa., 1896-99; assisted with econ. investigations Isthmian Canal Commn., 1899-1901; instr. commerce Wharton Sch. Finance and Commerce, U. Pa., 1903-06, asst. prof. geography and industry, 1906-09, prof. industry, 1909-19; prof. econ. geography Columbia, 1919-44, emeritus, 1944. Lectr. U.S. War College Pres. geog. sect. World Fedn. of Education Associations, 1929-33. Investigations for U. of Pa. in North Africa and Southern Europe as to extent and possibilities of a tree crop agriculture, 1913. Pres. Northern Nut Growers Assn., 1916, 17. Chmn. food commn. of Phila., Home Defense Com., 1917; spl. trade expert, War Trade Bd., Washington, 1918; geog. field work, Asia, 1925-26. Recipient Harmon Found. prize, 1927, Culium medal, American Geographic Society, 1956. President Association American Geographers 1941-42. Honorary mem. Swedish Society Geography and Anthropology. Mem. Soc. of Friends. Clubs: Cosmos (Washington); Franklin Inn. Author: The Organization of Ocean Commerce, 1905; The Story of Iron and Steel, 1908; The Ocean Carrier, 1908; industrial and Commercial Geography, 1913; Commerce and Industry, 1915; Elements of Industrial Management, 1916; Influence of the Great War on Shipping, 1918; The World's Food Resources, 1919; Human Geography (a grammar school text) Book I, Peoples and Countries, 1921, Book II, Regions and Trade, 1922; North America, 1925; Home Folks, a Geography for Beginners, 1926; Tree Crops, a Permanent Agriculture, 1929; Countries, Regions and Trade, a sixth grade geography, 1930; World Folks, an elementary geography, 1931; American Lands and Peoples, 1932; Foreign Lands and Peoples, 1933; Our Industrial World, 1934; Methods of Achieving Economic Justice, 1936; Men and Resources, a geography of North America, 1937; (with O. M. Phillips) North America, 1937; (with O. M. Phillips) North America, 1940; The Devil of the Machine Age, 1941; Neighbors Around the World, 1947; Neighbors at Home, 1947; Neighbors in the Americas, 1948; Neighbors in the U.S. and Canada, 1951; (with O.M. Phillips and Thomas R. Smith) Industrial and Commercial Geography, 1955. Contbr. to mags. and agrl. econ. and geog. jours. Home: Swarthmore, V1Pa.†

SMITH, JULES ANDRE, artist; b. of Am. parents at Hong Kong, China, Dec. 31, 1880; s. John Henry and Elizabeth (Connor) S.; prep. edn., Chauncey Hall Sch., Boston, Mass., and Columbia Grammar Sch., N.Y. City; B.Arch., Cornell U., 1902, resident fellow, 1903, M.S. in Architecture, 1904 traveling fellow, 1905-06; unmarried. Etcher, painter and architect, also designer of stage settings, and mural decorator. Represented in Congressional Mus., Washington, D.C.; Metropolitan Mus. of Art, Hispanic Soc., and New York Pub. Library (all N.Y. City); Mus. of Fine Arts, Boston; Detroit Mus. of Fine Arts. Awarded gold medal for etching, Panama-pacific Expn. Designer of U.S. Distinguished Service Medal. Served as 1st lt. Engr. Corps, U.S.A., later capt., 1917-18; official artist with A.E.F. (200 drawings in Nat. Mus., Washington, D.C.). Mem. Delta Upsilon. Club: Cornell (New York). Author: In France With the American Expeditionary Forces, 1919; The Scenewright, 1926. Illustrator: The Marne (by Maj. Hanson). Home: Pine Orchard, Conn.†

SMITH, LAWRENCE MEREDITH CLEMSON, b. Phila., Oct. 4, 1902; s. Lewis L. and Gertrude (Clemson) S.; A.B., U. Pa., 1923, LL.B., 1928; B.A., Magdalen Coll., Oxford U. (Eng.), 1925, M.A., 1946; m. Eleanor Houston, Feb. 23, 1933; children—Lewis Lawrence G., Eleanor K. (Mrs. James S. Morris), Samuel F. Houston, G.G. Meredith (Mrs. James H. Stevenson III), Sarah, Ludlow O., Mary Minor C. Admitted to the Pennsylvania State bar 1928; with firm Roberts & Montgomery, Phila., 1928-32, Montgomery & McCracken, Phila., 1932-33; asso. counsel RFC, 1932-33; gen. coordinator legal div. NRA, 1933-35; asso. counsel charge investigation and study investment trusts SEC, 1935-40; chief spl. war policies unit, war div. Dept. Justice 1940-43; chief econ. mission, French W. Africa, 1944; head U.S. purchasing mission, Switzerland, 1945; now pres. WFLN, Phila. Adviser U.S. delegation 3d meeting Minister Fgn. Affairs of Am. Republics, Rio de Janeiro, Brazil, 1942; mem. U.S. Nat. Commn. UNESCO, 1949-51, 54-60, 62-75, mem. exec. com., 1957-60, 63-75. Chmn. Bd. of Trade and Convs. Phila., 1955-63; past nat. treas., past chmn. Phila., Americans for Democratic Action, now mem. bd. dirs.; past mem. Phila. Com. Human Relations; bd. dirs. Phila. Housing Assn. Trustee, past pres. Am. Fedn. Arts; bd. dirs. Carson Coll.; asso. trustee U. Pa.; trustee Phila. Mus. Art. Mem. Phi Kappa Sigma. Democrat. Episcopalian. Clubs: Racquet, University Barge, Franklin Inn (Phila.); Chevy Chase, Sulgrave (Washington). Home: Philadelphia, Pa. Died Aug. 11, 1975.

SMITH, LAWRENCE WELD, med. cons.; b. Newton, Mass., June 20, 1895; s. William G. and Marian (Reynolds) S.; A.B., Harvard, 1916, M.D., 1920; m. Dorothy Matthews, Oct. 12, 1935; 1 dau. (by previous marriage), Shirley (Mrs. James Kilbreth). Instr. pathology Harvard Med. Sch., 1920-22, asst. prof. pathology, 1924-27; prof. pathology and bacteriology U. Philippines, 1922-23; asst. prof. Cornell Med. Coll., N.Y.C., 1928-33, asso. prof., 1934-35; prof. pathology and dir. labs. Temple U. Sch. of Medicine and Hosp., Phila., 1935-45, pathologist, asso. pathologist Lahey Clinic, Boston, Mass., 1924-28, Boston Floating Hosp., Boston Dispensary, Boston Infants and Childrens Hosp., New Eng. Deaconess Hosp., New Eng. Baptist Hosp., 1923-28, N.Y. Hosp., Nursery and Childs Hosp., N.Y.C., Willard Parker Hosp., 1928-38; med. cons. Med. Emergency Res. Corps during W.W.I. Cons. to sec. war on epidemic disease commn. World War II. Med. cons. R.I.S.T. Labs., N.Y., 1965. Corr. mem. Flemish Acad. Pathology and Medicine; mem. Suffolk County, N.Y. State med. socs., Am. Assn. Pathologists and Bacteriologists, Am. Soc. Cancer Research, A.M.A., Am. Soc. Clin. Pathologists, Am. Soc. Exptl. Pathology, N.Y. Heart Assn. (arteriosclerosis council). Author: Poliomyelitis (with John T. Landon), 1936; Essentials of Pathology (with Edwin S. Gault), 1938, 3d edit., 1948; Cardiovascular Renal Disease (with others), 1940. Home: Ridge, N.Y. Died Aug. 23, 1974; interred Pinelawn Meml. Cemetery, Suffolk County, N.Y.

SMITH, LEON EDGAR, educator, clergyman; b. Troup County, Ga., Oct. 25, 1884; s. John Everett and Mattie (Webb) S.; A.B., Elon (N.C.) Coll., 1910, D.D., 1922; grad. Princeton Theol. Sem., 1915; M.A., Princeton U., 1915; hon. LL.D., Marietta Coll., 1940; m. Ella Ora Brunk, Oct. 18, 1912; children—Rebecca Leon Edgar; m. 2d, Muriel C. Tuck, 1965 (dec.). Ordained ministry Christian Ch. 1905; began preaching as licentiate, 1906; pastor Huntington Ind., 1915-19. Third Ch., Norfolk, Va., 1919-31 (built the Christian Temple at Norfolk and increased membership from 236 to 1650); pres. Elon Coll., 1931-57, pres. emeritus, 1957-75, trustee, 1926-31. Mason (K.T.). Home: Virginia Beach, Va. Died Aug. 19, 1975; buried Elon College, N.C.

SMITH, LIVINGSTON, architect; b. Phila., Pa., Nov. 4, 1879; s. William Augustus and Margaret (Dulty) S.; Swartmore Prep. Sch., 1895-97, B.S., Arch., Univ. of Pa., 1901. Archtl. draftsman, N.Y. and Phila. offices, 1901-09; mem. firm Walter T. Karcher & Livingston Smith, Phila., from 1910; designs by firm include pub. bldgs., hosps., schools, churches, in eastern cities. Commd. 1st lt., F.A., 1917, captain, 1918; graduate School of Fire, and appointed instructor, F.A., 1918, with 108th F.A., 1919-21. Cresson traveling scholarship, Acad. Fine Arts, Phila., 1909-10. Fellow A.I.A.; pres. Phila. chapter, Pa. Soc. Architects, A.I.A., (1945-47); mem. Sigma Xi, Phi Kappa Psi. Mason Club: Union League (Phila., Pa.). Home: Philadelphia, Pa.†

SMITH, MARY CYNTHIA, religious work; b. Flandreau, S.D., May 8, 1882; d. Arthur J. and Henrietta Vail (Stevens) Smith; A.B., Smith Coll., 1906; M.S.S., Sch. for Social Work, Northampton, Mass., 1920; unmarried. High school teacher of English, 1907-11; instr. and med.-social case worker, U. of Minn., 1920-28; chmn. Woman's Dept., Minneapolis Church Fedn., Minneapolis, Minn., 1929-32; pres. Minn. Council Church Women, 1936-38; pres. Nat. Council Church Women, 1939-1941; vice pres. United Council of Ch. Women, 1941-44. Trustee Internat. Council of Religious Edn., 1942-44; trustee Minn. Council of Churches. Member American Assn. Univ. Women. Episcopalian. Club: Woman's of Minneapolis. Home: Minneapolis, Minn., Deceased.

SMITH, MELVIN MONTGOMERY, mfg. co. exec.; b. Onawa, Ia., Nov. 9, 1906; s. Claude M. and Mame (Smythe) S.; B.S., Wash. State U., 1928; m. Ruth Marie Muri, Oct. 15, 1937. Accoustical engr. Inland Insulating Co., Spokane, Wash., 1928-30, Asbestos Supply Co., Spokane, 1930-33; partner, pres. Spokane Pres-to-log Co., Inc., 1933-74; dir., v.p. Spokane Indsl. Park. Chmn. Mayor's Adv. Com. on Indsl. Devel., 1962-68; mem. Spokane Air Pollution Control Authority. Served from capt. to lt. col. USMCR, 1940-45; ret. brig. gen., 1959. Decorated Bronze Star with Combat V; recipient Spokane's Outstanding Salesman award Internat. Sales Marketing Execs., 1962. Mem. Spokane C. of C. (trustee 1960-62), Marine Corps Res. Officers Assn. (nat. v.p. 1958-62, vice chmn. bd. 1962-64), Wash. State Fedn. Clubs (pres. 1961-62, dir. 1961-65). Nat. Club Assn. (dir. 1962-65), Wine and Food Soc. Spokane (pres. 1962), Pi Kappa Alpha. Presbyn. Lion, Mason (Shriner). Clubs: Empire, The Spokane (pres. 1962-63), Spokane Country, Manito Golf, University (Spokane); Bohemian (San Francisco). Home: Spokane, Wash. Died July 27, 1974.

SMITH, MILDRED CATHARINE, mag. editor; b. Smethport, Pa.; d. Charles Abner and Jane (Haskell) Smith; B.A., Wellesley Coll., 1914, M.A., 1922. Asst. English lit. Wellesley Coll., 1915-17; tchr. English, Buffalo Sem., 1917-18; mem. staff Publishers Weekly, 1920-67, editor-in-chief, 1959-67; dir. R. R. Bowker Co., 1933-67, sec., 1936-67. Recipient Constance Lindsay Skinner award Women's Nat. Book Assn., 1944. Episcopalian. Author articles on book pub. Home: Great Neck, L.I. Died Aug. 30, 1973.

SMITH, MONROE WILLIAM, youth leader; b. Sunderland, Mass., Jan. 22, 1901; s. Carl Wm. and Mertie May (Loomis) S.; Ph.B., Wesleyan U., 1924; M.A., Columbia, 1928; m. Isabel Bacheler, 1924; children—Mertie Elizabeth, Stephen Bacheler, Jonathan Monroe. Instr. Germantown Friends' Sch., 1924-26, Peekskill Mil. Acad., 1926-27, Montclair Acad., 1927-28; Boy Scouts exec., Rochester, 1928-33; dir. Am. Youth Hostels, Inc., 1934-49; founder, pres. Youth Argosy, Inc.; ret., 1971. Led Internat. Friendship Group of Am. students to Europe, 1932; remained yr. to study youth hosteling in England, Norway, Holland, Belgium, Luxembourg, Germany, Switzerland. Opened 1st Am. Youth Hostel, Northfield, Mass., 1934 (now one of 250 in U.S.). Leader of groups traveling to Europe, Asia, S.Am., Mex. and Alaska. Leader 1st bicycle party over Pan-Am. Highway, 1945; leader group to Europe to rebuild war-destroyed hostels on invitation of ministers of edn. France, Luxembourg, Holland, 1946; leader Operation Crossroads Africa project, Nigeria, 1962. Am. rep. Internat. Youth Hostels Assn. (membership drawn from 64 countries sponsoring hosteling). Del. to internat. conventions at Godesburg, Germany, 1933, London, 1934, Copenhagen, 1936, Paris, 1937, Ardartan, Scotland, 1939 and 1946. Elected to Bicycle Hall of Fame, 1969. Mem. Soc. of Friends. Home: Delray Beach, Fla. Died Dec. 8, 1973.

SMITH, MORDON, supt. Puget Sound Naval Acad; b. Graham Co., Kan., June 10, 1881; s. Joseph Hamilton and Mary Hannah (Lochrie) S.; ed. pub. schs. of Downs, Kan.; m. Zillah Constance Stenger, of Herrington, Kan., Jan. 12, 1911; children—Robert Hamilton, Patricia. Rep. of newspaper syndicate, Washington, D.C., 1901-05; asso. for many years with newspapers in Kan. and Neb.; writer of spl. articles for Eastern publs.; mng. editor Grays Harbor Daily Washingtonian, Hoquiam, Wash., 1922-30; sec. to Congressman Albert Johnson, 1922-30; founder Puget Sound Naval Acad., 1938, and dir. and supt. Rep. State publicity dir., State of Wash., campaign of 1936. Republican. Episcopalian. Mason. Club: Professional and Business (Seattle, Wash.). Home: Bainbridge Island, Wash.†

SMITH, ORRIN HAROLD, prof. physics; b. Iveyville, Ia., Sept. 1, 1884; s. Howes and Frances Henrietta (Bosisto) S.; A.B., Knox Coll., Galesburg, Ill., 1908; A.M., U. of Ill., 1909, Ph.D., 1914; m. Jessie C. Lyon, June 15, 1911; children—Vernon Maurice, Marjorie Durling. Prof. physics, Cornell Coll., Mt. Vernon, Ia., 1914-25; prof. physics, DePauw U., Greencastle, Ind., from 1925; visiting prof. physics, under Rockefeller Foundation, at Nat. Southeastern U., Nanking, China, 1922-23. Mem. S.A.T.C., Ft. Sheridan, Ill., 1918. Received Oersted Medal, 1950. Fellow Ia. Acad. Science (pres. 1924-25); mem. Am. Assn. Physics Tchrs., Ia. Assn. Sci. Tchrs. (pres. 1923-24), Phi Beta Kappa, Sigma Xi, Kappa Delta Pi, A.A.A.S.; asso. mem. Am. Physical Soc. Nat. pres. Corda Fratres Assn. of Cosmopolitan Clubs. Methodist. Speaker writer on sci. subjects. Home: Everett, Wash. Died Sept. 12, 1973.

SMITH, PAUL GLEN, tube fabricating co. exec.; b. Sturgis, Mich., Aug. 9, 1930; s. Glen Hubert and Margaret (Straus) S.; student U. Lcycle (Chgo.), 1953. Underwriter, State Farm Ins. Co., Marshall, Mich., 1953-56; shipping and receiving clk. Doerr Products Corp., Barr Oak, Mich., 1958-64; v.p., gen. mgr. Precision Tube Corp., Bronson, Mich., 1964-71, also dir. Pres., Village of Burr Oak, 1966-69, trustee, 1965-66; township supr., 1970-71. Served with USNR, 1948-50. K.C. (4 deg.). Home: Burr Oak, Mich. Died Aug. 3, 1971.

SMITH, PERRY COKE, architect; b. Lynchburg, Va., Apr. 21, 1899; s. Alexander Coke and Kate (Kinard) S.; ed. Newberry (S.C.) Coll., 1914-16; University of Wis., 1916-17; B.Arch., Columbia University, 1920-23, McKim Fellow, 1923-24; married (2d) Sigrid Hovey, Sept. 9, 1938; children—(by 1st marriage) Joan Coke, Nancy Coke. Designer for Donn Barber, 1924; McKenzie, Voorhees & Gmelin, 1926; asso., Voorhees, Gmelin & Walker, 1930; partner of firm Smith, Haines, Lundberg & Waehler, and predecessor firms, 1938-68. Dir., mem. executive committee Regional Plan Association, Incorporated. Served 30th Engrs., 1st Gas Regt., A.E.F., 1917-19. Awarded Croix de Guerre with star, 1918. Fellow A.I.A. (ex-pres. N.Y. chpt.), Archti. League N.Y., Phi Kappa Sigma (Balt. Alpha Theta Chpt.). Clubs: Union League (N.Y.C.); Tarratine (Dark Harbor); Cruising of America. Home: Longboat Key, Fla. Died Nov. 10, 1973.

SMITH, ROBERT EDWIN, univ. ofcl.; b. Shabbona, Ill., Jan. 18, 1920; s. Harry E. and Harriet E. (Moore) S.; B.J., U. Mo., 1941; m. Sue Weiss, Nov. 20, 1941; 1 dau., Suzanne M. (Mrs, Alan McIntyre Fasoldt). Reporter A.P., 1945-46, St. Louis Globe-Dem., 1946-51; asst. to mayor St. Louis, 1951-56; exec. asst. to chmn. bd. and pres. McDonnell Aircraft Corp., 1956-67; asst. to chancellor U. Mo., St. Louis, 1967-74, dir. pub. information 1967-74. Mem. lay adv. bd. St. Louis Med. Soc., 1971-74; mem. planning commn. Marillac Coll., 1970-71. Trustee Lindell Hosp., St. Louis. Served with AUS, 1942-45. Decorated Bronze Star medal. Recipient Mayor's Civic award St. Louis, 1970. Mem. Pub. Relations Soc. Am. (chpt. bd. dirs.), Met. C. of C. St. Louis (mem. pub. relations com. 1970-71), Mo. Press Assn., Mo. Broadcasters Assn. Episcopalian. Clubs: Media, St. Louis Press. Home: Creve Coeur, Mo. Died Apr. 15, 1974.

SMITH, ROBERT WILLIAM, newspaper publisher; b. Austin, Minn., June 4, 1916; s. Jack and Norah (Gilbertson) S.; student Luther Coll., 1935-36; B.

Journalism, U. Mo., 1938; m. Margaret Ewing Cargill, July 13, 1944; m. 2d, Rosalie Heffelfinger Willkie, Aug. 26, 1968. Copy editor Mpls. Star, 1939-42, editorial writer, 1945-55, asso. editorial page editor, 1955-56, asso. editorial page editor Mpls. Star and Tribune, 1956-63, editorial page editor, 1963-67, exec. editor Mpls. Star, 1967-69, editor, 1969-72, asso. pub., 1972-73, pub., 1973-75; v.p. Mpls. Star and Tribune Co., 1969-75. Served to 1st lt. AUS, 1942-44; PTO. Mem. Am. Soc. Newspaper Editors, Council on Fgn. Relations, St. Paul-Mpls. Com. Fgn. Relations. Clubs: Minneapolis, Woodhill Country. Editor: Economics for You and Me, 1960. Home: Wayzata, Minn., Died Dec. 13, 1975.

SMITH, SHERMAN EVERETT, univ. adminstr.; b. Custer, S.D., Apr. 10, 1909; s. Charles Everett and Mabel (Dunham) S.; B.Sc. in chem. engring., S.D. Sch. Mines, 1930; Ph.D. in chemistry, Ohio State U., 1935; m. Rebecca Frances Jordan, Dec. 21, 1938; children—Burton Jordan, David Page. DuPont research asso. U. N.C., 1935-36; asst. prof. chemistry U. N.C., 1936-41, asso. prof., 1941-45; prof., chmn. dept. chemistry U. N.M., 1945-49, mem. adminstrn., 1949-73, adminstrv. v.p., 1965-73, also v.p. adminstrn., devel., 1969-73. Mem. adv. bd. Inst. Internat. Edn., Rocky Mountain region, 1954-73, Albuquerque Goals Com., 1969-73. Bd. dirs. United Conf. Christians and Jews, Internat. Folk Art Found. Mem. Am. Chem. Soc., Triangle fraternity, Sigma Xi, Phi Lambda Upsilon, Gamma Alpha. Democrat. Conglist. Author: (with E.C. Markham) General Chemistry, 1953. Contbr. chem. jours. Home: Albuquerque, N.M. Died Oct. 4, 1973.

SMITH, WESTON, news columnist; b. Bklyn., Jan. 28, 1901; s. Anson Weston and Clara (Sharp) S.; B.C.S., N.Y.U., 1925; m. Marjorie Ann Young, July 30, 1943; 1 son, Stuart; children by previous marriage—Joan Virginia (Mrs. Emile W. Achee), Robert. Statistician, Moody's Investors Service, N.Y.C., 1924-26; statistician Guenther Pub. Corp. pub. Financial World, N.Y.C., 1926-28; asso. editor Financial World, 1928-37, bus. editor and columnist, 1937-42, v.p. and pub. relations dir., 1943-48, exec. v.p. in charge pub. relations and advt., 1949-56, cons., 1956-61; organizer, pres. Weston Smith Assos., mgmt. consultants, N.Y.C., 1956-65; news columnist The Wall Street Transcript. Originator Annual Report Survey, 1941, dir., 1941-59; introduced Oscar of Industry Awards for 100 best annual reports each year, 1945; dir. Financial World Annual Awards Banquet, 1945-59; chmn. Investor Opinion Research Inst., 1963-69. Served with Signal Corps, N.Y. N.G., 1917-18; 2d lt., Res. Officers Tng. Corps., U.S. Army, 1919-20; capt. Aux. Police, O.C.D., 1943-45; 1st lt. Civil Air Patrol, N.Y., 1953-62. Awarded Anvil of Pub. Opinion trophy, Am. Pub. Relations Assn., 1946; Pub. Relations News Annual Achievement Award, 1950; certificate of Merit, Freedon Found., 1951; Blue Ribbon award United Shareholders Am., 1955; award Mark Twain Soc., 1968. Mem. N.Y.U. Men in Finance Club (dir. 1957-60), Pub. Relations Soc. Am. (dir. 1945-47, pres. N.Y. chpt. 1947-48), Pub. Relations Soc. N.Y., Am. Ordnance Assn., N.Y.U. Grad. Sch. Bus. Adminstrn. Alumni Assn. (dir. 1957-65, v.p. 1961-63), Soc. Profl. Mgmt. Consultants (sec. 1963-69), Soc. of Silurians, N.Y.U. Alumni Fedn. (past dir.) Soc. Am. Magicians, Air Force Assn., Internat. Platform Assn., Internat. Parental Assn. (chmn.), Soc. Am. Bus. Writers, Kappa Sigma, Sigma Alpha (grand master). Republican. Episcopalian (vestryman, treas.). Author: Stockholder Relations Guide book, 1950; compiler: Ann. Rev. of Shareholder Relations Policies of 1000 Indsl. Corps., 1952-54; pub.: Nat. Dir. of Financial Pub. Relations Counsel, 1953-64; editor: Shareholder Relations Yearbook, 1952-53, Financial Pub. Relations Confidential, 1958. Mng. editor Home: Stamford, N.Y. Deceased.

SMITH, WILLIAM ANTON, prof. education; b. Fruitgen, Bern, Switzerland, Dec. 2, 1880; s. Anton and Maria (Trachsel) Schmid; B.A., Wilamette U., Salem, Ore., 1909, B.O., 1910; M.A., U. of Wash., 1911; Ph.D., U. of Chicago, 1916; grad. study, U. of Calif., 1918-19, Stanford, 1919-20; unmarried. Teacher and prin. pub. schs., Ore., 1900-03, 1905-06; supt. schs. and prin. high sch., Wilbur, Wash., 1911-13; fellow Sch. of Edn., U. of Chicago, 1913-14; prof. ednl. adminstration, U. of Okla., 1914-19; asst. prof. edn., 1920-28, asso. prof., 1928-41, prof., from 1941-49, prof. emeritus, from 1949, U. of Calif.; visiting professor education, summer sessions, Univ. of Chicago, 1917, 18, U. of Calif., 1919, U. of Hawaii and Territorial Normal and Training Sch., 1927. Member American Assn. Univ. Profs., Calif. Soc. of Secondary Edn., Am. Edn., Am. Edn. Fellowship Soc. for Advancement of Edn., Phi Delta Kappa, Pi Gamma Mu, Kappa Delta Pi. Author: An Experimental Study in the Psychology of Reading (under name of William Anton Schmidt), 1917; The Reading Process, 1922; The Junior High School, 1925; Secondary Education in the United States, 1932. Asso. editor of, and contbr. to Calif. Jour. of Secondary Education. Home: Portland, Ore.†

SMOCK, HARRY BERDAN, printing co. exec.; b. Long Branch, N.J., Aug. 15, 1912; s. Harry Hendrickson and May (Busselle) S.; B.S., U. Ill., 1933; M.A., U. Chgo., 1952; m. Helen Brydia, May 3, 1941; children—John S., George B., Kathryn B. Lab. asst. W.F. Hall Printing Co., Chgo., 1933-35, asst. purchasing agt., 1935-38, sr. v.p., 1968-72; successively asst. prodn. mgr., plant engr., mfg. mgr. v.p., pres. Chgo. Rotoprint Co., 1938-68. Served as lt. comdr. USNR, 1942-46. Mem. Gravure Research Inst. (pres. 1961-63), Gravure Tech. Assn. (dir.), Sigma Chi. Home: Elmhurst, Ill. Died Mar. 11, 1972.

SMUTNY, RUDOLF, investment banker; b. Boston, Dec. 16, 1897; s. Josef and Adele (Meyer) S.; student N.Y. U., 1920; m. Florence Martin, Nov. 15, 1927; children—Florence Adele (Mrs. David D. King), Rudolf, Jr. With Salomon Bros. & Hutzler, 1916-57, sr. partner, chmn. finance com. until 1957, ret.; pres. R. W. Pressprich & Company, 1968-69; gen. partner Francis Garden duPont & Co., 1969-70, F.I. duPont, Glore Forgan Co., N.Y.C., 1970-74; past chmn. finance com. Rail-Trailer Co., subsidiary Van-Car Corp., Chgo.; dir. Trailer Train Co. Served USN, World War I; maj. USMC World War II; res. officer USMC. Mem. Investment Bankers Assn. Am. (gov.), Quiet Birdmen. Episcopalian. Clubs: Garden City Golf, Cherry Valley, Garden City, New York Athletic. Home: Garden City, NY. Died Nov. 1, 1974.

SNAITH, WILLIAM THEODORE, indsl. design exec.; b. N.Y.C., Mar. 26, 1908; s. Louis and Rose (Kaspar) S.; student N.Y. U., 1929-31, Ecole des Beaux Arts, Paris, 1931-32, Fountainbleau Acad. Fine Arts, 1932; m. Elizabeth Colman, Nov. 25, 1938; children—William MacLeod, Shepperd Francis, Jonathan Louis, Architect, Lawrence B. Emmons, Inc., 1927-29, Schultze & Weaver, 1929-31; archtl. designer for Elsie de Wolfe, 1933-35; with Raymond Loewy firm, 1936-74; dir. div. retail design and planning, 1940, partner 1944-56, managing partner, 1956-61; pres. Raymond Loewy-William Snaith, Inc., N.Y.C., 1961-74; pres., mem. bd. dirs. Market Concepts, 1964-74; treas., dir. Distbn. Systems, Inc.; lecturer on aesthetics and design Newcomen Soc. North Am., British Council Idustrial Design, others; exhibition paintings, New York City Whitney Museum, Pa. Acad. Arts, numerous traveling shows; pvt. collections. Bd. dirs. Flame of Hope, Inc., Mus. of Contemporary Crafts. Mem. A.I.A., Archtl. League N.Y., Indsl. Designers Soc. Am., Nat. Soc. Interior Designers, Am. Cratsmen's Council (trustee). Clubs: Stamford Yacht; Cruising of Am.; Royal Ocean Racing; Royal Swedish Yacht; Storm Trysail; Ocean Cruising; N.Y. Yacht, N.Y. Athletic, Lambs (N.Y.C.). Author: The Irresponsible Arts, 1964; Across the Western Ocean, 1965; On the Wind's Way, 1973. Stage designer Ode to Liberty; sets and costumes (ballet) Orestes and the Furies. Home: Weston, Conn. Died Feb. 19, 1974.

SNAVELY, GUY EVERETT, coll. ofcl.; b. Antietam, Md., Oct. 26, 1881; s. Charles Granville and Emma (Rohrer) S.; A.B., Johns Hopkins, 1901, Ph.D., 1908; Alliance Francaise, Paris, summer, 1905; hon. degress, from 23 univs., 1925-53; m. Ada Rittenhouse, Sept. 27, 1905 (died 1949); children—Guy Everett, Brant, Charles Albert; m. 2d, Louise Hutcheson, April 6, 1950 (died 1963); m. 3d, Madelyn Hale, July 17, 1964. Instr. Med. Nautical Acad., Easton, 1901-02; v. prin. Milton Acad., Balt., 1902-05; instr., 1906-07, asst. prof., 1907-09, prof. French, 1909, Romance langs. and lit., 1910-19, registrar, 1908-19, Allegheny Coll.; dean, Converse Coll., Spartanburg, S.C., 1919-21; pres. Birmingham-Soc. Coll., 1921-38, chancellor, 1955-74; interim pres. Lafayette Coll., 1957-58, Athens Coll., Athens, Ala., 1965; exec. dir. Assn. Am. Colleges, 1937-54; mem. bd. trustees Miles Coll., Hood Coll., Am. U.; chmn. Nat. Com. Colls. and Civilian Defense. Active Meth. Ch. orgn., del. gen. confs. Mem. Modern Lang. Assn. America, Nat. Advisory Com. on Education, Ala. Coll. Assn. (pres. 1926-27), Southern Assn. of Colleges and Secondary Schs. (sec., treas. 1926-37), Assn. Am. Colleges (pres. 1929-30), Am. Council on Edn. (vice chmn. 1937-38), Assn. Urban Univs. (pres. 1936-37); chmn. scholarship dept. of Presser Foundation; trustee and exec. com. Nat. Conf. Christian and Jews; v.p. Citizens Nat. Com.; Nat. Com. on UNESCO; trustee Sch. and Soc.; v.p. World Service Fund; mem. Nat. Com. on Accrediting Colls. and Univs. Mem. Phi Beta Kappa (past senator), Kappa Phi Kappa (nat. pres. 1927-31), Phi Gamma Delta, Omicron Delta Kappa (nat. pres. 1935-37), Phi Sigma Iota. Methodist. Decorated Officer d'Academie, 1914; Officer French Legion of Honor 1947. Clubs: Rotary, Kiwanis; Cosmos (Wash.). Author: Choose and Use Your College, History of Southern College Assn.; The Church and the Four Year College, 1955; A Search for Excellence: Memoirs of a College Administrator. Editor: Alarcon's El Capitáan Veneno, 1917; Valdéz, José (with R. C. Ward), 1919. Home: Birmingham, Ala. Died Mar. 12, 1974.

SNEDECOR, GEORGE W., statistician; b. Memphis, Tenn., Oct. 20, 1881; s. James George and Emily Alston (Estes) S.; B.S., U. of Ala., 1905; M.S., U. of Mich., 1913; m. Gertrude Douglas Crosier, Dec. 29, 1908; children—Edward Crosier (dec.), James George. Teacher Selma Mil. Acad., 1905-07; prof. mathemtics, Austin Coll., Sherman, Tex., 1907-11; asst. prof. mathematics, Iowa State Coll., 1913-16, asso. prof., 1916-33, prof. from 1933; dir. statistical lab., 1933-47; head statistical sect., Ia. Agrl. Expt. Sta., 1935-47, prof. statistics, from 1948. Fellow Am. Statis Assn. (pres. 1948), Inst. Math. Statistics, A.A.A.S.; mem. Iowa Academy of Science, Phi Beta Kappa, Sigma Xi, Gamma Alpha, Pi Mu Epsilon, Kappa Sigma. Author: Analysis of Variance, 1934; Statistical Methods, 1937, 1946; Everyday Statistics, 1950. Home: Ames, Ia.†

SNELL, ROY JUDSON, author; b. Laddonia, Mo., Nov. 12, 1878; s. James T. and Sarah A. (Knight) S.; A.B., Wheaton (Ill.) Coll., 1906; Harvard Div. Sch., 1907-08; B.D., Chicago Theol. Sem., 1916; M.A., U. of Chicago, 1917; m. Lucile Grace Ziegler, July 19, 1919; children—Francis Judson, John Ellis, James Laurie. Prin. Black Mountain Acad., Evarts, Ky., 1904-07; in charge Wales reindeer herd on Behring Straits, Alaska, 1908-09; with Y.M.C.A. in France, 1917-18. Conglist. Author numerous books from 1916; latest publs.; Destination Unknown, 1944; The Jet Plane Mystery, 1944. Lectr. to children; radio lectr. Home: Wheaton, Ill.†

SNODGRASS, SAMUEL ROBERT, neurosurgeon; b. Steubenville, O., Mar. 17, 1906; s. Samuel Robert and Florence (Sheldon) S.; B.S., Ind. U., 1927. M.D., 1929; m. Margaret Kinney, May 21, 1931; children—Samuel Robert, James Wilfred, Donald Kinney. Intern. Indpls. City Hosp., 1929-30; resident pathology Ind. U. Hosps., 1930-31; surg. intern Lakeside Hosp., Cleve., 1931-32; asst. resident surgeon Peter Bent Brigham Hosp., Boston, 1932-34, Harvey Cushing fellow, 1934; fellow neurosurgery Washington U. Med. Sch., St. Louis, 1934-36; fellow neurology Rockefeller Found., 1936-37; mem. faculty U. Tex. Med. Sch. at Galveston, 1937-72, prof. surgery, 1953-72, chmn. dept., 1968-70, Ashbel Smith prof. surgery, 1970-72; cons. USPHS Hosp., Galveston, Bur. Hearings and Appeals of Social Security Adminstrn. Mem. Am., Soc., Tex., Galveston County med. assns., Houston Neurol. Soc., Am. Acad. Neurosurgery (pres. 1961), Soc. Neurol. Surgeons (v.p. 1966), Am. Assn. Neurol. Surgeons, So. Neurosurg. Soc. (pres. 1968). Episcopalian. Club: Galveston Artillery. Home: Nashville, Tenn., Died Aug. 8, 1975.

SNOW, WILLIAM BENHAM, physician; b. Kingston, N.Y., May 6, 1895; s. William Benham and Adelaide Melvina (Smith) S.; M.D., L.I. Coll. Hosp., 1920; m. Mary Scott, Nov. 22, 1916; children—Edith, William, Elaine; m. 2d, Marie St. John Besekirsky, Oct. 15, 1961. Asst. dir. phys. medicine Beekman St. Hosp., 1930-33; dir. phys. med. coll., Presbyn. Med. Center, N.Y.C., 1935-60; supervisor phys. therapy Fifth Av. Hosp., 1931-35; dir. phys. medicine N.Y. Orthopedic Hosp., 1940-48; med. dir. phys. therapy and occupational therapy tng. courses, Columbia, 1941-60, prof. phys. medicine, 1945-60, prof. emeritus 1960; dir. phys. medicine and rehab. Doctors Hosp., N.Y.C.; clin. dir., asst. dir. N.Y. State Rehab. Hosp.; chief phys. medicine and rehab. Bath VA Med. Center. Mem. Am. Congress Phys. Medicine, Am. Acad. Cerebral Palsy, Am. Acad. Neurology, Am. Acad. Phys. Medicine and Rehabilitation. Kiwanian. Contbr. med. publs. Home: Madison, Conn. Died Nov. 16, 1974.

SNYDER, ADDISON HOGAN, editor; b. Barnesville, O., Jan. 30, 1879; s. Ephraim Hogan and Mary Ellen (Guthrie) S.; B.S., Ohio State U., 1901; m. Vara Hazard Dredge, Oct. 12, 1922. Scientific aid, Bur. of Plant Industry, U.S. Dept. Agr., Washington, 1901-02; scientific asst., Bur. of Soils, U.S. Dept. Agr., 1902-06; in charge soil extension work, Ia. State Coll. Agr. and Mech. Arts, 1906-12; editor Successful Farming, 1912-29, editor and specialist in journalism. U. of Md., from July 1, 1929; asst. dir. extension service, U. of Md., from 1948. Mem. Am. Agr. Editors Assn., Alpha Zeta, Phi Kappa Phi. Epsilon Sigma Phi. Republican. Methodist. Mason (32°, Shriner). Rotarian. Home: Washington, D.C.†

SNYDER, ERWIN PAUL, lawyer; b. Council Bluffs, Ia., Jan. 20, 1891; s. Samuel Bruce and Mary (McGlaughlin) S.; A.B., U. Neb., 1912; LL.B. cum laude, Harvard, 1916; m. Fern K. Bennett, July 28, 1917; children—Richard Bruce, John Bennett. Admitted to Mich. Bar. 1916, Ill. bar, 1920; practicing lawyer, Detroit, 1916-17, Chicago, 1920-75; partner and of counsel Chadwell, Keck, Kayser, Ruggles & McLaren, and predecessor firms; gen. counsel Kraft Foods division National Dairy Products Corp. and predecessors, 1922-75. Served as capt., U.S.R.C.A.C., 1917-19; adjutant, Anti-Aircraft Service, G.H.Q., A.E.F., France, 1918-19. Mem. Am., Ill., Chgo. bar assns. Republican. Conglist. Clubs: Legal, Law, University, Mid-Day, Indian Hill. Home: Wilmette, IL Died June 11, 1975.

SNYDER, GEORGE GORDON, physician, surgeon, b. Rosemont, Pa., Sept. 30, 1908; s. George Gordon and Elizabeth Montgomery (Anderson) S.; M.D., Temple, 1934; m. Lillian Christine Graham, June 24, 1936; children—George Gordon III, Jacqueline Graham. Postgrad. studies in otolaryngology U. Pa., 1935-36; intern Bryn Mawr (Pa.) Hosp., 1934-35, mem. staff, 1936-69, mem. exec. com., 1968-69, v.p. surg. staff, 1968; spl. course in endaural surgery Lempert Inst. div. Columbia-Presbyn. Med. Center, 1950; spl. course in facial plastic surgery Mt. Sinai Med. Center, 1953; mem. staff Misericordia Cons. Hosp., Phila., Paoli Meml. Hosp., others. courtesy staff Mt. Sinai Med. Center; otolaryngologist Villanova Coll., Swarthmore Coll., Rosemont Coll., Bryn Mawr Coll., Harcum Jr. Coll., Valley Forge Mil. Acad. and Jr. Coll., Malvern Prep. Sch.; asst. prof. otorhinogology Temple U.

Diplomate Am. Bd. Otolaryngology. Fellow A.C.S., Am. Laryngol., Rhinol. and Otol. Soc., Internat. Coll. Surgeons; mem. A.M.A., Am. Acad. Ophthalmology and Otolaryngology, Am. Acad. Facial Plastic and Reconstructive Surgery, Royal Soc. Medicine (London), Pan Am. Congress Bronchoesophalogy and Otorhinolaryngology, Pan Am. Med. Assn., Pan Pacific Surg. Assn., Internat. Congress Orolaryngologists, Pa. Acad. Ophthalmology and Otolaryngology, Pa. Hist. Soc., Montgomery County Med. Soc., Doctors Golf Assn., Royal Soc. Surgery (London), French Acad., Am. Triological Soc., Phila. Mus. Art, Pa. Acad. Fine Arts. Clubs: Merion Cricket, St. David's Golf (dir.), Seaview (N.J.) Country, Country of N.C. Home: Bryn Mawr, Pa. Died Mar. 21, 1969; buried St. Denis Cemetery, Havertown, Pa.

SOANS, CYRIL ARTHUR, lawyer; b. nr. Nottingham, Eng., May 31, 1884; s. John Isaac and Martha Anne (Campion) S.; grad. mech. and elec. engring., Univ. Coll., Nottingham, 1902; student N.Y., Law Sch., 1912-13; LL.B., John Marshall Law Sch., Chgo., 1915, LL.D., 1954, m. Mary Agnes Finn, June 14, 1913; children—Jacqueline, Tracy. Came to U.S., 1904, naturalized, 1911. Engr. mining projects, B.C., Nev., 1903-05; research telphone engring., mfr. elec. supplies, Chgo., 1906-10; research elec. starting and lighting of automobiles, N.Y.C., 1911-13; practice of law, specializing patent law, Chgo., from 1913; mem. firm Soans, Anderson, Luedeka & Fitch, and predecessors, 1918-65. Mem. Am. (chmn. patent sect. 1956), Chgo. bar assns., Assn. Bar City of N.Y., Chgo. Patent Law Assn. (pres. 1948), Am. Inst. of Electrical Engineers, Am. Patent Law Assn. Republican. Episcopalian. Mason (K.T., Shriner). Clubs: Oak Park (Ill.) Country; Union League (Chgo.). Home: Oak Park, Ill. Deceased.

SOBELOFF, SIMON E., judge; b. Dec. 3, 1894; s. Jacob and Mary (Kaplan) S.; LL.B., U. Md., 1915; m. Irene Ehrlich, May 19, 1918; children— Evva, Ruth. Asst. city solicitor, Balt., 1919-23, dep. city solicitor, 1927-31, city solicitor, 1943-47; U.S. atty. Dist. Md., 1931-34; resumed law practice; chmn. Commn. on Adminstrv. Orgn. of State Md., 1951-52; chief judge Md. Ct. of Appeals, 1952-54; solicitor gen. of U.S., 1954-55; judge U.S. Ct. of Appeals for 4th Circuit, 1956, chief judge, 1958-64, asso. judge. Home: Baltimore, Md. Died July 11, 1973.

SOBER, HERBERT ALEXANDER, biochemist; b. N.Y.C., Feb. 24, 1918; s. Casper C. and Sarah (Victor) S.; B.S., Coll. City N.Y., 1938; M.S., U. Wis., 1940, Ph.D., 1942; m. Eva Katzenelbogen, Aug. 27, 1941 (dec. Nov. 1972); children—Lillian Sara, Barbara Jane (Mrs. Daniel Rosvold). Civilian toxicologist C.W.S., U.S. Army, Edgewood, Md., 1942-45; research asso. gastroenterology lab. Mt. Sinai Hosp., N.Y.C., 1945-47; sr. asst. scientist, then scientist dir. Nat. Cancer Inst., NIH, USPHS, Bethesda, Md., 1947-59, chief lab. of biochemistry, 1959-68; chief lab. of nutrition and endocrinology Nat. Inst. Arthritis and Metabolic Diseases, NIH, Bethesda, 1968-74. Co-chmn. sect. proteins Gordon Research Conf., 1963. Recipient Hillebrand award Chem. Soc. Washington, 1970; Superior Service award Dept. Health, Edn. and Welfare, 1972. Mem. Am. Chem. Soc. (councilor), A.A.A.S., Am. Acad. Arts and Scis., Am. Soc. Cancer Research, Am. Soc. Biol. Chemists, Biochem. Soc. (Brit.), Israel Biochem. Soc., Soc. Exptl. Biology and Medicine, Found. Advanced Edn. in Scis., Biophys. Soc., Sigma Xi, Phi Lambda Upsilon. Asso. editor Biochemistry, Analytical Biochemistry, Preparative Biochemistry, Ann. Rev. of Biochemistry. Editor Handbook of Biochemistry. Home: Bethesda, Md. Died Nov. 26, 1974; buried Middletown, Md.

SOFFEL, JOSEPH AUGUST, surgeon; b. Pitts., Mar. 19, 1902; s. August and Anna Maroe (Sipe) S.; M.D., U. Pitts., 1924; m. Anna Jane Soderberg, Sept. 4, 1929; children—Andrew J., Jane (Mrs. Greg Connell), Joan (Mrs. Richard Carson). Intern, West Pa. Hosp., 1924-25; sr. surgeon; resident N.Y. Postgrad. Med. Sch.; pvt. practice medicine specializing in surgery, Pitts.; instr. surgery U. Pitts. Med. Sch. Served wtih M.C., AUS, 1943-45. Diplomate Am. Bd. Surgery. Fellow A.C.S.; mem. Indsl. Med. Assn., A.M.A. Home: Pittsburgh, Pa. Died Mar. 15, 1974; buried Homewood Cemetery, Pittsburgh, Pa.

SOGLOW, OTTO, cartoonist; b. N.Y.C., Dec. 23, 1900; ed. pub. schs., N.Y.C.; student Art Student's League, N.Y.C., 1919-25; m. Anna Rosen, Oct. 11, 1928; 1 dau., Tona. Began as cartoonist, 1925; cartoonist for leading mags. including New Yorker, Life, Judge, Collier's, Harper's Bazaar, etc.; with New York World, 1925-26; with King Features Synidate, 1933-75. Recipient Reuben award as outstanding cartoonist of the year Nat. Cartoonists Soc., 1967; Elzie Segar award for outstanding cartooning, 1972. Mem. Soc. Illustrators (N.Y.), Nat. Cartoonists Soc. Club: Dutch Treat. Author: Pretty Pictures, 1931; Everything's Rosy, 1932; The Little King, 1933 (with D. Plotkin) Wasn't the Depression Terrible?, 1934. Home: New York City, N.Y. Died Apr. 3, 1973.

SOLER, JUAN JOSÉ, Paraguayan diplomat; b. Asunción, Paraguay, June 24, 1880; s. Enrique and Francisca (Arévalo) S.; received bachelor's degree, Nat. Coll. of Asunción, Doctor of Law and Social Science, 1910; m. Mariana Sosa, Aug. 1906; children—Carlos Alberto, Ana Maria (wife of Dr. Julio Manuel Morales), Haidé (wife of Dr. Raúl Peña). Worked for supt. of elementary edn., 3 years; teacher Spanish and history, Nat. Coll. of Asunción; sec. of pres.'s office in govts. of Dr. Cecilio (Báez and Gen. Benigno Ferreira, 1905-08; became congressman, 1910, serving as v.p. of chamber; retired from political activity to devote self to legal profession and teaching of civil and internat. pvt. law at U. of Asunción; served as senator, 1925-31; then minister to Mexico; extraordinary envoy to Washington conf. on Bolivian non-aggression pact, 1931; mem. Nat. Delimitation Commn. and pres. Pilcomayan Commn. for Regulation of Paraguay-Argentina boundary, 1933; again senator, serving as mem. foreign rleations com. until dismissal of congress; Paraguayan minister to U.S., 1940-42. Mem.-founder Paraguayan Inst. of History and Geography; pres. Nat. Commn. for Codification of Internat. Pvt. Law; mem. Am. Inst. Internat. Law (Havana), Am. Inst. of Law and Comparative Legislation (Mexico), Inst. of History and Numismatics (Buenos Aires). Awarded hon. professorship of internat. pub. law and gold medal by U. of Mexico for lecture entitled "Doctrina Extrata," Author: International Pacifism of Paraguay, 1924; Foreign Law Status (senate bill), 1926; Bill for creation of Commn. of Jurists for redaction of the codices and explication of the motives, 1926; lectures on internat. pvt. law, 1927; University Reform, 1929; Estrata Doctrine, 1930; Mexico-Paraguay, 1930; White Book of Paraguayan Foreign Minister (containing Dr. Soler's work for Washington conf. on Bolivian non-aggression pact); Project For Commission for League and National Aspiration, 1934; The Liberal Party and the Defense of Chaco, 1935; also author numerous articles on Paraguayan nat. and foreign affairs. Address: Washington, D.C.*†

SOLLENBERGER, RICHARD TALBOT, educator; b. Balt., Feb. 1, 1907; s. Lawrence Randal and Ella (Morrow) S.; B.S., U. Va., 1930, M.S., 1933, Ph.D., 1936; m. Marian Worthington, Sept. 2, 1933; children—Richard W., Alice S. (Mrs. Erard Moore). Clin. psychologist U. Va. Hosp., 1933-36; research asst., instr. Inst. Human Relations, Yale, 1936-40; asst. prof. Mt. Holyoke Coll., South Hadley, Mass., 1940-42, asso. prof., 1946-50, prof., 1950-75, chmn. dept. psychology, edn., 1949-51; vis. lectr. Smith Coll., 1942, U. Va., summer 1951, U. Mich., summer 1959, U. Mass., 1963. Vice pres. bd. dirs. Area Mental Health Assn. Served to lt. col. USAAF, 1942-46. Mem. Am., Eastern, Mass. psychol. assns., A.A.A.S., Sigma Xi. Author: (with others) Frustration and Aggression, 1939. Editor: (with others) Psychol. Research on Operational Training in the Continental Air Forces, 1947. Contbr. articles profl. jours. Home: South Hadley, Mass. Died Aug. 21, 1975; buried St. Paul's Episcopal Ch., Ivy, Va.

SOLOMON, SIDNEY L., retail business exec.; b. Salem, Mass., Feb. 21, 1902; s. Samuel and Rose (Rosen) S.; B.S., Harvard, 1922, M.B.A., 1924; m. Jeanette Rabinovitz, Aug. 18, 1931; children—Richard, Peter. Pres., gen. mgr. Abraham & Straus, Bklyn., chief exec. officer, 1960-63, chmn. bd., chief exec. officer 1963-71, ret.; v.p. Federated Dept. Stores, N.Y.C., 1971-75. Home: New York City, N.Y. Died Sept. 24, 1975.

SOMERALL, JAMES BENTLEY, beverage co. exec.; b. Evergreen, Ala., Dec. 19, 1917; s. James Elhanon and Susan (Hanks) S.; student U. Ala., 1933-37, LL.D., 1971; m. Dorothy Jane Fiss, Feb. 21, 1942; children—Candace Jane (Mrs. Harvey S. Sherber), Stephen Robert. Vice pres., gen. mgr. Coca-Cola Bottling Co. of R.I. 1949-53; v.p. Pepsi-Cola Co., N.Y.C., 1953-55; pres. Pepsi-Cola Bottling Co. Cin., 1955-63; pres., chief exec. officer Pepsi-Cola Met. Bottling Co. N.Y.C., 1963-65; pres., chief exec. officer Pepsi-Cola, 1965-69, chmn. bd., chief exec. officer Pepsi-Cola, 1969-71; chief exec. officer, chmn. bd. Am. Pepsi-Cola Bottlers, Inc., N.Y.C. 1971-73; pres., chief exec. officer Champale, Inc., 1973-75. Served as 1st inf., AUS, 1942-45. Mem. Commerce Execs. Soc. of U. Ala. (chmn.). Episcopalian. Clubs: Sky, Raffles (N.Y.C.); Hope (Providence); Dunes, Point Judith Country (Narragansett, R.I.). Home: New York City, NY. Died Jan. 4, 1975; interred Evergreen, Ala.

SOMERS, JOSEPH PATRICK, steel co. exec.; b. Phila., 1919; ed. U. Notre Dame, 1941; m. Mary Hyland, Vice pres. Wyckoff Steel Co. div. AMPCO-Pitts. Corp., Pitts. Home: Pittsburgh, Pa. Died Sept. 23, 1974; interred Calvary Cemetery, Pittsburgh, Pa.

SOMERS, RICHARD H, army officer; b. Mantua, N.J., Dec. 8, 1881; s. Aaron B. and Lydia H. (Iredell) S.; B.S., U.S. Mil. Acad., 1907; grad. Ordnance Sch. of Tech., 1912, Army Industrial Coll., 1924; M.B.A., Harvard U., 1928; m. Sara Edith Shute, Aug. 28, 1907; children—Marion Sommers Foster, Dorothy Sommers Smith, Omar Herbert, Helen Somers Brown. Commd. 2d lt., Coast Arty. Corps, June 14, 1907; promoted through grades to brig. gen. (temp.) Oct. 1, 1940; retired for age, June 30, 1942, Sec. Army Ordnance Assn., 1922-25, exec. sec., 1942-44. Lecturer in math., Dartmouth Coll., from 1944. Mem. Am. Econ. Assn. Royal Econ. Soc. Club: National Press. Editor: Army Ordnance, 1922-25 and 1942-44. Address: Hanover, N.H.†

SOUERS, WARREN EARL, lawyer; b. Massillon, O., May 9, 1916; s. Franklin Earl and Mildred (Boice) S.; B.A., U. Pitts., 1941; J.D., Western Reserve U., 1948; m. Dorothy Jane Foltz, Nov. 6, 1948; children—Franklin E. II, Joseph W. Spl. investigator Retail Credit Co., Pitts., 1941-42; admitted to Ohio bar, 1948; research atty. Ohio Bur. Code Revision, Columbus, O., 1948-50; practiced in Marietta, O., 1950-75; spl. asst. to atty. gen. of Ohio, 1962-71. Dir., sec.-treas. Marietta Masonic Bldg. Co., 1953-71; dir. Marietta Food Center, Inc., Marble King Industries, Inc., Colonial Enterprises, Inc., Marietta Replica Arms, Inc., Alfco-Rokeby, Inc. City solicitor, Marietta, O., 1952-55, 58-59, councilman, 1956-57; mem. Marietta City Bd. Edn. 1960-67, pres., 1961, 62, 66, v.p., 1962-63. Mem. Marietta City Bd. Health, 1968-73; mem. Citizens Traffic Commn. Marietta City, 1966-67; council mem. at large Kootaga Area council Boy Scouts of America, 1967-69. Bd. trustees Ohio Eastern Star Home, 1961-63; trustee Clinic-Hosp. Fund, 1957-60; exec. bd. adv. com. Licensed Practical Nurse Assn. Ohio; pres. bd. trustees Washington County Library, 1967-68. Served with USAAF, 1942-45; ETO. Mem. Am., Ohio State, Washington County (pres. 1960-61) bar assns., Marietta Tourists and Conv. Bur. (pres. 1963), Ohio (trustee 1963), S.E. Ohio (trustee, exec. com. 1963-68) sch. bd. assns., Am. Legion, Washington County Law Library Assn. (trustee 1971, 72, 73, chmn. 1973), S.A.R., Ohio Library Trustees Assn. (mem. legislative com. 1971), Southeastern Ohio Library Orgn. (trustee, pres. 1971-73), Pi Sigma Alpha, Phi Delta Phi. Presbyn. (elder). Mason. Club: Marietta Advertising (pres. 1962-63). Home: Marietta, O. Died Jan. 17, 1975.

SOULES, MARY E. (MRS. POWELL J. BING), physician; b. Rochester, Minn., June 8, 1910; d. James and Wilhelmina (Neukom) Soules; B.A., U. N.D., 1931, B.S., 1932; M.D., U. Louisville, 1934; M.P.H., Harvard Sch. Pub. Health, 1942; m. Powell J. Bing, Jan. 22, 1938; children—Melvin D., Mary Ann, Jane E. Intern, New Eng. Hosp. for Women and Children, Boston, 1934-35; resident, N.D. State Sch. for Retarded, Grafton, 1934-40; dir. maternal, child health N.D. State Dept. Health, Bismarck, 1940-44; health officer Southwestern Dist. Health Dept., New Eng., N.D., 1945-47, Multnomah County, Ore, 1947-48, Clackamas County, Ore., 1948-52, Missoula County, Mont., 1952-56, Deschuttes County, Ore., 1956, Douglas County, Ore., 1956-59; dir. disease control Mont. State Dept. Health, 1959-71, chief health services, 1961-71. Home: Helena, Mont. Died Feb. 12, 1971.

SOUTH, LILLIAN H., (Mrs. H. H. Tye), bacteriologist; b. Bowling Green, Ky., 1880; d. J. F. (M.D.) and Martha Bell (Moore) South; ed. Potter Coll., Bowling Green, Paterson Gen. Hosp.; M.D., Woman's Med. Coll. of Pa.; m. Judge H. H. Tye, July 8, 1926 (dec.) Served as state bacteriologist of Ky. Made sanitary survey of Kentucky in reference to hookworms, and found it prevalent in 106 counties; also has made investigations as to agency of the house fly in spreading hookworm disease, and poliomyelitis; also made leprosy survey of the state. News editor Ky. Medical Journal. Now dir. of Labs., Ky.; directed Sch. for Lab. Tech., State Dept. of Health. Diplomate Am. Bd. Preventive Medicine, Pub. Health. Fellow A.M.A. (3d vice pres.), Association Southern Med. Women (ex-pres.; sec.-treas.), Tri-County Med. Soc. (v.p.), Whitley Co. (Ky.) Med. Soc. Presbyterian. Col. on Governor's Staff. Home: Williamsburg, Ky.†

SOUTHERLAND, CLARENCE ANDREW, lawyer; b. Baltimore, Apr. 10, 1889; s. Clarence and Amey (Fairbank) S.; student Friends Sch., Wilmington, Del., 1895-1905, Princeton, 1905-07; LL.B., Georgetown U., 1913; LL.D., U. Del., 1956; married Katharine Virden, Jan 11, 1923; children—Katherine Virden (Mrs. Stuart H. Johnson, Jr.), Clare Amey (Mrs. Charles B. Lenahan II). Admitted to Del. bar, 1914, practiced at Wilmington, 1914-51; atty. gen. State Del., 1925-29; chief justice Supreme Ct. Del., 1951-63; counsel Potter, Anderson & Corroon. Member of the Am., Del. State (pres. 1933-35), New Castle Co. and City of N.Y. bar assns. Republican. Clubs: Greenville Country; Wilmington. Home: Wilmington, Del. Died June 16, 1973.

SOYER, MOSES, artist; b. Russia, Dec. 25, 1899; s. Abraham and Bella (Schneyer) S.; came to U.S., 1913; naturalized, 1925; ed. Cooper Union Art Sch., N.A.D., Beaux Arts Inst., Ferrer Art Sch., Ednl. Alliance Art Sch.; study abroad; m. Ida Chassner, June 1926; 1 son, David. Artist, 1922-74. Represented by painting in numerous permanent collections including Met. Mus. of Art, Whitney Mus. Am. Art, New-York Hist. Soc., N.Y.C., Phillips Meml. Gallery, Washington, Toledo (O.) Mus., Congressional Library, Swope Mus., Terre Haute, Ind., Newark (N.J.) Mus., Brooklyn Mus., Modern Mus., N.Y.C., Butler Inst. Am. Art, and many private collections. Executed murals in post office at Phila., Pa. Mem. An Am. Group, Inc., Am. Soc. Painters, Gravers and Sculptors, Nat. Inst. Arts and Letters, N.A.D., Artists Equity. Home: New York City, N.Y. Died Sept. 2, 1974; cremated.

SPAATZ, CARL, army officer; b. Boyertown, Pa., June 28, 1891; s. Charles and Ann (Muntz) S.; B.S., U.S. Mil. Acad., 1914; student Aviation Sch., San Diego, Calif., 1915-16; grad. Tactical Sch., 1925, Command and Gen.

Staff Sch., 1936; m. Ruth Harrison, 1917; children—Katherine Harrison, Rebecca Wayne, Carla. Commd. 2d lt., U.S. Army, 1914, and advanced to brig. gen., 1940, general, 1945; with 25th Inf., Hawaii, 1914-15; with 1st Aero Squadron, N.M., 1916, later with Punitive Expdn., Mexican border; 3d Aero Squadron, Tex., 1917; became major, 31st Aero Squadron, A.E.F., Aug. 1917; officer in charge of training, Issoudon, France, Nov. 1917-Sept. 1918; became comdr. pursuit squadron; brought down 2 enemy planes in St. Mihiel offensive (awarded Distinguished Service Cross); asst. air officer Western Dept., San Francisco, 1919-20; charge Flying Circus, flying over U.S. in connection with Victory Loan drive, 1919; comd. Mather Field, Calif., July-Oct. 1920; comdg. officer Kelly Field, Tex., 1920-21; air officer 8th Corps Area, 1921; comd. 1st Pursuit Group, Selfridge Field, Mich., 1922-24; Office of Chief of Air Service, 1925-29; refueling flight, Los Angeles, 1929 (awarded Distinguished Flying Cross for record established); comdr. 7th Bombardment Group; Rockwell Field, Calif., later comdg. officer of Rockwell Field, 1929-31; comdg. officer 1st Bombardment Wing, March Field, Calif., 1931-33; chief of training and operations div., Office of Chief of Air Corps, 1933-35; exec. officer, 2d Wing, Air Force, 1936-39; chief Plans Div., Air Corps, 1940; chief of air staff, 1941; assigned chief air force Combat Command, 1942; chief air adviser to Gen. Eisenhower, N. Africa, Dec. 1942; dep. air comdr. N. Africa Theatre of Operations, 1943; comdr. N.W. African Air Forces, Sicily, 1943; apptd. comdr. in chief U.S. Strategic Air Force in Europe, Jan. 1944; apptd. comdr. in chief, U.S. Strategic Air Force against Japan, July 1945; assigned Hdqrs. A.A.F., Washington, Oct. 1945; Comdg. Gen. Army Air Forces, 1946; chief of staff, Air Force, Department of Defense, 1947-48; retired from Army Air Force July 1948. Decorated D.S.M. with 2 Oak Leaf Clusters, D.S.C., Legion of Merit, D.F.C., Bronze Star; Mexican Service, World War I and II Victory. European-African-Middle East, Asiatic-Pacific Campaign, American Defense and American Campaign Medals; Grand Officer Legion of Honor, Crois de Guerre (France); Order of Suvorov, 2d° (Russia); Comdr's. Cross with Star, Order of Polonia Restituta (Poland); Grand Comdr. of British Empire (Gt. Britain); Order of Orange-Nassau (Netherlands); Order of Crown with Palm, Croix de Guerre with Palm (Belgium). Contbg. editor Newsweek Mag. Club: Army and Navy (Washington). Home: Chevy Chase, Md. Died July 14, 1974.

SPACHNER, JOHN VICTOR, corp. ofcl.; b. Chgo., May 7, 1898; s. Joseph and Celia (Shore) S.; student pub. schs., Marengo, Ill.; m. Beatrice Teller, Oct. 17, 1926; children—Warren Roy, Carole Joy (Mrs. Mark B. Seelen, Jr.). Began as stenographer for the Chicago Mill & Lumber Co., 1918; gen. mgr. Chgo. Mill Paper Stock Co., 1921, vice pres., 1925-28; pres., gen. mgr. Pioneer Paper Stock Co., Chgo., 1928-42; dir. purchases, transportation Container Corp. Am., 1932-42, dir. from 1937, v.p., 1939-49, exec. v.p., dir., 1949, vice chmn., 1961-63, mem. exec. com., from 1961; dir. Carton Internacional (Panama), Carton y Papel de Mexico, S.A. Europa Carton, A.G., Germany, Bremer Papier und Wellpappen Fabrik, Germany, Europa Carton Italiana, Italy, Vosa, S.p.A., Italy, Cartoenvases de Mex. S.A., Carton de Columbia S.A., Corrugadora de Carton, S.A., Carton de Venezuela, S.A., Union Grafica, S.A., N.V. Mercurius Golf carton industrie, Holland, Grafiche Ripamonti, Italy, Celulosa y Papel de Colombia, S.A., Cartones Nacionales, S.A., Venezuela, Fibras Industriales de Venezuela, S.A. Mem. bd. trustees Sarah Lawrence Coll.; bd. dirs. Aspen Inst. Humanistic Studies. Clubs: Tavern, Standard, Mid-day (Chgo.); Lake Shore Country (Glencoe, Ill.); Harmonie (N.Y.). Home: Highland Park, Ill. Died May 1974.

SPARBER, JEAN LEAH WEINSTEIN (MRS. HOWARD SPARBER), social worker, journalist; b. N.Y.C., Nov. 23, 1923; d. Joseph F. and Ruth (Friedman) Weinstein; B.A. with honors, Skidmore Coll., 1944; M.S., Columbia, 1945; m. Howard Sparber, Mar. 25, 1945; children—Peter Garth, Andrew Glen, Richard Grant. Gag writer Timmy for H. Sparber, cartoonist, Chgo. Tribune-N.Y. News Syndicate, 1956-59; writing asst. Byrd House, N.Y. Herald Tribune Syndicate, 1960-61; youth page editor, columnist Morris County's Daily Record, 1961-67; edn. editor Crossroads Mag., 1965-66; writer feature Trix of Trade, Chgo. Tribune-N. Y. News Syndicate, 1965-68, writer Winnie Winkle comic strip, from 1965; psychiat. social worker N.J. State Hosp., Greystone Park, N.J., from 1967. Vice-pres. Shotzie Products Inc., from 1962; social work cons. for team research Morristown Meml. Hosp., 1960-66; cons. social work interpretation Sparber Advt. & Pub. Relations, Morristown, N.J., from 1967. Mem. adv. bd. Morris County P.T.A., 1961-63, Greater Morristown Youth Employment Service, 1962-66; sec. Morristown Coop. Nursery Sch., 1956-57; chmn. N.W. area Tb and Health Assn. Press Project, 1962-63; sec. Morris County Mental Health Assn., 1962-63; jud. appointee Morristown Juvenile Conf. Com., 1964-67; active various community drives. Recipient journalism award Toy Guidance Council, 1961, 3d prize N.J. Press Assn., 1962. Mem. Nat. Assn. Social Workers, Acad. Certified Social Workers. Home: Morristown, N.J. Died Feb. 1972.

SPAULDING, FREDERIC HENRY, univ. pres.; b. Norridgewock, Me., Dec. 20, 1892; s. Frank Willie and Ida May (Bell) S.; A.B., Bates Coll., 1916; Ed.M., Harvard, 1926; Ed.D., U. Tampa, 1936; m. Helen Margaret McKay, Sept. 8, 1924; children—Frederick William, David Butler. High sch. prin., Mass., 1916-20; teacher and prin. Hillsborough Sr. High Sch., Tampa, Fla., 1921-33; founder, 1921, University of Tampa, becoming president; later pres. Edgewood Park Sch., Briarcliff Manor, N.Y.; founder Tampa Junior College, 1931; founder and honorary director Fla. State Music Festival Assn. Served as chemist Chem. Warfare Service, U.S. Army, 1918. State del. World Fed. of Edn. Assns., Geneva, Switzerland, 1928. Mem. N.E.A., Fla. Edn. Assn., Am. Legion, Hillsborough County. Schoolmasters Club (founder; 1st pres.). Episcopalian. Mason (32°, K.T., Shriner). Clubs: Lions (pres. local chapt.), Fla. Bates (sec. and treas.), Fla. Harvard. Author: (monograph) The Teaching of English. Address: Briarcliff Manor, N.Y. Died Mar. 1974.

SPAULDING, JOHN PEARSON, book co. exec.; b. Cambridge, Mass., Aug. 22, 1923; s. William Ellsworth and Caroline Metcalf (Pearson) S.; grad. Williston Acad., 1941, Browne and Nichols Sch., 1942; B.A., Harvard, 1947; m. Anne Nute, Dec. 9, 1944; children—Martha Lee (Mrs. Joel Greenberger), Stephen John, Donald Richard. Fgn. service staff officer Dept. State, Washington, 1947; vice consul, Madras, India, 1948-50; asst. editor Reader's Digest Internat. Edits., N.Y.C., 1951-54; with Scholastic Mags., Inc., N.Y.C., from 1954, exec. v.p., 1967-71, pres., from 1971, also dir.; dir. Scholastic-TAB Publications, Ltd., Scholastic Publs. Ltd., H.J. Ashton Co., Ltd., H.J. Ashton Co. (Pty.), Ltd., Scholastic Japan, Ltd., Continental Field Services. Mem. Govt. Adv. Com. on Internat. Book and Library Programs from 1973; cons. Franklin Book Programs, Inc., Teheran, Iran, from 1964. Trustee Williston-Northampton Sch., Easthampton, Mass. Served to 1st lt. AUS, World War II; CBI. Decorated Bronze Star, Purple Heart. Mem. Assn. Am. Pubs. (vice chmn. from 1973). Clubs: Harvard (Westchester); Harvard Varsity, Harvard, Publishers' Lunch (pres. N.Y.C. 1973-74). Home: Armonk, N.Y. Died Sept. 3, 1974; buried Lake Winnepesaukee, N.H.

SPEAR, RAY, naval officer; b. Sept. 23, 1878; s. Joseph and Jennie B. (Ray) S.; entered U.S. Navy, Mar. 17, 1900; advanced through the grades to rear admiral, Supply Corps, Oct. 1929; m. Emilie Victorine, dau. of late Hon. Louis Piollet, Wysox, Pa.; children—Joseph Hornsby III (dec.), Mary (Mrs. R. S. Rooney), Louis P. (lt. comdr. U.S.N., Annapolis). Paymaster General, U.S. Navy; retired; recalled to active duty as gen. inspector Supply Corps. Awarded D.S.C. Navy D.S.M. Army, and other decorations. Home: St. Helena, Cal.†

SPEARE, MORRIS EDMUND, ednl. director; b. Boston, Mass.; s. Jacob and Marie (Rosen) S.; A.B., cum laude, Harvard U., 1908; A.M., 1909; Ph.D., Johns Hopkins U., 1923; m. Florence Jean Lewis, Nov. 2, 1915. Teacher, Fay Sch., Southboro, Mass., winter 1910; in charge English composition Colby Coll., Waterville, Me., 1910-11; instr. English. U. of Wis., 1911-14; substitute instr. English, Harvard, summer 1913; rep. in New England in behalf of the Permanent Tariff Commn. League of U.S. 1915-16, leading to establishment of the U.S. Tariff Commn. Bd.; mem. faculty of English of history and English, U.S. govt. schools, 1916-21; mem. faculty of English and History, University of California, summer 1923; head English dept. Baltimore schs. of U. of Md., 1922-25; with editorial dept., and dir. of ednl. dept. Oxford Univ. Press, 1925-29; lectured during 1928, 29, at U. of Oregon, U. of Wash., U. So. Cal., U. of Cal. So. Div., Duke U.; editorial staff of Alfred A. Knopf, Inc., pubs., 1929-30; ednl. editor Americana Encyclopaedia 1931-32; chmn., professor English St. John's U., N.Y.C., 1933-40; dir. ednl. dept. Funk & Wagnalls Co., 1936-37; editor of Pocket Books, Inc., publishers, New York, 1939-41 asso. editor World Publishing Co., Cleve., N.Y.C., Toronto, 1941-45; ednl. dir. Nat. Coal Assn. (Bituminous Institute), 1945-58. Mem. A.A.U.P., Nat. Sci. Teachers Assn., N.E.A., Am. Assn. Sch. Adminstrs., Bus.-Industry Orgn. of Harvard, Johns Hopkins alumni assns. Episcopalian Clubs: Harvard, Univ., Cosmos, Newcomen. Author or co-author: numerous books, from 1918 including: Coal and Coal Mining. monograph Am. Industries Series, 1957; Coal and Coal Mining articles Ency. Brit., 1951-57, Ency. Americana, 1956-57, Colliers Ency. Yearbooks, 1954, 57, World Scope Encyclopedia, 1946-52; Britannica Junior Ency., Fuels, 1954; Am. Peoples Ency., 1956-57; chpts. coal industry and coal mining in The Development of American Industries, 1951; Industrial Economic Geography, 1955; The Bituminous Coal Story booklet. 1952, rev. to 1957; Plant Life to Plastics, 1951-52. Gen. editor various anthologies including Chelsea Classics (46 vols.). Home: Washington, DC. Died Feb. 27, 1974.

SPEARS, LAWRENCE NAPOLEON, lawyer; b. Jasper, Tenn., Oct. 15, 1880; s. William Douglas and Lou (Hall) S.; student Pryor Instn., Vanderbilt U.; LL.B., Cumberland Law Sch.; m. Maude Stewart, Mar. 30, 1902; children—Jennie S. (Mrs. V.S. Welch), William Douglas, Mary Stewart (Mrs. W. W. Jacobs). Admitted to bar of Tenn., 1901 and practiced in Chattanooga, from 1910. Col. on Gov. Browning staff. Mem. Am., Tenn. and Chattanooga bar assns., Kappa Sigma. Elk. Mason, K.P. Democrat. Mem. Christian Ch. Home: Chattanooga, Tenn.*†

SPECHT, FREDERICK WILLIAM, business exec.; b. Lambertville, N.J. Jan. 6, 1890; s. Frederick Daniel and Gertrude (Sweeny) S.; student Springfield (Mass.) pub. schs., Springfield business coll.; m. Anne B. Moran, August 10, 1918 (deceased 1953); children—Annette, John Henry, Gerard Charles; married 2d, Dorothy Fagan, 1954. Student salesman, Armour and Co.'s Springfield br., Feb., 1910; mgr. of several br. houses, asst. dist. mgr., Phila., 1924, dist. mgr., Wilkes-Barre, 1925, dist. mgr., Phila., 1927, product sales mgr., Chicago, 1935, vice pres., 1936, gen. sales mgr., 1938, pres., 1947-57, dir., from 1948, chief executive officer, 1949, chmn. of board, 1952-61; dir. Am. National Bank and Trust Co. of Chicago, Pullman Company, American Industrial Leasing Company. Trustee Illinois Institute Tech. Decorated Knight of Malta. Member Nat. Assn. Mfrs. (dir.). Clubs: Economic, Tavern, Chicago, Chicago Athletic, Old Elm Country, and Racquet (Chicago); Chicago Golf (Wheaton, Illinois); Everglades (Palm Beach, Fla.). Home: Wheaton, Ill. Died May 27, 1973; interred St. Michaels Cemetery, Wheaton, Ill.

SPECTHRIE, SAMUEL WALDO, educator; b. Aug. 13, 1908; s. Meyer and Anna (Zahn) S.; B.S., U. Ill.; M.B.A., Northwestern U.; m. Mary Kleinerman, June 14, 1931; children—Jared, Ida Rae, Myra May. Faculty, Northwestern U., 1929-46; faculty 1946, chmn. dept., 1946-70; cons. accountant. C.P.A., Ill. Mem. Am. Assn. U. Profs., Financial Execs. Inst., Am. Accounting Assn., Ill. Soc. C.P.A.'s, Am. Inst. C.P.A.'s. Jewish religion. Author: Mathematics for the Accountant, 1940; Industrial Accounting, 1942, 47, 59, Basic Cost Accounting, 1950. Home: Skokie, IL. Died Nov. 8, 1973.

SPECTOR, BENJAMIN, physician; b. Bklyn., July 8, 1893; s. Maxwell and Ida (Schreiber) S.; M.D., N.Y.U. and Bellevue Hosp. Med. Coll., 1922; grad. study Mount Desert Island Biol. Lab., 1928, Mayo Clinic, 1930, der Rijks U., U. Groningen and Utrecht (Holland), 1932, Hunterian Mus., Royal Coll. Surgeons (London), 1932, Inst. Embryology Carnegie Inst., 1933; m. Bertha Burmann, July 5, 1919. Asst. anatomy N.Y.U. and Bellevue Hosp. Med. Coll., 1915-17, instr., 1917-22; asst. prof. Tufts U. Sch. Medicine, 1922-24, asso. prof., 1925-32, prof., chmn. dept. bioanatomy, after 1933, prof. hisotry of medicine, 1939, then emeritus; cons. bioantaomy New Eng. Center Hosp. Trustee Boston Med. Library; chmn. Friends of Armed Forces Med. Library, Washington. Fellow Royal Micros. Soc. London, Mass. Med. Soc. (mem. council); mem. Am. Assn. Anatomists, Am. Assn. History Medicine (treas. 1946-48-52, vice pres. 1953, president 1956-58, Garrison lectr. 1950), Hist. Sci. Soc. (council 1954-56), Med. Library Assn., Internat. Coll. Surgeons (Coll. of Electors), Internat. Assn. Dental Research, Am. Soc. Ophthal. and Otolaryngol. Allergy (hon.), Sigma Xi, Phi Delta Epsilon, Alpha Omega Alpha. Clubs: Biohistorical (pres. 1952), Boston Medical History (sec. 1935-45, pres. 1946-48), Author: A History of Tufts College Medical School, 1893-1943, 1943; One Hour of Medical History, 5 vols., 1931-36. 1931-36. Contbr. articles in field to tech. and lit. publs. Formerly hon. cons. Army Med. Library; formerly civil cons. U.S. Army. Home: Brookline, Mass., Died Feb. 17, 1976.

SPENCE, HOMER ROBERTS, judge, lawyer; b. San Francisco, Mar. 15, 1891; s. Clark and Grace Helene (Roberts) S.; A.B. Stanford U., 1913, J.D., 1915; LL.D., Williamette U., 1965; m. Helen Browne, May 22, 1929 (dec. 1951); children—Maynard Roberts, Schuyler Deloss; m. 2d, Mrs. Frances D. Horton, Nov. 15, 1952. Admitted to practice law before state and fed. courts, 1915; practiced in San Francisco and Alameda counties, 1915-27; judge of Superior Ct., Alameda County, 1927-30; asso. justice Dist. Ct. Appeals, 1930-45; asso. justice Supreme Ct., 1945-60. Mem. Cal. Legislature, 1921-27. Trustee Stanford U. Commd. 1st lt. F.A., U.S. Army, 1917; served with French 6th Army Corps during Aisne-Marne defensive, later with 314th F.A., 80th (Blue Ridge) Div., U.S. Army; instr. arty. O.T.C., Saumur, France; disch., 1919; capt. F.A. Res. Corps, until 1935. Pres., mem. adv. bd. Alameda council Boy Scouts Am.; recipient Silver Beaver award Nat. council Boy Scouts, 1943. Mem. Am., San Francisco, Alameda County Bar assns., Conf. of Cal. Judges (pres.), Stanford Law Soc. (pres.), Native Sons, Am. Legion, Am. Judicature Soc., Stanford Assos. (pres.), Cal. Alameda hist. socs., Chi Psi, Phi Delta Phi. Elk (exalted ruler and hon. life mem.). Club: Commonwealth (gov., pres., chmn. research com. San Francisco). Home: Oakland, Cal. Died July 1, 1973.

SPENCER, CLAYTON C(REE), univ. prof.; b. Plainfield, Vt., June 16, 1894; s. Maynard French and Laura (Cree) S.; B.S., Tufts Coll., Mass., 1916; Ph.D., Syracuse U., 1928; m. Esther Call, Sept. 1917 (dec. Nov. 1919); 1 dau., Esther Elizabeth (wife of Dr. W. L. VanHorne); m. 2d, Hazel Wood, June 9, 1924; 1 son, Maynard Frederick. Asst. prof. Syracuse U., 1928-31, asso. prof., 1931-34; prof. from 1934, acting chmn. chem. dept., 1946-47; vis. prof. chemistry Coll. Puget Sound, Tacoma, Wash., summer 1951, Edinboro (Pa.)

State Coll., 1960-62. Republican. Methodist. Member American Chemical Soc., Am. Assn. Univ. Profs., Phi Beta Kappa, Sigma Xi, Phi Lambda Upsilon, Alpha Epsilon Delta, Alpha Chi Sigma. Home: Syracuse, N.Y., Died Aug. 16, 1972; interred Oakwood Cemetery, Syracuse, N.Y.

SPENCER, GUY RAYMOND cartoonist; b. Jasepr Co., Mo., Sept. 1, 1878; s. Thomas Jefferson and Amelia (Haughawout) S.; grad. Falls City (Neb.) High Sch., 1896; m. Josephine McNulty, of Butte, Mont., Mar. 16, 1904; children—Steven Murray, Lois, Roger Steese, Kathleen. Cartoonist for Omaha World-Herald, 1899-1939; contributed cartoons regularly to The Commoner, Lincoln, Neb., 1902-08. Vice chmn. Neb. Game, Forestation and Parks Commn. Democrat. Unitarian. Home: Carter Lake Club, Omaha, Neb. Address: Lincoln, Neb.†

SPENCER, HARLEY ORTON, librarian; b. Detroit, July 21, 1916; s. Harley Orton and Harriet Fredonia (Hoeflinger) S.; A.B., U. Mich., 1939; B.L.S., U. N.C., 1947; m. Artheda Jean McFaul, June 18, 1949; 1 dau., Sarah Elizabeth. Head librarian Mishawaka (Ind.) Pub. Library, from 1947; dir. Ind. Library Film Circuit. Pres., bd. dirs. St. Joseph County Vis. Nurse Assn.; bd. dirs. South Bend Symphony Assn. Served with USAAF, World War II. Named Mishawaka citizen of the year, 1969. Mem Ind. Library Assn. (past pres.), Am. Heritage Round Table. Presbyn. (elder), Mason. Club: Mishawaka Garden. Home: Mishawaka, IN. Died Apr. 4, 1974.

SPENCER, HOWARD BONNELL, artist; b. Plainfield, N.J., Dec. 31, 1870; s. James Aborn and Anna Lewis (Bonnell) S.; student Art Student's League N.Y., 1904-07; m. Viola Winona Bogart, Nov. 18, 1903; children—Rev. Howard Bonnell, Eugene Bogart; m. 2d, Mary Isabel Coats, June 2, 1947. Exhibited Nat. Acad. Design, Nat. Arts Club, Allied Artists Am., Am. Artists Profl. League, Hudson Valley Art Assn., Nat. Soc. Pastel Painters, Nat. Soc. Casein Painters, Town Hall Club, Newton Gallery, N.Y.C.; paintings in permanent collections Wesleyan Coll., Macon, Ga., Ore. State chpt. Am. Artists Profl. League; also pvt. collections. Awarded prizes Allied Artists Am. exhbns., also Am. Artists Profl. League. Mem. Allied Artists Am., (pres. 1946-48, dir. 1948-51), Am. Artists Profl. League (dir. from 1949), Nat. Soc. Pastel Painters (v.p.), Nat. Soc. Painters Casein (dir.), S.R., Fine Arts Fedn. N.Y. Clubs: Salmagundi, Bernard (pres. 1944-47), Amateur Comedy (N.Y.C.) Home: Miami, Fla.†

SPENCER, IRENE KEYES (MRS. CHARLES TRUMAN SPENCER), retail druggist; b. Mariette, Mich., Nov. 21, 1892; d. Thomas Erwin and Alvira (Cooper) Keyes; B.A. in English and History, Mich. State U., 1929; m. Charles Truman Spencer, Sept. 28, 1915 (dec. 1924); children—George, Thomas Alvira Rose. Tchr. pub. schs., Williamston, Mich., 1913-14; substitute tchr. pub. schs., Lansing, Mich., 1930-40; owner-operator Coll. Drug Stores, East Lansing, 1924-45; pres. Campus Drug Corp., from 1950. Pres. Child Study Club, East Lansing, 1928; mem. Edward Sparrow Hosp. Aux., from 1949, treas., 1958-59, 1st v.p.; mem. Rehab. Hosp. Aux., from 1957, grey lady, 1946-51; mem. Social Welfare Bd., 1954-57, Mental Health Bd. Ingham County from 1964; pres. Practical Nurses Bd., 1960-61: pres. Coll. Women's Vols., 1959-60; v.p. Greater Lansing Panhellenic, chmn., 1962-63; member Mayors Beautification Com.; v.p. Women's War on Crime. Vice chmn. County Republicans, 1958-62; mem. Mich. Rep. Central Com., 1960-67, Ingham County Rep. Exec. Com., 6th Dist. Rep. Com., from 1964, Mich. Rep. Adv. Bd. 1961, State Rep. Fedn. Bd. Mem. East Lansing C. of C. Aux. (pres.), Am. Assn. Univ. Women (treas. 1946-47, from 1960, Irene Spencer grantee 1958), Bus. and Profl. Women's Club. Vis. Nurses Bd., Phi Mu (pres. corporating bd.). Mem. Peoples Ch. (mem. Spencer, Irene Keyes (Mrs. Charles Truman Spencer), inter-denomination planning bd.). Club: East Lansing Women's. Home: Lansing, Mich. Died Sept 23, 1971.

SPENCER, OMAR CORWIN, lawyer; b. Vernonia, Ore., Apr. 18, 1881; s. Israel Putnam and Sarah Ann (Tindall) S.; student Portland (Ore.) U. and Stanford; m. Laura V. Morgan, Jan. 1, 1907; children—Helen Elizabeth (Mrs. Thomas J. Mahoney, Jr.), John Alfred (dec.), Omar Corwin, Jr. Admitted to Calif. and Ore. bar 1905; in practice Portland; mem. firm Hart, Spencer, McCulloch, Rockwood & Davies; dir. Title & Trust Co., Portland Union Stock Yards, and others; trustee E. Henry Wemme Endowment Fund. Overseer Whitman Coll.; v.p. emeritus Portland council Boy Scouts America; director Oregon Historical Society; trustee, secretary Research Institute of Pacific Northwest; president Portland Community Chest, 1936-37. Member American Bar Assn., Phi Delta Phi. Republican. Clubs: Arlington, University, Author hist. brochures. Home: Portland, Ore.†

SPERLING, MELITTA, physician; b. Sniatyn, Austria, Oct. 15, 1899; d. Hirsch Lieb and Rachel (Biermann) Wojnilower; M.D., U. Vienna, 1924; m. Otto E. Sperling, Mar. 28,1929; came to U.S., 1938, naturalized, 1943; children—George, Eva Susan (Mrs. James D. Cockcroft). Intern, Allgemeines Krankenhaus, Hosp. of U. Vienna (Austria), 1925-26; resident Children's Hosp., Badhall, Austria, 1926-27; resident dept. psychiatry and neurology Vienna Gen. Hosp., 1927-29; postgrad. Psychoanalytic Inst., Vienna, N.Y.C.; chief child psychiatrist Bklyn. Jewish Hosp., 1940-53; cons. psychiatrist VA Hosp., Northport, N.Y.; clin. prof. psychiatry State U. N.Y. at Bklyn., tng. analyst and supr. div. psychiat. edn. Diplomate Am. Bd. Psychiatry and Neurology. Fellow Am. Psychiat. Assn., Am. Acad. Child Psychiatry; mem. A.M.A., Am. Psychoanalytic Assn., Psychoanalytic Assn. N.Y., Am. Ortho Psychiat. Assn., Am. Psychosomatic Soc. Author: The Major Neurosis and Behavior Disorders in Children, 1975. Home: New York City, N.Y., Died Dec, 28, 1973; buried Mt. Lebanon Cemetery, Queens, N.Y.

SPERO, STERLING D., educator; b. Bklyn., Nov. 20, 1896; s. Joseph and Sarah (Lewis) S.; A.B., Columbia, 1918, A.M., 1920, Ph.D., 1924; m. Louise T. Rothschild, June 2, 1921; children—Robert, James Sterling, Ellen Louise; m. Bertha Knappertsbusch, June 22, 1969. Fellow, New Sch. Social Research, 1924-25; research fellow Social Sic. Research Council, 1928-32, 20th Century Fund, 1934-35; cons. Commn. Inquiry on Pub. Service Personnel, 1935; research asso. Internat. Inst. Social Research, Columbia, 1936-37; lectr. grad. div. Bklyn. Coll., 1936; staff N.Y. State Constl. Conv. Com., 1938; prof. pub. adminstrn., Grad. Sch. Pub. Adminstrn. and Social Service, N.Y. U., from 1939, acting dean, 1959-60. Cons. N.Y. State Constl. Revision Commn., 1957-58, Ohio Legislative Service Commn., 1958; dir. Municipal Collective Bargaining study 20th Century Fund, 1967-68; mem. Mayor's Com. on Adminstrn., Tech. and Profl. Personnel, 1958. Dir. Civil Service Reform Assn. N.Y., Am. Council for Emigres in the Professions, Internat. Rescue Com., Consumers League Fair Labor Practices, League Indsl. Democracy, Labor Education Service; chmn. N.Y. N.J. regional trucking panel War Labor Bd., 1942-45; labor arbitrator's panel N.Y. Bd. Mediation. Mem. Citizens Union City of N.Y. Am. Soc. Pub. Adminstrn. (dir. N.Y. chpt. 1952-53). Am. Arbitration Assn. (mem. labor arbitrator's panel), Am. Polit. Sci. Assn., Acad. Polit. Sci., N.Y. State Polit. Sci. Assn. (dir.), Indsl. Relations Research Assn., Am. Assn. U. Profs. Author: Government as Employer, 1948; Labor Relations in British Nationalized Industry, 1955; (with Abram L. Harris) The Black Worker, 1931; (with John Carozzola) The Urban Community and Its Unionized Bureaucracies, 1973; others. Home: New York City, N.Y., Died Jan. 2, 1976.

SPERRY, PAUL, clergyman; b. Ashtabula, O., Jan. 11, 1879; s. Andrew Fuller and Hannah (Bassett) S.; A.B., George Washington U., 1902; grad. New Ch. Theol. Sch., Cambridge, Mass., 1905; m. Josephine Shallenberger, Nov. 7, 1906; 1 son, Arthur. Ordained ministry Gen. Conv. of the New Jerusalem (Swedenborgian), 1905; pastor Bath, Me., 1905-08, Brockton, Mass., 1908-15, Ch. of the Holy City, Washington, D.C., 1915-42, pastor emeritus, from 1942. Secretary Board of Missions, Swedenborgian Church, 1909-28; president General Conv. of the New Jerusalem, 1928-32. Dir. Nat. Library for the Blind, 1932, Library of Congress, 1946-49. Mem. Theta Delta Chi. Mason. Club: Cosmos. Author: Words of Life, 1917. Home: Washington, D.C.†

SPICER, ELEANOR W., (Mrs. Donald Spicer), orgn. exec.; b. Key West, Fla.; d. Raymond B. and Eleanor Russell (Chamberlin) Sullivan; m. Donald Spicer; children—Donald, Raymond, Rolf, Nancy Eleanor. Civilian supr. U.S. Naval Air Sta., San Diego, World War II. Active A.R.C. Successively chmn. geneal. records Cal. Soc. D.A.R., then corr. sec., vice regent, regent, 1966-68, historian gen., 1968-71, pres. gen., 1971-74, hon. life pres., 1974—. Mem. Coronado Women's Club (past pres.). Daus. Founders Patriots, Nat. Soc. Colonial Dames Am., Magna Carta Dames, Soc. Washington Family Descs., Mayflower Soc. Episcopalian. Address: McLean, Va., Died Sept. 13, 1974.

SPIEGEL, FREDERICK WILLIAM, business exec.; b. Chicago, Ill., July 19, 1898; s. Modie J. and Lena (Straus) S.; student pub. and pvt. schs., Ill., and Port Deposit, Md.; m. Clara Gatzert, Dec. 1, 1923; children—Frederick W., Andrew G.; married 2d, Ruth B. Hirsch, Dec. 18, 1949. with Spiegel, Inc., from 1920, pres., 1934-38, then exec. v.p., dir. President Valentine Boys Club. Served in Italy, World War I. Awarded Italian Croix de Guerra; captain, U.S. Army Air Corps, serving overseas, World War II. Clubs: Armed Forces Officer, Tavern, Central Manufacturing District, Standard, Lake Shore Country (Chgo.). Home: Chicago, Ill. Died Aug. 22, 1975.

SPINNING, JAMES M., supt. city schools; b. Rochester, N.Y., Mar. 5, 1892; s. Winfield Galoet and Helen Isabel (Martin) S.; A.B., U. of Rochester, 1913 LL.D., 1965; student U. of N.C., 1929-30; m. Mabel Hope Dunsford, Aug. 19, 1917, (dec.); m. 2d, Norma Burns Storey, Aug. 21, 1934. Teacher of English, Middletown High Sch., 1913; teacher of English, West High Sch., Rochester, N.Y., 1914-25, vice prin. 1925-31, prin. 1931-34; supt. of schools, Rochester N.Y., 1934-54; tchr. English, pub. speaking, 1954-65; author, lectr., 1954-72. Dir. Eastman Dental Dispensary; commissioner Museum Arts and Sciences; dir. Rochester Memorial Art Gallery, Rochester Y.M.C.A., Rochester Council of Social Agencies; commr. Commn. on Secondary Schs., Assn. of Colleges and Secondary Schs., Eastern States and Md., 1937-43. Served in U.S.N.R., 1918. Recipient Civic medal for community service Rochester Sci. Center, 1954. Mem. N.E.A., American Association School Adminstrs. (Year Book Commissioner, 1938, 1944, Distinguished Service award 1958). Mem. Ednl. Policies Commn., 1947-51. N.Y. State Council of Sch. Supts. (pres. 1940-41, Distinguished Service award 1964), N.Y. State Teachers Assn., Alpha Delta Phi, Phi Beta Kappa. Mason. Clubs: University, Rotary, Torch (Rochester, N.Y.). Home: Rochester, N.Y., Died Nov. 8, 1973.

SPOFFORD, GRACE HARRIET, music educator; b. Haverhill, Mass.; d. Harry H. and Sarah (Hastings) Spofford; B.A., Smith Coll., 1909; grad. in piano, 1913, organ, 1916, Peabody Conservatory Music, Balt.; Mus.D. (hon.), N.Y. Coll. Music, 1952. Instr. piano Heidelberg U., Tiffin, O., 1910-12; instr. piano Peabody Conservatory Music, 1913-18, exec. sec., 1917-24; music critic Balt. Eve. Sun, 1923-24; dean Curtis Inst. Music, Phila., 1924-31; dir. Music Sch. Henry St. Settlement, N.Y.C., 1935-54; asso. dir. N.Y. Coll. Music, 1934-38; lectr. music Katharine Gibbs Sch., N.Y.C., 1936-59, Auditioner, Fed. Music Project, 1934-39; head music div. Nat. Fedn. Settlements, 1938-42; ednl. cons. Nat. Youth Adminstrn., Radio Workshop, N.Y.C., 1941; instr. Julliard Summer Sch., 1942; counselor Vets. Music Service, N.Y.C. Center, 1945; U.S. Dept. State del. UNESCO Internat. Conf. on Music Edn., Brussels, 1953; exec. com., music com. People-to-People Program. Mem. bd. counselors Smith Coll., chmn. music com., 1954-58; del. Internat. Nongovtl. Orgns. Conf. UNESCO, 1960, Internat. Congress Profl. Music Edn., Bad Aussee and Salzburg, 1953, Internat. Council of Women Triennial, Helsinki, Finland, 1954, Montreal, Can., 1957, Istanbul, 1960, Washington, 1963, Teheran, Iran, 1966; del. Internat. Music Council, Hamburg, 1964, Rotterdam, 1966, N.Y., 1968; del. Internat. Musicol. Soc. Congress, 1958, Internat. Soc. Music Edn. Conf., Copenhagen, 1958, Budapest, 1964; Internat. Folk Music Confs., Oslo, 1955, Vienna, 1960, Que., 1961. Mem. Women's Nat. Republican Club. Recipient citiations Nat. Assn. Am. Composers and Condrs., 1954, Peabody Conservatory Alumni Assn., 1963, Mem. Internat. Council Women (past vice-convener Arts and letters, past chmn. music), Nat. Music Council (com. music in UNESCO), Nat. Guild Community Music Schs., Am. Symphony Orch. League, Friends of Philharmonic, Internat. Musicological Soc., Internat. Soc. Music Edn., Internat. Folk Music Council, (citation 1968, past chmn. internat. music relations, Presdl. citation 1971), N.Y. (dir.) fedns. music clubs, Internat. Soc. Contemporary Music, Music Tchrs. Nat. Assn., Nat. Council Women U.S. (past chmn. music), English Speaking Union, Women United UN, Nat. Council Arts and Govt., Met. Opera Guild, Am. Music Center, Am. Assn. U. Women, Soc. Asian Music, N.Y.C. Opera Guild (exec. com.), Mu Phi Epsilon. (citation 1970). Unitarian. Clubs: Cowdray (London); Musicians (N.Y.C.); Smith College; Women's City. Home: New York City, N.Y., Died June 5, 1974.

SPONBERG, HAROLD EUGENE, univ. adminstr.; b. New Richland, Minn., Sept. 26, 1918; s. Andrew F. and Hildah (Peterson) S.; B.A., Gustavus Adolphus Coll., 1940; M.A., U. Minn., 1942; Ph.D., Mich. State U., 1952; m. Grace Miller, Jan. 30, 1943; children—Arvid, Mary, Eric, Ingrid, Karl. Asst. prof. English, Mich. State U., 1946-48, asst. dean students, 1948-50, dir. Edn. Placement Bur., 1950-53, dirl univ. extension, 1954-56; exec. sec. Nat. 4-H Club Found., Chevy Chase, Md., 1953-54; v.p. No. Mich. U., 1956-61; pres. Washburn U., Topeka, 1961-65; pres Eastern Mich. U., Ypsilanti, 1965-75; asst. to pres. Mich. Technol. U., 1975. cons., State Dept., Somalia, 1965-71, mem. adv. commn., internat. programs AID, 1969-75. Charter mem. Mich. Art Train, 1968-75. Served to lt. (s.g.) USNR, World War II. Recipient Liberty Bell award. Mich Bar Assn., 1972, Outstanding Civilian award Army Dept., 1973, also distinguished service awards Mich. Assn. Sch. Adminstrs., Mich. Assn. Elementary Sch. Prins. Mem. Mich. Acad. Arts and Scis., Modern Lang. Assn., Nat. Assn. Tchrs. Coll. English, N.E.A., Coll. English, Mich. Edn. Assn., Am. Assn. U. Profs., Assn. Am. Colls., Jr. Classical League, Am. Assn. Sch. Adminstrs., Am. Personnel and Guidance Assn., Pi Gamma Mu, Pi Kappa Delta, Alpha Psi Omega, Alpha Phi Gamma, Omega Kappa, Phi Delta Kappa. Lutheran. Rotarian. Author: Rules For Parliamentary Procedure, 1948. Home: Houghton, Mich., Died Apr. 26, 1975.

SPORBORG, CONSTANCE A., (Mrs. William Dick Sporborg), civic leader; b. Cincinnati, O., July 11, 1880; d. Louis and Rose (Winkler) Amberg; B.S., Univ. of Cincinnati, 1901; L.H.D., Russell Sage Coll., 1939; m. William Dick Sporborg, June 5, 1902; children—Elizabeth (Mrs. Sidney Newton Morse), William Dick. Mem. seminar group studying conditions first hand in Germany, Poland, Russia, Gt.Britain, France, Scandinavian countries, 1937; mem. U.S. Nat. Commn. for UNESCO, 1946-49; orgnl. rep. UNRRA council meeting, Atlantic City, 1946; accredited observer U.N., from 1946. Mem. Union Women of the Americas (consultant from 1945), Inter-Am. Commn. of Women (mem. U.S. adv. com. of U.S. orgns. from 1944), Am.

Assn. for U.N. (mem. bd. from 1945), Nat. Council of Jewish Women (pres. 1926; pres. N.Y. sect. 1916-21, pres. N.Y. State Council, 1924-26), Nat. Com. Cause and Cure of War (recording sec. 1929-35, chmn. Pan-Am. commn. 1935-39; leader U.S. delegation to Inter-Am. Conf., Lima, Peru, 1938), Nat. Women's Forum (mem. adv. com. from 1945), Common Cause (adv. nat. com.), Women's Action Com. for Victory and Lasting Peace (vice chmn. from 1941), Women's Vol. Participation Defense Council (chmn. 1940), Women in World Affairs (mem. exec. nat. com. from 1942), City Fedn. Hotel Center for Self Supporting Students (v. chmn. from 1927), Women's Centennial Congress (exec. com.), Westchester Defense Council (appt. 1940). Jewish religion. Clubs: New York Federation of Women's (pres. 1925-27; chmn. dept. internat. relations, 1943-48), New York State Federation (pres. 1930-32); General Federation (chmn. resolution com. 1932-35; chmn. dept. legislation 1935-38; chmn. war housing com., 1941-44, chmn. dept. internat. relations 1944-47), Women's of Port Chester (pres. 1916-18), Women's Press of New York (chmn. internat. relations com. 1945-49), The Formers of New York State (pres. 1936-38), The Priors (pres. 1934-36). Home: New York City, N.Y.†

SPOTTSWOOD, STEPHEN GILL, bishop; b. Boston, July 18, 1897; s. Abraham Lincoln and Mary Elizabeth (Gray) S.; B.A., Albright Coll., Reading Pa., 1917; Th.B., Gordon Div. Sch., Boston, 1919; grad. study Yale, 1923-24; D.D. (hon.), Livingstone Coll., 1939; m. Viola Estelle Booker, June 10, 1919 (dec. Oct. 1953); children—Virginia Ruth (Mrs. Simon) Stephen Paul, Constance Booker (Mrs. Miller), Viola Stephanie (Mrs. Cabaniss), Alleyne Hankerson (Mrs. Hall); m. 2d, Mattie Brownita Johnson Elliott, Dec, 15, 1969. Ordained to ministry A.M.E. Zion Ch., 1920; pastor in West Newton and Lowell, Mass., 1918-20, Portland, Me., 1920-22, New Haven, 1922-25, Winston-Salem, N.C., 1925-28, Indpls., 1928-32, Buffalo, 1932-36, Washington 1936-52; elected bishop, 1952; presiding bishop West Tenn. and Miss., S. Miss., N. Ark., Ark., Okla., Tex and Colo. confs., 1952-56, Allegheny, Ohio, Mich. and Ind. confs., 1956-68, Guyana, Mich., New Eng., Phila. and Balt., V.I. confs., 1968-72. Chmn. bd. of finance, transp. and statistics, also commns. chaplains, A.M.E. Zion Ch.; mem. World Meth. Council, Nat. Council Churches; pres. Ohio Council of Churches, 1968-70 Frequent speaker on civil rights; mem. N.A.A.C.P. from 1919, pres. D.C. br., 1947-52, mem. nat. bd. dirs., from 1954, chmn. bd., from 1961. Home: Washington, D.C. Died Dec. 1, 1974.

SPRAGUE, EDWARD WHARTON, surgeon; b. New Centerville, N.Y., Apr. 6, 1880; s. Wharton Edward and Sarah Frances (Allen) S.; M.D., Coll. Physicians and Surgeons, Balt., 1903; m. Harriet Thorne Newman, Dec. 27, 1906 (dec. 1948); children—Doris S. Cusack (dec.), Janice S. Slattery; m. 2d, Mae Stone, Dec. 30, 1949 (dec. Nov. 1955), Practice of medicine, Newark, N.J., 1905-72, specializing surgery, 1919-72. Dir. Prudential Ins. Co. Am. Trustee, v.p. Welfare Fedn. Newark; gov. Med. Service Adminstrn. N.J.; trustee Hosp. Plan N.J. Med. Surg. Plan, N.J. Recipient Edward J. III award Acad. Med. No. N.J., 1945; Distinguished Service award Am. Coll. Surgeons, 1960. Diplomate Am. Bd. Surg. (founders group). Fellow A.C.S. (gov.); mem. Med. Soc. N.J., Soc. Surgeons N.J. (pres.), Acad. Medicine No. N.J. (pres.), Essex County Med. Soc. (pres.), A.M.A. Club: Essex County Country. Home: Orange, N.J. Died Feb. 21, 1974; interred Mt. Pleasant Cemetery, Newark, N.J.

SPRAGUE, PAUL EPWORTH, business exec.; b. Cleveland, Feb. 7, 1892; s. Frank M. and Josie (Griesmer) S.; B.S. in Chem.Engring., Ohio State U., 1914, M.S., 1915; m. Ruth E. Horrocks, June 20, 1918; children—Jean, Dorothea, Shirley. Chemist, sales engr., purchasing agent, Glidden Varnish Co., Cleveland, 1915-17, indsl. sales mgr., 1919-25; vice pes. Euston Lead Co., Scranton, Pa., 1925-30; v.p. Metals Refining Co., Hammond, Ind., 1930-35; v.p., dir. The Glidden Co., Clevleand, from 1935, mem. exec. com., chmn. research com.; vice pres. Growth Products Co., Pascagoula, Miss, v.p. Jacksonville (Fla.) Processing Corp. With U.S. Army, 1917-18. Apptd. mem. adv. coms. on lead, zinc, soy bean processing, and titanium industries WPB, also food advisory com. War Food Adminstrn. Pres. Soy Flour Assn., 1939; mem. Sigma Xi, Phi Lambda Upsilon, Phi Delta Chi, Republican. Mason. Club: Rowfant, Author: articles to tech. jours. Home: Shaker Heights, O., Died June 22, 1971.

SPRATT, NELSON TRACY, JR., educator, scientist; b. Atlanta, Dec. 26, 1911; s. Nelson Tracy and Katherine Elliott (Guerard) S.; A.B., Emory U., 1935; Ph.D., U. Rochester, 1940; m. Jacqueline Rae Dahl, June 8, 1952 (div. Mar. 1969); children—Nelson Tracy III, Jacquelita, Gwendolyn, Melinda, Jorgine; m. 2d, Gladys Aronson Wiener, June 1969. Instr. biology Emory U., 1935-36; research fellow U. Rochester, 1939-40; from research asst. to asst. prof. biology Johns Hopkins, 1940-49; faculty U. Minn., Mpls., 1949-75, prof. zoology, 1951-75, chmn. dept., 1958-66. Instr. embryology Marine Biol. Lab., summers 1955-61; vis prof. Gustavus Adolphus Coll., 1956, Inst. Nacional de Cardiologia, Mexico City, 1969, 71; program dir. devel. biology NSF, 1957-58; cons. NIH, from 1962. Served to capt. USAAF, 1943-46. Fellow Internat. Inst. Embryology, Acad. Zoology (India); mem. Soc. Devel. and Growth, Am. Soc. Zoologists, Am. Assn. Anatomists, Am. Soc. Naturalists (treas.), Phi Beta Kappa, Sigma Xi, Lambda Chi Alpha. Author: Development Biology. Contbr. articles to profl. jours. Home: St. Paul, Minn. Died Feb. 16, 1975.

SPRING, SAMUEL, lawyer; b. San Diego, Cal., Oct. 26, 1888; s. Abraham and Hannah (Glass) S.; student Phillips Acad., Andover, Mass., 1905-06; A.B., Harvard, 1910; LL.B., 1913; m. Imogene S. Morse, June 2, 1917; 1 son, Richard Lewis. Practiced law in Cal., 1913-18, moved to Boston, 1918; spl. asst. atty. gen., Mass., 1920; mem. spl. com. to investigate sale corporate securities, Mass., 1920-21; moved to N.Y.C., 1922; gen. counsel 1st Nat. Pictures, Inc., then elected treas., sec., v.p., 1925; now engaged in pvt. practice, N.Y.C.; also pres. Pasyl Corp., investments. Charge indsl. branch office Emergency Fleet Corp., San Francisco, 1918. Mem. Cal. Republican Com., 1916. Served with U.S. Army, World War I. Mem. Am., Cal., N.Y., Fed. bar assns. Jewish religion. Author: Blue Sky Laws, 1919; Taxable and Tax Exempt Securities, 1920; Insurance Investment Laws, 1921; Risks and Rights in Publications and Television, rev. edit., 1957; Tomorrow at the United Nations, 1967; also articles mags. Home: Larchmont, N.Y. Deceased.

SPRINGMEYER, GEORGE, lawyer; b. on ranch nr. Minden, Nev., September 28, 1881; s. H. H. and Wilhelmine (Heitman) S.; B.S., U. of Nevada,; A.B., Stanford University, 1903, LL.B., 1905; studied Harvard Law Sch., 1905-06; m. Sallie Maria Ruperti. Practiced law at Goldfield, Nev., 1906-11, at Reno from 1912. Asst. dist. atty., Goldfield, 1909-11; Rep. candidate for atty. gen. of Nevada three times, once for Congress, each time defeated; U.S. attorney for Nev., 1922-26; now mem. law firm of Springmeyer & Thompson. Served in U.S. Army, at front in France, as capt., later maj., World War. Mem. Am., Calif., Nev. State and Washoe Co. bar assns., Assn. Bar City of New York, Phi Gamma Delta Delta, Phi Delta Phi. Home: Reno, Nev.†

SPROGELL, HARRY E(DWARD), lawyer; b. Lansdale, Pa., Dec. 5, 1911; s. Francis E(dward) and Mary Coffman (Woodmansee) S.; A.B. with high honors, Swarthmore Coll., 1932; LL.B. (editor-in-chief Law Rev. 1934-35), U. Pa., 1935; m. Barbara Saul, June 24, 1939; children—Prudence (Mrs. Winston J. Churchill, Jr.), Carolyn (Mrs. Ross Van Denbergh). Robert, and Jonathan. Admitted to Pa. bar, 1935, practiced in Phila; partner firm Saul, Ewing, Remick & Saul, 1941-72. Dir. First Pa. Banking and Trust Co., Clarke Mortgage Co., Seaboard Agy., Inc.; sec. dir. Perfect Foods, Inc., Chipzels, Inc., 1951-66; vice president, director Foulkeways at Gwynedd, Incorporated, 1965-72. Member North Penn Joint School Board, 1953-59, president, 1955-57; member sch. bd. Upper Gwynedd Twp., 1953-59, pres., 1953-57; mem. Upper Gwynedd Twp. Zoning Comm., 1940-41. Zoning Rev. Commn., 1945-46; clk. Gwynedd Monthly Meeting Friends, 1951-62, 65-72, treasurer incorporated trustees, 1949-59; trustee Phila. Yearly Meeting Friends, 1952-72, v.p., 1966-68, pres., 1968-72. Trustee Wilmington Coll.; adv. bd. mgrs. Morris Arboretum; bd. dirs. N. Penn Hosp., Phila. Orch. Pension Fund, Grandom Instn., Pa. Civil Liberties Union, chmn. bd. dirs. Woodmere Gallery, Inc.; bd. dirs., v.p. Greater Phila. br. Am. Civil Liberties Union. Served to lt. USNR, 1943-45. Life mem. Pa. Acad. Fine Arts, Hist. Soc. Pa., Montgomery CountyHist. Soc.; mem. Am., Pa. Phila. (vice chmn. com. civil rights 1959-63) bar assns., Phi Beta Kappa, Delta Sigma Rho. Clubs: Union League, Sharswood Law, Rittenhouse (Phila.). Home: North Wales, Pa. Died Jan. 1, 1972.

SPROUL, ROBERT GORDON, educator; b. San Francisco, May 22, 1891; s. Robert and Sarah Elizabeth (Moore) S.; B.S., U. of Calif., 1913; LL.D., Occidental Coll., Los Angeles, 1926, U. of Southern Cal., 1930, U. of San Francisco, 1930, Pamona Coll., 1931, U. of Ore., 1932, U. of Neb., 1935, Yale, 1935, U. of Maine, 1938; Litt. D., Columbia U., 1938; LL.D., U. of N.M., 1940; Harvard, 1940; hon. fellow, Stanford U., 1941, LL.D., Mills Coll., 1943, Princeton 1947, Tulane U., 1949, St. Mary's Coll., 1949, U. Cal. at Berkeley, 1958, U.B.C., 1958, Rensselaer Polytech. Inst., 1958, Brigham Young U., 1959; L.H.D., U. of Cal. at Los Angeles, 1958; m. Ida Amelia Wittschen, Sept. 6. 1916; children—Marion Elizabeth Goodin, Robert Gordon, John Allan. Comptroller U. of Calif. and sec. of regents, 1920-30; v.p. 1925-30, pres. 1930-58, pres. emeritus, 1958-75. Mem. Cal. State Comm. Agrl. Edn., 1921-23; mem. Commn. Revision Cal. State Constn., 1929-30, 64-65, co-chmn., 1964; mem. Cal. State Bd. Social Welfare, 1928-31; treas. Save Redwoods League, 1921-71, treas, emeritus, 1971-75; mem. Saline Water Conservation Program, Dept. Interior, 1956-62; adv. bd. nat. parks, historical sites, buildings, monuments, 1959-65; bd. dirs. East Bay Regional Parks Cal., 1958-67, pres., 1963-67. Mem. exec. council Am. Cancer Soc., U.S. Naval Acad. Centennial Commn., 1945; mem. bd. of governors Philippine Found., World Affairs Council No. Cal.; trustee Pacific Sch. of Religion, 1921-75, chm. bd., 1966, chmn. emeritus, 1967-75; trustee Carnegie Found. for Advancement Teaching, 1939-58, Gen. Edn. Bd., Rockefeller Found., 1939-56; trustee Com. for Econ. Devel., 1945-55, hon. trustee, 1955-75; trustee Nat. Fund. Grad. Nursing Edn.; chmn. trustees Athenian Sch.; vice. chmn. Am. Heritage Found.; spl. cons., Office Sci. Research and Devel. 1943; sr. adviser, Am. Group on Allied Commn. on Reparations, 1945. Mem. Citizens Com. for the Marshall Plan; mem. Nat. Com. on Inter-Am. Intellectual Cooperation; dir. Calif. Assn. for Adult edn., Internat. House, Berkeley (dir.); formei mem. adv. com. utilization colls. and univs. War Manpower Commn.; Am. mem. Newcomen Soc. Eng.; mem. Nat. Red Cross Adv. Com. chmn., Cal. Adv. Com. U.S. Civil Rights Commn., 1958-60; mem. Cal. Citizens Adv. Com. on Pub. Edn. System, 1958-61; spl. ambassador to Korea, 1956; chmn. adminstrv. vocat. rehab. and edn. adv. com. VA, 1952-58; mem. Nat. Child Refugee Com., Nat. Com. Support Pub. Schs., 1962—. Bd. dirs. YMCA, Boy Scouts Am., trustee Inst. Internat. Edn. Elector Hall of Fame of Great Ams. Decorated chevalier Legion of Honnour, comdr. Crown of Roumania; officer Crown of Italy; officer Order Nat. Legion of Honnour; comdr. Royal Norwegian Order of St. Olav; comdr. 2d class Swedish Royal Order of the North Star. Fellow A.A.A.S., Am. (hon.), Internat. (hon.) colleges dentists; mem. Cal. C. of C. (dir. 1940-62), Abracadabra, Phi Beta Kappa, Tau Beta Pi, Delta Sigma Pi, Alpha Zeta. Republican. Presbyn. Clubs: Family (hon.), Bohemian (San Francisco); Faculty, Rotary (Berkeley); Lincoln (pres. 1945-45), Sunset (Los Angeles); Burlingame Country (hon.); Athenian-Nile (Oakland, Cal.); University (Los Angeles, hon., San Francisco, hon.). Home: Berkeley, Cal. Died Sept. 10, 1975.

SPURR, WILLIAM ALFRED, educator; b. Washington, Dec. 24, 1905; s. J. Edward and Sophie (Burchard) S.; A.B. magna cum laude, Harvard, 1925; M.B.A., 1928; Ph.D., Columbia, 1940; m. Elizabeth Mackey, 1935; m. 2d, Hallie Rucker, 1946; children—Diana E., Patricia R., Roberta B., Edward H., John L. Security analyst Clark Dodge & Co., N.Y.C., 1929-30; financial statistician Western Electric Co., 1930-35; asst., asso. prof. statistics, acting chmn. dept. bus. research U. Neb., 1937-41; sr. economist U.S. Dept. Commerce, 1941-42, prin. indsl. economist statistics div. WPB, 1942; asso. prof. statistics U. Chg., 1946; prof. bus. statistics Stanford Grad. Sch. Bus. 1946-69, prof. emeritus, 1969-75. Mem. Harvard Eclipse Expdn. to Sumatra, 1925-26, Geol. Survey Expdn. to Alaska, 1928, Rampart Dam Survey in Alaska, 1965. Served to lt. comdr. AC, USNR, 1942-45. Mem. Am. Statis Assn. (pres. San Francisco chpt. 1949), Nat. Assn. Bus. Economists, Am. Assn. U. Profs. (pres. Stanford chpt. 1957-58). Author: Seasonal Variations in the Economic Activities of Japan, 1940; (with Kellogg, Smith) Business and Economic Statistics, 1954, rev., 1961; (with Bonini) Statistical Analysis for Business Decisions, 1967, rev., 1973; also monographs. Contbr. articles to profl. jours. Home: Stanford, Cal., Died Mar. 8, 1975.

SQUIRES, DAVID DENTON, realtor; b. Bristol, Va., Aug. 11, 1906; s. William Henry Tappey and Anna (Hull) S.; B.S., Hampden-Sydney Coll., 1927; m. Sara Lee Cross, Oct. 24, 1931; children—Sara Lee (Mrs. Richard Culver Erickson), Emily Hull. With Standard Oil Co. (N.J.), 1927-37, advt. dept., Norfolk, Va., 1927-30, N.Y.C., 1931, Washington, 1932, sales dept., Hagerstown, Md., 1934-36, asst. dist. mgr. sales dept., Washington, 1936-37; owner retail petroleum products bus., Alexandria, Va., 1937-51; realtor Squires & Co., Alexandria, from 1951; dir. Alexandria 1st Fed. Savs. & Loan Assn., Alexandria Nat. Bank. Trustee Hampden-Sydney Coll., chmn. trustees, 1968-72; trustee Union Theol. Sem., Presbyn. Home, Lynchburg, Va.; bd. govs. St. Christophers Episcopal Sch. Mem. Theta Chi, Omicron Delta Kappa, Chi Beta Phl. Presbyn. (moderator Potomac Presbytery 1962). Home: Alexandria, Va. Died Oct. 19, 1973; interred Forest Lawn Cemetery, Norfolk, Va.

STAACK, JOHN GEORGE, topographic engr.; b. Middleton, Wis., Nov. 19, 1878; s. John Henry and Rosetta (Prien) S.; grad. State Teachers Coll., Platteville, 1900; B.S. in C.E., U. of Wis., 1904; m. L. Lenore Jones, Dec. 26, 1911; 1 dau., Elizabeth Roberts. With U.S. Geol. Survey, 1904-47, advancement through grades from jr. engr. to chief topographic engr., 1929-43, asst. chief topographic engr., 1943-47; retired July 1, 1947. Served as capt. Engr. Corps, U.S. Army, June 1917-Mar. 1919. Mem. Am. Congress on Surveying and Mapping. Mem. Am. Soc. C.E., Washington Soc. Engrs., Am. Soc. of Photogrammetry. Episcopalian (Register Transfiguration Parish). Home: Washington, D.C.†

STACEY, ALFRED EDWIN, JR. engr.; b. Elbridge, N.Y., Mar. 10, 1885; s. Alfred Edwin and Jessie (Rowe) S.; student Munro Collegiate Inst., Elbridge, N.Y., 1896-1902; M.E., Syracuse U., 1906; m. Hazel King, June 29, 1910; children—Alfred Edwin, Elizabeth Rowe (dec.), Janet King (Mrs. Stacey Simpson), John Markell (dec.). Research engr. Buffalo (N.Y.) Forge Co., 1906-07; chief engr. Carrier Air Conditioning Co., New York, N.Y., 1908-09; vice pres. Elbridge (N.Y.) Chair Co., 1909-11; western mgr. and engr. Carrier Air Conditioning Co., Chicago, 1911-15, Carrier Engring. Corp., 1915-19, chief of research at Newark (N.J.) plant, 1919-28, v.p. in charge research, 1928-31, v.p. in charge engring., 1931-33, v.p. and tech. sales advisor, 1934-35; v.p., chief engr. Buensod-Stacey Air

Conditioning, Inc., New York, N.Y., 1935-41; sr. consultant Carrier Corp., Syracuse, New York, 1946-57. Captain, U.S. Naval Reserve, ret. Recipient F. Paul Anderson medal, Am. Soc. Heating and Ventilating Engrs., 1946. Mem. A.A.A.S., Am. Soc. Heating and Ventilating Engrs. (p.p.), Am. Soc. Naval Engrs., Acoustical Soc. of Am., Am. Inst. of Physics, Am. Inst. of New York, Delta Upsilon. Republican. Episcopalain. Clubs: Army-Navy Country (Washington, D.C.); Military-Naval (New York, N.Y.). Author numerous papers on air conditioning to nat. tech. socs. Holds numerous patents covering application of heat and moisture in processing various materials. Home: Skaneateles, N.Y. Died Apr. 5, 1975.

STACEY, JOHN MARKELL, med. center dir.; Ilion, N.Y., Jan. 23, 1918; s. Alfred Edwin, Jr., and Hazel (King) S.; B.A., Wesleyan U., 1939; m. Charlotte Florence Smith, June 26, 1945; children—Pamela, John Markell, Ned Martin. Exec. asst. St. Luke's Hosp., N.Y.C. 1939-42; med. adminstr. Standard Oil Co. (N.J.), N.Y.C., 1946-51; cons. Booz, Allen & Hamilton, N.Y.C., 1951-53; dir. U. Va. Hosp., Charlotesville, 1953-64; dir. U. Va. Med. Center, 1964-72; lectr. U. Va. Med. Sch., 1953-72; Dir. Va. Hosp. Service Assn., from 1954; pres. Va. Council Health and Med. Care, from 1965, cons. Govt. of Aruba. Served from 1st lt. to maj, AUS, 1942-46. Fellow Am. Coll. Hosp. Adminstrs., Royal Society Health; mem. Va. Hosp. Assn. (pres. 1964-65), Am. Hosp. Assn. (del. at large from 1965), Assn. Am. Med. Colls., Psi Upsilon. Presbyn. Rotarian. Clubs: Torch, Farmington Country. Home: Charlottesville, Va. Died May 5, 1973; interred Charlottesville, Va.

STAFFORD, CLARENCE EUGENE, physician; b. Mountain View, Cal., Oct. 22, 1906; s. Francis Eugene and Nellie Ellen (Jessen) S.; M.D., Loma Linda U., 1932; m. Charlotte Martha Jackson, Aug. 11, 1930; children—Vernon L., Barbara (Mrs. Charles M. Landers, Jr.), Robert Eugene. Intern, White Meml. Med. Center, Los Angeles, 1931-32, resident in surgery, 1932-35, cons. staff; cons. staff Glendale Adventist Hosp.; emeritus prof. surgery Loma Linda U., also bd. dirs. Diplomate Am. Bd. Surgery. Fellow A.C.S.; mem. A.M.A., Pacific Coast Surg. Assn., Soc. Surgery Alimentary Tract, Collegium Internationale Chirurgiae Digestive, Soc. Internationale de Chirurgie. Mem. Seventh-day Adventist Ch. Rotarian (dir. East Los Angeles, Cal.). Contbr. numerous articles to med. jours. Home: Glendale, Cal. Died Aug. 4, 1974; buried Forest Lawn Cemetery, Glendale, Cal.

STAFFORD, DALE BERNARD, editor; b. St. Louis, Mich., Jan 25, 1908; s. James Gordon and Louise Mathilda (Wieck) S.; student Mich. State Coll., 1926-29; m. Vivian Leola Eaegle, May 5, 1931; 1 son John Bernard, Sports editor Lansing (Mich) Capital News, 1925-26; athletic publicity dir. Mich. State Coll., 1926-29; reporter Pontiac (Mich) Daily Press, 1929-37; reporter Asso. Press, 1937, 41; sports editor, Detroit (Mich) Free Press, 1941-45, asst. mng. editor, 1945, later mng. editor, editor and publisher Daily News, Greenville, Michigan. Member Michigan State College Athletic Board of Control, and dir. Mich. State Coll. Club (Detroit). Mem. Am. Soc. Newpaper Editors, Asso. Press Mng. Editors Assn., Sigma Delta Chi. Lutheran. Clubs: Red Run Golf (Royal Oak, Mich.), Yacht (Detroit). Home: Ferndale, Mich. Died 1973.

STAHLMAN, E. B., JR., newspaper exec.; b. Nashville, Tenn., Mar. 31, 1898; s. Edward Claiborne and Mary (Geddes) S.; student Webb Sch. for Boys and Wallace U. Sch.; student Vanderbilt U., 1917-19; m. Louise Kerrigan, Oct. 5, 1925. Exec. v.p., co-pub. Nashville Banner; sec., v.p., prodn. mgr. Newspaper Printing Corp., from 1940. Mem. So. Newspaper Pubs. Assn. (pres. 1946-47), Sigma Chi. Democrat. Clubs: Belle Meade Country, Kiwanis. Home: Nashville, Tenn. Died June 12, 1974; interred Calvary Cemetery, Nashville, Tenn.

STAIR, CHARLES AUGUSTUS, businessman; b. Knoxville, Tenn., June 19, 1879; s. William Farres and Martha Ann (Baxter) S.; ed. pub. schs.; m. Eva Manoque, Dec. 7, 1910; children—Marjorie (Mrs. James Caruthers Lancaster), Nancy (Mrs. Marvin Mitchell). Night operator with E. Tenn. Telephone and Telegraph Co., later mgr. at Danville, Ky.; continued in various capacities after company was absorbed by Cumberland Telephone and Telegraph, as mgr. Owensboro, Ky., Chattanooga, Tenn., Memphis, New Orleans (dist. supt. for La.) and Miss., later gen. mgr. for La.; exec. vice pres. and treas., Southern Bell Telephone & Telegraph Co., Atlanta, 1935-44, dir., from 1935. Served in Spanish-Am. war; notable for meeting communication emergencies during World War I. Chmn. Unemployment Relief of La. (received plaque from State therefore, Chmn. Atlanta Community Chest Fund, 1942-44; chmn. War Finance Com. for State of Ga., 1943-44. Chosen outstanding Atlanta citizen for 1942 by C. of C. Mem. Newcomen Society. Republican. Episcopalian. Clubs: Boston, Southern Yacht, Lake Shore (all New Orleans); Capital City (dir.) (Atlanta). Home: New Orleans, La.†

STALEY, AUGUSTUS EUGENE, JR., mfg. co. exec.; b. Balt., July 24, 1903; s. A.E. and Emma Louise (Tressler) S.; B.S., U. Pa., 1925; LL.D., Milikin U., 1950; m. Lenore Mueller, Sept. 15, 1926; children—Augustus Eugene, III, Henry M., William D.; m. 2d, Eva Coddington Turner, May 12, 1951, (dec. Feb. 1969); 1 son, Robert Coddington; m. 3d, Catherine A. Hull. With A.E. Staley Mfg. Co., Decatur, Ill., from 1925, pres., 1932-58, chief exec. officer, 1958-73, chmn. bd., from 1958; dir. Citizens Nat. Bank Decatur. Dep. chief Food Br., WPB, 1942; past chief Econ. Cooperation Adminstrn. spl. mission to Norway. Dir Decatur Meml. Hosp., 1932-53; mem. Ill. Bd. Unemployment Compensation and Free Employment Office Advisers, 1938-41; mem. Bus. Mgmt. Study Com. for Ill., 1966-67. Trustee Milikin U.; mem. bd. bus. edn. Wharton Sch., U. Pa., 1963-68. Decorated comdr. with star Order of St. Olav (Norway). Mem. Bus. Council, Ducks Unlimited, Kappa Sigma. Presbyn. Clubs: Decatur, Decatur Country; Tavern, University, Mid-America (Chgo.); Surf, Indian Creek Country (Miami Beach, Fla.); Augusta (Ga.) Nat. Golf. Home: Decatur, Ill. Died Mar. 1975.

STALKER, JOHN NELLIS, banker; b. Mt. Clemens, Mich., May 20, 1881; s. George Harrison and Georgiana (Nellis) S.; grad. high sch., Detroit; m. Edith L. Dailey, Nov. 25, 1908; children—Mary Emmaline, Harrison Dailey, Dake Egerton, Hester Nellis, John Nellis. Began with State Savings Bank, Detroit, 1899; pres. Union Trust Co., Jan. 1930, which merged with Guardian Trust Co., Mar. 1930; later vice chmn. bd. Union Guardian Trust Co.; later engaged in orgn. and development work of self and assos.; now trustee Wm. H. Hill estate. Formerly chmn. mortgage and finance div. and v.p. Nat. Assn. Real Estate Bds. Republican. Presbyterian. Home: St. Petersburg, Fla.†

STALL, ALBERT H., contractor; b. 1900; m. Engaged in oil field constrn. work, various cos. in La., 1921-34; individual contractor, 1934-39; partner Stall & McDermott, 1939-46; v.p. J. Ray McDermott & Co., Inc., 1946-64, v.p., vice chmn. bd., from 1964, also dir. Deceased

STALLARD, CARTON SHERMAN, mortgage banker; b. Elizabeth, N.J., May 27, 1905; s. George F. and Mabel (Cornella) S.; Ph.B., Brown U., 1927; m. M. Ruth Sefton, June 14, 1928; children—Sefton, Suzanne R. (Mrs. Richard Merrell). Accountant, Jersey Mortgage & Title Guaranty Co., Elizabeth, 1927-28, asst. treas., 1928-32, sec.-treas., 1932-37; sec.-treas. Jersey Mortgage Co., 1937-48, v.p., sec., dir., 1948-55, exec. v.p., 1955-57, pres., 1957-69, chief exec. officer, 1963-71, chmn. bd., 1969; dir., mem. exec. com. Union County Trust Co.; dir. Kenllworth State Bank. Instr. real estate and mortgage investment Upsala Coll., East Orange, N.J., extension div. Rutgers U.; lectr. Sch. Mortgage Banking, Stanford, Northwestern U. Trustee Elizabeth (N.J.) Gen. Hosp.; bd. dirs. Jr. Achievement Union County. Mem. Am. Inst. Real Estate Appraisers, Inst. Property Mgmt. of Nat. Assn. Real Estate Bds., Am. (chmn. bd. trustees Research and Ednl. Trust Fund), N.J. (bd. govs., trustee, pres.) mortgage bankers assns., Soc. Residential Appraisers (asso.), Bd. Realtors Eastern Union County (bd. govs.), Delta Upsilon. Mason (master). Clubs: Baltusrol Golf (gov., asst. treas. Springfield); Seaview Country (Absecon, N.J.); Mid-Ocean (Bermuda); Lost Tree (N. Palm Beach, Fla). Home: Springfield, N.J. Died Mar. 19, 1975.

STAMP, ADELE H., educator; b. Baltimore, Md., Aug. 9, 1893; d. Frederick and Anna (Harken) S.; B.A., Tulane U., 1921; M.A., U. MD., 1924; further postgrad. Am. U., Catholic U., Johns Hopkins, U. of Va. Teacher phys. edn. Catonsville High Sch., 1913-15; recreation and phys. edn. Alfred U. summer schools, 1915-16; recreation and pageantry U. of Md. summer schs., 1917; dir. recreation Old Hickory Munition Plant, Tenn. under war work council of nat. bd YWCA, 1918-19, dir. indsl. service center, New Orleans, La., 1919-20; field rep. Am. Red Cross, Oct., 1922; dean of women U. Md., 1922-60. Adviser Md. chpt. A.R.C.; mem. adv. com. UN Assn. Mem. Nat., Regional (exec. com.) assns. deans of women, Am. Assn. U. Women, Association of College Honor Societies (council), Md. Fedn. Women's Clubs, American Assn. Univ. Profs., Mortar Bd., Alpha Lambda Delta (nat. treas., exec. council), Delta Kappa Gamma (founder Md.), Phi Kappa Phi, Alpha Kappa Delta. Contbr. articles to profl. publs., assn. jours. Home: College Park, Md. Died Oct. 17, 1974.

STANBRO, WILLIAM WOODROW, physician; b. Ellicottville, N.Y., Mar. 13, 1913; s. Amos Karl and Jenny MacArthur (McGovern) S.; M.D., Washington U., St. Louis, 1938; m. Rosemary Muriel Conners, Oct. 10, 1940; children—William David, Mary Anne, Virginia Eleanor (Mrs. Harry Proctor, Jr.), Carol Jean. Intern, St. Louis City Hosp., 1938-39; resident Robert Koch Hosp., Koch, Mos., 1939-42; resident in radiology Barnes Hosp., St. Louis, 1945-47; prof., chmn. dept. radiology George Washington U., 1947-71, dir. radiology residency tng. program, 1947-71; radiologist Mowery Clinic, Salina, Kan., 1971-72; cons. in radiology Central Office, VA, Washington; sr. cons. Nuclear Inst., Cleve.; mem. adv. com. in radiology Washington Technol. Inst. Served to capt. M.C., AUS, 1942-45. Diplomate Am. Bd. Radiology. Fellow Am. Coll. Chest Physicians; mem. A.M.A., D.C. Med. soc., Am. Coll. Radiology, Soc. Nuclear Medicine, Soc. Chairmen Acad. Radiology Depts., A.A.U.P. Roman Catholic. Contbr. articles to profl. jours. Home: Salina, Kan. Died June 23, 1972; buried Gate of Heaven Cemetery, Silver Spring, Md.

STANDEVEN, JAMES WYLIE, hosp. supt.; b. Hancock, Ia., Jan. 25, 1916; s. John Frank and Elsie (Wylie) S.; B.S., State U. Ia., 1940, M.D., 1940; m. Jean E. Beckwith Apr. 30, 1960; children—John, Steven. Intern Neb. Meth. Hosp., Omaha; gen. practice medicine, Oakland, Ia., 1946-57; with VA, 1957-72, dir. VA Hosp., Montgomery Ala., 1968-70, then personnel physician VA Hosp., Tucson. Mem. Gov. Ala. Com. Employment Handicapped. Councilman, Oakland, Ia., 1950-54. Bd. dirs. local A.R.C. Served to capt. USAAF, 1941-45. Mem. Am. Coll. Hosp. Adminstrs., A.M.A., Aerospace Med. Assn., Fed. Execs. Assn., Alpha Omega Alpha, Alpha Kappa Kappa. Rotarian. Home: Tucson, Ariz., Died May 20, 1972.

STANGELAND, CHARLES EMIL, political economist; b. Sheldahl, Ia., May 1, 1881; s. Adolf and Thora Marie (Siqveland) S.; A.B., Abusburg Sem., Minneapolis, 1898; at U. of Wis., 1898-99; A.M., University of Minnesota, 1901; Democrat. Home: Henderson, Ky.†

STANNARD, ALBERT CLINTON, former president Southwestern Bell Telephone Co.; b. Greenfield, Mass., Dec. 14, 1881; s. Milton Shumway and Harriet (Sanborn) S.; grad. Greenfield (Mass.) High Sch., 1899; m. Grace S. Theodoropoulos, Nov. 18, 1931; children—Martha, George. Began as night operator Am. Telephone and Telegraph Co., Springfield, Mass., 1899-1901; with New Eng. Telephone and Telegraph Co., 1901-03, Southern Bell Telephone Co., Atlanta, Ga., 1903-06, Am. Telephone and Telegraph Co., Boston and New York, 1906-08. Pacific Telephone and Telegraph Co., San Francisco, 1908-19, Chesapeake and Potomac Telephone Co., Baltimore and Washington, 1919-21; gen. traffic mgr. Southwestern Bell Telephone Co. St. Louis, 1921-28, vice-pres., 1928-35, 1st vice-pres., 1935-37, pres. 1937-47; dir. and mem. exec. com. Southwestern Bell Co., director 1st National Bank (St. Louis). Presbyterian. Mason (K.T.). Clubs: Noonday, Racquet, Mo. Athletic (St. Louis). Home: Clayton, Mo.†

STANTON, ROBERT, clothing mfg. exec.; b. San Francisco, July 23, 1889; s. Adolph and Sophie (Steinberger) S.; student Stanford, 1911; m. Lilian Newbauer, Nov. 26, 1921; children—Barbara Davidson, Lari. With Aris Gloves, San Francisco, from 1930, chmn. bd., from 1960. Asst. dir. OPA, 1942-45. Served to 1st lt. USAAF, AUS, 1918-21. Rotarian. Clubs: Commonwealth, World Trade (San Francisco). Author: Forces for Freedom, 1961. Address: San Francisco, Cal. Died Oct. 16, 1974.

STANTON, THOMAS ELWOOD, engineering executive; b. Los Angeles, May 31, 1881; s. Thomas Elwood and Anna (Barthel) S.; B.S., A.B., M.S., M.A., St. Vincent's Coll., Los Angeles, 1892-99; B.S. in Mining Engring., U. of Calif., 1904; m. Leora Melrose Kimball, June 10, 1908; children—Patricia Wallace, Thomas Elwood, Roberta Melrose. Asst. engr., city engrs. office, Los Angeles, 1905-12; with Calif. State Div. of Highways, serving successively as asst. div. engr., asst. highway engr., asst. state highway engr. and chief dept. of materials and research, 1912-1951, ret.; mem. engring. adv. com., U. of Calif. Pres. bd. adminstrn. Calif. State Employees Retirement System, 1931-50; first pres. Calif. Employees Assn.; past dir. Sacramento Chamber of Commerce, Sacramento Council Boy Scouts of Am. Mem. Am. Concrete Inst. (dir. 6th Dist., 1943), Am. Soc. C.E. (nat. v.p. Zone IV, 1942-43; mem. nat. bd. of dirs., 1937-39); Am. Soc. for Testing Materials, Asphalt Paving Technologists Assn. (pres. 1942), Am. Assn. State Highway Officials, Highway Research Board, Native Sons of the Golden West, American Road Builders Assn. (v.p. western dist.). Awarded Wason Research medal, 1938; Norman medal, 1943. Republican. Roman Catholic, K.C., Rotary. Clubs: Serra, Sutter, Frequent contbr. to tech. jours. and proceedings of tech. orgns. Home: Sacramento, Cal.†

STARCK, TAYLOR, educator; b. Independence, Mo., Oct. 15, 1889; s. Christian and Conradine (Kaessmann) S.; A.B., Johns Hopkins, 1911, Ph.D., 1916; student U. Berlin, 1914-15, U. Madrid, 1919-20; A.M. (hon.), Harvard, 1942; Ph.D. (hon.), U. Saarland, 1960; m. Gretchen Todd, Sept. 16, 1921 (dec.); 1 dau., Elizabeth Manby. Asst. German, Johns Hopkins, 1913-14; instr. Smith Coll., 1915-18; acting asst. prof. N.Y. U., 1919; sec. and tchr. Ministry of Pub. Instrn., Madrid, Spain, 1919-20; instr. in German, Harvard, 1920-26, asst. prof., 1926-29, asso. prof., 1929-42. prof., 1942-52, chmn. dept. Germanic lang. and lit., 1927-32 and 1938-52. Kuno Francke prof. German art and culture, 1952-56, emeritus prof., from 1956, Fulbright vis. prof Germanic philology U. Leiden, 1956-57; vis. prof. Germanic philology U. Saarland, 1958-59, Harvard, 1959-60, Johns Hopkins, 1961; summer faculty N.Y. U., 1919, Columbia, 1920. Editor publs. Am. Acad. Arts and Scis., 1946-54. Served with AUS, 1918-19. Decorated knight Order of North Star (Sweden), 1955, Gold Goethe Medal, Goethe Inst., Munich, 1961; grand cross of merit Fed. Republic Germany, 1964. Fellow Mediaeval Acad. of Am., Am. Acad. of Arts and Scis.;

mem. Modern Lang. Assn. Am. (pres. 1957), Am. Dialect Soc., Am. Folkslore Soc., Mediaeval Acad. of Am., (clk. from 1957, Linguistic Soc. Am., Soc. for Advancement Akademie der Sprache und Dichtung (corr.). Clubs: Harvard (New York); Faculty (Cambridge). Author: Der Alraun, 1917; Notker, des Deutschen Werke (5 vols. with E. H. Sehrt), 1935-55. Contbr. to learn jours. Translator: The Inevitable War (F. Delaisi), 1915, Home: Cambridge, Mass. Died Jan 30, 1974.

STARCKE, VIGGO, Danish govt. ofcl., physician; b. Copenhagen, Denmark, Mar. 13, 1895; s. Carl Nicolai and Charlotte (Lorenzen) S.; student U. Copenhagen, 1931-21, Univs. Uppsala and Stockholm, 1927, U. Vienna, 1928; m. Lis Kristoffersen, Sept. 2, 1935; children—Vibeke, Asbjorn, Inge (Mrs. Poul Munk), Graa (Mrs. Steen Borup-Nielsen), Gunhild (Mrs. Ernst Kristoffersen), Ebbe. Demonstrator anatomy U. Copenhagen, 1917-18, lectr. pharmacology, 1923-25; chief physician Silkeborg, 1926-46; M.P. Denmark, 1945-60, mem. com. fgn. affairs, 1947-60, chmn. Parlimentary Group Justice Party, 1946-57, minister without portfolio, 1957-60; mem. Faeroe Delegation, 1946-47; mem. Commn. Icelandic Manuscripts; mem. bd. Royal Theatre, Cultural Found.; dep. prime minister, 1959; lectr. econ., polit. and hist. subjects in Gt. Britain, 1953, U.S.A., 1954. Mem. U. Rifles, Council Atlantic Treatice Assn., PEN Club. Author: Etiology of Polyarthritis, 1930; Induced Abortion, 1932; Hannibal Sehested, 1941; Danmark I Verdenshistorien, 1947; The Viking Danes, 1949; History of Land Taxation in Denmark, 1949; Our Daily Bread, 1949; Denmark in World History, 1962; Centuries of Experience with Land Taxation in Denmark, 1967; Triumf eller Flasco?, 1972; (with Borge Hjerl: Hansen Guldhorns Gäder, 1974. Home: Lyngby, Denmark. Died Mar. 22, 1974.

STARK, G. HAROLD, banker; b. Utica, N.Y., Mar. 9, 1894; s. George H. and Emma (Fredericks) S.; m. Emma Perrollaz, Sept. 26, 1922; children—Joan (Mrs. Philip J. Waldron), Jeanne (Mrs. Franklin Steffen). Pres., dir. Marine Midland Trust Co. of Mohawk Valley, Utica; dir. Foster Paper Co., Utica Box Co.; mem. adv. bd. Marine Midland Corp. Lutheran. Mason. Club: Ft. Schuyler (Utica). Home: Utica, N.Y., Died June 21, 1973.

STARK, PAUL CLARENCE, nurseryman; b. Louisiana, Mo., July 20, 1891; s. Clarence McDowell and Lilly (Crow) S.; student St. John's Coll., Annapolis, Md., 1907-08; B.S., Cornell, 1912; m. Theodosia Armstrong Barnett, Sept. 9, 1916; children—Paul C., Theodosia (Mrs. James Fitzmorris), Helen (Mrs. Alfred Lee Shapleigh II), Georgette. Asst. sec treas. Stark Bro's Nurseries & Orchards Co., Louisiana, Mo., 1912-22, treas. 1922-35, chmn. bd. 1936-41, v.p. from 1941, chmn. 150th Anniversary Celebration, 1966-67; dir. Stark-Burbank Inst. of Horticulture (supervised continuation of Luther Burbank exptl. work, 1927-48); vice pres. Bank of Louisiana (Mo.) from 1922; apptd. to agrl. adv. council, 1941; mem. fresh fruit and vegetable adv. com. W.P.B., 1942-45; mem. fresh fruit and vegetable shipping industry food adv. com., U.S. Dept. Agr., 1943-45. vice chmn. nat. garden adv. com., U.S. Dept. Agr., 1941-45; mem. nat. agrl. Jefferson bicentenary com., 1944; dir. Home Food Supply, May-Oct, 1945; dir. food distrbn. programs br. Prodn. and Marketing Adminstrn., U.S. Dept. Agr., Aug. 1945-June 1947; dir. nat. garden program and chmn. com. on home gardening, U.S. Dept. Agr., 1946-47; dir. Office of Emergency Food Program and exec. dir. Famine Emergency Com., U.S. Dept. Agr. 1946; consultant in prodn., marketing, U.S. Dept. Agr. from 1948, Member of Am. Pomological Society (pres. 1923-26), Apples for Health, Inc. (pres. 1926-28), Am. Assn. Nurserymen (pres. 1932-33), Mo. Hort. Soc. (pres. 1940-41), Nat. Apple Inst. (pres. 1940-41), Am. Farm Bur. Fedn. (mem. fruit and veg. com. 1939-41), Cornell Alumni Assn. (dir. 1939-40), Nat. Assn. Plant Patent Owners (pres. 1943-44), Nat. Victory Garden Inst. (pres. 1943-44), S.A.R., Alpha Tau Omega. Democrat Episcopalian. Clubs: Cornell University, Country (St. Louis). Selected as champion farmer rep. orcharding by Firestone Tire & Rubber Co., 1939; annual award National Apple Institute, 1951. Author: Stark Orchard Book, 1913: Simplified Landscaping, 1916; Stark Orchard and Spray Book, 1914. Asso. editor Am. Fruit Grower Mag., 1925-26. Active in organizing nat. programs and assns. for fruit growers and gardening, and community development through coordinated action by nat. assns. Home: Louisiana, Mo. Died Oct. 28, 1974.

STARK, WILLIAM EVERETT, educator; b. Cambridge, Mass., Feb. 12, 1873; s. William Frank and Sara Lavinia (Weeks) S.; A.B., Harvard, 1895, A.M., 1901; Teachers Coll., Columbia, 1910-11, 26-27; m. Eleanor Parker Fiske, Aug. 3, 1899. Instr. physics, Harvard Parker Fiske, Aug. 3, 1899. Instr. physics, Harvard and Radcliffe, 1895-96; civ. engr. Met. Water Bd., Boston, 1896-98; teacher physics, Rindge Manual Training School, Cambridge, Mass., 1898-1901; headmaster, Ferris Sch., Colorado Springs, Colo., 1901-03, also prin. Cutler Acad., and instr. surveying Colorado Coll., 1902-03; prin. Ethical Culture High Sch., New York, 1903-11; supt. pub. schs., Hackensack, N.J., 1911-23, Stamford, Conn., 1923-26; dean Collegiate Div. Hampton Inst., Va., 1927-32. Instr. ednl. adminstrn., Columbia U., summers 1923-34, U. of Buffalo, summer 1927. Served as supt. post and div. schs. and instr. Coll. of Edn., A.E.F. Univ., Beaune, France, Feb.-July 1919. Mem. N.E.A., A.A.A.S., Phi Beta Kappa. Club: University (Winter Park, Fla.) (sec., 1942-50). Unitarian. Author: Every Teacher's Problems, 1922. Address: Winter Park, Fla.†

STARKEY, HAROLD BELLAMY, savs. and loan assn. exec.; b. Grayville, Ill., Dec. 30, 1896; s. John B. and May B. (Chapman) S.; A.B., Stanford, 1920; L.H.D., Cal.-Western U., 1961; m. Augusta Bispham Witherow, Jan. 27, 1925; children—Harold B., John P., Hubert B., Craig A. Pres., Starkey Investment Co., San Diego, from 1956; exec. v.p. First Fed. Savs & Loan Assn., San Diego, 1934-46, pres., 1946-64, chmn. bd., 1964; pres. So. Mortgage Co., San Diego, 1950-57, chmn., from 1957; pres., dir. Fidelity & Guaranty Co., San Diego. Trustee, pres. U.S. Internat. U., San Diego. Mem. Cal. Savs. and Loan League (pres.), San Diego C. of C. (pres.), Navy League U.S. (pres. San Diego Council), Chi Psi. Mason. Presbyn. Clubs: Rotary, Country, Yacht, Cuyamaca, University, Kona Kai. Home: Chula Vista, Cal. Died Oct. 17, 1973; interred Greenwood Meml. Park, San Diego, Cal.

STARR, FRANCES (GRANT), actress; b. Oneonta, N.Y., 1886; d. Charles E. and Emma (Grant) S.; ed. Albany pub. schs.; m. Haskell Coffin, Made 1st appearance on stage in a stock co. at Leland Theatre, Albany, N.Y., June 1901; joined Murray Hill Stock Co., New York; played in Gallops with Charles Richman, spring of 1906; leading lady in The Music Master, fall of 1906; starring in The Rose of the Rancho, 1907, Easiest Way, 1909-11, Case of Becky, 1912-13, The Secret, 1914-15, Marie Odile, 1915-16, Little Lady in Blue, 1916-17, Tiger, Tiger, 1919-20, One, 1920-21, revival of Easiest Way, 1921-22; Shore Leave, 1922-23; Claudia, 1941. Home: Garden City, N.Y. Died June 1973.

STARR, H. DANFORTH, mining and smelting co. exec.; b. N.Y.C., March 2, 1905; s. Howard White and Henriette D. (Danforth) S.; grad. The Hill Sch., Pottstown, Pa., 1923; B.A., Williams Coll., 1927; M.B.A., Harvard, 1929; m. L. Kathryn Siedenburg, Oct. 10, 1931; children—Eleanor H. (Mrs. Cornelius P. Darcy), Natalie L. (Mrs. Charles H. Lee), K. Deborah (Mrs. Donald A. Shannon), Danforth W. With banks in London, Paris, Berlin, 1929-30, Fed. Res. Bank N.Y., 1931-35, Am. Gen. Corp. and affiliates, 1935-40; sec., asst. treas. Nat. Aviation Corp. also v.p., dir. Nat. Aviation Research Corp., 1940-43; dir., exec. v.p. Vidal Research Corp., 1942-43; dir. and asst. to pres. N.E. Airlines, Inc., 1943-44; successively co-ordinator mil. operations, dir. planning, sec.-treas. Am. Overseas Airlines, Inc., 1944-49; with Cerro Corp from 1949, asst. to pres. 1949-51, v.p., 1951-68, treas., 1955-65, dir., from 1956, vice chmn. bd., 1968-72, chmn. bd., from 1972; v.p., dir. Cerro de Pasco Ry. Co., 1950-58; dir. Atlantic Cement Co., Broad Street Investing Corp., Central and S.W. Corp., So. Peru Copper Corp., Union Capital Fund, Inc., Am. Reins. Co., Nat. Investors Corp., Whitehall Fund, Inc.; trustee Dry Dock Sav. Bank; mem. East Side adv. bd. Chem. Bank N.Y. Trust Co. Bd. dirs. Boys Club, Greenwich, Conn.; trustee St. Anthony Ednl. Found. Mem. S.R., Am. Inst. Mining Engrs., Squadron A Ex-Mems. Assn., Williams Coll. Alumni Soc. (exec. com. 1960-67, pres. 1965-67), Delta Psi. Mem. Community Church (ofcl. bd. Round Hill 1961-73, vice chmn. 1965-68, chmn. 1968-71). Clubs: St. Anthony, Mining, Williams, University (N.Y.C.); Round Hill (Greenwich); Portland (Me.) Yacht; Orleans Fish and Game (Montreal, Can.); Sharon (Conn.) Country. Home: Lakeville, Conn. Died Jan. 17, 1974; buried Round Hill Community Ch. Yard, Greenwich, Conn.

STARR, HELEN KNOWLTON, librarian; b. Algona, Ia., July 30, 1880; d. Milton and Kate (Krater) S.; A.B., Grinnell Coll., 1901; student U. of Ill. Library Sch., 1902-04. In catalog div. Library of Congress, 1904-18, in charge of bibliography and library science sect. of catalog div., 1908-18; head cataloger James J. Hill Reference Library, St. Paul, 1918-29, asst. librarian, 1929-30, librarian, 1930-49. Mem. A.L.A., Phi Beta Kappa. Republican. Conglist. Clubs: Women's City, New Century. Home: St. Paul, Minn.†

STARR, PAUL HART, physician; b. Falls City, Ore., July 31, 1908; s. Harie Eugene and Loretta Alice (Hart) S.; M.D., U. Ore., 1935; m. Helen Juanita Dreesen, Sept. 1, 1932; children—William Harie, Louanne Alice, James Eugene. Intern, Emanuel Hosp., Portland, Ore., 1935-36, mem. staff, 1951-71; resident in anesthesiology U. Ore. Hosps. and Clinics, 1949-51; mem. staff Cowlitz Hosp., Longview, Wash., 1946-49; pvt. practice gen. medicine, Clatsbanie, Ore., 1936-49. Diplomate Am. Bd. Anesthesiology. Mem. A.M.A., Am. Soc. Anesthesiologists, Ore. Med. Assn., Columbia County, Multnomah County med. socs., Lambda Chi Alpha. Republican. Home: Portland, Ore. Died Feb. 7, 1972; buried Rose City Cemetery, Portland, Ore.

STARRETT, VINCENT (CHARLES VINCENT EMERSON), author; b. Toronto, Ont., Can., Oct. 26, 1886; s. Robert Polk and Margaret Denniston (Young) S.; ed. pub. schs. Reporter Inter-Ocean, Chgo., 1905-06; staff Chgo. Daily News, 1906-16; war corr. in Mexico, 1914-15, with Gen Funston's expdn. and later with Mexican troops in the field; book Columnist Sunday Chgo. Tribune from 1942. Mem. Mystery Writers of America (pres. from 1961), Soc. Midland Authors (hon. pres.), Arthur Machen Soc. Author numerous books from 1918 including: Brillig, 1949; Poems, 1951; Best Loved Books of the Twentieth Centruy, 1956; Book Column, 1958; The Private Life of Sherlock Holmes, 1960, 71; Born in a Bookshop (autobiography), 1964, 221B: Studies in Sherlock Holmes, 1969; Ambrose Bierce, 1970; Buried Caesars, 1970; Stephen Crane (bibliography), 1970; The Old Dog and Other Essays, reissued 1971; Books Alive, reissued 1971; Bookman's Holiday, reissued 1971, Editor, compiler various other books. Home: Wilmette, Ill. Died Jan. 4, 1974.

STEADMAN, CHESTER CHANDLER, lawyer; b. Boston, Apr. 14, 1892; s. Alban Charles and Ethel M. (Chandler) S.; LL.B. cum laude, Northeastern U., 1918; m. Marguerite Granger, Aug. 30, 1919; Children—Marguerite Granger, Chester Chandler. Admitted to Mass. bar, practiced in Boston, 1923-71; mem. firm of Steadman & Thomason. Dir. Archer Rubber Co., Holihan Brewery. Mem. Corp. Northeastern U. Mem. Am., Mass., Boston (pres.), Cambridge (pres.) bar assns. Home: Wellesley Hills, Mass. Died Dec. 15, 1973; interred Newton Cemetery, Newton, Mass.

STEARNS, FREDERICK SWEET, business exec.; b. Detroit, Mich., July 12, 1881; s. Frederick K. and Helen Elizabeth (Sweet) S.; ed. Montclair (N.J.) Mil. Acad.; Lawrenceville (N.J.) Sch.; Univ. of Mich.; m. Therese Meyer, Mar. 24, 1915. Started with Frederick Stearns & Co., mfg. pharmacists (3d generation of Stearns family to be asso. with this co.), 1901-10; entered the banking business in N.Y. City, 1910; treas. Frederick Stearns & Co., Detroit, Mich., 1913, chairman of board, 1924, pres. and gen. mgr., 1930-40, chmn. bd., 1940-43. Served as captain, U.S. Army, World War I; remained in reserve and promoted to maj. Home: Grosse Point Farms, Mich.†

STEARNS, JOHN BARKER, educator; b. Norway, Me., Feb. 13, 1894; s. Seward Smith and Mary Eliza(Jordan) S.; A.B. Dartmouth Coll., 1916; M.A., Princeton, 1917; Ph.D. 1924; M. Elsie Huntting Thrall, July 8, 1922; 1 dau., Mary Cornelia (Mrs. William Albert Macdonald). Tchr. of classics Alfred U., 1920-22, Princeton, 1922-24, Yale 1924-27; with Dartmouth, 1927-61, successively asst. prof., prof. classics, also chmn. dept., 1949-51. Served as 1st lt. U.S. Army Ambulance Service, 1917-19, A.E.F. Mem. Archaeol. Inst. Am., Am. Philol. Assn., Classical Assn. New Eng., Phi Beta Kappa. Author: The Dream as a Technical Device in Latin Epic and Drama, 1927; Byzantine Coins in the Dartmouth Collection, 1952; The Assyrian Reliefs at Dartmouth, 1953; also articles for jours. Home: Hanover, N.H. Died July 14, 1973.

STEBBINS, HENRY ENDICOTT, U.S. ambassador; b. Milton, Mass., June 16, 1905; s. Roderick and Edith Endicott (Marean) S.; A.B., Harvard, 1927; m. Barbara Worthington, June 22, 1951. Clk. to comml. attache, Switzerland, 1929-30; asst. trade commr., Bern, 1930-32, Istanbul, 1932-33, London, 1933-36, Ottawa, Can., 1936, Vienna, 1937, asst. comml. attache, 1938; asst. trade commr., Paris, 1938-39, London, 1938-39; vice consul, London, 1939-41, 3d sec., 1941-43, 2d sec., 1941-43, consul and 2d sec., 1943-45, consul and 1st sec., 1945-50; assigned to Dept. State, 1950; with Nat. War Coll., 1950-51; consul gen., Melbourne, Australia, 1951-54; fgn. service insp. Dept. State, 1954-59; apptd. career minister, 1957; A.E. and P. to Kingdom of Nepal, 1959-66, Uganda, 1966-69. Clubs: Tavern, Harvard (Boston); Himalaya (Calcutta). Home: Milton, Mass. Died Mar. 28, 1973.

STEBBINS, JOEL, astronomer; b. Omaha, Neb., July 30, 1878; s. Charles Sumner and Sara Ann (Stubbs) S.; B.S., U. of Neb., 1899, LL.D., 1940; student U. of Wis., 1900-01, hon. Sc.D., 1920; Lick Obs., U. Cal., Ph.D., 1903, LL.D., 1953; student U. Munich, 1912-13; Sc.D., U. Chicago, 1954; married May Louise Prentiss, June 27, 1905; children—Robert P., Isabelle (Mrs. T. A. Dodge). Instructor in astronomy, University of Illinois, 1903-04, assistant professor, 1904-13, professor and dir. Obs., 1913-22; dir. Washburn Obs. and prof. astronomy, U. of Wis., 1922-48, emeritus, also research asso. Mt. Wilson Obs.; research asso. Lick Observatory from 1948. Recipient Royal Astronomical Soc. Gold Medal for 1950. Mem. National Academy Sciences, American Philosophical Society, Am. Acad. Arts and Sciences, A.A.A.S. (v.p.), Am. Astron. Soc. (sec., v.p., pres.); foreign asso. Royal Astron. Soc., Royal Astronomical Society Canada (hon.), Phi Delta Theta, Phi Beta Kappa, Sigma Xi. Was awarded Rumford premium, Am. Acad. Arts and Sciences; Draper medal, Nat. Acad. Sciences; Bruce medal, Astron. Soc. Pacific. Contbr. to astron. jours., principally on stellar photometry and interstellar space. Home: Menlo Park, Cal.†

STEBBINS, LUCY WARD, dean of women; b. San Francisco, Calif., May 24, 1880; d. Horatio and Lucy Elizabeth (Ward) Stebbins; student U. of Calif., 1899-1900; A.B., Radcliffe Coll., 1902; Litt.D., Mills Coll., 1933; unmarried. With Probation Dept. of Mass. State Industrial Sch. for Girls, 1903-07; dist. sec. Boston Associated Charities, 1908-10; dean of women, U. of Calif., July 1, 1912-Jan. 1941, also prof. social economics, dean of women, emeritus, from Jan. 1941. Unitarian. Mem. Am. Assn. Univ. Women, Am. Assn. Social Workers, Nat. Assn. Deans of Women. Clubs: Town and Country (San Francisco); Berkeley Women's City Club, Century Club of California. Home: Berkeley, Cal.†

STECHOW, WOLFGANG, educator; b. Kiel, Germany, June 5, 1896; s. Waldmar and Berta (Deutschmann) S.; student gymnasium Gottingen, Germany, 1905-14, U. Freiburg, 1914, U. Berlin, 1920; Ph.D., U. Gottingen 1921; m. Ursula Hoff, Dec. 16, 1932; children—Hans Axel, Barbara, Nicola. Came to U.S., 1936, naturalized, 1944. Assistantships and fellowships in Berlin, The Hague, Florence and Rome, 1921-31; instr. and asst. prof. history art U. Gottingen, 1926-35; acting asst. prof. history art U. Wis., 1936, asso. prof., 1937-40; prof. history art, Oberlin (O.) Coll., 1940-63; instr. Middlebury (Vt.) Coll. Sch. of German summers from 1942. Mem. adv. council dept. Germanic langs. and lit. Princeton U., Renaissance Soc. Am. mem. adv. selection com. for fine arts Fulbright Research Awards, 1950-52. Mem. Nat. Com. on History of Art, Am. Soc. for Aesthetics (trustee 1947), Coll. Art Assn. Am. (v.p. 1945-46), Archaeol. Inst. Am., Am. Assn. U. Profs., Phi Beta Kappa (hon.), Author: Apollo und Daphne (Leipzig), 1932; Salomon van Ruysdael (Berlin), 1938. Editor The Art Bulletin, 1950-52. Contbr. to art publs. in U.S., Belgium, England, Holland, Germany, Italy. Mem. consultive com. The Art Quar. Home: Overlin, O. Died Oct. 12, 1974.

STECIUK, BASIL W., educator, classicist; b. Hnylyiczky, Ukraine, Mar. 18, 1910; s. Simon I. and Anna F. (Bachynsky) S.; B.A., Classical Gymnasium, Ternopil, 1929; M.A., U. Lemberg, 1933; Ph.D., U. Prague, 1945; Ed.D., U.F.U., Munich, Germany, 1946; m. Maria K., Jan. 14, 1939; 1 son, George. Came to U.S., 1950, naturalized, 1955. Asst. prof. classics Cath. Classical Lyceum, Lemberg, 1933-38, asso. prof., pres., 1939-41; asso. prof., v.p. State Gymnasium Lyceum II, Lemberg, 1941-43; fellow U. Bratislava (Czechoslavakia), 1943-44; prof. classics Ukrain U., also v.p. Ukrain Cath. Coll., Munich, 1945-50; prof. Ukrainian Tech. Inst., N.Y.C., 1951-61; asso. prof. classics Seton Hall U., 1958-66, prof., 1967-75, chmn. dept., 1967-71. Mem. Am. Classics League, Am. Name Soc., Am. Polish philol. socs., Shevchenko Sci. Soc. (gen. learning sec.), Ukranian Tchrs. Assn. Internat. Platform Assn., Edn. Assn. Can. Contbr. to books, articles to profl. jours. Home: Jersey City, N.J., Died 1975.

STEEL, DAVID, physician; b. Rochester, N.Y., Mar. 30, 1893; s. William and Wilhelmena (Gray) S.; M.D., Johns Hopkins, 1920; m. Ruth Margaret Stewart, July 14, 1932; children—David, Jean. Intern. St. Vincent Charity Hosp., 1920-21, resident in surgery, 1921; resident in x-ray Mass. Gen. Hosp., Boston; roentgenologist Evang. Deaconess Hosp., St. Johns Hosp.; prof. roetgenology Case-Western Res. U. Sch. Medicine. Served to lt. U.S. Navy, World War I. Diplomate Am. Bd. Radiology. Mem. A.M.A., Am. Coll. Radiology, Radioll Soc. N.Am., Am. Roentgen Ray Soc., Mass. Med. Soc., Sigma Xi. Mason (32°, Shriner), Rotarian. Author: Roentgen Anatomy, 1951. Contbr. numerous articles to med. jours. Home: East Falmouth, Mass. Died Sept. 9, 1970.

STEELE, ALICE GARLAND, (Mrs. T. Austin-Ball), writer; b. N.Y. City, Mar. 7, 1880; d. Rev. William C. (D.D.) and Sarah Isles (DuBois) S.; diploma New York Collegiate Inst.; m. T. Austin-Ball, teacher, composer, July 1916. Regular contbr. to Munsey's publs., 1904-07; contbr. to mags. Specializes in psychol. work. Home: Rochester, N.Y.†

STEEN, FRED E, dental mfg. exec.; b. 1879; ed. Chicago-Kent Coll. of Law. Chmn. bd. S. S. White Dental Mfg. Co., Phila. Home: Haddonfield, N.J.*†

STEEN, MARGUERITE, novelist; b. Liverpool, Eng., 1894; educated privately. Instr., private sch., 1914-18; became instr. dancing; then began stage career; spent 3 yrs. with Fred Terry-Julia Neilson Co., British company of actors who toured England; U.S.; then became novelist. Fellow royal Soc. Lit. Author novels, including: The Sun is My Undoing, 1941; Shelter, 1942; William Nicholson, a biography, 1942; Bell Timson, 1946; Twilight on the Floods, 1949; Johovah Blues, 1952; The Swan, 1953; Anna Fitzalan, 1953; The Bulls of Parral, 1954; The Unquiet Spirit, 1956; The Woman in the Back Seat, 1959; The Tower, 1959; Candle in the Sun, 1964; Looking Glass I (autobiography), 1966; Pier Glass (autobiography), 1968. also several plays. Home: Berkshire, England. Died Aug. 1975.

STEERS, WILLIAM EDWARD, advt. exec.; b. N.Y.C., Oct. 26, 1906; s. Abraham and Ella Thompson S.; grad. Pawling Sch., 1926; A.B., Dartmouth, 1930; m. Hannah Elizabeth Leo, Apr. 29, 1933; children—Suzanne, William Edward, Michael Anthony. Media dir. Pedlar & Ryan, 1930-44; exec. v.p., sec. Doherty, Clifford, Steers & Shenfield, 1944-56, pres. 1956-64, chmn., chief exec. officer, 1964-65, chmn. bd. dir. N.Y. Div., 1965-76 (name changed to Needham, Harper & Steers, Inc.), chmn. policy com., 1967-76. Mem. Nat. Better Bus. Bur., Inc. (dir.), Audit Bur. Circulations (dir.), Assn. Better Bus. Burs. Internat. (gov.), Child Welfare League (dir.). Home: Hartsdale, N.Y., Died Feb. 23, 1976.

STEFFIAN, EDWIN THEODORE, architect; b. Mexico City, Mexico, Feb. 26, 1899 (parents Am. citizens); s. John and Tillie (Krakauer) S.; grad. Phillips Acad., Andover, Mass., 1917; student Mass. Inst. Tech., 1917-23; m. Lovina Fowler Smith, Dec. 29, 1928; children—John Ames, Peter. Practice architecture, San Antonio, 1924, Boston, 1924-26, N.Y.C., 1926-32; owner Edwin T. Steffian, architect, Boston, 1932-61, Edwin T. Steffian & Assos., Boston, 1961-65; pres., treas. Steffian, Steffian & Bradley, Inc., Boston, 1965-72. Instr. design Boston Archtl. Center, 1932-36. Mem. Cambridge (Mass.) Adv. Com., from 1967, gen. chmn., 1973; mem. Gov.'s Com. for Housing for Elderly for White House Conf., 1960, Mass. Designer Selection Bd. 1968-70; pres. Cambridge Center Adult Edn., 1956-59, treas., 1954-56. Served with U.S. Army, 1918. Recipient Prog. Architecture mag. award, 1960; award Boston Fine Arts Festival, 1964. Fellow A.I.A.; mem. Mass. State Assn. Architects, Boston Soc. Architects (pres. 1956-58), Phi Kappa Sigma. Clubs: St. Botolph (Boston); Cambridge; Mass. Institute of Technology; Harvard Faculty. Home: Cambridge, Mass. Died Apr. 26, 1974; buried Mt. Auburn Cemetery, Cambridge.

STEIN, HANNAH, assn. exec.; b. Berlin, Germany, Mar. 30, 1920; d. Arthur and Salome (Blumstein) Stein; student Ravensfield Coll., London, Eng., Ecole Benedict, Neuchatel, Switzerland; B.A., Pittman's Bus. and Adminstrv. Tng. Coll. London, 1945; L.H.D., Philathea Coll., London, Ont., Can., 1968. Came to U.S., 1952, naturalized, 1958. Pub. relations officer Children and Youth Aliyah, World Hdqrs., London, Eng., also adminstrv. sec. Brit. sect. World Jewish Congress, 1938-45; corr. Fgn. Press Assn. of Gt. Britain at Paris Peace Conf., Council Fgn. Ministers meeting, other European confs., 1945-48; coast-to-coast ednl. lecture tour for Canadian Hadassah, Zionist Women's Orgn. of Canada, 1948-49; pub. lectr. Zionist Orgn. Am., 1950-52, nat. fund-raising dir., asst. to exec. dir., 1952-59; exec. dir. Nat. Council Jewish Women, from 1959. Del. White House Conf. Children and Youth, 1959, White House Conf. on Aging, 1961; mem. President's Com. on Employment Physically Handicapped, 1963-73; bd. dirs. Am. Immigration Citizenship Conf., from 1959; mem. conf. execs. Nat. Social Welfare Assemly, from 1960; mem. planning com., ann. forum civil rights and intergroup relations Nat. Conf. Social Welfare, 1963. Bd. dirs. Nat. Found. Jewish Culture. Mem. Fedn. Zionist Youth Gt. Britain and Ireland (pres. 1944-46), Zionist Fedn. Gt. Britain (exec. com. 1946-48), Pub. Relations Soc. Am., Nat. Jewish Reconstructionist Found., Council on Social Work Edn. (ho. of dels. 1960-63), Zionist Orgn. Am., Women in Community Service, Inc., Internat. Platform Assn.; life mem. Hadassah, Nat. Council Jewish Women (dir. pub. relations). Address: New York City, N.Y. Died Sept. 11, 1973.

STEINBERGER, FRANKLIN JENNINGS, railroad ofcl.; b. Dawson, Yukon Ter., Can., Sept. 24, 1900; s. William J. and Jenny (McGarvey) S.; student Dawson City Coll.; m. Florinne M. Crawford, June 20, 1923; children—Norman, Donna (Mrs. Preston Grounds, Jr.), David. Came to U.S., 1918, naturalized, 1931. With A.T.&S. Ry. Co., 1920-68, gen. purchasing agt., 1955-58, v.p., gen. purchasing agt., 1959-68. Mem. Assn. Am. Railroads (chairman of purchases and stores div.), Association Commerce and Industry Chgo., Western Ry. Club. Republican. Club: Union League (Chgo.). Home: Evanston, Ill. Died June 18, 1973.

STEINBOCK, MAX, editor; b. N.Y.C., Feb. 18, 1917; s. Herman and Bertha (Beresner) S.; student Cooper Union Art Sch., 1933-34; m. Mildred M. Wolsky, June 26, 1941; children—Daniel J., Jean M. Mem. staff Retail Wholesale and Dept. Store Union, from 1940, editor union publ. Record, from 1954, asst. to union pres. from 1961. Asst. publicity dir. Labor League Human Rights, 1946; exec. dir. N.Y. County Liberal party, 1946-47; editor United Auto Workers publ. Labor Post, 1947-48, Local 338 News, 1949-54. Panelist, White House Conf. on Equal Employment Opportunity, 1965; labor mem. com. fair labor standards P.R. Dept. Labor, 1965; mem. nat. exec. com. Am. Trade Union Council for Histadrut. Bd. dirs. Workers Def. League, Nat. com. for Labor Israel. Served with USAAF, 1942-46. Mem Internat. Labor Press Assn. (v.p. 1965-72, pres. from 1973). Home: Valley Stream, N.Y. Died June 17, 1975.

STEINBRUGGE, EDWARD DONALD, judge Union County (N.J.); b. N.Y.C., June 3, 1917; s. Edward and Marjorie Cecily (MacDonald) S.; B.A., Amherst Coll., 1938; J.D., U. Va., 1941; m. Catherine A. Allen, Apr. 2, 1960; children—Edward Donald, Douglas Claude, Donald Allen. Admitted to N.J. bar, 1942, practiced in Morristown, 1942-43, Newark, 1946-50, East Orange, 1950-71; mem. firm Mills, Jeffers & Mountain, Morristown, 1942-43; judge dist. ct. Union County (N.J.), Elizabeth, 1972-73, County Ct., 1973-75. Mem. N.J. Mortgage Study Commn., 1971-72. Counsel, Union County Republican Com., 1969-70. Bd. dirs. N.J. Summit Area YMCA, N.J. Children with Learning Disabilities, Summit Playhouse, Garden State Art Ceneter. Served with USNR, 1943-45. Mem. Am., N.J. Summit bar assns., Am. Judicature Soc., St. Andrew's Soc. of N.Y. Republican. K.C. Clubs: Short Hills (N.J.); Canoe Brook Country (Summit). Home: Summit, N.J. Died 1975.

STEINER, BERNARD SIGFRIED, banker; b. Birmingham, Ala., Apr. 13, 1905; s. Leo Keith and Dian (Holzer) S.; B.S., U. Pa., 1926; m. Dorothy Levy, June 15, 1931; children—Bernard Sigfried, Arnold Levy. With Steiner Bank, Birmingham, from 1926, pres., chmn. bd., from 1944; pres. Gulf Holding Co., Cullman Property Co., Republic Properties, Inc. (all Birmingham); dir. Coplay (Pa.) Cement Mfg. Co., Old Republic Internat. Co.; exec. com. Old Republic Life Ins. Co., Chgo. Treas. Jefferson County Anti-Tb Assn. Jewish religion (past pres., life trustee temple). Clubs: The Club, Pinetree Golf and Country, Relay House (Birmingham). Home: Birmingham, Ala. Died Nov. 3, 1974.

STEINER, JESSE FREDERICK, educator; b. St. Paris, O., Feb. 25, 1880; s. of Rev. Jesse and Mary Emma (Norman) S.; A.B., Heidelberg U., Tiffin, O., 1901; grad. Heidelberg Theol. Sem., 1905; A.M., Harvard, 1913; Ph.D. (sociology), U. of Chicago, 1915; m. Ruth Schwartz, October 15, 1909; children—Charlotte Izora, Jesse Frederick, Herbert Norman, Miriam Bell. Professor English, North Japan College, Sendai, 1905-12; lecturer, University of Chicago, 1915-16. McCormick Theological Seminary, 1916; assistant supt. stockyards dist. United Charities of Chicago, 1915-16; asst. civic sec., City Club, Chicago, 1917; field rep. Am. Nat. Red Cross, Chicago, 1917; asst. prof. sociology, U. of Cincinnati, and asst. dir. Council of Social Agencies, Cincinnati, 1917-18; nat. dir. Bur. of Training for Home Service, 1918-19, nat. dir. ednl. service, 1919-20, Am. Red Cross, Washington; prof. social technology, U. of N.C., 1921-27; prof. sociology, Tulane University, 1927-30; mem. research staff of the President's Research Committee on Social Trends, 1931; professor sociology, University of Washington, 1931-48, emeritus; vis. prof. sociology, U. of Hawaii, 1948-49. Author: The Japanese Invasion, 1917; Education for Social Work, 1921; Community Organization, 1925; The North Carolina Chain Gang, 1927; The American Community in Action, 1928; Americans at Play, 1933; Recreation in the Depression, 1937; Recreation and Moral, 1942; Behind the Japanese Mask, 1943. Address: Honolulu, Hawaii.†

STEINERT, WILLIAM JOSEPH, judge; b. Versailes, Ky., Mar. 7, 1880; s. Philip Joseph and Katherine (Bretz) S.; B.A., Central U. of Ky., 1900; B.L., U. of Mich., 1905; m. Augusta Miller, June 24, 1914. Admitted to Ky. bar, 1906; in practice at Louisville, Ky., 1906-10, Seattle, Wash., 1910-27; judge Superior Court, King County, Wash., 1927-32; judge Supreme Court of Wash., 1932-49, ret.; regional counsel for O.P.S., from 1951. Dept. pros. atty., King Co., Seattle, 1918. Republican. Mason. Home: Seattle, Wash.†

STEINKRAUS, HERMAN W., indsl. exec.; b. Cleveland, O., Dec. 16, 1890; s. Herman F. and Wilhelmina (Lehnhardt) S.; A.B., Western Reserve U., 1914, LL.D.; LL.D., Boston U., 1950, Fairfield U., 1961; Litt.D., Univ. Miami, 1958; m. Gladys C. Tibbetts, Aug. 31, 1919; children—Ruth Constance, Marjorie Ann, William Clark, Exec., Osborn Mfg. Co., 1919-24; operated own metal and chem. business, 1924-28; vice pres. in charge sales Bridgeport Brass Co., 1928-41, v.p. and gen. mgr., 1941-42; pres. and gen. mgr., 1942-46, pres., chmn. bd., 1946-58, chmn. of bd., 1958-59; pres. Noranda Copper and Brass, Ltd., 1948-59, dir., 1959; prop. mgmt. cons. firm, N.Y.C.; dir. Bridgeport Gas Co., Carrier Corporation, Am. Mfrs. Mutual Insurance Co., Connecticut Nat. Bank, Bridgeport Hydraulic Co., Inc.; trustee Bridgeport Peoples Savings Bank. Chmn. bd. finance Town Westport, 1947. Trustee Twentieth Century Fund; Fairfield U., U. Bridgeport; bd. dirs. Bridgeport Hosp.; co-founder, president Conn. Symphony Orchestra, 1949-56, chmn. bd., 1956-58, dir., from 1958; pres. of the United States C. of C., 1949-50. Served from pvt. to capt. U.S. Army, World War I. Decorated Distinguished Service Cross; hon. Connecticut. Member UN Assn. of U.S.A. (pres. from 1959), Am. Legion, Disabled Am. Vets., Vets. Fgn. Wars, Sigma Chi. Past nat. comdr. Legion of Valor. Republican. Mem. Christ and Holy Trinity Ch. Mason (hon. 33°). Clubs: University, Algonquin, Brooklawn Country (Bridgeport); Union League (New York City); Metropolitan, National Press (Washington). Speaker and writer on labor mgmt. relations, pub. relations, etc. Home: Westport, Conn. Died May 9, 1974.

STEMMLER, THEODORE WASHINGTON, corp. official, cons. engr.; b. N.Y.C., Nov. 10, 1885; s. Theodore Washington and Jennie Taylor (Hunting) S.; ed. Cutler Sch., N.Y. and Columbia U.; m. Gertrude F. Williams, Apr. 24, 1924 (died Apr. 18, 1946); m. 2d, Charlotte H. Legget, Apr. 26, 1947. Sr. partner Stemmler & Co., investment bankers, from 1915; sr. partner Stemmler Engring. Co., chmn. bd. Peoples Bridge Corp.; receiver Columbia Mortgage Co.; chmn. various important bondholders' coms.; pres. Peoples Bridge Company of Harrisburg, Pa. Dumont Airplane and Marine Instruments, Inc., Ammonol Chemical Company; vice-president Albemarle Apartments, Inc.; dir. Phila. and Reading Coal and Iron Company. Served as captain constrn. service, U.S. Army, asst. to chief of constrn. div., later constrn. officer, Mexican border and coast defenses North Atlantic, World War. Mem. Am. com. to World Power Conf. Mem. Soc. Am. Mil. Engrs., N.Y. State Soc. of Professional Engrs., National Society Professional Engineers, National Geographic Society Huguenot Society of America, New York Society Mil. and Naval Officers World War, Mil. Order Foreign Wars, St. Nicholas Soc. of N.Y., Pilgrims of U.S., Order Colonial Lords of Manors in America, S.R., Soc. Colonial Wars, N.Y. State Chamber of Commerce, Rockaway Steeple Chase Assn., United Hunts Racing Assn.; hon. mem. Officers Club of 25th Inf., U.S. Army. Republican. Episcopalian. Clubs: Metropolitan, Engineers', Automobile Club America, Wall St., Atlantic Beach Club, Indian Harbor Yacht, Westchester Country, St. Nicholas; Regency; Lawrence Beach; Army and Navy (Washington, D.C.); Everglades, Bath and Tennis (Palm Beach); Seawane Country; Morris County Golf. Home: New York City, N.Y. Died Sept. 28, 1974.

STENGEL, (CHARLES DILLON) CASEY, baseball exec.; b. Kansas City, Mo., July 30, 1890; m. Edna Lawson, 1924. Profl. baseball player with following clubs: Kankakee, Ill., 1910, Maysville, Ky., 1910, Aurora, Ill., 1933, Montgomery, Ala., 1912, Bklyn., 1912-17, Pitts., 1918-19, Phila., 1920-21, N.Y., 1922-23, Boston, 1924-25; mgr. teams, Worcester, 1925, Toledo, 1926-31, Bklyn., 1934-36, Boston Braves, 1938-43, Milw., 1944, Kansas City, 1945, Oakland, 1946-48, N.Y. Yankees, 1949-60, N.Y. Mets, 1962-65; v.p. of New York Mets, 1965-75. Winner numerous pennants; mgr. of N.Y. Yankees in World Series, 1949-53, 55-58, 60. Dir. Valley Nat. Bank, Glendale, Cal. Died Sept. 29, 1975.

STENGEL, ERWIN, educator, psychiatrist; b. Vienna, Austria, Feb. 25, 1902; s. Marcus and Franziska (Popper) S.; M.D., U. Vienna; m. Anna Kohl, Dec. 22, 1935. Lectr. U. Vienna, 1938; research positions, Bristol, Eng., also Edinburgh, Scotland, 1938-45; mem. faculty U. London (Eng.), 1947-56; prof. psychiatry U. Sheffield (Eng.), 1956-67. Fellow Royal Coll. Physicians; mem. Royal Medico-Psychol. Assn. (pres.). Author: (with N. Cook) Attempted Suicide, 1958; Suicide and Attempted Suicide, 1964. Home: Sheffield, England. Died June 2, 1973.

STENTZ, JOHN CLYDE, business exec.; b. Mansfield, Ohio, May 25, 1880; s. Phillip M. and Mary E. (Reichard) S.; ed. business coll.; m. Effa Estelle Page, Jan. 1, 1907. With John Morrell & Co., Ottumwa, Ia., as stenographer, 1901-09, sales mgr., 1909-27, treas. and dir. sales, 1927. v.p. sales. Home: Ottumwa, Ia.†

STEPHAN, ARTHUR THEODORE, coll. adminstr.; b. Winfield, N.Y., Apr. 14, 1913; s. Arthur Theodore and Emma Taylor (Fountain) S.; diploma Pace Coll., 1937, postgrad., 1946; postgrad. Queens Coll., 1955; L.H.D., Philathea Coll., 1964; m. Margaret Corinne Meabon, Apr. 14, 1943; children—Marilyn Joy, Nancy (Mrs. William Piskothy), Arthur Theodore III, Douglas. Statistician, accountant Am. Surety Co. N.Y., 1927-37; gen. accountant Gen. Chem. Co., N.Y.C., 1937-38, traveling auditor W.Va. Ordnance Works, Point Pleasant, W.Va., 1941-45, resident auditor, 1941-45, supr. systems and internal auditing, 1945-47; accountant Greenman MacNicol & Co., N.Y.C., 1938-41; class A sr. accountant Peat, Warwich, Mitchel and Co., pub. accountants, 1947-52; sec., treas., controller FXR, Inc., Woodside, N.Y., 1952-60, 45th St. Realty, Woodside, 1952-60, Crosby Electronics, Inc., Syosset, N.Y., 1952-60, Crosby Teletronica, Inc., Syosset, 1960-61; treas., controller Indsl. Electronic Hardware Co., Inc., N.Y.C., 1962; asst. to pres. finance, registrar, bursar N.Y. Med. Coll., N.Y.C., from 1963; faculty mem. evening div. Pace Coll., 1945-46. Mem. N.Y. State Soc. C.P.A.'s, Order DeMolay (legion of honor). Episcopalian (jr. warden 1969-72, sr. warden from 1972, vestryman 1951-63; mem. finance com. Diocese L.I. 1952-54; exec. com. archdeaconry 1955-58). Mason (32 deg., K.T., Shriner). Home: Whitestone, N.Y. Died Mar. 14, 1973.

STEPHENS, A. E. S., state ofcl.; b. Wicomico Church, Va., Nov. 4, 1900; s. J. W. G. and Allie Tyson (Beane) S.; student Coll. of William and Mary, 1918-23; m. Anna Delk, Oct. 13, 1928; children—Jean S., Martha A., George D. Admitted to Va. bar, 1923, practiced in Smithfield; mem. Ho. of Dels. of Va., 1930-42, Senate, 1942-52; lt. gov. of Va., 1952-62. Mem. Va. Bar Assn., Omicron Delta Kappa. Episcopalian. Clubs: Ruritan, Commonwealth, Rotary. Home: Smithfield, Va. Died June 9, 1973; buried Old St. Luke's Ch. Cemetery, Smithfield.

STEPHENS, FRANK FLETCHER, coll. dean; b. Topeka, Kan., Aug. 8, 1878; s. Thomas White and Mary Elizabeth (Tyler) S.; Ph.B., U. of Chicago, 1904, Ph.M., 1905; Harrison fellow in Am. history, U. of Pa., 1905-07, Ph.D., 1907; m. Blanche Louise Howard, Sept. 20, 1905 (died Feb. 17, 1931); m. 2d, Louise Irby Trenholme, Feb. 20, 1933. With U. of Mo., from 1907, instr. in Am. history until 1912, asst. prof., 1912-19, asso. prof., 1919-20, prof., from 1920; also asst. dean Faculty of Arts and Science, 1924-29, dean underclassmen. Coll. Arts and Science, 1929-41, dean of students, 1941-48, emeritus. Mem. Am. Historical Assn., Miss. Valley Hist. Assn., State Hist. Society of Mo., Foreign Policy Assn., and Social Science, Alpha Pi Zeta, Phi Mu Alpha. Clubs: University, Kiwanis. Author: Transitional Period in the Government of the United States (1788-1789), 1909; The Monroe Doctrine—Its Origin, Development and Recent Interpretation, 1916; also pamphlets and articles on Am. history. Home: Columbia, Mo.†

STERLING, ERNEST ALBERT, forester; b. Brooklyn, Pa., June 27, 1878; s. Amos Gilbert and Inez Lucia (Titus) S.; ed. Bucknell U., 1898-1900; Cold Spring Biol. Lab., 1900; F.E. (Forest Engr.), Cornell U., 1902; studied at Forest Acad., Hann-Münden, Germany, and traveled in German and Swiss forests, 1903; m. Helen George Lee, Nov. 25, 1905; 1 dau., Mary Lee. Forester N.Y. State Forest, Fish and Game Commn., summer, 1902; forest asst. Bur. of Forestry, U.S. Dept. of Agr., 1903-05; asst. forester in charge office of Forest Extension, U.S. Forest Service, 1905-07; forester Pa. R.R., 1907-12; consulting forest and timber engr., 1912-15; mgr. trade extension dept. Nat. Lumber Mfg. Assn., 1915-17; eastern v.p., mgr. The James D. Lacey Co., Chicago, from 1917; also private consultant. Mem. Soc. Am. Foresters, Am. Wood Preservers Assn. (past pres.), Am. Forestry Assn., Phi Gamma Delta. Clubs: University (Washington); Cornell (New York). Writer of professional articles and papers. Home: Montrose, Pa.†

STERN, ADOLPH, physician, b. Eger, Austria, Nov. 4, 1878; s. Hermann and Rosalie (Klein) S.; came to U.S., 1886, naturalized, 1891; A.B., Coll. City of New York, 1898; M.D., Columbia, 1903; student psychoanalysis under Sigmund Freud, Vienna, 1920-21; m. Mamie Hallow, Apr. 18, 1914. Resident Kings Park (L.I.) State (N.Y.) Hosp., 1903-05; extern Mt. Sinai Hosp., New York, N.Y., 1905-06; staff out-patient dept., Mt. Sinai Hosp. and Vanderbilt Clinic, 1906-08; gen. practice, New York, N.Y., 1906-14; specialist in psychoanalysis, from 1921. Mem. A.M.A., Am. Psychoanalytic Assn. (past pres.), Am. Psychiatric Assn., New York State and County med. socs., N.Y. Acad. of Medicine, N.Y. Soc. for Clin. Psychiatry, N.Y. Psychoanalytic Soc. and Inst. (pres. 3 times). Contbr. short papers on psychoanalysis to N.Y. Med. Record, Internat. Jour. Psychoanalysis, N.Y. Med. Jour., Psychiatric Quarterly. Home: Flemington, N.J.†

STERN, CHARLES FRANK, banker; b. Arcata, Calif., May 8, 1880; s. Bernard Frank and Julia Frances (Hopkins) S.; grad. Union High Sch., Arcata; student U. of Calif., Class of 1903; m. True Aiken, June 12, 1905; children—William Wallace, Peter Bernard, Richard Martin. With Humboldt Commercial Co., wholesale grocers, Eureka, Calif., 1903-14; mem. Highway Commn., Calif., 1914-18; supt. Bank of Calif., 1918-21; exec. v.p., First Nat. Bank of Los Angeles, and Los Angeles Trust and Savings Bank, 1921-25; pres. Pacific Southwest Savings Bank, and exec. v.p. Los Angeles First Nat. Bank, 1925-29; pres. Occidental Gas Securities Co., 1931-38; dir. Calif. Seaboard Corp., from 1935; v.p. Dist. Bond Co., Deposited Bonds & Shares Corp. Pres. Oakwood Memorial Park. Mem. Calif. State Bd. Edn., 1913-14. Mem. Delta Upsilon. Mason (Shriner). Republican. Clubs: Sunset California (Los Angeles); Commonwealth (San Francisco). Author: Convict Labor Road Law in Calif. Home: Glendale, Cal.*†

STERN, EDITH MENDEL, writer; b. N.Y.C., June 24, 1901; d. Leon S. and Sadie (Jacobs) Mendel; student Calhoun Sch., 1907-18; A.B., Barnard Coll., 1922; m. William A. Stern, II, Aug. 18, 1923 (dec. May 1965); 1 dau., Monica Mary. Book publishers' editor, 1922-27; lectr. on current books, 1928-39. Dir. Epilepsy League, 1938. Mem. Md. Bd. Mental Hygiene, 1947, Nat. Com. for Mental Hygiene, 1946. Dir. Mental Hygiene Soc. Md., 1949. Spl. cons. Nat. Inst. Mental Health, 1958-63. Recipient Nat. Media award Family Service Assn. Am., 1965; Robert T. Morse writer's award Am. Psychiat. Assn., 1966. Fellow Am. Med. Writers Assn.; mem. Am. Assn. Mental Deficiency, Soc. Mag. Writers., Nat. Assn. Sci. Writers, Am. Gerontological Soc., Forum for Profls. and Execs. Clubs: Am. Newspaper Women's; Nat. Press Barnard (Washington). Author: Mental Illness; A Guide for the Family, 1942, 5th edit., 1968; The Attendant's Guide, 1943; The Housemother's Guide, 1947; The Mental Hospital: A Guide for the Citizen, 1947; The Handicapped Child: A Guide for Parents, 1950; You and Your Aging Parents, 1952, rev. edit. 1965; Notes for After Fifty, 1955; A Full Life After 65, 1963. Contbr. to govt. publs. and nat. mags. Home: Washington, D.C. Died Feb. 8, 1975.

STERN, GLADYS BERTHA, author; b. London, Eng., June 17, 1890; d. Albert and Elizabeth Stern; ed. Notting Hill High Sch. and Acad. of Dramatic Art; m. Geoffrey Lisle Holdsworth, 1919. Author numerous books; latest publs.: The Reasonable Shores 1946; No Son of Mine, 1948; A Duck to Water; Ten Days of Christmas, 1951; The Donkey Shore; A Name to Conjure With, 1953; Johnny Forsaken, 1954; For All We Know, 1956; Seventy Times Seven, 1957; And Did He Stop and Speak to You?, 1958; Travels With A Donkey, Unless I Marry, 1959; One is Only Human, Bernadette, 1960; Credit Title, 1961; All the Good Time; The Way it Worked Out; also short stories, film scripts, TV plays, revs. Home: England. Died Sept. 19, 1973.

STERN, LEO, stock broker; b. Bklyn., Dec. 21, 1895; s. Fred and Emma (Simon) S.; B.S. with honors, Columbia, 1915, M.A., 1916; m. Marjorie Phillips, Mar. 11, 1926; children—Robert L., Walter P., Richard D. Securities analyst Newburger, Henderson & Loeb, 1916-29; securities analyst Newburger, Loeb & Co., N.Y.C., 1930-35, partner, 1935-70. Pres., Westchester Ethical Soc. Trustee Leo and Marjorie Stern Found. Served with U.S. Army, 1917-18. Mem. Phi Beta Kappa. Home: Larchmont, N.Y. Died Aug. 13, 1973.

STERN, OSCAR DAVID, lawyer; b. Russia, Oct. 13, 1888; s. David O. and Rose (Handelman) S.; brought to U.S., 1897; student U. Chgo., 1905-06; LL.B., Northwestern U., 1910; m. Anne Preaskil, June 29, 1916; children—Darlene Geis, Jean Gottlieb. Admitted to Ill. bar, 1910, since practiced in Chgo.; with firm Judah, Willard, Wolf & Reichmann, 1910-27, mem. firm, 1927-72, firm became Judah, Reichmann. Trumbull, Cox & Stern, merged with Pam & Hurd to became Pam, Hurd & Reichmann, 1939, then Dallstream, Schiff, Stern & Hardin, now Schiff, Hardin, Waite, Dorschel & Dritton. Director of Rolands of Bloomington, Inc. Dir. second vice pres. Palm Springs Desert Mus. Mem. Art Inst. Chgo. (life), Field Mus. Natural History, Am., Ill. Chgo. bar assns., Northwestern U. Assos., Order of Coif. Clubs: Racquet (Palm Springs); Standard (pres. 1950-52, dir.), Art (trustee) (Chgo.). Home: Chicago, Ill., Died Nov. 28, 1973.

STERRETT, HENRY HATCH DENT, clergyman; b. Coudersport, Pa., Jan. 25, 1880; s. James Macbridge and Adlumia (Dent) S.; A.B., Harvard, 1899, A.M., 1900; B.D., Episcopal Theol. Sch., Cambridge, Mass., 1903; m. Helen Margaret Black, May 10, 1915; children—Ann, Henry Hatch Dent, Samuel Black. Deacon, 1903, priest, 1904, P.E. Church; formerly assistant at St. George's Church, New York City, then at Trinity Ch., New Haven, Conn., and rector St. Paul's Ch., Columbus, O.; rector All Souls Memorial Ch., Washington, 1917-48, ret. Mem. Theta Delta Chi. Democrat. Club: Chevy Chase. Home: Washington, D.C.†

STEVENS, FREDERIC HARPER, corp. official; b. Rowlett, Ky., Jan. 11, 1879; s. Peter Harper and Eliza (Faget) S.; ed. pub. and private schs., Chicago; m. Lucille Shield, Aug. 14, 1901; m. 2d, Martha Josephine Kuhen, Feb. 3, 1912 (dec.); children—Charlotte Louise, Lee Edward. Sales mgr. Lanston Monotype Co., Chicago, 1906-11; pres. McCullough Printing Co., Manila, P.I., 1912-29; dir. of imports Pacific Commercial Co., Manila, 1921-33; pres. F. H. Stevens & Co.; v.p. Zambales Chromite, Primo Mfg. Corp. Pres. Am. Sch., Inc., 1921-23. Hon. mem. and past pres. Manila Rotary Club; dir. Masonic Temple Assn., Y.M.C.A. (Manila), Pacific Inst.; hon. v.p. Hosp. for Crippled Children. Served with Troop F, 1st Ill. Vol. Cav., 1898; maj. U.S. Army Res. from 1917. Past dept. comdr. U.S. War Vets. Mason (33°, Shriner; past grand master of Masons in P.I.; deputy of Supreme Council in P.I.), Odd Fellow, Elk. Republican. Clubs: Army and Navy, Elks, Wack Wack Country, Manila Golf, Polo, University. Home: Manila, P.I.†

STEVENS, GEORGE, motion picture dir., producer; b. Oakland, Cal., 1905; s. Landers and Georgia (Cooper) S.; student pub. schs. Began career as cameramen, 1921; dir., from 1930, pictures include: Alice Adams, 1932, Annie Oakley, 1935, Quality Street, 1937; producer, dir. pictures including: Vivacious Lady, 1938; Gunga Din, 1939; Penny Serenade, 1941; Woman of the Year, 1942; The Talk of the Town, 1942; The More the Merrier, 1943; I Remember Mama, 1948; A Place in the Sun, 1951 (named Outstanding Picture of Year, Nat. Bd. Rev. Motion Pictures); Something to Live For, 1951; Shane, 1952; Giant, 1956; The Diary of Anne Frank, 1959; The Greatest Story Ever Told; The Only Game in Town. Pres., Screen Dir. Guild, 1946, bd., 1950. Recipient Acad. Motion Picture Arts and Scis. award for direction A Place in the Sun, 1952, Acad. and Look awards for Giant, 1956. Served from maj. to lt. col. Signal Corps, AUS, 1943-45; assigned as head spl. motion picture unit to photograph activities of 6th Army for nat. archives; recorded 6 major campaigns E.T.P.; also duty in Africa and Middle East. Home: Beverly Hills, Cal. Died Mar. 8, 1975.

STEVENS, JOHN MELIOR, banker; b. London, Eng., Nov. 7, 1913; s. Courtenay and Melior Frances (Barker) S.; student Winchester (Eng.) Coll., 1926-32; m. Frances Anne Hely Hutchinson, 1940; children—Jane Frances, Mary Anne Victoria, John Christopher Courtenay. Admitted as solicitor, 1937; adviser Bank Eng., 1946-54, exec. dir., 1957-65, dir., 1968—; dir. European dept. IMF, Washington, 1954-56; econ. minister Brit. embassy, Washington, also exec. dir. IMF and Internat. Bank Reconstrn. and Devel., 1965-67; mng. dir. Morgan Grenfell & Co. Ltd., 1967-72, chmn., 1972-73; dir. Suez Finance Co., Brit. Bank Middle East, Brit. Petroleum Co. Ltd. Mem. Council Fgn. Bondholders; mem. gen. adv. council BBC, 1963-64; chmn. East European Trade Council, 1970-73. Hon. treas. Army Benevolent Fund, 1963-64; Fellow Univ.

Coll. London, 1968, treas., 1970-73; mem. council Exeter U., 1971. High sheriff, County London, 1964. Served to col. British Army, 1939-45. Decorated Distinguished Service Order, officer Order Brit. Empire, Territorial Decoration, knight comdr. Order St. Michael and St. George. Home: London, England also Devon, England. Died Oct. 27, 1973; interred Devon, England.

STEVENS, SYLVESTER K(IRBY), author, historian, state ofcl.; b. Harrison Valley, Pa., July 10, 1904; s. Herbert Chester and Anna Elizabeth (Outman) S.; A.B., Pa. State Coll., 1926, M.A., 1927; Ph.D., Columbia, 1945; Litt. D., Lebanon Valley Coll., 1953; L.H.D., Susquehanna U.; LL.D., Moravian Coll., 1962; m. Crescence P. Miller, June 22, 1926; 1 son, James Harry. Asst. prof. history Pa. State Coll., 1926-37; state historian Commonwealth of Pa. 1937-56; exec. dir. Pa. Hist. and Mus. Commn., 1956-72; bus. mgr. Am. Heritage, 1950-54, mem. editorial bd., from 1954; dir. Am. Heritage Pub. Co. Cons. com. Historic Sights and Bldgs., Nat. Park Service; chmn. President's Adv. Council on Historic Preservation, from 1967. Recipient Distinguished Alumnus award, 1966; award of merit Am. Assn. State and Local History, 1969. Mem. Pa. Hist. Assn. (pres. 1948-51), Pa. Fedn. Hist. Socs. (exec. sec. 1937-72), Am. Assn. State and Local History (pres. 1946-50, treas. 1950-62, council mem. 1960-71), Am. Assn. Historic Sites Adminstrs. (pres. 1958-60, chmn. bd. 1960-66), Manuscript Soc. Am. (v.p. 1949-53), Nat. Park Service Historic Sites Survey (mem. adv. bd.), Theta Chi, Delta Sigma Rho, Pi Gamma Mu. Author: American Expansion in Hawaii, 1842-1898, 1945; Pennsylvania at War, 1941-45, 1946; Pennsylvania-Titan of Industry, 1948; Exploring Pennsylvania (with R.W. Cordier), 3 vols., 1953; Pennsylvania: The Keystone State, 2 vols. 1956; Pennsylvania, Birthplace of a Nation, 1964; Pennsylvania, Heritage of a Commonwealth, 1968; Pennsylvania Colony, 1969; Pennsylvania Portrait, 1969. Editor: Papers of Colonel Henry Bouquet (with Donald H. Kent), 1951; Travels in New Frances by J.C.B. (with Kent), 1942; Wilderness Chronicles of Northwestern Pennsylvania (with Kent), 1941; also pamphlets. Home: Camp Hill, Pa. Died Jan. 16, 1974.

STEVENS, WALTER E, banker; b. Minnehaha Co., S.D., Mar. 6, 1880; s. James E. and Nell (Bannister) S.; ed. common schs.; m. Myrtle Colburn, of Council Bluffs, Ia., Dec. 31, 1910. In banking business from 1899; pres. Security Nat. Bank, Sioux Falls, S.D., from 1910; v.p. and treas. Van Brunt-Overland Co. Republican. Episcopalian. Clubs: Dacotah, Minnehaha Country; Toledo (Toledo, O.). Home: Sioux Falls, S.D.†

STEVENS, WAYNE MACKENZIE, mgmt. cons., educator; b. Des Moines; s. Edwin Luther and Hattie Maude (Mackenzie) S.; B.S., U. Ill.; M.B.A., Northwestern U.; Ph.D., Am. U.; m. Phyla Marsh, Aug. 15, 1925. Mktg. specialist USDA; accountant, economist, prof. mktg. and financial mgmt. La. State U., 1924-37; dean Coll. Commerce, dir. bus. research U. Md., 1937-42; partner Mackenzie Stevens & Co., mgmt. cons., 1938—. Cons. economist; prin. orgn. expert Fed. Farm Bd., 1930; vis. prof. U. Nanking, China, cons. Shanghai Comml. & Savs. Bank, 1934-36; adviser Nat. Econ. Council, Govt. of China, 1934-36; cons. survey activities include spl. cons. on financial orgn. U.S. Bd. Econ. Warfare, 1942, U.S. Dept. State fgn. service res. officer, 1942-44, adviser Govt. China, Chunking, 1942-43, cons. Govt. Burma (Simia, India), Govt. India, Delhi, East Africa Govs. Conf., Nairobi, Kenya, West African War Council, Accra, Gold Coast, 1943; pres. Internat. div. Asso. Mfrs. Inc., 1946-49; Korean econ. commr., dir. trade and finance div. ECA, 1949-50; mem. State Dept. Far Eastern Conf., Tokyo, 1950; chmn. bus. div., dir. Sch. World Bus., cons. internat. devel. San Francisco State Coll., 1950-63; internat. economist, project evaluator Nat. Planning Office and Nat. Econ. Council, Govt. Nicaragua, 1965-67. Chmn., World Investment and Trade Corp., 1953-65, 68-75; project dir. Frederic Burk Found. and Devel. Improved Employment and More Effective Utilization Order Persons Project, San Francisco State U., 1968-75; mem. 7th ann. forum on finance Investment Bankers Assn. Am.; mem. Mem. U.S. Dept. Commerce Regional Export Expansion Council, cons. internat. trade devel., 1962-65. Mem. Am. Mgmt. Assn. (chmn. W. Coast conf. on setting up and administering internat. ops. 1958), Am. Econ. Assn., Assn. for Edn. in Internat. Bus. (v.p. 1959-61), World Affairs Council, Phi Kappa Phi, Beta Gamma Sigma, Delta Sigma Pi. Methodist. Mason. Clubs: Olympic Commonwealth. Author books on econ. devel., bus. mgmt.; prin. books include: Financial Organization and Adminstration; Structural Organization; Cooperative Organization and Management; Public Finance (with others). Died Oct. 17, 1975.

STEVENSON, COKE ROBERT, gov. of Tex.; b. Mason Co., Tex., Mar. 20, 1888; s. Robert M. and Virginia (Hurley) S.; studied law privately; m. Fay Wright, Dec. 24, 1912; 1 son, Coke; m. 2d, Marguerite King Heap, 1954; 1 dau., Jane; 1 stepson, Dennis Heap. With First State Bank and Junction State Bank, Junction, Tex., 1906-14; admitted to Tex. bar, 1913; county atty., Kimble County, 1914-18; county judge, 1919-21; pres. First Nat. Bank, Junction, 1921-27; mem. House of Reps., Tex. Legislature, 1929-39, speaker, 1933-37; lt. gov. of Tex., 1939-41; became gov. of Tex., Aug. 4, 1941 (to fill unexpired term of W. Lee O'Daniel); elected gov. for term beginning Jan. 19, 1943, Jan. 1945, term expired Jan. 1947; rancher, 62 yrs.; pvt. practice, Junction. Tex. Mem. Texas Bar Assn. Methodist. Mason (33°), Woodmen of the World, Praetorians, Elk, Rotarian. Home: nr. Junction, Tex. Died June 28, 1975; buried at ranch South Llano River, nr. Junction, Tex.

STEVENSON, DAVID LLOYD, educator; b. Escondido, Cal., June 10, 1910; s. Lloyd A. and Nellie (Baldridge) S.; A.B., U. Cal. at Berkeley, 1933, M.A., 1935; Ph.D., Columbia, 1941; m. Joan Thorsen, Sept. 4, 1937; children—John F.L. Instr. English, Cal. Inst. Tech., 1937-39, U. Wis., 1939-40, Wayne State U., 1940-41, U. Cal. at Berkeley, 1941-43; coordinator, then chief regional analyst, controlled materials compliance WPB, 1943-47; successively asso. prof. prof. Western Res. U., 1947-63, coordinator grad. Studies English, 1956-63; prof. English, Hunter Coll. fo City U. N.Y., 1963-75, chmn. dept., 1967-75. Mem. Modern Lang. Assn., Malone Soc., Renaissance Soc. Am., Phi Beta Kappa, Phi Kappa Sigma. Author: The Love Game Comedy, 2d edit., 1966; The Achievement of Shakespeare's Measure for Measure, 1967; The Elizabethan Age, 1967; also articles. Editor: (with Herbert Gold) Stories of Modern America, 1961; (Shakespeare) Much Ado About Nothing, 1964. Home: Falls Village, Conn. Died Apr. 28, 1975.

STEVENSON, ELMO NALL, educator; b. Calif., Feb. 25, 1904; s. Frank and Edith (Nall) S.; A.B., San Jose State Coll., 1927, A.M., Stanford Univ., 1929, Ed.D., 1938; m. Caroline M. Miles, Dec. 18, 1925; children—Rosemary, Vivian (Mrs. Raymond Lance Locke), Kenneth. Scout exec., Santa Clara, San Benito, Monterey Bay (Cal.) council, 1926-29; instr. biology, dean of men Eastern Ore. Coll. of Edn., La Grande, 1929-40; prof. of sci. edn. and coordinator of personnel Ore. State Coll., Corvallis, 1940-45; pres. So. Ore. Coll., from 1946. Bd. mem. A.R.C., Nat., Crater Lake councils Boy Scouts Am. Member adv. board Rogue National Forest. Member Assn. of State Colls. and Univs. past. sec.-treas.; rep. to nat. commn. accrediting 1965-67), A.A.A.S., Nat., Ore. edn. assns., Am. Nature Assn., Am. Biology Teachers Assn. Am. C. of C., Phi Delta Kappa, Kappa Delta Pi, Phi Sigma. Republican. Club: Lion's (past pres. 2 clubs, internat. counselor). Author: Nature Rambles in the Wallowas, 1937; Nature Games Book, 1941; Key to the Nests of the Pacific Coast Birds, 1943; Selected Procedures in Teaching Biology, 1950 Pets: Wild and Western, 1953; Contributor numerous magazine articles on natural history and edn. to various publications. Home: Ashland, Ore. Died Apr. 20, 1973.

STEVENSON, GEORGE STANLEY, ret. banker; b. Clinton, Maine, July 9, 1881; s. of George Stanley and Elizabeth (Whitten) S.; student Coburn Classical Inst., 1895-98, Colby Coll., Waterville, Me., 1898-1900; A.B., Harvard University, 1903, A.M., 1904; LL.D., Smith College, 1949; married Marjorie Elder, June 24, 1905; children—Elizabeth Elder (dec.), Sarah Elder. Teacher Greek and Latin Milton (Mass.) Acad., 1903-05; prin. Coburn Classical Inst., Waterville, Me., 1905-12; with Lee, Higginson & Co., Boston, 1913-15, Conn. mgr., 1915-21; treas. Society for Savings, Hartford, 1921-27; mem. Thomson, Fenn & Co. (later Stevenson, Gregory & Co.) 1927-38, member firm Putnam & Co., 1938-41; president The New Haven Savs. Bank, 1941-52, chmn. bd., 1952-56; dir. Hartford Accident & Indemnity Co., Hartford Fire Ins. Co., Arrow-Hart & Hegeman Electric Co., Conn. Light & Power Co.; hon. dir. Phoenix Mut. Life Ins. Co. Chmn. New Haven City Employees Retirement Fund. Bd. trustees Yale-New Haven Med. Center; trustee emeritus of Trinity Coll. Member board govs. Investment Bankers Conference, 1936-39, Investment Bankers Assn. of America, 1936-37; mem. bd. govs. exec. com. and treas. Nat. Assn. Security Dealers, Inc., 1939-40. Mem. Delta Upsilon, Phi Beta Kappa. Republican. Club: Graduates. Home: New Haven, Conn.†

STEVENSON, LIONEL, educator, author; b. Edinburgh, Scotland, July 16, 1902; s. Henry and Mabel Rose (Cary) S.; B.A., U.B.C., 1922; M.A., U. Toronto, 1923; Ph. D., U. Cal., 1925; B.Litt., U. Oxford, 1935, m. Lillian Sprague Jones, Apr. 10, 1954; 1 dau. Instr., U. Cal., 1925-30; prof. English, head dept. Ariz. State Coll., Tempe, 1930-37; asst. prof. English, U. So. Cal., 1937-41, asso. prof., 1941-44, prof., 1944-55, head dept., 1943-55; prof. English, Duke, 1955-72, chmn. dept. 1964-67. Vis. prof. summers U. B.C., 1930, 40, 54, N.Y. U., 1948, 62, U. Colo., 1950, U. Ill., 1952-53; vis. lectr. Oxford U., 1960; Berg vis. prof. N.Y. U., 1967-68. Mem. Western Coll. Assn., v.p., 1946-47. Fellow Royal Soc. Lit.; mem. Philol. Assn. Pacific Coast (pres. 1948-50), Coll. English Assn. (v.p. 1954), English Speaking Union (pres. Raleigh-Durham br. 1958-60). Clubs: Authors (London Eng.); Arts and Letters (Toronto); California Writers(pres. 1928-30); P.E.N. (del. Internat. Congresses, Vienna 1929, Edinburgh 1934, Paris 1937, Lausanne 1951, pres. Los Angeles chpt. 1943-53), Canadian Authors Assn. Author: Appraisals of Canadian Literature, 1926; A Pool of Stars (poetry), 1926; Darwin Among the Poets, 1932; The Rose of the Sea (poetry), 1932; The Wild Irish Girl, 1936; Doctor Quicksilver, 1939; The Showman of Vanity Fair, 1947; (with J.D. Cooke) English Literature of the Victorial Period, 1949; The Ordeal of George Meredith, 1953; The English Novel, a Panorama, 1960; History of the English Novel, Vol. XI, 1967. Editor: Victorian Fiction; A Guide to Research, 1964. Contbr. articles to lit. jours., U.S., Can. Eng. Home: Durham, N.C. Died Dec. 21, 1973.

STEWART, CHARLES LESLIE, educator, economist; b. Moweaqua, Ill., Sept. 3, 1890; s. James Gray and Tryphena Margaret (Brooks) S.; A.B., Ill. Wesleyan U., 1911, D.Sc., 1943; A.M., U. Ill., 1912, Ph.D., 1915, U. Berlin, 1914; m. Ruth Want, Aug. 12, 1916; children—Mary Margaret (Mrs. Richard A. Binfield), Charles Leslie, Barbara Jane (Mrs. McDonald), James Kinley (dec.). Instr. econs. U. Ill., 1915-18; prof. econs. U. Ark., 1918-20; asso. to agrl. economist Bur. Agrl. Econs., Dept. Agr., 1921-24; asso. prof. agrl. econs. U. Ill. Coll. Agr., Urbana, 1924-35, prof., 1935-59, emeritus prof. from 1959, also head div. land econs., dept. agrl. econs., chief in land econs. Agrl. Expt. Sta. Cons. nat., govt. orgns., 1931-59; supr. research project U. Ill. and Ill. Div. Hwys., 1959-60. Mem. nat. adv. com. Land Econs. Inst.; del. gen. assembly Internat. Inst. Agr., 1938; leader Land Use Statistics project Resources for Future, 1962-63. Mem. Am. Farm Econs. Assn., Land and Estate Cons. (mgr.), Am. Soc. Farm Mgrs. and Rural Appraisers, Am. Right-of-Way Assn. (nat. adv. com. on land econs.), Agrl. History Soc., Econ. History Assn., Internat. Conf. Agrl. Economists, Nabor House, Artus, Pi Kappa Delta, Kappa Delta Pi, Phi Eta, Phi Kappa Phi, Beta Gamma Sigma, Gamma Sigma Delta, Delta Phi. Methodist. Author nat. farm export debenture plan, books, bulls., from 1913; co-author Land Use Information, 1966. Co-editor Modern Land Policy, 1960. Mem. com. on 1958 yearbook Land (Dept. Agr.). Home: Urbana, Ill. Died Sept. 1, 1974; buried Woodlawn Cemetery, Urbana, Ill.

STEWART, HAROLD EDISON, univ. dean; b. Butler, O., May 24, 1903; s. Albert M. and Luella C. (Burger) S.; B.Sc., Ohio State U., 1925, M.A., 1927, Ph.D., 1937; m. Claire Margaret Ruescher, Sept. 5, 1924; children—Patricia Jean (Mrs. Robert Layton), Robert Arnold. Instr. dept. geography Coll. City of Detroit (now Wayne State U.), 1927, asst. prof. dept. geography Wayne State U., 1936-42, asso. prof., 1942-46, dir. student activities, 1946, asst. dean student affairs, 1947-52, dean students, 1953-75, dir. div. student personnel, 1953-75. Mem. Nat. Assn. Student Personnel Adminstrs. (v.p. 1961), Am. Personnel and Guidance Assn., Am. Coll. Personnel Assn., Am. Assn. U. Profs., Omicron Delta Kappa, Tau Kappa Epsilon. Author: (with James F. Chamberlin) Air-Age Geography and Society, 1945. Home: Detroit, Mich. Died July 14, 1975.

STEWART, JOHN HAMILTON, advt. exec.; b. Oklahoma City, June 14, 1917; s. Hamilton George and Ida (Shive) S.; B.A. in Journalism, U. Okla., 1939; m. Jonnie Lee Ingle, May 17, 1941; children—Susan (Mrs. Glenn Barnes), Linda (Mrs. Jeffrey Osgood). With Glenn Advt. Co., Dallas, from 1939, exec. v.p., 1947-57, pres., from 1957. Bd. dirs. Dallas County chpt. Am. Cancer Soc., Goodwill Industries. Served with AUS, 1940-45. Mem. Am. Assn. Advt. Agencies (past gov. S.W. council). Clubs: Dallas, Cipango, Brookhaven Country (Dallas). Home: Dallas, Tex., Deceased.

STEWART, MARSHALL BOWYER, clergyman, educator; b. Galveston, Tex., Sept. 4, 1880; s. John William and Alice Olin (Laney) S.; student Columbian (now George Washington) U., 1898-99; B.A., Trinity Coll., Hartford, Conn., 1902, A.M., 1906, D.D., 1927; B.D., Gen. Theol. Sem., 1905; D.D., Nashotah House, 1925; m. Katherine Corinne Keen, June 21, 1928; children—John Charles, Margaret Mary, Anne Marshall, Deacon, 1905, priest, 1905, P.E. Ch.; pastor St. John's Parish, Prince George and Charles counties, Md., 1905-07; prof. ecclesiastical history, Western Theol. Sem., at Chicago, Ill., 1909-13; prin. St. Martin's Sch., Salina, Kan., 1913-14; prof. dogmatic theology, Nashotah (Wis.) House, 1915-28; prof. dogmatic theology, Gen. Theol. Sem., from 1928. Mem. Phi Beta Kappa, Alpha Chi Rho. Author: God and Realty, 1926; In Other Words, 1941. Home: New York City, N.Y.†

STEWART, PAUL RICH, coll. ofcl.; b. Spraggs, Pa., Mar. 16, 1887; s. Ezra De Garmo and Lana Margaret (Waychoff) S.; grad. Waynesburg (Pa.) Coll. Acad., 1903; A.B., Waynesburg Coll., 1909, A.M., 1910, Sc.D., 1924; A.M., Columbia, 1916; LL.D., Grove City Coll., 1949; Sc.D., West Va. Wesleyan Coll., 1961; m. Dessie Knight Rush, Aug. 24, 1910; children—Ruth Harriett, Walter Alan. Prof. chemistry and geology, Waynesburg Coll., 1910-21, pres., 1921-63, chancellor coll., from 1963; asso. with Dr. B. K. Stewart in a survey of the fossil flora and fauna of the Dunkard Series of southwestern Pa. under Am. Philos. Soc. grant. Mem. A.A.A.S., Pa. Acad. Sci., So. Appalachian Botanical Club, Pitts. Geol. Soc., History of Sci. Soc., Soc. Vertebrate Paleontology, Delta Sigma Pi. Democrat. Presbyterian. Mason, Odd Fellow. Illustrated lectures: Wild Flowers of the Appalachia, Wild Flowers of the Rockies, Plants of the Past, Foods the Indians Gave Us; How the Earth Grew; Atomic Bombs in the Heavens. Home: Waynesburg, Pa. Died Jan. 27, 1974.

STEWART, ROLLAND MACLAREN, rural educator; b. Winslow, Ill., Nov. 27, 1878; s. James Alexander and Amanda (Rayhorn) S.; student Western Coll. (now Coe Coll.), 3 yrs.; A.B., State U. of Ia., 1904; B.Di., 1906, Ph.D., 1912; m. Hattie Philips, Dec. 22, 1904; children—Harold Philips, Ralph (dec.). Teacher rural schools of Illinois, 1897-98; professor of English and education, Graceland College, Lamoni, Iowa, 1904-08, president, 1905-08; with State U. of Iowa, 1908-18, asst. in edn., 1908-11, instr., Feb.-June 1911, asst. prof., 1912-18; prof. rural edn., Cornell U., from 1918, head dept. from 1944; acting dir. sch. edn. from Mar. 1, 1946, prof. rural edn. emeritus from July 1, 1946, dir. Porject for Presidents of Negro Land Grant Colls., Washington, D.C.; dir. N.Y. State summer session, Cornell, 1927-34, advisor vocational edn., 1937-46; teacher 3 summers, Purdue, U. of Ky. and Hampton Institute. Mem. Am. Vocational Assn. past chmn. research com. and editor Studies in Agr. Edn., for agrl. sec., N.E.A., Nat. Soc. College Teachers of Edn., Nat. Society for Study of Education; member Philippine educational committee, 1945. Kappa Phi Kappa, Phi Beta Kappa, Phi Delta Kappa. Republican. Methodist. Author: Cooperative Methods in the Development of School Support in the U.S., 1914; Teaching Agricultural Vocations (with Arthur K. Getman), 1927, 29. Contbr. to Book of Rural Life (10 vols.), and ednl. articles to mags. Home: Ithaca, N.Y.†

STEWART, ROSS, corp. exec.; b. Houston, Feb. 15, 1897; s. Cornelius James and Josephine (Calhoun) S.; student Tex. A. and M. Coll., 1915-18, Wash. U., 1918-19; m. Catherine Rial, Feb. 23, 1921; children—Nancy Jean (Mrs. Garth Bates), Cornelius James. Chmn. bd. emeritus C. Jim Stewart & Stevenson, Inc., Stewart & Stevenson Services, Inc.; v.p., dir. Internat. Switchboard Corp.; adv. dir. Tex. Commerce Bank; dir. Mangone Shipbldg. Co., Machinery Acceptance Corp.; v.p., sec. Lamb-McAshan Corp.; dir., chmn. bd. Houston br. Fed. Res. Bank of Dallas, 1945-54; indsl. adv. com. Fed. Res. Bank Dallas from 1954; dir. Peden Iron & Steel, Continental Airlines. Mem. Small Bus. Adv. Com., Sec. Commerce, 1945-50, chmn., 1947-48; mem. procurement policy council Office Def. Adminstrn., 1951; lt. Tex. N.G. Bd. govs. U. Houston, 1956-63; bd. dirs. Sam Houston area council Boy Scouts Am., Houston Speech and Hearing Center; trustee Merit Shop Found. Served as aviation cadet U.S. Naval Air Force, World War I. Mem. Houston C. of C. (dir. 1963, adv. mem. aviation com.), Navy League (pres. 1957-58), Am. Ordnance Assn. (council), Ross Vols. Tex. A. and M. Coll. Presbyn. Rotarian. Clubs: Country, Petroleum, Eagle Lake Rod and Gun; World Trade, Summit. Home: Houston, Tex. Died May 28, 1975; interred Forest Park Cemetery, Houston, Tex.

STEWART, RUSS, newspaper exec.; b. Holyoke, Mass., June 21, 1909; s. Alexander and Ellen (Moss) S.; ed. high sch.; m. 2d, Mildred Bradford Norris, Apr. 10, 1960; children (by previous marriage)—Sherry (Mrs. Donald Berger), Russell (dec. 1962). Successively reporter, columnist Bridgeport (Conn.) Times-Star, Bridgeport Post-Telegram; corr. United Press, N.Y. American, N.Y. Times; publicity man Fox theatres; scenario writer Hal Roach Studios, 1926-31; publicity man Metro-Goldwyn-Mayer pictures, 1932-35; promotion mgr. Chgo. Times, 1935-41, mng. editor, 1942-45, v.p., gen. mgr., 1946-47; v.p., gen. mgr. Chgo. Times Syndicate, Inc., 1939-47; vice pres., dir. Field Enterprises, Inc., exec. v.p. Chgo. Sun-Times, Chgo. Daily News; dir. Pubs. Newspaper Syndicate; chmn. bd. Manistique Pulp & Paper Co. (Mich.); pres. Paper Flotation, Inc.; dir. Gt. Lakes Paper Co., Ltd., This Week mag. Director bur. advt. Am. Newspaper Publishers Assn., chmn., 1960-62. Bd. dirs. Chgo. Boys Clubs, Immigrants Service League, Chgo. Com. Alcoholism, Chgo. Conv. Bur., Inc.; trustee La Rabida Jackson Park Sanitarium. Mem. adv. council war finance div. Treasury Dept., 1942-45; mem. newspaper industry adv. com. NPA, Dept. of Commerce, 1951-53; mem. adv. council on naval affairs Ninth Naval Dist., 1955. Mem. Chgo. Newspaper Pubs. Assn. (pres. 1954-59), City Press Assn., Chgo. (pres. 1952-54), Am. Soc. Newspaper Editors, Inter-Am. Press Assn., Navy League of U.S., Sigma Delta Chi. Clubs: Tavern, Mid-Am., Merchants and Manufacturers (Chgo.); Knollwood Country (Lake Forest); Nat. Press (Washington). Home: Chicago, Ill. Died Aug. 12, 1974.

STEWART, WALTER LESLIE, lawyer, banker; b. Tecumseh, Neb., Feb. 28, 1888; s. Joseph Alexander and Mary Jane (Rutledge) S.; A.B., State U. Ia., 1910, LL.B., 1912; m. Lucile Emerson, June 24, 1914; 1 dau., Susan Rebecca (Mrs. W. J. Alford, III). Head coach U. Ia. baseball and basketball team, 1911-12; football coach Simpson Coll., 1912, West Des Moines High Sch., 1913-16; admitted to Ia. Bar, 1912, practiced Des Moines, became sr. mem. Gibson, Stewart, Garrett, Heartney, Jones & Brodsky; vice chmn. bd. Central Nat. Bank & Trust Co., 1938-55, later dir. Dir., chmn. adv. com. State Automobile Ins. Assn. Chmn. Community Chest drive 1929, dir., 1929-32. Mem. athletic bd. State U. Ia. from 1931; adv. bd. YWCA; v.p., mem. bd. Tall Corn council Boy Scouts Am. (recipient Silver Beaver award 1950). Recipient certificate accomplishment U. Ia., 1947, Distinguished Service award, 1968; named mem. Ia. Sports Hall of Fame, 1965. Mem. Am., Ia. State and Polk Co. bar assns., Am. and Ia. State bankers assns., State U. Ia. Alumni Assn. (pres.), Des Moines Bus. Men's League (sec. 1912-22), Sigma Nu, Phi Delta Phi. Republican. Presbyn. (elder). Clubs: Wakonda, Des Moines (pres.), Rotary. Home: Des Moines, Ia. Died Aug. 15, 1974; interred Glendale Cemetery, Des Moines, Ia.

STIBBS, JOHN HENRY, univ. dean; b. Chgo., Feb. 10, 1909; s. Henry Howard and Bertha (Hemingway) S.; Ph.D., U. Mich., 1942; m. Phyllis Miner, May 25, 1941; children—Virginia Helen, Henry Howard II, John Henry. Teaching fellow U. Mich., 1937-42; instr. U.S. Naval Acad., 1946; with Tulane U., 1946—, successively asst. prof. English, asst. dean Coll. Arts and Scis., 1946-49, prof. and dean of students, 1949-75. Mem. exec. com. Assn. Naval R.O.T.C. Colls., 1967-70; acad. council Coll. Student Personnel Inst., 1966-70. Dir. Louise McGehee Sch. 1953-66. Served with USNR, 1942-46, now comdr. Mem. Nat. Assn. Student Personnel Adminstrs. (pres. 1954-55), Am. Personnel and Guidance Assn., Am. Coll. Health Assn., Am. Assn. U. Profs., Orleans Audubon Soc. (pres. 1951-69), Modern, South Central lang. assns., Renaissance Soc., S.R., Soc. War 1812, Delta Kappa Epsilon, Phi Kappa Phi, Omicron Delta Kappa. Clubs: Internat. House, Boston, South Louisiana Gun (dir.), Southern Yacht, New Orleans Lawn Tennis (New Orleans). Author short stories. contbr. articles to profl. jours. Home: New Orleans, La. Died Apr. 8, 1975.

STICKNEY, LOUIS R, clergyman; b. Newark, N.J., Feb. 26, 1879; s. George R. and Sylvia E. (De Wulf) S.; A.B., St. Charles Coll., Ellicott City, Md., 1896; S.T.L., North Am. Coll., Rome, 1902. Ordained priest R.C. Ch., 1902; sec. Apostolic Delegation, Ottawa, Can., 1903-04, Washington, D.C., 1904-08; sec. to Cardinal Gibbons, 1908-13; chancellor Archidiocese of Baltimore, 1913-19; apptd. consultor same, 1919; rector Cathedral, Baltimore, 1919-28; pastor Shrine of the Sacred Heart, Mount Washington, Baltimore, from 1928. Awarded medal Pro Ecclesia et Pontifice, by Pope Pius X, 1908; Chevalier Order of the Crown, Belgium, 1920; created domestic prelate by Pope Pius XI, 1922. Mem. Md. Hist. Soc. Home: Baltimore, Md.†

STIGNANI, EBE, mezzo-soprano. Appearances with leading opera companies in Rome, Milan (La Scala), also San Francisco Opera Assn.; roles include Adelgisa in Norma, also appearances in Mozart and Verdi requiems, Verdl operas; recording artist for Angel, Cetra records. Home: Imola, Italy., Died Oct. 5, 1974.

STILWELL, WILBER MOORE, educator, artist; b. Covington, Ind., Feb. 2, 1908; s. Wilber Fletcher and Sadie Eleanor (Moore) S.; student Kansas City (Mo.) Art Inst., 1929-33; B.S., Kan. State Teachers Coll., Emporia, 1940; M.A., U. of Ia., 1941; m. Gladys Louise Ferree, June 24, 1935; children—Elizabeth Ferree, Mary Ferree, Joan Ferree. Registrar Kansas City (Mo.) Art Inst., 1935-39, founder and dir. ann. high sch. competition in art, 1936-39; asst. prof. art, U. S.D., Vermillion, 1941-44, asso. prof., 1944-46, profs. art, from 1946; also head dept. art, 1941-67. Founder, dir. ann. S.D. high sch. competition in art, from 1942; founder, dir. Art Students Lecture Bur.; dep. nat. dir. Am. Art Week, 1966; state dir. for S.D. Am. Art Week, 1967, 68; judge art shows. Recipient bronze medal award in graphic arts Midwestern Artists' Exhibit, 1933, watercolor and pastel, 1936; 1st award for oil portrait Okla. Art Exhibit, Tulsa, 1939, water color, 1939, 40, water color portrait Kan. Art Exhibit, Topeka, 1940, sweepstakes award in prints and 1st award for color lithographs, 1942; 1st prize Am. Artists Profl. League for book co-designed, authored edited with wife, 1965; Nat. Gallery Art medal and Honorarium, 1966; gold medal Am. Artists Profl. League, 1966. Mem. Am. Assn. U. Profs. Mason. Clubs: Faculty Research and Scholarship of U. S.D. (pres. 1945-46). Co-author (with wife) articles in edn. jours. and mags. Co-inventor (with wife) printing processes in art; also mobile planning. Home: Vermillion, S.D. Died Mar. 8, 1974; interred Maple Hill Cemetery, Kansas City, Kan.

STINE, OSCAR CLEMEN, agrl. economist; b. Sandyville, Jackson County, W.Va., Nov. 13, 1884; s. Thomas and Emily Josephine (Boggess) S.; Ph.B., Ohio U., 1908; studied U. of Chicago, Harvard; Ph.D., U. of Wis., 1920; m. Ruth S. Speerstra, June 30, 1919; children—Ruth, Jane, Oscar, John. Supt. schs., Sparta, Wis., 1912-13; asst. instr. agrl. economics, U. of Wis., 1914-16; entered civil service, 1916; asst. in farm economics, 1916-19, asso. agrl. economist, 1920-21, agrl. economist in charge agrl. history, 1921-22, in charge of statis and hist. research Bur. of Agrl. Econimics, 1922-46, asst. chief in charge of hist. and statis. research and mktg., 1946-51, U.S. Dept. Agr.; vis. prof. agrl. econ. U. Fla., Gainesville, U.So. Ill., Carbondale; vis. prof. econs. Hampton Sydney Coll.; research aid congressional coms. Library of Congress; cons. econs; statistics Shepherd Coll., U. W.Va., Morgantown; mem. Central Statis. Bd. (v.p. 1933-35, 1937-40); mem. Statis. Adv. Com., Div. of Statis. Standards. Bur. of Budget. Mem. Social Science Advisroy Com. U.S. Civil Service Commn. Editor Jour. of Farm Economics, 1922-24; editor Agrl. History, 1927-31. Del. to Gen. Assembly Inernat. Inst. of Agr., Rome, 1926, 34. Pres. Agrl. Hist. Soc., 1924; fellow Am. Statis. Assn.; mem. Am. Econ. Assn., Am. Farm Econ. Assn. (pres. 1931), Agrl. Hist. Soc., Am. Statis. Assn., Social Science Research Council (sec., 1940-44). Internat. Conf. of Agrl. Economists, Council on Foreign Relations, Round Table, Phi Beta Kappa. Mem. Nat. Income and Nat. Price Confs. of Nat. Bur. Econ. Research, Club: Cosmos. Contbr. to Year Book and bulls., U.S. Dept. Agr., from 1921, to Book of Rural Life, 1925, to Ency. Britannica, reviews and articles in scientific jours. Home: Shepherdstown, W.Va., Died Mar. 29, 1974.

STIRLING, JOHN WILLIAM, elec. mfg. co. exec.; b. Pitts., July 3, 1910; s. John W. and Nellie (Stedeford) S.; B.S. in Elec. Engring., U. Pitts., 1932; grad. Advanced Mgmt. Program Harvard, 1959; m. Lois Rex, June 29, 1934. With Westinghouse Electric Corp., 1933-71, dep. gen. mgr. electric utility group, 1961-63, v.p., gen. mgr. transformer div., 1963-69, exec. v.p. transmission and distbn., 1969-71. Mem. I.E.E.E., Nat. Elec. Mfrs. Assn., Delta Tau Delta, Sigma Tau. Presbyn. Home: Pittsburgh, Pa. Died Apr. 9, 1975; interred Mt. Royal Cemetery, Pittsburgh, Pa.

STIRLING, MATTHEW WILLIAMS, anthropologist; b. Salinas, Cal., Aug. 28, 1896; s. John William and Ariana (Williams) S.; B.A., U. Cal., 1920; M.A., George Washington U., 1922, D.Sc., Tampa U., 1943; m. Marion Illig, Dec. 11, 1933; children—Matthew, Ariana. Tchr. anthropology U. Cal., 2 years; asst. curator, div. ethnology Nat. Mus., Washington, 1921-24; chief Bur. Am. Ethnology, Smithsonian Instn., 1928-47, dir., 1947-58, archaeologist emeritus, from 1958; collaborator in archeology Nat. Park Service, from 1958. Archaeol., ethnol. field work in various parts of N. Central, S.Am., Europe, East Indies; leader, Netherlands Am. expdn. to Central New Guinea, 1925-27, Nat. Geog. Soc.-Smithsonian Instn. archaeol. expdns. to So. Mexico, 1939-46, Nat. Geog. Soc. Smithsonian Instn. archaeol. expdns., Panama, 1948-53, Ecuador, 1957, Costa Rica, 1964. Served as ensign USN, World War I. Recipient Franklyn L. Burr award, 1939, 41, 58. Mem. Am. Anthrop. Assn. (v.p. 1935-36), A.A.A.S., Nat. Geog. Soc. (com. research and exploration from 1960), Washington Acad. Scis., Anthrop. Soc. Washington (pres. 1934-35), Washington Acad. Medicine, Soc. for Am. Archaeology, Sigma Xi. Clubs: Explorers, Cosmos. Lectr., N.Am. Indians. Author several books relating to field, also articles. Home: Washington, DC. Died Jan. 23, 1975; buried Gettysburg Nat. Mil. Park, Gettysburg, Pa.

STITES, RAYMOND SOMERS, educator; b. Passaic, N.J., June 19, 1899; s. Frederick Erskine and Marguerite (Adelhardt) S.; Ph.B., Brown U., 1921, A.M., 1922, Emma Josephone Arnold archeol. fellow, 1923, Morgan Edwards fellow classics; student R.I. Sch. Design, 1921-22; Ph.D., U. Vienna, 1927; m. Myrtle T. Fisk, Feb. 10, 1923 (dec.); children—Gretel (Mrs. Larry Friedman), Nan (Mrs. David Theonen); m. 2d, Mary Elizabeth Gaertner, July 29, 1938; 1 dau., Mary E. (Mrs. Paul Moyer). Art dir. Education Exhibition Co., Providence, 1922; dir. Davenport Art Mus., 1927; instr. U. Ia., 1927, U. Colo., 1928-29; asst. prof. Antioch Coll., 1930-32, prof., chmn. art dept., 1932-48; vis. prof. U. Chgo., 1932, Cornell U., 1934, Redlands U., 1946, U. N.M., 1947, U. Ariz., 1955, Kutztown State U., 1962; curator edn. Nat. Gallery Art, Washington, 1948-65, asst. to the dir. for edn. services, 1965-69; prof. art and religion Wesley Theol. Sem., 1968-74; president dir. Culture Films, Inc., from 1950. Served as pvt. U.S. Army, 1918. Mem. N.E.A., College Art Association, Archeological Institute of America, Phi Sigma Kappa. Member Soc. of Friends. Author: The Arts and Man, 1940; The Sublimations of Leonardo da Vinci, 1970. Home: Garrett Park, Md. Died Dec. 6, 1974; interred Cedar Lawn Cemetery, Paterson, N.J.

STOCK, LEO FRANCIS, hist. research; b. Gettysburg, Pa., July 31, 1878; s. George Edwin and Sarah (Noel) S.; A.B., Mount St. Mary's Coll., Emmitsburg, Md., 1896, A.M., 1898, LL.D., 1928; Ph.D., Catholic U. of America, 1920; m. Agnes Elizabeth Brooks, Dec. 30, 1902; children—Leo Francis, Elizabeth Queen (Mrs. J. Henry Cahill), Sarah Noel (Mrs. William Mong Murray), Mary Agnes (Mrs. Francis Bernard Kelly), Agnes Brooks (Mrs. John J. Scanlon), John Henry Brooks, William McSherry. Prof. of history and English, Pittsburgh (Pa.) Coll. (now Duquesne U.), 1899-1900; teacher, McGill Instn., Mobile, Ala., 1902-03, 1905-06; mem. staff Div. Hist. Research, Carnegie Instn. of Washington, 1910-45; recorder Nat. Bd. for Hist. Service, 1917-19; instr. in Am. history, Catholic U. of America, 1919-22, asso. prof., 1922-41; prof. Trinity Coll., Washington, D.C., 1945-49; lecturer, Catholic Summer School of America, Cliff Haven, N.Y., 1922-24, 30, 31, St. Joseph's Coll., Emmitsburg, Md., 1929-33. Co-editor Cath. Hist. Review, 1929-39. Benemcrent: medal conferred by Pope Pius XII, 1952. Mem. Am. Hist. Assn. (chmn. Com. on publs. 1928-34), Am. Catholic Hist. Assn. (pres. 1929; member exec. council 1930); fellow Royal Hist. Soc.; hon. fellow Knights of Columbus Hist. Commn. of Tex. Mem. K.C. (past grand knight). Author: Proceedings and Debates of the British Parliaments Respecting N.A. (5 vols.), 1924, 27, 30, 37, and 1941; List of American Journals. Devoted to the Humanistic and Soc. Scis., 1925, revised, 1928; United States Ministers to the Papal States, 1933; American Periodicals and Serial Publications in the Humanities and Social Sciences, 1933; Consular Relations between the United States and Papal States, 1945. Editor: Catholic Map of U.S., 1941.

Contbr. hist. and bibliog. articles, reviews, to Am. Hist. Review, Current Hist., Cath. Hist. Review, Hist. Outlook, etc. Home: Washington, D.C.†

STOCKHAUSEN, WILLIAM EDWARD, lawyer; b. Phila., Jan. 28, 1912; s. Thomas G. and Marguerite (Donovan) S.; grad. St. Paul's Sch., 1931; A.B., Yale, 1935, LL.B., 1938; LL.M., N.Y. U., 1948; m. Margaret Mabon Wise, Oct. 13, 1950; stepchildren—David M. Knott, Margaret M. Benham. Admitted to N.Y. bar, 1939, Vt. bar, 1971; partner Satterlee, & Stephens, N.Y.C., 1950-71; partner Campbell & Stockhausen, Manchester, Vt., 1971-74; dir. Moore & McCormack Co., Inc. Pres., bd. dirs. Nassau Hosp. Served to lt. comdr. USNR, 1942-46. Mem. Am. Bar Assn., Assn. Bar City N.Y. Republican. Roman Catholic. Clubs: University, Meadow Brook Golf, Grolier (N.Y.C.); Burning Tree (Washington); Paradise Valley (Phoenix) Royal and Ancient Golf (St. Andrews, Scotland). Home: Dorset, Vt. Died Apr. 4, 1974; buried Phila.

STOCKING, GEORGE WARD, economist; b. Clarendon, Tex., Sept. 24, 1892; s. Jerome Daniel and Sarah Maria (Ward) S.; grad. Clarendon Coll., 1910; B.A., U. Tex., 1918; M.A., Columbia (Garth fellow), 1921, Ph.D., 1925; m. Dorothé Reichard, June 23, 1923 (dec. Mar. 1973); children—George Ward, Myron Ralph, Sybil Ruth, Cynthia; m. 2d, Anne Fuendeling, Sept. 1, 1973. With Bur. Edn. Philippine Islands, 1915-16; supt. pub. schs., Clarendon, 1918-19; with geol. dept Empire Gas & Fuel Co., Fort Worth, 1919-20; asst. prof. econs. U. Vt., 1922-23; economist Nat. Indsl. Conf. Bd., N.Y.C., 1923-24; asst. prof. econs. Dartmouth, 1924-25; asso. prof. econs. U. Tex., 1925-26, prof., 1926-46; dir. Inst. Research in Social Scis., research prof. econs. Vanderbilt U., 1947-63, prof. emeritus, from 1963; research asso. dept. econs. U. Cal. at Berkeley, 1964-65. Vis. scholar Stanford, 1967-73; vis. prof. Am. U. Beirut, Lebanon, 1960-61; vis. distinguished prof. Mich. State U., 1965. Tech. adviser Labor Adv. Bd., NRA, 1933-35; mem. Petroleum Labor Policy Bd., NRA, 1933-34, chmn., 1934-35; chmn. Nat. Longshoremen's Mediation Bd., 1935-36; mem. nat. adv. council Social Security Bd., 1937-38; asst. dir. bur. research and statistics, adv. com. to Council Nat. Def., 1940; head consent degree sect., antitrust div. U.S. Dept. Justice, 1941; alternate Nat. Def. Mediation Bd., 1941; chmn. Pres.'s Emergency Bd. in Atlanta, Birmingham & Coast R.R. labor dispute, 1941; dir. fuels div. OPA, 1942; pub. mem. War Labor Bd., 1943; mem. Nat. Ry. Labor Panel, 1943-46; co-dir. Study in Internat. Cartels and Domestic Monopoly, Twentieth Century Fund, 1944-47; impartial arbitrator various labor disputes under Ry. Labor Act; dir. Social Sci. Research Council, N.Y.C., 1948-54, chmn. 1954. Served with U.S. Army, 1918. Guggenheim research fellow, 1932; Rockefeller Found. grantee, 1963-64; Ford Found. grantee, 1966-67. Mem. Am. (pres. 1958), So. (pres. 1952) econ. assns., Am. Assn. U. Profs., Phi Beta Kappa, Alpha Tau Omega. Club: Cosmos. Author: Middle East Oil: A Study in Political and Economic Controversy, 1970, others; articles in profl. jours. Home: Portola Valley, Cal. Died June 7, 1975.

STODDARD, ANNE, (MRS.), editor; b. Elizabeth. N.J., May 15, 1880; d. Charles Thorpe and Catharine Frances (Young) Glen; ed. Vail-Deane Sch., Elizabeth, N.J., 1890-97, Mt. Holyoke Coll., 1897-98. Teacher of primary classes, Vail-Deane Sch., 1898-1904; with Century Co. for over 20 yrs. in various editorial capacities including head manuscript reader of book dept., asst. editor on staff of Century Mag., head dept. of books for boys and girls; bus. mgr. American Girl, 1933-42, editor, 1933-45. Republican. Mem. P.E.N., International Society of Writers. Author: Young Heroes of the Bible, 1931; A Book of Marionette Plays (with Tony Sarg), 1927; A Good Little Dog, 1930; Bingo Is My Name, 1931; Here, Bingo!, 1932; Pussy, Pussy!, 1936. Editor: Discovering My Job; Topflight, 1946. Contbr. to mags. Author of puppet plays produced by Tony Sarg's Marionettes; Dramatization of Don Quixote, Dramatization of Hansel and Gretel, The Singing Lesson, etc. Home: East Orange, N.J.†

STOHLMAN, FREDERICK, JR., medical educator; b. Washington, Aug. 19, 1926; s. Frederick and Dorothy (Cahill) S.; student Georgetown Coll., 1943-44; M.D., Georgetown U., 1948; m. Bernadette Turner Bush, June 2, 1951; children—Bernadette M., Frederick III, Jeannine, John M. Intern Boston City Hosp., 1948-49, resident, 1949-51; fellow Georgetown U., 1951-53; sr. investigator NIH, Washington, 1953-60, chief sect. hematology, 1960-62; dir. medicine and research St. Elizabeth's Hosp., Boston, from 1962; asso. prof. Tufts Med. Sch., 1962-64, prof., from 1964; cons. NIH, Pan-Am. Health Orgn., A.R.C., Nat. Acad. Sci., Brookhaven Nat. Lab. Bd. dirs. Med. Found., Mass. div. Am. Cancer Soc., Leukemia Soc. Am. Served with USPHS, 1953-62. Mem. Assn. Am. Physicians, Am. Soc. Clin. Investigation, Am. Soc. Hematology, Internat. Soc. Hematology, Am. Soc. Exptl. Pathology (Parke Davis award 1964), Transplantation Soc. Author: Kinetics of Cellular Proliferation, 1959; Hemopoietic Cellular Proliferation, 1969; (with others) Modern Trends in Human Leukemia, 1974. Editor in chief Blood, Jour. Hematology. Contbr. articles profl. jours. Home: West Newton, Mass. Died Sept. 8, 1974.

STOICA, CHIVU, political ofcl.; b. Buzau, Romania, August 8, 1908; married; 1 dau. Apprentice r.r. co.; various positions metall. factories, Bucharest; assisted organizing ry. workers strike, 1933, imprisoned to 1944; indsl. labor relations work Romanian Communist Party; organizer, v.p. Gen. Confederation of Labor, 1945-47; mem. central com. Romanian Communist Party, 1945-48, mem. central com. and mem. polit. bur. of central com., 1948-65, mem. exec. com. and the permanent presidium of the central com., 1965-67; mem. nat. legislature Grand Nat. Assembly, 1946-67; gen. mgr. Romanian Railways Adminstrn., 1946-48; minister of industry Groza Cabinet, 1948-49, head ministry of metal and chem. industries, 1949-52; minister metall. industry Gheorghiu Dej's Cabinet, 1953-55, v.p. Council Ministers, 1950-54, 1st v.p. council, 1954; premier of Romania, 1955-61; sec. Central Com. Romanian Communist Party, 1960-65; pres. State Council of Socialist Republic of Romania, from 1965. Decorated Hero of Socialist Labor; Order of Star, Romanian People's Republic; Order of State Banner, Korean People's Republic. Home: Romania. Died Feb. 18, 1975.

STOKES, MILTON LONSDALE, educator; b. Sombra, Ont., Can., July 12, 1895; s. William Robert and Minnie Elizabeth (Cook) S.; B.A., U. Toronto. 1920, M.A., 1922, LL.B., 1926; grad. Osgoode Hall Law Sch., 1926; Ph.D., U. Pa., 1938; m. Janet May Miller, June 11, 1936; children—Ronald Miller, Robert Gordon. Came to U.S., 1926. Faculty, McMaster U., 1922, Lebanon Valley Coll., 1926-46; asso. prof. Pa. State U., 1946-47, prof. Wilson Coll., 1947-50; faculty Gettysburg Coll., 1950-65, prof. econs., 1950-65, chmn. dept., 1950-64; vis. prof. U. Toronto, 1943, Lebanon Valley Coll., Annville, Pa., 1965-67, Heidelberg Coll., Tiffin, O., 1967-68. Mem. Am. Econ. Assn., Ont. Bar, Pa. Polit. Sci. Assn. Presbyn. (elder). Mason (32°, Shriner). Clubs: Rotary, Torch. Author: Bank of Canada, 1938; (with Arlt) Money, Banking and the Economic System, 1955. Home: Gettysburg, Pa. Died Jan. 24, 1974; interred Evergreen Cemetery, Gettysburg.

STOKES, THOMAS, lawyer; b. N.Y.C., Nov. 24, 1906; s. Nicholas L. and Janet (O'Kane) S.; A.B., Dartmouth, 1929; LL.B., Harvard, 1932; m. Esther Bourneuf, Sept. 7, 1935; children—Jane d'E., Anne B., Margaret. Admitted to N.Y. bar, 1933, practiced in N.Y.C.; mem. firm Battle, Fowler, Stokes & Kheel and predecessor firms, 1947-74. Pres., dir. Stokes Industries, Inc. (N.Y.C.), Anderson Oil & Chem. Co. (Middletown, Conn.); pres. Hodson Corp. (Chgo.); dir. Van Stolk Commn. Co., Inc. (N.Y.C.). Mem. Am., N.Y. State bar assns., Assn. Bar City N.Y. Home: New York City, NY. Died Feb. 11, 1975.

STOKES, WILLIAM E, chemist; b. Scipio, Ind., Mar. 11, 1878; s. James Monroe and Elizabeth (James) S.; A.B., Miami U., Oxford, O., 1899; m. Rita Henderson, Sept. 30, 1910; 1 son James (dec.). Began as engr. in testing lab., C. & N.W. R.R. Co.; chemist Price Baking Powder Co., 1900-06, supt., 1906-14; chief chemist Royal Baking Powder Co., from 1914. Mem. Am. Chem. Soc., Soc. Cereal Chemists. Ind. Republican. Presbyn. Mason. Club: Adventurers. Home: Brooklyn, N.Y.†

STONE, JAMES CLIFTON, tobacco mcht.; b. Richmond, Ky., Jan. 3, 1878; s. Samuel Hanson and Pattie (Harris) S.; student Central University, Richmond, Ky., 1893-96. Centre College, Danville, Kentucky; m. Carrie C. Ferguson, November 5, 1913; 1 son. James Clifton. With insurance dept., State of Ky., 1896-99; established the Stone Tobacco Warehouse, Louisville, 1899; sold out to Louisville Tobacco Warehouse Co., 1902, and made dir. of co. and mgr. one of its houses; pres. and gen. mgr. Lexington (Ky.) Tobacco Warehouse Co., 1912-17; bought 2 loose leaf tobacco houses, 1917, and formed Central and Planters Tobacco Warehouse Co.; a founder, 1921, and pres. and gen. mgr. Burley Tobacco Growers Coöperative Assn. (over 100,000 members; abt. ¾,000,000 business yearly); owner of J. C. Stone & Co., Lexington, Ky., and Stone & Co., Louisville, Ky.; also farmer. Member of the Board of Public Safety, Louisville, 1910-11; ex-chmn. of the Federal Farm Bd.; pres. Thoroughbred Club of Am.; president, National Association Thoroughbred Club. Republican. Member Christian (Disciples) Church. Mason (K.T., Shriner), Elk. Clubs: University, Lexington Country; Louisville Country, Pendennis (Louisville). Home: Prospect, Ky.†

STONE, L(AWRENCE) JOSEPH, psychologist; b. Washington, May 20, 1912; s. Nahum and Esther Bertha (Levinson) S.; A.B., Cornell U., 1933; A.M., Columbia, 1934, Ph.D., 1937; m. Beatrice Berlin, June 23, 1933 (dec. Sept. 1962); children—Deborah (Mrs. Nelson), Susannah (Mrs. Eldridge), Miriam (Mrs. Robert Leavitt); m. 2d, Jeannette W. Galambos, May 9, 1970. Instr. psychology Columbia, 1935-37, Bklyn. Coll., 1938-39, Coll. City N.Y., 1940-42; research asso. Sarah Lawrence Coll., 1937-39; research editor dept. child study Vassar Coll., 1939-41, asst. prof., 1941-47, asso. prof., 1947-49, prof., 1949-65, prof. psychology, 1965-75, acting chmn. dept. child study, 1953-55, chmn., 1955-61, chmn. dept. psychology, 1966-70, dir. Vassar film series Studies of Normal Personality Development, 1942-75. Lectr., New Sch. Social Research, 1945-56; producer films on Israeli Kibbutz for Inst. Child Mental Health; dir. Com. for Certification Psychologists N.Y. State, 1954-57, mem. adv. bd. psychology bd. regents U. State N.Y., 1958-66; mem. research career award com. Nat. Inst. Mental Health, 1962-66. Served form lt. to lt. comdr., psychobiol. unit. USPHS, 1944-46, sci. dir. USPHS Res. Certified psychologist N.Y. Fulbright Research grantee U. Oslo, Norway, 1957-58; Nat. Inst. Mental Health spl. fellow, 1965; travel grantee Ford Found., Grant Found., 1970-71. Diplomate Clin. Psychology, Am. Bd. Examiners Profl. Psychology. Fellow Am. Psychol. Assn., Am. Orthopsychiat. Assn., Soc. Personality Assessment (past dir.), Soc. Research Child Devel. (past bd. govs.); mem. World Fedn. Mental Health, Eastern Psychol. Assn., Sigma Xi. Author: (with J. Church) Childhood and Adolescence: A Psychology of the Growing Person, 1957, 3d edit., 1973. Co-editor: The Competent Infant: Research and Commentary, 1937. Contbr. articles profl. jours.; many ednl. films. Home: Poughkeepsie, N.Y., Died Dec. 13, 1975.

STONE, LEE ALEXANDER, M.D., author; b. Louisville, Ky., Feb. 21, 1879; s. Walter Scott and Mattie Bell (Liter) S.; grammar and high sch.; M.D., Ky. U. (now U. of Louisville), 1902; m. Eva Nall, Memphis, Tenn., Sept. 10, 1902; children—Dorothy Mathilde, Eva Lucille. Practiced at Louisville, Ky., later Memphis, Tenn.; settled at Chicago, 1919; former head dept. of pub. health and prof. med. sociology, Gen. Med. Coll., Chicago; former prof. social hygiene, Chicago Training Sch. of Home and Pub. Health Nursing; former instr. social hygiene, Ill. Bell Telephone Co. Training Sch. and lecturer on social psychology, Sullin's Coll., Bristol, Va., Pvt. Res. Hosp., 1st Army Corps, Spanish-Am. War; maj. staff of Gov. Vardeman of Miss., 1907; capt. Med. Corps, U.S.A., 1917; maj. M.C., O.R.C., May 1919; lt. col. Mil. Intelligence, O.R.C., Sept. 1923; now lt.-col. Chem. Warfare Res., U.S. War Dept. lecturer to troops in field, 1917-18, attended U.S.A. War Coll., Sept.-Nov. 1923. Fellow A.M.A., Chicago Acad. Medicine; mem. Ill. State Med. Soc., Chicago Medical Soc., Alpha Mu Pi Omega. Mem. Volunteer Speakers' Com., "World's Fair" Chicago, 1933. Episcopalian. Mascn (32°, Shriner). Author: Eugenics and Marriage, 1915; The Woman of the Streets, 1919; An Open Talk with Mothers and Fathers, 1920; Sex Search Lights, 1922; The Power of a Symbol, 1925; Emerson Hough—His Place in American Letters, 1925; The Story of Phallicism, 1927; It Is Sex O'Clock, 1927; (pamphlets) Chicago's Birthday Party—a Story of Chicago, 1928; Chicago, the Best Advertised City—Not the Wickedest, 1929; The Child of a Swamp—or Chicago from 1830 to 1850, 1929. Lecturer. Home: Chicago, Ill.†

STONE, ULYSSES STEVENS, ex-congressman; b. Dewitt Co., Ill., Dec. 17, 1878; s. David Craig and Sarah Jane (Hollenbeck) S.; student U. of Okla., 1897-1901; m. Menor Minnie Butler, of Morley, Mo., June 1, 1903; 1 dau., Helena Butler (Mrs. Harney Cobb). Began in banking, 1902; pres. Bank of Jones, Okla., 1902-09, Spencer (Okla.) Bank, 1909-14; pres. U.S. Casulty Co., 1917-20; independent oil operator, from 1920. Rep. candidate for gov. of Okla., 1918; candidate for U.S. Senator, 1926; mem. 71st Congress (1929-31), 5th Okla. Dist.; Rep. candidate congressman at large, 1934. Presbyn. Kiwanian. Home: Oklahoma City, Okla.*†

STOOPS, JOHN DASHIELL, prof. philosophy; b. New Castle, Del., Jan. 26, 1873; s. William Thompson and Mary A. (Dashiell) S.; A.B., Dickinson Coll., Carlisle, Pa., 1894; A.M., Harvard, 1897; Ph.D., Boston U., 1899; post-grad. study Columbia and Clark University, 1901; LL.D., Grinnell College, 1945; married Mary E. Milner, December 25, 1901; m. 2d, Rose Edie Stoops, June 13, 1951. Prof. philosophy Mt. Union Coll., Alliance, O., 1899-1900; minister First Congl. Ch., Easthampton, Mass., 1901-04; prof. philosophy, Grinnell (Ia.) Coll., 1904-43, now retired from active teaching, Member American Philosophical Association (pres. Western div. 1933-34), Am. Assn. Univ. Profs., Phi Beta Kappa. Conglist. Mason (32°). Club: Poweshick. Author: Ideals of Conduct, 1926; The Kingdom of Jesus; The Integrated Life. Contbr. to jours. of philosophy. Address: Grinnell, Ia., Died Nov. 18, 1973.

STOPKA, ANDRZEJ WIESLAW, artist; b. Siedlec, Poland, Sept. 23, 1904; s. Andrzej and Marianne (Pruczek) S.; grad. Cracow Acad. Arts, 1924-29; m. Stefania Bando, Jan. 5, 1934 (div. 1939); 1 dau., Barbara; m. 2d, Wincentyna Wodzinowska, May 23, 1947. Painter, graphic artist Cracow, Poland, 1929-39; scenographer theaters, Cracow, Warsaw, Poland, Poznan, Poland, 1945-73; drawings jours. Poland and abroad; prof., dir. dept. scenography Cracow Acad. Arts, 1950-73. Decorated B. Cross Polonia Restituta, 1953, Comdr. Cross, 1959; recipient 1st prize exhbns. 15 Years Polish Artistic Achievements, 1962, Ministry Culture and Arts award, 1961, 67, State award, 1955, 72. Mem. Polish Artists Assn., Theater Authors and Composers Assn., Polish United Workers Party. Spl. work includes book illustrations. Home: Cracow, Poland. Died Aug. 11, 1973.

STORER, GEORGE BUTLER, radio, TV exec.; b. Champaign, Ill., Nov. 10, 1899; s. George Butler and Mabel (Mozier) S.; grad. Tome Sch., Port Deposit, Md.; stdent Cornell U., 1918-20; children—George Butler,

James Perley, Peter, Robert Mozier; m. 4th, Rita D. Storer, July 19, 1972. Pres., gen. mgr. Standard Tube Co., Toledo, 1921-26, pres. gen. mgr., Detroit, 1928-43, chmn. bd., 1946-65; v.p. steel and tubes div. Republic Steel Corp., Cleve., 1926-27; pres. Storer Broadcasting Co., 1927-61, chmn. Asst. chmn. Broadcasters Victory Council, 1941-43. Chmn. bd. dirs. Miami (Fla.) Heart Inst.; trustee U. Miami, Coral Gables, Fla. Served from lt. comdr. to comdr. UNSR, 1943-45. Mem. Nat. Assn. Radio and TV Broadcasters (past dir.), Delta Kappa Epsilon. Republican. Clubs: Detroit, Detroit Athletic; Indian Creek County (Miami Beach, Fla.); Cornell (Ithaca, N.Y.); Bloomfield Hills (Mich.) Country; La Gorce Country (Miami Beach); Old Baldy (Saratoga, Wyo.); Lyford Cay (Nassau). Home: Saratoga, Wyo., Died Nov. 4, 1975.

STORK, CHARLES WHARTON, critic, author; b. Phila., Pa., Feb. 12, 1881; s. Theophilus Baker and Hannah (Wharton) S.; A.B., Haverford Coll., 1902; A.M., Harvard, 1903; Ph.D., U. of Pa., 1905; research work in English univs., 1905; studied U. of Munich, 1907-08; m. Elisabeth, d. Franz von Pausinger (artist), Aug. 5, 1908; children—Rosalie, Francis Wharton, George Frederick, Carl Alexander. Asst. in English, U. of Pa., 1903-05, instr., 1906-14, asst. prof., 1914-16; resigned to engage in original literary work; resumed teaching of English, Harcum Junior College, Bryn Mawr, Pa., 1935. University Club, Philadelphia and P.E.N. Club, New York chapter Poetry Soc. America (former pres.), Phi Beta Kappa (Haverford). Clubs: Franklin Inn (Phila.); Harvard (New York). Author: (verse) Day Dreams of Greece, 1908; The Queen of Orplede, 1910; Sea and Bay, 1916; Sunset Harbor, 1933. Editor: Plays of William Rowley, 1910; Contemporary Verse Anthology, 1920; In the Sky Garden, Poems by Stephen Moylan Bird, 1922; Second Contemporary Verse Anthology, 1923. Translator: (from the Swedish) Selected Poems of Gustaf Fröding, 1916; Sweden's Laureate (poems of Verner von Heidenstam), 1919; (from the German) Hofmannthal's Lyrics, 1917; Anthology of Swedish Lyrics, 1917, 30; (from the Swedish) The Charles Men of Vernor von Heidenstam, 1920; Modern Swedish Masterpieces (short, stories), 1923; The Motherless, of Bengt Berg, 1924; The Swedes and Their Chieftains, of Verner von Heidenstam, 1925; Anthology of Swedish Stories, 1928; The Dragon and the Foreign Devils of J. G. Anderson (a book on modern China), 1928; Martin Birck's Youth of Hjalmar Söderberg, 1930; Short Stories of Hjalmar Söderberg, 1935; Tales of Ensign Stal (by J. L. Runeberg), 1938; I Sit Alone, from Norwegian of Waldemar Ager, 1931, Arcadia Borealis (poems from the Swedish of E. A. Karlfeldt). 1938; Anthology of Norwegian Lyrics, 1942. Contributor of article on Swedist literature in Collier's Encyclopedia. Contributor of play and numerous lyrics in transl. to The German Classics, 1914; also verse, transls., articles to Century, Harper's. Nation, New Republic, Yale Review, etc. Visited Sweden, 1920, 23, writing and lecturing on Am. poetry. Decorated Order of Gustaf Vasa, 1st class, 1922. Winner contest for original play offered by Plays and Players of Phila., 1925. Edited mag., Contemporary Verse, 1917-26. On board S.S. Athenia when torpedoed, Sept. 2, 1939; poem on the event in Saturday Evening Post, Nov. 4, 1939. Contbr. articles on Swedish lit. to Columbia Dictionary of Modern European Lit., 1945, 1947; Another Book of Danish Lyrics, 1947. Home: Philadelphia, Pa.†

STORM, JACK, pediatrician; b. N.Y.C., Dec. 23, 1927; s. Rudolf and Ida Storm; M.D., State U. N.Y., Bklyn., 1959; m. Barbara Storm, Aug. 30, 1960; children—Hilary, Jason. Intern, Einstein Med. Sch., N.Y.C., 1959-60; resident L.I. Jewish Hosp., 1960-62; practice medicine specializing in pediatrics; mem. staff L.I. Jewish Hosp., 1962-75; asst. attending physician North Shore Hosp.-Cornell Med. Sch., 1962-75; med. dir. Assn. for Help Retarded Children, Brookville, N.Y. Served to 2d lt. AUS, 1953-55. Diplomate Am. Bd. Pediatrics. Mem. A.M.A., Am. Acad. Pediatrics, Am. Assn. mental Deficiency. Home: Roslyn, N.Y. Died Mar. 26, 1975; buried Wellwood Cemetery, Long Island, N.Y.

STORMZAND, MARTIN JAMES, prof. education; b. Grand Rapids, Mich., Dec. 26, 1879; s. Anthony and Katherine (Schoonbeck) S.; student Hope Coll., Holland, Mich., 1897-1900; A.B., Alma (Mich.) Coll., 1904; B.D., Princeton Theol. Sem., 1908; studied U. of Wis., 1917-18; Ph.D., U. of Chicago, 1920; m. Leila Elizabeth Snowhook, Apr. 8, 1909. Maitland fellow, N.T. Greek, Princeton, 1908; newspaper work, Grand Rapids, 1900-03 and 1908-09; teacher high sch., Freeport, Ill., 1910-12, Davenport, Ia., 1912-15; prof. psychology and edn., State Normal Sch., Platteville, Wis., 1915-17; asst. in edn., U. of Wis., 1917-19; instr. in edn., U. of Ill., 1919-20; with U. of Southern Calif. as asso. prof. edn., 1920-23, prof. edn., 1923-26; prof. edn., Occidental Coll., from 1926; curriculum consultant Glendale schs., 1926-27, Santa Monica schools, 1927-32, Arcadie schools, 1929-30; ednl. adviser for Southern California Telephone Co., 1927. Member Phi Delta Kappa. Mason. Author several books relating to field. Home: Los Angeles, Cal.†

STOSKOPF, WILLIAM BREWSTER, clergyman; b. Freeport, Ill., July 26, 1878; s. Louis (M.D.) and Caroline Howard (Brewster) S.; student Beloit Coll., Acad.; B.A., Yale, 1900; B.D., Gen. Theol. Sem., 1903; D.D., Nashotah (Wis.) House, 1935. Deacon, 1903, priest, 1904, P.E. Ch.; curate Grace Ch., Oak Park, Ill., 1903-04, Ch. of the Advent, Boston, Mass., 1904-08; rector Trinity Ch., Bridgeport, Conn., 1908-09, Ch. of the Ascension, Chicago, from 1909. Chmn. Fedn. of Catholic Priests; vice-superior gen. Con-fraternity of the Blessed Sacrament; warden Guild of All Souls; pres. Chicago Clergy Round Table, 1920-22, Former gov. Ill. Soc. Mayflower Descendants; elder general, Society Mayflower Descendants U.S.A. Republican. Clubs: University, Yale. Home: Chicago, Ill.†

STOUFFER, VERNON BIGELOW, restaurant exec.; b. Cleve., Aug. 22, 1901; s. Abraham E. and Lena M. (Bigelow) S.; B.S., U. Pa., 1923; LL.D., Kenyon Coll., 1968; m. Gertrude Dean, Feb. 1928; children—Margery, James, Deanette. Chmn. Litton Industries, Food Services Group, Stouffer Foods Corp.; chmn. bd., prin. owner, later dir. Cleve. Indians, Inc.; dir. United Air Lines, Litton Industries, Inc., Soc. Nat. Bank of Cleve., Consol. Natural Gas Co. of N.Y., Republic Steel Corp. Trustee Nat. Recreation and Parks Bd., No. Ohio Opera Assn., YMCA of Cleve., University Hosps., Cleve. Mem. Cleve. Zool. Soc. (vice chmn. bd.), Cleve. Mus. Arts Assn. (trustee), Greater Cleve. Growth Assn. (dir.), Sigma Alpha Epsilon. Presbyn. Mason (33 deg.). Clubs: Union, Clevelander, Bluecoats (trustee), Question, 50, Clifton; Paradise Valley Country (Scottsdale, Ariz.). Home: Lakewood, O. Died July 26, 1974.

STOUGHTON, CLARENCE CHARLES, former coll. pres.; b. Rochester, N.Y., Feb. 8, 1895; s. George and Caroline (Lutz) S.; A.B., U. Rochester, 1918; A.M., Columbia, 1922; LL.D., Gettysburg Coll., 1941, Waterloo Luth. U., Can., 1963; Litt.D., Muhlenberg Coll., 1942, Wagner Coll., 1947; L.H.D., Thiel Coll., 1963, Wittenberg U., 1963; m. Hilda Spitz, Sept. 7th, 1920; children—Mrs. Jeanne F. Dagher, Donald William. Tchr. history Webster (N.Y.) High Sch., 1919; instr. history Wagner Coll., S.I., N.Y., 1919-23, prin. high sch. dept., 1923-27, treas., 1931-33, acting dean, 1933-35, pres. 1935-45; sec. Moffatt & Schwab, Inc., real estate, 1927-32; stewardship sec., exec. dir. laymen's movement United Luth. Ch., 1945-49; pres. Wittenberg U., Springfield, O., 1949-63, emeritus. Dir. N.Y. Alumni Assn. U. Rochester (pres. 1938); campaign chmn., dir. S.I. Community Chest; campaign chmn. United Appeals Fund, 1953; chmn. commn. on stewardship Luth. World Fedn.; United Luth. Ch. Am. del. Luth. World Fedn., Hanover, Germany, 1952, Mpls., 1957; mem. exec. bd. United Luth. Ch., 1954-62; bd. social ministry Luth. Ch. Am., 1963—; chmn. Nat. Luth. Edn. Council, 1957; chmn. joint dept. stewardship and benevolence Nat. Council Chs., 1951; del. World Council of Chs., Amsterdam, 1948, Evanston, 1954; sec. Ohio Found of Ind. Colls., 1956-59. Mem. Ohio Gov.'s Commn. on Edn. Beyond High Sch., 1959-62. Served with U.S. Army, 1918-19. Recipient Comdrs. Cross, Order of Merit, German Govt., 1958; Wichern medal Evang. Luth. Ch. Germany, 1963; alumni citation U. Rochester, 1963. Hon. fellow S.I. Inst. Arts and Scis.; mem. Delta Rho, Alpha Omicron Psi, Blue Key. Rotarian. Clubs: University (N.Y.C.). Author: Set Apart for the Gospel, 1946; Whatever You Do, 1948. Editor: Living Roots, 1955. Home: South Charleston, O. Died Aug. 31, 1975.

STOUT, IRVING WRIGHT, educator, author; b. Fall River, Wis., Dec. 15, 1903; s. Thomas Denzil and Etto Electa (Wright) S.; B.Ed., Platteville State Tchrs. Coll., 1936; M.A., Northwestern U., 1943, Ed.D., 1948; m. Grace June Brubaker, Jan. 20, 1934; 1 son, Thomas William. Tchr., prin. pub. schs., 1928-43; dir. guidance Milw. Pub. Schs., 1945-47; prof. edn. Milw. State Coll., 1947-49; asso. prof. edn. N.Y. U., 1949-51; prof. edn. So. Ill. U., 1951-53; dean Ariz. State U. Grad. Coll., Tempe, 1953-63, prof. edn., from 1953, dir. edn. tng. Head Start programs, from 1966. Sr. partner Wood & Stout Assos., from 1962; sr. cons. Rough Rock Demonstration Sch., from 1965. Mem. Gov.'s Com. Mental Health State Ariz.; chmn. adv. com. Navajo Community Coll. Recipient Children's Service award Am. Toy Inst., 1963. Fellow A.A.A.S.; mem. Newcomen Soc., N.E.A., Am. Assn. Sch. Supts., Assn. Supervision and Curriculum Devel., Assn. Childhood Edn., Internat. Soc. Research in Child Devel., Nat. Sch. Pub. Relations Assn. (pres.), Phoenix C. of C., Phi Delta Kappa, Alpha Kappa Delta. Republican. Conglist. Mason. Author: (with Grace Langdon) These Well Adjusted Children, 1952, Teacher-Parent Interviews, 1954, Telling Parents About Their Child's School, 1957, Teaching Moral and Spiritual Values, Teaching in the Primary Grades; Bringing Up Children; School Public Relations Issues and Cases; Homework; The Papago Educational Survey, 1966; Navajo Indian School Board Manual. Co-author daily newspaper column. Contbr. articles to profl. jours. Home: Tempe, Ariz. Died Aug. 9, 1972; interred East Resthaven Cemetery, Phoenix, Ariz.

STOUT, REX TODHUNTER, author; b. Nobelesville, Ind., Dec. 1, 1886; s. John Wallace and Lucetta Elizabeth (Todhunter) S.; student pub. schs.; m. Fay Kennedy, Dec. 16, 1916 (div.); m. 2d, Pola Hoffmann, Dec. 21, 1932; children—Barbara, Rebecca. Office boy, store clk., bookkeeper, sailor, hotel mgr., inventor sch. thrift system, 1916-27; enlisted USN, 1906, purchased discharge, 1908; master ceremonies, Speaking of Liberty radio program Council for Democracy, 1941; Voice of Freedom radio program Council for Democracy, 1941; Voice of Freedom radio program Freedom House, 1942; Our Secret Weapon radio prograprogram, 1942-43. Chmn., Writers's War Bd., 1941-46; pres. Friends Democracy, 1941-51; pres. Author's Guild, 1943-45; pres. Soc. Prevention World War III, 1943-46; chmn. Writer's Bd. World Govt., 1949—; pres. Author's League Am., 1951-55, 62-69, v.p., 1956-61; pres. Mystery Writers Am., 1958—; treas. Freedom House, 1957—. Author: How Like a God, 1929; Seed on the Wind, 1930; Golden Remedy, 1931; Forest Fire, 1933; Fer-de-Lance, 1934; The President Vanishes, 1934; The League of Frightened Men, 1935; O Carless Love, 1935; The Rubber Band, 1936; The Red Box, 1936; The Hand in the Glove, 1937; Too Many Cooks, 1938; Mr. Cinderella, 1938; Some Buried Caesar, 1939; Mountain Cat, 1939; Over My Dead Body, 1939; Red Threads, 1940; Double for Death, 1940; Bad for Business, 1940; Where There's a Will, 1941; The Broken Vase, 1941; Alphabet Hicks, 1942; Black Orchids, 1942; The Illustrious Dunderheads, 1942; Not Quite Dead Enough, 1944; The Silent Speaker, 1946; Too Many Women, 1947; And Be A Villain, 1948; Trouble in Triplicate, 1949; The Second Confession, 1949; Three Doors to Death, 1950; In the Best Families, 1950; Curtains for Three, 1951; Murder by the Book, 1951; Triple Jeopardy, 1952; Prisoner's Base, 1952; The Golden Spiders, 1953; Three Men Out, 1954; The Black Mountain, 1954; Before Midnight, 1955; Three Witnesses, 1956; Might as Well Be Dead, 1956; Three for the Chair, 1957; If Death Ever Slept, 1957; And Four to Go, 1958; Champagne for One, 1958; Plot It Yourself, 1959; Three at Wolfe's Door, 1960; Too Many Clients, 1960; The Final Deduction, 1961; Homicide Trinity, 1962; Gambit, 1962; The Mother Hunt, 1963; Trio for Blunt Instruments, 1964; A Right to Die, 1964; The Doorbell Rang, 1965; Death of a Doxy, 1966; The Father Hunt, 1968; Death of a Dude, 1969; Nero Wolfe Cookbook, 1973; Please Pass the Guilt, 1973; A Family Affair, 1975. Home: Brewster, N.Y., Died Oct. 27, 1975.

STOVER, JORDAN HOMER, III, lab. exec., inventor; b. Phila., June 25, 1911; s. Jordan Homer and Helen (Weeks) S. II; student Princeton, 1936; m. Shirley Vere-Smith, Sept. 20, 1941; 1 dau., Sandra. Founder, pres. Stover Lock Nut & Machinery Corp., Easton, Pa., 1942-54; mgr. Stover Sales, Lamson & Sessions Co., Cleve., 1954-64; owner Stover Labs., Tucson, 1964-74; inventor, 1954-74. Trustee Bloomfield Country Day Sch. Served with U.S. Army, 1936-39. Me. Indsl. Fasteners Inst. (chmn. lock nut standards and specifications com.), Am. Standards Assn. (vice chmn. lock nut standards com.), Soc. Automotive Engrs. Republican. Episcopalain. Kiwanian (dir.). Clubs: Princeton (N.Y.C., Tucson) (pres.); Greenwich (Conn.) Country; Detroit Athletic, Recess (Detroit); Oakland Hills Country (Birmingham, (Michigan); Old Pueblo (Tucson), Tucson Press, Skyline Country (Tucson). Inventor self-locking nut, mfg. machinery and processes, self-locking fasteners, torque tension fasteners, electronic and mech. clamp force measuring washers and systems. Patentee in U.S. and fgn. countries. Address: Tucson, Ariz. Died Dec. 8, 1974.

STOWELL, LEON CARL, corp. exec.; b. Keene, N.H., Nov. 1, 1891; s. Carlon N. and Hattie M. (Stratton) S.; ed. Phillips Andover Acad., and Harvard (A.B., 1914); LL.D. (hon.), Ithasca (N.Y.) Coll., 1951; married Ruth Powers, June 23, 1927; children—Samuel Curtis, Sally. Salesman Loose Wiles Biscuit Co. Boston, 1914-17; with Dictaphone div., Columbia Graphophone Co., 1919-23; sec. Dictaphone Corp., 1923-24, v.p., 1924-27, pres., 1927-36; exec. v.p. and dir. Underwood Elliott Fisher Co. from 1936; pres. Underwood Corp. (formerly Underwood Elliott Fisher Company), 1945-55, chairman of the board, 1955-56, also board directors; director Dictaphone Corp., Pitney Bowes, Inc. Served in U.S. Army Oct. 1917-Apr. 1919; discharged as captain Ordnance Dept. Mem. Commerce & Industry Assn. of N.Y., National Industrial Conf. Bd., Office Equipment Mfrs. Inst. Am. Soc. Sales Exec., Marketing Exec. Soc., Nat. Office Management Assn., Am. Management Assn. N.Y. Sales Mgrs. Club, Nat. Fedn. of Sales Executives, Council on Foreign Relatiions, Sigma Alpha Epsilon. Mason. Clubs: Union League, Harvard (New York); Bonnie Briar Country; Larchmont (N.Y.) Yacht. Contbr. to jours. Home: Larchmont, N.Y., Died Jan. 5, 1976.

STRACCIA, FRANK ALEXANDER, physician; b. Boston, Nov. 1, 1916; s. Joseph and Jenney Straccia; M.D., Tufts U., 1943; m. Ella Gilda Aucella, Sept. 2, 1946; children—Frank Joseph, Joseph Robert. Intern, Grace Hosp., Detroit, 1943-44; asst. physician Danvers State Hosp., 1946-49; sr. physician Worcester (Mass.) State Hosp., 1949-51; courtesy staff Valleyhead Hosp., Concord, Mass., Malden (Mass.) Hosp., Bournewood Hosp., Brookline, Mass.; staff Symmes Arlington Hosp., Carney Hosp., Boston; Glenside Hosp., Jamaica, Plain, Mass.; cons. Whidden Meml. Hosp., Everett, Mass., Lawrence Meml. Hosp., Medford, Mass., St. Elizabeth's Hosp., Brighton, Mass.; clin. instr. psychiatry Tufts U., 1952-57. Served to maj., M.C., AUS, 1944-46. Diplomate Am. Bd. Psychiatry and Neurology. Fellow Am. Psychiat. Assn.; mem. A.M.A., New Eng. Soc. Psychiatry, Ancient and Hon. Arty. Soc. Boston.

Contbr. articles to med. jours. Home: Arlington, Mass. Died Feb. 20, 1975; buried Woodlawn Cemetery, Everett, Mass.

STRALEM, DONALD S., investment banker; b. Port Washington, N.Y., June 28, 1903; s. Casimir I. and Edithe Alice (Neustadt) S.; A.B., Harvard, 1924; grad. work Cambridge U., Eng., 1925; m. Jean Lehman Ickelheimer, April 10, 1928; children—Sandra Jean, Sharon Lynn. Asso. with banking firms Pierson & Co., Amsterdam, Holland, 1926-27, Hardy & Co., Berlin, Germany, 1927-28; employed by investment bankers Hallgarten & Co., N.Y. City, 1928-32, partner, 1932-65, ltd. partner, 1965-66; pres., treas. director FICO Corp., 1958-62; chmn. bd. Stralem & Co., Inc., N.Y.C., 1966-76; dir. Conresco Corp., Columbia Pictures Corp. (chmn. finance com.), Continental Ind. Telephone Co., Ind. Telephone Corp. (chmn. executive committee), Atlantic Gulf Petroleum Corp., Conresco Corp., Screen Gems, Theatre Inc. Mem. of Commodity Exchange of New York, Trustee, chmn. finance com. Spence Sch., N.Y.; Corporate mem., founder, asso. mem., mem. development com. North Shore Hosp., L.I., N.Y.; mem. overseers com. to visit department fine arts and Fogg Museum Harvard U.; dir. Ingelnook Found., Cross Ridge Found., Inc., Lillian Emerson Terry Found., Nat. U.S.O., also mem. corp.; pres., U.S.O. Fund N.Y., Inc.; pres. Farfield Found., Shelter Rock Found., Inc. United Community Defense Services; member committee Armed Forces. Mem. bd. appeals Inc. Village North Hills, L.I. Awarded certificate commendation by United States Navy for contributing to welfare personnel, 1943. Chmn. finance com., 1950-53, chmn. activities committee, 1953-56, chairman of the executive committee, 1956-58, Nat. Travelers Aid Assn. (pres. dir.); mem. advisory bd. Girl Scout Am. Council of Greater N.Y.; trustee Kirk Douglas Found.; pres. George Jr. Republic Association. Incorporated: director Travelers Aid Society N.Y. Clubs: Harvard, Grolier, Bond, Wall Street, Sands Point Golf, Sands Point Bath and Tennis, Town Tennis, Harvor View, Stock Exchange Luncheon, Lambs (N.Y.C.); Tamarisk Country (Palm Springs, Cal.); Stockbridge (Mass.) Golf; Bucks (London, Eng.); Constitutional (Windsor, Eng.); Hawks (Cantab); Mid-Am. (Chgo.); Racquet (Montego Bay). Home: New York City, N.Y., Died Feb. 1, 1976.

STRAND, WILLIAM (CORNELIUS), editor; b. Chgo., July 16, 1911; s. William Cornelius and Grace Eleanor (Browne) S.; grad. Lake Forest Acad., 1930; student Brown U., 1930-31, Washington U., 1931-33; m. Florence Edna Talbot, Aug. 26, 1937; children—Dale William, Barbara (Mrs. Larroca). Reporter, rewrite man City News Bur., Chgo., 1934-37; reporter Chgo. Tribune, 1937-40, staff Washington Bur., 1940-43, 46-47, overseas war corr., 1943-45, with London Bur., 1944, corr. Western Front and Iceland, 1945; mng. editor Fairbanks Daily News-Miner, 1948-51; v.p. Tanana Pub. Co., 1949-51; exec. city editor Washington Times Herald, 1951-53; lectr. journalism George Washington U., 1952; dir. office territories Interior Dept., Washington, also adminstr. P.R. Reconstrn. Adminstrn., Roosevelt, P. R., 1953-55; asst. to Sec. Interior and dir. information Dept. of Interior, 1955-58; dir. pub. relations Rep. Nat. Com., 1958-61; mem. editorial staff Chicago Sun-Times, 1960-62; asst. to dir. communications A.M.A., Chgo., 1962-66; asst. to pres. Pharm. Mfrs. Assn., Washington, 1966-74. Decorated Purple Heart. Mem. Alpha Delta Phi. Republican. Clubs: National Press, Overseas Writers; Explorers (N.Y.), University (Washington). Home: Washington, D.C. Died Sept. 1, 1974.

STRANG, ROBERT HALLOCK WRIGHT, orthodontist; b. Bridgeport, Conn., Feb. 22, 1881; s. Dr. Clinton Wright and Ella Jane (Lewis) S.; student Wilbraham (Mass.) Acad., 1897-99; D.D.S., U. of Pa., 1902, M.D., 1904; post-grad. study, Angle Sch. of Orthodontia, St. Louis, 1906; Doctor of Sci., Temple Univ., Phila., 1963; Doctor of Laws, University of Bridgeport, 1965; m. Mary E. Dunlap, June 1, 1909; children—Marjorie Dunlap, Clinton Wright; m. 2d, Ruth Hancock, Mar. 15, 1922; children—Ruth Hancock, Dorothy Roberta. Began as intern Western Pa. Hosp., Pittsburgh, 1904; practiced dentistry in Bridgeport during 1905; specialized in orthodontia, from 1906 (first practitioner of this specialty in Conn.); lecturer on orthodontia in extension courses, Columbia U., Univ. of Toronto, Temple U., U. Brazil, Boston U., U. Oslo; founder and dir. Strang Post Graduate School of Orthodontia, Bridgeport; apptd. oral surgeon Bridgeport Hosp., 1906; dir. of the Fones School of Dental Hygiene, University of ridgeport. Received Alfred C. Fones Memorial Medal, Wilbraham Academy Alumni Award; Ketcham award, Am. Assn. of Orthodontists, 1959; award of merit, Conn. State Dental Assn.; Distinguished Sr. Alumnus, U. Pa. Sch. Medicine. Member of Med. Advisory Bd. of State of Conn., W.W. Mem. Am. Soc. Orthodontists, Edward H. Angle Soc. of Orthodontia, A.M.A., Am. Dental Assn., Delta Sigma Delta. Methodist. Clubs: University, Brooklawn Country. Author: A Text Book of Orthodontia, 1933, 4th edit., 1958. Asso. editor of The Angle Orthodontist. Home: Bridgeport, Conn.†

STRASSMANN, GEORGE SAMUEL, pathologist; b. Berlin, Germany, Feb. 22, 1890; s. Fritz and Rose Strassman; M.D., Heidelberg (Germany) U., 1913; m. Ilse Marwitz, Apr. 8, 1922; children—Fred P. Came to U.S., 1938, naturalized, 1943. Intern, Med. Clinic Charite and Inst. Forensic Medicine, Berlin, 1913-14; practice medicine specializing in pathology; asst. Inst. Legal Medicine, Berlin, also Vienna, Austria, 1919-25; med. examiner U. Breslau (Germany), 1922-35; cons. to chief med. examiner N.Y.C.; research fellow, chief med. examiner N.Y.U., 1963-68; asst. clin. prof. dept. psychiatry Tufts U., 1950-58. Diplomate Am. Bd. Pathology. Mem. Am. Assn. Pathologists and Bacteriologists, New Eng. Pathol. Soc. Home: Belmont, Mass. Died Oct. 5, 1972; buried Mt. Auburn Cemetery, Cambridge, Mass.

STRATH, WILLIAM, business exec.; b. New Cumnock, Scotland, Nov. 16, 1906; s. John and Elizabeth Strath; ed. Glasgow U.; m. Vera Brown, 1938. With Inland Revenue, 1929-38, Air Ministry, 1938-40, Ministry, Aircraft Prodn., 1940-45, Ministry of Supply, 1945-47,Central Econ. Planning Staff, 1947-55, Treasury, 1948-55; Mem. Econ. Planning Bd., 1949-55, U.K. Atomic Energy Authority, 1955-59; permanent sec. Ministry of Supply, 1959, Ministry of Aviation, 1959-60; a group mng. dir. tube Investments Ltd., 1961-70, dep. chmn., 1968—; also dir.; dir. Brit. Aluminum Co., 1961-72, chmn., 1962-72; dir. Legal and Gen. Assurance soc., 1963—. Address: London, England., Died May 8, 1975.

STRAUMANIS, MARTIN EDWARD, metallurgist; b. Krettingen, Lithuania, Nov. 23, 1898; s. Janis and Matilde (Sviders) S.; grad. Engring. Chemistry, U. Latvia, 1925, Dt. Chem., 1927; m. Ieva Reinhards, Apr. 25, 1927; children—Lilita, Mara, Andrejs, Ilze, Liene. Instr., asst. prof. U. Latvia, 1928-36, asso. prof., 1936-37, extraordinary prof., 1937-42, prof., 1942-44, dir. analytical lab., 1934-44; staff Inst. Metal Chemistry, U. Marburg, Germany, 1944-47; research prof. metallurgy U. Mo., Rolla., 1947-66, prof. metall. engring., research prof. materials, 1966-69, sr. investigator Grad. Center Materials Research, prof. emeritus, from 1969. Fellow Rockefeller Found., Göttingen, Germany, 1927-28; Fulbright vis. prof. Vienna Inst. Tech., 1957-58. Recipient Rodney Willis Whitney award Nat. Assn. Corrosion Engrs., 1968; Research award, U. Mo., 1967. Mem. Am. Crystallography Assn., Am. Chem. Soc., Electrochem. Soc., N.Y. Acad. Scis., Mo. Acad. Sci., Inst. Metals, Deutsche Bunsen Gesellschaft, Sigma Xi, Sigma Pi Sigma, Alpha Sigma Mu. Evang. Lutheran. Author: (with A. Jevins) Prazisonsbestimmung von Gitterkonstanten nach der asymmetrischen Methode, 1940, transl., 1959; (with B. Jirgensons) Lehrbuch der Kolloidchemie, 1949, rev. English edit., 1962, Spanish edit., 1965, Japanese edit., 1967. Contbr. articles to profl. jours. Home: Rolla, Mo. Died Mar. 19, 1973; cremated.

STRAUS, ROBERT E., bank exec.; b. Chgo., Aug. 29, 1903; s. Eli M. and Mattie H. (Horner) S.; student U. Wis., 1921-23; m. Marjorie Stern; 1 dau. Vice pres., syndicate mgr., underwriter S.W. Straus & Co., Chgo., 1922-31; exec. v.p., dir. Am. Nat. Bank & Trust Co., Chgo., 1932-55, pres., 1955-63, chmn. bd., 1963-69, chmn. exec. com. from 1969; dir. Brunswick Corp., UMC Industries. Bd. dirs. Lincoln Park Zool. Assn.; bd. dirs., v.p. Jewish Fedn. Met. Chgo.; bd. dirs., v.p. treas. Community Fund Chgo.; trustee, v.p. Chgo. Ednl. Television Assn.; trustee Northwestern U., Savs. and Profit Sharing Pension Fund Sears Roebuck. Clubs: Chicago, Tavern, Mid-Day, Mid-America, Standard; Lake Shore Country (Glencoe, Ill.). Home: Chicago, Ill. Died Nov. 1, 1973.

STRAUSS, HAROLD, editor; b. N.Y.C., June 18, 1907; s. Jack and Florence (Klauber) S.; student Horace Mann Sch. for Boys, 1919-24; B.S. magna cum laude, Harvard, 1928; m. Mildred Berstein, May 21, 1931. Editor, Alfred H. King, book pub., 1929-32; prodn. dir. Covici-Friede, Inc., book pub., 1932-34, editor-in-chief, 1934-38; dir. N.Y.C. Fed. Writers's project, editor N.Y.C. Guide, 1938-39; asso. editor Alfred A. Knopf, Inc., N.Y.C., 1939-42, editor in chief, 1942-66, cons. editor, 1966-75, dir., 1967-75. Mem. sci. writing adv. com. Columbia Sch. Journalism. Served to capt. USAAF, 1943-46. Winner Bowdoin prize Harvard, 1928. Clubs: P.E.N. (mem. exec. bd., chmn. com. on translation); Camera (trustee N.Y.C.). Contbr. book revs., articles, stories to N.Y. Times Book Rev., New Yorker, Atlantic, The Reporter. Home: New York City, N.Y., Died Nov. 27, 1975.

STRAUSS, LEO, educator, author; b. Kirchhain, Hesse, Germany, Sept. 20, 1899; s. Hugo and Jenny (David) S.; Ph.D., Hamburg U., 1921; m. Miriam Bernson, June 20, 1933; children—Jenny Ann, Thomas. Came to U.S., 1938, naturalized, 1944. Research asst. Acad. Jewish Research, Berlin, 1925-32; Rockefeller fellow social scis., France and Eng., 1932-34; lectr., asso. prof. prof. polit. sci. and philosophy New Sch. for Social Research, N.Y.C., 1938-48; prof. polit. philosophy U. Chgo., 1949-68, Robert Maynard Hutchins Distinguished Service Prof.; prof. polit. sci. Claremont Men's Coll., 1968-69; Scott Buchanan distinguised scholar-in-residence St. John's Coll., Annapolis, Md., from 1969. Vis. prof. philosophy, polit. sci. Hebrew U., Jerusalem, 1954-55, U. Cal., Berkeley, Cal., 1953. Author: The Political Philosophy of Hobbes, 1936; On Tyranny, 1950; Persecution and the Art of Writing, 1952; Natural Right and History, 1953; Thoughts on Machiavelli, 1958; What is Political Philosophy, 1959; The City and Man, 1964; Spinoza's Critique of Religion, 1965; Socrates and Aristophanes, 1965. Asso. editor Social Research, 1941-48; co-editor History of Political Philosophy, 1963. Home: Annapolis, Md. Died Oct. 18, 1973.

STRAUSS, LEWIS LICHTENSTEIN, govt. ofcl.; b. Charleston, W. Va., Jan. 31, 1896; s. Lewis and Rosa (Lichtenstein) S.; ed. pub. schs., Richmond; m. Alice Hanauer, Mar. 5, 1923; 1 son Lewis H. Associated with Kuhn, Loeb, & Co., N.Y., 1919-47, partner, 1929-47; member U.S. AEC, 1946-50; spl. asst. to Pres. on atomic energy matters, 1953; chmn. AEC, 1953-58; Sec. Commerce 1958-59; initiator Internat. Atomic Energy Agy. and internat. sci. confs. on peaceful uses of atomic energy. Sec. to Herbert Hoover, World War, 1917-19. Trustee George Washington U., Jewish Theol. Sem.; past pres. Inst. for Advanced Study. Commd. lt. comdr. USNR, 1926, rear admn., 1945. Decorated D.S.M., Legion of Merit with gold star (Navy), Oak Leaf Cluster (Army); Officer Legion of Honor (France); Medal of Freedom (U.S.); Grand Office Order of Leopold (Belguim). Jewish religion (past pres. congregation). Clubs: Century Assn. (N.Y.C.); Metropolitan (Washington). Author: Men and Decisions, 1962. Home: Brandy Station, Va. Died Jan. 21, 1974; interred Salem Fields Cemetery, Brooklyn, N.Y.

STRAUSS, MAURICE BENJAMIN, educator, physician; b. Bklyn., Mar. 5, 1904; s. Henry M. and Ida (Igleheimer) S.; A.B., Amherst Coll., 1924; M.D., Johns Hopkins, 1928; m. Ruth Franc, Sept. 8, 1927; children—Peter Franc, Barbara Franc. Intern Boston City Hosp., 1928-30; asst. in medicine Harvard Med. Sch., 1930-36, instr., 1936-39, asso., 1939-52, lectr., 1952-70; prof. medicine Boston U., 1952-66, lectr., 1967-70; prof. medicine Tufts U., from 1967, asso. dean, from 1967; resident physician Boston City Hosp., 1930-36, vis. physician, 1936-67, cons. physician, from 1968; chief medicine Cushing and Boston VA Hosps., 1946-66; cons. physician Faulkner Hosp., from 1939, New Eng. Center Hosp., from 1967. Mem. adv. com. Mass. Selective Service, 1950-60, mem. VA program com., 1960-68, physiology study sect. NIH, 1962-66, Nat. Acad. Sci. drug efficacy study, 1966-69; cons. FDA, from 1970; Peters lectr. Yale, 1959, Stoneburner lectr. Med. Coll. Va., 1968; Myers lectr. Washington Hosp. Center, 1971; Ratner lectr. Mt. Sinai Hosp. Cleve., 1972: Served to lt. col. AUS, 1943-46. Recipient citation Boston City Hosp., 1964. Mem. Assn. Am. Physicians, Am. Soc. Clin. Investigation, Am. Fedn. Clin. Research, A.C.P., Boylston Med. Soc. (pres. 1951-52), Phi Beta Kappa, Sigma Xi, Alpha Omega Alpha. Author: Clinical Management of Renal Failure, 1956; Body Water in Man, 1957; Diseases of the Kidney, 1963, 71; Familiar Medical Quotation, 1968. Home: Boston, Mass. Died Apr. 19, 1974.

STRAWBRIDGE, RUTH GAWTHORPE KNOWLES, civic interests; b. West Grove, Pa., Oct. 23, 1880; d. Joseph Gawthorpe and Sarah Mackey (Townsend) Moore; ed. Friend Sch., Rising Sun, Md.; student English dept., U. of Pa., 1897; m. Winthrop Curtis Knowles, 1903 (died 1909); m. 2d, George Holt Strawbridge, Feb. 19, 1913. Apptd. pres. Philadelphia. Help Bur., 1927, by late Chief Justice Taft; originator of the voluntary movement among society leaders, 1932, for observance of the Eighteenth Amendment; chmn. of "Flowers for Flowerless" of Phila.; mem. advisory bd. Salvation Army, Phila. also of advisory bd. Republican Women of Phiala. County and chmn. of welfare same; mem. bd. govs. Republican Women of Pa., Mem. English-Speaking Union (bd. govs.), Civic Assn. of Phila., Phila Art Alliance, Pa. Hort. Soc. Clubs: Women's City (bd. govs.), Print, Overbrook Golf. Compiler: Sunshine on Life's Way, 1910. Contbr. on law enforcement, also on welfare and social topics. Home: Philadelphia, Pa.†

STREETER, CARROLL PERRY, editor; b. Groton, S. D., Nov. 12, 1898; s. Wesley Simeon and Ada L. (Perry) S.; B.S. in agrl. economics. Ia. State Coll., 1923, B.S. in animal husbandry, 1923; m. Beulah K. Swilhart, Sept. 4, 1926; children—Joan, James W., John R. Farm editor The Cedar Rapids (Ia.) Evening Gazette, 1924-27; field editor The Farmers Wife mag., St. Paul, 1927-39; asso. editor Farm Jour., Phila. 1939-44, mng. editor, 1944-55, editor, 1955-68, contbg. editor, from 1968, also exec. v.p. Jour.; cons. Rockefeller Found., from 1968. Editor, Town Journal; consultant Farm Film Found. Sgt., 109th Field Signal Bn., 34th Div., U.S. Army, 1917-19. Recipient Reuben Brigham award for outstanding contributions toward a better agriculture Am. Assn. Agrl. Coll. Editors, 1947; Distinguished Achievement award Alumni Assn. Ia. State University, 1962. Mem. Nat. Bd. Christian Edn., Presbyn. Church U.S.A.; past mem. exec. com. Nat. Council Presbyn. Men. Member American Society of Farm Managers and Rural Appraisers, American Assn. of Agrl. Editors (pres. 1961), Sigma Delta Chi, Gamma Sigma Delta, Phi Kappa Phi. Alpha Zeta, Adelante. Republican. Presbyn. (elder). Clubs: National Press (Washington). Contbr. articles to nat. publs. Home: Swarthmore, Pa. Died Jan. 8, 1975.

STREIT, PAUL HENRY, physician, army officer b. officer; b. Seguin, Tex., Mar. 18, 1891; s. John and Louise (Weiss) S.; M.D., U. of Tex., 1916; interne John Sealy Hosp., Galveston, Tex., 1917; postgrad. nose and throat training, U. of Bordeaux, France, 1919; graduate of Army Medical Field Service School, 1923; nose and throat student, New York Post Graduate Hospital, 1925-26; student course in bronchoscopy under Dr. Chevalier Jackson, Phila., 1929; m. Metta Miller Megeath, Sept. 15, 1926; children—John Paul, Metta Elizabeth. Commd. 1st lt., Med. Corps, U.S. Army, 1917; promoted through grades to maj. gen., 1949. Mem. Thus Relief Expdn. in Poland, 1919-20; chief Eye, Ear, Nose and Throat Service, Army Dispensary, Washington, 1926-29, Sternberg Gen. Hosp., 1929-31, Ft. Leavenworth, Kan., 1931-35, A. & N. Gen. Hosp., 1935-38, Letterman Army Hospital, 1938-42;surg. Central Pacific Base Command, 1943-45; comdg. officer Dibble General Hospital, 1945-46, and Brooke General Hospital, 1946-49; commanded Army Medical Center and Walter Reed General Hospital, 1949-53; later cons. United Mine Workers of American Welfare and Retirement Fund. Diplomate Am. Bd. Otorhinolaryngol. Fellow A.C.S.; member Alpha Mu Pi Omega, Alpha Omega Alpha, Am. Med. Assn., Acad. medicine Medicine. Washington. Awarded Commemorative Cross of Poland; Legion of Merit with Oak Leaf Cluster, Republican. Episcopalian. Mason. Home: Chevy Chase, Md., Died Feb. 12, 1976.

STREIT, SAMUEL FREDERICK, stock broker; b. Newark, N.J., Aug. 15, 1870; s. Lewis Albert and Mary Elizabeth (Lyon) S.; ed. Poly Inst., Brooklyn; m. Helen Burt Holmes, of Orange, N.J., Feb. 1, 1913. With Samuel Streit & Co., wine importers, 1887-99; mem. H. T. Carey & Co., stock brokers, from 1899; mem. governing com. New York Stock Exchange, from May 1, 1906, also mem. arbitration com. and chmn. com. on clearing house; pres. Summit Mining Co. Episcopalian. Clubs: Metropolitan, Riding. Home: New York City, N.Y.†

STRENCH, DONALD DAVIS, r.r. exec.; b. Ketchikan, Alaska, Mar. 14, 1921; s. William Godfrey and Mary (Minthorne) S.; student U. Hawaii, 1939-41; B.S., W.Va. U., 1944; grad. in advanced mgmt. Northwestern U., 1961; grad. Advanced Mgmt. Program, Harvard, 1962; m. Mary Bibb Lamar, Jan. 14, 1956; children—Donald Davis, William Godfry, Bibb Lamar. With So. Ry. System, Atlanta, 1946-65, gen. mgr., 1962-65; exec. v.p. Atlanta's West Point, Western of Ala., Ga. R.R., Atlanta, 1965-66, pres., 1966-68; gen. mgr. Louisville & Nashville R.R., Louisville, 1968-69, v.p. operations, 1969-73, exec. v.p., 1973-74; dir. Louisville Trust Bank, Terminal R.R. St. Louis, Ky. and Ind. Terminal Co. Served as 1st lt. C.E., AUS, 1944-46. Republican. Episcopalian. Clubs: Hunting Creek Country, Pendennis (Louisville). Home: Louisville, Ky. Died May. 25, 1974.

STRENG, JESSE F., banker; b. Louisville, Aug. 25, 1880; s. Manvel John and Frances (Starr) S.; grad. high sch.; m. Marie Klauber, Jan. 5, 1910 (dec. 1952); children—Ray Merie, John L. Markstein; m. 2d, Louise Johnson Schaner, Sept. 4, 1959. Pres., Streng Shoe Store, until 1925; exec. v.p. Morris Plan Indsl. Bank, 1925-45; pres. Bank Louisville, from 1945, also chmn. bd. Mem. Central Western Consumer Bankers Assn. (pres.), Consumer Bankers Assn. (v.p.) Mason (Shriner), Optimist. Home: Louisville, Ky. Died Jan. 30, 1973.

STRETCH, OLIVE MINERVA (MRS. CARL HENRY RATHJEN), osteo. physician; b. Jersey City, Apr. 28, 1901; d. Edward Kirk and Margaret (Reiner) Stretch; D.O., Kirksville Coll. Osteopathy and Surgery, 1930; m. Herbert Stout, July 9, 1932 (div. 1942); 1 dau., Barbara Joy (Mrs. Herbert C. Miller); m. 2d, Carl Henry Rathjen, May 14, 1958. Practice medicine specializing in osteopathy, Union City, N.J., 1930-37, Alhambra, Cal., 1937-66, Meridian, Ida., from 1966; instr. London (Eng.) Coll. Osteopathy, 1967. Recipient Service award Internat. Rotary, 1966. Fellow Acad. Applied Osteopathy; mem. Ida. Osteopathic Assn. (sec., treas. 1967-71), Osteopathic Physicians and Surgeons Cal. (sec., treas. 1965-66; bd. dirs.), Nat. Assn. Music Therapists, Inc., Cranial Acad. (instr., lectr., from 1962, exec. sec., treas., editor news letter, from 1963), Sutherland Cranial Teaching Found. (instr., lectr. from 1962). Club: 750 Kirksville. Home: Meridian, Ida. Died Mar. 27, 1971.

STRICKLER, EARL T., assn. exec.; b. nr. Hellam, Pa., Nov. 27, 1908; s. A. Millard and Anna (Jacobs) S.; ed. bus. adminstrn. Internat. Corr. Schs., and horological tech. Brit. Horological Inst.; m. Mary Jane Kurtz, Apr. 25, 1969. Became owner A. M. Strickler & Son, Columbia, Pa., 1939; mem. adv. bd. Am. Bank, Selected Investment Corp., Am. Diversified Corp.; Americaid, Inc., Internat. Sci. Labs.; mng. dir., chief exec. officer Nat. Assn. Watch and Clock Collectors; founder with A. Millard Strickler, Columbia Mus. Horological Antiquities; exhibitor, lectr. Free Pub. Library, Phila., 1951; dir. Saito-Samelius Library, Hitotsubashi U., Tokyo; exhibited Japanese Clock Collection, 1954; lectr. Bd. dirs. Columbia Hosp. Corp.; treas., bd. dirs. Bowman Tech. Inst.; treas. Jeanne G. Parkhurst Fund Found. Served with F.A., U.S. Army, 1942-43. Named Ky. col. Fellow Royal Soc. Arts (London), Brit. Horological Inst.; mem. Ancient Monuments Soc., London, Suisse Societe de Chronometrie, Japanese Soc. Chronometry (hon. life dir.), Watchmaker's Assn. Pa. (hon. life), Japanese Horological Inst. (hon.), United Horological Assn. Am., Horol. Inst. Am. (hon. life), Nat. Assn. Watch and Clock Collectors (editor of bull, sec., mng. dir.) Asso. Japanese Horological Socs. (Am. rep.), A.I.M., Pa. Fuel Mchts. Assn. (dir.), Allemande-Korporation Zurich Switzerland (hon.), Masonic Sch. of Instrn. (life), 76th Div. Assn., Antiquarian Horological Soc. London, A.A.A.S., Assn. Watch and Clock Collectors, Smithsonian Instn. (asso.), Am. Soc. Assn. Execs., Am. Watchmakers Inst. Editor Am. Ency. Clocks and Watches. Contbg. editor Jour. Calendar Refrom. Contbr. articles to fgn. and domestic trade jours. Home: Columbia, Pa. Died May 26, 1974.

STRICKLER, WOODROW MANN, educator; b. Columbia, Pa., Sept. 8, 1912; s. Simon Frey and Ethel (Mann) S.; B.S., Bucknell U., 1934, Ped.D., 1956; M.B.A., U. Pa., 1935; postgrad. Northwestern U., 1935-38; LL.D., Bellarmine Coll., 1973; D. Social Scis., U. Louisville, 1974; m. Florence Gertrude MacLeod, Dec. 21, 1938. Research asst. Ill. Commerce Commn., Chgo., 1935; asst. dept. bus. orgn. and indsl. mgmt. Northwestern U., 1937-38; cons. Lord & Thomas, advt., Chgo., 1937-38; pub. utility cons., Harrisburg, Pa., Chgo., Louisville, 1937-43, instr. econs. U. Louisville, 1938, asst. prof., 1939-42, asso. prof., 1942-54, prof., 1954-75, dir. dept. coop. edn., 1942-43, dir. summer sch., acting dean Coll. Arts and Scis., 1946, dir. div. adult edn., 1946-51, v.p., 1951-58, exec. v.p., 1958-68, pres., 1968-72, emeritus, 1972-75; pres. U. Louisville Found., 1970-73, Kentuckiana Metroversity, 1969-73. Mem. adv. com. for econs. and bus. adminstrn. Bucknell U., 1960-68; dir. Center for Study Liberal Edn. for Adults, Chgo., 1951-56; v.p. So. U. Conf., 1962-63; mem. Ky. Commn. for Higher Edn. Ky. Council Pub. Higher Edn. Bd. dirs. Louisville Orch., Ky. Opera Assn., J.B. Speed Art Mus., Red Cross Hosp., Lions Eye Found. Ky. Served as lt. USNR, 1943-46. Recipient citation Nat. Soc. S.A.R., 1972; Ottenheimer award Jewish Community Center, 1972; Distinguished Educator award Spalding Coll., 1973; Ky. and Ind. Brotherhood award Nat. Conf. Christians and Jews, 1974. Mem. So. Econ. Assn., Newcomen Soc. N. Am., Am. Legion, Louisville C. of C. (dir.), Louisville Advt. Club (Man of Year 1972-73), Louisville Better Bus. Bur. (dir.), Louisville Credit Men's Assn. (dir.), English Speaking Union (hon. dir. Ky. br.), Ky. Region Nat. Conf. Christians and Jews, Omicron Delta Kappa, Delta Mu Delta, Kappa Delta Phi, Delta Alpha Epsilon, Alpha Phi Omega, Sigma Alpha Epsilon. Lion. Clubs: Pendennis, Salmagundi (Louisville). Contbr. articles to profl. publs. Home: Louisville, Ky. Died Aug. 21, 1975; interred Creswell (Pa.) Cemetery.

STRIGHT, HAYDEN LEROY, clergyman; b. Sheakleyville, Pa., Apr. 18, 1898; s. Leonard Marcus and Cora Ione (Palm) S.; A.B., Thiel Coll., 1919; M.R.E., Boston U., 1922, A.M., 1929; D.D., Carleton Coll., 1954; m. Ruth Harris Brown, June 25, 1928; children—Paul Leonard, Richard Hayden, Jean Louise (Mrs. Hale Davenport). Dir. young peoples work, weekday ch. schs. Ramsey County Sunday Sch. assn., St. Paul, 1922-24; dir. religious edn. Meth. Ch., Newtonville, Mass., 1924-29; isntr. Boston U., 1928-29; exec. sec. Minn. Council Religious Edn., Minn. Council Chs., Mpls., 1929-64, emeritus, 1964-75; dir. devel. Minn. Protestant Center, 1964-68; minister visitation John Calvin U.P. Ch., Apache Junction, Ariz., 1970-75. Mem. N.Am. adminstrv. com., mem. world assembly World Council Christian Edn.; past mem. gen. bd., bd. mgrs., exec. com. central dept. field adminstrn. Nat. Council Chs. Christ; mem. com. constituent membership, chmn., sec. state council execs. sect., div. Christian edn. Nat. Council Chs.; organizer Minn. Christian Rural Overseas Program, 1947. Mem. Minn. Gov.'s Com. on Refugees, Com. on Children and Youth; mem. Mayor's Com. to Preserve Old Fed. Cts. Bldg., 1969-70; mem. adv. council Am. Viewpoint. Sec. bd. dirs. Minn. Protestant Found. Recipient WCCO Radio Good Neighbor award, 1963; WTCN Radio award for Outstanding Community Service, 1963; Distinguished Alumni award Thiel Coll., 1966. Mem. Employed Council Officers Assn. (1st pres.), Assn. Council Secs. (past pres.), Mayflower Soc. (past gov. Minn.), S.A.R. (chaplain, bd. mgrs. Mpls., past pres. Minn.), Gen. Soc. Mayflower Descs. (elder gen. 1957-66, exec. com. 1966-72), Hennepin County (hon. life), Ramsey County (1st v.p. 1966-69, pres. 1969-71), Pinal County hist. socs., Mayflower Soc., Alden Kindred Am. Author: Together: the Story of Church Cooperation in Minnesota, 1971; A Stright Geneaology, 1973. Editor: Minnesota Messenger, 1929-64. Home: White Bear Lake, Minn., Died June 29, 1975; interred Sunset Meml. Park, Minneapolis, Minn.

STRINGER, HENRY DELPHOS, govt. ofcl.; b. Winfield, Tex., Nov. 18, 1907; s. Edward B. and Anna (Smith) S.; student Simmons U., 1924-25, U. Tex., 1925-27, U. Cal. at Los Angeles, 1927-28, Vanderbilt U., 1930; LL.B., Cumberland U., 1931; m. Glen Eyrie Faubion, July 30, 1927; children—Henry Delphos, Camille (Mrs. Donald L. Bloom), Cynthia (Mrs. J. Gregory Robertson); m. 2d, Mozelle Bernard, Sept. 30, 1953. Admitted to Tex. bar, 1931; practice in El Paso and Memphis, Tex., 1931-40; county atty. Hall County, Tex., 1941-43; with FTC, 1943-70, dir. Bur. Textiles and Furs, 1962-70. Recipient Superior Service award FTC, 1958, ofcl. commendation, 1960. Mem. State Bar Tex., Sigma Alpha Epsilon. Mason. Home: San Antonio, Tex. Died May 3, 1974; buried Winfield, Tex.

STRINGHAM, EDWIN JOHN, composer., author, b. Kenosha, Wis., July 11, 1890; s. Frank Dillingham and Anna (Jorgensen) S.; Mus.B., Northwestern U., 1914; Dr. Pedagogy, Cin. Conservatory, 1922; Mus.D. (hon.), Denver Coll. of Music, 1928; certificate in composition under Respighi, Royal Acad. Music, Rome, Italy, 1929; m. Alta Morrill Potts, Aug. 26, 1916; 1 son, Edward MacDowell. Tchr. violin North Shore Sch. Music, Hull House, 1910-14; dir. Grand Forks Sch. Music, 1914-15; lived in N.M., 1916-19; mem. staff music dept. U. Colo., 1919; organizer, dean Dener Coll. Music, 1920-29; chmn. music bd. Colo. State Bd. Edn., 1922-29; music critic Denver News and Denver Post, 1919-29; tchr. composition Union Theol. Sch. Sacred Music, Juilliard Sch. Music; prof. dept. music Tchrs. Coll. Columbia, 1930-38, instr. music criticism writing Pulitzer Sch. Journalism, 1933-35; founder music dept. Queens Coll., N.Y.C., 1938-44, prof. music, 1944; music editor Carl Fischer, Inc., 1930-31, Am. Book Co., 1932-39; dir., music editor Music Press, Inc., 1939-46; divisional head music U.S. Army Univ., Biarritz, France, 1945-46; vis. prof. music composition U. Cal., Los Angeles, 1946-47, U. Tex., 1947-48. Mem. organizing com. Nat. Assn. Schs. of Music and Am. Musicol. Soc. organizer 1st music festival of combined music depts. four city colls. City N.Y., 1941. Cromwell traveling fellow, Germany, 1936; scholar Royal Acad. Music Rome, Italy, 1929. Mem. Am. Assn. U. Profs., Acoustical Soc. Am., Renaissance Soc. Am., Phi Mu Alpha, Ki Kappa Lambda, Pi Gamma Mu, Phi Delta Kappa. Episcopalian. Composer: (for symphony orch.) The Phantom, Three Pastels, Visions, Ancient Mariner, Springtime Overture, Suite Dances Exotiques, Symphony No. 1 in B flat minor, Nocturne No. 1, Nocturne No. 2, Notturno for Woodwinds, Horns and Harp, Phantasy on an American Folk Tune for violin solo and orch., Childe Rowland, a symphonic narrative; (chamber music) String Quartet in F minor; (choral music) Pilgrim Fathers (mixed), Ave Maria (mixed), Dream Song, Longing, Tears (women's voices); (piano) Three Pastels; also many shorter works, songs. Author: listening to Music Creatively, rev. edit., 1959. Co-author: Creative Harmony and Musicianship. Contbr. editor various mus. works and books on music edn. Compositions performed by leading soloists and symphony orch. Author, co-author numerous items in field music. Home: Chapel Hill, NC. Died June 24, 1974.

STROHL, EVERETT LEE, pysician; b. Oblong, Ill., June 22, 1906; s. B. Lee and Lessa (Wilson) S.; A.B., U. Ill., 1929, B.S., 1930, M.D., 1932; M.S. In Surgery, U. Minn., 1936; m. Levinia Howells, Apr. 20, 1940 (dec. Mar. 1941); m. 1 son, Lee Howells; m. 2d, Margaret Perkins, Sept. 6, 1947; children—Kingman Perkins, Linda Keith. Intern, St. Luke's Hosp., Chgo., 1931-32, resident 1932-33; fellow in surgery Mayo Clinic, Rochester, Minn., 1933-37; practice medicine, specializing in surgery, Chgo., from 1937; sr. attending surgeon Presbyn.-St. Lukes Hosp., attending surgeon Cook County Hosp., from 1950; mem. Regional Com. Heart Disease, Stroke and Cancer; clin. prof. surgery U. Ill., Chgo., 1959-69; prof. surgery Rush Med. Coll., from 1969. Mem. Chgo. Bd. Health, from 1963. Pres. bd. dirs. Municipal Tb Sanitaruim, from 1959; treas., bd. govs. Inst. Medicine Chgo., 1949-65, v.p., 1965-66, pres., 1966-67; bd. dirs., treas. Central Service Chronically Ill, 1946-65; bd. dirs. Welfare Council Met. Chgo., Bishop Anderson Found. Served from capt. to col. M.C., AUS, 1942-46. Decorated Bronze Star, Soldiers medal; recipient Chgo. medal of honor, 1962; Tuberculosis Inst. medal, 1969; George Howell Coleman medal Inst. Medicine of Chgo., 1972; Community Service plaque Ill. Fedn. Women's Clubs. Fellow A.C.S. (vice-chmn. bd. govs. 1965-69); mem. Western, Central (pres. 1969-70, chmn. council from 1970) surg. assns., Societe International de Chirurgie, Nat. AORT (dir.), Theta Delta Chi, Nu Sigma Nu, Alpha Omega Alpha. Episcopalian. Clubs: Surgeons Travel (pres. 1950, 65); University Glen View; Quadrangle; Chicago Literary; Chickaming Country (Lakeside, Mich). Contbr. articles to profl. jours. Home: Chicago, IL. Died Dec. 23, 1973.

STROUSE, D. J., transportation exec.; b. Charles City, Ia., Nov. 6, 1879; s. Lewis and Emma (Trixler) S.; student Nora Springs (Ia.) Sem.; m. Mary Taylor, Apr. 30, 1903; children—Robert T., John C. Abstractor, Garner, Ia., 1897-1900; tax accountant, 1900-03; bookkeeper, later auditor and comptroller Twin City Rapid Transit Co., Minneapolis, Minn., 1903, vice pres. and sec., 1933, exec. vice pres., May 1936. pres and dir., from Oct. 1936; dir. Minneapolis St. Ry. Co., St. Paul City Ry. Co., Transit Supply Co., Minneapolis & St. Paul Suburban R.R. Co., Northwestern Nat. Bank & Trust Co. Clubs: Minneapolis, Minneapolis Athletic, Minikahda. Rotary, Six O'Clock (Minneapolis); Minnesota, St. Paul. Home: Minneapolis, Minn.†

STRUYE, PAUL, Belgian govt. ofcl.; b. Ghent, Belgium, 1896; s. Eugene and Jenny (Cinon) S.; ed. College Ste. Barbe (Belgium), U. Ghent; m. Suzanne Van de Heuvel, 1925; 3 sons, 2 daus. Adv., Ct. of Cassation; Senator, Belgium, 1946-74, pres. of Senate, 1950-54, 58-62, 63-74; minster justice, 1947-48; minister of state, 1958-74. Mem. Social Christian party. Author: Precis des Brevets Inventions, 1935; L'evolution du sentiment public sous l'occupation allemande, 1944; Taine, 1947; Nouveaux propos du

Conseiller Eudoxe, 1945; Melanges-Mengelingen, 1966; Problems internationaux, 1972. Brussels Belgium. Died Feb. 1974.

STRYKER, JOSIAH, lawyer; b. Plainville, N.J., Dec. 31, 1880; s. Abram VanDeripe and Mary Gertrude (Davison) S.; m. Hazel E. Benbrook, Aug. 11, 1908 (dec.); 1 dau., Dorothy (Mrs. David B. MacNeil). Admitted to N.J. bar, 1903 (counselor, 1906); legal asst. to atty. gen. of N.J., 1904-17, 2d asst., 1917-18; mem. law firm Lindabury, Depue & Faulks, 1918-67, sr. partner, 1936-67, firm now Stryker, Tams & Dill, counsel, from 1967; director emeritus Fidelity Union Trust Company, from 1961. Fellow Am. Bar Found.; mem. Am., N.J. (pres. 1934-35), Essex Co. bar assns. Republican. Episcopalian (former chancellor Diocese of Newark). Clubs: Essex, Downtown (Newark); Baltusrol Golf (Springfield). Home: South Orange, N.J.†

STUART, FRANCIS JOSEPH, mfr., banker; b. Bergen, Genesee Co., N.Y., Oct. 15, 1878; s. Adam McAdoo and Catherine Ann (Hiller) S.; ed. high sch., acad., business coll., Rochester, jr. yr. student U. of Rochester; m. Thelma Gwendolyn James, of N.Y. City; 1 daughter. Mfg. business, St. Louis, from 1906; pres. and treas. Plapao Laboratories, Inc.; propr. Stuart Plaster-Pad Co.; pres. Haight Orchard & Development Co.; owner Commercial Adv. & Exploitation Co. (hdqrs. in St. Louis with branches in Leamington, Ont., Can. and London, Eng.), Goodform Mfg. Co.; dir. Union Trust Co. Dir. U.S. Board of Trade; mem. St. Louis Chamber Commerce, Associated Industries of Mo., A.A.A.S., Am. Pharm. Assn., Am. Inst. of Banking; mem. Mo. Council Yenching Univ.; founder mem. Civil Legion. Republican. Methodist. Mason (32°, Shriner), K.T. Clubs: Missouri Athletic Assn., Amateur Athletic, Missouri Automobile, Sunset Hill Country, Pike County Country; Tucson; Mam-Thav Country. Has patented numerous mech. and chem. inventions, receiving gold medal, Grand Prix and other awards, also medal for excellence in chemistry. Home: University City, Mo.†

STUART, JAMES ARTHUR, newspaper editor; b. Bloomington, Ind., Sept. 2, 1880; s. John Wesley and Rachel E. S.; grad. high sch., Bloomington, 1897; A.B., Ind. U., 1901, LL.D., 1954; m. Moss Farr (dec.); m. 2d, Ruth L. Day, 1921; children—Rachel F. (Mrs. John A. Schumacher), James A., Edward Day (dec.), Lawrence Day. City editor Muncie (Ind.) Star, 1901; state editor, Sun. editor, city and news editor Indpls. Star, 1905-21, mng. editor, 1923-46, editor from 1946; editorial dir. Rocky Mtn. News and Denver Times, 1921-23. Pres. Ind. Heart Found., 1957. Bd. dirs. Indpls. YMCA; Am. Heart Assn., Nat. Council Chs. Christ, James Whitcomb Riley Meml. Assn., Meth. Hosp., A.R.C., Goodwill Industries, Boy Scouts of America. Member Am. Soc. Newspaper Editors, Ind. Soc. Chgo., Hoosier State Press Assn., Sigma Delta Chi (nat. pres. 1927-28). Mem. Christian (Disciples) Ch. (bd. dirs. unified promotion). Mason. Clubs: Press, Rotary, Indpls. Athletic (Indpls.); National Press (Washington). Home: Indianapolis, Ind. Died May 20, 1975.

STUART, MONTGOMERY ALEXANDER, naval officer; b. Detroit, Mich., Nov. 17, 1881; s. Alexander Joseph and Marie Louise (Christian) S.; M.D., U. of Mich., 1906, Detroit Coll. Medicine and Surgery, 1907; m. Nina Pauline Christian, Jan. 28, 1908 (dec.); children—Charles Watson (dec.), William Watson. Med. officer Camp Elliott, C.Z., 1908-09, Colon Hosp., Panama, 1909-11, U.S. Navy Hosp, at Norfolk, Va., 1911-12, at Las Animas, Colo., 1912-13, U.S. Legation Guard, Peking, China, 1913-16, U.S. Navy transport Martha Washington, 1917-18; 2d, Division, A.E.F., 1918; exec. officer, U.S. Navy Base Hospital, No. 1, Brest, France, 1918-19; medical officer U.S.S. Mississippi, 1925-27; in charge div. of preventive medicine, Bur. Medicine and Surgery, Washington, D.C.; instr. in hygiene, sanitation and preventive medicine, U.S. Navy Med. Sch., Washington, 1927-30; dir. gen. Nat. Pub. Health Service, Haiti, 1930-31; dir. Am. Scientific Mission to Haiti, 1931-33. Hospital Corps Sch., Portsmouth, Va., 1933-34; in charge of Division of Physical Qualifications and Medical Records, Bureau Medicine and Surgery, Washington, D.C., 1935-39; comd. Naval Medical Supply Depot, Brooklyn, N.Y., 1939-41; District Medical Officer, Tenth Naval Dist., May 1941-Jan. 1943; under orders to 3d Naval Dist., New York, N.Y.; capt. Med. Corps, U.S. Navy. Fellow Am. Coll. Surgeons; mem. Am. Med. Assn., Phi Alpha Gamma. Episcopalian. Clubs: Army and Navy, Army and Navy Country. Formerly contributor to U.S. Navy Med. Bull, Mil. Surgeon; contbr. chapter on tropical hygiene in Diagnostics and Treatment of Tropical Diseases, by Stitt. Home: Brooklyn, N.Y.*†

STUART, ROBERT DOUGLAS, food products exec.; b. Glencoe, Ill., Jan. 20, 1886; s. Robert and Margaret (Sharrar) S.; ed. Lawrenceville (N.J.) Sch., and Princeton; LL.D., Coe Coll., Northwestern U., Lake Forest Coll., U. Pitts.; m. Harriet McClure, June 10, 1913; children—Robert Douglas, Anne (Mrs. C.B. Batchelder), Margaret (Mrs. Augustin S. Hart, Jr.), Harriet (Mrs. Edson W. Spencer). With the Quaker Oats Co., from 1906, became pres., then vice chmn. bd., and in 1953 vice chmn. and pres., chmn. bd., 1956-62, then dir. emeritus; U.S. ambassador to Canada, 1953-56; dir. Canadian Corporate Mgmt. Co. Red Cross commr. for France, World War I; hon. pres. Chicago Council Boy Scouts Am., mem. nat. adv. bd.; mem. bd. mgrs. Presbyn.-St. Luke's Hosp.; mem. Bus. Council Rep. nat committeeman from Ill., 1948-53, from 1964. Mem. Nat. Planning Assn. Presbyn. Clubs: Commercial, Shoreacres, Onwentsia, Chicago, Old Elm; Capitol Hill, Metropolitan (Washington); Valley (Montecito, Cal.) Home: Lake Forest, Ill. Died Jan. 5, 1975.

STUCKEY, LORIN, educator; b. at Washington C.H., O., Aug. 16, 1879; s. Samuel N. and Mollie (Brown) S.; A.B., Miami U., Oxford, O., 1906; A.M., Columbia, 1907; Ph.D., State U. of Ia., 1915; m. Mae R. Ashton, of Philo, O., Dec. 24, 1906. Teacher pub. schs., Bloomingburg, O., 1897-1903; spl. teacher history, New Philadelphia, O., 1907-08; dean and prof. history, economics and sociology, Tri-State Coll., Angola, Ind., 1908-11; dean liberal arts and prof. history, economics and sociology, Highland Park Coll., Des Moines, Ia., 1911-13; instr. history, 1913-14, asst. prof. polit. economy and sociology, 1914-15, asst. prof. sociology, 1915-17, State U. of Ia.; pres. Sayre Coll., Lexington, Ky., 1917-18; dir. War Camp Community Service, Newark, N.J., and Camp Merritt, N.J., 1918-20; with Am. Colortype Co., Newark, N.J. Mem. Sigma Delta Chi. Mason, K.P. Author: The Iowa State Federation of Labor (State U. of Ia. Social Science Series), 1915. Lecturer on sociol. topics. Home: East Orange, N.J.†

STUDY, GUY, architect; b. Richmond, Ind., Nov. 29, 1880; s. Abel Lomax and Mary Alice (Hittle) S.; prep. edn., Phillips Exeter Acad., Exeter, N.H.; student Washington U., 1903-08, Atelier Laloux Ecole des Beaux Arts, Paris, 1908-11; studied architecture in France, Italy, Eng.; m. Georgette Avelin, Mar. 23, 1910 (divorced); 1 son, Lomax. Began as architect, St. Louis, Mo., 1912; mem. Study & Farrar from 1915. Prin. works: St. Paul's Episcopal Ch., Ch. of Our Lady of Lourdes, new Mary Inst. bldgs., bldgs. of Mo. River plant and filtration plant, Chain of Rocks Div., Long Art Gallery, St. Luke's R.C. Ch., Firmin Desloge Hosp., Municipal Service Bldg. (all in St. Louis), St. Paul's Ch., Paducah, Ky., high sch., Fort Scott, Kan.; St. Peter's Epis. Ch., Ladue, Mo.; restoration of Holy Family Parish Ch., Cahokia, Ill., Balduc House, St. Genevieve, Mo.; St. Paul's Epis. Ch., Alton, Ill.; new chancel St. John's Meth. Ch., St. Louis; First Meth. Ch. St. Charles, Mo.; Mesker Park Amphitheater, Evansville, Ind. Fellow A.I.A., Archaeol. Inst. Am. Mo. Hist. Soc., Phi Delta Theta. Episcopalian. Author: History of St. Paul's Church, Alton, Ill. Contributor to archtl. mags. Home: St. Louis, Mo.†

STUHR, WILLIAM S., lawyer, industrialist; b. Hoboken, N.J., Nov. 23, 1899; s. William S. and Marietta Lindsay (Miller) S.; student Stevens Hoboken Acad.; A.B., N.Y. U., 1914, LL.B., 1917; J.D., 1917; m. Margarete Marie Canning, Aug. 10, 1926; children—Thomas M., Bernard C., George M., Robert L. Admitted to N.J. bar, 1917, practiced in Hoboken; mem. Stuhr & Vogt later sr. partner Stuhr & Haas; judge Weehawken Recorder's Ct., 1922; corp. counsel, Weehawken, 1923-26; 1st v.p. United Board & Carton Corp. (formerly United Paperboard Co.), 1932-38, pres., chmn. bd., 1951-62, dir., from 1932, also cons.; pres. Stuhr Industries; pres., dir. Steel Castings, Inc., from 1942, Burco, Inc. (ASE) 1938-43, Densen Banner, Inc., Benton & Fairfield Ry., Upco Corp., Lowman Folding Box, other corporations; director Equity Financial Corporation, Bankers National Life Insurance Company, Sterling Precision Corporation. Chmn., Civil War Hall Fame Com., 1961. Bd. dirs. North Hudson chpt. A.R.C., from 1947, fund chmn., 1950-51, chpt. chmn., 1952-53; chmn. bd. govs., mem. bd. Syracuse U. Research Inst.; trustee Syracuse U. Research Corp.; chairman, board of managers Brooklyn Navy YMCA, 1963-65; chmn. Armed Forces Day Com., N.Y.C., 1954-64; bd. dirs., chmn. N.Y. Home for Homeless Boys, Inc.; trustee United Seamen's Service, Inc.; bd. dirs. USMC Youth Found., vice chmn. finance com.; bd. dirs. USCG Academy Found.; mem. Met. N.Y. chpt. USO, from 1970, mem. nat. council, from 1972; pres. Hudson County Bar Found., from 1969; trustee N.J. Bar Found.; chmn. bd. trustees Kingspoint Found., U.S. Mcht. Marine Acad. Served with USNR, 1943-46; comdr. Res. Recipient Alumni Achievement award N.Y. U., 1958; Outstanding Civilian awards from sec. of army, 1962, sec. of navy, 1963; Outstanding American award Jewish War Vets., 1961; N.J. Medal of Honor, Distinguished Mil. Service medal New Jersey; Centennial medal Syracuse U., 1969. Mem. N.A.M. (dir.), State Soc. U.S.S., N.J. (pres.), Nat. Paperboard Assn. (dir.), Folding Box Assn. Am. (dir.), T.A.P.P.I., Naval Order U.S. (historian; vice comdr. gen. from 1963), Am., N.J., Hudson County bar assns., Mil. Order Fgn. Wars, Mil. Order World Wars (N.J. comdr. 1952-58, comdr. N.J. chpt. 1960-61, treas. gen., mem. exec. com., nat. staff), Navy League. U.S. (nat. dir.; pres., dir. N.J. council), service scrolls, 1st Marine Div. Assn. (life; v.p.), Quartermaster Assn. (pres. 1961), Def. Supply Assn. (pres. N.Y. chpt. 1962, v.p., 1962-65, nat. pres., exec. com. from 1962), Naval Res. Assn. (v.p. finance 3d dist. 1963), Nat. Rifle Assn. Am. Legion, Marine Corps League (nat. staff from 1952; meritorious service award 1951, nat. naval liaison officer, trustee, distinguished service award), West Point Soc. (asso. life mem.), Am. Seaman's Friend Soc. N.Y. (pres., trustee), N.J. Hist. Soc., St. Andrew's Soc., Red Cross of Constantine, Syracuse, N.J., Ohio chambers commerce, N.Y. Bd. Trade, Newcomen Soc. Eng., Nat. Inst. Social Scis., Kappa Sigma, Theta Nu Epsilon. Independent Democrat. Presbyn. Mason. Clubs: Lawyers (Hoboken, N.J.); Essex (Newark); Advertising, Lotus, Union League (N.Y.C.); Letter (N.Y.U.); Ends of the Earth. Home: Weehawken, N.J. Died Sept. 24, 1973; interred L.I. Nat. Cemetery.

STUMPH, CALOWA WILLIAM, church official; b. Purdy, Tenn., Oct. 16, 1878; s. John Wesley and Louritta (Huddleston) S.; B.S., Union U., Jackson, Tenn., 1906; m. Delia Etta Beville, of Jackson, Nov. 14, 1906; 1 son, Roy Calowa. Ordained ministry Bapt. Ch., 1901; pastor successively Jackson, Tenn., Bunkie, La., Bloomfield, Mo., Charleston, Miss., Bastrop, La., Henderson, Tex., and Clovis, N.M., until 1923; corr. sec. Bapt. Conv. of N.M., from Dec. 1, 1922. Trustee Rusk Coll., 1915-21. Mem. Alpha Tau Omega. Home: Albuquerque, N.M.†

STYER, WILHELM D., army officer; b. Salt Lake City, July 22, 1893; s. Henry D. and Bessie (Wilkes) S.; student Nat. Prep. Acad., 1911-12; B.S., U.S. Military Academy, 1916; grad. Army General Staff Coll., AEF, 1917, Engr. Sch., 1919-20; B.S. in Civil Engring., Mass. Inst. Tech., 1922; grad. Army Indsl. Coll., 1940; Dr. Military Science, Pa. Mil. College, 1943; m. Dorothea Haeberle, Sept. 23, 1918; 1 son, George Delp. Commd. 2d lt., 1916, advancing through the grades to lt. gen., Nov. 7, 1944; assistant instructor N.J. National Guard, 1916; U.S. Punitive Expedition, Mexico, 1916-17; A.E.F., 1917-18; training section Office of Chief of Engrs., 1918-19; asst. instr. Nat. Guard of N.Y., 1920, of Mass., 1921-22; head of Marine Design Div., Office of Chief of Engrs., 1922-25; senior military asst. and exec. officer U.S. Dist. Engrs., with 1st New York Engr. Dist., then U.S. District Engineer, 1925-28; engineer American Battle Monuments Commission in Europe. 1928-31; U.S. district engineer, Pittsburgh, Pa., 1931-36; asst. engr., maintenance of Panama Canal, Panama R.R., 1936-39; comdr. Ft. McIntosh, Tex., 8th Engr. Squadron, 1940; deputy chief of construction, War Dept., 1940-42; mem. special com. on reorganization of War Dept., 1942; became chief of staff and dep. commander Army Service Forces. War Dept. 1942; comdg. general U.S. Army Forces of the Western Pacific, June 1945-July 1946; retired 1947. Mem. Am. Soc. C.E., Soc. Am. Mil. Engrs. Clubs: Army-Navy (Washington). Columbia Country (Chevy Chase, Md.); San Diego Country. Home: Coronado, Cal. Died Feb. 26, 1975.

SUFFERN, ARTHUR ELLIOTT, college prof.; b. Gilletts, Pa., Nov. 15, 1878; s. George K. and Hannah (Allen) S.; B.S., Columbia, 1909, M.A., 1910, Ph.D., 1915; m. Charlotte Catchpole, of Corning, N.Y., June 1, 1905. Lecturer on economics, Columbia, 1913-14; spl. investigator for U.S. Commn. on Industrial Relations, summer 1914; prof. economics, Beloit (Wis.) Coll., from Sept. 1914. Mem. Am. Econ. Assn. Conglist. Awarded 1st prize, $1,000, in Hart, Schaffner & Marx Econ. Prize Essay Contest, 1913. Author: Conciliation and Arbitration in the Coal Industry of America, 1915. Address: Beloit, Wis.†

SUHR, ROBERT CARL, banker; b. Chgo., Apr. 14, 1911; s. Carl. H. and Adelaide O. (Yager) S.; B.S., Northwestern U., 1932; student exec. program Columbia Grad. Sch. Bus., 1960; m. Grace Lyle Duerson, Aug. 4, 1936; children—Thomas Duerson, Kathryn Lyle. With Continental Ill. Nat. Bank & Trust Co., Chgo., from 1933, becoming exec. v.p.; dir. Libbey-Owens-Ford Co., Md. Cup Corp. Trustee Northwestern U. Mem. Newcomen Soc., Pi Kappa Alpha. Presbyn. (elder). Clubs: Yacht, Univ. Executives (Chgo.); Westmoreland Country, Sheridan Shore Yacht (Wilmette, Ill.). Home: Evanston, Ill. Died Dec. 12, 1974.

SULERUD, ALLEN CHRISTEN, state ofcl.; b. Halstad, Minn., May 11, 1903; s. John C. and Christine (Reiten) S.; B.A., U. Minn., 1926; m. Eleanor Blanche Monger, Oct. 25, 1941. With Grandin Land Trust, Boston, 1927-38, Minn. State Grain Bd., 1939-41; dept. sec., Minn. Dept. Taxation, St. Paul, 1941-56, adminstrv. asst., 1956-62, dir. spl. taxes, 1962-63, dir. property tax, from 1963. Dir. Sulerud Hardware Co., 1928-66, Halstad Elevator Co., 1935-39, Halstad Creamery Co., 1930-39; guest lectr. U. Minn., 1951-61. Div. comdr. St. Paul Community Chest, 1943-48; dir. Capitol Community Center, 1945-53; chmn. camp com. St. Paul YMCA, 1954; mem. budget com. United Fund, 1966-69; mem. St. Paul Urban League Bd., 1948-68. Trustee Minn. Masonic Home. Mem. Internat. Assn. Assessing Officers, Delta Chi, Alpha Kappa Psi. Republican. Episcopalian (vestryman 1943-68). Mason (33 deg., Shriner). Home: St. Paul, Minn. Died May 1974.

SULLIVAN, DAVID, trade union ofcl.; b. Cork City, Ireland, May 7, 1904; s. Stephen and Margaret (Fouhy) O'Sullivan; ed. Christian Bros. Sch., North Monastery, Cork City; m. Catherine Connaire, Feb. 12, 1930; children—Margaret (Mrs. William Reilly), Joan (Mrs. Edward Duffy), Stephen, Mary (Mrs. James Gonyon), John. Came to U.S., 1925, naturalized, 1932. From bus. rep. to pres. local 32B, Bldg. Service Employees

399 WHO WAS WHO

Internat. Union, 1936-60, gen. pres., 1960-76. Mem. N.Y.C. Bd. Welfare, 1963-76; N.Y. State Moreland Commn. Welfare, 1961-76; adv. com. Nat. Inst. Labor Edn., 1961-76. Recipient Equal Opportunity award Nat. Urban League, 1961. Mem. Am. Abritration Assn., United Housing Found. Home: Jackson Heights N.Y., Died Jan. 23, 1976.

SULLIVAN, EDWARD VINCENT, newspaper columnist, TV emcee; b. N.Y.C., Sept. 28, 1902; s. Peter Arthur and Elizabeth (Smith) S.; student St. Mary's Sch., Port Chester (N.Y.) High Sch.; m. Sylvia Weinstein, Apr. 28, 1930 (dec. Mar. 1973); 1 dau., Elizabeth (Mrs. Robert Henry Precht, Jr.). Reporter Port Chester Daily Item, 1918-19, Hartford (Conn.) Post, 1919; sportswriter N.Y. Evening Main (now N.Y. Sun), 1920-24, N.Y. World, 1924-25, N.Y. Morning Telegraph, Phila. Ledger, 1925-27; sports editor N.Y. Evening Graphic, 1927-29; Broadway columnist, 1929; columnist N.Y. Daily News, 1932-74; emcee Tabloid revue Down Patrol, Paramount Theatre, N.Y.C., 1932; introduced Jack Benny to radio as 1st radio entertainer sta. WABC, CBS, 1932; played vaudeville Lowe's State Theatre, N.Y.C., also Roxy Theatre, and Capitol Theatre, Chgo., 1933-50; emcee dance competition Harvest Moon Ball (sponsored by N.Y. Daily News at Madison Sq. Garden, N.Y.C.), 1936-52; own radio program Ed Sullivan Entertains, CBS, from 1942; emcee TV program The Ed Sullivan Show (formerly Toast of the Town), CBS-TV, 1948-71. Staged 46 benefit shows netting ¾ 0,000 for Army Emergency Relief and A.R.C., Madison Sq. Garden, World War II; recognized as 1st to organize and produce shows for wounded servicemen, N.Y. Pres. Damon Runyon-Walter Winchell Meml. Cancer Fund. Recipient LaSalle Coll. ann. journalism award, citations K.C., A.R.C., U. S. Navy, B'nai B'rith, Phila., Boston, N.Y.C., Cardinal Spellman, Cardinal Cushing, Am. Legion, Jewish War Vets., USAF, N.Y. Heart Fund, Sister Kenny; commendation distinguished service Halloran Gen. Hosp., S.I., 1945; cited by U.S. govt., 4 times; named TV Showman of Century, Boradcasting Execs. New Eng., 1968; Peabody award, 1968; Silver medal Poor Richard's Club, 1968. Clubs: Westchester Country, Winged Foot Golf. Author: Mister Lee, The Story of the Shuberts, 1948; TV biographies Rogers and Hammerstein, Helen Hayes, Beatrice Lillie, Walt Disney, Cole Porter, The Story of A.S.C.A.P., Story of Samuel Goldwyn, Story of Robert E. Sherwood; (comedy film) There Goes My Heart, 1938; (screenplay) Big Town Czar, 1939; (film) Ma, He's Making Eyes at Me, 1940. Home: New York City, N.Y. Died Oct. 13, 1974; buried Ferncliff Cemetery, Westchester County, N.Y.

SULLIVAN, FRANK (FRANCIS JOHN SULLIVAN), author; b. Saratoga Springs, N.Y., Sept. 22, 1892; s. Dennis and Catherine (Shea) S.; grad. high sch., Saraotga Springs, 1910; A.B., Cornell U., 1914; D. H. L. (honorary), Skidmore College, 1967; unmarried. Began newspaper work at Saratoga, 1910; later condr. of column in N.Y. World. Served as 2d lt. inf., World War. Mem. Corporation of Yaddo (Saratoga Springs). Clubs: Dutch Treat, The Players. Author: Life and Times of Martha Hepplethwaite, 1926; The Adventures of an Oaf (with Herb Roth), 1927; Innocent Bystanding, 1928; Broccoli and Old Lace, 1931; In One Ear, 1933; A Pearl in Every Oyster, 1938; Sullivan at Bay (pub. in England), 1939; A Rock in Every Snowball, 1946; The Night the Old Nostalgia Burned Down, 1953; Sullivan Bites News (with Sam Berman), 1954; A Moose in the Hoose, 1959. Contbr. New Yorker mag. Home: Saratoga Springs, N.Y., Died Feb. 19, 1976.

SULLIVAN, RUSSELL, amateur astronomer; b. Indianapolis, Ind., Nov. 23, 1881; s. George Robert and Annie Moore (Russell) S.; B.A., Yale, 1905; m. Marguerite Bowen, Oct. 21, 1916. Fellow A.A.A.S., Am. Geog. Soc., Royal Astron. Soc., England; mem. Am. Astron. Soc., Am. Assn. of Variable Star Observes, Societe Astronomique de France, S.A.R., Indiana Soc. Republican. Presbyn. Clubs: Indianapolis Literary, University, Dramatic, Contemporary, Columbia, Country, Woodstock; Royal Societies (London). Contbr. astron. articles in Popular Astronomy, Scientific American Supplement, etc. Home: Indianapolis, Ind.†

SUMMERS, CLEON AUBREY, lawyer; b. Hiseville, Ky., Dec. 9, 1881; s. Andrew Murray and Eliza Ann (Patterson) S.; student Liberty Coll., Glasgow, Ky., 1899-1902; A.B., Western Ky. State Teachers Coll., 1906; LL.B., Cumberland U., 1907; m. Josephine Beck, Dec. 16, 1914 (died July 9, 1926) m. 2d, Phyrne Hardy, Oct. 28, 1931; 1 son, Edward Hardy. Admitted to Ky. bar, 1907; began practice in Glasgow; county atty. Barren County 1910-14; admitted to Okla. bar, 1914; practiced in Wagoner, 1914-19; county atty. Wagoner County, 1916-19; asst. U.S. atty. Eastern Dist. of Okla., 1919-21; practiced in Muskogee, Okla., from 1921; actg. U.S. atty. Eastern District Oklahoma, 1934-35, U.S. atty., 1935-52; general practice of law, from 1952. Formerly chairman Oklahoma State Election Board; chairman Dem. Com. of Congressional Dist. Mem. Pi Kappa Alpha. Baptist (deacon). Mason (K.T., Shriner). Elk. Home: Muskogee, Okla.†

SUMMERS, LIONEL MORGAN, govt. ofcl., educator; b. Madrid, Spain, Nov. 20, 1905; s. Thomas Maddin and Natalia (Gorainoff) S.; B.S., Princeton, 1927; J.D., George Washington Law Sch., 1930; spl. courses (Am. Field Service fellow) Academie de droit internat., The Hague, 1930, Institut des hautes etudes Internationales, Paris, 1930-31; m. Lucy O'Bryan Bailey, Mar. 22, 1930; children—Lucy Bailey, Natalia. Research com. on Latin Am., Columbia, 1930; staff Law Library of Congress, 1931-33; with Burlingame, Nourse & Pettit, 1933-34; atty. on Am. Agy., Gen. Claims Arbitration, U.S.-Mexico, 1934-36; legal div. R.E.A. (later merged with Office of Solicitor of Dept. Agr.), 1936-43; apptd. Dept. State, 1943, to Fgn. Service, 1947, legal adviser to Am. embassy, Rome, 1947-52, agt. of U.S. before Italian-U.S. Conciliation Commn., 1949-52; fgn. service officer, 1952-62, counselor of legation, Tripoli and Benghazi, 1952-54; consul gen. Yokohama, 1955-59; counselor of embassy, Tokyo, Japan, 1959-60; U.S. mem. U.S.-Japanese Property Commn., 1957-60; dean Sch. Fgn. Affairs, Fgn. Service Inst., 1960-62; asso. prof. polit. sci. Rollins Coll., Winter Park, Fla., from 1962. Admitted to D.C. bar Mem. Am. Soc. Internat. Law, Order of Coif, Phi Delta Phi. Home: Winter Park, Fla. Died Mar. 29, 1975.

SUNDHEIM, TRIG, treas. Land O'Lakes Creameries, Inc. Address: Minneapolis, Minn. Deceased.

SUOZZO, JOHN, elec. mfg. co. exec.; b. N.Y.C., June 24, 1921; s. Xavier and Mary (Tolve) S.; B.E.E., Pratt Inst., 1942; postgrad. U. Pitts., 1942; m. Eileen L. Lavery, Sept. 18, 1948; children—John P., Marie, Diane, Thomas, Robert, Lorraine, Virginia, James. With Westinghouse Electric Corp., Jersey City, 1943-73, mgr. engring. dept., 1966-69, product mgr. escalators and hydraulic elevators, 1969-70, div. gen. mgr. high speed elevator div., 1970-73. Mem. Mayor's Adv. Com. Jersey City, 1971. Registered profl. engr., N.J. Mem. I.E.E.E. Patentee in field. Home: Hackensack, N.J. Died July 15, 1973.

SURRAN, EDNA M. WALSH, (Mrs. Carl Alger Surran), writer, clubwoman; b. Chgo., Jan. 27, 1895; d. Francis Walter and Ida May (Wiley) Walsh; grad. N.J. State Tchrs. Coll., 1912; m. Carl Alger Surran, Sept. 26, 1916 (dec. June 1970); 1 son, Carl Robert. Tchr., Atlantic City Pub. Sch., 1912-16, 18-19, Mem. hostess com. Miss. Am. Pageant, 1935-53; chmn. fund raising Children's Seashore House; founder Edna M. Surran Award for Good Citizenship, 1943; mem. Rent Control Bd.; pres. Women's Aux. Atlantic County Med. Soc., 1935-36; chmn. Atlantic unit Am. Woman's Vol. Services, 1943-45, v.p. N.J., 1944, nat. bd. dirs., 1944; pres. Beta Delphian, 1929-45. Worker, Republican Party; adviser Volusia County Rep. Club. Recipient awards for vol. services USAAF, City of Atlantic City, USO, A.R.C. Club: Atlantic City Woman's (charter mem., pres. 1956-57). Mem. Am. Mothers Assn., Am. Legion Aux., Internat. Platform Assn., Nat., Fla. Audubon socs. Clubs: Deland Women's, Deland Bridge, Deland Tourists. Home: DeLand Fla., Died June 1974.

SUSANN, JACQUELINE, author; m. Irving Mansfield. Early career as actress, appearing on TV programs including Studio One. Author: Every Night, Josephine, 1963; Valley of the Dolls, 1966; The Love Machine, 1969; One Is Not Enough, 1973. Home: Long Island, N.Y. Died Sept 21, 1974.

SUTHERLAND, ABBY ANN, (Mrs. William Furby Brown), educator; b. Cape Breton, N.S., Can., Jan. 6, 1871; d. John and Mary Ann (Gwinn) Sutherland; brought to U.S., 1892; A.B., Radcliffe Coll., 1899; hon. Ph.D., Temple U., Phila., 1916; A.M., U. Pa., 1950; Ph.D., U. of Pennsylvania, 1957; m. William Furby Brown, Sept. 20, 1916. Teacher Bradford (Mass.) Acad., 1899-1902; instr. English, Ogonitz Sch., Rydal, Pa., from 1902, prin., pres., from 1909; president Ogontz Junior College; director Ogontz White Mountain Camp. Member Progressive Edn. Assn. of Headmistresses, Foreign Policy Assn. Republican. Presbyterian. Clubs: Huntingdon Valley Golf, Art Alliance (v.p.), Republican Women of Pa. Author of pamphlets, Talks with Girls, General Information Guide, Increasing the Vocabulary; Orthography; Book of Devotions; 100 Years of Ogontz, 1958. Address: Ogontz Center, Pa.†

SUTHERLAND, EARL WILBUR, JR., physician, educator; b. Burlingame, Kan., Nov. 19, 1915; B.S., Washburn Coll., 1937; M.D., Washington U., St. Louis, 1942; div.; 3 children. Intern, Barnes Hosp., St. Louis, 1942; asst. in pharmacology Washington U. Sch. Medicine, 1940-42, instr., 1945-46, biochemist, 1946-50, asst. prof., 1950-52, asso. prof., 1952-53; with OSRD, 1943-45; prof. pharmacology, dir. dept. Case Western Res. U. Sch. Medicine, Cleve., 1953-63; prof. physiology Vanderbilt U. Sch. Medicine, Nashville, from 1963; Distinguished prof. biochemistry Sch. Medicine, U. Miami, Coral Gables, Fla. Mem. panel on metabolism sect. biochemistry com. on growth NRC, 1953-54; pharmacologists, exptl. therapeutist USPHS, 1954-58; mem. pharmacological tng. com. NIH, 1958-62, 63-65, mem. arthritis and metabolic disease program com., 1966—. Recipient Nobel prize in medicine and physiology for research in hormones, 1971. Mem. Nat. Acad. Sci., A.A.A.S., Soc. Biol. Chemists, Am. Chem. Soc., Soc. Pharmacology. Research on enzymatic and hormonal aspects of carbodhydrate metabolism, mechanism of action of hormones and drugs, intermediary carbohydrate metabolism, cyclic nucleotides. Died May 1974.

SUTHERLAND, ROBERT EDWARD LEE, coll. pres.; b. Booneville, Miss., May 1, 1878; s. W. W. (M.D.) and Anne Naomi (Nelson) S.; L.I., Peabody Coll. for Teachers, Nashville, Tenn., 1905, B.S., 1929, A.M., 1930; m. Ollie U. Wallace, Oct. 16, 1910; children—Bolivar Lee, Miriam Ursula, Annette. Prin. high sch., Pisgah, Miss., 1905, Wheeler, 1906; county supt. edn., Prentiss Co., 1908-16; supt. Alcorn County Agrl. High Sch., 1917-19, Hinds Co. Agrl. High Sch., 1919-23; pres. Hinds Co. Jr. Coll., 1923-30; pres. Miss. State Coll. for Women, 1930-35; dist. supervisor adult edn. program, Tupelo, Miss., from 1935. Home: Tupelo, Miss.†

SUTHERLAND, THOMAS HENRY, physician; b. Cin., July 11, 1898; s. Thomas Henry and Anne H. Sutherland; M.D., Johns Hopkins, 1923; m. Virginia Llewellyn, Aug. 21, 1950; 1 dau., Alice Anne. Intern, Grant Hosp., Columbus, O., 1923-24, B.F. Goodrich Hosp., Akron, O., 1924-25; lectr. med. law Ohio State U., Columbus, 1940-72. Served with U.S. Army, World War I. Diplomate Am. Bd. Preventive Medicine. Fellow Aerospace Med. Assn. (sec.-treas., bus. mgr. emeritus). Home: Marion, O. Died Jan. 12, 1972; buried Marion, O.

SUTTON, CHARLES EDWARD, physician; b. Flora, Ill., Apr. 26, 1914; s. Charles Edward and Della Leah Sutton; M.D., St. Louis U., 1937, M.Sc. in Obstetrics and Gynecology, 1952; m. Louise Bernice Chandler, Aug. 30, 1936; children—Salle (Mrs. Robert S. Mendelsohn), Charles Edward III. Intern, DePaul Hosp., St. Louis; U. in obstetrics and gynecology St. Louis U., 1949-52. Served as lt. (j.g.), M.C., USNR, 1942-43. Diplomate Am. Bd. Obstetrics and Gynecology. Mem. A.M.A. Home: Playa del Rey, Cal. Died July 4, 1974; buried Illmo, Mo.

SUTTON, DAVID NELSON, lawyer; b. King and Queen County, Va., July 14, 1895; s. David Covington and Mancha (House) S.; A.B., U. Richmond, 1915, LL.D., 1966; grad. legal dept. U. Va., 1921; LL.D., Atlantic Christian Coll., U. Richmond; m. Frances Lillard Shipman Oct. 4, 1924; children—David Nelson, Frances Witherspoon (Mrs. Raymond E. Oliver). Admitted to Va. bar, 1920; practiced law, West Point, Va., from 1921; dir., gen. counsel Citizens & Farmers Bank, West Point., from 1927; atty. Commonwealth King William County, 1928-46; asso. counsel prosecution Internat. Mil. Tribunal for Far East, in trial Tojo, other Japanese polit. leaders, 1946-48. Vice chmn. Va. commn. for study and report hospitalization of indigent persons, 1945, adv. legislative council to study hosp., med. care of indigents, 1952-53. Va. del. Nat. Dem. Convs., 1936, 40, 44. Trustee Lynchburg Coll., U. Richmond, Lexington Theol. Sem. Served as 1st lt., cav. U.S. Army, 1917-19. Fellow Am. Bar Found., Am. Coll. Trial Lawyers; mem. Soc. Internat. Law., Am., Va. (pres. 1948-49) bar assns., Va. State Bar (mem. council 1945-54, chmn. com. on continuing legal edn. 1949-52), Acad. Polit. Sci., Am Judicature Soc., Raven Soc. of U. Va., Gen. Alumni Soc. U. Richmond (pres. 1953-54), Phi Beta Kappa, Delta Sigma Rho, Sigma Upsilon. Mem. Disciples Christ Ch. (pres. Va. state conv. 1942, v.p. internat. conv. 1947). Clubs: West Point Country; Commonwealth (Richmond); Kiwanis (gov. Capital dist. 1940). Home: West Point, Va. Died Nov. 21, 1974.

SUTTON, FRANK SPENCER, actor; b. Clarksville, Tenn., Oct. 23, 1923; s. Frank Sims and Thelma Doris (Spencer) S.; B.S., Columbia, 1952; m. Toby M. Igler, Aug. 26, 1949; children—Joseph David, Amanda Lee. Actor appearing on stage and in motion pictures and television; stage credits include Barretts of Wimpole St., Andersonville Trial; motion pictures include Marty, Four Boys and a Gun, Town Without Pity, Satan Bug; appeared on all maj. networks, 1948-63; starred as Sgt. Carter in Gomer Pyle USMC, 1964-68; co-star Jim Nabors Variety Hour, 1969, 70-71. Served with AUS, 1943-46; PTO. Home: Beverly Hills, Cal. Died June 28, 1974.

SUTTON, JOSEPH WILSON, clergyman; b. Black, Md., June 6, 1881; s. John Carville and Susan Elizabeth (Heighe) S.; A.B., Washington Coll., Md., 1900, M.A., 1904, D.D., 1920; B.D., Gen. Theol Sem., 1905. Ordained priest, P.E. Ch., 1905; rector St. James' Ch., Port Deposit, Md., 1905-07; curate St. Paul's Ch., Baltimore, Md., 1907-10; Trinity Ch., New York, 1910-14; vicar Trinity Chapel, New York, 1914-43; rector St. Stephen's Church, N.Y., from 1943. Trustee Gen. Theological Sem.; trustee Church Army. Trustee Youth Consultation Service, Diocese of New York. Author: Peace Through the Cross, Our Life of Prayer, The Cross Our Hope. Home: New York City, N.Y.†

SVERDRUP, LEIF JOHN, civil engr.; b. Sulen, Norway, Jan. 11, 1898; s. John Edward and Agnes (Vollan) S.; came to U.S., 1914; B.A., Augsburg Coll., 1918; B.S. in C.E., U. Minn., 1921; D.Eng. (hon.) U. Mo. Sch. Mines and Metallurgy, 1952, Norwich U., 1969; D.Sc., Washington U., St. Louis, 1960; D. Aerospaceology (hon.), Air Force Systems Command, 1967; D.Litt. (hon.), Webster Coll., 1972; m. Helen L. Egilsrud, Nov. 26, 1924; 1 son, Johan Norman.

Designer and resident engr. Minn. Hwy. Dept., 1921-22; designer Mo. Hwy Dept., 1922-23, engr. in charge constrn. Mo. River bridges, 1922-23, chief bridge engr., 1924-28; partner Sverdrup & Parcel, cons. engrs., 1928-48; chmn. bd. Sverdrup & Parcel & Assos. Inc., St. Louis Sverdrup & Parcel Internat, Inc., Spire Corp.; chmn. bd., chief exec. officer Sverdrup & Parcel and Assos. N.Y. Inc., ARO, Inc., Inc; dir. First Union, Inc., St. Louis Nat. Baseball Club, Inc., Midcoast Aviation Services, Inc., 1st Nat. Bank St. Louis, Northwestern States Portland Cement Co., St. Louis Nat. Baseball Club, Inc., Midcoast Aviation Services, Inc., 1st Nat. Bank St. Louis, Northwestern States Portland Cement Co., St. Louis County Water Co., St. Louis Union Trust Co., Norwegian Am. Line Agy., Inc., Transp. Tech. Inc. Spl. cons. U.S. Corps Engrs. on airports in South Sea Islands, Australia and New Zealand, cons. on protable mil. bridges; spl. cons. Pub. Works Adminstrn. on Lake Washington Pontoon bridge, Seattle; mem. bd. inquiry into failure of Tacoma Narrows bridge, also mem. cons. bd. on re-design. Served in U.S. Army, 1918-19; col. to maj. gen. Engrs. Corps, AUS, 1942-46; chief engr. overseas duty PTO; comdg. gen. 102d Res. Inf. Div., 1947-58. Engr. adv. plan and devel. Ida. atomic reactor testing sta. Decorated Silver Star, D.S.M., Purple Heart, D.S.C., Legion of Merit, Philippine Distinguished Service Star; comdr. Order Bir. Empire, Croix de Guerre with palm; comdr. with star Order of St. Olav. Recipient Outstanding Achievement medal U. Minn., 1950; Honor award U. Mo., 1952; Man of Yr. award St. Louis Globe Democrat, 1956; Lloyd Kimbrough medal aAm. Inst. Steel Constrn., 1959; Golden Beaver award The Beavers, 1959 Outstanding Service award Nat. Soc. Profl. Engrs., 1961; Outstanding Tech. Achievement award Cons. Engrs. Council, 1964; Gold Medal Achievement award Engrs. Club St. Louis, 1966; Bronze Medal Meritorious Civilian Service award and lapel rosette Mobility Adv. Group, 1967; Distinguished Exec. award Sales & Marketing Executives-St. Louis, 1967; Citizen of Yr. award Mo. Moose Assn., 1967; Man of Yr. award Kiwanis, 1967; Silver Beaver award Boy Scouts Am., 1967, Silver Antelope award, 1968; Free Enterprise award Jr. Achievement, 1969; St. Louis award, 1970; Engr. of Yr. award Mo. Soc. Profl. Engrs., 1971; Distinguished Service medal Royal Arch Masons, 1971; Levee Stone award Downtown St. Louis, Inc., 1972. Mem. Am. Soc. Mil. Engrs. (award of appreciation 1970), Am. Soc. C.E. (hon.), Am. Inst. Cons. Engrs., Am. Ry. Engring. Assn. Lutheran. Clubs: St. Louis, St. Louis Country, Bogey, Old Warson Country, Racquet, Noonday, Engineers (St. Louis); Kansas City (Mo.); Links (N.Y.C.); Lyford Cay (Bahamas). Home: St. Louis, Mo., Died Jan. 2, 1976.

SVIEN, HENDRIK JULIUS, physician; b. Dennison, Minn., Feb. 28, 1911; s. Olaus J. and Caren (Bestul) S.; M.D., U. Minn., 1937, M.S. in Surgery, 1941; m. Nancy Weems Gatch, June 8, 1946; children—Karen Orytha, Dagny Elizabeth, Hendrik Thomas. Intern, U. Minn. Hosp., 1937-38; fellow in surgery Mayo Found. and Clinic, Rochester, Minn., 1938-42, fellow in neurosurgery, 1942, 46-48, cons. in neurosurgery, 1948-72; mem. faculty Mayo Grad. Sch. Medicine, 1949-72, prof. clin. neurosurgery, 1966-72. Chmn. Found for Internat. Edn. in Neurosurgery. Served to lt. comdr. M.C., USN, 1942-46. Recipient Distinguished Alumnus award St. Olaf Coll., Northfield, Minn., 1957. Diplomate Am. Bd. Neurol. Surgeons, N.Y. Acad. Scis., Phi Beta Kappa. Developer work on surg. treatment of torticollis and pituitary tumors; research in malignant lesions of the brain; use of steroids to control cerebral edema; circulatory problems involving the central nervous system; trigeminal neuralgia. Home: Rochester, Minn., Died June 29, 1972; buried Dennison, Minn.

SWAN, JAMES EDWARD, physician; b. Pitts., July 17, 1920; s. Frank Milton and Minnie Delilah (Clark) S.; M.D., Howard U., 1948; m. Elaine Manns, Sept. 27, 1941; 1 dau., Gail S. Cazenave. Intern, Freedmens Hosp., Washington, 1948-49, asst. resident in obstetrics and gynecology, 1949-52, resident, 1952-53, later jr. attending; jr. attending White Meml. Hosp., Temple Hosp., Los Angeles County Gen. Hosp.; asso. staff Queen of Angels Hosp.; courtesy staff Cedars of Lebanon Hosp. (all Los Angeles); former instr. obstetrics and gynecology Howard U.; asst. prof. Loma Linda U. Served to capt. M.C., USAF, 1954-56. Diplomate Am. Bd. Obstetrics and Gynecology. Fellow Am. Coll. Obstetrics and Gynecology; mem. A.M.A., Nat. Med. Assn., Kappa Pi, Omega Psi Phi. Home: Los Angeles, Cal. Died Nov. 27, 1972; buried Rosedale Meml. Cemetery, Los Angeles, Cal.

SWAN, NATHALIE HENDERSON, (Mrs. Joseph R.), trustee Teachers Coll., Columbia; b. N.Y. City, Dec. 7, 1881; d. Charles Rapallo and Jeanie Barham (North) Henderson; A.B., Barnard Coll., 1910; teaching diploma Columbia, 1910; m. Joseph R. Swan, Dec. 20, 1911. Report on visiting teachers included in 13th annual report N.Y. City Supt. Schs., 1910-11; trustee Teachers Coll., Columbia, from 1918; mem. sub-com. vocational training N.Y. City Mayor's Com. of Women; chmn. com. on edn. Women's City club, 1921-22, chmn. legislative com., 1925; mem. Com. of Mayors, Regents and Citizens apptd. to study adminstrn. city schs., 1920; mem. Friedsam Comm. governor's com. on sch. finance and adminstrn.), 1926; trustee Bennington Coll., 1926-32, 1938-43; member citizens com. on teachers salaries, N.Y. City, 1927; mem. governor's commn. on costs pub. edn. in N.Y. State, 1933; chmn. sch. defense aides under civilian defense volunteer orgn., Manhattan, 1941-42. Asst. dir. Child and Youth Services, in charge Youth Services, N.Y. City Civilian Defense Vol. Office. Life mem. N.E.A. Home: Farmington, Conn.†

SWARTHOUT, MAX VAN LEWEN, dean Coll. of Music; b. Pawpaw, Ill., Oct. 27, 1880; s. Teal and Ella Gladys (Smith) S.; student Balatka Musical Coll. and Gottschalk Musical Coll., Chicago, 1899-1902, Royal Conservatory of Music, Leipsig, Germany, 1902-05; Mus. D., Chicago Mus. Coll., 1943; m. Myrtle Edwards, Jan. 1, 1906; children—Rassele Edwards, John Max. Dorothy Jeanne (Mrs. Mark F. Jones, Jr.). Dir. music Oxford (O.) Coll. for Women, 1905-11; dir. music dept. Ill. Woman's Coll., Jacksonville, 1911-14; dir. Millilin Conservatory of Music, Decatur, Ill., 1914-23; prof. piano Coll. of Music, U. of Southern Calif., 1933-48, dean emeritus; trustee and mem. faculty, Los Angeles Conservatory of Music, from Sept. 1948. Mem. Music Teachers Nat. Assn. (sec. 1923). Calif. Music Teachers Assn. (pres. 1930-32), Phi Mu Alpha, Phi Kappa Phi. Democrat. Mason. Clubs: Musician's Guild of Los Angeles (pres. 1930-32). University. Home: Los Angeles, Cal.† 740270

SWARTZ, JACOB HYAMS, dermatologist; b. Russia, 1896; s. Aushur and Rose Schwartz; M.D., Harvard; m. Janet Heller, 1 son, Morton N. Intern, Boston City Hosp., 1920-21, resident in contagious diseases, 1921-22; tng. indermatology Mass. Gen. Hosp., Boston, 1922-23; fellow in mycology and histopathology, Harvard, 1923; practice medicine, specializing in dermatology, Boston, 1933-71; cons. dermatologist Addington Meml. Hosp., Jewish Meml. Hosp., Mass. Eye and Ear Infirmary; cons. dermatologist, also research and teaching hon. physician Mass. Gen. Hosp.; faculty clin. dermatology and mycology Harvard. Diplomate Am. Bd. Dermatology. Mem. Am. Acad. Dermatology, A.M.A., Am. Dermatol. Assn., New Eng. Dermatol. Soc., Soc. Investigative Dermatology. Author: Diagnosis and Treatment of Skin Diseases; Elements of Medical Mycology; Dermatology in General Practice. Home: Brookline, Mass., Died Aug. 17, 1971; buried Randolph, Mass.

SWARTZ, PETER WINFERD, univ. prof.; b. Bushton, Kan., July 15, 1880; s. Charles Wesley and Maggie (Rishel) S.; Life diploma Central State Coll., Edmond, Okla., 1905; A.B., Okla. U., 1910, A.M., 1911; A.M., Columbia, 1915; student U. of Chicago, summers 1907, 08, Northwestern, summers 1937, 38, Univ. Okla., 1935, 47; m. Edythe Belle Arnold, Aug. 17, 1913. Rural sch. teacher near Lahoma, Okla., 1899-1904, near Purcell, 1907-09; supt. Lindsay (Okla.) Schools, 1910-17, Okla. City Univ. Sept. 1927-49; vice pres. Farmers Exchange Bank, Lindsay, Okla., 1920-24; insp. farm products, Okla. State Market Commn., Okla. City, 1925-27; prof. psychol., Okla. City U., 1927-28, prof. bus. adminstrn., 1928-49, dean sch. of business, from 1951. Served in U.S. Army, 1917-19; disch. rank of 1st lt., Inf., 1919; capt. Q.M. Reserve Corps, from 1929, Rated training splist. in finance, World War II. Mem. Southwestern Econ. Assn., Okla. Ednl. Assn. Methodist. Home: Oklahoma City, Okla.†

SWEENEY, WILLIAM R., govt. ofcl.; b. Quaker Hill, Conn., July 11, 1911; s. Harry Clinton and Florence (Riley) S.; grad. Choats Sch., 1928; A.B., Harvard, 1932, student spl. program Bus. Sch., 1942-43; m. Doris Steffens, Aug. 12, 1949. Securities analyst, 1928-33; advt. exec., 1933-42, 46-47; with CIA, 1947-48; dep. asst. sec. mgmt. Dept. Air Force, 1948-52, also spl. cons. mgmt., 1952-62; pres. Wyo. Motors Corp., Melrose, Mass., 1952-54; mgmt. cons., Washington, 1954-57; v.p. Soundscriber Engring. Corp., North Haven, Conn., 1957-62; v.p. Daystrom, Inc., 1962-64; asst. dir. Adminstrv. Office of U.S. Cts., from 1964. Coordinator, USAF Advanced Mgmt. Program, George Washington U., 1954-59; industry adv. com. Dept. Def., 1960-62; chmn. small bus. com. Nat. Security Indsl. Assn., 1958-62; chmn. Fed. Records Council, from 1969. Served to col. USAAF, World War II; PTO. Decorated Bronze Star. Mem. Reformed Ch. Am. Clubs: Nat. Aviation (Washington); Leesburg (Va.) Country. Home: Bethesda, Md. Died July 12, 1974.

SWEET, FREDERIC E(LMORE), educator; b. Kirksville Mo., Jan. 13, 1900; s. Ralph A. and Ethel (Elmore) S.; Ph.B., Brown U., 1923, M.A., 1928; Docteur de L'universite, U. Strasbourg, 1934; m. Dorothy Myers, Aug. 21, 1933 (dec. Oct. 1946); children—John Lindsay, Geoffrey Ralph; m. Gertrude Evans, Aug. 27, 1955. Prof. German, Harwood Found., Beloit (Wis.) Coll., 1934-65, prof. emeritus, 1965—, vis. asso. prof. U. Wis. Rock County Center, Janesville, 1965-73. Mem. Modern Lang. Assn. Home: Beloit, Wis., Died Sept. 25, 1973; buried Beloit, Wis.

SWEETLAND, LEON HIRAM, clergyman, educator; b. Greene County, Ia., Mar. 25, 1880; s. William Albert and Celestia (McNall) S.; ed. Mo. State Normal Sch. (Warrensburg, Mo.), Carleton Coll. (Farmington, Mo.); A.B., Northwestern U., 1913, A.M., 1917; B.D., Garrett Bibl. Inst. (Northwestern U.), 1913; D.D., Southwestern Coll., 1936; LL.D., Kan. Wesleyan U., 1936; m. Ula Chandler, June 14, 1904; children—Leon Hiram, Jr., Paul Chandler, Emily Esther, Forrest Edward, Ralph Eugene, William Ernest, Ula Ruth. Teacher public and high schools, Missouri, 1898-1907; ordained to Methodist Episcopal ministry, 1907; pastor, Chitwood, Missouri, 1902-05, Moundville, 1907-08, Doe Run, 1908-10, Saint Luke's Church, Chicago, 1910-12, Zion City, Illinois, 1912-14, Lake Bluff, 1914-16, Maywood, Ill., 1916-17; pres. Mont. Wesleyan Coll., 1917-19; finance dept. M.E. Ch., 1919-20; pastor Havre, Mont., 1920-23. First Ch., El Paso, Tex., 1923-26, First Ch. and dir. Wesley Foundation, Hays, Kan., 1926-32, First Ch., McPherson, Kan., 1932-36; pres. Dakota Wesleyan U., 1936-37; pastor First Meth. Ch., Loveland, Colo., 1937-42, First Meth. Ch., La Junta, Colo., from 1942. Del. Gen. Conf. Meth. Ch., 1928, 1932. Progressive Republican. Mason, Odd Fellow, Lion. Address: La Junta, Colo.†

SWEITZER, J. MEARL, lawyer; b. Churchs Ferry, N.D., Apr. 16, 1900; s. Jpseph Studebaker and Mary (Barton) S.; LL.B., U. Minn., 1923; m. Margaret Orme, Nov. 10, 1932; children—James A., Mary (Mrs. John Porcella). With Employers Mutuals of Wausau (Wis.), from 1924, exec. v.p., 1959-60, pres., 1960-69; chmn., chief exec. officer Employers Ins. of Wausau, 1969-70, dir., mem. exec. com., from 1970; dir. Forward Communications Corp., 1st Am. Nat. Bank of Wausau, Wis., Central Wisconsin Bankshares, Wis. Valley Trust Co.; adv. council to bd. dirs. Am. Mut. Ins. Alliance, from 1970. Mem. Pres.'s Assn., Alpha Delta Phi, Phi Delta Phi. Home: Wausau, Wis. Died Feb. 13, 1975.

SWENSON, STANLEY PRESCOTT, educator; b. Wood Lake, Minn., Feb. 11, 1908; s. Walter and Tilda (Torgerson) S.; student St. Olaf Coll., 1926-27; B.S., U. Minn., 1932, M.S., 1935, Ph.D., 1936; m. Ollie Burris Veltum, June 19, 1936; children—Kathleen, Stanley Burris. Asso. prof. agronomy S.D. State U., 1936-41; asso. prof. agronomy Wash. State U., 1941-46, prof. agronomy, 1946-47, dean Coll. Agr., 1949-61, chief of party Exchange Program in Pakistan, 1958-63, dir. internat. programs, 1963-67; dean Faculty Agr., W. Pakistan Agrl. U., 1961-63; dean Faculty Agrl. Scis., Am. U., Beirut, Lebanon, 1967-73. Served with Mil. Govt., Germany, 1948. Mem. Am. Soc. Agronomy, A.A.A.S., Pullman C. of C., Lebanese Assn. for Advancement Sci., Sigma Xi, Phi Kappa Phi. Kiwanian. Contbr. articles profl. jours. Address: Sun City, Cal. Died Nov. 6, 1974.

SWICK, J. HOWARD, ex-congressman; b. New Brighton, Pa., Aug. 6, 1879; student Geneva Coll., Beaver Falls; M.D., Hahnemann Med. Coll., 1906, M.A., 1931; m. Esther Le Ethel Duncan, 1906; 1 son, J. Howard. Practiced at Beaver Falls many years; pres. Bur. of Health, Beaver Falls, 1907-14; pres. State Bank of Beaver Falls; dir. Moltrup Steel Products Co.; dir. Beaver Falls Thrift Corp., Peoples Bldg. and Loan Assn.; mem. 70th to 73 Congresses (1927-35), 26th Pa. Dist. Served in Med. Corps, U.S. Army, 18 mos., World War; with A.E.F., 12 mos.; col. Med. Res. Corps. Mem. Am. Legion, Vets. Foreign Wars. Republican. Methodist. Mason (32°, K.T., Shriner), K.P. Club: Lions. Home: Beaver Falls, Pa.†

SWIFT, EUGENE CLINTON, mfg. exec.; b. Ardmore, Pa., July 31, 1919; s. Archie Dean and Bernice (Thompson) S.; grad. Haverford Sch., 1938; A.B., Brown U., 1942; m. Mary Easton, Mar. 28, 1942; children—Eugene Clinton, Peter Easton, Stephen Evans, Paula Thompson. With Ins. Co. of N.Am., 1946-47; asst. sec.-treas. Sharples Corp., 1947-56, v.p. finance, 1956-58, pres., 1958-63, dir., 1956-63; v.p. Internat. Pennwalt Corp. (formerly Pennsalt Chems. Corp.), Phila., 1964-69, group v.p. equipment operations, 1970-73. Exec. bd., v.p. Valley Forge council Boy Scouts Am.; mem. Americans for Competitive Enterprise System. Trustee Brown U., The Haverford Sch. Served from pvt. to maj. USMC, 1941-46. Decorated Bronze Star medal. Mem. Machinery and Allied Products Inst., Planned Parenthood Assn. S.E. Pa. (dir.), Pa. Soc., Am. Mgmt. Assn. (dir. 1962-65, pres.'s mgmt roundtable 1961), Mfrs. Assn. Delaware Valley (v.p.), Process Equipment Mfrs. Assn. (pres. 1963). Presbyn. (trustee). Clubs: Union League, Racquet, Urban, Brown University (pres. Phila.); St. Davids Golf; Pine Valley Golf (Clementon, N.J.); Merion Golf (Ardmore, Pa.); Merion Cricket (Haverford, Pa); Midocean Golf (Bermuda). Home: Rosemont, Pa. Died July 28, 1973; buried Valley Forge Gardens, King of Prussia, Pa.

SWIFT, JOHN EDWARD, judge; b. Milford, Mass., Dec. 7, 1879; s. Thomas J. and Mary (McDonough) S.; A.B., Boston Coll., 1899, LL.D., 1933; LL.B., Boston University, 1902; LL.D., Loyola College, Baltimore, Md., 1948; m. Emily L. Lee, Apr. 18, 1917; children—John Edward, Marilyn Isobel, Francis Lee, Nancy Lee. Admitted to Mass, Bar, 1903; in gen. practice of law, Boston, 1903-33; mem. U.S. Supreme Court from 1917; apptd. to Superior Court of Mass. for life, 1933; prof. of law, Boston Coll. Law Sch., 1931-33; mem. adv. faculty Boston Coll. Sch. Social Work. Trustee St. Elizabeth's Hosp., Boston. Served on appeal bd. Selective Service, World War II. Decorated by Pope Pius XII as Knight Comdr. of the Order of St. Gregory the Great, 1942; Knight Grand Cross of the Order of St. Gregory the Great, 1946. Mem. Catholic Socality, Am. Bar Assn., Mass. State Bar Assn., Worcester Co. Bar Assn., Am. Irish Hist. Soc., Charitable Irish Soc.

K.C. (member supreme bd. dirs., 1927-39, dep. supreme knight, 1939-45, supreme knight from 1945). Home: Milford, Mass.*†

SWIFT, RAYMOND W(ALTER), educator; b. E. Longmeadow, Mass., June 12, 1895; s. Harry Brewster and Ida Marietta (Kibbe) S.; B.S., Univ. of Mass., 1920; M.S., Pa. State Coll., 1925; Ph. D., Univ. of Rochester, 1931; m. Laura Adams Dickinson, August 25, 1926; children—Raymond Emory, Elizabeth Dickinson. Analytical chemist, Mass. Exptl. Sta., 1920-23; asst. in animal nutrition, Pa. State Coll., 1923-28, asso., 1928-31; asst. in physiology, Univ. of Rochester, 1930-31 (on leave from Pa. State Coll.); asst. prof. animal nutrition, Pa. State Coll., 1931-35, asso. prof., 1935-38, prof., from 1938, head Dept. of Animal Nutrition from 1946. Served U.S. Army, A.E.F., 1917-19. Mem. Am. Inst. Nutrition, A.A.A.S., Am. Assn. Univ. Profs., Am. Soc. Animal Prodn., Kappa Gamma Psi, Phi Lambda Upsilon, Gamma Sigma Delta, Phi. Kappa Tau, Sigma Xi. Republican. Methodist. Contbr. numerous papers dealing with protein and energy metabolism, research in fundamental principles of nutrition to professional and tech. jours. Home: State College, Pa. Died July 11, 1975; buried Centre City Meml. Park, State College.

SWIGART, CLYDE ARTHUR, oil corp. ofcl.; b. Arroyo Grande, Cal., Nov. 5, 1888; s. Frank William and Mattie Susan (Rice) S.; A.B., Stanford, 1911; m. Blanche McCiel, May 21, 1937; children—Clyde Arthur, Jr., Wayne Woodman. Various positions pipeline dept. Standard Oil Co. (Cal.), 1911-43, mgr. pipeline dept., 1943-49, also v.p. Standard Pipeline Co.; v.p. Trans-Arabian Pipe Line Co., 1949-51, pres., 1951-56, chmn. bd. dirs. from 1956. Decorated officer Order of Cedars, Leganon. Mem. Am. Petroleum Inst. Clubs: Presidio Golf, Mchts. Exchange, (San Francisco); Univ. (N.Y.C.). Home: Beirut, Lebanon. Died June 1973.

SWIGART, LAVERN LAKE, surgeon; b. Maquon, Ill., Aug. 12, 1918; s. Arthur Lake and Ohnah Mae (Flinn) S.; M.D., Northwestern U., Northwestern U., 1945, M.S. in Anatomy, 1948; m. Charlene Gustat, Dec. 28, 1947; children—Peter Lake, Charyl Allison. Intern Wesley Meml. Hosp., Chgo., 1944-45; resident Passavant Meml. Hosp., Chgo., 1949-52, fellow in surgery, 1952-53; asso. surgeon Cook County Hosp., Chgo., 1953; practice medicine, specializing in surgery, 1954-70; attending staff St. Francis Sanitarium, Riverside Hosp., E.A. Conway Hosp. (all Monroe, La.), Williamson (W.Va.) Meml. Hosp., courtesy staff Crossett (Ark.) Health Center; asso. chief surgery Meml. Med. Center, Williamson, 1956-64. Served to lt. (j.g.) M.C., USNR, 1945-46. Named hon. Ky. col. Diplomate Am. Bd. Surgery. Fellow A.C.S.; mem. A.M.A. Home: Williamson, W.Va., Died Feb. 23, 1970; interred Mountain View Memory Gardens, Williamson, W.Va.

SWINFORD, MAC, judge; b. Cynthiana, Ky., Dec. 23, 1899; s. M.C. and Allie (McKee) S., LL.B., U. Va., 1925, postgrad. 1924-25; LL.D., Salmon P. Chase Law Sch.; m. Benton Peterson, Nov. 17, 1927; children—Mary (Mrs. McKay Reed, Jr.), John, Sally (Mrs. Hall Kinney), Alice (Mrs. Bruce Kolbe), Ann Gregg (Mrs. Delmer D. Dunn). Admitted to Ky. bar, 1922; practiced at Cynthiana from 1922; U.S. dist. atty. for Eastern Dist. of Ky., 1933-37; judge U.S. Dist. Ct. for Eastern and Western Dists. of Ky. from Sept. 11, 1937. Mem. Ky. Ho. of Reps., 1926-29 Mem. Jud. Conf. U.S., 1966-69. Mem. Am., Ky., Fed., Harrison County bar assns., Sigma Nu. Democrat. Presbyn. Club: Inquisitors. Author: Kentucky Lawyer. Home: Cynthiana, Ky. Died Feb. 3, 1975; buried Cynthiana, Ky.

SWINGLE, WILLIAM S., orgn. exec.; b. Kittanning, Pa., Oct. 11, 1891; s. William Martin and Lydia T. (Schmauk) S.; B.S., U. Pa., 1915; m. Helen Louise Thompson, 1925 (died 1940); m. 2d, Marion Bush Cross, 1944. Electrical engr. U.S. Cast Iron Pipe Co., 1915-19; asst. treas. Consolidated Steel Corp. (export), 1919-22; credit mgr. Asia Banking Corp., 1922-23, J. Henry Schroeder Banking Corp., 1923-25; mgr. fgn. credit interchange bur. and dir. fgn. dept., Nat. Assn. Credit Men, 1925-38, asst. treas., 1930-38, comptroller, 1931-38; vice pres. Nat. Fgn. Trade Council, 1938-47, vice chmn., 1943-45, director from 1943, executive vice pres., 1947-50, pres., 1950-62. Lectr. N.Y. U., Columbia, 1922-30. Mem. executive com. world trade center, N.Y. World's Fair, 1940; mem. adv. coms. Econ. Defense Bd., Bd. Econ. Warfare, Office Econ. Warfare, Lend-Lease Adminstrn., Fgn. Econ. Adminstrn., U.S. Dept. Interior, 1940-45; mem. Fgn. Commerce Com., U.S. C. of C., 1945-52, adv. com. Fgn. Service Depts., State and Commerce; adv. com. Export-Import Bank of Washington. Recipient Capt. Robert Dollar Memorial award, 1956. Member of Council of Foreign Relations, S.R., Phi Delta Theta, Eta Kappa Nu. Clubs: Wianno (Mass.); India House (member board of governors); Glen Ridge (New Jersey) Country; Suburban (U. of Pa.). Contbr. surveys and articles to professional publs. Home: Montclair, N.J. Died Aug. 2, 1973.

SWINNERTON, JAMES GUILFORD, artist; b. Eureka, Cal., Nov. 13. 1875; s. James Guilford and Cecile (Beauregard) S.; ed. pub. schs. and art sch.; m. 2d, Mrs. Gretchen Staples, Jan. 18, 1936. Began as cartoonist on San Francisco Examiner, 1892, continued as cartoonist and artist on various Hearst publs.; created comic strip "Little Jimmy," "Canyon Kiddies" in Good Housekeeping mag.; also portrayer of Am. Indians and painter of desert landscape. Clubs: Bohemian, Family, Calif. Art (San Francisco). Home: Los Angeles, Cal. Died Sept. 5, 1974.

SYLVESTER, ALBERT LENTHALL, finance co. exec.; b. Church Hill, Norwell, Mass., May 6, 1903; s. Albert Lenthall and Amy Winifred (Dinzey) S.; student St. Paul's Sch., Concord, N.H., 1916-20; A.B., Amherst Coll., 1924; M.B.A., Harvard, 1927; m. Elizabeth Edwards, May 5, 1933; children—Albert Lenthall, Susan E. (Mrs. Robert F. Hopwood), Amy D., Duncan P. Mem. research faculty Harvard Grad. Sch. Bus. Adminstrn., 1927-28; with Hornblower & Weeks, N.Y.C., 1928-32; v.p., dir. Cromwell & Cabot, Inc., Boston, 1935-38; pres., dir. Fidelity Fund, Inc., 1935-38; pres. W. Va. Water Service Co., 1952-60; pres. So. Gas & Water Co., 1960-65; chmn. bd. Acta Corp., Boston, 1965-73; trustee N.E. Gas & Elec. Assn.; dir. Fall River Gas Co. Trustee, treas. Retina Found. Mem. Alpha Delta Phi, Delta Sigma Rho. Republican. Episcopalian. Clubs: Harvard, Amherst (N.Y.C.); Cohasset Golf, Fort Hill. Home: Cohasset, Mass., Died June 16, 1973.

SYLVESTER, ROBERT, newspaper writer, columnist, author; b. Newark, Feb. 7, 1907; s. Robert Franklin and Edna (Brown) S.; spl. courses in journalism, lit. Yale and Columbia, 1925, 27; m. Bunty Pendleton, Oct. 1946; m. 2d, Kay Norton, May 14, 1956; m. 3d, Jane Meenan, July 31, 1965; children—Kathy Roberta, Karin Courtney. Editorial positions with New Haven Evening Register, N.Y. Post, N.Y. Evening World, N.Y. Am., N.Y. Daily News; pub. relations cons. for theatre, movies and individual theatrical stars, 1929-32; free-lance writer, 1927; drama and amusement writer N.Y. Daily News, from 1936; writer column Dream Street, from 1969; radio commentator WINS, NBC, 1962-63. Decorated officer Order of Carlos Manolo Cespedes (Cuba). Club: National Arts (N.Y.C.). Author: (novel and film) Dream Street, 1946; (novels) Rough Sketch, 1947, The Second Oldest Profession, 1949, Indian Summer, 1951, The Big Boodle, 1954; Tropical Paradise, 1958; No Cover Charge (history), 1955; Memoirs of an Unidentified Man, 1961; Notes of a Guilty Bystander, 1970; writer TV script Naked City, other scripts; (film) Joe Lewis Story, 1960; fiction and articles in Sat. Eve. Post, The New Yorker, Holiday, Esquire, other nat. mags.; non-ficition in nat. mags. Home: New York City, N.Y. Died Feb. 9, 1975.

SYMMES, LESLIE WEBB, business exec.; b. San Francisco, Calif., Oct. 13, 1879; s. Frank J. and Anna (Day) S.; B.S., U. of Calif., 1903; m. Grace M. Whittle, Aug. 14, 1912; children—Carol S. Kuechler, Day W. Spl. lecturer U. of Calif., Farmers Inst., 1903; on ranches, Nev., Calif. and Mex., 1904-05; with Forest Reserve, Bur. of Forestry and U.S. Reclamation Service, various periods; head of Leslie Symmes & Associates, agrl. engrs., San Francisco, V.p., gen. mgr. Poso Land & Products Co. (Hoover Farms), 1929-34. Spl. adviser to State of Yucatan, Mex., 1912; adviser Calif. Canning Peach Growers Assn., 1930-31; pres. Calif. Production Credit Corp., 1931-33. Dir. Calif. Cotton Cooperative Assn., Ltd. (pres. 1931-33); mem. Park and Playground Commn., Mill Valley; mem. Am. Soc. Agrl. Engrs., Delta Kappa Epsilon, Sigma Xi. Clubs: University (San Francisco); San Francisco Yacht (dir. 1939). Contbr. on agrl. topics. Home: Mill Valley, Cal.†

TAEUBER, IRENE BARNES (MRS. CONRAD TAEUBER), demographer, sociologist; b. Meadville, Mo., Dec. 25, 1906; d. Ninevah C. and Lily D. (Keller) Barnes; A.B., U. Mo., 1927; M.A., Northwestern U., 1928; Ph.D., U. Minn., 1931; LL.D., Smith Coll., 1960; D.Sc. (hon.), Western Coll. for Women, Oxford, O., 1965; m. Conrad Taeuber, July 1919; children—Richard Conrad, Karl Ernst. Instr. sociology, econs. U. Mo., 1923-27, Northwestern U., 1927-28, U. Minn., 1928-31, Mt. Holyoke Coll., 1931-34; research asso. Office Population Research, Princeton, 1936-61, sr. research demographer, 1962-74; vis. prof. Sch. Hygiene and Pub. Health, Johns Hopkins, 1962-64; cons. internat. statistics Bur. Census, 1940-50; cons. demography Pacific Sci. Bd., 1955-70, AID, 1963-70. Dir. census library project Library of Congress and Bur. of Census, 1941-44; manpower panel research and devel. bd. Dept. Def., 1947-53. Recipient Distinguished Achievement awards Univs. Mo., Minn. Fellow Am. Statis. Assn., A.A.A.S.; mem. Population Assn. Am. (pres. 1953-54), Am. Sociol. Soc. (sec. 1949), International Union for Sci. Study of Population (v.p.). Author: General Censuses and Vital Statistics in the Americas, 1943; (with F.W. Notestein) The Population of Europe and the Soviet Union, 1943; The Population of Tanganyika, 1949; (with Marshall C. Balfour) Public Health and Demography in the Far East, 1949; The Population of Japan, 1958; (with Conrad Taeuber) The Changing Population of the United States, 1958; (with Conrad Taeuber) People of the United States in the Twentieth Century, 1972. Home: Hyattsville, Md. Died Feb. 24, 1974; buried Md. Nat. Meml. Park, Laurel, Md.

TALIAFERRO, WILLIAM HAY, prof. microbiology; b. Portsmouth, Va., Feb. 10, 1895; s. William Hay and Mary Watkins (Leigh) T.; B.S., U. Va., 1915; Ph.D., Johns Hopkins, 1918; D.Sc. (hon.), U. N.C., 1946; LL.D. (hon.), Temple U., 1949; m. Lucy E. Graves, June 6, 1919. Instr., asso., and asso. prof. protozoology Johns Hopkins, 1919-24; asso. prof. parasitology U. Chgo., 1924-27, prof., 1927-39, Eliakim H. Moore Distinguished Service prof. parasitology 1939-54, prof. microbiology, 1954-60, prof. emeritus, 1960-73, chmn. dept. bacteriology and parasitology, 1932-54, chmn. dept. microbiology, 1954-60, asso. dean div. biol. scis., 1931-35, dean, 1935-44, adv. chancellor, 1944-48; sr. immunologist Argonne Nat. Lab., 1960-69, Mem. Com. on Biol. Warfare and Tropical Med., 1941-42, Panel of Pharmacology, 1942-45, Panel of Biochemistry of Antimalarials, 1942-45; mem. adv. bd. Gorgas Meml. Inst., Panama, 1936-69; bd. sci. dirs. Yerkes Labs. Primate Biology, 1942-69; mem. editorial com. on publs. in biology and medicine U. Chgo., 1941-60 Served to 2d lt. U.S. Army, 1917-19. Decorated Condecoracion al Mérito Bernardo O'Higgins 1st class (Chile); recipient Mary Kingsley medal Liverpool Sch. Tropical Medicine, 1949, Pasteur award Soc. Ill. Bacteriologists, 1962; hon. mem. faculty medicine U. Chile, 1953. Fellow Royal Soc. Tropical Medicine (hon.; Chalmers medal 1935); mem. Nat. Acad. Scis., Am. Philos. Soc., Am. Soc. Naturalists (v.p. 1939), Am. Soc. Parasitologists (council 1926-31, pres. 1933), Am. Soc. Tropical Medicine and Hygiene (pres. 1954-55), N.Y. Acad. Scis., Nat. Malaria Soc., Am. Assn. Immunologists, Brit. Soc. Immunology (hon.), Harvey Soc., Raven Soc., Phi Beta Kappa, Sigma Xi, Beta Theta Pi. Clubs: Quadrangle, University (Chgo.); Cosmos (Washington). Author: (with Dr. R. W. Hegner) Human Protozoology, 1924; Immunology of Parasitic Infections, 1929; (with L.G. Taliaferro and B.N. Jaroslow) Radiation and Immune Mechanisms, 1964. Editor: Medicine and the War, 1944. Contbr. articles on cytology and behavior of lower invertebrates, the cytology, genetics and immunology of animal parasites, cellular basis of immunity, the effects of X radiation on immunity, and the dynamics of antibody formation in biol. jours. Editor or joint editor Jour. Infectious Diseases, 1937-60; editorial com. Jour. Parasitology, 1934-43; joint editor (with J. H. Humphrey) Adv. Immunology, 1959-62; mem. editorial com. Ann. Rev. Microbiology, 1946-53; editorial bd. Revista di Malariologia, 1937-60. Home: LaGrange, Ill. Died Dec. 21, 1973; buried Presbyn. Cemetery, Alexandria, Va.

TALMADGE, CONSTANCE, actress; b. Bklyn., Apr. 19, 1900; d. Frederick and Margaret Talmadge; ed. Erasmus Hall, Bklyn.; m. John Pialogiou, Dec. 1921 (div.); m. 2d, Allaster MacIntosh (div. 1927); m. 3d. Townsend Netcher, May 8, 1929. Films include Intolerance; The Honeymoon; Who Cares; Mrs. Leffingwell's Boots; Romance and Arabella; Two Weeks; A Tempramental Wife; In Search of a Sinner; The Love Expert; The Perfect Woman; Mama's Affair; Woman's Place; Polly of the Follies; East is West; Dulcy; The Dangerous Maid. Address: Santa Monica, Cal. Died Nov. 23, 1973.

TAMM, IGOR, physicist; b. Vladivistok, USSR, July 8, 1895; s. Eugen and Olga (Davydova) T.; grad. Moscow State U., 1918, Dr. Physics and Math. Scis., USSR, 1933; m. Natalie Shuiskaia, Sept. 16, 1917; children—Irene, Eugen. Tchr. physics, univs. and tech. instns., Simpheropal and Odessa, 1919-22; with U. Moscow, 1924-71, prof., 1927-71, chair theoretical physics, 1930-37; head theoretical dept. Lebedev's Physical Inst., Acad. Scis. of USSR, Moscow, 1934-71, sr. physician virology and medicine Rockefeller U., 1967-71; research in quantum theory, also controlled thermonuclear reactions. Recipient (with P. Cerenkov, I. Frank), Nobel prize in physics for discovery and interpretation of Cerenkov's radiation, 1958; Lomonssov Medal, Academy Scis, USSR, 1968. Mem. Am. Acad. Arts and Scis. (foreign member), Acad. Scis. USSR, Acad. Scis. of Poland. Address: Moscow, Russia., Died Apr. 12, 1971.

TANAKA, KOTARO, ret. internat. jurist; b. Kagoshima, Japan, Oct. 25, 1890; s. Hideo and Kii (Iimori) T.; grad. faculty of law, Tokyo Imperial U., 1915; m. Mine Matsumoto, July 6, 1924; 1 son, Kozo. Student in U.S., Eng., France, Italy, Germany, 1919-22; asst. prof. law Tokyo Imperial U., 1917, prof., 1923-46, dean of faculty, 1937-39; minister of edn., Japan, 1946-47; mem. House of Peers, 1946; mem. House of Councillors, 1947-50; chief justice Supreme Ct. Japan, 1950-60; judge Internat. Ct. of Justice, The Hague, 1961-70; lectr. Italy, France, Belgium, 1936, Brazil, Argentina, Chile, Peru, Panama, Mexico, 1939. Mem. jury examiners for judicial career, Japan; collaborator with govt. for legislative matters of comml. law. Mem. Catholic Action (past pres.), Italo-Japanese Assn. (past pres.), Spanish-Japanese Cultural Assn. (past pres.), Japan Acad.; hon. mem. Am. Bar Assn. Author legal, cultural, ednl. and religious works. Home: Tokyo, Japan. Died Mar. 1974.

TANGLEY, EDWIN SAVORY (BARON TANGLEY OF BLACKHEATH), lawyer, business exec.; b. Egham, Surrey, Eng., June 29, 1899; s. Henry Herbert and Harriet (Elmes) T.; LL.B., LL.D. Queen's Coll., Taunton and Law Soc.'s Sch.; m. Gwendolen Judd, 1932; 4 children. Admitted solicitor, 1920; mem. firm Sydney Morse & Co., 1920-29, sr. partner, 1929-73; dir. Gen. Postal and Telegraph Censorship Dept., 1940-45; dir. Ultramar Co. Ltd., Imperial Continental Gas Assn.; dep. chmn. Rediffusion TV Ltd., Rediffusion Ltd. Mem.

Royal Commn. on Trade Unions and Employers Assn., 1965-68. Mem. Internat. C. of C. Home: Surrey, England. Died 1973.

TANSEY, PATRICK HENRY, army officer; b. Mt. Vernon, Ind., Jan. 26, 1894; s. Henry Stanislaus and Anna Katharine (Joest) T.; A.B., Christian Brothers Coll., 1914; B.S., U.S. Mil. Acad., 1918; grad. Army Engring Sch., 1925, Command and Gen. Staff Sch., 1936; m. Josephine Honora Baish. Dec. 28, 1918; children—Patrick Henry, Hubert E., Robert F., Mary Katharine, Philip Michael. Commd. 2d lt., 1918 and advanced through grades to maj. gen., 1944; instr. Engring. Sch., 1918; adj. 220th Engrs., 1919; troop comdr. 9th Mounted-Engrs., 1919; asst. prof. mil. sci., Ore. State Coll., 1920-24; instr. Dept. of Engring., U.S. Mil. Acad., 1928-32; asst. dist. engr., Honolulu, Hawaii, asst. public works adminstr. for Hawaii, 1932-35; asst. engr. commr. for Washington, 1936-40; comdr. 12th U.S. Engr., div. engr., 8th Div., Ft. Jackson, S.C., 1940-41; asst. engr., Gen. Hdqrs., 1941-42; War Dept. Gen. Staff, 1942-43; chief Logistics Group Operations Div., War Dept. Gen. Staff, 1943. Mem. Munitions Assignment Bd., Washington, 1944; mem. Com. of Combined Bds., Combined Chiefs of Staff, 1943-44; War Dept. mem. Logistic Staff of Joint Chiefs of Staff and Combined Chiefs of Staff; mem. Internat. Air Magellan Club, 1945; chief of engrs., G-4, and dep. comdr., and chief of operations, U.S. Army Service Command C., 8th Army, Philippine Island, Ryukus and Japanese home islands, 1945; civil property custodian, G.H.Q. SCAP, Tokyo, 1946-47; chief supply div. A.C. of S. G-4 Dept. of Army, 1949-53; field rep. Chief of Engrs., U.S. Army, 1953. Decorated D.S.M., Legion of Merit. Home: Blacksburg, Va., Died Feb. 3, 1976.

TAPP, ERNEST MARVIN, physician; b. West Mansfield, O., May 28, 1904; s. Ernest and Olive (Gilbert) T.; M.D., Ohio State U., 1930; m. Marjorie McIntosh, Nov. 26, 1931; children—Ernest George, Barbara (Mrs. Hal Freese). Intern, White Cross Hosp., Columbus, O., 1930-31; career physician VA, 1931-62; dir. VA Hosp., Poplar Bluff, Mo., 1952-57, 59-62, VA Hosp., Dearborn, Mich., 1957-59; health officer Butler County (O.), 1962; staff physician Kneibert Clinic, 1962-71. Dir., 1st Nat. Bank, Poplar Bluff. Served to col. M.C., AUS, 1944-46. Recipient certificate of appreciation Grand Junction lodge Elk Club, 1952, Presdl. certificate of appreciation, 1953. Diplomate Am. Bd. Internal Medicine. Fellow A.C.P.; mem. A.M.A., Am. Thoracic Soc., Am. Geriatrics Soc., Tri-County Med. Soc. (past sec.), Theta Kappa Psi (pres.). Presbyn. (elder, trustee). Rotarian (past pres. Poplar Bluff, certificate of gratitude 1957). Home: Poplar Bluff, Mo. Died Dec. 14, 1971; buried Meml. Gardens, Poplar Bluff, Mo.

TAPPERT, THEODORE GERHARDT, educator, editor; b. Meriden, Conn., May 5, 1904; s. Carl Reinhold and Magdalene (Drach) T.; student Wagner Coll., 1922-26, D.D., 1938; student Luth. Theol. Sem., 1926-29, fellow, 1930-31, D.D., Luther Coll., Pecorah, Ia., 1958; A.M., Columbia, 1931; postgrad. U. Pa., 1931-35; Litt.D., Muhlenberg Coll., 1943; D.D., U. Western Ont., 1959; m. Helen Louise Carson, May 29, 1937; children—Charles Carson, Frederick Drach, Eleanor Cochran, Paul Andrews. Instr., Luth Theol. Sem., Phila., 1931-36, asst. prof., 1936-38, prof. ch. history, 1938-73. Mng. editor Luth. Ch. Quar., 1938-49, 53-65; bd. publs. United Luth. Ch., 1944-56; editor Luth. World Rev., 1948-50; archivist Luth. Ministerium of Pa., 1940-73, Luth. Ch. in Am., 1962-73. Bd. dirs. Found. for Reformation Research, 1957-73. Author: (with H. Sasse) Here We Stand: Nature and Character of the Lutheran Faith, 1938; The Church in the Changing World, 1949; Our Neighbors' Churches, 1954; Luther's Letters of Spiritual Counsel, 1955; Luther in his Academic Role, 1959; Meaning and Practice of the Lord's Supper, 1961; Philip Jacob Spender's Pia Desideria, 1964; Luther's Table Talk, 1967. Editor, translator: (with J.W. Doberstein) The Journals of Henry Melchior Muhlenberg, 3 vols., 1942-58; Road to Reformation, 1946; The Book of Concord, 1959; Selected Writings of Martin Luther, 4 vols., 1967; Lutheran Confessional Theology in America, 1840-1880, 1972. Research cons. film Martin Luther. Home: Philadelphia, Pa. Died Dec. 25, 1973; inurned West Laurel Hill Cemetery, Philadelphia, Pa.

TARTAKOFF, JOSEPH, physician; b. Stoughton, Mass., Jan. 17, 1907; s. Abraham and Rose (Rodman) T.; M.D., Tufts U., 1929; m. Helen Herlihy, June 8, 1941; children—David Stephen, Alan Michael. Intern, Worcester (Mass.) City Hosp., 1930-32; resident in surgery Mt. Sinai Hosp., N.Y.C., 1932-33; resident in surgery Boston City Hosp., 1933-34, cons. surgery, until 1974; asso. div. surgery New Eng. Center Hosp., Boston; chief of surgery Mt. Auburn Hosp., Cambridge, Mass.; cons. Faulkner Hosp., Boston; thoracic surgeon Middlesex County Sanatorium; clin. prof. surgery Tufts U. Med. Sch., until 1974, clin. prof. surgery emetitus, 1974; lectr. in surgery Harvard. Diplomate Am. Bd. Surgery. Fellow A.C.S., Am. Coll. Chest Physicians; mem. Am. Thoracic Soc. Home: Cambridge, Mass. Died June 23, 1974; buried Mt. Auburn Cemetery, Cambridge, Mass.

TATUM, EDWARD LAWRIE, biochemist; b. Boulder, Colo., Dec. 14, 1909; s. Arthur Lawrie and Mabel (Webb) T.; A.B., U. Wis., 1931; M.S., 1932, Ph.D., 1934, also hon. degree; hon. degrees U. Notre Dame, Rutgers U., Trinity Coll., Gustavus Adolphus Coll., Yeshiva U., Northwestern U.; m. June Alton, 1934; children—Margaret Carol, Barbara Ann; m. 2d, Viola Kantor, 1956; m. 3d Elsie Bergland. Gen. Edn. Bd. fellow, U. Utrecht, Holland, 1936-37; research asso. biology Stanford, 1937-41, asso. prof. biology, 1942-45; asso. prof. botany Yale, 1945-46, prof. microbiology, 1946-48; prof. biology Stanford, 1948-56, prof. biochemistry, head dept., 1956-57; mem.-prof. Rockefeller U. 1957-75. Recipient Nobel prize for medicine and physiology, 1958. Mem. A.A.A.S., Am. Chem. Soc., Am. Philo. Soc., Am. Soc. Biol. Chemists, Bot. Soc. Am., Genetics Soc., Nat. Acad. Sci., Nat. Sci. Bd. Mem. editorial bds. profl. jours. Home: New York City, N.Y., Died Nov. 5, 1975.

TAUBENHAUS, LEON JAIR, physician; b. Newark, Del., Dec. 29, 1912; s. Jacob Joseph and Esther (Hirshenson) T.; A.B., Rice Inst., 1933; M.D., Tulane U., 1937; M.P.H., Harvard, 1955; L.H.D., Mass. Coll. Optometry, 1967; m. Marjorie Polon, Nov. 18, 1944 (div. 1966); children—Jair T. Pruitt, Marsha R.; m. 2d, Barbara B. Alpern, Sept. 6, 1969. Intern, Kings County Hosp., Bklyn., 1937-39; resident in surgery Mt. Sinai Hosp., N.Y.C., 1939-40; pvt. practice medicine, 1945-54; pub. health physician Mass. Dept. Pub. Health, 1955-57; dir. pub. health Brookline (Mass.) Health Dept., 1957-64; asso. in preventive medicine Beth Israel Hosp., Boston, 1959-68; asso. staff in medicine Peter Bent Brigham Hosp., Boston, 1962-68; dep. supt. for ambulatory services Boston City Hosp., 1964-66; dep. commr. for community health services Boston Dept. Health and Hosps., 1966-68; dir. community health services Beekman-Downtown Hosp., N.Y.C., 1968-73; lectr. pub. health Harvard Sch. Pub. Health, Boston, 1955-64; asst. clin. prof. pub. health Sch. Dental Medicine, Tufts U., Boston, 1960-62, lectr. preventive medicine Sch. Medicine, 1964-68; lectr. pub. health adminstrn. Florence Heller Grad. Sch. for Advanced Studies in Social Welfare, Brandeis U., Waltham, Mass., 1961-68; clin. prof. preventive medicine Boston U. Sch. Medicine, 1964-68; lectr. preventive medicine Harvard, 1964-68; lectr. pub. health and adminstrv. medicine Columbia Sch. Pub. Health and Adminstrv. Medicine, 1969-73. Mem. pub. edn. com. Nat. Found. for Kidney Disease, 1962-64; mem. day care center adv. com. Mass. Dept. Pub. Health, 1962-64, mem. glaucoma adv. com., 1964-66; mem. aging subcom. Mass. Task Force on Mental Health, 1964; mem. com. on nursing homes Mass. Hosp. Assn., 1965; mem. Mass. Legis. Study Commn. on Dental Health of Children, 1967, on Multiphasic Screening, 1968; N.Y. State Tech. Adv. Com. on Emergency Health Services, 1973; cons. in emergency services N.Y.C. Mayor's Organizational Task Force, 1971; mem. personal health services com. N.Y.C. Comprehensive Health Planning Agy., 1973; mem. emergency services adv. com. N.Y. Regional Med. Programs, 1972; mem. drug survey adv. com. Archeus Found., 1972; mem. program and budget com. Tb and Respiratory Disease Assn. N.Y., 1972-73; chmn. adv. group emergency med. tng. and information Paramount Pictures Corp., 1972-73. Bd. dirs. Norfolk County (Mass.) Tb and Health Assn., also chmn. research com., 1957-68; bd. dirs. Mass. Tb and Health League, 1964-68, Greater Boston chpt. Mass. Heart Assn., 1964-68, Lower Eastside Service Center, 1972-73; bd. dirs. Mass. Health Council, 1959-67, pres., 1964. Served from lt. (j.g.) to lt. comdr. M.C., USNR, 1941-45. Diplomate Am. Bd. Preventive Medicine. Fellow Am. Pub. Health Assn., Am. Coll. Preventive Medicine (com. on continuing edn. 1971); mem. A.M.A., N.Y. State (com. on hosp. and profl. relations 1971-73), New York County (pub. Health com. 1970-73) med. socs., Assn. Tchrs. Preventive Medicine, Am. Geriatrics Soc., Royal Soc. Health (London), Am. Assn. Pub. Health Physicians, A.A.A.S., Am. Coll. Emergency Physicians (charter, dir. 1972-73, sec.-treas. N.Y. State chpt. 1972-73, chmn. commn. on teaching hosps. 1971-72, com. on ednl. materials 1973, cons. editor jour. 1972-73), Indsl. Med. Assn., Am. Med. Writers Assn., Soc. for Total Emergency Programs (dir. 1973), Greater N.Y. Hosp. Assn., N.Y. C. of C. (mem. com. on health and welfare 1971), N.Y. Assn. for Ambulatory Care (pres. 1972-73), Mass. Health Officers Assn. (hon. life), Brookline Dental Soc. (hon.). Editor: Harvard Pub. Health Alumni Bull., 1958-62; mem. editorial bd. Clin. Medicine, 1963-66; contbg. editor Emergency Medicine, 1969-73. Contbr. articles to med. jours. Home: New York City, N.Y. Died Nov. 4, 1973; buried Sharon, Mass.

TAYLOR, ALAN CAREY, educator; b. Goulburn, Australia, Feb. 11, 1905; s. William Carey and Florence Mary (Boyhan) T.; B.A. with honours, Sydney U., 1926; D.U.P., Paris U., 1929, D. es L., 1938; m. Yvonne Antoinette Legal, Oct. 20, 1939; children—Jean-Claude, Patrick, Sabine (Mrs. Erich W. Hofmann). Lectr. French, Sydney U., 1933; lectr., then sr. lectr. French, Melbourne U., 1938-48; prof. French, Birkbeck Coll., U. London, 1948-72, U. Cape Coast (Ghana), 1972-75; French translator, announcer Radio Australia, 1941-48. Vice pres. French-Australian Assn. Victoria, 1944-48. Decorated chevalier Legion of Honor; laureate l'Académie Francaise. Mem. Assn. U. Profs. French (hon. sec. 1950-72). Author: Carlyle et la pensée latine, 1937; Le Président de Brosses et l'Australie, 1938; Non-French Admirers and Imitators of Balzac, 1950. Editor: Current Research in French Departments of British Universities, 1952-72. Home: London, England. Died Mar. 13, 1975; buried New Cemetery, Cape Coast.

TAYLOR, ARCHER, prof. emeritus; b. Phila., Aug. 1, 1890; s. Lowndes and Florence (York) T.; A.B., Swarthmore Coll., 1909; A.M., U. Pa., 1910; Ph.D., Harvard, 1915; m. Alice Jones, Sept. 9, 1915 (died June 16, 1930); children—Margaret B., Richard L., Cynthia; m. 2d, Hasseltine Byrd, June 17, 1932; children—Mary Constance, Ann Byrd. Instr. German, Penn. State College, 1910-12; instr., asst. prof., asso. prof. German, Washington U., St. Louis, Mo., 1915-25; also editor Washington Univ. Studies, 1919-25; ehrensenator, U. Giessen, Germany, 1925; prof. German lit., U. Chgo., 1925-39, chmn. dept. 1927-39; John Simon Guggenheim fellow, 1927, prof. medieval lit. and folklore, 1938-39; prof. German lit., U. Cal., Berkeley, 1939, prof. emeritus, 1957. Fellow of Newberry Library, 1945. Fellow Medieval Acad. Am., Am. Acad. Arts and Scis., Am. Philos. Soc.; mem. Modern Lang. Assn. (pres. 1951). Club Internacional de Folklore, Am. Folklore Soc. (pres. 1935-37), Phi Beta Kappa; hon. mem. Schweizerische Gesellschaft für Volkskunde, Finnish Lit. Soc. (Helsinki); Asociación folklórica Argentina (Buenos Aires), Kgl. Gustav Adolfs Akademi for Folklivsforskning (Uppsala), Société Finno-ougrienne (Helsinski), Folklore of Ireland Soc. (Dublin), Sociedad Folkórica (Mexico City), Finnish Academy of Science (Helsinki), Norsk Videnskapsselskab (Oslo). Author: The History of Bibliographies of Bibliographies, 1956; Book Catalogues: Their Varieties and Uses, 1957; The Shanghai Gesture, 1957. Home: Berkeley, Cal. Died Sept. 30, 1973.

TAYLOR, BURTON LEO, educator, planning cons.; b. Nephi, Utah, Feb. 10, 1926; s. Joel Elmer and Jessie V. (VanLeuven) T.; B.S., Utah State U., 1948; M.L.A., Harvard, 1951; spl. studies Cambridge Sch. Design, 1949, Mass. Inst. Tech., 1950; m. Eleanor Lois Baile, Sept. 3, 1950; 1 son, Joel Keene. Projects mgr. Pereira & Luckman, 1954-58; pvt. practice landscape architecture, 1958-62; cons., 1962-64; projects coordinator Victor Gruen Assos., 1962-64; head dept. landscape architecture and environmental planning Utah State U., 1964-72, prof., 1964. Cons. Pres.'s Office Utah State U. Master Plan, Utah Sec. of State's Office; mem. planning com. Utah Bd. Higher Edn. Cons. Cache Valley council Boy Scouts Am. Trustee J.T. Coit Estate. Licensed landscape architect, Cal., Colo., Utah. Fellow Royal Soc. Health; mem. Am. Inst. Planners, Am. Soc. Mil. Engrs., Am. Soc. Planning Ofcls., Nat. Rifle Assn. (life), Chatsworth C. of C. (past dir.). Clubs: Logan Golf and Country; Harvard (Salt Lake City). Contbr. articles to profl. publs. Home: Logan, Utah. Died Oct. 30, 1974; buried Nepmi, Utah.

TAYLOR, CHARLES KEEN, educator; b. Philadelphia, Pa., Dec. 4, 1879; s. Charles Tracy and Sophia Cramp (Davis) T.; B.S., U. of Pa., 1905, M.A., 1909; grad. study, Yale, 1906-07, Columbia, 1915-17; unmarried; adopted son, Michale!!Michael French. Asst. in psychology, U. of Pa., 1908-10; dean of Careret Acad., Orange, N.J., 1919-21; contbr. to and later mem. staff The Outlook, 1921-25; dir. Educational Records Bureau, New York City, 1926-30; director Vocational Research Bureau from 1931. Served with Engineer Corps U.S. Army, 1918-19. Trustee Foshay School District. Presbyterian. Clubs: Schoolmen's (New York). Author: Character Development of Children, 1911; Physical Examination and Training of Children, 1912; Physical Standards for Boys and Girls, 1919. Contbr. on edn. Home: Kent Cliffs, N.Y.†

TAYLOR, DANIEL ALBERT, lawyer; b. Casey County, Ky., Dec. 17, 1895; s. James David and Mintia Jane (Woodrum) T.; grad. Western Ky. State Normal and Tchrs. Coll., 1917; LL.B., Washington and Lee U., 1921; m. Margaret Gallegher, Dec. 26, 1928; children—Daniel Albert, Jane Carol. Admitted to Ky. bar, 1921, admitted to Ill., D.C. bars; practiced in Newport, 1921-28; spl. atty., trial and adminstrv. positions Office Gen. Counsel, Bur. Internal Revenue, 1928-42; pvt. practice specializing in fed. tax matters, Chgo., 1942-53; chief counsel Internal Revenue Service. Washington, 1953-54; partner firm Taylor & Kelly, Chgo., Washington, 1956-66. Served with AEF, World War I. Mem. Am., Fed., Chgo. bar assns. Mason. Clubs: Union League (Chgo.); Little, Delray Beach. Home: Delray Beach, Fla. Died Dec. 25, 1973; interred Parklawn Cemetery, Rockville, Md.

TAYLOR, DONALD WAYNE, univ. dean, psychologist; b. Boulder, Colo., May 9, 1919; s. Ralph O. and Mamie K. (Lauer) T.; A.B., Baker U., 1939, LL.D., 1963; M.A., U. Kan., 1940; M.A., Harvard, 1942, Ph.D., 1943; M.A. (hon.), Yale, 1955; m. Ruth I. Spence, Sept. 1, 1940; children—Laird E., Patricia A., Barbara K. (dec.), Roderic West. Spl. research asso. Radio Research Lab., Harvard, 1943-45, also part-time instr. psychology, 1943-44; civilian specialist radar countermeasures Am. embassy, London, Eng., 1944; asst. prof. psychology Stanford, 1945-48, asso. prof., 1948-55; prof. personnel adminstrn. Yale, 1955-60, prof. psychology, 1956-69, fellow Pierson Coll., 1956, chmn. dept. indsl. adminstrn., 1963-66, chmn. dept. psychology, 1966-69, dir. div. social scis., 1966-68,

Elizabeth S. and A. Varick Stout prof. social sci., 1968-69, dir. Inst. Social Sci., 1968-69, dean Grad Sch., Eugene Higgins prof. psychology, 1969-75; research fellow Cognitive Center Harvard, 1961-62. Mem. div. anthropology and psychology NRC, 1949-52; chmn. electronics tng. working group Research and Develop. Bd., Office Sec. Def., 1951-52; dir. study undergrad. edn. Stanford, 1954-55; mem. Grad. Record Exams. Bd., 1970-75; mem. exec. com. Council Grad. Schs., 1973. Rhodes Scholar, 1939. Fellow Am. Psychol. Assn. (publs. bd. 1960-66, policy and planning bd. 1965-68), A.A.A.S.; mem. Psychonomic Soc. Phi Beta Kappa, Sigma Xi (nat. lectr., 1960-61). Clubs: Yale (N.Y.C.); Mory's. Co-editor: Dorsey Series in Psychology, 1959-67; asso. editor Ann. Rev. Psychology, 1949-53; cons. editor Irwin Dorsey series Behavioral Science in Business, 1960-63. Contbr. numerous articles to profl. jours. Home: North Haven, Conn. Died Feb. 5, 1975; interred Alta Mesa Columbarium, Palo Alto, Cal.

TAYLOR, GEOFFREY INGRAM, educator; b. Mar. 7, 1886; s. Edward Ingram and Margaret (Boole) T.; student U. Coll. Sch., Cambridge U.; m. Grace Stephanie Francis Ravenhill, 1925 (dec. 1967). Yarrow research prof. Royal Soc.; meteorologist to Scotia Expdn. to N. Atlantic, 1913; engaged in exptl. aeronatuics and meteorology, 1914-18; worked with group making first nuclear explosion, Los Alamos, N.M., 1944-45; fellow Trinity Coll., Cambridge U. Created knight, 1944; recipient Order of Merit, 1969, Am. medal for Merit, Gold medal Royal Aeronaut. Soc., Exner medal, de Morgan medal, Internat. Panetti prize and medal, Kelvin Gold medal, Franklin medal, Platinum medal, James Watt Internat. Gold medal. Fellow Royal Soc. Contbr. articles on math., meteorology, aeronatuics and engring. to profl. jours.; collected sci. papers pub., 4 vols. Address: Cambridge, England. Died June 27, 1975.

TAYLOR, HENRY CHARLES, agrl. economist; b. Stockport. Ia., Apr. 16, 1873; s. Tarpley Early and Elmira (Martin) T.; Drake U., Des Moines, Ia., 1891-93; B.Agr., Ia. State Coll., Ames, 1896, M.S.A., 1898; Ph.D., U. of Wis., 1903, LL.D., 1933; studied London Sch. of Economics, 1899; Halle-Wittenberg U., U. of Berlin, each 1 sem., 1900-01; Dr. Polit. Sci. (hon.), Albert-Ludwig U., Freiburg, Germany, 1953; m. Elizabeth Bruner, June 17, 1904; 1 dau., Esther Elmira; m. 2d, Anne Dewees, June 24, 1941. Began as instr. of com., Univ. of Wisconsin, 1901, chmn. dept. agrl. economics, 1908-19; chief of Office of Farm Management, U.S. Dept. of Agr., 1919-21, and chief of Bur. Markets Bur. of Markets and Crop Estimates, 1921-22; chief of Bur. of Agrl. Economics, 1922-25; research associate Inst. Research Land Economics and Pub. Utilities, and prof. agrl. economics, Northwestern U., 1925-28; dir. comprehensive survey of rural Vt. and research profl. agrl. economics, U. of Vt., 1928-31; mem. Commn. of Laymen's Foreign Missions 1931-32; U.S. mem. permanent com. Internat. Inst. of Agr., Rome, Italy, 1933-35, pres. 13th Gen. Assembly of same inst., 1936; dir. of Farm Foundation, 1935-45; agricultural economist of same, from Oct. 1945. Mem. Presidents advisory Com. on Edn.,1936-39; mem. Am. Youth Commn., 1937-41. Mem. Royal Acad. of Agr. of Sweden, Am. Econ. Assn., Am. Farm Econ. Assn., Alpha Zeta, Phi Kappa Phi, Phi Beta Kappa. Mason (32°, K.T.); mem. Grange Author: Introc!duction to the Stydy!!Study of Agricultural Economics, 1905; Ot!utlines of Agricultural Economics, 1925; co-uat!!co-author: World Trade in Agricultural Products, 1943; The Story of Agricultural Economics in the United States, 1952; also bulletins. Home: U1Washington, D.C.†

TAYLOR, HUGH STOTT, educator; b. St. Helens, Lancashire, Eng., Feb. 6, 1890; s. James and Ellen (Stott) T.; B.Sc., Liverpool (Eng.) U., 1909, M.Sc., 1910, D.Sc., 1914; student Nobel Inst., Stockholm, 1912-13, Technische Hochschule, Hanover, Germany, 1913-14; m. Elizabeth Agnes Sawyer, June 12, 1919 (dec. July 1958); children—Joan (Mrs. Taylor Ashley), E. Sylvia (Mrs. M.F. Healy). Came to U.S., 1914. Prof. chemistry Princeton, 1922-58, chmn. chemistry dept., 1926-51, dean Grad. Sch., 1945-58, now emeritus. Pres. emeritus Woodrow Wilson Nat. Fellowship Found. With British Munitions Inventions Dept., 1917-19. Franklin medallist Am. Philos. Soc., 1941; recipient Nichols medal. Am. Chem. Soc., 1928; Mendel medal Villanova Coll., 1933; comdr. Order of Leopold II, 1937; recipient Research Corp. plague, 1939; Longstaff medal Chem. Soc. (London) 1942; 1st Priestley medallion Dickinson Coll., 1952; knight comdr. Order Brit. Empire, 1953; knight comdr. Order St. Gregory the Great, 1953; Franklin medal Franklin Inst., 1957; William Procter prize Sci. Research Soc. Am., 1964. Fellow Royal Soc. (London), Pontifical Acad. Scis., Am. Acad. Arts and Scis.; hon. mem. Soc. Chem. de Belgium, Chem. Soc. Eng., Polish Chem. Soc., Union d. Ingenieurs d. Louvain, Academy d. Scis. (Lyon); fgn. mem. Acad. Nazional dei Lincei (Rome), Acad. d. Scienze d. Institute Bologna, Belgian Acadamy Sci.; mem. Am. Pilos. Soc., Faraday Soc. (pres. 1952-53), Sigma Xi (nat. pres. 1951-53), Pax Romana (pres. 1952-55), several other profl. and sci. assns. Roman Catholic. Clubs: Nassau (Princeton); Century, Chemists, Princeton (N.Y.C.). Author, co-author and contbr. to numerous sci. books, after 1919. Home: Princeton, N.J. Died Apr. 17, 1974; interred, Princeton.

TAYLOR, JAMES SHERWOOD, physician, educator; b. Tallula, Ill., Jan. 30, 1904; s. Walter Sherwood and Lillian (Jack) T.; student Washington U., 1921-23; B.S., U. Ill., 1928, M.D., 1931; m. Elfleda May Murchie, Sept. 5, 1928 (dec. 1968). Intern U. Ill. Research and Ednl. Hosp., Chgo., 1930-31; practicing physician, 1931-33; commd. 1st lt. U.S.Army, 1933, advanced through grades to col., 1943; cardiologist various Army hosps., 1933-43; comdg. officer 90th Gen. Hosp., 1943-46; chief cardiology Walter Reed Gen. Hosp., 1946-51; ret., 1951; prof. medicine U. Ark. Med. Center, 1952-59, emeritus, 1969; cons. surgeons gen. army, USAAF, 1946-51; mem. nat. adv. heart council and study sect. U.S. Army, 1947-51. Decorated officer Couronne de Chene (Luxemburg); recipient Golden Apple award, 1967. Fellow A.C.P., Am. Coll. Cardiology, Am. Heart Assn.; mem. A.M.A., Ark., Pulaski County med. assns., Pi Kappa Alpha, Phi Rho Sigma, Alpha Omega Alpha. Clubs: Army and Navy (Washington); Capital (Little Rock). Episcopalian. Home: Little Rock, Ark. Died Jan. 16, 1975.

TAYLOR, JESSE READE, b. Spencer, Henry Co., Va., June 25, 1880; s. Ryland Reade and Jeannette (Read) T.; A.B., Rh!ichmond (Va.) Coll.; me!. Bessie Blair Ellyson, of Richmond, Oct. 12, 1904. Began with United Cigar Stores Co., 1901, elected pres. Aug.1919!!Aug. 1919; later treas., dir. Am. Tobacco Co.; dir. Chatham & Phenix Nat. Bank and Trust Co. Treas. Montclair (N.J.) Chapter Am. Red Cross Mem. Phi Gamma Delta. Republican. Baptist. Clubs: Union League; Montclair Golf. Home: !!Montclair, N.J.†

TAYLOR, JOHN MCNAY, naval ofcr.; b. Knoxville, Tenn., June 1, 1905; s. William (U.S. Army) and Margaret Graham (Dailey) T.; B.S. with distinction, U.S. Naval Acad., 1926, grad. student, 1933-36; student Nat. War Coll., Washington, 1950-51; m. Amelia Waugh Wade, June 30, 1928. Commd. ensign U.S.N., 1926, advanced through grades to vice adm., 1960; assigned U.S.S. Mississippi, 1926-27; staff CinC Battle Fleet, 1927; 12th Naval Dist., San Francisco, 1928-29; U.S.S. Parrott, 1929-31, U.S.S. Md., 1931-33; Ordnance postgrad. tng., 1933-36; ordnance repair officer U.S.S. Medusa, 1936-37; aide flag sec. Comdr. Battleship Div. One, 1937-39; asst. design officer Naval Gun Factory, Washington, 1939-42; gunnery officer U.S.S. Montpelier, 1942-43; gunnery officer, staff Comdr. Amphibious Forces Pacific Fleet, 1943-45; head design dept. Naval Gun Factory, 1945-48; comdg. officer U.S.S. George Clymer, 1948-49; chief staff Comdr. Amphibious Group One, 1949-50; comdr. Destroyer Sqdn. 6 Atlantic Fleet, 1951-52, chief staff Comdr. Amphibious Force Atlantic Fleet, 1952-53; dep. comdt. Armed Forces Staff Coll., 1953-55; comdt. Mil. Sea Transport Service East Atlantic and Med. Area, 1955-56; asst. chief naval operations (Naval Res.), 1956-59; comdr. Cruiser Force, Atlantic Fleet, 1959-60; Comdr. Amphibious Force, Atlantic Fleet, 1960-61, commander Second Fleet and NATO Striking Fleet, 1961-62; chief of staff, supreme allied comdr. Atlantic, 1962-64; comdt. 12th Naval Dist., 1964-65; comdr. Western Sea Frontier, 1965-67; retired, 1967. Decorated Silver Star, Legion Merit. Mem. Mil. Order of Carabao. Clubs: Bohemian, St. Francis Yacht (San Francisco); Army-Navy (Washington). Home: San Francisco, Cal. Died May 1973.

TAYLOR, LEA DEMAREST, social settlement and civic work; b. Hartford, Conn., June 24, 1883; d. Graham and Leah (Demarest) Taylor; student Lewis Inst., 1900; A.B., Vassar Coll., 1904. Resident of Chicago Commons since its founding, 1894, head resident, 1921-54, head resident emeritus, 1954-75 president of the Chicago Federation of Settlements, 1924-37 and 1939-40, National Fedn. of Settlements, 1930-34 and again 1950-52; vice president American Association of Social Workers, 1934, 1935 (v.p. Chicago Chapter 1935). Recipient Illinois Welfare Assn. Award Meritorious Service; 1954; Jane Addams Medal, Rockford College, 1953; Outstanding Achievement Award, National Fedn. Settlements & Neighborhood Centers, 1960; Jane Adams medallion, 1965. Member National Conference of Social Work (member executive committee 1932-34), Chicago Community Fund (bd. dirs. 1952-54), Chicago Council of Social Agencies (secretary 1935-41), Cook County Bureau of Public Welfare (advisory com.), Metropolitan Housing Council (bd. dirs.), Chicago Recreation Com. Immigrants Protective League of Chicago (bd. dirs.), Club: Woman's City (adv. bd.), Chicago Woman's, Chicago College. Contbr. article on Social Settlements in Social Works Year Book, 1935 and 1937. Home: Highland Park, Ill., Died Dec. 3, 1975.

TAYLOR, MARIAN YOUNG (PROFESSIONALLY MARTHA DEANE), radio commentator; b. Star Lake, N.Y., Nov. 21; d. Edwin and Mary Elizabeth (Zuber) Young; m. William Bolling Taylor, Mar. 6, 1937; children—William Bolling, Marian (Mrs. Robert Scott). Staff corr. NEA, Scripps-Howard Syndicate, 1930-34, women's editor, 1934-41, fgn. corr. 1936-37; radio commentator Martha Deane, 1941. Instr. journalism Centenary Jr. Coll., Hackettstown, N.J. 1938-40; merchandising cons. Krene div. Nat. Carbon Co., 1939-41. Trustee Internat. Rescue Com., Shelter Island (N.Y.) Pub. Library. Awarded Newspaper Women's Club prize "best column in specialized woman's field," 1937, radio columnists prize "best column in specialized woman's field," 1937, radio columnists prize "best radio program for women." 1942; award, Ohio State University's 16th Inst. for Edn. by Radio, as "best woman commentator," 1944, 48, 49, 52; McCall award pub. service, 1954; Broadcast Pioneers Distinguished Service award, 1968. Presbyn. Author: Cooking for Compliments, 1954. Address: New York City, N.Y. Died Dec. 9, 1973.

TAYLOR, MILLS JAMES, church official; b. Reeseville, O., May 6, 1879; s. John Manlove and Columbia (Mills) T.; grad. Washington (Ia.) Acad., 1898. post-grad. study, 1899; A.B., Monmouth (Ill.) Coll., 1905; grad. Xenia (O.) Theol. Sem., 1908, D.D., Tarkio (Mo.) Coll., 1922; m. Martha Slater Dill, June 11, 1908; children—Theophilus Mills, John Renwick, Martha (Dec.), George Dill. With U.S. mail service, 1900-03; ordained ministry U.P. Ch., 1908; pastor Ref. Presbyn. Ch., Cedarville, O., 1908-13, Second U.P. Ch., Monmouth, Ill., 1913-18; asso. sec. Bd. of Foreign Missions U.P. Ch. of N.A., 1918-48; asso. editor-mgr. United Presbyn., 1948-51; asso. pastor Christ United Presbyn. Ch., Drexel Hill, Pa., 1951-65, pastor emeritus, 1965-74; mem. com. sent by United Presbyns. to visit missions in Egypt, the Sudan, Abyssinia and India, 1921-22; mem. bd. United Presbyns. from 1925; Am. del. Internat. Missionary Conf., Madras, 1938; exec. sec. New World Movement, 1923-25, Republican. Home: Havertown, Pa., Died June 15, 1974.

TAYLOR, RALPH WESLEY, coll. dean; b. South Boston, Mass., Jan. 22, 1887; s. Albert Joseph and Emma Lulu (Nason) T.; A.B., Boston U., 1911, A.M., 1922; student Harvard, summers 1911, 12; m. Hortense Weed, Aug. 15, 1912 (died Jan. 7, 1941); children—Carl Weed (dec.), Paul Nason, Miriam Hortense (Mrs. John Houston), Martha Louise (Mrs. Frederick B. Lea); m. 2d, Elizabeth Stephan, July 23, 1944. Began as teaching principal of North Dartmouth (Massachusetts) High School, 1911-12, Medfield (Mass.) High Sch., 1912-18; registar, Boston Univ., 1918-37, instructor in English, 1922-37, prof. since 1937, sec. of faculty, 1919-37, dir. late afternoon, evening and Saturday courses, 1932-51, mem. adv. com. Boston U. eve. division since 1951; dean Boston U. Coll. of Liberal Arts since 1937; sec. Boston U. Convocation, 1924-26; sec. Boston Univ. Alumni Assn., 1926-28, dir., 1928-31. Trustee Morrill Memorial Library, Norwood, Mass., 1930-39, New Hampton Sch., New Hampton, N.H., 1952-73. Mem. New Eng. Assn. of Colls. and Secondary Schs., N.E. Deans Assn., Beta Theta Pi, Phi Beta Kappa. Conglist, Mason. Home: Norwood, Mass. Died May 1973.

TAYLOR, THELMA MARJORIE VOGT (MRS. JEAN LANDON TAYLOR), librarian; b. Battle Creek, Mich.; d. Herman Carl and S. Lillian (Balcom) Vogt; A.B., Western Mich. U., 1923; M.A., U. Chgo., 1930; M.L.S., Columbia U., 1941; m. Jean Landon Taylor, Aug. 26, 1923; 1 dau., Jane Ann (Mrs. James Armstrong). Critic tchr. Western Mich. U., Kalamazoo, 1923-29; instr. Spaids Sch. for Girls, Chgo., 1930-32; librarian Morgan Park Mil. Acad. and Jr. Coll., Chgo., 1933-45; library supr. Fullerton (Cal.) Elementary Schs., 1945-48; asst. dean, head librarian, Los Angeles City Coll., 1948-49; librarian and div. chmn., coordinator library services Los Angeles Harbor Coll., Wilmington, Cal., 1949-68; library cons. Antelope Valley Coll., Lancaster, Cal., 1956, Cal. Sch. Library Project, 1964. Mem. N.E.A., Cal. Tchrs. Assn. (hon. life), Assn. Coll. Research Librarians (constnl. revision com.), Am. Assn. U. Women. Democrat. Mem. United Ch. of Christ. Contbr. articles to profl. jours. Home: Palos Verdes Estates, Cal. Died Dec. 26, 1971.

TAYLOR, THOMAS IVAN, educator, chemist; b. Utah, Sept. 11, 1909; s. Thomas G. and Harriet Mae (Hill) T.; B.S., U. Ida., 1931, M.S., 1933; Ph.D., Columbia, 1938; D.Sc., U. Ida., 1972; m. Frances Rachel Nichols, Sept. 22, 1939; children—Mary, Arthur. Instr. chemistry U. Ida., 1931-35; teaching asst. Columbia, 1935-38; instr. chemistry U. Minn., 1938-40, asst. prof., 1940-42; chemist Nat. Bur. Standards, Washington, 1942-44; chemist research control group Manhattan Dist., Washington, Oak Ridge, N.Y.C., 1944-45; prof. chemistry U. Ia., 1945; asso. prof. chemistry Columbia. 1945-48, prof., 1949. Chmn., Gordon Conf. Physics and Chemistry of Isotopes, 1956; Chmn. adv. com. chemistry div. Nat. Bur. Standards, 1961-64; chmn. adv. com. chemistry dept. Brookhaven Nat. Lab., 1965. Mem. Am. Chem. Soc. (councilor 1950-54, chmn. N.Y. sect. 1957-58), Am. Nuclear Soc., Am. Phys. Soc., A.A.A.S., Soc. Applied Spectroscopy, Sigma Xi, Phi Lambda Upsilon, Gamma Alpha, Sigma Tau. Author: (with J.L. Maynard) Experiments in General Chemistry, 1944; (with H.H. Barber) Semimicro Qualitative Analysis, 1942. Editorial bd. Nucleonics, 1948-49. Contbr. research reports to sci. jours. Home: Leonia, N.J. Died July 27, 1973; buried George Washington Meml. Park, Paramus, N.J.

TAYLOR, W(ILLIAM) BAYARD, educator, economist; b. Red Wing, Minn., Sept. 21, 1896; s. William Edward and Clara Catherine (Gilmore) T.; A.B., Beloit Coll., 1918; A.M., U. Minn., 1923, Ph.D., 1928; LL.D., Claremont (Cal.) Men's Coll., 1961; m. Dorothy Beebe, Aug. 28, 1920; children—Joan (Mrs. Joseph C. Borton), James Carlton, Trainee, Western Electric Co., Chgo., 1919; bus. mgr. Windom Coll., 1919-21; teaching fellow econs. U. Minn., 1921-22, instr., 1922-26; instr. Carleton Coll., 1925-26; pvt. bus. as Surburban Devel. Co., Tulsa, instr. Am. Inst. Banking, 1926-27; prof. econs. Rockford (Ill.) Coll., 1927-28; asso. prof. econs. U. Kan., 1928-29, prof., 1929-30; researcher Kansas City Fed. Res. Bank, 1929, Halsey Stuart Co., Chgo., summer 1929; asso. prof. finance Western Res. U., 1930-31; asso. prof. U. Wis., 1931-36, prof., 1936-48; prof. finance Claremont Men's Coll. and Grad. Sch., 1948; dean faculty, 1949-61, dean Grad. Sch. and U. Center, 1962-63, dean emeritus, 1963, acting pres., 1954. Vis. lectr. summers U. Ill., 1950, U. Ida.,1954-65; vis. prof. U. Cal., 1962. Mem. U.S. Treasury Credit Survey, 1934-35; price officer Wis. OPA, 1942-43; regional price exec. Chgo. OPA, 1943-45; cons. Chgo. and Washington OPA, 1945-46; pvt. cons., 1936-65; econ. adviser SCAP, Tokyo, Japan, summer 1949. Served with U.S. Army, 1918-19; AEF. Mem. Am., Western, Midwest (founder 1934, v.p. 1938, pres. 1939) econs. assns., Am. Assn. U. Profs. (pres. Wis. chpt. 1946-47), Western Coll. Assn. (exec. com. 1958-61), Phi Beta Kappa, Artus, Beta Alpha Phi. Alpha Kappa Psi, Sigma Delta Chi, Tau Kappa Epsilon, Conglist. Author, co-author books in field; contbr. to econ., financial jours. Home: Claremont, Cal. Died June 8, 1975.

TAYLOR, WILLIAM DAVID, JR., educator; b. Hartford, Kan., Dec. 25, 1902; s. William David and Bessie (Johnston) T.; A.B., U. Wash., 1927, M.A., 1931; postgrad. U. So. Cal., Nat. U. Mexico, Northwestern U. Formerly reporter Spokane (Wash.) Daily Chronicle; asst. dean men. U. Wash., 1928-29, men's personnel dir., 1930-32; asst. prof. English Ariz. State U., Tempe, 1932-34, asso. prof. English and journalism, 1934-36; vis. prof. Medill Sch. Journalism Northwestern U., 1935-36; prof. journalism Kent (O.) State U., 1936-68, prof. emeritus, 1968-75, chmn. Sch. Journalism, 1936-63; dealer rare books; founder short courses news photography and other profl. adult insts. journalism. Spl. asst. to dir. indsl. relations Sperry Gyroscope Co., Inc., Bklyn., 1942-43, publicity dir., 1943, pub. relations counselor, 1956-68. Vice chmn. Ohio Crusade for Freedom, 1956-57; founding mem., vice chmn. Ohio Arts Council, 1956-67, chmn., 1967-74; mem. Ohio Hist. Site Preservation Bd., 1968-73; mem. Pres. Nixon's Adv. Com. Arts, 1970—; mem. Ohio Gov.'s Adv. Com. 1971 Festival Am. Folklore. Trustee Kent State U., 1971-79, Canton (O.) Art Inst., 1917-75, Ohio Outdoor Hist. Drama Assn., 1972-75, Canton Symphony Orch. Assn., 1972-75, Alliance for Arts Edn. com. Kennedy Center Performing Arts, 1973. Served to lt. col. U.S. Army, World War II; PTO. Decorated Bronze Star medal, campaign and unit citations. Recipient citation Nat. Press Photographers Assn., 1949, Gov.'s award Advancement Ohio Prestige, 1950, 60, Crusade for Freedom citation, 1953. First Pub. Relations Soc. Am. internat. fellow Timken Roller Bearing Co., Duston, Eng., 1964. Mem. Assn. U. Profs., Am. Assn. Tchrs. Journalism, Pub. Relations Soc. Am., Border Athletic Conf. (founder, pres.), Phi Gamma Delta, Sigma Delta Chi. Rotarian. Author: Vocational Information, 1931, also several monographs. Co-editor: Headlining America, 1937; A Guide to The Tagalog Dialect in the Philippines. Mem. two-man expdn. to South coast Isle of Pines to collect ednl. specimens, summer 1941. Home: Hartville, O., Died Nov. 3, 1975; interred Massillon (O.) Cemetery.

TEAD, ORDWAY, editor, teacher; b. Somerville, Mass., Sept. 10, 1891; s. Edward Sampson and Louise Moore (Ordway) T.; grad. Latin High Sch., Somerville, 1908; A.B., Amherst Coll., 1912, L.H.D., 1942; LL.D., St. Lawrence U., 1939, Keuka Coll., 1949, Am. Internat. Coll., 1950, Northwestern U., 1952; L.H.D., Bklyn. Coll., 1954, Columbia 1954; Litt.D., Bard Coll., 1953, Rollins Coll., 1961; m. Clara A. Murphy, July 29, 1915; 1 dau., Diana. Fellow Amherst Coll. South End House, Boston, 1912-14; mem. indsl. consultants, Valentine, Tead & Gregg, 1915-17; with Bur. Indsl. Research, N.Y.C., 1917-19; charge war emergency employment mgmt. courses of War Dept. at Columbia, 1917-18; lectr. personnel adminstrn. Columbia, 1920-50; mem. dept. industry, N.Y. Sch. Social Work, 1920-29; dir. bus. publns. McGraw-Hill Book Co., 1920-25; editor social and econ. books. Harper & Brothers, 1925-61; cons. editor Harper and Row, 1962. Chmn. N.Y.C. Bd. Edn., 1938-53; adj. prof. indsl. relations Columbia, 1951-56; hon. chmn. bd. Briarcliff Coll.; mem. Nat. Commn. for UNESCO, 1952-54; mem., cons. Pres. Commn. Higher Edn., 1946-47. Mem. Am. Econ. Assn., Am. Mgmt. Assn., Am. Psychol. Assn., Soc. Advancement Mgmt. (past pres.), Phi Beta Kappa, Alpha Delta Phi, Beta Gamma Sigma. Clubs: Century Assn. (N.Y.C.); Faculty (Columbia); Cosmos (Washington). Author: Instincts in Industry, 1918; The People's Part in Peace, 1918; Personnel Administration Its Principles and Practice (with H.C. Metcalf), 3d edit., 1933; A Course in Personnel Administration, 1923; Human Nature and Management, 2d edit., 1933; Labor Relations under the Recovery Act (with H.C. Metcalf), 1933; The Art of Leadership, 1935; Creative Management, 1935; The Case for Democracy, 1937; New Adventures in Democracy, 1939; Democratic Administration, 1945; Equalizing Educational Opportunities Beyond The Secondary School, 1947; The Climate of Learning, 1958; Administration; Its Purpose and Performance, 1959; co-author: Modern Education and Human Values, 1947; College Teaching and College Learning, 1949; The Art of Adminstration, 1951; Trustees, Teachers, Students, 1951; Character Building and Higher Education, 1953; The Climate of Learning, 1958; Administration: Its Purpose and Performance, 1959. Contbr. to mags. Home: Westport, Conn. Died Nov. 1973.

TEAGARDEN, FLORENCE M(ABEL), clin. psychologist; b. Dallas, W. Va., Sept. 5, 1887; d. William David and Sarah (Braddock) T.; A.B., of Pittsburgh, Pa., 1915, M.A., 1916; Ph.D., Columbia 1924; unmar Instr. pub. schs., Washington, Pa., 1908-13; instr., asst. prof., as prof. psychology, U. of Pittsburgh, 1916-31, prof. psychology from 9 1931 (leave of absence, 1922-24); staff psychol. clinic, after 1916; instr., Mills Coll., Calif., summer 1940; consultant for schs., social agencies and parents; clin. work with children having sensory emotional or intellectual handicaps. Fellow A.A.A.S., Am. Psychol. A (diplomate in clinical psychology), Am. Orthopsychiatric Ass Child Development Assn.; mem. Am. Assn. Univ. Profs., Pa.; Pitts psychological associations, Pa. State Edn. Assn. (past chmn. co on professional ethics), Sigma Xi, Pi Lambda Theta, Kappa Delta Pi. Club: South Hills College (Pittsburgh). Democrat. Presbyterian. Author Child Psychology for Professional Workers, 1940, revised edit. 1946. Contbr. to profl. jours. Home: Pittsburgh, Pa., Apr. 23, 1975.

TEAGUE, CHARLES MCKEVETT, congressman; b. Santa Paula, Cal., Sept. 18, 1909; s. Charles Collins and Harriet (McKevett) Teague; A.B., Stanford, 1931, LL.B., 1934; m. Marjorie Cowden, Apr. 27, 1929 (dec.); children—Norma (Mrs. James B. Potter, Jr.), Alan, Judith (Mrs. Robert Kenyon); m. 2d, Courtney Kempe Campbell, Nov. 6, 1970. Admitted to Cal. bar, 1934; practiced in Los Angeles and Ventura until 1954; dir. McKevett Corp., Teague-McKevett Co.; mem. 84th to 92d Congresses 13th Dist. Cal. Served in USAAF, 1942-46. Mem. Beta Theta Pi, Phi Delta Phi. Republican. Home: Santa Paula, Cal. Died Jan. 1, 1974.

TEELE, RAY PALMER, profl. engr.; b. Washington, July 12, 1903; s. Ray P. and Mary (Hazard) T.; B.S. in Elec. Engring., U. Mich., 1927; M.S. in Physics, George Washington U., 1929; m. Marion Beth Johnson, Apr. 12, 1927; 1 dau., Audrey (Mrs. Ronald A. Ryder). With Nat. Bur. Standards, Washington, 1923-65, physicist-in-charge research on photometry, 1965; cons. profl. engr., Washington, 1966-74; cons. Am. Assn. Motor Vehicle Adminstrs. Fellow Illuminating Engring. Soc., Optical Soc. Am., Washington Acad. Scis.; mem. Illuminating Engring. Soc. Gt. Britain, Soc. Automotive Engrs., Inst. Traffic Engrs. (affiliate). Address: Washington, D.C. Died Feb. 17, 1974; interred Rock Creek Cemetery, Washington, D.C.

TEESING, H(UBERT) P(AUL) H(ANS), educator; b. Amsterdam, Holland, Mar. 6, 1907; s. Hubert A.H. and Johanna (Hanewacker) T.; candiate's and doctoral exam. U. Groningen, 1929-35, Ph.D., 1948; student U. Heidelberg (Germany), 1933; m. Masha Polak, June 29, 1953; 1 dau., Erika (Mrs. Leo Schenck). Tchr. high schs., colls., Groningen, 1935-36; Middelburg, 1937-42, Amsterdam, 1942-52; asso. prof. Utrecht U., 1952-56, prof. German lit. and theory of lit. 1956-73, mem. univ. bd. Vis. prof., U. Cologne (Germany), 1956, U. Mich., Ann Arbor, 1961-62. Author: Das Problem der Perioden in der Literaturgeschichte, 1948; Literary History and Literary Theory, 1952; Irony in Literature, 1956. Co-editor jour. Neophilologus. Contbr. articles to profl. jours. and collections. Home: Utrecht, Netherlands. Died Aug. 19, 1973.

TEGTMEYER, WILLIAM HAHNE, bus. exec.; b. Chgo.; s. William O. and Elizabeth (Hahne) T.; B.S., Harvard; M.B.A., Northwestern U.; m. Constance Haig. Trader and salesman Paul II Davis & Co., Chgo., 1928-42; pres. (and or prin. or partner predeccessor firms) Wm. H. Tegtmeyer & Co., investment brokers, Chgo., 1946-65, investment mgrs., 1968; Chmn. C.I. Corp., investment mgr., 1973; sr. v.p., dir. The Chgo. Corp., investment brokers, Chgo., 1965-68; chmn. Super Food Services, Inc., 1957-68; chmn. bd. Automatic Burner Corp., 1963-72; dir. Stenographic Machines Corp. Served from pvt. to capt. AUS, 1942-45. Christian Scientist. Clubs: Mid-Day, Executives, University, Harvard, Svithiod Singing, Northwestern, Harvard (Chgo.). Home: Chicago, Ill. Died 1974.

TEMMEY, LEO ALBERT, lawyer; b. Onica, S.D., Nov. 6, 1894; s. Lawrence A. and Annie (O'Connor) T.; student S.D. State Coll., 1910-12; LL.B., U. Minn., 1915; m. Rose Tracy, Nov. 18, 1920; children—Larry A., Robert J. Admitted to Minn. bar, 1915; dep. states atty., Beadle County, S.D., 1926-30, states atty., 1930-35; mem. firm Temmey & Luby, Huron, S.D., 1936-75; atty. gen. State of S.D., 1939-42. Candidate for gov. of S.D., 1942; chmn. S.D. Republican Com.; mem. Rep. Nat. Com., 1960-66. Served with Co. I, 355th Inf., U.S. Army, World War I; AEF in France; commd. maj., U.S. Army, 1942; staff judge adv. gen., Washington; lt. col., mem. staff War Dept. Bd. Contract Appeals; staff under sec. war. Mem. Am., S.D., Beadle County bar assns., S.D. States Attys. Assn. (pres. 1933-35), S.D. Elks Assn. (pres. 1939-40), Am. Legion (state comdr. 1935-36, nat. vice-comdr. 1936-37), V.F.W., Phi Sigma Kappa. Home: Huron, S.D., Died Apr. 22, 1975.

TEMPKA, TADEUSZ, educator, physician; b. Cracow, Poland, Oct. 15, 1885; s. Bazej and Helena (Nowakowska) T.; Doctorate Medicine, Jagiellonian U., Cracow, 1911; m. Jakubowicz, Feb. 14, 1962. Docent Med. Faculty, Jagiellonian U., Cracow, 1926-45, prof. medicine, 1945—; head Med. Research Centre, Krynica. Decorated comdr.'s cross Order Polonia Restituta; State Sci. Prize 1st Class. Hon. Mem. Cracow Med. Soc., Lublin Med. Soc., Polish Soc. Internal Medicine, J.E. Purkyn Czechoslovak Med. Soc.; mem. Polish Acad. Learning, Polish Acad. Scis. Author textbook on diesases of hemogenous system; also articles. Pioneered biopsic examins. in Poland, biopsic exam. medulla and endocrines, astrohematic research, astrohematologic research. Home: Cracow, Poland, Died Mar. 14, 1974.

TENBULZEN, LESTER DALE, feed and hatcher exec.; b. Firth, Neb., Mar. 27, 1917; s. Henry John and Susanna (Obbink) T.; grad. high sch.; m. Lorraine Eloise Lister, Sept. 20, 1938; children—Judith (Mrs. Dennis Holm), Jane (Mrs. Ronald Olson), Jack L., Dale Lister, Cynthia (Mrs. Charles Dusenbury). Partner, Tenhulzen & Sons Hatchery, Denison, Ia., 1934-61; owner Tenhulzens Poultry Farms, Denison, 1954; pres. Tenhulzens' Hatchery & Feed Mill, Inc., Denison, 1961. Mem. bd. Indsl. Devel. Com., 1959. Served with USNR, 1944-45. Decorated Purple Heart. Named Man of Year, Poultry Industry, 1969. Mem. Ia. Poultry Assn. (pres. 1964-65). Republican. Presbyn. (mem. numerous coms.). Mason (Shriner), Odd Fellow. Clubs: Denison Country (sec. 1946-47), Exchange. Home: Denison, IA. Died May 6, 1973.

TENGGREN, GUSTAF ADOLF, illustrator, b. Magra Socken, Sweden, Nov. 3, 1896; s. Aron E. and Augusta (Andersdotter) T.; student Slodforening Art Sch., 1912-14. Valand Sch. of Fine Art, 1915-17; m. Malin Froberg, Sept. 21, 1927. Came to U.S., 1920, naturalized, 1936. One-man show Meden's Art Gallery, Gothenburg, 1916, U. Me., 1969; ann. Fairy tale Bland Tomtar o'Troll illustrator, Stockholm, 1917-26; exhibited in group shows Akron Art Inst., Me. Art Gallery, Tenggren Tellit Again, Carnegie Gallery-University of Maine, University Maine Traveling show, and others. Mem. Authors League of Am., Me. Art Gallery. Books illustrated: Tenggren Mother Goose, 1940; Stories from the Great Metropolitan Operas, 1943; Sing for Christman, 1943; Sing for America, 1944; Tenggren's Story Book, 1945; Farm Storie, 1946; Tenggren's Cowboys & Indians, 1948; Pirate Ships and Sailors, 1951; Tenggren's Arabian Nights, 1957; Canterbury Tales, 1961; King Arthur and the Knights of the Round Table, 1962. Home: West Southport, Me. Died Apr. 6, 1970; buried Spruce Lawn Cemetery, West Southport, Me.

TERAO, TAKEO, banker; b. Apr. 5, 1905; student Tokyo U. With Nomura Bank (name later changed to Daiwa Bank), 1929—, dir. 1947—, mng. dir., pres., 1950—. Mem. Fed. Bankers Assn. (v.p.), Osaka Bankers Assn. (v.p.). Address: Osaka, Japan., Died May 25, 1974.

TERRELL, CHARLES EVERETT, business exec.; b. Scarsboro, Ia., Dec. 4, 1880; s. Charles W. and Ida May (Evans) T.; student U. of Ia., 1901-02; m. Helen Mixer, Jan. 30, 1906; 1 dau. Nancy (Mrs. Brandon Carrell) With Dun and Bradstreet from 1930, became dir., v.p., 1931, executive vice pres., 1940-52, com., 1952, ret., 1956. Mem. Phi Delta Theta. Republican. Clubs: City, Brook Hollow (Dallas). Home: Dallas Tex.†

TERRELL, MARJORIE SMITH (MRS. WILLIAM SALE TERRELL), church assn. ofcl.; b. Toledo, Sept. 6, 1891; d. Willard Huntington and Rachel (Geddes) Smith; A.B., Mt. Holyoke Coll., 1913; certificate N.Y. Sch. Social Work, 1915; L.H.D., Keuka Coll., 1959, Mt. Holyoke Coll., 1962; m. William Sale Terrell, Oct. 30, 1918; children—John Rigby, Huntington, Robert Baynham. Pres. Hartford Council Ch. Women, 1944-46; pres. Conn. Council Ch. Women, 1947-51; v.p. Conn. Council Chs., 1947-51; mem. bd. mgrs. United Ch. Women, 1944-64; v.p. gen. dept. United Ch. Women, Nat. Council Chs., 1950-53, nat. pres. United Ch. Women, 1958-61; mem. planning com. for Nat. Council Chs., 1948-50, exec. bd. div. Christian life and work 1954-65, recording sec., 1957-60, mem. policy and strategy com., 1958-61; mem. gen. bd. Nat. Council Chs., 1950-63, v.p. Nat. Council Chs., 1960-63; mem. United Ch. Women Com. 100, 1964-67. Adv. com. Gov.'s Fact Finding Commn. on Edn., 1949-51; religious adv. council Pres.'s Com. on Govt. Contracts, 1959-60; mem. Nat. Women's Com. on Civil Rights, 1963-66; rep. Am. Bapt. Conv. to Evanston Assembly, World Council Chs., 1954; del. Bapt. World Alliance, London, 1955, Oberlin Conf. Faith and Order, 1957, Cleve. World Order Conf., 1953, 58, World Council Chs. Dept. on Coop. Men and Women in Church and Soc., Spittal, Austria, , 1959, World Council Chs. Conf. Christian Responsibility in Areas of Rapid Social Change, Salonika, Greece, 1959, World Council Chs. Central Com. in Rhodes, World Council Chs. Consultation Orthodox Women, Athens, 1959; mem. Internat. Leadership Team to Prayer Fellowship of Women from 21 Latin Am. countries, Lima, Peru, 1961. Bd. dirs, Hartford YWCA, 1946-52, Greater Hartford Community Council, 1946-49 Hartford Tb and Pub. Health Soc., 1947-49; adv. bd. Service Bur. for Women's

Orgns., Conn., 1947-51, 63-66; trustee Regional Community Colls. Conn., 1965-73, mem. budget and planning coms., academic policies com., bd. trustees. Mem. West Hartford League Women Voters, West Hartford Woman's Club (dir. 1948-50), Mt. Holyoke Coll. Club: Hartford. Address: West Hartford, Conn. Died May 11, 1973; buried Binghamton, N.Y.

TERRY, WILLIAM MICHAEL, radiologist; b. Prague, Czechoslovakia, July 16, 1916; came to U.S., 1948; s. Rudolf F. and Valeria K. Terry; M.D., Oxford (Eng.) U., 1943; m. Katherine Fischel; children—Barbara, Joan, Susan, Peter. Rotating intern Lawrence and Meml. Hosp., New London, Conn., 1949-50; resident in radiology Grace-New Haven Hosp., 1950-53, chief resident, 1952-53; practice medicine, specializing in radiology, Keene, N.H., 1954-69. Instr., Am. Cancer Soc., Yale, 1952-53. Active Monadnock Area Family Services, Planned Parenthood of Southwest N.H. Served to capt. M.C., Royal Army, 1943-45. Diplomate Am. Bd. Radiology. Mem. A.M.A., Am. Soc. Radiologists, Am. Coll. Radiology. Unitarian (pres., trustee). Home: Keene, N.H., Died Jan. 6, 1969; buried Munsonville, N.H.

TERTIS, LIONEL, viola player; b. W. Hartlepool, Eng., Dec. 29, 1876; student Leipzig, Germany, also Royal Acad. Music; m. Ada Gawthrop (dec. 1951) m. 2d, Lillian Florence Margaret Warmington, 1959. Tours of Europe and U.S. as soloist with orchestras and in concert; arranged various concertos for viola, also persuaded contemporary composers to write concertos for viola; designer Tertis model viola, Tertis model violoncello, Tertis model violin. Decorated comdr. British Empire, chevalier de l'Ordre de Couronne: recipient Gold medal Royal Philharmonic Soc.; Fritz Kreisler Award of Merit, 1950; Eugene Ysaye Medal (Brussels), 1968; hon. fellow Trinity Coll., London. Fellow Royal Acad. Music. Author: Beauty of Tone in String Playing 1938; Cinderella No More, an Autobiography, 1953; A Complete Autobiography, My Viola and I, 1974; also numerous articles, arrangements for viola. Club: Sesame. Address: London, Eng. Died Feb. 22, 1975.

THACKER, CARL GALE, fraternal order exec.; b. Ada, Okla., Feb. 27, 1907; s. Silas S. and Caraline (Johnson) T.; ed. pub. schs.; m. Mary Garnet Sanders, Aug. 1, 1929; children—Mary Jean (Mrs. Ewell Casey), Donald Robert. Mem. Fraternal Order of Eagles, 1934-75, grand worthy pres., after 1962, Northwest Aerie adviser, 1963-75. Home: Yakima, Wash., Died Apr. 21, 1975; interred Tahoma Cemetery, Yakima, Wash.

THANT, U, former sec.-gen. UN; b. Pantanaw, Burma, Jan. 1909; s. Pho Hnit and Daw Nan Thaung; student Univ. Coll., Rangoon, Burma; m. Daw Thein Tin, Nov. 17, 1934; 1 dau., Aye Aye Thant. Headmaster, Nat. High Sch., Pantanaw, Burma, 1931-42; sec. Bd. Edn. Burma, 1942-47, dir. press, 1947, dir. broadcasting, 1948, information sec., 1949-53, prime minister's sec., 1953-57; ambassador, permanent rep. UN, 1957-61; acting sec.-gen. UN, 1961, sec.-gen., 1962-71; sr. fellow Adlai Stevenson Inst. Internat. Affairs, Chgo., 1972-74. Adviser to prime minister of Burma internat. confs. including Bandung Conf., 1955. Mem. Burma Research Soc., Burma Text Book Com., Burma Translation Soc. (councillor). Author: Cities and their Stories, 1931; League of Nations, 1933; Toward a New Education, 1946. Home: Harrison, N.Y. Died Nov. 25, 1974.

THARP, MABEL FRANCES ROBINSON (MRS. VICTOR A THARP), bus. service exec.; b. Asheville, N.C., Apr. 19, 1899; d. Charles Edwin and Mary Lizzie (Ramsaur) Robinson; A.B., U. N.C., 1921; postgrad. King's Bus. Coll., 1923-24, Unity Sch. Christianity, Unity Village, Mo., 1936-72; m. Victor A. Tharp, Feb. 11, 1925 (dec. Apr. 1963); children—Arta (Mrs. J. C. Culbertson), Carl (dec.), Tchr., N.C., 1918, 21-22, W.Va., 1922-23; sec. Walla Walla (Wash.) Savs. & Loan, 1926; started steno office, Walla Walla, 1927; sec. to coop. specialist State of Washington, Hunt's Point, 1934; sec., bill collector for Victor A. Tharp, 1935-45; sec. to supt. Wash. State Penitentiary, Walla Walla, 1945-46; owner Harry Tharp Bus. Service, Walla Walla, 1950. Red Cross Grey Lady, VA Hosp., 1947-50. Mem. Walla Walla Bus. and Profl. Women's Club (state pub. relations chmn. 1936), Natural Foods Assos., Sr. Citizens Group, A.A.U.W., Am. Assn. Retired Persons. Democrat. Mem. Pythian Sisters. Address: Walla Walla, Wash. Died Mar. 1973.

THAYER, EDWIN FORCE, publisher; b. Newtonville, Mass., May 7, 1903; s. Edwin Montgomery and Maynard (Force) T.; B.S., Calif. Inst. Tech., Pasadena, Calif., 1925; m. Ruth Hubley, Nov. 29, 1930; 1 dau., Julie Clark. Asst. editor Electric Railway Journal, 1925; asst. editor McGraw-Hill Pub. Co., 1925-26; publicity mgr. Philadelphia Rapid Transit Co., 1927-30, also advt. mgr. Mitten Bank & Securities Corp., 1928-30; asst. to pres. St. Louis Pub. Service Co., 1930-33; central mgr. Retail Ledger Pub. Co., 1934-36; eastern mgr. Advertising Publications, Inc., 1937-43; pres. and pub. Tide Pub. Co., Inc., 1943-49; business manager of Quick Magazine 1949-63. Served as 1st lieut., Engrs., O.R.C., 1926-35. Chmn. bus. paper div. Am. Red. Cross War Fund, 1944-45. Dept. sector comdr. Air Warden Service, 1942-45. Trustee, Village of Ocean Beach, N.Y. 1946, mayor, 1946-47. Mem. Nat. Indsl. Advertisers Assn., Sales Execs. Club of N.Y.; chmn. bus. paper adv. com. of Advertising Council. Clubs: Western University, Advertising (New York, N.Y.), Nat. Press Club (Washington, D.C.). Home: Old Saybrook, Conn., Died Apr. 8, 1975.

THAYER, GEORGE CHAPMAN, JR., author; grad. U. Pa., also London (Eng.) Sch. Econs. Author: The British Political Fringe, 1965: The Farther Shores of Politics, 1967; The War Business, 1969; The American Political Fringe Today; others. Address: New York City, N.Y. Died Aug. 13, 1973.

THEOBALD, WALTER HENRY, otolaryngologist; b. Oconomowoc, Wis., Dec. 19, 1886; s. Peter A. and Sophia (Schudderkopf) T.; S.B., U. Chgo., 1909; M.D., Rush Med. Coll., 1911; m. Mildred Morkill, 1913; children—Pierce, Harriet M. (Mrs. Hugh M. Elwood). Specialist in diseases of ear, nose and throat, Chgo., 1913-69; intern St. Luke's Hosp., 1911-12; examining surgeon I.C. R.R., 1912; otolaryngologist Municipal Tb Sanitarium, 1914; became mem. sr. attending staff St. Luke's Hosp., 1915, emeritus staff Presbyn.-St. Luke's Hosp.; emeritus prof. dept. otolaryngology U. Ill., Research and Ednl. Hosp.; cons. Chgo. Bd. Health. V.p. Oconomowoc Canning Co.; dir. Champion Machinery Co., Joliet, Ill. Pres. Med. Center Commn. Ill., 1946-74. Mem. Procurement and Assignment Comm., 1944-45. Served as med. examiner Exemption Bd., SSS, Chgo., 1917-18. Recipient George Coleman medal Inst. Medicine, 1962. Fellow Inst. Medicine (pres. 1951); mem. A.M.A., Ill., Chgo. med. socs., Otolaryngology Soc., Am. Laryngol. Assn., Am. Acad. Ophthalmology and Otolaryngology (pres. 1954), Am. Laryngol., Rhinol. and Otol. Soc., Phi Beta Pi. Contbr. to med. lit. Home: Chicago, Ill., Died Dec. 1974.

THIBAUD, JACQUES, violinist; b. Brodeaux, France, Sept. 7, 1880; s. Georges and Reverdy T.; ed. Bordeaux Coll. and Paris Conservatory of Music (1st prize for violin, 1896); m. Marguerite Frankfort, of Paris, France, Sept. 30, 1902. First came to U.S., 1903. Composer for violin.†

THOMAS, BEAUMONT, chem. constrn. co. exec.; b. Llanelli, Wales, Nov. 23, 1910; s. John A. and Elizabeth A. (Lewis) T.; came to U.S., 1927, naturalized, 1933; B.A. in Chemistry, W. Va. U., 1933; m. Vera Catherine Finley, Jan. 14, 1939; children—Nancy (Mrs. Nicholas D. Morgia), Barry F. Chemist, Nat. Steel Co., Weirton, W. Va., 1933-37; research engr. Battelle Meml. Inst., Columbus, O., 1937-39; chief chemist Stebbins Engring & Mfg. Co., Watertown, N.Y., 1939-52, v.p. 1952-67, exec. v.p., 1967-72, also dir.; pres. Canadian Stebbins Engring. & Mfg. Co. Ltd., Montreal, Que. Fellow Am. Inst. Chemists; mem. Am. Soc. Testing and Materials (Merit award 1959). Am. Chem. Soc. T.A.P.P.I., Nat. Assn. Corrosion Engrs., Phi Beta Kappa. Contbr. articles to profl. jours., textbook. Patentee in field. Home: Watertown, N.Y. Died July 17, 1972; buried Brookside Cemetery, Watertown, N.Y.

THOMAS, EDWARD TRUDEAU, coll. dean; b. Balt., Oct. 9, 1901; s. Henry M. and Josephine Poe (Carey) T.; B.S., Princeton, 1923; certificate in edn. (Rhodes scholar), Oxford U., 1925; student Harvard Grad. Sch. Edn., Columbia Tchrs. Coll.; m. Martha Botsford, Sept. 2, 1932; children—James Carey, Henry Botsford, Patricia Carey. Tchr. various pvt. schs., 1925-34; headmaster Bedford-Rippawam Sch., N.Y., 1934-37, Shady Side Acad., Pitts., 1937-40; asst. admissions dir. Johns Hopkins, 1945-46; dean of admission Hofstra Coll., 1946; tchr. Knox Sch., 1961. Pres. Five Towns Community Council, Lawrence (N.Y.) Civic Assn. Trustee Knox Sch. Served to lt. comdr. USNR, 1940-45. Home: St James, N.Y. Died Aug. 24, 1973.

THOMAS, FAY MATHEW bank ofcl.; b. Creston, Ia., July 9, 1890; s. Lincoln and Fannie Elizabeth (Brenanstal) T.; m. Willa Mae Adams, July 19, 1919; children—Clinton L., Jean-Faye. Mgr. Richmond (Va.) Cafeterias, Inc., 1920-22; gen. mgr. United Hotels Corp. Cafeterias, Toronto and Montreal, Can., 1922-25; mgr. Cavalier Hotel, Virginia Beach, Va., 1925-27; gen. mgr. Hotel Roanoke (Va.), 1927-29, Motel Patrick Henry, 1929-32, Exchange Buffet Corp., N.Y.C., 1932-35; v.p., gen. mgr. Hotel Carter, Cleve., 1935-39; asst. to pres. Hotel New Yorker, N.Y.C., 1939-41; v.p., gen. mgr. Hotel Roosevelt, New Orleans, 1941-42, Hotel Book-Cadilla Detroit, 1942-52; v.p. for bus. devel. Broward Nat. Bank Ft. Lauderdale, Fla., 1955-72; dir. Key Biscayne Hotel and Villas, Miami, Jacksonville Coach Co., Jacksonville, Fla. Col. Civil Air Patrol, 1941-50, Mich. wing comdr., Midwest regional comdr., then mem. nat. exec. com.; dir. funding bd. Internat. Swimming Hall of Fame. Served with U.S. Army, World War 1. Mem. Am. Legion, D.A.V., Mil. Order World Wars, Detroit Bd. Commerce, So., Ohio, Ft. Lauderdale (hon. life). Detroit hotel assns., Mich. Aeros. and Space Assn. (hon. life). Mason. Clubs: Detroit Athletic; Aero of Michigan (hon. life); Wings (N.Y.C.); Army and Navy (Washington); Ft. Lauderdale (Fla.) Lauderdale Yacht (dir.); Lago Mar Country. Home: Fort Lauderdale, Fla. Died July 20, 1974.

THOMAS, FRANK WATERS, educator; b. Danville, Ind., May 14, 1878; s. Erasmus Darwin and Mary (Roseborough) T.; grad. Ind. State Normal, Terre Haute, 1902; A.B., Ind. U., 1905; A.M., U. of Ill., 1919; Ph.D., Stanford, 1926; LL.D. (honorary), Occidental College, 1945; married Ina Gregg, Sept. 2, 1908 (died Nov. 11, 1942); children—Lawrence, W. Craig. Franklin married 2d, Edith Archer Hover, December 4, 1957. Instructor at the Academy University of Ill., 1906-10, prin. Acad., 1910-11; prin. high sch., Santa Monica, Calif., 1911-13; prin. schs. Sacramento, Calif. 1913-17; head of dept. of edn., Fresno (Calif.) State Coll., 1917-27, pres., 1972-48; lecturer in summer sessions. Stanford, Univ. of Calif., U. of Hawaii U. of Southern California; cons. Pasadena Sch. Survey, 1951-52; visiting professor Claremont Graduate School., 1952-53. Pres. Am. Assn. of Teachers Colleges, 1938-39; mem. Nat. Commn. on Teacher Edn., 1939-43. Member NEA, Phi Beta Kappa, Phi Delta Kappa, Sigma Nu. Republican. Rotarian. Author: Training for Effective Study, 1921; Principles and Technique of Teaching, 1927; (with others) The Jr. Coll.-Its Organization and Adminstration, 1927; Principles of Modern Education (with A. R. Lang), 1937; An Experience in Health Education, 1950. in Health Education, 1950. Editor Calif. Jour. Secondary Edn., 1948-51. Home: Menlo Park, Cal.†

THOMAS, FREDDIE LEVY, research biologist; b. Norfolk, Va., Feb. 10, 1918; s. James Purnell and Hallie (Armstrong) T.; B.S., Wagner Coll., 1950; postgrad. Albany Med. Coll., 1950-52, U. Rochester, intermittently; m. Margaret Caroline Banks, Feb. 9, 1957. Research technologist Eastman Kodak, Rochester, N.Y., 1952-60; research asst. U. Rochester Sch. Medicine and Dentistry (N.Y.), 1961-66, research asso., 1966-74; owner pres. Original Researches. Vis. prof. Howard U., 1972-73. Recipient Award for Outstanding Achievement Nat. Assn. Negro Bus. and Profl. Women's Club, 1964; Wagner Coll. Alumni award, 1969; Imhotep-Ernest E. Just Sci. award, 1973; Nat. Dental Assn. award; Distinguished Service award Roxbury Tech. Inst., 1974; Community Service award Parents and Students Want to Know Group, 1968. Mem. Am. Acad. History Dentistry, A.A.A.S., Soc. Cryobiology, Pakistan Assn. Advancement Sci., Tissue Culture Assn., Math. Assn. Am., Rochester Acad. Sci., N.Y. Acad. Scis., Soc. Am. Historians, Inc., Am. Assn. for History of Medicine, Univ. Archaeol. Soc., Assn. for Study Negro Life and History, Royal Soc. Health (London), Royal Canadian Inst., Internat. Platform Assn., Ghana Assn., Sigma Xi. Mason. Editor Peoples Weekly, 1961-74, Evidence Newspaper. Contbr. articles to profl. jours. Inventor perfusion staining and photomicrography of viable cells in Thomas: Cramer chamber. Home: Rochester, N.Y. Died Feb. 1974.

THOMAS, HAROLD RUDOLPH, physician; b. Pine Forest, Hopkins County, Tex., Sept. 1907; s. Harry Raymond and Lela (Minter) T.; M.D., Baylor U., 1934; m. Elaine Warfield, Feb. 8, 1947; children—Randall (dec.), Lynn, Sharon (Mrs. Gerald S. Callaway). Intern, Baylor U. Hosp., Dallas, 1934-35, attending staff, 1951-74; intern Tampa (Fla.) Municipal Hosp., 1935-36; resident Brooke Army Hosp., San Antonio, 1947-50, Robert B. Green Hosp., San Antonio, 1950-51. Served to lt. col., M.C., AUS, 1940-50. Diplomate Am. Bd. Obstetrics and Gynecology. Mem. A.M.A. Home: Dallas, Tex., Died July 6, 1974; buried Hillcrest Meml. Park, Dallas, Tex.

THOMAS, JAMES SHELBY economist; b. Saltville, Va., Mar. 27, 1879; s. Samuel Morgan and Sarah (Vail) T.; B.A., Milligan Coll., 1900; M.A., Lynchburg College, 1904; graduate work, U. of Chicago, 1919; LL.D., Univ. of Alabama; m. Ethel McCartney, of New Castle, Va., June 18, 1902. Prof. history and Latin, Milligan Coll., 1900-03; prof. history, Lynchburg Coll., 1903-05; Va. state sch. examiner, 1905-08; state rural sch. supervisor of Va., 1908-10; dean of faculty, Lynchburg Coll., 1910-11; prof. secondary edn., U. of Ala., 1912-19; organized, and was dir. of extension div., U. of Ala., 1919-30; asso. dir. Ala. State Industrial Bd., 1928-29; chief economist Commonwealth & Southern Corpn., 1931-33; pres. Clarkson Coll. of Technology from June 1933; pres. Chrysler Inst. of Engring., Detroit. Mem. advisory council Vocational Edn. for N.Y. Civilian aide to sec. of War for Ala. Past dist. gov. Rotary Internat. and mem. Boy's Work Com., and economic advisory com. of N. America, Rotary Internat. Mem. NEA, Am. Acad. Polit. and Social Science, Newcomen Soc., Phi Beta Kappa, Sigma Chi. Democrat. Mem. Christian (Disciples) Ch. Clubs: Potsdam, Potsdam Country. Author: What machine Has Done to Mankind; New Frontiers for Smart People; This Thing Called Democracy. Contbr. to Engineering Opportunities, mags. and trade jours. Lecturer and traveler. Home: Potsdam, N.Y.†

THOMAS, PAUL HENWOOD, physician, coll. dean; b. Phila., May 8, 1926; s. John E. and Elizabeth (Henwood) T.; student U. Pa., 1949-51; D.O., Phila. Coll. Osteo. Medicine, 1955; B.S., Drexel U., 1962; Ph.D., Temple U., 1966; m. Miriam E. Gratz, June 25, 1960. Intern, Hosps. Phila. Coll. Osteo. Medicine, 1955-56, instr. physiology, 1956-62, asso. dean, prof. physiology, 1967, dean, 1969-72; gen. practice osteo. medicine, Hatboro, Pa., 1957-72; postdoctoral fellow Nat. Heart Inst., 1962-66; cons. div. physician manpower Dept. Health, Edn. and Welfare, 1969-72. Mem. Nat. Bd. Examiners Osteo. Physicians and Surgeons, 1965-72. Gov's. Task Force on Health Manpower, Commonwealth Pa., 1970-72. Served with

USMCR, 1944-47. Mem. Am. Assn. Osteo. Colls. (sec.-treas. 1968-72), A.A.A.S., Am. Heart Assn., Assn. Am. Med. Colls., Am., Pa. osteo. assns., N.Y. Acad. Sci., Franklin Inst. Phila., Phila. Physiol. Soc. Mason. Home: Media, Pa. Died June 18, 1972.

THOMAS, ROBERT DAVID, rubber co. exec.; b. Akron, O., Sept. 26, 1909; s. John Webster and Bertha Agnes (Hines) T.; grad. Asheville (N.C.) Sch., 1927; B.A., Amherst Coll., 1931; m. Mary Ann Morgenroth, Feb. 2, 1935; children—Susan (Mrs. Gary A. Kepler), Robert David, John Webster II, William Simon. With Firestone Tire & Rubber Co., Akron, 1931-73; gen. trade sales mgr., 1961-63, v.p. trade sales, 1963-66, exec. v.p. dir., 1966-70, pres., dir., 1970-71. Chief tire maintenance Office Def. Transp., Washington, 1942, regional dir., Cleve., 1942-45. Mem. Alpha Delta Phi. Episcopalian. Clubs: Portage Country, Firestone Country Sharon Country (Akron); Rolling Rock, Laurel (Lacrobe, Pa.). Home: Akron, Ohio. Died Oct. 1973.

THOMAS, ROBERT MCK., JR., formerly sr. v.p., gen. mgr., pres. and chief exec. officer Thomas & Betts Corp., Elizabeth, N.J. Home: Mendham, N.J. Died Dec. 23, 1973.

THOMAS, ROY ZACHARIAH, prof. chemistry; b. Frederick Co., Md., Mar. 19, 1897; s. George Zachariah and Louisa Elizabeth (Grove) T.; prep. edn. Frederick Male High Sch.; A.B., Western Md. Coll., 1900; postgrad. work, Johns Hopkins, 1900-02; M.A., West Lafayette (O.) Coll., 1902; Ph.D., Kansas City U., 1904; spl. work, Columbia; m. Alberta Clark Lingo, of Barton, Md., June 20, 1903; children—Louise, Albert (dec.), Helen Alberta, Roy Z., Goodwin Grove, James, Robert. V.p. and prof. science and mathematics, West Lafayette Coll., 1903-06; acting pres., 1906-07; prof. science and oratory, Newberry (S.C.) Coll., 1907-13; prof. chemistry Winthrop Coll., Rock Hill. S.C., 1913-26, also head of dept.; state food insp. for S.C., World War, also lecturer on war issues. Mem. Am. Chem. Soc., A.A.A.S., S.C. Chem. Soc. (pres.), S.C. Acad. Science (v.p.), Winthrop Science Club (pres.). Democrat. Presbyn. Rotarian. Commencement speaker; Chautauqua and lyceum lecturer. Author: A Laboratory Manual of General Chemistry, 1918; also brochures and articles on chem. topics. Contbg. editor Jour. of Chemical Education. Conductor of ednl. tours of Europe and America; pres. Thomas Tours, Inc. Home: Rock Hill, S.C.†

THOMAS, STANLEY POWERS ROWLAND, author; b. Castine, Maine, June 22, 1879; s. Rev. Lewis J. and Annie Frances (Powers) T.; A.B., Harvard, 1901; unmarried. Winner of Collier's $5,000 prize story, 1905. Author: The Little Gods, 1909; contbr. numerous short storeis. stories. Address: Milbrook Mass.†

THOMASON, ROBERT EWING, judge; b. Shelbyville, Tenn., May 30, 1879; s. Dr. Benjamin R. and Susan Olivia (Hoover) T.; B.S., Southwestern U., Georgetown, Tex., 1898; LL.B., U. of Tex., 1900; m. Belle Davis, Feb. 14, 1905 (now dec.); children—William Ewing, Isabelle; m. 2d, Abbie Long, Aug. 18, 1927. Began practice of law, Gainesville, Tex., 1900; dist. atty., Gainesville, 1902-06; practiced at El Paso, Tex., after 1912; mem. Tex. Ho. of Reps., 1917-21, speaker of House, 1920-21; mayor of El Paso, 1927-31; mem. 72d to 80th Congresses from 16th Tex. Dist.; U.S. Dist. judge, western dist., Tex. Mem. Kappa Sigma, Phi Delta Phi. Democrat. Presbyn. Mason (33°). Home: El Paso, Tex. Died Nov. 8, 1973; buried Restlawn Meml. Cemetery, El Paso, Tex,

THOMPKINS, LEONARD JOSEPH, physician; b. Phila., Sept. 27, 1934; s. Leonard Thomas and Alice Mary Thompkins; A.B. in Biology, LaSalle Coll., Phila., 1956; M.D., Jefferson Med. Coll., Phila., 1960. Intern, Misericordia Hosp., Phila., 1960-61, asso. pathologist, 1967-72, attending pathologist, 1972-74; resident in anat. pathology and clin. pathology Jefferson Med. Coll. Hosp., 1961-65; asst. chief pathology U.S. Naval Hosp., St. Albans, N.Y., 1965-67; instr. dept. pathology Jefferson Med. Coll., 1965-73, asst. prof. pathology, 1973-74; lectr. in pathology Phila. Coll. Pharmacy and Sci., 1971-74. Served as lt. comdr. M.C., USNR, 1965-69. Diplomate Am. Bd. Pathology. Fellow Coll. Am. Pathologists, Am. Soc. Clin. Pathologists, Phila. Coll. Physicians (fellowship com.); mem. Pa. Assn. Clin. Pathologists, Internat. Acad. Pathology, Assn. Clin. Scientists, Phila. Pathol. Soc., Am. Soc. Cytology, Am. Assn. Blood Banks, N.J. Soc. Pathologists. Contbr. articles to profl. jours. Home: Jenkintown, Pa. Died Sept. 25, 1974; buried Holy Sepulchre Cemetery, Glenside, Pa.

THOMPSON, HELEN MULFORD, orchestra exec.; b. Greenville, Ill.; d. Job Herbert and Lena (Henry) Mulford; student DePauw U., 1926-27; A.B. cum laude, U. Ill., 1932; Litt.D., Conservatory of Music Cin., 1961; Mus.D., Marshall U., 1967; m. Carl D. Thompson, Apr. 8, 1933; 1 son, Charles D. Agy. dir., casework supr. pub. and pvt. agys., Ill., Wis., N.Y., 1932-40; mgr. Charleston Symphony Orch., 1940-50; exec. sec. Am. Symphony Orch. League, 1950-63, exec. v.p., 1963-70; mgr. N.Y. Philharmonic, N.Y.C., 1970-74. Exec. vice chmn. Pres.'s music com. of People-to-People Program, 1956-59; mem. study panel Rockefeller Brothers Fund study on Performing Arts in U.S. Recipient Laurel Leaf award Am. Composers Alliance, 1961. Mem. Am. Fedn. Musicians, Nat. Music Council (mem. exec. com.), Phi Beta Kappa, Alpha Chi Omega, Sigma Alpha Iota. Presbyn. Author: The Community Symphony Orchestra — How to Organize and Develop it; also articles in field. Co-author: Organization and Presentation of Symphony Orchestra Concert Activities. Editor: Newsletter of Am. Symphony Orch. League, 1948-70. Home: New York City, N.Y. Died June 25, 1974.

THOMPSON, J. ERIC S., archaeologist; b. London, Eng., Dec. 31, 1898; s. George William and Mary (Cullen) T.; ed. Winchester Coll., Cambridge Univ.; m. Florence L. Keens, 1930; 1 son. Donald Enrique. Asst. curator, Central and South Am. archaeology, Chicago Natural History Mus., 1926-35; sr. archaeologist, dept. archaeology, Carnegie Inst. Washington, 1935; hon. prof. Museo Nacional de Mexico, 1941; research asso. Chicago Nat. Hist. Mus., 1942; numerous archaeological trips to C.A. and Mexico, 1941; specialist in Maya hierogyphic writing. Awarded Rivers Mem. Medal of Royal Anthropological Institute for field work in Maya area, 1945; recipient of Viking Fund medal, 1955. Protestant Episcopalian. Author numerous books and arts on Maya and Mexican archaeology and ethnology. Pres. Internat. Congress Americanists, Cambridge Eng., 1952. Home: Cambridge, England, Died Sept. 9, 1975.

THOMPSON, JAMES GOODHART, finance co. exec.; b. Lewistown, Pa., July 28, 1911; s. Charles M. and Martha (Goodhart) T.; B.S., Pa. State U., 1932; m. Natalle V. Lantz, Apr. 20, 1935; children—James Lantz, Phillp Gregg. Gen. ins. agt., 1932-34; mgr. local agy. Swigart Assos., 1934-36; sec., gen. mgr. Gen. Finance Co., 1936-38; sec., gen. mgr., dir. co-founder Gen. Finance Service, 1938, subsidiary cos. The Budget Plan, Inc., 1938, Keystone Consumer Discount Co., 1944; pres. Mary Ellen Coal Co., 1942-44, New Way Flying System, 1943-46; pres., dir. Gen. Finance Service Corp., The Budget Plan, Inc., 1946, Oneida Agy., 1950, The Budget Plan Consumer Discount Co., 1959; pres. Shirley Ayr Canning & Freezing Co., 1947-49; dir. Penn Central Nat. Bank, Huntingdon, Pa., Security of Am. Life Ins. Co., Reading, Pa. Select Risk Ins. Co. Pres., Huntingdon (Pa.) Community Chest, 1952. Served with USNR, 1945-46. Mem. C. of C. (past pres. Huntingdon), Pa. (dir., past pres., exec. com.), Nat. (state dir., pres.) consumer finance assns. Presbyn. Clubs: Union League, Rotary, Huntingdon Country (past pres., dir.), Seaview Country (Absecon, N.J.). Home: Huntingdon, Pa. Died Feb. 9, 1974.

THOMPSON, JOHN BERT, investigator in agrl.; b. in Indiana Co., Pa., Aug. 14, 1878; s. John Gray and Mary (Dilts) T.; B.S., Kan. State Agrl. Coll., Manhattan, Kan., 1905; unmarried. on fruit farm, San Bernardino Co., Cal., 1905-06; asst. in horticulture, N.M. Agrl. Coll., 4 mos., 1906; accepted position with Philippine Insular Govt., arriving in Manila, Dec. 24, 1906; successively agrl. insp., 1906-07; supt. Singalong Expt. Sta., 1907-09; dir. Guam Agrl. Expt. Sta., under U.S. Dept. Agr., from 1909. Life Mem. Am. Pomol. Soc. Home: San Bernardino, Cal.†

THOMPSON, JOHN KERWIN, banker; b. Paterson, N.J., Mar. 13, 1892; s. Frank and Sara Anne (Kerwin) T.; ed. public schools and high schools, Paterson, N.J.; student Sch. of Commerce, Accounts and Finance, New York U., 1911-12; m. Anne Louise Boyd, Feb. 11, 1918; children—Ruth Helen (Mrs. Walter E. Hoffman), Anne Boyd (Mrs. Hewitt A. Schoonover), Jr. clerk, accounting dept., Erie Railroad Co., 1907, gen. accountant, 1918-20, asst. to comptroller, 1920-23, asst. comptroller, 1923-31, comptroller, 1931-36, vice pres. and asst. to pres., 1936-38, vice pres. finance, accounting and purchase, 1938-44, dir., 1941-64; pres., dir. Union Commerce Bank, Cleve., 1944-55, chmn. bd., 1956-58, chmn. exec. com., 1959-63, hon. chmn., 1964-75; dir. U.S. Truck Lines, Inc. Trustee U. Hosps., John Carroll U., Cleve. Mason. Clubs: Union, Pepper Pike Country, The Country (Cleve.). Home: Cleveland, O., Died Jan. 3, 1975.

THOMPSON, M. GLADYS (Mrs. W. Stuart Thompson), club woman; b. N.Y.C.; d. John and Isabel (Rhind) Slade; B.A., Barnard Coll., 1913; student Am. Sch. Classical Studies (Athens, Greece), 1913-14, 22-25, N.Y. Sch. Social Work, 1934-35; m. W. Stuart Thompson, Aug. 22, 1913; children—W. Stuart, George C., Isabel F. (dec.). Exec. sec. Bklyn. League of Nations Assn., 1925-27. Worked with Greek Refugees, 1923-25; helped establish, mem. 1st bd. dirs., YWCA, Athens, Greece, 1922-24. Mem. Women's Aux. N.Y. Acad. Scis. (exec. bd. 1951-75), Am. Assn. U. Women. Presbyn. Clubs: Barnard and Greenwich College; Indian Harbor Yacht (Greenwich); Knollwood Garden; Women's Aux. Columbia U. Home: Greenwich, Conn., Died Sept. 4, 1975.

THOMPSON, RONALD BURDICK, univ. ofcl.; b. Chambersburg, Ill., Oct. 6, 1907; s. Grover C. and Nellie (Burdick) T.; A.B., Hastings Coll., 1929; M.A., U. Neb., 1933; Ph.D., 1939; LL.D., Marietta Coll., 1957; m. Alice Price, Aug. 24, 1930; children—Ruth Lauree, Marilyn Margaret, Kenneth Robert, Arthur Howard. Prin. high sch., Jansen, Neb., 1927-28, tchr. math. and music, Hastings, 1929-31; asst., dept. math. U. Neb., 1931-33, asst. tchrs. coll., 1935-36; supt. high sch., Beaver Crossing, 1933-35; instr. Sch. Edn., U. Utah, 1936-40, registrar, asso. prof. edn., 1940-44; registrar, univ. examiner and editor Ohio State U., Columbus, 1944-57, exec. dean, 1957-73; supr. instl. research Columbus Tech. Inst., 1973-75; cons. to registrar Punjab Agrl. U. and U. Udaipur, India, 1963-64. Cons. Pres.'s Com. on Edn. Beyond High Sch., 1956; hon. ednl. cons. 9th Service Command, Salt Lake City. Bd. dirs. Am. Coll. Testing Program, 1960-68. Mem. Am. Assn. Collegiate Registrars and Admissions Officer (pres. 1953-54), Sigma Xi, Phi Delta Kappa, Pi Mu Epsilon. Author: Remedial Arithmetic for High School Pupils, 1937; College Age Population Trends, 1940-1970, 1953; The Impending Tidal Wave of Students, 1954; The Problem of Rising College Enrollments, 1957; Enrollment Projections for Higher Education, 1961-1978, 1961; State of West Virginia Projection of Enrollment 1968-1985; Projected Enrollments College and Universities, Commonwealth of Kentucky, 1972-1985; Projected Enrollments Institutions of Higher Education State of Ohio, 1973-1989. Home: Columbus, Ohio. Died Sept. 15, 1975.

THOMPSON, STITH, educator, author; b. Bloomfield, Ky., Mar. 7, 1885; s. John Warden and Eliza (McClaskey) T.; student Butler Coll., Indianapolis; B.A., U. of Wis., 1909; M.A., U. of Calif., 1912; Ph.D., Harvard University, 1914; Litt.D., University of North Carolina, 1946; L.H.D., Indiana Central College, 1953; married to Louis Faust, June 14, 1918; children—Dorothy Cosette (Mrs. Robert L. Letsinger), Marguerite Frances (Mrs. David G. Hays). Secondary school teaching in Springfield, Kentucky, and Portland, Ore.; instr. English, U. of Tex., 1914-18; prof. English, Colorado Coll., 1918-20; asso. prof. English, U. of Me., 1920-21; asso. prof. English, Indiana University, 1921-29, prof., 1929-39, became professor of English and folklore, 1930, distinguished service professor of English and folklore, 1953-55, emeritus, 1955-76, dean grad. sch., 1947-50; Fulbright vis. prof. U. of Oslo, 1951-52. U.S. del. to Internat. Folklore Congress, Paris, 1937; official in various internat. folklore meetings; lectured throughout South America, 1947. Guggenheim fellow, 1956-57. Member of the American Folk-Lore Soc. (pres. 1937-40), Modern Language Assn. America, Medieval Acad. Am., Am. Philos. Soc., Internat. Commn. Folk Arts and Folklore (vice pres.), Delta Tau Delta, Phi Beta Kappa, Gustav Adolfs Akademi for Folklivsorskning, Société finnoougrienne (Helskinki), Norwegian Acad. Sci., Danish Acad. Letters and Science, hon. member folklore socities of various foreign countries. Unitarian. Author: Tales of the North American Indians, 1929; The Types of the Folk-Tale (with Antti Rarne; 1928; Motif-Index of Folk Literature, 6 vols, 1932-36, rev., 1955-57; Our Heritage of World Literature, 1938; The Folktale, 1946. Also author; co-author or translator numerous books, from 1912. contbr. articles on teaching of English and on folklore. Home: Columbus, Ind., Died Jan. 10, 1976.

THOMPSON, WILLIAM N., automobile mfr.; b. Indianapolis, Ind., Mar. 29, 1881; s. Thomas L. and Carrie E. (Zimmerman) T.; ed. pub. schs.; m. Jessie Helen Gilbert, of Indianapolis, Nov. 25, 1907. Has been identified with wholesale hardware business, wholesale lumber, banking and furniture mfg.; later pres. and gen. mgr. Stutz Motor Car Co. of America, Inc.; treas. The Gus Habich Co. Republican. Mason. Clubs: Columbia, Country, Canoe, Golf. Home: Indianapolis, Ind.†

THOMSON, SIR GEORGE PAGET, physicist; b. Cambridge, Eng., May 3, 1892; s. Sir Joseph John and Rose Elizabeth (Paget) T.; attended Perse Sch., Cambridge, B.A., Cantab (Trinity), 1913, M.A., 1916, D.Sc., Lisbon, Cambridge, Sheffield. Trinity Coll., Dublin, Reading, U. Wales, Westmister (Fulton); D.H.L., Ursinus; m. Kathleen Buchanan Smith, Sept. 18, 1924 (died); children—John Adam, Lilian Clare, David Paget, Caroline Rose Buchanan. Fellow, instr. Corpus Christi, Cambridge, 1914, 1919-22; prof. natural philosophy U. of Aberdeen, 1922; prof. physics Imperial Coll., S. Kensington, 1930-52; Baker lectr., Cornell, 1929-30; master Corpus Christi Coll. (Cambridge), 1952-62. Served with Inf. div. France, 1914-15, with R.A.F., 1915-19 on aeronautical research, chmn. (British) Com. on Atomic Energy, 1940-41, scientific liaison officer, Ottawa, 1941-42, dep. chmn. radio bd. (British), 1942-43, scientific adviser, Air Ministry, 1943-44); sci, adviser, British delegation Atomic Energy Commn., U.N., 1946-47. Fellow Royal Soc.; hon. fellow Corpus Christi (Cambridge); hon. fellow Trinity Coll. (Cambridge), 1952, Imperial Coll., 1955, Inst. of Physics (pres. 1958-60). Awarded Nobel Prize, 1937; Hughes medal Royal Soc., 1940, Royal Medal, 1949; Knighted 1943. Mem. British Assn. Advancement Sci. (pres. 1960). Mem. Am. Acad. Arts and Scis. Mem. Ch. of Eng. Club: Athenaeum (London). Author: Applied Aerodynamics, pub. 1919, The Atom, The Foreseeable Future, and similar works. Contbr. to sci. jours. Address: Cambridge, England. Died Sept. 1975.

THOMSON, PROCTER, educator, economist; b. Oak Park, Ill., June 14, 1919; s. Procter and Gladys (Craker) T.; B.A., Ohio State U., 1940, M.A., 1941; Ph.D., U. Chgo., 1951; m. Eugenie Gaines, Aug. 25, 1943 (div. 1957); m. 2d, Mary Jane Lening, Aug. 11, 1958.

Research asso. U. Chgo., 1947-49, asst. prof. econs. and edn., 1949-55; mem. faculty Clarement (Cal.) Men's Coll., 1955-75, John C. Lincoln prof. econs. and adminstrn., 1962-75; cons. joint com. econs. U.S. Congress, 1957, Com. Econ. Devel., 1958-59. Served with AUS, 1941-43, USAAF, 1944-46. Mem. Edn. Mgmt. and Evaluation Commn., Am. Econ. Assn., Am. Agrl. Econ. Assn., Econometric Assn., Nat. Soc. Study Edn., Inst. Studies in Federalism, Kappa Sigma, Phi Delta Kappa. Author: Economics in the Modern World, 1949; also articles; co-author: California Local Finance, 1960; Essays in Federalism, 1961; The American Property Tax, 1965. Home: Claremont, Cal., Died Jan. 26, 1975.

THOMSON, SAMUEL HARRISON educator, editor; b. Pasadena, Cal., Nov. 5, 1895; s. Williell and Clara F. (Thompson) T.; B.A., Princeton, 1923; Dr.Phil., Charles U., Prague, Czechoslovakia, 1925; B.Litt., Oxford U., 1926, D. Litt., 1942; m. Rosamund Vere Dargan, Jan. 30, 1936; children—Williell Riddett, Clara Day. Tutor modern langs. Princeton summer sch., 1922-31, co-prin., 1926-31; instr. Bibl. lit. Princeton, 1926-29; asst. prof. history Cal. Inst. Tech., 1929-31; fellow medieval history Huntington Library, 1929-30; traveling fellow Am. Council Learned Soc., 1931-33; asst. prof. modern history U. Chgo., 1934-35; asso. prof. European history and dir. admissions Carleton Coll., 1935-36; prof. history U. Colo., Boulder, from 1936, dir. Center for Slavic and East European Studies, 1960-64; vis. prof. U. Mich., 1941, Ind. U., 1950-51, U. Wash., 1964-65, U. Cal., Los Angeles, 1965-66; mem. Inst. Advanced Study, Princeton, 1955-56; Masaryk lectr. U. Toronto, Can., 1949; Fulbright prof. U. of Vienna, 1959. Served with U.S. Army in France, 1917-19; chief of outpost Office War Information, Czechoslovakia, 1945, spl. asst. to Am. ambassador to Czechoslovakia, 1945; dir. USIS, Warsaw, Poland, and pub. affairs officer Am. embassy, Warsaw, 1945-46. Recipient Czechoslovakia state prize for lit. 1944. Fellow Polish Acad. Scis., Mediaeval Acad. Am. (past 1st v.p. Haskins medal 1951); hon. fellow Polish Inst. Arts and Scis (council); mem. History Sci. Soc. (councillor 1947-53), Am. Council Learned Socs. and Social Sci. Research Council (mem. combined Slavic com. 1947-51, 1955-59; chmn. of the Western Slavic Conf., 1963), Am. His. Assn., Soc. Mediaeval Langs. and Lit. (Oxford) Am. Soc. Ch. History, Phi Beta Kappa; asso. Soc. Philosophique, Louvain. Republican. Presbyn. Club: Town and Gown (Boulder). Author or co-author books relating to field the latest being: Handbook of Slavic Studies (with others), 1949; Czechoslovakia in European History, rev. edit., 1953; M.J. Hus De Ecclesia, 1956; Guide to Historical Literature, 1961; Europe in Renaissance and Reformation, 1963, German edit., 1969; Latin Bookhands of the Later Middle Ages, 1969. Editor: Progress of Medieval and Renaissance Studies in United States and Canada, 1936; founder editor Jour. Central European Affairs, 1941-75, Medievalia et Humanistica, 1943-75; mem. editorial bd. Am. Slavic and East European Rev., 1941-61. Contbr. articles on cultural history to numerous Am. and European jours. Home: Boulder, Colo., Died Nov. 19, 1975; interred Boulder, Colo.

THOMSON, WILLIAM ARCHIBALD, JR., banker; b. New Haven, Conn., Nov. 9, 1905; s. William Archibald and Clara (Bogue) T.; E.E., Rensselaer Poly Inst., 1927; m. Isabel A. Johnson, Oct. 26, 1963; children—Diane T. (Mrs. Harold N. Bassett), Gail T. (Mrs. Thomas J. Norris). Investment analyst Chas. W. Scranton & Co., New Haven, Conn., 1928-41; with Union Trust Co., New Haven, also Stamford Conn., 1941-74, exec. v.p., dir. 1965-74. Treas., bd. dirs. Yale (N.H.) Hosp.; bd. dirs. Yale (N.H.) Med. Center, Gaylor Farm Assn. (Hosp.), Hosp. Cooperative Services, Vis. Nurse Assn. New Haven Childrens Center, Mem. Theta Xi. Episcopalian. Club: Quinnipack. Home: Killingworth, Conn., Died Nov. 7, 1974.

THOMSON, WILLIAM NOBEL, newspaper exec.; b. Ayr, Scotland, June 21, 1904; s. Roderick Nobel and Eliza Henderson (Wilson) T.; student pub. schs. Sherbrooke, Que.; m. Mabel A. Alderman, Feb. 22, 1927; children—Virginia Ruth (Mrs. A. Richard Gross), Roderick Nobel. Came to U. S., 1924, naturalized, 1927. Systematizer, Gen. Electric Co., 1924-30; chief accountant Albany (N.Y.) Times Union, 1930-35. Milw. Sentinel, 1935, bus. mgr., 1937, asst. pub., 1943-51; gen. mgr. N.Y. Mirror, 1951-64, Boston Record Am. and Sunday Advertiser, 1964-69. Republican. Conglist. Mason (32 deg., Shriner). Home: Whiting, N.J. Died Aug. 5, 1975.

THORNBURG, DELMAR LEON, lawyer; b. Beallsville, O., Aug. 15, 1881; s. Wilberforce and Miriam Luella (Daniel) T.; grad. Woodbine (Ia.) Normal Sch., 1897; B.Sc., U. of Neb., 1902; m. Alpha Emeline Sedgley, of Eureka, Calif., June 19, 1909; children—Delmar Sedgley, Destal Miriam. Instr. dept. of physics, U. of Neb., 1898-1902; head dept. of science Aberdeen (S.C.P. High Sch., 1902-03; prin. pub. schs., Newcastle, Wyo., 1903-05, Fortuna, Calif., 1905-06, city supt. schs., Eureka, Calif., 1906-11; supt. schs., Compton, Calif., 1912-13; practiced law, San Francisco and Oakland, 1913-1930; pres. Northern U., 1923-1930; practiced law in Washington, D.C., from 1930. Candidate for asso. justice Supreme Court of Calif., 1926. President Thornbury Family of America; president Sons and Daughters of Washington Fraternal Soc., 1925; pres. nat. Bird. Soc., from 1932; mem. Calif. Geneal. Soc. (pres. 1921).!, S.A.R. Democrat. Unitarian. Mason (32°, Shriner). Clubs: Univ. of Neb. Club (San Francisco); Press (Oakland). Author: California's Redwood Wonderland, 1924; California Geology, 1915. Composer: Songs of the Pacific, also hymns and instrumental pieces. Washington, D.C.†

THORNTON, CHARLES STEAD, educator, zoologist; b. Skipton, Eng., July 22, 1910; s. Stead and Frances Ann (Collier) T.; came to U.S., 1915, naturalized, 1922; A.B., Harvard, 1932; M.A., Princeton, 1936, Ph.D., 1937; m. Mary Grace Tyler, Dec. 29, 1937; children—Tyler Stead, Patricia Ann, Margaret. Mem. faculty Kenyon Coll., Gambier, O., 1936-62, prof. zoology, chmn. dept. Mich. State U., East Lansing, 1962. Fulbright prof. anatomy U. Cairo, 1952, 53; UNESCO lectr. Middle East, 1953. Mem. adv. bd. Kellogg Gull Lake Biol. Sta., 1962; commr. Commn. Undergrad Edn. Biol. Scis., 1967-69. Bd. dirs. Ohio Biol. Survey, 1940-50. Research grantee Am. Cancer Soc., 1949-51, NIH, 1954, NSF, 1955-61, 64-70; mem. cell biology study section NIH, 1964-68; Mem. Am. Soc. Zoologists (chmn. nominating com. devel. biology 1961-62). Internat. Soc. Developmental Biologists, Soc. Developmental Biology, Am. Soc. Antomists, Wilderness Soc., Sigma Xi, Sigma Pi. Contbr. articles to profl. jours. Asso. editor Jour. Exptl. Zoology , 1966-70, 72; editor: Regeneration in Vertebrates. 1959; Vertebrate Regeneration, 1974. Home: East Lansing, Mich. Died Jan. 14, 1974.

THORNTON, DAN, gov., corp. exec.; b. Tex., Jan. 31, 1911; s. Clay C. and Ida (Fife) T.; student Tex. Tech. Inst., 1930-31, U. Cal. at Los Angeles, 1932; m. Jessie Willock, Apr. 4, 1934. Ranch owner Ariz., 1936-41; former owner Thornton Hereford Ranch, Gunnison, Colo., dir. Financial Indsl. Fund, Inc., Cyclo Mfg. Co., Nat. Western Stock Show. Mem. Pres.' Econ. Com., Korea and Far East, 1954; mem. commn. on Intergovernmental Relations, 1954-55. Served as state senator, 11th Senatorial Dist. Colo.; gov. of Colo., 1950-54. Mem. C. of C. Republican. Mem. Community Ch. Elk, Rotarian. Home: Carmel Valley, Cal., Died Jan. 8, 1976.

THORNTON, ERIC LAURENCE, banker; b. Benson, Minn., Aug. 15, 1878; s. Frank M. and Elizabeth (Clague) T.; student St. Paul Coll. of Law; m. Jessie Dinsmoor, of Austin, Minn., Oct. 15, 1907. Admitted to Minn. bar; pres. Nat. Exchange Bank, St. Paul, Minn.; v.p. Benson Lumber Co., First Nat. Bank of Benson. Republican. Episcopalian. Clubs: Minnesota, St. Paul Athletic, Lions', Town & Country. Home: St. Paul, Minn.†

THORON, BENJAMIN WARDER, bank exec.; b. Washington, D.C., April 14, 1897; s. Ward and Ellen (Warder) T.; ed. St. Paul's Sch., Concord, N.H., 1910-15; A.B., Harvard, 1919; B.S. in C.E., Mass. Inst. of Tech., 1922; m. Violet Spencer, June 11, 1927; children—Ann Aston, Christopher, Samuel. Spl. asst. Am. Legation, The Hague, 1919; civil engr. with Fay, Spofford & Thorndike, cons. engrs., Boston, 1922-23; farmer, 1923-26; in banking and investment banking, Washington, 1926-33; in U.S. Govt. Service, Pub. Works Adminstrn., R.F.C., Interior Dept., 1933-46; director Div. of Territories and Island Possessions, 1942-45; treas., mem. bd. trustees P.E. Cathedral Found., 1947-67, hon. trustee, 1967-75; v.p., dir. Tenn. R.R. Co.; dir. Am. Security & Trust Co., Martha's Vineyard Nat. Bank (Mass.). Mem. Delta Psi. Clubs: Metropolitan; University (N.Y.C.). Author: Revenue Bond Financing by Political Subdivisions; Its Origin, Scope and Growth in the U.S., 1936; A Report on The Alaska Railroad (with G. Sundborg and E. Margolin), 1946. Home: Washington, D.C., Died Apr. 30, 1975.

THOROUGHMAN, JAMES CHANSLOR, physician; b. Ferguson, Mo., Aug. 25, 1904; s. James C. and Hattie (Manget) T.; B.S., Emory U., 1924, M.D., 1927, M.S., 1935; m. Verna Elizabeth Scarborough, May 6, 1929; children—Margaret (Mrs. James A. Callahan), James Chanslor, Thomas Vernon. Intern, Grady Meml. Hosp., Atlanta, 1927-28, resident, 1928-29; chief of surgery Changchow (China) Gen. 1930-36; supt., chief of surgery Soochow (China) Hosp., 1936-40, 46-50; chief surgery VA Hosp., Augusta, Ga., 1951-53; clin. prof. surgery Med. Coll. Ga., Augusta, 1951-53 chief surgery VA Hosp., Atlanta, 1953-69; prof. surgery Emory U. Sch. Medicine, 1953-69; staff Lee County Hosp., Opelika, Ala., 1969. Served to maj. M.C., AUS, 1942-46. Recipient award of honor Med. Alumni Assn. of Emory U., 1960, Assn. VA Surgeons, 1970; named Fed. Civil Servant of Greater Atlanta, 1960. Diplomate Am. Bd. Surgery. Fellow A.C.S., So. Surg. Assn., Southeastern Surg. Congress; mem. Ga. Surg. Soc., Assn. Mil. Surgeons, Assn. VA Surgeons (pres. 1968-69), Phi Beta Kappa, Alpha Omega Alpha, Sigma Alpha Epsilon, Alpha Kappa Kappa. Contbr. articles to profl. jours. Home: Opelika, Ala. Died July 14, 1972; buried Oak Hill Cemetery, Newnan, Coweta County, Ga.

THURMAN, AARON, physician; b. Boston, Nov. 16, 1897; s. Jacob Benjamin and Bella (Rabb) T.; M.D., Harvard, 1921; m. Julia G. Goodman, Mar. 10, 1932; children—Susan T. Klemman (Mrs. Philip Solomon), Daniel G. Intern, L.I. Hosp., 1921-22; intern Boston City Hosp., 1922-23, Boston Lying-In Hosp., 1924; resident in surgery Boston Sanitarium, 1924-26; surg. chief Jewish Meml. Hosp., Boston; asso. in surgery Beth Israel Hosp., Boston, Mt. Auburn Hosp., Cambridge, Mass., Faulkner Hosp., Boston, Newton-Wellesley Hosp.; asst. in surgery Tufts U. Med. Sch., cons. in field. Pres. Big Brother Assn. Boston. Ann. endowed lectureship Beth Israel Hosp. named in his honor. Diplomate Am. Bd. Surgery. Fellow A.C.S.; mem. A.M.A., Boston Med. Soc. (past pres.). Contbr. articles to profl. jours. Home: Brookline, Mass. Died Mar. 21, 1974; buried Wakefield, Mass.

THURSTON, ELLIOTT LADD, newspaper corr.; b. Fall River, Mass., Oct. 1, 1895; s. Thatcher Thayer and Ada D.; student Phillips Acad., Andover, Mass., Brown U.; m. Margaret Tucker, Nov. 8, 1919; children—Elliott Ladd, Virginia, Thatcher Tucker; m. 2d, Jane Mitchell Davis, June 20, 1947. Reporter, Providence Tribune, 1915, Providence Jour., 1916-18, N.Y. Sun, 1919-20; reporter N.Y. World, 1921-22, Washington corr., 1922-29, chief Washington Bur., 1929-31; Washington corr. Phila. Record, other newspapers, 1931-33; polit. editor Washington Post, 1933-35. Asst. to bd. govs. Fed. Res. System, 1935-60. Press officer Am. delegation Monetary and Econ. Conf., London, 1933. Mem. Psi Upsilon. Clubs: Gridiron, National Press. Home: Alexandria, Va. Died Sept. 2, 1975; buried Nat. Meml. Park, Falls Church, Va.

THURSTON, JOHN FOSTER, cons.; b. Denver, Aug. 13, 1910; s. Harry D. and Edna (Foster) T.; B.A., Colo. Coll., 1931; m. Marian L. Fee, June 10, 1931 (dec. Nov. 1960); 1 son, John Charles; m. 2d, Betty L. Shackleton, Oct. 6, 1961, step-children—R. Woodworth Shackleton, Leslie A. Shackleton. Eastern sales mgr. McQuay Norris Mfg. Co., St. Louis, 1936-52; merchandising mgr. replacement div. Thompson Products, Inc., Cleve., 1953-55; div. gen. mgr. electro dynamic div. Gen. Dynamics Corp., 1955-59, v.p. corp., 1957-61, pres. liquid carbonic div., also sr. v.p. corp., 1961-63; pres., chief exec. officer Mueller Co., Decatur, Ill., 1963-73; cons., 1973. Civilian cons. to sec. army, 1952-53. Trustee Milliken U. Served as maj. USAAF, 1942-46. Recipient Exceptional Civilian Service award Dept. Army 1954. Mem. Alpha Kappa Psi, Kappa Sigma. Club: Decatur Country. Home: Decatur, Ill. Died Oct. 15, 1974.

THURSTON, WALTER, diplomat; b. Colo., Dec. 5, 1895. Began as U.S. fgn. service officer, Mexico, 1914; subsequently in Guatemala, Nicaragua, Eng., Costa Rica, Brazil, Paraguay, Switzerland, Spain, Portugal, Soviet Union and U.S. State Dept.; served as ambassador to El Salvador, Bolivia, Mexico. Episcopalian. Club: Metropolitan (Washington). Address: Washington, D.C. Died Mar. 1974.

TIDEMANN, KARL, ins. dir.; b. Bremen, Germany, Jan. 24, 1878; s. Frederick Lawrence (M.D.) and Constance (Prott) T.; m. Pauline Wilkens, Mar. 9, 1904; children—Constance Elizabeth (wife John H. Fonvielle, U.S. Army), Karl Wilkens, Pauline Emily (Mrs. Svend Hansen), Fred Ernest, Richard Wilkens. Came to U.S., 1898, naturalized, 1921. Organizer firm K. Tidemann & Co., cotton mchts. and exporters, 1904, liquidated, 1928; dir. Am. Nat. Life Ins. Co., Galveston, Tex. Mem. Tex. Cotton Assn. (organizer, 1914). Home: Galveston, Tex.†

TIEDJENS, VICTOR ALPHONS, horticulturist, agronomist; b. Brillion, Wis., June 13, 1895; s. John Alfred and Anna M. (Nelesen) T.; B.S., U. Wis., 1921, M.S., 1922; postgrad. Harvard, 1928; Ph.D., Rutgers U., 1932; m. Dorothy Janet Dopp, June 2, 1923 (dec. June 1968); children—Dorothy Loraine, Penelope Emily; m. 2d, Edith Augustin, Sept. 19, 1968 (dec. Dec. 1975). Asst. research prof. Mass. State Coll., 1923-28; research specialist horticulture Rutgers U., 1928-32, asso. prof. vegetable gardening, 1934-45; dir. research Yoder Bros., Barberton, O., 1932-34; dir. Va. Truck Expt. Sta., Norfolk, Va., 1945-51; dir. research, chief chemist Nachurs Plant Food Co., 1951-55; v.p., dir. research Growers Chem. Corp., 1955-72, v.p., chmn. bd., 1972-75. Food survey Lago Oil & Transport Co., N.W. Indies, 1942. Mem. Va. Commn. on Research and Edn., 1945. Recipient Thomas Rowland award Mass. Hort. Soc., 1952. Mem. A.A.A.S. (v.p. 1951, chmn. Sect. O), Am. Chem. Soc., Va. Acad. Sci., Am. Assn. Hort Sci., Am. Soc. Agronomy, Alpha Zeta, Sigma Xi, Phi Sigma, Phi Kappa Phi. Presbyn. Clubs: Knights of the Round Table, Rotary. Author: Encyclopedia of Vegetable Gardening, 1943; Chemical Gardening for the Amateur (With C.M. Connors), 1939; A Practical Guide to Successful Farming with Wilkinson), 1950; More Food from Soil Science, 1966; Olena Farm, U.S.A., 1969; A Guy from Peshtigo (Bibliography). Inventor soilless window box, 1938. Home: Hamilton, O., Died July 26, 1975; interred Wood Lawn Cemetery, Norwalk, O.

TIEKEN, ROBERT, lawyer; b. Chgo., Dec. 8, 1903; s. Theodore and Bessie (Chapman) T.; Ph.B., U. Chgo., 1927, J.D., 1931; LL.D., John Marshall Law Sch., Chgo., 1955; married Dorothie Brentano, Apr. 16, 1936; children—Robin, Robert. Admitted to Ill. bar, 1931: mem. Winston, Strawn, Black & Towner, Chgo., 1929-54, beginning as clk., partner 1953; U.S. atty. No. Dist. of Ill., 1954-61; referee in bankruptcy No. Dist.

Ill., after 1962. Pres. Big Brothers Assn. of Chgo., 1931-39; dir. Young Republicans, Inc., of Ill., 1932-36; chmn. reviewing com. of protective agencies Council of Social Agencies, Chgo., 1937-39; dir. United Charities, Chgo., 1942; insp. Aero. Commn. of Ill., 1942; chmn. salvage com. Ill. State Council Def., 1941-42; dir. North Lake chpt. A.R.C., 1947-50. Alternate del. Rep. Nat. Conv., 1936; parliamentarian Rep. State Conv. Ill., 1938; v.p. Rep. Fedn. Lake County. Served as lt. comdr. USNR, 1942-45. Mem. Ill., Am., Lake County bar assns., U.S. Equestrian Team, Inc., Am. Horse Show Assn., Midwest Horse Soc. (pres.), Town and Country Equestrian Assn. (dir. 1948), Naval Order World Wars. Home: Libertyville, Ill. Died July 1973.

TILANDER, ARTUR GUNNAR, educator; b. Tranemo, Sweden, July 22, 1894; s. Alrik Gotthard and Levina (Larsson) T.; ed. U. Gothenburg (Sweden), U. Paris (France), U. Madrid (Spain), U. Lisbon (Portugal); Dr. phil, Dr. en droit, Docteur és lettres; m. Margareta Kruger, Jan. 28, 1939. Formerly prof. U. Lund (Sweden); prof. U. Stockholm (Sweden). Mem. Madrid, Lisbon, Barcelona acads., Institut de France (asso.), Stockholm Acad. Letters, Royal Acad. Lund, Hispanic Soc. Am., others. Author: Remarques sur le Roman de Renart, 1923; Lexique du Roman de Renart, 1924, 2d edit., 1970; Les Livres du rol Modus et de la reine Ratio, 1932; Cynegetica, 19 vols., 1953-71; Leges Hispanicae Medii Aeri, 10 vols., 1950-69, others. Home: Ulricehamn, Sweden. Died June 13, 1973; interred Tranemo, Sweden.

TILLETT, WILLIAM S., univ. prof.; b. Charlotte, N.C., July 10, 1892; s. Charles Walter and Carolyn (Patterson) T.; A.B., U. of N.C., 1913, D.Sc., 1942; M.D., Johns Hopkins, 1917; D.Sc. (hon.), U., Chgo., 1952, D.Sc. (hon.) Northwestern U., 1959; m. Dorothy Stockbridge, Sept. 8, 1928; 1 dau., Louise E. (Mrs. Douglas MacAgy). Asst. resident, resident physician, asso. Hosp. of Rockefeller Inst., 1922-30; asso. prof. of medicine Johns Hopkins Med. Sch., 1930-37; prof. bacterbiology, N.Y.U. Coll. Medicine, 1937-38, prof. medicine, 1938-58. emeritus, 1958-74; dir. research trainee grant USPHS, 1958-74. Dir. 3d med. div. and mem. exec. com. (sec. since 1941), Bellevue Hosp., N.Y. City, since 1938. Served as 1st lt. and capt., M. C., A.E.F., 1917-19. Cons. to sec. of war, epidemic diseases, 1941-46. Lasker award, Am. Pub. Health Assn., 1949; Borden Award Am. Assn. Med. Colls., 1952. Mem. Nat. Acad. Scis., Am. Assn. Physicians (pres. 1957-58), Soc. for Clinical Investigation (pres. 1936-37), Harvey Soc. (pres. 1957-58) N. Y. Acad. of Medicine (chmn. sect. on medicine, 1944-45), N.Y. Acad. Sciences, Am. Soc. of Bacteriology, Am. Assn. of Immunology (editorial bd. jour.), Soc. Exptl. Biology and Medicine (editorial bd. jour.), Interurban Clin. Club. (pres. 1946-47), A.A.A.S., Am. Med. Assn.; hon. mem Alpha Omega Alpha, Sigma Xi. Clubs: Players, Deer Island Yacht. Contbr. articles on exptl. research and clin. studies to tech. jours., including Jour. Exptl. Medicine, Jour. Clin. Investigation, Bull. Johns Hopkins Hosp. Home: New York City, N.Y. Died Apr. 4, 1974.

TILLEY, CECIL EDGAR, petrologist; b. Adelaide, South Australia, May 14, 1894; s. John Edward and Catherine Jane (Nicholas) T.; B.Sc., U. Adelaide, 1914. University Sydney, 1915; Ph.D., Univ. Cambridge, 1922; D.Sc. (hon.), U. Manchester, 1955, U. Sydney, 1964; m. Irene Doris Marshall, June 21, 1928; 1 daughter, Anne Demonstrator geology and mineralogy U. Sydney, 1916; chemist Dept. Explosives Supply, Queensterry, 1917-18; lectr. petrology U. Cambridge, 1928-31, prof. mineralogy and petrology, 1931-61; research asso. Carnegie Instn., Washington, 1956. Recipient Bigsby medal Geol. Soc. of London, 1937; Roebling medal Mineral. Soc. Am., 1954; Woolaston medal Geol. Soc. of London, 1960, President Geol. Society London, 1949-50. Mineral. Soc. Great Britain, 1948-51, 1957-60. Fellow Royal Soc. (hon.) (London, Edinburgh); corr. member Geol. Soc. America. Mineral. Soc. Am., Royal Soc. N.Z., Geol. Soc. Stockholm, Internat. Mineral Assn. (pres. 1964). Home: Cambridge, England., Died Jan. 24, 1973.

TILLMAN, ALBERT GALLATIN, III, physician; b. Vicksburg, Miss., Nov. 24, 1921; s. Albert Gallatin and Alice Polk (Banks) T.; student U. Miss., 1939-41; M.D., U. Tenn., 1944; m. Lucille M. Tack, June 9, 1951; children—Kathleen (Mrs. Robert L. Moody), Albert Gallatin IV, Alison (Mrs. David Simmons), Theodore, Suzanne, Marcia, Michael. Intern, Scott and White Hosp., Temple, Tex., 1945, resident in surgery, 1945-46; resident in Surgery Mercy Hosp., Vicksburg, 1948-50; teaching fellow in surgery Tulane U., 1950-51; asst. vis. surgeon Charity Hosp. La., New Orleans, 1950-51; mem. staff VA Hosp., Temple, 51-54, Tillman-West Surg. Clinic, 1954-72; mem. staff Gulfport (Miss.) Meml. Hosp., 1954-72, chief staff, 1961-62; cons. Keesler AFB, 1965-67. Served as lt. (j.g.) M.C., USNR, 1946-48. Diplomate Am. Bd. Surgery. Fellow A.C.S.; mem. A.M.A., Sigma Alpha Epsilon, Alpha Kappa Kappa. Episcopalian. Lion Clubs: Gulfport Yacht (gov. 1954-72, fleet surgeon), Century. Home: Gulfport, Miss. Died July 26, 1972; buried Gulfport.

TILLMAN, PAUL EDWARD, pharm. mfr.; b. Grand Rapids, Mich., Apr. 7, 1899; s. Louis and Mary (Every) T.; C.P.A., U. Ill., 1924; m. Margaret Bletsch, Aug. 9, 1924 (dec. Mar. 1949); children—Joan C., Wendy L.; m. 2d, Betty Van Winkle, Feb. 17, 1950 (div. 1966); m. 3d, Claire Labréche, Sept. 28, 1966. With G. D. Searle & Co., Chgo., 1931-75, beginning as office mgr., successively sec., treas., v.p., 1931-55, sr. v.p., 1955-75, also dir. Clubs: Chicago Athletic; Glenview Golf (Golf, Ill.). Home: Chicago, Ill. Died Jan. 9, 1975.

TINNON, THOMAS B., lawyer; b. Cotter, Ark., June 5, 1915; s. William Hugh and Pearl (Pitchford) T.; student Little Rock Jr. Coll., 1934-35, Ark. Tech. Coll. at Russellville, 1936; LL.B., U. Ark., 1949, J.D., 1969; m. T. Adele King, Feb. 24, 1942; 1 dau., Cynthia Ann (Mrs. Ed Cunningham). Admitted to Ark. bar, 1949, since practiced in Mountain Home, Ark.; mem. firm Thomas B. Tinnon, P.A.; organizer, 1st municipal judge, Mountain Home, 1960-61; incorporator, gen. counsel 1st Nat. Bank & Trust Co. Mountain Home, 1964-70; atty. North Ark. Elec. Coop., 1952-66; city atty., 1952; incorporator, gen. counsel, dir. 1st State Bldg. & Loan Assn., Mountain Home, 1960-73. Pres., Ark. Wildlife Fedn., 1955, 56. Served to capt. USAAF, 1940-46. Mem. Ark. (past pres., chmn. 1st spl. sect. for savs. and loan attys., mem. ho. of dels. 1973, fellow found.), Baxter-Marion Counties, Am. bar assns., Am. Trial Lawyers Assn., Am. Judicature Soc., D.A.V., Am. Legion, V.F.W., C. of C. (past pres.). Baptist. Mason. Home: Mountain Home, Ark. Died July 23, 1973; buried Cotter (Ark.) Cemetery.

TIPPY, WILLIAM BRUCE, ednl. adminstr., utilities cons.; b. Williamsport, Pa., Dec. 9, 1908; s. Charles Wesley and Mabel Margaret (Deacon) T.; A.B., Williams Coll., 1930; B.S., U. Mich., 1932; m. Margaret Louise Clarke, Apr. 8, 1933; children—Charles E., James W.; m. 2d, Marie Trabold, Feb. 4, 1965. With Detroit Edison Co., 1932-34, Gen. Electric Co., 1934-36, Consumers Power Co., 1936-45; asst. to v.p. Commonwealth & Southern Corp. (N.Y.), 1945-47, v.p., dir., 1947-49; v.p. Southern Ind. Gas & Electric Co., Evansville, Centrall Ill. Light Co., Peoria, 1947-49; v.p. Commonwealth Services, Inc. (formed after dissolution Commonwealth & Southern), 1949-53, exec. v.p., 1953-55, pres., 1955-67, chmn. bd., 1967-68; asst. to the pres. church Coll. of Hawaii, Lale, 1968-71. Mem. Sigma Xi (asso.), Phi Beta Kappa. Phi Kappa Phi, Theta Delta Chi. Republican. Mem. Ch. Jesus Christ Latter-Day Saints. Rotarian. Clubs: Players, Lambs, Amateur Comedy, Bras Coupe Hunting and Fishing (Can.). Author articles on economics, pub. utilities. Home: Rochester, N.Y., Died July 5, 1973.

TISHER, PAUL WINSLOW, ophthalmologist; b. Cedar Rapids, Ia., Sept. 17, 1909; s. Harry Franklin and Loshia Florence (Winslow) T.; M.D., U. Ia., 1935; m. Dorothy Jane Fluke, Aug. 29, 1934; children—Diane (Mrs. James G. McCulloh, Patricia (Mrs. Brendan T. Shea), Jane (Mrs. Robert P. Powell), Dorothy, Paul Winslow. Intern, Miller Hosp., St. Paul, 1935-36, Burch fellow, 1936-37; resident U. Minn. Hosps., Mpls., 1937-38; practiced medicine, specializing in ophthalmology, Conn.; sr. ophthalmic surgeon New Britain (Conn.) Gen. Hosp., Grenfell Mission Hosp. of St. Anthony, Nfld.; mem. courtesy staff Hartford (Conn.) Hosp.; cons. ophthalmology Bristol (Conn.) Hosp., Newington (Conn.) VA Hosp.; med. adviser Hope Found.; vol. Project HOPE, Indonesia and Ecuador. Bd. dirs. Eyes for Africa Found, Conn. unit Nat. Soc. for Prevention of Blindness. Diplomate Am. Bd. Ophthalmology. Fellow Oxford Ophthal. Cong. (England), Barraquer Inst. (Spain); mem. A.M.A., Am. Acad. Ophthalmology and Otolaryngology, New Britain Med. Soc. (pres., Man of Year award), Phi Rho Sigma, Sigma Phi Epsilon. Episcopalian (vestryman). Mason. Club: Shuttle Meadow Country (gov.) (New Britain). Home: New Britain, Conn. Died Dec. 22, 1974; buried West Lane Cemetery, Kensington, Conn.

TITCOMB, MIRIAM, educator; b. Augusta, Me., Dec. 19, 1879; d. and Ida Stone (Caldwell) T.; grad. high sch., Augusta, 1897; B.L., Smith Coll., 1901; postgrad. work, Radcliffe Coll. Teacher English, Abbott Acad., Andover, Mass., 1905-08, teacher mathematics high sch., Augusta, Me., 1908-09; teacher English and history, Miss May's Sch., Boston, 1909-15; prin. Bancroft Sch., Worcester, Mass., 1915-26; organizer and dir. from 1927, Hillsdale Country Day Sch., Cincinnati Chmn. Edn. Com. of Smith Coll. Alumnae Council, 1926—; mem. Council of Smith Coll., 1916, 17, 25, alumni trustee from 1930. Mem. Am. Assn. Univ. Women, Smith Coll. Alumni Assn., Nat. Assn. Principals of Schs. for Girls (charter mem.). Conglist. Address: Cincinnati, O.†

TOBIAS, NORMAN, physician; b. Elmira, N.Y., June 26, 1898; s. Sol and Jennie (Cohen) T.; M.D., N.Y.U., 1921; m. Agnes Blumberg, June 26, 1939; children—Sally and Susan (dec.) (twins). Intern, Hamot Hosp., Erie, Pa., 1922; resident Barnard Free Skin and Cancer Hosp., 1923; staff physician Deaconess Hosp., St. Louis; vis. physician St. Louis State Hosp., St. Mary's Hosp.; asso. prof. dermatology St. Louis U. Diplomate Am. Bd. Dermatology. Mem. Am. Acad. Dermatology, A.M.A., So. Med. Assn. Author: Essentials of Dermatology, 6th edit., 1963. Home: St. Louis Mo. Died May 8, 1974; buried Mt. Sinai Cemetery, St. Louis, Mo.

TOBIN, JAMES F(RANCIS), retail store exec.; b. Syracuse, N.Y., Apr. 7, 1912; s. Richard F. and Elizabeth B. (Whalen) T.; A.B., Niagara U., 1935; grad. student Syracuse U.; m. Anna C. O'Neill, July 6, 1940; children—Richard J., Monica A., Martha F., James Francis, Michael, Paul, Peter, Mary. With E. W. Edwards & Son, Syracuse, N.Y. 1935-52, gen. mgr. Edwards Store Buffalo, 1945-46; v.p. E. W. Edwards & Son, 1946-48, gen. mdse. mgr. three Edwards stores, 1948-52; exec. v.p. Wieboldt Stores, Inc., Chgo., 1952-54, pres., 1954-64; dir., 1954-75; dir. Central National Bank, (Chicago). Past lay trustee DePaul U. Mem. Nat. (dir.), Chgo. (dir.) retail mchts. assns., Ill. Fedn. Retail Assns. (dir.). Clubs: Union League (Chgo.); Butterfield Country (Hinsdale, Ill.); Oak Park (Ill.). Home: Oak Park, Ill. Died Feb. 4, 1975.

TODARO, VINCENT SETTIMO, architect; b. Catania, Italy, Jan. 1, 1891; s. Francesco and Teresa (Lobianco) T.; came to U.S., 1901, naturalized, 1914; m. Elena Rificl, Feb. 29, 1964. Architect, Comyns & Todaro, architects, N.Y.C., 1912-16, Lowinson & Todaro, architects, N.Y.C., 1916-36; pvt. practice as architect, Bklyn., 1936-64. Registered profl. architect, N.Y., N.J., Mass., Fla. Fellow Am. Registered Architects; mem. A.I.A. Prin. archtl. works include Mt. Alvernia Sem., Wappinger Falls, N.Y., 1952. Home: Brooklyn, N.Y. Died Dec. 27, 1972.

TODD, ROSCOE JOHNSON, bank examiner; b. Elgin, Ill., Mar. 17, 1895; s. Frank Murray and Nellie (Johnson) T.; B.S. in Commerce, U. of Ill., 1922. With Univ. State Bank, Champaign, Ill., (part time) 1919-22; Ill. Nat. Bank, Springfield, Ill., 1922-25; bank examiner State of Ill., 1925-27; liquidator state banks of Ill., 1929-35; asst. cashier Am. Nat. Bank Trust Co. Chgo., from 1935; (territorial officer for corr. bank div.); investigator U.S. Senate Com. on Banking and Currency (Insull situation in Chgo.); spl. examiner Merchants and Mfrs. Discount Corp., Chgo.; bank examiner Nat. Credit Assn.; examiner for R.F.C.; chmn. rev. bd. vets. claims, Hines Hosp., VA; bank examiner Chgo. and No. Ill. div.; auditor public accounts state Ill., 1951-58; sr. examiner banking dept. Chgo. No. Ill. div., Dept. Financial Instns. State Ill., 1959-66; sr. bank examiner, met. banking div., Ill. Commr. Banks and Trust Cos., 1967-72. Served with U.S. Army, 1917-19, overseas, 1918-19; battn. sgt. major, World War I. Mem. Camp Followers Assn. Ind. Bankers Assn. (chmn. constitutional com., 1947) Ill. Bankers Assn. (membership chmn. 1947), Am. Inst. Banking, Ill. Hist. Soc., U. Ill. Alumni Assn. (life), V.F.W., Am. Legion, Acacia. Methodist. Mason. Home: Elgin, Ill. Died Oct. 16, 1972.

TOLAN, EDWIN KIRKMAN, librarian; b. Montreal, Que., Can., Oct. 6, 1921; s. Michael Patrick and Amy (Wallwork) T.; B.A., McGill U., 1949, B.S. in L.S., 1954; M.A., U. Glasgow (Scotland), 1951; Ph.D., U. Montreal, 1959; m. Hannah Elizabeth MacLennan, July 7, 1956; children—Jennifer Ann, Joanne Elizabeth. Came to U.S., 1954. Reference librarian Hamilton Coll., 1954-57; librarian Washington and Jefferson Coll., 1957-62, Union Coll., Schenectady, 1962-76. Pres. bd. trustees Capital Dist. Library Council, 1966-68. Served with Canadian Army, 1941-46. Mem. N.Y. State Library Assn., Am. Assn. U. Profs., Societé Internationale pour l'Etude de la Philosophie Médiévale, Canadian Soc. Study History and Philosophy Sci. Home: Schenectady, N.Y., Died Feb. 1, 1976; interred Vale Cemetery, Schenectady, N.Y.

TOLANSKY, SAMUEL, physicist, educator; b. Newcastle-on-Tyne, Eng., Nov. 17, 1907; s. Barnet and Rose (Chait) T.; B.Sc., Newcastle U., 1928, Ph.D., 1931, London U., 1934; postgrad. U. Berlin (Germany), 1931-32; D.Sc., Manchester U. (Eng.), 1946; m. Ottilie Pincasovich, Apr. 7, 1935; children—Ann (Mrs. Stanley Saunders), Jonathan Paul. From lectr. to reader in physics Manchester U., 1934-47; prof. physics, head dept. Royal Holloway Coll., London U., 1947-73. Tolansky Lab., Royal Holloway Coll., London U., named in his honor, 1974. Fellow Royal Soc., Royal Astron. Soc.; hon. mem. A.A.A.S.; mem. Royal Soc. Arts (recipient Silver medal); hon. fellow Royal Microscopical Soc., Phys. Soc. London. Author 15 books on optics and structures of diamonds; contbr. articles to profl. jours. Home: Surrey, England. Died Mar. 4, 1973; buried Bushy Jewish Cemetery.

TOLKIEN, JOHN RONALD REUEL, author; educator; b. Jan. 3, 1892; s. Arthur Reuel Tolkien; M.A., Exeter Coll., Oxford (Eng.) U.; D. Litt. (hon.), Univ. Coll., Dublin, Ireland; Dr. en Phil. et Lettres (hon.), U. Liege; m. Edith M. Bratt, 1916 (dec. 1971); three sons, one dau. Reader in English, U. Leeds (Eng.), 1920, prof. English lang., 1924-25; Rawlinson and Bosworth prof. Anglo-Saxon, Oxford U., 1925-45, Merton prof. English lang. and lit., 1945-59, now fellow emeritus Merton Coll. and hon. fellow Exeter Coll.; Andrew Lang. lectr. St. Andrews U., 1939; W.P. Ker lectr. U. Glasgow, 1953. Served with British Army, 1915-18. Fellow Pembroke Coll., 1926-45; Leverhulme research fellow, 1934-36. Fellow Royal Soc. Lit.; mem. Philol. Soc. (v.p.); hon. mem. Hid Islenzka Bokmenntafelag. Author: A Middle English Vocabulary, 1922; Chaucer as a Philologist, 1934; Beowulf; The Monster and the Critics, 1936; The Hobbit, 1937; On Fairy Stories, 1938; Aotrou and Itroun, 1945; Farmer Giles of Ham, 1949; The Homecoming of Beorhrnoth, 1953; Ancrene Wisse, 1962; The Adventurers of Tom Bombadil, 1962; Tree and Leaf (reprint of On Fairy Stories and Leaf by Niggle), 1964; The Fellowship of the Ring; The Lord of the Rings, vol. I, 1954; The Two Towers, vol. II, 1965; The Return of the King, vol, III, 1955; (with Donald Swann) The Road Goes Ever On, 1968. Editor: (with E.V. Gordon) Sir Gawain and the Green Knight, 1925, rev. (N. Davis), 1968. Translator: Sit Gawain and the Green Knight, and Pearl, 1969. Home: London, England

TOLL, HENRY WOLCOTT, lawyer, founder Council State Govts.; b. Denver; s. Charles Hansen and Katharine Ellen (Wolcott) T.; B.A., Williams Coll., 1909, L.H.D., 1939; postgrad. Harvard Law Sch., 1909-11; LL.B., U. Denver, 1912; LL.D., Temple U., 1937; m. Cyrena Van Syckel Martin, Mar. 29, 1918; children—Karel (Mrs. Elwood Henneman), Henry Wolcott, Giles Darwin, Marcia (Mrs. Charles L. Saunders, Jr.). Admitted to Colo. bar, 1912; mem. firm Grant, Shafroth, Toll and McHendrie, and predecessors, 1927—; founder Council State Govts., 1924, exec. dir., 1924-38, hon. pres., mem. exec. com., 1938-75, organizer its interstate commns. on Delaware River Basin, conflicting taxation, others; founder its mag. State Govt. and ann. Book of the States and dir. publ. until 1939; mem. polit. sci. faculty U. Chgo., 1930-38; mem. Nat. Commn. Uniform State Laws, 1931-75. Dir. Titles, Inc. Mem. Denver Municipal Welfare Bd., 1946-62. Mem. Colo. Senate, 1923-31. Trustee Williams Coll., 1939-47; bd. regents Am. Coll. Probate Counsel; b. dirs. Webb-Waring Inst. for Med. Research, 1949—, Denver Library Found., 1961—. Decorated Order Brit. Empire, Mem. Am. (past v.p. Colo.), Colo., Denver (pres. 1929-30) bar asssns., Fgn. Policy Assn. (nat. bd. 1955-58), English Speaking Union (v.p. Denver, 1951-57). Clubs: Century (N.Y.C.); Colo. Harvard Law Assn. (1st pres. 1956-58), Denver (life), Press, Denver Country (life), Law (pres. 1936), Mile High (pres. 1930-31), Cactus (pres. 1942-44) (Denver). Home: Denver, Colo., Died Oct. 17, 1975.

TOLLES, FREDERICK BARNES, ret. educator; b. Nashua, N.H., Apr. 18, 1915; s. James Ulysses and Josie Hobson (Barnes) T.; Procter Acad., 1928-32; A.B. magna cum laude, Harvard, 1936, A.M., 1937, Ph.D., 1947; Litt.D., Haverford (Pa.) Coll., 1959; m. Elizabeth Ellen Smith, June 24, 1939; children—Ellen (Mrs. William Baker), James, Katharine (Mrs. Brian Smith). Asst. English, Harvard, 1937-41; dir. Friends Hist. Library, Swarthmore Coll., 1941-70, instr. history, 1941-47, asst. prof., 1947-50, asso. prof. on leave, 1950-54, Howard M. Jenkins prof. Quaker history and research, 1954-70, emeritus, 1970-75; vis. prof. history Harvard U., 1965; fellow Huntington Library, 1950-51, mem. permanent research group, 1951-54; asso. history Cal. Inst. Tech., 1951-54; vis. Lectr. history Bryn Mawr Coll., 1957-58. Fellow Soc. Religion in Higher Edn.; mem. Friends Hist. Soc. Eng. (pres. 1952), Am. Friends Service Com. (dir. 1945-50, 1954-58, 64-69, chmn. Am. sect. 1954-57, vice chmn. 1957), Inst. Early Am. History and Culture (council 1956- 59, 61-64), Am. Studies assn. (pres. Middle Atlantic States 1954-55), Hist. Soc. Pa. (council 1949-50, 55), Friends Hist. Assn. (dir. 1949, pres. 1968-69, editor Quaker History 1949-67), Am. Antiquarian Soc., Mass. Hist. Soc., Phi Beta Kappa. Mem. Soc. of Friends Author: Meeting House and Counting House: The Quaker Merchants of Colonial Philadelphia, 1948; Slavery and the Woman Question: Lucretia Mott's Diary, 1952; George Logan of Philadelphia, 1953; James Logan and the Culture of Provincial America, 1957; Quakers and the Atlantic Culture, 1960. Editor: (with E. Gordon Alderfer) The Witness of William Penn, 1957; Journal of John Woolman, 1961. Home: Swarthmore, Pa. Died Apr. 18, 1975; buried Nashua, N.H.

TOLSON, CLYDE ANDERSON, ret. govt. ofcl.; b. nr. Laredo, Mo., May 22, 1900; s. James William and Joaquin Miller (Anderson) T.; student Cedar Rapids (Ia.) Bus. Coll., 1917-18; A.B., George Washington U., 1925. LL.B., 1927. Confidential sec. to Secs. of War (Newton D. Baker, John W. Weeks, Dwight F. Davis), 1919-28; admitted to D.C. bar, 1928, U.S. Supreme Court bar, 1935; spl. agt. FBI, U.S. Dept. Justice, 1928, asst. dir., 1930, asst. to dir., 1938, asso. dir., 1947. Recipient Alumni Achievement award Geo. Washington U., 1947; Pres.'s award for distinguished fed. civilian service, 1965. Mem. Sigma Nu, Phi Delta Phi. Baptist. Mason. Address: Washington, D.C. Died Apr. 14, 1975.

TOMBALBAYE, FRANCOIS, pres. Republic of Chad; b. 1918. Formerly businessman, sch. ofcl.; territorial councilor, 1952, 57-59; mem. Grand Counseil, 1957-59, v.p., 1957-59; prime minister, 1959-75, minister of justice, 1959-62, minister defense, 1960-62; pres. Council of State, 1960-75; pres. Republic of Chad, 1960-75, minister interior, minister of nat. def. Address: Ft Lamy, Republic of Chad. Died Apr. 1975.

TOMKINS, GORDON MAYER, biochemist; b. Chgo., June 4, 1926; s. Howard Samuel and Jean (Gordon) T.; A.B., U. Cal. at Los Angeles, 1945; M.D., Harvard, 1949; Ph.D., U. Cal. at Berkeley, 1953; m. Millicent Hanson, July 19, 1951; children—Leslie Jean, Tanya Gordon. Intern, Peter Bent Brigham Hosp., Boston; investigator Nat. Heart Inst., 1953-55; investigator clin. br. Nat. Inst. Arthritis and Metabolic Diseases, 1955-58, chief sect, metabolic enzymes, 1958-62, became chief lab. molecular biology, 1962-69; Mider lectr. NIH, 1969; Jessup lectr. Columbia U., 1971; prof. biochemistry, vice chmn. dept. biochemistry and biophysics U. Cal. at San Francisco, 1969-75; Harvey Soc. lectr. Columbia, 1971; Prather lectr. Harvard, 1972. Mem. nat. adv. bd. Am. Cancer Soc., 1969-72; molecular biology study sect. NIH, 1971-74. Recipient award Washington Acad. Sci., 1965. Fellow Am. Acad. Arts and Scis.; mem. Am. Soc. Biol. Chemists, Am. Soc. Clin. Investigation, Am. Chem. Soc., Am. Soc. Human Genetics, Washington Philos. Soc., Endocrine Soc. Mem. editorial bd. Endocrinology, 1968-71, Developmental Biology, 1970, Ann. Rev. Biochemistry, Jour. Molecular Biology, 1972-74, Cell: Jour. of Cell Biology, 1972-74, Jour. of Cellular Physiology. Home: Mill Valley, Cal. Died July 22, 1975.

TOMLINSON, DOUGLAS, publisher; b. Bell Co., Tex., Mar. 3, 1888; s. J. D. and Sarah (Hand) T.; A.B., Tex. Christian U., 1909; LL.B., U. Tex., 1913; postgrad. in journalism, Columbia; LL.D., Tex. Christian U., 1967; m. Mar. 20, 1917 (wife dec. 1943); children—Douglas (dec.), Lambuth; m. 2d, Lottie Martin, May 26, 1946. Chmn. bd., founder All-Ch. Press Newspapers; pub. Dallas World, Ft. Worth Tribune, Houston Times, Memphis Mirror, Oklahoma City Star, Tulsa Herald, Wichita Light, Church Week. Chmn. bd. Brite Div. Sch., Tex. Christian U. Recipient Lambda Lambda award for Distinguished Service in Religious Journalism, Okla. Baptist U., 1954; Bronze medallion Columbia U., 1963; named to Journalism Hall of Fame, Mary Hardin-Baylor Coll., 1966. Mem. Christian Church. Clubs: Rotary, Fort Worth. Home: Fort Worth, Tex. Dec. Mar. 17, 1971.

TOMLINSON, EDWARD, lecturer, writer; b. Stockton, Ga., Sept. 27, 1892; s. John H. and Seapher (Touchtone) T.; student Ga. Normal Coll., Douglas, 1910-12, U. of Edinburgh, Scotland, 1918-19. Lecturer and writer on Inter-Am. affairs; Inter-Am. adviser, Nat. Broadcasting Co. Author: New Roads to Riches. In The Other Americas; The Other Americans; Battle for the Hemisphere; has reported all Pan-Am. Confs. since 1928; first to broadcast regular programs on Latin America; broadcast Pan-American confs.; has flown 400,000 miles in other Americas. Received Cabot Gold Medal from Columbia U. for Distinguished contribution Inter-Am. Relations. Awarded Order Southern Cross (Brazil), Order of Merit (Ecuador); Navy Commendation. Clubs: Dutch Treat, The Players (New York); Overseas Writers (Washington). Home: New York City, N.Y. Died Dec. 2, 1974.

TOOMEY, FLOYD F(RANCIS), lawyer; b. Independence, Ia., Mar. 31, 1894; s. Michael and Anna (Quirk) T.; student Ia. State Tchrs. Coll., 1913-14; LL.B., U. Wash., 1920, m. Ruth Holland, Aug. 2, 1924; children—Robert L., William D. Admitted to Wash. bar, 1920 and practiced in Seattle, 1921-24; atty., office Solicitor Internal Revenue, 1924-26; head, civil div. Office of Gen. Counsel, Bur. of Internal Revenue in charge of civil litigation in fed. cts., 1927-30, head, appeals div. in charge tax litigation before U.S. Bd. Tax Appeals, 1931-32; gen. asst. to gen. counsel Bur. Internal Revenue, 1933-34; partner Alvord & Alvord, Washington, in charge tax litigation, 1934-50, Lee, Toomey & Kent from 1950. Mem. Am. and D.C. bar assns., Phi Alpha Delta, Delta Sima Rho. Home: Pompano Beach, Fla. Died Mar. 27, 1975.

TOOPS, HERBERT ANDERSON, prof. psychology; b. Kiousville, Ohio, Sept. 18, 1895; s. John William and Leona Arvilla (Anderson) Toops; student Ohio Wesleyan University, 1912-14; A.B., Ohio State University, 1916, B.S. in education, 1916, A.M., 1917; Ph.D., Teachers College (Columbia University), 1921; married Laura Merrill Chassell, Dec. 31, 1922; children—Thorndike, Edward, Marian, Nona, Laurence. Research asso. of the Inst. of Ednl. Research, Teachers Coll. (Columbia), 1921-23; asst. prof. psychology, Ohio State U., 1923-27, prof. psychology, 1927-65, prof. emeritus, 1965-72; asso. prof. psychology, U. of Minn., summer 1927. Consultant in statistics, Secretary of War, Mar.-Sept. 1944; consultant to Nat. Roster of Scientific and Specialized Personnel, March-June 1945; consultant U.S. Navy, 1947-48, Nat. Research Council, Ohio Dept. Natural Resources, 1972. Fellow A.A.A.S., Ohio Academy of Science, American Psychol. Assn.; member Assn. for Computing Machinery, American Statistical Association, American Math. Soc., Math. Assn. America, American Ednl. Research Assn., National Society for Study of Edn., Sociometric Soc., Midwestern Psychological Assn., Inst. of Mathematical Statistics, Ohio State Horticulture Soc., Nat. Soc. Coll. Teachers of Edn., Ohio Ednl. Research Assn., Psychometric Soc., Royal Statis, Soc., American Sociological Society, Econometric Soc., O. Wesleyan Union, Phi Delta Kappa, Sigma Xi, Alpha Psi Delta. Writer on ednl. subjects. Home: Columbus, O., Died Aug. 12, 1972; buried Pleasant Township Cemetery of Madison County, Mount Sterling, O.

TOPPING, DANIEL REID, baseball exec.; b. 1912; s. Henry J. Topping; ed. Lawrenceville Sch., U. Pa.; m. Charlotte Ann Lillard; children—Rhea R., Tracey Anne, Daniel Reid, David Reid. Part-owner Bklyn. Profl. Football team, 1934; with Del Webb bought Yankee Stadium (purchase including the baseball team), N.Y.C., 1945; stadium sold to Arnold M. Johnson & Assos. of Chgo., then leased for long term by Messrs. Topping and Webb; past co-owner and exec. head of The Yankees; dir. Nat. Airlines, Inc., Automatic Canteen Co. of Am., Louis Sherry, Inc. Served as capt. USMC, World War II; lt. col. USMCR. Clubs: Brook; Nat. Golf Links; Deepdale; Seminole. Died May 18, 1974.

TORREY, CLARENCE EZRA, JR., govt. ofcl.; b. Milw., Jan. 16, 1913; s. Clarence Ezra and Frances (Williams) T.; B.A., M.A., U. Wis., 1934, grad. student, 1935-36; m. Dorothy Bowling Dyer, June 291946; children—Nancy, Pamela, Barbara. Asst. econs. U. Wis., 1935-36; with Lawrence Stern & Co., investments, Chgo., 1936-38; with Stern, Wampler & Co., Inc., investments, Chgo., 1938-42, comptroller, 1941-42; financial analyst Kebbon, McCormick & Co., Chgo., 1946-50; financial analyst A.G. Becker & Co., Chgo., 1950-57, v.p., 1958-60; v.p., Carrier Corp., Syracuse, N.Y., 1960-70, v.p., treas., 1961-62, v.p., chief financial officer, 1962-68, v.p. corporate devel., 1968-70; cons. econ. devel. adminstrn. U.S. Dept. Commerce, 1971-73. Served to capt. AUS, 1943-46. Recipient Army Commendation award. Mem. Financial Analysts Fedn. (v.p. 1958-59), Investment Analysts Soc. (pres. 1958-59), Am. Chgo. Finance Assn., N.Y. Soc. Security Analysts, Financial Execs. Inst., Phi Beta Kappa, Phi Kappa Phi, Delta Sigma Pi. Roman Catholic. Club: Union League (Chgo.). Home: Annandale, Va. Died July 7, 1973; buried Calvary Cemetery, Fairfax, Va.

TOUREL, JENNIE, opera singer; ed. in France and Switzerland. Came to U.S., 1941. Opera debut as Carmen, Opera-Comique, Paris, France, 1933; sang roles Carmen, Mignon, Charlotte 500 times, 1933-40; Am. concert debut with N.Y. Philharmonic under direction Arturo Toscanini, 1942; appeared with Boston Symphony under Serge Koussevitsky, N.B.C., under Leopold Stokowski, 1942; soloist with all maj. U.S. and Canadian orchs., 1942; joined Met. Opera Co., N.Y.C., 1944. Sang Carmen, Mignon, Adalgisa in Norma, Rosina in Barber of Seville; pioneer Met. mezzo-soprano coloratura version, Mar. 1945; S. Am. debut Theatro Municipal, Rio de Janiero, 1944, toured S. America 1945; London debut, Royal Albert Hall, 1947; appeared in major European Festivals, after 1948; Aspen Festival, after 1957; toured Israel, 1949, 50, 52, South Africa, 1954, Japan, 1962; Columbia Records; Odessey Records, mem. vocal dept. Julliard Sch. Music, 1963-73; head vocal dept. Rubin Acad. Music, Jerusalem, Israel, 1968-73. Decorated chevalier d l'Ordre des Art et des Lettres. Address: New York City, N.Y. Died Nov. 23, 1973.

TOWLE, LAWRENCE WILLIAM, educator; b. Saco, Me., May 24, 1902; s. Phillip Sheridan and Ilo Maud Cora Augusta (Innes) T.; A.B., Dowdoin Coll., 1924; A.M. (U. scholar), Harvard, 1927, Ph.D., 1932; m. Dorothy Storer Taylor, June 14, 1927; 1 son, William Geoffrey. With Fidelity Trust Co., Portland, Me., 1924-26; instr. Amherst Coll., 1927-29; instr. and tutor Harvard, 1930-33; instr. Williams Coll., 1933-34; instr. Colgate U., 1934-35; asso. prof. Lawrence Coll., 1935-42; prof. Trinity Coll., 1942-70, head dept. econs., 1942-67, sec. faculty, 1947-69, G. Fox & Co. prof. econs., 1957-67; Theodore Roosevelt prof. econs. Naval War Coll., Newport, R.I., 1970-71; vis. prof. U. Fla., 1942, Bowdoin Coll., summer 1947; adj. prof. Fla. Inst. Tech., 1973. Dir., cons. Hartford Fed. Savs. and Loan Assn., 1960. Prin. Econ. Office of Allen Property Custodian, 1942-43; mem. Commn. on City Plan, Hartford, Conn., 1949-54; adviser Hartford C. of C., 1944-45. Fellow Royal Econ. Soc.; mem. Am. Econ. Assn., Am. Assn. U. Profs., Phi Beta Kappa, Psi Upsilon (exec. council 1956-69), Pi Gamma Mu. Episcopalian. Author: Time Deposits, 1932; International Trade and Commercial Policy, 1947, rev. 1956. Contbr. to Ency. Brit., articles and reviews to profl. jours. Home: Indialantic, Fla. Died Jan. 21, 1974; buried Laurel Hill Cemetery, Saco, Me.

TOWNE, CHARLES WAYLAND, author; b. Dover, N.H., Nov. 14, 1875; s. T!Charles A. and Alice (Jordan) T.; A.B., Brown U., 1897; m. 3d, Priscilla Codner Sayre, Dec. 1, 1938; children—Betsy, Patricia, Richard S. Member of the staff of N.Y. Times, 1897-98, Boston Herald, 1898-1903; newspaper corr. and literary work, Boston, 1903; owner and pub. White Mountain Echo, Bethlehem, N.H., 1905-08; owner and editor Daily Evening Leader, Newburyport, Mass., and Newburyport Morning Herald, 1909; editor and pub. Cambridge Daily Standard, 1911. Publicity work, 5 years, with Ivy L. Lee; publicity dir. Anaconda Copper Mining Co. and Montana Power Company, 1920-41; later retired. Dramatic dir. 5 mos. at Camp Upton, N.Y., and 14 mos. in France, 1917-19, World War. mem. Am. Legion, Soc. for Preservation and Encouragement of Barber Shop Quarter Singing in Am., Delta Phi Clubs: Old Pueblo, Executives (pre.), Rotary. Episcopalian. Has written books and mag. articles (humorous) under pen-name of "Gideon Wurdz," Author: The Foolish Dictionary, 1904; Foolish Finance, 1905; Eediotic Etiquette, 1906; The New Foolish Dictionary, 1914; Her Majesty Montana, 1939; Shepherd's Empire (with E. N. Wentworth), 1945; Pigs, From Cave to Cornbelt, 1950; Cattle and Men, 1955; co-author: This Is the West, 1957. Address: Tucson Ariz†

TOYNBEE, ARNOLD JOSEPH, Brit. historian; b. London, Eng., Apr. 14, 1889; s. Harry Valpy and Sarah Edith (Marshall) T.; ed. Winchester Coll., 1902-07,

Balliol Col., Oxford (Engl.) U., 1907-11, Brit. Archaeol. Sch., Athens, 1911-12; D.Litt. (hon.), Oxford U., Cambridge (Eng.) U., Birmingham (Eng. and Ala.) U., D.C.L. (hon.), Princeton; LL.D., Columbia; m. Rosalind Murray, Sept. 1912 (marriage dissolved 1945); children—Theodore Philip, Lawrence Leif; m. 2d Veronica Boulter, Sept. 28, 1946. Fellow and tutor Balliol Coll., Oxford U., 1912-15; govt. work in connection with War, 1915-19, Polit. Intelligence Dept., Fgn. Office, 1918; mem. Middle Eastern sect. Brit. delegation to Peace Conf., Paris, 1919; prof. Byzantine and modern Greek lang., lit. and history U. London, 1919-24; dir. studies Royal Inst. of Internat. Affairs, London, 1925-55; research prof. internat. history U. of London, 1925-55, prof. emeritus; with Fgn. Office, 1939-46; mem. Brit. del. to Peace Conf., Paris, 1946; corr. Manchester Guardian (on leave of absence), 1921-22; lectr. Encounters Between Civiliation, Bryn Mawr Coll., 1947; vis. prof. numerous U.S. colls. and univs. Decorated Companion of Honor, 1956. Fellow Brit. Acad., 1937, mem. Philos. Soc. Am., Soc. Promotion Hellenic and Roman Studies, Great Britain, Inst. of France (asso.). Author: Nationality and War, 1915; The New Europe, 1915; The Western Question in Greece and Turkey, 1922; Greek Historical Thought, Greek Civilization and Character, 1924; The World After the Peace Conference, 1925; A Survey of International Affairs for 1920-23, 1924, contbr., editor series, until 1955; Turkey (with K.P. Kirwood), 1926; A Journey to China, 1931; A Study of History (vols. 1-111), 1934, (Volumes 1V-V1) 1939, and (Volumes V11-X) 1954. Vol. X1, Historical Atlas and Gazetteer, 1959, Vol. X11, Reconsiderations, 1961, illus. abridgement (with Jane Caplan, 1972; Civilization on Trial, 1948; War and Civilization, 1951; The World and the West, 1953; An Historian's Approach to Religion, 1956; East to West, 1958; Hellenism, 1959; Between Oxus and Jumna, 1961; Between Niger and Nile, 1965; Hannibal's Legacy, 1965; Change and Habit; Acquaintances, 1967; Between Naule and Amazon, 1967; Experiences; Some Problems of Greek History, 1969; Cities on the Move, 1970; Constantine Porphyrogenitus and His World, 1973; Mankind and Mother Earth, 1976. Editor: British Commonwealth Relations, 1934; Cities of Destiny; The Crucible of Christianity; Half the World (Eastern Asia). Contbr. various publications, including Internat. Affairs, (London) Nation, Asia, Contemporary Rev., New Republic, Atlantic Monthly, Harpers magazine, New York Times magazine, Observer Fgn. News Service, and others. Home: Terrington, York, England. Died Oct. 22, 1975.

TRACHTMAN, JOSEPH, lawyer; b. Phila., June 1, 1901; s. Max and Pauline (Glassman) T.; A.B., U. Pa., 1922; LL.B., Yale, 1926; m. Anne Neuhauser, Sept. 4, 1924. Admitted to N.Y. bar, 1927, since practiced in N.Y.C., specializing in wills, estates, trusts, taxation; lectr. Practising Law Institute, 1930-75; adjunct prof. grad. div. Sch. Law. N.Y.U., 1951-75; mem. law firm Hughes, Hubbard, & Reed, N.Y.C., 1964-75. Fell. Am. Bar Found.; mem. American (chmn. real property, probate and trust law sect., del. to ho. of dels.), Am. Coll. Probate Counsel (pres. 1966-67), N.Y. State bar assns., Bar Assn. City of N.Y., Bankers Club of Am. Clubs: Yale, The Players. Author: Estate Planning 1946-68. Home: Ridgefield, Conn. Died Oct. 15, 1975; interred Ferncliff, Westchester County, N.Y.

TRAISMAN, ALFRED STANLEY, physician; b. Russia, Sept. 22, 1896; s. Samuel and Ada Traisman; M.D., U. Ill., 1921; m. Sara Sevin, June 18, 1922; children—Howard S., Robert N. Intern, Cook County Hosp., Chgo., 1921-22; asso. attending physician Children's Mem. Hosp., Chgo.; asso. prof. pediatrics emeritus Northwestern U. Diplomate Am. Bd. Pediatrics. Mem. Am. Acad. Pediatrics, A.M.A., Am. Acad. Allergy. Home: Chicago, Ill. Died Dec. 7, 1974; buried Rosehill Cemetery, Chicago, Ill.

TRAPNELL, FREDERICK MACKAY, naval officer; b. Elizabeth, N.J., July 9, 1902; s. Benjamin and Ada (Probasco) T.; student Pingry Sch., Elizabeth, N.J., 1915-17, 19, Stevens Prep. Sch., Hoboken, N.J., 1917-18; B.S., U.S. Naval Acad., 1923; m. Alice Moffitt, June 10, 1936; two children—Frederick Mackay, Herbert Wallace. Commd. ensign U.S.N., 1923, advanced through grades to vice adm. ret., 1952; naval aviator, 1927-53; test pilot, 1930-32; chief flight test officer, 1940-43, World War II; comdg. officer U.S.S. Breton (escort carrier), 1943-44; chief staff, comdr. Carrier Div. 6, Pacific, 1944-45; comdr. Naval Air Test Center, Patuxent River, Md.; comdr. U.S.S. Coral Sea, 1950-51; dep. comdr. Sandia Base, 1951-52; now cons. engring. dept. Grumman Aircraft Engring. Corp. Received Octave Chanute award for outstanding tests jet aircraft, Inst. Aero. Sci., 1949; decorated Legion Merit, Bronze Star Medal, and also Presidential Unit Citation. Associate fellow of the Institute of Aeronautical Sci.; honorary fellow Soc. Experimental Test Pilots. Clubs: Army and Navy; Seawanhaka-Corinthian Yacht; New York Yacht. Home: Coronado, Cal. Died Jan. 30, 1975.

TRAPNELL, WILLIAM COLSTON, ret. ins. co. exec.; b. Phila., June 7, 1906; s. William and Elizabeth (Colston) T.; B.S., Va. Mil. Inst., 1927; m. Elsa Parma Bartlett, Sept. 1, 1931; children—Nancy White (Mrs. Andrew C. Holmes), William Colston. With E.I. duPont de Nemours & Co., Phila., 1927-29, Chase & Waring, cons. engrs., N.Y.C., 1929-34, U.S. Fed. Emergency Relief Adminstrn., Washington, 1934-36, Scudder, Stevens & Clark, N.Y.C., 1936-48; financial sec. Provident Mut. Life Ins. Co. Phila., 1948-56, 2d v.p., 1957-59, 2d v.p., sec., 1959-60, v.p., sec., 1961-67, v.p. investments, 1967-71; ret. 1971. Served to lieut. comdr. USNR, 1943-46. Mem. Financial Analysts Fedn. (dir. 1952-54, v.p. 1954, chmn. govt. relations com. 1959-64). Club: Racquet (Phila). Home: Front Royal, Va. Died Sept. 30, 1974; buried Zion Churchyard, Charles Town, W.Va.

TRAPNELL, WILLIAM HOLMES, utility exec.; b. Yonkers, N.Y., Jan. 19, 1905; s. Joseph and Laura Virginia (Kennedy) T.; B.S., Hobart Coll., 1927, LL.D., 1960; m. Sally Gordon, Mar. 26, 1930; children—William Holmes, Gordon, Sally Berkeley, Thomas Hall. Traffic supr. Chesapeake & Potomac Telephone Co. of Va., Richmond, 1927-29, dist. traffic mgr., Norfolk, 1929-34, gen. traffic mgr., Washington, 1939-46, v.p., 1946-51, gen. mgr., 1949-51; pres. Commonwealth Natural Gas Corp., 1951-70, chmn. bd., 1970; dir. First & Mchts. Nat. Bank, Chesapeake & Potomac Telephone Co. of Va., Va. Wood Preserving Corp., Richmond Corp., Life Ins. Co. of Va., First Mchts. Corp. Mem. Commn. on Higher Edn. Facilities. Trustee Va. Found. Ind. Colls.; b. visitors Wm. and Mary Coll. Mem. S.R. Va., Richmond (past pres.), U.S. chambers of commerce, Phi Beta Kappa, Sigma Phi, Kappa Beta Phi. Episcopalian (vestryman). Rotarian. Clubs: Country of Va., Commonwealth (pres.) (Richmond). Home: Sabot, Va. Died Aug. 12, 1973; buried St. Mary's Epis. Ch., Goochland County, Va.

TRAVIS, JUDSON COOPER, precious metals exec.; b. Mt. Vernon, N.Y., June 16, 1902; s. Judson Cooper and Mae (Loomis) T.; student high sch.; m. Helen Korth, Mar. 15, 1935; children—Jean Carol, Judith Mae. With Handy & Harman, N.Y.C., 1918-73, office boy asst. to pres., v.p., exec. v.p., pres., 1953-64, chmn., 1964-67, hon. chmn., 1967-73, dir., 1943-67; mem. exec. com., 1950-73. Presbyn. Clubs: 24 Karat, Economic, Manhattan (N.Y.C.); Canoe Brook Country (Summit, N.J.). Home: Summit, N.J. Died Nov. 3, 1973.

TREADWAY, WALTER LEWIS, physician; b. Arenzville, Ill., Jan. 15, 1886; s. Henry and Margaret Treadway; M.D., Barnes Med. Coll., 1907; D.D.S., U. Cal., 1930; Sc.D., U. So. Cal., 1945; m. Sylvia Houston, Aug. 5, 1908. Intern, St. Louis City Hosp., 1907-08; intern, resident physician Jacksonville (Ill.) State Hosp., 1909-11; clin. psychiatrist Ill. Psychol. Inst., Kankakee, 1912; resident physician Ill. State Hosp. Service, 1913, N.Y. State Psychol. Inst., 1914; chief neuropsychiatrist Wark Risk Ins. Bur. and Hosp., 1918-21; med. officer in charge VA Hosp., N.Y.C., 1922, Field Studies in Mental Hygiene, Boston, 1922-25, Western Europe Exam Prospective Immigrants Destined for U.S., 1925-27; resident Queens Sq. Hosp., London, 1928; asst. surg. gen. in charge mental hygiene div. USPHS, 1922-39; asst. in psychiatry Johns Hopkins, 1957-58. U.S. del. Internat. Neurol. Conf., Paris, 1925, 1st Pan Am. Conf., 1931, 3d Pan Am. conf., 1936; chmn. U.S. del. 2d Internat. Hosp. Conf. Served as capt., M.C., AUS, 1952-54. Diplomate Am. Bd. Psychiatry and Neurology. Fellow Am. Psychiat. Assn., Internat. Assn. Social Psychiatry, Am. Assn. Social Psychiatry (sec. 1971-73); mem. A.M.A., Pan Am. Med. Assn. Home: Santa Barbara, Cal. Died July 30, 1973; buried Santa Barbara Cemetery.

TREDTIN, WALTER C, clergyman, educator; b. Dayton, O., Sept. 15, 1881; s. Jacob and Elizabeth (Stoecklein) T.; ed. University of Dayton and U. of Fribourg, Switzerland. Taught in high schools, Chicago, and Cleveland; ordained Soc. of Mary, 1912; profl. Latin and Creek, U. of Dayton, 1912-16; prin. W. Phila. Catholic High Sch. for Boys, 1916-22; superior Mt. St. John Normal Sch., 1922-30; pres. Trinity Coll., Sioux City, Ia., 1930-32; pres. U. of Dayton, 1932-38; provincial eastern province, Soc. of Mary, from 1938. Address: Dayton, O.†

TREGASKIS, RICHARD, fgn. corr.; b. Elizabeth, N.J., Nov. 28, 1916; s. Archibald and Maude Madeline (Osterman) T.; ed. Peddie Sch., Hightstown, N.J., Pingry Sch., Elizabeth, N.J., 1932-34; A.B., Harvard, 1938; Litt.D., Hillsdale Coll., 1958; m. Marian Holmes, Aug. 30, 1941 (div.); m. 2d, Walton Jeffords, 1953 (div.); m. 3d, Moana Maharam, 1963. Harvard corr. Boston Record, Am. Advertiser, 1937-38, feature writer, 1938-41; rewrite man on fgn. desk Internat. News Service, 1942, Pacific Fleet corr., 1942-43, covering Coral Sea Battle, Doolittle-Tokyo task force, Battle of Midway, Battle for Guadalcanal, assigned MTO, covered invasions of Sicily, Italy, fall of Naples, wounded, 1943, assigned ETO, covered battle of Western front, 1944; Pacific war corr. Saturday Evening Post, 1945, covered surrender of Japan U.S.S. Missouri, 1945; staff writer, 1945-46; fgn. assignments for various mags., 1946-73. Decorated Purple Heart. Named one of America's 10 Outstanding Young Men, U.S. C. of C., 1942; recipient George R. Holmes award, 1942; Internat. News Service Medal of Honor for Heroic Devotion to Duty, 1942, 43; George Polk award hazardous reporting, 1964-65. Fellow Royal Geog. Soc., Acad. Motion Picture Arts and Scis.; mem. Authors League, Aviation Space Writers Assn. Author: Guadalcanal Diary, 1943; Invasion Diary, 1944; (novel) Stronger Than Fear, 1945; Round-The-World-Diary, 1948-49; (screen play) Force of Arms, 1951; (book) Seven Leagues to Paradise, 1951; (screen plays) The Wild Blue Yonder, 1951, Fair Wind to Java, 1952, Mission over Korea, 1953; (documentary film) Polar City, 1958; (book) X- 15 Diary, 1961; Last Plane to Shanghai 1961; John F. Kennedy and PT-109, 1962; Vietnam Diary, 1963 (George Polk award 1964); (poetry) Woman and the Sea, 1966; (novels) China Bomb, 1967, Warrior King: Hawaii's Kamehameha the Great, 1973; (history) Southeast Asia: Building the Bases, 1975; also numerous TV dramas. Contbr. nat. mags. Address: Honolulu, Hawaii. Died Aug. 1973.

TRESCOTT, PAUL HENRY, columnist; b. Millville, Pa., Aug. 19, 1898; s. Boyd and Annie (Potter) T.; student Wyo. Sem., Kingston, Pa., 1916-17, U. Akron, 1919-20; m. Stella H. Potts., Aug. 28, 1923; children—Paul B., Alfred P.; m. 2d, Louise A. Bachman, Mar. 10, 1948; 1 son, Clarke Bachman. Reporter Bloomsburg (Pa.) Press, 1914, city editor, 1921-37; reporter Wilkes-Barre (Pa.) Times Leader, 1916; city editor Berwick (Pa.) Enterprise, 1917-19; reporter Akron (O.) Times 1919-20; editorial writer Phila. Evening Bull., 1937-63; columnist Phila. Evening Bulletin, 1963-67, Charleston (S.C.) Evening Post, 1966-70; freelance columnist, 1970; tchr. creative writing Junto Sch., Phila., 1943-53; lectr. journalism schs. Mem. Nat. Conf. Editorial Writers (treas. 1951-53, vice chmn. 1953-54, chmn. 1954-55). Presbyn. Mason. Contbr. articles to mags. Address: Philadelphia, Pa. Died Apr. 9, 1974.

TRILLING, LIONEL, author, educator; b. N.Y.C., July 4, 1905; s. David W. and Fannie (Cohen) T.; A.B., Columbia, 1925, A.M., 1926, Ph.D., 1938; D.Litt., Trinity Coll., 1955, Harvard, 1963, Case Western Res. U., 1968, Durham U., Leicester U., 1973; L.H.D., Northwestern U., 1964; m. Diana Rubin, June 12, 1929; 1 son, James Lionel. Instr. English, U. Wis., 1926-27, Hunter Coll., 1927-30; mem. faculty English. Colubmia, 1931-75, prof., 1948-75; George Edward Woodberry prof. lit. and criticism, 1965-70, univ. prof., 1970-75. George Eastmen vis. prof. Oxford U., 1964-65; Charles Eliot Norton vis. prof. poetry Harvard, 1969-70; vis. fellow All Souls Coll., Oxford, 1972-73. Recipient Creative Arts award Brandeis U., 1968. Author: Matthew Arnold, 1939; E.M. Forster, 1943; The Middle of the Journey, 1947; The Liberal Imagination 1950; The Opposing Self, 1955; Freud and the Crisis of our Culture, 1955; A Cathering of Fugitives, 1956; Beyond Culture; Essays on Learning and Lit., 1965; The Experience of Literature, 1967; Sincerity and Authenticity, 1972; Mind in the Modern World, 1972; also stories, essays in various periodicals. Editor: The Portable Matthew Arnold, 1949; The Letters of John Keats, 1950; The Life and Work of Sigmund Freud; Literary Criticism, 1970; The Oxford Anthology of English Literature (with others), 1973. Fellow Am. Acad. Arts and Scis.; mem. Nat. Inst. Arts and Letters, Phi Beta Kappa. Club: Athenaeum (London); Century (N.Y.C.). Home: New York City, N.Y., Died Nov. 5, 1975.

TRIMBLE, SOUTH, JR., lawyer; b. Frankford, Ky., Aug. 21, 1896; s. South and Carrie Bell (Allan) T.; LL.B., Georgetown U., 1917, LL.M., 1919; m. Elaine A. Lazaro, Mar. 28, 1923; children—Elaine Lazaro Patterson, South III, Mary Allan Smith, Stephen Asbury, James L. Admitted to D.C. bar, 1917; atty. for U.S.R.R. Adminstrn., 1919, for Bur. of Internal Revenue, 1920-22; private practice, Washington, D.C., 1922-33, 53-73; solicitor U.S. Dept. Commerce, 1933-45; appointed chmn. adv. bd. Inland Waterways Corp., Dept. of Commerce, May 22, 1945; trustee U.S. Shipping Board Merchants Fleet Corp., 1933-36; chmn. Interdepartmental Shipping Policy Com., 1934; chmn. Bd. to Investigate Hindenburg Disaster; chmn. com. of alternates Fgn. Trade Zone Bd., 1939-45; gen. counsel Nat. Inventors Council, 1940-45; mem. 1st Fed. Maritime Bd., 1947-53. Served as lt. (j.g.) Supply Corps, U.S.N.R.F., World War. Mem. Am., Federal and D.C. bar assns., Barristers Club, Am. Legion (comdr. local post), Delta Theta Phi. Democrat. Roman Catholic. Elk. Home: Washington, D.C. Died Jan. 31, 1973.

TRIPP, LENA ELVINA FLACK, (Mrs. Elmer Tripp), author; b. Churdan, Ia., Sept. 30, 1899; d. Samuel Marion and Wilhelmina (Bjornson) Flack; A.B., U. Wash., 1923; M.A.,U. Cal. at Berkeley, 1924; m. Elmer Tripp, Aug. 24, 1935 (dec. Nov. 1959). First grade tchr., Plymouth, Cal., 1953-69. Author: Verses, 1968; More Verses, 1970; The Broken Tree, 1971; Those Pets of Mine 1971; Two Years Old, 1972; Words are Wonderful, 1972; Autumn Leaves, 1973. Contbr. poetry to profl. jours. Home: Plymouth, Cal., Deceased.

TRISSAL, JOHN MEREDITH, engr., r.r. exec.; b. Chgo., Dec. 30, 1903; s. Julius Ross and Sarah (Meredith) T.; B.S., U. Ill., 1925, Profl. Engr., 1940; m. Morva Jones, Aug. 27, 1932; children—Morva Joanne (Mrs. Park Kirk, Jr.), Sally Jeanne (Mrs. Stephen Spudich). With the Ill. Central Railroad, 1925-70, various positions engring. dept., supt. communication and elec. engr., 1945-50, asst. chief engr., 1950-56, chief engr., 1956-58, v.p., chief engr., 1958-64, v.p. devel. Ill. Central Industries, 1967-67, v.p. real estate and devel. I.C. R.R., also Ill. Central Industries, 1967-70. Mem. Am. Ry. Engring. Assn. (president), Assn. Am. R.R.,

Am. Soc. C.E., Am. Soc. Corrosion Engrs. Mason. Clubs: Chicago Athletic Assn., Engrs. (Chgo.); Flossmoor Country. Home: Flossmoor, Ill., Died Nov. 1, 1975.

TROTT, NORMAN LIEBMAN, sem. pres.; b. Balt., Sept. 25, 1901; s. Frank Bernard and Margaret (Tatum) T.; B.S., Johns Hopkins, 1931, postgrad., 1935; Balt. Rauschenbusch fellow, Md. Council Chs., 1935-38; D.D., Western Md. Coll., 1955; LL.D., Am. U., 1961; m. Lillain Durfee, Sept. 2, 1930. Ordained to ministry Methodist Ch., 1935; pastor in Arbutus, Md., 1926-33, Balt., 1933-39, Brunswick, Md., 1939-47, Hagerstown, Md., 1947-50; dist. supt., Balt., 1950-55; pres. Wesley Theol. Sem., Washington, 1955-67; now cons. on fund raising and pub. relations. Mem. gen. bd. evangelism Meth. Ch., 1956-64, gen. bd. social concerns, 1960-64, commn. ch. unity, 1960-68, mem. gen. conf., 1952, 56, 60, 64, 66, consultantion ch. union, joint com. Meth-Evang. U.B. merger, U.S. conf. World Council Chs.; del. World Meth. Conf., Oslo, 1961, London, 1966, Denver, 1971; bd. visitors Duke U. Div. Sch., 1969—; chmn. com. on publ. History Balt. Conf., 1968-72; chmn. planning and devel. com. Asbury Meth. Village, 1968—. Bd. dirs. Md. Gen. Hosp. Mason. Author: What Church People Think, 1937; Teen Agers Tell, 1948; contbg. author: Those Incredible Methodists, 1972; also verse, articles. Address: Gaithersburg, Md., Died Nov. 16, 1975.

TRUANT, ALDO PETER, pharm. co. exec.; b. Udine, Italy, Nov. 17, 1920; s. Liberale and Adele (Berarzzatti) T.; B.A., U. Western Ont., 1944; Ph.D., Yale, 1949; m. Lelia Serena, Oct. 4, 1947; children—Cynthia, Sandra, Marc, Alida. Came to U.S., 1948. Asst. prof. pharmacology George Washington U. Sch. Medicine, Washington, 1948-50. Tufts U. Sch. Medicine and Dentistry, Boston, 1950-53, asso. prof., 1953-55; v.p. research Astra Pharm. Products, Inc., Worcester, Mass., 1955-66; asso. prof. affiliate biology Clark U., 1959-63, prof. affiliate 1964-66; v.p. research and devel., pharm. div. Pennwalt Corp., Rochester, N.Y., 1966. Mem. A.A.A.S., Pharmacology Soc. Can., N.Y. Acad. Scis., Am. Soc. Pharmacology and Exptl. Therapeutics. Home: Rochester, N.Y. Died Sept. 5, 1973.

TRUDGIAN, ANDREW B., lawyer; born Washington, Nov. 17, 1895; s. Josiah Bassett and Margaret Frances (Van Vleck) T.; student U. of Pa. arts course class, 1914; LL.B., Georgetown U., 1918; LL.M. New York U., 1934; m. Emily Burton, May 5, 1924; 1 dau., Margaret Burton. Admitted to D. C. bar, 1919, N.Y. State bar, 1934; head tax dept., S.D. Leidesdorf & Co., certified pub. accountants, 1922-44; gen. counsel J. P. Stevens & Co. since 1944. Mem. Bar Supreme Court Dist. of Columbia, Bar of N.Y. State, Supreme Court of U.S., mem. Am. Bar Assn., New York County Lawyers Assn., Am. Arbitration Assn. (nat. panel) Lawyers' Assn. of Textile Industry (bd. govs.). Republican. Presbyn. Mason (past master). Clubs: Westchester Country (Rye, N.Y.); Union League (N.Y.C.). Home: Rye, N.Y. Died Sept. 16, 1974.

TRUEBLOOD, ROBERT MARTIN, accountant; b. Kindred, N.D., May 4, 1916; s. Samuel E. and Irene (Larsen) T.; B.B.A., U. Minn., 1937; postgrad. Northwestern U., 1939-40, Loyola U., Chgo., 1941; m. Florence Henry, Nov. 30, 1940; children—Ann Ames, Jane Blair. Accountant, Baumann, Finney & Co., 1937-42; partner Touche, Ross, Bailey & Smart, Pitts. and Chgo., 1946-74, policy group, 1961; vis. Ford distinguished research prof. Grad. Sch. Insdl. Adminstrn., Carnegie Inst. Tech., 1960-61; vis. lectr. Oxford (Eng.); Summer course, 1967; exec. in residence Stanford, 1969. Mem. Pres.'s Commn. Budget Concepts, 1967. Chmn. accountants group Chgo. Crusade of Mercy campaign, 1963. Councilman, Fox Chapel, Pa., 1957-61. Bd. dirs. Civic Club Allegheny County, Vis. Nurses Assn. Allegheny County. Served to lt. comdr. USNR, 1942-46. Recipient Outstanding Achievement award Bd. Trustees U. Minn., 1963, Gold medal Ill. Soc. C.P.A.'s, 1941, Silver medal in Elijah Watt Sells award Am. Inst. C.P.A.'s, 1941; Sec.'s Commendation award USN; laureate in finance Lincoln Acad. Ill. C.P.A., Ill., Pa. Mem. Am. Inst. C.P.A.'s (pres. 1965-66, mem. accounting principles bd. 1963-65, chmn. long range objectives com. 1961-65, chmn. accountants internat. study group 1966-68), Am. Acounting Assn., Inst. Mgmt. Scis., Inst. Internal Auditors, Nat. Assn. Accountants, Ill., Pa. (past pres.) socs. C.P.A.'s Beta Alpha Psi, Beta Gamma Sigma. Presbyn. (trustee). Author: (with Dean R.M. Cyert) Sampling Techniques in Accounting, 1958; (with others) The Future of Accounting Education, 1961, Auditing, Management Games, and Accounting Education, 1964; (with Sorter) William W. Werntz: His Accounting Thought, 1968. Contbr. article to profl. jours. Home: Northfield, Ill. Died Feb. 1974.

TRYON, CLARENCE ARCHER, JR., educator; b. Niagara Falls, N.Y., Nov. 15, 1911; s. Clarence Archer and Florence (Hough) T.; B.S., Cornell U., 1935, Ph.D., 1942; m. Jenette G. Rose, Dec. 28, 1935; children—Gayle (Mrs. George Gerald Shaw), Marilee (Mrs. John Hoskins). Asso. prof. biology Mont. State Coll., Bozeman, 1937-47; prof. biology, dir. Pymatuning Lab. Ecology, U. Pitts., 1947-73. Mem. Am. Assn. U. Profs., Am. Inst. Biol. Scis., Am. Soc. Mammologists, Assn. Inland Biol. Field Stas., Ecol. Soc. Am., Am. Ornithologists Union, Am. Soc. Ichthyologists and Herpetologists, Wildlife Soc. Contbr. articles to tech. jours. Home: Conneaut Lake, Pa. Died 1973.

TUCK, CLYDE EDWIN, author; b. nr. Springfield, Mo., Feb. 17, 1880; s. Edward C. and Mary Jane (Mitchell) T.; ed. Springfield High Sch. and Scarrett-Morrisville Coll.; unmarried. Reporter and editor various newspapers in different states until 1908; later editor for B. F. Bowen & Co., pubs., Indianapolis. Author: For Love of You, 1909; The Bald Knobbers, 1910. Home: Indianapolis Ind.†

TUCKER, CHESTER EVERETT, coll. adminstr.; b. Fitchburg, Mass., May 19, 1897; s. Fred and Catherine J. (Murray) T.; A.B., Harvard, 1919; m. Elizabeth Hopper, Nov. 16, 1929; children—Samuel Hopper, Elizabeth Robertson (Mrs. Edward F. Ripley). Served as a newspaper reporter, Massachusetts, 1914-15; fund raiser Harvard, 1919; staff mem. John Price Jones Co., N.Y.C., 1919-27, dir., 1925-54, v.p., 1927-51, pres., 1951-54; v.p. development and pub. relations U. Pa., 1955-65, consultant, since 1965, associate trustee; fund raising and pub. relations counsel, univs. and colls., A.R.C., U.S.O. Trustee Springside Sch., Phila., 1942-50, UN Council, Phila., 1948-50. Served as pvt., U.S. Army, 1918-19. Mem. Acad. Natural Scis. and U. Mus,, Am. Alumni Council, Am. Assn. Fund-Raising Counsel (treas. 1953-55). Clubs: Harvard (N.Y.C); Rittenhouse, Harvard (Phila.). Contbr. periodicals. Home: Philadelphia, Pa. Died June 21, 1975.

TUCKER, RICHARD, opera, concert singer, singer, tenor; b. Bklyn., s. Samuel and Fanny (Chippen) T.; ed. pub. schs.; A.F.D., Notre Dame U., 1967, Adelphi U., 1970, D.Mus. (hon.), Combs Coll., 1968, St. John's U., 1969; H.H.D., U. Miami, 1972; m. Sara Perelmuth, Feb. 11, 1936; children—Barry, David, Henry. Made operatic debut at Met. Opera House, N.Y.C., as Enzo in La Gioconda, 1945, and since has sung there as leading tenor, appearing in prodns. of 30 gt. operas. Makes extensive concert tours throughout U.S.; toured Far East, Nr. East, S.Am.; appeared Teatro Colon (Buenos Aires), Vienna Staatsoper, Naples, Verona, Rome Opera, La Scala (Milan), Covent Garden (London), Teatro Comunale (Florence), Teatro Reggio (Parma), appears on radio and TV; made recs. for Columbia, R.C.A. Victor, Angel records; toured Vietnam, Apr. 1967. Decorated comdr. Order Merit (Italy). Home: New York City, N.Y. Died Jan. 8, 1975.

TUCKER, ROBERT HENRY, economist; b. Lunenburg County, Virginia September 27, 1875; s Henry Williamson and Louisa Scott (Nelson) T.; A.B., Coll. of William and Mary, 1893, A.M., 1897, LL.D., 1926; studied Brunswick, Germany, U. Chgo., U. Wis., 1908-10, 15; LL.D., Washington and Lee U., 1956; m. Evelyn Page Edmunds. June 15, 1918. Instr. English and history, Coll. of William and Mary; asso. prof. German and English, Okal. A. and M. Coll., 1899-1902, prof., 1902-08, dean science and lit., 1904-08, v.p., 1906-08; asso. prof. economics and commerce, Washington and Lee U., 1915-19, prof. econs. and bus. adminstrn., 1919-49, acting pres. 1930, dean of College, 1930-32, emeritus, from 1950. Employment mgr. Am. Shipbuilding Co., World War I, 1918; chmn. Indsl. Commn. of Va., 1918-19; mem. Va. Commn. on Simplification of State and Local Govt., 1922-24, and other commns. on State reorgn.; mem. Va. Commn. State and Local Finance, 1948-50; chmn. Va. Commn. County Govt., 1930-32; public panel mem. Regional War abor Bd., 1943-44; econ. cons. Va. Dept. Hwys. 1952-57. Mem. Nat. Tax Assn., Am. Econ. Assn. (exec. com. 1931-34), Royal Econ. Soc. (London), Soc. of Cincinnati, S.R.; Sons of Colonial Wars, Kappa Sigma, Phi Beta Kappa, Omicron Delta Kappa.Democrat. Episcopalian. Club: Commonwealth (Richmond, Va.). Author articles, monographs on econs. subjects. Home: Halifax, Va.†

TUCKERMAN, JACOB EDWARD, surgeon; b. Austinburg, Ashtabula County, O., Aug. 23, 1876; s. Louis Bryant and Mary Ellen (Hopkins) T.; A.B., Adelbert Coll. (Western Reserve U.), Cleveland, O., 1897; M.D., Cleveland Coll. Physicians and Surgeons, 1902; m. Katherine Barton, May 30, 1913; children—Jacob Barton, Mary Katherine (dec.), Lois Elizabeth, William David, Margaret Isabel, Warner Whiton, Robert Gordon. Intern. St. Alexis Hosp., Cleveland, 1903; practiced, Cleveland, from 1903; chief, dept. surgery, Euclid-Glenville Hospital, 1957-59; member Charter Commn., Cleveland, 1913; mem. advisory com. Dept. of Pub. Health, Cleveland, 1915, 16, 17; mem. advisory com. Cleveland Foundation Recreation Survey, 1917; mem. Com. of Fifteen on advisability of city manager plan for City of Cleveland, 1917; pres. Cleveland Single Tax Club, 1916, 17; mem. Cleveland Council of Sociology (pres. 1916-17); dir. Bur. Municipal Research, 1925-28; trustee Cleveland Med. Library Assn., 1927-37, NeWelfare Assn., from 1935; mem. bd. dirs. Glenville Hosp.. Fellow Am. Coll. Surgeons; mem. Am. Acad. Medicine (pres. 1917-18), A.M.A., Ohio State Med. Assn. (c(chmn. com. on med. defense from 1916; mem. judicial and professional relations com., 1938-48), Cleveland Acad. Medicine (sec. 1912-17; pres. 1924; hon. sec. from 1935). Clubs: City (dir. 1915-17), Elysium Figure Skating (pres. 1938-39). Mem. Bd. of Appeal No. 8, group, 3, Ohio, 1942-45. Home: Euclid, O.†

TUGGLE, CHARLES SUMMEY, dentist; b. Stone Mountain, Ga., Aug. 7, 1899; s. Hilliard Cherry and Lena Brantley (Hodo) T.; B.A., Emory U., 1916; D.D.S., Atlanta So. Dental Coll., 1919; m. Bertie Louise Britt, July 20, 1917; children—Charles Summey, James Britt, H. Cherry. Practice dentistry, Stone Mountain, 1919-70; pres. Tuggle Investments, 1925-70; chmn. Tuggle Found., 1940-70; dir. Tuggle Enterprises. Active city, county govtl. adminstrn. Decorated Congl. Merit award. Life mem. Am., Ga. dental assns. Mason. Home: Stone Mountain, Ga. Died Jan. 24, 1972; interred Stone Mountain Cemetery.

TULLEY, DAVID HENRY, army ofcr.; b. Durango, Colo., Apr. 17, 1904; s. Thomas Henry and Victoria Lenore (Day) T.; B.S., U.S. Mil. Acad., 1925; student Cornell U., 1927-28, Command and Gen. Staff Sch., 1936-37, Nat. War Coll., 1949-50; m. Alice Gertrude Hannah, June 14, 1928; children—Gertrude Day, (Mrs. L.E. Surut), Mary Richards Grayeg, William Thomas, Alice Hannah Lively. Commd. 2d lt., U.S. Army, 1925, advanced through grades to maj. gen., 1956, dep. adminstr. paper and pulp sect. N.R.A., 1934; asst. engr. 3d Army, 1944-45; chief constrn. div. USAREUR, 1950-52, engr., 1952-53; asst. chief of engrs. for mil. constrn., 1953-56; comdg. gen. The Engr. Center and Ft. Belvoir, Va., 1956-58; comdg. gen. U.S. Army, Japan, 1958-61; ret., 1961. Decorated Legion of Merit, Bronze Star. Mem. Soc. Am. Mil. Engrs. Home: Aspen, Colo. Died Apr. 21, 1975.

TULP, ARNOLD, lawyer; b. Newark, Nov. 12, 1910; s. I. Peter and Anna (Behrens) T.; A.B. magna cum laude, Brown U., 1933; LL.B., Columbia, 1936; m. Mary Ellen Sheffield, Aug. 28, 1937; children—Arnold S., John S., Evelyn S., Claire S. Admitted to N.Y. bar, 1937, N.J. bar, 1944; with firm Burke & Burke, N.Y.C., 1936-40; with firm Kirlin, Campbell & Keating, N.Y.C., 1940-73, partner, 1948-73; pvt. practice, Red Bank, N.J., 1946-73. Dir. Argonaut Lines. Magistrate, Rumson, N.J., 1947-54. Trustee Oceanic Library, Rumson, 1952-56, Rumson Country Day Sch., 1953-63; bd. govs. Riverview Hosp., Red Bank, 1967-73. Served to lt. USNR, 1944-46. Mem. Am., N.J., Monmouth County (treas. 1967-70) bar assns., Phi Beta Kappa, Sigma Chi. Republican. Episcopalian (vestry 1960-66). Clubs: Rumson Country, Sea Bright Beach (Rumson); Bankers, Whitehall (N.Y.C.). Home: Rumson, N.J. Died Nov. 5, 1973.

TUNG PI-WU, Chinese polit ofcl.; b. 1886; student Tokyo Law Sch., Soviet Union. Joined Tungmeng-hui during Wuchang rising 1911; participant revolutionary activity; tchr. written coloquial Wuhan Middle Sch., 1920; founder Hupeh Chinese Communist Party, 1st Chinese Communist Party Congress, Shanghai, 1921; dir. agrl. and indsl. dept. Hupeh Provincial Govt.; del. San Francisco Conf.; Communist rep., Chungking and Nanking; Communist rep. Chinese People's Polit. Consultative Conf., 1949; mem. polit. bur. Chinese Communist Party, 1953; chmn. 2d Chinese People's Polit. Consultative Conf., 1954; Hupeh del. 1st Nat. People's Congress; sec. Central Control Commn. Chinese Communist Party, 1956; vice chmn. People's Republic of China, 1959-75. Address: Peking, China. Died Apr. 1975.

TUNSTALL, MRS., A(LFRED) M(OORE), dir. child welfare; b. Clarke Co., Ala., May 11, 1879; d. Travis Linyer and Martha (Goodman) Bedsole; ed. high sch., Thomasville, Ala., and the Atheneum, East Lake, Ala.; hon. LL.D., U. of Ala., 1930; .Dr. Charles Fletcher Bush, of Thomasville, Mar. 9, 1909 (dec.); m. 2d, Col. Alfred M. Tunstall, of Greensboro, Ala., Apr. 29, 1924. Dept. child labor insp., 1915-17; factory insp., Children's Bur., U.S. Dept. Labor, 1918-19; mem. Nat. Child Labor Com. of N.Y. City, 1918-19; dir. Ala. State Child Welfare Dept., 1919-24 and 1926-35. Home: Mobile, Ala.†

TUNSTILL, CLOVER DELL HILL (MRS. GARLAND ALBERT TUNSTILL), land devel. co. exec.; b. Houston, Sept. 10, 1909; d. John Elliot and Ella (Rodearmel) Hill; student Victoria Jr. Coll., 1928-29, U. Tex., 1932; B.A., Tex. Coll. Arts and Industries, 1936; m. Garland Albert Tunstill, Feb. 23, 1937. Tchr. pub. schs., Victoria, Tex., 1928-36; statis. clk. So. Pacific Ry., Houston, 1942-53; co-owner Tunstill Oil & Land Enterprises Tunstill Land Devel. Co., Houston, 1969-72; dir. Tunstill Oil & Land Enterprises, Ft. Worth. Christian Scientist. Home: Houston, Tex. Died July 19, 1972; buried Forest Park Lawndale Cemetery, Houston, Tex.

TURCK, RAYMOND CUSTER, surgeon; b. Alma, Mich., Oct. 12, 1874; s. William S. and Louise (Ely) T.; Alma Coll., 1890-91; grad. Mich. Mil. Acad., 1892; U. of Mich., med. dept., 1892-95; M.D., New York U., 1896; New York Post-Grad. Med. Sch., 1897; m. Bertha Bouton, Aug. 10, 1898; children—Mary Hanscomb, Eleanor Louise; m. 2d, Julia Maxwell Johnson, Jan. 17, 1934; 1 dau., Eleanor. Surgeon in charge Mich. Soldier's Home, 1897; practiced in Lansing, Mich., till 1898, in Chicago, 1998-1904; med. supt. and mgr. Alma Springs Sanitarium, 1904-05; removed to Fla., Jan. 1908. Instr., in surgery and demonstrator anatomy, Chicago Post-Grad. Med. Sch., 1898; prof. operative surgery, 1899-1908; surgeon in charge Chicago Hosp., 1900-02; adj. prof. surgery, U. of Ill., 1901-04; prof. gynecology,

Dearborn Md. Coll., 1904; attending surgeon Chicago, Post-Grad. and Samaritan hosps., and cons. surgeon Provident Hosp., Chicago, 1904; chief surgeon Provident Hosp., Chicago, 1904; chief surgeon St. Luke's Hosp., Jacksonville, Fla.; surgeon Fla. State Bd. of Health, 1910-16. Asst. surgeon, 1900, surgeon, 1901, Ill. Naval Reserves; lt. 4th div., same, 1901-04; lt. and ordnance officer, 1904-05; major Med. Corps. of Fla. comdg. 1st Fla. Field Hosp. on Tex. border, 1916; asst. div. surgeon 12th Div., Camp Wilson, Tex., 1917; adj. Med. Officers Training Camp, Ft. Oglethrope, Ga., 1917; div. sanitary insp., 31st Div., Camp Wheeler, Ga., 1917; lt. col., Med. Corps, div. surgeon, 35th Div. A.E.F., Apr. 10, 1918-Mar. 20, 1919; col., Feb. 26, 1919; base surgeon Base Sec. 2, A.E.F., Francce, 1919. Wounded in action, Argonne, Oct. 1, 1918; Croix de Guerre (France); citations for service in action from Marshal Petain, General Pershing and Maj. Gen. Traub; D.S.M., 1921; also awarded the Silver Star, Purple Heart, and University Palms, officer, grad., France, 1921. Col. comdg. 124th Inf., 1921-25. State health officer of Fla., 1921-25. Fellow Am. Coll. Surgeons; mem. Zeta Psi, Phi Rho Sigma. Democrat. Episco palian. Mason (K.T., Shriner). Clubs: Florida Yacht, Seminole. Author of various med. monographs, and contbns. to med. and mil. journals. Home: Jacksonville, Fla.†

TURIN, JOHN JOSEPH, educator; b. N.Y.C., Dec. 8, 1913; s. Samuel and Lena (Stein) T.; B.S., Wayne U., 1933; M.S., U. Mich., 1934, Ph.D., 1937; m. Gladys Marie Johnson, May 14, 1943; children—John Craig, Tally Johnson; m. 2d, Nancy G. Duryea, Oct. 18, 1956; children—Jennifer Davier, Beth Gould, David Gould; m. 3d, Sybil Briggs Walker, Dec. 21, 1963. Instr. U. Mich., 1935-37; research physicist Surface Combustion Corp., Toledo, 1937-44, cons., 1945; mem. faculty U. Toledo, 1945-73, prof. physics, engring. physics, 1946-73, chmn. dept. physics and astronomy, 1946, dir. nuclear sci. and engring., 1955-67, dir. Ritter Astrophysical Research Center, 1967, dean Grad. Sch., 1969; cons. Nat. Lead Co., 1948-50, Ill. Inst. Gas Tech., Chgo., 1962, Owens-Ill., Inc., Toledo, 1966. Served to lt. (j.g.) USNR, 1944-46. Mem. Am. Astron. Soc., Am. Phys. Soc., Am. Soc. Physics Tchrs., Am. Soc. Engring. Edn., A.A.A.S., Am. Soc. U. Profs., Council Grad. Deans, Sigma Xi, Phi Kappa Phi, Tau Beta Pi. Home: Toledo, Ohio. Died Dec. 18, 1973.

TURKINGTON, GRACE ALICE, (Miss.), educator; b. Woodstock, Conn., May 4, 1879; d. Rev. William Hyde and Anna M. (Esten) T.; ed. Tildon Sem., Boston Univ. (A. B., 1900, A.M., 1902). Mem. Nat. Geog. Soc., Coll. Club. Boston, Author of numerous mag. articles; co-editor of Blind's George 1904-16; Eliot, co-author The Exploration of the Mississippi Valley, in the Story of Exploration Series. Address: Cambridge, Mass.†

TURNBULL, HENRY RUTHERFORD, advt. co. exec.; b. Towson, Md., Aug. 19, 1905; s. Henry Rutherford and Elizabeth Risteau (Grason) T.; student Balt. City Coll., 1920-22; A.B., Johns Hopkins, 1926; m. Ruth L. White, Feb. 1931 (div. Apr. 1945); children—Henry Rutherford 3d, John Grason; m. 2d, Virginia Butler, July 12, 1945; 1 dau., Virginia Butler (Mrs. H.W. Scott, Jr.) With VanSant & Dugdale, Inc., Balt., 1927-34; copywriter Paris & Peart, N.Y.C., 1934-36; account exec. Blackett, Sample, Hummert, N.Y.C., 1936-40; v.p., account supr. Dancer, Fitzgerald Sample, N.Y.C., 1945-50; v.p., account supr. Biow Co., N.Y.C., 1950-56; v.p. for marketing Hamm Brewing Co., St. Paul, 1956-62; pres., chief exec. officer Turnbull & Allum, Inc., N.Y.C., 1962-69; sr. v.p., dir. gen. mgr. N.Y. office Clinton E. Frank, Inc. (merger with Turnbull & Allum, Inc.), 1970-75. Mgr. advt., broadcasting Thomas E. Dewey campaign for gov. N.Y., 1942, 46, 50; broadcast dir. presdl. campaign Republican. Nat. Com., 1944. Mem. alumni adv. com. for student recruiting Johns Hopkins, 1954-58. Mem. Am. Assn. Advt. Agys. (bd. govs. N.Y. council 1967-69). Episcopalian. Clubs: Johns Hopkins of New York; Boca Raton (Fla.) Country. Home: Boca Raton, Fla., Died Jan. 16, 1976.

TURNBULL, PHILLIPS ROOME, clothing co. exec., grad. Princeton, 1921; m. Aileen Timothy; children—Mrs. Eugene M. Geddes, Mrs. Richard T. Collier. Pres. Rogers Peet Co., N.Y.C., 1936-65; trustee Union Sq. Savs. Bank. Pres. Greenwich House, settlement house; v.p. Inst. Crippled and Disabled. Served with USN, World War I; dir. region War Prodn. Bd., World War II. Recipient Silver Beaver award Boy Scouts Am. Mem. U.S. Sr. Golf Assn. (past v.p.). Home: New York City, N.Y. also Juno Beach Fla. Died Mar. 1974.

TURNER, CLAIR ELSMERE, health educator; b. Harmony, Me., Apr. 28, 1890; s. Fred Orrison and Mary Frances (Chalmers) T.; B.A., Bates Coll., 1912, Sc.D., 1937; M.A., Harvard, 1913, M.P.H., 1947; C.P.H., Mass. Inst. Tech., 1917, Dr.P.H., 1928; Ed.M., Boston U., 1944; m. Naomi Elsie Cocke, Dec. 24, 1924; children—Mary Frances, Frederick Clair. Instr. biology Bates Coll., 1913-14; with Mass. Inst. of Tech., research asso., instr., asst. prof., prof. pub. health, head dept. Mass. Inst. Tech., 1914-44; cons. health edn. Boston Health Dept., 1941-46, Ill. Dept. Health, 1943-50, Kan. Bd. Health, 1944-50. Chief health edn. officer Div. Health and Sanitation, Office Coordinator of Inter-Am. Affairs 1944-45; vis. prof. health edn. Sch. Pub. Health U. Cal., 1945-46; asst. to pres. Nat. Found. for Infantile Paralysis, 1946-58; instr., asso. prof. hygiene Tufts Med. and Dental schs., 1917-29; mem. adminstrv. bd. Harvard Tech. Sch. Pub. Health, 1921-22; lectr. numerous univs., colls. and assns. Pub. health expert with overseas cons. to govt. Iran, 1949; cons. WHO, 1949, mem. expert panel Health Edn. Pub., 1951, chief health edn. WHO, 1962-64; chief adviser Internat. Union Health Edn., 1956-68, hon. pres. 1968. Trustee Bates Coll., 1922-73. Recipient gold medal Nat. Acad. Medicine, France, 1958; Grand Cross Order Merit, German Fed. Republic, 1959, Doyen Jacques Pariset medal Internat. Union for Health Edn., 1973; Lemuel Shattuck medal USPHS, 1969. Fellow A.A.H.P.E.R., Am. Pub. Health Assn., Am. Acad. Arts and Scis., Am. Acad. Phys. Edn., Am. Sch. Health Assn.; mem. nat., state, local profl. assns. Republican. Unitarian. Mason (32 deg.). Club: Harvard (Boston). Author several works in field, latest being: Personal and Community Health, 14th edit., 1971; also many papers, articles. Address: Arlington, Mass. Died Nov. 27, 1974; interred Mt. Auburn Cemetery, Cambridge, Mass.

TURNER, FRED HAROLD, educator; b. Hume, Ill., Mar. 22, 1900; s. John Frank and Louella (Connelly) T.; B.A., U. Ill., 1922, M.A., 1926, Ph.D., 1931; m. Elizabeth Weaver, June 1, 1924; children—Joanne, Sally. Asst. dean men. U. Ill., 1922-31, acting dean, 1931-32, dean, 1932-43, dean students, 1943-66, univ. dean students, chmn. U. Ill. Centennial Year, 1966-68, univ. dean students emeritus, 1968-75. Mem. S.A.T.C., U. Ill., 1918; capt. gov.'s staff, Ill. N.G., 1931-75; hon. mem. St. Louis Naval Aviation Cadet Selection Bd. 1942-75; civilian mem. com. which drafted Army Air Force Res. Plan, 1942. Trustee Levere Meml. Found. Recipient Gold Medal, Nat. Interfrat. Conf., 1955; Distinguished Service award, Coll. Frat. Secs. Assn., 1967; U. Ill. Alumni Achievement award, 1971. Mem. Nat. Interfrat. Conf. (pres. 1966-67), Nat. Assn. Deans and Advisers of Men, 1924-51; mem. Nat. Assn. Student Personnel Adminstrs. (sec., Treas. 1938-58, pres., 1958-59, exec. com. 1959-60, editor 1951), Am. Coll. Personnel Assn., Am. Council Edn., N.E.A., Save the Children Fedn. (nat. adv. com. 1954-75), Phi Delta Kappa, Phi Eta Sigma (historian, mem. exec. com.), Sigma Alpha Epsilon (scholarship commr. 1930-37, mem. supreme council 1937-45). Eminent Supreme Archon, 1943-45. Republican. Presbyn. Rotarian. Club: University (Urbana). Contbr. articles to current periodicals, ednl. jours. Editor Interfrat. Research and Adv. Council Bull., 1953-66. Home: Shelby, Mich. Died Sept. 6, 1975.

TURNER, NANCY BYRD, poet, eidtor; b. Boydton, Va., July 29, 1880; d. Rev. Byrd Thornton and Nancy Addison (Harrison) T.; grad. Hannah Moore Acad., Reisterstown, Md., 1898. Joined staff Youth's Companion, Boston, Mass., 1916; editor children's page, same, 1918-22; editorial staff The Independent, Boston, 1926; later mem. editorial staff Hougton Mifflin Co. Mem. N.E., Poetry Soc., Boston Authors' Club. Epsicopalian. Author: Zodiac Town, 1921; The Adventures of Ray Coon, 1923; Magpie Lane, 1927. Contbr. to mags. in America and Eng. Address: Boston, Mass.†

TURNIPSEED, B(ARNWELL) RHETT, Clergyman, educator; b. Columbia, S.C., Mar. 10, 1878; s. Barnwell Rhett and Matilda (Turner) T.; U.S., Clemson Coll. S.C., 1896; student Charleston Med. Coll., 1897-98; m. Emma Major Greene, of Greenwood, S.C., Mar. 8, 1900; children—Barnwell Rhett, Robert Edward. Ordained ministry M.E. Ch. S., 1900; pastor Granby Ch., Columbia, S.C., 1900-02, St. John's Ch., Aiken, 1903-06, Green St. Ch., Columbia, 1907-10, Trinity Ch., Darlingron, 1910-14, 1st Ch., Marion, 1914-16, Main St. Ch., Columbia, 1916-18, Main St. Ch., Greenwood, 1918-22, Central Ch., Spartanburg, 1922-23; pres. Lander Coll., 1923-27. Sec. Upper S.C. Conf., M.E. Ch., S.; mem. Gen. Conf., 1922, 26. Mason (K.T.), Odd Fellow, K.P. Club: Rotary (pres. 1925). Home: Grewnwich, S.C.†

TYLER, CARL HAMILTON, dentist; b. Springdale, Ky., Jan. 25, 1896; s. Charles Duncan and Addie T. (Ritter) T.; D.D.S., U. Louisville, 1920; m. Dewey Lee Arnsparger, Jan. 2, 1922. Dentist, Mental Retarded State Inst., 1920-28. Eastern State Mental Hosp., 1924-28; practice dentistry, Lexington, Ky., 1928. Mem. Acad. Internat. Dentistry, Internat. Coll. Dentistry, Pierre Fauchard Acad., Blue Grass Dental Soc. (Distinguished award for Outstanding Contbr. to Profession 1969, pres. 1943-44). Mem. Internat. Coll. Dentists. Democrat. Mem. Christian Ch. Mason. Club: Lexington Country. Pyramid, Optimist (life). Home: Lexington, Ky. Died June 22, 1973.

TYLER, EARL COTTLER, banker; b. Boston, Nov. 12, 1910; s. Almond Wesley and Ellen (Cottler) T.; A.B., Harvard, 1932, A.M., 1933; LL.B., Northeastern U., 1943; m. Priscilla Walmsley, July 3, 1936; children—Barbara Ellen (Mrs. J. Richard Soby), Robert Earl. Admitted to Mass. bar, 1943; with Nat. Shawmut Bank Boston, 1934, v.p., mgr. nat. div., 1960-73. Mem. Town Meeting. Fellow Nat. Inst. Credit; mem. Boston Bar Assn., Soc. Colonial Wars, S.A.R. Episcopalian. Mason (32D, Shriner). Clubs: Harvard, Downtown (Boston). Home: Needham, Mass. Died Oct 21, 1973.

TYSON, ROBERT CARROLL, ret. steel exec.; b. Thurmont, Md., Aug. 13, 1905; s. Robert Alexander and Effie May (Fleming) T.; grad. Mercersburg Acad., 1923; B.A., Princeton, 1927; C.P.A., N.Y., 1932; LL.D., Samford U.; m. Lucy Perry Bannar, Nov. 19, 1932; 1 dau., Virginia Carole (Mrs. Ralph E. Lawrence). Accountant, Remington Rand, Inc., N.Y.C., 1928; jr.-sr. supervising accountant Price, Waterhouse & Co., 1929-39; asst. audit supr. U.S. Steel Corp., 1939-41, gen. accountant, 1941-47, asst. comptroller, 1947-50, comptroller, 1950-55, v.p. 1951-52, vice chmn. finance com., dir., 1952-56, chmn. finance com., dir., 1956-70; dir. Chem. Bank, Chem. N.Y. Corp., Uniroyal Inc., Equitable Life Mortage and Realty Investors. Bd. dirs. Boys Clubs Am.; chmn. bd. dirs., bd. overseers Sweet Briar Coll.; chmn. bd. trustees Lahey Clinic Found.; trustee Va. Found. Ind. Colls. mem. bd. regents, finance com. Mercersburg Acad.; trustee Tax Found., Va. Found. for Ind. Colls.; adv. bd. Hoover Instn., Stanford, Cal. Recipient George Washington Honor medal Freedoms Found. Mem. Downtown-Lower Manhattan Assn. (dir.), Commerce and Industry Assn. N.Y. (dir., vice-chmn. exec. com.), Mason. Clubs: Princeton; Links (N.Y.C.); Nat. Golf Links, Links Golf (L.I.); Pine Valley Golf (N.J.); Connetquot River (N.Y.). Home: New York City, N.Y. Died Jan. 2 1974.

ULATE, OTILIO, pres. of Costa Rica; b. Alajuela, Costa Rica, Aug. 25, 1896; s. Ildefonso and Ermida (Blanco) U.; ed. Inst. de Alajuela, Liceo de Costa Rica. Dir. La Prensa Libre, La Tribuna, Diario de Costa Rica, since 1921. Dep., Asamblea Constituyente, 1917; sec. spl. mission to other Central Am. countries, 1920-21; sec. and chargé d'affaires, legation, Spain, 1928-29; dep. Congreso Constitucional, 1930-38; pres. Costa Rica since 1949. Address: San Jose, Costa Rica. Died Oct. 27, 1973.

ULINSKI, BRONISLAUS IGNATIUS, engr.; b. Buffalo, Apr. 26, 1902; s. Ignatius and Marcella (Butkiewicz) U.; student pub. schs.; m. Lorraine J. Carlson, June 17, 1939; children—Mary Ann (Mrs. Calvin Norris Hansen), Richard, Priscilla (Mrs. Fred Rinehart Klunk). Machine designer Automatic Transp. Co., 1922-31; chief engr. McKeown Co., Buffalo, 1932-33; chief engr. Automatic Transp. Co., Chgo., 1933-51, dir. engring. 1951-56, dir. devel. and design, 1956-65; project mgr. Advanced Engring. Center, Yale & Towne, Inc., Phila., 1965-67. Registered profl. engr., Ill. Mem. Soc. Automotive Engrs. Patentee. Home: Palm Beach, Fla. Died Apr. 4, 1973.

UMSTATTD, WILLIAM EARLE, roller bearing co. exec.; b. Bristol, Tenn., Aug. 17, 1894; s. John William and Alice Rogers (Mitchell) U.; student pub. schs.; m. Doris Bowman. Chmn. exec. com. Timken Co. Home: Canton, Ohio. Died Dec. 2, 1973.

UNDEN, BO OSTEN, lawyer; b. Karistad, Sweden, Aug. 25, 1886; s. Victor and Beate (Kaijser) U.; LL.D., Univ. of Lund, Sweden, 1912; LL.D. (hon.), University of Oslo, 1938, U. Sophia, 1939, University of Copenhagen, 1945; University of Toulouse, 1952; Ph.D. (honorary), Univ. of Uppsala, 1945; married Agnes Jacobsson, June 23, 1912 (died 1935); children—Karin Agnes (Mrs. Arne Brunnberg), Inger Gunnel (Mrs. Bengt Skanse). Prof. of law Uppsala Univ., 1917-37, rector of univ., 1929-32; chancellor univs. of Sweden, 1937-51; minister without portfolio, 1917-20, and 1932-36, minister of justice, 1920, minister of fgn. affairs, 1924-26, 45-62. Chief Swedish delegation to UN, 1946-61. Home: Stockholm, Sweden. Died Jan. 1974.

UNDERWOOD, E. VICTOR, corp. exec.; b. Buffalo, Sept. 12, 1889; s. George Farwell and Hattie (BeauJean) U.; B.S., Cornell U., 1913; m. Violet Ruth Stewart, June 16, 1916 (dec.); 1 son, Victor Stewart; m. 2d, Ella S. Salisbury, Apr. 10, 1954 (dec.). Agrl. tchr. Moravia (N.Y.) High Sch., 1913-14; county agrl. agt., Oswego County, N.Y., 1914-18, Erie County, N.Y., 1918-20; sec. N.Y. State Farm Bur. Fedn., 1920-29, sec.-treas., 1929-35; pres. Coop. G.L.F. Holding Corp., Ithaca, N.Y., 1935-54; hon. chmn., dir. Allegheny Airlines, Inc.; sec.-treas. Coop. G.L.F. Exchange, Inc., until 1954; past dir. Tompkins Co. Trust Co., Ithaca; former vice chmn. Ithaca Savs. & Loan Assn.; pres. Am. Agriculturist. Mem. Newcomen Soc. N. Am. Republican. Methodist. Mason. Clubs: Rotary (past pres.), Cornell (Ithaca). Home: Ithaca, N.Y. Deceased.

UNDERWOOD, JULIUS GAY, mfg. co. exec.; b. Los Angeles, Apr. 10, 1915; s. Roy A. and Lillian (Foster) U.; evening student U. Cin.; m. Helen Selvaggio, Apr. 1, 1965; children by previous marriage—Herbert J., Julia Anne (Mrs. Stanley Coniff), Charles T.; 1 stepson, Frank Caliguri, Jr. With H. & S. Pogue Co., Cin., 1933-35; sec., treas., dir. M. Werk Soap Co., Cin., 1935-51; with Harsco Corp., Harrisburg, Pa., 1951-75, exec. v.p., 1965-68, pres., 1968-75, also chief exec. officer, dir.; dir. Dauphin Deposit Trust, Harrisburg. Trustee Harsco Corp. Fund, Community Gen. Osteo. Hosp. Mem. Nat. Assn. Accountants (past nat. pres.), Pa. C. of C. (dir.), Harrisburg Execs. Club. Home: Mechanicsburg, Pa., Died May 5, 1975; interred St. Joseph's Mausoleum, Cincinnati, O.

UNDERWOOD, PAUL HALLADAY, coll. prof.; b. Ludlowville, N.Y., Dec. 29, 1881; s. Harlan Page and Inez Aritta (Halladay) U.; C.E., Cornell U., 1907;

student Grad. Sch,e[!!Sch., Cornell U., 1910-11; m. Eva Frances Humphreys, Oct. 25, 1919; 1 son, Robert Humphreys. Rodman, Dept. of State Engr. and Surveyor, N.Y., 1907; instr. incivil engring., Coll. of Engring., Cornell U., 1907-11, 1911-12; asst. engr. Isthmian Canal Commn., Culebra, Panama, Feb.-Sept. 1911; asst. prof. of topographic and geodetic engring., Cornell U., 1912-22, prof., 1922-49, charge dept. of surveying, 1920-49, acting dir. Sch. of Civil Engring., 1937-38; professor of civil engineering emeritus from 1949. Member advisory committee on maps and surveys, Div. State Planning, N.Y., from 1937. Fellow A.A.A.S.; Am. Soc. C.E. (pres. Ithaca Sect. 1938-39), Soc. Photogrammetry, Am. Soc. for Engring. Education, Cornell Soc. Engrs., Am. Geophys. Union (vice chmn. sect. of geodesy 1935-38), Chi Epsilon. Republican. Presbyterian (elder). Contbr. to professional jours. Home: Ithaca, N.Y.†

UPCHURCH, VERNON HILL, educator; b. Tamaha, Okla., Mar. 3, 1918; s. James Arch and Valora Elaine (Cole) U.; B.S., Okla. U., 1942, M.B.A., 1947; Ph.D., Tex. U., 1954; m. Gloria Hornbeak, Nov. 27, 1941; children—Paul Douglas, Melinda Marie. Partner with father in mercantile bus., 1936-40; faculty East Central State Coll., Ada. Okla., 1947-55; faculty U. Okla., 1955-75, prof. accounting, chmn. dept., 1959-75. Served with AUS, 1942-46. C.P.A., Okla. Mem. Am. Inst. C.P.A.'s, Am. Accounting Assn., Okla. Soc. C.P.A.'s, Delta Sigma Pi, Beta Alpha Psi, Beta Gamma Sigma. Home: Norman, Okla. Died Mar. 5, 1975.

UPJOHN, HUBERT S, supt. of schools; b. Kalamazoo, Mich., Jan. 4, 1881; s. Henry U. and Pamelia (Kirby) U.; Ph.B., Kalamazoo Coll., 1903, U. of Chicago, 1903; m. Della DeLano of Bellevue, Ida., Dec. 30, 1906 (died 1909); children—Richard Delano, Janet Pamelia; m. 2d, Estelle Leach, of Pasadena, Calif., June 28, 1913. Teacher high schs., Mich. and Ida., 1903-08, Riverside (Calif.) High Sch., 1908-12; prin.S! prin. S. Pasadena High Sch., 1912-16; asst. supt. Los Angeles Co. Schs., 1916-27, supt., 1927-31; supt. Long Beach Schs., 1932-35. Club: Oneonta. Home: S. Pasadena, Calif.†

UPSON, WILLIAM HAZLETT, writer; b. Glen Ridge, N.J., Sept. 26, 1891; s. William Ford and Grace (Hazlett) U.; B.S., Cornell U., 1914; hon. Litt.D., Middlebury College, 1950; m. Marjory Alexander Wright, Aug. 18, 1923; children—John Wright, Polly Wright (Mrs. Polly Upson Kahler). Farmer, Leesburg, Va., 1914-17; with service dept. Caterpillar Tractor Co., Peoria, Ill., 1919-24; contbr. short stories to Saturday Evening Post, 1924-75; also Colliers, Esquire, Reader's Digest, others. Chmn. bd. trustees Thorpe Camp for Crippled Children, Goshen, Vt. Del. Republican Nat. Conv., San Francisco 1956. Served as pvt. 13th F.A., 4th Div., U.S. Army, 1917-19; participated in Marne-Aisne, St. Mihiel and Meuse-Argonne offensives; Army Occupation. Clubs: Rotary (Middlebury); University (Winter Park, Fla.). Author: The Piano Movers, 1927; Me and Henry and the Artillery, 1928; Alexander Botts Earthworm Tractors, 1929; Earthworms in Europe, 1931; Keep 'Em Crawling; Earthworms at War, 1943; Botts in War, Botts in Peace, 1944; How to Be Rich Like Me, 1947; Earthworms Through the Ages, 1947; Hello, Mr. Henderson, 1949; No Rest for Botts, 1951; Earthworm Tractors (motion picture starring Joe E. Brown) 1936; Middlebury Parade (musical comedy), 1949; The Best of Botts, 1961; Original Letters of Alexander Botts, 1963. Home: Middlebury, Vt. Died Feb. 1975.

URBAN, PERCY LINWOOD, clergyman, dean; b. Phila., June 3, 1886; s. Rev. Abram Linwood and Emma Louise (Trexler) U.; student William Penn Charter Sch., Phila.; A.B., Princeton, 1906, A.M., 1907, fellow, 1907-10; S.T.D. (hon.), Berkeley Div. Sch., 1935; D.D. (hon.), Kenyon Coll., 1954; m. Mary Robinson Hodge, June 10, 1922; children—Percy Linwood, Margaret Hodge, Hugh Bayard. Formerly prof. philosophy St. John's U., Shanghai, China, master St. Paul's Sch., Concord, N.H.; ordained to ministry, P.E. Ch., 1914, asst. minister St. Peter's Ch., Germantown, Phila.; rector St. John's Ch., North Haven, Conn., 1924-41; lectr. theology Berkeley Div. Sch., Yale, 1923-35, asso. prof., 1935-41, prof. systematic theology, 1941, dean since 1947; vis. prof. theology Phila. Div. Sch., 1944-46; hon. canon Christ Ch. Cathedral, Hartford, Conn., 1950-74; mem. theol. commn. Gen. Conv. P.E. Ch. Mem. Am. Theol. Soc., Am. Philos. Assn., Phi Beta Kappa. Republican. Club: Graduates (New Haven). Home: New Haven Conn. Died Aug. 16, 1974.

URE, MARY, actress; b. Glasgow, Scotland, Feb. 18, 1933; d. Colin McGregor and Edith H.E. (Willis Swinburne) Ure; ed. Mount Sch., York Eng., Central Sch. Speech Tng. and Dramatic Art; m. John James Osborne, 1957; m. 2d, Robert Shaw, 1963; m. 4 children. Stage appearances include Simon and Laura, 1954; Time Remembered, 1954; Hamlet, 1955; View from the Bridge, 1956; Look Back in Anger, 1958; Othello, 1959; A Midsummer Night's Dream, 1959; Duel of Angels, 1960; Trials, 1960; The Changeling, 1961; motion pictures include Wisdom's Way, Look Back in Anger, Sons and Lovers, The Mindbenders, The Luck of Ginger Coffey, Where Eagles Dove, Custer of The West, Where Eagles Dare, 1968; TV appearances in U.S. and Eng. Home: London, England. Died Apr. 3, 1975.

URRIOLAGOITIA, H. MAMERTO, president Bolivia; b. Sucre, Bolivia, Dec. 5, 1895; s. Mamerto Urriolagiotia T. and Corina Harriague M.; ed. Escuela, Benjamin Guzman, Sucre; student Penssionat de Passy (Christian Brothers, Paris, France, Jesuit Coll., Sucre; Univ. Law Sch., San Francisco Xavier, Sucre; m. Juana Hernandez, Jan. 10, 1940. Civil adjunct to Legation in England, 1918, second sec., 1918, first sec., 1922, counselor of legation, 1933; ad interim charge d'affaires, 1921-22, 1924, 1926-27, 1929, 1930-33. 1934-39; pres., del. of Bolivia to Eighth Cong. Universal Postal Union at Stockholm, 1924; del. of Bolivia to Ninth World Cong. of Prisons, London, 1925; del. to the World Cong. of Autoridades Locales, 1932. Cong. of Comml. Edn., London, 1932, World Econ. and Monetary Cong., London, 1933; del. to Univ. of Oxford Cong., 1935; nat. senator from Chuquisaca, 1940-44; convencional senator, 1944, 1945; chancellor of Republic, 1947, vice pres., since 1947, interim president, 1947 and 48; president of Republic of Bolivia since 1949. Decorated Grand Cross Order of the Condor of the Andes (Bolivia), Grand Cross Royal Order of Isabel the Catholic, Don Alfonso XIII; Knight Comdr. First Class Royal Order of the Polar Star, conferred by His Majesty the King of Sweden; Knight Comdr. Royal Order of St. Olav, conferred by His Majesty the King of Norway; citation and star of the Royal Spanish-American Acad. of Cadiz; Medal of First Class of the Spanish Red Cross; Commemorative medal of Cinquecentenial of the Universal Postal Union; Commemorative Medal of Jubilee of His Britannic Majesty George V. Mem. Nat. Geographic Soc. of Washington (corr. mem.), Internat. Diplomatic Acad. of Paris, Geographic Soc. of Sucre. Author: Official Handbook of Bolivia, 1924; Bolivia 1825-1925, 1925. Home: Sucre, Bolivia. Died June 4, 1974.

USHER, ROLAND GREENE, prof. history; b. Lynn, Mass., May 3, 1880; s. Edward Preston and Adela Louise (Payson) U.; A.B., summa cum laude, Harvard, 1901, A.M., summos honores in historia, 1902; studied Oxford, Paris and Cambridge, Eng., 1902-04; Ph.D., Harvard, 1905; m. Florence Wyman Richardson, June 9, 1910; children—Florence, Roland G., Dorothea, Richardson. Asst. in history, Harvard, 1904-07; instr. in history, 1907-10, asst. prof., 1910-12, asso. prof. in charge of Dept. of History, 1912-14, and professor history, 1914-50, Washington U., St. Louis. Mem. Nat. Inst. Social Sciences, Am. Hist. Assn., Mo. Soc. Teachers History and Govt., Mo. Hist. Soc.; fellow Royal Hist. Soc. of England, 1926; coor!!corr. mem. Mass. Hist. Assn. Republican. Episcopalian. Author books relating to field, News analyst for radio sta. KSD, N.B.C., 1941-49. Home: St. Louis, Mo.†

UTLEY, FRANCIS LEE, educator; b. Watertown, Wis., May 25, 1907; s. Philip Lee and Hannah (Arbeiter) U.; student St. John's Mil. Acad., Delafield, Wis., 1920-21; A.B. with honors, U. Wis., 1929; A.M., Harvard, 1934, Ph.D., 1936; m. Ruth Alice Scott, June 27, 1936; children—Philip Lee, Andrew Scott, Jean Marie. Asst. in English, U. Wis., 1929, Harvard, 1933-34; with Ohio State U., 1935, successively instr. in English, asst. and asso. prof., prof., 1947-74, prof. English and folklore, 1973-74, dir. Ohio State Center Medieval and Renaissance Studies, 1965-69; vis. prof. Columbia, 1950, U. Cal. at Los Angeles, 1963, Harvard, 1965, Berkeley, 1967, Pa. State U., 1973, U. Va., 1973; Fulbright lectr. U. Padua, also Instituto Universitario di Economia e Commercio (Venice), 1954-55. Mem. Fulbright Commn. for U.K., 1955-58. Dir. Ohio State U. Medieval Conf., 1958, Ohio State Archives of Primitive, Ethnic and Folk Music, 1962-74. Recipient Festschrift vol. entitled Medieval Literature and Folklore Studies, Essays in Honor of Francis Lee Utley, 1970. Dexter fellow Harvard, 1934, Guggenheim fellow, 1946, 48, 52. Mem. Am. (pres. 1951-52, del. internat. congress 1959, mem. exec. bd. 1959-62), Ohio (pres. 1950, 62-63) folklore socs., Am. Council Learned Socs. (fellowship panel 1961-62), Mediaeval Acad. Am. (council 1951-54), Modern Lang. Assn. (exec. council 1969-74), Am. Anthrop. Assn., Linguistic Soc. Am., Ohio Acad. Sci., Coll. Eng. Assn. U.S.A. (pres. 1969), Am. Name Soc. (pres. 1964), Folklore Soc. Gt. Britain (hon. mem. council), Internat. Folk Narrative Soc. (chmn. credentials commn.), Am. Dialect Soc. (exec. bd.), Phi Beta Kappa, Kappa Sigma. Episcopalian. Author: The Crooked Rib, 1944; Ninth Supplement to Wells' Manual of the Writings in Middle English, 1951; also articles. Editor: The Forward Movement of the Fourteenth Century, 1961; Old Slack's Reminiscence, 1973, Pocket History of the Colored Profession, 1973. Co-editor: Studies in Biblical and Jewish Folklore, 1960; Bear, Man, and God, 1964, 71; Place names of Georgia: Essays in honor of John H. Goff, 1975. Former mem. editorial bd. Names. Cons. in lit. Random House Dictionary, 1963-64; cons. folklore and mythology Ency. Americana, 1960-70, Dictionary of the History of Ideas, 1973. Home: Columbus, Ohio. Died Mar. 8, 1974.

UTUDJIAN, EDOUARD, architect; b. France, Nov. 12, 1905; s. Baptist and Elisa U.; diploma Higher Financial and Comml. Studies, Coll. Mekhitarist Fathers, Constantinople (now Istanbul), Turkey; postgrad. civil engring. Am. Robert Coll. Constantinople (now Istanbul), 1921, archtl. engring., architecture Ecole Nationale Superieure des Beaux Arts (Paris), 1931; diploma Town Planning, Paris U., 1945; m. Suzanne Marle Renee Esnaulit (dec. 1961); 1 dau., Elaine Saint Andre. Founding editor Underground World rev., Paris, France, 1936; profl. lectr. Ecole Nationale Superieure des Beaux Arts, 1948-68, Ecole Speciale d'Architecture, 1948-68, Conservatoire Nationale des Arts et Metiers, 1949-65, others; practice architecture, Paris. Vice pres. nat. council French Soc. Civil Def. Served with 24th Inf., other units, French Army. Recipient Grand Prix for underground layout of Paris capitol Paris Exhbn., 1937; decorated knight Legion Honor, officer, 1970; officer Nat. Order Merit, comdr., 1970. Fellow A.I.A. (hon.); mem. Group for Study and Coordination of Underground Planning (founder, gen. sec.), Internat. Standing Com. for Underground Techniques and Town Planning (sec. gen.). Contbr. articles to profl. jours. Works include equipment, sanitation for Baghdad, Basrah (Iraq); restoration of 4th C. Armenian Etchmiadzine Cathedral; Basilica of Holy Sepulchre, Jerusalem, Armenian Cathedral, N.Y.C., St. John's Cathedral, Southfield, Mich.. Home: Paris, France., Died July 28, 1975.

VAGTBORG, HAROLD, research adminstr.; b. Copenhagen, Denmark, Sept. 17, 1904; s. Christian Peter Vagtborg; B.S., U. Ill., 1926; M.S., Armour Inst. Tech., 1934; D.Sc., Park Coll., 1947; LL.D., Mo. Valley Coll., 1950; m. Maurine Jones, June 3, 1926; children—Harold, Phyllis Maurine. Dir. Armour Research Found., Chgo., 1937-45, Inst. Gas. Tech., Chgo., 1942-44; pres., dir. Midwest Research Inst., Kansas City, Mo., 1945-48; pres. S.W. Research Inst.; dir. S.W. Found. Research and Edn., Inst. Inventive Research San Antonio, 1948-59; pres. S.W. Research Center, 1950-76, S.W. Agrl. Inst., 1957-59; pres. S.W. Research Center comprising S.W. Research Inst., S.W. Agrl. Inst. S.W. Found. Research and Edn., San Antonio, 1959-76; mem. tech. adv. bd. Commerce Dept., 1956-69; dir. San Antonio br. Fed. Res. Bank. Mem. bd. San Antonio Med. Found., South Tex. Methodist Hosp.; vice chmn. bd. trustees Lady of Lake Coll.; trustee St. Mary's U., Am. Inst. Character Edn.; nat. councilor U. Okla. Research Inst. Fellow A.A.A.S., Am. Soc. M.E.; mem. Chem. Soc. London, Am. Soc. C.E., Sci. Research Soc. Am. (gov.), Soc. Chem. Industry of London, Am. Chem. Soc., Am. Phys. Soc. Methodist. Clubs: Oak Hills Country, San Antonio. Home: San Antonio, Tex., Died Jan. 18, 1976.

VAIL, ALBERT ROSS, clergyman; b. Wisner, Neb., June 27, 1880; s. Irving Hamilton and Carrie Eliza (Ames) V.; Ph.B., U. of Chicago, 1903; S.T.B., Harvard Div. Sch., 1906; m. Emily McClellan, June 23, 1909. Ordained Unitarian ministry, 1906; organizer, 1907, and pastor Unitarian Ch., Urbana, Ill., until 1918; later lecturer and writer on history of religions. Mem. Phi Beta Kappa. Delta Sigma Rho, Pi Gamma Mu. Joint Author: (with wife) HeroicLives in Uniersal Religion (in Beacon Course in Religious Education). Editor, contributor to periodicals and encylopedias. Home: St. Joseph, Mich.†

VAIL, DAVID JAMESON, physician; b. Cin., Jan. 16, 1926; s. Derrick Tilton and Elizabeth (Yeiser) V.; M.D., Harvard, 1948; m. Joane Pauline Rand, Nov. 24, 1956; children—Belinda, Martha (Mrs. Thomas Sputal), David Rand, Garrett Murphy, Sara Jameson, Michael Walsh. Intern, St. Luke's Hosp., Chgo., 1948-49; resident in psychiatry John Hospkins Hosp., Balt., 1949-52; psychoanalytic tng. Balt. Psychoanalytic Inst., 1950-55; staff psychiatrist Rosewood Tng. Sch., Owings Mills, Md., 1952-56, dir. psychiat. edn., 1952-55, clin. dir., 1955-56; dir. outpatient services N.H. State Hosp., 1956, asst. supt., 1956-59; asst. med. dir. Minn. Dept. Pub. Welfare, 1959-60, med. dir., 1960-71; instr. in psychiatry Johns Hopkins, 1953-56; clin. prof. psychiatry U. Minn. Past bd. dirs. Nat. Assn. State Mental Health Program Dirs. Recipient Posthumous award Minn. Civil Liberties Union. Diplomate Am. Bd. Psychiatry and Neurology. Mem. Minn. Assn. Hosp. Adminstrs. (hon.). Author: The British Mental Hospital System, 1965; Dehumanization and the Institutional Career, 1966; Mental Health System in Scandinavia, 1968. Home: White Bear Lake, Minn. Died Oct. 21, 1971; buried Cincinnati, O.

VAKIL, NUSSERVANJI KAVASJI, univ. adminstr.; b. Bhavnagar, India, May 17, 1908; s. Kavasji Burjorji and Meherbal (Kaikhushru) V.; B.A., Elphinstone Coll., Bombay, India, 1929; LL.B., Govt. Law Coll., 1931; m. Perin Kaikhushru Davur, Dec. 18, 1937 (dec.); children—Burjor, Homi, Veera. Began practice law, Surant, India, 1931; spl. officer to organize city civil, small causes and city magistrates cts., State of Gujarat, Ahmedabad, India, 1961; 1st prin. judge City Civil Ct., 1961; judge High Ct. of Gujarat, 1962-70; vice chancellor Maharaja Sayajiraeo U. of of Baroda, India, 1970-74. Mem. exec. bd. Indian Law Inst.; mem. standing com. Inter-Univ. Bd. India; pres. bd. trustees Surat Parsi Panchayat, 1950-61; pres. Indian U. Assn. for Continuing Edn. Mem. Sarvajanik Edn. Soc. (mem. mng. and exec. bodies, pres.). Rotarian (hon. mem. Surat and Baroda). Home: Gujarat, India. Died May 4, 1974.

VAKIL, RUSTOM JAL, cardiologist; b. Bombay, India, July 17, 1911; s. Jal r. and Jebanoo (Sethna) V.; student Elphinstone Coll., Bombay, 1927, Royal Inst. Sci., Bombay, 1928; M.B.B.S., St. Thomas Hosp., London; M.D., U. London, 1937, diploma Tropical Medicine and Hygiene, 1938. Student, house physician St. Thomas Hosp., London, 1928-34; Tata Med. Research scholar, Bombay, 1939-40; hon. cons. physician, also charge cardiological dept. King Edward Meml. Hosp., Bombay, 1941-58; lectr. medicine G.S. Med. Coll., Bombay, 1941-58, Grant Med. Coll.; hon. physician Gov. Bombay, 1950-74; cons. physician, cardiologist, 1938-74. Del., 1st World Conf. Cardiology, Paris, 1950, 2d European Congress of Cardiology, Sweden, 1956; internat. adv. panel WHO, 1955-74. Recipient Solly medal and prize, 1935; Mead medal, 1936; Seymour Graves Toller medal, 1936; Wainwright medal, 1936; Lalcaca Univ. Gold medal, 1938, London U.; Albert Lasker award Am. Pub. Health Assn., 1957; 1st Dr. B.C. Roy Nat. award Indian Med. Council, 1969; numerous others; awarded padma bhusan Pres. Republic India, 1958. Licentiate Royal Coll. Physicians. Fellow Acad. Scis. (India), Coll. Physicians and Surgeons (Bombay), Royal Geog. Soc. (London), Royal Faculty Physicians and Surgeons (Glasgow), Royal Coll. Physicians (London), Am. Coll. Cardiology, Am. Coll. Chest Physicians, A.C.P., Royal Soc. Promotion Health, Am. Pub. Health Assn., Royal Soc. Medicine, Nat. Inst. Sci. (India), Royal Soc. Tropical Medicine, Royal Soc. Arts; mem. Royal Coll. Surgeons (Eng.). Cardiological Soc. India (pres. 1955-56), Am. Heart Assn., A.A.A.S. Author: The Romance of Healing and Other Essays, 1961; The Heart in Health and Disease, 1964; Our Glorious Heritage, 1966; Textbook of Medicine, 1969; Medical Emergencies, 1972. Contbr. to Indian, internat. med. jours. Mem. editorial bd. med. jours. Home: Bombay, India. Died Nov. 20, 1974.

VALYI, PETER, Hungarian govt. ofcl.; b. Szombathely, Dec. 25, 1919; s. Mano and Rosa (Pollak) V.; Chem. Engr., Tech. U. Budapest, 1942; m. Vilma Schäfer, Sept. 15, 1945; 1 son, Istvan. Engr. leather factory, Simontornya, 1943-47; dir. leather factory, Budapest, 1947; referent Nat. Planning Office, Budapest, 1947-49, 54-67; dir. Chinoin Pharm. Works, Budapest, 1953; chief dept. organic chemistry Ministry of Heavy Industries, 1954; minister Ministry Finance, 1967-71, dep. premier, 1971-73. Home: Budapest, Hungary, Died Sept. 18, 1973.

VAN ACKER, ACHILLE H., Belgian prime minister; b. 1898. Became mem. Chamber of Deputies, 1927; minister of econ. affairs, also for coal prodn., 1946; minister of communications, 1947-49; prime minister, 1945-46 and 1957-75. Address: Westmeersch Bruges, Belgium.*

VAN BEUREN, ARCHBOLD, publishing co. exec.; b. N.Y.C., Dec. 21, 1905; s. Michael Murray and Mary (Archbold) van B.; grad. St. George's Sch., Newport, R.I., 1923; A.B. cum laude, Williams Coll., 1927; postgrad. Columbia Law Sch., 1928-29; m. Margaret P. Ziegler, June 12, 1929; children—Michael C., J. Archbold, Mary, Marilla. Asso. Scudder, Stevens & Clark, investment counsel, Boston, N.Y.C., 1930-36; treas., chmn. bd. dirs. Cue Pub. Co., 1938-43, pres., dir., 1944-54, chmn. bd. dirs., 1959-70; chmn. bd. dirs. Continental Communications Corp., 1963-75, Conresco Corp., 1966-75; pub. Cue mag., 1955-58. Served with OSS, Washington, 1942-45. Mem. English Speaking Union U.S. (pres. 1966), Phi Beta Kappa, Delta Sigma Rho, Psi Upsilon. Republican. Episcopalian. Mason. Home: Newport, R.I., also New York City, N.Y. Died Dec. 8, 1974.

VAN BIESBROECK, GEORGE (ACHILLE), astronomer; b. Ghent, Belgium, Jan. 21, 1880; s. Louis and Pharaïlde (Colpaert) Van B.; ed. Athenaeum, Ghent; spl. degree in astronomy, U. of Ghent, 1902, Dr. Engring., 1902, Lauréat du concours Universitaire, 1903; studied astronomy, Heidelberg, 1905, Potsdam, 1906; m. Julia Sterpin, May 7, 1910; children—Simone, Micheline, Edwin. Engr. Belgian Govt., 1903-08; astronomer Royal Obs., Belgium, 1908-17; came to U.S. as visiting prof., 1915, naturalized citizen, 1922; with University of Chicago from 1917, professor astronomy, 1924-45; professor emeritus from 1945; with lunar and planetary lab. U. Ariz., 1963-74. Mem. Nat. Geog. Soc. expdns. Brazil, 1947, Korea, 1948, Sudan, 1952; conducted site survey in Congo for Belgian govt., 1949. Fellow A.A.A.S.; member Am. Astron. Soc., Royal Astron. Soc. (London), Astron. Gesellschaft, Soc. belge d'astron., History of Science Soc., Royal Astron. Soc. Can. (hon.). Awarded gold medal by Royal Soc. of Copenhagen, 1912; Mailly prize, Belgium Acad. Sciences, 1920; Valz prize, Acad. Sciences, Paris, 1928; Burr prize Nat. Geog. Soc., 1952, Watson prize, 1958. Protestant. Contbr. to Am. and European jours. Has specialized in studies of double stars, comets and asteroids. Home: Tucson, Ariz. Died Feb. 23, 1974.

VAN BUREN, ALBERT WILLIAM, prof. archaeology; b. Milford, Conn., 1878; s. James Heartt and Annie Maria (Smith) Van B.; prep. edn., Phillips Acad., Andover, Mass.; A.B., Yale, 1900, grad. study, 1900-02, Ph.D., 1915; grad. study, Am. Sch. Classical Studies in Rome, 1902-06; m. Elizabeth Douglas, Aug. 19, 1914; instr. in Latin, Yale, 1906-07, instr. in Roman religion, 1907-08; librarian Am. Acad. in Rome, 1913-26, asso. prof. archaeology, 1912-23, professor, 1923-46, also editor of publs. and curator of Museum, 1927-46. Jurdicial custodian of Library and Museum of Am. of Am. Academy in Rome, during World War II. Fellow Royal Numismatic Society (London); member Society for Promotion Hellenic Studies; regular member German Archaeological Institute, Pontifical Acad. Archaeology; honorary member Virtuosi al Pantheon; mem. com., Keats-Shelley Memorial, Rome. Episcopalian. Club: Club: Curzon (London). Author: A Bibliographical Guide to Latium and Southern Etruria (4th edit.), 1938; A Companion to the Study of Pompeii and Herculaneum, 1938; Ancient Rome as revealed by Recent Discoveries, 1936. Compiler (with Sir James George Frazer) Graecia Antiqua, maps and plans to illustrate Pausanias's Description of Greece, 1930. Contbr. to publs. Am. Acad. in Rome, also to Am. Jour. Archaeology, Am. Jour. Philology, Classical Review, Jour. Roman Studies, etc. Home: Rome, Italy.†

VANCE, JOHN EDWARD, educator; b. Dayton, O., May 21, 1905; s. Edward Delmar and Kathleen (Phillips) V.; B.S., Yale, 1926, Ph.D., 1929; m. Esther Christensen, July 3, 1931; children—Joan, Philip. Instr. Yale, 1929-30, 31-35, asst. prof., 1935-40, asso. prof., 1940-48; prof. N.Y. U., chmn. dept. chemistry Washington Square Coll. and Grad. Sch. Arts and Sci., 1948-51, head dept., 1951-57, on leave as chief scientist and dep. chief research and devel. Office Chief of Staff, 1953-55. Mem. Army Sci. Adv. Panel, 1956-69; mem. Chem. corps Adv. Council, 1958-60, U.S. Army Research Office Adv. Council, 1962-72, Test and Evaluation Command Sci. Adv. Group, 1962-75, Missile Command Sci. Adv. Group, 1965-75 sr. staff to rep. UNAEC. Served as maj. C.W.S., 1942-43, lt. col. C.E., 1943-46; col. Army Res., 1956-62, brig. gen., 1962-66. Sterling fellow Yale for Study in Copenhagen, Denmark, 1930-31. Fellow N.Y. Acad. Scis.; mem. Am. Chem. Soc., Sigma Xi. Clubs: Yale, Chemists (N.Y.C.). Contbr. articles on analytical, inorganic, phys. chemistry to sci. jours. Home: New York City, N.Y. Died Mar. 19, 1975; buried Arlington Nat. Cemetery.

VANCE, RUPERT BAYLESS, sociologist, author; b. Plumerville, Ark., Mar. 15, 1899; s. Walter Johnson and Lula Mary (Bayless) V.; A.B., Henderson-Brown Coll., Arkadelphia, Ark., 1920; A.M., Vanderbilt U., Nashville, Tenn., 1921; Ph.D., U. of N.C., 1928; LL.D., Hendrix Coll., 1938; m. Rheba Ceceile Usher, June 5, 1930; children—David Rupert, Donald Ernest, and Victor Stuart, Principal of high school, Talikina, Okla., from 1921 to 1923. Instructor of English, S. Ga. Coll., McRae, Ga., 1923-25; teaching fellow sociology, Univ. of N.C. 1927-28, research asso., 1929-37; prof. U. of Texas summer school, 1936; visiting prof La. State U., 1942; research prof., Inst. for Research in Social Science, U. of N.C., since 1937, Kenan prof. sociology from 1945; mem. board govs. Univ. of N.C. Press. Served in various research capacities with Nat. Resources Commn., Study of Population, Redistribution, Social Security Bd., Rosenwald Fund, Social Science Research Council. Rosenwald fellow, 1945. Mem. Am. Sociol. Soc. (exec. com. 1942-49, pres. 1944), Am. Acad. Polit. and Social Science, Population Assn. of America, Am. Econ. Assn., Southern Regional Com. of Social Science Research Council, Southern Sociol. Soc. (sec.-treas. 1935-37; pres. 1938), Phi Beta Kappa, Alpha Kappa Delta, Alpha Psi Delta, Pi Kappa Delta, and also Lambda Chi Alpha. Democrat Author: books relating to field; co-author: New Farm Homes for Old, 1946. Exploring the South, 1949; Urban South, 1954. Asso. editor Social Forces; contbg. editor Rural Sociology. Home: Chapel Hill N.C. Died Aug. 25, 1975

VANCE, WILLIAM FORD, city commr.; b. nr. Hattiesburg, Miss., Dec. 20, 1909; s. Angus Nicholson and Carrie Pearl (Ford) V.; grad. high sch.; m. Anna Sue Lacey, Oct. 28, 1944; children—Gene Ford, Cindy Sue (Mrs. W. J. McLaughlin, Jr.). Safety patrolman Miss. Hwy. Dept., 1941-43, 45-46; owner-mgr. Vance Dairy, 1947-56; sheriff, tax collector Forrest County, Miss., 1956-60; pres. Fla. Vance Corp., v.p. Brokers Devel. Corp., sec.-treas. Deep South Investments, Hattiesburg, Miss., 1960; city commr., Hattiesburg, 1969-72. Served with USNR, 1932-36, USAAF, 1943-45. Decorated Bronze Star medal with oak leaf cluster, Air medal with four oak leaf clusters. Mem. Am. Legion, V.F.W., Aircraft Owners and Pilots Assn. Democrat. Methodist. Elk, Rotarian. Home: Hattiesburg, Miss. Died Feb. 21, 1972.

VAN CLEAVE, HARLEY WILLIAM, lawyer; b. Davis, Okla., July 21, 1907; s. Thomas Jefferson and Bessie (Henderson) Van C.; B.S., Okla. State U., 1931; asso. B. Comml. Sci., Okla. Sch. Accountancy and Finance, 1934; LL.B., Tulsa U., 1939; m. Thelma Florence Smith, Aug. 5, 1933. Accountant, atty. Tidewater Asso. Oil Co., Tulsa, 1932-50; admitted to Okla. bar, 1940, since practiced in Tulsa; partner Van Cleave, Gresham, Liebier, Dalton & Bivens, 1950-73; chmn. Okla. Bar Seminars. Mem. Civilian Prodn. Adminstrn. Bd., 1947-48; chmn. N.C. Armory Bd., 1950-51; chmn. Multiple Sclerosis Soc., 1954-64; chmn. Tulsa City Athletic Commn., 1959-64; pres. Whitaker Orphan Homes Found., 1958-62; chmn. War Meml. Services, Tulsa, 1950-70. Pres. League Young Democrats, 1940-41. Served to capt. USAAF, 1942-46; PTO. Recipient Distinguished Service awards City of Tulsa, 1959, V.F.W., 1949, Okla. Bar Assn., 1964, Multiple Sclerosis Soc., 1958. Mem. Am., Okla., Tulsa County bar assns., Tulsa Law Club (Past pres.), Am. Legion, V.F.W., (past pres.), Delta Kappa Chi (past nat. v.p.), Phi Beta Gamma. Methodist. Mason (32 °, Shriner), Elk. Home: Tulsa, Okla., Died Feb. 1973.

VAN CLEEF, EUGENE, geographer, author; b. Chgo., Jan. 17, 1887; s. Adolphe and Marie (Pollock) Van C.; S.B., U. Chgo., 1908; student Leipzig U. (Germany), 1913-14; Ph.D., Clark U., 1926; m. Frieda Miller, Apr. 3, 1915. Spl. investigator Rand, McNally & Co., Chgo., 1908-11; in charge geography dept. State Tchrs. Coll., Duluth, Minn., 1911-18; climatologist Latin-Am. div. House Inquiry, 1918; mgr. fgn. trade dept. Van Cleef Bros., Chgo., 1919-21; prof. geography, in charge fgn. trade curriculum Ohio State U., 1921-57, prof. bus. orgn., 1946-57, prof. emeritus, 1957-73. Export cons. geog. research div. Mil. Intelligence Service, 1942-44. Vice chmn. city plan commn., Columbus, O., 1949-53, Upper Arlington, O., 1960-62. Decorated knight Order of White Rose, comdr. Order of White Rose (Finland); recipient Geog. Writing award Nat. Council for Geog. Edn., 1962. Fellow A.A.A.S. (life mem.), Am. Meteorol. Soc. (profl. mem.), Ohio Acad. Sci. (pres. 1941-42), hon. life mem.), Am. Geog. Soc.; mem. Am. Soc. Planning Ofcls. (hon.), Am. Relief Adminstrn., Assn. Am. Geographers, Nat. Council Geography Tchrs., Sigma Xi, Phi Beta Kappa, Beta Gamma Sigma, Delta Sigma Pi, Delta Phi Epsilon, Geog. Soc. Finland (corr.). Author: Precipitation Map of the United States, 1924; The Story of the Weather, 1929; Finland, The Republic Farthest North, 1929; Trade Centers and Trade Routes, 1937; Geography for the Businessman, 1943; Getting Into Foreign Trade, 1946; Global Geography, 1963; Cities in Action, 1970. Contbr. articles to profl. jours. Home: Columbus, Ohio. Died Nov. 7, 1973.

VAN CLEEF, FRANK C., financial counsel; b. Wellington, O., Dec. 5, 1881; s. Edward Anson and Josephine (Chapman) Van C.; A.B., Oberlin (O.) Coll., 1904; LL.B., Columbia, 1907; m. Grace Langeland, Nov. 1906 (dec.); children—Esther (Mrs. Jabez H. Wood), John H. (capt. A.A.F.), Frank C., Langeland (capt. A.A.F.); m. 2d, Coila Stemple Algeo, June 28, 1941. Admitted to Ohio and N.Y. bars, 1907; practice of law with Hoyt, Dustin, Kelley, McKeehan & Andrews, Cleveland, O., 1907-16; counsel, sec., dir. and mem. exec. com., B. F. Goodrich Co., Akron, O., 1916-27; with buying dept., Guaranty Co. of New York, 1928-30; mem. firm Van Cleef, Jordan and Wood, N.Y.C., from 1930. director of Elyria Savs. and Trust Nat. Bank (O.). Spl. asst. to W.P.B., 1941-42. Trustee Oberlin College. Trustee Allen Meml. Hospital, Oberlin. Mem. Oberlin Hist. and Improvement Orgn. (pres.), Phi Beta Kappa, Phi Delta Phi, Alpha Tau Omega. Home: Oberlin, O.†

VAN CLEVE, THOMAS CURTIS, professor history; b. Malden, Mo., May 1, 1888; s. George Thomas (M.D.) and Vera Ella (James) Van C.; A.B., U. of Mo., 1911, A.M., 1912; Ph.D., U. of Wis., 1921; Litt.D., Bowdoin College, 1954. Instructor in history University of Missouri, 1912-13; assistant in history, Univ. of Wis., 1913-15; instr. in history, Bowdoin Coll., 1915-17, asst. prof. history, 1917-20, prof., 1920-25, Frank Munsey prof. history, 1925-26, Thomas Brackett Reed prof. history and polit. science, 1926-54, emeritus; visiting professor University of S.Carolina, 1955. Served as lt. later capt., inf., U.S. Army, with Intelligence Sect., 1st Div., A.E.F., 1917-18; citation for "distinguished and efficient services"; attached to 2d Sec., Gen. Staff, until July 1919. Re-enteredmilitary intelligence service Sept. 1942, as lt. col., later col. M.I., serving in North Africa, Italy, France, Luxembourg and Germany, and in Washington, D.C. Received War Dept. citation "for meritorious and exceptional service to the Military Intelligence Service." Mem. Council on Fgn. Relations. Fellow Royal History Soc., London; mem. Am. Hist. Soc., Mediaeval Acad. Am., Phi Beta Kappa. Republican. Author: Markward of Anweiler and the Sicilian Regency; A Study of Hohenstaufen Policy in Sicily during the Minority of Frederick II, 1937; the Emperor, Frederick II of Hohenstaufen, 1972. Contbr. to Am. Hist. Review, Dictionary of Am. Biography; Speculum. Home: Brunswick, Me., Died Feb. 10, 1976; interred Malden, Mo.

VANCURA, ZDENEK, lit. historian, translator; b. Prague, Czechoslovakia, Jan. 11, 1903; Ph.D., Charles U., Prague, 1926, D.Sc., 1959; postgrad. Columbia, 1926-28. Tchr., Comml. Acad., Prague, 1929-45, asst. prof. Sch. Commerce, 1937-45; prof. Philos. Faculty, Charles U., from 1946, dean, 1953-55; dir. Inst. Langs. and Lit., Czechoslovak Acad. Scis., Prague, 1964-69. Recipient award for outstanding work, 1963. Mem. Czechoslovak Union Writers, Internat. Assn. U. Profs. English, (corr.) Czechoslovak Acad. Scis. Author: Walt Whitman, Poet of Democracy, 1955; The Art of G.B. Shaw, 1958; The Pilgrim Fathers and the Beginnings of American Literature, 1965; Twenty Years of the English Novel, 1945-1964; Ency. of American Authors. Chief editor: Modern Philology; Philologica Pragensia; Anglistics. Translator 10 English novels and 40 English plays. Home: Prague, Czechoslovakia., Died May 5, 1974.

VANDEGRIFT, ALEXANDER ARCHER, Marine Corps officer; b. Charlottesville, Va., Mar. 13, 1887; s. William Thomas and Sarah Agnes (Archer) V.; grad. Charlottesville High Sch.; student U. of Va., 2 years; grad. Marine Officers Sch., Advanced Base Course and Field Officers Course, U.S. Marine Corps; m. Mildred Strode, June 29, 1910; 1 son, Alexander Archer. Commissioned 2d lt., U.S. Marine Corps, Jan. 22, 1909, and advanced to brig. gen., 1940, maj. gen., 1942, lt. gen., 1943, gen., 1945; duty Marine Barracks, Paris Island, S.C., Portsmouth, N.H., Phila., Norfolk, Va., Quantico, Va., Washington, D.C., San Diego, Calif.; also in Haiti, Nicaragua, Mexico, Cuba, and China; comdg. 1st Marine Div. on Guadalcanal-Tulagi, Aug. 7-Dec. 9, 1942; comdg. 1st Marine Amphibious Corps in landing on Bougainville, Northern Solomon Islands, Nov. 1, 1943; comdt. Marine Corps since Jan. 1, 1944. Decorated Medal of Honor, Distinguished Service Medal, Navy Cross. Received hon. LL.D., Columbia U., 1947. Home: Lynchburg, Va. Died May 1973.

VANDEN BERG, HENRY JOHN surgeon; b. Zeeland, Mich., July 6, 1879; s. John William and Dena (DeKruif) Vanden B.; student Hope Coll., Holland Mich., 1909; M.D., U. of Mich., 1905, post grad. work, U. of Vienna, 1909-10; m. Edn. Gibson, 1908; children ° Anna Jean, Henry John; m. 2d, Sabra Oliver, Jan. 1, 1921; children ° William Oliver, Marianne, Diane. On surgical staff Butterworth Hosp., 1910-24. Blodgett Memorial Hosp., from 1917 (chief of staff, 1935-39, chief of cancer and tumor clinic, 1935-41); spl. lecturer in Post-Grad. Medicine, U. of Mich., 1935, 36, 39, 42. Mem. Vol. Med. Service Corps; chmn. Med. Adv. Bd. Dist. No. 9, State of Michigan; now mem. Advisory Board No. 9. Chmn. State Executive Committee Women's Field Army of Am. Cancer Soc., 1936-46, resigned chairmanship, 1946 (mem. bd. dirs. of soc. 1941-46); chmn. fact-finding com. Am. Coll. Surgeons, and counselor Mich. exec. com. Member Planning Commn., East Grand Rapids. Received for ten consecutive years, award for distinguished service in the war against cancer from American Society for Control of Cancer; award for outstanding service in developing program for cancer control from Michigan division Am. Cancer Society. Mem. Inst. Trop. and Preventive Medicine, American Medical Writers Association, New York Academy of Science. Michigan (mem. cancer control com. and mem. fact-finding com. of the com.), Kent Co. med. socs., A.M.A., Am. Assn. for the Study of Goiter, Founder's Group of Am. Bd. of Surgery, founder member of Central Surg. Assn., American Geriatrics Soc., American Goiter Assn.; mem. Grand Rapids Symphony Soc. (1st v.p.). Fel. Am. Coll. Surgeons; mem. Phi Gamma Delta. Protestant. Clubs: Kent Country, University, Torch, Rotary, Grand Rapids Yacht, Peninsular. Contbr. numerous tech. articles. Home: Grand Rapids, Mich.†

VANDERBILT, AMY, author, journalist; b. S.I., N.Y.; d. Joseph Mortimer and Mary Estelle (Brooks) Vanderbilt; student Inst. Heubl, Lausanne, Switzerland, Packer Collegiate Inst., Bklyn.; spl. student sch. journalism N.Y. U., 1926-28; m. Robert S. Brinkerhoff, 1929; m. 2d, Morton G. Clark, 1935; 1 son, Lincoln Gill Clark; m. 3d, Hans Knopf, 1945 (div.); children—Paul Vanderbilt, Stephen John; m. 4th, Curtis B. Kellar, Mar. 1, 1968. Soc., feature writer S.I. Advance, 1927-29; asst. advt., publicity dir. H.R. Mallison Co., 1929-30, advt., account exec., N.Y.C., 1930-33; columnist Internat. News Service, bus. mgr., lit. mag. Am. Spectator, 1933; home service dir. Tower mags., 1934; 1st v.p. Publicity Assos., N.Y.C., 1937-40, pres., 1940-45; cons. design Bristol, Inc., 1960-65; syndicated columnist Amy Vanderbilt's Etiquette, United Feature Syndicate, 1954-68, Los Angeles Times Syndicate, 1968-74; television artist, etiquette program It's Good Taste, 1954-60; radio program The Right Thing To Do, 1960-62; monthly page McCall's mag., 1963, Ladies Home Jour., 1965-74; etiquette authority World Book Ency. Mem. N.Y. Acad. Scis. (bd. woman's aux.), Screen Actors Guild, Authors League Am., Authors Guild. Democrat. Episcopalian. Author: Amy Vanderbilt's Complete Book of Etiquette, 1952; Amy Vanderbilt's Everyday Etiquette, 1956, rev., 1974; Amy Vanderbilt's Complete Cook Book, 1961; Amy Vanderbilt's New Complete Book of Etiquette, 1963; Amy Vanderbilt's Etiquette, 1972. Contbr. articles to newspapers, nat. mags., 1930-74. Address: New York City, N.Y. Died Dec. 27, 1974; buried the Evergreens, N.Y.

VANDERBILT, CORNELIUS, JR., author, lectr., cinematographer, televiser; b. N.Y.C., Apr. 30, 1898; s. Cornelius and Grace Graham (Wilson) V.; ed. St. Paul's Sch. (Concord, N.H.), Harstrom's Tutoring Sch. (Norwalk, Conn.); m. Rachel Littleton, Apr. 29, 1920 (div. Nov. 26, 1927); m. 2d, Mary Weir Logan, July 1928 (div. Aug. 1931); m. 3d. Helen Varner Anderson, Jan. 4, 1935 (div. Dec. 1940); m. 4th, Feliza Loraine Pablos, Sept. 3, 1946 (div. Apr. 29, 1948); m. 5th, Patricia Murphy Wallace, Sept. 2, 1948 (div. June 1953); m. 6th, Ann Needham, 1957 (div. May 1960); m. 7th, Mary Lou Gardner Bristol, Nov. 4, 1967. Reporter New York Herald, 1919-20; Albany corr. N.Y. Times, winter, 1920, United Press, in Far West, summer 1921, Universal Service, Wash., D.C., 1921-22; independent corr., Washington, D.C., 1923; founder, 1923, and pres. Vanderbilt Newspapers, Inc.; formerly pub;. Illustrated Daily News, Los Angeles, Illustrated Daily Herald, San Francisco, Illustrated Daily Tab, Miami; asso. editor N.Y. Mirror, July 1925-Sept. 1929; pub. Nomad Mag., 1927, 28, 29; columnist Western Newspaper Union, Am. Press Assn., Liberty, Script, Click, Photoplay, and Radio Guide; travel columnist New York Post, 1943-47; travel columnist Affiliated News Features, 1948. Producer Germany Bounces Back, 1952, Africa Unrehearsed, 1956, Israel Today (film), 1958; pres. Vagabonding with Vanderbilt. Inc., 1962; editor, pub. Vagabonding with Vanderbilt Newsletter, 1950-65; v.p. public services Am. Film Prodns., Inc.; v.p. Chuckhall Travel Bur., Miami Beach, Fla. Mem. Nevada Adv. Com. on Arts. Served as pvt. U.S. Army, 1917-19; dispatch driver 27th Div., A.E.F., 1918; attended U.S. Army War Coll., 1922; lt. U.S.R., 1920-23; capt. N.Y. Nat. Guard, 1923-27; major U.S.R., 1927-42; major Intelligence, AUS, 1942-43; Walter Reed Hosp., for phys. disability, 1942-43. Decorated Croix de la Croix Rouge (France); Distinguished Service Cross of Federal Bureau of Investigation, 1942; Abdon Calderon (Ecuador), 1944. Mem. Am. Legion, World War I Veterans (trustee 1965), Hist. and Landmark Soc. (pres.), Historic Am. Landmards Soc. (adv. com.), French Soc. of Am., Authors League, Authors Guild, La Cave Des Boys. Episcopalian. Clubs: National Press, Overseas Press, Overseas Correspondents, American Automobile Association (Washington); Royal Automobile Association, Caravan (London); Auto Club de France (Paris); Nev. Press, Reno Press; Palm Bay (Miami, Fla.). Author: Symposium of Public Opinion on Japanese-American Question, 1921; Personal Experiences of a Cub Reporter, 1922; Experiences of a Washington Correspondent, 1924; Reno, 1929; Park Avenue, 1930; Palm Beach, 1931; Farewell to Fifth Avenue, 1935; Woman of Washington, 1937; Vagabonding Through Europe Today, 1949; My Fabulous Mother; All Roads Lead to Rome (1st colored travelogue for TV shown for FCC); Personal European Travel Directory, 1954; The Living Past of America, 1955; Queen of the Golden Age, 1956; The Vanderbilt Feud, 1956; Man Of The World, 1959; Ranches and Ranch Life On America, 1968. Home: Reno, Nev. Died July 7, 1974.

VAN DER MERWE, HENDERIK JOHANNES JAN MATTHYS, educator; b. Morgenzon, S. Africa, Oct. 27, 1913; s. Henderik and Anna (Nel) van der M.; B.A., U.S. Africa, 1936; Diploma in Edn., Tchrs. Tng. Coll. Pretoria, S. Africa, 1937; D.Litt. U. Pretoria, 1946; m. Gesina S.W. de Klerk, July 4, 1942; 1 step-son, Nicolaas Johnannes Smit. Mem. faculty arts and sci., head dept. Afrikaans and Netherlands, head dept. gen. linguistics U. S. Africa, Pretoria, 1946—, prof., 1954—, dean faculty arts and scis., 1964—;. Mem. council U. Durban-Westville, U. West-Cape Mem. South African Acad. Sci. and Arts, Linguistic Soc. S. Africa (founder, 1965), Dutch, Belgian assns. for lang., literature and history, Afrikaans Lang. Commn. Author 30 books in linguistics, 4 on African politics. Home: Pretoria, Republic of South Africa., Died Feb. 25, 1974.

VAN DER STRATEN PONTHOZ, COUNT, ROBERT, ambassador; b. Brussels, Belgium, Sept. 12, 1879; s. Charles and Marie (d'Offignies) Van Der Straten P.; Dr. in Law, Brussels Univ.; m. Henriette Devoto, April 21, 1912. Enlisted Belgian diplomatic service, 1901; sec. of legation at The Hague, Copenhagen, Oslo, Berne, Paris, 1912-17; counselor of legation at Madrid, 1917-18; charge d&23affaires at Buenos Aires, 1918-21, E.E. and M.P., 1921-34; E.E. and M.P. to Denmark and Norway, 1934; ambassador to and the U.S. from 1934; Decorated comdr. Order of Leopold; comdr. Order of the Crown (Belgium); Grand Cross of St. Olaf of Norway, Catholic. Address: Belgium†

VANDER VEER, MILTON T., banker; b. Asbury Park, N.J., Mar. 31, 1901; s. Thaddeus and Frances (Nutt) Vander V.; student Peddie Inst., Hightstown, N.J.; m. Mary Hutchinson, June 21, 1924; 1 dau., Eleanor Jean (Mrs. John Franklin Shaak, Jr.), With Home Title Guaranty Co., Bklyn., 1922, clk., appraiser, loan officer, v.p., 1922-56, pres., 1956-57, chmn. bd., chief exec. officer, 1957-60; dir. Lafayette Nat. Bank, Bklyn., 1944, chmn. bd., chief exec. officer, pres., 1958-65; chmn. bd., trustee Kings Lafayette Bank, 1965; dir., mem. exec. com. Kings Lafayette Corp., 1969. Home Title div. Chgo. Title Ins. Co. Dir. Bklyn. Region Nat. Conf. Christians and Jews, 1958; v.p., trustee Indsl. Home for Blind, 1952; trustee Adelphi Hosp., 1955, Jersey Shore Med Center, Neptune, N.J.; bd. dirs., exec. com. Bklyn. chpt. A.R.C., exec. bd. Greater N.Y.; bd. dirs., N.Y.C. cancer com. Am. Cancer Soc.; bd. dirs. Urban Am., Inc. Mem. Nat. Assn. Real Estate Bds., L.I., Bklyn. (dir) real estate bds., L.I. Soc. Real Estate Appraisers, Am. Inst. Real Estate Appraisers, Holland Soc. of N.Y., Bklyn. C. of C. (dir., exec. com.); Downtown Bklyn. Assn. (dir.) Presbyn. Mason (K.T.) Clubs: Union League, Downtown Assn. (N.Y.C.); Brooklyn; Spring Lake Golf and Country; Montauk; Baltrusol Golf. Home: Short Hills, N.J. Died May 1973.

VANDERVELDE, CONRAD, educator; b. Brandon, Wis., Dec. 9, 1879; s. Marten and Adrianna Jeanette (De Swarte) V.; A.B., Ripon (Wis.) College, 1904, D.D., 1919; A.M., Princeton, 1906; B.D., Princeton Theological Seminary, 1907; studied University of Chicago Chicago, summers, 1909, 1910, 1919; married Kate Annelia Cross, September 6, 1909; children—Cornelia, Benjamin Stoddert. Porf. philosophy and student pastor, Hatings (Nebr.) Coll., 1907-09; ordained Presbyn. ministry, 1908; prof. philosophy and edn., Westminster Coll., Fulton, Mo., 1909-11; professor philosophy, College of Emporia, Kansas, 1911-1941, also registrar, 1913-14, dean, 1916-1941, dean emeritus, from 1941, acting president, 1918; teacher psychology, Kansas State Teachers Coll., Emporia, summers 1920-32, teacher of philosophy of religion, 1947; teacher abnormal psychology, Coll. of Emporia, 1947; pastor, Sardis Congregational Church, from 1943. Active in Liberty Loan and American Red Cross work during World War I. Mem. bd. of dirs. Community Training School of Religious Edn., 1916-18. Mem. Mid-western Psychol. Assn., Kansas Mental Hygiene Soc., Pi Gamma Mu (sec. 1927-34, 1937-39). Clubs: Forum, Rotary (pres. 1929-30, sec., 1944-46). Contbr. articles to current religious and ednl. mags. Home: Emporia, Kans.†

VANDER VELDE, LEWIS GEORGE, univ. prof.; b. Grandville, Mich., Oct. 17, 1890; s. George and Katherine (Lubbers) V.; student Hope Coll., 1908-10; A.B., U. of Mich., 1913, A.M., 1921; Ph.D., Harvard, 1931; LL.D., Eastern Michigan University, 1961. Head history dept., State Teachers College, St. Cloud, Minn., 1921-26; instr. in history, U. of Mich., 1928-31; asst. prof., 1931-36; asso. prof., 1936-40, prof. of history, from 1940. chmn. history dept., 1946-53. Dir. Mich. Hist. Collections, U. of Mich., from 1938. Member Michigan State Hist. Commn. from 1950. Mem. Am. Hist. Assn., Miss. Valley Hist. Assn. Soc. of Am. Archivists, Am. Assn. for State and Local History, Hist. Soc. of Mich. (pres. 1958-59). Presbyterian. Author: The Presbyterian Churches and the Federal Union, 1861-69 (Harvard Historical Studies), 1932; contbr. articles to Miss. Valley Historical Review, Church History, The Am. Archivist, Dictionary of Am. Biography, various encys.; editor: Mich. and the Cleveland Era (With Earl D. Babst), 1948. Specialism; Am. constitutional history, history of Mich. Home: Ann Arbor, Mich., Died Oct. 31, 1975.

VAN DONGEN, CORNELIUS THEODORE MARIE, painter; b. Delfshaven, Holland, Jan. 26, 1877; s. Johannes and Helene (Geurts) Van D.; m. Marie Claire Huguen; 1 son, Jean-Marie. Home: Monaco.†

VAN DRESSER, JASMINE STONE, author; b. St. St. Louis, Mo., Oct. 1878; d. Charles Henry and Margaret Manson (Barber) Stone; ed. Randolph Macon Coll., Lynchburg, Va., 1895-97; studied art in Paris and St. Louis; m. William Van Dresser, of Memphis, Tenn., June 3, 1903; children—Cleland S., Peter H. Founder Stone, Van Dresser Co., commercial artists; gave up art after marriage to devote attention to writing; dir. Little Theatre, Bronx, New York, and in acted in own plays in vaudeville. Mem. Authors' League America. Author: How to Find Happyland, 1907; Gibby of Clamshell Alley, 1917; The Little Pink Pig and the Big Road, 1924; Jimsey, 1925; also short stories in Metropolitan Mags., Delineator and Green Book. Home: Palm Beach, V1Fla.†

VAN DUSEN, HENRY PITNEY, clergyman, educator; b. Phila., Pa., Dec. 11, 1897; s. George Richstein and Katherine James (Pitney) Van D.; A.B., Princeton, 1919; B.D., Union Theol. Sem., 1924; Ph.D., Edinburgh U., 1932, D.D., 1946; S.T.D., N.Y.U., 1945, Westminster Theol. Sem., 1956, Columbia, 1956; D.D., Amherst Coll., 1946, Oberlin Coll., 1947, Yale, 1947, Heidelberg Coll., 1950, Queen's U., 1952, Harvard, 1954, Dertmouth, 1956, Colgate U., 1960, Va. Theol. Sem., 1963, Pacific Sch. Religion, 1963, Bucknell U., 1964, Assumption Coll., 1968; Litt.D., Jewish Theol. Sem. 1958; L.H.D., Bates Coll., 1959; m. Elizabeth Coghill Bartholomew, June 19, 1931; children—John George, Henry Hugh, Derek Bartholomew. Ordained to ministry Presbyn. Ch., 1924; instr. Union Theol. Sem., N.Y.C., 1926, asst. prof. systematic theology and philosophy of religion, 1928-31, asso. prof., 1931-36, prof. systematic theology, 1936-63, dean of students, 1931-39, pres., 1945-63; pres. faculty, Auburn Theol. Sem., 1945-63. Trustee Princeton; trustee Found. Theol. Edn. S.E. Asia, chmn., 1952; trustee Millbrook Sch., 1939-48, Vassar Coll., 1937-41, Smith Coll., 1945-50, Elizabeth Morrow Sch. Mem. United Board Christian Higher Edn. In Asia pres., 1953-64; mem. bd. Fgn. Missions, United Presbyn. Ch., U.S.A.; past pres. Union Settlement Assn. Trustee Rockefeller Found., Gen. Edn. Bd.; dir. Fund for Republic; dir. Fund Theol. Edn., also chmn. exec. com. Fellow Nat. Council on Religion in Higher Edn.; mem. Am. Theol. Soc., Council on Fgn. Relations, World Council Chs. and Internat. Missionary Council. Clubs: Century, Princeton, Nassau, Author numerous books in field of religion, latest being: Life's Meaning, 1951; Spirit, Son and Father, 1958; One Great Ground of Hope, 1961; The Vindication of Liberal Theology, 1963; Christanity on the March, 1963; Dag Hammarskjoid: The Statesman and his Faith, 1967. Editor: The Spiritual Legacy of John Foster Dulles, 1960; editor, contbr. compilations to religious works; mem. editorial bd. Christianity and Crisis, Christendom, 1945-48; Ecumenical Rev. Home: Princeton, N.J. Died Feb. 1975.

VAN EVERY, WILLIAM STANLEY, newspaperman, assn. exec.; b. Fenwick, Ont., Can., Dec. 18, 1892; s. Horace Murray and Stella Maud (Page) Van E.; student St. Catharine's Bus. Coll., 1909-10; B.S.A., Ont. Agrl. Coll., 1922; m. Clara Ethel Burgoyne, June 18, 1929. Agrl. rep. Ont. Dept. Agr., Lincoln County, 1923-26; rep. Can. Life Assurance Co., St. Catharines, Ont., 1926-31; farm editor St. Catharines Standard, 1932-69; pres., United Empire Loyalist Assn. Can., St. Catharines, 1966-72; owner, operator farm and nursery, 1917-67. Bd. dirs. Pickering Coll., Newmarket, Ont. Life mem. Agrl. Inst. Can. Mem. Soc. of Friends (pastor 1924-56). Address: St Catharines, Ont., Can. Died Nov. 14, 1972.

VAN FLEET, DICK SCOTT, botanist, educator; b. Trenton, N.J. Mar. 23, 1912; s. Peter and Stella Susan (Kise) Van F.; A.B., Ind. U. 1936; M.A., 1937, Ph.D., 1940; Sterling fellow Yale, 1943-44; m. Clara Mootz, Sept. 4, 1939; children—Peter Scott, Susan Jo. Grad. asst. Ind. U., 1937-40; instr. biology Heidelberg Coll., 1940-42, asst. prof., 1942-43; asst. prof. botany U. Mo., 1944-47, asso. prof. 1947-52, prof., 1952-57; chmn. botany dept. U. Toronto, 1957-59; head botany dept. U. Mass., 1959-62, U. Ga., Athens, 1962-68, prof., 1968-75. Mem. Bot. Soc. Am. Phytochemical Soc., Histochem. Soc. Contbr. articles to profl. jours. Home: Athens Ga., Died Oct. 29, 1975.

VAN HAERSOLTE, WILIEM (BARON), Dutch diplomat; b. Arnhem, Netherlands, Sept. 3, 1909; s. J.C. and E.T.J. (van Heemstra) van H.; Dr.Law, U. Utrecht (Netherlands); m. Emilie Saxild, Feb. 26, 1952; 1 son, Johan Christiaan. Ambassador to Montevideo, 1953-58, Lima, Peru, 1959-64, Madrid, Spain, 1965-71, Stockholm, Sweden, 1971-74. Served with cav. Netherlands Army; now capt. Res. Decorated Grand Cross Isabella la Catolica; Grand Cross Sol del Peru. Club: Haagse (The Hauge). Address: Stockholm, Sweden. Died July 14, 1974.

VAN HAGAN, LESLIE FLANDERS, coll. prof.; b. Hyde Park, Chicago, Ill., Sept. 13, 1878; s. Edward Isaac and Margaretta (Flanders) Van H.; B.S. in C.E., U. of Wis., 1904, C.E., 1919; m. M(ary) Ethel Caine, July 8, 1908, children—E(thel) Jean (wife of Dr. John Carroll McCarter), Robert Leslie, Charles Edward. Instr. drawing, U. of Wis., 1904-05; teaching in coll. of engring., 1911-49, chmn. dept., 1930-49; engr. with Nat. Lines of Mexico, 1905-11. Served with S.A.T.C., Fort Sheridan, 1918. Mem. Am. Soc. C.E., Am. Ry. Engrs. Assn., Society for Engineering Education, Tau Beta Pi, Chi Epsilon. Protestant. Republican. Club: University (Madison). Home: Madison, Wis.†

VAN KEUREN, FLOYD, clergyman; b. Sioux City, Ia., 1880; s. Robert Scott and Delia Louise (Baker) Van K.; A.B., Hobart Coll., 1904, D.D., 1931; student Gen. Theol. Sem., 1904-07; m. Helen Huey, 1910. Ordained deacon P.E. Ch., 1907, priest, 1908; rector Trinity Memorial Ch., Erie, Pa., 1907-10, Christ Ch., New Brighton, Pa., 1910-12, All Saints Ch., Denver, Colo., 1912-15, Christ Ch., Canon City, Colo., 1915-17; dist. mgr. Am. Red Cross Relief Work, France, 1917-19; exec. dir. Family Service Soc., Columbus, O., 1919-22; lecturer in sociology, Ohio State U., 1920-23; asso. rector Trinity Ch., Columbus, 1922-25; rector Christ Ch., Indianapolis, Ind., 1925-31; exec. sec. N.Y. Diocesan Social Service Commn., 1931-43; rector St. Barnabas' Church, Irvington-on-Hudson N.Y., 1943-49, emeirtus, from 1949; registrar Diocese of N.Y., 1933-49; dep. Gen. Convention, 1928. Decorated Reconnaissance Francaise, and Medaille de Secours aux Blesses Militaries, also Medaille de l'Union Des Femmes De France (France). Mem. Theta Delta Chi. Author: Outfitting for Spirtual Marriage, 1935; The Open Door, 1942; Christian Marriage, 1947; The Game of Living, 1953. Home: Kent, Conn.†

VANNASSE, EDWARD THEOPHILE, transp. exec.; b. Cambridge, Mass., Apr. 14, 1905, s. Henry John and Amanda (Verrette) V.; student pub. schs.; m. Anne Barnes, May 9, 1928; children—Dana Edward, Judith Anne. Br. mgr. Am. Oil Co., Springfield, Mass., 1934-41,, supt. stations, Boston, 1941-45; pres. Met. Coach Service Inc., Belmont, Mass., 1941-69; co-owner Waverley Taxi (Mass.), 1941-47; partner Belmont Motors, 1949-69; pres. Tri-Town Assos., 1955-58; v.p. Beacon Hill Travel Service, Inc., Boston, 1968-71. Notary public, 1937-71. Mem. New Eng., Mass. bus. assns., New Eng. Transit Club. Kiwanian (past pres. Belmont). Home: Waltham, Mass. Died Sept. 18, 1971.

VANNECK, JOHN, corp. exec.; b. Paris, France, Jan. 14, 1906; s. John Torrance and Sarah (Brookman) V.; brought to U.S., 1912, naturalized 1927; ed. Buckley and Fay Schs.; LL.D., Union Coll., 1973; m. Barbara Bailey, May 17, 1930; children—Marion Louise, John Bailey, William Prentice, Barbara Anne. Pres., dir. Equitable Holding Corp., 1927; dir. L.I. Lighting Co.; trustee Dime Savs. Bank of N.Y. Mem. N.Y. Stock Exchange, Am. Stock Exchange. Pres., dir. Vanneck-Bailey Found., 1949-74. Life trustee Union College, Schnectady. Clubs: Lawrence Beach (N.Y.); Athletic, Pinnacle, River, Turf and Field, West Side Tennis (N.Y.C.); Manursing Island (N.Y.); Bath and Tennis Everglades (Palm Beach, Fla.); Apawamis (Rye, N.Y.); Am. Yacht (Rye); Blind Brook (Port Chester). Home: Rye, N.Y. Died May 26, 1974; buried The Green-Wood Cemetery, Brooklyn, N.Y.

VAN ROYEN, WILLIAM, geographer; b. Utrecht, Netherlands, June 22, 1900; s. Willem and Christina (Schmelling) Van R.; M.A., Rijksuniversteit Utrecht, 1925; Ph.D., Clark U., 1928; m. Mary Shipman, 1931 (dec.); children—Charles Putnam, William Shipman; m. 2d, Irene Fetty, 1947 (div.); 1 son, John Francis; m. 3d, Wilhelmina Adriana de Bruyn, 1958, 1 dau., Annalisa Jeanne. Came to U.S., 1926, naturalized, 1937. Under-sec. Netherlands C. of C., N.Y.C., 1928-30; asst. prof. geography U. Neb., 1930-40; asst. prof. econs. Bklyn. Coll., 1940-44 (partial leave); acting chief timber unit., div. supply and resources Bd. Econ. Warfare, 1942-43, chief plant foods unit, 1943-44; prof. geography U. Md., 1944-66, head dept. geography, 1951-66; dir. div. environmental scis. U.S. Army Research Office, 1966-70. Dir. research, editor Atlas of the World's Resources, 1944-51 (on leave, 1950-51); sr. staff mem. Operations Research Office, Dept. of Army and Johns Hopkins, 1950-51, former mem. publ. and review bd.; operations analyst Hdqrs. 8th Army, Seoul, Korea, 1950-51; collaborator Bur. Agrl. Econs. USDA, 1944-66; former cons. Office Q.M. Gen.; vice chmn. Army Sci. Adv. Panel, 1961-65; cons. U.S. Dept. Commerce, 1957-66. Mem. Am. Soc. Profl. Geographers (past pres.), Assn. Am. Geographers, Geol. Soc. Am., Am. Assn. U. Profs., Royal Netherlands Geog. Soc. (past dir.), Am. Geog. Soc., Am. Congress Surveying and Mapping. Author: Atlas of the World's Resources, Vol. I.; The Agricultural Resources of the World, 1954, Vo. II; (with O. Bowles) The Mineral Resources of the World, 1952; (with N.A. Bengtson) Fundamentals of Economic Geography, 5th edit., 1964; The Low Countries between the Great Powers, in Political Geography (R. H. Fifield and G. E. Pearcy), 1948; numerous articles, reviews. Home: Bilthoven, The Netherlands. Died 1973.

VAN RYN VAN ALKEMAUDE, MARIUS ANNE, justice; b. Netherlands, Dec. 30, 1902; LL.D., U. Amsterdam (Netherlands); m. M.M. Countess van Randwyck, 1927; children—Jacob, Cornelle Henriette. Judge. Ct. Justice Haarlem, 1931-36, The Hague, 1936-47; councillor Ct. Appeal, The Hague, 1947-49; mem. Supreme Ct. Justice, The Hague, 1949—, chief justice, 1971—. Created knight Order Netherlands Lion. Home: The Hague, Netherlands., Died Nov. 4, 1974.

VAN SLYKE, LUCILLE BALDWIN (MRS. G. M.), author; b. Mannsville, N.Y., Sept. 28, 1880; d. William Edward and Jeannette (Fish) Bladwin; A.B., yracuse U., 1902; m. George Martin Van Slyke, of New York, Dec. 31, 1903. Author: Eve's Other Children, 1912. Contbr. short stories to mags. Home: Larchmont, N.Y.†

VAN WATERS, MIRIAM, social work; b. Greensburg, Pa., Oct. 4, 1887; d. George Browne and Maude (Vosburg) Van Waters; grad. St. Helens Hall, Portland, Ore., 1904; A.B., U. of Ore., 1908, A.M., 1910, LL.D., 1944; fellow in anthropology, Clark University, Worcester, Mass., Ph.D., 1913; LL.D., Smith Coll., 1934. Supt. Juvenile Court Detention Home, Los Angeles, 1917-20; supt. El Retiro, school for delinquent girls,. San Fernando, Calif., 1919-20; referee Los Angeles County (Calif.) Juvenile Court, 1920-30; now supt. State Reformatory for Women, Framingham, Mass.; dir. juvenile delinquency sect. Harvard Law School Crime Survey since 1926; consultant in juvenile delinquency Nat. Com. on Law Observance and Enforcement, 1928-31. Mem. bd. dirs. Nat. Assn. Travelers Aid Socs., Nat. Probation Assn.; v.p. Internat. Assn. Juvenile Court Magistrates since 1930; sec. Am. Youth Commn.; president American League to Abolish Capital Punishment; member Calif. Conf. Social Work (pres. 1926, 1944), Nat. Conf. of Social Work (pres. 1929-30), Southern Calif. Soc. for Mental Hygiene (pres. 1925-26), Parent-Teachers Assn. (nat. chmn. juvenile protection), Mass. Conf. Social Workers (pres. 1945), Phi Beta Kappa, Pi Lambda Theta. Author: Youth in Conflict, 1925; Parents on Probation, 1927. Contbr. to Ency. Brit. and Ency. of Social Sciences. Framingham, Mass. Died Jan. 1974.

VASSALIO, EDWARD ANDREW, business exec.; b. Ardmore, Pa., July 20, 1916; s. Andrew M. and Ragnhild (Nielsen) V.; student Pa. State U.; m. Mickey McCollum, Mar. 4, 1950; children—Andrea Hamilton, Allison Hood. Exec. v.p., gen. sales mgr. Campbell Soup Co., Camden, N.J., 1957-58; mng. dir. Campbell Soups Ltd., King's Lynn, Eng., 1958-69; v.p. research and taxation subsidiaries R.J. Reynolds Tobacco Co., Winston-Salem, N.C., 1969-70; v.p. R.J. Reynolds Industries, 1970; chmn. bd. RJR Foods Mem. Salem Arts Council, 1969. Winston-Salem Symphony, 1969. Served to capt. USAAF, 1941-46; PTO. Decorated Bronze Star, Air medal. Mem. English Speaking Union, C. of C. (v.p. 1973). Rotarian. Clubs: Old Town Country (Winston-Salem); Bermuda Run; Directors (London). Home: Winston-Salem, N.C. Died Feb. 22, 1974.

VAVRUSKA, FRANK, artist specializing in rubbings of manhole covers. Guggenheim fellow, also Ryerson fellow. Address: Chicago, Ill. Died July 29, 1974.

VEATCH, NATHAN THOMAS, cons. engr.; b. Rushville, Ill., Aug. 25, 1886; s. Nathan Thomas and Lizzie (Montgomery) V.; prep. edn. Lewis Acad., Wichita; student U. Kan., 1905-09, B.S. and C.E.; D.Engring. (hon.), U. Mo. at Rolla, 1973; m. Amarette Weaver, Oct. 8, 1912; children—Nancy (dec.), Jane (Mrs. Richard A.Barber), Aileen (Mrs. Redman Callaway). Began in engring., 1909; instr. U. Kan., and asst. State Bd. Health, 1910-11; with Worley & Black, 1911-12, 13-14, Am. Water Works & Guarantee Co., 1912-13; co-founder Black & Veatch, cons. engrs., Kansas City, Mo., 1915-75. Mem. exec. com. Automobile Club Mo.; bd. dirs. Bus. Men's Assurance Co., Plaza Bank & Trust Co., Kansas City, Starlight Theatre Assn., Kansas City, Mo.; trustee Midwest Research Inst., Kansas City, U. Kan. Endowment Assn., Kan. 4H Found., bd. govs. Am. Royal Assn. Kansas City. Recipient citation for distinguished service U. Kan., 1943, Fred Ellsworth medallion for unique and significant Service (posthumously), 1975; award for distinguished service in engring. U.Mo., 1966. Diplomate Am. Acad. Environmental Engrs. Fellow Am. Soc. M.E.: mem. A.A.A.S., Am. Concrete Inst., Am. Cons. Engrs. Council, Am. Pub. Works Assn. Am. Soc. C.E. (past dir.), Am. Soc. Testing and Materials, Am. Water Works Assn. (hon., past pres., Fuller award 1951, Diven award 1965, Harry Jordan Achievement award 1968), Nat., Mo. socs. profl. engrs., Soc. Mil. Engrs., Water Pollution Control Federation, Sigma Xi, Tau Beta Pi, Sigma Tau, Kappa Eta Kappa, Chi Epsilon. Republican. Presbyn. Mason. (Shriner). Clubs: Kansas City, Mission Hills Country, Saddle and Sirloin. Contributor to tech. mags. Avocation farming. Home: Kansas City, Mo., Died Oct. 8, 1975.

VENABLE, EMERSON, educator; b. Cin., Dec. 22, 1875; s. William Henry and Mary Ann (Vater) V.; grad. Woodward High Sch., Cin., 1893; B.A., U. Cin., 1898; m. Dolores Cameron, Dec. 24, 1912; 1 dau., Evelyn. Prin., Cin. Summer Sch., 1897; instr. Latin and physics Eclectic Med. Inst., Cin., 1897-1902; librarian and teacher mathematics Ohio Mechanics Inst., 1899-1900; head dept. English, Walnut Hills High Sch., Cin., 1900-34. Lectr., writer on lit. and ednl. topics. Served in Spanish-Am. War, Troop H. 1st Ohio Vol. Cav., 1898; captain Co. X, Cin. Home Guard, 917. Div. Dir. war issues course, S.A.T.C., Ohio Coll. Dental Surgery, 1918. Mem. United Spanish War Veterans, Authors Club (London). Author: A Speculation Regarding Shakespeare, 1905; Poets of Ohio, 1909; The Hamlet Problem and Its Solution, 1912; Scense from the Life of Joan of Arc (with dau.), 1935; The Hamlet Problem and its Solution; An Interpretative Study, 1946, students' edition, 1954; Joan of Arc: A Drama (with daughter), 1956. Editor: The Poems of William Henry Venable, 1925. Presented D.C. Venable meml. collection letters and mss to Ohio State Archaeol. and Hist. Soc., 1931; presented the Golden Book of American American Verse (1800-1925) to U. Cin., 1953. Home: Los Angeles, Cal.†

VENABLE, WILLIAM WEBB, congressman; b. Clinton, Miss., Sept. 25, 1880; s. Dr. R. A. and Fannie A. (Webb) V.; ed. pub. schs.,; m. Gowdyloch Johnston, of Meridian, Miss., Mar. 25, 1914. Served as county atty., Lauderdale Co., Miss.; was dist. atty., 10th Jud. Dist., and judge Circuit Court, same dist.; elected to Congress to serve unexpired term of Hon. S. A. Witherspoon (deceased), 1916-17, and reelected 65th and 66th Congresses (1917-21), 5th Miss. Dist. Democrat. Home: Meridian, Miss.†

VERLENDEN, JACOB SERRILL, business exec.; b. Darby, Pa., mar. 17, 1879; s. William Lane and Mary (Serrill) Verlenden; B.S., Swarthmore Coll., 1899; M. Jean Bell Parker, 1909. Pres. First Nat. Bank, Darby, Pa., 1921-33; pres. Sharon Bldg. Assn., Darby, Pa., 1921-33; pres. Standard-Coosa-Thatcher Co., chmn. bd., from 1933; treas. Verlenden Bros., Inc., Darby, Pa. Home: Landsdowne, Pa.†

VERNADSKY, GEORGE, historian; b. St. Petersburg, Russia, Aug. 20, 1887; s. Vladimir and Natalie (Staritsky) V.; student Moscow (Russia) Fifth Classical Gymnasium, 1899-1905, U. of Moscow, 1905-10; Magister (Equivalent to Ph.D.) of Russian History, U. of St. Petersburg, Russia, 1917; M.A., Yale, 1946; H.H.D. honoris causa, Columbia U., 1959; m. Nina Ilyinsky, Nov. 9, 1908. Came to U.S. 1927, naturalized, 1933. Asst. prof. (privatdocent) U. of St. Petersburg, 1914-17; acting prof. U. of Perm, Russia, 1917-18; prof. U. of Taurida, Simferopol, Crimea, Russia, 1918-20; prof. Russian Sch. Law, Prague, Czechoslovakia, 1922-27; research asso. in history (prof. rank), Yale U., 1927-46; prof. Russian History, Yale, 1946-56, then emeritus; lectr. history, Stanford U., 1931; Harvard U., 1931-32; Columbia U., 1944-45; Henry E. Bourne Lectr., Mather Coll., Western Reserve U., 1945; lectr. history, Johns Hopkins U., summers 1948 and 49, vis. prof. Columbia, spring 1949 and 50. Recipient spl. award Am. Council of Learned Socs., 1958. Fellow Medieval Acad. Am.; mem. Am. Hist. Assn., Am. Oriental Soc., Conn. Acad. Arts and Scis., Am. Assn. Advancement Slavic Studies (hon. life pres. 1965), Societe Asiatique, Paris (France), Mem. Greek Orthodox Ch. Club: Yale (N.Y.C.). Author: Lenin, Red Dictator, 1931; The Russian Revolution, 1932; Political and Diplomatic History of Russia, 1936; Bohdan: Hetman of Ukraine, 1941; Ancient Russia, 1943; Medieval Russian Laws, 1947; Kievan Russia, 1948; The Mongols and Russia, 1953; A History of Russia, 1954, rev. edit., 1969; The Origins of Russia, 1959, reprinted, 1975; Russia at The Dawn of the Modern Age, 1959; Tsardom of Moscow, 1969. Editor: Dictionary of Russian Historical Terms from the Eleventh Century to 1917, 1970; Source Book for Russian History, 3 vols., 1972. Home: New Haven, Conn. Died June 12, 1973; buried Beaverdale Meml. Park, New Haven, Conn.

VERNON, ROBERT ORION, geologist; b. Montevallo, Ala., Mar. 30, 1912; s. William Sturdevant and Marion Virginia (Allen) V.; B.S. Birmingham So. Coll., 1935; M.S., U. Ia., 1938; Ph.D., La. State U., 1942; m. Kathryn Tyler Winters, Sept. 15, 1937; children—Sara Katherine, Judith Anne, Robert Russell, Hilton Scott, Virginea Anthony. Asst. geology U. Ia., 1935-38; geologist Phillips Petroleum Co., summers 1937-38, La. State U., summers 1938-39; research geologist Fla. Geol. Survey, 1938-40, asst. geologist, 1941-43, asso. geologist, 1946-55, asst. dir., 1955-58, dir., state geologist, 1958-71, dir. div. interior resources, 1971-74. Cons. geologist. Served to lt. USNR, World War II. Fellow Geol. Soc. Am. (councillor 1966-68, chmn. Southeastern sect. 1968-69, asso. editor 1969-72); mem. Southeastern Geol. Soc. (pres. 1953), Assn. Am. State Geologists (pres. 1967-68), Am. Assn. Petroleum Geologists, Am. Water Works Assn., Am. Geophys. Union, Am. Inst. Mining and Metall. Engrs., Gulf Coast Assn. Geol. Socs. (pres. 1969), Fla. Well Drillers Contractors Assn. (hon.). Presbyn. Lion (pres. 1953, zone chmn., dep. dist. gov.). Author bulls. in field. Home: Tallahassee, Fla. Died June 19, 1974.

VERRILL, ELMER RUSSELL, educator; b. Wyane, Me., Nov. 5, 1881; s. Millard Filmore and Harriett Blake (Larrabee) V.; grad. Oak Grove Sem., 1901; A.B., Bates Coll. 1906; post-grad. work, U. of Me. and Columbia; m. Abbie E. Burgess, of N. Vassalbore, Me., Aug. 7, 1907; children—Helen M., Clair B., (dec.), Clayton L., Maurice L. (dec.), Ruth, Elmer R., John Alden Margaret (dec.), Donald E. Prin. Island Falls High Sch., 1906-09, Lee Normal Acad., 1909-14, East Maine Conf. Sem., 1914-21, Me. Central Inst., 1921-25, Rockland High Sch., from 1925. Baptist. Home: Rockland, Me.†

VIALL, RICHMOND, mfr. machinery; b. Providence, June 26, 1896; s. William Angell and Harriet Elizabeth (Warner) V.; grad. Phillips Exeter Acad., 1915; student Williams Coll., 1915-17; m. Adelaide M. Brown, Sept. 6, 1919; children—Richmond, William Angell, Adelaide Maybury (Mrs. N.R. Tingley). With Brown & Sharpe Mfg. Co., Providence, 1919—, v.p., sec., dir., 1942—; pres., treas. Marshall & Williams Corp., Providence, 1946-61, chairman of the board, 1961-65; member board of dirs. Plantations Bank of R.I., Providence Washington Ins. Co.; trustee Peoples Savs. Bank. Trustee Rhode Island Sch. Design. Served as lt. Royal Air Force, 1917-19. Mem. Am. Soc. M.E., S.A.R., Soc. Colonial Wars. Republican. Episcopalian. Clubs: Hope, Turks Head (Providence). Home: Providence, R.I., Died July 16, 1973.

VIAUT, ANDRÉ JULES ARMAND, French govt. ofcl.; b. Civry, France, Oct. 16, 1899; s. Armand and Berthe (Tavoillot) V.; B.S. College de Tonnerre (Yonne), 1917; m. Marcelle Moreau, Sept. 21, 1921; 1 son, Michel. Meteorologist, Nat. Meteorol. Bur. France, 1921-28, chief meteorologist, 1928-36, head tech. dept., 1936-42, asst. dir., 1942-44, dir. nat. meteorology, 1944-64. Pres. 6th regional commn. Europe, Internat. Meteorol. Orgn., 1946-51, mem. synoptical and aero commns., 1946-51, 1st v.p., 1947-51; 1st v.p. World Meteorol. Orgn., 1951, pres., 1955-64; chmn. study commn. Global Atlas of Clouds, 1949-56; expert Meteorol. meteorol. div. Internat. Civil Aviation Orgn., 1952-64; mem. Internat. Union Geodesy and Geophysics, 1946-64. Decorated comdr. Order of Cambodia; comdr. Cedar of Lebanon; comdr. Legion d'Honneur (France); comdr. Touristic Merit; recipient Prix Academia des Sciences, Grelaud, 1950, Hirn, 1965; Grand Gold medal Aeroclub France, 1965. Mem. Société Meteo de France (sec. gen. 1946-64), Aeroclub France. Author: du Vol a Voile, 1948; La Mer et le Vent, 1963; Meteorology of the Navigator, 1949; Meteorology, 1942. Home: Meudon, France, Died Aug. 11, 1973.

VILLANI, RALPH A., lawyer; born Elizabeth, New Jersey, September 11, 1901; s. Carmine and Anna (Fontanarosa) V.; LL.B., Syracuse U., 1924; m. Theresa Galante, June 19, 1929; 1 dau., Alyce. Admitted to N.J. bar, 1924 and since practiced in Newark; police magistrate City of Newark, 1933-37, city commr., 1941-49, mayor, 1949-53. Recipient Pilgrim Degree of Merit, L.O.M., 1940, Mem. Griffith Music Found.; Gov. Columbus Hosp. civic, charitable and frat. orgns. K.C., Elk, Eagle, Moose (past gov., pres. N.J. assn., 1934; chief justice supreme Forum, mem. Surpeme Council. Supreme Gov. 1957-58) trustee Moosehaven. Clubs: Newark Athletic, Columbia Civic. Home: Newark, N.J. Died Mar. 1974.

VILLA-REAL, ANTONIO, judge; b. Arayat, Pampanga, P.I., Jan. 17, 1880; s. Luis Enciso and Francisca (Ochangco) Villa-R.; prep. edn. at Manila and Tokyo; grad. Imperial U., Tokyo, 1904; grad. in law, La. Jurisprudencia Sch., Manila, 1909; m. Paz Doronila, of Jaro, Iloilo, Aug. 17, 1917; children—Alicia, Carlos, Interperter and translator, Bur. of Justice, P.I., 1904-10; asst. atty. same, 1910-16; auxiliary judge of First Instance, 1916-20; dist. judge First Instance, 1920-21; assty. gen. P.I., 1921-25; asso. justice Supreme Court of P.I., from Mar. 1925; also professional lecturer on criminology and penology, criminal law, statutory construction, and dir. Practice Court, U. of Philippines and Nat. Univ. Mem. Am. Judicature Soc., Am. Sociol. Soc., Assn. Internat. de Droit Penal. Catholic. Clubs: Filipino, Cosmos, Philippine Columbian. Home: Manila, Philippines.†

VINAL, WILLIAM GOULD, teacher; b. S. Scituate (Norwell), Mass., Nov. 29, 1881; s. William Raymond and Mary Ellen (Farrar) V.; Bridgewater Normal Sch., 1899-1904; S.B., Lawrence Scientific Sch. (Harvard), 1906; A.M., Harvard, 1907; Ph.D., Brown U., 1922; m. Lillie Hale Downing, of Medford, Mass., Dept. 2, 1908; children—Raymond Gould, Meriel HaleHale. Laboratory asst. in botany, Harvard, 1906-07; head dept. biology and geology, Marshall College, Huntington, W.Va., 1907-09; instr. geography, State Normal Sch., Salem, Mass., 1910; prof. nature study, R.I. Coll of Edn., 1911-25; govt. nature guide, Yosemite Nat. Park, 1924; prof. nature study, N.Y. State Coll. of Forestry (Syracuse U.), 1925-27; dir. of Nature Guide School, Western Reserve U., 1928-31, ranger naturalist, Glacier National Park, 1931, Crater Lake Nat. Park, 1933. Granted leave as nature specialist Nat. Recreation Assn. to hold insts. in nature recreation for leaders in principal cities, 1936-37. Assistant biologist, Masssachusetts Fish and Game Commission, summers, 1907-13, Dir. Camp Chequesset for Girls, 1914-26; founder, and dir. Nature-lore School for Nature Counsellors, 1920-26. Prof. nature Edn. Sch. of Edn. Western Reserve Univ., 1927-37; dir. Nature Guide Sch. and prof. Nature Edn., Mass. State Coll., from 1937. Fellow A.A.A.S., 1933. Author: Guide for Laboratory and Field Studies in Botany, 1910; Camp and Field Notebook (Comstock and Vinal); Nature Guiding, 1927; Nature Almanac, 1927; Naturalist Diary, 1930, Lecturer on biol. subjects. Home: Amherst, Mass.†

VINAVER, CHEMJO, musician; b. Warsaw, Poland, July 10, 1900; pupil H. Ruedel, S. Ochs, Berlin, Germany; m. Mascha Kaleko. Debut State Acad. Music, Berlin, 1926; dir. Hanigun choir; concert tour, Europe, Palestine, 1934-35; dir. Vinaver chorus, 1935-38; concerts U.S.A., 1938-54; editor Anthology of Jewish Music, 1954. Compositions include The Seventh Day, 1946; Oratorio Shabbat, 1957; Chassidic Cantata, 1967. Contbr. articles mags., newspapers. Address: Jerusalem, Israel. Died Dec. 12, 1973.

VIOLETTE, EBAL E., clergyman, traveler, writer; b. nr. Jacksonville, Ill., Feb. 17, 1880; s. Leroy and Sarah Mitilda (Lee) V.; ed. North Prairie Sem., rn. Winchester, Ill., and abroad 2 yrs.; D. Litt., Canton U., 1903; LL.D., Transylvania Coll., Lexington, Ky., 1930; m. Hazel Dove Bonnell, of Loveland, Colo., Sept. 29, 1904. Ordained Christian (Disciples) ministry, 1899; pastor Whitehall, Ill., 1899, Roseville, 1900-01, Loveland, Colo., 1901-04, Shelbyville, Tenn., 1904-06; gen. evangelistic work, traveling, writing, lecturing, 1906-18; pastor Independence Boul. Ch., Kansas City, Mo., 1918, Central Ch., Kansas City, from Sept. 1919. Dir. speakers' bur. 10th Federl Reserve Dist., during World War, 1917-18. Republican. Clubs: City, Knife and Fork (Kansas City); Mo. Athletic (St. Louis); Los Angeles (Calif.) Country; Hellenic Travellers' (London). Author: Training for Soul-Winning, 1915; My Pledge to America, 1917; in Palestine with the 23d Psalm, 1918; Vanitas Vanitatis, 1918; In Palestine at the Empty Tomb, 1920; The Uncanny Abner Wiseman, 1920; Nature of Contents of Bible Books, 1916; Notes on Moffat's New Testament, 1923; In Palestine on the Shores of Galilee, 1924; Myra-of-the-Mountains, 1924; Night on the River Styx and Other Poems, 1924; Paul Temperli and Other Orations, 1925; The Goal of History, 1926; The Evolution of Peace, 1926; Memory and Self-Education, 1927; Palestine Across the Ages, 1929; Twilight in God's Acre, 1930; The Days With God, 1930; Meditations on Growing Old, 1931; Pen Portraits of World Wonders, 1931; Interviews with Great Men and Women, 1931; Sketches From a Traveller's Diary,1933; Romance and Lineage of the American Presidency, 1934; Auto-biography of an Average American, 1935. Contbr. on internat. politics. Traveled extensively in Europe, Asia, Africa and the Arcitc regions; made tour of the Far East, spring and summer 1921, as newspaper corr. Address: Loveland, Colo.†

VIPOND, KENNETH C(LINTON), govt. ofcl.; b. Montreal, Can., Mar. 16, 1880; s. Benjamin Salkeld and Rosana Selina (Parent) V.; came to U.S., 1881, naturalized 1901; ed. Troy (N.H.) pub. schs., 1877-95, Troy Bus. Sch., 1895-97. Pvt. bus., 1897-04; with U.S. Civil Service Commn., Washington, 1904-51, asst. chief examiner, 1921-49, assistant executive director, 1949-51, retired 1951; general chairman coms. on hours of labor, annual and sick leave of Fed. employees, 1936; 1 of 3 mems. of 1st com. on deferment of Fed. employees under Selective Service Act, 1943-44; mem. Fed. Personnel Council from 1940; later nat. mem. Bd. Examiners to Fgn. Service of U.S. Dept. of State, from 1946. Mem. Soc. for Personnel Adminstrn., Civil Service Assembly of U.S. and Can. Republican. Methodist. Republican. Methodist. Home: Washington, D.C.†

VIRTANEN, ARTTURI ILMARI, educator; b. Helsinki, Finland, Jan. 15, 1895; s. Kaarlo and Serafiina (Isotalo) V.; grad. Classical Lyceum, Viipuri, 1913; M.Sc., U. Helsinki, 1916, Ph.D., 1919; Dr. Medicine honoris causa, U. Lund, 1936; Dr. honoris causa, Royal Tech. Coll., Stockholm 1949; Finland Inst. Tech., 1949, U. Paris, 1952; Dr. Agr., U. Justus-Liebig, Giessen, 1955; Dr. Agr. and Forestry, U. of Helsinki, 1955; m. Lilja Moisio, Feb. 29, 1920; children—Kaarlo Ilmari, Artturi Olavi. First asst. Central Lab. of Industry, 1916-17; chem. asst. state butter and cheese control sta., 1919; chemist lab. Butter Export Assn., Valio, 1919-20, dir. since 1921; dir. Biochem. Research Inst. (including lab. Valio and lab. Found. for Chem. Research) 1931-73; docent chemistry U. Helsinki, 1924-39; prof. biochemistry Finland Inst. Tech., 1931-39; prof. biochemistry U. Helsinki, 1939-48; mem. and pres. Acad. Finland, 1948-65. Mem. Editorial staff Karjantuote, 1924-73, Suomen Kemistilehti, 1928-73, Enzymologia, 1936-73, Acta Physiologia Scandinavica, 1940-73, Annales Scientiarum Fennicae Series Chemica, 1945-73, Acta Chemica Scandinavica, 1946-73, Annales Medicinae Experimentalis et Biologiae Fenniae, 1947-73, Acta Endocrinologica, 1948-73, Plant and Soil, 1948-73. Mem. state com. on popular nutrition, 1936-40, state com. on prodn., 1940-42; rep. of Finland, League of Nations com. on nutrition, 1938; mem. com. chem. industry, 1942-73; expert of Ministry of Supply, 1942-44. Decorated Scheele medal Swedish Chem. Soc., 1938; Adelsköld medal Swedish Acad. Scis., 1943; Prize of Honor, Fund of Wihuri, 1943; Nobel Prize for chemistry, 1945; Golden Plaque of Mjolkpropagandan, Stockholm, 1946; Plaque of Finnish Tech. Soc., 1946; Great Medal of U. Ghent, 1946; Gadolin-Medal of Finnish Chem. Soc., 1949, Kairamo-Medal of Societas Zoologica Botanica Fennica Vanamo, 1950; comdr. 2d class Order White Rose of Finland, 1943; Cross of Liberty 2d class, 1945; Comdr. 1st class Order Lion of Finland, 1945; Comdr. 1st class Royal Order of Danebrog (Denmark), 1951; Grand Cross Civil Order Agrl. Merits (Spain), 1951; Emanuele Paternó medal of Societa Chimica Italiana, 1957; medal of University of Pavia, 1957, U. Helsinki, 1960, Faber Foundation, 1964, Friesland Prize, Holland, 1967, W. O. Atwater Meml. lectr. and prize, 1968, Siegfried Thannhauser medal, 1969, honor diploma Associazione Italiana per il Progresso dell' Industria dell' Latte, 1969, golden cross and fgn. mem. Order pour le Merite für Wissen Schaften und Künste, Bonn, 1971, Golden Egg, Italy, 1973; 1st Fundacion F. Cuenca Villoro lectr., prize and gold medal, 1972. Fellow A.A.A.S.; mem. Nat. Acad. Scis., European Nutritionists, Am. Soc. Microbiology, German Acad. Leopoldina, Am. Soc. Biol. Chemists (hon.), German Soc. Nutrition, Finnish Acad. Sciences (chairman 1944-45), Swedish Acad. Agrl., Brit. Assn. Advancement, Finnish Acad. Agr., Royal Sci. Soc. Uppsala, Royal Sci. Acad. Sweden, Swedish Acad. Engring. Sci., Pontifical Acad. Sci., U.S. Nat. Acad. Scis., hon. mem. Finnish Chem. Soc., Finnish Soc. Dairy Sci., Sci. Agr. Soc. Finland, Finnish Soc. Agronomists, Finnish Econ. Soc., Austrian Chem. Soc., Viipuri Student Union, Biochem. Soc. Stockholm, Finnish Med. Soc. Duodecim, Finnish Tech. Soc., Central Assn. Chemists (bd. and working com.), Royal Soc. Edinburgh, Am. Inst. Nutrition, Academia Pugliese delle Scienze, Bari Italia, Higher Council Sci. Research, Madrid (hon. councillor). German Soc. for Quality Research. Finnish Acad. Scis. Author: Cattle Fodder and Human Nutriton, 1938; AIV System as the Basis of Cattle Feeding, 1943. Contbr. articles to tech. jours. Address: Helsinki, Finland. Died Nov. 11, 1973.

VISCONTI, LUCHINO, motion picture dir.; b. Milan, Italy, Nov. 2, 1906. Set designer asst. to Jean Renoir in France for prodns. Une Partie de campagne, 1935; Le bas-fonds; dir. first film in Italy, Obsession, 1941; returned to set designing for Teatro Eliseo, Rome, Italy, until 1941; recent prodns. include La terra Trema, 1948; Bellissima, 1951; Siamo donne, Senso, 1955; Le notti blanche, 1957; Rocco and His Brothers, 1961; Boccacio '70 (one sketch), 1961; The Leopard, 1962; Vaghe Stella del Orsa; Streghe; Lo Straniero; The Damned; Death in Venice, 1971; Conversation Piece; also dir. ballets. Address: Rome, Italy. Died Mar. 17, 1976.

VISHNIAC, WOLF VLADIMIR, educator, biologist; b. Berlin, Germany, May 20, 1922; s. Roman and Lea (Bagg) V.; came to U.S., 1940, naturalized, 1946; A.B., Bklyn. Coll., 1945; M.S., Washington U., St. Louis, 1946; Ph.D., Stanford, 1949; m. Helen Frances Simpson, Aug. 18, 1951; children—David Obadiah (dec.), Ethan Tecumseh, Ephraim Meriwether. USPHS fellow biochemistry N.Y. U. Sch. Medicine, 1949-52; asst. prof., then asso. prof. microbiology Yale Sch. Medicine, 1942-61; prof. biology U. Rochester, 1961-73, chmn. dept., 1965-69; asso. dir. Space Sci. Center, 1966-71. CONS. NASA, Nat. Acad. Scis.; chmn. life sci. working group mem. exec. com. COSPAR; lectr. USSR Acad. Scis., 1969; Am. Chem. Soc. lectr., 1969, 72; Microbiology Found. lectr., 1972. Del. Conn. Democratic Convs., 1958. Recipient Distinguished Alumnus award Bklyn. Coll., 1970, Apollo Achievement award NASA, 1970, Lunar Quarantine Operations award NASA, 1971. Fellow A.A.A.S.; mem. Am. Soc. Microbiology, Rochester Acad. Scis. (hon.), Soc. Gen. Microbiology, Am. Soc. Biol. Chemists. Mem. editorial bd. jours. in field. Research on photosynthesis, bacterial physiology, devel. instruments for exobiology, Antarctic soil microbiology. Home: Rochester, N.Y., Died Dec. 10, 1973.

VITETTL, LEONARDO, govt. ofcl. Italy; b. Locri, Italy, Dec. 15, 1894; s. Ernesto Vitetti and Jemma Carmelita; J.D., U. Rome, 1922; m. Natalie Mai Coe, May 19, 1934; 1 son, Ernesto Guglielmo. Entered diplomatic service, 1923; 1st sec. Italian Embassy, Washington, 1925-31; mem. Italian delegation League Nations, also agt. Italian Govt. to Internat. Ct. Justice, 1931-32; mem. Italian delegation Disarmament Conf., Geneva, Naval Conf., London, 1933; counsellor Italian Embassy, London, 1933-36; minister plenipotentiary, dir. legal and cultural affairs Italian Fgn. Office, 1936-43; Italian del. FAO Assembly, 1949, UN Assembly and Trusteeship Council, 1950-51; ambassador-at-large, 1952-55; adviser Ministry Fgn. Affairs, Italian permanent del. Orgn. European Econ. Coop., Paris, 1955; Italian permanent representative to UN, 1956-73; ambassador to France, 1958-73. Decorated Knight of Malta, Knight Comdr. Order St. Maurice and Lazarus, Knight Great Cross Order of Merit, Knight Great Cross Order Crown of Italy; Knight Great Cross Order St. Gregory and Holy Sepulchre (Holy See); Knight Great Cross Order of Isabelle (Spain); Order of Christ (Portugal); Knight Great Cross Order Polar Star (Sweden); Knight Comdr. Order Rising Sun (Japan); Knight Cmdr. Order Leopold I (Belgium) Knight Commander Legion d'Honneur (France). Clubs: Knickerbocker (N.Y.C.); Piping Rock (Locust Valley, N.Y.); Circolo della Caccia, Polo (Rome). Home: Rome, Italy. Died May 1973.

VOEGTLIN, CARL, pharmacologist; b. Switzerland, July 28, 1879; s. Carl V.; ed. univs. of Basel, Munich, Geneva and Freiburg; Ph.D., Freiburg, 1903; studied Victoria U., Manchester, Eng., 1903-04; D.Sc., Rochester, 1947; m. Lillian Kreuter, December 21, 1912; 1 son, Hugh Stewart. Instructor chemistry, University of Wisconsin, 1905; assistant in med.; associate and asso associate prof. pharmacology, Johns Hopkins Med. Sch., 1906-13; chief Div. of Pharmacology, Nat. inst. of Health, U.S.P.H.S., 1913-39; chief Nat. Cancer inst., 1938-42; lecturer in pharmacol. U. of Rochester, Med. Sch. from 1943, now sr. consultant in cancer research. toxicology; cons. Manhattan Dist. Herter lecturer N.Y. U. Med. Coll., 1938, Barnard Hosp., 40. Research. in physiol. and pathology of nutrition, beri beri, pellagra, function of the parathyroid gland, pharmacol. action of serum preservatives, anaphylaxis, cancer, indsl. poisoning, chemotherapy, biol. oxidation-reduction, etc. Mem. com. in drug addiction Nat. Research Council. Mem. A.M.A., Am. Chem. Soc., A.A.A.S., Soc. Biol. Chemists, Am. Physiol. Soc., Soc. Pharmacology and Exptl. Therapeutics (pres 1927-30), Am. Fed. for Exptl. Biology (chmn. 1928), Acad. Sciences (Washington), Clinico-Pathol. Soc. Washington, Harvey Soc., Phi Beta Kappa, Sigma Xi. Mem. o!1st, 2d Internat. Conf. for Biol. Standardization of Drugs, Edinburgh and Geneva, Permanent Commn. on Biol. Standardization of League of Nations, Acad. of Med. of Washington, D.C., (pres. 1938-40), Soc. Exptl. Biology and Medicine, Am. Assn. Cancer Research (pres. 1941), m. Soc. for the Control of Cancer (dir.) Club: Chevy Chase. Home: Washington, D.C.†

VOGEL, EDWIN CHESTER, born New York City, Sept. 21, 1883; s. Heyman and Mathilda (Sherrick) V.; B.A., Columbia, 1904; LL.B., N.Y. Law Sch., 1906; m. Florence Goldman, Apr. 19, 1911; 1 dau., Betsy (Mrs. Evans), Admitted to N.Y. bar, 1906, practiced N.Y.C. until 1918; dir. C.I.T. Financial Corp. Trustee, mem. exec. com. Mt. Sinai Hosp.; hon. chmn. bd. United Hosp. Fund of N.Y.C.; past dir. Greater N.Y. Fund, Mem. Columbia Coll. Council. Served as capt., ordnance dept., U.S. Army, World War I. Mem. Bar Assn. City N.Y. Clubs: Century Country (White Plains, N.Y.); Columbia U., Harmonie (N.Y.C.). Home: New York City, N.Y. Died May 1973.

VOGELER, RUDOLF FREDERICK, univ. adminstr.; b. N.Y.C., Sept. 29, 1902; s. Rudolf and Martha (Kaiser) V.; student Cornell U., 1921-24, Ithaca Coll., 1924-26; A.B., U. Neb., 1928, M.A., 1930; m. Alice Elziabeth Leslie, Jan. 25, 1930; children—Martha (Mrs. Howard Adler), Gretchen (Mrs. John Pennybacker), Susan (Mrs. James Heerin), Alice (Mrs. Richard Meyer). Dir. intramural athletics U. Neb., 1926-33; with USES, 1933-42, dir. Phila. area War Manpower Commn., 1942-43; mgr. indsl. council, exec. dir. Phila. C. of C., 1943-56; asst. to pres., v.p. devel. also v.p. for student affairs Drexel U., 1956-69, asso. prof. bus. adminstrn., 1956-69. Arbitrator, Am. Arbitration Assn., 1950; mem. appeals com. NWLB, 1946, regional Wage Stblzn. Bd., 1950; sec. Nat. Invest in Am. Council, 1950. Bd. dirs. Phila. council Girl Scout U.S.A., 1962-65; trustee Ardmore Library. Mem. Sigma Xi, Delta Sigma Phi. Republican. Presbyn. Mason. Contbr. to profl. jours. Home: Wynnewood, Pa. Died June 18, 1974.

VOGT, HENRY F., business exec.; b. Milwaukee, Wis., Nov. 24, 1879; s. Henry A. F. and Helene (Devere) V.; ed. pub. schs.; m. Abbie M. Scofield; children—Janet V. Lowry, Margaret V. Rose, Lucile V. Coerper. Started as timekeeper and cost clk. Cutler-Hammer, Inc., 1900, advanced through various offices and became chief accountant, 1905, became aduitor, asst. treas., office mgr. and comptorller, 1920, dir., 1920, treas., 1928, v.p. and treas., 1931, 1934 v.p. operations, vice pres. and treas., 1934, chmn. board, form 1947; dir. Louis Allis Co., Safway Steel Products Co., Globe Union, Inc., Koehring Co., Marine Nat. Exchange Bank Clubs: Milwaukee, Milwaukee Country, University, Electrical Manufacturers. Home: Milwaukee, Wis.†

VOGT, PAUL LEROY, sociologist; b. Upper Sandusky, Ol, May 28, 1878; s. William Allen and Sarah Jane (Ewart) V.; A.B., Ohio Northern U., Ada, 1901; A.B., Butler Coll., Indianapolis, 1903; A.B., U. of Chicago, 1903; studied Columbia, 1904-06; Ph.D., U. of Pa., 1907; m. Caroline Ada Pennell, of Lima, O., 1905. With bur. of advice and information, New York Charity Orgn. Soc., 1907-08; spl. agt. U.S. Bur. Labor and of Corpns., 1908-09; prof. economics, State Coll. of Wash., 1909-11; prof. sociology, Miami U., 1911-15; prof. and head dept. rural economics, Ohio State U., 1915-17; supt. rural work, Bd. of Home Missions and Ch. Extension M.E. Ch., from 1917. Pres. social welfare sect. Ohio State Charities Assn., 1912-14. Mem. Am. Econ. Assn., Am. Sociol. Soc., Am. Country Life Assn., Delta Tau Delta. Democrat. ethodist. Mason. Author: The Sugar Refining Industry in United States, 1908; Introduction to Rural Sociology, 1918; The Church Coöperating in Community Life, 1921; also various brochures, articles, etc., on sociol. topics. Home: Lima, O.†

VOLZ, EDWARD J., labor union ofcl.; b. Cin., Aug. 22, 1879; s. Nicholas and Gertrude (Roth) V.; student pub. schs. on Cin.; m. Winifred Flannery, July 16, 1913. Local pres. N.Y. Photo Engravers Union, 1916-28; pres. Internat. Photo Engravers Union, from 1929. Home: Mt. Vernon, N.Y.†

VONDER HAAR, EDWARD P., univ. ofcl.; b. Hamilton, O., Nov. 3, 1908; s. Edward J. and Mary Gertrude (Brown) Vonder Haar; B.A., Xavier U., 1931. Alumni sec. Xavier U., 1932-47, news bur. mgr., 1932-42, bus. mgr. athletics 1940-47, editor, 1942-48, dir. pub. relations, 1942-46, asst. to pres., 1946-66, v.p. for pub. relations and devel., 1966. Trustee Found. Pub. Relations Edn. and Research. Mem. Am. Coll. Pub. Relations Assn. (pres.). Pub. Relations Soc. Am. (pres. Cin. chpt.). Pub. Relations Soc. Am. (dir. 1960-63, 66-69, pres. 1968), Internat. Pub. Relations Association, Soc. Colonial Wars, S.A.R. Clubs: Cincinnati, Cuvier Press. Home: Cincinnati, Ohio. Died Oct. 1, 1973; interred St. Mary Cemetery, Hamilton, Ohio.

VON DER HEYDE, MATTHEW JENNINGS, investment counsel; b. N.Y.C., July 22, 1906; s. Ernst and Abbey (Jennings) von der H.; A.B., Columbia, 1928, student Grad. Sch. Bus., 1928-29; student N.Y.U. Grad. Sch. Bus., 1939-41; m. Camilla Cowan, Aug. 9, 1934; children—Sarah, Abby, Jane. With Douglas T. Johnston & Co., Inc., N.Y.C., 1936-74, v.p., 1945-61, pres., 1961-68, chmn., dir., 1968-74; with Johnston Mut. Fund Inc., N.Y.C., 1947, pres., 1956-68, chmn., 1968-74; also dir. Bd. dirs. Knapp Fund Charitable. Served lt. comdr. USNR, 1942-46. Mem. N.Y. Soc. Security Analysts, Investment Counsel Assn. Am. (gov.), Ex-Mens. Assn. Squadron A. Clubs: Columbia Univ. (N.Y.C.); New Canaan Country; Norwalk Yacht. Home: New Canaan, Conn. Died June 8, 1974.

VON DEWALL, HANS WERNER, mining co. exec.; b. Celle, Germany, Sept. 14, 1901; s. Hans and Emmy (Mertens) von D.; student Berlin Tech. High Sch., 1920-25; Dr.Ing., Berlin, 1927; Dipl.Ing., 1925; m. Ursula Weigel, May 9, 1940; children—Hans, Anne. Mines ofcl. Prussian Ministry for Trade and Commerce, 1928-32; with Bergwerksgesellschaft Hibernia, Herne, 1932-33; with Bergrevier, Duisburg, 1934; mining dir. Saargruben A.G., 1935-40; head, tech. dir. Oberschlesien Mining Adminstrn., 1940-45; mining dir., mem. Bd. Hibernia, 1948-68, chmn., 1966-69; mem. Bd. VEBA AG, 1965-68. Mem. German del. European High Commn. for Coal and Steel, 1950-51. Decorated chevalier de la Légion d'Honneur. Home: Essen-Werden, Federal Republic of Germany., Died 1974.

VON ENGELKEN, FRIEDRICH JOHANNES HUGO, b. Schleswig-Holstein, Germany, Apr. 26, 1881; s. Lousi H. and Emilie (Döderlein) V.; grad. high sch. Winona, Minn., 1899; m. Lonisiana Breckinridge Hart Gibson, of Lexington, Ky., Feb. 2, 1906. Represented State of Fla. on Am. Commn. for the Study of Rural Credits in Europe, 1913,and co-author, with Gordon Jones, of Denver, Colo., of the minority report of the commn.; dir. of the Mint, Sept. 20, 1916-Feb.20, 1917; pres. Federal Land Banks, Columbia, S.C., by appmt. of Pres. Wilson, Feb. 21, 1917-Apr. 1918; resigned to assist in promotion of sale of farm loan bonds. Author of "The German Farmer and Cooperation" (Senate Doc. 201, 63d Congress). Home: U1Columbia S.C.†

VON ENGELN, OSKAR DEITRICH, geologist, geographer; b. Dayton, O., July 3, 1880; s. Dietrich and Elizabeth (Adam) von E.; A.B., Cornell U., 1908, Ph.D., 1911; m. Maude Graham Hewitt, Sept. 7, 1910. Asst. instr. in dynamic geology, Carnell U., 1905-07, instr. in physical geography, 1907-19, assistant professor, 1919-21, professor, 1921-39, professor geology, 1939-49, emeritus (chmn. dept. from 1944); chief examiner in physicial geography, coll. entrance examination bd., 1923-36; mem. U.S. Geol. Survey Expdn. to Alaska, 1906, Nat. Geog. Soc. Expdn. to Alaska, 1909; scientific expert N.Y. State Geol. Survey, 1922. Del. from Cornell University to the Centennial of the Geological Society of France, 1930; from U.S. Department State and National Research Council to Internat. Geological Congress, Warsaw, 1934; travel, West Indies and South America, 1919; round the world, 1929-30; Scandinavia, 1934; Mexico, 1936; mem. Internat. Commn. of Snow since 1937; Bownocker Lectures Geology, Ohio State Univ., 1943. Awarded Barnes Shakespeare prize. 1905, Walker Natural History FelFellow Am. Assn. Advancement of Sci., Assn. Am. Geographers, Geol. Soc. Am.; Am. Geog. Soc., Sigma Xi,Sigma Phi Epsilon, hon. mem. Sigma Gamma Epsilon. Author: (with R.S. Tarr) La. Manual of Phys. and Comml. Geog., 1910, revised edition, 1932; Dynamic Geology, 1913; Concerning Cornell, 1917; Inheriting the Earth, 1922; (with J. McK. Urquhart) Story Key to Geographical Names, 1924; (wtih R. S. Tarr) New Physical Geography, rev., 1926; Geomorphology, 1942; Geology (with K. E. Caster), 1951. Contributor articles to scientific jours. Home: Ithaca, N.Y.†

VON MINDEN, WILLIAM JOHN, accountant; b. Secaucus, N.J., Aug. 31, 1901; s. William and Elizabeth (Kane) von M.; B.C.S., N.Y.U., 1926, M.C.S., 1932; m. Helen A. Jersey, Sept. 8, 1927; children—Ann (Mrs. Kjell Kosberg), William H., Martha. Asst. to treas. J. C. Penny-Gwinn Corp., 1926-31; lectr. finance Sch. Commerce N.Y.U., 1929-38; sr. accountant Joseph E. Freund & Co., accountants and auditors, N.Y.C., 1931-34, partner, 1934-37; partner William J. von Minden & Co., C.P.A.'s, N.Y.C., 1937-47; asso. prof. accounting Sch. Bus. Adminstrn., U. Newark, 1938-42, prof., chmn. dept. accounting, 1942-46; prof., chmn. dept. accounting Sch. Bus. Adminstrn., Rutgers U., 1946-73; dir. Grad. Sch. Pub. Accounting, 1956-73, partner von Minden & Bruneau, C.P.A.'s, Ridgewood, N.J. and N.Y.C., 1947-73. Mem. bd. edn., Saddle River, N.J., 1942-56. Trustee Mills Coll. Edn., N.Y.C., 1938-53; trustee, mem. finance com. Internat. Soc. Christian Endeavor, 1928. Mem. Am. Inst. C.P.A.'s (council and trial bd.), Am. Accounting Assn., Am. Mgmt. Assn., N.J. (past pres.), N.Y. State socs. C.P.A.'s, Nat. Assn. Accountants, Controllers Inst. Am. (asso.), Accountants Club Am., Beta Gamma Sigma, Delta Sigma Pi, Beta Alpha Psi. Mem. Reformed Church in America. Mason. Club: Downtown (Newark). Author: (with D. D. Kennedy and George R. Esterly) Principles of Accounting, 1940; (with same) Introductory Accounting, 1942. Home: Saddle River, N.J. Died May 15, 1973.

VON MISES, LUDWIG EDLER, economist; b. Lemberg, Austria, Sept. 29, 1881; s. Arthur Edler and Adele (Landau) von M.; Dr. in Canon and Roman Law, U. Vienna, Feb. 20, 1906; m. Margit Sereny, July 6, 1938. Came to U.S., 1940, naturalized, 1946. Econ. advisor Austrian C. of C., Vienna, 1909-34; prof. econs. U. Vienna, 1913-38; founder, exec. v.p. Austrian Inst. Bus. Cycle Research, Vienna, 1926-38; prof. internat. econ. relations Grad. Inst. Internat. Studies, Geneva, Switzerland, 1934-40; vis. prof. Nat. U. Mexico, 1942, N.Y.U. 1945-69. Author: The Theory of Money and Credit, 1912; Socialism, 1922; Omnipotent Government, 1944; Bureaucracy, 1944; Human Action, A Treatise on Economics, 1949, Planning for Freedom, 1952; The Anticapitalistic Mentality. 1956; Theory and History, 1957; The Ultimate Foundation of Economic Science, 1962; others. Home: New York City N.Y. Died Oct. 10, 1973; interred Ferncliff Cemetery, Hartsdale, N.Y.

VON SALLMANN, LUDWIG, physician; b. Vienna, Austria, June 8, 1892; s. Ludwig and Josephine (Scheid) Von S.; M.D., U. Vienna, 1919; Dr.(hon.), U. Aix, Marseille, 1952; m. Henriette Sommerman, Mar. 28, 1929. Attending ophthalmologist U. Vienna, 1923-30, docent for ophthalmology, 1931-38; asso. prof. ophthalmology, head dept. Med. Sch., Peking Union, 1930-31; head eye dept. Empress Elizabeth Hosp., Vienna, 1939; dir. lab. Herman Knapp Eye Hosp., N.Y.C., 1939; research asso. dept. ophthalmology Columbia Coll. Phys. and Surg., 1940-41, asst. prof. to prof., 1941-46, head research dept., 1946-55; asst. attending ophthalmologist Vanderbilt Eye Clinic, Presbyn. Hosp., N.Y.C., 1941-45, asso. attending, 1946-55, attending ophthalmologist, 1955-56; vis. sci. Nat. Inst. Neurol. Diseases and Blindness, Nat. Insts. Health. Bethesda, Md., 1955-56, chief ophthalmology br., 1956-70, sr. research neurophysiologist, 1970-75. Recipient Proctor medal, 1951; Braille award Soc. Prevention of Blindness, 1959; Superior Service award U.S. Dept. Health, Edn. and Welfare, 1968; award Internat. Com. for Eye Research, 1972. Mem. Am., Greek ophthalmological socs., Pan-Am. Assn. ophthalmology, Assn. Research in Ophthalmology (hon.; Lucien Howe medal), Am. Acad. Ophthalmology and Otolaryngology, A.A.A.S., N.Y. Med. Soc., A.M.A., N.Y. Acad. Scis. Home: Bethesda, Md. Died Sept. 24, 1975; interred Vienna, Austria.

VOORHEES, BOYNTON STEPHEN, railroad exec.; b. Hackensack, N.J., Apr. 29, 1886; s. Edwin Walton and Matilda (Paulison) V.; Ph.B., Yale, 1907; m. Marjorie D. Crandall, July 16, 1912; 1 son, Darrell Graham. Rodman, insp. maintenance of way dept. N.Y.,

N.H. & H. R.R., 1907-08; rodman, instrumentman, insp. constrn. dept. N.Y.C. R.R. System, 1908-12, asst. engr. grade crossings, engring. dept., 1912-16, engr. grade crossings, 1916-20, dist. engr. eastern div., 1920, gen. office engr., 1920-24, engring. asst. to v.p., 1924-42, asst. v.p., 1942-48, v.p., 1949-53, ret.; asst. to chmn. bd. dirs. Am. Ry. Car Inst., N.Y.C., since 1953. Mem. Yale Engring. Assn., Am. Ry. Engring. Assn., Am. Soc. C.E Clubs: Yale, Railroad (N.Y.C.). Home: Yonkers, N.Y. Died July 14, 1973.

VOORHEES, MELVIN HAROLD, newspaper pub.; b. Marysville, Kan., Feb. 17, 1880; s. James Rockefeller and Martha (Bailey) V.; ed. pub. schs.; m. Ora. Belle Smith, July 14, 1901; children; Melvin B., Elsie Jane. Advertising dir. Seattle (Wash.) Star, 1905-06; founder, 1906, pub. until 1901, Portland (Ore.) News; gen. mgr. Seattle Star, 1910-13; founder, 1913, and pub., Mont.. Mag.; gen. mgr. Tacoma (Wash.) Times (mem. Scripps League of Newspapers), 1919-34; served as pres. same and Tacoma Times Pub. Co.; gen. mgr. Dallas (Tex.) Dispatch, Boise (Ida.) Capital News. San Luis Obispo (Calif.) Telegram, Provo (Utah) Herald, Logan (Utah) Herald, 1934-38. Club: Fircrest Golf and Country. Home: Seattle, Wash.†

VOORHEES, TRACY S., lawyer; b. New Brunswick, N.J., June 30, 1890; s. John Schenck and Mary Hinman (Stebbins) V.; A.B., Rutgers U., 1911, A.M., 1914; LL.B., Columbia Law Sch., 1915; LL.D., Rutgers U., 1950; m. Josephine Ludlow Palmer, Dec. 19, 1918; children—Mrs. Mary Van Wilson, John Schenck. Admitted to N.J. bar, 1915, N.Y. bar, 1918; asso., firm Satterlee, Canfield & Stone, N.Y., 1917; asst. to dir., Bur. of Imports, War Trade Bd., 1918; practicing atty. as mem. of firms, Ewing, Alley & Voorhees and Ewing & Voorhees, 1919-28; mem. firm Blake & Voorhees 1939-42. Served as col. AUS, 1942-46; spl. asst. to Sec. War, 1946-47; War Dept. Food Adminstr. for Occupied Areas, 1947-48; Asst. Sec. Army, 1948-49; Under-Sec. Army, 1949-50; vice chmn. com. on present danger, 1951-53; L.I. Transit Authority, 1951-54; Def. Adv. to U.S. Mission to NATO with rank of minister and dir. offshore procurement in Europe for sec. of def., 1953-54; cons. to sec. of def., 1954-61; the President's rep. Hungarian refugee affairs and chmn. President's Com. for Hungarian Refugee Relief, 1956-57; Pres.' Personal Rep. for Cuban Refugees, 1960-61. Bd. regents L.I. Coll. Hosp., Bklyn., 1932-48, pres. bd., 1938-43, and 1945-48; trustee Rutgers U., 1942-43, 1947, bd. govs., 1957-65, vice chmn., 1959-65. Recipient Rutgers U. award, 1941; Park Assn. (N.Y. City), Citation of Merit, 1942; D.S.M. (Army), 1946; Dept. Army Distinguished Civilian Service award, 1959; Department Def. award for Distinguished Pub. Service, 1960; Alumni Trustee award Rutgers U., 1971, section of Queens Campus of Rutgers U. designated Voorhees Campus, 1974. Mem. Beta Theta Pi, Phi Beta Kappa. Home: Brooklyn, N.Y. Died Sept. 25, 1974.

VORBERG, MARTIN PHILIP, business cons.; b. Rochester, N.Y., Sept. 12, 1901; s. Rev. Robert T. and Salome A. (Ungerer) V.; student Marietta Coll., 1919-22; m. Mildred E. Johnson, May 23, 1927; 1 dau., Mary M. (Mrs. Alan W. Joslyn, Jr.). Mgr., Ford agy., Marietta, O., 1922-28; mgr. Logan TO Co., Parkersburg, W.Va., 1928-31; asst. sales promotion mgr. Oldsmobile div. Gen. Motors Corp., Lansing, Mich., 1931-33, sales promotion mgr., 1933-39; account exec. Stirling Gitchell Advt., Detroit, 1939-42; mgr. Compton Advt., Inc., 1945-46; v.p., dir., gen. sales mgr. Ia. Ford Tractor Co., Des Moines, 1947-52; pres., treas., dir. United-Hagie Hybirds, Inc., 1952-68; bus. cons., Marietta, O., 1969-73. Bd. fellows Marietta Coll.; mem. adv. bd. Salvation Army. Served from maj. to lt. col. Ordnance Dept., AUS, 1942-46. Mem. Alpha Tau Omega. Epsicopalian. Clubs: Des Moines, Parkersburg Country. Home: Marietta, O. Died Aug. 22, 1973.

VORWALD, ARTHUR JOHN, physician, ret. educator; b. Dubuque, Ia., Apr. 12, 1904; s. Dr. Theodore Francis and Rose (Wilkey) V.; B.A., Columbia Coll., Dubuque, Ia., 1925; M.D., U. Chgo., 1931, Ph.D. in Pathology, 1932, D.Sc. (hon.), Hobart and William Smith Colls., 1949; LL.D., Loras Coll., Dubuque, 1950; m. Madeleine Foeller, June 22, 1931. Asst. pathology U. Chgo., 1928-31, instr. pathology, 1931-32; intern Presbyn. Hosp., Chgo., 1932, Henry Ford Hosp., Detroit, 1932-33; fellow NRC, Cambridge U., Eng., 1933-34; lectr. and pathologist Trudeau Sch., 1934-42; dir. Edward L. Trudeau Found. and Saranac Lab., Saranac Lake, N.Y., 1947-54, dir. silicosis and beryllium symposia Saranac Lab., 1947-54; pathologist Trudeau (N.Y.) Sanatorium, 1934-42; pathologist active staff Gen. Hosp., Saranac Lake, 1947-54; asso. dept. pathology U. Rochester Med. Sch., 1936-42, 47-54; postgrad. Meml. Hosp., N.Y.C., 1938, Mallory Inst., Boston, 1939; asso. clin. prof. indsl. medicine N.Y.U. Postgrad. Med. Sch., 1949-54; prof., chmn. dept. occupational, environmental health Coll. Medicine, Wayne State U., 1954-72, prof. emeritus, 1972, dir. Summer Inst. Radiation Biology High Sch. Sci. Tchrs., AEC and Nat. Sci. Found., 1957-60. Served from lt. comdr. to capt. M.C., USNR, 1942-47. Recipient Howard Taylor Ricketts award bacteriology and pathology U. Chicago, 1930, distinguished service award U. of Chicago Medical Alumni, 1957; citation for excellence in medical authorship Indsl. Med. Assn., 1951, ann. award of honor, Am. Acad. Occupational Med., 1961; award Am. Cancer Soc., 1963. Diplomate Am. Bd. Clin. Pathology, Pathol. Anatomy, Am. Bd. Occupational Medicine. Fellow A.A.A.S., Am. Assn. Thoracic Surgery, Am. Coll. Chest Physicians, A.M.A., Indsl. Med. Assn., Royal Soc. Health, Am. Coll. Preventive Medicine; mem. Coll. Am. Pathologists, A.C.P., Am. Coll. Preventive Medicine, Royal Soc. Med. of Eng.; hon. mem. European and S.A. Med. and Tb Socs., Franklin County Med. Soc. (pres. 1938-39), Saranac Lake Med. Soc. N.Y. (pres. 1941-42), Pan Am. Med. Assn., Mich. and Detroit Med. Socs., Am. Assn. Pathologists and Bacteriologists, Am. Indsl. Hygiene Assn., Am. Pub. Health Assn., Am. Soc. Exptl. Pathology, Am. Thoracic Soc., Assn. Mil. Surgeons U.S., Nat. Tb Assn., N.Y. Acad. Medicine, Soc. Exptl. Biology and Medicine, Soc. Med. Jurisprudence, Am. Assn. Cancer Research, Internat. Assn. on Occupational Health (mem. permanent commn.), Am. Acad. Occupational Medicine, Internat. Acad. Pathology, Ramazzini Soc., Sigma Xi, Phi Beta Kappa. Clubs: Army-Navy, Cosmos (Washington); Oneida (Green Bay, Wis.). Contbr. med. articles profl. jours. Home: Green Bay, Wis. Died Nov. 29, 1974; buried Alloney Cemetery, Green Bay, Wis.

VOSE, JAMES WILSON, educator; b. Ashburnham, Mass., June 5, 1881; s. James Edward and Lois Elizabeth (Stickney) V.; grad. Cushing Acad., Ashburnham, 1899; A.C., Williams Coll., 1903; grad. study Columbia, Stanford and Boston univs.; Ed.M., Harvard Grad. Sch. of Edn., 1928; hon. A.M., Williams Coll., 1929; m. Lorna Craig Fowler, June 7, 1905; m. 2d, Rose Elizabeth, Berg, June 25, 1949. Teacher of science, Ky. Military Institute, Lyndon, Ky., 1903-07; head of science dept., Cushing Acad., 1907-12; prin. Ky. Mil. Inst., 1912-15; prin. Arms Acad., Shelburne Falls, Mass., 1915-17, 1919-24; prin. Drury High Sch., North Adams, Mass., 1924-26; prin. Cushing Acad., 1926-33; supt. schs., Marblehead, Mass., 1934-48. War camp community service, Chattanooga, Tenn., Anniston, Ala., and N.Y. City, 1917-19. em. N.E.A., New Eng. Assn. School Supts., Merrimac Valley Supts. Assn., Nat.Assn. Sch. Supts., Mass. Sch. Supts. Assn., Mass. Teachers Fedn., Essex County Teachers' Assn., Marblehead Teachers Assn., Nat. Assn. for Childhood Edn., Phi Delta Kappa, Delta Kapa Kappa. Epsilon. Rotarian. Republican. Conglist. Mason. Home: Marblehead, Mass.*†

VOSHELL, ALLEN FISKE, physician; b. Providence, Oct. 28, 1893; M.D., Johns Hopkins, 1919; m. Frances R. Voshell. House officer Johns Hopkins Hosp., Balt., 1919-20, asst. dispensary surgeon, instr. orthpaedic surgery, resident in orthopaedic surgery, 1920-21; adviser crippled children services Md. Dept. Health; mem. adv. com. Balt. Bd. Health; surgeon-in-chief James Lawrence Kernan Hosp. and Indsl. Sch. for Crippled Children, 1931-68, dir. emeritus, 1971-73; vis. orthopedist Hosp. for Women of Md., Mercy Hosp., Union Meml. Hosp., South Balt. Gen. Hosp.; instr. orthopaedic surgery U. Va., 1921-23, chief orthopaedic service, 1921-31, asst. prof., 1923-26, asso. prof., 1926-31; prof. orthopaedic surgery U. Md., 1931-64. Died July 22, 1973; buried Druid Ridge Cemetery.

VREELAND, ALBERT LINCOLN, lawyer, congressman; b. East Orange, N.J., July 2, 1901; s. James Henry and Martha (Blackmore) V.; ed. N.Y. Elec. Sch., 1919, Peddie Sch., Hightstown, N.J., to 1922; LL.B., N.J. Law Sch., 1925; m. Helen Aeschbach, June 27, 1923; children—Elizabeth (dec.), James Albert. Admitted to N.J. bar as atty., 1927, counsellor, 1931; in gen. practice of law at East Orange since 1927; mem. firm Vreeland, Aeschbach & Duffy since 1938; spl. master in chancery, 1931; asst. city counsel, East Orange, 1931-34; judge East Orange Recorder's Court, 1934-38; admitted to practice before the Supreme Court of the U.S., 1939; member 76th and 77th Congresses (1939-43), 11th N.J. Dist.; police commr., East Orange. Served with A.R.C., Ambulance Corps, 1918; lt. col., Inf., overseas in S.W.P.A. 1941-45; lt. col. J.A.G.D. Res. Mem. Am. and Essex County bar assns., Delta Theta Phi. Res. Officers Assn. (p. pres. Dept. of N.J.; p. pres. Southern Essex Chap.), Nat. Sjourners (pres. Northern N. J. Chap.), Holland Soc., S.A.R., Am. Legion, V.F. W. Republican. Bapt. Mason (K.T.), Elk. Home: East Orange, N.J. Died May 1975.

VURSELL, CHARLES W., Congressman; b. Salem, Ill., 1881; s. Henry and Nancy (Young) V.; ed. pub. schs.; m. Besse Brasel, Apr. 18, 1904; children—Charles E., Harold D. Hardware merchant, 1904; served in Ill. Legislature, 1915-17; sheriff, Marion County, 1910-14; entered publishing business, 1918; mem. 78th to 82d Congress, 24th Ill. Dist., 83d to 85th Congresses, 23d Ill. Dist. Republican. Mason. Elk. Home: Salem, Ill. Died Sept. 1974.

WACKERNISTER, WILLIAM, coll. prof.; b. Basel, Switzerland, Sept. 25, 1880; s. Wilhelm W. (Ph.D., LL.D.) and Louise (Bluntschly) W.; ed. in Basel; hon. A.M., Muhlenberg Coll., 1922, LL.D., 1938, D.D., U. of Pa., 1940. Missionary in Holy Land, 1910-1930; asst. editor, Der Pilger, Hope, Pa., 1930-35; ordained Luth. ministry, 1901, pastor Piston, Pa., 1901-12; prof. modern langs. and lit., Madeline Coll., Lake Forest, Ill., 1912-28, acting pres. from 1938; pastor St. Stephen's, Kenilworth, 1940-41. Editor, Der Jugend Freund; editor German Sunday School lessons. German sec. Ministerium of Ill., 1930-37. Compiler: Die Liedergeschichten. Author: Dr. Martin Luther; Hans. Egede. Home: Chicago, Ill.*†

WACKMAN, KENNETH B., business exec.; b. 1912; Ph.B., U. Wis., 1935; m. Henrietta Beach; children—Christopher, John, Ann Oros. With Alexander Grant & Co., 1935-65; pres. James Talcott Inc., 1965-74; pres. dir. Talcott Nat. Corp., 1968-73, vice chmn., 1973-74. Home: Scarsdale, N.Y. Died May 7, 1974.

WADDINGTON, CONRAD HAL, biologist, educator, author; b. Evesham, Eng., Nov. 8, 1905; s. Hal and Mary Ellen (Warner) W.; student Clifton Coll., 1919-23, Cambridge U., 1923-27; D.Sc. (hon.), Montreal, 1958, Trinity Coll., Dublin, 1965, Prague, 1966, Geneva, 1967; LL.D., Aberdeen, 1966; m. C. Elizabeth Lascelles, July 11, 1927 (div. Jan. 1936); 1 son, Cecil Jake; m. 2d Justin Blanco White, Aug. 25, 1936; children—Caroline, Margaret Dusa. Lectr. zoology, embryologist Strangeways Lab., Cambridge U., 1933-45, fellow Christ's Coll., 1942-45; prof. animal genetics, hon. dir. epigenetics research group Med. Research Council, Edinburgh U., 1946-75; vis. Einstein prof. State U. N.Y., Buffalo, 1969; traveling fellow Rockefeller Found., Germany, 1932, N.Y.C. and Pasadena, Cal., 1938; Jesup lectr. Columbia, 1961. Pres., Internat. Union Biol. Scis., 1961-67. Served with RAF, 1942-45. Fellow Center Advanced Studies Wesleyan U., Middletown, Conn., 1961. Decorated comdr. Brit. Empire. Fellow Royal Soc. London, N.Y. Acad. Sci.; mem. Am. Acad. Arts and Scis. Author: Introduction to Modern Genetics, 1939; Organisers and Genes, 1940; Science and Ethics, 1942; The Epigenetics of Birds, 1952; The Scientific Attitude, rev. edit., 1948; Quantitative Inheritance, 1952; Principles of Embryology, 1956; The Strategy of the Genes, 1957; Biological Organization, 1959; The Ethical Animal, 1960; The Nature of Life, 1961; New Patterns in Genetics and Development, 1962; How Animals Develop, rev. edit., 1962; Biology for the Modern World, 1962; Principles of Development Differentation, 1966; Behind Appearance, 1969. Editor: Towards a Theoretical Biology, vols. 1-3, 1967-69. Contbr. articles to sci. jours. Home: Edinburgh, Scotland. Died Sept. 28, 1975.

WADE, HARRY VINCENT, editor; born in Boston, Mass., Mar. 26, 1894; s. Arthur Dudley and Kate Elizabeth (Masters) W.; grad. Boston Latin Sch., 1910; studied law, 1911-15; m. Mary Isabel Olson, June 14, 1924; children—Mary Caroline (Mrs. Wymann D. Barrett, Jr.), Cecily (Mrs. John P. Steiketee). Writer on Boston newspapers, 1915-16; editor Gangplank News, Army daily, St. Nazaire, France, 1919; reporter, asst. city editor, editorial writer Detroit Journal, 1920-22; editorial writer, paragrapher Detroit News, from 1922; writer of paragraph feature The Newsreel, 1936-53, asso. editor, 1951-53, editor, 1953-59, cons. to pub., from 1959; writer daily humorous feature Senator Soaper Says (syndicated to 80 papers in U.S. and Can. 1930-53. Commd. 2d lt. infantry O.R.C., 1916, 1st lt. inf., with A.E.F., 1918-19. Mem. Boston Latin Assn. Episcoplian. Club: Detroit. Home: Grosse Pointe Farms, Mich. Died Sept. 1973.

WADSTED, OTTO, diplomatist; b. Copenhagen, Denmark, Aug. 19, 1881; s. Otto and Augusta (Goos) R.; LL.M., Copenhagen, 1904, Master Political Sciences, 1911; m. Maria ConcepciÓn Carafi, Sept. 22, 1926. Sec. to Ministry of Foreign Affairs, Copenhagen, 1906-07, 1908-10; sec. to consul gen., New York, 1907-08; studied in Paris, 1909-10; asst. chief, Ministry of Foreign Affairs, Copenhagen, 1910; acting conusl gen. and chargé d'affaires, Buenos Aires, 1912; consul at San Francisco, 1914-16, also resident commr. Panama Pacific Internat. Expn.; consul gen. Australia and New Zealand, 1917; chargé d'affaires, Buenos Aires, 1919; M.P. and E.E., Buenos Aires, 1921; spl. mission to Centennial, Peru, 1921; accredited to Montevideo, 1923; asst. sec. of state for legal div., Denmark, 1925, for polit. and legal div., 1928; dep. del. to Assembly of League of Nations, 1928; E.E. and M.P. to U.S. from Dec. 1930. Knight Comdr. Order of Dannebrog, also Danish Cross of same. Address: Denmark.†

WADSWORTH, ALICE HAY, (Mrs. James Wolcott Wadsworth); b. Cleveland, O., Jan. 6, 1880; d. Hon. John and Clara Louise (Stone) Hay; ed. the Misses Masters' Sch., Dobbs Ferry, N.Y.; m. James Wolcott Wadsworth, Sept. 30, 1902; children—Evelyn (Mrs. Stuart Symington), James Jeremiah, Reverdy. Pres. Nat. Assn. Opposed to Woman Suffrage, 1917-19, elected hon. pres. for life; mem. League for National Unity (exec. com.). War Camp Service Commn. (exec. com.), War Work Council Y.W.C.A. (exec. com.); nat. pres. Am. Women's Legion, 1921-23; mem. Nat. Playground and Recreation Assn. America, Churchwomen's League for Patriotic Serfice (exec. com.), Sentinels of America; trustee Wakefield Nat. Memorial Assn.; v.p. and mem. of Bd. of Layd Vistors, Children's Hospital of Washington. Republican. Presbyterian. Clubs: Colony, Woman's Republican (New York). Mem. Am. Women's Voluntary Services, D.C. Unit. Home: Geneseo, N.Y.†

WAGER, RALPH EDMOND, prof. edn.; b. Grooms, N.Y., Mar. 31, 1881; s. Frank and Julia (Brust) W.; A.B., Syracuse U., 1902, A.M., 1905; Ped.B., State Teachers'

Coll., Albany, N.Y., 1904; Ph.D., U. of Chicago, 1922; m. Irma Rasmussen, August 12, 1909 (now deceased); children—Ralph Waldo, Harold Edmond, Robert Franklin (deceased), William Francis; m. 2d, Lillian Pierpont, Sept. 4, 1940; 1 son, John Pierpont. Began as teacher of mathematics high school, Esconaba, Michigan, 1902-03; supervision prinv. public schs., Clayton, N.H., 1906-08; head dept. natural science, State Normal Sch., Potsdam, N.Y., 1908-10; head dept. natural Teachers' Coll., DeKalb, Ill., 1910-19; cience, State U. of Chicago, summers, 1920, 21 and 26; prof. edn., 1921-50, also head of dept.; mem. faculty Northwestern, summer, 1928. Chmn. State Social Hygiene Council; president Atlanta Mental Hygiene Society; member A.A.A.S., National Society for Study of Edn., Nat. Soc. Coll. Teahcers of Edn., Southern Assn. Philsophy and Psychology, Phi Kappa Psi, Phi Beta Kappa, Sigma Xi, Phi Delta Kappa, Pi Gamma Mu, Kappa Phi Kappa. Methodist. Mason. Clubs: Civitan, Torch. Contbr. on biol., scientific and ednl. subjects. Address: Stone Mountain Ga.†

WAGNER, H. HUGHES, clergyman, univ. trustee; b. Nora Springs, Ia., Mar. 22, 1903; s. James Elvin and Mary Catherine (Britt) W.; A.B., Ohio Wesleyan U., 1925, D.D. (hon.), 1950; S.T.B., Boston U., 1928; D.D. (hon.), Am. Internat. Coll., 1942; LL.D., Western New England Coll., 1968; m. Justine Isobel Heasley, June 11, 1929; children—James Edward, Mary Jo (Mrs. Robert Manley), Hughes Heasley. Ordained to ministry Methodist Ch., 1928; pastor in Medford, Mass., 1926-27, East Kingston, N.H., 1927-28, McMechen, W.Va., 1928-34, Elkins, W.Va., 1934-36, Trinity Meth. Ch., Springfield, Mass., 1936-68, minister emeritus, 1968-75, Mem. Gen. Conf. Meth. Ch., 1952, 56, 60, 64, Northeastern Jurisdictional Conf., 1948, 52, 56, 60, 64, alternate mem. Jud. Council, 1961-64; mem. World Meth. Council, 1961-73; pres. Springfield Council Chs., 1939-40, Springfield Ministerial Assn., 1948-49; v.p., dir. Mass. Council Chs., 1952-56. Trustee Boston U., Wilbraham (Mass.) Acad.; corporator Deaconess Hosp., Boston; bd. dirs. Cummings Meml., Springfield. Recipient Distinguished Alumnus award Boston U., 1964. Mem. U.S. Power Squadron, Sigma Alpha Epsilon, Pi Delta Epsilon. Republican. Mason (33°), Kiwanian (pres. Springfield 1955). Clubs: Longmeadow (Mass.) Country; Springfield Yacht. Author: Trinity's First Century, 1945; The Word in Season, 1950. Home: Springfield, Mass. Died Oct. 1, 1973.

WAGNER, KIP LOWELL, historian, researcher; b. Montgomery, O., Dec. 4, 1905; s. William H. and Clara E. (Kuhns) W.; student pub. schs., Ohio; D.Sc., Westminster Coll., New Wilmington, Pa., 1966; m. Alice Louise Stocker, Apr. 4, 1931; 1 son, Thomas Lee. Self employed historian researcher Mexico, Barcelona, Madrid, Sevilla, London and Paris pertaining to 1715 Spanish Plate Fleet, 1951-71; chief research Civil Service, Wright AFB, Dayton, 1938-44; pres., chmn. bd. Real 8 Corp., 1960-70; owner, operator research library Foul Anchor Archives. Pres. Wabasso P.T.A., 1951-54; scoutmaster Gulf Stream council Boy Scouts Am., 1951-54; Mgr. Little League Baseball, 1951-54. Recipient Diving award of Year, 1962; plaque for Treasure Hunter of 1962. Mason. Author: Pieces of 8, 1966. Home: Sebastian, Fla. Died Feb. 26, 1972; buried Hillcrest Meml. Gardens, Vero Beach, Fla.

WAGNER, MYRON LEROY, educator, chemist; b. Oak Park, Ill., Nov. 11, 1923; s. Otto G. and Amy (Schultz) W.; A.B., Carthage Coll., 1948; M.S., State U. Ia., 1952, Ph.D., 1954; m. Adelaide Maas, Dec. 21, 1947; children—Judith Ann, Amy Marie, Mark Myron. Postdoctoral research asso. Cornell U., 1954-56; instr. State U. Ia., 1956-57; mem. faculty U. Mo. at Kansas City, 1957-75. prof. chemistry, 1964-75, chmn. dept., 1960-71. Served with AUS, 1943-45. Mem. Am. Chem. Soc. (chmn. Kansas City sect. 1964), Sigma Xi. Contbr. profl. jours. Home: Kansas City, Mo. Died Mar. 3, 1975; buried Mt. Moriah Cemetery, Kansas City, Mo.

WAGSTAFF, ROBERT MCALPINE, lawyer; b. Abilene, Tex., Sept. 2, 1892; s. John Miles and Bessie (McAlpine) W.; B.A., Simmons Coll., Abilene, 1913; J.D., U. Tex., 1916; m. Texas Orms, Feb. 14, 1931; children—Marnie (Mrs. Robert E. Mueller), John Morris. Admitted to Tex. bar, 1916, since practiced in Abilene; partner firm Wagstaff, Alvis, Alvis & Leonard and predecessor law firms, 1919-73; prof. business adminstrn. Hardin-Simmons U., 1947-51. Mem. Tex. Civil Jud. Council, 1953-59. Mem. Tex. Ho. of Reps. from 116th Dist., 1931-35; mem. Tex. Democratic Exec. Com., 1954-56. Served to capt., inf., Mexican Border and World War I, U.S. Army, 1916-19; maj. Tex. N.G., 1921-26. Fellow Am. Coll. Probate Counsel; mem. Am., Tex., Abilene bar assns., Am. Judicature Soc., Tex. and Southwestern Cattle Raisers Assn., Tex. Sheep and Goat Raisers Assn., Am. Farm Bur., Ind. Petroleum Assn. Am., West Central Tex. Oil and Gas Assn., Mid Continent Petroleum Assn., S.A.R., Am. Legion, Vets. Fgn. Wars, Vets. World War I., Tex. State, West Tex. hist. assns. Republican. Presbyn. Mason (K.T., 32, Shriner). Clubs: Abilene Petroleum, Abilene Country. Home: Abilene, Tex. Died Apr. 9, 1973.

WAILLY, JACQUES WARNIER DE, landscape architect; b. Abbeville, Somme, France, Mar. 12, 1903; s. Paul Warnier de and Marthe de Mesnil (de Maricourt) W.; ed. Instn. Sainte-Croix, Neuilly-sur-Seine, France; diploma, certified landscape gardener Nat. Superior Sch. Fine Arts and Decorative Arts; m. Monique de Senneville-Grave, July 6, 1930; children—Marthe (Mrs. Osmond de la Belliere), Henri. Specialist in architecture of parks and gardens; v.p. French Soc. Garden Architecturel pres. bd. examiners, sec. 2d Internat. Congress Landscape Gardeners, 1950; v.p. com. honor gardening art Internat. Flower Show, Nantes, France, 1958—; prin. works include parks, playing fields, cities and surroundings of groups of apts. bldgs. in Amiens, Abbeville, also pvt. parks and gardens, France and abroad. Decorated officer Agrl. Merit and Social Merit, chevailer Arts and Letters, Order Holy Sepulchre; laureate Acad. Fine Arts; recipient Bronze medal soc. French Artists; 1st, 2d, 3d prizes competitive exam. parks and gardens, Algiers, Algeria; Gold medal Nat. Hort. Soc.; 1st medal Internat. Monumental Art Festival Masterpieces in Peril prize. Mem. French Soc. Town Planners. Author: Parks and Gardens; Structure and Technique; The Garden and Its Problems; also articles. Home: Abbeville, France. Died May 15, 1971.

WAKASUGI, SUEYUKI, trading co. exec.; b. Japan, Feb. 22, 1903; s. Suehachi and Taka Wakasugi; grad. Nagasaki (Japan) Comml. Coll., 1925; m. Fujiko Awamura, Nov. 5, 1934; children—Takatoshi, Kiyoteru, Sumiko (Mrs. Koichi Iwado). With Mitsui & Co., Tokyo, Japan, 1925, with N.Y.C. office, 1934-41, gen. mgr., N.Y.C., 1964-66, pres. Mitsui & Co. (U.S.A.), N.Y.C., 1966-67, exec. v.p., Tokyo, 1967, pres., 1969-73. Dir. Japan Fgn. Trade Council; mem. Customs Tariff Council, Japan; mem. Japan Ministry Finance. Mem. Fedn. Econ. Orgns. (councillor). Home: Tokyo, Japan. Died May 10, 1973.

WAKEFIELD, HENRIETTE (MRS. GREEK EVANS), contralto; b. New York, N.Y.; d. Herman Bangs and Elizabeth (Guthrie) Wilson; desc. of James Wilson, signer of Declaration of Independence, from Pa.; ed. Miss Moore's Sch., N.Y. City; m. Greek Evans, Apr. 11, 1921; 1 son, David Black. Entered Metropolitan Opera Sch. at 17, and made debut a year later with Metropolitan Opera Co., continuing 5 yrs.; owner and dir. of Theatre-in-the-Woods, Norwalk, Conn. Appeared in leading role in operetta, "Dove of Peace," by Walter Damrosch; returned to Metropolitan Opera Co., now retired. Sang part of Gertrude in Haensel and Gretel in first radio broadcast made directly from stage of Metropolitan, Dec. 25, 1931. Prin. rôles: Magdelene in "Meistersinger"; Carmen in "Carmen"; Nancy in "Martha"; Delila in "Samson and Delila"; Amneris in "Aida"; Azucena in "Trovatore," etc. Republican. Presbyterian. Home: Norwalk, Conn. Died Oct. 23, 1974.

WAKEFIELD, MILTON C., chem. co. exec.; Cleve., Nov. 28, 1917; s. Vernon Lloyd and Pauline Margaret (Reich) W.; B.S., Purdue U., 1939, M.S., 1940; m. Helen Jane Pierce, Dec. 4, 1943; children—Susan (Mrs. David W. Mandt), Marion (Mrs. David L. Griffiths). Project engr. Harshaw Chem. Co. div. Kewanee Oil Co., Cleve., 1946-47, plant engr., Gloucester City, N.J., 1947-55, asst. chief engr., Cleve., 1955-65, chief engr., 1966-69, dir. engring., 1969-74; cons. Vari-Systems, Inc. Served to capt. AUS, 1942-46. Decorated Bronze Star medal. Mem. Am. Assn. Cost Engrs. (pres. N.E. Ohio sect. 1964-65), Cleve. Tech. Socs. Council (pres. 1969-70), Cleve. Engring. Soc., Pi Tau Sigma. Home: South Euclid, O. Died May 13, 1974.

WAKEMAN, EARL SEELEY, lawyer; b. Howard County, Ia., Apr. 11, 1881; s. Edward James and Lucy A. (Robbins) W.; prep. edn., Oberlin Acad.; A.B., Stanford University, 1910; J.D., same university, 1912; married Harriett Alice Stillson, August 1, 1906; children—Dorothea (Mrs. Robert H. Howe), Norman Hammond, Gwendolyn (Mrs. R. Joseph Kincaid), Geraldine (Mrs. Robert Bowlus). Admitted to 1912, and since practiced at Los Angeles; with land and title dept., Title Ins. and Trust Co., Los Angeles, 1912-14; city atty. San Gabriel, Calif., 1912-16; mem. Montgomery & Wakeman, 1922-26; sr. mem. Wakeman, Rogers & Brown from 1928; dir. Berkeley Thousand Oaks. Mem. Am. Calif. State and Los Angeles bar assns., Alhambra Dist. Bar Assn. (organizer), Los Angeles hamber Commerce (statis com.), S.R., Stanford U. Alumni Assn. Republican. Episcopalian. Mason. lubs: Altadena Town and Country University (Pasadena); Alhambra (Calif.) Gun; Dos Robles Tennis, Al Malarikah Shrine Club. Home: San Gabriel, Cal.†

WAKSMEN, SELMAN ABRAHAM, educator; b. Priluka, Kiev, Russia, July 22, 1888; s. Jacob and Fradia (London) W.; came to U.S., 1910, naturalized 1916; B.S., Rutgers U., 1915, M.S., 1916, hon. D.Sc., 1943; Ph.D., U. Cal., 1918, Hebrew U. (hon.), 1958; M.D. (hon.), U. Liege, Belgium, 1946; D.Sc. (hon.) Princeton U., 1947, U. of Madrid, 1950, R.I. State Coll., 1950, Pe. Mil. Coll., Phila. Coll. Pharmacy and Sci., 1953, Brandeis Univ., 1954; LL.D., Yeshiva Univ., 1949, Keio Univ., Japan, 1953; D.H.L., Hebrew Union Coll., 1951; Dr. honoris causa U. Athens, 1952; D.Sc. (hon.), U. Brazil, 1963, U. Strassbourg (France), and others; m. Deborah B. Mithik, Aug. 5, 1916; 1 son, Byron H. Research asst. in soil microbiology, 1915; research biochemist Cutter Laboratories, 1917-18; bacteriologist Takamine Laboratories, 1919-20; lectr. soil microbiology Rutgers Univ., 1918-24, asso. prof., 1924-30; prof. soil microbiology, 1930, prof. microbiology, 1942-58, prof. emeritus, 1958-73; microbiologist N.J. Agri. Expt. Sta., New Brunswick, 1921-54; marine bacteriologist Woods Hole Oceanographic Inst., 1930-42; past dir. Inst. Microbiology Rutgers Univ. Fellow A.A.A.S.; mem. Soc. Am. Bacteriol. (pres. 1942), Soil Science Soc. Am., Mycol. Soc., Soc. Exptl. Biology and Med., Internat. Soc. Soil Sci. (pres. 3d com.), Am. Chem. Soc., Nat. Acad. Sci., Nat. Research Council, Phi Beta Kappa. Sigma Xi; fgn. asso. French Acad. Sci., Swedish Acad. Agr., Indian Chem. Soc. and others. Recipient Nitrate of Soda Research award of Am. Soc. of Agronomy for 1930; Passano Foundation Award, 1947; Emil Chr. Hansen Prize, 1947, Nobel prize in physiology and med., 1952; decorated commander French Legion of Honor; and numerous other awards and honors. Author or co-author books relating to field; latest; Streptomycin, Its Nature and Application, 1949; Soil Microbiology, 1952; Guide to the Actinomycetes and Their Antibiotics, 1953; My Life with the Microbes, 1954; Neomycin, Nature and Application, 1958; The Actinomycetes, Vol. I, 1959, Vol. II, 1961, Vol. III, 1962; The Conquest of Tuberculosis, 1964. Contbr. to tech. jours. Home: New Haven, Conn. Died Aug. 16, 1973; buried Woods Hole, Mass.

WALES, JULIA GRACE, peace advocate; b. at Bury, P.Q., July, 1881; d. Benjamin Nathaniel (M.D.) and Emmeline Theodosia (Osgood) W.; B.A., McGill U., Montreal, 1903; M.A., Radcliffe Coll., Cambridge, Mass., 1904. Teacher in Trafalgar Inst., Montreal, 1904-08; asst. and instructor English, U. of Wis., from 1909. Del. from U. of Wis. and Wis. Peace Soc. to International Congress of Women at The Hague, 1915; sec. of envoys from the Congress to govts. of Denmark, Norway Lang. Assn. America. Club: Century, and Sweden. Mem. Modern Wrote: (pamphlet) Continuous Meditation Without Armistice, Feb., 1915. Plan as presented in pamphlet was adopted by Nat. Peace Conf., Chicago, in Feb. 1915, by State of Wis., in Mar., Internat. Congress of Women, at The Hague, Apr., Internat. Peace Conf., San Francisco, Oct., and during the yr. was presented by envoys to govts. of all the leading countries of Europe. Studied problems of constructive internationalism in Sweden, 1916. Home: Madison, Wis.†

WALES, ROYAL LINFIELD, coll. dean; b. Groveland, Mass., Nov. 24, 1878; s. James Lawrence and Mary Chase (Ordway) W.; grad. Haverhill (Mass.) High Sch., 1898; B.S. in Chem. Engring., Mass., Inst. Tech., 1902; Dr. Eng. (hon.), Rhode Island State Coll., 1945; m. Rose M. Blake, Aug. 15, 1904; children—Lawrence Blake, Linwood Ordway, Royal Thayer. Asst. in gas, oil and fuel anaylsis, Mass. Inst. Tech., 1902-04; instr. in mech. engring., Agrl. and Mech. Coll. of N.C., 1904-05; asst. prof. exptl. engring., U. of Tenn., 1905-08; prof. mech. engring., R.I. State Coll., from 1908, dean engring. depts., 1909-45, dean emeritus from June 1945; on leave of absence and mech. engr. in carburetor research, U.S. Bur. of Standards, 1921. Mem. Am. Soc. Mech. Engrs., Soc. Promotion Engring. Edn., Providence Engring. Soc.; hon. mem. Nat. Assn. Stationary Engrs. Home: Kingston, R.I.†

WALKER, AARON THIBAUD (T-BONE), jazz musician; b. Linden, Tex., May 22, 1909; m. Vida; 1 son, 2 daus. Player family act in early career; toured with Ida Cox, B.B. Medicine Show, Ma Rainey, Les Hite; solo performer, 1940; toured Europe, 1950; rec. artist Columbia Records, Polydor Records. Died Mar. 16, 1975.

WALKER, CHAPMAN JOHNSTON, mech. engr.; b. McComas, W.Va., Dec. 16, 1909; s. John Tracy and Barbara (Emmons) W.; B.S. in Elec. Engring., Va. Mil. Inst., 1930; M.M.E., Rensselaer Poly. Inst., 1934, D.M.E., 1936; m. Mathea Cornelia Copeland, May 14, 1936; children—Michael John, Deborah Ann. With Gen. Electric Co., 1930-57, mgr. advanced design nuclear power, Schenectady, 1955-57; chief engr. Curtiss-Wright Corp., Woodridge, N.J., 1957-63, dir. research and tech., 1963-71. Nuclear power cons., 1952-71; mem. research adv. com. NASA, 1963. Recipient Rensselaer Poly. Inst. fellowship, 1933-36. Registered profl. engr., N.Y. Mem. Am. Soc. M.E., Am. Inst. Aeros. and Astronautics, A.A.A.S., Nat. Soc. Profl. Engrs., Air Force Assn., Am. Ordnance Assn., Smithsonian Assos., Sigma Xi. Patentee in field. Home: Saddle River, N.J. Died Dec. 1971.

WALKER, CHARLES RUMFORD, writer; b. Concord, N.H., July 31, 1893; s. Charles Rumford and Frances (Sheafe) W.; B.A., Yale, 1916; m. Adelaide Haley George, Oct. 28, 1928; children—Charles Rumford, Daniel Sheafe. Served as 1st lt. C.A.C., during World War; with A.E.F., Sept. 1918-Feb. 1919; worked in steel mills; asst. editor Atlantic Monthly, 1922-23; asso. editor Independent, 1924-25; asso. editor The Bookman, 1928-29. Sec. Yale U. War Council, 1942; asst. sec. Yale U., 1942-45, dir. research in technol. and indsl. relations, 1945-62, ret., 1962, fellow emeritus Berkeley Coll., Yale, 1962, curator tech., soc. collection U. library, Yale, 1962-74. Cons. automation WHO, 1957. Guggenheim fellow in history, 1938-39; sr. research fellow Yale, 1956; Bollingen fellow, 1959. Mem. Soc. Applied Anthropology (pres.), Phi Beta Kappa, Psi Upsilon. Club: Tavern (Boston). Author: Steel-The Diary of a Furnace Worker, 1922; Bread and

Fire (novel), 1927; Our Gods Are Not Born (short stories), 1931; American City, 1937; American Productivity, 1946; Human Relations in an Expanding Company (with F. L. W. Richardson), 1948; Steeltown, An Industrial Case History, 1950; The Man on the Assembly Line (with Robert H. Guest), 1952; Toward the Automatic Factory, 1957; co-author: The Foreman on the Assembly Line, 1956; Modern Technology and Civilization, 1962. Translator Sophocles' Oedipus the King and Oedipus at Colonus, 1964; Technology, Industry and Man: The age of acceleration, 1968; Aeschylus' Prometheus Bound, 1970. Home: Wellfleet, Mass. Died Nov. 26, 1974; buried Concord, N.H.

WALKER, DARRELL E., educator; b. Hubbell, Neb., June 7, 1920; s. Robert Stephen and Rosa Alma (Slagle) W.; B.S. in Ed., Neb. State Tchrs. Coll., Kearney, 1941; Ph.D., U. Cal. at Berkeley, 1952; m. Margaret Louise Creswell, June 26, 1943; children—Ann Elizabeth, Stephen Creswell. Tchr., Hubbell High Sch., 1941-42; tchr., prin. Hebron (Neb.) High Sch., 1946-48; research asst. U. Cal. at Berkeley, 1948-50; research asso. Rod McLellan Co., orchid growers, 1950-53; mem. faculty Pa. State U., 1954-73, prof. horticulture, head dept., 1963-73. Mem. A.A.A.S., Am. Soc. Hort. Sci., Sigma Xi, Gamma Sigma Delta, Pi Alpha Xi. Home: State College Pa. Died July 7, 1973; buried Centre County Meml. Park, State College, Pa.

WALKER, EDWIN RUTHVEN, educator; b. Rockwall, Tex., Nov. 9, 1906; s. Charles J. and Alona B. (Keahey) W.; A.B., Southwestern U., 1926; B.D., Vanderbilt U., 1928; Ph.D., U. Chgo., 1939; LL.D., Southwestern U., 1957; m. Pherba Thomas, Dec. 28, 1925; children—Martha Ann, Edwin Ruthven. Prof. philosophy Central Coll., Mo., 1935-42; asso. prof. philosophy U. Colo., 1942-47; prof. philosophy, dir. gen. edn. Okla. A. & M. Coll., 1947-48; dean coll. arts and sci. Fla. State U., Tallahassee, 1948-52; dean Rollins Coll., Winter Park, Fla., 1952-54; pres. Queens Coll., Charlotte, N.C., 1954-67, chancellor, 1967-69; writer and ednl. cons., 1969-74. Consultant Federal Civil Defense Adminstrn., 1951. Mem. Am. Philos. Assn., Southwestern Philos, Conf., Pi Kappa Delta, Phi Kappa Phi, Phi Delta Theta. Democrat. Author articles on philosophy. Home: Tallahassee Fla. Died Sept. 19, 1974; interred Tallahassee, Fla.

WALKER, FRANCIS JOHN HARWELL, clergyman, educator; b. London, Eng., Oct. 25, 1881; s. Thomas and Catherine (Barwell) W.;ed. U. of Cambridge local, 1896; 1st and 2d class in chemistry, U. of London (Hastings Branch School of Science and Art), 1898; arts and theology, U. of Durham (Univ. Coll.), 1903; B.A., U. of Southern Minn., 1910; M.A., Highland (Kan.) U., 1912, Ph.D., 1913; M.A., Muskingum Coll., New Concord, O., 1915; D.C.L., Lincoln-Jefferson U., 1914, B.D., 1915, S.T.D., 1917; D.C.L., Chicago Law Sch., 1916; B.D., Manitoba Coll. (U. of Manitoba), 1924; hon. D. Litt. and Ph.D., U. of Southern Minn., 1914; D.D., Campbell Coll., Holton, Kan., 1914; LL.D., Lanier U., tlanta, Ga., 1921; m. Amy Louisa Largen, of London, Eng., July 8, 1908. Organist and lay preacher, 1896-11, deacon, 1911, priest, 1912, P.E. Ch.; rector Ascension Ch., Ontonagon, and St. George's Ch., Hancock, Mich., 1911-15, St. Mark's Ch., Chester, and vicar Holy Trinity ., Murphysboro, Ill., 1915-16; curate, then priest in charge St. Bartholomew's Ch., Chicago, 1916-18; rector St. Bartholomew's Ch., Chicago, 1916-18; rector St. Paul's Ch., Chicago, 1916-18; rector St. Paul's Ch., LaPorte, Ind., from Feb. 1918. Examining Chaplain to Bishop of N. Ind., from 1921. 1919; mem. standing com., Diocese of Ind., 1920-21, from 1923; mem. bishop and council from 1921. Pres. Lincoln-Jefferson U. (a coorespondence school), Chicago from 1917. Founder, 1910. and superior gen. Am. br. Guild of the Holy Ghost, 1910-20. Fellow Philos. Soc. Eng., 1914, Royal Geog. Soc., 1921; mem. Royal Soc. of Lit., 1922, Société Académique d'Historie Internationale, Paris, 1922, Academia Internazionale di applic. Med.-Antro. Soc., Italy, 1921. Epsilon Tau.eC!!Tau Chi. Awarded Grand Cross 2d class, Acadmeia Internazionale di Lettere e Scienze di Napoli, 1921; Grand Commandeur L'Ordre Chev. et E Rel. De!!de la Couronne d'Epines, 1922; gold medal in Arts and Sciences of Saxe-Coburg-Gotha, 1918; Grand Cross Order Danilo I (Montenegro), 1924. Republican. Mason (32°), Moose. Home: LaPorte, Ind.†

WALKER, GEORGE ROWLAND, lawyer; b. Oxford, Me., Aug. 28, 1879; s. George Franklin and Frances M. (Chadbourne) W.; A.B., summa cum laude, Bowdoin Coll., 1902, hon. A.M., 1932; LL.D., Harvard, 1905; m. Ruth Bradley Steinthal, Apr. 30, 1919; children—Ruth, George R., Frances. Admitted to N.Y. bar, 1906, and thereafter practiced in N.Y. City for many years; head of the firm of Walker & Redman for over 20 years; later pres. and dir. Huron Holding Corp., Huron Mines, Inc.; also dir. General Public Utilities Corp. Mem. bd. overseers, Bowdoin Coll. from 1919. (pres. 1939-43). Member Provident Loan Society of New York, American Bar Association, Maine Society of New York, Bowdoin Assn. of N.Y.; Phi Beta Kappa, Delta Kappa Epsilon. Clubs: University, The Creek, The Recess. Home: Manhasset, L.I. N.Y.†

WALKER, IRWIN NOLAN, lawyer; b. Franklin, La., s. Edward Marcus and Kate (Wood) W.; student U. Chgo., 1905-10; m. Gladys Louise Labarthe, May 7, 1925; 1 dau., Marieange (Mrs. Robert J. Harmon). Admitted to Ill. bar, 1911, practiced in Chgo.; cons. corporate, estate and tax matters; asst. states atty. Cook County, Ill., 1912-17, 18-19, gen. corp. practice. Vice pres. Chgo. Bd. Edn., 1933-42; mem. Tchrs. Pension Bd., 1933-42. Trustee Maremount Coll., Boca Raton, Fla. Served as 2d lt., U.S. Army, 1917-18. Recipient Fifty Year award Am. Bar Assn., 1971; decorated knight St. Gregory the Great (Pope John XXIII). Mem. Serra Internat., Am. Ill., Chgo. bar assns., Holy Name Soc., Phi Kappa Sigma. Clubs: Chicago Athletic, Skyline, Tavern (Chgo.); Everglades, Bath and Tennis (Palm Beach, Fla.). Author: Facts About the Chicago Public Schools, 1938; Facts about the Superintendent of Chicago Public Schools, 1938. Home: Lake Bluff, Ill., Died Sept. 28, 1973.

WALKER, JOHN FRANKLIN, physician; b. Chgo., June 2, 1925; s. Frank Elliott and Frederica Emma (Gaertner) W.; B.S., Emory U., 1942, M.D., 1948; m. Betty Louise Brown, June 11, 1948; children—John Franklin, Betsy Ellen, Stephen Brown. Intern Providence Hosp., Detroit, 1948-49; resident radiology Lawson and Grady hosps., Atlanta; pvt. practice medicine, Atlanta, 1953; mem. staff Grady, Ponce de Leon, Atlanta, Peachtree, Park Wood hosps.; clin. asso. prof. radiology Emory U. Sch. Medicine. Trustee Med. Benevolence Found.; bd. visitors Emory U.; Atlanta bd. counselors Oxford (Ga.) Coll. of Emory U. Served to capt. M.C., AUS, 1948-50. Diplomate Am. Bd. Radiology. Mem. A.M.A. (speaker ho. dels. 1972, speaker emeritus 1973), Fulton County (past pres.), 5th Dist. (past pres.) med. socs., Atlanta Clin. Soc. (past pres.), Ga. Radiol. Soc. (past pres.), Am. Coll. Radiology (past pres., past chmn. bd. chancellors, Gold medal 1974), Emory U. Alumni Assn. (past pres.; award honor 1972), Med. Assn. Ga. (speaker ho. dels.), World Med. Assn. (del.), Phi Delta Theta, Omicron Delta Kappa, Phi Chi. Presbyn. (elder). Rotarian. Clubs: Piedmont Driving, Cherokee Town and Country (Atlanta). Home: Atlanta, Ga. Died Oct. 6, 1973; buried Oakland Cemetery, Atlanta.

WALKER, ROBERT SPARKS, author; b. Chickamauga, Tenn., Feb. 4, 1878; s. William Thomas and Mary Elizabeth (Moore) W.; student Maryville (Tenn.) Coll., 1900; LL.B., U. of Chattanooga, 1905; m. S. Elberta Clark, Aug. 16, 1904 (died Feb. 26, 1924); children—Robert Sparks (dec.), Wendell Clark. Editor Southern Fruit Grower, and pres. Fruit Grower Pub. Co., 1900-21; dept. editor New South Mag., 1926-27; editor Nature Dept. of The Flower Grower, 1923-34. Founder Elberta Clark Walker fund for 2 ann. cash prizes in nat. nature poetry contest, through Chattanooga Writers' Club. Pres. Tenn. State Hort. Soc., 1915; life mem. Tenn. Acad. Science, Chattanooga Writers' Club (hon.), The International Mark Twain Society (hon.), The Tennessee State Garden Clubs (hon.). Congregationalist. Organized and was leader Chattanooga-Lookout Mountain Hiking Clubs, with 1000 members and 40 units, and leader of the Master's Hiking Club, 1932-32; dir. and leader Cumberlands Hiking Club, 1932-38 (hon. pres.). Naturalist and lecturer Boy Scouts and Girl Scouts from 1920. The Robert Sparks Walker Audubon Society named for him, 1944, with program including the Elise Chapin Wildlife Sanctuary containing over 100 acres. Author books from 1926; latest; States Flowers and State Birds, 1950. Editor nature dept. Chattanooga Times, from 1933; editor Flower and Feather mag. Editor and compiler Prize-Winning Nature Poems, an anthology, 1937. Home: Chattanooga, Tenn.†

WALKER, WILLIAM ALEXANDER, physician; b. Chester, S.C., Nov. 1, 1894; s. William Alexander and Jannie Harriet (Anderson) W.; B.A., Meharry Med. Sch., 1923, M.D., 1927; m. Ada Louise Givens, June 1, 1941. Pvt. practice gen. medicine, Lewisburg, Tenn., 1927-59, 62-75; dir. phys. medicine VA Hosp., Tuskegee, Ala., 1959-62; mem. staffs Brown's Hosp., Gordon's Hosp., Taylor's Hosp. (all in Lewisburg, Tenn.). Mem. Tenn. Med. Assn., Nat. Med. Assn., Marshall County Med. Soc., Am. Acad. Gen. Practice, N.A.A.C.P., Omega Psi Phi. Democrat. Methodist. Mason (32°). Home: Lewisburg Tenn. Died Jan. 7, 1975.

WALKER, WILLIAM G(EORGE), army officer; b. New York, June 28, 1890; s. James and Mary Ann (Reid) W.; grad. Army War Coll., 1938, Command and Gen. Staff Sch., 1935; m. Jeanne Smith Haight, Mar. 27, 1919; children—William G., James H., Jean Mary, Margaret L., Barbara R. Commanded Co. K, 350th Inf., 88th div., A.E.F., World War I; staff duties in U.S. and abroad, 1920-40; with GHQ, Washington, Headquarters, Army Ground Forces in charge of equipment and supply, hdqrs. Western Pacific, operations and equipment, World War II; advanced through successive ranks to brig. gen.; retired, 1946; later in real estate and farming. Presbyterian. Home: Kensington, Md., also Jefferson County, W.Va. Died Dec. 31, 1974.

WALKER, WILLIAM MAY, circuit judge; b. Crawfordsville, Fla., May 2, 1905; s. Nat R. and Alice (Tully) W.; J.D., Samford U., 1927; m. Pansy Mavis Crosby, Feb. 22, 1937; children—William May, Joseph Stanley. Admitted to Fla. bar, 1927; practiced in Tallahassee, 1927-40; judge Leon County Ct., 1933-40, 2d. Jud. Circuit Ct., Tallahassee, 1940-74. Mem. examining bd. Fla. Parole Commn., 1960. Mem. Fla. Bar, Am., 2d Jud. Circuit, Tallahassee, Gadsden County (hon.) bar assns., Am. Judicature Soc., Nat. Conf. State Trial Judges, Fla. Circuit Judges Conf. (past pres.), Tallahassee C. of C. (past dir.), Woodmen of World, Phi Alpha Delta. Democrat. Baptist (deacon). Mason (32°, Shriner), Lion (past Tallahassee pres., past Fla. dep. dist. gov.). Club: Nat. Seminole. Home: Tallahassee, Fla. Died Sept. 16, 1974; buried Oakland Cemetery, Tallahassee.

WALL, HARRY RUTHERFORD, electric and gas utility exec.; b. Shreveport, La., July 24, 1909; s. Clarence and Alto (Brantley) W.; B.S. in Elec. Engring., Carnegie Inst. Tech., 1931; m. Jean Larsen, Apr. 11, 1942; 1 dau. Nancy (Mrs. John W. Reif); m. 2d, Margaret Holmes, July 24, 1961; stepchildren—Stephen, John; 1 dau., Suzanne. Operating engr. Cleve. Electric Illuminating Co., 1933-37; elec. designer Tenn. Electric Power Co., 1937-39; electric power system planner Commonwealth & So. Corp., 1939-42, 46-51; with Consumers Power Co., Jackson, Mich., 1951-73, v.p., 1954-68, sr. v.p., 1968-72, vice chmn. bd., 1972-73. Mem. adv. com. nat. power survey FPC, 1962-64. Pres. Mich. Safety Conf., 1958. Served to lt. comdr. USNR, 1942-46. Registered profl. engr., Mich., Mass. Fellow I.E.E.E.; mem. Edison Electric Inst. (nat. coms.), N.A.M., Assn. Edison Illuminating Cos. (nat. coms.), Nat. Soc. Profl. Engrs., Ret. Officers Assn. Clubs: Jackson Country, Hidden Valley, Sea Pines Plantation, Grandfather Golf. Home: Jackson, Mich. Died Dec. 9, 1973.

WALLACE, GEORGE SELDEN, lawyer; b. Greenwood Station, Va., Sept. 6, 1871;s. Charles Irving and Maria Logan (Sclater) W.; ed. pub. sch. and Mechanics' Inst., Richmond; LL.B., W. Va. U., 1897; m. Frances Bodine Gibson, Oct. 4, 1905 (deceased June 25, 1951); children—Frances Gibson, Champe Carter (Mrs. Huddleston Haynes). Elizabeth Logan (Mrs. J. A. Cook), Margaret Sclater (Mrs. Buel B. Whitehill), William, and George Selden. Began law practice, 1897; was dir., pres. and 1st v.p. Union Bank & Trust Co., Huntington, 30 years; prs. of Rockbottom Land Co.; sec. and treasurer Blackberry, Ky., and West Virginia Coal & Coke Co.; vice-president Jeff Newberry Shoe Co.; city attorney, Central City, W.Va., 1902-04; pros. atty., Cabell County, 1905-08; mem. Dem. city, county and state commns.; del. Dem. Nat. Conv., Baltimore, 1912. Spl. judge of Circuit Court (Cabell) Co.) 1937-41. Pres. bd. park commrs., Huntington, W. Va., 1925-50. Served as 2d and 1st lt 2d W.Va. Vol. Inf., Spanish-Am. War, 1898-99; div. q.m., Dec. 1898-Apr. 1899; mem. W.Va., Nat. Guard, 1900-16, advancing to lt. col.; actg. J.A.G.'s office, Washington, D.C.; promoted lt. col.; went to France, June 1918; sr. asst. to acting J.A.G. for France; honorably discharged, June 16, 1919. Mem. Am. Bar Assn., Cabell County Bar Assn. (ex-pres.), Soc. of Cincinnati in Va., Phi Sigma Kappa. Democrat. Episcopalian. Clubs: Army and Navy, Army, Navy and Marine Corps Country (Washington, D.C.). Author: The Need, Basis and Propriety of Martial Law, 1916; Genealogical Data Pertaining to the Descendants of Peter Wallace and Elizabeth Woods; The Sclater Family in Virginia; The Carters of Blenheim; Cabell County Annals and Families; and Huntington Through Seventy-Five Years. Home: Huntington, W.Va.†

WALLACE, KARL RICHARDS, univ. prof.; born Hubbardsville, N.Y., Nov. 10, 1905; s. Lew and Rena (Dart) W.; B.A., Cornell U., 1927, M.A., 1931, Ph.D., 1933; m. Dorothy M. Peirce, Aug. 27, 1929; children—Margit (Mrs. Edwin Gerow), Elizabeth (Mrs. Joseph Empen), Peter. Instr. and assistant prof. speech la. State Coll., 1927-30, 1933-36; asst. and instr. pub. speaking Cornell U., 1931-33; asst. prof. English U. of Mo., summers 1933, 1934; asst. prof. English in charge of speech, Washington U., St. Louis, 1936-37; asso. prof. and prof. speech U. of Va., 1937-47, chmn. Sch. of Speech, 1937-44, chmn. Sch. Speech and Drama, 1944-47; prof. speech and head dept. of speech U. of Ill., 1947-68; prof. speech U. Massachusetts, Amherst, from 1968. Mem. Speech Association America (exec. council 1944-57, editor 1945-47, president 1954), National Council Tchrs. English, Delta Sigma Phi, Phi Kappa Phi, Omicron Delta Kappa, Phi Beta Kappa. Methodist. Clubs: University, Rotary. Author or co-author books and articles relating to field. Home: Amherst, Mass. Died Oct. 16, 1973.

WALLACE, LAWRENCE WILKERSON, mech. engr.; b. Webberville, Tex., Aug. 5, 1881; s. William Davis and Caledonia Clementine (Fowler) W.; B.S., Agrl. and Mechanical College of Texas, 1903; Dr. Engrineering, 1943; Mechanical Engineering, Purdue University, 1912, Dr. Engring., 1932; m. 2d, Lula Arey, June 7, 1934; children (by first marriage)—Ouida Kathryn, Marjorie Louise (Mrs. Carder Welles). Special apprentice, Gulf, Colorado & Santa Fe Ry., Cleburne, 1903-06; asst. prof. railway and indsl. management, Purdue, 1906-13, prof., 1913-17; asst. gen. mgr. Diamond Chain & Mfg. Co., Indianapolis, Ind., 1917-19; dir. Red Cross Inst. for Blind (training men blinded in World War I), Baltimore, Md., 1919-21; exec. sec. Am. Engring. Council, Washington, D.C., 1921-34; v.p. W. S. Lee Engring. Corp., 1934; dir. Engring. Research Assn. of Am. R.R.'s., 1935-37; dir. engring. and research Crane Co., 1937-41; v.p. Trundle Engring. Co., Cleveland, 1941-47; pres. Wallace, Wright & Van

Fossen, Inc. 1947-49; owner Lawrence W. Wallace Assos. from 1949-53; chief transp. materials handling and instruments sect. Machinery br. OPS, 1951-52; conf. leader Top Management Seminar, Army Mgmt. Engring. Tng. Agency Rock Island Arsenal 1952-66. Dir. Purdue Research Foundation; indsl. councilor, Texas A. & M. Research Foundation, 1944-72; mem. div. engring. and indusl. research Nat. Research Council. Mem. Ind. State Council Defense, World War I, also U.S. Fuel Adminstrn. for Indianapolis, Indianapolis War Chest. Chmn. bd. Eyesight Conservation Council of America, 1920-30; sec. com. on Patent Office Procedure, Dept. Commerce, 1925; mem. advisory com. Washington br. Internat. Labor Office, 1925; del. 1st Internat. Mgmt. Congress, Prague, Czechoslovakia, 1924, World Power Conf., London, 1924. Recipient Meritorious Service award Dept. Def., 1959, Exceptional Service award, 1966. Fellow Am. Inst. Indsl. Engrs., Am. Soc. M.E. (v.p. 1938-39); mem. Am. Soc. Pub. Adminstrn., Academy of Organizational Service, Am. Acad. Polit. and Social Science, Soc. for Promotion of Engring. Edn., A.A.A.S., Soc. Advancement of Management (pres. Cleveland chapter 1941-42), Industrial Research Inst. (chmn. 1941), Pi Tau Sigma, Tau Beta Pi, Acacia; hon. mem. Masaryk Acad. of Work, Prague, Inst. of Scientific Mgmt. Poland. Decorated Knight Order of White Lion (Czechoslovakia). Methodist. Mason (Shriner). Club: Cosmos (Washington, District of Columbia). Author of Car Design, 1913; Fire Losses-Locomotive Sparks, 1923. Editor various repts. of Am. Engring. Council Contbr. many articles on ry. and indusl. engring. problems; also chpts. in books. Home: Davenport, Ia., Died Jan. 19, 1973; interred Greenwich, Va.

WALLACE, MARY KENT, educator; b. Steubenville, O.; d. William Henry and Mary (Stuart) W.; grad. Wolfe Hall, Denver, Colo.; A.B., Colorado Coll., Colorado Springs, Colo., 1896; post-grad. work, Columbia; traveled and studied in France, Italy, Germany, Greece and Constantinople, 1906, 12. Head Dept. of Latin and Greek, Wolcott Sch., Denver, Colo., 1897-1921, prin. 1921-22; pres. Kent Sch. for Girls, 1922-36. Episcopalian. Home: Denver, Colo. Died Apr. 30, 1948; buried Fairmont Cemetery, Denver, Colo.

WALLACE, S(AMUEL) MAYNER, lawyer; b. Woodford Co., Ky., Dec. 25, 1886; s. Robert and Margaret Brudette (Alford) W.; LL.B., U. Va., 1907; m. Gladys Lucille Penn. Sept. 15, 1926; 1 dau., Margaret Penn (Mrs. Carl Trauernicht, Jr.). Admitted to Ky. bar, 1908, Mo., 1911; practiced in Lexington, Ky., 1908-11, St. Louis, 1911-75. Home: St. Louis, Mo., Died Feb. 23, 1975.

WALLACE, SEBON RAINS, psychologist, educator; b. Knoxville, Tenn., Dec. 19, 1913; s. Sebon Rains and Margaret (Donaldson) W.; B.S., U. Va., 1934, M.S., 1935, Ph.D., 1937; m. Sarah Fidelia Hahn, Sept. 21, 1934; children—Sarah Gray, David Rains. Instr., Ohio State U., 1936-37; asso. prof. Tulane U., New Orleans, 1937-42, prof., chmn. dept. psychology, 1946-47; chief behavioral and social scis. Dept. Def., 1965-66; pres. Am. Inst. for Research, Pitts., 1967-70; prof., chmn. dept. psychology Ohio State U., Columbus, 1970-73. Vis. lectr. Yale, 1952-54. Served from 1st lt. to lt. col. USAAF, 1942-46. Mem. Am. Psychol. Assn. (pres. div. indsl. psychology, 1964), Life Ins. Agy. Mgmt. Assn. (v.p. 1947-67), Sigma Xi. Editor; Personnel Psychology, 1973. Home: Columbus, O. Died Aug. 28, 1973.

WALLER, EDWIN JAMES, educator; b. Tiawah, Okla., July 16, 1925; s. William Russell and Nelle Lou (Beeman) W.; B.S., Okla. State U., 1949, M.S., 1951, Ph.D. (NSF-Sci. faculty fellow), 1968; Engr. (NSF-Sci. faculty fellow), Stanford, 1959; m. George Ann Vernon, Aug. 9, 1953; 1 son, Reed Vernon. Asst. prof. Okla. State U., 1951-55, asso. prof., 1956-64; research engr. Carter Oil Co. Research Lab., Tulsa, 1955-56; asso. prof. U.S. Naval Acad., Annapolis, 1964-68, prof., 1968-75, sr. prof. systems engring., 1968-70, chmn. weapons and systems engring. dept., 1970—; cons. pressure surges, noise and vibrations, 1955-75. systems engring., 1959-75. Served with AUS, 1942-45. Registered profl. engr., Okla. Mem. Am. Soc. Engring. Edn., Am. Soc. M.E., Sigma Xi. Research and publs. in pressure surges in pipelines, liquid borne noise, nonlinear control, analog computer simulation. Home: Arndol, Md., Died Mar. 26, 1975.

WALLS, WILLIAM JACOB, bishop; b. Rutherford, N.C., May 8, 1885; s. Edward and Hattie (Edgerton) W.; A.B., Livingstone Coll., Salisbury, N.C., 1908, B.D., 1913, D.D., LL.D.; postgrad. Columbia, 1922; A.M., U. Chgo., 1941. m. Dorothy L. Jordon, Dec. 6, 1956. Evangelist, 1899-1905; pastor Cleveland, N.C., 1905-07, Lincolnton, N.C., 1908-10, Salisbury, N.C. (built Soldiers Meml. Ch.), 1910-13, Louisville (built Broadway Temple), 1913-20; editor Star of Zion, Charlotte, N.C., 1920-24; bishop A.M.E. Zion Ch. Am., 1924-75, sr. bishop 1951-68, chmn. bd. religious edn., 1924-68. Chmn., A.M.E. Zion Sesquicentennial, 1946; del. gen. Conf. M.E. Ch., South, 1918, M.E. Church, 1928; del. Eumenical Meth. Conf., 1921-71; v.p. World Meth. Conf., 1951; historian A.M.E. Zion Ch., 1968-75. Mem. pres.'s and war sec.'s Am. Clergymen's Commn. to occupied countries in Europe, 1947; mem. commn. cultural and human relations, 1954; del. World Council of Chs., Amsterdam, Holland, 1948, Evanston, Ill., 1954, New Delhi, India, 1961, Uppsala, Sweden, 1968, mem. message and central coms., 1948-54; exec. com. World Meth. Council, 1956; del. World Christian Edn. and Sunday Sch. Conv., Tokyo, 1958; past v.p. Div. Sch. Alumni, U. Chgo. Trustee United Internat. Christian Endeavor Soc.; chmn. trustees Livingstone Coll., 1941-73; chmn. Harriet Tubman Found. Served as chaplain, World War I. Mem. Religious Ednl. Assn. Internat. Council Religious Edn., World's Sunday Sch. Assn., Nat. Council Ch. Christ Am. (co-founder, past v.p.), N.A.A.C.P. (past v.p.), Am. Bible Soc. (adv. council 1941-70), Am. Acad. Polit. Sci., Nat. Negro Bus. League (life, past chaplain), Phi Beta Sigma. Mason, Odd Fellow, K.P., Elk. Author: J.C. Price Educator and Race Leader, The Romance of A College, The African Methodist Episcopal Zion Church-Reality of the Black Church, Pamphlets, Pastorates and Reminiscences, What Youth Wants, The Dream of Youth, Living Essentials of Methodism, Harriet Tubman; also works pub. posthumously. Founder Camp Dorothy Walls, Black Mountain, N.C., 1958. Home: Yonkers, N.Y., Died Apr. 23, 1975.

WALSH, SIR, CYRIL AMBROSE, justice High Ct. Australia; b. Sydney, Australia, June 15, 1909; s. M.J. Walsh; ed. Sydney U.; m. Mary Smyth, Nov. 28, 1942; 3 sons. Admitted to New South Wales bar, 1934; judge Supreme Ct., New South Wales, from 1954; later justice High Ct. Australia. Fellow St. John's Coll., U. Sydney, 1956-73. Decorated Knight Brit. Empire. Address: Mosman, Australia. Died Nov. 29, 1973; interred No. Suburbs Roman Catholic Lawn Sect.

WALSH, EDWARD ANTHONY, educator; b. Newport, R.I., Aug. 7, 1900; s. John and Margaret (Shea) W.; B.Ph., Holy Cross Coll., 1924; M.Ed., R.I. Coll. Edn., 1949; profl. diploma communication, Columbia Tchrs. Coll., 1953. Newspaper reporter, editorial writer, corr., 1925-48; faculty journalism div., dept. communication arts Fordham U., from 1949, Patterson prof. journalism, vice chmn. dept., 1954-69, emeritus, 1969, cons. dept. communication arts, 1969; asst. dir. N.Am. sect. Vatican Radio, 1967-68, cons. N.Am. Adv. committee, from 1968. K.C. fellow U. Notre Dame, 1924-25. Fellow Royal Soc. Arts, London; mem. International Association Mass Communications Research, National Conf. Editorial Writers, Inter-Am. Press Assn. Internat. Press Inst., Assn. Edn. in Journalism, Am. Soc. Journalism Sch. Adminstrs., Am. Assn. U. Profs., Am. Acad. Advt. (regional dean). Internat. Radio and TV Soc. Inc., Sigma Delta Chi. Club: Overseas Press (N.Y.C.). Asso. editor Jour. of Communication. Home: New York City, N.Y. Died Oct. 24, 1973.

WALSH, J(OSEPH) HARTT, educator; b. Boston, Apr. 23, 1902; s. Joseph J. and Laura A. (Hartt) W.; B.E., U. Wis., Eau Claire, 1927; Ph.B., Ripon (Wis.) Coll., 1927; A.M., U. Minn., 1934; Ph.D., U. Wis., 1945; m. Nettie L. Stokes, Sept. 29, 1930. Prin. schs., Arkansaw, Wis., 1924-26, Jr.-Sr. High Sch., Lake Geneva, Wis., 1928-29; prodn. mgr. Textile Mill., Nashville, 1929-30; supt. schs., Fulda, Minn., 1931-34; sr. high sch. tchr., Wauwatosa Wis., 1927-28, 34-35; supt. schs., Lancaster, Wis., 1935-40; chief ednl. cons. USAAF Tech. Tng. Command. Truax Field, 1942-43; USN V-12 coll. tng. program Univs. of Pa., and Wis., Ia. State Coll.; comdg. officer S.E. Mo. State Coll., Washington and St. Louis univs., 1943-46; dir. curriculum research USAFI, 1946; asso. prof. edn. Washington U., 1946-48; dean Butler U. Coll. Edn., Indpls., 1948-68, dean emeritus, 1968-75. Cons. to George F. Crame Map & Globe Co.; former editor Croft publs., Child Life mag. Chmn. finance com. Ind. White Ho. Conf. on Edn., 1955; mem. exec. bd. Ind. Congress P.T.A., 1955-58. Mem. Wis. Edn. Assn. (v.p. 1938). Ind. Schoolmen's Club (pres. 1954), Res. Officers Assn., A.A.A.S., Ind. Assn. Supervision and Curriculum Devel. (pres. 1957), Am. Acad. Polit. and Social Sci., Nat. Soc. Coll. Tchrs. Edn., Am. Ednl. Research Assn., Nat. Soc. for Study Edn., Am. Assn. Sch. Adminstrs., Wis. U. Alumni Assn., Ind., Ind. Ret. tchrs. assns., Am. Legion, Phi Delta Kappa (emeritus), Kappa Delta Pi. Mason (32 deg., Shriner), K.P. Author: Teaching in a Divided World, 1950; Education in 2000 A.D.; Wither American Higher Education?; Geography in the World Beyond Tomorrow, 1961, rev.; The Curriculum and the World Beyond Tomorrow, 1961; Cram Student Atlas of Earth Science and Outer Space, 1971; others. Contbr. and editor to Child Life mag., World Book Ency., articles to ednl. jours. Home: Indianapolis, Ind. Died June 30, 1975; buried Oak Hill Cemetery, Waterloo, Wis.

WALSH, JOSEPH LEONARD, educator; b. Washington, Sept. 21, 1895; s. John Leonard and Sallie Ellicott (Jones) W.; grad. Baltimore Poly. Inst., 1912; student Columbia, 1912-13; S.B., lHarvard, 1916, Ph.D., 1920; S.M., U. of Wis., 1917; sutdent U. of Chicago, 1916, U. of Paris, 1920-21, U. of Munich, 1925-26; m. Aline Natalie Burgess, July 16, 1931 (divorced); m. 2d Elizabeth Cherry Strayhorn, Apr. 2, 1946; children—Sallie Elizabeth, Elizabeth Hildegarde. Mem. faculty Harvard, 1915-66. Sheldon traveling fellow, 1920-21, prof. mathematics since 1935. chmn. dept., 1937-42. Perkins prof. of math., 1946-66, Perkins prof. emeritus, 1966-73; prof. math. U. Md. 1965; acting master Adams House, Harvard U., 1956-57; fellow Internat. Edn. Board, 1925-26, Inst. for Advanced Study, 1934-35. Mem. U.S.N.R.F., World War I; ensign, 1918-19; lt (j.g.) 1919, Lt. comdr., capt. USNR (ret. 1955), active duty 1942-46, including 2 yrs. as navigator of combatant escort aircraft carrier, Fellow A.A.A.S. (v.p. 1944, 1961), Am. Academy of Arts and Sciences; member Am. Math. Soc. (president 1949-50; v.p. 1937-38), Mathematical Association of America (trustee 1934-36, visiting lecturer in 1957), Nat. Acad. Sciences, Deutsche Math. Verein, Phi Beta Kappa. etc. Methodist. Author or co-author books relating to field, latest publ.; (with A.H. Ahlberg and E. N. Nilson) Spline Functions, 1967. Originator Walsh Orthogonal functions. Home: University Park, Md. Died Dec. 10, 1973.

WALSH, PHILIP F., utility exec.; grad. Temple U. With So. Cal. Water Co., from 1938, becoming pres., chief exec. officer; dir. Pacific Employers Ins. Co. Mem. Gov.'s Utilities Adv. Com. Trustee, Los Angeles Tech. Services Corp. Mem. Los Angeles Area C. of C. (pres. 1971), Cal. State C. of C. Address: Los Angeles, Cal. Died Dec. 28, 1973.

WALSH, WILLIAM CONCANNON, lawyer; b. Cumberland, Md., Apr. 2, 1890; s. William Edward and Mary (Concannon) W.; A.B., Mt. Saint Mary's Coll., Emmitsburg Md., 1910; LL.B. Cath. U. Law Sch., Washington, 1913; hon. LL.D., Mt. Saint Mary's Coll., 1930; m. Sarah Elizabeth Nee, June 1, 1929; children—William, Sarah Elizabeth. Admitted to Md. bar, 1913, engaged in practice at Cumberland from 1913 except when otherwise engaged; served as city atty., 1920-21; asso. judge 4th jud. circuit Md., 1921, chief judge and men. Court of Appeals, Md., 1924-26; state ins. commr. Md., 1931-35; atty. gen. Md. for term 1938-42 and re-elected in 1942 for a 4-year term; resigned June 1945, to become mem. firm Miles, Walsh & Stockbridge, Cumberland, Miles & Stockbridge, Balt.; later mem. law firm Walsh & Walsh, Cumberland; Walsh, Walsh & Reinhart, Cumberland; chmn. Liberty Trust Co.; dir. Kelly-Springfield Tire Co., Cumberland, Nat. Jet Co., Nat. Jet. Drill Co. Served as pvt. and cpl. infantry Md. Nat. Guard, on Mexican border, 1916; sgt. to 1st lt. inf., U.S. Army, 1917-19; with A.E.F. in France; served in machine gun co., 113th Inf., 29th Div. Del. to Dem. Nat. Convs., 1924, 28, 32, 40, 44, 64; chmn. Dem. state conv., 1922. Mem. A.R.C. Bd. for Allegany County, Md. Mem. regional bd. Nat. Conf. Christians and Jews; regent U. Md., 1959-67. Pres. Allegany County United Fund, 1959. Fellow Am. Bar Found.; mem. Am. (ho. dels. 1948-49, 1952-55), Md. State (pres. 1948-49), Baltimore City, Allegany County bar assns., Am., Md. bar founds., Am. Judicature Soc., Md. Hist. Soc. Democrat. Roman Catholic K.C. Elk. Clubs: Country, Maryland (Balt.). Home: Cumberland, Md. Died June 17, 1975; buried Sts. Peter and Paul Catholic Cemetery, Cumberland, Md.

WALSH, WILLIAM EDWIN, lawyer; b. Oswego, N.Y., Jan. 29, 1903; s. William Edwin and Mary (Schneider) W.; LL.B., J.D., Willamette U., 1927; m. Marian Kardell, Aug. 6, 1932; 1 son, William Edwin III. Admitted to Ore. bar, 1927; practiced in Coos Bay, from 1929; mem. firm Walsh, Chandler, Walberg and Whitty, from 1968; dist. atty. Coos County, 1930-32. Pres. owner radio sta. KWRO, Coquille, 1949. Dir. Southwestern Ore. Area Edn. Dist., 1966-70; mem. Statute Revision Council Ore., 1949-51; pres. Ore. Emergency Bd., 1949-50; mem. Ore. Bd. Higher Edn., 1953-64, pres., 1961-64; mem. travel adv. com. Ore. Hwy. Commn., 1965-75. Mem. Ore. Senate, 1941-52, pres., 1949-51; acting gov. Ore. intermittently, 1949-51; del. Republican Nat. Conv., 1952; chmn. Ore. Rockefeller for Pres., 1964. Trustee Williamette U., 1953-68, life trustee, 1970-75. Mem. Am., Coos-Curry County bar assns., Ore. State Bar (bd. govs. 1951-54), Ore. Motor Assn. (bd. dirs., v.p.). Mason (Shriner); mem. Order Eastern Star. Home: Coos Bay, Ore. Died Apr. 9, 1975; buried Sunset Meml. Park Cemetery Coos Bay, Ore.

WALTER, PAUL ALFRED FRANCIS, JR., univ. prof.; b. Santa Fe, N.M., Apr. 23, 1901; s. Paul A. F. and Clara (Stauffer) W.; A.B., Stanford, 1921, M.A., 1933, Ph.D., 1937; m. Valyne Gazley, Jan. 28, 1923; children—Paul A. F., III, Constance (Mrs. J. K. Culbertson). Newspaper reporter, 1921-29; asst. dir. Sch. of Am. Research, Santa Fe, N.M., 1929-30; instr. journalism U. of N.M., 1930-37, asst. prof. sociology, 1937-45, asso. prof., 1945-46, prof. sociology from 1946, founder U.N.M. Press, 1931; vis. prof. Boston U. and Oberlin Coll., 1945, Stanford, 1959, Mich. State Univ., 1956. State information officer, O.P.A., N.M., 1943-44. Principal investigator AF office Sci. Research, 1957. Fellow A.A.A.S.; mem. of the Am. and Southwestern Sociol. Socs., Soc. Study Social Problems. Am. Assn. U. Profs., Phi Kappa Phi, Alpha Kappa Delta, Alpha Sigma Phi. Author: (with J. C. Knode) An American Philosophy of Education, 1942; (with J. S. Roucek and assos.) Sociological Foundations of Education, 1942, Social Control, 1947; The Social Sciences, 1949; Race and Culture Relations, 1952; also numerous articles. Home: Albuquerque, N.M., Died Nov. 3, 1973; buried Sunset Meml. Park, Albuquerque, N.M.

WALTERS, BASIL L., newspaper cons.; b. Frankfort, Ind., May 3, 1896; s. Fred and Nancy (Fisher) W.; student Ind. U., 1914-17, LL.D., 1954; m. Reah

Elizabeth Handy, Oct. 3, 1923; children—Nancy Elizabeth, Tom Frederick, James Handy. Reporter, Richmond (Ind.) Palladium, 1915; editor U.S. Army Newspaper, Camp Crane, 1917, Milan, Italy, 1918; telegraph editor Indpls. Star, 1920-21, Milw. Jour., 1921-28; asst. mng. editor Des Moines Register and Tribune, 1928-31, mng. editor, 1931-37; editor Mpls. Star, 1937-39; editor Mpls. Star-Jour., 1939-41; exec. editor, v.p. Mpls. Star-Jour. and Tribune, 1941-44; exec. editor, dir. Knight Newspapers, Inc. (Chgo. Daily News), 1944-59; editor Chgo. Daily News, 1959-61; pres. Newspaper Research Assos., Chgo., 1961-75. Lyle Spencer prof. journalism Syracuse U., from 1972. Mem. exec. com. A.P. Mng. Editors Assn., 1936, 1940-41; pres. 1941-43, regent, 1971-75; dir. Am. Soc. Newspaper Editors (pres. 1953-54); mem. Allied Newspaper Council, 1943. Served with U.S. Ambulance Service, attached to Italian Army, World War I. Recipient Peter Zenger award U. Ariz., 1956; named to Ind. Newspaper Hall of Fame, 1973. Fellow Sigma Delta Chi, Lambda Chi Alpha; mem. Ind. Acad. Conglist. Mason. Club: Commercial (Chgo.). Home: Frankfort, Ind. Died Aug. 29, 1975; interred Frankfort, Ind.

WALTERS, HERBERT SANFORD, banker, Dem. Nat. committeeman; b. Leadville, Tenn., Nov. 17, 1891; s. John Milo and Lula (Franklin) W.; student Carson Newman Coll., Jefferson City, Tenn., 1907-08. Castle Heights, 1909-10, Univ. of Tenn., 1917; m. Sarah Ruckman Lockridge, July 23, 1928. Engring. dept. C.M. & St.P. Ry., Milwaukee, 1911-14, Ill. Central R.R., Chicago, 1914-16; partner, Harrison Walters & Prater, Morristown, Tenn., 1926, pres. Walters & Prater, Inc., gen. contractors, from 1922; pres. Hamilton Nat. Bank, Morristown, Tenn., from 1946 (dir. from 1933, pres. 1934-35, chmn. bd. 1936-45); commr. State Dept. Highways and Pub. Works, Nashville, 1934-35; v.p., dir. Concrete Materials, Inc., from 1947; dir. C&S Constn. Co., Tenn. Natural Gas Lines, Inc., Hamilton Nat. Bank Knoxville from 1947, Hamilton Nat. Associates, Chattanooga from 1945, E. Tenn. Natural Gas Co. from 1947, Nashville Gas & Heating Company; executive vice pres., 1949-50, chmn. bd., from 1962. Nat. Dem. Committeeman from Tenn., 1945-47, 1956; mem. state Dem. exec. com., 1934-37, chmn., 1940-44, and since 1953. Chairman Morristown Water & Electric Light Commrs., 1944-47. Mem. Morristown Chamber of Commerce (pres. 1945). Trustee King Coll., Bristol, Tenn., treas. King Coll. endowment funds. Trustee U. Tenn., Knoxville, from 1962, mem. devel. council from 1955. Presbyn. Mason. Elk, Kiwanian. Home: Morristown, Tenn. Died Aug. 17, 1973; interred Jarnagin Cemetery, Morristown, Tenn.

WALTERS, ORVILLE SELKIRK, med. educator; b. Enid, Okla., July 17, 1903; s. Frank Simpson and Marjory Pollock (Hynde) W.; A.A., Central Coll., McPherson, Kan., 1922; A.B., U. Kan., 1927, A.M., 1932; Ph.D., 1934; M.D., St. Louis U., 1939; m. Geneva Fern Faley, Aug. 27, 1930; children—Stanley David, Richard Paul, Margery Jean (Mrs. George Douglas Browning). Instr. biology Central Coll., McPherson, 1927-28, pres., 1939-44; instr. chemistry Enid High Sch., 1928-29; mgr. Garber Tool Co. (Okla.), 1929-30; instr. physiology U. Kan., 1930-34, St. Louis U., 1934-39; intern Wesley Hosp., Wichita, Kan., 1943-44; family physician, Buhler, Kan., 1944-45, McPherson, 1945-53; fellow Menninger Sch. Psychiatry, staff psychiatrist VA Hosp., Topeka, 1953-56; staff psychiatrist VA Hosp., Danville, Ill., lectr. psychology with rank asso. prof. U. Ill., 1956-58, dir. health services, med. dir. State Univs. Retirement System, prof. health sci., lectr. psychiatry U. Ill., Urbana, 1958-68, research prof. health sci., lectr. psychiatry, 1968-71; asst. med. dir. for psychiatry Meth. Hosp., Peoria, Ill., 1971-74; clin. prof. psychiatry Peoria Sch. Medicine, U. Ill., 1971-75; vis. prof. Union Bibl. Sem., Yeotmal, India, 1969-70. Sec.-treas., dir. Inst. for Advanced Christian Studies, 1970-74, pres., 1974-75; dir. Free Meth. Found., U. Ill., 1958-71; chmn. bd. trustees Greenville (Ill.) Coll., 1957-64; dir. leadership tng. Free Meth. Ch. N.Am., 1937-59. Diplomate Am. Bd. Psychiatry and Neurology. Fellow A.C.P.; mem. A.M.A., Am. Psychiat. Assn., Acad. Religion and Mental Health, Christian Med. Soc. (v.p. 1965-66), Am. Physiol. Soc., Soc. for Exptl. Biology and Medicine, Sigma Xi, Alpha Omega Alpha. Republican. Free Methodist (deacon, elder). Rotarian. Editor: Recent Books for Ministers, 1959-63. Contbr. articles to profl. and reliqious jours. Home: Peoria, Ill. Died Feb. 16, 1975; interred Parkview Cemetery, Peoria, Ill.

WALTON, CHARLES SPITTALL, JR., leather co. exec.; b. St. Davids, Pa., July 26, 1S93; s. Charles Spittall and Martha (England) W.; grad. Haverford Sch., 1911; B.S., U. Pa., 1915; LL.D. (hon.), Eastern Bapt. Coll., 1958; m. May Potts, April 1, 1915 (dec. 1961); children—Virginia (Mrs. John A. Baird, Jr.), Barbara (Mrs. Elbert K. St. Claire); m. 2d, Elsie Virginia Stout, Sept. 15, 1962. Founder, Chas. S. Walton & Co., Inc., tanners, Phila., Balt., 1919, past pres., dir.; dir. Central Penn Nat. Bank, Phila. Bourse, Hunt Mfg. Co., Hires-Turner Glass Co., Inc., Walton-Gibb Leather Co. Former dir., incorporator Presbyn. Ministers' Fund, Phila.; dir. Tb and Health Soc., Phila., Phila. YMCA (former pres.); dir. Neighborhood League; chmn. bd. Bapt. Orphanage, Phila.; trustee Eastern Bapt. Theol. Sem., Phila., Eastern Bapt. Coll. St. Davids, Pa.; former trustee U. Pa.; trustee Evans Dental Inst. at U. Pa.; life trustee Tanners Research Found., U. Cin.; past dir. Haverford (Pa.) Sch.; past pres., dir. Pa. Theol. Sem. Found., Phila.; Pitts.; dir. Mchts. Fund, Phila.; mem. gen. bd. dirs. Bapt. Conv., Atlantic City, 1940. Mem. Polit. Sci. Acad., Colonial Soc. Pa., Loyal Legion of U.S.A., Phila. Skating and Humane Soc., Pa. Soc. N.Y., Welcome Soc. Pa., Soc. Four Arts English-Speaking Union, Phi Delta Theta. Baptist. Republican. Mason. Clubs: Union League, Art Alliance, Rittenhouse, Peale (Phila.); Merion Cricket (Haverford, Pa.); Everglades, Bath and Tennis (Palm Beach, Fla.). Home: Rosemont Pa., also Palm Beach, Fla. Died Feb. 15, 1973.

WALTON, DUANE EDWARD, pump co. exec.; b. Battle Creek, Mich., June 9, 1915; s. John B. and Elsie L. (Race) W.; grad. Argubright Bus. Coll., Battle Creek, 1937; m. Lura I. Ash, Sept. 4, 1937; children—Julie, Susan. With Duplex Printing Press, Battle Creek, 1937-38, Standard Oil of Ind., Battle Creek, 1938-41; with Union Pump Co., Battle Creek, 1942-73, sec.-treas., 1962-69, v.p., treas., 1969-73, dir., 1970-73. Treas., dir. Battle Creek Symphony Orch. Assn. Mem. Nat. Assn. Accountants. Home: Battle Creek, Mich. Died Nov. 5, 1973; interred Meml. Park Cemetery.

WALTON, JOHN FAWCETT, JR., investment management; born Pitts., Feb. 28, 1893; s. John Fawcett and Annie (Farley) W.; student St. Paul's Sch., Concord, N.H., 1908-12; Ph.B., Yale, 1915; m. Rachel Larimer Mellon, Mar. 30, 1922; children—Anne Farley (Mrs. Joshua C. Whetzel, Jr.), Mary Taylor (Mrs. Walter J. P. Curley, Jr.), John Fawcett, III, James Mellon. With Aluminum Co. of Am., 1919-32; sec.-treas. Aluminum Goods Mfg. Co., 1932-37; v.p. M. B. Sydam Co., 1937-41; dir. Gulf Oil Corp.; bd. govs. T. Mellon & Sons, Pitts., from 1949. Trustee Carnegie Inst., Carnegie Library, Carnegie Inst. Tech., St. Margaret Hosp., Western Pa. Assn. for Blind. Served as ensign USNRF, 1917-19. Presbyn. (trustee). Home: Pittsburgh Pa Died Nov. 1974.

WALTZ, ARTHUR DAVID, physician; b. Williamsport, Pa., Feb. 9, 1884; s. Pierce E. and Emma (Ulmer) W.; B.S., Bucknell U., 1912, M.S., 1914; M.D., U. Pa., 1916; m. Sarah Mary Davies, Oct. 10, 1918. Tng. in clin. pathology Phila. Gen. Hosp., 1920-23; cons. pathologist Delaware County Hosp., Drexel Hill, Pa.; pathologist emeritus Childrens Hosp., Phila.; asso. path. Grad. Sch. Med., U. Pa. Served to lt., M.C., U.S. Army, World War I. Diplomate Am. Bd. Pathology. Mem. A.M.A., Am. Soc. Clin. Pathologists, Coll. Am. Pathologists. Baptist (life deacon). Home: Lansdowne, Pa. Died Nov. 4, 1974; cremated.

WALZER, ELMER C., news consultant, columnist; b. Rochester, N.Y.; student U. Rochester, Columbia U. Tchr. English and history Wagner Luth. Coll., Staten Island, N.Y., 1924-26; with United Press, from 1926, financial editor, 1926-60, consultant United Press Internat. News Dept., from 1960, also writer stock market news and daily column, Financial Gossip, and contbr. two columns weekly to the radio service. Charter mem. and past pres. N.Y. Writers Assn.; mem. Silurians, Sigma Delta Chi (past pres.). Mason, Elk. Home: Clermont, Fla. Died May 18, 1974.

WAMPLER, CLOUD, corporation executive; born Hallsville, Ill., June 7, 1895; s. Thomas Calvin and Elizabeth (Cloud) Wampler; B.S.; Knox Coll., 1916; LL.D. (honoary), Hobart College, 1944, Knox College, 1946, Syracuse University, 1951; L.H.D. (honary), LeMoyne College, 1958; married to Eugenia Trask, June 29, 1918; children—Elizabeth (Mrs. William Macfarlane Jones), Eleanor (Mrs. E. Charles Majer). With Harris Trust & Savings Bank, Chicago, 1916; sales mgr. Taylor, Ewart & Co., investments, Chicago, 1920-29, vice pres., 1921-29; vice pres. and dir. Lawrence Stern & Co., Chicago, 1929-38; pres. Stern, Wampler & Co., Inc., Chicago, 1938-41; dir. Carrier Corp., Syracuse, N.Y., 1935-65, chmn. finance com., 1938-65, chmn. exec. com., 1953-65, exec. v.p., 1941-42, pres., 1942-52, pres. and chmn., 1952-56, chmn. bd. 1956-65; dir. Marine Midland Trust Co., Marine Midland Corp. Mem. bd. govs. Nat. Indsl. Conf. Bd.; trustee Tax Found., Inc.; founding dir. Nat. Found. for Advanced Econ. Research; trustee Nat. Fund for Grad. Nursing Education; dir. Empire State Found. Ind. Liberal Arts Colls.; founding mem. Citizens Found., Inc. Served as capt. Hdqrs., 86th Div., asst. chief of staff, G-2, 1917-19. Mem. Mfrs. Assn. Syracuse (dir.), Pilgrims of U.S., Phi Gamma Delta, Delta Sigma Rho, Beta Gamma Sigma. Clubs: Century, Onondago Golf and Country (Syracuse); Links (N.Y.C.); Cloud (Phoenix). Presbyn. Home: Scottsdale, Ariz. Died Nov. 14, 1973.

WANGLER, THEODORE JOSEPH, clergyman, b. St. Louis, Aug. 8, 1905; s. Joseph A. and Magdalen (Fehlig) W.; A.M., St. Mary's Sem., Perryville, Mo., 1932; M.S., Columbia, 1937; student De Paul U., Chgo., 1932-35. Entered Soc. of Congregation of the Mission, 1923; ordained priest Roman Catholic Ch., 1932; mem. faculty DePaul U., 1932, instr. math., 1932-35, instr. chemistry, 1937, later asst. prof., prof. chemistry 1943, chmn. dept. chemistry, 1943, dean Coll. Liberal Arts and Scis., 1945-55, trustee 1945-70, v.p. student affairs, 1955-70, then adviser to pres. in community relations. Mem. exec. com., dir. Lincoln Park Conservation Assn.; mem. Conservation Community Council; mem. adv. com. Chgo. Dept. Human Relations. Mem. N.E.A., Nat. Cath. Ednl. Assn., Phi Kappa Alpha, Delta Epsilon Sigma (past nat. pres.). Home: Chicago, Ill. Died Nov. 28, 1973; interred All Saints Cemetery, Des Plaines, Ill.

WANKOWICZ, MELCHIOR, author; b. Kaluzyce, Byelorussia, USSR; Jan 10, 1892; s. Melchior and Maria (Szwoynicka) W.; magister luris, U. Warsaw, 1923; m. Zofia Malagowska, Feb. 8, 1916; children—Krystyna (dec.), Marta (Mrs. Jan. Erdman). War corr. World War II. Served with Polish Army, World War I, Polish-Russian War, 1920. Decorated Casino cross; comdr. Polonia Restitua; cross Independent Polish Lit. Acad. Mem. Polish Writers Assn., PEN Club. Author: Tatters of an Epos, 1922; The Field Hospital at Cichinicze, 1923; (children) O Matej Matgosi, 1924; In the Churches of Mexico, 1927; The Puppy Years, 1934; The Feathered Revolution, 1935; On the Trail of Nazi Devil, 1936; C.O.P., 1937; The Relay, 1939; De Profundis, 1943; Golgotha Road, 1944; The Battle of Monte Cassino, 3 vols., 1947; The Club of the Third Place, 1949; Sprouts on the Volcano, 1951; Poles in America, 1955; Here and There, 1961; The Fighting Griffon, 1964; From the Horse's Mouth, 1965; Broth on Nails, 1967; Atlantic-Pacific, 1967; Rabbit and the Oceans, 1968; Sketches from Monte Cassino, 1969; In the Navel of U.S.A., 1969; From Stolpce to Cairo, 1969; Four Climates, 1971; The War and the Pen, 1972; Lafontaine's Decanter, 1972, others. Contbr. mags. Home: Warsaw, Poland. Died Sept. 1974.

WANSTROM, RUTH CECILIA, physician; b. Rockford, Ill., Apr. 10, 1893; d. Gustavus Adolphus and Emma C. (Anderson) Wanstrom; M.D., U. Mich., 1918, M.A. in Pathology, 1924. Intern, Meml. Hosp., Worcester, Mass., 1918-19; research asst. dept. pathology U. Mich., Ann Arbor, 1922-24, asst. prof. pathology, 1925, later prof.; postgrad. in pathology U. Vienna, 1927-28. Recipient spl. scroll U. Mich. Med. Sch. Faculty, 1958. Diplomate Am. Bd. Pathology. Fellow A.C.P.; mem. Am. Assn. Pathologists and Baceriologists, Internat. Acad. Pathology, Mich. Soc. Pathologists (pres. 1938), Alpha Omega Alpha. Episcopalian. Research on spirochetes. Home: San Angelo, Tex. Died Dec. 23, 1971, buried Scandanavian Cemetery, Rockford, Ill.

WARBURG, FREDERICK MARCUS, banking; b. New Yok, N.Y., Oct. 14, 1897; s. Felix Moritz and Frieda (Schiff) W.; ed. Middlesex Sch., Concord, Massachusetts, 1910-15; A.B., Harvard University, 1919; married Wilma L. Shannon, March 4, 1946. Asso. with Am. Internat. Corp., 1919-21, M.M. Warburg & Co., Hamburg, Germany, 1921-22, Kuhn, Leob & Co., 1922-27, Lehman Bros., 1927-30; partner Kuhn, Loeb & Co., 1931-73; dir. Los Angles & Salt Lake R.R.; trustee Union Pacific Railroad Foundation. Servid as lt. inf. United States Army Res., 1918-37; Col. U.S. Army Spl. Service Div., 1941-46. Vice president of New York Foundation; director Boy Scout Council of Greater New York; chairman of The Fresh Air Fund, Trustee Middlesex Sch., Nat. Recreation Assn., Fedn. Jewish Philanthropies. Jewish religion. Clubs: River, Harvard, Century Assn. (N.Y.C.); Tavern (Boston). Home: New York City, N.Y., also Middleburg, Va., also Cos Cob, Conn. Died July 10, 1973.

WARBURTON, CLYDE WILLIAMS, agronomist; b. Independence, Ia., Dec. 7, 1879; s. William Henry and Ellen Clarissa (Irvine) W.; B.S. in Agr., Ia. State Coll. Agr. and Mechanic Arts, 1902, D.Sc., 1925; m. Anne Eliza Draper, Oct. 16, 1907. With U.S. Dept. Agr. from 1903, except 1911-12; successively asst. agr., Office Of Farm Management, 1903-07, in charge oat investigations. Bur. Plant Industry, 1907-10, and 1912-20, in charge cereal agronomy experiments, 1920-23, dir. extension work, U.S. Dept. Agr., Sept. 1923-Jan. 1940; deputy gov., Farm Credit Adminstrn. February 1940-September 1945; retired October 1945; editor book department Webb Publishing company, St. Paul, Minn., 1911-12. Fellow A.A.A.S.; mem. Am. Soc. Agronomy (sec. 1915-18, pres. 1925), Washington Acad. Science, Beta Theta Pi, Phi Kappa Phi, Gamma Sigma Delta (pres. Nat. Council, 1925-26). Episcopalian. Club: Cosmos. Author: (with A. D. Wilson) Field Crops, 1912. Editor Jour. Am. Soc. Agronomy, 1915-21. Home: Washington, D.C.†

WARD, CHARLES BONNELL, ex-congressman, financier; b. Newark, N.J., Apr. 27, 1879; s. Elias Sayre and Anna Dickerson (Bonnell) W.; B.S., Pa. Mil. Coll., Chester, 1898; m. Anachen Katherin Heller, of Newark, N.J., Dec. 11, 1905. Editor Liberty (N.Y.) Register, from 1910, also pres. Liberty Register Co.; dir. Nat. Bank of Liberty; pres. Livingston Manor (N.Y.) Nat. Bank. Mem. 64th to 68th Congresses (1915-25), 27th N.Y. Dist. Republican. Episcopalian. Mason. Home: De Bruce, N.Y.†

WARD, FRANK TRENWITH, JR., Naval officer; b. Raleigh, N.C. Dec. 25, 1901; s. Frank Trenwith and Lulu Tucker (Holden) W.; student N.C. State Coll., 1917-18; B.S., U.S. Naval Acad., 1923; m. Thelma Phelps, Sept. 3, 1932; children—Jane C., Anne Elizabeth, Frank Trenwith. Commd. ensign, U.S. Navy, 1923, and advanced through grades to rear adm., 1950; comd. VP 11, 1939-40; director U.S. Naval Aviation Training, 1943; comd. U.S.S. Shamrock Bay (CVE84), 1944-45, U.S.S. Wright (CVL 49), 1947; comdt. of Midshipmen, 1947-49; chief of staff, Compair Jax,

1949-50; chief Navy adv. group Air U. from 1950, ret., 1958. Awarded Legion of Merit with gold star (combat), Letter of Commendation (combat). Decorated Honorary Knight Comdr. of British Empire (mil. div.), 1947; Officer, Order of Leopold, 1948. Mem. U.S. Naval Inst. Episcopalian. Home: Coronado, Cal., Died Feb. 8, 1976.

WARD, GORDON BERT, ins. co. exec.; b. Pine Forest, Fla., Apr. 7, 1909; s. Aulsie A. and Alice (Strickland) W.; grad. pub. schs.; m. Mary Nash, June 3, 1933; children—G. Bert, Sharon Ward Henderson. With Life of Ga., Mobile, Ala. and Little Rock, 1933-57, state mgr., 1948-57; v.p. Nat. Investors Life, Little Rock, 1957-59; pres., chmn. bd. dirs. Investors Preferred Life, Little Rock, 1959-68; chmn. bd. Western Preferred Life, Denver, 1962-74; chmn. Nat. Preferred Life, Great States Life, Royal Am. Life, Am. Preferred Life, Great Mo. Life, Tenn. Nat. Life, Ward-Douglass Distbg. Co. Served with AUS, 1943-45. Mem. Ark. Life Underwriters Assn. (dir. 1948-68), Nat. Assn. Life Cos., Ark. Life Conv. Democrat. Baptist. Mason (32 deg., Shriner). Clubs: Little Rock; Pleasant Valley Country. Home: Little Rock, Ark. Died Mar. 26, 1974; interred Pinecrest Cemetery Mauseleum, Little Rock, Ark.

WARD, HOLCOMBE, textile mfr.; b. New York, N.Y. Nov. 23, 1878; s. Robert and Mary Elizabeth (Snedekor) W.; A.B. Harvard Univ., 1900; m. Louise Palen Conway, Apr. 16, 1905; children—Elizabeth E., Helen L. (Mrs. Richard M. Hurd, Jr.). Began with French & Ward, textile mfrs., New York, 1900, mem. of firm, 1901 to liquidation, 1983. Pres. U.S. Lawn Tennis Assn., from 1937. Mem. Fly Club (Harvard). Republican. Episcopalian. (vestryman St. Peters Ch., Galilee, N.J.). Clubs: Harvard (New York); Seabright (N.J.) Lawn Tennis & Cricket (hon.), Heights Casino of Brooklyn (hon.); Orange Lawn Tennis (hon.) Home: Red Bank, N.J.†

WARD, JOHN HARRIS, co. dir.; b. Kansas City, Mo., Mar. 17, 1908; s. Hugh C. and Vassie (James) W.; A.B., Harvard, 1930, M.B.A., 1932; m. Mary Godwin Van Etten, Aug. 18, 1931; children—David Harris, John Anthony. Staff NRA, Washington, 1933-35; joined Commonwealth Edison Co., 1938, sec., 1948-55, v.p., 1951-55, exec. v.p., 1955-59, pres., 1959, pres., chmn., chief exec. officer, 1961, chmn., chief exec. officer, 1964-73, also dir.; dir. No. Trust Co., Internat. Harvester Co., Union Carbide Corp., N.Y. Life Ins. Co. Pres., Community Fund Chgo., 1959-60; mem. Chgo. Central Area Com., 1964-73, Com. Econ. and Cultural Devel. Chgo.; bus. adv. com. Chgo. Urban League; exec. dir. compliance div. WPB, 1940-42, exec. dir. organizational control, 1942. Trustee Mus. Sci. and Industry, U. Chgo.; mem. vis. com. Harvard Bus. Sch. Served as maj., ordnance dept. AUS, 1944; staff strategic bombing survey ETO. Decorated Bronze Star. Mem. Asso. Harvard Alumni (past pres.). Clubs: Onwentsia, Old Elm (Lake Forest); Commercial, Commonwealth, Chicago (Chgo.). Home: Lake Forest, Ill. Died July 28, 1974.

WARD, ROBERT STAFFORD, educator; b. Waltham, Mass., Dec. 20, 1906; s. George Liggett and Huldah Jane (Barnes) W.; grad. Phillips Acad., Andover, Mass., 1925; B.A., Yale, 1929; M.A., Boston U., 1932, Ph.D., 1951; LL.B., Harvard, 1937; m. Anne Caverly Connally, Mar. 31, 1944; children—Thomas C., Linda Elizabeth Ward Jacobsen, Anne Calhoun. Head coach football, master English, Blair Acad., Blairstown, N.J., 1929-32; asst. football coach Yale, 1932-33; admitted to Mass. bar, 1937; pvt. practice, Boston, 1937-42; faculty U. Miami (Fla.), 1946-72, asso. prof. English, 1951-56, prof., 1956-72, chmn div. humanities, 1962-68, chmn. grad. Am. studies, 1968-72. Mem. Sch. Com. Waltham, Mass., 1937-43. Served to comdr. USNR, 1942-46. So. Fellowship Fund grantee, 1968-69. Mem. Modern Lang. Assn., So. Modern Lang. Assn., Psi Upsilon. Club: Yale (Miami). Editor Longfellow's jours. Home: Miami, Fla. Died May 22, 1975.

WARDEN, JAMES, banker; b. Mt. Pleasant, Pa., May 15, 1907; s. Eugene and Pleasant (Glessner) W.; B.S., Washington and Jefferson Coll., 1928; J.D., Duquesne U., 1931; Litt. M., U. Pitts., 1951; m. Emily Bryce, Jan. 30, 1933; children—Mary Bryce, James Bryce, Gerard Bryce. With Pitts. Nat. Bank and predecessors, 1929, v.p., trust officer, 1935-46, v.p., sec., 1959-69, v.p. comml. banking div., 1969-73; dir. Washington Steel Corp., Newcomer Products, Inc. Mem. City Pitts. Bd. Edn., 1958-70. Mem. Am., Pa., Allegheny County bar assns., Am. Soc. Corporate Secs., Newcomen Soc. N.Am., Civil War Roundtable, Pitts. Junta, Phi Delta Theta, Phi Delta Phi. Episcopalian (vestryman). Clubs: Duquesne, University, Fox Chapel Golf (Pitts.); Laurel Valley Golf, Rolling Rock (Ligonier, Pa.); Pinehurst (N.C.) Country. Home: Jones Mills, Pa. Died Jan. 24, 1973; interred Mt. Pleasant (Pa.) Cemetery.

WARE, ALLISON, educator; b. Santa Rosa, Cal., Apr. 2, 1880; s. Allison Burr and Lilla (Werlein) W.; B.L., U. of Cal., 1903; m. Maud Boyne, of Sacramento, Cal. Instr. in high sch., 1903-05; supervisor San Francisco State Normal Sch., 1905-10; candidate for state supt. pub. instrn. on first Progressive ticket, 1910; prs. State Normal Sch., Chico, from 1910. Mem. Cal. State Bd. Edn., 1910-12. mem. Cal. Teacher's Assn. (pres. northern sect. 1913). Clubs: Cal. Schoolmasters', Scholia, Commonwealth, etc. Author: Map Geography, 1908; The Common Literature of Life, 1909; Common Essentials in Spelling, 1914. Lecturer on ednl. topics. Commd. capt., Inf. U.S.R., Nov. 8, 1917 (on leave of absence from State Noraml Sch.). Address: Chico, Cal.†

WAREHAM, JOHN HAMILTON DEE, art dir., Rookwood Pottery Co.; b. Grand Ledge, Mich., January 27, 1881;s. Hamilton and Julia Ellen (Delaney) W.; grad. Grand Ledge High School; student Cincinnati Art Acad.; awarded 2 foreign travel scholarships; unmarried. Began as artist, 1900; awarded diploma and bronze medal, St. Louis; trustee, under will of Wm. Watts Taylor, Rookwood Pottery Company, 1913-34, v.p. and treas., 1913-34, pres. and treas. from 1934; mem. bd. of dirs. The Crafters Company, President Municipal Art Soc., Cincinnati, from 1913; trustee Cincinnati Music Hall Association, Cincinnati Union Bethal; dir., Cemetery of Spring Grove; mem. visiting committee Dept. of Art and Archeology, Princeton. Mem. Duveneck Soc. of Painters, Cincinnati MacDowell Soc. Clubs: Cincinnati Art, Commonwealth (president 1931), Commercial, Queen City, Cincinnati Country. Home: Cincinnati O.†

WARFIELD, ETHELBERT, lawyer; b. Easton, Pa., Feb. 28, 1898; s. Ethelbert D. and Nellie Frances (Tilton) W.; LL.B., Dickinson Sch. Law, 1922; m. Dorothy Lewis Marshall, Apr. 14, 1927; m. 2d, Alice Blum Taliaferro, Nov. 11, 1967. Admitted to N.Y. bar, 1928, Pa. bar, 1923, U.S. Supreme Ct. bar, 1941; practiced in N.Y.C., 1922-23, 1926-71, Phila., 1923-26, Oyster Bay, N.Y., 1971-74; partner Kellogg, Emery & Inness-Brown, 1929-41; partner Satterlee, Warfield & Stephens, 1941-69, counsel, 1969-71. Dir. ASG Industries Inc., Edie Instl. Fund, Inc., Edie Spl. Growth Fund, Inc., Gen. Reins. Corp.; pres. Lin Processing Corp., mem. adv. com. Chem. Bank. Mem. Am., N.Y. State, Phila., Nassau County bar assns., Assn. Bar City N.Y., Mural Artists Guild (hon.). Home: Oyster Bay, N.Y. Died July 23, 1974.

WARK, GEORGE H., army officer; b. Kansas, Dec. 19, 1878; LL.B., U. of Kansas, 1903; apptd. 1st lt. Inf. Kan. Nat. Guard, May 1909; entered Fed. service, World War I; commd. capt. F.A., Kan. Nat. Guard 1922, and advanced to brig. gen. of the line, Feb. 1933; entered Fed. service Dec. 1940, in command of 60th Arty. Brigade, 35th Div. in training at Camp Joseph T. Robinson, Ark.; relieved of assignment June 25, 1941, and continued at Camp Joseph T. Robinson. Address: Camp Joseph T. Robinson, Ark.†

WARNACH, PAUL VICTOR, clergyman; b. Metz, France, July 28, 1909; s. Paul-Wilhelm and Elisabeth (Schoppmann) W.; student State U. Bonn and Cologne (Germany), 1927; Dr. Phil., Sant'Anselmo, U. Rome (Italy), 1935. Joined Benedictine Order, 1927; lectr. philosophy Benedictine Monastery Maria Laach, Rhineland, 1936-58, lectr. Bibl. theology, 1938-42; chaplain Benedictine nunnery Herstelle, Weser, Westphalia, 1951-57; tchr. philosophy State Faculty Theology, Salzburg, Austria, 1958; prof. U. Salzburg, 1962-70, pres. Inst. Philosophy, 1963-69, dean faculty theology, 1967-68; mem. Protestant-Cath. Circle for Ecumenical Work, Paderborner Kreis, Germany, 1946-70. Active in resocialization of former prisoners. Mem. Philosophische Gesellschaft Salzburg (v.p.), Abt-Herwegen Inst., Benedictine Acad. Munich. Author: Erkennen und Sprechen bel Thomas von Aquin, 1938, 2d edit., 1941; (with H. Schlier) Die Kirche im Epheserbrief, 1949; Agape. Die Liebe als Grundmotiv der neutestamentlichen Theologie, 1951; Contbr. profl. jours. Editor Salzburger Jahrbuch fur Philosophie, 1959-60; founding editor Salzburger Studien zur Philosophie, 1962-70. Home: Salzburg, Austria. Died May 6, 1970.

WARNER, BRADFORD NEWMAN, pub. relations exec.; b. Fairfield, Conn., June 27, 1924; s. Bradford G. and Eunice (Newman) W.; student Choate Sch., 1940-43, Yale, 1943, Brown U., 1944-47; m. Marilyn Hammond, Nov. 29, 1947; children—Bradford Hammond, Victoria Hammond. Expediter, Warnaco Inc., Bridgeport, historian, 1947-50, asst. personnel mgr., 1950-57, mgr. pub., employee relations, 1957-62, dir. corporate community & employee relations, 1962-71, historian, 1964-71, also dir.; pres. Warnaco Fund, Inc., 1964; dir. Fairfield br. City Trust Co. Chmn., A.R.C. fund drive, Fairfield, 1960-62, Chmn. Fairfield chpt., 1964-66; v.p. Barnum Festival Soc., 1962 ringmaster 1961, pres., 1963; chmn. Park City Hosp. fund drive, 1965-69. Past chmn. Conn. YMCA Indsl. Recreation council; chmn. pub. relations com. Bridgeport YMCA capital fund drive; campaign chmn. United Fund, 1963; regional rep. Am. Social Health Assn., 1969. Bd. dirs. United Fund of Eastern Fairfield County, Mus. Art. Sci. and Industry; Pres. Park City Hosp., 1969-71; bd. dirs. Greater Bridgeport YMCA, Bridgeport Community Chest and Council, Mountain Grove Cemetery Assn.; bd. assos. U. Bridgeport, 1964-71, indsl. adv. com., 1965-71, 3d v.p., 1969; bd. dirs. Jr. Achievement S.W. Conn., Goodwill Industries, Bridgeport; trustee Woodfield Children's Village, Fairfield. Mem. bd. finance Town of Fairfield, 1965-67, bd. selectmen, 1967-69, sewer commr., 1970; mem. Fairfield Charter Revision Com., 1970. Named Young Man of Year, Jr. C. of C., 1960. Mem. Bridgeport C. of C. (past chmn. comml. relations com., vice chmn. pub. affairs com.), Pub. Relations Soc. Am. (pres. Conn. chpt. 1964-66), Greater Bridgeport. Personnel Assn., Bridgeport Mfrs. Assn. (chmn. community relations). Conglist. Rotarian. Club: Exchange (past pres., Bridgeport). Home: Fairfield, Conn. Died July 16, 1971.

WARNER, FRANKLIN HUMPHREY, business exec.; b. New York City, June 6, 1875; s. Lucien Calvin and Karen Sarah Tersa (Osborne) W.; tutored in Lausanne, Switzerland; B.S., Oberlin Coll., 1898, A.B., 1907; LL.D., Pacific Univ., 1945; m. Estelle Dunn Hynes, Apr. 25, 1899; children—Lucien Hynes, Douglas Calvin. Founder, dir., pres., Warner Chemical Co., 1901, Westvaco Chlorine Products Corp. from 1910; pres. and dir. Citizens Nat. Bank, Claremont, Calif. from 1930. Served in various offices for educational, religious and philanthropic advancement. Asso. moderator, General Council of Conglist-Christian Churches, 1929-31, mem. exec. com., 1927-33, treas., 1923-27; mem. commn. of status of ministry, 1919-22, evangelism and devotional life, 1921-27 (treas. 1923-29), seminar on worship, 1925-29; del. to Internat. Council of Conglist. Churches, Bournmouth, Eng., 1930; mem.-at-large Am. B. of Commissioners for Fgn. Missions, from 1917, prudential com., 1923-32, also mem. subcoms.; mem. Conglist. Church Building Soc. (dir. 1915-21); trustee, v.p., pres., Yenching U., Peiping, China; trustee. Also Bd. of Christian Colls. in China, 1934-39; treas. trustees Am. Coll., Madura, India; corporate mem. Kobe Coll., Japan; turstee trustee. Also Bd. of Christian Colls. in China, 1934-39; treas. trustees Am. Coll., Madura, India; corporate mem. Kobe Coll., Japan; trustee Pacific U., Forest Grove, Ore., 1943-54; dir., pres. White Plains (New York), Y.M.C.A.; dir. Casa Colina Home for Crippled Children, Chino, Calif. from 1930. (v.p., 1937-44, pres. 1944-46). Served in U.S. Army Air Force as ground observer, 1942-43. Conglist. Clubs: University, Chemical (New York); Union (Boston); Red Hill Country (Upland, Calif.) Mem. Mayflower Soc., New England Soc. Republican. Home: Claremont, Cal.†

WARNER, JACK F., physician; b. St. Louis, 1912; s. Ben and Sarah Warner; M.D., Wayne State U., 1942; m. Edith Zloatnick, July 18, 1943; children—Rachel, Deborah, Elizabeth. Intern, Pontiac (Mich.) Gen. Hosp., 1941-42; tng. Pontiac State Hosp., 1942-45, Eloise Hosp., 1945-46; clin. dir. Detroit Med. Hosp.; instr. clin. psychiatry Wayne State U. Diplomate Am. Bd. Psychiatry and Neurology. Mem. A.M.A., Am. Psychiat. Assn. Home: West Los Angeles, Cal. Died Oct. 12, 1967; buried Hillside Meml. Park, Los Angeles, Cal.

WARNER, JAMES EDWARD, writer, editor; born Providence, Dec. 17, 1905; s. Edward George and Mary Ann (Worthy) W.; student pub. schs., Providence; m. Marion Steele, Sept. 16, 1933; dau., Marion (Mrs. John W. Bogle). Reporter, Providence Jour., 1923-29, asst. Washington corr., 1929-31, city staff, 1931-36, staff Washington br., 1936-42; press div. Office of Censorship, Washington, also N.Y.C., 1942-45; bur. news editor, asst. chief Washington bur. N.Y. Herald Tribune, 1945-57, White House corr., 1957-64; free-lance writer, editor; cons. adminstrn. on aging U.S. Dept. Health. Edn. and Welfare, 1966-67; assistant editor, later editor Aging magazine, 1967-75. Decorated Chevalier Ordre Coronne (Belgium). Mem. White House corrs. Assn., Overseas Writers Washington. Sigma Delta Chi (past pres. Washington). Club: Nat. Press (past sec., bd. govs.) (Washington). Home: Washington, D.C. Died Sept. 14, 1975; interred St. Joseph Cemetery, Boston, Mass.

WARNER, ROBERT FORESMAN, hotel cons.; b. Newark, May 13, 1909; s. Bartley Shuster and Edith (Gray) W.; student Northwestern U., 1927-31; m. Josephine Cadman, Oct. 8, 1936; children—Lois Suzanne (Mrs. Malcolm Dean Williams), Robert Cadman, Jody Gray (Mrs. John Winfield Stumpf). Founder, chmn. Robert F. Warner, Inc., internat. hotel sales cons., N.Y.C., 1934-73; pioneer sales devel., representation, mgmt. cons. for ind. owned operated resorts and hotels; originated Distinguished Hotels, de luxe ind. owned city hotels, 1952; pres. Hotel Ednl. Bur., Inc., N.Y.C., 1939-73, Warner Publs, N.Y.C., pubs. Digest of Distinguished Resorts, Digest of Conv. Locations, Warner Reservation and Information Manual; chmn. Whiteface Inn Corp.; dir. Glen W. Fawcett, Inc., Koehl, Landis, Landan, Inc., advt. Mem. Am. Hotel and Motel Assn., Am. Soc. Travel Agts., Hotels Sales Mgmt. Assn., Internat. hotel assns. Presbyn. Clubs: Sky, Lake Placid, Rockefeller Center Luncheon, Internat. (N.Y.C.); Ardsley Country (Ardsley-on-Hudson, N.Y.); Sleepy Hollow Country (ScarboroughN.Y.). Home: Lolly's Hill, Bermuda, also Ardsley-on-Hudson, N.Y. Died May 1973.

WARNER, W. LLOYD, univ. prof., anthropologist and sociologist; born in Redlands, California, October 26, 1898; son of William Taylor and Clara Belle (Carter) W.; A.B., University of Calif., 1925, postgrad., 1925-26 m. Mildred Hall, Jan. 12, 1932; children—Ann Covington Warner Arlen, Caroline Hall (Mrs. John B. Hightower), William Taylor. Research for Rockefeller Foundn. and Australia, Nat. Research Council, Australia, 1926-29; instr., then asst. prof. anthropology Harvard, 1929-35; asso. prof. and prof. anthropology, Sociology and human devel. U. Chgo., 1935-59; Univ.

Prof. Social Research, Michigan State University, 1959-70; research on N.E., Deep South, Chgo. Negro, Middlewestern communities, also on careers of Am. big bus. leaders and Am. industry, Am. Fed. execs., Am. large-scale orgns. and mass media and symbolic behavior. Member American Academy of Arts and Sciences, Am. Anthrop. Assn., American Sociological Society, also mem. Sigma Xi. Author or co-author: Black Civilization (Australia); Yankee City Series, 5 vols.; Social Class in America; American Life, Dream and Reality; Big Business Leaders in America; Occupational Mobility in American Business and Industry; The Living and The Dead; Industrial Man; The Corporation in the Emergent American Society; The American Federal Executive; the Emergent American Society. Home: Chesterton, Ind. Died May 20, 1970; inurned Borrego Springs, Cal.

WARNOCK, ERNEST HENRY, physician; b. Portland, Ind., Dec. 3, 1903; s. William Heenan and Anna (Sommers) W.; M.D., Ind. U., 1932; m. Mary Frances Ogle, May 20 1933; children—William, Nancy (Mrs. Richard Sombrano). Intern, Ind. U. Hosps., 1932-33; sr. resident in anesthesiology Hartford (Conn.) Hosp., 1937-38; head anesthesiologist Hartford Municipal Hosp., 1939; head dept. anesthesiology Hoff Hosp., Santa Barbara, Cal., 1942-44, Letterman Hosp., San Francisco, 1944-45, Walter Reed Hosp., Washington, 1945-46; sr. staff Hosp. of Good Samaritan, Los Angeles past vice chmn. med. staff, past chmn. sect. anesthesiology; courtesy staff St. Vincent's Hosp., Los Angeles; cons. VA Hosp., Los Angeles, 1946-49; founder, anesthesiologist Methodist Hosp., Arcadia, Cal. Served to maj., M.C., AUS, 1942-46. Diplomate Am. Bd. Anesthesiology. Fellow Am. Coll. Anesthesiology (gov. 1948-52); mem. A.M.A., Am. Soc. Anesthesiologists (dir. 19th dist. 1949-51), Los Angeles Acad. Medicine, Cal., Los Angeles County med. assns., Phi Rho. Presbyn. Clubs: City (San Marino, Cal.); Pasadena (Cal.) Casting. Pioneer cardiac anesthesiology. Home: San Marino, Cal. Died Oct. 1, 1974; buried Rose Hills, Whittier, Cal.

WARREN, CASPER CARL, clergyman; b. Sampson Co., N.C., May 28, 1896; s. Richard Moore and Rosella (Strickland) W.; B.A., Wake Forest Coll., 1917, LL.B., 1920, D.D., 1948; Th.M., So. Bapt. Sem., Louisville, 1925, Th.D., 1928; D.D., Ouachita Coll., Ark., 1944; m. Mary Lashbrook Strickland, Aug. 26, 1925. Ordained to ministry, Bapt. Ch., 1922; pastor Lexington Av. Bapt. Ch., Danville, Ky., 1928-38, Immanuel Bapt. Ch., Little Rock, Ark., 1938-43, First Bapt. Ch., Charlotte, 1943-58; dir. 30,000 Movement, So. Bapt. Conv., from 1958; guest preacher Bapt. Hour and Columbia Ch. of Air, 1948; pres. N.C. Bapt. State Conv., 1946-47; 1st v.p. So. Baptist Conv., 1953, pres. pastor's conf. 1952-53; pres. N.C. Bapt. Gen. Bd. 1950-54; pres. So. Bapt. Exec. Com., 1953; president of Southern Baptist Convention, 1955. Served as 2d lt. CAC, World War I. Club: Charlotte Executives. Address: Charlotte, N.C. Died May 20, 1973.

WARREN, EARL, chief justice U.S.; b. Los Angeles, Mar. 19, 1891; s. Methias H. and Chrystal (Hernlund) W.; B.A. U. Cal., 1912, J.D., 1914, LL.D.; recipient numerous hon. degrees; m. Nina P. Meyers, Oct. 14, 1925; children—James C., Virginia (Mrs. John Charles Daly), Earl, Dorothy (Mrs. Harry Van Knight), Nina Elizabeth (Mrs. Stuart Brien), Robert. Admitted to Cal. bar, 1914, practiced in San Francisco, Oakland, 1914-17; clk. assembly judiciary com. Cal. Legislature, 1919; dep. city atty., Oakland, 1919-20; dep. dist. atty. Alameda County, 1920-23, chief dep., 1923-25, dist. atty., 1925-39; atty. gen. Cal., 1939-43; gov. Cal., 1943-53; spl. U.S. ambassador to coronation Queen Elizabeth II, 1953; chief justice U.S., 1953-69. Research asso. Bur. Pub. Adminstrn., U. Cal., 1932-40; pres. Nat. Assn. Attys. Gen., 1940-41. Chancellor. bd. regents Smithsonian Instn., 1953-69; chmn. bd. trustees Nat. Gallery Art, 1953-69. Alternate del. Republican Nat. Conv., 1928, del., 1932; chmn. Rep. Nat. Conv., 1944; Rep. candidate for v.p. U.S., 1948. Served as 1st lt., inf. U.S. Army, 1917-18; capt. res. until 1936. Mem. State Bar Cal., Alameda County and Sacramento County bar assns., Am. Acad. Arts and Scis., Nat. Geog. Soc. (trustee), Am. Philos. Soc., Selden Soc., Phi Delta Phi, Sigma Phi. Republican. Mason (33 deg., grand master Cal. 1935-36). Clubs: Olympic, Bohemian (San Francisco): Athens Athletic, Claremont Country (Oakland): Jonathan, California (Los Angeles); Sutter, Del Paso Country (Sacramento). Home: Washington, D.C. Died July 9, 1974; buried Arlington National Cemetery.

WARREN, FULLER, gov. Florida; b. Blountstown, Fla., Oct. 3, 1905; s. Charles Ryan and Grace (Fuller) W.; grad., Thomas indsl. Inst., 1922; student, Univ. of Fla., 1922-27; LL.B., Cumberland University, 1928; married Barbara Manning., June, 1949. Admitted to Florida State bar, 1929, and practiced in Jacksonville, 1929-48; elected to Fla. legislature from Calhoun Co., 1926-28; del. to Democratic Nat. Conv., 1928; mem. Jacksonville City Council, 1931-37; elected to State legislature from Duval Co., 1938-40; elected chief exec. of Fla. for term, 1949-53; dir., Riverside Bank, Jacksonville. Served as gunnery officer with rank of lt. j.g., U.S. Navy, 1942-45. Mem. Fla. Bar Assn., Am. Legion, Vets. of Fgn. Wars, Theta Chi. Democrat. Baptist. Elk. Author: Speaking of Speaking, 1943; How To Win In Politics, 1948l Died Sept. 23, 1973.

WARREN, GEORGE EARLE, banker; b. Brooklyn, N.Y., Jan. 9, 1881; s. Walter S. and Marguerite (Reyrer) W.; student Columbia U., 1903; M.A. (hon.), Middlebury Coll.; LL.D., Tuskegee Inst., 1963; m. Anna Kearney, Nov. 25, 1916. Dir. Chgo Title Guaranty Co., Inter Ocean Isn. Co., Am. Re-Ins. Co., Seaboard Fire & Marine Ins. Co., Yorkshire Ins. Co., also dir. Commercial Investment Trust (C.I.T.) Corp.; trust advisory committee, vice president Chase Manhattan Bank. Trustee Columbia; Trustee and mem. finance com. Tuskegee Inst.; trustee N.Y. Infirmary; member board of trustees and treasurere Ladd Found.; treas. and dir. The Andrew Freedman Home. Member Down Town Assn. Clubs: University, Washington, Men's Faculty (Columbia U.); Columbia University. Mem. Chamber of Commerce of State of N.Y. Home: Washington, Conn.†

WARREN, JOHN DAVOCK, investment banker; b. Buffalo, June 11, 1904; s. William Candee and Clara Sizer (Davock) W.; grad. Hill Sch., 1923; B.A., Yale, 1927; m. Helen G. Lynch, May 29, 1948; 1 son, Thomas Davock. With Marine Trust Co., Buffalo, 1928-29; mem. N.Y. Stock Exchange, 1930-31; partner Gammack & Co., N.Y.C., 1932-44, G.H. Walker & Co., N.Y.C., 1944-75; dir. Conrae Corp., Nat. Licorice Co. Bd. govs. Am. Stock Exchange, 1960-66. Clubs: Yale, Links (N.Y.C.). Home: Essex, Conn. Died Oct. 26, 1975; interred Buffalo, N.Y.

WARRINER, REUEL EDWARD, metal co. exec.; b. Johnannesburg, South Africa, Apr. 19, 1910; s. Ruel Chaffee and Suzanne (Gutherz) W.; grad. Hill Sch., 1929; B.A., Yale, 1933; m. Doris Stanley, June 6, 1936 (dec. Feb. 1967); children—Reuel Edward, Alma Timolat, Robert Stanley; m. 2d, Ellen H. Saltus, Feb. 24, 1968. Came to U.S., 1918. With Western Mining Corp., 1933-34, Lake View & Star, Kalgoofie, West Australia, 1934-35, Internat. Nickel Co., Huntington, W.Va., 1935-42; with civilian ordnance dept. U.S. Army, 1942-43; charge steel and iron sec. nickel sales dept. Internat. Nickel Co., N.Y.C., 1943-54; v.p. sales Am. Metal Climax, Inc., 1954-68, v.p. nickel project, 1968-72. Mem. Am. Iron and Steel Inst., Am. Inst. Mining and Metall. Engring., Am. Soc. Testing Materials, Am. Ordnance Assn. Episcopalian. Clubs: Yale, Mining, Farm (N.Y.C.); Duquesne (Pitts); American Cattle (N.H.); Field (Morristown, N.J.). Home: Redding Ridge, Conn., Died Nov. 8, 1972.

WARTHEN, WILLIAM HORACE FRANKLIN, physician; b. Balt., Dec. 8, 1897; s. Franklin Filmore and Minnie Lee (Blake) W.; B.A., Johns Hopkins, 1919, M.D., 1922, M.P.H., 1940; m. Blenda Ellen Smith, Jan. 19, 1936; 1 son, William Horace Franklin. Intern, Johns Hopkins Hosp., Harriet Lane Home, 1922-23; resident physician children's Hosp., Akron, O., 1923-24; dir. bur. child hygiene City of Balt., 1924-34; asst. comr. health Md. and Baltimore County Dept. Health, 1934-74; asso. in hygiene and pub. health U. Md., 1935-47, asso. prof., 1947-74; lectr. health edn. U. Cal. at Berkeley, 1937; lectr. pub. health adminstrn. Johns Hopkins Sch. Hygiene and Pub. Health. Mem. med. care com. Md. Planning Commn., 1950-74; dir. med. services Civil Def., Balt., 1951-74; del. White House Conf. Child Health and Protection, 1930, White House Conf. on Aging, 1961. Bd. dirs. Md. Soc. Prevention of Blindness, 1927-74. Named Man of Yr., Towson (Md.) Town Assn., 1950. Diplomate Am. Bd. Preventive Medicine. Fellow Am. Pub. Health Assn.; mem. A.M.A., Md. Pub. Health Assn. (chmn. founders group, past pres.), Baltimore County Med. Assn. (pres. 1947), Delta Omega, Gamma Alpha Phi. Rotarian (pres. Towson 1947). Author: (with Ira V. Hiscock) Ways to Community Health Education. Contbr. articles to profl. jours. Home: Townson, Md. Died Mar. 26, 1974; buried Lorraine Cemetery, Baltimore, Md.

WARWICK, EDWARD, artist; b. Phila., Pa., Dec. 10, 1881; s. Charles F. and Katherine (Griesemer) W.; prep. edn., Friends Central Sch. and Delancy Sch., Phila.; student U. of Pa.; studied at Phila. Museum School of Indsl. Art; Dr. Letters, Beaver College, Jenkintown, Pa., 1949; m. Ethel Herrick, June 19, 1912; 1 son, Edward Worthington. Began instr., Phila. Museum Sch. Indsl. Art, 1914, dean from 1933; lecturer on period constume and furniture; has specialized on wood blocks, pen and ink and pastels. Mem. Phila. Art Alliance (mem. bd.), Phila. Water Color Club (vice pres.), Phila. Sketch Club, Phila. Print Club: Fleisher Foundation (mem. bd.), The Franklin Inst. (mem. bd.), Phi Kappa Psi. Clubs: Arms and Armourers (New York); Sketch (Phila.). Author: Early American Costume, 1929. Home: Philadelphia, Pa.†

WASHBURN, WATSON, lawyer; b. N.Y.C., June 13, 1894; s. William Tucker and Mary (Doughty) W.; A.B. summa cum laude, Harvard, 1914; LL.B., Columbia, 1917; unmarried. Admitted to N.Y. bar, 1920; partner Washburn & Gray and predecessor, from 1920; asst. atty. gen. N.Y., 1929-31; dir. Osborne Assn., Citizens for Freedom, Inc.; trustee Ballet Found.; pres. Reading Reform Found., from 1962. Acting sec. to Gov. Dewey, 1948. Served as capt. F.A., U.S. Army, with A.E.F., 1918-19. Mem. Assn. Bar City N.Y., Spee Club (Harvard). Republican. Episcopalian. Clubs: Racquet and Tennis, Harvard, West Side Tennis (N.Y.C.); Pine Valley Golf (Clementon, N.J.); Edgewood (Tivoli, N.Y.). Author: High and Low Financiers (with Edmund S. deLong), 1932. Tennis player: mem. U.S. Davis Cup Team, 1920, 21. Home: New York City, N.Y. Died Dec. 2, 1973.

WASSON, ALONZO, newspaper correspondent; b. Ft. Smith, Ark., Apr. 13, 1870; s. Alonzo and Sarah Jane (Fealy) W.; ed. St. Vincent's Coll., Cape Girardeau, Mo.; m. Loretto Smith, Nov. 21, 1906. Began newspaper work in Gainesville, Tex., 1891; successively with Ft. Worth Gazette, San Antonio Express, Kansas City Times, St. Louis Globe Democrat and Dallas Morning News; with Dallas News successively as Washington corr., editorial writer, editor and Capital corr. Lay mem. Tex. Civil Jud. Council. Mem. legislative com. State Child Welfare Assn. Mem. Tex. State Philos. Soc. Independent Democrat. Catholic. Home: Austin, Tex.†

WATERFALL, WALLACE, acoustical engr.; b. Columbia City, Ind., May 27, 1900; s. William H. and Zadie (Wallace) W.; B.S., U. Ill., 1923, Engring. Physicist, 1931; m. Fern Riley, Dec. 24, 1923; 1 son, Wallace Knapp. Acoustical engr., dir. research Celotex Corp., 1925-42; with div. of war research Columbia, 1943-47; dir. research Celotex Corp. 1947-49; sec. Acoustical Soc. Am., 1929-69, treas., from 1969; exec. sec. Acoustical Materials Assn., 1949-68; sec. governing bd. Am. Inst. Physics, 1946-49, exec. sec., 1949-58, sec., treas., 1958-64, sec., dep. dir., 1964-67, sec., from 1967. Recipient 1st gold medal Acoustical Soc. Am., 1954. Fellow Am. Phys. Soc., A.A.A.S., Sigma Xi; mem. Tau Beta Pi. Club: Cosmos (Washington). Home: Bronxville, N.Y. Died Aug. 21, 1974.

WATERMULDER, LOUIS F., bus. exec. b;. Chicago, Aug. 17, 1901; s. Gustave A. and Frances (Verbeck) W.; student Hope Prep. Sch.; A.B., Yale, 1923, postgrad. law sch., 1923-24; m. Helen Dawes, May 23, 1936. With No. Trust Co., Chgo., 1924-39, asst. cashier, 1928-30, 2d v.p., 1930-39; asst. treas. Quaker Oats Co., 1939-42, treas., 1942-49; adminstrv. v.p., dir. Lever Bros., 1949-50; v.p. dir., W.R. Grace & Co., N.Y.C.; 1951; chmn. bd. Electric Sprayit Co., Sheboygan, Wis., 1952; pres. L.F. Watermulder & Assos., Chgo.; chmn. Buckner Corp. Presbyn. Clubs: Onwentsia, Attic, Racquet (Chgo.); Pinnacle (N.Y.C.). Home: Chicago, Ill., Died Nov. 20, 1975.

WATERS, VINCENT S., bishop. Ordained priest Roman Cath. Ch., 1931; bishop of Raleigh, N.C., from 1945. Home: Raleigh, N.C. Died Dec. 1974.

WATKINS, ARTHUR V., senator, govt. official; b. Midway, Utah, Dec. 18, 1886; s. Arthur and Emily A. (Gerber) W.; student, Brigham Young Univ., 1903-06, N.Y. U., 1909-10; LL.B. Columbia University, 1912; LL.D., U. Utah, 1959; m. Andrea Rich, June 18, 1913; children—Nedra Reese, Arthur Rich, Don Rich, Venna Swalberg, Jeanene Scott, Nina Palmer. Dist. judge, 1928-33; asst. co. (Salt Lake) atty., 1914-17; commr. Utah State Bar; counsel Provo River Water Users Assn. from 1935. U.S. Senator from Utah, 1947-58, co-sponsor Colo. River Storage Project and numerous other reclamation projects; associate member of the Indian Claims Commission, 1959-60, became chmn., 1960, later chief commr. Pub. Orem-Geneva Times, Utah Valley News; fruit farmer; rancher. Mem. platform com., Rep. Nat. Conv., 1944, 56. Republican. Mem. ch. of Latter Day Saints. Kiwanian (life mem.). Home: Orem, Utah. Died Sept. 1, 1973.

WATKINS, DWIGHT EVERETT, prof. pub. speaking; b. Deavertown, O., Jan. 7, 1878; s. Edmund Daugherty and Mary Augusta (Malster) W.; A.B., U. of Mich., 1901, post-grad. work, Harvard, 1912-13; A.M., 1908; m. Ada Grace Lennox, of Ithaca, Mich., Apr. 4, 1906 (died July 12, 1925); children—Genevieve Augusta, Gertrude Irene, Robert Edmund. Prin. high sch., Union City, Mich., 1901-03; instr. pub. speaking, Mich. Mil. Acad., Orchard Lake, 1905-06; same, high sch., Akron, O., 1906-08; prof. pub. speaking, Knox Coll., Galesburg, Ill., 1908-18; asso. prof. pub. speaking, from 1918, chairman of dept., 1922-24, U. of Calif. Served as instr. pub. speaking at Harvard, and in summer session of Columbia, U. of Colo., Ill. State Normal U., U. of Calif. Mem. Nat. Assn. of Teachers of Speech. Presbyterian. Mason. Author: Public Speaking for High Schools, 1913; The Forum of Democracy, 1917. Joint editor of School Poetry for Oral Expression, 1925; Best Dog Stories, 1925; Effective Speech (6 vols.), 1927. Home: Berkeley, Cal.†

WATKINS, MARK HANNA, educator, anthropoligist; b. Huntsville, Tex., Nov. 23, 1903; s. Walter and Laura (Williams) W.; S.B. in Edn., Prairie View State Coll., 1926; A.M., in Anthropology, U. Chgo., 1930, Ph.D., 1933; m. Charlotte Elizabeth Crawford, June 16, 1951. Asst. prof. sociology Louisville Municipal Coll., 1933-34; asst. prof., then prof. anthropology Fisk U., 1934-47; Lichtstern research asst., part-time vis. prof. anthropology U. Chgo., 1944-45; vis. prof. linguistics Escuela Nacional de Antropologia e Historia, Mexico, 1945; vis. prof. anthropology U. de San Carlos (Guatemala). summer 1948; prof. anthropology Howard

U., 1947-72, emeritus, 1972-76, head dept. sociology and anthropology, 1959-64, dir. African Lang. and Area Center, 1959-65. Field work, C.Am., Africa. Gen. Edn. bd. fellow, 1930-32; Rosenwald Fund fellow, 1946. Fellow Am. Anthrop. Assn., A.A.A.S., Am. Sociol. Assn., African Studies Assn., Soc. Applied Anthropology; mem. Am. Assn. Phys. Anthropologists, Linguistic Soc. Am., Anthrop. Soc. Washington, Washington Linguistic Club, Am. Acad. Polit. and Social Sci., Internat. African Inst., Am. Assn. U. Profs., Internat. Linguistic Assn., Modern Lang. Assn. Author: A Grammar of Chichewa, A Bantu Language of British Central Africa, 1937. Contbr. numerous articles to profl. jours., also to encys. Home: Washington, D.C., Died Feb. 24, 1976; buried Evergreen Cemetery, New Haven, Conn.

WATKINS, THOMAS FRANKLIN, lawyer; born Sandy Springs, S.C., Aug. 2, 1881; s. John C. and Elizabeth Jane (Smith) W.; A.B., Wofford Coll., 1902; LL.B., U. of Va., 1904; m. Agnes D. Law, Nov. 14, 1906; 1 son, William Law. Admitted to S.C. bar, 1904, practiced in Anderson; mem. Watkins, Vandiner, Kirven, Long & Gable; spl. judge S.C. Supreme Ct., 1934; dir. Piedmont & No. Ry. Co., Ross Builders Supplies, Inc. Trustee Presbyn. Coll. of South Carolina, Anderson Memorial Hospital. Mem. Am., S.C. (pres. 1935) bar assns., Cotton Mfrs. Assn. of S.C. (gen. counsel 1928-52). Served as state senator S.C., 1919-23. Chmn. bd. trustees Anderson Sch. Dist. 1941-57. Democrat (pres. Anderson Co. conv.; pres. S.C. Conv.). Home: Anderson, S.C. Died Feb. 2, 1973; buried Silverbrook Cemetery, Anderson, S.C.

WATSON, ARTHUR CLINTON, educator, inventor; b. Petrolia, Ont., 1878; s. Arthur John and Lucy (Allen) W.; B.A., McMaster U., Toronto, 1901; Ph.D., U. of Chicago, 1915; m. Ethel B. Speller, 1907. Ordained Bapt. ministry, 1906; asso. pastor First Ch., Dayton, O., 1906-08; pastor Victoria, Ont., 1909-12, Big Rock, Ill., 1912-13, Mendota, 1913-14; prof. philosophy and psychology, Rockford Coll., 1914-17; asso. field dir. Am. Red Cross, Camp Grant, Ill., 1917-18; prof. philosophy and psychology, Marietta Coll., from 1918; founder, 1926, later pres. Marietta Apparatus Co., mfrs. psychol. lab. equipment; pres. Cineon Corp., mfrs. luminous advertising equipment, from 1931. Mem. Optical Soc. America, Am. Philos. Assn. (western div.), Am. Assn. Univ. Profs. Ba Mason. Author: The Logic of Religion, 1918. Inventor of differential color mixers, etc. Member of research staff, Paint and Varnish Production Manager (mag.), from 1930. Home: Marietta, O.†

WATSON, ARTHUR KITTREDGE, business exec., U.S. ambassador; b. Summit, N.J., Apr. 23, 1919; s. Thomas J. and Jeanette (Kittredge) W.; grad. Yale, 1942; m. Ann C. Hemingway, July 10, 1948; children—Ann Carroll, Jane White, Caroline Trowbridge, Arthur Kittredge, Stuart Hemingway, David John. With IBM Corp., 1947-70, v.p., group exec., dir., 1959-70, mem. exec. com., 1961, v.p., group exec., corp. staff, 1963-64, sr. v.p., 1964-66, vice chmn., 1966-70; v.p. IBM World Trade Corp., 1949-54, pres., 1954-63, chmn. bd., 1963-70; U.S. ambassador to France, 1970-72. Trustee Ethel Walker Sch., Hotchkiss Sch., Presbyn. Hosp. N.Y.C.; fellow Corp. of Yale. Served to maj. Ordnance Corps, AUS, 1941-46. Decorated comdr. Order of Merit (Chile); officer Legion of Honor (France); commenda Al Merito Della Republica (Italy); officer Order So. Cross (Brazil); comdr. Peruvian Order of Merit; officer Belgian Order of Leopold II; grand cross Equestrian Order St. Sylvester; Grand Silver Medal of Honor (Austria); comdr. Swedish Order of Vasa; Grand Cross of Boyaca (Columbia); comdr. Order of Orange Nassau (Netherlands), Order of Golden Heart (Philippines), pres.). Clubs: Elibu (Yale); River, Union, Yale (N.Y.C.); New Canaan Country; St. Cloud Golf; Indian Harbor Yacht. Home: New Canaan, Conn. Died July 1974.

WATSON, BENJAMIN PHILIP, gynecologist; b. Anstruther, Scotland, Jan. 4, 1880; s. David and Elizabeth (Philp) W.; M.B., Ch.B., U. of Edinburgh, 1902, M.D., 1905; M. Angfele Hamendt, June 17, 1917; children—Monique, David. Prof. obstetrics and gynecology, U. of Toronto, Can., 1912-22; prof. same, Columbia, 1926-46, emeritus, from 1946; dir. Sloane Hosp. for Women; consultant. Served as capt. Med. Corps, Canadian Army, 1914-17. Fellow Am. Coll. Surgeons, Royal Coll. Surgeons; apst pres. Am. Gynecol. Soc.; pres. N.Y. Academy of Medicine from 1949. Presbyterian. Clubs: University (New York); University (Edinburgh). Contributor numerous articles to med. jours. Home: New York, N.Y.†

WATSON, BURL STEVENS, business exec.; b. Talledega Co., Ala., Nov. 7, 1893; s. Byron S. and Mary Elizabeth (Huff) W.; B.S.E.E., Univ. of Ala., 1916; m. Emitom Burns, June 2, 1920; children—Burl Stevens, Angie Burns (Mrs. John D'Albora, Jr.). Entire career with Cities Service orgn. dir. Cities Service Co., 1940-75, pres., 1953-59, chairman bd., 1959-66, continuing as chairman executive committee, also officer and director numerous subsidiaries; bd. dirs. Richfield Oil Corp. Mem. Commerce and Industry Assn. N.Y., Am. Inst. Mining and Metall. Engrs., Am. Gas Assn., Am. Petroleum Institute, Newcomen Soc. N.A. Clubs: Bankers, Downtown Athletic, Economic, Metropolitan, New York Southern Society, Pinnacle, North Hempstead Country. Home: Port Washington, N.Y. Died Aug. 2, 1975.

WATSON, EDWARD HANN, educator, geologist; b. Balt., July 31, 1902; s. Edward Louis and Edith (Hann) W.; student Balt. Poly. Inst., 1921; A.B., Johns Hopkins, 1925, Ph.D., 1929; m. Isabella McDowell Hannan, Mar. 25, 1944; children—Martha, Edward, Susannah. Instr. Johns Hopkins, 1928-30; asst. prof. Bryn Mawr Coll., 1930-39, prof., 1940-71, chmn. dept. geology, 1930-71, research asso., 1971-74; lectr. La Salle Coll., 1971; geologist U.S. Geol. Survey, Mont., 1927, Md. Geol. Survey, 1928-30, Pa. Geol. Survey, 1935-75, U. Mich. Expdn. to Mexico, 1930, Atlantic Refining Co., Mont., 1944-45, Brazilian govt. Goias, 1954; leader NSF conf. geology Appalachians, 1960-67; cons. cement rock, metall. limestone, water supply. Fellow Geol. Soc. Am., Mineral. Soc. Am.; mem. Am. Inst. M.E., Geol. Soc. Phila. (pres. 1939, 64-66). Phi Beta Kappa, Sigma Xi, Phi Gamma Delta. Author tech. papers. Home: Bryn Mawr, Pa. Died Feb. 21, 1975; buried Church of the Redeemer, Bryn Mawr, Pa.

WATSON, JAMES FRAUGHTMAN, director Atlanta Inst. of Speech and Expression; b. Sellers, S.C., June 3, 1879; s. James Robert and Flora Ellen (Lane) W.; B.A., Furman U., 1902; teacher's diploma, Sch. of Expression, Boston, 1909; B.D., Newton Theol. Instn., 1917; Ph.D., Webster U., Atlanta, Ga., 1930; m. Lillian Olivia Lee, July 30, 1913; children—Robert Lee, Fraughtman Lane. Prin. Gaddys Mill high sch., Dillon, S.C., 1902-04; supt. high sch. North, S.C., 1904-07; organizer, and supt. high sch., Lake View, S.C., 1909-12; supply pastor First Bapt. Ch., Lake View, 1911-12; supt. Dacusville High Sch., Pickens County, S.C., 1913-14; pastor Friendship Bapt. Ch., Friendship, Me., summer, Me., summer 1915, Immanuel Bapt. Ch., Ipswich, Mass., 1915-16; prin. Mechanicsville High Sch., Darlington, S.C., 1918; pres. Piedmont Inst., Waycross, Ga., 1918-19; teacher, Curry Sch. of Expression, Asheville, summer terms, 1917, 19; founder, pression, Asheville, summer terms, 1917-19; founder, 1920, and pres. Atlnata School of Oratory and Expression until 1939; teacher of public speaking, Atlanta chap. Am. Inst. of Banking, 1926-33, Atlanta Assn. Baptist Training Union, from 1939. S. Eastern Bible Inst. from 1941, Atlanta Bible Inst., from 1945; lecturer on pub. speaking, Evening Sch. of Commerce, Ga. Sch. of Tech. summers 1927-29; teacher personality and pub. speaking Jr. Chamber Commerce, Atlanta, 1927-34; prof. pub. speaking and all phases of expression and speech. Salvation Army Southern Training Coll., 1946. Mem. Am. Philos. Research Soc. (pres. 1927-30; v.p.). Democrat. Author: Basic Principles of Education and Expression, 1929; Effective Speaking and Selling, 1940; also "Five Diamonds" (personality play), "Speech Drills for Effective Speaking," "Parliamentary Law in Action," "Effective Speaking through Panel Discussion," "Conversation Through Conversation," "Story Building" and "Hormiletics and Public Speaking , Oral Reading and Praying, 1942; Key to Effective Speakingand Oral Reading, 1945; Speech Democracy, 1945; Voice and Speech Correction, 1946; Public Ideation, Types of Speeches and Success Hints, 1946. Home: Atlanta, Ga.†

WATSON, LEROY HUGH, army officer; b. St. Louis, Mo., Nov. 3, 1893; s. George W. and Sarah Ann (Callahan) W.; B.S., U.S. Mil. Acad., 1915; grad. Inf. Sch., 1921, Command and Gen. Staff Sch., 1930, Army War Coll., 1934, Tank Sch., 1940; m. Alice Virginia Furey, June 16, 1915 (dec.); children—Sarah Virginia, Leroy Hugh, Margareta Maria, Robert Bartley; m. 2d, Elizabeth Livingston, Apr. 10, 1943 (div.); m. 3d, Libouse Besin, Dec. 25, 1946 (dec.); 1 dau., Antoinette Besin (Mrs. John Sanderson); m. 4th, Beulah Beatrice Von Holst Pellikan, August 9, 1950. Commd. 2d lieutenant, United States Army, 1915, and advanced through the grades to brig. gen., Feb. 16, 1942, major gen., Sept. 1942; served in 11th and 22d. Inf., Douglas, Ariz., and Ft. Oglethorpe, 1915-17; with 6th Div., A.E.F., France and Germany, 1918-20 (batn. comdr. 1 year); instr. Inf. Sch., 1921-25; batn. comdr., 42d and 32d Inf., Panama, C.Z., 1925-28; instr. Command and Gen. Staff Sch., 1930-33; batn. comdr., 33d Inf., Ft. McPherson, Ga., 1934-36; War Dept. Gen. Staff, 1936-40; G-1, 2d Army Div., later comdr. 66th Armored Regt., 2d Armored Div., Ft. Bennington, 1940-41; comdr. 40th Army Regt., 3d Armored Div., Camp Beauregard and Camp Polk, 1941-42; comdr. Combat Command No. 1, 3d Armored Div., 1942; comdg. gen. Fort MacArthur, Calif. and of the Southern Mil. Dist., 1948-50; comdg. gen. Fort Lewis, 1950-51; chief civil affairs sect. G.H.Q., F.E.C., 1951-53; comdg. gen. Safety Adv. Group, Japan, from 1953. Active Brit. United Service Club, Ft. MacArthur, United Crusade, Opera Guild So. Cal., Los Angeles Philharmonic Orch., others. Mem. Beverly Hills Council, 8 yrs.; mayor, Beverly Hills, lyr. Awarded Silver Star, Bronze Star with 2 clusters, Legion of Merit; fgn. decorations. Home: Beverly Hills, Cal. Died Feb. 12, 1975. Buried U.S. Mil. Acad. Cemetery, West Point, N.Y.

WATSON-WATT, SIR ROBERT, (ALEXANDER), sci. adv.; b. Apr. 13, 1892; s. Patrick and Mary (Matthew) W.W.; Student U. Coll., Dundee in U. of St. Andrews; LL.D., St. Andrews, 1943; D.Sc., U. Toronto, 1943; D.Sc., Laval U., 1952; m. Margaret Robertson, 1916 (div. 1952); m. 2d, Mrs. Jean Smith 1952 (dec. Dec. 1964); stepchildren—Anthony, Dennie (Mrs. Douglas Reburn); m. 3d, Dame Katherine Trefusis Forbes. Engaged as asst. to prof. natural philosophy Univ. Coll., Dundee, 1912-21; various posts in meteorology, radio and radar in meteorol. office Dept. Sci. and Indsl. Research, Air Ministry, Ministries of Aircraft Prodn., Supply, Civil Aviation and Transport, 1915-52; dep. chmn. radio bd. of War Cabinet, 1943-46; adv. bd. Axe Sci. Corp.; cons. to the Sterling Forest Research Center. Created Knight, 1942, Decorated Companion of the Bath, 1941; U.S. Medal of Merit, Valdemar Poulsen medal Danish Acad. Tech. Scis., Hughes medal Royal Soc., Elliott Cresson medal, Franklin Institute, French Republic gold medal Soc. Encouragement Progress. Fellow Royal Meterological Soc. (past pres.), Royal Aero. Soc., Inst. Physics, Am. Phys. Soc.; mem. Inst. Nav. (past pres.). I.R.E. (past v.p.). Club: Athenaeum. Author: Through the Weather House; Three Steps to Victory; The Pulse of Radar; Man's Means to His End (with others), The Cathode Ray Oscillograph in Radio Research. Home: London, England. Died Dec. 1973.

WATTERSON, JOSEPH, architect; b. Cleve., Aug. 7, 1900; s. William Ruggles and Mary (Batchelor) W.; grad. Mt. Hermon (Mass.) Sch., 1920; student Sch. Architecture U. Pa., 1924; m. Kathleen T. Howes, June 6, 1923 (dec.); children—David S., Stephen W., Joseph; m. 2d, Gertrude Harris, Dec. 30, 1948. Draftsman, Abram Garfield, Cleve., 1922-24; with Frederick L. Ackerman, N.Y.C., 1924-27; travel study abroad, 1926; designer Schultze & Weaver, N.Y.C., 1927-30, Reinhard & Hoffmeister, 1931; head art dept. Nassau Collegiate Center, Garden City, L.I., 1932-36; instr. art appreciation Coll. City N.Y., 1936; propr. own office, Mineola, N.Y., 1936-56; chief engr. Dade Bros., Inc., Mineola, 1941-45. Cons. to sec. interior, 1965-66, spl. asst., 1966-67; chief div. historic architecture Office Archeology and Historic Preservation, Nat. Park Service, 1968-71; lectr. univs. and confs. Fellow A.I.A. (editor Jour. 1957-65, past sec., v.p. L.I. chpt., Kempar award 1965; mem. Soc. Archtl. Historians (former dir.), Nat. Trust Historic Preservation, Archtl. League N.Y., Nassau County Hist. Soc. (hon. trustee), World Soc. for Ekistics, Am. Assn. State and Local History, Delta Kappa Epsilon. Episcopalian. Club: Cosmos (Washington). Author: Architecture-5000 Years of Building, 1950; Architecture A Short History, 1968; author-editor: The Growth of the Architect, 1971. Editor: Urban Design-The Planning of Towns and Cities, 1965; The Restoration Manual, 1966; (with others) with Heritage So Rich, 1966. Contbr. to Elementary School Self-Taught, 1940. Home: Titusville, Fla. Died May 30, 1971; buried Pine Forest Cemetery, Mount Dora, Fla.

WATTIE, JAMES, canning co. exec.; b. Mar. 23, 1902; s. William John and Annie Elizabeth Wattie; ed. pub. schs., New Zealand; m. Gladys Madeline Henderson, 1925; 2 sons. Jr. clk. HB Farmers Meat Co. Ltd., 1917-19, asst. accountant, 1919-24; accountant Roachs Ltd., 1924-25; sec. H.B. Fruit-growers Ltd., 1926-27, mgr., 1927-34; chmn., mng. dir. J. Wattie Canneries Ltd., 1934-74. Mem. New Zealand Trade Promotion Council. Life mem. Hawke's Bay Med. Research Found. Decorated comdr. Order Brit. Empire, 1963; created knight, 1966. Mem. Hastings C. of C. Clubs: Wellesley (Wellington, New Zealand); Auckland; Poverty Bay (Gisborne, New Zealand); Havelock North (Havelock, New Zealand); Hawke's Bay, Napier (Napier, New Zealand); Hastings, County. Home: Hawke's Bay, New Zealand. Died June 8, 1974.

WATTS, ALAN WILSON, author, philosopher; b. Chislehurst, Eng., Jan. 6, 1915; s. Laurence Wilson and Emily Mary (Buchan) W.; student King's Sch., Canterbury, Eng., 1928-32; S.T.M., Seabury-Western Theol. Sem., Evanston, Ill., 1948; D.D., U. Vt., 1958; m. Eleanor Everett, Apr. 2, 1938 (div. 1950); children—Joan Watts-Tabernik, Ann (Mrs. Joel Andrews); m. 2d, Dorothy DeWitt, June 29, 1950 (div. 1963); children—Tia, Mark, Richard, Lila, Diane; m. 3d, Mary Jane Yates King, Dec. 4, 1963. Came to U.S., 1938, naturalized, 1943. Editor, The Middle Way, London, Eng., 1934-38; religious counselor, also Episcopal chaplain Northwestern U., 1944-50; prof. comparative philosophy Am. Acad. Asian Studies, U. Pacific, San Francisco, 1951-57, dean, 1953-56; ind. writer and lectr.; guest lectr. at univs., U.S., Can., Europe, Japan, Ceylon, also C.G. Jung Inst., Switzerland, and other psychiat. and mental health instns.; co-editor Wisdom of the East series, 1938-41; program series Eastern Wisdom and Modern Life, Nat. Ednl. TV, 1959; research cons. Md. Psychiat. Research Center, 1969. Mem. council, exec. com. World Congress of Faiths, 1937-39. Bollingen Found. research fellow, 1951-53, 62-64; research fellow Harvard, 1962-64; vis. scholar San Jose State Coll., 1968. Mem. Am. Oriental Soc., Soc. for Comparative Philosophy (pres.). Author: The Sprit of Zen, 1936; The Legacy of Asia and Western Man, 1937; The Meaning of Happiness, 1940; The Theologia Mystica of St. Dionysius, 1946; Behold the Spirit, 1947; Zen, 1948; Easter-Its Story and Meaning, 1950; The Supreme Identity, 1950; The Wisdom of Insecurity, 1951; Myth and Ritual in Christianity, 1953; The Way of Liberation in Zen Buddhism, 1955; The Way of Zen, 1957; Nature, Man and Woman, 1958; This is It, 1960; Psychotherapy East and West, 1961;

The Joyous Cosmology, 1962; The Two Hands of God, 1963; Beyond Theology, 1964; The Book On the Taboo Against Knowing Who You Are, 1966; Does it Matter?, 1970; Erotic Spirituality, 1970. Home: Sausalito, Cal. Died Nov. 16, 1973.

WATTS, MAY PETREA THEILGAARD, (Mrs. Raymond Watts), naturalist; b. Chgo., May 1, 1893; d. Hermann and Claudia (Andersen) Theilgaard; B.S., U. Chgo., 1918; m. Raymond Watts, Dec. 27, 1924; children—Erica, Tom, Nancy, Peter. Staff naturalist Morton Arboretum, Lisle, Ill., 1942-61, naturalist emeirtus, from 1961; lectr. TV programs. Hon. mem. Friends of Our Native Landscape, 1950; chmn. emeritus, founder Ill. Prairie Path., from 1965. Recipient Douglas medal for conservation edn. Garden Club. Am., 1954; May Theilgaard Watts Reading Garden named for her Morton Arboretum, 1963; Du Page Audubon Soc. Pres.'s award, 1965; spl. citation Ill. Parks and Recreation, 1966; citation award for teaching Am. Hort. Soc., 1971; Book of Year award Chgo. Geog. Soc., 1972; citation Ill. Ho. of Reps., 1972; Hutchinson medal Chgo. Hort. Soc., 1972; Arthur Hoyt Scott Garden and Hort. award and medal, 1972. Mem. Soc. Interpretive Naturalists (hon.). Phi Beta Kappa. Democrat. Conglist. Clubs: Garden (hon.) (Ravinia and Naperville). Author: Reading the Landscape, 1957; Trees, 1964; Reading the Landscape of Europe, 1971; also handbooks; weekly Nature column Chicago Tribune, 1966. Home: Naperville, Ill., Died Aug. 20, 1975.

WATTS, RIDLEY, cotton textile exec.; b. Morristown N.J., May 12, 1901; s. Ridley and Gertrude (Hoy) W.; grad. St. Paul's Sch., 1919; Harvard, 1923; m. Mary Stuart Cottrell, Feb. 26, 1928; children—Ridley, David. Mem. N.Y. Stock Exchange, 1931-37; exec. v.p. Spartan Mills, Inc., N.Y. City, from 1948; dir. Phila. Life Ins. Co. Pres. The Lighthouse, N.Y. Association for the Blind. Mem. Assn. Cotton Textile Merchants (director, treasurer). Served as lt., USNR, 1942-45. Home: Stonington, Conn. Died June 10, 1975.

WAUGH, COULTON, author, artist; b. St. Ives, Eng. (parents U.S. citizens), Mar. 10, 1896; s. Frederick Judd and Clara Eugenie (Bunn) W.; brought to U.S., 1908; ed. Upton Sch., London, Art Students League, N.Y., 1917-18, New Paltz (N.Y.) Tchrs. Coll., Orange County Community Coll.; m. Elizabeth Dey Jenkinson, May 18, 1919 (dec. 1944); m. 2d, Mabel Odin Burwick, Jan. 17, 1945; children—Phyllis Elizabeth, John Coulton. Cartoonist N.Y. World, N.Y. Tribune, 1918-19; wrote and drew comic strip "Dickie Dare," Associated Press, New York, 1934-44 and from 1949, "Hank" for newspaper P.M., 1945; wrote and drew quiz feature Junior Editors, A.P., 1960-70. Author: The Comics, 1947, reprinted, 1975; How To Paint With A Knife, 1971; Landscape Painting With A Knife (finished by wife). 1974; The Golden Whale. Contbr. of various articles to Yachting, Boys Life Mag. Exhibited Nat. Acad. of Design, 1918, Carnegie Internat. Show (Pittsburgh), 1939-40, Golden Gate Exhibition, San Francisco; one-man shows, Grand Central Galleries, N.Y., 1931, Hudson D. Walker Galleries, N.Y., 1938, 460 Park Av. Galleries, N.Y., 1940, 1942, others. Mem. Nat. Cartoonists Soc., Pioneer Galliers. Home: Newburgh, N.Y. Died May 23, 1973.

WAY, GORDON L., mining co. exec.; b. Mpls., July 31, 1913; s. Elwood J. and Justina (Rhea) W.; S.B., Mass. Inst. Tech., 1934; m. Georgeanna Hamilton; children—Stephen F., Peter V., Lindsay Ann, David G., Scott H. Rhoden. With Bechtel Corp., San Francisco, 1946-64; v.p. engring. Hanna Mining Co., Cleve., 1965-74. Served from lt. to lt. col. USAAF, 1940-46. Home: Westlake, O. Died Jan. 11, 1974.

WAYMAN, DOROTHY C., (Pseudonym Theodate Geoffrey) author; b. San Bernardino County, Cal., Jan. 7, 1893; d. Charles Washington and Sarah Lauretta Ida Vincent (Park) Godfrey; prep. edn. Mt. St. Mary's (convent), Manchester, N.H.; student Bryn Mawr. Coll., 1914; grad. Sch. for Social Workers, Boston, 1914; Litt.D., Holy Cross Coll., Worcester, 1954; m. Charles Stafford Wayman, July 10, 1915; children—John Godfrey, Charles Stafford, Richard Park. Began as contbr. to newspapers and periodicals; spent 4 years in Japan (1918-22), learned to speak, write Japanese; mng. editor Falmouth Enterprise, 1929-33; mem. editorial staff Boston Globe 1933-53; reference librarian St. Bonaventure (N.Y.) U., 1955-62; on staff Olean (N.Y.) Times-Herald Mem. Olean Bd. Edn. Mem. Meml. Gallery Living Cath. Authors, Guild of Our Lady of Ransom (v.p.), Am. Cath. Hist. Assn. (exec. council), Falmouth Hist. Soc. Roman Catholic. Club: Bryn Mawr (Boston). Author: An Immigrant in Japan, 1926; Powdered Ashes, 1926; Suckanesset, A History of Falmouth, 1929; Dumaine of New England, 1958; (with V.H. Godfrey) John Holmes at Annapolis, 1927; (with Willis Fitch) Wings in the Night, 1938; co-author: Edward Sylvester Morse: A Biography, 1942; Bite the Bullet (autobiography), 1948; David I. Walsh: Citizen-Patriot, 1952; Cardinal O'Connell of Boston, 1955; Quaker Pioneers in Quaker History, 1962; Franciscan Illumination in John Rylands Library, vol. 21, Franciscan Studies, 1962; Friends on the Frontier in Quaker History, 1965. Contbr. articles to Am. Heritage, Folklore, The Cord. Home: Olean, N.Y., Died Oct. 27, 1975.

WAYMAN, HARRY CLIFFORD, clergyman, educator; b. Kenton Co., Ky., Apr. 19, 1881; s. George Stanton and Jennie (French) W.; A.B., Georgetown (Ky.) Coll., 1900, D.D., 1916; Th.M., Southern Bapt. Sem., 1915, Th.D., 1926; m. Margaret Biggerstaff, of Lexington, Ky., 1907; children—Margaret, Harry Clifford. Ordained Bapt. ministry, 1910; pastor at Walton, LaGrange, and Louisville, Ky.; prof. Hebrew and archaeology, Southern Bapt. Theol. Sem., 1914-23; pres. William Jewell Coll., 1923-28; pres. Des Moines U., 1928-29; pastor at Newport, Ky., from 1929. Studied and traveled abroad, 2 yrs. Mason (32°, Shriner). Home: Newport, Ky.†

WAYSON, JAMES THOMAS, physician; b. Port Townsend, Wash., June 16, 1870; s. James Thomas and Mary Elizabeth (Riley) W.; M.D., U. of Calif., 1891; m. Delia Walcott Sheeby, Nov. 25, 1897; children—India Walcott (Mrs. Walter J. L. Wilson), Eleanor Hodgins (Mrs. Robert Paul Sroat). Surgeon U.S. Cutter Service, 1892-95; attending physician Kalihi Hosp. for Lepers, Honolulu, 1895-96; me. Bd. of Health, Hawaii, 1905-09, asst. adminstr., 1931-32; city and county physician to Honolulu, 1911-18; gen. health officer of Hawaii, 1918-31; physician Bd. of Leper Hosps., from 1932. Served as capt and surgeon Nat. Guard of Hawaii, in revolution of 1895-96; later mem. Old Guards. Mem. Territorial, Honolulu and Baltimore City med. socs. Mason, Odd fellow, Elk. Contbr. med. articles to jours. Address: Bd. of Hospitals and Settlement, Honolulu, Hawaii.*†.

WEAD, (MARY) EUNICE, librarian; b. Ann Arbor, Mich., May 26, 1881; d. Charles Kasson and Sarah Walton (Pease) Wead; A.B., Smith Coll., 1902; certificate, N.Y. State Library Sch., Albany, N.Y., 1903; A.M., U. of Mich., 1927. Asst. in catalogue div. Library of Congress, 1904-06; reference librarian, Smith Coll. Library, 1906-11; cataloger of private libraries, 1911-17; asst. curator, later curator, of rare books, U. of Mich. Library, 1917-24; asst. custodian, William L. Clements Library, U. of Mich., 1924-26, successively instr., asst. prof. and asso. prof., Dept. Library Science, Univ. of Mich., 1926-45; visiting prof., Sch. Library Service, Columbia U., summers, 1940, 1944. Recipient Carnegie Corp.-Am. Library Assn. grant-in-aid for foreign study, 1932. Mem. Assn. of College and Research Libraries (dir. 1944-46), American Library Assn., Bibliog. Soc. America, Phi Beta Kappa. Compiler: Catalogue of Samuel A. Jones Carlyle Collection, 1919. Contbr. articles to professional periodicals. Address: Hartford, Conn.†

WEAR, SAMUEL MCCONNELL, lawyer; b. Cassville, Mo., 1880; grad. Drury Coll., Springfield, Mo., 1902; LL.B., Cumberland U., Lebanon, Tenn., 1904; m. Susan M. Wear; children—Hunter, William A., Charles W., Susan (Mrs. Mills). Admitted to bar, 1904; mem. firm Wear & Wear, Springfield; pros. atty., Greene County, Mo., 1912, 1914; U.S. dist. atty., from 1945. Address: Kansas City, Mo.*†

WEART, DOUGLAS LAFAYETTE, army officer; b. Chicago, Ill., Aug. 10, 1891; s. Edward Nickelson and Mary (Subers) W.; student Armour Sci. Acad., 1906-09, Armour Inst. of Tech., 1909-11; B.S., U.S. Mil. Acad., 1915; m. Gertrude Keith Spoor, Feb. 19, 1916 (dec. Apr. 1975); children—Gertrude Spoor, George Spoor, Maryada Spoor, Douglas Spoor. Commd. 2d lt. U.S. Corps Engrs., 1915, and advanced through the grades to maj. gen. 1945; served on Mexican Border, 1916; with 1st Div. and Gen. Hdqrs. in France, 1917-18; exec. officer, Office Pub. Bldgs. and Grounds, Washington, D.C., 1921-24; U.S. dist. engr., Savannah, Ga., 1928-32; asst. to pres. Mississippi River Commn., 1932-34; student and instructor Command and Gen. Staff Sch., 1934-38; student Army War Coll., 1938-39; asst. engr. of maintenance, The Panama Canal, 1939-42; chief of staff, Caribbean Defense Command, 1942-44, comdg. gen. rear eschelon, Tactical Hdqrs., and Shanghai base comdg. China Theater; dir. engr. New Eng. div., dir. engr. Ohio River div., 1946-48; later comdg. officer, Ft. Belvoir, Va. Decorations: D.S.M., Legion of Merit with cluster (U.S.), also from China, Panama, Colombia, Ecuador, Peru, Chile. Mem. Soc. of Am. Mil. Engrs., Delta Tau Delta. Mason, Shrine. Home: Chicago, Ill. Died Apr. 5, 1975.

WEATHERED, ROY BISHOP, physician; b. Norwich, Kan., Aug. 19, 1911; s. Pleasant Bush and Helen (Bishop) W.; M.D., U. Kan., 1937; m. Olivia Kate Pott, May 1, 1959. Intern, Kansas City Gen. Hosp., 1937-38; fellow and resident in radiology Garfield Hosp., Washington, 1942-45, Warwick Clinic, Washington, 1942-45; active staff Good Samaritan Hosp., Los Angeles, 1946-62, St. Mary Desert Valley Hosp., Apple Valley, Cal., 1962-65, Barstow (Cal.) Community Hosp., 1962-72. Diplomate Am. Bd. Radiology. Mem. A.M.A., Am. Coll. Radiology, Cal., Inland radiol. socs., Radiol. Soc. So. Cal. Home: Barstow, Cal. Died Sept. 7, 1972; buried Mountain View Cemetery, Barstow, Cal.

WEAVER, JOSEPH B., marine consultant; b. Philadelphia, Pennsylvania, June, 19, 1880; s. of Clement and Caroline (Sloan) W.; M.E., Cornell University, 1902; m. Charlotte K. Hubbell, May 6, 1929. With Newport News Shipbuilding & Drydock Co., serviing as draftsman, asst. to v.p., supt. of hull constrn. and gen. supt. of plant, 1902-17; v.p. and gen. mgr. Harlan & Hollingsworth Shipbuilding Co., Wilmington, Del. (later mergeed with Bethlehem Shipbuilding Co.), 1917; v.p. Pullman Co., in charge of tech. matters, 1918-22; in cons. engring. work in London and New York, made surveys in various European countries, 1922-34; dep. adminstr. for shipbuilding and shipping with NRA, Washington, 1934; dir. Bur. of Navigation and Steamboat Inspection, U.S. Dept. of Commerce, Washington, 1934-37; later marine consultant. Home: Washington, V1D.C.†

WEAVER, JUNIUS VADEN, steel co. exec.; b. Colonial Heights, Va., June 22, 1927; s. Thomas Joseph and Daisy Dean (Vaden) W.; B.S., Va. Poly. Inst., 1954; m. Frances Elizabeth McKnight, Nov. 27, 1954; children—Martha Ann, Mary Elizabeth, Joseph David. Sales engr. Wallace & Tiernan, Inc., Roanoke, Va., 1954-55; field engr. Am. Bridge Co., Roanoke, Chgo., Lynchburg, Va., 1955-59; design engr., sales engr. Montaque-Betts Co., 1959-66; pres. J.V. Weaver Steel Co., Lynchburg, 1967-72. Served with USAAF, 1945-47. Registered profl. engr., Va., N.C. Mem. Nat., Va. socs. profl. engrs. Methodist (trustee). Pioneer staggered truss system for constrn. high rise bldgs. Home: Lynchburg, Va. Died Nov. 18, 1972.

WEAVER, PHILIP TENNANT, physician; b. St. Paul, Mar. 24, 1922; s. Luther and Reba (Tennant) W.; M.D., U. So. Cal., 1947; m. Helen-Marie Kelley; children—Nancy Kellene, Wendy Clark; m. 2d, Roberta Ann Wray, Dec. 30, 1969. Intern, Los Angeles County Gen. Hosp., 1947-48; resident Huntington Meml. Hosp., Pasadena, Cal., 1949-50, Long Beach (Cal.) VA Hosp., 1951-52; practice medicine specializing in internal medicine, Cal.; mem. staff Los Angeles County Gen. Hosp., Little Company of Mary Hosp., Torrance, Cal., South Bay Dist. Hosp., Redondo Beach, Cal.; asso. clin. prof. internal medicine U. So. Cal. Sch. Medicine. Served to capt., M.C., AUS. Diplomate Am. Bd. Internal Medicine. Fellow A.C.P.; mem. A.M.A. Home: Manhattan Beach, Cal. Died Apr. 13, 1973; buried Inglewood Park, Inglewood, Cal.

WEAVER, R(ALPH) H(OLDER), bacteriologist; born Khedive, Pa., Jan. 13, 1903; s. Albert and Dora (Holder) W.; B.S., Allegheny Coll., 1922, M.S., 1923; Ph.D., Mich. State Coll., 1926; m. Grace Wells, Mar. 11, 1927; 1 son, Robert. Instr. in bacteriology U. of Ky., 1926-28, asst. prof., 1928-31, asso. prof., 1931-37, prof. of bacteriology from 1937. Fellow A.A.A.S.; mem. Soc. Am. Bacteriologists (councillor since 1947), Am. Pub. Health Assn., Ky.-Tenn. branch Soc. Am. Bacteriologists (pres. 1942), Ky. Acad. Sci. (treas. from 1947), Phi Beta Kappa, Sigma Xi, Phi Sigma, Phi Beta Phi, Semmarius Botanicus. Democrat. Contbr. to sci. jours. in fields of fundamental bacteriology, water bacteriology and food bacteriology. Home: Lexington, Ky. Died Sept. 25, 1973.

WEBB, DEL E., bus. exec.; b. Fresno, Cal., May 17, 1899; s. Ernest Griffith and Henrietta Susan (Forthcamp) W.; m. Hazel L. Church, June 25, 1919; married 2d, Toni Ince, 1961. Carpenter, Oakland, Cal., 1917-28, Phoenix, 1928-29; played baseball, 1916-26; started bus. as bldg. contractor, 1929, becoming chmn. bd., chief exec. officer Del E. Webb Corp.; part owner Am. League Baseball Club (Yankees), 1945-65, v.p., dir., 1945-65. Clubs: Phoenix Country (Phoenix, Arizona); Paradise Valley Country; also Beverly Hills (Cal.); Los Angeles Country; Lakeside Country (North Hollywood, Cal.); Burning Tree (Bethesda, Md.). Home: Scottsdale, Ariz. Died July 4, 1974.

WEBB, JAMES RUFFIN, author; b. Denver, Oct. 4, 1909; s. Browne Ruffin and Verna (Monarch) W.; A.B., Stanford, 1930; D.H.L., Mt. Mercy Coll., 1973; m. Susan Noble, Jan. 25, 1936; children—James Cox, Helen Catherine. Fiction writer for nat. mags., including Sat. Eve. Post, Colliers, Cosmopolitan, from 1936; screenwriter, from 1938. Founder, ass. Hollywood Museum, Los Angeles Music Center; trustee of Motion Picture Relief Fund. Served to maj. AUS, 1942-46; ETO. Decorated Invasion Arrowhead, Commendation; recipient Valentine Davies award for contbn. to motion picture community, 1962. Mem. Screen Writers Guild (sec. 1950), Writers Guild Am. (pres. screen br. 1961), Writers Guild Am. West (pres. 1962-63, nat. chmn. 1964-65), Internat. Writers Guild (pres. 1964-67, chmn. 1967-69), Writers Guild Found. (pres. 1966), Producers-Writers Pension Plan (bd. dirs., past chmn.), Acad. Motion Picture Arts and Scis., Navy League, Alpha Tau Omega. Republican. Episcopalian. Film scripts include: Apache, 1953; Vera Cruz, 1954; Trapeze, 1956; The Big Country, 1958; Port Chop Hill, 1959; Cape Fear, 1961; How the West Was Won (Acad. writing award), 1963; Cheyenne Autumn (Western Heritage writing award), 1964; Sinful Davey, 1969; The Hawaiians, 1970; The Organization, 1971. Home: Beverly Hills, Cal. Died Sept. 27, 1974.

WEBB, THOMPSON, tchr.; b. Bell Buckle, Tenn., Oct. 24, 1887; s. William Robert and Emma (Clary) W.; Grad. Webb Sch. Bell Buckle, Tenn., 1907; A.B., U. of N.C.; 1911; D. of Pedagogy, Coll. of Pacific 1949; LL.D., Occidental Coll., 1962, Pomona Coll., 1962; m. Vivian Howell, June 22, 1915 (dec. 1971); children—Thompson, Robert Howell, William Robert, John Lambuth. Dir Webb Sch. Camp, Bell Buckle, summers 1900-11; ranching in Cal., 1911-18; teacher Webb Sch.,

Bell Buckle, 1918-22, and asso. dir. its summer camp; settled at Claremont, Cal., 1922, and founder, head Webb Sch. of Cal., until 1962. Dir. Cal. Jr. Republic, 1926-53; hon. chmn. bd. Cal. Boys Republic; dir. Scripps Coll., Webb Sch. (Bell Buckle), Cal. Ednl. Aid Found; pres. bd. Pilgrim Place, Claremont, Cal., 1947-58, then hon. pres. bd. Trustee Midland Sch., Los Olivos, Cal., Chandler Sch., Pasadena, Girls Collegiate, Claremont, Cal. Mem. Nat. Assn. Ind. Schs., Cal. Assn. Ind. Schs. Headmasters Assn. Delta Kappa Epsilon, Phi Beta Kappa. Democrat. Methodist. Home: Claremont, Cal. Died Jan. 13, 1975.

WEBER, FREDERICK CLARENCE, chemist; b. Columbus, O., Oct. 1, 1878; s. Herman Philip and Medora Isabelle (Maize) W.; B.Sc., Ohio State U., 1901; M.D., George Washington U., 1908; m. Alice Louise Baker, of Hyattsville, Md., June 20, 1908. Asst. chemist., Kan. Expt. Sta., Manhattan, 1901-02; Bur. of Chemistry, U.S. Dept. of Agr., Washington, 1902-22, scientific asst., 1902-06, chemist in charge Animal Physiol. Chem. Laboratory, 1906-22; research chemist, The Fleischmann Co., New York, from 1923. Mem. Am. Chem. Soc., A.A.A.S., Sigma Xi, Delta Tau Delta. in biol. and physiol. chemistry, foods and nutrition. Home: New York City, N.Y.†

WEBER, GUSTAVE FREDERICK, physician; b. New Orleans, June 3, 1910; s. Gustave Adolph and Elizabeth Susan (Wambsganss) W.; M.D., Tulane U., 1936; m. Shirley Scales, Aug. 1, 1936; 1 dau., Elizabeth W. Galloway. Intern, Charity Hosp., Shreveport, La., 1936-37, resident, 1937-39; Staff Fraser Sanitarium, Mang, La., 1939-50; fellow in internal medicine Ochsner Clinic, New Orleans, 1950-53, staff internal medicine; staff internal medicine Ochsner Found. Hosp., New Orleans; clin. asso. prof. medicine Tulane U., New Orleans. Served to lt. col., M.C. AUS, 1954-56. Diplomate Am. Bd. Internal Medicine. Fellow A.C.P.; mem. A.M.A., Pi Kappa Phi. Lutheran. Home: New Orleans, La. Died Mar. 21, 1971; buried Marshall, Tex.

WEBER, WILLIAM A, prof. religious edn.; b. Cincinnati, O., July 30, 1880; s. John and Frederique (Opperman) W.; A.B., Otterbein Coll., Ohio, 1906, D.D., 1919; B.D., Bonebrake Theol. Sem., Dayton, O., 1909; studied Berlin and Marburg univs., 1910-11, U. of Chicago, summers, 1912-16, and Yale University, 1923-24; Ph.D., Yale Univ.; m. Justina A. Lemmerman, Sept. 27, 1910; 1 son, Robert L. Ordained U.B. ministry, 1909; pastor in Cleveland and Dayton, O., 4 yrs.; prof. religious edn., Bonebrake Theol. Sem., 1911-25; prof. religious edn., Theol Sem., New Brunswick, New Jersey, from 1925; also registrar and secretary of the faculty; teacher, summer sessions, Rutgers University, 1926-31, prof. extension courses from 1951. Member Internat. Council Religious Edn., (member research advisory section), member board control Sunday Schools of United Brethren Ch., 1920-29; chmn. com. Week Day Sch. Religion, Dayton, O.; mem. exec. com. N.J. Council Religious Edn. (chmn. com. on week-day and vacation ch. schs.; also chmn. com. on ednl. program and policies). Mem. Bd. of Edn. (com. on institutions and students). Reformed Church in America, also chairman hymn book committee; member Board of Education, Dayton, Ohio, 1921-25 (twice president); member Department of Internat. Justice and Goodwill, Federal Council of Chs., of Christ in America. Mem. Religious Edn. Assn., A.A.A.S., Phi Beta Kappa. Club: Clergy. Author: The Daily Vacation Bible School; (joint) The Progressive Training Course; Theological Education in the Reformed Church in America. Contbr. numerous articles in religious and ednl. journals. Home: New Brunswick, N.J.†

WEBSTER, BENJAMIN FRANCIS, jazz musician; b. Kansas City, Mo., Feb. 27, 1909. Tenor saxophonist with many swing bands including Benny Carter, Fletcher Henderson, Cab Calloway; asso. with Duke Ellington, 1939-43, 48; later lived and worked in Los Angeles, N.Y.C.; moved to Eng., 1965, later played clubs and concerts, Eng. and the continent. Records include: Webster-Oscar Peterson, Webster & Assos. (with Coleman Hawkins), Soul of Ben Webster (with Art Farmer), Warm Moods (with String quartet), See You at the Fair, Webster-Sweets Edison, Sophisticated Lady, Soulville. Home: Jamaica, N.Y. Died July 1973.

WEBSTER, BRUCE PECK, physician; b. Lansdowne, Ont., Can., Nov. 1, 1901; s. Thomas Amos and Bertha (Peck) W.; M.D., C.M., McGill U., 1925. Came to U.S., 1927, naturalized, 1932. Intern. asst. resident medicine Montreal Gen. Hosp., 1925-27; asst. resident medicine, Jacques Loeb fellow Johns Hopkins Hosp. and U., 1927-29; fellow medicine NRC, 1929-31; asst. prof. medicine Tulane U., 1931-32; asst. prof. medicine Cornell U. Med. Sch., 1932-46, asso. prof. clin. medicine, 1946-66, clin. prof. medicine, 1966-76; pvt. practice medicine, 1946-76; attending physician N.Y. Hosp.; med. dir. Time, Inc., 1947-67. Mem. pub. adv. com. to surgeon gen. USPHS; cons. Dept. Army; exec. com. Japanese Christian U. Found., St. Luke's Hosp., Tokyo; med. adv. bd. Am. Hosp., Paris; past pres. Internat. Union Against Trepanomatoses; chmn. nat. commn. venereal disease Dept. Health, Edn. and Welfare. Served from lt. col to col. AUS, 1942-46. Decorated Legion of Merit. Mem. Soc. Exptl. Biology and Medicine, Soc. Clin. Investigation, Am. Inst. Nutrition, Harvey Soc., Soc. Research Child Devel., N.Y. Acad. Medicine. Am. Soc. Hygienne (past prs., chmn. internat. com.), Soc. Med. Consultants to Armed Forces (past pres.). Clubs: University, Century Assn., Nippon (N.Y.C.); Maidstone (Easthampton, N.Y.). Home: New York City, N.Y., Died Jan. 5, 1976.

WEBSTER, EDWARD JEROME, clergyman; b. Hardwick, Vt., Jan. 11, 1881; s. Noble Elderkin and Dora Mary (Schoolcraft) W.; B.A., Yale, 1913; B.D., Union Theol. Sem., 1917; M.A., Columbia, 1918; m. Elsie Brooks, of Chester, N.Y., Feb. 12, 1918. Ordained Congl. ministry, 1917; asso. pastor, First Congl. Ch., New Haven, Conn., 1918; pastor Aurora, Ill., from Apr. 1919. Accused of speaking too plainly; vote of 90 to 59, Sept. 1921, in favor of his remaining in charge. Sec. Com. of 100, New Haven, 1918; organizer and chmn. Com. of 12, Aurora. Mem. Phi Beta Kappa, Beta Theta Pi. Club: Kiwanis. Home: Aurora, Ill†

WEBSTER, JEROME PIERCE, plastic surgeon; b. Ashland, N.H., Aug. 2, 1888; s. Rev. Lorin and Jennie Josephine (Adams) W.; grad. Holderness Sch., Plymouth, N.H., 1906; A.B., Trinity Coll., Hartford, Conn., 1910, M.S. (hon.), 1937, D.Sc. (hon.), 1968; M.D., Johns Hopkins, 1914; M.D. (hon.) U. Bologna, Italy, 1952; m. Geraldine Rockefeller McAlpin, July 14, 1934 (dec.); m. 2d, Emily Brune Randall, Mar. 24, 1951 (dec.) Intern Johns Hopkins Hosp., 1914-15, asst. resident in surgery, 1915-16, 1920-21; spl. asst. to Am. ambassador, Berlin, Germany, inspecting prison camps, 1916-17; jr. fellow Trinity Coll., 1917-20 and 1934-39; instr. surgery, Johns Hopkins Sch. of Nursing, 1920-21; resident in surgery, Union Med. Coll., Peking, China, 1921-22, asso. in surgery, 1922-23, asst. prof., 1923-25, asso. prof., 1925-26; practiced in N.Y.C., from 1928; fellow in surgery, Presbyn. Hosp., 1928-31, asst. attending surg., 1931-38, asso. attending surgeon, 1938-45, attending surgeon, 1945-54, cons., 1954; asso. in surgery coll. phys. and surg. Columbia, 1931-35, asst. prof. surgery, 1935-38, asst. prof. clin. surgery, 1938-48, prof., 1948-54, prof. emeritus, 1954-74; in charge of plastic surgery Vanderbilt Clinic, 1928-54; 1s5 1st vis. prof. plastic surgery, U. Rochester, 1958; fellow Cesare Barbieri Center of Italian Studies, Trinity Coll., Hartford, Conn., from 1959; Albert Kuntz lectr. St. Louis U. Sch. Medicine, 1958; dir. courses in plastic surgery, 1942-43. Trustee Holderness Sch., Trinity Coll.; v.p., trustee Watkinson Library. Insp. plastic surgery facilities Office Surgeon Gen. AUS, 1944-46. Pres. Am. Bur. Med. Aid. to China, 1956-60. Served as 1st lt. M.C., U.S. Army, 1917-19, with British on Lens Sector, French and A.E.F. on Toul, Chateau-Thierry and St. Mihiel sectors and through Argonne-Meuse drive. Awarded plate with British seal (acceptance authorized by U.S. Congress); Croix de Guerre (gold star); cited for bravery on Toul Sector, June 1918; twice decorated by Chinese Govt., twice Greek Govt.; recipient spl. hon. citation. Am. Soc. Plastic and Reconstructive Surgery, 1958; citation for distinguished services Columbia U. Libraries, 1971. Fellow Am. Med. Assn., Am. Coll. of Surgeons; mem. A.A.A.S., Am. Assn. Plastic Surgeons (pres. 1941-42, award medal 1972), Soc. Plastic and Reconstructive Surgeons, Am. Surgical Assn., Med. Library Assn., Harvey Soc., N.Y. Acad. Medicine (editorial bd.; v.p. 1954-57, plaque 1973), Am. Assn. History of Medicine Welch Medal 1954, Sociedad Latino-americana de Cirugia Plastica (hon.), Académie Internationale d.Histoire de la Medécine, Societa Italiana della Scienze Mediche e naturali; Am. Geog. Soc., Halsted Soc., Am. Soc. for Surgery of The Hand (v.p. 1956), Assn. Internationale de Bibliophilie, Psi Upsilon; hon. mem. Sociedad Chilena de Cirugia Plastica y Reparadoro. Clubs: St. Andrews Golf, Riverdale Yacht, Grolier, Century Assn., Charaka. Home: Riverdale-on-Hudson, N.Y. Died Nov. 14, 1974.

WEED, CLYDE E., mining exec.; b. Moorestown, Mich., Aug. 8, 1890; s. Herbert Moores and Emma (Van Aiken) W.; student Mich. State State Coll., 1906-07; B.S., Michigan College of Mines and Technology, E.M., 1911, Doctor Engineering, 1946; Dr. Engring., Mont. Sch. Mines, 1959; D.Sc., University of Ariz., 1962; LL.D. (hon.), Michigan State University, 1963; m. Albertine Milan, June 17, 1930; 1 son, Herbert Morrison. Miner Calumet & Hecla Mining Co., Mich., 1911-12; mines supt. Victoria Copper Mining Co., Ontonagon County, Mich., 1913-15; supt. Lake Copper Company, same county, 1915-17; manager Hancock (Michigan) Consolidated Copper Company, 1917-20; foreman Live Oak Division, Inspiration (Arizona) Consolidated Copper Co., 1921-23, assistant mgr. same co., 1924-29; gen. mgr. Cananea Consolidated Copper Co., Cananea, Sonora, Mex., 1930-35, pres. and gen. mgr., 1935-38; gen. mgr. mines Anaconda Copper Mining Co., 1938-42, v.p. in charge mining operations, 1942-52; v.p. charge operations 1952-56, (name changed to Anaconda Co.); pres. Anaconda Co., 1956-58, chmn. bd., dir., 1958-65, chairman executive committee, director, from 1965; dir. Andes Copper Mining Co., Chile Copper Co., Chile Exploration Co.; mem. bd., dirs. Anaconda Am. Brass Company, Greene Cananea Copper Company, Anaconda Aluminum Co., Anaconda Sales Company, Anaconda Wire & Cable Company. Pres., director Am. Mining Congress. Mem. bd. dirs. United Cerebral Palsy Research and Edn. Found., Inc. Decorated knight comdr. Order of Merit Gen. Bernardo O'Higgins (Govt. of Chile), 1955. Recipient ANKH award, Copper Club N. Y., 1962. Mem. Nat. Indsl. Conf. Bd., Am. Inst. Mining, Metall. and Petroleum Engrs. (William L. Saunders medal for achievement in mining 1951), Copper Inst. (pres., dir.), Am. Arbitration Assn., The Pilgrims of U.S., Fed. Hall Meml. Assos. Clubs: Mining, University, River, India House (N.Y.C.); Butte (Mont.) Country; The Creek (Locust Valley, N.Y.); Clove Valley Rod and Gun; Cat Key (Cat Cay, The Bahamas); Lyford Cay (Bahamas). Home: New York City, N.Y. Died May 5, 1973.

WEEKS, HARRY CURTIS, lawyer; b. Arlington, Tex., Sept. 25, 1890; s. W.C. and Ella (Potter) W.; student Carlisle Mil. Acad., 1902-06, Hanover Coll., 1909, U. Tex., 1906-11; m. Ethel Gill, Nov. 26, 1912 (dec.); 1 son, Harry Curtis; m. 2d, Mrs. Martha Cantey Teas, Feb. 9, 1952 (dec.). Admitted to Tex. bar, 1915, practiced in Witchita Falls and Ft. Worth; sr. mem. Weeks, Bird, Appleman, from 1937. Mem. Newcomen Soc. N.Am., State Bar Tex., Am., Ft. Worth bar assns., Ft. Worth Art Assn., Beta Theta Pi. Episcopalian. Clubs: Shady Oaks Country, Ft. Worth, River Crest Country (Ft. Worth); Petroleum (Dallas). Home: Fort Worth, Tex. Died Jan. 29, 1973.

WEGEMANN, CARROLL HARVEY, geologist; b. Lake Mills, Wis., Mar. 26, 1879; s. August Henry and Susannah Isabel (Harvey) W.; student Beloit (Wis.) Coll., 1899-1901; U. of Wis., 1901-05, B.S., 1903, M.A., 1907; m. Mrs. Louise Presbury (Cook) Hiss, April 8, 1911; one daughter, Isabel Harvey (Mrs. R. C. Becker). Exploration for iron, Ontario, 1904; land development, Isle of Pines W.I., 1905-06; instructor geology, University of Illinois, 1906-07; geologist, U.S. Geol. Survey, 1907-17; mem. Oil Land Bd., same, 1911-17; geol exploration in Cuba, 1916; chief geologist, Franco Wyo. Oil Co. and affiliated cos., 1917-19. Western States Oil & Land Co., 1919-20. Midwest Refining Co., 1921-25, Pan-Am. Petroleum & Transport Company (exploration in Mexico and Central America), 1925-31; chief geologist Crown Central Petroleum Corp., 1933, cons. geologist Wintershall Corp., Germany, 1934; regional geologist Nat. Park Service, 1935-42; lecturer in geology, University of Oamaha, 1936-42; sr. geologist Petroleum Adminstration for War, 1942-45, consulting geologist from 1945. Mem. Geol. Soc. Am., Rocky Mountain Assn. of Geologists, Colo. Archaeological Society, Am. Assn. Petroleum Geologists, Am. Inst. Mining and Metall. Engrs., Soc. Econ. Geologists. Conglis. Author of about 20 govt. reports on petroleum, coal, gen. geology of Western U.S.; also popular articles. Latest publication: Guide to the Geology of Rocky Mt. Nat. Park, Govt. Printing Office, 1944. Home: Denver, Colo.†

WEHLING, LOUIS ALBERT, educator; b. Chgo., Aug. 20, 1910; s. Louis Christian and Katharine (Schosser) W.: A.B., U. Ill., 1932; J.D., U. Chgo., 1935; A.M., U. So. Cal., 1940; m. Mildred Buls, Oct. 26, 1956; children—Katharine, Caroline, Jefferson. Admitted to Ill. bar, 1935; mem. law faculty Valparaiso U., 1936-74, prof. govt., 1949-74, head dept., 1949-70. Served as officer USNR, 1942-45; comdr. Res. Mem. Am. Polit. Sci. Assn., Valparaiso C. of C. (past bd. dirs.), Delta Theta Phi, Pi Sigma Alpha. Rotarian (past dir. Valparaiso). Home: Valparaiso Ind. Died May 9, 1974.

WEHRHAN, NELSON W., clergyman; b. Wis., May 3, 1878; s. G. L. and Matilda (Paley) W.; Ph.B., Grinnell (Ia.) Coll., 1906; student Hartford (Conn.) Theol. Sem., 1906-07; B.D., Chicago Theol. Sem., 1908; D.D., Tabor Coll., 1918; m. Anna Penrose, Oct. 14, 1910; 1 dau., Lois Rachel. Ordained Congl. ministry, 1903; home missionary in Mont., 1908-09; pastor 1st Ch., Ft. Dodge, Ia., 1909-13; dean Tabor (Ia.) Coll., 1913, acting pres., 1914-16, and pres., 1916-21; pastor Dodge Memorial Ch., Council Bluffs, Ia., 1921-23; asst. to pres. Grinnell Coll., 1923-33; Naperville, 1933-37, Alameda Park Congl. Ch. from 1938. Home: Portland, Ore.*†

WEIDMAN, CHARLES, dancer, choreographer, instr.; b. Lincoln, Neb., July 22, 1901; s. Charles Edward and Vesta (Hoffman) W.; studied dance with Ruth St. Denis, Ted Shawn, Theodore Kosliff. Tchr., Eleanor Frampton, 1931; toured in vaudeville with Martha Graham, later with Denishawn Dancing Co., touring Eng., U.S., Orient; with Doris Humphrey established own dancing sch. and co., 1929; pioneer devel. modern dance in U.S.; established own dance co., 1941, since touring U.S. yearly; producer ballet Fables For Our Time, 1948; former choreographer N.Y.C. Center Opera; established with Mikhail Santoro, Expression of Two Arts Theatre, 1960. Guggenheim fellow, 1947. Home: New York City N.Y. Died July 15, 1975.

WEIGEL, EUGENE JOHN, coll. prof.; b. Cleveland, O., Sept. 6, 1894; s. John Michael and Emma (Bankhardt) W.; student Columbia U., 1919-21, Hochschule für Musik, Berlin, 1923. Western Reserve U., 1924, Cleveland Law Coll., 1916-17; B.S., Ohio State U., 1928 M.A., 1939; m. Nina Clemens Gunn, Aug. 17, 1929 (dec.); children—MaryRuth, Nina Jean. Eugene John, Jr.; married 2d, Margaret W. Banning. Mar. 16, 1957. Tchr. violin, professional musician, conductor, 1914-29; teacher instrumental music, Cleveland Pub. Schs., 1923-24, supervisor in secondary schs., 1924-29; asst. prof., Ohio State U., summer 1928, prof. of music, from 1929, chairman of the department of music, 1940-44, dir. School of Music, from 1945; condr. symphonic and marching bands, 1929-39, also

Ohio State Symphony Orchestra, 1929-46; music director Columbus Civic Opera, 1933-37. Served with U.S. Navy Band, 1918-19. Mem. bd. directors Columbus Philharmonic Orchestra Assn., editorial bd. Music Educators Nat. Conf., Nat. Com. on Music Appreciation North Central com. on music in higher edn., music curriculum com., State Dept. Edn., Ohio, Nat. Music in War Time Committee; past president National Association Music Executives of State Univs., Ohio Music Educators Association, Mem. Phi Mu Alpha, Kappa Kappa Psi, Phi Delta Kappa, Beta Theta Pi, Sphinx, Varsity "O," Am. Legion (past comdr. Mason. Presbyterian. Republican. Clubs: Rotary, Faculty, Musicians, Univ. Golf. Address: Columbus, O. Died Aug. 11, 1973; interred Union Cemetery, Columbus.

WEIGLE, LUTHER ALLEN, univ. prof.; b. Littlewtown, Pa., Sept. 11, 1880; s. Elias Daniel (D.D.) and Hannah (Bream) W.; B.A., Gettysburg Coll., 1900, M.A., 1903, LL.D., 1934; student Lutheran Theol. Sem., Gettysburg, 1900-02; Yale, 1902-05, Ph.D., 1905; D.D., Carleton, 1916, Gettysburg Coll., 1917; Litt.D., Muhlenberg Coll., 1925; Doctor of Laws, Dickinson College, 1933, Wittenburg Coll., 1949; S.T.D., Ohio U., 1934. Berkeley Div. Sch., 1950; J.U.D., Boston U., 1939; D.D., Queen's U., 1941, Princeton, 1946, Yale, 1950; L.H.D., Otterbein Coll., 1952. Lambuth Coll., 1960; m. Clara Boxrud, June 15, 1909; children—Richard, Luther Allan, Margare (Mrs. W.F. Quillian, Jr.), Ruth (Mrs. A.C. Guyton). Ordained Luth. ministry, 1903; pastor, Bridgeport, Connecticut, 1903-04; assistant in psychology, Yale, 1904-05; professor philsoophy, Carleton College, Northfield, Minn., 1905-16, dean, prof. of 1910-15; Horace Bushnell Christian nuture, Yale, 1916-24, Sterling prof. of religious edn., 1924-49, dean of Yale Divinity Sch., 1928-49, now emeritus; had held lectureships at many sems. and univs. Prs. Conf. Theol. Sems., 1929, chmn. exec. com., 1930-49; chmn. adminstrv. com. Fed. Council Chs., 1939-32, pres., 1940-42; chmn. planning com. orgn. Nat. Council Chs. Christ, U.S.A., 1941-50; chmn. World Council Christian Edn. and Sunday Sch. Assn., 1928-58; chmn. com. which edited Revised Standard Version of the Bible from 1930; chmn. com. revising Apocrypha, from 1953. Trustee Northfield Schools. Hazen Found., Yale-in China (pres. 1946-56). Decorated Knight of St. Gregory the Great (Pope Paul VI); recipient citation distinguished service Cong. Chs., A.M.E. Zion Ch., Nat. Councils Chs., Boy Scouts; Gutenberg award, Chgo. Bible Soc., 1959; Wilbur Cross medal Yale University, 1967. Author numerous books, from 1911, same being, The Living Word, 1956; A Bible Word Book (with Ronald Bridges), 1959; The New Testament Octapla, 1961; The Genesis Octapla, 1965. Home: New Haven, Conn.†

WEIL, ROBERT T., JR., ednl. adminstr.; B.S. in Elec. Engring., Poly. Inst. Bklyn., 1930; M.S., Columbia; m. Helen Marshall. Joined faculty Manhattan Coll., 1932, prof. elec. engring., 1945, dean Sch. Engring., 1961-71. Registered profl. engr., N.Y. Office: Bronx, N.Y. Died Oct. 30, 1974; interred St. Charles Cemetery, Pinelawn, N.Y.

WEILL, MILTON, mfg. exec.; b. N.Y.C., Oct. 21, 1891; s. Charles and Rose (Straus) W.; A.B., Columbia, 1913; m. Teresa Jackson, Mar. 5, 1922. Partner Weil-Blow-Weill (became Blow Co.), advt. agy., 1916-20; v.p., A. J. Donahue Sales Corp., 1920-23; v.p. Arrow Mfg. Co., 1926-42, pres., 1942-61, chmn., 1961-75; chmn. bd. Arrow Case Mfg. Co. Ltd., Toronto; Mem. bd. United Jewish Appeal Greater N.Y.; pres. Fedn. Jewish Philanthropies N.Y., 1951-54, now asso. chmn., hon. trustee; bd. Nat. Jewish Welfare Bd.; mem. bd. overseers Brandeis U. Grad. Sch. Social Welfare; fellow Brandeis U., 1965; hon. chmn. bd. Asso. YM-YWHA's Greater N.Y., 1957-58, exec. bd. 1959; hon. v.p. N.Y. YM-YWHA; gov., trustee Am. Jewish Com., 1946-75. Clubs: Twenty-four Karat, City Athletic, Harmonie (N.Y.C.); Old Oaks Country (pres. 1939-40) (Purchase, N.Y.). Home: Sarasota, Fla. Died Oct. 2, 1975.

WEINBERG, ROBERT CHARLES, architect, planning cons., author; b. N.Y.C., Dec. 18, 1901; s. Charles and Lily (Hayman) W.; A.B., Harvard, 1923, postgrad. Sch. Arch., 1924-26, Sch. City Planning, 1930-31; m. Marian King Himes, Dec. 15, 1951. Architect, site planner Gen. Houses, Inc., Chgo., 1932-35; cons. Mayor's Com. on City Planning, N.Y.C., 1935-38; asso. city planner N.Y.C. Dept. Planning, 1938-42; cons. Chgo. Plan Commn., 1941; sr. housing specialist Nat. Housing Agy., 1942-43; research asso. Com. on Hygiene of Housing, 1943; planning cons. Chgo. Housing Authority, 1943-44, Cleve. Planning Commn., 1943-48; pvt. practice architecture and planning, N.Y.C., 1946-70; dir., planning cons. Hancock Little Calvert, Inc., 1970-74. Critic-at-large architecture, planning for radio sta. WNYC, 1966; dir. Pantheon Books, Inc., 1943-63; adj. prof. urban planning N.Y. U. Grad. Sch. Pub. Adminstrn., from 1944; lectr., critic New Sch. for Social Research, Yale, Pratt Inst.; lectr. on city planning under Fulbright program Germany, Norway, 1954; A.W. Mellon distinguished vis. prof. Carnegie Inst. Tech., Pitts., 1960-61. Dir. Citizens Union, N.Y.C., Washington Sq. Assn., N.Y.C., v.p., from 1967; chmn., Greenwich Village Community Planning Bd., 1950-56. Bd. dirs. Citizens Housing and Planning Council, Encampment for Citizenship; bd. dirs. Vinmont Found., from 1947, pres., 1964-71, treas., from 1971; mem. Harvard Grad. Sch. Design Alumni Council, 1959-66, pres., 1961-64. Recipient Bard award Citizens Union N.Y., 1973; Posthumous award N.Y. Met. chpt. Am. Inst. Planners, 1974. Fellow A.I.A.; mem. Am. Inst. Planners, Real Estate Bd. N.Y. Book rev. editor Jour. Am. Inst. Planners, 1948-60; editor City Planning: Housing, vol. III (Werner Hegemann), 1938. Author: Planning and Community Appearance, 1957. Contbr. articles to profl. jours. Home: New York City, N.Y. also Ridgefield, Conn. Died Jan. 25, 1974; buried Hawthorne, N.Y.

WEINBERGER, JACOB, judge; b. Czechoslovakia (formerly a part Austria-Hungary) Jan. 4, 1882; brought to U.S. 1889; s. Herman and Nettie (Flaster); LL.B., U. of Colo., 1904; LL.D. (hon.), U. Ariz., 1959; m. Blanche Ruth Solomon, June 11, 1907; children—Adrienne (Mrs. Herbert H. Hafter), Richard. Admitted to Colo. bar, 1904, Ariz. bar, 1905, Cal. bar, 1911; practiced in Denver, 1904, Globe, Ariz., 1905-11; asst. dist. atty. Gila County, Ariz., 1907-09; del. from Gila County to Ariz. Constl. Conv., 1910; practice in San Diego, 1911-41; city atty. San Diego, 1941-43; judge Superior Ct., San Diego County, 1943-45; U.S. dist. judge So. Dist. Cal., from 1946; sr. judge U.S. Dist. Ct., from 1958. Mem. bd. edn., City San Diego 21 years. Mason (32, Shriner), Eagle, Lion; mem. B'nai B'rith. Home: San Diego Cal. Died May 1974.

WEINER, JOSEPH LEE, lawyer; b. Dombrowitz, Russia, Mar. 16, 1902; s. Morris and Anna (Levine) W.; A.B., Columbia U., 1923, LL.B., 1926; m. Ruth Lessall, Dec. 26, 1923; children—Elizabeth, Stephen Arthur. Admitted to New York bar, 1926; practiced and taught law, N.Y. bar, 1926; practiced and taught law, N.Y. City, 1926-33; asst. corp. counsel in charge of franchises and utilities, N.Y. City, 1933-37; counsel Bd. of Transportation, 1937-38; spl. counsel reorganization div. Securities and Exchange Commn., 1938-39, dir. pub. utilities div., 1939-41; asst. adminstr. Office of Price Adminstration and Civilian Supply, in charge civilian allocation, later director of Civilian Supply, War Production Board, 1941-43. Private practice of law 1943-76; lectr. in finance, adj. prof. finance Columbia, N.Y.C., 1947-56; spl. counsel SEC, 1961; adj. prof. law N.Y.U., 1970-76. Dir. Bankers Security Life Ins. Soc., Boise Cascade Corp., Internat. Controls Corp. Home: New York City, N.Y., Died Jan. 15, 1976.

WEINGARTEN, LAWRENCE A., motion picture producer; m. Jessie Marmorston; children—Elizabeth (Mrs. Harold Horowitz), Norma (Mrs. Sam Pisar), Lailee (Mrs. W. Momerts). Producer in assn. with E.J. Banks, series bibl. films, 1921; dir. Babylonian expdn. U. Chgo., 1921; dir. publicity for Jackie Coogan, 1923-26; joined Metro-Goldwyn-Mayer Studios, 1927; producer 75 films, including A Day at the Races, Adam's Rib, Pat and Mike, When Ladies Meet, Libeled Lady, I'll Cry Tomorrow, The Tender Trap, Cat On a Hot Tin Roof, Unsinkable Molly Brown. Mem. Producers Guild Am. (pres. 1963-65). Home: Los Angeles, Cal. Died Feb. 6, 1975.

WEINHANDL, FERDINAND, educator; b. Gudenburg, Austria, Jan. 31, 1896; s. Ferdinand and Lucia (Matzun) W.; ed. U. Graz (Austria), 1914-19; Dr.phil.; m. Margarete Slantocknigg, Aug. 5, 1919. Lectr. publ., Munich, 1919-21; dozent, prof. U. Kiel, 1921-42; prof. U. Frankfurt (Germany), 1942-45; prof. U. Graz, 1952-65, prof. emeritus, 1965—. Served with Armed Forces, 1914-16. Mem. Austrian Acad. Arts and Sci., Austrian Acad. Science. Author: Die Gestaltanalyse, 1927; Die Metaphysik Goetkes, 1932. Home: Graz, Austria., Deceased.

WEINSTEIN, JACOB JOSEPH, clergyman; b. Stephin, Poland, June 6, 1902; s. Benjamin and Shaindel (Weinstein) W.; came to U.S., 1907, naturalized, 1925; A.B., Reed Coll., 1923; Rabbi, Hebrew Union Coll., 1929, D.D., 1955; D.H.L., Spertus Coll. Jewish Studies, 1971; m. Janet Harris, Aug. 10, 1931; children—Ruth, Daniel, Judith, Deborah. Ordained, 1929; rabbi Congregation Beth Israel, Austin, Tex., 1929-30, Congregation Sherith Israel, San Francisco, 1930-32, Kehillat Anshe Mayriv Temple, Chgo., 1939-70 (emeritus from 1967); adviser Jewish students Columbia, 1932-33; dir. Adult Sch. Jewish Studies, N.Y.C., 1933-35, Sch. Jewish Studies, San Francisco, 1935-39. Mem. bd. Jewish Welfare Bd. Chgo., 1963-65; nat. chmn. Nat. Com. Labor Israel, 1958-70; mem. bus. ethics adv. com. Dept. Commerce, Pres.'s Com. on Equal Employment Opportunity, 1961-65; mem. Ill. Commn. Human Relations, 1953-56; pres. Central Conf. Am. Rabbis, 1965-67. Recipient award Mayor Chgo. Commn. on Human Relations, 1947; Daniel Burnham award Roosevelt U., 1962; award Immigrant Service League, 1963. Mem. Chgo. Bd. Rabbis (pres. 1947-49), Hyde Park Council Chs. and Synagogues (pres. 1959-61), Union Am. Hebrew Congregations (mem. bd. 1961), Am. Forestry Assn., Central Conf. Am. Rabbis (pres.), Lincoln Acad. Ill. Mem. B'nai B'rith. Editorial bd. Jewish Frontier, 1933. Home: San Francisco, Cal. Died Nov. 2, 1974.

WEINTRAUB, ABRAHAM ALLEN, hosp. adminstrn.; b. Phila., Sept. 15, 1917; s. Morris and Celia (Levine) W.; B.S., LaSalle Coll., 1940; student Cornell U., 1960, U.Cal. at Berkeley, 1968; Mass. Inst. Tech., 1972; m. Mildred Strauss, Apr. 2, 1944; Children—Cynthia (Mrs. Sidney A. Galton), Alvin, Tracy. Asst. adminstr. St. Vincent Infirmary, Little Rock, Ark., 1954-61, asso. adminstr., 1961-67, adminstr., 1967-73, asst. to pres., 1973-74. Bd. dirs. Central Ark. Radiation Therapy Inst., Ark. chpt. Nat. Conf. Christians and Jews, Little Rock chpt. A.R.C., vis. Nurses Assn.; exec. bd. Quapaw Area council Boy Scouts Am.; bd. dirs. Little Rock Boys Club, St. Joseph's Home for Children. Served to lt. col., med. adminstrv. corps, AUS, 1941-46. Fellow Am. Coll. Hosp. Adminstrs.; mem. Am. Hosp. Assn. (trustee 1970-74); Catholic (trustee 1970-74), Ark. (pres. 1961-62) hosp. assns., Am. Assn. Hosp. Accountants (pres. Ark. chpt. 1956-57), Ark. Soc. Med. Technologists, Little Rock Hosp. Council, Little Rock C. of C. (dir. 1964-67), Ark. Assn. Mental Health, Ark. Bd. Edn. Home: Little Rock, Ark., Died May 3, 1974.

WEISIGER, KENDALL, b. in Richmond, Virginia, February 14, 1880; s. of Samuel Carter and Bettie Collier (Martin) Weisiger; B.S. in E.E., Virginia Polytechnic Inst., 1899; m. Rose Drayton Woodruff, June 1, 1904. Began telephone work in 1900; served as installer, insp., engr., asst. chief engr., gen. information mgr. Southern Bell Tel. & Telegraph Co., Atlanta, Ga. Retired Feb. 28, 1945, to become treas. Oglethorpe U. Mem. com. on classification of personnel in army, World War, also conducted schs. for army personnel officers, now lt. col. O.R.C. (ret.). Founder-chmn. trustees Rotary Ednl. Foundation of Atlanta; mem. Assn. for International Office of Education, member National Housing Association, mem. American Arbitration Association; treasurer Southern Area Council Y.M.C.A.; chmn. Bd. trustees Morehouse College; trustee, Atlanta University, Atlanta Univ. School of Social Work, Piedmont College, National Council Y.M.C.A., Univ. Housing Project; adminstrator of unemployment relief work, Atlanta, 1932; member Regional Compliance Council NRA, 1935; special consultant to adminstr., Farm Security Adminstrn., 1935; pres. Family Welfare Soc., Tuberculosis Assn., Council of Social Agencies; dir. Nat. Tuberculosis Assn., Dir. Soc. Friends of the Land; mem. Regional Loyalty Bd. of Civil Service. Mem. Telephone Pioneers (life mem.), O.D.K., Pi Sigma Alpha. Democrat. Episcopalian. Mason. Rotarian. Author: The Youngfellow's Book, Background for Brotherhood; Getting Along Together. Home: Atlanta, Ga.†

WEISS, RICHARD ALEXANDER, sci. adminstr.; b. Port Washington, L.I., N.Y., Jan. 23, 1910; s. Robert Oswald and Bertha (Schwabe) W.; B.S. in Physics and Math., Randolph-Macon Coll., 1934; M.S. in Physics, U. Va., 1938, Ph.D., 1940; m. Marie E. Jehne, July 30, 1937; children—Katherine D. (Mrs. Frank E. Cook), Carolyn E. (Mrs. Chalmers J. Gorman), Stephen J. Research physicist Magnolia Metals Co., Bayway, N.J., 1940-41; with Signal Corps Engring. Labs., U.S. Army, Ft. Mommouth, N.J., 1941-55, chief phys. scis. div., 1952-55; sci. adviser, then acting chief scientist Office Chief Research and Devel., Dept. Army, 1955-58, dep. and sci. dir. U.S. Army Research Office, 1958-72. Chmn. bd. edn., Highlands, N.J., 1947-53. Recipient Nat. Civil Service League Career Service award, 1959, Metritorious Civilian Service award Dept. Army, 1962, Exceptional Civilian Service award Dept. Army, 1972. Senior member I.E.E.E.; mem. Washington Acad. Scis., Am. Phys. Soc., A.A.A.S., Association of U.S. Army, Phi Beta Kappa, Sigma Xi, Omicron Delta Kappa. Home: Arlington Va. Died Mar. 18, 1974.

WEITZ, RUDOLPH WILSON, constrn. exec.; b. Des Moines, Jan. 5, 1901; s. Frederick William and Alice Carey (Wilson) W.; A.B., Grinnell Coll., 1921; grad. study, Harvard Sch. Bus. Adminstrn., 1923; m. Sarah Stevenson, Sept. 30, 1926; children—Frederick William II, Stevenson. Various positions Weitz Co., Inc., Des Moines, 1923-33, pres., dir., 1935-60, chmn. bd., 1960; dep. asst. sec. def., 1954-55; v.p. Valley Bank & Trust Co., 1933-35; chmn. bd. Weitz-Hettelsater Engrs., Kansas City; pres., dir. Weitz Bros., Inc.; dir. Bankers Trust Co., Des Moines, Employers Mut. Casualty Co., Des Moines. Civilian aide for Ia. to sec. army, 1958-64; mem. Gov.'s Commn. Econ. and Social Trends. Pres., dir. Des Moines Community Chest, 1950-53, Weitz Found., Christian Home Services, Inc.; trustee Grinnell Coll. Mem. Asso. Gen. Contractors Am. (dir.), Des Moines Indsl. Bur. (dir.), Am. Concrete Inst., U.S., Des Moines (past pres. dir.) chambers commerce, Cons. Constructors Council Am., Master Builders Ia. (past pres., dir.), Sigma Delta Chi. Clubs: University (Chgo.); Des Moines, Wakonda (Des Moines); International (Washington); Kansas City (Mo.). Home: Des Moines, Ia. Died May 26, 1974.

WELCH, DALE DENNIS, corp. exec.; born Clayton County, Ia., Apr. 19, 1896; s. Oscar Eugene and Nora Ianthia (Stalnaker) W.; A.B., U. of Dubuque, 1921; A.M., Cornell U., 1928; LL.D., Coe Coll. (Ia.), 1936; grad. work Northwestern U., 1923; D.D., U. of Dubuque, 1947; m. Margaret Lucile Aitchison, June 25, 1920; 1 dau., Margaret Jean. Instr. in Epworth (Ia.) Sem., 1918-20, U. of Dubuque, 1922-28; ordained ministry, 1923; mgr. Dubuque Clinic, 1928-36; pres. U. Dubuque, 1936-47; pres. Alma (Mich.) Coll., 1947-50; v.p. Whitworth Coll., Spokane, Wash., 1950-51; pres. Hastings (Neb.) Coll., 1952-57; v.p. First of Ia. Corp., Des Moines. Republican. Mason. Rotarian. Address: Dubuque, Ia. Died Sept. 8, 1975; buried Dubuque, Ia.

WELCH, LIVINGSTON, educator; b. New Rochelle, N.Y., Aug. 8, 1901; s. Charles James and Elizabeth (Livingston) W; B.A., Columbia, 1931, M.A., 1932, Ph.D., 1935; student Cambridge (Eng.) U., 1933-35; m. Helen Sharp, 1936 (dec. Oct. 1969); Children—Basilia, Deirdre (dec.), Pamela Welsh Trumper. Instr. Hunter Coll., N.Y.C., 1936-42, asst. prof., 1942-47, asst. prof., dir. inst. research in clin. and child psychology, 1948, prof. psychology, 1952-72, chmn. dept., 1954-68; asso. prof. Cornell U., 1952; sr. psychologist Payne Whitney Clinic, New York Hosp., N.Y.C. Exhibited sculptor works at Carlebach, Ferragile, 1949, Portraits, Inc., 1950 Caravan, 1957, Mus. City N.Y., 1958; one man show Wellons, 1956, World House Galleries, 1962, 64, New Sch. Social Research, 1962, Robert Shuster Gallery, Tasca Gallery, others. Fellow Am., Eastern psychol. assns., A.A.A.S., N.Y. Acad. Sci.; mem. Am. Psychopathol. Assn. Author: Imagination and Human Nature, 1935; From Boring Dinosaur to Passionate Computer (poetry), 1968; also numerous articles in scientific jours.; included in anthologies; numerous recordings in Archive of Recorded Poetry and Lit., Library of Congress, 1961. Home: New York City, N.Y., Died Apr. 18, 1973.

WELD, LEROY DOUGHERTY, physicis; b. Cresco, Ia., Mar. 6, 1880; s. LeRoy Tryon and Nancy Rose (Dougherty) W.; B.S., State University of Iowa, 1899, M.S., 1902, Ph.D., 1922; D.Sc., Coe College, 1974; married Lulu A. Graff, June 24, 1903; children—Rose Esther (Dec.) Virginia Lloyd. Teacher Ia. secondary schs., 1898-1902; prof. physics, Coe Coll., 1902-45. Chief physicist, The Turner Company (manufacturers electrical equipment), 1943-48. Lecturer on physics, Columbia, 4 mos. 1912. University of Iowa, summer 1915. Member Acoustical Soc. of America, Iowa Academy Science (president 1927), Sigma Xi, Phi Kappa Phi. Presbyterian. Author: The Theory of Errors and Least Squares (textbook), 1916; (with prof. Frederic Palmer, Jr.) A Textbook of Modern Physics, 1925; A Textbook of Heat, 1948. Joint translator: Helmholtz's Physiological Optics (from the German), 1924. Compiler and editor: Glossary of Physics, 1937. Contbg. editor: Van Nostrand Scientific Ency. (physics), 1938, 1945. Home: Cedar Rapids, Ia.†

WELDON, JAMES BREWER, clergyman, educator; b. Denton Co., Tex., Nov. 3, 1878; s. Abram James and Martha L. (Lindsay) W.; A.B., A.M., Christian U. (now Culver-Stockton Coll.), Canton, Mo., 1904, B.D., 1906; studied U. of Chicago, summer 1922; m. Mary Lena Hottel, of Canton, July 9, 1901; children—John Brewer, james Oliver, Ada Lorine (dec.), Ida Louise. Ordained ministry Christian (Disciples of Chirst) Ch., 1902; teacher Greek and history, Culver-Stockton Coll., 1906-07; pastor Boonville, Mo., 1908-18, during which time became widely known as prohibition advocate; dist. supt. missions, Disciples of Christ, 1918-20; v.p. Culver-Stockton Coll., 1920-24; asso. sec. Dept. of Endowments, same ch., 1924-26; pres. Cotner Coll., from Jan. 1926. Mem. bd. dirs. Nat. Bd. of Edn., Disciples of Christ. Mason, Kiwanian. Home: Bethany, Neb.†

WELLES, DONALD PHELPS, banker; b. Chicago, Nov. 7, 1898; s. Edward Phelps and Emelyn (Munch) W.; grad. St. Paul's Sch., Concord, N.H., 1917; Ph.B., Sheffield Sci. Sch., Yale, 1920; post grad. work, Magdalene Coll., Cambridge U., England, 1921; m. Barbara Scott, Sept. 23, 1925; children—Donald Phelps, Jr., Robert C., Frederic L., James Stuart. With Chicago Trust Co., 1921-23; with Harris Trust & Savs. Bank, Chgo., 1923-63, exec. v.p., dir., until 1963; director of Besly-Welles Corp., Beloit, Wisconsin. Served as 2d lt., F.A., U.S. Army, World War I; comdr., U.S.N.R., 1942-45. Former dir. Northwestern U. Settlement (pres., 1936-39); mem. bd. mgrs., trustee YMCA, Chgo.; trustee Taxpayers Fedn. of Ill., Nat. Bd. of the YMCA's; trustee Episcopal Ch. Found., Keep America Beautiful, Inc., Seabury Western Theological Seminary, George Williams Coll., Chicago. Member of St. Anthony Hall, Delta Psi, Aurelian Honor Society (Yale). Republican. Episcopalian. Clubs: University, Yale, Chicago, The Attic, The Casino Commercial (Chicago); Old Elm (Ft. Sheridan, Ill.); Onwentsia (Lake Forest, Ill.). Home: Lake Forest Ill. Died Apr. 5, 1974.

WELLESZ, EGON JOSEPH, composer; b. Vienna, Austria, Oct. 21, 1885; s. S. Wellesz and Ilona; D.Phil., U. Vienna, 1908; fellow Lincoln Coll.; Mus.D. (hon.), Oxford U., 1932; Harvard vis. scholar, Dumbarton Oaks, 1954, 56-57; m. Emmy Stross, Aug. 23, 1908; children—Magda Pole, Elizabeth Marla Kessler. Privat dozent U. Vienna, 1913-29, prof., 1929-38; lectr., reader faculty of music Oxford U., 1938-56; lectr. Yale, Columbia, U. Cal., U. So. Cal., 1954, Princeton, Library Congress, 1957. Vice pres. Consociation Internat. Musicae Sacrae, 1964. Decorated Comdr. Order Brit. Empire; Great Golden Insignia of Honor (Austria); Knight Commander of Order St. Gregory; recipient Great Austrian State prize, 1961. Fellow of the Royal Danish Academy, British Acad. Composer operas: Die Prinzessin Girnara, 1921, Alkestis, 1924, Die Bakchantinnen, 1931, Incognita, 1951, others, also symphonic music, 9 string guartets, 9 symphonies. Author: Eastern Elements in Western Chant, 1947; A History of Byzantine Music and Hymnography, 1949, rev. edit., 1962. Editor: New Oxford History of Music Vols. I, VII. Home: Oxford England. Died Nov. 9, 1974; interred Vienna, Austria.

WELLINGTON, RICHARD, horticulturist; b. Waltham, Mass., Oct. 10, 1884; s. Edward and Mary (Worcester) W.; B.S. Mass. Agr. Coll., 1906; M.S., Harvard, 1911; m. Minerva Collins, Oct. 10, 1912; children—Marylizabeth, John Clark. Asst. and asso. horticulturist N.Y. Agrl. Expt. Sta., 1906-13; head of section of fruit and vegetable investigations, U. of Minn., 1913-19; prof. vegetable gardening, U. of Md., 1919-20; asso. horticulturist and chief in research, N.Y. Agrl. Expt. Sta., from 1920, also head div. of pomology from 1929. Fellow A.A.A.S.; mem. Am. Soc. for Hort. Science. Home: Geneva, N.Y. Died June 15, 1975; interred Mt. Peake Cemetery, Waltham, Mass.

WELLIVER, LESTER ALLEN, clergyman; b. Stockton, Pa., Feb. 2, 1896; s. Daniel and Mary Ann (East) W.; A.B., Dickinson Coll., 1918, M.A., 1922, D.D., 1940; B.D., Drew Theol. Sem., 1922; LL.D., Western Md. Coll., 1944; m. Eleanor Frances Frieda Yeaworth, Oct. 2, 1923; children—Lester Allyn, Daniel Irvin, Kenneth Bruce, Paul Wesley, Glenn Edwin. Ordained to ministry Methodist Ch., 1918; pastor in Altoona, Pa., 1922-24, Bellwood, Pa., 1924-28, Lewisburg, Pa., 1928-33, Clearfield, Pa., 1933-36, Williamsport, Pa., 1942-43, Stevens Meml. Ch., Harrisburg, Pa., 1961-65. Supt. Harrisburg Dist. Meth. Ch., 1936-42, Williamsport Dist., 1955-61; trustee Westminster (Md.) Theol. Sem., 1940-55, pres., 1943-55; mem. Judicial Council Meth. Ch., 1954-68, v.p., 1956-60, pres., 1960-64, mem. Gen. Conf., 1940, 48, 52, mem. Jurisdictional Conf., 1940, 44, 48, 52; mem. World Meth. Council, 1951-66; del. World Meth. Conf., Oxford, 1951, Lake Junaluska, N.C., 1956; mem. gen. bd. edn. Meth. Ch., 1940-54. Member of the bd. trustees Dickinson Coll. Served with U.S. Army, World War I. Mem. Assn. Meth. Hist. Socs. (v.p., past pres. N.E. jurisdiction), Phi Beta Kappa, also mem. Kappa Sigma. Research editor: The Journal and Letters of Francis Asbury, 1958. Home: Gaithersburg Md. Died Nov. 13, 1973.

WELLMAN, HOLLEY GARFIELD, foundry exec.; b. Cleve., May 19, 1881; s. Samuel Thomas and Julia Almina (Ballard) W.; student mechanical engineering, Cornell U., 1901-04; m. Clara Kennedy, Nov. 7, 1905; children—John H. (dec.), Bertah, Helen (Mrs. David V. Stickle). Prodn. mgr., part owner The Wellman Bronze and Alumnium Co., Cleve., 1912-53, vice chmn. bd., sec., from 1953. Trustee Cleve. Rehabilitation Centre. Mem. Cleve. Chamber of Commerce Am. Magnesium Assn. (mem. committee fire prevention and safety). Cleveland Engring. Soc. Rotarian. Home: Chagrin Falls, O.†

WELLMAN, WILLIAM AUGUSTUS motion picture dir.; b. Brookline, Mass., Feb. 29, 1896; s. Arthur Gouverneur and Cecelia (McCarthy) W.; grad. high sch.; m. Dorothy Coonan, May 9, 1933; children—Patti, Bill, Kitty, Tim, Cissy, Mike, Maggie. Began in wool bus., Boston; actor, asst. property man, asst. film editor, asst. dir. Goldwyn Studies (motion picures) pictures), Hollywood, Cal., 1919-23; dir. Fox Studio, Paramount Famous Lasky Corp., 1923-30, Warner Bros.-1st Nat. Prodns., 1930-33, 20th Century Pictures, Metro-Goldwyn-Mayer Corp., Inc., Paramount Pictures, United Artists-Selznick, Paramount, United Artists, 20th Century-Fox Prodns., Columbia Pictures, RKO Radio Pictures, Wayne-Fellows-Warner Bros., Batjac-Warners, Universal-Internat., 1933-60; dir. Wings, Public Enemy, Star Witness, Frisco Jenny, Wild Boys of the Road, So-Big, The Conquerors, The President Vanishes, Call of the Wild, Robin Hood of Eldorado, Small Town Gril, A Star Is Born, Nothing Sacred, Men with Wings, Beau Geste, The Light That Failed, Reaching for the Sun, The Great Man's Lady, Roxy Hart, Lady of Burlesque, Thunder Birds, Buffalo Bill, The Ox-Bow Incident, G.I. Joe, Gallant Journey, Magic Town, The Iron Curtain, Yellow Sky, Battle Ground, The Next Voice You Hear, Across the Wide Missouri, Westward the Women, Island in the Sky, The High and the Mighty. Joined Norton-Harjes Amublance Corps, N.Y., 1917; trans. to French Fgn. Legion, June 1917; joined Lafayette Flying Corps, Escadrille 87, and became pursuit pilot and was shot down in battle; 1st lt. U.S. Aviation Service, at Rockwell Field, Cal. Decorated Croix de Guerre with 4 gold palm leaves (France), also 5 citations. Republican. Episcopalian. Author: (book) Go, Get 'Em, 1918; (autobiography) A Short Time for Insanity, 1974; Growing Old Disgracefully, 1975; also motion pictures, A Star Is Born, 1936; The Last Gangster, 1937; Home: Los Angeles, Cal., Died Dec. 9, 1975.

WELLS, CHARLES J(OSEPH), physician; b. Onondoga Hill, N.Y., May 21, 1881; s. Rev. Melville James and Louisa Mary (Underhill) W.; prep. edn. Cazenovia (N.Y.) Sem., 1898-1901; Ph.B., Suracuse U., 1905, M.D., 1908; m. Lela Pauline Brewster, Oct. 4, 1910; children—Evalyn Juliette (Mrs. WaAngell), Constance Louise (Mrs. Frederick W. Fehling), Lt. Brewster Joseph (pilot, A.A.C.; killed in action, Italy, April 25, 1944), Barbara Jean (Mrs. F. Richard Bornhurst). Practicing physician, Syracuse, from 1908; anesthetist St. Joseph's Hosp. unitl 1910, Good Shepherd Hospital, from 1911. City Hospital, from 1927, Onondaga General Hospital, from 1947; lecturer in anesthesia, Syracuse U. Medicial Coll., 1938-45. Member bd. dirs. International Anesthesia Research Soc. (pres. 1947); sec. Associated Anesthetists U.S. and Can.; pres. World's Congress of Anesthetits, Boston, 1935; Certified by Am. Bd. of Anesthesiology; mem. S.A.R., Delta Kappa Epsilon, Nu Sigma Nu. Republican. Methodist. Mason (K.T., Shriner, 32°). Home: Syracuse, N.Y.†

WELLS, GEORGE HARLAN, M.D.; b. Elkton, Md., May 28, 1880; s. Joseph Lumm and Florence (Harlan) W.; grad. Elkton Acad., 1895; B.S., U. of Del., 1899; M.D., Hahnemann Med. Coll., 1902, LL.D., 1930; hon. Dr. Med. Science, U. of Delaware, 19m. Martha Parr Scott, Apr. 11, 1907 (died July 19, 1922); m. 2d, Emma E. Mertz, Feb. 12, 1925; children—William Henry Scott, Florence Harlan, Virginia. Began practice at Phila., 1902; instr. in medicine, Hahnemann Med. Coll. of Phila., 1902-16, asso. prof. of medicine, 1916-25, prof. of clinical medicine, 1925-31, prof. of medicine, 1931-48, emeritus; editor Hahnemann Monthly, 1913-18; visiting physician, Hahnemann Hospital; cons. physician Broad St., Women's Homeopathic, Crozier, Wilmington Homeopathic and West Jersey Homeopathic hosps. Chief of a Div. of Medicine, Philadelphia Gen. Hosp., 1946. Contract surgeon, U.S. Army, 1918. Fellow Am. Coll. Physicians; mem. Am. Inst. Hemeopathy (ex-pres.), Homeo. Med. Soc. Pa. (pres.). Homeo. Med. Soc. of Phila. (trustee), Pa. Hist. Soc., A.M.A. Repbulican. Presbyn. Clubs: Union League, Penn Club. Contbr. to Hahnemannian Monthly, Jour. Am. Inst. of Homeopathy. Home: Philadelphia, Pa.†

WELLS, HARRY LUMM, univ. ofcl.; b. Coshocton. O, June 23, 1889; s. Charles Howard and Fannie T. (Lumm) W., B.S., Northwestern U., 1913, LL.D., 1960; LL.D., Lawrence Coll., 1949; D.Litt., Rockford Coll., 1958; m. Viola E. Shearer, Oct. 6, 1915; children—David Howard, Richard Grant, Virginia Ruth, Harry Shearer. Mfg. exec. B. Kuppenheimer & Co., clothing mfr., 1915-16; operating exec., Hart Schaffner & Marx, clothing mfrs., 1917-29, on leave 1917-18, as asst. and acting chief Uniform div. U.S. Army; v.p., gn. mgr. Bauer & Black div. Kendall Co., 1929-34; became bus. mgr. Northwestern U., 1934, v.p., bus. mgr., 1937, turstee, 1932-34; hon. chmn. John Evans Club, Northwestern U., 1964-76. Trustee H. R. Kendall Estate; chmn. bd. Wells Badger Corp. Milw.; dir. Hart Schaffner & Marx, Washington Nat. Ins. Co. Former mem. Northeastern Ill. Met. Governmantal Services Commn.; mem. bd. Evanston (Ill.) Devel. Corp. Mem. Delta Sigma Rho. Alpha Delta Phi, Deru, Beta Gamma Sigma. Protestant. Club: University. Author: Higher Education is Serious Business. Home: Evanston, Ill., Died Feb. 10, 1976.

WELLS, LINTON, writer, traveler, aviator, radio broadcaster; b. Louisville, Apr. 1, 1893; s. Rufus Coleman and Minnie Belle (Tindel) W.; ed. Louisville and Denver pub. schs., also U.S. Naval Acad.; children—Barbara Jeanne, Patricia; m. 2d, Fay Gillis (traveler, aviztrix, writer, broadcaster), Apr. 1, 1935; 1 son, Linton II. Fgn. war corr. and staff writer for newspapers, syndicates and mags., 1911-76; dir. Storer Broadcasting Co., Washington, 1962-69. Established circumnavigation of bglobe record, 28 days, 14 hours and 36 minutes, in 1926. Headed Govt. Mission Portuguese West Africa, 1942-46. Served with U.S. Navy, World War I; foreign decorations. Mem. Radio and TV analysts N.Y.C. (founder). Clubs: Nat. Pres. International (founder), Georgetown (Washington); Overseas Press (N.Y.C.). Author: Around the World in 28 Days, 1926; Jumping Meridians, 1926; Blood on the Moon, 1937; Salute to Valor, 1942; (play) Second Guesses. Home: Washington, D.C., Died Jan. 31, 1976; cremated.

WELLS, MARY EVELYN, coll. prof.; b. LeRaysville, Pa., Pa., Aug. 20, 1818; d. William Henry and Delphine (Whitford) Wells; A.B., Mt. Holyoke Coll., 1904; M.S., U. of Chicago, 1907, Ph.D., 1915; attended U. of Italy, 1927-28; unmarried. Instr., Mt. Holyoke Coll., 1907-12; acting asst. prof., Oberlin Coll., 1914-15; instr. mathematics, Vassar Coll., 1915-20, asst. prof., 1920-22, asso. prof., 1922-28, prof., 1928-48, emeritus; exchange prof., Women's Christian Coll., U. of Madras, India, 1926-27, 1936-37. Awarded Mt. Holyoke fellowship for study at U. of Chgo., 1912-13, U. of Chicago fellowship, 1913-14. Dir. St. Christopher's Coll. (Madras, India), 1928-37, Women's Christian Coll. (India), 1927-37, from 1948, Women's Christian Coll. (Tokyo, Japan), 1930-37. Fellow A.A.A.S.; mem. Am. Math. Soc., Math. Assn. of Am., Phi Beta Kappa, Sigma Xi. Contbr. to math. jour. Translations of math. articles. Home: Southport, Me.†

WELLS, RALPH GENT, reasarch, mgmt. consultant, b. Lawrenceburg, Ind., July 15, 1879; s. Martin Lemuel and Mattie Wilderson (Gent) W.; ed. Manual Training High Sch., Indianapolis, Harvard Law Sch.; m. Fanny Larcom Abbot, Apr. 18, 1904; children—Winifred (dec.), Katharine Abbot, Dane Ellingwood, Salesman Globe Wernicke Co., Cincinnati, (N.Y. and Boston offices); spl. orgn. and research work Arkwright Club Commercial Agency, Boston Chamber of Commerce, Bureau of University Travel, Employment Managers Assn., Boston Rotary Club, 1906-17; secretary last two organizations, 1912-17; with E. I. du Pont de Nemours Co., Wilmington, Del., 1917-19; instr., Boston U. Coll. of Business Adminstrn., 1919-24, prof. and head of management dept. 1924-49, dir. Bur. of Business Research, from 1928, asst. to pres., 1926-28. Mem. Univ. Post War Planning Com. Mem. Am. marketing Assn., Soc. Advancement of Management. Rep. Unitarian. Mason. Co-author, editor of publs. relating to field; latest; Ratio Analysis of 1947 Census of Manufactures, 1950. Contbg. editor Am. Bus. Practice. Home: Needham, Mass.*†

WELSH, GEORGE A., judge; b. Bay View, Cecil County, Md., Aug. 9, 1878; s. George and Sarah (Pickering) W.; student Temple U., 1892-94, LL.B., 1906, LL.D., 1939; m. Nellie Ross Wolff, June 27, 1906 (died Feb. 18, 1920); children—William, Conwell; m. 2d, Helen Reed Kirk, Oct. 31, 1921; children—Margaret, Patrick, Deborah, Sec. to ayor of Phila., 1904-06; asst. city solicitor of Phila., 1906-07; asst. disty. atty. of Phila., 1907-22; mem. law firm Welsh & Bluett; mem. 68th to 72d Congresses (1923-33), 6th Pa. Dist.; resigned May 31, 1932, served as U.S. dist. judge, Eastern Dist. of Pa., later sr. judge. Dir. and sec. Temple U. many yrs., v.p., from 1939, later mem. exec. bd. board trustees. Mem. Bd. of Edn., Phila. County, 11 yrs. Republican. Mason (K.T.). Club: Mid-Day. Home: Lima, Pa.†

WELSH, GEORGE WILSON, publisher; born Glasgow, Scotland, Mar. 27, 1883; s. Joseph and Elizabeth (Wilson) W.; brought by parents to U.S., 1891; ed. pub. schs.; m. Shirlie Louise Smith, Oct. 4, 1906; 1 dau., Jean Frances Elizabeth (Mrs. Chester Nelson Weldon). Began publication of "The Fruit Belt" (later Fruits and Gardens), at Grand Rapids, 1905; pub. Grand Rapids Shopping News; pres. George W. Welsh Co., pubs. and printers. Alderman, Grand Rapids, 1912-16; mem. Mich. Ho. of Rep., 1917-24 (speaker of House, 1923-24); lt. gov. of Mich., 1925-26; candidate for Rep. nomination for gov. of Mich., 1928; chosen city mgr. of Grand Rapids, 1929 (refusing salary of 1,000 to serve for $1.00). Mason (32°, K.T., Shriner), Elk. Presbyn. Candidate for gov. of Mich., 1932; elected mayor of Grand Rapids, 1938, 1940, 42, 44, 46, 48; pres. U.S. Conference of Mayors, 1947-48. Decorated comdr. House of Orange-Nassau, 1948; Officer French Legion of Honor, 1950. Home: Grand Rapids Mich. Died June 29, 1974.

WELSH, JOHN RUSHING, III, educator; b. Monroe, N.C., May 19, 1916; s. John Rushing and Hallie Hamilton (Benton) W.; A.B., U. of South, 1939; M.A., Syracuse U., 1941; Ph.D. (teaching fellow), Vanderbilt U., 1951; m. Ruth Elizabeth Davis, Aug. 9, 1941 (div. Sept. 1962); children—Nancy Benton, John Rushing IV; m. 2d, Sevena Molair, Dec. 20, 1963; 1 adopted son, William L. Instr. English, head dept. Linsly Inst., Wheeling, W.Va., 1941-42; mem. faculty U. S.C., 46-74, prof. English, 1960, head dept., 1973-74, v.p. for instrn., 1974; founding mem. bd. dirs. Ednl. Found., 1958. Served with AUS, 1943-46: PTO. Recipient Distinguished Teaching award U. S.C., 1958, Achievement award Wingate Coll., 1963. Mem. Modern Lang. Assn., S. Atlantic Modern Lang. Assn., Soc. Study So. Lit., Southeastern Coll. English Assn. (adv. council 1953-54), South Caroliniana Soc., Phi Beta Kappa, Am. Assn. U. Profs. (pres. 1954-55), Blue Key, Pi Gamma Mu, Kappa Sigma. Author: The Mind of William Gilmore Simms: His Social and Political Thought, 1951. Asso. editor South Atlantic Bulletin, 1969. Contbr. profl. jours. Home: Columbia S.C. Died Oct. 4, 1974; buried Monroe, N.C.

WELTMER, (CYRUS) ERNEST, mental scientist; b. Morgan Co., Mo., Nov. 23, 1880; s. Didney A. and Mary G. (Stone) W.; ed. under father; m. at St. Louis, Mo., Dorothea J. M. H. Hoffmann, of Ghent, Belgium, Sept. 14, 1912; children—Sidney Pierre, Dorothee Denise. Teacher suggestive therapeutics from 1899; sec. Weltmer Inst. of Suggestive Therapeutics, pres. Weltmer Foundation; licensed by State Bd. to practice suggestion therapy in State of Wash., 1919. Author: Realization, 1909; Text-Book of Hypnotism, 1911; The Practice of Sugggestive Therapeutics (Vol. I), 1913; Ernest Weltmer's Man Power Development Lessons, 1919; A Brief Course of Lessions in Practice Healing, 1921; The Weltmer Brief Cours in Practical Psychology (with father), 1924; Sex, Love and Life, 1925; also Spiritual Unfoldment, Introduction to Metapsychology, assage for Suggestion Therapists, Healing by Thought, Word and Hand, Psychoanalysis and Suggestion Therapy—all 1926; Special Interpretative Lessons in Christian Healing; Heirs of the King, 1927; Relaxation, Health, and Happiness, 1928; (booklet) As I See Myself, 1930; The Message of Freedom, 1934; Primary Lessons in Christian Freedom, 1934; Practical Magnetic Healing, Outlines, 1935; Magnetic Massage, 1935. Editor Weltmer's Magazine. Home: Nevada. Mo.†

WENDT, GERALD (LOUIS), chemist, lectr., author; b. Davenport, Ia., Mar. 3, 1891; s. Johannes Heinrich and Dora (Albrecht) W.; grad. high sch., Davenport; A.B., Harvard, 1913, A.M., 1914, Ph.D., 1916; Sc.D., MacMurray Coll., Jacksonville, Ill., 1958; m. Elsie Paula Lerch, Sept. 5, 1916 (div. 1938); 1 son, Robert Louis; m. 2d, Anne D. Powers, Feb. 22, 1947. Jr. chemist U.S. Bur. Mines, 1916; instr. chemistry Rice Inst., 1916-17; instr. U. Chgo., 1917-18, asst. prof. chemistry, 1918-21, asso. prof., 1921-22; asst. dir. research Standard Oil Co. Ind., 1922-24; dean Sch. of Chemistry and Physics, Pa. State Coll., 1924-28; dir. Battelle Meml. Inst., Columbus, O., 1927-28; asst. to pres. charge research Pa. State Coll., 1928-29; pres. Coffee Products Corp., 1929-35; dir. Am. Inst. of City N.Y., 1936-38; dir. research Gen. Printing Ink Corp., 1937-38; dir. sci. and edn. N.Y. World's Fair, 1938-40; sci. editor Time, Inc., 1942-45; editorial dir. Sci. Illus., 1946-49; head div. teaching and dissemination Dept. Natural Scis., UNESCO, Paris, 1952-54; pres. Nat. Agy. Internat. Publs., Inc., 1956-67; chmn. N.Am. Commn. Internat. Humanist and Ethical Union, 1965-68; editor Chem. Revs., 1927-38. Served as capt. research div., Chem. Warfare Service, U.S. Army, 1918. Fellow A.A.A.S.; mem. Am. Chem. Soc., Phi Beta Kappa, Sigma Xi. Club: Harvard (N.Y.C.). Author: Matter and Energy, 1930; Science for the World of Tomorrow, 1939; Chemistry, 1942; The Atomic Age Opens, 1945; Atomic Energy and the Hydrogen Bomb, 1950; You and the Atom, 1955; Prospects of Nuclear Power and Technology, 1957; Atoms for Industry, World Survey, 1960. Editor: The Humanist, 1959-64; editor-in-chief United Nations Conference on Science and Technology, 1963. Home: New York City, N.Y. Died Dec. 22, 1973; buried Forest Hills Cemetery, Jamaica Plains, Mass.

WENNAGEL, LEONARD ALVIN, banker; b. Balt., July 25, 1911; s. George F. and Mary (Batchelor) W.; grad. Balt. Poly. Inst., 1929; A.B., Johns Hopkins, 1933; m. Margaret Colburn, Nov. 15, 1947; children—Leonard L., Robert W. With Equitable Trust Co., Balt., 1934-75, v.p., 1956-66, sr. v.p., chmn. loan com., 1966-75, vice-chmn. exec. com., 1973-75, also dir.; pres., dir. Commodity Credit Co., Inc.; sr. v.p., dir. Equitable Bancorp. Mem. St. George's Soc. Balt., Presbyn. (trustee). Mason. Clubs: Johns Hopkins; Merchants. Home: Baltimore, Md., Died May 29, 1975.

WENTZ, PETER LELAND, lawyer; b. Provo Bench, Utah, Sept. 23, 1903; s. Ray Vernon and Eliza Catherine (Wilson) W.; B.S., Brigham Young U., 1923; J.D. cum laude, U. Chgo., 1925; spl. courses mining and accounting, U. Cal. at Berkeley, U. Utah, Northwestern U.; m. Vida Broadbent, Sept. 10, 1925; children—Carol, Helen. Admitted to Ill. bar, 1926, practiced in Chgo.; partner firm Hopkins, Sutter, Owen, Mulory, Wentz & Davis and predecessor firms, Chgo., from 1935; engaged in mining and oil exploration operations, from 1926. Served from pvt. to capt. AUS, 1942-46. Member Am., Ill., Chgo. bar assns., Order of Coif. Clubs: Mid-Am., Legal, Law, Mid-Day, Executives. Home: Chicago, Ill., Deceased.

WENZEL, THOMAS PHILIP, physician; b. Indpls., Aug. 6, 1917; s. William Sebastian and Helen (Dobson) W.; M.D., U. Cin., 1941; m. Shirley Anne Eisele, Sept. 7, 1942; children—William E., Thomas Philip, Robert J., Barbara A., John S., Richard C. Intern, Good Samaritan Hosp., Cin., 1941-42, Mercy Hosp., Hamilton, O., 1946-47; resident in anesthesiology Huron Road Hosp., East Cleveland, O., 1951-53; mem. staff anesthesiology Middletown (O.) Hosp., 1948-71; asst. to county coroner, 1949-53, asst. to city physician, 1949-53. Served as capt. M.C., AUS, 1942-46. Decorated Bronze Star. Diplomate Am. Bd. Anesthesiology. Fellow Am. Soc. Anesthesiologists, Internat. Assn. Anesthesia; mem. A.M.A., Ohio Med. Assn. Republican. Roman Catholic. Home: Middletown, O. Died June 8, 1971; buried Woodside Cemetery, Middletown, O.

WERMUTH, BURT, editor; b. Ithaca, Mich., Aug. 20, 1879; s. Frederick and Rosetta (Wiseman) W.; B.S., Mich. State Coll., 1902, A.B., 1911; student Detroit Coll. of Law, 1911; m. Katherine Stevenson, June 23, 1909 (died 1934); children—Rosetta Jane, Arthur Burt; m. 2d, Ida Leonard, Sept. 6, 1935. County school teacher, 1897-98; admitted to the bar, 1911; horticultural editor Michigan Farmer, 1904-19, editor, 1919-32, mgr. from 1932. Republican. Methodist. Clubs: Kiwanis, High Twelve, Home: Detroit, Mich.†

WERNER, EDWIN H., utilities exec.; b. Wernersville, Pa., 1890; Pa. State Coll., 1911. Pres. and dir. Jersey Central Power & Light Co. Home: Asbury Park N.J. Died Oct. 1, 1973.

WERNER, JOSEPH GUSTAVE, lawyer; b. Friendship, Wis., May 21, 1911; s. Theodore Michael and Christina Cecilia (Seger) W.; B.A., U. Wis., 1933, LL.B., 1936, S.J.D., 1937; m. Elizabeth Helen Tormey, Sept. 13, 1941; children—Thomas Joseph, Stephen Cole, Richard Theodore, David Weston, Philip William. Admitted to Wis. bar, 1936; lawyer Thomas & Orr, Madison, 1937-42; legal rationing OPA, Washington, 1942-43; head patent sect. Office Gen. Counsel, Office Alien Property Custodian, Washington, 1943-46; partner Isaksen, Werner, Lathrop & Heaney, Madison, 1946-73. Dir. Prescription Pharmacy, Inc., Mem. City of Madison Bd. Health, 1951-53; chmn. Madison Commn. for Youth, 1958-63; chmn. Study for Prevention and Control of Delinquency, Madison, 1960-61. Alderman, City Council Madison, 1951-53. Bd. dirs. Madison Community Chest, Dane County chpt. A.R.C., U. Wis. YMCA; trustee U. Wis. Meml. Union Bldg. Assn. Mem. Am., Wis. (past sect. chmn.), Dane County (past pres.), 7th Fed. Circuit (past bd. govs.) bar assns., Am., Milw., Chgo. patent law assns., Order of Coif, Phi Beta Kappa, Phi Delta Phi. Roman Catholic. K.C. (4 deg.), Rotarian (past pres. Madison, past dist. gov., internat. dir.). Clubs: Serra International (past dist. gov.), Serra of Madison (past pres.), Madison (dir.), Maple Bluff Country, Madison Technical (dir.) (Madison). Contbr. chpts. to West's Federal Practice Manual, 1970; also articles profl. jours. Home: Madison, Wis. Died Nov. 27, 1973; buried Madison, Wis.

WESSON, MILEY BARTON, urologist; b. Sedalia, Mo., Oct. 12, 1881; s. Miley Barton and Alice Bush (Proctor) W.; B.S., U. of Tex., 1902; M.D., Johns Hopskins University, 1910. Assistant in chemistry, University of Texas, 1902; taught science in secondary schools and colleges, 1902-06; asst. in anatomy, Johns Hopkins, 1907-18; resident surgeon Hudson St. Hosp., New York 1910-12; suregon, El Paso, Tex., 1912-17; asst. to Dr. Hugh H. Young, Johns Hopkins Hosp., 1919-21; instr. urology, U. of Calif., 1921-23; later in practice at San Francisco; prof. anatomy school of dentistry, College Physicians and Surgeons, U. of the Pacific, from 1928. Captain Med. Corps, U.S. Army, with A.E.F., 1917-19. Mem. A.M.A., Am. Urol. Assn. (ex-pres.), Western br. soc. A.U.A. (ex-pres.), Internat. Urol. Assn., Societa Italiano Urologia (hon.), Cal. Med. Assn., San Francisco Med. Soc., Cal. Acad. Medicine, Pan Pacific Surgical Association, American Assn. Physicians and Surgeons, American Fertility Society, A.A.A.S., Am. Geriatrics Soc., Law-Sci. Acad., Am. Bd. Urology (founder), S.A.R., Omicron Kappa Upsilon, Nu Sigma Nu. Mason (Shriner). Awarded Carnegie silver medal. Clubs: Olympic, Lakeside Golf. Author: "Urological Roentgenology"; "Early History of Urology on the West Coast" in History of Urology, Vol. 1; "Antomical Variations of the Bladder," in The Cyclopedia of Medicine, Vol. 2, Urologic Roentgenology. Founder and first editor of Southwestern Medicine. Contbr. numerous papers to Am. and fgn. med. jours. Home: San Francisco Cal.†

WEST, BEN, lawyer; born Columbia, Tennessee, Mar. 31, 1911; s. J. Watt and Martha Melissa (Wilson) W.; LL.B., Cumberland U., 1930; B.A., Vanderbilt U., 1934; m. Mary Humes Meadors, Aug. 31, 1935; children—Ben, John Meadors. Reporter Nashville Banner, 1928-34; admitted to Tenn. bar, 1932, practiced in Nashville, 1932-51; asst. atty. gen. 10th Jud. Dist. Tenn., 1934-43; atty.-gen. pro tem. Jackson, Tenn., 1942; vice mayor, Nashville, 1947-51, mayor, 1951-63; state senator 16th Senatorial Dist. 1949-51; lectr. 6th Ann. Inst. Race Relations, Fisk U., Nashville, 1949. Vice pres. Nat. Safety Council, Chgo., from 1964. Chmn. Nat. Com. Urban Transp., 1958, 59; joint chmn. com. hwys, Am. Municipal Assn. and Am. Assn. State Hwy. Ofcls., 1958, 59, 60; panel mem. Pres.'s Commn. Nat. Goals, 1960; dir. Nat. Conf. Traffic, 1960; mem. Pres.'s Com. on Traffic Safety, 1962; bd. dirs. Am. council to Improve Our Neighborhoods, Inc. State chmn. Nat. Found. Infantile Paralysis, 1942. Mem. State Dem. Exec. Com., 1944-48, 55-56, vice chmn., 1946-48. Mem. Nashville Bar Assn. (bd. dirs. 1942-45, 1st v.p. 1945), Tenn. Municipal League (v.p. 1951-53, pres. 1955), Am. Municipal Assn. (pres. 1957), Davidson Co. Assn. Masonic Lodges (pres. 1942), Am. Pub. Works Assn. (dir. 1960), Pan-Am. Assn. Tenn. (pres. 1964-65). Mem. Church of Christ. Mason (Shriner, K.T.). Home: Nashville Tenn. Died Nov. 20, 1974.

WEST, CHRISTOPHER, operatic and theatrical dir.; b. Weston-Super-Mare, Eng., July 27, 1915; s. Edward and Alice Wlizabeth (Whitehead) W.; ed. Royal Acad. Dramatic Art. With Sir Barry Jackson's Co. Stratford-on-Avon, Eng., 1946-48, Old Vic Co., London, 1949-50; resident state dir. Royal Opera Covent Garden, London, 1950-59; dir. prodns. Dublin Nat. Ballet, 1959-62; mem. staff Nat. Sch. Opera, London, 1957-62; dir. Opera Theatre of Juilliard Sch. Music, 1962-71; operatic prodns. Covent Garden include: Salome, Fairy Queen (with Constant Lambert), Der Rosenkavalier (with Kleiber), Der Freischutz, world premiere Midsummer Marriage, Bartered Bride, Magic Flute, Jenufa and Tristan and Isolde (last four with Kubelik); Albert Herring for Wiesbaden Festival, 1953, world premiere Hidden King (verse play), Edinburgh Festival, 1957; U.S. prodns. include Jenufa, 1959, Don Carlo, Le Nozze de Figaro, Die Walkure and Madama Butterfly, 1960, all for Chgo. Lyric Opera; Katya Kabonva for Empire State Music Festival, 1960; Orfeo, The Prisoner (with Stokowski) for N.Y.C. Opera, 1960; Fidello (with Klemperer), Covent Garden, 1961; Il Trittico and the Wings of the Dove (world premiere) for N.Y.C. Opera; Gosi fan Tutte, Fidelio for Chgo. Lyric Opera, 1961; Die Zauberflöte (with Klemperer) for Covent Garden; Louise for N.Y.C. Opera; Orfeo ed Euridice for Chgo. Lyric Opera, 1962, Ballo in Maschera, 1964; Capriccio for N.Y.C. Opera, 1966; Rape of Lucretia for Washington Opera Soc., 1966; also various prodns. for Juilliard Opera Theatre 1963-71; others. Served with RAF, World War II. Contbr. articles to theatrical mus. jours. Home: New York City, N.Y., Deceased.

WEST, GEORGE V., radiologist; b. Woburn, Mass., 1919; M.D., Tufts U., 1944. Intern, Worcester (Mass.) City Hosp., 1944-45; resident Lawrence (Mass.) Gen. Hosp., 1947-49; practice medicine specializing in radiology, Mass.; mem. staff Melrose (Mass.)-Wakefield Hosp.; dir. radiology Lawrence Gen. Hosp.; cons. in roentgenology Isham Infirmary, Phillips Acad.,

Andover, Mass. Served to capt., M.C., AUS, 1945-47. Diplomate Am. Bd. Radiology. Mem. A.M.A., Am. Coll. Radiology, New Eng. Roentgen Ray Soc., Radiol. Soc. N.Am., A.A.A.S. Home: Lawrence, Mass. Died Sept. 8, 1974.

WEST, HERBERT FAULKNER, educator, pub. co. exec., writer; b. Jamaica Plain, Mass., Jan. 6, 1898; s. Arthur Richard and Annie Leila (Faulkner) W.; student Pa. State Coll., 1917-19; A.B., Dartmouth, 1922, A.M., 1924; postgrad. London and Berlin, 1924-25; A.M., Harvard, 1933; m. Carin af Robson, May 23, 1925; 1 son, Herbert Faulkner. Instr. English, Dartmouth, 1925-28, asst. prof. comparative lit., 1928-37, prof., 1937-64, prof. emeritus comparative lit., 1964-74, chmn. dept., 1953-57; Kate Hurd Mead lectr., 1959; founder pres., treas., Westholm Publs., 1955. Book reviewer for New York Times Sunday Book Mag. Served with 73d Arty., U.S. Army, with A.E.F., 1918-19. Dir. Friends The Dartmouth Coll. Library. Mem. Thoreau Soc. (pres.), Boston Soc. Ind. Artists, Delta Upsilon. Episcopalian. Clubs: Book of California; The Century (New York City); American (London). Author: Robert Boutine Cunninghame Graham 1932; Modern Book Collecting for the Impecunious Amateur, 1936; The Nature Writers, 1939; The George Matthew Adam Vachel Lindsay Collection, 1945; The Mind on the Wing, 1947; W. H. Hudson's Reading, 1947; A Stephen Crane Collection, 1948; John Sloan's Last Summer 1952; Rebel Thought, 1953; The Coronary Club, 1956; What Price Teaching, 1957; Learning My ABC's, 1958; For a Hudson Biographer, 1958; Here's To Togetherness, pub. 1961; The Impecunious Amateur Looks Back: A Bookman's World, 1966; Notes from a Bookman, 1968; HMS Cephalonia, 1969; Sunny Intervals, 1972. Editor: Two Letters on an Albatross (by W. H. Hudson, R. B. Cunningham Graham), 1955; Emerson at Dartmouth, 1956; Three Fugitive Pieces (by R. B. Cunningham Graham), 1960. Home: Hanover N.H. Died Nov. 9, 1974.

WEST, THOMAS HECTOR, physician; b. San Marcial, N.M., Apr. 29, 1905; s. Drew Hector and Maude (Rawlings) W.; M.D., U. Tenn., 1928; m. Margaret La Follette, Dec. 24, 1935; children—Thomas La Follette, Robert Rawlings, Margaret Suzanne (Mrs. David D. Dubois), William Hoath. Intern, S.I. (N.Y.) Hosp., 1929-31; asst. resident in pathology Memphis Gen. Hosp., 1931-32, resident, 1932-33, asst. resident in surgery and gynecology, 1933-34, res in surgery and gynecology, 1934-35; fellow in surgery Lahey Clinic, Boston, 1935-36; attending surgeon John Gaston Hosp.; sr. surgeon Baptist Meml. Hosp.; vis. surgeon Methodist Hosp., St. Josephs Hosp. (all Memphis); asst. prof. surgery U. Tenn. Thomas H. West Meml. lectr. in surgery established at Bapt. Meml. Hosp. Diplomate Am. Bd. Surgery. Fellow A.C.S.; mem. A.M.A., So. Med. Assn., Am. Thyroid Assn. Methodist. Home: Memphis, Tenn. Died June 3, 1973. Buried La Follette, Tenn.

WESTCOTT, HARRY R., cons. engr.; b. Dighton, Mass., Dec. 2, 1881; s. Alvin T. and Lydia H. (Bowen) W.; student Brown U., 1908-11, Yale, 1920-22; M.E., Stevens Inst. Tech., 1934; m. Margaret L. Rusden, May 31, 1932; 1 son, Allan R. Draftsman, Jenks & Ballou, 1900-09; engr. in charge, Atlantic Mills, 1909-12; asst. to pres. Hood Rubber Co., 1912-14; supt. of construction, United Illuminating Co., 1914-16; pres. Westcott & Mapes, Inc., New Haven, Conn., from 1916. Mem. bd. dirs. New Haven Y.M.C.A., 1923-28; New Haven Chamber of Commerce, 1928-34. Fellow American Soc. M.E. Mason (32°). Clubs: Lions, Quinnipiack (New Haven); University (Bridgeport). Home: Woodbridge, Conn.†

WESTCOTT, RICHARD NUTTER, physician; b. Providence, Aug. 7, 1918; s. Charles Hapgood and Hazel (Nutter) W.; M.D., Harvard, 1943; m. Patricia Bosworth Ranney, June 20, 1944; children—Mark Ranney, Bruce Austin, Anne Nutter. Intern, Presbyn. Hosp., N.Y.C., 1943; jr. asst. resident in medicine Cin. Gen. Hosp., 1947-48, sr. asst. resident, 1948-49, Nat. Heart Inst., research fellow Cardiac Lab., 1949-51, asst. vis. physician, 1951; staff physician dept. clin. cardiology Cleve. Clinic Hosp., 1951-73; head sect. electrocardiography Cleve. Clinic Found.; instr. medicine U. Cin., 1949-51. Served from 1st lt. to capt., M.C., AUS, 1944[46. Diplomate Am. Bd. Internal Medicine. Fellow A.C.P., Am. Coll. Cardiology; mem. A.M.A., Am. Fedn. Clin. Research, Am. Heart Assn., Ohio Med. Assn., Ohio Soc. Internal Medicine (trustee), Aesculapian Soc. Cleve., Boylston Med. Soc., Nu Sigma Nu, Sigma Alpha Epsilon. Episcopalian. Club: Aesculapian (Boston). Home: Pepper Pike, O. Died Mar. 10, 1973.

WESTERMEYER, H(ARRY) E(DWARD), coll. prof.; b. Bison, Kan., Jan. 25, 1896; s. Jacob and Katherine (Eitel) W.; A.B., Clinton (Mo.) Theol. Sem., 1917; A.M., Coll. of Pacific, 1934; Ph.D., Stanford, 1946; m. Clara Helen Reinmuth, Aug. 28, 1918; children—Harry, Darlene (wife of Dr. Arthur Carleton), Claribel, Robert. Dean of boys, Enterprise (Kan.) Acad., 1919-20; prin. Campion Acad., Acad., Loveland, Colo., 1920-23, Laurelwood Acad., Gaston, Ore., 1923-30, Lodi (Calif.) Acad., 1930-37, Mountain View (Calif.) Acad., 1937-41; head history dept. Walla Walla (Wash.) Coll., 1942-62. Mem. of the Sherwood Eddy Seminar to Russia, 1957. Mem. Am. Hist. Assn. (Pacific br.), Wash. State Hist. Soc., Walla Walla Archaeol. Soc. Republican. Mem. Seventh Day Adventist Ch. Author: The Fall of the German Gods, 1950. Home: Riverside, Cal., Died Feb. 27, 1974.

WESTERVELT, ESTHER JULIA MANNING, (Mrs. Andrew Castle Westervelt), educator; b. N.Y.C.; d. Hiram Terry and Emma (Wilson) Manning; B.A., Vassar Coll., 1935; M.A., Tchrs. Coll., Columbia, 1956; E.D., Columbia, 1961; m. Ira Hart Koenig, 1937 (div. 1939); m. 2d, Marvin Rothfielder, 1942 (div. 1944); 1 son, John Terry; m. 3d, Harold E. Shively, Oct. 24, 1944 (div. June 1961); children—Bonnie, Robin, Julie; m. 4th Andrew Castle Westervelt, July 3, 1961. Exec. dir. Orange County Council Community Services, 1953-60; instr., research asso. Tchrs. Coll., Columbia, 1961-63, asst. prof. edn., 1964-67, adj. asso. prof. edn., 1967-69; dir. N.Y. State Guidance Center for Women, Suffern, N.Y., 1966-68, dir. research, 1969-70; exec. co-dir. Nat. Coalition for Research for Women's Edn. and Devel., State U. N.Y. at Stony Brook, 1970-72; holder alumnae endowed chair, dir. instl. studies Simmons Coll., Boston, 1973-75. Lectr., cons., workshop leader to numerous colls., univs., and orgns. Mem. com. on home and community Pres.'s Commn. on Status of Women, 1962-63; mem. Woman's Council$ of N.Y. State Dept. Commerce Women's Program, 1963-75, co-chmn. com. on edn., 1964-75. Bd. dirs. Orange County Council for Community Services, Inc. Served with WAFS, 1942-44. Fellow Assn. for Applied Anthropology; mem. Am. Assn. U. Women, Am. Ednl. Research Assn., Am. Personnel and Guidance Assn. (mem. finance com. 1963-65), Nat. Vocational Guidance Assn. (commn. on occupational status of women, 1969-75), Nat. Assn. Women Deans and Counselors, Am. Assn. for Higher Edn., Am. Coll. Personnel Assn., N.E.A., Internat. Oceanographic Found., League Women Voters, Am. Civil Liberties Union, Nat. Council Negro Women, Nat. Council on Day Care of Children, Nat. Council on Family Relations, Pi Lambda Theta, Kappa Delta Pi. Author: (with D.A. Fixter) Women's Higher and Continuing Education, 1971. Editor: (with Esterh Lloyd-Jones) Behavioral Science and Guidance: Perspectives and Proposals, 1963. Contbr. to books, also articles to profl. jours. Home: Goshen, N.Y., Died Dec. 18, 1975.

WESTFELDT, GEORGE G(USTAF), corp. ofcl.; b. Fletcher, N.C., July 12, 1880; s. Gustaf R. and Marie L. (Dugan) W.; B.S., Tulane U., 1901; m. Martha V. Gasquet, Oct. 28, 1905 (dec.); children—Ethel Jane (Mrs. F. H. Bunting), Martha (Mrs. W. H.Fitzpatrick). Partner Westfield Bros., New Orleans, from 1904, sr. partner, from 1916; v.p. Miss. Shipping Co., from 1923, New Orleans Cold Storage Co., from 1910; treasurer and director D. H. Holmes Co., from 1916; director New Orleans & Northeastern R.R., Southdown, Inc. (New Orleans). Pres. Bd. Liquidatin, City Debt, New Orleans, Pres. Soc. Relief Destitute Orphan Boys; dir. Schlieder Found Clubs: Boston (past pres.), Country (past pres.). Home: New Orleans, La.†

WESTMORE, GEORGE BUD, cosmetic mfr.; b. New Orleans, Jan. 13, 1918; s. George Henry and Ada Florence (Savage) W.; student St. John's, Golden State, Pacific mil. acads.; m. Martha Raye, 1938; m. 2d, Rosemary Lane, 1941 (div. 1955); 1 dau., Susan Bridget; m. 3d, Jeanne Shores, Apr. 1, 1955; children—Robert, Melinda, Timothy, Charles. Make-up artist Warner Bros. Studios, 1934-37, Paramount Studios, 1937-40, 20th Century Fox Studios, 1940; dir. make-up and hairstyling Producers Releasing Corp. studios Eagle Lion Studio, 1945-47, Universal-Internat. Studio, from 1947; owner House of Westmore, from 1947. Mem. Soc. Make-Up Artist. Author: (with Ern Westmore) So You Want to Be Beautiful, 1941; (with others) Westmore Beauty Book, 1955. Author articles on make-up. Home: Sherman Oaks, Cal. Died June 23, 1973; interred Valhalla Meml. Park North Hollywood, Cal.

WESTON, ELIZABETH STEWART, mag. editor; b. Chgo.; d. Stewart and Doris (Templeton) Weston; student Vassar Coll.; A.B., U. Chgo.; m. Jefferson Berryman, Jan. 8, 1949 (div. Sept. 1958); m. 2d, Archibald Gaulocher, Mar. 25, 1971. Features editor Glamour mag., N.Y.C., 1945-51; chief staff writer Good Housekeeping mag., N.Y.C., 1951-58; asst. to editor McCall's mag., N.Y.C., 1958-61, mng. editor, 1961-63, exec. editor, 1963-70; mng. editor Harper's Bazaar, from 1970. Mem. Fashion Group, N.Y. Travel Writers Assn. Republican. Episcopalian. Home: New York City N.Y. Died Nov. 18, 1973.

WETTERAU, OLIVER GEORGE, food distbg. co. exec.; b. St. Louis, June 7, 1908; s. Otto J.C. and Ida A. (Schuttenhelm) W.; B.S. in Bus. Adminstrn., Washington U., St. Louis, 1929; LL.D. (hon.), Elmhurst Coll., 1970; m. Virginia A. Kretschmar, June 11, 1932; 1 dau., Sandra V. (Mrs. Richard Nieman). With Southwestern Bell Telephone Co., 1929-30; with Wetterau, Inc., St. Louis, 1930-73, pres., 1963-70, chmn. bd., 1970-73; trustee Tom Haggaii and Assos. Active local United Fund drive; past v.p. Deaconess Hosp., St. Louis. Bd. dirs. March of Dimes, Conv. Bur. City St. Louis, Inner City Missions of United Ch. Christ; trustee Elmhurst Coll.; bd. govs. Washington U. Mem. Allied Food Club St. Louis, Sigma Phi Epsilon, Alpha Kappa Psi, Beta Gamma Sigma. Mason (Shriner). Clubs: St. Louis, Missouri Athletic, Sunset Country (St. Louis). Home: St. Louis Mo. Died Dec. 21, 1973.

WEXLER, JACOB, physician; b. Kishinef, Russia, June 18, 1904; s. Samuel and Minnie (Kaminsky) W.; came to U.S., 1905; student U. Tenn., 1924-26; M.D., Middlesex U., 1931; evening student Boston Coll. Law, 1935-39; J.D., Calvin Coolidge Law Sch., 1940; m. Edith Seidle, July 7, 1935; children—Stanley, Larry, Sherwin. Intern Trinity Hosp., Bklyn., 1931-32; resident Warren County Hosp., Phillipsburg, N.J., 1932-33; practiced medicine, specializing in genito-urinary diseases, Boston, 1934; staff Boston, Forest Hills, Kenmore hosps.; sch. physician Boston City schs., 1945-71. Served as capt. M.C., AUS, 1942-45. Decorated Bronze Star medal. Diplomate Am. Bd. Legal Medicine. Fellow Am. Coll. Legal Medicine, Am. Geriatric Soc., A.A.A.S.; mem. A.M.A., Mass. Med.-Legal Soc., Mass. Med. Soc., Mass. Sch. Physicians Assn., Assn. Mil. Surgeons, Charles River Med. Soc., Assn. Am. Physicians and Surgeons, Am. Acad. Gen. Practice. Home: Newton Highlands Mass. Died July 5, 1972; buried Sharon Meml. Park, Sharon, Mass.

WEYL, WOLDEMAR ANATOL, scientist, educator; b. Darmstadt, Germany, June 13, 1901; s. Wladimir and Auguste (Blech) W.; Diploma Ingenieur, Tech. U., Darmstadt, 1923; Dr. Chem.E., Tech. U., Aachen, 1931; m. Ilse Rudow, Oct. 29, 1937; 1 dau., Karin Gisela. Came to U.S., 1936, naturalized, 1943. Head dept. glass tech. Kaiser Wilhelm Inst. Silicate Research, 1926-36; vis. prof. U.S., 1936-37; prof. glass tech. Pa. State U., 1938-66, chmn. div. mineral tech. Coll. Mineral Industries, 1948-60, Evan Pugh research prof. in phys. scis., 1960-66, emeritus, 1966-75. Fellow Brit., German socs. glass tech.; mem. Am. Chem. Soc., Am. Ceramics Soc (hon. life), Geochem. Soc. (charter), Sigma Xi (hon.). Mem. Keramos (hon.). Editor: French jour. Verre at Refractaire. Home: State College, Pa. Died July 30, 1975; interred Graysville, (Pa.) Cemetery.

WHALING, HORACE MORLAND, JR., clergyman, educator; b. Memphis. Tenn., July 15, 1881; s. Horace M. and Alice (Heiskell) W.; A.B., U. of Tex., 1903; B.D., Vanderbilt, 1907; D.D., Centenary Coll., 1926; m. Annie Byrd Ward, Mar. 14, 1911; children—Anne, Horace M. III, Ward. Ordained ministry M.E. Ch., S., 1907; pastor McKee St. Ch., Houston, Tex., 1909-13, Marlin, 1914, Highland Park Ch., Dallas, 1918-19; prof. church history, Sch. of Theology, Southern Meth. U., 1916; became v.p. Southern Meth. U., 1917; pastor Oak Lawn Ch., Dallas, 1931-36, Houston Dist, 1936-42; editor Southwestern Advocate, 1942-46. Democrat. Address: Dallas, Tex.†

WHALLON, WALTER LOWRIE, clergyman; b. Vincennes, Ind., Sept. 23, 1878; s. Edward P. (Rev. Dr.) and Margaret Ellen (Kitchell) W.; A.B., Hanover (Ind.) Coll., 1899, A.M., 1903, D.D., 1916; grad. Princeton Theol. Sem., 1903; m. Irene Snyder, Oct. 26, 1905; children—Edward Valentine, John Montgomery. Ordained ministry Presbyn. Ch. U.S.A., 1903; pastor Broad Av. Ch., Altoona, Pa., 1903-10, Central Ch. Zanesville, O., 1910-25, Roseville Av. Ch., Newark, N.J., from 1925; exchange preacher in London and England, 1928. Mem. Permanent Jud. Commn. of Presbyn. Ch., 1916-19; moderator Synod of Ohio, 1922; mem. Gen. Assembly's Com. on Princeton Theol. Sem., 1926-28; mem. bd. mgrs. and pres. Lord's Day Alliance of U.S.; mem. bd. of Foreign Missions Presbyn. Ch., U.S.A.; mem. Bd. of Corporators of the Presbyn. Ministers' Fund (Phila.). Trustee Coll. of Wooster (O.), 1916-25, Princeton and Bloomfield Theol. sems., Presbyn. Hosp., Newark, Pres. bd. dirs. Bloomfield Coll. and Sem. Mem. Princeton Theol. Sem. Alumni Assn. of N.Y. City and Vicinity (pres. 1927-28, 1938-40), S.A.R., Beta Thete Pi, Pi Gamma Mu. Mason (K.T.); Grand Chaplain Masonic Grand Lodge of N.J., 1931-32, 1947-48. Home: Newark, N.J.†

WHARTON, WILLIAM P, b. Beverly, Mass., Aug. 12, 1880; s. William F. and Fanny (Pickman) W.; prep. edn., Groton (Mass.) Sch.; A.B., Harvard, 1903; grad. study, Harvar Law Sch., 1904-05; m. Ruth Gerrish, Feb. 16, 1915; m. 2d, Elizabeth M. Wiggin, Aug. 29, 1922. Engaged in farming nr. Groton from 1905. Selectman, Groton, 1921-24. Actively identified with movements for conservation of natural resources. Chmn. Mass. State Forestry Committee; former chmn. Mass. Conservation Council; mem. standing com. Trustees of Public Reservations (Mass.) Mem. bd. dirs. New England Forestry Foundation. Mem. Mass. Farm Bureau Fedn. (ex-pres.). American Forestry Association (dir.), Society Am. Foresters, Mass. Forest and Park Assn. (pres.), Soc. for Portection, N.J. Forests, Nat. Audubon Society, National Parks Association (president), Mass. Audubon Soc., Am. Ornithologists Union, Northeastern Bird Banding Assn., Am. Bison-Soc., (ex-sec.) Episcopalian. Clubs: Harvard (New York); Harvard (Boston); Cosmos (Washington). Home: Groton, Mass.†

WHEAT, HARRY G(ROVE), prof. edn.; born Berkeley Springs, W.Va., April 8, 1890; s. Alfred Asbury and Tamson Bell (Shockey) W.; A.B., W.Va. U., 1912; A.M., U. of Chicago, 1917; Ph.D., Columbia, 1929; m. Florence Bodey, Aug. 20, 1919 (died Feb. 6, 1945); 1 dau., Mary Eleanor (Mrs. Harold Piggott);

married Margaret Leckie, December 19, 1949. Teacher, high school, Davis, W.Va., 1912-13; supt. schs., Williamstown, W.Va., 1913-16; instr. edn., State Normal Sch., Glenville, W.Va., 1917, 1919-24, State Teachers Coll., Milwaukee, 1924-25; prof. edn., Marshall Coll., Huntington, W.Va., 1925-35; prof. edn., W.Va. U., from 1935; summer teacher, Duke U., 1940, U. of Alberta, 1947; spl. lecturer, U. of Pa., U. of Chicago, Temple U. Served in F.A., U.S. Army with A.E.F., 1918-19, grad. Saumur Arty. Sch., France, 1919. Mem. com. to prepare yearbooks on arithmetic in pub. schs. Nat. Council Teachers of Mathematics and Nat. Soc. for the Study of Edn. Mem. N.E.A., State Edn. Assn., Phi Beta Kappa, Phi Delta Kappa, Sigma Phi Epsilon. Republican. Methodist. Mason. Club. Kiwanis. Author: The Teaching of Reading, 1923; The Relative Merits of Arithmetic Problems, 1929; Psychology of the Elementary School, 1931; The Psychology and Teaching of Arithmetic, 1937; Practice Books for Arithmetic, 1936; Foundations of School Learning, 1955; sr. author The Row-Peterson Arithmetics, 1951; How to Teach Arithmetic, 1951. Home: Morgantown, W.Va. Died Mar. 29, 1975; buried East Oak Cemetery, Morgantown.

WHEELER, BURTON KENDALL, senator; b. Hudson, Mass., Feb. 27, 1882; s. Asa Leonard and Mary Elizabeth (Tyler) W.; grad. Hudson High Sch., 1900; LL.B., U. of Mich., 1905; m. Lulu M. White, Sept. 7, 1907; children—John Leonard, Elizabeth Hale, Edward Kendall, Frances Lulu, Richard Burton, Marion Montana. Admitted to Mont. bar, 1906, and practiced at Butte. Mem. Mont. Ho. of Reps., 1911-13; U.S. atty. Dist. of Mont., by appointment of Pres. Wilson, 1913-18 (resigned); mem. U.S. Senate, 4 terms, 1923-47; practice of law, with son, Washington, after 1947. Progressive Party candidate for vice-pres. of U.S. with Robert M. LaFollette, 1924. Democrat. Mem. Mont. Bar Assn. Methodist. Mason (Shriner), Elk. Home: Washington, D.C. Died Jan. 1975.

WHEELER, CHARLES FRANCIS, educator; b. Cin., May 19, 1906; s. James Fleming and Mary Etheldreda (Sweeney) W.; A.B., Xavier U., Cin., 1928; student Cin. Coll. Music, 1925-27; A.M., U. Cin., 1929, Ph.D., 1935; m. Esther Therese Spaeth, June 11, 1950. Mem. faculty Xavier U., 1929-70, prof. of English, chmn. dept., 1940-65, prof. English, dean summer sessions, 1965-70, dir. summer sessions, 1951-61; pres. N. Central Conf. Summer Schs., 1956-57; choir dir. and organist St. Patrick Ch. 1923-52. Mem. Nat. Council Tchrs. English, Ohio Council Tchr. Edn., Xavier U., U. Cin. alumni assns., Am. Assn. U. Profs., Cin. Schoolmasters Club. Author: Classical Mythology in Jonson, 1938. Contbr. articles mags. Lectr. lit. and the arts. Home: Cincinnati O. Died Dec. 28, 1974.

WHEELER, CHARLES (REGINALD), business exec.; b. London, Eng., Dec. 5, 1904; s. Henry and Nellie Bowdler (Healing) W.; grad. St. Paul's Sch., 1922; m. Frieda Close, Sept. 5, 1929; 1 son, 2 daus. With Baldwins Ltd., 1922-46; mng dir. Guest Keen Iron & Steel Co., 1946-59, chmn. 1959-60; chmn. Asso. Elec. Industries Ltd., 1964-67; chmn. Sheerness Steel Co. Ltd.; dir. Rudolf Wolff (Holdings) Ltd., Phoenix Assurance Co. Ltd., George Wimpey & Co. Ltd., Triumph Investment Trust Ltd., Oceanic Securities Ltd. Mem. ct. govs. Univ. Coll. South Wales and Monmouthshire Coll. Mem. English-Speaking Union (joint hon. treas., gov.), Brit. Elec. Allied Mfrs. Assn. (past pres.). Created knight 1966; decorated chevalier Legion d' Honneur; officer Legion d'Honneur; comdr. Order Brit. Empire. Clubs: Garrick, Rowing (London); Leander (Henley-on-Thames). Home: Bellington near Chesham, England., Died Nov. 25, 1975.

WHEELER, DANIEL EDWIN, editor, writer; b. New York, N.Y., Mar. 1, 1880; s. Leonard and Elizabeth (Gorman) W.; ed. pub. schs. and under private tutors; m. Mercy Dorothy Willson, Mar. 11, 1914. Began with Cosmopolitan Mag., 1898, later asso. editor Collier's Weekly; did work for Ency. Britannica, also hist. research; with Popular Mag., 1912-20; editorial dir. with the Edison Phonograph Co., 1920-22. Episcopalian. Author: Life and Writings of T. Paine, 1907; Abraham Lincoln, 1916; Autobiography, 1917. Editor: Writings of Thomas Jefferson, 1903; Great Events by Famous Historians, 1905; Lincoln, 1906. Mng. editor Outline of Christianity, 1923-26; on editorial staffs of New York Times, 1926-27, and Cosmopolitan Mag., 1927; editor McClure's Magazine, 1928-29, of Smar Set. 1929-30; fiction editor of Liberty Magazine, 1931-33, mem. editorial staff, 1935-46. Home: Briarcliff Manor, N.Y.†

WHEELER, EARLE GILMORE, army officer; b. Washington, Jan. 13, 1908; s. Clifton Freeman and Ida (Gilmore) W.; B.S., U.S. Mil. Acad., 1932; LL.D., U. Akron, 1964, U. R.I., 1965, Washington and Jefferson Coll., 1965; Sc.D. (hon.), Norwich U., 1966; m. Betty Rogers Howell, June 10, 1932; 1 son, Gilmore Stone. Commd. 2d lt., inf., U.S. Army, 1932, advanced through grades to maj. gen., 1955, gen., 1962; chief staff 63d Inf. Div., World War II; with Allied Forces So. Europe, 1952-55; dir. plans Office Dep. Chief Staff for Mil. Operations, Dept. Army, 1955-58; comdg. gen. 2d Armored Div., 1958-60; dir. joint staff Orgn. Joint Chiefs Staff, 1960-62; dep. comdr.-in-chief U.S. European Command., 1962; chief staff U.S. Army 1962-64; chmn. Joint Chiefs Staff, Dept. Def., 1964-70; ret., 1970. Dir. Monsanto Co. Decorated D.S.M. with 2 oak leaf clusters, Legion of Merit, Bronze Star medal with oak leaf cluster, D.S.M. (Navy), D.S.M. (USAF), Joint Services Commendation medal, Def. Distinguished Service medal; grand comdr. Legion of Honor, Croix de Guerre with palm (France); Order of Abdon Calderon (Ecuador); grand cross Order of Merit (Fed. Republic Germany); Order White Rose (Finland); Decoration of Mil. Merit (Mexico); knight grand cross Royal Order of Sword (Sweden); Exalted Order White Elephant (Thailand); Order Service medal (Korea); comdr. Legon Honor (Philippines); Nat. Order grand officer Gallantry Cross with palm (Vietnam); grand officer Order Mil. Merit (Brazil). Home: Martinsburg, W.Va., Died Dec. 18, 1975.

WHEELER, JOHN NEVILLE, newspaperman; b. Yonkers, N.Y., Apr. 11, 1886; s. Charles W. and Kate (Neville) W.; A.B., Columbia, 1908; m. Elizabeth Wood Thompson, Jan. 30, 1918; 1 dau., Elizabeth N. (Mrs. William McLaren Ellison) (dec.). With N.Y. Herald, 1908-12; est. Wheeler Syndicate, 1913, sold out, 1916; est. Bell Newspaper Syndicate, Inc., 1916, former pres., dir. The Bell Syndicate, Inc., N. Am. Newspaper Alliance, Inc., 1931-64; later consultant to the United Feature Syndicate; pres., dir. Wheeler Development Corp.; was exec. editor Liberty Weekly. Served as 2d lt., later 1st lt. F.A., U.S. Army, Aug. 1917-Feb. 1919, with A.E.F. in France, May 1918-Feb. 1919. Mem. Sigma Chi. Episcopalian. Clubs: Maidstone Peachtree (Atlanta); University, Dutch Treat Club, Coffee House, National Golf Links of America, Artists and Writers. Author: I've Got News for You, 1961. Home: Ridgefield Conn. Died Oct. 13, 1973.

WHEELER, RAYMOND ALBERT, army officer, cons. civil engr.; b. Peoria, Ill., July 31, 1885; s. Stephen Andrew and Margaret (Maple) W.; B.S., U.S. Mil. Acad., 1911; grad. Army Sch. Engring., 1913, Command and Gen. Staff Sch., 1927, Army War Coll., 1937; D.Sc. (hon.), Bradley U., 1961, U.N.C., 1962; m. Olive Keithley, June 29, 1912 (dec. 1954); 1 dau., Margaret Irene (Mrs. William C. Wilkinson, Jr.); m. 2d, Virginia Morsey, June 17, 1959. Commd. 2d lt., C.E., U.S. Army, 1911, advanced through grades to lt. gen., 1944; wartime service in Vera Cruz (Mexico) Expdn., 1914, in France, Germany and Italy, World War I, in Persian Gulf area, China, Burma, India and S.E. Asia, World War II; dep. supreme allied comdr. S.E. Asia Command, 1944; comdg. gen. India-Burma theatre, 1945; peacetime service in Panama Canal, Hawaiian Islands, various engr. dists. in U.S.; chief engrs. U.S. Army, 1945-49; retired, 1949; engring. adviser Internat. Bank Reconstrn. and Devel., 1949-64; rep. Internat. Bank Reconstrn. and Devel. in water dispute negotiations with India and Pakistan over waters of Indus Basin, 1952-60; spl. UN assignments include clearance Suez Canal, 1956-57, chief Mekong River Survey Mission, Asia, 1957-58, operation Congo, 1960, 63; mem., chmn. adv. bd. Mekong Coordination Com., Cambodia, Laos, Thailand, Vietnam, 1960-69; mem. Columbia Bd. Rev., B.C. Hydro and Power Authority, Vancouver, 1963-71. Decorated D.S.M. with 3 oak leaf clusters, Silver Star, Air medal, Legion of Merit; created hon. knight Great Britain, 1944, Indian Empire, 1947, Thailand, 1945; Hoover gold medal Am. Soc. C.E., Am. Inst. Mining, Metall. and Petroleum Engrs., Am. Soc. M.E., I.E.E.E., 1958. Mem. Am. Inst. Cons. Engrs., A.I.A. (hon.), Soc. Am. Mil. Engrs. (v.p. 1949). Address: Washington, D.C. Died Feb. 8, 1974; buried Arlington Nat. Cemetery.

WHEELER, WALTER HEBER, JR., mfg. exec.; b. N.Y.C. Feb. 21, 1897; s. Walter Heber and Charlotte (Dutton) W.; student Worcester Acad., 1910-14; A.B., Harvard, 1918; m. Florence Chilton, Nov. 12, 1917 (dec. Sept. 1967); children—Walter H., Thomas C.; m. 2d, Marjorie Bradshaw Foster, June 7, 1969. With Pitney-Bowes, Inc., and predecessor firm, Stamford Conn., 1919, salesman, 1920-22, spl. European rep., 1922, N.Y. br. mgr., 1923-24, gen. mgr., 1924-31, v.p., 1931-38, pres., 1938-60, dir., from 1938, chmn. bd., 1960-69, chmn. exec. com., 1969-73, hon. chmn., dir. emeritus, 1973-75; dir. Arwood Corp. Mem. patent adv. com. Dept. Commerce, 1938-44, Business Council, from 1937; dep. dir., div. contract distbn. OPM, Washington, 1941; chief contract distbn. br. WPB, 1942, N.E. regional dir., Boston, 1942-44; past chmn. Council World Tensions; past employer-mem. Fed. Adv. Council Employment security; past pres. New Eng. Council; past mem. bus. leadership adv. council Office Econ. Opportunity; trustee U.S. council Internat. C. of C.; dir. Com. Nat. Trade Policy; hon. trustee Com. Econ. Devel.; past mem. Citizens Com. Internat. Devel., Nat. Com. Internat. Devel.; past pres., dir., past chmn. nat. corps. participation com. United Community Funds and Councils Am., past chmn. nat corps. participation com. Trustee Old Sturbridge Village, Profit Sharing Research Found., Worcester Acad.; mem. emeritus council Stamford Hosp. (past pres.); hon. dir. Stamford Boys' Club; trustee, past pres. Stamford Found. Served with French as mem. Am. Ambulance Field Service, 1916; with USN, 1917-18, lt., comdr. submarine chaser in Adriatic. Decorated Croix de Guerre (France); Navy Cross (U.S.). Nat. Asso. Boys Club Am.; mem. Nat. Urban League, U.S. C. of C. (past nat. councillor), Fgn. Policy Assn. (past vice chmn. bd., chmn. nat. council, dir.), UN Assn. (past dir. U.S.), Nat. Indsl. Conf. Bd., Council Profit Sharing Industries (founding trustee), Yacht Racing Assn. L.I. Sound (past pres.), Council Fgn. Relations. Clubs: Cruising of Am., N.Y. Yacht, Harvard (N.Y.C.); Harvard (Boston); Halloween Yacht, Ponus Yacht, Yacht (Stamford); Royal Bermuda Yacht. Home: Stamford Conn. Died Dec. 11, 1974.

WHEELWRIGHT, MARY CABOT, dir. Museum of Navajo Ceremonial Art; b. Boston, Mass., 1878; d. Andrew C. and Sarah (Cabot) Wheelwright; unmarried. Founder Museum of Navajo Ceremonial Art, Sante Fe, N.M., and dir. from 1938. Recorder of Navajo Indian religion, from 1919; one of the founders South Edn Music Sch., Boston, Mass., 1912. Author: Navajo Creation Myth (Mus. Navajo Ceremonial Art), 1941; Hail and Water Chants (Mus. Navajo Ceremonial Art), 1946. Address: Alcalde, N.M.†

WHELCHEL, CLARENCE ANTHONY, banker; b. Dawsonville, Ga., Sept. 9, 1899; s. Jeff D. and Margaret (Boone) W.; student Ga. Sch. Tech., 1920-24; m. Sibyl Esther Aiken, June 28, 1923; 1 dau., Sibyl Ann (Mrs. C. W. Nestor, Jr.). Pub. accountant, Gainesville, Ga., 1929-32; examiner Fed. Res. Bank of Atlanta, 1932-39; v.p. Commerce Union Bank, Columbia, Tenn., 1939-44; pres., chmn. bd. First Farmers & Mchts. Nat. Bank, Columbia, 1944-72; dir. Nashville br. Fed. Res. Bank Atlanta, 1959-61. Mem. Columbia Pub. Service Commn., 1943-49. Trustee Maury County Hosp., Columbia. Episcopalian (jr. and sr. warden). Home: Columbia, Tenn. Died Nov. 4, 1972; buried St. John's, Mt. Pleasant Pike.

WHELCHEL, JOHN ESTEN, naval officer; b. Hogansville, Ga., Apr. 1, 1898; s. Jasper Esten and Louise (Longstreet) W.; A.B., U.S. Naval Acad., 1919; m. Virginia Hoover, May 29, 1920 (dec. Feb. 28, 1941); children—Laurel Denmead, Louise Longstreet, John Esten; m. 2d, Marion Payne, Oct. 20, 1946. Served in U.S.S. Rochester, Atlantic convoy duty, World War I; chief of staff to comdr. service squadrons U.S.S. San Francisco, South Pacific, World War II; advanced through grades to rear adm., Aug. 1947; retired as vice adm., Aug. 1949; engaged in real estate and farming, 1950-73. Asst. coach football U.S. Naval Acad., head coach, 1942-43, dir. athletics, 1943; head coach Washington Redskins, Nat. League team, 1949. Mem. Sweet Potato Growers Assn. (pres.). Home: Virginia Beach Va. Died Nov. 5, 1973; buried Arlington (Va.) Nat. Cemetery.

WHERRY, FRANK GILBERT, ednl. adminstr.; b. St. Louis, Oct. 25, 1922; s. Gilbert and Florence Elizabeth (Schall) W.; B.S., St. Louis U., 1943, M.S., 1953, Ph.D., 1957. Mem. faculty Sch. Commerce and Finance, St. Louis U., 1947-53, asst. regent, 1948-51, exec. sec. grad. programs commerce and finance, 1951-53; dean Sch. Econs. and Bus. Adminstrn., dir. dept. journalism Gonzaga U., 1953-56; dir. bus. research, prof. econs. Marquette U., 1956-58; asst. sec., asst. comptroller Terminal R.R. Assn. St. Louis, 1958-61, comptroller, sec., 1961-63, v.p., comptroller, sec., 1963-64; v.p. Merc. Trust Co., from 1964; v.p., dir. St. Louis Bridge Co., from 1961, Tunnel Railroad of St. Louis, from 1961; sec., dir. Wiggins Ferry Co., from 1958, Terminal Realty Co., from 1958; chief financial officer, sec. Fla. Palm-Aire Corp., 1967-69; comptroller Tose Inc., 1969-71, asst. to pres., 1971; dir. div. econs. and bus. adminstrn. Community Coll. Phila., from 1972. Originator, coordinator, Indsl. Relations Inst. series, Spokane, Wash.; ednl. adviser Am. Inst. Banking, Spokane. Mem. Am. Statis. Assn., Nat. Sales Execs. Assn., Advt. Assn., Econ. Assn., Cath. Econ. Assn., Northwest Personnel Assn., Assn. Am. Railroads (hon.), Delta Sigma Pi, Alpha Delta Gamma, Sigma Delta Psi. Club: Missouri Athletic. Past editor Marquette Bus. Rev. Home: Philadelphia, Pa. Died Oct. 28, 1974; interred Sunset Burial Park, Affton, Mo.

WHIDDEN, RAY ALLEN, pres. Bauer & Black; b. Oakland, Calif., Oct. 14, 1878; s. George Ackerman and Mary Bell (Allen) W.; Ph.G., U. of Calif., 1902; m. Laura A. Harvey, Mar. 28, 1902; children—Dorothy, Ray Harvey, Lola Ann. Began career as druggist's clk., 1896; salesman, 1904-09; Pacific coast salesman, Eli Lilly & Co., Indianapolis, 1909-13, mgr. Chicago dist., 1914-23, western sales mgr., 1923-27; v.p. and gen. mgr. Bauer & Black, Chicago, 1927-30, pres. from 1930. v.p. and dir. The Kendall Co., Boston. Mem. Am. Soc. Sales Executives, Phi Delta Chi. Republican. Presbyterian. Mason (32°, Shriner). Clubs: Lake Shore Athletic (Chicago); 100,000 Mile. Home: Kenilworth, Ill.†

WHIPPLE, GEORGE HOYT, pathologist; b. Ashland, N.H., Aug. 28, 1878; s. Ashley Copper and Frances Anna (Hoyt) W.; A.B., Yale, 1900, M.A. (hon.), 1927, D.Sc. (hon.), 1947; M.D., Johns Hopkins, 1905, LL.D. (hon.), 1947; D.Sc. (hon.), Colgate, 1927, Wesleyan U., 1935, Trinity Coll., Hartford, 1936, Western Reserve Med. Sch., 1943, U. Chgo., 1952; LL.D. (hon.) Tulane U., 1935, U. Cal., 1935, U. Buffalo, 1946, U. Rochester, 1950, U. Glasgow, 1951; honorary doctorate, U. of Athens, 1937; m. Katherine Ball Waring, June 24, 1914; children—George Hoyt, Barbara (Mrs. Grant Heilman). Asst. in pathology Johns Hopkins, 1905-06, instr., 1906-07; pathologist Ancon Hosp., Panama, 1907-08, also Bay View Hosp., Balt., 1908; asso. in pathology Johns Hopkins, 1909-11, asso. prof., 1911-14, resident pathologist, Johns Hopkins Hosp., 1910-14;

prof. research medicine, U. of Cal., and dir. Hooper Found. Med. Research, Med. Sch., U. Cal., 1914-21; dean U. of Cal. Med. Sch., 1920-21; dean Sch. Medicine and Dentistry, U. Rochester, 1921-53, prof. pathology, 1921-55, prof. pathology emeritus, 1955. Trustee Rockefeller Found., 1927-43; mem. bd. sci. dirs. Rockefeller Inst. for Med. Research, 1936-53, bd. trustees, 1939-60; mem. and trustee Gen. Edn. Bd; 1936-43. Recipient Nobel prize in medicine, joint award, 1934; William Wood Gerhard gold medal, 1934; Kober medal Georgetown U., 1939; Rochester Civic medal, 1943; Gold-Headed Cane award Am. Assn. Pathologists and Bacteriologists, 1961; Kovalenko medal National Academy Scis., 1962; Distinguished Service award A.M.A., 1973; Pres.'s medal U. Rochester, 1975. Charles Mickle fellow U. Toronto, 1938. Fellow Am. Acad. Oral Pathology (hon.); mem. Internat. Assn. Dental Research (hon.), Pathol. Soc. Gt. Britain. and Ireland (hon.), Am. Soc. Exptl. Pathology (pres. 1925), Assn. Am. Physicians, Am. Physiol. Soc., A.M.A., Am. Assn. Pathologists and Bacteriologists (pres. 1930), Nat. Acad. Scis., Am. Philos. Soc., Brit. Med. Assn. (fgn. corr.), Sigma Xi, Alpha Omega Alpha, Phi Beta Kappa, Beta Theta Pi, Phi Chi. Home: Rochester, N.Y. Died Feb. 1, 1976.

WHIPPLE, HOWARD GREGORY, banker; b. Northfield, Minn., Aug. 18, 1881; s. Abram Olin and Mary Josephine (Ten Broeck) W.; grad. Carleton Acad., Northfield, 1899; A.B., Williams Coll., 1903; m. Eugenie Valeska Fink, of Milwaukee, Wis., Sept. 11, 1915; children—Gregory Ten Broeck, Gerald Howard, Janice Marr. Began with First Nat. Bank, Devils Lake, N.D., 1903; traveled in U.S. and Europe, 1910-14; in banking business, Turlock, Calif., from 1914; pres. First Nat. Bank from 1914; pres. Commercial Bank of Turlock; dir. Federal Reserve Bank of San Francisco. Mem. Theta Delta Chi. Republican. Club: Turlock Country. Home: Turlock, Cal.†

WHIPPLE, JAY NORTHAM, investment banker; b. Chicago, Ill., July 28, 1897; s. Arthur Jay and Myrtle (Northam) W.; grad. Phillips Exeter Acad., 1915; student Yale University, 1915-17; married Marjorie Cox, Jan. 17, 1925 (div.); children—Margaret Cox, (Mrs. Gordon R. Wright), Jay N.; married Hollis Letts McLaughlin, Apr. 21, 1950. With Chgo. Trust Co., 1919-26; mem. firm Bacon, Whipple & Co., investment securities, Chicago, 1926-73; pres. Investment Bankers Assn. of America, 1942-43. Served as lt. (j.g.), on U.S.S. Agamemnon, World War I. Mem. 7th Federal Reserve Dist. Victory Fund Com., and Nat. Com. on Securities Industry for War Finance; chmn. 2d War Loan Drive, Met. Chgo.; vice chmn. Ill. War Finance Com. Gov. N.Y. Stock Exchange, 1947-52. Term trustee Phillips Exeter Academy, 1944-50. Trustee Lake Forest Acad., 1945-54. Mem. Delta Kappa Epsilon. Clubs: University, Chicago, Commercial, Attic, Shoreacres, Old Elm, Onwentsia. Home: Lake Forest Ill. Died Nov. 26, 1973.

WHITAKER, BENJAMIN PALMER, educator; b. Newburgh, N.Y., July 30, 1899; s. Lewis Samuel and Mary Elizabeth (Palmer) W.; A.B., Colgate U., 1921; L.H.D., Union Coll., Schenectady, 1946; M.A., Yale, 1925, Ph.D., 1931; m. Helen Frances Johnson, Sept. 5, 1925; children—Jeanne (dec.), Mary Ann (Mrs. James S. Dolliver), Benjamin P., Robert L. Salesman bonds Harris, Furhes & Co. and J.G. White & Co., N.Y.C., 1921-24; instr. Yale, 1925-31, also tax cons.; mem. sr. staff Brookings Instn., Washington, 1931-33; research dir. State of Conn., Hartford, 1933-37, budget dir., 1937-39; prof. econs. Union Coll., Schenectady, 1939-65, comptroller, 1943-45, acting pres., 1945-46, prof. emeritus, 1965-74. Dir. Schenectady Indsl. Corp., Schenectady Indsl. Devel. Corp. Cons. tax and adminstrn. City Schenectady, 1940; sec. ways and means com. Assembly State N.Y., Albany, 1949-50; fiscal aid, majority leader N.Y. Senate, 1957-64; hwy. toll studies and others State N.Y., 1959-64. Bd. mgrs. Ellis Hosp., Schenectady, 1945-72; bd. dirs. Schenectady Found., 1963-71, chmn. 1969-71; trustee YMCA. Fulbright lectr. Kelo U. (Japan), Sophia U., Tokyo, 1957. Mem. Phi Beta Kappa, Lambda Chi Alpha. Home: Schenectady, N.Y. Died June 25, 1974; interred Chapel St. George's Ch., Schenectady.

WHITAKER, DOUGLAS, inst. exec.; b. Stanford U., Calif., Mar. 5, 1904; s. Albert C. and Mary E. (Merritt) W.; A.B., Stanford U., 1926; Ph.D., 1928; attended Columbia U., 1927; m. Edith Morgan, Aug. 2, 1928; children—Nancy, Douglas Hunt. Research Asso. Carnegie Tortugas Lab., summer 1926; instr. physiology, Stanford U., 1928-29; Nat. Research fellow, Harvard U., 1929-30; asst. prof. zoölogy, Columbia U., 1929-31; asso. prof. biology, Stanford U., 1931-32, prof. biology, 1932-55, dean School of Biol. Sci., 1946-49; acting v.p., 1948-49, dean graduate study, 1948-51, dean humanities and scis., 1951-52, provost, 1952-55; v.p. for adminstrn. Rockefeller Inst., 1955-61, vice president for academic adminstrn., 1961-64; instr. embryol., Marine Biol. Lab., Woods Hole, Mass., summer 1938; exec. sec., div. biology and agr., Nat. Research Council, 1943, chmn., 1950-51; chief sci. sect., Shrivenham Am. U. of U.S. Army, 1945; biologist Bikini Sci. Resurvey, USN, 1947. Mem. sci. adv. bd. Fels Research Inst., Inst. Advanced Learning Med. Scis. Fellow Cal. Acad. Sci.; mem. Assn. Aid Crippled children, N.Y. (dir.), A.A.A.S., Am. Soc. Zoologists (pres. 1950), Am. Naturalists, Western Soc. Naturalists; trustee Bermuda Biol. Sta., Sci. Service. Editor: Jour. Exptl. Zoology. Contbr. sci. publs. Home: San Antonio Tex. Died Oct. 5, 1973.

WHITAKER, ELBERT COLEMAN, physician; b. Lexington, Ky., 1919; M.D., U. Louisville, 1943; m. Ruby Keeton, Sept. 21, 1971. Intern, St. Elizabeth Hosp., Covington, Ky., 1944; jr. asst. resident in gen. surgery Louisville Gen. Hosp., 1944-45, asst. resident, 1945-46; resident in surgery VA Hosp., Louisville, 1949-51; asst. chief surgeon VA Hosp., Lake City, Fla., 1951-56. Served to capt. M.C., AUS, 1946-48. Diplomate Am. Bd. Surgery. Fellow A.C.S.; mem. A.M.A., So. Surg. Assn. Home: Madison, Ind. Died Dec. 25, 1971; buried Winchester Cemetery, Winchester, Ky.

WHITAKER, LEWIS ALFRED, physician; b. Dravosburg, Pa., Aug. 21, 1881; s. William McClure and Elizabeth (Corey) W.; A.B., Allegheny Coll. at Meadeville, Penn., 1903; M.D., Univ. Pittsburgh, 1908; m. Jennie M. Jones, Mar. 16, 1909; children—Dr. Darrell W., Dr. Paul J., Dr. Theodore R. Licensed to practice med. and surgery, State Pa., 1908, State W.Va., 1909; pvt. practice med. and surgery, City Weirton, W.Va., from 1909, practiced limited to indsl. med. and surg. from 1929; med. dir. Weirton Steel Co. from 1935; staff (Steubenville) Ohio Valley Hosp. Fellow Am. Assn. Iron and Steel Inst. (mem. com. indsl. health), W.Va. and Hancock County Med. Assn. Presbyn. Mason. Home: Weirton, W.Va.†

WHITAKER, U.A., mfg. exec.; b. Lincoln, Kan., Mar. 22, 1900; s. Oliver Barr and Annetta Ruth (Boyle) W.; B.S. in Mech. Engring., Mass. Inst. Tech., 1923; B.S. in Elec. Engring., Carnegie Inst. Tech., 1929; J.D., Cleve. Law Sch., 1935; Sc.D., Elizabethtown Coll., 1954; LL.D., Gettysburg Coll., 1967; m. Helen Margaret Fisher, Sept. 26, 1944; children—Ruth (Holmes), Portia (Shumaker). Spl. engr. Westinghouse Air Brake Co., 1923-29; dir. devel. and design Hoover Co., 1939-38; dir. research and engring. Am. Machine & Foundry Co., 1938-41; founder, pres., dir. AMP Inc. (formerly Aircraft-Marine Products, Inc.), 1941-62, chmn. bd., 1962-75; chmn. bd. operating subsidiaries in France, Australia, Germany, Italy, Holland, Eng., Japan, Mexico, Spain, Sweden, Can., U.S., Argentine, Brazil, Switzerland, 1962—; chmn. bd. affiliate Pamcor, Inc., Rio Piedras, P.R., 1962-75. Life mem. corp. Mass. Inst. Tech., 1966-75; distinguished fellow Cleve. Clin. Found., 1972-75. Recipient Eli Whitney Meml. award Soc. Mfg. Engrs., 1970; Distinguished Achievement award Carnegie-Mellon U. Fellow I.E.E.E. (life mem.), Am. Soc. M.E.; mem. A.A.A.S. Clubs: N.Y. Yacht (N.Y.C.); Stamford Yacht; Key Largo Anglers; Ocean Reef; Port Royal Beach; Metropolitan. Died Sept. 16. 1975.

WHITCOMB, DAVID, builder; b. Worcester, Mass., Jan. 22, 1879; s. George Henry and Abbie (Estabrook) W.; B.A. Amherst, 1900. M.A., 1905; student Harvard Law Sch., 1902-04; LL.B., George Washington U., 1905; m. Mildred Osgood, Sept. 13, 1911 (dec. 1939); 1 son, David; m. 2d, Mary Louise Robinson, August 2, 1944. Engaged in construction and management of buildings, at Seattle, Wash., from 1909; later pres. Arcade Building & Realty Co., Garage Building Co. Woodway Park Corp., Arlington Investment Co.; director and president of the Ranier National Park Co. Federal Fuel adminstr. for State of Wash., 1917-18; exec. sec. U.S. Fuel Adminstrn., Washington, D.C., 1918-19. Pres. Seattle Chamber Commerce, 1924-26; mem. Phi Beta Kappa, Psi Upsilon. Republican. Conglist. Home: Edmonds, Wash.†

WHITCOMB, DAVID TWINING, physician; b. Charles City, Ia., Jan. 18, 1928; s. Ward Almon and Ruth (Twining) W.; M.D., Ohio State U., 1952; m. Barbara Brown, Dec. 26, 1950; children—Matthew Ward, Julia Monnett, Wendolyn Ruth. Intern, Detroit Receiving Hosp., 1952-53; resident in psychiatry Walter Reed Army Hosp., 1955-58; med. dir. Brook Lane Psychiat. Center, Hagerstown, Md., 1963-68; instr. psychiatry W.Va. U. Served to capt. M.D., AUS, 1954-61. Diplomate in psychiatry Am. Bd. Psychiatry and Neurology. Mem. Am. Psychiat. Assn., A.M.A., Phi Gamma Delta. Episcopalian (vestryman). Home: Hagerstown, Md. Died Mar. 25, 1968; buried Hiram, O.

WHITE, CHARLES ALEXANDER, variety store exec.; b. Greenville, N.C., Sept. 3, 1899; s. Samuel Tilden and Annie (Sheppard) W.; student Mars Hill Coll., 1913, Randolph-Macon Acad., 1914-15, U.N.C., 1916-18; m. Nancy Rogers Lay, June 23, 1925; children—Samuel Tilden II, Barbara Sheppard (Mrs. A. Ward Peacock), Charles Alexander, Elizabeth Atkinson (Mrs. Robert F. Clayton), George Lay, Anna Louise (Mrs. Errol Haun). Ins. adjuster N.J. Fidelity & Plate Glass Ins. Co., N.Y.C., 1919-23; asso. Thomas A. Edison, Inc., East Orange, N.J., 1924-25, Hassell-Dupree Co., Miami, Fla., 1925-26; owner brokerage Charles A. White, Greenville, 1927-29; partner, mgr.-buyer White's Stores, Inc., Greenville, 1930-75, pres., 1966-75; treas. Carolina Mills Fabrics, Inc. Comdr., Civil Def., Greenville, 1942-55; chmn. Pitt County chpt. N.C. Symphony Soc., 1947-50; mem. adv. bd. East Carolina U. Summer Theatre, 1964-65, 66-68, East Carolina U. Artists Series, 1967-70, chmn., 1971-72; v.p. Pitt County United Fund, 1966-67. Bd. dirs. East Carolina U. Sch. Music Fund, 1971-72. Mem. Greenville (pres. 1952, dir. 1950-60, 64), N.C. (dir. 1966-72) mchts. assns., C. of C. (pres. 1960; dir. 1957-63, 64), Pitt County Hist. Soc. (pres. 1968-70). Episcopalian. Rotarian. (pres. 1951-52, dir. 1948-56, 65-66). Club: Greenville Music (pres. 1949). Home: Greenville, N.C. Died Mar. 2, 1975; interred Greenville, N.C.

WHITE, EGBERT, advt. exec., publisher; b. Kansas City, Mo., Mar. 7, 1894; s. Benjamin Porter and Ina (Miles) W.; student pub. schs.; m. Estelle Shepard, July 10, 1919; children—Marian Estelle, Elizabeth Anne, John Shepard. Asso. with Batten, Barton, Durstine & Osborn, Incorporated, advertising agency, as v.p. and dir., 1916-46. Served with American Expeditionary Forces, World War I, 2 years; commd. lt. col., U.S. Army, May 1942, and apptd. officer in charge of Yank, Army newspaper, Officer in charge Stars and Stripes, Mediterranean, Nov. 1942-July 1944. Promoted col., Feb. 1944; inactive status, March, 1945; special consultant, Department of State, 1945; dir. Regional Service Center, Internat. Information Adminstrn., Manila, Dept. of State, 1951-53, permanent mem. Plans Bd., Internat. Information Adminstrn., from 1953; treas., dir. Bus. Internat. Corp., 1955-70. Pub. United Nations World, 1947-50. Dir. tech. assistance div. E.C.A., 1950-51. Awarded divisional citation, Battle of Seicheprey; decorated Order of Purple Heart, Silver Star; awarded Legion of Merit, Aug. 1943; received numerous advt. awards. Mem. Yankee Div. Vets. Assn., Stars and Stripes Assn., Am. Legion, A.V.C. Methodist. Clubs: Chemists, Overseas Press (N.Y.); Nat. Press (Washington). Home: New Milford, Conn., Died Jan. 29, 1976.

WHITE, FRANK THOMAS MATTHEWS, educator; b. Melbourne, Australia, Sept. 16, 1909; s. Frank Kenworthy and Edith (Matthews) W.; B.E. in Metallurgy, U. Melbourne, 1931, B.E. in Mining, 1931; m. Tessa Marian Nunn, May 18, 1935; children—Hilary Joceln Matthews, Franklin Marshall Matthews. Came to Can., 1966. Employed in mining industry, Western Australia, 1931-36; employed with H.M. Colonial Service, 1937-44; tech. adviser mining rehab., Malaya also active in mining industries rehab. in Far East, 1945-49; prof. mining and metall. engring. U. Queensland, Australia, 1950-65; Macdonald prof. mining engring., chmn. dept. mining engring. and applied geophysics McGill U., Montreal, Que., 1966-71, dir. Inst. for Mineral Industry Research, 1968-71. Cons. numerous mining cos., also S. Africa Chamber of Mines, Colombo Plan, others. Served to capt. Fiji Mil. Forces, 1940-44. Decorated Coronation medal. Recipient Florence Taylor medal Australian Inst. Metals, 1961. Nuffield Found. fellow 1952; Carnegie Found. fellow 1957, Fellow Inst. Mining Engrs. (London), Inst. Metallurgists (London); mem. Am. Inst. Mining, Metall. and Petroleum Engrs., A.A.A.S., Inst. Mining and Metallurgy (London), Canadian Inst. Mining and Metallurgy, Australian Inst. Mining and Metallurgy, Mines Ventilation Soc. (South Africa). Contbr. articles to profl. jours. Home: Montreal Que. Canada. Died Nov. 26, 1971.

WHITE , (HUTCHINS) MARK, M.D., endocrinologist; b. Winchester, Tenn., Jan. 15, 1879; s. Mark Hutchins and Nannie (Ransom) W.; B.S., Winchester Normal Coll., 1900; M.D., Univ. of Pa., 1904; m. Pauline, d. of the late Washington Porter, of Chicago, 1922. Made extensive research of the glands of internal secretion; discovered the Mark White endocrine gland serum therapy; practiced at Denver, Colo., 10 yrs.; came to Chicago, 1914. Mason. Home: Chicago, Ill.†

WHITE, JOAN FULTON, educator; b. Geneseo, Ill., Sept. 7, 1923; d. William and Madeline (Atkins) Fulton; A.B., U. Ia., 1945; postgrad. Columbia, 1947-49; Ph.D., Bryn Mawr Coll., 1953; m. Robert F. White, Jr., Feb. 19, 1949 (div. Mar. 1969); children—Stephen Augustus, Christopher McKinney. Predoctoral fellow Nat. Cancer Inst., 1951-53, postdoctoral fellow, 1953-55; lectr. Bryn Mawr (Pa.) Coll., 1955-56; instr. zoology Cornell U., Ithaca, N.Y., 1956-60; asst. prof. zoology Eastern Ill. U., Charleston, 1960-62, 68-73. Mem. bd. Eastern Ill. chpt. Am. Civil Liberties Union. NIH fellow U. Ill., 1963-67; USPHS fellow, Canberra, Australia, 1967-68. Mem. Am. Assn. Anatomists, N.Y. Acad. Sci., Tissue Culture Assn., Am. Soc. Cell Biology, League Women Voters (mem. bd. 1963-66), Sigma Xi, Pi Beta Phi. Contbr. articles to profl. jours. Home: Charleston, Ill. Died Mar. 26, 1973; cremated.

WHITE, KATHLEEN MERELL, clergywoman; b. Millstone, N.J., Nov. 28, 1889; d. William Merrell and Anna Field (Garretson) Staats; A.B., Alma White Coll., 1932, M.A., 1952; m. Arthur Kent White, Sept. 6, 1915; children—Arlene Hart (Mrs. Evan Jerry Lawrence), Horace Merell, Constance Juanita (Mrs. David Koewing Brown), Pauline Alma (Mrs. Robert Dallenbach). Ordained to ministry Pillar of Fire Ch., 1924; asst. supt., 1946; v.p., sec. Pillar of Fire, Inc. of Colo., 1946-57; lectr., 1924-57; program dir., lectr. on radio stations N.J. and Denver; pres. Zarephath Bible Sem., 1946-57, Belleview Bible Sem., 1946-57. Trustee Pillar of Fire Ch., 1946-57. Republican. Author: Drunk Stuff, 1952; Think on These Things, 1968. Home: Zarephath, N.J., also Denver, Colo. Died Apr. 19, 1973.

WHITE, LESLIE ALVIN, educator, anthropologist; b. Salida, Colo., Jan. 19, 1900; s. Alvin Lincoln and Mildred (Millard) W.; student La. State U., 1919-21; A.B., Columbia, 1923, A.M., 1924; student U. Cal. at Los Angeles, summer 1923, Universite de Dijon, summer 1924, New Sch. Social Research, 1922-24; Ph.D., U. Chgo., 1927; Sc.D., U. Buffalo, 1962; LL.D., U. Colo., 1970; m. Mary Augusta Pattison, Feb. 9, 1931 (dec.). Instr. sociology and anthropology U. Buffalo, 1927-28, asst. prof., 1928-30; asst. prof. anthropology U. Mich., 1930-32, asso., prof., 1932-43, prof., from 1943, chmn. dept., 1945-57; asst. prof. anthropology U. Chgo., summer 1931; guest lectr. Yenching U., Peiping, China, fall 1936; vis. lectr. with rank prof. Yale, fall 1947-48; vis. prof. anthropology Harvard, fall 1949-50, U. Cal. at Berkeley, 1957, Rice U., 1970, San Francisco State Coll., 1970-71, U. Cal. at Santa Barbara, from 1973; curator anthropology Buffalo Mus. of Sci., 1927-30; prof. anthropology Columbia, summer 1948. Mem. div. anthropology and psychology NRC, 1948-49; leader ethnologic field party Lab. Anthropology, Santa Fe, 1932; numerous field trips to Pueblo Indians, 1926-57. Served with U.S.N., 1918-19. Recipient Faculty award U. Mich., 1957, Viking medal gen. anthropolgy, 1959; fellow Center for Advanced Study in Behavioral Scis. Mem. Am. Anthrop. Assn. (pres. 1963-64), Am. Folk Lore Soc. (treas. 1931, 2d v.p. 1941-42), A.A.A.S. (v.p., chmn. sect. H 1957), Mich. Acad. Sci., Arts and Letters, Am. Assn. U. Profs., Phi Beta Kappa, Sigma Xi, Phi Sigma. Club: Research (U. Mich.). Author or editor books relating to field. Address: Santa Barbara, Cal. Died Mar. 31, 1975.

WHITE, LEWIS CHARLES, govt. ofcl.; b. Morrison, Ill., Dec. 27, 1915; s. Lewis Woody and Reka (Laman) W.; ad. high sch., Holland, Mich.; m. Lillian May Ard, Nov. 26, 1936; children—Daniel Lyman, Paul Judson. Personnel officer, civilian personnel sect. Hdqrs. SCAP, Dept. Army, Tokyo, Japan, 1946-54; personnel officer U.S. Operations Mission, New Delhi, India, 1954-56; regional personnel officer ICA, Washington, 1956-58; exec. officer U.S. Operations Mission to Iran, Tehran, 1958-61; personnel office AID, Washington, 1961-65; exec. officer U.S. AID Mission to Afghanistan, Kabul, 1965-67, asst. dir. mgmt., 1967-68; dep. dir. fgn. service personnel Office Personnel and Mgmt., AID, Washington, 1968-73. Named Civic Leader of Am., 1968. Episcopalian. Mason. Club: American, Home: Alexandria, Va. Died Feb. 2, 1973; interred Sault Ste. Marie, Mich.

WHITE, LUCIEN, librarian; b. Hillsdale, Ill., Nov. 16, 1914; A.B., Augustana Coll., 1935; M.A., U. Ill., 1944, Ph.D., 1947, M.S. in L.S., 1954; postgrad. U. Grenoble (France), 1949-50; m. Lois Sanuelson. Prof. modern langs. Augustana Coll., 1939-53, librarian, 1954-58; asso. dir. pub. service depts. U. Ill., 1958-65, dir. pub. service depts., 1965-68, asso. dean library adminstrn., 1968-71, univ. librarian, 1971-75. Mem. Ill. State Library Adv. Council, 1965-75. Mem. A.L.A., Phi Beta Kappa, Beta Phi Mu. Editorial bd. Library Trends, 1958. Address: Champaign Ill Died Mar. 6, 1975.

WHITE, PAUL DUDLEY, physician; b. Roxbury, Mass., June 6, 1886; s. Herbert Warren (M.D.) and Elizabeth A. (Dudley) W.; prep. edn. Roxbury (Mass.) Latin Sch.; A.B., Harvard, 1908, M.D., 1911, D.Sc., 1950; postgrad. Univ. Coll. Hosp. Med. Sch., London, 1913-14; honoris causa, Charles U., Prague, 1948, Athens U., Greece, 1948, Salonica U., Greece, 1948, Brazil, 1960; D.Sc., U. So. Cal., 1953, U. Montreal, 1960; LL.D., St. Johns U., 1961, U. Mass., 1962; Litt. D., Ithaca Coll., 1962, Jagellonian U. (Poland), 1964, Boston U., 1964; m. Ina Reid, June 28, 1924; children—Penelope Dudley, Alexander Warren. Intern Mass. Gen. Hosp., 1911-13; study abroad as Harvard traveling fellow, in london, 1913-14, in Vienna, 1928-29; resident in medicine, Mass. Gen. Hosp., 1914-17, 19-20; asst. to physician to cons. medicine, Mass. Gen. Hosp., after 1920; teaching fellow to clin. prof. medicine Harvard Med. Sch., after 1914; engaged in research, practice, and teaching, especially in the field of heart disease; vis. lectr. Australia, 1958, South Africa, 1959. Served as med. officer Base Hosp., No. 22, B.E.F., France, 1916, with A.E.F., France, 1917-19; med. officer A.R.C., Greece, 1919; honored by Greek decorations, 1919; chmn. Am. Med. teaching mission to Czechoslovakia, 1946; honored by Czech. and Cuban decorations; decorated Legion d'Honneur; Order of Lion (Finland); Freedon Medal, U.S.A., 1964; also recipient Lasker award for distinguised achievement in field of cardiovascular diseases; Herrick award, 1973; chmn. Am. Med. Teaching Mission to Greece and Italy, 1948; mission to Pakistan, India, Israel, and Greece, 1952, USSR, 1956. Chmn. com. cardiovascular disease NRC, 1940-46. Exec. dir. Nat. Advisory Heart Council, 1948-56. Mem. Am. Acad. Arts and Scis., A.M.A., (distinguised service medal, 1952), Am. Heart Assn. (past pres.), Royal Soc. Medicine (England), Royal College of Physicians (London, Ireland), Internat. Soc. Cardiology (past pres.; pres. found. 1957), Nat. Acad. Medicine of France, Cardiac Soc. of Great Britain and Ireland, also cardiol. socs. of France, Mexico, Czechoslovakia, Brazil, Chile, South Africa, Australia, Italy, Belgium and Argentina, Soviet Acad. of Med. Scis., Assn. Am. Physicians, Am. Clin. and Climatol. Assn., Am. Soc. Clin. Investigation, Am. Coll. Physicians, N.E. Heart Assn., Mass. Med. Soc., Aesculapian Club, Alpha Omega Alpha. Clubs: Harvard (Boston); St. Botolph, Saturday (Boston). Author: Heart Disease, 1931, 4th edit., 1951; Heart Disease in General Practice, 1937; Electrocardiography in Practice (with Ashton Graybiel), 3d edit., 1952; Coronary Heart Disease in Young Adults (with Menard Gertler), 1954; Clues in the Diagnosis and Treatment of Heart Disease, 1955; Fitness for the Whole Family (with Curtis Mitchell), 1964; Hearts: Their Long Follow-Up (with Helen Donovan), 1966; My Life and Medicine, 1971; (with Gertler) Coronary Heart Disease: A. Twenty-Five Year Study in Retrospect, 1976. Contbr. articles to jours. Home: Belmont, Mass. Died Oct. 31, 1973.

WHITE, S. ETELKA, educator; Dayton, O.; d. William Elmer and Alice Elizabeth (Saner) White; B.A., U. Toledo, 1928; M.A., U. Mich., 1949, postgrad. Inst. Confs. Aging, 1956-64. Tchr., Wernerts, Lucas County, 1928-30; intake and dist. Lucas County Relief Adminstrn., 1930-42; tchr. Willard (O.) Pub. Schs., 1942-43, Carleton (Mich.) Schs., 1943-46; tchr. counselor North Baltimore (O.) Schs., 1946-49; tchr. Swanton Twp., Lucas County, 1950-51; personnel dir. Goodwill Industries, Toledo, 1952-54; family visitor, counselor sr. citizens North Toledo Community House, 1954-64; tchr., St. Johns, Toledo, 1965, St. Teresa, 1966-67, St. James, Toledo, 1967; substitute tchr. Toledo Bd. Edn., 1968; acting dir. North Toledo Community House, 1959; directress Federated Sr. Citizen's Chorus, 1959-71; exec. bd. Fedn. Toledo Sr. Citizen Clubs, 1967-73. Counselor, Jr. Red Cross, 1965. Mem. Nat. Assn. Social Work, Adult Edn. Assn., Speech Assn. Am., Sr. Citizens Am., Am. Assn. U. Women, Nat. Bus. and Profl. Women. Author, poet. Home: Toledo, O. Died Aug. 21, 1973; buried Toledo Memorial Park and Mausoleum.

WHITE, WENDELYN FLORENCE WHEELER, (Mrs. Edwin Donnell White), med. editor, writer; b. Tyler, Tex., May 7, 1939; d. Ronald Wendell, Jr. and Mary Florence (Cogswell) W.; B.A. magna cum laude, Tex. Christian U., 1960, M.A., 1961; m. Edwin Donnell White, Sept. 1, 1962; 1 dau., Wendelyn Anne-Ingram. Instr. psychology U. Tex. at Arlington, 1961-62; research asst. psychollgy Tex. Christian U., 1961-62; asst. editor U. Tex. M.D. Anderson Hosp. and Tumor Inst., Houston, 1962-67, asso. editor, 1968-71; writer Cancer Bull, Houston, 1966-71, asso. editor, 1968-71; free lance med. writer, editor, 1971-73; cons. Med. Arts Pub. Found., Oncological Word Bank Div., 1968-71. Mem. Harris County Heritage Soc. (docent), Delta Gamma, Psi Chi, Alpha Chi. Mem. Disciples of Chirst (program chmn. jr. Matrons). Club: Houston College Women's Contbr. articles to profl. jours. Home: Houston, Tex., Died June 2, 1973.

WHITE, WILLIAM HENRY, JR., ret. prof. of law; b. Norfolk, Va., June 9, 1881; s. William Henry and Emma (Gray) W.; LL.B., Univ. of Va., 1905; B.A., S.J.D., National U., 1934; m. Mary Stamps Royster, Jan. 11, 1911; children—Mary (Mrs. W.G. Subling) (dec.), Emma (Mrs. Charles C. Hillyer), Frances Webb (Mrs. Laurence A. Sykes), Hilah (Mrs. Charles C. Craddock), William Henry 3. Admitted to Va. var, 1905; private practice of law, 1905-17; assistant counsel, law dept., U.S. Shipping Bd. Emergency Fleet Corp., later asst. gen. counsel and gen. counsel, 1917-19; private practice, Washington, D.C., 1919-36; professor law Univ. Va., 1936-51, acting dean, 1942-45, later prof. emeritus; dir. F. S. Royster Guane Co., Norfolk, Virginia, Peoples National Bank of Charl ottesville, Va., Jackson Park Realty Co., Monticello Hotel Co.; formerly secretary Electoral Bd. of Norfolk, Virginia. Trustee emeritus Woodberry Forest (Va.) Sch.; sec.-treas. Alumni Bd. Trustees of U. of Va. Endowment Fund. Mem. Am., Virginia bar assns., U.S. Maritime law Association, Delta Psi Alumni Assn. of University of Virginia (past pres.). Democrat. Clubs: Metropolitan (Washington); Farmington, Colonnade (U. of Va.); St. Anthony (New York). Home: Charlottesville, Va.†

WHITE, WILLIAM LINDSAY, newspaperman; b. Emporia, Kan., June 17, 1900; s. William Allen and Sallie (Lindsay) W.; student Kansas U., 1918-20; A.B., Harvard, 1924; m. Kathrine Klinkenberg, Apr. 29, 1931; 1 dau., Barbara. Reporter on Emporia Gazette, 1914, later circulation mgr., mng. editor, editorial writer, asso. editor pub., editor, 1944-73; staff Washington Post, 1935, Fortune Mag., 1937; war corr. for 40 Am. daily newspapers, also rep. CBS as European corr., 1939-40; Christmas, 1939, broadcast from Mannerheim Line in Finland; awarded first prize by Nat. Headliners Club as year's best European broadcast; went to England on one of 50 former Am. destroyers to represent North Am. Newspaper Alliance and Reader's Digest in London winter of 1940-41; becam roving editor The Reader's Digest, 1942. Chmn. Rep. County Com., Lyon County, 1933-34; mem. Kansas State Legislature, 1931-32. Dir. Am. Friends of Middle East, Am. Com. for Liberation, Am. Assn. Indian Affairs, Overseer Harvard, 1950-56. Fellow Am. Numis. Soc.; mem. A.C.L.U. (dir.), Theodore Roosevelt Meml. Assn. (dir.), Freedom House (dir.), Am. Soc. of Newspaper Editors, Nat. Assn. Newspaper Editors, Internat. Press Inst., Inter-Am. Press Inst. Conglist. Clubs: Century Club, Harvard Club, Overseas Press Club, Coffee House (N.Y.C.); National Press (Washington). Author: What People Said (novel), 1938; co-author Zero Hour (fgn. affiars), 1940; author Journey for Margaret (war-time travel), 1941; They Were Expendable, 1942; Queens Die Proudly, 1943; Report on the Russians, 1945; Report of the Germans, 1947; Lost Boundaries, 1948; Land of Milk and Honey, 1949; Bernard Baruch, 1951; Back Down The Ridge, 1953; The Captives of Korea, 1957; The Little Toy Dog, 1962; Report on the Asians, 1969. Contbr. to numerous popular mags. Home: New York City, N.Y., Died July 26, 1973.

WHITE, WILSON HENRY STOUT, educator; b. Lewis County, W.Va., Dec. 1, 1881; s. Remington Breckenridge and Malinda Ellen (Knight) W.;grad. Glenville (W.Va.) Normal Sch.,1904; A.B., W.Va. Univ., 1912, A.M., 1921; studied Johns Hopkins U.; Ped.D., from Salem (W.Va.) College, 1933; m. Grace Eliza Yoke, Aug. 22, 1908; children—Dorothy Jo. Wilson Henry Stout, James Solomon (killed in the line of dity, France, June 22, 1914), Helinda Elizabeth, Patricia Grace. Principal Cowen (W.Va.) High Sch., 1908-09, supt. schs., Kingwood, 1910-11; supt. Piedmont district and city schools, 1913-18; superintendent schools, Logan City, 1918-19; pres. Shepherd College, 1920-27, president emeritus, from July 1947. Alderman on Shepherdstown (West Virginia) City Council; mem. Jefferson County Relief Adminstration; chairman W.Va. Ednl. Assn. (pres. 1927), Am. Assn. Teachers' Colleges, S.A.R., Pi Kappa Alpha, Kappa Delta Pi, Alpha Psi Omega, Phi Beta Kappa. Chmn. Eastern Panhandle of W.Va. Bicentennial Commn. for Celebration of 200th Anniversary of Birth of George Washington. Democrat. Methodist. Mason (K.T., 32°, K.C.C.H.); grand master Grand Lodge A. F. and A.M. of W.Va., 1936; grand sec. R.A.M. from 1916; Odd Fellow, Kiwanian (gov. W.Va. Dist. 1930). Home: Shepherdstown, W.Va.†

WHITEHEAD, ASA CARTER lawyer, judge; b. Lynchburg, Va., Apr. 15, 1904; s. Thomas and Sally Oliver (Carter) W.; student Roanoke (Va.) Coll., 1922-24, law sch. U. Va., 1925, 1930; m. Charlotte Klocke, Feb. 23, 1935; children—Asa Carter, Robert, Nell. Tchr. Pittsylvania Co., Va., 1925; prin. Brookneal High Sch., 1926-29; admitted to Va. bar, 1930, Supreme Ct. Va. 1934, U.S. Dist. Ct., 1937, Circuit Ct. Appeals, 1937; mem. Whitehead & Whitehead, Amherst, 1930-33, Blackwell, Ozlin & Whitehead, Kenbridge, 1933-40; apptd. spl. asst. U.S. atty., Eastern Dist. Va., 1942-51, U.S. atty., 1951-53; mem. Richard, Moncure & Whitehead, and predecessor firm, from 1953. Mem. C. of C. (past pres.), Am., Fed., Va., Alexandria bar assns. Democrat. Methodist. Mason. Clubs: Young Democrats (past pres. Lun engurg Co.), Alexandria, Kiwanis. Home: Alexandria, Va., Died Feb. 20, 1976.

WHITEHEAD, HAROLD, author; b. Birmingham, Eng., Jan. 10, 1880; s. Joseph Frederick and Caroline Mary W.; ed. Birmingham Coll. (non-grad.); B.A. from Boston University in 1922; m. Muriel Parker, of Birmingham, June 27, 1904; 1 dau., Lona May. Came to United States, 1907; sales agent, later business consultant; prof. and head dept. of sales relations, Coll. of Business Adminstration, Boston U., many yrs. from 1916, also vocation counsellor at the College and adviser on sales relations courses; later head of Harold Whitehead & Staff, Ltd., market research and business management, London, Eng. Mem. English-Speaking Union. Episcopalian. Clubs: Royal Automobile, Ranelagh (London). Author: Bond Salesmanship, 1915; Rexall Course in Drug Merchandising, 1915; Principles of Salesmanship, 1916 (revised 1923); Dawson Black—Retail Merchant, 1917; Bruno Duke, Solver of Business Problems, 1918; The Business Career of Peter Flint, 1919; Your Job, 1920; How to Run a Store, 1921; J. C. Penney Business Training Course, 1921; Common Sense in Business, 1922; The Business of Selling, 1923; A Simple Explanation of the Constitution of the United States, 1923; Problems of the Executive, 1927; Adminstration of Marketing and Selling. Home: Working, Surrey, England.†

WHITING, ALMON CLARK, architect and artist; b. at Worcester, Mass., Mar. 5, 1878; s. of M. Albert and Samanthy (Greene) W.; studied at Mass. Normal Art Sch., Boston; Académie Julien. Paris, under Constant and Laurens; pupil of Whistler, Paris. Mem. Am. Art Assn., Paris; dir. 1901-03, Toledo Museum of Art. Mural Decoration: "The Goose Girl," residence of W. W. Windle, Millbury, Mass. Mem. Commn. for Relief in Belgium during World War. Mem. Nat. Geographic Soc. Club: Salmagundi Address: New York City, N.Y.†

WHITING, EDWARD CLARK, landscape architect; b. Bklyn., Aug. 8, 1881; s. Edward May and Sue (Thayer) W.; student Brwone & Nichols Sch., 1897-99; A.B., Harvard, 1903, grad. study landscape architecture, 1904-05; m. Winifred Hanus, Sept. 29, 1906; 1 dau., Charlotte (wife of Dr. William Page Reed). With Olmsted Bros., from 1905, 1950; partner, 1920-50, sr. partner, from 150; works include Fine Arts Garden at Cleve. Mus. Art, Phillips Andover Acad., grad. sch. bus. adminstrn. Harvard, Rock Creek Park in Md. and Washington, D.C., Oyster Harbors on Cape Cod and Khakum Wood in Greenwich, Conn., residential subdivs., Am. Cemetery, ambridge, Eng. Dir. Hubbard Trust, Inc., res.,rom 1954; mem. overseers com. to visit Grad. Sch. Design, Harvard. Served with camp planning sect. constrn. div. U.S. Army, 1918. Fellow Am. Soc.

Landscape Architects; mem. Boston Soc. Landscape Architects (past pres.), Mass. Hort. Soc., Greater Boston C. of C. Republican. Unitarian. Clubs: Harvard (N.Y.C.); Harvard Faculty (Cambridge, Mass.). Contbr. profl. jours. Home: Cambridge, Mass.†

WHITING, LAWRENCE HARLEY, banker, industrialist, mil. historian; b. Plattsmouth, Neb., Jan. 29, 1890; s. Harley Edwin and Ada Augusta (Simpson) W.; U. Chgo., 1918; m. Eleanor Robinson Countiss, Apr. 30, 1925 (dec. 1931); children—Lawrence Harley, Barbar Eleanor (Mrs. W. Ashton Lee). With A. B. Leach & Co., investment bankers, 1915-21; founder, with father and brother, 1921, Whiting & Co., investment bankers, Chgo., pres., from 1921; founder Boulevard Bridge Bank (now Nat. Boulevard Bank), 1921, pres., 1921-32; founder Am. Furniture Mart Corp., 1923, chmn., pres., vice chmn. bd. founder Indiana Limestone Company. 1926. chmn., 1926-32; chmn. exec. com. Forman Realty Corp.; dir. Acme Steel Co., 333 N. Michigan Av. Bldg., Bismarck Hotel Corp., Am. Publs., Inc. (all Chgo.) Trustee Passavant Meml. Hosp., Chgo. Latin Sch. Found; mem. citizens bd. U. Chgo.; chmn. exec. com. Northwestern Mil. and Naval Academy. Served as pvt. O.T.C., 1917; commd. capt. cav., 1917; lt. col., engrs. (Res.), 1919; col., 1941; brig. gen. U.S. Army Res., from 1949; assigned div. personnel officer 86th Div. to assist in installation army personnel system (pioneer active div. personnel system in U.S. Army), also mem. div. hdqrs. staff, 1917; assigned as chief Classification of Personnel System, U.S. Army, and detailed to Adj. Gen.'s Dept., Washington; chief personnel officer AEF, G.H.Q., France, and mem. comdg. gen.'s G.H.Q. staff, 1918; exec. officer finance bur. A.E.F. Peace Conf., Paris, 1918; spl. asst. to U.S. commr. finance in Europe, Am. Mission to Negotiate Peace, also Am. mem. Allied Exchange Commn. (banking and exchange operations in Europe), Peace Conf., 1919; mem. adv. bus. council to sec. of war until 1939; spl. asst. and adviser in matters relating to army personnel and pay system to adj. gen. of army, 1939; expert cons. to sec. of war, 1941-47; mem. adv. com. on mil. service pay Office Sec. Def., 1947-49; comdg. gen. 5500th Logistical Div. (Tng.). 5th Army, U.S. Army. 1949. Recipient distinguished alumni citation U. Chgo., 1944, certificate of appreciation Nat. Mil. Establishment. Mem. Paris caucus, 1919, and one of founders of Am. Legion. Mem. Inst. Am. Strategy, American Mil. Inst., Soc. Colonial Wars, several hist. socs., Phi Kappa Psi. Republican. Episcopalian. Clubs: Racquet. Casino (Chgo.); Lake Geneva (Wis.) Country. Lake Geneva Yacht; Army and Navy (Washington). Home: Chicago Ill. Died Sept. 9, 1974.

WHITING, PERCY HOLLISTER, ednl. adminstr.; b. Great Barrington, Mass., Apr. 10, 1880; s. John Fred and Annie Hitchcock (Hollister) W.; student Harvard, 1898-99, Vanderbilt U., 1900-02; m. Elise Warren Polk, Nov. 27, 1909; children—Percy Hollister, Dorothy Polk (Mrs. T. G. owland); m. 2d Genevieve Celeste Bearmore, Oct. 19, 1946. Editor sports pages Nashville News, Memphis News-Scimitar and Atlanta Georgian, 1902-13; advt. mgr. Comfort, Augusta, Me., 1913-18; mgr. securities dept. Central Maine Power Co., 1918-23; gen. retail sales mgr. securities dept., Henry L. Doherty & Co., 1923-27; pres. P. H. Whiting & Co., Inc., 1927-32; v.p. W. R. Bull & Co., Inc., 1933-37; with Dale Carnegie Inst., N.Y. City, from 1937, mng. dir., 1943-52; later mng. dir Dale Carnegie Sales Courses. Mem. Sigma Chi Club: Sales Executive (charter mem., N.Y.C.). Author: How to Sell Securities, 1918; Manual for Sales Managers, 1924; The Five Great Rules of Selling, 1946; How to Speak and Write with Humor; also articles in various trade mags. Home: Chappaqua, N.Y.†

WHITLEY, MARY THEODORA, author, educator; b. London, Eng., Oct. 4, 1878; d. Thomas and Emma Bradley (Rooke) Whitley; came to U.S., 1901, naturalized citizen, 1922; B.S., Teachers Coll. (Columbia), 1905, M.A., 1906, Ph.D., 1911. Asst. in psychology, 1908-09, lecturer in psychology, 1909-11, instr., 1911-14, asst. prof. edn., 1914-30, asso. prof., 1930-43, ret., 1943. Teachers Coll., Columbia. Fellow A.A.A.S.; mem. Am. Psychol. Assn., Child Study Assn. America. Republican. Baptist. Club: Faculty (Columbia U.); Author: Psychology of Childhood (Norsworthy and Whitley), 1933; A Study of the Little Child, 1921; A Study of the Primary Child, 1922; A Study of the Junior Child, 1923; Boys and Girls in Other Lands, and Manual, 1925. Home: Yonkers, N.Y.†

WHITLOCK, DOUGLAS, lawyer; b. Terre Haute, Oct. 3, 1904; s. Charles Chester and Birdella (Smith) W.; B.S., Ind. U., 1926, LL.B., 1928; m. Mary Ellen Jenkins, June 18, 1929; children—Douglas II, Marilyn (Mrs. Robert Long), Sandra (Mrs. Theodore G. Dirscoll, Jr.). Admitted to Ind. bar, 1929, D.C. bar, 1929, also U.S. Supreme Ct.; asso. Sanders, Childs, Bobb & Wescott, 1929-36; partner Sanders, Gravelle, Whitlock & Howrey, 1936-53, Sanders, Gravelle, Whitlock & Markey, 1953-55, Gravelle, Whitlock, Howrey and Markey, Washington, 1955-56, then Whitlock, Markey & Tait; partner firm Reed, Smith, Shaw & McClay, Washington. Chmn. Young Republicans Ind., 1928-30; pres. Young Rep. Nat. Fedn., 1930-32; exec. dir. Eisenhower Campaign Tour Com., 1952, 56, also Goldwater Campaign Tour Com. Dir. Devereux Found., 1964-70. Decorated Knight comdr. Liberia; Order of Merit (Haiti). Mem. Structural Clay Products, Inst., U.S. C. of C., Brick Inst. Am., Producers Council (pres. 1943-45; dir.), Bldg. Products Inst. (chmn.), Am., D.C. bar assns., Ind. Soc. Washington, Alpha Tau Omega, Gamma Eta Gamma. Episcopalian. (chancellor Diocese of Washington) Home: Washington, D.C., Died May 16, 1973; buried Rock Creek Cemetery, Washington, D.C.

WHITLOCK, PAUL CAMERON, lawyer; b. Richmond County, N.C., Jan. 16, 1878; s. Eli Davidson and Caroline (Cameron) W.; prep. edn., Rockingham (N.C.) Acad. and Davis Mil. Sch., Winston-Salem, N.C.; B.S., U. of N.C., 1898; m. Maude Crosland, June 5, 1901; children—Maude (dec.), Virginia LeGrand (Mrs. James Orr Cobb), Paul Cameron, Elizabeth Caroline (Mrs. Douglas Duff Connah), Neill. Admitted to North Carolina bar 1899, and began practice at Rockingham; moved to Charlotte, N.C., 1906; mem. firm Whitlock, Dockery, Ruff & Perry; trust officer Am. Trust Co., 1911-22, dir., corp. counsel, Charlotte, 1911. Pres. N.C. Orthopedic Hosp., GAstonia, N.C., 1923-41. Pres. Charlotte C. of C., 1918; mem. American, N.C. and Mecklenburg County bar assns. Democrat. Methodist. Home: Charlotte, N.C.†

WHITMAN, HOWARD, journalist; b. Cleve., May 6, 1914; s. Lawrence Alvin and Bettie (Goldman) W.; A.B. magna cum laude, Western Res. U., 1935; m. Suzanne Marcia Desberg, Mar. 9, 1938; children—Constance Marcia, Kenneth Jay. Mem. staff N.Y. Herald Tribune, Paris edit., 1936, London Daily Express, 1936-37, N.Y. Daily News, 1937-45; war corr. ETO, World War II; specialist on articles on social problems, from 1945; pres. Howard Whitman Prodns., nat. newspaper syndicate, from 1970. Mem. commn. mental health edn. Internat. Congress on Mental Health, 1948; lectr. sex. edn., mental health, social problems; pres. Grand Bahama Mental Health Assn., 1968-69. Joint winner Sigma Delta Chi profl. journalism award for pub. service for series articles in Collier's, Terror In Our Cities, 1949-50; winner Freedoms Found. award for article The Truth About Patriotism, 1952, also for TV series A Time to Remember, 1956, for TV program The American Flag, 1971, Blakeslee award Am. Heart Assn., 1956; TV award Nat. Assn. Mental Health, 1957; winner 1st award Ohio State U. Inst. for Radio and TV for program Nervous Tension, 1961. Clubs: Saugatuck Harbor Yacht (commodore 1965); Palm Beach Golf. Author: Let's Tell The Truth About Sex, 1948; Terror in the Streets, 1951; A Reporter in Search of God, 1953; Success Is Within You, 1956; A Brighter Later Life, 1961; The Sex Age, 1962; syndicated news series, Vandalism, 1953, The Divorce Dilemma, 1954; Parenthood Without Hokum, 1955; Keeping Our Sanity, 1957; Our Moral Crisis, 1958; Our Drinking Habits, 1958; New Frontiers in Living, 1959; Your Middle Years, 1961; Making Marriage More Rewarding, 1962; Don't Be Nervous, 1963; The American Way of Love, 1964; Our Family Crisis, 1968; The Sleeping Pill Nightmare, 1971; Reducing Your Chances of a Heart Attack, 1972. Appeared NBC-TV series Howard Whitman Talks, 1953; News of Medicine and Health, NBC-TV, 1956; roving editor NBC-TV Home Show, 1957; Dumont TV series Probe, 1957-58; Collier's series The Struggle for our Children's Minds, 1954; Better Home and Gardens series America's Moral Crisis, 1957. Producer nat. TV series Medical Special Events, 1958-61; News of Your Life, NBC-TV, 1962-64; NBC radio Emphasis, 1964-66; NBC Monitor, 1967-70; A Better Life from Fifty On, radio syndication, 1968-69; News About You, TV syndication, 1970. Columnist Palm Beach Life, 1972; author travel articles. Address: Palm Beach Fla. Died Jan. 29, 1975.

WHITMAN, STEPHEN F(RENCH), author; b. Phila., Pa., Jan. 10, 1880; s. Rowland and Jeannette (Tresize) W.; prep. edn., Exeter and Lawrenceville schs.; A.B., Princeton, 1901; unmarried. Spl. writer New York Evening Sun, 1901-03; writer short stories, screen plays and novels, from 1903. Served in U.S.N.R.F., World War. Mem. various assns. and clubs. Address: New York City, N.Y.†

WHITMAN, WALTER GORDON, govt. ofcl.; b. Winthrop, Mass., Nov. 30, 1895; s. John Turner and Ida May (Alexander) W.; B.S., Mass. Inst. Tech., 1917, M.S., 1920; D.Sc. (hon.), Northeastern U., 1954, Centre Coll., 1956, U. Pa., 1956; m. Martha Thurmond Key, June 7, 1921; children—Elizabeth Ann, John Turner, 2d, William Key. Engaged as asst. in chem. engring., Mass. Inst. Tech., 1917-18, instr., 1918-20, asst. prof., 1920-25, dir. of station, Sch. of Chem. Engring. Practice, 1920-22, asst. dir. Research Lab. Applied Chemistry, 1922-25; asst. dir. research Standard Oil Co. of Ind., 1925-29, asso. dir. research, 1929-34; prof., head dept. chem. engring., Mass. Inst. Technology, 1934-60; science adviser to Sec. of State from 1960; National Advisory Commn. for Aeronautics (chmn. sub. com. on Aircraft Fuels and Lubricants, 1940-45; dir. Basic Chems. Div. War Prodn. Bd.; dir. Lexington Project, A.E.C., 1948, gen. adv. com., 1950-56; conf. sec.-gen. UN Conf. on peaceful use of atomic energy, 1955. Chmn. research and development bd., Dept. Defense, 1951-53; mem. Nat. Adv. Com. for Aero., 1951-53. Mem. American Institute Chemical Engineers (president 1956), American Chemical Society, American Acad. Arts and Sci., Am. Philos. Soc., Tau Beta Pi, Sigma Xi. Unitarian. Clubs: Chemists (N.Y.C.); Cosmos (Washington), Social Circle (Concord). Home: Washington DC. Died Apr. 6, 1974.

WHITMAN, WILLIAM R., surgeon; b. 1876; A.B., Roanoke Coll., 1896; M.D., Columbia, 1901. Chief Surgeon Norfolk & Western Ry.; surgeon Lewis-Gale Hosp. Fellow Am. Coll. Surgeons; member Am. Med. Assn. Address: Roanoke, Va.*†

WHITNEY, DAVID DAY, prof. zoology; b. Brookfield, Vt., Aug. 6, 1878; s. Cryus Hall and Luthera Samantah (Sprague) W.; A.B., Wesleyan U., Conn., 1904; A.M., Columbia, 1906, Ph.D., 1909; m. Kathryn Stillman Bunce, June 17, 1914; 1 dau., Elizabeth Instr. in zoology, Wesleyan U., 1908-11, asso. prof., 1911-16; prof. zoology, U. of Neb., 1916-48, chmn. dept., 1934-46. Spl. work in regulation of sex in rotifers and heredity in man. Fellow A.A.A.S.; mem. Am. Soc. Zoologists, Am. Soc. Naists, Corp. Marine Biol. Lab. (Woods Hole, Mass.), Am. Genetic Assn., Delta Tau Delta, Sigma Xi. Republican. Methodist. Home: Lincoln, Neb.†

WHITNEY, JASON F(RANKLIN); b. Westminster, Mass., Sept. 3, 1878; s. Aaron F. and Almira S. (Gleason) W.; ed. pub. schs., Mass.; m. June Bandler, July 1, 1921; children—Jason F., June B., II. Asst. to. pres. Phenix Cheese Corp., 1912-24, pres., 1924-28; pres. Kraft-Phenix Cheese Corp., 1928-31; chmn. Blue Moon Cheese Products Inc., Blue Moon Foods, Inc. Pres. Chicago City Opera Co. 1936-39. Mason (K.T.). Home: Chicago, Ill.†

WHITNEY, LEON FRADLEY, veterinarian, biologist; b. Bklyn., Mar. 29, 1894; s. Leon Augustine and Geneva (Fradley) W.; B.S., Mass. Agrl. Coll., 1916; student Yale, 1937-38; D.V.M., Ala. Poly. Inst., 1940; m. Katharine Carroll Sackett, Feb. 12, 1916; children—Julia Mead, George Dana, Exec. sec. Am. Eugenics Soc., 1924-34; clin. instr. pathology Yale Sch. Medicine, 1946-60. Mem. Am. Genetics Assn., Eugenics Research Assn. Am. Soc. Mammalogists, Am. Psychol. Assn., A.A.A.S., Am. Vet. Med. Assn., Kappa Sigma, Phi Kappa Phi (hon.), Omega Tau Sigma. Republican. Unitarian. Kiwanian. Author: (with Ellsworth Huntington) The Builders of America (an intensive study of the persons named in Who's Who in America, Vol. 14, 1926-27), 1927; The Basis of Breeding, 1928; Pigeon City (for boys), 1931; The Partner Series (boys' books), 1932; Sex and Birth Control, 1933; The Case for Sterilization, 1934 (pub. Eng. 1935); How to Breed Dogs, 1937; Bloodhounds and How to Train Them, 1937; Feeding Our Dogs, 1949; The Complete Book of Home Pet Care, 1950; That Useless Hound (juvenile), 1950; The Raccoon, 1952; The Coon Hunter's Handbook, 1952; That's My Dog (juvenile), 1952; All About Guppies, 1952; The Complete Book of Dog Care, 1953; The Distemper Complex, 1953; The Complete Book of Cat Care, 1953; First Aid For Pets, 1954; Your Puppy, 1955; This is the Cocker Spaniel, 1956; Dollars in Dogs, 1956; The Complete Guide to Tropical Fishes, 1957; The Truth about Dogs, 1959; Wonders of the Dog World, 1959; Birth Control Today, 1960; Keep Your Pigeons Flying, 1960; Breed Your Dog, 1960; Feed Your Dog, 1960; Groom Your Dog, 1960; The Natural Method of Dog Training, 1965; The Farm Veterinarian, 1964; Dog Psychology, 1964; People and Pets, 1967; Training You to Train Your Cat, 1968; How to Select, Train and Breed Your Dog, 1968; The Basis of Breeding Racing Pigeons, 1968; Pets, 1971; Animal Doctor, 1973; also scientific papers and articles, Original studies in human genetics, populations problems, also genetic characteristics and metal aptitudes in dogs; mating cycle in dogs; worked with cancer in dogs; studied new methods of eradication of canine parasites; discovered new canine disease (Housedog disease); performed successful ovarian transplantation in dogs; founder Leon F. Whitney collection of dogs, Peabody Museum, Yale; discovered fetal resorptive qualities of yeast extract, Malucidin. Home: Orange Conn. Died Apr. 11, 1973.

WHITNEY, RICHARD, pres. N.Y. Stock Exchange; b. Beverly, Mass., Aug. 1, 1888; s. George and Elizabeth W.; pre edn., Groton Sch., Mass.; A.B., Harvard, 1911; m. Gertrude Sheldon, May 27, 1916; children—Nancy, Alice. Head of Richard Whitney & Co., dealers in stocks and bonds. Mem. New York Stock Exchange (pres. 1930-35). Home: Far Hills N.J. Died Dec. 5, 1974.

WHITTAKER, CHARLES E(VANS), lawyer b. Troy, Kansas, February 22, 1901; son of Charles E. and Ida E. (Miller) W.; LL.B., U. Kansas City, 1924; m. Winifred R. Pugh, July 7, 1928; children—Charles Keith, Kent E., Gary T. Admitted to Mo. bar, 1923, practiced in Kansas City until 1954; judge U.S. Dist. Ct. for Western Dist. Mo., 1954-56, U.S. Ct. of Appeals for 8th Circuit, 1956-57; asso. justice U.S. Supreme Ct., 1957-62; dealer relations umpire Gen. Motors. Mem. Am., Mo. (pres. 1953-54), Kansas City bar assns., Lawyer Assn. Kansas City. Home: Shawnee Mission Kan. Died Nov. 26, 1973.

WHITTON, CHARLOTTE, mayor; b. Renfrew, Ont.; d. John and Elizabeth (Langin) Whitton; student Renfrew Collegiate Inst.; M.A., Queen's U., 1917, grad. pedagogy, 1918, LL.D. (hon.), 1941; D.C.L., U. King's Coll., Halifax, N.S., 1939, Acadia U., 1948; LL.D., U. Rochester, 1952. Asst. sec. Social Service Council Can.,

1918-22; pvt. sec. Minister Trade and Commerce, Ottawa, 1922-25; exec. dir. Canadian Welfare Council, 1925-42; dir. Alberta Welfare Study, 1947; columnist Ottawa Citizen, Thomson Dailies, Halifax Herald Chronicle, 1950; controller City of Ottawa, 1950, mayor, 1951-56, 60-64. Assessor Commn. on Child Protection, League of Nations, Geneva; del. Social Questions Commn. Decorated Comdr. Order Brit. Empire, 1934; awarded Jubilee medal, 1936, Coronation medal, 1937. Mem. Queen's U. Alumni Assn. (past pres.), Imperial Order Daughters Empire (nat. exec.). Mem. Church of Eng. (mem. council social service). Clubs: Canadian Women's Press, Themis (Montreal); Ladies (Toronto); Overseas (London). Author: A Hundred Years A-Fellin', 1942; The Dawn of Ampler Life, 1943. Contbr. articles profl. publs. Home: Ottawa Ont., Canada. Died Jan. 25, 1975.

WHOLBERG, GERALD WALTER, physician; b. Bklyn., Mar. 4, 1939; s. Joseph and Hedwig Wohlberg; M.D., Albert Einstein Coll. Medicine, 1964; m. Janet Wasserman, Mar. 27, 1966; children—Ilana Hilorie, Shira Lynn. Med. intern Jackson Meml. Hosp. U., Miami (Fla.), 1965; resident div. psychiatry Boston U., 1965-68, research tng. fellow in psychiatry, 1968-70, teaching asst. in psychiatry, 1967-68, instr. psychiatry, 1970-71, asst. prof., 1971-73; cons. neuropsychiatrist VA Hosp., Bedford, Mass., 1967-68, Bridgewater (Mass.) State Hosp., 1967-68; cons. alcoholic outpatient dept. New Eng. Hosp., Boston, 1967-68; sr. psychiatrist Boston State Hosp. Chmn. Middle East affairs com. New Eng. Jewish Community Council. Diplomate Am. Bd. Psychiatry and Neurology. Mem. A.M.A., Am. Psychiat. Assn., A.A.U.P., Am. Profs. for Peace in Middle East. Home: Wayland, Mass., Died Dec. 30, 1973; buried Natick, Mass.

WICKES, HARVEY RANDALL, mfg. exec.; b. Saginaw, Mich., Sept. 1, 1889; s. Harry Tuthill and Fanny (Hamilton) W.; A.B., U. Michigan, 1911; m. Ruth Brady, Feb. 15, 1915; 1 dau., Nancy Hamilton (Mrs. R. H. Blanford). Entire business career with Wickes Corp. and affiliated cos.; served as v.p. Wickes Boiler Co., pres. 1941-47, U.S. Graphite Co., 1930-47, Wickes Brothers, 1931-47, the three firms merged into Wickes Corp., Saginew, 1947, pres., 1947-64, chmn. bd. dirs., 1964-69, hon. chmn. bd., 1969-74; dir. Mich. Nat. Bank, Lobdell Emery Co. Mem. Am. Legion. Mason (Shriner), Elk. Address: Saginaw, Mich. Died Oct. 6, 1974; buried Forest Lawn Cemetery, Saginaw.

WICKLOW, NORMAN LOUIS, banker; b. Owatonna, Minn., Aug. 15, 1906; s. Fred William and Louise Wilhelmina (Jahreiss) W.; grad. high sch.; m. Harriette Leona Carter, Aug. 4, 1940. Wtih Nat. Farmers Bank, Owatonna, Minn., 1924-26, First Nat. Bank, Owatonna, 1926-35; ins. salesman Travelers Ins. Co., Owatonna, 1935-36; with Security Bank & Trust Co., Owatonna, 1936-73, trust officer, 1962-73, sr. v.p., 1969-73, also dir.; dir. Owatonna Elevator Co. (Minn.). Bd. dirs. Forest Hill Cemetery Assn., Owatonna, 1945-73, pres., 1955-73, sec., 1965-73; bd. dirs. Indsl. Devel. Corp., Owatonna. Served with AUS, 1943-45. Decorated Purple Heart with two oak leaf clusters. Named Boss of Year, Owatonna Jr. C. of C., 1970. Minn. Cemeterian of Year, Midwest Monument Dealers, 1968. Mem. Owatonna C. of C. (dir.), V.F.W., Am. Legion. Lutheran (pres. 1950). Mem. DeMolay. Rotarian. Home: Owatonna Minn. Died Apr. 1, 1973; buried Forest Hill Cemetery, Owatonna.

WICKWIRE, THEODORE HARRY, JR., mfr.; b. Cortland, N.Y., Apr. 6, 1879; s. Theldore H. and Emma V. (Woodmansee) W.; student State Normal Sch., Cortland, N.Y.; grad. Andover Acad., 1898; A.B., Yale, 1903; m. Sophie Brenner Hedge, Oct. 1, 1903; children—Theodore H., Hedge. Began with Wickwire Bros., Cortland, 1903, as chemist, later supt. open hearth, asst. treas.; moved to Buffalo, 1907; assisted in forming Wirkwire Steel Co. and was v.p. and treas., later merged with Clinton Wright Wire Co., which was merger of Clinton Wire Cloth Co., Wright Wire Co. and Morgan Spring Co. (all of Mass.) and Spencer Wire Co., forming Wickwire Spencer Steel Corp., of which was pres. until June 1925; pres. Weldwire Corp.; pres. Welded Fabrics Corp.; chmn. bd. Trent, Inc. Republican. Presbyn. Clubs: The Leash, Blooming Grove Hunting and Fishing, Yale Club: Racquet, Merion Cricket (Phila.). Home: Narbeth, Pa. Address: Philadelphia, Pa.†

WIDTMANN, ARTHUR ALBERT, risk mgmt. co. exec.; b. Chgo., Dec. 20, 1917; s. Max and Anna (Brey) W.; B.S. (with honors), Northwestern U., 1941; C.P.C.U., Am. Inst. Property and Liability Underwriters, 1968; Asso. in Risk Mgmt. certificate Ins. Inst. Am., 1969; postgrad. U. Wis., 1941-43, Marquette U., 1946; m. Mildred Louise Duderstadt, May 30, 1941; children—Mary Anne (Mrs. John R. Phillips), Judith Marie (Mrs. William J. Tetu), Christine Louise, Margaret Mary. Corporate risk mgr. A.O. Smith Corp., Milw., 1941-70; sr. cons. risk mgmt. Ebasco Services, Inc., Chgo., 1970-73, cons. risk mgmt. services The Wyatt Co., Chgo., 1973-74; conducted chairs risk mgmt. seminars Ins. Sch. Chgo., 1970-74, U. Wis., 1968-70. Served as officer USN, 1943-46. Mem. Soc. C.P.C.U.'s, Am. Soc. Ins. Mgmt. (regional v.p. 1962, nat. bd. dirs. 1960, pres. Wis. chpt. 1958-59), Milw. Ins. Buyers Inc. (chmn. 1956). Home: Glenview, Ill. Died Apr. 7, 1974; buried All Saints, Des Plaines, Ill.

WIEBOLDT, WERNER A., chmn. bd. Wieboldt Stores, Inc.; b. Feb. 26, 1884; s. William A. and Anna L. (Krueger) W.; grad. Lewis Institute, Chicago, 1902; LL.B., Northwestern U., 1908; m. Pearl O. Pomy, Mar. 25, 1909; children—William H., Werner A., Pearl Anne, Robert. With Wieboldt Stores, Inc. (department stores), Chicago, 1905-64, chmn. bd., 1932-64. Presbyterian. Clubs: Commercial, Exmoor Country; University (Chgo). Home: Lake Forest Ill. Died Nov. 29, 1973.

WIECK, FRED DERNBURG, editor; b. Berlin, Germany, Dec. 3, 1910; s. Otto August and Louise (Dernburg) W.; LL.B., U. Berlin, 1932; m. Teresa Reidy, Dec. 31, 1942; children—David, Peter. Came to U.S., 1935, naturalized, 1942. Asso. editor U. Chgo. Press, 1946-50; dir. U. Mich. Press, 1954-61; sr. editor Harper & Row, 1962-67; dir. U. Pa. Press, 1969-73. Office: Philadelphia Pa. Died Nov. 13, 1973.

WIEDMANN, FRANCIS EDWARD, physician; b. Phila., Nov. 22, 1925; s. John August and Marie Magdalen (Roppelt) W.; M.D., Jefferson Med. Coll., 1952; m. Bertha Helene Willis, Nov. 7, 1953; children—Francis Edward, Marie Elizabeth, Theresa Anne, Dennis John, John Paul. Rotating intern Nazareth Hosp., Phila., 1952-53; resident in clin. and anat. pathology Pa. Hosp., 1957-61; attending pathologist VA Hosp., Coatesville, Pa.; clin. asst. in ear, nose and throat Episcopal Hosp., Phila.; courtesy staff Jean's Hosp., Phila.; asso. pathologist, active staff No. div. Albert Einstein Med. Center; instr. pathology Temple U. Served with USNR, 1944-46. Francis E. Wiedmann Surg. Pathology Lab. at Albert Einstein Med. Center No. Div. dedicated and named in his honor, 1971. Diplomate Am. Bd. pathology. Mem. A.M.A., Coll. Am. Pathologists. Developer ethyl chloride freezing method of preserving and staining surg. slides. Home: Huntingdon Valley, Pa., Died Oct. 28, 1970; buried Holy Sepulchre Cemetery, Wyncote, Pa.

WIEGAND, ERNEST HERMAN, educator; b. Danville, Ill., July 10, 1886; s. Herman and Elise (Boettiger) W.; B.S., U. of Mo., 1914; m. Josephine Fritz, June 22, 1918; children—Robert Ernest, Jean Elise. Prodn. lemons, poultry, mfg. olive oil, National City Calif., 1914-17; agt. Bur. of Animal Industry, U.S. Dept. Agr., prodn. specialist Manhattan, Kan., 1917-19; mem. staff Ore. State Coll., Corvallis, since 1919, became prof. and head dept. food technology, 1919, food technologist in charge Agr. Expt. Sta. from 1919, later prof. emeritus; pvt. cons. food technologist; cons. Corn Industries Research Found., Washington, Ross Packing Co., Selah, Wash., Hudson House. Inc., Portland; technical consultant California Hawaiian Sugar Refining Corp., Ltd., San Francisco, 1931-32; member tech. adv. com. Western Regional Research Lab. Recipient Distinguished Service to Ore. Agrl. award, Ore. Farm Bur. Fedn., 1955. Fellow A.A.A.S.; mem. American Trade Association Executives. American Chemical Soc. (mem. exec. com. agrl. and food chemistry div.), Nat. Farm Chemurgic Council, Inst. Food Technologists, Northwest Cherry Briners Assn. (1st pres., sec. since 1936), Cherry Growers and Industries Found. (sec.-treas., trustee), Assos. Food and Container Inst. (instnl. mem.), Q.M. Food and Container Inst. for Armed Forces (liaison and adv. bd.), Produce Prepackaging Assn., C. of C. Sigma Xi, Phi Kappa Phi, Alpha Zeta, Gamma Sigma Delta. Clubs: Century, Faculty, Triad, Country, Republican. Authority in fields of canning, freezing and dehydration of fruits and vegetables. Developed recirculating dehydrator; also method of brining cherries used by U.S. barreling plants. Speaker tech. and profl. groups. Author numerous bulls. and articles on food mfr. in trade and sci. mags. Home: Corvallis, Ore. Died Apr. 30, 1973; buried Oaklawn Cemetery, Corvallis.

WIEMAN, HENRY NELSON, educator; b. Richhill, Mo., Aug. 19, 1884; s. William Henry and Alma (Morgan) W.; B.A., Park Coll., Parkville, Mo., 1907, D.D., 1929; student San Francisco Theol. Sem., 1907-10, U. Jena (Germany), U. Heidelberg (Germany), 1910-11; Ph.D., Harvard, 1917; Litt. D., Occidental Coll., 1930; D. Litt., Grinnell Coll., 1964; D.D., Meadville Theol. Sch., Chgo., 1966; L.H.D. So. Ill. U. 1966, Coll. Osteo. Medicine and Surgery, Des Moines, 1968; m. Anna M. Orr, Jan. 15, 1912 (dec. 1931); children—Florence Margaret, Nelson Orr, Marion Isabelle, Robert Morgan, Eleanor Brunhilde; m. 2d, Regina H. Westcott, 1932 (div. 1948); m. 3d, Laura Matlack, 1948. Prof. philosophy Occidental Coll., Los Angeles, 1917-27; prof. philosophy of religion U. Chgo. Div. Sch., 1927-47, emeritus; prof. So. Ill. U., 1956-66, prof. emeritus, 1966-75; prof. philosophy U. Ore., 1949-51; prof. philosophy U. Houston, 1951-53; lectr. McCormick Theol. Sem., 1926-27; Nathaniel William Taylor lectr. Yale, 1939; Mendenhall lectr. DePauw U., 1930; Swander lectr. Theol. Sem. Ref. Ch., 1930; Earl Found. lectr. Pacific Sch. Religion, 1932; Carew lectr. Harford Sem. Found., 1938; Ayer lectr. Colgate-Rochester Sem., 1947. Mem. Am. Philos. Assn., Am. Theol. Assn., Am. Assn. U. Profs. Unitarian. Club: Quadrangle. Author: Religious Experience and Scientific Method, 1st edit., 1926; Normative Psychology of Religion, 1st edit., 1935; Man's Ultimate Commitment, 1958; Source of Human Good, 1964. Contbr. to Contemporary Am. Theology, New Nat. Ency., Ency. Religion. Address: Grinnell, Ia. Died June 19, 1975.

WIEST, EDWARD, prof. economics; b. Citrus County, Fla., Apr. 28, 1878; Das. Daniel Clayton and Katherine (Snyder) W.; A.B., George Washington U., 1912; A.M., Columbia, 1913, Ph.D., 1916; m. Sidney Pierce Crews, Dec. 14, 1913; 1 dau., Marjorie Sidney. Teaching and in business until 1906; with U.S. Weather Bur., Washington, D.C., 1906-14; instr. economics, U. of Vt., 1915, asst. prof., 1916; prof. economics, U. of Ky., from 1918, also acting dean Grad. Sch., 1924, dean Coll. Commerce, 1925-48, emeritus, Chmn. Ky. Employment Com., 1930. Mem. Am. Econ. Assn., Southen Econ. Assn., Acad. Polit. Science, Ky. Ednl. Assn., Delta Sigma Pi, Phi Sigma Kappa. Presbyterian. Author: The Butter Industry in the United States, 1916; Agricultural Organization in the United States, 1923. Contbr. to Ency. of the Social Sciences and Dictionary of Am. Biography. Home: Lexington, Ky.†

WIESTLING, HELEN MERWIN, physician; b. Wheeling, W.Va., 1889; M.D., Boston U., 1926. Intern, Mass. Meml. Hosp., Boston, 1926-28; resident Worchester (Mass.) Hosp. for Contagious Disease, 1928-36; resident physician Reformatory for Women, Framingham, Mass., 1936-44; ward physician Northampton (Mass.) State Hosp., 1936-44, dir. outpatient clinic, 1944-49; psychiatrist, sr. med. officer VA Clinic, Wheeling, 1949-69. Diplomate Am. Bd. Psychiatry and Neurology, Nat. Bd. Med. Examiners. Mem. A.M.A., Am. Psychiat. Assn. Home: Wheeling, W.Va. Died Apr. 28, 1969.

WILCOX, CARL C(LIFFORD), prof., engr.; b. Busti, N.Y., May 24, 1880; s. Abram F. and Sally M. (Meade) W.; M.E., Ohio State U., 1903, M.E. in Elec. Engring., 1907; m. Hazel E. Marsh, Aug. 6, 1909; 1 dau., Carl Carol L. Apprentice engr., Columbus, O., Ry. and Light Co., 1902-03; with Bartlett Illuminating Co., Saginaw, Mich., 1903-05, Tenn. Coal, Iron R.R. Co., Birmingham, Ala., 1905-06; fellow in mech. engring., Ohio State U., 1907; asst. in mech. engring., Mich. Agrl. Coll., Lansing, 1907-10; asst. cons. engr., Hodenpyle Hardy and Co., Inc., N.Y., in charge of construction and operation of electric and heating plants-Peoria, DeKalb, Sycamore, Springfield, Ill., Springfield, O., Johnstown, Pa. Evansville, Ind., Cadillac, Mich., etc., 1910-19; chief engr., Gen. Motors Bldg. Corp., 1919-22; supt. power div., Studebaker Corp., South Bend, Ind., 1922-37; pvt. cons. practice, from 1937; head dept. mech. engring., Notre Dame U., 1938-50 (on leave on govt. work in Can., 1943; chief engr. "Canal" project, 1942-44), also spl. consultant Sverdrup & Parcel, St. Louis, Mo., 1946-47. Mem. (life) American Soc. M.E., Pi Tau Sigma. Republican. Mason. Club: St.Joseph Valley Engrs. Address: South Bend, Bend, Ind.†

WILCOX, ELGIN ROSCOE, univ. prof.; b. Seattle Wash., Mar. 15, 1892; s. Elgin and Lenora Jane (Stookey) W.; B.S., U. of Washington, 1915, Metall. Engr., 1919; m. Ruth Begg, May 6, 1916; children—Ruth (Mrs. John Ellis Mylroie), Rosalea (Mrs. Stanley Donald Vanek). With engr. dept., Alaska Gold, Juneau, Alaska, summers 1913-14; mining engr., Overlook Mining and Development Co., Idaho, 1915; millman, Butte-Superior Mining Co., Butte Mont., 1916; supt., Big Thing Mine, Carcross, Yukon Territory, Can., 1917; assayer and engr., Venus Mine, Carcross, 1918; supt. and engr., Northern Copper Co., Wrangell, Alaska, 1919-20; instr. civil engring., Coll. of Engring., U. of Wash., 1921-24, asst. prof., 1924-28, asso. prof. gen. engring., 1928-36, head of dept., 1924-59, prof., from 1936; instr., American Univ. Shrivenham, England, 1945-46. Fellow U.S. Bureau of Mines, 1918-19. Mem. Am. Inst. Mining and Metall. Engrs., Am. Soc. Engring. Edn., Sigma Xi, Tau Beta Pi, Alpha Delta Phi. Home: Seattle Wash. Died May 14, 1974.

WILCOX, GRAFTON STILES, newspaperman; b. Griggsville, Ill., Aug. 2, 1879; s. Seth Morrell and Cornelia C. (Cokerly) W.; ed. pub. schs.; m. Carey C. Shipley, Jan. 1910. Reporter and city editor Daily Sun, Waukegan, Ill., 1898-99; successively reporter Chicago Chronicle, Chicago Record Herald, Associated Press (Chicago) to 1909, Associated Press (Washington, D.C.), and chief of Capitol staff same, 1910-17; with Washington Bur., Chicago Tribune, 1917-24, Washington Bur., New York Herald Tribune, 1924-26; asst. mng. editor New York Herald Tribune, 1926-31, mng. editor Oct. 1931-Feb. 1941. Republican. Episcopalian. Clubs: Gridiron, Nat. Press (ex-pres.) Home: Mt. Vernon, N.Y.†

WILCOX, ROY C., b. Meriden, Conn., Dec. 24, 1891; s. George Horace and Nettie Barker (Curtis) W.; ed. pub. schs., Meriden, Hotchkiss Sch., Yale; m. Katherine Smith, Oct. 23, 1920; 1 dau., Charlotte Smith. With Internat. Silver Co. from 1913, sucessively as sales helper, 1913-14, workman bench order chaser, 1914-15, salesman, 1915-16, hotel dept., 1916-17, asst. mgr., 1919-20, mgr., 1920-28, dir. from 1921, sec., 1928-35, exec. v.p., 1935-57; dir. Meriden br. Connecticut Bank and Trust Co., Waterbury Buckle Co., Aetna Life Ins. Co., Aetna Casualty & Surety Co., Underwood Corp. Dir. Meriden Hosp.; trustee Meriden Y.M.C.A., First

Congl. Ch., Meriden. Mem. Meriden City Council and Bd. Aldermen, 1922-26. Mem. Conn. Senate, 1927 and 1929, pres. protem. 1929; treas. State of Conn., 1931-32; lt. gov. State of Conn., 1933-34. Served with French Army, World War I. Chevalier French Legion of Honor, Croix du Guerre. Mem. Am. Legion, Veterans Fgn. Wars. Republican. Clubs: Metabetchouan, Clove Valley Rod and Gun, Hammonassett, Shuttle Meadow; The Links (N.Y.); Boone and Crockett, Moose, Eagle, Elk, Mason (32°). Home: Meriden, Conn. Died Mar. 30, 1975.

WILCOX, WAYNE AYRES, govt. ofcl.; b. Pendleton, Ind., July 13, 1932; s. John Milo and Magdalen (Curran) W.; B.S., Purdue U., 1954; M.A., Columbia, 1958, Ph.D., 1960; m. Ouida Neill, July 21, 1956; children—Kailan, Clark, Shelly, Spencer. Mem. faculty Columbia, 1960-71, prof., 1968-71, chmn. dept. polit. sci., 1968-71; sr. analyst RAND Corp., Santa Monica, Cal., 1967-68, cons., 1967-74; U.S. cultural attache, London, Eng., 1971-74; cons. Dept State, 1964-71, AID, 1968-71, Ford Found., 1969-74. Trustee Am. Inst. Indian Studies, Acad. Polit. Sci., Am. Sch. in London. Served with USNR, 1954-56; ETO. Ford Found. fellow, 1956-57; Rockefeller Found. fellow, 1962-63; Guggenheim Found. fellow, 1970-71. Mem. Assn. Asian Studies, Am. Polit. Sci. Assn., Inst. Strategic Studies, Royal Acad. Arts, Acad. Polit. Sci., A.A.U.P., Internat. Studies Assn. Club: Athenaeum (London). Author: Pakistan the Consolidation of a Nation, 1963; India, Pakistan and the Rise of China, 1964; Asia and U.S. Policy, 1968; Asia and the World System, 1971; also numerous articles in profl. jours. Died Mar. 3, 1974.

WILD, NORMAN RUSSELL, electronic engr.; b. Hartford, Conn., Mar. 9, 1921; s. Otto and Amalie I. (Killer) W.; student U. Conn., 1939-40, Northwestern U., 1940-41, Mass. Inst. Tech., 1942-43; m. Lois Lund, June 11, 1960; children—Bradford, James. Elec. engr. Mandel Bros., Chgo., 1940-41; research chem. engr. Cardox Corp., Chgo., 1941-42; elec. engr. Power tube div. Raytheon Mfg. Co., Waltham, Mass., 1942-43, head test equipment engr., 1943-45, project engr. elec. div., 1945-47, head microwave dept. radar Div., 1947-51; with microwave dept. Sanders Assos., Inc., Nashua, N.H., 1951-57, chief engr., electronic C/M div., 1958-60, gen. mgr., 1960-61, corp. sci., 1961-68, v.p. tech. devel., 1968, asso. co., 1951-71, dir., 1963-71. Mem. Am. Ordnance Assn., Navy League (Nashua chpt., Nat. Geographic Soc. Conglist. Clubs: Mt. Sunapee ski (past pres., dir.), Mt. Mansfield ski (Vt.); Governors Island (Laconia, N.H.); Rotary (Nashua). Contbr. articles to profl. jours. Patentee in field. Home: Laconia, N.H. Died Mar. 14, 1971; buried Union Cemetery, Laconia.

WILDER, ROBERT INGERSOLL, author, journalist; b. Richmond, Va., Jan. 25, 1901; s. William Wallace and Estrella (Mendoza) W.; student John B. Stetson U., DeLand Fla., 1918, Columbia, 1920-22; m. Sarah Adams Peters, 1928; 1 son, Robert Wallace. Began with Internat. Press Bur., then did theatrical publicity for 6 years; asso. with NBC, was dir. publicity for sta. WOR; with N.Y. Sun, 1935-44; writing column On the Sun Deck, 1936-44; asso. with MGM, Paramount, Warner Bros. Studios, 1944-48; corr. in Mexico for the Miami Herald, 1950-54. Served in U.S. Army, 1918. Mem. Theta Xi. Author: (plays) Sweet Chariot (produced in N.Y.C. with Frank Wilson), 1928; Stardust (produced in N.Y.C. with Frances Starr), 1937; (books) God Has A Long Face, 1940; Flamingo Road, 1942; Mr. G. Strings Along; Out of the Blue; Written on the Wind, Bright Feather, Wait for Tomorrow; (screen play) Flamingo Road; And Ride A Tiger, 1951; Autumn Thunder, 1952, Thread for Arladne, 1953; The Wine of Youth, 1954; Redemption Cay, 1955; Shadow in Copper, 1956; Walk with Evil, 1957; The Big Country (screenplay), 1958; A Handful of Men, 1960; The Sun is My Shadow, 1960; Plough the Sea, 1961; Wind from the Carolinas, 1963; Fruit of the Poppy, 1965; The Sea and the Stars, 1967; An Affair of Honor, 1969; The Sound of Drums and Cymbals, 1974. Contbr. articles to mags. Died Aug. 22, 1974.

WILDER, THORNTON NIVEN, author; b. Madison, Wis., Apr. 17, 1897; s. Amos P. (Ph.D.) and Isabella Thronton (Niven) W.; prep. edn., high schs., Berkeley, Cal., Chefoo, China, and Thacher Sch., Ojai, Cal.; student Oberlin Coll., 1915-17; A.B., Yale, 1920; grad. study, Am. Acad. in Rome, 1920-21; A.M., Princeton, 1925; Litt.D., N.Y.U., Yale, Kenyon, Wooster, Harvard, Northeastern, Oberlin, Goethe U., Frankfurt-am-Main, Germany, 1957, U. Zürich, U. N.H. Tchr. Lawrenceville (N.J.) Sch., 1921-28; mem. faculty U. Chgo., 1930-36; Charles E. Norton prof. poetry Harvard, 1950-51. Served in U.S. Air Corps Intelligence, 1942, lt. col. Awarded Legion of Merit, Bronze Star, Mil. Order Brit. Empire, Legion d'Honneur; Order of Merit, W. Germany; Peace Prize, Frankfurt-am-Main, 1957; Gold Medal for fiction Nat. Inst. Arts and Letters. Am. Acad. Arts and Letters, 1952. Medal of Honor, Sci. and Art, Austria, 1959; Edward MacDowell media for contbn. to letters, 1960; Order of Merit (Peru); Goethe Plakette, 1959; Presdl. award, 1963; Nat. Book Com. prize, 1965. Mem. Am. Acad. Arts and Letters, Actors Equity Assn., Authors League Am., Alpha Delta Phi, Elizabethan; corr. mem. Bayr Akad., Deutsche Akad. (Mainz). Conglist. Clubs: Century, Graduate. Author: The Cabala, 1925; The Bridge of San Luis Rey, 1927 (Pulitzer prize); The Angel That Troubled the Waters, 1928; The Woman of Andros, 1930; The Long Christmas Dinner, 1931; Heaven's May Destination, 1935; Our Town, 1938 (Pulitzer prize); The Merchant of Yonkers, 1938; The Skin of Our Teeth, 1942 (Pulitzer prize); The Ides of March, 1948; The Matchmaker, 1954; The Alestiad (play), Edinburgh Festival, 1955; The Long Christmas Dinner, 1961; Piay For Bleeker Street, 1962; Hello Dolly (musical comedy based on his play The Matchmaker), 1964; The English Day (nat. (Nat. Book award 1968), 1967; Theophilus North, 1973. Home: Hamden, Conn., Died Dec. 7, 1975.

WILDERMUTH, JOE HENRY, architect; b. Pulaski County, Ind., July 6, 1897; s. Elias and Olive (Herrick) W.; student U. Ariz., 1917-18; B.A., U. Ill., 1920; postgrad. real estate valuation U. Chgo. 1935; m. Madeleine Havens, Jan. 5, 1923; children—Richard Lee, Dorthy Ann (Mrs. Mike Vekasl). Architect pub. schs., Gary, Ind., 1921-39; prin. Joe H. Wildermuth & Co., Architects, 1921-46, Wildermuth & Wildermuth, Gary, Ind., 1946-60, Joe H. Wildermuth Emeritus, Marathon Shores, Fla., from 1960; pres. Washington & 7th Corp., from 1931;. Vesta Ct. Corp.; with Gary Fed. Savs. & Loan Assn., 1935-60, v.p., pres., 1958-61. Chief appraiser, asst. mgr. Fed. Home Owners Loan Corp., N.W. Ind., 1933-37; chmn. FHA N.W., Ind., 1934-40; mem. fed. com. sch. house design Interior Dept., 1933-44; chmn. Ind. Bd. Architects, 1933-45. Del., Democratic Ind. Conv., 1932, 36, 40. Served with U.S. Army, 1917-18. Mem. A.I.A., Ind. Soc. Architects (v.p. 1934-36), Am. Legion, Nat. Assn. Real Estate Appraisers, Sigma Chi, Alpha Rho Chi. Elk. Author: Real Estate Valuation, 1934; Treatise on School House Design, 1935. Home: Marathon Shores Fla. Died Dec. 30, 1972

WILDT, RUPERT, astrophysicist; b. Munich, Germany, June 25, 1905; s. Gero and Hertha Wildt; Ph.D., U. Berlin, 1927; m. Katherine Eldredge, Oct. 26, 1962. Came to U.S., 1935, naturalized, 1942. Mem. faculty Bonn U., 1928-29, U. Goettingen, 1930-34; Rockefeller fellow Mt. Wilson Obs., 1935-36; mem. Inst. for Advanced Study, Princeton, N.J., 1936-37; research asso. Princeton, 1937-42; asst. prof. U. Va., 1942-46; mem. faculty Yale, 1946-76, prof. emeritus, 1973-76, chmn. astronomy dept., 1966-68; vis. prof. Basel U. (Switzerland), 1947, U. Cal. at Berkeley, 1956, Nat. U. Mexico, 1963. Recipient Bronze medal U. Liege (Belgium), 1962, Eddington Gold medal Royal Astron. Soc. (London), 1966. Mem. Am., Royal astron. socs., Internat. Astron. Union, Assn. Univs. for Research in Astronomy (pres. 1965-68, 71-72, chmn. bd. 1973-76, dir., 1958-76). Home: Orleans, Mass., Died Jan. 9, 1976; interred Orleans (Mass.) Cemetery.

WILE, FRANK SLOAN, govt. ofcl.; b. Ann Arbor, Mich., July 13, 1925; s. Udo Julius and Katharine Eleanor (Work) W.; B.A., Princeton, 1947; m. Virginia Katherine DerGarry, Sept. 15, 1951; children—Sara Sloan, Susan Bowman, Katherine Taylor. Consular asst. Port of Spain, Trinidad, 1949-51; vice consul Rotterdam, Netherlands, 1951-54; econ. officer, 2d sec., Monrovia, also vice consul, Freetown, Sierra Leone, 1954-56; internat. economist State Dept., 1956-61; consul, comml. officer, Amsterdam, Netherlands, 1961-65; mgr. personnel State Dept., 1965-69; dep. exec. dir. Bur. European Affairs, State Dept., 1969-71; consul gen., Zurich, Leichtenstein, 1971-73. Served with AUS, 1943-46. Recipient Pres.'s award for mgmt. improvement certificate. Mem. Am. Fgn. Service Assn. (mem. bd. 1968-70). Home: Kensington Md. Died Oct. 7, 1974

WILKES, CHARLES S., ins. co. exec.; b. Montgomery, Ala., Dec. 25, 1920; s. Frank Cornelius and Evie (Boutwell) W.; B.S., Sanford U., 1947. With Old Republic Life Ins. Co., Chgo., from 1948, adminstrv. v.p., sec., 1960-73, treas., 1962, sr. v.p., from 1973; sec. Old Republic Life Ins. Co. N.Y., from 1964, sr. v.p. from 1973; v.p. asst. sec., dir. Old Republic Ins. Co., Greensburg, Pa., from 1955; v.p. asst. sec., dir. Motorists Beneficial Ins. Co., Chgo., 1961; treas. asst. sec. Old Republic Lloyds Tex., Dallas, from 1966; sr. v.p., treas., dir. Old Republic Internat. Corp., from 1969; treas. asst. sec., dir. Home owners Life Ins. Co., from 1971. Served with USAAF, 1942-45. Home: Chicago Ill. Deceased.

WILKINSON, ALBERT EDMUND, horticulturist; b. Boston, July 17, 1879; s. Richard and Lizzie Robinson (Barney) W.; B.S., R.I. State Coll., 1906, M.Agr., 1916; m. Maude Lucy Owen, of Bangor, Me., Sept. 12, 1906. Farm mgr. and supt. until 1910; horticulturist, Lyndon Agrl. Sch., Lyndon Center, Vt., 19112, Cornell U. Agrl. Coll., from 1912. Republican. Conglist. Author: Modern Strawberry Growing, 1913; The Apple, 1915; Sweet Corn Growing, 1915; Muck Land Crops, 1916; Vegetable Gardening Series; also bulletins for Cornell U. and many articles in agrl. mags. Address: Ithaca, N.Y.†

WILKINSON, ELIZABETH HAYS, author; b. Pittsburgh, Feb. 29, 1880; d. James M. and Virginia (Hart) Wilkinson; A.B., U. of Pittsburgh, 1925; unmarried. Assistant in English at University of Pittsburgh. Clubs: Authors', Twentieth Century. Author: The Lane to Sleepy Town, 1910; Peter and Polly, 1912; Little Billy 'Coon, 1914; Storyland (children's operetta), 1923. Home: Pittsburgh, Pa.†

WILKINSON, JAMES CUTHBERT, clergyman; b. Brooks County, Ga., Oct. 26, 1880; s. William Lee and Mary Frances (Bentley) W.; student Mercer U., 1896-98, D.D., 1921; Th.B., Southern Bapt. Theol. Sem., 1900; D.D., U. of Ga., 1924; m. Rachel Thompson Baldwin, Oct. 23, 1902; children—Velma Juanita (dec.), James Frances (dec.), Began as pastor country chs.; prss. Bapt. Acad., Lakeland, Ga., 1905-12; pastor Eastern Heights Ch., Columbus, 1912-14, Rose Hill Ch., Columbus, 1914-18, Milledgeville, 1918-21, First Ch., Athens, from 1921. Taught trigonometry, Ga. Mil. Coll.; later teaching Bible, Summer Sch. for Negroes. Pres. exec. com. Ga. Bapt. Conv. (pres. 1944-46); dir. The Christina Index; trustee Mercer Univ., Shorter College; mem. Southern Baptist Exec. Com. Democrat. Mason (Prelate Grand Commandery of Ga.). Clubs: Kiwanis (Milledgeville); Athens County, Athens Rotary (pres.). Home: Athens, Ga.*†

WILKINSON, JOHN, painter; b. Berkeley, Cal., July 2, 1913; s. James William and Amelia Catherine (Wyser) W.; student U. Ore., 1932-34, Cal. Sch. Fine Arts, San Francisco, 1934-36, Acad. Ronson, Paris, France, 1938-39; m. Una McCann, Sept. 21, 1940; 1 dau. Catherine Marie. Exhbns. include Chgo. Art Inst., 1937, San Francisco Mus. Art. 1939-41, Portland Art Mus., 1945-59, other museums throughout U.S.; joined faculty U. Ore., 1941, named prof. art, 1959, head dept. fine and applied arts, 1963-68; prof., head dept. fine arts La. State U., Baton Rouge, 1968-74. Fellow Royal Soc. Arts; mem A.A.U.P., Royal Soc. London, Coll. Art Assn. Home: Baton Rouge La., Died Aug. 4, 1974.

WILLARD, CHARLES J(ULIUS), educator; b. Manhattan, Kan., Feb. 14, 1889; s. Julius T. and Lydia P. (Gardiner) W.; B.S., Kan. State Coll., 1908; B.S. in Agr., U. Ill., 1910, M.S., 1917; Ph.D., Ohio State U., 1926; m. Vivien Ullmer, Oct. 28, 1911; m. 2d, Jacqueline Ullmer, June 19, 1937; 1 dau., Charlene Marie (Mrs. Robert Steven Wilkinson). Farmer, Bradford, Kan., 1911-13, Williamsburg, Va., 1913-16; asst. prof. farm crops Ohio State U., 1917-26, prof., 1926-33, prof. agronomy, 1933-59, emeritus, from 1959; associate agronomy Ohio Agrl. Expt. Sta., 1925-51, prof. agronomy, 1951-59, emeritus, from 1959; senior scientist London Embassy, Dept. State, 1948. Recipient Nat. award, Gamma Sigma Delta, 1955. Fellow A.A.A.S., Am. Soc. Agronomy (pres. 1954); mem. Soil Sci. Soc. Am., North Central Weed Control Conf. (pres. 1948), Ecol. Soc., Am., Am. Soc. Plant Physiologists, Weed Soc. Am., Conf. Biol. Editors, Soil Conservation Soc., Ohio Acad. Sci., Sigma Xi, Gamma Sigma Delta, Phi Kappa Phi, Alpha Zeta. Editor: N. Central Weed Control Conf. Proceedings, 1957—; Weeds, 1958—. Contbr. profl. publs. Home: Columbus, O., Died Sept. 13, 1974.

WILLARD, EDWARD LAWRENCE, lawyer; b. State College, Pa., Aug. 31, 1904; s. Joseph Moody and Henrietta (Nunn) W.; B.A., Pa. State U., 1927; LL.B. Harvard, 1930; m. Julia Mary Hill, Feb. 9, 1935; children—Joseph Hill, James Peter. Admitted to Pa. bar, 1933, also U.S. Supreme Ct.; with firm Haight, Smith, Griffin & Deming, admiralty lawyers, N.Y.C., 1930-34; sr. partner firm Willard, Dunaway & Mazza, State College, 1935-67; individual practice law State College, from 1967; dist. atty. Centre County, Pa., 1946-52; pub. defender Centre County, from 1970. Dir. Chemcut Corp. Pres. Dist. Attys. Assn. Pa., 1951. Incorporator, bd. dirs. Am. Philatelic Research Library. Mem. Inter-Am., Philatelic Soc. (v.p.) Am. Philatelic Society (dir. at large 1960-65, pres. 1965-69), Acacia. Decorated York Cross of Honor (Mason); Red Cross Constantine (Mason). Republican Presbyn. Mason, Kiwanian. Author: Two Cent Red Brown 1883-1887, 1970. Home: State College Pa. Died May 1973.

WILLARD, HOBART HURD, prof. chemistry; b. Erie, Pa., June 3, 1881; s. James Richard and Julia Maria (Hobart) W.; A.B., U. of Mich., 1903, A.M., 1905; Ph.D., Harvard, 1909; m. Margaret A. Sheppard, June 27, 1927; children—Ann Hobart, Nancy Margaret. With U. of Michigan from 1904, instr. in analytical chemistry, 1905-10, asst. prof., 1911-17, asso. prof., 1918-23, prof. chemistry, from 1923. Served as dir. Chem and Metall. Lab., Bur. of Aircraft Production, Detroit dist., 1918, World War. Recipient Fisher award Am. Chem. Soc., 1951, Henry Russel award U. Mich., 1948. Mem. Am. Chem. Soc. (dir. 1934-40), Electrochemical Soc., A.A.A.S., Nat. Research Council (div. of chemistry and chem. technology 1933-36), Delta Tau Delta, Sigma Xi, etc. Republican. Author: Elementary Quantitative Analysis (with N. H. Furman), 1933, 3d edit., 1940; Advanced Quantitative Analysis (with H. C. Diehl), 1943; Short Course in Elementary Quantitative Analysis (with N. H. Furman and J. F. Flagg), 1943; Instrumental Methods of Analysis (with L. L. Merritt and J. A. Dean), 1948; also numerous paper concerning results of research since 1909, in analytical and inorganic chemistry. Asso. editor Jour. American Chemical Society, 1922-31, Industrial and Engineering Chemistry since 1934. Home: Ann Arbor, Mich. Died May 7, 1974; buried Washtenong Meml. Park.

WILLCOX, WALTER FRANCIS, univ. prof., statistician; b. Reading, Mass., Mar. 22, 1861;s. William Henry and Annie Holmes (Goodenow) W.; brother of Mary Alice Willcox; A.B., Amherst College, 1884, A.M., 1888; LL.B., Columbia. 1877, Ph.D., 1891; Doctor of Laws, Amherst College, 1906; married Alice E. Work, Mar. 30, 1892 (deceased September 18, 1952); children—Bertram Francis, Mary Goodenow,Work, William Bradford. Prof. economics and statistics, Cornell U., 1891-1931, emeritus, 1931; was dean College Arts and Sciences, 1902-07, faculty rep. on bd. of trustees, 1916-20. Statis. expert for War Dept. upon Censuses of Cuba and P.R., 1899-1900; chief statistician 12th U.S., Census, 1899-1901; spl. agt. U.S. Census Bur., 1902-31; mem. Census Advisory Com. (representing Am. Econ. Assn. 1921-28; chmn. 1928-31); mem. N.Y. State Bd. of Health, 1899-1902, and cons. statistician for same, 1907-20. Mem. Am. Econ. Assn., from 1892 (sec. 1896-99; pres. 1915); mem. Am. Statis. Assn., from 1892 (pres. 1912; fellow from 1917); mem. Internat. Statis Inst., from 1899 (v.p. 1923-47, president 1947, hon. pres., from 1947; hon. mem., from 1935, U.S. delegate to its sessions, Berlin, 1903, London, 1905, Paris, 1909, Brussels 1923, Rome, 1925, Warsaw 1929, Tokyo 1930, Madrid 1931, Mexico 1933, London 1934, Athens 1936, Prague 1938, Washington, 1947, New Delhi, India, 1951, Petrolis, Brazil, 1955, Stockholm, 1957), vice chairman executive committee and president section on demography. International Congress on Hygiene and Demography, Washington, D.C., 1912; member American Council Learned Socs. (rep. Am. Econ. Assn. 1925; exec. com. 1925-28; v. chmn. 1926-28); fellow Royal Statis. Soc., from 1897 (hon. from 1918); hon. mem. Statis. Soc. of Hungary, Czechoslovak Statis. Soc., Mexican Soc. Geography and Statistics; mem. World Statis. Congress (pes.), Social Science Research Council (pre. Am. Statistical Assn., 1925-26); mem. Psi Upsilon, Phi Beta Kappa, Sigma Xi. Clubs: Century City (New York); Cosmos (Washington). Author: The Divorce Problem-a Study in Statistics, 2 edit., 1897; Supplementary Analysis and D Derivative Tables, 12th Census, 1906; Introduction to the Vital Statistics of the United States (1900-1930), 1933; Studies in American Demography (with bibliography), 1940. Home: Ithaca, N.Y.†

WILLETTS, ERNEST WARD, physician; b. Pittsburgh, Pa., Sept. 20, 1879; s. Jesse and Sarah (Dunn) W.; M.D. U. of Pa., 1902; grad. study, U. of Vienna, Austria, 1902-03, 1904-05; m. Anne Beattie, May 10, 1905; children—Agnes Beville, Ernest, Arthur T. Interne U. of Pa. Hosp., Phila., 1903-04; pathologist Pittsburgh Hosp., 1905-07, Columbia Hosp., 1906-09, Western Pa. Hosp., 1906-14, St. Francis Hosp., 1909-11, Pittsburgh Eye and Ear Hosp., 1906-24, Dixmont Hosp., 1908-12; med. consultant St. Margaret's Hosp.; physician-in-chief Allegheny Gen. Hosp.; consultant Pittsburgh Eye and Ear Hosp.; asso. pathology, U. of Pittsburgh Med. Sch., 1910-11. Fellow Am. Coll. Physicians, Am. Soc. Clin. Pathologists; mem. A.M.A, Assn Am. Bacteriologists, Med. Soc. State of Pa. (ex-v.p.), Allegheny County Med. Soc. (ex-pres.), Pittsburgh Acad. Medicine (ex-pres.). Club: University. Home: Verona, Pa.†

WILLEY, MALCOLM MACDONALD, sociologist, univ. adminstr.; b. Portland, Me., Nov. 13, 1897; s. Carlton Bartlett and Helen Marr (Macdonald) W.; A.B., Clark U., 1920, L.H.D., 1945; A.M., Columbia U., 1921, Ph.D., 1926; LL.D., U. Me., 1952; m. Nancy Burnham Boyd, Feb. 6, 1924 (div.); m. 2d Betty Washburn, Aug. 1, 1955 (dec. June 1962); m. 3d, Delores T. Miller, Sept. 7, 1963; 1 son, Anil; stepchildren—Christine, George, Dolores. Instr. sociology, Dartmouth, 1923-24, asst. prof., 1924-27; asso. prof., U. of Minn., 1927-29, prof., 1929-34; univ. dean and asst. to the pres., U. of Minn., 1934-43, v.p. acad. adminstrn., 1943-63; ednl. cons. Ford Found., U. Calcutta (India), 1963; prof. sociology Maryville (Tenn.) Coll.; visiting lecturer in sociology, U. of Chicago, winter quarter, 1929-30. Member U.S. Nat. Commn. for UNESCO, 1953-59. Investigator Pres. Research Com. on Social Trends, 1931, and author (with S. A. Rice) of the section on communication in the committee's report; dir. of studies for Com. on Effect of Depression and Recovery on Higher Education, Am. Assn. Univ. Profs., 1934-35. Mem. com. on faculty research fellowships, 1950-56, mem. P. and P. com., 1952-56, 59-63, Social Sci. Research Council, dir., 1950-63, chmn. bd. dirs., 1959-63; sci. adv. com. specialized personnel Nat. SSS, 1949-52. Dir. Midwest Inter-Library Corporation (chmn. bd. 1958-59). Bd. dirs. Calcutta YMCA 1966. Fellow Am. Sociol. Soc., A.A.A.S.; mem. Newcomen Soc., several profl. assns. Clubs: Columbia University (N.Y.C.); Cosmos (Washington); Tollygunge, Calcutta Swimming (Calcutta, India). Author and co-author several books in field, 1926-50. Contbr. to profl. jours. Home: Maryville Tenn Died Feb. 12, 1974.

WILLIAM, MAURICE, dentist, author; b. Kharkov, Russia, April 12, 1881; s. Robert Samuel and Pearl (Herbel) W.; brought to U.S., 1889, naturalized 1902; D.D.S., N.Y.U., 1907; m. Marie B. Kresky, Dec. 20, 1910; children—Robert Samuel, Esther (Mrs. Anthony Garat). Practice dentistry, N.Y. City, 1907-59. Writer and lectr. on social, polit. and econ. questions, from 1912. Past mem. advisory bd. Guggenheim Dental Found. Past. sec. dental adv. bd. Dept. of Health, N.Y.C. Past v.p. American Bur. Med. Aid to China; chmn. exec. com. Help Korean Orphans; vice chmn. Sino-Am. Amity, Inc.; dir. Am.-Korean Found., Inc. Life mem. Kuomintang (only non-Chinese so honored; chmn. U.S. pub. relations com.). Recipient Order of the Jade (China), 1940; Decoration of Honor, Third Order (Korea), 1950. Fellow Am. Coll. Dentists; mem. King's County Dental Soc. (pres. 1914), Allied Dental Council N.Y. (pres. 1913, 24; chmn. oral hygiene com. Greater N.Y., 1927, 29), Am. Dental Assn., 1st Dist. Dental Soc. State of N.Y., East and West Assn. (bd. dirs.), China Soc. Am., Omicron Kappa Upsilon, Jewish religion. Club: Town Hall (New York). Author: The Social Interpretation of History; A Refutation of the Marxian Economic Interpretation of History, 1921, Brit. edit., 1922, German transl. with introduction of Oswald Spengler, Berlin, 1924, Chinese transl. by Liu Lu-in, Shanghai, 1926, rev. Am. edit. in preparation; Sun Yat-sen Versus Communism, 1932; The Cause and Cure of the Sino-Japanese Conflict (monograph submitted to League Nations), 1932; Biography of Maurice William (Sun Yat-sen and Maurice William) by Maurice Zolotow, (pub. London, 1948). The Social Interpretation of History is credited with converting Dr. Sun Yat-sen and China from pro-Marxian to pro-democratic ideology and has received recent internat. publicity. Home: Los Angeles Cal. Died Sept. 1973.

WILLIAMS, ALAN MEREDITH, Brit. diplomat; b. London, Aug. 22, 1909; s. Thomas and Margaret (McGregor) W.; ed. Pembroke Coll. of U. Cambridge; m. Masha Poustchine, 1946; 1 son, 1 dau. Served with Brit. consular service in San Francisco, Colon, Panama, Paris, Hamburg, Rotterdam, Reykjavik, Dakar, 1932-43; vice-consul, Leopoldville, 1943, acting consul-gen., 1943; chief Brit. econ. rep., 1944; consul, Vienna, 1945-47, Baghdad, 1947-49; served in fgn. office, 1949-50, 56-60; counsellor and dep. counsul-gen., N.Y.C., 1950-53; consul-gen., Tunis, 1963-56, N.Y.C., 1960-64; ambassador to Panama, 1964-66, to Spain, 1966-69. Decorated knight comdr. Order St. Michael and St. George. Address: London, England. Died Dec. 1972.

WILLIAMS, ALFRED HECTOR, bus. exec.; b. Horatio, Pa., Feb. 28, 1893; s. Joseph and Elizabeth (Powell) W.; B.S. in Economics, U. of Pa., 1915, A.M., 1916, Ph.D., 1924, LL.D. 1951; LL.D., Hahnemann Med. Coll. and Hosp., 1950, Gettysburg College, 1952, U. Del., 1955, Franklin and Marshall College, 1955; married Mabel Baker Fisher, November 28, 1917. Instr. in industry, U. of Pa., 1915-16; asst. gen. mgr. J. Franklin Miller, Inc., Philadelphia, 1916-17; staff, research div., U. S. Shipping Bd., 1919; asst. prof. in industry, Wharton Sch. of Finance and Commerce, U. of Pa., 1920-21, prof., 1921-41, dean, 1939-41; pres. Federal Reserve Bank of Philadelphia, 1941-58; dir. Armstrong Cork Co., Internat. Resistance Co., Selas Corporation of America; finance chairman Pa.-N.J.-Del. Metropolitan Project, Inc.; assistant dir. consumers advisory board, NRA, 1933; exec. sec. Automobile Labor Bd., 1934; dir. (Class C) Fed. Res. Bank of Phila., 1939-41. Trustee Eisenhower Exchange Fellowships, Inc. Dir. The Laymen's Movement for a Christian World, Inc. Member board managers of Swarthmore College; chmn. bd. trustees, U. Pa., 1956-61; trustee State Teachers College at Cheyney; dir. Hering Found., New School of Music, United Fund; director The Philadelphia Award, Samuel S. Fels Fund, Penn. State Planning Bd. Served as 2d lt. ordnance dept., U.S. Army, 1917-19, with American Expeditionary Forces. Recipient Gold Medal Award, Nat. Planning Assn. Mem. American Academy Political and Social Science, and Alpha Tau Omega. Republican. Methodist. Clubs: Rolling Green Golf, Midday (Phila.). Author: Analysis of Production of Worsted Sales Yarns (with A.M. Brunbaugh and H. S. Davis), 1929. Editor: The Marketing of Textiles, 1938; Textile Costing, 1938; Management of Textile Business, 1938; The Textile Industries-An Economic Analysis. Home: Wallingford Pa. Died July 3, 1974.

WILLIAMS, BEATTY BRICKER, engine mfr.; b. Shelby, O., Aug. 22, 1876; s. Benjamin J. and Ida (Whiting) W.; grad. Oberlin Acad., 1895; A.B., Oberlin Coll., 1899; LL.D., Grove City Coll., 1954; married Amy Fairchild, October 24, 1900 (deceased November 30, 1952); 1 son, Lawrence Fairchild; married second, Mrs. Edith McLeon Hindley, November, 14, 1953. Resident engineer with the Shelby Steel Tube Co., 1899-1900; sales engr. The C. & G. Cooper Co. (now Cooper Bessemer Corp.), Engine uilders, Mt. Vernon, 190-108; dir. and mgr. sales, 1908-12, sec., 1912-16, v.p. and gen. mgr., 1916-20. prs. and gen. mgr., 1920-35; pres and dir., 1935-43; chmn. bd., dir., 1943-56, director, chairman exec. com., 1956-59, ret, 1959. Chmn. bd., dir. First-Knox Nat. Bank, Mt. Vernon. O. Mem. Nat. War Work Council, YMCA, World War I; pres. Nat. Council YMCA's of U.S.A., 1935-36; delegate to World Conf. Y.M.C.A., 1926 (mem. world com.). Trustee emeritus Oberlin Coll. Chmn. distbn. com. Mt. Vernon Community Trust. Recipient of Oberlin Alumni medal, 1953. Mem. U.S. and Ohio senior golfers assns. Republican. Conglist. Clubs: Mt. Vernon Country; Union (Cleveland). Home; Mt. Vernon, O.†

WILLIAMS, BENJAMIN HARRISON, author; b. Eugene, Ore., Mar. 23, 1889; s. John Monroe and Jennie Mary (Gwin) W.; A.B., U. Ore., 1910, A.M., 1912; student Harvard Law Sch., 1912-13; Ph.D., U. Cal., 1921; m. Helen Frances Ogsbury, Nov. 18, 1917 (dec. 1948); children—Patricia (Mrs. Robert C. McMann), Stanton M.; m. 2d, Evelyn Ernestine Allemong, 1951. Statistician, Ore. Indsl. Accident Commn., 1914-16; sec. social welfare U. Ore. extension div., 1916-17; teaching fellow polit. sci. U. Cal., 1920-21; instr. polit. sci. U. Pa., 1921-23; lectr. politics Bryn Mawr Coll., 1923; asst. prof. U. Pitts., 1923-27, asso. prof., 1927-30, prof., 1930-43; vis. prof. U. Ore., summers 1921, 23, 25, 27. Sec. U. Ore. Alumni Assn., 1914; prin. research analyst Office Chief Staff, War Dept., 1943; div. asst. State Dept., 1943-44; mem. staff and faculty Indsl. Coll. Armed Forces, 1944-59; cons. USIA, 1960. Treas. Pisgah council Girl Scouts, 1963-66. Served as 1st it., arty., U.S. Army, 1918-19; AEF. Recipient Dept. Army Exceptional Civilian Service medal, 1959. Fellow A.A.A.S. (v.p. chmn. sect. K, 1956); mem. Nat. Acad. Econs. and Polit. Sci. (chmn. 1948-59). Democrat. Unitarian. Club: Civitan (scholarship chmn. 1964-70) (Asheville). Author: Economic Foreign Policy of the United States, 1929; The London Naval Conference, 1930; The United States and Disarmament, 1931; American Diplomacy-Policies and Practice, 1936; Foreign Loan Policy of the United States since 1933, 1939; The United States in the Nuclear Age, 1970; Humbug, Brainwash, and Other Verse, 1972. Editor: The Search for National Security, 1951; asso. editor The Scholastic, 1927-28, Social Sci., 1955; contbr. jours. Address: Asheville, N.C. Died Sept. 11, 1974; interred Mt. Olivet Cemetery, Washington, D.C.

WILLIAMS, CHARLES HAMILTON, university prof.; b. Mayfield, Mo., July 2, 1880; s. Marshall H. and Emily (Tallent) W.; A.B., B.S. in Edn., U. of Mo., 1907; scholar, Sage Sch. of Philosophy, Cornell U., 1907-08, fellow, 1908; m. Helen E. Davault, of Marble Hill, Mo., Dec. 29, 1916; 1 dau., Helen Emily. Asst. in ethics, Cornell U., 1908-10; Sage fellow same, 1910-11; asst. prof. of edn., U. of Colo., 1911-13, also state high sch. insp. of Colo.; dir. Univ. Extension, U. of Mo., 1913-31; dir. summer session and prof. history and principles of edn., same, 1918. Spl. rep. of N.E.A. in Europe, summer 1922; del. of N.E.A. to World Conf. on Edn., San Francisco, summer 1923, Edinburgh, Scotland, 1925, Toronto, Can., 1927, Geneva, Switzerland, 1929, Denver, 1931; sec. World Federation of Edn. Assns., 1923-31. Home: Columbia, Mo.†

WILLIAMS, CHARLES IRA, mfg. co. exec.; b. Quincy, Mass., Oct. 8, 1900; s. Frederick William and Elizabeth Cole (Litchfield) W.; B.S., Northeastern U., 1922; m. Martha Evelyn Markham, Sept. 7, 1937; 1 dau., Nancy (Mrs. James W. Pollack). Service engr. Worthington Corp., N.Y.C., 1922-31; with Swanson-Nunn Electric Co., Evansville, Ind., from 1932, v.p., from 1958. Mem. Elec. Apparatus Service Assn. (pres. 1958-59). Methodist. Clubs: Evansville Scientec, Central Topners (Evansville). Home: Evansville Ind. Deceased.

WILLIAMS, CHARLES RICHARD, chem. engr.; b. Texas County, Okla., Nov. 5, 1907; s. Charles Calvin and Clara (Houston) W.; B.S. in Chem. Engring., U. Okla., 1930; student gas tech., Johns Hopkins, 1932-33; m. Stella Disney, Apr. 25, 1931; children—Charles Richard, Robert Lee. With Conoco Co., 1930-39, process engr., 1936-39; gen. mgr. oil and gas div., then v.p. charge operations Chicago Corp., 1942-51; pres., then vice chmn. bd. Pacific N.W. Pipeline Corp., 1951-57; ind. cons. engr., bus. investor, 1961—; dir. Belco Petroleum Corp., El Paso Natural Gas Co., Northwest Prodn. Corp., v.p. Fish Internat. Corp., Fish Northwest Contructors, Inc. Trustee Tex. Christian U., Inst. Religion. Registered profl. engr., Tex. Mem. Am. Petroleum Inst., Natural Gas Assn. Am. (pres. 1948-49), Cal. Natural Gas Assn., Am. Gas Assn., Am. Inst. M.E., Tex. Soc. Profl. Engrs., Alpha Chi Sigma. Mem. Christian Ch. Clubs: River Oaks, Petroleum, Internat. (Houston). Home: Houston, Tex., Died Feb. 24, 1975.

WILLIAMS, DANIEL DAY, clergyman, educator; b. Denver, Sept. 12, 1910; s. Wayne Cullen and Lena Belle (Day) W.; A.B., U. Denver, 1931; A.M., U. Chgo., 1933; B.D., Chgo. Theol. Sem., 1934, D.D. (hon.), 1966; Ph.D., Columbia, 1940; D.D. (hon.), Colo. Coll., 1965, Bloomfield Coll., 1973; m. Eulalia Westberg, June 15, 1935. Ordained to ministry Congl. Ch., 1936; pastor First Congl. Ch., Colorado Srpings, Colo., 1936-38; dean Shove Meml. Chapel, instr. religion Colo. Coll., 1938-39; Rauschenbush lectr. Colgate-Rochester Div. Sch., 1947; Mead-Swing lectr. Oberlin Coll., 1951; lectr. gen. council Congl. Chs., 1952, mem. commn. on basis of social action, 1953; Nathaniel Taylor lectr. Yale Div. Sch., 1953; prof. Christian theology Chgo. Theol. Sem., also Federated Theol. Faculty, U. Chgo., 1939-54; asso. dir. Theol. Edn. Survey, 1954-55; prof. systematic theology Union Theol. Sem., N.Y.C., 1954-59, Roosevelt prof. systematic theology, 1959-73; Alden-Tuthill lectr. Chgo. Theol. Sem., also Earl lectr. Pacific Sch. Religion, 1959; lectr. Theol. Faculties Inst., Singapore, 1960. Congregational del. Faith and Order Conf., Lund, Sweden, 1952; del. of United Ch. Christ to faith and order com. World Council Chs., 1971-73. Mem. Am. Theol. Soc. (pres. 1966), Sigma Alpha Epsilon. Author: The Andover Liberals, 1941; God's Grace and Man's Hope, 1949; What Present-Day Theologians Are Thinking, 1952 (published in Eng. as Interpreting Theology, 1918-52), 1953; The Minister and the Care of Souls, 1961; The Spirit and the Forms of Love, 1968; co-author: The Advancement of Theological Education, 1957. Contbr. The Theology of Reinhold Niebuhr: A Companion to the Study of St. Augustine, 1954; The Shaping of American Religion, 1961; The Empirical Theology of H. N. Wieman, 1963; Alfred North Whitehead: Essays on His Philosophy, 1963. Contbr. profl. publs. Home: New York City N.Y. Died Dec. 3, 1973.

WILLIAMS, EDGAR IRVING, architect; b. Rutherford, N.J., Oct. 5, 1884; s. William George and Raquel Helen (Hoheb) W.; student Chateau De Lancy (Geneva, Switzerland), 1898-99; B.S., Mass. Inst. Tech., 1908, M.S., 1909; student Am. Acad. in Rome, 1909-12 (fellow, 1912); m. Hulda Gustafva Olson, Sept. 16, 1913; children—Ingrid Helen (Mrs. Fred W. Wackernagle II), Hulda Palamona (Mrs. Jeffrey Ferris), Edith Maria (Mrs. Edward Horn), Christina Nilsson (Mrs. James E. Koegel). Archtl. designer for Welles, Bosworth, N.Y.C., 1912-15; Guy Lowell, Boston, 1915-16, E. P. Mellon, N.Y.C., 1916-37; instr. Mass. Inst. Tech., 1912-13, asso. prof., 1913-14; dir. A.R.C., Genoa, 1917-19; partnership Williams and Barratt, 1920-28; own office from 1928; on staff Columbia, asso. in design, 1921-29, 37-46. Prin. works: Manton B. Metcalf Meml., Orange, N.J.; K. D. Pierson residence, Milw.; C. R. Holmes Estate, Port Washington, N.Y.; Donnell Bldg. of N.Y. Pub Library. Cons. architect N.Y. Pub. Library, Ebasco Services, Inc., Dept. State. Recipient Prix de Rome, 1909; decorated Knight, Royal Order of Vasa 1st class, Sweden, 1944, Fellow Am. Acad. in Rome, 1912, A.I.A. 1942 (regional dir. 1942-45; chmn. jury of fellows, 1946-48; vice chancellor coll. of fellows 1954, chancellor 1956). Mem. Bergen County, (N.J.) Park Commn., 1947-49. Trustee, Am. Scenic and Historic Preservation Soc., Am. Archtl. Found., Am. Acad. in Rome, 1919-37, Am. Fine Arts Soc., 1938-40, Met. Mus. Art. Benjamin Franklin fellow Royal Soc. of Arts, 1962. Mem. N.A.D. (pres. 1962-66), Archtl. League (pres. 1939-41), Fine Arts Fedn. of N.Y. (v.p. 1941-43), N.Y. Bldg. Congress (bd. govs. 1942), Nat. Sculpture Soc. (council, 1942, v.p. 1945-47), Municipal Art Soc. N.Y. (pres. 1950-51). Club: Century. Contbr. to profl. journals. Home: New Milford Conn. Died Jan. 1, 1974.

WILLIAMS, EDWIN BUCHER, educator, writer, lexicographer; b. Columbia, Pa., Sept. 20, 1891; s. Thomas Allison and Alice Jane (Bucher) W.; grad. Reading (Pa.) High Sch., 1910; student Internat. Corr. Schs., also U. Dijon (France), 1911; A.B., U. Pa., 1914, A.M., 1916, Ph.D., 1924, LL.D., 1958; Dr. honoris causa, U. Montpellier (France), 1946; L.H.D. (hon.), Bucknell U., 1959; m. Leonore Rowe, Jan. 29, 1921. Asst. prof. Romance langs. U. Pa., 1925-32, prof., 1932-61, prof. emeritus, 1961-75, chmn. dept. 1931-38, dean Grad. Sch. Arts and Scis., 1938-52, provost univ., 1951-56, provost emeritus, 1973; vis. prof. U. Colo., summer 1935. Served with M.C., U.S. Army, Camp Greenleaf, Ga., 1918-19. Mem. Mediaeval Acad. Am., Linguistic, Soc. Am., Modern Lang. Assn. Am., Am. Assn. Tchrs. Spanish and Portuguese, Am. Philos. Soc., Hispanic Soc. Am., Phi Beta Kappa. Clubs: Union League, Art Alliance (Phila.); Faculty (U. Pa.). Author or editor numerous books relating to field, latest being: Spanish-English Dictionary, rev. 1973; Diccionario del idioma español, rev. edit., 1967; (with Alfred Senn) The New College Multilingual Dictionary - A Seven-language Dictionary, 1967; The New College Spanish and English Dictionary 1968; From Latin to Portuguese, rev. edit., 1968; Williams' Handbook of Modern Spanish, 1969. Gen. editor Bantam New College Dictionary series, 1964. Contbr. to profl. publs. Home: Philadelphia, Pa. Died Apr. 28, 1975; buried Charles Evans Cemetery, Reading, Pa.

WILLIAMS, EUGENE E., corp. exec.; b. 1913; grad. U. Buffalo; married. With Nat. Gypsum Co., 1944-75, treas., 1964-75. Address: Buffalo, N.Y. Died Apr. 1975.

WILLIAMS, GUY YANDALL, chemist; b. Cook Co., Tex., Sept. 7, 1881; s. John Archer and Molly M. (Dickson) W.; B.A., U. of Okla., 1906, M.A., 1910; M.S., U. of Chicago, 1911; Ph.D., U. of Ill., 1913; m. Ella Rae Thomas, of Norman, Okla., Aug. 12, 1906; children—Guy Herson, Robert Thomas. Instr. chemistry, 1906-08, asso. prof., 1908-18, prof. physical chemistry, 1918-23, head chem. dept. and dir. Sch. Chem. Engring., from 1923, U. of Okla.; fellow U. of Ill., 1911-13. Served as 1st lt. Co. A, Okla. Engrs., Mexican border, 1916-17; pvt. Co. 20, S.A.T.C., comdt. mil. science, U. of Okla., 1918. Mem. American Chemical Society, American Association Univ. Profs., Okla. Acad. Science, Phi Beta Kappa, Alpha Chi Sigma, Phi Lamdba Upsilon, Phi Delta Chi, Rho Chi. Democrat. Mson. Presbyn. Club: Faculty. Home: Norman, Okla.*†

WILLIAMS, HAROLD WESLEY, psychiatrist; b. Schenectady, Sept. 6, 1904; s. James and Annie (Thompson) W.; A.B., Syracuse U., 1926, M.D., 1929; m. Dorothy Turner, Aug. 26, 1929. Intern, St. Joseph Hosp., Syracuse, 1928-29; intern pathology R.I. Hosp., Providence, 1929-30, resident pathology, 1930-31; Rockefeller fellow neuropathology Research Inst. Physicians, Munich, Germany, 1933-34; Rockefeller fellow clin. psychiatry Anstalt Burgholzi, Zurich, Switzerland, 1935, Maudsley Hosp., Eng., 1935, Phipps Psychiat. Clinic Johns Hopkins Hosp., 1935-36; practice medicine specializing in psychiatry, from 1941; mem. cons. staff, asso. neuropathologist R.I. Hosp., from 1941. Served to comdr. USNR, until 1946. Diplomate Am. Bd. Psychiatry and Neurology, Mem. A.M.A., Am. Psychiat. Assn., Am. Acad. Neurology, Assn. for Research in Nervous and Mental Diseases. Home: Providence R.I. Deceased.

WILLIAMS, HENRY, naval officer; born Hagerstown, Md., Aug. 12, 1877; s. Thomas John Chew and Cora (Maddox) W.; student Johns Hopkins, 1892-94; B.S., U.S. Naval Acad., 1898; diploma Ingenieur Civil des Construction Navales, Ecole d'Application du Genie Maritime, Paris, 1901; m. Anna Maud Steers, Mar. 12, 1906 (died July 1947); 1 son, Henry; m. 2d, Hazel Forrest, Nov. 1948. Commd. U. S. Navy, and advanced through grades to rear adm., 1940; service at sea, Spanish Am. War, 1898-1901; commd. in construction corps, U. S. Navy, 1900; mgr. Navy Yard, Norfolk, Va., 1923-28, Phila., Pa., 1935-37; asst. chief of bur. of construction and repair, U.S. Navy Dept., 1937-40; administrative officer, Bur. of Ships, U.S. Navy Dept., 1940-42; Navy Dept. rep. with W.P.B., 1942-45; spl. asst. to chmn., U.S. Maritime Commn., 1945-46; ret. from active service, May 1946. Awarded spl. letter of commendation from comdr. in chief, U.S. Navy, World War II. Mem. Am. Soc. of Naval Engrs. (pres. 1939-40), Soc. of Am. Mil. Engrs. (pres., 1946-47), Soc. of Naval Architects and Marine Engrs. (v.p., 1948), United Spanish War Vets., Naval and Mil. Order of Spanish Am. War. Democrat. Episcopalian. Clubs: Yacht (N.Y. City), Army Navy (Washington). Home: Washington D.C. Died July 6, 1973.

WILLIAMS, HERMANN WARNER, JR., museum dir.; b. Boston, Nov. 2, 1908; s. Hermann Warner and Helen Chilton (French) W.; A.B., Harvard, 1931, A.M., 1933; Ph.D., Courtauld Inst. Art, U. London (Eng.), 1935; postgrad. Inst. Fine Arts, N.Y. U., 1935-41; m. Alice Barrett Farley, Aug. 30, 1942; children—Susan, Penelope, Richard. Intern Bklyn. Mus. grantee Rockefeller Found., 1935; asst. curator Renaissance and modern art Bklyn. Mus., 1936; asst. dept. paintings Met. Mus. Art, 1937, asst. curator, 1942; asst. dir. Corcoran Gallery Art, Washington, 1946, dir., sec., 1947-68, dir. emeritus, cons. to bd. trustees, 1968-74; adviser to bd. trustees Lauren-Rogers Mus., Laurel, Miss., 1970-74. Served in AUS, 1942-46; chief hist. properties sect. War Dept., lt. col. Res. ret. Recipient Corcoran Gold medal, 1969. Fellow Co. Mil. Historians; mem. Am. Assn. Museums, Am. Soc. Arms Collectors. Unitarian. Clubs: Harvard, Armor and Arms, Century Assn. (N.Y.C.); Cosmos, Harvard (Washington). Author: (with Bartlett Cowdrey) William Sidney Mount, 1944; The Civil War: The Artists' Record, 1961; Mirror to the American Past, A Survey of American Genre Painting 1750-1900, 1973. Contbr. articles on art subjects to art and ednl. jours., Ency. Am. Art. Home: Washington, D.C., also Ocean Point, Me. Died Nov. 3, 1974; interred Mount Auburn Cemetery, Cambridge, Mass.

WILLIAMS, HOWARD REES, b. Bangor, Me., Nov. 10, 1881; s. David Thomas and Esther (Rees) W.; Marietta (O.) Coll., 1900-1902; A.B., Western Reserve U., 1904; studied Union Theol. Sem., 1914-16, Columbia, 1915-16; m. Edna Jean Mitchell, of New York, 1907 (died 1912); 1 dau., Judith Mitchell; m. 2d, Sara Mildred Strauss, of New York City, 1922. In business, N.Y. City, until 1914; minister Unitarian Ch., Concord, N.H., 1917-18; with Foyer du Soldat, French Army, Mar.-Sept. 1918; speaker War Work Drive, U.S., Oct.-Dec. 1918; with Army Ednl. Corps, A.E.F., in France, 1919; vice chmn. Com. of 48; later v.p. Business Training Corpn., New York. Mem. League for Industrial Democracy, Civil Liberties Union, Free Religious Assn., League for Independent Political Action. Clubs: Newspaper, Meeting Place. Home: New York City, N.Y.†

WILLIAMS, JAMES MICKEL, sociologist; b. Sangerfield, N.Y., June 22, 1876; s. Riley Walter and Mary Turnbull (Mickel) W.; A.B., Brown U., 1898; B.D., Union Theol. Sem., 1901; Ph.D., Columbia, 1906; LL.D., Hobart, 1941; m. Lucinda Chamberlain Noyes, Jan. 22, 1913; 1 son, Henry Noyes. Lecturer in economics at Vassar College, 1907-08; professor of sociology, Hobart Coll., 1908-41, prof. emeritus from 1941. Author: The American Town, 1906; The Foundations of Social Science, 1920; Principles of Social Psychology, 1922; Our Rural Heritage, 1925; The Expansion of Rural Life, 1926; Children and the Depression, 1932; Human Aspects of Unemployment and Relief, 1933; The Police School-An Experiment in Adult Education, 1936. Home: Geneva N.Y. Died Aug. 7, 1973.

WILLIAMS, JESSE RAYMOND, educator; b. Noble, Ill., Oct. 13, 1878; s. Elbert Singleton and Lizzie (Edmondson) W.; A.B., B.S., U. of Mo., 1906; grad. student, U. of Chicago, 1908; m. Bertah Lucetta McKibben, Dec. 21, 1907; children—Raymond Gaylord, Franklin Reed. Supt. schs., Waukesha, Wis., 1918-21; pres. Advance Acad., Ft. Smith, Ark., 1921-24; founder, 1924, and pres. Miami Military Academy, Served as 1st lt. vols., Spanish-Am. War; mem. O.T.C., Ft. Sheridan, Ill., 1971. Mem. Miami Chamber Commerce. Republican. Episcopalian. Address: Miami, Fla.†

WILLIAMS, JOHN SCOTT, artist; b. Liverpool, Eng.; s. Richard and Mary Jane (Scott) W.; student pub. schs., Chgo., Art. Inst. of Chgo.; m. Clara Elsene Peck; children—Aynard Scott, Conway Scott; m. 2d, Mina Van Bott, June 30, 1930. Designer stained glass, mural, painter, art tchr., lectr., porcelain enamelist, 1937-75; asso. prof. U. Wyo. Coll. Edn., 1946-49; projects include porcelain enamel panel Cleveland Union Terminal, windows and murals Indiana State Liberary, library windows U. Ill., Johns Hopkins, set of military maps in procelain enamel American Battle Mounments Commn., stained glass and murals Milo H. Stuart Memorial. N.A., Mem. Am. Atrtists Profl. League (pres.), Am. Watercolor Soc., Architl. League N.Y. (past acting pres.), Allied Artists Am., Nat. Soc. Mental Painters (past pres., sec.-treas.), Phi Beta Kappa. Clubs: Salmagundi (past v.p.); Nat. Arts (gov.). Home: Gettysburg, Pa., Died Nov. 4, 1975.

WILLIAMS, JOSEPH TUTTLE, educator; b. Calhoun Co., Ill., June 1, 1878; s. Martin and Mary (Hamilton) W.; A.B., Washington U., 1902; Ph.D., Columbia, 1907; m. Mary A. Johnson, of Seattle, Wash., Aug. 10, 1911; children—Robert Martin, Marian. Instructor English, U. of Nev., 1902-03, in edn., State U. of Ia., 1907-08; lecturer on child psychology, Whitman Coll., 1909-10, on pedagogy, Brooklyn Inst. Arts and Sciences, 1910-11; social service sec. Charities Societies of N.Y. City, 1910-15; prof. edn., Wilmington Coll., 1915-17, Drury Coll., 1917-14, Whittier Coll., 1924-31; prof. polit. science, Los Angeles Jr. Coll., from 1931. Mem. Am. Acad. Polit. and Social Science, Pacific Southwest Acad. Polit. and Social Science, Am. Sociol. Soc., Am. Assn. Univ. Profs., Municipal League. Clubs: University, Kiwanis. Democrat. Author: Social Equality, 1907; Education in Recent Sociology, 1921. Home: Vista, Cal.†

WILLIAMS, KATHLEEN MARY, educator; b. Briton Ferry, S. Wales; d. Cecil Reginald and Rachel (Davey) Williams; B.A. with 1st class honours, Somerville Coll., Oxford (Eng.) U., 1941, M.A., 1946; D.Litt., U. Wales, 1967. Came to U.S., 1964. Lectr., then sr. lectr. U. Wales, 1946-54; mem. faculty U. Cal. at Riverside, 1964-66, and from 1967, prof. 18th century and Renaissance Eng., from 1967; prof. Rice U., 1966-67. Author: Jonathan Swift and the Age of Compromise, 2d edit., 1959; Spenser's World of Glass: The Faerie Queene, 1966; Erasmus Praise of Folly; Swift, 1970. Home: Riverside Cal. Died Dec. 5, 1974; buried Olivewood Cemetery, Riverside, Cal

WILLIAMS, LAURENS, lawyer; b. Pottsville, Pa., Dec. 14, 1906; s. Henry Laurens and Marian (Mortimer) W.; A.B., Hastings Coll., 1928; LL.B., Cornell U., 1931; LL.D. (hon.), U. Neb., 1968; m. 2d, Irene Benson, Mar. 22, 1958; children previous marriage—Henry L. IV, Catharine (Mrs. Michael B. Adler). Admitted to Neb. bar, 1931, D.C., bar, 1956, Ga. bar, 1957; practice of law, Omaha, 1931-54; partner Young, Williams & Holm, 1936-54; asst. to sec. reasury Dept., head legal adv. staff, 1954-56; sr. partner Sutherland, Asbill & Brennan, specializing fed. tax matters. Recipient Alexander Hamilton medal for distinguished leadership Treasury Dept. Mem. Am., Neb. (pres. 1953), Fed. (nat. council 1954-63) bar assns., Am. Law Inst. (council mem. 1955—, mem. exec. com. 1966—, treas. 1968—), Am. Judicature Soc., Nat. Tax Assn., D.C. Bar Assn. Clubs: Omaha; Metropolitan, Columbia Country (Washington). Author articles on legal subjects. Home: Washington, D.C., Died June 7, 1975.

WILLIAMS, LESLIE BENJAMIN, assn. exec.; b. Kinston, N.C., Sept. 3, 1914; s. Brown and Alice (Stroud) W.; B.S. in Chem. Engring., N.C. State U., 1935; postgrad. Harvard, Mass. Inst. Tech., 1941, U. Pa., 1946; M.S. in Physics, U. N.C., 1950; m. Christine Underwood Derby, Mar. 28, 1936; children—Leslie Benjamin, Rodger Derby, David Brown. Research engr., physicist Socony Vacuum Oil Co. (now Mobil Oil Co.), 1936-41, 46-47; commd. lt. col. USAF, 1947, advanced through grades to col., 1952; chief Aerospace Research Labs., USAF, 1950-55; dir. research Air Research and Devel. Command, 1955-57; chief research br., reactor devel. div. AEC, 1958-61; ret., 1963; dir. research U. Del., 1963-68; with Am. Soc. Engring. Edn., Washington, from 1968, exec. dir., from 1969. Exchange officer Dept. Def. to Dept. State, 1961-63; chmn. 22d Nat. Conf. Adminstrn. Research, 1968. Asso. fellow Am. Inst. Aeros. and Astronautics; mem. Am. Soc. Engring. Edn., Sigma Xi, Gamma Sigma Epsilon, Delta Sigma Phi. Home: Washington, D.C. Died May 14, 1974, buried Arlington Nat. Cemetery.

WILLIAMS, LESTER ALONZO, educator; b. Hampstead, N.H., June 11, 1880; s. Caleb Washington and Martha Hannah (Gordon) W.; student Am. Internat. Coll., Springfield, Mass., 1898-1901; A.B., Dartmouth, 1903, A.M., 1908; Pd.D., New York Univ., 1913; m. Charlene Augusta Tenney, Dec. 31, 1908 (died 1937); m. 2d, Elizabeth Louise Bishop, June 18, 1938. principal of West Dennis, Mass., 1903-04, North Brewster, 1904-05,Groveland, 1905-08, Laconia, N.H., 1908-09, Plymouth, Mass., 1909-11; supervising prin., Leonia, N.J., 1912-13; professor school adminstrn., School of Edn., University of N.C., 1913-22; prof. edn., University of Calif., from 1922, emeritus, from 1945. Associate director of Relations with Schools, 1936-40.

Fellow A.A.A.S.; mem. American Psychol. Association, N.E.A., Nat. Assn. Dirs. of Ednl. Research, Alpah Psi Delta, Phi Delta Kappa. Presbyterian. Mason. Club: Faculty. Author: The Making of High School Curricular; Secondary Schools for American Youth; (with G.A. Rice) Principles of Secondary Education; The Person-Consciousness of High School Pupils. Contbr. to mags. Home: Carmel, Cal.†

WILLIAMS, LLOYD THOMAS, lawyer; b. Jackson, O., May 31, 1874; s. William E. and Anna (Hughes) W.; Ph.B., Ohio State U., 1896, LL.B., 1900; LL.D., Defiance Coll., 1905; m. Frances Elizabeth Baker, Sept. 14, 1912; children—Frances Williams (Mrs. Lawrence Cathles), Alice (Mrs. Samuel Carson), Lloyd T., William, Arthur B. Admitted to Ohio bar, 1900, practiced in Toledo, 1900-03; asso. Brown & Geddes, 1903-04, partner Brown, Geddes, Schmettau & Williams, 1905-23; joined successor firm Williams Eversman & Black, Toledo, 1923, now mem. firm Williams, Robison & Curphey, Toledo. Mem. Am. Ohio, Toledo bar assns., Phi Beta Kappa, Phi Delta Phi, Beta Theta Pi. Clubs: Toledo, Toeldo Country. Home: Toledo, O.†

WILLIAMS, ROBERT SEATON, metallurgist; b. Hartford, Conn., July 11, 1880; s. Robert Edwards and Helen Elizabeth (Seaton) W.; S.B., Mass. Institute Tech., 1902; Ph.D., Göttingen, 1907; m. Bertha M. Downes, Jan. 29, 1910; children—Robert Downes, Seton Sawyer. Asst. in chemistry, 1902, instr., 1907, asst. prof., 1911, asso. prof., 1917-21, asso. prof. chemistry and metallography, 1921-24, prof. analyt. chemsitry and metallography, 1924-26, prof. phys. metallurgy, 1926-46, and head of dept. of metallurgy 1937-46, dep. dean engring., 1942-45, dean of Army and Navy Students, 1945-46, later emeritus, Massachusetts Inst. Tech. Fellow Am. Acad. Arts and Sciences, A.A.A.S.; member Mining and Metallurgical Society of America, Am. Institute Mining and Metall. Engrs., Am. Soc. for Metals, Am. Soc. for Testing Materials. Am. Foundrymen's Assn. Republican. Episcopalian. Author: Principles of Metallography, 1919, 5th edit. 1948. The Examination of Iron, Steel and Brass (with Prof. W. T. Hall), 1924. Translater; Ostwald's Introduction to Chemistry (with Prof. William T. Hall), 1911; Bauer and Deiss' Sampling and Analysis of Iron and Steel (with same), 11915. Home: Belmont, Mass.†

WILLIAMS, SAMUEL ROBINSON, prof. physics; b. Marengo, Ia., Mar. 2, 1879; s. John Dockray and Alma Porter (Davis) W.; Ph.B., Grinnell (Ia.) Coll., 1901, hon. D.Sc., 1928; M.A., U. of Neb., 1903; U. of Berlin, 1903-05; Ph.D., Columbia University, 1906; honorary D.Sc., Oberlin College, 1904; m. Ella Adelheid Mehlin, June 17, 1908; children—Ralph Mehlin, Paul Roger. Pvt. research asst. to Prof. F. Nichols, of Colubmia, 1905-06; lecturer in physics, Barnard Coll. (Columbia), 1906-07, tutor, 1907-08; asso. prof. physcis, Oberlin, 1908-10, prof., 1910-24; prof. physics, Amherst, 1924-47, later emeritus; cons. magnetism Gen. Motors Research Laboratories, Engr., Bur. Air Craft Prond., 1918. Fellow Am. Phys. Society, A.A.A.S.; mem. Am. Soc. of Metals, Phi Beta Kappa, Sigma Xi. Conglist. Author: Magnetic Phenomena, Foundations of College Physics, Experimental Physics, Hardness and Hardness Testing. Contbr. on magnetic and hardness phenomena. Home: Amherst, Mass.†

WILLIAMS, THOMAS R., business exec.; b. N.Y.C., 1881. Proprietor Ichabod T. Williams & Sons, N.Y.C.; pres., dir. George D. Emery Co., N.Y.C., Edgewater Saw Mills Co.; pres. Astoria Importing & Mfg. Co., N.Y.C.; chairman Astoria Pan Americana Co.; mem. adv. com. bd. Chem. Bank and N.Y. Trust Co. Home: Lawrence, N.Y.†

WILLIAMS, WHITING, author, lecturer, consultant; b. Shelby, O., Mar. 11, 1878; s. B. J. and Ida (Whiting) W.; A.B., Oberlin, 1899, A.M., 1909; U. of Berlin, 1899-1900, U. of Chicago (dept. of theology), 1900-01; m. Caroline Harter, Sept. 5, 1906 (died July 2, 1938), children—Carl R. (dec.), Harter Whiting, m. 2d, Dorothy Rogers, Aug. 4, 1941. Manager of Bureau University Travel, 1901-04; asst. to president Oberlin Coll., 1904-12; exec. sec. Cleveland Welfare Fed., 1912-16; special (group) agent, Equitable Life Assurance Soc., 1916-18; personnel dir. and v.p. Hydraulic Steel Co., 1918-20. Laborer in coal mines, steel plants, etc., in U.S. Germany, France and Gt. Britain, 1919-23, also studied workers' conditions in Russia (twice), Italy, Central and South American and unemployment and prohibition conditions in mid-west and Canadian industrial cities, various times, 1925-38. Speaks French, German, Spanish, Italian. Lecturer on labor and management problems orgns. in the U.S. and Canada. Adviser to large employers on personnel and public relations. Trustee Cleveland School of Art, Hiram House, Bur. U. Travel. Mem. Nat. Panel Arbitrators from 1940. Fellow Royal Geog. Society (London); mem. Am. Acad. Polit. and Social Science, Soc. for Advancement of Management, Am. Management Assn., Am. Econ. Assn., Personnel Research Federation. Decorated Order St. Sava (Servian). Republican. Presbyterian. Clubs: Union, Philos., City. Chamber of Commerce (Cleveland); Harvard, Dutch Treat (N.Y. City); Cosmos (Washington). Author books and articles relating to indsl. and sociol. questions. Home: Cleveland, Heights, O., Died Apr. 14, 1975.

WILLIAMS, WILLIAM ALFRED, geologist, mining engr.; b. San Francisco, Aug. 25, 1880; s. William Alfred and Lucy Addie (Goodell) W.; A.B., in geology and mining engring., U., 1903; Stanford m. Winifred H. Wright, of San Francisco, June 7, 1911. Asst. in geology, Stanford U., 1903-04; field asst. U.S. Geol. Survey, 1903, 04; mining in western states, Mexico and South America, 1904-08; geologist and chief geologist, Associated Oil Co., 1908-13; cons. geologist Gen. Petroleum Co., 1913-14; chief petroleum technologist, U.S. Bur. of Mines, in charge of petroleum investigations, 1914-16; asst. gen. mgr. Henry L. Doherty & Co., oil and gas properties, in mid-continent fields, 1917; with oil div. U.S. Fuel Adminstration, 1918; v.p. Henry L. Doherty & Co., 1919-20; v.p. Pierce Oil Corpn., 1920-22; pres. Crown Central Petroleum Corpn., 1925-32; later cons. engr. Address: San Francisco Cal.†

WILLIAMSON, EDWIN MOORE, physician; b. Tecumseh, Mich., Oct. 18, 1910; s. Charles and Naomi Williamson; M.D., U. Mich., 1937; m. Mary Eleanor Anderson, June 25, 1938. Rotating intern Toledo Hosp., 1937-38; staff psychiatrist Kalamazoo (Mich.) State Hosp., 1938-39; Nat. Com. for Mental Hygiene fellow in mental hygiene and child psychiatry Children's Center, Detroit, 1939-41; dir. Child Guidance Clinic, Kalamazoo, 1946-52; civilian cons. in psychiatry Percy Jones Gen. Hosp., 1946-49; psychiatrist in chief Plainwell (Mich.) Sanatarium, 1946-68. Served with armed Forces, 1941-46. Diplomate Am. Bd. Psychiatry and Neurology. Fellow Am. Psychiat. Assn.; mem. A.M.A., World Med. Assn. Bd. dirs. Lakeside Home for Boys and Girls, pres., 1963-65. Home: Kalamazoo, Mich. Died May 12, 1972; buried Tecumseh, Mich.

WILLIAMSON, PAULINE BROOKS, civic worker, educator; b. Glad Springs, Va., Mar. 28, 1887; d. John L. and Ellen (Brooks) Williamson; student U. Chgo., 1916; B.S., Columbia, 1918; diploma State Normal Sch., 1906. State rural supr. charge health work State Dept. Pub. Instrn. and State Dept. Health, Richmond, Va., 1922-25; chief sch. health bur. Health and Welfare div. Met. Life Ins. Co., N.Y.C., 1925-47; chmn. bd. dirs. Am. Assn. for Gifted Children, N.Y.C., 1947-72; spl. lectr. grad. course Tchrs. Coll., Columbia, 1948. Bd. dirs., hon. v.p. Nat. Soc. for Prevention of Blindness. M.B.L.S. Fellow Am. Pub. Health Assn., A.A.A.S., Am. Sch. Health Assn., Am. Assn. Sch. Adminstrs., Soc. Pub. Health Edn.; mem. Internat. Platform Assn., Kappa Delta Pi, Phi Delta Gamma (hon.). Democrat. Club: National Arts. Author: (with C. E. A. Winslow) The Laws of Health and How to Teach Them, 1925; also numerous articles on health and edn. Home: New York City, N.Y. Died July 22, 1972

WILLIBRAND, WILLIAM ANTHONY, educator; born Westphalia, Mo., June 30, 1892; s. John H. and Gertrude (Schwartze) W.; A.B., Warrensburg Mo. Tchrs. Coll., 1919; A.M., U. Chicago, 1921; Ph.D., U. Ia., 1940; student U. Montpellier, 1919, Nat. U. Mexico, 1922-23, Stanford, 1924-32, U. Heidelberg, 1930, U. Strasbourg, 1930-31; m. Thelma Whaley, May 31, 1936 (dec. Sept. 2, 1937); m. 2d Rosa Stimpert, Aug. 20, 1942; children—Ann, Mary. Tchr. pub. sch., Freeburg, Mo., 1909-14, St. Elizabeth, Mo., 1910-12; supt. Worthington (Mo.) Consol. Sch., 1916-17; instr. French and Spanish William Warren Sch., Menlo Park, Calif., 1921-22, Warrensburg Mo. State Tchrs. Coll., summer 1923; instr. Spanish San Jose (Calif.) State Tchrs. Coll., summer 1922. Ia. State Coll., 1923-24; asst. prof. U. Okla., 1924-35, asso. prof., 1935-45, prof. modern langs. from 1945; broadcaster in German radio sta. WNAD, University, Norman, Okla., 1938-51. Served as sgt., A.E.F., Europe, 1918-19. Mem. Modern Lang. Assn. of Am., S. Central Modern Lang. Assn., Am. Assn. Tchrs. German, Modern Humanities Research Assn., Okla Hist. Soc., Delta Phi Alpha. Roman Catholic. Author: Ernst Toller, Product of Two Revolutions, 1941; Ernst Toller and his Ideology, 1945; articles various publs. Research and articles on German settlements in Mo., Okla. Asst. and cons. editor of Books Abroad from 1928. Contbr. book reviews various periodicals. Home: Norman Okla. Died Sept. 10, 1973

WILLINGER, ALOYSIUS J(OSEPH), clergyman; b. Baltimore, Apr. 19, 1886; s. Louis J. and Ana Regina (Helrank) W.; student St. James Parochial Sch., Baltimore, St. Mary's Coll., N. East, Pa. and Mount St. Alphonsus, Esopus, N.Y. Ordained priest, Roman Cath. Ch., July 2, 1911; priest Mount St. Alphonsus Ch., 1911, redemptorist Mission House, Boston, redemptorist Missionary parishes in San Juan and Mayaguez, P.R.; bishop of Ponce, 1929-46, Diocese of Monterey-Fresno, Cal., from 1946. Commendador de Numero de la Orden de Isabel la Catolica. Mem. Phi Beta Gamma. Author: The Eucharist in Christian Life; Eucharist and Christian Life, 1958. Home: Fresno Cal. Died July 1973

WILLIS, WILLIAM DARRELL, army officer, physician b. Bryan, Tex., Jan. 29, 1907; s. William Eugene and Mary Etta (Wilcox) W.; M.D., Baylor U., 1931; student Grad. Sch. U. Pa., 1947-48; m. Dorcas Frances Chamberlain, Oct. 7, 1933; children—William Darrell, James E., Mary Louise (Mrs. C.W. Hale). with M.C.U.S. Army, 1931-58, advanced through grades to col.; intern, Brooke Gen. Hosp., Ft. Sam Houston, Tex., 1931-32; clin. tng. Sch. Aviation Medicine, Randolph Field, Tex., 1937-38, Army Med. Sch., Washington, 1938-39, Army Field Med. Sch., Carlisle, Pa., 1939; comdg. officer sta. hosp. Grenler Field, Manchester, N.H., 1941-42, Sta. Hosp. Mitchel Field, Long Island, N.Y., 1942-43, Air Force Hosp., Breaker's Hotel, Palm Beach, Fla., 1943, Biltmore Hosp., Coral Gables, Fla., sta. hosp. Hammer Field, Fresno, Cal., 308th Gen. Hosp., Tinian Island, Mariannas and Japan, 1945; surgeon, Seoul; Korea, 1946; chief of medicine Valley Forge Gen. Hosp.; mem. staff Phoenixville, Pa., 97th Gen. Hosp., Frankfurt, Germany, 1952-54, U.S. Army Hosp., Ft. Carson, Colo., 1954-56; staff U.S. Army Hosp., Ft. Hood, Tex., 1956-58; comdg. officer 1957-58; ret. 1958; physician Tex. A. and M. Coll., 1958-61. Diplomate Am. Bd. Internal Medicine. Mem. A.M.A. Home: San Antonio, Tex. Died Oct. 26, 1973; buried Ft. Sam Houston Nat. Cemetery, San Antonio,

WILLIUS, FREDERICK ARTHUR, physician; b. St. Paul, Nov. 24, 1888; s. Gustav Otto Conrad and Emma (Klausmayer) W.; M.D., U. Minn., 1914, M.Sc. in Medicine, 1920; m. Stella Popple, Sept. 26, 1917; children—Jane (Mrs. R.M. Landry), Betty (Mrs. T.J. Kirby), Dorothy (Mrs. Charles Knight). Intern, U. Minn. Hosp., Mpls., 1914-15; fellow in medicine Mayo Found., 1915-20; founder heart sect. Mayo Clinic, Rochester, Minn., 1922, head sect. cardiology, 1922, sr. cons., until 1972; prof. medicine emeritus Mayo Found. Grad. Sch. Diplomate Am. Bd. Internal Medicine. Fellow A.C.P.; mem. Am. Heart Assn., A.M.A., Central Soc. Clin. Research. Author numerous books including Cardiac Classics. Contbr. articles to med. jours. Home: Rochester, Minn. Died Oct. 19, 1972; buried Oakwood Cemetery, Rochester, Minn.

WILLKIE, PHILIP HERMAN, lawyer, banker; b. Rushville, Ind., Dec. 7, 1919; s. Wendell Lewis and Edith (Wilk) W.; A.B., Princeton, 1940; A.M. in History, Harvard, 1941; LL.B., Columbia, 1947; LL.D., Salem Coll., 1960; grad Stonier Grad. Sch. Banking, Rutgers U., 1957; L.H.D., Rider Coll., 1966; m. Virginia Z. Adamson; children—Wendell II, Philip H., Frank P., Benjamin J., David Wilk. Vice pres., dir. Rushville Nat. Bank, 1947-55, pres., atty., 1956-74; pres. So. Indiana, Inc., 1969-74; dir. Radio Liberty, Inc., Santee Utilities, Inc., Water Refining Corp.; admitted to Ind., N.Y. and D.C. bars, 1948; chief counsel U.S. Senate subcom. on morals and ethics, 1951. Republican rep. from Rush and Henry Counties to Ind. Legislature, 1949-55; alt. del. Rep. Nat. Conv., 1948, 60; del. Rep. State Conv., 1950; asst. chmn. Rep. Nat. Senatorial campaign com., 1949-50; Rep. candidate Ind. Supt. Pub. Instrn., 1960; mem. Rush County Rep. Com., 1963-66. Nat. chmn. Council for Advancement Small Colls., 1959-61; mem. U.S. bd. fgn. scholarships, 1953-58. Served from apprentice seaman to lt. USN, 1941-45. Mem. Beta Theta Pi. Presbyn. Mason. Lion. Clubs: Elks (Rushville); Press, Columbia (Indpls.); University (N.Y.C.). Author articles. Home: Rushville, Ind. Died Apr. 10, 1974; buried East Hill Cemetery, Rushville,

WILLS, BOB, composer, musician; b. Kosse, Tex., Mar. 6, 1905; s. John and Emmaline (Foley) W.; ed. schs., Tex.; m. Betty Anderson, Aug. 10, 1942; children—James Robert, Diane, Carolyn, Cindy. Organized music group Light Crust Doughboys, 1931, Tex. Playboys, 1933; appeared in numerous movies; rec. artist Columbia, MGM, Decca, others; compositions include San Antonio Rose, Faded Love, Maiden's Prayer, Spanish Two Step, Big Beaver. Served with AUS, World War II. Named to Country Music Hall of Fame, 1968, Cowboy Hall of Fame, 1969. Mem. Am. Soc. Composers Authors and Publishers. Address: Fort Worth, Tex. Died May 13, 1975; interred Meml. Park, Tulsa, Okla.

WILLSON, JAMES MCCRORRY, lumber dealer; b. Boonesville, Tex., Dec. 21, 1887; s. David and Sarah Eugenia (Strange) W.; A.B., Southwestern U., 1912; LL.D., Tex. Wesleyan Coll., 1947; L.H.D., McMurry Coll., Abilene, Tex., 1956; m. Mavis Louis, June 14, 1919; children—James McCrorry, Mavis Louis, (Mrs. Louis Arnold), Ora Eugenia Addis, David R. Owner lumber yards, 1908-72; line yard operator Willson & Son, 1916-72. Trustee So. Meth. U., Dallas, 1930-69; trustee McMurry Coll., Abilene, 1936-72, chmn. bd., 1951; established founds. numerous colls. and univs.; v.p. bd. trustees Meth. Hosp., Lubbock, Tex. Served with U.S. Army, World War I. Awarded Purple Heart Accolade. Mem. Gen. Conf. Meth. Ch., 1934-68, Uniting Conf., 1939; chmn. jurisdictional bd. hosp. and homes of Meth. Ch., 1949; trustee Western Meth. Assembly, v.p., 1934-66; trustee, chmn. camp bds. N.W. Tex. Conf. Meth. Ch., 1960-66; v.p. bd. trustees Meth. Hosp., Lubbock. Recipient Humanities awards Southwestern Coll., Wayland Coll.; Freedoms Found. award, 1960; named Ky. Col., 1967-72. Mem. Nat. council Boy Scouts Am. (Silver Beaver award), W. Tex. C. of C. (past pres.), Am. Legion (vice comdr.) (Tex.), V.F.W. (life). Mason (Shriner), Rotarian (dist. gov. 1935-36). Home: Floydada Tex. Died June 5, 1972.

WILMER, RICHARD HOOKER, lawyer; b. Washington, Oct. 20, 1892; s. William Holland and Re Lewis (Smith) W.; A.B., Yale, 1915; LL.B., Columbia,

1917, J.D., 1969; m. Margaret Van Dyke Grant, June 2, 1917; children—Richard H., John Grant. Admitted to D.C. bar, 1917, State of N.Y. bar, 1929; asso. Minor, Gatley & Rowland, Washington, 1919-24, Cravath, de Gersdorff, Swaine & Wood, N.Y.C. and Washington, 1924-29, partner, 1929-42; sr. partner Wilmer & Broun, 1946-62; sr. partner Wilmer, Cutler & Pickering, 1962-76. Chmn. A.R.C. campaign met. area Washington, 1946. Served to 1st lt. C.A.C., U.S. Army, 1917-19, to col. C.A.C. AUS, 1942-46; chief legal adviser Allied Commn. (Italy), 1944. Decorated Legion of Merit with oak leaf cluster, comdr. Order Saints Mauritius and Lazarus (Italy), Chevalier Legion Honor (France). Mem. Soc. Cin. (past pres., gen.), Am. Legion, Mil. Order World Wars, Am., D.C. bar assns. Bar Assn. City N.Y., Am. Law Inst. Mem. Chapter Washington Cathedral. Episcopalian. Clubs: Metropolitan. Chevy Chase, International (Washington). Home: Washington, D.C., Died Mar. 3, 1976.

WILSON, CHARLES HENRY, orthopedic surgeon; b. Coffeeville, Ala., 1908; M.D., Tulane U., 1935. Intern, Lloyd Noland Hosp., Fairfield, Ala., 1935-36. resident, 1936-40; practice medicine specializing in orthopedic surgery, Birmingham, Ala., 1947-74; mem. staff St. Vincent's Hosp., Univ. Hosp., Bapt. Hosp., Children's Hosp.; asso. prof. orthopedic surgery Med. Coll. Ala. Served to lt. col. M.C., AUS, 1942-47. Diplomate Am. Bd. Orthopedic Surgery. Fellow A.C.S.; mem. A.M.A., So. Med. Assns., Am. Acad. Orthopedic Surgeons. Home: Birmingham, Ala., Died Dec. 22, 1974.

WILSON, CHARLES STUART, physician; b. Detroit, Sept. 12, 1884; M.D., U. Mich., 1907; m. Myssel Hanover. Cons. medicine Grace Hosp.; chief med. sect. Alpena (Mich.) Gen. Hosp.; clin. prof. medicine Wayne State U. Sch. Medicine, 1920-34. Served to lt. col., M.C., AUS. Diplomate Am. Bd. Internal Medicine. Fellow A.C.P.; mem. A.M.A. Home: Alpena, Mich. Died May 19, 1972; buried Woodmere Cemetery, Detroit, Mich.

WILSON, EARL B., business exec.; b. Winchester, Mass., May 30, 1891; s. John Thomas and Pleasantine (Cushman) W.; m. Margaret Pew, Sept. 14, 1920; children—Pleasantine Cushman (Mrs. Robert G. Drake), Earl Boden, Margaret Pew (Mrs. Robert D. Kershaw). Engaged in surveying general land office, Southwestern United States and Alaska, 1910-15; entered sugar business with Ham & Seymour, N.Y. City, 1920; v.p. Nat. Sugar Refining Co., 1940-43; pres. and dir. Calif. and Hawaiian Sugar Refining Corp., Ltd., San Francisco, 1946-51; chmn. Sterling Sugars Inc., from 1952; dir. Commercial Bank and Trust Company, Franklin, La. Served U.S. Army, 1916-19, resigning as maj., cav., 1919. Prin. indsl. specialist, War Prodn.-Bd., consultant, Bd. Econ. Warfare, 1942; dir. sugar div., Commodity Credit Corp., U.S. Dept. Agr., 1943-45, dir. sugar branch, 1945-46. Mem. Soc. Mayflower Descendants, S.A.R., Am. Legion. Conglist. Mason. Clubs: Explorers (N.Y.C.); Boston. Author: Sugar and Its Wartime Controls, 1941-47. Home: Franklin La. Died Aug. 1973.

WILSON, ERNEST THEODORE, life ins. co. exec.; b. Fayetteville, Tenn., Nov. 14, 1908; s. Harmon Harrison and Margaret Vera (Sumners) W.; B.S. in Commerce, U. Tenn., 1930; m. Kathryn L. Jameson, Mar. 18, 1939; children—Kathryn Henrietta (Mrs. William J. Shasteen), Linda Margaret. Auditor, TVA, Knoxville, 1935-37; revenue agt. Bur. Internal Revenue, Nashville, 1937-42; successively home office auditor, asst. treas., asst. v.p. and treas., treas. Nat. Life and Accident Ins. Co., Nashville, 1942-64, v.p., treas., 1964-73. Served with USNR, 1944-46. C.P.A., Tenn. Mem. Am. Inst. C.P.A.'s, Tenn. Soc. C.P.A.'s. Methodist. Home: Nashville Tenn. Died May 11, 1973; interred Alexander Cemetery, Spring Hill, Tenn.

WILSON, EUGENE EDWARD, author, ret. naval officer; b. Dayton, Wash., Aug. 21, 1897; S. Eugene Talmadge and Clara (Pomeroy) W.; student U.S. Naval Academy 1904-08; A.M., Columbia, 1915; D.Sc. (honorary), Trinity College (Hartford), 1942; Eng.D. (honorary), Rensselaer Poly. Institute, Troy, N.Y., 1945, Worcester Poly. Inst., 1946; m. Genevieve Speer, Feb. 7, 1911. Commd. ensign, U.S. Navy, 1910, and advanced through grades to comdr.; resigned, 1930, to become pres. Hamilton Standard Propeller Corp., then pres. Sikorsky Aviation Corporation, Chance Vought Corporation; president and vice chairman United Aircraft Corporation, 1940-46; hon. dir. Hartford Nat. Bank & Trust Co.; dir. Dime Savs. Bank. Chmn. bd. govs. Aircraft Industries Assn. of Am., 1944-48. Republican. Conglist. Clubs: Army and Navy (Washington); Hartford, Anglers (hon.), New York Yacht (New York); Hobe Sound Yacht. Author: Air Power for Peace; Slipstream; A Pilgrimage of Anglers; Northwood's Rendezvous; Wings of the Dawn; On Eagles' Wings; Kitty Hawk to Sputnik to Polaris; The Gift of Foresight; Hawks & Doves in the Nez Perce Indian War of 1877. Home: Hartford Conn. also Palm Beach Fla. Died July 10, 1974.

WILSON, FRANK ROBERT, editor, pub.; b. Woodbury Co., Ia., Oct. 18, 1881; s. Milton R. and Anna G. (Roath) W.; grad. high sch., Sioux City, 1902; m. Philena Yutzv, of Sioux City, June 26, 1907. Editor and pub. Sioux City Daily News and pres. Sioux City News Co., 1906-15; publicity dir. Federal Farm Labor Bur., Washington, D.C., 1916-18; nat. dir. publicity of the 3d, 4th, and Victory liberty loans, 1918-19; financial dir. for D.W. Griffith, Inc, 1919-21; pres. Motion Picture Capital Corpn., 1923; pres. North American Theaters, Inc., Talking Picture Epics, Inc.; v.p. Principal Distributing Corpn. Chief of organization, Bur. of Pub. Relations, Nat. Recovery Adminstrn., Washington, D.C., Mem. Beta Theta Pi. Democrat. Clubs: Newspaper (New York), National Press (Washington). Author: The Farm Loan Primer; Borrowers' Bulletin; also newspaper and mag. articles. Address; Washington, D.C.†

WILSON, HAROLD J, lawyer; b. Monmouth, Ill., Aug. 20, 1879; s. Robert A. and Luella (Joss) W.; A.B., Monmouth College, 1901, M.A., 1906; J.D., Blackstone Law Institute, Chicago, 1904; married Lucia Blake, February 4, 1904; children—Richard Blake (deceased), Robert Edgar (foreign service officer), Lucia Hurd Simons. Admitted to Iowa bar, 1904, Circuit Court of Appeals 1905; practiced in Burlington from 1904; senior partner Wilson & Jackson; president Burlington Security Company, mgr. and sec. Ia. Posting Service; treas. and dir.; Outdoor Advertising Assn. of Ia.; local atty., adjuster western Ill. and eastern Iowa, Am. Surety Co., N.Y., Am. Auto Ins. Co., St. Louis, Eagle and Globe Indemnity, Aetna Casulaty. Served as secretary, local board, Selective Service, World War I; chmn. Appeal Board No. 4, Selective Service, Dir. Des Moines County Legal Library Assn.; trustee Burlington Municipal Golf Assn. Mem. Civil Legion, Y.M.C.A. (State exec. com.), Am. and Ia. State bar assn. Republican. Presbyn. (elder; clk. of session). Mason. Elks. Club: Kiwanis (pres. 1940). Author: (brochure) Were I A Boy Again, 1912 (21 editions); Behold Burlington, 1943 (3 21 editions). Editor Harold's Column, "The Antlers" B.P.O.E. No. 84; also contbr. "Cocklebur," Omaha, Neb., "The Lawyer," Brooklyn, N.Y., "Underwriters Review," Des Moines, Iowa. Weekly broadcasts over KBUR. Home: Burlington, Ia.†

WILSON, J. CHRISTY, clergyman, educator, missionary; b. Columbus, Neb., July 22, 1891; s. Charles and Lilly Gray (Moore) W.; A.B., U. Kan., 1914; A.M., Princeton, 1919, Th.M., 1926; D.D., Emporia (Kan.) Coll., 1934, Lafayetta (Pa.) Coll., 1934; m. C. Fern Wilson, Apr. 7, 1917; children—John Brenton, J. Christy, Stanley Donald, Nancy Carol. Ordained to ministry Presbyn. Ch., 1918; evanglistic missionary under Presbyn. Bd. Fgn. Missions stationed Tabriz, Azerbaijan, Iran, 1919-40; chmn. Near East Relief Com. for Persia, 1921-23; chmn. Near East Christian Council, 1937-40; tchr. defense courses Persian Columbia, 1941-42; became dir. field work and asso. prof. ecumenics Princeton Theol. Sem., 1941, past dean of field service; dir. Princeton Inst. of Theology, 1942-56; resource leader Winona Lake Sch. Theology Flying Seminar to Middle East and Russia, 1958; pastor of visitation 1st Presbyn. Ch., Princeton, 1962-65, 1st Presbyn. Ch., Monrovia, Cal., 1965-70; prof. missions Mary Stewart Internat. U., Monrovia, 1970-73. Interpreter, piegraphist two expdns. of Iranian Inst. of N.Y.; interpreter, lang. aid to Dr. Frank Laubach in Literacy Campaign in Afghanistan, 1951. Mem. exec. com. World Literacy and Christian Literature div. Fgn. Missions, Nat. Council of Chs. in U.S. Dir. YMCA of Princeton and Mercer County. Mem. Waldensain Aid Soc. (pres. Princeton br.), Phi Beta Kappa, Delta Chi. Club: New York Oriental (N.Y.C.). Author: (books in the Persian language) Commentary on the Epistle to the Hewbrews, 1933; The Bible and Evangelism, 1936; The History of Iranian Art (at request of Imperial Ministry of Edn. of Iran), 1938; (books in English) Introducing Islam, 1950; The Christian Message to Islam, 1950; Apostle to Islam, biography of Samuel M. Zwemer, 1952; Flaming Prophet, 1970. Missionary editor and writer weekly missionary column, the Presbyterian, 1935-48; adv. editor: The Muslim World. Contbr. articles on the Near East for New Collier's Ency. and Schaff-Herzog Ency. of Religious Knowledge. Contbr. Christian Century, World Dominion, Orient and Occident and others. Radio speaker on Middle East. Editor: Ministers in Training: Textbook on Field Education, 1957. Home: Duarte Cal. Died Apr. 8, 1973.

WILSON, ROBERT CHRISTIAN, banker; b. Mudgee, Australia, Nov. 11, 1896; grad. high sch.; m. Gertrude Brooks, May 7, 1932; 1 son, 2 daus. Chmn., Tooheys Ltd., 1962-73; dir. Bank of N.S.W., Allied Mills Ltd., Australian Guarantee Corp. Ltd., Scottish Australian Co. Ltd., Sydneey bd. Union Fidelity Trustee Co. Ltd. With Royal Flying Doctor Service. Served with Australian Imperial Forces, World War I. Decorated comdr. Order St. Michael and St. George, MLC; created knight, 1966. Clubs: Australian, Elanora, Queensland (Brisbane). Address: Sydney, Australia. Died 1973.

WILSON, ROBERT WILBAR, army officer; b. Harrisburg, Pa., Aug. 26, 1893; s. Edwin Ellsworth and Loretta (Wilbar) W.; A.B., Yale, 1916; grad. Command and Gen. Staff Sch., Ft. Leavenworth, Kan., 1941; m. Edith Lyle Miller, Apr. 16, 1919; children—Robert Wilbar, Charlotte Ann. Engaged in sales and sales promotion of pharm. products, 1922-41. Commd. 2d lt., F.A., U. S. Army, 1917, capt. 1922; commd. lt. col., F.A., Army U.S., 1941; apptd. A.C. of S. G-4, II Corps, 1943; apptd. brig. gen., 1944, maj. gen. 1949; regional mgr. VA to 1958; v.p. Macon Smith & Company, mgmt. cons. from 1958. Chairman Southeastern Pennsylvania chapter A.R.C. Decorated Legion of Merit with Oak Leaf Cluster; Distinguished Service Medal; Legion of Honor (France); Croix de Guerre (France); Order of Kutusov 2d Class (Russia). St. Andrews Soc., Pa. Hist. Soc. Union League. Clubs: Penn, Yale (Phila.), Army and Navy (Washington). Home: Drexel Hill Pa. Died Feb. 13, 1975; buried Arlington National Cemetery.

WILSON, RUTH DANENHOWER (MRS. ALBERT FREDERICK WILSON), author; b. Annapolis, Md., Feb. 10, 1887; d. Lt. John Wilson (U.S. Navy) and Helen (Sloan) Danenhower; B.A., Vassar, 1911 (Phi Beta Kappa); M.A., N.Y. U., 1947; m. Albert Frederick Wilson, June 10, 1916 (dec. June 1940); children—Mary Sherwood (Mrs. Rowley Bialla), Sloan, Geoffrey. Extensive research in psychology and sociology. Pres., Ticonderoga (N.Y. Arts and Crafts Soc., 1931-36, Alliance Francaise of Volusia County, Fla., 1938-39, North Country Arts and Crafts Soc., Ticonderoga, 1941-56, Rogers Rock Club, Ticonderoga, 1941-65. Trustee Bethune-Cookman Coll., 1944-55. Mem. Am. Assn. U. Women (1st v.p. N.Y.C. br. 1949-55), Essex County Adirondeck Garden Club (pres. 1952-55). Episcopalian. Author: Giving Your Child the Best Chance, 1924; Jim Crow Joins Up, A Study of Negroes in the Armed Forces of the U.S., 1944, 1945; Here is Haiti, 1957. Contbr. spl. articles to mags. Address: Ticonderoga N.Y. Died Nov. 2, 1974.

WILSON, SOL, artist; b. Vilno, Poland, Aug. 23, 1896; s. Herman and Ida (Volk) W.; student Cooper Union Art. Sch., 1918-20 Beaux Arts Sch., N.Y.C., 1919, Nat. Acad. Design, 1920-22; studied with Robert Henri, George Bellows; m. Dora Packriss, Sept. 1921; 1 dau., Jacqueline. Came to U.S., 1911, naturalized, 1927. Instr. Y.M.H.A. New Haven, 1926-27, Am. Artists Sch., 1936-40, Sch. Art Studies, N.Y.C., 1946; teacher at the Art Students League, N.Y.C. One man exhbns. Civic Art Club, N.Y.C., 1926, New Haven, 1927, Paris, 1931. Babcock Galleries, N.Y.C., 1932, 36, 40, 42, 1944-45, 47, 51, 53, Currier Gallery Manchester, N.H., 1945, Cowie Gallery, Los Angeles, Shore Studio Galleries, Boston and Provincetown, Mass., Garelick Galleries, Detroit; Athena Galleries, New Haven, East End Gallery, Provincetown, Fine Arts Gallery, Boston, North Truro (Mass.) Art Center, Provincetown Art Group Gallery, Foster Harmon Galleries, Sarasota and Naples, Fla.; works represented nat. exhibits N.Y.. World's Fair, 1939, Carnegie Inst., Corcoran Galleries, Pa. Acad., Nat. Acad., Chgo. Art Inst., Va. Mus., Clearwater Mus., Montclair Mus., Critic's Choice, Arts and Antiques Show, N.Y.C., 1945, Whitney Mus., Addison Gallery, Neb. Art. Assn., St. Louis City Mus., U. Ia., Walker Art Center, Newark Mus., Bklyn Mus., State Dept. Exhbn., Met. Mus., Akron Art Inst.; represented collections Seattle Mus., U. Ia. Mus., St. Louis City Mus., Telfair Acad., Savannah, Ga., Balt. Mus., Bklyn Coll., Library Congress, Bklyn. Mus., Met Museum of Art, A.R.C., U. Minn., N.Y.U., Provincetown Art Assn., Smithsonian Instn., Worcester (Mass.) Mus., Newark Mus., Bezalel Mus., Israel, Living Arts Found., N.Y.C., Brandeis U., Butler Art Inst., Youngstown, O., Syracuse U. Mus., others; also represented in pvt. collections. Mem. Artists Equity Assn., Audubon Artists, also National Academy of Design, 1968. Awarded purchase prize A.R.C. competition, 1942; Artists for Victory prize, 1943; Pepsi-Cola prize, 1944; Audubon Artists prize, 1947, 50, 63, 69; Corcoran Biennial award, 1947; Carnegie Annual award, 1947; Medal of Honor Pepsi-Cola, 1948; Am. Acad. Arts and Letters Grant, 1950; First prize Cape Cod Art Assn., 1954, 56; Child Hassam Fund Purchase prize, 1954; Soc. Paintersin Casein award, 1955; Adolph and Clara Obrig prize, Nat. Acad. Design, 1958; Ranger Fund Purchase prize, 1958; Audubon Medal of Honor, 1959; Andrew Carnegie prize N.A.D., 1966. Mem. Provincetown Art Assn. Home: New York City N.Y. Died Nov. 23, 1974; interred Wellwood Cemetery, Long Island, N.Y.

WILSON, STANLEY KIDDER, writer; b. Madions, N.J., Apr. 16, 1879; s. James Oliver (D.D.) and Evalina Elizabeth (Kidder) W.; A.B., Columbia, 1902, Proud fit fellow in letters, Columbia, 1903-05. A.M., Harvard, 1903; m. Marguerite Kitchenman Scanlin, of Phila., Feb. 3, 1906; children—Stanley Kidder, Patricia (Mrs. Auguste Jean Charles Vaurie), irginia Gordon (Mrs. William Baker Miller). Advertising and publicity work, 1918-22; copy dir. Erickson Co., advertising, 1922-30, Newell-Emmett Co., 1930-34; vice pres. Chase Dallas Reach Co., 1935-36; creative dir. Erwin, Wasey & Co., Ltd., London, Eng. and mem. bd. of dirs. from 1936. Mem. Phi Beta Kappa, Phi Gamma Delta. Republican. Clubs: Columbia University (New York); Philobiblon (Phila.); American Club of London; Royal Automobile (London). Author: John Leech, Introduction and Bibliography (Grolier Club), 1914; Winning and Holding in Advertising and Selling, 1930; (novel) The Scream of the Doll, 1931; Guess Who (pseud. Pliny the Youngest), 1934. Contbr. to mags. Home: London, England.†

WILSON, THOMAS R(ICHARD), educator; b. Seattle, Sept. 29, 1897; s. Thomas H. and Mary J. (Contraman) W.; B.S., U. Cal., 1922; B.F.S., Georgetown U., 1923, Ph.D., 1932; M.A., George Washington U., 1924; m. Gladys M. Cockerille, June 28, 1929; children—Thomas Richard, Ralph Gregory.

Staff U.S. Dept. Commerce, 1922-57; professor San Francisco State Coll., 1957-70, prof: emeritus, 1970, asst. director Center World Bus. Chief Brit. Sect. Western European div., 1923-25, asst. trade commr. Ottawa, 1925-26, chief Brit. and Orient sect., fgn. tariffs div., 1926-29, chief European sect., finance div., 1929-41, chief Brit. Empire unit div. internat. economy, 1942-45, asst. dir. areas br. Office Internat. Trade, 1946, dir. areas div., 1948-51, asst. to dir. Bur. Fgn. Commerce, 1951-55; special assistant to asst. sec. for international affairs, Foreign Service Operations, 1955-57. Mem. World Affairs Council, No. Cal. Mem. Am. Legion, San Francisco Bay World Trade Assn., Pi Gamma Mu, Alpha Kappa Lambda, Delta Sigma Pi, Beta Gamma Sigma, Phi Sigma Pi. Baptist. Mason. Clubs: Commonwealth (Cal.); Propellar (hon.) (San Francisco). Address: San Francisco, Cal. Died Sept. 21, 1970.

WILSON, VINCENT EDWARD, elec. contractor; b. Mpls., Oct. 31, 1920; s. Vincent Edward and Inga (Tomte) W.; student U. Minn., 1938-41; m. Jeanne Engstrom, July 26, 1944; children—Candyce (Mrs. David D. Bartol), Brian Vincent. Vice pres. Wilson Electric Co., Mpls., 1955-60, pres., 1960-74. Chmn. com. Viking council Boy Scouts Am., 1968-74. Mem. Nat. Elec. Contractors Assn. (bd. dirs., head marketing com. 1968, pres. 1971-73), Soc. Illuminating Engrs. Club: S.W. Exchange (pres. Mpls. 1968-69). Home: Minnetonka, Minn. Died Mar. 17, 1974; buried Lakewood Cemetery, Mpls.

WILSON, WALTER LEWIS, physician, mfr.; preacher, lecturer; b. Aurora, Ind., May 27, 1881; s. Albert Miller (M.D.) and Emma (Dyke) W.; grad. high sch., Kansas City, Mo., 1899; studied medicine, Northwestern Univ., 1902; M.D., U. of Kan., 1904; L.H.D., Bob Jones Coll., Cleveland, Tenn., 1937; m. Marion Ruth Baker, 1904; children—Emma Elizabeth, Walter Lewis, Margaret Esther, Marion Ruth, Norman Albert, Nathaniel Dyke, Martha Frances, Catherine Jeanne. Practiced in Kansas City from 1904, giving much time to gratuitous service; gen. mgr. Baker Lockwood Mfg. Co., tents and awnings, 1912-20, pres., 1926-28; specialized in lagrge tents for circuses, theatricals, chautauquas, and the U.S. Govt. A founder, 1932, director and president Kansas City Bible Institute; conductor daily Bible radio broadcast over station WDAP, Kansas City, 1926-35, station WHB, Kansas City, 1943-44; undenominational preacher at Central Bible Hall, Kansas City, in churches and at Bible conferences throughout U.S. Trustee Bob Jones Coll., Cleveland, Tenn. Republican. Mem. Plymouth Brethren Ch. Author of numerous brochures and other publs., also med. and religious articles. Lectr. Home: Kansas City, Mo.*†

WILSON, WEBSTER HILL, electronics co. exec.; b. Wollaston, Mass., Apr. 5, 1913; s. Walton Wesley and Ethel May (Jones) W.; grad. Phillips Acad., Andover, Mass., 1932; B.S., Mass. Inst. Tech., 1936; m. Marguerite Von Lenz Brandt, June 10, 1939 (dec. Apr. 1947); children—Joan Wesley, Lee Webster; m. 2d, Annabelle d'Arche, Nov. 16, 1951. Engr., Boston Edison Co., 1936-42; with Hazeltine Corp., Little Neck, L.I., N.Y., 1946-63, v.p. electronics div., 1955-57, exec. v.p. div., 1957-60, dir., 1958-63, pres., 1960-63, chmn., 1961-63; pres. Hazeltine Research, Inc., 1962-63; dir. Western Union Co. Mem. U.S. delegation 1st Internat. Meeting Radio Aids to Marine Nav., London, Eng., 1946. Served to lt. comdr. USNR, 1942-46, Mem. Inst. Electronic and Elec. Engrs., Nat. Security Indsl. Assn., Armed Forces Communications and Electronics Assn., Am. Soc. Naval Engrs., Air Force Assn., Am. Ordnance Assn., Nat. Aviation Club, Delta Kappa Epsilon. Home: New York City, N.Y. Died Apr. 2, 1974.

WILSON, WILLARD, coll. adminstr., writer; b. Hansen, Ky., June 29, 1904; s. William C. and Sarah (Ragsdale) W.; A.B., Occidental Coll., 1929, LL.D., 1961; M.A., Columbia U., 1930; Ph.D., U. So. Cal., 1939; m. Magreita Livingston, June 13, 1942; 1 dau., Martha Ann. Free-lance writer, 1928-35; instr. English U. Hawaii, 1930, asst. prof., 1939-42, asso. prof. 1943-47, prof., 1948-50, sr. prof., 1950-70, chmn. dept., 1941-47, dean students, 1948-51, dean coll. arts and scis., 1951-55, v.p. dean faculties, 1955-57, acting pres., 1957-58, provost, 1958-63, sec. univ., 1963-70, emeritus sr. prof. and adminstr., 1969; free lance writer, 1970-74; exec. Office Censorship; dist. postal censor, Hawaii, 1944-45. Bd. mgrs. Mid-Pacific Inst. Chmn. Western Interstate Commn. for Higher Edn., 1965; chmn. Hawaii Com. on Alcoholism, 1963-66. Dir. Honolulu Symphony Soc., Hawaii Med. Service Assn. (pres. 1963-64). Mem. N.E.A., Am. Assn. U. Profs., Western Interstate Commn, Higher Edn. (exec. com.), Social Science Assn., Newcomen Soc. N. Am., Hawaiian Hist. Soc., Phi Beta Kappa, Phi Kappa Phi. Conglist. Clubs: Oahu Country. Author: Represented in Pacific Era, 1948; Sherlock Holmes: Master Detective, 1952; also numerous articles. Home: Kula, Maui, Hawaii Died Dec. 1974

WILSON, WILLIAM JOSEPH physician; b. Lowndesville, S.C., Aug. 4, 1909; s. Joseph D. and Ella (Sherard) W.; M.D., U. Colo., 1940; m. Bernice M. MacDonald, Sept. 23, 1944; children—Marshall, Margaret (Mrs. Johnnie Ravan). Intern, N.Y.C. Hosp., 1940-41; polio researcher Colo. Bd. Health, 1941-42; resident Johns Hopkins Hosp., 1945-48, Children's Hosp., Balt., 1945-48; staff James Walker Meml. Hosp., Wilmington, N.C., Babies Hosp., Wilmington; chief orthopaedic surgery VA Hosp., Lake City, Fla., 1955-57; orthopaedic surgeon S.C. State Hosp., Columbia; St. Lukes Hosp., Tryon, N.C.; instr. in orthopaedics Johns Hopkins U. Sch. Medicine, 1946-48. Served to maj. M.C., AUS, 1942-45; PTO. Diplomate Am. Bd. Orthopaedic Surgery. Mem. A.M.A., Am. Acad. Orthopaedic Surgeons. Contbr. articles to profl. jours. Home: Tryon, N.C. Died Oct. 10, 1974; buried Asheville, S.C.

WILSON, WILLIAM RALPH, physician; b. Rochester, N.Y., Nov. 18, 1924; s. Clair Van Deusen and Bertha (Gilfillan) W.; B.A., Hamilton Coll., 1948; M.D., State U. N.Y. at Syracuse, 1952; m. Charlotte Ann York, June 24, 1950; 1 son, Jeffrey Scott. Intern, Ind. U. Hosps., 1952-53; resident Univ. Hosps., Iowa City, 1953-56, research fellow, 1956-59; staff, 1956-75; practice medicine specializing in internal medicine, Iowa City; mem. staff VA Hosp., 1956-75; asst. prof. internal medicine U. Ia., 1959-63, asso. prof., 1963-64, asso. prof. pharmacology, 1964-68, prof. internal medicine and pharmacology, 1968-75. Served to 1st lt. M.C., AUS, 1952-56. Diplomate Am. Bd. Internal Medicine. Fellow A.C.P.; mem. Am. Heart Assn., Am. Fedn. for Clin. Research, A.A.A.S., Ia. Med. Soc., A.M.A., A.A.U.P., N.Y. Acad. Scis., Central Soc. for Clin. Research, Am. Soc. for Clin. Investigation, Soc. for Exptl. Biology and Medicine, Am. Soc. for Pharmacology and Exptl. Therapeutics, Central Clin. Research Club, Johnson County Med. Soc., Ia. Heart Assn. (pres. 1970-72), Ia. Soc. Internal Medicine, Sigma Xi, others. Home: Iowa City, Ia. Died May 1, 1975; buried Oakland Cemetery, Iowa City, Ia.

WILT, NAPIER, educator; b. Hillsboro, Ind., Dec. 20, 1896; s. John A. and Susie (Napier) W.; A.B., Indiana University, 1917, Litt.D., 1954; A.M., University of Chicago, 1921, Ph.D., 1923; unmarried. Instructor, asst. prof., asso. professor University of Chicago, 1923-40, prof. of English from 1940, also chmn. English dept. 1947-51, dean dvision of division of the humanities, 1951-61. Served with Battery F, 150th F.A., United States Army, 1917-19. Member Modern Lang. Assn. of Am. Democrat. Episcopalian. Clubs: Quadrangle (University of Chicago), Tavern (Chicago). Author: Some Nineteenth Century American Humorists, 1928; The Plays of Bartley Campbell, 1945. Contbr. articles and revs. on Am. literature. Home: Chicago, Ill., Died Nov. 12, 1975.

WIMSATT, WILLIAM KURTZ, educator; b. Washington, Nov. 27, 1907; s. William K. and Bertha (McSherry) W.; A.B., Georgetown U., 1928, M.A., 1929; postgrad. Cath. U. Am., 1935-36; Ph.D., Yale, 1939; Litt.D., Vilanova U., 1962, U. Notre Dame, 1963; LL.D., St. Louis U., 1964; D.H.L., Le Moyne Coll., 1965, Kenyon Coll., 1970; m. Margaret Elizabeth Hecht, Sept. 1944; children—William Alexander (dec. 1965), James Christopher. Head dept. English, Portsmouth (R.I.) Sch., 1930-35; instr. English, Yale, 1939-43, asst. prof., 1943-49, asso. prof., 1949-55, prof., 1955-75. Guggenheim fellow, 1946-47; Fund for Advancement of Learning fellow, 1953-54. Mem. Modern Lang. Assn. Am. (exec. council 1955-58), English Inst. (chmn. 1954), Conn. Acad. Arts and Scis. (pres. 1969-70). Author: The Prose Style of Samuel Johnson, 1941; Philosophic Words, 1948; The Verbal Icon, 1954; (with Cleanth Brooks) Literary Criticism, A Short History, 1957; Hateful Contraries, 1965; The Portraits of Alexander Pope, 1965. Editor: The Idea of Comedy, 1969; Versification, Major Language Types, 1972; Day of the Leopards: Essays in Defense of Poems, posthumous publ., 1976. Co-editor; Boswell for the Defence, 1769-1774, 1959. Home: New Haven, Conn., Died Dec. 17, 1975; buried All Saints Cemetery, North Haven, Conn.

WINANS, WILFRED HUGHES, corp. indsl. relations exec.; b. Port Henry, N.Y., Oct. 1, 1889; s. William Robert and Ida M. (Lansing) W.; A.B., Ohio Wesleyan U., 1909; m. Beatrice Coby, June 15, 1911; children—Dorothy Coby (Mrs. H. J. Jensen), Robert Coby. Supt. Asso. Charities, 1913; sec. Dept. Pub. Welfare, Cleve., 1914; commr. Charities and Correction, 1915-16; employment mgr. Nat. Carbon Co., 1916-19 (all Cleveland); industrial relations manager Union Carbide & Carbon Corporation, 1919-50, vice president industrial relations from 1950, Linde Air Products Co.; vice president National Carbon Co., Electro Metall. Co. (all N.Y. City). Mem. Nat. Assn. Mfrs. (mem. bd. dirs.), Sigma Alpha Epsilon. Clubs: Shore (Larchmont, N.Y.). Uptown (N.Y. City); Timber Trails (Sherman, Conn.). Home: Larchmont, N.Y., Died June 11, 1975.

WINDGASSEN, WOLFGANG FRIEDRICH HERMANN, tenor; b. Annemasse, Haute Savoie, Germany, June 26, 1914; s. Fritz and Vally (von der Osten) W.; ed. Württemberg Acad. Music, Stuttgart, 1934-37; m. Charlotte Schweikher, Nov. 20, 1939; (dec. July 1961); children—Peter, Verena; m. 2d, Lore Wissmann, Dec. 29, 1961; Appeared Municipal; Theatre, Pforzheim, 1939-44, State Opera Stuttgart, 1945, Festival Performance, Bayreuth, 1951, State Opera Vienna, 1953; performances with oepra houses in Milan, Rome, Naples, Venice, Paris, Brussels, Amsterdam, London, N.Y.C., Lisbon, Barcelona, Zürich, Budapest, otehrs. Pres. Assn. German Theatres Members in German Trade Union, 1963-74. Served with German Army, 1937-39. Named Court Singer in Württemberg, 1951, Austrian Court Singer, 1964; recipient Golden Orpheus medal (Italy), 1957, Golden medal of theatre, Liceo, Barcelona, 1958. Home: Stuttgart, Federal Republic of Germany.

WINEMAN, HENRY, merchant; b. Cincinnati, Dec. 12, 1878; s. Leopold and Henrietta (Bettman) W.; B.A., U. Mich., 1901; m. Gertrude Friedman, Nov. 30, 1911; children—James, Mary (Mrs. Arthur Davis). Pres. Wineman Realty Co.; chmn. Peoples Outfitting Co. (both Detroit). Co.-chmn. Detroit Round Table Catholics, Jews and Protestants; dir. Jewish Welfare Fedn. of Detroit; hon. chmn. Detroit, 1952; Allied Jewish Campaign, Dir. United Found. (Detroit). Mem. bd. Am. Friends of Hebrew U. in Palestine. Trustee v.p., Sinal Hosp. Mem. U.S. C. of C., Detroit Bd. Commerce. Clubs: Golf (Detroit); Franklin Hills Golf (Franklin, Mich.). Home: U1Detroit, Mich.†

WINKENWERDER, HUGO AUGUST, forester; b. Watertown, Wis., Mar. 16, 1878; s. Henry and Sophia (Kusel) W.; student Northwestern Coll., Watertown, Wis.; B.Sc., U. of Wis., 1902; M.F., Yale Sch. of Forestry, 1907; m. Adeline Clark, Nov. 27, 1909. Instr. Sheboygan High Sch., 1902-05; Sch., 1902-05; in charge of edn., U.S. Forest Service, July 1, 1907-Jan. 16, 1908; asst. prof. of forestry, Colorado Coll., Colorado Springs, Colo., 1908-09; asso. prof. forestry, 1909-12, prof. forestry and dean College of Forestry, Aug. 1, 1912, Feb. 28, 1945; dean emeritus, from Mar. 1, 1945; Univ. of Wash., acting prs., Apr. 1, 1933-Aug. 1, 1934; dir. Wash. State Arboretum, 1934-38, Collaborator United States Forest Service, 1908-14. Chmn. Wash. State Forestry Conf., 1922-24. pres. 1925-45; vice chmn. Wash. State Forest Service, 1908-14, Chmn. Wash. State Forestry Conf., 1922-24, pres. 1925-45; vice chmn. Wash. State Forest Bd., 1923-45. Trustee Pack. Forest Educational trustee Puget Sound Acad. Science, Arboretum Foundation of Wash.; fellow Soc. Am. Foresters (council mem. 1932-38), A.A.A.S.; mem. Am. Forestry Assn., Sigma Xi; hon. life mem. Seattle Chapter Garden Club of America. Clubs: Faculty, Seattle Rod and Gun (hon. life). Author: Migration of Birds, 1902; Forestry in the Public Schools, 1907; Forests and American History, 1912; Exercises in Forest Mensuration (with E. T. Clark), 1915, etc. Home: Seattle, Wash.†

WINNER, PERCY, author, journalist; b. N.Y.C., Oct. 16, 1899; s. David N. and Rose L. (Chavin) W.; student Columbia, 1916-18, Sorbonne, Paris, France, 1919-21; m. Fale Jarmel, Sept. 29, 1925 (div. 1933); 1 son Anthony; m. 2d. Giselle de Libohova; 1 son, Christopher Percy. With Chgo. Tribune, Paris, 1920-21, N.Y. Sun, 1922, N.Y. Herald, 1922-23, A.P., N.Y.C., 1923, corr. London, Eng., Paris, 1924, Rome, 1924-28; news, fgn. editor, editorial writer, polit. columnist N.Y. Evening Post, 1928-32; asso. N.Y. corr. Manchester (Eng.) Guardian, 1930-31; polit. columnist N.Y. Jour., 1932-33; radio commentator sta. WINS, 1933; chief N. Am. corr. Havas News Agy., Paris, 1934-36; commentator CBS, 1936, fgn. commentator, 1936-37; dir. internat. div. short wave NBC, 1937-38; fgn. staff Internat. News Service, 1938-40, dir. Italy, 1939-41; co-ordinator information O.W.I., London, 1941-42, dep. dir., 1942-44; various assignments U.S. Army, Europe, Africa, 1942-44; sr. editor New Republic, 1948, fgn. affairs editor, 1949-50, corr. Western Europe, 1956-58; sr. writer UNESCO, 1950-56; dep. dir. research Fgn. Area Studies, Am. U., Washington, from 1958. Staff lectr. Mil. Assistance Inst., Arlington Va.; spl. rep. in Spain, Interpub., N.Y.C., 1962-63. Author: Dario, 1947, Scene in the Ice-Blue Eyes, the Mote and the Beam, 1948. Contbr. polit. psychol. articles to jours. Home: Washington, D.C. Died Jan. 5, 1974.

WINNETT, PERCY G(LEN), retail store exec.; b. Winnipeg, Can., Apr. 3, 1881; s. John W. And Lydia (Roe) W.; student pub. schs., Can.; LL.D., Occidental Coll.; m. Helen Hutton, June 7, 1905. With Broadway Dept. Store, 1896-1906; with Bullocks, Inc., Los Angeles, from 1907, pres., 1933-50, chairman, from 1950. Mem. exec. com. and director Greater Los Angeles Plans, Inc., President Santa Anita Foundation, Winnett Foundation, trustee California Institute of Technology, Claremont Men's College; member board governors Welfare Federation of Los Angeles Area Mem. Downtown Business Men's Assn., Los Angeles Area Bldg. Funds (v.p.). Mason. Clubs: Sunset, Los Angeles Country, California. Home: Los Angeles, Cal.†

WINSHIP, LAURENCE LEATHE, newspaperman; b. Somerville, Mass., Feb. 19, 1890; s. Albert Edward and Ella Rebecca (Parker) W.; grad. Sommerville Latin Sch.; A.B., Harvard, 1911; m. Ruth Spindler, Oct. 15, 1915; children—John Spindler, Thomas, Joanna. With Journal of Edn., Boston, 1911-12; mem. staff Boston Globe, from 1912, mng. editor, 1937-55, editor, 1955-65. Mem. Am. Acad. Arts and Scis. Club: Tavern. Home: Sudbury Mass. Died Mar. 3, 1975

WINSTON, PATRICK HENRY, prof. law; b. Chapel Hill, N.C., Oct. 10, 1881; s. George Tayloe and Caroline Sophia (Taylor) W.; prep. edn., Norner Mil. Sch., Oxford (Now Charlotte), N.C.; student U. U. of Tex.,

1897-98; student U. of N.C., 1899-1900, later studied law there; grad. U.S. Mil. Acad., 1905; spl. work law depts. Harvard and U. of Mich.; m. Josephine Wilkinson, of Port Gibson, Miss., Oct. 10, 1907; children—Elizabeth Harding, George Tayloe, Carolyn, Patrick Henry. Served as 2d lt. 18th Battery, Field Artillery, 1905-06 (resigned); began law practice at Asheville, N.C., 1906; associated in practice with Gov. Locke Craig, 1906-09; prof. law. U. of N.C., from Sept. 1909. Apptd. maj. Judge Advocate Gen.'s R.C., July 25, 1917; assigned as judge advocate to 83d Div. N.A., Camp Sherman, O., Aug. 1917; hon. discharged, 1918. Mem. N.C. Bar Assn., Phi Delta Theta; pres. N.C. Tennis Assn., 1919. Democrat. Episcopalian. Home: Chapel Hill, N.C.†

WINTERS, ALLEN CHARLES, radiologist; b. Jacksonville, Fla., Mar. 28, 1907; s. Harry Sunderland and Mabel Winifred (Allen) W.; M.D., U. Tenn., 1933; m. Vernice Paschal, Apr. 15, 1933 (dec. Apr. 1952); m. 2d, Dorothy Irene Schneider, Apr. 11, 1953. Intern. Spartanburg (S.C.) Gen. Hosp., 1932-34, Mayo Clinic; resident U. Ga., VA Hosp., Denver; practice medicine specializing in radiology; chief staff of radiology VA Hosp., Alexandria, La., 1946-63; cons. charity Hosp., Pineville, La., 1948-62, Volusia County Health Dept., 1967-73; instr. radiology Tulane U. Sch. Medicine, 1960-62; hon. mem. staff Fish Meml. Hosp., New Smyrna Beach, Fla. Bd. dirs. Vis. Nurse Assn., A.R.C. Served to maj., M.C. U.S. Army, 1934-38, also World War II. Diplomate Am. Bd. Radiology. Mem. A.M.A., So. Med. Assn., Theta Kappa Psi. Methodist. Elk. Home: New Smyrna Beach, Fla. Died Dec. 11, 1974; buried Oakdale Cemetery, DeLand, Fla.

WIRKA, HERMAN WENZEL, physician; b. Madison, Wis., July 24, 1903; s. Joseph A. and Amelia (Harbort) W.; M.D., U. Wis., 1930; m. Mildred N. Engler, Apr. 10, 1929; children—Herman Wenzel, Julia (Mrs. Camille Bauer). Intern, Wis. Gen. Hosp., 1930-31, resident in orthopedic surgery, 1931-34, then asst. in orthopedic surgery; asst. in orthopedic surgery Wis. Orthopedic Hosp. for Children; cons. staff St. Mary's Hosp., Madison; cons. in orthopedic surgery VA Hosp., Madison; prof. orthopedic surgery U. Wis., chmn. dept. orthopedics, 1962-71. Recipient commendation Wis. Dept. Industry, Labor and Human Relations, 1973. Diplomate Am. Bd. Orthopedic Surgery. Fellow A.C.S.; mem. Am. Acad. Orthopedic Surgeons, Central Orthopedic Soc. (V.P. 1969-70), Soc. Internat. Chirurgie Orthopedique et Traumatologie, Am. Trauma Soc. (founding mem.), Dane County Med. Soc., Soc. Univ. Surgeons, Madison Wis. orthopedic socs., Chi Phi. Republican. Roman Catholic. Rotarian. Home: Madison, Wis. Died Dec. 26, 1974; buried Resurrection Cemetery, Madison, Wis.

WIRTH, WILLIAM JOSEPH, physician; b. Allentown, Pa., Nov. 11, 1908; s. Frank and Julia Wirth; M.D., Temple U., 1936; m. Miriam Dempsey, Aug. 28, 1941; 1 son, Christopher Alan. Rotating intern Allentown Gen. Hosp., 1936-37; postgrad. tng. Johns Hopkins, Balt.; med. idr. Remington Arms Co., Ilion, N.Y. Diplomate Am. Bd. Preventive Medicine, Nat. Bd. Med. Examiners. Fellow Am. Acad. Occupational Medicine; mem. A.M.A., N.Y. State, Herkimer County med. socs., Utica Acad. Medicine. Home: Ilion, N.Y. Died Apr. 23, 1973; buried Ilion, N.Y.

WISE, JENNINGS CROPPER, lawyer; author; b. Richmond, Va., Sept. 10, 1881; s. John Sergeant and Evelyn Bryd Beverley (Douglas) W.; B.S., Va. Mil. Inst., 1903, M.A., 1916; B.L., U. of Va., 1909; m. Elizabeth Lydecker Anderson, Oct. 4, 1905; m. 2d, Lucy Carmack Smith, May 18, 1939. Pres. Kamargo Supply Co., Inc., Watertown, 1906-17; practiced law at Richmond, Va., 1909-12; prof. economics, polit. science and law, Va. Mil. Inst., 1912-15; spl. asst. atty. gen. of United States, 1930-38; private practice New York and Washington. 2d lt., U.S. Army, 1902-05 (resigned); 1st lt. and batt. adj. N.G., N.Y., 1905-07; col. engrs. Va. Vols., 1912-15; comdt. cadets Va. Mil. Inst., 1912-14; raised regt. for proposed Roosevelt Div., 1916-17; maj. Inf., U.S. Army, May 15, 1917; lt. col., Apr. 16, 1919; hon. discharged. June 28, 1919. Temporarily attached to British and French armies; grad. Army Gen. Staff Coll., A.E.F.; Operations Sect., May 31, 1918; grad. M.G. School, British G.H.Q., Camiéres, France; reassigned to 318th Inf., U.S. Army, July 1918; served with regt. in Picardy and in St. Mihiel and Meuse-Argonne offensives; wounded at Nantillois, Oct. 4, 1918; twice cited and awarded D.S.C. "for extraordinary heroism in battle, retaining command though wounded." Decorated Legion of Honor, Republic of France. Was mem. of bd. of contract adjustment of War Dept. and spl. mem. War Dept. Claims Bd. for transportational service and constrn. div.; spl. counsel for agent of U.S., Mixed Claims Commission, U.S., and Germany; special asst. atty. gen. of U.S., 1930-33. Historian N.Y. Soc. Order of Founders and Patroits. Mem. Va. Historical Commission. Mem. A.A.A.S., Virginia Academy of Science, S.A.R., Social Colonial Wars Southern and Va. hist. socs., Va. Audubon Soc., Kappa Alpha (Southern), Phi Delta Phi, Phi Beta Kappa, etc. Republican. Episcopalian. Mason. Clubs: Keswick Hunt, Country of Va.; Metropolitan (Washington); Authors (London). Founder and president Monticello Publishers. Author numerous books, brochures and articles from 1912. Home: Cloverdale, Va.*†

WISEMAN, JOSEPH R(OSENFELD), physician; b. Syracuse, N.Y., Dec. 16, 1881; s. Gates and Fannie (Rosenfeld) W.; A.B., Harvard, 1902; M.D., Syracuse Coll. of Medicine, 1906; m. Emma May Jacobson, Apr. 29, 1909; children—Gerald N., Nathan J., Richard D. House officer, Boston City Hosp., 1906-08; practice of medicine, Syracuse, N.Y., from 1908; prof. of clin. medicine, Syracuse U.; later prof. clin. medicine emeritus; senior attending physician, St. Joseph Hosp., Syracuse Memorial Hosp., (both Syracuse, N.Y.), Mem. Mayor's Med. Advisory Com., from 1934, Fellow Am. Coll. Physicians A.M.A. Am. Acad. of Allergy, American College of Allergists; member Onodaga County Med. Soc., Syraccuse Acad. Medicine, Alpha Omega Alpha, Nu Sigma Nu. Republican. Jewish religion. Contbr. many articles to med. jours. Home: Syracuse, N.Y.†

WISHARD, WILLIAM NILES, JR. physician; b. Indpls., July 29, 1898; s. William Niles and Frances Cornelia (Scoville) W.; B.A., Williams Coll., 1921; M.D. cum laude, Harvard, 1925; m. Carolyn Louise Davis, Oct. 10, 1938; children—Susan (Mrs. David S. Poston), William Niles III, Gordon Davis. Intern, E. surg. house officer Mass. Gen. Hosp., Boston, 1926-27; individual practice genito urinary surgery, Indpls., 1928-73; mem. staff Meth. Hosp., 1928-73, chmn. urol. staff, 1938, chmn. med. adv. com., 1938-40, pres. med. staff, 1940-41, chmn. research com. 1965-73, chmn. profl. standards com., 1970; mem. staff St. Vincents, Ind. U. Med. Center hosps.; cons. staff Marion County Gen., Community hosps.; chmn. urol. staff Marion County Gen. Hosp., 1950-53; faculty Ind. U. Sch. Medicine, 1928-73, clin. prof. urology, 1953-73, William Niles Wishard, Jr. vis. prof. urology, 1969-73; pres. Drs. Wishard, Nourse, Mertz & Newman, Inc., 1964-73, Mem. Bd. Med. Registration and Exam. Ind., 1945-57. Recipient Distinguished Tchr. award Meth. Hosp. Grad. Center, 1966-73. Spl. award for Meritorious Service Am. Bd. Urology, 1969. Diplomate Nat. Bd. Med. Examiners, Am. Bd. Urology (sec.-treas. 1955-68, chmn. credentials com. 1955-68, pres. 1968-69). Mem. Am. Urol. Assn. (pres. N. central sect. 1951), Am. Assn. Genito Urinary Surgeons (council 1963-66, pres. 1965-66), A.M.A., Indpls. (pres. Council 1946), Ind. (chmn. surg. sect. 1948) med. assns., Am. Assn. Med. History, Assn. Am. Med. Colls., A.C.S., Internat. Urol. Soc., S.A.R., Mass. Gen. Hosp., Harvard Med. Sch., Ind. U. alumni assns., Delta Upsilon, Phi Beta Pi. Republican. Presbyn. (elder 1941-59). Clubs: Literary (v.p. 1961), Contemporary (pres. 1937), Harvard, Woodstock Country, Indiana University (Indpls.). Home: Indianapolis, Ind. Died Oct. 27, 1973.

WISTRAND, KARL KNUTSSON, politician; b. Karlskoga, Sweden, Apr. 9, 1889; s. Knut and Louise (Strokirk) W.; Jur. Kand., U. Uppsala (Sweden), 1911; M.D. h.c., Stockholm (Sweden) U., 1951; m. Louise Follin, Sept. 23, 1936 (dec. Aug. 1954). Dir. Jarnbruksforbundet, Stockholm 1918-36; mem. Consultative Assembly, European Council, 1949-59; chmn. bd. Med. Mus., Stockholm, also Friends of Med. Mus. Chmn. Belgo-Swedish Soc., 1950-59. Mem. Town Council Stockholm 1930-37; Conservative senator, 1936-54. Decorated comdr. 1st class Swedish Vasa, Order North Star, grand officer Order Leopold 11 (Belgium), comdr. Legion Honor (France), mem. 1st class White Rose Order, comdr. Lion Order (Finland). Mem. Acad. Sci. (Uppsala U.). Author: Hort Och Upplevat, 1962. Address: Stockholm, Sweden. Died Dec. 27, 1974.

WITHAM, HENRY BRYAN, educator; b. Orient, Ia., Oct. 17, 1894; s. Martin Woodman and Mary Jane (Reed) W.; A.B., University of Iowa, 1919, J.D., 1925; married Elsa Dethlefs, Oct. 11, 1918; children—Barbara Ann (Mrs. Herbert Harrington). Henry Bryan, Peter Martin, Prin, Frankfort (Kan.) High Sch., 1921-22, supt. schs., Ocheyedan, Ia., 1922-24; admitted to Ia. bar, 1922; practiced at Davenport, 1924-26; asst. prof. law and sec. Law College, Univ. of Tenn., 1926-28, prof. law, 1928-44, acting dean, 1930-33, dean 1933-44. Prof. law, asso. dean and in charge Indianapolis div., Sch. of Law, Indiana Univ., from 1944. Pres., dir. Tenn. Law Review, Inc., 1930-44; mem. Tenn. Judicial Council 1942-44. Secretary-treasurer of the Indiana Bar Foundation. Public panel mem. War Labor Board, 1943-44. Served in U.S.N.R., 1918-19. Mem. Ia., Tenn., and U.S. Supreme Court bars, Indiana State and Am. bar assns., Am. Law Inst., Phi Kappa Phi, Phi Delta Phi, Kappa Sigma, Order of Coif. Presbyterian. Contbr. legal articles. Home: Indianapolis Ind. Died May 17, 1973

WITHEY, HENRY FRANKLIN, architect; b. Lynn, Mass., Feb. 4, 1880; s. John Franklin and Martha Brooks (Peckham) W.; ed. pub. schs., Mass.; m. Elsie Dickenson Rathburn, Oct. 14, 1916. Draftsman archtl. firms, Boston and Los Angeles; partner Withey & Davis, architects, Los Angeles, 1910-20; pvt. practice, Los Angeles and Sherman Oaks, Cal., from 1920; prin. works include Artesia (Cal.) Grammar Sch., 1912, also additions, 1920-31, Chino Grammar Sch., 1913, Santa Ana (Cal.), also 17 intermediate schs., Los Angeles, 1914-58, Farmers & Merchants Bank, Saticoy, 1924, First Nat. Bank of Artesia, 1930, John Muir Pub. Library, Los Angeles, 1930, Marine Bank Bldg., Santa Minica, 1932, Ascot Pub. Library, Los Angeles, 1939, other comml. and residential bldgs. Mem. Los Angeles City Planning Commn., 1921-24; supr. hist. Am. bldg. survey program in So. Cal. for Dept. Interior, 1934-47. Fellow A.I.A. (sec., v.p. So. Cal. 1918-21). Author: (with wife) Biographical Dictionary of American Arthitects, 1956. Home: Sherman Oaks, Cal.†

WITHROW, JAMES RENWICK, chem. engr.; b. Phila., Pa., Aug. 29, 1878; s. David Daniel and Margaret McCool (Stewart) W.; B.S., Univ. of Pa., 1899, Ph.D., 1905; hon. D.Sc., Geneva College, Beaver Falls, 1935; m. Alice Steelman, 1906; children—Mrs. Alice W. Field, James Renwick, David Daniel, Chemist, Barret Mfg. Co., Phila., 1899-1900; in charge benzol and light oil mfg. depts., also research lab. for general co., 1900-03; asst. instr. gen. chemistry and instr. analyt. chemistry, 1905-06; asst. prof. chemistry, 1906-09, asso. prof., 1909-12, prof., 1912-24, in charge industrial and applied electro chemistry, head dept. of chem. engring, from 1923—, prof. of chem. engring. from 1924, all Ohio State U. Consultant on chem. engring and patent work to various industries, U.S., France and England, Member U.S. Naval Consulting Bd. for Ohio, 1915-17; con. chem. engr. on war-gas, U.S. Bur. Mines and trench warfare sect., Ordnance Bur., War Dept., 1917; lecturer explosives, Ground Sch., Signal Corps, U.S. Army, Columbus, 1917; with C.W.S., 1917-19. Fellow A.A.A.S., Ohio Acad. Sci., Am. Inst. Chemists (councillor), Am. Geog. Soc.; past councillor, and chmn. lime and sugar-ash com., Am. Chemical Soc.; director Am. Inst. Chem. Engrs.; past pres. Phila. Mineral. Soc. Sigma Xi (Ohio), Ohio State U. Scientific Soc. and Columbus Engineers' Club; mem. Am. Engring. Council Assembly, Am. Soc. for Testing Materials, Federation Am. Engring. Soc., Am. Electrochem. Soc., Am. Assn. Univ. Profs., Soc. Promotion Engring. Edn., Alliance Francaise, Foreign Foreign Policy Assn.; hon. mem. Chinese Student Alliance America, American Academy Political and Social Science, etc. Clubs: Faculty (Columbus); Chemists' (New York); Torch. Joint r of Nat. Research Council Repts. Editor: Indsl. Chemistry, Chemical Engring., Am. Year Book, 1912-19. Progress of Chemistry in America, 1926, 27. Mem. Am. Advisroy C Council, Yenching U., Peiping, China. Ref. Presbhn. Home: Columbus, O.†

WITMER, DAVID JULIUS, architect; b. Los Angeles, Aug. 29, 1888; s. Joseph Myer and Josephine Smith (Sullivan) W.; A.B., Harvard, 1910, student Grad. Sch. Architecture, 1910-12; m. Helen Elizabeth Williams, June 7, 1917; children—David Williams, Mrs. James A. Kendall, Peter Charlton. Draftsman with C.H. Blackall, Boston, 1911, 1912-14; in practices in Los Angeles, Cal., 1915-19; formed partnership with Loyall F. Watson, 1919, became sr. partner; active partner Witmer, Watson & Pidgeon; pres. Allied Architects Assn. of Los Angeles; v.p. Witmer Bros. Co.; chief archtl. supr. FHA, So. Cal. Dist., 1934-38; co-chief architect U.S. War Dept. for Pentagon bldg. 1941-42, chief architect, 1942-43; chief control civil affairs div. Hdqrs. European Command 1948-50. Chmn. adv. com. Coll. Architecture, U. So. Cal., 1925-41. Dir. Library Architecture and Allied Arts, Los Angeles, from 1938, pres. bd. dirs., from 1952. Mem. commn. architects for Asso. Colleges at Claremont, Cal., from 1956; mem. adv. council Coll. Architecture, U. Cal. at Berkeley. Served as 1st lt. Signal Corps, Aviation Sect., 1917-18, and capt. Air Service, 1918-19; capt. Air Service Officers Res. Corps, 1919-29. Served as maj. to col. AUS, 1943-48. Decorated Bronze Star, Legion of Merit (U.S.); Chevalier de la Légion d-Honneur, Croix de Guerre avec Etoile Vermeille, Officer de l'Ordre Merit Maritime (France); Officer de l'Ordre du Courrone du Chéne (Luxembourg) Croix Militaire, Premier Classe; (Belgium). Fellow A.I.A. (pres. So. Cal. chpt. 1926-27; regional dir., 1933-36, mem. nat. com. for observance of centennial (1955-57). Clubs: Harvard (Southern Cal.); Ellis, Orpheus (Los Angeles). Home: Los Angeles Cal. Died May 5, 1973; buried Evergreen Cemetery, Los Angeles, Cal.

WITT, EDGAR E., lawyer; b. Texas, Jan. 28, 1879; s. James Monreo and Elizabeth (Simons) W.; A.B., U. of Tex., LL.B., 1903; m. Gwynne Johnstone, June 6, 1904. Admitted to Tex. bar, and later practiced in Waco; mem. firm Witt, Terrell, Lincoln, Jones & Riley from 1918. Served as state senator, 1918-30; lt. gov. of Tex., 1930-34; chmn. special Mexican Claims Commn., 1935-38; chmm. chmn. Am.-Tex. Claims Commn., 1943-47; chief, Indian Claims Commission, from 1947. Served as captain, Army Service Corps, 1918. Chmn. Selective Service Board, Waco, Tex., 1941-43. Mem. Tex. Bar Assn., Am. Legion, Phi Delta Theta. Knight of Pythias, Woodman of World, Rotarian. Author, with others, of Letters of Harry Steger, 1920; also of reports to sec. to state, Decisions of Special Mexican Claims Commission, 1940. Home: Waco, Tex.†

WITTY, PAUL ANDREW, psychologist; b. Terre Haute, Ind., July 23, 1898; s. William L. and Margaret (Kerr) W.; A.B., Ind. State Tchrs. Coll., 1920; postgrad. U. Chgo., 1920-22; M.A., Columbia, 1923, Ph.D., 1931. Sch. psychologist, Scarborough-on-Hudson, 1922; asso. prof. ednl. psychology U. Kan., 1924-25, prof., 1925-30; prof. edn., dir. Psycho-Educational Clinic, Northwestern U., 1930-66, prof. emeritus edn., 1966-76. Chief ednl. cons. D.C. Heath & Co., 1940-76; cons. Western Pub. Co. Served as maj. AUS, 1942-44. Fellow A.A.A.S., Am. Psychol. Assn.; mem. Am. Childhood Edn. Assn., Am. Ednl. Research Assn., Assn. for

Supervision and Curriculum Devel., Internat. Council Exceptional Children, Soc. Advancement Edn., Internat. Soc. for Study Semantics, Nat. Council Tchrs. English, Nat. Soc. Study Edn. (dir.), N.E.A., Internat. Council Improvement Reading Instrn. (pres. 1954), Am. Assn. Gifted Children (v.p.), Sigma Nu, Phi Delta Kappa, Kappa Delta Pi. Author: Study of Deviates in Play; Reading in Modern Education, 1949; Freedom and Our U.S. Family; Streamline Your Reading; Helping Children Read Better; You Can Read Better; (with Edith Grotberg) Helping the Gifted Child, 1970; (with Thomas Barensfeld) The Life and Times of Eight Presidents, 1970; also numerous articles in jours. of pscyhology and education. Co-author: Psychology of Play Activities; Reading and the Educative Process; You and The Constitution, 1948; Teaching the People's Language; Educational Psychology; Elementary Educational Psychology; It's Fun to Find Out Series of Film Readers; Your Child and Radio, TV, Comics and Movies. Editor: Mental Hygiene in Modern Education; The Gifted Child; Reading for Interest and Reading Caravan Series of Readers. Former adv. editor My Weekly Reader; editorial bd. Exceptional Children, Parent Tchrs. Mag.; asso. editor Highlights for Teachers, Highlights for Children mag. Author: How to Improve Your Reading; How to Become a Better Reader. Co-author: The Teaching of Reading—A Developmental Process, 1966; Developing Your Vocabulary; The Educationally Retarded and the Disadvantaged, 1967; editor, author chpts. 1 and 6 Reading for the Gifted and the Creative Student, 1971. Home: Chicago, Ill., Died Feb. 11, 1976.

WODEHOUSE, PELHAM GRENVILLE, author; b. Guildford, Surrey, Eng., Oct. 15, 1881; s. Henry Ernest and Eleanor (Deane) W.; student Dulwich Coll., 1894-1900; m. Ethel Rowley Wayman, Sept. 30, 1914. Writer of humorous column By The Way, London Globe, 1903-09; first came to U.S., 1909. Interned by Germany during World War II. Author 96 books, from 1910; latest publs.: Nothing Serious, 1951; Old Reliable, 1951; adapted: Play's the Thing (Ferenc Molnar), 1951; Angel Cake, 1952; American I Like You, 1956; French Leave, 1958; Barmy in Wonderland, Few Quick Ones (short stories), Laughing Gas, Money for Nothing, Over Seventy, Very Good, Jeeves (all 1959); Jeeves in the Offing, 1960; Most of P. G. Wodehouse, 1960; Author! Author!, 1961; Stiff Upper Lip, Jeeves, 1962; Code of the Woosters, 1962; Nothing Serious, 1964; Frozen Assets, 1964; Galahad at Blandings, 1965; Company for Henry, 1967; Do Butlers Burgle Banks?, 1968; Uncle Fred in the Springtime, i969; Fish Preterred, 1969; Miheand Psmith, 1969; No Nudes Is Good Nudes, 1970; Girl in Blue, 1971; Jeeves and the Tie that Birds, 1971. Home: Remsenburg N.Y. Died Feb. 1975

WOELK, NORMA MARIE, air force civilian; b. Belleville, Ill.; d. Robert D. and Mary (Beineke) Woelk; high sch. grad. Sec. Bd. Edn. Dist. No. 118, Belleville, 1947-53; dep. chief staff operations, Tng. Div., Air Weather Service, 1953-72. Mem. Marquis Biog. Library Soc. Charter mem. Zonta Club Belleville (bd. dirs.). Presbyn. Home: Belleville, Ill. Died Sept. 7, 1972; interred Valhalla Cemetery, Belleville.

WOLCOTT, DANIEL FOOKS, judge; b. Wilmington, Del., Jan. 29, 1910; s. Josiah Ollver and Mary Rebecca (Fooks) W.; A.B., Yale, 1933; LL.B., , U. Pa., 1936; LL.D. U. Del., 1967; m. Eliza Rodney, Mar. 31, 1941; children—Eliza, Daniel Fooks, Mary Fooks. Admitted to Del. bar, 1936; asso. Southerland, Berl & Potter. Wilmington, 1937-47, partner, 1948-49; asso. Judge at large Superior Ct. Del., 1949; chancellor Del., 1950; asso. justice Supreme Ct. Del., 1950-64, chief justice Supreme Ct. Del., 1964-73. Dem. candidate for atty. gen. Del., 1946; chmn. New Castle Co. Dem. Com., 1947-49. Trustee, pres. New Castle Common. Served with AUS, 1941; from lt. (j.g.) to lt. USNR 1942-45. Mem. Am., Del. bar assns., Del. Hist. Soc. (dir.), New Castle Hist. Soc. (dir.), Library Assos. (past pres.), Beta Theta Pl. Episcopallan (vestryman, sr. warden). Clubs: Wilmington. Home: New Castle, Del. Died July 10, 1973; buried Immanuel Ch. Churchyard, New Castle, Del.

WOLCOTT, HENRY MERRILL, consular service; b. Colchester, Vt., Nov. 8, 1879; s. Elijah Wilbur and Ellen (Kent) W.; ed. Chicago Atheneum, Chicago, and under pvt. tutors; m. Jessie E. Lord, Sept. 7, 1918. Apptd. v. and dep. consul, Santiago de Cuba, June 1906; v. and dep. oconsul gen., Mexico City, Mexico, 1912-13; at consulate gen., Havana, Cuba, 1913-15; appts. consul, 1915, and filled various assignments; assigned to Bilbao, Spain, 1919, to Caracas, Venezuela, 1926, to Adelaide, Australia, 1930, to London, 1937; consul. Plymouth, England, 1938-42, Nassau, Aug. 1942; consul gen., Tenerife, Canary Islands, 1943; retired Nov. 1944. Address: Woodstock, Vt.†

WOLF, ARNOLD VERYL, physiologist, educator; b. N.Y.C., Dec. 3, 1916; s. Paul and Anna E. (Greenfield) W.; B.S., Coll. City N.Y., 1938; Ph.D., in Physiology, U. Rochester, 1942; m. Orietta L. Behrens, May 18, 1944; children—Paula D., Robyn L., Rodney A. Asst., physiology expdn. in desert S.W., U.S., U. Rochester, 1942; from instr. to asso. prof. physiology Albany (N.Y.) Med. Coll., 1942-52; chief renal sect. dept. cardiorespiratory diseases Walter Reed Army Inst. Research, 1952-58; prof. physiology, head dept. U. Ill. Coll. Medicine, 1958-73; dean Grad. Coll., U. Ill. at Med. Center, Chgo., 1973-75. Cons. Am. Optical Co.; mem. adv. com. gen. medicine Office Surgeon Gen. Mem. Am. Physiol. Soc., A.A.A.S., Am. Soc. Artificial Internal Organs, Soc. Exptl. Biology and Medicine, Sigma Xi. Author: The Urinary Function of the Kidney, 1950, Thirst: Physiology of the Urge to Drink and Problems of Water Lack, 1958; (with N.A. Crowder) An Introduction to Body Fluid Metabolism, 1964; Aqueous Solutions and Body Fluids: Their Concentrative Properties and Conversion Tables, 1966; also papers in field water metabolism. A developer TS meter for refractometric determination of water and total solids content of body fluids. Home: Highland Park Ill. Died Feb. 27, 1975

WOLF, HENRY JOHN, mining engr.; b. Phila., Feb. 6, 1881; s. Henry John and Emma Regina (Goldbeck) W.; E.M., Colo. Sch. Mines, 1903, M.S., 1913; m. Carolyn Alice Wright, Jan. 19, 1908; children—Harry Joh, William Robert, George Edward. Began as assayer and chemist San Miguel Consol. Gold Mining Co. Colo., 1902, later mining engr. same and for other corps.; engr. Telluride Power Co. 1904, alter (Colo.), asst. elec. engr., power line supt.; chief engr. Camp Bird Mine, Colo., 1906; supt. Stanley Mines Co., 1907; gen. mgr. Japan-Flora Mines Co., 1909; prof. mining Colo. Sch. Mines, 1912-18, head dept., 1913-18; formerly county surveyor and engr. San Miguel County, Colo., also city engr., Telluride, Colo.; formerly asso. editor Engring. and Mining Jour.; pres. H. J. Wolf Assos., mem. The Malm-Wolf Co.; cons. engr., financial adviser pvt. clients; cons. cadmium, copper-zinc br., also chief cadmium sect. prodn. div. OPM, 1941; prin. tech. cons., chief cadmium sect., micagraphite br. WPB, 1942, chief Cadmium-bismuth sect., zinc div., 1942, chief cadmium-bismuth Cadmium-bismuth sect., zinc div., 1942, chief cadmium-indium and miscellaneous metals sect., zinc div., 1943-44, lead and mineral specialist, metals div. F.E.A., 1944-45; engr. Renolds Research, Glen Cove, L.I., 1945-47; mem., sec. Behre, Dolbear & Co., 1947-48; pvt. practice mining and cons. engr., N.Y.C., from 1948; cons. engr. Lajo Mines, Ltd., from 1949; Surinam Development Corp., from 1958; cons. engr. gen. mgr. Lajo Surinam Associates, from 1959. Active member, treasurer Long Island Symphony Orchester; active member of the Washington Civic Orchestra and War Production Bd. Orchestra. Recipient of the distinguished achievement medal Colo. Sch. Mines, 1949; Legion of Honor, Am. Inst. Mining EnrEngrs. Fellow A.A.A.S.; mem. Am. Inst. Mining and Metall Engrs., Am. Electrochem. Soc., Soc. Promotion Engring. Edn., Mining and Metall. Soc. Am., Am. Mining Congress, Colo. Sci. Soc., Pan Am. Inst. Mining Engring. and Geology, Tau Beta Pi, Pi Gamma Mu. Republican. Mason (K.T., Shriner, 32°). Clubs: Rocky Mountain, Mining (N.Y.C.); Teknik (Denver); Cosmos (Washington). Author: Studies in Stock Speculation; The Ten Cardinal Principles of Trading; A Treatise on Cadmium; Pitfalls inthe New Stock Market, also numerous tech. and financial articles. Home: Little Neck, N.Y.†

WOLFE, HARRY DEANE, educator; b. Lawrence, Mass., Oct. 15, 1901; s. Samuel J. and Katherine (Gould) W.; student Mass. Inst. Tech., 1919-21; B.S., Darmouth, 1924; M.A., U. Wis., 1936, Ph.D., 1938; m. Dorothy Nelson, Feb. 1, 1958; 1 dau., Isabel (Mrs. Allan Bacon). Asst. mgr. Montgomery Ward, Balt., 1927-27; mdse. mgr. S. Kann Sons Co., Washington, 1927-35; prof. Kent (O.) State U., 1938-42; economist WPB, Washington, 1942-43; dir. marketing research Colgate Palmolive Co., N.Y.C., 1943-57; prof. bus. U. Wis.-Madison, 1958-72; dir. Bergstrom Paper Co., Am. Family Ins. Co., Madison. Bd. dirs. Cancer Soc., Madison. Mem. Market Research Council N.Y., Am. Marketing Assn., Newcomen Soc. N. Am. Republican. Presbyn. (trustee). Club: Maple Bluff Country (Madison). Author: Business Forecasting Methods, 1966; (with others) Measuring Advertising Results, 1962; Pretesting Advertising, 1963; Evaluating Media, 1966; Essentials of the Promotional Mix, 1970. Home: Madison, Wis. Died Mar. 28, 1975.

WOLFE, JOHN MARCUS, supt. Archdiocesan schs.,; b. Chickasaw County Ia., Feb. 4, 1881; s. Dominic and Susanna (Scheuer) W.; A.b., A.B., St. Joseph's (Columbia) Coll., Dubuque, 1901; S.T.D., Propaganda U., Rome, Italy, 1905; Ph.D., Luceum of St. Thomas, Rome, 1905; A.M., Columbia Coll., Dubuque, 1915. Ordained to ministry R.C. Ch., 1905; business mgr. Columbia Coll., 1915-18; dir. The Society for the Propagation of the Faith, Inc., from 1921; supt. of Archdiocesan schs., Dubuque, from 1921; Archdiocesan dir. of Catholic action and same of mission activities. Chairman of Dubuque Planning and Zoning Commn.; mem. Dubuque Adjustment Board; dir. Boy Scouts of America, Boys Club, Conservation Soc. Mem. Nat. Cath. Edn. Assn. N.E.A. (dept. superintendence), Ia. State White House Conf., Cath. Anthrop. Assn. Cath. Assn. Internat. Peace, Nat. Educational Research Assn., Nat. Soc. for the Study of Edn. Chmn. Dubuque Coordinating Council of Social Welfare Agencies, Ia. Conf. of Family Relations, Made a domestic prelate by Pope Pius XI, 1932; made Prothonotary Apostolic, 1939. Author books relating to field; contbr. ednl. articles to Cath. jours. Address: Dubuque, Ia.*†

WOLFE, WILLIAM HENRY, lawyer; b. Parkersburg, W.Va., Mar. 3, 1879; s. William Henry and Joanna M. (Cook) W.; A.B., Marietta (O.) Coll., 1899; A.M., Columbia, 1901, LL.B., 1902; m. Katherine V. White, Feb. 16, 1905; children—Elizabeth, Albert B., Agnes W. (dec.). Admitted to N.Y. bar, 1903, and began practice at N.Y. City; in practice at Parkersburg, from 1903; pres. 2d Nat. Bank of Parkersburg, 1910-27; v.p. and atty. First Nat. Bank of Parkersburg, 1927-31. Atty. Parkersburg, 1909-11. Trustee Marietta Coll., Davis and Elkins Coll., Elkins, W.Va. Mem. Am. Bar Assn., Phi Beta Kappa. Republican. Presbyterian. ason, Elk. Clubs: Parkersburg Country. Home: Parkersburg, W.Va.†

WOLFKILL, GUY FONTELLE, coll. pres. b. Lincoln, Neb., Dec. 29, 1881; s. Ware S. and Minno (Cornell) W.; A.B., Walla Walla Coll., 1913; M.A., Pacific Union Coll., 1917, U. of Neb., 1925; studied U. of Calif., U. of Chicago and Whitman Coll.; m. Lydia Jane Kime, of College Pl., Wash., Sept. 5, 1906. Prin. Forest Home Acad., Wash., 1907-09; with science dept. Walla Walla Coll., 1910-12; head science dept. Pacific Union Coll. Calif., 1913-20, Washington Missionary Coll., Washington, D.C., 1921, Union Coll., Neb., 1922-24; pres. Emmanuel Mission Coll., Berrien Springs, Mich., 1925-30; chmn. dept. of psychology and secondary edn., Pacific Union Coll., from 1931. Seventh-Day Adventist. Home: Angwin, Cal.†

WOLFMAN, AUGUSTUS, editor; b. Bklyn., Apr. 28, 1908; s. David and Ethel (Kogel) W.; Ph.G. with honor, Bklyn. Coll. Pharmacy, 1928; student N.Y. Inst. Photography, 1929, Coll. City N.Y., 1942, 43; m. Lydia Sandra Turner, Aug. 14, 1938; children—Leslie Miriam, Neil Turner, Carol Ruth. Advt. mgr. E. Leitz, Inc., 1935-44; editor Leica Photography, 1935-44, Universal Photo Almanac, 1945; editor-in-chief Photo Dealer, 1944-65, Modern Photography, 1951-64. Dir. Photo. Industry, ann., 1945-65, Photo Fun, quar., 1949-57, Photo Methods for Industry, 1958-65, Reprodn. Methods for Industry, 1961-65, Training in Business and Industry, 1964-65; editorial cons. Modern Photography, Photog. Trade News, 1965-68. Recipient Certificate for work on Am. Standards Assn. war project 252, establishing standard on photog. products, 1946; Photokina awards, 1954, 56, 58, 60, 63, 66. Mem. Profl. Photographers Am., Photography Soc. Am. (asso.), Soc. Motion Picture and TV Engrs., Soc. Photog. Scientists and Engrs., Photog. Industry Adminstrs. Author: The Fine Grain Negative, 1935; also chpts. photography books. Editor; pub.; The Wolfman Report on the Photographic Industry in the United States. Contbr. articles to various publs. Home: Bayside N.Y. Died Oct. 21, 1974

WOLFSON, HARRY AUSTRYN, educator; b. Austryn, Wilna, Russia, Nov. 2, 1887; s. Mendel and Sarah Deborah (Savitsky) W.; came to U.S. at 16; A.B., Harvard, 1911 (as of 1912), A.M., 1912, Ph.D., 1915; Harvard Sheldon traveling fellow, studying in Germany, France and Eng., 1912-14; D.H. Litt., from Jewish Inst. of Religion, 1935, Jewish Theological Seminary, 1937; D.H.L., Hebrew Union Coll., 1945; L.H.D., Yeshiva University, 1950, University of Chicago, 1953; Litt.D., Dropsie College, 1952, Harvard, 1956. Instructor Hebrew lit. and philosophy, Harvard, 1915-21, asst. prof., 1921-25. became Nathan Littauer prof., later Nathan Littauer prof. Hebrew lit. and philosophy, also hon. curator Hebraica and Judaica in Harvard Coll. Library; prof. Jewish Inst. Religion, N.Y.C., 1923-25. Fellow Mediaeval Acad. America. Mem. Am. Oriental Soc., Soc. Bibl. Lit. and Exegesis, Am. Philos Assn., Am. Hist. Assn., History of Science Soc.; fellow Am. Acad. for Jewish Research (pres. 1935-37), Am. Acad. of Arts and Sciences, Polish Institute Arts and Scis. in Am., Am. Philos. Soc. Served as pvt. U.S. Army, 1918-19. Author: Crescas' Critique of Aristotle, 1929; The Philosophy of Spinoza, 2 vols., 1934; The Internal Senses, 1935; Philo, 2 vols., 1947; The Philosophy of the Church Fathers, Vol. I, 1956; (essays) Religious Philosophy, 1961; Studies in the History of Philosophy and Religion, vol. I, 1973, vol. II, 1976; the Philosophy of the Kalam, 2 vols. 1976; Kalam Repercussions in Jewish Philosophy, 1976. Home: Cambridge, Mass. Died Sept. 19, 1974.

WOMACK, ENNIS BRYAN, chemist, educator; b. Marietta, Tex., Oct. 4, 1899; s. Andrew M. and May Belle (Floyd) W.; B.A., Union U., 1920, M.A., 1921; grad. study U. Wis., 1927-28; Ph.D., U. Chgo., 1931; m. Marie Rutledge, Oct. 5, 1925; 1 son, Robert M. Tchr. mathematics, athletic coach, Columbus (Miss.) High Sch., 1921-23; prin., coach Comanche (Tex.) High Sch., 1923-24; tchr. chemistry, coach Jonesboro Coll., 1924-27; asst. professor phys. sci. Middlebury Coll., 1930-36, asso. prof., 1936-39, prof., chmn. div., 1939, dean coll., 1940-46; prof. chemistry, head dept. Fresno State Coll., 1947-61, prof., 1961-67, prof. emeritus, 1967—. vis. scholar Brookhaven National Laboratory and Harvard University 1961. Dir. Central Cal. Valleys Science Fair, 1963—. Served as commander USNR, World War II; supervisor vets. rehabilitation and edn. VA, Dallas, 1946-47. Fellow A.C.S.; mem. A.A.A.S., Pacific S.W. Assn. Chemistry Tchrs., Am. Assn. U. Profs., Sigma Xi. Mason (Shriner). Contbr. articles profl. jours. Home: Fresno, Cal., Died Oct. 17, 1974; buried Belmont Meml. Park, Fresno, Cal.

WOMACK, NATHAN ANTHONY, physician; b. Reidsville, N.C., May 24, 1901; s. James Henry and Susan Margaret (Norman) W.; B.S., U. N.C., 1922; M.D., Washington U., 1924; traveling European fellow, 1929-30; m. Margaret Elizabeth Richardson, Jan. 23, 1937; children—James Anthony, Sarah Richardson. Intern, asst. resident surgery Barnes Hosp., 1924-26, resident, 1927-29; asst. surgery Washington U., 1926-27, 30-32, instr., 1932-34, instr. clin. surgery, 1934-36, asst. prof. surgery, 1936-37, clin. surgery, 1937-39, asso. prof. clin. surgery, 1939-47, prof., 1947-48; prof. surgery, head dept. U. Ia., 1948-51, surgeon-in-chief, Hosps., 1948-51; prof., chmn. dept. surgery Sch. Medicine U. N.C., Chapel Hill, 1951-67, chmn. dept. surgery emeritus 1967-75, Kenan prof. surgery. Vis. surgeon-in-chief protem Cleve, Clinic, 1952; vis. prof. surgery U. Mich., 1943, U. Cin., 1959, Ochsner Clinic, New Orleans, 1965, U. Miami (Fla.) Sch. Medicine, 1968; vis. prof. Vanderbilt U., 1969, U. Ariz., U. Ky., 1970; Samuel Harvey vis. prof. surgery Yale, 1954; nat. sci. adv. com. City of Hope, Los Angeles, 1954-57; Selig: lectr., St. Louis, 1955, Hodgen lectr., 1965; Gundersen vis. prof. surgery U. Wis., 1966; Tompkins lectr. Wash., 1958; cons. Los Alamos Med. Center. Fellow A.C.S., A.A.A.S.; mem. Nat. Bd. Med. Examiners exec. com. nat. bd. 1956, pres. 1960-63, treas. 1966-70), Am. Bd. Surgery (founder), N.Y. Acad. Scis., A.M.A., So. Med. Assn., Am. (sec. 1948-53), So., Central States surg. assns., Am. Cancer Research, Soc. Exptl. Biology and Medicine, Soc. Clin. Surgeons, Soc. U. Surgeons, Societe Internationale de Chirurgie, United Med. Research Found. N.C. (pres. 1960-62), Golden Fleece, Assn. Am. Med. Colls., Southeastern Surg. Congress, Durham-Orange County N.C. med. socs., Ia. Clin. Surg. Soc., Sigma Xi, Beta Theta Pi, Phi Chi, Alpha Omega Alpha. Contbr. articles to profl. jours. Editorial bd. Annals of Surgery. Home: Chapel Hill, N.C. Died Feb. 2, 1975; buried Reidsville, N.C.

WONDERLEY, ANTHONY WAYNE, educator; b. Columbus, O., Dec. 19, 1913; s. William Vincent and Sarah Pearl (McFee) W.; B.A. cum laude, Ohio State U., 1935; certificate Heidelberg U. (German), 1935; M.A., U. Wis., 1936, Ph.D., 1941; m. Gladys Larson, July 9, 1945; children—Linda, Anthony, Patricia, Wendy. Instr. French andGerman, Ala. Poly. Inst., 1936-38; from instr. to asso. prof., acting chmn. dept. German, Ohio State U., 1947-60; prof. German, Hiram Coll., 1960-61; prof., head dept. lang. Western Mich. U., 1961-66; prof. chmn. dept. Germanic langs. and lit. U. Ky., 1966-75. Fulbright research fellow U. Munich, 1955-56; Served to col. AUS, 1941-47; Mem. Modern Lang. Assn., Ohio (sec.-treas., v.p. 1957-61), Central States modern lang. tchrs. assns., Am. Assn. Tchrs. German (pres. Ohio chpt. 1954-55, Ky. chpt. 1971-73), S. Atlantic Modern Lang. Assn., Phi Beta Kappa. Lutheran. Author: (with R. O. Röseler) Altes und Neues, 1960; Sein und Schein, 1966. Translater novel: Schmelmuffsky, 1962. Editor text dit. German novella: Harmonie (E. Keyserling), 1964; editor Lyrica Germanica, 1965-75, Germanic Notes, 1970—, Germanistische Forschungs-Ketten, 1974-75. Contbr. articles and revs. to profl. jours. Home: Lexington, Ky., Died July 26, 1975; buried Lexington (Ky.) Cemetery.

WONNACOTT, NORMAN, indsl. equipment mfg. co. exec.; b. Ireland, 1903. Vice chmn. dir. Willcox & Gibbs Sewing Machine Co.; dir. Wilcox & Gibbs Sewing Machine Co., Ltd., London, Eng. Home: Scarsdale N.Y. Died Sept. 12, 1974.

WOOD, ANN VAN CLEEF, govt. ofcl.; b. Glenwood, Fla., Nov. 17, 1902; d. Elmer Squires and Nina (Booth) Van Cleef; m. Anderson Wood, Aug. 6, 1938 (div. 1941). Owner Ann Van Cleef Ins. and Secretarial Office, Deland, Fla., 1935-38; sec. to city atty. Middlesboro, Ky., 1938-41; sec., ins. rating clk. Hall Bros., W.R. O'Neil, O'Neil, Lee & West, 1941-43; sec. to v.p. and trust officer 1st Nat. Bank, Orlando, Fla., 1947-49; sec. Orlando AFB, 1943-47; sec.-clk. Statis. Services Air Force Missile Test Center, Cocoa Beach, Fla., 1951-59; sci. and tech. info. officer Air Force Eastern Test Range, 1959-73. Mem. alumni fund raising com. John B. Stetson U., Deland, Fla., 1971. Recipient Outstanding award Air Force Missile Test Center and Air Force Eastern Test Range, 1957, 62, 1968. Mem. Cocoa Beach Bus. and Profl. Women's Club, Tri Delta Alliance, Delta Delta Delta. Democrat. Presbyn. Home: Cocoa Fla. Died May 4, 1973

WOOD, ARTHUR EVANS, sociology; b. Boston, Mass., Oct. 19, 1881; s. William Harvey and Sarah Mercia (Kendall) W.; A.B., Harvard, 1906; S.T.B., Harvard Divinity Sch., 1911; Harrison fellow in sociology, U. of Pa., 1915-17, Ph.D. in Sociology, 1920; m. Julia Lewis Bishop, Sept. 5, 1911; children—Arthur Lewis, Kendall Bishop. Instr. in social sciences, Reed Coll., Portland, Ore., 1911-15; with U. of Mich., from 1917, advancing through various ranks to prof. sociology, 1928, also dir. curriculum in social work, retired; John Hay Whitney vis. professor sociology Wittenberg College, Springfield, Ohio, 1952-53. Pres. Mich. Conf. on Family Relations from 1945; chmn. Mich. State Council on Corrections from 1948; president Michigan Corrections Assn., from 1946. Mem. President Hoover's Conf. on Home Building and Home Ownership; mem. Com. to Revise Mich. Penal Sytem, 1937, Am. Parole Assn. (com. on principles and standards), Am. Sociol. Soc., Nat. Com. on Prisons and Prison Labor (exec. council), U. of Mich. Research Club, Phi Beta Kappa, etc. Author: Community Problems, 1928; Crime and Its Treatment (with Prof. John B. Waite), 1941; also numerous articles and repts. pertaining to sociol. subjects. In Germany Studying problems relating to housing, social work and penology, 1932-33. Contbg. editor Dictionary of Sociology, 1943; Dictionary of Religion, 1945. Mem. editorial staff, Am. Sociol. Review, Address: Springfield, O.†

WOOD, AUSTIN VOORHEES, publisher; b. Athens, O., Apr. 22, 1893; s. James Perry and Mary Ellen (Voorhees) W.; A.B., Ohio U., 1915; postgrad., Ohio State State U., 1915-16, W.Va., U., 1917; m. Vashti P. Flesher, June 19, 1927. Admitted to W.Va. bar, 1917; practiced in Wheeling, 1917-43; pub. Ogden Newspapers, Inc., Wheeling, also 2 other pub. corps. pub. 10 newspapers, W.Va., N.Y., Ia., Mo., 1943-73; hon. chmn. bd. Half Dollar Trust & Savs. Bank, Wheeling, 1943-73. Bd. govs. W.Va. U., 1940-43; hon. trustee Bethany Coll. Mem. Phi Delta Theta, Phi Delta Phi. Republican. Presbyn. Club: Fort Henry (Wheeling). Home: Wheeling, W.Va., Died Sept. 19, 1973.

WOOD, J(OHN) PERRY, lawyer; b. Baltimore, Md., Mr. Mar. 30, 1879; s. John Allen and Ida Lewis (Perry) W.; A.M., Dickinson Coll., 1901; LL.B., Yale, 1902; m. Claudine Hazen, June 17, 1911 (dec.) children—Wallbridge, Dana; m. 2d, Elizabeth Monroe, July 18, 1933. Admitted to Calif. bar, 1912, and began practice at Los Angeles; city atty. Pasadena, 1906-10; in charge proceedins while city atty., resulting in establishment of the city water system; also establishing municipal power and light system; handled litigation for city vs. Bell Telephone interests, resulting in consolidation of local telephone cos. and establishment of rights of telephone and telegraph cos. in streets of cities of Calif.; judge Superior Ct., Los Angeles County, Calif., 1910-25; presiding judge, 1918; resigned; later practicing in Los Angeles, mem. firm Wood, Crump, Rogers & Arndt. Rep. of Calif. State Bar Association, 1928, in proceedings in Superior Court for liberal interpretation of constitutional provisions for judicial council; initiated movement in Calif. for reform of judicial selection and tenure, 1932; chairman committee, conference bar association delegates on judicial selection and tenure, 1935, 36, and of lie Com., Am. Bar Assn., 1937-44; pres. Judicial Sec. Calif. Bar Assn., 1924-26; mem. bd. of govs. of Calif. State Bar, 1931-34, (v.p. 1933); rep. Los Angeles Bar Assn. to House of Dels. Am. Bar Assn., 1936-42; elected by assembly Am. Bar Assn., del. to House of Dels., Am. Bar Assn., 1940-42; mem. Internat. Law Assn. League of Nations Assn. of Southern Calif. (pes. 1923-24), World Court Com. of Southern Calif., English-Speaking Union; pres. Yale Alumni Assn. of Calif., 1912-14. Trustee, Scripps College, Republican. Author of law establishing civil proceedings in municipal courts of Calif. Contbr. to legal jours. Clubs: University, City (Los Angeles); Overland (Pasadena). Home: Claremont, Cal.†

WOOD, LAURENCE IRVEN, lawyer; b. Rochester, Minn., Oct. 10, 1914; s. Irven B. and Frances (Palmer) W.; A.B., DePauw U., 1936, LL.D., 1967; J.D., Northwestern U., 1939; grad. student Harvard, 1951; m. Thalia Banning, June 17, 1938 (div. 1967); children—Thalia L. (Corral), Madeleine B. (Arnheim); m. 2d, Elizabeth Beam, 1968. Admitted to Ill. bar, 1939, N.Y. bar, 1948, D.C. bar, 1970; asso. firm Banning and Banning, Chgo., 1939-41; price atty. CPA, Chgo., 1941-42; atty. Continental Casualty Co., Chgo., 1942-43; office gen. counsel Navy Dept., Washington, 1943-44; atty. Gen. Electric Co., 1945-60, v.p., 1960-70, gen. counsel, sec., 1960-64, mgr. Washington corporate affairs, 1964-70; partner Vedder, Price, Kaufman & Kammholz, 1971; lectr. Rutgars U., 1947-48, N.Y.U., 1959-60, Am. U., 1967-70. Corp. Conferes, Pres.'s Com. on Civil Rights, 1946-47; mem. Atty. Gen.'s Nat. Com. to Study Antitrust Laws, 1953-55; pres. Food and Drug Law Inst., 1970. Recipient Alumni citation DePauw U., 1961, named Alumnus of Year, 1963. Mem. Am. (chmn. Sherman Act com. 1955-56,), Fed. bar assns., Bar Assn. City N.Y. (chmn. com. corp. law depts. 1961-63), Nat. Legal Aid & Defender Assn., N.Y. State, Inter-Am., Internat. bar assns., Assn. Gen. Counsel, Bus.-Govt. Relations Council (pres. 1966-69), Harvard Advanced Mgmt. Assn. (permanent sec.), Order of Coif, Phi Beta Kappa, Pi Epsilon Delta, Alpha Tau Omega, Phi Delta Phi. Author: Patents and Antitrust Law, 1942; United State Patent System—A Survey, 1946. Home: Washington, D.C. Died June 9, 1973; buried Dulaney Valley Meml. Gardens, Cockeysville, Md.

WOOD, LEONARD EARLE, food mfr.; b. Leadville, Colo., June 27, 1881; s. Tingley S. and Leonora (Chestnut) W.; ed. pub. schs. of Springfield, Ill.; m. Gertrude Scott Hewtit, Mar. 30, 1910; children—Leonard Earle, Charles Tingley; m. 2d, Claudine C. Gillespie, Jan. 22, 1937. Began as office boy with J. K. Armsby Co., San Francisco, and continued with same until 1916, when company was merged into the Calif. Packing Corp., makers of Del Monte and Sunkist brands of foods, of which later dir (resigned -as pres., Jan. 11, 1940); trustee George N. Armsby Trust; dir. Bank of Calif. Member Alaska Packers Assn. Mem. bd. govs. San Francisco Symphony Orchestera. Clubs: Pacific Union, Press. Home: San Francisco, Cal.†

WOOD, MEREDITH, publisher; b. Bklyn., Sept. 19, 1895; s. John Scott and Elizabeth King (Barrow) W.; A.B., Williams Coll., 1916; m. Helen A. Martin, Apr. 30, 1930; children—Meredith, Kingsley, Christopher Martin (dec.). Mem. staff Vanity Fair mag., 1916-17; credit rep. Chem. Bank N.Y. Trust Co. (formerly Chem. Nat. Bank), N.Y.C., 1919-24, asst. cashier, 1924-27, asst. v.p., 1927-38, v.p., 1928-29, mem. adv. bd., 1929-73, chmn. W. Side adv. bd., 1958-60; dir., treas. Book-of-the-Month Club, Inc., 1929-31, exec. v.p., dir., treas., 1929-50, pres., 1950-60, then dir.; dir. treas. Book-of-the-Month Club (Can.) Ltd., 1929-31, exec. v.p., dir., treas., 1931-47, exec. v.p., dir., 1947-60, now dir.; dir. Franklin Publs., Inc., Grosset & Dunlap, Inc., Bantam Books, Inc., 1944-68. Bd. dirs. Scherman Found., N.Y.C.; trustee Williams Coll., 1947-52. Chmn. book pubs. div. Com. Econ. Devel. Fund Campaign, 1955, U.S. Treasury War Bond drive, World War II, United Hosp. Fund Campaign of N.Y., 1948; dir. Council on Books in Wartime during World War II. Served from 2d lt. to capt. 308 Inf., 77 div. AEF, U.S. Army, 1917-19. Decorated D.S.C., Verdun medal, Corps and Divl. citations, Purple Heart, Croix de Guerre with Silver Star (France), recipient Conspicuous Service medal State of N.Y. Mem. Am. Bood Publs. Council (dir.), Order Lafayette, Beta Theta Pi. Clubs: Williams of New York (pres. 1943-45), Fox Meadow Tennis (Scarsdale, N.Y.); University (N.Y.C.); Shenorock Shore (Rye, N.Y.). Home: Scarsdale, N.Y. Died May 14, 1974; interred Sleepy Hollow Cemetery, Tarrytown, N.Y.

WOOD, WILLIAM CARLETON, Clergyman, educator; b. Farmington, N.Y., Apr. 24, 1880; s. Charles Henry and Adelaide (Hallock) W.; A.B., Penn Coll., Oskaloosa, Ia., 1905, A.M., 1970; student Princeton Theol. Sem., 1905-06; B.D., Hartford Theol. Sem., 1909, Ph.D., 1911; m. Alice Cook, of Oskaloosa, Ia., Sept. 27, 1907. Prof. Bibl. lit., Penn Coll., Oskaloosa, 1906-08; ordained minister Soc. of Friends, 1907; Porter Ogden Jacobus fellow, Hartford Theol. Sem., 1909-10; Thayer fellow, at Jerusalem Sch. of Oriental Research, Palestine, 1910-11; pastor Friends Ch., Winthrop Center, Me., 1911-14, Plymouth Ch., Hartford, Conn., 1914-15; classical master and Bibl. instr., Pickering Coll., Newmarket, Ont., Can., 1915-17; pastor Friends Ch., Fall River, Mass., 1917-19, also supt. evangelistic and ch. extension work for Southern N.E., for N.E. Yearly Meeting of Friends; prof. Bibl. philosophy, Whittier (Calif.) Coll., from Sept. 1919. Mem. Soc. Bibl. Lit. and Exegesis. Author: The Religion of Canaan, 1917. Home: Whittier, Cal.†

WOODBERY, D. HOYT, cigar co. exec.; b. 1892; married. With Havatampa Cigar Corp., 1910-73, pres., chief exec. officer, treas., 1947-73, also chmn. and dir.; dir. Exchange Nat. Bank, Tampa. Bd. dirs. Fla. State Fair, Gasparilla Assn. Address; Tampa, Fla. Died Mar. 16, 1973.

WOODBRIDGE, FREDERICK JAMES, architect; b. Mpls., May 18, 1900; s. Frederick J.E. and Helena Belle (Adams) W.; grad. Philips Exeter, 1917; A.B., Amherst, 1921; B.Arch, Columbia, 1923; M.A. (hon.), Amherst Coll., 1951; m. Catherine Baldwin, Oct. 15, 1927; children—John M., Jane (Mrs. A.F. Sieverts). Vis. student Am. Acad. Rome, 1923-25; Boyer research fellow in classical archaeology U. Mich., 1924-25; architect for excavations at Antioch of Pisidia Carthage, Tunisia, 1924-25; partner Evans Moore & Woodbridge, architects, 1929-42, Adams & Woodbridge, 1945-74; faculty mem. extension Columbia Sch. Architecture, 1934-42; Fulbright grantee, architect in residence Am. Acad. Rome, 1951-52; lectr. Tchrs. Coll., 1938-42; architect to corp. Trinity Ch., N.Y.C.; faculty Salzburg Seminar in Am. Studies, 1966. Architect mem. Art Commn. City N.Y., 1956-59; vice chmn. Landmarks Preservation Commn. N.Y., 1962-65, mem., 1962-68. Trustee St. Luke's Hosp. Center; bd. dirs. Bethlehem Day Nursery, N.Y.C. Served at lt. comdr. USNR, naval avaition observer (nav.), World War II. Registered architect, N.Y., Conn., N.J., Pa. Prin works: Adirondack Mus., Blue Mountain Lake, N.Y.; St. Andrews Ch., Bronx, St. Mark's Tower, St. John's Chapel And Demarest Library, Hobart Coll.; Alumnae House of Smith Coll; Keene Valley (N.Y.) Ch; House Libraries, Amherst Coll.; Mission Ch., Liberia, Africa; office bldg. Mfrs. Assn. N.J. (Trenton); chapel and parish house Brick Presbyn, Ch., N.Y.C.; parish house St. Augustine Chapel, N.Y.C.; Trinity Ch., Newtown, Conn.; Episcopal Ch. Center, N.Y.C.; hdqrs. Girl Scount council Greater N.Y.; others; cons. architect Columbia, 1947-70. Fellow A.I.A. (pres. N.Y. chpt. 1961-62); mem. N.A.D. (asso.), Archtl. League N.Y. (pres. 1941-43, 48-49 sec. 1939-41), Nat. Inst. Archtl. Edn., Municipal Art Soc. N.Y. (dir.), Fine Arts Fedn. N.Y. (pres.), Sch. Art League N.Y.C. (past pres.), Phi Beta Kappa, Alpha Delta Phi. Episcopalian (sec.-treas. joint commn. on architecture and allied arts P.E. Ch. 1958-68). Clubs: Coffee House, Century (N.Y.C.). Home: New York City N.Y. Died Jan. 17, 1974

WOODBURN, WILLIAM, lawyer; b. Virginia City, Nev., Jan. 1, 1880; s. William and Mary (Duffy) W.; LL.B., Georgetown U., 1903; m. Mary Kervin, Aug. 31, 1909; children—William K., Mary Barbara (Mrs. P. Paul Vlautin), John K. Admitted to Nev. bar, 1907; mem. of firm Thathcer, Woodburn & Forman attys. at law, Reno, Nev.; v.p. and dir. The Goldfield Consolidated Mines Co., from 1925; dist. atty., Washoe

County, Nev., 1909-13; U.S. atty., State of Nev., 1914-22. Served as yeoman, U.S. Navy, 1899-99. Democrat. Catholic. Home: Reno Nev.†

WOODBURY, MILDRED FAIRCHILD, welfare consultant; b. Tabor, Iowa, April 30, 1894; d. James Thome and Emma Louise (Dickinson) Fairchild; A.B. Overlin College, 1916, A.M., 1925; Ph.D., Bryn Mawr College; married Robert Morse Woodbury, July 24, 1947. Member staff, Fisk University, 1916-18; with Playground and Recreation Association of America, 1920-22; campaign field organizer Oberlin Coll., 1923; fellow social economy and social research, Bryn Mawr Coll., 1925-27, research asst. grad dept. 1927-28; student London (Eng.) Sch. Econs., 1928-29; research fellow in U.S.S.R., of Am. Russian Inst., 1929-30; asso. in social economy and social research Bryn Mawr Coll., 1930-34; asso. prof. 1934-36; dir. grad. dept. of social economy, 1936-46; chief of section on Women's Work and Protection of Young Workers, Internat. Labour Office, 1947-54; consultant in child welfare and youth employment. Served in War Camp Community Service, 1918-20; Mem. State Adv. Council, Bur. of Employment Service and Unemployment Compensation, Dept. of Labor and Industry of Pa., 1938-39, chmn 1941-42. Mem. bd. directors Pa. Public Edn. and Child Labor Assn., exec. com. Pub. Charities Assn. of Pa.; chmn. sub-com. on woman power, War Man Power Commn., Phila. area, 1944; bd. dirs. Nat. Child Labor Com., 1954-70, chairman of the board, 1958-64; chairman technical advisory com. on assistance standards Pa. Dept. Public Assistance, 1956; v.p. Health and Welfare Council, Philadelphia, 1966-67. Bd. trustees Community Resources Pa., 1968-69. Recipient Distinguished Dau. of Pa. award, 1963. Mem. Phila. Art Alliance, Am. Sociol. Society, Am. Econ. Association, American Assn. U. Woman, Pa. Citizen's Association for Health and Welfare (member of the board of dirs. 1958-66), Phi Beta Kappa. Club: Women's University (Philadelphia), Author: The Needs of Children in the World, 1956. Co-author (with Susan M. Kingbury), Factory, Family and Woman in Soviet Russia, 1935. Contbr. articles and surveys. Home: Bryn Mawr Pa. Died Feb. 1975

WOODING, HUGH OLLIVIERE BERESFORD, business exec.; b. Trinidad, Jan. 14, 1904; s. Iddo Arthur Reginald and Rosina Ethelinda (Cadogan) W.; ed. (Trinidad and Tobago scholar, Gold medallist), Queen's Royal Coll., Trinidad, 1915-23, Middle Temple, London, Eng., 1924-27; LL.D., U. W.I., 1967; m. Anne Marie Coussey, Jan. 14, 1928; children—Hugh Arthur Selby Ambah Rose (Mrs. Max Matthew Thomas), Anne Daphne (Mrs. Garnet Roosevelt Woodham), Henley Orbah Beresford. Practice law, Commonwealth Caribbean, 1927-62; chief justice Trinidad and Tobago, 1962-68; mem. judicial com. Privy Council in Britain, 1967; past vice chmn. Caribbean Devel. Co. Ltd.; past chmn. Brit. West Indian Airways, Trinidad Broadcasting Co. Ltd., Rediffusion Trinidad Ltd., Internat. Aeradio (Caribbean) Ltd.; chmn. Trinidad and Tobago bd. Furness, With & Co. Ltd., Trinidad Trading Co., Swan Hunter (Trinidad) Ltd., Furness & Gordon Ltd., Furness & Watson Ltd., Diversey (Caribbean) Ltd., Metalock (Caribbean) Ltd., also Brokers-West Indies Ltd., 1969-74, Reed Trinidad Ltd., 1971-74, Caribbean Telecoms Ltd., 1972-74, Caribbean Devel. Co. Ltd.; dir. Carib Glassworks Ltd., Texaco Trinidad, Inc., Internat. Trust of Washington (Caribbean) Ltd., West Indian Tobacco Co. Ltd., Barbados Telephone Co. Ltd., Grenada Telephone Co. Ltd., Bank of Nova Scotia (Trinidad & Tobago) Ltd. Chmn., Little Carib Theatre, 1948-74, Assn. Child Care of Trinidad and Tobago, 1969-74; mem. Judicial and Legal Service Commn., 1969-74; chmn. Trinidad and Tobago Constrn. Commn., 1971; chmn. Princess Alice Appeal Fund in Trinidad and Tobago, U. W.I., 1959-74, chmn. Friends of U. In Trinidad and Tobago, 1969-74, chmn. coms. advising on establishment law faculty, 1963-64, 67, mem. West Indian council legal edn., 1971-74, mem. univ. council, 1967-74, chmn., chancellor, 1971-74. City councillor Port of Spain, Trinidad, 1941-43, mayor, 1943-44, alderman, 1944-47. Trustee Trust Corp. Methodist Ch. in Caribbean and Americas. Decorated comdr. Order Brit. Empire (U.K.); Trinity Cross (Trinidad and Tobago); created knight bachelor, 1963; named Hon. Bencher, Inner Temple, 1968. Fellow Inst. Dirs.; mem. Bar Assn. Trinidad and Tobago (v.p. until 1962), Caribbean Bar Assn. (pres. until 1962), Methodist (sr. circuit steward until 1971). Mason. Clubs: Maple, Queen's Park, Union (Trinidad); Jamaica; West Indian (London). Author: A Collection of Addresses, 1968. Home: Maraval, Trinidad. Died July 26, 1974.

WOODRUFF, ISAAC OGDEN, physician; b. N.Y. City Feb. 13, 1881; s. Isaac Ogden and Charlotte(Coburn) W.; A.B., Coll. of the City of New York, 1900; M.D., Columbia, 1904; m. Mabel G. Compton, June 18, 1908 (div.); children—Ogden Compton and Charlotte Van Camp (twins); m. 2d, Phyllis I. Temple, Aug. 16, 1947. Emeritus prof. clinical medicine, Columbia U.; cons. physician Bellevue Hosp.; pres. Helath Council of New York City; cons. physciian Otisville Sanatorium, Greenwich and St. Francis hosps., Port Jervis; mem. com. on medicine in the changing order, New York Acad. of Medicine. Awarded Alumni Service award, Townsend Harris medal (Coll. City of New York), 1937 and 1939. Diplomate Am. Bd. of Internal Medicine. Fellow Am. Coll. of Physcisians; Physicians; mem. A.M.A., Am. Trudeau Soc., Nat. Tuberculosis Assn., New York Acad. of Medicine, Am. Assn. Adv. Sci. (Research Council on Alcohol, an asso. soc.), sr. surg. (reserve) U.S.P.H. Service, Sigma Alpha, Phi Beta Kappa, Delta Kappa Epsilon, Alpha Omega Alpah. Republican. Episcopalian. Author: Report of Committee on Open Air Class (Bd. of Edn., New York), 1941. Contbr. articles to books and med. jours. Home: NEw York City, N.Y.†

WOODRUFF, MARSTON TRUE, physician; b. Webster Groves, Mo., Mar. 13, 1905; s. Charles Lincoln and Julia (Hodgdon) W.; M.D., Jefferson Med. Coll., 1930; m. Viola Estelle Habel, June 26, 1930; children—Charles Lawrence, Constance (Mrs. Robert Atwell), Stephen Marston. Intern, Frankford Hosp., Phila., 1930-31; past pres med. staff, radiologist emeritus; resident in radiology Mt. Sinai Hosp., N.Y.C., 1936-37; radiologist Friends Hosp.; cons. in radiology Ft. Dix Army Hosp., until 1973, Frankford Arsenal, until 1973; instr. radiology Grad. Hosp., Phila. Active Phila. div. Am. Cancer Soc., sec., until 1973, hon. life mem. Served to lt. col. M.C., AUS, 1941-45. Recipient Spl. award for outstanding service Phila. div. Am. Cancer Soc. Diplomate Am. Bd. Radiology. Mem. A.M.A., Am. Coll. Radiology, Radiol. Soc. N.Am., Pa. Radiol. Soc. (past v.p.), Phila. Roentgen Ray Soc. (past pres.), Philadelphia County Med. Soc., (past v.p., treas.). Episcopalian (vestryman). Home: Jenkintown, Pa. Died Sept. 8, 1973; buried Whitemarsh Meml. Park, Prospectville, Pa.

WOODS, BILL MILTON, publishing cons.; b. Pottawattamie County, Ia., May 26, 1924; s. Fred Cline and Mary Ellen (Hughes) W.; A.B., Peru (Neb.) State Coll., 1945; B.S., U. Ill., 1947, M.S., 1953; postgrad. U. Neb., 1945-46, 47-48; m. Janice Thumm, June 12, 1948; children—Suzanne Marie (Mrs. Douglas E. Kelley), David Owen, Steven Alan. Circulation asst. library U. Neb., 1945-46, asst. librarian social studies, curator maps, 1947-49; acting map librarian U. Ill., 1946-47, map librarian, 1949-56, map and geography librarian, 1956-58, instr. library sci., 1951-55, asst. prof. 1955-58; head proccessing sect. map div. Library of Congress, 1958-59; exec. sec. Spl. Libraries Assn., 1959-63, exec. dir., 1963-67; cons. Nat. Adv. Commn. on Libraries, 1967; with Engring Index, Inc., 1967-73, exec. dir., pub., sec.-treas., 1968-73; cons., 1973. Vis. lect. Drexel Inst., 1962, 66-68, adj. prof. L.I. U., 1972. Sec., N. Y. Met. Reference and Research Agy., 1966-68, chmn., 1964, trustee, 1962-73. Mem. Council Nat. Library Assns. (trustee 1960-62, sec.-treas. 1962-64, chmn. 1964-67), Nat. Assn. Exhibit Mgrs. (dir. 1963-65), Am. Soc. Information Sci., Information Industry Assn., Fedn. Mgmt. Orgns. (treas. 1st v.p. 1962-64), Assn. Am. Geographers, Am. Soc. for Engring. Edn., N.Y., Soc. Assn. Execs., A.A.A.S., Nat. Fedn. Abstracting and Indexing Services (dir., sec. 1969-70, pres. elect 1970-71, pres. 1971-72), Beta Phi Mu (pres. 1950-51), Kappa Delta Pi, Sigma Tau Delta. Democrat. Methodist. Contbr. articles to profl., other jours. Home: New York City N.Y. Died May 1, 1974.

WOODS, GEORGE HERBERT, b. Sept. 28, 1878; pres. Bridgeport Peoples Savings Bank, from 1924. Address: Bridgeport, Conn.†

WOODS, GRANVILLE CECIL, financial adviser; b. Shelbyville, Tenn., June 17, 1900; s. George A. and Fannie (Sandusky) W.; student Sewanee Mil. Acad.; student U. South, 1917-18, D.C.L., 1965; m. Katherine Elizabeth Greer, Sept. 8, 1921; 1 son, Granville Cecil. Bookkeeper, Farmers Nat. Bank, Shelbyville, 1919-22; gen. agt. for State of Tenn., Bankers Life Co. of Des Moines, 1922-37; mgr. real estate and mortgage loan dept. nat. Life & Accident Ins. Co., Nashville, 1937-39; pres, dir. Vol. State Life Ins. Co., Chattanooga, 1939-63, chmn. bd., 1963-68, then dir.; dir. Am. Nat. Bank & Trust Co. Mem. exec. com. Am. Life Conv., Chgo., 1950, pres., 1951. State chmn. War Finance Com. of Tenn., 1943-45. Past. dir. Life Ins. Med. Research Fund; former trustee S. Research Inst.; bd regents, trustee U. of South, bd. dirs. United Fund, Community Found. Greater Chattanooga. Mem. Life Ins. Assn. Am. (past dir.), Inst. Life Ins. (past dir.), Sigma Alpha Epsilon. Presbyn. Clubs: Mountain City (Chattanooga); Fairyland (Lookout Mountain, Tenn.). Home: Chattanooga, Tenn., Died June 16, 1975.

WOODS, TIGHE EDWARD, govt. ofcl., realtor; b. Chicago, Aug. 2, 1910; s. Clifton F. and Frances (Tighe) W.; A.B. in journalism, U. of Notre Dame, 1933; grad. student Northwestern U., 1935-36; m. Lucy Beasley, Jan. 12, 1935; children—Bryan, Margaret, Hope. Worked for real estate firm, Chicago, 1933-36; operated and owned property management office, Chicago, 1936-42; examiner rent control office, O.P.A., Chicago, 1942-44, rent dir. 1946, regional rent dir., 1947; dep. housing expediter Office of Rent Control, Washington, 1947, apptd. housing expediter, Dec. 20, 1947; director of office Rent Stabilization, 1952; later pvt. realtor, real estate appraiser and land developer. Served with United States N. R. F. as lt. (j.g.) on active duty, 1944-46 radar officer U.S.S. Hanover, Pacific. Mem. Inst. Real Estate Management, Nat. Assn. Real Estate Bds. Democrat. Roman Catholic Club: South Shore Country (Chicago). Editor of Chicago Apt. House Operaiing Cost Manual, 1940-41. Home: Washington D.C. Died July 9, 1974

WOODWARD, CARL RAYMOND, univ. pres.; b. Tennent, N.J., July 20, 1890; s. William Henry and Edith Augusta (Reid) W.; B.S., Rutgers U., 1914; A.M., 1919, Litt.D., 1941; Ph.D., Cornell U., 1926; D.Sc., R.I., Coll. Phar., 1943, Bryant Coll., 1943; LL.D., Boston U., 1947, Univ. of Maine, 1948; Providence Coll., 1950, Brown U., 1955; Ed.D., R.I., Coll. of Edn., 1954; m. Lulu Altha Ryno, April 5, 1916; children—Carl Raymond, Mildred Ryno (Mrs. James A. Stackhouse, Jr.), William Van Neste. Teacher in rural schools, Monmouth County, N.J., 1908-10; teacher Rutgers Coll., summer 1914; teacher science and mathematics, Madison (N.J.) High Sch., 1914-15; editor and librarian N.J. Agrl. Expt. Station and Coll. of Agr., Rutgers U., 1915-16, editor and sec., 1916-27, instr. in English, 1920-26, asst. prof., 1926-27; Alumni Assn. work, Rutgers U., 1927-28, asst. to pres., 1928-36, dir. ednl. research, 1930-32, sec. U., 1936-41; pres. University of Rhode Island, from 1941; bd. mgrs. Wakefield br. Indsl. National Bank Providence. Mem. N.J. State Bd. Edn., 1936-41; pres. Kiwanis, New Brunswick, 1929; pres. Community Chest, New Brunswick, 1935-36; trustee N.J. Hist. Soc., 1940-41; mem. adv. bd. overseers Old Sturbridge Village. Lecturer Franklin Institute, 1940. Recipient Freedoms Found. award, 1953, 57; R.I. World Affairs Council award, 1954; Rutgers Alumni award, 1956. Mem. New Eng. Council (dir.), American Assn. of Agricultural Coll. Editors (pres. 1921-22), Agrl. History Soc. (pres. 1942-43), N.J. Press, Assn. (life), R.I. and N.J. hist. assns., Barnard Club (pres. 1945-46). R.I. Inst. Instrn. (exec. com.), Nat. Commn. on Accrediting, Nat. Assn. State Univs. (pres. 1955-56), Assn. Land Grant Colleges and Univs. (chmn. pres.' council 1955-56), Alpha Zeta, Phi Alpha Theta, Phi Kappa Phi, Phi Gamma Delta, Phi Beta Kappa, Phi Delta Kappa; hon. mem. R.I. Agrl. Conf., Future Farmers of Am. Trustee Phi Gamma Delta Ednl. Foundation. Ind. Republican. Congregationalist. Mason, Grange. Hon. mem. University Club and British Empire Club, Providence, Providence Art Club. Author or co-author several books from 1924. Home: Kingston R.I. Died Oct. 2, 1974

WOODWARD, DONALD BOSLEY, economist; b. Clayton, Ind., Dec. 17, 1905; s. Alvin and Sarah (Bosley) W.; A.B., Ind. U., 1928; m. Jean Davis, Feb. 8, 1930; 1 dau., Penelope; m. 2d, Ethel P. Hutcheson, Dec. 22, 1961; m. 3d, Frances H. Milnes, Dec. 26, 1969. Staff mem. Wall St. Jour., 1927-29; financial editor Bus. Week., 1929-32; economist Moody's Investors Service, 1933-40; mem. research staff NRA, 1933; cons. to bd. govs. FRS, 1939; instr. bank investments Columbia, 1939-41; cons. expert Treasury Dept., 1942-44; cons. to U.S. Dept State, 1947-48; research asst. to pres. Mut. Life Ins. Co. of N.Y.C., 1940-46, 2d v.p., 1946-52, v.p. research, 1952-53; economist, dir. Richardson Merrill, Inc., 1953-61; mng. partner A. W. Jones & Co., 1961-69; trustee Lincoln Savs. Bank Bklyn.; dir. Piedmont Mgmt. Co. Staff dir. Pres.'s Citizen Advisers on Mut. Security Program, 1956-57. Trustee Brookings Inst.; bd. dirs. Perrot Meml. Library, Old Greenwich, Conn., Nat. Bur. Econ. Research. Fellow Wilton Park (Eng.); mem. Conf. Bus. Economists. Conglist. Clubs: University (N.Y.C.); Cosmos (Washington). Author: (with M.A. Rose) Primer of Money 1932, Inflation 1933; (with Murray Shields) Prosperity: We Can Have It If We Want It 1945. Home: Riverside, Conn. Died Sept. 23, 1974; interred 1st Congregational Ch. Cemetery, Old Greenwich, Conn.

WOODWARD, DUDLEY KEZER, JR., lawyer; b. Uvalde County, Tex., July 19, 1881; s. Dudley Kezer and Anna (Russell) W.; A.B., U. of Tex., Texas, 1901; J.D. cum laude, U. of Chicago, 1907; m. Mary Lee Thomson, Jan. 4, 1911; children—Elizabeth (Mrs. Robert H. Jones), Mary Virginia (Mrs. Thomas R. Hougton). Began in civil engring. work, railroad location and construction, southwestern U.S., 1902-04; admitted to bar, 1907, and practiced, Austin, Tex., 1907-32; special legal and adminstrative work, Dallas, Tex., from 1932; chmn. bd. dirs. Oak Lawn Nat. Bank, Dallas. Mem. Bd. regents U. Texas (former chmn.). Mem. Am., Tex. and Dallas County bar assns., Philos. Soc. Tex. (pres.), Sigma Alpah Epsilon, Phi Delta Phi. Mason (33°). Clubs: City, Dallas Country, Critic (Dallas.) Home: Dallas, Tex.†

WOODWARD, ELIZABETH ASH, lecturer, educator; b. Atglen, Pa., Aug. 9, 1878; d. George Wilmer and Adeline (Doan) Ash W.; grad. Phila. (Pa.) Normal Sch.; B.S., Columbia, 1910, A.M., 1917; post-grad. study U. of Pa., Dartmouth, New Sch. of Social Research, etc.; unmarried. Teacher pub. chs., N.Y. City, 1900-10; lecturer on science, Froebel League Training Sch. for Teachers, N.Y. City, 1908-12; prin. pvt. country day sch., Germantown, Pa., 1912-14; lecturer on methods and literature, Pratt Ins., and supervisor Brooklyn Free Kindergarten Soc., 1914-19; N.Y. State supervisor adult edn. of foreign-born, from 1919; organizer, 1921, and later supervisor of pvt. demonstration in adult end., edn., Neighborhood Teacher Assn., N.Y. City; lecturer, Hunter Coll. extension from 1922, Teachers Coll., New York, from 1924. Mem. exec. bd. Council on Adult Edn., of Foreign-Born, N.Y. City, Nat. Conf. on Immigration Policy. Life mem. N.E.A.; mem. Administrative Women in Edn., Am. Assn. Univ. Women. Republican.

Mem. Society of Friends. Clubs: Women's City, Town Hall. Writer of many pamphlets and repts. on adult edn. Home: New York City, N.Y.†

WOODWARD, JACK EDWARD, utility exec.; b. Lewis, Ia., Mar. 29, 1921; s. Edward Charles and Stella (Pierce) W.; B.S., Ia., State U., 1950; m. Marjorie Cochran, May 8, 1943; children—Kathleen Sue, Richard Mark. Gen. foreman substation dept. Omaha Pub. Power Dist., Omaha, 1961-72; mem. adv. com., chmn. insulating fluids com. Doble Engring. Co. Served to 1st lt. AUS, 1942-46. Registered profl. engr., Neb. Mem. I.E.E.E. (sr.), C. of C. Methodist. Mason (32 deg., Shriner). Home: Omaha, Neb. Died Apr. 15, 1972; buried Forest Lawn Cemetery, Omaha.

WOODWARD, KARL WILSON, prof. forestry; b. Detroit, Mich., July 24, 1881; s. Robert Simpson and Martha Gretin (Bond) W.; A.B., Cornell U., 1904; M.F., Yale, 1904; m. Olive Smith, Sept. 11, 1909; children—Karl Wilson, William Smith. With U.S. Forest Service, Washington, D.C., 1904-15; prof. forestry, U. of N.H., 1915-40; prof. forestry, Mass., State Coll., 1942-43; forest working plans in Minn. and N.H. from 1943. Member executive committee D. Webster Council, Boy Scouts of America, Recerived Beaver Award, Oct. 1939. Mem. Soc. Am. Foresters, Soc. for Protection of N.H. Forests (exec. com. 1929), A.A.A.S., N.H. Acad. Science, Phi Kappa Phi. Republican. Unitarian. Club: Rotary (Dover, N.H.). Author: Valuation of American Timberlands, 1921. Home: Durham, N.H.*†

WOODWARD, THOMAS MULLEN, lawyer; b. Phila., Mar. 2, 1884; s. Winfield Scott and Katharine Carroll Dun (Mullen) W.; A.B., Princeton, 1906; LL.B. U. of Pa., 1910; m. Constance Goodnow Perry, June 2, 1917; children—Constance, Katharine Carroll, Anne Perry, Thomas Mullen, Jr. Admitted to Pa. bar, 1910, Supreme Court of U.S., 1921; in practice at Phila., 1910-14; atty. Interstate Commerce Commn., 1914-20; atty. for dir. gen. of railroads, 1920-24; in practice at Washington, 1924-33, and from 1946; atty. A.A.A., dept. of Agr., 1933; vice pres. U.S. Shipping Board Merchant Fleet Corp. and mem. advisory committee to Sec. Commerce, 1933-35; consumers' counsel of Nat. Bituminous Coal Commn., 1935-37; member U.S. Maritime Commn., Apr. 1937-45, vice chmn., 1938-42; chmn. Price Adjustment Bd. of Maritime Commn. Mem. Washington Lit. Soc. Club: Cosmos (Washington). Home: Washington, D.C. Died May 2, 1975.

WOOLF, HERBERT M, merchant; b. Kansas City, Mo., Oct. 11, 1880; s. Alfred S. and Phoebe (Davis) W.; ed. Central High Sch., Kansas City; unmarried. Pres. Woolf Brothers, Inc., men's and women's ready to wear, Kansas City (5 branch stores); pres. Midland Theatre & Realty Co., Midland Investment Co. Mem. staff of Gov. Hyde, 1920-24. Deputy police commr. of Kansas City, 1922-24; mem. Jackson County (Mo.) Park Bd. Dir. Am. Royal Live Stock Show. V.p. Menorah Hosp. Mem. Nat. Assn. Retail Clothiers and Furnishers, Kansas City C of C (dir.). Clubs: Kansas City Athletic, Oakwood Country. Owner of "Lawrin," winner of 1938 Kentucky Derby; also large stables of racing horses. Home: Kansas City, Mo.†

WOOLMAN, C. E., pres., gen. mgr. Delta Air Lines, Inc. Address: Atlanta, Ga., Died Sept. 11, 1966.

WOON, BASIL (DILLON), author; The Real Sarah Bernhardt, 1925; The Frantic Atlantic, 1927; When It's Cocktail Time in Cuba, 1928; From Deauville to Monte Carlo, 1929; Paris That's Not in the Guide Books, 1931; Incredible Land, 1933; San Francisco and the Golden Empire, 1935. Died June 1974

WOOSLEY, WILLIAM BRYANT, investor, ret. poultry industry exec.; b. Shelbyville, Tenn., Jan. 14, 1904; s. Harry Lee and Mattie (Bryant) W.; B.S. in Textile Engring., Ga. Inst. Tech., 1926; m. Lula Lewis, Oct. 5, 1926; children—William Bryant, Harry Lee II. Pres., Woosley Knitting Mills, 1927-63, Nat. Pencil Co., 1940-63; v.p. Dixie Grain Co., 1935-69; pres. Dixie Home Corp., 1958-61, chmn. bd. 1961-69 (all Shelbyville); v.p. Dixie Home Feed Mills of Ala., Albertville, 1957-69; dir. Forrest Life Ins. Co., 1965-70, Synercon Corp., 1970-72. Trusteee Webb Sch., Bell Buckle, Tenn. Mem. Tenn. Mfrs. Assn. (gov. 1936-63, pres. 1964-65), Kappa Sigma. Methodist (trustee). Rotarian (past pres.). Home: Shelbyville, Tenn. Died Dec. 28, 1972.

WORLEY, FRANCIS EUGENE, judge; b. Lone Wolf, Okla., Oct. 10, 1908; s. John B. and Idelle (Johnson) W.; student Tex. A. & M. Coll., 1927-29; academic, law student U. Tex., 1930-36; m. Ann Spivy, Sept. 15, 1937; children—Gene, Sam, Morgan. Admitted to Texas bar, 1936; mem. Tex. House of Reps., 1935-40; mem. 77th-81st Congresses, 18th Tex. Dist.; asso. judge U.S. Ct. Customs and Patent Appeals, 1950-59, chief judge, 1959-72, sr. judge, 1972-74. Del. Dem. Nat. Conv., 1936. Mem. Am., Tex. bar assns., Am. Legion, V.F.W. Methodist. Mason. Home: Shamrock, Tex. Died Dec. 17, 1974; interred Columbia Gardens, Arlington, Va.

WORRILOW, GEORGE MELVILLE, adnl. adminstr.; b. Zion, Md., May 25, 1904; s. Joseph M. and Georgia (Vandergrift) W.; B.S., U. Md., 1927, D.Agr., 1954; m. Lucie Griest, Aug. 23, 1930; 1 dau., Stephanie (Mrs. Rodney H. Dann, Jr.). Mem. county and state extension staff U. Del., 1927-38, prof. dairy husbandry U. Del., 1938-41, asso. dir. extension, 1941-43, dir. Extension and Expt. Sta., 1943-54; dean Sch. Arg., 1954-65, v.p. univ. relations, 1961-72; asst. to chmn. bd. Farmers Bank State of Del., 1972-75, also dir. Chmn. Gov.'s Interstate Liaison Com. on Water Resources, 1954-60; sec. Del. Poultry Commn., 1950-64; chmn. Del. Coastal Zone Indsl. Bd., 1971-75. Bd. Dirs. Greater Wilmington Devel. Council, Community Services Council Del., Del. Safety Council, Union Hosp., Elkton, Md. chmn. Del Soil Conservation Commn., 1954-65; trustee Del. Inst. Med. Edn. and Research 1969-72, trustee, bd. dirs. Wilmington Med. Center, Inc., 1972. Recipient Distinguished Service award Del. Grange, 1957; 50th Anniversary Gold Medal award, Balt. Dist. Fed. Land Bank and Fed. Intermediate Credit Bank of Balt. for prominent role agr., 1967; Gold Medal award Phila. Soc. Promoting Agr., 1964; Gold Good Citizenship award Del. soc. S.A.R., 1972; State's Gold medal for meritorious service, also named to Del. Hall of Fame, 1973. Mem. Am. Assn. Land Grant Colls. and State Univs., Am Dairy Sci. Assn., Del. Grange, Eastern Guernsey Breeders Assn. (dir. mem. exec. com. 1958), Am. Coll. Pub. Relations Assn., Alpha Tau Omega, Omicron Delta Kappa, Alph Zeta, Epsilon Sigma Phi. Presbyn. Contbg. editor The Delaware Citizen, 1952, Delaware Interstate Water Survey, 1960. Contbr. articles profl. jours. Home: Oaklands, Newark, Del. Died Feb. 27, 1975; interred Head of Christiana Cemetery, Newark, Del.

WORRILOW, WILLIAM HENRY, mfr.; b. Chester, Pa., Mar 8, 1877; s. Charles Franklin and Elizabeth (Andrew) W.; ed. Chester pub. schs., LL.D., Annville, Pa., Lebanon Valley Coll., 1948; m. Ethel Brooks Ledward, Sept. 29, 1903 (died 1915); m. 2d, Pauline Emma Light, April 11, 1917; children—Emily Louise (Mrs. George Brubaker Gaul), William Henry, John Light, Polly Ann (Mrs. Allen Henry Ehrgood, Jr.). With Am. Steel Casting Co., Chester, 1891-1903, advanced from jr. clerk to asst. dist. mgr.; sales mgr. Solid Steel Casting Co., Chester, 1903-07; asles mgr. Lebanon (Pa.) Steel Casting Co., 1907-11; pres. Lebanon (Pa.) Steel Foundry from 1911; dir. Armstrong Cork Company, Lancaster, Pa., 1931-32; later member board of directors. President of Steel Founders Soc. of Am., 1931-32. Alloy Casting Assn., N.Y.C., 1933, Alloy Casting Inst., N.Y.C., 1940-44. Mem. steel and alloy casting adv. com. to W.P.B. during World War II. Recipient Distinguished Service Award, Am. Soc. Metals, 1948. Dir. Research Inst. of Temple U., Phila.; mem. bd. trustees Lebanon Valley Coll., Annville, Pa. Mem. American Ordnance Association (pres.), Newcomen Soc. Eng., Pa. German Folklore Society, Pa. German Soc., Hugunot Soc. Pa. Republican. Episcopalian. Mason (K.T., Shriner). Club: Lebanon (Pa.) Country. Home: Lebanon, Pa.†

WORSHAM, WILLIAM A(RCHER), college prof.; b. Monroe County, Ga., Mar. 9, 1878; s. William A. and Emma (Zellner) W.; B.S., Univ. of Ga., 1903; A.M., Harvard, 1908; Ph.D., Columbia, 1924; m. Bessie Stanley, Dec. 29, 1922. Teaching fellow, Harvard, 1908-09; asst. Ga. State chemist, Atlanta, Ga., 1909-10; asst. prof. agrl. chemistry, Univ. of Ga., 1910-11, prof. agrl. chemistry, 1911-21; lecturer Hunter Coll., New York, 1921-22, asso. prof., 1922-28, prof., 1928-47, emeritus chmn. dept. of chemistry, 1945-47. Mem. A.A.A.S. (sec. council, 1913, gen. sec., 1914), Am. Chem. Soc., Phi Beta Kappa, Sigma Nu. Democrat. Club: Chemists. Home: Jackson Heights, N.Y.†

WORTHINGTON, MARJORIE, author; b. N.Y.C.; d. Oscar and Rose (Samuels) Muir; m. Lyman Worthington, Mar. 10, 1923 (div. 1932); m. 2d, William B. Seabrook, Feb. 2, 1935 (div. 1941). Author books, 1930-76, latest being: The House on the Park, 1946; The Enchanted Heart, 1949; Miss Alcott of Concord, 1958; (biography) Abelard and Heloise, 1960; Bouboukar, 1962; The Strange World of Willie Seabrook, 1966; books pub. also in England, Germany, Italy. Contbr. nat. mags., encys. Story, Hunger, included in O'Henry Prize Stories of 1942, O'Brien Anthology of Best Short Stories, 1942. Mem. Authors League. Home: Ft Fort Lauderdale, Fla., Died Feb. 17, 1976.

WOTRUBA, FRITZ, sculptor; b. Vienna, Austria, Apr. 23, 1907; s. Adolf W.; pupil of Anton Hanak; m. Lucy Vorel, 1955. Sculptor, 1927-75; prof. Acad. Fine Arts, Vienna, Austria, 1945-75; prin. works include Torso (marble), 1929-30, Sitting Figures (limestone), 1949, Reclining Figure (conglomerate), 1951, Figures in Relief (bronze) 1958, Standing Figure (limestone), 1957-59, Kneeling Figure 1960, Large Figure (limestone), 1963, Figures in Relife (marble relief at Philipps U., Marburg, 1964; exhibited Germany, Zurich, Venice, London, Paris, Vienna, Winterthur, Basle, Berne, Göteborg, Phila., Brussels, N.Y.C., Sao Paulo, Milan, Rome, Boston, Florence; designer scenery and costumes for Der Ring des Nibelungen, Berlin Opera Festival, 1967. Home: Vienna, Austria., Died Aug. 28, 1975.

WRAY, JAMES BAILEY, orthopedic surgeon, educator; b. Knoxville, Tenn., Apr. 1, 1926; s. James Bailey and Elizbeth (Hobson) W.; B.S., U. Tenn., 1947, M.D., 1950; m. Margaret Mustoe, Apr. 9, 1950; children—Nancy Elizabeth, David James, Jonathan Lee. Intern U. Mich. Hosp., 1950-51; resident orthopedic surgery Duke Med. Center, 1955-57; instr. orthopedic surgery Bowman Gray Med. Sch., 1957-60; asso. prof., chmn. orthopedic sect. Upstate Med. Center, Syracuse, N.Y., 1960-62, prof. chmn. dept. orthopedic surgery, 1963-66; prof., chmn. dept. Orthopedic Surgery Ind. U. Sch. Medicine, 1966-73; cons. VA, Indpls. Mem. Gov. Ind. Commn. Handicapped; bd. dirs. Cerebral Palsy Assn. Indpls. Served with USNR, 1943-45, USAF, 1951-53. Recipient Kappa Delta award research orthopedic surgery, 1962; Angiology Research Found. award, 1964; Nicholas Andry award research orthopedic surgery, 1966. Mem. Am. Acad. Orthopedic Surgeons, Am. Orthopedic Assn., Am. Soc. Surgery Hand, Am. Assn. Anatomists, Orthopedic Research Soc., A.C.S. Home: Indianapolis Ind. Died Feb. 6, 1973

WRIGHT, ALBERT HAZEN, zoölogist; b. Hilton, N.Y., Aug. 15, 1879; s. Delos C. and Emily A. (Hazen) W.; grad. State Normal and Training Sch., Brockport, N.Y., 1899; A.B., Cornell U., 1904, A.M., 1905, Ph.D., 1908; m. Anna Allen (Cornell 1909), June 25, 1910. Asst. in vertebrate zoölogy, Cornell U., 1905-08, instr., 1908-15, asst. prof., 1915-25, prof., 1925-46, emeritus; temp. asst. U.S. Bur., Fisheries, 1915. Recipient Eminent Ecologist award, 1955. Fellow A.A.A.S., Am. Geog. Soc., Acad. Zoology India; hon. mem. Am. Fish Soc.; mem. Am. Soc. Zoologists, Biol. Soc. Washington, Ecol. Soc. Am. Am. Soc. Mammalogists, Am. Soc. Ichthyologists and Herpetologists, American Ornithologists Union, American Fisheries Society, Sigma Xi, Gamma Alpha (nat. pres.), Phi Kappa Phi. Author: North American Anura, 1914; Biol. Reconnaissance of the Okefinokee Swamp, Ga.; Old Northampton, N.Y., 1928; Life Histories of Okefinokee Frogs, 1931; Handbook of Frogs and Toads, 1933, 1942; History and Catography of Okefinokee Swamp, Vol. I, 1945; also Studies in History Nos., 1-32; Handbook of U.S.A. Snakes, 2 Vols., 1958. Home: Ithaca, N.Y.†

WRIGHT, BERNICE M. (MRS. DONALD G. WRIGHT), coll. dean; undergrad. and master's degrees Syracuse U.; Ph.D., U. Edinburgh (Scotland); children—David, Deborah, Douglas, Richard. Formerly woman's student counselor Hendricks Chapel staff Syracuse U., case worker Mass. Soc. Prevention Cruelty to Children, and staff mem. nat. bd. YWCA; tchr. Syracuse U., head dept. family relations and child devel., later became dean Coll. Human Devel. Chmn. Eastern region Nat. Council Adminstrs. Home Econs. Mem. nat. bd. dirs. Girls' Clubs Am. Mem. Am. Home Econs. Assn., Child Study Assn., Nat. Council on Family Relations, N.Y. State P.T.A. (hon. life mem., named twice and all-time Post Standard Woman of Achievement for work in family life edn.), Am. League Pan Woman, Zonta Internat., Pi Lambda Theta, Theta Chi Beta, Delta Sigma Rho, Zeta Phi Eta, Ete Pi Upsilon. Author: (with Donald G. Wright) Into Parenthood. Home: Syracuse, N.Y. Died Feb. 17, 1975; interred Oakwood Cemetery, Syracuse.

WRIGHT, BURTON HARRY, fire chief; b. Syracuse, N.Y., Aug. 23, 1905; s. Harry Oscar and Maude (Spencer) W.; ed. State N.Y. Fire Coll., 1928-31; m. Helen June Shauer, Feb. 13, 1925; children—Barbara (Mrs. Charles S. May), Burton, Raymond, Peter Joy, Susan, Jane. Apptd. fireman, Syracuse, 1930-40, lt. 1940, apptd. dep. chief, 1960, 1st dep. chief, 1963, chief, 1966-71; liaison officer civil def., Syracuse. Bd. dirs. A.R.C., Syracuse. Recipient Arthur Jenkins medal. Author: Fire Fighters Medal, 1966. Home: DeWitt N.Y. Died Jan. 12, 1971

WRIGHT, CARROLL MARYOTT, instnl. adminstr.; b. Baltimore, Md. July 6, 1887; s. John Nowell and Ann Elizabeth (Tipton) W.; student Baltimore City Coll.; studied bus. law U. of Md.; m. Martha A. Webb, Nov. 8, 1910 (dec. 1970); children—Rev. Maryott Webb, Lillian Frances (Mrs. Paul A. Northrop), and Anne Elizabeth (Mrs. Charles Earle Snyder); m. 2d, Gertrude C. Patriquin, Oct. 29, 1970. Accountant in field of banking and finance, 1905-19; exec. sec. Internat. Soc. of Christian Endeavor, 1920, supt. dept. of travel and recreation, 1927-31, financial sec. and mgr., travel dept., 1931-34, exec. sec. and treas. World's Christian Endeavor Union, 1941-47; exec. sec. and asst. treas. Nat. Council of the Service Men's Christian League, 1942-46; dir. pub. relations Christian Herald Assn., 1947-57; resident dir. Christian Herald's Meml. Home Community 1957—, dir. Christian Herald Travel Bur., 1954—. Mem. Acad. Polit. Sci. Conglist. Mason. Clubs: Congregational (Boston); Advertising of N.Y.; Travel of America, Rotary. Home: Green Cove Springs, Fla., Died Dec. 16, 1972.

WRIGHT, DUDLEY HUGH ALOYSIUS, banker; b. London, Eng., Nov. 4, 1912; s. Clarence A.J. and Emma (Taylor) W.; student St. Francis Xavier's Coll., Liverpool, Eng.; m. Helen Marguerite Carroll, Aug. 17, 1940; children—Vernon, Wilfred, Harper. With Barclays Bank D.C.O., 1930-56, mng. dir. Bahamas Internat. Trust Co. Ltd., Nassau, 1957-72, chmn., 1972-73; chmn. Cayman Internat. Trust Co. Ltd.; dep. chmn. bd. Tanganyika Concessions Ltd.; dir. Internat. Trust Co. Bermuda Ltd., Melanesia Internat. Trust Co. Ltd., New Hebrides. Treas. Boy Scouts Assn. Bahamas, 1958-

67, chmn., 1969-70. Served with RAF, 1943-47. Mem. Assn. Inst. Bankers. Roman Catholic. Rotarian. Home: Nassau, Bahamas. Died 1973.

WRIGHT, EDMOND FLEMING, U.N. official; b. Davis, Mass., Aug. 7, 1898; s. Arthur and Elizabeth (Hayes) W.; B.S., Harvard, 1924, M.B.A., 1926; m. Louisa Hopkins Murray, Sept. 21, 1946; step-children—Louisa G. Murray, Patricia, Elizabeth. Instr. manufacturing and finance, asst. dean, dir. placement, Harvard Bus. Sch., 1926-36; engaged in finance, investment banking, N.Y. City, Boston, 1936-41; management engr., exec. selection dept., McKinsey & Co., N.Y. City, 1941-42; exec. placement officer, sec. prodn. exec. com., W.P.B., 1942-43; asst. dean, lecturer on personnel relations, dir. alumni relations, dir. of placement, Harvard Bus. Sch. 1942-48; exec. asst. to asst. sec. gen. in charge of administrative and financial services, U.N., 1946-48; sec. Fifth Com., Gen. Assembly, Oct.-Dec. 1946; exec. asst. to pres. of John Hancock Mutual Life Ins. Co., Boston. Mem. regional com. on administrative; personnel, Boston Dist., U.S. Civil Service Commn. Served with U.S. Army in U.S. and France, World War I. Presbyterian. Clubs: Harvard (New York City and Boston). Co-author of books on personnel management. Home: Cambridge Mass. Died Feb. 1974

WRIGHT, ERNEST LINWOOD, educator; b. Tappahannock, Va., Mar. 9, 1893; s. William Ernest and Emma (Campbell) W.; B.A., Coll. of William and Mary, Williamsburg, Va., 1915; M.A., U. Va., 1927; Dr. of Pedagogy, Davidson (N.C.) College, 1945; m. Elizabeth Pope Ramey, Dec. 20, 1930; children—Alice (Mrs. John Turner), Betty (Mrs. Robert H. Ledbetter). Prin. high school, Heathsville, Va., 1915-17, 19-20; became headmaster Darlington Sch., Rome, Ga., 1920, pres., 1954-63, pres. emeritus, 1963-73. Mem. Ga. Accrediting Commn., 1951-52, Pres., Rome chpt. A.R.C. rep. on Coll. Entrance Exam. Bd., 1951-54; Bd. dirs. Rome Community Center; bd. regents Ga. U. System, 1959-65; trustee Shorter Coll., Thornwood Sch. Served as 1st lt. USMC, 1917-19. Recipient Alumni medallion Coll. William and Mary, 1969. Mem. Am. Legion, Va. Hist. Soc., Mid-South (pres. 1953-54), Ga. (pres. 1958-59) assns. ind. schs., Soc. of Alumni Coll. William and Mary (dir.), S.A.R. (pres. Rome chpt. 1958-66, v.p. Ga. Soc., 1958), So. Assn. Coll. and Secondary Schs., (chmn. Ga. state com., 1951-53, mem. exec. com., 1953-54), Ga. Assn. Sch. Adminstrs., Acad. Polit. Sci., Headmasters Assn., No. Neck Va., Hist. Soc., Rome Jr. C. of C. (hon.), M.B.L.S., Phi Beta Kappa, Pi Kappa Alpha, Pi Gamma Mu. Baptist. Kiwanian (pres. 1931-32). Club: Coosa Country. Author: Reading for Comprehension, 1941; Read A While, Books I and II, 1947; The South's Predicament; A National Problem, 1960; The State-The People, 1964. Home: Rome, Ga. Died Feb. 11, 1974; interred Mrytle Hill Cemetery, Rome, Ga.

WRIGHT, G(EORGE) ERNEST, educator; b. Zanesville, O., Sept. 5, 1909; s. Rev. Ernest Johnson and Caroline Lucretia (Shedd) W.; A.B., Wooster Coll., 1931, D.D., 1949; B.D., McCormick Theol. Sem., Chgo., 1934, A.M., Johns Hopkins, 1936, Ph.D., 1937; A.M. (hon.), Harvard U., 1958; Litt.D., Alma (Mich.) Coll., 1968; L.H.D., Dropsie U., 1972, St. Anselm Coll., 1973; LL.D., Widener Coll., 1973; m. Emily E. DeNyse, July 31, 1937; children—George Ernest, David DeNyse, Daniel Shedd, Carolynn Arria (Mrs. Ted A. Lester). Ordained to ministry Presbyn. Ch. 1934; Nettie F. McCormick fellow McCormick Theol. Sem., 1934-36; field sec. Am. Schs. Oriental Research 1938; instr. in O.T., asst. prof., asso. McCormick Theol. Sem., 1939-45, prof. O.T. history and theology, 1945-58; Parkman prof. div. Harvard, 1958-74; archeol. dir. Drew-McCormick Archeol. Expn. to Palestine, 1956-64; dir. Hebrew Union Coll. Excavation at Gezer, 1964-65, Am. Expdn. to Idalion, Cyprus, 1971-74. Curator Harvard Semitic Mus. Fellow Soc. Antiquaries, Am. Acad. Arts and Scis.; mem. Archeol. Inst., Am. Acad Religion, Am. Schs. Oriental Research (pres. 1966-74), Soc. Bibl. Lit. and Exegesis, Phi Beta Kappa. Author: Pottery of Palestine from Earliest Times to End Early Bronze Age: The Old Testament Against Its Environment, 1950; God Who Acts; Biblical Archaology; The Rule of God, 1960; The Biblical Doctrine of Man In Society, 1954; Shechem; Biography of a Biblical City, 1965; Isaiah in Laymen's Bible Commentaries, 1964; The old Testament and Theology, 1969; co-author: Ain Shems Excavations Pts. IV, V, Westminister Historical Atlas to the Bible; The Book of the Acts of God, 1957; Gezer I, 1970. Editor: The Bible and the Ancient Near East, 1961. Founder Studies in Bibl. Theology, 1948; founder, mem. editorial bd. Biblical Archaeologist. Co-editor: The Biblical Archaeologist Reader, 1961; Ecumenical Dialogue at Harvard: The Roman Catholic-Protestant Colloquium, 1964. Prin. advisor, editorial cons. Reader's Digest Book--Great People of the Bible, 1974. Home: Lexington, Mass. Died Aug. 29, 1974; interred Jaffrey Center, N.H.

WRIGHT, GEORGE MANN, cotton mfr.; b. Cumberland County, Va., Dec. 14, 1879; s. George Mann and Josephine (Leitch) W.; student Randolph-Macon Coll., Ashland, Va., 1894-95; m. Jeanie Wardlaw White, Jan. 21, 1903; children—Jeanie Wardlaw, George Mann, Thomas Perrin, Joseph Leitch. Began in cotton mfg. at Union, S.C., 1897; pres. and gen. mgr. Banna Mfg. Co., Goldville, S.C., 1906-18; pres. and treas. Watts Mills, Laurens, 1919-27; pres. Lucas Bank of Laurens, 1919-27; later pres. Republic Cotton Mills, Great Falls, S.C. Mem. Laurens County Highway Commn., 1915-20. Trustee U. of S.C., 1928-33. Democrat. Methodist. Clubs: Rotary (ex-pres); Charlotte (N.C.) Country; Merchants (New York). Home: Great Falls, S.C.†

WRIGHT, HENRY WILKES, educator, author; b. St. James, Mich., Aug. 16, 1878; s. Henry and Jessie Victoria (Wilkes) W.; Ph.B., Cornell U., 1899, Ph.D., 1904; m. Celia Evelyn Morgan, of Charlotte, Mich., Sept. 4, 1903; children—Sherman Wilkes, Henry Wilkes, Fidelia Ann, Morgan Wilkes. Instr. philosophy, Cornell U., until 1907; prof. philosophy, from Sept. 15, 1907, acting pres. 1981, Lake Forest (Ill.) College; later professor of psychology in (Provincial) U. of Manitoba. Fellow A.A.A.S.; mem. Am. Philos. Assn., Western Philos. Assn., Sigma Alpha Epsilon. Presbyn. Author: Self-Realization, 1938; Faith Justified by Progress, 1916. Collaborated in writing Philosophical Essays in Honor of J. E. Creighton, 1917. The Moral Standards of Democracy, 1925; The Religious Response, 1929. Contbr. numerous articles in Philos. Rev. Jour. of Philosophy, etc. Investigations looking to wear harmony of science and religion. Home: Winnipeg, Can.†

WRIGHT, JAMES ELWIN, religious exec.; writer; b. Corinth, Vt., July 9, 1890; s. Joel Adams and Mary Melissa (Goodwin) W.; grad Missionary Inst., Nyack, N.Y., 1921; LL.D., Bob Jones U., 1945; m. Florence Daisy Dunkling, July 8, 1911; 1 dau. Muriel Virginia (wife of Rev. David J. Evans). Ordained to ministry, 1919; founder New Eng. Fellowship, 1929; co-secretary Commission for World Evangelical Fellowship, 1951-59, honorary secretary, 1959-73. Official delegate various conferences of church leaders in 51 countries, 1946-56; dir. Chinese Native Evangelistic Crusade, 1961. Member Nat. Assn. Evangelicals (founded 1943). Author: Old Fashioned Revival Hour, 1939; Manna in the Morning, 1943; Evangelical Action, 1942. Compiler; Story of the Lord Jesus, 1938. Home: Tujunga Cal. Died June 29, 1973; interred Rumney, N.H.

WRIGHT, JAMES FREDERICK, govt. ofcl.; b. Volga, S.D., Aug. 31, 1914; s. James Cady and Clara (Whymes) W.; student U. S.D., 1930-31; Asso. in Adminstrn., Am. U., 1952; m. Eula Page Hockett, Apr. 11, 1950; children—James Oliver, Clara Lynn. Various positions Naval Communications, Navy Dept., Washington, 1941-48; budget analyst, budget officer Office Navy Comptroller, 1948-53; dep. fiscal dir. Marine Corps, 1953-62, fiscal dir., 1962-73. Served with AUS, em. Am. Soc. Mil. Comptrollers, V.F.W. Presbyn. Home: Sterling, Va., Deceased.

WRIGHT, LOUIS CLINTON, coll. pres.; b. Virgil, Cortland County, N.Y., Feb. 3, 1879; s. Wallace Eugene and Phoebe (Webber) W.; A.B., Syracuse U., 1904; S.T.B., Boston U. Sch. of Theology, 1907; Ph.D., Boston U. Sch. of Theology, 1907; Ph.D., Boston U., 1917; (hon.) LL.D., Ohio Wesleyan U., 1936, Syracuse U. 1944; D.Sc., in Education, Boston U., 1946; m. Flora Greenlees, Aug. 8, 1906; children—Robert Wallace, Donald Greenlees, Esther Louise. Ordained ministry M.E. Ch., 1908; pastor Fernwood, N.Y., 1902-04. First Congl. Ch., Somerville, Mass., 1905-08, Meth. Ch., Gardner, Mass., 1908-10, Melrose, 1910-16. Springfield, 1916-20, Cleveland, Epworth-Euclid Ch., 1920-34; pres Baldwin-Wallace Coll., Berea, O., 1934-38, emeritus 1948. Dir. Y.M.C.A. work, British Zone, France, 1918. Trustee St. Luke's Hosp., Cleveland. Mem. Pi Gamma Mu, Phi Mu Alpha, Sinfonia, Sigma Phi Epsilon. Exchange preacher in England 1938. Republican. Mason (33°). Club: Alathian. Author: Trails for Climbing Youth, 1939. Contbr. to ednl. journals and Christian Advocates of Mech. Ch. Home: Lakewood O.†

WRIGHT, LOYD, lawyer; b. San Jacinto, Cal., Dec. 24, 1892; s. Lucius A. and Naamah Pauline (Hank) W.; LL.B., U. Southern Cal. 1915; LL.D., Ottawa U.; m. Julia M. Kingsbury, Sept. 7, 1918; children—Loyd, Dudley, Pauline (Mrs. Long Ellis), Clarissa Jane (Mrs. James E. Sergeant). Admitted to Cal. bar 1945, practiced law in Los Angeles; mem. firm Wright, Rodi, Wright, Talton & Van Zyl; lectr. at U. of Southern Cal. Sch. of Law, 1921-36; dir. of various corps. Served overseas as 1st lt., 8th Inf., U.S. Army in command Co. D., 1917-19; grad from Command and Gen. Staff Sch., Fort Leavenworth, Kan., Jan. 1943. Served as mem. Bd. of Appeals of the Atty. Gen. of U.S. in connection with hearings of enemy aliens, World War II. Chmn. avaition project com., State of Cal., 1944; chmn. Calif. Horse Racing Bd., 1944-51; mem. Water and Power Commn., City of Los Angeles; chmn. nat. strategy com. Am. Security Council. Fellow U. of Southern Cal. Pres. State Bar of Cal., 1940-41. Mem. Am. (pres. 1954-55, chmn commn. on govt. security 1955-57), Los Angeles County (past pres.) bar assns., Nat. Assn. State Racing Commrs. (past pres.), Gen. Alumni Assn. of U. of Southern Cal. (past pres.), Order of Coif, Phi Delta Phi (Beatty Inn). Mason (32, K.T., Shriner). Clubs: California, Los Angeles Country. Home: Los Angeles Cal. Died Oct. 22, 1974

WRIGHT, MURIEL HAZEL, historian; b. Lehigh, Indian Ty.; d. Eliphalet Nott and Ida Belle (Richards) Wright; grad. E. Central State Normal, Ada, Okla., 1912; postgrad. Barnard Coll., Columbia, 1916-17; L.H.D., Oklahoma City U., 1964. Tchr. high sch. and elementary sch. Johnston and Coal counties (Okla.), 1912-24; hist. researcher, writer state histories and articles Okla. Hist. Soc., 1924-75, editor The Chronicles of Oklahoma, editor, 1955-73. Mem. hist. adv. panel Gov's Council for Cultural Devel., 1964; pres. Nat. Hall of Fame for Famous Am. Indians, Anadarko, Okla., 1965-75; mem. Okla. bd. geog. names Okla. Geol. Survey, 1965. Recipient Distinguished Service citation U. Okla., 1948; MacDowell Club award, 1948; named Woman of Year, Oklahoma City Bus. and Profl. Women, 1951; named to Okla. Hall of Fame, 1940; Matrix award Theta Sigma Phi, 1941. Mem. Women in Communications Oklahoma City, Nat. League Am. Pen Women (pres. Oklahoma City br. 1962-64), Am. Historians, Oklahoma City Civil War Round Table (pres. 1963-64), Am. State and Local History, So. Hist. Assn., Soc. Mayflower Descs., U.D.C., D.A.R., Colonial Dames XV11 Century, Okla. Hist. Society (hon. life), Alpha Gamma Delta, Delta Kappa Gamma (hon.). Presbyn. Clubs: Red Bud, Women's Dinner, Westerner's Indian Terr. Women's Posse. Author: A Guide to the Indian Tribes of Oklahoma, 1951; The Story of Oklahoma, 1929; Our Oklahoma, 1939; The Oklahoma History, 1955; (with J.B. Thoburn) Oklahoma: A History of the State and Its People, 1929; (with George H. Shirk) Rambler in Oklahoma, 1956; (W. LeRoy H. Fischer) Civil War Sites in Oklahoma, 1967. Address: Oklahoma City, Okla. Died Feb. 27, 1975.

WRIGHT, ORA CAMPBELL, church official; b. Orleans, Ind., Jan. 30, 1872; s. Jonathan Hugh and Polly Jane (Hardman) W.; B.S., Southern Ind. Normal Coll., 1891; A.B., Franklin Coll., 1895, D.D., 1916; grad. Rochester Theol. Sem., 1898; A.M., U. of Ore., 1905; m. Sarah Richards Reed, Sept. 7, 1897 (dec.); children—Clarence Cuthbert, Hugh William (dec.), Ordained Baptist minitry, 1898; pastorates, First Ch., Defiance, O., Calvary Ch., Evansville, Ind., First Ch., Madison, S.Dak., First Ch., Ogden, Utah, First Ch., Eugene, Ore., unitl 1910; chaplain Wash. State Reformatory, 1910-12; exec. sec. (supt.) Ore. Bapt. State Conv., 1912-33. Mem. Bd. Missionary Coöperation, Northern Bapt. Conv., and Linfield Coll. until 1933; trustee Berkeley (Calif.) Bapt. Div. Sch., Western Bapt. Theol. Sem.; hist. sec. Ore. Bapt. State Conv. from 1934; later Ad Interim pastor in Bapt. chs. in Wash., Ore., Cal. Mem. Phi Delta Theta, Pi Gamma Mu. Republican. Now writing history of Baptist in Ore; lectr. and field rep. Bapt. orgns. Address: Burlingame, V1Cal.†

WRIGHT, WIRT, banker; b. Libertyville, Ill., June 6, 1878; s. Caleb Frank and Emma Jane (Price) W.; A.B., Beloit (Wis.) Coll., 1901; m. Addie Wiswell Stafford, Oct. 15, 1901; 1 dau., Katherine. Teller, N.W. Harris & Co., Chicago, 1901-04; cashier First Nat. Bank, Edgerton, Wis., 1904-07; cashier Nat. Stock Yards, Nat. Bank, East St. Louis, Ill., 1907-10, pres., 1910-25; v.p. State Bank & Trust Co., Evanston, Ill., 1925-26, pres. from 1926. Chmn. Liberty Loan Drive, St. Clair Co., Ill., World War. Dir. Evanston Council Boy Scouts of America; chmn. Advisory Com. of NRA; pres. Evanston Community Chest, Inc., Mem. Am. Bankers Assn., Ill. Bankers Assn. (ex-pres.), Evanston (Chamber Commerce, North Shore Festival Assn. Phi Kappa Psi. Republican. Episcopalian. Clubs: Bankers (Chicago); University, Evanston. Home: Evanston, Ill.†

WRINCH, DOROTHY, sci. research, molecular biologist; b. Rosario, Argentina, S.Am.; d. Hugh Edward Hart and Ada Minnie (Souter) Wrinch; scholar Girton Coll., Cambridge, Eng., 1913, wrangler, math. tripos, 1916, moral sciences tripos, 1917; B.A., M.A., Cmabridge U.; M.A., D.Sc., Oxford U.; M.Sc., D.Sc., London U.; student Univs. Cambridge, London, Vienna, Paris; m. J. W. Nicholson, 1922 (div. 1938); 1 dau., Pamela; m. 2d, Otto Charles Glaser, 1941 (dec. 1951). Lectured pure math. Univ. Coll. London, 1918-20; research fellow Girton Coll., 1920-24, 30-34, Oxford U., 1931-33, 39-41, Rockefeller Found. fellow, 1935-41; teaching mem. faculty pres. phys. scis. Oxford, 1923-39; lectr. chemistry Johns Hopkins, 1939-41 vis. prof. Amherst, Mt. Holyoke and Smith colls., 1941-42; lectr. physics Smith Coll., 1942-54, vis. prof. physics, 1954-59, vis. research prof., 1959-66, Sophia Smith fellow, from 1966; hon. research asso., dept. biohcemistry U. Coll., London, 1962. Mem. Internat. Commn. Teachers Math., 1932-39; mem. corp. Marine Biology Lab., Woods Hole, Mass., 1943. Fellow Am. Phys.Soc.; mem. Am. Chem. Soc., Math. Sect. British Assn. (sec. 1932-38). Author: Fourier Transforms and Structure Factor, 1946, 67; Chem. Aspects of the Structures of Small Peptides: An Introduction, 1960; Chemical Aspects of Polypeptide Chain Structures and the Cyclol Theory, 1965. Contbr. sci. jours. Home: Woods Hole, Mass., Died Feb. 11, 1976.

WURSTER, WILLIAM WILSON, architect; b. Stockton, Calif., Oct. 20, 1895; s. Frederick William and Maude Evelyn (Wilson) W.; A.B., Univ. of Cal., 1919; LL.D., 1964; m. Catherine Bauer, Aug. 13, 1940 (dec. Nov. 1964); 1 dau., Sarah. Began as office boy for E. B. Brown, architect, Stockton, Cal., 1910; with John

Reid, Jr., architect, San Francisco, 1920; asso. with Charles Dean on Sacramento filtration plant, 1921-22; traveled in Europe, 1922-23; with Delano & Aldrich, architects, New York, 1923-24, East Bay Water Co. filtration plant, 1924-25; practicing alone 1926-43; fellow in Grad Sch. of Design, Harvard U., 1943; dean of Sch. of Arch. and Planning, Mass. Inst. of Tech., 1944-50; dean sch., now coll. architecture U. Cal., Berkeley, 1950-59, dean College of Environmental Design, 1959-63, dean emeritus, 1963-73, acting dean, 1965; practicing architect as partner with Theodore C. Bernardi and Donn Emmons. Principal works include Golden Gateway Redevelopment Project, San Francisco, Center for Advanced study in Behavioral Sciences, Palo Alto, Ghirardelli Sq., San Francisco, Cowell Coll., U. Cal., Santa Cruz, also office buildings. Chmn. architects' adv. com. Nat. Housing Agency, 1942; mem. Nat. Capitol Park and Planning Commn., 1948. chmn., 1949-50; mem. Capitol Bldg. and Planning Commn., State Cal., 1959-67; mem. archtl. adv. panel. office foreign buildings U.S. Dept. of State. 1958-63; cons. to board, 1964. Recipient Merit certificate National Academy of Design, 1968, Gold Medal award A.I.A., 1969. Fellow Am. Acad. Arts and Scis., Royal Acad. Fine Arts, Copenhagen, A.I.A.; mem. Royal Inst. British Architects (corr. mem.), The Berkeley Fellow of Univ. of California, Am. Inst. Planners (affiliate), Akademie der Kunsta, Berlin, Tau Beta Pi. Home: Berkeley, Cal. Died Sept. 19, 1973.

WYATT, ROBERT H., assn. exec.; b. Allen Co., Ind., Nov. 4, 1903; s. James Louis and Joanna (Hall) W.; A.B., Indiana U., Jan. 1925, A.M., Oct. 1925, grad. fellow, 1925-26; grad, study U. of Chicago, 1929. U. of Southern Calif., 1935-36; LL.D., Ball State Tchrs. Coll., Taylor U., 1962; m. Margaret Lambert, Dec. 31, 1941. Teacher Noble County (Ind.). schs., 1920-23, Ft. Wayne (Ind.) Jr. High Sch., 1926-29; teacher Central High Sch., Ft. Wayne, 1929-38, head dept. of social studies, 1934-38, dir. of guidance, 1937-38; exec. sec. Ind. State Teachers Assn., 1938-71, also editor of Indiana Teacher, official mag. of assn. from 1938; dir. Brotherhood Mutual Life Ins. Co., Ft. Wayne, from 1939; pub. Brown County Democrat (weekly), Nashville, Ind.; dir. Secured Fire and Marine Ins. Co., Indpls., 1942-43, Mut. Security Life Ins. Co., Ft. Wayne, Investment Corp. Am., Indpls., NEA Mut. Fund, Washington, Blue Cross Hospital Service, from 1944; chmn. edn. div. Ind. War Finance Com., 1944-45; pres. bd. trustees, Ind. State Teachers Retirement Fund from 1941; mem. Governor's Tax Study Commission from 1946; mem. Indiana Army Advisory Com. from 1946; apptd. council of advisors U.S. Commr. of Edn., 1950. Mem. N.E.A. (chmn. legislative commn.; pres. 1963-64), Fort Wayne Tchrs. Assn. (pres. 1931-35), Ind. State Fedn. Public Sch. Teachers (pres., 1935-38), Ind. Soc. of Chgo., Am. Assn. for Adult Edn., Am. Assn. Sch. Administrs., Nat. Assn. Secs. State Tchrs. Assns. (pres. 1952-54), Nat. Council Tchr. Retirement (executive committee), Phi Delta Kappa, Phi Sigma Sigma. , Mem. English Luth. Ch. Clubs; Indiana Schoolmen's Indianapolis Press, Executives, Kiwanis. Contbr. numerous ednl. monographs, mag. and newspaper articles. Home: Greenwood Ind. Died July 23, 1975

WYKA, KAZIMIERZ, historian, lit. critic; b. Krzeszowice, Poland, Mar. 19, 1910; s. Wojciech and Maria (Pietakiewicz) W.; m. Dec. 31, 1935; children—Marta, Malgorzata. Prof., Jagellone U., Cracow, 1949; mem. Polish Acad. Scis., 1952, dir. Inst. Lit. Research. Decorated Order of Standard of Work 1st and 2d Class, comdr. with star Polish Order Restituta. Author: La Vie Apparente, 1957; The Case of Imagination, 1959; Literary Modernism in Poland, 1969; Concerning the Necessity of History of Literature, 1969; J. Malczewski and his Epoch, 1970; In Search of Themes, Historic, Literary and Artistic Essays, Vols. 1-111, 1970. Address: Cracow, Poland. Died Jan. 19, 1975.

WYLIE, JAMES RENWICK, JR., petroleum engr.; b. Wilkinsburg, Pa., Sept. 12, 1897; s. James Renwick and Laura (Steele) W.; B.S., Dartmouth, 1919; M.S., U. Pitts., 1921; m. Alice Virginia Bell, Feb. 26, 1927; children—Virginia (Mrs. William P. Barber), James Renwick III, John S. Partner, Huntley & Huntley, petroleum geologists and engrs., Pitts., 1926; dir. prodn. Dist. 1, Petroleum Adminstrn. for War, 1941-45; v.p., gen. mgr. Hiawatha Oil & Gas Co., 1946-61, pres., 1961-64; v.p., gen. mgr. Penn Ohio Gas Co., 1946-61; pres., 1961-64; v.p., gen mgr. Benedum Trees Oil Co.; pres. Sunflower Royalties Co.; dir. Colonial Royalties Co. Mem. Pa. Oil and Gas Conservation Commn., from 1961. Served with U.S. Army, World War I. Mem. Am. Assn. Petroleum Geologists, Phi Kappa Psi. Republican. Presbyn. Rotarian. Home: Pittsburgh Pa. Died Jan. 8, 1974.

WYLIE, MAX, author TV exec.; b. Beverly, Mass.; s. Edmund M. and Edna (Edwards) W.; A.B., Hamilton Coll., 1928; grad. student U. Pa., 1931-32; L.H.D., Rollins Coll., Winter Park, Fla., 1967; m. Isabel W. Lamb, Nov. 11, 1933; children—Pamela Cleveland, Janice Lamb (dec.). Prof. English novel Forman Coll., Punjab U., Lahore, India, 1929-31; instr. English U. Pa., 1931-32; jr. editor for Johathan Cape and Robert Ballous, 1932; successively producer, writer, dir. script and continuity CBS, 1933-40; TV program supr. Lennen & Newell. Exec. editor TV program Omnibus (Ford Found.); writer Wide Wide World (NBC-TV), March of Time (radio); creator TV series The Flying Nun. Lectr. on radio writing N.Y.U., creative writing Temple U. Mem. Author's League Dramatists' Guild, Delta Upsilon. Club: Dutch Treat (N.Y.C.). Author: Hindu Heaven (novel), 1933; Radio Writing, 1939; (radio ann. anthologies) Best Broadcasts; Radio and Television Writing, 1950; (novel) Go Home and Tell Your Mother, 1951; Clear Channels, 1955; Assignment: Churchill, 1955; (novel) Trouble in the Flesh, 1959; Never the Twain (novel), 1961; The Gift of Janice, Career Girl, Watch Your Step; Writing for Television (texbook), 1970; Courts, Chaos, and Public Conscience, 1971; (plays) The Greatest of These, (with Milton Geiger) Everywhere a Chick-Chick; (with Lester H. Loble) Delinquency Can Be Stopped, 1967. Editorial bd., life mem. Television Acad. quar. Home: Richmond, Va. Died Sept. 22, 1975.

WYLIE, SAMUEL JOSEPH, clergyman; b. N.Y.C., Nov. 5, 1918; s. Samuel John and Mary (Little) W.; B.S., Wheaton Coll., 1938; S.T.B., Bibl. Sem. in N.Y., 1942; S.T.M., Union Theol. Sem., 1952; M.A. (hon.), Brown U., 1958, D.D., 1967; D.D., Va. Sem., 1967, Huron Coll., 1968; m. Beatrice Irene Browne, Aug. 31, 1942; children—Irene (Mrs. Daniel Rodgers), Mary (Mrs. Raymond C Carter), John, Jean. Ordained to ministry Presbyn. Ch., 1942; pastor John Hall Meml. Presbyn. Ch., 1946-49; chaplain Protestant students Columbia, 1949-51; ordained deacon Episcopal Ch., 1951, priest, 1952; Episcopal coll. chaplain U. Va., 1951-54, Brown U., 1954-58; mem. staff div. coll. work exec. council Episcopal Ch., N.Y.C., 1958-60; rector Ch. of the Advent, Boston, 1960-66; dean Gen. Theol. Sem., N.Y.C., 1966-72; bishop Episcopal Diocese No. Mich., Menominee, 1972-74. Served to lt. as chaplain USNR, 1943-46. Author: New Patterns for Christian Action, 1960; Precede the Dawn, 1963; The Celebration of Smallness, 1973. Contbg. author: New Canterbury Pilgrims, 1952; Living Thankfully, 1964. Home: Menominee, Mich. Died May 6, 1974.

WYLLIE, IRVIN GORDON, ednl. adminstr.; b. Pitts., Jan. 3, 1920; s. Gordon William and Anna Margaret (Skiles) W.; B.A. magna cum laude, Westminster Coll., Pa., 1941; M.A., Oberlin Coll., 1942; Ph.D., U. Wis., 1949; m. Harriet Elizabeth Fairley, Sept. 4, 1945; children—Gordon William, Kay Ann, Laura Sue. Instr. history Westminster Coll. Pa., 1943-44; grad research asst. U. Wis., 1944-46, univ. fellow, 1946-47, lectr. history, summer 1951, asso. prof. history 1957-60, prof. history, 1960; chmn. dept. history, 1964-66, Gordon Fox prof. Am. Instn., 1962-66, chancellor U. Wis.-Parkside Kenosha, 1966-74; instr. history U. Md., 1947-48; instr. history U. Mo., 1948-49, asst. prof., 1949-52, asso. prof., 1952-57. Ford faculty fellow Cornell U., 1954-55; vis. prof. U. Del., summer 1955; Fulbright lectr. Am. history Univs. Gothenburg and Lund, Sweden, 1961-62. Commr., North Central Assn. Colls. and Secondary Schs., 1969-73; mem. commn. on instnl. affairs Assn. Am. Colls., 1969-72; visitor German univs. as ofcl. guest Fed. Republic, 1973. Served with AUS, 1942-43. Mem. Am., So. hist. assns., Orgn. Am. Historians, Am. Assn. U. Profs. (pres. U. Mo. chpt. 1956-57), Am. Studies Assn. (exec. council 1959-61), Wis. Hist. Soc. (editorial com. 1959-64). Author: The Self-Made Man In America, 1954. Am. history editor Dorsey Press, 1961. Home: Kenosha, Wis. Died Oct. 25, 1974; buried Oakwood Cemetery, Somers, Wis.

WYNN, JAMES OSCAR, lawyer; found. exec.; b. Dallas, July 30, 1897; s. James Oscar and Orlena (Norwood) W.; student U. Tex., 1915-17; LL.B., Georgetown U., 1921; LL.D., Clemson Coll., 1955, Cornell Coll., Mt. Vernon, Ia., 1961, Colo. Coll., 1962, Macalester Coll., 1965, U. So. Cal., 1963; D.C.L., Bucknell Univ., 1955; J.D., Lafayette Coll., 1956; D.Sc., Worcester Poly Inst., 1959; L.H.D., Neb. Wesleyan U., 1968; m. Margaret Farrar, Sept. 2, 1921 (dec. Apr. 26, 1964) children—Peggy Jane (Mrs. Arthur Price), James Oscar, William Farrar; m. 2d, Kathryn W. Sheridan, June 12, 1965. Code clk. State Dept., 1918-19; spl. agt. Bur. Investigation, Dept. Justice, 1919-21; pvt. sec. to Col. Robert H. Montgomery, 1921-22; admitted to D.C. bar, 1922, N.Y. bar, 1924, U.S. Supreme Ct., 1935, also other fed. cts.; mem. tax dept. Lybrand, Ross Bros. & Montgomery, .P.A.'s N.Y.C., 1922-24; asso., then partner in pratice law of Col. Robert H. Montgomery, 1925-49; mem. firm, Wynn, Blattmachr, Campbell & Milas, and predecessors, N.Y.C. Bd. dirs. Olin Found., 1938-75, v.p., gen. counsel, 1951-75; dir. mem. sec. com. N.Y. U. Law Sch. Center Found., 1955-75; bd. dirs. Armstrong Meml. Research Found. Fellow Pierpont Mongay Library. Mem. Am. N.Y. State, New York County bar assns., Assn. Bar City N.Y., Am. Judicature Soc., C. of C. State N.Y., Delta Chi. Episcopalian. Republican. Mason. Clubs: University, Coffee House, Accountants of Am. (N.Y.C.). Home: Darien, Conn., Died Oct. 16, 1975.

WYNTER, BRYAN HERBERT, artist; b. Sept. 8, 1915; s. James Harold and Dora (Judd) W.; student Haileybury, Slade Sch. Fine Art; m. Suzanne Lethbridge. 1949; 2 children; m. 2d, Monica Harman, 1959; 2 children. Exhibited one-man shows Redfern Gallery, 1947-57, Waddington Gallery, 1959-74; exhibited major cities of the world; represented in permanent collections Tate Gallery, Mus. Modern Art, N.Y.C., Victoria and Albert Mus., Brit. Arts councils, Contemporary Art Soc., Gulbenkian Found., Stuyvesant Found., City Art Galleries of Bristol, Manchester, Bradford, Birmingham, Coventry, Lincoln, Fitzwilliam Mus. Cambridge, Towner Art Gallery, Whitworth Art Gallery, Rutherstone Collection. Address: Penzance, England. Died Feb. 11, 1975.

YACKER, JULIUS S., lawyer; b. Chgo., Feb. 20, 1923; s. Samuel and Jeanne (Rubin) Y.; B.S., U. Chgo., 1948, M.B.A., 1951, J.D., 1951; m. Zinette Solomonique, Aug. 17, 1947; children—Daniel, David. Admitted to Ill. bar; practice law, Chgo.; sr. partner firm Yacker and Gerson. Lectr. U. Chgo. Center for Urban Studies; cons. Dept. State, AID. Served to 1st lt. AUS, 1942-46. Home: Park Forest Ill. Died Feb. 18, 1975.

YADEN, JAMES GARFIELD, b. Claiborne County, Tenn., Oct. 20, 1880; s. Joseph Hunter and Esther (Van Rebber) Y.; grad. Normal Dept., Sue Bennett Sch., London, Ky., 1905; m. Nellie Hammock, Aug. 13, 1911; children—Audry Virginia, James Edward. Teacher pub. schs., Ky., until 1905; mem. Ky. Ho. of Rep., 1906-08; teacher Sue Bennett Sch., 1907-10; employed by Census Bur., Washington, D.C., 1910-12; with U.S. Civ. Service Commission, 1912-48, chief of Examining Div., 1920-38, mem. bd. Appeals and Review; pres. Am. Fedn. Govt. Employees, from 1948. Served as pvt. 2d Ky. Vols. Spanish-American War, 1898. Baptits. Mason Odd Fellow, K.P. (Grand Chancellor) Club: Press (Washington), Home: Washington, D.C.†

YANCEY, GEORGE RICHARD, investment banker; b. Co Bluffs, Ia., Jan. 25, 1898; s. Charles C. and Lucy E. (Linebarger) Y B.S., Whitman Coll., 1921; m. Ruth M. Yenney, Aug. 21, 1925; children—Richard C., Robert G. Chmn. Murphey Favre. Inc., Composite Research & Mgmt. Co.; pres. Composite Fund, Inc., Composite Bond and Stock Fund, Inc. (all Spokane). Trustee Deaconess Hosp.; hon. overseer Whitman Coll. Home: Spokane, Wash., Died Mar. 11, 1974.

YANKWICH, LEON RENE, judge; b. Jassy, Roumania, Sept. 25, 1888; prep. edn. in Roumania; LL.B., Willamette U., 1909; J.D., Loyola U., Los Angeles, 1926, LL.D., 1929; m. Helen Werner, Jan. 22, 1919; children—Peter, Ilyana. Came to U.S. 1907, naturalized, 1912. Admitted to Ore. bar, 1909, Cal. bar. 1909; engaged in practice, Modesto, Cal., 1909-16, Los Angeles, 1916-27; judge Superior Ct. Los Angeles County, 1927-35; judge U.S. Dist. Ct. Central Dist. Cal. 1935-64, chief judge 1951-59, sr. judge, 1964-75. Lectr. on pleading and practice, St. Vincent School Law, Loyola U., 1925-34. Author with Hon Thomas F. Griffin of Cal. women's 8 hour law, successfully defending its constitutionality. Served in World War I, hon. disch. as sergt., 1918. Mem. Am., Cal., Los Angeles bar assns., Southwest Acad., Am. Legion, Order of the Coif, Kappa Tau Alpha, Phi Delta Phi. Mason (32 deg., K.T., Shriner). Club: Jonathan. Author numerous books, including: Commentary on New Federal Criminal Rules, 1946; It's Libel or Contempt if You Print It, 1950; The Nature of our Freedom, 1951. Contbr. articles on state and fed. procedure and on libel; also on subjects ranging from the Code of Hammurabi to the French Revolution and Religion. Contbr. to So. Cal. Law Review, Am. Bar Jour., Georgetown U. Law Quar., Notre Dame Lawyers, Pa., Va., La. law reviews, others. In a child custody case, 1928, he uttered the sentence now become famous: There are no illegitimate children, there are only illegitimate parents. Presided numerous notorious cases including peacetime espionage, wartime espionage, mineral rights, riparian rights, and others. Home: Los Angeles, Cal. Died Feb. 9, 1975; interred Inglewood, Cal.

YARBROUGH, WILLIAM THOMAS (TOM), journalist; b. Chickasha, Okla., May 22, 1910; s. William Ambrus and Maude (Morton) Y.; student d. Okla., 1932; m. Mulia Martha Fisher, Oct. 19, 1941; children—John, Julie, Mary. Reporter, Oklahoma City Times, 1932-35; reporter-editor A.P., 1935-50; adminstrv. asst. to. U.S. Senator Hennings, 1951; spl. asst. to chmn. Nat. Security Resources Bd., 1951-52; reporter St. Louis 1953-75, book editor, 1965-69. Asst. dir. publicity Democratic Nat. Com., 1952-53. Mem. Phi Beta Kappa (hon), Sigma Chi. Home: Webster Groves, Mo. Deceased.

YARMOLINSKY, AVRAHM(ABRAHAM), author, librarian; b. Russia, Jan. 1 (O.S.), 1890; s. Bezaleel and Malka (Nemoy) Y.; ed. U. Neuchatel (Switzerland) 1913; A.B., Coll. City N.Y., 1916; Ph.D., Columbia U., 1921; m. Babette Deutsch; 2 sons. Came to U.S., 1913, naturalized, 1922. Instr. Russian evening session Coll. City N.Y., 1917-18; instr. Russian lang. and lit. extension div. Columbia, 1919-20; chief Slavonic div. N.Y. Pub. Library, 1918-55. Recipient Townsend Harris medal, 1939. Alumnus mem. Phi Beta Kappa. Author: Turgenev The Man, His Art and His Age, 1926, rev. edit., 1959; The Jews and Other Minor Nationalities Under the Soviets, 1928; Picturesque United States of America, a Memoir on Svinin, 1930; Russian Literature, 1931; Dostoevsky, A Life, 1934, rev. edit., 1957; Early Polish Americana, 1937; Russian Americana, 1943; Road to Revolution, 1957, transl. into German, 1968; Literature Under Communism, 1960; A Russian's American Dream, 1965; The Russian Literary Imagination, 1969; Dostoevsky, Works and Days, 1971; others. Translator: The Russian School of Painting,

1916; Memoirs of Count Witte, 1921; (with Babette Deutsch) Modern Russian Poetry, an Anthology, 1921, Contemporary German Poetry, 1923, Russian Poetry, an Anthology, 1927, The Twelve, 1931; others. Editor: The Brothers Karamazov (by Dostoevsky, Garnett's transl. revised), 1933; The Possessed (Dostoevsky, Garnett's transl.), 1936; The Works of Alexander Pushkin, 1936; (with Baroness Moura Budberg) A Book of Short Stories by Maxim Gorki, 1939; (with B. Deutsch) Eugene Onegin by Alexander Pushkin, 1943, rev., 1965; A Treasury of of Great Russian Short Stories, 1944; Chichikov's Journeys by Nikolai Gogol (transl B. G. Gwernsey), 1944; The Portable Chekhov, 1947; (with B. Deutsch) A Treasury of Russian Verse, 1949, rev. edit., 1963; Crime and Punishment (Dostoevsky, Garnett's transl. revised), 1951; The Unknown Chekhov, 1954; The Idiot (Dostoevsky), 1956; Russians Then and Now, 1963; (with B. Deutsch) Two Centuries of Russian Verse, 1966, Tales of Faraway Folk, 1952, More Tales of Faraway Folk, 1963, Leskov, The Steel Flea, 1943, rev. edit., 1964; three Short Novels (Dostoevsky, Garnett's transl. revised); 1960; Letters of Anton Chekhov, 1973. Co-editor: The Heritage of European Literature, 2 vols., 1948-49. Home: New York City, N.Y. Died Sept. 28, 1975.

YARNALL, D. ROBERT, mechanical engr.; b. Delaware County, Pa., June 28, 1878; s. Edward S. and Sidney S. (Garrett) Y.; B.S. in M.E. University of Penna., 1901; M.E., 1905; Dr. Engring., Lehigh University, 1942; D.Sc., Haverford College, 1947; married Elizabeth R. Biddle, 1923; children—D. Robert, James Biddle, Nancy Hutton, With Coatesville Boiler Works, 1902-07, Stokes & Smith Co., 1907-12; vice pres., general manager Nelson Valve C. Co., Phila., 1912-18; organizer, 1912, dir. and president Yarnall-Waring Company, mfrs. power plant specialties, chmn. bd., from 1957; chmn. James G. Biddle Co. until 1963, now director. Member Commn. in Europe having charge of feeding German children, 1920, and chmn. during later part of time with hdqrs. in Berlin, again in 1924 for Am. Friends Service Com. and the Gen. Allen Com.; mem. Austrian Refugee Commn., 1938; mem. commn. to England to make survey of relief needs due to war,1941. Presiding officer Phila. Yearly Meeting (Quaker), 1929-40. Chmn. bd. Pendle Hill, 1931-54; chmn. Westtown Sch. Com., 1936-48; mem. bus. adv. council U.S. Dept. of Commerce, 1940-42, Phila. City Planning Commn., 1942-55, vice chmn., 1945-55. Associate trustee University Pa., until 1962; dir. American Engring. Council, 1928-34; vice chmn. Engring. Found., 1934-37, dir. United Engring. Trustees, 1934-37, president, 1938-39. Fellow American Society M.E. (mgr. 1917-20; pres. 1946); Hoover medal award, 1941. Mem. Franklin Inst., Engineers Club of Phila. (pres. 1929-30), Am. Friends Service Com. (dir.; v.p. 1941-46), Sigma Xi, Quaker, Clubs: Engineers, Phila. Cricket. Home: Philadelphia, Pa.†

YARNELLE, EDWARD RALPH, mfr.; b. Ft. Wayne, Ind., Dec. 16, 1879; s. Edward Franklin Wayne, Ind., Dec. 16, 1879; Edward Franklin and Alice (Moffatt) Y.; A.B., Williams Coll., 1902; hon. M.A., Lafayette Coll., 1925; m. Margaret d. John M. Coulter, U. of Chicago, Sept. 20, 1904. Sec. and dir. Mossman Yarnelle, Ft. Wayne, 1902-11; v.p. Am. Horse Shoe Co., Phillipsburg, N.J., 1912-19, pres. from 1919, pres. Galvanized Products Co., Watson Silk Co., v.p. Lafayette Trust Co., (Easton, Pa.), Gronner Foundry Co., Easton Coll. Co., Leighton's Restaurant Corporation; treasurer, dir. Mandarin Silk Co.; dir. Phillipsburg Trest Co.; organizer of all above named companies except the first and last. Member Easton Board Edn., 1922-30; v.p. Community Welfare Chest; v.p. Boy Scouts America; trustee Social Service League; pres. Easton Board of Trade, 1925-26. Mem. Am. Acad. Polit. Science, Iron and Steel Inst., Northampton Co. Hist. Soc., Chi Psi. Republican. Presybn. (elder). Mason (32°, Shriner). Clubs; Clubs: Pomfret, Rotary, Northampton Country; William Coll. (New York). Home: White Plains, N.Y.†

YATES, GILBERT E., UN ofcl.; b. Manchester, Eng., Sept. 20, 1907; s. A.E. and Jessie Yates; student George Watson's Coll., Edinburgh, 1913-25; grad. U. Edinburgh (1st class honors in history), 1929; m. Janine May-Lawrence Herbert, 1949; 1 dau. Served in Ministry of Health, London, 1930-38, Imperial Def. Coll., 1938, Ministry of Home Security, London, 1939-40, Office of the British Minister of State in the Middle East, Cairo, 1942-46; became sec. Econ. and Social Council, UN, 1946, dir. narcotics div. UN, 1952; UN rep. Malta, from 1965. Cons., UN Fund for Drug Abuse control. Clubs: Athenaeum (London); also Casino Maltese (Vallets). Contbr. articles on drug problems to profl. jours. and newspapers. Deceased.

YATES, KYLE MONROE, theologian; b. Apex, N.C., Feb. 7, 1895; s. William Charles Manly and Della (Jones) Y.; diploma Campbell Coll., Buies Creek, N.C., 1911; A.B., Wake Forest (N.C.) Coll., 1916, A.M., 1917, Th.M., So. Bapt. Theol. Sem., 1920, Th.D., 1922; D.D., Mercer U., Macon, Ga., 1930; Ph.D., U. Edinburgh, 1932; LL.D., Union U., 1939; Litt.D., Baylor U., Waco, Tex., 1948; m. Margaret Webb Sharp, Aug. 24, 1922; children—Kyle M., Margaret Jean, Ellen. Ordained ministry. So. Ch., 1916; pastor successively Ft. Barnwell, N.C., New Castle, Ky., New Salem, and Beechmont Ch., Louisville, 1920-28; prof. O.T., So. Bapt. Theol. Sem., 1922-42; pastor Walnut St. Bapt. Ch., Louisville, 1942-46; pastor 2d Bapt. Ch., Houston, 1946-56; Distinguished prof. Bible, Baylor U., 1956-71, prof. emeritus, 1917-75. Mason (K.T., Shriner), Rotarian. Mem. Com. on Revision of Bible, 1938-75. Author books relating to field, including Preaching from the Prophets; Preaching from the Psalms; Preaching from the Great Chapters of the Bible; Preaching from the Gospel of John; Genesis in the Wycliffe Bible Commentary. Home: Waco, Tex., Died Feb. 15, 1975; buried Oakwood Cemetery, Waco, Tex.

YEISER, JOHN OTHO, III, inventor; b. Omaha, Apr. 13, 1923; s. John Otho and Gertrude Almeda (Sturm) Y.; student Omaha U., 1940-41, U. N.D., 1942, Ore. State U., 1943, U. Ore., 1945-46; m. Patsy de Merce Burkhardt, Aug. 26, 1961; children—James Dana, John Otho IV, Debra, Mark. Head biomed. support group U.S. Naval Radiol. Def. Lab., Hunters Point, Cal., 1949-50; mgr. instruments div. Mandrel Industries, Houston, 1958-60; owner Yeiser Labs., Costa Mesa, Cal., 1961-74; dir. Nesco Instruments, Newport Beach, Cal.; cons. to Beckman, Teledyne, Ralph M. Parsons Co., Lockheed, Milton Roy, Inc. Served with AUS, 1942-45. Mem. I.E.E.E., Instrument Soc. Am., S.A.R. (chpt. pres. 1965-66), S.R., Baronial Order of Magna Charta. Republican. Presbyn. Patentee aerospace, electronic instrumentation. Home: Mission Viejo Cal. Died Jan. 21, 1974

YERUSHALMY, JACOB, bio-statistician; b. Vienna, Austria, Aug. 5, 1904; s. Zev and Anna (Ziev) Y.; B.A., Johns Hopkins, 1927, M.A., 1929, Ph.D., 1930; m. Eva R. Zemil, Sept. 4, 1934; children—Zeva Anne, Paul Zev. Came to U.S., 1924, naturalized, 1931, Instr. math. Johns Hopkins, 1932-35; statistician N.Y. State Dept. Health, 1934-38, NIH, 1938-41; dir. div. statis research Children's Bur., Dept. Labor 1941-43; prin. statistician USPHS, 1943-48; prof. biostatistics U. Cal. at Berkeley, 1948-73; dir. child health and devel. studies Kaiser Found. Research Inst., 1959-73; cons. WHO, USPHS, Cal. Dept. Pub. Health. NRC fellow mathematics, 1930-32. Mem. Nat. Adv. Neurol. Diseases and Blindness Council, Am. Pub. Health Assn., Am. Statis. Assn., Population Assn. Am., Internat. Union Sci. Study Population, Phi Beta Kappa, Sigma Xi. Contbr. articles sci. jours. Home: Berkeley Cal. Died Oct. 15, 1973

YESKO, ELMER GEORGE, dentist; b. Wilkes-Barre, Pa., Nov. 23, 1918; s. George and Mary (Switch) Y.; B.A., Harvard U., 1940; D.D.S., Temple U., 1961; M.P.H., U. Pitts., 1969; student U. Scranton, 1937, U. Detroit, 1955, Wayne U., 1955-57, U. N.C., 1964-66, 67, U. Mich., 1966, Temple U., 1967-71, U. Pa., 1967, Georgetown U., 1971; m. Edith Eleanora Koski, Nov. 14, 1970; 1 son, George Cluny-Brown. Commd. ensign, U.S. Navy, 1942, advanced through grades to lt. comdr., 1942-55, spl. intelligence, Washington, 1951-53, assigned to state health depts. Va., 1962-66, Mich., 1966-67, Pa., 1967-72, personal pilot for sec. of navy, 1946-48, adminstrv. officer, Chief of Naval Air Training, 1945-46, personnel war planning, Washington, 1948, watch com., Washington, 1951-53, ret., 1955); individual practice dentistry, Harrisburg, Pa., 1967-74; cons. spl. patient care, Harrisburg, 1967-73, VA Hosp., 1973-74. Decorated Air medal with two oak leaf clusters. Fellow Am. Pub. Health Assn., Am. Orthopedic Soc., Fedn. Dental Internat., Royal Soc. Health, Soc. Oral Physiology and Occlusion, Am. Soc. Preventive Dentistry, Harrisburg Dental Soc., Am. Soc. Dentistry Children (pres.-elect), Phila., Montgomery, Bucks dental socs. Republican. Roman Catholic. Home: Duncansville,

YI, HA-YUN, poet; b. Ichon, Korea, Apr. 9, 1906; s. Yi Chong-Seok Lee and Cheong-Sun; Y.; B.A., Faculty of Lit., Hosei U., Tokyo, Japan, 1929; m. Kim Eule-Ye, Apr. 18, 1928; children—Don-Sik, Chang-Sik, Chung-Sik, Young-Sik, Eun-Sik. Prof. Tong-Kuk U., 1945-49; prof. Coll. Edn., Seoul (Korea) Nat. U., 1949-71; prof. Duksung Woman's Coll., Seoul, 1971-74. Recipient Nat. Merit Medal, 1970. Mem. Comparative Lit. Soc. Korea (chmn.), Internat. P.E.N. Author: Waterwheel, 1939; Poems from English and French, 1933, 48, 54; Anthologies, 1939, 1946, 1949, 1955; Irish Literary Renaissance. Home: Seoul, Republic of Korea. Died Mar. 12, 1974.

YOCHUM, H(AROLD) L(ELAND), clergyman; b. Fostoria, O., June 7, 1903; s. William Henry and Ida Aemelia (Heiserman) Y.; A.B., Capital U., Columbus, O., 1923, B.D., 1928, D.D., 1943; A.M., Ohio State U., 1924; m. Agatha Emilie Pfeiffer, July 5, 1928; children—Doris Christine, Marilyn Agatha, Faith Elizabeth. Tchr. high sch., 1924-25; ordained Lutheran minister, 1928; instr., Capital U., 1925-28; minister Emanuel Luth. ch., Hessville, O., 1928-34, Holy Trinity Ch., Detroit, 1934-39; full time pres. Mich. Dist., Am. Luth. Ch., 1939-46; v.p. Am. Luth. Ch., 1940-46; commr. to Nat. Luth. Council from 1940; pres. Am. Luth. Conf., 1942-46; pres. Capital Univ., 1946-69; minister to shut-ins Christ Luth. Ch., Columbus. Mem. Kappa Sigma Upsilon. Author: Confirmation Sermons, 1933; Confessional Sermons and Addresses, 1936. Home: Columbus O. Died Sept. 1, 1974.

YODER, ANNE ELIZABETH, educator; b. South Bend, Ind., Nov. 7, 1879; d. Samuel and Elizabeth (Woods) Y.; high sch. Elkhart, Ind.; grad. Sch. of Oratory, Northwestern U., 1903, post-grad., 1906. Teacher Goshen (Ind.) Coll., 1902-05, Cornell Coll., Mt. Vernon, Ia., 1906-08; with U. of Southern Calif., 1908-29, dean Sch. of Speech, 1981-29; dir. Elizabeth Yoder School (collegiate sch. for Am. girls), Villa Ramberg gia della Stufa, Florence, Italy, from Sept. 1929. Lecturer and dramatic reader. Mem. Kappa Alpha Theta, Zeta Phi Eta, Collegiat Players. Republican. Christian Scientist. Home: Los Angeles, Calif. Address: Florence, Italy.†

YONGE, JULIEN C(HANDLER), editor; b. Pensacola, Fla., Jan. 20, 1879; s. Philip Jeyes and Lucie Cairns (Davis) Y.; student Ala. Poly. Inst., 1895-98; unmarried. Editor, Florida Historical Quarterly, 1924-56, editor emeritus, from 1956; director Florida Historical Society, from 1925; vice president, 1935-36. Dir. and curator P. K. Yonge Library of Florida History, U. of Fla., from 1944; established Julien C. Yonge graduate research professorship in history, U. of Fla., from 1958; established Julien C. Yong Chair of Florida History, from 1959. Member of Southern Hist. Assn., Pi Kappa Alpha, Phi Alpha Theta. Episcopalian. Democrat. Home: Pensacola, Fla.†

YOOK, YOUNG-SOO, first lady Republic Korea; b. North Chungohong Province, Korea, Nov. 29, 1925; ed. Paehwa Girls' High Sch.; m. Pres. Park Chung-hee, 1950. Hon. chmn. Yangji Hoe women's soc. Home: Seoul, Republic Korea., Died Aug. 15, 1974.

YORAN, GEORGE FRANCIS, naval officer; b. Eugene, Ore., Dec. 25, 1892; s. George Oliver and Annie Laurie (Dunn) Y.; student U. Ore., 1918; M.B.A., Harvard, 1925; m. Lucile Greenleaf, Apr. 20, 1918; 1 son, Ensign George Francis, Jr., U.S. Navy. Entered U.S. Navy, 1917, commd. ensign, 1917, and advanced through grades to rear admiral, 1949; served on U.S.S. Oregon and U.S.S. Kon der Nederlanden, 1917-19; U.S.S. Camden, 1920-23; accounting officer, Mare Island, Calif., 1925-26; supply officer Shanghai, China, 1926-29; supply officer Bur. Navigation, Washington, 1929-32; U.S.S. Saratoga, 1932-35; supply officer U.S.S. Colorado, 1936-39; purchasing officer Bur. Supplies and Accounts, Washington, 1939-43; staff Comdr. Naval Group CHINA, 1944; staff of comdr. in chief, Pacific Fleet, 1944-45; staff CinC Atlantic Fleet, 1948-49; dir. of Cost Inspection Service, 1951-53; insp. gen. supply corps Bur. Supplies and Accountants, Navy, 1953-55, ret. Home: Washington D.C. Died Sept. 10, 1974.

YORK, MILES FREDERICK, ins. exec.; b. Cayucos, Cal., Dec. 28, 1901; s. Walter G. and Lily F. (Peterson) Y.; A.B., U. Cal., 1922; m. Myrtle Glenn, Dec. 17, 1923; children—Steven W. (dec.), Alice. Employee Fireman's Fund Ins. Co., San Francisco, 1922-42, asst. mgr. Atlantic marine dept., N.Y.C., 1942-45; v.p., gen. mgr. Pacific Coast operations Atlantic Mut. Ins. Co., San Francisco, 1945-51, v.p., trustee, 1950; executive v.p. Atlantic Mutual Ins. Co., 1951-53, pres., 1953-66, chmn. bd., chief exec. officer, 1966-69; pres., dir. Centennial Ins. Co.; dir. Home Life Ins. Co. Mem. bd. mgrs. Am. Bur. Shipping. Mem. Maritime Assn. Port New York (director, treasurer), American Institute Marine Underwriters (president 1958-60), Bd. Underwriters New York (president 1959-60), Insurance Society of New York (trustee), also Alpha Sigma Phi, Phi Phi, Pi Delta Epsilon. Clubs: University, India House, Bohemian, Economic. Home: New York City N.Y. Died May 12, 1973.

YORK, ROBERT, cartoonist; b. Mpls., Aug. 23, 1909; s. Raymond and Nelle (Johnston) Y.; student Drake U., 1927-28, Cummings Sch. Art, 1928, Chgo. Acad. Fine Arts, 1930; m. Lillian Lossin, Apr. 11, 1936; 1 dau., Robin Lee. Asst. comic strip artist Chicago Tribune, Chgo., 1930-35; polit. cartoonist Nashville Banner, 1936-37, Louisville Times, 1937-43, 45-74. Served as sgt. artist, USAAF, 1943-45. Recipient Pulitzer prize, 1956. Home: Louisville Ky. Died May 21, 1975.

YOSHIDA, TOMIZO, physician, educator; b. Fukushima, Japan, Feb. 10, 1903; s. Kilchiro and Nao Y.; ed. Imperial U., Tokyo; m. Kimiko Yoshida, Mar. 6, 1931; children—Naoya, Yasuko (Mrs. Ichiro Anzai), Syohei, Kazuko (Mrs. Tadashi Sugano). Asst. prof. Nagasaki Med. Coll., 1935-38, prof., 1938-44; prof. Tohoku Imperial U., Sendai, Japan, 1944-52; prof. medicine Tokyo U., 1952-73, dir. Sasaki Inst., 1953-73, dean Faculty of Medicine, 1958; dir. Cancer Inst. Japanese Found. for Cancer Research, 1963-73. Adviser, Minister of Edn., 1963-73; v.p. Sci. Council Japan, 1963-65; pres. Internat. Cancer Congress, 1966. Decorated Order of Cultural Merit. Recipient Imperial prize Japanese Acad., 1931, 1953, Scheele medal, 1956, Koch medal (Germany), 1963. Contbr. articles to profl. lit. Home: Tokyo, Japan. Died Apr. 27, 1973; interred Tokyo, Japan.

YOST, LENNA LOWE, (Mrs. Ellis A.); b. Basnettville, W.Va., Jan. 25, 1878; d. Jonathan and Columbia (Basnett) Lowe; ed. W.Va. Wesleyan Coll., and Ohio Northern U.; L.H.D., W.Va., Wesleyan Coll., 1929; m. Ellis A. Yost, 1899; 1 son, Leland Lowe. Pres. W.Va. Equal Suffrage Assn. as chmn. of com. directed campaign for ratification of the 19th Amendment; nat.

rep. and corr. in Washington, 1918-30, and pres., W.Va. Woman's Christian Temperance Union. First woman teller Rep. Nat. Conv., 1920; first woman to preside over a Rep. State Conv., and first woman to serve as chmn. Platform Com. in a Rep. State Conv.; chmn. Rep. Women's Exec. Com. of W.Va., 1920-22; mem. Rep. Nat. Com., 1924-32, exec. com., 1928-32; director women's div. Rep. Nat. Committee, 1930-35. Mem. State Board of Edn., W.Va., 1921-33; trustee West Virginia Wesleyan College, 1928-42. United States delegate to International Congress Against Alcoholism, Lausanne, Switzerland, 1921, Copenhagen, Denmark, 1923. Member American Association University Women, League of Am. Pen. Women, D.A.R., Woman's Nat. Farm and Garden Assn. (exec. com.), Pi Sigma Alpha. Club: Nat. Woman's Country. Home: Huntington, W.Va.*†

YOUNG, AGATHA (MRS. GEORGE BENHAM YOUNG), author; b. Cleve., Nov. 18, 1898; d. Edward Howard and Agnes (Chapin) Brooks; grad. Dana Hall, Wellesley, Mass., 1916; ed. in art Cleve. Sch. of Art, 1918, Sch. of Arts and Design, 1919, Columbia, 1919, L'Ecole Francaise, Paris, 1920; m. George Benham Young, Nov. 27, 1920. Executed bas relief of Florence Nightingale, now in St. Thomas' Hosp., London; costume dir. The Playhouse, Cleve., 1923-27; head. dept. of costuming Yale Theatre, 1928-29; mem. faculty depts. of fine arts and adult edn. Western Res. U., 1930-32; lectr. art and psychology of dress; in charge of preparing weekly summary of editorial opinion for War Dept., 1940-41; cons. to War Manpower Commn., 1941; cons. Retng. and Reemployment Adminstrn., 1944; mem. staff Mt. Ascutney Hosp. and Med. Center (Agatha Young Med. Library there named in her honor); hon. staff Ottauquechee Health Center. Trustee Edward R. Murrow Found. Mem. Fashion Group, Am. Statis. Assn. Episcopalian. Club: Overseas of Am. Author: Stage Costuming, 1927, Recurring Cycles of Fashion, 1937; (under name Agatha Young): Light In the Sky, 1948, Blaze of Glory, 1950, Clown of the Goos, 1954, Scalpel, 1956, The Women and the Crisis: Women of the North in the Civil War, 1960, Men Who Made Surgery 1961, Manual of Statistics, 1964, The Town and Dr. Moore, 1966, I Swear by Apollo, 1968, The Hospital, 1970, Dr. Moore's Legacy, 1973, Contbr. articles to mags. Home: New York City N.Y. Died Feb. 6, 1974.

YOUNG, CHIC, (Murat Bernard Young), cartoonist; b. Chgo., Jan. 9, 1901; s. James Luther and Martha (Techen) Y.; ed. pub. schs. of St. Louis, also arts schs. in Chgo., N.Y.C., Cleve.; m. Athel L. Lindorff, Oct. 4, 1927; children—Wayne Roy (dec.), Dean Wayne, Jeanne Athel. With Newspaper Enterprise Assn., 1920-21, Bell Syndicate, New York, 1921-23, King Features Syndicate, from 1923; originated comic strip Dumb Dora, 1924, and drew it 6 yrs.; originated comic strip "Blondie", 1930, and drew this strip daily for 1600 Am. and fgn. newpspaers. Home: New York City, N.Y., Died Mar. 14, 1973.

YOUNG, D. PHILIP, newspaper pub.; b. York, Pa., June 11, 1887; s. John Frederick and Tene Etta (Stahle) Y.; student Pa. State Coll.; m. Anna May Myers, July 5, 1910; children—Pauline T. (Mrs. N. Richard Gallatin), Philip H. (dec.), Robert L. With The Dispatch Pub. Co., pubs. York (Pa.) Dispatch, 1906-75, gen. mgr., 1942, v.p., dir. 1942-47, pres., pub., 1947-75, Mem. Pa. Newspaper Pubs. Assn., Inter Am. Press Assn., York County Agrl. assn., Internat. Typog. Union, Asso. Press, S.A.R., Pa. Soc., YMCA, Mason (32 K.T., Shriner), Tall Cedars, Elk. Clubs: Rotary, Country, Lafayette (York); Sun City (Ariz.) Country; Bon Air Country. Home: York Pa. Died Oct. 1975.

YOUNG, GLADWIN E(LLIS), agrl. economist; b. Frankfort, Ind., Dec. 24, 1900; s. Claude A. and Lucy (Bozworth) Y.; B.S.A., Prudue, U., 1923, M.S. A., 1926; m. Mildred Kline, July 3, 1925; children—Jean (Mrs. Robert E. Schmidt), Keith K., Roger E., Lynn E. Agrl. economist Purdue Agrl. Exptl. Sta., 1923-34; regional cons. corn belt states Nat. Resources Planning Bd., 1935-36; regional chief north central states and land use planning. Resettlement Adminstrn., 1937-38; field rep. north central states bur. agrl. econs. U.S. Dept. of Agr., 1938-45; agrl. rehabilitation specialist White Russian Mission, UN RRA, 1946; mem. Mo. River Basin Inter-Agency Com., 1947-52, asst. to Asst. Sec. Agr., 1953, dep. adminstr. Soil Conservation Service, 1954-63, asso. adminstr., 1963-67; chmn. Fed. Interagy. Com. Water Resources, 1962-73. Mem. Arlington Com. Parks, Nature Areas and Open Space. Fellow Soil Conservation Soc. Am.; mem. Farm Econs. Assn., Phi Kappa Sigma. Home: Arlington, Va., Died June 13, 1973; buried Nat. Meml. Park, Falls Church, Va.

YOUNG, HORACE AUTREY, lawyer; b. Nashville, Ark., Jan. 14, 1899; s. George A. and Margaret (Hooker) Y.; A.B., Hendrix Coll., Conway, Ark., 1921; J.D., U. Chgo. 1924; m. Mabel Turner, Aug. 25, 1921. Admitted to Ill. bar, 1925; law clk. Ill. Bell Telephone Co., 1924-25, asst. atty., 1925-28; asso. Sonnenschein, Berkson, Lautmann, Levinson & Morse, 1928-32, specializing real estate and mortgage law; with Fisher, Boyden, Bell, Boyd & Marshall, real estate and mortgage law, corporate reorgns., 1932-37; gen. pvt. practice, Chgo., 1938; dir. Benefit Trust Life Ins. Co., Electro-Matic Products Co. Bd. dirs. N.W. Harris-Methodist Found. Served with AUS, 1918; from capt. to lt. col. AUS, 1943-46. Fellow Am. Bar. Found. (life fellow); mem. Am. (ho. dels. 1962-66), Fed., Ill. (pres. 1963-64), Chgo. bar assns., U. Chgo. Law Sch. Alumni Assn. (pres. 1939-40), Phi Delta Phi. Republican. Methodist. Mason. Clubs: Michigan Shores (Wilmette) Law (Chgo.). Home: Wilmette Ill. Died 1973.

YOUNG, HOWARD SLOAN, lawyer; b. Indianapolis, Ind., Aug. 7, 1879; s. Archibald A. and Georgia (Sloan) Y.; Ph.B., U. of Chicago, 1901; LL.B., Ind. Law Sch., 1903; m. Elsie Street, Oct. 26, 1909 (dec.); children—Lillian (Mrs. J. S. Pearson, Jr., dec.), Dorothy (Mrs. Frederick G. Johns), Howard Sloan. Admitted to Ind. bar, 1903; in office Addison C. Harris, Indianapolis, Ind., 1902-04; practiced alone, 1904-15; mem. firm Elam, Fesler, Elam & Young, 1915-16, Fesler, Elam & Young, 1916-32, Fesler, Elam, Young & Fauvre, 1932-44; judge Supreme Court of Indiana, 1945-51. U.S. Commr., 1903-44. Counsel for Ind. Special Coal and Food Commn., 1920-21. Elected Indianapolis School Board, 1942. Mem. Indianapolis (pres. 1931) and Ind. State Bar Assns., Phi Kappa Psi. Mason. Clubs: Kiwanis, Contemporary (Indianapolis). Home: Indianapolis, Ind.†

YOUNG, KIMBALL, educator; b. Provo, Utah, Oct. 26, 1893; s. Oscar Brigham and Anna Marie (Roseberry) Y.; A.B., Brigham Young U., 1915; A.M., U. of Chicago, 1918; Ph.D., Stanford, 1921; m. 2d, Lillian D. Jackson, April 6, 1940; 1 dau. Helen Anderson (Mrs. R. D. Willey) (by first marriage). Began as teacher high school, 1915; asst., later asso. professor psychology, Univ. of Oregon, 1920-22, 1923-26; asst. prof. psychology, Clark U., Worcester, Mass., 1922-23; asso. prof. sociology, U. of Wis., 1926-30, prof. social psychology, 1930-40; chmn. dept. of sociology, Queens Coll., Flushing, N.Y., 1940-47; chairman department sociology Northwestern U., from 1947; Guggenheim fellowship, 1951-52; Expert consultant War Dept., 1944; head sociology branch Shrivenham Am. Univ. (U.S. Army), 1945. Mem. American Psychological Association, American Anthropological Assn., Am. Sociol. Soc. (pres. 1945), Sigma Xi, Alpha Kappa Delta (nat. pres. 1928-30), Theta Chi. Author or co-author books relating to field. Gen. editor American Sociology Series (Am. Book Co.). Contbr. books and jours. of social sci. Address: Evanston Ill. Died Sept. 1, 1973.

YOUNG, ROBERT WINTHROP, business exec., lawyer; b. Boston, Feb. 16, 1887; s. Aaron Winthrop and Maria Louise (Plimpton) Y.; LL.B., Northeastern U., 1909; m. Amanda H. Phillips, Oct. 10, 1910; children—Andrew Plimpton, Robert Winthrop. Admitted to Mass. bar, 1908; chmn. bd., pres., dir. The Durex Corp., The Durex Abrasives Corp., and pres., dir. Baeder Adamson Co.; chmn. bd. Minn. Mining & Mfg. Internat. Co.; pres., dir. Minco Corp., Ltd., Can.; asso. Minn. de France S.A.R.L., Minn. Manufactura Mercantil, S.A., Argentina; dir. Minn. Mining & Mfg. of Can., Ltd., Minn. Mining & Mfg. Co., Ltd., Eng. Mem. Assn. Bar City N.Y. Club: Greenwich (Conn.) Country. Home: Greenwich Conn. Died Sept. 19, 1974.

YOUNG, RODNEY STUART, archaeologist; b. Bernardsville, N.J., Aug. 1, 1907; s. Henry and Alice I. (Ballantine) Y.; A.B., Princeton, 1929, Ph.D., 1940; M.A., Columbia, 1932. Asso. curator U. Mus., U. Pa., 1949-50; curator, 1950; dir. excavations Gordion, Phrygla, 1950-74, also prof. classical archaeology U. Pa. Chief Greek desk OSS, 1942-44; spl. asst. to chief Greek mission UNRRA, 1944-45. Decorated Bronze Star (U.S.); Croix de Guerre (Greece); Agora fellow Am. Sch. Classical Studies, Athens, 1933-40; Fulbright fellow, 1947-49. Mem. Archaeol. Inst. Am. (pres. 1968-72), German Archaeol. Inst., Am. Philos. Soc. Contbr. articles tech., popular jours. Home: Chester Springs Pa. Died Oct. 25, 1974.

YOUNG, STANLEY (PRESTON), author, pub.; b. Greencastle, Ind., Feb. 3, 1906; s. Augustus and Martha (Watson) Y.; Ph.B., U. Chgo., 1929; spl. student U. Grenoble, 1927-28; grad. student U. Munich, 1929-30; A.M., Columbia, 1931; m. Margaret Elneth Linde, Dec. 20, 1929 (div.); children—Margaret Roper Aline, Martha Cecily Heron, Christopher Augustus; m. 2d, Nancy Wilson Ross, 1942. Fgn. corr., 1927-28; instr. in English, Bklyn. Poly. Inst., 1930-31, Williams Coll., 1931-34; lit. adviser Macmillan Co., 1934-36; lit. critic N.Y. Times Sunday book sect., from 1936; mem. editorial bd. Harcourt, Brace & Co., 1939-42; mng. dir. Bollingen Found., 1942-47; dir. Farrar, Straus & Co., from 1945; mng. dir. Farrar, Straus and Young, 1950-55; exec. dir. Am. Nat. Theatre and Acad.; prof. drama, asst. to pres. Hofstra U., 1965-71, prof. emeritus, 1971-75. Mem. Nat. Council on Arts, from 1965. Rockefeller Found. fellow, 1936-37; John Golden fellow for playwriting, 1938. Mem. Author's League (council), Owl and Serpent, Sigma Nu. Conglist. Clubs: Century Assn., Players (N.Y.C.); Adirondack League. Author: Robin Landing (verse drama), 1938; Ship Forever Sailing, 1938; Sons Without Anger (novel), 1939; Young Hickory (children's book), 1940; My Sister and I (pseudonym Dirk van der Heide), 1941; Mayflower Boy, 1944. Plays Produced: Robin Landing, 1937; Bright Rebel, 1938; Night Between the Rivers, 1939; Farmer Brown's Pig (in Best Plays of 1940); Ask My Friend Sandy, 1943; A Bunyan Yarn (in Best One-acts, 1945); Mystery Story (To Walk the Night), 1948; the Big People, 1948; Mr. Pickwick, 1952; Tippecanoe and Tyler, Too!, 1957; The Sound of Apples (verse-play: recipient prize Acad. Am. Poets and CBS), 1957; Laurette, 1965; The World Next Door. Contbr. articles and verse to periodicals; war corr., 1945. Home: Old Westbury, N.Y. Died Mar. 22, 1975.

YOUNGBLOOD, BONNEY, b. Milam County, Tex., July 31, 1881; s. Thomas Bunyan and Mattie (Sivils) Y.; B.S., Tex. Agrl. and Mech. Coll., 1902, M.S., 1907; Ph.D., U. of Wis., 1921; m. Lotus Shamburger, May 16, 1907. Pvt. Co. I, 1st Tex. Vol. Inf., Spanish-Am. War, May 6-Oct. 20, 1898. Manager Smith Ranch, Grayson County, Tex., 1903; prin. high sch., Henderson, Tex., 1903-05, Mineola, 1905-06; supt. schs., Paul Valley, Okla., 1906-07; agriculturist, Office of Farm Management, U.S. Dept. Agr., 1907-11; dir. Tex. Expt. Sta., 1911-28; recommended located and developed first State Ranch Expt. Station, Sutton County, Texas, 1915; on leave from Texas Station serving as senior agrl. economist U.S. Dept. Agr., to organize its cotton marketing economics program, 1926-28; principal agrl. economist, U.S. Dept. Agr., from 1928; advisor to U.S. Indian Service on economic and social problems of the Navajo Indians, 1934-44; made report on Navajo trading, 1935; recommended, 1934, and later helped develop Southwestern Range and Sheep Breeding Laboratory, Ft. Wingate, N.M. Member Farm Econ. Assn., Alpha Gamma Rho (Iota Chapter); fellow Am. Geog. Soc. Mason (K.T., Shriner). Author of "An Economic Study of a Typical Ranching Area on the Edwards Plateau of Texas," other bulls., and professional papers of the Tex. Agrl. Sta. and U.S. Dept. Agr. Home: Harpers Ferry, W.Va.†

YUNG, JULIUS RUDOLPH, surgeon; b. Terre Haute, Ind., Mar. 23, 1878; s. Carl and Elizabeth (Fox) Y.; M.D., U. of Ill., 1900; grad. work, N.Y. Post Grad. Sch., 1905; Harvard, 1916; m. Jane Marsten Kimball. Interne Hosp. St. Anthony de Padua, Chicago, 1900-02; further study of thyroid diseases and operation techniques, Lahey (Boston), Crile (Cleveland), Mayo (Rochester, Minn.) clinics, 1919; studied in European clinics, Berne, Switzerland; Paris, France; Brussels, Belgium; The Hague, Holland; Vienna, Austrai; Munich, Germany, 1921-27; mem. med. and surg staff St. Anthony Hosp., Terre Haute, Ind., from 1904, past pres., chief goiter service, also chief surg. service, from 1947, mem. exec. staff, from 1940. Del. and mem. publ. com., 1st and 2d Internat. Goiter confs., Berne, Switzerland, 1927, 3d conference, Washington, 1938. Diplomate International Board of Surgery. Charter fellow Am. chapter Internat. Coll. Surgeons (past pres. study guild State of Ind., now regent); fellow A.M.A.; mem. Terre Haute Acad. Medicine, Vigo County Med. Soc., Ind. State Med. (pres. 1944-45), Am. Assn. for Study of Goiter (pres. 1936), Nu Sigma Nu. Club: Surgeons of Mayo Clinic (life mem., from 1917). Contbr. numerous articles to med. jours. Home: Terre Haute, Ind.†

YURKA, BLANCHE, actress, author; b. St. Paul, June 19, 1887; d. Anton and Karolina (Novak) Jurka; student Inst. Musical Art, N.Y.C., also Met. Opera Sch., N.Y.C., 1904-07; L.H.D. (hon.), U. Tampa, 1967. Broadway productions include Hamlet with John Barrymore, Lucrece, also Romeo and Juliet with Katherine Cornell, Goat Song with the Lunts, Electra, Lysistrata; motion picture appearances include A Tale of Two Cities, 1934, Song of Bernadette, Woman From Hell; theatrical dir. one woman show throughout U.S. and Hawaii. Author: Dear Audience, 1954. Died June 1974.

ZABINSKI, JAN FRANCISZEK, zoologist; b. Warsaw, Poland, Apr. 8, 1897; s. Jozef and Helena (Strazeszewska) Z.; M.Sc. in Agr., Higher Sch. Agrl. Economy, Warsaw, 1917; Ph.D., U. Warsaw, 1921; Phil. Docant, Curie-Sklodowska U., Lublin, Poland, 1946; m. Jadwiga Moxzydiowska, 1918; children—Helena, Jozef; m. 2d, Antonia Erdman, 1931; children—Ryszard, Teresa. Asst. chair zoology Higher Sch. Agr., 1918-29; dir. Warsaw Zool. Gardens, 1929-51; insp.-in-chief State Supervision Polish Zoos, 1949-52; prof. animal physiology Higher Sch. Pedagogy, 1952-53; radio author; lectr. Clandestine Warsaw U., 1941-44. Served as 1st lt. Inf. Polish Army, 1918-20, 41, lt., 1943-45. Decorated Independence Cross; Gold-Cross of Merit; Medal for Liberty and Victory; comdr.'s cross Order of Potonia Restituta; recipient award for best sci. publ. in agr., 1931; award of Radio, 1959; award City of Warsaw, 1960; Bruno Winawer award, 1961, 68; award Warsaw Sci. Soc., 1962; award Polish Radio, 1967. Mem. Polish Physiol. Soc., Polish Zool. Soc., Polish Sci. Soc., Union Polish Writers, Internat. Union for Preservation of Nature (pres. European bison com.), Polish Acad. Scis. (mem. zoology com.). Author: Cockroach (monograph), 1928; Przekroj przez Zoo, 1953; Wildlife, 6 vols., 1953-69; Zagadka ewolucjonizmu, 1968; also numerous other books, articles. Editor: European Bison Pedigree Books, 1947-74. Home: Warsaw, Poland. Died July 26, 1974; buried Powazki Cemetery, Warsaw.

ZACHER, CLARENCE HENRY, educator; b. Blue Island, Ill., Oct. 27, 1908; s. August R. and Lena (MueMouse) Z.; B.S. in Civil Engring., Ill. Inst. Tech., 1932, postgrad. 1935-37, 53; student Chgo. Tchrs. Coll., 1933; m. Eileen Curry, Apr. 12, 1947; 1 son, Alan

Robert. Draftsman, designer Lakeside Engring. Corp., Chgo., 1934-36; jr. engr., surveyor U.S. Corps. Engrs., War Dept., 1936-41; tchr. St Rita High Sch., Chgo., 1941-42, Luther Inst., Chgo., 1942-44, Bloom Twp. (Ill.) High Sch., 1944-48; instr. Purdue U., Calumet Center, Hammond, Ind., 1948-53, asst. prof., 1953-63, asso. prof., 1963-74, posthumous prof. emeritus, 1974, chmn. mech. engring. tech. and civil engring. programs, 1963-64, charge civil engring. and engring. graphics programs, 1964-74; mem. firm Springer & Zacher Engrs., 1958-61, Zacher Engring., 1961-71, Bevins & Zacher Engring., 1971-74. Cons. Lake County Surveyors Office, 1965-71. Sponsor student chpt. profl. engrs. Purdue U.-Calumet Campus, Hammond, Ind., 1967-74. Recipient service award Ind. Soc. Profl. Engrs., 1970, student chpt. profl. engrs. Purdue U., 1973. Registered land surveyor, Ind. Registered profl. engr., Ind., Ill. Mem. Western Soc. Engrs. (life), Am. Soc. Engring. Edn., Am. Assn. U. Profs., Nat., Ind. (state dir. 1972-73, trustee scholarship fund, state scholarship com. 1972-74, state chmn. edn. and scholarship com. 1968-70, chmn. guidance and scholarship com. Calumet chpt. 1962, pres. 71-72; Order Engr.), Ill. (state chmn. edn. and scholarship com. 1969-70, alternate chpt. rep. Sauk Trail chpt. 1968-70) socs. profl. engrs., Alpha Sigma Lambda. Lutheran (elder). Club: Calumet Country (Ill.). Club: Youche Country (Crown Point). Author: Problems in Isometric Sketching Drawing: Problems in Development and Intersections, 1954; Descriptive Geometry problems, 1962. Home: Crown Point, Ind. Died Jan. 22, 1974; interred Homewood (Ill.) Meml. Gardens.

ZAIN, REBYL (MRS. GEORGE K. ZAIN), publicity and pub. relations leader; b. nr. Findlay, O., Sept. 7, 1909; d. Peter and Rebecca (Gossman) Silver; student pub. schs.; m. George K. Zain, Feb. 21, 1935 (dec. Sept. 1966). Vice-pres. newspaper campaigns The Zain Advt. System, N.Y.C., 1930-41; publicist varied civic activities Coral Gables, Fla., 1942-44; v.p. charge publicity and promotion Miracle Mile Coral Gables, 1944, chmn. bd., 1966; publicity, promotion, pub. relations dir. Zain Plans Beautification Cities downtown shopping sts., 1944, parking, 1950, residential sts., pkwys., 1962. Recipient (with husband) bronze plaque city Coral Gables, Fla., 1961. Episcopalian. Clubs: Coral Gables (Fla.) Country. Home: Coral Gables, Fla. Died July 9, 1973.

ZALESKI, ALEXANDER, bishop; b. Laurel, N.Y.; June 24, 1906; s. Anthony and Bertha (Janulewicz) A.; student Don Bosco Prep. Sch., Ramsey, N.J.; student St. Mary's Coll., Orchard Lake, Mich., 1924-27, U. Louvain, 1927-31; S.S.L., Pontifical Bibl. Inst., Rome, 1935. Ordained priest Roman Cath. Ch., 1931; asst. pastor Ressurrection, St. Thomas the Apostle, Detroit, 1931-32; instr. St. Mary's Coll., 1935-37; vice chancellor Archdiocese of Detroit, 1937-49; pastor St. Vincent de Paul Parish, Pontiac, 1949-56; aux. bishop, Detroit, 1950-64; vicar gen., 1954-64; bishop, Lansing, Mich., 1964-75; formerly pastor St. Alphonsus Parish, Dearborn, Mich. Chmn. com. on doctrine Nat. Council Cath. Bishops, 1966-70. Vice chmn. bd. trustees Cath. U. Am., 1968—. Home: Lansing, Mich., Died May 16, 1975.

ZANDER, ARNOLD SCHEUER, orgn. exec.; b. Two Rivers, Wis., Nov. 26, 1901; s. Arnold and Anna (Scheuer) Z.; B.S., U. Wis., 1923, M.S., 1929, Ph.D., 1931; m. Lola Dynes, June 15, 1929; children—Ann, Karla, Stephen. Draftsmen, Wis. Telephone Co., Milw., 1923-24; bridge draftsmen B. & O. R.R., Balt., 1924-25; structural steel draftsman Manitowoc (Wis.) Shipbldg. Corp., 1925-27 faculty asst. and grad. student U. Wis., 1927-29; sec. League of Wis. Municipalities, 1929; prin. examiner Wis. Civil Service Dept. Bur. Personnel, 1930-34; exec. sec. Wis. Civil Service Employees Union, 1933-35; founder and formerly pres. Am. Fedn. of State, County and Municipal Employees, A.F. of L., CIO, hdqrs. Washington; pres. United World Federalists, 1966-67; professorial lectr. U. Wis., Green Bay, 1968-73. Vis. expert OMGUS, Germany, 1949; A.F. of L. rep. to Swedish Public Employees Congress, Stockholm, 1946; frat. del. A.F. of L. to Brit. Trades Union Congress, 1947; gen. bd. AFL-CIO, mem. com. on Security through Arms Control, NPA, 1957, vice chmn., chmn. labor com.; mem. internat. study team to Africa, 1958. Vice pres. World Congress Profl. Employees, Brussels, 1951; cmn. Labor Delegation to Argentina, 1947; mem. council of Nat. Civil Service League; mem. exec. com. internat. trade secretariat for pub. employees, Pub. Services Internat. Chmn. local chpt. Ams. Democratic Action, Washington, 1965. Mem. Pub. Personnel Assn., Wis. Profl. Civil Engrs., Am. Soc. Pub. Adminstrn., Nat. Municipal League, Nat. Planning Assn. (sec.; mem. exec. com. of Canadian-Am. and Brit.-N.Am. coms.), Am. Polit. Sci. Assn., Am. Acad. Polit. and Social Sci. Club: Cosmos (Washington). Home: Green Bay, Wis. Died July 17, 1975.

ZANETTI, JOAQUIN ENRIQUE, professor chemistry; b. St. Domingo, Dominican Republic, Jan. 20, 1885; s. Enrique Lucas and Isabel (Hernandez) Z.; student Roxbury Latin Sch., Boston, Mass., 1901-02; A.B., magna cum laude, Harvard, 1906; A.M., 1907, Ph.D., 1909; m. Esperanza Conill, Apr. 23, 1913 (dec.); 1 son, Juan Conill (died Apr. 24, 1915); m. 2d, Elizabeth Kathryn Born, July 1967. Came to U.S., 1900 naturalized citizen, 1906. Instr. in chemistry, Columbia, 1909-12; dir. Inst. Industrial Chemistry, Montevideo, Uruguay, 1912-13; asst. prof. chemistry, Columbia, 1913-22, asso. prof., 1922-29, professor, 1929-53, professor emeritus from 1953, director of laboratories, 1939-53, associate provost, 1948-50. Served as capt. Ordnance, A.U.S., 1917, captain, lt. col. C.W.S., 1918-19; lt. col. C.W. Res., U.S. Army, 1922-26, col., 1926-74; called to active duty Washington, D.C., July 14, 1941, at Office of Chief Chemical Warfare Service; military observer, London, Aug. 1941; chief Incendiaries Branch, C.W.S., Sept. 1941-June 1942; asst. mil. attache, London, July 1942-Mar. 1944; chief, Special Projects Division, C.W.S., April-Sept. 1944; returned inactive status Nov. 10, 1944; retired June 28, 1948, Honorary Reserve, since 1948. Army War College, 1930; mem. Board Consulting Experts, C.W.S., U.S. Army. Liaison officer French C.W.S., 1917-18; sec. for U.S. of Inter-Allied Congress for Chem. Warfare, Paris, 1918; officer in charge C.W.S., Dist. of Paris 1919. Del. to Internat. Union Pure and Applied Chemistry, Paris 1919, Cambridge, Eng., 1923, Copenhagen, 1924; cons. expert on chem. warfare to League of Nations, 1922-26. Mem. Am. Chem. Soc. Nat. Research Council (chmn. div. chemistry and chem. tech., 1923-24; exec. com. 1924-25). Decorated D.S.M. (U.S.), Legion Merit (U.S.) Distinguished Service Order, Order Brit. Empire (Eng.); Chevalier Legion d'Honneur (France); Officer Crown of Italy. Author: The Significance of Nitrogen, 1932; Fire From the Air, The ABC of Incendiaries, 1941; also tech. papers. Home: Germantown, N.Y. Died Jan. 26, 1974; buried Woodlawn Cemetery, N.Y.C.

ZELLER, HARRY A, v.p., treas. W.Va. Rail Co.; b. Girard, O., Oct. 25, 1871; s. Louis and Rosina (Hahn) Z.; ed. pub. and high schs., Girard; m. Evalyn May Probst, Oct. Oct. 15, 1896; children—Sylvia, Margaret (dec.). Clerk in store Girard, 1885-88; asst. postmaster, Girard, 1888-90; office boy and yard clk. Trumbull Iron Co., 1890-92; paymaster Union Iron & Steel Co., 1892-93; shipping clk. same and O Pomeroy (O.) Iron & Steel Co., 1893-99; supt. Am. S. H. Carnegie Steel Co., 1899-1902, Schonthal Iron & Steel Co., Cumberland, Md., 1902-05; gen. supt. Md. Rail Co., Cumberlband, 1905-06; traveled for Schonthal Iron Co., Columbus, O., 1906-07; organizer, 1907, treas. and gen. mgr. The W.Va. Rail Co., 1907-12; v.p. and gen. mgr. from 1912. Dist. chmn. four-minute men, 2d tr. camp, Ft. Benjamin Harrison; mem. War Labor and War Resources bds., Council of Defense, Liberty Loan, Thrift Stamps, Am. Red Cross, Salvation Army, Y.M.C.A., Jewish and Catholic drives, World War; chmn. Citizen's Corp. com., "flu" epidemic, 1918; dir. Community Chest, Park Bd., Boys' Work; dir. Salvation Army Bd.; Y.M.C.A. Bd., Cabell County War Memorial Arch Assn. Mem. W.Va. Mfrs. Assn. (dir.), Jobbers and Mfrs. Bureau (dir., pres.), Huntington Chamber of Commerce (ex-pres.), W.Va. State Chamber Commerce (dir.). Republican. Episcopalian. Clubs: Rotary (pres.), Huntington Manufacturers' (pres.), Guyandot, Guyan Country. Home: Huntington, W.Va†

ZERAN, FRANKLIN ROYALTON, educator; b. Chgo., Dec. 13, 1906; s. Roy and Anna (Henricks) Z.; A.B., U. Wis., 1930, A.M., 1932, Ph.D., 1937; m. Margaret A. Fritschier, June 27, 1936 (dec. Sept. 9, 1953); 1 dau., Mary Kay. Asst. dean U. of Wis., 1930-32; dir. testing and guidance, Manitowoc, Wis., 1932-40; specialist in occupational information and guidance U.S. Office Edn., Washington, 1940-45, 1946-Feb. 1947, for counseling pupil personnel and work program, Feb.-Nov. 1947; registrar, dir. admissions and dir. testing bur. U. N.M., 1945-46; became asso. dean Sch. of Edn., Ore. State U., 1947, dean, 1948-68, prof. edn., 1968-72, prof. emeritus, dean emeritus, 1972-74, dir. summer sessions, 1948-64; mem. staff U. of N.C., summer 1940, N.C. State Coll. Agr. and Engring., summers 1940-41. George Washington U., summer 1941, 1941-42, Utah State Coll. Agr., summer 1942, La. State U., summer 1943, also Marshall Coll., U. of N.D., S.D. State Coll. Agr., U. of Ky., U. of Mo., 1945, Ore. State Coll., U. of Ga., 1947, dept. edn. workshop, B.C. Provincial Govt., 1948, 49, 53. Franklin R. Zeran Meml. Loan Fund established in his honor Ore. State U. Mem. Am. Psychol. Assn., Am. Personnel and Guidance Assn., Am. Vocational Assn., Kappa Delta Pi, Phi Delta Kappa, Pi Sigma Alpha, Phi Eta Sigma, Phi Kappa Phi. Chmn. Kiwanis Internat. com. on vocational guidance, 1940. Editor series of guidance books, How to Do, for McGraw Hill Book Co., 1945; gen. editor for Chartwell House, Inc. Author varies forms of publs. relating to field. Home: Corvallis, Ore. Died May 1, 1974.

ZHUKOV, GEORGI KONSTANTNOVICH, Russian marshall, govt. ofcl.; b. Strelkova, Russia, 1895; student pub. schs., Moscow; tng. mechanized warfare Frunze Mil. Acad. for Soviet Officers, 1932; married; two daughters. Apprentice leather dresser and furrier; noncommissioned officer Novgorod Dragons, Army of Czar, 1915; cavalry officer Red Army, 1917; mil. observer for USSR, civil war in Spain, 1936; comdr. Soviet forces Outer Mongolia against 6th Japanese Army, 1938-39; officer Russo-Finnish War, 1939-40; chief gen. staff, vice commissar of def., USSR, 1941; comdr. in chief def. of Soviet capital, 1941; comdr.-in-chief western front, 1941-42; 1st dep. commissar for def., 1942; Soviet mil. adminstr., Germany, also mem. Allied Control Commn., 1945-46; comdr.-in-chief Soviet ground forces, also mem. Supreme Soviet Presidium, 1946; head Soviet mil. mission, Poland, 1948; 1st dep. minister of def., 1953-55, minister def., 1955-57; mem. Central Com. Communist Party, 1953-57. Named gen., 1940, Marshall of Soviet Union, 1943. Decorated Cross of St. George (2), Order of Lenin (5), Order of Suroror, Order Red Banner, Hero of Soviet Union (4), others. Address: Moscow USSR. Died June 18, 1974.

ZIEGLER, KARL, chemist; b. Helsa nr. Kassel, Germany, Nov. 26, 1898; s. Karl and Luise (Rall) Ziegler; student Marburg U.; m. Maria Kurtz, 1922; children—Marianne, Erhart. Lectr., Marburg U., 1923; prof. Heidelberg U., 1927; prof. chemistry, dir. Chem. Inst. U. Halle, 1936, dir. Max Planck Inst. Coal Research, Mülheim-Ruhr, 1943-69, sci. mem. inst., 1969; guest prof. U. Chgo., 1936; Carl Folkers lectr., Madison, Wis., also Urbana, Ill., 1952. Recipient Liebig medal German Chemists' Soc., 1935, Carl Duisberg plaque, 1953; Lavoisier medal French Chem. Soc., 1955; Carl Engler plaque, 1958; Siemens ring, 1961; Nobel prize chemistry, 1963; Swinburne medal Plastics Inst., London, 1964; Pour le mérite for Scis. and Arts, 1969; also numerous other awards for discoveries in chemistry of carbon compounds, devel. of plastics. Mem. German Chemists' Soc., N.Y. Acad. Scis., Royal Soc. (London), Royal Soc. (Edinburgh), other sci. acads. Home: Müiheim-Ruhr Germany. Died Aug. 11, 1973; interred Mülheim-Ruhr, Germany.

ZIELKE, GEORGE ROBERT, newspaper corr.; b. LaCrosse, Wis., Apr. 15, 1911; s. Otto C. and Hulda (Ulrich) Z.; student La Crosse Tcrs. Coll., 1928-30; A.B., U. Wis., 1932; m. Ruth Hungate, July 3, 1936; 1 dau., Betty. Reporter editor LaCrosse (Wis.) Tribune, 1927-36; with A. P., 1936-44; Washington corr. Toledo Blade, Pitts. Post-Gazette, 1944-73. Mem. Sigma Delta Chi, Phi Mu Alpha Sinfonia. Clubs: National Press (Washington). Home: Alexandria Va. Died Sept. 10, 1973.

ZIGROSSER, CARL, museum curator; b. Indpls., Sept. 28, 1891; s. Hugo A. and Emma (Haller) Z.; B.A., Columbia, 1911, postgrad., 1911-12; Litt.D., Temple U., 1961; m. Florence King 1915 (dec. 1945); 1 dau., Carola; m. 2d, Laura Canade, 1946. With Keppel & Co., N.Y.C., 1912-17; research at United Engring. Socs. Library, 1917-18; dir. Weyhe Gallery, N.Y., 1919-40; curator prints, drawings, rare books Phila. Mus. Art, 1941-63; vice dir., 1955-63, curator emeritus, from 1964; cons. graphic art Carnegie Study of Arts in U.S. Exhbn. curatorial retrospective Phila. Mus. Art, 1964. Trustee Solomon R. Guggenheim Mus., from 1952. Guggenheim fellow, 1939, 40, Recipient medal Phila. Watercolor Club. 1945; Distinguished Achievement medal Phila. Art Alliance, 1959. Mem. Print Club Phila. (hon. pres.), Print Council Am. (life), Phi Beta Kappa. Editor (with introduction): Twelve Prints by Contemporary Am. Artists, 1919; Lithographs by Lautrec, 1946. Author: Fine Prints, Old and New, 1937; Six Centuries of Fine Prints, 1937; The Artist in America, 1942; Kaethe Kollwitz, 1946; Book of Fine Prints, 1948; Caroline Durieux, 1949; Masterpieces of Drawing, 1950; Ars Medica, 1955, 59; The Expressionsits: A Survey of their Graphic Art, 1957; Mauricio Lasansky, 1960; Misch Kohn, 1961; Guide to the Collecting and Care of Original Prints, 1965; Multum in Parvo, 1965; The Complete Etchings of John Marin, 1969; Prints and Drawings of Kaethe Kollwitz, 1969; Medicine and the Artist, 1970; The Appeal of Prints, 1970; My Own Shall Come to Me, a Personal Memoir, 1971. Editor and contbr. to Prints; Thirteen Essays, 1962. Home: Montagnola, Switzerland., Died Nov. 26, 1975.

ZIMMERMAN, EDWARD AUGUST, physician; b. Dayton, O., Nov. 29, 1906; B.S., U. Dayton, 1929; M.D., St. Louis U., 1931; m. Katherine Janice Matlockee, Apr. 8, 1932; children—Dolores Z. Randerson, Doris Z. Lampe, Norman, Paul. Intern, St. Elizabeth Hosp., Dayton, 1931-32, preceptorship in obstetrics and gynecology, 1932-38; preceptorship in obstetrics and gynecology St. Ann Maternity Hosp., Dayton, 1932-38; postgrad. in obstetrics and gynecology Boston Lying-In Hosp., Harvard, 1938; commd. officer U.S. Army, 1941, advanced through grades to col.; chief obstetrics and gynecology sect. Brooke Gen. Hosp., San Antonio, 1945-46, fellow, 1947-48; chief obstet. and gynecol. service Gorgas Hosp., C.Z., Panama, 1946-50, Letterman Gen. Hosp., San Francisco, 1950-58, Tripler Gen. Hosp., Honolulu, 1958-61, Walter Reed Gen. Hosp., Washington, 1961-68; ret., 1968; asso. clin. prof. George Washington U., Washington, 1961-68, Georgetown U., 1961-68; prof. dept. obstetrics and gynecology U. N.M. Sch. Medicine, Albuquerque, 1969-74; also chief gynecologic oncology service; cons. Indian Health Service, St. Joseph's, Presbyn., VA, Sandia Base, Meml., Gallup, Osteo. hosps. (all Albuquerque); former cons. to surgeon gen. Decorated Legion of Merit; recipient award N.M. chpt. Am. Cancer Soc., 1973, Profl. Service award Bernalillo County Unit. Edward A. Zimmerman Meml. Chapel, Bernalillo County U. N.M. Affiliated Hosp. named in his honor. Diplomate Am. Bd. Obstetrics and Gynecology (former examiner). Mem. A.M.A. (vice chmn. sect. council on obstetrics and gynecology, rep.

from nat. council on obstetrics and gynecology to intersplty. com. 1967-70), Am. Coll. Obstetricians and Gynecologists (chmn. armed forces dist. hist. com. 1963-66, mem. exec. bd. 1962-68, 1st v.p. 1967-68, 2d v.p. 1973-74, mem. ad hoc com. on Indian affairs, adv. com.), Assn. Mil. Surgeons U.S. Roman Catholic. Contbr. articles to med. jours. Home: Albuquerque, N.M.

ZOBEL, HAROLD, physician; b. Grodna, Russia, June 30, 1899; s. Charles and Tessie Zobel; M.D., State U. N.Y., Bklyn., 1921; m. Natalie Fishman, Nov. 21, 1925; children—Gloria, Rosalie, James Stuber, Rovert Silver. Intern, Beth Moses Hosp., Bklyn., 1921-23; postgrad. in psychiatry, 1946-47; chief continued treatment service VA Hosp., Northport, N.Y. Served from capt. to maj. M.C., AUS, 1944-46. Diplomate Am. Bd. Psychiatry and Neurology. Mem. A.M.A., Am. Psychiat. Assn. Home: New York City, N.Y. Died Mar. 4, 1967; buried Beth David Cemetery, Elmont, N.Y.

ZORBACH, WILLIAM WERNER, educator; b. Sandusky, O., June 15, 1916; s. William and Helen (Werner) Z.; B.S., Bowling Green State U., 1947; Ph.D., McGill U., 1951; m. Betty Canfield June 28, 1946; 1 dau., Judy Lynne. Instr. Bowling Green (O.) State U., 1951-52; asst. prof. chemistry Georgetown U., Washington, 1952-56; research chemist SIM, Bethesda, Md., 1957-58; asso. prof. chemistry Georgetown U., Washington, 1958-64, prof., 1964-67; dir. bio-organic chemistry Gulf South Research Inst., New Iberia, La., 1967-69; prof. chemistry Mich Tech. U., Boughton, 1969-70. Served with C.E., AUS, 1943-45. Fellow Am. Inst. Chemists; mem. Am. Chem. Soc., Am. Amaryllis Soc., Nat. Wildlife Fedn., N.Y. Acad. Scis., Sigma Xi, Alpha Chi Sigma. Home: Houghton Mich. Died June 28, 1970.

ZUCKERBROD, MORRIS, physician; b. Bklyn., 1914; M.D., State U. N.Y., Bklyn., 1938. Intern, L.I. Coll. Hosp., Bklyn., 1938-39, Kings County Hosp., Bklyn., 1939-40; resident in medicine Goldwater Meml. Hosp., Welfare Island, N.Y.C., 1946-47, research fellow in medicine, 1947-48; attending physician Maimonides Hosp., Bklyn.; clin. asst. prof. medicine State U. N.Y., Bklyn. Served to maj. M.C., AUS, 1942-46. Diplomate Am. Bd. Internal Medicine. Fellow A.C.P.; mem. A.M.A. Home: Brooklyn, N.Y. Died 1971; interred Beth David Cemetery, Elmont, N.Y.

ZUCKERMAN, HARRY, physician; b. N.Y.C., Sept. 20, 1899; s. Ignatz and Hannah (Klein) Z.; M.D., Fordham U., 1920; m. Anne Wiener, Aug. 18, 1929; children—Frederick W., Harriet A. Intern, Harlem Hosp., 1920-22; Gouverneur Hosp., 1922-23; tng. in gen. pediatrics Mt. Sinai Hosp., 1927, tng. in child psychiatry, 1928; emeritus prof. pediatrics, cons. pediatrician Polyclin. Hosp. and Med. Sch., N.Y.C.; asst. vis. physician Willard Parker Hosp. for contagious Disease, N.Y.C.; attending pediatrician, mem. med. bd. Med. Arts Center Hosp. Chmn. N.Y. County Certified Milk Commn. Served with U.S. Army, World War I. Diplomate Am. Bd. Pediatrics. Fellow Am. Acad. Pediatrics; mem. A.M.A. Home: New York City, N.Y. Died Apr. 20, 1973; buried Westchester Hills, Hastings-on-Hudson, N.Y.

ZUKOR, ADOLPH, motion picture mfr.; b. Ricse, Hungary, Jan. 7, 1873; s. Jacob and Hannah (Lieberman) Z.; ed. in Hungary, and evening schs., New York; m. Lottie Kaufman, Jan. 10, 1897; children—Eugene James, Mrs. Mildred Loew. Came to U.S., 1888; engaged in hardware, upholstery and fur business, New York and Chicago; assoc., 1904, with Mitchell Mark, who was owner of the Strand Theatre, New York, and with Marcus Loew, presenting vaudeville and motion pictures; founder of Famous Players Film Co., 1912; chmn. bd. emeritus Paramount Pictures Corp. Jewish religion. Mason. Clubs: Lambs, City Athletic (N.Y.) Address: New York City, N.Y.†

ZUR BURG, FREDERICK WILLIAM, educator; b. Asheville, N.C., Sept. 7, 1905; s. William Harmon and Rose (Green) zur B.; B.S., U. N.C., 1927, M.S., 1928; Ph.D., Va. Poly. Inst., 1943; m. Pheme Blanton, June 20, 1931; children—Peggy (Mrs. John H. Fry), Frederick W. Instr. Miss. State Coll., 1928-29; successively instr., asst. prof., asso. prof., head dept. chem. engring. Clemson U., 1929-42; head dept of chemical engring. to dean of engring., dir. research Southwestern Louisiana Inst. (name now changed to U. of Southwestern La.), 1942-70, also dir. radiation laboratories cons. Dept. Commerce and Industry State La., 1943 Lafourche Sugar Co., 1945, U.S. Dept. Agr., 1946, U.C. C.E., 1947, 53, 58-59, Gamma Industries, 1952-53; dir. research problem control aquatic weeds in navigable inland waters U.S. C.E., 1959-70; cons. water purification problems; mem. Lafayette Auditorium Commn., 1960, La Industry Engring. Coll. Council. Bd. dirs., council trustees Gulf South Research Inst. Mem. La. State Bd. Registration Profl. Engrs. and Land Surveyors, sec., 1966, chmn., 1968. Registered profl. engr., La., Ga. Member Am. Chem. Soc., Engring. Edn., Am. Inst. Chem. Engrs., La. Engring. Soc. (recipient Technical Achievement medal 1966), La. Tchrs. Assn., Nat. Soc. Profl. Engrs., Nat. Council State Bd. Engring. Examiners. Sigma Xi, Phi Kappa Phi, Tau Beta Pi, Phi Eta Sigma. Presbyn. Home: St. Augustine Fla. Died Mar. 17, 1974; buried Anderson, S.C.

ZURCHER, ARNOLD JOHN, educator, writer; b. S. Amherst, O., Oct. 20, 1902; s. John and Elizabeth (Berger) Z.; A.B., Oberlin Coll., 1924; A.M., Cornell U., 1926; Ph.D., Princeton, 1928; m. Marie Moore Elder, June 27, 1929; children—Arnold John, Elizabeth Anne (Mrs. Carl H. Janzen). Instr., Sulphur Springs (O.) High Sch., 1924-25; Andrew D. White fellow in social sci. Cornell U., 1925-26; Charlotte E. Procter fellow in politics Princeton, 1927-28; instr. history and govt. Emory U., summer 1928; instr. N.Y.U., 1928, prof. politics emeritus; v.p., exec. dir., trustee Alfred P. Sloan Found., 1945-68; lectr. politics Princeton, 1938; vis. prof. govt. Yale, 1943-44; civilian lectr. War Dept. Sch. Mil. Govt., Charlottesville, Va., 1943-44; occasional lectr. Indsl. Coll. Armed Forces, Naval War Coll., Inter-Am. Def. Coll. Dir. Inst. Postwar Reconstrn., N.Y. U., 1943-45. Mem. adv. council Sch. Indsl. Mgmt., Mass. Inst. Tech.; trustee, past pres. Taraknath Das Found.; past trustee, mem. exec. com. Found. Library Center; past mem. vis. com. Grad. Sch. Edn., Harvard; trustee Nat. Council on Philanthropy. Decorated Golden Cross Order of Phoenix (Greece). Mem. Polish Inst. Arts and Scis. in Am. (council), N.Y. Council Fgn. Relations, Am. Polit. Sci. Assn., Am. Assn. U. Profs., Phi Beta Kappa Assos. (life), Phi Beta Kappa. Club: The Century Association. Author: Experiment with Democracy in Central Europe, 1933; Propaganda and Dictatorship (with H.L. Childs and others), 1936; The Governments of Continental Europe (with J.T. Shotwell et al.), 1940, 2d edit., 1952; Postwar European Federation (with Count R.N. Coudenhove-Kalergi et al), 1943; Dictionary of Economics (with H. S. Sloan), 1949, 5th edit., 1970; The Struggle to Unite Europe 1940-58, 1959, Italian edit., 1964. Co-author: The Dictionary of Am. Politics, rev. edits., 1949, 55, 68; co-editor: Postwar Goals and Economic Reconstruction, 1944; Postwar Economic Society, 1944; America's Place in the World Economy, 1945; editor and contbr. Constitutions and Constitutional Trends, 1951, German edit. 1956; (with Elmer Plischke et al.) Systems of Integrating the International Community, 1964; The Management of American Foundations, 1972; (with Jane Dustan) The Foundation Administrator, 1972. Editor or co-author of textbooks on polit. sci.; contbr. to encys., periodicals. Home: Pelham N.Y. Died July 9, 1974.

ZWEIG, BEN, fgn. service officer; b. Columbia, Ill., Mar. 8, 1898; s. Fred and Magdalene (Rehg) Z.; m. Lia Robert, June 24, 1933; children—Caroline (Mrs. Frank J. Dudzienski, Jr.), Charles, Robert, Frederick. Clk. fgn. service, Guatemala City, also San Jose, Costa Rica, 1924-36; vice consul, Tegucigalpa, San Jose, then Nogales, 1936-46; consul. Nogales, Havana, Rome, Mexico City, then Nuevo Laredo, 1946-63; exec. dir. OEO, Santa Cruz County City of Nogales, 1964-67, dir. Santa Cruz County Neighborhood Youth Corps, 1969-70. Mem. adv. bd. Salvation Army, Laredo, Tex. Served with USMC, 1916-20, 21-24. Home: Tucson, Ariz., Died Mar. 24, 1973.

ZWICKY, FRITZ, astrophysics; b. Varna, Bulgaria (citizen of Switzerland), Feb. 14, 1898; s. Fridolin and Franziska (Wreck) Z.; B.S. in Physics, Federal Inst. of Tech., Zurich, Switzerland, 1920, Ph.D., 1922; m. Margaritha Anna Zuercher, Oct. 15, 1947; children—Margrit, Franziska, Barbara. Came to the United States in 1925. Research assistant Fed. Inst. Tech., Zurich, 1920-25; internat. research fellow Calif. Inst. Tech., Rockefeller Foundation, 1925-27, asst. prof., theoretical physics, 1927-29, asso. prof., 1929-41, prof. of astrophysics, 1942-68, professor emeritus, 1968-74; dir. research Aerojet Engring. Corporation, Azusa, Calif., 1943-49, technical adviser, chief research cons., 1949-61; astronomer Mount Wilson and Palomar Observatories, from 1948. Chmn. bd. trustees Pestalozzi Found. Am., 1958. Recipient Presidential Medal of Freedom, 1949. Mem. Am. and Swiss phys. socs., Am. Astron. Soc., Internat. Acad. Astronautics (v.p. 1967), Soc. for Morphological Research (pres., founder 1961). Clubs: Swiss Alpine (Glarus, Switzerland); French Alpine (Lyons, France). Author: Morphological Astronomy, 1957; Morphology of Propulsive Power, 1962; Discovery, Invention, Research, 1969. Contbr. numerous articles to Am., Swiss and German sci. mags. Inventor aeropulse, hydropulse, hydroturbojet, monopropellants, coruscatives. Patentee in field. Home: Pasadena, Cal. Died Feb. 8, 1974; interred Mollis, Switzerland.

A

ADAMS, Myron Winslow 1
ADAMS, Nathan 5
ADAMS, Nehemiah H
ADAMS, Nicholson Barney 5
ADAMS, Numa Pompilius 2
  Garfield
ADAMS, Oliver Stephen 1
ADAMS, Oscar Fay 1
ADAMS, Oscar Sherman 4
ADAMS, Otto Vincent 5
ADAMS, Parmenio 1
ADAMS, Philip 6
ADAMS, Porter Hartwell 2
ADAMS, R. R. 3
ADAMS, Ralph Snyder 1
ADAMS, Randolph 3
  Greenfield
ADAMS, Raymond Fletcher 3
ADAMS, Robert Jr. 1
ADAMS, Robert Brooks 3
ADAMS, Robert H
  Huntington
ADAMS, Robert J. 4
ADAMS, Robert Morton 5
ADAMS, Robert Newton 4
ADAMS, Robert Simeon 3
ADAMS, Roger 3
ADAMS, Romanzo 2
ADAMS, Samuel H
ADAMS, Samuel * 1
ADAMS, Samuel Barnard 1
ADAMS, Samuel Hopkins 3
ADAMS, Samuel Shugert 1
ADAMS, Silas H
ADAMS, Stephen H
ADAMS, Suzanne 5
ADAMS, Thomas H
ADAMS, Thomas Sewall 4
ADAMS, Thurston Madison 4
ADAMS, Walter Sydney 3
ADAMS, Warren Austin 1
ADAMS, Washington Irving 2
  Lincoln
ADAMS, Wayman 3
ADAMS, Weston Woollard 6
ADAMS, Wilbur Louis 4
ADAMS, William H
ADAMS, William II 1
ADAMS, William A. 1
ADAMS, William Edward 6
ADAMS, William Forbes 1
ADAMS, William Grant 1
ADAMS, William H. 3
ADAMS, William Henry 1
ADAMS, William Jackson 1
ADAMS, William Milton 3
ADAMS, William 4
  Montgomery
ADAMS, William Taylor H
ADAMS, William Wirt H
ADAMS, Winston Davis 1
ADAMSON, Alfred 1
ADAMSON, Charles 1
ADAMSON, J. E. 4
ADAMSON, Robert 2
ADAMSON, William 1
  Charles
ADANK, J. L. 5
ADCOCK, Clarence Lionel 6
ADCOCK, Edmund David 3
ADDAMS, Clifford Isaac 2
ADDAMS, Jane 1
ADDAMS, William H
ADDEMAN, Joshua 1
  Melancthon
ADDERLEY, Julian Edwin 6
ADDICKS, Frank F. 3
ADDICKS, George B. 1
ADDICKS, John Edward 1
ADDICKS, Lawrence 6
ADDICKS, Walter Robarts 1
ADDINGTON, Keene 1
  Harwood
ADDINGTON, Sarah 1
ADDIS, Thomas 4
ADDISON, Daniel Dulany 1
ADDISON, James Thayer 1
ADDISON, Julia de Wolf 4
ADDISON, William H. F. 4
ADE, George 2
ADEE, Alvey Augustus 1
ADENAUER, Konrad 4
ADERHOLD, Arthur 6
  Chairrier
ADERHOLD, Omer Clyde 5
ADERS, Oral Madison 6
ADGATE, Andrew H
ADGATE, Asa H
ADGATE, Frederick 1
  Whitney
ADIE, David Craig 2
ADKINS, Charles 1
ADKINS, Curtis D. 5
ADKINS, Galen Horatio 4
ADKINS, Homer 3

ADKINS, Homer Martin 4
ADKINS, Jesse Corcoran 3
ADKINS, John Scudder 1
ADKINS, Leonard Dawson 4
ADKINS, William H. 4
ADLER, Alfred H
ADLER, Alfred 4
ADLER, Betty 6
ADLER, Buddy M. 4
ADLER, Clarence 5
ADLER, Cyrus 1
ADLER, Dankmar 1
ADLER, David 3
ADLER, Elmer 1
ADLER, Emanuel Philip 2
ADLER, F. Charles 3
ADLER, Felix 1
ADLER, Frederick Henry 4
  Herbert
ADLER, Freyda Nacque 5
ADLER, George J. 1
ADLER, Herman Morris 1
ADLER, Isaac 4
ADLER, Joel B. 6
ADLER, Julius Ochs 3
ADLER, Leopold 5
ADLER, Max 3
ADLER, Samuel H
ADLER, Simon Louis 1
ADLERBLUM, Nima H. 4
ADLUM, John H
ADNEY, Edwin Tappan 3
ADOLPHE, Albert Jean 1
ADOUE, Jean Baptiste Jr. 3
ADRAIN, Garnett Bowditch H
ADRAIN, Robert H
ADRIAN, G. 3
ADRIAN, William 5
  Lawrence
ADRIANCE, John Sabin 4
ADSON, Alfred Washington 3
AEBERSOLD, Paul C. 4
AFFEL, Herman Andrew 6
AFFELDER, William L. 4
AFFLECK, Benjamin 2
  Franklin
AFFLECK, James Gelston 5
AFRICA, John Simpson 1
AGA KHAN, Aga Sultan 3
  Mohamad Shah
AGAR, John Giraud 1
AGAR, William 5
  Macdonough
AGASSIZ, Alexander 1
AGASSIZ, Elizabeth Cabot 1
AGASSIZ, George Russell 3
AGASSIZ, Jean Louis H
  Rodolphe
AGASSIZ, Rodolphe Louis 1
AGATE, Alfred T. H
AGATE, Frederick Styles H
AGEE, Alva 2
AGEE, James H
AGEE, James 4
AGER, Waldemar 1
AGERSBORG, H. P. K. 5
AGETON, Arthur Ainslie 5
AGG, Thomas Radford 2
AGGELER, William Tell 1
AGGER, Eugene Ewald 4
AGNELLI, Joseph B. 5
AGNEW, Andrew Davison 3
AGNEW, Benjamin Lashells 4
AGNEW, Cornelius Rea H
AGNEW, Daniel 1
AGNEW, David Hayes H
AGNEW, Eliza H
AGNEW, George Harvey 5
AGNEW, Hugh Elmer 5
AGNEW, Janet Margaret 4
AGNEW, P. G. 2
AGNEW, Peter Lawrence 5
AGNEW, Walter D. 5
AGNEW, William Henry 1
AGNEW, William John 3
  Clarke
AGNON, Shmuel Yosef 5
  Halevi
AGNUS, Felix 1
AGOOS, Solomon 3
AGRAMONTE, Aristides 1
AGRY, Warren C. 3
AGUILAR, Roberto 3
  Trigueros
AGUINALDO, Emilio H
AGUINALDO, Emilio 4
AHALT, Arthur M. 3
AHERN, Eugene Leslie 4
AHERN, Leo James 6
AHERN, Mary Eileen 1
AHERN, Michael Joseph 4
AHL, Henry Hammond 5
AHL, John Alexander H
AHL, Orville Walter 4
AHLPORT, Brodie E. 5

AHLQUIST, Miriam Sweet 6
  (Mrs. Carl Gustaf
  Ahlquist)
AHLQUIST, Robert 4
  Wilhelm
AHMAD, King of Yemen 4
AHMANSON, Howard 5
  Fieldstead
AHRENS, Edward Hamblin 2
AHRENS, Mary A. 4
AHRENS, Theodore 1
AID, George Charles 1
AIELLO, Gaetan Rudolph 6
AIGLER, Ralph William 5
AIKEN, Alfred Lawrence 2
AIKEN, Charles Augustus H
AIKEN, Charles Avery 1
AIKEN, Charles Francis 1
AIKEN, Charles Sedgwick 1
AIKEN, Conrad Potter 6
AIKEN, David Wyatt H
AIKEN, E. Clarence 4
AIKEN, Ednah (Mrs. 5
  Charles Sedgwick Aiken)
AIKEN, Frank Eugene 1
AIKEN, Gayle 4
AIKEN, George L. H
AIKEN, Howard Hathaway 5
AIKEN, John Adams 1
AIKEN, Paul C. 6
AIKEN, Robert Leon 5
AIKEN, William H
AIKEN, William Appleton 1
AIKEN, William Hamblen 6
AIKEN, William Martin 1
AIKEN, Wyatt 2
AIKENS, Andrew Jackson 1
AIKENS, Charles Thomas 1
AIKIN, Wilford Merton 4
AIKINS, Herbert Austin 4
AIKMAN, Walter Monteith 2
AIKMAN, William 1
AILES, John William III 3
AILES, Milton Everett 1
AILSHIE, James Franklin 4
AILSHIE, Margaret Cobb 3
AILSHIE, Robert 2
AIME, Valcour H
AIMES, Hubert Hilary 5
  Suffren
AINEY, William David 1
  Blakeslee
AINSLIE, George 1
AINSLIE, George 2
AINSLIE, Hew H
AINSLIE, James Stuart 4
AINSLIE, Peter 1
AINSWORTH, Edward 5
  Maddin
AINSWORTH, Frank 2
  Kenley
AINSWORTH, Fred 1
  Crayton
AINSWORTH, John 3
  Churchill
AINSWORTH, Walden L. 4
AINSWORTH, William 2
  Newman
AIRD, Alexander N. 3
AIREY, Charles Theodore 1
AIREY, John 1
AIREY, Richard 1
AIRHART, John C. 5
AISHTON, Richard Henry 2
AITCHISON, Clyde Bruce 4
AITCHISON, John Young 1
AITCHISON, Robert J. 4
AITKEN, David D. 1
AITKEN, Peter 4
AITKEN, Robert H
AITKEN, Robert Grant 3
AITKEN, Robert Ingersoll 3
AKAR, John J. 6
AKE, Russell Everett 4
AKED, Charles Frederic 1
AKELEY, Carl Ethan 1
AKELEY, Healy Cady 1
AKELEY, Lewis Ellsworth 4
AKELEY, Mary L. Jobe 4
AKERBERG, Herbert 4
  Vestner
AKERMAN, Alexander 4
AKERMAN, Amos Tappan H
AKERMAN, John D. 5
AKERS, Benjamin Paul H
AKERS, Elizabeth 1
AKERS, Lewis Robeson 6
AKERS, Milburn Peter 5
AKERS, Oscar Perry 5
AKERS, Sheldon 6
  Buckingham
AKERS, Thomas Peter 4
AKERSON, George Edward 1
AKHARAJ VARADHARA, 4
  Phya
AKIN, John 4

AKIN, Margaret Catherine 6
  Rouse (Mrs. Austin
  Franklin Akin)
AKIN, Spencer Ball 6
AKIN, Theron 1
AKIN, Thomas Russell 2
AKINS, Zoe 3
ALA, Hussein 4
ALABASTER, Francis 3
  Asbury
ALANSON, Bertram 3
  Edward
ALARCON, Hernando H
ALBACH, George H. 4
ALBANI, Emma H
ALBANI, Emma 4
ALBANI, Madame 3
ALBARDA, Horatius 4
ALBAUGH, George 5
  Sylvanus
ALBAUGH, John W. 1
ALBEE, Edward F. 1
ALBEE, Ernest 1
ALBEE, Fred Houdlett 3
ALBEE, John 1
ALBEE, Percy F. 4
ALBER, David O. 5
ALBER, Louis John 4
ALBERS, George 5
ALBERS, Henri 4
ALBERS, Homer 2
ALBERS, Joseph H. 4
ALBERS, William Henry 4
ALBERT, A(braham) 5
  Adrian
ALBERT, Allen Diehl 1
ALBERT, Allen Diehl Jr. 5
ALBERT, Aristides 1
  Elphonso Peter
ALBERT, Calvin Dodge 5
ALBERT, Charles Stanley 1
ALBERT, Charles Sumner 1
ALBERT, Clifford Edmund 4
ALBERT, Elma Gates 3
ALBERT, Ernest 2
ALBERT, Henry 1
ALBERT, Brother Sylvester 4
ALBERT, William Julian H
ALBERTS, Joseph Ortan 4
ALBERTSON, Abraham 1
  Horace
ALBERTSON, Charles 3
  Carroll
ALBERTSON, George 1
  Roger
ALBERTSON, J. MARK 4
ALBERTSON, James 1
  Herbert
ALBERTSON, Nathaniel H
ALBERTSON, Ralph 3
ALBERTY, (Bernard) 5
  Harold
ALBERY, Bronson James 3
ALBERY, Faxon Franklin 4
  Duane
ALBIG, John William 4
ALBING, Otto Frederick 1
ALBION, James Francis 4
ALBREN, Edward Joseph 6
ALBRIGHT, Adam Emory 3
ALBRIGHT, Charles H
ALBRIGHT, Charles 6
  Clinton
ALBRIGHT, Charles Edgar 2
ALBRIGHT, Charles H
  Jefferson
ALBRIGHT, Edward 1
ALBRIGHT, Edwin 1
ALBRIGHT, Frank Herman 1
ALBRIGHT, Fuller 5
ALBRIGHT, Guy Harry 5
ALBRIGHT, Jacob H
ALBRIGHT, Jacob 5
  Dissinger
ALBRIGHT, John Joseph 1
ALBRIGHT, Percy R. 1
ALBRIGHT, Raymond Wolf 4
ALBRIGHT, Robert Choate 6
ALBRIGHT, William 5
  Foxwell
ALBRIZIO, Humbert 5
ALBRO, Addis 1
ALBRO, Mrs. Curtis 3
  Sanford
ALCIATORE, Roy Louis 4
ALCOCK, Nathaniel 1
  Graham
ALCORN, Douglas Earle 4
ALCORN, Hugh Mead 3
ALCORN, James Lusk H
ALCORN, Roy Anvil 6
ALCOTT, Amos Bronson H
ALCOTT, Carroll Duard 4
ALCOTT, Louisa May H
ALCOTT, William Andrus H
ALDEN, Bertram F. H

ALDEN, Carlos Coolidge 4
ALDEN, Carroll Storrs 5
ALDEN, Charles Henry 1
ALDEN, Charles Henry 3
ALDEN, Ebenezer 3
ALDEN, Edward S. 3
ALDEN, Ezra Hyde 2
ALDEN, George Henry 4
ALDEN, Henry Mills 1
ALDEN, Herbert Watson 3
ALDEN, Ichabod 1
ALDEN, Isabella 1
  Macdonald
ALDEN, James H
ALDEN, John H
ALDEN, John 1
ALDEN, John B. 1
ALDEN, Joseph H
ALDEN, Mrs. Cynthia May 1
  Westover
ALDEN, Raymond 1
  Macdonald
ALDEN, Timothy H
ALDEN, William Clinton 4
ALDEN, William Livingston 1
ALDEN, William Tracy 3
ALDER, Byron 3
ALDER, Kurt 4
ALDERMAN, Edward 4
  Sinclair
ALDERMAN, Edwin 1
  Anderson
ALDERMAN, Frank 6
ALDERMAN, Grover 1
  Henry
ALDERMAN, Rhenas 5
  Hoffard
ALDERMANN, Lewis R. 5
ALDERSON, Victor Clifton 2
ALDERSON, Wroe 4
ALDINGTON, Richard 4
ALDIS, Arthur Taylor 1
ALDIS, Dorothy Keeley 4
ALDIS, Graham 4
ALDIS, Mary Reynolds 2
ALDIS, Owen Franklin 1
ALDRED, John Edward 2
ALDREY Y MONTOLIO, 1
  Pedro de
ALDRICH, Anne Reeve H
ALDRICH, Auretta Roys 1
ALDRICH, Bess Streeter 3
ALDRICH, Charles 1
ALDRICH, Charles 2
  Anderson
ALDRICH, Charles Henry 1
ALDRICH, Charles John 1
ALDRICH, Charles 6
  Spaulding
ALDRICH, Chester Hardy 1
ALDRICH, Chester Holmes 1
ALDRICH, Chilson Darragh 2
ALDRICH, Cyrus H
ALDRICH, Darragh 4
ALDRICH, Donald 4
  Bradshaw
ALDRICH, Edgar 1
ALDRICH, Edward Burgess 3
ALDRICH, George Ames 1
ALDRICH, Henry Clay 1
ALDRICH, Herbert Lincoln 4
ALDRICH, James H
ALDRICH, John Gladding 1
ALDRICH, John Gladding 5
ALDRICH, John Merton 1
ALDRICH, Kildroy Philip 5
ALDRICH, Leander 4
  Jefferson
ALDRICH, Louis 1
ALDRICH, Louise Banister 6
  (Mrs. Truman Aldrich)
ALDRICH, Loyal Blaine 4
ALDRICH, Lynn Ellis 6
ALDRICH, Mary Jane 1
ALDRICH, Mildred 1
ALDRICH, Morton Arnold 3
ALDRICH, Nelson 1
  Wilmarth
ALDRICH, Orlando W. 4
ALDRICH, Perley Dunn 1
ALDRICH, Richard 1
ALDRICH, Richard S. 1
ALDRICH, Richard S. 2
ALDRICH, Sherwood 1
ALDRICH, Thomas Bailey 1
ALDRICH, Truman 1
  Heminway
ALDRICH, William H
ALDRICH, William 1
  Farrington
ALDRICH, William Sleeper 4
ALDRICH, William Truman 4
ALDRICH, Winthrop 6
  Williams
ALDRIDGE, Clayson 2
  Wheeler

456

ALDRIDGE, George Washington 4
ALDRIDGE, Ira Frederick H
ALDRIDGE, Walter Hull 3
ALDUNATE, Don Santiago 1
ALEMANY, Jose Sadoc H
ALENCASTRE, Stephen Peter 2
ALERDING, Herman Joseph 1
ALESHIRE, Arthur William 1
ALESHIRE, Edward 4
ALESHIRE, James Buchanan 1
ALESSANDRI-PALMA, Arturo 5
ALESSANDRONI, Walter Edwin 4
ALEXANDER, Abraham H
ALEXANDER, Adam H
ALEXANDER, Adam Rankin H
ALEXANDER, Albert Victor 4
ALEXANDER, Armstead Milton H
ALEXANDER, Barton Stone H
ALEXANDER, Ben 2
ALEXANDER, Carter 4
ALEXANDER, Charles 5
ALEXANDER, Charles Beatty 1
ALEXANDER, Charles McCallon
ALEXANDER, Charles Tripler
ALEXANDER, Charlton 1
ALEXANDER, Christine 6
ALEXANDER, Clyde C. 4
ALEXANDER, Clyde H. 6
ALEXANDER, Cosmo H
ALEXANDER, DeAlva Stanwood 1
ALEXANDER, Donald 3
ALEXANDER, Douglas 2
ALEXANDER, Eben 1
ALEXANDER, Edward Albert 2
ALEXANDER, Edward Porter 1
ALEXANDER, Evan Shelby H
ALEXANDER, Francesca 1
ALEXANDER, Francis H
ALEXANDER, Franz 4
ALEXANDER, Frederick 5
ALEXANDER, George 1
ALEXANDER, George F. 2
ALEXANDER, Grace 5
ALEXANDER, Gross 1
ALEXANDER, Harold David 5
ALEXANDER, Hartley Burr
ALEXANDER, Hattie Elizabeth 5
ALEXANDER, Henry Clay 5
ALEXANDER, Henry Martyn
ALEXANDER, Henry Martyn 3
ALEXANDER, Henry Porteous H
ALEXANDER, Herbert G. B.
ALEXANDER, Hooper 1
ALEXANDER, Hubbard Foster 3
ALEXANDER, James H
ALEXANDER, James Jr. H
ALEXANDER, James F. 1
ALEXANDER, James Patterson 2
ALEXANDER, James Strange
ALEXANDER, James Waddel H
ALEXANDER, James Waddell 1
ALEXANDER, James Waddell II 5
ALEXANDER, Jerome 3
ALEXANDER, John H
ALEXANDER, John 3
ALEXANDER, John Brevard 4
ALEXANDER, John E.
ALEXANDER, John Henry H
ALEXANDER, John L. 1
ALEXANDER, John Macmillan 3
ALEXANDER, John Romich
ALEXANDER, John White 1

ALEXANDER, Joseph Addison H
ALEXANDER, Joshua W. 1
ALEXANDER, Julian Power 3
ALEXANDER, Leigh 2
ALEXANDER, Lester Fisher 3
ALEXANDER, M. Moss 3
ALEXANDER, Magnus Washington 1
ALEXANDER, Maitland 1
ALEXANDER, Mark H
ALEXANDER, Minnie (Rebecca) 5
ALEXANDER, Moses 1
ALEXANDER, Nathaniel 1
ALEXANDER, Oakey Logan 2
ALEXANDER, Paul W. 4
ALEXANDER, Raymond Pace 6
ALEXANDER, (Richard) Thomas 5
ALEXANDER, Robert H
ALEXANDER, Robert 1
ALEXANDER, Robert C. 1
ALEXANDER, Samuel Davies H
ALEXANDER, Samuel Nathan 5
ALEXANDER, Sir William 3
ALEXANDER, Stephen H
ALEXANDER, Suydenham B. 4
ALEXANDER, Taliaferro 1
ALEXANDER, Truman Hudson 2
ALEXANDER, Vance J. 4
ALEXANDER, Wallace 1
ALEXANDER, Walter R. 3
ALEXANDER, Wilford S. 3
ALEXANDER, Will Winton 3
ALEXANDER, William H
ALEXANDER, William 1
ALEXANDER, William Albert 2
ALEXANDER, William DeWitt
ALEXANDER, William Henry
ALEXANDER, William Leidy 5
ALEXANDER, William McFaddin 1
ALEXANDER, William Valentine 3
ALEXANDERSON, Ernst Frederick Werner 6
ALEXIS, Algert Daniel 4
ALEXY, Janko 5
ALEY, Robert Judson 1
ALFANO, Vincenzo
ALFARO, Colon Eloy 3
ALFARO, Ricardo Joaquin 5
ALFARO, Victor Ricardo 6
ALFONCE, Jean H
ALFORD, Julius Caesar H
ALFORD, Leon Pratt 1
ALFORD, Leon Pratt 2
ALFORD, Mrs. Nell 3
ALFORD, Theodore Crandall 2
ALFORD, William Hays 4
ALFRED, Frank H. 4
ALFREDSON, Bernard V(ictor) 5
ALFRIEND, Edward Morrisson 4
ALGER, Cyrus H
ALGER, Frederick M. Jr. 4
ALGER, George William 4
ALGER, Horatio Jr. H
ALGER, John Lincoln 4
ALGER, Philip Rounseville 1
ALGER, Russell Alexander 1
ALGER, William Rounseville 1
ALI, Anwar 6
ALI, Mohammed 4
ALI KHAN, Liaquat 3
ALINSKY, Saul * David 5
ALISON, Francis H
ALLAIRE, James Peter H
ALLAIRE, William Herbert 1
ALLAN, Chilton H
ALLAN, Denison Maurice 6
ALLAN, John H
ALLAN, John J. 4
ALLARD, John S. 4
ALLARDICE, Robert Edgar 1
ALLDERDICE, Norman 4
ALLDREDGE, Eugene Perry
ALLDREDGE, J. Haden 4

ALLEE, James Frank 1
ALLEE, Marjorie Hill 2
ALLEE, Warder Clyde 3
ALLEFONSCE, Jean H
ALLEMAN, Gellert 2
ALLEMAN, Herbert Christian
ALLEMANG, Herbert John 4
ALLEN, Abel Leighton
ALLEN, Addison 4
ALLEN, Alexander John 5
ALLEN, Alexander Viets Griswold 1
ALLEN, Alfred 2
ALLEN, Alfred Gaither 1
ALLEN, Alfred Reginald 1
ALLEN, Amos Lawrence 1
ALLEN, Andrew H
ALLEN, Andrew Aniel 4
ALLEN, Andrew Hussey 1
ALLEN, Andrew Jackson 1
ALLEN, Andrews 1
ALLEN, Anthony Benezet 1
ALLEN, Arch Turner 1
ALLEN, Arthur Augustus 4
ALLEN, Arthur Francis 2
ALLEN, Arthur Moulton 3
ALLEN, Arthur Watts 3
ALLEN, Arthur Wilburn 3
ALLEN, Austin Oscar 4
ALLEN, Benjamin 1
ALLEN, Benjamin 3
ALLEN, Benjamin Franklin 5
ALLEN, Benjamin Leach 1
ALLEN, Bennet Mills 4
ALLEN, Beverly Sprague 1
ALLEN, Calvin Francis 2
ALLEN, Carlos Eben 3
ALLEN, Charles H
ALLEN, Charles 1
ALLEN, Charles Claffin 1
ALLEN, Charles Claflin 6
ALLEN, Charles Curtis 1
ALLEN, Charles Dexter 1
ALLEN, Charles Edward 1
ALLEN, Charles Elmer 3
ALLEN, Charles Herbert 1
ALLEN, Charles Julius 1
ALLEN, Charles Lucius 1
ALLEN, Charles Metcalf 3
ALLEN, Charles Morse 1
ALLEN, Charles Ricketson 2
ALLEN, Charles Warrenne 1
ALLEN, Chester Arthur 4
ALLEN, Claxton Edmonds 3
ALLEN, Clay 1
ALLEN, Clinton L. 4
ALLEN, Courtney 5
ALLEN, Crombie 2
ALLEN, David Oliver H
ALLEN, Devere 3
ALLEN, Don B. 4
ALLEN, Don Cameron H
ALLEN, Dudley Peter 1
ALLEN, Duff S. 1
ALLEN, Edgar 2
ALLEN, Edgar Van Nuys 4
ALLEN, Edmund Thompson 1
ALLEN, Edward Archibald 4
ALLEN, Edward Bartlett 4
ALLEN, Edward Ellis 3
ALLEN, Edward Mortimer 4
ALLEN, Edward Normand 5
ALLEN, Edward Patrick 1
ALLEN, Edward Tyson 3
ALLEN, Edwin Brown 6
ALLEN, Edwin Madison 2
ALLEN, Edwin West 1
ALLEN, Eliot Dinsmore 5
ALLEN, Elisha Hunt 1
ALLEN, Eric William 2
ALLEN, Ernest Bourner 1
ALLEN, Ethan 3
ALLEN, Ethan 1
ALLEN, Eugene Thomas 4
ALLEN, Ezra Griffen 3
ALLEN, F. Sturges 1
ALLEN, Florence Ellinwood 4
ALLEN, Frances 1
ALLEN, Francis Henry 4
ALLEN, Francis Richmond 1
ALLEN, Frank 1
ALLEN, Frank Bigelow 3
ALLEN, Frank G. 5
ALLEN, Frank Philip Jr. 2
ALLEN, Frank Waller 1
ALLEN, Fred 3
ALLEN, Fred Hovey 1
ALLEN, Fred William Jr. 6
ALLEN, Frederic De Forest H
ALLEN, Frederic Winthrop 1
ALLEN, Frederick Baylies 1
ALLEN, Frederick Hobbes 4
ALLEN, Frederick Innes 1

ALLEN, Frederick James 1
ALLEN, Frederick Lewis 3
ALLEN, Frederick Madison 6
ALLEN, Freeman Harlow 1
ALLEN, Gardner Weld 2
ALLEN, Geo A. Jr. H
ALLEN, George H
ALLEN, George Edward 5
ALLEN, George Garland 5
ALLEN, George Henry 3
ALLEN, George Venable 5
ALLEN, George Walton 6
ALLEN, George Washington Holker
ALLEN, George 1
ALLEN, George Whiting 1
ALLEN, Glover Morrill 2
ALLEN, Gordon 5
ALLEN, Gordon Forrest 6
ALLEN, Gracie 2
ALLEN, Grant 1
ALLEN, Grosvenor Noyes 5
ALLEN, Guy Fletcher 3
ALLEN, Hamilton Ford 4
ALLEN, Hans H
ALLEN, Harris Campbell 5
ALLEN, Harrison H
ALLEN, Heman * H
ALLEN, Henry Jr. 4
ALLEN, Henry Butler 4
ALLEN, Henry Crosby 5
ALLEN, Henry D. 4
ALLEN, Henry Justin 2
ALLEN, Henry Tureman H
ALLEN, Henry Watkins H
ALLEN, Hope Emily 4
ALLEN, Horace Eugene 5
ALLEN, Horace Newton H
ALLEN, Horatio H
ALLEN, Howard Cameron 4
ALLEN, Hubert A. 2
ALLEN, Ida Bailey 6
ALLEN, Ira H
ALLEN, Ira Wilder 1
ALLEN, J. Weston 1
ALLEN, James 1
ALLEN, James E. 4
ALLEN, James Edward 2
ALLEN, James Edward Jr. 1
ALLEN, James Henry 3
ALLEN, James Lane 1
ALLEN, James Turney 2
ALLEN, Jean Malven (Mrs. Frederick H. Allen) 6
ALLEN, Jeremiah Mervin H
ALLEN, Joel Asaph 1
ALLEN, John * H
ALLEN, John Alpheus 6
ALLEN, John Beard 1
ALLEN, John Clayton 3
ALLEN, John Denby 4
ALLEN, John Eliot 2
ALLEN, John F. H
ALLEN, John James H
ALLEN, John Johnson 4
ALLEN, John Kermott 4
ALLEN, John Mills 1
ALLEN, John Rex 5
ALLEN, John Robert 4
ALLEN, John Stevenson 4
ALLEN, John Wesley 4
ALLEN, John Weston 2
ALLEN, John William 1
ALLEN, Joseph H
ALLEN, Joseph Dana 4
ALLEN, Joseph Henry H
ALLEN, Joseph Holmes 5
ALLEN, Judson H
ALLEN, Julian 1
ALLEN, Junius 4
ALLEN, Kenneth 1
ALLEN, Laurence Edmund (Larry) 6
ALLEN, Leo Elwood 5
ALLEN, Leon Menard 1
ALLEN, Leroy 2
ALLEN, Lewis Falley H
ALLEN, Lewis George 1
ALLEN, Louis J. 1
ALLEN, Lucy Ellis 1
ALLEN, Lyman Whitney 1
ALLEN, M. Marshall 3
ALLEN, Mrs. Marion Boyd 1
ALLEN, Martha Meir 1
ALLEN, Maryland 1
ALLEN, Milton Irving 4
ALLEN, Nat Burtis 2
ALLEN, Nathan H
ALLEN, Nathaniel 1
ALLEN, Nellie Burnham 5
ALLEN, Paul H
ALLEN, Paul S. 6
ALLEN, Perry S. 1
ALLEN, Philip H
ALLEN, Philip Loring 1
ALLEN, Philip Ray 4

ALLEN, Philip Schuyler 1
ALLEN, Ralph 4
ALLEN, Ralph Clayton 4
ALLEN, Ray 1
ALLEN, Richard H
ALLEN, Richard Day 2
ALLEN, Richard Frazer H
ALLEN, Richard Lamb H
ALLEN, Riley Harris 4
ALLEN, Robert * H
ALLEN, Robert E. Lee 4
ALLEN, Robert Emmet 3
ALLEN, Robert Gray 4
ALLEN, Robert H. 2
ALLEN, Robert I. 4
ALLEN, Robert McDowell 4
ALLEN, Robert Porter 4
ALLEN, Roderick Random 5
ALLEN, Rolland Craten 2
ALLEN, Russell Morton 4
ALLEN, Samuel Clesson H
ALLEN, Samuel Edward 1
ALLEN, Samuel G. 3
ALLEN, Samuel James McIntosh 5
ALLEN, Sherman 2
ALLEN, Sidney J. 3
ALLEN, Stephen Haley 1
ALLEN, Sturges 3
ALLEN, Thomas H
ALLEN, Thomas 1
ALLEN, Thomas Grant 4
ALLEN, Thomas M. H
ALLEN, Thomas Stinson 2
ALLEN, Timothy Field 1
ALLEN, Viola 2
ALLEN, Walter 1
ALLEN, Walter Barth 2
ALLEN, Walter Cleveland 2
ALLEN, William * H
ALLEN, William Fitch 3
ALLEN, William Francis H
ALLEN, William Frederick 1
ALLEN, William H. Jr. 2
ALLEN, William Henry * H
ALLEN, William Hervey 2
ALLEN, William Joshua 1
ALLEN, William Orville 1
ALLEN, William Ray 1
ALLEN, William Reynolds 1
ALLEN, William Sims 3
ALLEN, William Vincent 1
ALLEN, Willis H
ALLEN, Willis Boyd 1
ALLEN, Wilmar Mason 3
ALLEN, Wyeth 5
ALLEN, Zachariah H
ALLENDOERFER, Carl 6
ALLENDOERFER, Carl W. 3
ALLENSON, Hazel Sandiford 6
ALLER, Howard Lewis 3
ALLERTON, Isaac H
ALLERTON, Samuel Waters 1
ALLERUP, Paul Richard 6
ALLEY, Calvin Lane 5
ALLEY, Charles Edwin (C. Ed) 5
ALLEY, James Pinckney 1
ALLEY, John Bassett H
ALLEY, Rayford W. 4
ALLEZ, George Clare 3
ALLGOOD, Dwight Maurice
ALLGOOD, Miles Clayton 6
ALLIBOXE, Samuel Austin H
ALLIN, Arthur 1
ALLIN, Bushrod Warren 5
ALLIN, Cephas Daniel 1
ALLIN, George Litchfield 5
ALLIN, George R. 6
ALLIN, Roger H
ALLINE, Henry H
ALLING, Arthur Nathaniel 2
ALLING, Asa Alling 1
ALLING, Harold Lattimore 4
ALLING, John Wesley 1
ALLING, Joseph Tilden 1
ALLING, Paul Humiston 2
ALLINGTON, Homer C. 4
ALLINSON, Anne Crosby Emery 1
ALLINSON, Francis Greenleaf 1
ALLIOT, Hector 1
ALLIS, Edward Phelps H
ALLIS, Edward Phelps Jr. 4
ALLIS, James Ashton 6
ALLIS, Louis 3
ALLIS, Oscar Huntington 1
ALLIS, Oswald Thompson 5
ALLISON, Fred 6
ALLISON, James Jr. H
ALLISON, James Boyd

ALLISON, James Edward 5
ALLISON, James Nicholls 1
ALLISON, John H
ALLISON, John 2
  Maudgridge Snowden
ALLISON, John P. 4
ALLISON, Nathaniel 1
ALLISON, Noah Dwight 5
ALLISON, Richard H
ALLISON, Robert H
ALLISON, Robert Burns 6
ALLISON, Samuel King 4
ALLISON, William Boyd 5
ALLISON, William Henry H
ALLISON, William Henry 2
ALLMAN, David Bacharach 5
ALLMAN, Justin Paul 5
ALLMAN, Leslie Coover 4
ALLMOND, Marcus Blakey 4
ALLOUEZ, Claude Jean H
ALLPORT, Fayette Ward 3
ALLPORT, Frank 4
ALLPORT, Gordon Willard 4
ALLPORT, Gordon Willard 5
ALLRED, James V. 3
ALLSOPP, Clinton Bonfield 4
ALLSOPP, Frederick 2
  William
ALLSTON, Robert Francis H
  Withers
ALLSTON, Washington H
ALLTON, James Miller 6
  (Tom)
ALLWARDT, Henry 1
  Augustus
ALLWORK, Eleanor Bloom 5
  (Mrs. Ronald Allwork)
ALLYN, Arden Lacey 4
ALLYN, Arthur Cecil 4
ALLYN, Harriett May 3
ALLYN, Robert H
ALLYN, Stanley Charles 5
ALMACK, John C. 3
ALMAND, Claude Marion 3
ALMERT, Harold 3
ALMON, Edward Berton 1
ALMOND, James Edward 3
ALMOND, Nina 4
ALMSTEDT, Hermann 5
  Benjamin
ALMY, Frederic 1
ALMY, John Jay H
ALMY, Robert Forbes 5
ALONSO, Amado 3
ALPERS, William Charles 1
ALPHONSA, Mother 1
ALPHONSA, Mother 4
ALRICH, Samuel Nelson 1
ALSBERG, C. Lucas 1
ALSCHULER, Alfred S. 1
ALSCHULER, Benjamin 5
  Philip
ALSCHULER, Samuel 1
ALSOP, George H
ALSOP, John H
ALSOP, Joseph Wright 3
ALSOP, Reese Fell 4
ALSOP, Richard H
ALSOP, Stewart Johonnot 6
  Oliver
ALSTON, Angus Sorensen 6
ALSTON, George L. 4
ALSTON, Joseph H
ALSTON, Lemuel James H
ALSTON, Philip Henry 6
ALSTON, Robert Cotten 1
ALSTON, William Jeffreys H
ALSTON, Willis H
ALSTORK, John Wesley 5
ALT, Howard Lang 5
ALTE, Visconde de 3
ALTER, David H
ALTER, Dinsmore 5
ALTER, George Elias 1
ALTER, Lucien Weaver 4
  Scott
ALTER, Nicholas M(ark) 5
ALTER, Wilbur McClure 6
ALTERMAN, Zipora 6
  Stephania Balaban
ALTGELD, John Peter 1
ALTGLASS, Max Mayer 3
ALTHAM, John 4
ALTHAUS, Edward 4
ALTHAUSER, Norman Ray 4
ALTHER, Joseph G. 6
ALTHERR, Alfred 5
ALTHOFF, Henry 2
ALTHOUSE, Harry Witman 1
ALTHOUSE, Howell 5
  Halberstadt
ALTHOUSE, Paul Marcks 4
ALTHOUSE, Paul Shearer 3
ALTMAIER, Clinton John 3
ALTMAN, Benjamin 2
ALTMAN, Benjamin 4

ALTMAN, Julian Allen 6
ALTMAN, Oscar Louis 5
ALTMEYER, Arthur Joseph 5
ALTON, Alfred Edward 4
ALTON, Charles De Lancey 4
ALTROCCHI, Julia Cooley 6
  (Mrs. Rudolph Altrocchi)
ALTROCCHI, Rudolph 3
ALTSCHULER, Modest 5
ALTSHELER, Joseph H
  Alexander
ALTVATER, H. Hugh 4
ALVARADO, Juan Bautista H
ALVAREZ, Alejandro 5
ALVERSON, Claude B. 1
ALVEY, Henry F(red) 5
ALVEY, Richard Henry 1
ALVORD, Benjamin H
ALVORD, Benjamin 1
ALVORD, Clarence 1
  Walworth
ALVORD, Corydon Alexis H
ALVORD, Elisworth 5
  Chapman
ALVORD, Henry Elijah 1
ALVORD, Idress Head 5
  (Mrs. Clarence W.
  Alvord)
ALVORD, James Church H
ALVORD, James Church 4
ALVORD, John Watson 2
ALVORD, Katharine 5
  Sprague
ALWARD, Herbert 6
  Vaughan
ALWAY, Frederick James 5
ALWOOD, Olin Good 3
ALWOOD, William 1
  Bradford
ALWORTH, Royal D. 4
ALWYNE, Horace 6
ALY KHAN, Shah 4
AMADAS, Phillip H
AMATEIS, Louis H
AMATEIS, Louis 4
AMATO, Pasquale 2
AMBAUEN, Andrew 4
  Joseph
AMBERG, Emil 2
AMBERG, Harold Vincent 4
AMBERG, Julius H. 3
AMBERG, Richard Hiller 4
AMBERG, Samuel 5
AMBLER, Benjamin Mason 1
AMBLER, Charles Henry 3
AMBLER, Chase P. 1
AMBLER, Frank Rhoades 4
AMBLER, James Markham H
  Marshall
AMBLER, James Murray 4
AMBLER, Mason Gaither 2
AMBLER, Sara Ellmaker 1
AMBROSE, Arthur Warren 3
AMBROSE, Paul 4
AMBRUSTER, Howard 1
  Watson
AMBRUSTER, Watson 1
AMDUR, Isadore 5
AMELI, Howard Wilmurt 4
AMELIA H
AMELL, Howard Wilmurt 6
AMEN, Harlan Page 1
AMEN, John Harlan 3
AMEND, Bernhard 3
  Gottwald
AMEND, Edward Bernard 1
AMENT, James E. 1
AMERMAN, Lemuel 1
AMERMAN, Ralph Alonzo 1
AMES, Adelbert Jr. 3
AMES, Butler 3
AMES, Charles Bismark 1
AMES, Charles Gordon 1
AMES, Charles Wilberforce 1
AMES, Edgar 2
AMES, Edward Elbridge 3
AMES, Edward Raymond 4
AMES, Edward Scribner 3
AMES, Eleanor Kirk 1
AMES, Ezra H
AMES, Fisher H
AMES, Fisher 1
AMES, Frederick Lothrop H
AMES, Herman Vandenburg 1
AMES, Hobart 2
AMES, James Barr H
AMES, James Barr 1
AMES, James Barr 4
AMES, James Tyler H
AMES, Jesse Hazer 5
AMES, John Griffith 1
AMES, John Griffith H
AMES, John Lincoln 4
AMES, John Ormsbee 1
AMES, Joseph Alexander H

AMES, Joseph Bushnell 1
AMES, Joseph Sweetman 2
AMES, Knowlton Lyman 1
AMES, Lewis Darwin 5
AMES, Louis Annin 3
AMES, Mary Lesley 1
AMES, Nathan Peabody H
AMES, Nathaniel H
AMES, Norman Bruce H
AMES, Oakes H
AMES, Oakes 3
AMES, Oliver * H
AMES, Oliver H
AMES, Robert Parker Marr 4
AMES, Samuel H
AMES, Susie M(ay) 5
AMES, William 1
AMES, William Lafayette 3
AMES, Winthrop 1
AMEY, Harry Burton 3
AMEZAGA, Juan Jose 3
AMHERST, Jeffery H
AMICK, Erwin Hamer Jr. 1
AMIDON, Beulah 3
AMIDON, Charles Fremont 1
AMIDON, Samuel Barker 1
AMIGER, William Thomas 4
AMMANN, Othmar 4
  Hermann
AMMAR, Abbas Moustafa 6
AMMEN, Daniel H
AMMEN, Jacob H
AMMEN, Samuel Zenas 4
AMMIDOWN, Edward 4
  Holmes
AMMONS, Elias Milton 1
AMMONS, Eugene (Gene) 6
AMMONS, Teller 5
AMORY, Arthur 1
AMORY, Charles Walter 1
AMORY, Harcourt 5
AMORY, John James 1
AMORY, Robert 1
AMORY, Robert 5
AMORY, Thomas H
AMORY, William H
AMOS, Frank R. 4
AMOS, Thyrsa Wealhtheow 4
AMOS, William Frederick 5
AMOSS, Harold L. 3
AMRINE, William 5
  Frederick
AMSBARY, Frank C. Jr. 4
AMSBARY, Wallace Bruce 4
AMSLER, Henry Moore 6
AMSTER, Nathan Leonard 1
AMSTUZ, John O. 4
AMWEG, Frederick James 1
AMYOT, Louis Joseph 5
  Adjutor
ANAGNOS, Julia Romana H
  Howe
ANAGNOS, Michael H
ANAGNOS, Michael 4
ANAST, James Louis 4
ANASTASSY, 5
ANCENEY, Charles L. 1
ANCERL, Karel 6
ANDEREGG, Frederick 1
ANDERES, Robert L. 3
ANDERLEDY, Anthony 1
  Maria
ANDERMAN, William 4
ANDERS, James Meschter 1
ANDERS, John Daniel 1
ANDERS, Paul R. 4
ANDERS, Thomas Jefferson 1
ANDERSEN, Albert M. 3
ANDERSEN, Andreas 6
  Storrs
ANDERSEN, Arthur 2
  Edward
ANDERSEN, Arthur Olaf 1
ANDERSEN, Bjorn 5
ANDERSEN, Christian 5
  Schmidt
ANDERSEN, Hendrik 1
  Christian
ANDERSEN, Hendrik 2
  Christian
ANDERSEN, James Roy 5
ANDERSEN, John Dlbos 5
ANDERSEN, Joyce 5
  Marilyn Off (Mrs. Chester
  W. Andersen)
ANDERSON, Abraham H
  Archibald
ANDERSON, Abraham 2
  Archibald
ANDERSON, Ada 4
  Woodruff
ANDERSON, Alan Ross 6
ANDERSON, Albert 5
ANDERSON, Albert 2
ANDERSON, Albert Barnes 1
ANDERSON, Alden 2

ANDERSON, Alexander H
ANDERSON, Alexander H
  Outlaw
ANDERSON, Alexander 2
  Pierce
ANDERSON, Alvin George 6
ANDERSON, Amabel A. 1
ANDERSON, Amos Carey 5
ANDERSON, Andrew 4
  Freeman
ANDERSON, Andrew 3
  Runni
ANDERSON, Andrew 2
  Work
ANDERSON, Anton 6
  Bennett
ANDERSON, Arch W. 2
ANDERSON, Archibald 4
  Watson
ANDERSON, Arthur Julius 5
ANDERSON, Arthur 4
  Marvin
ANDERSON, Asher 1
ANDERSON, Axel Gordon 6
ANDERSON, Axel Henry 5
ANDERSON, Benjamin 2
  McAlester
ANDERSON, Carl C. 1
ANDERSON, Carl Harold 6
ANDERSON, Carl Magnus 5
ANDERSON, Carl Thomas 2
ANDERSON, Carlotta 1
  Adele
ANDERSON, Chandler 1
  Parsons
ANDERSON, Charles 4
  Albert
ANDERSON, Charles 5
  Hardin
ANDERSON, Charles 6
  Joseph
ANDERSON, Charles 5
  Loftus Grant
ANDERSON, Charles 1
  Palmerston
ANDERSON, Clifford Le 1
  Conte
ANDERSON, Clinton 6
  Presba
ANDERSON, David Allen 5
ANDERSON, Dice Robins 2
ANDERSON, Dillon 6
ANDERSON, Donald 3
  Brown
ANDERSON, Douglas 3
  Smith
ANDERSON, Dwight 3
ANDERSON, Dwight 4
ANDERSON, Earl W. 5
ANDERSON, Edgar 5
ANDERSON, Edward 4
ANDERSON, Edward 3
  Delmar
ANDERSON, Edward Lee 5
ANDERSON, Edward 1
  Lowell
ANDERSON, Edward 4
  Wharton
ANDERSON, Edwin 1
  Alexander
ANDERSON, Edwin 4
  Hatfield
ANDERSON, Elam 2
  Jonathan
ANDERSON, Elbert Ellery 4
ANDERSON, Elbridge R. 2
ANDERSON, Elizabeth 1
  Preston
ANDERSON, Elsie Grace 1
ANDERSON, Ernest 3
ANDERSON, Esther L. 5
ANDERSON, Eva Greenslit 6
ANDERSON, F. Paul 1
ANDERSON, Frank 1
ANDERSON, Frank Bartow 1
ANDERSON, Frank 4
  Leonard
ANDERSON, Frank Maley 6
ANDERSON, Frederick 2
  Irving
ANDERSON, Frederick L. 5
ANDERSON, Frederick 4
  Lincoln
ANDERSON, Galusha 1
ANDERSON, George 5
ANDERSON, George A. 5
ANDERSON, George H
  Alburtus
ANDERSON, George 5
  Edward
ANDERSON, George 1
  Everett
ANDERSON, George 6
  LaVerne
ANDERSON, George 1
  Lucius

ANDERSON, George 3
  Minor
ANDERSON, George Smith 1
ANDERSON, George H
  Thomas
ANDERSON, George 1
  Weston
ANDERSON, George 5
  Wood
ANDERSON, Harold 5
ANDERSON, Harold 3
  Durbin
ANDERSON, Harold H
  MacDonald
ANDERSON, Harold V. 4
ANDERSON, Harry 1
  Bennett
ANDERSON, Harry 1
  Reuben
ANDERSON, Harry 3
  William
ANDERSON, Helen Natalie 4
  Johnson
ANDERSON, Henry Clay 1
ANDERSON, Henry Hill H
ANDERSON, Henry James H
ANDERSON, Henry 3
  Tompkins
ANDERSON, Henry 3
  Watkins
ANDERSON, Henry 1
  William
ANDERSON, Howard B. 4
ANDERSON, Hugh H
  Johnston
ANDERSON, Isaac H
ANDERSON, Isabel 2
ANDERSON, J(efferson) 5
  Randolph
ANDERSON, Jacob Nelson 4
ANDERSON, James Arthur 4
ANDERSON, James Cuyler 5
ANDERSON, James 5
  Howard
ANDERSON, James 2
  Nesbitt
ANDERSON, James Patton H
ANDERSON, James R. H
ANDERSON, John H
ANDERSON, John * 3
ANDERSON, John Albert 4
ANDERSON, John 3
  Alexander
ANDERSON, John August 3
ANDERSON, John 3
  Benjamin
ANDERSON, John 1
  Crawford
ANDERSON, John Edward 2
ANDERSON, John Edward 4
ANDERSON, John F. 3
ANDERSON, John Francis 1
ANDERSON, John George 2
ANDERSON, John Hargis 2
ANDERSON, John Jacob 1
ANDERSON, John Murray 3
ANDERSON, John Quincy 6
ANDERSON, John Will 1
ANDERSON, John William 5
ANDERSON, John 6
  W(illiam)
ANDERSON, Joseph H
ANDERSON, Joseph 1
ANDERSON, Joseph 1
  Gaudentius
ANDERSON, Joseph H
  Halstead
ANDERSON, Joseph Reid H
ANDERSON, Joseph Starr 3
ANDERSON, Josiah 1
  McNair
ANDERSON, Karl 3
ANDERSON, Karl Leopold 5
ANDERSON, Larz 5
ANDERSON, Lee 5
ANDERSON, Lee William 6
ANDERSON, Leroy 6
ANDERSON, Leroy Dean 4
ANDERSON, Lewis Flint 1
ANDERSON, Louis Francis 3
ANDERSON, Martin 3
ANDERSON, Martin H
  Brewer
ANDERSON, Mary * H
ANDERSON, Mary * 5
ANDERSON, Mary 5
  Mortlock (Mrs. Walter
  Anderson)
ANDERSON, Maxwell 5
ANDERSON, Melville Best 1
ANDERSON, Merle 5
  Hampton
ANDERSON, Neal Larkin 1
ANDERSON, Nelson Paul 3

ANDERSON, Newton Mitchell
ANDERSON, Nils 4
ANDERSON, Oscar V. 5
ANDERSON, Paul Lewis 4
ANDERSON, Paul N(athaniel) 5
ANDERSON, Paul Vernon 5
ANDERSON, Paul Y. 1
ANDERSON, Peirce 1
ANDERSON, R. T. 4
ANDERSON, Ralph J. 4
ANDERSON, Rasmus Bjorn 1
ANDERSON, Richard Clough H
ANDERSON, Richard Clough Jr. H
ANDERSON, Richard Heron H
ANDERSON, Richard James 5
ANDERSON, Robert H
ANDERSON, Robert Campbell 3
ANDERSON, Robert Earle 4
ANDERSON, Robert Edward Jr. 5
ANDERSON, Robert Gordon 3
ANDERSON, Robert Hargis 4
ANDERSON, Robert van Vleck 2
ANDERSON, Rose 4
ANDERSON, Roy Nels 6
ANDERSON, Rudolph John 4
ANDERSON, Rudolph Martin 4
ANDERSON, Rufus H
ANDERSON, Samuel H
ANDERSON, Samuel Wagner 4
ANDERSON, Sherwood 4
ANDERSON, Simeon H. H
ANDERSON, Sophie H
ANDERSON, Stonewall 1
ANDERSON, Sydney 2
ANDERSON, Thomas Davis 1
ANDERSON, Thomas H. 1
ANDERSON, Thomas Joel Jr. 4
ANDERSON, Thomas Lilbourne H
ANDERSON, Thomas McArthur 1
ANDERSON, Troyer Steele 2
ANDERSON, Victor E. 4
ANDERSON, Victor Emanuel 4
ANDERSON, Victor Vance 2
ANDERSON, W. C. 1
ANDERSON, Walter H
ANDERSON, Walter Alexander 4
ANDERSON, Walter Williams 6
ANDERSON, Wells Foster 3
ANDERSON, Wendell W. 3
ANDERSON, William H
ANDERSON, William 6
ANDERSON, William A. 1
ANDERSON, William A. 3
ANDERSON, William Allison 2
ANDERSON, William Beverly 5
ANDERSON, William Brennan 1
ANDERSON, William Clayton H
ANDERSON, William D. 3
ANDERSON, William Downs 5
ANDERSON, William Dozier 5
ANDERSON, William Franklin 2
ANDERSON, William Gilbert 2
ANDERSON, William Hamilton 3
ANDERSON, William Harry 5
ANDERSON, William Henry 1
ANDERSON, William Joseph Jr. 4
ANDERSON, William Ketcham 2
ANDERSON, William Madison 1
ANDERSON, William Otto 4
ANDERSON, William Thomas 2

ANDERSON, William Thompson 4
ANDERSON, William Wallace H
ANDERSON, Winslow 1
ANDERSON, Winslow Samuel 2
ANDERSSON, Alfred Oscar 3
ANDERTON, Stephen Philbin 2
ANDRADE, Cipriano 1
ANDRE, Floyd 5
ANDRE, John H
ANDRE, Louis H
ANDREA, Frank A. D. 4
ANDREASEN, Milian Lauritz 5
ANDREEN, Gustav Albert 1
ANDRESEN, Albert Frederick Ruger 4
ANDRESEN, August Herman 3
ANDRESS, James Mace 1
ANDRESS, James Mace 2
ANDRESS, Robert Joseph 4
ANDRETTA, S. A. 4
ANDREW, A. Piatt 1
ANDREW, Edwin Lee 6
ANDREW, Hardage L. 1
ANDREW, Harriet White Fisher 1
ANDREW, Henry Hersey 1
ANDREW, James Osgood H
ANDREW, John Albion H
ANDREW, John Forrester H
ANDREW, Joseph Atkins 5
ANDREW, Samuel H
ANDREWES, Sir William (Gerrard) 6
ANDREWS, Addison Fletcher 1
ANDREWS, Adolphus 2
ANDREWS, Alexander Boyd 1
ANDREWS, Alexander Boyd 2
ANDREWS, Alexander Speer 5
ANDREWS, Ambrose H
ANDREWS, Annulet 2
ANDREWS, Arthur Leonard 1
ANDREWS, Avery DeLano 3
ANDREWS, Bert 3
ANDREWS, Charles H
ANDREWS, Charles 1
ANDREWS, Charles Bartlett 1
ANDREWS, Charles Cecil 4
ANDREWS, Charles Edgar Jr. 3
ANDREWS, Charles Henry 2
ANDREWS, Charles McLean 2
ANDREWS, Charles Oscar 2
ANDREWS, Charles Oscar Jr. 5
ANDREWS, Charlton 6
ANDREWS, Chauncey Hummason H
ANDREWS, Christopher Columbus 1
ANDREWS, Clarence Edward 1
ANDREWS, Clarence L. 5
ANDREWS, Clayton Farrington 4
ANDREWS, Clement Walker 1
ANDREWS, Daniel Marshall 1
ANDREWS, Donald Hatch 6
ANDREWS, E. Benjamin 1
ANDREWS, E. Wyllys 1
ANDREWS, Edmund 1
ANDREWS, Edward Gayer 1
ANDREWS, Eliphalet Frazer 1
ANDREWS, Eliza Frances 1
ANDREWS, Elmer Frank 4
ANDREWS, Ethan Allen 1
ANDREWS, Eugene Plumb 4
ANDREWS, Evangeline Walker 4
ANDREWS, Fannie Fern 3
ANDREWS, Frank 1
ANDREWS, Frank L. 6
ANDREWS, Frank Maxwell 2
ANDREWS, Frank Mills 2
ANDREWS, Frank Taylor 1
ANDREWS, Garnett 1
ANDREWS, Garnett 1
ANDREWS, George 1
ANDREWS, George Leonard H

ANDREWS, George 1 Leonard
ANDREWS, George Lippitt 1
ANDREWS, George Pierce 1
ANDREWS, George Rex H
ANDREWS, George Whitfield 1
ANDREWS, George William 5
ANDREWS, Gwendolen Foulke 4
ANDREWS, Harry Eugene 1
ANDREWS, Herbert Marston 1
ANDREWS, Hiram Bertrand 4
ANDREWS, Horace Ellsworth H
ANDREWS, Irene Osgood 5 (Mrs. John B. Andrews)
ANDREWS, Israel DeWolf H
ANDREWS, Israel Ward H
ANDREWS, J. Warren 1
ANDREWS, James DeWitt H
ANDREWS, James Parkhill 1
ANDREWS, Jesse 4
ANDREWS, John 4
ANDREWS, John 3
ANDREWS, John Bertram 1
ANDREWS, John Newman 1
ANDREWS, John Tuttle H
ANDREWS, John Williams 6
ANDREWS, Joseph H
ANDREWS, Julia Lincoln Ray 4
ANDREWS, Justin M. 4
ANDREWS, Landaff Watson H
ANDREWS, Launcelot 1
ANDREWS, Leila Edna 1
ANDREWS, Leland Stanford 5
ANDREWS, Lewis Whiting 4
ANDREWS, Lincoln Clark 3
ANDREWS, Lorrin 1
ANDREWS, Marie Scherer 6
ANDREWS, Marietta Minnigerode 1
ANDREWS, Marshall 6
ANDREWS, Martin Register 1
ANDREWS, Mary Raymond Shipman 1
ANDREWS, Matthew Page 2
ANDREWS, Matthew Thomas 1
ANDREWS, Newton Lloyd 1
ANDREWS, Paul Shipman 2
ANDREWS, Philip 2
ANDREWS, Robert Christie 4
ANDREWS, Robert Day 1
ANDREWS, Robert Macon 5
ANDREWS, Robert Robbins 1
ANDREWS, Roger Mercein 3
ANDREWS, Roland Franklyn 1
ANDREWS, Roy Chapman 3
ANDREWS, Samuel George H
ANDREWS, Samuel James 1
ANDREWS, Schofield 5
ANDREWS, Sherlock James H
ANDREWS, Sidney H
ANDREWS, Sidney Francis 1
ANDREWS, Steffan 3
ANDREWS, Stephen Pearl H
ANDREWS, T. Wingate 1
ANDREWS, Thomas G. 1
ANDREWS, Thomas Galphin 2
ANDREWS, Timothy Patrick H
ANDREWS, Vernon Daniel 1
ANDREWS, W. Earle 4
ANDREWS, Walter Gresham 2
ANDREWS, Walter Pemberton 1
ANDREWS, Wilfred Leslie 3
ANDREWS, William E. 1
ANDREWS, William Given 1
ANDREWS, William Loring 1
ANDREWS, William Noble 5
ANDREWS, William Page 1
ANDREWS, William Shankland 1
ANDREWS, William Watson H
ANDREWS, William Symes 1
ANDREWS, William Williams 1
ANDRIC, Ivo 6
ANDRIEU, Mathuren Arthur H
ANDROS, Sir Edmund H
ANDRUS, Clift 5
ANDRUS, John Emory 1
ANDRUSS, E. Van Arsdale 1

ANFUSO, Victor L. 4
ANGAS, W. Mack 4
ANGEL, Benjamin Franklin H
ANGEL, Franz 6
ANGEL, John 4
ANGEL, William G. 4
ANGELA, Mother H
ANGELESCO, Constantin 2
ANGELI, Pier (Anna Marie 5 Pierangeli)
ANGELL, Alexis Caswell 1
ANGELL, Emmett Dunn 6
ANGELL, Ernest 5
ANGELL, Frank 1
ANGELL, George Thorndike 1
ANGELL, Henry Clay 1
ANGELL, Israel H
ANGELL, James Burrill 1
ANGELL, James Rowland 2
ANGELL, Joseph Kinnicutt H
ANGELL, L(isbeth) 5
ANGELL, Martin Fuller 1
ANGELL, Montgomery B. 3
ANGELL, Sir Norman 4
ANGELL, Norman (Ralph 1 Norman Angell Lane)
ANGELL, Robert Henderson 1
ANGELL, Walter Foster 4
ANGELL, William Gorham H
ANGELL, William Robert 2
ANGELLOTTI, Frank M. 1
ANGER, Sister Mary Alacoque 5
ANGERT, Eugene Henry 1
ANGEVINE, Jay B(ernard) 5
ANGIER, Roswell Parker 2
ANGIER, Walter Eugene 1
ANGLAND, Emmett Cyril 5
ANGLE, Edward Hartley 1
ANGLE, Edward John 1
ANGLE, George Keyser 1
ANGLE, Glenn D(ale) 5
ANGLE, Jay Warren 3
ANGLE, Paul McClelland 6
ANGLE, Wesley Motley 4
ANGLEMAN, Sydney Winfield 5
ANGLIN, Margaret (Mary) 2
ANGLY, Edward 3
ANGOOD, Sidney Bernard 5
ANHEUSER, Eberhard 4
ANISFELD, Boris 6
ANJARIA, Jashwantrai Jayantilal 5
ANKCORN, Charles M. 3
ANKENEY, John Sites 2
ANKENY, John D'Art 2
ANKENY, Levi 1
ANNADOWN, Ruth Vivian 5
ANNAND, Percy Nicol 3
ANOKHIN, Petr Kusmich 6
ANSBERRY, Timothy Thomas 2
ANSCHUTZ, Karl H
ANSEL, Martin Frederick 4
ANSELL, Samuel Tilden 5
ANSERMET, Ernest Alexandre 5
ANSHEN, S. Robert 5
ANSHUTZ, Edward Pollock 1
ANSHUTZ, Thomas Pollock 1
ANSLEY, Clarke Fisher 1
ANSLINGER, Harry Jacob 6
ANSLOW, Gladys Amelia 5
ANSLOW, W. Parker Jr. H
ANSON, Adrian Constantine H
ANSON, Adrian Constantine 4
ANSORGE, Martin Charles 4
ANSPACH, Brooke Melancthon 5
ANSPACHER, Louis Kaufman 2
ANSPRENGER, Aloys George 6
ANSTADT, Henry 1
ANSTED, Harry Bidwell 3
ANSTICE, Henry 1
ANTES, Henry H
ANTES, John H
ANTHEIL, George 3
ANTHON, Charles H
ANTHON, Charles Edward H
ANTHON, John H
ANTHONY, Alfred Williams 1
ANTHONY, Andrew Varick Stout 1
ANTHONY, Ann 1
ANTHONY, Arthur Cox 3
ANTHONY, Benjamin Harris 1

ANTHONY, Brayman William 4
ANTHONY, Daniel Read 1
ANTHONY, Daniel Read Jr. 1
ANTHONY, Donald Elliot 6
ANTHONY, Earle C. 4
ANTHONY, Edward 5
ANTHONY, Ernest Lee 5
ANTHONY, Gardner Chace 1
ANTHONY, George Tobey H
ANTHONY, Henry Bowen H
ANTHONY, John Gould H
ANTHONY, Joseph Biles H
ANTHONY, Katharine Susan 4
ANTHONY, Katharine Susan 5
ANTHONY, Lovick Pierce 5
ANTHONY, Luther B. 3
ANTHONY, Norman (Hume) 5
ANTHONY, Sister Brownell H
ANTHONY, Susan Brownell 1
ANTHONY, William Arnold 1
ANTIN, Mary (Mary Antin 6 Grabau)
ANTISDALE, Louis Marlin 1
ANTISDEL, Clarence Baumes 2
ANTOINE, Josephine Louise 5
ANTOINE, Pere H
ANTON, Mark 5
ANTON, Roberta Charlotte 6 Weiss (Mrs. Aaron Anton)
ANTONIA, Sister 2
ANTONIEWICZ, Wlodzimierz 6
ANTRIM, Doron Kemp 4
ANTRIM, Ernest Irving 3
ANTRIM, Eugene Marion 3
ANTRIM, Minna Thomas 4
ANTROBUS, John H
ANTROBUS, John 4
ANUNDSEN, Brynild 1
ANZA, Juan Bautista de H
AOKI, Viscount Siuzo 4
APES, William H
APGAR, Austin Craig 1
APGAR, Virginia 6
APLIN, Henry Harrison 4
APP, Frank 4
APPEL, Daniel Frederick 1
APPEL, George F(rederick) 5 Baer
APPEL, John Wilberforce Jr. 2
APPEL, Joseph Herbert 2
APPEL, Leon Howard 6
APPEL, Monte 5
APPEL, Theodore 1
APPEL, Theodore Burton 1
APPELT, Frank R. 1
APPENZELLAR, Paul 3
APPENZELLER, Alice Rebecca 3
APPENZELLER, Henry Gerhard H
APPLBAUM, Karl 6
APPLE, Andrew Thomas Geiger 1
APPLE, Henry Harbaugh 2
APPLE, Joseph Henry 2
APPLE, Thomas Gilmore H
APPLEBY, Frank 1
APPLEBY, Thomas Henry 4 Montague Villiers
APPLEBY, Troy Wilson 2
APPLEBY, William Remsen 1
APPLEGATE, Frank G. 1
APPLEGATE, H. W. 4
APPLEGATE, Irvamae Vincent 5
APPLEGATE, Jesse H
APPLEGATE, John Stilwell 1
APPLEGATE, Paul Ray 4
APPLEMAN, Charles Orville 4
APPLESEED, Johnny H
APPLETON, Charles W. 2
APPLETON, Daniel H
APPLETON, Edward Victor 4
APPLETON, Floyd 1
APPLETON, Francis Henry 1
APPLETON, Francis Randall 1
APPLETON, Francis Randall Jr. 6
APPLETON, James H
APPLETON, Jesse H
APPLETON, John * H
APPLETON, John Adams 4

APPLETON, John Howard 1
APPLETON, L. Estelle 1
APPLETON, Nathan H
APPLETON, Nathaniel H
  Walker
APPLETON, Samuel H
APPLETON, Thomas Gold H
APPLETON, William H
APPLETON, William 5
  Channing
APPLETON, William Henry H
APPLETON, William Henry 1
APPLETON, William Hyde 3
APPLETON, William 2
  Sumner
APPLETON, William
  Worthen
APTHORP, William Foster 4
ARAKI, Eikichi 3
ARAMBURU, Pedro 5
  Eugenio
ARANETA, Gregorio 4
ARANNA, Oswaldo 3
ARANT, Herschel Whitfield 1
ARBEELY, Abraham 4
  Joseph
ARBUCKLE, Charles 3
  Nathaniel
ARBUCKLE, Howard Bell 2
ARBUCKLE, John 4
ARBUCKLE, John D. 4
ARBUCKLE, Maclyn 5
ARBUCKLE, Matthew H
ARBUCKLE, Roscoe 1
  Conkling
ARBUS, Diane 5
ARBUTHNOT, Charles 4
  Criswell
ARBUTHNOT, Charles 5
  Criswell
ARBUTHNOT, May Hill 5
  (Mrs. Charles C.
  Arbuthnot)
ARBUTHNOT, Thomas 5
  Shaw
ARBUTHNOT, Wilson S. 1
ARCAYA, Pedro Manuel 5
ARCE, Jose 5
ARCHAMBAULT, A. 3
  Margaretta
ARCHBALD, James VI 1
ARCHBALD, Robert 1
  Wodrow
ARCHBOLD, John Dustin 1
ARCHDALE, John H
ARCHER, Allen Thurman 4
ARCHER, Belle 1
ARCHER, Branch Tanner 5
ARCHER, Clifford Paul 5
ARCHER, Franklin Morse 2
ARCHER, Frederic 4
ARCHER, Gleason Leonard 4
ARCHER, James J. 4
ARCHER, John H
ARCHER, John Clark 3
ARCHER, Julian Lawrence 4
ARCHER, Peter 4
ARCHER, Ralph Curtis 3
ARCHER, Shreve MacLaren 2
ARCHER, Stevenson * H
ARCHER, Thomas P. 2
ARCHER, William Segar 1
ARCHIBALD, Andrew 1
  Webster
ARCHIBALD, Frank C. 1
ARCHIBALD, James 5
  Francis Jewell
ARCHIBALD, Maynard 3
  Brown
ARCHIBALD, Mrs. George 1
ARCHIBALD, Raymond 3
  Clare
ARCHIPENKO, Alexander 4
ARCTOWSKA, Adrian Jane 5
ARCTOWSKI, Henryk 3
ARDEN, Edwin Hunter 1
  Pendleton
ARDEN, Elizabeth 4
ARDERY, William 4
  Breckenridge
ARDISON, Robert Joseph 4
AREF, Abdul Salam 5
ARENALES CATALAN,
  Emilio
ARENBERG, Albert Lee 5
AREND, Harry O. 4
ARENDT, Hannah 6
ARENDT, Morton 5
ARENS, Egmont 5
ARENS, Franz Xavier 1
ARENS, Henry 5
ARENS, Richard 5
ARENSBERG, Walter 3
  Conrad
ARENTS, Albert 4
ARENTS, George 4

ARENTZ, Frederic C. H. 4
AREY, Hawthorne 5
AREY, Melvin Franklin 1
ARGALL, Philip 1
ARGALL, Samuel H
ARGETSINGER, J. C. 3
ARGUELLO, Jose Dario H
ARGUELLO, Leonardo 2
ARGUELLO, Luis Antonio H
  Robertson
ARGYLE, William 4
ARJONA, Jaime Homero 4
ARKELL, Bartlett 2
ARKELL, William Clark 4
ARKELL, William J. 1
ARKUSH, Ralph 4
  Montgomery
ARKWRIGHT, George 5
  Alfred
ARKWRIGHT, Preston 2
  Stanley
ARLEN, Michael 3
ARLISS, George 2
ARMAS, Carlos Castillo 3
ARMBRECHT, William 2
  Henry
ARMBRISTER, Victor 4
  Stradley
ARMBRUSTER, Adolph 3
  Henry
ARMES, William Dallam 4
ARMISTEAD, George H
ARMISTEAD, Henry 3
  Beauford
ARMISTEAD, Henry 3
  Marshall
ARMISTEAD, Jesse Warren 3
ARMISTEAD, Lewis H
  Addison
ARMITAGE, Albert T. 5
ARMITAGE, Merle 6
ARMITAGE, Paul 2
ARMOR, Mrs. Mary 4
  Elizabeth Harris
ARMOUR, A. Watson 3
ARMOUR, Allison Vincent 1
ARMOUR, Bernard R. 2
ARMOUR, Herman Ossian 1
ARMOUR, J. Ogden 1
ARMOUR, Laurance 3
  Hearne
ARMOUR, Lester 5
ARMOUR, Philip Danforth 1
ARMOUR, Philip Danforth 3
ARMS, Frank Thornton 2
ARMS, John Taylor 3
ARMS, Samuel Dwight 4
ARMS, Thomas Seelye 5
ARMSBY, George Newell 2
ARMSBY, Henry Prentiss 1
ARMSTEAD, George 3
  Brooks
ARMSTEAD, Henry Howell 1
ARMSTRONG, A. Joseph 3
ARMSTRONG, Alexander 1
ARMSTRONG, Andrew 1
  Campbell
ARMSTRONG, Anne 3
  Wetzell
ARMSTRONG, Arthur 1
  Henry
ARMSTRONG, Barbara 6
  Nachtrieb
ARMSTRONG, C. Dudley 1
ARMSTRONG, Charles 4
  Dickey
ARMSTRONG, Charles 1
  Wallace
ARMSTRONG, Charles 5
  (Mrs. Jack Lewi)
ARMSTRONG, Clare Hibbs 5
ARMSTRONG, Clyde 6
  Allman
ARMSTRONG, D. 1
  Maitland
ARMSTRONG, Dallas 5
  Warren
ARMSTRONG, David H
  Hartley
ARMSTRONG, David 4
  William
ARMSTRONG, DeWitt 1
  Clinton
ARMSTRONG, Donald 5
  Budd
ARMSTRONG, Edward 1
  Ambler
ARMSTRONG, Edward 2
  Cooke
ARMSTRONG, Edwin H. 3
ARMSTRONG, Frank 5
  Alton Jr.
ARMSTRONG, Frank C. 1
ARMSTRONG, Gayle 1
  Geard

ARMSTRONG, George H
  Buchanan
ARMSTRONG, George H
  Dod
ARMSTRONG, George 1
  Dodd
ARMSTRONG, George 4
  Simpson
ARMSTRONG, George W. 4
  Jr.
ARMSTRONG, George H
  Washington
ARMSTRONG, George 1
  William Jr.
ARMSTRONG, H. C. 5
ARMSTRONG, Hamilton 5
  Fish
ARMSTRONG, Harris 6
ARMSTRONG, Helen 2
  Maitland
ARMSTRONG, Herbert 6
  Deuel
ARMSTRONG, Houston 5
  Churchwell
ARMSTRONG, J. P. Taylor 4
ARMSTRONG, James H
ARMSTRONG, James 1
ARMSTRONG, James 5
  Edward
ARMSTRONG, James 5
  Reverdy
ARMSTRONG, Jesse Evan 4
ARMSTRONG, John * H
ARMSTRONG, John Irvine H
ARMSTRONG, John 2
  Nelson
ARMSTRONG, Joseph 4
  Gillespie 3rd
ARMSTRONG, Leroy 1
ARMSTRONG, Lilian 5
  Harden
ARMSTRONG, Louis 5
ARMSTRONG, Lyndon 2
  King
ARMSTRONG, Lyndon 4
  King
ARMSTRONG, Margaret 2
  Neilson
ARMSTRONG, Maurice 5
  Whitman
ARMSTRONG, Moses 3
  Kimball
ARMSTRONG, Paul 1
ARMSTRONG, Paul 3
  Galloway
ARMSTRONG, Philander 4
  Banister
ARMSTRONG, Richard H. 3
ARMSTRONG, Robert H
ARMSTRONG, Robert 1
  Allen
ARMSTRONG, Robert 2
  Burns
ARMSTRONG, Robert 5
  Hayden
ARMSTRONG, Robert 4
  Helms
ARMSTRONG, Robert 3
  John
ARMSTRONG, Samuel H
  Chapman
ARMSTRONG, Samuel 2
  Treat
ARMSTRONG, Samuel H
  Turell
ARMSTRONG, Thomas Jr. 1
ARMSTRONG, Walter 2
  Preston
ARMSTRONG, William 1
ARMSTRONG, William 2
ARMSTRONG, William C. 1
ARMSTRONG, William 5
  Gilbert
ARMSTRONG, William 4
  Jackson
ARMSTRONG, William 2
  Park
ARMSTRONG, William 1
  Wright
ARMSTRONG-HOPKINS, 4
  Geroge Franklin
ARMSTRONG-HOPKINS, 4
  Saleni
ARN, Elmer Raymond 3
ARN, William Godfrey 5
ARNAL, Leon E. 4
ARNDT, C. O. 4
ARNDT, Elmer Jacob 5
  Frederick
ARNDT, Karl M. 3
ARNDT, Robert Norton 6
  Downs
ARNDT, Walter Tallmadge 1
ARNDT, William Frederick 3
ARNEILL, James Rae 1
ARNESEN, Sigurd J. 4

ARNESON, Ben 3
ARNETT, Alex Mathews 2
ARNETT, Benjamin William 1
ARNETT, Clare Newton 1
ARNETTE, D. W. 4
ARNEY, C. E. Jr. 3
ARNHEIM, Ralph Leroy 6
ARNHOLTZ, Arthur 6
ARNN, Charles Edward 4
ARNO, Peter 4
ARNOLD, Abraham Kerns 4
ARNOLD, Alfred Colburn 4
ARNOLD, Alma Cusian 5
ARNOLD, Almon Al 3
ARNOLD, Arthur 4
ARNOLD, Arthur Z. 4
ARNOLD, Augusta Foote 1
ARNOLD, Aza H
ARNOLD, Ben 3
ARNOLD, Benedict * H
ARNOLD, Benjamin 5
  William Jr.
ARNOLD, Bion Joseph 1
ARNOLD, Bion Joseph 2
ARNOLD, Birch 1
ARNOLD, Carl Franklin 2
ARNOLD, Carl Raymond 4
ARNOLD, Charles 6
ARNOLD, Constantine 1
  Peter
ARNOLD, Conway Hillyer 1
ARNOLD, Earl Caspar 3
ARNOLD, Edmund Samuel 1
  Foster
ARNOLD, Edward 3
ARNOLD, Edwin Gustaf 1
ARNOLD, Eliza Almy 4
  Peckham
ARNOLD, Ernst Hermann 1
ARNOLD, Felix 3
ARNOLD, Felix 5
ARNOLD, Francis A(rthur) 1
  Jr.
ARNOLD, Francis Joseph 3
ARNOLD, Frank Atkinson 3
ARNOLD, Frank Russell 5
ARNOLD, George H
ARNOLD, George Stanleigh 1
ARNOLD, George Stanleigh 2
ARNOLD, Harold DeForest 1
ARNOLD, Harry Wayne 4
ARNOLD, Hazen S. 3
ARNOLD, Henry H. 2
ARNOLD, Henry J. 3
ARNOLD, Horace David 2
ARNOLD, Howard Payson 1
ARNOLD, Isaac Newton H
ARNOLD, James E. 5
ARNOLD, James Loring 1
ARNOLD, James Newell 4
ARNOLD, John Jr. 4
ARNOLD, John A. 6
ARNOLD, John Anderson 4
ARNOLD, John Carlisle 3
ARNOLD, John Hampton 6
ARNOLD, John Himes 4
ARNOLD, John Jacob 1
ARNOLD, Jonathan 4
ARNOLD, Joseph Addison 4
ARNOLD, Julean (Herbert) 4
ARNOLD, Julian Biddulph 4
ARNOLD, Lauren Briggs H
ARNOLD, Laurence F. 4
ARNOLD, Lemuel Hastings H
ARNOLD, Leslie Philip 4
ARNOLD, Lewis Golding H
ARNOLD, Lloyd 3
ARNOLD, Lois J. 5
ARNOLD, Lynn John 4
ARNOLD, Maurice 2
ARNOLD, Morris Allen 4
ARNOLD, Newton Darling 5
ARNOLD, Olney 6
ARNOLD, Oswald James 2
ARNOLD, Peleg H
ARNOLD, Ralph 4
ARNOLD, Remmie Leroy 5
ARNOLD, Reuben Rose 4
ARNOLD, Richard H
ARNOLD, Richard 4
ARNOLD, Richard Dennis H
ARNOLD, Samuel H
ARNOLD, Samuel Greene H
ARNOLD, Samuel 4
  Tomlinson
ARNOLD, Sarah Louise 1
ARNOLD, Thomas Dickens H
ARNOLD, Thomas Jackson 1
ARNOLD, Thurman Wesley 5
ARNOLD, W. F. 3
ARNOLD, Waldo Robert 2
ARNOLD, Walter P. 4
ARNOLD, William C. 3
ARNOLD, William 2
  Hendrick

ARNOLD, William Joseph 4
ARNOLD, William Richard 4
ARNOLD, William 1
  Rosenzweig
ARNOLD, William Wright 3
ARNOLD, Winifred 5
ARNOLDSON, Sigrid 5
  (Mme. Fischof)
ARNOTE, Walter James 5
ARNOUX, William Henry 1
ARNSTEIN, Albert 4
ARNSTEIN, Henry 1
ARNSTEIN, Karl 6
ARNSTEIN, Margaret G. 5
ARNY, Henry Vinecome 2
ARON, Albert William 2
ARONOVICI, Carol 6
ARONOWITZ, Leon 5
ARONSON, Albert Y. 5
ARONSON, Jacob 3
ARONSON, Maurice 5
ARONSON, Robert Louis 5
ARONSON, Rudolph 1
ARONSTAM, Noah 3
  Ephraim
AROSEMENA, Carlos C. 1
ARP, Jean 4
ARPS, George Frederick 1
ARRASMITH, John W. 4
ARREL, George F. 1
ARRICITIVA, Juan H
ARRICK, Clifford 1
ARRIGHI, Antonio Andrea 4
ARRINGTON, Alfred W. H
ARRINGTON, Archibald H
  Hunter
ARRINGTON, Kenneth 5
  Barton
ARRINGTON, Richard 4
  Olney
ARROWOOD, Charles 3
  Flinn
ARROWSMITH, Robert 1
ARROYO DEL RIO, Carlos 5
ARSCOTT, A. E. 3
ARTER, Charles Kingsley 5
ARTER, Frank Asbury 4
ARTERS, John Manley 1
ARTHUR, Alfred 1
ARTHUR, Alfred Franklin 1
ARTHUR, Chester Alan H
ARTHUR, Franklin Kilnore 6
  Jr.
ARTHUR, Harold John 5
ARTHUR, James B. Mckee 4
ARTHUR, John Morris 4
ARTHUR, Joseph Charles 1
ARTHUR, Julia 5
ARTHUR, Paul Harrison 4
ARTHUR, Peter M. 1
ARTHUR, Thomas 1
ARTHUR, Timothy Shay H
ARTHUR, W(illiam) 5
  C(athcart)
ARTHUR, William H
ARTHUR, William Evans H
ARTHUR, William Hemple 1
ARTHUR, William Reed 6
ARTHURS, Stanley M. 1
ARTIN, Emil 4
ARTOM, Camilio 5
ARTOM, Eugenio 6
ARTZYBASHEFF, Boris 5
ARUNDELL, Charles 5
  Rogers
ARVIN, Newton 4
ARVINE, Earlliss Porter 1
ARY, Henry H
ASAKAWA, Kwanlchi 2
ASBOTH, Alexander Sandor H
ASBURY, Francis H
ASBURY, Herbert 4
ASBURY, Wilbur Francis 6
ASCH, Morris Joseph 4
ASCH, Nathan 4
ASCH, Sholem 5
ASCHAM, John Bayne 3
ASCHER, Abraham Harry 6
ASCHER, Hans Albert 5
ASCHWARZ, William Tefft 4
ASDALE, William James 4
ASELTINE, Walter Morley 5
ASH, Louis Russell 4
ASH, Nichael Woolston H
ASH, Percy H
ASHBRIDGE, Samuel H. 1
ASHBROOK, Ernest 3
  Shepardson
ASHBROOK, M(ilan) 5
  Forest
ASHBROOK, William 1
  Albert
ASHBURN, Percy Moreau 1
ASHBURN, Thomas Quinn 1
ASHBURNER, Charles H
  Albert

ASHBURTON, 1st baron H
ASHBY, George Franklin 3
ASHBY, Samuel 2
ASHBY, Thomas Almond 4
ASHBY, Turner H
ASHBY, Winifred Mayer 6
ASHCRAFT, Lee 3
ASHCRAFT, Leon Thomas 2
ASHE, Bowman Foster 3
ASHE, Edmund Marion 5
ASHE, Edward Joseph 5
ASHE, George B(amford) 5
ASHE, John H
ASHE, John Bapista * H
ASHE, Samuel H
ASHE, Samuel A'Court 1
ASHE, Thomas Samuel H
ASHE, William Francis Jr. 4
ASHE, William Shepperd H
ASHFORD, Bailey Kelly 1
ASHFORD, Emma Louise 1
ASHFORD, Mahlon 3
ASHHURST, Astley Paston Cooper 1
ASHHURST, John 1
ASHHURST, John Jr. 1
ASHHURST, Richard Lewis 1
ASHLEY, Barnas Freeman 4
ASHLEY, Charles Sumner 1
ASHLEY, Chester H
ASHLEY, Clarence Degrand 1
ASHLEY, Clifford Warren 2
ASHLEY, Daniel W. 2
ASHLEY, Delos Rodeyn H
ASHLEY, Edward 1
ASHLEY, Frederick William 3
ASHLEY, George Hall 3
ASHLEY, Henry H
ASHLEY, James Mitchell H
ASHLEY, John Pritchard 1
ASHLEY, Maurice C. 4
ASHLEY, Ossian D. 1
ASHLEY, Roscoe Lewis 4
ASHLEY, William Henry H
ASHMAN, James Ernest 6
ASHMEAD, Isaac H
ASHMEAD, William Harris 1
ASHMORE, Frank Leon 6
ASHMORE, John Durant H
ASHMORE, Otis 4
ASHMORE, Sidney Gillespie 1
ASHMORE, William H
ASHMORE, William 4
ASHMUN, Eli Porter H
ASHMUN, George H
ASHMUN, George Coates 1
ASHMUN, Jehudi H
ASHMUN, Margaret Eliza 1
ASHTON, Albert A. 6
ASHTON, Eve 4
ASHTON, Henry Rusling 5
ASHTON, John H
ASHTON, John 4
ASHTON, John William 5
ASHTON, Joseph Hubley 1
ASHTON, Raymond J. 6
ASHTON, William 4
ASHTON, William Easterly 1
ASHTON, Winifred 4
ASHURST, Henry Fountain 4
ASHWORTH, Hattie Tiller (Mrs. Eugene Marvin Ashworth) 5
ASHWORTH, John H. 2
ASHWORTH, Robert Archibald 3
ASHWORTH, Walter C. 4
ASKENSTEDT, Fritz Conrad 2
ASKEW, Ralph Kirk Jr. 6
ASKEW, Sarah Byrd 2
ASKEW, Thyrza Simonton 3
ASKEY, Edwin Vincent 6
ASKIN, Robert J. 4
ASKREN, William David 4
ASPEGREN, John 1
ASPER, Joel Funk H
ASPINALL, Joseph 1
ASPINALL, Richard 6
ASPINWALL, Clarence Aikin 4
ASPINWALL, Glenn William 5
ASPINWALL, J. Lawrence 4
ASPINWALL, Thomas 1
ASPINWALL, William H
ASPINWALL, William Billings 3
ASPINWALL, William Henry H
ASPLUND, Rupert Franz 3
ASPLUNDH, E. T. 6
ASQUITH, Anthony 5
ASSMUTH, Joseph 3
ASSUM, Arthur Louis 6
ASTAUROV, Boris Lvovich 6
ASTON, Anthony H
ASTON, James 4
ASTON, Ralph 1
ASTON, Richard Douglas 5
ASTOR, John Jacob * H
ASTOR, John Jacob 1
ASTOR, Vincent 3
ASTOR, Viscountess 4
ASTOR, William Backhouse H
ASTOR, William Waldorf 1
ASTOR OF HEVER, Baron (John Jacob Astor) 5
ASTURIAS, Miguel Angel 6
ASWELL, Edward C. 3
ASWELL, James Benjamin 1
ATCHESON, George Jr. 2
ATCHISON, David Rice H
ATCHISON, Thomas Cunningham 1
ATEN, Fred N. 3
ATHEARN, Fred Goodrich 3
ATHEARN, Walter Scott 1
ATHENAGORAS, His All Holiness 5
ATHERTON, Charles Gordon H
ATHERTON, Charles Humphrey H
ATHERTON, Edwin Newton 2
ATHERTON, Frank Cooke 2
ATHERTON, George W. 1
ATHERTON, Gertrude Franklin 2
ATHERTON, Gibson H
ATHERTON, Henry Francis 2
ATHERTON, John C. 3
ATHERTON, Joseph Ballard 4
ATHERTON, Joshua H
ATHERTON, Louis M. 3
ATHERTON, Percy Lee 2
ATHERTON, Ray 3
ATKESON, Clarence Lee Conner 6
ATKESON, Floyd Warnick 3
ATKESON, Thomas Clark 1
ATKESON, William Oscar 2
ATKIELSKI, Roman R. 5
ATKIN, Isaac Cubitt Raymond 3
ATKINS, Albert Henry 3
ATKINS, Arthur 4
ATKINS, Arthur Kennedy 6
ATKINS, Charles Duke 4
ATKINS, Edwin F. 1
ATKINS, George Tyng 2
ATKINS, George Washington Ely 4
ATKINS, Harry T. 1
ATKINS, Harry Thomas 5
ATKINS, Henry Hornby 5
ATKINS, James 1
ATKINS, Jearum H
ATKINS, John De Witt Clinton 1
ATKINS, Joseph Alexander 6
ATKINS, Joseph Preston 6
ATKINS, Mrs. Louise Allen 3
ATKINS, Smith Dykins 1
ATKINS, Willard Earl 5
ATKINSON, Albert Algernon 5
ATKINSON, Archibald H
ATKINSON, Arthur Kimmins 4
ATKINSON, Benjamin Searcy 3
ATKINSON, Charles Edwin 4
ATKINSON, Charles R. 5
ATKINSON, Christoper Joseph 1
ATKINSON, Donald Taylor 3
ATKINSON, Edward 1
ATKINSON, Eleanor 2
ATKINSON, Fred Washington 4
ATKINSON, Geoffrey 4
ATKINSON, George Francis 1
ATKINSON, George Henry H
ATKINSON, George Wesley 1
ATKINSON, Guy F. 5
ATKINSON, Harry Hunt 5
ATKINSON, Henry H
ATKINSON, Henry Avery 3
ATKINSON, Henry Morrell 1
ATKINSON, Herbert Spencer 3
ATKINSON, Herschel C. 4
ATKINSON, Isaac Edmondson 1
ATKINSON, J. Robert 4
ATKINSON, John H
ATKINSON, John Bradshaw 4
ATKINSON, Joseph Story 5
ATKINSON, Louis Evans 1
ATKINSON, Ralph 2
ATKINSON, Ralph Waldo 4
ATKINSON, Samuel C. 2
ATKINSON, Thomas H
ATKINSON, Thomas Edgar 4
ATKINSON, Thomas Wilson 1
ATKINSON, William Biddle 4
ATKINSON, William Brockliss 4
ATKINSON, William E. 1
ATKINSON, William Elrie 1
ATKINSON, William Sackston 1
ATKINSON, William Walker 1
ATKINSON, William Yates H
ATKINSON, William Yates 1
ATKINSON, William Yates 3
ATKINSON, Wilmer 1
ATLASS, H. Leslie 4
ATLEE, John Light H
ATLEE, John Light 3
ATLEE, Samuel John H
ATLEE, Washington Lemuel H
ATTEBERY, Olin Moody 3
ATTERBURY, Anson Phelps 1
ATTERBURY, Grosvenor 3
ATTERBURY, William Wallace 1
ATTERIDGE, Harold Richard 1
ATTERIDGE, Harold Richard 2
ATTLEE, Earl 4
ATTRIDGE, Richard 4
ATTUCKS, Crispus H
ATTWILL, Henry Converse 1
ATTWOOD, Frederic 5
ATTWOOD, Stephen S. 4
ATWATER, Caleb H
ATWATER, David Hay 2
ATWATER, Edward Perrin 5
ATWATER, Francis 1
ATWATER, George Parkin 1
ATWATER, Helen Woodard 2
ATWATER, Henry G. 3
ATWATER, John Wilbur 4
ATWATER, Lyman Hotchkiss H
ATWATER, Mary Meigs 3
ATWATER, Reginald Myers 3
ATWATER, Richard Mead 1
ATWATER, Wilbur Olin 1
ATWATER, William Cutler 1
ATWELL, Charles Beach 1
ATWELL, William Hawley 4
ATWILL, Douglass Henry 4
ATWILL, Edward Robert 1
ATWILL, Lionel 2
ATWILL, William 1
ATWOOD, Albert William 6
ATWOOD, Arthur R. 3
ATWOOD, Charles B. H
ATWOOD, Charles Edwin 1
ATWOOD, David H
ATWOOD, Edward Leland 5
ATWOOD, Edwin Byron 1
ATWOOD, Elmer Bugg 3
ATWOOD, Felix 6
ATWOOD, Frank Ely 2
ATWOOD, George Edward 4
ATWOOD, Harrison 3
ATWOOD, Harry 1
ATWOOD, Henry 3
ATWOOD, Hinckley Gardner 2
ATWOOD, Isaac Morgan 1
ATWOOD, James Arthur 2
ATWOOD, Jesse H
ATWOOD, John Harrison 1
ATWOOD, John Murray 3
ATWOOD, Julius Walter 2
ATWOOD, Lemuel True 1
ATWOOD, Millard V. 1
ATWOOD, Millard V. 2
ATWOOD, Oscar 1
ATWOOD, Roy Franklin 4
ATWOOD, Wallace Walter 2
AUB, Joseph Charles 6
AUBERT, Lloyd Lees 5
AUBREY, Edwin Ewart 3
AUBREY, Henry George 5
AUBREY, James Thomas 4
AUBREY, John Edmond 5
AUBREY, William 1
AUCH, John F. 4
AUCHINCLOSS, Charles C. 4
AUCHINCLOSS, Gordon 2
AUCHINCLOSS, John Winthrop 1
AUCHINCLOSS, William Stuart 1
AUCHMUTY, Richard Tylden H
AUCHMUTY, Robert * H
AUCHMUTY, Samuel H
AUCHTER, Eugene Curtis 3
AUCOCK, Arthur Morgan 5
AUD, Guy 4
AUDEN, Wystan Hugh 6
AUDRIETH, Ludwig Frederick 4
AUDSLEY, George Ashdown 4
AUDUBON, John James H
AUDUBON, John Woodhouse H
AUDUBON, Victor Gifford H
AUDY, Jack Ralph 6
AUER, Harry Anton 6
AUER, John 2
AUER, Joseph Lawrence 4
AUER, Leopold 1
AUERBACH, Beatrice Fox 5
AUERBACH, Erich 3
AUERBACH, Frank Ludwig 4
AUERBACH, Herbert S. 2
AUERBACH, Joseph S. 2
AUERBACH-LEVY, William 4
AUF DER HEIDE, Oscar Louis 2
AUGENSTEIN, Leroy George 5
AUGER, Charles L. 1
AUGHINBAUGH, William Edmund 1
AUGSPURGER, Owen Beal 5
AUGUR, Christopher Columbus H
AUGUR, Hezekiah H
AUGUR, Jacob Arnold 1
AUGUST, Harry Wirt 5
AUGUSTINE, Harry Hamill 4
AUGUSTINE, William Franklin 2
AUGUSTUS, Ellsworth Hunt 4
AUGUSTUS, John H
AUGUSTYN, Godfrey William 2
AULD, George P. 4
AULD, John Maxwell 4
AULT, Bromwell 5
AULT, James Percy 1
AULT, Nelson Allen 4
AULT, Otto Thurman 3
AULTMAN, Dwight Edward 1
AUMAN, Orrin W. 3
AUMAN, Russell Frank 5
AUMAN, William 1
AURAND, Samuel Herbert 4
AURELL, Alvin Karl 4
AURELL, George Emanuel 5
AURINGER, Obadiah Cyrus 1
AURIOL, Vincent 4
AUSE, Orval Hope 6
AUSLEY, Charles Saxon 6
AUSTELL, Adelaide Roberts 6
AUSTELL, Alfred H
AUSTEN, Benjamin H
AUSTEN, Peter Townsend 1
AUSTIN, Albert E. 1
AUSTIN, Albert E. 2
AUSTIN, Archibald H
AUSTIN, Benjamin Fish 4
AUSTIN, Calvin 1
AUSTIN, Charles Burgess 6
AUSTIN, Clyde Bernard 4
AUSTIN, Cyrus Brooks 1
AUSTIN, David H
AUSTIN, Dwight Bertram 3
AUSTIN, Edward Thompson 6
AUSTIN, Ennis Raymond 3
AUSTIN, Eugene Munger 4
AUSTIN, Francis Marion 1
AUSTIN, Fred Thaddeus 1
AUSTIN, Frederick Carleton 1
AUSTIN, George Curtis 4
AUSTIN, Henry H
AUSTIN, Henry 4
AUSTIN, Herbert Douglas 5
AUSTIN, Howard 4
AUSTIN, Howard Albert Jr. 5
AUSTIN, Isabella McHugh 1
AUSTIN, James Harold 3
AUSTIN, James Trecothick H
AUSTIN, Jane Goodwin H
AUSTIN, John Corneby Wilson 5
AUSTIN, John Langshaw 4
AUSTIN, John Osborne 1
AUSTIN, John Turnell 5
AUSTIN, Jonathan Loring H
AUSTIN, Leonard S. 1
AUSTIN, Lloyd Lewis 5
AUSTIN, Louis Winslow 1
AUSTIN, Mary 1
AUSTIN, Moses H
AUSTIN, Oscar Phelps 1
AUSTIN, Richard Loper 2
AUSTIN, Richard Wilson 1
AUSTIN, Samuel H
AUSTIN, Samuel Yates 5
AUSTIN, Stephen Fuller H
AUSTIN, Warren Robinson 4
AUSTIN, Wilbert John 1
AUSTIN, William H
AUSTIN, William Lacy 3
AUSTIN, William Lane 2
AUSTIN, William Liseter 1
AUSTIN-BALL, Thomas 5
AUSTRIAN, Alfred S. 1
AUSTRIAN, Carl Joseph 5
AUSTRIAN, Charles Robert 3
AUSTRINS, Emilija Pone (Mrs. Peteris Austrins) 6
AUTEN, James Ernest 2
AUTHIER, George Francis 5
AVANCENA, Ramon 5
AVELLANUS, Arcadius 1
AVENT, Joseph Emory 3
AVERBACH, Albert 6
AVERELL, William Woods H
AVERETT, Thomas Hamlet H
AVERILL, George G. 3
AVERILL, Glenn Mark 1
AVERILL, John H. 5
AVERILL, John Thomas H
AVERITT, George Alfred 5
AVERS, Henry Godfrey 2
AVERY, Alphonso Calhoun 4
AVERY, Benjamin Parke H
AVERY, Catherine Hitchcock Tilden 1
AVERY, Christopher Lester 3
AVERY, Clarence Willard 2
AVERY, Coleman 1
AVERY, Cyrus Stevens 5
AVERY, Daniel H
AVERY, Delos 4
AVERY, Elroy McKendree 1
AVERY, George C. 1
AVERY, George True 2
AVERY, Henry Ogden H
AVERY, Isaac Wheeler H
AVERY, Isaac Wheeler 1
AVERY, John * H
AVERY, John 1
AVERY, John 4
AVERY, Johnston 5
AVERY, Milton 4
AVERY, Moses Nathan 2
AVERY, Nathan Prentice 2
AVERY, Oswald Theodore 3
AVERY, Rachel Foster 1
AVERY, Robert 1
AVERY, Samuel 1
AVERY, Samuel Putnam 1
AVERY, Sewell Lee 4
AVERY, Susan Look 1
AVERY, Thomas Burt 4
AVERY, William Tecumsah H
AVERY, William Waightstill H
AVERY, Willis Frank 6
AVES, Dreda 2
AVES, Henry Damerel 1
AVILDSEN, Clarence 4
AVINOAM, Reuben 6
AVINOFF, Andrew 2
AVIS, John Boyd 2
AVIS, Samuel Brashear 1
AVITABILE, Salvatore 3
AVNET, Lester Francis 5
AVNSOE, Thorkild 3
AVRAM, Mois H(erban) 6
AWL, William Maclay H
AXE, Emerson Wirt 4
AXE, Ruth Houghton 4
AXEL, Hans H
AXELRAD, Sidney 6
AXELROD, Haim Izchak 5
AXELROD, Leonard Richardson 6
AXELSON, Charles Frederic 5
AXLINE, George Andrew 1
AXSON, Stockton 1
AXTELL, Decatur 1
AXTELL, Edwin Rodarmel 1
AXTELL, Frances Cleveland 4
AXTELL, Harold Lucius 3
AXTELL, John Thomas 1

* Indicates More Than One Such Name Listed

AXTELL, Samuel Beach H
AXTELLE, George Edward 6
AXTON, John Thomas 1
AYALA, Juan Manuel de
AYARS, George 5
  W(ashington)
AYCOCK, Charles Brantley 1
AYCRIGG, John Bancker 1
AYDELOTT, James 4
  Howard
AYDELOTTE, Dora 5
AYDELOTTE, Frank 3
AYDLETT, Edwin Ferebee 1
AYER, Benjamin F. 1
AYER, Charles Fanning 3
AYER, Charles Frederick 5
AYER, Clarence Walter 1
AYER, Edward Everett 1
AYER, F. Wayland 1
AYER, Franklin Deming 4
AYER, Fred Carleton 6
AYER, Frederic Eugene 4
AYER, Frederick 1
AYER, Frederick Fanning 1
AYER, Harriet Hubbard 4
AYER, James Bourne 4
AYER, James Cook H
AYER, John 4
AYER, Joseph Cullen 2
AYER, Nathaniel Farwell 6
AYER, Richard Small H
AYER, Winslow B. 4
AYERS, Allan Farrell 5
AYERS, Clarence Edwin 5
AYERS, Edward Everett 4
AYERS, Fred Wesley 4
AYERS, Harry Mell 4
AYERS, Howard 1
AYERS, Joseph Burton 6
AYERS, Lemuel 3
AYERS, Roy E. 3
AYERS, Rufus Adolphus 5
AYERS, William 6
  P(endergast)
AYETA, Francisco de H
AYLER, Albert 5
AYLESWORTH, Barton 1
  Orville
AYLESWORTH, Merlin 3
  Hall
AYLING, Charles Lincoln 1
AYLLON, Lucas Vasquez H
  De
AYLSWORTH, Leon 5
  Emmons
AYLSWORTH, Nicholas 4
  John
AYLSWORTH, William 5
  Prince
AYLWIN, John Cushing H
AYME, Louis Henri 1
AYME, Marcel 4
AYNESWORTH, Kenneth 2
  Hazen
AYRES, Albert Douglass 2
AYRES, Anne H
AYRES, Atlee Bernard 5
AYRES, Brown 1
AYRES, Burt Wilmot 5
AYRES, Edward 1
AYRES, Eugene Edmond 5
AYRES, Frank C. 3
AYRES, Franklin Herman 4
AYRES, George Frederic 4
AYRES, Harry Morgan 4
AYRES, Joseph Gerrish 1
AYRES, Leonard Porter 2
AYRES, Louis 2
AYRES, Milan Church 1
AYRES, Milan Valentine 1
AYRES, Philip Wheelock 5
AYRES, Quincy Claude 4
AYRES, Romeyn Beck H
AYRES, Samuel Gardiner 1
AYRES, Samuel Loring 1
  Percival
AYRES, Stephen Cooper 1
AYRES, Steven Beckwith 1
AYRES, Thomas A. H
AYRES, William Augustus 3
AYUB KHAN, Mohammed 6
AZAD, Abul Kalam 3
  Maulana
AZARIAS, Brother
AZCARATE Y FLOREZ, 5
  Pablo de
AZEVEDO, Philadelpho 3
AZUELA, Mariano 5
AZUOLA, Eduardo 3

B

BAAB, Otto J. 3
BAADE, Walter 4
BAAR, Arnold R. 3

BABASINIAN, V. S. 1
BABB, Clement Edwin 1
BABB, Cyrus Cates 1
BABB, James Elisha 1
BABB, James T(inkham) 5
BABB, Max Wellington 1
BABB, Washington Irving 1
BABBITT, Benjamin Talbot H
BABBITT, Charles James 4
BABBITT, Edwin Burr 1
BABBITT, Edwin Dwight 4
BABBITT, Elijah 1
BABBITT, Eugene Howard H
BABBITT, Frank Cole 1
BABBITT, George Franklin 1
BABBITT, Irving 1
BABBITT, Isaac H
BABBITT, Juliette M. 3
BABBITT, Kurnal R. 1
BABBITT, Lawrence 1
  Sprague
BABBOTT, Frank Lusk 1
BABBS, Arthur Vergil 1
BABBS, Charles Frederick 6
BABCOCK, Albert 4
BABCOCK, Alfred 5
BABCOCK, Allen 5
BABCOCK, Bernie 5
BABCOCK, Birton E. 1
BABCOCK, Charles 1
BABCOCK, Charles Henry 1
BABCOCK, Charles Henry 4
BABCOCK, Charles Henry 5
BABCOCK, Earle Brownell 1
BABCOCK, Earle Jay 4
BABCOCK, Edward Vose 1
BABCOCK, Ernest Brown 4
BABCOCK, George Herman H
BABCOCK, Harold Delos 5
BABCOCK, Harriet 4
BABCOCK, Harry Allan 4
BABCOCK, Havilah 4
BABCOCK, Howard 3
  Edward
BABCOCK, Irving Brown 4
BABCOCK, James Chester 6
BABCOCK, James Francis 1
BABCOCK, James Woods 1
BABCOCK, John 1
  Breckinridge
BABCOCK, John Pease 4
BABCOCK, Joseph Weeks 1
BABCOCK, Kendric Charles 1
BABCOCK, Leander H
BABCOCK, Louis Locke 5
BABCOCK, Maltbie 1
  Davenport
BABCOCK, Orville Elias H
BABCOCK, Richard Earle 3
BABCOCK, Robert Hall 1
BABCOCK, Robert Weston 4
BABCOCK, Samuel Denison 1
BABCOCK, Samuel Gavitt 2
BABCOCK, Stephen 1
  Moulton
BABCOCK, Warren La 2
  Verne
BABCOCK, Washington 1
  Irving
BABCOCK, William H
BABCOCK, William Henry 1
BABCOCK, William 4
  Waterman
BABCOCK, William Wayne 5
BABCOCK, Winnifred 6
  Eaton (Onoto Watanna)
BABER, George W. 5
BABER, Ray Erwin 4
BABIN, Hosea John 4
BABIN, Victor 5
BABLER, Bernard Joseph 4
BABLER, Jacob L. 2
BABSON, Herman 1
BABSON, Paul Talbot 5
BABSON, Roger Ward 4
BABST, Earl D. 4
BACCALONI, Salvatore 4
BACH, Harry 6
BACH, Oscar Bruno 3
BACH, Ralph Edward 4
BACH, Richard F. 4
BACH, Thomas Cumming 4
BACHARACH, Eric 5
  William
BACHARACH, Isaac 3
BACHE, Alexander Dallas H
BACHE, Benjamin Franklin H
BACHE, Dallas 1
BACHE, Franklin 1
BACHE, Harold L. 5
BACHE, Jules Semon 2
BACHE, Leopold Semon 1
BACHE, Louise Franklin 1
BACHE, Rene 4
BACHE, Richard H
BACHE, Theophylact H

BACHE-WILG, Jens 6
BACHE, William H
BACHELDER, John Badger H
BACHELDER, Nahum 1
  Josiah
BACHELLER, Irving 2
  Addison
BACHELLER, Joseph 1
  Henry
BACHEM, Albert 3
BACHER, Otto Henry 1
BACHE-WIIG, Jens 6
BACHKE, Halvard Huitfeldt 3
BACHMAN, Absalom 4
  Pierre
BACHMAN, Allan 5
  Earnshaw
BACHMAN, Frank 1
  Puterbaugh
BACHMAN, Ingeborg 6
BACHMAN, John H
BACHMAN, Jonathan 1
  Waverly
BACHMAN, Nathan 1
BACHMAN, Nathan Lynn 1
BACHMAN, Paul Stanton 3
BACHMAN, Robert 5
  Abraham
BACHMANN, Raphael 5
  Otto
BACHMANN, Werner 3
  Emmanuel
BACHMEYER, Arthur 3
  Charles
BACHOUR, Rafic Jibrail 6
BACHRACH, Louis Fabian 4
BACHRACH, Walter 4
  Keyser
BACIGALUPI, James 3
  Augustus
BACIGALUPI, Tadini 4
BACK, Ernest Adna 6
BACK, George Irving 5
BACKER, George 6
BACKES, John H. 1
BACKHAUS, Wilhelm 5
BACKMAN, Kenneth B. 4
BACKSTRAND, Clifford J. 5
BACKUS, August Charles 4
BACKUS, Azel 1
BACKUS, Edward 1
  Wellington
BACKUS, Edwin Burdette 3
BACKUS, Isaac H
BACKUS, Louise Burton 6
  Laidlaw (Mrs. Dana
  Converse Backus)
BACKUS, Manson Franklin 1
BACKUS, Samuel Woolsey 1
BACKUS, Standish 2
BACKUS, Truman Jay 1
BACKUS, Wilson Marvin 2
BACOATS, J. Alvin 6
BACON, Albert Williamson 1
BACON, Alexander Samuel 1
BACON, Alice Mabel 1
BACON, Augustus Octavius 1
BACON, Benjamin Wisner 1
BACON, Charles Sumner 2
BACON, Clara Latimer 4
BACON, David H
BACON, David William H
BACON, Delia Salter H
BACON, Edgar Mayhew 1
BACON, Edward Payson 1
BACON, Edward Rathbone 1
BACON, Edwin Munroe 1
BACON, Edwin Munroe 2
BACON, Ezekiel H
BACON, Francis 1
BACON, Francis Leonard 4
BACON, Francis R. 4
BACON, Frank 1
BACON, Frank Rogers 2
BACON, Gaspar Griswold 2
BACON, George Andrew 5
BACON, George Morgan 5
BACON, George P. 1
BACON, George Wood 3
BACON, Henry 1
BACON, John H
BACON, John Harwood 1
BACON, John Mosby 1
BACON, John Watson H
BACON, Josephine Dodge 5
  Daskam
BACON, Leonard 1
BACON, Leonard 3
BACON, Leonard Woolsey H
BACON, Mary Elizabeth 6
  (Mrs. Philip Bacon)
BACON, Mary Schell Hoke 5
  ("Dolores Marbourg")
BACON, Nathaniel H
BACON, Raymond Foss 3

BACON, Robert 1
BACON, Robert Low 1
BACON, Robert Stillwell 5
BACON, Selden 2
BACON, Thomas H
BACON, Walter W. 4
BACON, William Johnson H
BACON, William Stevens 3
BADAWI PASHA, Abdel 4
  Hamid
BADE, William Frederic 1
BADEAU, Adam H
BADENBERGER, Henry 4
BADER, Jesse Moren 4
BADER, Ralph Hedrick 1
BADER, Richard George 5
BADGER, Charles Johnston 1
BADGER, Dewitt Clinton 4
BADGER, George Edmund H
BADGER, George Henry 4
BADGER, Joseph * H
BADGER, Luther H
BADGER, Oscar Charles 1
BADGER, Oscar Charles 3
BADGER, Philip Owen 5
BADGER, Walter Irving 1
BADGER, Walter Lucius 3
BADGLEY, Maxwell 5
  Forrest
BADGLEY, Sidney Rose 1
BADIN, Stephen Theodore H
BADING, Gerhard Adolph 2
BADLEY, Brenton Thoburn 4
BADT, Milton B. 4
BAEHR, Carl Adolph 5
BAEHR, Max Joseph 4
BAEHR, William Alfred 2
BAEHR, William Frederick 5
  Otto
BAEKELAND, Celine 3
BAEKELAND, George 4
BAEKELAND, Leo 2
  Hendrik
BAENSCH, Emil 3
BAENSCH, Willy E. 5
BAEPLER, Walter A. 3
BAER, Arthur A. 6
BAER, George Jr. H
BAER, George Frederick 1
BAER, Jean Hitchcock 6
BAER, John M(iller) 5
BAER, John Willis 1
BAER, Joseph Augustus 6
BAER, Joseph Louis 3
BAER, Libbie C. 4
BAER, Sidney R. 3
BAER, Townsend W. 6
BAER, William Bush 3
BAER, William Jacob 1
BAERWALD, Paul 5
BAETJER, Edwin G. 2
BAETJER, Frederick Henry 1
BAEZ, Cecilio 4
BAEZA, Marco A. 4
BAGAR, Robert 3
BAGBY, Albert Morris 4
BAGBY, Arthur Pendleton H
BAGBY, George Franklin 4
BAGBY, George William H
BAGBY, John Courts 1
BAGBY, John Hampden 1
  Chamberlayne
BAGBY, William Buck 4
BAGDATOPOULOS, 5
  William Spencer
BAGG, Lyman Hotchkiss 1
BAGG, Rufus Mather 5
BAGGER, Henry Horneman 4
BAGGETT, Samuel Graves 4
BAGGS, Arthur Eugene 2
BAGGS, Mae Lacy 1
BAGGS, William Calhoun 4
BAGLEY, Charles Leland 5
BAGLEY, Clarence Booth 1
BAGLEY, David Worth 4
BAGLEY, William Chandler 2
  Clark
BAGLEY, Willis Gaylord 2
BAGNELL, Robert 3
BAGOT, Sir Charles H
BAGSTAD, Anna Emilia 5
BAGSTER-COLLINS, 1
  Elijah William
BAGWELL, Paul D(ouglas) 6
BAHL, William Edgar 5
BAHN, Chester Bert 4
BAHNSON, Agnew Hunter 4
BAHR, Emory J. 4
BAHR, Walter Julien 4
BAHRENBURG, Louis P. 1
  H.
BAIER, Victor 1
BAILEY, Albert Edward 5
BAILEY, Alexander H
  Hamilton

BAILEY, Alfred Halsey 3
BAILEY, Alice Ward 4
BAILEY, Ann H
BAILEY, Anna Warner H
BAILEY, Arthur Low 1
BAILEY, Arthur Scott 5
BAILEY, Benjamin Franklin 1
BAILEY, Bert Heald 1
BAILEY, Bertha 1
BAILEY, Calvin Weston 5
BAILEY, Carl Edward 2
BAILEY, Cassius Mercer 1
BAILEY, Charles Franklin 3
BAILEY, Charles Justin 2
BAILEY, Charles Langdon 5
BAILEY, Charles Olin 1
BAILEY, Charles Reuben 1
BAILEY, Charles William 4
BAILEY, Clarence Mitchell 1
BAILEY, David Jackson H
BAILEY, E. Stillman 1
BAILEY, Ebenezer H
BAILEY, Edgar Henry 1
  Summerfield
BAILEY, Edward 1
BAILEY, Edward Monroe 2
BAILEY, Elijah Prentiss 1
BAILEY, Ervin George 6
BAILEY, Everett Hoskins 1
BAILEY, Florence Augusta 2
  Merriam
BAILEY, Francis H
BAILEY, Frank 3
BAILEY, Frank Harvey 1
BAILEY, Frank Moye 4
BAILEY, Fred Oliver 1
BAILEY, Frederick 1
  Randolph
BAILEY, Gamaliel 1
BAILEY, George Davis 4
BAILEY, George 2
  Washington
BAILEY, George Wicks 1
BAILEY, Gilbert Ellis 1
BAILEY, Goldsmith Fox H
BAILEY, Guy Winfred 1
BAILEY, Hannah Johnston 1
BAILEY, Harold Harris 6
BAILEY, Harold Wood 6
BAILEY, Harry Louis 4
BAILEY, Henry Turner 1
BAILEY, Hollis Russell 1
BAILEY, Irving Widmer 4
BAILEY, Ivon Arthur 4
BAILEY, Jacob 1
BAILEY, Jacob Whitman H
BAILEY, James Anthony 1
BAILEY, James Edmund 1
BAILEY, James Garfield 1
BAILEY, James H
  Montgomery
BAILEY, Jennings 4
BAILEY, Jeremiah H
BAILEY, Jessie Emerson 6
BAILEY, John H
BAILEY, John Hays 5
BAILEY, John Moran 6
BAILEY, John Mosher 1
BAILEY, John Ora 3
BAILEY, John Wendell 4
BAILEY, Joseph * H
BAILEY, Joseph T. 1
BAILEY, Joseph Weldon 1
BAILEY, Joseph Weldon Jr. 2
BAILEY, Josiah William 2
BAILEY, Leonard Henry 4
BAILEY, Lewis W. 6
BAILEY, Liberty Hyde 3
BAILEY, Loring Woart 1
BAILEY, Louis Jonathan 4
BAILEY, Lydia R. H
BAILEY, Margaret Emerson 3
BAILEY, Mark Jr. 4
BAILEY, Mercer Silas 1
BAILEY, Mervyn J. 3
BAILEY, Milus Kendrick 4
BAILEY, Morton 1
BAILEY, Morton Shelley 1
BAILEY, Pearce 4
BAILEY, Percival 6
BAILEY, Ralph Edward 4
BAILEY, Ralph Emerson 6
BAILEY, Ray W. 3
BAILEY, Rufus William H
BAILEY, Solon Irving 1
BAILEY, Steele 1
BAILEY, Temple 4
BAILEY, Theodore Mead 1
BAILEY, Theodorus * H
BAILEY, Thomas L. 2
BAILEY, Thomas Pearce 2
BAILEY, Vernon 2
BAILEY, Vernon Howe 3
BAILEY, Warren Worth 1
BAILEY, William Arthur 5
BAILEY, William Bacon 3

BAILEY, William Whitman 1
BAILEY, William Whitman 4
BAILEY, Willis J. 1
BAILHACHE, Preston 1
  Heath
BAILIE, Earle 1
BAILIE, Virginia 1
BAILIE, William 4
BAILIE, William Lamdin 1
BAILLARGEON, Cebert 4
BAILLIE, Archie Fraser 3
BAILLIE, Hugh 4
BAILLIE, John 4
BAILLOT, Edouard Paul 4
BAILLY, Joseph Alexis H
BAILLY-BLANCHARD, 1
  Arthur
BAILOR, Edwin Maurice 5
BAILY, Alfred William 4
BAILY, Elisha Ingram 1
BAILY, Harold James 4
BAILY, Joshua L. 1
BAIN, Charles Wesley 4
BAIN, Edgar Collins 5
BAIN, Ferdinand R. 2
BAIN, Fred B. 5
BAIN, George Grantham 4
BAIN, George Luke Scobie H
BAIN, George Washington 1
BAIN, Harry Foster 4
BAIN, Jarvis Johnson 6
BAIN, Robert Edward 1
  Mather
BAINBRIDGE, Alexander 1
  Gilbert
BAINBRIDGE, Lucy 1
  Seaman
BAINBRIDGE, William H
BAINBRIDGE, William 2
  Seaman
BAINES, Edward Richards 5
BAINES-MILLER, Minnie 5
  Willis
BAINTER, Fay Okell 5
BAIRD, Absalom 1
BAIRD, Andrew D. 1
BAIRD, Andrew McClung 4
BAIRD, Bruce 4
BAIRD, Cameron 4
BAIRD, Charles Washington H
BAIRD, Cora 5
BAIRD, David 1
BAIRD, David Jr. 3
BAIRD, David W. E. 6
BAIRD, Edward Rouzie 6
BAIRD, Frank Burkett 1
BAIRD, George Washington 1
BAIRD, George William 1
BAIRD, Henry Carey 1
BAIRD, Henry Martyn 1
BAIRD, Henry W. 4
BAIRD, James 3
BAIRD, Jean Katherine 1
BAIRD, John L. 4
BAIRD, John Wallace 1
BAIRD, Joseph Edward 2
BAIRD, Julian William 1
BAIRD, Louise 5
BAIRD, Lucius Olmsted 2
BAIRD, Matthew H
BAIRD, Phil C. 1
BAIRD, Raleigh William 1
BAIRD, Richard F. 3
BAIRD, Robert 1
BAIRD, Robert W. 5
BAIRD, Samuel John H
BAIRD, Spencer Fullerton 1
BAIRD, Thomas H. H
BAIRD, William Jesse 1
BAIRD, William Raimond 1
BAITER, Richard Englis 1
BAITS, Vera Burridge 4
BAITY, George Perry 4
BAITY, Herman Glenn 6
BAITY, James L. 5
BAJPAI, Sir Girja Shankar 4
BAKENHUS, Reuben 4
  Edwin
BAKER, A. George 4
BAKER, Abijah Richardson H
BAKER, Albert 2
BAKER, Albert C. 1
BAKER, Albert Rufus 1
BAKER, Alfred Brittin 1
BAKER, Alfred Landon 1
BAKER, Alfred Zantzinger 5
BAKER, Alton Fletcher 4
BAKER, Archibald Eachern 1
  Mountford
BAKER, Arthur Josiah 4
BAKER, Arthur Latham 1
BAKER, Arthur Mulford 1
BAKER, Asa George 1
BAKER, Asher Carter 1
BAKER, Benedict J. 2
BAKER, Benjamin Franklin H

BAKER, Benjamin Webb 1
BAKER, Bernard Nadal 1
BAKER, Bertha Kunz 2
BAKER, Bertha Kunz 5
BAKER, Bryant 5
BAKER, Caleb H
BAKER, Charles Fuller 1
BAKER, Charles Henry H
BAKER, Charles Hinckley 1
BAKER, Charles Samuel 4
BAKER, Charles Whiting 1
BAKER, Charles William 1
BAKER, Chauncey Brooke 1
BAKER, Claude Milem 4
BAKER, Cora Warman 5
BAKER, Cornelia 1
BAKER, Crosby Fred 3
BAKER, Daniel 1
BAKER, Daniel Clifton Jr. 6
BAKER, Darius 1
BAKER, David 4
BAKER, David Dudrow 3
BAKER, David Floyd 5
BAKER, David Jewett H
BAKER, Dorothy 5
BAKER, Earl Dewey 1
BAKER, Earle A. 4
BAKER, Edgar Campbell 6
BAKER, Edgar Robey 5
BAKER, Edna Dean 3
BAKER, Edward Dickinson 1
BAKER, Edwin George 4
BAKER, Elbert H. 1
BAKER, Elizabeth Bradford 5
  Faulkner
BAKER, Elizabeth Gowdy 1
BAKER, Ellis Crain 2
BAKER, Emilie (Addoms) 5
  Kip (Mrs. Franklin
  Thomas Baker)
BAKER, Eric Wilfred 6
BAKER, Ernest Hamlin 6
BAKER, Everett Moore 5
BAKER, Ezra H
BAKER, Ezra Flavius 5
BAKER, Ezra Henry 4
BAKER, Francis Asbury 1
BAKER, Francis Elisha 1
BAKER, Frank * 1
BAKER, Frank Collins 2
BAKER, Frank E. 5
BAKER, Frank Kline 4
BAKER, Frank S. 4
BAKER, Franklin Jr. 1
BAKER, Franklin Thomas 2
BAKER, Frederick Cecil 4
BAKER, Frederick Storrs 4
BAKER, Frederick Van 5
  Vliet
BAKER, George 6
BAKER, George Augustus H
BAKER, George Augustus 1
BAKER, George Barr 1
BAKER, George Bramwell 1
BAKER, George Claude Jr. 6
BAKER, George Danielson 1
BAKER, George Fisher * 1
BAKER, George Hall 1
BAKER, George Holbrook H
BAKER, George Holbrook 1
BAKER, George L. 4
BAKER, George Merrick 4
BAKER, George Pierce 1
BAKER, George Randolph 1
BAKER, George Randolph 2
BAKER, George Theodore 4
BAKER, George Titus 6
BAKER, Gladden 6
  Whetstone
BAKER, Gordon Harrington 4
BAKER, Harold Bruss 5
BAKER, Harold Griffith 3
BAKER, Harriette Newell 1
  Woods
BAKER, Harry B. 4
BAKER, Harvey Almy 1
BAKER, Harvey Humphrey 1
BAKER, Henry Dunster 1
BAKER, Henry Moore 1
BAKER, Henry Moore 4
BAKER, Herbert 1
BAKER, Herbert Abram 1
BAKER, Herbert Madison 1
BAKER, Hollis 5
BAKER, Holmes Davenport 3
BAKER, Horace 4
BAKER, Horace Forbes 5
BAKER, Howard H. 4
BAKER, Hugh Benton 4
BAKER, Hugh Potter 3
BAKER, Ira Osborn 1
BAKER, Isaac Due 1
BAKER, J. Thompson 1
BAKER, James H
BAKER, James Addison 1
BAKER, James Andrew 6

BAKER, James Barnes 1
BAKER, James Chamberlain 6
BAKER, James Heaton 1
BAKER, James Hutchins 1
BAKER, James Marion 1
BAKER, James Norment 2
BAKER, Jehu 1
BAKER, John H
BAKER, John Daniel 4
BAKER, John Earl 3
BAKER, John Harris 1
BAKER, John Hopkinson 6
BAKER, John Stewart 4
BAKER, Joseph Dill 1
BAKER, Joseph Richardson 2
BAKER, Josephine 6
BAKER, Josephine Turck 4
BAKER, Julia Wetherill 1
BAKER, Karle Wilson 4
BAKER, La Fayette Curry H
BAKER, Lawrence Simons 1
BAKER, Leonard Theodore 3
BAKER, Lewis H
BAKER, Lucien 1
BAKER, Lucius K. 1
BAKER, Marcus 1
BAKER, Marjorie 3
  Montgomery Ward
BAKER, Martha Susan 1
BAKER, Mary Francis 5
BAKER, Morton 6
BAKER, Moses Nelson 4
BAKER, Murray M. 4
BAKER, Murray M. 4
BAKER, Naaman Rimmon 4
BAKER, Newman Freese 1
BAKER, Newton Diehl 1
BAKER, Oliver Edwin 2
BAKER, Orlando Harrison H
BAKER, Osman Cleander H
BAKER, Osmyn H
BAKER, Page M. 1
BAKER, Peter Carpenter 1
BAKER, Phil 4
BAKER, Purley A. 1
BAKER, Ralph Jackson 4
BAKER, Ray Stannard 2
BAKER, Raymond T. 1
BAKER, Remember 1
BAKER, Robert 4
BAKER, Robert Homes 4
BAKER, Roland Morris 5
BAKER, Roy Newsom 5
BAKER, S. Josephine 2
BAKER, Sam A. 1
BAKER, Samuel Garland 6
BAKER, Sarah 1
  Schoonmaker
BAKER, Simon Strousse 4
BAKER, Smith 1
BAKER, Stephen H
BAKER, Stephen 1
BAKER, Tarkington 1
BAKER, Thomas Rakestraw 1
BAKER, Thomas Stockham 1
BAKER, Virginia 1
BAKER, W. Browne 5
BAKER, Walter Browne 6
BAKER, Walter Cummings 1
BAKER, Walter Hudson 1
BAKER, Walter Ransom 4
  Gail
BAKER, Wilder DuPuy 6
BAKER, William B. 1
BAKER, William Clyde Jr. 4
BAKER, William Edgar 1
BAKER, William Gideon Jr. 2
BAKER, William Henry 1
BAKER, William Jesse 3
BAKER, William L. 1
BAKER, William Mumford 1
BAKER, William Pimm 6
BAKER, William Reginald 6
  Jr.
BAKER, William Taylor 1
BAKER, William W. 4
BAKETEL, H. Sheridan 3
BAKETEL, Oliver Sherman 1
BAKEWELL, Charles 1
  Montague
BAKEWELL, Donald 3
  Campbell
BAKEWELL, Paul 4
BAKHMETEFF, Boris 3
  Alexander
BAKHMETEFF, George 1
BAKHSHI, Chulam 1
  Mohammad
BAKKE, E. Wight 5
BAKKEN, Clarence John 5
BAKKEN, Herman Ernst 4
BAKKUM, Glenn A(lmer) 5
BAKLANOFF, Georges 1
BAKST, Henry Jacob 5
BAKWIN, Harry 6

BALABAN, Abraham 4
  Joseph
BALABAN, Barney 5
BALABAN, Emanuel 5
BALABAN, John 3
BALASSONE, Francis 6
  Salvatore
BALATKA, Hans H
BALBACH, Edward 4
BALBOA, Vasco Nunez de H
BALCH, Allan Christopher 2
BALCH, Edwin Swift 1
BALCH, Emily Greene 4
BALCH, Ernest Berkeley 1
BALCH, Franklin Greene 3
BALCH, George Beall 1
BALCH, Thomas Willing 1
BALCH, William Monroe 5
BALCHEN, Bernt 6
BALCOM, Max Fenton 4
BALD, J. Dorsey H
BALD, Robert Cecil 4
BALDANZI, George 5
BALDENSPERGER, 5
  Fernand
BALDERSTON, John Lloyd 3
BALDERSTON, Lydia Ray 5
BALDES, Edward James 5
BALDES, Raymond Charles 5
BALDINGER, Albert 5
  Henry
BALDINGER, Lawrence H. 5
BALDOMIR, Alfredo 2
BALDRIDGE, H. Clarence 4
BALDRIDGE, Howard 1
  Hammond
BALDRIDGE, Kenneth 5
  Ferguson
BALDRIDGE, Thomas 4
  Jackson
BALDWIN, A. Stuart 1
BALDWIN, Abel Seymour 4
BALDWIN, Abraham 1
BALDWIN, Abram Martin 1
BALDWIN, Albertus 4
  Hutchinson
BALDWIN, Alexander 3
  Richards
BALDWIN, Alice Mary 4
BALDWIN, Arthur Charles 3
BALDWIN, Arthur Douglas 5
BALDWIN, Arthur J. 1
BALDWIN, Asa Columbus 2
BALDWIN, Asa Fred 4
BALDWIN, Benjamin James 1
BALDWIN, Benjamin James 2
BALDWIN, Bird Thomas 1
BALDWIN, Calvin Benham 6
BALDWIN, Charles Jacobs 1
BALDWIN, Charles Sears 1
BALDWIN, Clarke Edward 3
BALDWIN, Daniel Pratt 1
BALDWIN, Edward 5
  Chauncey
BALDWIN, Edward J. H
BALDWIN, Edward 2
  Robinson
BALDWIN, Elbert Francis 1
BALDWIN, Elihu H
  Whittlesey
BALDWIN, Evelyn Briggs 1
BALDWIN, F. Spencer 4
BALDWIN, Francis Everett 3
BALDWIN, Francis Marsh 3
BALDWIN, Frank A. 3
BALDWIN, Frank Conger 2
BALDWIN, Frank Dwight 1
BALDWIN, Frank F. 4
BALDWIN, Geoffrey P. 3
BALDWIN, George Colfax 1
BALDWIN, George Johnson 1
BALDWIN, Hadley 4
BALDWIN, Harmon Allen 4
BALDWIN, Harry Streett 3
BALDWIN, Henry 1
BALDWIN, Henry 1
BALDWIN, Henry de 1
  Forest
BALDWIN, Henry 2
  Alexander
BALDWIN, Henry Perrine 4
BALDWIN, Henry Porter H
BALDWIN, Howard C. 4
BALDWIN, James 1
BALDWIN, James Fairchild 1
BALDWIN, James Fosdick 1
BALDWIN, James Fowler H
BALDWIN, James H. 1
BALDWIN, James Hewitt 5
BALDWIN, James Mark 5
BALDWIN, Jane North 5
BALDWIN, Jesse A. 1
BALDWIN, John * H
BALDWIN, John Brown H
BALDWIN, John Denison H
BALDWIN, John Finley Jr. 4

BALDWIN, John Thomas 6
  Jr.
BALDWIN, Joseph Clark 3
BALDWIN, Joseph Clark Jr. 1
BALDWIN, Joseph Glover H
BALDWIN, Lawrence 5
  (Counsell) Martin
BALDWIN, LaVerne 5
BALDWIN, Le Roy Wilbur 1
BALDWIN, Lewis 2
  Warrington
BALDWIN, Loammi H
BALDWIN, Loammi Jr. H
BALDWIN, Maitland 5
BALDWIN, Marshall 6
  Whithed
BALDWIN, Martin 3
  Mortimer
BALDWIN, Matthias H
  William
BALDWIN, Minor Coe 4
BALDWIN, Neilson Abeel 1
BALDWIN, Nellie Elizabeth 4
BALDWIN, Noyes 5
BALDWIN, Oliver Hazard 5
  Perry
BALDWIN, Ralph Lyman 5
BALDWIN, Raymond 5
  Peacock
BALDWIN, Robert James 5
BALDWIN, Roger Sherman H
BALDWIN, Roger Sherman 2
BALDWIN, Roland Dennis 3
BALDWIN, Samuel 4
  Atkinson
BALDWIN, Samuel Prentiss 1
BALDWIN, Sherman 5
BALDWIN, Simeon H
BALDWIN, Simeon Eben H
BALDWIN, Sylvanus H
BALDWIN, Theodore 1
  Anderson
BALDWIN, Theron H
BALDWIN, Thomas Scott 1
BALDWIN, Wesley 6
  Manning
BALDWIN, Wilbur 1
  McIntosh
BALDWIN, William H
BALDWIN, William 3
  Alpheus
BALDWIN, William Ayer 2
BALDWIN, William 1
  Delevan
BALDWIN, William 4
  Edward
BALDWIN, William 5
  Edward
BALDWIN, William Henry 1
BALDWIN, William Henry 1
  Jr.
BALDWIN, William James 1
BALDWIN, William Lester 4
BALDWIN, William Wright 2
BALDY, Christopher 1
BALDY, Edward Vincent 4
BALDY, John Montgomery 2
BALENCIAGA, Cristobal 5
BALES, James Anthony H
BALESTIER, Charles H
  Wolcott
BALEWA, Alhaji Abubaker 4
  Tafawa
BALFOUR, Donald Church 4
BALFOUR OF 4
  BURLEIGH, Lord
BALK, Robert 3
BALKE, Clarence William 4
BALKEN, Edward Duff 4
BALL, A. Brayton 1
BALL, Alice Worthington 1
BALL, Caroline Peddle 1
BALL, Charles Backus 1
BALL, Charles Thomas 4
BALL, Edward H
BALL, Elmer Darwin 2
BALL, Ephraim 1
BALL, Farlin Q. 1
BALL, Francis Kingsley 2
BALL, Frank Clayton 2
BALL, Frank Harvey 4
BALL, Fred Samuel 1
BALL, Frederick Joseph 4
BALL, George Alexander 3
BALL, George Harvey 1
BALL, Gordon Reginald 4
BALL, Helen Elizabeth 6
  Voellmig
BALL, Henry Price 2
BALL, Herman Frederick 1
BALL, James Moores 1
BALL, John Rice 1
BALL, L. Heisler 1
BALL, Louise Charlotte 2
BALL, Max W. 3
BALL, Michael Valentine 2

* Indicates More Than One Such Name Listed

BALL, Norman T(ower) 5
BALL, Oscar Melville 2
BALL, Otho Fisher 3
BALL, Raymond Nathaniel 4
BALL, Robert Bruce 6
BALL, Robert Lee 5
BALL, Sydney Hobart 2
BALL, Thomas 1
BALL, Thomas Henry 2
BALL, Thomas Raymond 2
BALL, William David 5
BALL, William Lee H
BALL, William Sherman 5
BALL, William Watts 5
BALL, Willis Manville 2
BALLAGH, James Curtis 2
BALLAINE, Francis Knight 4
BALLANTINE, Arthur Atwood 4
BALLANTINE, Edward 5
BALLANTINE, Henry Winthrop 3
BALLANTINE, Joseph William 5
BALLANTINE, Stuart 2
BALLANTINE, William Gay 1
BALLANTYNE, John 2
BALLARD, Aaron Edward 1
BALLARD, Addison 5
BALLARD, Bland Williams H
BALLARD, Charles William 4
BALLARD, Edward Lathrop 5
BALLARD, Ellis Ames 1
BALLARD, Ernest Schwefel 2
BALLARD, Frederic Lyman 4
BALLARD, Harlan Hoge 1
BALLARD, James Franklin 1
BALLARD, Nathaniel Harrison 3
BALLARD, Russell Henry 1
BALLARD, S. Thruston 1
BALLARD, Sam M. 4
BALLARD, Sumner 1
BALLARD, W. C. Jr. 3
BALLARD, William 5
BALLENGER, Edgar Garrison 5
BALLENGER, George Walter 1
BALLENGER, Howard C. 1
BALLENGER, William Lincoln 1
BALLENGER, William Sylvester 3
BALLENTINE, George Andrew 5
BALLENTINE, John Jennings 5
BALLER, Stuart Taylor 6
BALLIET, Thomas M. 2
BALLIN, Hugo 3
BALLIN, Max 1
BALLINGER, Charles L. 6
BALLINGER, John H. 6
BALLINGER, Richard Achilles 2
BALLINGER, Robert Irving 6
BALLMANN, Martin 1
BALLOCH, Edward Arthur 2
BALLOU, Adin Augustus H
BALLOU, Charles Clarendon 1
BALLOU, Frank Washington 3
BALLOU, Hosea H
BALLOU, Hosea II H
BALLOU, Hosea Starr 2
BALLOU, Levi Herbert 1
BALLOU, Maturin Murray H
BALLOU, Sidney 1
BALLOU, William Hosea 2
BALLY, Louis Henry 1
BALMANNO, Charles Gorden 1
BALMER, Edwin 3
BALMER, Frank Everett 3
BALMER, Thomas 3
BALOUGH, Charles 4
BALSAM, Aldo R. 4
BALTES, Peter Joseph H
BALTIMORE, 1st baron H
BALTIMORE, 3d baron H
BALTIMORE, 1st lord H
BALTIMORE, 2nd lord H
BALTZ, William N. 4
BALTZELL, Maude Day 4
BALTZELL, Robert C. 3
BALTZELL, Winton James 4
BALTZLY, Oliver Daniel 5
BALUTIS, Bronius Kasimir 6
BALZ, Albert George Adam 3
BALZAR, Frederick Bennett 4
BAMBERGER, Ernest 3
BAMBERGER, Louis 2
BAMBERGER, Ralph 5

BAMBERGER, Simon 1
BAMBOROUGH, William H
BAMBOSCHEK, Giuseppe 5
BAMFORD, Mary Ellen 5
BANAY, Ralph Steven 5
BANCROFT, Aaron H
BANCROFT, Cecil Franklin Patch 1
BANCROFT, Charles Grey 3
BANCROFT, Charles Parker 1
BANCROFT, Edgar Addison 1
BANCROFT, Edward H
BANCROFT, Francis Sydney 3
BANCROFT, Frederic 2
BANCROFT, George H
BANCROFT, Howland 4
BANCROFT, Hubert Howe 1
BANCROFT, Hugh 1
BANCROFT, J. Sellers 1
BANCROFT, Jessie Hubbell 5
BANCROFT, Joseph 1
BANCROFT, Levi Horace 3
BANCROFT, Milton H. 2
BANCROFT, Philip 6
BANCROFT, Thomas Moore 5
BANCROFT, Wilder Dwight 3
BANCROFT, William Amos 1
BANCROFT, William H. 1
BANCROFT, William Poole 1
BAND, Charles Shaw 5
BANDARANAIKE, Solomon West Ridgeway Dias 3
BANDELIER, Adolph Francis Alphonse 1
BANDHOLTZ, Harry Hill 1
BANDLER, Clarence G. 3
BANDMANN, Daniel Edward H
BANDY, Orville Lee 6
BANE, Juliet Lita 3
BANFIELD, Richard Wallace 4
BANFIELD, Thomas Harry 4
BANGHAM, Ralph Vandervort 4
BANGS, Francis Nehemiah H
BANGS, Francis Reginald 1
BANGS, George Archer 1
BANGS, Isaac Sparrow 1
BANGS, J. Edward 4
BANGS, John Kendrick 1
BANGS, L. Bolton 1
BANGS, Nathan H
BANGS, Outram 1
BANGS, Tracy R. 1
BANGSBERG, Harry Frederick 4
BANISTER, John * H
BANISTER, Marion Glass 3
BANISTER, William Brodnax 4
BANISTER, Zilpah Grant H
BANKER, Howard James 2
BANKER, Walter 6
BANKHEAD, Henry McAuley 5
BANKHEAD, John Hollis 1
BANKHEAD, John Hollis 5
BANKHEAD, Tallulah Brockman 5
BANKHEAD, William Brockman 1
BANKS, A. A. 3
BANKS, Alexander French 4
BANKS, Alexander Robinson 4
BANKS, Aloysius Burton 4
BANKS, Charles Eugene 4
BANKS, E. S. 3
BANKS, Edgar James 4
BANKS, Elizabeth 1
BANKS, Frank Arthur 4
BANKS, George B. 4
BANKS, Harry Pickands 3
BANKS, James Jones 3
BANKS, John H
BANKS, John Henry 1
BANKS, John Wallace 3
BANKS, Linn 1
BANKS, Louis Albert 1
BANKS, Nathan H
BANKS, Nathanial Prentiss H
BANKS, Theodore H. 1
BANKS, William Nathaniel 4
BANKSON, Virgil Lee 4
BANNARD, Otto Tremont 1
BANNEKER, Benjamin H
BANNER, John 5
BANNER, Peter H

BANNERMAN, Arthur Marling 6
BANNING, Ephraim 1
BANNING, Henry Blackstone 1
BANNING, Kendall 2
BANNING, Pierson Worrall 1
BANNING, William Vaughn 6
BANNISTER, Edward M. 1
BANNISTER, Harry Ray 4
BANNISTER, Henry Martyn 4
BANNISTER, Lucius Ward 3
BANNISTER, Nathaniel Harrington 1
BANNISTER, Robert James 6
BANNON, Henry Towne 3
BANNON, John Joseph Jr. 6
BANNOW, Rudolph F. 4
BANOV, Leon 6
BANTA, Arthur Mangun 2
BANTA, N. Moore 1
BANTA, Parke Monroe 5
BANTEL, Edward Christian Henry 5
BANVARD, John H
BANVARD, Joseph H
BANZHAF, Henry Leo 3
BAPST, John H
BAPST, Robert Thomas 3
BARA, Theda 4
BARACH, Frederica Pisek 6
BARACH, Joseph H. 3
BARACK, Louis Barry 6
BARAGWANATH, John Gordon 4
BARAKAT, Mohammad Zaki Taha Ibrahim 6
BARANOV, Alexander Andreivich H
BARAZA, Frederic H
BARBA, Charles Elmer 5
BARBE, Waitman 1
BARBEE, David Rankin 3
BARBEE, Hugh Arthur 5
BARBEE, James Thomas 4
BARBEE, William Randolph H
BARBELIN, Felix Joseph H
BARBER, Amzi Lorenzo 1
BARBER, Charles Newell 4
BARBER, Charles Williams 2
BARBER, Daniel H
BARBER, Donn 1
BARBER, Edward John 3
BARBER, Edwin AtLee 1
BARBER, Francis H
BARBER, George Garfield 2
BARBER, George Holcomb 5
BARBER, Gershom Morse 1
BARBER, H(oratio) 5
BARBER, Henry A. Jr. 4
BARBER, Henry Hervey 4
BARBER, Herbert Goodell 3
BARBER, Joel Allen 1
BARBER, John Warner H
BARBER, Levi H
BARBER, Mary I. 4
BARBER, Milton Augustus 1
BARBER, Muriel V. (Mrs. J.S. Barber) 6
BARBER, Noyes H
BARBER, Ohio Columbus 1
BARBER, Orion Metcalf 5
BARBER, Raymond Jenness 3
BARBER, Sidman I(ra) 1
BARBER, Virgil 5
BARBER, William A. 2
BARBER, William Harley 6
BARBER, William Henry 4
BARBEY, Daniel Edward 5
BARBEY, John Edward 3
BARBIROLLI, Sir John 5
BARBORKA, Clifford Joseph 5
BARBOT, Louis J. H
BARBOUR, Anna Maynard Mrs. 1
BARBOUR, Clarence Augustus 1
BARBOUR, Erwin Hinckly 5
BARBOUR, Frank Alexander 1
BARBOUR, George Harrison 1
BARBOUR, Henry Ellsworth 2
BARBOUR, Henry Gray 3
BARBOUR, Henry Merlin 4
BARBOUR, James H
BARBOUR, James Joseph 5
BARBOUR, John Carlyle 4
BARBOUR, John Humphrey 1
BARBOUR, John S. 3
BARBOUR, John Strode H
BARBOUR, John Strode Jr. H

BARBOUR, Lola Diehl 4
BARBOUR, Lucien H
BARBOUR, Oliver Lorenzo H
BARBOUR, Percy E. 2
BARBOUR, Philip Foster 2
BARBOUR, Philip Pendleton H
BARBOUR, Ralph Henry 2
BARBOUR, Thomas 2
BARBOUR, Thomas Seymour 1
BARBOUR, W. Warren 2
BARBOUR, William 1
BARBOUR, William Rinehart 4
BARBOUR, William Tefft 3
BARCELLA, Ernest Lawrence 6
BARCHFIELD, Andrew Jackson 1
BARCK, Carl 4
BARCLAY, Bertram Donald 3
BARCLAY, Charles Frederick 1
BARCLAY, Charles James 4
BARCLAY, David H
BARCLAY, George A. 4
BARCLAY, James Edward 4
BARCLAY, McClelland 2
BARCLAY, McKee 5
BARCLAY, Robert 4
BARCLAY, Shepard 1
BARCLAY, Thomas H
BARCLAY, Wade Crawford 5
BARCLAY, William Franklin 4
BARCLAY, William Kennedy Jr. 3
BARCUS, James Samuel 5
BARCUS, John M. 1
BARCUS, Norman 5
BARD, A. T. 3
BARD, Albert Sprague 5
BARD, Cephas L. 1
BARD, David H
BARD, Guy Kurtz 4
BARD, Harry Erwin 3
BARD, John H
BARD, Ralph A. 6
BARD, Roy Emerson 5
BARD, Samuel H
BARD, Sara Foresman 5
BARD, Thomas Robert 1
BARD, William H
BARDEEN, Charles Russell 1
BARDEEN, Charles Valde 1
BARDEEN, Charles William 1
BARDEL, William 1
BARDEN, Graham Arthur 4
BARDEN, Roderick Dudley 6
BARDGETT, Edward Russell 5
BARDO, August John 6
BARDO, Clinton Lloyd 1
BARDON, Thomas 1
BARDON, Thomas 4
BARDWELL, Rodney Jewett 3
BARDWELL, Winfield William 2
BARGER, Floyd 6
BARGER, Milton Sanford 4
BARGER, Samuel F. 4
BARGERON, Carlisle 6
BARHAM, Charles 3
BARHAM, Frank Forrest 4
BARHAM, John A. 4
BARING, Alexander H
BARING, Maurice 5
BARING, Walter Stephan 6
BARJA, Cesar 4
BARK, John Daly H
BARKAN, Adolf 1
BARKAN, Otto 3
BARKDULL, Charles J. 3
BARKDULL, Howard L. 4
BARKER, Albert Smith 1
BARKER, Albert Winslow 2
BARKER, Benjamin Fordyce H
BARKER, B(urrill) Devereux 6
BARKER, Burt Brown 6
BARKER, Charles Whitney Tillinghast 1
BARKER, Clare Wright 4
BARKER, David 1
BARKER, David Jr. H
BARKER, David R. H
BARKER, Ellen Blackmar ("Ellen Blackmar Maxwell") 5
BARKER, Elsa 3
BARKER, Ernest Franklin 5
BARKER, Franklin Davis 1

BARKER, Frederick William 2
BARKER, George 1
BARKER, George Frederick 1
BARKER, Harold Richard 4
BARKER, Harry 6
BARKER, Helen Morton 1
BARKER, Henry Ames 1
BARKER, Henry Stites 1
BARKER, Howard Hines 1
BARKER, Jacob H
BARKER, James L(ouis) 6
BARKER, James Madison 6
BARKER, James Madison 1
BARKER, James Nelson 3
BARKER, James William H
BARKER, Jeremiah H
BARKER, John Jr. 5
BARKER, John Marshall 1
BARKER, John Tull 3
BARKER, Joseph H
BARKER, Joseph Warren 6
BARKER, Josiah H
BARKER, Lewellys Franklin 2
BARKER, LeBaron R. Jr. 6
BARKER, Lillian Marion 4
BARKER, M. Herbert 2
BARKER, Nelson W(aite) 4
BARKER, Prelate Demick 4
BARKER, Ralph Hollenback 5
BARKER, Ralph Malcolm 3
BARKER, Reginald Charles 1
BARKER, Reginald Charles 2
BARKER, Samuel Haydock 5
BARKER, Theodore Gaillard 4
BARKER, Walter R. 3
BARKER, Wendell Phillips 1
BARKER, Wharton 1
BARKER, William Morris 1
BARKHORN, Henry Charles 1
BARKLEY, Alben William 3
BARKLEY, Henry L. 1
BARKLEY, James Morrison 1
BARKLEY, Jane Rucker 4
BARKLEY, William Elliot 2
BARKSDALE, Alfred Dickinson 5
BARKSDALE, Ethelbert 1
BARKSDALE, Ethelbert Courtland 6
BARKSDALE, John Woodson 5
BARKSDALE, Joseph Downs 1
BARKSDALE, William H
BARLEY, Rex 5
BARLOW, Arthur J. 2
BARLOW, Bradley H
BARLOW, Claude Heman 5
BARLOW, De Witt Dukes 2
BARLOW, Elmer Elbert 2
BARLOW, Francis Channing 1
BARLOW, Fred Jr. 3
BARLOW, Harry Elmore 3
BARLOW, Howard 5
BARLOW, Joel H
BARLOW, John 1
BARLOW, John Quincy 1
BARLOW, John Whitney 1
BARLOW, Maximillan A. J. 4
BARLOW, Milton Theodore 1
BARLOW, Samuel Kimbrough 1
BARLOW, Samuel Latham Mitchill 1
BARLOW, Stephen H
BARLOW, T. Noble 4
BARLOW, W. JARVIS 1
BARLOW, William Edward 1
BARLOW, William Harvey 5
BARNABAS, Brother 1
BARNABEE, Henry Clay 1
BARNARD, Charles 1
BARNARD, Charles Francis H
BARNARD, Charles Inman 2
BARNARD, Chester Irving 4
BARNARD, Daniel Dewey H
BARNARD, Edward Chester 1
BARNARD, Edward Emerson 1
BARNARD, Ernest Sargent 4
BARNARD, Frederick Augustus Porter H
BARNARD, George Grey 1
BARNARD, George M. 2
BARNARD, Harrison Bernard 5
BARNARD, Harry Eliot 3
BARNARD, Harry Everett 2
BARNARD, Henry H
BARNARD, Isaac Dutton H
BARNARD, James Lynn 2

BARNARD, Job 4
BARNARD, John H
BARNARD, John Gross H
BARNARD, Joseph Folger 1
BARNARD, Kate 6
BARNARD, William 2
  Nichols
BARNARD, William O. 3
BARNASON, Charles 2
  Frederick
BARNDS, William Paul 5
BARNDT, Milton A. 4
BARNES, Albert H
BARNES, Alfred Edward 2
BARNES, Alfred Victor 2
BARNES, Amos 1
BARNES, Annie Maria 4
BARNES, Benjamin F. 1
BARNES, Cassius 4
  McDonald
BARNES, Charles Albert 3
BARNES, Charles Benjamin 5
BARNES, Charles P. 3
BARNES, Charles Reid 5
BARNES, Charlotte Mary H
  Sanford
BARNES, Clarence Alfred 5
BARNES, Clifford Webster 2
BARNES, Demas H
BARNES, Dewey Loyd 4
BARNES, Donald C. 6
BARNES, Donald Lee Jr. 6
BARNES, Earl 1
BARNES, Earl Brandon * 4
BARNES, Eric Wollencott 4
BARNES, Floyd Morgan 3
BARNES, Frances Julia 4
BARNES, Francis George 5
BARNES, Frank Haslehurst 6
BARNES, Fred Asa 3
BARNES, Fuller Forbes 4
BARNES, George Anthony 4
BARNES, George Edward 5
BARNES, George Emerson 2
BARNES, George O. 2
BARNES, Gilbert Hobbs 4
BARNES, Gladeon Marcus 4
BARNES, Harlan Ward 2
BARNES, Harold Arthur 3
BARNES, Harry George 4
BARNES, Helen Florence 3
BARNES, Henry A. 5
BARNES, Henry Burr 1
BARNES, Henry Whitmer 5
BARNES, Hiram Putnam 4
BARNES, Howard 5
BARNES, Howel Henry Jr. 6
BARNES, Irving Franklin 3
BARNES, James 5
BARNES, James 1
BARNES, James Martin 3
BARNES, James Phillips 6
BARNES, Jasper Converse 1
BARNES, John 1
BARNES, John Beaumont 1
BARNES, John Bryson 3
BARNES, John Hampton 3
BARNES, John Peter 5
BARNES, John Potts 5
BARNES, John Wilcox 4
BARNES, Joseph Fels 5
BARNES, Joseph K. H
BARNES, Julius Howland 4
BARNES, Lemuel Call 1
BARNES, Margaret Ayer 4
BARNES, Margaret 4
  Campbell
BARNES, Mary Clark 2
BARNES, Mary Downing H
  Sheldon
BARNES, Maynard Bertram 5
BARNES, Morgan 1
BARNES, Mortimer Grant 1
BARNES, Mrs. John 4
BARNES, Nathan 6
BARNES, Nathaniel Waring 3
BARNES, Oliver Weldon 4
BARNES, Parker Thayer 5
BARNES, Parry 1
BARNES, Ralph W. 1
BARNES, Raymond Flatt 5
BARNES, Raymond Joseph 5
BARNES, Roswell Parkhurst 2
BARNES, Stephen 4
  Goodyear
BARNES, Stuart Knowlton 4
BARNES, Stuart Knowlton 5
BARNES, Thomas Robert 1
BARNES, Thurlow Weed 1
BARNES, Will Croft 1
BARNES, William * 1
BARNES, William H. 1
BARNES, William Henry 1
BARNES, William Preston 2
BARNET, Herbert L. 5

BARNETT, Augustus 4
  Edward
BARNETT, Bion Hall 3
BARNETT, Charles Condit 6
BARNETT, Charles 1
  Eldridge
BARNETT, Claribel Ruth 3
BARNETT, Claude A. 4
BARNETT, Claude A. 5
BARNETT, Eugene 5
  Epperson
BARNETT, Evelyn Scott 1
  Snead
BARNETT, Frank Willis 2
BARNETT, George 5
BARNETT, George Ernest 5
BARNETT, Harry 3
BARNETT, Herbert Phillip 5
BARNETT, James 1
BARNETT, James Foote 3
BARNETT, John T. 2
BARNETT, Joseph W. 6
BARNETT, Otto Raymond 2
BARNETT, R(obert) J(ohn) 5
BARNETT, Samuel Jackson 5
BARNETT, Stanley Pugh 5
BARNETT, Stephen Trent 1
BARNETT, Tom P. 1
BARNETT, William H
BARNETTE, William Jay 3
BARNEY, Austin Dunham 5
BARNEY, Charles Neal 3
BARNEY, Charles Tracy 1
BARNEY, Edgar Starr 1
BARNEY, John H
BARNEY, Joshua H
BARNEY, Mrs. Alice Pike 1
BARNEY, Samuel Stebbins 1
BARNEY, William Joshua 3
BARNHARDT, George 1
  Columbus
BARNHARDT, Jesse 2
  Homer
BARNHART, Henry A. 1
BARNHART, John 5
  D(onald)
BARNHART, Thomas 3
  Frederick
BARNHART, William Gray 1
BARNHILL, John Finch 2
BARNHILL, John Henry 6
BARNHORN, Clement J. 4
BARNHOUSE, Donald 4
  Grey
BARNICKEL, William 1
  Sidney
BARNITZ, Albert 4
BARNITZ, Charles H
  Augustus
BARNOUW, Adriaan Jacob 5
BARNOWE, Theodore 5
  Joseph
BARNS, William Eddy 1
BARNUM, Charlotte 1
  Cynthia
BARNUM, Dana Dwight 2
BARNUM, Gertrude 3
BARNUM, Hedrick Ware 4
BARNUM, Henry A. H
BARNUM, Henry Samuel 1
BARNUM, Herman Norton 1
BARNUM, Jerome 4
BARNUM, Malvern-Hill 2
BARNUM, Phineas Taylor H
BARNUM, Samuel Weed H
BARNUM, William Henry H
BARNUM, William Milo 1
BARNUM, Zenus H
BARNWELL, Charles 4
  Heyward
BARNWELL, Henry 6
  Stepehn
BARNWELL, John H
BARNWELL, John Blair 4
BARNWELL, Middleton 3
  Stuart
BARNWELL, Robert H
  Woodward
BARNWELL, Robert H
  Woodward
BARON, Herman 4
BARON, Joseph Louis 4
BARR, Albert J. 1
BARR, Alfred Hamilton 4
BARR, Alton Parker 4
BARR, Amelia Edith 1
BARR, Arvil S. 4
BARR, Charles H
BARR, Charles 4
BARR, Charles Elisha 1
BARR, David Goodwin 5
BARR, Frank 1
BARR, G. Walter 1
BARR, George Andrew 2
BARR, James Adam 5

BARR, James M. 4
BARR, John Henry 1
BARR, John W. 1
BARR, Joseph Seaton 5
BARR, Lyman 5
BARR, Norman B. 4
BARR, Richard Alexander 3
BARR, Robert 2
BARR, Roy Evan 6
BARR, Samuel Davis 3
BARR, Samuel Fleming 5
BARR, Thomas Francis 1
BARR, Thomas Jefferson 5
BARR, Thomas T. 4
BARR, William A. 4
BARR, William Alexander 1
BARR, William Francis 1
BARRADALL, Edward 4
BARRALET, John James H
BARRAS, Harry Watson 5
BARRATT, Norris Stanley 1
BARRELL, Joseph 1
BARRERE, Claude 4
BARRERE, Georges 2
BARRERE, Granville 5
BARRERE, Nelson H
BARRETT, Albert Moore 5
BARRETT, Alva Pearl 6
BARRETT, Benjamin Fiske 4
BARRETT, Channing 3
  Whitney
BARRETT, Charles D. 2
BARRETT, Charles F. 4
BARRETT, Charles J. 4
BARRETT, Charles 5
  Raymond
BARRETT, Charles Simon 1
BARRETT, Clifford Leslie 5
BARRETT, Darwin 1
  Sherwood Jr.
BARRETT, Don Carlos 2
BARRETT, Edward F. 3
BARRETT, Edward Ware 1
BARRETT, Frank A. 4
BARRETT, Fred Dennett 5
BARRETT, George Carter 4
BARRETT, George Horton H
BARRETT, Harrison D. 1
BARRETT, Harry 1
  McWhirter
BARRETT, Jay Amos 4
BARRETT, Jesse W. 3
BARRETT, John 1
BARRETT, John Ignatius 2
BARRETT, John Patrick 1
BARRETT, Joseph Hartwell 1
BARRETT, Kate Waller 1
BARRETT, Lawrence H
BARRETT, Leonard 2
  Andrew
BARRETT, Lillian Foster 4
BARRETT, Linton Lomas 5
BARRETT, Michael Thomas 1
BARRETT, Oliver Rogers 2
BARRETT, Oscar Fitzallen 1
BARRETT, Otis Warren 5
BARRETT, Raymond F. 5
BARRETT, Reginald 4
BARRETT, Reginald 4
BARRETT, Richard 4
  Cornelius
BARRETT, Richard Warren 2
BARRETT, Robert South 3
BARRETT, Samuel Alfred 4
BARRETT, Stephen Melvil 4
BARRETT, W. Franklin 4
BARRETT, Wilbert 3
  Hamilton
BARRETT, William E. 1
BARRETT, William Felton 3
BARRETT, William Hale 1
BARRETT, William Henry 6
BARRETT, William M. 1
BARRETT, Wilson H
BARRETTE, John 1
  Davenport
BARRETTO, Joseph (Marie) 5
  Antonio
BARRETTO, Laurence 5
  Brevoort (Larry)
BARRIENTOS, Rene 5
  Ortuno
BARRIER, Joseph Henry 5
BARRIERE, Hippolite H
BARRIGER, John Walker 5
BARRIGER, William Lillard 6
  Laurens
BARRINGER, Daniel H
  Moreau
BARRINGER, Daniel 4
  Moreau
BARRINGER, Edwin C. 6
BARRINGER, Paul 1
  Brandon

BARRINGER, Paul 5
  Brandon Jr.
BARRINGER, Rufus H
BARRON, Carter Tate 4
BARRON, Clarence Walker 1
BARRON, E. S. Guzman 3
BARRON, Elbert Macby 5
BARRON, Elwyn Alfred 1
BARRON, Ernest R. 4
BARRON, George Davis 2
BARRON, James H
BARRON, Joseph Day 4
BARRON, Leonard 1
BARRON, Mark 4
BARRON, Minerva Crowell 6
  Rogers (Mrs. Robert
  Eglinton Barron)
BARRON, Robert E. 4
BARRON, Samuel H
BARRON, William Andros 4
  Jr.
BARROW, Alexander H
BARROW, David 4
BARROW, David Crenshaw 1
BARROW, Elizabeth N. 5
BARROW, Frances H
  Elizabeth Mease
BARROW, Pope 1
BARROW, Washington H
BARROWS, Anna 3
BARROWS, Arthur 4
  Stanhope
BARROWS, Charles Clifford 1
BARROWS, Charles Henry 1
BARROWS, Chester Willard 1
BARROWS, David Prescott 5
BARROWS, Edwin 1
  Armington
BARROWS, Harlan H. 4
BARROWS, Harold Kilbrith 3
BARROWS, Isabel Chapin 1
BARROWS, John Chester 4
BARROWS, John Henry 1
BARROWS, John Otis 1
BARROWS, Lewis Orin 4
BARROWS, Morton 4
BARROWS, Nathaniel 4
  Albert
BARROWS, Nathaniel 3
  Haven
BARROWS, Raymond H. 3
BARROWS, Samuel June 1
BARROWS, Stanley Hill 1
BARROWS, Thomas 4
  Nichols
BARROWS, Wayne Groves 6
BARROWS, William 2
  Morton
BARROWS, William Stanley 1
BARRUS, Clara 1
BARRUS, George Hale 1
BARRY, David Sheldon 1
BARRY, Edward Buttevant 1
BARRY, Etheldred Breeze 5
BARRY, Frederick Lehrle 4
BARRY, Henry W. H
BARRY, Herbert 2
BARRY, James Henry 1
BARRY, John * H
BARRY, John Daniel 2
BARRY, John H. 3
BARRY, John Stewart H
BARRY, Joseph Gayle Hurd 1
BARRY, Leland Clifford 4
BARRY, Maggie W. 4
BARRY, Maurice Joseph 6
BARRY, Patrick H
BARRY, Patrick 1
BARRY, Peter 5
BARRY, Philip 2
BARRY, Thomas Henry 1
BARRY, Walter R. 1
BARRY, William Bernard 2
BARRY, William Farquhar 1
BARRY, William Taylor H
BARRY, William Taylor H
  Sullivan
BARRYMORE, Ethel 3
BARRYMORE, Georgiana 1
  Emma Drew
BARRYMORE, John 2
BARRYMORE, Lionel 3
BARRYMORE, Maurice 1
BARSANTI, Olinto Mark 5
BARSE, George Randolph 1
  Jr.
BARSS, John Edmund 5
BARSTOW, Edith 6
BARSTOW, Edwin Ormond 5
BARSTOW, Frank Quarles 4
BARSTOW, Gamaliel Henry H
BARSTOW, George Eames H
BARSTOW, Gideon H
BARSTOW, John Lester 1
BARSTOW, Robbins 4
  Wolcott

BARSTOW, William H
  Augustus
BARSTOW, William Slocum 2
BARTCH, George 1
  Washington
BARTEL, William Edwin 3
BARTELL, Floyd Earl 4
BARTELS, Vernon C. 3
BARTELT, Edward F. 3
BARTH, Carl G. 1
BARTH, Charles H. 1
BARTH, Charles H. JR. 2
BARTH, George Bittman 5
BARTH, Karl 5
BARTH, Theodore H. 4
BARTH, Theodore Nott 4
BARTH, William George 4
BARTHBERGER, Charles 4
BARTHEL, Oliver Edward 5
BARTHELMESS, Richard 4
BARTHOLD, Robert M. 6
BARTHOLDT, Richard 1
BARTHOLF, John Charles 5
  Palmer
BARTHOLOMAY, 6
  Anthony Francis
BARTHOLOMEH, George 4
  Kellam
BARTHOLOMEW, Abram 1
  Glenni
BARTHOLOMEW, Allen 1
  R.
BARTHOLOMEW, Charles 2
  L.
BARTHOLOMEW, Edward 2
  Fry
BARTHOLOMEW, Edward H
  Sheffield
BARTHOLOMEW, J. M. 1
BARTHOLOMEW, Pliny 1
  Webster
BARTHOLOMEW, 5
  Rudolph A.
BARTHOLOMEW, Tracy 3
BARTHOLOMEW, Truman H
  C.
BARTHOLOMEW, William 2
  Henry
BARTHOLOMEW, William H
  Newton
BARTHOLOW, Roberts 1
BARTINE, Horace F. 4
BARTKY, Adolph John 6
BARTKY, Walter 3
BARTLE, H(arold) Roe 6
BARTLEMAN, Richard 4
  Milne
BARTLESON, John H
BARTLET, William H
BARTLETT, Adolphus Clay 1
BARTLETT, Albert LeRoy 4
BARTLETT, Alden Eugene 5
BARTLETT, Alice Elinor 4
BARTLETT, Alice Hunt 4
  (Mrs. William Allen
  Bartlett)
BARTLETT, Allan Charles 5
BARTLETT, Arthur Charles 4
BARTLETT, Bailey H
BARTLETT, Boyd Wheeler 4
BARTLETT, Charles 3
  Lafayette
BARTLETT, Charles Ward 1
BARTLETT, Charles 4
  William
BARTLETT, Clarence 3
BARTLETT, Craig Scott 4
BARTLETT, Dana Webster 4
BARTLETT, Edgar Elliott 1
BARTLETT, Edmund 1
  Morgan
BARTLETT, Edward 4
  Everett Jr.
BARTLETT, Edward Lewis 5
BARTLETT, Edward 3
  Randolph
BARTLETT, Edward 1
  Theodore
BARTLETT, Edwin Julius 1
BARTLETT, Edwin Rice 3
BARTLETT, Elisha H
BARTLETT, Frank Leslie 4
BARTLETT, Frank W. 4
BARTLETT, Franklin 1
BARTLETT, Frederic Clay 3
BARTLETT, Frederic 4
  Huntington
BARTLETT, Frederic 5
  Pearson
BARTLETT, Frederick 1
  Bethune
BARTLETT, Frederick Orin 1
BARTLETT, George A. 5
BARTLETT, George 5
  Griffiths
BARTLETT, George True 2

BARTLETT, Harley Harris 4
BARTLETT, Homer Lyman 4
BARTLETT, Homer 4
  Newton
BARTLETT, Ichabod H
BARTLETT, J. Gardner 1
BARTLETT, John 1
BARTLETT, John Frank 5
BARTLETT, John Henry 4
BARTLETT, John Pomeroy 1
BARTLETT, John Russell 1
BARTLETT, John Russell H
BARTLETT, John S. 1
BARTLETT, John Sherren 4
BARTLETT, John Thomas 2
BARTLETT, John W. 4
BARTLETT, Joseph 1
BARTLETT, Joseph Warren 4
BARTLETT, Josiah 1
BARTLETT, Josiah Jr. H
BARTLETT, Louis 1
BARTLETT, Lynn Mahlon 1
BARTLETT, Maitland 2
BARTLETT, Margaret 3
  Abbott
BARTLETT, Murray 2
BARTLETT, Paul Dana 4
BARTLETT, Paul Wayland 1
BARTLETT, Robert Abram 4
BARTLETT, Samuel H
  Colcord
BARTLETT, Sir Charles 3
  John
BARTLETT, Thomas Jr. 1
BARTLETT, Walter Manny 5
BARTLETT, Willard 1
BARTLETT, William Henry 4
BARTLETT, William Henry 1
BARTLEY, Donald 5
BARTLEY, Elias Hudson 1
BARTLEY, Mordecai
BARTMAN, Russell C(lyde) 6
BARTOK, Bela H
BARTOK, Bela 4
BARTOL, Cyrus Augustus H
BARTOL, Cyrus Augustus 1
BARTOL, George E. 1
BARTOL, John Washburn 5
BARTOL, William Cyrus 1
BARTON, Andrew H
BARTON, Arthur James 2
BARTON, Benjamin Smith H
BARTON, Bruce 4
BARTON, Carlyle 1
BARTON, Charles Harmon 1
BARTON, Charles William 3
BARTON, Clara 1
BARTON, David H
BARTON, Donald Clinton 1
BARTON, Edmund Mills 1
BARTON, Enos M. 1
BARTON, Francis Brown 5
BARTON, George 1
BARTON, George Aaron 4
BARTON, George Hunt 1
BARTON, James 1
BARTON, James Levi 1
BARTON, James Moore 1
BARTON, John Kennedy 1
BARTON, John Rhea H
BARTON, John Wynne 1
BARTON, Joseph Wesley 6
BARTON, Lela Viola 5
BARTON, Levi Elder 1
BARTON, Olive Roberts 3
BARTON, Philip Price 4
BARTON, Ralph 1
BARTON, Ralph Martin 2
BARTON, Randolph 1
BARTON, Richard Walker H
BARTON, Robert 1
  McKinney
BARTON, Robert T. 1
BARTON, Samuel H
BARTON, Samuel Marx 1
BARTON, Silas Reynolds 1
BARTON, Stephen Emory 1
BARTON, Thomas Harry 4
BARTON, Thomas Pennant H
BARTON, Wilfred Mason 4
BARTON, William H
BARTON, William Edward 5
BARTON, William Eleazar 1
BARTON, William Henry 2
  Jr.
BARTON, William Paul H
  Crillon
BARTOW, Charles K. 1
BARTOW, Edward 4
BARTOW, Francis Dwight 3
BARTOW, Harry Edwards 4
BARTRAM, John H
BARTRAM, William 3
BARTSCH, Edward 4
BARTSCH, Paul 3
BARUCH, Bernard Mannes 4

BARUCH, Dorothy Walter 4
BARUCH, Emanuel de 1
  Marnay
BARUCH, Herman 3
  Benjamin
BARUCH, Simon 1
BARUCH, Sydney Norton 4
BARUH, Joseph Y. 4
BARUS, Annie Howes 5
BARUS, Carl 4
BARUTH, Ralph Howard 2
BARWELL-WALKER, 6
  Francis John
BARZINI, Luigi 5
BARZYNSKI, Joseph E. 5
BARZYNSKI, Vincent H
BASALDELLA, Mirko 5
BASCH, Antonin 5
BASCOM, Florence 4
BASCOM, Henry Bidleman H
BASCOM, John 1
BASDEVANT, Jules 5
BASDEVANT, Pierre Jules 4
BASE, Daniel 1
BASH, Louis Hermann 3
BASHEV, Ivan Hristov 5
BASHFORD, Coles H
BASHFORD, Herbert 1
BASHFORD, James 1
  Whitford
BASHIR, Antony 4
BASHORE, Harry William 5
BASHORE, Harvey Brown 5
BASILE, Anthony Robert 6
BASING, Charles 4
BASINGER, William S. 3
BASKERVILL, Charles 5
  Read
BASKERVILL, William 3
  Malone
BASKERVILLE, Charles 1
BASKETT, James Newton 1
BASKETTE, Gideon Hicks 1
BASKIN, Robert N. 5
BASQUIN, Olin Hanson 2
BASS, Charles Cassedy 5
BASS, Edgar Wales 1
BASS, Edward 3
BASS, Elizabeth 3
BASS, Frederic Herbert 3
BASS, George Arthur 4
BASS, George Arthur 5
BASS, Ivan Ernest 3
BASS, John Foster 1
BASS, John Meredith 3
BASS, Joseph Parker 1
BASS, Leo 3
BASS, Lyman Kidder H
BASS, Lyman Metcalfe 3
BASS, Ray Spurgeon 6
BASS, Robert Perkins 1
BASS, Sam H
BASS, Ula LeHentz 4
BASS, William Capers 3
BASSE, Jeremiah H
BASSET, Norman Leslie 1
BASSET, William Rupert 3
BASSETT, Adelaide 4
  Florence
BASSETT, Austin Bradley 1
BASSETT, Burwell H
BASSETT, Carroll Phillips 3
BASSETT, Charles A. II 4
BASSETT, Charles Nebeker 2
BASSETT, Ebenezer Don 1
  Carlos
BASSETT, Edward Murray 2
BASSETT, George Jarvis 4
BASSETT, Harry Winfred; 5
BASSETT, J. D. Jr. 4
BASSETT, John 3
BASSETT, John David Sr. 1
BASSETT, John Spencer 1
BASSETT, Lee Emerson 5
BASSETT, Louis D. 6
BASSETT, Neal 3
BASSETT, Richard H
BASSETT, Royal 4
BASSETT, Samuel Eliot 1
BASSETT, Sara Ware 5
BASSETT, Thomas J. 4
BASSETT, W. M. 3
BASSETT, William Austin 1
BASSETT, William Hastings 1
BASSFORD, Homer S. 1
BASSFORD, Horace 5
  Richardson
BASSI, Amadeo 5
BASSILL, John E. 3
BASSLER, Anthony 1
BASSLER, Ray Smith 6
BASSO, Hamilton 4
BASTEDO, Paul Henry 4
BASTIAN, Robert Owen 5
BASTIAN, Walter 6
  Maximillian

BASTIANINI, Ettore 4
BASTIN, Edson Sunderland 3
BASYN, Thomas 4
BATCHELDER, Ann 3
BATCHELDER, Charles 2
  Clarence
BATCHELDER, Charles 3
  Foster
BATCHELDER, Edward 3
  Trumbull
BATCHELDER, Ernest 5
  Allen
BATCHELDER, Frank 1
  Charles
BATCHELDER, John H
  Putnam
BATCHELDER, Loren 4
  Harrison
BATCHELDER, Nathaniel 3
  Horton
BATCHELDER, Richard N. 1
BATCHELDER, Roger 2
BATCHELDER, Samuel H
BATCHELDER, Wallace 1
BATCHELLER, George 1
  Clinton
BATCHELLER, George 1
  Sherman
BATCHELLER, Hiland 4
  Garfield
BATCHELOR, Tryphosa 3
  Bates
BATCHELOR, George 1
BATCHELOR, Horace 4
BATCHELOR, James 5
  Madison
BATDORF, Grant David 3
BATE, William Brimage 4
BATEMAN, Alan Mara 5
BATEMAN, Charles Heisler 4
BATEMAN, E. Allen 4
BATEMAN, Ephraim 1
BATEMAN, George Cecil 4
BATEMAN, George F. 2
BATEMAN, George 1
  Monroe
BATEMAN, Harry 2
BATEMAN, Herbert D. 3
BATEMAN, John 3
BATEMAN, John H. 3
BATEMAN, Newton 1
  Johnston
BATEMAN, Robert 2
BATEMAN, Sidney Frances H
  Cowell
BATEN, Anderson Edith 1
BATEN, Anderson Monroe 2
BATES, Albert Carlos 3
BATES, Albert H. 3
BATES, Alexander Berry 1
BATES, Alfred Elliott 1
BATES, Arlo 1
BATES, Arthur Laban 1
BATES, Barnabas H
BATES, Blanche 1
BATES, Blanche 2
BATES, Charles Austin 4
BATES, Charlotte Fiske 1
BATES, Clement 1
BATES, Clinton Owen 4
BATES, Daniel Moore H
BATES, David Stanhope H
BATES, E. D. 3
BATES, Edward H
BATES, Emma Frances 1
  Duncan
BATES, Ernest Sutherland 1
BATES, Frederick H
BATES, Frederick 3
BATES, George Andrew 1
BATES, George Dennis 1
BATES, George Handy H
BATES, George Handy 4
BATES, George Joseph 4
BATES, George W. 1
BATES, George Williams 1
BATES, Harriet Hegar 6
BATES, Harriet Leonora H
  Vose
BATES, Harry C. 5
BATES, Harry Cole 4
BATES, Henry Clay 1
BATES, Henry Liberty 6
BATES, Henry Moore 2
BATES, Herbert 1
BATES, Herbert Ernest 6
BATES, Isaac Chapman H
BATES, James 1
BATES, James L. 4
BATES, James Woodson 4
BATES, Jefferson Blakey 6
BATES, John H
BATES, John Coalter 1
BATES, John Lewis 2

BATES, Josephine White 5
  (Mrs. Lindon Wallace
  Bates)
BATES, Joshua H
BATES, Katharine Lee 1
BATES, Lewis Elon 6
BATES, Lindon Jr. 1
BATES, Lindon Wallace 1
BATES, Margret Holmes 4
BATES, Marston 6
BATES, Mary Elizabeth 1
BATES, Miner Lee 1
BATES, Onward 1
BATES, Oric 1
BATES, Phaon Hilborn 6
BATES, Putnam Asbury 5
BATES, Richard Waller 6
BATES, Samuel Penniman 1
BATES, Sanford 5
BATES, Theodore Cornelius 5
BATES, Theodore Lewis 5
BATES, Vyrl Raymond 6
BATES, Walter H
BATES, Walter Irving 1
BATES, William Albert 4
BATES, William H. 5
BATES, William Nickerson 2
BATES, William Oscar 1
BATES, William Wallace 1
BATH, Albert Alcus 5
BATHON, Wingrove 5
BATHRICK, Ellsworth R. 1
BATISTA (Y Zaldivar), 5
  Fulgencio
BATJER, Lawrence Paul 5
BATLLE BERRES, Luis 4
BATMAN, Levi Gordon 5
BATSON, David William 4
BATSON, William Howard 3
BATT, William Loren 4
BATTELL, Joseph 1
BATTELLS, Sarah M. E. 1
BATTEN, Charles Edward 4
BATTEN, Harry Albert 4
BATTEN, Joseph Minton 3
BATTEN, Loring Woart 1
BATTEN, Percy Haight 4
BATTEN, Samuel Zane 1
BATTENHOUSE, Henry 4
  Martin
BATTERSHALL, Fletcher 4
  Williams
BATTERSHALL, Walton 1
  Wesley
BATTERSON, Hermon 1
  Griswold
BATTERSON, James 1
  Goodwin
BATTEY, Robert H
BATTIN, Charles Reginald 3
BATTIN, Charles Thomas 4
BATTLE, Archibald John 1
BATTLE, Burrill Bunn 1
BATTLE, Cullen Andrews 1
BATTLE, George Gordon 2
BATTLE, Henry Wilson 1
BATTLE, Herbert Bemerton 1
BATTLE, Hyman Llewellyn 5
BATTLE, John S(tewart) 5
BATTLE, John Thomas 1
  Johnson
BATTLE, Kemp Davis 6
BATTLE, Kemp Plummer * 1
BATTLE, Richard Henry 1
BATTLE, S. Westray 1
BATTLE, Thomas Hall 1
BATTLE, William Horn H
BATTLE, William James 3
BATTLEY, Joseph F. 5
BATTS, Arthur Alanson 3
BATTS, Robert Lynn 1
BATTS, William Oscar 6
BAUCUM, A. W. 5
BAUDER, Reginald I. 4
BAUDOIN, Michael H
BAUER, Augustus H
BAUER, Benjamin F. 4
BAUER, Branz Karl 1
BAUER, Charles Christian 2
BAUER, Eugene Casper 6
BAUER, Franz Karl 1
BAUER, George Neander 5
BAUER, H(ans) G(ustav) 1
BAUER, Harold 3
BAUER, Johannes Henrik 4
BAUER, L. A. 1
BAUER, Leland Mason 5
BAUER, Louis Hopewell 4
BAUER, Marion Eugenie 3
BAUER, Ralph S. 1
BAUER, Ralph Stanley 3
BAUER, Walter 4
BAUER, William Charles 4
BAUER, William Hans 5
BAUER, William Waldo 4
BAUGHER, A. Charles 4

BAUGHER, Henry Louis H
BAUGHER, Norman J. 5
BAUGHMAN, L. Victor 1
BAUGHMAN, Lyle Lynden 4
BAUGHMAN, Roland 1
  Robert
BAUKHAGE, Hilmar 6
BAUM, Dwight James 1
BAUM, Ellis Conrad 4
BAUM, Frank George 1
BAUM, Harry 3
BAUM, Henry Mason 4
BAUM, Isidor 4
BAUM, L. Frank 1
BAUM, Mary Helen 6
BAUM, Morton J. 4
BAUM, Paull Franklin 4
BAUM, Vicki 4
BAUM, Walter Emerson 3
BAUM, William Miller Jr. 4
BAUMAN, Edward H
BAUMAN, Val Samuel 4
BAUMANN, Gustave 6
BAUMANN, Rudolf 5
BAUMBERGER, James 6
  Percy
BAUME, James Simpson 1
BAUMER, Bertha 3
BAUMES, Caleb Howard 1
BAUMGARDNER, Evelyn 6
  Julia Groves
BAUMGARDT, B. R. 1
BAUMGARTEN, Gustav 1
BAUMGARTNER, 5
  Apollinaris
BAUMGARTNER, 6
  Josephine Mae
BAUMGARTNER, Warren 4
  William
BAUMGARTNER, William 5
  Jacob
BAUR, Bertha 1
BAUR, Bertha E. 3
BAUR, Bertha E. 4
BAUR, Clara 1
BAUSCH, Edward 2
BAUSCH, John Jacob 1
BAUSCH, William 2
BAUSLIN, David Henry 1
BAUSMAN, Benjamin 1
BAUSMAN, Frederick 1
BAUSMAN, J. W. B. 1
BAWDEN, Samuel Day 2
BAWDEN, William Thomas 5
BAXENDALE, Esther 4
  Minerva
BAXLEY, Henry Willis H
BAXTER, Batsell 3
BAXTER, Bruce Richard 2
BAXTER, Clarence 1
  Hughson
BAXTER, Dow Vawter 4
BAXTER, Earl Hayes 5
BAXTER, Edmund 1
  Dillabunty
BAXTER, Edmund Francis 4
BAXTER, Elisha H
BAXTER, George Edwin 4
BAXTER, George Edwin 5
  M.D.
BAXTER, George Strong 1
BAXTER, Gregory Paul 5
BAXTER, H. R. 4
BAXTER, Henry H
BAXTER, Irving Franklin 1
BAXTER, James Phinney 1
BAXTER, James Phinney 6
  3d
BAXTER, Jere H
BAXTER, John H
BAXTER, John Babington 2
  Macaulay
BAXTER, Lionel David 3
  MacKenzie
BAXTER, Norman 3
  Washington
BAXTER, Percival Proctor 5
BAXTER, Portus H
BAXTER, Sylvester 1
BAXTER, Warner 3
BAXTER, William H
BAXTER, William Joseph 5
BAY, Charles Ulrick 4
BAY, Jens Christian 4
BAY, William Van Ness H
BAYARD, Edwin Stanton 3
BAYARD, Fairfax 5
BAYARD, James Asheton * H
BAYARD, John Bubenheim H
BAYARD, Nicholas 2
BAYARD, Richard Henry H
BAYARD, Samuel H
BAYARD, Thomas Francis H
BAYARD, Thomas Francis 1
BAYARD, William H
BAYDUR, Huseyin Ragip 3

BAYER, Lloyd Felch 3
BAYLES, Edwin Atkinson 5
BAYLES, George James 1
BAYLES, James Copper 4
BAYLES, Theodore Floyd 3
BAYLESS, William Silver 1
BAYLEY, Edward Bancroft 1
BAYLEY, Francis Reed 5
BAYLEY, Frank Tappan 3
BAYLEY, James Roosevelt H
BAYLEY, Richard 2
BAYLEY, Warner Baldwin 1
BAYLEY, William Shirley 3
BAYLIES, Edmund Lincoln 1
BAYLIES, Edwin 4
BAYLIES, Francis H
BAYLIES, Walter Cabot 1
BAYLIES, William H
BAYLIS, Charles T. 5
BAYLIS, Robert Nelson 2
BAYLISS, Alfred 1
BAYLISS, Clara Kern H
BAYLISS, Major William 3
BAYLOR, Adelaide Steele 1
BAYLOR, Frances Courtenay H
BAYLOR, Frances Courtenay 4
BAYLOR, George H
BAYLOR, James Bowen 1
BAYLOR, John Roy 3
BAYLOR, Robert Emmett H Bledsoe
BAYLOR, William Henry 5
BAYLY, Thomas H
BAYLY, Thomas Henry 4
BAYLY, Thomas Monteagle H
BAYMA, Joseph 3
BAYNE, Howard 3
BAYNE, Howard Randolph 1
BAYNE, Hugh Aiken 4
BAYNE, Reed Taft 3
BAYNE, Samuel Gamble 1
BAYNE, Stephen Fielding 6 Jr.
BAYNE, Thomas McKee H
BAYNE, William 3
BAYNE-JONES, Stanhope 5
BAYNES, Ernest Harold 2
BAYNES, John 1
BAYNHAM, William 4
BAYOL, Edgar Sansom 5
BAYS, Alfred William 3
BAYUK, Samuel 3
BAZETT, Henry Cuthbert 4
BAZIN, John Stephen H
BAZIOTES, William 4
BEA, Augustin Cardinal 5
BEACH, Albert Isaac 1
BEACH, Alfred Ely H
BEACH, Amy Marcy Cheney 2
BEACH, Arthur Grandville 1
BEACH, Charles Fisk * 1
BEACH, Charles Lewis 1
BEACH, Chester 3
BEACH, Daniel 1
BEACH, Daniel Magee 2
BEACH, David Nelson 5
BEACH, Earl Edward 6
BEACH, Edward Latimer 4
BEACH, Francis Asbury 1
BEACH, Frederick Converse 4
BEACH, George Corwin Jr. 2
BEACH, Harlan Page 1
BEACH, Harrison L. 1
BEACH, Harry Prescott 2
BEACH, Henry Harris 1 Aubrey
BEACH, John Kimberly 1
BEACH, John Newton 4
BEACH, Joseph Warren 5
BEACH, King D. 3
BEACH, Lansing Hoskins 2
BEACH, Lewis H
BEACH, Miles 1
BEACH, Moses Sperry H
BEACH, Moses Yale H
BEACH, R. Clyde 3
BEACH, Rex Ellingwood 4
BEACH, S. Judd 5
BEACH, Seth Curtis 4
BEACH, Spencer Ambrose 4
BEACH, Stanley Yale 5
BEACH, Sylvester 1 Woodbridge
BEACH, Walter Greenwood 2
BEACH, William Augustus H
BEACH, William Dorrance 4
BEACH, William Harrison 4
BEACH, William Mulholland 1
BEACH, William Mulholland 2
BEACH, Wooster H
BEACHAM, Joseph Jr. 3

BEACHLEY, Charles E. 3
BEACHLEY, Ralph Gregory 5
BEACOM, Thomas H. 3
BEACOM, Thomas H. 4
BEADLE, Chauncey Delos H
BEADLE, Erastus Flavel H
BEADLE, William Henry Harrison H
BEAHAN, Willard 1
BEAHM, William Mc Kinley 4
BEAIRD, Pat 4
BEAKE, Harold Carnes 5
BEAKES, Crosby Jordan 2
BEAKES, Samuel Willard 2
BEAL, Alvin Casey 1
BEAL, Carl H. 2
BEAL, Foster Ellenborough Lascelles H
BEAL, Francis Leavitt 4
BEAL, George Denton 5
BEAL, Gerald F. 5
BEAL, Gifford Reynolds 4
BEAL, Harry 2
BEAL, Henry C. 3
BEAL, James Hartley 4
BEAL, John M. 3
BEAL, Junius Emery 4
BEAL, Mary Barnes 4
BEAL, Reynolds 2
BEAL, Royal 5
BEAL, Thomas Andrew 4
BEAL, Thomas Prince 1
BEAL, Walter Henry 2
BEAL, William James 1
BEALE, Arthur Stanley 1
BEALE, Charles Hallock 2
BEALE, Charles Willing 4
BEALE, Edward Fitzgerald H
BEALE, Frank D. 5
BEALE, George William 3
BEALE, Howard Kennedy 4
BEALE, James Madison H Hite
BEALE, Joseph G. 4
BEALE, Joseph Henry 3
BEALE, Leonard Tillinghast 4
BEALE, Maria Taylor 4
BEALE, Richard Lee H Turberville
BEALE, Stephen 3
BEALE, Truxtun 1
BEALE, William Gerrish 3
BEALER, Alexander 3 Winkler
BEALES, C. William 1
BEALES, LeVerne 5
BEALL, Elias James 4
BEALL, Forest Wade 5
BEALL, Jack 1
BEALL, Jack 4
BEALL, James Glenn 5
BEALL, John Yates H
BEALL, Mary Stevens 1
BEALL, Reasin H
BEALL, Samuel Wootton 4
BEALS, Charles Edward 1
BEALS, David Thomas 4
BEALS, Edward Alden 1
BEALS, Frank Lee 5
BEALS, Ralph Albert 4
BEALS, Robert Diggs 5
BEALS, Walter Burges 4
BEAM, Francis H. 4
BEAM, Harry Peter 4
BEAM, Walter Irvin 3
BEAMAN, Alexander 2 Gaylord Emmons
BEAMAN, Bartlett 2
BEAMAN, Charles 1 Cotesworth
BEAMAN, Fernando Cortez H
BEAMAN, George William 1
BEAMAN, Robert Prentis 3
BEAMAN, William Major 1
BEAMER, Elmer A. 4
BEAMER, George Noah 6
BEAMER, John V. 4
BEAMISH, Richard Joseph 2
BEAMSLEY, Foster Gilman 3
BEAN, Arthur John 1
BEAN, Barton A. 4
BEAN, Benning Moulton H
BEAN, Charles Homer 5
BEAN, Francis Atherton 3
BEAN, George W. 3
BEAN, Henry J. 4
BEAN, Holly Marshall 4
BEAN, L. L. 4
BEAN, Richard 6
BEAN, Robert Bennett 2
BEAN, Robert Sharp 2
BEAN, Tarleton Hoffman 4
BEAN, William (Gleason) 6
BEAN, William Smith

BEANBLOSSOM, Moody Lewis 1
BEANE, Fred Emery 1
BEANE, John G. 1
BEAR, Firman Edward 5
BEAR, Harry 3
BEAR, Joseph Ainslie 3
BEARCE, Henry Walter 3
BEARCE, Ralph King 5
BEARD, Adelia Belle 4
BEARD, Augustus Field 1
BEARD, Charles Austin 2
BEARD, Charles Heady 2
BEARD, Cyrus 1
BEARD, Daniel Carter 1
BEARD, Edward E. 1
BEARD, George Miller H
BEARD, Gerald Hamilton 2
BEARD, James Carter 1
BEARD, James Henry H
BEARD, James Randolph 3
BEARD, James Thom 2
BEARD, James Thom 2
BEARD, John Grover 2
BEARD, Joseph Howard 3
BEARD, Lina 2
BEARD, Mary 2
BEARD, Mary Ritter 3
BEARD, Oliver Thomas 4
BEARD, Reuben Alview 2
BEARD, Richard 1
BEARD, Thomas Francis 1
BEARD, W. D. 1
BEARD, William Holbrook 1
BEARD, Wolcott Le Clear 4
BEARDALL, John Reginald 4
BEARDSHEAR, William Miller 1
BEARDSLEE, Clark Smith 1
BEARDSLEF, John Walter 4 Jr.
BEARDSLEE, Lester Anthony 1
BEARDSLEY, Arthur 2 Lehman
BEARDSLEY, Charles 4 Alexander
BEARDSLEY, Charles 4 Sumner
BEARDSLEY, Eben H Edwards
BEARDSLEY, Frank 3 Grenville
BEARDSLEY, Glover 4
BEARDSLEY, Grenville 4
BEARDSLEY, Guy Erastus 5
BEARDSLEY, Harry M. 3
BEARDSLEY, Henry 1 Mahan
BEARDSLEY, James 2 Wallace
BEARDSLEY, Samuel H
BEARDSLEY, Samuel 1 Arthur
BEARDSLEY, William 2 Agur
BEARDSLEY, William H. 1
BEARDSLEY, William S. 3
BEARDWOOD, Joseph 5 Thomas A.
BEARDWOOD, Matthew H
BEARY, Donald Bradford 4
BEASLEY, Frederick H
BEASLEY, Jean Tallman 6
BEASLEY, John 1
BEASLEY, Mercer H
BEASLEY, Rex Webb 4
BEASLEY, Ronald Storey 5
BEASLEY, Rowland Fowler 3
BEATES, Henry Jr. 1
BEATH, Robert Burns 1
BEATLEY, Clara Bancroft 1
BEATON, David 1
BEATON, Kenneth Carrol 5
BEATON, Lindsay Eugene 6
BEATON, Ralph Hastings 2
BEATTIE, Charlton Reid 1
BEATTIE, Fountain Fox 6
BEATTIE, Francis Robert 1
BEATTIE, James A. 4
BEATTIE, John Walter 3
BEATTIE, R. Leslie 3
BEATTIE, Robert Brewster 2
BEATTIE, Ronald Hanna 5
BEATTY, Adam 1
BEATTY, Alfred Chester 4
BEATTY, Alfred Chester 4
BEATTY, Arthur 2
BEATTY, Bessie 1
BEATTY, Charles Clinton 1
BEATTY, Clara Smith (Mrs. 5 Jesse O. Beatty)
BEATTY, Frank Edmund 1
BEATTY, Henry Russell 1
BEATTY, Hugh Gibson 4
BEATTY, James Helmick 5

BEATTY, James Laughead 5
BEATTY, Jerome 4
BEATTY, John H
BEATTY, John 1
BEATTY, John W. 1
BEATTY, Morgan 6
BEATTY, Paul Cousart 6
BEATTY, Richmond Croom 4
BEATTY, Sir Edward 1
BEATTY, Troy 1
BEATTY, Willard Walcott 4
BEATTY, William H
BEATTY, William Henry 1
BEATTYS, George Davis 2
BEATY, Amos Leonidas 1
BEATY, John Owen 4
BEATY, John Yocum 3
BEATY, Julian Bonar 6
BEATY, Martin H
BEATY, Richard A. D. 3
BEAU, Jonathan H
BEAUBIEN, De Gaspe 6
BEAUCHAMP, Edwin 4
BEAUCHAMP, Emerson 5
BEAUCHAMP, James K. 4
BEAUCHAMP, Lou Jenks 1
BEAUCHAMP, William 2
BEAUCHAMP, William Benjamin 1
BEAUCHAMP, William Martin 1
BEAUDETTE, F. R. 3
BEAUDOIN, L. Rene 5
BEAUJOLAIS, Louis H Charles D'Orleans
BEAUMONT, Andre Alden 6
BEAUMONT, Andrew 1
BEAUMONT, Campbell 3 Eben
BEAUMONT, Edmond 5 Eckhart
BEAUMONT, John Colt H
BEAUMONT, John Colt 2
BEAUMONT, Lilian Adele 1
BEAUMONT, William H
BEAUPRE, Arthur Matthias 1
BEAUREGARD, Augustin 3 Toutant
BEAUREGARD, Elie 3
BEAUREGARD, Marie H Antoinette
BEAUREGARD, Pierre H Gustave Toutant
BEAUX, Cecilia 2
BEAVEN, Albert William 2
BEAVEN, J. C. 3
BEAVEN, Thomas Daniel 1
BEAVER, Harry C. 4
BEAVER, James Addams 1
BEAVER, Sandy 5
BEAVERBROOK, Lord 6
BEAVERS, Thomas N. 4
BEAZELL, William Preston 2
BEAZLEY, George Grimes 6 Jr.
BEBAN, George 1
BEBB, Charles Herbert 2
BEBERMAN, Max 5
BECH, Georg 3
BECH, George 6
BECHDOLT, Frederick 3 Ritchie
BECHET, Paul Esnard H
BECHET, Sidney 3
BECHET, Sidney 4
BECHMAN, William 1 George
BECHT, J. George 1
BECHTEL, Edward 5 Ambrose
BECHTEL, Edwin De 3 Turck
BECHTEL, George M. 3
BECK, Adam L. 1
BECK, Brooks 1
BECK, Carl 1
BECK, Carl 1
BECK, Carol H. 4
BECK, Charles H
BECK, Claude Schaeffer 5
BECK, D. Elden 4
BECK, Edward Adam 1
BECK, Edward Scott 2
BECK, George 2
BECK, Herbert Wardle H
BECK, James Burnie H
BECK, James Montgomery 1
BECK, Jean-Baptiste 4
BECK, Johann Heinrich 1
BECK, Joseph David 1
BECK, Lewis Caleb H
BECK, Marcus Wayland 2
BECK, Martin H
BECK, Martin 4
BECK, Mary H

BECK, Robert McCandlass 5 Jr.
BECK, Theodric Romeyn H
BECK, Thomas Hambly 3
BECK, Victor Emanuel 4
BECK, Walter 4
BECK, William 1
BECK, William A. 4
BECK, William Henry 1
BECK, William Hopkins 3
BECKER, Alfred Le Roy 4
BECKER, Arthur Charles 6
BECKER, Arthur Dow 2
BECKER, Benjamin V. 3
BECKER, Carl Lotus 2
BECKER, Charles E. 5
BECKER, Charles 5 W(ashington)
BECKER, Elery Ronald 4
BECKER, Elizabeth H. 5 (Mrs. Richard F. Becker)
BECKER, Florence Hague 5 (Mrs. William A. Becker)
BECKER, Frederic Harry 3
BECKER, George Ferdinand 1
BECKER, Gustave Louis 3
BECKER, Harry J. 6
BECKER, Howard 4
BECKER, Isidor Schultz 4
BECKER, James Herman 5
BECKER, Joseph 4
BECKER, Lawrence 4
BECKER, May Lamberton 4
BECKER, Neal Dow 4
BECKER, Nils Folke 4
BECKER, Owen Chauncey 3
BECKER, P. L. 4
BECKER, Raymond 6 Herman
BECKER, Robert 4
BECKER, Sherburn Merrill 5
BECKER, Thomas A. 1
BECKER, Tracy Chatfield 1
BECKER, Washington 1
BECKER, William Dee 2
BECKERS, William Gerard 2
BECKET, Frederick Mark 2
BECKET, Welton David 5
BECKETT, Percy Gordon 4
BECKETT, Peter Gordon 6 Stewart
BECKETT, Richard 5 Creighton
BECKETT, Thomas Gervus 5 Jr.
BECKETT, Wesley Wilbur 1
BECKETT, William Wesley 4
BECKHAM, Clifford Myron 5
BECKHAM, J. Crepps 1 Wickliffe
BECKHART, Benjamin 6 Haggott
BECKINGTON, Alice 4
BECKJORD, Walter 1 Clarence
BECKLER, William 5 Alexander
BECKLEY, Quitman F. 4
BECKLEY, Zoe 4
BECKMAN, Francis Joseph 2
BECKMAN, Frederick 3 William
BECKMAN, Henry 5 Frederick
BECKMAN, L. J. 5
BECKMAN, Nils Arvid 5 Teodor
BECKMAN, P. E. 4
BECKMAN, Theodore N. 5
BECKMAN, Vincent Henry 1
BECKMANN, Max 4
BECKNELL, William H
BECKNER, Lucien 5
BECKWAY, Harvey George 6
BECKWITH, Charles 1 Minnigerode
BECKWITH, Clarence 1 Augustine
BECKWITH, Edward Anson 6
BECKWITH, Frederick 6 Downey
BECKWITH, Isbon 2 Thaddeus
BECKWITH, J. Carroll 1
BECKWITH, Paul Edmond 1
BECKWITH, Theodore Day 4
BECKWOURTH, James P. H
BECTON, Joseph D. 1
BÉDARD, Pierre (Pierre- 6 Armand Bédard de La Perriere)
BEDARD, Pierre (Pierre- 5 Armand Bedard de La Perriere)
BEDAUX, Charles E. 2
BEDDALL, Edward Fitch 4

---

* Indicates More Than One Such Name Listed

BEDDOWS, Charles Roland 5
BEDE, J. Adam 2
BEDELL, Arthur J. 6
BEDELL, Frederick
BEDELL, Gregory Thurston H
BEDELL, Gregory Townshend
BEDFORD, Alfred Cotton 1
BEDFORD, Edward 1
  Thomas
BEDFORD, F. H. Jr. 3
BEDFORD, Frederick
  Thomas
BEDFORD, Gunning * H
BEDFORD, Gunning S. H
BEDFORD, Henry Clark 5
BEDFORD, Homer F. 6
BEDFORD, Paul 5
BEDFORD, Scott Elias 5
  William
BEDFORD-JONES, Henry 2
  James O'Brien
BEDINGER, George H
  Michael
BEDINGER, Henry H
BEDLE, Joseph Dorsett H
BEDSOLE, Joseph Linyer 6
BEE, Barnard Elliott H
BEE, Hamilton Prioleau H
BEE, Thomas H
BEEBE, Brooks Ford 1
BEEBE, Frederick Sessions 5
BEEBE, James Albert 1
BEEBE, James Lyndon 4
BEEBE, Katherine 3
BEEBE, Kenneth John 5
BEEBE, Lewis C. 3
BEEBE, Lucius Morris 5
BEEBE, Murray Charles 2
BEEBE, Philip S. 5
BEEBE, Raymond Nelson 5
BEEBE, Royden Eugene Jr. 3
BEEBE, William 1
BEEBE, William 4
BEEBER, Dimner 1
BEECH, Walter Herschel 3
BEECHAM, Sir Thomas 4
BEECHE, Octavio H
BEECHER, Amariah H
  Dwight
BEECHER, Catharine H
  Esther
BEECHER, Charles 1
BEECHER, Charles 1
  Emerson
BEECHER, Edward H
BEECHER, Eunice White H
  Bullard
BEECHER, George Allen H
BEECHER, Henry Ward H
BEECHER, Laban S. H
BEECHER, Lyman H
BEECHER, Philemon H
BEECHER, Thomas H
  Kinnicut
BEECHER, Willis Judson H
BEECHLER, Glenn Curtis 3
BEECKMAN, R. Livingston 1
BEECROFT, John William 4
  Richard
BEEDE, Frank Herbert 1
BEEDE, Herbert Gould 2
BEEDE, Joshua William 1
BEEDY, Carroll Linwood 5
BEEHLER, William Henry 1
BEEK, Alice D. Engley 5
BEEKEY, Cyrus Ezra 6
BEEKMAN, Charles K. 1
BEEKMAN, Fenwick 4
BEEKMAN, Frederick 5
  Warren
BEEKMAN, Henry Rutgers 4
BEEKMAN, John K. H
BEEKMAN, Thomas 4
BEELER, Helen Marion 6
BEELER, John Allen 2
BEELER, Roy Hood 3
BEELEY, Arthur Lewton 6
BEER, George Louis 1
BEER, Thomas 1
BEER, William 1
BEERBOHM, Sir Max 3
BEERS, Alfred Bishop 1
BEERS, Barnet William 5
BEERS, Clifford
  Whittingham
BEERS, Cyrus H
BEERS, Edward M. 1
BEERS, Ethel Lynn H
BEERS, Frederick 3
BEERS, George Emerson 2
BEERS, Henry Augustin 2
BEERS, Lucius Hart 1
BEERS, William Harmon 5
BEESE, Charles William 3
BEESLEY, Eugene Nevin 6

BEESON, Charles Henry 2
BEESON, Henry White H
BEESON, Jasper Luther 4
BEESON, Malcolm Alfred 6
BEEST, Albert Van H
BEETLE, David Harold 5
BEETS, Henry 2
BEEUWKES, Adelia Marie 4
BEFFA, Harvey Arthur 6
BEGEMAN, Louis 2
BEGG, Alexander Swanson 1
BEGG, James Thomas 5
BEGG, John Alfred 6
BEGG, Robert Burns 6
  Haldane
BEGGS, George Erle 1
BEGGS, Gertrude Harper 5
BEGGS, Lyall T. 6
BEGICH, Nicholas Joseph 5
BEGIEN, Ralph Norman 2
BEGLEY, Ed 4
BEGLEY, John Patrick 6
BEGOLE, George Davis 5
BEGOLE, Josiah Williams H
BEHAN, Brendan Francis 4
BEHAN, Helen Peters 4
BEHAN, Joseph C. 3
BEHAN, Richard Joseph 4
BEHAN, Warren Palmer 3
BEHAN, William James 1
BEHARRELL, Sir George H
BEHM, Walter Henry John 4
BEHN, Hernand 1
BEHN, Sosthenes 3
BEHNCKE, David L. 4
BEHNER, Albert Jacob 1
BEHOUNEK, Frantisek 5
BEHREND, Bernard Arthur 1
BEHREND, Ernst Richard 1
BEHREND, Ernst Richard 2
BEHREND, Genevieve A. 4
  (Mrs. Hugo W. Behrend)
BEHRENDS, Adolphus 1
  Julius Frederick
BEHRENDT, Walter Curt 4
BEHRENS, Charles August 3
BEHRENS, Charles 6
  Frederick
BEHRENS, H. Frederick 1
BEHRENS, Henry H
BEHRENS, Herman Albert 4
BEHRENS, William 4
  Wohlsen
BEHRMAN, Martin 1
BEHRMAN, Samuel 6
  Nathaniel
BEHYMER, Arthur 5
  Livingstone
BEHYMER, Francis Albert 3
BEHYMER, Lynden 3
  Ellsworth
BEIDERBECKE, Leon Bix 4
BEIDERBECKE, Leon Bix 4
BEIDLER, Jacob Atlee 4
BEILSTEIN, Edward Henry 6
BEINECKE, Edwin John 5
BEINECKE, Frederick 5
  William
BEINECKE, Richard Sperry 4
BEINECKE, Walter 3
BEIRNE, Andrew H
BEIRNE, Joseph Anthony 4
BEISSEL, Johann Conrad 1
BEITLER, Harold 6
  Bornemann
BEK, William Godfrey 2
BEKINS, Melvin 4
BEKKER, Leander J. de 1
BELANGER, John W. 5
BELASCO, David 1
BELAUNDE, Victor Andres 4
BELAVAL, José S. 6
BELCHER, Edwin Newton 5
  Jr.
BELCHER, Frank 1
  Garrettson
BELCHER, Frank J. Jr. 3
BELCHER, Hilda 4
BELCHER, Hiram H
BELCHER, James Elmer 5
BELCHER, Jonathan H
BELCHER, Nathan H
BELCHER, Supply H
BELCHER, Wallace Edward 4
BELCOURT, George H
  Antoine
BELDEN, Charles Dwight 1
BELDEN, Charles Francis 1
  Dorr
BELDEN, Ellsworth Burnett 1
BELDEN, George Oglivie H
BELDEN, Henry Marvin 4
BELDEN, James Jerome 1
BELDEN, Jessie Van Zile 1
BELDEN, Josiah H

BELDEN, William 5
  Burlingame
BELDING, Alvah Norton 1
BELDING, Anson Wood 6
BELDING, David Lawrence 4
BELDING, Don 5
BELDING, Frederick 1
  Norton
BELDING, Milo Merrick Jr. 1
BELDING, Milo Merrick 1
  Sr.
BELDOCK, George J. 5
BELFIELD, Henry Holmes 1
BELFIELD, William 1
  Thomas
BELFORD, James B. 1
BELFORD, John L. 3
BELFOUR, C(ampbell) 5
  Stanton
BELGRANO, Frank N. Jr. 3
BELIN, Ferdinand Lammet 6
BELIN, G. d'Andelot 3
BELISLE, Hector Louis 2
BELK, Henry 5
BELK, William Henry 3
BELKNAP, Charles 3
BELKNAP, Daniel H
BELKNAP, Edwin Star 1
BELKNAP, George Eugene 1
BELKNAP, Henry Wychoff 2
BELKNAP, Jeremy H
BELKNAP, Morris Burke 1
BELKNAP, Paul Edward 6
BELKNAP, Raymond H. 4
BELKNAP, Reginald Rowan 3
BELKNAP, William 1
  Richardson
BELKNAP, William Worth H
BELL, Agrippa Nelson 1
BELL, Alexander Graham 1
BELL, Alexander Melville 1
BELL, Alfred Lee Loomis 6
BELL, Alphonzo Edward 2
BELL, Archie 5
BELL, Bennett D. 4
BELL, Bernard Iddings 3
BELL, Bert 2
BELL, Brian 2
BELL, Charles Henry H
BELL, Charles James * 1
BELL, Charles S. 2
BELL, Charles S. 3
BELL, Charles Webster 2
BELL, Clark 1
BELL, Daniel Wafena 5
BELL, Digby 1
BELL, E. T. 4
BELL, Earl Hoyt 4
BELL, Edward 1
BELL, Edward August 3
BELL, Edward Price 2
BELL, Edward Theodore 4
BELL, Enoch Frye 2
BELL, Frank Breckenridge 2
BELL, Frederic Somers 1
BELL, Frederic Somers 1
BELL, George 1
BELL, George Alfred 3
BELL, George Fisher 4
BELL, George Jr. 1
BELL, George Kennedy 3
  Allen
BELL, George L. 3
BELL, George Maxwell 5
BELL, Graham Bernat 5
BELL, Harmon 1
BELL, (Harold) Idris 1
BELL, Helene S. 1
BELL, Henry Gough 4
BELL, Henry Haywood H
BELL, Herbert Clifford 4
  Francis
BELL, Hill McClelland 1
BELL, Hillary 1
BELL, Hiram H
BELL, Hiram Parks H
BELL, Howard James Jr. 2
BELL, Hugh McKee 5
BELL, Isaac 1
BELL, J. Franklin 1
BELL, J. Spencer 4
BELL, Jack L. 6
BELL, Jacob H
BELL, James H
BELL, James Carleton 2
BELL, James Ford 4
BELL, James Madison H
BELL, James Martin H
BELL, James Montgomery 1
BELL, James Munsie 1
BELL, James S. 1
BELL, James Warsaw 5
BELL, James Washington 1
BELL, John * H
BELL, John C. 1
BELL, John Cromwell 1

BELL, John Cromwell Jr. 6
BELL, John G. 3
BELL, John Lewis 5
BELL, John W. 4
BELL, Joseph A(sbury) 5
BELL, Joseph B. 4
BELL, Joseph Clark 4
BELL, Joseph Milligan 5
BELL, Joshua Fry H
BELL, Kenneth C. 3
BELL, L. Nelson 6
BELL, Laird 4
BELL, Laura Joyce 1
BELL, Lawrence Dale 3
BELL, Lilian 1
BELL, Louis 1
BELL, Luther Vose H
BELL, Major Townsend 5
BELL, Marcus Lafayette 2
BELL, Mary Adelaide Fuller 4
BELL, Miller Stephens 2
BELL, Neil 4
BELL, Nicholas 4
  Montgomery
BELL, Ovid 3
BELL, Peter Hansborough H
BELL, Rae Floyd 5
BELL, Raley Husted 1
BELL, Reason Chesnutt 4
BELL, Rex 4
BELL, Robert 4
BELL, Robert Cook 4
BELL, Robert Edward 6
BELL, Roscoe Rutherford 1
BELL, Samuel H
BELL, Samuel Newell 4
BELL, Samuel Paris 4
BELL, Solomon H
BELL, Stoughton 6
BELL, Theodore Arlington 1
BELL, Thomas Montgomery 1
BELL, Ulric 3
BELL, Wilbur Cosby 1
BELL, William Allen 3
BELL, William Augustus 2
BELL, William Bonar 2
BELL, William Brown 3
BELL, William Constantine 5
BELL, William H. 4
BELL, William Hemphill 1
BELL, William Melvin 1
BELL, William Roe 4
BELL, William Yancy 4
BELLAH, Mildred Marie 6
BELLAIRE, Robert Thomas 2
BELLAMAH, Jeanne Lees 5
  (Mrs. Dale John
  Bellamah)
BELLAMANN, Henry 2
BELLAMANN, Katherine 3
BELLAMY, Blanche Wilder 4
BELLAMY, Charles Joseph 1
BELLAMY, Edward 1
BELLAMY, Elizabeth 1
  Whitfield
BELLAMY, F. Wilder 3
BELLAMY, Francis H
BELLAMY, Francis 4
BELLAMY, Francis Rufus 5
BELLAMY, Gladys Carmen 6
BELLAMY, John Dillard 1
BELLAMY, Joseph H
BELLAMY, Leslie Burgess 4
BELLAMY, Paul 3
BELLAMY, Raymond 4
  (Flavius)
BELLAMY, William 4
BELLANCA, Guiseppe 4
  Mario
BELLATTI, C. Robert 3
BELLATTY, Charles E. 5
BELLEW, Frank Henry H
  Temple
BELLEW, Kyrle 1
BELLEZZA, Russell G. 3
BELLEZZA, Vincenzo 4
BELLINGER, Charles 1
  Byron
BELLINGER, John 1
  Bellinger
BELLINGER, Joseph H
BELLINGER, Martha 1
  Fletcher
BELLINGER, Patrick 4
  Niesen Lynch
BELLINGER, William 2
  Whaley
BELLINGHAM, Richard H
BELLIS, Leon Robert 5
BELLMAN, Lawrence 5
  Stevens
BELLMAN, Russell 6
BELLOC, Hilaire 1
BELLOMONT, 1st earl H
BELLOWS, Albert Fitch H
BELLOWS, George Wesley 1

BELLOWS, Henry Adams 1
BELLOWS, Henry Whitney H
BELLOWS, Howard Perry 1
BELLOWS, Johnson 2
  McClure
BELLOWS, Robert Peabody 3
BELMONT, Alva E. Smith 1
BELMONT, August H
BELMONT, August 1
BELMONT, Morgan 3
BELMONT, Mrs. O. H. P. 1
BELMONT, Oliver Hazard 1
  Perry
BELMONT, Perry 2
BELNAP, LaMonte Judson 6
BELO, Alfred H. 1
BELO, Alfred Horatio 1
BELSER, James Edwin 6
BELSTERLING, Charles 3
  Starne
BELT, Benjamin Carleton 4
BELT, Harry H. 3
BELT, William Bradley 5
  Tyler
BELTZ, William Ray 6
BELVISO, Thomas Henry 4
BELYAYEV, Pavel 4
  Ivanovich
BELZ, Mrs. Henry (Dorothy 6
  Pershall Belz)
BEMAN, Nathan Sidney H
  Smith
BEMAN, Solon Spencer 1
BEMAN, Wooster Woodruff 1
BEMELMANS, Ludwig 4
BEMENT, Alburto 4
BEMENT, Alon 3
BEMENT, Caleb N. H
BEMENT, Clarence Edwin 4
BEMENT, Howard 1
BEMIS, Albert Farwell 1
BEMIS, Edward Webster 1
BEMIS, George H
BEMIS, Harold Medberry 5
BEMIS, Judson Stephen 1
BEMIS, Samuel Flag 6
BEMIS, Thomas Frederick 4
BEMISS, Samuel Merrifield 4
BENADE, James Arthur H
BENARD, Henri Jean Emile H
BENBRIDGE, Henry H
  Antony
BENCHLEY, Robert 2
  Charles
BENCHOFF, Howard 3
  Johnston
BENCHOFF, Robert 5
  J(ohnston)
BENCKENSTEIN, Leonard 4
  Julius
BENDA, Harry Jindrich 5
BENDA, Wladyslaw 2
  Theodor
BENDELARI, Arthur 6
  Enrico
BENDELARI, George 1
BENDER, Albert Maurice 1
BENDER, Eric J. 4
BENDER, George H. 4
BENDER, Harold H. 3
BENDER, Jack I. 5
BENDER, John Frederick 6
BENDER, Melvin T. 5
BENDER, Prosper 4
BENDER, Walter 3
BENDER, Wilbur H. 1
BENDER, Wilbur Joseph 5
BENDINER, Alfred 4
BENDIRE, Charles E. H
BENDIX, Ella Crosby (Mrs. 1
  Ella Crosby Bendix)
BENDIX, Max 2
BENDIX, Vincent 2
BENDIX, William 4
BENECKE, Adelbert 4
  Oswald
BENEDICT, A. L. 1
BENEDICT, Alfred Barnum 1
BENEDICT, Andrew Bell 3
BENEDICT, Anne 4
BENEDICT, Asa Gardiner 4
BENEDICT, C. Harry 5
BENEDICT, Cleveland 4
  Keith
BENEDICT, Cooper Procter 5
BENEDICT, Crystal 6
  Eastman
BENEDICT, David 1
BENEDICT, Elias Cornelius 4
BENEDICT, Erastus 1
  Cornelius
BENEDICT, Francis Gano H
BENEDICT, Frank Lee 1
BENEDICT, George 1
  Grenville

BERNARD, Victor Ferdinand 4
BERNARD, William Bayle H
BERNARDIN, Joseph Mariotte 4
BERNARDY, Amy Allemand 6
BERNATOWICZ, Albert John 5
BERNAYS, Augustus Charles 1
BERNBAUM, Ernest 3
BERNE, Eric Lennard 5
BERNE-ALLEN, Allan 5
BERNECKER, Edward M. 3
BERNEKER, Louis Frederick
BERNER, Harry M. 3
BERNET, John J. 1
BERNET KEMPERS, Karel Phillipus 6
BERNHARD, Alva Douglas 3
BERNHARD, Dorothy Lehman 5
BERNHARD, Joseph 3
BERNHARD, Richard J. 4
BERNHARD, William 5
BERNHARDT, Sarah 1
BERNHARDT, Wilhelm 5
BERNHEIM, Bertram Moses 3
BERNHEIM, Oscar Frederick 4
BERNHEIMER, Charles L. 2
BERNHEIMER, Charles Seligman 5
BERNHISEL, John Milton H
BERNIE, Ben 5
BERNIER, Paul 4
BERNINGHAUS, Oscar Edmund 3
BERNO, Jack Charles 6
BERNSTEIN, Aline 3
BERNSTEIN, Charles 2
BERNSTEIN, David 2
BERNSTEIN, Herman 1
BERNSTEIN, Jacob Lawrence 5
BERNSTEIN, Louis 1
BERNSTEIN, Louis 4
BERNSTORFF, Count Johann 1
BERNSTROM, Victor 1
BEROL, Alfred C. 6
BEROLZHEIMER, Edwin Michael 2
BEROUJON, Claude H
BERRES, Albert Julius 5
BERRESFORD, Arthur William
BERRETH, Herbert Raymond 6
BERREY, Rhodes Clay 6
BERREY, Ruth Robertson 6
BERRI, Wililam 1
BERRIEN, Cornelius Roach 5
BERRIEN, Frank Dunn 3
BERRIEN, John Macpherson H
BERRIGAN, Thomas Joseph 5
BERRY, Albert Edgar 1
BERRY, Albert Gleaves 1
BERRY, Albert Seaton 1
BERRY, Cecil Ralph 5
BERRY, Charles Harold 4
BERRY, Charles Scott 6
BERRY, Charles White 3
BERRY, Edward Wilber 2
BERRY, Edward Willard 5
BERRY, Frank 4
BERRY, Frank Allen 4
BERRY, George Leonard 2
BERRY, George Ricker 2
BERRY, George Titus 5
BERRY, Gilbert Milo 1
BERRY, Gordon Lockwood 1
BERRY, Harold Haile 4
BERRY, Harold Lee 4
BERRY, Hiram Gregory H
BERRY, Howard 3
BERRY, James Berthold 6
BERRY, James Edward 4
BERRY, James Henderson 1
BERRY, John H
BERRY, John Cutting 4
BERRY, Joseph Flintoft 1
BERRY, Joseph Francis 6
BERRY, Kearie Lee 5
BERRY, Lillian Gay 5
BERRY, Mark Perrin Lowrey 6
BERRY, Martha McChesney 2
BERRY, Mervin Albert 6
BERRY, Nathaniel Springer H

BERRY, Nixon T. 6
BERRY, Raymond Hirst 5
BERRY, Robert Mallory 1
BERRY, Robert W. 4
BERRY, Thomas 3
BERRY, Wallace 2
BERRY, Walter Van Rensselaer 1
BERRY, Ward Leonard 4
BERRY, Wilbur Fisk 4
BERRY, William Franklin 1
BERRY, William H. 2
BERRY, William H. 5
BERRYMAN, Clifford Kennedy 2
BERRYMAN, James Thomas 5
BERRYMAN, Jerome Woods 1
BERRYMAN, John 5
BERRYMAN, John Brondgeest 2
BERRYMAN, W. A. 3
BERSELL, Petrus Olof Immanuel 5
BERSTED, Alfred 1
BERTALANFFY, Ludwig von 6
BERTHOLF, Ellsworth Price 1
BERTOLET, William S(chaeffer) 5
BERTRAM, Helen (Lulu May Burt) 5
BERTRAM, James 1
BERTRAM, John H
BERTRAND, Ernest 3
BERTRANDIAS, Victor Emile 4
BERTRON, Samuel R. 1
BERTRON, Samuel Reading 1
BERTSCH, Howard 5
BERWALD, William 4
BERWIN, Franklin 6
BERWIND, Edward Julius 1
BESEMER, Howard Burhans 1
BESHLIN, Earl Hanley 5
BESLER, William George 4
BESLEY, Fred Wilson 5
BESLEY, Frederic Atwood 2
BESOSA, Harry Felipe 6
BESS, Demaree Caughey 4
BESS, Elmer Allen 4
BESSE, Arthur 3
BESSEY, Charles Edwin 1
BESSEY, Ernst Athearn 3
BESSON, Harlan 2
BESSON, Waldemar Max 4
BEST, Alfred M. 4
BEST, Clarence L. 3
BEST, Ernest Maurice 4
BEST, George Newton 1
BEST, Gertrude Delprat 2
BEST, Harry 4
BEST, Henry Riley 1
BEST, Howard Richard 4
BEST, James Irvin 4
BEST, James MacLeod 4
BEST, John G(arvin) 5
BEST, Nolan Rice 1
BEST, William 3
BEST, William Hall 4
BEST, William Parker 5
BESTIC, John Brereton 5
BESTON, Henry 5
BESTOR, Arthur Eugene 2
BESTOR, Paul 4
BESTROM, Leonard L. 5
BETELLE, James O. 6
BETH, Hilary Raymond 4
BETHEA, Jack 3
BETHEA, Oscar Walter 6
BETHEA, Solomon Hicks 1
BETHEL, George Emmett 1
BETHEL, John P. 4
BETHEL, Lawrence L. 4
BETHELL, Frank Hartsuff 3
BETHELL, Frank Hopkins 5
BETHELL, Union Noble 1
BETHKE, William 4
BETHUNE, George Washington H
BETHUNE, Lauchlin H
BETHUNE, Louise H
BETHUNE, Marion H
BETHUNE, Mary McLeod 3
BETTELHEIM, Edwin Summer J. 3
BETTEN, Cornelius 5
BETTEN, Francis Salesius 2
BETTENDORF, Joseph William 1
BETTENDORF, William Peter

BETTENDORF, William Peter 4
BETTERIDGE, Walter Robert 1
BETTERS, Paul V. 3
BETTI, Ugo 4
BETTMAN, Alfred 2
BETTMAN, Gilbert 2
BETTMANN, Bernhard 1
BETTON, Silas H
BETTS, Albert Deems 4
BETTS, B. Prank 1
BETTS, Charles Henry 1
BETTS, Craven Langstroth 1
BETTS, Edgar Hayes 3
BETTS, Edward C. 2
BETTS, Frederic H. 1
BETTS, Frederick A. 4
BETTS, Frederick William 1
BETTS, George Herbert 1
BETTS, George Whitefield Jr. 3
BETTS, James A. 1
BETTS, Louis 4
BETTS, Philander III 2
BETTS, Rome Abel 6
BETTS, Samuel Rossiter H
BETTS, Thaddeus 1
BETTS, William James 4
BETTY, Frank F. 6
BETZ, Robert Milton 5
BEUGLER, Edwin James 5
BEUKEMA, Herman 4
BEURY, Charles E. 3
BEUTEL, Albert Phillip 5
BEUTENMULLER, William 1
BEVAN, Arthur Dean 2
BEVAN, Charles Frederick 2
BEVAN, Laurence A. 4
BEVAN, Lynne J. 3
BEVAN, Ralph Hervey 6
BEVAN, Thomas Horatio 1
BEVAN, W. Lloyd 1
BEVEN, John Lansing 2
BEVERIDGE, Albert Jeremiah 1
BEVERIDGE, Andrew Bennie 5
BEVERIDGE, Frank Stanley 1
BEVERIDGE, Hugh Raymond 4
BEVERIDGE, John Harrie 1
BEVERIDGE, John Lourie 1
BEVERIDGE, Kuhne 5
BEVERIDGE, Lord William Henry 4
BEVERLY, Robert H
BEVIER, Isabel 2
BEVIER, Louis 1
BEVIN, Ernest 3
BEVIS, Howard Landis 4
BEWER, Julius August 3
BEWLEY, Anthony H
BEWLEY, Edwin Elmore 2
BEWLEY, Luther Boone 5
BEXELL, John Andrew 2
BEYE, Howard Lombard 1
BEYE, William 1
BEYEA, Herbert Writer 5
BEYER, Frederick Charles 4
BEYER, George Eugene 4
BEYER, Gustav 4
BEYER, Henry Gustav 1
BEYER, Otto Sternoff 2
BEYER, Samuel Walker 1
BEYERS, Henry Wendell 1
BEYL, John Lewis 4
BEYMER, William Gilmore 6
BEZANSON, Osborne 4
BEZANSON, Philip Thomas 6
BEZIAT, Andre 1
BHABHA, Homi Jehangir 4
BIANCHI, Julio Domingo 3
BIANCHI, Martha Dickinson 2
BIANCHI-BANDINELLI, Ranuccio 6
BIANCO, Margery Williams (Mrs. Francesco Bianco) 6
BIARD, Pierre H
BIAS, Randolph 3
BIBB, George Motier H
BIBB, William Wyatt H
BIBBY, James Harry 5
BIBERMAN, Herbert J. 5
BIBIGHAUS, Thomas Marshal H
BIBLE, Frank William 1
BIBLE, George Albert 3
BICKEL, Alexander Mordecai 6
BICKEL, Karl August 5
BICKEL, Shlomo 5
BICKELHAUPT, Carroll Owen 3

BICKELHAUPT, George Bernard 5
BICKERDYKE, Mary Ann Ball H
BICKET, James Pratt 1
BICKETT, Fanny Neal Yarborough 3
BICKFORD, Thomas Walter 1
BICKFORD, Thomas 1
BICKFORD, Walter Mansur 1
BICKHAM, Warren Stone 1
BICKING, Ada Elizabeth 4
BICKLE, Edward William 4
BICKLEY, George Harvey 1
BICKLEY, Howard Lee 2
BICKMORE, Albert Smith 1
BICKNELL, Bennet H
BICKNELL, Ernest Percy 1
BICKNELL, Frank Alfred 2
BICKNELL, Frank Martin 1
BICKNELL, George Augustus H
BICKNELL, George Augustus 1
BICKNELL, Lewis Williams 3
BICKNELL, Thomas Williams 1
BICKNELL, Warren Jr. 6
BICKNELL, Warren Moses 1
BICKNELL, William Harry Warren 4
BICKS, Alexander 4
BICKSLER, W. Scott 1
BIDDINGER, Noble Lycester 1
BIDDLE, A. J. Drexel 4
BIDDLE, Alexander 5
BIDDLE, Andrew Porter 2
BIDDLE, Anthony Joseph Drexel 2
BIDDLE, Arney Sylvenus 1
BIDDLE, Charles J. 5
BIDDLE, Charles John H
BIDDLE, Clement H
BIDDLE, Clement Miller Sr. 5
BIDDLE, Edward 1
BIDDLE, Edward William 1
BIDDLE, Francis 5
BIDDLE, George 6
BIDDLE, Henry Chalmers 1
BIDDLE, Horace P. H
BIDDLE, James H
BIDDLE, James 1
BIDDLE, James Stokes 1
BIDDLE, John 1
BIDDLE, John 1
BIDDLE, Nicholas * H
BIDDLE, Nicholas 1
BIDDLE, Richard H
BIDDLE, Ward Gray 2
BIDDLE, William Baxter 1
BIDDLE, William Phillips 1
BIDLACK, Benjamin Alden H
BIDWELL, Annie Ellicott Kennedy 1
BIDWELL, Barnabas H
BIDWELL, Charles Clarence 1
BIDWELL, Daniel Doane 4
BIDWELL, Edwin Curtis 1
BIDWELL, George Rogers 4
BIDWELL, John H
BIDWELL, Marshall Spring 1
BIDWELL, Marshall Spring H
BIDWELL, Percy Wells 5
BIDWELL, Walter Hilliard 4
BIEBEL, Franklin Matthews 4
BIEBER, Charles L. 4
BIEBER, Sidney 5
BIEDERBICK, Henry 1
BIEDERMANN, August Julius 1
BIEDERWOLF, William Edward 1
BIEFELD, Paul Alfred 2
BIEGLER, Philip Sheridan 2
BIELASKI, Alexander Bruce 4
BIEN, Julius 1
BIEN, Morris 1
BIENSTOCK, David Paul 6
BIENVILLE, sieur de H
BIERBAUM, Christopher Henry 2
BIERBOWER, Austin 1
BIERCE, Ambrose 1
BIERCE, Ambrose Gwinett H
BIERD, William Grant 2
BIERER, Andrew Gordon Curtin Jr. 3
BIERER, Andrew Gregg Curtin 1
BIERI, Bernhard Henry 5
BIERRING, Walter Lawrence 1
BIERS, Howard 4

BIERSTADT, Albert 1
BIESECKER, Frederick Winters 1
BIESTERFELD, Chester H. 3
BIFFLE, Leslie L. 4
BIGELOW, Abijah H
BIGELOW, Albert Francis 6
BIGELOW, Archibald Pierce 3
BIGELOW, Bruce Macmillan 3
BIGELOW, Charles C. 3
BIGELOW, Daniel Folger H
BIGELOW, Daniel Folger 4
BIGELOW, Edith Evelyn 4
BIGELOW, Edward Fuller 1
BIGELOW, Erastus Brigham H
BIGELOW, Florence 3
BIGELOW, Francis Hill 1
BIGELOW, Frank Hagar 1
BIGELOW, Frank Hoffnagel 1
BIGELOW, Frederic Russell 2
BIGELOW, Frederick Southgate 1
BIGELOW, George Hoyt 1
BIGELOW, Harriet Williams 1
BIGELOW, Harry Augustus 2
BIGELOW, Henry Bryant 4
BIGELOW, Henry Forbes 1
BIGELOW, Henry Jacob H
BIGELOW, Herbert Seely 3
BIGELOW, Jacob H
BIGELOW, John * 1
BIGELOW, John Milton 4
BIGELOW, John Ogden 6
BIGELOW, Lewis H
BIGELOW, Marshall Train 1
BIGELOW, Mason Huntington 5
BIGELOW, Maurice Alpheus 3
BIGELOW, Melville Madison 1
BIGELOW, Poultney 3
BIGELOW, Prescott 1
BIGELOW, Robert 5
BIGELOW, Robert Payne Mansfield 1
BIGELOW, Samuel Lawrence 2
BIGELOW, Willard Dell 1
BIGELOW, William Frederick 4
BIGELOW, William Sturgis 1
BIGGAR, Frank 6
BIGGAR, Hamilton Fisk 1
BIGGAR, Oliver Mowat 2
BIGGER, Frederick 4
BIGGER, Isaac Alexander 3
BIGGER, Robert Rush 4
BIGGERS, Earl Derr 1
BIGGERS, George Clinton 4
BIGGERS, John David 6
BIGGIN, Frederic Child 2
BIGGS, Albert Welburne 1
BIGGS, Asa H
BIGGS, Benjamin T. 1
BIGGS, Benjamin Thomas H
BIGGS, David Clifton 1
BIGGS, Hermann Michael 1
BIGGS, J. Crawford 3
BIGGS, Kate Britt (Mrs. Furnam Kenneth Biggs) 4
BIGGS, Walter 4
BIGGS, William Richardson 6
BIGHAM, Madge Alford 1
BIGHAM, Truman C. 3
BIGLER, Henry William H
BIGLER, John H
BIGLER, John Adolph 4
BIGLER, Regina Marie 4
BIGLER, William H
BIGLER, William H. 1
BIGLOW, Lucius Horatio 4
BIJUR, Nathan 1
BIKLE, Henry Wolf 1
BIKLE, Philip Melanchthon 1
BIKRAM, Tribhubana Bir 3
BILBO, Theodore Gilmore 3
BILBY, George N. 1
BILDER, Nathaniel 6
BILDERSEE, Adele 5
BILES, George Phineas 1
BILGRAM, Hugo 1
BILL, Alfred Hoyt 4
BILL, Earl Gordon 2
BILL, Edward Lyman 1
BILL, Harry Leon 6
BILL, John G. 3
BILL, Ledyard 1
BILL, Nathan D. 1
BILL, Raymond 4
BILLADO, Francis William 4
BILLANY, Harry Hilton 1

BILLER, George Jr. 1
BILLHARDT, Fred A. 5
BILLIKOPF, Jacob 3
BILLINGHURST, Benson 1
  Dillon
BILLINGHURST, Charles H
BILLINGS, Charles Ethan 4
BILLINGS, Cornelius 1
  Kingsley Garrison
BILLINGS, Edmund H
BILLINGS, Edward Everett 4
BILLINGS, Frank 5
BILLINGS, Frank Seaver 4
BILLINGS, Franklin Swift 5
BILLINGS, Frederic Church 5
BILLINGS, Frederick H
BILLINGS, Frederick 5
  Horatio
BILLINGS, George Herrick 1
BILLINGS, J(ohn) Harland 5
BILLINGS, John Shaw 1
BILLINGS, John Shaw 6
BILLINGS, Josh 1
BILLINGS, Luther Guiteau 1
BILLINGS, Stephen 5
  Ellsworth
BILLINGS, Thomas Henry 6
BILLINGS, W. Chester 1
BILLINGS, William H
BILLINGSLEY, Allen 3
  Loren
BILLINGSLEY, Paul 4
BILLINGSLEY, Sherman 5
BILLINGSLEY, William
  Newton
BILLMAN, Carl 6
BILLNER, Karl Paul 4
BILLOCK, George D(onald) 6
BILLOW, Clayton Oscar 4
BILLS, Hubert Leo 6
BILLSON, William Weldon 1
BILLUPS, Richard
  Alphonzo
BILLY THE KID H
BILMANIS, Alfred 2
BILOTTI, Anton 4
BILTZ, John Fredric 6
BILTZ, Norman Henry 4
BIMELER, Joseph Michael H
BIMSON, Lloyd A. 4
BIN ISHAK, Inche Yusoff 5
BIN-NUN, Dov 5
BINCH, Wilfred Reese 5
BINDER, Carroll 3
BINDER, Rudolph Michael 3
BINDERUP, Charles Gustav 3
BINES, Thomas 4
BINFORD, Jessie Florence 4
BINFORD, Lloyd Tilghman 3
BINFORD, Raymond 3
BINFORD, Thomas Howell 6
BINGAY, Malcolm Wallace 3
BINGHAM, Albert Young 6
BINGHAM, Amelia 1
BINGHAM, Anne Willing H
BINGHAM, Caleb H
BINGHAM, David Judson 1
BINGHAM, Edward 4
  Franklin
BINGHAM, Eugene Cook 2
BINGHAM, Florence 5
  Cornell
BINGHAM, George Caleb H
BINGHAM, George 5
  Hutchins
BINGHAM, Gonzalez 4
  Sidney
BINGHAM, Guy Morse 5
BINGHAM, Harry 4
BINGHAM, Henry Harrison 1
BINGHAM, Herbert
  Mackay
BINGHAM, Hiram H
BINGHAM, Hiram 1
BINGHAM, Hiram 3
BINGHAM, Joel Foote 1
BINGHAM, John Armor H
BINGHAM, Joseph Walter 6
BINGHAM, Kinsley Scott H
BINGHAM, Millicent Todd 5
  (Mrs. Walter V. Bingham)
BINGHAM, Norman 3
  Williams
BINGHAM, Ralph 1
BINGHAM, Robert 4
BINGHAM, Robert Fry 2
BINGHAM, Robert Worth 1
BINGHAM, Stillman 5
BINGHAM, Theodore
  Alfred
BINGHAM, Theodore 6
  Clifton
BINGHAM, Walter Van
  Dyke
BINGHAM, Wheelock
  Hayward

BINGHAM, William * H
BINGHAM, William II 3
BINGHAM, William J. 5
BINGHAM, William
  Theodore
BINING, Arthur Cecil 3
BINKLEY, Almond 5
  M(adison)
BINKLEY, Christian 5
  Kreider
BINKLEY, Robert Cedric 1
BINKLEY, Wilfred 4
  Ellsworth
BINKLEY, William 5
  Campbell
BINNEY, Amos H
BINNEY, Arthur 1
BINNEY, Charles Chauncey 1
BINNEY, Edwin 1
BINNEY, Horace H
BINNEY, John 1
BINNICKER, Richard 4
  Johnson
BINNIE, John Fairbairn 4
BINNION, Randolph 1
BINNS, Archie 5
BINNS, Charles Fergus 1
BINNS, Jack 3
BINNS, John H
BINNS, John Alexander H
BINNS, Walter Pope 4
BINSSE, Louis Francis de H
  Paul
BINSTED, Norman Spencer 4
BINYON, Robert Laurence 2
BIOLETTI, Frederic 4
  Theodore
BIOSSAT, Bruce 6
BIOW, Milton H. 6
BIPPUS, Rupert Frederick 3
BIRCH, Alexander Clitherall 6
BIRCH, David Robert 5
BIRCH, Frank Victor 6
BIRCH, Raymond Russell 6
BIRCH, Reginald Bathurst 2
BIRCH, Stephen 1
BIRCH, T. Bruce 6
BIRCH, Thomas H
BIRCH, Thomas Howard 1
BIRCH, William Russell H
BIRCHARD, Clarence C. 4
BIRCHARD, Glen Robbins 4
BIRCKHEAD, Hugh 1
BIRCKHEAD, Oliver W. 4
BIRD, Abraham Calvin 4
BIRD, Anna Child 4
BIRD, Anna Pennock 5
BIRD, Arthur 3
BIRD, Charles 1
BIRD, Charles 3
BIRD, Charles Sumner 4
BIRD, Eugene Hunt 4
BIRD, Frederic Mayer 4
BIRD, George Emerson 1
BIRD, Hobart Stanley 4
BIRD, James Pyper 3
BIRD, John 1
BIRD, John E. 1
BIRD, Paul Percy 5
BIRD, Philip Smead 2
BIRD, Reginald William 3
BIRD, Remsen du Bois 5
BIRD, Richard Ely 6
BIRD, Robert Montgomery 1
BIRD, Robert Montgomery 4
BIRD, Wallace Samuel 5
BIRD, Winfield Austin Scott 4
BIRDSALL, Benjamin P. 1
BIRDSALL, Carl A. 3
BIRDSALL, James H
BIRDSALL, Samuel H
BIRDSALL, William M. 1
BIRDSEYE, Clarence 3
BIRDSEYE, Claude Hale 3
BIRDSEYE, Victory H
BIRDWELL, Alton William 3
BIRDZELL, Luther Earle 4
BIRGE, Edward Asahel 2
BIRGE, Edward Bailey 5
BIRGE, Henry Warner H
BIRGE, Julius 3
BIRK, Newman Peter 4
BIRKBECK, Morris H
BIRKE, William D. 4
BIRKENMEYER, Carl 1
  Bruce
BIRKHEAD, Claude Vivian 3
BIRKHEAD, Leon Milton 3
BIRKHIMER, William
  Edward
BIRKHOFF, George David 2
BIRKINBINE, John 1
BIRKMIRE, William Harvey 1
BIRMINGHAM, Henry 1
  Patrick
BIRNBAUM, Martin 5

BIRNBAUM, Nathan 6
BIRNEY, Arthur Alexis 1
BIRNEY, David Bell H
BIRNEY, Hoffman 3
BIRNEY, James H
BIRNEY, James Gillespie 1
BIRNEY, Lauress J. 1
BIRNEY, William 1
BIRNEY, William Verplanck 1
BIRNIE, Rogers 1
BIRNIE, Upton Jr. 3
BIRNKRANT, Michael 4
  Charles
BIRREN, Joseph P. 1
BIRTLEY, Robert Lewis 2
BIRTWELL, Charles Wesley 1
BISBEE, Eldon 4
BISBEE, Frederick Adelbert 1
BISBEE, Horatio 4
BISBEE, Joseph Bartlett 4
BISBEE, Marvin Davis 1
BISBEE, Spaulding 3
BISBEE, William Henry 2
BISBING, Henry 1
  Singlewood
BISCH, Louis Edward 5
BISCHOFF, Henry Jr. 1
BISCOE, Alvin B. 4
BISCOE, Howard Morton 1
BISCOE, Thomas Dwight 3
BISEY, Sunker Abaji 1
BISGYER, Maurice 6
BISHOP, Abraham H
BISHOP, Arthur Giles 2
BISHOP, Arthur Vaughan 3
BISHOP, Avard Longley 4
BISHOP, Bruce Clay 5
BISHOP, Charles Alvord 4
BISHOP, Charles McTyeire 2
BISHOP, Charles Reed H
BISHOP, Charles Reed 4
BISHOP, Curtis Vance 4
BISHOP, Daniel Sanborn 3
BISHOP, David Horace 5
BISHOP, Eben Faxon 2
BISHOP, Edwin Whitney 2
BISHOP, Elias B. 1
BISHOP, Emily Montague 1
BISHOP, Ernest Simons 1
BISHOP, Eugene Lindsay 3
BISHOP, Everett L. 4
BISHOP, Farnham 1
BISHOP, Frederic Lendall 2
BISHOP, Geo(rge) Lee 5
BISHOP, George Sayles 1
BISHOP, George Taylor 1
BISHOP, Harry Gore 1
BISHOP, Heber Reginald 1
BISHOP, Henry Alfred 1
BISHOP, Hubert Keeney 6
BISHOP, Inez Shannon 6
BISHOP, Irving Prescott 4
BISHOP, James H
BISHOP, James 1
BISHOP, James Robert 3
  Thoburn
BISHOP, Joel Prentiss H
BISHOP, John Peale 2
BISHOP, John Remsen 4
BISHOP, Joseph Bucklin 1
BISHOP, Judson Wade 4
BISHOP, Louis Faugeres 4
BISHOP, Morris Gilbert 6
BISHOP, Mrs. L. Brackett 1
BISHOP, Nathan H
BISHOP, Percy Poe 4
BISHOP, Phanuel 1
BISHOP, Robert H. 4
BISHOP, Robert Hamilton 4
BISHOP, Roswell P. 1
BISHOP, Samuel A. 5
BISHOP, Samuel Henry 1
BISHOP, Sereno Edwards 1
BISHOP, Seth Scott 1
BISHOP, William Darius 4
BISHOP, William Henry 1
BISHOP, William Samuel 2
BISHOP, William Warner 4
BISHOPP, Fred Corry 5
BISPHAM, David Scull 1
BISPHAM, George Tucker 1
BISSELL, Arthur Douglas 1
BISSELL, Charles Spencer 5
BISSELL, Clayton Lawrence 5
BISSELL, Dougal 1
BISSELL, E. Perot 2
BISSELL, Edwin Cone 1
BISSELL, French Rayburn 5
BISSELL, George Edwin 1
BISSELL, George Henry 4
BISSELL, George Welton H
BISSELL, Herbert Porter 1
BISSELL, Hezekiah 1
BISSELL, Hillary Rarden 6
  (Mrs. Wadsworth Bissell)
BISSELL, Howard 1

BISSELL, John Henry 1
BISSELL, John William 4
BISSELL, Mary Taylor 5
BISSELL, Pelham St George 2
BISSELL, Richard Mervin 1
BISSELL, Walter Henry 1
BISSELL, William 1
  Grosvenor
BISSELL, William Henry H
BISSELL, Wilson Shannon 1
BISSELLE, Hulbert T. 4
BISSET, Andrew G(ustave) 2
BISSET, George 6
BISSETT, Clark Prescott 1
BISSHOPP, Kenneth 6
  Edward
BISSIER, Julius 4
BISSIKUMMER, Charles 4
  Hills
BISSONNETTE, T. Hume 3
BISSOT, Francois Marie 4
BISSOT, Jean Baptiste H
BISTLINE, Francis M. 5
BITNER, Harry Murray 4
BITTER, Francis 4
BITTER, Karl Theodore 1
  Francis
BITTING, William Coleman 1
BITTINGER, Charles 6
BITTINGER, John 1
  Lawrence
BITTINGER, Lucy Forney 4
BITTNER, John Joseph 4
BITTNER, Van Amburg 2
BIXBY, Anna Pierce Hobbs H
BIXBY, Augustus Rufus 4
BIXBY, Edson Kingman 1
BIXBY, Harold McMillian 4
BIXBY, Horace Ezra 5
BIXBY, Horace Ezra 4
BIXBY, James Thompson 1
BIXBY, Kenneth Roberts 5
BIXBY, Tams 1
BIXBY, Walter Edwin 6
BIXBY, William Herbert 1
BIXBY, William Keeney 1
BIXER, Edmond P. 5
BIXLER, Edward Clinton 5
BIXLER, James Wilson 2
BIZE, Louis A. 5
BIZZELL, James Adrian 2
BIZZELL, William Bennett 2
BJERKNES, Jacob Aall 6
  Bonneive
BJERREGAARD, Carl 1
  Henry Andrew
BJOERLING, Jussi 4
BJORK, David Knuth 4
BJORK, Eskil Von 6
BJORKMAN, Edwin 3
BJORNSSON, Sveinn 3
BJORNSTAD, Altrea 1
  William
BLABON, Joseph Ward 1
BLACHER, Boris 4
BLACHLY, Clarence Dan 6
BLACHLY, Frederick Frank 6
BLACK, Albert Gain 4
BLACK, Alexander 1
BLACK, Alfred Lawrence 5
BLACK, Arthur Davenport 1
BLACK, Barron Foster 6
BLACK, Benjamin Warren 4
BLACK, Carl E. 4
BLACK, Carlyle H. 4
BLACK, Charles Clarke 2
BLACK, Charles E. 3
BLACK, Chauncey Forward 1
BLACK, Clinton R. Jr. 4
BLACK, Dugald 4
BLACK, E. Charlton 1
BLACK, Edward Junius H
BLACK, Eli M. 6
BLACK, Ernest Bateman 2
BLACK, Eugene 6
BLACK, Eugene Robert 4
BLACK, Forrest Revere 2
BLACK, Frank B. 1
BLACK, Frank Swett 1
BLACK, Garland C. 3
BLACK, George Harold 5
BLACK, George Robison H
BLACK, Greene Vardiman 1
BLACK, Harold Alfred 5
BLACK, Harry Alfred 1
BLACK, Harry S. 1
BLACK, Henry 4
BLACK, Henry Campbell 1
BLACK, Howard 4
BLACK, Hugh 2
BLACK, Hugh S. 3
BLACK, Hugo La Fayette 5
BLACK HAWK H
BLACK, James * H
BLACK, James Augustus H

BLACK, James Byers 4
BLACK, James C. C. 1
BLACK, James Dixon 1
BLACK, James Harvey 3
BLACK, James William 1
BLACK, Jenny O. 1
BLACK, John H
BLACK, John Charles 1
BLACK, John Clarke 1
BLACK, John Donald 3
BLACK, John Donald 4
BLACK, John Janvier 1
BLACK KETTLE H
BLACK, Leon Harold 6
BLACK, Lloyd Llewellyn 3
BLACK, Loring M. 1
BLACK, Malcolm Stuart 4
BLACK, Marian Watkins 5
BLACK, Melville 5
BLACK, Mrs. Madeleine 5
  Elmer
BLACK, Newton Henry 5
BLACK, Newton Wade 3
BLACK, Norman David 2
BLACK, Norman David Jr. 5
BLACK, Robert Fager 6
BLACK, Robert Lounsbury 3
BLACK, Ruby Aurora 3
BLACK, Ryland Melville 5
BLACK, S(amuel) Bruce 5
BLACK, Samuel Charles 1
BLACK, Samuel Duncan 3
BLACK, Samuel Luccock 4
BLACK, Van-Lear 1
BLACK, Walter Joseph 4
BLACK, William 1
BLACK, William Harman 5
BLACK, William Henry 1
BLACK, William Joseph 4
BLACK, William Murray 1
BLACK, William Wesley 2
BLACK, Winifred 1
BLACK, Witherbee 3
BLACKALL, Christopher 1
  Rubey
BLACKALL, Clarence 1
  Howard
BLACKALL, Clarence 2
  Howard
BLACKALL, Frederick 1
  Steele
BLACKALL, Frederick 4
  Steele Jr.
BLACKARD, James 1
  Washington
BLACKBEARD H
BLACKBURN, Alexander 1
BLACKBURN, Armour 5
  Jennings
BLACKBURN, Edmund 4
  Spencer
BLACKBURN, Frederick 5
  George
BLACKBURN, George 1
  Andrew
BLACKBURN, George 4
  Stebbins
BLACKBURN, Gideon H
BLACKBURN, John Henry 3
BLACKBURN, John 4
  Simpson
BLACKBURN, Joseph H
BLACKBURN, Joseph Clay 1
  Styles
BLACKBURN, Joseph E. 4
BLACKBURN, K. Wilde 5
BLACKBURN, Luke Pryor H
BLACKBURN, Merrill H
  Mason
BLACKBURN, Robert 1
BLACKBURN, Walter 1
  Evans
BLACKBURN, William J. 2
BLACKBURN, William 1
  Jasper
BLACKBURN, William 1
  Maxwell
BLACKBURN, William 4
  Wallace
BLACKBURN, Willis 5
  Clifford
BLACKBURNE, Mary 5
  Frances
BLACKER, Daniel James 5
BLACKERBY, Philip Earle 2
BLACKETT, Patrick 6
  Maynard Stuart
BLACKFAN, Kenneth D. 1
BLACKFORD, Eugene 1
  Gilbert
BLACKFORD, Katherine 5
  M(elvina) H(untsinger)
BLACKFORD, Launcelot 1
  Minor

BLACKFORD, Staige Davis 2
BLACKHAM, George 1
Edmund
BLACKLEDGE, William H
BLACKLEDGE, William H
Salter
BLACKMAN, Edward 5
Bernard
BLACKMAN, William 1
Fremont
BLACKMAN, William 2
Waldo
BLACKMAR, Abel Edward 1
BLACKMAR, Charles 4
Maxwell
BLACKMAR, Esbon H
BLACKMAR, Frank Wilson 1
BLACKMARR, Frank 5
Hamlin
BLACKMER, Henry M. 5
BLACKMER, Samuel 3
Howard
BLACKMER, Sydney 6
BLACKMON, Frederick 1
Leonard
BLACKMORE, Emil A. 4
BLACKMORE, George 2
Augustus
BLACKMORE, Henry 4
Spencer
BLACKMORE, Simon 1
Augustine
BLACKMUR, Richard 4
Palmer
BLACKNEY, William 4
Wallace
BLACKSTOCK, Ira Burton 1
BLACKSTONE, A. E. 3
BLACKSTONE, Richard 1
BLACKSTONE, Timothy B. 1
BLACKSTONE, William H
BLACKTON, J. Stuart 1
BLACKWELDER, Charles 4
Davis
BLACKWELDER, Elliot 6
BLACKWELDER, Paul 6
BLACKWELL, Alice Stone 2
BLACKWELL, Antoinette 1
Louisa Brown
BLACKWELL, Ashby 6
Carlyle
BLACKWELL, Elizabeth 1
BLACKWELL, Emily 1
BLACKWELL, George 4
Lincoln
BLACKWELL, Hubert 3
Charles Hansard
BLACKWELL, James 4
Shannon
BLACKWELL, Julius W. H
BLACKWELL, Mary B. 6
(Mrs. Edward F.
Joehrendt)
BLACKWELL, Otto 5
Bernard
BLACKWELL, Robert 1
Emory
BLACKWELL, Thomas 4
Joseph
BLACKWOOD, Alexander 1
Leslie
BLACKWOOD, Andrew 4
Watterson
BLACKWOOD, Ibra C. 1
BLACKWOOD, Norman 1
Jerome
BLACKWOOD, Oswald 3
BLADEN, William H
BLAESS, August F. 5
BLAFFER, Robert Lee 2
BLAGDEN, Augustus 4
Silliman
BLAGONRAROV, Anatoli 6
Arkadyevich
BLAHD, Mose Emmett 1
BLAIKIE, William 1
BLAIN, Alexander William 4
BLAIN, Hugh Mercer Sr. 5
BLAINE, Helen Louise 1
Townsend
BLAINE, James Gillespie H
BLAINE, James Gillespie 5
BLAINE, John J. 4
BLAINE, Mrs. Emmons 3
BLAIR, Albion Zelophehad 4
BLAIR, Algernon 3
BLAIR, Andrew Alexander 1
BLAIR, Apolline Madison 4
BLAIR, Austin 1
BLAIR, Bernard H
BLAIR, C. Ledyard 4
BLAIR, Charles Austin 1
BLAIR, Chauncey J. 1
BLAIR, Cowgill 5
BLAIR, David Ellmore 3
BLAIR, David H. 2

BLAIR, Edwin Foster 5
BLAIR, Eliza Nelson 1
BLAIR, Emily Newell 3
BLAIR, Emma Helen 1
BLAIR, Eugenie (Mrs. 5
Robert L. Downing)
BLAIR, Floyd Gilbert 4
BLAIR, Francis Grant 1
BLAIR, Francis Grant 1
BLAIR, Francis Preston H
BLAIR, Francis Preston Jr. H
BLAIR, Frank Warrenner 3
BLAIR, Frederic Howes 4
BLAIR, Harry Wallace 4
BLAIR, Henry Alexander 5
BLAIR, Henry Augustus 2
BLAIR, Henry Patterson 2
BLAIR, Henry William 1
BLAIR, Herbert Francis 5
BLAIR, Hugh McLeod 4
BLAIR, Jack F. 5
BLAIR, James * H
BLAIR, James A. Jr. 1
BLAIR, James Carroll 3
BLAIR, James Lawrence 1
BLAIR, James T. Jr. 4
BLAIR, James Thomas 5
BLAIR, John * H
BLAIR, John Halsey 1
BLAIR, John Insley 1
BLAIR, John Leo 1
BLAIR, Joseph Cullen 1
BLAIR, Joseph Paxton 2
BLAIR, Margaret Josephine 4
BLAIR, Montgomery H
BLAIR, Paxton 6
BLAIR, Samuel H
BLAIR, Samuel Steel H
BLAIR, Vilray Papin 3
BLAIR, Walter Dabney 3
BLAIR, Watson Franklin 1
BLAIR, William Allen 2
BLAIR, William Reid 1
BLAIR, William Richards 6
BLAIR, William Wightman 1
BLAIR-SMITH, Robert M. 5
BLAISDELL, Albert 1
Franklin
BLAISDELL, Anthony 1
Houghtaling
BLAISDELL, Daniel H
BLAISDELL, Gideon 5
Moores
BLAISDELL, James Arnold 1
BLAISDELL, Thomas 2
Charles
BLAISDELL, Warren Carl 5
BLAKE, A. Harold 3
BLAKE, Charles S. 1
BLAKE, Chauncey 2
Etheridge
BLAKE, Clarence John 1
BLAKE, Clinton Hamlin 2
BLAKE, Edgar 2
BLAKE, Edgar Jr. 2
BLAKE, Edward Everett 2
BLAKE, Eli Whitney H
BLAKE, Emily Calvin 3
BLAKE, Francis 1
BLAKE, Francis Gilman 3
BLAKE, Frederic Columbus 5
BLAKE, George H. 5
BLAKE, Harold Hamilton 5
BLAKE, Harrison Gray Otis H
BLAKE, Henry Nichols 3
BLAKE, Henry Seavey 3
BLAKE, Henry William 1
BLAKE, Homer Crane H
BLAKE, James Henry 4
BLAKE, James Vila 1
BLAKE, John Charles 5
BLAKE, John George 1
BLAKE, John Jr. H
BLAKE, John Lauris H
BLAKE, John Walter 4
BLAKE, Joseph Augustus 1
BLAKE, Katherine 1
Alexander Duer
BLAKE, Lillie Devereux 1
BLAKE, Lucien Ira 1
BLAKE, Luther Lee 3
BLAKE, Lyman Reed 1
BLAKE, Lynn Stanford 4
BLAKE, Mary Elizabeth 1
BLAKE, Mary Katharine 4
Evans
BLAKE, Maxwell 3
BLAKE, Monroe Williams 3
BLAKE, Ralph Mason 3
BLAKE, Robert Pierpont 3
BLAKE, Sidney Fay 4
BLAKE, Theodore 2
Evernghim
BLAKE, Thomas H
Holdsworth
BLAKE, Tiffany 2

BLAKE, Warren Everett 4
BLAKE, William Phipps 1
BLAKE, William Rufus H
BLAKELEY, George Henry 2
BLAKELOCK, David 6
Hazen
BLAKELOCK, Ralph Albert 1
BLAKELY, Bertha Eliza 5
BLAKELY, Charles Adams 6
BLAKELY, Edward 6
Bradford
BLAKELY, George 5
BLAKELY, John Russell 2
Young
BLAKELY, Johnston H
BLAKEMAN, Edward 6
William
BLAKEMORE, Arthur 5
Hendley
BLAKENEY, Albert 1
Alexander
BLAKESLEE, Albert 3
Francis
BLAKESLEE, Arthur 4
Lyman
BLAKESLEE, Clarence 4
BLAKESLEE, Dennis A. 1
BLAKESLEE, Edwin 4
Mitchell
BLAKESLEE, Erastus 1
BLAKESLEE, Francis 2
Durbin
BLAKESLEE, Fred Gilbert 2
BLAKESLEE, George 3
Hubbard
BLAKESLEE, Howard 3
Walter
BLAKESLEE, Raymond 1
Ives
BLAKEY, Roy Gillispie 5
BLAKLEY, William A. 6
BLAKSLEE, James I. 5
BLALOCK, Alfred 4
BLALOCK, Jesse Marion 5
BLALOCK, Myron Geer 3
BLALOCK, U(riah) Benton 5
BLAMER, DeWitt 5
BLANC, Antoine 5
BLANCH, Arnold 5
BLANCHARD, Amy Ella 1
BLANCHARD, Arthur 5
Alphonzo
BLANCHARD, Arthur 5
Horace
BLANCHARD, Charles 1
Albert
BLANCHARD, Clarence 4
John
BLANCHARD, Ferdinand 5
Quincy
BLANCHARD, Frank 1
LeRoy
BLANCHARD, Frederic 2
Thomas
BLANCHARD, George 1
Roberts
BLANCHARD, Grace 2
BLANCHARD, Harold 5
Hooper
BLANCHARD, Harold M. 4
BLANCHARD, Henry 1
BLANCHARD, James 1
Armstrong
BLANCHARD, John H
BLANCHARD, Jonathan H
BLANCHARD, LaFayette 1
Randall
BLANCHARD, Lucy 1
Mansfield
BLANCHARD, Murray 1
BLANCHARD, Nathan 1
Weston
BLANCHARD, Newton 1
Crain
BLANCHARD, Ozro Seth 3
BLANCHARD, Ralph 5
Harris
BLANCHARD, Ralph 6
Harrub
BLANCHARD, Raoul 5
BLANCHARD, Rufus 1
BLANCHARD, Thomas H
BLANCHARD, William H. 4
BLANCHARD, William 2
Martin
BLANCHET, Clement 4
Theophilus
BLANCHET, Francois H
Norbert
BLANCHET, John Baptiste 3
BLANCK, Jacob Nathaniel 6
BLANCKE, Leo Mulford 4
BLANCKE, William Henry 5
BLANCKE, Wilton Wendell 5
BLANCO, Jose G. 6

BLANCO-FOMBONA, 5
Rufino
BLAND, Henry Meade 1
BLAND, John Randolph 1
BLAND, Oscar E. 3
BLAND, Pascal Brooke 1
BLAND, Richard H
BLAND, Richard Howard 3
BLAND, Richard Parks 1
BLAND, Schuyler Otis 2
BLAND, Theodorick H
BLAND, Thomas H
BLAND, William Thomas 1
BLANDEN, Charles 1
Granger
BLANDFORD, John 5
Bennett Jr.
BLANDIN, Charles 3
Kenneth
BLANDING, Albert Hazen 5
BLANDING, Don 3
BLANDY, William Henry 3
Purnell
BLANEY, Dwight 2
BLANEY, Henry R. 4
BLANEY, Isabella Williams 1
BLANEY, William Osgood 1
BLANK, Abe H. 6
BLANKENBUEHLER, 4
John H.
BLANKENBURG, Lucretia 2
Longshore
BLANKENBURG, Rudolph 1
BLANKENHORN, Marion 3
Arthur
BLANKINSHIP, Leslie 6
Charles
BLANKS, Robert Franklin 3
BLANN, John Edward 6
BLANTON, Annie Webb 2
BLANTON, John Diell 1
BLANTON, Joseph Philip 4
BLANTON, Lindsay 5
Hughes
BLANTON, Smiley 4
BLANTON, Thomas 3
Lindsay
BLANTON, Wyndham 4
Bolling
BLASDEL, Henry Goode H
BLASH, Rudolph F. 3
BLASHFIELD, Albert Dodd 1
BLASHFIELD, Edwin 1
Howland
BLATCH, Harriet Stanton 1
BLATCHFORD, Charles 2
Hammond
BLATCHFORD, Eliphalet 1
Wickes
BLATCHFORD, Richard 1
Milford
BLATCHFORD, Richard 1
Milford
BLATCHFORD, Samuel H
BLATCHLEY, Willis 1
Stanley
BLATT, William M(osher) 5
BLATTEIS, Simon Risefeld 5
BLATTENBERGER, 5
Raymond
BLAU, Max Friedrich 1
BLAUCH, Lloyd E. 6
BLAUER, William E. 3
BLAUSTEIN, Jacob 5
BLAUSTEIN, Louis 1
BLAUVELT, Bradford 1
BLAUVELT, Charles F. 1
BLAUVELT, Lillian Evans 2
BLAUVELT, Martin Post 1
BLAUVELT, Mary Taylor 5
BLAVATSKY, Helena H
Petrovna Hahn
BLAXTER, Henry Vaughan 2
BLAYLOCK, Louis 1
BLAYNEY, John McClusky 1
BLAYNEY, Lindsey 6
BLAYNEY, T(homas) 5
Lindsey
BLAZER, Paul Garrett 4
BLAZER, Rexford Sydney 6
BLEAKLEY, William 5
Francis
BLEASE, Coleman 1
Livingston
BLEASE, Coleman 2
Livingston
BLECKLEY, Logan E. 1
BLECKWENN, William 4
Jefferson
BLEDSOE, Albert Taylor H
BLEDSOE, Benjamin 1
Franklin
BLEDSOE, Jesse H
BLEDSOE, Samuel Thomas 1
BLEECKER, Ann Eliza 1
BLEECKER, Harmanus H

BLEECKER, John Van 1
Benthuysen
BLEGEN, Carl William 5
BLEICH, Clements Harry 5
BLEICHER, Clarence E. 3
BLEININGER, Albert 2
Victor
BLENDER, Dorothea Klotz 5
BLENDINGER, Fred L. 1
BLENK, James Hubert 1
BLENKINSOP, Peter H
BLENNER, Carle John 3
BLENNERHASSETT, H
Harman
BLESH, Abraham Lincoln 1
BLESSE, Frederick Arthur 3
BLESSING, Edgar M. 5
BLESSING, George 1
Frederick
BLESSING, Lewis Greene 5
BLESSING, Riley Andrew 5
BLETHEN, Alden Joseph 1
BLETHEN, Clarence 2
Brettun
BLETHEN, Frank Alden 5
BLETHEN, William 4
Kingsley
BLEWER, Clarence 5
Frederick
BLEWETT, Ben 1
BLEWETT, William E. Jr. 4
BLEYER, Herman 3
BLEYER, J. Mount 4
BLEYER, Willard 1
Grosvenor
BLICHFELDT, Emil Harry 5
BLICHFELDT, Hans 2
Frederik
BLICKENSDERFER, 4
Joseph Patrick
BLICKENSDERFER, 4
Robert
BLIEM, Milton Jacob 1
BLIGHT, Reynold E. 3
BLIM, Miles G. 6
BLINN, Charles Payson Jr. 6
BLINN, Holbrook 1
BLINN, Randolph 2
BLISS, A. Richard Jr. 1
BLISS, Aaron Thomas 1
BLISS, Arthur 6
BLISS, Charles Bemis 4
BLISS, Collins Pechin 2
BLISS, Cornelius Newton 1
BLISS, Cornelius Newton 1
BLISS, D. Spencer 3
BLISS, Daniel 1
BLISS, Don Alfonso 4
BLISS, Don C. 4
BLISS, Edwin Elisha H
BLISS, Edwin Munsell 1
BLISS, Eliakim Raymond 1
BLISS, Eliphalet Williams 1
BLISS, Elmer Jared 4
BLISS, Eugene Frederick 4
BLISS, Frederick Jones 1
BLISS, George * H
BLISS, George Laurence 5
BLISS, George Yemens 1
BLISS, Gilbert Ames 5
BLISS, Harding 4
BLISS, Harry Hayner 1
BLISS, Henry Evelyn 1
BLISS, Howard Sweetser 1
BLISS, James Harris 3
BLISS, John Carlton 1
BLISS, Jonathan H
BLISS, Louis Denton 4
BLISS, Louis G. 5
BLISS, Malcolm Andrews 1
BLISS, Mildred 6
BLISS, Paul Southworth 1
BLISS, Philemon 1
BLISS, Philip Elijah 1
BLISS, Phillip Paul H
BLISS, Porter Cornelius 1
BLISS, Ralph Kenneth 6
BLISS, Raymond Whitcomb 4
BLISS, Robert Pratt 4
BLISS, Robert Woods 4
BLISS, Tasker Howard 1
BLISS, Walter Phelps 1
BLISS, William 1
BLISS, William Carpenter 5
BLISS, William Dwight 1
Porter
BLISS, William Henry 1
BLISS, William J. 1
BLISS, William Julian Albert 1
BLISS, William Lancer 6
BLISS, William Root 1
BLISS, Zenas Randall 1
BLISS, Zenas Work 3
BLITZ, Anne Dudley 3
BLITZ, Antonio H
BLITZSTEIN, Marc 4

BLIXEN-FINECKE, Karen 4
Christentze
BLIZZARD, Reese 4
BLIZZARD, Warren Lale 3
BLOCH, Albert 4
BLOCH, Alexander 1
BLOCH, Bernard 4
BLOCH, Charles Julian 6
BLOCH, Claude Charles 4
BLOCH, Ernest 3
BLOCH, Herbert Aaron 4
BLOCH, Jesse A. 3
BLOCH, Julius 3
BLOCH, Louis 3
BLOCH, Monroe Percy 5
BLOCH, Robert Gustav 6
BLOCK, Adriaen H
BLOCK, Edward 4
BLOCK, Karl Morgan 3
BLOCK, Leopold E. 3
BLOCK, Louis James 1
BLOCK, Melvin A. 4
BLOCK, Paul 1
BLOCK, Philip Dee 2
BLOCK, Ralph 6
BLOCK, Rudolph 1
BLOCK, Samuel
Westheimer
BLOCKER, Dan 5
BLOCKER, Daniel James 3
BLOCKER, William Preston 2
BLOCKLINGER, Gottfried 1
BLOCKSOM, Augustus 1
Perry
BLODGET, Lorin 1
BLODGETT, Benjamin 1
Colman
BLODGETT, Francis 5
Branch
BLODGETT, Frank 5
Dickinson
BLODGETT, Henry 1
Williams
BLODGETT, Hugh Carlton 5
BLODGETT, Isaac N. 1
BLODGETT, John Taggard 2
BLODGETT, John Wood 3
BLODGETT, Mabel Louise 3
Fuller
BLODGETT, Rufus 1
BLODGETT, Samuel * H
BLODGETT, Thomas 4
Harper
BLODGETT, Thurston 5
P(ond)
BLODGETT, Wells Howard 1
BLOEDE, Gertrude 1
BLOEDE, Victor Gustave 1
BLOEDEL, Julius Harold 5
BLOEDORN, Fernando 6
Germane
BLOIS, Marsden Scott 4
BLOM, Frans 4
BLOMGREN, Carl August 4
BLOMQUIST, Edwin Oscar 4
BLOMQUIST, Hugo 4
Leander
BLONDEL, Jacob D. H
BLOOD, Charles H. 4
BLOOD, Henry Ames 1
BLOOD, Henry Hooper 2
BLOOD, Robert 3
McCutchins
BLOOD, Robert Oscar 6
BLOOD, William Henry Jr. 1
BLOODGOOD, Clare 4
Sutton
BLOODGOOD, Delavan 4
BLOODGOOD, Joseph Colt 1
BLOODGOOD, Wheeler 1
Peckham
BLOODWORTH, Andrew 3
Dunn Franklin
BLOODWORTH, Timothy 4
BLOOM, Charles James 2
BLOOM, Edgar Selden 3
BLOOM, Issac H
BLOOM, Melvin Harold 6
BLOOM, Sol 2
BLOOM, W. Knighton 1
BLOOMBERG, Maxwell 5
Hillel
BLOOMER, Amelia Jenks H
BLOOMER, Edgar Nelson 4
BLOOMER, Millard J. Jr. 6
BLOOMER, Millard J. 5
BLOOMFIELD, Arthur 5
Collier
BLOOMFIELD, Daniel 4
BLOOMFIELD, Joseph H
BLOOMFIELD, Leonard 2
BLOOMFIELD, Maurice 1
BLOOMFIELD, Meyer 1
BLOOMINGDALE, Charles 2
BLOOMINGDALE, 1
Emanuel Watson

BLOOMINGDALE, Samuel 5
Joseph
BLOOMSTEIN, Max Jr. 4
BLOOR, Alfred Janson 4
BLOOR, Walter Ray 4
BLOSS, James Ramsdell 3
BLOSSOM, Francis 5
BLOSSOM, George W. Jr. 4
BLOSSOM, Harold Hill 1
BLOSSOM, Henry Martyn 1
Jr.
BLOSSOM, Robert Alden 6
BLOUGH, Earl 5
BLOUGH, Elijah Robert 6
BLOUGH, Sanford P. 6
BLOUNT, George Dexter 4
BLOUNT, Henry Fitch 4
BLOUNT, James Henderson 1
BLOUNT, Roy A. 6
BLOUNT, Thomas H
BLOUNT, William H
BLOUNT, William 1
Alexander
BLOUNT, William Grainger H
BLOUNT, Willie 1
BLOW, Allmand M. 2
BLOW, Henry Taylor H
BLOWERS, Sampson Salter H
BLOXHAM, William D. 1
BLUCHER, Franz 3
BLUE, Burdette 2
BLUE, Frederick Omar 4
BLUE, John Howard 5
BLUE, Rupert 2
BLUE, Victor 1
BLUETT, John Joseph 4
BLUFORD, Ferdinand 3
Douglas
BLUGERMAN, Lee N. 5
(Leonid)
BLUM, Daniel 4
BLUM, Edward Charles 2
BLUM, Elias 4
BLUM, Harry 5
BLUM, Harry H. 4
BLUM, Leon 2
BLUM, Robert 4
BLUM, Robert Frederick 1
BLUM, Samuel J. 3
BLUM, William 5
BLUMBERG, Hyman 5
BLUMBERG, Nathan J. 4
BLUME, Clinton Willis 6
BLUME, Fred H. 5
BLUMENBERG, Marc A. 1
BLUMENFELD, Ralph 2
David
BLUMENFIELD, Samuel 5
M.
BLUMENSCHEIN, Ernest 4
L.
BLUMENSCHEIN, Mary 3
Shepard Greene
BLUMENSCHEIN, William 1
Leonard
BLUMENSCHINE, Leonard 5
G.
BLUMENTHAL, George 1
BLUMENTHAL, Gustave 1
Adolph
BLUMENTHAL, Sidney 2
BLUMER, G. Alder 4
BLUMER, George 4
BLUMEYER, Arthur 3
Adolphus
BLUN, Henry 1
BLUNT, Edmund March H
BLUNT, George William H
BLUNT, Hugh Francis 4
BLUNT, James Gillpatrick H
BLUNT, John Ellsworth 1
BLUNT, John S. H
BLUNT, Katharine 3
BLUNT, Matthew M. 1
BLUNT, Stanhope English 1
BLUSTEIN, Herman 4
BLY, Eleanor Schooley 5
BLY, John Marius 1
BLY, Nelly H
BLY, Nelly 4
BLY, Robert Stewart 5
BLYDE, Lewis J(ohn) 5
N(ewbery)
BLYDEN, Larry (Ivan 6
Lawrence Blieden)
BLYDENBURGH, Charles 1
Edward
BLYLEY, Katherine Gillette 4
BLYNN, Lloyd Ross 5
BLYTH, Charles R. 4
BLYTHE, David Gilmour H
BLYTHE, Joseph L. 5
BLYTHE, Joseph William 1
BLYTHE, Samuel George 2
BLYTHIN, Edward 4
BLYTHIN, Robert 5

BOAK, Arthur Edward 4
Romilly
BOAL, Pierre de Lagarde 4
BOARDMAN, Albert 1
Barnes
BOARDMAN, Charles 3
Willis
BOARDMAN, Elijah H
BOARDMAN, George 1
Dana
BOARDMAN, George 5
Henry
BOARDMAN, George Nye 1
BOARDMAN, Harold 5
Sherburne
BOARDMAN, Harry Clow 3
BOARDMAN, Harry L. 4
BOARDMAN, Henry 1
Augustus
BOARDMAN, Henry 1
Bradford
BOARDMAN, Mabel Thorp 4
BOARDMAN, Paul 6
Lawrence
BOARDMAN, Samuel Lane 1
BOARDMAN, Samuel 1
Ward
BOARDMAN, Thomas H
Danforth
BOARDMAN, Waldo Elias 1
BOARDMAN, William 4
Bradford
BOARDMAN, William 1
Henry
BOARDMAN, William H
Whiting
BOARMAN, Aleck 3
BOARTS, Robert Marsh 4
BOAS, Emil Leopold 1
BOAS, Ernst Philip 3
BOAS, Franz 2
BOATNER, Victor Vincent 4
BOATRIGHT, Byron B. 5
BOATRIGHT, Mody 5
Coggin
BOATRIGHT, William 1
Louis
BOATWRIGHT, Frederic 3
William
BOATWRIGHT, Gertrude 5
Floyd Harris
BOAZ, Hiram Abiff 4
BOAZ, Hiram Abiff 5
BOBB, Byron Arthur 4
BOBB, Clyde S. 3
BOBB, Earl Victor 3
BOBBITT, Franklin 3
BOBBITT, Joseph Matthew 5
BOBBITT, Mary Lavinia 6
Reed (Mrs. Vernon L.
Bobbitt)
BOBBS, William Conrad 1
BOBER, Sam Henry 5
BOCHER, Maxime 1
BOCK, Harold Pattendon 5
BOCK, Otto 2
BOCKEE, Abraham H
BOCKMAN, Marcus Olaus 2
BOCKUS, Charles E. 1
BOCOCK, Clarence Edgar 4
BOCOCK, John Holmes 3
BOCOCK, Thomas S. H
BOCOCK, Willis Henry 4
BOCQUERAZ, Leon 6
Edward
BODANSKY, Meyer 1
BODANZKY, Artur 1
BODDE, John R. 5
BODDINGTON, Ernest 1
Fearby
BODDIS, George 4
BODDY, E. Manchester 4
BODDY, William Henry 1
BODE, Boyd Henry 3
BODE, Frederick 2
BODECKER, Carl Friedrich 4
Wilhelm
BODELL, David Eugene 5
BODELL, Joseph James 3
BODEN, Andrew 4
BODEN, Reynold 4
Blomerley
BODENHAMER, Osee Lee 1
BODENHEIM, Maxwell 3
BODENWEIN, Theodore 1
BODER, Bartlett 5
BODER, David Pablo 4
BODFISH, Morton 4
BODINE, A(ldine) Aubrey 5
BODINE, Alfred Van Sant 4
BODINE, James Morrison 1
BODINE, Joseph Hall 3
BODINE, Joseph Lamb 3
BODINE, Roy L. 6
BODINE, Samuel Louis 3
BODINE, Samuel Taylor 1

BODINE, William Budd 3
BODINE, William Warden 3
BODLE, Charles H
BODLEY, Temple H
BODMAN, Ernest James 3
BODMAN, Henry Edward 4
BODMER, Karl H
BODMER, Walter 6
BODY, Charles William 1
Edmund
BODY, Ralph C. 6
BOE, Lars Wilhelm 2
BOECKLIN, Roland 5
BOEGNER, Marc 5
BOEHLER, Peter H
BOEHM, Edward Marshall 5
BOEHM, Henry H
BOEHM, John Philip H
BOEHM, Martin H
BOEHME, Ernest Adolph 4
BOEHMER, Max 1
BOEING, William Edward H
BOELEN, Jacob H
BOELTER, Llewellyn 4
Michael Kraus
BOERICKE, Garth 5
Wilkinson
BOERNSTEIN, Ralph 5
A(ugustus)
BOERUM, Simon H
BOESCHENSTEIN, Charles 3
BOESCHENSTEIN, Harold 5
BOESEL, Frank Tilden 4
BOETTCHER, Charles 2
BOETTCHER, Charles II 4
BOETTCHER, Claude 5
Kedzie
BOETTGER, Theodore 6
BOETTIGER, John 3
BOEYE, John Franklin 4
BOEYNAEMS, Libert 3
Hubert John Louis
BOFINGER, D. T. 2
BOGAN, Louise 5
BOGAN, R. A. L. 4
BOGAN, William Joseph 1
BOGARDUS, Emory 6
Stephen
BOGARDUS, Everardus H
BOGARDUS, James H
BOGART, Ernest Ludlow 3
BOGART, Humphrey 5
DeForest
BOGART, John 1
BOGART, Paul Nebeker 4
BOGART, Walter 5
Thompson
BOGART, William Henry H
BOGARTE, Martin Eugene 1
BOGEN, Emil 4
BOGEN, Jules Irwin 4
BOGER, Glen Alvin 5
BOGER, Robert Forrester 5
BOGERT, Edward Strong 1
BOGERT, George H. 2
BOGERT, Marston Taylor 5
BOGERT, Walter Lawrence 5
BOGGESS, Arthur Clinton 5
BOGGS, Carroll Curtis 1
BOGGS, Charles Stuart 5
BOGGS, Earl Huffner 5
BOGGS, Frank Cranstoun 5
BOGGS, Frank M. 1
BOGGS, Gilbert Hillhouse 1
BOGGS, Lillburn W. 1
BOGGS, Robert 4
BOGGS, S. Whittemore 2
BOGGS, Sara E. 3
BOGGS, Thomas Hale 5
BOGGS, Thomas Richmond 1
BOGGS, William Brenton H
BOGGS, William Ellison 1
BOGGS, William Robertson 1
BOGIE, Mord M. 3
BOGLE, James H
BOGLE, Robert Boyd 1
BOGLE, Sarah Comly 1
Norris
BOGLE, Thomas Ashford 1
BOGLE, Walter Scott 1
BOGOSIAN, Ares George 5
BOGOSLOVSKY, Boris 4
Basil
BOGUE, Harold J. 4
BOGUE, Jesse Parker 4
BOGUE, Morton Griswold 3
BOGUE, Virgil Gay 1
BOGUSLAWSKI, Molssaye 2
BOGY, Lewis Vital H
BOHACHEVSKY, 6
Constantine
BOHAN, Merwin Lee 5
BOHAN, Peter Thomas 5
BOHANNON, Eugene 3
William

BOHANNON, William 1
Everette
BOHART, Philip Harris 4
BOHEN, Frederick Owen 6
BOHLEN, Charles Eustis 6
BOHLEN, Diedrich A. H
BOHLEN, Francis Hermann 2
BOHLMAN, Herbert 5
William
BOHLMANN, Henry 4
Frederic Theodore
BOHM, Max 1
BOHN, Charles B. 3
BOHN, Donald George 5
BOHN, Ernest John 6
BOHN, Frank 6
BOHN, Frank Probasco 4
BOHN, Gebhard C. 6
BOHN, William Frederick 4
BOHR, Frank 5
BOHR, Niels Henrik David 4
BOHUNE, Lawrence H
BOICE, James Young 4
BOIES, Henry Martyn 1
BOIES, Horace 1
BOIES, William Artemas 5
BOIES, William Dayton 1
BOIFEUILLET, John 1
Theodore
BOILEAU, Philip 1
BOISE, Otis Bardwell 1
BOISOT, Emile Kellogg 4
BOISOT, Louis 1
BOISSEVAIN, Charles 2
Hercules
BOISSEVAIN, Inez 1
Milholland
BOJER, Johan 3
BOK, Cary William 5
BOK, Curtis 4
BOK, Edward William 1
BOKAT, George 6
BOKEE, David Alexander H
BOKER, George Henry 4
BOKHARI, Ahmed Shah 3
BOKOR, Margit 3
BOLAND, Francis Joseph 4
BOLAND, Frank Kells 3
BOLAND, George Bernard 4
BOLAND, John J. 6
BOLAND, John Peter 5
BOLAND, Mary 4
BOLAND, Patrick J. 2
BOLDEN, Charles H
BOLDEN, Charles 1
BOLDT, George C. 1
BOLDT, Hermann Johannes 2
BOLDUAN, Charles 3
Frederick
BOLE, Benjamin Patterson 5
BOLE, William McLure 1
BOLEND, Floyd Jackson 1
BOLES, Edgar Howard 2
BOLES, H(enry) Leo 5
BOLES, John 5
BOLGER, Henry Joseph 4
BOLIN, Rolf Ling 6
BOLIVAR, Simon H
BOLL, Jacob H
BOLLAN, William H
BOLLENGIER, Albert 6
Emile Jr.
BOLLER, Alfred Pancoast 1
BOLLES, Albert Sidney 1
BOLLES, Edwin Cortlandt 1
BOLLES, Frank 1
BOLLES, Frank Crandall 5
BOLLES, Stephen 1
BOLLING, Alexander 4
Russell
BOLLING, George Melville 5
BOLLING, Raynal 1
Cawthorne
BOLLINGER, James Wills 3
BOLLMAN, Justus Erich H
BOLOTOV, Ivan Il'ich H
BOLSTAD, Milo Myrum 6
BOLSTER, Stanley Marshall 5
BOLSTER, Wilfred 2
BOLSTER, William Wheeler 4
BOLT, Richard Arthur 4
BOLTE, William John 4
BOLTON, Abby H
BOLTON, Benjamin Meade 1
BOLTON, Charles Edward 1
BOLTON, Charles Knowles 1
BOLTON, Chester Castle 1
BOLTON, Elmer Keiser 5
BOLTON, Ethel 1
BOLTON, Frederick Elmer 5
BOLTON, Henry Carrington 1
BOLTON, Herbert Eugene 5
BOLTON, J. Gray 1
BOLTON, John H
BOLTON, (John) Whitney 5
(French)

BOUCICAULT, Ruth 5
  Baldwin Holt (Mrs.
  Aubrey Boucicault)
BOUCK, Francis Eugene 1
BOUCK, Joseph H
BOUCK, William C. H
BOUCK, Zeh 2
BOUCKE, Ewald Augustus 5
BOUCKE, O. Fred 1
BOUDE, Thomas H
BOUDEMAN, Dallas 4
BOUDEMAN, Robert 6
  Meier
BOUDET, Dominic W. H
BOUDET, Nicholas Vincent H
BOUDIN, Louis B. 3
BOUDINOT, Elias * H
BOUDINOT, Elias H
  Cornelius
BOUDINOT, Jane J. 5
BOUDINOT, Truman 2
  Everett
BOUGHNER, Leroy John 6
BOUGHTON, George
  Henry
BOUGHTON, George 1
  Henry
BOUGHTON, Martha 1
  Arnold
BOUGHTON, Willis
BOUGUEREAU, Elizabeth 4
  Gardner
BOUILLON, Lincoln 5
BOULDIN, James Wood H
BOULDIN, Thomas Tyler H
BOULDIN, Virgil 5
BOULIGNY, Dominique
BOULIGNY, John Edward
BOULT, William Thomas 2
BOULTER, Howard 3
  Thornton
BOULTER, Thornton
BOULTON, Payne Augustin 4
BOUNETHEAU, Henry H
  Brintell
BOUQUET, Henry H
BOUQUILLON, Thomas 1
BOURDIER, Lillian Blanche 6
BOURGADE, Peter 1
BOURGEOIS, Lionel John 4
  Sr.
BOURGMONT, sieur de H
BOURGOINE, Joseph John 3
BOURKE, John Gregory
BOURKE-WHITE, 5
  Margaret
BOURLAND, Albert Pike 1
BOURLAND, Benjamin 2
  Parsons
BOURLAND, Caroline 5
  Brown
BOURN, Augustus Osborn
BOURNE, Benjamin H
BOURNE, Edward Gaylord 1
BOURNE, Frank Augustus 1
BOURNE, Frederick Gilbert 1
BOURNE, George
BOURNE, Henry Eldridge 2
BOURNE, Jonathan Jr. 1
BOURNE, Nehemiah H
BOURNE, Randolph 1
BOURNE, Shearjashub H
BOURQUIN, George M. 3
BOURSKAYA, Ina 3
BOUSCAREN, Louis 1
  Frederic Gustave
BOUSCAREN, Louis H. G. 4
BOUSFIELD, Midian 2
  Othello
BOUSH, Clifford Joseph
BOUTELL, Henry Sherman 1
BOUTELLE, Charles 1
  Addison
BOUTELLE, De Witt H
  Clinton
BOUTELLE, Richard Schley 4
BOUTON, Archilbald Lewis 2
BOUTON, Burrett Beebe 4
BOUTON, Charles Leonard 1
BOUTON, Edward Henry 4
BOUTON, Emily St. John 5
BOUTON, John Bell H
BOUTON, Nathaniel H
BOUTON, Rosa 4
BOUTON, S(tephen) Miles 5
BOUTWELL, George Sewall 1
BOUTWELL, John M(ason) 5
BOUTWELL, Paul Winslow 5
BOUTWELL, William Rowe 1
BOUVE, Clement Lincoln 2
BOUVE, Pauline Carrington 1
BOUVET, Jeanne Marie 4
BOUVET, Marie Marguerite 1
BOUVIER, John H
BOUVIER, Maurice 5
BOVARD, Charles Lincoln 1

BOVARD, Freeman Daily 1
BOVARD, George Finley 1
BOVARD, John Freeman 6
BOVARD, Warren Bradley 1
BOVARD, William Sherman 1
BOVEE, Christian Nestell 1
BOVEE, J. Wesley 1
BOVEE, Matthias Jacob H
BOVENIZER, George 4
  Wallace
BOVEY, Charles Cranton 3
BOVIE, William T. 3
BOVING, Adam Giede 5
BOVING, Charles B(rasee) 5
BOW, Frank Townsend 5
BOW, Jonathan Gaines 4
BOW, Warren E. 2
BOWATER, Sir Eric 4
  Vansittart
BOWDEN, Aberdeen 2
  Orlando
BOWDEN, Garfield Arthur 2
BOWDEN, George Edwin 4
BOWDEN, John H
BOWDEN, Laurens Reeve 4
BOWDEN, Lemuel Jackson H
BOWDITCH, Charles 1
  Pickering
BOWDITCH, Henry H
  Ingersoll
BOWDITCH, Henry 1
  Pickering
BOWDITCH, Nathaniel H
BOWDITCH, Richard Lyon 3
BOWDITCH, Vincent 1
  Yardley
BOWDLE, Stanley Eyre 4
BOWDOIN, George E. 3
BOWDOIN, George 1
  Sullivan
BOWDOIN, James * H
BOWDOIN, William H
  Goodrich
BOWDON, Franklin Welsh H
BOWE, Augustine J. 4
BOWEN, Abel H
BOWEN, Albert E. 3
BOWEN, Arthur John 5
BOWEN, Asa Bosworth
BOWEN, Benjamin Lester 1
BOWEN, Catherine Drinker 6
BOWEN, Christopher
  Columbus
BOWEN, Clarence 1
  Winthrop
BOWEN, Clayton Raymond 1
BOWEN, Daniel H
BOWEN, Earl 4
BOWEN, Edwin Winfield 3
BOWEN, Elizabeth 5
  Dorothea Cole
BOWEN, Ezra 2
BOWEN, Francis H
BOWEN, George H
BOWEN, Harold Gardiner 4
BOWEN, Harry 2
BOWEN, Henry Chandler 4
BOWEN, Herbert Wolcott H
BOWEN, Ira Sprague 5
BOWEN, Ivan 3
BOWEN, John C. 3
BOWEN, John Campbell 5
BOWEN, John Henry H
BOWEN, John Templeton 1
BOWEN, John Wesley 4
  Edward
BOWEN, Joseph Henry 1
BOWEN, Lem Warner 1
BOWEN, Louise de Koven 3
BOWEN, Marcellus 1
BOWEN, Norman Levi 3
BOWEN, Rees Tate 1
BOWEN, Reuben Dean 1
BOWEN, Richard LeBaron 6
BOWEN, Thomas M. 1
BOWEN, Wilbur Pardon 1
BOWEN, William 1
BOWEN, William Abraham 1
BOWEN, William Miller 1
BOWER, Alexander 3
BOWER, Bertha Muzzy 1
BOWER, George Hoyle 1
BOWER, Gustavus Miller 4
BOWER, Joseph Augustus 6
BOWER, Lucy Scott 1
BOWER, Raymond G. 4
BOWERMAN, George 4
  Franklin
BOWERMAN, Guy 2
  Emerson
BOWERS, Alphonzo 1
  Benjamin
BOWERS, Claude G. 3
BOWERS, Eaton Jackson 1
BOWERS, Edgar 4
BOWERS, Edison Louis

BOWERS, Edward Augustus 4
BOWERS, Elizabeth H
  Crocker
BOWERS, Elsworth 6
BOWERS, George Meade 1
BOWERS, Henry Francis 1
BOWERS, Henry Smith 6
BOWERS, Herbert Edmund 1
BOWERS, John Hugh 1
BOWERS, John Myer H
BOWERS, Larkin Bruce 1
BOWERS, LaMont 1
  Montgomery
BOWERS, Lloyd Wheaton 1
BOWERS, Robert Graves 5
BOWERS, Robert Hood 1
BOWERS, Theodore Shelton H
BOWERS, Thomas Wilson 1
BOWERS, Walter Abraham 6
BOWERS, William Gray 2
BOWERSOCK, Donald 3
  Curtis
BOWERSOCK, Justin 1
  DeWitt
BOWES, Edward Major 2
BOWES, Frank B. 4
BOWES, Joseph 4
BOWES, Theodore F. 4
BOWES, Theodore F. 1
BOWIE, Clifford Pinckney 3
BOWIE, Edward Hall 4
BOWIE, James H
BOWIE, Oden H
BOWIE, Richard Johns H
BOWIE, Robert H
BOWIE, Sydney Johnston 1
BOWIE, Thomas Fielder H
BOWIE, Walter H
BOWIE, Walter Russell 5
BOWIE, William 1
BOWKER, Horace 3
BOWKER, Richard Rogers 1
BOWLBY, Harry Laity 6
BOWLBY, Joel Morgan 3
BOWLEN, John James 4
BOWLER, Edmond Wesley 4
BOWLER, James B. 3
BOWLER, John Pollard 6
BOWLER, John William 1
BOWLER, Metcalf H
BOWLER, William Howard 3
BOWLES, Charles 4
BOWLES, Charles Phillips 4
BOWLES, Elliott A. 1
BOWLES, Francis Tiffany 1
BOWLES, Frank Hamilton 6
BOWLES, Gilbert 5
BOWLES, Henry Leland 1
BOWLES, Oliver 3
BOWLES, Phillip Ernest 1
BOWLES, Pinckney Downie 1
BOWLES, Samuel H
BOWLES, Samuel 1
BOWLES, Samuel II H
BOWLES, Sherman Hoar 3
BOWLES, William Augustus H
BOWLEY, Albert Jesse 2
BOWLEY, Arthur Lyon 5
BOWLIN, Jamer Butler H
BOWLIN, William Ray 6
BOWLING, Edgar Simeon 3
BOWLING, William 2
  Bismarck
BOWMAN, Albert Chase 4
BOWMAN, Alpheus Henry 1
BOWMAN, Charles Calvin 1
BOWMAN, Charles Grimes 4
BOWMAN, Charles Henry 5
BOWMAN, Clellan Asbury 1
BOWMAN, Crete Dillon 5
  (Mrs. John W. Boman)
BOWMAN, Edward J. 4
BOWMAN, Edward Morris 1
BOWMAN, Frank 1
  Llewellyn
BOWMAN, Frank Otto 3
BOWMAN, George Ernest 1
BOWMAN, George Lynn 4
BOWMAN, George T. 3
BOWMAN, Gus Karl Jr. 6
BOWMAN, Harold Leonard 4
BOWMAN, Harold Martin 2
BOWMAN, Harry Lake 4
BOWMAN, Harry Samuel 5
BOWMAN, Howard 1
  H(iestand) M(innich)
BOWMAN, Isaiah * 2
BOWMAN, James H
BOWMAN, James Clinton 5
BOWMAN, James Cloyd 4
BOWMAN, John Brady 1
BOWMAN, John Bryan H
BOWMAN, John Calvin 1
BOWMAN, John Fife 1
BOWMAN, John Gabbert 4
BOWMAN, John McEntee 1

BOWMAN, John R. 4
BOWMAN, Joseph Merrell 5
  Jr.
BOWMAN, Karl Murdock 5
BOWMAN, Lloyd David 4
BOWMAN, Milo Jesse 5
BOWMAN, Robert A. 1
BOWMAN, Robert Jay 3
BOWMAN, Roland Claude 3
BOWMAN, Rufus Samuel 1
BOWMAN, Samuel Henry 1
  Jr.
BOWMAN, Thomas * 1
BOWN, Ralph 5
BOWNE, Borden Parker 1
BOWNE, John H
BOWNE, Obadiah H
BOWNE, Samuel Smith H
BOWNE, William Rainear 6
BOWNOCKER, John 1
  Adams
BOWRA, Cecil Maurice 5
BOWRON, Arthur John Jr. 4
BOWRON, Fletcher 5
BOWRON, James 1
BOWSER, Edward Albert 1
BOWSFIELD, Colvin C. 1
BOWYER, John Marshall 1
BOWYER, John Wilson 5
BOX, John Calvin 5
BOXER, Harold Horton 6
BOXLEY, Calvin Peyton 1
BOYAJIAN, Setrak Krikor 1
BOYCE, Charles Meredith 5
BOYCE, Charles Prevost 5
BOYCE, Fred Grayson Jr. 4
BOYCE, Heyward E. 5
BOYCE, James 1
BOYCE, James Petigru H
BOYCE, John H
BOYCE, Sir Leslie 3
BOYCE, William A. 6
BOYCE, William D. 2
BOYCE, William H. 1
BOYCE, William Waters H
BOYD, A. Hunter 1
BOYD, Adam 2
BOYD, Alexander 1
BOYD, Alfred H
BOYD, Augusto Samuel 3
BOYD, Belle 5
BOYD, Bernard Henry 6
BOYD, Charles Arthur 4
BOYD, Charles Morgan 3
BOYD, Colin Macnicol 4
BOYD, D. Knickerbacker 2
BOYD, Darrell Sully 5
BOYD, David French 4
BOYD, David Ross 1
BOYD, Donald Lewis 4
BOYD, Edwin Forrest 5
BOYD, Ellen Wright 4
BOYD, Ernest 2
BOYD, Everett Marion 3
BOYD, Fiske 6
BOYD, Francis R(aymond) 6
BOYD, George Adams 5
BOYD, George H. 4
BOYD, George Washington 1
BOYD, Harry Burton 3
BOYD, Harry Hutcheson 5
BOYD, Henry W. Jr. 3
BOYD, James 1
BOYD, James 1
BOYD, James Churchill 5
BOYD, James E. 1
BOYD, James Edmund 1
BOYD, James Ellsworth 2
BOYD, James Harrington 2
BOYD, James Oscar 2
BOYD, James P. 1
BOYD, John Frank 3
BOYD, John Hardgrove H
BOYD, John Huggins H
BOYD, John Parker H
BOYD, Joseph Milton 4
BOYD, Louise Arner 6
BOYD, Lynn H
BOYD, Mary Brown 5
  Sumner (Mrs. Mark Boyd)
BOYD, Paul Prentice 5
BOYD, Ralph E. 5
BOYD, Ralph Gates 5
BOYD, Robert 5
BOYD, Sempronius H
  Hamilton
BOYD, Thomas 1
BOYD, Thomas Alexander H
BOYD, Thomas Duckett 4
BOYD, Thomas M. 4
BOYD, William 5
BOYD, William (Hopalong 5
  Cassidy)
BOYD, William H. 2
BOYD, William Kenneth 1
BOYD, William Robert 3

BOYD, William Robert 4
BOYD, William Rufus Jr. 3
BOYD, William Sprott 3
BOYD, William Waddell 1
BOYD, William Young 1
BOYD-CARPENTER 6
BOYDEN, Albert H
BOYDEN, Albert Augustus 1
BOYDEN, Albert Gardner 1
BOYDEN, Arthur Clarke 1
BOYDEN, Elbridge H
BOYDEN, Frank Learoyd 5
BOYDEN, Guy Lee 2
BOYDEN, Nathaniel H
BOYDEN, Roland William 1
BOYDEN, Seth H
BOYDEN, Uriah Atherton H
BOYDEN, William Cowper 1
BOYDEN, William Cowper H
BOYE, Martin H. 1
BOYER, Benjamin Markley H
BOYER, C. Valentine 6
BOYER, Charles Clinton 3
BOYER, Emanuel Roth 1
BOYER, Francis 5
BOYER, John F. 6
BOYER, Joseph 1
BOYER, Lewis Leonard 3
BOYER, Pearce Fowler 3
BOYER, Willis Boothe 6
BOYES, Kurwin Robert 3
BOYESEN, Hjalmar Hjorth H
BOYKIN, Frank William 5
BOYKIN, Garland Lester 4
BOYKIN, James Chambers 1
BOYKIN, Richard Manning 6
BOYKIN, Samuel Francis 3
BOYLAN, Grace Duffie 1
BOYLAN, John J. 1
BOYLAN, John J. 3
BOYLAN, John Patrick 4
BOYLAN, Murtha Joseph 3
BOYLAN, Richard Joseph 4
BOYLAN, Robert P. 4
BOYLAN, William A. 1
BOYLE, Albert Clarence Jr. 1
BOYLE, Andrew Joseph 6
BOYLE, Charles A. 3
BOYLE, Charles Edmund 1
BOYLE, Emmet D. 1
  Lee
BOYLE, Ferdinand Thomas H
  Lee
BOYLE, Ferdinand Thomas 4
  (Hal)
BOYLE, Harold Vincent 6
BOYLE, Hugh Charles 3
BOYLE, James 1
BOYLE, James Ernest 1
BOYLE, Jeremiah Tilford H
BOYLE, John 1
BOYLE, John J. 1
BOYLE, Leo Martin 5
BOYLE, Murat 1
BOYLE, Thomas 1
BOYLE, Thomas Newton 1
BOYLE, Virginia Frazer 1
BOYLE, W. H. Wray 4
BOYLE, Walter Fabien 3
BOYLE, Wilbur Fisk 1
BOYLE, William Marshall 4
  Jr.
BOYLEN, Matthew James 5
BOYLES, Aubrey 6
BOYLES, Emerson 6
  R(ichard)
BOYLON, Francis Oscar 4
BOYLSTON, Zabdiel H
BOYNTON, Arthur Jerome 1
BOYNTON, Ben Lynn 6
BOYNTON, Charles Albert 5
BOYNTON, Charles 1
  Augustus
BOYNTON, Charles H
  Brandon
BOYNTON, Charles Homer 5
BOYNTON, Charles 1
  Hudson
BOYNTON, Charles 1
  Theodore
BOYNTON, Edward H
  Carlisle
BOYNTON, Edward Young 4
BOYNTON, Frank David 1
BOYNTON, George Mills 1
BOYNTON, George Rufus 2
BOYNTON, Henry Van 1
  Ness
BOYNTON, Henry Walcott 5
BOYNTON, James 1
  Stoddard
BOYNTON, Melbourne 2
  Parker
BOYNTON, Morrison 3
  Russell

BOYNTON, Nathan Smith 1
BOYNTON, Nehemiah 1
BOYNTON, Paul L. 3
BOYNTON, Percy Holmes 2
BOYNTON, Richard Wilson 4
BOYNTON, Thomas 2
  Jefferson
BOYNTON, William Pingry 3
BOYSEN JENSEN, Peter 4
BOYTON, Neil 3
BOZELL, Harold Veatch 5
BOZELL, Leo B. 2
BOZEMAN, John M. H
BOZMAN, John Leeds H
BRAASCH, William 6
  Frederick
BRABSON, Reese Bowen H
BRACE, Charles Loring H
BRACE, Charles Loring 1
BRACE, DeWitt Bristol 3
BRACE, Donald Clifford 3
BRACE, John Pierce 1
BRACE, Jonathan H
BRACE, Theodore 4
BRACELEN, Charles 1
  Michael
BRACH, Edwin J. 4
BRACH, Emil J. 2
BRACH, Frank Vincent 5
BRACKEN, Clio Hirton 1
BRACKEN, Edward P. 1
BRACKEN, Henry Martyn 1
BRACKEN, John 5
BRACKEN, Stanley 1
BRACKENRIDGE, 4
  Alexander
BRACKENRIDGE, Henry H
  Marie
BRACKENRIDGE, Hugh H
  Henry
BRACKENRIDGE, William 1
  Algernon
BRACKENRIDGE, William H
  D.
BRACKER, Milton 4
BRACKETT, Anna 1
  Callender
BRACKETT, Byron Briggs 1
BRACKETT, Charles Albert 1
BRACKETT, Cyrus Fogg 1
BRACKETT, Dexter 1
BRACKETT, E(lmer) 5
  E(ugene)
BRACKETT, Elliott Gray 1
BRACKETT, Frank 5
  Parkhurst
BRACKETT, Gustavus 1
  Benson
BRACKETT, Haven Darling 5
BRACKETT, J. Raymond 1
BRACKETT, Jeffery 4
  Richardson
BRACKETT, John Quincy 1
  Adams
BRACKETT, Ledru Joshua 5
BRACKETT, Richard 4
  Newman
BRACKETT, Walter M. 1
BRACKETT, William Oliver 2
BRACQ, Jean Charlemagne 1
BRADBURY, Albert 1
  Williams
BRADBURY, George H
BRADBURY, Howard 4
  William
BRADBURY, James Ware 1
BRADBURY, Joseph P. 1
BRADBURY, Robert Hart 2
BRADBURY, Samuel 2
BRADBURY, Theophilus H
BRADBURY, William 4
BRADBURY, William H
  Batchelder
BRADBURY, William 1
  Frothingham
BRADBURY, Woodman 1
BRADDOCK, Edward H
BRADDOCK, Robert Louis 5
BRADEN, Arthur 6
BRADEN, George Walter 5
BRADEN, J. Noble 3
BRADEN, James Andrew 4
BRADEN, John 1
BRADEN, William 6
BRADFIELD, George 6
  Herndon
BRADFIELD, William D. 4
BRADFORD, Alexander H
  Warfield
BRADFORD, Allen H
BRADFORD, Allen H
  Alexander
BRADFORD, Amory Howe 1
BRADFORD, Andrew H
BRADFORD, Augustus H
  Williamson

BRADFORD, Charles 1
BRADFORD, Edward 1
  Anthony
BRADFORD, Edward H
  Green
BRADFORD, Edward 1
  Green
BRADFORD, Edward 1
  Hickling
BRADFORD, Ernest Smith 4
BRADFORD, Fancis Scott 4
BRADFORD, Gamaliel * 1
BRADFORD, George 2
  Henry
BRADFORD, Gerard 3
BRADFORD, Harry E. 6
BRADFORD, John 1
BRADFORD, John Ewing 1
BRADFORD, Joseph 1
BRADFORD, Joseph 3
  Nelson
BRADFORD, Karl 5
  Slaughter
BRADFORD, Lindsay 3
BRADFORD, Roark 2
BRADFORD, Robert D. 5
BRADFORD, Royal Bird 1
BRADFORD, Saxton 4
BRADFORD, Taul H
BRADFORD, Thomas H
BRADFORD, Thomas 1
  Lindsley
BRADFORD, William * H
BRADFORD, William 4
  Brooks
BRADFUTE, Oscar Edwin 1
BRADISH, Alvah H
BRADISH, Luther H
BRADLEE, Arthur Tisdale 1
BRADLEE, Caleb Davis H
BRADLEE, Henry G. 2
BRADLEE, Nathaniel J. 1
BRADLEY, Alexander 4
  Stuart
BRADLEY, Alfred Eugene 1
BRADLEY, Alice 2
BRADLEY, Alva 3
BRADLEY, Andrew Coyle 1
BRADLEY, Bernard James 1
BRADLEY, Carolyn 3
  Gertrude
BRADLEY, Charles 1
BRADLEY, Charles Burnet 4
BRADLEY, Charles Clark 1
BRADLEY, Charles Harvey 1
BRADLEY, Charles Henry 1
BRADLEY, Charles 2
  Leininger
BRADLEY, Charles 1
  Schenck
BRADLEY, Charles William H
BRADLEY, Cornelius Beach 3
BRADLEY, Dan Freeman 1
BRADLEY, Denis M. 1
BRADLEY, Dorothy 6
  Winchester
BRADLEY, Dwight 3
BRADLEY, Edward H
BRADLEY, Edward Elias 1
BRADLEY, Edward 1
  Lounsberry
BRADLEY, Elizabeth 4
  Ganse
BRADLEY, Follett 4
BRADLEY, Francis 1
BRADLEY, Frank Howe H
BRADLEY, Frederick Van 2
  Ness
BRADLEY, Frederick 1
  Worthen
BRADLEY, George 1
  Beckwith
BRADLEY, George Edgar 6
BRADLEY, Glenn Danford 1
BRADLEY, Guy M. 4
BRADLEY, Harold 6
  Cornelius
BRADLEY, Harry L. 4
BRADLEY, Henry D. 6
BRADLEY, Henry Stiles 5
BRADLEY, Herbert Edwin 4
BRADLEY, Herbert Edwin 5
BRADLEY, J. Kenneth 5
BRADLEY, James L. 3
BRADLEY, Jay D. 3
BRADLEY, John Davis 4
BRADLEY, John Edwin 1
BRADLEY, John Hodgdon 4
BRADLEY, John Jewsbury 2
BRADLEY, John Robins 1
BRADLEY, Joseph Gardner 6
BRADLEY, Joseph P. H
BRADLEY, Joseph Sladen 4
BRADLEY, Kenneth 3
  McPherson

BRADLEY, Laura May 5
  Thompson (Mrs. William
  Pickering)
BRADLEY, Lee Carrington 2
BRADLEY, Lucas H
BRADLEY, Luke C. 2
BRADLEY, Luther Prentice 1
BRADLEY, Lydia Moss 1
BRADLEY, Mark Edward 6
BRADLEY, Milton 1
BRADLEY, Otis T. 3
BRADLEY, Peter Butler 1
BRADLEY, Philip Read 2
BRADLEY, Robert L. 2
BRADLEY, Robert Stow 5
BRADLEY, Samuel Stewart 2
BRADLEY, Stephen Row H
BRADLEY, Theodore James 1
BRADLEY, Thomas J. 5
BRADLEY, Thomas W. 1
BRADLEY, Walter Parke 5
BRADLEY, Warren Ives H
BRADLEY, Will 4
BRADLEY, William 1
  Aspenwall
BRADLEY, William Clark 2
BRADLEY, William Czar 1
BRADLEY, William 1
  Harrison
BRADLEY, William 5
  O'Connell
BRADLEY, Willis W. 3
BRADMAN, Frederic 6
  Leison
BRADNER, Lester 1
BRADSHAW, Charles 3
  Sullivan
BRADSHAW, De Emmett 1
BRADSHAW, Frederick 5
  Joseph Jr.
BRADSHAW, Jean Paul 5
BRADSHAW, John 2
  Hammond
BRADSHAW, Leslie 3
  Havergal
BRADSHAW, Michael 5
BRADSHAW, Robert 4
  Wallace
BRADSHAW, Samuel Carey H
BRADSHAW, Sidney 1
  Ernest
BRADSHAW, William 1
  Francis
BRADSHAW, William L. 4
BRADSHER, Earl 6
  L(ockridge)
BRADSTREET, Anne H
  Dudley
BRADSTREET, John H
BRADSTREET, Simon H
BRADT, Charles Edwin 1
BRADT, Peter Edward III 5
BRADWELL, James B. 1
BRADWELL, Myra Colby H
BRADY, Alice 1
BRADY, Anthony Nicholas 1
BRADY, Cyrus Townsend 1
BRADY, Francis M. 5
BRADY, Francis X. 1
BRADY, James Boyd 1
BRADY, James Buchanan H
BRADY, James Buchanan 4
BRADY, James Cox H
BRADY, James Cox 5
BRADY, James H. 1
BRADY, James Harry 6
BRADY, James Topham H
BRADY, Jasper Ewing 1
BRADY, John 1
BRADY, John Everett 3
BRADY, John Green 1
BRADY, John J. 1
BRADY, John Leeford 1
BRADY, Jules Longmore 4
BRADY, Lionel Francis 4
BRADY, Matthew B. 4
BRADY, Matthew Francis 4
BRADY, Nicholas Frederic 1
BRADY, Robert Alexander 4
BRADY, Thomas Allan 4
BRADY, Thomas Francis 5
BRADY, Thomas Jefferson 1
BRADY, Thomas Jr. 2
BRADY, Thomas Pickens 5
BRADY, William 1
BRADY, William A. 4
BRADY, William Gage Jr. 4
BRADY, William Otterwell 4
  Ignatius
BRAGA, Bernardo 4
BRAGDON, Charles 1
  Cushman
BRAGDON, Claude 2
BRAGDON, John Stewart 4
BRAGDON, Merritt 3
  Caldwell

BRAGDON, Olive Hurd 1
BRAGG, Braxton H
BRAGG, Edward Milton 5
BRAGG, Edward 1
  Stuyvesant
BRAGG, George 4
BRAGG, George Freeman 3
BRAGG, John H
BRAGG, Sir (William) 5
  Lawrence
BRAGG, Thomas H
BRAGINTON, Mary 6
  Victoria
BRAHANY, Thomas W. 4
BRAHENEY, Bernard F. 3
BRAID, Andrew 4
BRAIN, Belle Marvel 1
BRAIN, Walter Russell 5
BRAINARD, Clinton Tyler 1
BRAINARD, Daniel H
BRAINARD, David Legge 2
BRAINARD, John Gardiner H
  Calkins
BRAINARD, Morgan B Jr. 5
BRAINARD, Morgan 3
  Bulkeley
BRAINARD, Morgan 4
  Bulkeley Jr.
BRAINARD, Newton Case 6
BRAINARD, Owen 1
BRAINE, Clinton Elgin Jr. 3
BRAINE, Robert D. 4
BRAINERD, Arthur 1
  Alanson
BRAINERD, Cephas 1
BRAINERD, Chauncey 1
  Cory
BRAINERD, David H
BRAINERD, Eleanor Hoyt 2
BRAINERD, Erastus 1
BRAINERD, Ezra 1
BRAINERD, Ezra Jr. 1
BRAINERD, Frank 1
BRAINERD, Henry Dean 5
  Sr.
BRAINERD, Henry Green 1
BRAINERD, John H
BRAINERD, Lawrence 1
BRAINERD, Thomas H
BRAISLIN, Edward 1
BRAISLIN, William C. 2
BRAISTED, William 1
  Clarence
BRAITHWAITE, William 4
  Stanley Beaumont
BRAITMAYER, Otto 1
  Ernest
BRAKELEY, George 4
  Archibald
BRAKENSIEK, Clifton 6
  Mack
BRALEY, Berton 4
BRALEY, Henry King 1
BRALLEY, Francis Marion 1
BRALLIAR, Floyd Burton 3
BRAM, Joseph 5
BRAMAN, Dwight 1
BRAMER, Samuel Eugene 2
BRAMHALL, Edith 4
  Clementine
BRAMHALL, Howard 4
  Wellington
BRAMHAM, William 2
  Gibbons
BRAMKAMP, John Milton 5
BRAMLETTE, Thomas E. H
BRAMMER, George 2
  Edward
BRAMSON, Leo 6
BRAMUGLIA, Juan Atilio 4
BRANCH, Anna Hempstead 1
BRANCH, Charles Henry 5
  Hardin
BRANCH, Ernest A. 3
BRANCH, Ernest William 4
BRANCH, Harllee 4
BRANCH, Harold Francis 4
BRANCH, Houston 5
BRANCH, Irving Lewis 4
BRANCH, James Ransom 4
BRANCH, John 1
BRANCH, John B. 1
BRANCH, John Patteson H
BRANCH, Joseph Gerald 4
BRANCH, Lawrence H
  O'Bryan
BRANCH, Mary Lydia 1
  Bolles
BRANCH, Oliver Ernesto 1
BRANCH, Oliver Winslow 4
BRANCUSI, Constantin 3
BRAND, Charles 4
BRAND, Charles Hillyer 1
BRAND, Charles John 2
BRAND, Charles L. 2
BRAND, Edward Alexander 6

BRAND, Edward Parish 1
BRAND, Harrison Jr. 5
BRAND, James Tenney 4
BRAND, John W. B. 1
BRAND, Louis 5
BRAND, Robert Henry 4
BRAND, William Henry 3
BRANDE, Dorothea 2
  Thompson
BRANDEBERRY, John 3
  Benjamin
BRANDEGEE, Frank 1
  Bosworth
BRANDEIS, Erich 3
BRANDEIS, Frederic H
BRANDEIS, Frederick 1
BRANDEIS, Louis Dembitz 1
BRANDEL, S. W. 3
BRANDELLE, Gustaf 1
  Albert
BRANDEN, Paul Maerker 2
BRANDENBURG, Earnest 4
  Silas
BRANDENBURG, Edwin 1
  Charles
BRANDENBURG, 1
  Frederick Harmon
BRANDENBURG, George 1
  Clinton
BRANDENBURG, Mort 5
BRANDENBURG, Samuel 6
  J.
BRANDENBURG, William 1
  A.
BRANDENBURG, William 6
  Aaron Jr.
BRANDES, Elmer Walker 4
BRANDHORST, Otto 6
  William
BRANDI, Hermann 6
  Theodor
BRANDJORD, Iver 3
  Martinson
BRANDON, Edgar Ewing 3
BRANDON, Edmund John 2
BRANDON, Gerard H
  Chittocque
BRANDON, Jesse DeWitt 3
BRANDON, Morris 1
BRANDON, Rodney Howe 6
BRANDON, Samuel George 5
  Frederick
BRANDON, William 1
  Woodward
BRANDT, Allen Demmy 5
BRANDT, Carl Gunard 5
BRANDT, Carl Ludwig H
BRANDT, Carl Ludwig 1
BRANDT, Erdmann 4
  Neumiester
BRANDT, George Louis 5
BRANDT, Harry 5
BRANDT, Herman Carl 1
  George
BRANDT, John 3
BRANDT, John Lincoln 2
BRANDT, Joseph Granger 4
BRANDT, Karl 6
BRANDT, Nils 1
BRANDT, Olaf Elias 4
BRANDT, Raymond Peter 6
BRANDT, William Earle 4
BRANGWYN, Sir Frank 3
BRANHAM, Sara Elizabeth 4
BRANHAM, William 1
  Charles
BRANIFF, Thomas E. 3
BRANIGIN, Roger Douglas 6
BRANN, Donald W. 4
BRANN, Henry Athanasius 1
BRANN, Louis Jefferson 2
BRANN, William Cowper H
BRANNAN, John Milton H
BRANNAN, John Winters 1
BRANNAN, Joseph 1
  Doddridge
BRANNAN, Samuel 3
BRANNAN, William 3
  Forrest
BRANNEN, Burton 4
  Alexander
BRANNER, John Casper 1
BRANNER, Martin Michael 5
BRANNER, Robert 6
BRANNON, Henry 1
BRANNON, Melvin Amos 4
BRANNON, Peter 4
  Alexander
BRANNON, William W. 4
BRANNT, William 1
  Theodore
BRANOM, Mendel Everett 4
BRANSBY, Carlos 1
BRANSCOMB, John W. 3

BRANSCOMB, Lewis Capers 1
BRANSCOMBE, Gena (Mrs. John Ferguson Tenney) 6
BRANSFORD, Clifton Wood 1
BRANSHAW, Charles E. 2
BRANSON, Edwin Bayer 3
BRANSON, Eugene Cunningham 1
BRANSON, Frederick Page 4
BRANSON, John William 3
BRANSON, Taylor 1
BRANSON, William Henry 4
BRANSTROM, William Jeremiah 4
BRANT, Gerald Clark 6
BRANT, Joseph 4
BRANTINGHAM, Charles Simonson 4
BRANTLEY, William Gordon 1
BRANTLY, Theodore 1
BRANTLY, Theodore Lee 4
BRANTLY, William Theophilus 4
BRANTON, James Rodney 5
BRANZELL, Karin 6
BRAQUE, Georges 4
BRAS, Harry Leonard 1
BRASCH, Frederick Edward 6
BRASE, Hagbard 3
BRASHEAR, John Alfred H
BRASHEAR, John Alfred 1
BRASHEAR, John Alfred 1
BRASHEAR, Peter Cominges 2
BRASHEARS, Edwin Lawrence 6
BRASHER, Rex 3
BRASKAMP, Bernard 4
BRASLAU, Sophie 1
BRASOL, Boris 4
BRASSERT, Herman Alexander 5
BRASTED, Alva Jennings 5
BRASTED, Fred 3
BRASTOW, Lewis Orsmond 1
BRASWELL, James Craig 4
BRATENAHL, George Carl Fitch 1
BRATNEY, John Frederick 6
BRATT, Elmer Clark 6
BRATTLE, Thomas H
BRATTLE, William H
BRATTON, John H
BRATTON, John Walter 4
BRATTON, Leslie Emmett 3
BRATTON, Robert Franklin 1
BRATTON, Sam Gilbert 4
BRATTON, Samuel Tilden 1
BRATTON, Theodore DuBose 2
BRATTON, Walter Andrew 2
BRAU, Charles Frederick 6
BRAUCHER, Frank 5
BRAUCHER, Howard S. 2
BRAUDE, Jacob Morton 5
BRAUFF, Herbert D. 3
BRAUER, Alfred 4
BRAUER, George R. 1
BRAUER, John Charles 5
BRAUN, Arthur E. 6
BRAUN, Carl Franklin 3
BRAUN, John F. 2
BRAUN, Maurice 2
BRAUN, Robert 3
BRAUN, Werner 4
BRAUNE, Gustave Maurice 1
BRAUNER, Julius Frederick 6
BRAUNER, Olaf Martinius 2
BRAUNSCHWEIGER, Walter J. 6
BRAUSE, Edward 4
BRAWLEY, Benjamin 1
BRAWLEY, Frank 4
BRAWLEY, William H. 3
BRAXTON, A. Caperton 1
BRAXTON, Carter H
BRAXTON, Elliott Muse H
BRAY, Charles I. 3
BRAY, Frank Chapin 2
BRAY, Harold Bryan 5
BRAY, Henry Truro 1
BRAY, John Leighton 3
BRAY, John P. 1
BRAY, Patrick Albert 4
BRAY, Robert Stuart 1
BRAY, Stephen 6
BRAY, Thomas H
BRAY, Thomas Joseph 1
BRAY, William Crowell 2
BRAY, William L. 1
BRAYMAN, Mason H
BRAYMER, Daniel Harvey 1

BRAYTON, Aaron Martin 2
BRAYTON, Alembert Winthrop 1
BRAYTON, Charles Ray 1
BRAYTON, Israel 1
BRAYTON, William Daniel H
BRAZEAU, Theodore Walter 5
BRAZELTON, William Buchanan 1
BRAZER, Clarence Wilson 3
BRAZER, John H
BRAZIER, Miss Marion Howard 1
BREADON, Sam 2
BREADY, Charles J. 5
BREAN, Herbert 6
BREARLEY, David H
BREARLEY, Harry Chase 6
BREARLEY, William Henry 1
BREASTED, James Henry 1
BREAUX, Joseph A. 1
BREAZEALE, Phanor 1
BREBNER, John Bartlet 3
BRECHT, Bertoit Eugen Friedrich 4
BRECHT, Bertolt Eugen Friedrich H
BRECHT, Robert Paul 5
BRECK, Daniel H
BRECK, Edward 1
BRECK, George William 1
BRECK, James Lloyd H
BRECK, John H. 4
BRECK, Joseph 1
BRECK, Samuel H
BRECK, Samuel 1
BRECKENRIDGE, Clifton Rodes 1
BRECKENRIDGE, Hugh Henry 1
BRECKENRIDGE, James H
BRECKENRIDGE, James Miller 4
BRECKENRIDGE, John 1
BRECKENRIDGE, John C. 4
BRECKENRIDGE, Lester Paige 3
BRECKENRIDGE, Ralph W. 1
BRECKINRIDGE, Aida de Acosta 4
BRECKINRIDGE, Desha 1
BRECKINRIDGE, Henry 4
BRECKINRIDGE, James Carson 2
BRECKINRIDGE, James Douglas H
BRECKINRIDGE, Jefferson H
BRECKINRIDGE, John Cabell H
BRECKINRIDGE, John Cabell 1
BRECKINRIDGE, Joseph Cabell 1
BRECKINRIDGE, Madeline McDowell 1
BRECKINRIDGE, Mary 4
BRECKINRIDGE, Sophonisba Preston 2
BRECKINRIDGE, William Campbell Preston 1
BRECKINRIDGE, William Lewis 1
BRECKONS, Robert W. 1
BREDIN, R. Sloan 1
BREED, Charles Blaney 3
BREED, Charles Henry 3
BREED, David Riddle 1
BREED, Dwight Payson 1
BREED, Ebenezer H
BREED, Mary Bidwell 6
BREED, R. E. 1
BREED, Robert Stanley 3
BREED, William Constable H
BREED, William Constable Jr. 6
BREEDEN, Harvey Oscar 1
BREEDING, Glenn Edward 5
BREEN, Aloysius Andrew 4
BREEN, Joseph Ignatius 4
BREEN, Patrick 1
BREEN, Robert A. 3
BREEN, William John Jr. 5
BREEN, William P. 1
BREENE, Frank Thomas 1
BREES, Herbert Jay 5
BREESE, Burtis Burr 1
BREESE, Edmund 1
BREESE, Randolph Kidder H
BREESE, Sidney H
BREESE, William Llywelyn 3
BREG, W. Roy 3
BREGY, Francis Amedee 1
BREGY, Katherine Marie Cornelia 4

BREHAN, Marquise de H
BREHM, Cloide Everett 5
BREHM, John S. 2
BREHM, Marie Caroline 1
BREIDENBAUGH, Edward Swoyer 1
BREIDENTHAL, John W. 1
BREIDENTHAL, John W. 5
BREIDENTHAL, Maurice L. 4
BREIDENTHAL, Maurice Lauren Jr. 5
BREIDENTHAL, Willard J. 4
BREIL, Joseph Carl 1
BREISACH, Paul 3
BREISACHER, Leo M. D. 4
BREITENBACH, Edward Victor 6
BREITHAUPT, Louis Orville 4
BREITHUT, Frederick Ernest 6
BREITUNG, Charles Adelbert 3
BREITUNG, Edward H
BREITUNG, Edward Nicklas 1
BREITWIESER, Joseph Valentine 3
BRELSFORD, Charles Henry 4
BRELSFORD, Millard 2
BREM, Walter Vernon 1
BREMER, Adolf 1
BREMER, George A. 3
BREMER, John Lewis 3
BREMER, Otto 3
BREMNER, George Hampton 1
BREMNER, William Hepburn 1
BRENDEL, Otto Johannes 6
BRENDLER, Charles 4
BRENDLINGER, Margaret Robinson 5
BRENEMAN, Abram Adam 1
BRENGLE, Francis H
BRENGLE, Henry Gaw 2
BRENKE, William Charles 5
BRENNAN, Alfred Laurens 4
BRENNAN, Andrew James 3
BRENNAN, Edward James 4
BRENNAN, Frederick Hazlitt 4
BRENNAN, George E. 1
BRENNAN, George M. 3
BRENNAN, Gerald Leo 4
BRENNAN, James Dowd 3
BRENNAN, John Francis 3
BRENNAN, Martin Adlai 1
BRENNAN, Martin S. 2
BRENNAN, Robert 3
BRENNAN, Thomas Francis 4
BRENNAN, Walter Andrew 6
BRENNAN, William Henry 4
BRENNECKE, Cornelius G. 3
BRENNECKE, Ernest 5
BRENNECKE, Henry 4
BRENNEMANN, Joseph 2
BRENNER, John L. 4
BRENNER, Mortimer 5
BRENNER, Otto 5
BRENNER, Ruth Marie (Mrs. Chester T. Mellinger) 6
BRENNER, Victor David 1
BRENON, Herbert 3
BRENT, Charles Henry 1
BRENT, Frank Pierce 4
BRENT, Henry Johnson H
BRENT, Joseph Lancaster 1
BRENT, Margaret H
BRENT, Meade Stith 6
BRENT, Richard H
BRENT, Theodore 3
BRENT, William Leigh H
BRENTANO, Arthur 2
BRENTANO, Lorenz H
BRENTANO, Lowell 3
BRENTANO, Theodore 1
BRENTON, Charles Richmond 1
BRENTON, Clyde Edward 1
BRENTON, Cranston 1
BRENTON, Samuel H
BRENTON, Woodward Harold 5
BRERETON, Lewis Hyde 4
BRES, Edward Sedley 5
BRESCHARD 1
BRESKY, Otto 6
BRESLICH, Arthur Louis 4
BRESLICH, Ernst Rudolph 5
BRESLIN, James H. 1
BRESNAHAN, Thomas F. 5

BRESNAHAN, William H. 2
BRESSLER, Raymond G. JR. 4
BRESSLER, Raymond George 2
BRESTELL, Rudolph Emile 5
BRETHERTON, Sidney Elliott 1
BRETHORST, Alice Beatrice 6
BRETON, Andre 4
BRETON, Ruth 4
BRETT, Agnes Baldwin 3
BRETT, Alden Chase 5
BRETT, Axel 3
BRETT, George Platt 1
BRETT, Homer 1
BRETT, Lloyd M. 1
BRETT, Philip Milledoler 4
BRETT, Rutherford 3
BRETT, Sereno E. 3
BRETT, William Howard 1
BRETT, William Pierce 4
BRETZ, Julian Pleasant 3
BREUER, Bessie 6
BREUER, Carl A. 5
BREUER, Henry Joseph 4
BREUER, Louis Henry 1
BREUNINGER, Lewis Talmage 6
BREVARD, Joseph H
BREVOORT, James Carson H
BREVOORT, James Renwick 1
BREWBAKER, Cassie Leta (Mrs. William Styne Brewbaker) 6
BREWBAKER, Charles Warren 5
BREWER, Abraham T. 1
BREWER, Arthur Allen Jr. 6
BREWER, Basil H
BREWER, Charles H
BREWER, Charles Edward 3
BREWER, Charles S. 1
BREWER, Clara Tagg 6
BREWER, D. Chauncey 1
BREWER, David Josiah 1
BREWER, Earl LeRoy 2
BREWER, Edward Vere 6
BREWER, Francis Beattie 1
BREWER, Franklin Nourse 1
BREWER, George 1
BREWER, George Emerson 1
BREWER, George St P. 4
BREWER, Hugh Graham 4
BREWER, James Arthur 3
BREWER, John Bruce 4
BREWER, John Hyatt 1
BREWER, John Marks 4
BREWER, Leigh Richmond 1
BREWER, Leo 4
BREWER, Luther Albertus 1
BREWER, Mark Spencer 1
BREWER, Nicholas Richard 2
BREWER, Oby T. 5
BREWER, Robert Du Bois 1
BREWER, Robert Paine 1
BREWER, Thomas Mayo 6
BREWER, William A. Jr. 4
BREWER, William Henry 1
BREWER, Willis 5
BREWSTER, Albert Vincent 3
BREWSTER, Andre Walker 2
BREWSTER, Benjamin 1
BREWSTER, Benjamin Harris H
BREWSTER, Benjamin Harris 4
BREWSTER, Benjamin Harris Jr. 1
BREWSTER, Chauncey Bunce 1
BREWSTER, David Lukens 2
BREWSTER, David P. H
BREWSTER, Edward Lester 1
BREWSTER, Edwin Tenney 3
BREWSTER, Elisha Hume 2
BREWSTER, Ethel Hampson 2
BREWSTER, Eugene Valentine 1
BREWSTER, Few 3
BREWSTER, Frances Stanton 1
BREWSTER, Frederick Carroll 1
BREWSTER, George Thomas 2
BREWSTER, George Washington Wales 1
BREWSTER, Henry Colvin 1
BREWSTER, James H
BREWSTER, James Henry 1

BREWSTER, James Henry Jr. 3
BREWSTER, Osmyn H
BREWSTER, Owen 4
BREWSTER, Raymond 5
BREWSTER, Reginald R. 2
BREWSTER, Sardius Mason 1
BREWSTER, Walter Stanton 3
BREWSTER, William H
BREWSTER, William 1
BREWSTER, William Nesbitt 1
BREWSTER, William Roe 4
BREWSTER, William Tenney 4
BREYER, Henry W Jr. 5
BREYFOGEL, Sylvanus Charles 1
BREZING, Herman 2
BRIAN, Donald 2
BRICE, Calvin Stewart 1
BRICE, Charles Rufus 4
BRICE, Fanny 3
BRICE, John A. 2
BRICHER, Alfred Thompson 3
BRICK, Abraham Lincoln 1
BRICK, Alyea M. 4
BRICK, Nicholas William 1
BRICKELL, Henry Herschel 5
BRICKELL, Robert Coman 1
BRICKELL, William David 4
BRICKEN, Carl Ernest 5
BRICKER, Edwin Dyson 4
BRICKER, Garland Armor 6
BRICKER, Luther Otterbein 2
BRICKER, Mead L. 4
BRICKLEY, Bartholomew A. 3
BRICKNER, Barnett Robert 3
BRICKNER, Walter M. 1
BRIDE, William Witthaft 1
BRIDGE, Ann (Lady O'Malley) 6
BRIDGE, Gerard 5
BRIDGE, James Howard 1
BRIDGE, Norman 1
BRIDGER, James H
BRIDGERS, Robert Rufus H
BRIDGES, Calvin Blackman 1
BRIDGES, Charles Higbee 2
BRIDGES, Charles Scott 1
BRIDGES, Edson Lowell 1
BRIDGES, Fidelia 1
BRIDGES, George Washington H
BRIDGES, Hedley Francis Gregory 2
BRIDGES, Horace James 3
BRIDGES, James Robertson 1
BRIDGES, Jesse B. 1
BRIDGES, Milton Arlanden 1
BRIDGES, Robert * H
BRIDGES, Robert 1
BRIDGES, Ronald 4
BRIDGES, S. Russell 4
BRIDGES, Samuel Augustus H
BRIDGES, Styles 4
BRIDGES, Thomas Henry 4
BRIDGES, Thomas Reed 2
BRIDGES, Willson Orton 4
BRIDGMAN, Elijah Coleman H
BRIDGMAN, Frederic Arthur 1
BRIDGMAN, George Henry 4
BRIDGMAN, George Herbert 4
BRIDGMAN, Grenville Temple 3
BRIDGMAN, Helen Bartlett (Mrs. Herbert L. Bridgman) 5
BRIDGMAN, Herbert Lawrence 1
BRIDGMAN, Howard Allen 1
BRIDGMAN, Laura Dewey H
BRIDGMAN, Lewis Jesse 1
BRIDGMAN, Olga Louise 6
BRIDGMAN, Percy Williams 4
BRIDGMAN, Raymond Landon 1
BRIDGWATER, William 4
BRIDPORT, Hugh H
BRIEFS, Goetz A(ntony) 6
BRIEN, William Given 4
BRIER, Ernest 3
BRIER, Royce 6
BRIER, Warren Judson 1
BRIERLEY, Wilfrid Gordon 5
BRIERLY, James Leslie 6
BRIERTON, John H

BRIESEN, Arthur von 1
BRIETZKE, June Oneson 6
　(Mrs. Charles H. Brietzke)
BRIGANCE, W. Norwood 3
BRIGGS, Arthur Hyslop 1
BRIGGS, Asa Gilbert 2
BRIGGS, Austin Eugene 6
BRIGGS, Charles 1
BRIGGS, Charles Augustus 1
BRIGGS, Charles Frederick H
BRIGGS, Charles S. 4
BRIGGS, Clare A. 1
BRIGGS, Clay Stone 1
BRIGGS, Corona Hibbard 4
BRIGGS, Edward Cornelius 3
BRIGGS, Elizabeth Darling 3
BRIGGS, Ellis O. 6
BRIGGS, Frank Alonzo 1
BRIGGS, Frank Obadiah 1
BRIGGS, Frank Richmond 5
BRIGGS, Frederic 3
　Melancthon
BRIGGS, George H
BRIGGS, George Ernest 5
BRIGGS, George Isaac 2
BRIGGS, George Nathaniel 1
BRIGGS, George Nixon H
BRIGGS, George Waverley 3
BRIGGS, George Weston 2
BRIGGS, Gordon Dobson 3
BRIGGS, Henry Birdice 1
　Richmond
BRIGGS, Henry Harrison 1
BRIGGS, J. Emmons 1
BRIGGS, John De 4
　Quedville
BRIGGS, John Ely 3
BRIGGS, L. Vernon 1
BRIGGS, Le Baron Russell 1
BRIGGS, Lucia Russell 3
BRIGGS, Lyman James 4
BRIGGS, Raymond 6
　Westcott
BRIGGS, Robert Aldrich 4
BRIGGS, Roswell Emmons 4
BRIGGS, Stephen Albro 4
BRIGGS, Thomas Henry 5
BRIGGS, Thomas Roland 3
BRIGGS, Walter Owen 3
BRIGGS, Walter Owen Jr. 5
BRIGGS, Warren Richard 2
BRIGGS, William Harlowe 5
BRIGHAM, Albert Perry 1
BRIGHAM, Amariah 4
BRIGHAM, Arthur Amber 4
BRIGHAM, Carl Campbell 2
BRIGHAM, Clarence 4
　Saunders
BRIGHAM, Claude Ernest 6
BRIGHAM, Elbert Sidney 4
BRIGHAM, Elijah H
BRIGHAM, Gertrude 5
　Richardson ("Viktor
　Flambeau")
BRIGHAM, Harold 5
　Frederick
BRIGHAM, Henry 4
　Randolph
BRIGHAM, Johnson 1
BRIGHAM, Joseph Henry 1
BRIGHAM, L. Ward 4
BRIGHAM, Lewis H
　Alexander
BRIGHAM, Mary Ann 1
BRIGHAM, Nat Maynard 1
BRIGHAM, Richard 3
　Douglas
BRIGHAM, Sarah Jeannette 1
BRIGHAM, William Erastus 1
BRIGHAM, William Tufts 1
BRIGHT, Alfred Harris 1
BRIGHT, David Edward 4
BRIGHT, Edward H
BRIGHT EYES H
BRIGHT, James Wilson 1
BRIGHT, Jesse David H
BRIGHT, John 2
BRIGHT, J(oseph) S(hirley) 6
BRIGHT, Louis Victor 4
BRIGHT, Marshal 1
　Huntington
BRIGHTLY, Frank 4
　Frederick
BRIGHTLY, Frederick H
　Charles
BRIGHTMAN, Alvin 1
　Collins
BRIGHTMAN, Edgar 3
　Sheffield
BRIGHTMAN, Horace 1
　Irving
BRIGHTMAN, Horace 2
　Irving
BRIGMAN, Bennett 1
　Mattingly
BRILES, Charles Walter 5

BRILL, Abraham Arden 2
BRILL, George Mackenzie 5
BRILL, George Reiter 1
BRILL, Harvey Clayton 5
BRILL, Hascal Russel 3
BRILL, Joseph Eugene 6
BRILL, Nathan Edwin 1
BRILL, William Hascal 1
BRILLHART, David H. 3
BRIM, Kenneth Milliken 6
BRIMHALL, George Henry 1
BRIMSON, William George 1
BRINCKE, William Draper H
BRINCKERHOFF, Arthur 4
　Freeman
BRINCKERHOFF, Henry 1
　Morton
BRIND, Charles Albert 5
BRIND, Sir Patrick 4
BRINDLEY, John Edwin 6
BRINDLEY, Paul 3
BRINEY, Paul Wallace 6
BRINEY, Russell 1
BRINGHURST, Robert 1
　Porter
BRININSTOOL, Earl 3
　Alonzo
BRINK, Charles Bernard 6
BRINK, Francis G. 3
BRINK, Gilbert Nicholas 1
BRINKEN, Carl Ernest 5
BRINKER, Howard Rasmus 4
BRINKER, Josiah Henry 1
BRINKERHOFF, Henry H
　Roelif
BRINKERHOFF, Jacob H
BRINKERHOFF, Robert 3
　Moore
BRINKERHOFF, Roeliff 1
BRINKMAN, Oscar H. 5
BRINKMAN, William 1
　Augustus
BRINLEY, Charles A. 4
BRINLEY, Charles Edward 6
BRINLEY, Daniel Putnam 4
BRINLEY, Katherine 4
　Gordon Sanger
BRINSER, Harry Lerch 2
BRINSMADE, John 1
　Chaplin
BRINSMADE, Robert 4
　Bruce
BRINSMADE, William 4
　Barrett
BRINSON, Samuel Mitchell 1
BRINSTAD, Charles 2
　William
BRINTON, Christian 2
BRINTON, Daniel Garrison 1
BRINTON, Howard T. 4
BRINTON, Jasper Yeates 6
BRINTON, John Hill 1
BRINTON, Paul Henry 4
　Mallet-Prevost
BRINTON, Willard Cope 3
BRISBANE, Albert H
BRISBANE, Arthur 2
BRISBIN, Clarence Franklin 5
BRISBIN, James S. H
BRISBIN, John H
BRISBINE, Annie M'Iver 4
BRISCO, Norris Arthur 2
BRISCOE, Birdsall 5
　Parmenas
BRISCOE, Herman T. 4
BRISCOE, John Parran 4
BRISCOE, Robert Pearce 5
BRISKIN, Samuel Jacob 5
BRISSENDEN, Paul 6
　Frederick
BRIST, George Louis 6
BRISTED, Charles Astor H
BRISTED, John H
BRISTER, Charles James 3
BRISTER, John Willard 4
BRISTOL, Arthur E. 3
BRISTOL, Arthur LeRoy 2
BRISTOL, Augusta Cooper 1
BRISTOL, Charles 1
　Lawrence
BRISTOL, Edward Newell 2
BRISTOL, Frank Milton 1
BRISTOL, George Prentiss 1
BRISTOL, Henry P. 3
BRISTOL, John Bunyan 1
BRISTOL, John Isaac Devoe 1
BRISTOL, Lee Hastings 4
BRISTOL, Leverett Dale 3
BRISTOL, Mark Lambert 1
BRISTOL, Theodore Louis 5
BRISTOL, William Henry 1
BRISTOW, Algernon 1
　Thomas
BRISTOW, Benjamin Helm H
BRISTOW, Francis Marion H
BRISTOW, George F. 4

BRISTOW, George H
　Frederick
BRISTOW, George 4
　Washington
BRISTOW, Joseph Little 2
BRISTOW, Louis Judson 5
BRITAN, Halbert Hains 2
BRITT, James J. 1
BRITT, Walter Stratton 6
BRITTAIN, Carlo Bonaparte 1
BRITTAIN, Charles Mercer 2
BRITTAIN, Frank Smith 1
BRITTAIN, Joseph I. 1
BRITTAIN, Marion Luther 3
BRITTAN, Belle H
BRITTEN, Edwin Franklin 4
　Jr.
BRITTEN, Flora Phelps 4
　Harley
BRITTEN, Fred Albert 2
BRITTEN, Fred Ernest 1
BRITTIN, Lewis Hotchkiss 5
BRITTINGHAM, Thomas 2
　Evans
BRITTINGHAM, Thomas 4
　Evans Jr.
BRITTON, Alexander 1
　Thompson
BRITTON, Edgar C. 4
BRITTON, Edward Elms 1
BRITTON, Elizabeth 1
　Gertrude
BRITTON, Frank Hamilton 3
BRITTON, Frederick O. 4
BRITTON, John Alexander 1
BRITTON, Mason 6
BRITTON, Nathaniel Lord 1
BRITTON, Wilton Everett 1
BRIZZOLARA, Ralph 5
　Dominic
BROADBENT, James 5
　Thomas
BROADDUS, Bower 3
BROADFOOT, Grover L. 4
BROADHEAD, Garland 1
　Carr
BROADHEAD, James H
　Overton
BROADHURST, Edward T. 3
BROADHURST, Edwin 1
　Borden
BROADHURST, George H. 3
BROADHURST, Jean H
BROADUS, John Albert H
BROADWATER, J. A. B. 3
BROCH, Hermann Joseph 4
BROCK, Charles Robert 1
BROCK, Charles William 1
　Penn
BROCK, Clifford Edward 4
BROCK, Elmer Leslie 4
BROCK, George William 2
BROCK, Henry Irving 6
BROCK, James Ellison 4
BROCK, Larry 5
BROCK, Loring Stewart 5
BROCK, Robert Alonzo 1
BROCK, Sidney Gorham 4
BROCK, Thomas Sleeper 5
BROCK, William Emerson 4
BROCKENBROUGH, H
　William Henry
BROCKETT, Linus Pierpont H
BROCKHAGEN, Carl 2
　Homer ·
BROCKIE, Arthur H. 2
BROCKLESBY, John 4
BROCKMAN, Fletcher 2
　Sims
BROCKSON, Franklin 4
BROCKWAY, Albert 1
　Leverett
BROCKWAY, Fred John 1
BROCKWAY, George A. 5
BROCKWAY, Hobart 6
　Mortimer Jr.
BROCKWAY, Howard 3
BROCKWAY, John Hall 4
BROCKWAY, Zebulon 1
　Reed
BRODA, Frederick Martin 6
BRODBECK, Andrew R. 4
BRODE, Charles Geiger 4
BRODE, Howard Stidham 4
BRODE, Wallace Reed 6
BRODEK, Charles Adrian 2
BRODERICK, Bonaventure 2
　Finnbarr
BRODERICK, Carroll 5
　Joseph
BRODERICK, Case 3
BRODERICK, David H
　Colbreth
BRODERICK, Henry 6
BRODERICK, John P. 6
BRODERICK, John T. 1

BRODERICK, Joseph A. 3
BRODERICK, William 4
　Stephen
BRODERS, Albert Compton 4
BRODESSER, Roman 4
　Adolph
BRODEUR, Clarence 1
　Arthur
BRODHEAD, Daniel H
BRODHEAD, George 5
　Livingston
BRODHEAD, George 4
　Milton
BRODHEAD, J. Davis 1
BRODHEAD, John H
BRODHEAD, John Curtis H
BRODHEAD, John Romeyn H
BRODHEAD, Richard 1
BRODIE, Alexander Oswald 1
BRODIE, Allan Gibson 6
BRODIE, Andrew Melrose 1
BRODIE, Donald M. 6
BRODIE, Edward Everett 1
BRODIE, Gandy 6
BRODIE, Israel B. 4
BRODNEY, Spencer 6
BRODRICK, Lynn 3
　Rosegrant
BRODRICK, Richard 1
　Godfrey
BRODSKY, Nathan 5
BRODSKY, Paul 5
BRODY, Clark Louis 4
BRODY, Daniel Anthony 6
BRODY, Joseph Isaac 4
BRODY, Samuel 3
BROEDEL, Max 1
BROEDEL, Max 2
BROEK, Jan Otto Marius 6
BROEK, John Yonker 4
BROEKMAN, David 3
　Hendrines
BROENING, William 3
　Frederick
BROGAN, Sir Denis 6
　William
BROGAN, Francis Albert 5
BROGAN, James M. 1
BROGAN, Thomas J. 4
BROGDEN, Wilfred John 6
BROGDEN, Willis James 1
BROGHAMER, George P. 6
BROGLIE, Duc de 4
BROIDY, Edward William 3
BROKAMP, Frank William 4
BROKAW, Charles 1
　Livingston
BROKAW, Howard Crosby 4
BROKENSHIRE, Charles 3
　Digory
BROKENSHIRE, Norman 4
BROKENSHIRE, William 4
　Samuel Jr.
BROKMEYER, Henry C. H
BROKMEYER, Henry C. 4
BROMBERG, Frederick 1
　George
BROMER, Edward 3
　Sheppard
BROMER, Ralph Shepherd 3
BROMFIELD, John H
BROMFIELD, Louis 3
BROMILOW, Frank 4
BROMLEY, Charles 5
　Dunham
BROMWELL, Charles 1
　Summers
BROMWELL, Jacob Henry 4
BRONDEL, John B. 1
BRONFENBRENNER, 3
　Jacques Jacob
BRONFMAN, Samuel 5
BRONK, Detlev W. 6
BRONK, Isabelle 2
BRONK, Mitchell 3
BRONLEM, Isaac Hill H
BRONNER, Augusta Fox 6
　(Mrs. William Healy)
BRONNER, Edmond D. 1
BRONNER, Harry 1
BRONOWSKI, Jacob 6
BRONSON, Bennet 4
BRONSON, Charles Eli 4
BRONSON, David H
BRONSON, Dillon 2
BRONSON, Francis 4
　Woolsey
BRONSON, Harrison 2
　Arthur
BRONSON, Henry H
BRONSON, Isaac Hopkins H
BRONSON, Samuel Lathrop 1
BRONSON, Solon Cary 1
BRONSON, Thomas 3
　Bertrand

BRONSON, Walter 1
　Cochrane
BRONSON, William 5
　Howard
BRONSON, William 4
　Sherlock
BROOK, Charles Henry 4
BROOK, Clive 6
BROOKE, Ben C. 5
BROOKE, Flavius Lionel 1
BROOKE, Francis Key 1
BROOKE, Francis Taliaferro H
BROOKE, Franklin 4
　Ellsworth
BROOKE, James J. 1
BROOKE, John Mercer 1
BROOKE, John Rutter 1
BROOKE, Mary Myrtle 5
BROOKE, Richard Norris 1
BROOKE, St George 1
　Tucker
BROOKE, Thomas Preston 4
BROOKE, Tucker 2
BROOKE, Walter H
BROOKE, William 4
　Ellsworth
BROOKE, William 5
　Ellsworth
BROOKEBOROUGH, 6
　Viscount (Brooke)
BROOKER, Charles 1
　Frederick
BROOKER, John William 3
BROOKE-RAWLE, William 1
BROOKES, John St Clair Jr. 4
BROOKES, Samuel 1
　Marsdon
BROOKHART, Smith W. 2
BROOKINGS, Robert 1
　Somers
BROOKINGS, Walter 3
　DuBois
BROOKINGS, Walter 4
　DuBois
BROOKINS, Homer De 3
　Wilton
BROOKS, Alfred Hulse 1
BROOKS, Alfred Mansfield 5
BROOKS, Allerton Frank 3
BROOKS, Alonzo Beecher 2
BROOKS, Anson Strong 1
BROOKS, Arbie Leroy 3
BROOKS, Arthur H
BROOKS, Arthur Alford 1
BROOKS, Arthur Thomas 2
BROOKS, Arthur Wolfort 2
BROOKS, Benjamin Talbott 4
BROOKS, Bryant Butler 2
BROOKS, C. Wayland 4
BROOKS, Charles 3
BROOKS, Charles Alvin 1
BROOKS, Charles Edward 1
BROOKS, Charles F. 3
BROOKS, Charles Hayward 5
BROOKS, Charles Stephen 1
BROOKS, Charles Timothy H
BROOKS, Christopher 1
　Parkinson
BROOKS, Clarence Richard 5
BROOKS, David 1
BROOKS, Edward 1
BROOKS, Edward 1
　Schroeder
BROOKS, Edwin B. 4
BROOKS, Elbridge Streeter 1
BROOKS, Erastus 1
BROOKS, Eugene Clyde 2
BROOKS, Florence 1
BROOKS, Frank Hilliard 1
BROOKS, Frank Wilks 1
BROOKS, Franklin Eli 1
BROOKS, Fred Emerson 1
BROOKS, Frederick A. 5
BROOKS, George Merrick 1
BROOKS, George Sprague H
BROOKS, George 4
　Washington
BROOKS, Geraldine 5
BROOKS, Harlow 1
BROOKS, Harry Sayer 5
BROOKS, Henry Luesing 5
BROOKS, Henry S. 5
BROOKS, Henry Turner 4
BROOKS, J. Wilton 3
BROOKS, Jabez 1
BROOKS, James H
BROOKS, James Byron 1
BROOKS, James Gordon 1
BROOKS, Jesse Wendell H
BROOKS, John H
BROOKS, John B. 6
BROOKS, John G(aunt) 1
BROOKS, John Graham 4
BROOKS, John Pascal 4
BROOKS, Joseph Hudson 3
BROOKS, Joshua Loring 2

BROOKS, Laurance Waddill 5
BROOKS, LaVerne W. 5
BROOKS, Leon Richard 4
BROOKS, Maria Gowen H
BROOKS, Mary Willard 5
BROOKS, Micah H
BROOKS, Morgan 2
BROOKS, Ned 5
BROOKS, Neil 5
BROOKS, Noah 1
BROOKS, Olin L. 4
BROOKS, Overton 4
BROOKS, Paul David 3
BROOKS, Peter Anthony H
BROOKS, Peter Chardon H
BROOKS, Phillips H
BROOKS, Phillips 6
BROOKS, Phillips Moore 5
BROOKS, Preston Smith 1
BROOKS, Ralph Gilmour 4
BROOKS, Raymond 2
  Cummings
BROOKS, Richard E. 1
BROOKS, Robert Blemker 5
BROOKS, Robert Clarkson 1
BROOKS, Robert Mary 2
BROOKS, Robert Nathaniel 3
BROOKS, Robert Preston 6
BROOKS, Rodney Joseph 3
BROOKS, Roelif Hasbrouck 6
BROOKS, Samuel Palmer 1
BROOKS, Sarah Warner 1
BROOKS, Stewart 5
BROOKS, Stratton Duluth 2
BROOKS, Summer Cushing 1
BROOKS, Thomas Benton 3
BROOKS, Van Wyck 4
BROOKS, Victor Lee 5
BROOKS, Walter Rollin 3
BROOKS, Wendell Stanton 1
BROOKS, William Benthall 4
BROOKS, William E. 5
BROOKS, William F. 6
BROOKS, William Keith 1
BROOKS, William Myron 1
BROOKS, William Penn 1
BROOKS, William Robert 1
BROOKS, William Thomas H
  Harbaugh
BROOKS, Winfield Sears 4
BROOKSHER, William 6
  Riley
BROOKSHIRE, Elijah 1
  Voorhees
BROOM, Jacob H
BROOM, James Madison 1
BROOMALL, John Martin H
BROOME, Edwin Cornelius 4
BROOME, Harvey 4
BROOME, Harvey 5
BROOME, Isaac 1
BROOME, Robert Edwin 4
BROGMELL, I. Norman 1
BROOMFIELD, John 2
  Calvin
BROONZY, William Lee 4
  Conley
BROPHY, C. Gerald 3
BROPHY, Daniel Francis 4
BROPHY, Ellen Amelia 1
BROPHY, Thomas D'Arcy 4
BROPHY, Truman William 1
BROPHY, William Henry 1
BROREIN, Carl D. 6
BROREIN, William G. 1
BROSE, Louis D. 1
BROSIUS, Marriott 1
BROSMAN, Paul William 3
BROSMITH, William 1
BROSNAHAN, Patrick 5
  Edward
BROSNAHAN, Timothy 1
BROSS, Ernest 1
BROSS, William H
BROSSART, Ferdinand 4
BROSSEAU, Alfred J. 1
BROTHER, Doran Palmer 4
BROTHERTON, Alice
  Williams
BROUGH, John H
BROUGH, William 4
BROUGHAM, John H
BROUGHER, J. Whitcomb 6
BROUGHER, J(ames) 5
  Whitcomb
BROUGHTON, Carrie 6
  Loungee
BROUGHTON, Charles 3
  Elmer
BROUGHTON, Charles 6
  Frederic
BROUGHTON, Joseph 2
  Melville
BROUGHTON, Leonard 1
  Gaston

BROUGHTON, Leslie 5
  Nathan
BROUGHTON, Levin 2
  Bowland
BROUGHTON, William R. 4
BROUGHTON, William S. 3
BROUILLETTE, T. Gilbert 5
BROULLIRE, John Merlin 5
BROUN, Heywood 1
BROUN, William Le Roy 1
BROUNOFF, Platon 1
BROUSE, Edwin Walter 4
BROUSSARD, Edwin 1
  Sidney
BROUSSARD, James 2
  Francis
BROUSSARD, Robert F. 1
BROUSSEAU, Kate 1
BROUWER, Dirk 4
BROUWER, Luitzen 4
  Egbertus Jan
BROWARD, Napoleon 1
  Bonaparte
BROWDER, Basil David 3
BROWDER, Earl (Russel) 5
BROWER, Alfred Smith 5
BROWER, Daniel 6
BROWER, Daniel Roberts 1
BROWER, Harriette Moore 1
BROWER, Jacob
  Vradenberg
BROWER, Reuben Arthur 6
BROWER, Walter Scott 4
BROWER, William Leverich 1
BROWERE, Albertus D. O. H
BROWERE, John Henri H
  Isaac
BROWN, A. Curtis 2
BROWN, A. Luther 3
BROWN, A. Page H
BROWN, Aaron Switzer 5
BROWN, Aaron Venable H
BROWN, Abbie Farwell 1
BROWN, Abram English 1
BROWN, Addison 1
BROWN, Alanson David 1
BROWN, Albert Edmund 5
BROWN, Albert Frederic 4
BROWN, Albert Gallatin H
BROWN, Albert Oscar 1
BROWN, Albert Sidney 5
BROWN, Alexander H
BROWN, Alexander 1
BROWN, Alexander 2
BROWN, Alexander 4
  Cushing
BROWN, Alexander
  Ephraim
BROWN, Alfred Hodgdon 5
BROWN, Alfred Seely 5
BROWN, Alice 2
BROWN, Alice Cooke 6
BROWN, Allen Van 2
  Vechten
BROWN, Alvin (McCreary) 5
BROWN, Amanda Elizabeth 1
BROWN, Ames 2
BROWN, Ames Thorndike 4
BROWN, Amos Peaslee 1
BROWN, Ann Mary 5
  Marothy (Mrs. Ernest M.
  Brown)
BROWN, Anson H
BROWN, Archer 1
BROWN, Archibald 3
  Manning
BROWN, Arlo Ayres 4
BROWN, Armstead 4
BROWN, Arthur 1
BROWN, Arthur Charles 2
  Lewis
BROWN, Arthur Edward 1
BROWN, Arthur Erwin 1
BROWN, Arthur Jr. 3
BROWN, Arthur Judson * 1
BROWN, Arthur Lewis 1
BROWN, Arthur Morton 2
BROWN, Arthur Voorhees 2
BROWN, Arthur William 4
BROWN, Arthur Winton 3
BROWN, Ashmun Norris 4
BROWN, Barnum 4
BROWN, Baxter Lamont 3
BROWN, Bedford H
BROWN, Benjamin 4
BROWN, Benjamin 2
  Beuhring
BROWN, Benjamin 1
  Chambers
BROWN, Benjamin Gratz H
BROWN, Benjamin Henry 4
  Inness
BROWN, Bernard 3
BROWN, Bolton 1
BROWN, Brian 6
BROWN, Buford Mason 4

BROWN, Burdette 5
  Boardman
BROWN, C. Foster Jr. 4
BROWN, C. Henry 1
BROWN, Calvin Luther 1
BROWN, Calvin Smith 2
BROWN, Carleton 1
BROWN, Caxton 3
BROWN, Cecil Kenneth 3
BROWN, Charles H
BROWN, Charles Allen 1
BROWN, Charles Brockden H
BROWN, Charles Carroll 2
BROWN, Charles Edward 1
BROWN, Charles Francis 1
BROWN, Charles H. 2
BROWN, Charles Harvey 3
BROWN, Charles Ira 1
BROWN, Charles Irwin 5
BROWN, Charles Leonard 4
BROWN, Charles Reynolds 3
BROWN, Charles Rufus 1
BROWN, Charles Sumner 1
BROWN, Charles Walter 1
BROWN, Charles William 1
BROWN, Charles Wilson 5
BROWN, Charlotte H
  Emerson
BROWN, Charlotte Harding 3
BROWN, Clarence J. 4
BROWN, Clarence 3
  Montgomery
BROWN, Clyde 1
BROWN, Colvin W. 3
BROWN, Cyrus Jay 5
BROWN, Cyrus Perrin 3
BROWN, D. J. 3
BROWN, Daniel Russell 1
BROWN, David Abraham 5
BROWN, David Chester 2
BROWN, David Paul H
BROWN, Demarchus 1
  Clariton
BROWN, Demetra Vaka 2
BROWN, Donald C. 1
BROWN, Donald Lamont 1
BROWN, Donald Lee 4
BROWN, Donaldson 4
BROWN, Downing P. 3
BROWN, Dudley 6
B(radstreet) W(illiams)
BROWN, Earl Theodore 3
BROWN, Earle Godfrey 4
BROWN, Ebenezer H
BROWN, Edgar 5
BROWN, Edith 5
BROWN, Edna Adelaide 2
BROWN, Edward Eagle 3
BROWN, Edward Fisher 6
BROWN, Edward Killoran 3
BROWN, Edward Lee 4
BROWN, Edward Miles 1
BROWN, Edward Norphlet 3
BROWN, Edward Osgood 1
BROWN, Edward Scott 2
BROWN, Edward Vail 5
  Lapham
BROWN, Edwin Hacker 1
BROWN, Edwin Perkins 1
BROWN, Edwin Pierce 5
BROWN, Edwin Putnam 1
BROWN, Edwy Rolfe 1
BROWN, Eli Huston Jr. 2
BROWN, Elias H
BROWN, Eliphalet M. Jr. H
BROWN, Elliott Wilber 1
BROWN, Elmer 1
BROWN, Elmer Ellsworth 1
BROWN, Elon Rouse 1
BROWN, Elzear Joseph 5
BROWN, Emma Elizabeth 1
BROWN, Enoch 4
BROWN, Eric Gore 4
BROWN, Ernest G(ay) 6
BROWN, Ernest William 1
BROWN, Estelle Aubrey 5
BROWN, Ethan Allen H
BROWN, Everett Chase 1
BROWN, Everett J. 2
BROWN, F. E. 3
BROWN, F. E. 4
BROWN, Fay (Cluff) 4
BROWN, Fayette 1
BROWN, Fayette 3
BROWN, Fletcher 1
BROWN, Foster Vincent 1
BROWN, Francis H
BROWN, Francis 1
BROWN, Francis Cabell 4
BROWN, Francis Henry 1
BROWN, Francis James 1
BROWN, Francis Shunk 1
BROWN, Frank H
BROWN, Frank Chilton 3
BROWN, Frank Chouteau 2
BROWN, Frank Clyde 2

BROWN, Frank Llewellyn 1
BROWN, Frank Xavier 5
BROWN, Franklin Q. 3
BROWN, Franklin Stewart 1
BROWN, Fred 6
BROWN, Fred Comings 3
BROWN, Fred Herbert 3
BROWN, Frederic Kenyon 1
BROWN, Frederic L. 6
BROWN, Frederick Anson 1
BROWN, Frederick Harvey 1
BROWN, Frederick Ronald 6
BROWN, Frederick 5
  Walworth
BROWN, Frederick William 1
BROWN, Frederick 5
  Winfield
BROWN, Fredric 5
BROWN, George * H
BROWN, George 1
BROWN, George Francis 1
BROWN, George Garvin 1
BROWN, George Granger 3
BROWN, George H. 1
BROWN, George Houston H
BROWN, George Lincoln 3
BROWN, George Loring H
BROWN, George M. 1
BROWN, George Marion 1
BROWN, George Newland 4
BROWN, George Pliny 1
BROWN, George Rothwell 4
BROWN, George Rowland 5
  III
BROWN, George Samson 2
BROWN, George Stewart 1
BROWN, George Stewart 3
BROWN, George Tiden 4
BROWN, George Van Ingen 2
BROWN, George W. 1
BROWN, George Warren 1
BROWN, George 1
  Washington
BROWN, George William H
BROWN, George William 2
BROWN, George Woodford 5
BROWN, Gertrude Foster 4
BROWN, Gilmor 5
BROWN, Glen David 3
BROWN, Glenn 1
BROWN, Goold H
BROWN, Grace Marn 4
BROWN, H. Martin 1
BROWN, Harold Eugene 6
BROWN, Harold Haven 4
BROWN, Harry Alvin 6
BROWN, Harry B. 5
BROWN, Harry Fletcher 2
BROWN, Harry Gunnison 6
BROWN, Harry Joe 5
BROWN, Harry Sanford 1
BROWN, Harry Winfield 2
BROWN, Harvey H. Jr. 3
BROWN, Helen Dawes 1
BROWN, Helen Gilman 2
BROWN, Henry B. 1
BROWN, Henry Bascom 1
BROWN, Henry Billings 1
BROWN, Henry Collins 4
BROWN, Henry Daniels 1
BROWN, Henry Harrison 1
BROWN, Henry Kirke 5
BROWN, Henry Matthias 5
BROWN, Henry Seymour 1
BROWN, Herbert Daniel 4
BROWN, Herbert Daniel 5
BROWN, Herbert J. 2
BROWN, Herman 4
BROWN, (Herman) LaRue 5
BROWN, Hilton Ultimus 3
BROWN, Hiram Chellis 4
BROWN, Hiram Staunton 5
BROWN, Holcombe James 3
BROWN, Homer Caffee 5
BROWN, Horace 1
  Manchester
BROWN, Howard Benner 4
BROWN, Howard Junior 6
BROWN, Howard 1
  Nicholson
BROWN, Hugh Auchincloss 6
BROWN, Hugh B. 6
BROWN, Hugh Elmer 1
BROWN, Hugh Henry 1
BROWN, Hugh S. 4
BROWN, Isaac Eddy 1
BROWN, Isaac Van Arsdale H
BROWN, Ivor John 1
  Carnegie
BROWN, J. Appleton 1
BROWN, J. Hammond 3
BROWN, J. Hay 1
BROWN, J. Stanley 1
BROWN, J. Thompson 3
BROWN, J. Vallance 1

BROWN, Jacob Jennings H
BROWN, James * H
BROWN, James * 1
BROWN, James B. 5
BROWN, James Barrett 5
BROWN, James Dorsey 3
BROWN, James Elwyn Jr. 4
BROWN, James F. 1
BROWN, James F. 3
BROWN, James Greenlief 3
BROWN, James Henry 4
BROWN, James R. 1
BROWN, James Salisbury H
BROWN, James Sproat H
BROWN, James Thomas 3
BROWN, James Wright 3
BROWN, James Wright Jr. 5
BROWN, Jeremiah H
BROWN, Joe Evan 5
BROWN, Joel Bascom 5
BROWN, John * H
BROWN, John A. H
BROWN, John Albert 2
BROWN, John Bernis 3
BROWN, John C. 1
BROWN, John Calvin H
BROWN, John Carter H
BROWN, John Crosby 1
BROWN, John Elward 3
BROWN, John Franklin 1
BROWN, John George 1
BROWN, John Griest 2
BROWN, John Hamilton 4
BROWN, John Henry H
BROWN, John Herbert Jr. 4
BROWN, John Howard 1
BROWN, John Jacob 3
BROWN, John Mackenzie 3
BROWN, John Marshall 1
BROWN, John Mifflin H
BROWN, John Newton H
BROWN, John Pinkney 1
BROWN, John Porter H
BROWN, John Richard H
BROWN, John W. H
BROWN, John Young * 1
BROWN, Joseph H
BROWN, Joseph 6
BROWN, Joseph Alleine 1
BROWN, Joseph Clifton 2
BROWN, Joseph Eckford 1
BROWN, Joseph Emerson H
BROWN, Joseph Gill 1
BROWN, Joseph M. 1
BROWN, Joseph Real 1
BROWN, Joseph Rogers H
BROWN, Julius L. 1
BROWN, Junius Calvin 1
BROWN, Justus Morris 1
BROWN, Kate Louise 1
BROWN, Katharine Holland 1
BROWN, Kenneth 4
BROWN, Kenneth Rent 3
BROWN, Lathrop 2
BROWN, Lawrason 1
BROWN, Leigh A. 3
BROWN, Levant Frederick 1
BROWN, Lew 3
BROWN, Lewis H. 4
BROWN, Lloyd Arnold 4
BROWN, Lloyd Davidson 3
BROWN, Louis M(yron) 5
BROWN, Louise Fargo 3
BROWN, Lucius 1
BROWN, Lucius Polk 1
BROWN, Lucy Hall 1
BROWN, Lyndon Osmond 4
BROWN, Lytle 2
BROWN, M. McClellan 1
BROWN, M(ary) Belle 5
BROWN, Manuel Nicholas 5
BROWN, Margaret Wise 3
BROWN, Mark A. 4
BROWN, Marshall 1
BROWN, Marshall Stewart 3
BROWN, Mather H
BROWN, Maxine 5
  McFadden (Mrs. Jack T.
  Brown)
BROWN, May Belleville 1
BROWN, Milton 1
BROWN, Milton Wilbert 5
BROWN, Montreville Jay 6
BROWN, Morris H
BROWN, Moses * H
BROWN, Moses True H
BROWN, Nathaniel Smith 2
BROWN, Neal 1
BROWN, Neill Smith H
BROWN, Nicholas * H
BROWN, Norriw H
BROWN, Obadiah H
BROWN, Olympia H
BROWN, Orville Harry 2
BROWN, Orvon Graff 4
BROWN, Oswald Eugene 1

BROWN, Owen Clarence 5
BROWN, Owsley 3
BROWN, Parke 2
BROWN, Paul 4
BROWN, Paul Goodwin 1
BROWN, Paul Winthrop 1
BROWN, Percy 3
BROWN, Percy A. 4
BROWN, Percy Edgar 1
BROWN, Percy W. 3
BROWN, Philip E. 1
BROWN, Philip Greely 1
BROWN, Philip King 1
BROWN, Philip King 2
BROWN, Philip Marshall 4
BROWN, Phoebe Hinsdale H
BROWN, Prentiss Marsh 6
BROWN, Preston 1
BROWN, R. Lewis 2
BROWN, Ralph Hall 2
BROWN, Ray 2
BROWN, Ray Andrews 4
BROWN, Ray Everett 6
BROWN, Raymond Dwight 3
BROWN, Rexwald 1
BROWN, Reynolds Driver 5
BROWN, Rezeau Blanchard 3
BROWN, Richard Evan 6
BROWN, Robert 1
BROWN, Robert Abner 1
BROWN, Robert Alexander 1
BROWN, Robert Arthur Jr. 5
BROWN, Robert Burns 1
BROWN, Robert Elliott 1
BROWN, Robert Frederick 5
BROWN, Robert K. 2
BROWN, Robert Marshall 6
BROWN, Robert Rankins 1
BROWN, Robert Sater 2
BROWN, Robert Woodrow 6
BROWN, Robert Young 4
BROWN, Rollo Walter 3
BROWN, Rome G. 2
BROWN, Roscoe Conkling 2
    Ensign
BROWN, Roy 3
BROWN, Roy Howard 6
BROWN, Rufus Everson 4
BROWN, Ruth Mowry 3
BROWN, Samuel H
BROWN, Samuel Alburtus 3
BROWN, Samuel Gilman 1
BROWN, Samuel Horton Jr. 1
BROWN, Samuel Robbins 1
BROWN, Sanford Miller 1
BROWN, Sanger 1
BROWN, Selden Stanley 1
BROWN, Seth W. 1
BROWN, Sevellon Ledyard 3
BROWN, Simon 1
BROWN, S(impson) Leroy 6
BROWN, Solyman H
BROWN, Stanley Doty 4
BROWN, Stanley L. 4
BROWN, Stimson Joseph 1
BROWN, Sydney Barlow 3
BROWN, Sydney 3
    MacGillvary
BROWN, Sylvanus H
BROWN, Thaddeus Harold 1
BROWN, Thatcher M. 3
BROWN, Theodore Henry 6
BROWN, Theophilus 6
BROWN, Theron 1
BROWN, Theron Adelbert 4
BROWN, Thomas Allston 4
BROWN, Thomas Cook 4
BROWN, Thomas Edwin 1
BROWN, Thomas F. 4
BROWN, Thomas Jefferson 1
BROWN, Thomas 3
    Richardson
BROWN, Titus H
BROWN, Vandyke 1
BROWN, Volney Mason 6
BROWN, W. Cabell 1
BROWN, W. Kennedy 1
BROWN, W(illiam) L(ee) 5
    Lyons
BROWN, Wade Hampton 2
BROWN, Wade R. 4
BROWN, Waldron Post 1
BROWN, Wallace Elias 1
BROWN, Wallace Winthrop 4
BROWN, Walter Folger 4
BROWN, Walter Folger 5
BROWN, Walter Franklin 3
BROWN, Walter L. 6
BROWN, Walter Lewis 1
BROWN, Warwick Thomas 4
BROWN, Webster Everett 1
BROWN, Wilbur Vincent 1
BROWN, Willard Dayton 5
BROWN, William * H
BROWN, William 1
BROWN, William Adams 2

BROWN, William Adams 3
    Jr.
BROWN, William Atwell Jr. 5
BROWN, William Averell 4
BROWN, William C. 1
BROWN, William C. 4
BROWN, William Carey 4
BROWN, William Channing 5
BROWN, William Edward 1
BROWN, William G. Jr. 1
BROWN, William Garl Jr. H
BROWN, William Garrott 1
BROWN, William Gay 1
BROWN, William George 1
BROWN, William Henry H
BROWN, William Henry * 1
BROWN, William Hill 1
BROWN, William Horace 1
BROWN, William John H
BROWN, William Lee 1
BROWN, William Liston 1
BROWN, William 1
    Montgomery
BROWN, W(illiam) Norman 6
BROWN, William O. 3
BROWN, William Perry 2
BROWN, William Thayer 3
BROWN, William Thurston 4
BROWN, William Wallace 1
BROWN, William Wells H
BROWN, Wilson 4
BROWN, Wrisley 2
BROWN, Wylie 1
BROWN, Zaidee 5
BROWNE, Aldis Birdsey 1
BROWNE, Alfred David 6
BROWNE, Arthur Wesley 1
BROWNE, Belmore 3
BROWNE, Benjamin H
    Frederick
BROWNE, Bennet Bernard 1
BROWNE, Beverly 6
    F(ielding)
BROWNE, Byron 4
BROWNE, Causten 1
BROWNE, Charles 2
BROWNE, Charles Albert 2
BROWNE, Charles Farrar H
BROWNE, Charles Francis 1
BROWNE, Daniel Jay H
BROWNE, Duncan Hodge 4
BROWNE, Edward Everts 2
BROWNE, Edward Tankard 3
BROWNE, Francis Fisher 1
BROWNE, Frederick 4
    William
BROWNE, George Elmer 2
BROWNE, George Henry 1
BROWNE, George H
    Huntington
BROWNE, George Israel 3
BROWNE, George Waldo 1
BROWNE, Harry C. 3
BROWNE, Herbert 2
    Wheildon Cotton
BROWNE, Irving H
BROWNE, J. Lewis 1
BROWNE, Jefferson Beale 1
BROWNE, John H
BROWNE, John Ross H
BROWNE, Junius Henri H
BROWNE, Lewis 2
BROWNE, Lewis Allen 1
BROWNE, Louis Edgar 3
BROWNE, Margaret 5
    Fitzhugh
BROWNE, Maurice 3
BROWNE, Nina Eliza 4
BROWNE, Page 2
BROWNE, Porter Emerson 1
BROWNE, Ralph Cowan 1
BROWNE, Rhodes 1
BROWNE, Robert Bell 1
BROWNE, Robert H. 4
BROWNE, Roger J. 6
BROWNE, Rollin 1
BROWNE, Thomas H
BROWNE, Thomas Henry H
    Bayly
BROWNE, Thomas H
    McLelland
BROWNE, Waldo Ralph 3
BROWNE, William H
BROWNE, William Hand 1
BROWNE, William 1
    Hardcastle
BROWNELL, Atherton 1
BROWNELL, Baker 4
BROWNELL, Clarence 1
    Ludlow
BROWNELL, Eleanor 5
    Olivia
BROWNELL, Emery Albert 4
BROWNELL, Francis 1
    Herbert

BROWNELL, George 1
    Francis
BROWNELL, George 1
    Griffin
BROWNELL, Harry 1
    Franklin
BROWNELL, Harry Gault 4
BROWNELL, Henry H
    Howard
BROWNELL, Jane Louise 4
BROWNELL, Kenneth C. 3
BROWNELL, Silas B. 1
BROWNELL, Thomas H
    Church
BROWNELL, Walter A. 4
BROWNELL, William 1
    Crary
BROWNING, Arthur 6
    Montcalm
BROWNING, Charles 1
    Clifton
BROWNING, Charles 1
    Henry
BROWNING, Eliza Gordon 5
BROWNING, George 2
    Landon
BROWNING, Grace 1
BROWNING, John Hull 1
BROWNING, John M. 1
BROWNING, Matthew 1
    Sandefur
BROWNING, McPherson 3
BROWNING, Miles 3
BROWNING, Orville H
    Hickman
BROWNING, Philip 1
    Embury
BROWNING, Ralph 4
    Rushton
BROWNING, Robert 5
    Turner
BROWNING, Webster E. 1
BROWNING, William 1
BROWNING, William Hull 4
BROWNING, William J. 1
BROWNLEE, Frederick 4
    Leslie
BROWNLEE, James F. 4
BROWNLEE, James 1
    Leaman
BROWNLEE, William Craig H
BROWNLOW, Louis 4
BROWNLOW, Walter 1
    Preston
BROWNLOW, William H
    Gannaway
BROWNRIGG, Dorothy 6
    Ruth Akin (Mrs. Robert
    Charles Brownrigg)
BROWNSCOMBE, Jennie 1
BROWNSON, Carleton 2
    Lewis
BROWNSON, Henry 4
    Francis
BROWNSON, James Irwin 1
BROWNSON, Marcus 1
    Acheson
BROWNSON, Mary Wilson 5
BROWNSON, Nathan H
BROWNSON, Orestes 1
    Augustus
BROWNSON, Truman 4
    Gaylord
BROWNSON, Willard 1
    Herbert
BROY, Charles Clinton 2
BROYDE, Isaac 4
BROYLES, Joseph Warren 2
    Royer
BRUBACK, Theodore 1
BRUBACHER, Abram 1
BRUBAKER, Albert Philson 4
BRUBAKER, Howard 1
BRUCE, Alexander 4
    Campbell
BRUCE, Andrew Alexander 1
BRUCE, Andrew Davis 5
BRUCE, Archibald H
BRUCE, Blanche Kelso H
BRUCE, Charles Arthur 1
BRUCE, Charles Morelle 1
BRUCE, Donald Cogley 5
BRUCE, Dwight Hall 1
BRUCE, Edward 2
BRUCE, Eugene Sewell 1
BRUCE, Frank M. Sr. 1
BRUCE, Frank M. Sr. 3
BRUCE, George H
BRUCE, Gustav Marius 4
BRUCE, H. Duane 4
BRUCE, H(enry) Addington 5
    (Bayley)
BRUCE, Harold Lawton 1
BRUCE, Helm 1
BRUCE, Henry William 2

BRUCE, Horatio 1
    Washington
BRUCE, Howard 4
BRUCE, Jackson Martin 4
BRUCE, James Deacon 2
BRUCE, James Douglas 1
BRUCE, James Latimer 6
BRUCE, John 1
BRUCE, John Edgar 3
BRUCE, John Edward 4
BRUCE, John Eldridge 1
BRUCE, Lenny 4
BRUCE, Logan Lithgow 5
BRUCE, Matthew Linn 1
BRUCE, Philip Alexander 1
BRUCE, Phineas H
BRUCE, Robert H
BRUCE, Robert Glenn 1
BRUCE, Roscoe Conkling 6
BRUCE, Saunders Dewees 1
BRUCE, Wallace 1
BRUCE, William Cabell 1
BRUCE, William George 2
BRUCE, William Herschel 1
BRUCE, William Paterson 1
BRUCE OF MELBOURNE, 4
    Viscount
BRUCKER, Joseph 4
BRUCKER, Wilber M(arion) 5
BRUCKNER, Aloys L. 4
BRUCKNER, Henry 1
BRUCKNER, Jacob Herbert 5
BRUDNO, Ezra Selig 1
BRUECKMANN, John 4
    George
BRUECKNER, Leo John 4
BRUEGGEMAN, Bessie 1
    Parker
BRUEGGER, John 4
BRUENING, Edward 6
    H(enry)
BRUENING, Heinrich 5
BRUENING, William 4
    Ferdinand
BRUERE, Henry 3
BRUERE, Robert Walter 5
BRUES, Charles Thomas 3
BRUESTLE, George 1
    Matthew
BRUFF, Joseph H
    Goldsborough
BRUFF, Lawrence 1
    Laurenson
BRUGGMANN, Charles 4
BRUHL, Gustav 5
BRUHN, Carl 1
BRUHN, Wilhelm L. 3
BRUHN, Wilhelm L. 4
BRUINS, John H. 3
BRULE, Etienne H
BRUMAGIM, Robert Smith 6
BRUMBAUGH, Clement 2
BRUMBAUGH, Gaius 5
    Marcus
BRUMBAUGH, I. Harvey 1
BRUMBAUGH, Martin 1
    Grove
BRUMBAUGH, Roy 3
    Talmage
BRUMBY, Frank Hardeman 5
BRUMBY, Richard Trapier H
BRUMBY, Thomas Mason 1
BRUMIDI, Constantino 1
BRUMLEY, Benjamin Basil 5
BRUMLEY, Daniel Joseph 4
BRUMLEY, Oscar Victor 2
BRUMM, Charles Napoleon 3
BRUMM, George Franklin 1
BRUMM, John Lewis 3
BRUMMITT, Dan Brearley 1
BRUMMITT, Dennis G. 1
BRUN, Constantin 1
BRUNAUER, Esther 3
    Caukin
BRUNCKEN, Ernest 4
BRUNDAGE, Albert 1
    Harrison
BRUNDAGE, Avery 6
BRUNDAGE, Charles 5
    Edwin
BRUNDAGE, Edward 1
    Jackson
BRUNDAGE, William 1
    Milton
BRUNDIDGE, Oscar Dean 3
BRUNDIDGE, Stephen Jr. 4
BRUNE, Adolf Gerhard 1
BRUNE, Frederick W. 5
BRUNER, Henry Lane 2
BRUNER, Herbert Bascom 4
BRUNER, James Dowden 4
BRUNER, Lawrence 1
BRUNER, Raymond 5
    Alphonse
BRUNER, Weston 4
BRUNER, William Evans 5

BRUNIA, William Frans 5
BRUNING, Walter Henry 6
BRUNIS, Georg (George 6
    Brunies)
BRUNKER, Albert Ridgley 1
BRUNNER, Arnold William 1
BRUNNER, David B. 1
BRUNNER, Edmund de 6
    Schweinitz
BRUNNER, Henry George 4
BRUNNER, John 1
BRUNNER, John Hamilton 3
BRUNNER, Nicholaus H
    Joseph
BRUNNER, William F. 4
BRUNNOW, Rudolph 1
    Ernest
BRUNO, Frank J. 3
BRUNOT, Harney Felix 1
BRUNS, Friedrich 6
BRUNS, Henry Dickson 1
BRUNS, Henry Frederick 2
BRUNS, Thomas Nelson 4
    Carter
BRUNSCHWIG, Alexander 5
BRUNSCHWIG, Roger E. 4
BRUNSON, James Edwin 4
BRUNSON, May Augusta 5
BRUNSWICK, Mark 5
BRUNSWIG, Lucien 2
    Napoleon
BRUNTON, David William 1
BRUSH, Alvin G. 4
BRUSH, Charles Francis 1
BRUSH, Daniel Harmon 1
BRUSH, Edward Nathaniel 1
BRUSH, Florence 4
BRUSH, Frank Spencer 1
BRUSH, Frederic (Louis) 4
BRUSH, George de Forest 1
BRUSH, George Jarvis 1
BRUSH, George Washington 1
BRUSH, Henry H
BRUSH, Henry Raymond 1
BRUSH, Howard Grafton 5
BRUSH, Jacob Henry 1
BRUSH, Katharine 3
BRUSH, Louis Herbert 2
BRUSH, Matthew Chauncey 1
BRUSH, Murray Peabody 5
BRUSH, William Whitlock 1
BRUSHINGHAM, John 1
    Patrick
BRUSIE, Charles Frederick 4
BRUSKE, Augustus Fredrich 4
BRUST, Peter 2
BRUTE de REMUR, Simon H
    William Gabriel
BRUTON, John Fletcher 5
BRUYN, Andrew De Witt 1
BRUYN, Charles DeWitt 3
BRYAN, Adolphus Jerome 3
BRYAN, Beauregard 4
BRYAN, Benjamin 1
    Chambers
BRYAN, Charles Page 1
BRYAN, Charles W. Jr. 4
BRYAN, Charles Wayland 3
BRYAN, Claude S. 3
BRYAN, Daniel Bunyan 4
BRYAN, Edward Payson 1
BRYAN, Elmer Burritt 1
BRYAN, Enoch Albert 1
BRYAN, Enoch Albert 2
BRYAN, Ernest Rowlett 3
BRYAN, Frederick Carlos 1
BRYAN, George H
BRYAN, George 1
BRYAN, George Sands 2
BRYAN, Guy Morrison 1
BRYAN, Henry Francis 3
BRYAN, Henry H. H
BRYAN, Henry Lewis 1
BRYAN, Henry Ravenscroft 4
BRYAN, James Wesley 3
BRYAN, James William 3
BRYAN, John Heritage H
BRYAN, John P. Kennedy 1
BRYAN, John Stewart 2
BRYAN, Joseph H
BRYAN, Joseph Hammond 4
BRYAN, Joseph Hunter H
BRYAN, Joseph Roberts 1
BRYAN, Julien 6
BRYAN, Kirk 3
BRYAN, L. R. Jr. 3
BRYAN, Lewis Randolph 1
BRYAN, Louis Allen 4
BRYAN, Malcolm Honroe 4
BRYAN, Mary Edwards 1
BRYAN, Mrs. William 1
    Jennings
BRYAN, Nathan H
BRYAN, Nathan Philemon 1
BRYAN, Oscar Eugene 1
BRYAN, O(val) N(elson) 6

* Indicates More Than One Such Name Listed

BRYAN, Ralph 4
BRYAN, Robert Coalter 1
BRYAN, Sheldon Martin 5
BRYAN, Shepard 6
BRYAN, Thomas Barbour 1
BRYAN, W. S. Plumer
BRYAN, William Alanson 2
BRYAN, William James 1
BRYAN, William Jennings 1
BRYAN, William Lowe 3
BRYAN, William Shepard Jr.
BRYAN, Winfred Francis 5
BRYAN, Worcester Allen 1
BRYAN-JONES, Noel D. 6
BRYANS, Henry Bussell 5
BRYANS, William Alexander III 4
BRYANS, William Remington 6
BRYANT, Anna Burnham 5
BRYANT, Arthur Peyton 1
BRYANT, Daniel Pennington 6
BRYANT, David E. 1
BRYANT, De Witt Clinton 4
BRYANT, Donald H. 6
BRYANT, Edgar Reeve 1
BRYANT, Edwin Eustace 1
BRYANT, Eliot H. 3
BRYANT, Emmons 6
BRYANT, Ernest Albert 1
BRYANT, Eugene 5
BRYANT, Floyd Sherman 4
BRYANT, Frank Augustus 1
BRYANT, Frederick Howard 2
BRYANT, George Archie 4
BRYANT, Gridley H
BRYANT, Henry H
BRYANT, Henry Edward Cowan 5
BRYANT, Henry Grier 1
BRYANT, John H. 1
BRYANT, John Howard 1
BRYANT, Joseph Decatur 1
BRYANT, Lorinda Munson 1
BRYANT, Louise Stevens 3
BRYANT, Ralph Clement 1
BRYANT, Randolph 3
BRYANT, Samuel Hollinger 6
BRYANT, Samuel Wood 5
BRYANT, Sara Cone 5
BRYANT, Thomas Wallace 1
BRYANT, Victor Silas 1
BRYANT, W. Sohier 3
BRYANT, Waldo Calvin 1
BRYANT, William Cullen H
BRYANT, William Cullen McKendree
BRYCE, James 1
BRYCE, Lloyd 1
BRYCE, Robert Alexander 4
BRYCE, Ronald 1
BRYCE, Wilson Bartlett 6
BRYDEN, Helmer Halvorsen 3
BRYN, Andrew H
BRYNE, Edward H
BRYNE, John H
BRYNE, Richard H
BRYNE, William H
BRYSON, Charles Lee 2
BRYSON, Charles William 1
BRYSON, Gladys 3
BRYSON, John Paul 1
BRYSON, Joseph Montgomery 2
BRYSON, Joseph Raleigh 3
BRYSON, Lyman 1
BRYSON, Olive Flora 5
BRYSON, Robert Hamilton 4
BRYSON, Robert Hassey 1
BUBB, Henry Clay 4
BUBB, John Wilson 1
BUBER, Martin
BUCH, Joseph Godfrey 2
BUCHANAN, Andrew H
BUCHANAN, Andrew Hays 1
BUCHANAN, Arthur Stillingfleet 1
BUCHANAN, Benjamin Franklin 1
BUCHANAN, Daniel Houston 3
BUCHANAN, David H. 5
BUCHANAN, Ella 3
BUCHANAN, Frank 1
BUCHANAN, Frank 3
BUCHANAN, Franklin H
BUCHANAN, Georgre Sidney
BUCHANAN, George Edward 1

BUCHANAN, Herbert Earle 6
BUCHANAN, Hugh H
BUCHANAN, James H
BUCHANAN, James Anderson
BUCHANAN, James Isaac 1
BUCHANAN, James L. 3
BUCHANAN, James P. 1
BUCHANAN, James Shannon
BUCHANAN, James William 3
BUCHANAN, John H
BUCHANAN, John Alexander
BUCHANAN, John Jenkins 1
BUCHANAN, John Lee 1
BUCHANAN, John P. 3
BUCHANAN, Joseph 1
BUCHANAN, Joseph Ray 1
BUCHANAN, Joseph Ray 4
BUCHANAN, Joseph Rodes 1
BUCHANAN, Kenneth 4
BUCHANAN, Kenneth B. 3
BUCHANAN, Leonard Brown
BUCHANAN, Malcolm Griswold
BUCHANAN, Norman Sharpe
BUCHANAN, Oswald C. 4
BUCHANAN, Roberdeau 1
BUCHANAN, Robert Christie H
BUCHANAN, Scott 5
BUCHANAN, T. Drysdale 1
BUCHANAN, Thomas H
BUCHANAN, Thomas C. 3
BUCHANAN, Thompson H
BUCHANAN, Mrs. Vera Daerr 3
BUCHANAN, W. C. 5
BUCHANAN, Walter Duncan 1
BUCHANAN, William Asbury 3
BUCHANAN, William Insco
BUCHBINDER, Jacob Richter 3
BUCHEN, Walther 4
BUCHER, August Johannes 1
BUCHER, John Calvin 2
BUCHER, John Conrad H
BUCHER, John Emery 5
BUCHER, Walter H. 4
BUCHER, William Henry 4
BUCHHOLZ, Heinrich 3
BUCHHOLZ, John Theodore
BUCHHOLZ, Ludwig Wilhelm 1
BUCHHOLZ, William 3
BUCHMAN, Frank N. D. 4
BUCHNER, Edward Franklin
BUCHANAN, Mrs. Vera Daerr
BUCHSER, Frank H
BUCHTA, J. Williams H
BUCHTEL, Henry Augustus 1
BUCHTEL, John Richards H
BUCK, Albert Henry 1
BUCK, Alfred Eliab 1
BUCK, Beaumont Bonaparte 3
BUCK, Benjamin F. 1
BUCK, C. Douglas 4
BUCK, Carl Darling 3
BUCK, Carl E. 4
BUCK, Cassius M. 4
BUCK, Charles Henry 1
BUCK, Charles Neville 6
BUCK, Charles William 1
BUCK, Clarence Frank 2
BUCK, Daniel 1
BUCK, Daniel 4
BUCK, Daniel Azro Ashley H
BUCK, Dudley 1
BUCK, Ellsworth Brewer 5
BUCK, Ernest Ferguson 4
BUCK, Florence 1
BUCK, Foster 5
BUCK, Frank 2
BUCK, Frank Henry 1
BUCK, Frank Henry 2
BUCK, George Machan 1
BUCK, George Sturges 4
BUCK, Gertrude 1
BUCK, Gurdon H
BUCK, Harold Winthrop 3
BUCK, Harry Lambert 5
BUCK, Henry William 4
BUCK, Jirah Dewey 1
BUCK, John Lossing 6
BUCK, John Ransom 4

BUCK, Leffert Lefferts 1
BUCK, Norman Sydney 4
BUCK, Oscar MacMillan 1
BUCK, Pearl Sydenstricker (Mrs. Richard J. Walsh)
BUCK, Peter Henry 3
BUCK, Phillip Earl 4
BUCK, Philo Melvin 1
BUCK, Philo Melvin Jr. 3
BUCK, Raymond Elliott 5
BUCK, Richard Sutton 6
BUCK, Samuel Jay 1
BUCK, Solon Justus 4
BUCK, Walter Albert 4
BUCK, Walter E. 5
BUCK, Walter Hooper 4
BUCK, William Bradford 6
BUCKALEW, Charles H. 1
BUCKBEE, Anna 4
BUCKBEE, John T. 1
BUCKELEY, Peter H
BUCKENDALE, L. Ray 3
BUCKHAM, James 1
BUCKHAM, John Wright 4
BUCKHAM, Matthew Henry 1
BUCKHOUT, Isaac Craig 1
BUCKINGHAM, Burdette Ross 5
BUCKINGHAM, Charles Luman 1
BUCKINGHAM, David Eastburn 5
BUCKINGHAM, Edgar 1
BUCKINGHAM, Edward Taylor 5
BUCKINGHAM, George Tracy 1
BUCKINGHAM, Joseph Tinker H
BUCKINGHAM, Norman S. 1
BUCKINGHAM, Theophilus Nash 6
BUCKINGHAM, Walter Jr. 1
BUCKINGHAM, William Alfred H
BUCKLAND, Albert William James 3
BUCKLAND, Charles Clark 5
BUCKLAND, Cyrus H
BUCKLAND, Edward Grant 1
BUCKLAND, Ralph Pomeroy H
BUCKLAND, William H
BUCKLE, John Franklin 5
BUCKLER, Richard Thompson 3
BUCKLER, Thomas Hepburn H
BUCKLER, William Hepburn 3
BUCKLEY, Albert Coulson 1
BUCKLEY, Charles A. 4
BUCKLEY, Edmund 1
BUCKLEY, Edwin M. 3
BUCKLEY, Ernest Robertson 1
BUCKLEY, George Wright 4
BUCKLEY, Harry D. 3
BUCKLEY, Homer John 6
BUCKLEY, James Monroe 1
BUCKLEY, James R. 5
BUCKLEY, James V. 4
BUCKLEY, Jere D. 4
BUCKLEY, John Peter 2
BUCKLEY, Leo Jerome 4
BUCKLEY, May 5
BUCKLEY, Oliver Ellsworth 3
BUCKLEY, Samuel Botsford H
BUCKLEY, Tim 6
BUCKLIN, Edward C. 1
BUCKLIN, George Augustus 5
BUCKLIN, James C. H
BUCKLIN, James W. 1
BUCKLIN, Walter Stanley 4
BUCKMAN, C. B. 3
BUCKMAN, Harry Oliver 4
BUCKMAN, Henry Holland II 5
BUCKMASTER, Leland Stanford 4
BUCKMINSTER, Joseph Stevens H
BUCKNAM, Ransford D. 1
BUCKNELL, Howard Jr. 5
BUCKNELL, William 1
BUCKNER, Albert Gallatin 4
BUCKNER, Alexander H
BUCKNER, Aylett Hawes H
BUCKNER, Aylette 1
BUCKNER, Chester Arthur 6
BUCKNER, David Ernest 5
BUCKNER, E. C. 4

BUCKNER, Emory Roy 1
BUCKNER, George Washington 4
BUCKNER, Mortimer Norton 2
BUCKNER, Richard Aylett H
BUCKNER, Simon Bolivar H
BUCKNER, Simon Bolivar Jr.
BUCKNER, Thomas Aylette 2
BUCKNER, Walker 3
BUCKNER, Walter Coleman
BUCKS, William Henry 4
BUCKSTONE, John B. H
BUCKWALTER, Tracy V. 3
BUCKY, Gustav 4
BUCKY, Philip Barnett 3
BUCOVE, Bernard 6
BUDA, Joseph 5
BUDD, Britton Ihrie 4
BUDD, Charles Henry 3
BUDD, Charles Jay 1
BUDD, Edward G. 2
BUDD, Edward G Jr. 4
BUDD, Henry 4
BUDD, James Herbert 1
BUDD, Nathan P. 5
BUDD, Ralph 4
BUDDY, Charles F. 4
BUDENZ, Louis Francis 4
BUDER, Gustavus Adolphus 3
BUDGE, Alfred 3
BUDGE, David Clare 2
BUDGE, Ross A. 3
BUDGE, Walter Lyttleton 4
BUDGETT, Sidney Payne 4
BUDINA, Adolph Otto 6
BUDINGER, John Michael 1
BUDINGTON, Robert Allyn 3
BUDLONG, Frederick Grandy 3
BUDROW, Lester Rusk 5
BUEHLER, Albert Carl 5
BUEHLER, Alfred Grether 5
BUEHLER, Henry Andrew 2
BUEHLER, Huber Gray 1
BUEHLER, William Emmett
BUEHLER, William George 1
BUEHNER, Carl William 5
BUEHR, Karl Albert 3
BUEHRER, Theophil Frederic 6
BUEHRING, Paul Henry 3
BUEHRMAN, Peter A. 4
BUEK, Gustave Herman 1
BUEL, Alexander Woodruff H
BUEL, Clarence Clough 1
BUEL, James William 1
BUEL, Jesse H
BUEL, Walker Showers 3
BUELL, Abel H
BUELL, Alexander Hamilton H
BUELL, Augustus C. 1
BUELL, Caroline Brown 1
BUELL, Charles Edward 1
BUELL, Don Carlos 1
BUELL, Marcus Darius 1
BUELL, Murray F. 6
BUELL, Raymond Leslie 2
BUELL, Robert Catlin Jr. 5
BUELL, Robert Lewis 4
BUENGER, Theodore 2
BUENTING, Otto Wilhelm 4
BUESCHING, Charles Henry
BUESSER, Frederick G. 3
BUETOW, Herbert P(aul) 5
BUFFALO CHILD LONG LANCE 1
BUFFETT, Howard 4
BUFFINGTON, Adelbert Rinaldo
BUFFINGTON, Eugene Jackson 1
BUFFINGTON, Joseph H
BUFFINGTON, Joseph 2
BUFFINTON, James 1
BUFFINTON, Merrill 4
BUFORD, John H. H
BUFFUM, Arnold H
BUFFUM, Burt C. H
BUFFUM, Douglas Labaree 4
BUFFUM, George Tower 1
BUFFUM, Hugh Straight H
BUFFUM, Joseph Jr. H
BUFFUM, Robert Earle 1
BUFORD, Abraham * H
BUFORD, Charles Homer 4
BUFORD, Elizabeth Burgess 4
BUFORD, John H
BUFORD, Lawrence B. 6

BUFORD, Napoleon Bonaparte H
BUFORD, Rivers Henderson 6
BUGAN, Thomas Gregory 3
BUGBEE, Benjamin C. 3
BUGBEE, Henry Greenwood 2
BUGBEE, Lester Gladstone 1
BUGBEE, Lucius Hatfield 2
BUGBEE, Percy Isaac 3
BUGG, Benjamin Lamar 5
BUGG, Lelia Hardin 5
BUGG, Robert Malone H
BUGGE, Sven Brun 2
BUGGELLI, Blanche Swett (Mowry) 5
BUGNIAZET, G. M. 3
BUHL, Arthur Hiram 1
BUHL, Lawrence D. 3
BUHLER, Charlotte 6
BUICK, James McNair 1
BUIE, Louis Arthur Sr. MN 6
BUISSERET STEENBECQUE DE BLAREGHIEN, Count Conrad de 4
BUIST, Archibald Johnston 2
BUIST, George Alexander 4
BUIST, George L. 4
BUIST, George Lamb 1
BUIST, Harold J. 3
BUIST, Henry 2
BUIST, John Somers 1
BUKOFZER, Manfred F. 3
BUKOWSKI, Peter Ivan 3
BULEY, R. Carlyle 5
BULFINCH, Charles H
BULFINCH, Thomas H
BULGAKOW, Michael Afanasievich 4
BULGANIN, Nikolai Aleksandrovich 6
BULKELEY, Harry Clough 2
BULKELEY, Morgan Gardner
BULKELEY, William E. A. 3
BULKLEY, Frank 1
BULKLEY, George Grant 1
BULKLEY, Harry Conant 2
BULKLEY, John Williams 1
BULKLEY, L. Duncan 1
BULKLEY, Robert Johns 4
BULL, Alfred Castleman 1
BULL, Carroll Gideon 1
BULL, Charles Livingston 1
BULL, Charles Stedman 1
BULL, Dorothy 1
BULL, E. Myron 3
BULL, Ephraim Wales H
BULL, Ernest M. 2
BULL, Frank Kellogg 1
BULL, George Mairs 5
BULL, James Henry 1
BULL, John * H
BULL, Ludlow 3
BULL, Melville 1
BULL, Sara Chapman 1
BULL, Storm 1
BULL, William * H
BULL, William Lanman 1
BULL, William Rutledge 6
BULL, William Tillinghast 1
BULLA, Charles Dehaven 1
BULLA, Robert Nelson 1
BULLARD, Arthur 1
BULLARD, Daniel R. 5
BULLARD, Edward Clarke 5
BULLARD, Edward Payson Jr. 3
BULLARD, Ernest Luther 1
BULLARD, F. Lauriston 3
BULLARD, Frank Dearborn 1
BULLARD, Frederic Field 1
BULLARD, Henry Adams H
BULLARD, James Atkins 3
BULLARD, Otis A. H
BULLARD, Ralph Hadley 5
BULLARD, Robert Felton 5
BULLARD, Robert Lee 2
BULLARD, Stanley Hale 1
BULLARD, Washington Irving 2
BULLARD, William Hannum Grubb 1
BULLARD, William Norton 1
BULLEN, Percy Sutherland 4
BULLENE, Egbert Frank 3
BULLIET, Clarence Joseph 4
BULLINGTON, John P. 2
BULLIS, Harry Amos 4
BULLIS, John Lapham 1
BULLITT, Alexander Scott H
BULLITT, Henry Massie 1
BULLITT, John C. 1
BULLITT, Scott 1

BULLITT, Thomas W. 1
BULLITT, William Christian 4
BULLITT, William Marshall 3
BULLOCH, Archibald H
BULLOCH, Joseph Gaston 4
  Baillie
BULLOCH, William H
  Bellinger
BULLOCK, A. George 1
BULLOCK, Alexander H
  Hamilton
BULLOCK, Alexander 4
  Hamilton
BULLOCK, Calvin 2
BULLOCK, Chandler 5
BULLOCK, Charles Jesse 1
BULLOCK, Harry Elmer 3
BULLOCK, James H
  Dunwoody
BULLOCK, Motier Acklin 1
BULLOCK, Stephen H
BULLOCK, Theodore 3
BULLOCK, Thomas Seaman 4
BULLOCK, William A. 4
BULLOCK, Wingfield H
BULLOWA, Jesse G. M. 2
BULMAN, John Noel 5
  Thompson
BULMAN, Olvier Meredith 6
  Boone
BULOVA, Arde 3
BULOW, William John 3
BULWINKLE, Alfred Lee 3
BUMBY, John Harold 6
BUMGARDNER, Helen 6
  Ayers
BUMGARNER, Ray 5
  Quincy
BUMP, Charles Weathers 1
BUMP, Milan Raynard 1
BUMPOUS, E. T. 4
BUMPUS, Hermon Carey 2
BUMSTEAD, Charles W. 5
BUMSTEAD, Freeman H
  Josiah
BUMSTEAD, Henry H
  Andrews
BUMSTEAD, Horace 4
BUNCE, Allen Hamilton 4
BUNCE, Arthur C. 3
BUNCE, Edgar F. 6
BUNCE, Francis Marvin 1
BUNCE, J. Oscar 4
BUNCE, Oliver Bell H
BUNCE, W. Gedney 1
BUNCH, Samuel H
BUNCHE, Ralph Johnson 5
BUNDEL, Charles Michael 1
BUNDESEN, Herman Niels 4
BUNDLIE, Gerhard 4
BUNDY, Edwin S. 4
BUNDY, Harvey Hollister 4
BUNDY, Hezekiah Sanford 4
BUNDY, John Elwood 1
BUNDY, Jonas Mills H
BUNDY, Omar 1
BUNDY, Solomon 4
BUNDY, William Edgar 1
BUNGE, Helen Lathrop 5
BUNIM, Joseph J. 4
BUNIN, Ivan Alekseevich 3
BUNKER, Alonzo 1
BUNKER, Arthur H. 4
BUNKER, Charles C. 6
BUNKER, Charles Waite 1
  Orville
BUNKER, Frank Forest 2
BUNKER, Harry Surfus 4
BUNKLEY, Joel William 4
BUNKLEY, Joel William Jr. 5
BUNN, Charles 1
BUNN, Charles Wilson 1
BUNN, Clinton Orrin 1
BUNN, Edward Bernard 5
BUNN, Edward Schaible 5
BUNN, George Lincoln 1
BUNN, Henry Gaston 4
BUNN, Howard Stolpp 4
BUNN, Jacob 1
BUNN, Paul Axtell 5
BUNN, Romanzo 1
BUNN, William Hall 4
BUNNELL, Charles Ernest 4
BUNNELL, Edward Horace 3
BUNNELL, Sterling Haight 5
BUNNER, Henry Cuyler H
BUNNER, Rudolph 1
BUNTING, Charles Henry 4
BUNTING, George Avery 5
BUNTING, Guy J. 1
BUNTING, Martha 4
BUNTING, Russell Welford 4
BUNTLINE, Ned H
BUNTS, Frank Emory 1
BUNZELL, Herbert Horace 1
BURBA, Edwin Hess 5

BURBA, George Francis 1
BURBAGE, William Henry 4
BURBANK, Elbridge Ayer 2
BURBANK, Harold 3
  Hitchings
BURBANK, James Brattle 1
BURBANK, Luther 1
BURBANK, Mortimer 3
  Lincoln
BURBANK, Wilbur Swett 6
BURBIDGE, Frederick 4
BURBIDGE, Sir Richard 4
  Grant Woodman
BURBRIDGE, Stephen H
  Gano
BURCH, Albert 5
BURCH, Angelus Teague 4
BURCH, Charles Bell 3
BURCH, Charles Newell 1
BURCH, Charles Sumner 1
BURCH, Edward Parris 2
BURCH, Ernest Ward 1
BURCH, Frank Earl 3
BURCH, George Bosworth 6
BURCH, Guy Irving 4
BURCH, H(ubert) Wendel 5
BURCH, Henry Reed 5
BURCH, John Chilton H
BURCH, Lowell R. 4
BURCH, Lucius Edward 1
BURCH, Newton Dexter 1
BURCH, Rousseau Angelus 3
BURCH, Thomas Granville 3
BURCHARD, Edward 2
  Lawver
BURCHARD, Ernest 5
  Francis
BURCHARD, Horatio 1
  Chapin
BURCHARD, John Ely 6
BURCHARD, Samuel H
  Dickinson
BURCHETT, George 4
  Jerome
BURCHFIELD, A. H. J. 4
BURCHFIELD, Albert 2
  Horne
BURCHFIELD, Charles 4
  Ephraim
BURCHILL, Thomas F. 3
BURCHKHARDT, Charles 6
  Jacob
BURCKHALTER, Charles 1
BURCKHALTER, Frank 1
  Lucien
BURD, George H
BURD, George Eli 1
BURDELL, William 2
  Frederick
BURDEN, Harry P. 5
BURDEN, Henry H
BURDEN, James 1
  Abercrombie *
BURDEN, Oliver D. 4
BURDETT, Everett Watson 1
BURDETT, Fred Hartshorn 1
BURDETT, George Albert 4
BURDETT, Herbert C. 4
BURDETT, Samuel Swinfin 1
BURDETT, William Carter 2
BURDETTE, Clara Bradley 1
  (Mrs. Robert J. Burdette)
BURDETTE, Franklin L. 6
BURDETTE, Robert Jones 1
BURDGE, Franklin 1
BURDGE, Howard Griffith 3
BURDICK, Alfred Stephen 1
BURDICK, Charles Baker 3
BURDICK, Charles Kellogg 1
BURDICK, Charles Kellogg 3
BURDICK, Charles Williams 1
BURDICK, Clark 4
BURDICK, Clinton De Witt 1
BURDICK, Donald 5
  Langworthy
BURDICK, Eugene L. 4
BURDICK, Francis Marion 1
BURDICK, Harold Ormond 6
BURDICK, Joel Wakeman 1
BURDICK, Usher L. 4
BURDICK, Willard DeLure 1
BURDICK, William Livesey 2
BUREAU, E. A. 1
BURES, Charles Edwin 6
BURFORD, Archie Dean 2
BURFORD, Bernard Boyd 4
BURFORD, Cyrus Edgar 4
BURFORD, John Henry 1
BURG, Alfred William 3
BURGAN, John 4
BURGE, Flippen D. 2
BURGE, J. H. Hobart 1
BURGEE, Clyde Elmore 5
BURGEE, Joseph Zeno 5
BURGER, John D. 2

BURGER, Kathryn 3
  Reynolds
BURGER, Owen Francis 1
BURGER, William Henry 4
BURGER, William Henry 5
BURGES, Dempsey H
BURGES, Richard Fenner 2
BURGES, Tristam H
BURGES, William Henry 2
BURGESS, Albert Franklin 3
BURGESS, Alexander 1
BURGESS, Charles 1
  Frederick
BURGESS, Charles 5
  McFetridge
BURGESS, Cora Louise 4
  Turney
BURGESS, Edward H
BURGESS, Edward 1
  Sandford
BURGESS, Elizabeth 2
  Chamberlain
BURGESS, Ellis Beaver 1
BURGESS, Ernest Watson 5
BURGESS, Frank H. 1
BURGESS, Frederick 1
BURGESS, Gaven D. 1
BURGESS, Gelett 3
BURGESS, George H
BURGESS, George Farmer 1
BURGESS, George 5
  Heckman
BURGESS, George Kimball 1
BURGESS, Harry 1
BURGESS, Ida Josephine 1
BURGESS, John Albert 5
BURGESS, John William 1
BURGESS, Kenneth Farwell 4
BURGESS, May Ayres 3
BURGESS, Mrs. Samuel 5
  Rostron
BURGESS, Perry 4
BURGESS, Philip 5
BURGESS, Rembert 1
  Bennett
BURGESS, Robert Wilbur 5
BURGESS, Roy Howard Jr. 3
BURGESS, Ruth Payne 1
  Jewett
BURGESS, Theodore 1
  Chalon
BURGESS, Theodore 4
  Herbert
BURGESS, Thomas M. 1
BURGESS, Thornton Waldo 4
BURGESS, William * 1
BURGESS, William Starling 5
BURGEVINE, Henry H
  Andrea
BURGHALTER, Daniel 2
BURGIN, Henry T. 3
BURGIN, Samuel H. C. 5
BURGIN, William Garner 5
BURGIN, William Olin 5
BURGIS, William H
BURGISS, William Wesley 3
BURGOYNE, John H
BURHOP, William Henry 4
BURK, Frederic Lister 1
BURK, Henry 1
BURK, Jesse Young 1
BURK, Joseph Edwill 2
BURK, W. Herbert 1
BURKE, Aedanus H
BURKE, Andrew H. 4
BURKE, Arthur Devries 3
BURKE, B. Ellen 4
BURKE, Billie 5
BURKE, Charles Henry 1
BURKE, Charles St Thomas H
BURKE, Daniel 5
BURKE, Daniel Webster 4
BURKE, Edmund * H
BURKE, Edmund 5
BURKE, Edmund Whitney 5
BURKE, Edward M. 4
BURKE, Edward Raymond 5
BURKE, Edward Timothy 1
BURKE, Ellen Coolidge 6
BURKE, Eugene Paul 4
BURKE, George James 3
BURKE, Haslett Platt 3
BURKE, James Francis 1
BURKE, James Owen 4
BURKE, Jeremiah Edmund 1
BURKE, John H
BURKE, John Edmund 5
BURKE, John J. 1
BURKE, John P. 5
BURKE, John Stephen 4
BURKE, John Woolfolk 3
BURKE, Joseph A. 4
BURKE, Joseph Henry 1
BURKE, Kendall Edwards 2
BURKE, Maurice Francis 1
BURKE, Michael E. 3

BURKE, Milo Darwin 4
BURKE, N. Charles 4
BURKE, Patrick H. 3
BURKE, Raymond H. 6
BURKE, Robert Belle 1
BURKE, Robert Emmet 1
BURKE, Stephen Patrick 2
BURKE, Stevenson 1
BURKE, Thomas H
BURKE, Thomas 1
BURKE, Thomas A. 6
BURKE, Thomas Henry 3
BURKE, Thomas Joseph 4
BURKE, Thomas Martin 1
  Aloysius
BURKE, Timothy Farrar 1
BURKE, Victor 3
BURKE, Vincent John 6
BURKE, Webster H. 3
BURKE, William J. 1
BURKET, Harlan Fessenden 3
BURKET, Jacob F. 1
BURKETT, Charles William 5
BURKETT, Charles William 5
BURKETT, Elmer Jacob 2
BURKHALTER, Edward 1
  Read
BURKHALTER, Everett 6
  Glen
BURKHALTER, Frank 6
  Elisha
BURKHALTER, John 5
  Thomas
BURKHARDT, Samuel Jr. 1
BURKHARDT, Wilbur Neil 1
BURKHART, Harvey Jacob 2
BURKHART, Roy Abram 4
BURKHART, Samuel 6
  Ellsworth
BURKHART, Summers 1
BURKHEAD, Margaret 6
BURKHOLDER, Charles 4
  Bristow
BURKHOLDER. Charles 5
  Harvey
BURKHOLDER, Charles 5
  Irvine
BURKHOLDER, Paul Rufus 5
BURKLIN, Robert Reyburn 4
BURKLUND, Carl Edwin 4
BURKS, Jesse Desmaux 4
BURKS, Martin Parks 1
BURLEIGH, Charles H
  Calistus
BURLEIGH, Clarence 1
BURLEIGH, Clarence 1
  Blendon
BURLEIGH, Edwin Chick 1
BURLEIGH, George 1
  Shepard
BURLEIGH, George 1
  William
BURLEIGH, Harry T. 2
BURLEIGH, John Holmes H
BURLEIGH, May Halsey 1
  Miller
BURLEIGH, Nathaniel 5
  George
BURLEIGH, Sydney 1
  Richmond
BURLEIGH, Walter H
  Atwood
BURLEIGH, William 1
BURLEIGH, William Henry H
BURLESON, Albert Sidney 1
BURLESON, Edward H
BURLESON, Hugh Latimer 1
BURLESON, Rufus 1
  Columbus
BURLEW, Ebert Keiser 2
BURLEY, Clarence 1
  Augustus
BURLIN, Natalie Curtis 1
BURLIN, Paul 5
BURLING, Albert E. 4
BURLING, Edward H
BURLING, Edward 1
  Burnham
BURLING, (Fred) Temple 6
BURLINGAME, Anson H
BURLINGAME, C. Charles 3
BURLINGAME, Edward 1
  Livermore
BURLINGAME, Eugene 1
  Watson
BURLINGAME, Leonas 5
  Lancelot
BURLINGAME, Leroy J. 4
BURLINGAME, Luther D. 1
BURLINGAME, Roger 4
BURLINGHAM, Aaron 1
  Hale
BURLINGHAM, Charles C. 3
BURLINGHAM, Louis 2
  Herbert
BURLIUK, David 4
  Davidovich

BURMA, John Harmon 1
BURMEISTER, Richard 1
BURN, Belle Sumner Angier 5
BURNAM, Anthony Rollins 1
BURNAM, Curtis Field 2
BURNAM, John Miller 1
BURNAP, George 2
  Washington
BURNELL, Barker H
BURNELL, Edward John 3
BURNELL, Edward John Jr. 1
BURNELL, Max Ronald 3
BURNES, Alonzo D. 4
BURNES, James Nelson 1
BURNES, Matthews James 4
BURNET, David H
  Gouverneur
BURNET, Duncan 5
BURNET, Jacob H
BURNET, W. Everit 3
BURNET, William * H
BURNETT, Charles 1
BURNETT, Charles Henry 5
BURNETT, Charles Hoyt 5
BURNETT, Charles Hugh 5
  Jr.
BURNETT, Charles 2
  Theodore
BURNETT, Cordas Chris 6
BURNETT, Dana 4
BURNETT, Edgar Albert 1
BURNETT, Edmund Cody 2
BURNETT, Edwin Clark 1
BURNETT, Frances 1
  Hodgson
BURNETT, George Henry 1
BURNETT, George Jackson 5
BURNETT, Henry Cornelius H
BURNETT, Henry 1
  Lawrence
BURNETT, Jesse McGarrity 5
BURNETT, John Lawson 1
BURNETT, John Torrey 1
BURNETT, Joseph H
BURNETT, Joseph Herndon 4
BURNETT, Leo 5
BURNETT, Leo 6
BURNETT, Paul Moreton 1
BURNETT, Peter Hardeman H
BURNETT, Robert M. 1
BURNETT, Rogers Levering 4
BURNETT, Swan Moses 1
BURNETT, Whit 5
BURNETTE, Wells Dewey 6
BURNHAM, Alfred Avery H
BURNHAM, Charles Edwin 4
BURNHAM, Clara Louise 1
BURNHAM, Claude George 1
BURNHAM, Daniel Hudson 1
BURNHAM, Daniel Hudson 4
BURNHAM, E(noch) Lewis 1
BURNHAM, Frederic 1
  Lynden
BURNHAM, Frederick 5
  E(dwin)
BURNHAM, Frederick 2
  Russell
BURNHAM, Frederick 5
  William
BURNHAM, George 1
BURNHAM, George Jr. 1
BURNHAM, Henry Eben 1
BURNHAM, Hubert 5
BURNHAM, John Bird 1
BURNHAM, Michael 1
BURNHAM, Ralph W. 4
BURNHAM, Roger Noble 1
BURNHAM, Sherburne 1
  Wesley
BURNHAM, Silas Henry 1
BURNHAM, Smith 2
BURNHAM, Sylvester 1
BURNHAM, Walter Henry 5
BURNHAM, William Henry 1
BURNHAM, William Power 1
BURNIGHT, Ralph Fletcher 6
BURNITE, Caroline 5
BURNQUIST, Joseph Alfred 4
  Arner
BURNS, Allen Tibbals 3
BURNS, Andrew J. 3
BURNS, Anna Letitia 5
BURNS, Anthony H
BURNS, Bob 3
BURNS, Charles Wesley 1
BURNS, Clyde Edwin 4
BURNS, Cornelius F. 1
BURNS, Daniel M. 5
BURNS, David 1
BURNS, Dennis Francis 6
BURNS, Donald Bruce 3
BURNS, Edward H. 4
BURNS, Edward McNall 5
BURNS, Elmer Ellsworth 1
BURNS, Francis Highlands 1
BURNS, Frank 2

BURNS, George Plumer 3
BURNS, Hendry Stuart 5
  Mackenzie
BURNS, Henry B. 4
BURNS, Herbert Deschamps 3
BURNS, Howard Fletcher 5
BURNS, James Aloysius 1
BURNS, James Austin 1
BURNS, James J. 1
BURNS, John Anthony 6
BURNS, John Horne 4
BURNS, John Joseph 3
BURNS, Joseph H
BURNS, Kevin 3
BURNS, Lee 3
BURNS, Louis Henry 1
BURNS, Matthew D. 4
BURNS, Melvin P. 1
BURNS, Michael Anthony 1
BURNS, Murray Edwin 6
BURNS, Otway H
BURNS, Owen McIntosh 3
BURNS, P. P. 3
BURNS, Ralph Arthur 6
BURNS, Robert H
BURNS, Robert Edward 1
BURNS, Robert Emmett 5
BURNS, Robert Whitney 4
BURNS, Walter Noble 1
BURNS, William Henry 1
BURNS, William John 1
BURNSIDE, Ambrose H
  Everett
BURNSIDE, Thomas H
BURPEE, Charles Winslow 4
BURPEE, George William 4
BURPEE, Lucien Francis 1
BURPEE, W. Atlee 5
BURPEE, William Partridge 4
BURQUE, Henri Alphonse 2
BURR, Aaron * H
BURR, Albert George 1
BURR, Alexander George 3
BURR, Alfred Edmund 1
BURR, Allston 2
BURR, Anna Robeson 1
BURR, Borden 3
BURR, C. B. 1
BURR, Charles Walts 3
BURR, Edward 3
BURR, Enoch Fitch 1
BURR, Eugene Wyllys 4
BURR, Freeman F. 5
BURR, George Elbert 1
BURR, George Howard 4
BURR, George Hutchison 4
BURR, George L(indsley) 5
BURR, George Lincoln 1
BURR, George Washington 1
BURR, Hanford Montrose 4
BURR, Harold S(axton) 3
BURR, Henry Turner 5
BURR, Hudson C. 3
BURR, I. Tucker 4
BURR, Joseph Arthur 1
BURR, Karl Edward 2
BURR, Leslie L. 4
BURR, Nelson Beardsley 1
BURR, Theodosia H
BURR, William Henry 1
BURR, William Hubert 1
BURR, William P. 1
BURR, William Wesley 4
BURRAGE, Albert 1
  Cameron
BURRAGE, Champlin 4
BURRAGE, Charles Dana 1
BURRAGE, Dwight Grafton 5
BURRAGE, Guy Hamilton 4
BURRAGE, Henry Sweetser 1
BURRAGE, Walter Lincoln 1
BURRALL, William Porter H
BURRELL, David de Forest 5
BURRELL, David James 1
BURRELL, Edward Parker 1
BURRELL, Frederick 1
  Augustus Muhlenberg
BURRELL, George Arthur 3
BURRELL, George W. 5
BURRELL, H. Cayford 3
BURRELL, Herbert Leslie 1
BURRELL, John Angus 3
BURRELL, Joseph Dunn 1
BURRETT, Claude Adelbert 1
BURRILL, Alexander H
  Mansfield
BURRILL, Harvey D. 1
BURRILL, James H
BURRILL, Stanley Stinton 3
BURRILL, Thomas 1
  Jonathan
BURRINGTON, George H
BURRINGTON, Howard 4
  Rice
BURRIS, Benjamin J. 1
BURRIS, Quincy Guy 5

BURRIS, William Paxton 2
BURRITT, Bailey Barton 3
BURRITT, Eldon Grant 1
BURRITT, Elihu H
BURRITT, Henry W. 4
BURROUGH, Edmund 4
  Weldmann
BURROUGHS, Bryson 1
BURROUGHS, Charles 4
  Franklin
BURROUGHS, Edgar Rice 2
BURROUGHS, Edith 1
  Woodman
BURROUGHS, George 1
  Stockton
BURROUGHS, George W. 3
BURROUGHS, Harry 2
  Ernest
BURROUGHS, John 1
BURROUGHS, John Curtis 4
  Edington
BURROUGHS, Marie 4
BURROUGHS, Prince 2
  Emmanuel
BURROUGHS, Sherman 1
  Everett
BURROUGHS, Silas H
  Mainville
BURROUGHS, W(illiam) 5
  Dwight
BURROUGHS, William H
  Seward
BURROW, James Randall 1
BURROW, Joel Randall 1
BURROW, Trigant 3
BURROWES, Alexander J. 1
BURROWES, Alonzo 3
  Moore
BURROWES, Arthur Victor 5
BURROWES, Edward 1
  Thomas
BURROWES, Katharine 1
BURROWES, Peter Edward 1
BURROWES, Thomas 6
BURROWES, Thomas H
  Henry
BURROWS, Charles 1
  William
BURROWS, Daniel H
BURROWS, Daniel Chapel 5
BURROWS, Frederick 4
  Nelson
BURROWS, Julius C. 1
BURROWS, Lansing 1
BURROWS, Lorenzo H
BURROWS, Mark 4
BURROWS, Montrose 2
  Thomas
BURROWS, Robert Jay 1
BURROWS, Warren Booth 3
BURROWS, William 1
BURROWS, William Russell 3
BURRUS, John Perry 4
BURRUS, John T. 5
BURRUSS, Julian Ashby 2
BURRY, George W. 4
BURRY, William 1
BURSE, Walter Morrill 3
BURSLEY, Herbert Sidney 4
BURSLEY, Joseph Aldrich 3
BURSUM, Holm O. 5
BURT, Alonzo 1
BURT, Andrew Sheridan 1
BURT, Armistead H
BURT, Austin 5
BURT, Charles Kennedy H
BURT, Charles Morrison 4
BURT, Clayton Raymond 3
BURT, David Allan 2
BURT, Edward Angus 1
BURT, Frank 4
BURT, Frank Henry 4
BURT, Frederic Percy 4
BURT, George Haskell 4
BURT, Glenn Brigham Jr. 6
BURT, Henry Jackson 1
BURT, Horace Greeley 1
BURT, John H
BURT, Joseph Bell 5
BURT, Mary Elizabeth 1
BURT, Silas Wright 1
BURT, Stephen Smith 1
BURT, Struthers 3
BURT, Thomas Gregory 1
BURT, William 1
BURT, William Austin H
BURTIN, Will 5
BURTIS, Arthur 1
BURTNESS, Olger B. 4
BURTON, Alfred Edgar 1
BURTON, Andrew Mizell 4
BURTON, Asa 1
BURTON, Charles Emerson 1
BURTON, Charles 1
  Germman

BURTON, Charles Luther 4
BURTON, Charles Pierce 4
BURTON, Clarence Monroe 1
BURTON, Edgar Gordon 5
BURTON, Edward Francis 1
BURTON, Ernest DeWitt 1
BURTON, Frederick Russell 1
BURTON, George Dexter 1
BURTON, George Hall 1
BURTON, George William 4
BURTON, Harold Hitz 4
BURTON, Harry Edward 2
BURTON, Harry Edwin 2
BURTON, Hazen James 1
BURTON, Henry Fairfield 1
BURTON, Hiram Rodney 3
BURTON, Hutchings H
  Gordon
BURTON, James 1
BURTON, Jean 3
BURTON, Joseph Ralph 1
BURTON, Laurence 5
  V(reeland)
BURTON, Lewis William 1
BURTON, Marion LeRoy 1
BURTON, Myron Garfield 1
BURTON, Nathaniel Judson H
BURTON, Oliver Milton 3
BURTON, Richard 1
BURTON, Robert H
BURTON, Robert Allen 5
BURTON, Robert Mitchell 1
BURTON, Spence H
BURTON, Theodore Elijah 1
BURTON, Virgil Lee 5
BURTON, Warren H
BURTON, William H
BURTON, William Evans H
BURTON, William Henry 4
BURTON-OPITZ, Russell 1
BURTS, Charles Elford 1
BURTT, Wilson Bryant 1
BURWELL, Armistead 1
BURWELL, Arthur Warner 2
BURWELL, Benjamin 1
  Franklin
BURWELL, Charles Sidney 4
BURWELL, John 1
  T(ownsend), Jr.
BURWELL, William 1
  Armisted
BURWELL, William Russell 5
BURWELL, William 1
  Turnbull
BUSBEE, Charles Manly 1
BUSBEE, Charles Manly 5
BUSBEE, Fabius Haywood 1
BUSBEE, Jacques 5
BUSBEY, Fred E. 4
BUSBEY, Hamilton 1
BUSBEY, Katherine Graves 5
BUSBEY, L. White 1
BUSBY, George Henry H
BUSBY, Leonard Asbury 1
BUSBY, Orel 4
BUSCH, Adolf Georg 3
  Wilhelm
BUSCH, Adolphus 1
BUSCH, Adolphus III 3
BUSCH, Francis Xavier 6
BUSCH, Fritz 3
BUSCH, H. A. 4
BUSCH, Henry Miller 5
BUSCH, Joseph Francis 1
BUSCH, Joseph Peter 6
BUSCHEMEYER, John 1
  Henry
BUSCHMAN, S. L. 2
BUSEY, Paul Graham 3
BUSEY, Samuel Clagett 1
BUSEY, Samuel Thompson 1
BUSH, Albert Peyton 1
BUSH, Alvin Ray 4
BUSH, Archibald Granville 4
BUSH, Asahel 1
BUSH, Benjamin Franklin 1
BUSH, Benjamin Jay 3
BUSH, Charles G. 1
BUSH, Earl J. 4
BUSH, Florence Lilian 1
BUSH, George H
BUSH, Gordon Kenner 4
BUSH, Henry Tatnall 2
BUSH, Ira Benton 4
BUSH, Irving T. 1
BUSH, John A. 4
BUSH, Katharine Jeannette 1
BUSH, Leonard T. 3
BUSH, Lincoln 1
BUSH, Prescott Sheldon 5
BUSH, Robert R(ay) 5
BUSH, Royal Robert 1
BUSH, Thomas Greene 1
BUSH, Vannevar 6
BUSH, Wendell T. 1

BUSH-BROWN, Henry 1
  Kirke
BUSHBY, Wilkie 5
BUSHEE, Frederick 5
  Alexander
BUSHER, George Dewey 6
BUSHFIELD, Harlan J. 4
BUSHMAN, Francis X. 4
BUSHNELL, Asa Smith 1
BUSHNELL, Asa Smith 6
BUSHNELL, Charles Joseph 3
BUSHNELL, David 1
BUSHNELL, David I Jr. 5
BUSHNELL, Edward 1
BUSHNELL, George 1
  Edward
BUSHNELL, George Ensign 1
BUSHNELL, Henry Allen 1
BUSHNELL, Henry Davis 5
  Martin
BUSHNELL, Herbert 2
  Martin
BUSHNELL, Horace 1
BUSHNELL, John Edward 4
BUSHNELL, Leland David 6
BUSHNELL, Madeline 5
  Vaughan (Abbott)
BUSHNELL, Robert T. 2
BUSHNELL, Winthrop 1
  Grant
BUSHONG, Robert Grey 3
BUSICK, Adrien Fowler 5
BUSIEL, Charles Albert 1
BUSKIN, Martin 6
BUSSER, Ralph Cox 3
BUSSEWITZ, Maxillian 2
  Alfred
BUSSEY, Cyrus 1
BUSSEY, Gertrude Carman 3
BUSSEY, William Henry 6
BUSSOM, Thomas 3
  Wainwright
BUSTARD, William Walter 1
BUSWELL, Arthur Moses 1
BUSWELL, Henry Clark 4
BUSWELL, Henry Foster 1
BUTCHER, Edwin 6
BUTCHER, Howard Jr. 6
BUTCHER, Thomas 1
  Campbell
BUTCHER, Thomas Walter 5
BUTCHER, William Lewis 1
BUTIN, Romain Francois 1
BUTLER, Alford Augustus 1
BUTLER, Amos William 1
BUTLER, Andrew Pickens H
BUTLER, Arthur Pierce 3
BUTLER, Benjamin 1
  Franklin *
BUTLER, Bert S. 4
BUTLER, Burridge Davenal 2
BUTLER, Charles 1
BUTLER, Charles 3
BUTLER, Charles C. 1
BUTLER, Charles Henry 1
BUTLER, Charles St John 2
BUTLER, Charles 3
  Thompson
BUTLER, Charles William 5
BUTLER, Chester Pierce H
BUTLER, Clement Moore H
BUTLER, Dan B. 3
BUTLER, Doris Lane 4
BUTLER, Edmond Borgia 4
BUTLER, Edward Burgess 1
BUTLER, Edward H. 1
BUTLER, Mrs. Edward H. 6
BUTLER, Edward Hubert 1
BUTLER, Edward Hubert 3
BUTLER, Ellis Parker 1
BUTLER, Elmer Grimshaw 5
BUTLER, Ethan Flagg 4
BUTLER, Ezra H
BUTLER, Frank Osgood 5
BUTLER, Fred Mason 1
BUTLER, George Alfred 6
BUTLER, George Bernard 1
BUTLER, George Frank 1
BUTLER, George Harrison 1
  Jr.
BUTLER, Glentworth Reeve 1
BUTLER, G(ordon) 6
  Montague
BUTLER, Harold Lancaster 3
BUTLER, Harold Lancaster 5
BUTLER, Henry Varnum 4
BUTLER, Howard Crosby 1
BUTLER, Howard Russell 1
BUTLER, Hugh 4
BUTLER, Hugh Alfred 6
BUTLER, J. Glentworth 4
BUTLER, J. Vernon 4
BUTLER, James Davie 1
BUTLER, James Gay 1
BUTLER, James Joseph 2
BUTLER, James Orval 5
BUTLER, Jerome Ambrose 3

BUTLER, Joe Beaty 3
BUTLER, John 1
BUTLER, John Ammi 1
BUTLER, John Cornelius 3
BUTLER, John Gazzam 1
BUTLER, John George 1
BUTLER, John Jay H
BUTLER, John Wesley 1
BUTLER, John Winchel 3
  Spencer
BUTLER, Joseph Green Jr. 1
BUTLER, Josiah 1
BUTLER, Louis Fatio 1
BUTLER, Marion 1
BUTLER, Mary 2
BUTLER, Matthew 1
  Calbraith
BUTLER, Nathaniel 1
BUTLER, Nicholas Murray 2
BUTLER, Ovid 4
BUTLER, Paul M. 4
BUTLER, Peter Walton 1
BUTLER, Pierce H
BUTLER, Pierce 1
BUTLER, Pierce * 3
BUTLER, Pierce Mason 1
BUTLER, Ralph H
BUTLER, Richard 3
BUTLER, Richard 1
BUTLER, Robert 3
BUTLER, Robert Gordon 1
BUTLER, Robert Paul 5
BUTLER, Robert Reyburn 1
BUTLER, Rush Clark 3
BUTLER, Sampson Hale H
BUTLER, Samuel R. 4
BUTLER, Scot 1
BUTLER, Simeon 1
BUTLER, Smedley 1
  Darlington
BUTLER, Tait 1
BUTLER, Thomas H
BUTLER, Thomas Baldwin 5
BUTLER, Thomas Belden 1
BUTLER, Thomas S. 1
BUTLER, Walter N. H
BUTLER, William * H
BUTLER, William 1
BUTLER, William Allen * 1
BUTLER, William Frederick 1
BUTLER, William John 2
BUTLER, William Mill 1
BUTLER, William Morgan 2
BUTLER, William Morris 1
BUTLER, William Orlando H
BUTLER, Willis Howard 1
BUTLER, Zebulon H
BUTMAN, Arthur Benjamin 3
BUTMAN, Samuel 1
BUTNER, Henry W. 1
BUTT, Archibald 1
  Willingham
BUTT, John D. 4
BUTT, William 4
BUTTE, George Charles 1
BUTTENHEIM, Edgar J. 4
BUTTENHEIM, Harold S. 4
BUTTENWIESER, Moses 1
BUTTERFIELD, Consul 1
  Willshire
BUTTERFIELD, Daniel H
BUTTERFIELD, Daniel 1
BUTTERFIELD, Ernest 5
  Warren
BUTTERFIELD, John 1
BUTTERFIELD, Kenyon 1
  Leech
BUTTERFIELD, Martin H
BUTTERFIELD, Ora Elmer 1
BUTTERFIELD, Victor 6
  Lloyd
BUTTERICK, Ebenezer 1
BUTTERWORTH, Benjamin H
BUTTERWORTH, Charles 3
  Fred
BUTTERWORTH, G. 3
  Forrest
BUTTERWORTH, George 1
  Forrest
BUTTERWORTH, Hezekiah 1
BUTTERWORTH, Julian 4
  Edward
BUTTERWORTH, William 1
BUTTERWORTH, William 6
  Walton
BUTTFIELD, W. J. 2
BUTTLES, John S. 2
BUTTON, Frank 1
  Christopher
BUTTON, Stephen D. H
BUTTRAM, Frank 4
BUTTRE, John Chester H
BUTTRICK, James Tyler 4
BUTTRICK, Wallace 1
BUTTS, Alfred Benjamin 4

BUTTS, Annice Esther Bradford 1
BUTTS, Arthur Clarkson 4
BUTTS, Charles 3
BUTTS, Edmund Luther 1
BUTTS, Edward 4
BUTTS, Isaac H
BUTZ, Henry Anson 1
BUTZ, Jesse Samuel Cooper 4
BUTZ, Reuben Jacob 3
BUTZEL, Fred M. 2
BUTZEL, Henry Magnus 4
BUTZEL, Leo Martin 4
BUTZER, Albert George 3
BUWALDA, John Peter 3
BUXTON, Albert 1
BUXTON, Charles Lee 5
BUXTON, Edwin Orlando 4
BUXTON, Frank W. 5
BUXTON, G. Edward 2
BUXTON, John A. 3
BUXTON, L. Haynes 1
BUXTON, Robert William 4
BUYS, John L. 3
BUZBEE, Thomas Stephen 5
BUZBY, George Carroll 5
BUZZI, Alfred Antoni 4
BUZZNELL, Reginald W. 3
BYARS, Louis Thomas 5
BYARS, William Vincent 4
BYAS, Hugh 2
BYE, Carl R. 4
BYE, Frank Paxson 1
BYER, Herman Bailey 4
BYERLY, William Elwood 1
BYERS, Clovis E. 6
BYERS, Gordon Leslie 6
BYERS, John Frederic 2
BYERS, John Winford 5
BYERS, Joseph Perkins 4
BYERS, Maxwell Cunningham 1
BYERS, Mortimer W. 4
BYERS, Samuel Hawkins Marshall 1
BYERS, Vincent Gerard 4
BYERS, Walter Louis 5
BYERS, William Newton 1
BYFIELD, Ernest Lessing 4
BYFIELD, Joseph 1
BYFORD, Henry Turman 1
BYFORD, William Heath 3
BYINGTON, Cyrus H
BYINGTON, Edwin Hallock 2
BYINGTON, Ezra Hoyt 1
BYINGTON, Homer Morrison 4
BYINGTON, Spring 5
BYINGTON, Steven Tracy 4
BYLES, Axtell J. 1
BYLES, Mather H
BYLLESBY, Henry Marison 1
BYNE, Arthur 4
BYNNER, Edwin Lassetter H
BYNNER, Witter 5
BYNUM, Curtis 4
BYNUM, Jesse Atherton H
BYNUM, Marshall Francis 5
BYNUM, William Dallas 1
BYNUM, William Preston 1
BYOIR, Carl 3
BYRAM, George Logan 1
BYRAM, Harry E. 2
BYRD, Adam Monroe 1
BYRD, Anderson Floyd 4
BYRD, Elon Eugene 6
BYRD, Harry Clifton 5
BYRD, Harry Flood 4
BYRD, Richard Evelyn 1
BYRD, Richard Evelyn 3
BYRD, Samuel Craig 4
BYRD, William * H
BYRD, William Clifton 6
BYRER, Charles Emory 5
BYRER, Harry Hopkins 5
BYRNE, Alice Hill 2
BYRNE, Amanda Austin 5
BYRNE, Austin Thomas 4
BYRNE, Barry 4
BYRNE, Bernard Albert 1
BYRNE, Charles Alfred 1
BYRNE, Charles Christopher 1
BYRNE, Christopher 3
BYRNE, Cornelius James 6
BYRNE, Edwin Vincent 4
BYRNE, Frank M. 1
BYRNE, Harry Vincent 6
BYRNE, James 1
BYRNE, John 1
BYRNE, John Baird 4
BYRNE, Joseph 2
BYRNE, Joseph M. Jr. 1
BYRNE, Sister Marie Jose 3

BYRNE, Sister Marie Jose 5
BYRNE, Thomas Sebastian 1
BYRNE, William 1
BYRNE, William Matthew 6
BYRNE, William Thomas 3
BYRNES, Allen William 5
BYRNES, Charles Metcalfe 1
BYRNES, Clifford Hamilton 6
BYRNES, Eugene Alexander 4
BYRNES, James Francis 5
BYRNES, Ralph Leonidas 5
BYRNES, Robert Dennison 5
BYRNES, Timothy Edward 2
BYRNES, William M. 4
BYRNS, Clarence Franklin 4
BYRNS, Joseph W. 1
BYRON, Arthur William 2
BYRON, Charles Loomis 4
BYRON, Joseph Wilson 3
BYRON, Robert Burns Jr. 5
BYRON, William Devereux 4
BYRUM, Enoch Edwin 4

C

CABANA, Oliver Jr. 1
CABANISS, Edward Harman 1
CABANISS, Edward M. 4
CABANISS, Henry Harrison 1
CABANISS, Thomas Banks 4
CABEEN, Charles William 1
CABEEN, David Clark 4
CABELL, Benjamin Francis 4
CABELL, Charles Pearre 5
CABELL, De Rosey Carroll 1
CABELL, Earle 6
CABELL, Edward Carrington H
CABELL, George Craghead 1
CABELL, Isa Carrington 4
CABELL, James Alston 1
CABELL, James Branch 3
CABELL, James Lawrence 4
CABELL, Joseph Carrington H
CABELL, Nathaniel Francis H
CABELL, Robert Hervey 2
CABELL, Royal Eubank 4
CABELL, Samuel Jordan H
CABELL, William H
CABELL, William H. 4
CABELL, William Lewis 1
CABELL, Wymond 3
CABET, Etienne H
CABLE, Benjamin Stickney 1
CABLE, Benjamin Taylor 1
CABLE, Emmett James 5
CABLE, Frank T. 2
CABLE, George Washington 1
CABLE, John L. 5
CABLE, John Ray 3
CABLE, Joseph H
CABLE, Ransom R. 1
CABOT, Arthur Tracy 1
CABOT, Carolyn Sturgis 4
CABOT, Edward 4
CABOT, Edward Clarke H
CABOT, Ella Lyman 4
CABOT, Francis Higginson 4
CABOT, Frederick Pickering 1
CABOT, George H
CABOT, George E. 4
CABOT, Godfrey Lowell 4
CABOT, Henry B. 4
CABOT, Henry Bromfield 1
CABOT, Hugh 2
CABOT, John H
CABOT, Philip 1
CABOT, Richard Clarke 1
CABOT, Sebastian H
CABOT, Stephen Perkins H
CABOT, Ted 5
CABOT, William Brooks 2
CABRILLO, Juan Rodriguez H
CABRINI, Saint Frances Xavier H
CABRINI, Saint Frances Xavier 4
CADBURY, Henry Joel 6
CADDELL, Albert D. 4
CADDOO, William Henry 6
CADDY, Edmund Harrington Homer 5
CADE, Cassius Marcellus 3
CADE, George Newton 3
CADEK, Ottokar T. 3
CADILLAC, Sieur de H
CADISCH, Gordon Francis 1
CADMAN, Charles Wakefield 2
CADMAN, Paul Fletcher 2
CADMAN, S. Parkes 1
CADORIN, Ettore 6

CADWALADER, Charles Evert 1
CADWALADER, John * H
CADWALADER, John 1
CADWALADER, John Lambert H
CADWALADER, Lambert H
CADWALADER, Richard McCall 1
CADWALADER, Thomas H
CADWALADER, Thomas Francis 5
CADWALLADER, Isaac Henry 1
CADWALLADER, Starr 1
CADWELL, Charles Stewart 5
CADY, Calvin Brainerd 4
CADY, Claude E. 6
CADY, Daniel H
CADY, Daniel Leavens 1
CADY, Edward Hammond 4
CADY, Everett Ware 1
CADY, George Luther 1
CADY, Hamilton Perkins 2
CADY, J. Cleveland 1
CADY, John Hutchins 5
CADY, John Watts H
CADY, Jonathan Rider 4
CADY, Philander Kinney 1
CADY, Putnam 1
CADY, Samuel Howard 4
CADY, Walter Guyton 5
CAESAR, Doris 5
CAESAR, Kathleen 4
CAESAR, Orville Swan 4
CAETANI, Gelasio 1
CAFFEE, Robert Henderson 3
CAFFERTY, James H. H
CAFFERY, Donelson 1
CAFFERY, Eldon Lee 6
CAFFERY, Jefferson 6
CAFFEY, Eugene Mead 4
CAFFEY, Francis Gordon 3
CAFFIN, Charles Henry 1
CAFFREY, James Joseph 4
CAGE, Harry H
CAGLE, Alvah Penn 4
CAGLE, Fred Ray 5
CAHAN, Abraham 3
CAHEN, Alfred 1
CAHILL, Arthur James 5
CAHILL, Bernard J. S. 1
CAHILL, Edward 1
CAHILL, Edward A. 4
CAHILL, Edward Cornelius 4
CAHILL, George Francis 1
CAHILL, Holger 4
CAHILL, Isaac Jasper 4
CAHILL, James Christopher 2
CAHILL, John Thomas 4
CAHILL, Marie 1
CAHILL, Michael Harrison 1
CAHILL, Michael Henry 4
CAHILL, Thaddeus 1
CAHN, Bertram Joseph 3
CAHN, Edmond 4
CAHN, Gladys D. Freeman 4
CAHOON, Edward Augustus 1
CAHOON, William H
CAILLE, Augustus 1
CAILLOUET, Adrian Joseph 2
CAIN, George R. 5
CAIN, James William 1
CAIN, Joseph E. 4
CAIN, Richard Harvey H
CAIN, Rolly Morton 1
CAIN, Walter 1
CAIN, William 1
CAINE, John Thomas III 3
CAINE, Milton A. 3
CAINES, George 1
CAIRNS, Alexander 3
CAIRNS, Anna Sneed 1
CAIRNS, Charles Andrew 1
CAIRNS, Frederick Irvan 2
CAIRNS, W. D. 3
CAIRNS, William B. 1
CAJORI, Florian 1
CAKE, Ralph Harlan 5
CAKE, Wallace Ellwood 4
CALABRESE, Giuseppe 4
CALDER, Alexander 4
CALDER, Alexander Milne 1
CALDER, Alexander Stirling 2
CALDER, Curtis Ernest 3
CALDER, Helen Barnetson 3
CALDER, Hugh Gordon 5
CALDER, Louis 5
CALDER, Louis Jr. 4
CALDER, Robert Scott 5
CALDER, William M. 2
CALDERHEAD, William Alexander 1

CALDERON GUARDIA, Rafael Angel 5
CALDERON, Ignacio 4
CALDERON, Luis 6
CALDERON, Manuel Alvarez 4
CALDERWOOD, Alva John 2
CALDWELL, Alexander 4
CALDWELL, Ben Franklin 1
CALDWELL, Benjamin Palmer 1
CALDWELL, Bert Wilmer 3
CALDWELL, Burns Durbin 1
CALDWELL, Capt Billy H
CALDWELL, Charles H
CALDWELL, Charles Henry Bromedge H
CALDWELL, Charles * 1
Pope
CALDWELL, Clarence B. 4
CALDWELL, Clifford Douglass 1
CALDWELL, Daniel Templeton 3
CALDWELL, David H
CALDWELL, Edwin Valdivia 4
CALDWELL, Eugene Craighead 1
CALDWELL, Eugene Wilson 1
CALDWELL, Francis Cary 3
CALDWELL, Frank Congleton 4
CALDWELL, Frank Merrill 1
CALDWELL, Fred T. 3
CALDWELL, George Alfred H
CALDWELL, George Brinton 1
CALDWELL, George Chapman 1
CALDWELL, Greene Washington H
CALDWELL, Henry Clay 1
CALDWELL, Howard Walter 1
CALDWELL, Hugh Milton 5
CALDWELL, J. G. 5
CALDWELL, James 1
CALDWELL, James E. 2
CALDWELL, James H. H
CALDWELL, James Henry 4
CALDWELL, Jesse Cobb 4
CALDWELL, John Curtis 1
CALDWELL, John Handly 3
CALDWELL, John Kenneth 6
CALDWELL, John Lawrence 1
CALDWELL, John Livy 5
CALDWELL, John Williamson 1
CALDWELL, Joseph H
Pearson
CALDWELL, Joseph H
Pearson
CALDWELL, Joseph 1
Pearson
CALDWELL, Joshua William 1
CALDWELL, Josiah S. 4
CALDWELL, Lisle Bones 4
CALDWELL, Louis Goldsborough 3
CALDWELL, Mary Letitia 5
CALDWELL, Morley Albert 1
CALDWELL, Orestes Hampton 4
CALDWELL, Orestes Hampton 5
CALDWELL, Otis William 2
CALDWELL, Patrick H
CALDWELL, Patrick Calhoun 1
CALDWELL, Robert Breckenridge 1
CALDWELL, Robert J. 4
CALDWELL, Robert Porter H
CALDWELL, Robert Tate 6
CALDWELL, Samuel Cushman 1
CALDWELL, Samuel Hawks 4
CALDWELL, Samuel Lunt H
CALDWELL, Stephen Adolphus 3
CALDWELL, Thomas Jones 4
CALDWELL, Victor Bush 1
CALDWELL, Waller Cochran 1
CALDWELL, Walter Lindsay 4
CALDWELL, William 3
CALDWELL, William Edgar 2
CALE, Thomas 4

CALEF, Robert H
CALEY, Katharine 1
CALEY, Llewelyn N. 1
CALFEE, John Edward 1
CALFEE, Robert Martin 6
CALHANE, Daniel Francis 3
CALHERN, Louis 3
CALHOON, John H
CALHOON, Solomon Saladin 1
CALHOUN, Abner Wellborn 1
CALHOUN, Alexander McConnell 1
CALHOUN, Byron E. 3
CALHOUN, David Randolph 3
CALHOUN, Fred Harvey Hall 1
CALHOUN, Galloway 4
CALHOUN, George Miller 4
CALHOUN, Hall Laurie 1
CALHOUN, John H
CALHOUN, John 1
CALHOUN, John Caldwell H
CALHOUN, John Calwell 1
CALHOUN, John Darr 1
CALHOUN, John William 2
CALHOUN, Joseph H
CALHOUN, Joseph Painter 4
CALHOUN, Newell Meeker 1
CALHOUN, Patrick 2
CALHOUN, Philo Clarke 4
CALHOUN, Ralph Emerson 5
CALHOUN, William Barron H
CALHOUN, William James 1
CALHOUN, William Lowndes 4
CALIFF, Joseph Mark 1
CALIFORNIA JOE H
CALIGA, Issac Henry 4
CALISCH, Edward N. 2
CALIVER, Ambrose 4
CALKINS, Allard A. 6
CALKINS, Earnest Elmo 4
CALKINS, Franklin Welles 1
CALKINS, Gary Nathan 2
CALKINS, Harvey Reeves 1
CALKINS, Howard W. 6
CALKINS, James E. 5
CALKINS, L. A. 4
CALKINS, Lyman Darrow 1
CALKINS, Mary Whiton 1
CALKINS, Norman Allison 1
CALKINS, Ransom M. 1
CALKINS, Raymond 5
CALKINS, Truesdel Peck 2
CALKINS, William Henry 1
CALKINS, Wolcott 1
CALL, Arthur Deerin 2
CALL, Charles Warren Jr. 6
CALL, Edward Payson 1
CALL, Jacob H
CALL, Leland Everett 6
CALL, Manfred 1
CALL, Margaret Fleming 6
CALL, Norman 1
CALL, Rhydon Mays 1
CALL, Richard Ellsworth 1
CALL, Richard Keith H
CALL, S. Leigh 3
CALL, Wilkinson 1
CALLAGHAN, Alfred 3
CALLAGHAN, Stephen 3
CALLAHAN, Donald A. 3
CALLAHAN, Ethelbert 1
CALLAHAN, Henry White 4
CALLAHAN, James Yancy 4
CALLAHAN, Jeremiah Joseph 5
CALLAHAN, John 3
CALLAHAN, Patrick Henry 1
CALLAHAN, William Paul Jr. 1
CALLAN, Albert Stevens 4
CALLAN, Charles Jerome 4
CALLAN, John Gurney 1
CALLAN, Peter A. 1
CALLAN, Robert Emmet 1
CALLANAN, Carolyn Williams 1
CALLANDER, Edward A. 4
CALLANDER, Cyrus N. 1
CALLANDER, Cyrus N. 1
CALLANDER, William Forrest 4
CALLAWAY, Cason Jewell 4
CALLAWAY, Ely Reeves Sr. 3
CALLAWAY, Enoch Howard 1
CALLAWAY, Fuller Earle 3
CALLAWAY, Llewellyn Link 3
CALLAWAY, Merrel Price 3
CALLAWAY, Morgan Jr. 1

CALLAWAY, Samuel Rodger 1
CALLAWAY, Trowbridge 4
CALLBREATH, James Finch 1
CALLCOTT, Wilfrid Hardy 5
CALLEN, Alfred Copeland 3
CALLEN, J. Spencer 4
CALLENDER, Edward Belcher 1
CALLENDER, George Russell 5
CALLENDER, Guy Stevens 1
CALLENDER, Harold 3
CALLENDER, James Thomson H
CALLENDER, John H
CALLENDER, Romaine 4
CALLENDER, Sherman D. 3
CALLENDER, Walter Reid H
CALLER, Mary Alice 5
CALLERY, Francis Anthony 5
CALLERY, James Dawson 1
CALLES, Plutarco Elias 2
CALLEY, Walter 1
CALLIERES BONNEVUE, Louis Hector de H
CALLISON, Tolliver Cleveland 4
CALLISTER, Edward Henry 1
CALLOS, George John 4
CALLOW, John Michael 1
CALLOWAY, Alfred W. 1
CALLOWAY, Thomas Clanton 6
CALLOWAY, Walter Bowles 5
CALLVERT, Ronald Glenn 3
CALTHROP, Samuel Robert 1
CALVE, Emma 1
CALVE, Emma 2
CALVER, George Wehnes 5
CALVER, Homer Northup 5
CALVERLEY, Charles 1
CALVERT, Cecil H
CALVERT, Charles H
CALVERT, Charles Benedict H
CALVERT, George H
CALVERT, George Henry H
CALVERT, John Betts 1
CALVERT, John F. 4
CALVERT, Leonard 1
CALVERT, Philip Powell H
CALVERT, Richard Creagh Mackubin 5
CALVERT, Robert 5
CALVERT, Thomas Elwood 1
CALVERT, William Jephtha 5
CALVERTON, Victor Francis H
CALVERY, Herbert Orion 2
CALVIN, Edgar Eugene 1
CALVIN, Henrietta Willard 5
(Mrs. John H. Calvin)
CALVIN, Samuel H
CALVIN, Samuel 1
CALVIN, William Austin 4
CALVO, Joaquin Bernardo 1
CALWELL, Charles Sheridan 1
CALYO, Nicolino H
CAM, Helen Maud 4
CAMAC, Charles Nicoll Bancker 1
CAMACHO, Manual Avila 3
CAMAK, David English 6
CAMBRELENG, Churchill Caldom H
CAMDEN, Harry Poole 2
CAMDEN, Johnson Newlon 1
CAMDEN, Johnson Newlon H
CAMERON, Adam Kirk 5
CAMERON, Albert Barnes 5
CAMERON, Alexander H
CAMERON, Andrew Carr H
CAMERON, Angus H
CAMERON, Archibald H
CAMERON, Arnold Guyot 2
CAMERON, Augustus Garfield 6
CAMERON, Benjamin Franklin 4
CAMERON, Charles Conrad 3
CAMERON, Charles Raymond 5
CAMERON, D(onald) Ewen 5
CAMERON, Donald Forrester 6
CAMERON, Edgar Spier 2
CAMERON, Edward Herbert

CAMERON, Edwin J. 3
CAMERON, Francis 6
CAMERON, Frank Kenneth 3
CAMERON, George Hamilton 2
CAMERON, George Toland 3
CAMERON, Gordon Wyatt 3
CAMERON, Harold William 5
CAMERON, Henry Clay 1
CAMERON, J. Walter 6
CAMERON, James Donald 1
CAMERON, John H
CAMERON, John Andrew 4
CAMERON, John M. 1
CAMERON, Norman W. 2
CAMERON, Ossian 4
CAMERON, Ralph Henry 3
CAMERON, Robert Alexander H
CAMERON, Roderick William 1
CAMERON, Shelton Thomas 2
CAMERON, Simon H
CAMERON, Thomas Brown 6
CAMERON, Turner Christian Jr. 5
CAMERON, William Donald 4
CAMERON, William Evelyn 1
CAMERON, William J. 4
CAMERON, William John 3
CAMERON, William McC. 3
CAMILLO, Michael Francis 5
CAMINETTI, Anthony 1
CAMM, John H
CAMMACK, Edmund Ernest 3
CAMMACK, Ira Insco 1
CAMMACK, James William 1
CAMMACK, James William 3
CAMMACK, John Walter 5
CAMMERHOFF, John Christopher Frederick H
CAMP, Albert Sidney 3
CAMP, Charles Lewis 6
CAMP, Charles Wadsworth 1
CAMP, David Nelson 1
CAMP, Edgar Whittlesey 4
CAMP, Frederic Edgar 4
CAMP, Hiram H
CAMP, Hugh Douglas 6
CAMP, Irving Luzerne 4
CAMP, John Henry 1
CAMP, John Lafayette H
CAMP, John Spencer 2
CAMP, Lawrence Sabyllia 2
CAMP, Mortimer Hart 4
CAMP, Thomas James 6
CAMP, Thomas Ringgold 5
CAMP, Walter 1
CAMP, Walter John Richard 4
CAMP, Wendell H. 4
CAMP, William Bacon 6
CAMP, William McCutcheon 4
CAMPANARI, Giuseppe 1
CAMPANINI, Cleofonte 1
CAMPANIUS, John H
CAMPAU, Daniel J. 1
CAMPAU, Francis Denis 3
CAMPAU, Joseph H
CAMPA Y CARAVEDA, Miguel Abgel 4
CAMPBELL, Albert H. H
CAMPBELL, Albert James 1
CAMPBELL, Alexander * H
CAMPBELL, Alexander Boyd 4
CAMPBELL, Alexander Morton 5
CAMPBELL, Alfred Hills 1
CAMPBELL, Allan H
CAMPBELL, Allan B. 4
CAMPBELL, Andrew 4
CAMPBELL, Archibald Brush 4
CAMPBELL, Archibald Duncan 6
CAMPBELL, Archibald Murray 4
CAMPBELL, Arthur Griffith 3
CAMPBELL, Bartley 1
CAMPBELL, Benjamin 4
CAMPBELL, Brookins H
CAMPBELL, Bruce Alexander 3
CAMPBELL, Bruce Jones H
CAMPBELL, Chandler 3
CAMPBELL, Charles 1
CAMPBELL, Charles Atwood

CAMPBELL, Charles Diven 1
CAMPBELL, Charles E. 4
CAMPBELL, Charles King 5
CAMPBELL, Charles L. 3
CAMPBELL, Charles Macfie 2
CAMPBELL, Charles S. 3
CAMPBELL, Charles Sherman 3
CAMPBELL, Chesser M. 4
CAMPBELL, Chester I. 1
CAMPBELL, D. Scott 4
CAMPBELL, Daisy Rhodes 4
CAMPBELL, Dan Hampton 6
CAMPBELL, Daniel A. 4
CAMPBELL, Delwin Morton 3
CAMPBELL, Doak 5
CAMPBELL, Donald Francis 5
CAMPBELL, Donald J. 2
CAMPBELL, Donald Malcolm 2
CAMPBELL, Douglas Houghton 3
CAMPBELL, Dwight 4
CAMPBELL, E(rnest) Ray 5
CAMPBELL, Edmond Ernest 3
CAMPBELL, Edmund Schureman 3
CAMPBELL, Edward De Mille 1
CAMPBELL, Edward Hale 5
CAMPBELL, Edward Hastings 4
CAMPBELL, Edward K. 1
CAMPBELL, Eldridge 3
CAMPBELL, Elizabeth 4
CAMPBELL, Elmer Grant 5
CAMPBELL, Felix 4
CAMPBELL, Floyd D. 4
CAMPBELL, Frank 4
CAMPBELL, Frank L. 4
CAMPBELL, Gabriel 4
CAMPBELL, George 2
CAMPBELL, George Alexander 4
CAMPBELL, George Ashley 3
CAMPBELL, George Hollister 1
CAMPBELL, George Washington * H
CAMPBELL, Gerald 4
CAMPBELL, Gilbert Whitney 1
CAMPBELL, Gordon Hensley 6
CAMPBELL, Gordon Peter 4
CAMPBELL, H. Wood 5
CAMPBELL, H. Donald 5
CAMPBELL, Hardy Webster 4
CAMPBELL, Harold Denny 3
CAMPBELL, Harold George 2
CAMPBELL, Harry Huse 4
CAMPBELL, Helen Stuart 4
CAMPBELL, Henry Colin 1
CAMPBELL, Henry Donald 1
CAMPBELL, Henry Fraser H
CAMPBELL, Henry Munroe 1
CAMPBELL, Herbert Grant 1
CAMPBELL, Ira Alexander 4
CAMPBELL, J. W. 3
CAMPBELL, Jacob Miller H
CAMPBELL, James H
CAMPBELL, James A. 1
CAMPBELL, James Alexander 2
CAMPBELL, James Archibald 1
CAMPBELL, James C. 4
CAMPBELL, James Daniels 1
CAMPBELL, James E. 1
CAMPBELL, James Hepburn H
CAMPBELL, James Hobart 5
CAMPBELL, James LeRoy 2
CAMPBELL, James Mann 2
CAMPBELL, James Philander 1
CAMPBELL, James Romulus H
CAMPBELL, James U. 1
CAMPBELL, James Valentine 1
CAMPBELL, James Watson 5
CAMPBELL, John * H
CAMPBELL, John * H
CAMPBELL, John A. H
CAMPBELL, John Allen H

CAMPBELL, John Archibald H
CAMPBELL, John A(rthur) Jr. 6
CAMPBELL, John Bayard Taylor 3
CAMPBELL, John Bradford 1
CAMPBELL, John Bulow 4
CAMPBELL, John Charles 1
CAMPBELL, John Henry 1
CAMPBELL, John Hull H
CAMPBELL, John Logan 4
CAMPBELL, John Lorne 4
CAMPBELL, John Lyle 4
CAMPBELL, John Neal 4
CAMPBELL, John Pendleton 4
CAMPBELL, John Pierce H
CAMPBELL, John Preston 4
CAMPBELL, John TenBrook 1
CAMPBELL, John Thomas 1
CAMPBELL, John Wilson H
CAMPBELL, Johnston B. 3
CAMPBELL, Josiah A. Patterson
CAMPBELL, Kathleen Roseanne 6
CAMPBELL, Killis 1
CAMPBELL, L. j. 5
CAMPBELL, Leon 3
CAMPBELL, Lewis Davis H
CAMPBELL, LeRoy Brotzman 3
CAMPBELL, LeRoy Walter 5
CAMPBELL, Lily Bess 4
CAMPBELL, Lucien Quitman 2
CAMPBELL, Luther A. 2
CAMPBELL, Macy 1
CAMPBELL, Marcus B. 1
CAMPBELL, Marguerite 4
CAMPBELL, Marius Robison
CAMPBELL, M(ary) Edith 6
CAMPBELL, Oscar James Jr. 5
CAMPBELL, Mrs. Patrick 1
CAMPBELL, Patrick Thomas
CAMPBELL, Persia (Mrs. Edward Rice Jr.) 6
CAMPBELL, Philip Pitt 1
CAMPBELL, Price 1
CAMPBELL, Prince Lucian 1
CAMPBELL, R. Granville 1
CAMPBELL, Ralph Emerson
CAMPBELL, Richard 1
CAMPBELL, Richard Kenna
CAMPBELL, Robert H
CAMPBELL, Robert Blair H
CAMPBELL, Robert Donald 4
CAMPBELL, Robert Fishburne 2
CAMPBELL, Robert Morrell 6
CAMPBELL, Robert Willis 2
CAMPBELL, Ronald Neil 4
CAMPBELL, Ross Turner 2
CAMPBELL, Rowland 2
CAMPBELL, Roy Davies 4
CAMPBELL, Roy Hilton 6
CAMPBELL, Sam 4
CAMPBELL, Samuel H
CAMPBELL, Theodorick Pryor 1
CAMPBELL, Thomas H
CAMPBELL, Thomas A. 5
CAMPBELL, Thomas Donald
CAMPBELL, Thomas Edward
CAMPBELL, Thomas Huffman 2
CAMPBELL, Thomas Jefferson
CAMPBELL, Thomas Joseph
CAMPBELL, Thomas Mitchell
CAMPBELL, Thomas W. H
CAMPBELL, Thompson 3
CAMPBELL, Wallace 3
CAMPBELL, Wallace Edwin
CAMPBELL, Walter Gilbert 5
CAMPBELL, Walter Stanley 3
CAMPBELL, Wayne 5
CAMPBELL, William * H
CAMPBELL, William 1
CAMPBELL, William Alexander

CAMPBELL, William Bowen H
CAMPBELL, William Carey 4
CAMPBELL, William Francis 1
CAMPBELL, William Henry H
CAMPBELL, William James 2
CAMPBELL, William Lyman 4
CAMPBELL, William Neal 2
CAMPBELL, William Purnell 5
CAMPBELL, William Rogers 1
CAMPBELL, William Taggart 1
CAMPBELL, William W. H
CAMPBELL, William W. 4
CAMPBELL, William Wallace 1
CAMPBELL, William Wilson 5
CAMPBELL, Willis Cohoon 1
CAMPBELL, Worthington 4
CAMPELLO, Count Solone Di 5
CAMPHOR, Alexander Priestly 1
CAMPNEY, Ralph Osbourne 4
CAMPOS, Maria E. 3
CAMROSE, 1st Viscount of Hackwood Park 3
CAMSELL, Charles 3
CAMUS, Albert 3
CANADA, John Walter 3
CANADA, John William 3
CANADA, John William 3
CANADA, Robert Owen Jr. 5
CANADA, William Wesley 1
CANADAY, Paul O'Neal 2
CANARUTTO, Angelo 2
CANARY, Martha Jane H
CANARY, Martha Jane 4
CANBY, Edward Richard Sprigg H
CANBY, Henry Seidel 4
CANBY, Richard Sprigg H
CANBY, William Marriott 1
CANDEE, Charles Lucius 5
CANDEE, Helen Churchill 2
CANDEE, Leverett H
CANDEE, Lyman 2
CANDLER, Allen Daniel 1
CANDLER, Asa G. 1
CANDLER, Charles Howard 3
CANDLER, Charles Murphey 1
CANDLER, Ezekiel Samuel Jr. 2
CANDLER, Henry E. 5
CANDLER, John Slaughter 2
CANDLER, Samuel Charles 5
CANDLER, Thomas Slaughter
CANDLER, Warren A. 1
CANDLER, William 1
CANDY, Albert Luther 2
CANEVIN, J. F. Regis 1
CANFIELD, Arthur Graves 2
CANFIELD, Edward 4
CANFIELD, George Folger 1
CANFIELD, Harry C. 2
CANFIELD, James Hulme 1
CANFIELD, Roy Bishop 1
CANFIELD, William Walker H
CANHAM, Charles Draper William 4
CANJAR, Lawrence Nicholas 5
CANN, James Ferris 2
CANN, Norman D. 3
CANNAN, Robert Keith 4
CANNIFF, William Henry H
CANNING, George H
CANNON, A. Benson 3
CANNON, Annie Jump 1
CANNON, Austin Victor 1
CANNON, Cavendish Welles 4
CANNON, Charles A. 5
CANNON, Charles James H
CANNON, Clarence 4
CANNON, Cornelia James 5
(Mrs. Walter Bradford Cannon)
CANNON, Frank Jenne 1
CANNON, George Lyman Jr. 5
CANNON, George Quayle H
CANNON, Grant Groesbeck 5
CANNON, Harriet Starr H

* Indicates More Than One Such Name Listed

CANNON, Henry White 1
CANNON, James Jr. 2
CANNON, James III 3
CANNON, James Graham 1
CANNON, Jimmy 6
CANNON, John 1
CANNON, John Franklin 1
CANNON, John Kenneth 3
CANNON, Joseph Gurney 1
CANNON, Le Grand 1
Bouton
CANNON, Martin L. 3
CANNON, Newton H
CANNON, Raymond J. 3
CANNON, Sylvester 2
Quayle
CANNON, Walter Bradford 2
CANNON, William H
CANNON, William 5
Cornelius
CANONCHET H
CANONGE, Louis Placide H
CANONICUS H
CANOVA, Leon Joseph 4
CANRIGHT, Dudley 1
Marvin
CANSE, John Martin 5
CANT, William Alexander 1
CANTACUZENE, Mme 6
CANTELLI, Guido 1
CANTER, Howard Vernon 5
CANTER, Joshua 1
CANTEY, Morgan Sabb 4
CANTILLON, William 1
David
CANTILO, Jose Maria 5
CANTOR, Eddie 4
CANTOR, Jacob Aaron 1
CANTOR, Nathaniel 5
CANTRALL, Arch Martin 5
CANTRELL, Charles E. 4
CANTRELL, Deaderick 1
Harrell
CANTRIL, A(lbert) Hadley 5
CANTRILL, James 1
Campbell
CANTRILL, James E. 1
CANTWELL, Alfred W. 4
CANTWELL, James 1
William
CANTWELL, John Joseph 2
CANTWELL, Robert 3
Murray
CANTY, Thomas 4
CAPA, Robert 4
CAPARO, Jose Angel 3
CAPE, Emily Palmer 4
CAPEK, Thomas 3
CAPEN, Charles Laban 1
CAPEN, Edward Warren 5
CAPEN, Elmer Hewitt 1
CAPEN, Nahum H
CAPEN, Oliver Bronson 3
CAPEN, Samuel Billings 1
CAPEN, Samuel Paul 3
CAPERS, Ellison 1
CAPERS, John G. 1
CAPERS, Walter Branham 5
CAPERS, William H
CAPERS, William 2
Theodotus
CAPERTON, Allen Taylor H
CAPERTON, Hugh H
CAPERTON, William Banks 1
CAPES, William Parr 2
CAPLES, Martin Joseph 1
CAPLES, Russell B. 5
CAPOGROSSI, Gulseppe 6
CAPPELLUCCI, Gabriel 6
Orazio
CAPPER, Arthur 3
CAPPS, Charles R. 1
CAPPS, Edward 3
CAPPS, Joseph Almarin 4
CAPPS, Stephen Reid 1
CAPPS, Washington Lee 1
CAPRON, Adin Ballou 1
CAPRON, Charles 3
Alexander
CAPRON, Horace H
CAPSTAFF, Albert L. 4
CAPSTAFF, John George 5
CAPSTICK, John Henry 1
CAPT, James Clyde 2
CAPTAIN JACK H
CARAWAY, Hattie Wyatt H
CARAWAY, Thaddeus H. 1
CARBAJL, Fernando 6
CARBEE, Scott Clifton 4
CARBO, Luis Felipe 5
CARBONARA, E(mil) 5
Vernon
CARBONE, Agostino 1
CARBONNIER, Claes Cecil 4
CARD, Benjamin Cozzens 1
CARD, Ernest Mason 5

CARDELLI, Pietro H
CARDEN, Cap R. 1
CARDEN, Edward Walter 3
CARDEN, George 2
Alexander
CARDEN, William Thomas 1
CARDENAS, Garcia Lopez H
de
CARDENAS, Lazaro 5
CARDER, Eugene Clayton 6
CARDEW, Emily Craske 6
CARDIFF, Ira D. 5
CARDOFF, Thomas H. 4
CARDON, Philip Vincent 4
CARDOZO, Benjamin 1
Nathan
CARDOZO, Jacob Newton H
CARDWELL, James R. 3
CARDY, Samuel 4
CARENS, Thomas Henry 4
CAREW, Harold David 2
CAREW, James 1
CAREW, John F. 3
CAREY, Archibald 3
CAREY, Archibald James 1
CAREY, Arthur Astor 1
CAREY, Asa Bacon 1
CAREY, Charles Emerson 3
CAREY, Charles Henry 1
CAREY, Charles Irving 5
CAREY, Eben James 2
CAREY, Eustace W. 4
CAREY, Francis King 2
CAREY, Hampson 3
CAREY, Henry Charles H
CAREY, Henry Westonrae 1
CAREY, James Barron 6
CAREY, James F. 4
CAREY, James William 5
CAREY, John Joseph 5
CAREY, Joseph 1
CAREY, Joseph Maull 1
CAREY, Lawrence Bernard 6
CAREY, Liguori John 4
CAREY, Mathew H
CAREY, Miriam Eliza 1
CAREY, Peter Bernard 2
CAREY, Robert 4
CAREY, Robert Davis 1
CAREY, Robert Lincoln 4
CAREY, William Francis 3
CAREY, William Gibson Jr. 2
CARGILL, Frank Valentine 5
CARGILL, Oscar 5
CARHARDT, Raymond T. 6
CARHART, Daniel 1
CARHART, Frank Milton 4
CARHART, Henry Smith 1
CARHART, Winfield Scott 4
CARHARTT, Hamilton 1
CARHARTT, John Ernest 4
CARIANI, Anthony 6
CARIAS ANDINO, 5
Tiburcio
CARIS, Albert Garfield 6
CARKIN, Seth Ballou 1
CARKNER, James W. 4
CARL, Francis Augustus 1
CARL, Katharine Augusta 1
CARL, Melvin Latshaw 3
CARL, William Crane 1
CARLAND, John Emmett 1
CARLE, E. E. 4
CARLE, Frank Austin 1
CARLE, Nathaniel Allen 1
CARLE, Richard 1
CARLES, Arthur B. 3
CARLETON, Bukk G. 1
CARLETON, Clifford 4
CARLETON, Edward 1
Hercules
CARLETON, Guy 3
CARLETON, Henry H
CARLETON, Henry Guy 1
CARLETON, Mark Alfred 1
CARLETON, Murray 1
CARLETON, Peter H
CARLETON, Philip 6
Greenleaf
CARLETON, Robert 6
Andrew Wood
CARLETON, Sprague 6
CARLETON, Will 1
CARLEY, Henry Thompson 4
CARLEY, Patrick J. 1
CARLEY, W. F. 4
CARLILE, John Snyder H
CARLILE, William Buford 5
CARLIN, Andrew B. 1
CARLIN, Charles Creighton 1
CARLIN, Charles L. 5
CARLIN, George Andrew 4
CARLIN, Henry A. 4
CARLIN, James Joseph 1
CARLIN, John H
CARLIN, Thomas H

CARLIN, Walter Jeffreys 3
CARLIN, William Passmore 1
CARLIN, William Worth H
CARLISLE, Charles Arthur 1
CARLISLE, Chester Lee 4
CARLISLE, Clifton Hugh 3
CARLISLE, Floyd Leslie 2
CARLISLE, G. Lister Jr. 1
CARLISLE, Harold Walter 4
CARLISLE, Helen Grace H
CARLISLE, Howard Bobo 5
CARLISLE, James Henry 1
CARLISLE, James H
Mandeville
CARLISLE, James McCoy 4
CARLISLE, John Griffin 1
CARLISLE, John Nelson 1
CARLISLE, Marcus Lee 5
CARLL, John Franklin 1
CARLOCK, John Bruce 4
CARLOUGH, David 4
Jacobus
CARLSEN, Carl Laurence 4
CARLSEN, Clarence J. 4
CARLSEN, Dines 4
CARLSEN, Emil 1
CARLSEN, Niels Christian 3
CARLSON, Albert Sigfrid 5
CARLSON, Anders Johan 5
CARLSON, Anton Julius 4
CARLSON, Chester 5
CARLSON, Clarence Erick 3
CARLSON, E(rnest) Leslie 5
CARLSON, Evans Fordyce 2
CARLSON, George Alfred 1
CARLSON, Gunard Oscar 5
CARLSON, Harry Johan 5
CARLSON, James Alfred 4
CARLSON, John Fabian 2
CARLSON, Loren Daniel 4
CARLSON, T(horgny) 5
C(edric)
CARLSON, Wally 4
CARLSTON, Kenneth S. 5
CARLSTROM, Oscar E. 2
CARLTON, A. C. 3
CARLTON, Albert E. 1
CARLTON, Caleb Henry 1
CARLTON, Caleb Sidney 5
CARLTON, Clarence Clay 3
CARLTON, Doyle Elam 5
CARLTON, Ernest W. 4
CARLTON, Frank Tracy 5
CARLTON, Leslie Gilbert 1
CARLTON, Newcomb 3
CARLTON, Richard Paul 4
CARLTON, Romulus Lee 6
CARLTON, William 2
Newnham Chattin
CARLYLE, Irving Edward 5
CARLYLE, William Levi 5
CARMACK, Edward Ward 1
CARMALT, James Walton 1
CARMALT, William Henry 1
CARMAN, Albert Pruden 3
CARMAN, Augustine 1
Spencer
CARMAN, Bliss 1
CARMAN, Ezra Ayers 1
CARMAN, George Noble 2
CARMAN, Harry James 4
CARMELIA, Francis Albion 2
CARMICHAEL, Archibald 3
Hill
CARMICHAEL, Francis 6
Abbott Jr.
CARMICHAEL, George 1
Edgar
CARMICHAEL, George T. 4
CARMICHAEL, Henry 1
CARMICHAEL, James 6
Vinson
CARMICHAEL, John Hugh 5
CARMICHAEL, Leonard 4
CARMICHAEL, Oliver 4
Cromwell
CARMICHAEL, Omer 3
CARMICHAEL, Richard 1
Bennett
CARMICHAEL, Robert 4
Daniel
CARMICHAEL, Robert 6
Daniel
CARMICHAEL, Thomas 2
Harrison
CARMICHAEL, William H
CARMICHAEL, William 4
Donald Jr.
CARMICHAEL, William 2
Perrin
CARMODY, John 3
CARMODY, John Michael 4
CARMODY, Martin Henry 4
CARMODY, Terence 2
Francis
CARMODY, Thomas 1

CARMODY, Thomas 2
Edward
CARMONA, Antonio Oscar 3
de Fragoso
CARNAHAN, A.S.J. 5
CARNAHAN, David 5
Hobart
CARNAHAN, George 1
Holmes
CARNAHAN, Herschel L. 1
CARNAHAN, James H
CARNAHAN, James 1
Richards
CARNAHAN, Paul Harvey 4
CARNAHAN, Wendell 4
CARNAP, Rudolf 5
CARNEGIE, Andrew 1
CARNEGIE, Dale 3
CARNEGIE, Hattie 3
CARNEGIE, Louise 2
Whitfield
CARNEGIE, T(homas) 5
Morris(on)
CARNELL, Edward John 4
CARNELL, Laura Horner 1
CARNES, Cecil 3
CARNES, Thomas Petters H
CARNEY, Francis Joseph 1
CARNEY, Frank 1
CARNEY, Harry Howell 6
CARNEY, James Lorring 1
CARNEY, Leonard T. 4
CARNEY, Thomas 1
CARNEY, Thomas Joseph 2
CARNEY, William Roy 3
CARNOCHRAN, John H
Murray
CARO, Marcus Rayner 4
CAROL, Kate 1
CARONDELET, Baron H
Francisco Luis Hector de
CAROTHERS, Wallace H. 1
CARPENDER, Arthur S. 3
CARPENTER, Aaron 5
Everly
CARPENTER, Alfred Saint 6
Vrain
CARPENTER, Allen Fuller 2
CARPENTER, Allen 1
Harmon
CARPENTER, Alva Edwin 1
CARPENTER, Arthur 3
DeVere
CARPENTER, Arthur 3
Howe
CARPENTER, B. Platt 1
CARPENTER, Benjamin 1
CARPENTER, Charles 1
Carroll
CARPENTER, Charles 5
Colcock Jones
CARPENTER, Charles E. 1
CARPENTER, Charles 2
Ernest
CARPENTER, Charles 1
Lincoln
CARPENTER, Clarence 5
CARPENTER, Clarence 6
Ray
CARPENTER, Clinton E. 2
Cornelius
CARPENTER, Coy 5
CARPENTER, Cyrus Clay H
CARPENTER, Davis 1
CARPENTER, Decatur H
Merritt Hammond
CARPENTER, Delph E. 3
CARPENTER, Edmund 1
Janes
CARPENTER, Edward 5
Childs
CARPENTER, Elbert 1
Lawrence
CARPENTER, Ellen Maria H
CARPENTER, Eugene R. 1
CARPENTER, Fanny 5
Hallock
CARPENTER, Ford 2
CARPENTER, Francis 1
Bicknell
CARPENTER, Frank 1
George
CARPENTER, Frank Oliver 4
CARPENTER, Frank Pierce 1
CARPENTER, Frank 1
Watson
CARPENTER, Franklin 1
Reuben
CARPENTER, Fred Green 4
CARPENTER, Fred Warner 5
CARPENTER, Frederic Ives 1
CARPENTER, Frederic 1
Walton
CARPENTER, George 4
Albert

CARPENTER, George 1
Oliver
CARPENTER, George Rice 1
CARPENTER, Gilbert 1
Saltonstall
CARPENTER, H. Beach 3
CARPENTER, Homer 6
Wilson
CARPENTER, Horace 1
Francis
CARPENTER, Hubert 2
Vinton
CARPENTER, J. Henry 3
CARPENTER, James D. 5
CARPENTER, James W. * 4
CARPENTER, John Alden 3
CARPENTER, John 1
Slaughter
CARPENTER, John 6
William
CARPENTER, Julia 1
Wiltberger
CARPENTER, Leslie E. 6
CARPENTER, Levi D. H
CARPENTER, Louis 1
George
CARPENTER, Louis Henry 1
CARPENTER, Matthew H
Hale
CARPENTER, Miriam 6
Feronia
CARPENTER, Myron Jay 4
CARPENTER, Newton 1
Henry
CARPENTER, Ralph 4
Emerson
CARPENTER, Ray Wilford 4
CARPENTER, Reid 1
CARPENTER, Robert 2
Ruliph Morgan
CARPENTER, Robert 5
Wilfred
CARPENTER, Rolla 1
Clinton
CARPENTER, Samuel H. H
CARPENTER, Stephen H
Cullen
CARPENTER, Stephen H
Haskins
CARPENTER, W. T. 6
Coleman
CARPENTER, Walter 6
Samuel Jr.
CARPENTER, William E. 1
CARPENTER, William H. 1
CARPENTER, William 1
Henry
CARPENTER, William 1
Leland
CARPENTER, William Seal 3
CARPENTER, William 5
Weston
CARPENTIER, Charles 4
Francis
CARR, Albert Zolotkoff 5
CARR, Alexander 2
CARR, Arthur R. 3
CARR, Benjamin 1
CARR, Camillo Casatti 1
Cadmus
CARR, Ceylon Spencer 1
CARR, Charlotte 5
CARR, Clarence Alfred 1
CARR, Clark E. 1
CARR, Clyde Mitchell 1
CARR, Dabney H
CARR, Dabney Smith 1
CARR, Elias 1
CARR, Emma Perry 5
CARR, Eugene Asa 1
CARR, Floyd LeVerne 2
CARR, Francis 3
CARR, Gene 3
CARR, George H. 1
CARR, George Wallace 1
CARR, Harry 1
CARR, Harry C. 3
CARR, Harvey 3
CARR, Henry James 1
CARR, Herbert Wildon 1
CARR, Irving J. 5
CARR, James H
CARR, James O. 2
CARR, James Ozborn 1
CARR, John H
CARR, John Foster 1
CARR, John Wesley 3
CARR, Joseph Bradford 1
CARR, Julian Shakespeare 1
CARR, Lawrence 5
CARR, Leland Walker 5
CARR, Lewis E. 1
CARR, Lucien 1
CARR, Nathan Tracy H
CARR, Ossian Elmer 1
CARR, Ralph L. 3

486

CARR, Reid Langdon 2
CARR, Robert Franklin 2
CARR, Samuel 1
CARR, Sarah Pratt 4
CARR, Sterling Douglas 5
CARR, Thomas Matthew H
CARR, Walter Lester 4
CARR, Walter Scott 4
CARR, Wilbert Lester 5
CARR, Wilbur John 2
CARR, William Jarvis 6
CARR, William John 1
CARR, William Kearny 1
CARR, William Phillips 4
CARR, Wooda Nichols 3
CARRE, Henry Beach 1
CARRE, Jean Marie 3
CARREL, Alexis 2
CARRELL, George Aloysius H
CARRELL, William Beall 2
CARRERE, John Merven 1
CARRICK, Alice Van Leer 5
 (Mrs. Prescott Orde
 Skinner)
CARRICK, Lynn 4
CARRICK, Manton Marble 1
CARRICK, Samuel 1
CARRICO, Joseph Leonard 2
CARRIER, Augustus Stiles 1
CARRIER, Wilbur Oscar 1
CARRIER, Willis Haviland 3
CARRIGAN, Clarence 1
CARRIGAN, Edward 2
CARRIGAN, William L. 1
CARRINGTON, Alexander 6
 Berkeley Jr.
CARRINGTON, Edward H
CARRINGTON, Edward 1
 Codrington
CARRINGTON, Elaine 2
CARRINGTON, FitzRoy 3
CARRINGTON, Frances 1
 Courtney
CARRINGTON, Francis 6
 Louis
CARRINGTON, Gordon de 2
 L.
CARRINGTON, Henry 1
 Beebee
CARRINGTON, Hereward 6
 (Hubert Lavington)
CARRINGTON, James 1
 Beebee
CARRINGTON, Paul H
CARRINGTON, Richard 3
 Adams Jr.
CARRINGTON, William 2
 John
CARRINGTON, William 1
 Thomas
CARRIS, Lewis Herbert 3
CARRITHERS, Howard 4
CARROLL, Anna Ella H
CARROLL, Augustus John 5
CARROLL, B. Harvey 1
CARROLL, Ben 2
CARROLL, Benajah Harvey 1
CARROLL, Beryl F. 1
CARROLL, Caroline 5
 Moncure Benedict (Mrs.
 Mitchell Carroll)
CARROLL, Charles * H
CARROLL, Charles 1
CARROLL, Charles 1
 Chauncey
CARROLL, Charles Eden 2
CARROLL, Charles Hobart H
CARROLL, Daniel H
CARROLL, Dudley DeWitt 5
CARROLL, Earl 2
CARROLL, Edward 2
 Ambrose
CARROLL, Francis Patrick 4
CARROLL, Francis X. 2
CARROLL, Frederick 2
 Aloysius
CARROLL, George W. 4
CARROLL, Henry 1
CARROLL, Henry King 1
CARROLL, Horace Bailey 2
CARROLL, Horace Bailey 5
CARROLL, Howard 1
CARROLL, Howard Joseph 3
CARROLL, James H
CARROLL, James 1
CARROLL, James Bernard 1
CARROLL, James E. 5
CARROLL, James F. 3
CARROLL, James Jordan 1
CARROLL, James Milton 1
CARROLL, John H
CARROLL, John 1
CARROLL, John D. 1
CARROLL, John E. 6
CARROLL, John F. 1
CARROLL, John Francis 1

CARROLL, John Haydock 1
CARROLL, John Joseph 1
CARROLL, John Lee 1
CARROLL, John P. 2
CARROLL, Joseph Francis 3
CARROLL, Leo G. 5
CARROLL, Louis Francis 5
CARROLL, Mitchell 1
CARROLL, Monroe 5
 Spurgeon
CARROLL, Paul E. 6
CARROLL, Paul Thomas 3
CARROLL, Paul Vincent 5
CARROLL, Phil 5
CARROLL, Philip A. 3
CARROLL, Raymond G. 2
CARROLL, Richard 3
 Augustine
CARROLL, Robert Paris 3
CARROLL, Robert Sproul 3
CARROLL, Samuel Sprigg H
CARROLL, Thomas Claude 4
CARROLL, Thomas F. 1
CARROLL, Thomas Henry 4
 II
CARROLL, Thomas Patrick 4
CARROLL, William H
CARROLL, William Henry 1
CARROON, Frank 5
CARROTHERS, George 4
 Ezra
CARROW, Fleming 4
CARRUTH, Arthur Jay Jr. 4
CARRUTH, Charles 1
 Theodore
CARRUTH, Hayden 1
CARRUTH, Louis 1
CARRUTH, William 1
 Herbert
CARRUTHERS, John 3
 Franklin Bruce
CARRUTHERS, Thomas 4
 Neely
CARRY, Edward Francis 1
CARRYL, Charles Edward 2
CARRYL, Guy Wetmore 1
CARSE, Elizabeth 5
CARSE, Matilda Bradley 4
CARSON, Adam Clarke 1
CARSON, Cale Wellman 6
CARSON, Charles Averette 3
CARSON, Charles Clifton 2
CARSON, Charles L. H
CARSON, Christopher 1
CARSON, Clifford 5
CARSON, Frank L. 3
CARSON, George Prentice 4
CARSON, Hampton 1
 Lawrence
CARSON, Harry Roberts 2
CARSON, Howard Adams 1
CARSON, James Carlton 4
CARSON, James Oliver 1
CARSON, James S. 5
CARSON, Jessie M(ay) 1
CARSON, John Fleming 1
CARSON, John Hargadine 5
CARSON, John Miller 1
CARSON, John Miller 3
CARSON, John Renshaw 1
CARSON, Joseph H
CARSON, Joseph Kirtley Jr. 3
CARSON, Luella Clay 1
CARSON, Matthew 5
 Vaughan Jr.
CARSON, Norman Bruce 1
CARSON, Rachel L. 4
CARSON, Robert 3
CARSON, Samuel Price 4
CARSON, Walter Lapsley 4
CARSON, William E. 2
CARSON, William Henry 4
CARSON, William Pierce 5
CARSON, William Waller 1
CARSS, William Leighton 1
CARSTARPHEN, Frederick 3
 Charles
CARSTARPHEN, William 1
 Turner
CARSTENS, Christian Carl 1
CARSTENS, Henry Rohnert 6
CARSTENS, J. Henry 1
CARSTENSEN, Gustav 1
 Arnold
CARSTENSEN, John 1

CARTER, A. F. 4
CARTER, Alan 1
CARTER, Albert Edward 6
CARTER, Albert Paine 5
CARTER, Amon Giles 3
CARTER, Arthur Hazelton 4
CARTER, Asher 2
CARTER, Benjamin Estes 2
CARTER, Bernard 1
CARTER, Bernard Shirley 4
CARTER, Boake 2

CARTER, C. C. 4
CARTER, Charles David 1
CARTER, Charles Francis 1
CARTER, Charles Frederick 1
CARTER, Clarence Edwin 3
CARTER, Clifton Carroll 3
CARTER, Creed Fulton Jr. 6
CARTER, DeWitt 3
CARTER, Edward Carlos 1
CARTER, Edward Clark 3
CARTER, Edwin A. 2
CARTER, Edwin Farnham 3
CARTER, Elias H
CARTER, Emma Smuller 1
CARTER, Emmet 4
 Thoroughman
CARTER, Ernest Trow 3
CARTER, Francis 1
 Beauregard
CARTER, Francis Graves 4
CARTER, Franklin 1
CARTER, Fred Afton 2
CARTER, Fred G. 3
CARTER, Fred Mason 3
CARTER, Gale H. 4
CARTER, Gardner Lloyd 4
CARTER, George 1
CARTER, George Calvin 5
CARTER, George Henry 2
CARTER, George Milton 3
CARTER, George Robert 1
CARTER, George William 1
CARTER, Harold Samuel 4
CARTER, Henry Alpheus H
 Pierce
CARTER, Henry Holland 3
CARTER, Henry Rose 1
CARTER, Herbert 1
 DeWayne
CARTER, Herbert Swift 1
CARTER, Hodding 5
CARTER, Homer Munroe 6
 Sr.
CARTER, Horace A. 3
CARTER, Hubert Lazell 3
CARTER, James 2
CARTER, James Coolidge 1
CARTER, James Francis 5
CARTER, James Gordon H
CARTER, James Madison 1
 Gore
CARTER, James Richard 1
CARTER, Jesse Benedict 1
CARTER, Jesse Francis 2
CARTER, Jesse McIlvaine 1
CARTER, Jesse Washington 3
CARTER, John * H
CARTER, John 6
CARTER, John Wayn Flete 4
CARTER, John Franklin Jr. 4
CARTER, John H. 4
CARTER, John Ridgely 4
CARTER, John S. 3
CARTER, Joseph Newton 1
CARTER, Landon H
CARTER, Mrs. Leslie 1
CARTER, Leyton E. 3
CARTER, Louise Wilson 6
 Lamica
CARTER, Luther Cullen 1
CARTER, Lyndall Frederic 6
CARTER, Mary Elizabeth 4
CARTER, Morris 6
CARTER, Nathan A. Sr. 3
CARTER, Oberlin 2
 Montgomery
CARTER, Oliver Clinton 3
CARTER, Oma Belle Bixler 6
 (Mrs. W. Taylor Carter)
CARTER, Orrin Nelson 1
CARTER, Philips John 4
CARTER, Randall Albert 5
CARTER, Raymond Lanson 3
CARTER, Richard Burrage 2
CARTER, Robert * H
CARTER, Robert Allen 4
CARTER, Robert Inglee 4
CARTER, Russell Gordon 3
CARTER, Samuel Fain 1
CARTER, Samuel Powhatan H
CARTER, Seth May 4
CARTER, Steven V. 3
CARTER, Thomas Coke 1
CARTER, Thomas Henry 1
CARTER, Timothy Jarvis 1
CARTER, Walter Steuben 1
CARTER, Warren Ray 6
CARTER, Wilbert James 5
CARTER, William 2
CARTER, William Blount 1
CARTER, William Curtis 1
CARTER, William Daniel 6
CARTER, William Francis 3
CARTER, William Harding 1
CARTER, William Harrison 6
CARTER, William Henric 1

CARTER, William Henry 3
CARTER, William Samuel 1
CARTER, William Spencer 2
CARTER, William V. 5
CARTER, Winthrop Lakey 4
CARTER, Worrall Reed 6
CARTERET, Philip H
CARTERET, Sir George H
CARTIER, Jacques H
CARTLAND, Donald Lee 4
CARTLIDGE, Harold 6
 Tyndale
CARTON, Alfred Thomas 4
CARTON, John Jay 1
CARTOTTO, Ercole 2
CARTTER, David Kellogg H
CARTWRIGHT, Alexander H
 Joy
CARTWRIGHT, C. Hawley 4
CARTWRIGHT, Frank 4
 Thomas
CARTWRIGHT, James 1
 Henry
CARTWRIGHT, Morse 6
 Adams
CARTWRIGHT, Peter H
CARTY, Donald Joseph 3
CARTY, John J. 1
CARTY, Roland Kenneth 5
CARUANA, George J. 3
CARUS, Emma 1
CARUS, Paul 1
CARUSI, Charles Francis 1
CARUSO, Enrico 1
CARUTHERS, Robert H
 Looney
CARUTHERS, Samuel 1
CARUTHERS, William H
 Alexander
CARVAJAL, Manuel 6
CARVALHO, David Nunes 1
CARVALHO, Solomon H
 Nunes
CARVALHO, Solomon Solis 2
CARVER, Clifford Nickels 4
CARVER, George 3
 Washington
CARVER, George H
 Washington
CARVER, George 2
 Washington
CARVER, George 4
 Washington
CARVER, Jay Ward 2
CARVER, John H
CARVER, John Stuart 3
CARVER, Jonathan H
CARVER, Thomas Nixon 4
CARVER, Walter 4
 Buckingham
CARVER, Walter Lexor 3
CARVER, Williard 3
CARVETH, Hector Russell 2
CARVILLE, E. P. 3
CARY, Alice 1
CARY, Annie Louise 1
CARY, Archibald H
CARY, Austin 1
CARY, Charles 1
CARY, Charles Preston 3
CARY, Charles Reed 6
CARY, Edward 1
CARY, Edward Henry 3
CARY, Edward Richard 1
CARY, Elisabeth Luther 1
CARY, George H
CARY, George 2
CARY, George Booth H
CARY, George Foster 1
CARY, George Lovell 1
CARY, Glover H. 1
CARY, Guy 3
CARY, Harry Francis 5
CARY, Henry Nathaniel 1
CARY, Jeremiah Eaton H
CARY, Joyce 3
CARY, Lott H
CARY, Lucian 5
CARY, Melbern Brinckerhoff 2
CARY, Phoebe 1
CARY, Robert John 1
CARY, Robert Webster 4
CARY, Russell Singer 6
CARY, Shepard H
CARY, William Joseph 1
CASADAY, L(auren) 5
 W(ilde)
CASADESUS, Robert 5
CASADY, Thomas 4
CASALS, Pablo (Pau Carlos 6
 Salvador Defillo de)
CASAMAJOR, George 4
 Holberton
CASAMAJOR, Louis 6
CASANOWICZ, Immanuel 1
 Moses
CASE, Albert Hermon 5

CASE, Arthur Ellicott 2
CASE, Carl Delos 1
CASE, Charles H
CASE, Charles Clinton 4
CASE, Charles Orlando 4
CASE, Clarence Edwards 4
CASE, Clarence Marsh 2
CASE, Clifford Philip 1
CASE, Dwight Samuel 4
CASE, Eckstein 1
CASE, Ermine Cowles 5
CASE, Francis Higbee 4
CASE, Francis Owen 5
CASE, George Sessions 1
CASE, George Wilkinson 6
CASE, Harold Claude 4
CASE, Harold Clayton M. 4
CASE, Howard Gregory 2
CASE, J(ames) Herbert 4
CASE, James Herbert Jr. 4
CASE, James Thomas 4
CASE, Jerome Increase H
CASE, John Francis 4
CASE, Leonard * H
CASE, Lorenzo Dow 5
CASE, Mary Emily 4
CASE, Maurice 5
CASE, Nelson 1
CASE, Norman Stanley 4
CASE, Ralph E. 5
CASE, Rolland Webster 3
CASE, Shirley Jackson 2
CASE, Theodore Spencer 1
CASE, Walter H
CASE, Walter Summerhayes 1
CASE, William Scoville 1
CASEMENT, Dan Dillon 3
CASER, Ettore 3
CASESA, Philip Robert 5
CASEY, Charles Clinton 4
CASEY, Daniel Vincent 5
CASEY, Douglas 4
CASEY, Edward Pearce 1
CASEY, Francis de Sales 1
CASEY, George J. 4
CASEY, John Francis 2
CASEY, John J. 1
CASEY, John Schuyler 2
CASEY, Joseph H
CASEY, Lee 3
CASEY, Levi H
CASEY, Lyman R. 1
CASEY, Robert Joseph 4
CASEY, Robert Pierce 4
CASEY, Samuel Brown 4
CASEY, Silas 1
CASEY, Silas 1
CASEY, Thomas Lincoln 1
CASEY, William Joseph 3
CASEY, Zadoc H
CASH, Albert D. 3
CASH, James (Robert) 6
CASH, Wilbur Joseph 2
CASH, William Thomas 3
CASHEN, Thomas Cecil 1
CASHIN, John Martin 5
CASHMAN, Earl William 3
CASHMAN, Edwin James 5
CASHMAN, Joseph Thomas 1
CASHMORE, John 4
CASILEAR, John William 4
CASKEY, John Fletcher 4
CASKIE, John Samuels H
CASKIE, Marion Maxwell 1
CASKODEN, Edwin 1
CASLER, Lester Alonzo 6
CASON, Hulsey 3
CASPARI, Charles Edward 2
CASPARI, Charles Jr. 1
CASS, Alonzo Beecher 1
CASS, Charles Anderson 1
CASS, George Washington H
CASS, Joseph Kerr 1
CASS, Lewis H
CASS, Louis S. 4
CASSADY, John Howard 4
CASSADY, Morley Franklin 5
CASSADY, Thomas Gantz 4
CASSANDRA 3
CASSATT, Alexander 1
 Johnston
CASSATT, Mary 1
CASSEDY, George H
CASSEDY, John Irvin 1
CASSEL, Henry Burd 1
CASSEL, John H. 5
CASSELBERRY, William 1
 Evans
CASSELL, Wallace Lewis 1
CASSELMAN, Arthur Vale 3
CASSELS, Edwin Henry 2
CASSELS, Louis Welborn 6
CASSERLY, Eugene H
CASSIDY, George 4
 Livingston

CASSIDY, George Washington — 1
CASSIDY, George Williams — H
CASSIDY, Gerald — 1
CASSIDY, James E. — 3
CASSIDY, James H. — 5
CASSIDY, Leslie Martin — 4
CASSIDY, Lewis Cochran — 2
CASSIDY, M. Joseph — 3
CASSIDY, Massilon Alexander —
CASSIDY, William — H
CASSIDY, William Joseph — 6
CASSIL, Hurd Alexander — 6
CASSILL, Harold E. — 3
CASSILLY, Francis —
CASSILLY, Philip Jacquemn — 6
CASSIN, John — H
CASSIN, Rene — 6
CASSINGHAM, John W. — 4
CASSINGHAM, Roy B. — 4
CASSINO, Samuel Edson — 4
CASSIRER, Ernst — 4
CASSODAY, John B. —
CASSON, Herbert Newton — 5
CASTANEDA, Carlos Eduardo — 3
CASTEGNIER, Georges —
CASTELLANI, Aldo (Count of Chisimaio) — 5
CASTELLO, Eugene — 1
CASTELLO BRANCO, Humberto de Alencar — 4
CASTELLOW, Bryant Thomas — 5
CASTELNUOVO-TEDESCO, Mario — 5
CASTEN, Daniel Francis — 6
CASTER, George Brown — 5
CASTIGLIONI, Arturo — 4
CASTILLO, Ramon S. — 2
CASTILLO NAJERA, Francisco — 3
CASTLE, Alfred L. — 6
CASTLE, Edward Sears — 6
CASTLE, Eugene Winston — 3
CASTLE, Frederick Albert — 1
CASTLE, Harold Kainalu Long — 4
CASTLE, Henry Anson —
CASTLE, Homer Levi — 4
CASTLE, John H Jr. — 5
CASTLE, Kendall Brooks — 5
CASTLE, Lewis Gould — 4
CASTLE, Nicholas —
CASTLE, Samuel Northrup — 6
CASTLE, Vernon — 4
CASTLE, William —
CASTLE, William Ernest — 4
CASTLE, William Richards — 1
CASTLE, William Richards — 4
CASTLEBERRY, John Jackson —
CASTLEBERRY, Winston — 6
CASTLEMAN, Francis Lee Jr. — 3
CASTLEMAN, John Breckinridge — 1
CASTLEMAN, Virginia Carter — 3
CASTLEMON, Harry — 1
CASTLES, Alfred Guldo Rudolph — 2
CASTNER, Joseph Compton — 2
CASTO, C. Everett — 3
CASTON, Saul — 5
CASTRO, Americo — 5
CASTRO, Frank Monroe — 6
CASTRO, Hector David — 6
CASTRO, Jose — H
CASTRO, Matilde (Mrs. James H. Tufts) — 6
CASWELL, Albert Edward — 3
CASWELL, Alexis — H
CASWELL, Edward C. — 6
CASWELL, Irving A. — 4
CASWELL, Lucien B. —
CASWELL, Mary S. — 1
CASWELL, Richard — H
CASWELL, Thomas Hubbard — 1
CASWELL, Thomas Thompson — 1
CATCHINGS, Thomas Clendinen — 4
CATCHINGS, Waddill — 4
CATE, Horace Nelson —
CATE, Roscoe Simmons Jr. — 4
CATES, Charles Theodore Jr. — 1
CATES, Clifton Bledsoe — 5
CATES, Gordon Dell — 5
CATES, Junius Sidney — 3
CATES, Louis Shattuck — 3
CATES, Walter Thruston — 5

CATESBY, Mark — H
CATHCART, Arthur Martin — 2
CATHCART, Charles Sanderson — 2
CATHCART, Charles William — H
CATHCART, James Leander — H
CATHCART, Robert Spann — 2
CATHCART, Stanley H. — 3
CATHCART, Thomas Edward (Tom Cathcart) — 5
CATHCART, Wallace Hugh — 4
CATHCART, William — 1
CATHCART, William Ledyard —
CATHELL, Daniel Webster — 4
CATHELL, William T. — 4
CATHER, David Clark — 4
CATHER, Willa Sibert — 2
CATHERWOOD, Mary Hartwell — 1
CATHLES, Lawrence Maclagan — 5
CATLIN, Albertus Wright — 1
CATLIN, Charles Albert — 1
CATLIN, George — H
CATLIN, George Smith — 1
CATLIN, Henry Guy — 4
CATLIN, Isaac Swartwood — 1
CATLIN, Louise Ensign — 4
CATLIN, Randolph — 1
CATLIN, Robert Mayo — 1
CATLIN, Roy George — 1
CATLIN, Theron Ephron — 1
CATLIN, Warren Benjamin — 5
CATON, Arthur J. — 1
CATON, Harry Anderson — 6
CATON, John Dean — H
CATOR, George — 1
CATRON, Charles Christopher — 4
CATRON, John — H
CATRON, Thomas Benton — 1
CATT, Carrie Chapman — 2
CATT, George William — 1
CATTELL, Alexander Gilmore — H
CATTELL, Edward James — 1
CATTELL, Henry Ware — 1
CATTELL, James McKeen — 2
CATTELL, Jaques — 4
CATTELL, Richard Bartley Channing — 4
CATTELL, William Ashburner — 1
CATTELL, William Cassaday — H
CATTELLE, Wallis Richard — 1
CATTERALL, Ralph Charles Henry —
CATTO, Thomas Sivewright, Lord — 6
CATTON, Charles Jr. — H
CATTS, Sidney Johnston — 1
CAUFFMAN, Frank Guernsey — 4
CAULDWELL, Frederic Wadsworth — 5
CAULDWELL, John Britton — 4
CAULDWELL, Leslie Giffen — 1
CAULDWELL, Oscar Ray — 3
CAULFIELD, Bernard Gregory — H
CAULFIELD, Henry Stewart — 4
CAULFIELD, John Francis — 6
CAULK, John Roberts —
CAULLERY, Maurice Jules Gaston Corneille — 3
CAUSEY, James Campbell Jr. — 6
CAUSEY, William Bowdoin — 1
CAUSIN, John M. S. — H
CAUTHORN, Joseph Lurton — 5
CAVADAS, Athenagoras — 4
CAVAGNARO, James Francis — 5
CAVAGNARO, Robert John — 5
CAVALIERI, Lina (Mrs. Lucien Muratore) — 5
CAVALLARO, Joseph B. — 3
CAVALLITO, Albino — 4
CAVAN, Marie (Mary Cawein) — 5
CAVANA, Martin — 4
CAVANAGH, C. J. — 5
CAVANAGH, John Alexis — 6
CAVANAUGH, James Michael — H
CAVANAUGH, John William —

CAVANAUGH, John William — 5
CAVANAUGH, Robert Joseph — 4
CAVE, Edward Powell — 3
CAVE, H. W. — 3
CAVE, Henry Wisdom — 4
CAVE, Reuben Lindsay — 4
CAVELIER, Robert — H
CAVERNO, Charles — 1
CAVICCHIA, Peter Angelo — 4
CAVINS, Lorimer Victor — 2
CAWEIN, Madison Julius — 1
CAWL, Franklin Robert — 4
CAWLEY, Edgar Moore — 5
CAWLEY, Robert Ralston — 6
CAWTHORN, Joseph Bridger — 2
CAYCE, Edgar — 4
CAYLOR, John — 4
CAYTON, Horace Roscoe — 6
CAYVAN, Georgia — 1
CAYWOOD, Roland Blanchard — 3
CAZEDESSUS, Eugene Romain — 1
CAZENOVE, Theophile — H
CAZIARC, Louis Vasmer — 1
CECIL, Charles Purcell — 3
CECIL, George W. — 5
CECIL, James McCosh — 3
CECIL, John Giles — 1
CECIL, Lamar — 3
CECIL, Russell — 1
CECIL, Russell LaFayette — 3
CECIL OF CHELWOOD, Viscount — 3
CEDERBERG, William Emanuel — 5
CEDERGREN, Hugo — 5
CEDERSTROM, Albert Gustaf — 4
CEHRS, Charles Harold — 5
CEKADA, Emil Bogomir — 5
CELENTANO, William C. — 5
CELERON DE BLAINVILLE, Pierre Joseph de — H
CELINE, Louis Ferdinand — 4
CELL, George C. — 1
CELL, John W(esley) — 5
CELLA, John G. — 5
CELLINI, Renato — 4
CERACCHI, Guiseppe — H
CERF, Barry * — 2
CERF, Bennett Alfred — 5
CERF, Edward Owen — 3
CERF, Jay Henry — 6
CERMAK, Anton Joseph — 1
CERRACCHIO, Enrico Filiberto —
CERRE, Jean Gabriel — H
CESNOLA, Louis Palma Di — 1
CESPEDES Y ORTIZ, Carlos Miguel — 3
CESSNA, John — H
CESSNA, Orange Howard — 1
CESTARO, Michael Paul — 6
CHABRAT, Guy Ignatius — H
CHACE, Arnold Buffum — 1
CHACE, Arthur Freeborn — 1
CHACE, Elizabeth Buffum — H
CHACE, George Hart — 3
CHACE, Jonathan — 1
CHACE, Malcolmn Greene — 5
CHACE, William N(iels) — 6
CHADBOURN, Erlon R. — 4
CHADBOURN, William Hobbs Jr. — 4
CHADBOURNE, George Storrs — 1
CHADBOURNE, Paul Ansel — H
CHADBOURNE, Thomas Lincoln — 1
CHADBOURNE, William Merriam — 4
CHADDOCK, Charles Gilbert — 1
CHADDOCK, Robert Emmet — 1
CHADSEY, Charles Ernest — 1
CHADWICK, Charles Wesley — 3
CHADWICK, Charles — H
CHADWICK, Clarence Wells —
CHADWICK, E. Wallace — 4
CHADWICK, French Ensor — 1
CHADWICK, George Halcott — 3
CHADWICK, George Whitefield — 1
CHADWICK, Henry Dexter — 5
CHADWICK, James — 6
CHADWICK, James Carroll — 6

CHADWICK, James Read — 1
CHADWICK, John Raymond — 4
CHADWICK, John White — 1
CHADWICK, Lee Sherman — 5
CHADWICK, Leigh E(dward) — 6
CHADWICK, Stephen Fowler — 6
CHADWICK, Stephen James —
CHAFEE, Adna Romanza — 1
CHAFEE, Henry Sharpe — 4
CHAFEE, Zechariah Jr. — 5
CHAFER, Lewis Sperry — 3
CHAFFE, Henry Hansell — 5
CHAFFEE, Adna Romanza — 4
CHAFFEE, Arthur Billings — 4
CHAFFEE, Calvin Clifford — H
CHAFFEE, Emory Leon — 6
CHAFFEE, Jerome Bunty — H
CHAFFEE, Jerome Stuart — 5
CHAFFEE, Robert Emory — 6
CHAFFEE, Roger B. — 4
CHAFFEY, Andrew M. — 1
CHAFFEY, George — 1
CHAFFIN, Lucien Gates — 1
CHAFIN, Eugene Wilder — 1
CHAILLE, Stanford Emerson —
CHAILLE-LONG, Charles — 1
CHAINEY, George — 4
CHAISSON, John Robert — 5
CHALFANT, Alexander Steele — 4
CHALFANT, Harry Malcolm — 1
CHALIAPIN, Feodor — 1
CHALIFOUR, Joseph Onesime — 3
CHALKLEY, Lyman — 1
CHALKLEY, Otway H. — 3
CHALKLEY, Thomas — H
CHALLENER, William Albert — 4
CHALLIS, John — 6
CHALMERS, Allan Knight — 5
CHALMERS, Gordon Keith — 3
CHALMERS, Harvey 2d — 5
CHALMERS, Henry — 3
CHALMERS, Hugh — 1
CHALMERS, James — 1
CHALMERS, James Ronald — H
CHALMERS, Joseph — H
CHALMERS, Louis Henry — 4
CHALMERS, Robert Scott — 1
CHALMERS, Stephen — 1
CHALMERS, Thomas — 1
CHALMERS, Thomas Clark — 4
CHALMERS, Thomas Hardie —
CHALMERS, Thomas Mitchell — 2
CHALMERS, Thomas Stuart —
CHALMERS, William Everett —
CHALMERS, William James —
CHALMERS, William Wallace — 4
CHAMBELLAN, Rene Paul — 3
CHAMBERLAIN, Abiram — 1
CHAMBERLAIN, Alexander Francis — 1
CHAMBERLAIN, Allen — 1
CHAMBERLAIN, Arthur Henry — 2
CHAMBERLAIN, Arthur Van Doorn — 5
CHAMBERLAIN, Charles Joseph —
CHAMBERLAIN, Clark Wells — 2
CHAMBERLAIN, Clarke E. S. —
CHAMBERLAIN, Daniel Henry — 1
CHAMBERLAIN, Dwight Lincoln — 3
CHAMBERLAIN, Ebenzer Mattoon — H
CHAMBERLAIN, Eugene Tyler —
CHAMBERLAIN, Francis Asbury —
CHAMBERLAIN, Frank — 1
CHAMBERLAIN, Frederick Stanley — 1
CHAMBERLAIN, George Agnew — 4
CHAMBERLAIN, George Earle —
CHAMBERLAIN, Glenn R. — 3
CHAMBERLAIN, Henry — 1

CHAMBERLAIN, Henry Richardson — 1
CHAMBERLAIN, Henry Thomas — 4
CHAMBERLAIN, Herbert Marvin — 3
CHAMBERLAIN, Hiram Sanborn —
CAMBERLAIN, Mrs. Hope Summerell — 5
CHAMBERLAIN, Isaac Dearborn — 1
CHAMBERLAIN, Jacob — 1
CHAMBERLAIN, Jacob Payson — H
CHAMBERLAIN, James Franklin — 2
CHAMBERLAIN, James Mortimer Wills — 6
CHAMBERLAIN, John Curtis — H
CHAMBERLAIN, John Loomis — 2
CHAMBERLAIN, John M. — 3
CHAMBERLAIN, Joseph Perkins — 3
CHAMBERLAIN, Joseph Scudder — 5
CHAMBERLAIN, Joshua Lawrence — 1
CHAMBERLAIN, Leander Trowbridge — 1
CHAMBERLAIN, Lucy Jefferies — 5
CHAMBERLAIN, Mary Crowninshield Endicott —
CHAMBERLAIN, Mellen — 1
CHAMBERLAIN, Montague — 1
CHAMBERLAIN, Nathan Henry — H
CHAMBERLAIN, Orville Tryon — 4
CHAMBERLAIN, Oscar Pearl —
CHAMBERLAIN, Paul Mellen — 1
CHAMBERLAIN, Richard Hall — 6
CHAMBERLAIN, Robert F. — 4
CHAMBERLAIN, Samuel — 6
CHAMBERLAIN, Samuel Selwyn — 1
CHAMBERLAIN, W. Lawrence — 4
CHAMBERLAIN, William — H
CHAMBERLAIN, William Isaac — 1
CHAMBERLAIN, William W. — 2
CHAMBERLAIN, Winthrop Burr — 4
CHAMBERLAINE, William — 1
CHAMBERLAYNE, Catharine Jane — 1
CHAMBERLAYNE, Churchill Gibson —
CHAMBERLAYNE, Lewis Parke —
CHAMBERLIN, Chester Harvey — 1
CHAMBERLIN, Clayton Jenkins — 4
CHAMBERLIN, Edson Joseph — 4
CHAMBERLIN, F. Tolles — 1
CHAMBERLIN, Frederick — 2
CHAMBERLIN, George Ellsworth — 5
CHAMBERLIN, Harry Dwight — 2
CHAMBERLIN, Henry Barrett —
CHAMBERLIN, Henry Harmon — 3
CHAMBERLIN, Joseph Edgar — 1
CHAMBERLIN, Joseph Hanson — 3
CHAMBERLIN, McKendree Hypes — 4
CHAMBERLIN, Ralph Vary — 6
CHAMBERLIN, Rollin Thomas — 2
CHAMBERLIN, Stephen J. — 5
CHAMBERLIN, Thomas Chrowder — 1
CHAMBERLIN, Walter Howard — 4
CHAMBERLIN, William H(enry) — 4
CHAMBERLIN, Willis Arden — 4

488

CHATBURN, George Richard 1
CHATFIELD, Thomas Ives 1
CHATFIELD, Walter Henry 1
CHATFIELD, William Hayden 5
CHATFIELD-TAYLOR, Hobart C. 2
CHATHAM, 1st earl H
CHATHAM, Thurmond 3
CHATTERS, Carl Hallack 4
CHATTERTON, Fenimore 3
CHATTERTON, Ruth 4
CHAUMONOT, Pierre Joseph Marie H
CHAUNCEY, Isaac H
CHAUNCY, Charles * H
CHAUTEMPS, Camille 4
CHAUVENET, Regis 1
CHAUVENET, William H
CHAUVENET, William Marc 4
CHAVE, Ernest J. 4
CHAVEZ, Dennis 4
CHAVIS, John 4
CHEADLE, John Begg 4
CHEATHAM, Benjamin Franklin 4
CHEATHAM, Elliott Evans 5
CHEATHAM, John Henry 3
CHEATHAM, Owen Robertson 5
CHEATHAM, Richard H
CHEATNAM, B. Frank 2
CHEATNAM, Joseph J. 2
CHEATUM, Elmer Philip 4
CHEAVENS, David Anderson 5
CHECKLEY, John H
CHEEK, F. J. Jr. 3
CHEEK, Robert Stanley 4
CHEER, Miss H
CHEESMAN, Forman H
CHEESMAN, William James 6
CHEETHAM, James H
CHEEVER, David 3
CHEEVER, David Williams 1
CHEEVER, Ezekiel H
CHEEVER, George Barrell H
CHEEVER, Harriet A. 1
CHEEVER, Henry Theodore H
CHEFFETZ, Asa 4
CHEFFEY, John Howard 5
CHEHAB, Fuad 5
CHEKIB, Bey 4
CHELDELIN, Vernon H. 4
CHELEY, Frank Howbert 4
CHEN, Yi 5
CHENERY, Christopher Tompkins 5
CHENERY, William Elisha 5
CHENERY, William Ludlow 6
CHENERY, Winthrop Holt 3
CHENEY, Albert Nelson 1
CHENEY, Archibald Myron 3
CHENEY, Azio E. 1
CHENEY, Benjamin Austin 5
CHENEY, Benjamin Pierce H
CHENEY, Charles 2
CHENEY, Charles Baldwin 3
CHENEY, Charles Edward 1
CHENEY, Charles Henry 2
CHENEY, Clarence Orion 2
CHENEY, Clifford D. 2
CHENEY, Ednah Dow 1
CHENEY, Elmer Erwood 1
CHENEY, Frank D. 6
CHENEY, Frank Jr. 5
CHENEY, Frank Woodbridge 1
CHENEY, Harold Clark 4
CHENEY, Howell 3
CHENEY, James William 1
CHENEY, Jerome Lucius 4
CHENEY, John H
CHENEY, John Moses 1
CHENEY, John Richard 4
CHENEY, John Vance 1
CHENEY, Louis Richmond 2
CHENEY, Monroe George 6
CHENEY, Orion Howard 2
CHENEY, Person Colby 1
CHENEY, Russell 2
CHENEY, Seth Wells H
CHENEY, Sherwood Alfred 2
CHENEY, Thomas Perkins 2
CHENEY, Ward H
CHENEY, Ward 4
CHENEY, Warren 1
CHENEY, William Atwell 1
CHENEY, William Fitch 4
CHENG, Chen 5
CHENNAULT, Claire Lee 4

CHENOWETH, Alexander Crawford 1
CHENOWETH, Caroline van Deusen 4
CHENOWETH, Catherine Richardson 1
CHENOWETH, David Macpherson 5
CHENTUNG, Liang-Cheng Sir 5
CHERINGTON, Charles Richards 4
CHERINGTON, Paul Terry 3
CHERINGTON, Paul Whiton 6
CHERNICK, Jack 6
CHERONIS, Nicholas Dimitrius 4
CHERRIE, George Kruck 2
CHERRINGTON, Ernest Hurst 2
CHERRINGTON, Virgil Arthur 6
CHERRY, C. Waldo 2
CHERRY, Charles 4
CHERRY, Francis A. 4
CHERRY, Henry Hardin 1
CHERRY, Howard H. 6
CHERRY, James William 2
CHERRY, Kathryn Evelyn 1
CHERRY, Lloyd Benjamin 6
CHERRY, Robert Gregg 3
CHERRY, Thomas Crittenden 4
CHERRY, Ulysses Simpson Grant 2
CHERRY, Walter L. 2
CHERRY, Wilbur Harkness 3
CHERRY, William Stamps 6
CHERWELL, 1st Baron of Oxford 3
CHESEBROUGH, Caroline H
CHESEBROUGH, Robert Augustus 1
CHESEN, Doris Schimmel 6
CHESHIRE, Fleming Duncan 1
CHESHIRE, Joseph Blount 1
CHESLEY, Albert Justus 4
CHESNEY, Alan Mason 4
CHESNEY, Cummings C. 2
CHESNUT, James Jr. H
CHESNUT, James Lyons 2
CHESNUT, Victor King 1
CHESNUT, William Calvin 4
CHESNUTT, Charles Waddell 1
CHESNUTT, Nelson Alexander 5
CHESSIN, Alexander 4
CHESTER, Albert Huntington 1
CHESTER, Alden 1
CHESTER, Colby Mitchel * 4
CHESTER, Colby Mitchell 1
CHESTER, Colby Mitchell 4
CHESTER, Edmund A(lbert) Sr. 6
CHESTER, Eliza 1
CHESTER, Frank Dyer 1
CHESTER, Frederick Dixon 2
CHESTER, George Randolph 1
CHESTER, Hawley Thomas 3
CHESTER, John Needels 5
CHESTER, Joseph Lemuel H
CHESTER, K(enneth) Starr 4
CHESTER, Samuel Hall 1
CHESTER, Wayland Morgan 3
CHESTER, William Merrill 4
CHESTERMAN, Francis John 4
CHESTERMAN, William Dallas 1
CHESTON, J. Hamilton 4
CHESTON, Radcliffe Jr. 5
CHETLAIN, Arthur Henry 4
CHETLAIN, Augustus Louis 1
CHETTA, Nicholas John 5
CHETWOOD, Charles Howard 5
CHETWOOD, John 4
CHETWOOD, William H
CHEVALIER, John B. 3
CHEVALIER, Maurice (Auguste) 5
CHEVALIER, Stuart 4
CHEVALIER, Willard Townsend 4
CHEVEE, Charles Humbert 4
CHEVER, James W. H
CHEVERTON, Cecil Frank 3

CHEVERUS, Jean Louis Anne Magdelene Lefebre de H
CHEVES, Langdon H
CHEVIGNY, Hector 4
CHEVRIER, Edgar Rodolphe Eugene 4
CHEW, Benjamin H
CHEW, Beverly 1
CHEW, Ng Poon 1
CHEW, Oswald 2
CHEW, Samuel Claggett 1
CHEW, Samuel Claggett 3
CHEWNING, Edmund Taylor 5
CHEYDLEUR, Frederic Daniel 2
CHEYNEY, Barton 4
CHEYNEY, Edward Gheen 2
CHEYNEY, Edward Potts 2
CHEZ, Joseph 5
CHIANG KAI-SHEK (CHIANG CHUNG-CHENG) 6
CHICHESTER, Richard Henry Lee 1
CHICHESTER, Sir Francis 5
CHICKERING, Allen 3
CHICKERING, Charles A. 1
CHICKERING, John White 1
CHICKERING, Jonas H
CHICKERING, William Elbridge 3
CHIDESTER, John Young 3
CHIDLEY, Howard James 4
CHIDSEY, Thomas McKeen 3
CHIDWICK, John Patrick Sylvester 1
CHIEF JOSEPH H
CHIERA, Edward 1
CHIFLEY, The Rt Hon Joseph Benedict 4
CHILBERG, John Edward 3
CHILCOTE, Sanford Marshall 6
CHILCOTT, Ellery Channing 1
CHILCOTT, George Miles H
CHILD, Charles Manning 3
CHILD, Clarence Griffin 2
CHILD, Clement Dexter 1
CHILD, David Lee H
CHILD, Edwin Burrage 1
CHILD, Eleanor Dodge 2
CHILD, Elias Earle 6
CHILD, Francis James H
CHILD, Frank Samuel 1
CHILD, Fred S. 4
CHILD, George Newport 1
CHILD, Katherine Blake 3
CHILD, Lydia Maria Francis H
CHILD, Richard Washburn 1
CHILD, Thomas Jr. H
CHILDE, John H
CHILDERS, James Saxon 4
CHILDERS, Marvin Alonzo 4
CHILDERS, Sylvester Earl 2
CHILDRESS, John Whitsitt 1
CHILDRESS, Levi Wade 2
CHILDS, Arthur Edward 1
CHILDS, C. Frederick 3
CHILDS, Cephas Grier H
CHILDS, Donald Smythe 4
CHILDS, Edward Powell 5
CHILDS, Eleanor Stuart 1
CHILDS, Eversley 1
CHILDS, Francis Lane 6
CHILDS, Frank Aiken 4
CHILDS, Frank Hall 3
CHILDS, Geoffrey Stafford 3
CHILDS, George Theodore 4
CHILDS, George William H
CHILDS, Harwood Lawrence 5
CHILDS, Henry A. 1
CHILDS, John Lewis 4
CHILDS, Joseph William 4
CHILDS, Prescott 3
CHILDS, Ross Renfroe 2
CHILDS, Samuel Beresford 4
CHILDS, Thomas H
CHILDS, Thomas Spencer 4
CHILDS, Timothy H
CHILDS, William Hamlin 1
CHILES, Harry Linden 2
CHILES, James Alburn 5
CHILES, Joseph B. H
CHILES, Wilma Klein 6
CHILLMAN, James Jr. 5
CHILTON, Arthur Bounds 4
CHILTON, Cecil Hamilton 5
CHILTON, Cleo Madison 5
CHILTON, Horace 1
CHILTON, J. Matt 6

CH!LTON, Robert S. 2
CHILTON, Samuel H
CHILTON, Thomas H
CHILTON, Thomas Hamilton 5
CHILTON, William Edwin 1
CHILTON, William Edwin Jr. 3
CHILTON, William Paris 1
CHILTON, William Ransdell 6
CHINARD, Gilbert 5
CHINDBLOM, Carl Richard 3
CHING, Cyrus Stuart 4
CHING, Cyrus Stuart 5
CHINLUND, Edwin F. 3
CHINN, Armstrong 3
CHINN, C. B. 3
CHINN, Joseph William H
CHINN, Joseph William 4
CHINN, Thomas Withers H
CHINOY, Ely 6
CHIPERFIELD, Burnett Mitchell 1
CHIPERFIELD, Robert Bruce 5
CHIPMAN, Daniel H
CHIPMAN, John Logan H
CHIPMAN, John Smith 1
CHIPMAN, John Sniffen 1
CHIPMAN, Nathaniel H
CHIPMAN, Norris Bowie 3
CHIPMAN, Norton Parker 1
CHIPMAN, Ward H
CHIPMAN, William Pendleton 1
CHIRSMEN, James Stone H
CHIRSTIE, Gabriel H
CHIRUG, James Thomas 5
CHISHOLM, Hugh J. 1
CHISHOLM, Hugh J. 3
CHISHOLM, Julian J. 5
CHISHOLM, Sir Joseph Andrew 3
CHISHOLM, William 1
CHISHOLM, William Sr. 1
CHISLETT, Howard Roy 1
CHISOLM, Alexander Robert H
CHISOLM, Alexander Robert 4
CHISOLM, John Julian H
CHISUM, John Simpson H
CHITTENDEN, Frank Hurlbut 1
CHITTENDEN, Hiram Martin 1
CHITTENDEN, J. Brace 1
CHITTENDEN, Kate S. 2
CHITTENDEN, Martin H
CHITTENDEN, Russell Henry 2
CHITTENDEN, Simeon Baldwin H
CHITTENDEN, Thomas H
CHITTENDEN, Thomas Cotton H
CHITTENDEN, William Lawrence 1
CHITWOOD, Joseph Howard 1
CHITWOOD, Oliver Perry 5
CHIVERS, Elijah Eynon 1
CHIVERS, Thomas Holley H
CHIVINGTON, John Milton H
CHOATE, Augusta 5
CHOATE, Charles Francis 1
CHOATE, Charles Francis Jr. 1
CHOATE, Emett Clay 6
CHOATE, Isaac Bassett 4
CHOATE, Isaac W. 4
CHOATE, Joseph Hodges 4
CHOATE, Joseph Hodges Jr. 4
CHOATE, Joseph Kittredge 1
CHOATE, Nathaniel 4
CHOATE, Robert Burnett 4
CHOATE, Rufus H
CHOATE, Washington 4
CHOATE, William Gardner 1
CHODORCOFF, William 4
CHODOROV, Frank 4
CHOLMELEY-JONES, R. G. 1
CHOMMIE, John Campbell 6
CHOPIN, Kate 1
CHOQUETTE, Charles Auguste 4
CHORIS, Ludovik H
CHORLEY, Kenneth 6
CHORPENNING, George H
CHOTINER, Murray M. 6
CHOTZINOFF, Samuel 4

CHOU EN-LAI 6
CHOUINARD, Carroll 5
CHOUINARD, Mrs. Nelbert Murphy 5
CHOULES, John Overton H
CHOUTEAU, Jean Pierre H
CHOUTEAU, Pierre H
CHOUTEAU, Pierre 1
CHOUTEAU, Pierre Auguste H
CHOUTEAU, Rene H
CHOVET, Abraham H
CHOW, Bacon Field 6
CHREITZBERG, Augustus McKee 5
CHRESTMAN, Marion Nelson 2
CHRISMAN, Arthur Bowie 3
CHRISMAN, Edward Robert 3
CHRISMAN, Lewis Herbert 4
CHRISMAN, Oscar 1
CHRIST, Harding Simon 5
CHRISTENBERRY, Charles W. 6
CHRISTENBERRY, Herbert William 6
CHRISTENBERRY, Robert Keaton 5
CHRISTENSEN, Asher Norman 4
CHRISTENSEN, Bernard Victor 3
CHRISTENSEN, Erwin Ottomar 6
CHRISTENSEN, George Francis 5
CHRISTENSEN, J. J. 5
CHRISTENSEN, John Cornelius 3
CHRISTENSEN, Niels Anton 5
CHRISTENSEN, Niels Parker 3
CHRISTENSEN, Parley 1
CHRISTENSON, Carroll Lawrence 6
CHRISTENSON, John August 2
CHRISTENSON, Louis P. 4
CHRISTENSON, Walter E. 5
CHRISTIAN, Andrew Dunscomb 2
CHRISTIAN, Edmund Adolph 1
CHRISTIAN, Eugene 1
CHRISTIAN, Frank Lamar 4
CHRISTIAN, George Busby Jr. 5
CHRISTIAN, George Eastland 1
CHRISTIAN, George Llewellyn 1
CHRISTIAN, Henry Asbury 4
CHRISTIAN, John L. 5
CHRISTIAN, John Tyler 1
CHRISTIAN, Palmer 2
CHRISTIAN, Robert J. 4
CHRISTIAN, Sanders Lewis 2
CHRISTIAN, William H
CHRISTIAN, William Peter 2
CHRISTIANCY, Isaac Peckham H
CHRISTIANS, William F. 3
CHRISTIANSEN, Arthur 4
CHRISTIANSEN, Edward S IV 5
CHRISTIANSEN, F. Melius 3
CHRISTIANSEN, N. Woodruff 4
CHRISTIANSON, Adolph Marcus 5
CHRISTIANSON, John Oscar 6
CHRISTIANSON, Theodore 3
CHRISTIANSON, Theodore Clarissa 6
CHRISTIE, Agatha Mary 6
CHRISTIE, Alexander 1
CHRISTIE, Alexander Graham 4
CHRISTIE, Arthur Carlisle 3
CHRISTIE, Charles Johnson 4
CHRISTIE, Dan Edwin 6
CHRISTIE, Francis Albert 4
CHRISTIE, George Irving 5
CHRISTIE, James 1
CHRISTIE, Jane Johnstone 1
CHRISTIE, John Watson 2
CHRISTIE, Lansdell Kisner 4
CHRISTIE, Luther Rice 6
CHRISTIE, R. E. 3
CHRISTIE, Robert 1
CHRISTIE, Robert James 4
CHRISTIE, Thomas Davidson 1

CHRISTIE, William Wallace 1
CHRISTISON, J. Sanderson 1
CHRIST-JANER, Albert 6
  William
CHRISTMAN, Charles E. 4
CHRISTMAN, Henry Jacob 2
CHRISTMAN, W. W. 1
CHRISTMAN, Warren 2
  Ursinus
CHRISTOL, Carl
CHRISTOPHER, Frederick 4
CHRISTOPHER, George H. 3
CHRISTOPHER, George T. 3
CHRISTOPHER, William 6
  Rodolphus
CHRISTOPHERSON, 3
  Charles Andrew
CHRISTY, David H
CHRISTY, Earl 4
CHRISTY, Edwin P. 6
CHRISTY, Howard 3
  Chandler
CHRISTY, Samuel Benedict 1
CHRISTY, William C. 3
CHRITTON, George Alvah 2
CHRYSLER, Jack Forker 3
CHRYSLER, Mintin Asbury 5
CHRYSLER, Walter Percy 1
CHRYST, Robert D. 3
CHRYSTIE, Thomas 3
  Ludlow
CHRYSTIE, Thomas Witter 3
CHU, Lan Jen 6
CHUBB, Chester Niles 5
CHUBB, Edwin Watts 4
CHUBB, Hendon 4
CHUBB, Lewis Warrington 3
CHUBB, Percival 4
CHUBB, Thomas Caldecot 5
CHUBBUCK, Thomas 3
CHUJOY, Anatole 5
CHUNDRIGAR, Ismail 4
  Ibrahim
CHUPP, Charles David 5
CHURCH, Alonzo H
CHURCH, Alonzo 1
CHURCH, Aloysius 6
  Stanislaus
CHURCH, Angelica 3
  Schuyler
CHURCH, Archibald 4
CHURCH, Arthur Latham 1
CHURCH, Augustus 1
  Byington
CHURCH, Benjamin * H
CHURCH, Benjamin Butler 3
CHURCH, Denver Samuel 3
CHURCH, Earl D. 1
CHURCH, Edward Bentley 1
Jr.
CHURCH, Edwin Fayette 6
CHURCH, Elihu 6
CHURCH, Francis 1
  Pharcellus
CHURCH, Frank Henry 1
CHURCH, Frederick Edwin 1
CHURCH, Frederick Stuart 1
CHURCH, George Dudley 6
CHURCH, George Hervey 1
CHURCH, Henry Ward 4
CHURCH, Irving Porter 1
CHURCH, James Edward 1
CHURCH, John Adams 1
CHURCH, John Fertig 1
CHURCH, John Huston 3
CHURCH, Melville 1
CHURCH, Pharcellus H
CHURCH, Ralph Edwin 2
CHURCH, Randolph 6
CHURCH, Richard Cassius 6
CHURCH, Samuel Harden 1
CHURCH, William Conant 1
CHURCH, William E. 1
CHURCH, William Howell 1
CHURCHILL, Alfred Vance 2
CHURCHILL, Charles 1
  Samuel
CHURCHILL, Edward 5
  Delos
CHURCHILL, Everett 3
  Avery
CHURCHILL, Frank Edwin 2
CHURCHILL, Frank 4
  Spooner
CHURCHILL, George 1
  Bosworth
CHURCHILL, George 5
  Morton
CHURCHILL, Henry Stern 4
CHURCHILL, John Charles 1
CHURCHILL, John Wesley 1
CHURCHILL, Joseph 1
  Richmond
CHURCHILL, Julius Alonzo 4
CHURCHILL, Lady 1
  Randolph Spencer

CHURCHILL, Lida A. 5
CHURCHILL, Marlborough 2
CHURCHILL, Ralph Loren 6
CHURCHILL, Sir Winston 4
CHURCHILL, Thomas J. 1
CHURCHILL, Thomas 1
  William
CHURCHILL, William 1
CHURCHILL, Winston 2
CHURCHMAN, John 1
  Woolman
CHURCHMAN, Philip 5
  Hudson
CHURCHMAN, William H
  Henry
CHURCHWELL, William H
  Montgomery
CHUTE, A(aron) Hamilton 5
CHUTE, Arthur Hunt 1
CHUTE, Arthur Lambert 1
CHUTE, Charles Lionel 3
CHUTE, Horatio Nelson 1
CHWOROWSKY, Martin 6
  Philip
CIANCA, Bernard Joseph 6
CICOGNANI, Amleto 6
  Giovanni
CILLEY, Bradbury H
CILLEY, C. C. 5
CILLEY, Gordon Harper 1
CILLEY, Greenleaf 1
CILLEY, Jonathan 1
  Longfellow
CILLEY, Jonathan Prince 1
CILLEY, Joseph * H
CIMIOTTI, Gustave 5
CINELLI, Albert Arthur 6
CIOBANU, Ioan 5
CIOCCO, Antonio 5
CIPOLLARO, Anthony 6
  Caesar
CIST, Charles * 1
CIST, Henry Martyn 1
CIST, Jacob 1
CLAASSEN, Peter Walter 1
CLABAUGH, Harry M. 1
CLABAUGH, Hinton 2
  Graves
CLAESSENS, Maria 6
CLAFLIN, Arthur Whitman 1
CLAFLIN, Horace Brigham H
CLAFLIN, John 1
CLAFLIN, W(alter) Harold 6
CLAFLIN, William 1
CLAGETT, Clifton 1
CLAGETT, John Rozier 1
CLAGETT, Wyseman H
CLAGHORN, George 1
CLAGHORN, Kate 1
  Holladay
CLAGUE, Frank 3
CLAIBORNE, John H
CLAIBORNE, John Francis H
  Hamtramck
CLAIBORNE, John Herbert 1
CLAIBORNE, Nathaniel H
  Herbert
CLAIBORNE, Thomas * H
CLAIBORNE, William H
CLAIBORNE, William H
  Charles Coles
CLAIBORNE, William 1
  Stirling
CLAIR, Edward L. 3
CLAIR, Matthew Wesley 2
CLAIRE, Richard Shaw 5
CLAMER, Guilliam Henry 4
CLANCY, Albert 4
  Worthington
CLANCY, Frank J. 3
CLANCY, Frank Willey 1
CLANCY, George 4
  Carpenter
CLANCY, John Richard 1
CLANCY, John W. 5
CLANCY, Robert H. 4
CLAP, Nathaniel H
CLAP, Thoms H
CLAPHAM, Thomas 4
CLAPP, Asa H
CLAPP, Asa William Henry H
CLAPP, Augustus Wilson 2
CLAPP, Charles Horace 1
CLAPP, Clift Rogers 1
CLAPP, Clyde Alvin 3
CLAPP, Cornelia Maria 1
CLAPP, Earle Hart 5
CLAPP, Edward Bull 1
CLAPP, Edwin Jones 1
CLAPP, Elmer Frederick 1
CLAPP, Frank Leslie 1
CLAPP, Franklin Halsted 2
CLAPP, Frederick Gardner 4
CLAPP, Gordon Rufus 4
CLAPP, Harold L. 4
CLAPP, Henry Austin 1

CLAPP, Herbert Codman 1
CLAPP, Jacob Crawford 4
CLAPP, John Mantle 5
CLAPP, Margaret 6
CLAPP, Moses Edwin 1
CLAPP, Paul Spencer 3
CLAPP, Philip Greeley 3
CLAPP, Verner Warren 5
CLAPP, William Warland H
CLAPPER, Raymond 2
CLAPPER, Samuel Mott 1
  Duryea
CLARAHAN, Leo E. 4
CLARDY, John D. 4
CLARDY, Kit 4
CLARE, Arthur James 1
CLARE, Israel Smith 1
CLARITY, Frank Edmund 4
CLARK, A. Howard 1
CLARK, Abraham H
CLARK, Addison 4
CLARK, Albert 3
  Montgomery
CLARK, Albert Warren 1
CLARK, Alden Hyde 4
CLARK, Alfred Edward 3
CLARK, Allan 3
CLARK, Allan Jay 3
CLARK, Allen Culling 2
CLARK, Alson Skinner 2
CLARK, Alva Benson 5
CLARK, Alvan H
CLARK, Alvan Graham H
CLARK, Ambrose Williams H
CLARK, Andrew Hill 6
CLARK, Anne Kinnier 4
CLARK, Annie Maria 4
  Lawrence
CLARK, Anson Luman 3
CLARK, Arthur Bridgman 2
CLARK, Arthur Bryan 1
CLARK, Arthur Elwood 2
CLARK, Arthur Henry 1
CLARK, Austin Hobart 1
CLARK, B. Preston 1
CLARK, Badger 1
CLARK, Barrett H. 1
CLARK, Barzilla Worth 2
CLARK, Bennett Champ 3
CLARK, Bert Boone 5
CLARK, Bobby 5
CLARK, Bonnell Wetmore 5
CLARK, C. P. 4
CLARK, Calvin Montague 2
CLARK, Cameron 3
CLARK, Caroline Richards 5
CLARK, Champ 1
CLARK, Charles H
CLARK, Charles Benjamin 1
CLARK, Charles Cleveland 5
CLARK, Charles Dickson 1
CLARK, Charles Edgar 1
CLARK, Charles Edward 4
CLARK, Charles Finney 2
CLARK, Charles Heber 1
CLARK, Charles Hopkins 1
CLARK, Charles Martin 1
CLARK, Charles Upson 4
CLARK, Charles Walker 1
CLARK, Charles William 1
CLARK, Chase Addison 4
CLARK, Chester Frederic 3
CLARK, Christopher H
  Henderson
CLARK, Clarence Don 1
CLARK, Clarence Munroe 5
CLARK, Clarence Sewall 4
CLARK, Claude Lester 4
CLARK, Clifford Pease 3
CLARK, Cyrus J. 3
CLARK, D. Worth 3
CLARK, Dan Elbert 3
CLARK, Daniel * H
CLARK, David L. 1
CLARK, David Wasgate 1
CLARK, Davis Wasgatt 1
CLARK, Derral LeRoy 5
CLARK, Donald Lemen 4
CLARK, Duncan Campbell 4
CLARK, Dwight Edwin 1
CLARK, Edgar Erastus 1
CLARK, Edith Kirkwood 6
  Ormsby
CLARK, Edson Lyman 1
CLARK, Edward 1
CLARK, Edward Brayton 5
CLARK, Edward Gay 2
CLARK, Edward Hardy 1
CLARK, Edward L. 4
CLARK, Edward Lee 4
CLARK, Edward Lord 1
CLARK, Edward P. 1
CLARK, Edward W. 2
CLARK, Elijah H
CLARK, Eliot Round 4
CLARK, Ellery Harding 2

CLARK, Elmer Talmage 4
CLARK, Elroy Newton 4
CLARK, Emily 3
CLARK, Emmons 1
CLARK, Emory W. 3
CLARK, Eugene Bradley 4
CLARK, Eugene Francis 1
CLARK, Ezra Jr. H
CLARK, Ezra Westcote 2
CLARK, F. Lewis 1
CLARK, Felicia Buttz 4
CLARK, Felton Grandison 5
CLARK, Fontaine Riker 5
CLARK, Francis Edward 1
CLARK, Frank 1
CLARK, Frank Hodges 3
CLARK, Frank Sylvester 3
CLARK, Frank William 2
CLARK, Franklin H
CLARK, Franklin Jones 1
CLARK, Fred 5
CLARK, Fred Emerson 5
CLARK, Fred George 5
CLARK, Fred Pope 1
CLARK, Frederic 4
  Huntington
CLARK, Frederick John 1
CLARK, Frederick M. 1
CLARK, Frederick Pareis 5
CLARK, Frederick Timothy 1
CLARK, Friend Ebenezer 5
CLARK, Gaylord Parsons 1
CLARK, George 4
CLARK, George Archibald 4
CLARK, George Campbell 4
CLARK, George Crawford 1
CLARK, George Halford 5
CLARK, George Hardy 4
CLARK, George Harlow 5
CLARK, George J. 3
CLARK, George Larkin 4
CLARK, George Lindenberg 5
CLARK, George Luther 5
CLARK, George Ramsey 2
CLARK, George Rogers H
CLARK, George Thomas 1
CLARK, George Whitefield 1
CLARK, Glenn W(hitmire) 6
CLARK, Grenville 5
CLARK, Grenville 5
CLARK, Grover 1
CLARK, Hamilton Burdick 1
CLARK, Hannah Belle 5
CLARK, Harold Benjamin 3
CLARK, Harold Johnson 3
CLARK, Harold Terry 4
CLARK, Harry Camp 1
CLARK, Harry Granville 1
CLARK, Harry Henderson 5
CLARK, Harry Willard 4
CLARK, Harvey Cyrus 1
CLARK, Henry A. 3
CLARK, Henry Benjamin 5
CLARK, Henry Hunt 5
CLARK, Henry James 1
CLARK, Henry Selby H
CLARK, Henry W. 2
CLARK, Herbert W. 4
CLARK, Herma N. 3
CLARK, Homer Pierce 5
CLARK, Horace Francis H
CLARK, Horace Spencer 4
CLARK, Horatio David 3
CLARK, Howard J. 1
CLARK, Howard V. 4
CLARK, Hubert Lyman 2
CLARK, Imogen 1
CLARK, Isaac 5
CLARK, Isaiah Raymond 1
CLARK, J. Reuben Jr. 4
CLARK, J. Ross 1
CLARK, J. Scott 1
CLARK, James H
CLARK, James Edward 5
CLARK, James Edwin 4
CLARK, James G. 1
CLARK, James Truman 4
CLARK, James Waddey 5
CLARK, James West H
CLARK, Janet Howell 5
CLARK, Jesse Redman 1
CLARK, John H
CLARK, John Alden 6
CLARK, John Arvine 3
CLARK, John Bates 1
CLARK, John Brittan 2
CLARK, John Bullock H
CLARK, John Bullock 1
CLARK, John Chamberlain H
CLARK, John Cheesman 2
CLARK, John Edward 1
CLARK, John Emory 6
CLARK, John Goodrich 1
CLARK, John Howe 1
CLARK, John Jesse 1

CLARK, John Lewis 5
CLARK, John Marshall 4
CLARK, John Maurice 4
CLARK, John Robert 3
CLARK, John Spencer 4
CLARK, Jonas H
CLARK, Jonas Gilman H
CLARK, Joseph Bourne 5
CLARK, Joseph James 5
CLARK, Joseph Leon 4
CLARK, Joseph Sylvester 1
CLARK, Josephine Adelaide 4
CLARK, Julian Jerome 5
CLARK, Kate Upson 1
CLARK, Keith 3
CLARK, L. Pierce 1
CLARK, Lee Hinchman 4
CLARK, Lester Williams 1
CLARK, Lewis Gaylord H
CLARK, Lewis Whitehouse 1
CLARK, Lincoln H
CLARK, Lindley Daniel 1
CLARK, Linwood L. 5
CLARK, Lloyd Montgomery 5
CLARK, Lot H
CLARK, Lucius Charles 2
CLARK, Mallie Adkin 1
CLARK, Marguerite 1
CLARK, Melville 1
CLARK, Melville 3
CLARK, Melvin Green 1
CLARK, Meriwether Lewis H
CLARK, Myron H. 3
CLARK, Myron Holley H
CLARK, Nathaniel Walling 1
CLARK, Olynthus B. 1
CLARK, Paul Burroughes 4
CLARK, Faul Dennison 5
CLARK, Paul Foster 4
CLARK, Percy Hamilton 4
CLARK, Randolph 4
CLARK, Ray Henry 3
CLARK, Reed Paige 3
CLARK, Rensselaer Weston 4
CLARK, Richard Francis 6
  Maplestone
CLARK, Robert H
CLARK, Robert Bruce 5
CLARK, Robert Cariton 1
CLARK, Robert Fry 6
CLARK, Robert Lanier 1
CLARK, Robert Thomas Jr. 3
CLARK, Roe Sidney 3
CLARK, Roland Eugene 3
CLARK, Rollin M. 3
CLARK, Roy Wallace 2
CLARK, Rufus Wheelwright H
CLARK, Rufus Wheelwright 1
CLARK, Rush 1
CLARK, Sam L. 4
CLARK, Samuel H
CLARK, Samuel M. 1
CLARK, Samuel Orman Jr. 6
CLARK, Samuel Wesley 3
CLARK, Sheldon H
CLARK, Sheldon 1
CLARK, Solomon Henry 1
CLARK, Stephen Carlton 1
CLARK, Stephen Cutter 3
CLARK, Taliaferro 2
CLARK, Theodore 4
CLARK, Theodore Minot 1
CLARK, Thomas Arkle 1
CLARK, Thomas Collier 4
CLARK, Thomas Curtis 1
CLARK, Thomas Frederic 4
CLARK, Thomas Harvey 3
CLARK, Thomas March 1
CLARK, Victor Selden 3
CLARK, Virginius E. 4
CLARK, W. A. Graham 2
CLARK, Wallace 2
CLARK, Walter * 1
CLARK, Walter Appleton 1
CLARK, Walter Eli 2
CLARK, Walter Ernest 1
CLARK, Walter Eugene 4
CLARK, Walter Loane 1
CLARK, Walter VanTilburg 5
CLARK, Walton 1
CLARK, Washington A. 1
CLARK, Wilbur 4
CLARK, Will L. 5
CLARK, William * H
CLARK, William 1
CLARK, William Andrews 1
CLARK, William Andrews 1
  Jr.
CLARK, William Anthony 1
CLARK, William Arthur 1
CLARK, William Braddock 1
CLARK, William Bullock 1
CLARK, William Clifford 3
CLARK, William E. 1
CLARK, William Francis 4
CLARK, William Heermans 1

* Indicates More Than One Such Name Listed

493

COHEN, Andrew Benjamin 5
COHEN, Archie H. 3
COHEN, Barnett 3
COHEN, Benjamin A. 3
COHEN, Charles Joseph 1
COHEN, David Solis 4
COHEN, Dolly Lurie (Mrs. 5
  A. B. Cohen)
COHEN, Felix S. 3
COHEN, George Harry 2
COHEN, Harry 5
COHEN, Henry 1
COHEN, Herbert Spencer 4
COHEN, Irvin Joseph 5
COHEN, Jacob Solis 1
COHEN, John Sanford 1
COHEN, Julius Henry 3
COHEN, Katherine M. 1
COHEN, Lewis 1
COHEN, Lily Young 1
COHEN, Louis 2
COHEN, Mendes 1
COHEN, Merrill Morris 4
COHEN, Morris Raphael 2
COHEN, Murray 4
COHEN, Nathaniel A. 6
COHEN, Octavus Roy 5
COHEN, Paul 5
COHEN, Paul Pincus 1
COHEN, Sara Barr 6
COHEN, William Nathan 1
COHEN, William W. 1
COHILL, Edmund 2
  Pendleton
COHN, Adolphe 1
COHN, Alfred Einstein 1
COHN, Alfred I. 4
COHN, Charles Mittendorff 2
COHN, Edwin Joseph 3
COHN, Harry 3
COHN, Jack 3
COHN, Joseph Hoffman 3
COHN, Morris M. 1
COHN, Ralph Morris 3
COHN, Saul 3
COHON, Morris 1
COHON, Samuel Solomon 4
COHU, La Motte T. 5
COIL, Everett Johnston 3
COILE, Samuel Andrew 1
COINER, Beverly Waugh 4
COIT, Alfred 2
COIT, Arthur Clinton 1
COIT, Henry Augustus H
COIT, J. Milnor 1
COIT, John Clarke 5
COIT, J(ohn) Eliot 6
COIT, John Knox 5
COIT, John McLean 1
COIT, Joseph Howland 1
COIT, Joshua H
COIT, Joshua 1
COIT, Judson Boardman 1
COIT, Olin Burr 4
COIT, Ruth 1
COIT, Stanton 4
COIT, Thomas Winthrop H
COKE, Henry Cornick 1
COKE, James L. 5
COKE, John Story 5
COKE, Richard H
COKE, Richard Jr. H
COKE, Thomas H
COKENOWER, James W. 3
COKER, David Robert 1
COKER, Francis William 4
COKER, James Lide 1
COKER, James Lide 4
COKER, Robert E(rvin) 5
COKER, William Chambers 2
COLACCI, Mario 5
COLAHAN, John Barron Jr. 1
COLAW, John Marvin
COLBERT, Carl Cato 3
COLBERT, Charles Francis 5
  Jr.
COLBERT, James William 6
  Jr.
COLBERT, Leo Otis 5
COLBERT, Richard Gary 6
COLBERT, Richard Victor 4
COLBRON, Grace Isabel 2
COLBURN, Albert E. 3
COLBURN, Allan Philip
COLBURN, Burnham 3
  Standish
COLBURN, Dana Pond H
COLBURN, Warren H
COLBURN, Zerah H
COLBY, Albert Ladd 3
COLBY, Bainbridge 3
COLBY, Branch Harris
COLBY, Charles Carlyle 4
COLBY, Clara Bewick 1
COLBY, Everett 2

COLBY, Frank C. 1
COLBY, Frank Harvey 4
COLBY, Frank Moore 1
COLBY, Franklin Green 1
COLBY, Gardner H
COLBY, Gardner 1
COLBY, Harrison Gray Otis 1
COLBY, Henry Francis 1
COLBY, Irving Harold 5
COLBY, J. Rose 1
COLBY, James Fairbanks 1
COLBY, Joseph Milton 6
COLBY, Leonard Wright 1
COLBY, Luther 1
COLBY, Nathalie Sedgwick 2
COLBY, Walter Francis 5
COLBY, William Edward 4
COLBY, William Edward 5
COLBY, William Irving 1
COLBY, Willoughby Amos 4
COLCLOUGH, Otho 6
  Thomas
COLCOCK, F. Horton 1
COLCOCK, William H
  Ferguson
COLCORD, Bradford C. 1
COLCORD, Charles Francis 1
COLCORD, Frank Forest 3
COLCORD, Joanna Carver 4
COLCORD, Lincoln Ross 2
COLCORD, Roswell Keyes 1
COLDEN, Cadwallader H
COLDEN, Cadwallader H
  David
COLDEN, Charles J. 1
COLDEN, Charles S. 4
COLDEN, Jane H
COLDREN, Philip 3
COLE, Aaron Hodgman 1
COLE, Alfred Dodge 1
COLE, Ashley Trimble 4
COLE, Betty Joy 5
COLE, Carlos Merton 1
COLE, Charles Cleaves 1
COLE, Charles F. 1
COLE, Charles H. 5
COLE, Charles Knox 1
COLE, Charles Nelson 1
COLE, Chester Cicero 1
COLE, Clarence Alfred 4
COLE, Cornelius 1
COLE, Cyrenus 1
COLE, Cyrus W(illard) 5
COLE, David 1
COLE, Douglas Seaman 4
COLE, Edward Smith 2
COLE, Eli Kelley 1
COLE, Elmer E. 4
COLE, Ernest E. 2
COLE, Fay-Cooper 5
COLE, Felix 5
COLE, Francis Watkinson 4
COLE, Frank Nelson 1
COLE, Franklin 1
COLE, George Clarence 5
COLE, George Douglas 3
  Howard
COLE, George E. * 1
COLE, George Lamont 1
COLE, George Lee 6
COLE, George W. 1
COLE, George Watson 1
COLE, Glen Walker 1
COLE, Harold Mercer 5
COLE, Harry Outen 3
COLE, Henry Tiffany 1
COLE, Howard Ellsworth 3
COLE, Howard I. 4
COLE, Howard Ware 5
COLE, Jack 6
COLE, Jean Dean 1
COLE, John Adams 4
COLE, John Nelson 1
COLE, John Tupper 6
COLE, Joseph Foxcroft 1
COLE, Lawrence Thomas 5
COLE, Lawrence Wooster 2
COLE, Leon Jacob 1
COLE, Lewis Gregory 3
COLE, Louis Maurice 1
COLE, Nat King 4
COLE, Nathan Jr. 1
COLE, Nelson 1
COLE, Ralph Dayton 1
COLE, Ralph R. 3
COLE, Redmond Selecman 6
COLE, Richard Beverly 1
COLE, Rossetter Gleason 4
COLE, Roy 6
COLE, Rufus 5
COLE, Rufus 5
COLE, Russell D. 4
COLE, Samuel Valentine 1
COLE, Samuel Winkley 1
COLE, Theodore Lee 1
COLE, Thomas H

COLE, Thomas F. 4
COLE, Thomas (Raymond) 6
COLE, Timothy 1
COLE, Walton Adamson 4
COLE, Whitefoord R. 1
COLE, Willard W. 6
COLE, William Carey 1
COLE, William H. 4
COLE, William Hinson H
COLE, William Isaac 1
COLE, William Morse 4
COLE, William Purrington 3
  Jr.
COLE, Wilson Giffin 3
COLEBAUGH, Charles 2
  Henry
COLEGROVE, Chauncey 4
  Peter
COLEGROVE, Frederick 4
  Welton
COLEGROVE, Kenneth 6
  Wallace
COLEMAN, Algernon 1
COLEMAN, Alice 1
  Blanchard
COLEMAN, Arch 4
COLEMAN, Arch 5
COLEMAN, Arthur 6
  Prudden
COLEMAN, Benjamin 1
  Wilson
COLEMAN, Chapman 1
COLEMAN, Charles Caryl 1
COLEMAN, Charles Elliott 4
COLEMAN, Charles Philip 1
COLEMAN, Charles 1
  Washington
COLEMAN, Christopher 2
  Bush
COLEMAN, Claude C. 3
COLEMAN, Cornelius 5
  Cunningham
COLEMAN, Cynthia 1
  Beverley Tucker
COLEMAN, Cyril 3
COLEMAN, D'Alton Corry 3
COLEMAN, Frank Joseph 1
COLEMAN, Frederick W. 2
  B.
COLEMAN, Frederick 2
  William
COLEMAN, George 2
  Preston
COLEMAN, George 1
  Whitfield
COLEMAN, George 3
  William
COLEMAN, Gilbert Payson 4
COLEMAN, James Daniel 6
  Stetson
COLEMAN, James Melville 4
COLEMAN, John 4
COLEMAN, John Dawson 4
COLEMAN, John Francis 2
COLEMAN, John Hamline 4
COLEMAN, John Shields 5
COLEMAN, John Strider 3
COLEMAN, Kathleen Blake 4
COLEMAN, Leighton 1
COLEMAN, Lewis Minor 1
COLEMAN, Lyman H
COLEMAN, Nicholas H
  Daniel
COLEMAN, Philip Frantz 3
COLEMAN, Ralph Pailen 5
COLEMAN, Richard B. 4
COLEMAN, Robert 6
COLEMAN, S. Waldo 6
COLEMAN, Satis Narrona 4
COLEMAN, Sidney 6
COLEMAN, Stewart P. 5
COLEMAN, Sydney Haines 3
COLEMAN, Thomas 1
  Davies
COLEMAN, Thomas 4
  Emmet
COLEMAN, Thomas Wilkes 1
COLEMAN, Walter Moore 1
COLEMAN, Warren 2
COLEMAN, William H
  Caldwell
COLEMAN, William Coffin 3
COLEMAN, William 1
  Emmette
COLEMAN, William 4
  Harold
COLEMAN, William Henry 3
COLEMAN, William John 5
COLEMAN, William 1
  Magruder
COLEMAN, William Tell H
COLEMAN, William 4
  Wheeler
COLER, Bird Sim 1

COLES, Alfred Porter 2
COLES, David Smalley 4
COLES, Edward H
COLES, Isaac H
COLES, J. Ackerman 1
COLES, Walter H
COLESTOCK, Henry 4
  Thomas
COLETTE 3
COLETTI, Joseph Arthur 4
COLEY, Bradley Lancaster 4
COLEY, Edward 2
  Huntington
COLEY, Francis Chase 1
COLEY, William Bradley 1
COLFAX, Schuyler H
COLFELT, Lawrence 4
  Maclay
COLFLESH, Robert William 4
COLFORD, William 5
  Edward
COLGATE, Gilbert 1
COLGATE, Henry A. 3
COLGATE, James Boorman 1
COLGATE, James Colby 2
COLGATE, Russell 1
COLGATE, S. Bayard 4
COLGATE, Sidney Morse 1
COLGATE, William H
COLGROVE, Philip Taylor 1
COLHOUN, John Ewing H
COLIE, Edward Martin 1
COLIE, Rosalie Littell 5
COLKET, Edward Burton 5
COLL, Raymond S. 4
COLLADAY, Edward 4
  Francis
COLLADAY, Samuel 2
  Rakestraw
COLLAMER, Jacob H
COLLAMORE, Harry 6
  Bacon
COLLAR, William Coe 1
COLLBRAN, Henry 1
COLLEDGE, William A. 1
COLLENS, Arthur Morris 6
COLLENS, Charles 3
COLLENS, Clarence Lyman 5
COLLENS, Thomas H
  Wharton
COLLER, Frederick Amasa 4
COLLER, Julius A. 4
COLLES, Christopher H
COLLET, John Caskie H
COLLETT, Armand René 6
COLLETT, George Richard 1
COLLETT, John 1
COLLETT, Robert Arthur 6
COLLIE, George Lucius 3
COLLIER, Barron 1
COLLIER, Daniel Lewis 1
COLLIER, David Charles 1
COLLIER, Edward 1
  Augustus
COLLIER, Frank Wilbur 2
COLLIER, George Haskell 1
COLLIER, Harry D. 3
COLLIER, Henry Watkins H
COLLIER, James William 1
COLLIER, John 5
COLLIER, John Allen 1
COLLIER, John Howard 5
COLLIER, Marie Elizabeth 5
COLLIER, Peter 1
COLLIER, Peter Fenelon 1
COLLIER, Price 1
COLLIER, Robert Joseph 1
COLLIER, Theodore 4
COLLIER, William 2
COLLIER, William 1
  Armistead
COLLIER, William Miller 3
COLLIGAN, Francis James 6
COLLIN, Alonzo 1
COLLIN, Charles Avery 1
COLLIN, Frederick 1
COLLIN, Harry E. 5
COLLIN, John Francis 1
COLLINGE, Patricia 6
COLLINGS, Clyde Wilson 1
COLLINGS, Crittenden 1
  Taylor
COLLINGS, Gilbert Hooper 4
COLLINGS, Harry Thomas 1
COLLINGS, Howard 1
  Paxton
COLLINGS, John Ayres 1
COLLINGS, Kenneth 1
  Brown
COLLINGS, Samuel Posey 1
COLLINGWOOD, Francis 1
COLLINGWOOD, G. 3
  Harris
COLLINGWOOD, Herbert 1
  Winslow

COLLINS, A(rchie) 5
  Frederick
COLLINS, Alan Copeland 4
COLLINS, Albert Hamilton 2
COLLINS, Alfred Morris 1
COLLINS, Alfred Quinton 1
COLLINS, Atwood 1
COLLINS, Bertrand Robson 4
  Torsey
COLLINS, Carter 6
COLLINS, Charles Bertine 6
COLLINS, Charles E. 5
COLLINS, Charles Edwin 4
COLLINS, Charles Wallace 6
COLLINS, Charles William 1
COLLINS, Clifford Ulysses 2
COLLINS, Clinton DeWitt 1
COLLINS, Conrad Green 5
COLLINS, Cornelius 1
  Vallance
COLLINS, Cornelius Van 1
  Santvoord
COLLINS, Edgar Thomas 1
COLLINS, Edward Day 1
COLLINS, Edward Knight H
COLLINS, Edwin R. 1
COLLINS, Ela H
COLLINS, Everell Stanton 1
COLLINS, Foster K. 1
COLLINS, Francis Arnold 1
COLLINS, Francis Dolan H
COLLINS, Frank Shipley 3
COLLINS, Franklin Wallace 2
COLLINS, Frederick Lewis 1
COLLINS, George Lewis 1
COLLINS, George Stuart 1
COLLINS, George W. 5
COLLINS, George William 1
COLLINS, Gilbert 1
COLLINS, Guy N. 1
COLLINS, Harold 3
  Moorman
COLLINS, Henry W. 5
COLLINS, Herman LeRoy 1
COLLINS, Howard Dennis 4
COLLINS, Hubert Edwin 1
COLLINS, J. Franklin 1
COLLINS, James Franklin 1
COLLINS, James H(iram) 1
COLLINS, James Lawton 4
COLLINS, John H
COLLINS, John Anderson 1
COLLINS, John 1
  Bartholomew
COLLINS, John Joseph 1
COLLINS, John Martin 1
COLLINS, John Mathewson 1
COLLINS, John Timothy 1
COLLINS, Joseph 5
COLLINS, Joseph Henry 4
COLLINS, Joseph Howland 1
COLLINS, Joseph Martin 1
COLLINS, Joseph Victor 1
COLLINS, Joseph William 1
COLLINS, Joshua 1
COLLINS, Laura G. 4
COLLINS, Loren Warren 1
COLLINS, Lorin Cone 1
COLLINS, Mark 1
COLLINS, Matthew Garrett 1
COLLINS, Mauney D. 4
COLLINS, Michael Francis 5
COLLINS, Napoleon H
COLLINS, Patrick A. 1
COLLINS, Paul Fisk 5
COLLINS, Paul Valorous 1
COLLINS, Philip Sheridan 1
COLLINS, Ralph L. 4
COLLINS, Robert 1
  Alexander
COLLINS, Robert Moore 1
COLLINS, Ross Alexander 5
COLLINS, Ross Alexander 5
COLLINS, Roy Charles 5
COLLINS, Stewart G. 2
COLLINS, Truman W. 4
COLLINS, Varnum Lansing 1
COLLINS, Virgil Dewey 4
COLLINS, Vivian 1
COLLINS, Whitley Charles 4
COLLINS, Wilbur M(ausly) 1
COLLINS, William H
COLLINS, William 1
COLLINS, William 1
COLLINS, William Dennis 1
COLLINS, William Henry 3
COLLINS, Winifred 1
COLLINS, Yvonne 6
  Deakins (Mrs. Carr P.
  Collins Jr.)
COLLIP, James Bertram 4
COLLIS, Charles H. T. 1
COLLISON, Wilson 1
COLLISSON, Norman 1
  Harvey
COLLITZ, Hermann 1

COLLITZ, Klara 2
Hechtenberg
COLLYER, Robert 1
COLM, Gerhard 5
COLMAN, Benjamin H
COLMAN, Henry H
COLMAN, James Douglas 5
COLMAN, John H
COLMAN, Norman Jay 1
COLMAN, Ronald 1
COLMAN, Samuel H
COLMORE, Charles 3
Blayney
COLNON, Aaron 3
COLONNA, Paul Crenshaw 4
COLPITTS, Edwin Henry 2
COLPITTS, Walter William 3
COLQUHOUN, Walter 4
Alexander
COLQUITT, Alfred Holt H
COLQUITT, Oscar Branch 1
COLQUITT, Walter T. 1
COLQUITT, Walter Terry H
COLSON, Clyde Lemuel 4
COLSON, David Grant 1
COLSTON, Edward H
COLSTON, Edward 1
COLSTON, Raleigh Edward H
COLSTON, William Ainslie 5
COLT, Harris Dunscomb 3
COLT, Le Baron Bradford 1
COLT, Samuel H
COLT, Samuel Pomeroy 1
COLT, Samuel Sloan 6
COLTER, Frederick Tuttle 1
COLTER, John H
COLTMAN, Robert 4
COLTMAN, William 4
George
COLTON, A. M. F. H
COLTON, Arthur Willis 1
COLTON, Calvin H
COLTON, Charles Adams 1
COLTON, Charles Henry 1
COLTON, Don Byron 5
COLTON, Elizabeth Avery 1
COLTON, Elizabeth 3
Sweetser
COLTON, Ethan Theodore 5
COLTON, Ferry Barrows 1
COLTON, Gardner Quincy H
COLTON, George Henry 1
COLTON, George Radcliffe 1
COLTON, Harold Sellers 5
COLTON, James Hooper 6
COLTON, Julia M. 5
COLTON, Walter H
COLTON, Winfred Rufus 6
COLTRANE, Eugene J. 4
COLTRANE, John William 4
COLUM, Mary M. 3
COLUM, Padraic 5
COLUMBUS, Christopher H
COLUMBUS, Diego H
COLUMBUS, Fernando H
Colon
COLVER, Benton Noble 3
COLVER, Nathaniel 1
COLVER, William Byron 1
COLVIN, Addison Beecher 1
COLVIN, Allan DeWitt 3
COLVIN, D. Leigh 3
COLVIN, Fred Herbert 4
COLVIN, George 1
COLVIN, H. Milton 3
COLVIN, James G. 5
COLVIN, Mamie White 3
COLVIN, Oliver Dyer 4
COLVIN, Stephen Sheldon 1
COLVIN, Verplanck 1
COLVIN, W. H. Jr. 3
COLVOCORESSES, George H
Musalas
COLVOCORESSES, George 1
Partridge
COLWELL, Ernest Cadman 6
COLWELL, Felton 6
COLWELL, Nathan Porter 1
COLWELL, Robert Talcott 4
COLWELL, Stephen 1
COLYER, Douglas 3
COLYER, Vincent H
COMAN, Charlotte Buell 1
COMAN, Edwin Truman 5
COMAN, Henry Benjamin 1
COMAN, Katharine 1
COMAN, Mary Meriam 4
COMAN, Wilber Edmund 1
COMAR, Jerome Morton 2
COMBA, Richard 1
COMBEST, Earl Edgar 6
COMBS, Everett Randolph 5
COMBS, George W. 3
COMBS, Gilbert Raynolds 1
COMBS, J. M. 2
COMBS, James Horton 3

COMBS, Leslie H
COMBS, Leslie H
COMBS, Morgan Lafayette 3
COMBS, Moses Newell H
COMBS, Pat (William 6
Malone)
COMBS, Thomas Selby 4
COMEAUX, C. Stewart 3
COMEGYS, Joseph Parsons H
COMER, Braxton Bragg 1
COMER, Edward Trippe 4
COMER, George Legare 4
COMER, Harry D. 4
COMER, Hugh Moss 4
COMER, James McDonald 4
COMERFORD, Frank 1
COMERFORD, Frank 2
Dowd
COMEY, Arthur Coleman 3
COMEY, Arthur Messinger 1
COMFORT, Anna Manning 1
COMFORT, Charlotte 5
Walrath
COMFORT, Frank J. 3
COMFORT, George Fisk 1
COMFORT, Mandred 3
Whitset
COMFORT, Walter R. 4
COMFORT, Will Levington 1
COMFORT, William Wistar 3
COMINGO, Abram H
COMINS, Linus Bacon H
COMINSKY, Jacob 5
R(obert)
COMLY, Samuel Pancoast 1
COMMONS, John Rogers 2
COMPARETTE, T. Louis 1
COMPERE, Ebenezer 6
Lattimore
COMPHER, Wilber G. 4
COMPTON, Alfred 2
Donaldson
COMPTON, Alfred George 1
COMPTON, Arthur H. H
COMPTON, Arthur H. 4
COMPTON, Charles Elmer 1
COMPTON, Elias 1
COMPTON, George 1
Brokaw
COMPTON, Karl Taylor 3
COMPTON, Lewis 2
COMPTON, Loulie 1
COMPTON, Ranulf 6
COMPTON, Richard J. 3
COMPTON, Walter 3
COMPTON, William 6
Randall
COMPTON, William 3
Randolph
COMPTON, Wilson 4
Martindale
COMPTON-BURNETT, Ivy 5
COMSTOCK, A. Barr 4
COMSTOCK, Ada Louise 6
COMSTOCK, Albert H. 4
COMSTOCK, Alzada 3
COMSTOCK, Anna 1
Botsford
COMSTOCK, Anthony 1
COMSTOCK, Clarence 2
Elmer
COMSTOCK, Cyrus Ballou 1
COMSTOCK, Daniel Frost 5
COMSTOCK, Elizabeth L. H
COMSTOCK, Elting 5
Houghtaling
COMSTOCK, F. Ray 4
COMSTOCK, Frank Mason 1
COMSTOCK, George Cary 1
COMSTOCK, George H
Franklin
COMSTOCK, Harriet 5
Theresa
COMSTOCK, Henry H
Tompkins Paige
COMSTOCK, John Henry 1
COMSTOCK, Louis Kossuth 4
COMSTOCK, Oliver H
Cromwell
COMSTOCK, Ralph J. 4
COMSTOCK, Sarah 3
COMSTOCK, Solomon 1
Gilman
COMSTOCK, Theodore 1
Bryant
COMSTOCK, William 2
Alfred
COMTOIS, Paul 4
CONAGHAN, Brian 6
Francis
CONANT, Alban Jasper 1
CONANT, C. Everett 1
CONANT, Charles Arthur 1
CONANT, Charlotte 1
Howard
CONANT, Ernest Bancroft 5

CONANT, Frederick Odell 1
CONANT, Gordon Daniel 4
CONANT, Hannah O'Brien H
Chaplin
CONANT, Harold Wright 4
CONANT, Helen Peters 1
Stevens
CONANT, Henry Dunning 4
CONANT, Hezekiah 1
CONANT, John Willis 4
CONANT, Levi Leonard 1
CONANT, Roger H
CONANT, Thomas H
Jefferson
CONANT, Thomas Oakes 1
CONARD, Frederick 3
Underwood
CONARD, Henry 5
Shoemaker
CONARD, John 1
CONARRO, Harry Wiborg 4
CONARROE, George W. H
CONATY, Thomas James 1
CONAWAY, Charles 3
Herman
CONAWAY, Paul Brewer 6
CONBOY, Martin 2
CONBOY, Sara Agnes 1
CONCANNON, Charles 5
Cuthbert
CONCHESO, Aurelio 3
Fernandez
CONDE, Bertha 5
CONDEE, Robert Asa 1
CONDICT, George Herbert 1
CONDICT, Lewis H
CONDICT, Silas H
CONDIT, Blackford 1
CONDIT, John H
CONDIT, Kenneth 6
Hamilton
CONDIT, Silas H
CONDO, Gus S. 3
CONDON, Eddie (Albert 6
Edwin Condon)
CONDON, Edward J. 4
CONDON, Edward U. 6
CONDON, Francis Bernard 4
CONDON, Herbert Thomas 3
CONDON, John Thomas 1
CONDON, Randall Judson 1
CONDON, Richard William 4
CONDON, Thomas Gerald 4
CONDRA, George Evert 1
CONDRON, Theodore 5
Lincoln
CONE, Burtis Octavius 4
CONE, Frederick Preston 2
CONE, Helen Gray 2
CONE, Herman 3
CONE, Hutchinson Ingham 1
CONE, Martin 4
CONE, Marvin Dorwart 4
CONE, Orello 1
CONE, Russell G. 4
CONE, Spencer Houghton 4
CONEY, Aims Chamberlain 4
CONEY, Jabez H
CONEY, John H
CONFREY, Edward Elzear 5
(ZEZ)
CONGDON, Charles Harris 1
CONGDON, Charles 1
Howard
CONGDON, Charles Taber H
CONGDON, Chester 1
Adgate
CONGDON, Clement 4
Hilman
CONGDON, Edward 5
Chester
CONGDON, Ernest Arnold 4
CONGDON, Gilbert 4
Maurice
CONGDON, Harriet Rice 5
CONGDON, Joseph 1
William
CONGER, Abraham 3
Benjamin
CONGER, Albert C. 5
CONGER, Edward A. 4
CONGER, Edwin Hurd 1
CONGER, Everett Lorentus 1
CONGER, George Perrigo 4
CONGER, Harmon 1
Sweatland
CONGER, James Lockwood H
CONGER, John Leonard 1
CONGER, John William 1
CONGER, John William 4
CONGER, Robert Alan 4
CONGER, Seymour Beach 1
CONGER, (Seymour) Beach 5
III
CONGLETON, Jerome 1
Taylor

CONICK, Harold C. 4
CONKEY, Elizabeth A. 4
CONKEY, Henry Phillips 4
CONKLIN, Abram 4
CONKLIN, Arthur Stewart 4
CONKLIN, Charles 1
CONKLIN, Clifford 3
Tremaine
CONKLIN, Edmund Smith 2
CONKLIN, Edwin Grant 1
CONKLIN, Franklin Jr. 4
CONKLIN, Jennie Maria 1
Drinkwater
CONKLIN, John F. 5
CONKLIN, Roland Ray 1
CONKLIN, Viola A. 4
CONKLIN, William 1
Augustus
CONKLIN, William Judkins 1
CONKLING, Alfred H
CONKLING, Alfred Ronald 4
CONKLING, Donald 6
Herbert
CONKLING, Frederick H
Augustus
CONKLING, Grace Hazard 3
CONKLING, Mark Le Roy 4
CONKLING, Roscoe H
CONKLING, Roscoe 3
Powers
CONLAND, Henry H. 2
CONLEN, William J. 3
CONLEY, Alonzo Theodore 4
CONLEY, Carey Herbert 4
CONLEY, Clyde 5
CONLEY, Clyde G. 6
CONLEY, Dudley Steele 6
CONLEY, Edgar Thomas 3
CONLEY, Elmo Hansford 3
CONLEY, George J. 3
CONLEY, John Wesley 1
CONLEY, William Gustavus 1
CONLEY, William H. 6
CONLEY, William Maxwell 3
CONLIN, Earl Edgar 6
CONLON, Mrs. William F. 6
(Sara Frances Smith
Conlon)
CONN, Donald Deans 3
CONN, George Chester 4
CONN, Granville Priest 1
CONN, Harry L. 1
CONN, Herbert William 1
CONN, Ulysses Sylvester 1
CONNAH, Douglas John 1
CONNALLY, Ben C. 6
CONNALLY, Elijah L. 1
CONNALLY, Tom 4
CONNELL, Albert James 2
CONNELL, Arthur J. 4
CONNELL, Carl W. 2
CONNELL, Charles R. 1
CONNELL, Francis J. 4
CONNELL, George Boyce 3
CONNELL, Horatio 1
CONNELL, James Mark 4
CONNELL, Karl 1
CONNELL, Kenneth Hugh 6
CONNELL, Richard 2
CONNELL, Richard E. 1
CONNELL, Wilfrid Thomas 4
CONNELL, William 1
CONNELL, William Henry 2
CONNELL, William 1
Lawrence
CONNELL, William Phillips 1
CONNELL, Wilson Edward 1
CONNELLEY, Clifford 1
Brown
CONNELLEY, Earl John 3
CONNELLEY, William 1
Elsey
CONNELLY, Celia Logan 1
CONNELLY, Cornelia H
CONNELLY, Edward 2
Michael
CONNELLY, Emma Mary 5
CONNELLY, Henry H
CONNELLY, James H. 1
CONNELLY, John R. 5
CONNELLY, Pierce Francis H
Francis
CONNELY, Emmett 4
CONNELY, Willard 4
CONNER, Albert Holmes 6
CONNER, Benjamin 1
Coulbourn
CONNER, Benjamin Howe 4
CONNER, Bruce 5
CONNER, David 1
CONNER, Eli Taylor 1
CONNER, Fox 1
CONNER, James 4
CONNER, James Keyes 1
CONNER, James Moyer 4
CONNER, James Perry 4

CONNER, John Coggswell H
CONNER, Lewis Atterbury 3
CONNER, Martin Sennett 1
CONNER, Phineas Sanborn 1
CONNER, Samuel Shepard 4
CONNER, Walter Thomas 5
CONNERS, William James 1
CONNERS, William James 3
Jr.
CONNERY, Lawrence J. 1
CONNERY, Thomas 4
Bernard Joseph
CONNERY, William Patrick 1
Jr.
CONNESS, John 1
CONNESS, Leland Stanford 2
CONNICK, Arthur Elwell 4
CONNICK, Charles Jay 2
CONNICK, Harris De 4
Haven
CONNIFF, Frank 5
CONNIFF, Paul R. 5
CONNING, John Stuart 3
CONNOLLY, Brendan 6
CONNOLLY, Christopher 1
Powell
CONNOLLY, Daniel Ward H
CONNOLLY, Francis X. 4
CONNOLLY, James Austin 1
CONNOLLY, James 3
Brendan
CONNOLLY, James J. 3
CONNOLLY, John * H
CONNOLLY, Joseph Peter 2
CONNOLLY, Joseph 2
Vincent
CONNOLLY, Louise 1
CONNOLLY, Maurice 1
CONNOLLY, Michael 1
William
CONNOLLY, Mike 4
CONNOLLY, Robert 3
Emmet
CONNOLLY, Terence Leo 4
CONNOLY, Theodore 1
CONNOR, Aloysius J. 4
CONNOR, Charles Ashley 6
Richard
CONNOR, Charles Francis 6
CONNOR, Edward 5
CONNOR, George L. 1
CONNOR, George 1
Whitfield
CONNOR, Guy Leartus 2
CONNOR, Henry Groves 1
CONNOR, Henry William H
CONNOR, Jacob Elon 4
CONNOR, Louis George 4
CONNOR, Patrick Edward H
CONNOR, Ray 1
CONNOR, Robert Digges 2
Wimberly
CONNOR, Seldon 1
CONNOR, Washington 1
Everett
CONNOR, William 4
Durward
CONNOR, William Neil 4
CONNOR, William Ott 1
CONNORS, James Joseph * 6
CONNORS, John P. 4
CONNORS, Joseph Mathew 4
CONOLLY, Richard L. 4
CONOVER, Adams Jewett 1
CONOVER, Charles H. 1
CONOVER, Elbert Moore 3
CONOVER, Harvey 2
CONOVER, (James) Milton 5
CONOVER, Obediah H
Milton
CONOVER, Samuel 4
Seymour
CONQUEST, Ida 1
CONRAD, Arcturus Z. 1
CONRAD, Carl Nicholas 1
CONRAD, Casper Hauzer 3
Jr.
CONRAD, Charles H
CONRAD, Charles Magill 1
CONRAD, Charles Wearne 3
CONRAD, Cuthbert Powell 3
CONRAD, Frank 1
CONRAD, Frank L. 2
CONRAD, Frederick H
CONRAD, Frowenus 1
CONRAD, G. Miles 4
CONRAD, Henry Clay 1
CONRAD, James Lawson 6
CONRAD, Lowell Edwin 4
CONRAD, Marus Edward 4
CONRAD, Nicholas John 1
CONRAD, Paul C. 4
CONRAD, Robert Taylor H
CONRAD, Stephen 1
CONRAD, Timothy Abbot H

CONRAD, Victor Allen 4
CONRADI, Edward 2
CONRIED, Heinrich 1
CONROW, Wilford Seymour 3
CONROY, John Joseph H
CONROY, Joseph H. 1
CONROY, Peter Joseph 3
CONROY, Thomas Francis 3
CONROY, Thomas Michael 5
CONRY, Michael Francis 1
CONRY, Thomas 2
CONS, Louis 2
CONSIDERANT, Victor Prosper H
CONSIDINE, James W(illiam) 5
CONSIDINE, Robert Bernard 6
CONSTABLE, Albert H
CONSTABLE, William George 6
CONSTANGY, Frank Alan 5
CONSTANT, Frank Henry 2
CONSTANT, Samuel Victor 1
CONSTANTINE, Earl Gladstone 3
CONSTANTINOPLE, Panaglotes S. 4
CONTE, Richard 6
CONTEE, Benjamin H
CONVERSE, Amasa R. H
CONVERSE, C. Crozat 1
CONVERSE, Costello C. 1
CONVERSE, Edmund Cogswell 1
CONVERSE, Florence 6
CONVERSE, Francis Bartlett 1
CONVERSE, Frederick Shepherd 1
CONVERSE, George Albert 1
CONVERSE, George Leroy H
CONVERSE, George Peabody 4
CONVERSE, Harriet Maxwell 1
CONVERSE, Harry E. 1
CONVERSE, Harry Pollard 3
CONVERSE, James Booth 1
CONVERSE, John Heman 1
CONVERSE, Marquis Mills 1
CONVERSE, Miriam Sewall 6
CONVERSE, Myron Frederick 3
CONVERY, Neil Joseph 4
CONWAY, Albert 5
CONWAY, Barret 2
CONWAY, Carle Cotter 3
CONWAY, Edwin Stapleton 1
CONWAY, Elias Nelson H
CONWAY, Frederick Bartlett H
CONWAY, Henry Wharton H
CONWAY, Herbert 5
CONWAY, James Ignatius 4
CONWAY, James Sevier H
CONWAY, John Edward 2
CONWAY, John Sebastian 6
CONWAY, John Severinus 1
CONWAY, Joseph M. 4
CONWAY, Joseph W. 2
CONWAY, Katherine Eleanor 1
CONWAY, Martin Franklin H
CONWAY, Moncure Daniel 1
CONWAY, Patrick 1
CONWAY, Thomas H
CONWAY, Thomas Jr. 4
CONWAY, Walter 3
CONWELL, Hugh Earle 6
CONWELL, Russell Herman 1
CONWELL, Walter Lewis 2
CONYNGHAM, Gustavus H
CONYNGHAM, William Hillard 2
COOGAN, Edward Francis 4
COOGAN, Thomas James 6
COOK, Albert John 1
COOK, Albert Samuel 3
COOK, Albert Stanburrough 1
COOK, Alfred A. 2
COOK, Alfred Newton 1
COOK, Alice Rice 5
COOK, Allan Nehrands 4
COOK, Alton 4
COOK, Andrew Bruce 5
COOK, Ansel Granville 1
COOK, Arthur Leroy 6
COOK, Burton Chauncey H
COOK, Carroll Blaine 1
COOK, Cary Wilson 4
COOK, Charles Alston 1
COOK, Charles Augustus 1
COOK, Charles Emerson 5
COOK, Charles R. 3
COOK, Charles Sumner 1
COOK, Charles T. 1
COOK, Chauncey William 2
COOK, Chester Aquila 3
COOK, Clarence Chatham H
COOK, Clinton Dana 5
COOK, Daniel Pope H
COOK, David C. 1
COOK, Donald 4
COOK, Ebenezer H
COOK, Edward Noble 5
COOK, Elmer Jay 4
COOK, Ermond Edson 1
COOK, Ernest Fullerton 4
COOK, Eugene 4
COOK, Everett Richard 6
COOK, Fannie 2
COOK, Fayette Lamartine 1
COOK, Francis Augustus 1
COOK, Frank Gaylord 2
COOK, Frederic White 3
COOK, Frederick Albert 1
COOK, George Brinton 1
COOK, George Cram 1
COOK, George Crouse 4
COOK, George Fox 4
COOK, George Frederick 1
COOK, George Hammell H
COOK, George Roy 5
COOK, George Washington 4
COOK, George Wythe 4
COOK, Gilbert Richard 4
COOK, Grant L. 3
COOK, H. Earl 5
COOK, Harold James 4
COOK, Henry Clay 1
COOK, Henry Mudd 4
COOK, Henry Webster 4
COOK, Irving Winthrop 3
COOK, Isaac H
COOK, J. Clinton Jr. 4
COOK, James H
COOK, James Henry 2
COOK, James Merrill H
COOK, Joe 4
COOK, Joel 1
COOK, John 1
COOK, John 3
COOK, John Belmont 6
COOK, John Henry 5
COOK, John Parsons H
COOK, John Williston 1
COOK, Joseph 1
COOK, Joseph Platt H
COOK, Marc H
COOK, Martha Elizabeth Duncan Walker H
COOK, May Elizabeth 6
COOK, Melville Thurston 3
COOK, Orator Fuller Jr. 3
COOK, Orchard H
COOK, Otis Seabury 1
COOK, Paul 1
COOK, Peter Jr. 5
COOK, Philip H
COOK, Philip 1
COOK, Raymond Mack 4
COOK, Richard Briscoe 1
COOK, Richard Yerkes 1
COOK, Robert George 1
COOK, Robert Harvey 2
COOK, Roy Bird 4
COOK, Roy H. 4
COOK, Russell S. H
COOK, Samuel A. 1
COOK, Samuel C. 1
COOK, Samuel E. 4
COOK, Samuel Richard 4
COOK, Sidney Albert 2
COOK, Theodore Augustus 4
COOK, Vernon 3
COOK, Virgil Y. 1
COOK, Waldo Lincoln 3
COOK, Walter 1
COOK, Walter W. 4
COOK, Walter Wheeler 2
COOK, Walter William Spencer 4
COOK, William Cassius 3
COOK, William Henry * 1
COOK, William Locke 2
COOK, William Wallace 1
COOK, William Wilson 1
COOK, Willis Clifford 1
COOK, Willis Clifford 2
COOK, Zadock H
COOK, Zebedee H
COOKE, A. Wayland 1
COOKE, Alexander Bennett 2
COOKE, Arthur Bledsoe 5
COOKE, Bates H
COOKE, Charles Maynard Jr. 5
COOKE, Charles Montague Jr. 2
COOKE, Clarence Hyde 2
COOKE, Douglas H. 2
COOKE, Ebenezer H
COOKE, Edmund Vance 1
COOKE, Edward Dean H
COOKE, Elbridge Clinton 4
COOKE, Eleutheros H
COOKE, Elisha * H
COOKE, Flora Juliette 3
COOKE, George H
COOKE, George Anderson 1
COOKE, George Henry 1
COOKE, George Willis 1
COOKE, Grace MacGowan 4
COOKE, Harold Groves 3
COOKE, Harrison Rice 5
COOKE, Helen Temple 3
COOKE, Henry D. 3
COOKE, Henry David H
COOKE, Hereward Lester 2
COOKE, James Francis 3
COOKE, Jay 1
COOKE, Jay 4
COOKE, John Daniel 5
COOKE, John Esten * H
COOKE, John Rogers H
COOKE, Joseph Brown 4
COOKE, Joseph Platt 3
COOKE, Josiah Parsons H
COOKE, Juan Isaac 3
COOKE, Leslie Edward 4
COOKE, Lorenzo Wesley 1
COOKE, Lorrin Alanson 1
COOKE, Lucy Finkel (Mrs. S. Jay Cooke) 6
COOKE, Marjorie Benton 1
COOKE, Morris Llewellyn 3
COOKE, Philip Pendleton H
COOKE, Philip St George H
COOKE, Richard Dickson 3
COOKE, Richard Joseph 1
COOKE, Robert Anderson 4
COOKE, Robert Locke 3
COOKE, Rose Terry H
COOKE, Samuel 4
COOKE, Thomas Burrage H
COOKE, Thomas Turner 4
COOKE, Thornton 3
COOKE, Walter Platt 1
COOKE, William Parker 1
COOKMAN, Alfred H
COOKSEY, George Robert 2
COOKSON, Walter John 1
COOLBAUGH, Melville Fuller 3
COOLBRITH, Ina Donna 1
COOLE, Thomas Henry 1
COOLEY, Alford Warriner 1
COOLEY, Anna Maria 5
COOLEY, Arthur Henderson 5
COOLEY, Charles Horton 1
COOLEY, Charles Parsons 5
COOLEY, Charles Parsons Jr. 6
COOLEY, Edwin Gilbert 1
COOLEY, Ethel Halcrow (Mrs. John B. Cooley) 5
COOLEY, Frederick Boyden 2
COOLEY, Harold Dunbar 6
COOLEY, Hollis Eli 1
COOLEY, LeRoy Clark 1
COOLEY, Lyman Edgar 1
COOLEY, McWhorter Stephens 6
COOLEY, Mortimer Elwyn 2
COOLEY, Robert Allen 5
COOLEY, Robert Lawrence 3
COOLEY, Roger William 1
COOLEY, Stoughton 1
COOLEY, Thomas Benton 2
COOLEY, Thomas MacIntyre H
COOLEY, Thomas Ross 3
COOLEY, William Forbes 4
COOLIDGE, Algernon 1
COOLIDGE, Amory 3
COOLIDGE, Archibald Cary 1
COOLIDGE, Arthur William 3
COOLIDGE, Calvin 1
COOLIDGE, Charles Allerton 1
COOLIDGE, Charles Austin 1
COOLIDGE, Cora Helen 1
COOLIDGE, Cornelius H
COOLIDGE, Dane 1
COOLIDGE, Edgar D. 6
COOLIDGE, Elizabeth Sprague 3
COOLIDGE, Emelyn Lincoln 2
COOLIDGE, Emma Downing 4
COOLIDGE, George Greer 3
COOLIDGE, Grace Goodhue 3
COOLIDGE, Harold Jefferson 1
COOLIDGE, Herbert 5
COOLIDGE, J. Randolph 1
COOLIDGE, James Henry 4
COOLIDGE, John Gardner 1
COOLIDGE, Joseph Bradford 4
COOLIDGE, Julian Lowell 3
COOLIDGE, Lawrence 3
COOLIDGE, Louis Arthur 1
COOLIDGE, Marcus Allen 2
COOLIDGE, Mary Roberts 2
COOLIDGE, Richard Bradford 4
COOLIDGE, Sherman 1
COOLIDGE, Sidney 1
COOLIDGE, T. Jefferson 1
COOLIDGE, T. Jefferson 3
COOLIDGE, T. Jefferson Jr. 1
COOLIDGE, William David 6
COOLIDGE, William Henry 1
COOM, Charles Sleeman 4
COOMARASWAMY, Ananda Kentish 2
COOMBE, Harry E. (James) 5
COOMBE, Thomas H
COOMBES, Ethel Russell 6
COOMBS, C. Whitney 1
COOMBS, Frank L. 1
COOMBS, George Holden 2
COOMBS, Harrison S. 5
COOMBS, William Jerome 1
COOMBS, Zelotes Wood 2
COON, Charles Lee 1
COON, J. R. 4
COON, Jesse Drake 3
COON, John Sayler 4
COON, Owen L. 2
COON, Stephen Mortimer 1
COONAN, Frederick Leo 4
COONE, Henry Herbert 1
COONEY, Charles Edwin 3
COONEY, Frank H. 1
COONEY, James 4
COONEY, James D. 5
COONEY, Michael 1
COONEY, Percival John 1
COONEY, Russell Conwell 4
COONLEY, Howard 4
COONLEY, Lydia Avery 1
COONLEY, Prentiss Loomis 5
COONRADT, Arthur C. 3
COONS, Albert 3
COONS, Arthur Gardiner 5
COONS, Henry N. 4
COONS, James Ephraim 5
COONS, Leroy Wilson 2
COONS, Samuel Warwick 4
COONTZ, Robert Edward 1
COOPE, George Frederick 6
COOPER, Albert Hudlburgh 6
COOPER, Alfred Duff 3
COOPER, Allen Foster 4
COOPER, Armwell Lockwood 5
COOPER, Brainard 4
COOPER, Bryant Syms 3
COOPER, Charles Champlin 1
COOPER, Charles Hermance 4
COOPER, Charles Lawrence 1
COOPER, Charles Phillips 3
COOPER, Charles Proctor 4
COOPER, Clayton Sedgwick 1
COOPER, Colin Campbell 1
COOPER, Courtney Ryley 1
COOPER, Cyril Bernard 5
COOPER, David Acron 6
COOPER, Douglas Harold 4
COOPER, Drury W. 3
COOPER, Edward 1
COOPER, Edward 3
COOPER, Edward Nathan 5
COOPER, Elias Samuel H
COOPER, Elisha Hilliard 2
COOPER, Elizabeth (Mrs. Clayton Sedgwick Cooper) 5
COOPER, Ellwood 4
COOPER, Emma Lampert 1
COOPER, Ezekiel H
COOPER, Frank 2
COOPER, Frank B. 4
COOPER, Frank Edward 5
COOPER, Frank Irving 1
COOPER, Frederic Taber 1
COOPER, Gary 4
COOPER, George 3
COOPER, George Bryan H
COOPER, George Franklin 3
COOPER, George Victor H
COOPER, Gladys 5
COOPER, Harold 5
COOPER, Henry H
COOPER, Henry Allen 1
COOPER, Henry Elliott 3
COOPER, Henry Ernest 1
COOPER, Herman Charles 5
COOPER, Homer Eber 3
COOPER, Homer H. 4
COOPER, Hugh Lincoln 1
COOPER, Irving Steiger 1
COOPER, Isabelle Mitchell 5
COOPER, Jacob 1
COOPER, James H
COOPER, James Fenimore H
COOPER, James Graham H
COOPER, James Wesley 1
COOPER, Jere 3
COOPER, Job A. 1
COOPER, John H
COOPER, John Cobb 4
COOPER, John Gordon 5
COOPER, John Montgomery 3
COOPER, Joseph David 6
COOPER, Kent 4
COOPER, Lane 3
COOPER, Linton Leander 6
COOPER, Mark Anthony H
COOPER, Merian C. 5
COOPER, Myers Y. 3
COOPER, Myles H
COOPER, Oscar Henry 1
COOPER, Peter H
COOPER, Philip 6
COOPER, Philip Henry 1
COOPER, Prentice 5
COOPER, Richard Matlack H
COOPER, Richard Watson 3
COOPER, Robert Archer 3
COOPER, Robert Franklin 4
COOPER, Robert Muldrow 4
COOPER, Russell Morgan 6
COOPER, Sam Bronson 1
COOPER, Samuel * H
COOPER, Samuel Inman 6
COOPER, Samuel Williams 1
COOPER, Sanson Milligan 4
COOPER, Sarah Brown Ingersoll H
COOPER, Susan Fenimore H
COOPER, Theodore 1
COOPER, Thomas * H
COOPER, Thomas Abthorpe H
COOPER, Thomas Buchecker H
COOPER, Wade Hampton 4
COOPER, Wade Hampton 5
COOPER, William * H
COOPER, William Albert 4
COOPER, William Alpha 1
COOPER, William Goodwin 5
COOPER, William Irenaeus 1
COOPER, William John 1
COOPER, William Knowles 1
COOPER, William Lee 6
COOPER, William Raworth H
COOPER, Wyllis 3
COOPER-POUCHER, Matilda S. H
COOPERRIDER, George T. 1
COORS, D. Stanley 4
COOTE, Richard H
COOTER, James Thomas 4
COOVER, John Edgar 1
COOVER, Melanchthon 3
COPASS, Benjamin Andrew 5
COPE, Alexis 4
COPE, Arthur Clay 4
COPE, Caleb H
COPE, Edward Drinker H
COPE, Gilbert 3
COPE, Henry Frederick 1
COPE, Millard 4
COPE, Quill Evan 5
COPE, Robert S. 3
COPE, Thomas Pym H
COPE, Walter H
COPELAN, Robert W. 4
COPELAND, Alfred Bryant 4
COPELAND, Arthur H(erbert), Sr. 5
COPELAND, Charles 2
COPELAND, Charles Townsend 3
COPELAND, Charles W. H
COPELAND, Edward Rivers 3
COPELAND, Edwin Bingham 5
COPELAND, Fayette 4
COPELAND, Foster 1
COPELAND, Frederick Kent 1

COPELAND, Guild Anderson 1
COPELAND, Kenneth Wilford 6
COPELAND, Lennie Phoebe 3
COPELAND, Manton 6
COPELAND, Melvin Thomas 6
COPELAND, Oren S. 3
COPELAND, Paul L. 4
COPELAND, Royal Samuel 1
COPELAND, Theodore 1
COPELAND, Walter Scott 1
COPELAND, William Adams 4
COPELAND, William Franklin 3
COPLAND, Douglas Berry 5
COPLEY, Ira Clifton 2
COPLEY, James Strohn 6
COPLEY, John Singleton H
COPLEY, Lionel H
COPLIN, William Michael Late 1
COPP, Arthur Woodward 1
COPP, Owen 1
COPPEE, Henry H
COPPEE, Henry St Leger 1
COPPENS, Charles 1
COPPER, Joseph Benjamin 5
COPPERNOLL, William D. 4
COPPERS, George Henry 4
COPPIN, Levi J. 3
COPPINGER, John Joseph 1
COPPINI, Pompeo 5
COPPOCK, Fred Douglass 6
COPPOCK, William Homer 6
COPPRIDGE, William Maurice 3
COPWAY, George H
COQUARD, Leon 4
COQUELIN, Benoit Constant H
COQUELIN, Benoit Constant 4
COQUILLETT, Daniel William 1
COQUILLETTE, St. Elmo 5
CORAM, Joseph A. 5
CORAM, Thomas * H
CORBALEY, Gordon Cook 4
CORBE, Zenan M. 5
CORBETT, Gail Sherman (Mrs. Harvey Corbett C.)
CORBETT, Gerald Robert 6
CORBETT, Harvey Wiley 3
CORBETT, Henry L. 4
CORBETT, Henry Winslow 1
CORBETT, Hunter 1
CORBETT, James John H
CORBETT, James Jerome 4
CORBETT, Jim 3
CORBETT, Lamert Seymour 2
CORBETT, Laurence Jay 5
CORBETT, Lee Cleveland 1
CORBETT, Robert James 5
CORBETT, Timothy 1
CORBETTA, Roger Henry 6
CORBIN, Alvin LeRoy 5
CORBIN, Arthur Linton 4
CORBIN, Arthur Linton Jr. 5
CORBIN, Austin H
CORBIN, Caroline Fairfield 1
CORBIN, Charles Russell 2
CORBIN, Clement K. 4
CORBIN, Daniel C. 1
CORBIN, Henry Clark 1
CORBIN, Henry Pinkney 1
CORBIN, Horace Kellogg 3
CORBIN, John 3
CORBIN, Joseph Carter 4
CORBIN, Margaret 1
CORBIN, Philip 1
CORBIN, William Herbert 2
CORBIN, William Lee 3
CORBIND, Jon 4
CORBIT, John Darlington Jr. 6
CORBIT, Ross 6
CORBITT, Charles Linwood 1
CORBITT, James Howard 2
CORBLY, Lawrence Jugurtha 4
CORBUS, Budd Clarke 3
CORBY, William H
CORCORAN, Brewer 5
CORCORAN, Francis Vincent 1
CORCORAN, George Fancis 4
CORCORAN, John William 1
CORCORAN, Katherine
CORCORAN, Michael H
CORCORAN, Sanford William 2

CORCORAN, Thomas J. 3
CORCORAN, William Warwick 4
CORCORAN, William Wilson H
CORCOS, Lucille 6
CORD, Errett Lobban 6
CORDELL, Wayne Wellington 4
CORDES, Frank 3
CORDES, Frederick Carl 6
CORDIER, Andrew Wellington 6
CORDINER, Ralph Jarron 6
CORDLEY, Arthur Burton 1
CORDON, Guy 5
CORDOVA, Gabriel 3
CORDOVA-DAVILA, Felix 4
COREA, George Claude Stanley 4
COREA, Luis Felipe 1
CORETTE, John Earl 4
COREY, Albert B. 4
COREY, Alfred Adams Jr. 5
COREY, Charles Henry 1
COREY, Fred Daniel 1
COREY, Herbert 3
COREY, Horace Harold 4
COREY, James William 3
COREY, Lester Spaulding 6
COREY, Robert Brainard 5
COREY, Stephen Jared 5
COREY, Wendell Reid 5
COREY, William Ellis 1
CORFMAN, Elmer 5
CORGAN, Joseph Aloysius 6
CORI, Gerty Theresa 4
CORIAT, Isador Henry 2
CORIELL, Louis Duncan 6
CORK, James M. 3
CORKER, Stephen Alfestus 4
CORKERY, Francis E. 5
CORKEY, Alexander 1
CORKILL, James Frederick 4
CORLE, Edwin 3
CORLETT, George Milton 3
CORLETT, Webster David 5
CORLETT, William Thomas 2
CORLETT, William Wellington H
CORLEY, Frederick Dexter 4
CORLEY, James Henry 6
CORLEY, Jesse Lee 2
CORLISS, Augustus Whittemore 1
CORLISS, Charles Albert 1
CORLISS, Frederick William 4
CORLISS, George Henry 6
CORLISS, Guy Carleton Haynes 3
CORLISS, John Blaisdell 1
CORLISS, Leland Marchant 5
CORMENY, Alvin E(ugene) 5
CORN, Herbert F. 4
CORN, N. S. 4
CORN, Samuel Thompson 1
CORNBROOKS, Thomas Mullan 2
CORNBURY, Viscount H
CORNE, Michel Felice H
CORNEAU, Barton 6
CORNELIUS, Adam E. 3
CORNELIUS, Charles Le Sueur 5
CORNELIUS, Charles Over 1
CORNELIUS, Martin Phelps 3
CORNELIUS, Mary Ann 1
CORNELIUS, Ralph E. 5
CORNELIUS, Samuel Anderson 1
CORNELIUS, Willard M. 3
CORNELL, Alonzo B. 1
CORNELL, Ezekiel H
CORNELL, Ezra H
CORNELL, Irwin H. 4
CORNELL, Joseph 5
CORNELL, Katharine 5
CORNELL, (Sarah) Hughes 5
CORNELL, Thomas 1
CORNELL, Walter Stewart 5
CORNELL, William Bouck 3
CORNELSON, George Henry 1
CORNER, George Washington Jr.
CORNER, Thomas Cromwell 1
CORNETET, Noah E. 1
CORNICK, Howard 2
CORNICK, Philip H. 5
CORNING, Charles Robert H
CORNING, Edwin 2
CORNING, Erastus H

CORNING, Frederick Gleason 1
CORNING, Hobart M. 5
CORNING, J. Leonard 1
CORNISH, Albert Judson 4
CORNISH, Ed 4
CORNISH, Edward Joel 1
CORNISH, Gertrude Eleanor 6
CORNISH, Leslie Colby 1
CORNISH, Lorenzo Dana 1
CORNISH, Louis Craig 2
CORNISH, William D. 1
CORNMAN, Daniel 3
CORNMAN, Noel 2
CORNMAN, Oliver Perry 1
CORNOYER, Paul 1
CORNSTALK H
CORNWALL, Edward Everett 1
CORNWALL, Henry Bedinger 1
CORNWALLIS, Charles H
CORNWALLIS, Kinahan 1
CORNWELL, Alfred L. 5
CORNWELL, Dean 4
CORNWELL, Forest Augustus 1
CORNWELL, John J. 3
CORNWELL, William Caryl 4
CORNYN, John Hubert 1
COROMILAS, Lambros A. 4
CORONADO, Francisco Vazquez de H
CORP, Paul Metzger 6
CORPER, Harry John 6
CORRADO, Gaetano 1
CORRE, Joseph H
CORREGAN, Charles Hunter 2
CORRELL, Charles J. 5
CORRIE, Walter Samuel 4
CORRIGAN, Emmett 3
CORRIGAN, Francis Patrick 4
CORRIGAN, John 3
CORRIGAN, Jones Irwin Joseph 2
CORRIGAN, Joseph Moran 2
CORRIGAN, Leo Francis 6
CORRIGAN, Michael Augustine 1
CORRIGAN, Owen Bernard 1
CORRIGAN, Severinus John 4
CORRIGAN, Walter Dickson Sr. 3
CORRIGAN, William John 4
CORROON, Richard Aloysius 2
CORROTHERS, James David 5
CORRUCCINI, Roberto 1
CORRY, Edgar Clayton 5
CORSE, John Murray H
CORSE, William Malcolm 2
CORSER, Harry Prosper 1
CORSI, Edward 4
CORSON, Caroline Rollins 1
CORSON, David Birdsall 1
CORSON, Dighton 1
CORSON, Eugene Rollin 4
CORSON, Harry Herbert 5
CORSON, Hiram 1
CORSON, Juliet H
CORSON, Oscar Taylor H
CORSON, William Russell Cone 2
CORT, Stewart J. 3
CORTAMBERT, Louis Richard H
CORTELYOU, George Bruce 1
CORTESI, Arnaldo 4
CORTEZ, Hernando H
CORTHELL, Arthur Bateman 1
CORTHELL, Elmer Lawrence 1
CORTHELL, Nellis Eugene 4
CORTILET, Michael P. 3
CORTISSOZ, Ellen Mackay Hutchinson 1
CORTISSOZ, Royal 2
CORTNEY, Philip 5
CORTRIGHT, Ernest Everett 5
CORUM, Martene Windsor 3
CORWIN, Arthur Frank 3
CORWIN, Arthur Mills 1
CORWIN, Charles Edward 3
CORWIN, Edward Samuel 4
CORWIN, Edward Tanjore 1
CORWIN, Franklin 1
CORWIN, George B. 5
CORWIN, Moses Biedso H

CORWIN, Richard Warren 1
CORWIN, Robert Gilbert 1
CORWIN, Robert Nelson 2
CORWIN, Thomas H
CORWINE, Aaron H. H
CORWITH, Howard Post 4
CORWITH, James Carlton 4
CORY, Abram Edward 5
CORY, Charles Barney 1
CORY, Charles Edward 5
CORY, Clarence Linus 1
CORY, David 4
CORY, Harry Thomas 5
CORY, Thomas J. 4
CORY, Virgil 1
CORYELL, Charles DuBois 5
COSBY, Frank Carvill 1
COSBY, George Blake 1
COSBY, Spencer 4
COSBY, William H
COSDEN, Jeremiah H
COSDEN, Joshua S. 1
COSENZA, Mario Emilio 4
COSGRAVE, George 2
COSGRAVE, Jessica Garretson 2
COSGRAVE, John O'Hara 1
COSGRAVE, John O'Hara II 5
COSGRAVE, William Thomas 4
COSGRIFF, James E. 1
COSGRIFF, Walter Everett 4
COSGROVE, Edward Bradley 4
COSGROVE, Emilie Dohrmann (Mrs. John Charles Cosgrove) 5
COSGROVE, Henry 1
COSGROVE, James J. 4
COSGROVE, John Phillips 3
COSGROVE, Michael Frank 4
COSGROVE, Terence 3
COSHOW, Oliver Perry 1
COSS, John J. 2
COSSON, George 4
COSTAIN, Thomas Bertram 4
COSTANSO, Miguel H
COSTE, Paul F. 4
COSTELLO, Frederick Hankerson 1
COSTELLO, Harry Todd 4
COSTELLO, J. F. 3
COSTELLO, John A(loysius) 6
COSTELLO, John Cornelius 6
COSTELLO, Lou 4
COSTELLO, Louis B. 3
COSTELLO, Peter E. 4
COSTELLO, William Aloysius 5
COSTER, Frank Donald 1
COSTIGAN, Edward Prentiss 1
COSTIGAN, Francis 1
COSTIGAN, George Purcell Jr. 1
COSTIGAN, John Edward 5
COSTIKYAN, S. Kent 2
COSTLEY, Elizabeth Christine 6
COSTOLOW, William Evert 4
COTE, Alcide 3
COTHERN, Leland 4
COTHRAN, Frank Harrison 2
COTHRAN, James Sproull H
COTHRAN, Perrin Chiles 3
COTNAREANU, Leon 5
COTT, Ted 6
COTTAM, Clarence 6
COTTAM, Gilbert Geoffrey 2
COTTEN, Sallie Southall 1
COTTER, Carl Henry 4
COTTER, Charles F. 3
COTTER, James Edward 1
COTTER, John F. 3
COTTER, John W. 4
COTTER, Joseph B. 1
COTTER, William 1
COTTER, William Edward 1
COTTERAL, John Hazleton 1
COTTERILL, George Fletcher 2
COTTERMAN, Charles Mason 4
COTTING, John Ruggles H
COTTINGHAM, Claybrook 4
COTTINGHAM, George W. 2
COTTINGHAM, Irven A. 1
COTTIS, George W. 3
COTTLE, Brooks 4
COTTMAN, James Hough 1

COTTMAN, Joseph Stewart H
COTTMAN, Vincendon Lazarus 1
COTTON, Alfred Cleveland 1
COTTON, Charles Stanhope 1
COTTON, Edward Howe 6
COTTON, Elizabeth Jane 4
COTTON, Fassett Allen 4
COTTON, Francis Ridgely 1
COTTON, Frederic Jay 1
COTTON, Henry Andrews 1
COTTON, Jesse Lee 1
COTTON, John H
COTTON, Joseph Bell 1
COTTON, Joseph Potter 1
COTTON, William Edwin 3
COTTON, William H. 3
COTTON, William Joseph Henry 1
COTTON, William Wick 1
COTTRELL, Calvert Byron H
COTTRELL, Donald C. 3
COTTRELL, Edwin Angell 4
COTTRELL, Elias 1
COTTRELL, Frederick Gardner 2
COTTRELL, James La Fayette H
COTTRELL, Jesse Samuel 2
COTTRELL, Leonard 6
COTTRELL, Mary James 3
COTTRELL, Samuel 6
COTTRELL, Will Rea Jr. 5
COTY, Rene 4
COUCH, Albert Irving 1
COUCH, Benjamin Warren 2
COUCH, Charles Peter 4
COUCH, Darius Nash H
COUCH, George W. Jr. 6
COUCH, Harvey Crowley 1
COUCH, Harvey Crowley Jr.
COUCH, Herbert Newell 3
COUCHMAN, Charles Bennington 4
COUDEN, Albert Reynolds 1
COUDEN, Henry Noble 1
COUDERT, Amalia Kussner 5
COUDERT, Frederic Rene 1
COUDERT, Frederic Rene 3
COUDERT, Frederic Rene Jr. 5
COUDREY, Harry Marcy 4
COUES, Elliott 1
COUES, Samuel Franklin 1
COUEY, James Henry Jr. 5
COUGHLAN, Robert Edward Jr.
COUGHLIN, Clarence Dennis 3
COUGHLIN, Edward Joseph Jr. 6
COUGHLIN, John William 1
COUGHLIN, Timothy J. 3
COUGHLIN, W. G. 4
COUGHLIN, Walter James 4
COUGHLIN, William Thomas 1
COULDOCK, Charles Walter H
COULSON, Charles Alfred 6
COULSON, Edwin Ray 5
COULSON, Robert E. 4
COULSTON, John Bishop 1
COULSTON, Melvin Herbert 3
COULTAS, Andrew Jackson 1
COULTER, Charles M. 3
COULTER, John Lee 3
COULTER, John Merle 1
COULTER, John Stanley 2
COULTER, Mary Geigus 1
COULTER, Merle Crowe 3
COULTER, Richard 4
COULTER, Sidney Beech 5
COULTER, Stanley 1
COULTER, William S(ummy) 6
COULTHARD, George William 5
COULTON, George A. 1
COULTON, Thomas Evans 4
COUNCIL, Carl C. 4
COUNCIL, Walter Wooten 2
COUNCILL, William Hooper 1
COUNCILMAN, William Thomas 1
COUNCILOR, James Allan 2
COUNSELMAN, Charles 1
COUNTERMINE, John Donnan 4
COUNTRYMAN, Edwin 1
COUNTRYMAN, Gratia Alta 3
COUNTRYMAN, J. E. 5

* Indicates More Than One Such Name Listed

COUNTRYMAN, Marcellus 4
L.
COUNTRYMAN, Willis 4
Arthur
COUNTS, George Sylvester 6
COUNTS, Gerald Alford
COUNTWAY, Francis A. 3
COUNTY, Albert John 2
COUPAL, James Francis
COUPER, James Hamilton H
COUPER, William 2
COURANT, Richard 5
COURCHESNE, Georges 3
COURNAND, Edward L. 6
COURSAULT, Jesse 1
Harliaman
COURSEY, Oscar William 3
COURT, Frank Willard 4
COURTENAY, William 1
Ashmead
COURTENAY, William 1
Howard
COURTER, Claude V. 4
COURTIS, Frank 1
COURTIS, Stuart Appleton 5
COURTIS, William Munroe 1
COURTLEIGH, William 1
Louis
COURTNEY, Frederick 1
COURTNEY, Joseph 1
William
COURTNEY, Luther Weeks 6
COURTNEY, Thomas 5
J(ames)
COURTNEY, Walter 1
COURTS, Malon Clay 3
COURVILLE, Cyril Brian 5
COUSE, E. Irving
COUSENS, John Albert 1
COUSINS, Arthur George 3
COUSINS, Frank 4
COUSINS, Ralph P. 4
COUSINS, Robert Bartow 1
COUSINS, Robert Gordon 1
COUSLEY, Stanley W. 3
COUTANT, Frank 6
Raymond
COUTURIER, Hendrick H
COUZENS, Frank 3
COUZENS, James 1
COUZINS, Phoebe 4
COVARRUBIAS, Miguel 3
COVELL, Louis Chapin 5
COVENEY, Charles Carden 5
COVER, Ralph 5
COVER, Rodney Addison 4
COVERDALE, William 3
Hugh
COVERLEY, Robert 4
COVERT, Charles Edward 5
COVERT, John Cutler 1
COVERT, Lloyd W. 4
COVERT, William Chalmers 1
COVEY, Arthur Sinclair 3
COVILLE, Frederick V. 1
COVINGTON, Euclid M. 6
COVINGTON, Harry 1
Franklin
COVINGTON, Harry 3
Stockdell
COVINGTON, J. Harry 1
COVINGTON, Leonard H
COVODE, John H
COWAN, Andrew 1
COWAN, Clyde Lorrain 6
COWAN, Edgar H
COWAN, Edward Payson 1
COWAN, Frank 1
COWAN, Frank Augustus 3
COWAN, Frank Irving 2
COWAN, Jacob Pitzer H
COWAN, James Raymo 3
COWAN, John Franklin 1
COWAN, Robert Ernest 2
COWAN, Samuel Kinkade 5
COWARD, Edward Fales 5
COWARD, Noel Peirce 4
COWARD, Thomas 3
Ridgway
COWART, Harry 6
Maciemore
COWDEN, Howard Austin 6
COWDEN, John Brandon 4
COWDEN, Robert E. Jr. 5
COWDERY, Edward 1
Gilmore
COWDERY, Robert Holmes 6
COWDIN, J. Cheever 4
COWDRY, Edmund 6
Vincent
COWELL, Alfred Lucius 5
COWELL, Henry Dixon 4
COWELL, Hervey Sumner 1
COWELL, Joseph Leathley 6
COWELL, Sylvester E. 5
COWEN, Benjamin Rush 1

COWEN, Benjamin Sprague H
COWEN, Benjamin Sprague 1
COWEN, John King 1
COWEN, Joshua Lionel 4
COWEN, Lawrence 5
COWEN, Myron Melvin 4
COWEN, William B. 4
COWGER, William Owen 5
COWGILL, George 6
Raymond
COWHERD, William 1
Strother
COWIE, David Murray 4
COWIE, Jack Baron 4
COWIE, Thomas Jefferson 1
COWIN, John Clay 4
COWING, Hugh Alvin 2
COWL, Jane 3
COWLES, Alfred 4
COWLES, Alfred 1
Hutchinson
COWLES, Augustus 1
Woodruff
COWLES, Cheney 2
COWLES, Dudley Redwood 6
COWLES, Edward 4
COWLES, Edward Spencer 4
COWLES, Edwin H
COWLES, Emma Milton 4
COWLES, Eugene Chase 4
COWLES, Frederic Albert 1
COWLES, Gardner 2
COWLES, Henry Booth H
COWLES, Henry Chandler 1
COWLES, James Lewis 1
COWLES, John Guiteau 1
Welch
COWLES, John Henry 3
COWLES, Mrs. Josiah 4
Evans
COWLES, Julia Darrow 1
COWLES, LeRoy Eugene 4
COWLES, Maude Alice 4
COWLES, Percival William 6
COWLES, Torris Zalmon 1
COWLES, Walter Cleveland 1
COWLES, William 2
Hutchinson
COWLES, William 5
Hutchinson
COWLES, William Lyman 1
COWLES, William Sheffield 1
COWLEY, Charles 2
COWLEY, Matthew 3
COWLING, Donald J. 4
COWPER, Harry Mattingly 1
COWPERTHWAITE, Allen 4
Corson
COX, Abraham Beekman 1
COX, Albert Lyman 4
COX, Albert Scott 4
COX, Allen 6
COX, Alonzo Bettis 5
COX, Archibald 4
COX, Argus 4
COX, Attilla 2
COX, Benjamin 2
COX, C(larence) Brown 5
COX, Channing Harris 5
COX, Charles Elbridge 1
COX, Charles Finney 1
COX, Charles Raymond 5
COX, (Charles) Hudson 5
Baynham
COX, Creed Fulton 2
COX, Creed Fulton 5
COX, Daniel Hargate 3
COX, Douglas Farley 5
COX, Edward Eugene 4
COX, Edward Weston 5
COX, Eleanor Rogers 1
COX, Forrest Dale 4
COX, Frank P. 4
COX, Frederick Irving 1
COX, G. Howland 1
COX, Garfield V. 5
COX, George Bryan 1
COX, George Clarke 4
COX, George Howland Jr. 2
COX, George James 2
COX, Guy Henry 4
COX, Guy Wilbur 3
COX, Hannah Pierce H
COX, Harvey Warren 4
COX, Henry Hamilton H
COX, Henry Joseph 4
COX, Hugh 6
COX, Isaac Joslin 4
COX, J. Elwood 5
COX, Jacob H
COX, Jacob Dolson 1
COX, Jacob Dolson 4
COX, James H
COX, James B. 4
COX, James C. 1
COX, James Franklin 6

COX, James M. 3
COX, James Middleton Jr. 1
COX, James Monroe 2
COX, Jocelyn Meridith 5
Nolting (Mrs. Rowland
Cox III)
COX, John Harrington 4
COX, Joseph Winston 1
COX, Katherine Hamilton 1
Cabell
COX, Kenyon 1
COX, Leander Martin H
COX, Leilyn Munns 5
COX, Lemuel H
COX, Leonard Martin 2
COX, Lester Edmund 5
COX, Linton A. 5
COX, Louis Sherburne 1
COX, Louise Howland King 4
COX, Millard F. 4
COX, Nellie I. McMaster 5
(Mrs. William Cox)
COX, Nicholas Nichols 4
COX, Oscar Larken 5
COX, Oscar Sydney 4
COX, Palmer 1
COX, Philip Wescott 6
Lawrence
COX, Raymond Benjamin 3
COX, Rowland H
COX, Samuel Hanson H
COX, Samuel Sullivan H
COX, Taylor H. 4
COX, Theodore Sullivan 4
COX, W(illiam) Rowland 5
COX, Wally 5
COX, Walter Smith 1
COX, William Elijah 4
COX, William Ruffin 1
COX, William Stakely 3
COX, William Van Zandt 1
COX, William Wesley 4
COX, Wilson Naylor 5
COXE, Alfred Conkling 1
COXE, Alfred Conkling 3
COXE, Arthur Cleveland 1
COXE, Daniel H
COXE, Eckley Brinton 1
COXE, Frank Morrell 1
COXE, James Clarke 1
Watson
COXE, John Redman H
COXE, Lewis Crocker 6
COXE, Macgrane 1
COXE, Richard Smith 1
COXE, Tench H
COXE, William H
COXE, William Briscom 1
COXE, William Ellery C. 1
COXETTER, Louis Mitchell H
COXEY, Jacob S. 3
COY, Edward Gustin 1
COY, Eliah Washburn 1
COY, Wayne 3
COYE, William Henry 1
COYKENDALL, Frederick 3
COYL, Horace Edward 4
COYLE, David Cushman 5
COYLE, Eugene 4
COYLE, Frank J. 5
COYLE, Henry 4
COYLE, James Edwin 1
COYLE, Marvin E. 4
COYLE, Robert Francis 1
COYLE, Robert McCurdy 1
COYLE, William Radford 4
COYNE, Frederick E. 4
COYNE, John Nicholas 1
COYNER, Charles Luther 5
COZART, Reed 6
COZENS, Frederick Warren 3
COZIER, Robert V. 4
COZZENS, Frederick H
Swartwout
CRABB, George Whitfield H
CRABB, Jeremiah H
CRABBE, George William 3
CRABBE, John Grant 1
CRABBS, George Dent 2
CRABITES, Pierre 4
CRABTREE, Charlotte 1
CRABTREE, Ernest 2
Granville
CRABTREE, Frederick 1
CRABTREE, Harold Roy 4
CRABTREE, James 4
Anderson
CRABTREE, James William 2
CRABTREE, Nate L. 4
CRACCHI, Guiseppe H
CRADDOCK, Charles 1
Egbert
CRADDOCK, John Derrett 6
CRADLEBAUGH, John 1
CRAFT, Clarence Christian 1
CRAFT, E. A. 3

CRAFT, Edward Beech 1
CRAFT, Frost 1
CRAFTON, Allen 4
CRAFTS, Annetta Stratford 4
CRAFTS, Clayton Edward 4
CRAFTS, James Mason 1
CRAFTS, Leland Whitney 5
CRAFTS, Leo Melville 1
CRAFTS, Samuel Chandler H
CRAFTS, Sara Jane 5
CRAFTS, Walter 1
CRAFTS, Wilbur Fisk 1
CRAFTS, William H
CRAGHAN, George H
CRAGIN, Edwin Bradford 1
CRAGIN, Francis 4
Whittemore
CRAGO, Alfred 6
CRAGO, Thomas Spencer 1
CRAGUN, John Wiley 5
CRAIG, Alexander Kerr H
CRAIG, Alexander Righter 1
CRAIG, Alfred Edwin 1
CRAIG, Alfred M. 1
CRAIG, Asa Hollister 1
CRAIG, Austin H
CRAIG, Austin 3
CRAIG, Charles 4
CRAIG, Charles Curtis 4
CRAIG, Charles Franklin 4
CRAIG, Charles Patton 1
CRAIG, Clarence Tucker 3
CRAIG, Daniel Frank 3
CRAIG, Daniel H. 1
CRAIG, Donald Alexander 1
CRAIG, Edward Chilton 3
CRAIG, Edwin Wilson 5
CRAIG, Elisabeth May 4
CRAIG, Frank 1
CRAIG, George M. 4
CRAIG, Hardin 5
CRAIG, Hardin Jr. 6
CRAIG, Hector H
CRAIG, James H
CRAIG, James Alexander 1
CRAIG, James Edward 5
CRAIG, John 1
CRAIG, Joseph Davis 1
CRAIG, Joseph Edgar 1
CRAIG, Jubal Early 6
CRAIG, Katherine L. 1
CRAIG, Locke 1
CRAIG, Lyman C. 6
CRAIG, Malin 2
CRAIG, Oscar John 3
CRAIG, Palmer Hunt 6
CRAIG, Paul Frederick 6
CRAIG, Robert H
CRAIG, Robert B. 6
CRAIG, Robert S(pencer) 5
CRAIG, Samuel G. 4
CRAIG, Thomas H
CRAIG, Thomas Bigalow 1
CRAIG, Wallace 5
CRAIG, Walter 1
CRAIG, William Bayard 1
CRAIG, William Benjamin 1
CRAIG, William Edward 1
CRAIG, Willis Green 1
CRAIG, Winchell 3
McKendree
CRAIGE, Francis Burton 1
CRAIGE, Francis Burton 2
CRAIGHEAD, Edwin 3
Boone
CRAIGHEAD, Erwin 4
CRAIGHILL, George 5
Bowdoin Sr.
CRAIGHILL, William Price 1
CRAIGIE, Andrew H
CRAIGIE, David Johnston 1
CRAIGIE, Pearl Mary- 1
Teresa
CRAIGIE, William 3
Alexander
CRAIK, James H
CRAIK, William H
CRAIL, Joe 1
CRAIN, G.D. Jr. 6
CRAIN, James Kerr 5
CRAIN, John Hillier 4
CRAIN, William Henry H
CRAM, Franklin Webster 4
CRAM, George F. 1
CRAM, Harold Edgerly 2
CRAM, Ralph Adams H
CRAM, Ralph Adams 1
CRAM, Ralph Adams 4
CRAM, Ralph Warren 5
CRAM, Willard Gliden 5
CRAM, William Everett 5
CRAM, Wingate Franklin 3
CRAMBLET, Thomas E. 1
CRAMBLET, Wilbur 5
Haverfield
CRAMER, Frederic 5

CRAMER, Harriet Laura 1
CRAMER, John H
CRAMER, John Francis 5
CRAMER, John Luther 4
CRAMER, John Wesley 4
CRAMER, Kenneth Frank 3
CRAMER, Michael John H
CRAMER, Myron Cady 4
CRAMER, Sterling B. 3
CRAMER, Stuart Warren 1
CRAMER, Stuart Warren 1
Jr.
CRAMER, W. Stuart 1
CRAMER, William 2
CRAMP, Arthur Joseph 5
CRAMP, Charles Henry 1
CRAMP, Walter Concemore 1
CRAMP, William 3
CRAMPTON, Albert M. 3
CRAMPTON, C. Ward 4
CRAMPTON, Charles 1
Albert
CRAMPTON, George S. 5
CRAMPTON, Guy Chester 3
CRAMPTON, Henry 3
Edward
CRAMTON, Louis C. 5
CRANCH, Christopher H
Pearse
CRANCH, John H
CRANCH, William H
CRANDALL, Albert Rogers 3
CRANDALL, Andrew 4
Wallace
CRANDALL, Arthur Fitz 3
James
CRANDALL, Bruce Verne 2
CRANDALL, Charles 1
Henry
CRANDALL, Charles Lee 1
CRANDALL, Charles 1
Spencer
CRANDALL, Clifford 5
Waldorf
CRANDALL, Floyd Milford 1
CRANDALL, Francis 1
Asbury
CRANDALL, George 4
Strachen
CRANDALL, H. Burr 4
CRANDALL, Lathan 1
Augustus
CRANDALL, Lee Saunders 5
CRANDALL, Prudence H
CRANDALL, Shannon 5
CRANDALL, Shannon Jr. 4
CRANDELL, A. William 6
CRANDON, Franklin Philip 4
CRANDON, Le Roi 1
Goddard
CRANE, A. W. 1
CRANE, Aaron Martin 1
CRANE, Albert Sears 2
CRANE, Anne Moncure H
CRANE, Arthur Griswold 1
CRANE, Arthur Henry 4
CRANE, Augustus 4
CRANE, Bruce 1
CRANE, Caroline Bartlett 1
CRANE, Cephas Bennett 1
CRANE, Charles Alva 1
CRANE, Charles Howard 4
CRANE, Charles Kittredge 1
CRANE, Charles P. 5
CRANE, Charles Richard 1
CRANE, Charles Richard II 3
CRANE, Clinton Hoadley 3
CRANE, Cyrus 3
CRANE, Earl H(oward) 4
CRANE, Edward Andrew 4
CRANE, Edward Matthews 4
CRANE, Elvin Williamson 4
CRANE, Evan Jay 4
CRANE, Frank 1
CRANE, Frederick Evan 2
CRANE, Frederick Lea 3
CRANE, G. Stewart 3
CRANE, George Francis 1
CRANE, Hart 1
CRANE, Jason George 1
CRANE, Jasper Elliot 5
CRANE, Jay Everett 5
CRANE, Jefferson Davis 1
CRANE, John 1
CRANE, John Alden 3
CRANE, Jonathan Townley H
CRANE, Joseph Halsey 1
CRANE, Lawrence Gordon 5
CRANE, Leo 1
CRANE, Louis Burton 1
CRANE, Martin McNulty 2
CRANE, Michael Joseph 1
CRANE, Oscar W. 5
CRANE, R. B. 1
CRANE, R. Newton 1
CRANE, Ralph Thompson 1

CRANE, Raymond E. 3
CRANE, Richard 1
CRANE, Richard Teller 1
CRANE, Richard Teller Jr. 1
CRANE, Robert Clark 4
CRANE, Robert Treat 4
CRANE, Ronald Salmon 1
CRANE, Ronald Salmon 5
CRANE, Ross 4
CRANE, Stephen H
CRANE, Stephen 1
CRANE, Theodore 4
CRANE, Thomas Frederick 1
CRANE, Verner Winslow 6
CRANE, W. Murray 1
CRANE, Walter Richard 5
CRANE, William G. 3
CRANE, William H. 1
CRANE, William Iler 1
CRANE, William Montgomery H
CRANE, Winthrop Murray Jr. 5
CRANE, Zenas Marshall 1
CRANE-GARTZ, Kate 1
CRANFILL, James Britton 1
CRANFORD, William Ivey 4
CRANMER, Gibson L. 1
CRANMER, William H. H. 4
CRANNELL, Elizabeth Keller Shaule (Mrs. Winslow Crannell) 5
CRANNELL, Philip Wendell 1
CRANSTON, Claudia 2
CRANSTON, Earl 1
CRANSTON, Earl 5
CRANSTON, Henry Young H
CRANSTON, John H
CRANSTON, Robert Bennie H
CRANSTON, Samuel H
CRANWELL, James Logan 4
CRANWELL, Thomas George 1
CRAPO, Philip M. 1
CRAPO, Stanford Tappan 1
CRAPO, William Wallace 1
CRAPSEY, Algernon Sidney 1
CRARY, George Waldo 1
CRARY, Gordon B. 4
CRARY, Isaac Edwin H
CRASSWELLER, Frank 2
CRATHORNE, Arthur Robert 1
CRATTY, Mabel 1
CRATTY, Robert Irvin 1
CRAVATH, Erastus Milo 1
CRAVATH, Paul Drennan 4
CRAVEN, Alex 4
CRAVEN, Alfred 1
CRAVEN, Braxton H
CRAVEN, Charles Edmiston 4
CRAVEN, Elijah Richardson 1
CRAVEN, Frank 2
CRAVEN, George Warren 1
CRAVEN, Hermon Wilson 4
CRAVEN, James Braxton 1
CRAVEN, John Joseph H
CRAVEN, Leslie 5
CRAVEN, Thomas 3
CRAVEN, Thomas Tingey 1
CRAVEN, Thomas Tingey H
CRAVEN, Tunis Augustus Macdonough 5
CRAVEN, Tunus Augustus Macdonough H
CRAVEN, William Reno 4
CRAVENS, Ben 1
CRAVENS, Du Val Garland 5
CRAVENS, James Addison H
CRAVENS, James Harrison 1
CRAVENS, John William 1
CRAVENS, Kenton Robinson 5
CRAVENS, Oscar Henry 5
CRAVER, Harrison Warwick 1
CRAVER, Samuel Porch 1
CRAWFORD, Andrew Murray 1
CRAWFORD, Andrew Wright 1
CRAWFORD, Angus 4
CRAWFORD, Angus 5
CRAWFORD, Arch 1
CRAWFORD, Arthur 1
CRAWFORD, Charles 3
CRAWFORD, Charles Wallace 3
CRAWFORD, Clarence K. 4
CRAWFORD, Coe Isaac 4
CRAWFORD, David A. 3

CRAWFORD, David McLean 4
CRAWFORD, Earl Stetson 5
CRAWFORD, Eben G. 2
CRAWFORD, Edward Grant 1
CRAWFORD, Edwin Robert 1
CRAWFORD, Eugene Lowther 1
CRAWFORD, F. Stuart 1
CRAWFORD, Finia Goff 5
CRAWFORD, Francis Marion 1
CRAWFORD, Fred Lewis 3
CRAWFORD, George Gordon 1
CRAWFORD, George Washington H
CRAWFORD, Harry Clement 6
CRAWFORD, Harry J. 1
CRAWFORD, Harry Jennings 3
CRAWFORD, Isabel 4
CRAWFORD, Ivan Charles 4
CRAWFORD, Jack Randall 5
CRAWFORD, J(ames) C(hamberlain) 6
CRAWFORD, James Pyle Wickersham 1
CRAWFORD, James Stoner 4
CRAWFORD, Jerry Tinder 1
CRAWFORD, Joel H
CRAWFORD, John H
CRAWFORD, John Forsyth 5
CRAWFORD, John Jones 4
CRAWFORD, John M. 3
CRAWFORD, John Martin 1
CRAWFORD, John Raymond 1
CRAWFORD, John Wallace 4
CRAWFORD, Joseph 5
CRAWFORD, Leonard Jacob 1
CRAWFORD, Leonidas Wakefield 3
CRAWFORD, Martin Jenkins H
CRAWFORD, Mary Caroline 1
CRAWFORD, Mary Sinclair 4
CRAWFORD, Medorem 1
CRAWFORD, Meriwether Lewis 4
CRAWFORD, Milo Hicks 6
CRAWFORD, Morris Barker 1
CRAWFORD, Morris Barker 2
CRAWFORD, Nelson Antrim 4
CRAWFORD, Porter James 2
CRAWFORD, Ralph Dixon 3
CRAWFORD, Robert A. 1
CRAWFORD, Russell Tracy 3
CRAWFORD, Samuel Johnson 1
CRAWFORD, Stanton Chapman 4
CRAWFORD, Thomas H
CRAWFORD, Thomas Dwight 1
CRAWFORD, Thomas Hartley 1
CRAWFORD, Thomas Henry 1
CRAWFORD, Walter Joshua 1
CRAWFORD, William * H
CRAWFORD, William Alfred 1
CRAWFORD, William Campbell 4
CRAWFORD, William Harris 1
CRAWFORD, William Henry 2
CRAWFORD, William Hopkins 4
CRAWFORD, William L. 1
CRAWFORD, William T. 4
CRAWFORD, William Thomas 1
CRAWFORD, William Walt 6
CRAWFORD, William Webb 1
CRAWFORD-FROST, William Albert
CRAWLEY, Clyde B. 3
CRAWLEY, David Ephraim 2
CRAWLEY, Edwin Schoffield 1
CRAWSHAW, Fred Duane 5

CRAWSHAW, William Henry 1
CRAYTON, Jenkins Street 6
CRAZY HORSE 1
CREAGER, Charles E. 5
CREAGER, John Oscar 2
CREAGER, Marvin H. 3
CREAGER, Rentfro Banton 3
CREAGER, William Pitcher 1
CREAL, Edward Wester 2
CREAMER, David 1
CREAMER, Thomas J. 4
CREAN, Robert 4
CREASER, Charles W. 4
CREASEY, John 1
CREASY, William Neville 6
CREATH, Jacob * H
CREBS, John Montgomery 1
CRECRAFT, Earl Willis 3
CREE, Archibald Cunningham 2
CREECH, Harris 2
CREECH, John W. 1
CREECH, Oscar Jr. 4
CREECH, Oscar Jr. 5
CREED, Thomas Percival 5
CREED, Wigginton Ellis 1
CREEDE, Frank J. 4
CREEDEN, Daniel W. 3
CREEGAN, Charles Cole 1
CREEK, Herbert LeSourd 6
CREEL, Enrique C. 1
CREEL, George 3
CREEL, Robert Calhoun 5
CREELMAN, Harlan 3
CREELMAN, James 1
CREESE, James 4
CREESE, Wadsworth 5
CREESY, Josiah Perkins H
CREEVEY, Caroline Alathea Stickney 1
CREHORE, Albert Cushing 4
CREHORE, William Williams 1
CREIGHTON, Albert Morton 4
CREIGHTON, Edward H
CREIGHTON, Elmer Ellsworth Farmer 1
CREIGHTON, Frank Whittington 2
CREIGHTON, James Edwin 1
CREIGHTON, John Thrale 1
CREIGHTON, Martha Gladys 4
CREIGHTON, William H
CREIGHTON, William Henry 1
CREIGHTON, William J. 3
CREIM, Ben Wilton 1
CREITZ, Charles Erwin 1
CRELLIN, Edward Webster 2
CREMER, Jacob Theodoor 1
CRENIER, Henri 2
CRENSHAW, Bolling Hall 1
CRENSHAW, H. F. 1
CRENSHAW, James Llewellyn 1
CRENSHAW, Ollinger 5
CRENSHAW, Thomas C. 4
CRERAR, Henry Duncan 4
CRERAR, John H
CRESAP, Mark W. Jr. 4
CRESAP, Mark Winfield 2
CRESAP, Michael H
CRESAP, Thomas H
CRESON, Larry Barkley 5
CRESPI, Juan H
CRESPO Y MARTINEZ, Gilberto 4
CRESS, George Clifford 3
CRESS, George Oscar 1
CRESSEY, George Babcock 4
CRESSEY, George Croswell 1
CRESSLER, Alfred Miller 1
CRESSLER, Isabel Bonbrake 3
CRESSON, Elliott H
CRESSON, Ezra Townsend 4
CRESSON, Margaret French 6
CRESSON, W. Penn 1
CRESSWELL, Robert 2
CRESSY, Warren Francis 1
CRESSY, Wilfred Wesley 4
CRESSY, Will Martin 1
CRESWELL, Edward J. 3
CRESWELL, Harry I. T. 5
CRESWELL, John Angel James 1
CRESWELL, Mary E. 6
CRET, Paul Philippe 2
CRETIN, Joseph H
CREVECOEUR, Michel-Guillaume Jean De H

CREW, Henry 3
CREW, William Binford 1
CREWS, Floyd Houston 4
CREWS, Leslie F. 5
CREWS, Ralph 1
CRICHTON, Alexander Fraser 1
CRICHTON, Kyle S. 4
CRIDER, Blake 6
CRIDER, John Henshaw 4
CRIDLAND, Charles 5
CRIDLER, Thomas Wilbur 4
CRILE, Austin Daniel 3
CRILE, Dennis Rider Wood 4
CRILE, George Washington 2
CRILLEY, A. Cyril 5
CRIM, John William Henry 1
CRIMI, James Ernest 6
CRIMMINS, Harry Benedict 4
CRIMMINS, John Daniel 1
CRIMONT, Joseph Raphael 2
CRINKLEY, Matthew S. 4
CRIPPA, Edward David 4
CRIPPEN, Henry Durrell 1
CRIPPEN, Lloyd Kenneth 5
CRIPPS, Sir Stafford 3
CRISCUOLO, Luigi 3
CRISFIELD, John Woodland H
CRISP, Arthur 6
CRISP, Charles Frederick 1
CRISP, Charles R. 1
CRISP, Donald 6
CRISPIN, M. Jackson 3
CRISS, Clair C. 3
CRISS, Neil Louis 5
CRISSEY, Forrest 2
CRISSINGER, Daniel Richard 2
CRIST, Bainbridge 5
CRIST, Harris McCabe 2
CRIST, Henry 1
CRIST, Raymond Fowler 2
CRISTY, Albert Barnes 4
CRISTY, Albert Moses 1
CRISWELL, George Stuart 1
CRITCHFIELD, Howard Emmett 6
CRITCHLOW, Francis B. 3
CRITES, Lowry Hyer 6
CRITTENBERGER, George Dale 4
CRITTENDEN, Christopher 5
CRITTENDEN, Eugene Casson 1
CRITTENDEN, George Bibb 4
CRITTENDEN, John Jordan H
CRITTENDEN, Thomas Leonidas 1
CRITTENDEN, Thomas Theodore 1
CRITTENDEN, Walter Hayden 1
CRITZ, Hugh 5
CRITZ, Richard 1
CROASDALE, Jack Finch 4
CROASDALE, Stuart 1
CROCE, Benedetto 3
CROCHERON, Henry H
CROCHERON, Jacob 1
CROCKARD, Frank Hearne 3
CROCKER, Alvah 1
CROCKER, Arthur W. 4
CROCKER, Augustus Luther 4
CROCKER, Bosworth 2
CROCKER, Charles 1
CROCKER, Charles Henry 1
CROCKER, Edward Savage 5
CROCKER, Francis Bacon 1
CROCKER, Frank Longfellow 2
CROCKER, George 1
CROCKER, George Glover 1
CROCKER, Hannah Mather H
CROCKER, Henry E. 1
CROCKER, Samuel Leonard H
CROCKER, Sarah G. H
CROCKER, Stuart Miller 2
CROCKER, Templeton 2
CROCKER, Theodore D. 2
CROCKER, Uriel H
CROCKER, Uriel Haskell 1
CROCKER, Walter James 4
CROCKER, William 2
CROCKER, William Henry 1
CROCKER, William Willard 4
CROCKETT, Albert Stevens 5
CROCKETT, Arthur Jay 4
CROCKETT, Charles Winthrop 1
CROCKETT, David H

CROCKETT, Eugene Anthony 1
CROCKETT, Franklin Smith 6
CROCKETT, Horace Guy 4
CROCKETT, Ingram 4
CROCKETT, John Wesley H
CROCKETT, Montgomery Adams 4
CROCKETT, Walter Hill 1
CROCKETT, William Day 1
CROCKETT, William Goggin 1
CROES, John James Robertson 1
CROFFUT, William Augustus 1
CROFT, Albert Jefferson i
CROFT, Delmer Eugene 1
CROFT, Edward 1
CROFT, George William 1
CROFT, Harry William 2
CROFT, Richard Graham 1
CROFTAN, Alfred Careno 1
CROFTS, Frederick Sharer 3
CROGHAN, George H
CROGHAN, Hubert McLeod 4
CROGMAN, William Henry Sr. 1
CROISSANT, De Witt Clinton 2
CROIX, Teodoro de H
CROKER, Richard 1
CROLL, Morris William 2
CROLL, Philip C. 4
CROLL, William M. 1
CROLY, David Goodman H
CROLY, Herbert 1
CROLY, Jane Cunningham 1
CROMELIN, Paul Bowen 3
CROMER, George Benedict 1
CROMER, George Washington 4
CROMER, S. S. 4
CROMIE, William James 5
CROMMELIN, Henry 5
CROMPTON, George H
CROMPTON, George 3
CROMPTON, William 5
CROMWELL, Arthur Dayton 5
CROMWELL, Bartlett Jefferson 1
CROMWELL, Emma Guy 4
CROMWELL, Frank H. 6
CROMWELL, Frederic 1
CROMWELL, Frederick 1
CROMWELL, George 1
CROMWELL, Lincoln 3
CROMWELL, Michael Jenkins 5
CROMWELL, Paul Crawford 6
CROMWELL, William Nelson 2
CRONAU, Rudolf 1
CRONBACH, Abraham 5
CRONE, Frank Linden 5
CRONE, R. Bertram 5
CRONEIS, Carey 5
CRONIN, Con P. 1
CRONIN, David Edward 4
CRONIN, Edward Joseph 3
CRONIN, John J. 3
CRONIN, John William 3
CRONIN, Marcus Daniel 1
CRONIN, Ralph Marvin 6
CRONIN, Timothy T. 3
CRONIN, William Francis 4
CRONKHITE, Adelbert 1
CRONKHITE, Leonard Wolsey 1
CRONSTEDT, Val 6
CRONYN, George William 5
CROOK, Alja Robinson 1
CROOK, George H
CROOK, Isaac 1
CROOK, James King 1
CROOK, James Walter 1
CROOK, Jere Lawrence 1
CROOK, William McKissack 2
CROOKE, Philip Schuyler H
CROOKER, Florence Kollock 1
CROOKER, Joseph Henry 1
CROOKS, Alexander Richard 1
CROOKS, Arthur H
CROOKS, Ezra Breckenridge 1
CROOKS, Ezra Breckenridge 2
CROOKS, George Richard H
CROOKS, Harry Means 6

CROOKS, Ramsay H
CROOKS, Richard M. 5
CROOKSHANK, Angus 4
James
CROPLEY, Charles Elmore 3
CROPPER, Walter V. 2
CROPSEY, James Church 1
CROPSEY, Jasper Francis 1
CROPSEY, Nebraska Miss 5
CROSAS, Andres 5
Bernardino
CROSBY, Alpheus H
CROSBY, Charles Noel 3
CROSBY, Dick J. 4
CROSBY, Edward Harold 1
CROSBY, Edwin L. 5
CROSBY, Edwin Stanislau 3
CROSBY, Ernest Howard 1
CROSBY, Evan 2
CROSBY, Everett Nathaniel 5
CROSBY, Everett Uberto 4
CROSBY, Fanny 1
CROSBY, Franklin Muzzy 2
CROSBY, Frederic Van 1
Schoonhoven
CROSBY, George 1
Harrington
CROSBY, George Heman 4
CROSBY, H. E. 3
CROSBY, Harley N. 3
CROSBY, Henry Lamar 6
CROSBY, Herbert Ball 3
CROSBY, Howard H
CROSBY, James Ott 4
CROSBY, John 4
CROSBY, John Crawford 4
CROSBY, John Schuyler 1
CROSBY, Nathan 3
CROSBY, Oscar Terry 2
CROSBY, Peirce 1
CROSBY, Pierce H
CROSBY, Raymond Moreau 2
CROSBY, Sheldon Leavitt 1
CROSBY, Stephen Moody 1
CROSBY, Walter Wilson 5
CROSBY, William Dorr 4
CROSBY, William Hugh 5
CROSBY, William Otis 4
CROSE, William Michael 4
CROSIER, Edwin Neil 3
CROSKEY, John Welsh 3
CROSLAND, John Everett 5
CROSLEY, Powel Jr. 1
CROSLEY, Walter Selwyn 1
CROSMAN, Charles 1
Sumner
CROSMAN, Henrietta 2
CROSS, Anson Kent 4
CROSS, Arthur Chester 3
CROSS, Arthur Lyon 1
CROSS, Asa Beebe 1
CROSS, Cecil Frank 4
CROSS, Charles Robert 1
CROSS, Charles Whitman 4
CROSS, Clarence Eland 4
CROSS, Claude B. 6
CROSS, E(than) A(llen) 5
CROSS, Earle Bennett 4
CROSS, Edward H
CROSS, Edward Makin 4
CROSS, Edward Weeks 1
CROSS, George 6
CROSS, Hardy 3
CROSS, Harold L. 3
CROSS, Harry Parsons 1
CROSS, Henry H. H
CROSS, Henry H. 4
CROSS, John W(alker) 5
CROSS, John Walter 2
CROSS, Joseph 1
CROSS, Judson Lewis 2
CROSS, Judson Newell 1
CROSS, Lewis Josephus 5
CROSS, Louis John 2
CROSS, Michael Hurley H
CROSS, Milton 6
CROSS, Morton Robinson 6
CROSS, Oliver Harlan 3
CROSS, Peter F. H
CROSS, Richard James 1
CROSS, Roselle Theodore 4
CROSS, Roy 2
CROSS, Samuel Hazzard 4
CROSS, Thomas Joseph 4
CROSS, Tom Peete 6
CROSS, Walter Snell 4
CROSS, Wilbur Lucius 2
CROSS, William Campbell 2
CROSSE, Charles Washburn 2
CROSSE, Mentor 1
CROSSEN, George Edward 3
CROSSEN, Harry Sturgeon 5
CROSSER, John Roach 1
CROSSER, Robert 4
CROSSETT, Edward C. 4
CROSSETT, Lewis Abbott 1

CROSSFIELD, Richard 3
Henry
CROSSKEY, William 4
Winslow
CROSSLAND, Edward H
CROSSLAND, Paul Marion 5
CROSSLAND, Weldon 4
Frank
CROSSLEY, Arthur 5
Webster
CROSSLEY, Frederic Beers 1
CROSSLEY, James Judson 5
CROSSLEY, Robert J. 3
CROSSLEY, Robert Pierce 5
CROSSMAN, Edgar Gibson 4
CROSSMAN, Edgar O. 4
CROSSMAN, Jerome 5
Kenneth
CROSSMAN, Richard 6
Howard Stafford
CROSSWELL, William H
CROSWELL, Edwin H
CROSWELL, Harry H
CROSWELL, James 1
Greenleaf
CROTHERS, Austin L. 1
CROTHERS, Bronson 3
CROTHERS, George 3
Edward
CROTHERS, Harold 4
Marion
CROTHERS, Rachel 3
CROTHERS, Samuel 1
McChord
CROTHERS, Thomas 1
Davison
CROTT, Homer Daniel 5
CROTTI, Andre 3
CROTTY, Homer Daniel 6
CROTTY, Sister M. 6
Madeleine
CROUCH, Austin 3
CROUCH, Calvin Henry 4
CROUCH, Charles T. 3
CROUCH, Courtney Chet 6
CROUCH, Edward H
CROUCH, Leonard 3
Callender
CROUCH, Ralph B. 6
CROUCH, Richard Edwin 4
CROUCH, Sydney James 5
Leonhardt
CROUNSE, Lorenzo 1
CROUNSE, Robert Mabie 6
CROUSE, George Nellis 2
CROUSE, Mary Elizabeth 5
CROUSE, Russel 4
CROUTER, A. L. Edgerton 1
CROW, Charles Augustus 3
CROW, Charles Langley 1
CROW, Herbert Carl 2
CROW, Martha Foote 1
CROW, Orin Faison 3
CROW, Randolph Fairfax 3
CROW, William E. 1
CROWDER, Enoch Herbert 1
CROWDER, Frank Warfield 1
CROWDER, John Batte 5
CROWDER, Render Lewis 5
Jr.
CROWDER, Thomas Reid 5
CROWE, Francis Trenholm 2
CROWE, John A. 4
CROWE, R. L. 3
CROWE, Thomas Bennett 4
CROWE, William 4
CROWELL, Bowman 3
Corning
CROWELL, Chester 1
Theodore
CROWELL, Edward Payson 1
CROWELL, Grace Noll 5
(Mrs. Norman H. Crowell)
CROWELL, Henry Coleman 4
CROWELL, Henry Parsons 1
CROWELL, James Foster 1
CROWELL, James 1
McMullin
CROWELL, John * H
CROWELL, John 1
CROWELL, John Franklin 1
CROWELL, John Stephen 1
CROWELL, Katharine 1
Roney
CROWELL, Lester Avant 3
Sr.
CROWELL, Luther Childs 1
CROWELL, Merle 1
CROWELL, Thomas Irving 4
Jr.
CROWLEY, Charles Francis 3
CROWLEY, Henry J. 1
CROWLEY, John Dennis 5
CROWLEY, Joseph Burns 4
CROWLEY, Karl Allen 2

CROWLEY, Leo T. 5
CROWLEY, Mary 1
Catherine
CROWLEY, Patrick Edward 3
CROWLEY, Patrick F. 6
CROWLEY, Xavier 3
CROWN, Edward A. 6
CROWN, James Evans 2
CROWNE, John H
CROWNE, William H
CROWNFIELD, Gertrude 1
CROWNHART, Charles 1
Henry
CROWNHART, Charles 6
Henry
CROWNHART, Jesse 2
George
CROWNINSHIELD, Arent 1
Schuyler
CROWNINSHIELD, H
Benjamin Williams
CROWNINSHIELD, 1
Bowdoin Bradlee
CROWNINSHIELD, Caspar 1
Schuyler
CROWNINSHIELD, Frank 2
CROWNINSHIELD, 1
Frederic
CROWNINSHIELD, 1
George
CROWNINSHIELD, Jacob 1
CROWNINSHIELD, Mary 1
Bradford
CROWNOVER, Arthur Jr. 4
CROWNOVER, Arthur Sr. 2
CROWSON, Benjamin 1
Franklin
CROWTHER, Cyril Irwin 5
CROWTHER, Frank 3
CROWTHER, James Edwin 2
CROWTHER, Samuel 2
CROXTON, Fred C. 4
CROY, Homer 4
CROY, Homer 5
CROZER, John Price 1
CROZER, Samuel Aldrich 1
CROZET, Claude 1
CROZIER, Herbert William 1
CROZIER, John 6
CROZIER, John Hervey 1
CROZIER, Norman Robert 1
CROZIER, Robert H
CROZIER, W. J. 3
CROZIER, William 2
CRUCE, Lee 1
CRUCHAGA-TOCORNAL, 5
Miguel
CRUDUP, Josiah H
CRUGER, Daniel H
CRUGER, Henry H
CRUGER, John H
CRUGER, Mary 1
CRUICKSHANK, H. W. 4
CRUIKSHANK, Alfred B. 1
CRUIKSHANK, Margaret 3
CRUIKSHANK, R. J. 3
CRUIKSHANK, Russell V. 4
CRUIKSHANK, William 2
Mackey
CRULL, Harry Edward 4
CRUM, Bartley Cavanaugh 3
CRUM, Roy W. 3
CRUM, William Demos 1
CRUM, William Leonard 4
CRUMB, Frederick Waite 4
CRUMBACKER, William 3
Pollock
CRUMBINE, Samuel Jay 3
CRUMLEY, Thomas 3
CRUMLEY, Thomas 2
Ralston
CRUMMER, Le Roy 1
CRUMMEY, John D. 6
CRUMP, Edward Hull 3
CRUMP, George William H
CRUMP, Rousseau O. 1
CRUMP, Walter Gray 2
CRUMP, William Wood H
CRUMPACKER, Edgar 1
Dean
CRUMPACKER, Maurice 1
Edgar
CRUMPTON, Washington 1
Bryan
CRUNDEN, Frederick 1
Morgan
CRUNELLE, Leonard 2
CRUSE, Thomas 2
CRUSINBERRY, William 3
Alfred
CRUTCHFIELD, James 3
Stapleton
CRUTCHFIELD, William H
CRUTCHFIELD, William 5
Gayle

CRUTHCER, Lewis 5
Pinkerton
CRUTTENDEN, Walter 2
Barnes
CRUZ, Anibal 1
CRUZE, James 1
CRYDERMAN, Mackie 5
Macintyre (Mrs. Clifford William)
CRYER, George Edward 4
CRYER, Matthew Henry 1
CSANADL, György 6
CSATORDAY, Karoly 5
CUBBERLEY, Ellwood 1
Patterson
CUBBERLY, Fred 1
CUBBINS, William Robert 3
CUCKSON, John 1
CUDAHY, Edward A. 4
CUDAHY, Edward Aloysius 1
Sr.
CUDAHY, John 1
CUDAHY, John 2
CUDAHY, Joseph M. 2
CUDAHY, Michael 1
CUDAHY, Michael Francis 5
CUDAHY, Patrick 1
CUDDEBACK, Allan W. 1
CUDDEBACK, William 1
Herman
CUDDIHY, Herbert Lester 3
CUDDY, Warren N. 4
CUDLIP, Merlin A. 5
CUENY, Elizabeth 4
CUFFE, Paul H
CUFFE, Thomas E. 4
CULBERSON, Charles A. 1
CULBERSON, David 1
Browning
CULBERTSON, Albert L. 3
CULBERTSON, Alexander H
CULBERTSON, Anne 4
Virginia
CULBERTSON, Ely 3
CULBERTSON, Emma 1
Valeria Bicknell
CULBERTSON, Henry Coe 1
CULBERTSON, James Coe 1
CULBERTSON, James 5
Gordon
CULBERTSON, John J. 1
CULBERTSON, William 5
CULBERTSON, William 6
H(oward)
CULBERTSON, William 1
Smith
CULBRETH, David Marvel 4
Reynolds
CULBRETH, Thomas H
CULIG, Ivan Conrad 4
CULIN, Alice Mumford 5
(Mrs. Stewart Culin)
CULIN, Frank Lewis 4
CULIN, Stewart 1
CULKIN, Francis D. 2
CULKINS, William Clement 1
CULLEN, Countee 2
CULLEN, Edgar 1
Montgomery
CULLEN, Elisha Dickerson H
CULLEN, Frederick John 5
CULLEN, Glenn E. 1
CULLEN, Hugh Roy 3
CULLEN, James Aloysius 2
CULLEN, Richard J. 2
CULLEN, Thomas Ernest 1
CULLEN, Thomas H. 2
CULLEN, Thomas Joseph 4
Vincent
CULLEN, Thomas Stephen 3
CULLEN, Vincent 1
CULLEN, William George 6
CULLER, Arthur Jerome 2
CULLER, Arthur Merl 4
CULLER, Joseph Albertus 1
CULLIMORE, Allan 3
Reginald
CULLIMORE, Clarence 4
CULLINAN, Craig Francis 3
CULLINAN, Edith Phillips 3
CULLINAN, Joseph 1
Stephen
CULLIS, Charles H
CULLISON, James 1
Buchanan
CULLMAN, Howard S(tix) 5
CULLOM, Alvan 1
CULLOM, Marvin 4
McTyeire
CULLOM, Shelby Moore 1
CULLOM, William H
CULLOP, William Allen 5
CULLUM, George H
Washington
CULMER, Henry L. A. 1

CULP, Charles Cantrell 4
CULP, John M. 1
CULPEPER, John H
CULPEPER, Thomas H
CULPEPPER, James Henry 6
CULPEPPER, John H
CULTER, Mary McCrae 4
CULVER, Bernard Mott 3
CULVER, Bertram Beach 3
CULVER, Charles Aaron 6
CULVER, Charles Beach 1
CULVER, Charles Mortimer 1
CULVER, Erastus Dean 1
CULVER, Frank Pugh 2
CULVER, Harry Hazel 2
CULVER, Helen 1
CULVER, Henry S. 4
CULVER, John Yapp 4
CULVER, Montgomery 3
Morton
CULVER, Raymond B. 1
CULVER, Romulus Estep 1
CUMBERLAND, William 3
Wilson
CUMING, Fortescue H
CUMING, Sir Alexander H
CUMINGS, Edgar Roscoe 5
CUMMER, Clyde Lottridge 3
CUMMING, Alfred 1
CUMMING, Charles 1
Atherton
CUMMING, Hugh S. 2
CUMMING, Thomas H
William
CUMMING, William H
CUMMINGHAM, William 2
Burgess
CUMMINGS, Amos 1
CUMMINGS, Bertrude 4
Fields Mrs.
CUMMINGS, Charles Amos 1
CUMMINGS, Clara Eaton 1
CUMMINGS, D. Mark 1
CUMMINGS, Edward 4
CUMMINGS, Edward 1
Estlin
CUMMINGS, George Bain 6
CUMMINGS, George 4
Donald
CUMMINGS, George W. 1
CUMMINGS, Gordon H
Parker
CUMMINGS, Harold Neff 4
CUMMINGS, Henry 1
Johnson Brodhead
CUMMINGS, Henry 4
Johnson Brodhead
CUMMINGS, Homer Stille 3
CUMMINGS, James Howell 1
CUMMINGS, Jeremiah H
Williams
CUMMINGS, Joe Brown 3
CUMMINGS, John 1
CUMMINGS, John 1
CUMMINGS, Joseph 1
CUMMINGS, Marshall 5
Baxter
CUMMINGS, Marvin Earl 5
CUMMINGS, O. Sam H
CUMMINGS, Thomas Seir H
CUMMINGS, Walter J. 4
CUMMINS, Albert Baird 1
CUMMINS, Albert Wilson 1
CUMMINS, Alexander H
CUMMINS, Alexander H
Griswold
CUMMINS, Claude 4
CUMMINS, Claude 1
CUMMINS, Clessie Lyle 5
CUMMINS, George David H
CUMMINS, John 1
CUMMINS, John D. 6
CUMMINS, Joseph Michael 3
CUMMINS, Maria Susanna H
CUMMINS, Ralph 1
CUMMINS, Robert Rankin 3
CUMMINS, William 1
Fletcher
CUMMINS, William J. 1
CUMMINS, William Taylor 3
CUMMINS, William Taylor 6
CUMNOCK, Robert 1
McLean
CUNHA, Felix 4
CUNINGGIM, Jesse Lee 3
CUNLIFFE, John William 2
CUNLIFFE-OWEN, 1
Frederick
CUNLIFFE-OWEN, Sir 2
Hugo
CUNNIFF, Michael Glen 1
CUNNINGHAM, Albert 4
Benjamin
CUNNINGHAM, Andrew 1
Chase

CUNNINGHAM, Andrew Oswald 1
CUNNINGHAM, Ann Pamela H
CUNNINGHAM, Augustine Joseph 3
CUNNINGHAM, Benjamin B. 2
CUNNINGHAM, Benjamin Frazier 5
CUNNINGHAM, Bert 2
CUNNINGHAM, Burris Bell 5
CUNNINGHAM, C. Frederick 5
CUNNINGHAM, Charles Barnard 6
CUNNINGHAM, Charles Henry 2
CUNNINGHAM, Cornelius Carman 3
CUNNINGHAM, David West 1
CUNNINGHAM, Donnell LaFayette 2
CUNNINGHAM, Edward Henry 1
CUNNINGHAM, Edwin Sheddan 3
CUNNINGHAM, Edwin W. 4
CUNNINGHAM, Elijah William 4
CUNNINGHAM, Eugene 3
CUNNINGHAM, Firman 6
CUNNINGHAM, Francis Alanson H
CUNNINGHAM, Frank 4
CUNNINGHAM, Frank Harrison 5
CUNNINGHAM, Frank Simpson 1
CUNNINGHAM, George A. 4
CUNNINGHAM, George William 3
CUNNINGHAM, Gustavus Watts 6
CUNNINGHAM, Harrison Edward 6
CUNNINGHAM, Harry A. 4
CUNNINGHAM, Henry Vincent 1
CUNNINGHAM, Holly Estil 3
CUNNINGHAM, Horace Herndon 5
CUNNINGHAM, I. A. 1
CUNNINGHAM, James A. 4
CUNNINGHAM, James Dalton 4
CUNNINGHAM, John Charles 5
CUNNINGHAM, John Ferguson 3
CUNNINGHAM, John Henry 5
CUNNINGHAM, John Lovell 4
CUNNINGHAM, Joseph Oscar 1
CUNNINGHAM, Julian W. 5
CUNNINGHAM, Louis Wyborn 1
CUNNINGHAM, Milton Joseph 1
CUNNINGHAM, Paul 4
CUNNINGHAM, Paul Davis 1
CUNNINGHAM, Richard Hoope 1
CUNNINGHAM, Robert Sydney 4
CUNNINGHAM, Ross MacDuffee 4
CUNNINGHAM, Russell McWhorter 1
CUNNINGHAM, Solomon M. 4
CUNNINGHAM, Sumner Archibald 1
CUNNINGHAM, Thomas F. 1
CUNNINGHAM, Thomas Mayhew 5
CUNNINGHAM, Wallace McCook 6
CUNNINGHAM, Warren W. 3
CUNNINGHAM, Wilfred Harris 5
CUNNINGHAM, William 4
CUNNINGHAM, William Francis 4
CUNNINGHAM, William James 5
CUNZ, Dieter 5
CUPPIA, Jerome Chester 4
CUPPLES, Samuel 1
CUPPY, Hazlitt Alva 1
CUPPY, William Jacob 2
CURETON, Calvin Maples 2
CURIE, Robert James 6
CURL, Robert Floyd 5
CURLEE, Francis M. 3
CURLESS, Howard Marion 6
CURLEY, Daniel J. 1
CURLEY, Edward W. 1
CURLEY, Frank E. 1
CURLEY, James H
CURLEY, James Michael 3
CURLEY, Michael Joseph 2
CURLEY, Walter J. 5
CURLEY, William A. 3
CURME, George Oliver 2
CUROE, Philip R(aphael) V(incent) 5
CURRAN, Charles Courtney 2
CURRAN, Edward Lawrence 6
CURRAN, Henry Hastings 4
CURRAN, Kenneth James 5
CURRAN, Peter Ferguson 6
CURRAN, Thomas Jerome 3
CURRAN, William Reid 4
CURRELL, William Spenser 2
CURREY, Brownlee Own 3
CURREY, J. Seymour 1
CURREY, John 1
CURRICK, Max Cohen 2
CURRIE, Barton Wood 4
CURRIE, Brainerd 4
CURRIE, Donald Herbert 1
CURRIE, Edward James 4
CURRIE, George Graham 1
CURRIE, Gilbert Archibald 4
CURRIE, John S. 3
CURRIE, Thomas White 2
CURRIER, Albert Dean 1
CURRIER, Albert Henry 4
CURRIER, Amos Noyes 1
CURRIER, Charles Francis Adams 1
CURRIER, Charles Warren 1
CURRIER, Frank Dunklee 1
CURRIER, George Harvey 5
CURRIER, J. Frank 1
CURRIER, John C. 4
CURRIER, Moody H
CURRIER, Nathaniel H
CURRIER, Raymond Pillsbury 5
CURRIER, Richard Dudley 2
CURRIER, Thomas Franklin 2
CURRY, Albert Bruce 1
CURRY, Allen 5
CURRY, Arthur Mansfield 4
CURRY, Charles Forrest 1
CURRY, Charles Madison 2
CURRY, Edward Rufus 1
CURRY, George 2
CURRY, George Law H
CURRY, Jabez Lamar Monroe 1
CURRY, James Bernard 1
CURRY, James J. 4
CURRY, James Rowland 5
CURRY, John F. 3
CURRY, John Francis 6
CURRY, John Steuart 2
CURRY, Michael John 3
CURRY, Neil James 4
CURRY, Peter H. 3
CURRY, R. Granville 4
CURRY, Samuel Silas 1
CURRY, William Melville 1
CURTICE, Harlow Herbert 4
CURTIN, Andrew Gregg H
CURTIN, Austin 4
CURTIN, D. Thomas 4
CURTIN, Jeremiah 1
CURTIN, Roland Gideon 1
CURTIS, A. J. R. 3
CURTIS, Alfred Allen 1
CURTIS, Arthur Melvin 2
CURTIS, Asahel 5
CURTIS, Augustus Darwin 1
CURTIS, Benjamin Robbins H
CURTIS, C. Densmore 1
CURTIS, Carlton Brandaga H
CURTIS, Carlton Clarence 2
CURTIS, Charles 1
CURTIS, Charles Albert 1
CURTIS, Charles Boyd 1
CURTIS, Charles Clarence 4
CURTIS, Charles Gordon 3
CURTIS, Charles Minot 2
CURTIS, Charles Pelham 2
CURTIS, Charles Pelham 3
CURTIS, Constance 3
CURTIS, Cyrus Hermann Kotzschmar 1
CURTIS, David A. 1
CURTIS, Earl A. 6
CURTIS, Edward H
CURTIS, Edward 1
CURTIS, Edward Gilman 5
CURTIS, Edward Glion Jr. 5
CURTIS, Edward Harvey 4
CURTIS, Edward Lewis 1
CURTIS, Edward S. 4
CURTIS, Edwin Upton 1
CURTIS, Eugene Judson 3
CURTIS, Eugene Newton 2
CURTIS, F. Kingsbury 1
CURTIS, Florence Rising 2
CURTIS, Francis 4
CURTIS, Francis Joseph 4
CURTIS, Frederic Colton 4
CURTIS, Frederick Smillie 1
CURTIS, George H
CURTIS, George Carroll 1
CURTIS, George Lenox 4
CURTIS, George Lewis 3
CURTIS, George Martin 1
CURTIS, George Martin II 5
CURTIS, George Milton 1
CURTIS, George Morris 4
CURTIS, George Munson 1
CURTIS, George Ticknor H
CURTIS, George William H
CURTIS, Georgina Pell 1
CURTIS, Gerald Beckwith 3
CURTIS, H. Holbrook 1
CURTIS, Harry Alfred 4
CURTIS, Harvey Lincoln 3
CURTIS, Heber Doust 1
CURTIS, Henry G. 1
CURTIS, Henry Stoddard 3
CURTIS, Howard James 5
CURTIS, Howard Junior 1
CURTIS, Isabel Gordon 1
CURTIS, James Freeman 3
CURTIS, Jesse William 5
CURTIS, John Green 1
CURTIS, John Jay 1
CURTIS, John Talbot 3
CURTIS, John Thomas 4
CURTIS, Mattoon Monroe 4
CURTIS, Melville Goss 3
CURTIS, Moses Ashley H
CURTIS, Nathaniel Cortlandt 6
CURTIS, Newton Martin 1
CURTIS, Oakley Chester 1
CURTIS, Olin Alfred 1
CURTIS, Otis Freeman 2
CURTIS, Richard Cary 3
CURTIS, Roy Emerson 4
CURTIS, Samuel Ryan H
CURTIS, Sumner 1
CURTIS, Vivian Critz 5
CURTIS, Wardon Allan 1
CURTIS, William Buckingham 1
CURTIS, William Edmond 1
CURTIS, William Eleroy 1
CURTIS, William Franklin 1
CURTIS, William Fuller 5
CURTIS, William John 1
CURTIS, William Rodolph 6
CURTIS, William Samuel 1
CURTIS, Winterton Conway 5
CURTISS, Charles Chauncey 1
CURTISS, Charles Franklin 2
CURTISS, David Raymond 3
CURTISS, George Boughton 4
CURTISS, Glenn Hammond 1
CURTISS, Julian Wheeler 2
CURTISS, Lawrence Meredith 5
CURTISS, Philip 4
CURTISS, Ralph Hamilton 1
CURTISS, Richard Sydney 4
CURTISS, Samuel Ives 1
CURTISS, William Hanford 3
CURTISS, William John 3
CURTIZ, Michael 4
CURTS, Lewis 1
CURTS, Maurice Edwin 6
CURWEN, John 1
CURWEN, Samuel H
CURWEN, Samuel M. 1
CURWOOD, James Oliver 1
CURZON, Mary Victoria 1
CUSACK, Thomas Francis 1
CUSHING, Caleb H
CUSHING, Charles C. S. 1
CUSHING, Charles Phelps 6
CUSHING, Edward Harvey 5
CUSHING, Ernest Watson 1
CUSHING, Frank Hamilton H
CUSHING, George Holmes 5
CUSHING, Grafton Dulany 1
CUSHING, Harry Alonzo 3
CUSHING, Harry Cooke 4
CUSHING, Harvey 1
CUSHING, Henry Platt 1
CUSHING, Herbert Howard 5
CUSHING, Howard Gardiner 1
CUSHING, John E. 3
CUSHING, John Pearsons 1
CUSHING, John Perkins H
CUSHING, John Thayer 1
CUSHING, Luther Stearns H
CUSHING, Oscar K. 2
CUSHING, Richard Cardinal 5
CUSHING, Samuel Tobey 1
CUSHING, Stephen S. 3
CUSHING, Thomas H
CUSHING, William H
CUSHING, William Barker H
CUSHING, William Erastus 1
CUSHING, William Lee 1
CUSHMAN, Allerton Seward 1
CUSHMAN, Arlon Vannevar 3
CUSHMAN, Austin Sprague 1
CUSHMAN, Beulah 4
CUSHMAN, Charlotte Saunders H
CUSHMAN, Edward Everett 4
CUSHMAN, Francis W. 1
CUSHMAN, Frank 3
CUSHMAN, George Hewitt H
CUSHMAN, Henry W. 4
CUSHMAN, Herbert Ernest 4
CUSHMAN, Horace O. 5
CUSHMAN, John Paine H
CUSHMAN, Joseph Augustine 2
CUSHMAN, Joshua H
CUSHMAN, Lewis Arthur 4
CUSHMAN, Pauline H
CUSHMAN, Ralph Spaulding 4
CUSHMAN, Robert H
CUSHMAN, Robert Eugene 5
CUSHMAN, Samuel H
CUSHMAN, Susan Webb H
CUSHMAN, William Michael 4
CUSHWA, Charles B. Jr. 6
CUSICK, James Francis 6
CUSTER, Elizabeth Bacon 1
CUSTER, George Armstrong H
CUSTER, Omer Nixon 2
CUSTIS, George Washington Parke H
CUSTIS, John Trevor 2
CUSTIS, Marvin A. 3
CUSTIS, Vanderveer 4
CUSUMANO, Stefano 6
CUTBUSH, James H
CUTCHEON, Byron M. 1
CUTCHEON, Franklin W. M. 1
CUTHBERT, Alfred H
CUTHBERT, John Alfred H
CUTHBERT, Lucius Montrose 1
CUTHELL, Chester Welde 2
CUTHRELL, Hugh H. 3
CUTLER, Anna Alice 3
CUTLER, Arthur Hamilton 1
CUTLER, Augustus William H
CUTLER, Bertram 3
CUTLER, Carroll H
CUTLER, Charles Frederic 1
CUTLER, Condict Walker 1
CUTLER, Condict Walker Jr. 3
CUTLER, Elbridge Gerry 1
CUTLER, Elliott Carr 2
CUTLER, Everett Alonzo 1
CUTLER, Frederick Morse 2
CUTLER, Garnet Homer 4
CUTLER, George Chalmers 3
CUTLER, Harry Morton 1
CUTLER, Henry Edwin 3
CUTLER, Henry Franklin 4
CUTLER, Ira Eugene 1
CUTLER, James Elbert 3
CUTLER, James Goold 1
CUTLER, James Gould H
CUTLER, James Gould 4
CUTLER, John Christopher 1
CUTLER, John W. 3
CUTLER, Lizzie Petit H
CUTLER, Manasseh H
CUTLER, Otis Henderson 1
CUTLER, Ralph William 1
CUTLER, Robert 6
CUTLER, Timothy H
CUTLER, William Frye 3
CUTLER, William Parker H
CUTRIGHT, Harold Glen 4
CUTSHALL, H. Walton Jr. 4
CUTTEN, Arthur W. 1
CUTTEN, George Barton 4
CUTTEN, Ruloff Edward 4
CUTTER, Benjamin 1
CUTTER, Charles Ammi 1
CUTTER, Ephraim 1
CUTTER, Mrs. George Albert (Florence Maxim Cutter) 5
CUTTER, George Washington H
CUTTER, Irving Samuel 2
CUTTER, John Ashburton 4
CUTTER, K. K. 1
CUTTER, Robert Kennedy 6
CUTTER, Victor Macomber 3
CUTTER, Victor Macomber Jr. 4
CUTTER, William Dick 1
CUTTER, William Parker 4
CUTTING, Bronson 1
CUTTING, Charles Sidney 1
CUTTING, Charles Suydam 5
CUTTING, Churchill Hunter 1
CUTTING, Elisabeth Brown 2
CUTTING, Francis Brockholst H
CUTTING, Hiram Adolphus H
CUTTING, James Ambrose H
CUTTING, Mary Stewart 1
CUTTING, R. Pulton 1
CUTTING, Starr Willard 1
CUTTING, W. Bayard 1
CUTTING, Windsor Cooper 5
CUTTLE, Francis 5
CUTTS, Charles H
CUTTS, Elmer Henry 4
CUTTS, Marsena Edgar H
CUTTS, Richard H
CUTTS, Richard Malcolm 6
CUYLER, Cornelius Cuyler 1
CUYLER, T. DE Witt 1
CUYLER, Theodore H
CUYLER, Theodore Ledyard 1
CYBIS, Jan 6
CYBULSKI, Waclaw Boleslaw 6
CYR, Paul Narcisse 2
CZARNOMSKA, Marie Elizabeth Josephine 1
CZERNIK, Stanislaw 6
CZERWONKY, Richard Rudolph 2

D

DABLON, Claude H
DABNEY, Charles William 2
DABNEY, Edwin 1
DABNEY, Francis Lewis 6
DABNEY, Julia Parker 4
DABNEY, Lewis Stackpole 1
DABNEY, Richard H
DABNEY, Richard Heath 2
DABNEY, Robert Lewis H
DABNEY, Samuel Gordon 2
DABNEY, Thomas Smith Gregory H
DABNEY, Virginius H
DABNEY, William C. 4
DABO, Leon 4
DABO, Theodore Scott 1
DABOLL, Nathan H
DABROWSKI, Joseph H
DACOSTA, Albert Lloyd 5
DA COSTA, Chalmers 1
DA COSTA, Jacob M. 1
DA COSTA, John C. Jr. 1
DACSO, Michael Mihaly 6
DADANT, Camille Pierre 1
DADE, Alexander Lucien 1
DADMUN, Frances May 5
DADOURIAN, Haroutune Mugurdich 6
DAEGER, Albert Thomas 1
DAFOE, Carmie R. Jr. 6
DAFOE, John Wesley 2
DAFT, Leo H
DAFT, Leo 4
DA GAMA, Vasco H
DAGER, Forrest Eugene 1
DAGG, John Leadley H
DAGGETT, Aaron Simon 1
DAGGETT, Athern Park 5
DAGGETT, David H
DAGGETT, Ellsworth 1
DAGGETT, Harriet Spiller 4
DAGGETT, Leonard Mayhew 2
DAGGETT, Mabel Potter 1
DAGGETT, Mary Stewart 1
DAGGETT, Naphtali H

* Indicates More Than One Such Name Listed

DAGGETT, Parker Hayward 4
DAGGETT, Robert Frost 3
DAGGETT, Stuart 3
DAGGY, Maynard Lee 5
DAGUE, Paul Bartram 6
DAGWELL, Benjamin Dunlap 4
DAHL, Francis W. 5
DAHL, George 4
DAHL, Gerhard Melvin 3
DAHL, Myrtle Hooper 3
DAHL, Theodore H. 1
DAHLBERG, Arthur Chester 4
DAHLBERG, Bror Gustave 3
DAHLE, Herman B. 3
DAHLE, Herman Bjorn H
DAHLE, Herman Bjorn 4
DAHLERUP, Ioost Baron 2
DAHLGREEN, Charles W. 3
DAHLGREN, B. E. 4
DAHLGREN, John Adolphus Bernard H
DAHLGREN, Sarah Madeleine Vinton H
DAHLGREN, Ulric 2
DAHLMAN, James Charles 1
DAHLQUIST, John E. 6
DAHLQUIST, Thomas Wilford 4
DAICOVICIU, Constantin 6
DAIGNEAU, Ralph H. 3
DAILEY, Morris Elmer 1
DAILY, Francis L. 4
DAILY, Joseph Earl 4
DAILY, Samuel Gordon H
DAINE, Robert 3
DAINES, Lyman Luther 2
DAINGERFIELD, Elliott 1
DAINGERFIELD, Foxhall Alexander 1
DAINS, Frank Burnett 2
DAISH, John Broughton 1
DAISLEY, Robert Henry 4
DAKE, Charles 2
DAKE, Charles Laurence 1
DAKIN, Henry Drysdale 3
DAKINS, John Gordon 4
DALAND, Judson 1
DALAND, William Clifton 1
DALBEY, Josiah T. 4
DALBY, Zachary Lewis 5
DALE, Alan 1
DALE, Albert Ennis 3
DALE, Chester 4
DALE, Coudoashia Bernice Watts (Mrs. Luther W. Dale) 5
DALE, Edward Everett 5
DALE, Essie Rock 6
DALE, Frank 1
DALE, Harry Howard 1
DALE, Sir Henry Hallett 5
DALE, James Wilkinson H
DALE, Nelson Clark 6
DALE, Porter Hinman 1
DALE, Richard H
DALE, Samuel H
DALE, Thomas H
DALE, Thomas Henry 1
DALE, Thomas Nelson 1
DALE, Warren Jefferson 4
DALESIO, Carmine 4
DALEY, Arthur John 6
DALEY, John F. 4
DALEY, John Phillips 4
DALEY, Robert Morris 3
DALEY, William Raymond 5
DALGLEISH, Oakley Hedley 4
DALL, Caroline Healey 4
DALL, William Healey 1
DALLAPICCOLA, Luigi 6
DALLAS, Alexander James H
DALLAS, Charles Donald 3
DALLAS, George Mifflin H
DALLAS, George Mifflin 4
DALLAS, Jacob A. H
DALLAS, John Thomson 4
DALLAS, Trevanion Barlow 4
DALLA VALLE, Joseph Maria 3
DALLENBACH, Karl M. 5
DALLIN, Cyrus Edwin 2
DALLIN, David Julievich 4
DALLMAN, Vincent Y. 4
DALLMANN, William 3
DALLSTREAM, Andrew John 4
DALMORES, Charles 1
DALRYMPLE, Louis 1
DALRYMPLE, William Haddock 1
DALSIMER, Philip T. 6
DALSIMER, Samuel 5
DALSTROM, Oscar Frederick 5
DALTON, Albert Clayton 5
DALTON, Henry George 1
DALTON, James L. 2
DALTON, John Call H
DALTON, John Henry 6
DALTON, John M(ontgomery) 5
DALTON, Joseph N. 4
DALTON, Mary Louise 1
DALTON, Robert H
DALTON, Sidna Poage 4
DALTON, Test 2
DALTON, Tristram H
DALTON, W. R. Inge 1
DALTON, William 5
DALY, Arnold 1
DALY, Augustin 1
DALY, Brenton L. 3
DALY, Carroll John 3
DALY, Sister Cecilia 5
DALY, Charles Frederick 1
DALY, Charles Patrick 1
DALY, David 6
DALY, Edward C. 4
DALY, Edward James 3
DALY, Edwin King 3
DALY, Howard J. Sr. 4
DALY, Ivan de Burgh 6
DALY, J. Burrwood 1
DALY, J. J. 2
DALY, John Fidlar 5
DALY, John Francis 6
DALY, John J. 4
DALY, John Wallace 4
DALY, Joseph Francis 1
DALY, Kay Frances 6
DALY, Marcus 1
DALY, Reginald Aldworth 3
DALY, Thomas Augustine 2
DALY, William Barry 2
DALY, William D. 1
DALZELL, John 1
DALZELL, Lloyd Howland 4
DALZELL, Robert M. H
DALZELL, William Sage 1
DAM, Henry Jackson Wells 1
DAMBACH, Charles Arthur 5
DAME, Elizabeth L. 5
DAME, Frank Libby 1
DAME, Harriet Patience 1
DAME, J. Frank 5
DAMESHEK, William 5
DAMIANO, Celestine Joseph 4
DAMIANOV, Georgi 3
DAMM, Henry Christian Augustus 1
DAMM, Walter J. 4
DAMMANN, John Francis 4
DAMMANN, Milton 4
DAMMANN, Theodore 3
DAMON, Alexander Martin 2
DAMON, Alonzo Willard 1
DAMON, Frank Hardy 5
DAMON, George Alfred 1
DAMON, Howard Franklin H
DAMON, Lindsay Todd 1
DAMON, Norman Clare 5
DAMON, Ralph Shepard 3
DAMON, Robert Hosken 3
DAMON, S(amuel) Foster 5
DAMON, Samuel Mills 3
DAMON, William Emerson 1
D'AMOURS, Ernest R. 4
DAMRELL, William Shapleigh H
DAMROSCH, Frank Heino 1
DAMROSCH, Leopold H
DAMROSCH, Walter Johannes 3
DANA, Amasa H
DANA, Charles Anderson H
DANA, Charles Anderson 6
DANA, Charles Edmund 1
DANA, Charles Loomis 1
DANA, Edward Salisbury 1
DANA, Floyd G. 4
DANA, Francis H
DANA, Francis E. 1
DANA, Frank M. 5
DANA, Harvey Eugene 2
DANA, Henry Wadsworth Longfellow 3
DANA, Israel Thorndike 1
DANA, James H
DANA, James Dwight H
DANA, James Dwight 3
DANA, James Freeman H
DANA, John Cotton 1
DANA, John Fessenden 4
DANA, Judah H
DANA, Lynn Boardman 1
DANA, Marvin 4
DANA, Myron T. 4
DANA, Napoleon Jackson Tecumseh 1
DANA, Paul 1
DANA, Richard H
DANA, Richard Henry * H
DANA, Richard Henry 1
DANA, Richard Turner 1
DANA, Samuel H
DANA, Samuel Luther H
DANA, Samuel Whittelsey H
DANA, Stephen Winchester 1
DANA, William Franklin 1
DANA, William Henry 1
DANA, William Parsons Winchester 1
DANCEL, Christian H
DANCER, H. M. 3
DANCKAERTS, Jasper H
DANCY, Alexander Brown 1
DANDRIDGE, Danske 4
DANDRIDGE, Dorothy 4
DANDRIDGE, N. Pendleton 1
DANDY, George Brown 1
DANDY, John Percy 6
DANDY, Walter Edward 2
DANE, Ernest Blaney 2
DANE, Joseph H
DANE, Nathan H
DANE, Walter Alden 5
DANELY, Alfred Marion 4
DANENHOWER, John Wilson H
DANEY, Eugene 2
DANFORD, Lorenzo 1
DANFORD, Robert Melville 6
DANFORTH, Charles H
DANFORTH, Charles H. 5
DANFORTH, Donald 6
DANFORTH, Elliott 1
DANFORTH, George Jonathan 3
DANFORTH, George Washington 4
DANFORTH, Henry Gold 1
DANFORTH, Isaac Newton 1
DANFORTH, Joshua Noble H
DANFORTH, Loomis Le Grand 4
DANFORTH, Moseley Isaac H
DANFORTH, Thomas H
DANFORTH, William H. 3
DANGAIX, William Joseph 2
DANGERFIELD, Royden (James) 6
DANHOF, John James 6
DANHOF, Ralph John 5
DANIEL, Charles Ezra 4
DANIEL, Charles William 5
DANIEL, Cullen Coleman 6
DANIEL, David R. 4
DANIEL, Ferdinand Eugene 1
DANIEL, Henry H
DANIEL, J. McTyeire 5
DANIEL, John 2
DANIEL, John Franklin 2
DANIEL, John Moncure H
DANIEL, John Reeves Jones H
DANIEL, John Warwick 1
DANIEL, Lewis C. 3
DANIEL, Peter Vivian H
DANIEL, Richard Potts 5
DANIEL, Robert Norman 3
DANIEL, Robert Prentiss 4
DANIEL, Walter Fletcher 6
DANIELIAN, Noobar Retheos 6
DANIELL, Francis Raymond 5
DANIELL, Moses Grant 1
DANIELLS, Arthur Grosvenor 2
DANIELLS, William Willard 1
DANIEL-ROPS, Henry 4
DANIELS, Arthur Hill 1
DANIELS, Arthur Simpson 4
DANIELS, Benjamin 3
DANIELS, Charles H
DANIELS, Charles Herbert 1
DANIELS, Charles Nelson 1
DANIELS, Cora Linn 4
DANIELS, Farrington 5
DANIELS, Francis Cummings 3
DANIELS, Francis Potter 2
DANIELS, Frank 1
DANIELS, Fred Harris 1
DANIELS, George Henry 1
DANIELS, Harold Kennan 4
DANIELS, Henry H. 3
DANIELS, John 3
DANIELS, John Karl 5
DANIELS, Joseph J. 5
DANIELS, Joseph Leonard 1
DANIELS, Josephus 2
DANIELS, Josephus Jr. 4
DANIELS, Lilla Wood 4
DANIELS, Mark (Roy) 6
DANIELS, Milton J. 2
DANIELS, William S. 1
DANIELS, Winthrop More 2
DANIELSON, Clarence Hagbart 3
DANIELSON, Jacques 3
DANIELSON, Reuben Gustaf 3
DANIELSON, Richard Ely 3
DANIELSON, Wilmot Alfred 4
DANLEY, William L. 4
DANN, Alexander William 4
DANN, Hollis Ellsworth 1
DANNAT, William T. 1
DANNELLY, John Milton 1
DANNENBAUM, Walter 4
DANNER, Arthur Vincent 5
DANNER, Harris Leslie 1
DANNER, Joel Buchanan H
DANNER, Peter C. 1
DANNREUTHER, Gustav H
DANNREUTHER, Gustav 4
DANNREUTHER, Walter T. 3
DANSINGBERG, Paul 2
DANTON, George Henry 6
D'ANTONI, Salvador 3
DANTZIG, Henry Poincare 6
DANTZLER, Lehre L(ivingston) 6
DANZIGER, Henry 1
DA PONTE, Lorenzo H
DA PONTE, Lorenzo Brooke 3
DAPPING, William Osborne 5
DARBY, Ada Claire 3
DARBY, Edwin Tyler 1
DARBY, Ezra H
DARBY, John * H
DARBY, John Eaton 1
DARBY, John Fletcher H
DARBY, John Frederick 3
DARBY, William H
DARBY, William Johnson 1
DARBY, William Lambert 3
DARBYSHIRE, Leonard 4
D'ARCY, William Cheever 2
DARDEN, Thomas Francis 2
DARE, Virginia H
DARGAN, Edmond Strother H
DARGAN, Edwin Charles 1
DARGAN, Edwin Preston 1
DARGAN, Henry McCune 5
DARGAN, Olive Tilford 5
DARGAVEL, John William 4
DARGEON, Harold William 5
DARGUE, Herbert Arthur 2
DARGUSCH, Carlton Spencer Jr. 6
DARIN, Bobby 6
DARKE, William H
DARKENWALD, Gordon Gerald 4
DARLEY, Felix Octavius Carr H
DARLEY, Jane Cooper H
DARLING, Arthur Beebe 5
DARLING, Arthur Burr 5
DARLING, C. Coburn 4
DARLING, Charles Ellett 6
DARLING, Charles Hial 2
DARLING, Charles Kimball 1
DARLING, Charles William 1
DARLING, Chester Arthur 6
DARLING, Edward 6
DARLING, Flora Adams 1
DARLING, Henry H
DARLING, Herbert Franklin 5
DARLING, Jay Norwood 4
DARLING, John Augustus 1
DARLING, Joseph Robinson 5
DARLING, Louis Jr. 5
DARLING, Mary Greenleaf 4
DARLING, Mason Cook H
DARLING, Philip Grenville 6
DARLING, Robert Ensign 5
DARLING, Samuel Taylor 1
DARLING, Sid L(ouis) 5
DARLING, William Augustus H
DARLING, William Lafayette 1
DARLINGTON, Charles Francis 1
DARLINGTON, Charles Goodliffe 4
DARLINGTON, Charles Joseph 4
DARLINGTON, Edward H
DARLINGTON, Frederick 3
DARLINGTON, Henry 3
DARLINGTON, Isaac H
DARLINGTON, James Henry 1
DARLINGTON, Joseph James 1
DARLINGTON, Thomas 1
DARLINGTON, Thomas 2
DARLINGTON, Urban Valentine W. 3
DARLINGTON, William H
DARLOW, Albert Edward 4
DARMS, John Martin George 2
DARNALL, Carl Rogers 1
DARNALL, Marcy Bradshaw 4
DARNALL, William Edgar 1
DARNELL, Henry Faulkner 1
DARNELL, Linda 4
DARNTON, Eleanor Choate 5
DARR, Earl A. 4
DARR, Edward A. 3
DARR, John Whittier 5
DARR, Loren Robert 5
DARRACH, William 2
DARRAGH, Ann Sophia Towne H
DARRAGH, Archibald Bard 4
DARRAGH, Cornelius H
DARRAH, Thomas W. 3
DARRAH, William Lee 6
DARRIN, Erwin N. 4
DARROW, Chester William 5
DARROW, Clarence 1
DARROW, Daniel Cady 4
DARROW, George Potter 2
DARSEY, Joseph Frederick 6
DARSIE, Darsie Lloyd 4
DARSIE, Marvin Lloyd 1
DARST, Joseph Miltenberger 3
DARST, Thomas Campbell 2
DART, Carlton Rollin 1
DART, Edward Dupaquier 6
DART, Henry Plauche 1
DART, Raymond Osborne 6
DARTON, Nelson Horatio 2
DARVAS, Lili 6
D'ARVILLE, Camille 1
DARWIN, Charles Carlyle 1
DARWIN, Charles Galton 4
DARWIN, Gertrude Bascom 1
DARWIN, Sir Robin (Robert Vere Darwin) 6
DAS, Rajani Kanta 6
DAS, Taraknath 3
D'ASCENZO, Nicola 3
DASCH, George 3
DASHER, Benjamin Joseph 5
DASHER, Charles Lanier Jr. 5
DASHIELL, Alfred Sheppard 5
DASHIELL, John Frederick 6
DASHIELL, Paul Joseph 3
DASHIELL, William Robert 1
DASKAM, Walter Duryee 1
DATER, Alfred Warner 1
DATES, Henry Baldwin 5
DATTNER, Bernhard 3
DAU, William Herman Theodore 2
DAUBIN, Freeland Allen 3
DAUGETTE, Clarence William 2
DAUGHERTY, Arthur Cornelius 5
DAUGHERTY, Charles M. 1
DAUGHERTY, Duncan W(ilmer) 5
DAUGHERTY, Edgar Fay 3
DAUGHERTY, Harry Kerr 3
DAUGHERTY, Harry Micajah 1
DAUGHERTY, James Alexander 4
DAUGHERTY, James Henry 6
DAUGHERTY, Jerome 4
DAUGHERTY, Lewis Sylvester 1
DAUGHTERS, Freeman 3
DAULTON, Agnes McClelland 2
DAULTON, George 1
DAUMONT, Simon Francois H
D'AUNOY, Rigney 1

DAUZVARDIS, Petras Paulius 5
DAVANT, Thomas S. 5
DAVEE, Henry A. 3
DAVEE, Thomas H
DAVEIS, Charles Stewart H
DAVEISS, Joseph Hamilton H
DAVELER, Erle Victor 3
DAVENPORT, Basil 4
DAVENPORT, Bennett Franklin 1
DAVENPORT, Charles Benedict 2
DAVENPORT, Edward Loomis H
DAVENPORT, Erwin R. 4
DAVENPORT, Eugene 1
DAVENPORT, Fanny Lily Gypsy H
DAVENPORT, Frances Gardiner 1
DAVENPORT, Franklin H
DAVENPORT, Frederick M. 3
DAVENPORT, Frederick Parker 1
DAVENPORT, George H
DAVENPORT, George Edward 1
DAVENPORT, George William 5
DAVENPORT, Gideon I. 4
DAVENPORT, Henry Joralemon 4
DAVENPORT, Herbert Joseph 1
DAVENPORT, Holton 4
DAVENPORT, Homer Calvin 1
DAVENPORT, Ira 1
DAVENPORT, Ira Erastus H
DAVENPORT, Ira Erastus 4
DAVENPORT, James * 1
DAVENPORT, James Henry 1
DAVENPORT, James LeRoy 1
DAVENPORT, James Sanford 1
DAVENPORT, John * H
DAVENPORT, John Gaylord 1
DAVENPORT, Leroy Benjamin 4
DAVENPORT, Louis M. 5
DAVENPORT, R. Briggs 1
DAVENPORT, Richard Graham 1
DAVENPORT, Roy Leonard 4
DAVENPORT, Russell 3
DAVENPORT, Samuel Arza 4
DAVENPORT, Stanley Woodward 1
DAVENPORT, Thomas * H
DAVENPORT, Walter 5
DAVENPORT, Walter Rice 2
DAVENPORT, William Henry Harrison 1
DAVES, Jessica 6
DAVEY, James Charles 1
DAVEY, John 1
DAVEY, Martin L. 4
DAVEY, Randall 4
DAVEY, Robert C. 1
DAVEY, Wheeler P. H
D'AVEZAC, Auguste Genevieve Valentin H
DAVID, Edward Wandell 4
DAVID, John Baptist Mary 1
DAVID, Vernon Cyrenius 4
DAVIDGE, John Beale 1
DAVIDGE, William Pleater H
DAVIDOFF, Leo Max 6
DAVIDOW, H. M. 3
DAVIDS, James H
DAVIDSON, Alexander Caldwell 1
DAVIDSON, Alfred James 1
DAVIDSON, Anstruther 1
DAVIDSON, Arnold 4
DAVIDSON, Augustus Cleveland 1
DAVIDSON, Benjamin 1
DAVIDSON, Carter 4
DAVIDSON, Charles 1
DAVIDSON, David J. 2
DAVIDSON, De Witt A. 6
DAVIDSON, Donald (Grady) 5
DAVIDSON, Donald Miner 4
DAVIDSON, Edwin Lee 1
DAVIDSON, George 1
DAVIDSON, George 1
DAVIDSON, George A. 4

DAVIDSON, Hannah Amelia 1
DAVIDSON, Harlan Page 1
DAVIDSON, Henry Alexander 6
DAVIDSON, Irville Fay 1
DAVIDSON, Israel 1
DAVIDSON, J. Brownlee 1
DAVIDSON, James Edward 2
DAVIDSON, James Edward 3
DAVIDSON, James Hamilton 2
DAVIDSON, James Henry 1
DAVIDSON, James O. 1
DAVIDSON, James Wheeler 1
DAVIDSON, James Wood 1
DAVIDSON, Jo 3
DAVIDSON, John Wynn 4
DAVIDSON, Joseph G. 5
DAVIDSON, Joseph Quentin 5
DAVIDSON, Laura Lee 5
DAVIDSON, Levette Jay 5
DAVIDSON, Loucretia Isobel 5
DAVIDSON, Louis Rogers 1
DAVIDSON, Lucretia Maria H
DAVIDSON, Lyal Ament 3
DAVIDSON, Margaret Miller H
DAVIDSON, Mary Blossom (Mrs. Charles S. Davidson) 5
DAVIDSON, Maurice P. 3
DAVIDSON, Robert * H
DAVIDSON, Robert James 1
DAVIDSON, Roy Elton 4
DAVIDSON, Royal Page 2
DAVIDSON, Samuel Presley 1
DAVIDSON, Theodore Fulton 1
DAVIDSON, Thomas 1
DAVIDSON, Thomas Green H
DAVIDSON, Thomas Whitfield 6
DAVIDSON, Thomas William 4
DAVIDSON, Victor H. 3
DAVIDSON, Ward Follett 4
DAVIDSON, Wilbur Leroy 1
DAVIDSON, William 1
DAVIDSON, William Andrew 3
DAVIDSON, William Lee H
DAVIDSON, William Mehard 1
DAVID-WEILL, Pierre Sylvain Desire Gerard 6
DAVIE, Maurice R. 4
DAVIE, Preston 6
DAVIE, William Richardson H
DAVIES, Acton 1
DAVIES, Arthur B. 1
DAVIES, Arthur Ernest 4
DAVIES, Arthur Powell 3
DAVIES, Caroline Stodder 4
DAVIES, Charles H
DAVIES, Charles Frederick H
DAVIES, David Charles 1
DAVIES, Edward H
DAVIES, Ernest Coulter 4
DAVIES, George Reginald 5
DAVIES, Harry William 3
DAVIES, Henry Eugene 1
DAVIES, Hywel 1
DAVIES, James 1
DAVIES, James William Frederick 4
DAVIES, John Newton 6
DAVIES, John Rumsey 1
DAVIES, John Vipond 1
DAVIES, Joseph Edward 3
DAVIES, Julian Tappan 1
DAVIES, Marion 4
DAVIES, Martin 4
DAVIES, Paul Lewis 6
DAVIES, Percy Albert 4
DAVIES, Rodger Paul 6
DAVIES, Samuel H
DAVIES, Thomas Frederick * 1
DAVIES, Thomas Stephen 5
DAVIES, Thurston Jynkins 4
DAVIES, Valentine 5
DAVIES, William Gilbert 1
DAVIES, William Preston 2
DAVIES, William Rupert 1
DAVIES, William Walter 1
DAVIESS, Maria Thompson 1
DAVILA, Carlos 3
DAVILA, Charles Alexander 4

DAVILA, Céleo 6
DAVIN, John Wysor 2
DAVIS, A. M. 5
DAVIS, Abel 1
DAVIS, Achilles Edward 4
DAVIS, Addison D. 4
DAVIS, Adelle (Mrs. Frank V. Sieglinger) 6
DAVIS, Albert Gould 1
DAVIS, Alexander Jackson H
DAVIS, Alexander Macdonald 4
DAVIS, Alexander Mathews H
DAVIS, Alfred Cookman 2
DAVIS, Alton Frank 3
DAVIS, Alva Raymond 4
DAVIS, Amos 1
DAVIS, Andrew Jay 3
DAVIS, Andrew McFarland 1
DAVIS, Arlene 4
DAVIS, Arlene (Mrs. Max T. Davis) 5
DAVIS, Arnold Lyman 1
DAVIS, Arthur Cayley 5
DAVIS, Arthur Kyle 3
DAVIS, Arthur Marshall 4
DAVIS, Arthur Newton 5
DAVIS, Arthur Powell 1
DAVIS, Arthur Vining 4
DAVIS, Arthur Vining 5
DAVIS, Arthur William 2
DAVIS, Asa Barnes 1
DAVIS, Beale 1
DAVIS, Benjamin Marshall 4
DAVIS, Benson Willis 3
DAVIS, Bergen 3
DAVIS, Bernard George 5
DAVIS, Bert Byron 2
DAVIS, Boothe Colwell 1
DAVIS, Bradley Moore 1
DAVIS, Brinton Beauregard 5
DAVIS, Bruce Gregory 6
DAVIS, Byron Bennett 1
DAVIS, Calvin Olin 3
DAVIS, Cameron Josiah 3
DAVIS, Carl Braden 3
DAVIS, Carlisle R. 4
DAVIS, Carroll Melvin 1
DAVIS, Cecil Clark 3
DAVIS, Champion McDowell 6
DAVIS, Charles Albert 1
DAVIS, Charles B. 2
DAVIS, Charles Belmont 1
DAVIS, Charles Edward Law Baldwin 1
DAVIS, Charles Ernest Jr. 5
DAVIS, Charles Gilbert 1
DAVIS, Charles Harold 1
DAVIS, Charles Henry H
DAVIS, Charles Henry 1
DAVIS, Charles Henry Stanley 1
DAVIS, Charles Hubbard 6
DAVIS, Charles K. 4
DAVIS, Charles Lukens 4
DAVIS, Charles Moler 5
DAVIS, Charles Palmer 1
DAVIS, Charles Russell 1
DAVIS, Charles Strout 4
DAVIS, Charles Thornton 4
DAVIS, Charles Wellington 5
DAVIS, Chester Charles 6
DAVIS, Chester R. 4
DAVIS, Clarence Alba 6
DAVIS, Claude Jefferson 4
DAVIS, Clifford 5
DAVIS, Clinton Wildes 3
DAVIS, Clyde Brion 4
DAVIS, Cushman Kellogg 1
DAVIS, D. Dwight 4
DAVIS, Daniel Franklin H
DAVIS, Darrell Haug 4
DAVIS, David H
DAVIS, David Jackson 1
DAVIS, David John 1
DAVIS, David William 5
DAVIS, Donald Derby 4
DAVIS, Donald W. 4
DAVIS, Dwight Filley 2
DAVIS, E. Asbury 1
DAVIS, E. Gorton 1
DAVIS, E. Asbury 1
DAVIS, Earl Fred 4
DAVIS, Earl J. 4
DAVIS, Edith Smith 1
DAVIS, Edmund Jackson H
DAVIS, Edward 1
DAVIS, Edward C. P. 3
DAVIS, Edward E. 5
DAVIS, Edward Everett 3
DAVIS, Edward Parker 1
DAVIS, Edwin 4
DAVIS, Edwin G. 5
DAVIS, Edwin Hamilton H

DAVIS, Edwin Weyerhaeuser 4
DAVIS, Effa Vetina 1
DAVIS, Ellery Williams 1
DAVIS, Elmer 3
DAVIS, Elmer Joseph 5
DAVIS, Emerson H
DAVIS, Ewin Lamar 1
DAVIS, Fay 2
DAVIS, Francis Breese Jr. 4
DAVIS, Frank De Montbirt 4
DAVIS, Frank Garfield 3
DAVIS, Frank Jr. 1
DAVIS, Frank Parker 3
DAVIS, Fred Henry 1
DAVIS, Frederick Barton 6
DAVIS, Frederick Henry 3
DAVIS, Garret H
DAVIS, Gaylord 5
DAVIS, George H
DAVIS, George Arthur 6
DAVIS, George Breckenridge 1
DAVIS, George Burwell 4
DAVIS, George Gilman 4
DAVIS, George H. 3
DAVIS, George Harvey 3
DAVIS, George Royal 1
DAVIS, George Russell 4
DAVIS, George Samler 1
DAVIS, George Thomas 5
DAVIS, George Thompson Brown 5
DAVIS, George Washington 4
DAVIS, George Whitefield 1
DAVIS, George William 4
DAVIS, Gladys Rockmore 6
DAVIS, Graham Lee 3
DAVIS, Gwilym George 1
DAVIS, H. L. 4
DAVIS, Hal Strange 3
DAVIS, Hallie Flanagan 5
DAVIS, Harold Thayer 6
DAVIS, Harry Ellerbe 5
DAVIS, Harry Lyman 3
DAVIS, Harry Orville 1
DAVIS, Harry Phillips 1
DAVIS, Harvey Henry 5
DAVIS, Harvey Nathaniel 3
DAVIS, Hassoldt 3
DAVIS, Hayne 1
DAVIS, Helen Clarkson Miller (Mrs. Harvey Nathaniel Davis) 5
DAVIS, Henry H
DAVIS, Henry 4
DAVIS, Henry Edgar 1
DAVIS, Henry Gassaway 1
DAVIS, Henry Gassett H
DAVIS, Henry Winter H
DAVIS, Herbert Burnham 1
DAVIS, Herbert John 4
DAVIS, Herbert Spencer 5
DAVIS, Herman S. 1
DAVIS, Horace 1
DAVIS, Howard 4
DAVIS, Howard Clarke 6
DAVIS, Howland Shippen 5
DAVIS, Hugh Orton 5
DAVIS, Ira Cleveland 4
DAVIS, Irving Gilman 4
DAVIS, J. Dewitt 4
DAVIS, J. Frank 4
DAVIS, J. Mccan 1
DAVIS, J. F. 1
DAVIS, J(ohn) Lionberger 5
DAVIS, Jackson 2
DAVIS, Jacob Cunningham H
DAVIS, James 1
DAVIS, James Cox 1
DAVIS, James Harvey 4
DAVIS, James John 2
DAVIS, James Sherman 5
DAVIS, James Thomas 3
DAVIS, Jeanne Frances West 6
DAVIS, Jeff 1
DAVIS, Jefferson H
DAVIS, Jefferson Columbus H
DAVIS, Jess Harrison 5
DAVIS, Jesse Buttrick 3
DAVIS, Jesse Duke 4
DAVIS, Joan 4
DAVIS, Joe L. 2
DAVIS, Joe Lee 6
DAVIS, John * H
DAVIS, John 1
DAVIS, John A. G. H
DAVIS, John Chandler Bancroft 1
DAVIS, John Charles 1
DAVIS, John D. 1
DAVIS, John Francis 1
DAVIS, John Givan 1
DAVIS, John Kennerly Sr. 6
DAVIS, John Ker 5

DAVIS, John Lee H
DAVIS, John Marcus 2
DAVIS, John Merrill 1
DAVIS, John Moore Kelso 1
DAVIS, John Patterson 1
DAVIS, John Rose Wilson 1
DAVIS, John Staige 2
DAVIS, John Wesley H
DAVIS, John William 1
DAVIS, John William 3
DAVIS, John Williams 1
DAVIS, John Woodbridge 1
DAVIS, Jonathan McMillan 2
DAVIS, Joseph Baker 1
DAVIS, Joseph Jonathan H
DAVIS, Joseph Phineas 1
DAVIS, Joseph Robert H
DAVIS, Joseph Smith 5
DAVIS, Joseph Stancliffe 6
DAVIS, Joshua A. 4
DAVIS, Kary Cadmus 1
DAVIS, Katharine Bement 1
DAVIS, Lemuel Clarke 1
DAVIS, Leonard Moore 1
DAVIS, LeCompte 3
DAVIS, Lyman Edwyn 1
DAVIS, Malcolm McTear 5
DAVIS, Malvin Edward 4
DAVIS, Manton 3
DAVIS, Manvel 3
DAVIS, Mary Evelyn Moore 1
DAVIS, Mary Gould 3
DAVIS, Matthew Livingston H
DAVIS, Mervyn 6
DAVIS, Michael Marks 5
DAVIS, Milton Fennimore 1
DAVIS, Minnie S. 4
DAVIS, Monnett Bain 3
DAVIS, Nathan Smith * 1
DAVIS, Nathan Smith 5
DAVIS, Nathaniel French 1
DAVIS, Neal Balbach 5
DAVIS, Nelson Fithian 1
DAVIS, Newton Eads 3
DAVIS, Noah 1
DAVIS, Noah Knowles 1
DAVIS, Norah 6
DAVIS, Norman H. 2
DAVIS, Olive Bell 1
DAVIS, Oscar Franklyn 4
DAVIS, Oscar King 1
DAVIS, Owen 3
DAVIS, Ozora Stearns 1
DAVIS, Paul (Alexander) 6
DAVIS, Paul A. 2
DAVIS, Paul Arthur 4
DAVIS, Paul Hazlitt 5
DAVIS, Paulina Kellogg Wright H
DAVIS, Philip 5
DAVIS, Phineas H
DAVIS, Pierpont 3
DAVIS, Pierpont V. 4
DAVIS, R. C. 3
DAVIS, Ralph Waldo 4
DAVIS, Raymond Cazallis 1
DAVIS, Rebecca Harding 1
DAVIS, Reuben H
DAVIS, Reuben Nelson 4
DAVIS, Richard Beale 4
DAVIS, Richard Bingham 1
DAVIS, Richard David H
DAVIS, Richard Hallock 5
DAVIS, Richard Harding 1
DAVIS, Richard J. 1
DAVIS, Richmond Pearson 6
DAVIS, Robert 1
DAVIS, Robert Courtney 2
DAVIS, Robert Fisher 6
DAVIS, Robert Hobart 1
DAVIS, Robert McNair 3
DAVIS, Robert Stewart 1
DAVIS, Robert W. 4
DAVIS, Roblin Henry 2
DAVIS, Roger H
DAVIS, Roger Wolcott 3
DAVIS, Roland Parker 6
DAVIS, Rowland Lucius 1
DAVIS, Roy H
DAVIS, Roy Tasco 6
DAVIS, Royal Jenkins 1
DAVIS, Royall Oscar Eugene 2
DAVIS, Sam H
DAVIS, Samuel H
DAVIS, Samuel T. 1
DAVIS, Sheldon Emmer 4
DAVIS, Stephen Brooks 1
DAVIS, Stuart 5
DAVIS, Sturgis Brown 5
DAVIS, Susan Topliff 5
DAVIS, T. Lawrence 4
DAVIS, Tenney Lombard H
DAVIS, Theodore Russell H
DAVIS, Thomas 1

DAVIS, Thomas Archibald 4
DAVIS, Thomas Bealle 2
DAVIS, Thomas Crawley 1
DAVIS, Thomas Davis 1
DAVIS, Thomas Edward 1
DAVIS, Thomas Francis 1
DAVIS, Thomas Harold 6
DAVIS, Thomas Jefferson 3
DAVIS, Thomas Latham 3
DAVIS, Thomas Terry H
DAVIS, Thomas Treadwell H
DAVIS, Thomas Walker 3
DAVIS, Timothy * H
DAVIS, Titus Elwood 4
DAVIS, Tobe Coller 4
DAVIS, Tom J. 3
DAVIS, Varina Anne H
Jefferson
DAVIS, Varina Jefferson 1
DAVIS, Vernon Mansfield 1
DAVIS, Wallace McRae 5
DAVIS, Walton 4
DAVIS, Warren Bartlett 1
DAVIS, Warren Blair 1
DAVIS, Warren Johnson 4
DAVIS, Warren Ransom H
DAVIS, Watson 4
DAVIS, Webster 1
DAVIS, Westmoreland 2
DAVIS, Whitman 6
DAVIS, Will J. 1
DAVIS, William Augustine H
DAVIS, William Church 3
DAVIS, William Francis Jr. 3
DAVIS, William Garland 4
DAVIS, William H. 4
DAVIS, William H. 4
DAVIS, William Hammatt 4
DAVIS, William Harper 5
DAVIS, William Hersey 3
DAVIS, William Holmes 5
DAVIS, William Horace 1
DAVIS, William Morris H
DAVIS, William Morris 1
DAVIS, William Philip 3
DAVIS, William R. 1
DAVIS, William Rees 2
DAVIS, William Stearns 1
DAVIS, William Thomas 1
DAVIS, William Thornwall 4
DAVIS, William Warren 1
DAVIS, William Watts Hart 4
DAVIS, William Whiting 4
DAVIS, William Z. 2
DAVIS, Wirt 1
DAVIS, Wirt 2
DAVISON, Albert Watson 4
DAVISON, Archibald 4
Thompson
DAVISON, Charles 1
DAVISON, Charles Stewart 2
DAVISON, Donald Angus 2
DAVISON, Edward 5
DAVISON, Francis Lyle 6
DAVISON, Frank Elon 4
DAVISON, F(rederick) 6
Trubee
DAVISON, George Stewart 2
DAVISON, George Willets 3
DAVISON, Harry P. 4
DAVISON, Henry Pomeroy 1
DAVISON, Mrs. Henry 5
Pomeroy
DAVISON, Homer R(eese) 5
DAVISON, John A. 2
DAVISON, Peter Weimer 1
DAVISON, Sarah Margaret 6
DAVISON, Thomas 3
Callahan
DAVISON, Wilburt Cornell 5
DAVISON, William 1
Anthony
DAVISSON, Albert Eugene 1
DAVISSON, Clinton Joseph 3
DAVOL, Ralph 5
DAVY, John M. 1
DAWBARN, Charles 4
DAWE, George Grosvenor 2
DAWE, Helen Cleveland 5
DAWES, Anna Laurens 3
DAWES, Beman Gates 3
DAWES, Charles Gates 1
DAWES, Chester Mitchell 1
DAWES, Henry Laurens 1
DAWES, Henry May 3
DAWES, Irving D. 5
DAWES, James William 3
DAWES, Norman James 4
DAWES, Rufus Cutler 1
DAWES, William H
DAWES, William Ruggles 1
DAWKINS, Benjamin 6
Cornwell
DAWKINS, Henry H
DAWLEY, Frank E. 1

DAWLEY, Thomas 1
Robinson Jr.
DAWSON, Albert Foster 5
DAWSON, Allan 1
DAWSON, Allan 2
DAWSON, Archie Owen 4
DAWSON, Arthur 1
DAWSON, Benjamin Elisha 1
DAWSON, Cecil Forrest 4
DAWSON, Charles I. 5
DAWSON, Claude Ivan 5
DAWSON, Clyde C. 1
DAWSON, Edgar 2
DAWSON, Edward 2
DAWSON, Francis H
Warrington
DAWSON, (Francis) 6
Warrington
DAWSON, Fred 4
DAWSON, George 1
DAWSON, George 1
Ellsworth
DAWSON, George Louis 4
DAWSON, George Walter 1
DAWSON, Henry Barton H
DAWSON, J. Douglas 6
DAWSON, James Frederick 5
DAWSON, John 1
DAWSON, John Bennett 1
DAWSON, John Charles 6
DAWSON, John Littleton 1
DAWSON, John Shaw 4
DAWSON, Joseph Martin 6
DAWSON, Lemuel Orah 1
DAWSON, Marion Lindsay 5
DAWSON, Mary 1
DAWSON, Miles Menander 2
DAWSON, Thomas Cleland 1
DAWSON, Thomas S. 4
DAWSON, William 5
DAWSON, William Crosby H
DAWSON, William James 1
DAWSON, William H
Johnston
DAWSON, William L. 5
DAWSON, William Leon 1
DAWSON, William Mercer 1
Owens
DAWSON, William Warren 2
DAWSON-WATSON, 1
Dawson
DAY, Albert Edward 6
DAY, Arthur Louis 4
DAY, Benjamin Franklin 1
DAY, Benjamin Henry 1
DAY, Bernard Pope 4
DAY, Charles 1
DAY, Charles Ivan 3
DAY, Charles Manley 2
DAY, Charles Orrin 1
DAY, Clarence 1
DAY, Clifford Louis 4
DAY, Clive 5
DAY, Cyrus Lawrence 4
DAY, David Alexander H
DAY, David Sheldon 4
DAY, David Talbot 1
DAY, Edmund 1
DAY, Edmund Ezra 3
DAY, Edward 4
DAY, Edward Cason 1
DAY, Edward Charles 2
DAY, Edward Marvin 1
DAY, Erastus Sheldon 2
DAY, Ewing Wilber 2
DAY, Fisk Holbrook 1
DAY, Florence Roberts 3
DAY, Francis 1
DAY, Frank Leighton 4
DAY, Frank Leslie 1
DAY, Frank Miles 1
DAY, Frank Parker 3
DAY, G. Z. 2
DAY, George Armstrong 1
DAY, George Calvin 1
DAY, George Edward * 1
DAY, George Parmly 3
DAY, Harold Briggs 4
DAY, Henry H
DAY, Henry Noble 1
DAY, Herbert James 3
DAY, Holman Francis 1
DAY, Horace H. 4
DAY, James E. 4
DAY, James Gamble H
DAY, James Roscoe 1
DAY, James W. 4
DAY, Jeremiah B. 1
DAY, Jerome J. 1
DAY, Jesse Erwin 1
DAY, John Boynton Wilson 1
DAY, John Boynton Wilson 4
DAY, John Dabney 1
DAY, John Francis 1
DAY, John William 1

DAY, Joseph Paul 2
DAY, Karl S. 5
DAY, Kenneth 5
DAY, L. B. H
DAY, Leigh Gross 4
DAY, Luther 1
DAY, Luther H
DAY, Mary Anna 4
DAY, Oscar Fayette Gaines 4
DAY, Ralph E. 2
DAY, Richard Edwin 1
DAY, Richard Ellsworth 4
DAY, Robert Henry 4
DAY, Rowland H
DAY, Sarah J. 1
DAY, Stephen H
DAY, Stephen A. 2
DAY, Thomas Fleming 1
DAY, Thomas Franklin 4
DAY, Timothy Crane H
DAY, William A. 1
DAY, William A. 3
DAY, William Baker 1
DAY, William Cathcart 4
DAY, William Cyrus 1
DAY, William Horace 2
DAY, William L. 1
DAY, William Louis 1
DAY, William Plummer 1
DAY, William Rufus 1
DAYAN, Charles H
DAY-LEWIS, Cecil 5
DAYTON, Alston Gordon 1
DAYTON, Arthur Spencer 4
DAYTON, Charles 1
Willoughby
DAYTON, Ellas H
DAYTON, George Draper 4
DAYTON, Hughes 5
DAYTON, James Henry 1
DAYTON, John Havens 3
DAYTON, Jonathan H
DAYTON, Lewis Seeley 1
DAYTON, Roy 3
DAYTON, William A. 3
DAYTON, William Lewis 1
DAYTON, William Lewis 1
DAZEY, Charles Turner 1
DEADERICK, William 2
Heiskell
DEADY, Matthew Paul H
DEAK, Francis 5
DEAKIN, Gerald 1
DEAKYNE, Herbert 2
DEAL, Edson H. 4
DEAL, Erastus Charles 5
DEAL, Herbert L. 3
DEAL, Joseph T. 2
DEAL, Roy Walter 4
DE ALARCON, Hernando H
DE ALBA, Pedro 4
DEALEY, Edward 5
Musgrove (Ted)
DEALEY, George 2
Bannerman
DEALEY, James Quayle 1
DEALEY, Patrick Francis H
DEAM, Arthur Francis 6
DE AMORIM FERREIRA, 6
Herculano
DEAN, Alexander 4
DEAN, Amos H
DEAN, Arthur Davis 2
DEAN, Arthur Lyman 3
DEAN, Bashford 1
DEAN, Basil 4
DEAN, Ben 3
DEAN, Benjamin 1
DEAN, Charles H
DEAN, Edward N. 6
DEAN, Edwin Blanchard 1
DEAN, Ezra 1
DEAN, Francis Winthrop 1
DEAN, George Adam 5
DEAN, George Reinald 4
DEAN, Gilbert H
DEAN, Gordon Evans 3
DEAN, Graham M. 6
DEAN, H. Trendley 4
DEAN, Howard B. 4
DEAN, Hugh 4
DEAN, James 4
DEAN, James Renwick 1
DEAN, James Theodore 4
DEAN, John 4
DEAN, John Candee 1
DEAN, John Marvin 1
DEAN, John Ward 1
DEAN, Josiah 1
DEAN, Julia 1
DEAN, Lee Wallace 4
DEAN, Myron E. 5
DEAN, Reginald Scott 4
DEAN, Richard Crain 1
DEAN, Richard Doggett 4
DEAN, Richmond 1

DEAN, Robert Augustus 1
DEAN, Samuel E. Jr. 6
DEAN, Sara 5
DEAN, Sidney H
DEAN, Sidney Butler 6
DEAN, Vera Micheles 5
DEAN, Walter Carleton 5
DEAN, Walter Lofthouse 1
DEAN, William Blake 1
DEAN, William John 1
DEAN, William Laird 1
DEAN, Willis Johnson 2
DEAN, Willis Leonard 2
DEANDRADE, Anthony J. 5
James Felix Bartholomew
DEANE, Charles Bennett 5
DEANE, Charles J. 4
DEANE, Gardiner Andrus 4
Armstrong
DEANE, John Hall 1
DEANE, Ruthven 1
DEANE, Samuel H
DEANE, Silas H
DEANE, Walter 1
DE ANGELIS, Jefferson 1
DE ANGELIS, Pascal H
Charles Joseph
DE ANZA, Juan Bautista H
DEAR, J. Albert 3
DEAR, J. Albert 4
DEAR, Joseph Albert 2
DEAR, Walter Moore 4
DE ARAUJO CASTRO, 6
Joao Augusto
DEARBORN, Benjamin H
DEARBORN, Donald 4
Curtis
DEARBORN, Earl 5
Hamilton
DEARBORN, George Van 1
Ness
DEARBORN, Henry H
DEARBORN, Henry H
Alexander Scammell
DEARBORN, Henry M. 1
DEARBORN, John 1
DEARBORN, Nathaniel 4
DEARBORN, Ned 1
DEARBORN, Ned Harland 4
DEARBORN, Richard H
Harold
DEARBORN, Walter Fenno 3
DEARDORFF, Neva Ruth 3
DEARHOLT, Hoyt E. 1
DEARING, Charles Lee 5
DEARING, Fred Morris 6
DEARING, John Lincoln 1
DEARING, William 1
Prentice
DE ARMOND, David A. 1
DEARMONT, Russell Lee 4
DEARMONT, Washington 1
Strother
DEARTH, Henry Golden 1
DEAS, Charles 4
DEAS, Zachariah Cantey H
DEASY, John Francis 3
DEASY, Luere B. 1
DEAVER, Bascom S. 2
DEAVER, George Gilbert 6
DEAVER, John B. 1
DEAVOURS, Stone 4
DE AYALA, Juan Manuel H
DE AYLLON, Lucas H
Vasquez
DEBARDELEBEN, Charles 2
Fairchild
DE BARDELEBEN, Henry H
Fairchild
DE BARDELEBEN, Henry 4
Fairchild
DEBARDELEBEN, Henry 1
Ticknor
DE BARR, Edwin 4
DE BASTOS, Emil 5
DE BEAUMONT, Guerin 1
Jean Michel du Bosco
DE BECK, William 2
DE BELLEVILLE, Frederic 1
DE BENEVIDES, Alonzo 1
DE BERARD, Wilford 4
Willis
DE BERDT, Dennys H
DEBERRY, Edmund H
DEBERRY, William Nelson 2
DEBEVOISE, Kendall Bush 6
DEBEVOISE, P. Leroy 4
DEBEVOISE, Thomas 3
DEBEY, Cornelia Bernarda 4
DEBISSCHOP, Frank J. 4
DE BLOIS, Austen 1
Kennedy
DE BLOIS, George Lewis 1
DEBOARD, Elmer H. 4
DEBOE, William J. 1

DE BOER, John J. 5
DE BOER, Joseph Arend 1
DE BOER, Saco Rienk 6
DEBOEST, Henry Frulan 4
DEBOLT, John T. 5
DE BOLT, Rezin A. H
DE BONNEVILLE, 1
Benjamin Louis Eulalie
DE BOOY, Theodoor 1
DE BOST, William Ludlam 3
DEBOW, Charles Louis 4
DE BOW, James Dunwoody H
Brownson
DE BOWER, Herbert 1
Francis
DE BRA, Harvey Rufus 4
DE BRAHM, William H
Girard
DE BREHAN, Marquise H
DEBS, Eugene Victor 1
DEBUCHI, Katsuji 2
DEBUSK, Burchard 1
Woodson
DEBUYS, Laurence Richard 3
DEBYE, Peter Joseph 4
William
DE CALLIERES H
BONNEVUE, Louis
Hector
DE CAMP, George 5
DE CAMP, John A. 3
DE CAMP, Joseph Rodefer 1
DE CAMP, William Scott 1
De CAPRILES, Jose Rafael 5
DE CARDENAS, Garcia 1
Lopez
DE CARDENAS Y 6
RODRIGUEZ DE
RIVAS, Juan Francisco
DE CARONDELET, H
Francisco Luis Hector
DE CARTIER DE 2
MARCHIENNE, Baron
Emile
DE CARVALHO, Estevao 6
Leitao
DECASSERES, Benjamin 2
DE CASTRO, Hector 1
DECASTRO, Josue 6
DE CASTRO, Morris F. 4
DECATUR, Emmett Daniel H
DECATUR, Stephen H
DE CELERON DE H
BLAINVILLE, Pierre
Joseph
DECELL, John Lloyd 2
DE CHAMPLAIN, Samuel H
DECHANT, John Aloysius 6
DE CHARLEVOIX, Pierre H
Francois Xavier
DE CHAVANNE, Countess 4
Loveau
DECHERD, H. Ben 5
DECHERD, Henry Martyn 1
DECHERT, Henry Taylor 1
DECHERT, Robert 5
DE CHEVERUS, Jean Louis H
Anne Magdelen Lefebre
DE CISNEROS, Eleonora 1
DE CISNEROS, Eleonora 2
DECKER, Alonzo Galloway 5
DECKER, Benton Clark 1
DECKER, Charles Elijah 4
DECKER, Clarence 5
Raymond
DECKER, Edward William 3
DECKER, Edward William 5
DECKER, Floyd F. 2
DECKER, Marion Emory 5
DECKER, Martin Snyder 4
DECKER, Orlady Paul 4
DECKER, Perl D. 5
DECKER, Sarah Platt 1
DE CLORIVIERE, Joseph- H
Pierre Picot de Limoelan
DECORMIS, Louis 1
DE COSTA, Benjamin 1
Franklin
DE COU, Branson 1
DE COU, Edgar Ezekiel 2
DE COURCY, Charles A. 1
DE CREVECOEUR, H
Michel-Guillaume Jean
DEDERICK, Peter Kells 1
DEEB, Paul Harold 6
DEEDMEYER, Frank 4
DEEDS, Edward Andrew 4
DEEGAN, William Joseph 2
DEEKS, William Edgar 1
DEEMER, Elias 1
DEEMER, Horace Emerson 1
DEEMS, Charles Force H
DEEMS, Edward Mark 1
DEEMS, J. Harry 1
DEEN, Joshua Lee 1
DEEPING, Werwick 3

504

DEER, George Harvison 4
DE ERDELY, Francis 4
DEERE, Charles Henry 1
DEERE, John
DEERFOOT H
DEERING, Charles 1
DEERING, Frank Prentiss 1
DEERING, James 1
DEERING, Nathaniel
DEERING, Nathaniel Cobb H
DEERING, Robert Waller
DEERING, William 1
DEES, Randall Euesta 5
DEESZ, Louis A. 3
DEETER, Paxson
DEETJEN, Rudolph Henry 4
DEETZ, Charles Henry 3
DEFAUW, Desire 4
DEFEBAUGH, James 1
Elliott
DEFENBACH, Byron;
DEFERRARI, Roy Joseph 5
DEFFENBAUGH, Walter 5
Sylvanus
DE FLOREZ, Luis 4
DEFOE, Harry Joseph 3
DE FOE, Louis Vincent 1
DE FONTIANE, Felix H
Gregory
DEFORD, Miriam Allen 6
DE FOREST, Alfred Victor 2
DE FOREST, Charles Mills 2
DE FOREST, David Curtis 4
DE FOREST, Erastus H
Lyman
DE FOREST, Henry 3
Lockwood
DE FOREST, Henry 2
Pelouze
DE FOREST, Henry S. 1
DE FOREST, Henry 1
Wheeler
DE FOREST, John William H
DE FOREST, John William 4
DE FOREST, John Williams 4
DEFOREST, Johnston 3
DE FOREST, Katharine 5
DE FOREST, Lee 4
DE FOREST, Lockwood 1
DE FOREST, Marian
DE FOREST, Robert Weeks 1
DE FRANCA, Manuel H
Joachim
DE FRANCESCO, Italo
Luther
DE FRANCISCI, Anthony 4
DEFREES, Donald 5
DEFREES, Joseph Holton
DEFREES, Joseph Hutton
DEFREES, Joseph Rollie 3
DE FREYRE Y 2
SANTANDER, Manuel
DE GALVEZ, Bernardo H
DE GARMO, James M. 4
DE GARMO, William
DEGAS, Hilaire Germain H
Edgar
DEGAS, Hillaire Germain 4
Edgar
DE GASPERI, Alcide 3
DE GAULLE, Charles 5
Andre Joseph Marie
DE GELLEKE, Gerrit
Jacob
DEGENER, Edward H
DEGERING, Edward
Franklind
DE GERSDORFF, Carl 2
August
DEGETAU, Federico 4
DE GHELDERODE, 4
Michel
DEGLMAN, George 5
Anthony
DE GOGORZA, Emilio
Eduardo
DE GOGORZA, Emilio 3
Eduardo
DE GOLYER, E. L. 3
DE GOLYER, Robert 3
Seeley
DE GRAEFF, Dr. A. C. D. 3
DE GRAFF, John Isaac H
DE GRAFF, Lawrence 1
DE GRAFF, Mark H. 4
DE GRAFFENRIED, H
Christopher
DE GRAFFENRIED,
Edward
DE GRAFFENRIED, Mary 4
Clare
DE GRAFFENRIED, Reese 1
Calhoun
DE GRASSE, Francois H
Joseph Paul
DE GRAW, Peter Voorhees 1

DEGROAT, George Blewer 5
DEGROAT, Harry DeWitt 5
DE GROOT, William A. 1
DE HAAN, John Jr. 2
DE HAAS, Jacob Jaudah 4
Aaron
DE HAAS, Jacob Judah H
Aaron
DE HAAS, John Philip H
DE HART, John H
DE HART, William Henry 1
DE HART, William Mathias 4
DE HASS, Mauritz H
Frederick Hendrick
DE HASS, Wills 1
DE HAVEN, David William 2
DE HAVEN, Edwin Jesse H
DE HAVEN, Frank 4
DE HAVEN, Franklin 1
DEHAVEN, John B.
DE HAVEN, John Jefferson 1
DE HAVILLAND, Sir
Geoffrey
DE HEVESY, George 4
Charles
DEHN, Adolf 5
DEHON, Theodore H
DEIBLER, Frederick Shipp 4
DEICHMAN, Carl F.
DEIGERT, Robert Campbell 6
DEILER, John Hanno
DEILY, Curtis R. 6
DEIMEL, Henry L. 4
DEIMLER, Paul Ellas 5
DEINES, Ernest Hubert 5
DEININGER, William
DEISS, Charles F. 3
DEITRICH, Theodore C. 1
DEITRICK, Elizabeth Platt 5
DEITRICK, Frederick 3
Simpson
DEITRICK, James 4
DEITRICK, William Henley 6
DEITZ, Archibald Edwin 5
DEITZLER, George
Washington
DE JARNETTE, Daniel H
Coleman
DEJARNETTE, Joseph 5
Spencer
DE JESOS, Angel Roman 3
DE JONG, David Cirnel 4
DEJONG, Yvonne 6
Germaine
DE JURENEV, Nicholas 3
DE KALB, Courtenay 1
DEKALB, Frances Douglas 4
(Mrs. Courtenay DeKalb)
DE KAY, Charles 1
DE KAY, George Colman H
DE KAY, James Ellsworth H
DE KAY, John Wesley 5
DEKKER, Albert 4
DE KLEINE, William 3
DEKNATEL, Frederick 6
Brockway
DEKNATEL, William 6
Ferguson
DE KNIGHT, Clarence
Woods
DE KOVEN, Anna Farwell 4
DE KOVEN, James H
DE KOVEN, Reginald 1
DEKRAFFT, William 4
DE KROYFT, S. Helen A. 1
DE KRUIF, Paul 6
DE LA BARRA, Francisco 4
Leon
DE LA BARRE, Cecil 3
Franzen
DELABARRE, Edmund 2
Burke
DELABARRE, Frank 1
Alexander
DE LABOULAYE, Ander 4
Lefebvre
DE LABOULAYE, Andre 5
Lefebure
DELACOUR, Reginald 2
Beardsley
DE LACY, Walter H
Washington
DELAFIELD, E. M. 2
DELAFIELD, Edward 1
DELAFIELD, Francis 1
DELAFIELD, John H
DELAFIELD, John Ross 4
DELAFIELD, Lewis 2
Livingston
DELAFIELD, Lewis 3
Livingston
DELAFIELD, Maturin 2
Livingston
DELAFIELD, Richard H
DELAFIELD, Richard 1
DE LA HABA, Gabriel

DELAHANTY, William 5
John
DELAHAY, Mark William H
DELAMANO, William H
DE LAMAR, Joseph 1
Raphael
DE LAMAR, Joseph 4
Raphael
DE LA MARE, Walter 3
DELAMARTER, Eric 3
DELAMATER, Cornelius H
Henry
DELAMATER, Nicholas B. 1
DE LA MATYR, Gilbert H
DE LA MOTHE, Antoine 1
DE LANCEY, Darragh 1
DE LANCEY, Edward 1
Floyd
DE LANCEY, James H
DE LANCEY, Oliver H
DE LANCEY, William H
Heathcote
DE LAND, Charles 3
Edmund
DE LAND, Charles Victor 1
DE LAND, Clyde Osmer 2
DELAND, Ellen Douglas
DELAND, Margaretta 2
Wade
DELAND, Paul Stanley 1
DELANDER, N. Paul 3
DELANEY, George A. 6
DELANEY, George Philip 5
DELANEY, John J. 1
DELANEY, Matthew A. 1
DE LANEY, Paul 4
DELANEY, Peter A. 1
DELANEY, Sadie Peterson 3
DE LANGLADE, Charles H
Michel
DELANO, Aline P. 4
DELANO, Amassa H
DELANO, Charles H
DELANO, Columbus H
DELANO, Edith Barnard 2
DELANO, Eugene 1
DELANO, Frances Jackson 4
DELANO, Francis Henry 1
DELANO, Frederic Adrian 3
DELANO, Jane Arminda H
DELANO, Jane Arminda 1
DELANO, Lyman 2
DELANO, William Adams 5
DELANY, John Bernard 1
DELANY, John Joseph 1
DELANY, Joseph Francis 2
DELANY, Martin Robinson H
DELANY, Patrick Bernard 1
DELANY, Selden Peabody 1
DE LA OSSA, Ernesto
DELAPLAINE, Isaac H
Clason
DE LA PUENTE, Don Juan H
Joseph Eligio
DE LARGE, Robert Carlos H
DE LARGENTAYE, Jean 5
DE LA RICHARDIE, H
Armand
DE LARME, Alonzo Alvin 1
DE LA ROCHE, Mazo 4
DE LA RONDE, Louis 4
Denis
DELATOUR, Henry 1
Beeckman
DE LAUBENFELS, Max 3
W.
DE LAUDONNIERE, Rene H
Goulaine
DELAUP, Sidney Philip 1
DELAVAN, David Bryson 2
DELAVAN, Edward 1
Cornelius
DE LA WARR, baron 4
DELBOS, Julius 5
DE LEE, Joseph Bolivar 1
DE LE MONTANYA, H
James
DE LEON, Daniel 1
DE LEON, Edwin 1
DE LEON, Edwin Warren 1
DE LEON, Pablo Ocampo 1
DE LEON, Thomas Cooper 1
DE LEQUERICA Y 4
ERQUIZA, Jose Felix
DELERY, Francois Charles H
DE LERY, Joseph Gaspard H
Chaussegros
DE LESTRY, Edmond 1
Louis
DELEUW, Charles Edmund 5
DEL GAUDIO, Matthew 4
William
DE L'HALLE, Constantin H
DE LIMA E. SILVA, R. 2
DE LISSER, Horace 1
DELIUS, Frederick H

DELIUS, Frederick 4
DELK, Edward Buehler 3
DELK, Edwin Heyl 1
DELL, Floyd 5
DELL, Francis William 2
DELL, Roger LeRoy 4
DELL, Roger LeRoy 5
DELLA PIETRA, Alfonso 5
DELLA TORRE ALTA, Il 5
Marchese (Albert-Felix
Schmitt)
DELL'AGNESE, F. 6
DELLENBAUGH, 1
Frederick Samuel
DELLENBAUGH, Harriet 1
Rogers Otis
DELLET, James H
DELLINGER, John Howard 4
DELLPLAIN, Morse 5
DEL MAR, Alexander 1
DEL MAR, Algernon 5
DEL MAR, Eugene 2
DEL MAR, William Arthur 6
DELMAS, Delphin Michael 1
DELMONICO, Lorenzo H
DELOACH, Robert John 5
Henderson
DE LOM D'ARCE, Louis- H
Armand
DE LONG, George 2
Washington
DE LONG, Ira Mitchell 2
DE LONG, Irwin Hoch 5
DE LONGPRE, Paul 1
DE LOS RIOS, Fernando 2
DELOUGAZ, Pinhas Pierre 6
DE LOUTHERBOURG, H
Annibale Christian Henry
DELSASSO, Leo Peter 5
DEL SESTO, Christopher 6
DEL SOLAR, June Eckart 6
De Gonzalez
DEL TUFO, Raymond Jr. 5
DELUCA, Giuseppe 3
DE LUNA Y ARELLANO, H
Tristan
DELUREY, Laurence 4
Augustine
DEL VALLE, Manuel 5
Angel
DELWICHE, Edmond 2
Joseph
DELZELL, James Ellis 4
DELZELL, Thomas White 5
DE MAR, John L. 2
DE MARE, Jeanne 6
DEMAREE, Albert Lowther 4
DEMAREST, George Stuart 5
DEMAREST, Henry Samuel 1
DEMAREST, William 3
Henry Steele
DEMAREST, William 1
Thomas
DEMARTINO, Nobile 3
Giacomo
DE MARTINO, Nobile 4
Giacomo
DEMBITZ, Lewis Naphtali 1
DEMBO, Leon H 4
DEMBY, V. E. Thomas 3
DEMEISSNER, Sophie 4
Radford
DE MENASCE, Jacques 3
DE MENIL, Alexander 1
Nicolas
DE MENIL, John 6
DE MENT, Byron Hoover 1
DEMEREC, Milislav 4
DE MERITTE, Edwin 1
DE MERRALL, Leo Cyril 6
DE MERRY DEL VAL, 6
Alfonse
DEMERS, Albert Fox 2
DEMERS, Pierre Paul 5
DE MEZIERES Y H
CLUGNY, Athanase
DEMIASHKEVICH, 3
Michael John
DE MILHAU, Louis John 5
de Grenon
DE MILLE, Cecil Blount 3
DE MILLE, Henry 1
Churchill
DE MILLE, William 3
Churchill
DE MILT, Aida Rodman 6
DEMING, Benjamin F. H
DEMING, Clarence 1
DEMING, Edwin Willard 2
DEMING, Harold S. 3
DEMING, Henry Champion H
DEMING, Horace Edward 1
DEMING, Judson Keith 4
DEMING, Lucius 4
Parmenias
DEMING, Philander 1

DEMING, Therese O. 2
DEMING, Thomas Harlan 3
DEMING, William Chapin 2
DE MIRANDA, Francisco H
DEMME, Charles Rudolph H
DEMMON, Isaac Newton 1
DE MOKCSA, Agoston H
Haraszthy
DE MONCHY, W. H. 5
DEMOREST, Frederic Coe 4
DEMOREST, William 4
Curtis
DEMOREST, William 6
Jennings
DEMOS, Raphael 5
DE MOSCOSO DE H
ALVARADO, Luis
DE MOTT, John H
DEMOTT, Richard Hopper 5
DE MOTTE, Harvey 1
Clelland
DE MOTTE, Mark L. 1
DEMPSEY, Clarence 1
Haines
DEMPSEY, Edward John 4
DEMPSEY, Edward Joseph 3
DEMPSEY, Edward 6
Wheeler
DEMPSEY, Elam Franklin 2
DEMPSEY, F(rancis) 6
Kenneth
DEMPSEY, James Howard 1
DEMPSEY, John Bourne 1
DEMPSEY, John J. 3
DEMPSEY, John Stanley 3
DEMPSEY, K. Mary 6
DEMPSEY, Michael Ryan 4
DEMPSEY, Stephen 2
Wallace
DEMPSIE, Ephraim 1
DEMPSTER, Arthur Jeffrey 2
DEMPSTER, John H
DEMPSTER, William John 1
DEMPWOLF, Reinhardt 2
DEMUTH, Charles H
DEMUTH, Charles 4
DEMUTH, Laurence 4
Wheeler
DE NANCREDE, Paul H
Joseph Guerard
DENARI, Andrew F. 3
DE NARVAEZ, Panfilo H
DENBIGH, John Halliday 2
DENBY, Charles * 1
DENBY, Edwin 1
DENCH, Edward Bradford 1
DENDRAMIS, Vassill 3
DENE, Shafto Henry 1
Monckton
DENECHAUD, Charles 3
Isidore
DE NECKERE, Leo H
Raymond
DENEEFE, Robert 3
DENEEN, Charles Samuel 1
DENEGRE, Walter Denis 1
DENFELD, Louis Emil 5
DENFELD, Robert Edward 1
DENHAM, Edward 1
DENHAM, Henry 5
Henderson
DENHAM, Robert Newton 3
DENHAM, Thomas Palmer 4
DENHAM, William Ernest 6
DENHARD, Charles 1
Edward
DENHARDT, Henry H. 1
DENIG, Robert Gracey 1
DENIG-MANOE, Rudolf 4
Karl Moor
DENIO, Francis Brigham 1
DENIOUS, Jess C. 3
DENIOUS, Wilbur Franklin 3
DENISE, Larimore Conover 5
DENISON, A. Rodger 4
DENISON, Arthur Carter 2
DENISON, Charles 1
DENISON, Charles 1
DENISON, Charles Simeon 1
DENISON, Edward Everett 5
DENISON, Frederic 1
DENISON, George H
DENISON, Henry Willard 1
DENISON, James Henry 6
DENISON, John Henry 1
DENISON, John Hopkins 1
DENISON, John Ledyard 1
DENISON, Lindsay 1
DENISON, Mary Andrews 1
DENISON, Robert Charles 1
DENISON, Robert Fuller 5
DENISON, Thomas Stewart 1
DENISON, William Cecil 1
DENISON, Winfred Thaxter 1
DE NIZA, Marcos H
DENMAN, Burt J. 1

DENMAN, Ira O. 1
DENMAN, Leroy Gilbert 1
DENMAN, William H
DENMAN, William 3
DENNEN, Ernest Joseph 1
DENNEN, Jeanne Whitney 1
DENNETT, Carl Pullen 3
DENNETT, Edward Power 1
DENNETT, Fred 2
DENNETT, John Richard H
DENNETT, Raymond 4
DENNETT, Roger Herbert 1
DENNETT, Tyler 2
DENNEY, Charles Eugene 6
DENNEY, James Arlando 4
DENNEY, Joseph Villiers 1
DENNEY, Lawrence 5
Vincent
DENNEY, Oswald Evans 1
DENNEY, William du 4
Hamel
DENNIE, Charles Clayton 5
DENNIE, Joseph 4
DENNING, Forrest Wayne 4
DENNING, James Edwin 5
DENNING, Joseph M. 1
DENNING, Reynolds 5
McConnell
DENNING, William * H
DENNIS, Alfred Lewis 1
Pinneo
DENNIS, Alfred Pearce 1
DENNIS, Charles Henry 2
DENNIS, David Worth 1
DENNIS, E. Willard 4
DENNIS, Edward Wimberly 6
DENNIS, Fred L. 3
DENNIS, Frederic Shepard 1
DENNIS, Gabriel Lafayette 3
DENNIS, George Robertson H
DENNIS, Graham Barclay 1
DENNIS, James Shepard 1
DENNIS, James Teackle 1
DENNIS, John * H
DENNIS, John Cobb 3
DENNIS, John Hancock 4
DENNIS, John M. 1
DENNIS, Joseph Charles 5
DENNIS, Lindley Hoaq 2
DENNIS, Littleton Purnell H
DENNIS, Louis Munroe 1
DENNIS, Ralph Brownell 2
DENNIS, Samuel K. 4
DENNIS, Samuel Shepard 1
DENNIS, William B. 1
DENNIS, William Cullen 1
DENNIS, William Henry 1
DENNIS, William Henry Jr. 4
DENNISON, Aaron Lufkin 1
DENNISON, Clare 3
DENNISON, E. Haldeman 1
DENNISON, Ethan Allen 3
DENNISON, Henry Strugis 1
DENNISON, Henry Sturgis 5
DENNISON, Jackson 3
Belden
DENNISON, Walter 1
DENNISON, William H
DENNISTON, Henry 1
Martyn
DENNY, Charles Eugene 4
DENNY, Collins 2
DENNY, Collins Jr. 4
DENNY, Ebenezer 1
DENNY, Frank Lee 1
DENNY, George Hutcheson 3
DENNY, George Vernon Jr. 3
DENNY, Harmar 1
DENNY, Harmar Denny 4
DENNY, Harold Norman 2
DENNY, James W. 5
DENNY, Ludwell 5
DENNY, Reginald Leigh 4
DENNY, Robert H. 3
DE NOGALES, Pedro 6
Rafael (y Mendez)
DE NORMANDIE, James 1
DE NORMANDIE, Robert 3
L.
DE NOYAN, Pierre-Jacques H
Payen
DENOYELLES, Peter H
DENOYER, L. Philip 4
DENSLOW, Dorothea 5
Henrietta
DENSLOW, Herbert 1
McKenzie
DENSLOW, William 1
Wallace
DENSMORE, Emmet 1
DENSMORE, Frances 3
DENSMORE, Harvey Bruce 6
DENSMORE, Hiram D. 1
DENSMORE, John B. 3
DENSMORE, John Hopkins 2
DENSON, Nimrod Davis 1

DENSON, Samuel Crawford 1
DENSTEDT, Orville 6
Frederick
DENT, Frederick Rodgers 5
Jr.
DENT, Frederick Tracy H
DENT, George 3
DENT, Hawthorne K. 3
DENT, John Marshall Jr. 6
DENT, Louis Addison 1
DENT, Marmaduke Herbert 1
DENT, Stanley Hubert 1
DENT, William Barton H
Wade
DENTON, George 1
Kirkpatrick
DENTON, J. Furman 5
DENTON, James Clarence 2
DENTON, James Edgar 1
DENTON, Lyman Morse 3
DENTON, Minna Caroline 3
DENTON, Winfield K. 5
DENVER, James William 1
DENVER, Matthew 3
Rombach
DENYES, John Russell 1
DE ONATE, Juan H
DE ONIS, Federico 4
DE OTERMEN, Antonio H
DE PADILLA, Juan H
DE PAOLIS, Alessio 4
DE PARIS, Wilbur 5
DE PAUGHER, Adrien H
DE PAULA GUTIERREZ, 6
Don Francisco
DEPAUW, Washington H
Charles
DE PENA, Carlos Maria 1
DE PENALOSA 1
BRICENO, Diego Dionsio
DE PERALTA, Pedro H
DEPEW, Chauncey Mitchell 1
DEPEW, Claude Ira 3
DEPEW, Joseph William 5
DE PEYSTER, Abraham 1
DE PEYSTER, Frederic 1
James
DE PEYSTER, John Watts 1
DEPINET, Ned E. 6
DEPONAI, John Martin 1
DE PORTOLA, Gaspar H
DE POUILLY, Jacques H
Nicholas Bussiere
DE POURTALES, Louis H
Francois
DEPPERMANN, William 5
Herman
DE PRIEST, Oscar 1
DEPUE, David A. 1
DEPUTY, Manfred Wolfe 2
DE PUY, William Harrison 1
DE QUILLE, Dan H
DERAMUS, William Neal 4
DERBIGNY, Irving A. 3
DERBIGNY, Pierre Auguste H
Charles Bourguignon
DERBY, Ashton Philander 6
DERBY, Donald 5
DERBY, Elias Hasket H
DERBY, George Horatio 1
DERBY, George McClellan 3
DERBY, George Strong 1
DERBY, Jeanette Barr 4
DERBY, Orville Adelbert 1
DERBY, Richard H
DERBY, Richard 4
DERBY, Samuel Carroll 1
DERBY, Stephen Hasket 2
DERCUM, Francis X. 1
DE REMER, John A. 1
DE RESZKE, Edouard 1
DE RESZKE, Jean 1
DERICKSON, Donald 4
DERICKSON, Samuel 3
Hoffman
DERIEUX, Samuel Arthur 1
DERLETH, August 5
(William)
DERLETH, Charles Jr. 5
DERN, Alfred L. 2
DERN, George Henry 1
DERN, John 1
DERN, John 1
DE ROALDES, Arthur 1
Washington
DE ROSE, Peter 3
DE ROSSET, Frederick 1
Ancrum
DE ROSSET, Moses John 4
DE ROSSET, William Lord 3
DE ROUEN, Rene L. 2
DEROULET, Vincent W. 6
DE ROUSSY DE SALES, 3
Raoul
DERR, Cyrus George 1
DERR, Homer Munro 5

DERR, Louis 1
DERRICK, Samuel 5
Melanchthon
DERRICK, Sidney Jacob 2
DERRY, George Hermann 2
DERSE, Alexander Anthony 4
DERSHEM, Franklin Lewis 4
DERTHICK, Frank A. 4
DERTHICK, Henry J. 5
DERTINGER, Georg 4
DERUJINSKY, Gleb W. 6
DE RUSSY, Isaac H
Denniston
DERWENT, Clarence 3
DERY, D. George 3
DE ST. AUBIN, Percival 1
Ovide
DE ST. DENIS, Louis H
Juchereau
DE SAINT EXUPERY, 2
Antoine
DE ST. VRAIN, Ceran De H
Hault Delassus
DE SAINT-MEMIN, H
Charles Balthazar Jullen
Fevret
DE SALVIO, Alfonso 5
DESANCTIS, Adolph 4
George
DE SANTILLANA, Giorgio 6
Diaz
DE SAULLES, Charles 5
August Heckscher
DE SAUSSURE, Henry H
William
DE SAUZE, Emile Blais 6
DE SAVITSCH, Eugene 4
Constantine
DESCHAMPS, Paul 6
DE SCHWEINITZ, H
Edmond Alexander
DE SCHWEINITZ, Karl 6
DE SCHWEINITZ, Paul H
DESHA, Joseph H
DESHA, Mary 1
DESHA, Robert H
DESHON, George 1
DE SICA, VITTORIO 6
DESIDERIO, Anthony 5
DESJARDINS, Arthur 4
Ulderic
DESLOGE, Joseph 5
DE SMET, Pierre Jean H
DESMOND, Daniel Francis 2
DESMOND, Humphrey 1
Joseph
DESMOND, Thomas 5
Charles
DESMOND, Thomas Henry 4
DE SOLLAR, Tenney Cook 4
DE SOTO, Hernando H
DE SOTO, Hernando 1
DESPARD, Clement L. 3
DES PLANCHES, Baron 4
Ed Mayor
DES PORTES, Fay Allen 2
D'ESPOSITO, Joshua 3
DESPRADELLE, Constant 1
Desire
DESPRES, Emile 6
DESPRES, Maurice Samuel 3
DESSAR, Leo Charles 1
DESSAR, Louis Paul 3
DESSES, Jean 5
DESSEZ, Mrs. Elizabeth 6
Richey
DESSION, George 3
Hathaway
DE STEIGUER, Louis 2
Rodolph
DESTINN, Emmy 1
DESTREHAN, John Noel H
DESVERNINE, Raoul 4
Eugene
DE SYLVA, George Gard 4
DETCHON, Adelaide 5
DETELS, Martin Paul 5
DETHMERS, John R. 5
DETMER, Julian Francis 4
DETMOLD, Christian H
Edward
DE TOCQUEVILLE, Alexis H
Henri Maurice Clerel
DE TONTY, Henry H
DE TORRENTE, Henry 4
DE TOUSARD, Anne Louis H
DETRE, László 6
DE TREVILLE, Yvonne 1
DETRICK, Jacob Stoll 4
DE TROBRIAND, Regis H
Denis de Kereden
DETT, Robert Nathaniel 2
DETWEILER, A(lbert) 5
Henry
DETWEILER, Charles 4
Samuel

DETWEILER, Frederick 3
German
DETWEILER, George H. 3
DETWILER, Frederick 3
Knecht
DETWILER, Samuel 3
Randall
DETWILER, W. Frank 3
DEUEL, Alanson Chase 1
DEUEL, Harry James Jr. 3
DEUEL, Wallace Rankin 6
DE ULLOA, Antonio H
DEUPREE, John Greer 4
DEUPREE, Richard 6
Redwood
DE URSO, James Joseph 6
DEUSSEN, Alexander 4
DEUTSCH, Adolph 6
DEUTSCH, Albert 4
DEUTSCH, Alcuin Henry 3
DEUTSCH, Bernard 1
Seymour
DEUTSCH, Gotthard 1
DEUTSCH, Henry 5
DEUTSCH, Monroe 3
Emanuel
DEUTSCHER, Isaac 5
DEVALERA, Eamon 6
DE VAULT, Samuel H. 6
DEVAN, Harriet Beecher 5
Scoville
DE VANE, William Clyde 6
DEVANEY, John Patrick 1
DEVANEY, Michael R. 5
DE VARGAS ZAPATA Y H
LUJAN PONCE DE,
Leon Diego
DE VEGH, Imrie 4
DEVENDORF, Irving R. 1
DEVENDORF, James 2
Franklin
DEVENS, Charles H
DEVER, Paul Andrew 3
DEVER, William Emmett 1
DEVEREAUX, Helena 6
Trafford
DEVEREUX, F. Ramsey 4
DEVEREUX, John C. H
DEVEREUX, John Henry 1
DEVEREUX, Mary 1
DEVEREUX, Nicholas 1
DEVILBISS, Howard P. 5
DEVIN, Thomas Casimer 1
DEVIN, William Augustus 3
DEVINE, David Francis 1
DEVINE, Edward Thomas 2
DEVINE, James Gasper 5
DEVINE, James Herbert 3
DEVINE, John M. 5
DEVINE, Joseph McMurray 4
DEVINE, Thomas Hume 1
DE VINNE, Theodore Low 1
DEVINS, John Bancroft 1
DEVINY, John Joseph 4
DE VLIEG, Ray Albert 5
DEVLIN, Robert Thomas 1
DEVLIN, Thomas Francis 1
DEVOE, Alan 3
DEVOE, Emma Smith 1
DEVOE, Frederick William 1
DE VOE, John M. 4
DEVOE, Ralph Godwin 4
DEVOE, Robert W. 5
DE VOE, Walter 5
DEVOE, William Beck 5
DEVOL, Carroll Augustine 1
DE VOLL, F. Usher 6
DEVOORE, Ann (Mrs. 5
Reginald Prescott Walden)
DEVOR, Donald Smith 4
DEVORE, Daniel Bradford 4
DEVORE, Harry S. 2
DE VORE, Rebecca Jane 5
DE VOS, Julius Emilius 4
DEVOSS, James Clarence 3
DE VOTO, Bernard 3
Augustine
DEVOY, John H
DEVOY, John 1
DEVREE, Howard 4
DE VRIES, David Pieterson H
DEVRIES, Herman 2
DEVRIES, Louis 3
DE VRIES, Marion 1
DE VRIES, Tiemen 1
DE VRIES, William 1
Levering
DEW, Louise E. 4
DEW, Thomas Roderick H
DEW, Thomas Roderick H
DE WAHA, Baron 5
Raymond
DEWALT, Arthur Granville 1
DEWAR, Henry Hamilton 6
DEWART, Frederick 1
Wesley

DEWART, Lewis H
DEWART, Murray Wilder 1
D'EWART, Wesley Abner 6
DEWART, William Herbert 1
DEWART, William Lewis H
DEWART, William 2
Thompson
DEWEERD, James A. 5
DEWEES, William Potts H
DE WEESE, Truman 4
Armstrong
DEWESSE, Arville Ottis 5
DEWEY, Bradley 6
DEWEY, Byrd Spilman 5
DEWEY, Charles 1
DEWEY, Charles Almon 1
DEWEY, Charles Melville 1
DEWEY, Charles Schuveldt 6
DEWEY, Chester 1
DEWEY, Chester Robert 6
DEWEY, Daniel 1
DEWEY, Davis Rich 2
DEWEY, Francis Henshaw 1
DEWEY, Frederic Perkins 1
DEWEY, George 1
DEWEY, Harry Pinneo 1
DEWEY, Henry Bingham 1
DEWEY, Henry Sweetser 1
DEWEY, James F. 3
DEWEY, John 3
DEWEY, Julian Hiland 1
DEWEY, Lloyd Ellis 1
DEWEY, Lyster Hoxie 2
DEWEY, Malcolm Howard 4
DEWEY, Mary Elizabeth 1
DEWEY, Melvil 1
DEWEY, Orville H
DEWEY, Richard 1
DEWEY, Stoddard 1
DEWEY, Thomas Edmund 6
DEWEY, W. A. 1
DEWHURST, Frederic Eli 1
DEWHURST, J. Frederic 4
DEWILDE, Brandon 6
DE WINDT, Delano 4
DEWINDT, Harold Clifford 5
DEWING, Arthur Stone 4
DEWING, Francis 1
DEWING, Maria Oakey H
DEWING, Thomas Wilmer 1
DE WITT, Alexander 1
DE WITT, Benjamin Parke 4
DE WITT, Calvin 1
DE WITT, Charles 1
DE WITT, Charles Gerrit 1
DE WITT, David Miller 1
DE WITT, George Ashley 5
DE WITT, Jacob Hasbrouck H
DE WITT, John 1
DE WITT, John 4
DEWITT, John Doyle 1
DEWITT, John Hibbett 1
DE WITT, John Lesesne 4
DE WITT, Julia Woodhull 1
DE WITT, Lydia Maria 1
DEWITT, Norman Johnston 4
DEWITT, Simeon 1
DEWITT, Wallace 6
DE WITT, William 4
Converse
DE WITT, William Hedges 1
DE WOLF, Frank 3
Walbridge
DE WOLF, James 1
DE WOLF, John 1
DEWOLF, Richard Crosby 2
DE WOLF, Wallace Leroy 1
DEWOLFE, Donald Joseph 4
DE WOLFE, Elsie 4
DE WOLFE, James 4
Pernatte
DEWOODY, Charles 1
Frederick
DE WOSKIN, Morris R. 5
DEWSNUP, Ernest Ritson 5
DEWSON, Mary Williams 4
DEXTER, Byron 6
DEXTER, Clarence Sawyer 2
DEXTER, Edwin Grant 1
DEXTER, Franklin 1
DEXTER, Franklin 1
DEXTER, Franklin 1
Bowditch
DEXTER, Gordon 1
DEXTER, Gregory 1
Mumford
DEXTER, Henry H
DEXTER, Henry 1
DEXTER, Henry Martyn 1
DEXTER, Morton 1
DEXTER, Philip 1
DEXTER, Robert Cloutman 3
DEXTER, Robert E. 3
DEXTER, Samuel * H
DEXTER, Seymour 1

DEXTER, Timothy H
DEXTER, Walter Friar 2
DEXTER, William 2
DEXTER, Wirt
DEY, Benjamin Clifford 6
DEY, William Morton 6
DEYMANN, Clementine H
DE YO, Anna Marden 3
DEYO, C. W. 3
DEYO, Donald Edmund 5
DEYO, Morton Lyndholm 6
DEYOE, Albert M. 4
DEYOE, George P. 4
DE YOUNG, Chris 5
Anthony
DE YOUNG, Frederic 1
Robert
DEYOUNG, Harry 3
Anthony
DE YOUNG, Meichel 1
Harry
DE YTURRALDE, Mariano 4
DEZENDORF, John H
Frederick
D'HARNONCOURT, Rene 5
D'HERELLE, Felix 5
D'HUMY, Fernand Emile 3
DIAL, Nathaniel Barksdale
DIAMANTOPOULOS,
Cimon P.
DIAMOND, Tobias 5
Ellsworth
DIAS, Bartholomeu de H
Novaes
DIAZ, Abby Morton 1
DIAZ, Eduardo Acevedo 4
DIBARTOLOMEO, Robert 6
Edward
DIBBLE, Barry 4
DIBBLE, Charles Lemuel 1
DIBBLE, Roy Floyd 1
DIBELIUS, Otto Friedrich 4
Karl
DIBELL, Homer B. 1
DIBRELL, George Gibbs H
DIBRELL, James Anthony 1
DICE, Agnew Thomson 1
DICE, Charles Amos 6
DICE, J. Howard 1
DI CELLERE, Count V. 1
Macchi
DICK, Albert Blake 1
DICK, Albert Blake Jr. 3
DICK, Charles 2
DICK, Elisha Cullen H
DICK, George Alexander 2
DICK, George Frederick 4
DICK, Gladys Henry 4
DICK, Henry Kissinger 3
DICK, Homer T.
DICK, Hugh Gilchrist 5
DICK, John H
DICK, Paul Stephens 1
DICK, Robert P. 1
DICK, Robert Paine 4
DICK, Samuel H
DICK, Samuel Bernard 4
DICK, Samuel Medary 1
DICK, William Henry 3
DICK, William K. 3
DICKASON, John Howard 4
DICKEN, Charles Ernest 5
DICKEN, Clinton Orr 3
DICKENS, Albert
DICKENS, Charles H
DICKENS, John Lunsford 4
DICKENS, Samuel H
DICKENSON, Melville 5
Pierce
DICKENSON, Robert 5
Edward
DICKER, Samuel Byron 3
DICKERMAN, Charles 4
Heber
DICKERMAN, George 1
Sherwood
DICKERMAN, Sherwood 1
Owen
DICKERMAN, William
Carter
DICKERSON, Charles 1
Estell
DICKERSON, Denver S. 1
DICKERSON, Edward H
Nicoll
DICKERSON, James 1
Spencer
DICKERSON, John J. 4
DICKERSON, Luther L. 3
DICKERSON, Mahlon H
DICKERSON, Mary
Cynthia
DICKERSON, Oliver 4
Morton
DICKERSON, Philemon H
DICKERSON, Robert Carl 3

DICKERSON, Roy Ernest 4
DICKERT, David Augustus 4
DICKEY, Adam Herbert 1
DICKEY, Arthur W.
DICKEY, Charles Andrews 1
DICKEY, Charles Emmet 5
DICKEY, Charles Hadley 1
DICKEY, Donald Ryder 1
DICKEY, Herbert Spencer 2
DICKEY, James Allen 2
DICKEY, James Edward 4
DICKEY, Jesse Column 4
DICKEY, John H
DICKEY, John Lindsay 1
DICKEY, Lincoln Griffith 1
DICKEY, Lloyd Blackwell 6
DICKEY, Lyle Alexander 4
DICKEY, Marcus 4
DICKEY, Oliver James 4
DICKEY, Robert W(illiam) 5
DICKEY, Samuel 2
DICKEY, Samuel Jackson 4
DICKEY, Solomon Cravens 4
DICKEY, Theophilus Lyle H
DICKEY, Walter S. 1
DICKEY, William 1
Donaldson
DICKIE, Alexander Jack 2
DICKIE, George William 1
DICKIE, J. Roy 4
DICKIE, James Francis 4
DICKIE, Samuel 1
DICKINS, Francis William 4
DICKINS, John H
DICKINSON, Albert 1
DICKINSON, Alfred Elijah 1
DICKINSON, Alfred James 4
DICKINSON, Anna 1
Elizabeth
DICKINSON, Anson H
DICKINSON, Asa Don 4
DICKINSON, Augustus 5
Edwin
DICKINSON, Calvin L. 5
DICKINSON, Charles 1
Henry
DICKINSON, Charles 1
Monroe
DICKINSON, Clarence 5
DICKINSON, Clement 1
Cabell
DICKINSON, Clinton Roy 2
Stevens
DICKINSON, Daniel H
DICKINSON, David W. H
McDonald
DICKINSON, Don 1
McDonald
DICKINSON, Dwight 4
DICKINSON, Edward H
DICKINSON, Edward 2
DICKINSON, Edward 5
Everett Jr.
DICKINSON, Edward H
Fenwick
DICKINSON, Edward T. Jr. 4
DICKINSON, Edwin 4
DeWitt
DICKINSON, Edwin Henry 4
DICKINSON, Emily H
Elizabeth
DICKINSON, Frances
DICKINSON, George 4
Sherman
DICKINSON, Helena Adell 3
DICKINSON, Hobart Cutler 2
DICKINSON, Horace 1
Danforth
DICKINSON, Hunt Tilford 4
DICKINSON, James Taylor 1
DICKINSON, John 1
DICKINSON, John 3
DICKINSON, John Dean 1
DICKINSON, John Quincy 1
DICKINSON, John H
Woodbridge
DICKINSON, Jonathan H
DICKINSON, Lester Jesse 5
DICKINSON, Levi Call 6
DICKINSON, Lucy 5
Jennings (Mrs. La Fell
Dickinson)
DICKINSON, Luren 2
Dudley
DICKINSON, Marquis
Fayette
DICKINSON, Mary Low 4
DICKINSON, May Bliss 5
DICKINSON, Oliver Booth 1
DICKINSON, Philemon 1
DICKINSON, Robert Latou 4
DICKINSON, Robert Smith 5
DICKINSON, Rodolphus H
DICKINSON, Roscoe 3
Gilkey
DICKINSON, Selden 4
Stratton

DICKINSON, Thomas H. 4
DICKINSON, William 1
Frederick
DICKINSON, William Hale 5
Jr.
DICKINSON, Zenas Clark 4
DICKMAN, John William 1
DICKMAN, Joseph 1
Theodore
DICK-READ, Grantly 3
DICKSEE, Sir Francis 4
Bernard
DICKSON, David * H
DICKSON, Earl Ensign 4
DICKSON, Edward 3
Augustus
DICKSON, Frank Dake 4
DICKSON, Frank Stoddard 3
DICKSON, Frederick 1
Stoever
DICKSON, Harris 5
DICKSON, John H
DICKSON, Joseph H
DICKSON, Leonard Eugene 3
DICKSON, R. L. 4
DICKSON, R. S. 4
DICKSON, Reid Stuart 4
DICKSON, Robert 1
DICKSON, Robert Barnes 3
DICKSON, Samuel 1
DICKSON, Samuel 1
DICKSON, Samuel Henry H
DICKSON, Samuel Henry 1
DICKSON, Thomas H
DICKSON, Tracy Campbell 1
DICKSON, William 4
Alexander
DICKSTEIN, Samuel 3
DIDAMA, Henry D. 1
DIDCOCT, John Joseph 1
DIDIER, Eugene Lemoine 4
DIDUSCH, James Francis 3
DIDUSCH, Joseph Stephen 6
DIECKMANN, Johannes 3
DIECKMANN, William 3
Joseph
DIEDERICH, Henry 1
William
DIEDERICH, John Thomas 6
DIEDERICH, William Hunt 3
DIEDERICHS, Herman 1
DIEFENBACH, Elmer G. 2
DIEFENDORF, Allen Ross 5
DIEFENDORF, Dorr Frank 5
DIEFFENBACH, Albert 5
Charles
DIEGO, Jose de 1
DIEGO Y MORENO, H
Francisco Garcia
DIEHL, Charles Edward 5
DIEHL, Charles Sanford 2
DIEHL, Conrad 4
DIEHL, Edith 3
DIEHL, Harold Sheely 6
DIEHL, Jacob 2
DIEHL, John Casper 4
DIEHL, Samuel Willauer 1
Black
DIEHL, William Wells 6
DIEKE, Gerhard Heinrich 4
DIEKEMA, Gerrit John 1
DIELMAN, Frederick 4
DIELMAN, Louis Henry 5
DIELS, Otto Paul Hermann 3
DIEM, William Roy 4
DIEMER, George Willis 3
DIEMER, Hugo 1
DIENER, William Lewis 4
DIENST, George Elias 1
DIERKS, DeVere 3
DIERKS, Frederick Henry 4
DIES, Martin 3
DIES, Martin 5
DIESEL, William F. 1
DIESTEL, Hermann 4
DIETER, Berthold B. 1
DIETERICH, William H. 4
DIETERICH, William 1
Herbert
DIETERLE, William 5
DIETL, Ernest Lawrence 6
DIETRICH, Charles Henry 1
DIETRICH, Frank Sigel 1
DIETRICH, Herman 3
Rudolph
DIETRICH, John Hassler 6
DIETRICHSON, Gustav 3
Johan Fredrik
DIETRICK, Charles Robert 6
DIETRICKSON, Johannes H
Wilhelm Christian
DIETSCH, C(larence) 6
Percival
DIETZ, Arthur O. 4
DIETZ, Carl F. 3

DIETZ, Gould Cooke 5
DIETZ, Joseph F. 4
DIETZ, Sherl Melvin 4
DIETZ, William H
DIETZMAN, Richard Priest 2
DIFENDERFER, Robert E. 1
DIFFENDERFER, George 2
M.
DIFFENDERFER, Lloyd 4
Herr
DIFFENDERFFER, Frank 4
Ried
DIFFENDORFER, Ralph 3
Eugene
DIGGES, Dudley 2
DIGGES, Isaac Watlington 3
DIGGES, Thomas Atwood 4
DIGGES, Walter Mitchell 1
DIGGLE, Roland 3
DIGGS, Annie LePorte 1
DIGGS, James Robert 4
Lincoln
DIGGS, Marshall Ramsey 5
DI GIORGIO, Joseph 3
DIGNAN, Thomas G. 4
DIKE, Chester Thomas 5
DIKE, George Phillips 6
DIKE, Henry B. 4
DIKE, Norman Staunton 3
DIKE, Samuel Warren 1
DILES, Dorothy Vernon 5
DILGER, Walter Linnell 5
DILKS, Walter Howard A. 2
DILL, Franklin Geselbracht 1
DILL, Homer Ray 4
DILL, James Brooks 1
DILL, Leonard Carter Jr. 6
DILL, Lewis
DILLARD, Allyn 5
DILLARD, Frank Clifford 4
DILLARD, George 6
Henderson Lee
DILLARD, James Edgar 3
DILLARD, James Hardy 1
DILLARD, Paul 1
DILLAYE, Blanche 1
DILLE, John Flint 3
DILLEHUNT, Richard 3
Benjamin
DILLER, George E. 5
DILLER, Joseph Silas 1
DILLER, Neal V. 3
DILLER, Theodore 2
DILLEY, Arthur Urbane 5
DILLINGHAM, Albert 1
Caldwell
DILLINGHAM, Charles 1
Bancroft
DILLINGHAM, Frances 5
Bent
DILLINGHAM, Frank 4
DILLINGHAM, Frank 1
Ayer
DILLINGHAM, James 4
Darius
DILLINGHAM, John Hoag 1
DILLINGHAM, Paul Jr. H
DILLINGHAM, W. O. 6
DILLINGHAM, Walter 4
Francis
DILLINGHAM, William 1
Paul
DILLON, Charles 2
DILLON, Charles Hall 1
DILLON, Edmond Bothwell 1
DILLON, Edmond Bothwell 2
DILLON, Fannie Charles
DILLON, George 5
DILLON, J. Clifford 3
DILLON, James 1
DILLON, Jesse William 5
DILLON, John Forest 1
DILLON, John Irving 1
DILLON, John J. 2
DILLON, John Jordan 2
DILLON, John Richard 2
DILLON, John Thomas 3
DILLON, Mary 1
DILLON, Philip Robert 1
DILLON, Richard Charles 4
DILLON, Robert E. 5
DILLON, Sidney H
DILLON, Thomas J. 2
DILLON, Thomas Joseph 4
DILLON, William Thomas 4
DILNOT, Frank 5
DILWORTH, Richardson 6
DIMAN, Jeremiah Lewis 1
DIMAN, John Hugh 2
DIMITROFF, George 4
Zakharieff
DIMITROV, Georgi 3
DIMITRY, Alexander 1
DIMITRY, Charles Patton 1
DIMITRY, John Bull Smith 1
DIMMICK, Eugene Dumont 1

DIMMICK, Milo H
Melankthon
DIMMICK, William H
Harrison
DIMMITT, Lillian English 4
DIMMOCK, George 1
DIMNENT, Edward D. 5
DIMOCK, Anthony Weston 1
DIMOCK, Davis Jr. H
DIMOCK, Hedley S. 4
DIMOCK, William Wallace 3
DIMON, Raymond Clark 4
DIMOND, Anthony Joseph 3
DINAND, Joseph Nicholas 2
DINEHART, Alan 2
DINERMAN, Helen 6
Schneider
DINES, Homer Duncan 3
DINES, Thomas A. 6
DINES, Tyson S. 1
DINGELL, John David 3
DINGER, Harold Eugene 6
DINGLE, John Holmes 6
DINGLEY, Edward Nelson 1
DINGLEY, Frank Lambert 1
DINGLEY, Nelson H
DINGS, Peter Conrad 1
DINKELSPIEL, Lloyd W. 3
DINKEY, Alva Clymer 1
DINKINS, James 1
DINKINS, Philip M. 5
DINKLER, Carling 4
DINKMEYER, Henry 3
William
DINNEEN, Fitz-George 1
DINSMOOR, Robert H
DINSMORE, Samuel H
DINSMORE, Carlos 2
Millson
DINSMORE, Charles Allen 1
DINSMORE, Frank F. 6
DINSMORE, Hugh 1
Anderson
DINSMORE, John Walker 1
DINSMORE, John Wirt 4
DINSMORE, Joseph 5
Campbell
DINSMORE, Robert Scott 3
D'INVILLIERS, Edward 1
Vincent
D'INVILLIERS, Edward 4
Vincent
DINWIDDIE, Albert 1
Bledsoe
DINWIDDIE, Courtenay 2
DINWIDDIE, Edwin 1
Courtland
DINWIDDIE, George 5
Summey
DINWIDDIE, John Ekin 4
DINWIDDIE, Robert H
DINWIDDIE, William 1
DIOR, Christian 3
DIPALMA, Joseph Alfred 6
DIPPEL, Andreas 1
DIRKS, Louis Herman 4
DIRKSEN, Everett 5
McKinley
DIRR, Peter George 4
DISERENS, Paul 3
DISHMAN, John Wesley Jr. 4
DISKIN, Carlton Fine 1
DISMUKES, Douglas 2
Eugene
DISNEY, David Tiernan H
DISNEY, Roy O. 5
DISNEY, Walter E. 4
DISNEY, Wesley Ernest 4
DISQUE, Brice P. 3
DISQUE, Robert Conrad 5
DISSTON, Henry H
DISTLER, Carl Martin 2
DISTURNELL, John H
DITCHY, Clair William 4
DITHMAR, Edward 1
Augustus
DITISHEIM, Hanns 4
DITMARS, Raymond Lee 2
DITMARS, Walter Earl 4
DITRICHSTEIN, Leo 1
DITSON, Charles Healy 1
DITSON, George Leighton H
DITSON, Oliver H
DITTEMORE, John 1
Valentine
DITTENHAVER, Sarah 6
Louise
DITTENHOEFER, Abram 1
Jesse
DITTER, J. William 2
DITTMAR, George Walter 2
DITTO, Rollo C. 2
DITTRICK, Howard 3
DITZLER, Charlotte Weber 5
DIVEN, Alexander Samuel H
DIVEN, George Miles 1

DIVEN, Robert Joseph 5
DIVINE, Frank Henry 1
DIX, Dorothea Lynde H
DIX, Edwin Asa H
DIX, John Adams H
DIX, John Alden 1
DIX, John Homer H
DIX, Morgan 1
DIX, Otto 5
DIX, William Frederick 2
DIXEY, Henry E. 2
DIXEY, John H
DIXON, Amzi Clarence 1
DIXON, Archibald H
DIXON, Arminius Gray 5
DIXON, Brandt Van Blarcom
DIXON, Edgar H. 4
DIXON, Frank 1
DIXON, Frank Haigh 2
DIXON, Frank Joseph 4
DIXON, Frank Murray 4
DIXON, Frederick 1
DIXON, George Dallas 1
DIXON, George Hall 4
DIXON, George Peleg 3
DIXON, George W. Jr. 1
DIXON, George William H
DIXON, Henry Aldous 4
DIXON, James H
DIXON, James M. 1
DIXON, James Main 1
DIXON, John 4
DIXON, John Edward 4
DIXON, Joseph * H
DIXON, Joseph Andrew 6
DIXON, Joseph Moore 1
DIXON, L. A. Sr. 5
DIXON, Lincoln 1
DIXON, Luther Swift H
DIXON, Mary Quincy Allen 4
DIXON, Maynard 2
DIXON, Nathan Fellows * H
DIXON, Pierson 4
DIXON, Robert M. 1
DIXON, Rolland Burrage 1
DIXON, Royal 5
DIXON, Russell Alexander 6
DIXON, Sam Houston 4
DIXON, Samuel Gibson 1
DIXON, Sherwood 6
DIXON, Susan Bullitt 1
DIXON, Thomas 1
DIXON, Wesley Moon 5
DIXON, William H
DIXON, William 4
DIXON, William Palmer 1
DIXON, William Palmer 5
DIXON, William Wirt H
DIXON, Zella Allen 1
DIXWELL, John H
DJUANDA 4
KARTAWIDJAJA, Raden Hadji
DOAK, Samuel H
DOAK, William Nuckles 1
DOAN, Fletcher Morris 1
DOAN, Frank Carleton 1
DOAN, Gilbert Everett 5
DOAN, James Burton 5
DOAN, Leland Ira 6
DOAN, William H
DOANE, George Hobart 1
DOANE, George Washington H
DOANE, Ralph Harrington 2
DOANE, Richard Congdon 5
DOANE, Samuel Everett 1
DOANE, Thomas H
DOANE, William Croswell 1
DOANE, William Howard 1
DOBBIE, Elliott Van Kirk 5
DOBBIE, George Alexander 3
DOBBIN, Carroll Edward 5
DOBBIN, George W. 1
DOBBIN, James 1
DOBBIN, James Cochran H
DOBBINS, Donald Claude 2
DOBBINS, Harry Thompson 5
DOBBINS, James T(almage) 5
DOBBINS, Samuel Atkinson H
DOBBS, Arthur H
DOBBS, Hoyt McWhorter 5
DOBBS, John Francis 2
DOBBS, Samuel Candler 5
DOBBS, Stuart Piper 4
DOBERSTEIN, John Walter 4
DOBI, Istvan 5
DOBIE, Armistead Mason 4
DOBIE, Charles Caldwell 1
DOBIE, James Frank 4
DOBIE, Kendall Dyer 4
DOBLE, Budd *
DOBRINER, Konrad 3
DOBSON, George Frederick 1
DOBSON, Mason Henry 3

DOBSON, Sir Roy Hardy 5
DOBYNS, Ashbel Webster 2
DOBYNS, Fletcher 2
DOBYNS, John Robert 1
DOBYNS, William Ray 1
DOBZHANSKY, Theodosius 6
DOCHEZ, Alphonse Raymond 4
DOCK, Christopher H
DOCK, George 3
DOCK, Lavinia L. H
DOCKERAY, Floyd Carlton 6
DOCKERY, Alexander Monroe 1
DOCKERY, Alfred H
DOCKING, George 4
DOCKING, James Tippet 4
DOCKWEILER, Isidore Bernard 2
DOCKWEILER, John Francis 2
DOCKWEILER, Thomas A. J. 4
DOCTOROFF, John 5
DOD, Albert Baldwin H
DOD, Daniel H
DOD, Thaddeus H
DODD, Alvin Earl 3
DODD, Amzi 1
DODD, Anna Bowman 2
DODD, Charles Harold 6
DODD, Charles Hastings 1
DODD, Edward 1
DODD, Edward Howard 4
DODD, Edwin Merrick 3
DODD, Francis Joseph 4
DODD, Frank Courtenay 4
DODD, Frank Howard 1
DODD, George Allan 1
DODD, Henry Martyn 1
DODD, Ira Seymour 4
DODD, John Morris 1
DODD, Lee Wilson 1
DODD, Monroe Elmon 3
DODD, Norris E. 5
DODD, Samuel C. T. 1
DODD, Thomas Joseph 5
DODD, Verne Adams 6
DODD, Walter Fairleigh 4
DODD, William Clifton 1
DODD, William Edward 1
DODD, William George 4
DODDRIDGE, Joseph H
DODDRIDGE, Philip H
DODDRIDGE, William Brown 4
DODDS, Alexander 1
DODDS, B. L. 3
DODDS, Chauncey Y. 3
DODDS, Eugene Maxwell 4
DODDS, Francis Henry 4
DODDS, George William 2
DODDS, Ozro John 2
DODDS, Robert J. 5
DODDS, Samuel 2
DODDS, Warren 4
DODGE, Augustus Ceasar H
DODGE, Barnett Fred 5
DODGE, Bayard 5
DODGE, Bernard Ogilvie 4
DODGE, Charles Richards 1
DODGE, Charles Wright 1
DODGE, Clarence Phelps 1
DODGE, Cleveland Hoadley 1
DODGE, D. Stuart 1
DODGE, Daniel Kilham 1
DODGE, David Child 1
DODGE, David Low H
DODGE, Ebenezer H
DODGE, Francis Safford 1
DODGE, Frederic 1
DODGE, Grace Hoadley 1
DODGE, Grenville Mellen 1
DODGE, H. Percival 1
DODGE, Harris T. 4
DODGE, Henry 1
DODGE, Henry Irving 1
DODGE, Henry Nehemiah 1
DODGE, Jacob Richards 1
DODGE, James Mapes 1
DODGE, Jeremiah H
DODGE, John Wood 1
DODGE, Joseph Morrell 4
DODGE, Josephine Marshall Jewell 1
DODGE, Joshua Eric 1
DODGE, Kern 6
DODGE, Louis 5
DODGE, M. Hartley 4
DODGE, Martin * 3
DODGE, Mary Abigail H
DODGE, Mary Mapes 1
DODGE, Melvin Gilbert 3
DODGE, Murray Witherbee 1

DODGE, Nathan Phillips 3
DODGE, Omenzo George 4
DODGE, Philip Tell 1
DODGE, R. E. Neil 1
DODGE, Raymond 2
DODGE, Raynal 4
DODGE, Richard Elwood 3
DODGE, Robert Gray 5
DODGE, Sherwood 5
DODGE, Theodore Ayrault 1
DODGE, Walter Phelps 5
DODGE, William De Leftwich 1
DODGE, William Earl H
DODGE, William Earl 1
DODGE, Willis Edward 4
DODS, John Bovee H
DODSHON, Joseph Henry 2
DODSON, George Rowland 1
DODSON, Harry Lea 3
DODSON, John E. 1
DODSON, John Milton 1
DODSON, Loren Ralph 5
DODSON, Martha Ethel 5
DOE, Charles 1
DOE, Edward M. 1
DOE, Joseph Bodwell 1
DOE, Nicholas Bartlett H
DOE, Thomas Bartwell H
DOERFLER, Christian 1
DOERFLINGER, Charles Hermann 1
DOERFLINGER, Jon Arno 6
DOERING, Edmund Janes 4
DOERMANN, Henry John 1
DOERR, John Edward 4
DOERSCHUK, Anna Beatrice 6
DOESCHER, Waldemar Oswald 4
DOETSCH, James F. 4
DOGAN, Matthew Winfred 2
DOGGETT, John L. 1
DOGGETT, Laurence Locke 3
DOGLIOTTI, Achille Mario 4
DOHAN, Edward G. 5
DOHENY, Edward Laurence 1
DOHERTY, Edward J. 6
DOHERTY, Henry Latham 1
DOHERTY, Philip Joseph 1
DOHERTY, Robert Ernest 3
DOHERTY, Robert Remington 4
DOHME, Alfred Robert Louis 5
DOHNANYI, Erno (Ernest von Dohnanyi) 5
DOIDGE, Frederick Widdowson 3
DOIG, Andrew Wheeler H
DOIG, James Rufus 5
DOIG, Thomas W. 3
DOING, Mahlon B. 4
DOLAK, Michael Charles 3
DOLAN, Arthur W. 2
DOLAN, Daniel Leo 4
DOLAN, Elizabeth Honor 1
DOLAN, Francis James 1
DOLAN, George W. 2
DOLAN, James Edward 4
DOLAN, Margaret Baggett (Mrs. Charles E. Dolan) 6
DOLAN, Robert Emmett 5
DOLAN, Thomas 1
DOLAN, Tom 5
DOLAND, James Joseph 4
DOLBEAR, Amos Emerson 1
DOLCHO, Frederick H
DOLD, Jacob C. 1
DOLE, Arthur Jr. 5
DOLE, Charles Fletcher 1
DOLE, Edmund Pearson 1
DOLE, Helen James Bennett 2
DOLE, James Drummond 3
DOLE, Margaret Femald (Mrs. John S. Dole) 4
DOLE, Nathan Haskell 1
DOLE, Sanford Ballard 1
DOLGE, Alfred 1
D'OLIER, Franklin 3
DOLKART, Leo 4
DOLL, Alfred W. 3
DOLL, William DeBerge 2
DOLLAR, R. Stanley 3
DOLLAR, Robert 1
DOLLAR, Paul M. 4
DOLLARD, Stewart Edward 6
DOLLARD, William H
DOLLENS, Burl Austin 3
DOLLEY, Charles Sumner 4
DOLLEY, David Hough 1
DOLLIVER, George Benton 6

DOLLIVER, Jonathan Prentiss 1
DOLLIVER, Margaret Gay 4
DOLMAN, John Jr. 3
DOLOWITZ, Francis Marie Fleisher (Mrs. David A. Dolowitz) 5
DOLPH, John H. 1
DOLPH, Joseph Norton H
DOLPHY, Eric Allan 4
DOMAGK, Gerhard 4
DOMENEC, Michael H
DOMERATZKY, Louis 6
DOMERS, Henry Russell 5
DOMINIAN, Leon 1
DOMINICI, Santos Anibal 5
DOMINICK, Frank 1
DOMINICK, Fred H. 5
DOMINICK, Gayer Gardner 4
DOMINICK, James Robert 5
DOMONOSKE, Arthur B(oquer) 6
DONAGHEY, Frederick 1
DONAGHEY, George W. 1
DONAGHY, William Andrew 6
DONAHEY, James Harrison 2
DONAHEY, John William 4
DONAHEY, Mary Dickerson 4
DONAHEY, Vic 2
DONAHOE, Daniel Joseph 1
DONAHOE, Patrick H
DONAHUE, Charles 5
DONAHUE, Charles Henry 5
DONAHUE, John Bartholomew 5
DONAHUE, Joseph Michael 4
DONAHUE, Joseph P. 3
DONAHUE, Maurice H. 1
DONAHUE, Patrick James 1
DONAHUE, Peter H
DONALD, George H. 5
DONALD, Joseph Marion 5
DONALD, Norman Henderson 5
DONALD, William Goodricke 3
DONALD, William John Alexander 5
DONALDSON, Albert Eeley 6
DONALDSON, Allyn Capron 6
DONALDSON, Charles M. 6
DONALDSON, Fred Kermit 4
DONALDSON, Henry Herbert 1
DONALDSON, J. A. 5
DONALDSON, James Rider 6
DONALDSON, Jesse Monroe 5
DONALDSON, John 3
DONALDSON, John M. 1
DONALDSON, Kenneth Hume 5
DONALDSON, Norman Vaux 4
DONALDSON, Robert Golden 5
DONALDSON, Thomas Quint 1
DONALDSON, Walter Foster 6
DONALDSON, William Raymond 4
DONALSON, Erle Meldrim 6
DONALSON, John Ernest 4
DONAT, Robert 3
DONATI, Pine 6
DONATO, Giuseppe 4
DONDERO, George Anthony 5
DONDLINGER, Peter Tracy 3
DONDO, Mathurin 5
DONDORE, Dorothy Anne 2
DONEGAN, Edmund Joseph 3
DONEGAN, Harold Hand 4
DONEGAN, Maurice Francis 3
DO-NE-HO-GA-WA H
DONEHOO, George Patterson 1
DONEHUE, Vincent Julian 4
DONELSON, Andrew Jackson H
DONEY, Carl Gregg 3
DONGAN, Thomas H

DONGES, Ralph Waldo Emerson 5
DONGES, Theophilus Ebenaezer 4
DONHAM, C. R. 3
DONHAM, Harold Gregory 2
DONHAM, Wallace Brett 3
DONHAUSER, J. Lewi 4
DONIGER, William 5
DONIPHAN, Alexander William H
DONKIN, McKay 5
DONLEVY, Alice Heighes 1
DONLEVY, Harriet Farley 1
DONLEY, Charles Sherman 4
DONLEY, William Henry 1
DONLON, Alphonsus John 1
DONN, Edward Wilton Jr. 3
DONNAN, Elizabeth 3
DONNELL, Annie Hamilton 3
DONNELL, Ben Dobyns 3
DONNELL, Harold Eugene 4
DONNELL, James J. 1
DONNELL, Otto Dewey 4
DONNELL, Philip Stone 4
DONNELL, Richard H
DONNELL, Robert H
DONNELLEY, Elliott 6
DONNELLEY, Thomas Elliott 3
DONNELLON, James Augustine 5
DONNELLY, Arthur Barrett 1
DONNELLY, Charles Agnes
DONNELLY, Dorothy 1
DONNELLY, Edward Terence 1
DONNELLY, Eleanor Cecilia 1
DONNELLY, Frederick William 1
DONNELLY, George J. 3
DONNELLY, Harold Irvin 1
DONNELLY, Henry Edmund 5
DONNELLY, Horace James 6
DONNELLY, Ignatius 1
DONNELLY, James L(eonard) 5
DONNELLY, John C. 1
DONNELLY, Joseph Gordon 1
DONNELLY, June Richardson 5
DONNELLY, Lucy Martin 2
DONNELLY, Phil M. 4
DONNELLY, Richard Carter 5
DONNELLY, Samuel Bratton 2
DONNELLY, Simon Peter 1
DONNELLY, Thomas Frederick 1
DONNELLY, Thomas James 4
DONNELLY, Walter Joseph 5
DONNER, George 1
DONNER, Tamsen H
DONNER, William Henry 3
DONOGHUE, Thomas J. 5
DONOHO, Ruger 1
DONOHOE, Denis 1
DONOHOE, James A. 1
DONOHOE, Michael 4
DONOHOE, Thomas Joseph 1
DONOHOE, William A. 4
DONOHUE, Charles 1
DONOHUE, Francis Michael 1
DONOHUGH, Thomas Smith 4
DONOVAN, Edward Francis 2
DONOVAN, George Francis 5
DONOVAN, Herman Lee 4
DONOVAN, James Britt 5
DONOVAN, James J. 5
DONOVAN, Jeremiah 1
DONOVAN, Jerome Francis 2
DONOVAN, John Joseph 1
DONOVAN, Richard 2
DONOVAN, Richard Joseph 1
DONOVAN, Thomas Leroy 6
DONOVAN, William Joseph 3
DONOVAN, Winfred Nichols 4

508

DONWORTH, George 2
DONWORTH, Grace 2
D'OOGE, Benjamin 3 Leonard
D'OOGE, Martin Luther 1
DOOLAN, John Calvin 2
DOOLAN, Leonard 2 Weakley
DOOLEY, Channing Rice 3
DOOLEY, Henry 1 Williamson
DOOLEY, Joseph Brannon 4
DOOLEY, Lucy 3
DOOLEY, M. S. 3
DOOLEY, Michael F. 1
DOOLEY, Thomas Anthony 4 III
DOOLEY, Virginia Perrin 6 Corttis
DOOLEY, William Francis 1
DOOLEY, William Henry 2
DOOLIN, John B. 1
DOOLING, Maurice T. 1
DOOLING, Peter J. 1
DOOLITTLE, Amos H
DOOLITTLE, Charles H Camp
DOOLITTLE, Charles 1 Leander
DOOLITTLE, Dudley 3
DOOLITTLE, Eric 1
DOOLITTLE, Frederick 3 William
DOOLITTLE, Hilda 4
DOOLITTLE, Hooker 4 Austin
DOOLITTLE, James Rood H
DOOLITTLE, Roscoe 1 Edward
DOOLITTLE, Thomas 1 Benjamin
DOOLY, Oscar Earle 5
DOORLY, Henry 4
DOPP, Katherine Elizabeth 5
DORAN, James M. 2
DORAN, Joseph Ingersoll 1
DORAN, Thomas Francis 1
DORAN, William Thomas 1
DORCHESTER, Daniel 1
DORCHESTER, Daniel 2
DORCHESTER, Liverus 3 Hull
DORE, John F. 1
DOREMUS, Charles Avery 1
DOREMUS, Frank 2 Ellsworth
DOREMUS, Henry M. 4
DOREMUS, Robert Ogden 1
DOREMUS, Sarah Platt H Haines
DOREN, Electra Collins 1
DORESAM, Charles Henry 2
DORETY, Frederic Gerber 4
DORGAN, Thomas H Aloysius
DORGAN, Thomas 4 Aloysius
DORIA, Clara 1
DORIAN, Harry William 1
DORIGAN, Harry William 5
DORION, Eustache Charles 1 Edouard
DORION, Marie H
DORLAND, Ralph E. Sr. 1
DORLAND, William 4 Alexander Newman
DORMAN, Edmund 4 Lawrence
DORMAN, William Edwin 1
DORMER, Charles Joseph 6
DORN, Harold F. 1
DORN, John Emil 6
DORNE, Albert 4
DORNIN, Bernard 1
DORNIN, Thomas Aloysius H
DOROSHAW, Jennis 4 Milford
DORR, Carl E. 6
DORR, Dudley Huntington 4
DORR, Edward Monroe 4
DORR, George Bucknam 2
DORR, Harold M. 5
DORR, John Van Nostrand 4
DORR, Julia Caroline 1 Ripley
DORR, Rheta Childe 2
DORR, Robert East 1 Apthoep
DORR, Robert John 4
DORR, Thomas Wilson H
DORRANCE, Arthur 2 Calbraith
DORRANCE, George 2 Morris
DORRANCE, Gordon 3

DORRANCE, John 1 Thompson
DORRANCE, Sturges Dick 5
DORRELL, William H
DORROH, John Hazard 6
D'ORSAY, Lawrance 1
DORSCH, Eduard H
DORSET, Marion 2
DORSETT, P. H. 4
DORSETT, Walter 1 Balckburn
DORSEY, Charles Howard 6 Jr.
DORSEY, Clarence Wilbur 5
DORSEY, Clayton 2 Chauncey
DORSEY, Clement 1
DORSEY, Ella Loraine 4
DORSEY, Francis Oswald 1
DORSEY, Frank J. G. 2
DORSEY, George Amos 1
DORSEY, Harry Woodward 5
DORSEY, Herbert Grove 4
DORSEY, Hugh Manson 2
DORSEY, Jack Sidney 6
DORSEY, James Emmet 3
DORSEY, James Owen 1
DORSEY, John Syng H
DORSEY, Leo Patrick 6
DORSEY, LeRoy Howard 3
DORSEY, Maxwell J. 4
DORSEY, Sarah Ann Ellis 1
DORSEY, Stephen Palmer 4
DORSEY, Stephen W. 1
DORSEY, Susan M. 4
DORSEY, Thomas Francis 4
DORSEY, W. Roderick 4
DORSHEIMER, William H Edward
DORST, Joseph Haddox 2
DORT, J. Dallas 1
DORWARD, William 4 Thompson
DORWIN, Oscar John 6
DOS PASSOS, John 5 (Roderigo)
DOSDALL, Chester Arthur 3
DOSKER, Henry E. 1
DOS PASSOS, John 1 Randolph
DOSS, Clay 3
DOSS, Roscoe James 2
DOSTER, Frank 1
DOSTER, James Jarvis 2
DOSTERT, Leon Emile 5
DOTEN, Carroll Warren 2
DOTEN, Samuel Bradford 3
DOTSON, Floyd D. 5
DOTSON, George Edgar 6
DOTTERWEICH, June 5 (Mrs. Frank Henry Dotterweich)
DOTY, Alvah Hunt 4
DOTY, Carl Babcock 6
DOTY, Douglas Zabriskie 1
DOTY, Elihu H
DOTY, James Duane 1
DOTY, John Williams 6
DOTY, Madeleine Zabriskie 6 (Mrs. Roger N. Baldwin)
DOTY, Paul 1
DOTY, Robert Clark 6
DOTY, William Furman 5
DOUBLEDAY, Abner H
DOUBLEDAY, Frank 1 Nelson
DOUBLEDAY, George 3
DOUBLEDAY, Nelson 2
DOUBLEDAY, Netje De 1 Graff
DOUBLEDAY, Russell 2
DOUBLEDAY, Ulysses H Freeman
DOUDNA, Edgar George 2
DOUDOROFF, Michael 6
DOUGAL, William H. H
DOUGHERTY, Blanford 3 Barnard
DOUGHERTY, Curtis 1
DOUGHERTY, Denis J. 3
DOUGHERTY, Edward 5 Archer
DOUGHERTY, Edward E. 2
DOUGHERTY, George A. 1
DOUGHERTY, George S. 1
DOUGHERTY, Hugh 1
DOUGHERTY, J. Hampden 1
DOUGHERTY, John 1 P(atrick)
DOUGHERTY, Joseph 5
DOUGHERTY, Lee J. 6
DOUGHERTY, Paul 1
DOUGHERTY, Proctor 5 Lambert
DOUGHERTY, Raymond 1 Philip

DOUGHERTY, Richard 4 Erwin
DOUGHERTY, Thomas 6 Francis
DOUGHERTY, William 1 Edgeworth
DOUGHERTY, William H. 6
DOUGHTON, Robert L. 3
DOUGHTY, Howard 2 Waters
DOUGHTY, Mrs. Alla 1
DOUGHTY, Thomas H
DOUGHTY, Walter Francis 1
DOUGHTY, William Ellison 5
DOUGHTY, William Henry 1
DOUGHTY, William Henry 1 Jr.
DOUGLAS, of Kirtleside 5 Lord (William Sholto Douglas)
DOUGLAS, Albert 4
DOUGLAS, Alexander 4
DOUGLAS, Alice May 2
DOUGLAS, Amanda 1 Minnie
DOUGLAS, Archibald 2
DOUGLAS, Arthur F. 3
DOUGLAS, Benjamin H
DOUGLAS, Beverly Browne H
DOUGLAS, Bruce 2 Hutchinson
DOUGLAS, Charles A. 1
DOUGLAS, Charles Henry 3
DOUGLAS, Charles 2 Winfred
DOUGLAS, Clarence 5 Brown
DOUGLAS, David Dwight 3
DOUGLAS, Davison 1 McDowell
DOUGLAS, Donald B. 6
DOUGLAS, Ernest 4
DOUGLAS, Fred James 2
DOUGLAS, Frederic 3 Huntington
DOUGLAS, Frederick A. 4
DOUGLAS, George Bruce 1
DOUGLAS, George William 1
DOUGLAS, George William 1
DOUGLAS, Grace Parsons 6
DOUGLAS, Hamilton 1
DOUGLAS, Henry Kyd 1
DOUGLAS, Henry Trovert 4 Jr.
DOUGLAS, James 1
DOUGLAS, James H. 1
DOUGLAS, James Stuart 2
DOUGLAS, John 1
DOUGLAS, John Francis 3
DOUGLAS, John Frederick 4 Howard
DOUGLAS, John Gray 6
DOUGLAS, Julia S. 1
DOUGLAS, Kenneth 6 Wallace
DOUGLAS, Lee 3
DOUGLAS, Lewis Williams 6
DOUGLAS, Lloyd C. 3
DOUGLAS, Orlando 1 Benajah
DOUGLAS, Oscar Berry 4
DOUGLAS, Percy 4 Liningston
DOUGLAS, Richard 4
DOUGLAS, Robert Martin 1
DOUGLAS, Silas Hamilton H
DOUGLAS, Stephen Arnold H
DOUGLAS, Stephen Arnold 1
DOUGLAS, Thaddeus 2
DOUGLAS, Theodore 4 Wayland
DOUGLAS, Wallace Barton 4
DOUGLAS, Walter 2
DOUGLAS, Walter G. 5
DOUGLAS, Walter John 6
DOUGLAS, William H
DOUGLAS, William Archer 3 Sholte
DOUGLAS, William Harris 2
DOUGLAS, William Lewis 1
DOUGLAS, William 1 Wilberforce
DOUGLASS, Andrew 1 Ellicott
DOUGLASS, Andrew 4 Ellicott
DOUGLASS, Aubrey 3 Augustus
DOUGLASS, Benjamin 1 Wallace
DOUGLASS, Dana Carroll 3
DOUGLASS, David Bates H
DOUGLASS, Earl 1
DOUGLASS, Earl Leroy 6
DOUGLASS, Edwin 4 Herbert

DOUGLASS, Frank Harvey 4
DOUGLASS, Frederick H
DOUGLASS, Frederick 3 Melvin
DOUGLASS, Gaylord 5 William
DOUGLASS, George C. 1
DOUGLASS, George 3 Shearer
DOUGLASS, H. Paul 3
DOUGLASS, H(erbert) 5 Ellwood
DOUGLASS, John Joseph 3
DOUGLASS, John 1 Watkinson
DOUGLASS, Joseph Henry 6
DOUGLASS, Lucille 1 Sinclair
DOUGLASS, Mabel Smith 5
DOUGLASS, Matthew Hale 2
DOUGLASS, Robert M. J. H
DOUGLASS, Rufus Collins 4
DOUGLASS, Thomas 4 VanKirk
DOUGLASS, Truman 5 Bartlett
DOUGLASS, Truman 1 Orville
DOUGLASS, William H
DOULL, James Angus 4
DOUNCE, Harry Esty 3
DOUTHIRT, Walstein F. 3
DOUTHIT, Claude 3
DOUTHIT, Harold 4
DOUTHIT, Jasper L. 4
DOUTRICH, Isaac H. 1
DOUTY, Nicholas 5
DOVE, David James H
DOVE, W(illiam) Franklin 5
DOVELL, Ray C. 5
DOVENER, Blackburn 4 Barrett
DOVER, Elmer 1
DOW, Alex 2
DOW, Allan Wade 3
DOW, Arthur Wesley 1
DOW, Blanche Hinman 6
DOW, Caroline Bell 1
DOW, Charles Mason 1
DOW, Earle Wilbur 4
DOW, Edward Albert 2
DOW, Fayette Brown 4
DOW, Frederick Neal 1
DOW, George Francis 1
DOW, Henry H
DOW, Herbert Henry 1
DOW, Howard Malcolm 1
DOW, John Reneau 6
DOW, Lorenzo H
DOW, Neal H
DOW, Roger 4
DOW, Willard Henry 1
DOWD, Charles Ferdinand 1
DOWD, Charles North 1
DOWD, David L(loyd) 5
DOWD, Fred A. 6
DOWD, James Edward 4
DOWD, Jerome 4
DOWD, John Worthington 1
DOWD, W. Carey Jr. 3
DOWD, Wallace Rutherford 4
DOWD, William 1
DOWDALL, Edward 4
DOWDALL, Guy Grigsby 1
DOWDELL, James 1 Ferguson
DOWDELL, James Render 1
DOWDNEY, Abraham 1
DOWE, Jennie Elizabeth 1 Tupper
DOWELL, Alvis Yates 5
DOWELL, Benjamin B. 3
DOWELL, Carr Thomas 6
DOWELL, Cassius C. 1
DOWELL, Floyd Dee 4
DOWELL, Greensville H
DOWELL, Spright 4
DOWER, Walter H. 4
DOWLING, Alexander 1
DOWLING, Austin 1
DOWLING, Eddie 6
DOWLING, Edward C. 6
DOWLING, Emmett 1 Patrick
DOWLING, George 4 Thomas
DOWLING, John Joseph 2
DOWLING, John William 1
DOWLING, Judson Davie 6
DOWLING, Michael John 1
DOWLING, Noel Thomas 5
DOWLING, Oscar 1
DOWLING, Robert Whittle 6
DOWLING, Victor James 1
DOWLING, William E. 4

DOWMAN, Charles 1 Edward
DOWNER, Alan Seymour 5
DOWNER, Charles Alfred 1
DOWNER, Eliphalet H
DOWNER, James Walker 1
DOWNER, Samuel H
DOWNES, Anne Miller 4
DOWNES, Bruce 4
DOWNES, Dennis Sawyer 6
DOWNES, James R. 3
DOWNES, John H
DOWNES, John 3
DOWNES, Olin 3
DOWNES, William 2 Augustus
DOWNES, William Howe 1
DOWNEY, David George 1
DOWNEY, Francis X. 4
DOWNEY, Francis Xavier 2
DOWNEY, George Eddy 1
DOWNEY, George Faber 1
DOWNEY, Hal 3
DOWNEY, Hermon Horatio 5
DOWNEY, John H
DOWNEY, John Florin 1
DOWNEY, June E. 1
DOWNEY, Mary Elizabeth 3
DOWNEY, Sheridan 4
DOWNEY, Stanley Wilson 1 Crowell
DOWNEY, Walter Francis 4
DOWNEY, William H. 3
DOWNIE, Robert C. 4
DOWNING, Andrew H Jackson
DOWNING, Augustus 1
DOWNING, Charles * 1
DOWNING, Elliot Rowland 2
DOWNING, Frances H Murdaugh
DOWNING, George H
DOWNING, Harold Kemp 2
DOWNING, John Franklin 1
DOWNING, John Robert 1
DOWNING, Lewis King 5
DOWNING, Maj Jack H
DOWNING, Paul M. 2
DOWNING, Robert 3 Everard
DOWNING, Robert L. 2
DOWNING, Russell 5 Vincent
DOWNING, Warwick 4 Miller
DOWNS, Francis Shunk 1
DOWNS, George Sheldon H Mrs.
DOWNS, John Ayman 4
DOWNS, John William Sr. 4
DOWNS, Joseph 1
DOWNS, Lawrence 1 Aloysius
DOWNS, Le Roy Donnelly 5
DOWNS, Solomon H Weathersbee
DOWNS, William Findlay 4
DOWNS, William Smith 1
DOWRIE, George William 2
DOWS, Sutherland 5
DOWSE, Edward 1
DOWSE, Thomas 1
DOWSE, William Bradford 1 Homer
DOX, Charles E. 5
DOX, Peter Myndert H
DOXIADIS, Constantinos 6 Apostolos
DOXTATER, Lee Walter 1 Edward
DOYLE, Albert Pryor 5
DOYLE, Alexander 1
DOYLE, Alexander P. 1
DOYLE, Bernard Wendell 1
DOYLE, C. W. 1
DOYLE, Clyde Gilman 4
DOYLE, Cornelius James 1
DOYLE, Edward H. 1
DOYLE, Edward John 1
DOYLE, Gregory 1
DOYLE, Henry Grattan 4
DOYLE, Howard L. 3
DOYLE, James Harold 1
DOYLE, John Hardy 1
DOYLE, John T. 1
DOYLE, Martha Claire 5 MacGowan ("Martha James")
DOYLE, Michael Francis 3
DOYLE, Price 5
DOYLE, Rhederick Elwood 5 Jr.
DOYLE, Richard Smith 5
DOYLE, Robert Morris 1
DOYLE, Sarah Elizabeth 1
DOYLE, Sherman Hoadley 5

* Indicates More Than One Such Name Listed

DOYLE, Sister Mary Peter 5
DOYLE, Thomas Aloysius 1
DOYLE, Thomas Henchion 5
DOYNE, John James 3
DOZER, Russell Shinnick 4
DOZIER, Curtis Merry 4
DOZIER, Elizabeth Gist 4
DOZIER, James Corde 6
DOZIER, Melville 4
DOZIER, Orion T. 4
DRAA, Charles Clifton
DRABKIN, Israel Edward 4
DRABKIN, Stella Molly 6
  Friedman (Mrs. David L. Drabkin)
DRACH, Edmund L. 5
DRACHMAN, Bernard 2
DRACHSLER, Julius 4
DRAEMEL, Milo Frederick 5
DRAFFAN, George 4
  Livingston
DRAGER, Walter Louis 5
DRAGSTEDT, Lester 6
  Reynold
DRAHMS, August 4
DRAIN, James Andrew 2
DRAIN, Jesse Cyrus 6
DRAKE, Alexander Wilson 4
DRAKE, Archie Augustus 4
  Jr.
DRAKE, Benjamin H
DRAKE, C. St Clair
DRAKE, Charles Daniel H
DRAKE, Daniel H
DRAKE, Durant 1
DRAKE, Edwin Laurentine H
DRAKE, Emma Frances 4
  Angell
DRAKE, Emmet Addis 4
DRAKE, Frances Ann H
  Denny
DRAKE, Francis Marion 1
DRAKE, Francis Samuel 1
DRAKE, Franklin Jeremiah 1
DRAKE, Fred Raymond 1
DRAKE, Frederic Nelson 4
DRAKE, Harry Trevor 4
DRAKE, Helen Virginia 6
  Frederick
DRAKE, James Calhoun 1
DRAKE, J(ames) Frank 6
DRAKE, James Madison 1
DRAKE, Jeannette May 3
DRAKE, John Burroughs H
DRAKE, John Poad H
DRAKE, John Reuben H
DRAKE, John Walter 2
DRAKE, Joseph Horace Sr. 1
DRAKE, Joseph Rodman 1
DRAKE, Lauren J. 3
DRAKE, Milton Jay 6
DRAKE, Nathan Lincoln 4
DRAKE, Noah Fields 1
DRAKE, Russell Payson 5
DRAKE, Samuel 1
DRAKE, Samuel Adams 1
DRAKE, Samuel Gardner 1
DRAKE, Sir Francis H
DRAKE, Tracy Corey 1
DRAKE, William A. 4
DRAKE, William Henry 1
DRANE, Herbert Jackson 1
DRANSFIELD, Jane 5
DRANT, Patricia 6
DRAPANAS, Theodore 6
DRAPER, Alfred Pearman 3
DRAPER, Andrew Sloan 1
DRAPER, Benjamin Helm 2
  Bristow
DRAPER, Daniel 1
DRAPER, Dorothy 5
  (Tuckerman)
DRAPER, Eben Sumner 1
DRAPER, Edward Bailey 2
DRAPER, Ernest Gallaudet 3
DRAPER, Frank Winthrop 1
DRAPER, George Otis 1
DRAPER, Henry H
DRAPER, Ira H
DRAPER, John H
DRAPER, John William H
DRAPER, Joseph H
DRAPER, Lyman Copeland H
DRAPER, Margaret Green H
DRAPER, Norman 4
DRAPER, Richard H
DRAPER, Ruth H
DRAPER, Warren Fales 5
DRAPER, William Franklin 1
DRAPER, William H. 4
DRAPER, William Henry 1
DRAPER, William Henry 6
  Jr.
DRAPER, William Kinnicutt 1
DRAUGHON, Ralph Brown 5
DRAYER, Clarence Earl; 6

DRAYTON, Charles O. 1
DRAYTON, Grace Gebbie 1
DRAYTON, Henry 1
  Shipman
DRAYTON, John H
DRAYTON, Percival H
DRAYTON, Samuel 2
DRAYTON, Thomas H
  Fenwick
DRAYTON, William * H
DRAYTON, William Henry H
DREES, Charles William 1
DREFS, Arthur George 3
DREHER, Julius Daniel 1
DREHER, LeRoy Herbert 4
DREHER, Monroe Franklin 5
DREHER, William Counts 1
DREIER, Mary Elisabeth 4
DREIKURS, Rudolph 5
DREISER, Theodore 2
DRELLER, Louis 3
DRENNAN, Michael C. 1
DRESBACH, Glenn Ward 5
DRESBACH, Melvin 3
DRESCHER, Theodore 3
  Bausch
DRESDEN, Arnold 3
DRESEL, Ellis Loring 1
DRESEL, Otto 1
DRESEN, Oswald Mathew 4
DRESLER, Earl Louis 5
DRESSEL, Edwin Henry 4
DRESSEN, Charles Walter 4
DRESSER, Daniel Le Roy 1
DRESSER, Horatio Willis 3
DRESSER, Louise 2
DRESSER, Paul H
DRESSER, Paul H
DRESSER, Raymond H. 5
DRESSER, Solomon Robert 1
DRESSLAR, Fletcher 1
  Bascom
DRESSLAR, Frank A Sr. 5
DRESSLER, Louis Raphael 1
DRESSLER, Marie 1
DREVER, Thomas 4
DREVES, Walter Julius 4
DREW, Alfred Stanislaus 5
DREW, Charles Richard 3
DREW, Daniel H
DREW, Frank Gifford 1
DREW, Franklin Mellen 1
DREW, George Alexander 5
DREW, Gerald Augustin 5
DREW, Gilman Arthur 1
DREW, Ira Walton 5
DREW, Irving Webster 1
DREW, James Byron 5
DREW, John H
DREW, John H
DREW, John Graham 4
DREW, Louisa Lane 1
DREWES, Alfred H. 4
DREWES, Alfred H(erman) 5
DREWRY, Patrick Henry 2
DREWRY, William Francis 1
DREXEL, Anthony Joseph H
DREXEL, Francis Anthony H
DREXEL, Francis Martin H
DREXEL, George W. 2
  Childs
DREXEL, Joseph William H
DREYER, George Peter 1
DREYER, Jorgan Christian 2
DREYER, Leslie Hayes 4
DREYER, Russell Paul 4
DREYER, Walter 4
DREYFUS, Felix Julius 6
DREYFUS, Camille 3
  Edouard
DREYFUS, Carl 3
DREYFUS, Louis Goethe 6
  Jr.
DREYFUS-BARNEY, 6
  Laura (Mme. L. Dreyfus-Barney)
DREYFUSS, Henry 5
DREYFUSS, Leonard 5
DREYSPRING, Adolphe 1
DREYSTADT, Nicholas 2
DRIEMEYER, Henry 4
DRIGGS, Edmund Hope 2
DRIGGS, Frank Howard 4
DRIGGS, Frank Milton 5
DRIGGS, Howard Roscoe 4
DRIGGS, John Fletcher H
DRIGGS, Laurence La 2
  Tourette
DRILL, Lewis L. 5
DRINKER, Cecil Kent 3
DRINKER, Henry Sandwith 6
DRINKER, Henry Sturgis 1
DRINKER, Philip 5
DRIPPS, Isaac L. H
DRIPPS, Joseph Frederick 4
DRIPPS, Robert Dunning 6

DRISCOLL, Alfred E. 6
DRISCOLL, Arthur Francis 4
DRISCOLL, Charles 3
  Benedict
DRISCOLL, Clara 2
DRISCOLL, Daniel Angelus 5
DRISCOLL, Denis J. 3
DRISCOLL, Donald 6
  Gotzian
DRISCOLL, Frederick 1
DRISCOLL, George Walter 4
DRISCOLL, Joseph 3
DRISCOLL, Louise 3
DRISCOLL, Michael 1
  Edward
DRISCOLL, William H. 3
DRISLER, Henry H
DRIVER, Godfrey Rolles 6
DRIVER, James 1
DRIVER, John Merritte 1
DRIVER, Leeotis Lincoln 4
DRIVER, Samuel Marion 3
DRIVER, William J. 5
DRIVER, William Raymond 4
DROEGE, John Albert 5
DROKE, George Wesley 4
DROKE, Maxwell 4
DROMGOOLE, George H
  Coke
DROMGOOLE, Will Allen 1
DRONE, Eaton Sylvester 1
DROPPERS, Garrett 1
DROSSAERTS, Arthur 1
DROUET, Robert 1
DROUGHT, Arthur Bernard 5
DROUGHT, Henry Patrick 5
DROUIN, Mark Robert 4
DROWN, Edward Staples 1
DROWN, Thomas 1
  Messinger
DROZNIAK, Edward 4
DRUCKENMILLER, 4
  Barton W.
DRUCKER, Arthur Ellert 2
DRUECK, Charles 4
DRUFFEL, John Henry 4
DRUILLETTES, Gabriel H
DRUKKER, Dow Henry 1
DRUKKER, Dow Henry 5
DRUKKER, Richard 5
DRUM, A. L. 1
DRUM, Augustus H
DRUM, Hugh Aloysius 3
DRUM, John Sylvester 1
DRUM, Richard Coulter 1
DRUM, Walter 1
DRUMGOOLE, John H
  Christopher
DRUMHELLER, Joseph 5
DRUMHELLER, Roscoe 2
  Maxson
DRUMM, Thomas W. 1
DRUMMOND, Alexander 3
  M.
DRUMMOND, Harrison 5
  Irwin
DRUMMOND, Huntly 3
  Redpath
DRUMMOND, I. Wyman 1
DRUMMOND, James 1
  Herbert
DRUMMOND, Josiah 1
  Hayden
DRUMMOND, Sara King 1
  Wiley
DRUMMOND, Thomas 5
  Russell
DRUMMOND, Wilbert 1
  Ivanhoe
DRURY, Alexander Greer 1
DRURY, Aubrey 5
DRURY, Augustus Waldo 1
DRURY, Francis Keese 3
  Wynkoop
DRURY, John 5
DRURY, John Benjamin 1
DRURY, Lacy H
DRURY, Marion 1
  Richardson
DRURY, Philo Walker 6
DRURY, Samuel Smith 1
DRURY, Victor Montague 1
DRURY, Walter Maynard 2
DRURY, Wells 1
DRUSHEL, J. Andrew 4
DRYDEN, Forrest Fairchild 1
DRYDEN, George Bascomb 3
DRYDEN, Hugh Latimer 4
DRYDEN, James 1
DRYDEN, John Fairfield 1
DRYDEN, John Lester 3
DRYDEN, John N. 3
DRYER, Charles Redway 1
DRYER, George William 3
DRYER, Joseph Edward 6
DRYFOOS, Orvil Eugene 4

DRYSDALE, Matthew Watt 4
DRYSDALE, Robert A. 4
DRYSDALE, Thomas 1
  Murray
DRYSDALE, William 1
DU HAMEL, William 5
DU MOUCHEL, Leandre 5
  Arthur
DU PONT, Alfred Rhett 5
DUANE, Alexander 1
DUANE, James H
DUANE, James Chatham 1
DUANE, James May 1
DUANE, Russell 1
DUANE, William H
DUANE, William J. 2
DUANE, William John H
DU BARRY, Beekman 1
DUBARRY, William H. 3
DUBBINK, Gerrit Hendrik 1
DUBBS, Henry A. 1
DUBBS, Joseph Henry 1
DUBILIER, William 5
DUBOC, Frank Windsor 5
DU BOIS, Augustus Jay 1
DUBOIS, Charles Gilbert 4
DU BOIS, Coert 3
DUBOIS, Durwood Carl 4
DU BOIS, Edward Church 1
DUBOIS, Eugene Floyd 3
DUBOIS, Fred Thomas 1
DUBOIS, Gaston Frederic 3
DUBOIS, Guy Pene 3
DU BOIS, James T. 1
DUBOIS, Jean Joseph 1
DUBOIS, John H
DU BOIS, John Ezekiel 1
DUBOIS, Jules 4
DU BOIS, Julian Arthur 3
DU BOIS, Mary Constance 4
DU BOIS, Patterson 1
DUBOIS, Samuel F. 1
DU BOIS, William Edward 4
  Burghardt
DU BOIS, William Ewing 1
DUBORD, Richard Joseph 5
DU BOSE, Catherine Anne 4
DU BOSE, Dudley McIver 1
DUBOSE, Francis Goodwin 1
DU BOSE, Henry Wade 3
DU BOSE, Horace Mellard 1
DU BOSE, Joel Campbell 4
DU BOSE, John 1
  Witherspoon
DUBOSE, Marion 6
DU BOSE, William Haskell 1
DU BOSE, William Porcher 1
DU BOSE, William 4
  Richards
DU BOSQUE, Francis 1
  LeBrun
DU BOURG, Louis H
  Guillaume Valentin
DUBOURJAL, Savinien H
  Edme
DUBRAY, Charles Albert 5
DUBUIS, Claude Mary H
DUBUQUE, Julien H
DUCASSE, Curt John 5
DUCE, Hugh Marlo 4
DUCE, James Terry 5
DUCEY, Thomas James 1
DU CHAILLU, Paul Belloni 1
DUCHE, Jacob H
DUCHESNE, Rose H
  Philippine
DUCKER, Edward Augustus 2
DUCKWORTH, George 5
  Eckel
DUCKWORTH, Roy 6
  Demarest
DUCKWORTH, William 1
  Henry
DUCOMMUN, Edmond 1
  Frederick
DUCOMMUN, Jesse 1
  Clarence
DU COUDRAY, Philippe 1
  Charles Jean Tronson
DUCRUE, Francis Bennon H
DUDA, Herbert Wilhelm 6
DUDDY, Edward Augustin 4
DUDGEON, Matthew S. 3
DUDLEY, A. Dean 4
DUDLEY, Albert Henry 3
DUDLEY, Albertus True 1
DUDLEY, Augustus Palmer 1
DUDLEY, Benjamin 1
  Winslow
DUDLEY, Bide 2
DUDLEY, Carl Ward 6
DUDLEY, Charles Ashman 4
DUDLEY, Charles Benjamin 1
DUDLEY, Charles Edward H

DUDLEY, Charles Rowland 1
DUDLEY, Edgar Swartwout 1
DUDLEY, Edgar Swartwout 4
DUDLEY, Edward Bishop H
DUDLEY, Emelius Clark 1
DUDLEY, Frank Alonzo 2
DUDLEY, Frank Virgil 6
DUDLEY, Frederick Merritt 4
DUDLEY, Guilford Swathel 4
DUDLEY, Helena Stuart 3
DUDLEY, Henry C. H
DUDLEY, Henry H(olden) 6
DUDLEY, Irving Bedell 1
DUDLEY, James Benson 1
DUDLEY, James G. 4
DUDLEY, John Benton 4
DUDLEY, John Gant 1
DUDLEY, Joseph H
DUDLEY, Joseph Grassie 5
DUDLEY, Lucy Bronson 1
DUDLEY, Mrs. Guilford 3
  Monroe
DUDLEY, Nathan Augustus 1
DUDLEY, Paul H
DUDLEY, Pemberton 1
DUDLEY, Pendleton 4
DUDLEY, Plimmon Henry 1
DUDLEY, Samuel Madison 2
DUDLEY, Samuel William 4
DUDLEY, Thomas H
DUDLEY, Thomas 1
  Underwood
DUDLEY, Wesley Coleman 4
DUDLEY, William Lofland 1
DUDLEY, William Russel 1
DUDLEY, William Wade 1
DUDLEY, Winfield Ware 1
DUDYCHA, George J(ohn) 5
DUEL, Arthur Baldwin 1
DUELL, Charles Halliwell 5
DUELL, Charles Holland 3
DUELL, Prentice 4
DUELL, Robert Holland 1
DUEMLING, Hermann 4
DUER, Caroline King 3
DUER, Edward Louis 2
DUER, John H
DUER, William * H
DUER, William Alexander H
DUERR, Alvan Emile 3
DUFF, Alexander Wilmer 3
DUFF, Edward Aloysius 1
DUFF, G. Lyman 3
DUFF, James H. 5
DUFF, Mary Ann Dyke 4
DUFF, Philip Grandy 4
DUFF, Philip Sheridan 1
DUFF, Sir Lyman Poore 3
DUFF, William McGill 1
DUFFEE, Warren S(adler) 5
DUFFELL, William 1
  R(aymond)
DUFFEY, George Wallace 6
DUFFEY, Warren Joseph 1
DUFFIELD, Edward 1
  Dickinson
DUFFIELD, Eugene Schulte 6
DUFFIELD, George * 1
DUFFIELD, Henry Martyn 1
DUFFIELD, Howard 1
DUFFIELD, John Thomas 1
DUFFIELD, Marcus 5
  McCampbell
DUFFIELD, Pitts 2
DUFFIELD, Samuel H
  Augustus Willoughby
DUFFIELD, Samuel Pearce 4
DUFFIELD, William Ward 1
DUFFUS, Robert Luther 5
DUFFY, Bernard Cornelius 5
DUFFY, Charles 4
DUFFY, Edmund 5
DUFFY, Francis Patrick H
DUFFY, Francis Patrick 1
DUFFY, Frank H. 3
DUFFY, Herbert Smith 4
DUFFY, James Albert 4
DUFFY, James Albert 5
DUFFY, James O. G. 1
DUFFY, James Patrick 6
  Bernard
DUFFY, John A. 2
DUFFY, Joseph Alexander 1
DUFFY, Phillip B. 6
DUFFY, Richard 1
DUFFY, Ward Everett 4
DUFNER, Edward 2
DUFOUR, Frank Oliver 4
DUFOUR, John James 1
DUFOUR, William Cyprien 5
DUFOURCQ, Edward 1
  Leonce
DUFY, Raoul 3
DUGAN, Caro Atherton 1
DUGAN, Howard Francis 4
DUGAN, James 4

DUGAN, Larry Hull 5
DUGAN, Raymond Smith 1
DUGAN, Thomas Buchanan 1
DUGANNE, Augustine
Joseph Hickey H
DUGARDIN, Herve 5
DUGDALE, Ralph E. 4
DUGDALE, Richard Louis H
DUGGAN, B. O. 3
DUGGAN, Charles F. 4
DUGGAN, John J. 3
DUGGAN, Laurence 2
DUGGAN, Mell L. 1
DUGGAN, Sherman 6
DUGGAN, Stephen 3
DUGGAN, Walter Teeling 1
DUGGAN, William H. 4
DUGGAR, Benjamin Minge 3
DUGGAR, John Frederick 2
DUGGAR, Reuben Henry 3
DUGMORE, Arthur
Radclyffe 5
DUGRO, P. Henry 1
DUGUE, Charles Oscar H
DUHRING, Louis Adolphus 1
DUJARDIN, Rosamond
Neal 4
DUKE, Basil Wilson 1
DUKE, Benjamin Newton 1
DUKE, Charles Wesley 3
DUKE, Claude Walter 1
DUKE, James Buchanan 4
DUKE, James Thomas 5
DUKE, Nathaniel 4
DUKE, Richard Thomas
Walker Jr. 1
DUKE, Samuel Page 3
DUKE, T. Seddon 4
DUKE, Vernon 5
DUKE, Victor LeRoy 1
DUKE, William Mark 6
DUKE, William Richard 1
DUKE, William Waddell 2
DUKELOW, Charles
Thomas 1
DUKES, Charles Alfred 2
DUKES, Richard Gustavus 3
DULANEY, Benjamin
Lewis 1
DULANEY, Henry Stier 1
DULANEY, William Leroy 4
DULANY, Daniel * H
DULANY, George William
Jr. 3
DULANY, Henry Rozier Jr. 2
DULANY, William Henry 2
DULCAN, Charles B. 1
DULING, G. Harold 1
DULL, Floyd Norman 6
DULLES, Allen Macy 1
DULLES, Allen Welsh 5
DULLES, Charles Winslow 1
DULLES, John Foster 1
DULLES, Joseph Heatly 1
DULUTH, Daniel Greysolon H
DULZELL, Paul 4
DUMAINE, Frederic 3
Christopher
DUMAS, Gustave 3
DUMAS, Walter A. 1
DUMAS, William Thomas 4
DUMBA, Constantin 1
Theodor
DUMBAULD, Horatio 3
Snyder
DUMBLE, Edwin Theodore 1
DU MEZ, Andrew Grover 2
DUMLER, Martin George 1
DUMM, Benjamin Alfred 5
DUMMEIER, Edwin F. 2
DUMMER, Edwin Heyse 1
DUMMER, Jeremiah * H
DUMOND, Frank Vincent 4
DU MONT, Allen Balcom 1
DUMONT, Ebenezer H
DUMONT, Frederick 1
Theodore Frelinghuysen
DUMONT, Paul Emile 6
DUMONT, Wayne 1
DU MOULIN, Frank 2
DUN, Angus 5
DUN, Edwin 1
DUN, James 1
DUN, Robert Graham 1
DUNAWAY, John Allder 5
DUNAWAY, Thomas F. 4
DUNBAR, Arthur White 5
DUNBAR, Charles Edward 4
Jr.
DUNBAR, Charles Franklin 1
DUNBAR, Duke Wellington 5
DUNBAR, Erroll 1
DUNBAR, Flanders 2
DUNBAR, James Robert 1
DUNBAR, James Whitson 2

DUNBAR, John H. 1
DUNBAR, Moses H
DUNBAR, Newell 1
DUNBAR, Paul Laurence 4
DUNBAR, Ralph O. 1
DUNBAR, Robert 1
DUNBAR, Saidie Orr (Mrs.) 6
DUNBAR, Ulric Stonewall 1
Jackson
DUNBAR, William * H
DUNBAR, William Harrison 1
DUNBAUGH, Harry Joy 5
DUNCA, Frederick S. 2
DUNCALF, Frederic 4
DUNCAN, Albert Greene 1
DUNCAN, Alexander H
Edward
DUNCAN, Alexander 5
Edward
DUNCAN, Alexander 6
Edward
DUNCAN, Carson Samuel 3
DUNCAN, Charles H
DUNCAN, Charles Miguel 4
DUNCAN, Daniel H
DUNCAN, David Shaw 1
DUNCAN, Edward Carlton 1
DUNCAN, Edwin 6
DUNCAN, Frances (Mrs. 5
John L. Manning)
DUNCAN, Garnett H
DUNCAN, George Brand 2
DUNCAN, George Martin 1
DUNCAN, Gerald 1
DUNCAN, Glenn A. 3
DUNCAN, Greer Assheton 4
DUNCAN, Herschel Mills 3
DUNCAN, Isadora H
DUNCAN, Isadora 1
DUNCAN, James H
DUNCAN, James 1
DUNCAN, James Cameron 1
DUNCAN, James Floyd 5
DUNCAN, James Henry 1
DUNCAN, James R. 4
DUNCAN, John Harris 1
DUNCAN, Joseph H
DUNCAN, Joseph Wilson 1
DUNCAN, Lewis Johnston 5
DUNCAN, Louis 1
DUNCAN, Luther Noble 2
DUNCAN, Norman 1
DUNCAN, Oscar Dibble 2
DUNCAN, Richard M. 6
DUNCAN, Robert Kennedy 1
DUNCAN, Ruth Henley 5
(Mrs. Isaac Greenwood
Duncan)
DUNCAN, Samuel Edward 1
DUNCAN, Stuart 3
DUNCAN, Thomas Shearer 4
DUNCAN, W. Butler 1
DUNCAN, Walter Jack 1
DUNCAN, Walter Wofford 2
Tucker
DUNCAN, Warren W. 1
DUNCAN, Watson Boone 1
DUNCAN, William Addison H
DUNCAN, William Cary 2
DUNCAN, William 2
McKinley
DUNCAN, William Wallace 1
DUNCAN-CLARK, Samuel 1
John
DUNCANSON, Robert S. 6
DUNCANSON, Thomas 5
Sherriff
DUNCKLEE, John Butler 1
DUNDEY, Charles L. 5
DUNFORD, Edward 1
Bradstreet
DUNFORD, Ralph Emerson 5
DUNGAN, Albert Wallace 4
DUNGAN, David Roberts 4
DUNGAN, Paul Baxter 2
DUNGAY, Neil Stanley 3
DUNGLISON, Richard H
James
DUNGLISON, Robley H
DUNHAM, Arthur 1
DUNHAM, Charles Little 6
DUNHAM, Cyrus 1
Livingston
DUNHAM, Daniel H. 1
DUNHAM, Edward Kellogg 1
DUNHAM, Franklin 4
DUNHAM, Frederic 2
Gibbons
DUNHAM, George Earl 1
DUNHAM, Henry 4
Goodrich
DUNHAM, Henry Kennon 2
DUNHAM, Henry Morton 1
DUNHAM, Howard Potter 6
DUNHAM, James Henry 3
DUNHAM, James Webb 4
DUNHAM, John Dudley 1

DUNHAM, Ransom H
Williams
DUNHAM, Robert James 3
DUNHAM, Russell H. 3
DUNHAM, Samuel Clarke 4
DUNHAM, Sturges Sigler 2
DUNHAM, Sylvester Clark 1
DUNHAM, William Russell 4
DUNIWAY, Abigail Scott 1
DUNIWAY, Clyde 2
Augustus
DUNKEL, Joel Ambrose 2
DUNKIN, Damon Duffield 1
DUNKLEY, Ferdinand Luis 3
DUNLAP, Andrew 1
DUNLAP, Arthur Ray 6
DUNLAP, Boutwell 1
DUNLAP, Charles Bates 1
DUNLAP, Charles Edward 4
DUNLAP, Charles Graham 1
DUNLAP, Charles Kephart 2
DUNLAP, David 5
Richardson
DUNLAP, Elbert 1
DUNLAP, Frederick 6
DUNLAP, Frederick Levy 1
DUNLAP, George H
Washington
DUNLAP, Harry 4
DUNLAP, Hiram J. 1
DUNLAP, James Boliver 1
DUNLAP, John H
DUNLAP, John Bettes 4
DUNLAP, John Robertson 1
DUNLAP, John T. 6
DUNLAP, Knight 1
DUNLAP, Millard Fillmore 4
DUNLAP, Orrin Elmer Jr. 5
DUNLAP, Renick William 1
DUNLAP, Robert 1
DUNLAP, Robert Finley 1
DUNLAP, Robert Henry 5
DUNLAP, Robert Pinckney H
DUNLAP, Roy J. 1
DUNLAP, Roy John Jr. 5
DUNLAP, William H
DUNLAP, William H
Claiborne
DUNLAVY, Edwin Wesley 5
DUNLEVY, Robert Baldwin 3
DUNLOP, James 4
DUNLOP, Walter Scott 6
DUNMIRE, Glenn DeWitt 6
DUNMORE, 4th earl H
DUNMORE, Walter 2
Thomas
DUNN, Alan 6
DUNN, Alexander Gordon 1
DUNN, Arthur Wallace 1
DUNN, Arthur William 1
DUNN, Ballard 5
DUNN, Beverly Charles 1
DUNN, Byron Archibald 4
DUNN, Charles H
DUNN, Charles Gwyllym 4
DUNN, Charles John 1
DUNN, Charles Putnam 4
DUNN, Charles Wesley 3
DUNN, Edward Gregory 2
DUNN, Elias Bound 4
DUNN, Emmett Reid 5
DUNN, Fannie Wyche 2
DUNN, Frank Harold 4
DUNN, Frank Kershner 4
DUNN, Frederick Julian 4
DUNN, Frederick Sherwood 4
DUNN, Gano 3
DUNN, George Grundy 1
DUNN, George Hedford H
DUNN, George M. 4
DUNN, Harris Ashton 4
DUNN, Harry Thatcher 5
DUNN, Harvey 3
DUNN, Henry Wesley 5
DUNN, Herbert Omar 1
DUNN, Ignatius J. 3
DUNN, Jacob Piatt 1
DUNN, James Phillip 1
DUNN, Jesse James 1
DUNN, John Joseph 1
DUNN, John Randall 2
DUNN, Joseph 3
DUNN, Joseph Allan 1
DUNN, Leslie Clarence 6
DUNN, Martha Baker 4
DUNN, Matthew A. 2
DUNN, R. Roy 6
DUNN, Ray A. 6
DUNN, Richard J. 1
DUNN, Robert 3
DUNN, Robert A. 2
DUNN, Samuel O. 3
DUNN, Sir James Hamet 2
DUNN, Thomas B. 1
DUNN, Waldo Hilary 5

DUNN, William Edward 4
DUNN, William Frank 5
DUNN, William Le Roy 1
DUNN, William McKee 1
DUNN, William Warren 4
DUNN, Williamson H
DUNNACK, Henry E. 1
DUNNE, Charles D. 4
DUNNE, Edmond M. 1
DUNNE, Edward 1
Fitzsimons
DUNNE, Edward Joseph 1
DUNNE, Finley Peter 1
DUNNE, James Edward 1
DUNNE, James Edward 4
Craven
DUNNE, Peter Francis 1
DUNNELL, Elbridge Gerry 1
DUNNELL, Mark Boothby 1
DUNNELL, Mark Hill 1
DUNNETT, Alexander 1
DUNNING, Albert Elijah 1
DUNNING, Alden W. 4
DUNNING, Charles A. 3
DUNNING, Edwin James 1
DUNNING, George 1
Freeman
DUNNING, Harrison F. 6
DUNNING, Harry 5
Westbrook
DUNNING, Henry Armitt 4
Brown
DUNNING, Henry Sage 3
DUNNING, James Edmund 3
DUNNING, James Edwin 3
DUNNING, John Ray 6
DUNNING, John Sullivan 5
DUNNING, John Wirt 3
DUNNING, Lehman H. 1
DUNNING, Morton Dexter 5
DUNNING, N. Max 2
DUNNING, Philip 5
DUNNING, Robert 5
M(ackenzie)
DUNNING, Stewart N. 3
DUNNING, William 1
Archibald
DUNNINGER, Joseph 6
DUNNINGTON, Francis 4
Perry
DUNNINGTON, Walter 5
Grey
DUNOYER DE 6
SEGONZAC, Andre
DUNPHY, Charles 1
DUNPHY, William Henry 1
DUNSCOMB, Charles 1
Ellsworth
DUNSCOMB, Samuel 1
Whitney Jr.
DUNSHEE, Jay Dee 3
DUNSMORE, Andrew B. 1
DUNSMORE, John Ward 2
DUNSMORE, Philo Cordon 5
DUNSTAN, Arthur St. 5
Charles
DUNSTAN, Edmund 5
Fleetwood
DUNSTER, Henry H
DUNTLEY, John Wheeler 1
DUNTON, Edith Kellogg 3
DUNTON, Frank Holt 4
DUNTON, Larkin 1
DUNTON, Lewis Marion 4
DUNTON, William Herbert 1
DUNWELL, Charles 1
Tappan
DUNWELL, James Winslow 1
DUNWODY, Thomas Edgar 4
DUNWODY, William 3
Elliott
DUNWOODY, Henry 3
Harrison Chase
DUNWOODY, William 1
Hood
DUPALAIS, Virginia H
Poullard
DUPEE, John 5
DUPIUS, Charles W(illiam) 6
DUPLESSIS, Maurice L. 3
DUPONCEAU, Pierre H
Etinne
DU PONT, A. Felix 2
DU PONT, Alfred I. 1
DU PONT, Eleuthere Irenee H
DUPONT, Emile Francis 6
DUPONT, Francis V. 4
DU PONT, Henry 4
DU PONT, Henry Algernon 1
DUPONT, Henry B. 1
DUPONT, Henry Francis 5
DUPONT, Irenee 1
DUPONT, Irenee 5
DUPONT, Jessie Ball (Mrs. 5
Alfred Irenee DuPont)
DU PONT, Lammot 3

DU PONT, Pierre Samuel 3
DU PONT, Samuel Francis H
DU PONT, T. Coleman 1
DU PONT, Victor Marie H
DU PONT, William Jr. 4
DUPRATZ, Antoine Simon H
Le Page
DU PRE, Arthur Mason 2
DU PRE, Daniel Allston 4
DUPRE, Henry Garland 1
DUPRE, Marcel 5
DUPUIS, Raymond 5
DUPUY, Eliza Ann H
DUPUY, Herbert 1
DU PUY, Pierre 5
DU PUY, Raymond 1
DUPUY, R(ichard) Ernest 6
DUPUY, Samuel Stuart 1
DU PUY, William Atherton 1
DUQUE, Henry O'Melveny 1
DUQUESNE DE
MENNEVILLE, Marquis H
DURAN, F. Mutis 4
DURAN, Narcisco H
DURAND, Asher Brown H
DURAND, Cyrus H
DURAND, David 5
DURAND, E(dward) Dana 5
DURAND, Elias Judah 1
DURAND, Elle Magioire H
DURAND, G(eorge) 5
Harrison
DURAND, James Harrison 6
DURAND, Loyal Jr. 5
DURAND, Sir Henry 2
Mortimer
DURAND, William 3
Frederick
DURANT, Charles Person H
DURANT, Frederick Clark 1
Jr.
DURANT, Henry H
DURANT, Henry Fowle H
DURANT, Thomas Clark H
DURANT, Thomas 1
Jefferson
DURANT, William Crapo 2
DURANTE, Oscar 2
DURANTY, Walter 3
DURAS, Victor Hugo 6
DURBIN, Elisha John H
DURBIN, John Price H
DURBIN, Winfield Taylor 1
DURBROW, Chandler 6
Wolcott
DURELL, Daniel Meserve 1
DURELL, Edward Henry 1
DURELL, Edward Hovey 4
DURELL, George B. 1
DU RELLE, George 4
DURET, Miguel Lanz 4
DUREY, Cyrus 1
DUREY, John C. 5
DURFEE, Edgar Noble 4
DURFEE, Herbert Augustus H
DURFEE, Job 1
DURFEE, Nathaniel Briggs H
DURFEE, Thomas 1
DURFEE, Walter 6
Hetherington
DURFEE, William Franklin 1
DURFEE, William Pitt 1
DURFEE, William Pitt 2
DURFEE, Winthrop Carver 1
DURFEE, Zoheth Sherman H
DURFREY, John Cooper 1
DURGIN, Calvin Thornton 4
DURGIN, Cyrus W. 4
DURGIN, George Francis 4
DURGIN, Samuel Holmes 4
DURHAM, Caleb Wheeler H
DURHAM, Calen Wheeler 1
DURHAM, Carl Thomas 6
DURHAM, Charles Love 1
DURHAM, Donald B. 3
DURHAM, Edward 1
DURHAM, Edward Miall 3
Jr.
DURHAM, Fred Stranahan 3
DURHAM, Henry Welles 3
DURHAM, Hobart Noble 5
DURHAM, Isreal W. 1
DURHAM, James Ware 4
DURHAM, John Stephens 1
DURHAM, Knowlton 5
DURHAM, Milton Jamison 1
DURHAM, Nelson Wayne 1
DURHAM, Plato Tracy 1
DURHAM, Robert Lee 2
DURIER, Antoine H
DURIVAGE, Francis H
Alexander
DURKEE, Charles H
DURKEE, Frank Williams 1
DURKEE, J(ames) Stanley 5
DURKEE, John H

DURKIN, Martin 3
DURLAND, Kellogg 1
DURLING, Edgar Vincent 3
DURR, Clifford Judkins 6
DURRELL, Joseph H. 4
DURRETT, Reuben Thomas 1
DURRIE, Daniel Steele H
DURRIE, George Henry H
DURST, William Arthur 1
DURSTINE, Roy Sarles 4
DURSTON, John Hurst 1
DURY, Charles 4
DURYEA, Charles Edgar 4
DURYEA, Charles Edgar 4
DURYEA, Dan(iel) (Edwin) 5
DURYEA, Edwin 1
DURYEA, Hiram 4
DURYEA, Nina Larrey 3
DURYEA, Wright 4
DURYEE, Abram 1
DU SABLE, Jean Baptiste H
  Point
DU SACRE COEUR, 4
  Mother Marie
DUSCHAK, Lionel Herman 2
DUSE, Eleonora H
DUSE, Eleonora 4
DUSHAM, E(dward) 6
  H(enry)
DU SHANE, Donald 2
DUSHANE, Graham 4
DUSHMAN, Saul 3
DU SIMITIERE, Pierre H
  Eugene
DUSSER DE BARENNE, 1
  Joannes Gregorius
DUSTIN, Hannah H
DUTCHER, Charles Mason 1
DUTCHER, Francis Edward 6
DUTCHER, George 3
  Matthew
DUTCHER, Silas Belden 1
DUTCHER, William 1
DUTRA, Eurico Gaspar 6
DUTREMBLAY, Pamphile- 3
  Real
DUTROW, Howard Victor 6
DUTTON, Benjamin F. 1
DUTTON, Charles Judson 4
DUTTON, Clair C. 6
DUTTON, Clarence Edward 1
DUTTON, Edward A. 3
DUTTON, Edward Payson 1
DUTTON, Emily Helen 2
DUTTON, George Burwell 1
DUTTON, George Elliott 2
DUTTON, Henry H
DUTTON, Joseph 1
DUTTON, Richard King 5
DUTTON, Samuel Train 1
DUTTON, Walter C. 4
DUTTON, William Jay 4
DUVAL, Charles Warren 4
DU VAL, Frederic Beale 4
DUVAL, H. Rieman 1
DUVAL, Isaac Harding 1
DUVAL, Laurel 3
DUVAL, William Pope H
DUVALIER, Francois 5
DUVALL, Charles Raymond 1
DUVALL, Donald 5
  Chauncey
DUVALL, Gabriel H
DUVALL, James William 4
DUVALL, Trumbull Gillette 4
DUVALL, William Penn 1
DUVEL, Joseph William 2
  Tell
DUVENECK, Frank 1
DUVERNAY, Ludger H
DUWE, George E. 5
DUXBURY, George H. 3
DUYCKINCK, Evert H
  Augustus
DUYCKINCK, George H
  Long
DUYCKINCK, Gerrit H
DVORAK, Antonin 6
DVORNIK, Francis 6
D'VYS, George Whitefield 1
DWAN, Ralph Hubert 5
DWENGER, Joseph 1
DWIGGINS, Clare Victor 3
DWIGGINS, William 3
  Addison
DWIGHT, Arthur Smith 2
DWIGHT, Benjamin H
  Franklin
DWIGHT, Benjamin 1
  Woodbridge
DWIGHT, Edmund H
DWIGHT, Edmund 1
DWIGHT, Edwin Welles 1
DWIGHT, Francis H
DWIGHT, Harrison 3
  Griswold

DWIGHT, Henry Otis 1
DWIGHT, Henry Williams H
DWIGHT, Jeremiah Wilbur H
DWIGHT, John Sullivan H
DWIGHT, John Wilbur 1
DWIGHT, Jonathan 1
DWIGHT, Mabel 5
DWIGHT, Minnie Ryan 3
DWIGHT, Nathaniel H
DWIGHT, Ogden Graham 5
DWIGHT, Richard Everett H
DWIGHT, Sereno Edwards H
DWIGHT, Theodore * H
DWIGHT, Theodore H
  William
DWIGHT, Thomas H
DWIGHT, Thomas 1
DWIGHT, Timothy H
DWIGHT, Timothy 1
DWIGHT, William H
DWIGHT, William Buck 1
DWINELL, Justin H
DWINNELL, Clifton 1
  Howard
DWIRE, Henry Rudolph 2
DWORKIS, Martin B. 4
DWORSHAK, Henry 4
  Clarence
DWYER, Charles 1
DWYER, Edward Martin 3
DWYER, Florence 6
DWYER, James A. 3
DWYER, James Francis 4
DWYER, Jeremiah 4
DWYER, John B. 3
DWYER, John William 4
DWYER, Robert Arthur 4
DWYER, Robert E. 4
DWYER, William Joseph 3
DWYRE, Dudley G. 2
DYAR, Harrison Gray 1
DYAS, Ada H
DYAS, Ada 4
DYCHE, Howard Edward 3
DYCHE, Louis Lindsay 1
DYCHE, William Andrew 1
DYE, Alexander Vincent 3
DYE, Clair Albert 2
DYE, Eugene Allen 4
DYE, Eva Emery 3
DYE, John T. 1
DYE, John Walter 6
DYE, William Holton 4
DYER, Albert Joseph 6
DYER, Alexander Brydie H
DYER, Alexander Brydie 3
DYER, Catherine Cornelia 1
DYER, Clifton G. 3
DYER, David Patterson 1
DYER, Eliphalet H
DYER, Elisha 1
DYER, Everett R. 6
DYER, Francis John 4
DYER, Frank 5
DYER, Frank Lewis 1
DYER, Franklin Benjamin 4
DYER, Frederick Rainey 1
DYER, George Leland 1
DYER, Gustavus Walker 4
DYER, Heman 1
DYER, Hezekiah Anthony 2
DYER, Isaac Watson 1
DYER, Isadore 1
DYER, James Ballard 4
DYER, James Edward 5
DYER, Jesse Farley 1
DYER, John H. 4
DYER, John LaFayette 1
DYER, John Lewis 5
DYER, John Napier 3
DYER, Joseph Henry 2
DYER, Leonard Huntress 3
DYER, Leonidas 3
  Carstarphen
DYER, Louis 1
DYER, Mary H
DYER, Nehemiah Mayo 1
DYER, Oliver 1
DYER, Sallie 6
DYER, Samuel Eugene 6
DYER, Walter Alden 2
DYETT, Herbert Thomas 5
DYHRENFURTH, Gunter 6
  Oskar
DYKE, Charles Bartlett 5
DYKE, Herbert H. 4
DYKEMA, Karl W(ashburn) 3
DYKEMA, Peter William 3
DYKEMA, Raymond K. 3
DYKEMAN, King 1
DYKHUIZEN, Harold 5
  Daniel
DYKSTRA, Clarence 4
  Addison
DYKSTRA, Gerald Oscar 5
DYKSTRA, John 5

DYKSTRA, Ralph 6
DYLANDER, John H
DYM, Aaron 3
DYMENT, Colin Victor 1
DYMOND, Florence 6
DYNES, Owen William 5
DYOTT, Thomas W. 1
DYRENFORTH, Robert St H
  George
DYSINGER, Holmes 4
DYSON, Charles Wilson 1
DYSON, James Lindsay H
DYSON, Verne 6

E

EACHES, Hector H
EACHES, Owen Philips 1
EADE, Charles 4
EADS, James Buchanan 1
EAGAN, Charles Patrick 1
EAGAN, Edward Patrick 5
  Francis
EAGAN, John Joseph 1
EAGELS, Jeanne 1
EAGER, George Boardman 1
EAGER, George Eugene 4
EAGER, Helen 3
EAGER, Henry Gossett 5
EAGER, John M. 3
EAGER, Samuel Watkins H
EAGLE, J. Frederick 4
EAGLE, James Phillip 1
EAGLE, Joe Henry 4
EAGLE, Joe Henry 5
EAGLE, Mary Kavanaugh 1
EAGLE, The H
  Montgomery
EAGLE, Vernon Ainsworth 6
EAGLES, Theophilus 1
  Randolph
EAGLESON, Freeman 1
  Thomas
EAGLESON, James Beaty 1
EAGLESON, Thomas R. H
EAGLETON, Clyde 5
EAGLETON, Wells Phillips 2
EAKIN, Robert 1
EAKINS, Thomas 1
EAKLE, Arthur Starr 1
EAMAN, Frank Dwight 4
EAMES, Alfred Warner 3
EAMES, Arthur Johnson 6
EAMES, Charles H
EAMES, Charles Holmes 3
EAMES, Edward Williams 6
EAMES, Emma 1
EAMES, Hayden 1
EAMES, Henry Purmort 3
EAMES, John Capen 4
EAMES, Wilberforce 1
EAMES, William S. 1
EARDLEY, Armand John 5
EARHART, Amelia 1
EARHART, Harry Boyd 3
EARHART, Lida Belle 4
EARHART, Robert Francis 1
EARHART, Will 5
EARL, Augustus H
EARL, Charles 2
EARL, Edward 1
EARL, Edwin T. 1
EARL, Mrs Elizabeth 1
  Claypool
EARL, George Goodell 1
EARL, George H. 4
EARL, Guy Chaffee 1
EARL, Harley J. 5
EARL, John Arthur 1
EARL, N. Clark Jr. 1
EARL, Ottis M. 4
EARL, Ralph Eleaser 1
  Whiteside
EARL, Robert 1
EARL, Robert 2
EARLE, Alice Morse 1
EARLE, Clarence Edwards 3
EARLE, Edward Mead 3
EARLE, Elias 1
EARLE, Frank Breckenridge 1
EARLE, Franklin Sumner 1
EARLE, Genevieve Beavers 5
EARLE, George Howard 1
EARLE, George Howard 6
EARLE, James 1
EARLE, John Baylis 1
EARLE, Joseph Haynsworth H
EARLE, Lawrence 1
  Carmichael
EARLE, Mortimer Lamson 1
EARLE, Pliny * H
EARLE, Ralph H
EARLE, Ralph 1
EARLE, Robert L. 6
EARLE, Samuel 1
EARLE, Samuel Broadus 6

EARLE, Samuel T. Jr. 1
EARLE, Swenson 6
EARLE, Thomas H
EARLE, Walter Frank 1
EARLE, Walter Keese 5
EARLE, William Hughes 4
EARLEY, John Joseph 4
EARLING, Albert J. 1
EARLING, Herman B. 5
EARLL, Jonas Jr. H
EARLL, Nehemiah H
  Hezekiah
EARLY, Eleanor 5
EARLY, Gilbert Garfield 2
EARLY, John 1
EARLY, John Jacob 2
EARLY, John Jacob 3
EARLY, Jubal Anderson H
EARLY, Maurice 3
EARLY, Peter 1
EARLY, Robert Lee 4
EARLY, Stephen 3
EARLY, William Wallace 1
EARNEST, Herbert Ludwell 5
EARNHEART, Harold 3
EARNSHAW, Manuel 1
EARP, Edwin Lee 1
EARP, James William 3
EARP, John Rosslyn 1
EARP, Wyatt Berry Stapp 1
EARP, Wyatt Berry Stapp H
EASBY-SMITH, James S. 5
EASCH, Albertina 4
EASLEY, Claudius Miller 4
EASLEY, Gertrude Beeks 2
EASLEY, Katherine 1
EASLEY, Ralph 1
  Montgomery
EASON, George Millar 4
EAST, Edward Murray 1
EASTBURN, L. A. 3
EASTER, Charles 5
  Whittlesey
EASTER, De la Warr 1
  Benjamin
EASTERBROOK, Arthur E. 3
EASTERBROOK, Edmund 1
  Pepperell
EASTERBY, James Harold 4
EASTERWOOD, William 1
  Edward Jr.
EASTIN, Bertrand P. 4
EASTLAND, Florence 4
  Martin
EASTMAN, Annis Ford 1
EASTMAN, Arthur 1
  MacArthur
EASTMAN, Barrett 1
EASTMAN, Ben C. H
EASTMAN, Charles 4
  Alexander Ohiyesa
EASTMAN, Charles H
  Gamage
EASTMAN, Charles 1
  Rochester
EASTMAN, Clarence Willis 3
EASTMAN, Edwin Gamage 1
EASTMAN, Enoch 1
  Worthen
EASTMAN, Fred 4
EASTMAN, George 1
EASTMAN, Hal Pond 3
EASTMAN, Harry L. 4
EASTMAN, Harvey Gridley H
EASTMAN, Helen 3
EASTMAN, Ira Allen 1
EASTMAN, John Coates 1
EASTMAN, John Robie 1
EASTMAN, Joseph 1
EASTMAN, Joseph Bartlett 2
EASTMAN, Joseph Rilus 2
EASTMAN, Julia Arabella 1
EASTMAN, LeRoy 5
  Emerson
EASTMAN, Linda Anne 4
EASTMAN, Lucius Root 3
EASTMAN, M. Gale 3
EASTMAN, Max 5
  (Forrester)
EASTMAN, Nehemiah 1
EASTMAN, Nicholson 6
  Joseph
EASTMAN, Rebecca Lane 5
  Hooper (Mrs. William
  Franklin)
EASTMAN, Samuel Coffin 1
EASTMAN, Samuel Palmer 1
EASTMAN, Seth H
EASTMAN, Timothy H
  Corser
EASTMAN, William Reed 4
EASTON, Burton Scott 2
EASTON, Edward Denison 1
EASTON, John 1
EASTON, Morton William 1
EASTON, Nicholas H

EASTON, Robert Eastman 6
EASTON, Rufus H
EASTON, Stanly Alexander 4
EASTVOLD, Carl Johan 4
EASTVOLD, Seth Clarence 4
EASTWOOD, A. J. 3
EASTWOOD, Alice 3
EASTWOOD, Everett 5
  Owen
EASTWOOD, George 4
  Anderson
EATON, Amasa Mason 1
EATON, Amos 1
EATON, Arthur Wentworth 1
  Hamilton
EATON, Barney Edward 2
EATON, Benjamin Harrison 1
EATON, C. Harry 1
EATON, Charles Aubrey 3
EATON, Charles Frederick 4
EATON, Charles H. 2
EATON, Charles H. 1
EATON, Charles Warren 1
EATON, Cyrus 1
EATON, D. Cady H
EATON, Daniel Cady H
EATON, Dorman 1
  Bridgeman
EATON, Edward Dwight 2
EATON, Elon Howard 1
EATON, Emma Florence 3
EATON, Ephraim Llewellyn 4
EATON, Ernest Theophilus 3
EATON, Fred Laurine 1
EATON, Frederick Heber 1
EATON, George Daniel 1
EATON, George Francis 2
EATON, George Franklin 3
EATON, Harvey Doane 3
EATON, Henry William 1
EATON, Homer 1
EATON, Horace Ainsworth 5
EATON, Hubert 1
EATON, James Briggs 4
EATON, James Murchie 3
EATON, James Shirley 3
EATON, James Tucker 5
EATON, James Webster 1
EATON, John 1
EATON, John David 6
EATON, John Henry H
EATON, John Wallace 1
EATON, Joseph Giles 1
EATON, Joseph Horace H
EATON, Joseph Oriel 1
EATON, Joseph Oriel 3
EATON, L. Mckendree H
EATON, Lewis 1
EATON, Lewis Tillson 3
EATON, Lucien 3
EATON, Marquis 1
EATON, Marquis G. 3
EATON, Melvin Carr 4
EATON, Nathaniel H
EATON, Paul B. 4
EATON, Philip Bentley 3
EATON, Russell 5
EATON, Samuel H
EATON, Seymour 1
EATON, Theodore Hildreth 4
EATON, Theophilus H
EATON, Thomas Treadwell 1
EATON, Walter Prichard 3
EATON, William 1
EATON, William Colgate 1
EATON, William H. 4
EATON, William Hanmer 3
EATON, William Robb 2
EATON, Wyatt H
EAVENSON, Howard 3
  Nicholas
EAVES, George 1
EAVES, Lucile 5
EBAUGH, Franklin 5
  Gessford
EBBERT, Frank Baker 6
EBBOTT, Percy John 6
EBEL, William K. 5
EBELING, Philip Calvin 4
EBELING, Willi Henry 4
EBERBACH, Carl Walter 4
EBERHARD, Ernst 4
EBERHARDT, Charles 4
  Christopher
EBERHARDT, Charles 5
  Christopher
EBERHARDT, Frederick L. 2
EBERHART, Nelle 2
  Richmond
EBERHARTER, Herman 3
  Peter
EBERLE, Abastenia St 2
  Leger
EBERLE, E. G. 4
EBERLE, Edward Walter 1

EBERLE, Frederick J. 4
EBERLE, J. Louis 4
EBERLE, John H
EBERLEIN, Harold Donaldson 4
EBERLY, George Agler 5
EBERSOLE, Ezra Christian 1
EBERSOLE, J(acob) Scott 5
EBERSOLE, John Franklin 2
EBERSOLE, William Stahl 3
EBERSTADT, Ferdinand 5
EBERSTADT, Rudolph 4
EBERT, Edmund Francis 5
EBERT, Robert Edwin 4
EBERT, Rudolph Gustav 5
EBLE, Frank Xavier A. 6
EBRIGHT, Homer Kingsley 6
EBY, Frederick 1
EBY, Frederick 5
EBY, Ivan David 4
EBY, Kermit 4
EBY, Kerr 2
EBY, Robert Killian 5
ECCLES, James A. 3
ECCLES, Robert G. 1
ECCLESTON, Samuel H
ECHOLS, Angus B. 1
ECHOLS, Charles Patton 1
ECHOLS, John H
ECHOLS, John Warnock 1
ECHOLS, Leonard Sidney 5
ECHOLS, Oliver P. 3
ECHOLS, Robert 3
ECHOLS, William Holding Jr. 1
ECHOLS, William Joseph 1
ECIJA, Juan de H
ECKARD, Elisabeth Ellen Gilliland 5
ECKARD, James Read H
ECKARD, Leighton Wilson 1
ECKARDT, Lisgar Russell 2
ECKART, Carl 6
ECKART, E. Albert 5
ECKEL, Clarence Lewis 5
ECKEL, Edwin Clarence 2
ECKELS, James Herron 1
ECKENRODE, Hamilton James 1
ECKER, Enrique E. 4
ECKER, Frederic W. 4
ECKER, Frederick H. 4
ECKERSALL, Edwin Robert
ECKERSALL, Walter H. 1
ECKERT, Charles R. 4
ECKERT, George Nicholas H
ECKERT, Howard Haines 4
ECKERT, Thomas Thompson
ECKERT, Wallace J. 5
ECKERT, William D(ole) 5
ECKFELDT, Howard 4
ECKFELDT, Thomas Hooper 1
ECKFORD, Henry H
ECKHARD, George Frederick 2
ECKHART, Bernard Albert 1
ECKHART, Percy Bernard 5
ECKHOUSE, Joseph L. 4
ECKLES, Clarence Henry 1
ECKLES, Isabel Lancaster 5
ECKLEY, William Thomas 4
ECKMAN, Donald Preston 4
ECKMAN, George Peck 1
ECKMANN, Janos 6
ECKOFF, William Julius 1
ECKRICH, Richard P. 6
ECKSTEIN, Frederick H
ECKSTEIN, John H
ECKSTEIN, Louis 1
ECKSTEIN, Nathan 1
ECKSTORM, Fannie Hardy 2
ECKSTROM, Lawrence Joel 4
ECTON, Zales Nelson 5
ED, Carl Frank Ludwig 3
EDBROOKE, Willoughby J. H
EDDINS, Henry A. 4
EDDIS, William H
EDDLEMAN, Thomas Stricker 6
EDDY, Alfred Delavan 1
EDDY, Allen 3
EDDY, Arthur Jerome 1
EDDY, Brayton 3
EDDY, Charles Brown 3
EDDY, Clarence 1
EDDY, Condit Nelson 4
EDDY, Daniel Clarke H
EDDY, David Brewer 2
EDDY, Forrest Greenwood 1
EDDY, Frank Woodman 1
EDDY, Harrison Prescott 1
EDDY, Henry Brevoort 5

EDDY, Henry Stephens 2
EDDY, Henry Turner 1
EDDY, Isaac H
EDDY, Lee Moin 6
EDDY, Manton S. 4
EDDY, Mary Baker Glover 1
EDDY, Milton Walker 5
EDDY, Nathan Browne 5
EDDY, Nelson 4
EDDY, Norman H
EDDY, Oliver Tarbell 5
EDDY, Paul Dawson 6
EDDY, Richard 1
EDDY, Samuel H
EDDY, Sherwood 4
EDDY, Spencer 1
EDDY, Thomas H
EDDY, Thomas Mears 1
EDDY, Walter Hollis 3
EDDY, William Abner 1
EDDY, William Alfred 4
EDDY, Zachary 1
EDEBOHLS, George Michael 1
EDELHERTZ, Bernard 1
EDELMAN, John W. 5
EDELMAN, Maurice 6
EDELMAN, Nathan 5
EDELSTEIN, Ludwig 4
EDELSTEIN, M. Michael 2
EDEN, Charles H
EDEN, Robert 4
EDENBORN, William 1
EDENS, Arthur Hollis 4
EDENS, James Benjamin 5
EDENS, William Grant 1
EDER, Phanor James 5
EDES, Benjamin 2
EDES, Henry Herbert 1
EDES, Robert Thaxter 1
EDES, William Cushing 4
EDESON, Robert 1
EDGAR, Alvin Randall 6
EDGAR, Charles Bloomfield 1
EDGAR, Charles Leavitt 1
EDGAR, Graham 3
EDGAR, J. Clifton 1
EDGAR, Randolph 1
EDGAR, Randolph 2
EDGAR, Robert Franklin 5
EDGAR, Thomas Delbert 1
EDGAR, William Crowell 1
EDGCOMB, Ernest Isaac 4
EDGE, Rosalie (Mrs. Charles Noel) 6
EDGE, Walter Evans 3
EDGECOMBE, Samuel 3
EDGELL, George Harold 3
EDGERLY, Beatrice (Mrs. J. Havard MacPherson) 6
EDGERLY, Winfield Scot 1
EDGERTON, Alfred Peck 4
EDGERTON, Alice Craig 4
EDGERTON, Alonzo Jay H
EDGERTON, Charles Eugene
EDGERTON, Edward Keith 6
EDGERTON, Franklin 4
EDGERTON, Halsey Charles 4
EDGERTON, Henry White 5
EDGERTON, Herbert Oliver 5
EDGERTON, Hiram H. 1
EDGERTON, James Arthur 1
EDGERTON, John Emmett 1
EDGERTON, John Warren 1
EDGERTON, Justin Lincoln 5
EDGERTON, William Franklin 5
EDGETT, Edwin Francis 2
EDGINGTON, Thomas Benton 1
EDGREN, John Alexis 1
EDHOLM-SIBLEY, Mary G. Charlton 4
EDIE, Guy Lewis 4
EDIE, John Rufus H
EDIE, Lionel Danforth 4
EDINGS, William Seabrook 4
EDINGTON, Arlo Channing 3
EDISON, Charles 5
EDISON, Charles B. 4
EDISON, Harry 4
EDISON, Mark Aaron 5
EDISON, Oskar E. 4
EDISON, Samuel Bernard 5
EDISON, Thomas A. 1
EDMAN, Irwin 2
EDMAN, V. Raymond 4
EDMANDS, John 1
EDMANDS, John Wiley 5
EDMANDS, Samuel Sumner 1

EDMISTER, Floyd (Harris) 6
EDMISTON, Andrew 4
EDMISTON, R. W. 4
EDMISTON, William Sherman 5
EDMOND, William H
EDMONDS, Dean Stockett 5
EDMONDS, Douglas Lyman 4
EDMONDS, Francis William H
EDMONDS, Franklin Spencer 2
EDMONDS, George Washington 1
EDMONDS, Harry Marcus Weston 2
EDMONDS, Henry Morris 4
EDMONDS, Ira Clement 6
EDMONDS, James E. 6
EDMONDS, John Worth 4
EDMONDS, Richard Hathaway 1
EDMONDS, Thomas Sechler 6
EDMONDSON, Cathrine Elizabeth 5
EDMONDSON, Clarence Edmund 2
EDMONDSON, James Howard 5
EDMONDSON, Thomas William 1
EDMONDSON, William John 5
EDMUNDS, Albert Joseph 1
EDMUNDS, Albert Joseph 2
EDMUNDS, Charles Carroll 4
EDMUNDS, Charles Keyser 1
EDMUNDS, Charles Wallis 1
EDMUNDS, George Franklin 1
EDMUNDS, Harry Nicholas 1
EDMUNDS, James Richard Jr. 3
EDMUNDS, Samuel Henry 1
EDMUNDS, Sterling Edwin 2
EDMUNDS-HEMINGWAY, Mme 3
EDMUNDSON, Henry Alonzo H
EDMUNDSON, James Depew 1
EDOUART, Alexander H
EDOUART, Auguste H
EDRINGTON, William Reynolds 1
EDROP, Percy T. 5
EDSALL, David Linn 2
EDSALL, Joseph E. H
EDSALL, Preston William 5
EDSALL, Samuel Cook 1
EDSFORTH, Charles Dugdale 4
EDSON, Andrew Wheatley 1
EDSON, Carroll Everett 1
EDSON, Cyrus 1
EDSON, Franklin 1
EDSON, Gus 4
EDSON, Howard Austin 5
EDSON, Job Adolphus 1
EDSON, John Joy 1
EDSON, Katherine Philips 1
EDSON, Merritt Austin 3
EDSON, Robert Clay 4
EDSON, Stephen Reuben 5
EDSON, Tracy R. H
EDSON, Winfield 3
EDSTROM, David 1
EDWARD, Harvey 2
EDWARDS, Alanson W. 1
EDWARDS, Alba M. 5
EDWARDS, Alfred Shenstone 4
EDWARDS, Arthur Robin 1
EDWARDS, Bela Bates H
EDWARDS, Benjamin H
EDWARDS, Benjamin D. 1
EDWARDS, Benjamin Franklin 4
EDWARDS, Charles 1
EDWARDS, Charles Gordon 1
EDWARDS, Charles Lincoln 1
EDWARDS, Charles Vernon 5
EDWARDS, Charles William 3
EDWARDS, Chauncey Theodore 5
EDWARDS, Clarence Ransom 1
EDWARDS, Clement Stanislaus 5
EDWARDS, David Frank 4

EDWARDS, David George 4
EDWARDS, David Morton 1
EDWARDS, Deltus Malin 5
EDWARDS, Don Calvin 1
EDWARDS, Edward B. 2
EDWARDS, Edward Irving 1
EDWARDS, Edward William 1
EDWARDS, Elisha Jay 4
EDWARDS, Everett Eugene 3
EDWARDS, F. Boyd 2
EDWARDS, Frank 4
EDWARDS, Frederick 5
EDWARDS, George Herbert 2
EDWARDS, George Lane 5
EDWARDS, George Porter 1
EDWARDS, George Thornton 1
EDWARDS, George Wharton 2
EDWARDS, George William 3
EDWARDS, Gordon L. 3
EDWARDS, Granville Dennis 3
EDWARDS, Gurney 3
EDWARDS, Harrison Griffith 5
EDWARDS, Harry Stillwell 1
EDWARDS, Heber L. 4
EDWARDS, Henry Waggaman H
EDWARDS, Howard 1
EDWARDS, Howard Wesley 4
EDWARDS, Ira 2
EDWARDS, James Thomas 1
EDWARDS, John * H
EDWARDS, John Cummins H
EDWARDS, John Harrington 4
EDWARDS, John Homer 1
EDWARDS, John Palmer 4
EDWARDS, John Richard 1
EDWARDS, John Rogers 2
EDWARDS, Jonathan * H
EDWARDS, Joseph Lee 1
EDWARDS, Joseph Lee 5
EDWARDS, Julian 1
EDWARDS, Justin H
EDWARDS, Landon Brame 1
EDWARDS, Le Roy Mallory 4
EDWARDS, Leroy D. 3
EDWARDS, Linden Forest 5
EDWARDS, Loren McClain 2
EDWARDS, Louise Betts 1
EDWARDS, Margaret Messenger 4
EDWARDS, Morgan 1
EDWARDS, Murray French 4
EDWARDS, Myrtle Sassman (Mrs. Harlan H. Edwards) 5
EDWARDS, Nathaniel Marsh 1
EDWARDS, Ninian 1
EDWARDS, Ninian Wirt H
EDWARDS, Ogden Matthias 1
EDWARDS, Paul Kenneth 3
EDWARDS, Percy Noyes 4
EDWARDS, Philip R. 4
EDWARDS, Pierpont 1
EDWARDS, Ray Gwyther 5
EDWARDS, Richard 1
EDWARDS, Richard Henry 3
EDWARDS, Richard Stanislaus 3
EDWARDS, Robert Ernest 5
EDWARDS, Robert Wilkinson 1
EDWARDS, Ronald Stanley 6
EDWARDS, Samuel 1
EDWARDS, Samuel 1
EDWARDS, Stephen Ostrom 1
EDWARDS, Talmadge Allison H
EDWARDS, Thomas Cynonfardd 3
EDWARDS, Thomas McKey H
EDWARDS, Thomas H
EDWARDS, Thomas Owen 1
EDWARDS, Velma Green (Mrs. Lowell Wayne Edwards) 5
EDWARDS, Vere Buckingham 2
EDWARDS, Victor Everett 1
EDWARDS, Walter Alison H
EDWARDS, Weldon Nathaniel 1

EDWARDS, Willard Eldridge 6
EDWARDS, William H
EDWARDS, William A. 3
EDWARDS, William Augustus 1
EDWARDS, William Cunningham 6
EDWARDS, William Hanford 5
EDWARDS, William Henry 1
EDWARDS, William Seymour 1
EELLS, Dan Parmelee 1
EELLS, Elsie Eusebia Spicer 4
EELLS, Hastings 5
EELLS, Howard Parmelee 1
EELLS, Myron 1
EELLS, Stillman Witt 1
EELLS, Walter Crosby 4
EERDMANS, William Bernard 4
EFFINGER, John Robert 1
EFFLER, Erwin R. 3
EFNER, Valentine 1
EFROYMSON, Abram B. 4
EFROYMSON, Gustave A. 2
EGAN, Hannah M. 2
EGAN, John M. 4
EGAN, Joseph B(urke) 6
EGAN, Joseph L. 2
EGAN, Louis Henry 3
EGAN, Martin 1
EGAN, Maurice Francis 1
EGAN, Michael H
EGAN, Thomas Aloysius 3
EGAR, John Hodson 4
EGAS, Camilo 4
EGBERT, Albert Gallatin H
EGBERT, Donald Drew 5
EGBERT, James Chidester 1
EGBERT, Joseph 1
EGBERT, Percy T. 5
EGBERT, Seneca 1
EGBERT, Sherwood Harry 5
EGBERT, W. Grant 1
EGE, George H
EGE, Hattie B. 5
EGELSON, Louis I. 3
EGERTON, Graham 1
EGGERS, Albert Herman 6
EGGERS, George William 4
EGGERS, Harold Everett 4
EGGERS, Otto R. 5
EGGERSS, H. A. 5
EGGERT, Carl Edgar 4
EGGERT, Charles Augustus 1
EGGERT, Harry T. 5
EGGIMANN, Edward Daniel 5
EGGLESTON, Allan Arthur 4
EGGLESTON, Benjamin H
EGGLESTON, Cary 5
EGGLESTON, David Quinn 1
EGGLESTON, Edward 1
EGGLESTON, George Cary 1
EGGLESTON, Joseph H
EGGLESTON, Joseph Dupuy 3
EGGLESTON, Sir Frederic William 3
EGGLETON, Frank E(gbert) 5
EGLE, William Henry 1
EGLESTON, Thomas 1
EGLIN, William Charles Lawson 1
EGLOF, Warren K. 4
EGLOFF, Gustav 5
EGLOFFSTEIN, Frederick W. Von H
EGLY, Henry Harris 3
EGNER, Arthur Frederick 2
EGNER, Frank 3
EGTVEDT, Clairmont Leroy 6
EHLERS, Henry Edward 6
EHNES, Morris Wellington 2
EHRENFELD, Charles Hatch 1
EHRENFELD, Charles Lewis 1
EHRENFRIED, Albert 3
EHRENREICH, Joseph 5
EHRENSVARD, Johan Jacob Albert 4
EHRENZWEIG, Albert Armin 6
EHRHARDT, Julius George 1
EHRHORN, Edward Macfarlane 1
EHRICH, Harold Louis 1
EHRICH, Louis R. 1
EHRICH, Walter Louis 6

EHRICH, William E(rnst) 5
(Hermann Heinrich)
EHRINGHAUS, John 2
Christoph Blucher
EHRLICH, Harry 3
EHRLICH, Jacob W. 5
EHRLICHMAN, Ben B. 5
EHRMAN, Frederick L. 6
EHRMAN, Mary H
Bartholomew
EHRMAN, Sidney M(yer) 5
EHRMANN, Herbert 6
Brutus
EHRMANN, Max 5
EICHBERG, Julius H
EICHELBERGER, Robert 4
Lawrence
EICHELBERGER, William 5
Snyder
EICHELBRENNER, Ernest 6
A.
EICHENAUER, Charles 3
Frederick
EICHENLAUB, Frank 6
Joseph
EICHER, Edward Clayton 2
EICHER, Henry Martin 3
EICHHEIM, Henry 2
EICHHOLTZ, Jacob H
EICHHORN, William A. 3
EICKEMEYER, Rudolf H
EICKEMEYER, Rudolf 1
EIDEM, Olaf 5
EIDLITZ, Charles Leo 1
EIDLITZ, Otto Marc 1
EIDMANN, Frank Lewis 1
EIELSEN, Elling H
EIESLAND, John (Arndt) 5
EIFERT, Virginia Snider 4
EIGENMANN, Carl H. 1
EIKENBARY, Charles 1
Franklin
EIKENBERRY, Dan 4
Harrison
EIKENBERRY, William 3
Lewis
EILENBERGER, Clinton B. 1
EILERS, Anton 1
EILERS, Karl 1
EILERT, Ernest Frederick 4
EILSHEMIUS, Louis 1
Michel
EILSHEMIUS, Louis 2
Michel
EIMBECK, William 4
EINAUDI, Luigi 4
EINHORN, David H
EINHORN, Max H
EINSIDEL, D. H
EINSTEIN, Albert 3
EINSTEIN, Alfred 3
EINSTEIN, Lewis 3
EINUM, Lucille Grace 6
Johnson
EIS, Frederick 4
EISELEN, Frederick Carl 1
EISEMAN, Frederick 6
Benjamin
EISEN, Gustavus A. 1
EISENBERG, David Berton 6
EISENBERG, Irwin 5
Weinman
EISENBERG, Maurice 5
EISENDRATH, Daniel 1
Nathan
EISENDRATH, Maurice 6
Nathan
EISENHARDT, Raymond 4
EISENHARDT, Raymond 5
F.
EISENHART, Charles 4
Marion
EISENHART, Luther 4
Pfahler
EISENHART, Martin 6
Herbert
EISENHOWER, Arthur B. 3
EISENHOWER, Dwight 5
David
EISENHOWER, Edgar 5
Nuton
EISENMAN, William Hunt 3
EISENSCHIML, Otto 4
EISFELD, Theodor H
EISNER, J. Lester 3
EISNER, Mark 3
EISNER, Monroe 6
EITEL, George Gotthilf 1
EKBLAW, Walter Elmer 2
EKBLOM, John Olof 1
EKEBERG, Lars Birger 6
EKELEY, John Bernard 1
EKENGREN, Wilhelm 1
August Ferdinand
EKERN, Herman Lewis 3
EKIN, John Jamison 6

EKINS, H. R. 4
EKLUND, Fred Nils 3
EKSERGIAN, Rupen 4
EKWALL, William 3
Alexander
EL AZHARI, Ismail 5
ELA, David Hough 4
ELA, Jacob Hart H
ELA, John Whittier 1
ELAM, Emma Lee 1
ELAM, John Babb 1
ELAM, Joseph Barton H
ELAN, Meir 5
ELANDER, Albin Eskel 4
ELBERT, John Aloysius 4
ELBERT, Samuel H
ELDEN, John Aten 1
ELDER, Alfonso 6
ELDER, Bowman 1
ELDER, Cyrus 1
ELDER, Frank Ray 4
ELDER, George 1
ELDER, John Adams H
ELDER, Joseph Freeman 1
ELDER, Orr Jay 1
ELDER, Paul 2
ELDER, Robert Henry 5
ELDER, Samuel James 1
ELDER, Susan Blanchard 4
ELDER, William 1
ELDER, William Henry 1
ELDER, William Line 1
ELDERKIN, George Wicker 4
ELDERKIN, John 4
ELDERKIN, Karl Osler 4
ELDERKIN, Noble Strong 4
ELDRED, Byron E. 3
ELDRED, Lewis 4
ELDREDGE, Arch Bishop 1
ELDREDGE, Charles H
Augustus
ELDREDGE, Charles 1
Henry
ELDREDGE, Joseph U. Jr. 1
ELDREDGE, Nathaniel H
Buel
ELDREDGE, Zoeth Skinner 1
ELDRERGE, Elliott Minton 3
ELDRIDGE, Edward Henry 5
ELDRIDGE, Francis 2
Howard
ELDRIDGE, Frank Harold 1
ELDRIDGE, Frederick L. 4
ELDRIDGE, Frederick 1
William
ELDRIDGE, George 1
Homans
ELDRIDGE, Maurice Owen 5
ELDRIDGE, Muriel Tilden 6
(Mrs. Richard Burdick
Eldridge)
ELDRIDGE, Seba 3
ELDRIDGE, Shalor H
Winchell
ELDRIDGE, William 3
Angevine
ELGHAMMER, H. William 5
ELIAS, Albert Barnes 1
ELIAS, Harold Lee 3
ELIASBERG, Wladimir G. 5
ELIASON, James Bayard 4
ELIOT, Amory 3
ELIOT, Charles 1
ELIOT, Charles William 1
ELIOT, Christopher Rhodes 2
ELIOT, Douglas Fitch 5
Guilford
ELIOT, Edward Cranch 1
ELIOT, Frederick May 1
ELIOT, George Fielding 5
ELIOT, Jared 1
ELIOT, John H
ELIOT, Samuel H
ELIOT, Samuel Atkins 1
ELIOT, Thomas Dawes 1
ELIOT, Thomas Lamb H
ELIOT, Thomas Stearns 4
ELIOT, Walter Graeme 1
ELIOT, William Greenleaf H
ELIOT, William Greenleaf 3
Jr.
ELIOT, Van Courtlandt 5
ELISOFON, Eliot 5
ELIZALDE, Rafael Hector 5
EL-KHOURY, Bechara 4
ELKIN, Daniel Collier 3
ELKIN, John Pratt 1
ELKIN, William Lewis 1
ELKIN, William Simpson 1
ELKINS, Davis 3
ELKINS, George W. 1
ELKINS, James Anderson 5
ELKINS, Stephen Benton 1
ELKINS, William Lukens 1
ELKINS, William McIntire 2
ELKUS, Abram I. 2

ELKUS, Charles de Young 4
ELLABARGER, Daniel 3
Rudolph
ELLARD, Roscoe Brabazon 4
ELLEFSON, Bennett 5
Stanley
ELLEGOOD, Robert 1
Griffith
ELLENDER, Allen Joseph 5
ELLENDER, Raphael 5
Theodore
ELLENSTEIN, Meyer C. 4
ELLENWOOD, Frank 2
Oakes
ELLENWOOD, Fred Alden 2
ELLER, Adolphus Hill 2
ELLERBE, Alma Martin 5
ELLERBE, James Edwin 4
ELLERBE, William 1
Haselden
ELLERHUSEN, Florence 3
Cooney
ELLERHUSEN, Ulrich 3
Henry
ELLERMAN, Ferdinand 1
ELLERY, Christopher H
ELLERY, Edward 5
ELLERY, Eloise 5
ELLERY, Frank 5
ELLERY, William H
ELLET, Charles H
ELLET, Elizabeth Fries H
Lummis
ELLET, Henry Thomas H
ELLETT, Edward Coleman 2
ELLETT, Thomas Harlan 5
ELLETT, Walter Beal 2
ELLICK, Alfred George 2
ELLICKSON, Raymond 6
Thorwald
ELLICOTT, Andrew H
ELLICOTT, Benjamin H
ELLICOTT, Eugene 4
ELLICOTT, John Morris 3
ELLICOTT, Joseph H
ELLIFF, Edgar Alonzo 5
ELLIFF, Joseph Doliver 5
ELLIMAN, Douglas Ludlow 5
ELLIMAN, Lawrence 3
Bogert
ELLING, Christian 6
ELLING, Henry 1
ELLINGER, Moritz 4
ELLINGHAM, Lewis 1
Glendale
ELLINGSON, Carl Herman 3
ELLINGTON, Buford 5
ELLINGTON, Edward 6
Kennedy (Duke)
ELLINGTON, Jesse 5
Thompson
ELLINGWOOD, Albert 1
Russell
ELLINGWOOD, Finley 1
ELLINWOOD, Everett E. 2
ELLINWOOD, Frank Field 1
ELLINWOOD, Ralph 1
Everett
ELLINWOOD, Truman 1
Jeremiah
ELLIOT, Charles H
ELLIOT, Daniel Giraud H
ELLIOT, George Thomson 1
ELLIOT, Henry Rutherford 1
ELLIOT, James H
ELLIOT, John Wheelock 1
ELLIOT, Jonathan H
ELLIOTT, A. Marshall 1
ELLIOTT, Alfred J. 5
ELLIOTT, Arthur Richard 4
ELLIOTT, Benjamin 1
ELLIOTT, Byron Kosciusko 1
ELLIOTT, Charles Addison 1
ELLIOTT, Charles Burke 1
ELLIOTT, Charles Gleason 1
ELLIOTT, Charles Herbert 6
ELLIOTT, Charles Loring 1
ELLIOTT, Claude 5
ELLIOTT, Curtis Miller 5
ELLIOTT, Daniel Stanley 4
ELLIOTT, Edward 2
ELLIOTT, Edward Charles 4
ELLIOTT, Edward Loomis 1
ELLIOTT, Ernest Eugene 1
ELLIOTT, Francis Perry 1
ELLIOTT, Frank Rumsey 4
ELLIOTT, George 1
ELLIOTT, George Blow 2
ELLIOTT, George Frank 1
ELLIOTT, George Frederick 4
ELLIOTT, Gertrude 3
ELLIOTT, Harold Hirsch 4
ELLIOTT, Harriet Wiseman 2
ELLIOTT, Harrison Sacket 5
ELLIOTT, Henry Wood 4
ELLIOTT, Homer 3

ELLIOTT, Howard 1
ELLIOTT, Huger 2
ELLIOTT, J. M. 2
ELLIOTT, Jackson S. 2
ELLIOTT, James H
ELLIOTT, James Douglas 1
ELLIOTT, James Lewis 1
ELLIOTT, James Robert 4
ELLIOTT, James Thomas 1
ELLIOTT, Jesse Duncan H
ELLIOTT, John H
ELLIOTT, John 1
ELLIOTT, John Asbury 1
ELLIOTT, John B. 4
ELLIOTT, John Barnwell 5
ELLIOTT, John Henry * 1
ELLIOTT, John Lovejoy 2
ELLIOTT, John M. 4
ELLIOTT, John Mackay 1
ELLIOTT, John Milton 1
ELLIOTT, John Stuart 4
ELLIOTT, John Wesley 1
ELLIOTT, John Wesley 5
ELLIOTT, Joseph 4
Alexander
ELLIOTT, Lewis Grimes 2
ELLIOTT, Martin Kelso 2
ELLIOTT, Maud Howe 2
ELLIOTT, Maxine 1
ELLIOTT, Middleton Stuart 3
ELLIOTT, Milton 1
Courtright
ELLIOTT, Oliver Morton 1
ELLIOTT, Orrin Leslie 1
ELLIOTT, Philip Lovin 4
ELLIOTT, Phillips Packer 4
ELLIOTT, Richard 5
Hammond
ELLIOTT, Richard Nash 2
ELLIOTT, Robert Brown H
ELLIOTT, Robert Irving 2
ELLIOTT, Robert Michael 4
ELLIOTT, Roy Gordon 3
ELLIOTT, Sarah Barnwell 1
ELLIOTT, Shelden Douglass 5
ELLIOTT, Simon Bolivar 4
ELLIOTT, Stephen 1
ELLIOTT, Stuart Rhett 5
ELLIOTT, Thompson Coit 2
ELLIOTT, Walter 1
ELLIOTT, Washington H
Lafayette
ELLIOTT, William H
ELLIOTT, William 1
ELLIOTT, William 2
ELLIOTT, William Arthur 4
ELLIOTT, William Henry 1
ELLIOTT, William John 6
ELLIOTT, William Sanders 3
ELLIOTT, William Swan 1
ELLIS, Alexander Caswell 1
ELLIS, Alston 1
ELLIS, Anderson Nelson 1
ELLIS, Anna M. B. 1
ELLIS, Arthur McDonald 1
ELLIS, Caleb H
ELLIS, Calvin H
ELLIS, Carleton 1
ELLIS, Carlyle 6
ELLIS, Challen Blackburn 2
ELLIS, Charles Alton 2
ELLIS, Charles Calvert 3
ELLIS, Charles S. 4
ELLIS, Chesselden 1
ELLIS, Crawford Hatcher 4
ELLIS, David Abram 1
ELLIS, Don Carlos 3
ELLIS, Edgar Clarence 2
ELLIS, Edward Sylvester 1
ELLIS, Edwin Erastus 1
ELLIS, Ezekiel John H
ELLIS, Frank Burton 5
ELLIS, G. Corson 4
ELL!S, George Adams 3
ELLIS, George David 4
ELLIS, George Edward H
ELLIS, George Edwin 4
ELLIS, George Price Sr. 1
ELLIS, George Washington 1
ELLIS, George William 4
ELLIS, Gordon 6
ELLIS, Griffith Ogden 4
ELLIS, H. Bert 1
ELLIS, Harold Milton 3
ELLIS, Harvey 1
ELLIS, Hayne 5
ELLIS, Henry H
ELLIS, Horace 1
ELLIS, Howard 1
ELLIS, Howard 4
ELLIS, Ira Howell 4
ELLIS, J. Breckenridge 3
ELLIS, James 6
ELLIS, James Tandy 4
ELLIS, Job Bicknell 1
ELLIS, John Dayhuff 3

ELLIS, John Henry 6
ELLIS, John Washington H
ELLIS, John Washington 4
ELLIS, John William 1
ELLIS, John Willis H
ELLIS, Katharine Ruth 6
ELLIS, Leighton Arthur 4
ELLIS, Mary 1
ELLIS, Max Mapes 3
ELLIS, Milton Andrew 4
ELLIS, Overton Gentry 1
ELLIS, Perry Canby 1
ELLIS, Powhatan H
ELLIS, Ralph 3
ELLIS, Robert Walpole 1
ELLIS, Rudolph 1
ELLIS, Samuel Mervyl 2
ELLIS, Seth H. 1
ELLIS, Tharon J. 4
ELLIS, Theodore Thaddeus 4
Warner
ELLIS, Thomas Cargill 4
ELLIS, Thomas David 3
ELLIS, W. R. 3
ELLIS, Wade H. 2
ELLIS, Willard Drake 2
ELLIS, William Cox H
ELLIS, William D. 4
ELLIS, William Hull 2
ELLIS, William John 2
ELLIS, William Russell 1
ELLIS, William Thomas 3
ELLISON, Andrew H
ELLISON, Everett Monroe 1
ELLISON, George Robb 3
ELLISON, Joseph Roy 5
ELLISON, Robert S(purrier) 5
ELLISON, Thomas Emmet 1
ELLISON, William Bruce 1
ELLISTON, George 2
ELLISTON, Grace 3
ELLISTON, Herbert 3
Berridge
ELLITHORP, John Stafford 4
Jr.
ELLMAKER, Amos H
ELLMAKER, Lee 3
ELLS, Arthur Fairbanks H
ELLSBERRY, William H
Wallace
ELLSLER, Effie 1
ELLSLER, Effie 2
ELLSWORTH, Albert 3
LeRoy
ELLSWORTH, Elmer H
Ephriam
ELLSWORTH, Franklin 1
Fowler
ELLSWORTH, Fred 3
Winthrop
ELLSWORTH, Henry 1
Leavitt
ELLSWORTH, James H
Drummond
ELLSWORTH, James 1
William
ELLSWORTH, John Jay 1
ELLSWORTH, John Orval 6
ELLSWORTH, Lincoln 3
ELLSWORTH, Oliver H
ELLSWORTH, Oliver B. 5
ELLSWORTH, Samuel H
Stewart
ELLSWORTH, Sidney 4
Ernest
ELLSWORTH, William 1
Webster
ELLSWORTH, William H
Wolcott
ELLWANGER, George 1
Herman
ELLWANGER, William De 1
Lancey
ELLWOOD, Charles Abram 4
ELLWOOD, Isaac Leonard 4
ELLWOOD, John Kelley 4
ELLWOOD, Reuben H
ELLYSON, J. Taylor 1
ELMAN, Mischa 4
ELMAN, Robert 6
ELMEN, Gustaf Waldemar 3
ELMENDORF, Dwight 1
Lathrop
ELMENDORF, Francis 5
Littleton
ELMENDORF, Henry 1
Livingston
ELMENDORF, Joachim 1
ELMENDORF, John E. Jr. 4
ELMENDORF, Lucas 4
Conrad
ELMENDORF, Theresa 1
Hubbell
ELMER, Ebenezer H
ELMER, Henry Whiteley 1
ELMER, Herbert Charles 4

ELMER, Jonathan H
ELMER, Lucius Quintius Cincinnatus H
ELMER, S. Lewis 4
ELMER, S(amuel) Lewis 5
ELMER, William 1
ELMER, William 3
ELMER, William Price 3
ELMHIRST, Leonard Knight 6
ELMORE, Franklin Harper H
ELMORE, George Sutherland 3
ELMORE, Jefferson 1
ELMORE, Samuel Edward 1
ELMORE, Wilber Theodore 1
ELMQUIST, Axel Louis 2
ELMSLIE, George Grant 3
ELOESSER, Leo 6
ELOFSON, Carl L. 3
ELROD, Morton John 4
ELROD, Ralph 3
ELROD, Samuel Harrison 1
ELSBERG, Charles Albert 2
ELSBERG, Louis H
ELSENBAST, Arthur S. 6
ELSER, Frank B. 1
ELSER, Maximilian Jr. 4
ELSER, William James 5
ELSEY, Charles 6
ELSNER, Henry Leopold 1
ELSOM, James Claude 4
ELSON, Alfred Walter 2
ELSON, Arthur 1
ELSON, Henry William 3
ELSON, Louis Charles 1
ELSON, William Harris 1
ELSSFELDT, Otto Hermann Wilheim Leonhard 6
ELSTAD, Rudolph T. 3
ELSTON, Dorothy Andrews (Mrs. Walter L. Kabis) 5
ELSTON, Isaac Compton 1
ELSTON, Isaac Compton Jr. 4
ELSTON, John Arthur 1
ELSWORTH, Edward 1
ELTHON, Leo 4
ELTING, Arthur Wells 2
ELTING, Howard 3
ELTING, Victor 3
ELTING, Winston 5
ELTINGE, Julian 1
ELTINGE, LeRoy 1
ELTON, Frederic Garfield 6
ELTON, J. O. 3
ELTON, James Samuel 1
ELTON, John Prince 2
ELTZHOLTZ, Carl Frederick 1
ELVEHJEM, Conrad Arnold 4
ELVERSON, James 1
ELVEY, Christian Thomas 5
ELVINS, Politte 2
ELWELL, Charles Clement 1
ELWELL, Clarence Edward 6
ELWELL, Francis Edwin 1
ELWELL, Herbert 6
ELWELL, John Johnson H
ELWELL, Levi Henry 1
ELWELL, Richard E. 6
ELWOOD, Everett Sprague 6
ELWOOD, John Worden 4
ELWOOD, Philip Homer Jr. 4
ELWOOD, Robert Arthur 3
ELWYN, Alfred Langdon H
ELY, Albert Heman 1
ELY, Alfred H
ELY, Charles Russell 1
ELY, Charles Wright 1
ELY, Elizabeth L. 5
ELY, Frederick David 1
ELY, Grosvenor 4
ELY, Hanson Edward 3
ELY, John H
ELY, John Hugh 1
ELY, John Slade 1
ELY, Joseph Buell 3
ELY, Lafayette G. 4
ELY, Leonard Wheeler 4
ELY, Richard R(oyal) 5
ELY, Richard Theodore 2
ELY, Robert Erskine 2
ELY, Roy J. W. 4
ELY, Sims 3
ELY, Smith 1
ELY, Sterling 4
ELY, Sumner Boyer 5
ELY, Theodore Newel 1
ELY, Thomas Southgate 6
ELY, Wayne 3
ELY, William H
ELY, Wilson C. 3
ELZAS, Barnett Abraham 1
ELZEY, Arnold H
ELZNER, Alfred Oscar 1
EMANUEL, Victor 4
EMBER, Aaron 1
EMBLETON, Harry 3
EMBODY, George Charles 1
EMBREE, Charles Fleming 1
EMBREE, Edwin Rogers 2
EMBREE, Elihu H
EMBREE, Elisha H
EMBRIE, Jonas Reece H
EMBRY, John 4
EMBURY, Aymar II 4
EMBURY, David A. 4
EMBURY, Philip H
EMCH, Arnold 5
EMERICH, Ira 6
EMERICH, Martin 4
EMERICK, Charles Franklin 1
EMERICK, Edson James 3
EMERMAN, David 6
EMERSON, Benjamin Kendall 1
EMERSON, Charles Franklin 1
EMERSON, Charles Phillips 1
EMERSON, Charles Wesley 1
EMERSON, Cherry Logan 4
EMERSON, Chester Burge 6
EMERSON, Edward Randolph 1
EMERSON, Edward Waldo 1
EMERSON, Edwin 4
EMERSON, Edwin Jr. 5
EMERSON, Ellen Russell 1
EMERSON, Evalyn (stage name Evalyn Earle) 5
EMERSON, Frank Collins 1
EMERSON, Frank Nelson 5
EMERSON, George Barrell H
EMERSON, George H. 5
EMERSON, Gouverneur H
EMERSON, Guy 5
EMERSON, Harold Logan 4
EMERSON, Harrington 1
EMERSON, Haven 3
EMERSON, Henry Pendexter 1
EMERSON, Jabez Oscar 5
EMERSON, James Ezekiel 1
EMERSON, Jay Noble 2
EMERSON, John 3
EMERSON, Joseph H
EMERSON, Justin Edwards 4
EMERSON, Kendall 5
EMERSON, Linn 5
EMERSON, Lousis W. 4
EMERSON, Luther Orlando 1
EMERSON, Merton Leslie 2
EMERSON, Nathaniel Bright 1
EMERSON, Nathaniel Waldo 1
EMERSON, Oliver Farrar 1
EMERSON, Paul 1
EMERSON, Philip 4
EMERSON, Ralph H
EMERSON, Ralph 1
EMERSON, Ralph Waldo H
EMERSON, Robert 3
EMERSON, Robert Alton 4
EMERSON, Robert Stephen 1
EMERSON, Rollins Adams 2
EMERSON, Sam W. 6
EMERSON, Samuel Franklin 1
EMERSON, Summer Brooks 5
EMERSON, Susan Mabel 4
EMERSON, Willard I. 4
EMERSON, William H
EMERSON, William 3
EMERSON, Willis George 1
EMERTON, Ephraim 1
EMERTON, James H. 1
EMERY, Albert Hamilton 1
EMERY, Alden H(ayes) 6
EMERY, Ambrose R. 2
EMERY, Charles Edward H
EMERY, DeWitt McKinley 3
EMERY, Edward Kellogg 1
EMERY, Fred Azro 4
EMERY, Fred Parker 1
EMERY, Grenville C. 1
EMERY, Henry Crosby 1
EMERY, Ina Capitola 1
EMERY, James Augustan 3
EMERY, John Garfield 6
EMERY, John Runkle 1
EMERY, Lewis Jr. 1
EMERY, Lucilius Alonzo 1
EMERY, Matthew Gault 1
EMERY, Natt Morrill 1
EMERY, Richard Runkel 4
EMERY, Roe 3
EMERY, Sarah Anna 1
EMERY, Stephen Albert H
EMERY, Susan L. 1
EMERY, William Marshall * 4
EMERY, William Morrell 4
EMERY, William Orrin 3
EMERY, Z. Taylor 1
EMHARDT, William Chauncey 3
EMIG, Arthur S. 3
EMIG, Elmer Jacob 3
EMIL, Allan D. 6
EMISON, John C. 4
EMISON, John C. 5
EMKEN, Cecil Wheeler 5
EMLAW, Harlan Stigand 3
EMMERICH, F.J. 5
EMMERICH, Herbert 5
EMMERSON, Henry Read 3
EMMERSON, Louis Lincoln 1
EMMERT, John Harley 2
EMMET, Grenville Temple 1
EMMET, John Patten H
EMMET, Lydia Field 3
EMMET, Thomas Addis H
EMMET, Thomas Addis 1
EMMET, William LeRoy 1
EMMET, William Temple 1
EMMETT, Daniel Decatur H
EMMETT, Daniel Decatur 2
EMMONS, Arthur Brewster III 4
EMMONS, Charles Demoss 1
EMMONS, Delos Carleton 4
EMMONS, Ebenezer H
EMMONS, George Foster H
EMMONS, George Thorton 2
EMMONS, Grover Carlton 2
EMMONS, Harold Hunter 4
EMMONS, Lloyd C. 3
EMMONS, Nathanael H
EMMONS, Samuel Franklin 1
EMMONS, William Harvey 2
EMORY, Frederic 1
EMORY, Frederick Lincoln 1
EMORY, John H
EMORY, Samuel T. 3
EMORY, William Hemsley H
EMORY, William Hermsley 1
EMOTT, James * H
EMPEY, Arthur Guy 4
EMPRINGHAM, James 5
EMRICH, Frederick Ernest 1
EMRICH, Jeannette Wallace 2
EMSWELLER, Samuel Leonar 5
ENANDER, John Alfred 1
ENCKELL, Carl J. A. 3
ENDALKACHEW, Makonnen 6
ENDALKATCHOU, Bitwoded Makonnen 4
ENDECOTT, John H
ENDELMAN, Julio 2
ENDERS, George Christian 4
ENDERS, Howard Edwin 5
ENDERS, John Ostrom 3
ENDICOTT, Charles Moses H
ENDICOTT, George H
ENDICOTT, H. Wendell 3
ENDICOTT, Henry 1
ENDICOTT, Mordecal Thomas 1
ENDICOTT, William H
ENDICOTT, William 1
ENDICOTT, William Crowninshield * 1
ENDLICH, Gustav Adolf 1
ENDORE, (Samuel) Guy 5
ENELOW, Heman Gerson 1
ENESCO, Georges 3
ENFIELD, Gertrude Dixon (Mrs. John Enfield) 5
ENGBERG, Carl Christian 1
ENGEL, Albert Joseph 3
ENGEL, Carl 2
ENGEL, Carl Henry 5
ENGEL, Edward J. 2
ENGEL, K. August 4
ENGEL, Katharine Asher 3
ENGEL, Michael Martin 5
ENGEL, Peter 1
ENGELHARDT, Francis Ernest 4
ENGELHARDT, Fred 2
ENGELHARDT, Nickolaus Louis 3
ENGELHARDT, William R. 6
ENGELHARDT, Zephyrin 1
ENGELKEMEIR, Donald William 5
ENGELMANN, George H
ENGELMANN, George Julius 1
ENGELMORE, Irwin B. 6
ENGEN, Hans Kristian 4
ENGER, Melvin Lorenius 3
ENGERRAND, George C. 4
ENGERUD, Edward 1
ENGLAND, Edward Theodore 5
ENGLAND, George Allan 1
ENGLAND, John H
ENGLAND, William Henry 5
ENGLAR, D. Roger 3
ENGLE, Clair 4
ENGLE, Earl T. 3
ENGLE, Jesse A. 4
ENGLE, John Summerfield 5
ENGLE, Wilbur Dwight 5
ENGLEBRIGHT, Harry Lane 2
ENGLEBRIGHT, William F. 4
ENGLEHARD, Charles William 5
ENGLEHART, Robert William 4
ENGLEMAN, James Ozro 2
ENGLER, Edmund Arthur 1
ENGLIS, Charles Mortimer 1
ENGLIS, John H
ENGLISH, Charles Henry 2
ENGLISH, Conover 4
ENGLISH, David Combs 1
ENGLISH, Earle Walter 4
ENGLISH, Elbert Hartwell H
ENGLISH, Frank A. 3
ENGLISH, Frank Clare 5
ENGLISH, George Bethune H
ENGLISH, George Letchworth 2
ENGLISH, George Washington 4
ENGLISH, Harry David Williams 1
ENGLISH, Horace Bidwell 4
ENGLISH, James Edward H
ENGLISH, John Francis 5
ENGLISH, John Mahan 1
ENGLISH, Merle Neville 2
ENGLISH, Robert Byrns 3
ENGLISH, Robert Henry 2
ENGLISH, Sara John (Mrs. Henry W. English) 5
ENGLISH, Thomas Dunn 1
ENGLISH, Virgil P. 4
ENGLISH, William Eastin 1
ENGLISH, William Hayden H
ENGMAN, Martin Feeney 3
ENGSTROM, Adolph (Hiaimer) 6
ENGSTROM, Howard Theodore 4
ENGSTROM, Sigfrid Emanuel 3
ENGSTROM, William Weborg 6
ENLOE, Benjamin Augustine 1
ENLOW, Robert Cooke 4
ENMAN, Horace Luttrell 4
ENNEKING, John Joseph 1
ENNIS, Alfred 4
ENNIS, George Pearse 1
ENNIS, H. Robert 2
ENNIS, Joseph 3
ENNIS, Luna May 1
ENNIS, Thomas Leland 3
ENNIS, William Duane 2
ENO, William Phelps 2
ENOCHS, Herbert Alexander 5
ENOCHS, William Henry H
ENOS, George M. 3
ENRIETTO, John 6
ENRIGHT, Earl F. 4
ENRIGHT, Elizabeth 5
ENRIGHT, Richard Edward 3
ENRIGHT, Walter J(oseph) 5
ENSEY, Lot 5
ENSIGN, Forest Chester 5
ENSIGN, Josiah Davis 1
ENSIGN, Mary Jane 6
ENSIGN, Orville Hiram 1
ENSIGN, Willis Lee 6
ENSLEN, Eugene F. 2
ENSLEY, Enoch H
ENSLOW, Linn Harrison 3
ENSOR, James 4
ENSOR, Lowell Skinner 6
ENSTROM, William N. 3
ENT, Uzal Girard 2
ENTIZMINGER, Louis 6
ENTRATTER, Jack 5
ENTRIKIN, John Bennett 4
ENTWISTLE, James 1
ENTZ, John A. 6
ENWALL, Hasse Octavius 2
EPES, Louis Spencer 1
EPES, Sydney P. 1
EPLER, Percy H(arold) 5
EPLEY, Lloyd L. 5
EPP, George Edward 5
EPPERLY, James Melvin 6
EPPES, John Wayles H
EPPLEY, Eugene C. 3
EPSTEIN, Abraham 2
EPSTEIN, Henry 4
EPSTEIN, Jacob 2
EPSTEIN, Jacob 3
EPSTEIN, Joseph Hugo 4
EPSTEIN, Louis M. 2
EPSTEIN, Max 3
EPSTEIN, Paul Sophus 4
EPSTEIN, Ralph C. 3
EPSTEIN, Stephan 6
EQUEN, Murdock 4
ERB, Carl Lee Jr. 5
ERB, Donald Milton 2
ERB, Frank Otis 3
ERB, John Lawrence 2
ERB, John Warren 2
ERB, Newman 1
ERBEN, Henry Vander Bogert 3
ERBES, Philip Henry 5
ERDLAND, Bernard August 5
ERDMAN, Charles Rosenbury 4
ERDMAN, Frederick Seward 5
ERDMAN, Helga Mae 6
ERDMAN, Jacob H
ERDMAN, John Frederic 3
ERDMANN, Charles Albert 4
ERDMANN, William Lawrence 4
ERHARDT, Joel Benedict 5
ERHARDT, John George 3
ERIC THE RED H
ERICHSEN, Hugo 2
ERICKSON, Alfred William 1
ERICKSON, Arvel Benjamin 6
ERICKSON, Charles Watt 6
ERICKSON, Clifford E. 4
ERICKSON, Cyrus 3
ERICKSON, E(dwin) R. 6
ERICKSON, Frank Morton 3
ERICKSON, J(ulius) L(yman) E(dward) 5
ERICKSON, John E. 2
ERICKSON, Knut Eric 4
ERICKSON, Peter W. 6
ERICKSON, Reinhart H
ERICSON, Charles John Alfred 1
ERICSON, John Ernst 1
ERICSSON, Frans August 3
ERICSSON, John H
ERICSSON, Leif H
ERIKSON, Carl Anthony 3
ERIKSON, David Junkin 4
ERIKSON, Henry Anton 3
ERIKSSON, Erik McKinley 1
ERIKSSON, Herman 2
ERK, Edmund Frederick 3
ERLANGER, Abraham Lincoln 1
ERLANGER, Joseph 4
ERLANGER, Milton S. 5
ERLANGER, Mitchell Louis 1
ERMATINGER, Francis H
ERMENTROUT, Daniel 1
ERMINGER, Howell B. Jr. 3
ERN, Henri 4
ERNEST, Albert 4
ERNEST, John Henry 6
ERNSBERGER, Millard Clayton 1
ERNST, Alwin Charles 2
ERNST, August Frederic 3
ERNST, Bernard Morris Lee 1
ERNST, Carl Clark 4
ERNST, Carl Wilhelm 4
ERNST, Clayton Holt 2
ERNST, Edward Cranch 2
ERNST, Edwin Charles 5
ERNST, Fritz B. 3
ERNST, George Alexander Otis 1
ERNST, Harold Clarence 1
ERNST, Henry 1
ERNST, Oswald Herbert 1
ERNST, Richard Pretlow 1
ERNSTENE, Arthur Carlton 5
ERNY, Charles G. 4
ERPF, Armand Grover 5
ERRETT, Edwin Reader 2
ERRETT, Isaac H
ERRETT, Russell H
ERSKINE, Albert Russel 1
ERSKINE, Ebenezer 1

* Indicates More Than One Such Name Listed

ERSKINE, Emma Payne 1
ERSKINE, George Chester 6
ERSKINE, Graves Blanchard
ERSKINE, Howard Major 4
ERSKINE, John H
ERSKINE, John 3
ERSKINE, Robert H
ERTEGUN, Mehmet Munir 2
ERTZ, R. B. A. Edward 4
ERVIN, Charles Edwin 2
ERVIN, James H
ERVIN, James S. 4
ERVIN, Jee W. 2
ERVIN, Morris Donaldson
ERVIN, Paul Revere 6
ERVIN, Robert Tait 4
ERVINE, St. John Greer 5
ERVING, George William H
ERVING, Henry Wood 4
ERVING, William Gage 1
ERWAY, Richard Eugene 5
ERWIN, Claude Mayo 5
ERWIN, Clyde Atkinson 3
ERWIN, George Jr. JR. 2
ERWIN, Guy Burton 1
ERWIN, Henry Parsons 3
ERWIN, Howell Cobb 5
ERWIN, James Brailsford 1
ERWIN, Marion Corbett 3
ERWIN, Richard Kenney 1
ERWIN, Robert Gallaudet 1
ESAREY, Logan 5
ESBERG, Milton Herman 1
ESBJORN, Lars Paul H
ESCALANTE, Diogenes 4
ESCALANTE, Silvestre Velez de H
ESCH, John Jacob 1
ESCHER, Franklin 3
ESCHOLIER, Raymond 6
ESCHWEILER, Franz Chadbourne 1
ESCOBAR, Adrian C. 3
ESCOBOSA, Hector 4
ESENWEIN, Joseph Berg 2
ESHBACH, Ovid Wallace 3
ESHELMAN, Elmer T. 6
ESHELMAN, Walter Witmer 5
ESHKOL, (Shkolnik) Levi 5
ESHLEMAN, Charles L(everich) 6
ESHLEMAN, Fred Koontz 4
ESHLEMAN, John Morton 2
ESHNER, Augustus Adolph 2
ESKEW, Samuel W(illiams) 1
ESKILDSEN, Clarence Raymond 4
ESKOLA, Pentti Eelis 4
ESKRIDGE, J. T. 1
ESKRIDGE, James Burnette 3
ESLICK, Edward Everett 1
ESLING, Charles Henry Augustine
ESMAY, Rhodolph Leslie 4
ESPEJO, Antonio de H
ESPELAGE, Bernard Theodore 6
ESPENSHADE, Abraham Howry 3
ESPIL, Felipe A. 5
ESPINA, Concha 3
ESPINOSA, Aurelio Macedonio 3
ESPINOSA Y SAN MARTIN, Antonio 5
ESPINOSA DE LOS MONTEROS, Antonio 3
ESPOSITO, Vincent Joseph 4
ESPOSITO, Vincent Joseph 5
ESPY, James Pollard H
ESQUIROL, John Henry 5
ESS, Henry N. 4
ESSARY, Jesse Frederick 2
ESSELEN, Gustavus John 3
ESSER, Sigurd Emanuel 3
ESSERY, Carl Vanstone 3
ESSEX, William Leopold 3
ESSIG, Benjamin C(lark) 5
ESSIG, Edward Oliver 4
ESSINGTON, Thurlow Gault
ESTABROOK, Arthur F. 1
ESTABROOK, Experience H
ESTABROOK, Fred Watson 1
ESTABROOK, Henry Dodge
ESTABROOK, John D. 5
ESTABROOK, Joseph 6
ESTABROOK, Leon Moyer 1
ESTABROOK, Merrick Gay 3 Jr.
ESTABROOK, Robert Francis 6

ESTABROOKS, George Hoben 6
ESTAING, Charles Hector H
ESTAUGH, Elizabeth Haddon H
ESTBERG, Edward Robert 2
ESTEE, James Borden 1
ESTEE, Morris M. 1
ESTENSON, Lyle Osbern 5
ESTEP, Preston 5
ESTERBROOK, Richard H
ESTERLINE, Blackburn 1
ESTERLY, Calvin Olin 1
ESTERLY, George H
ESTERLY, Henry Minor 1
ESTERQUEST, Ralph Theodore 5
ESTERS, Bernard E. 4
ESTES, Charles Thompson 4
ESTES, Dana 1
ESTES, David Foster 1
ESTES, George Henson 5
ESTES, Ludwell H. 4
ESTES, Ludwell Hunter 6
ESTES, Maurice James 6
ESTES, Webster Cummings 1
ESTES, William Lawrence 1
ESTES, William Lee 1
ESTEY, Alexander R. H
ESTEY, Jacob H
ESTEY, James Arthur 4
ESTEY, Stephen Sewall 1
ESTIGARRIBIA, Jose Felix 2
ESTIL, Benjamin 4
ESTILL, George Castleman 3
ESTILL, Harry Fishburne 2
ESTILL, John Holbrook 1
ESTOPINAL, Albert 1
ESTREM, Herbert William 6
ESTREM, Thomas Sabin 4
ESTY, Edward Tuckerman 2
ESTY, William 1
ESTY, William Cole 1
ESTY, William Cole III 3
ETCHEVERRY, Bernard Alfred 3
ETCHISON, Page McKendree 3
ETHEL, Agnes 4
ETHEREDGE, M(ahion) P(adgett) 5
ETHERIDGE, Emerson 1
ETHRIDGE, George H. 6
ETHRIDGE, Willaim Nathaniel Jr. 5
ETLER, Alvin Derald 6
ETLING, Carl D. 6
ETS-HOKIN, Louis 5
ETTER, William Kirby 2
ETTINGER, George Taylor 2
ETTINGER, Richard Prentice
ETTINGER, William L. 2
ETTWEIN, John H
ETZ, Roger Frederick 5
ETZELL, George Ferdinand 6
EUBANK, Earle Edward 2
EUBANK, Jessie Burrall 4
EUBANK, John Augustine 3
EUBANK, Victor 1
EUBANKS, Elinor Mae 6
EUBANKS, Sam B. 4
EULER, Ralph Stapleton 6
EULER, William D. 4
EULER, William Gilman Badger 3
EUMENES H
EUNSON, Robert Charles Romaine
EUSDEN, Ray Anderson 5
EUSTACE, Bartholomew Joseph
EUSTIS, Allan Chotard Jr. 6
EUSTIS, Arthur Galen 3
EUSTIS, Augustus Hemenway
EUSTIS, Frederic Augustus 5
EUSTIS, George * H
EUSTIS, Henry Lawrence H
EUSTIS, James 1
EUSTIS, James Biddle H
EUSTIS, John Edward 1
EUSTIS, Percy Sprague 4
EUSTIS, William 1
EUSTIS, William H. 4
EUWER, Anthony Henderson 5
EVALD, Emmy 2
EVANS, Alexander 1
EVANS, Alexander William 3
EVANS, Alice Catherine 4
EVANS, Allan 5
EVANS, Alvin 1
EVANS, Alvin Eleazer H
EVANS, Andrew Wallace 1
EVANS, Anthony Harrison 4

EVANS, Anthony Walton Whyte H
EVANS, Arthur Grant 1
EVANS, Arthur Maybury 4
EVANS, Arthur Thompson 2
EVANS, Aurelius Augustus 4
EVANS, Austin Patterson 4
EVANS, Beverly Daniel 1
EVANS, Britton Duroc 1
EVANS, Cadwallader Jr. 4
EVANS, Cecil Eugene 6
EVANS, Charles 4
EVANS, Charles 5
EVANS, Charles Napoleon 1
EVANS, Charles Robley 4
EVANS, Charles Rountree 1
EVANS, Clement Anselm 1
EVANS, Clinton Buswell 5
EVANS, Curtis Alban 2
EVANS, Dafydd Joshua 1
EVANS, Daniel 2
EVANS, Daniel Henry 4
EVANS, David Ellicott H
EVANS, David Reid H
EVANS, De Scott 4
EVANS, Donald 1
EVANS, Donald 3
EVANS, Dudley 4
EVANS, Earle Wood 1
EVANS, Edgar Hanks 4
EVANS, Edith Brazwell 4
EVANS, Edward 4
EVANS, Edward Andrew 1
EVANS, Edward Baker 4
EVANS, Edward Benjamin 5
EVANS, Edward Payson 4
EVANS, Edward Steptoe 2
EVANS, Elizabeth Edson 1
EVANS, Elizabeth Gardiner 4
EVANS, Elwyn 2
EVANS, Ernestine 4
EVANS, Evan Alfred 4
EVANS, Everett Idris 3
EVANS, Frank 4
EVANS, Frank Edgar 2
EVANS, Fred(eric) M(aurice)
EVANS, Frederic Dahl 3
EVANS, Frederick 4
EVANS, Frederick Noble 4
EVANS, Frederick Walter 1
EVANS, Frederick William H
EVANS, George 3
EVANS, George 4
EVANS, George Ballentine 1
EVANS, George E. 1
EVANS, George Edward 2
EVANS, George Henry 4
EVANS, George L. 6
EVANS, George Watkin 3
EVANS, Griffith Conrad 6
EVANS, H. Clay 1
EVANS, H(enry) David 5
EVANS, Harold Sulser 3
EVANS, Harry Carroll 4
EVANS, Harry G. 1
EVANS, Harry Marshall Erskine
EVANS, Henry 1
EVANS, Henry Clay 3
EVANS, Henry Ridgely 4
EVANS, Herbert Francis 4
EVANS, Herbert P. 3
EVANS, Hiram Kinsman 4
EVANS, Hiram Wesley 6
EVANS, Howard Rector 4
EVANS, Howell Gershom 4
EVANS, Hugh Ivan 4
EVANS, Ira Hobart 1
EVANS, Isaac Blair 1
EVANS, James 4
EVANS, Jervice Gaylord 1
EVANS, Jessie Benton 5
EVANS, John * H
EVANS, John 4
EVANS, John Brooke 3
EVANS, John C. 3
EVANS, John Fairhurst 3
EVANS, John Gary 2
EVANS, John Henry 2
EVANS, John Morgan 4
EVANS, John Morris 4
EVANS, John Norris 3
EVANS, John William 3
EVANS, Joseph E(arly) 5
EVANS, Joseph Spragg 2
EVANS, Joshua Jr. H
EVANS, Joshua Jr. 5
EVANS, Josiah James H
EVANS, Lawrence Boyd 1
EVANS, Lawton Bryan 4
EVANS, Lemuel Dale H
EVANS, Letitia Pate H
EVANS, Lewis Orvis 1
EVANS, Marcellus Hugh 3

EVANS, Marshall Blakemore 5
EVANS, Mary 4
EVANS, Milton G. 1
EVANS, Montgomery 4
EVANS, Nathan 1
EVANS, Nelson Wiley 1
EVANS, Newton Gurdon 2
EVANS, Oliver H
EVANS, Percy Henriques 5
EVANS, Peyton Randolph 5
EVANS, Ray O. 3
EVANS, Richard Bunton 4
EVANS, Richard Joseph 1
EVANS, Richard Louis 5
EVANS, Robert Emory 1
EVANS, Robert Kennon 1
EVANS, Robert T. 5
EVANS, Robley Dunglison 1
EVANS, Rudolph Martin 4
EVANS, Rudulph 3
EVANS, Silas 3
EVANS, Silliman H
EVANS, Silliman Jr. 4
EVANS, Thomas H
EVANS, Thomas 4
EVANS, Thomas 6
EVANS, Thomas Crain 4
EVANS, Titus Carr 4
EVANS, Walker 6
EVANS, Walter 1
EVANS, Walter Chew 1
EVANS, Walter Harrison 5
EVANS, Walter Howard 3
EVANS, Ward Vinton 3
EVANS, William 3
EVANS, William Augustus 3
EVANS, William D. 1
EVANS, William Dent Jr. 1
EVANS, William E. 3
EVANS, William Frank 1
EVANS, William Gray 1
EVANS, William John 4
EVANS, William Lloyd 3
EVANS, William Ney 6
EVANS, William Prentice 1
EVANS, Wilmot Roby 1
EVANS, Wilmoth Duane 6
EVARTS, Allen Wardner 1
EVARTS, Edward Mark 1
EVARTS, Hal G. 1
EVARTS, Maxwell 1
EVARTS, Richard Conover 5
EVARTS, William Maxwell H
EVATT, Herbert V. 4
EVATT, William Steinwedell 5
EVE, Duncan 1
EVE, Henry Prontaut 5
EVE, Joseph H
EVE, Paul Fitzsimons H
EVELAND, Samuel S. 1
EVELAND, William Perry 4
EVELEIGH, Nicholas H
EVELETH, True Ballentine 5
EVELYN, Judith 4
EVELYN, Sister Mary 3
EVENDEN, Edward Samuel 3
EVENS, Alfred 6
EVERARD, Lewis Charles 2
EVERENDON, Walter H
EVEREST, David Clark 3
EVEREST, Frank Fort 1
EVEREST, Harold Philip 4
EVERETT, Alexander Hill H
EVERETT, Arthur Greene 1
EVERETT, Charles Carroll 1
EVERETT, Charles Horatio 3
EVERETT, Edward H
EVERETT, Francis Dewey 6
EVERETT, George Abram 3
EVERETT, Harry Harding 4
EVERETT, Henry A. 1
EVERETT, Herbert Edward 1
EVERETT, Horace 1
EVERETT, Howard 4
EVERETT, Louellea Dorothea
EVERETT, Robert Ashton 5
EVERETT, Sidney Johnston 2
EVERETT, Walter Goodnow
EVERETT, William 1
EVERETT, William Henry 1
EVERETT, William Wade 4
EVERETT, Willis Mead 2
EVERGOOD, Philip (Howard Francis Dixon)
EVERHART, Benjamin Matlack 1
EVERHART, James Bowen H
EVERHART, Mahlon Thatcher
EVERHART, William H
EVERILL, Royal Burdette 5
EVERIT, Edward Hotchkiss 5

EVERITT, Charles Raymond 2
EVERITT, George Bain 1
EVERMANN, Barton Warren
EVERSMAN, Alice 6
EVERSMAN, Walter A. 4
EVERSON, William Graham 3
EVERSULL, Frank Lissenden 4
EVERSULL, Harry Kelso 3
EVERSZ, Moritz Ernst 4
EVERTS, Orpheus 1
EVERWIJN, Jan Charles August 5
EVETT, Robert 6
EVINS, John Hamilton H
EVINS, Robert Benson 1
EVISON, Frances Millicent Marion (Mrs. Frank D. McEntee) 6
EVITT, James Edward Jr. 6
EVJEN, John Oluf 1
EVJUE, William Theodore 5
EVVARD, John Marcus 2
EWALD, Henry Theodore 4
EWART, Frank Carman 2
EWART, Hamilton Glover 1
EWART, J. Kaye 3
EWBANK, Henry Lee 4
EWBANK, Louis B. 5
EWBANK, Thomas H
EWELL, Arthur Woolsey 5
EWELL, Elliott Gordon 4
EWELL, Ervin Edgar 1
EWELL, Glenn Blackmer 6
EWELL, James 1
EWELL, Marshall Davis 1
EWELL, Richard Stoddert H
EWEN, Edward C. 3
EWEN, John Meiggs 1
EWEN, Melvin M. 4
EWEN, W. C. 3
EWER, Bernard Capen 4
EWER, Ferdinand Cartwright H
EWER, Warren Baxter 1
EWERS, Ezra Philetus 1
EWERS, John Ray 5
EWING, Alfred Cyril 6
EWING, Alonzo B(yron) 5
EWING, Andrew H
EWING, Arthur Eugene 1
EWING, Arthur Henry 1
EWING, Charles H
EWING, Charles A. 6
EWING, Charles H. 1
EWING, Cortez A. M. 4
EWING, David L. 1
EWING, Emma Pike 4
EWING, Fayette Clay 3
EWING, Finis 2
EWING, Henry Ellsworth 3
EWING, Hugh Boyle 4
EWING, James H
EWING, James 1
EWING, James Caruthers Rhea 1
EWING, James Dunlop 4
EWING, James Stevenson 1
EWING, John * H
EWING, John 1
EWING, John Dunbrack 2
EWING, John Gillespie 4
EWING, John Hoge 1
EWING, John Thomas 1
EWING, Lynn Moore 3
EWING, Majl 6
EWING, Maurice 6
EWING, Nathaniel H
EWING, Philemon H
EWING, Presley Kittredge 1
EWING, Presley Underwood H
EWING, Robert 1
EWING, Robert Legan 1
EWING, Russell Charles 5
EWING, Samuel Edgar 2
EWING, Sherman 3
EWING, Thomas * H
EWING, Thomas 2
EWING, William 3
EWING, William 4
EWING, William F. C. 4
EWING, William Lee Davidson H
EWOLDT, Harold Boaden 5
EXALL, Henry 1
EXCELL, Edwin Othello 1
EXLINE, Frank 4
EXMAN, Eugene 6
EXNER, Max Joseph 2
EXTON, James Anderson 4
EXTON, William Gustav 2
EYANSON, Charles Louis 4

EYCLESHYMER, Albert Chauncey 1
EYERLY, Elmer Kendall 4
EYERLY, James Bryan 4
EYERMAN, John 4
EYMAN, Frank P. 4
EYMAN, Henry C. 1
EYRE, Laurence 3
EYRE, Wilson 2
EYRING, Carl Ferdinand 4
EYSMANS, Julien L. 5
EYSTER, George Senseny 3
EYSTER, John Augustine English 6
EYSTER, Nellie Blessing 1
EYSTER, William Henry 5
EYTINGE, Rose 1
EZEKIEL, Mordecai Joseph Brill 6
EZEKIEL, Moses 1
EZEKIEL, Walter Naphtali 4
EZELL, B. F. 4

F

FABENS, Joseph Warren H
FABER, Eberhard 2
FABER, John Eberhard H
FABER, John Lewis 5
FABER, Lothar W. 2
FABER, William Frederic 5
FABIAN, Simon H. 5
FABIANI, Aurelio 5
FABING, Howard Douglas 5
FABRI, Ralph 6
FABRICIAN, Rev. Brother 4
FABYAN, George 1
FACCIOLI, Giuseppe 4
FACKENTHAL, Benjamin Franklin Jr. 1
FACKENTHAL, Frank Diehl 5
FACKLER, David Parks 1
FACKLER, Edward Bathurst 3
FADDIS, Charles I. 5
FAELTEN, Carl 1
FAELTEN, Reinhold 4
FAESCH, John Jacob H
FAESI, Robert 5
FAGAN, Charles Aloysius 1
FAGAN, Irving 6
FAGAN, James Fleming H
FAGAN, James J. 1
FAGAN, James Octavius 4
FAGAN, William Long 3
FAGERBURG, Dewey Frank
FAGERGREN, Fred C. 5
FAGES, Pedro H
FAGET, Guy Henry 2
FAGET, Jean Charles H
FAGG, John Gerardus 1
FAGGI, Alfeo 4
FAGIN, N. Bryllion 5
FAGLEY, Frederick Louis 5
FAGNANI, Charles Prospero 1
FAHEY, John H. 3
FAHNESTOCK, Harris Charles 1
FAHNESTOCK, James Frederick 1
FAHNESTOCK, James Murray 5
FAHNESTOCK, Karol James 5
FAHNESTOCK, William 1
FAHNESTOCK, Zephine Huphrey 3
FAHS, David Wesley 1
FAIG, John Theodore 3
FAIGLE, Eric H. 5
FAILLA, Gioacchino 4
FAILOR, Isaac Newton 4
FAINSOD, Merle 5
FAIR, Eugene 1
FAIR, Gordon Maskew 5
FAIR, H. H. 4
FAIR, James Graham H
FAIRBAIRN, Henry Arnold 1
FAIRBANK, Alfred 5
FAIRBANK, Arthur Boyce 1
FAIRBANK, Calvin H
FAIRBANK, Herbert Sinclair 4
FAIRBANK, Janet Ayer 3
FAIRBANK, Kellogg 1
FAIRBANK, Leigh Cole 5
FAIRBANKS, Arthur 2
FAIRBANKS, Charles Warren 1
FAIRBANKS, Cornelia Cole 1
FAIRBANKS, Douglas 1

FAIRBANKS, Edward Taylor 1
FAIRBANKS, Erastus H
FAIRBANKS, Frank Perley 4
FAIRBANKS, Frederick Cole 1
FAIRBANKS, George Rainsford 4
FAIRBANKS, Harold Wellman 4
FAIRBANKS, Henry 1
FAIRBANKS, John Leo 5
FAIRBANKS, Richard 2
FAIRBANKS, Thaddeus H
FAIRBANKS, Warren Charles 1
FAIRBURN, William Armstrong 1
FAIRCHILD, Arthur Wilson 3
FAIRCHILD, Benjamin Lewis 2
FAIRCHILD, Charles Stebbins 1
FAIRCHILD, Clarence A. 5
FAIRCHILD, David 3
FAIRCHILD, David Sturges 1
FAIRCHILD, Edward Thomson 1
FAIRCHILD, Fred Rogers 4
FAIRCHILD, George Thompson 1
FAIRCHILD, George Winthrop 1
FAIRCHILD, Henry Pratt 5
FAIRCHILD, Herman Le Roy 1
FAIRCHILD, Hoxie N. 6
FAIRCHILD, James Harris 1
FAIRCHILD, Joseph Schmitz 4
FAIRCHILD, Julian D. 1
FAIRCHILD, Lucius H
FAIRCHILD, Milton 1
FAIRCHILD, Muir Stephen 2
FAIRCHILD, Raymond Wilber 3
FAIRCHILD, Salome Cutler 1
FAIRCHILD, Sherman M. 5
FAIRCHILD, Thomas Everett 1
FAIRCLOTH, James M. 1
FAIRCLOTH, William Tyson 1
FAIRCLOUGH, George Herbert 5
FAIRCLOUGH, Henry Rushton 1
FAIRES, Virgil Moring 6
FAIRFAX, Albert Kirby 5
FAIRFAX, Donald McNeill H
FAIRFAX, Thomas H
FAIRFIELD, Arthur Philip 2
FAIRFIELD, Edward George 1
FAIRFIELD, John H
FAIRFIELD, Louis W. 1
FAIRFIELD, Sumner Lincoln 1
FAIRFIELD, Wynn Cowan 4
FAIRHURST, William 3
FAIRLAMB, James Remington 1
FAIRLEIGH, David William 1
FAIRLESS, Benjamin F. 4
FAIRLEY, Edwin 1
FAIRLEY, William 1
FAIRLIE, John Archibald 3
FAIRMAN, F. E. Jr. 3
FAIRMAN, Gideon 1
FAIRMAN, James H
FAIRMAN, James Ferdinand 4
FAIRMAN, Seibert 3
FAIRWEATHER, Clement Wilson 3
FAIRWEATHER, Jack Hall 3
Alliger Lee
FAISAL, Ibn Abdul Aziz Al Saud 6
FAISAL II, King of Iraq 3
FAISON, John Miller 1
FAISON, Samson Lane 1
FAITH, Percy 6
FAITHORN, John Nicholson 1
FAJANS, Kasimir 6
FAKE, Guy Leverne 3
FALAYI, Samual Oladeie 6
FALCK, Alexander Diven 4
FALCKNER, Daniel H
FALCKNER, Justus H
FALCONER, Douglas Platt 5
FALCONER, Jacob Alexander 5

FALCONER, John Ironside 1
FALCONER, John Ironside 4
FALCONER, John Mackie 1
FALCONER, Robert Clemons 1
FALCONER, William Armistead 1
FALCONIO, Diomede 1
FALES, De Coursey 4
FALES, Frederick Sayward 5
FALES, Herbert Peck 5
FALES, Jonathan Cilley 4
FALES, Winnifred (Shaw) 5
FALK, Elmer M. 6
FALK, Harold Sands 3
FALK, K. George 3
FALK, Louis 1
FALK, Maurice 2
FALK, Myron Samuel 4
FALK, Otto Herbert 2
FALK, Ralph 4
FALK, Sawyer 5
FALKNER, Jefferson Manly 4
FALKNER, Roland Post 1
FALL, Albert Bacon 2
FALL, Bernard B. 4
FALL, Charles Gershom 1
FALL, Clifford Pervines 1
FALL, Delos 1
FALL, Frank Andrews 3
FALL, Gilbert Haven 3
FALL, Henry Clinton 1
FALLERS, Lloyd Ashton Jr. 6
FALLEY, George Frederick 4
FALLIGANT, Robert 1
FALLIS, Iva Campbell Doyle 3
FALLIS, Laurence Sidney 6
FALLIS, William David 6
FALLON, Bernard Joseph 2
FALLON, Lester (Raymond) 5
FALLOWS, Alice Katharine 1
FALLOWS, Edward Huntington 1
FALLOWS, Samuel 1
FALLS, Charles Buckles 4
FALLS, Charles Buckles 5
FALLS, DeWitt Clinton 1
FALLS, Frederick Howard 6
FALLS, Raymond Leonard 3
FALSEY, William J. 4
FALVEY, Daniel Patrick 4
FALVEY, Timothy J. 2
FALVEY, Wallace 3
FANCHER, Bertram Hull 1
FANCHER, Elvadore R. 1
FANCHER, Frederick Bartlett 4
FANCIULLI, Francesco 1
FANE, Frances Gordon 4
FANER, Robert Dunn 5
FANEUIL, Peter H
FANNIN, James Walker H
FANNING, Alexander Campbell Wilder H
FANNING, Cecil 1
FANNING, David H
FANNING, Edmund * H
FANNING, John Thomas 1
FANNING, Lawrence Stanley 5
FANNING, Nathaniel H
FANNING, Ralph 5
FANNING, Raymond Joseph 6
FANNING, Tolbert 1
FANSLER, Michael Louis 4
FANT, Clyde Edward 6
FANT, John Clayton 1
FANT, Lester Glenn 2
FARABEE, Samuel Howard 1
FARABEE, William Curtis 1
FARAGHER, Donald Qualtrough 5
FARAGHER, Warren Fred 4
FARAN, James John H
FARBER, John Clarke 1
FARBER, Sidney 5
FARBER, William Sims 4
FARDWELL, Harry R(inggold) 6
FARENHOLT, Ammen 5
FARENHOLT, Oscar Walter 1
FARGO, Charles 1
FARGO, James Congdel 1
FARGO, Lucile Foster 6
FARGO, William George 1
FARIBAULT, Jean Baptist H
FARILL, Juan Solares 6
FARIS, Barry 5
FARIS, Charles Breckenridge 1
FARIS, Ellsworth 3
FARIS, George Washington 1

FARIS, Herman Preston 1
FARIS, James Edge 3
FARIS, John Thomson 2
FARIS, Paul Patton 5
FARIS, Robert Lee 1
FARISH, Frederick Garesche 2
FARISH, Hunter Dickinson 2
FARISH, William Stamps 2
FARLEE, Isaac Gray H
FARLEY, Edward Philip 3
FARLEY, Eliot 3
FARLEY, Ephraim Wilder 1
FARLEY, Eugene Shedden 6
FARLEY, Frank Edgar 2
FARLEY, Frederic Henry Morton Stanley 4
FARLEY, Hugh D. 4
FARLEY, J. W. 3
FARLEY, James I. 1
FARLEY, James Thompson H
FARLEY, John Murphy 1
FARLEY, Joseph Francis 6
FARLEY, Joseph Pearson 1
FARLEY, Michael F. 1
FARLEY, Richard Blossom 5
FARLEY, Robert E. 1
FARLIN, Dudley 1
FARLOW, Alfred 1
FARLOW, Arthur Clark 4
FARLOW, William Gilson 1
FARMAN, Elbert Eli 1
FARMER, Alfred Gibson 2
FARMER, Arthur Lafayette 4
FARMER, August Neustadt 5
FARMER, Chester Jefferson 5
FARMER, Clyde F. 3
FARMER, Donald Francis 5
FARMER, Edward 5
FARMER, Edward McNeil 5
FARMER, F. Malcolm 5
FARMER, Fannie Merritt 1
FARMER, Ferdinand H
FARMER, Garland Sr. 2
FARMER, Gene 5
FARMER, Harry 5
FARMER, James Eugene 4
FARMER, John * 1
FARMER, Leslie P. 1
FARMER, Lydia Hoyt 1
FARMER, Moses Gerrish H
FARMER, S. J. 3
FARMER, Sarah Jane 1
FARMER, Silas 1
FARMER, Thomas Harris 1
FARMER, William Burton 1
FARMER, William M. 1
FARNAM, Henry H
FARNAM, Henry Walcott 1
FARNAM, Ruth Stanley 3
FARNAM, William Whitman 1
FARNDON, Walter 4
FARNELL, Frederic James 5
FARNESS, Orin Jocevious 5
FARNHAM, Charles Chittenden 1
FARNHAM, Charles Haight 4
FARNHAM, Charles Wells 1
FARNHAM, Dwight Thompson 3
FARNHAM, Edwin Pickett 4
FARNHAM, Eliza Woodson H
Burnhans
FARNHAM, Mateel Howe 4
FARNHAM, Robert 5
FARNHAM, Roswell 1
FARNHAM, Russel H
FARNHAM, Sally James 2
FARNHAM, Thomas Jefferson H
FARNSWORTH, Charles Hubert 2
FARNSWORTH, Charles Stewart 3
FARNSWORTH, Elon John H
FARNSWORTH, Frederick Eugene 1
FARNSWORTH, George Low 4
FARNSWORTH, Helen Elliott Cherington 6
FARNSWORTH, Joseph Eastman 4
FARNSWORTH, Louis Henderson 1
FARNSWORTH, Philo Judson 4
FARNSWORTH, Philo Taylor 5
FARNSWORTH, Ray D. 4
FARNSWORTH, Sidney Woods 5
FARNSWORTH, Wilson Amos 1

FARNUM, Dustin 1
FARNUM, George Rossiter 5
FARNUM, Loring Nelson 1
FARNY, Henry F. 1
FAROUK, I. 4
FARQUHAR, Arthur B. 1
FARQUHAR, Edward 1
FARQUHAR, Francis Peloubet 6
FARQUHAR, Henry 1
FARQUHAR, John Hanson H
FARQUHAR, John McCreath 1
FARQUHAR, Norman von Heldreich 1
FARQUHAR, Samuel Thaxter 3
FARQUHAR, Silas Edgar 2
FARQUHAR, Thomas Lippincott 5
FARQUHARSON, James 3
FARR, Albert George 1
FARR, Clifford Bailey 5
FARR, Evarts Worcester H
FARR, Finis King 1
FARR, Frederic William 1
FARR, Harry Willson 4
FARR, Henry Bartow 4
FARR, Hilda Butler 5
FARR, John Richard 1
FARR, Marcus Stults 2
FARR, Newton Camp 4
FARR, T. J. 4
FARRAGUT, David Glasgow H
FARRAGUT, George H
FARRAGUT, Loyall 4
FARRAH, Albert John 2
FARRAH, Clarence B. 5
FARRAND, Beatrix 5
FARRAND, George E. 3
FARRAND, Livingston 2
FARRAND, Max 2
FARRAND, Roy Felton 6
FARRAND, Wilson 2
FARRAR, Clarence B. 5
FARRAR, Edgar Howard 1
FARRAR, Fred 2
FARRAR, Geraldine 4
FARRAR, Gilbert Powderly 3
FARRAR, James McNail 1
FARRAR, John H
FARRAR, John Chipman 4
FARRAR, Roy Montgomery 2
FARRAR, Thomas James 5
FARRAR, Timothy H
FARRAR, William Edmund 1
FARREL, Franklin Jr. 6
FARRELL, Benjamin Peter 2
FARRELL, Charles LeRoy 6
FARRELL, Francis David 6
FARRELL, Gabriel 5
FARRELL, Glenda 5
FARRELL, Henry Edward 4
FARRELL, J. Fletcher 1
FARRELL, James Augustine 1
FARRELL, James Charles 1
FARRELL, John D. 4
FARRELL, John J. 1
FARRELL, Joseph D. 5
FARRELL, Patrick Joseph Hoshie 5
FARRELL, Thomas Francis 4
FARRELL, William Elliston 2
FARRELLY, John P. 1
FARRELLY, John Wilson H
FARRELLY, Patrick H
FARREN, George P. H
FARREN, Marie Ann Russell H
FARRER, Henry 1
FARRINGTON, Carl Coleman 5
FARRINGTON, Donald H. 4
FARRINGTON, Dora Davis 6
FARRINGTON, Edward Holyoke 1
FARRINGTON, Edward Irving 5
FARRINGTON, Edward Silsby 1
FARRINGTON, Ernest Albert 1
FARRINGTON, Frank 4
FARRINGTON, Frank George 1
FARRINGTON, Frederic Ernest 1
FARRINGTON, Harold P. 4
FARRINGTON, Harry Webb 1
FARRINGTON, Isabelle Scudder (Mrs. F. E. Farrington) 5

FARRINGTON, James H
FARRINGTON, John D.
FARRINGTON, Joseph 3
Rider
FARRINGTON, Oliver 1
Cummings
FARRINGTON, Robert I. 3
FARRINGTON, Wallace 1
Rider
FARRINGTON, William 1
George
FARRINGTON, William 4
Giddings
FARRIS, Edmond J. 4
FARRIS, Frank Mitchell 3
FARRIS, John Wallace de 5
Beque
FARRIS, Ralph W. 5
FARRIS, Robert Perry 1
FARRISEE, William James 4
FARRISS, Charles
Sherwood
FARROW, Edward Samuel 1
FARROW, Edward Samuel 4
FARROW, John Villiers 4
FARROW, Miles 5
FARROW, Samuel H
FARSON, John 1
FARWELL, Arthur 3
FARWELL, Arthur Burrage 1
FARWELL, Charles 1
Benjamin
FARWELL, Frederick 4
Marcus *
FARWELL, John Villiers 1
FARWELL, John Villiers 2
FARWELL, John W. 1
FARWELL, Nathan Allen 1
FARWELL, Thomas Abbot 1
FARYON, Reginald Richard 4
FASSO Guido 6
FASSETT, Charles Marvin 1
FASSETT, Cornelia Adele H
Strong
FASSETT, Helen Mary 2
Revere
FASSETT, Jacob Sloat 1
FASSETT, James Hiram 1
FASSETT, Norman C. 3
FASSETT, William M. 5
FASSIG, Oliver Lanard 1
FAST, Gustave 2
FASTEN, Nathan 3
FATH, Edward Arthur 6
FATH, Jacques F. 3
FAUBEL, Arthur Louis 4
FAUCETTE, William 2
Dollison
FAULCONER, Albert 5
FAULEY, Wilbur Finley 2
FAULK, Andrew Jackson H
FAULK, C. E. 3
FAULKES, James Nelson 3
FAULKES, William Fred 4
FAULKNER, Barry 4
FAULKNER, Charles James H
FAULKNER, Charles James 1
FAULKNER, Charles James 3
FAULKNER, Georgene 5
("The Story Lady")
FAULKNER, Harold 5
Underwood
FAULKNER, Harry Charles 4
FAULKNER, Herbert 4
Nelson
FAULKNER, Herbert 1
Waldron
FAULKNER, John Alfred 1
FAULKNER, Leon Charles 2
FAULKNER, Lester 5
Bradner
FAULKNER, Roy H. 3
FAULKNER, William 4
FAULKNER, William 5
Harrison
FAULKS, Theodosia 2
FAULL, Joseph Horace 4
FAUNCE, Daniel Worcester 1
FAUNCE, William Herbert 1
Perry
FAUQUIER, Francis H
FAUST, Albert Bernhardt 3
FAUST, Allen Klein 3
FAUST, Charles Lee 1
FAUST, Clarence Henry 6
FAUST, John Bernard 3
FAUST, Paul E. 3
FAUST, Samuel D. 1
FAUST, Walter Livingston 3
FAUSTMANN, Edmund C. 2
FAUVER, Edgar 2
FAUVER, Edwin 5
FAVERSHAM, William 1
FAVILL, Henry Baird 1
FAVILLE, Alpheus Davis 6
FAVILLE, David Ernest 1

FAVILLE, Frederick F. 5
FAVILLE, Henry 4
FAVILLE, John 1
FAVILLE, William Baker 2
FAVOUR, Alpheus Hoyt 5
FAVREAU, Guy 4
FAVROT, Charles Allen 1
FAVROT, George Kent 2
FAVROT, Laurence 4
Harrison
FAVROT, Leo Mortimer 5
FAW, Walter Wagner 3
FAWCETT, Angelo Vance 1
FAWCETT, Edgar 1
FAWCETT, George D. 1
FAWCETT, Harold Pascoe 6
FAWCETT, Howard Samuel 2
FAWCETT, Jacob 4
FAWCETT, M. Edward 1
FAWCETT, Owen 1
FAWCETT, Wilford 5
Hamilton Jr.
FAWCETT, William H. 3
FAWCETT, William Vaughn 4
Moody
FAXON, Charles Edward 1
FAXON, Frederick 1
Winthrop
FAXON, Henry Darlington 5
FAXON, Nathaniel Wales 6
FAXON, Walter 1
FAXON, William Bailey 1
FAXON, William Otis II 5
FAY, Albert Hill 1
FAY, Amy 3
FAY, Arthur Cecil 4
FAY, Charles Ernest 1
FAY, Charles Norman 2
FAY, Charles Robert 3
FAY, Charles W. 5
FAY, Edward Allen 1
FAY, Edwin Whitfield 1
FAY, Francis Ball H
FAY, Frederic Harold 2
FAY, George Morris 3
FAY, Henry 4
FAY, Irving Wetherbee 1
FAY, James H. 5
FAY, John H
FAY, Jonas H
FAY, Lucy Ella 5
FAY, Oliver James 2
FAY, Sidney Bradshaw 3
FAY, Sidney Bradshaw 5
FAY, Temple 4
FAY, Theodore Sedgwick 1
FAY, Waldo Burnett 6
FAY, William Patrick 5
FAYANT, Frank H. 4
FAYER, Margaret Wilson 1
FAYERWEATHER, Daniel H
Burton
FAYSSOUX, Peter H
FEAD, Louis H. 2
FEAGIN, Noah Baxter 1
FEAGIN, William Francis 5
FEARING, Daniel Butler 1
FEARING, Kenneth 4
Flexner
FEARING, Paul H
FEARN, John Walker 1
FEARN, Richard Lee 4
FEARON, Henry Dana 2
FEATHERS, William C. 2
FEATHERSTON, Winfield H
Scott
FEATHERSTONE, Robert 6
Marion
FEATHERSTONE, William 3
B.
FEBIGER, Christian H
FECHET, James Edmond 2
FECHNER, Robert 1
FECHTELER, Augustus 1
Francis
FECHTELER, William 4
Morrow
FECHTER, Charles Albert H
FECHTER, Oscar Augustus 1
FEDERBUSH, Simon 5
FEDERSPIEL, Matthew 3
Nicholas
FEDIGAN, John J. 1
FEE, Charles S. 1
FEE, Chester Anders 3
FEE, James Alger 4
FEE, Jerome John 5
FEE, John Gregg 1
FEE, William Thomas 1
FEEHAN, Daniel F. 1
FEEHAN, Patrick A. 1
FEELEY, James Patrick 4
FEELEY, William P. 5
FEELY, Edward Francis 4
FEELY, John Joseph 1
FEEMAN, Harlan Luther 3

FEEMSTER, Robert M. 4
FEENEY, Daniel J. 5
FEENEY, Joseph Gerald 5
FEGAN, Hugh J. 3
FEGAN, Joseph Charles 2
FEGTLY, Samuel Marks 2
FEHLANDT, August 1
Frederick
FEHR, Arthur 5
FEHR, Harrison Robert 1
FEHR, Herman 5
FEHRENBACH, John 4
FEIBELMAN, Herbert U. 5
FEIBUS, Arthur 6
FEIDELSON, Charles N. 4
FEIERABEND, Raymond 5
H.
FEIGL, Hugo 4
FEIKER, Frederick Morris 4
FEILCHENFELD, Ernst H. 3
FEINBERG, Louis 6
FEINBERG, Samuel 6
Maurice
FEININGER, Lyonel 3
Charles Adrian
FEIS, Herbert * 5
FEISAL II 3
FEISS, Paul Louis 5
FEJOS, Paul 4
FEKE, Robert H
FELAND, Faris Robison II 3
FELAND, Logan 1
FELCH, Alpheus 5
FELD, Jacob 6
FELDBERG, Morris 5
FELDBUSH, Harry A. 4
FELDER, C. S. 3
FELDER, John Myers H
FELDER, Samuel Demeritt 1
FELDMAN, A. Harry 6
FELDMAN, Charles K. 5
FELDMAN, Herman 2
FELDMAN, William 4
H(ugh)
FELDMANN, Charles 6
Russell
FELDMANN, Leonard G. 5
FELDMANN, Markus 3
FELDMANN, Robert 6
Lincoln
FELDMANS, Jules 3
FELDSTEIN, David 6
FELGAR, James Huston 2
FELITTO, Raymond 5
Nicholas
FELIX, Anthony G. 3
FELIX, Elizabeth Rachel H
FELKEL, Herbert 1
FELKER, Samuel Demeritt 1
FELL, Alpheus Gilbert 1
FELL, Charles Albert 1
FELL, D. Newlin 1
FELL, Frank J. Jr. 4
FELL, George Edward 1
FELL, Harold Bertels 3
FELL, John H
FELL, John R. 4
FELL, Thomas 2
FELLAND, Ole Gunderson 1
FELLER, Abraham Howard 4
FELLER, Alto Edmund 4
FELLER, William 5
FELLERS, Bonner Frank 4
FELLERS, Carl Raymond 3
FELLHEIMER, Alfred 3
FELLINGHAM, John 5
Henry
FELLOWS, C. Gurnee 1
FELLOWS, Dorkas 1
FELLOWS, Eugene Hilpert 6
FELLOWS, Frank 3
FELLOWS, George Emory 1
FELLOWS, Grant 1
FELLOWS, Harold E. 3
FELLOWS, John Ernest 4
FELLOWS, John R. H
FELLOWS, Oscar F. 1
FELLOWS, William 1
Bainbridge
FELLOWS, William Kinne 2
FELMLEY, David 1
FELS, Joseph 1
FELS, Mary 3
FELS, Samuel S. 3
FELS, William Carl 4
FELSING, William August 3
FELT, Charles Frederick 1
Wilson
FELT, Dorr Eugene 1
FELT, Edward Webster 3
FELT, Edwin Porter H
FELT, Joseph Barlow H
FELT, Truman Thomas 4
FELTER, Harvey Wickes 4
FELTES, Nicholas Rudolph 3
FELTIN, Maurice 3
FELTON, Charles 1

FELTON, Cornelius H
Conway
FELTON, Edgar Conway 1
FELTON, George Hurlburt 4
FELTON, Lloyd Derr 3
FELTON, Rebecca Latimer 1
FELTON, Samuel Morse H
FELTON, Samuel Morse 1
FELTON, Samuel Morse 5
FELTON, William Hamilton 1
FENDALL, Josias H
FENETRY, Clare Gerald 3
FENGER, Christian 1
FENHAGEN, George 3
Corner
FENHAGEN, James Corner 3
FENKELL, George 3
Harrison
FENLEY, Oscar 1
FENLON, John F. 2
FENN, E. Hart 1
FENN, George Karl 4
FENN, Harry 1
FENN, Stephen Southmyd H
FENN, Wallace Osgood 5
FENN, William Wallace 1
FENNELL, Earle James 6
FENNELL, James 1
FENNELL, William George 1
FENNELLY, John 6
Fauntleroy
FENNEMAN, Nevin M. 1
FENNER, Arthur H
FENNER, Burt L. 1
FENNER, Charles E. 1
FENNER, Charles Erasmus 1
FENNER, Charles Payne 1
FENNER, Clarence Norman 3
FENNER, Edward Blaine 2
FENNER, Erasmus Darwin 2
FENNER, Harlan K. 4
FENNER, Hiram Walter 1
FENNER, James 1
FENNER, Robert Coyner 5
FENNING, Frederick 2
Alexander
FENNO, John H
FENOLLOSA, Ernest 1
Francisco
FENOLLOSA, Mary 3
McNeill
FENSHAM, Florence 1
FENSKE, Merrell Robert 5
FENSKE, Theodore H. 4
FENSTERMACHER, R. 1
FENSTERWALD, Bernard 3
FENSTON, Earl J. 3
FENTON, Hector Tyndale 1
FENTON, Howard Withrow 4
FENTON, Jerome D. 1
FENTON, Joseph Clifford 5
FENTON, Lucien Jerome 1
FENTON, Ralph Albert 4
FENTON, Reuben Eaton 1
FENTON, William David 1
FENTRESS, Calvin 5
FENWICK, Charles 6
Ghequiere
FENWICK, Benedict Joseph H
FENWICK, Charles G. 5
FENWICK, Charles Philip 4
FENWICK, Edward H
Dominic
FENWICK, Edward Taylor 2
FENWICK, George 1
FENWICK, John H
FERBER, Edna 5
FERBERT, Adolph Henry 2
FERDON, John William 4
FEREBEE, Enoch Emory 4
FERENBAUGH, Claude 6
Birkett
FERGER, Roger H(enry) 6
FERGUSON, Alexander 1
Hugh
FERGUSON, Charles 5
FERGUSON, Charles 6
FERGUSON, Charles 4
Eugene
FERGUSON, DeLancey 4
FERGUSON, Edmund 1
Sheppard
FERGUSON, Edward 5
FERGUSON, Elsie 4
FERGUSON, Emma Henry 1
FERGUSON, Everard D. 1
FERGUSON, Farquhar 1
FERGUSON, Fenner H
FERGUSON, Finlay Forbes 1
FERGUSON, Frank 4
Cardwell
FERGUSON, Frank William 1
FERGUSON, Franklin La 4
Du
FERGUSON, Fred 3
Swearengin

FERGUSON, Garland 4
Sevier Jr.
FERGUSON, George Albert 1
FERGUSON, Georgia 4
Ransom
FERGUSON, Harley 5
B(ascom)
FERGUSON, Harriet R. 4
FERGUSON, Harry George 4
FERGUSON, Henry 1
FERGUSON, Henry A. 1
FERGUSON, Henry 1
Gardiner
FERGUSON, Hill 5
FERGUSON, Homer Lenoir 3
FERGUSON, Ira Alfred 5
FERGUSON, James Edward 2
FERGUSON, John Calvin 1
FERGUSON, John Donald 1
FERGUSON, John Lambuth 3
FERGUSON, John William 1
FERGUSON, Kenneth 3
Reinhard
FERGUSON, Louis 1
Aloysius
FERGUSON, Margaret Clay 3
FERGUSON, Melville 5
Foster
FERGUSON, Milton James 3
FERGUSON, Miriam A. 4
FERGUSON, Olin Jerome 4
FERGUSON, R. J. 3
FERGUSON, Robert 5
Gracey
FERGUSON, Robert 5
Gracey
FERGUSON, Roy King 6
FERGUSON, Samuel 2
FERGUSON, Samuel David 1
FERGUSON, Smith Farley 3
FERGUSON, Thomas 4
Ewing
FERGUSON, Thompson B. 1
FERGUSON, Walter 1
FERGUSON, William Blair 6
Morton (William Morton)
FERGUSON, William H. 4
FERGUSON, William J. 1
FERGUSON, William Law 4
FERGUSON, William 1
Porter Frisbee
FERGUSON, William Scott 3
FERGUSSON, Arthur 1
Walsh
FERGUSSON, E. Morris 1
FERGUSSON, Frank Kerby 1
FERGUSSON, Harvey 1
Butler
FERLAINO, Frank Ralph 3
FERM, Vergilius Ture 6
Anselm
FERMAN, Joseph Wolfe 6
FERMI, Enrico 3
FERN, Fanny H
FERNALD, Bert M. 1
FERNALD, Charles Henry 1
FERNALD, Chester Bailey 1
FERNALD, Frank Lysander 1
FERNALD, Gustavus 1
Stockman
FERNALD, Henry Barker 4
FERNALD, Henry Torsey 3
FERNALD, James 1
Champlin
FERNALD, Merritt 1
Caldwell
FERNALD, Merritt Lyndon 3
FERNALD, Robert Foss 4
FERNALD, Robert 1
Heywood
FERNALD, Walter Elmore 1
FERNANDEL, (Ferdinand 5
Joseph Desire Contandin)
FERNANDEZ, Antonio M. 4
FERNANDEZ, John D. 4
FERNBACH, R(obert) 5
Livingston
FERNBERGER, Samuel 3
Weiller
FERNLEY, George 5
Anderson
FERNOW, Bernhard 1
Eduard
FERNOW, Berthold 1
FERNSTROM, Henning 1
FERON, Madame H
FERRARA, Orestes 5
FERRARI, Louis 3
FERRARI-FONTANA, 1
Edoardo
FERRATA, Giuseppe 1
FERRE, Nels Fredrik 5
Solomon
FERREE, Barr 1
FERREE, Clarence Errol 2
FERREE, John Willard 6

FERREL, William H
FERRELL, Chiles Clifton 1
FERRELL, John Appley 1
FERRELL, John Atkinson 1
FERREN, John (Millard) 5
FERRERO, Edward 1
FERRI, Antonio 6
FERRIER, Kathleen 1
FERRIER, Kathleen 4
FERRIER, William Warren 4
FERRIN, Augustin William 5
FERRIN, Dana Holman 4
FERRIN, William Nelson 4
FERRIS, Albert Warren 1
FERRIS, Charles Edward 5
FERRIS, Charles Goadsby H
FERRIS, Cornelius 1
FERRIS, David 1
FERRIS, David Lincoln 2
FERRIS, Elmer Ellsworth 4
FERRIS, Eugene B. Jr. 3
FERRIS, George Floyd 4
FERRIS, George Hooper 1
FERRIS, George Washington Gale H
FERRIS, Harry Burr 1
FERRIS, Helen (Josephine) 5
FERRIS, Isaac H
FERRIS, Jean Leon Gerome 1
FERRIS, Joel Edward 6
FERRIS, John Mason 1
FERRIS, John Wallace de Beque 6
FERRIS, Mary Lanman Douw 1
FERRIS, Morris Patterson 1
FERRIS, Ralph Hall 3
FERRIS, Scott 5
FERRIS, Theodore Parker 5
FERRIS, Walter Rockwood 5
FERRIS, Walton C. 3
FERRIS, Woodbridge Nathan 1
FERRISS, Franklin 1
FERRISS, Hugh 4
FERRISS, James Henry 1
FERRISS, Orange H
FERRY, David William 3
FERRY, Dexter Mason 1
FERRY, Dexter Mason Jr. 3
FERRY, E. Hayward 1
FERRY, Elisha Peyre H
FERRY, Ervin Sidney 3
FERRY, Frederick Carlos 5
FERRY, George Bowman 1
FERRY, George Francis 3
FERRY, Hugh J. 5
FERRY, Orris Sanford 1
FERRY, Thomas White H
FERRY, William Mont H
FERSON, Merton Leroy 4
FERST, Monie Alan 4
FERST, Simeon D. 1
FESS, Simeon D. 1
FESSENDEN, Edwin Allan 5
FESSENDEN, Francis 1
FESSENDEN, Franklin Goodridge 1
FESSENDEN, Frederick J. 4
FESSENDEN, James Deering H
FESSENDEN, Laura Dayton 3
FESSENDEN, Reginald Aubrey 1
FESSENDEN, Russell Green 2
FESSENDEN, Samuel H
FESSENDEN, Samuel 1
FESSENDEN, Samuel Clement H
FESSENDEN, Thomas Amory Debois H
FESSENDEN, Thomas Green H
FESSENDEN, William Pitt H
FEST, Francis B. 4
FETHERS, Ogden Hoffman 1
FETHERSTON, Edith Hedges 6
FETHERSTON, John Turney 4
FETTER, Elizabeth Lean Fields Head (Mrs. Ferdinand Fetter) 6
FETTER, Frank Albert 2
FETTER, Norman 4
FETTERMAN, John Davis 6
FETTERMAN, William Judd H
FETTEROLF, Adam H. 1
FETZER, Frank L. 3
FETZER, Gottlob 4
FETZER, Lewis William 6
FETZER, Wade 3
FETZER, Wade Jr. 5
FEUCHTWANGER, Lion 4

FEUER, Mortimer 5
FEUILLERAT, Albert Gabriel 3
FEURT, Seldon Dick 6
FEUSTEL, Robert M. 1
FEW, Ignatius Alphonso H
FEW, William H
FEW, William Preston 1
FEWKES, J. Walter 1
FEWSMITH, Joseph 3
FEYERHERM, Harvey August 6
FEZANDIE, Clement 4
FFOULKE, Charles Mather 1
FFRENCH, Charles Dominic H
FIALA, Anthony 4
FIALA, Sigmund Nicholas 5
FICHTE, Harold O. 5
FICK, George Henry 4
FICK, Henry H. 1
FICKE, Arthur Davison 2
FICKEL, Jacob Earl 3
FICKEN, Clarence Elwood 4
FICKEN, George John 4
FICKEN, H. Edwards 1
FICKEN, Henry Horlbeck 3
FICKES, Robert O. 5
FICKLEN, John Rose 1
FICKLIN, Orlando Bell H
FICSHER, Mario McCaughin 5
FIDLER, Harry L. 1
FIEANDT, Rainer von 5
FIEBACH, Albert H. 3
FIEBEGER, Gustav Joseph 1
FIEDLER, Edward Henry 6
FIEKERS, Bernard Albert 5
FIELD, Allan Bertram 5
FIELD, Allen W. 4
FIELD, Archelaus G. 4
FIELD, B. Rush 1
FIELD, Benjamin Hazard H
FIELD, Betty 6
FIELD, Caroline Leslie 1
FIELD, Carter 3
FIELD, Charles Neale 3
FIELD, Charles William H
FIELD, Cortlandt de Peyster 1
FIELD, Crosby 5
FIELD, Cynthia 6
FIELD, Cyrus West 1
FIELD, Daniel F. 1
FIELD, David Dudley 4
FIELD, David Mason 4
FIELD, E. B. 4
FIELD, Edward 1
FIELD, Edward Davenport 6
FIELD, Edward Pearsall Jr. 4
FIELD, Elisha C. 1
FIELD, Erastus Salisbury H
FIELD, Eugene H
FIELD, F(rances) Bernice 6
FIELD, Frank Harvey 4
FIELD, Fred Tarbell 3
FIELD, George Wilton 1
FIELD, Hamilton Easter 1
FIELD, Harry Ashby 1
FIELD, Harry Hubert 2
FIELD, Heman H. 4
FIELD, Henry 2
FIELD, Henry Alonzo 1
FIELD, Henry Martyn 1
FIELD, Herbert H. 4
FIELD, Herbert Haviland 1
FIELD, Hugh W. 4
FIELD, Isaac S. 1
FIELD, Jacob 4
FIELD, James Alfred 1
FIELD, James Gaven 1
FIELD, Joseph M. H
FIELD, Marshall 1
FIELD, Marshall 3
FIELD, Marshall IV 4
FIELD, Mary Katherine Keemie 1
FIELD, Maunsell Bradhurst H
FIELD, Moses Whelock H
FIELD, Neill Brooks 1
FIELD, Oliver Peter 3
FIELD, Rachel 2
FIELD, Richard Stockton 1
FIELD, Richard Stockton 3
FIELD, Robert 1
FIELD, Robert E. Lee 4
FIELD, Robert Michael 2
FIELD, Robert Patterson 4
FIELD, Roswell Martin 1
FIELD, Scott 5
FIELD, Stanley 6
FIELD, Stephen Dudley 1
FIELD, Stephen Johnson H
FIELD, Theron Rockwell 1
FIELD, Thomas Warren 1
FIELD, Walbridge Abner H

FIELD, Walter Taylor 1
FIELD, Wells Laflin 1
FIELD, William Henry 1
FIELD, William Hildreth 4
FIELD, William Jefferson 4
FIELD, William Lusk Webster 4
FIELD, William Perez 5
FIELD, Winston Joseph 5
FIELDE, Adele Marion 1
FIELDER, Clarence Hunt 4
FIELDER, James Fairman 1
FIELDER, William 1
FIELDING, Mantle 1
FIELDING, Michael Farlow 4
FIELDING, William John 6
FIELDNER, Arno Carl 4
FIELDS, Annie Adams 2
FIELDS, Dorothy 1
FIELDS, Ernest Seymour 4
FIELDS, Harold 4
FIELDS, Herbert 3
FIELDS, James Thomas H
FIELDS, John 1
FIELDS, Joseph E. 3
FIELDS, Lew 3
FIELDS, Louis Glenn 4
FIELDS, Mitchell 4
FIELDS, W. C. 2
FIELDS, William Craig 5
FIELDS, William Henry 3
FIELDS, William Jason 4
FIENE, Ernest 4
FIERO, J. Newton 1
FIESER, James Louis 4
FIFE, George Buchanan 1
FIFE, James 4
FIFE, Joseph Paul 2
FIFE, Ray 3
FIFE, Robert Herndon 3
FIFER, Joseph Wilson 1
FIFER, Orien Wesley 2
FIFIELD, Albert Frank 4
FIFIELD, Benjamin F. 1
FIFIELD, Henry Allen 4
FIFIELD, Lawrence Wendell 4
FIFIELD, Lawrence Wendell 4
FIFIELD, Samuel Stillman 1
FIGGATT, Tinney Cavenaugh 6
FIGGE, Frank Henry John 4
FIGGINS, Jesse Dade 4
FIGGIS, Dudley Weld 4
FIGL, Leopold 4
FIGUERAS-CHIQUES, Jose Maria 5
FIHN, Joseph Adam 6
FIKE, Charles Laird 3
FIKE, Pierre Hicks 3
FILBERT, Ludwig S. 1
FILBERT, William J. 2
FILBEY, Edward Joseph 3
FILBEY, Edward Joseph 4
FILENE, Edward A. 1
FILENE, Lincoln 4
FILER, Harry Lambert 5
FILER, Herbert Augustus 5
FILES, Howard W. 3
FILIPOWICZ, Tytus 5
FILLEBROWN, Charles Bowdoin 1
FILLER, Mervin Grant 1
FILLEY, Chauncey Ives 1
FILLEY, Everett R. 1
FILLEY, Horace Clyde 6
FILLION, Francis 4
FILLIS, Ben Earle 5
FILLMORE, Charles 2
FILLMORE, John Comfort 1
FILLMORE, Millard H
FILLMORE, Parker 2
FILLMORE, Waldo Rickert 4
FILSINGER, Ernst B. 2
FILSON, John H
FIMPLE, John H. 4
FINAN, Joseph B. 4
FINCH, Edward Ridley 4
FINCH, Francis Miles 1
FINCH, Frederick L. 3
FINCH, George Augustus 3
FINCH, Henry LeRoy 3
FINCH, Herbert Isaac 3
FINCH, Isaac H
FINCH, James Kip 4
FINCH, John Aylard 1
FINCH, John Wellington 5
FINCH, Morton Easley 5
FINCH, Opal Clair Lane (Mrs. Ralph Finch) 6
FINCH, Peyton Newell Jr. 5
FINCH, Royal George 4
FINCH, Ruy Herbert 3
FINCH, Stanley Wellington 5

FINCH, Thomas Austin 2
FINCH, Vernor Clifford 3
FINCH, Volney Cecil 3
FINCH, William Albert 1
FINCH, William Rufus 1
FINCHER, Edgar Franklin 5
FINCK, Edward Bertrand (Bert Finck) 5
FINCK, Henry Theophilus 1
FINCKE, Clarence Mann 4
FINCKEL, Martin Luther 1
FINDENEGG, Ingomar 6
FINDLAY, Hugh 5
FINDLAY, James H
FINDLAY, John H
FINDLAY, John Van Lear 1
FINDLAY, William 1
FINDLEY, Alvin Irwin 1
FINDLEY, Earl Nelson 4
FINDLEY, Palmer 4
FINDLEY, Thomas Maskell 4
FINDLEY, Thomas Palmer Jr. 6
FINDLEY, William H
FINE, Benjamin 5
FINE, Henry Burchard 1
FINE, Irving Gifford 5
FINE, John H
FINEGAN, James Emmet 1
FINEGAN, Thomas Edward 1
FINER, Herman 5
FINERTY, John Frederick 1
FINESILVER, Benjamin 6
FINESINGER, Jacob Ellis 5
FINFROCK, Clarence Millard 2
FINGER, Aaron 5
FINGER, Charles Joseph 1
FINGER, Henry James 4
FINGERHOOD, Boris 2
FINGOLD, George 5
FINGOLD, Samuel 5
FINK, A. J. 4
FINK, Albert H
FINK, Bruce 1
FINK, Colin Garfield 3
FINK, David N. 4
FINK, Denman 4
FINK, Emil C. 2
FINK, Francis A. 4
FINK, Frank Wolfe 6
FINK, George R. 4
FINK, Henry 1
FINK, Homer Bernard 6
FINK, Joseph Lionel 4
FINK, Louis Maria 1
FINK, Ollie Edgar 5
FINK, Reuben 4
FINK, William Green 3
FINKE, George 5
FINKE, Walter William 5
FINKE, William F. 5
FINKEL, Benjamin Franklin 2
FINKELNBURG, G. A. 1
FINKELSTEIN, Jacob Joel 6
FINKLE, Frederick Cecil 3
FINKLER, Rita V. Sapiro 5
FINKS, Nettie Velier 4
FINLAY, Charles John 1
FINLAY, George Irving 5
FINLAY, Hugh H
FINLAY, James Ralph 5
FINLAY, John Jerome 5
FINLAY, Kirkman George 1
FINLAY, Walter Stevenson Jr. 5
FINLAYSON, Frank Graham 2
FINLAYSON, John Duncan 3
FINLEY, Charles 1
FINLEY, Charles William 3
FINLEY, David Edward 1
FINLEY, Emmet 3
FINLEY, Ernest Latimer 4
FINLEY, Harold Eugene 6
FINLEY, James H
FINLEY, James Bradley H
FINLEY, John Huston 1
FINLEY, John Huston 2
FINLEY, Joseph William 4
FINLEY, Lorraine Noel (Mrs. Theodore Frank Fitch) 6
FINLEY, Martha 1
FINLEY, Robert H
FINLEY, Ruth Ebright 3
FINLEY, Samuel H
FINLEY, Solomon Henderson 2
FINLEY, William Henry 1
FINLEY, William Lovell 1
FINLEY, William Wilson H
FINN, Francis James 1
FINN, Henry James William H
FINN, Howard Joseph 4
FINN, John F. X. 3

FINN, William Joseph 4
FINNEGAN, Edward Rowan 5
FINNEGAN, James A. 3
FINNEGAN, James Edward 4
FINNEGAN, James Francis 6
FINNEGAN, Joseph Francis 4
FINNEGAN, Philip J. 3
FINNEGAN, Richard James 3
FINNEGAN, William A. 4
FINNELL, Woolsey
FINNEY, Benjamin Ficklin 2
FINNEY, Charles Grandison H
FINNEY, Darwin Abel H
FINNEY, Edward Clingan 5
FINNEY, Frederick Norton 1
FINNEY, James Imboden 5
FINNEY, John Miller Turpin 2
FINNEY, Ross Lee 1
FINNEY, William Parker 2
FINNIGAN, George Joseph 1
FINOTTI, Joseph Maria H
FINTA, Alexander 3
FINTY, Tom Jr. 1
FIORIO, Franco Emilio 6
FIPPIN, Elmer Otterbein 3
FIREMAN, Peter 4
FIRESTEIN, Alfred 5
FIRESTONE, Charles E. 6
FIRESTONE, Clark Barnaby 3
FIRESTONE, Harvey Samuel 1
FIRESTONE, Harvey Samuel Jr. 5
FIRESTONE, Ray Ernest 4
FIRESTONE, Roger Stanley 5
FIRING, Thoralf Otmann 5
FIRKINS, Oscar W. 1
FIRM, Joseph Lannison 4
FIRMIN, Albert Bancroft Wilcox 4
FISCHEL, Victor Arnold 5
FISCHEL, Walter Joseph 6
FISCHEL, Washington Emil 1
FISCHER, Ann Kindrick (Mrs. John L. Fischer) 5
FISCHER, Anton Otto 4
FISCHER, Arthur Frederick 4
FISCHER, Earl Britzius 4
FISCHER, Earl W. 5
FISCHER, Edward Louis 5
FISCHER, Ernst Georg 1
FISCHER, Frederic Philip 6
FISCHER, George Alexander 1
FISCHER, George August 2
FISCHER, Henry W. 4
FISCHER, Herman Arthur 4
FISCHER, Hermann Otto Laurenz 4
FISCHER, Israel F. 4
FISCHER, Jacob 3
FISCHER, Karl 5
FISCHER, Kermit 5
FISCHER, Leo H. 5
FISCHER, Leo J. 2
FISCHER, Louis 2
FISCHER, Louis 4
FISCHER, Louis Albert 1
FISCHER, Martin Henry 4
FISCHER, Mary Ellen Sigsbee (Mary Sigsbee Fischer) 5
FISCHER, Maurice Ritz 6
FISCHLER, Peter K. 3
FISET, Sir Eugene (Marie-Joseph)
FISH, Alfred Lawrence 3
FISH, Bert 2
FISH, C. W. 4
FISH, Carl Russell 1
FISH, Daniel 1
FISH, Edwards R. 1
FISH, Frank Leslie 1
FISH, Fred Alan 1
FISH, Frederick Perry 1
FISH, Frederick Samuel 1
FISH, Hamilton H
FISH, Herbert Henry 5
FISH, Horace 1
FISH, Irving Andrews 2
FISH, John Charles Lounsbury 5
FISH, Mayer Alvin 6
FISH, Milton Ernest 5
FISH, Nicholas H
FISH, Nicholas 1
FISH, Pierre Augustine 1
FISH, Preserved H
FISH, Stuyvesant 1
FISH, Walter Clark 4

FISH, William Hansell 1
FISH, William Henry 1
FISH, Williston 1
FISHBACK, George Welton 4
FISHBACK, William Meade 1
FISHBERG, Maurice 1
FISHBURN, John Eugene 1
FISHBURN, Junius Blair 3
FISHBURN, Junius Parker 3
FISHBURN, Randolph 1
  Eugene
FISHBURNE, Edward Bell 5
FISHBURNE, John Wood H
FISHER, Albert Kenrick 2
FISHER, Alphonse Louis 3
FISHER, Alvan H
FISHER, Anna 3
FISHER, Anne B. 4
FISHER, Anne B(enson) 5
FISHER, Arthur 4
FISHER, Arthur William 5
FISHER, Ben S. 3
FISHER, Bud 3
FISHER, Cassius Asa 1
FISHER, Charles * H
FISHER, Charles A. 1
FISHER, Charles Asbury 2
FISHER, Charles E. 4
FISHER, Charles Thomas 3
Jr.
FISHER, Charles Willis 6
FISHER, Clara H
FISHER, Clarence Stanley 1
FISHER, Daniel C. 4
FISHER, Daniel Webster 1
FISHER, David H
FISHER, Dorothy Canfield 3
FISHER, Dorsey Gassaway 4
FISHER, Ebenezer H
FISHER, Edgar Jacob 5
FISHER, Edmund Drew 4
FISHER, Edward Dix 4
FISHER, Edward F. 5
FISHER, Edwin 2
FISHER, Edwin Lyle 6
FISHER, Elam 1
FISHER, Elizabeth Florette 5
FISHER, Emory Devilla 5
FISHER, Frank Cyril 5
FISHER, Franklin L. 3
FISHER, Fred Douglas 5
FISHER, Frederic John 1
FISHER, Frederick Bohn 1
FISHER, Frederick Charles 5
FISHER, Frederick Vining 4
FISHER, Galen Merriam 3
FISHER, Genevieve 6
FISHER, Geoffrey Francis 5
FISHER, George H
FISHER, George Clyde 2
FISHER, George Egbert 5
FISHER, George J. 4
FISHER, George Jackson H
FISHER, George Park 1
FISHER, George Purnell H
FISHER, Gordon 3
FISHER, Haldane S. 4
FISHER, Hammond Edward 3
FISHER, Harold Henry 6
FISHER, Harrison 1
FISHER, Harry Linn 4
FISHER, Henry C. 5
FISHER, Henry Johnson 4
FISHER, Henry Wright 5
FISHER, Herman Guy 6
FISHER, Horace Newton 4
FISHER, Horatio Gates H
FISHER, Hubert Frederick 1
FISHER, Irving 2
FISHER, James Blaine 3
FISHER, James Maxwell 5
McConnell
FISHER, John H
FISHER, John Dix H
FISHER, John Frederick 1
FISHER, John S. 1
FISHER, John Wesley 3
FISHER, Jonathan H
FISHER, Joseph Anton 5
FISHER, Joshua Francis H
FISHER, Lawrence 6
Frederick
FISHER, Lawrence Peter 4
FISHER, Lewis Beals 1
FISHER, Lindale Carson 6
FISHER, Lucius George 1
FISHER, Lyle Harris 5
FISHER, Mahlon Leonard 2
FISHER, Martin Luther 1
FISHER, Mary 4
FISHER, Miles Bull 5
FISHER, Oscar Louis 1
FISHER, Ralph Talcott 2
FISHER, Richard Thornton 4
FISHER, Robert 4

FISHER, Robert Farley 4
FISHER, Robert John 6
FISHER, Robert Jones 1
FISHER, Robert Joseph 1
FISHER, Robert Joseph Jr. 4
FISHER, Robert Welles 1
FISHER, Robert Welles 1
FISHER, Russell Todd 3
FISHER, Samuel Brownlee 1
FISHER, Samuel Herbert 5
FISHER, Samuel Jackson 1
FISHER, Samuel Ware H
FISHER, Sidney George H
FISHER, Stanley Ross 6
FISHER, Stokely S. 1
FISHER, Sydney George 1
FISHER, Theodore Willis 4
FISHER, Thomas Edward 5
FISHER, Thomas Kaufman 4
FISHER, Thomas Russell 4
FISHER, Vardis 4
FISHER, Waldo Emanuel 4
FISHER, Walter Kenrick 6
FISHER, Walter L. 1
FISHER, Willard Clark 1
FISHER, William A(ndrew) 5
FISHER, William Alexander 6
FISHER, William Arms 2
FISHER, William Cummings 1
FISHER, William H. 4
FISHER, William Orris 5
FISHER, William Victor 5
FISHER, (William) Mark 5
FISHER, Willis Richardson 1
FISHER, Woolf 6
FISHMAN, Leo 6
FISHPAW, Kenneth B. 4
FISK, Bradley 4
FISK, Charles Henry 1
FISK, Charles Joseph 1
FISK, Clinton Bowen 4
FISK, Daniel Moses 4
FISK, Eugene Lyman 1
FISK, Everett Olin 1
FISK, Frederick Mewborn 4
FISK, George Mygatt 4
FISK, Harlan Wilbur 1
FISK, Harold N. 4
FISK, Herbert Franklin 1
FISK, James * H
FISK, Jessie (Gladys) 5
FISK, Jonathan H
FISK, Katharine 4
FISK, Kerby H. 4
FISK, Louisa Holman 3
Richardson
FISK, Samuel Augustus 1
FISK, Wilbur H
FISKE, Adam Hastings 3
FISKE, Amos Kidder 1
FISKE, Arthur Irving 4
FISKE, Asa Severance 1
FISKE, Augustus Henry 6
FISKE, Bradley Allen 2
FISKE, Charles 1
FISKE, Charles Parker 4
FISKE, Daniel Willard 4
FISKE, Edmund Walter 1
FISKE, Eugene Allen 1
FISKE, Fidelia 1
FISKE, George Converse 5
FISKE, George McClellan 5
FISKE, George Walter 2
FISKE, Gertrude 4
FISKE, Haley 1
FISKE, Harold Benjamin 5
FISKE, Harrison Grey 2
FISKE, Horace Spencer 1
FISKE, James Porter 1
FISKE, John H
FISKE, John 1
FISKE, Lewis Ransom 1
FISKE, Minnie Maddern 1
FISKE, Stephen 1
FISKE, Thomas Scott 2
FISKE, William F. 5
FISKE, William Mead 1
Lindsley
FISKE, Wyman P(arkhurst) 5
FISKEN, John Barclay 2
FISKER, Kay 4
FISTELL, Harry 5
FITCH, Albert Parker 4
FITCH, Asa * H
FITCH, Ashbel Parmelee 1
FITCH, Cecil 4
FITCH, Charles Elliott 1
FITCH, Charles Hall 1
FITCH, Clifford Penny 4
FITCH, Clyde 1
FITCH, Edward 1
FITCH, Ezra Charles 1
FITCH, Florence Mary 4
FITCH, Frank E. 1
FITCH, George 1
FITCH, George Hamlin 4

FITCH, Graham Newell H
FITCH, Grant 1
FITCH, James Burgess 4
FITCH, John H
FITCH, John Andrews 3
FITCH, John Hall 5
FITCH, Joseph Henry 4
FITCH, Rachel Louise 4
FITCH, Ralph Roswell 6
FITCH, Samuel H
FITCH, Tecumseh Sherman 5
FITCH, Thomas H
FITCH, Thomas Davis H
FITCH, Thomas F. 4
FITCH, Walter H
FITCH, William Edward 2
FITCH, William Foresman 1
FITCH, William Kountz 5
FITE, Alexander Green 1
FITE, Emerson David 3
FITE, Warner 3
FITE, William Benjamin 4
FITE, William Conyers 4
FITHIAN, Edward 4
FITKIN, Abraham Edward 1
FITLER, Edwin Henry H
FITTERER, John Conrad 2
FITTON, James 1
FITTS, Alice Evelina 4
FITTS, Charles Newton 5
FITTS, Dudley 5
FITTS, George Henry 1
FITTS, William Cochran 3
FITTZ, Austin Hervey 5
FITZ GERALD, Leslie 5
Maurice
FITZ, Henry H
FITZ, Hugh Alexander 5
FITZ, Reginald 3
FITZ, Reginald Heber 2
FITZGERALD, A. Ann 6
Strayer
FITZ-GERALD, Aaron 4
Ogden
FITZGERALD, Adolphus 4
Leigh
FITZGERALD, Barry 4
FITZ-GERALD, Daniel 6
Michael
FITZGERALD, David 2
Edward
FITZGERALD, Desmond 1
FITZGERALD, E. Roy 3
FITZGERALD, Edward 1
FITZGERALD, Edward 5
Aloyslus
FITZGERALD, Francis 1
Alexander James
FITZGERALD, Francis 1
Scott Key
FITZGERALD, Frank 1
Dwight
FITZGERALD, Harrington 1
FITZ GERALD, James 1
FITZGERALD, James J. 2
FITZGERALD, James 1
Merlin
FITZ GERALD, James 1
Newbury
FITZGERALD, James 6
Robert
FITZGERALD, James 4
Wilford
FITZ-GERALD, John 2
Driscoll II
FITZGERALD, John 1
Francis
FITZGERALD, John Joseph 3
FITZGERALD, John 3
Morton
FITZGERALD, Joseph 1
FITZGERALD, Leo David 3
FITZGERALD, Louis 1
FITZGERALD, Matthew 1
Joseph
FITZGERALD, Maurice A. 3
FITZGERALD, Michael 2
Edward
FITZGERALD, Oscar Penn 1
Mullins
FITZGERALD, Robert 1
FITZGERALD, Roy Gerald 4
FITZGERALD, Rufus 4
Henry
FITZGERALD, Ruth 1
FITZ GERALD, Susan 2
Walker
FITZGERALD, Theodore 5
FITZGERALD, Thomas * H
FITZGERALD, Thomas 3
FITZGERALD, Thomas 1
Edward
FITZGERALD, W. Thomas 1
FITZGERALD, Walter 1
James

FITZGERALD, William H
FITZGERALD, William A. 1
FITZGERALD, William 2
Joseph
FITZGERALD, William 3
Joseph
FITZ GERALD, William 1
Sinton
FITZGIBBON, Catherine H
FITZGIBBON, John Harold 3
FITZGIBBON, Thomas 4
O'Gorman
FITZ GIBBON, William 4
FITZGIBBONS, John 1
FITZGIBBONS, John 4
Joseph
FITZHENRY, Louis 1
FITZHUGH, Edwin A. 5
FITZHUGH, George H
FITZHUGH, Guston 1
Thomas
FITZHUGH, Millsaps 5
FITZHUGH, Percy Keese 3
FITZHUGH, Thomas 4
FITZHUGH, William * H
FITZHUGH, William Wyvill 5
FITZMAURICE, Edmond J. 4
FITZMAURICE, John E. 3
FITZPATRICK, Benedict 6
(James Benedict Ossory)
FITZPATRICK, Benjamin 1
FITZPATRICK, Berchmans 6
Tanner
FITZPATRICK, Clyde J. 6
FITZPATRICK, Daniel 5
Robert
FITZPATRICK, Edward 4
Augustus
FITZ-PATRICK, Gilbert 1
FITZ-PATRICK, Herbert 4
FITZ-PATRICK, Hugh 4
Louis
FITZPATRICK, John H
Bernard
FITZPATRICK, John 1
Clement
FITZPATRICK, John 1
Francis
FITZPATRICK, John Tracy 1
FITZPATRICK, Morgan C. 3
FITZPATRICK, Paul 1
Edward
FITZPATRICK, Ray Erian 6
FITZPATRICK, Thomas 1
FITZPATRICK, Thomas 1
Vanhook
FITZPATRICK, Thomas Y. 4
FITZPATRICK, William 5
Samuel
FITZ-RANDOLPH, Corliss 3
FITZROY, Herbert William 5
Keith
FITZSIMMONS, Cortland 1
FITZSIMMONS, Thomas H
FITZSIMON, Laurence 3
Julius
FITZSIMONS, Charles 1
FITZ SIMONS, Ellen 2
French
FITZWATER, Perry B. 3
FITZWILLIAM, Fanny H
FLACCUS, Doris H
FLACK, Joseph 3
FLACK, Marjorie 3
FLACK, William Henry 1
FLAD, Edward 5
FLAD, Henry 1
FLAGET, Benedict Joseph H
FLAGG, Azariah Cutting H
FLAGG, Burton Sanderson 6
FLAGG, Charles Allcott 1
FLAGG, Charles Noel 1
FLAGG, Edmund 1
FLAGG, Edward Octavus 1
FLAGG, Ernest 2
FLAGG, George Whiting 1
FLAGG, Isaac 4
FLAGG, James Chester 4
FLAGG, James 4
Montgomery
FLAGG, Jared Bradley 1
FLAGG, Josiah H
FLAGG, Josiah Foster H
FLAGG, Josiah Foster 1
FLAGG, Montague 5
FLAGG, Paluel Joseph 5
FLAGG, Rufus Cushman 1
FLAGG, Thomas Wilson H
FLAGLER, Clement 1
Alexander Finley
FLAGLER, Harry Harkness 5
FLAGLER, Henry M. 1
FLAGLER, Isaac Van Vleck 1
FLAGLER, John Haldane 1
FLAGLER, Thomas Thorn H
FLAGSTAD, Kirsten 4

FLAHERTY, Frederick H. 1
FLAHERTY, J.L. 6
FLAHERTY, Lawrence J. 1
FLAHERTY, Robert Joseph 3
FLANAGAN, Dan Collins 4
FLANAGAN, Edward 2
Joseph
FLANAGAN, Harold 4
Francis
FLANAGAN, Henry 4
Clinton
FLANAGAN, James 3
Wainwright
FLANAGAN, James H
Winfrip
FLANAGAN, John 3
FLANAGAN, Thomas 4
Edmund
FLANAGIN, Harris 1
FLANDERS, Alvan H
FLANDERS, Benjamin H
Franklin
FLANDERS, Fred C. 3
FLANDERS, George Lovell 4
FLANDERS, Henry 1
FLANDERS, James Greeley 1
FLANDERS, Michael 6
FLANDERS, Ralph Edward 5
FLANDERS, Ralph Lindsay 5
FLANDERS, Ruth Stone 6
(Mrs. Phillip Ray
Flanders)
FLANDRAU, Charles 1
Eugene
FLANDRAU, Charles 5
Macomb
FLANDRAU, Grace 5
Hodgson
FLANIGAN, Edward 1
Joseph
FLANIGAN, Howard 4
Adams
FLANNAGAN, John 3
William Jr.
FLANNELLY, Joseph F. 6
FLANNERY, Harry 4
William
FLANNERY, John 4
FLANNERY, John Rogers 2
FLANNERY, John Spalding 3
FLANNERY, Vaughn 3
FLANNIGAN, Richard 1
Charles
FLASCH, Kilian Casper H
FLATH, Earl Hugo 5
FLATHER, Frederick 5
Arthur
FLATHER, John Joseph 1
FLATTERY, M. Douglas 1
FLAVEN, Allan Ervin 6
FLAVIN, Martin 4
FLAVIN, Thomas J. 6
FLEBBE, Beulah Marie Dix 5
(Mrs. George H. Flebbe)
FLECK, Alexander 5
FLECK, Henry Thomas 4
FLECK, Wilbur H. 5
FLEEGER, George H
Washington
FLEEK, John Sherwood 3
FLEESON, Doris 3
FLEESON, Howard Tebbe 3
FLEET, Alexander 1
Frederick
FLEET, Reuben Hollis 6
FLEET, Thomas H
FLEETWOOD, Benjamin 1
Franklin
FLEETWOOD, Frederick 1
Gleed
FLEGENHEIMER, Albert 5
FLEISCHER, Charles H
FLEISCHMANN, Charles H
Louis
FLEISCHMANN, Julius 1
FLEISCHMANN, Max C. 3
FLEISCHMANN, Raoul H. 5
FLEISCHMANN, Simon 2
FLEISHER, Benjamin 1
Wilfrid
FLEISHER, Samuel S. 2
FLEISHER, Walter Louis 4
FLEISHHACKER, Herbert 3
FLEISHHACKER,
Mortimer
FLEMER, John Adolph 5
FLEMING, Adrian 1
Sebastian
FLEMING, Aretas Brooks 1
FLEMING, Arthur Henry 1
FLEMING, Bryant 2
FLEMING, Burton Percival 1
FLEMING, Charles A. 1
FLEMING, Daniel Johnson 5
FLEMING, Dewey Lee 3

* Indicates More Than One Such Name Listed

FORD, Emory M. 5
FORD, Ford Madox H
FORD, Ford Madox 2
FORD, Ford Madox 4
FORD, Francis Chipman 1
FORD, Francis J.W. 6
FORD, Frank Richards 1
FORD, Frazer L. 3
FORD, George Alfred 4
FORD, George Burdett 1
FORD, George Michael 4
FORD, Gordon Lester H
FORD, Guy Stanton 4
FORD, H. Clark 1
FORD, Harriet French 3
FORD, Henry 2
FORD, Henry Clinton H
FORD, Henry Clinton 1
FORD, Henry Jones 1
FORD, Henry P. 5
FORD, Hiram Church 5
FORD, Howard Egbert 6
FORD, Hugh 5
FORD, Isaac Nelson 1
FORD, Jacob H
FORD, James H
FORD, James 1
FORD, James Buchanan 2
FORD, James Lauren 1
FORD, James W. H
FORD, Jeremiah Denis Matthias 3
FORD, John 1
FORD, John Baptiste H
FORD, John Battice 2
FORD, John Donaldson 1
FORD, John (Sean O'Feeney) 6
FORD, John Thompson H
FORD, Joseph C. 3
FORD, Julia Ellsworth 5 (Mrs. Simeon Ford)
FORD, Leland Merritt 4
FORD, Leonard Augustine 5
FORD, Mary Elizabeth 6 Forker (Mrs. Harland B. Ford)
FORD, Mary Hanford 4
FORD, Mason 3
FORD, Melbourne Haddock H
FORD, Nancy Keffer 4
FORD, Nicholas H
FORD, Nixola Greeley-Smith 6 (Mrs. Andrew Watres Ford)
FORD, Patrick 1
FORD, Paul Charles 5
FORD, Paul Leicester 1
FORD, Peter J. 4
FORD, Peyton 5
FORD, Richard 5
FORD, Richard Clyde 3
FORD, Sallie Rochester 4
FORD, Samuel Clarence 4
FORD, Samuel Howard 1
FORD, Sewell 4
FORD, Shirley Samuel 2
FORD, Simeon 1
FORD, Smith Thomas 1
FORD, Stanley Myron 5
FORD, Sumner 4
FORD, Thomas H
FORD, Thomas Francis 3
FORD, Tirey Lafayette 1
FORD, Walter Burton 5
FORD, Willard Stanley 3
FORD, William D. 5
FORD, William Ebenezer 1
FORD, William Henry 4
FORD, William Jesse 6
FORD, William Miller 1
FORD, William Webber 1
FORD, Worthington Chauncey 1
FORDHAM, Herbert 3
FORDNEY, Joseph Warren 1
FORDYCE, Charles 3
FORDYCE, Claude Powell 6
FORDYCE, James Paul 6
FORDYCE, John Addison 1
FORDYCE, Samuel Wesley 1
FORDYCE, Samuel Wesley 2
FOREHAND, Brooks 3
FOREMAN, Albert Watson 3
FOREMAN, Alvan Herbert 3
FOREMAN, Grant 3
FOREMAN, Harold Edwin 3
FOREMAN, Henry Gerhard 1
FOREMAN, Lester B. 5
FOREMAN, Milton J. 4
FOREMAN, Oscar G. 1
FOREPAUGH, Adam 1
FORESMAN, Hugh Austin 3
FOREST, John Anthony 4
FORESTER, Cecil Scott 4
FORESTER, Frank

FORESTER, John B. H
FORESTI, Eleutario Felice H
FORGAN, David Robertson 1
FORGAN, James Berwick 1
FORGAN, James Russell 6
FORGASH, Morris 4
FORIO, Edgar Joseph 5
FORKER, John Norman 3
FORKNER, Hamden 6 Landon
FORMAN, Allan 1
FORMAN, David H
FORMAN, Henry James 4
FORMAN, Joshua H
FORMAN, Justus Miles 1
FORMAN, Samuel Eagle 1
FORMAN, William St John 1
FORMENTO, Felix 4
FORMES, Karl Johann 4
FORNANCE, Joseph H
FORNELL, Earl Wesley 5
FORNES, Charles Vincent 1
FORNEY, Daniel Munroe 4
FORNEY, James H
FORNEY, John H. 1
FORNEY, John Wien H
FORNEY, Peter 1
FORNEY, William 1
FORNEY, William R(ufus) 5
FORNIA, Rita 1
FORREST, Aubrey Leland 3
FORREST, Edwin H
FORREST, French H
FORREST, Jacob Dorsey 5
FORREST, Nathan Bedford H
FORREST, Nathan Bedford 4
FORREST, Thomas H
FORREST, Uriah H
FORREST, William Mentzel 4
FORREST, William Sylvester H
FORRESTAL, Frank Vincent 3
FORRESTAL, James 2
FORRESTAL, James 4
FORRESTER, D. Bruce 3
FORRESTER, Elijah Lewis 5
FORRESTER, Graham 2
FORRESTER, Henry 4
FORRESTER, James Joseph 1
FORREY, George C. Jr. 3
FORRY, John Harold 4
FORSANDER, Nils 1
FORSCH, Albert 6
FORSE, Charles Thomas 1
FORSTALL, Armand William 2
FORSTER, Alexius Mador 4
FORSTER, E(dward) 5 M(organ)
FORSTER, Frank Joseph 2
FORSTER, James Franklin 5
FORSTER, Rudolph 5
FORSTER, Weidman 5 Wallace
FORSTER, William Blair 1
FORSTMANN, Curt Erwin 3
FORSTMANN, Julius G. 4
FORSYTH, David Dryden 1
FORSYTH, George Alexander 1
FORSYTH, Henry Hazlett 1
FORSYTH, James McQueen 1
FORSYTH, James W. 1
FORSYTH, Jessie 1
FORSYTH, John * H
FORSYTH, Robert 1
FORSYTH, Thomas H
FORSYTH, William 1
FORSYTHE, George Elmer 5
FORSYTHE, Newton 4 Melville
FORSYTHE, Robert Stanley 1
FORSYTHE, W. B. 3
FORT, Carl Allen 6
FORT, Franklin William 1
FORT, George Franklin H
FORT, George Hudson 6
FORT, Gerrit 1
FORT, Greenbury Lafayette H
FORT, J. Franklin 1
FORT, Jardine Carter 1
FORT, Joel B. Jr. 3
FORT, Marion Kirkland Jr. 4
FORT, Rufus Elijah 2
FORT, Tomlinson 1
FORTEN, James 6
FORTENBAUGH, Abraham 4
FORTENBAUGH, Robert 4
FORTESCUE, Granville 3
FORTH, Edward Walter 4
FORTIER, Alcee 1
FORTIER, Louis J. 6
FORTIER, Michel J. 3
FORTIER, Samuel 1

FORTMILLER, Hubert 6 Clare
FORTUNE, Alonzo Willard 3
FORTUNE, J(ohn) Robert 5
FORTUNE, William 1
FORWARD, Chauncey H
FORWARD, John F. Jr. 5
FORWARD, Walter H
FORWOOD, William Henry 1
FOSBROKE, Gerald Elton 4
FOSBROKE, Hughell Edgar 3 Woodall
FOSCO, Peter 6
FOSCUE, Edwin Jay 5
FOSDICK, Charles Austin 1
FOSDICK, James William 1
FOSDICK, Lucian John 4
FOSDICK, Nicoll H
FOSDICK, Raymond Blaine 5
FOSDICK, William 1 Whiteman
FOSHAG, William 3 Frederick
FOSHAY, James A. 1
FOSKETT, James Hicks 4
FOSS, Claude William 1
FOSS, Cyrus David 1
FOSS, Eugene Noble 1
FOSS, Feodore Feodorovich 5
FOSS, George Edmund 1
FOSS, George Ernest 3
FOSS, Martin Moore 6
FOSS, Noble 1
FOSS, Sam Walter 1
FOSS, Wilson Jr. 3
FOSSEEN, Carrie S. (Mrs. 5 Manley L. Fosseen)
FOSSLER, Laurence 1
FOSTER, A. Lawrence H
FOSTER, Abiel H
FOSTER, Abigail Kelley H
FOSTER, Addison Gardner 1
FOSTER, Adriance S. 6
FOSTER, Agnes Greene 1
FOSTER, Albert Douglas 5
FOSTER, Alexis Caldwell 2
FOSTER, Alfred Dwight 1
FOSTER, Allyn King 1
FOSTER, Ardeen 4
FOSTER, Arthur Borders 4
FOSTER, Austin Theophilus 4
FOSTER, Ben 1
FOSTER, Bernard Augustus 5 Jr.
FOSTER, Cassius G. 1
FOSTER, Cedric 6
FOSTER, Charles 1
FOSTER, Charles Elwood 1
FOSTER, Charles Henry 3 Wheelwright
FOSTER, Charles James H
FOSTER, Charles Kendall 2
FOSTER, Charles Richard 1
FOSTER, Clyde Tanner 6
FOSTER, David Johnson 1
FOSTER, David Nathaniel 1
FOSTER, David Skaats 1
FOSTER, Dwight H
FOSTER, Edna Abigail 2
FOSTER, Edward K. 4
FOSTER, Ellsworth D. 1
FOSTER, Enoch 1
FOSTER, Ephraim Hubbard H
FOSTER, Ernest Le Neve 4
FOSTER, Eugene Clifford 1
FOSTER, Fay 4
FOSTER, Finley M. K. 3
FOSTER, Francis Apthorp 5
FOSTER, Frank Hugh 1
FOSTER, Frank Keyes 1
FOSTER, Frank Pierce 1
FOSTER, George Burgess 3 Jr.
FOSTER, George Burman 1
FOSTER, George Nimmons 3
FOSTER, George P. 4
FOSTER, George Sanford 3
FOSTER, Glen Edward 4
FOSTER, Hannah Webster H
FOSTER, Harry Ellsworth 4
FOSTER, Harry LaTourette 1
FOSTER, Henry Allen H
FOSTER, Henry Bacon 3
FOSTER, Henry Donnel 1
FOSTER, Henry Hubbard 2
FOSTER, Herbert Darling 1
FOSTER, Herbert Hamilton 2
FOSTER, Horatio Alvah 1
FOSTER, Irving Lysander 4
FOSTER, Israel Moore 1
FOSTER, James Peers 4
FOSTER, James William 4
FOSTER, Jeanne Robert 5 (Mrs. Matlack Foster)
FOSTER, John H
FOSTER, John Early 1

FOSTER, John Gilman 1
FOSTER, John Gray H
FOSTER, John Hopkins 1
FOSTER, John McGaw 1
FOSTER, John Morrell 3
FOSTER, John Morton 5
FOSTER, John Pierrepont 1 Codrington
FOSTER, John Shaw 2
FOSTER, John Watson 1
FOSTER, John Wells 1
FOSTER, John Winthrop 6
FOSTER, Joseph 1
FOSTER, Joseph C. 6
FOSTER, Joseph Franklin 6
FOSTER, Joshua Hill 5
FOSTER, Judith Ellen 1 Horton
FOSTER, Julian Barringer 2
FOSTER, Laurence 5
FOSTER, LaFayette Sabine 1
FOSTER, Luther 4
FOSTER, Mabel Grace 1
FOSTER, Major Bronson 3
FOSTER, Marcellus Elliott 2
FOSTER, Martin D. 1
FOSTER, Matthias 4 Lanckton
FOSTER, Maximilian 5
FOSTER, Milton Hugh 6
FOSTER, Murphy James 1
FOSTER, Nathaniel Greene H
FOSTER, Nellis Barnes 2
FOSTER, Paul F. 5
FOSTER, Paul Hadley 5
FOSTER, Paul Pinkerton 5
FOSTER, Percy Semple 1
FOSTER, Randolph Sinks H
FOSTER, Reginald 2
FOSTER, Richard Clarke 2
FOSTER, Robert Arnold 4
FOSTER, Robert Frederick 1
FOSTER, Robert Sandford 1
FOSTER, Robert Verrell 1
FOSTER, Roger 1
FOSTER, Rufus Edward 2
FOSTER, Rufus James 4
FOSTER, Samuel Monell 1
FOSTER, Scott 5
FOSTER, Sheppard Walter 2
FOSTER, Stephen Clark H
FOSTER, Stephen Collins H
FOSTER, Stephen Symonds 4
FOSTER, T. Stewart 4
FOSTER, Ted 6
FOSTER, Theodore 1
FOSTER, Theodosia Toll 1
FOSTER, Theodosia Toll 3
FOSTER, Thomas Arnold 5
FOSTER, Thomas Flournoy 3
FOSTER, Thomas Henry 3
FOSTER, Thomas Jefferson H
FOSTER, Thomas Jefferson H
FOSTER, Vernon Whit 6
FOSTER, Virgll Elwood 5
FOSTER, Volney William 1
FOSTER, W(alter) 5 Bert(ram)
FOSTER, Walter Herbert 6
FOSTER, Warren William 2
FOSTER, Wilder De Ayr H
FOSTER, William 1
FOSTER, William Davis 1
FOSTER, William Eaton 1
FOSTER, William Edward * 1
FOSTER, William Frederick 2
FOSTER, William Garnett H
FOSTER, William Heber 2 Thompson
FOSTER, William Henry 3
FOSTER, William James 3
FOSTER, William Trufant 2
FOSTER, William Wallace 4
FOSTER, William Wilson 1 Jr.
FOSTER, William Z. 4
FOTHERGILL, John 3 Vincent
FOTITCH, A. Constantin 3
FOUGNER, Ernest Hjalmar 5
FOUGNER, G. Selmer 1
FOUILHOUX, Jacques 2 Andre
FOUKE, Philip Bond H
FOUKE, William Hargrave 1
FOULDS, Henry W. 3
FOULK, Charles William 5
FOULK, Claude Claude 5
FOULK, George Clayton 5
FOULK, William Henry 4
FOULKE, Elizabeth E. 5
FOULKE, William Dudley 1
FOULKROD, Harry 5 Ellsworth
FOULKROD, William W. 1

FOULOIS, Benjamin 4 Delahauf
FOUNTAIN, Claude Russell 2
FOUNTAIN, Percy 3 Coleman
FOUNTAIN, Reginald 5 Morton
FOUNTAIN, Richard 2 Tillman
FOUNTAIN, Samuel 1 Warren
FOUNTAIN, William 3 Alfred Sr.
FOURNIER, Alexis Jean 2
FOURNIER, Alphonse 4
FOURNIER, Leslie Thomas 4
FOUSE, Levi Garner 1
FOUSE, Winfred Eugene 3
FOUST, Julius Isaac 2
FOUT, Henry H. 4
FOWKE, Gerard 1
FOWLE, Daniel H
FOWLE, Frank Fuller 2
FOWLE, Luther Richardson 5
FOWLE, William Bentley H
FOWLER, Alfred 3
FOWLER, Arthur Thomas 5
FOWLER, Benjamin Austin 1
FOWLER, Burton Philander 4
FOWLER, C. Lewis 5
FOWLER, Carl Hitchcock 2
FOWLER, Charles Evan 1
FOWLER, Charles Henry 1
FOWLER, Charles Newell 1
FOWLER, Charles Rollin 3
FOWLER, Charles Wesley 4
FOWLER, Chester Almeron 2
FOWLER, Clifton Lefevre 4
FOWLER, David 1
FOWLER, Edmund P. Jr. 4
FOWLER, Edmund Prince 4
FOWLER, Elbert Hazelton 1
FOWLER, Elbert Hazelton 2
FOWLER, Elting Alexander 1
FOWLER, Frank 1
FOWLER, Frederick Curtis 5 II
FOWLER, Frederick Hall 2
FOWLER, Gene 4
FOWLER, George Little 1
FOWLER, George Ryerson 1
FOWLER, George S. 5
FOWLER, H. Robert 1
FOWLER, Harold North 3
FOWLER, Harry Atwood 5
FOWLER, Helen Frances 5 Wose (Mrs. Albert Vann Fowler)
FOWLER, Henry Thatcher 3
FOWLER, James Alexander 3
FOWLER, Jessie Allen 1
FOWLER, John H
FOWLER, John 1
FOWLER, Joseph Smith 1
FOWLER, Laura 6
FOWLER, Laurence Hall 4
FOWLER, Leonard Burke 2
FOWLER, Ludlow Sebring 4
FOWLER, Nathaniel Clark 1 Jr.
FOWLER, Orin H
FOWLER, Orson Squire H
FOWLER, Raymond Foster 2
FOWLER, Rex H. 5
FOWLER, Richard Labbitt 3
FOWLER, Robert Lambert 3
FOWLER, Robert Ludlow 1
FOWLER, Russell Story 3
FOWLER, Samuel 1
FOWLER, Thomas Powell 1
FOWLER, Trevor Thomas H
FOWLER, Walter William 1
FOWLER, William Charles 1
FOWLER, William Edward 5
FOWLER, William Eric 6

FOX, Abraham Manuel 2
FOX, Albert Charles 1
FOX, Alex P. 4
FOX, Andrew Fuller 3
FOX, Augustus Henry 6
FOX, Austen George 1
FOX, Carl 3
FOX, Charles Eben 1
FOX, Charles Eli 1
FOX, Charles James 5
FOX, Charles Kemble H
FOX, Charles Shattuck 1
FOX, Charles Welford 6
FOX, Daniel Frederick 2
FOX, Della 1
FOX, Dixon Ryan 2
FOX, Donald L. 2
FOX, Donald Richard 6
FOX, Early Lee 2
FOX, Edward J. 1
FOX, Emma Augusta 2

FOX, Fayburn L. 4
FOX, Felix 2
FOX, Fontaine Talbot Jr. 4
FOX, Francis Morton 5
FOX, Fred C. 4
FOX, Fred Lee 3
FOX, Frederick S(hartle) 5
FOX, Genevieve 3
FOX, George Henry 1
FOX, George Levi 1
FOX, George Washington Lafayette H
FOX, Gilbert H
FOX, Gustavus Vasa H
FOX, Harry H
FOX, Henry 5
FOX, Herbert 2
FOX, Herbert Henry Heywood 2
FOX, Howard 3
FOX, Jabez 1
FOX, James Butler 4
FOX, James D. 1
FOX, James Harold 5
FOX, Jared Copeland III 5
FOX, Jesse William 2
FOX, John 1
FOX, John Jr. 1
FOX, John McDill 1
FOX, John Pierce 1
FOX, Joseph John 1
FOX, L. Webster 1
FOX, Luther Augustine 4
FOX, Margaret H
FOX, Matthew 4
FOX, Norman 1
FOX, Norman Arnold 3
FOX, Oscar Chapman 1
FOX, Philip 2
FOX, Robert Myron 6
FOX, Sherwood Dean 5
FOX, Victor Samuel 3
FOX, Walter Dennis 1
FOX, Walter Gordon 1
FOX, William 3
FOX, William Freeman 1
FOX, William H. 1
FOX, William Henry 3
FOX, William Joseph 2
FOX, Williams Carlton 1
FOXALL, Henry H
FOXCROFT, Frank 1
FOY, Byron Cecil 5
FOY, Eddie 1
FOY, Mary Emily 5
FOY, Robert Cherry 2
FOYE, Andrew Jay Coleman 1
FOYE, Wilbur Garland 1
FRACHON, Benoit 6
FRACHTENBERG, Leo Joachim 1
FRACKER, Stanley Black 5
FRACKLETON, Susan Stuart 4
FRADENBURGH, Adelbert Grant 1
FRADENBURGH, J. N. 4
FRAILEY, Carson Peter 5
FRAILEY, Leonard August 1
FRAIN, Andrew Thomas 4
FRAKER, George W. 3
FRALEIGH, Arnold 5
FRALEY, Frederick H
FRAME, Alice Browne 1
FRAME, Andrew Jay 4
FRAME, James Everett 3
FRAME, Nat Terry 4
FRAME, Norman Renville 6
FRANCA, Manuel Joachim de H
FRANCE, Beulah Sanford 5
FRANCE, Charles E. 3
FRANCE, Evalyn Smith 1
FRANCE, Harry Clinton 5
FRANCE, Jacob 4
FRANCE, Joseph Irwin 1
FRANCE, Lewis B. 4
FRANCE, Mary Adele 6
FRANCE, Melville Jefferson 3
FRANCE, Mervin B. 5
FRANCE, Royal Wilbur 4
FRANCHERE, Gabriel H
FRANCHOT, Charles Pascal 3
FRANCHOT, Richard 1
FRANCINE, Albert Philip 1
FRANCIS, Arthur J. 2
FRANCIS, Brother Clement 4
FRANCIS, Charles Edward 1
FRANCIS, Charles Inge 5
FRANCIS, Charles Spencer 1
FRANCIS, Charles Stephen H
FRANCIS, Convers 1
FRANCIS, David Rowland 1
FRANCIS, Edward 1

FRANCIS, Emily A. 4
FRANCIS, G. Churchill 5
FRANCIS, George Blinn 1
FRANCIS, Herbert Cadogan 4
FRANCIS, James A. 1
FRANCIS, James Bicheno 6
FRANCIS, James Draper 3
FRANCIS, John Brown H
FRANCIS, John F. H
FRANCIS, John Haywood 1
FRANCIS, John Jr. 3
FRANCIS, John Miller 1
FRANCIS, John Morgan 1
FRANCIS, John Morgan 1
FRANCIS, John Wakefield 1
FRANCIS, Joseph H
FRANCIS, Joseph G. 6
FRANCIS, Joseph Marshall 1
FRANCIS, Kay 5
FRANCIS, Lee Masten 5
FRANCIS, Mark 1
FRANCIS, Parker B. 3
FRANCIS, Richard Clarence 4
FRANCIS, Richard J. 5
FRANCIS, Samuel Ward 1
FRANCIS, Sarah Dimon Chapman 4
FRANCIS, Sir Josiah 4
FRANCIS, Tench H
FRANCIS, Thomas Jr. 5
FRANCIS, W. A. 3
FRANCIS, Warren Briggs 5
FRANCIS, William Bates 6
FRANCIS, William Howard 2
FRANCIS, William Howard Jr. 4
FRANCIS, William Mursell 3
FRANCISCO, Don 6
FRANCISCO, John Bond 5
FRANCK, Charles 5
FRANCK, Harry Alverson 4
FRANCK, James 1
FRANCKE, Kuno 1
FRANCO, Bahamonde 6
FRANCOIS, Samson 5
FRANCOIS, Victor Emmanuel 4
FRANCOLINI, Joseph Nocola 4
FRANDSEN, Julius Herman 4
FRANDSEN, Peter 5
FRANGES, Ivan 5
FRANK, Abraham 1
FRANK, Alfred 2
FRANK, Alfred Swift 4
FRANK, Arthur Albert 4
FRANK, Augustus H
FRANK, Eli 3
FRANK, Everett 5
FRANK, Fritz John 4
FRANK, Glenn 1
FRANK, Graham 1
FRANK, Helen Sophia 6
FRANK, Henry 1
FRANK, Isaac William 1
FRANK, Jerome N. 3
FRANK, John Mayer 5
FRANK, Joseph Otto 1
FRANK, Lawrence Kelso 5
FRANK, Lawrence Louis 5
FRANK, Lewis Crown Jr. 5
FRANK, Maude Morrison 5
FRANK, Nathan 1
FRANK, Nelson 4
FRANK, Pat Harry Hart 4
FRANK, Royal Thaxter 5
FRANK, Selby Harney 6
FRANK, Tenney 1
FRANK, Theodore 3
FRANK, Theodore McConnell 1
FRANK, Waldo 5
FRANK, Walter 5
FRANKAU, Pamela 5
FRANKE, Ann 6
FRANKE, Gustav Henry 3
FRANKE, Louis 1
FRANKEL, Bernard Louis 4
FRANKEL, Emil 4
FRANKEL, Joseph Jerome 4
FRANKEL, Lee Kaufer 1
FRANKEL, Max 6
FRANKEL, Rudolf 5
FRANKEL, William Victor 5
FRANKENBERG, Lloyd 5
FRANKENBERG, Theodore Thomas 1
FRANKENFELD, Frederick 6
FRANKENFIELD, Harry Crawford 1
FRANKENSTEIN, Godfrey N. H

FRANKENSTEIN, John Peter H
FRANKENTHAL, Adolph Levy 4
FRANKFORT, Henri 3
FRANKFORTER, George Bell 3
FRANKFURTER, Felix H
FRANKL, Paul Theodore 3
FRANKLAND, Frederick Herston 4
FRANKLAND, Frederick William 1
FRANKLAND, Lady Agnes Surriage H
FRANKLIN, Alfred 5
FRANKLIN, Benjamin * H
FRANKLIN, Benjamin A. 1
FRANKLIN, Charles Thomas 6
FRANKLIN, Chester Arthur 3
FRANKLIN, Edward Curtis 1
FRANKLIN, Ezra Thomas 6
FRANKLIN, Fabian 1
FRANKLIN, Frank George 4
FRANKLIN, James 1
FRANKLIN, James Henry 4
FRANKLIN, Jesse 1
FRANKLIN, John Eddy 4
FRANKLIN, John Merryman 6
FRANKLIN, John Rankin H
FRANKLIN, Leo M. 2
FRANKLIN, Lewis Battelle 3
FRANKLIN, Lindley Murray 1
FRANKLIN, Lucy Jenkins 5
FRANKLIN, Lynn Winterdale 3
FRANKLIN, Marvin Augustus 5
FRANKLIN, Melvin M. 1
FRANKLIN, Meshack H
FRANKLIN, Philip 4
FRANKLIN, Philip Albright Small 1
FRANKLIN, Samuel Petty 3
FRANKLIN, Samuel Rhoads 1
FRANKLIN, Sidney Arnold 5
FRANKLIN, Thomas Levering 1
FRANKLIN, Wallace Collin 3
FRANKLIN, Walter Alexander 1
FRANKLIN, Walter Simonds 1
FRANKLIN, Walter Simonds 5
FRANKLIN, William H
FRANKLIN, William Buel 1
FRANKLIN, William Suddards 1
FRANKLIN, Wirt 4
FRANKS, E. T. 4
FRANKS, John B. 2
FRANKS, Robert A. 4
FRANT, Samuel 4
FRANTZ, Edward 1
FRANTZ, Frank 1
FRANTZ, Frank Flavius 4
FRANTZ, Joseph Henry 5
FRANTZ, Oswin Stricker 6
FRANTZ, Robert Benjamin 4
FRANTZ, Virginia Kneeland 4
FRANTZ, Virginia Kneeland 6
FRANZ, Elmer Franklin 5
FRANZ, Shepherd Ivory 1
FRANZEN, August 1
FRANZEN, Carl G. F. 3
FRANZHEIM, Kenneth 3
FRANZONI, Charles William 4
FRAPRIE, Frank Roy 3
FRAPS, George Stronach 5
FRARY, Ihna Thayer 5
FRASCA, William Robert 4
FRASCH, Herman H
FRASCH, Herman 1
FRASER, Abel McIver 1
FRASER, Alexander David 3
FRASER, Arthur McNutt 5
FRASER, Blair 5
FRASER, Carlyle 5
FRASER, Cecil Eaton 2
FRASER, Charles 1
FRASER, Chelsea Curtis 3
FRASER, Daniel 1
FRASER, Duncan William 3
FRASER, Elisha Alexander 1
FRASER, Forrest L. 4
FRASER, Frank Edwin 5
FRASER, Harry Wilson 3
FRASER, Horace John 5
FRASER, Horatio Nelson 4

FRASER, Hugh John 3
FRASER, Hugh Wilson Jr. 6
FRASER, James Earle 3
FRASER, John Falconer 5
FRASER, Laura Gardin 3
FRASER, Leon 2
FRASER, Malcolm 1
FRASER, Melvin 1
FRASER, Peter 3
FRASER, Samuel 3
FRASER, Thomas Boone 1
FRASER, Wilber John 2
FRASER, William Alexander 1
FRASER, William Jocelyn Ian 6
FRASER, William Lewis 1
FRASIER, George Willard 3
FRASIER, Waldo 6
FRASSINELLI, Attilio 4
FRATER, George Ellsworth 4
FRAUDENDORFER, Alfred 6
FRAUENHEIM, George Meyer 5
FRAUNCES, Samuel H
FRAWLEY, John Edward 4
FRAWLEY, John Milan 5
FRAWLEY, Michael P. 5
FRAYNE, Hugh 1
FRAZAR, Everett Welles 4
FRAZAR, Lether Edward 4
FRAZEE, Harry Herbert 1
FRAZEE, John H
FRAZER, David Ruddach 1
FRAZER, Elizabeth 4
FRAZER, George Enfield 5
FRAZER, John 4
FRAZER, John Fries 4
FRAZER, John G. 2
FRAZER, John Stanley 1
FRAZER, Joseph Christie Whitney 5
FRAZER, Joseph Washington 5
FRAZER, Leslie 2
FRAZER, Oliver H
FRAZER, Oscar Bryant 6
FRAZER, Persifor H
FRAZER, Persifor 1
FRAZER, Robert Sellers 1
FRAZER, Spaulding 6
FRAZER, William Henry 4
FRAZIER, Arthur Hugh 4
FRAZIER, Benjamin West 1
FRAZIER, Charles Harrison 1
FRAZIER, Chester North 4
FRAZIER, Clarence Mackay 3
FRAZIER, Edward Franklin 4
FRAZIER, Fred Brennings 6
FRAZIER, George Harrison 4
FRAZIER, James B. 1
FRAZIER, John Robinson 4
FRAZIER, Kenneth 2
FRAZIER, Lynn Joseph 2
FRAZIER, Raymond Robert 3
FRAZIER, Robert Thomas 1
FRAZIER, William Fiske 4
FREAR, James A. 1
FREAR, Walter 2
FREAR, Walter Francis 2
FREAR, William 1
FREAS, Howard George 5
FREAS, Thomas Bruce 1
FREAS, William Streeper 1
FREASE, Donald William 5
FRECHETTE, Annie Howells 5
FREDENTHAL, David 3
FREDERIC, Harold H
FREDERICK, Daniel Alfred 1
FREDERICK, George Aloysius 1
FREDERICK, Karl Telford 4
FREDERICK, Pauline 5
FREDERICK, Robert Tryon 5
FREDERICK, Russell Adair 4
FREDERICKS, John Donnan 2
FREDERICKS, Mary Pate (Mrs. George W. Fredericks) 6
FREDERICKS, R. N. 4
FREDERICKSON, Charles Richard 3
FREDERICKSON, George 4
FREDERIK, Christian Frederik Franz Michael Carl Valdemar 5
FREDERIKSEN, Ditlew Monrad 4
FREDRICK, John E. 2
FREDRICK, Leopold 1
FREDRIKS, Gerrit James 6

FREE, Arthur Monroe 3
FREE, Edward Elway 1
FREE, Joseph Paul 6
FREE, Lincoln Forrest 4
FREE, Montague 4
FREE, Spencer Michael 1
FREE, Walter Henry 4
FREEBORN, Stanley B. 4
FREEBOURN, Harrison J. 1
FREEBURG, Victor Oscar 1
FREEBURNE, Cecil Max 6
FREED, Arthur 5
FREED, Charles Abram 4
FREED, Emerich Burt 3
FREED, Fred 6
FREED, Isadore 4
FREED, Nettie S(chwer) 6
FREEDLANDER, A.L. 3
FREEDLANDER, Joseph Henry 2
FREEDLEY, Angelo Tillinghast 1
FREEDLEY, Edwin Troxell 1
FREEDLEY, George 5
FREEDLEY, John H
FREEDLEY, Vinton 5
FREEDMAN, Andrew 1
FREEDMAN, Emanuel R(alph) 5
FREEDMAN, John Joseph 1
FREEDMAN, M. Joel 6
FREEDMAN, William Horatio 1
FREEHILL, Joseph Hugh 4
FREELING, Sargent Prentiss 5
FREEMAN, A. F. Patrick 4
FREEMAN, Abraham Clark 1
FREEMAN, Albert Howard 4
FREEMAN, Alden 1
FREEMAN, Alfred Bird 3
FREEMAN, Allen Weir 1
FREEMAN, Arthur Merriman 6
FREEMAN, Bernardus H
FREEMAN, Charles Seymour 5
FREEMAN, Charles West 4
FREEMAN, Charles Yoe 4
FREEMAN, Clarence Campbell 1
FREEMAN, Clayton E. 5
FREEMAN, Douglas Southall 3
FREEMAN, Edmond Wroe 2
FREEMAN, Edward Monroe 4
FREEMAN, Ernest Bigelow 5
FREEMAN, Ernest Harrison 3
FREEMAN, Francis Breakey 2
FREEMAN, Frank Nugent 4
FREEMAN, Fulton 6
FREEMAN, George 1
FREEMAN, George Fouche 1
FREEMAN, Hadley Fairfield 3
FREEMAN, Harrison Barber 2
FREEMAN, Henry Blanchard 1
FREEMAN, Henry Raymond 1
FREEMAN, Henry Varnum 1
FREEMAN, James H
FREEMAN, James Crawford 1
FREEMAN, James Edward 2
FREEMAN, James Edwards H
FREEMAN, James Midwinter 1
FREEMAN, John Charles 1
FREEMAN, John D. H
FREEMAN, John D. Jr. 6
FREEMAN, John Dolliver 1
FREEMAN, John Ripley 1
FREEMAN, John William 1
FREEMAN, John William 6
FREEMAN, Jonathan 4
FREEMAN, Joseph 4
FREEMAN, Joseph Hewett 4
FREEMAN, Julia S. Wheelock 1
FREEMAN, Leonard 1
FREEMAN, Leonard 4
FREEMAN, Lewis Ransome 6
FREEMAN, Luther 4
FREEMAN, Mary E. Wilkins 1
FREEMAN, Miller 3
FREEMAN, Monroe Edward 5
FREEMAN, Nathaniel H
FREEMAN, Nathaniel Jr. H

FREEMAN, Ralph Evans 5
FREEMAN, Richard Austin 2
FREEMAN, Richard D. 5
FREEMAN, Richard Patrick 2
FREEMAN, Robert 1
FREEMAN, Rowland Godfrey
FREEMAN, Talbot Otis
FREEMAN, Thomas H
FREEMAN, Thomas J. A. H
FREEMAN, Thomas Jones 1
FREEMAN, W(eldon) Winans 5
FREEMAN, Walker Burford 1
FREEMAN, Walter
FREEMAN, Will 4
FREEMAN, William Perry 3
FREEMAN, Winfield 5
FREEMAN, Y(oung) F(rank) 5
FREER, Charles Lang 1
FREER, Eleanor Everest 2
FREER, Frederick Warren 1
FREER, Hamline Hurlburt 1
FREER, Otto 1
FREER, Paul Caspar 2
FREER, Robert Elliott 4
FREER, Romeo Hoyt 3
FREER, William Davis 5
FREESE, John Henry 5
FREESTON, William D(enney) 5
FREEBERG, Albert Henry 1
FREIBERG, Joseph Albert 6
FREIBERG, Leonard Henry 3
FREIBERG, Maurice 1
FREIBERGER, Isadore Fred 5
FREIDIN, Jesse 5
FREILER, Abraham J. 4
FREIMAN, Henry David 3
FREIMANN, Frank Michael 5
FREIN, Pierre Joseph 3
FREITAG, Joseph Kendall 5
FREITAG, Walter 3
FRELEY, Jasper Warren 4
FRELINGHUYSEN, Frederick H
FRELINGHUYSEN, Frederick 4
FRELINGHUYSEN, Frederick Theodore H
FRELINGHUYSEN, Joseph Sherman 2
FRELINGHUYSEN, Theodore H
FRELINGHUYSEN, Theodorus Jacobus H
FREMMING, Morris A. 3
FREMONT, Jessie Benton 1
FREMONT, John Charles 1
FREMONT, John Charles 1
FREMONT-SMITH, Frank 6
FREMSTAD, Olive 3
FRENCH, Aaron H
FRENCH, Alice 1
FRENCH, Allen 1
FRENCH, Amos Tuck 1
FRENCH, Amos Tuck 2
FRENCH, Anne Warner 1
FRENCH, Arthur Willard 4
FRENCH, Asa Palmer 1
FRENCH, Augustus C. H
FRENCH, Burton Lee 3
FRENCH, Calvin Hervey 1
FRENCH, Charles Wallace 1
FRENCH, Daniel Chester 1
FRENCH, Edward L(ivingstone) 5
FRENCH, Edward Sanborn 5
FRENCH, Edward Vinton 5
FRENCH, Edwin Davis 1
FRENCH, Ezra Bartlett 1
FRENCH, Ferdinand Courtney 1
FRENCH, Frances Graham 1
FRENCH, Francis Henry 1
FRENCH, Frank 1
FRENCH, Frank Chauncey 3
FRENCH, George 1
FRENCH, Harlan Page 1
FRENCH, Harley Ellsworth 5
FRENCH, Henry Willard 4
FRENCH, Herbert Greer 1
FRENCH, Hollis 1
FRENCH, Horace S. 4
FRENCH, Howard Barclay 1
FRENCH, J. Milton 4
FRENCH, Jacob 1
FRENCH, James Adolphus 1
FRENCH, James J. 1
FRENCH, John Robert H
FRENCH, John Shaw 5

FRENCH, John Stewart 5
FRENCH, Joseph Lewis 1
FRENCH, Leigh Hill 4
FRENCH, Lillie Hamilton 4
FRENCH, Lucy Virginia Smith H
FRENCH, Mary Adams 4
FRENCH, Mary Montagu Billings 3
FRENCH, Nathaniel Stowers 1
FRENCH, Owen Bert 4
FRENCH, Paul Comly 4
FRENCH, Pinckney 4
FRENCH, Ralph Lines 2
FRENCH, Richard H
FRENCH, Robert Dudley 3
FRENCH, Roy LaVerne 5
FRENCH, Samuel Gibbs 1
FRENCH, Seward Haight Jr.
FRENCH, Thomas H
FRENCH, Thomas Ewing 2
FRENCH, Willard 1
FRENCH, Willard S. 3
FRENCH, William 4
FRENCH, William Henry H
FRENCH, William Henry 4
FRENCH, William John 1
FRENCH, William John 2
FRENCH, William Merchant Richardson 1
FRENCH, William W. Jr. 5
FRENEAU, Philip Morin H
FRENZEL, John Peter Jr. 2
FRENZENY, Paul H
FRERET, James H
FRERET, William Alfred 4
FRERI, Joseph 4
FRERICHS, William Reinhard 3
FRERKING, Herbert William 6
FRESEMAN, William Langfitt 5
FRESHWATER, Robert Marquis 4
FRETTER, Frank B. 1
FRETWELL, Elbert Kirtley 4
FRETZ, Franklin Kline 2
FREUCHEN, Peter 3
FREUD, Sigmund H
FREUD, Sigmund 4
FREUDENBERGER, Clay Briscoe
FREULER, John Rudolph 1
FREUND, Ernst 3
FREUND, Erwin O. 3
FREUND, Hugo Abraham 3
FREUND, Jules 4
FREUND, Sanford H. E. 3
FREUTEL, Guy Scott 3
FREVERT, Harry Louis 6
FREW, Walter Edwin 1
FREW, William 2
FREW, William Nimick 1
FREY, Adolf 3
FREY, Albert R. 1
FREY, Calvin Alexander 2
FREY, Charles Daniel 3
FREY, Erwin Mortimer 5
FREY, John Philip 3
FREY, John Walter 4
FREY, John Weaver 5
FREY, Joseph Samuel Christian Frederick
FREY, Oliver W. 1
FREY, Walter Guernsey Jr. 4
FREYBERG, Sir Bernard H
FREYER, William Norman 4
FREYVOGEL, Charles Ernest Cecil
FRICK, Frank 1
FRICK, Henry H
FRICK, Henry Clay 1
FRICK, John Henry 3
FRICK, Joseph E. 1
FRICK, Philip Louis 5
FRICK, William Jacob 2
FRICK, William Keller 1
FRICKE, William A. 4
FRICKS, Lunsford Dickson 2
FRIDAY 1
FRIDAY, Charles Bostwick 6
FRIDAY, David 2
FRIDEN, John H. 4
FRIDENBERG, Percy 4
FRIDGE, Benjamin Franklin 3
FRIEBOLIN, Carl D(avid) 6
FRIED, George 2
FRIEDEL, Francis Joseph 4
FRIEDEN, Alexander 1
FRIEDEN, John Pierre 1
FRIEDEN, Pierre 3
FRIEDENBERG, Albert Marx 6

FRIEDENWALD, Aaron H
FRIEDENWALD, Harry 3
FRIEDENWALD, Herbert 2
FRIEDENWALD, Jonas Stein 3
FRIEDENWALD, Julius 1
FRIEDLAENDER, Israel 1
FRIEDLAENDER, Walter 4
FRIEDLANDER, Alfred 1
FRIEDLANDER, Israel 2
FRIEDLANDER, Jackson H. 6
FRIEDLANDER, Leo 4
FRIEDLANDER, Theodore 4
FRIEDMAN, Bernard 4
FRIEDMAN, Elisha Michael 3
FRIEDMAN, Emanuel David
FRIEDMAN, Francis Lee
FRIEDMAN, Harry G. 4
FRIEDMAN, Herbert Jacob 3
FRIEDMAN, Isaac Kahn 1
FRIEDMAN, Jacob Henry 6
FRIEDMAN, Lee Max 3
FRIEDMAN, Moses 3
FRIEDMAN, Samuel 5
FRIEDMAN, Sol H. 3
FRIEDMAN, Stanleigh Pohly 4
FRIEDMAN, William Frederick 5
FRIEDMAN, William Henry 4
FRIEDMAN, William Sterne 2
FRIEDMANN, Max E. 3
FRIEDMANN, Wolfgang Gaston 5
FRIEDRICH, Ferdinand August 6
FRIEDSAM, Michael 1
FRIEES, Horace Leland 6
FRIEL, Arthur Olney 1
FRIEL, Francis de Sales 3
FRIEL, Henry Craig 5
FRIELDS, Eva Christine 2
FRIEND, Albert Mathias Jr. 3
FRIEND, Albert Wiley 5
FRIEND, Emil 1
FRIEND, Oscar Jerome 3
FRIEND, Robert Ellas 4
FRIENDLY, Edwin Samson 5
FRIENDLY, Oscar Nathan 6
FRIERSON, Horace 3
FRIERSON, James Nelson 3
FRIERSON, John Woods 3
FRIERSON, William Little 1
FRIES, Adelaide Lisetta 2
FRIES, Amos Alfred 5
FRIES, Archibald 1
FRIES, Elmer Plumas 3
FRIES, Francis H
FRIES, Francis Henry 1
FRIES, George 2
FRIES, J. Elias 1
FRIES, John 1
FRIES, John William 1
FRIES, William Otterbein 1
FRIESEKE, Frederick Carl 1
FRIESELL, H. Edmund 2
FRIESEN, Abraham Penner 3
FRIESNER, Ray Clarence 3
FRIETCHIE, Barbara 4
FRIEZE, Henry Simmons 4
FRILEY, Charles Edwin 3
FRIMI, Rudolf 5
FRINK, Fred Goodrich 3
FRINK, John Samuel Hatch 3
FRIPP, William J. 4
FRISBIE, Alvan Lillie 1
FRISBIE, Guy Stoddard 5
FRISBIE, Henry Samuel 4
FRISBIE, Levi H
FRISBIE, Robert Dean 2
FRISBIE, William Albert 4
FRISBY, Edgar 1
FRISCH, Hartvig 2
FRISCH, Martin 3
FRISCH, Ragnar Anton Kittil 5
FRISCH, William 1
FRISHMUTH, Harriet Whitney 6
FRISON, Theodore Henry 2
FRISSELL, Algernon Sydney 1
FRISSELL, Hollis Burke 1
FRITCH, Louis Charlton 5
FRITSCH, Homer Charles 4
FRITSCHEL, Conrad Sigmund H
FRITSCHEL, George John 4
FRITSCHEL, Gottfried Leonhard Wilhelm H

FRITSCHEL, Herman L(awrence) 5
FRITTS, Carl Emerson 5
FRITZ, Herbert Daniel 5
FRITZ, John 1
FRITZ, John Henry Charles 3
FRITZ, Lawrence G(eorge) 5
FRITZ, Oscar Marion 3
FRITZSCHE, Carl Ferdinand 4
FRIZELL, Joseph Palmer 1
FRIZOL, Sylvester M. 5
FRIZZELL, Albert Burnett 1
FRIZZELL, Donald Leslie 5
FROBISHER, Sir Martin H
FROEDTERT, Kurtis R. 3
FROEHLICH, Jack E. 4
FROEHLINGER, Richard Anthony
FROELICHER, Francis Mitchell 4
FROELICHER, Hans 1
FROHLICH, Ludwig William 5
FROHMAN, Charles 1
FROHMAN, Daniel 1
FROHMAN, Philip Hubert 5
FROHMAN, Sidney 5
FROHRING, William Otto 3
FROLICH, Finn Haakon 4
FROMENTIN, Eligius H
FROMKES, Maurice 1
FROMMELT, Henry Julius 5
FROMUTH, Charles Henry 4
FRONING, Henry Bernhardt
FRONTENAC, Louis de Baude H
FROST, Albert D. 2
FROST, Albert Ellis 1
FROST, Alfred Sidney 1
FROST, Arthur Burdett 1
FROST, Charles Sumner 1
FROST, Edward J. 2
FROST, Edward Wheeler 4
FROST, Edwin Brant 1
FROST, Eliott Park 1
FROST, Frances 3
FROST, Frederick George 1
FROST, Fredric Worthen 2
FROST, George H
FROST, George Frederick 1
FROST, George Henry 1
FROST, Harry Talfourd 2
FROST, Henry Atherton 3
FROST, Henry Weston 3
FROST, Hildreth 6
FROST, James Marion 1
FROST, Joel H
FROST, John 1
FROST, John Edward 1
FROST, Joseph H. 4
FROST, Leslie Miscampbell 5
FROST, Norman 4
FROST, Norman Burke 6
FROST, Robert 4
FROST, Rufus Smith H
FROST, Stanley 2
FROST, Thomas C. 5
FROST, Thomas Gold 3
FROST, Timothy Prescott 1
FROST, Wade Hampton 1
FROST, Walter Archer 4
FROST, Wesley 4
FROST, William Dodge 3
FROST, William Goodell 1
FROST, William Henry 1
FROTHINGHAM, Arthur Lincoln 1
FROTHINGHAM, Channing 3
FROTHINGHAM, Ellen 1
FROTHINGHAM, Eugenia Brooks 5
FROTHINGHAM, James 1
FROTHINGHAM, James 1
FROTHINGHAM, Jessie Peabody 2
FROTHINGHAM, Louis Adams
FROTHINGHAM, Nathaniel Langdon H
FROTHINGHAM, Octavius Brooks H
FROTHINGHAM, Paul Revere 1
FROTHINGHAM, Richard H
FROTHINGHAM, Robert 1
FROTHINGHAM, Theodore Longfellow
FROTHINGHAM, Thomas Goddard
FRUEAUFF, Frank W. 1
FRUEAUFF, Harry Day 3
FRUEHAUF, Harry Richard 4

FRUEHAUF, Harvey Charles 5
FRUEHAUF, Roy A. 4
FRUIT, John Phelps
FRUITNIGHT, John Henry 1
FRUMESS, Gerald Myron 6
FRY, Alfred Brooks
FRY, Anson Clifton 5
FRY, Birkett Davenport H
FRY, C. Luther 1
FRY, Carl
FRY, Clements Collard 3
FRY, Francis Rhodes 5
FRY, Franklin Clark 5
FRY, Franklin Foster 1
FRY, Georgiana Timken 4
FRY, Harry Shipley 3
FRY, Henry Davidson 1
FRY, Jacob 1
FRY, Jacob Jr. H
FRY, James Barnet H
FRY, John A.B. 5
FRY, John Hemming 2
FRY, Joseph Jr. H
FRY, Joshua H
FRY, Lawford H. 2
FRY, Morton Harrison 5
FRY, Richard H
FRY, Samuel Roeder 5
FRY, Sherry Edmundson 6
FRY, Wilfred Washington 1
FRY, William H. 6
FRY, William Henry H
FRY, William Wallace 3
FRYBERGER, Agnes Moore 1
FRYDLER, William Wladyslaw 6
FRYE, Alexis Everett 1
FRYE, Benjamin Porter 5
FRYE, Frank Augustus 5
FRYE, Jack 3
FRYE, James Albert 1
FRYE, John H. 2
FRYE, Joseph H
FRYE, L. Arnold 4
FRYE, Louise Alexander (Mrs. Royal M. Frye) 5
FRYE, Newton Phillips 3
FRYE, Prosser Hall 1
FRYE, Theodore Christian 5
FRYE, William H
FRYE, William Clinton 3
FRYE, William Pierce 1
FRYE, William Wesley 6
FRYER, Douglas 5
FRYER, Eli Thompson 5
FRYER, Eugenie Mary 6
FRYER, Jane Eayre (Mrs. John Gayton Fryer) 5
FRYER, John 4
FRYER, Robert Livingston 1
FRYXELL, Roald H. 6
FTELEY, Alphonse 1
FTHENAKIS, Emmanuel 6
FUCHS, Emil 1
FUERBRINGER, Ludwig Ernest 2
FUERST, P. Placidus 3
FUERTES, Estevan Antonio 1
FUERTES, James Hillhouse 1
FUERTES, Louis Agassiz 1
FUESS, Claude Moore 4
FUESS, John Cushing 5
FUESSLE, Newton Augustus 1
FUGARD, John Reed 5
FUJKHOUSER, Raymond Joseph 4
FULBRIGHT, James F. 2
FULCHER, George Cordon 6
FULCHER, Paul Milton 3
FULD, Leonhard Felix 4
FULDA, Carl Herman 6
FULEIHAN, Anis 5
FULKERSON, Frank Ballard 4
FULKERSON, Monroe 3
FULLAM, James Edson 3
FULLAM, William Freeland 1
FULLBROOK, Earl S. 4
FULLER, Abraham Lincoln 4
FULLER, Alfred Carl 6
FULLER, Alfred Howard 3
FULLER, Alvin Tufts 3
FULLER, Andrew S. H
FULLER, Anna 1
FULLER, Arthur Davenport 4
FULLER, Ben Hebard 1
FULLER, Caroline Macomber
FULLER, Charles E. 1
FULLER, Charles E. 5
FULLER, Charles Gordon 5
FULLER, Claude A. 4
FULLER, Claude A(lbert) 5

FULLER, Clyde Dale 5
FULLER, Edgar 6
FULLER, Edward 1
FULLER, Edward Hawley 1
  Laton
FULLER, Ellis Adams 3
FULLER, Emily Guillon 4
FULLER, Eugene 1
FULLER, Frank Lanneau 3
FULLER, Frank Manly 3
FULLER, George H
FULLER, George Freeman 5
FULLER, George Gregg 5
FULLER, George Newman 5
FULLER, George R.
FULLER, George Warren 1
FULLER, George 1
  Washington
FULLER, H. Harrison 4
FULLER, Harold deWolf 3
FULLER, Harry James 6
FULLER, Hector 4
FULLER, Helen 5
FULLER, Henry Amzi 1
FULLER, Henry Blake 1
FULLER, Henry Brown 1
FULLER, Henry Jones 3
FULLER, Henry Mills H
FULLER, Henry Starkey 4
FULLER, Hiram H
FULLER, Homer Taylor 4
FULLER, Howard G.
FULLER, Hulbert 1
FULLER, J(ohn) Douglas 1
FULLER, John Wallace H
FULLER, Leo Charles 4
FULLER, Leslie Elmer 1
FULLER, Levi Knight H
FULLER, Loie 1
FULLER, Lucia Fairchild 1
FULLER, Lucius Eckstein 5
FULLER, Marcellus Bunyan 1
FULLER, Margaret 3
FULLER, Melville Weston 1
FULLER, Myron Leslie 1
FULLER, Olive Beatrice 5
  Muir
FULLER, Oliver Clyde 2
FULLER, Paul Jr. 2
FULLER, Philo Case H
FULLER, Raymond 4
  Garfield
FULLER, Richard H
FULLER, Robert Higginson 1
FULLER, Robert Stevens 5
FULLER, Samuel L.
FULLER, Sarah Margaret H
FULLER, Stuart Jamieson 1
FULLER, Teddy Ray 5
FULLER, Thomas H
FULLER, Thomas Charles 4
FULLER, Thomas James H
  Duncan
FULLER, Thomas Staples 1
FULLER, Timothy 1
FULLER, Walter Deane 4
FULLER, Warner 3
FULLER, Warren Graham 4
FULLER, Wiley Madison 3
FULLER, William David 4
FULLER, William Eddy 4
FULLER, William Elijah 1
FULLER, William Hayes 5
FULLER, William Kendall 1
FULLER, William Oliver 1
FULLER, William Parmer 5
  Jr.
FULLER, Williamson 1
  Whitehead
FULLERTON, Anna M. 5
FULLERTON, Baxter P. 1
FULLERTON, Charles 3
  Alexander
FULLERTON, David H
FULLERTON, Edith Loring 1
FULLERTON, George 1
  Stuart
FULLERTON, Hugh Stuart 5
FULLERTON, Kemper 1
FULLERTON, Mark A. 1
FULLERTON, Samuel 5
  Clyde
FULLERTON, William 4
  Morton
FULMER, Clark Adelbert 1
FULMER, Ellis Ingham 3
FULMER, Elton 1
FULMER, Hampton Pitts 2
FULMORE, Zachary Taylor 4
FULP, James Douglas 5
FULTON, Albert Cooley 1
FULTON, Andrew Steele 4
FULTON, Charles Herman 5
FULTON, Charles William 1
FULTON, Chester Alan 1
FULTON, Elmer Lincoln 4

FULTON, Frank Taylor 4
FULTON, Hugh 4
FULTON, James A. 3
FULTON, James Grove 5
FULTON, John 1
FULTON, John Allen 1
FULTON, John Farquhar 1
FULTON, John Hall H
FULTON, John Hamilton 1
FULTON, John Samuel 1
FULTON, Joseph Samuel 1
FULTON, Justin Dewey 1
FULTON, Kerwin Holmes 3
FULTON, Maurice Garland 5
FULTON, Robert H
FULTON, Robert Burwell 1
FULTON, Robert Irving 1
FULTON, Samuel 3
  Alexander
FULTON, Wallace H. 6
FULTON, Walter Scott 5
FULTON, Weston Miller Sr. H
FULTON, Weston Miller Sr. 4
FULTON, William H
FULTON, William John 4
FULTON, William Pomeroy 1
FULTON, William Savin 1
FULTON, William Shirley 4
FULTON, William Stewart 1
FULTZ, Francis Marion 4
FULWOOD, Charles Allen 4
FUMASONI-BIONDI, 1
  Peter
FUNCHESS, Marion Jacob 3
FUNDERBURK, James 6
  Ernest
FUNK, Casimir 4
FUNK, Charles Earle 3
FUNK, Clarence Sidney 1
FUNK, Erwin Charles 5
FUNK, Eugene Duncan 2
FUNK, Frank Hamilton 1
FUNK, Henry Daniel 1
FUNK, Isaac Kaufman 1
FUNK, John Clarence 3
FUNK, Miles Conrad 5
FUNK, Wilfred 4
FUNK, Wilhelm Heinrich 4
FUNK, William R. 1
FUNKE, Erich (Alfred) 6
FUNKHOUSER, Abram 4
  Paul
FUNKHOUSER, George A. 1
FUNKHOUSER, John 6
  William
FUNKHOUSER, William 2
  Delbert
FUNSTEN, Benjamin Reed 5
FUNSTEN, James Bowen 1
FUNSTON, Edward Hogue 1
FUNSTON, Frederick 1
FUQUA, Henry 1
FUQUA, Isham W. 6
FUQUA, James Henry 4
FUQUA, Stephen Ogden 2
FURAY, James Henry 3
FURAY, John Baptist 5
FURBER, Fred Nason 3
FURBER, Henry Jewett 4
FURBER, Pierce T. H
FURBERSHAW, Virginia 6
  Lawton
FURBRINGER, Max Henry 4
FURBUSH, Charles Lincoln 1
FURCHES, David Moffatt 1
FURER, Julius Augustus 4
FURER, William Charles 4
FUREY, Francis Thomas 4
FUREY, John Vincent 1
FURGUSON, Elizabeth H
  Graeme
FURLONG, Atherton 4
  Bernard Sr.
FURLONG, Charles 4
  Wellington
FURLONG, Thomas J. H
FURLONG, William Rea 6
FURLOW, Floyd Charles 4
FURMAN, Bess (Mrs. 5
  Robert B. Armstrong Jr.)
FURMAN, Franklin De 2
  Ronde
FURMAN, James Cement H
FURMAN, John Myers 1
FURMAN, Lucy 3
FURMAN, N. Howell 4
FURMAN, Richard H
FURNALD, Henry Natsch 2
FURNAS, Clifford Cook 5
FURNAS, Elwood 1
FURNAS, Robert Wilkinson 1
FURNESS, Caroline Ellen 1
FURNESS, Clifton Joseph 3
FURNESS, Horace Howard 1
FURNESS, Horace Howard 1
  Jr.

FURNESS, James Wilson 5
FURNESS, William Henry H
FURNESS, William Henry 1
  III
FURNISS, Edgar 5
  Stephenson
FURNISS, Edgar 4
  Stephenson Jr.
FURNISS, Henry Dawson 1
FURR, Roy 6
FURRER, Rudolph 5
FURROW, Clarence Lee 3
FURRY, William Davis 4
FURST, Clyde 1
FURST, Joseph 4
FURST, Moritz H
FURST, Sidney Dale 5
FURSTENBERG, Albert 5
  Carl
FURTH, Albert Lavenson 5
FURTSEVA, Yekaterina 6
  Alekseevna
FURTWANGLER, Wilhelm 3
FURUSETH, Andrew 1
FUSON, Samuel Dillard 4
FUSSELL, Bartholomew H
FUSSELL, Joseph Hall 1
FUSSELL, Lewis 1
FUSSELL, M. Howard 1
FUSTING, Frederick Erwin 4
FUTCHER, Thomas Barnes 1
FUTHEY, Bruce 4
FUTHEY, John Smith H
FUTRALL, John Clinton 5
FUTRELL, Junius Marion 3
FUTRELLE, Jacques 1
FUTRELLE, May 5
FYAN, Robert Washington H
FYFE, John William 4
FYLES, Franklin 1

G

GAARDE, Fred William 2
GABA, Meyer Grupp 4
GABALDON, Isauro 4
GABB, William More H
GABBARD, Elmer Everett 5
GABBERT, Mont Robertson 3
GABBERT, William Henry 1
GABEL, Carl W. 4
GABLE, Clark 3
GABLE, George Daniel 1
GABLE, Morgan Edwards 1
GABLE, William Russell 6
GABLEMAN, Edwin 3
  Wilson
GABRIEL, Charles L. 3
GABRIEL, Gilbert Wolf 4
GABRIEL, John Huston 4
GABRIEL, Mgrditch 4
  Simbad
GABRIELS, Henry 1
GABRILOWITSCH, Ossip 1
GABUZDA, George Joseph 6
  Jr.
GADDIS, Cyrus Jacob 4
GADE, John Allyne 3
GADLOW, David Berman 4
GADSBY, Edward Northup 6
GADSBY, George M. 1
GADSBY, Robert Charles 4
GADSDEN, Philip Henry 1
GADSEN, Christopher H
GADSEN, James H
GADSKI, Madame Johanna 1
GAEBELEIN, Arno 2
  Clemens
GAEDE, William R. 4
GAEHR, Paul Frederick 4
GAENSLEN, Frederick 1
  Julius
GAERTNER, Carl 3
  Frederick
GAERTNER, Fred Jr. 4
GAERTNER, Herman 3
  Julius
GAERTNER, William 2
GAERTTNER, Erwin 6
  Rudolf
GAFFEY, Hugh J. 2
GAFFNEY, Dale V. 3
GAFFNEY, Emmett 4
  Lawrence
GAFFNEY, Hugh H. 4
GAFFNEY, John Jerome 2
GAFFNEY, John Marshall 5
GAFFNEY, Leo Vincent 5
GAFFNEY, Matthew Page 4
GAFFNEY, Thomas St 2
  John
GAG, Wanda 2
GAGARIN, Yuri 6
  (Alekseyevich)
GAGE, Alfred Payson 1

GAGE, Brownell 2
GAGE, Charles Amon 5
GAGE, Elbert Mauney 5
GAGE, Frances Dana H
  Barker
GAGE, George Williams 1
GAGE, Harry Morehouse 4
GAGE, Henry Tifft 1
GAGE, Homer 1
GAGE, John Bailey 5
GAGE, John Bailey 6
GAGE, John H. 4
GAGE, Joshua H
GAGE, Lyman Judson 1
GAGE, Matilda Joslyn 1
GAGE, Simon Henry 2
GAGE, Susanna Phelps 1
GAGE, Thomas H
GAGE, Thomas Hovey 1
GAGE, Walter Boutwell H
GAGE-DAY, Mary M. D. 1
GAGEL, Edward 1
GAGER, Charles Stuart 2
GAGER, Curtis H. 4
GAGER, Edwin Baker 1
GAGGIN, Edwin Hall 3
GAGLIARDI, Tommaso H
GAGNON, J-Romeo 5
GAGNON, Onesime 4
GAGNON, Wilfrid 4
GAHN, Harry C. 4
GAIGE, Crosby 2
GAIL, William Wallace 3
GAILLARD, David Du 1
  Bose
GAILLARD, Edwin Samuel H
GAILLARD, Edwin White 1
GAILLARD, Felix 5
GAILLARD, John H
GAILLARD, William 6
  Dawson
GAILLARDET, Theodore H
  Frederic
GAILOR, Frank Hoyt 3
GAILOR, Thomas Frank 1
GAINE, Hugh H
GAINER, Denzil Lee 6
GAINER, Joseph Henry 2
GAINES, Charles Kelsey 1
GAINES, Clement 4
  Carrington
GAINES, Edmund H
  Pendleton
GAINES, Edward Franklin 2
GAINES, Francis Pendleton 4
GAINES, Frank Henry 1
GAINES, George Strother H
GAINES, James Marshall 1
GAINES, John Pollard H
GAINES, John Wesley 1
GAINES, John William 5
GAINES, Joseph Holt 1
GAINES, L. Ebersole 3
GAINES, Lewis McFarland 1
GAINES, Paschal Clay 1
GAINES, Reuben Reid 1
GAINES, Robert Edwin 4
GAINES, Ruth 6
GAINES, Wesley John 1
GAINEY, Percy Leigh 5
GAIR, George West 1
GAISMAN, Henry Jacques 6
GAITHER, Frances 3
GAITHER, H. Rowan Jr. 4
GAITHER, Nathan H
GAITHER, P(erry) Stokes 2
GAITHER, William Cotter 1
  Jr.
GAITSKELL, Hugh Todd 5
  Naylor
GAITSKILL, Bennett S. 1
GALARNEAULT, John 5
  Toan
GALATTI, Stephen 4
GALBERRY, Thomas H
GALBRAITH, Anna Mary 1
GALBRAITH, Archibald 5
  Victor
GALBRAITH, Clinton 1
  Alexander
GALBRAITH, John H
GALBRAITH, Nettie May 2
GALBREATH, John 1
  Morrison
GALBREATH, Robert 4
  Ferguson
GALE, Arthur Sullivan 5
GALE, Benjamin H
GALE, Clement Rowland 4
GALE, Edward Chenery 2
GALE, Edward Justus 5
GALE, Esson McDowell 4
GALE, George H
GALE, George Washington H
GALE, Henry Gordon 2
GALE, Hoyt Stoddard 3

GALE, Joseph Wasson 5
GALE, Laurence Edward 4
GALE, Levin H
GALE, Minna K. 5
GALE, Noel 4
GALE, Oliver Marble 5
GALE, Philip Bartlett 2
GALE, Richard Pillsbury 6
GALE, Samuel Chester 1
GALE, Stephen Henry 1
GALE, William Holt 1
GALE, Willis Donald 4
GALE, Zona 1
GALEN, Albert John 1
GALER, Roger Sherman 3
GALES, George M. 3
GALES, Joseph * H
GALITZEN, Elizabeth H
GALL, H
GALL, John Christian 3
GALLAGHER, Charles 3
  Eugene
GALLAGHER, Charles 1
  Theodore
GALLAGHER, Charles 1
  Wesley
GALLAGHER, Daniel J. 3
GALLAGHER, Edward 6
  George
GALLAGHER, Francis 3
  Edward
GALLAGHER, Henry M. 4
GALLAGHER, Howard 5
  William
GALLAGHER, Hugh 5
GALLAGHER, Hugh 1
  Clifford
GALLAGHER, Hugh H
  Patrick
GALLAGHER, John James 5
GALLAGHER, Louis 5
  Joseph
GALLAGHER, Michael 3
GALLAGHER, Michael 1
  James
GALLAGHER, Nicholas 1
  Aloysius
GALLAGHER, Ralph 4
  Aloysius
GALLAGHER, Ralph W. 3
GALLAGHER, Sears 3
GALLAGHER, Thomas 1
GALLAGHER, William 1
GALLAGHER, William H
  Davis
GALLAGHER, William J. 1
GALLAHER, Ernest Yale 5
GALLAHUE, Dudley 5
  Richard
GALLAHUE, Edward 5
  Francis
GALLALEE, John Morin 4
GALLAND, Joseph 2
  Stanislaus
GALLANT, Albert Ernest 1
GALLATIN, Albert H
GALLATIN, Albert Eugene 3
GALLATIN, Francis 1
  Dawson
GALLAUDET, Bern Budd 1
GALLAUDET, Edward 1
  Miner
GALLAUDET, Thomas 1
GALLAUDET, Thomas H
  Hopkins
GALLAWAY, Robert Macy 1
GALLEGOS, Jose Manuel H
GALLEN, John James 6
GALLICO, Poole 3
GALLI-CURCI, Amelita 4
GALLIE, William Edward 3
GALLIER, James 1
GALLIGAN, Matthew 4
  James
GALLIHER, William 1
  Thompson
GALLINGER, Jacob H. 1
GALLISON, Henry 1
  Hammond
GALLITZIN, Demetrius H
  Augustine
GALLIVAN, James 1
  Ambrose
GALLIVER, George Alfred 1
GALLIZIER, Nathan 4
GALLO, Fortune 5
GALLOWAY, Beverly 1
  Thomas
GALLOWAY, Charles 3
  Anderson
GALLOWAY, Charles Betts 1
GALLOWAY, Charles 1
  Henry
GALLOWAY, Charles Mills 5
GALLOWAY, Charles 1
  William

GALLOWAY, David Henry 3
GALLOWAY, Floyd 3
  Emerson
GALLOWAY, Irene Oṭi'lia 4
GALLOWAY, J. J. 4
GALLOWAY, John Stuart 4
GALLOWAY, Joseph H
GALLOWAY, Lee 4
GALLOWAY, Robert E. 4
GALLOWAY, Samuel H
GALLOWAY, Thomas 1
  Walton
GALLOZZI, Tommaso 3
GALLUP, Albert 4
GALLUP, Anna Billings 3
GALLUP, Clarence Mason 2
GALLUP, Edward Hatton 5
  Jr.
GALLUP, Frank Amner 3
GALLUP, Joseph Adams H
GALLUP, William Arthur 1
GALPIN, Charles Josiah 4
GALPIN, Kate Tupper 1
GALPIN, Perrin C. 6
GALPIN, Stanley Leman 4
GALPIN, William Freeman 4
GALSTON, Clarence G. 4
GALT, Alexander H
GALT, Arthur Thomas 6
GALT, Herbert Randolph 4
GALT, Howard Spilman 5
GALT, John Randolph 1
GALUSHA, Hugh Duncan 5
  Jr.
GALVEZ, Bernardo de H
GALVIN, John 2
GALVIN, John E. 6
GALVIN, John Francis 1
GALVIN, Joseph A. 3
GALVIN, Leroy Spahr 3
GALVIN, Michael Joseph 4
GALVIN, Paul Vincent 3
GAMA, Domicio da H
GAMACHE, George Paul 5
GAMAGE, Frederick 3
  Luther
GAMBEL, William H
GAMBER, Branson Van 3
  Leer
GAMBLE, Cecil Huggins 5
GAMBLE, Donald Phelps 5
GAMBLE, E. Ross 4
GAMBLE, Eleanor Acheson 1
  McCulloch
GAMBLE, Hamilton Rowan H
GAMBLE, James H
GAMBLE, James Lawder 4
GAMBLE, James Norris 1
GAMBLE, John Rankin 4
GAMBLE, Millard Gobert 6
GAMBLE, Ralph Abernethy 5
GAMBLE, Robert Bruce 1
GAMBLE, Robert Howard 4
GAMBLE, Robert Jackson 1
GAMBLE, Roger Lawson H
GAMBLE, Samuel Walter 5
GAMBLE, Sidney David 4
GAMBLE, Theodore Robert 5
GAMBLE, Theodore 4
  Roosevelt
GAMBLE, William Elliott 4
GAMBRELL, James Bruton 1
GAMBRELL, Joel Halbert 4
GAMBRELL, Mary Latimer 6
GAMBRILL, Charles D. 5
GAMBRILL, J. 3
  Montgomery
GAMBRILL, James Henry 3
  Jr.
GAMBRILL, Stephen 1
  Warfield
GAME, Josiah Bethea 1
GAMEL, W. Warren 5
GAMER, Helena Margaret 1
GAMERTSFELDER,
  Solomon Jacob
GAMERTSFELDER, 4
  Walter Sylvester
GAMEWELL, Francis 3
  Dunlap
GAMLEN, James Eli 6
GAMMACK, Arthur James 5
GAMMACK, James 3
GAMMAGE, Grady 4
GAMMELL, Robert Ives 1
GAMMELL, William 2
GAMMON, Burton 6
  Osmond
GAMMON, Edgar Graham 4
GAMMON, Elijah Hedding H
GAMMON, George Davis 6
GAMMON, Landon Haynes 6
GAMMON, Robert William 2
GAMMONS, Charles 4
  Clifford
GAMON, Wylena Clarissa 5

GAMORAN, Emanuel 4
GAMOW, George 5
GANDEK, Charles 6
GANDHI, Mohandas 2
  Karamchand Mahatma
GANDY, Charles Moore 4
GANDY, Harry L. 6
GANDY, John Manuel 5
GANDY, Joseph Edward 5
GANEV, Dimiter 4
GANEY, J. Cullen 5
GANFIELD, William 1
  Arthur
GANGEL, Martha 6
  O'Donnell (Mrs.
  Alexander Gangel)
GANGEWERE, Earnest 6
  Paul
GANIERE, George Etienne 1
GANIODAIIO H
GANLY, James Vincent 1
GANN, Edward Everett 4
GANNAM, John 4
GANNETT, Anne 3
  Macomber
GANNETT, Barzillai H
GANNETT, Ezra Stiles H
GANNETT, Farley 3
GANNETT, Frank Ernest 3
GANNETT, Guy Patterson 3
GANNETT, Henry 1
GANNETT, Lewis Stiles * 4
GANNETT, Thomas Brattle 1
GANNETT, William 1
  Channing
GANNETT, William 2
  Howard
GANNON, Anna 5
GANNON, Frank Stanislaus 1
GANNON, Fred Hall 6
GANNON, John Mark 5
GANNON, Sinclair 2
GANNON, Thomas Joseph 1
GANO, John H
GANO, Roy A. 5
GANO, Seth Thomas 3
GANO, Stephen H
GANOE, William Addleman 5
GANONG, William Francis 1
GANS, Edgar Hilary 4
GANSEVOORT, Leonard 1
GANSEVOORT, Peter H
GANSON, John H
GANT, Samuel Goodwin 5
GANTENBEIN, Calvin 1
  Ursinus
GANTENBEIN, James 4
  Watson
GANTT, Ernest Sneed 2
GANTT, Henry Laurence 4
GANTT, James Britton 1
GANTT, Nicholas Jourdan 6
  Jr.
GANTT, Robert Anderson 6
GANTVOORT, Arnold 1
  Johann
GANTZ, Hallie George 5
GANUS, Clifton L. 3
GANZ, Albert Frederick 1
GANZ, Rudolph 5
GARAKONTHIE, Daniel 4
GARAND, John C. 6
GARBER, Daniel 3
GARBER, Earl Augustus 4
GARBER, Frederick 2
  William
GARBER, Harvey C. 4
GARBER, J(ames) Otis 5
GARBER, John Palmer 1
GARBER, Milton Cline 5
GARBER, Paul Neff 5
GARCELON, Alonzo 1
GARCELON, William Frye 2
GARCES, Francisco Tomas H
  Hermenegildo
GARCIA, Carlos P. 5
GARCIA, Fabian 3
GARCIA LORCA, Federico 4
GARCIA-VELEZ, Carlos 4
GARD, Warren 1
GARD, Willis Lloyd 5
GARDEN, Alexander * H
GARDEN, Hugh Mackie 4
  Gordon
GARDEN, Hugh 4
  Richardson
GARDEN, Mary 4
GARDENER, Cornelius 1
GARDENER, Helen 1
  Hamilton
GARDENHIRE, Samuel 1
  Major
GARDENIER, Barent H
GARDINER, Arthur Z. 6
GARDINER, Asa Bird 1

GARDINER, Charles 1
  Alexander
GARDINER, Sir H
  Christopher
GARDINER, Curtiss C. 2
GARDINER, Frederic 1
GARDINER, George 1
  Schuyler
GARDINER, Glenn L. 4
GARDINER, Harry 1
  Norman
GARDINER, James 4
  Garfield
GARDINER, James L. 3
GARDINER, James Terry 1
GARDINER, John * H
GARDINER, John Hays 4
GARDINER, John Sylvester H
GARDINER, Lion H
GARDINER, Robert H
  Hallowell
GARDINER, Robert 1
  Hallowell
GARDINER, Silvester H
GARDINER, Sylvester H
GARDINER, T. Momolu 1
GARDINER, William 3
  Howard
GARDINER, William Tudor 3
GARDNER, Addison 5
  Leman
GARDNER, Albert 4
  TenEyck
GARDNER, Archibald K. 4
GARDNER, Arthur 4
GARDNER, Augustus 1
  Peabody
GARDNER, Bertie Charles 5
GARDNER, Caleb H
GARDNER, Celia 4
  Emmeline
GARDNER, Charles Henry 4
GARDNER, Charles Kitchel H
GARDNER, Charles M. 3
GARDNER, Charles 2
  Spurgeon
GARDNER, Dillard Scott 4
GARDNER, Donfred Huber 6
GARDNER, Earl 5
  Wentworth
GARDNER, Edward 4
  Frederic
GARDNER, Edward Joseph 3
GARDNER, Edward Tytus 3
GARDNER, Erie Stanley 6
GARDNER, Eugene C. 1
GARDNER, Eugene Elmore 3
GARDNER, Francis H
GARDNER, Frank 2
GARDNER, Frank Duane 4
GARDNER, Frank Saltus 1
GARDNER, Frederick 1
  Dozier
GARDNER, George 1
  Peabody
GARDNER, George W. 1
GARDNER, Gideon H
GARDNER, Gilson 1
GARDNER, Grandison 5
GARDNER, Halbert Paine 5
GARDNER, Harold Ward 5
GARDNER, Harry 5
  Wentworth
GARDNER, Helen 2
GARDNER, Henry A. 4
GARDNER, Henry Brayton 1
GARDNER, Henry Joseph H
GARDNER, Herbert 1
  Spencer
GARDNER, Herman 2
GARDNER, Hilton Bowen 4
GARDNER, Horace Chase 1
GARDNER, Horace John 3
GARDNER, Horace 4
  Tillman
GARDNER, Hugh Miller 2
GARDNER, Irvine C(lifton) 5
GARDNER, Isabella 1
  Stewart
GARDNER, James 1
  Augustus
GARDNER, James Henry 4
GARDNER, John 5
GARDNER, John Henry 4
GARDNER, John Howland 2
GARDNER, John J. 1
GARDNER, John Lane H
GARDNER, Joseph H
GARDNER, Karl Dana 2
GARDNER, Kirtland C. 5
GARDNER, Leroy Upson 2
GARDNER, Lester Durand 3
GARDNER, Mary Sewell 2
GARDNER, Matthias 6
  Bennett

GARDNER, Mrs. O. Max 5
  (Fay Webb Gardner)
GARDNER, Obadiah 1
GARDNER, Oliver Max 2
GARDNER, Percy W. 3
GARDNER, Rathbone 1
GARDNER, Robert Abbe 3
GARDNER, Robert 1
  Waterman
GARDNER, Trevor 4
GARDNER, Vernon 5
  O(race)
GARDNER, Wallace John 1
GARDNER, Walter Edwin 1
GARDNER, Walter Pennett 2
GARDNER, Washington 1
GARDNER, William A. 1
GARDNER, William 5
  Edward
GARDNER, William 5
  Edward
GARDNER, William Henry 1
GARDNER, William Sisson 1
GARDNER, Wright Austin 6
GARESCHE, Claude 4
  Francis
GARESCHE, Edward 4
  Francis
GAREY, Enoch Barton 3
GAREY, Eugene Lester 3
GARFIELD, Abram 3
GARFIELD, Charles Fowler 1
GARFIELD, Charles 1
  William
GARFIELD, Harry 2
  Augustus
GARFIELD, Irvin 3
  McDowell
GARFIELD, James Abram H
GARFIELD, James Rudolph 2
GARFIELD, Lucretia 1
  Rudolph
GARFIELDE, Selucius H
GARFORD, Arthur L. 1
GARIBALDI, Guiseppe H
GARIBI Y RIVERA, Jose 6
GARIS, Charles Frederick 3
  Fleming
GARIS, Howard Roger 4
GARIS, Lilian C. 3
GARLAND, Augustus Hill H
GARLAND, Cecil 5
  Raymond
GARLAND, Charles 5
  Stedman
GARLAND, Daniel Frank 1
GARLAND, David 4
  Shepherd
GARLAND, Frank Milton 4
GARLAND, Hamlin 1
GARLAND, James H
GARLAND, James A. 4
GARLAND, James Powell 4
GARLAND, Joseph 6
GARLAND, Judy 5
GARLAND, L. Henry 4
GARLAND, Landon Cabell H
GARLAND, Mahlon M. 1
GARLAND, Mary J. 1
GARLAND, Rice H
GARLAND, Robert 2
GARLAND, Robert 3
GARLAND, Thomas James 4
GARLAND, William May 2
GARLICK, Henry M. 1
GARLICK, Theodatus H
GARLINGTON, Creswell 2
GARLINGTON, Ernest 1
  Albert
GARMAN, Charles Edward 1
GARMAN, Harrison 4
GARMAN, Harry Otto 6
GARMAN, Raymond 5
  LeRoy
GARMAN, Samuel 1
GARMHAUSEN, Erwin 4
  John
GARNER, Alfred 5
  Buckwalter
GARNER, Harry Hyman 6
GARNER, James Bert 5
GARNER, James Wilford 2
GARNER, John Nance 4
GARNER, Richard Lynch 1
GARNER, Robert 6
  Livingston
GARNER, Wightman Wells 5
GARNET, Henry Highland H
GARNETT, Alexander H
  Yelverton Peyton
GARNETT, George 1
  Harrison
GARNETT, James Mercer 1
GARNETT, James Mercur H
GARNETT, Judith 1
  Livingston Cox

GARNETT, Louise Ayres 1
GARNETT, Muscoe Russel H
  Hunter
GARNETT, Porter 3
GARNETT, Robert Selden H
  *
GARNETT, Theodore 1
  Stanford
GARNSEY, Daniel Greene H
GARNSEY, Elmer 2
  Ellsworth
GARRABRANT, Arthur 3
  Anderson
GARRAN, Frank W. 2
GARRARD, James H
GARRARD, Jeanne 6
GARRARD, Jeptha 1
GARRARD, Kenner 4
GARREAU, Armand H
GARRECHT, Francis 4
  Arthur
GARRELS, Arthur 2
GARRETSON, Abram 1
  Quick
GARRETSON, Arthur 4
  Samuel
GARRETSON, Austin 1
  Bruce
GARRETSON, Cornelius 5
  David
GARRETSON, Garret 1
  James
GARRETSON, George 1
  Armstrong
GARRETSON, James H
  Edmund
GARRETSON, Joseph 1
  Kelleam
GARRETSON, Oliver 6
GARRETT, Alexander 1
  Charles
GARRETT, Alfred Cope 2
  Deane
GARRETT, Campbell 4
  Deane
GARRETT, Clyde D. 6
GARRETT, Daniel Edward 1
GARRETT, David 1
  Claiborne
GARRETT, Donald Wallace 5
GARRETT, Edmund Henry 1
GARRETT, Edward Isaiah 6
GARRETT, Eileen Jeanette 5
GARRETT, Erwin Clarkson 3
GARRETT, Finis James 3
GARRETT, Garet 3
GARRETT, George Angus 5
GARRETT, Harry Freeland 5
GARRETT, Henry 6
  E(dward)
GARRETT, J. Tracy 2
GARRETT, James Madison 5
  Jr.
GARRETT, James William 5
GARRETT, John Biddle 1
GARRETT, John Clifford H
GARRETT, John Work 1
GARRETT, John Work 2
GARRETT, Leroy Allin 4
GARRETT, Paul Loos 3
GARRETT, Philip C. 1
GARRETT, Ray 5
GARRETT, Robert 1
GARRETT, Robert 4
GARRETT, Robert Edwin 6
GARRETT, Rufus Napoleon 2
GARRETT, Thomas H
GARRETT, William Abner 1
GARRETT, William Adelor 5
GARRETT, William 1
  Robertson
GARRETTSON, Freeborn H
GARREY, George Henry 2
GARREY, Walter Eugene 3
GARRICK, James P. 6
GARRIGA, Mariano Simon 5
GARRIGAN, Philip Joseph 1
GARRIGUE, Jean 5
GARRIGUES, Henry 1
  Jacques
GARRIGUES, James 2
  Edward
GARRIOTT, Edward 1
  Bennett
GARRISON, Carl Louise 5
GARRISON, Charles Grant 1
GARRISON, Cornelius H
  Kingsland
GARRISON, Daniel H
GARRISON, Daniel 1
  Mershon
GARRISON, F(rank) H
  Lynwood
GARRISON, Fielding 1
  Hudson
GARRISON, Francis 1
  Jackson

GARRISON, George Pierce 1
GARRISON, George H
 Tankard
GARRISON, Harrell 5
 Edmond
GARRISON, Homer Jr. 5
GARRISON, James Carr 1
GARRISON, James Harvey 4
GARRISON, John Boggs 3
GARRISON, John R. 1
GARRISON, Lemuel 1
 Addison
GARRISON, Lindley Miller 1
GARRISON, Lloyd Amos 6
GARRISON, Mabel 4
GARRISON, Sidney 2
 Clarence
GARRISON, Walter 4
 Raymond
GARRISON, Wendell 1
 Phillips
GARRISON, William Hart 1
GARRISON, William Lloyd H
GARRISON, William Lloyd 1
GARRISON, William Re H
 Tallack
GARRISON, Winfred 5
 Ernest
GARROW, Nathaniel H
GARRY, Harold Bernard 1
GARRY, Spokane H
GARSIDE, Charles 4
GARST, Perry 1
GARST, Warren 1
GARSTANG, John 4
GARTH, Schuyler Edward 2
GARTH, Thomas Russell 1
GARTHE, Louis 1
GARTIN, Carroll 4
GARTLAND, Joseph 3
 Francis
GARTLEY, Harold 5
 McKinley
GARTON, Will Melville 2
GARTRELL, Lucius H
 Jeremiah
GARVAN, Francis Patrick 1
GARVER, Austin Samuel 1
GARVER, Chauncey 5
 Brewster
GARVER, Earl S. 5
GARVER, Francis Marion 5
GARVER, Frank Harmon 5
GARVER, Frederic 2
 Benjamin
GARVER, John Anson 1
GARVER, John Newton Jr. 3
GARVER, William Henry 4
 Harrison
GARVER, William Lincoln 4
GARVEY, Eugene A. 1
GARVEY, Helen Marie 5
GARVEY, James Allen 5
GARVEY, John L. 4
GARVEY, Marcus Moziah H
GARVEY, Marcus Moziah 4
GARVEY, Mary Patricia 3
 Sister
GARVIN, Edwin Louis 4
GARVIN, George Kinne * 5
GARVIN, Jay Earle 3
GARVIN, Joseph F. 4
GARVIN, Lucius Fayette 1
 Clark
GARVIN, Margaret Root 2
GARVIN, William Swan H
GARWOOD, Hiram 1
 Morgan
GARWOOD, Irving 3
GARWOOD, Sterling 1
 Marion
GARY, E. Stanley 4
GARY, Elbert Henry 1
GARY, Eugene Blackburn 1
GARY, Frank Boyd 1
GARY, Hampson 1
GARY, Hunter Larrabee 2
GARY, J. Vaughan 6
GARY, James Albert 1
GARY, Joseph Easton 1
GARY, Martin Witherspoon H
GARY, Theodore 3
GASAWAY, Howard 4
 Hamilton
GASCOYNE, John J. 1
GASKILL, Alfred 3
GASKILL, Francis Almon 1
GASKILL, Harold Vincent 6
GASKILL, Harvey Freeman H
GASKINS, Lossie Leonard 1
GASQUE, Allard Henry 1
GASS, Howard Allan 1
GASS, Patrick H
GASS, Sherlock Bronson 2
GASSAWAY, Percy Lee 1
GASSER, Herbert Spencer 4

GASSER, Lorenzo Dow 3
GASSER, Roy Cullen 4
GASSNER, John Waldhorn 4
GASSON, Thomas Ignatius 1
GAST, Charles E. 1
GAST, Frederick Augustus 1
GAST, Paul Frederick 6
GAST, Robert Shaeffer 2
GASTON, Arthur Lee 3
GASTON, Athelston 4
GASTON, Charles Robert 2
GASTON, Edward Page 1
GASTON, Ernest B. 1
GASTON, Everett Thayer 5
GASTON, George Albert 5
GASTON, James McFadden 4
GASTON, John 5
 Montgomery
GASTON, Joseph Alfred 1
GASTON, Lloyd H. 4
GASTON, Lucy Page 1
GASTON, William * H
GASTON, William 1
 Alexander
GATCH, Lee 4
GATCH, Thomas Leigh 3
GATCH, Thomas Milton 3
GATCH, Willis Dew 4
GATCHELL, Charles 4
GATCHELL, George 1
 Washington
GATELY, James Hayes 5
GATENBY, John William 6
 Jr.
GATES, Albert R. 5
GATES, Arthur Irving 5
GATES, Caleb Frank 2
GATES, Caleb Frank 3
GATES, Cassius Emerson 4
GATES, Charles Cassius 4
GATES, Charles Gilbert 1
GATES, Charles Winslow 1
GATES, Clarence Ray 1
GATES, Clifford Elwood 5
GATES, Earle Winslow 4
GATES, Edmund O. 5
GATES, Eleanor 3
GATES, Ellen M. 1
 Huntington
GATES, Elmer 1
GATES, Errett 5
GATES, Fanny Cook 1
GATES, Frederick Taylor 1
GATES, George Augustus 1
GATES, Herbert Wright 2
GATES, Horatio H
GATES, Isaac Edgar 4
GATES, Jasper Calvin 4
GATES, John Howard 1
GATES, John Warne 1
GATES, Joseph Wilson 4
GATES, Josephine Scribner 4
GATES, Kermit Hoyt 4
GATES, Lewis Edwards 1
GATES, Merrill Edwards 1
GATES, Milo Hudson 1
GATES, Moody Bliss 6
GATES, Owen Hamilton 1
GATES, Paul Hayden 3
GATES, Philetus Warren 1
GATES, Robert McFarland 4
GATES, Robert Moores 5
GATES, Robert S. 5
GATES, Seth Merrill H
GATES, Susa Young 4
GATES, Sylvester Govett 6
GATES, Sir Thomas H
GATES, Thomas Sovereign 2
GATES, W. Francis 4
GATES, William Benjamin 3
GATES, William Byram Jr. 6
GATES, William Frederick 1
GATESON, Daniel Wilmot 4
GATEWOOD, Arthur 5
 Randolph
GATEWOOD, James 1
 Duncan
GATEWOOD, James Edwin 4
 Norris
GATHERCOAL, Edmund 3
GATHMANN, Louis 4
GATLEY, George Grant 1
GATLEY, H. Prescott 4
GATLIN, Alfred Moore H
GATLING, Richard Jordan 1
GATSCHET, Albert Samuel 1
GATTI-CASAZZA, Giulio 1
GATTON, Roy Harper 4
GATTS, Robert Roswell 4
GATY, Lewis Rumsey 4
GAUCH, Donald Eugene 6
GAUCHAT, Robert David 6
GAUDIN, Antoine Marc 4
GAUGENGIGL, Ignaz 1
 Marcel
GAUGLER, Ray C. 3

GAUL, Gilbert William 1
GAUL, Harvey B. 2
GAULEY, Robert David 3
GAULIN, Alphonse Jr. 5
GAULT, Arthur Eugene 6
GAULT, Franklin Benjamin 1
GAULT, James Sherman 1
GAULT, Mark R. 5
GAULT, Norman Cox 3
GAUNT, Alfred Calvin 3
GAUS, Charles H. 1
GAUSE, Frank Ales 5
GAUSE, Fred C. 2
GAUSE, Lucien Coatsworth H
GAUSEWITZ, Alfred 4
 LeRoy
GAUSS, Christian 3
GAUSS, Clarence Edward 3
GAUT, John McReynolds 1
GAUTHIER, Eva 1
GAUVREAU, Emile Henry 3
GAVAGAN, Joseph 5
 Andrew
GAVEGAN, Edward James 4
GAVER, Harry Hamilton 4
GAVER, Jack 6
GAVIN, Frank Stanton 1
 Burns
GAVIN, Leon Harry 4
GAVISK, Francis Henry 1
GAVIT, Bernard Campbell 3
GAVIT, John E. H
GAVIT, John Palmer 3
GAVIT, Joseph 5
GAVRILOVIC, Stoyan 4
GAW, Allison 4
GAW, Cooper 3
GAW, Esther Allen 6
GAWTRY, Harrison E. 1
GAY, Carl Warren 5
GAY, Charles Richard 2
GAY, Ebenezer H
GAY, Edward 1
GAY, Edward James H
GAY, Edward Randolph 1
GAY, Edwin Francis 2
GAY, Frank Butler 1
GAY, Frederick Lewis 1
GAY, Frederick Parker 1
GAY, Frederick Parker 1
GAY, George Washington 1
GAY, H. Nelson 1
GAY, John Longdon 4
GAY, Maria 3
GAY, Maude Clark 3
GAY, Norman Russell 4
GAY, Robert Malcolm 4
GAY, Sydney Howard H
GAY, Taylor Scott 4
GAY, W. Allan 1
GAY, Walter 1
GAYARRE, Charles H
 Etienne Arthur
GAYER, Arthur David 3
GAYLE, John H
GAYLE, R. Finley Jr. 3
GAYLER, Charles H
GAYLEY, Charles Mills 1
GAYLEY, Henry Clifford 6
GAYLEY, James 1
GAYLORD, Charles Seely H
GAYLORD, Clifford 3
 Willard
GAYLORD, Edward King 6
GAYLORD, Franklin 2
 Augustus
GAYLORD, Harvey Russell 1
GAYLORD, James Madison H
GAYLORD, Joseph Searle 4
GAYLORD, Truman 1
 Penfield
GAYLORD, Willis H
GAYNOR, Frank R. 1
GAYNOR, Jessie Smith 1
GAYNOR, Paul Sr. 6
GAYNOR, William Jay 1
GAYOSO DE LEMOS, H
 Manuel
GAZLAY, P. M. 4
GAZLEY, James William H
GAZZAM, Joseph M. 1
GEAR, Harry Barnes 3
GEAR, Hiram Lewis 4
GEAR, John Henry 1
GEAR, Joseph 1
GEARE, Randolph Iltyd 1
GEARHART, Bertrand 4
 Wesley
GEARHART, Ephraim 6
 Maclay
GEARIN, John M. 1
GEARY, George Reginald 5
GEARY, John White H
GEARY, Joseph James 2
GEBELEIN, George 2
 Christian

GEBERT, Herbert George 4
GEBHARD, Heinrich 6
GEBHARD, John H
GEBHARD, Willrich 4
GEBHARDT, Ernest A. 4
GEBHARDT, George 5
 Frederic
GEBHARDT, Raymond L. 3
GEDDES, Alice Spencer 3
GEDDES, Sir Auckland 3
 Campbell
GEDDES, Frederick Lyman 1
GEDDES, George H
 Washington
GEDDES, James H
GEDDES, James Jr. 2
GEDDES, James Loraine H
GEDDES, John Joseph 2
GEDDES, Norman Bel 3
GEDDES, Ross Campbell 6
GEDDES, William Findlay 4
GEDDES, Williamson 1
 Nevin
GEDDY, Vernon Meredith 3
GEDYE, George Eric Rowe 4
GEE, A.M. 6
GEE, Edward 3
GEE, Nathaniel Gist 1
GEE, Wilson 3
GEER, Bennette Eugene 4
GEER, Curtis Manning 1
GEER, Danforth 4
GEER, E. Harold 4
GEER, Everett Kinne 3
GEER, George Jarvis H
GEER, Theodore Thurston 1
GEER, Walter 1
GEER, William Chauncey 4
GEER, William Clarke 2
GEER, William Henry 1
GEER, William Montague 1
GEERY, William Beckwith 4
GEHAN, John Francis 4
GEHL, Edward J. 3
GEHLBACH, Herman 4
 Hunter
GEHLE, Frederick W. 4
GEHLKE, Charles Elmer 5
GEHRES, Leslie Edward 6
GEHRIG, Lou 4
GEHRING, Albert 1
GEHRING, John George 1
GEHRMANN, Adolph 1
 John
GEHRMANN, Bernard 3
GEHRMANN, George 3
 Howard
GEHRON, William 3
GEHRS, John Henry 1
GEIBEL, Adam 1
GEIBEL, Victor B. 4
GEIER, Frederick August 1
GEIER, Philip Otto 3
GEIER, Philip Otto 1
GEIFFERT, Alfred Jr. 3
GEIGER, Alfred B. 3
GEIGER, C. Harve 6
GEIGER, Ferdinand A. 1
GEIGER, Jacob 1
GEIGER, Marlin George 4
GEIGER, Roy Stanley 2
GEIGER, William Frederick 5
GEIGLE, Francis R. 6
GEIJSBEEK, John Bart 5
GEIL, William Edgar 1
GEIS, George (Sherman) 4
GEISEL, Carolyn 1
GEISER, Karl Frederick 1
GEISLER, John George 1
GEISSINGER, James Allen 1
GEISSLER, Arthur H. 2
GEISSLER, Ludwig 1
 Reinhold
GEIST, Clarence Henry 1
GEIST, Emil Sebastian 4
GEIST, Samuel Herbert 2
GEIST, Walter 3
GELBACH, Loring Lusk 4
GELEERD, Elisabeth 1
 Rozetta (Mrs. Rudolph M.
 Loewenstein)
GELERT, Johannes Sophus 1
GELLATLY, John Arthur 5
GELLER, David 4
GELLERMANN, William 4
GELLERT, N. Henry 1
GELLES, Paul P. 4
GELLHORN, Ernst 4
GELLHORN, George 1
GELMAN, Samuel Joseph 6
GELSTON, David H
GEMMELL, Robert 1
 Campbell
GEMMELL, William Henry 4
GEMMILL, Benjamin 1
 McKee

GEMMILL, Willard 1
 Beharrell
GEMMILL, William 3
 Headrick
GEMMILL, William Nelson 1
GEMUNDER, August H
 Martin Ludwig
GENET, Arthur Samuel 5
GENET, Edmond Charles H
GENGEMBRE, Charles H
 Antoine Colomb
GENGLER, Leonard 6
GENIN, John Nicholas H
GENIN, Sylvester H
GENNET, Charles Westcott 2
 Jr.
GENNETT, Nathaniel 6
 Chapman Weems Jr.
GENSMAN, Lorrain M. 6
GENT, Mrs. Sophia S. H
 Daniell
GENTELE, C. Goran H.A. 5
GENTH, Frederick H
 Augustus
GENTH, Frederick 1
 Augustus Jr.
GENTH, Lillian 3
GENTHE, Arnold 2
GENTHE, Karl Wilhelm 5
GENTILE, Edward 5
GENTILE, Felix Michael 3
GENTLE, Alice True 3
GENTRY, Charles Burt 4
GENTRY, Cyrus S. 4
GENTRY, Martin Butler 3
GENTRY, Meredith H
 Poindexter
GENTRY, North Todd 2
GENTRY, Thomas George 4
GENTRY, William Lee 4
GENTRY, William Richard 4
GENUNG, George 1
 Frederick
GENUNG, John Franklin 1
GEOFFROY, W. J. 4
GEOGHAN, William F. X. 3
GEOGHEGAN, Anthony 4
 Vincent Barrett
GEOGHEGAN, William 1
 Anthony
GEORG, Walter Ferdinand 5
GEORGE, Albert Eugene 4
GEORGE, Albert Joseph 4
GEORGE, Andrew Jackson 1
GEORGE, Andrew Jackson 1
GEORGE, Charles Albert 3
GEORGE, Charles Carlton 1
GEORGE, Charles P. 2
GEORGE, Edgar Jesse 1
GEORGE, Edwin Black 4
GEORGE, Harold Coulter 1
GEORGE, Henry H
GEORGE, Henry 1
GEORGE I H
GEORGE II H
GEORGE III H
GEORGE, James Zachariah H
GEORGE, Jennings Burton 6
GEORGE, John J. 4
GEORGE, Joseph Henry 1
GEORGE, Joseph Johnson 6
GEORGE, Joseph Warren 4
GEORGE, Manfred 4
GEORGE, Robert James 1
GEORGE, Robert Mabry 4
GEORGE, Rufus Lambert 4
GEORGE, Russell D. 4
GEORGE, Vesper Lincoln 1
GEORGE, VI H
GEORGE, W. Kyle 6
GEORGE, W. Perry 4
GEORGE, Walter Franklin 3
GEORGE, William 1
GEORGE, William Reuben 1
GEORGESON, Charles 1
 Christian
GEOTHALS, George 1
 Washington
GEPPERT, Otto Emil 5
GEPSON, John Morgan 6
GERAGHTY, James M. 1
GERAGHTY, Martin John 1
GERALD, Mother Mary 1
GERAN, Elmer 3
 Hendrickson
GERARD, Felix Roy 2
GERARD, James Watson H
GERARD, James Watson 1
GERARD, Ralph Waldo 6
GERARDI, Joseph A. 4
GERASIMOV, Mikhail 1
 Mikhaylovich
GERBER, Daniel F. 6
GERBER, Frank 3

GERBERDING, George 1
Henry
GERBERDING, Richard 5
Henry
GERBRANDY, P. S. 4
GERCKE, Daniel James 4
GERDEMANN, Herbert 5
Edmund
GERDES, John 3
GERDINE, Thomas 1
Golding
GERE, Brewster Huntington 6
GERE, Charles Henry 1
GERE, George Grant 3
GERE, George Washington 4
GEREN, Paul Francis 5
GERGEN, John Jay 4
GERHARD, Gerhard 5
Russell
GERHARD, William Paul 2
GERHARD, William Wood H
GERHARDT, August 4
Edward
GERHARDT, Karl 4
GERHARDT, Paul Jr. 4
GERHART, Emanuel Vogel 1
GERHAUSER, William 3
Henry
GERICKE, Wilhelm 1
GERIG, John Lawrence 3
GERIG, William 2
GERITY, James Jr. 6
GERKEN, Rudolph A. 2
GERKEN, Walter Diedrick 5
GERLACH, Arch C. 5
GERLACH, Charles L. 2
GERLACH, George W. 4
GERLACH, John Joseph 1
GERLAUGH, Paul 2
GERLING, Henry Joseph 3
GERMAIN, George H
GERMAN, John S. 2
GERMAN, Obadiah H
GERMAN, William J. 2
GERMANE, Charles E. 2
GERMANN, Frank E(rhart) 6
E(mmanuel)
GERMANOS 2
GERMANY, Eugene 5
Benjamin
GERMER, Lester Halbert 5
GERMUTH, Frederick 4
George
GERNERD, Fred Benjamin 2
GERNON, Frank E. 1
GERNSBACK, Hugo 4
GERONIMO H
GERONIMO 4
GEROULD, Gordon Hall 3
GEROULD, James Thayer 4
GEROULD, John Hiram 4
GEROULD, Katharine 1
Fullerton
GEROULD, Winifred 3
Gregory
GEROW, Leonard 5
Townsend
GERRER, Gregory 3
GERRISH, Frederic Henry 1
GERRISH, Theodore 4
GERRISH, Thornton 3
GERRISH, Willard Peabody 5
GERRITY, Thomas Patrick 5
GERRY, Elbridge * H
GERRY, Elbridge Thomas 1
GERRY, James H
GERRY, Louis Cardell 4
GERRY, Margarita Spalding 4
GERRY, Martin Hughes Jr. 2
GERRY, Peter Goelet 3
GERSBACHER, Eva Nina 5
Oxford (Mrs. W.M.
Gersbacher)
GERSHON-COHEN, Jacob 5
GERSHOVITZ, Samuel D. 4
GERSHOY, Leo 6
GERSHWIN, George 5
GERSON, Felix Napoleon 2
GERSON, Oscar 5
GERSON, Theodore 5
Perceval
GERST, Francis Joseph 5
GERSTELL, Robert Sinclair 5
GERSTEN, E. Chester 5
GERSTENBERG, Charles 2
William
GERSTENBERGER, Henry 3
John
GERSTENFELD, Norman 5
GERSTER, Arpad Geyza 1
GERSTER, Jack Alan 5
GERSTLE, Lewis H
GERSTLE, Mark Lewis 5
GERTKEN, Severin (James) 6
GERVAIS, John Lewis 4
GERWIG, George William 3

GESELL, Arnold 4
GESELL, Robert 3
GESNER, Anthon Temple 1
GESNER, Bertram Melvin 5
GESSLER, A(lbert) 5
E(dward)
GESSLER, Theodore A. K. 1
GESSNER, Hermann 2
Bertram
GESSNER, Robert 5
GEST, John Marshall 1
GEST, Joseph Henry 1
GEST, Morris 2
GEST, William Purves 1
GESTEFELD, Ursula 1
Newell
GESTIDO, General Oscar 4
GETCHELL, Charles 4
Munro
GETCHELL, J. Stirling 5
GETCHELL, Noble 5
Hamilton
GETHOEFER, Louis Henry 2
GETHRO, Fred William 5
GETLER, Charles 4
GETMAN, Frederick 2
Hutton
GETSCHOW, Roy Martin 5
GETSINGER, Edward 4
Christopher
GETTELL, Raymond 3
Garfield
GETTEMY, Charles Ferris 1
GETTY, George Franklin II 6
GETTY, George 3
Washington
GETTY, Jean Paul 6
GETTY, Robert 5
GETTY, Robert N. 1
GETZ, Forry Rohrer 4
GETZ, George Fulmer 4
GETZ, Hiram Landis 4
GETZ, James Lawrence 1
GEYER, Bertram Birch 5
GEYER, Ellen M. 3
GEYER, Henry Sheffie 1
GEYER, Lee Edward 1
GEYL, Pieter 5
GHALI, Paul 5
GHEEN, Edward Hickman 1
GHENT, William James 2
GHEORGHIU-DEJ, 4
Gheorghe
GHERARDI, Bancroft * 1
GHERARDI, Walter 1
Rockwell
GHOLSON, James Herbert H
GHOLSON, Samuel 1
Jameson
GHOLSON, Thomas Jr. H
GHOLSON, Thomas H
Saunders
GHOLSON, William Yates H
GHORMLEY, Alfred M. 4
GHORMLEY, John Wallace 5
GHORMLEY, Ralph K. 3
GHORMLEY, Robert Lee 3
GHULAM, Mohammed 3
GIACCONE, John S. 6
GIACOMETTI, Alberto 4
GIANELLONI, Vivian 3
Joseph
GIANNINI, Amadeo Peter 2
GIANNINI, Attilio H. 2
GIANNINI, Lawrence 3
Mario
GIANNINI, Vittorio 5
GIAUQUE, Florien 1
GIAVER, Joachim G. 1
GIBAULT, Pierre H
GIBB, Arthur Norman 3
GIBB, Frederick William 5
GIBB, Hamilton Alexander 5
Rosskeen
GIBBES, Heneage 1
GIBBES, Robert Wilson H
GIBBINS, Henry 2
GIBBON, John H
GIBBON, John Heysham 3
GIBBON, John Heysham Jr. 5
GIBBON, Thomas Edward 1
GIBBONEY, Stuart 2
Gatewood
GIBBONS, Abigail Hopper H
GIBBONS, Cedric 5
GIBBONS, Charles David 5
GIBBONS, Douglas 4
GIBBONS, Edmund F. 4
GIBBONS, Edmund F. 1
GIBBONS, Floyd 1
GIBBONS, George Rison 3
GIBBONS, Henry H
GIBBONS, Henry 1
GIBBONS, Henry Jr. 1
GIBBONS, Herbert Adams 1
GIBBONS, James Cardinal 1

GIBBONS, James Edmund 3
GIBBONS, James Sloan H
GIBBONS, John 1
GIBBONS, Stephen B. 3
GIBBONS, Thomas H
GIBBONS, Walter Bernard 5
GIBBONS, William * H
GIBBONS, William Cephus 4
GIBBONS, William Futhey 4
GIBBS, A. Hamilton 4
GIBBS, Alfred Wolcott 1
GIBBS, Carey A. 5
GIBBS, Edwin C. 1
GIBBS, Frederick Seymour 1
GIBBS, George * H
GIBBS, George 1
GIBBS, George 2
GIBBS, George Couper 3
GIBBS, George Sabin 2
GIBBS, Harry Drake 1
GIBBS, James Ethan Allen H
GIBBS, Jeannette Phillips 5
GIBBS, John Sears Jr. 1
GIBBS, Josiah Willard H
GIBBS, Josiah Willard 1
GIBBS, Lincoln Robinson 2
GIBBS, Sir Philip 4
GIBBS, Ralph A. 4
GIBBS, Robert Adams 3
GIBBS, Roswell Clifton 6
GIBBS, William Francis 4
GIBBS, William Hasell 1
GIBBS, Willis Benjamin 1
GIBBS, Winifred Stuart 1
GIBBS, Wolcott 1
GIBBS, Wolcott 3
GIBIER, Paul 1
GIBLIN, Walter M. 4
GIBNEY, Virgil Pendleton 1
GIBSON, Anna Lemira 4
GIBSON, Axel Emil 1
GIBSON, Ben J. 2
GIBSON, Cable Morgan 5
GIBSON, Carleton Bartlett 1
GIBSON, Charles Brockway 4
GIBSON, Charles Dana H
GIBSON, Charles Donnel 4
GIBSON, Charles 3
Hammond
GIBSON, Charles Hopper 1
GIBSON, Charles Langdon 2
GIBSON, Edgar J. 1
GIBSON, Edwin T. 3
GIBSON, Ernest Willard 3
GIBSON, Ernest William 5
GIBSON, Eva Katherine 1
Clapp
GIBSON, Finley F. 5
GIBSON, Frank Markey 1
GIBSON, George H
GIBSON, George Miles 1
GIBSON, Harvey Dow 3
GIBSON, Henry Richard 1
GIBSON, Horatio Gates 1
GIBSON, Hugh 3
GIBSON, J(ohn) J(oseph) 5
GIBSON, James Alexander 1
GIBSON, James Edgar 4
GIBSON, James King H
GIBSON, James Lambert 2
GIBSON, John H
GIBSON, John Bannister H
GIBSON, Joseph Thompson 1
GIBSON, Lorenzo P. 1
GIBSON, Louis Henry 1
GIBSON, Norman Rothwell 6
GIBSON, Paris 1
GIBSON, Paul Emil 4
GIBSON, Preston 1
GIBSON, Randall Lee H
GIBSON, Robert Atkinson 1
GIBSON, Robert Edward 4
Lee
GIBSON, Robert Murray 2
GIBSON, Robert Newcomb 4
GIBSON, Robert Williams 1
GIBSON, Samuel Carrol 1
GIBSON, Stanley 3
GIBSON, Thomas L. 6
GIBSON, Truman Kella 1
GIBSON, Walter Murray 3
GIBSON, William H
GIBSON, William Campbell 1
GIBSON, William Hamilton H
GIBSON, William Meredith 1
GIBSON, William Richie 1
GIBSON, William Wesley 1
GIDDINGS, Franklin 1
Henry
GIDDINGS, Howard 2
Andrus
GIDDINGS, Joshua Reed H
GIDDINGS, Napoleon H
Bonaparte
GIDE, Andre Paul 3
Guillaume

GIDEON, Abram 4
GIDEON, Dave 2
GIDEON, Peter Miller H
GIDEON, Valentine 3
GIDLEY, James Williams 1
GIDNEY, Herbert Alfred 4
GIE, Stefanus Francois 5
Naude
GIEDION, Siegfried 5
GIEGENGACK, Augustus 6
E.
GIEGERICH, Leonard 1
Anthony
GIELNIAK, Jozef 5
GIELOW, Martha Sawyer 1
GIERING, Eugene Thomas 1
GIERULA, Jerzy Kazimierz 6
GIES, William John 3
GIESE, Augustus Albert 5
GIESE, Herman Robert 5
GIESE, Oscar W. 3
GIESE, William Frederic 5
GIESECKE, Frederick 5
Ernest
GIESECKE, Friederich 5
Ernst
GIESEKING, Walter 3
Wilhelm
GIESEL, Frederick W. 2
GIESLER, Jerry 4
GIESLER-ANNEKE, H
Mathilde Franziska
GIESY, John Ulrich 2
GIFFEN, James Kelly 1
GIFFEN, John Kelly 1
GIFFIN, William M. 4
GIFFORD, Augusta Hale 1
GIFFORD, Charles L. 2
GIFFORD, Frances Eliot 4
GIFFORD, Franklin Kent 4
GIFFORD, George 1
GIFFORD, George 3
GIFFORD, Glen J. 3
GIFFORD, Harold 4
GIFFORD, James Meacham 1
GIFFORD, John Clayton 2
GIFFORD, Kenneth C. 4
GIFFORD, L. C. 5
GIFFORD, Livingston 1
GIFFORD, Miram 5
Wentworth
GIFFORD, Orrin Philip 1
GIFFORD, Ralph Clayton 5
GIFFORD, Ralph Waldo 1
GIFFORD, Robert Ladd 4
GIFFORD, Robert Swain 1
GIFFORD, Roy Wellington 3
GIFFORD, Sanford H
Robinson
GIFFORD, Sanford 2
Robinson
GIFFORD, Seth Kelley 1
GIFFORD, Sidney Brooks 4
GIFFORD, Walter John 3
GIFFORD, Walter Sherman 4
GIFFORD, William Logan 5
Rodman
GIGLI, Benjimino 3
GIGNILLIAT, Leigh 5
R(obinson) Jr.
GIGNILLIAT, Leigh 1
Robinson
GIGNOUX, Regis Francois H
GIGOT, Francis Ernest 1
GIHON, Albert Dakin 5
GIHON, Albert Leary 1
GILBER, James Henry 5
GILBERT, Abijah 1
GILBERT, Albert Clark 5
GILBERT, Alexander 1
GILBERT, Alfred Carlton 5
GILBERT, Alfred Carlton 4
Jr.
GILBERT, Arthur Hill 5
GILBERT, Arthur Witter 1
GILBERT, Benjamin Davis 1
GILBERT, Carol Jeanne 6
GILBERT, Cass 1
GILBERT, Charles Allan 4
GILBERT, Charles Benajah 1
GILBERT, Charles Calvin 3
Sr.
GILBERT, Charles Henry 1
GILBERT, Charles Kendall 4
GILBERT, Charles 5
Pierrepont H.
GILBERT, Clinton Wallace 1
GILBERT, Donald Wood 3
GILBERT, Earl C. 4
GILBERT, Edward H
GILBERT, Edward 5
Martinius
GILBERT, Eliphalet H
Wheeler
GILBERT, Ezekiel H
GILBERT, Frank Bixby 1

GILBERT, Frederick 6
Augustus
GILBERT, Frederick 5
Spofford
GILBERT, George Blodgett 2
GILBERT, George Burton 3
GILBERT, George Gilmore 1
GILBERT, Mrs. George 1
Henry
GILBERT, George Holley 1
GILBERT, Grove Karl 1
GILBERT, Harvey 3
Wilbarger
GILBERT, Henderson 4
GILBERT, Henry Franklin 1
Belknap
GILBERT, Hiram Thornton 1
GILBERT, Horace Mark 1
GILBERT, Sir Humphrey H
GILBERT, James Eleazer 1
GILBERT, James Henry 6
GILBERT, John 1
GILBERT, John 4
GILBERT, John Gibbs H
GILBERT, John Ingersoll 5
GILBERT, Joseph Oscar 5
GILBERT, Joseph Walter 2
GILBERT, Katharine 3
GILBERT, L(ouis) Wolfe 4
GILBERT, Levi 1
GILBERT, Linda H
GILBERT, Lyman D. 1
GILBERT, Mahlon Norris 1
GILBERT, Marie Dolores H
Eliza Rosanna
GILBERT, Marion L. 4
GILBERT, Matthew William 1
GILBERT, Nelson Rust 4
GILBERT, Newell Clark 3
GILBERT, Newton Whiting 1
GILBERT, Osceola 2
Pinckney
GILBERT, Prentiss Bailey 2
GILBERT, Ralph 1
GILBERT, Robert Randle 5
GILBERT, Rufus Henry H
GILBERT, S. Price 3
GILBERT, Samuel T. 2
GILBERT, Seymour Parker 1
GILBERT, Sylvester H
GILBERT, Vedder Morris 5
GILBERT, Virgil O. 4
GILBERT, Walter Bond 1
GILBERT, William H
Augustus
GILBERT, William Ball 1
GILBERT, William Edward 2
GILBERT, William Lewis H
GILBERT, William Marshall 4
GIL-BORGES, Esteban 6
GILBOY, Glennon 3
GILBREATH, James 4
Richard
GILBREATH, Sidney 1
Gordon
GILBREATH, W(illiam) 5
Sydnor Jr.
GILBRETH, Frank Bunker 1
GILBRETH, Lillian Moller 5
GILBRETH, Lillian Moller 6
GILCHRIST, Albert Waller 1
GILCHRIST, Alexander 1
GILCHRIST, Beth Bradford 1
GILCHRIST, Clarence 6
Thomas
GILCHRIST, Donald Bean 1
GILCHRIST, Fred C. 3
GILCHRIST, Harry Lorenzo 2
GILCHRIST, Huntington 6
GILCHRIST, Jack Cecil 5
GILCHRIST, John Foster 4
GILCHRIST, John 1
Raymond
GILCHRIST, Robert H
GILCHRIST, T. Caspar 1
GILCHRIST, Thomas Byron 4
GILCHRIST, William 1
Wallace
GILCREASE, Thomas 4
GILDER, Jeannette Leonard 1
GILDER, John Francis 1
GILDER, Joseph B. 1
GILDER, Richard Watson 1
GILDER, Robert Fletcher 1
GILDER, Rodman 3
GILDER, William Henry 1
GILDERSLEEVE, Basil 1
Lanneau
GILDERSLEEVE, 1
Ferdinand
GILDERSLEEVE, Henry 1
Alger
GILDERSLEEVE, Oliver 1
GILDERSLEEVE, Virginia 4
Crocheron
GILE, John Fowler 3

GILE, John Martin 1
GILE, M. Clement 1
GILES, Chauncey H
GILES, Dorothy 4
GILES, Howard Everett 3
GILES, J. Edward 4
GILES, Malcolm R. 3
GILES, William Alexander 1
GILES, William Branch H
GILES, William Fell H
GILHAMS, Clarence C. 3
GILKEY, Charles Whitney 5
GILKEY, Geraldine Gunsaulus Brown 3
GILKINSON, Howard 4
GILKISON, Frank E. 3
GILKYSON, (Thomas) Walter 5
GILL, Adam Capen 1
GILL, Augustus Herman 1
GILL, Benjamin 1
GILL, Bennett Lloyd 1
GILL, Charles Clifford 2
GILL, Corrington 2
GILL, Elbyrne Grady 4
GILL, Everett 3
GILL, George Carleton 4
GILL, Henry Z. 1
GILL, James Presley 4
GILL, Joe Henry 2
GILL, John H
GILL, John Edward 1
GILL, John Goodner 4
GILL, John Jr. 1
GILL, Joseph A. 1
GILL, Joseph J. 4
GILL, Joseph Kaye 1
GILL, Kermode Frederic 5
GILL, Laura Drake 1
GILL, Patrick Francis 1
GILL, Paul Ludwig 1
GILL, Richard C. 3
GILL, Theodore Nicholas 1
GILL, Thomas Augustus 1
GILL, Thomas Harvey 5
GILL, Waltus Hughes 1
GILL, William Andrew 1
GILL, William Fearing 1
GILL, William Francis 1
GILL, William Hanson 6
GILL, William Hugh 1
GILL, Wilson Lindsley 1
GILLAM, Bernhard H
GILLAM, Manly Marcus 4
GILLAN, Silas Lee 4
GILLANDERS, John Gordon 2
GILLEAUDEAU, Raymond 3
GILLEM, Alvan Cullem H
GILLEM, Alvan Cullom Jr. 5
GILLEN, Charles P. 3
GILLEN, Courtland C. 3
GILLEN, Wilfred Donnell 5
GILLES, Verner Arthur 3
GILLESPIE, Alexander Garfield 3
GILLESPIE, Barnes 1
GILLESPIE, Charles Bowen 1
GILLESPIE, Dean Milton 2
GILLESPIE, George H
GILLESPIE, George Benjamin 3
GILLESPIE, George De Normandie 1
GILLESPIE, George Lewis 1
GILLESPIE, James H
GILLESPIE, James Edward 4
GILLESPIE, James Frank 3
GILLESPIE, Julian Edgeworth 1
GILLESPIE, Louis Frank 5
GILLESPIE, Mabel H
GILLESPIE, Mabel 4
GILLESPIE, Neal Henry H
GILLESPIE, Oscar William 4
GILLESPIE, Richard Thomas 1
GILLESPIE, Thomas A. 1
GILLESPIE, William 2
GILLESPIE, William Lane 3
GILLESPIE, William Mitchell H
GILLET, Charles 5
GILLET, Charles William 1
GILLET, Guy Mark 5
GILLET, Joseph Eugene 3
GILLET, Paul 5
GILLET, Ransom Hooker H
GILLETT, Arthur Dudley Samuel 2
GILLETT, Arthur Lincoln 1
GILLETT, Charles Ripley 4
GILLETT, Ezra Hall H
GILLETT, Frederick Huntington 1
GILLETT, James Norris 1
GILLETT, John Henry 1
GILLETT, Leonard Godfrey 3
GILLETT, Philip Goode 1
GILLETT, William Kendall 1
GILLETTE, Albert Cooley 3
GILLETTE, Clarence Preston 1
GILLETTE, Edward Hooker 1
GILLETTE, Fanny Lemira 4
GILLETTE, Francis H
GILLETTE, Frank Edward 4
GILLETTE, Gene 6
GILLETTE, Guy Mark 6
GILLETTE, Halbert Powers 3
GILLETTE, John Morris 3
GILLETTE, King Camp 1
GILLETTE, Leon N. 2
GILLETTE, Lewis Singer 1
GILLETTE, Walter Robarts 1
GILLETTE, William 1
GILLETTE, Wilson D. 3
GILLHAM, Robert 1
GILLIAM, David Tod 4
GILLIAM, Donnell 4
GILLIARD, E. Thomas 4
GILLICK, James T. 3
GILLICK, Laurance Henry 5
GILLIE, George W. 6
GILLIES, Andrew 2
GILLIES, Donald B. 3
GILLIES, James Lewis 2
GILLIES, John A. 2
GILLIG, Edward M. 1
GILLIGAN, Edmund 6
GILLILAN, Strickland 3
GILLILAND, Charles Edward Jr. 6
GILLILAND, Clarence Vosburgh 1
GILLILAND, Edwin R. 6
GILLILAND, John W. 3
GILLIN, John Lewis 3
GILLIN, John P(hilip) 6
GILLINGHAM, Anna 6
GILLINGHAM, Clinton Hancock 5
GILLIS, James Henry 1
GILLIS, James Lisle H
GILLIS, James Louis 1
GILLIS, James Martin 3
GILLISPIE, Robert Wallace 4
GILLISS, James Melville H
GILLMAN, Henry 1
GILLMAN, Robert Winthrop 4
GILLMER, Gipson P. 1
GILLMOR, Horatio Gonzalo 4
GILLMOR, Horatio Gonzalo 5
GILLMOR, Reginald E. 3
GILLMORE, Frank 2
GILLMORE, James Clarkson 1
GILLMORE, Quincy Adams H
GILLMORE, Quincy Adams 3
GILLMORE, Rufus 1
GILLMORE, William E. 2
GILLON, Alexander H
GILLON, John William 1
GILLPATRICK, Wallace 4
GILLS, Joe Pitzer 6
GILLSON, Joseph Lincoln 4
GILMAN, Albert Franklin 3
GILMAN, Alfred Alonzo 4
GILMAN, Andrew L. 6
GILMAN, Arthur 1
GILMAN, Arthur Delevan H
GILMAN, Benjamin Ives 1
GILMAN, Bradley 1
GILMAN, Caroline Howard H
GILMAN, Charlotte Perkins 1
GILMAN, Daniel Colt 1
GILMAN, Harry A. 5
GILMAN, James Henry 5
GILMAN, John E. 1
GILMAN, John Ellis 1
GILMAN, John R. 3
GILMAN, John Taylor H
GILMAN, Lawrence 1
GILMAN, Luthene Clairmont 2
GILMAN, Margaret 3
GILMAN, Mary Rebecca Foster 2
GILMAN, Max M. 4
GILMAN, Nicholas H
GILMAN, Nicholas Paine 1
GILMAN, Roger 5
GILMAN, Samuel H
GILMAN, Samuel P. 1
GILMAN, Stella Scott (Mrs. Marion Vaughn) 5
GILMAN, Stephen Warren 1
GILMAN, Theodore 1
GILMAN, W. Stewart 2
GILMARTIN, Eugene Richard 4
GILMER, Albert Hatton 3
GILMER, Elizabeth Meriwether 3
GILMER, Elizabeth Meriwether (Dorothy Dix) 5
GILMER, Francis Walker H
GILMER, George Rockingham H
GILMER, John Adams H
GILMER, Thomas H
GILMER, Thomas Lewis 1
GILMER, William Wirt 4
GILMOR, Harry H
GILMORE, Albert Field 2
GILMORE, Alfred H
GILMORE, Charles Whitney 2
GILMORE, Eddy Lanier King 4
GILMORE, Edward 4
GILMORE, Eugene Allen 3
GILMORE, Eugene Allen Jr. 5
GILMORE, George William 1
GILMORE, James Roberts 1
GILMORE, John H
GILMORE, John Curtis 1
GILMORE, John Washington 2
GILMORE, Joseph Albree H
GILMORE, Joseph Henry H
GILMORE, Joseph Henry 1
GILMORE, Joseph Henry 4
GILMORE, Joseph Michael 4
GILMORE, Maurice E. 3
GILMORE, Melvin Randolph 1
GILMORE, Myron T. 4
GILMORE, Pascal Pearl 4
GILMORE, Patrick Sarsfield H
GILMORE, Robert 2
GILMORE, Samuel Louis 1
GILMORE, Thomas Francis 3
GILMORE, Thomas Mador 1
GILMOUR, Abram David Pollock 3
GILMOUR, George Peel 4
GILMOUR, Ray Bergantz 2
GILMOUR, Richard H
GILPATRIC, Guy 3
GILPATRICK, John Lord 4
GILPIN, C. Monteith 5
GILPIN, Charles Sidney 1
GILPIN, Edward Woodward H
GILPIN, Henry Dilworth H
GILPIN, Joseph Elliott 1
GILPIN, William H
GILROY, Thomas F. 1
GILROY, William Edgar 6
GILRUTH, Irwin Thoburn 3
GILSON, Roy Rolfe 1
GILTNER, Frank Carlton 1
GILTNER, Leigh Gordon 3
GILTNER, Ward 3
GIMBEL, Adam Long 5
GIMBEL, Benedict Jr. 5
GIMBEL, Bernard F. 4
GIMBEL, Charles 1
GIMBEL, Ellis A. 2
GIMBEL, Jacob 2
GIMBREDE, Thomas H
GIMMESTAD, Lars Monson 2
GIMSLEY, George Perry 4
GINDER, Philip DeWitt 5
GINGER, Ray 6
GINGRICH, Curvin Henry 3
GINGRICH, John Edward 4
GINN, Curtiss Jr. 4
GINN, Edwin 1
GINN, Frank Hadley 1
GINN, James Theda 4
GINOTT, Haim G. 6
GINSBURG, William Irving 4
GINSBURGH, A. Robert 3
GINTER, Lewis H
GINTER, Ribert McNiel 5
GINTHER, Mrs. Pemberton 3
GINZBERG, Louis 3
GIORDANO, Alfred S. 3
GIPPRICH, John L. 3
GIPSON, James Herrick 4
GIPSON, Lawrence Henry 6
GIRARD, Alfred Conrad 1
GIRARD, Andre 5
GIRARD, Charles Frederic H
GIRARD, Joseph Basil 1
GIRARD, Stephen H
GIRARDEAU, John Lafayette H
GIRARDIN, Ray 5
GIRD, Richard 4
GIRDLER, Tom Mercer 4
GIRDLER, Walter Higgins Jr. 4
GIRDNER, John Harvey 2
GIRL, Christian 2
GIRSCH, Frederick H
GIRTY, George Herbert 1
GIRTY, Simon H
GIRVETZ, Harry Kenneth 6
GIST, Arthur Stanley 3
GIST, Christopher H
GIST, Joseph H
GIST, Mordecai H
GIST, Nathan Howard 4
GIST, William Henry H
GITCHELL, Mazie 6
GITELSON, M. Leo 4
GITELSON, Maxwell 4
GITHENS, Alfred Morton 5
GITHENS, Perry 4
GITLIN, Irving Joseph 4
GITLOW, Benjamin 4
GITT, Charles Moul 5
GITT, Josiah William 6
GITTINGER, Roy 3
GITTINGS, J. Claxton 3
GITTINS, Robert Henry 5
GIVAGO-GRISHINA, Nadeshda 1
GIVAN, Thurman Boyd 6
GIVEN, John LaPorte 3
GIVEN, Josiah 1
GIVEN, Leslie Emmett 4
GIVEN, William Barns Jr. 5
GIVENS, Raymond L. 5
GIVENS, Spencer Hollingsworth 5
GIVENS, Willard Earl 5
GIVLER, J. P. 3
GJELSNESS, Rudolph H. 5
GJERSET, Knut 1
GLACKENS, William J. 1
GLADDEN, George 1
GLADDEN, Washington 1
GLADDING, Albert F. 1
GLADDING, Ernest Knight 3
GLADDING, Timothy H
GLADSON, Guy Allen 5
GLADSON, William Nathan 4
GLADSTONE, Robert William 3
GLADWIN, Henry H
GLADWIN, Mary Elizabeth 1
GLADWIN, William Zachary 1
GLAENZER, Richard Butler 1
GLAESER, Martin Gustave 4
GLAMAN, Eugenie Fish 3
GLANCY, Alfred Robinson 3
GLARNER, Fritz 5
GLASCOCK, Hugh Grundy 1
GLASCOCK, Thomas H
GLASCOFF, Donald G. 4
GLASER, Lulu 3
GLASER, Otto 3
GLASGOW, Arthur Graham 3
GLASGOW, Benjamin Bascom 6
GLASGOW, Ellen 2
GLASGOW, Frank Lawson 5
GLASGOW, Hugh H
GLASGOW, Hugh 2
GLASGOW, William Anderson Jr. 1
GLASGOW, William Hargadine 2
GLASGOW, William Jefferson 4
GLASIER, Gilson Gardner 5
GLASOE, Paul Maurice 5
GLASPELL, Susan 2
GLASS, Carter 2
GLASS, Carter Jr. 3
GLASS, Franklin Potts 1
GLASS, Gilbert 1
GLASS, Henry 1
GLASS, Hiram 1
GLASS, Hugh H
GLASS, James H. 1
GLASS, James William Jr. H
GLASS, Joseph Sarsfield 1
GLASS, Marvin 6
GLASS, Meta 4
GLASS, Montague 1
GLASS, Powell 2
GLASS, Robert Camillus 3
GLASSCOCK, Carl Burgess 2
GLASSCOCK, Samuel Sampson 4
GLASSCOCK, William Ellsworth 1
GLASSER, Otto 4
GLASSFORD, William Alexander II 3
GLASSIE, Henry Haywood 1
GLASSMAN, Oscar 5
GLASSON, William Henry 2
GLATFELTER, Samuel F. 1
GLATFELTER, William Lincoln 1
GLAVIN, Charles C. 5
GLAVIS, Louis Russell 5
GLAZEBROOK, Otis Allan 1
GLAZEBROOK, Otis Allan Jr. 3
GLAZIER, Robert Cromer 3
GLAZIER, Willard 1
GLAZIER, William S. 4
GLEASON, Archie Leland 6
GLEASON, Arthur Huntington 1
GLEASON, Carlisle Joyslin 1
GLEASON, Clarence Willard 2
GLEASON, Daniel Angell 1
GLEASON, Edward Baldwin 1
GLEASON, Elliott Perry 1
GLEASON, Frederic Grant 1
GLEASON, Gay 3
GLEASON, Herbert Wendell 4
GLEASON, James 3
GLEASON, James E. 4
GLEASON, Kate 1
GLEASON, Lafayette B. 1
GLEASON, Ralph Joseph 6
GLEASON, Sarell Everett 6
GLEASON, William Palmer 1
GLEASON, William Thomas 6
GLEAVES, Albert 1
GLEDHILL, Franklin 6
GLEED, Charles Sumner 1
GLEED, James Willis 1
GLEESON, Joseph Michael 1
GLEIS, Paul G. 3
GLEISS, Henry Crete 1
GLEISSNER, John M. 1
GLEN, Henry H
GLEN, Irving Mackey 1
GLEN, James Allison 3
GLENDINNING, Malcolm 5
GLENDINNING, Robert 1
GLENN, Charles Bowles 5
GLENN, Edgar Eugene 3
GLENN, Edwin Forbes 1
GLENN, Garrard 2
GLENN, Gustavus Richard 3
GLENN, J. Lyles 1
GLENN, James Dryden 3
GLENN, James W. 4
GLENN, John Brodnax 4
GLENN, John Mark 3
GLENN, John McGaw 1
GLENN, Leonidas Chalmers 3
GLENN, Mary Willcox 1
GLENN, Milton Willits 4
GLENN, Oliver Edmunds 6
GLENN, Otis Ferguson 3
GLENN, Robert Brodnax 1
GLENN, Thomas Kearney 2
GLENN, Thomas L. 4
GLENN, William Schaeffer 1
GLENNAN, Arthur Henry 4
GLENNON, James Henry 1
GLENNON, John Joseph 2
GLESSING, Thomas B. H
GLESSNER, John Jacob 1
GLICK, Carl 5
GLICK, George Washington 1
GLICKMAN, Irving 5
GLICKMAN, Mendel 4
GLICKSMAN, Harry 6
GLIDDEN, Charles Jasper 1
GLIDDEN, Joseph Farwell H
GLIDDEN, Joseph Farwell 4
GLIDDEN, Minnie Maud 4
GLINES, Earle Stanley 4
GLINSKY, Vincent 6
GLINTENKAMP, Hendrik 2
GLOCK, Carl 4
GLOGAUER, Fritz 1
GLONINGER, John H
GLORE, Charles Foster 3
GLORIEUX, Alphonsus Joseph 1
GLOSE, Adolf 4
GLOSSBRENNER, Adam John H
GLOTZBACH, William Edward 1
GLOVER, Arthur James 2
GLOVER, Charles 1
GLOVER, Charles Carroll 1
GLOVER, David D. 3
GLOVER, Frederic Samuel 3
GLOVER, George Henry 5

* Indicates More Than One Such Name Listed

GLOVER, James Waterman 1
GLOVER, John George 5
GLOVER, John H
  Montgomery
GLOVER, Lyman Beecher 1
GLOVER, Robert Hall 2
GLOVER, Roy Henry 3
GLOVER, Townend H
GLOVER, W(arren) Irving 6
GLOVER, William Howard H
GLUCK, Alma 1
GLUECK, Bernard 5
GLUECK, Eleanor Touroff 5
  (Mrs. Sheldon Glueck)
GLUECK, Nelson 5
GLUHAREFF, Michael E. 4
GLYNDON, Howard 4
GLYNN, James H
GLYNN, James P. 1
GLYNN, Martin H. 3
GMEINER, John 1
GOAN, Orrin S. 4
GOBBLE, Aaron Ezra 4
GOBEIL, Samuel 4
GOBEILLE, Harrold Le
  Fevre
GOBER, William Mathis 5
GOBETZ, Wallace 6
GOBIN, Hillary Asbury 1
GOBIN, John Peter Shindel 1
GOBLE, George
  Washington
GOBRECHT, Christian H
GOCK, A. J. 4
GODARD, George Seymour 1
GODBE, William Samuel H
GODBEER, George H. 4
GODBEY, Allen Howard 2
GODBEY, Earle 2
GODBEY, John Campbell 1
GODBEY, John Emory 1
GODBOLD, Edgar 3
GODBOLD, Norman
  Dosier
GODBOUT, Joseph Adelard 3
GODCHARLES, Frederic 2
  Antes
GODCHAUX, Charles 3
GODCHAUX, Frank A. 4
GODCHAUX, Jules 3
GODDARD, Calvin H
GODDARD, Calvin Hooker 3
GODDARD, Calvin Luther H
GODDARD, Charles 3
  William
GODDARD, Christopher 4
  Marsh
GODDARD, Edwin C. 2
GODDARD, Harold Clarke 2
GODDARD, Harry 1
  Williams
GODDARD, Henry Herbert 4
GODDARD, Henry Newell 4
GODDARD, Henry Warren 3
GODDARD, John H
GODDARD, John Calvin 2
GODDARD, Karl B. 4
GODDARD, Leroy Albert 2
GODDARD, Loring 4
  Hapgood
GODDARD, Luther M. 1
GODDARD, Morrill 1
GODDARD, O. Fletcher 4
GODDARD, Oscar Elmo 3
GODDARD, Paul Beck H
GODDARD, Pliny Earle 1
GODDARD, Ralph Bartlett 1
GODDARD, Ralph Willis 1
GODDARD, Robert Hale H
  Ives
GODDARD, Robert Hales 1
  Ives
GODDARD, Robert 2
  Hutchings
GODDARD, William H
GODDARD, William 1
GODDING, Adelaide M. 4
  Smith
GODDING, John Granville 1
GODDING, William 1
  Whitney
GODEFROY, Maximilian 1
GODEHN, Paul M. 3
GODEY, Louis Antoine H
GODFREY, Alfred 1
  Laurance
GODFREY, Benjamin H
GODFREY, Edward Settle 1
GODFREY, Fletcher 4
GODFREY, Hollis 2
GODFREY, Lincoln 1
GODFREY, Stuart C. 2
GODFREY, Thomas * H
GODING, Frederic Webster 1
GODKIN, Edwin Lawrence 1

GODLEY, Frederick 4
  Augustus
GODLOVE, Isaac Hahn 3
GODMAN, John Davidson H
GODOLPHIN, Francis 6
  Richard Borroum
GODOWSKY, Leopold 1
GODOY, Jose Francisco 4
GODSHALK, William H
GODSHALL, Lincoln 5
  Derstine
GODSHALL, Wilson Leon 3
GODWIN, Earl 3
GODWIN, Edward Allison 1
GODWIN, Hannibal La 5
  Fayette
GODWIN, Harold 1
GODWIN, Herbert 5
GODWIN, Parke 1
GOEBEL, Frank J. 4
GOEBEL, Herman Philip 1
GOEBEL, Julius 1
GOEBEL, Julius Jr. 6
GOEBEL, Louis William 6
GOEBEL, Peter W. 1
GOEBEL, William H
GOEKE, John Henry 1
GOELET, Augustin Hardin 1
GOELET, Robert 4
GOELET, Robert Walton 1
GOEPP, Philip Henry 1
GOERKE, Lenor Stephen 5
GOERTNER, Francis B. 4
GOERTZ, Raymond C. 5
GOESSMANN, Charles 1
  Anthony
GOESSMANN, Helena 3
  Theresa
GOETCHIUS, Henry 1
  Richard
GOETHE, Charles Matthias 4
GOETSCHIUS, John Henry H
GOETSCHIUS, Percy 4
GOETTE, John 6
GOETZ, Albert Gillies 4
GOETZ, George H
  Washington
GOETZ, Norman S. 5
GOETZ, Philip Becker 3
GOETZ, William 5
GOETZE, Albrecht 5
GOETZE, Arthur Burton 4
GOETZE, Frederick Arthur 3
GOETZMANN, Jule 3
  Lawrence
GOFF, Charles Weer 6
GOFF, Emmet Stull H
GOFF, Ernest Lucius 4
GOFF, Frederick Harris 1
GOFF, Guy Despard 1
GOFF, Harold 1
GOFF, John W. 1
GOFF, Nathan 1
GOFF, Thomas Theodore 2
GOFFE, J. Riddle 1
GOFFE, William H
GOFORTH, William H
GOGARTY, Oliver St John 3
GOGGIN, Catharine 5
GOGGIN, William Leftwich H
GOHDES, Conrad Bruno 3
GOHEN, Charles Marsh 5
GOIN, Sanford Williams 5
GOING, Charles Buxton 5
GOING, Jonathan H
GOING, Maud 1
GOLATKA, Walter Francis 4
GOLAY, John Ford 5
GOLD, Harry 5
GOLD, Howard R. 3
GOLD, Nathan Jules 5
GOLD, Pleasant Daniel Jr. 1
GOLD, Thomas Ruggles H
GOLD, William Henry 4
GOLD, William Jason 1
GOLDBECK, Albert 5
  Theodore
GOLDBECK, Edward 5
GOLDBECK, Robert 1
GOLDBERG, Abraham 6
  Isaac
GOLDBERG, Isaac 1
GOLDBERG, Leo 5
GOLDBERG, Reuben 6
  Lucius (Rube)
GOLDBERG, Samuel 6
  Auron
GOLDBERGER, Isidore 5
  Harry
GOLDBERGER, Joseph 1
GOLDBLATT, Maurice 4
  Henry
GOLDBLATT, Nathan 2
GOLDEN, Ben Hale 5
GOLDEN, Clinton Strong 4
GOLDEN, Grace 5

GOLDEN, James S. 5
GOLDEN, John 3
GOLDEN, Michael Joseph 4
GOLDEN, Richard 5
GOLDEN, Ross 6
GOLDEN, S. Herbert 1
GOLDEN, S. M. 3
GOLDENBERG, Morris 5
GOLDENWEISER, 1
  Alexander
GOLDENWEISER, 3
  Emanuel Alexander
GOLDER, Benjamin M. 2
GOLDER, Frank Alfred 1
GOLDESBERRY, John 5
  Milford
GOLDET, Antoine Gustave 4
GOLDFOGLE, Henry M. 1
GOLDFORB, Abraham 6
  Jules
GOLDING, Frank Henry 1
GOLDING, Jerrold R. 4
GOLDING, Louis 3
GOLDING, Louis Thorn 4
GOLDING, Samuel H. 5
GOLDMAN, Albert 4
GOLDMAN, Alfred 6
GOLDMAN, Alvin 4
  D(amascus)
GOLDMAN, Edward 2
  Alphonse
GOLDMAN, Edwin Franko 3
GOLDMAN, Emma H
GOLDMAN, Emma 4
GOLDMAN, Frank 4
GOLDMAN, Hetty 5
GOLDMAN, Leon 6
GOLDMAN, Maurice 4
  Harry
GOLDMAN, Mayer C. 1
GOLDMAN, Morris H. 6
GOLDMAN, Samuel P. 5
GOLDMAN, Solomon 3
GOLDMANN, Franz 5
GOLDMARK, Pauline 4
  Dorothea
GOLDMARK, Pauline 5
  Dorothea
GOLDMARK, Rubin 1
GOLDNER, Jacob Henry 5
GOLDSBERRY, Louise 5
  Dunham
GOLDSBOROUGH, H
  Charles
GOLDSBOROUGH, Laird 3
  S.
GOLDSBOROUGH, Laird 2
  Shields
GOLDSBOROUGH, Louis H
  Malesherbes
GOLDSBOROUGH, 2
  Phillips Lee
GOLDSBOROUGH, 1
  Richard Francis
GOLDSBOROUGH, Robert H
GOLDSBOROUGH, Robert H
  Henry
GOLDSBOROUGH, T. 3
  Alan
GOLDSBOROUGH, W. 3
  Elwell
GOLDSBOROUGH, 5
  Washington Laird
GOLDSBOROUGH, 1
  Worthington
GOLDSCHMIDT, Jakob 3
GOLDSCHMIDT, Richard 3
  Benedict
GOLDSCHMIDT, Samuel 1
  Anthony
GOLDSMITH, Alan 4
  Gustavus
GOLDSMITH, Brooks P. 5
GOLDSMITH, Clifford 5
GOLDSMITH, Deborah 5
GOLDSMITH, Goldwin 5
GOLDSMITH, Grace 6
  Arabell
GOLDSMITH, Jonothan 1
GOLDSMITH, Middleton H
GOLDSMITH, Milton 3
GOLDSMITH, Philip H. 3
GOLDSMITH, Robert 1
GOLDSPOHN, Albert 1
GOLDSTEIN, Benjamin 6
  Franklin
GOLDSTEIN, Irving 5
GOLDSTEIN, Louis 4
GOLDSTEIN, Max Aaron 1
GOLDSTEIN, Molse 5
  Herbert
GOLDSTEIN, Sidney 3
  Emanuel
GOLDSTINE, Harry 3
GOLDSTON, Eli 6

GOLDSWORTHY, William 6
  Arthur
GOLDTHWAIT, James 2
  Walter
GOLDTHWAIT, Joel 5
  Ernest
GOLDTHWAIT, Nathan 3
  Edward
GOLDTHWAIT, Sheldon 4
  Forrest
GOLDTHWAITE, du Val 3
  R.
GOLDTHWAITE, Anne 2
GOLDTHWAITE, George H
GOLDTHWAITE, George 4
  Edgar
GOLDTHWAITE, Henry H
  Barnes
GOLDTHWAITE, Nellie 2
  Esther
GOLDTHWAITE, Vere 5
GOLDWATER, Richard M. 5
GOLDWATER, Robert 5
GOLDWATER, Sigismund 2
  Schultz
GOLDWYN, Samuel 6
GOLER, George W. 1
GOLER, William Harvey 4
GOLLADAY, Edward Isaac H
GOLLADAY, Jacob Shall H
GOLLOMB, Joseph 3
GOLOVIN, Nicholas 5
  Erasmus
GOLSCHMANN, Vladimir 5
GOLTMAN, Maximilian 1
GOLTRA, Edward Field 1
GOLUB, Jacob Joshua 3
GOMBERG, Morris 6
GOMBERG, Moses 2
GOMBROWICZ, Witold 5
GOMEZ, Laureano 4
GOMEZ-MORENO 5
  MARTINEZ, Manuel
GOMORL, Pal 6
GOMPERS, Samuel 1
GOMPERT, William Henry 2
GONCE, John Eugene Jr. 3
GONDELMAN, Sidney 5
GONGWER, Lillian May 5
GONS, James Walker H
GONZALES, Ambrose 1
  Elliott
GONZALES, William 1
  Elliott
GONZALEZ, Bienvenido 3
  M.
GONZALEZ, Mario Flores 6
GONZALEZ, Rosa Mangual 4
GOOCH, D. Linn 4
GOOCH, Daniel H
  Wheelwright
GOOCH, Frank Austin 1
GOOCH, Tom Carbry 3
GOOCH, Sir William H
GOOD, Adolphus Clemens H
GOOD, Alice Campbell 4
GOOD, Charles Winfred 3
GOOD, Edward Ellsworth 5
GOOD, Edwin Stanton 5
GOOD, Fredrick Hopkins 4
GOOD, Howard Harrison 4
GOOD, Irby J. 2
GOOD, James Isaac 1
GOOD, James William 1
GOOD, Jeremiah Haak 1
GOOD, John Walter 6
GOOD, Paul Francis 5
GOODALE, Charles 1
  Warren
GOODALE, Dora Read 4
GOODALE, George 1
  Lincoln
GOODALE, George 5
  Pomeroy
GOODALE, Greenleaf 1
  Austin
GOODALE, Hubert Dana 6
GOODALE, Joseph Lincoln 4
GOODALE, Joseph Lincoln 5
GOODALE, Stephen H
  Lincoln
GOODALE, Stephen 3
  Lincoln
GOODALL, Albert Gallatin H
GOODALL, Charles 5
  Edward
GOODALL, Harvey L. 4
GOODALL, Louis Bertrand 1
GOODBAR, Joseph Ernest 3
GOODCHILD, Frank 1
  Marsden
GOODE, Clement Tyson 4
GOODE, George Brown H
GOODE, George William H
GOODE, J. Paul 1
GOODE, John 1

GOODE, Patrick Gaines H
GOODE, Richard 1
  Livingston
GOODE, Richard Urquhart 1
GOODE, Samuel H
GOODE, William 5
  Athelstane Meredith
GOODE, William Osborne H
GOODELL, Charles Elmer 1
GOODELL, Charles Le Roy 1
GOODELL, David Harvey 1
GOODELL, Henry Hill 1
GOODELL, Raymond 3
  Batchelder
GOODELL, Reginald 2
  Rusden
GOODELL, Roswell Eaton 1
GOODELL, Thomas 1
  Dwight
GOODELL, William * H
GOODEN, Robert Burton 6
GOODENOUGH, Erwin 4
  Ramsdell
GOODENOUGH, George 1
  Alfred
GOODENOUGH, Luman 3
  W.
GOODENOW, John Milton H
GOODENOW, Robert 1
GOODENOW, Rufus King H
GOODERHAM, Melvill 3
  Ross
GOODFELLOW, Edward 1
GOODFELLOW, Millard 6
  Preston
GOODHARTZ, Abraham 6
  Samuel
GOODHEART, William 4
  Raymond Jr.
GOODHUE, Benjamin H
GOODHUE, Bertram 1
  Grosvenor
GOODHUE, Edward Solon 4
GOODHUE, Everett 6
  Walton
GOODHUE, Francis Abbot 4
GOODHUE, James H
  Madison
GOODHUE, William Joseph 5
GOODIER, James Norman 5
GOODIN, John Randolph H
GOODING, Frank R. 1
GOODKIND, Gilbert E. 3
GOODKIND, Maurice 1
  Louis
GOODKNIGHT, James 1
  Lincoln
GOODLAND, Walter 2
  Samuel
GOODLOE, Daniel Reaves H
GOODLOE, Don Speed 6
  Smith
GOODLOE, William H
  Cassius
GOODMAN, Benedict Kay 4
GOODMAN, Charles H
GOODMAN, Charles 1
GOODMAN, Daniel Carson 3
GOODMAN, David 5
GOODMAN, Frank Bartlett 3
GOODMAN, Frank Croly 3
GOODMAN, George Hill 5
GOODMAN, Jack Arthur 3
GOODMAN, James E. 4
GOODMAN, Mrs Jean R. 1
GOODMAN, Jess Dee 5
GOODMAN, John 4
GOODMAN, John Forest 2
GOODMAN, Jules Eckert 3
GOODMAN, Louis Earl 4
GOODMAN, Mary Ellen 5
GOODMAN, Nathan 1
  Gerson
GOODMAN, Paul 5
GOODMAN, William 4
  Edward
GOODMAN, William M. 3
GOODMAN, William Owen 1
GOODNIGHT, Charles H
GOODNIGHT, Charles 1
GOODNIGHT, Cloyd 1
GOODNIGHT, Isaac 1
  Herschel
GOODNIGHT, Scott 5
  Holland
GOODNO, William Colby 1
GOODNOW, Charles Allen 1
GOODNOW, Frank 1
  Johnson
GOODNOW, Isaac H
  Tichenor
GOODNOW, John 1
GOODNOW, Minnie 5
GOODPASTURE, Ernest 4
  William

GOODPASTURE, Wendell 5
  Williamson
GOODRELL, Mancil Clay 1
GOODRICH, Alfred John 4
GOODRICH, Alva Curtis 6
GOODRICH, Annie 3
  Warburton
GOODRICH, Arthur 1
GOODRICH, Ben 4
GOODRICH, Benjamin H
  Franklin
GOODRICH, Carter 6
GOODRICH, Caspar 1
  Frederick
GOODRICH, Charles H
  Augustus
GOODRICH, Chauncey * H
GOODRICH, Chauncey 1
GOODRICH, Chauncey H
  Allen
GOODRICH, Chauncey 3
  William
GOODRICH, David Marvin 3
GOODRICH, Donald 2
  Reuben
GOODRICH, Edgar 5
  Jennings
GOODRICH, Elizur H
GOODRICH, Elizus H
GOODRICH, Ernest Payson 3
GOODRICH, Foster 5
  Edward
GOODRICH, Francis Lee 5
  Dewey
GOODRICH, Frank 1
GOODRICH, Frank Boott H
GOODRICH, Frederick 4
  William
GOODRICH, Hale Caldwell 5
GOODRICH, Herbert F. 4
GOODRICH, Hubert Baker 4
GOODRICH, James 3
  Clarence
GOODRICH, James 3
  Edward
GOODRICH, James Putnam 1
GOODRICH, John 1
  Ellsworth
GOODRICH, John Zacheus H
GOODRICH, Joseph King 5
GOODRICH, L(awrence) 5
  Keith
GOODRICH, Levi H
GOODRICH, Lowell Pierce 2
GOODRICH, Milo H
GOODRICH, Nathaniel 3
  Lewis
GOODRICH, Pierre Frist 6
GOODRICH, Ralph 6
  Dickinson
GOODRICH, Ralph Leland 4
GOODRICH, Robert 5
  Eugene
GOODRICH, Samuel H
  Griswold
GOODRICH, Wallace 3
GOODRICH, William H
  Marcellus
GOODRICH, William W. 1
GOODRIDGE, John 4
GOODRIDGE, Malcolm 3
GOODRIDGE, Sarah H
GOODSELL, Charles True 1
GOODSELL, Charles True 2
GOODSELL, Daniel Ayres 1
GOODSELL, Fred Field 6
GOODSELL, Henry Guy 4
GOODSELL, Willystine 5
GOODSON, Edward 4
  Fletcher
GOODSPEED, Arthur 4
  Willis
GOODSPEED, Charles 2
  Barnett
GOODSPEED, Charles Ten 2
  Broeke
GOODSPEED, Edgar 4
  Johnson
GOODSPEED, Frank 1
  Lincoln
GOODSPEED, George 1
  Stephen
GOODSPEED, Thomas 4
  Harper
GOODSPEED, Thomas 1
  Wakefield
GOODSPEED, Walter 1
  Stuart
GOODWILLIE, David 3
  Herrick
GOODWILLIE, David 1
  Lincoln
GOODWIN, Angier Louis 6
GOODWIN, Arthur C. 1
GOODWIN, Cardinal 2
  Leonidas

GOODWIN, Charles 3
  Archibald
GOODWIN, Charles Jaques 1
GOODWIN, Clarence 3
  Norton
GOODWIN, Daniel 1
GOODWIN, Daniel Raynes H
GOODWIN, E. Mckee 1
GOODWIN, Edward C. 1
GOODWIN, Edward Jasper 1
GOODWIN, Edward Jewett 1
GOODWIN, Elijah H
GOODWIN, Elliot H. 1
GOODWIN, Ernest Vance 4
GOODWIN, Francis M. 6
GOODWIN, Frank Judson 3
GOODWIN, Frederick C. 2
GOODWIN, Godfrey G. 1
GOODWIN, Grace Duffield 5
  (Mrs. Frank J. Goodwin)
GOODWIN, Hannibal H
  Williston
GOODWIN, Harold 1
GOODWIN, Harry Manley 3
GOODWIN, Henry Charles H
GOODWIN, Ichabod H
GOODWIN, J. Cheever 1
GOODWIN, James Junius 1
GOODWIN, John Benjamin 1
GOODWIN, John Edward 2
GOODWIN, John Noble H
GOODWIN, Kathryn 5
  Dickinson
GOODWIN, Lavinia Stella 1
GOODWIN, Leo Sr. 5
GOODWIN, Mark London 5
GOODWIN, Maud Wilder 1
GOODWIN, Nat C. 1
GOODWIN, Philip Arnold 5
GOODWIN, Philip 3
  Lippincott
GOODWIN, Richard 3
  Vanderburgh
GOODWIN, Robert Eliot 6
GOODWIN, Russell Parker 4
GOODWIN, Wilder 3
GOODWIN, Willard T. 3
  Archer Rutherford
GOODWIN, William Hall 1
GOODWIN, William N. 6
GOODWIN, William 1
  Watson
GOODWYN, Peterson H
GOODYEAR, Anson 4
  Conger
GOODYEAR, Charles * H
GOODYEAR, Charles 1
  Waterhouse
GOODYEAR, John 4
GOODYEAR, William 1
  Henry
GOODYKOONTZ, Colin 3
  Brummitt
GOODYKOONTZ, Wells 2
GOOKIN, Daniel H
GOOLD, Marshall Newton 1
GOOLRICK, C. O'CONOR 4
GOOLSBY, Robert Edwin 4
  Moorman
GOOSSENS, Eugene Sir 4
GORBACH, Alfons 5
GORBY, Paul Ford 5
GORDIN, Harry Mann 4
GORDINIER, Charles H. 4
GORDINIER, Hermon 4
  Camp
GORDON, Adoniram H
  Judson
GORDON, Alfred 5
GORDON, Andrew 4
GORDON, Anna Adams 1
GORDON, Archibald D. H
GORDON, Armistead 1
  Churchill
GORDON, Armistead 3
  Churchill Jr.
GORDON, Arthur Horace 1
GORDON, Charles 2
GORDON, Charles A. 6
GORDON, Charles Henry 1
GORDON, Clarence 4
GORDON, Clarence 5
  McCheyne
GORDON, Colin Stuart 4
GORDON, David Stuart 1
GORDON, Donald 5
GORDON, Dorothy 5
GORDON, Douglas 2
GORDON, Edward Clifford 1
GORDON, Edwin Seamer 1
GORDON, Eleanor 4
  Elizabeth
GORDON, Eleanor Kinzie 1
GORDON, Elizabeth 1
GORDON, Ernest (Barron) 5

GORDON, Francis 1
  Edmond
GORDON, Frank Malcolm 2
GORDON, Fred George 4
  Russ
GORDON, Frederic Sutterle 3
GORDON, Frederick 1
  Charles
GORDON, George 3
  Anderson
GORDON, George Angier 1
GORDON, George Breed 5
GORDON, George Byron 1
GORDON, George C. 4
GORDON, George Henry 1
GORDON, George Phineas H
GORDON, George 1
  Washington
GORDON, Gurdon Wright 5
GORDON, Hirsch Loeb 5
GORDON, Irwin Leslie 3
GORDON, Jacques 2
GORDON, James H
GORDON, James 1
GORDON, James Herndon 1
GORDON, James Logan 1
GORDON, James Marcus 3
GORDON, John 1
GORDON, John 3
GORDON, John Brown 1
GORDON, Joseph 1
  Claybaugh
GORDON, Julien 1
GORDON, Laura De Force H
GORDON, Laura De Force 1
GORDON, Leon 2
GORDON, Louis 1
GORDON, M. Lafayette 1
GORDON, Margaret 4
GORDON, Merritt J. 4
GORDON, Neil Elbridge 2
GORDON, Ney Kingsley 4
GORDON, Peter Benjamin 6
GORDON, Peyton 2
GORDON, Ray P(ercival) 5
GORDON, Richard 5
  Sammons
GORDON, Robert 3
GORDON, Robert Loudon 2
GORDON, S. D. 1
GORDON, Samuel 1
GORDON, Seth Chase 1
GORDON, Thomas Sylvy 3
GORDON, Thurlow 6
  Marshall
GORDON, Walter Henry 1
GORDON, William * H
GORDON, William 1
GORDON, William 2
GORDON, William Duncan 4
GORDON, William H
  Fitzhugh
GORDON, William Knox 2
GORDON, William 5
  Lawrence Sanford
GORDON, William Robert H
GORDON, William St Clair 4
GORDON, William W. 1
GORDON, William H
  Washington
GORDON-DAVIS, Alfred 5
  Burwell (Davis Brinton)
GORDY, J. P. 1
GORDY, Wilbur Fisk 1
GORE, Christopher H
GORE, Claude 3
GORE, Elbert Brutus 4
GORE, Herbert Charles 5
GORE, Howard Mason 2
GORE, James Howard 4
GORE, John Kinsey 1
GORE, Joshua Walker 1
GORE, Quentin Pryor 4
GORE, Robert Hayes 6
GORE, Thomas Pryor 2
GORE, W. A. 1
GORGAS, Ferdinand James 4
  Samuel
GORGAS, Josiah H
GORGAS, William 1
  Crawford
GORGES, Sir Ferdinando H
GORHAM, Benjamin 1
GORHAM, Frederic Poole 4
GORHAM, George 1
  Congdon
GORHAM, Jabez H
GORHAM, John 1
GORHAM, Nathaniel H
GORHAM, Willis Arnold 1
GORIN, Orville B. 1
GORKY, Arshile 4
GORMAN, Arthur Pue 1
GORMAN, Arthur Pue Jr. 1
GORMAN, Charles 1
  Edmund
GORMAN, Daniel M. 1

GORMAN, George 1
  Edmond
GORMAN, Herbert 3
  Sherman
GORMAN, James Edward 2
GORMAN, Lawrence 3
  Clifton
GORMAN, Michael Arthur 3
GORMAN, Robert Nestor 4
GORMAN, Thomas J. 5
GOROSTIZA, Jose 5
GORRELL, Edgar Staley 4
GORRELL, Faith Lanman 6
GORRIE, John H
GORRINGE, Henry H
  Honeychurch
GORSKI, Martin 2
GORTATOWSKY, Jacob 4
  Dewey
GORTHY, Willis Charles 4
GORTNER, Ross Aiken 3
GORTON, David Allyn 4
GORTON, Eliot 1
GORTON, Samuel H
GOSA, Robert Earl 6
GOSE, Mack F. 3
GOSE, Thomas Phelps 5
GOSHEN, Elmer Isaac 4
GOSHORN, Alfred Traber 1
GOSHORN, Clarence Baker 1
GOSHORN, Lenore Rhyno 3
GOSHORN, R. C. 3
GOSLEE, Hart John 1
GOSLINE, William A. Jr. 2
GOSLING, Glenn Donald 6
GOSLING, Thomas 4
  Warrington
GOSNELL, John Ansley 5
GOSNEY, Ezra Seymour 2
GOSNOLD, Bartholomew H
GOSS, Albert S. 3
GOSS, Arthur 4
GOSS, Bert Crawford 5
GOSS, Charles A. 1
GOSS, Charles Frederic 1
GOSS, Chauncey P. 1
GOSS, Chauncey Porter 4
GOSS, Edward Otis 1
GOSS, Elbridge Henry 1
GOSS, Evan Benson 1
GOSS, Francis Webster 1
GOSS, Harvey Theo 3
GOSS, John Henry 2
GOSS, Nathaniel Stickney H
GOSS, Robert Whitmore 5
GOSS, Warren Lee 1
GOSS, William Freeman 1
  Myrick
GOSS, William Middlebrook 4
GOSSARD, George Daniel 1
GOSSARD, Harry Clinton 3
GOSSETT, Alfred Newton 2
GOSSETT, Benjamin Brown 3
GOSSETT, Earl J. 4
GOSSETT, John Taylor 1
GOSSETT, Robert Kenneth 5
GOSSLER, Philip Green 2
GOSTELOWE, Jonathan H
GOTSCH, Arthur Edward 5
GOTSHAL, Sylvan 5
GOTSHALK, Dilman Water 6
GOTSHALL, William 1
  Charles
GOTT, Charles 1
GOTT, Daniel H
GOTT, Edgar Nathaniel 2
GOTT, William Thomas 1
GOTTESMAN, D. Samuel 3
GOTTFRIED, Louis Elio 5
GOTTHEIL, Gustave 1
GOTTHEIL, Richard James 1
  Horatio
GOTTHEIL, William 4
  Samuel
GOTTLIEB, Adolph 6
GOTTLIEB, James E. 6
GOTTLIEB, Polly Rose 6
  (Mrs. Alex Gottlieb)
GOTTSCHALK, Alfred 6
GOTTSCHALK, Alfred L. 1
  Moreau
GOTTSCHALK, Louis 6
GOTTSCHALK, Louis 1
  Ferdinand
GOTTSCHALK, Louis H
  Moreau
GOTTSCHALL, Morton 5
GOTTSCHALL, Oscar M. 4
GOTTWALD, Klement 3
GOTWALD, Luther 1
  Alexander
GOTWALS, John C. 3
GOUCHER, John Franklin 1
GOUDY, Frank Burris 2
GOUDY, Franklin Curtis 5
GOUDY, Frederic William 2

GOUDY, William Charles H
GOUGAR, Helen M. 1
GOUGE, William M. H
GOUGH, Emile Jefferson 2
GOUGH, John H
  Bartholomew
GOUGH, Lewis Ketcham 4
GOUGH, Robert E. 5
GOULD, Anna Laura 5
GOULD, Arthur Robinson 1
GOULD, Augustus Addison H
GOULD, Benjamin Apthorp H
GOULD, Carl Frelinghuysen 1
GOULD, Charles Newton 2
GOULD, Charles Winthrop 1
GOULD, Clarence 5
  Pembroke
GOULD, Edward Sherman 1
GOULD, Edward Shuman H
GOULD, Edwin 1
GOULD, Edwin Miner 3
  Lawrence
GOULD, Edwin Sprague 1
GOULD, Elgin Ralston 1
  Lovell
GOULD, Elizabeth Lincoln 1
GOULD, Ezra Palmer 1
GOULD, Frank 4
GOULD, Frank Horace 1
GOULD, Frank Jay 3
GOULD, Frank Miller 2
GOULD, George Jay 1
GOULD, George Milbry 1
GOULD, Hannah Flagg H
GOULD, Harris Perley 2
GOULD, Harry 2
GOULD, Harry Edward 5
GOULD, Herman Day H
GOULD, Howard 1
GOULD, James H
GOULD, Jay H
GOULD, Kenneth Miller 5
GOULD, Kingdon 2
GOULD, Laura Stedman 1
GOULD, Moses Joseph 4
GOULD, Nathaniel Duren 4
GOULD, Norman Judd 2
GOULD, Norman Judd 5
GOULD, Samuel 1
  Wadsworth
GOULD, Theodore Pennock 4
GOULD, Thomas Ridgeway 1
GOULD, William Edward 3
GOULDEN, Joseph 1
  Augustus
GOULDER, Harvey 1
  Danforth
GOULDER, Harvey 4
  Danforth
GOULDING, Edmund 3
GOULDING, Francis H
  Robert
GOULETT, Paul R. 4
GOULEY, John William 4
  Severin
GOUPIL, St Rene H
GOURDIN, Theodore H
GOURLEY, Joseph Harvey 2
GOURLEY, Louis Hill 3
GOURLEY, Robert John 6
GOURLEY, William B. 1
GOUVERNEUR, Marian 1
GOVAN, Andrew Robison 1
GOVE, Aaron 1
GOVE, Charles Augustus 1
GOVE, Frank Edward 4
GOVE, George 1
GOVE, George 6
GOVE, Philip Babcock 5
GOVIN, Rafael R. 1
GOW, Arthur Sidney 1
GOW, Charles R(ice) 5
GOW, George Coleman 1
GOW, James Steele 5
GOW, John Russell 1
GOW, Robert Macgregor 1
GOWANS, Ephraim Gowan 4
GOWANS, William H
GOWDY, John Kennedy 1
GOWDY, Robert Clyde 3
GOWDY, Roy Cotsworth 5
GOWEN, Francis Innes H
GOWEN, Franklin 1
  Benjamin
GOWEN, Herbert Henry 5
GOWEN, Isaac William 1
GOWEN, James 3
  Bartholomew
GOWEN, James Emmet 5
GOWEN, John Knowles Jr. 4
GOWEN, John Wittemore 4
GOWEN, Robert Fellows 4
GOWEN, Samuel Emmett 6
GOWENLOCK, Thomas 4
  Russell

* Indicates More Than One Such Name Listed

GOWER, John Henry 4
GOWMAN, T. Harry 4
GRABAU, Amadeus 5
William
GRABAU, Johannes H
Andreas August
GRABAU, Martin 4
GRABER, Edward Darwin 1
GRABFELDER, Samuel 1
GRABILL, Ethelbert 5
Vincent
GRABLE, Betty (Elizabeth 5
Ruth)
GRABLE, E. F. 4
GRABLE, Errett Marion 4
GRACE, Atonzo G. 5
GRACE, Carl Guy 4
GRACE, Edward Raymond 4
GRACE, Eugene Gifford 4
GRACE, Francis Mitchell 1
GRACE, Frank W. 2
GRACE, Harry Holder 4
GRACE, James Thomas Jr. 5
GRACE, John Joseph 5
GRACE, Joseph Peter 5
GRACE, Louise Carol 5
GRACE, Thomas 1
GRACE, Thomas L. 5
GRACE, Thomas Langdon H
GRACE, William 1
GRACE, William Joseph 3
GRACE, William Russell 1
GRACE, William Russell 2
GRACEY, Samuel Levis 1
GRACEY, Wilbur Tirrell 5
GRACEY, William Adolphe 2
GRACIE, Archibald 1
GRADLE, Harry Searls 3
GRADLE, Henry 1
GRADY, Daniel Henry 3
GRADY, Eleanor Hundson 5
GRADY, Henry Francis 3
GRADY, Henry W. 4
GRADY, Henry Woodfin 5
GRAEBNER, August 3
Lawrence
GRAEBNER, Martin 3
Adolph Henry
GRAEBNER, Theodore 3
GRAEFFE, Edwin O(tto) 5
GRAESSER, Roy French 5
GRAESSL, Lawrence H
GRAF, Herbert 5
GRAF, Homer William 5
GRAF, Oskar Maria 5
GRAF, Robert Joseph 2
GRAFF, Ellis U. 4
GRAFF, Everett D. 4
GRAFF, Frederic H
GRAFF, Frederick 1
GRAFF, Fritz William 3
GRAFF, George E. 1
GRAFF, Joseph Verdi 1
GRAFFENRIED, H
Christopher
GRAFFLIN, Douglas 3
Gordon
GRAFLY, Charles 1
GRAFTON, Charles 1
Chapman
GRAFTON, Robert 1
Wadsworth
GRAHAM, Albert D. 3
GRAHAM, Alexander 2
William
GRAHAM, Allen Jordan 1
GRAHAM, Arthur Butler 6
GRAHAM, B.A. 5
GRAHAM, Balus Joseph 5
Windsor
GRAHAM, Ben George 2
GRAHAM, Charles H
Kinnaird
GRAHAM, Charles 4
Vanderveer
GRAHAM, Christopher 3
GRAHAM, Clarence Henry 5
GRAHAM, Dale 3
GRAHAM, David H
GRAHAM, David Wilson 1
GRAHAM, Donald Earl 6
GRAHAM, Donald 5
Goodnow
GRAHAM, Dorothy 3
GRAHAM, Edward Kidder 1
GRAHAM, Edwin Charles 3
GRAHAM, Edwin Eldon 1
GRAHAM, Edwin R. 5
GRAHAM, Ernest Robert 1
GRAHAM, Evarts Ambrose 3
GRAHAM, Frank 4
GRAHAM, Frank Dunstone 2
GRAHAM, Frank Porter 5
GRAHAM, Frederick J. 6
GRAHAM, George Edward 4
GRAHAM, George Rex H

GRAHAM, George Scott 1
GRAHAM, Gwethalyn 4
GRAHAM, Henry Tucker 3
GRAHAM, Horace French 1
GRAHAM, Horace French 2
GRAHAM, Horace 3
Reynolds
GRAHAM, Hoyt Conlin 1
GRAHAM, Hugh 3
GRAHAM, Inez 4
GRAHAM, Isabella H
Marshall
GRAHAM, James * H
GRAHAM, James B. 4
GRAHAM, James Duncan H
GRAHAM, James Francis 4
GRAHAM, James Harper 4
GRAHAM, James Hiram 4
GRAHAM, James M. 2
GRAHAM, John * H
GRAHAM, John Andrew 4
GRAHAM, John Howard 3
GRAHAM, John Hugh 1
GRAHAM, John Joseph 6
GRAHAM, John Meredith 5
GRAHAM, John William Jr. 6
GRAHAM, Jonathan 1
Thomas
GRAHAM, Joseph H
GRAHAM, Joseph 4
Alexander
GRAHAM, Kelley 4
GRAHAM, Lawrence Pike 1
GRAHAM, Lena Forney 4
Reinhardt (Mrs. Joseph
Graham)
GRAHAM, Louis Edward 4
GRAHAM, Malbone 4
Watson
GRAHAM, Margaret Collier 1
GRAHAM, Mary Owen 4
GRAHAM, Neil F. 4
GRAHAM, Philip L. 4
GRAHAM, Ray Austin 4
GRAHAM, Robert Cabel 4
GRAHAM, Robert Henry 5
GRAHAM, Robert Orlando 1
GRAHAM, Robert X. 3
GRAHAM, Samuel Jordan 4
GRAHAM, Stephen A. 4
GRAHAM, Stephen Victor 5
GRAHAM, Sterling Edward 5
GRAHAM, Sylvester 4
GRAHAM, Thomas Wesley 5
GRAHAM, Walter James 2
GRAHAM, Walter Waverly 6
Jr.
GRAHAM, Willard J. 4
GRAHAM, William H
GRAHAM, William H
Alexander
GRAHAM, William 3
Alexander
GRAHAM, William 4
Harrison
GRAHAM, William 1
Johnson
GRAHAM, William Joseph 4
GRAHAM, William 1
Montrose
GRAHAM, William Pratt 4
GRAHAM, William Tate 5
GRAHAME, Laurance Hill 4
GRAIG, Frank Andrew 6
GRAINGER, Percy 4
GRAMBLING, Allen 5
Rowell
GRAMLICH, Francis 6
W(illiam)
GRAMMER, Allen L(uther) 5
GRAMMER, Carl Eckhardt 2
GRAMMER, Elijah 1
Sherman
GRAMMER, Jacob 1
GRANAHAN, William 3
Thomas
GRANBERRY, C. Read 4
GRANBERY, John Cowper 4
GRANBERY, John Cowper 5
GRAND, Gordon Jr. 5
GRANDFIELD, Charles 1
Paxton
GRANDGENT, Charles 4
Hall
GRANDIN, Egbert Henry 1
GRANDJANY, Marcel 6
GRANFIELD, William 3
Joseph
GRANGER, Alfred Hoyt 3
GRANGER, Amédéé 6
GRANGER, Amos Phelps H
GRANGER, Armour 1
Townsend
GRANGER, Arthur Otis 1
GRANGER, Barlow 1

GRANGER, Bradley H
Francis
GRANGER, Charles 1
Trumbull
GRANGER, Daniel Larned 1
Davis
GRANGER, Francis H
GRANGER, Frank Butler 1
GRANGER, Gideon 1
GRANGER, Gordon H
GRANGER, Lester B. 6
GRANGER, Miles Tobey 1
GRANGER, Moses 1
Moorhead
GRANGER, Sherman 5
Moorhead
GRANGER, Walter 1
GRANGER, William 1
Alexander
GRANIK, Theodore H
GRANJON, Henry Regis 4
GRANNAN, Charles P. 4
GRANNIS, Elizabeth 1
Bartlett
GRANNIS, Robert Maitland 5
GRANNISS, Anna Jane 4
GRANNISS, Robert 1
Andrews
GRANT, Abraham 1
GRANT, Abraham Phineas H
GRANT, Albert Weston 1
GRANT, Alsie Raymond 4
GRANT, Amy (Allison) 6
GRANT, Arthur Rogers 2
GRANT, Asahel H
GRANT, Bishop F(ranklin) 5
GRANT, Carroll Walter 5
GRANT, Charles Henry 4
GRANT, Charles Leon 6
GRANT, Claudius Buchanan 1
GRANT, David Elias 5
GRANT, David Norvell 4
Walker
GRANT, DeForest 5
GRANT, Duncan Campbell 4
GRANT, Elihu 2
GRANT, Elliott Mansfield 5
GRANT, Frederick Clifton 6
GRANT, Frederick Dent 1
GRANT, George Barnard H
GRANT, George Barnard 4
GRANT, George Camron 3
GRANT, George Ernest 3
GRANT, Gordon 4
GRANT, Harry Johnston 4
GRANT, Heber J. 2
GRANT, Henry Horace 4
GRANT, Henry William 5
GRANT, Hugh John 4
GRANT, James Benton 1
GRANT, James Benton 4
GRANT, James Richard 3
GRANT, Jesse R. 4
GRANT, John Black 4
GRANT, John Cowles 4
GRANT, John Gaston 4
GRANT, John Henry 1
GRANT, John MacGregor 4
GRANT, John Prescott 2
GRANT, John Thomas 4
GRANT, Joseph Donohoe 2
GRANT, Joseph Henry 4
GRANT, Julia Dent 1
GRANT, Lester Strickland 5
GRANT, Lewis Addison 1
GRANT, Madison 4
GRANT, Margaret 4
GRANT, Percy Stickney 1
GRANT, Richard Frank 5
GRANT, Richard Ralph 3
Hallam
GRANT, Robert 1
GRANT, Robert John 2
GRANT, Roderick 4
McLellan
GRANT, Rollin P. 1
GRANT, Thomas McMillan 3
GRANT, Ulysses S. III 5
GRANT, Ulysses S. Jr. 1
GRANT, Ulysses Sherman 1
GRANT, Ulysses Simpson H
GRANT, Walter Bruce 4
GRANT, Walter Schuyler 6
GRANT, Whit McDonough 5
GRANT, William Daniel 1
GRANT, William Thomas 3
GRANT, William Thomas 4
GRANT, William West 2
GRANT, William West 3
GRANTHAM, Edwin 1
Lincoln
GRANTLAND, Seaton H
GRANT-SMITH, U. 4
GRANVILLE, 4th earl 3
GRANVILLE, William 1
Anthony

GRANVILLE-SMITH, W. 1
GRANVILLE-SMITH, 6
Walter Jr.
GRASON, C. Gus 3
GRASS, John H
GRASS, John 4
GRASSE, Edwin 3
GRASSE, Francois Joseph H
Paul de
GRASSELLI, Caesar 1
Augustin
GRASSELLI, Thomas Fries 5
GRASSELLI, Thomas 2
Saxton
GRASSHAM, Charles C. 1
GRASSHOFF, Frank O. 3
GRASSIE, Herbert J. 6
GRASTY, Charles Henry 1
GRASTY, John Sharshall 1
GRATACAP, Louis Pope 1
GRATIOT, Charles H
GRATKE, Charles Edward 2
GRATON, L(ouis) C(ary) 6
GRATZ, Bernard H
GRATZ, Michael H
GRATZ, Rebecca H
GRATZ, W. Edward J. 3
GRAU, Maurice 1
GRAU SAN MARTIN, 5
Ramon
GRAUDAN, Nikolai 5
GRAUEL, George Edward 4
GRAUER, A. E. 5
GRAUER, Natalie Eynon 5
GRAUER, Theophil Paul 4
GRAUPNER, Adolphus 2
Earhart
GRAUPNER, Johann H
Christian Gottlieb
GRAUSTEIN, Archibald 5
R(obertson)
GRAUSTEIN, William 1
Caspar
GRAVATT, John James 6
GRAVATT, William Loyall 2
GRAVE, Caswell 2
GRAVE, Frederick David 4
GRAVELY, Joseph Jackson H
GRAVEN, Bruce 6
GRAVEN, Henry Norman 5
GRAVES, Abbott Fuller 1
GRAVES, Alvin C. 4
GRAVES, Anson Rogers 1
GRAVES, Bibb 2
GRAVES, Charles 1
GRAVES, Charles Alfred 1
GRAVES, Charles Burleigh 4
GRAVES, Charles Hinman 1
GRAVES, Charles Marshall 4
GRAVES, Eli Edwin 4
GRAVES, Eugene Silas 1
GRAVES, Frank Pierrepont 3
GRAVES, Frederick Rogers 1
GRAVES, George Keene 2
GRAVES, Grant Ostrander 5
GRAVES, Harold Nathan 4
GRAVES, Henry Solon 4
GRAVES, Herbert Cornelius 1
GRAVES, Ireland 5
GRAVES, Jackson Alpheus 1
GRAVES, James Robinson H
GRAVES, James Wesley 3
GRAVES, Jay P. 1
GRAVES, John 4
GRAVES, John Temple 1
GRAVES, John Temple 4
GRAVES, Louis 4
GRAVES, Lulu Grace 4
GRAVES, Mark 2
GRAVES, Marvin Lee 4
GRAVES, Mary Wheat 1
(Mrs. Billy Z. Graves)
GRAVES, Nelson Zuingle 4
GRAVES, Ralph A. 1
GRAVES, Ralph H. 1
GRAVES, Robert John 1
GRAVES, Schuyler Colfax 1
GRAVES, Waller W. 1
GRAVES, William Blair 1
GRAVES, William Jordan H
GRAVES, William Lucius 2
GRAVES, William Phillips 1
GRAVES, William Sidney 1
GRAVES, William 3
Washington
GRAVES, Zuinglius Calvin H
GRAVETT, Joshua 5
GRAVIER, Charles H
GRAVIER, Jacques 1
GRAWE, Oliver Rudolph 4
GRAWN, Charles Theodore 4
GRAY, Albert F(rederick) 5
GRAY, Alexander 1
GRAY, Alfred Leftwich 1
GRAY, Alfred Walter 1
GRAY, Andrew Caldwell 1

GRAY, Arthur Irving 4
GRAY, Arthur Romeyn 1
GRAY, Asa H
GRAY, Baron De Kalb 2
GRAY, Bowman 1
GRAY, Bowman 2
GRAY, Campbell 2
GRAY, Carl Raymond 1
GRAY, Carl Raymond Jr. 4
GRAY, Charles Harold 3
GRAY, Charles Oliver 4
GRAY, Charlotte Elvira 1
GRAY, Chester Earl 2
GRAY, Chester H. 4
GRAY, Clarence Truman 5
GRAY, Clifton Daggett 2
GRAY, Clifton Merritt 1
GRAY, Cyrus S. 1
GRAY, Daniel Thomas 6
GRAY, David 1
GRAY, David 5
GRAY, David L. 4
GRAY, Donald Joseph 5
GRAY, Dudley Guy 1
GRAY, Duncan 4
Montgomery
GRAY, E. Mcqueen 1
GRAY, Earle * 5
GRAY, Edward Winthrop 2
GRAY, Edwin 1
GRAY, Elisha 1
GRAY, Ernest Weston 4
GRAY, Finly H. 3
GRAY, Francis Calley H
GRAY, George 1
GRAY, George Edward 4
GRAY, George Herbert 4
GRAY, George William 4
GRAY, George Zabriskie 1
GRAY, Giles Wilkeson 5
GRAY, Gordon 5
GRAY, Harold (Lincoln) 5
GRAY, Harold Edwin 5
GRAY, Harold Parker 4
GRAY, Henry David 5
GRAY, Henry G. 3
GRAY, Henry Peteers 1
GRAY, Hiram 5
GRAY, Hob 1
GRAY, Horace 1
GRAY, Howard Adams 4
GRAY, Howard Kramer 3
GRAY, Isaac Pusey 1
GRAY, J. P. 4
GRAY, J. S. 5
GRAY, James Alexander 3
GRAY, James Burdis 1
GRAY, James M. 1
GRAY, James Richard 1
GRAY, Jessie 5
GRAY, John Chipman 1
GRAY, John Clinton 1
GRAY, John Cowper H
GRAY, John Henry 1
GRAY, John Pinkham 1
GRAY, John Purdue H
GRAY, Joseph M. M. 3
GRAY, Joseph Phelps 4
GRAY, Joseph Preston 5
GRAY, Joseph W. H
GRAY, Joslyn 1
GRAY, Leon Fowler 5
GRAY, Lewis Cecil 2
GRAY, Louis Herbert 3
GRAY, Maria Freeman 5
GRAY, Mat 4
GRAY, Morris 1
GRAY, Oscar Lee 1
GRAY, Prentiss Nathaniel 1
GRAY, Ralph Weld 5
GRAY, Richard J. 4
GRAY, Robert 5
GRAY, Roland 1
GRAY, Thomas 6
GRAY, Walter H. 4
GRAY, Willard Franklin 6
GRAY, William 1
GRAY, William C. 1
GRAY, William H. 4
GRAY, William John 4
GRAY, William Price Jr. 4
GRAY, William Rensselaer 1
GRAY, William Scott 5
GRAY, William Steele 1
GRAYDON, Alexander 1
GRAYDON, James Weir 4
GRAYDON, Joseph 5
Spencer
GRAYDON, William H
GRAYSON, Cary Travers 1
GRAYSON, Charles Prevost 1
GRAYSON, Clifford 1
Prevost
GRAYSON, Theodore J. 1

GRAYSON, Thomas Jackson 4
GRAYSON, Thomas Wray 1
GRAYSON, William
GRAYSON, William Bandy 4
GRAYSON, William John H
GREACEN, Edmund 2
GREATHOUSE, Charles A. 4
GREATHOUSE, Clarence R. 1
GREATHOUSE, Clarence Ridgeby H
GREATON, John H
GREATON, Joseph H
GREATOREX, Eliza Pratt H
GREATOREX, Kathleen Honora 3
GREAVES, Frederick Clarence 6
GREAVES, Joseph Eames 3
GREBE, Marguerite Luckett 5
GREBENSTCHIKOFF, George 4
GREBLE, Edwin St John 1
GREBLE, John T. H
GREEAR, Fred Bonham 4
GREEF, Robert Julius 4
GREELEY, Edwin Seneca 4
GREELEY, Horace H
GREELEY, Louis May 4
GREELEY, Mellen Clark 6
GREELEY, Samuel Arnold 5
GREELEY, William B. 3
GREELEY, William Roger 4
GREELY, Adolphus Washington 1
GREELY, Antoinette 6
GREELY, Edward 2
GREELY, John Nesmith 4
GREEN, Abel 6
GREEN, Addison Loomis 2
GREEN, Adolphus Williamson 1
GREEN, Adwin Wigfall 4
GREEN, Adwin Wigfall 5
GREEN, Alexander Little Page H
GREEN, Allen Percival 3
GREEN, Andrew Haswell 1
GREEN, Arthur Laurence 4
GREEN, Asa H
GREEN, Ashbel H
GREEN, Bartholomew H
GREEN, Beriah H
GREEN, Bernard Richardson 1
GREEN, Berryman 1
GREEN, Bert 2
GREEN, Byram H
GREEN, Charles Boden 5
GREEN, Charles Carrol 4
GREEN, Charles Edward 4
GREEN, Charles Henry 1
GREEN, Charles Henry 3
GREEN, Charles Montraville 1
GREEN, Conant Lewis 1
GREEN, Constance McLaughlin 6
GREEN, Crawford Richmond 6
GREEN, Darrell Bennet 3
GREEN, David Edward 1
GREEN, David I. 1
GREEN, Duff H
GREEN, Dwight H. 3
GREEN, Dwight Phelps 6
GREEN, Edward Averill 4
GREEN, Edward Brodhead 3
GREEN, Edward Howland Robinson 1
GREEN, Edward Melvin 1
GREEN, Edwin Luther 3
GREEN, Estill I. 6
GREEN, Fitzhugh 2
GREEN, Francis Harriet Whipple H
GREEN, Francis Harvey 1
GREEN, Francis Mathews 1
GREEN, Frank Russell 1
GREEN, Fred Warren 1
GREEN, Frederick 1
GREEN, Frederick Robin 1
GREEN, Frederick William H
GREEN, Garner Leland 6
GREEN, George Rex 2
GREEN, George Walter 2
GREEN, Grafton 2
GREEN, H. T. S. 2
GREEN, Harold L. 3
GREEN, Harold Roy 3
GREEN, Harry E. 6
GREEN, Harry Joseph 4
GREEN, Henry 1
GREEN, Henry Irvin 3

GREEN, Henry Woodhull H
GREEN, Henry Woodhull 1
GREEN, Hetty Howland Robinson 1
GREEN, Horace H
GREEN, Horace 1
GREEN, Howard Whipple 3
GREEN, Innis H
GREEN, Isaiah Lewis H
GREEN, Jacob * H
GREEN, James H
GREEN, James Benjamin 5
GREEN, James F. 4
GREEN, James Gilchrist H
GREEN, James Monroe 1
GREEN, James Stephen H
GREEN, James Woods 1
GREEN, Jerome Joseph 1
GREEN, Jesse Cope 1
GREEN, John * 4
GREEN, John 2
GREEN, John 4
GREEN, John Cleve H
GREEN, John Edgar Jr. 2
GREEN, John F. 1
GREEN, John Garside 4
GREEN, John M. 6
GREEN, John Orne 1
GREEN, John Pugh 1
GREEN, John Webb 3
GREEN, Jonas 1
GREEN, Joseph H
GREEN, Joseph Andrew 4
GREEN, Joshua 6
GREEN, Julia M. 4
GREEN, Leslie H. H
GREEN, Lewis Warner H
GREEN, Lot 4
GREEN, Marcellus 2
GREEN, Nathan H
GREEN, Nathan 1
GREEN, Nathan Williams 3
GREEN, Norvin H
GREEN, Norvin Hewitt 3
GREEN, Paul Martin 6
GREEN, Percy Warren 1
GREEN, Perry Luther 3
GREEN, Robert Gladding 2
GREEN, Robert McCay 4
GREEN, Robert N. 4
GREEN, Robert Stockton 1
GREEN, Rolland Lester 5
GREEN, Roy Monroe 2
GREEN, Rufus Lot 1
GREEN, Samuel H
GREEN, Samuel Abbott 1
GREEN, Samuel Bowdlear 1
GREEN, Samuel Swett 1
GREEN, Seth H
GREEN, Theodore Francis 4
GREEN, Theodore Meyer 5
GREEN, Thomas H
GREEN, Thomas Dunbar 3
GREEN, Thomas Edward 1
GREEN, Walter Lawrence H
GREEN, Walton Atwater 3
GREEN, Warren Everett 1
GREEN, Wharton Jackson 1
GREEN, William H
GREEN, William 1
GREEN, William 3
GREEN, William Charles 4
GREEN, William Elza 1
GREEN, William Henry 1
GREEN, William Joseph Jr. 4
GREEN, William Marvin 2
GREEN, William Mercer H
GREEN, William Mercer 2
GREEN, William Raymond 2
GREEN, Willis H
GREEN, Wyman Reed 3
GREENAWALD, Paul Benjamin
GREENBAUM, David 6
GREENBAUM, Edward S. 5
GREENBAUM, Leo 1
GREENBAUM, Max 1
GREENBAUM, Samuel 1
GREENBAUM, Sigmund Samuel 2
GREENBERG, Bernard Samuel 4
GREENBERG, Noah 4
GREENBERG, Sarah K. 6
GREENBERRY, Nicholas 4
GREENBIE, Marjorie Barstow 1
GREENBIE, Marjorie Barstow 6
GREENBLATT, Jacob 6
GREENBLATT, Louis 5
GREENDLINGER, Leo 3
GREENE, A. Crawford 4
GREENE, Aella 1
GREENE, Albert Collins H
GREENE, Albert Gorton H

GREENE, Anne Bosworth 6
GREENE, Arthur Maurice 5 Jr.
GREENE, Benjamin Allen 1
GREENE, Charles Arthur 5
GREENE, Charles Ezra 1
GREENE, Charles Jerome 2
GREENE, Charles Lyman 1
GREENE, Charles Samuel 1
GREENE, Charles Warren 4
GREENE, Charles Wilson 4
GREENE, Chester W. 4
GREENE, Christopher 1
GREENE, Clay Meredith 1
GREENE, Condon Lorntz 6
GREENE, D. Crosby 1
GREENE, Daniel Crosby 1
GREENE, David Maxson 1
GREENE, Edward Belden 3
GREENE, Edward Lee 1
GREENE, Edward Martin 3
GREENE, Edwin Farnham 3
GREENE, Evarts Boutell 2
GREENE, Flora Hartley 4
GREENE, Floyd L. 1
GREENE, Francis Vinton 1
GREENE, Frank Lester 1
GREENE, Fred T. 4
GREENE, Frederick Stuart 1
GREENE, Gardiner 1
GREENE, George C. 1
GREENE, George Francis 1
GREENE, George Louis 5
GREENE, George Sears 1
GREENE, George Sears Jr. 1
GREENE, George H
GREENE, George Washington 1
GREENE, George Wellington H
GREENE, George Woodward 1
GREENE, Harry Irving 4
GREENE, Harry Sylvestre Nutting 5
GREENE, Henry Alexander 1
GREENE, Henry Copley 3
GREENE, Henry Fay 1
GREENE, Henry Vincent 3
GREENE, Herbert Eveleth 2
GREENE, Herbert Wilber 1
GREENE, Homer 1
GREENE, Howard 1
GREENE, Isabel Catherine 4
GREENE, Jacob L. 1
GREENE, James E(dward) 5
GREENE, James H. 1
GREENE, James Leon 1
GREENE, James Nicholas 5
GREENE, James Sonnett 3
GREENE, Jerome Davis 3
GREENE, John 1
GREENE, John Ernest 1
GREENE, John Holden H
GREENE, John Morton 1
GREENE, John Priest 1
GREENE, Joseph Ingham 3
GREENE, Joseph Nathaniel 5
GREENE, Katherine Glass 2
GREENE, Laurence Whitridge 6
GREENE, Lionel Y. 4
GREENE, M(aria) Louise 4
GREENE, Marc Tiffany 4
GREENE, Mary Anne 4
GREENE, Myron Wesley 1
GREENE, Nathanael 1
GREENE, Nathaniel H
GREENE, Oliver D. 1
GREENE, Patterson 5
GREENE, Raleigh W. 3
GREENE, Ray 1
GREENE, Richard Gleason 1
GREENE, Richard Thurston 3
GREENE, Robert Holmes 1
GREENE, Roger Sherman 1
GREENE, Roger Sherman 2
GREENE, S. Harold 2
GREENE, Sam 1
GREENE, Samuel Dana H
GREENE, Samuel Harrison 4
GREENE, Samuel Stillman 1
GREENE, Samuel Webb 5
GREENE, Sarah Pratt 1
GREENE, Theodore Ainsworth 3
GREENE, Thomas L. 1
GREENE, Thomas Marston H
GREENE, Ward 3
GREENE, Warwick 1
GREENE, William * H
GREENE, William Brenton 4
GREENE, William Cornell 1
GREENE, William Houston 1
GREENE, William L. 1
GREENE, William Milbury 4
GREENE, William Stedman 1

GREENE, Winfield Wardwell 4
GREENEBAUM, Henry Everett 1
GREENEBAUM, Leon Charles 5
GREENEBAUM, Moses Ernest 1
GREENEBAUM, Samuel Lewis 6
GREENEFIELD, Nathan R. 1
GREENER, John Hunter 5
GREENER, Richard Theodore 4
GREENFIELD, Albert Monroe 4
GREENFIELD, Eric Viele 1
GREENFIELD, Joseph A. 6
GREENFIELD, Kent Roberts 1
GREENHALGE, Frederick Thomas H
GREENHILL, J. P. 6
GREENHOW, Robert 1
GREENING, Harry Cornell 5
GREENLAW, Edwin 1
GREENLAW, Lowell M. 5
GREENLEAF, Benjamin H
GREENLEAF, Carl Dimond 3
GREENLEAF, Charles Ravenscroft 1
GREENLEAF, Edmund H
GREENLEAF, Georgie H. Franck 1
GREENLEAF, James Leal 1
GREENLEAF, Jonathan 1
GREENLEAF, Moses * H
GREENLEAF, Simon H
GREENLEAF, Thomas H
GREENLEE, John Reece 6
GREENLEE, Karl B. 4
GREENLEY, Howard 1
GREENMAN, A. V. 4
GREENMAN, Frederick Francis 4
GREENMAN, Jesse More 3
GREENMAN, Milton J. 1
GREENMAN, Walter Folger 2
GREENOUGH, Allen Jackson 6
GREENOUGH, Chester Noyes 1
GREENOUGH, George Gordon 1
GREENOUGH, Henry H
GREENOUGH, Horatio H
GREENOUGH, James Bradstreet 1
GREENOUGH, James Carruthers 1
GREENOUGH, Jeanie Ashley Bates 4
GREENOUGH, John 1
GREENOUGH, Robert Battey 1
GREENOUGH, William 2
GREENQUIST, Kenneth Lloyd 5
GREENSFELDER, Albert Preston 3
GREENSHIELDS, Donn D. 4
GREENSLADE, John Wills 2
GREENSLET, Ferris 1
GREENSTEIN, Jesse P. 3
GREENSTONE, Julius Hillel 1
GREENUP, Christopher H
GREENWALD, Emanuel H
GREENWALD, Herbert S. 3
GREENWALT, Elmer Ellsworth 1
GREENWAY, Charles Moore 1
GREENWAY, Isabella Selmes 3
GREENWAY, James Cowan 5
GREENWAY, John Campbell 1
GREENWAY, Walter Burton 1
GREENWELL, Darrell J. 4
GREENWELL, Hiliary Johnson 4
GREENWOOD, Alfred Burton 1
GREENWOOD, Allen 2
GREENWOOD, Arthur H. 4
GREENWOOD, Elizabeth Ward 1
GREENWOOD, Ernest 3
GREENWOOD, Ethan Allen 1

GREENWOOD, Grace 1
GREENWOOD, Isaac 6
GREENWOOD, James M. 4
GREENWOOD, John H
GREENWOOD, John Joseph 5
GREENWOOD, Marion 5
GREENWOOD, Miles H
GREENWOOD, Thomas Benton 2
GREER, Benjamin Brinton 1
GREER, David Hummell 1
GREER, Frank U. 2
GREER, Herbert Chester 2
GREER, Hilton Ross 3
GREER, Isaac Garfield 6
GREER, James Agustin 1
GREER, Lawrence 1
GREER, Margaret R. 3
GREER, Samuel Miller 2
GREET, William Cabell 5
GREEVER, Garland 4
GREEVER, Walton Harlowe 4
GREGERSEN, Magnus Ingstrup 5
GREGG, Alan 3
GREGG, Alexander H
GREGG, Alexander White 1
GREGG, Alexander White Jr. 3
GREGG, Andrew H
GREGG, Curtis Hussey 4
GREGG, David 1
GREGG, David McMurtrie 1
GREGG, Earl Lamont 6
GREGG, Florence Clara 6
GREGG, Francis Whitlock 5
GREGG, Frank Moody 4
GREGG, Fred Marion 4
GREGG, Godfrey Robert 4
GREGG, J. A. 3
GREGG, James Bartlett 1
GREGG, James Edgar 2
GREGG, James Madison H
GREGG, John H
GREGG, John Andrew 3
GREGG, John B. 4
GREGG, John Price 3
GREGG, John Robert 2
GREGG, John William 6
GREGG, Josiah H
GREGG, Maxcy H
GREGG, Paul L. * 3
GREGG, Russell Taaffe 6
GREGG, William H
GREGG, William C. 3
GREGG, William Henry 4
GREGG, Willis Ray 1
GREGOR, Elmer Russell 2
GREGORY, Carl C. 1
GREGORY, Caspar Rene 1
GREGORY, Charles Noble 2
GREGORY, Chester Arthur 3
GREGORY, Clifford V. 2
GREGORY, Daniel Seelye 1
GREGORY, David Thomas 3
GREGORY, Dudley Sanford H
GREGORY, Edmund Bristol 4
GREGORY, Eliot 1
GREGORY, Elisha Hall 1
GREGORY, Herbert Bailey 3
GREGORY, Herbert E. 3
GREGORY, Jackson 2
GREGORY, John 3
GREGORY, John Goadby 3
GREGORY, John Henry 1
GREGORY, John Herbert 3
GREGORY, John Milton H
GREGORY, Laurence Wilcoxson 6
GREGORY, Leslie Roscoe 3
GREGORY, Louis Hoyt 2
GREGORY, Luther Elwood 4
GREGORY, L.H. 6
GREGORY, Martin LeRoy 5
GREGORY, Maurice Clinton 6
GREGORY, Menas Sarkis 1
GREGORY, Noble Jones 5
GREGORY, Oliver Fuller 3
GREGORY, Raymond William 3
GREGORY, Samuel H
GREGORY, Stephen Strong 1
GREGORY, Tappan 4
GREGORY, Thomas B. 3
GREGORY, Thomas T. C. 1
GREGORY, Thomas Watt 1
GREGORY, Virginia 6
GREGORY, Warren 1
GREGORY, Warren Fenno 1
GREGORY, William 1

GREGORY, William Benjamin 2
GREGORY, William Edward 3
GREGORY, William Hamilton Jr. 4
GREGORY, William K(ing) 5
GREGORY, William Logan 3
GREGORY, William Mumford 5
GREGORY, William Voris 1
GREHAN, Bernard H. 3
GREIG, Alexander Simpson 4
GREIG, John H
GREINER, John E. 2
GREINER, Tuisco 4
GREIS, Henry Nauert 2
GRELL, Louis 4
GRELLET, Stephen H
GRENELL, Zelotes 1
GRENFELL, Helen Loring 1
GRENFELL, Nicholas Pirie Jr. 6
GRENFELL, Sir Wilfred Thomason 1
GRENIER, Arthur Sylvester 1
GRENNELL, George Jr. H
GRESHAM, James Wilmer 3
GRESHAM, LeRoy 3
GRESHAM, Thomas Dew 6
GRESHAM, Walter Quintin H
GRESS, Ernest Milton 5
GREUSEL, John Hubert 2
GREVE, Charles Theodore H
GREVILLE, Mr. H
GREVSTAD, Nicolay Andrew
GREW, Henry S. 3
GREW, Joseph Clark 4
GREW, Theophilus
GREY, Benjamin Edwards H
GREY, Elmer 4
GREY, Samuel Howell 1
GREY, Zane 1
GRIBBEL, John
GRICE, David Stephen 4
GRICE, Warren 2
GRIDER, Henry H
GRIDLEY, Charles O. 4
GRIDLEY, Charles Vernon H
GRIDLEY, Jeremiah
GRIDLEY, Marion Eleanor 6 (Mrs. Robinson Johnson)
GRIDLEY, Richard H
GRIER, Albert Oliver 3 Herman
GRIER, Alvan Ruckman
GRIER, Boyce McLaughlin 6
GRIER, Francis Ebenezer 3
GRIER, Harry Dobson 6 Miller
GRIER, James Alexander 4
GRIER, James Harper 1
GRIER, Norman 3 MacDowell
GRIER, Robert Cooper H
GRIER, Robert Maxwell 6
GRIER, William 1
GRIER, William Moffatt 1
GRIERSON, Benjamin H. 4
GRIERSON, Benjamin 1 Henry
GRIERSON, John 5
GRIES, John Matthew 3
GRIESEDIECK, Alvin 4
GRIEST, Theodore Reed 6
GRIEST, William Walton 4
GRIEVE, Miller H
GRIFFES, Charles Tomlinson H
GRIFFES, Charles Tomlinson 4
GRIFFIN, Angus MacIvor 5
GRIFFIN, Anthony Jerome 1
GRIFFIN, Appleton Prentiss 1 Clark
GRIFFIN, Bulkley 5 Southworth
GRIFFIN, Cardinal Bernard 3
GRIFFIN, Carroll Wardlaw 3
GRIFFIN, Charles H
GRIFFIN, Cyrus H
GRIFFIN, Daniel J. 1
GRIFFIN, Delia Isabel 4
GRIFFIN, Edward Dorr 1
GRIFFIN, Edward Herrick 1
GRIFFIN, Emmet D. 5
GRIFFIN, Eugene 1
GRIFFIN, Eugene Leonard 6
GRIFFIN, Frank Loxley 5
GRIFFIN, Frederick 5 Robertson
GRIFFIN, Henry Lyman 1
GRIFFIN, Isaac H
GRIFFIN, James Aloysius 2

GRIFFIN, James Arthur 3
GRIFFIN, James H. 1
GRIFFIN, James Owen 4
GRIFFIN, John H
GRIFFIN, John Howard 3
GRIFFIN, John Joseph 1
GRIFFIN, John King H
GRIFFIN, John W. 4
GRIFFIN, Lawrence 5 Edmonds
GRIFFIN, Lee Henry 4
GRIFFIN, Levi Thomas 1
GRIFFIN, Mark Alexander 5
GRIFFIN, Martin Eugene 1
GRIFFIN, Martin Ignatius 1
GRIFFIN, Martin Luther 2
GRIFFIN, Michael 1
GRIFFIN, Nathaniel 1 Edward
GRIFFIN, Robert Melville 6
GRIFFIN, Robert Stanislaus 1
GRIFFIN, Samuel H
GRIFFIN, Simon Goddell 1
GRIFFIN, Solomon Bulkley 1
GRIFFIN, Thomas 1
GRIFFIN, Walter 1
GRIFFIN, William Aloysius 2
GRIFFIN, William Richard 3
GRIFFIN, William Vincent 3
GRIFFING, Josephine 1 Sophie White
GRIFFIS, Elliot 4
GRIFFIS, Lawrence W. 4
GRIFFIS, Stanton 6
GRIFFIS, William Elliot 4
GRIFFITH, Armond 4 Harrold
GRIFFITH, Benjamin 1 Whitfield
GRIFFITH, Benjamin 1
GRIFFITH, C. J. 4
GRIFFITH, Chauncey H. 3
GRIFFITH, Clark 4 Roberts
GRIFFITH, Coleman 1
GRIFFITH, David Lewelyn 2 Wark
GRIFFITH, David Wark H
GRIFFITH, David Wark 4
GRIFFITH, Earl L. 4
GRIFFITH, Elmer 1 Cummings
GRIFFITH, Francis Marion 1
GRIFFITH, Frank Carlos 1
GRIFFITH, Frank Leslie 5
GRIFFITH, Franklin 3 Thomas
GRIFFITH, Frederic 5 Richardson
GRIFFITH, George 1
GRIFFITH, George Cupp 6
GRIFFITH, Griffith Jenkins 1
GRIFFITH, Griffith 4 Pritchard
GRIFFITH, Hall McAlister 3
GRIFFITH, Harry Elmer 4
GRIFFITH, Harry Melvin 5
GRIFFITH, Heber Emlyn 5
GRIFFITH, Helen Sherman 4
GRIFFITH, Herbert Eugene 1
GRIFFITH, Ivor 4
GRIFFITH, J. P. Crozer 1
GRIFFITH, John 5
GRIFFITH, John L. 2
GRIFFITH, M. Dison 6
GRIFFITH, P. MERRILL 1
GRIFFITH, Paul Howard 6
GRIFFITH, Reginald 3 Harvey
GRIFFITH, Richard 1
GRIFFITH, Robert H Eglesfield
GRIFFITH, Samuel H
GRIFFITH, Samuel 5 Henderson
GRIFFITH, Thomas Stuart 4
GRIFFITH, Virgil A. 5
GRIFFITH, W. M. 3
GRIFFITH, Wendell Horace 5
GRIFFITH, William 1
GRIFFITH, William 1
GRIFFITH, William G. 4
GRIFFITHS, Arthur Floyd 1
GRIFFITHS, David 1 Patterson
GRIFFITHS, Edwin 6
GRIFFITHS, Edwin Stephen 1
GRIFFITHS, Farnham Pond 3
GRIFFITHS, Frederick J. 2
GRIFFITHS, James Henry 4
GRIFFITHS, John Lewis 1
GRIFFITHS, John Willis H
GRIFFITHS, William John 4 Jr.
GRIGEBY, Hugh Blair H

GRIGGS, Chauncey Wright 1
GRIGGS, David Cullen 3
GRIGGS, David Tressel 6
GRIGGS, Edward Howard 3
GRIGGS, Everett Gallup 1
GRIGGS, Frederick 5
GRIGGS, Herbert Lebau 2
GRIGGS, James M. 1
GRIGGS, John William 1
GRIGGS, Nathan Kirk 1
GRIGGS, Thomas Newell 5
GRIGGS, William Cornelius 4
GRIGSBY, Bertram James 3
GRIGSBY, William Fred 3
GRIM, Allan K. 4
GRIM, David H
GRIM, Paul Ridgeway 3
GRIMBALL, Elizabeth 3 Berkeley
GRIME, Sarah Lois 4
GRIMES, Charles 3 Pennebaker
GRIMES, Donald Robert 5
GRIMES, Fern Edith 6 Munroe (Mrs. William Schuyler Grimes)
GRIMES, Frances 4
GRIMES, Frank 4
GRIMES, George 1
GRIMES, George Simon 1
GRIMES, J. Bryan 1
GRIMES, J. Frank 6
GRIMES, James Stanley H
GRIMES, James Wilson H
GRIMES, John 1
GRIMES, Waldo Ernest 2
GRIMES, William Henry 5
GRIMES, William 3 Middleton
GRIMKE, Angelina Emily 6
GRIMKE, Angelina Weld 6
GRIMKE, Archibald Henry 1
GRIMKE, Francis James 4
GRIMKE, Frederick H
GRIMKE, John Faucheraud H
GRIMKE, Sarah Moore H
GRIMKE, Thomas Smith H
GRIMM, Carl William 4
GRIMM, Jacob Luther 1
GRIMM, John Crawford 5 Milton
GRIMM, John Hugo 4
GRIMM, John Murchison 5
GRIMMELSMAN, Henry 1 Joseph
GRIMMELSMAN, Joseph 1
GRIMMER, Ward Chipman 2 Hazen
GRIMSHAW, Austin 4
GRIMSHAW, Robert 4
GRIMSTON, John (6th Earl 6 of Veruiam)
GRINDAL, Herbert W. 3
GRINDALL, Charles 1 Sylvester
GRINDLEY, Harry Sands 4
GRINDON, Joseph Sr. 4
GRINER, John F. 6
GRINNELL, Charles 1 Edward
GRINNELL, Elizabeth 1
GRINNELL, Frank 4 Washburn
GRINNELL, Frederick 1
GRINNELL, George Bird 1
GRINNELL, George 3 Morton
GRINNELL, Harold C. 5
GRINNELL, Henry H
GRINNELL, Joseph 1
GRINNELL, Joseph H
GRINNELL, Josiah H Bushnell
GRINNELL, Morton 1
GRINNELL, Moses Hicks H
GRINNELL, Russell 2
GRINNELL, William 1 Morton
GRINSFELDER, H. J. 4
GRISCOM, Clement Acton 1 *
GRISCOM, John H
GRISCOM, Lloyd Carpenter 5
GRISCOM, Ludlow 3
GRISCOM, Rodman Ellison 3
GRISER, John Millen 3
GRISMER, Joseph Rhode 1
GRISMORE, Grover 3 Cleveland
GRISSOM, Irene Welch 1 (Mrs. Charles Meigs Grissom)
GRISSOM, Pinkney 6
GRISSOM, Richard H. 6
GRISSOM, Virgil Ivan 4
GRISWOLD, A. Whitney 4

GRISWOLD, Alexander H Viets
GRISWOLD, Alphonso 4 Miner
GRISWOLD, Augustus H. 1
GRISWOLD, Benjamin 2 Howell Jr.
GRISWOLD, Casimir 1 Clayton
GRISWOLD, Clayton Tracy 5
GRISWOLD, Dwight 3 Palmer
GRISWOLD, Edith Julia 1
GRISWOLD, F. Gray 1
GRISWOLD, Gaylord 1
GRISWOLD, Glenn 1
GRISWOLD, Glenn 3
GRISWOLD, Hattie Tyng 1
GRISWOLD, Hervey 3 DeWitt
GRISWOLD, James F. 3
GRISWOLD, John Augustus H
GRISWOLD, Latta 4
GRISWOLD, Leon Stacy 4
GRISWOLD, Matthew H
GRISWOLD, Merrill 3
GRISWOLD, Morley 3
GRISWOLD, Oscar 3 Woolverton
GRISWOLD, Rettig Arnold 5
GRISWOLD, Roger 1
GRISWOLD, Rufus Wilmot H
GRISWOLD, Sheldon 1 Munson
GRISWOLD, Stanley H
GRISWOLD, Stephen 1 Benham
GRISWOLD, Thomas Jr. 1
GRISWOLD, Victor Moreau H
GRISWOLD, William 4 Edward Schenck
GRISWOLD, William H McCrillis
GRISWOLD, William 1 McCrillis
GROAT, Benjamin Feland 2
GROAT, Carl D. 3
GROAT, George Gorham 4
GROAT, William Avery 2
GROCHOWSKI, Leon M. 5
GRODZINS, Morton 4
GROEDEL, Franz 3 Maximillian
GROEL, Frederick Henry 4
GROESBECK, Alexander J. 3
GROESBECK, Clarence 1 Edward
GROESBECK, Herman V. 3 S.
GROESBECK, Stephen 4 Walley
GROESBECK, William H Slocum
GROEZINGER, Leland 6 Becker
GROFE, Ferde (Ferdinand 1 Rudolph von Grofe)
GROFF, George G. 1
GROFF, George Weidman 3
GROGAN, James J. 2
GROGAN, Starke 6 McLaughlin
GROLL, Albert Lorey 5
GROMAIRE, Marcel 5
GROMER, Samuel David 3
GRONDAHL, Jens Kristian 1
GRONDAHL, Lars Olai 6
GRONER, Duncan 5 Lawrence
GRONER, Frank Shelby 2
GRONER, John Vaughan 5
GRONLUND, Laurence 1
GRONLUND, Lawrence H
GRONNA, A. J. 4
GRONNA, Asle J. 1
GRONWALL, Thomas 1 Hakon
GROOM, Thomas J. 4
GROOMBRIDGE, William H
GROOME, James Black H
GROOVER, Paul 3
GROPIUS, Walter Adolf 5
GROS, John Daniel H
GROSE, Clyde Leclare 2
GROSE, George Richmond 3
GROSE, George Richmond 5
GROSE, Howard Benjamin 1
GROSE, William H
GROSEILLIERS, sieur de H
GROSS, A. Haller 1
GROSS, Alfred Otto 5
GROSS, Charles H
GROSS, Charles Edward 1
GROSS, Charles Philip 6
GROSS, Charles Welles 3
GROSS, Christian 1

GROSS, Ezra Carter H
GROSS, Fred Louis 2
GROSS, Harold Judson 1
GROSS, John E. 4
GROSS, Joseph Leonard 1
GROSS, Mervin E. 2
GROSS, Milt 3
GROSS, Myra Geraldine 6
GROSS, Nathan L. 4
GROSS, Nels 6
GROSS, Oskar 4
GROSS, Robert Ellsworth 4
GROSS, Samuel H
GROSS, Samuel David 4
GROSS, Samuel Elbely 4
GROSS, Samuel Weisscll 5
GROSS, Sidney 6
GROSS, Walter W. 5
GROSS, William Jennings 2
GROSSCUP, Benjamin 1 Sidney
GROSSCUP, Peter Stenger 1
GROSSCUP, Walter T. 3
GROSSET, Alexander H
GROSSET, Alexander 4
GROSSI, Carmine James 6
GROSSINGER, Jennie 5
GROSSMAN, Georg Martin H
GROSSMAN, Marc Justin 5
GROSSMAN, Mary Belle 6
GROSSMAN, Moses Henry 2
GROSSMANN, Louis 1
GROSSMANN, Rudolph 1
GROSVENOR, Abbie 4 Johnston
GROSVENOR, Charles H Henry
GROSVENOR, Edwin 1 Augustus
GROSVENOR, Edwin H Prescott
GROSVENOR, Gilbert 4 Hovey *
GROSVENOR, Graham 2 Bethune
GROSVENOR, Lemuel 1 Conant
GROSVENOR, Thomas H Peabody
GROSVENOR, William H Mason
GROSVENOR, William 3 Mason
GROSVENOR, William H Mercer
GROSZ, George 3
GROSZMANN, Maximilian 1 Paul Eugen
GROTE, August D. 3
GROTE, Augustus Radcliffe H
GROTE, Irvine Walter 5
GROTEWOHL, Otto 4
GROTH, Arnold William 5
GROTHJEAN, Francesca 1 C. R.
GROTON, William 1 Mansfield
GROUARD, Frank H
GROUITCH, Slavko Y. 5
GROUT, Abel Joel 1
GROUT, Daniel Alexander 4
GROUT, Edward Marshall 1
GROUT, Frank F. 2
GROUT, John Henry 4
GROUT, Jonathan 1
GROUT, Josiah 1
GROUT, Lewis 1
GROUT, William Wallace 1
GROVE, Asa Porter H
GROVE, Charles Gordon 4
GROVE, James Harvey 4
GROVE, Lon Woodfin 6
GROVE, Philip Harvey 6
GROVE VALLEJO, 6 Marmaduke
GROVE, William Barry 1
GROVER, Cuvier H
GROVER, Delo Corydon 3
GROVER, Eulalie Osgood 5
GROVER, Frederick Orville 4
GROVER, Frederick 5 Warren
GROVER, James Hamilton 1
GROVER, La Fayette 1
GROVER, Martin 1
GROVER, Nathan Clifford 4
GROVER, Oliver Dennett 1
GROVER, Wayne C(layton) 5
GROVES, Charles Stuart 5
GROVES, Ernest 1 Rutherford
GROVES, Frank Malvon 4
GROVES, Leslie Richard 5
GROVES, Owen Griffith H
GROVES, Robert Walker 4
GROW, Galusha Aaron 1

GROWER, Roy William 3
GROWOLL, Adolf 1
GROZA, Petre 3
GROZIER, Edwin Atkins 3
GROZIER, Richard 2
GRUBB, Edward Burd 4
GRUBB, Eugene Housel 4
GRUBB, George Albert 3
GRUBB, Ignatius Cooper 1
GRUBB, William Irwin 1
GRUBBE, Emil Herman 4
GRUBBS, Samuel Bates 2
GRUBE, Bernhard Adam 4
GRUBER, John Lewis 3
GRUBER, L. Franklin 1
GRUBER, Leo Ray 4
GRUBER, Lewis 1
GRUEHR, Anatole Rodolph 4
GRUEN, Frederick 2
  Gustavus
GRUEN, George John 3
GRUENBERG, Benj C. 4
GRUENBERG, Louis 4
GRUENBERG, Sidonie 6
  Matsner (Mrs. Benjamin
  C. Gruenberg)
GRUENER, Gustav 1
GRUENER, Hippolyte 5
GRUENING, Ernest 6
GRUENSTEIN, Siegfried 3
  Emanuel
GRUENTHANER, Michael 4
  J.
GRUGER, Frederic Rodrigo 5
GRUHL, Edwin 1
GRUITCH, Jerry M. 5
GRULEE, Clifford Grosselle 4
  G.
GRUMBINE, Grant 6
  Bartholomew
GRUMBINE, Harvey 2
  Carson
GRUMM, Arnold Henry 4
GRUND, Francis Joseph H
GRUNDY, Felix 4
GRUNDY, Joseph R. 4
GRUNERT, Francis Eugene 1
GRUNERT, George 6
GRUNERT, Robert W. 4
GRUNEWALD, Gustavus H
GRUNEWALD, Max 5
  Eugene
GRUNITZKY, Nicholas 5
GRUNN, Homer 3
GRUNSFELD, Ernest Alton 6
  Jr.
GRUNSKY, Carl Ewald 1
GRUNWALD, Kurt 4
GRUPPE, Charles Paul 1
GRUSKIN, Alan Daniel 5
GRUVER, Harvey Snyder 5
GRUWELL, Hugh Clifton 5
GRUZEN, Barnett Sumner 6
GRYLLS, Humphry John 2
  Maxwell
GUARD, Samuel R. 4
GUARD, Samuel R. 5
GUARESCHI, Giovanni 6
GUASTI, Secondo III 4
GUBB, Larry E. 6
GUCK, Homer 2
GUCKER, Frank Thomson 5
GUDAKUNST, Donald 2
  Welsh
GUDDE, Erwin Gustav 5
GUDE, Ove 1
GUDEBROD, Louis Albert 5
GUDEMAN, Alfred 2
GUDEMAN, Edward 1
GUDEMAN, Edward 6
GUDGEN, Marjorie Gloria 6
GUDGER, Eugene Willis 3
GUDGER, Hezekiah A. 1
GUDGER, James Cassius 4
  Lowry
GUDGER, James Madison 4
  Jr.
GUE, Benjamin F. 1
GUEDALLA, Philip 2
GUENDLING, J. H. 4
GUENTHER, August 5
  Ernest
GUENTHER, Francis 1
  Luther
GUENTHER, Louis 3
GUENTHER, Richard 1
GUENTHER, Rudolph 4
GUEPIN, Felix Alouis 4
  Caspar
GUERARD, Albert Leon * 3
GUERBER, Helene Adeline 1
GUERIN, Anne-Therese H
GUERIN, Jules 2
GUERIN, William Estil 1
GUERIN, William Eugene 4
GUERLAC, Othan Goepp 1

GUERNSEY, Alice 1
  Margaret
GUERNSEY, Egbert 1
GUERNSEY, Frank Edward 1
GUERNSEY, Henry Newell H
GUERNSEY, James Seeley 4
GUERNSEY, Lucy Ellen 1
GUERNSEY, Nathaniel 1
  Taylor
GUERNSEY, Peter Buel 4
GUERNSEY, Rocellus 1
  Sheridan
GUERNSEY, Samuel James 1
GUERNSEY, Sarah 1
  Elizabeth
GUERRANT, Edward 1
  Owings
GUERRERO, Jose Custavo 3
GUERRIER, Edith 4
GUERRY, Alexander 2
GUERRY, Dupont 4
GUERRY, Le Grand 2
GUERRY, William 1
  Alexander
GUERTIN, George Albert 1
GUESS, George H
GUESS, Harry Adelbert 2
GUESS, Walter Eugene 6
GUEST, Edgar Albert 3
GUEST, Harold Walter 3
GUEST, Richard Clarence 4
GUEVARA, Ernesto 4
GUEVARA, Pedro 6
GUFFEY, James McClurg 1
GUFFEY, Joseph F. 3
GUFFY, Bayless Leander 1
  Durant
GUFLER, Bernard 6
GUGGENHEIM, Daniel 4
GUGGENHEIM, Edmond 5
  Alfred
GUGGENHEIM, Isaac 1
GUGGENHEIM, M. Robert 3
GUGGENHEIM, Murry 4
GUGGENHEIM, Olga H. 5
  (Mrs. Simon Guggenheim)
GUGGENHEIM, Simon 1
GUGGENHEIM, Solomon 2
  R.
GUGGENHEIM, William 1
GUGGENHEIMER, 3
  Charles S.
GUGGENHEIMER, Minnie 4
GUGGENHEIMER, 1
  Randolph
GUGLER, Eric 6
GUGLER, Henry H
GUGLIELMI, Louis O. 3
GUIGNAS, Michel 1
GUIHER, James Morford 4
GUILBERT, Frank 1
  Warburton
GUILBERT, Yvette 4
GUILD, Courtenay 2
GUILD, Curtis * 1
GUILD, George A. 2
GUILD, Henry J. 4
GUILD, Josephus Conn 1
GUILD, LaFayette H
GUILD, Lewis Thurber 1
GUILD, Reuben Aldridge H
GUILD, Reuben Aldridge 1
GUILD, Roy Bergen 4
GUILD, William Alva 6
GUILD, William Huntoon 2
GUILDAY, Peter 2
GUILER, Henry Anderson 1
GUILFOILE, Francis 5
  Patrick
GUILFORD, Nathan H
GUILFORD, Simeon 1
  Hayden
GUILL, John Hudson 3
GUILLE, Andrew J. 1
GUILLE, Frances Vernor 6
GUILLE, Peter 5
GUILLEBEAU, Joseph 1
  Edwin
GUINEE, William Fenton 1
GUINEY, Louise Imogen 1
GUINEY, Patrick Robert H
GUINEY, Patrick William 1
GUINTHER, Robert 3
GUINZBURG, Harold K. 4
GUINZBURG, Ralph K. 3
GUINZBURG, Roland Hay 4
GUION, Connie M. 5
GUION, Lewis 1
GUION, Walter 1
GUIRAUD, Ernest 1
GUITEAU, Charles Julius H
GUITERAS, Gregario Maria 1
GUITERAS, Juan 1
GUITERAS, Ramon 4
GUITERMAN, Arthur 2

GUITTEAU, William 4
  Backus
GUIZADE, Jose Ramon 4
GULICK, Archibald A. 4
GULICK, Charles Burton 4
GULICK, Charles P. 3
GULICK, Edward Leeds 1
GULICK, John Thomas 1
GULICK, John W. 1
GULICK, Lee Nelson 6
GULICK, Luther Halsey 1
GULICK, Luther Halsey 4
GULICK, Sidney Lewis 2
GULICK, Thomas Lafon 1
GULLAGER, Christian 6
GULLETTE, George Albert 5
GULLEY, Needham Yancey 4
GULLION, Allen Wyant 2
GULLIVER, Ashbel Green 6
GULLIVER, Frederic 4
  Putnam
GULLIVER, Julia Henrietta 1
GUM, Walter Clarke 5
GUMBEL, Irving 4
GUMMERE, Amelia Mott 4
GUMMERE, Francis Barton 1
GUMMERE, John H
GUMMERE, Samuel James H
GUMMERE, Samuel Rene 1
GUMMERE, William 1
  Stryker
GUMMEY, Henry Riley Jr. 5
GUMP, Louis Franklin 5
GUMPERT, Martin 4
GUNBY, Andrew Augustus 4
GUNCKEL, John Elstner 1
GUNCKEL, Lewis B. 1
GUND, George 4
GUNDELL, Glenn 4
GUNDER, Dwight Francis 4
GUNDERSEN, Adolf 1
GUNDERSEN, Henrik 1
GUNDERSON, B. Harry 5
GUNDERSON, Carl 1
GUNDERSON, Clark 4
  Young
GUNDRY, Richard Fitz 1
  Harris
GUNLOCK, V. E. 4
GUNN, Alexander Hunter 4
  III
GUNN, Archibald 4
GUNN, E. L. Jr. 4
GUNN, Frederick William H
GUNN, George Purnell 6
GUNN, Glenn Dillard 6
GUNN, Herbert Smith 4
GUNN, James H
GUNN, James Newton 1
GUNN, James Newton 1
GUNN, John Edward 1
GUNN, John W. 5
GUNN, John William 4
GUNN, Ross 4
GUNN, Selskar Michael 2
GUNN, Walter Thomas 3
GUNNELL, Francis M. 1
GUNNELL, George 1
GUNNISON, Almon 1
GUNNISON, Binney 4
GUNNISON, Foster 4
GUNNISON, Frederic 1
  Everest
GUNNISON, Herbert 1
  Foster
GUNNISON, John Williams H
GUNNISON, Raymond M. 5
GUNNISON, Royal Arch 1
GUNNISON, Royal Arch 4
GUNNISON, Walter 1
  Balfour
GUNSAULUS, Edwin 1
  Norton
GUNSAULUS, Frank 1
  Wakeley
GUNSETT, Helen Tossey 5
GUNSETT, Helen Tossey 6
GUNTER, Archibald 1
  Clavering
GUNTER, Clarence 3
GUNTER, Felix Eugene 5
GUNTER, Julius Caldeen 1
GUNTER, Richmond Baker 6
GUNTHER, Charles 1
  Frederick
GUNTHER, Charles Otto 3
GUNTHER, Ernest Ludolph 2
GUNTHER, Franklin Mott 1
GUNTHER, John 6
GUNTHROP, Horace 4
GUNTON, George 1
GUNTON, Rebecca 1
  Douglas (Mrs. George
  Gunton)
GUPTILL, Arthur Leighton 3
GUPTON, William 5

GURD, Fraser Baillie 2
GUREWITSCH, Arno 6
  David
GURIAN, Waldemar 3
GURKOFF, Eugene 5
GURLER, Henry Benjamin 1
GURLEY, Boyd 6
GURLEY, Henry Hosford 1
GURLEY, John Addison H
GURLEY, Ralph Randolph 1
GURLEY, William Fitzhugh 1
GURLEY, William Wirt 1
GURNEY, Augustus M. 4
GURNEY, Charles Henry 4
GURNEY, Deloss Butler 4
  (D. B.)
GURNEY, E. Floyd 6
GURNEY, Ephraim H
  Whitman
GURNEY, James Paul 1
GUROWSKI, Adam H
GURSEL, Cemal 4
GURWITSCH, Aron 6
GUSHEE, Edward Manning 1
GUSHEE, Edward T. 4
GUSS, Uriah Cloyd 3
GUST, John Lewis 3
GUSTAFSON, Airik 6
GUSTAFSON, Axel Carl 4
  Johan
GUSTAFSON, Carl Henry 5
GUSTAFSON, Frank 5
  August
GUSTAFSON, G(ustaf) 5
  Joseph
GUSTAFSON, Gilbert 3
  Eugene
GUSTAFSON, Wesley A. 6
GUSTAFSON, William 1
GUSTAFSON, Zadel Barnes 1
GUSTAV, Adolf VI 6
GUSTAVSON, Reuben 6
  Gilbert
GUSTAVUS V 3
GUSTE, William Joseph Sr. 3
GUSTIN, Albert Lyman Jr. 4
GUSTINE, Amos H
GUTELIUS, Frederick 4
  Passmore
GUTENBERG, Bene 4
GUTERMAN, Carl Edward 3
  Frederick
GUTH, William Westley 1
GUTHE, Carl Eugen 6
GUTHE, Karl Eugen 1
GUTHEIL, Emilian Arthur 3
GUTHERZ, Carl 1
GUTHMANN, Walter S. 6
GUTHNER, William Ernest 3
GUTHRIE, Alfred H
GUTHRIE, Anna Lorraine 4
GUTHRIE, Charles Claude 1
GUTHRIE, Charles 1
  Ellsworth
GUTHRIE, David Vance 4
GUTHRIE, Donald 1
GUTHRIE, Edward Sewall 4
GUTHRIE, Ernest Graham 2
GUTHRIE, George Wilkins 1
GUTHRIE, Hunter 4
GUTHRIE, James H
GUTHRIE, James Alan 1
GUTHRIE, James Alan 5
GUTHRIE, John Dennett 6
GUTHRIE, Joseph Edward 1
GUTHRIE, Kenneth Sylvan 1
GUTHRIE, Lewis Van 4
  Gilder
GUTHRIE, Marshall Crapon 6
GUTHRIE, Mary J(ane) 4
GUTHRIE, Ramon 6
GUTHRIE, Robert R. 6
GUTHRIE, S(eymour) 5
  Ashley
GUTHRIE, Samuel H
GUTHRIE, Stanley Walter 3
GUTHRIE, Thomas Joseph 3
GUTHRIE, Walter James 1
GUTHRIE, William 1
  Anderson
GUTHRIE, William Buck 4
GUTHRIE, William 1
  Dameron
GUTHRIE, William Norman 2
GUTHRIE, William Tyrone 6
GUTHRIE, Woody 4
GUTHUNZ, Henry 6
GUTIERREZ ROSS, 6
  Francisco de Paula
GUTMAN, Monroe C. 6
GUTMANN, Addis 5
GUTSCH, Milton Rietow 6
GUTSTADT, Richard E. 4
GUTT, Camille 3
GUTTERSON, George H. 4
GUTTERSON, Henry H. 3

GUTTERSON, Herbert 4
  Lindsley
GUTTMACHER, Alan 6
  Frank
GUTTMACHER, Manfred 4
  S.
GUTTRIDGE, G(eorge) 5
  H(erbert)
GUY, Charles Lewis 1
GUY, Francis H
GUY, Harvey Hugo 1
GUY, J. Sam 3
GUY, Seymour Joseph 1
GUY, William Evans 1
GUY, William George 5
GUYER, Michael Frederic 5
GUYER, Ulysses Samuel 2
GUYER, William Harris 1
GUYON, James Jr. H
GUYOT, Arnold Henry H
GUYTON, David Edgar 4
GUZE, Henry 5
GWALTNEY, Leslie Lee 4
GWATHMEY, Edward 3
  Moseley
GWATHMEY, Edward 6
  Smith
GWATHMEY, James 2
  Tayloe
GWIN, Earl Stimson 1
GWIN, William McKendree H
GWINN, Joseph Marr 5
GWINN, Ralph W. 4
GWINNETT, Button H
GWYN, Herbert Britton 1
GWYN, Thomas Lenoir 6
GWYNN, J(ohn) Minor H
GWYNNE, Charles Thomas 2
GWYNNE, Walker 1
GYGER, Edgar Grant 1

H

HAACKE, Henry 1
HAAG, Harvey B. 4
HAAG, Joseph Jr. 3
HAAKE, Alfred Paul 4
HAAKON VII 3
HAAN, William George 1
HAANEL, Charles Francis 4
HAANSTRA, John Wilson 5
HAAS, Francis Joseph 3
HAAS, George Christian 1
  Frederick
HAAS, Gustav 1
HAAS, Harry J. 6
HAAS, Jacob Judah Aaron H
  de
HAAS, Jacob Judah Aaron 4
  de
HAAS, John A. W. 1
HAAS, Leonard 5
HAAS, Otto 3
HAAS, Samuel 5
HAAS, Sidney Valentine 5
HAAS, William David 4
HAAS, William H. 5
HAASE, Ferdinand Jr. 6
HAASS, Julius Henry 1
HABBERTON, John 1
HABER, Ernest Straign 4
HABERMAN, Phillip 5
  William Jr.
HABERMAN, Sol 1
HABERSHAM, Alexander H
  Wylly
HABERSHAM, James H
HABERSHAM, John H
HABERSHAM, Joseph H
HABERSHAM, Richard H
  Wylly
HABOUSH, Edward Joseph 6
HACK, Elizabeth Jane 4
  Miller
HACK, George 1
HACK, Gwendolyn Dunlevy 5
  Kelley
HACK, Roy Kenneth 2
HACKEMANN, Louis 1
  Frederick
HACKENBURG, William 4
  Bower
HACKER, Fred A. 3
HACKER, Newton 3
HACKETT, Arthur 5
HACKETT, Charles 1
HACKETT, Charles 5
  Megginson
HACKETT, Charles Wilson 3
HACKETT, Chauncey 3
HACKETT, E. Byrne 3
HACKETT, Francis 4
HACKETT, Frank D. 3
HACKETT, Frank S. 3

HACKETT, Frank Warren 1
HACKETT, Horatio Balch 1
HACKETT, James 5
  Dominick
HACKETT, James Henry H
HACKETT, James J. 6
HACKETT, James Keteltas 1
HACKETT, Karleton 1
  Spalding
HACKETT, Lewis Wendell 4
HACKETT, Richard 3
  Nathaniel
HACKETT, Robert Phillip 4
HACKETT, Samuel Everett 5
HACKETT, Thomas C. H
HACKETT, Wallace 4
HACKETT, William 1
  Stormont
HACKH, Ingo W. D. 1
HACKL, George F. Jr. 1
HACKLER, Victor 6
HACKLEY, Aaron Jr. H
HACKLEY, Charles Elihu 1
HACKLEY, Charles H. 1
HACKMAN, Abe 1
HACKMAN, Pearl E(stella) 6
HACKNEY, Ed T. 1
HACKNEY, Leonard J. 4
HACKNEY, Thomas 2
HACKNEY, Walter S. 1
HADAMARD, Jacques 5
  Salomon
HADAS, Moses 4
HADDEN, Alexander 1
HADDEN, Archibald 1
HADDEN, Charles 3
HADDEN, Crowell 1
HADDEN, Maude Miner 4
HADDOCK, Charles H
  Brickett
HADDOCK, Frank 1
  Channing
HADDOCK, John Courtney 4
HADDOW, Alexander 6
HADEN, Annie Bates (Mrs. 5
  Charles J. Haden)
HADEN, Charles Jones 5
HADEN, Russell Landram 5
HADER, Berta Hoerner 6
HADFIELD, Barnabas 4
  Burrows
HADFIELD, George H
HADING, Hane 4
HADJIMARKOS, 6
  Demetrios Markos
HADLEY, Arthur Twining 1
HADLEY, Carleton 1
  Sturtevant
HADLEY, Cassius Clay 1
HADLEY, Chalmers 3
HADLEY, Charles William 3
HADLEY, Edwin Marshall 3
HADLEY, Ernest Elvin 3
HADLEY, Everett Addison 1
HADLEY, Hamilton 6
HADLEY, Henry 1
  Harrison *
HADLEY, Henry K. 1
HADLEY, Herbert Spencer 1
HADLEY, Hiram 1
HADLEY, Hiram Elwood 1
HADLEY, James H
HADLEY, John Vestal 1
HADLEY, Lindley Hoag 2
HADLEY, Philip Bardwell 1
HADSALL, Harry Hugh 5
HADSELL, Irving W. 4
HADZSITS, George Depue 3
HAEBERLE, Arminius T. 5
HAEBERLE, Frederick 6
  Edward
HAECKER, Theophilus Levi 1
HAENSEL, Fitzhugh 2
  William
HAENSEL, Paul 2
HAERING, George John 4
HAERTLEIN, Albert 4
HAESCHE, William Edwin 1
HAESHMAN, Walter Scott 1
HAESSLER, Carl 6
HAEUSSLER, Armin 1
HAFEN, Ann Woodbury 5
  (Mrs. LeRoy R. Hafen)
HAFEY, William Joseph 3
HAFF, Delbert James 2
HAFFENREFFER, Rudolf 3
  Frederick
HAFNER, John A. 3
HAGA, Oliver Owen 2
HAGAN, Edward James 3
HAGAN, Horace Henry 1
HAGAN, John Campbell Jr. 3
HAGAN, William Arthur 4
HAGAR, Edward McKim 1
HAGAR, George Jotham 1
HAGAR, Gerald Hanna 4

HAGAR, Stansbury 5
HAGEBOECK, Alfons 1
  Ludwig
HAGEDORN, Hermann 4
HAGEMAN, Harry Andrew 5
HAGEMAN, Richard 4
HAGEMANN, Harry H. 5
HAGEMEYER, Jesse 6
  Kalper
HAGEN, Harold C. 3
HAGEN, Hermann August H
HAGEN, Jere 5
HAGEN, John George 4
HAGEN, Oskar Frank 3
  Leonard
HAGEN, Sam 3
HAGENAH, William John 6
HAGENBARTH, Francis 4
  Joseph
HAGER, Albert Davis H
HAGER, Albert Ralph 5
HAGER, Alice Rogers 6
HAGER, Clint Wood 2
HAGER, Eric Hill 6
HAGER, George Caldwell 1
HAGER, John Sharpenstein H
HAGER, Luther George 2
HAGERMAN, Edward 4
  Thomson
HAGERMAN, Frank 1
HAGERMAN, Herbert 1
  James
HAGERMAN, James 1
HAGERTY, Christian Dane 1
HAGERTY, Edward Daniel 5
HAGERTY, George James 4
HAGERTY, James Edward 2
HAGGARD, Alfred Martin 4
HAGGARD, Fred Porter 4
HAGGARD, Sir Godfrey 5
  Digsby Napier
HAGGARD, Howard 3
  Wilcox
HAGGARD, Sewell 1
HAGGARD, William David 1
HAGGE, Hans Jergen 3
HAGGERSON, Fred H. 4
HAGGERTY, Cornelius J. 5
HAGGERTY, James E. 5
HAGGERTY, John James 6
HAGGERTY, Melvin 1
  Everett
HAGGERTY, William J. 6
HAGGETT, Arthur Sewall 1
HAGGIN, Ben Ali 3
HAGGIN, James B. 1
HAGGIN, Louis Terah 1
HAGGOTT, Warren 4
  Armstrong
HAGIN, Fred Eugene 1
HAGNER, Alexander 1
  Burton
HAGNER, Francis Randall 1
HAGNER, Peter H
HAGOOD, Johnson H
HAGOOD, Johnson 2
HAGSPIEL, Bruno Martin 4
HAGSTROM, G. Arvid 1
HAGUE, Arnold 1
HAGUE, Eliott Baldwin 6
HAGUE, Frank 3
HAGUE, James Duncan 1
HAGUE, Louis Marchand 4
HAGUE, Maurice Stewart 2
HAGUE, Parthenia 1
  Antoinette Vardaman
HAGUE, William H
HAGY, Henry B. 3
HAHN, Adolf 1
HAHN, Albert George 5
HAHN, Benjamin Daviese 1
HAHN, Calvin 6
HAHN, Conrad Velder 1
HAHN, E. Adelaide 4
HAHN, Frederic Halsted 5
HAHN, Frederick E. 2
HAHN, George Philip 1
HAHN, Herman F. 1
HAHN, J. Jerome 1
HAHN, John H
HAHN, Lew 3
HAHN, Michael Georg H
  Decker
HAHN, Nancy Coonsman 6
HAHN, Otto 5
HAHN, Paul M. 4
HAHN, Willard E. 4
HAHNE, Ernest Herman 3
HAID, Leo 1
HAID, Paul L. 2
HAIDT, John Valentine H
HAIG, John T. 1
HAIG, Robert Murray 3
HAIG, Vernon Lester 1
  Hague)
HAIGHT, Albert 1

HAIGHT, Cameron 5
HAIGHT, Charles H
HAIGHT, Charles Coolidge 1
HAIGHT, Charles S. 5
HAIGHT, Edward H
HAIGHT, Elizabeth 4
  Hazelton
HAIGHT, George Ives 3
HAIGHT, H. W. 5
HAIGHT, Henry Huntly H
HAIGHT, Raymond LeRoy 2
HAIGHT, Thomas Griffith 2
HAIGIS, John William 4
HAILE, Columbus 1
HAILE SELLASSIE 6
HAILE, William 1
HAILES, Patrick Buchan- 6
  Hepburn
HAILEY, Orren Luico 1
HAILEY, Thomas Griffin 4
HAILMANN, William 4
  Nicholas
HAILPERIN, Herman 5
HAILS, Raymond Richard 4
HAIN, Edward Wiles 6
HAIN, Jacob L. 5
HAINDS, John Robert 6
HAINER, Bayard Taylor 1
HAINES, Charles Glidden 1
HAINES, Charles Grove 2
HAINES, Charles Henry 4
HAINES, Daniel 1
HAINES, Edmund Thomas 6
HAINES, Elwood Lindsay 5
HAINES, Frank David 3
HAINES, Harry B. 5
HAINES, Harry L. 2
HAINES, Helen 1
HAINES, Helen Elizabeth 5
HAINES, Henry Cargill 1
HAINES, Jennie Day 4
HAINES, John Allen 1
HAINES, John Michener 1
HAINES, John Peter 1
HAINES, Matthias Loring 4
HAINES, Robert Terrel 5
HAINES, Thomas Harvey 3
HAINES, Walter Stanley 1
HAINES, William T. 1
HAINS, Peter Conover 1
HAINS, Thornton Jenkins 4
HAIRE, Andrew J. 3
HAISH, Jacob H
HAISH, Jacob 1
HAISLIP, Wade Hampton 5
HAISS, Catherine Nugent 6
  (Mrs. John D Haiss)
HAJI ALI H
HAKANSSON, Erik Gosta H
HAKE, Harry 3
HAKLUYT, Richard 4
HALBERSTADT, Baird 1
HALBERT, Henry Sale 1
HALBERT, Homer Valmore 1
HALD, Henry Martin 4
HALDANE, William 6
  George
HALDEMAN, Bruce 2
HALDEMAN, Frederick 4
  Dwight
HALDEMAN, Harry 1
  Marston
HALDEMAN, Isaac Massey 1
HALDEMAN, Richard H
  Jacobs
HALDEMAN, Samuel H
  Steman
HALDEMAN, Walter 1
  Newman
HALDEMAN, William 1
  Birch
HALDEMAN-JULIUS, E. 3
HALDEN, Alfred A. 3
HALDEN, Leon Gilbert 5
HALDERMAN, John A. 1
HALE, Albert 4
HALE, Albert Cable 1
HALE, Anne Gardner 1
HALE, Annie Riley 2
HALE, Artemas H
HALE, Benjamin H
HALE, Chandler 3
HALE, Charles H
HALE, Charles Reuben 1
HALE, Clarence 1
HALE, David 1
HALE, David C. H
HALE, Earl Melvin 4
HALE, Edward Everett * 1
HALE, Edward Joseph 1
HALE, Edward Russell 4
HALE, Edwin Moses 1
HALE, Edwin Moses 1
HALE, Ellen Day 1
HALE, Enoch H
HALE, Eugene 1

HALE, Fletcher 1
HALE, Florence 3
HALE, Floyd Orlin 1
HALE, Frank J. 6
HALE, Frank Judson 5
HALE, Franklin Darius 1
HALE, Fred Douglas 4
HALE, Frederick 4
HALE, Gardner 1
HALE, George Ellery 4
HALE, Harris Grafton 4
HALE, Harrison 6
HALE, Harry Clay 2
HALE, Horatio Emmons H
HALE, Hugh Ellmaker 3
HALE, Irving H
HALE, James Tracy 4
HALE, John Howard 1
HALE, John Parker 4
HALE, John Philetus 1
HALE, Ledyard Park 1
HALE, Lillian Westcott 4
HALE, Lincoln Bell 5
HALE, Louise Closser 1
HALE, Lucretia Peabody 1
HALE, Marshal 2
HALE, Matthew 1
HALE, Morris Smith 2
HALE, Nathan * H
HALE, Nathan Wesley 4
HALE, Oscar 3
HALE, Philip 1
HALE, Philip Leslie 1
HALE, Philip Thomas 1
HALE, Prentis Cobb 1
HALE, Ralph Tracy 3
HALE, Reuben Brooks 1
HALE, Richard Walden 2
HALE, Robert Lee 5
HALE, Robert Safford H
HALE, Salma 1
HALE, Sarah Josepha Buell H
HALE, Susan 1
HALE, Walter 1
HALE, Will T. 4
HALE, William * H
HALE, William Barton 1
HALE, William Bayard 1
HALE, William Benjamin 1
HALE, William Browne 2
HALE, William Gardner 1
HALE, William Green 3
HALE, William Harlan 6
HALE, William Henry 1
HALE, William J. 3
HALE, William Thomas 1
HALE, Willis H. 4
HALE, Wyatt Walker 2
HALECKI, Oscar 6
HALEY, Andrew Gallagher 4
HALEY, Dennis C. 4
HALEY, Elisha H
HALEY, George Franklin 1
HALEY, James Frederick 5
HALEY, Jesse James 1
HALEY, Mrs. Lovick 6
  Pierce;
HALEY, Ora 1
HALEY, William J. 3
HALFHILL, James Wood 1
HALFORD, Albert James 1
HALFORD, Elijah Walker 1
HALFORD, John Henry 5
HALIFAX, Earl of 3
HALL, A. Cleveland 1
HALL, A. Neely 1
HALL, Abraham Oakey H
HALL, Alaistair Cameron 5
HALL, Alexander Wilford 1
HALL, Allen Garland 1
HALL, Alton Parker 3
HALL, Alvin Percy 6
  McDonald
HALL, Alvin William 5
HALL, Ansel Franklin 4
HALL, Arethusa H
HALL, Arnold Bennett 1
HALL, Arthur Benedict 6
HALL, Arthur Crawshay 1
  Alliston
HALL, Arthur Fletcher 1
HALL, Arthur Graham 1
HALL, Arthur Jackson 2
HALL, Arthur Pinckney 1
HALL, Asaph 1
HALL, Asaph Jr. 1
HALL, Augustus H
HALL, Baynard Rush 1
HALL, Benjamin Mortimer 1
HALL, Benton Jay H
HALL, Bolling 1
HALL, Bolton 1
HALL, C. Lester 5
HALL, Chaffee E(arl) 5
HALL, Chapin 1
HALL, Charles Badger 1

HALL, Charles Cuthbert 1
HALL, Charles Edward 4
HALL, Charles Francis 1
HALL, Charles Henry H
HALL, Charles Hershall 1
HALL, Charles Martin 1
HALL, Charles Mercer 1
HALL, Charles Philip 3
HALL, Charles Winslow 4
HALL, Chester Wallace 1
HALL, Christopher Webber 1
HALL, Claude Caleb 5
HALL, Colby Dixon 6
HALL, Damon Everett 1
HALL, Daniel 1
HALL, David 1
HALL, David McKee Jr. 3
HALL, Dominick Augustin H
HALL, Edmond 4
HALL, Edward Bigelow 5
HALL, Edward Hagaman 1
HALL, Edward Henry 1
HALL, Edward Kimball 1
HALL, Edwin Herbert 1
HALL, Edwin S. 3
HALL, Elmer Edwards 1
HALL, Emery Stanford 1
HALL, Ernest 1
HALL, Everett Wesley 4
HALL, Fitzedward H
HALL, Fitzgerald 1
HALL, Florence Marion 1
  Howe
HALL, Ford Poulton 3
HALL, Francis Joseph 1
HALL, Frank A. 5
HALL, Frank Herbert 3
HALL, Frank Hillman 3
HALL, Frank Lucas 1
HALL, Frank M. 1
HALL, Frank Oliver 1
HALL, Franklin 5
HALL, Fred Smith 5
HALL, Fred(erick) L. 5
HALL, Frederic Aldin 1
HALL, Frederic Byron 1
HALL, G. Stanley 1
HALL, G(eorge) Edward 1
HALL, Gene W. 3
HALL, George H
HALL, George Edward 4
HALL, George Eli 1
HALL, George Elisha 2
HALL, George Gilman 4
HALL, George Henry 1
HALL, George Martin 1
HALL, George Washington 1
HALL, Gertrude 4
HALL, Grover Cleveland 1
HALL, Grover Cleveland Jr. 5
HALL, Harold 4
HALL, Harry Hinckley 1
HALL, Harry Melville 1
HALL, Harvey Monroe 1
HALL, Henry * 1
HALL, Henry B. 4
HALL, Henry Bryan H
HALL, Henry Clay 1
HALL, Henry Harrington 4
HALL, Herbert Edwin 4
HALL, Herbert James 1
HALL, Herman 4
HALL, Hilland 1
HALL, Holworthy 1
HALL, Homer William 5
HALL, Howard 1
HALL, Howard Judson 2
HALL, Isaac Harry 4
HALL, Isaac Hollister H
HALL, James * 1
HALL, James 1
HALL, James Alexander 1
HALL, James Glenn 3
HALL, James Jabez 1
HALL, James King 2
HALL, James Knox Polk 1
HALL, James Morris 4
  Whiton
HALL, James Norman 3
HALL, James Parker 1
HALL, James Pierre 1
HALL, James Whitney 1
HALL, Jennie 1
HALL, John * H
HALL, John Dean H
HALL, John Elihu H
HALL, John Ellsworth 2
HALL, John H. 1
HALL, John L. 4
HALL, John Lesslie 1
HALL, John Raymond 1
HALL, John William H
HALL, Joseph H
HALL, Joseph Kevin 4

HAMM, William Jr. 5	HAMMOND, Thomas 3	HANDWORK, Bentley S. 3	HANNA, Richard Henry 2	HANSON, Victor Henry 2

HAMM, William Jr. 5
HAMMAKER, Wilbur 5
  Emery
HAMMAN, Louis 2
HAMMARSKJOLD, Dag 4
  Hjalmar Agne Carl
HAMMEL, Wilbert C. 4
HAMMEL, William Charles 3
  Adam
HAMMELL, Alfred Lawson 4
HAMMELL, George M. 4
HAMMER, Edwin Wesley 3
HAMMER, John 1
  Schackelford
HAMMER, Kenneth S. 5
HAMMER, Trygve 2
HAMMER, William C. 1
HAMMER, William Joseph 1
HAMMERLING, Louis 1
  Nicholas
HAMMERSTEIN, Oscar 1
HAMMERSTEIN, Oscar 2d 4
HAMMETT, Edward 5
HAMMETT, Henry H
  Pinckney
HAMMETT, Samuel Adams H
HAMMETT, Samuel 4
  Dashiell
HAMMETT, William H. H
HAMMILL, Fred H. 1
HAMMILL, John 1
HAMMITT, Jackson Lewis 1
HAMMON, Jupiter H
HAMMOND, Alonzo John 2
HAMMOND, Andrew B. 1
HAMMOND, Bray 5
HAMMOND, Charles 5
  Herrick
HAMMOND, Charles 3
  Parker
HAMMOND, Creed 1
  Cheshire
HAMMOND, Datus Miller 6
HAMMOND, Dean B(urt) 2
HAMMOND, Edward H
HAMMOND, Edward 1
  Payson
HAMMOND, Edward 5
  Sanford
HAMMOND, Edwin H
HAMMOND, Edwin 1
  Pollock
HAMMOND, Eleanor 1
  Prescott
HAMMOND, Eli Shelby 1
HAMMOND, Frank Clinch 5
HAMMOND, George 4
  Francis
HAMMOND, George H
  Henry
HAMMOND, George 4
  Young
HAMMOND, Godfrey 5
HAMMOND, Graeme 2
  Monroe
HAMMOND, Harold 1
HAMMOND, Harry Parker 3
HAMMOND, Jabez Dean 1
HAMMOND, Jabez Delano H
HAMMOND, Jack 1
HAMMOND, James Jr. 3
HAMMOND, James H
  Bartlett
HAMMOND, James 4
  Bartlett
HAMMOND, James Henry H
HAMMOND, Jason E. 4
HAMMOND, John H
HAMMOND, John Dennis 1
HAMMOND, John Hays 1
HAMMOND, John Hays Jr. 4
HAMMOND, John Henry 2
HAMMOND, John Wilkes 1
HAMMOND, John 1
  Winthrop
HAMMOND, Laurens 6
HAMMOND, Lily Hardy 1
HAMMOND, Lyman Pierce 3
HAMMOND, Matthew 1
  Brown
HAMMOND, Monroe 1
  Percy
HAMMOND, Nathaniel Job H
HAMMOND, Norma Mae 4
HAMMOND, Ogden 3
  Haggerty
HAMMOND, Percy 1
HAMMOND, Robert H
  Hanna
HAMMOND, Roland 4
HAMMOND, Samuel 1
HAMMOND, Stevens Hill 3
HAMMOND, Theodore 1
  Augustus

HAMMOND, Thomas 3
  Stevens
HAMMOND, William 6
HAMMOND, William 1
  Alexander
HAMMOND, William 4
  Alexander
HAMMOND, William 2
  Churchill
HAMMOND, William H
  Gardiner
HAMMOND, Winfield 1
  Scott
HAMMONS, David H
HAMMONS, Earle 4
  Wooldridge
HAMMONS, Earle 1
  Woolridge
HAMMONS, Joseph H
HAMMONS, Paul Edward 6
HAMP, Sidford Frederick 1
HAMPDEN, Walter 3
HAMPSON, Alfred Aubert 2
HAMPSON, Philip F. 1
HAMPTON, Aubrey Otis 3
HAMPTON, Benjamin 1
  Bowles
HAMPTON, Edgar Lloyd 1
HAMPTON, George 4
HAMPTON, Ireland 2
HAMPTON, James Giles H
HAMPTON, Moses H
HAMPTON, Wade H
HAMPTON, Wade 1
HAMRIN, Shirley Austin 3
HAMSUN, Knut 3
HAMSUN, Knut 4
HAMTRAMCK, John H
  Francis
HAMUDA PASHA H
HANAN, John H. 1
HANAN, Kenneth John 3
HANAUER, Jerome J. 1
HANAW, Henry 1
HANBACK, Lewis 1
HANBY, Albert Thatcher 6
HANBY, Benjamin Russel H
HANCEY, Carlos 1
HANCH, Charles Connard 2
HANCHER, John William 4
HANCHER, Virgil Melvin 4
HANCHETT, Benton 1
HANCHETT, Edwin Lani 6
HANCHETT, George 5
  Tilden
HANCHETT, Henry 1
  Granger
HANCHETT, Lafayette 3
HANCHETT, Luther 5
HANCOCK, Albert Elmer 1
HANCOCK, Arthur Boyd 5
HANCOCK, Clarence 2
  Eugene
HANCOCK, Elizabeth 1
  Hazlewood
HANCOCK, G. Allan 4
HANCOCK, George H
HANCOCK, Glover Dunn 1
HANCOCK, H. IRVING 1
HANCOCK, Harris 4
HANCOCK, James Cole 1
HANCOCK, John * 1
HANCOCK, John M. 3
HANCOCK, La Toucha 1
HANCOCK, Theodore E. 1
HANCOCK, Thomas 1
HANCOCK, Thomas 2
  Hightower
HANCOCK, W(alter) Scott 5
HANCOCK, William Wayne 4
HANCOCK, Winfield Scott H
HAND, Alfred 1
HAND, Augustus 1
  Cincinnatus
HAND, Augustus Noble 3
HAND, Chauncey Harris 4
HAND, Daniel H
HAND, Edward H
HAND, George Trowbridge 5
HAND, Harold Curtis 5
HAND, John Pryor 1
HAND, Learned 4
HAND, Richard Lockhart 1
HAND, Thomas Millet 3
HAND, William Flowers 1
HANDBURY, John D. 5
HANDERSON, Henry 1
  Ebenezer
HANDFORTH, Thomas 2
HANDLEY, Carroll Alfred 4
HANDLEY, Harold Willis 5
HANDLEY, William White 1
HANDLIN, Frank 3
  Augustine
HANDMAN, Max Sylvius 1
HANDSCHIN, Charles H. 4

HANDWORK, Bentley S. 3
HANDY, Alexander H
  Hamilton
HANDY, Anson Burgess 2
HANDY, Burton 3
HANDY, Henry Hunter 1
  Smith
HANDY, James A. 1
HANDY, Parker Douglas 1
HANDY, Ray D. 1
HANDY, William 3
  Christopher
HANECY, Elbridge 1
HANEMAN, Frederick 4
  Theodore
HANES, Frederic Moir 5
HANES, James Gordon 5
HANES, Leigh (Buckner) 2
HANES, P(leasant) H(uber) 6
HANES, Ralph Philip 6
HANES, Robert March 5
HANES, S. B. Jr. 4
HANES, Thomas Andrews 6
HANEY, Bart Emory 5
HANEY, Carol 4
HANEY, Dick 2
HANEY, George Jacob 6
HANEY, James Parton 1
HANEY, John Louis 5
HANEY, Lewis Henry 5
HANFORD, A(lfred) 6
  Chester
HANFORD, Ben 1
HANFORD, Charles 1
  Barnum
HANFORD, Cornelius 1
  Holgate
HANFORD, Franklin 1
HANFORD, James Holly 5
HANGER, Franklin 1
  M(cCue)
HANGER, G. Wallace 1
  William
HANGER, Harry Baylor 1
HANGER, Robert Kittrell 5
HANGER, William A. 2
HANIFAN, Lyda Judson 1
HANISCH, Arthur Oscar 4
HANK, Frederick Borter 4
HANK, Oscar Charles 4
HANKINS, Frank Hamilton 5
HANKS, Abbott Atherton 1
HANKS, Mrs. Bernard 4
HANKS, Bryan Cayce 5
HANKS, Charles Stedman 1
HANKS, Henry G. 1
HANKS, Lucien Mason 2
HANKS, Marshall Bernard 2
HANKWITZ, Arthur Walter 5
HANLEY, DeLoss Reed 6
HANLEY, Elijah Andrews 5
HANLEY, Herbert Russell 4
HANLEY, James Hugh 6
HANLEY, John Chaney 1
HANLEY, Joseph Rhodes 3
HANLEY, Miles L. 3
HANLEY, Sarah Bond 5
HANLEY, Stewart 1
HANLEY, Thomas James 5
  Jr.
HANLEY, William Andrew 4
HANLEY, William Scott 6
HANLIN, Merton L. 3
HANLON, Edward I. 4
HANLON, Edward K. 3
HANLON, Lawrence 5
  Wilson
HANLON, Thomas J. Jr. 4
HANLY, J. Frank 1
HANMER, Lee Franklin 5
HANN, Charles 4
HANNA, Charles Augustus 3
HANNA, Dan R. 1
HANNA, Daniel Rhodes Jr. 4
HANNA, Edward J. 2
HANNA, Frank Willard 2
HANNA, Guy Carleton 4
HANNA, Howard Melville 2
HANNA, Hugh Henry 1
HANNA, Hugh Sisson 2
HANNA, James Robert 3
HANNA, John H
HANNA, John 4
HANNA, John Andre H
HANNA, John Hunter 2
HANNA, Mrs John M. 3
HANNA, Kathryn Abbey 5
HANNA, Leonard Colton 1
  Jr.
HANNA, Louis Benjamin 1
HANNA, Marcus Alonzo 1
HANNA, Margaret M. 3
HANNA, Matthew Elting 2
HANNA, Philip C. 1
HANNA, Philip Sidney 3

HANNA, Richard Henry 2
HANNA, Robert H
HANNA, Septimus James 1
HANNA, William Brantly 1
HANNAFORD, Charles 1
  Edward
HANNAFORD, Jule Murat 1
HANNAGAN, Stephen 1
  Jerome
HANNAH, Harvey Horatio 2
HANNAN, Frederick 1
  Watson
HANNAN, Jerome Daniel 4
HANNAY, Neilson 4
  Campbell
HANNEGAN, Edward H
  Allen
HANNEGAN, Robert E. 2
HANNIGAN, Francis 1
  James
HANNIKAINEN, Tauno 5
HANNON, W. H. 4
HANNON, William Garrett 4
HANNUM, Warren Thomas 6
HANOVER, Clinton DeWitt 4
  Jr.
HANRAHAN, Edward 3
  Mitchell
HANSBERRY, Lorraine 4
HANSBROUGH, Henry 1
  Clay
HANSCOM, Charles 1
  Ridgely
HANSCOM, Elizabeth 3
  Deering
HANSCOM, Frank Edward 1
HANSCOM, John Forsyth 1
HANSEL, Charles 1
HANSEL, John Washington 1
HANSEL, John Washington 3
HANSELL, Granger 5
HANSELL, Howard Forde 1
HANSELMAN, Joseph 1
  Francis
HANSEN, A. B. 2
HANSEN, Alice G. 3
HANSEN, Alvin Harvey 6
HANSEN, Arild Edsten 3
HANSEN, Armin Carl 3
HANSEN, Augie Louis 4
HANSEN, Carl Ludwig Jr. 6
HANSEN, Carl W. 4
HANSEN, Einar A. 4
HANSEN, Eric H. 4
HANSEN, Eric H. 5
HANSEN, Florence Froney 5
HANSEN, George 4
HANSEN, George 5
HANSEN, George Troup 4
HANSEN, Hans Christian 3
  Svane
HANSEN, Hans Christian 4
  Svane
HANSEN, John Robert 6
HANSEN, Niels Ebbesen 3
HANSEN, Oskar J. W. 5
HANSEN, Paul 2
HANSEN, Walter William 4
HANSEN, William W. 3
HANSMANN, William H. 4
HANSON, Albert Hoit 5
HANSON, Alexander H
  Contee *
HANSON, Arthur Edwin 4
HANSON, Bert 1
HANSON, Burton 1
HANSON, Charles Lane 5
HANSON, Elisha 4
HANSON, Ephraim 5
HANSON, Felix Valentine 2
HANSON, Frank Blair 3
HANSON, George Charles 1
HANSON, George M. 1
HANSON, Henry W. A. 4
HANSON, James Christian 1
  Meinich
HANSON, John H
HANSON, John Fletcher 1
HANSON, Joseph Miles 1
HANSON, Karl P(eter) 5
HANSON, Leonard G. 4
HANSON, Loring Outbier 4
HANSON, Martin Gustav 4
HANSON, Martin H. 1
HANSON, Michael Francis 4
HANSON, Miles 1
HANSON, Murray 5
HANSON, Norwood Russell 4
HANSON, O. B. 4
HANSON, Ole 1
HANSON, Paul M. 6
HANSON, Richard Burpee 2
HANSON, Richard Locke 4
HANSON, Roger H
  Weightman
HANSON, Thomas Grafton 2

HANSON, Victor Henry 2
HANUS, Paul Henry 1
HANUS, Paul Henry 2
HANWAY, J. E. 2
HANZLIK, Paul John 3
HANZSCHE, William 3
  Thomson
HAPGOOD, Hutchins 2
HAPGOOD, Isabel Florence 1
HAPGOOD, Marshall Jay 1
HAPGOOD, Neith Boyce 3
HAPGOOD, Norman 1
HAPPER, Andrew Patton H
HARADA, Tasuku 4
HARADEN, Jonathan H
HARAHAN, James 1
  Theodore
HARAHAN, William 1
  Johnson
HARALSON, Hugh H
  Anderson
HARALSON, Jonathan 1
HARBACH, Abram 1
  Alexander
HARBACH, Otto Abels 4
HARBAUGH, Charles 5
  William
HARBAUGH, Henry H
HARBAUGH, James 4
  Fleming Linn
HARBAUGH, Thomas 1
  Chalmers
HARBEN, Will N. 1
HARBER, Giles Bates 1
HARBER, Winford Elmer 6
HARBERT, Elizabeth 1
  Morrisson Boynton
HARBESON, William Page 5
HARBISON, E. Harris 4
HARBISON, Ralph Warner 1
HARBISON, Robert Cleland 1
HARBISON, William Albert 3
HARBO, Elias Peter 1
HARBOLD, Peter Monroe 5
HARBORD, James Guthrie 2
HARBOROUGH-
  SHERARD, Mrs. Robert
HARBOTTLE, John 6
HARBOUR, Jefferson Lee 1
HARBY, Isaac H
HARBY, Lee Cohen 4
HARCOURT, Alfred 3
HARCUM, Edith Hatcher 4
HARD, Gideon 1
HARD, William 4
HARDAWAY, William 1
  Augustus
HARDEE, Cary Augustus 3
HARDEE, Theodore 4
HARDEE, William Joseph H
HARDEMAN, Nicholas 5
  Brodie
HARDEMAN, Thomas Jr. 1
HARDEN, Edward Walker 5
HARDEN, John Henry 4
HARDEN, Komuria Albert 6
HARDEN, Orville 3
HARDEN, William 1
  Janeway
HARDENBERGH, Henry 1
  Janeway
HARDENBERGH, Jacob H
  Rutsen
HARDENBERGH, John 4
  Gerard
HARDENBURGH, H
  Augustus Albert
HARDER, Howard Charles 6
HARDESTY, Frederick A. 3
HARDESTY, Irving 2
HARDESTY, Marshall 6
  Glade
HARDESTY, Shortridge 3
HARDEY, Mother Mary H
  Aloysia
HARDGROVE, George P. 4
HARDGROVE, John 5
  Gilbert
HARDIE, George Robert 1
HARDIE, James Allen 1
HARDIE, James Finley 6
HARDIE, Robert Gordon 1
HARDIE, William Vincent 6
HARDIN, Benjamin 1
HARDIN, Charles Henry H
HARDIN, Charles Roe 3
HARDIN, Everitt C. 1
HARDIN, George A. 1
HARDIN, John H
HARDIN, John J. H
HARDIN, John Ralph 3
HARDIN, John Ralph 5
HARDIN, John Wesley H
HARDIN, Martin D. H
HARDIN, Martin D. * 1
HARDIN, Robert Allen 5
HARDIN, Willett Lepley 4

HARDING, Aaron H
HARDING, Abner Clark H
HARDING, Albert Austin 3
HARDING, Alfred 1
HARDING, Alfred 5
HARDING, Arthur 2
  McCracken
HARDING, Carroll Rede 4
HARDING, Charles Francis 2
HARDING, Charles L. 5
HARDING, Chester H
HARDING, Chester 1
HARDING, Edwin Forrest 5
HARDING, Garrick M. 4
HARDING, George 1
HARDING, George 1
  Franklin
HARDING, George M. 3
HARDING, Harry Alexis 5
HARDING, Harry Patrick 5
HARDING, Henry 1
HARDING, J. Horace 4
HARDING, J. M. 4
HARDING, Jesper H
HARDING, John Cowden 4
HARDING, John Eugene 5
HARDING, John Francis 1
HARDING, John Thomas 2
HARDING, John William 4
HARDING, Louis A. 3
HARDING, Nelson 5
HARDING, Robert H
HARDING, Robert Ellison 3
HARDING, Russell 1
HARDING, Samuel 1
  Bannister
HARDING, Seth H
HARDING, Warren G. 1
HARDING, William Barclay 4
HARDING, William Lloyd 1
HARDING, William P. G. 1
HARDING, William White H
HARDINGE, Hal Williams 2
HARDISON, Allen Crosby 6
HARDISON, Osborne 3
  Bennett
HARDMAN, Lamartine 1
  Griffin
HARDT, Frank McCulley 2
HARDT, John William 3
HARDT, Walter Keller 6
HARDWICK, Charles
  Cheever Jr.
HARDWICK, Charles Z. 4
HARDWICK, Clifford 5
  Emerson
HARDWICK, Katharine 6
  Davis
HARDWICK, Thomas 2
  William
HARDWICKE, Cedric 4
  Webster Sir
HARDY, Alexander George 6
HARDY, Arthur Sherburne 1
HARDY, Ashley Kingsley 1
HARDY, Caldwell 1
HARDY, Charles J. 3
HARDY, Charles J. Jr. 6
HARDY, Charles Oscar 2
HARDY, David Keith 6
HARDY, David Phillip 1
HARDY, Edward Lawyer 5
HARDY, Edwin Noah 3
HARDY, Ewing Lloyd 5
HARDY, George Erastus 4
HARDY, George Fiske 2
HARDY, Guy U. 2
HARDY, H(arrison) Claude 6
HARDY, Irene 4
HARDY, James Graham 3
HARDY, John Crumpton 1
HARDY, John Henry 1
HARDY, Joseph Johnston 1
HARDY, Josiah H
HARDY, Kenneth Burnham 5
HARDY, Lamar 4
HARDY, Le Grand Haven 3
HARDY, Marjorie 2
HARDY, Martha Eugenia 5
  Sidebottom (Mrs. Donald
  Hardy)
HARDY, Mary Earle 1
HARDY, Oscar J. 3
HARDY, Ralph W. 3
HARDY, Robert Marion 4
HARDY, Rufus 1
HARDY, Samuel H
HARDY, Summers 3
HARDY, Thomas Walter 4
HARDY, Warren Follansbee 1
HARDY, William Adams H
HARE, Arley Munson (Mrs. 5
  James Hare)
HARE, Clifford LeRoy 2
HARE, Darius Dodge H
HARE, Emlen Spencer 4

HARE, George Andrew 1
HARE, George Emien H
HARE, Hobart Amory 4
HARE, Hugh F. 4
HARE, James H. 2
HARE, James Madison 4
HARE, John Innes Clark 4
HARE, Marmaduke 1
HARE, Robert H
HARE, S. Herbert 4
HARE, T(homas) Truxtun 6
HARE, William Hobart 1
HARER, William Benson 5
HARGADON, I. Leo 3
HARGER, Charles Moreau 1
HARGEST, William Milton 2
HARGETT, Ira Mason 6
HARGIS, Thomas Frazier 1
HARGITT, Charles Wesley 1
HARGITT, George Thomas 6
HARGRAVE, Frank Flavius 6
HARGRAVE, Homer 4
  Pearson
HARGRAVE, Thomas Jean 4
HARGRAVE, William 6
  Loftin
HARGREAVES, John 3
  Morris
HARGREAVES, Richard 5
  T(heodore)
HARGROVE, Reginald 3
  Henry
HARGROVE, Robert 1
  Kennon
HARING, Alexander 1
HARING, Clarence Henry 4
HARING, Clarence Melvin 3
HARING, Douglas Gilbert 5
HARING, John H
HARING, Philip Erwin 5
HARISON, Beverly Drake 1
HARK, J. Max 1
HARKER, Catherine 1
HARKER, Joseph Ralph 1
HARKER, Oliver Albert 1
HARKER, Ray Clarkson 5
HARKEY, Simeon Walcher H
HARKINS, Edward Francis 5
HARKINS, Henry Nelson 4
HARKINS, Matthew 1
HARKINS, Thomas J. 4
HARKINS, William Draper 3
HARKNESS, Albert 1
HARKNESS, Albert 1
  Granger
HARKNESS, Charles 1
  William
HARKNESS, Edward 1
  Stephen
HARKNESS, Georgia Elma 6
HARKNESS, Gordon 4
  Follette
HARKNESS, Harvey W. 1
HARKNESS, James Stewart 4
HARKNESS, William 1
HARKNESS, William Hale 3
HARL, Maple Talbot 6
HARLAN, Aaron H
HARLAN, Byron Berry 2
HARLAN, Campbell Allen 5
HARLAN, Edgar Rubey 1
HARLAN, George Cuvier 1
HARLAN, Henry David 2
HARLAN, James * 1
HARLAN, James 1
HARLAN, James Elliott 1
HARLAN, James S. 1
HARLAN, John Marshall 1
HARLAN, John Marshall 5
HARLAN, John Maynard 1
HARLAN, Josiah H
HARLAN, Otis 1
HARLAN, Richard H
HARLAN, Richard 1
  Davenport
HARLAN, Rolvix 5
HARLAND, Edward 1
HARLAND, Henry 1
HARLAND, James Penrose 5
HARLAND, Lewis E. 6
HARLAND, Thomas H
HARLEY, Charles Richard 1
HARLEY, Lewis Reifsneider 4
HARLING, W. Franke 3
HARLLEE, William Curry 6
HARLOW, Alvin Fay 4
HARLOW, Jean H
HARLOW, Jean 1
HARLOW, John Brayton 4
HARLOW, Louis Kinney 4
HARLOW, Ralph Volney 5
HARLOW, Richard Cresson 4
HARLOW, S. Ralph 5
HARLOW, Victor 3
  Emmanuel
HARLOW, William Burt 1

HARLOW, William Elam 3
HARLOW, William Page 1
HARMAN, Arthur Fort 2
HARMAN, Harvey John 5
HARMAN, Henry Elliott 1
HARMAN, Jacob Anthony 1
HARMAN, James Lewie 5
HARMAN, Pinckney Jones 1
HARMAN, Pinckney Jones 4
HARMANSON, John H
  Henry
HARMAR, Josiah H
HARMATI, Sandor 1
HARMELING, Henry 4
HARMELING, Stephen 3
  John
HARMER, Alfred C. 1
HARMON, Andrew 3
  Davidson
HARMON, Arthur Loomis 3
HARMON, Austin Morris 5
HARMON, Benjamin Smith 1
HARMON, Cameron 5
HARMON, Claude Moore 3
HARMON, Daniel Williams H
HARMON, Darrell Victor 6
HARMON, Frank Wilson 1
HARMON, Harold Elliott 4
HARMON, Henry Gadd 4
HARMON, Hubert Reilly 3
HARMON, John Francis 3
HARMON, John Millard 6
HARMON, Judson 1
HARMON, Leo Clinton 5
HARMON, Miliard Fillmore 2
HARMON, Paul M. 4
HARMON, William Elmer 1
HARMONY, David Buttz 1
HARMS, John Henry 2
HARN, Orlando Clinton 1
HARNDEN, William H
  Frederick
HARNED, Perry L. 4
HARNED, Robert Ellsworth 5
HARNED, Thomas Biggs 1
HARNED, Virginia 2
HARNER, Nevin Cowger 3
HARNETT, Cornelius H
HARNEY, George Edward 1
HARNEY, John Milton 1
HARNEY, William Selby H
HARNLY, Andrew Hoerner 4
HARNO, Albert James 4
HAROLD, Raymond Paget 5
HAROUTUNIAN, Joseph 5
HARPER, Alexander H
HARPER, Carrie Anna 1
HARPER, Cornelius Allen 2
HARPER, Donald 3
HARPER, Earl Enyeart 4
HARPER, Edward Thomson 1
HARPER, Fletcher 1
HARPER, Floyd Arthur 5
HARPER, Fowler Vincent 4
HARPER, Francis Jacob 1
HARPER, George Andrew 1
HARPER, George McLean 2
HARPER, George 3
  Washington Finley
HARPER, H. Mitchell 4
HARPER, Harold 2
HARPER, Harry F. 2
HARPER, Harvey W. 3
HARPER, Herbert E. 6
HARPER, Henry Winston 2
HARPER, Ida Husted 1
HARPER, Jacob Chandler 1
HARPER, James * H
HARPER, James Clarence H
HARPER, James Patterson 1
  Jr.
HARPER, James R. 5
HARPER, John Adams H
HARPER, John Erasmus 1
HARPER, John Lyell 1
HARPER, Joseph Morrill H
HARPER, Mary McKibbin 5
HARPER, Merritt Wesley 4
HARPER, Paul Tompkins 1
HARPER, Paul Vincent 2
HARPER, Robert Almer 2
HARPER, Robert Francis 1
HARPER, Robert Goodloe H
HARPER, Robert N. 1
HARPER, Robert S. 4
HARPER, Roland M. 4
HARPER, Samuel Northrup 2
HARPER, Samuel Williams 1
HARPER, Theodore Acland 3
HARPER, Thomas Henry 4
HARPER, Wilhelmina 6
HARPER, William H
HARPER, William Allen 1
HARPER, William Rainey 1
HARPER, William St John 1
HARPER, William Wade 1

HARPHAM, Gertrude 5
  Tressel Rider
HARPSTER, Charles 1
  Melvin
HARPSTER, John Henry 1
HARPUR, Robert H
HARR, Luther 3
HARR, William R. 3
HARRAH, Charles Jefferson H
HARRAH, Charles Jefferson 4
HARRAH, William 3
  Ferguson
HARRAL, Jared Alphonso 4
HARRAL, Stewart 4
HARRAR, Ellwood Scott 6
HARRE, T. Everett 2
HARRELD, John William 5
HARRELL, Alfred 2
HARRELL, Joel Ellis 5
HARRELL, John H
HARRELL, Linwood Parker 5
HARRELL, Mack 4
HARRELSON, John 3
  William
HARRER, Gustave 2
  Adolphus
HARRIES, George Herbert 1
HARRIGAN, Edward 1
HARRIGAN, Nolan 1
HARRIMAN, Alice 1
HARRIMAN, Alonzo Jesse 5
HARRIMAN, Charles 1
  Conant
HARRIMAN, Edward 5
  Avery
HARRIMAN, Edward 1
  Henry
HARRIMAN, Florence 4
  Jaffray
HARRIMAN, Frank Black 4
HARRIMAN, Frederick 1
  William
HARRIMAN, Henry 3
  Ingraham
HARRIMAN, Job 1
HARRIMAN, John Walter 5
HARRIMAN, Joseph 1
  Wright
HARRIMAN, Karl Edwin 5
HARRIMAN, Lewis 5
  Gildersleeve
HARRIMAN, Mary W. 1
HARRIMAN, Oliver 1
HARRIMAN, Raymond 5
  Davis
HARRIMAN, Walter H
HARRINGTON, Arthur 4
  William
HARRINGTON, Charles 1
HARRINGTON, Charles A. 5
HARRINGTON, Charles 1
  Kendall
HARRINGTON, Charles 1
  Medbury
HARRINGTON, Daniel 6
HARRINGTON, David L. 4
HARRINGTON, Emerson 4
  Columbus
HARRINGTON, Francis 1
  Bishop
HARRINGTON, Francis 1
  Clark
HARRINGTON, Frank 1
  Annibal
HARRINGTON, George 4
  Bates
HARRINGTON, Harry 1
  Franklin
HARRINGTON, Henry Hill 4
HARRINGTON, Henry 1
  William
HARRINGTON, Howard 1
  DeWitt
HARRINGTON, John Lyle 2
HARRINGTON, John T. 1
HARRINGTON, John 2
  Thomas
HARRINGTON, John 3
  Walker
HARRINGTON, Joseph 5
HARRINGTON, Karl 4
  Pomeroy
HARRINGTON, Leon W. 4
HARRINGTON, Louis 1
  Clare
HARRINGTON, Mark 5
  Raymond
HARRINGTON, Mark H
  Walrod
HARRINGTON, Mark 4
  Walrod
HARRINGTON, Philip 2
HARRINGTON, Purnell 1
  Frederick
HARRINGTON, Russell 5
  Chase

HARRINGTON, Samuel H
  Maxwell
HARRINGTON, Samuel 2
  Milby
HARRINGTON, Stuart 5
  William
HARRINGTON, Thomas F. 3
HARRINGTON, Thomas 1
  Francis
HARRINGTON, Vincent 2
  Francis
HARRINGTON, William 5
  Watson
HARRINGTON, Willis F. 4
HARRIOTT, Frank 4
HARRIS, Abram Lincoln 4
HARRIS, Abram 1
  Winegardner
HARRIS, Addison C. 1
HARRIS, Agnes Ellen 3
HARRIS, Albert Hall 1
HARRIS, Albert Mason 2
HARRIS, Albert Wadsworth 5
HARRIS, Alexander 5
HARRIS, Alfred F. 2
HARRIS, Alfred S. 2
HARRIS, Amanda Bartlett 1
HARRIS, Andrew Lintner 1
HARRIS, Arthur Emerson 3
HARRIS, Arthur I. 4
HARRIS, Arthur M. 1
HARRIS, Arvil Ernest 4
HARRIS, Basil 2
HARRIS, Benjamin H
HARRIS, Benjamin Bee 4
HARRIS, Benjamin Franklin 1
HARRIS, Benjamin Gwinn H
HARRIS, Beverly Dabney 2
HARRIS, Bravid 4
  Washington
HARRIS, Caleb Fiske H
HARRIS, Carlton Danner 1
HARRIS, Chapin Aaron H
HARRIS, Charles 2
HARRIS, Charles Butler 4
HARRIS, Charles Cuthbert 4
HARRIS, Charles Joseph 2
HARRIS, Charles K. 1
HARRIS, Charles Murray 4
HARRIS, Charles Tillman 4
  Jr.
HARRIS, Charles Willis 4
HARRIS, Christopher C. 4
HARRIS, Cicero Richardson 1
HARRIS, Corra May 1
HARRIS, Credo Fitch 3
HARRIS, D. D. 6
HARRIS, Daniel Lester H
HARRIS, Dawson Bailey 3
HARRIS, Duncan G. 5
HARRIS, Edwin Ewell 2
HARRIS, Elijah Paddock 1
HARRIS, Elisha H
HARRIS, Ella Isabel 5
HARRIS, Emerson Pitt 1
HARRIS, Eugene Dennis 5
HARRIS, Everett Earl 3
HARRIS, Frank 1
HARRIS, Franklin Stewart 4
HARRIS, Frederic Robert 4
HARRIS, Frederick Brown 5
HARRIS, Garrard 1
HARRIS, George 1
HARRIS, George B. 1
HARRIS, George Barnes 1
HARRIS, George Ellsworth 1
HARRIS, George Simmons 2
HARRIS, George Stiles 5
HARRIS, George Upham 1
HARRIS, George Waldo 1
HARRIS, George H
  Washington
HARRIS, George William 3
HARRIS, George William 1
HARRIS, Gilbert Dennison 3
HARRIS, Grady DeWitt Jr. 6
HARRIS, Guy W(alter) 5
HARRIS, Hamilton 1
HARRIS, Harry Ezekiel Sr. 6
HARRIS, Heaton W. 4
HARRIS, Henry Burkhardt 1
HARRIS, Henry Fauntleroy 1
HARRIS, Henry Hiter 1
HARRIS, Henry Tudor 4
  Brownell
HARRIS, Herbert Eugene 5
HARRIS, Hugh Henry 5
HARRIS, Ira H
HARRIS, Isham Green H
HARRIS, J. Andrews Jr. 1
HARRIS, J. Arthur 2
HARRIS, James A. 2
HARRIS, James Coffee 1
HARRIS, Joel Chandler 1
HARRIS, John * H
HARRIS, John Andrews 4

HARRIS, John Augustus 3
HARRIS, John Burke 3
HARRIS, John Harper 5
HARRIS, John Howard 1
HARRIS, John Peter 5
HARRIS, John Royall 1
HARRIS, John Warton 3
HARRIS, John Woods H
HARRIS, Joseph H
HARRIS, Joseph 1
HARRIS, Joseph B. 4
HARRIS, Joseph Hastings 1
HARRIS, Joseph Smith 1
HARRIS, Julia Collier 5
HARRIS, Julia Fillmore 6
HARRIS, Julian LaRose 4
HARRIS, Lancelot Minor 4
HARRIS, Leslie Huntington 1
HARRIS, Lloyd Webb 6
HARRIS, Loe A. 2
HARRIS, Louis Israel 1
HARRIS, Louis Marshall 3
HARRIS, M. Anstice 3
HARRIS, Malcolm LaSalle 3
HARRIS, Mark H
HARRIS, Mary Belle 3
HARRIS, Mattie Powell 5
HARRIS, Maurice Henry 1
HARRIS, May 5
HARRIS, Maynard 6
Lawrence
HARRIS, Merriman Colbert 1
HARRIS, Miriam Coles 4
HARRIS, Monteflore M. 3
HARRIS, Morris Bedford 2
HARRIS, Moses H
HARRIS, Moses Henry 1
HARRIS, Nathaniel Edwin 1
HARRIS, Newton Megrue 5
HARRIS, Norman Dwight 5
HARRIS, Norman W. 4
HARRIS, Norman Wait 1
HARRIS, Overton 1
HARRIS, Paul Percy 2
HARRIS, Peter Charles 3
HARRIS, Philip H. 5
HARRIS, Pierce 5
HARRIS, Mrs. Ralph A. 3
HARRIS, Ralph Scott 4
HARRIS, Robert H
HARRIS, Robert Alfred 5
HARRIS, Robert Le Roy 2
HARRIS, Robert Orr 1
HARRIS, Rollin Arthur 1
HARRIS, Ruth Miriam 5
HARRIS, Sam H. 1
HARRIS, Sampson Willis H
HARRIS, Samuel 1
HARRIS, Samuel 1
HARRIS, Samuel Henry 1
HARRIS, Samuel Smith H
HARRIS, Seale 3
HARRIS, Seymour Edwin 6
HARRIS, Sherwin Bentley 5
HARRIS, Stanley G. 5
HARRIS, Thaddeus Mason H
HARRIS, Thaddeus William H
HARRIS, Thomas Green 4
HARRIS, Thomas Jefferson 2
HARRIS, Thomas K. H
HARRIS, Thomas Langrell H
HARRIS, Thomas LeGrand 1
HARRIS, Thomas Luther 4
HARRIS, Titus Holliday 5
HARRIS, Townsend H
HARRIS, Uriah Rose 1
HARRIS, Victor 5
HARRIS, W. Hall 1
HARRIS, W. John 3
HARRIS, Wade Hampton 1
HARRIS, Wade N. 5
HARRIS, Walter Alexander 3
HARRIS, Walter Butler 1
HARRIS, Walter Edward 1
HARRIS, Walter William 3
HARRIS, Wiley Pope H
HARRIS, William H
HARRIS, William Alexander H
HARRIS, William Alexander 1
HARRIS, William Charles 1
HARRIS, William Fenwick 1
HARRIS, William Jr. 1
HARRIS, William Julius 1
HARRIS, William Laurel 1
HARRIS, William Littleton H
HARRIS, William Logan H
HARRIS, William Torrey H
HARRIS, William Welton H
HARRIS, Willis Overton 1
HARRIS, Winder Russell 5
HARRISON, Albert H
Galliton
HARRISON, Alexander 1
HARRISON, Alfred Craven 5
Jr.

HARRISON, B. George 3
HARRISON, Belle 4
Richardson
HARRISON, Benjamin H
HARRISON, Benjamin 1
HARRISON, Benjamin 4
HARRISON, Benjamin 5
Franklin
HARRISON, Benjamin 4
Inabnit
HARRISON, Birge 1
HARRISON, Bruce Magill 6
HARRISON, Burr Powell 4
HARRISON, Carter Bassett H
HARRISON, Carter Henry H
HARRISON, Carter Henry 3
HARRISON, Charles A. 3
HARRISON, Charles Custis 1
HARRISON, Charles Yale 3
HARRISON, Christopher H
HARRISON, Constance 1
Cary
HARRISON, DeSales 5
HARRISON, Earl Grant 3
HARRISON, Edith Ogden 5
HARRISON, Edward Tyler 4
HARRISON, Edwin 1
HARRISON, Elizabeth 1
HARRISON, Fairfax 1
HARRISON, Floyd Reed 4
HARRISON, Francis Burton 3
HARRISON, Fred 1
HARRISON, Gabriel 1
HARRISON, George 5
Billingsley
HARRISON, George L. 3
McGregor
HARRISON, George 1
Moffett
HARRISON, George Paul 4
HARRISON, Gessner H
HARRISON, Hall 1
HARRISON, Hamlett 5
HARRISON, Harold Everus 6
HARRISON, Harry P. 5
HARRISON, Harvey 2
Thomas
HARRISON, Henry Sydnor 1
HARRISON, Horace H
Harrison
HARRISON, Ida Withers 1
HARRISON, Ike H(enry) 5
HARRISON, James H
HARRISON, James Albert 1
HARRISON, James D. 5
HARRISON, James Jabez 1
HARRISON, James 6
Leftwich
HARRISON, Jamison 4
Richard
HARRISON, Jay Smolens 6
HARRISON, John H
HARRISON, John B. 2
HARRISON, John Ellis 4
HARRISON, John Green 1
HARRISON, John Higgins 1
HARRISON, John Scott 5
HARRISON, John Smith 5
HARRISON, Jonathan 1
Baxter
HARRISON, Joseph H
HARRISON, Joseph Le Roy 3
HARRISON, Leland 3
HARRISON, Leon 1
HARRISON, Lester Stanley 4
HARRISON, Luther 1
HARRISON, Lynde 1
HARRISON, Mark Robert H
HARRISON, Mary Scott 2
Lord
HARRISON, Maurice 3
Edward
HARRISON, Milton 2
Whately
HARRISON, Orla Ellsworth 1
HARRISON, Pat 1
HARRISON, Peleg Dennis 1
HARRISON, Perry G. 3
HARRISON, Peter 1
HARRISON, Ralph 1
Chandler
HARRISON, Ray 3
HARRISON, Raymond 4
Leyden
HARRISON, Richard 1
Almgill
HARRISON, Richard B. 1
HARRISON, Roland H
Rathbun
HARRISON, Roland 4
Wendell
HARRISON, Ross Granville 3
HARRISON, Russell 1
Benjamin
HARRISON, Samuel Smith H

HARRISON, Shelby Millard 5
HARRISON, Stephen Noble 4
HARRISON, Thomas Perrin 2
HARRISON, Thomas 1
Skelton
HARRISON, Thomas 1
Walter
HARRISON, W. Vernon 1
HARRISON, Walter 4
Munford
HARRISON, Ward 5
HARRISON, William 2
Benjamin
HARRISON, William Groce 5
HARRISON, William Henry H
HARRISON, William Henry 3
HARRISON, William Jr. H
HARRISON, William 6
Moore
HARRISON, William 4
Mortimer
HARRISON, William Pope H
HARRISON, William 1
Preston
HARRISON, William 1
Robert
HARRISON, Zadok Daniel 4
HARRITY, William Francis 1
HARROD, Benjamin 1
Morgan
HARROD, James H
HARROFF, Fred F. 5
HARROLD, Charles Cotton 2
HARROLD, Orville 1
HARRON, Marion Janet 5
HARROP, George Argale 2
Jr.
HARROP, Leslie DeVottie 5
HARROW, Benjamin 5
HARRY, Joseph Edward 2
HARSH, David Newby 5
HARSH, James Birney 1
HARSH, Philip Whaley 4
HARSHA, William McIntire 2
HARSHA, William Thomas 3
HARSHAW, William Jacob 4
HARSHBARGER, William 4
Asbury
HARSHBERGER, John 1
William
HARSHE, Robert Bartholow 1
HARSON, M. Joseph 1
HARSTROM, Carl Axel 1
HART, Abraham H
HART, Albert Bushnell 2
HART, Alden Leonard 4
HART, Archibald Chapman 1
HART, Boies Chittenden 2
HART, Burdett 1
HART, Charles A. 3
HART, Charles Allan 6
HART, Charles Arthur 3
HART, Charles Edward 1
HART, Charles Henry 1
HART, Edmund Hall H
HART, Edward 1
HART, Edward J. 4
HART, Edward Payson 4
HART, Edwin Bret 3
HART, Elizur Kirke 4
HART, Emanuel Bernard H
HART, Ernest Eldred 1
HART, Frances Noyes 2
HART, Francis Russell 1
HART, Franklin Augustus 4
HART, Freeman H. 4
HART, George H. 5
HART, George Overbury 1
HART, H. Martyn 1
HART, Harris 5
HART, Hastings Hornell 1
HART, Henry Clay 4
HART, Henry Hersch 5
HART, Henry Joseph 6
HART, Henry Melvin Jr. 5
HART, Hornell 2
HART, Howard Stanley 2
HART, Irving Harlow 3
HART, James A. 4
HART, James Hill 6
HART, James MacDougall 1
HART, James Morgan 1
HART, James Norris 1
HART, Jerome Alfred 1
HART, Jesse Cleveland 5
HART, Joel Tanner H
HART, John H
HART, John Francis 4
HART, John Marion 5
HART, John Nathaniel 5
HART, John Seely H
HART, John William 2
HART, Joseph Kinmont 2
HART, Lasher 4
HART, Lorenz 4
HART, Louis Bret 1

HART, Louis Folwell 1
HART, Luke Edward 4
HART, Marion Weddell 1
HART, Merwin Kimball 4
HART, Michael James 3
HART, Moss 4
HART, Oliver Philip 3
HART, Percie (William 5
Edward)
HART, Ringgold 4
HART, Roswell H
HART, Samuel 1
HART, Simeon Thompson 5
HART, Simeon Thompson 6
HART, Sophie Chantal 2
HART, Theodore Stuart 3
HART, Thomas 6
HART, Thomas Charles 5
HART, Thomas Norton 1
HART, Thomas Patrick 5
HART, Walter Morris 5
HART, William H
HART, William H. 1
HART, William Henry 4
Harrison
HART, William Lee 3
HART, William Lincoln 1
HART, William Michael 4
HART, William Octave 4
HART, William Richard 4
HART, William S. 2
HARTE, Bret 4
HARTE, Emmet Forrest 5
HARTE, Houston 5
HARTE, Richard 5
HARTE, Richard Hickman 1
HARTE, Thomas John 4
HARTENSTEIN, Robert 4
Franklin
HARTER, Dow W(atters) 5
HARTER, George Abram 2
HARTER, Isaac 3
HARTER, J. Francis 2
HARTER, Michael Daniel H
HARTFIELD, John 4
McCallum
HARTFIELD, Joseph 4
Manuel
HARTFORD, Fernando 1
Wood
HARTFORD, George H
Huntington
HARTFORD, George 4
Huntington
HARTFORD, George L. 3
HARTFORD, John A. 3
HARTHORN, Drew 5
Thompson
HARTIGAN, Charles 1
Conway
HARTIGAN, Raymond 5
Harvey
HARTINGER, William 5
Calvert
HARTLEY, Charles 5
Pinckney
HARTLEY, Ellis Taylor 1
HARTLEY, Eugene Fuller 4
HARTLEY, Frank 1
HARTLEY, Fred Allan Jr. 4
HARTLEY, Harold H. 4
HARTLEY, Henry 1
Alexander Saturnin
HARTLEY, Isaac Smithson 1
HARTLEY, James Joseph 2
HARTLEY, Jonathan Scott 1
HARTLEY, Leslie Poles 5
HARTLEY, Lowrie C. 5
HARTLEY, Robert Willard 1
HARTLEY, Roland H. 4
HARTLEY, Thomas H
HARTMAN, Carl G. 5
HARTMAN, Charles S. 1
HARTMAN, Charles 5
William
HARTMAN, Douglas 4
William
HARTMAN, Edwin Mitman 2
HARTMAN, Ernest 5
Herman
HARTMAN, Frank 1
Alexander
HARTMAN, Gertrude 4
HARTMAN, Harold Hoover 4
HARTMAN, Harvey 4
Clarence
HARTMAN, Henry 4
HARTMAN, Howard 1
Russell
HARTMAN, Jesse L. 4
HARTMAN, John A. 5
HARTMAN, John Clark 5
HARTMAN, John Daniel 6
HARTMAN, John Peter 2
HARTMAN, Lee Foster 4
HARTMAN, Leon Wilson 4

HARTMAN, Lewis Oliver 3
HARTMAN, Louis Francis 4
HARTMAN, Louis H. 4
HARTMAN, Paul William 6
HARTMAN, Robert S. 6
HARTMAN, Sara 5
HARTMAN, Siegfried 3
Frisch
HARTMANN, Alexis Frank 4
HARTMANN, (Carl) 5
Sadakichi
HARTMANN, F. M. 1
HARTMANN, F. Norman 6
HARTMANN, George W. 3
HARTMANN, Jacob 2
Wittmer
HARTMANN, Reina Kate 6
Goldstein;
HARTMANN, William V. 5
HARTNESS, James 1
HARTNETT, Timothy V. 5
HARTNEY, Harold Evans 2
HARTRANFT, Chester 1
David
HARTRANFT, John H
Frederick
HARTRATH, Lucie 4
HARTREE, Douglas Rayner 3
HARTRIDGE, Clifford 4
Wayne
HARTRIDGE, Emelyn 2
Battersby
HARTRIDGE, John Earle 1
HARTRIDGE, Julian H
HARTS, William Wright 4
HARTSFIELD, William 5
Berry
HARTSHORN, Edwin 6
Simpson
HARTSHORN, William 1
Henry
HARTSHORN, William 1
Newton
HARTSHORNE, Charles 1
HARTSHORNE, Charles 1
Hopkins
HARTSHORNE, Henry H
HARTSHORNE, Hugh 4
HARTSUFF, Albert 1
HARTSUFF, George Lucas H
HARTT, Charles Frederick H
HARTT, George 3
Montgomery
HARTT, Mary Bronson 5
HARTT, Rollin Lynde 2
HARTUNG, Albert Michael 6
HARTWELL, Alfred 1
Stedman
HARTWELL, Burt Laws 4
HARTWELL, Edward 1
Mussey
HARTWELL, Ernest Clark 4
HARTWELL, Henry Walker 3
HARTWELL, John 1
Augustus
HARTWELL, Shattuck 3
Osgood
HARTWICH, Herman 2
HARTWIG, Johann H
Christoph
HARTY, Jeremiah J. 1
HARTZ, William Homer 5
HARTZELL, Charles 1
HARTZELL, J. Culver 1
HARTZELL, Joseph Crane 1
HARTZELL, Milton Bixler 1
HARTZELL, Thomas B. 1
HARTZLER, Henry Burns 1
HARTZLER, John 4
Ellsworth
HARTZOG, Henry Simms 1
HARTZOG, Justin R. 4
HARVARD, John H
HARVEY, Alexander 2
HARVEY, Andrew Magee 2
HARVEY, Basil Coleman 1
Hyatt
HARVEY, Byron 4
HARVEY, Byron 3
Schermerhorn
HARVEY, Charles Henry 1
HARVEY, Charles Milton 1
HARVEY, Charles Mitchell 1
HARVEY, Daniel Robert 4
HARVEY, Edmund Newton 3
HARVEY, Eli 3
HARVEY, Ethel Browne 6
HARVEY, Ford 1
HARVEY, Frederick Loviad 1
HARVEY, George H
HARVEY, George 1
HARVEY, George 1
Cockburn
HARVEY, George U. 2
HARVEY, Harold Brown 2

540

HARVEY, Haywood Augustus — H
HARVEY, Holman — 5
HARVEY, Horace — 3
HARVEY, I. J. Jr. — 4
HARVEY, James Madison — H
HARVEY, Jean Charles — 5
HARVEY, Sir John
HARVEY, John (Lacey) — 5
HARVEY, Jonathan
HARVEY, Kenneth G. — 5
HARVEY, Laurence — 6
HARVEY, Lawson Moreau — 4
HARVEY, Leo M. — 6
HARVEY, LeRoy
HARVEY, Lillian A. (Mrs. Raymond F. Harvey) — 5
HARVEY, Lorenzo Dow — 1
HARVEY, Louis Powell — H
HARVEY, Matthew — H
HARVEY, P(aul) Casper — 6
HARVEY, Philip Francis — 1
HARVEY, Ralph Hicks — 3
HARVEY, Ray Forrest — 5
HARVEY, Rodney Beecher — 2
HARVEY, Roger Allen — 6
HARVEY, Roland Bridendall — 1
HARVEY, Rowland Hill — 4
HARVEY, Samuel Clark — 3
HARVEY, W(illiam) W(est) — 5
HARVEY, William Edwin
HARVEY, William Hope — 4
HARVEY, William Lemuel — 1
HARVEY, William Patrick — 4
HARVEY, William Riggs — 3
HARVIE, Eric Lafferty — 6
HARVIE, John — H
HARVIE, John Bruce — 2
HARVIE, Peter Lyons — 2
HARWOOD, Andrew Allen — H
HARWOOD, Charles — 3
HARWOOD, Charles McHenry — 4
HARWOOD, Cole Leslie
HARWOOD, Edwin — 1
HARWOOD, Frank James — 1
HARWOOD, George Alexander — 1
HARWOOD, John — H
HARWOOD, John E. — H
HARWOOD, Thomas A. — 4
HARWOOD, William Sumner — 1
HARZA, Leroy Francis — 3
HASBROUCK, Abraham Bruyn — H
HASBROUCK, Abraham Joseph — H
HASBROUCK, Alfred — 1
HASBROUCK, Charles Alfred — 4
HASBROUCK, Gilbert D. B. — 2
HASBROUCK, Henry Cornelius — 1
HASBROUCK, Josiah — H
HASBROUCK, Lydia Sayer — H
HASBROUCK, Lydia Sayer — 4
HASCALL, Augustus Porter — H
HASCALL, Milo Smith — 1
HASCALL, Wilbur — 1
HASCHE, Rudolph Leonard — 3
HASE, William Frederick — 1
HASELDEN, Kyle Emerson — 5
HASELTINE, Burton — 2
HASELTINE, George — 1
HASELTINE, Herbert — 4
HASELTINE, Nathan Stone — 5
HASELTON, Page Smith — 5
HASELTON, Seneca — 1
HASEMAN, Charles — 1
HASENCLEVER, Peter — H
HASKELL, Charles Nathaniel — 1
HASKELL, Clinton Howard — 3
HASKELL, Duane Hedrick — 6
HASKELL, Dudley Chase — H
HASKELL, Earl Stanley — 1
HASKELL, Edward Howard — 1
HASKELL, Edwin Bradbury — 1
HASKELL, Ella Louise Knowles — H
HASKELL, Ella Louise Knowles — 4
HASKELL, Eugene Elwin — 1
HASKELL, Freda Rew (Mrs. George S. Haskell) — 5
HASKELL, Frederick Tudor — 1
HASKELL, Glenn Leach — 5
HASKELL, Harold Clifford — 3
HASKELL, Harriet Newell — 1
HASKELL, Harry Garner — 1
HASKELL, Harry Leland — 1
HASKELL, Helen Eggleston — 5

HASKELL, Henry Joseph — 3
HASKELL, Horace Bray — 5
HASKELL, J. Amory — 1
HASKELL, Lewis Wardlaw — 4
HASKELL, Llewellyn Frost — 4
HASKELL, Mellen Woodman — 2
HASKELL, Reuben L. — 6
HASKELL, Thomas Hawes — 1
HASKELL, William Edwin — 1
HASKELL, William Edwin Jr.
HASKELL, William Nafew — 3
HASKELL, William T. — H
HASKET, Elias — H
HASKIN, Frederic J. — 2
HASKIN, John Bussing
HASKIN, William Lawrence — 1
HASKINS, Caryl Davis — 1
HASKINS, Charles Homer — 1
HASKINS, Charles Nelson — 2
HASKINS, Charles Waldo — 1
HASKINS, Kittredge
HASKINS, Samuel Moody — 3
HASLAM, Charles Raymond — 4
HASLAM, Robert Thomas — 4
HASLER, Frederick Edward — 5
HASLER, Henry — 4
HASLUP, Lemuel A. — 3
HASPEL, Joseph — 4
HASSAM, Childe — 1
HASSAM, John Tyler — 1
HASSARD, John Greene
HASSAUREK, Friedrich — H
HASSE, Adelaide — 3
HASSEL, Karl Elmer — 6
HASSELBRING, Heinrich — 5
HASSELMANS, Louis — 3
HASSELQUIST, Tuve Nilsson — H
HASSELTINE, Hermon Erwin — 5
HASSETT, William D. — 6
HASSKARL, Joseph F. — 1
HASSLER, Elizabeth Emily — 4
HASSLER, Ferdinand Augustus — 1
HASSLER, Ferdinand Rudolph — H
HASSLER, Russell Herman — 5
HASSLER, Simon — 1
HASTINGS, Charles Douglas
HASTINGS, Charles Harris — 5
HASTINGS, Charles Sheldon — 1
HASTINGS, Daniel — 1
HASTINGS, Daniel O. — 4
HASTINGS, Earl Freeman — 4
HASTINGS, Edgar Morton — 4
HASTINGS, Edwin George — 5
HASTINGS, Francis William — 4
HASTINGS, Frank Seymour — 1
HASTINGS, Frank Warren — 1
HASTINGS, George — 1
HASTINGS, George Aubrey — 3
HASTINGS, George Buckland — 1
HASTINGS, George Everett — 2
HASTINGS, George Henry — 1
HASTINGS, Harry George — 4
HASTINGS, Hugh — 1
HASTINGS, John — H
HASTINGS, John Russel — 2
HASTINGS, Lansford W. — H
HASTINGS, Paul Pardee — 2
HASTINGS, Reuben C. M. — 4
HASTINGS, Samuel Dexter — 1
HASTINGS, Samuel Miles — 4
HASTINGS, Serramus Clinton
HASTINGS, Seth — H
HASTINGS, Thomas — 1
HASTINGS, Thomas — 1
HASTINGS, Thomas Samuel
HASTINGS, Thomas Wood — 5
HASTINGS, Wells Southworth
HASTINGS, William Granger
HASTINGS, William Soden — H
HASTINGS, William Walter — 4
HASTINGS, William Wirt — 1
HASWELL, Alanson Mason — 1
HASWELL, Anthony — H
HASWELL, Charles Haynes — 1
HASWELL, Kanah — 1
HASWELL, Elizabeth Marcum (Mrs. Harold Alanson)
HATATHLI, Ned — 6
HATCH, Abram — H
HATCH, Albert Sydney — 4

HATCH, Alden — 6
HATCH, Carl A. — 4
HATCH, Edward — H
HATCH, Edward Jr. — 4
HATCH, Edward Wingate — H
HATCH, Edwin Glentworth — 1
HATCH, Emily Nichols — 3
HATCH, Everard E. — 1
HATCH, Francis March — 1
HATCH, Frederick Thomas — 1
HATCH, Harry C. — 2
HATCH, Henry James — 1
HATCH, Israel Thompson — H
HATCH, James Noble — 4
HATCH, John Fletcher — 6
HATCH, John Porter — H
HATCH, John Wood — 4
HATCH, L. Boyd — 5
HATCH, Leonard Williams — 3
HATCH, Lloyd A. — 4
HATCH, Louis Clinton — 5
HATCH, Pascal Enos — 3
HATCH, Philander Ellsworth — 4
HATCH, Robert Seymour — 5
HATCH, Roy Winthrop — 4
HATCH, Rufus — H
HATCH, Samuel Grantham — 1
HATCH, Stephen D. — H
HATCH, Vermont — 3
HATCH, William Henry — H
HATCHER, Eldridge Burwell — 2
HATCHER, James Fulton — 3
HATCHER, John Bell — 1
HATCHER, John Henry — 5
HATCHER, Julian Sommerville — 4
HATCHER, Orle Latham — 2
HATCHER, Robert Anthony — H
HATCHER, Robert Anthony — 2
HATCHER, Samuel Claiborne — 3
HATCHER, William Bass — 2
HATCHER, William E. — 1
HATCHER, Wirt Hargrove — 6
HATFIELD, Charles Albert — 4
HATFIELD, Charles Phelps — 1
HATFIELD, Charles Folsom
HATFIELD, Charles James — 3
HATFIELD, Charles Sherrod — 2
HATFIELD, Edwin Francis — H
HATFIELD, George — 3
HATFIELD, George Juan — 3
HATFIELD, Henry Drury — 4
HATFIELD, Henry Rand — 2
HATFIELD, James Taft — 1
HATFIELD, James Tobias — 1
HATFIELD, Joseph Clayton — 3
HATFIELD, Joshua Alexander — 1
HATFIELD, Lansing — 3
HATFIELD, Marcus Patten — 1
HATFIELD, Oliver Perry — H
HATFIELD, R. G. — H
HATHAWAY, Arthur Stafford — 1
HATHAWAY, Charles Montgomery Jr. — 3
HATHAWAY, Evangeline — 5
HATHAWAY, Fons A. — 5
HATHAWAY, Forrest Henry — 1
HATHAWAY, George Henry — 1
HATHAWAY, Harle Wallace — 2
HATHAWAY, Joseph Henry — 5
HATHAWAY, King — 2
HATHAWAY, Lester Gordon — 6
HATHAWAY, Robert Joseph — 3
HATHAWAY, Samuel Gilbert — H
HATHAWAY, Stewart Southworth — 4
HATHAWAY, Warren — 3
HATHAWAY, William Lee — 4
HATHORN, Henry Harrison — H
HATHORN, John — H
HATHORNE, George — H
HATHORNE, William — H
HATHWAY, Calvin Sutliff — 6
HATHWAY, George W. — 5
HATHWAY, Marion — 4
HATLO, Jimmy — 4
HATOYAMA, Ichiro — 6
HATT, Paul Kitchener — 3
HATT, William Kendrick — 5

HATTON, Augustus Rutan — 2
HATTON, Charles Harold — 1
HATTON, E. Roy — 4
HATTON, Frank — H
HATTON, Moses Wesley — 4
HATTON, Robert Hopkins — H
HATTON, T. Chalkley — 1
HATTSTAEDT, John James — 1
HAUBERG, John Henry — 3
HAUBOLD, Herman A. — 1
HAUCK, Fred — 4
HAUCK, Louise Platt — 2
HAUCK, Minnie — H
HAUGAN, Henry Alexander — 1
HAUGE, Hjalmar Christian — 4
HAUGEN, Gilbert N. — 1
HAUGEN, Nils Pederson — 1
HAUGH, Jesse Lee — 4
HAUGHEY, Thomas — H
HAUGHT, Benjamin Franklin — 4
HAUGHT, Thomas William — 3
HAUHART, William Frederic — 5
HAUK, Minnie — H
HAUK, Minnie — H
HAUKE, Robert Charles — 6
HAULENBEEK, P. Raymond — 4
HAUN, Burton Oliver — 5
HAUN, Henry Peter — H
HAUPERT, Raymond Samuel — 5
HAUPT, Alexander James Derbyshire — 1
HAUPT, Charles Elvin — 1
HAUPT, Herman — H
HAUPT, Ira — 4
HAUPT, Lewis Muhlenberg — 1
HAUPT, Paul — 1
HAUPT, Sarah Minerva — 5
HAUPTMANN, Gerhart — 2
HAUSDORFER, Walter — 5
HAUSER, Charles R(oy) — 5
HAUSER, Conrad Augustine — 2
HAUSER, Ernst A. — 3
HAUSER, Harry — 4
HAUSER, Samuel Thomas — 1
HAUSER, Walter — 4
HAUSERMAN, Fredric Martin — 5
HAUSKENS, Peter Bert — 5
HAUSMAN, Leon Augustus — 4
HAUSMAN, Louis — 3
HAUSMAN, William A. Jr. — 2
HAUSMANN, Erich — 4
HAUSSERMANN, John William — 4
HAUSSERMANN, Oscar William — 6
HAUSSLER, Arthur Glenn — 6
HAUSSMANN, Alfred Carl — 4
HAUT, Irvin Charles — 5
HAUTECOEUR, Louis — 6
HAUXHURST, Henry Austin — 6
HAVARD, Valery — 1
HAVAS, George — 4
HAVELL, Robert — H
HAVEMEYER, Henry Osborne — H
HAVEMEYER, Henry Osborne — 1
HAVEMEYER, Horace — 3
HAVEMEYER, John Craig — 5
HAVEMEYER, Loomis — 5
HAVEMEYER, Theodore Augustus — 1
HAVEMEYER, William Frederick — H
HAVEMEYER, William Frederick — 1
HAVEN, Emily Bradley Neal — H
HAVEN, Erastus Otis — H
HAVEN, Franklin — 1
HAVEN, George Griswold — 1
HAVEN, Gilbert — H
HAVEN, Henry Philemon — H
HAVEN, Joseph — H
HAVEN, Joseph Emerson — 1
HAVEN, Nathaniel Appleton — H
HAVEN, Solomon George — H
HAVEN, William Ingraham — 1
HAVENHILL, L. D. — 3
HAVENNER, Franck Roberts — 5
HAVENNER, George Clement — 5
HAVENS, Donald — 3
HAVENS, Frank Colton — H
HAVENS, James Dexter — 4
HAVENS, James Smith — 1

HAVENS, Jonathan Nicoll — H
HAVENS, Paul Egbert — H
HAVENS, Raymond Dexter — 3
HAVENS, Valentine Britton — 3
HAVERLY, Christopher — H
HAVERSTICK, Edward Everett — 3
HAVERTY, Clarence — 4
HAVIGHURST, Freeman Alfred — 5
HAVILAND, Clarence Floyd — H
HAVILAND, James Thomas — 3
HAVILAND, John — H
HAVNER, Horace Moore — 3
HAW, George Edwin — 5
HAWES, Albert Gallatin — H
HAWES, Austin Foster — 6
HAWES, Aylett — H
HAWES, Charles Henry — 2
HAWES, Elizabeth — 5
HAWES, George Edward — 4
HAWES, Harriet Boyd — 3
HAWES, Harry Bartow — 2
HAWES, James William — 1
HAWES, Joel — H
HAWES, John Bromham II — 3
HAWES, Richard — H
HAWES, Richard S. — 2
HAWES, Stewart S. — 4
HAWES, Stewart S(tarks) — 5
HAWES, William Post — H
HAWGOOD, Harry — 1
HAWK, Eugene Blake — 6
HAWK, Philip Bovier — 4
HAWK, Robert Moffett Allison — H
HAWK, Wilbur C. — 1
HAWKE, James Albert — 1
HAWKES, Albert Wahl — 6
HAWKES, Benjamin Carleton — 1
HAWKES, Clarence — 3
HAWKES, Elden Earl — 5
HAWKES, Forbes — 1
HAWKES, Herbert Edwin — 2
HAWKES, James — H
HAWKES, McDougall — 1
HAWKES, William F. — 5
HAWKESWORTH, Alan Spencer — 2
HAWKINS, Alvin — 1
HAWKINS, Arthur Hanson — 3
HAWKINS, Benjamin — H
HAWKINS, Benjamin Waterhouse — H
HAWKINS, Charles Martyr — 4
HAWKINS, Chauncey — 1
HAWKINS, Coleman — 6
HAWKINS, Dexter Arnold — H
HAWKINS, Dexter Clarkson — 4
HAWKINS, Earle T(aylor) — 5
HAWKINS, Edward Russell — 4
HAWKINS, George K. — 1
HAWKINS, George Sydney H. — 1
HAWKINS, Hamilton Smith — 1
HAWKINS, Hamilton Smith — 3
HAWKINS, Henry Gabriel — 4
HAWKINS, Horace Norman — 2
HAWKINS, Ira — 1
HAWKINS, Isaac Roberts — H
HAWKINS, J. Dawson — 4
HAWKINS, J. E. — 4
HAWKINS, Jack — 5
HAWKINS, John J. — 1
HAWKINS, John Parker — 1
HAWKINS, Joseph — H
HAWKINS, Joseph H. — H
HAWKINS, Laurence Ashley — 3
HAWKINS, Layton S. — 4
HAWKINS, Micajah Thomas — H
HAWKINS, Morris Seymour — 2
HAWKINS, Prince Albert — 1
HAWKINS, Rush Christopher — 1
HAWKINS, Thomas Hayden — 5
HAWKINS, William Bruce — 6
HAWKINS, William Edward — 1
HAWKINS, William George — 4
HAWKINS, William John — 4
HAWKINS, William Waller — 3
HAWKS, Charles Jr. — 4
HAWKS, Francis Lister — H
HAWKS, Frank Monroe — 1
HAWKS, James Dudley — 4
HAWKS, John — H
HAWLEY, Alan Ramsay — 1
HAWLEY, Albert Henry — 1
HAWLEY, Bostwick — 1

HAWLEY, Cameron 5
HAWLEY, Charles Anthony 4
HAWLEY, Charles B. 4
HAWLEY, Donly Curtis 4
HAWLEY, Edwin 1
HAWLEY, Fred Vermillia 1
HAWLEY, Frederick 3
William
HAWLEY, Gideon * H
HAWLEY, Harry Franklin 5
HAWLEY, James H. 1
HAWLEY, John Baldwin H
HAWLEY, John Blackstock 1
HAWLEY, John Mitchell 1
HAWLEY, Joseph H
HAWLEY, Joseph Boswell 1
HAWLEY, Julius Sargent 1
HAWLEY, Margaret Foote 6
HAWLEY, Newton 1
Fremont
HAWLEY, Paul Ramsey 4
HAWLEY, Ralph Chipman 5
HAWLEY, Ransom Smith 6
HAWLEY, Thomas Porter 1
HAWLEY, Willis Chatman 1
HAWN, Henry Gaines 1
HAWORTH, Erasmus 1
HAWORTH, Joseph 1
HAWORTH, Paul Leland 1
HAWORTH, Sir Walter 2
Norman
HAWS, John Henry Hobart H
HAWTHORNE, Charles 1
Webster
HAWTHORNE, Hildegarde 3
HAWTHORNE, Hugh 4
Robert
HAWTHORNE, Julian 1
HAWTHORNE, Nathaniel H
HAWTHORNE, Rose H
HAWTHORNE, Rose 4
HAWTREY, Charles Henry 1
HAWTREY, Sir Ralph 6
George
HAWXHURST, Robert Jr. 5
HAXO, Henry Emile 6
HAY, Andrew Kessler H
HAY, Arthur Douglas 3
HAY, Charles Augustus 1
HAY, Charles Martin 1
HAY, Clarence Leonard 5
HAY, Earl Downing 1
HAY, Eugene Gano 1
HAY, George H
HAY, Henry Clinton 1
HAY, James 1
HAY, James Jr. 1
HAY, John 1
HAY, John W. 3
HAY, Logan 2
HAY, Malcolm 5
HAY, Marion E. 1
HAY, Mary Garrett 1
HAY, Oliver Perry 1
HAY, Samuel Ross 2
HAY, Stephen John 1
HAY, Thomas Abraham 1
Horn
HAY, William Henry 2
HAY, William Perry 2
HAYAKAWA, Sessue 6
(Kintaro Hayakawa)
HAYCOX, Ernest 3
HAYCRAFT, Julius 5
Everette
HAYDEN, Amos Sutton H
HAYDEN, Arthur 4
Gunderson
HAYDEN, Austin Albert 1
HAYDEN, Carl (Trumbull) 5
HAYDEN, Carl (Trumbull) 6
HAYDEN, Charles 1
HAYDEN, Charles H. 1
HAYDEN, Charles Sidney 1
HAYDEN, Edward Everett 1
HAYDEN, Ferdinand H
Vandiveer
HAYDEN, Frank 1
HAYDEN, Frederick Smith 4
HAYDEN, Horace Edwin 1
HAYDEN, Horace H. H
HAYDEN, Jay G. 5
HAYDEN, Joel Babcock 2
HAYDEN, John Louis 1
HAYDEN, Joseph H
HAYDEN, Joseph Ralston 2
HAYDEN, Josiah Willard 5
HAYDEN, Merrill A. 6
HAYDEN, Moses 1
HAYDEN, Philip Cady 4
HAYDEN, Velma Denison 4
HAYDEN, Warren Sherman 1
HAYDEN, William H
HAYDN, Hiram 6
HAYDN, Hiram Collins 1
HAYDOCK, George Sewell 5

HAYDON, Albert Eustace 6
HAYDON, Glen 4
HAYES, Alfred 4
HAYES, Anson 4
HAYES, Arthur Badley 1
HAYES, Augustus Allen H
HAYES, C. Willard 4
HAYES, Carlton Joseph 4
Huntley
HAYES, Charles Harris 1
HAYES, Clifford Barron 4
HAYES, Daniel Webster 1
HAYES, David J. A. 3
HAYES, Doremus Almy 1
HAYES, Edward Arthur 3
HAYES, Edward Cary 1
HAYES, Edward Francis 6
HAYES, Edward Mortimer 1
HAYES, Ellen 1
HAYES, Everis Anson 4
HAYES, Francis Little 1
HAYES, Frederick Albert 4
HAYES, George Miller 3
HAYES, Hammond Vinton 2
HAYES, Harold M. 4
HAYES, Harvey Cornelius 5
HAYES, Helen Hayden 6
HAYES, Henry 4
HAYES, Henry Reed 3
HAYES, Isaac Israel 1
HAYES, James Edward 2
HAYES, James Leo 5
HAYES, Jay Orley 2
HAYES, John Herman 4
HAYES, John Lord H
HAYES, John Russell 3
HAYES, John William 1
HAYES, Johnson Jay 5
HAYES, Joseph 4
HAYES, Joseph P.; 5
HAYES, Lucy Webb 4
HAYES, Mary Sanders 5
(Mrs. William Henry
Hays)
HAYES, Max S. 2
HAYES, Montrose W. 1
HAYES, Myron J. 3
HAYES, Patrick Joseph 1
HAYES, Philip 2
HAYES, Philip Cornelius 1
HAYES, R. S. 5
HAYES, Rutherford H
Birchard
HAYES, Samuel Perkins 3
HAYES, Samuel Walter 1
HAYES, Simeon Mills 4
HAYES, Stephen Quentin 1
HAYES, Thomas Gordon 1
HAYES, Thomas Sumner 1
HAYES, Wade Hampton 3
HAYES, Warren Howard 1
HAYES, Watson McMillan 2
HAYES, Wayland J(ackson) 5
HAYES, Webb Cook 1
HAYES, Webb Cook II 3
HAYFORD, John Fillmore 2
HAYGOOD, Atticus Green H
HAYGOOD, Laura Askew H
HAYHOW, Edgar Charles 3
HAYHURST, Emery Roe 4
HAYKIN, David Judson 3
HAYLER, Guy Wilfrid 5
HAYLEY, John William 1
HAYMAKER, Jesse N. 1
HAYMAN, Al 1
HAYMOND, Frank Cruise 5
HAYMOND, Thomas S. 5
HAYMOND, Thomas H
Sherwood
HAYMOND, William H
Summerville
HAYNE, Arthur Peronneau H
HAYNE, Coe 5
HAYNE, Isaac H
HAYNE, James Adams 5
HAYNE, Paul Hamilton 1
HAYNE, Robert Young H
HAYNE, William Hamilton 1
HAYNER, Rutherford 1
HAYNES, Arthur Edwin 1
HAYNES, Benjamin 4
Rudolph
HAYNES, Carlyle Boynton 5
HAYNES, Charles Eaton H
HAYNES, Charles H(enry) 3
HAYNES, Daniel H. 2
HAYNES, David Oliphant 1
HAYNES, Eli Stuart 1
HAYNES, Elizabeth A. 3
Ross
HAYNES, Elwood 1
HAYNES, Emory James 1
HAYNES, Evan 3
HAYNES, Fred Emory 4
HAYNES, George Edmund 4
HAYNES, George Henry 2

HAYNES, Harley A(rmand) 5
HAYNES, Henry 1
Williamson
HAYNES, Ira Allen 3
HAYNES, Irving Samuel 2
HAYNES, John H
HAYNES, John Randolph 1
HAYNES, Joseph Walton 5
HAYNES, Justin O'Brien 5
HAYNES, Myron Wilbur 1
HAYNES, Nathaniel Smith 1
HAYNES, Robert Blair 5
HAYNES, Rowland 4
HAYNES, Roy Asa 1
HAYNES, Thornwell 3
HAYNIE, Henry 1
HAYS, Albert Theodore 6
HAYS, Alexander 1
HAYS, Arthur Alexander 3
HAYS, Arthur Garfield 3
HAYS, Calvin Cornwell 1
HAYS, Charles H
HAYS, Charles Melville 1
HAYS, Charles Thomas 2
HAYS, Daniel Peixotto 1
HAYS, Edde K. 4
HAYS, Edward D. 1
HAYS, Edward Retilla H
HAYS, Elmer D. 1
HAYS, Frank Lazmer 3
HAYS, Frank W. 1
HAYS, George Washington 1
HAYS, Harry Thompson H
HAYS, Howard H. 5
HAYS, I. Minis 1
HAYS, Isaac H
HAYS, Jack Newton 5
HAYS, John 1
HAYS, John Coffee H
HAYS, Margaret Gebbie 1
HAYS, Mortimer 4
HAYS, Samuel H
HAYS, Samuel Lewis 1
HAYS, Silas B. 4
HAYS, Walter Lee 4
HAYS, Will H. 3
HAYS, Willet Martin 4
HAYS, William Charles 4
HAYS, William Jacob H
HAYS, William Jacob 1
HAYS, William Shakespeare 1
HAYT, Charles D. 1
HAYWARD, Benjamin 3
Dover
HAYWARD, Edward 1
Farwell
HAYWARD, Florence 1
HAYWARD, Fred Preston 5
HAYWARD, George H
HAYWARD, Harry 1
HAYWARD, Harry Taft 1
HAYWARD, Joseph Warren 1
HAYWARD, Monroe 1
Leland
HAYWARD, Nathan 2
HAYWARD, Nathaniel H
Manley
HAYWARD, Ralph A. 3
HAYWARD, Susan 6
HAYWARD, Walter 1
Brownell
HAYWARD, William 2
HAYWARD, William Jr. 1
HAYWARD, William Leete 3
HAYWOOD, Allen S. 3
HAYWOOD, Harry LeRoy 3
HAYWOOD, John 1
HAYWOOD, John Kerfoot 1
HAYWOOD, John Wilfred 5
HAYWOOD, Marshall De 1
Lancey
HAYWOOD, Marshall Jr. 5
HAYWOOD, William 1
Dudley
HAYWOOD, William 4
Dudley
HAYWOOD, William H
Henry Jr.
HAZARD, Augustus George H
HAZARD, Caroline 2
HAZARD, Clifton T. 1
HAZARD, Daniel Lyman 3
HAZARD, Ebenezer 1
HAZARD, Elmer Clarke; 6
HAZARD, Frederick 1
Rowland
HAZARD, Henry Bernard 3
HAZARD, Jonathan J. H
HAZARD, Lauriston 1
Hartwell
HAZARD, Marshall Curtiss 1
HAZARD, Rowland Gibson H
HAZARD, Rowland Gibson 1
HAZARD, Samuel 1
HAZARD, Spencer Peabody 3
HAZARD, Thomas 1

HAZARD, Thomas 5
Pierrepont
HAZARD, Thomas H
Robinson
HAZARD, Willis Hatfield 1
HAZEL, John Raymond 4
HAZELBAKER, Norval 5
Denver
HAZELIUS, Ernest Lewis H
HAZELRIGG, James 4
Hervey
HAZELTINE, Abner H
HAZELTINE, Alan 4
HAZELTINE, George 1
Cochrane Jr.
HAZELTINE, Harold 5
Dexter
HAZELTINE, Horace 4
HAZELTINE, Mary 2
Emogene
HAZELTINE, Mayo 1
Williamson
HAZELTON, John H. 3
HAZELTON, John Wright 1
HAZELWOOD, John H
HAZEN, Allen 1
HAZEN, Azel Washburn 1
HAZEN, Charles Downer 2
HAZEN, Henry Allen * H
HAZEN, Henry Honeyman 4
HAZEN, John Vose 1
HAZEN, Joseph Chalmers 5
HAZEN, Marshman 1
Williams
HAZEN, Maynard 4
Thompson
HAZEN, Moses 1
HAZEN, William Babcock H
HAZEN, William Livingston 2
HAZLET, Stewart 6
E(merson)
HAZLETT, Harry Fouts 4
HAZLETT, Robert 2
HAZLETT, Samuel M. 3
HAZLEWOOD, Craig 3
Beebe
HAZZARD, Charles 1
HAZZARD, Jesse Charles 5
HAZZARD, John Edward 1
H'DOUBLER, Francis Todd 4
HEACOCK, Frank Ahern 5
HEACOX, Roger Lee 4
HEACOX, Arthur Edward 5
HEAD, Franklin Harvey 1
HEAD, Henry Oswald 1
HEAD, James Butler 1
HEAD, James Marshall 1
HEAD, James Milne 1
HEAD, Jerome Reed 6
HEAD, John Benedict 1
HEAD, John Frazier 1
HEAD, Leon Oswald 4
HEAD, Mabel 1
HEAD, T. Grady 4
HEAD, Walter Dutton 1
HEAD, Walter William 1
HEAD, Walton O. 1
HEADDEN, William Parker 1
HEADE, Martin Johnson 6
HEADLAND, Isaac Taylor 2
HEADLEE, Thomas J. 2
HEADLEY, Cleon 1
HEADLEY, Joel Tyler H
HEADLEY, John William 1
HEADLEY, Leal Aubrey 4
HEADLEY, Phineas Camp 1
HEADLEY, Roy 3
HEAFFORD, George Henry 4
HEAL, Gilbert B. 1
HEALD, Daniel Addison 1
HEALD, Frederick De 1
Forest
HEALD, Henry Townley 6
HEALD, Kenneth Conrad 1
HEALD, William Henry 1
HEALE, Charles J. 2
HEALEY, Arthur Daniel 2
HEALEY, Charles C. 1
HEALEY, Michael J. 5
HEALY, A. Augustus 1
HEALY, Daniel Joseph 1
HEALY, Daniel Joseph 6
HEALY, Daniel Ward Jr. 5
HEALY, Ezra Anthony 1
HEALY, Fred Albert 2
HEALY, George Peter H
Alexander
HEALY, James Augustine 1
HEALY, Joseph 1
HEALY, Patrick Joseph 1
HEALY, Robert E. 4
HEALY, Robert Wallace 1
HEALY, Thomas Henry 1
HEALY, William 4
HEANEY, John William 3
HEANEY, Noble Sproat 3

HEAP, David Porter 1
HEAP, Samuel Davies H
HEAPS, William James 5
HEARD, Arthur Marston 1
HEARD, Augustine H
HEARD, Augustine 1
HEARD, Bill James 5
HEARD, Dwight Bancroft 1
HEARD, Franklin Fiske H
HEARD, Gerald 5
HEARD, James Delavan 1
HEARD, Oscar Edwin 1
HEARD, William H. 1
HEARD, William Wright 1
HEARE, Clayton 5
HEARN, Clint Calvin 1
HEARN, David William 1
HEARN, Hardie B. 4
HEARN, Lafcadio 1
HEARNE, Edward Dingle 4
HEARNE, John J(oseph) 5
HEARON, Charles Oscar 5
HEARST, Charles Ernest 1
HEARST, George H
HEARST, George Randolph 5
Sr.
HEARST, John Randolph 3
HEARST, Phoebe Apperson 1
HEARST, William Randolph 3
HEATH, Clyde J(ames) 5
HEATH, Daniel Collamore 1
HEATH, Edwin Joseph 3
HEATH, Ferry Kimball 1
HEATH, Fred H. 5
HEATH, Frederic Carroll 1
HEATH, Harold 1
HEATH, Hubert A. 4
HEATH, Hugh Austin 1
HEATH, James Ewell H
HEATH, James P. H
HEATH, John H
HEATH, Perry Sanford 1
HEATH, S. Burton 2
HEATH, William H
HEATH, William Ames 1
HEATH, William Womack 5
HEATHCOTE, Caleb H
HEATHCOTE, Charles 4
William
HEATLEY, Stuart Alden 4
HEATON, Arthur B. 3
HEATON, Augustus 1
Goodyear
HEATON, David H
HEATON, Harry Clifton 3
HEATON, Herbert 3
HEATON, John Langdon 1
HEATON, Lucia Elizabeth 1
HEATON, Percy 4
HEATON, Robert Douglas 1
HEATWOLE, Cornelius 1
Jacob
HEATWOLE, Joel Prescott 1
HEATWOLE, Lewis James 1
HEATWOLE, Timothy 1
Oliver
HEAVEY, John William 2
HEBARD, Arthur Foster 2
HEBARD, Grace Raymond 1
HEBARD, William H
HEBBERD, John Bailey 6
HEBDEN, John Calder 1
HEBEL, John William 1
HEBERT, Felix 5
HEBERT, Paul Octave H
HEBRARD, Jean 4
HECHT, Ben 4
HECHT, David Stanford H
HECHT, Hans H. 5
HECHT, Julius Lawrence 3
HECHT, Moses S. 3
HECHT, Rudolf S. 2
HECHT, Selig 3
HECHT, Wilbur Hudson 6
HECK, Barbara Ruckle H
HECK, Nicholas Hunter 3
HECK, Robert Culbertson 3
Hays
HECK, William Harry 1
HECKE, G. H. 4
HECKEL, Albert Kerr 6
HECKEL, Edward Balthasar 1
HECKEL, George Baugh 1
HECKEL, Norris Julius 4
HECKER, Frank Joseph 1
HECKER, Friedrich Karl H
Franz
HECKER, Isaac Thomas 4
HECKER, John Valentine 4
HECKERT, Charles Girven 1
HECKERT, John Walter 4
HECKETT, Eric Harlow 4
HECKEWELDER, John H
Gottlieb Ernestus
HECKLER, Edwin Little 4
HECKMAN, James Robert 2

HECKMAN, Samuel B. 3
HECKMAN, Wallace 1
HECKSCHER, August 1
HECKSCHER, August 1
HECKSCHER, Celeste Delongpre 1
HEDBACK, Axel Emanuel 3
HEDBLOM, Carl Arthur 1
HEDBROOKE, Andrew H
HEDENSTROM, Paul Henry 5
HEDERMAN, T. M. 2
HEDGCOCK, George Grant 4
HEDGE, Charles Gorham 1
HEDGE, Frederic Henry 4
HEDGE, Frederic Henry H
HEDGE, Henry Rogers 5
HEDGE, Levi H
HEDGE, Thomas 4
HEDGE, William Russell 2
HEDGES, Benjamin Van Doren 5
HEDGES, Frank Hinckley 1
HEDGES, J. Edward 4
HEDGES, James Blaine 4
HEDGES, Job Elmer 4
HEDGES, Joseph Harold 3
HEDGES, Marion Hawthorne 3
HEDGES, Samuel Hamilton 2
HEDLESTON, Winn David 4
HEDLEY, Frank 3
HEDLY, Arthur Howard 4
HEDRICH, Kenneth 5
HEDRICK, Bayard Murphy 4
HEDRICK, Charles Baker 2
HEDRICK, Charles Embury 3
HEDRICK, E. H. 1
HEDRICK, Earle Raymond 2
HEDRICK, Ira Grant 4
HEDRICK, Lawrence E. 6
HEDRICK, Tubman Keene 5
HEDRICK, Ulysses Prentiss 4
HEDRICK, Wyatt Cephas 4
HEDSTROM, Carl Oscar 5
HEDTOFT, Hans 3
HEEBNER, Charles 3
HEED, Thomas D. 3
HEEKIN, Albert Edward Jr. 1
HEELAN, Edmond 2
HEELY, Allan Vanderhoef 3
HEENAN, John Carmel H
HEENEHAN, James T. 3
HEENEY, Arnold Danford Patrick
HEERMAN, Ritz Edwin 4
HEERMANCE, Edgar Laing 5
HEERMANN, Adolphus L. H
HEERMANS, Augustyn A
HEERMANS, Charles Abram 4
HEERMANS, Forbes 1
HEERMANS, Josephine Woodbury 4
HEES, William Rathbun 2
HEETER, Silvanus Laurabee 5
HEFELBOWER, Samuel Gring 3
HEFFELFINGER, Frank Totton 3
HEFFELFINGER, George W. P. 5
HEFFERAN, Thomas Hume 5
HEFFERAN, W. S. Jr. 4
HEFFERLINE, Ralph Franklin 6
HEFFERN, Andrew Duff 1
HEFFERNAN, James Joseph 4
HEFFRON, John Lorenzo 1
HEFFRON, Patrick Richard 1
HEFLIN, Aubrey Newbill 6
HEFLIN, J. Thomas 4
HEFLIN, Van 5
HEFLING, Arthur William 6
HEFNER, Ralph A(ubrie) 4
HEFTY, Thomas R. 4
HEG, Elmer Ellsworth 4
HEGEMAN, John Rogers 1
HEGER, Anthony 1
HEGGEN, Thomas Orlo 2
HEGLAND, Martin 4
HEGNER, Bertha Hofer Mrs.
HEGNER, Robert William 2
HEHER, Harry 5
HEHIR, Martin A. 4
HEIDEGGER, Martin 6
HEIDEL, William Arthur 4
HEIDEN, Konrad 4
HEIDER, Raphael 5
HEIDINGER, James Vandaveer 2

HEIDINGSFIELD, Myron S(amuel) 5
HEIFETZ, Benar 6
HEIKES, Victor Conrad 2
HEIL, Charles Emile 3
HEIL, Julius Peter 2
HEIL, William Franklin 1
HEILBRONNER, Louis 5
HEILBRUNN, Lewis Victor 4
HEILEMAN, Frank A. 4
HEILIG, Sterling 4
HEILMAN, Fordyce R. 4
HEILMAN, Ralph Emerson 4
HEILMAN, Russell Howard 4
HEILMAN, William H
HEILMAN, William Clifford
HEILNER, Samuel 1
HEILNER, Van Campen 5
HEILPRIN, Angelo 1
HEILPRIN, Louis 1
HEILPRIN, Michael H
HEIM, Herbert E. 5
HEIM, Jacques 4
HEIMANN, Henry Herman 3
HEIMBACH, Arthur E. 3
HEIMBACH, Howard Anders 5
HEIMERICH, John James 5
HEIMKE, William 1
HEIMROD, George 4
HEIN, Carl 2
HEIN, Carl Christian 1
HEIN, Otto Louis 1
HEIN, Walter Jacob 4
HEINBERG, John Gilbert 3
HEINDEL, Augusta Foss 4
HEINE, Peter Bernard William H
HEINEMAN, Walter Ben 1
HEINEMANN, E. 1
HEINER, Gordon Graham 2
HEINER, Moroni 5
HEINGARTNER, Robert Wayne 2
HEINICKE, Arthur John 5
HEINISCH, Don 6
HEINITSH, George W. Jr. 6
HEINL, Robert D. 3
HEINLEIN, Mary Virginia 4
HEINMILLER, Louis Edward 1
HEINMULLER, John P. V. 1
HEINO, Albert Frederic 3
HEINRICH, Antony Philip H
HEINRICH, Edward Oscar 3
HEINRICH, Wilhelm 1
HEINRICHS, Charles E. 4
HEINRICHS, Jacob 2
HEINROTH, Charles 5
HEINS, George Lewis 1
HEINSHEIMER, Edward Lewis 1
HEINSOHN, Alvin Frederick 5
HEINTZ, Philip Benjamin 2
HEINTZELMAN, Arthur William 4
HEINTZELMAN, Samuel Peter H
HEINTZELMAN, Stuart 2
HEINTZLEMAN, Percival Stewart 2
HEINZ, Fred C. 4
HEINZ, Henry John 1
HEINZ, Howard 1
HEINZ, John Bernard 4
HEINZE, F. Augustus 1
HEINZE, Otto Charles 5
HEINZEN, Karl Peter H
HEISCHMANN, John J. 1
HEISE, Fred H. 2
HEISEL, Thomas Bayard 1
HEISEN, Aaron Jonah 5
HEISENBERG, Werner 4
HEISER, Victor George 5
HEISERMAN, Arthur Ray 4
HEISERMAN, Clarence Benjamin 3
HEISING, Raymond Alphonsus 4
HEISKELL, Frederick Hugh 1
HEISKELL, Henry Lee 1
HEISKELL, John Netherland 5
HEISKELL, Samuel G. 1
HEISLER, John Clement 1
HEISS, Austin Elmer 4
HEISS, Gerson Kirkland 4
HEISS, Marion Welch 4
HEISS, Michael H
HEISSENBUTTEL, John Diedrich
HEISTAND, Henry Olcot Sheldon

HEITFELD, Henry 1
HEITMAN, Charles Easton 3
HEITMAN, Francis Bernard 4
HEITSCHMIDT, Earl T. 5
HEIZER, Oscar Stuart 4
HEIZMANN, Charles Lawrence 4
HEKKING, William Mathews 5
HEKMA, Jacob 2
HEKMAN, John 3
HEKTOEN, Ludvig 3
HELBRON, Peter H
HELBURN, Theresa 3
HELD, Anna 1
HELD, John Jr. 3
HELDER, H. A. 1
HELFEN, Mathias 3
HELFENSTEIN, Edward Trail 1
HELFENSTEIN, Ernest H
HELFFENSTEIN, John Albert Conrad H
HELGESEN, Henry T. 1
HELLAND, Andreas 5
HELLBAUM, Arthur Alfred 4
HELLEMS, Fred Burton Renney 1
HELLENTHAL, John Albertus 2
HELLER, A. Arthur 4
HELLER, Edmund 1
HELLER, Edward Hellman Grunsfeld 4
HELLER, Florence 5
HELLER, Frank Henry 5
HELLER, Frank Morley 3
HELLER, George 3
HELLER, Helen West 4
HELLER, James Gutheim 5
HELLER, Joseph Milton 2
HELLER, Maximilian 1
HELLER, Otto 1
HELLER, Robert 6
HELLER, Victor H. 4
HELLER, Walter E. 4
HELLER, William 4
HELLIER, Charles Edward 1
HELLINGER, Ernst David 2
HELLINGER, Mark 2
HELLMAN, C(larisse) Doris (Mrs. Morton Pepper) 6
HELLMAN, F. J. 4
HELLMAN, George Sidney 3
HELLMAN, Hugo Edward 6
HELLMAN, Isias William 1
HELLMAN, Isias William Jr. 1
HELLMAN, Marco H. 6
HELLMAN, Maurice S. 4
HELLMAN, Milo 4
HELLMUND, Rudolph Emil 2
HELLSTROM, Carl Reinhold 4
HELLWEG, J. F. 6
HELM, Harry Sherman 2
HELM, Harvey 1
HELM, James Meredith 1
HELM, John Charles H
HELM, John Larue H
HELM, Joseph Church 1
HELM, Nathan Wilbur 6
HELM, Nelson 4
HELM, Roy 1
HELM, Thaddeus Geary 4
HELM, Thomas Kennedy 1
HELM, Wilbur 5
HELM, William P. 3
HELMER, B. Bradwell 1
HELMER, Frank Ambrose 1
HELMHOLZ, Henry Frederic 4
HELMICK, Eli Alva 2
HELMICK, Milton John 3
HELMICK, William H
HELMING, Oscar Clemens 1
HELMLE, Frank J. 1
HELMPRAECHT, Joseph H
HELMS, Edgar James 4
HELMS, Elmer Ellsworth 4
HELMS, Paul Hoy 3
HELMS, William 4
HELMSLEY, William H
HELMUTH, Justus Henry Christian H
HELMUTH, William Tod * 1
HELPER, Hinton Rowan 1
HELPMAN, Dell A. 1
HELSER, Albert D. 5
HELSER, Maurice David 3
HELTMAN, Harry Joseph 4
HELVERING, Guy Tresillian 2
HELYAR, Frank G. 4

HEMANS, Lawton Thomas 1
HEMBDT, Phil Harold 1
HEMBORG, Carl August 4
HEMENWAY, Alfred 1
HEMENWAY, Augustus 1
HEMENWAY, Charles Clifton 5
HEMENWAY, Charles Reed 2
HEMENWAY, Henry Bixby 1
HEMENWAY, Herbert Daniel 2
HEMENWAY, James Alexander 1
HEMENWAY, Mary Porter H
HEMING, Arthur 1
HEMINGTON, Francis 2
HEMINGWAY, Allan 5
HEMINGWAY, Ernest 4
HEMINGWAY, Harold Edgar 4
HEMINGWAY, Harry J. 4
HEMINGWAY, James S. 4
HEMINGWAY, Samuel Burdett 3
HEMINGWAY, Walter Clarke 3
HEMINGWAY, Wilson Edwin 1
HEMINGWAY, Wilson Linn 3
HEMLEY, Cecil 4
HEMLEY, Cecil 5
HEMLEY, Samuel 5
HEMMETER, Henry Bernard 2
HEMMETER, John Conrad 1
HEMPEL, Charles Julius H
HEMPEL, Frieda 3
HEMPHILL, Alexander Julian 1
HEMPHILL, Charles Robert 1
HEMPHILL, Clifford 4
HEMPHILL, James Calvin 1
HEMPHILL, John H
HEMPHILL, John James 1
HEMPHILL, Joseph H
HEMPHILL, Joseph Newton 1
HEMPHILL, Victor Herman 3
HEMPHILL, William Arnold 1
HEMPHILL, William P. 4
HEMPL, George 1
HEMPSTEAD, Clark 3
HEMPSTEAD, Edward 1
HEMPSTEAD, Fay 1
HEMRY, Charles W. 4
HEMSTREET, Charles 1
HENCH, Atcheson Laughlin 6
HENCH, Jay Lyman 4
HENCH, Philip Showalter 4
HENCHMAN, Daniel H
HENCK, John Benjamin 1
HENDEE, George Ellsworth 1
HENDEL, John William H
HENDELSON, William H. 6
HENDERLITE, James Henry 3
HENDERSON, Alexander Iselin 4
HENDERSON, Alfred Edwin 5
HENDERSON, Archibald H
HENDERSON, Archibald 4
HENDERSON, Bennett H. H
HENDERSON, Byrd 4
HENDERSON, C. Hanford 1
HENDERSON, Charles Belknap 3
HENDERSON, Charles English 1
HENDERSON, Charles J. 4
HENDERSON, Charles Richmond 1
HENDERSON, Charles William 2
HENDERSON, Daniel 3
HENDERSON, David 1
HENDERSON, David Bremner 1
HENDERSON, David E. 6
HENDERSON, David English H
HENDERSON, Earl C. 3
HENDERSON, Edward 5
HENDERSON, Eldon Hazelton 5
HENDERSON, Elmer Lee 3
HENDERSON, Ernest 4
HENDERSON, Ernest Flagg 1

HENDERSON, Ernest Norton 1
HENDERSON, George Bunsen 5
HENDERSON, George Logan 4
HENDERSON, Gerard C. 1
HENDERSON, Grace Mildred 5
HENDERSON, Harold Gould 6
HENDERSON, Harry Peters 6
HENDERSON, Helen Weston 5
HENDERSON, Howard Andrew Millet 1
HENDERSON, Isaac 1
HENDERSON, James Fletcher 4
HENDERSON, James Henry Dickey H
HENDERSON, James Monroe 4
HENDERSON, James Pinckney H
HENDERSON, John Armstrong H
HENDERSON, John Brooks * 1
HENDERSON, John H. 4
HENDERSON, John Joseph 1
HENDERSON, John Moreland 1
HENDERSON, John O. 6
HENDERSON, John Steele 1
HENDERSON, John Thompson 3
HENDERSON, Joseph H
HENDERSON, Joseph Lindsey 4
HENDERSON, Joseph W. 1
HENDERSON, Junius 1
HENDERSON, Kenneth Manning 5
HENDERSON, Lawrence Joseph 1
HENDERSON, Leland John 5
HENDERSON, Leon N. 4
HENDERSON, Leonard H
HENDERSON, Lizzie George 4
HENDERSON, Mary N. 4
HENDERSON, Melvin Starkey 3
HENDERSON, Peronneau Finley 5
HENDERSON, Peter H
HENDERSON, Philip Eldon 3
HENDERSON, Richard H
HENDERSON, Robert 2
HENDERSON, Robert 3
HENDERSON, Robert Burns 1
HENDERSON, Robert Miller 1
HENDERSON, Samuel 1
HENDERSON, Theodore Sommers 1
HENDERSON, Thomas H
HENDERSON, Thomas Howard 5
HENDERSON, Thomas Jefferson 1
HENDERSON, Thomas Stalworth 1
HENDERSON, Vivian Wilson 6
HENDERSON, Walter Brooks Drayton 2
HENDERSON, Walter C. 3
HENDERSON, William D. 2
HENDERSON, William James 1
HENDERSON, William Olin 1
HENDERSON, William Penhallow 2
HENDERSON, William Price 2
HENDERSON, William Thomas 5
HENDERSON, William Williams 2
HENDERSON, Yandell 4
HENDLER, L. Manuel 4
HENDREN, Linville Laurentine 6
HENDREN, Paul 3
HENDREN, William Mayhew 1
HENDRICK H

HENDRICK, Archer 1
  Wilmot
HENDRICK, Burton Jesse 2
HENDRICK, Calvin 4
  Wheeler
HENDRICK, Ellwood 1
HENDRICK, Frank 5
HENDRICK, Ives 5
HENDRICK, John Thilman 2
HENDRICK, Michael J. 4
HENDRICK, Peter Aloysius 1
HENDRICK, Thomas 1
  Augustine
HENDRICK, William 4
  Jackson
HENDRICKS, Allan 5
  Barringer Jr.
HENDRICKS, Eldo Lewis 3
HENDRICKS, Francis 4
HENDRICKS, Ira King 5
HENDRICKS, Thomas H
  Andrews
HENDRICKS, Thomas 2
  Armstrong
HENDRICKS, William H
HENDRICKSON, Charles 1
  Elvin
HENDRICKSON, George 4
  Lincoln
HENDRICKSON, Homer 3
  O.
HENDRICKSON, Robert 4
  C.
HENDRICKSON, William 1
  Woodbury
HENDRIX, Eugene Russell 1
HENDRIX, Jimi 5
HENDRIX, Joseph Clifford 1
HENDRIX, William Samuel 2
HENDRIXSON, Walter 1
  Scott
HENDRYX, James 4
  Beardsley
HENEY, Francis Joseph 1
HENGST, James McCleery 4
HENICAN, Joseph Padrick 1
  Jr.
HENIE, Sonja 5
HENIGAN, George Francis 6
HENING, Benjamin Cabell 2
HENING, William Waller H
HENIUS, Max 1
HENKE, Frederick 4
  Goodrich
HENKEL, Paul H
HENKLE, Charles Zane 4
HENKLE, Eli Jones H
HENKLE, Rae DeLancey 1
HENLE, James 5
HENLEY, Robert 1
HENLEY, Robert E. 4
HENLEY, Thomas Jefferson H
HENLEY, Walter Ervin 6
HENMON, Vivian Allen 3
  Charles
HENN, Albert William 3
HENN, Bernhart 4
HENNEMAN, John Bell 1
HENNEMUTH, Robert 6
  George
HENNEPIN, Louis H
HENNEQUIN, Alfred 4
HENNESSEY, Thomas 6
  Michael
HENNESSY, Frank J. 6
HENNESSY, John 1
HENNESSY, John Francis 5
HENNESSY, John Joseph 1
HENNESSY, John 3
  Lawrence
HENNESSY, Michael 3
  Edmund
HENNESSY, Roland Burke 5
HENNESSY, William John 1
HENNESSY, William 4
  Thomas
HENNEY, William Franklin 1
HENNI, John Martin 4
HENNING, Arthur Sears 4
HENNING, Edward J. 1
HENNING, George Neely 3
HENNINGS, E. Martin 3
HENNINGS, Thomas Carey 6
  Sr.
HENNINGS, Thomas Carey 4
  Jr.
HENNINGSEN, Charles H
  Frederick
HENNISEE, Argalus Garey 4
HENNOCK, Frieda B. 4
HENNRICH, Kilian Joseph 2
HENNY, David Christian 4
HENRETTA, James Edward 5
HENRI, Robert 1
HENRICH, V. C. 4

HENRICHS, Henry 6
  Frederick
HENRICI, Arthur 2
  Trautwein
HENRICKS, Coleman 5
  Bresee
HENRICKS, Harold H. 5
HENRIQUES, Robert 4
  David Quixano
HENRIQUEZ-URENA, 5
  Max
HENRIQUEZ-URENA, 2
  Pedro
HENROTIN, Charles 1
HENROTIN, Ellen M. 1
  Martin
HENROTIN, Fernand 1
HENRY, Albert P. H
HENRY, Alexander 1
HENRY, Alexander 1
HENRY, Alfred Hylas 4
HENRY, Alfred Judson 1
HENRY, Andrew H
HENRY, Arnold Kahle 5
HENRY, Arthur 1
HENRY, Barklie McKee 4
HENRY, Bayard 1
HENRY, Caleb Sprague H
HENRY, Carl French 1
HENRY, Charles Lewis 1
HENRY, Charles William 1
HENRY, Claude Morrison 1
HENRY, David W. 3
HENRY, Douglas Selph 5
HENRY, E. Stevens 1
HENRY, Edward Atwood 6
HENRY, Edward Lamson 1
HENRY, Eugene John 4
HENRY, Frederick 2
  Augustus
HENRY, Frederick Porteous 4
HENRY, George Francis 1
HENRY, George Frederick 2
HENRY, George McClellan 5
HENRY, George William 4
HENRY, Guy Vernor 1
HENRY, Guy Vernor 4
HENRY, Heth 1
HENRY, Horace Chapin 1
HENRY, Howard James 1
HENRY, Howell Meadors 3
HENRY, Hugh Carter 2
HENRY, Hugh Thomas 4
HENRY, J. Norman 1
HENRY, J(ohn) Porter H
HENRY, James H
HENRY, James Addison 1
HENRY, James McClure 3
HENRY, Jerry Maurice 6
HENRY, John * H
HENRY, John Flournoy H
HENRY, John Robert Jr. 6
HENRY, John Robertson 1
HENRY, Joseph H
HENRY, Jules 5
HENRY, Kate Kearney 1
HENRY, Langdon C. 4
HENRY, Lemuel H. 1
HENRY, Matthew George 6
HENRY, Morris Henry H
HENRY, Myron Ormell 3
HENRY, O. 1
HENRY, Patrick H
HENRY, Patrick 3
HENRY, Philip Solomon 1
HENRY, Philip Walter 2
HENRY, Ralph Coolidge 5
HENRY, Robert H
HENRY, Robert K. 2
HENRY, Robert Lee 1
HENRY, Robert Llewellyn 5
  Jr.
HENRY, Robert Patterson 6
HENRY, Robert Pryor 1
HENRY, Robert Selph 5
HENRY, Samuel Clements 2
HENRY, Sidney Morgan 3
HENRY, Stuart 3
HENRY, Thomas H
HENRY, Thomas P. 2
HENRY, Waights Gibbs 4
HENRY, William * H
HENRY, William Arnon 1
HENRY, William Elmer 1
HENRY, William M. (Bill) 4
HENRY, William Thomas 3
HENRY, William Wirt 1
HENSCHEL, George . 2
HENSCHEL, Lillian June H
  Bailey
HENSEL, William Uhler 1
HENSHALL, James 1
  Alexander
HENSHAW, Albert Melville 3
HENSHAW, David H

HENSHAW, Frederic Rich 1
HENSHAW, Frederick 1
  William
HENSHAW, Henry 1
  Wetherbee
HENSHAW, Samuel 2
HENSHEL, Harry Davis 4
HENSLEY, Adelia Gates 5
HENSLEY, Richard Gibson 4
HENSLEY, Samuel J. H
HENSLEY, Sophia Almon 4
HENSLEY, Walter Lewis 2
HENSLEY, William 1
  Nicholas Jr.
HENSON, Aubrey Eugene 5
HENSON, Clarence 5
  Cherrington
HENSON, Elmer D. 6
HENSON, John O'neal 3
HENSON, Josiah 1
HENSON, Poindexter Smith 1
HENTHORNE, Norris 4
  Gifford
HENTZ, Caroline Lee H
  Whiting
HENTZ, Nicholas Marcellus H
HENWOOD, Berryman 3
HENYEY, Louis G(eorge) 5
HENZE, Henry Rudolf 6
HEPBURN, A. Barton 1
HEPBURN, Andrew Dousa 1
HEPBURN, Andrew 4
  Hopewell
HEPBURN, Arthur Japy 4
HEPBURN, Charles Keith 5
HEPBURN, Charles 1
  McGuffey
HEPBURN, Frederick 3
  Taylor
HEPBURN, James Curtis 1
HEPBURN, Neil Jamieson 4
HEPBURN, Samuel 6
HEPBURN, William 3
  McGuffey
HEPBURN, William Murray 4
HEPBURN, William Peters 1
HEPNER, Walter Ray 6
HEPPENHEIMER, Ernest 3
  J.
HEPPENHEIMER, William 1
  Christian
HEPPENSTALL, Robert B. 4
HEPPENSTALL, Thomas 3
  Earl
HEPWORTH, Barbara 6
HEPWORTH, George 1
  Hughes
HERBEIN, B. William 5
HERBEN, Stephen Joseph 4
HERBERMANN, Charles 1
  George
HERBERT, Addier Hibler 6
HERBERT, Sir A(lan) 5
  Patrick
HERBERT, Albert 1
HERBERT, F. Hugh 3
HERBERT, F. M. Jr. 5
HERBERT, Frederick Davis 3
HERBERT, Hilary Abner 1
HERBERT, J. Joseph 3
HERBERT, James Cassidy 5
HERBERT, James M. 1
HERBERT, John Carlyle 1
HERBERT, John F. J. 1
HERBERT, John I. H. 4
HERBERT, John Kingston 5
HERBERT, John Warne 1
HERBERT, Louis H
HERBERT, Philemon H
  Thomas
HERBERT, Thomas J(ohn) 6
HERBERT, Victor 1
HERBERT, Walter 6
HERBERT, William Henry H
HERBST, Josephine Frey 5
HERBST, Stanislaw 6
HERDER, Ralph Barnes 3
HERDIC, Peter H
HERDMAN, William James 1
HEREFORD, Frank 4
HEREFORD, William 1
  Richard
HERFORD, Beatrice 5
HERFORD, Oliver 1
HERGESHEIMER, Joseph 3
HERHOLZ, Alfred 4
HERHOLZ, Ottilie 4
HERING, Carl 1
HERING, Constantine H
HERING, Daniel Webster 1
HERING, Frank Earl 2
HERING, Henry 2
HERING, Hermann S. 1
HERING, Hollis Webster 2
HERING, Oswald 2
  Constantin

HERING, Rudolph 1
HERIOT, George H
HERKIMER, John H
HERKIMER, Nicholas H
HERLANDS, William 5
  Bernard *
HERLIHY, Charles Michael 2
HERLIHY, John Albert 4
HERLY, Louis 3
HERMAN, Abraham 1
HERMAN, Alexander C. 6
HERMAN, Henry Edson 3
  Todd
HERMAN, James R. 3
HERMAN, Lebrecht 1
  Frederick
HERMAN, Leon Emerson 3
HERMAN, Raphael 2
HERMAN, Stewart Winfield 6
HERMAN, Theodore 2
  Frederick
HERMANCE, William 1
  Ellsworth
HERMANN, Binger 1
HERMANN, Edward 4
  Adolph
HERMANNSSON, Halldor 3
HERMS, William Brodbeck 3
HERMSEN, Edward 5
  Herman
HERNANDEZ, Benigno 1
  Cardenas
HERNANDEZ, Jose 1
  Conrado
HERNANDEZ, Joseph H
  Marion
HERNANDEZ, Roberto 4
HERNDON, Charles 3
  Traverse
HERNDON, James B. Jr. 3
HERNDON, John Goodwin 3
HERNDON, Thomas Hord H
HERNDON, William Henry H
HERNDON, William Lewis H
HERNE, James A. 1
HERNE, Katherine H
  Corcoran
HERNON, William Seton 3
HERO, Andrew Jr. 1
HEROD, William 1
HEROD, William Pirtle 1
HEROD, William Pirtle H
HEROD, William Rogers 6
HEROLD, Don 4
HEROLD, Jean Christopher 4
HERON, James Henry 5
  (Jamie Heron)
HERON, Matilda Agnes H
HERON, S. D. 4
HERON, William H
HEROY, James Harold 3
HEROY, William Bayard 5
HERR, Edwin Musser 1
HERR, Herbert Thacker 1
HERR, Hiero Benjamin 1
HERR, John H
HERR, John Knowles 6
HERR, Vincent V. 5
HERRE, Albert W. C. T. 6
HERREID, Charles N. 1
HERREID, Myron Tillman 4
HERRESHOFF, Charles 1
  Frederick
HERRESHOFF, J. B. 1
  Francis
HERRESHOFF, James 1
  Brown
HERRESHOFF, John 1
  Brown
HERRESHOFF, Nathaniel 1
  Greene
HERRICK, Albert Bledsoe 1
HERRICK, Anson H
HERRICK, Charles Judson 3
HERRICK, Cheesman Abiah 3
  Terhune
HERRICK, Christine 2
  Terhune
HERRICK, Clarence Luther 1
HERRICK, Clinton B. 4
HERRICK, Curtis James 5
HERRICK, D-Cady 1
HERRICK, Ebenezer 1
HERRICK, Edward H
  Claudius
HERRICK, Elinore 4
  Morehouse
HERRICK, Elizabeth 1
HERRICK, Everett Carleton 3
HERRICK, Francis Hobart 1
HERRICK, Frederick 2
  Cowles
HERRICK, Genevieve 5
  Forbes (Mrs. John Origen
  Herrick)
HERRICK, George 1
  Frederick

HERRICK, George Marsh 4
HERRICK, Glenn 5
  Washington
HERRICK, Harold 1
HERRICK, Henry W. 1
HERRICK, Huldah 4
HERRICK, James Bryan 3
HERRICK, John Origen 5
HERRICK, Joshua H
HERRICK, Lott Russell 1
HERRICK, Lucius Carroll 1
HERRICK, Manuel 5
HERRICK, Marvin 4
  Theodore
HERRICK, Myron T. 1
HERRICK, Parmely Webb 1
HERRICK, Paul Murray 5
HERRICK, Ray W. 5
HERRICK, Richard Platt H
HERRICK, Robert 1
HERRICK, Robert 2
  Frederick
HERRICK, Samuel H
HERRICK, Samuel Jr. 1
HERRICK, Samuel Edward 1
HERRICK, Sophia 1
  M'Ilvaine Bledsoe
HERRICK, Stephen Solon 1
HERRICK, Walter R. 5
HERRICK, Wirt 4
HERRIDGE, William 4
  Duncan
HERRIN, William Franklin 1
HERRING, Clyde LaVerne 2
HERRING, Herbert James 5
HERRING, Hubert Clinton 5
HERRING, Hubert Clinton 5
HERRING, James H
HERRING, Silas Clark 1
HERRING, William H
HERRINGTON, Arthur 5
  William Sidney
HERRINGTON, Cass E. 2
HERRINGTON, Lewis 6
  Butler
HERRIOT, Edouard Marie 3
HERRIOTT, Frank Irving 2
HERRIOTT, Irving 3
HERRIOTT, James Homer 5
HERRIOTT, Maxwell 3
  Haines
HERRLE, Colin 3
HERRMAN, Augustine H
HERRMANN, Esther 1
HERRMANN, Alexander H
HERRMANN, Bernard 3
HERRMANN, Ernest 3
  Edward
HERRMANN, Henry 4
  Francis
HERRMANN, Richard 2
HERROLD, Gordon 5
  William
HERRON, Charles 2
HERRON, Charles Douglas 1
HERRON, Clark Lincoln 1
HERRON, George Davis 1
HERRON, James Hervey 4
HERRON, John S. 3
HERRON, Rufus Hills 1
HERSCHDORFER, Manuel 1
HERSCHEL, Clemens 1
HERSCHELL, William 1
HERSEY, George Dallas 1
HERSEY, Heloise Edwina 1
HERSEY, Henry Blanchard 2
HERSEY, Henry Johnson 1
HERSEY, Ira Greenlief 2
HERSEY, Jacob Daniel 1
  Temple
HERSEY, Mark Leslie 1
HERSEY, Samuel Freeman H
HERSH, A. H. 3
HERSHEY, Amos Shartle 1
HERSHEY, Burnet 5
HERSHEY, Charlie Brown 1
HERSHEY, Harry Bryant 4
HERSHEY, John Willard 5
HERSHEY, Milton Snavely 1
HERSHEY, Omer F. 4
HERSHEY, Oscar H. 1
HERSHEY, Paris N. 3
HERSHEY, Robert Landis 6
HERSHEY, Scott F. 1
HERSHMAN, Oliver 1
  Sylvester
HERSHOLT, Jean 3
HERSKOVITS, Melville 4
  Jean
HERSMAN, Charles 4
  Campbell
HERSMAN, Christopher C. 4
HERSMAN, Hugh Steel 3
HERT, Alvin Tobias 1
HERT, Sally Aley 2
HERTEL, Robert Russell 4

HERTER, Albert 3
HERTER, Christian H
HERTER, Christian Archibald 1
HERTER, Christian Archibald 4
HERTERICK, Vincent Richard 5
HERTS, B. Russell 3
HERTY, Charles Holmes 1
HERTY, Charles Holmes Jr. 3
HERTZ, Alfred 2
HERTZ, Emanuel 1
HERTZ, Gustav Crane 4
HERTZ, John Daniel 4
HERTZ, John Jr. 5
HERTZ, Richard Otto 4
HERTZBERG, Hans Rudolph Reinhart 1
HERTZKA, Wayne Solomon 6
HERTZLER, Arthur Emanuel 2
HERTZLER, Charles William 4
HERTZOG, Charles D(emetrius) 5
HERTZOG, Walter Scott 5
HERTZOG, Walter Sylvester 6
HERVAS Y PANDURO, Lorenzo H
HERVEY, Alpheus Baker 1
HERVEY, Daniel E. 4
HERVEY, Donald Franklin 6
HERVEY, Harcourt 5
HERVEY, Harcourt Jr. 5
HERVEY, Harry Clay 3
HERVEY, James Madison 5
HERVEY, Walter Lowrie 3
HERVEY, William Addison 1
HERVEY, William Rhodes 3
HERZBERG, Max J. 3
HERZIG, Charles Simon 5
HERZOG, Anna Edes 3
HERZOG, Felix Benedict 1
HERZOG, Maximilian Joseph 1
HERZSTEIN, Joseph 5
HESCHEL, Abraham Joshua 5
HESLIN, Thomas 1
HESS, Alfred Fabian 1
HESS, Elmer 4
HESS, Finley B. 5
HESS, Frank L. 3
HESS, Franklin 1
HESS, Harry Hammond 5
HESS, Henry 1
HESS, Herbert William 2
HESS, Jerome Sayles 5
HESS, Julius Hays 3
HESS, Leslie Elsworth 3
HESS, Max 5
HESS, Myra 4
HESS, Victor Francis 4
HESS, Walter J. 6
HESS, Walter Rudolf 6
HESS, Wendell Frederick 3
HESSBERG, Albert 1
HESSBERG, Irving Kapp 2
HESSE, Bernard Conrad 1
HESSE, Frank McNeil 3
HESSE, Herman Carl 6
HESSE, Hermann 4
HESSE, Richard 6
HESSE, Seymour David 4
HESSELBERG, Edouard Gregory 1
HESSELIUS, Gustavus H
HESSELIUS, John H
HESSELLUND-JENSEN, Aage 6
HESSELTINE, William Best 4
HESSER, Frederic William 3
HESSLER, John Charles 2
HESSLER, William Henry 4
HESSON, Samuel Moodie 6
HESTER, Clinton Monroe 5
HESTER, John Hutchison 6
HESTER, John Kenton 4
HESTER, St Clair 1
HESTER, William 1
HESTER, William John 3
HESTER, William Van Arden 1
HESTON, J(ohn) Edgar 5
HESTON, John William 1
HETERICK, Robert Hynton 3
HETERICK, Vincent Richard 5
HETH, Henry H
HETHERINGTON, John Aikman 6
HETHERINGTON, John Edwin 1
HETLER, Donald McK 3
HETTINGER, Frederick C. 4
HETTINGER, Herman Strecker 6
HETTRICK, Elwood Harrison 5
HETZEL, Ralph Dorn 2
HETZLER, Howard George 1
HETZLER, Theodore 2
HEUCHLING, Fred G. 5
HEUER, George J. 3
HEUER, John Harland 5
HEUER, William Henry 4
HEUSER, Emil 3
HEUSER, Frederick William Justus 4
HEUSER, Gustave A. 5
HEUSNER, William Samuel 5
HEUSS, John 4
HEUSS, Theodor 4
HEUSTIS, Charles Herbert 4
HEVESY, George de 4
HEWAT, Alexander H
HEWE, Laurence Ilsey 3
HEWES, Amy 5
HEWES, Clarence Bussey 4
HEWES, Fletcher Willis 1
HEWES, Joseph H
HEWES, M. Lewin 1
HEWES, Robert H
HEWES, Thomas 3
HEWETSON, H. H. 5
HEWETT, Donnel Foster 5
HEWETT, Edgar Lee 2
HEWETT, Edwin Crawford 1
HEWETT, Hobart 4
HEWETT, Waterman Thomas 1
HEWETT, William Wallace 4
HEWETT-THAYER, Harvey Waterman 4
HEWINS, Caroline Maria 1
HEWIT, Augustine Francis H
HEWITT, A. 2
HEWITT, Abram Stevens 1
HEWITT, Charles Nathaniel 1
HEWITT, Clarence Horace 3
HEWITT, Edward Ringwood 3
HEWITT, Edward Shepard 4
HEWITT, Edwin Hawley 1
HEWITT, Emma Churchman 4
HEWITT, Erastus Henry 5
HEWITT, Erskine 1
HEWITT, Fayette 1
HEWITT, George Ayres 4
HEWITT, Goldsmith Whitehouse H
HEWITT, H. Kent 5
HEWITT, Harvey 3
HEWITT, Henry Jr. 1
HEWITT, Herbert Edmund 2
HEWITT, James H
HEWITT, John Haskell 1
HEWITT, John Hill H
HEWITT, John Napoleon Brinton 4
HEWITT, Joseph William 1
HEWITT, Leland Hazelton 4
HEWITT, Ogden Blackfan 4
HEWITT, Peter Cooper 1
HEWITT, Richard Miner 5
HEWITT, Theodore Brown 3
HEWITT, William 1
HEWITT, William Keesey H
HEWLETT, A. Walter 1
HEWLETT, James Howell 3
HEWLETT, James Monroe 1
HEWSON, Addinell 1
HEXAMER, Charles John 1
HEXNER, Ervin Paul 5
HEXTER, Irving Bernard 4
HEXTER, Joseph 3
HEYBURN, Weldon Brinton 1
HEYDECKER, Edward Le Moyne 4
HEYDLER, Charles 5
HEYDON, Henry Darling 1
HEYDRICK, Benjamin Alexander 5
HEYDT, Herman A. 1
HEYE, Carl T. 2
HEYE, George Gustav 3
HEYER, Georgette 6
HEYER, John Christian Frederick H
HEYKE, John Ericson Jr. 6
HEYL, Bernard Chapman 4
HEYL, Henry Livingston 6
HEYL, Paul Renno 5
HEYMAN, Clarence Henry 4
HEYMANN, Edgar 5
HEYMANN, Hans 2
HEYMANS, Corneille (Jean) (Francois) 5
HEYMSFELD, Ralph Taft 4
HEYNE, Maurice 5
HEYNE, Roland 4
HEYNS, Garrett 5
HEYROVSKY, Jaroslav 4
HEYSHAM, Theodore 1
HEYSINGER, Isaac Winter 4
HEYWARD, Dorothy 4
HEYWARD, Duncan Clinch 2
HEYWARD, DuBose 1
HEYWARD, Thomas H
HEYWOOD, Abbot Rodney 1
HEYWOOD, Alba 1
HEYWOOD, Albert Samuel 1
HEYWOOD, Charles 1
HEYWOOD, Ezra Hervey H
HEYWOOD, Gene Bryant 5
HEYWOOD, Levi H
HEYWORTH, James Omerod 1
HIACOOMES H
HIATT, Walter Sanders 3
HIBBARD, Addison 2
HIBBARD, Aldro Thompson 5
HIBBARD, Angus Smith 2
HIBBARD, Benjamin Horace 3
HIBBARD, Carlisle V. 3
HIBBARD, Claude William 6
HIBBARD, David Sutherland 4
HIBBARD, Ellery Albee 1
HIBBARD, Frank 3
HIBBARD, Frederick Cleveland 3
HIBBARD, Freeborn Garrettson H
HIBBARD, George 1
HIBBARD, George Albee 1
HIBBARD, H. Wade 1
HIBBARD, Rufus Percival 5
HIBBEN, John Grier 1
HIBBEN, Paxton 1
HIBBEN, Samuel Galloway 5
HIBBERD, James Farquhar 1
HIBBINS, Ann H
HIBBS, Ben 6
HIBBS, Harold Dickson 5
HIBBS, Henry C. 2
HIBBS, Louis E. 5
HIBSHMAN, Jacob H
HICHBORN, Franklin 5
HICHBORN, Philip 1
HICKAM, John Bamber 5
HICKENLOOPER, Andrew 1
HICKENLOOPER, Bourke Blakemore 5
HICKENLOOPER, Smith 1
HICKERNELL, Latimer Farrington 4
HICKEY, Andrew J. 2
HICKEY, James Burke 1
HICKEY, Jeremiah Griffin 3
HICKEY, John F. 4
HICKEY, John Joseph 5
HICKEY, Joseph Aloysious 3
HICKEY, Lee Cole 5
HICKEY, Leo J. 1
HICKEY, Matthew (Joseph Jr.) 5
HICKEY, Philip J. 4
HICKEY, Preston Manasseh 1
HICKEY, Turner Paul 5
HICKEY, William Augustine 1
HICKLING, D. Percy 1
HICKMAN, Adam Clark 1
HICKMAN, Cuthbert Wright 3
HICKMAN, Emily 2
HICKMAN, Eugene Christian 1
HICKMAN, Herman Michael 3
HICKMAN, John H
HICKMAN, John Edward 4
HICKMAN, Norman 3
HICKMAN, William Howard 4
HICKOK, Charles Thomas 3
HICKOK, James Butler H
HICKOK, Laurens Perseus H
HICKOK, Paul Robinson 2
HICKOK, Ralph Kiddoo 2
HICKOX, Ralph W. 1
HICKS, Ami Mali 5
HICKS, Archie Ray Jr. 6
HICKS, Clarence John 2
HICKS, Clifford E(rving) 5
HICKS, Douglas Mallory 4
HICKS, Edward H
HICKS, Elias H
HICKS, Francis Marion 4
HICKS, Frank M. 3
HICKS, Frederick Charles 3
HICKS, Frederick Cocks 1
HICKS, George 4
HICKS, Hanne John 5
HICKS, John 1
HICKS, John Donald 5
HICKS, Joseph Emerson 5
HICKS, Joseph Winstead 4
HICKS, Josiah Duane 4
HICKS, Lawrence Emerson 3
HICKS, Leonard 4
HICKS, Lewis Ezra 4
HICKS, Lewis Wenman 6
HICKS, Marshall 1
HICKS, Robert Emmet 4
HICKS, Thomas H
HICKS, Thomas E. 4
HICKS, Thomas Holliday H
HICKS, Thomas Holliday 3
HICKS, W. B. 5
HICKS, William Arthur 3
HICKS, William Minor 5
HICKS, William Norwood 6
HICKS, Wilson 5
HICKS, Xenophon 3
HICKSON, William James 1
HIDDEN, William Earl 1
HIDER, Arthur 1
HIEBERT, Joelle C. 2
HIEBERT, Peter Cornelius 4
HIERONYMUS, Robert Enoch 2
HIERONYMUS, William Peter 3
HIESTAND, Edgar Willard 5
HIESTAND, Jean Carter 3
HIESTAND, John Andrew H
HIESTER, Anselm Vinet 1
HIESTER, Daniel * H
HIESTER, Isaac Elimaker H
HIESTER, John H
HIESTER, Joseph H
HIESTER, William H
HIGBEE, Albert Enos 1
HIGBEE, Frederic Goodson 6
HIGBEE, Harry 1
HIGBEE, Irving Jackson 3
HIGBIE, Carlton M. 3
HIGBIE, Edgar Creighton 2
HIGBIE, Robert Winfield 1
HIGBY, Chester Penn 4
HIGBY, Gilbert C. 3
HIGBY, William H
HIGGINBOTHAM, Alfred Leslie 4
HIGGINBOTHAM, Jay Cee 6
HIGGINBOTTOM, Sam 3
HIGGINS, A. Foster 1
HIGGINS, Aldus Chapin 2
HIGGINS, Alice Louise 1
HIGGINS, Allan Herbert Webster 4
HIGGINS, Alvin McCaslin 1
HIGGINS, Andrew Jackson 3
HIGGINS, Anthony 1
HIGGINS, Archibald Thomas 2
HIGGINS, Charles H. 4
HIGGINS, Charles Melbourne 4
HIGGINS, Daniel Paul 3
HIGGINS, Edward 1
HIGGINS, Edwin Werter 3
HIGGINS, Elmore Fitzpatrick 1
HIGGINS, Eugene 3
HIGGINS, Francis G. 4
HIGGINS, Frank James 1
HIGGINS, Frank Wayland 1
HIGGINS, George Frederick 4
HIGGINS, George Thomas 5
HIGGINS, Harry B. 4
HIGGINS, Herbert Newton 4
HIGGINS, James Bennett 5
HIGGINS, James Henry 1
HIGGINS, James Henry Jr. 6
HIGGINS, John Clark 3
HIGGINS, John Martin 6
HIGGINS, John Patrick 3
HIGGINS, John W. 4
HIGGINS, John Wilfred 1
HIGGINS, Joseph 2
HIGGINS, Katharine Elizabeth Chapin 1
HIGGINS, Marguerite 4
HIGGINS, Milton Prince 1
HIGGINS, Montgomery Earle 6
HIGGINS, Richard Thomas 1
HIGGINS, Robert Barnard 1
HIGGINS, Robert William 4
HIGGINS, Rodney Gonzales 4
HIGGINS, Samuel 4
HIGGINS, Stanley Carmen Jr. 5
HIGGINS, Victor 2
HIGGINS, William Edward 1
HIGGINS, William Lincoln 3
HIGGINSON, Ella 1
HIGGINSON, Francis H
HIGGINSON, Francis John 1
HIGGINSON, Francis Lee 1
HIGGINSON, Francis Lee 5
HIGGINSON, Henry Lee 1
HIGGINSON, John H
HIGGINSON, Mary P. Thacher 1
HIGGINSON, Nathaniel H
HIGGINSON, Stephen H
HIGGINSON, Thomas Wentworth 1
HIGH, Robert King 4
HIGH, Stanley 4
HIGHFILL, Robert David 4
HIGHLAND, Cecil Blaine 3
HIGHLAND, Virgil Lee 1
HIGHSMITH, J. Henry 3
HIGHSMITH, Jacob Franklin 1
HIGHT, Clarence Albert 2
HIGHTOWER, Emmett 1
HIGHTOWER, Louis Victor 5
HIGHTOWER, Robert E. 4
HIGHTOWER, William Harrison 2
HIGINBOTHAM, Harlow Niles 1
HIGINBOTHAM, John U. 4
HIGLEY, Adelbert Pankey 2
HIGLEY, Albert Maltby 5
HIGLEY, Brodie Gilman 2
HIGLEY, Cyrus Martin 5
HIGLEY, Henry Grant 5
HIGLEY, Miles M. 3
HIGLEY, Walter Maydole 5
HIGLEY, Warren 1
HILAND, James H. 1
HILBERSEIMER, Ludwig Karl 4
HILBERT, George H(enry) 6
HILBRANT, Robert Edward 5
HILBUN, Ben Frank 4
HILBUN, William Bryan 6
HILD, Frederick Henry 5
HILD, Oscar F. 3
HILDEBRAND, Daniel Munroe 2
HILDEBRAND, H. Edward 4
HILDEBRAND, Ira Polk 2
HILDEBRAND, Jesse Richardson 3
HILDEBRANDT, Fred H. 3
HILDEBRANDT, Harvey Thornton 4
HILDEBRANDT, Howard L. 3
HILDEBRANT, Charles Quinn 4
HILDEBURN, Charles Swift Riche 1
HILDER, Howard 1
HILDER, John Chapman 1
HILDINGER, Wade Wheeler 4
HILDRETH, David Merrill 1
HILDRETH, Harold Mowbray 4
HILDRETH, John Lewis 1
HILDRETH, Joseph S. 4
HILDRETH, Melvin Andrew 2
HILDRETH, Melvin Davis 3
HILDRETH, Richard H
HILDRETH, Samuel Prescott H
HILDRETH, William Sobieski 4
HILDT, John Coffey 1
HILDUM, Clayton Edward 3
HILGARD, Eugene Woldemar 1
HILGARD, Ferdinand Heinrich Gustav H
HILGARD, Julius Erasmus H
HILGARTNER, Henry Louis 1
HILKEY, Charles Joseph 4
HILL, Adams Sherman 1
HILL, Agnes Leonard 1
HILL, Albert Hudgins 1
HILL, Albert Ross 2
HILL, Alferd J. 3
HILL, Alfred Gibson 5
HILL, Ambrose Powell H
HILL, Arthur B. 6
HILL, Arthur Dehon 2
HILL, Arthur Edward 1
HILL, Arthur Joseph 4
HILL, Arthur Middleton 5
HILL, Arthur Turnbull 1
HILL, Bancroft 3
HILL, Benjamin Harvey H

* Indicates More Than One Such Name Listed

HILL, Bert Hodge 3
HILL, Carlton 5
HILL, Mrs. Caroline Miles 3
HILL, Carolyn Bailey 4
HILL, Charles 4
HILL, Charles Edward 1
HILL, Charles Leander 1
HILL, Charles Lewis 3
HILL, Charles Shattuck 4
HILL, (Charles) Francis 5
HILL, Chester James Jr. 5
HILL, Claiborne Milton 3
HILL, Claude Eugene 3
HILL, Clyde Milton 4
HILL, Crawford 1
HILL, Daniel Harvey H
HILL, Daniel Harvey 4
HILL, David Bennett 5
HILL, David Garrett 5
HILL, David Jayne 1
HILL, David Spende 3
HILL, Donald MacKay 6
HILL, Eben Clayton M. D. 1
HILL, Ebenezer J. 1
HILL, Edgar Preston 5
HILL, Edmund Walton 6
HILL, Edward Burlingame 4
HILL, Edward Curtis 4
HILL, Edward Gurney 1
HILL, Edward Lee 6
HILL, Edward Llewellyn 3
HILL, Edward Yates 1
HILL, Edwin Conger 3
HILL, Emory 4
HILL, Ernest Rowland 2
HILL, Ernest W. 5
HILL, Ernie 3
HILL, Eugene Lott 6
HILL, Felix Robertson Jr. 5
HILL, Frank Alpine 1
HILL, Frank Davis 1
HILL, Frank Ernest 5
HILL, Frank Pierce 1
HILL, Fred Burnett 1
HILL, Frederic Stanhope H
HILL, Frederic Stanhope 5
HILL, Frederick Sinclair 3
HILL, Frederick Thayer 5
HILL, Frederick Trevor 1
HILL, G. Albert 4
HILL, George Alfred Jr. 2
HILL, George Andrews 1
HILL, George Anthony 1
HILL, George Griswold 1
HILL, George Handel H
HILL, George Robert 6
HILL, George Washington 4
HILL, George William * 1
HILL, Gershom Hyde 5
HILL, Grace Livingston 2
HILL, Grover Bennett 4
HILL, Harold O. 4
HILL, Harry Granison 3
HILL, Harry Harrison 4
HILL, Harry W. 5
HILL, Henry Albert 3
HILL, Henry Alexander 4
HILL, Henry Barker 1
HILL, Henry Clarke 3
HILL, Henry Wayland 5
HILL, Herbert Wynford 2
HILL, Hiram Warner 4
HILL, Horace Greeley 2
HILL, Howard Copeland 1
HILL, Hugh Lawson White H
HILL, Irving 4
HILL, Isaac H
HILL, Isaac William 4
HILL, J. B. P. Clayton 1
HILL, J. Gilbert 1
HILL, J. Murray 4
HILL, J. Stacy 1
HILL, James H
HILL, James 4
HILL, James Jr. 3
HILL, James Brents 4
HILL, James Ewing 1
HILL, James J. 4
HILL, James Langdon 3
HILL, James Michael 4
HILL, James Norman 1
HILL, James Perminter 3
HILL, James W. 3
HILL, Janet McKenzie 1
HILL, Joe H
HILL, Joe 4
HILL, John * H
HILL, John A. 3
HILL, John Alexander 1
HILL, John Calvin 6
HILL, John Edward 4
HILL, John Ethan 4
HILL, John Fremont 1
HILL, John Godfrey 5
HILL, John Henry H
HILL, John Leonard 6

HILL, John Lindsay 4
HILL, John Sprunt 4
HILL, John Wesley 1
HILL, John William H
HILL, Joseph Adna 1
HILL, Joseph Henry 1
HILL, Joseph Knoerle 5
HILL, Joseph Morrison 5
HILL, Joseph St Clair 5
HILL, Joshua H
HILL, Judson Sudborough 4
HILL, Julien Harrison 2
HILL, Knute 5
HILL, Lamar 1
HILL, Laurance Landreth 1
HILL, Lawrence 6
HILL, Lee H. 6
HILL, Leslie Pinckney 3
HILL, Louis A. 4
HILL, Louis Clarence 4
HILL, Louis Warren 2
HILL, Lysander 1
HILL, Mabel Jones 1
HILL, Marion 1
HILL, Mark Langdon H
HILL, Max 2
HILL, Mozell Clarence 5
HILL, Nathaniel Peter H
HILL, Nathaniel Peter 1
HILL, Noble 4
HILL, Norman Stewart 5
HILL, Owen Aloysius 1
HILL, Owen Duffy 4
HILL, Patty Smith 2
HILL, Percival Smith 1
HILL, Pierre Bernard 4
HILL, Ralph Waldo
Snowden 3
HILL, Randolph William 3
HILL, Reese Franklin 5
HILL, Reuben L. 3
HILL, Richard H
HILL, Robert Andrews H
HILL, Robert Carmer H
HILL, Robert E. Lee 2
HILL, Robert Potter 1
HILL, Robert Thomas 1
HILL, Robert William 4
HILL, Rolla Bennett 4
HILL, Roscoe R. 4
HILL, Samuel 1
HILL, Sherwin A. 4
HILL, Theophilus Hunter 1
HILL, Thomas H
HILL, Thomas 1
HILL, Thomas Edie 1
HILL, Thomas Guthrie
Franklin 1
HILL, Thomas Russell 6
HILL, Tom Burbridge 3
HILL, Ureli Corelli H
HILL, Vassie James 3
HILL, Walker 1
HILL, Walter Barnard 1
HILL, Walter Clay 4
HILL, Walter Henry 1
HILL, Walter Newell 3
HILL, Warren E. 4
HILL, Whitmel H
HILL, William H
HILL, William A. 1
HILL, William Austin 2
HILL, William Bancroft 1
HILL, William Edwin 1
HILL, William Free 1
HILL, William H. 4
HILL, William Henry H
HILL, William Henry 1
HILL, William S. 1
HILL, William Silas 5
HILL, Wilson Shedric 4
HILLARD, Charles W. 1
HILLARD, George Stillman H
HILLARD, Mary Robbins 1
HILLAS, Robert M. 3
HILLBRAND, Earl K. 4
HILLE, Gustav 1
HILLE, Hermann 4
HILLEARY, Edgar D. 5
HILLEBOE, Herman
Ertresvaag 4
HILLEBRAND, Harold
Newcomb 3
HILLEBRAND, William
Francis 1
HILLEGAS, Howard
Clemens 1
HILLEGAS, Michael H
HILLEN, Solomon Jr. H
HILLENMEYER, Louis
Edward 4
HILLER, Alfred 1
HILLER, Hiram Milliken 3
HILLES, Charles Dewey 1
HILLES, Frederick Vantyne 5
Holbrook

HILLES, Frederick Whiley 6
HILLES, William Samuel 1
HILLHOUSE, James H
HILLHOUSE, James
Abraham H
HILLHOUSE, William H
HILLIARD, Benjamin Clark 3
HILLIARD, Benjamin Clark 5
Jr.
HILLIARD, Curtis Morrison 5
HILLIARD, Edmund 6
Bayfield
HILLIARD, Francis H
HILLIARD, Henry H
Washington
HILLIARD, Isaac 1
HILLIARD, John Northern 1
HILLIARD, Raymond 4
Marcellus
HILLIARD, Robert Cochran 1
HILLIARD, Thomas C. 4
HILLINGER, Raymond 5
Peter
HILLIS, David H
HILLIS, Mrs. Newell 1
Dwight
HILLIS, Newell Dwight 1
HILLMAN, Alex L. 5
HILLMAN, Christine Huff 6
(Mrs. Howard S. Hillman)
HILLMAN, James Frazer 5
HILLMAN, John Hartwell 3
Jr.
HILLMAN, John William 5
HILLMAN, Lucy Rosaltha 4
HILLMAN, Sidney 2
HILLMAN, William 4
HILLQUIT, Morris 1
HILLS, Ada A. 1
HILLS, Elijah Clarence 1
HILLS, Franklin Grant 4
HILLS, Joseph Lawrence 5
HILLS, Laura Coombs 1
HILLS, Laurence 1
HILLS, Lewis Samuel 1
HILLS, Oscar Armstrong 3
HILLS, Richard Charles 1
HILLS, Thomas McDougall 6
HILLS, Victor Gardiner 1
HILLS, William Henry 1
HILLYER, H. Stanley 4
HILLYER, Homer Winthrop 2
HILLYER, Junius 1
HILLYER, Robert Silliman 4
HILLYER, Thomas Arthur 4
HILLYER, Virgil Mores 1
HILLYER, William Hurd 4
HILMER, William Charles H
HILPERT, Elmer Ernest 1
HILPRECHT, Herman 1
Volrath
HILSBERG, Alexander 4
HILSON, Edwin I. 3
HILTMAN, John Wolfe 1
HILTON, Alexander 1
HILTON, Clifford L. 1
HILTON, David Clark 2
HILTON, Henry Hoyt 1
HILTON, Hugh Gerald 5
HILTON, James 3
HILTON, Warren 1
HILTON, William Atwood 6
HIMEBAUGH, Keith 4
HIMES, Charles Francis 1
HIMES, Charles Francis 1
HIMES, John Andrew 1
HIMES, Joseph Hendrix 4
HIMES, Joshua Vaughan H
HIMES, Norman Edwin 2
HIMLER, Leonard E. 5
HIMMEL, Joseph 1
HIMMELBLAU, David 1
HIMMELWRIGHT, 1
Abraham Lincoln Artman
HIMSTEAD, Ralph E. 3
HIMSWORTH, Winston E. 5
HINCHEE, Fred Lee 4
HINCHMAN, Walter Swain 6
HINCKLE, William 1
HINCKLEY, Allen Carter 1
HINCKLEY, Edwin Smith 3
HINCKLEY, Frank Erastus 1
HINCKLEY, Frank L. 2
HINCKLEY, Frederic Allen 1
HINCKLEY, Frederick 1
Wheeler
HINCKLEY, George Lyman 1
HINCKLEY, George W. 4
HINCKLEY, Robert 1
HINCKLEY, Thomas 1
HINCKS, Carroll Clark 4
HINCKS, Clarence 4
Meredith
HINCKS, Edward Young 1
HINDEMITH, Paul 4

HINDERLIDER, Michael 5
Creed
HINDLE, Norman 4
Frederick
HINDLEY, George 4
HINDLEY, Howard Lister 2
HINDMAN, Albert Clare 1
HINDMAN, Baker Michael 5
HINDMAN, James Edward 4
HINDMAN, Thomas H
Carmichael
HINDMAN, William H
HINDMARSH, Harry 3
Comfort
HINDS, Anthony Keith 4
HINDS, Asher Crosby 1
HINDS, Ernest 1
HINDS, Frederick Wesley 4
HINDS, Henry 1
HINDS, James H
HINDS, John Iredelle 1
Dillard
HINDS, Julian 6
HINDS, Thomas H
HINDS, Warren Elmer 1
HINDS, William Alfred 1
HINDS, William Lawyer 4
HINDUS, Maurice 5
Gerschon
HINE, Charles Daniel 1
HINE, Charles De Lane 1
HINE, Clint C. 1
HINE, Francis Lyman 1
HINEBAUGH, William 4
Henry
HINERFELD, Benjamin 3
HINES, Charles 4
HINES, Duncan 3
HINES, Earle Garfield 1
HINES, Edgar Alphonso 4
HINES, Edward 1
HINES, Edward Norris 1
HINES, Edward Warren 1
HINES, Frank Thomas 1
HINES, Harry Matlock 1
HINES, James Kollock 1
HINES, John Fore 1
HINES, John Leonard 1
HINES, Laurence Edward 1
HINES, Linnaeus Neal 1
HINES, Murray Arnold 1
HINES, Ralph J. 3
HINES, Richard H
HINES, Walker Downer 1
HINGELEY, Joseph 1
Beaumont
HINITT, Frederick William 1
HINKE, Frederick William 1
HINKE, William John 2
HINKLE, Beatrice M. 1
HINKLE, Elmer Forry 3
HINKLE, Frederick Wallis 2
HINKLE, James Fielding 4
HINKLE, Ross Oel 3
HINKLE, Thomas Clark 1
HINKLE, Thornton Mills 1
HINKLEY, H. Lawrence 4
HINKLEY, J. William III 2
HINKLEY, John 1
HINMAN, Alice Hamlin 1
HINMAN, Dale Durkee 1
HINMAN, E(dgar) Harold 5
HINMAN, Elisha H
HINMAN, George Elijah 1
HINMAN, George Warren 1
HINMAN, George Wheeler 1
HINMAN, Harold J. 3
HINMAN, Harvey 3
DeForest
HINMAN, Joel H
HINMAN, Russell 1
HINMAN, Thomas Philip 1
HINRICHS, Carl Gustav 6
HINRICHS, Gustavus 4
Detlef
HINRICHS, Gustavus 4
Detlef
HINRICHSEN, Walter 5
HINRICHSEN, William H. 4
HINSCH, Charles Arthur 4
HINSDALE, Burke Aaron 1
HINSDALE, Ellen Clarinda 4
HINSDALE, Grace Webster 4
HINSDALE, Guy 2
HINSDALE, John Wetmore 1
HINSDALE, Wilbert B. 2
HINSHAW, Carl 3
HINSHAW, David 3
HINSHAW, Edmund 4
Howard
HINSHAW, Joseph Howard 5
HINSHAW, Melvin 6
Taliaferro
HINSHAW, Virgil 1
Goodman

HINSHAW, William Wade 2
HINSHELWOOD, Sir Cyril 4
HINSHELWOOD, Sir Cyril 5
(Norman)
HINSMAN, Carl B. 5
HINSON, M. R. 4
HINSON, Noel Bertram 3
HINSON, Walter Benwell 3
HINTON, Charles Louis 3
HINTON, Edward Wilcox 4
HINTON, H. D. 4
HINTON, Harold B. 3
HINTON, James William 5
HINTON, L. W. 6
HINTON, Raymond J. 4
HINTZ, Alfred Edward 4
HINTZ, Howard William 4
HIPPLE, Alpheus Hugh 1
HIPPLE, Frank K. 1
HIPSHER, Edward 2
Ellsworth
HIPSLEY, Elmer R. 5
HIRE, Chas 3
HIRES, Charles Elmer H
HIRES, Charles Elmer 1
HIRES, Harrison Streeter 1
HIRONS, Frederic C. 1
HIRONS, Frederic Charles 5
HIRSCH, Alcan 1
HIRSCH, Edwin Frederick 5
HIRSCH, Emil Gustav 1
HIRSCH, Frank E. 4
HIRSCH, Gustav 3
HIRSCH, Harold 1
HIRSCH, Irene Dorothea 5
HIRSCH, Isaac E. 2
HIRSCH, I(saac) Seth 6
HIRSCH, John Frederick 4
HIRSCH, Julius 4
HIRSCH, Max 3
HIRSCHBERG, Michael 1
Henry
HIRSCHBERG, Sanford 4
Leon
HIRSCHFELD, Hans M. 2
HIRSCHFELDER, Arthur 2
Douglass
HIRSCHFELDER, Joseph 1
Oakland
HIRSCHHORN, Fred 1
HIRSCHLER, Frederic Salz 5
HIRSCHMAN, Louis Jacob 4
HIRSH, Herbert William 5
HIRSH, Hugo 1
HIRSHBERG, Albert Simon 6
HIRSHBERG, Herbert 3
Simon
HIRSHBERG, Leonard 5
Keene
HIRSHFELD, Clarence 1
Floyd
HIRST, Barton Cooke 1
HIRST, Henry Beck H
HIRST, Robert Lincoln 4
HIRTH, Emma P. 2
HIRTH, Friedrich 1
HISAW, Frederick Lee 5
HISCOCK, Frank 1
HISCOCK, Frank Harris H
HISE, Elijah 1
HISGEN, Thomas Louis 1
HITCH, Arthur Martin 5
HITCH, Calvin Milton 1
HITCH, Robert Mark 1
HITCHCOCK, Abner 4
Edward
HITCHCOCK, Albert Spear 1
HITCHCOCK, Alfred H
HITCHCOCK, Alfred 3
Marshall
HITCHCOCK, Alvirus 4
Nelson
HITCHCOCK, Caroline 4
Hanks
HITCHCOCK, Charles A. 1
HITCHCOCK, Charles 5
Baker
HITCHCOCK, Charles 1
Henry
HITCHCOCK, Curtice 2
HITCHCOCK, Edward H
HITCHCOCK, Edward 1
Asbury
HITCHCOCK, Embury 4
HITCHCOCK, Enos H
HITCHCOCK, Ethan Allen H
HITCHCOCK, Ethan Allen 1
HITCHCOCK, Frank Harris 1
HITCHCOCK, Frank 3
Lauren
HITCHCOCK, Frederick 1
Collamore
HITCHCOCK, Frederick 1
Hills
HITCHCOCK, George 1

HITCHCOCK, George Collier 5
HITCHCOCK, Gilbert Monell 1
HITCHCOCK, Henry 1
HITCHCOCK, Henry Booth 1
HITCHCOCK, Herbert E. 4
HITCHCOCK, Lauren Blakely 5
HITCHCOCK, Lucius Wolcott 2
HITCHCOCK, Peter H
HITCHCOCK, Phineas Warrener H
HITCHCOCK, Ripley 1
HITCHCOCK, Romyn 4
HITCHCOCK, Roswell Dwight H
HITCHENS, Arthur Parker 2
HITCHLER, Theresa 3
HITCHLER, Walter Harrison 3
HITE, Bert Holmes 1
HITE, George E. Jr. 3
HITE, Jost H
HITE, Lewis Field 2
HITER, Frank Ambrose 3
HITLER, Adolf H
HITREC, Joseph George 5
HITT, R. S. Reynolds
HITT, Robert Melvin Jr. 5
HITT, Robert Roberts 1
HITTEL, Charles J. 4
HITTELL, John Sherzer 1
HITZ, John 1
HITZ, Ralph 1
HITZ, William 1
HIX, Asa Witt 4
HIX, Charles H. 1
HIXON, Ernest Howard 5
HIXSON, Arthur Warren 6
HIXSON, Fred White 1
HIXSON, William Aase 6
HLAVATY, Vaclav 5
HO CHI-MINH 5
HOAD, William Christian 4
HOADLEY, David H
HOADLEY, George Arthur 3
HOADLEY, John Chipman H
HOADLY, Leigh 6
HOADLY, George H
HOAG, Clarence Gilbert 6
HOAG, David Doughty 1
HOAG, Ernest Bryant 1
HOAG, Frank Stephen 4
HOAG, George Grant 5
HOAG, Gilbert Thomas 3
HOAG, Joseph H
HOAG, Junius Clarkson 1
HOAG, Truman Harrison H
HOAG, William Ricketson 4
HOAGE, Robert J. 5
HOAGLAND, Denis Robert 3
HOAGLAND, Henry E. 6
HOAGLAND, John Hurle 4
HOAGLAND, Moses H
HOAGLAND, Warren Eugene 5
HOAN, Daniel Webster 4
HOAR, Ebenezer Rockwood H
HOAR, George Frisbie 1
HOAR, Leonard H
HOAR, Rockwood 1
HOAR, Samuel H
HOARD, Charles Brooks 1
HOARD, William Dempster 1
HOARE, Elmer Joseph 5
HOBAN, Edward Francis 4
HOBAN, James H
HOBAN, Michael John 1
HOBART, Aaron H
HOBART, Alice Tisdale 4
HOBART, Alvah Sabin 1
HOBART, Franklin Gatfield 4
HOBART, Garret Augustus 1
HOBART, George Vere 1
HOBART, Henry Metcalf 1
HOBART, Horace Reynolds 1
HOBART, John Henry H
HOBART, John Sloss H
HOBART, Lewis Parsons 1
HOBART, Mrs. Lowell Fletcher (Edith Liela) 5
HOBART, Marie Elizabeth Jefferys
HOBBIE, Henry Martin 3
HOBBIE, Selah Reeve H
HOBBINS, James R. 3
HOBBLE, Deborah Sharp 5
HOBBS, Alfred Charles
HOBBS, Allan Wilson 4
HOBBS, Charles Seright 5
HOBBS, Charles Wood 5
HOBBS, Edward H. 1
HOBBS, Franklin Warren 3
HOBBS, George Sayward

HOBBS, Gustavus Warfield Jr. 3
HOBBS, Ichabod Goodwin 1
HOBBS, James Randolph 2
HOBBS, John Edward 1
HOBBS, John Weston 4
HOBBS, Leland Stanford 4
HOBBS, Lewis Lyndon 4
HOBBS, Morris Henry 4
HOBBS, Perry L. 4
HOBBS, Ralph Waller 1
HOBBS, Roe Raymond 4
HOBBS, Roscoe Conklin 6
HOBBS, Sam Francis 3
HOBBS, William Herbert 4
HOBBS, William J. 4
HOBBY, William Pettus 4
HOBDY, John Buford 5
HOBEN, Allan 1
HOBEN, Lindsay 4
HOBGOOD, Charles Goyne 6
HOBGOOD, Frank P. 5
HOBLER, Atherton W. 6
HOBLITZELL, John Dempsey Jr. 4
HOBLITZELLE, Harrison 2
HOBLITZELLE, Karl 4
HOBSON, A(lphonzo) Augustus 5
HOBSON, Alfred Norman 1
HOBSON, Benjamin Lewis 4
HOBSON, Edward Henry 1
HOBSON, Jesse Edward 5
HOBSON, John Peyton 1
HOBSON, Joseph Reid Anderson 4
HOBSON, Richmond Pearson 1
HOBSON, Robert Louis 5
HOBSON, Robert P. 4
HOBSON, Sarah Matilda 4
HOBSON, Stanley H. 4
HOBSON, T. Francis 4
HOBSON, Thayer 4
HOBSON, Wilder 4
HOBSON, William Andrew 5
HOBSON, William Horace 4
HOCA, Myron Myroslaw 5
HOCH, August 1
HOCH, Daniel K. 5
HOCH, Edward Wallis 1
HOCH, Homer 2
HOCH, Paul H. 4
HOCHBAUM, Hans Weller 5
HOCHDOERFER, Richard 4
HOCHE, Herman Emanuel 4
HOCHMUTH, Bruno Arthur 4
HOCHSTETTER, Robert William 5
HOCHWALD, Fritz G(abriel) 5
HOCHWALT, Albert Frederick 1
HOCHWALT, Frederick G. 4
HOCKADAY, Ela 5
HOCKEMA, Frank C. 3
HOCKENBEAMER, August Frederick 1
HOCKENSMITH, Wilbur Darwin 3
HOCKER, Lon O. 2
HOCKER, William Adam 4
HOCKETT, Homer Carey 4
HOCKING, Brian 5
HOCKING, William Ernest 4
HOCKLEY, Chester Fox 4
HOCKSTADER, Leonard Albert 4
HODDER, Alfred 1
HODDER, Frank Heywood 1
HODDINOTT, Mary Loretta 5
HODELL, Charles Wesley 1
HODES, Henry Irving 4
HODGDON, Charles 3
HODGDON, Frank Wellington 1
HODGDON, Frank Wilbert 4
HODGE, Archibald Alexander H
HODGE, Bachman Gladstone 4
HODGE, Caspar Wistar 1
HODGE, Charles H
HODGE, Clifton Fremont 4
HODGE, Edward B. 1
HODGE, Edward Blanchard 2
HODGE, Edwin Rose Jr. 4
HODGE, Frederick Webb 3
HODGE, Henry Wilson 1
HODGE, Hugh Lenox H
HODGE, Hugh Lenox 4
HODGE, John Aspinwall 1
HODGE, John R. 4
HODGE, Kenneth LaVern 5

HODGE, Oliver 4
HODGE, Richard Morse 4
HODGE, Tobe 1
HODGE, Walter Hartman 5
HODGE, Walter Roberts 1
HODGE, Willard Wellington 4
HODGE, William 1
HODGE, William Irvine 5
HODGE, William Vallance Douglas 6
HODGEN, John Thompson H
HODGES, Arthur H
HODGES, Brandon Patton 3
HODGES, Campbell Blackshear 2
HODGES, Charles 4
HODGES, Charles Drury H
HODGES, Charles H. 1
HODGES, Charles Libbens 5
HODGES, Courtney H. 4
HODGES, Frank 5
HODGES, George 1
HODGES, George Hartshorn 1
HODGES, George Tisdale H
HODGES, Gilbert 5
HODGES, Gilbert Tennent 3
HODGES, Harry Foote 1
HODGES, Harry Marsh 4
HODGES, Henry Clay 1
HODGES, James Leonard H
HODGES, John Cunyus 4
HODGES, John Cunyus 5
HODGES, John Sebastian Bach 1
HODGES, Johnny 5
HODGES, Joseph Gilluly 5
HODGES, Leigh Mitchell 3
HODGES, LeRoy 4
HODGES, Louise Threete 5
HODGES, Luther Hartwell 6
HODGES, Nathaniel Dana Carlile 1
HODGES, Richard Edward 4
HODGES, Richard Gilbert 6
HODGES, Thomas Edward 4
HODGES, Walter Edward 2
HODGES, William Franklin 3
HODGES, William Thomas 2
HODGES, William V. 4
HODGHEAD, Beverly Lacy 1
HODGIN, Charles Elkanah 4
HODGIN, Cyrus Wilburn 1
HODGINS, Eric 5
HODGKIN, Henry Theodore 1
HODGKIN, Wilfred Reginald Haughton 6
HODGKIN, William Newton 4
HODGKINS, Alton Ross 3
HODGKINS, Howard Lincoln 1
HODGKINS, Louise Manning 1
HODGKINS, William Candler 1
HODGKINSON, Francis 2
HODGKINSON, John H
HODGMAN, Burns P. 1
HODGMAN, T. Morey 1
HODGMAN, William Lansing 1
HODGON, Anderson Dana 2
HODGSDON, Daniel Bascome 1
HODGSON, Albert James 2
HODGSON, Carey Vandervort 1
HODGSON, Caspar Wistar 1
HODGSON, Frank Corrin 5
HODGSON, Fred Grady 5
HODGSON, Harry 5
HODGSON, Joseph Frederick 1
HODGSON, Joseph Park 5
HODGSON, Laurence Curran 1
HODGSON, Marshall 5
HODGSON, Morton Strahan 3
HODGSON, Richard 1
HODGSON, Robert Willard 4
HODGSON, Thekla Roese 1
HODGSON, William Brown H
HODGSON, William Roy 6
HODNETTE, John K. 4
HODOUS, Lewis 2
HODSON, Clarence 1
HODSON, William 2
HODUR, Francis H
HOE, Richard March H
HOE, Robert H
HOE, Robert 1

HOE, Robert 3
HOEBER, Arthur 1
HOECHST, Edward John 5
HOECK, Theodor Albert 4
HOECKEN, Christian H
HOEFELD, Norman 3
HOEFER, Charles Wenzel 3
HOEHLER, Fred Kenneth 5
HOEHLING, Adolph August 1
HOEHLING, Adolph August 2
HOEHN, Kenneth William 5
HOEING, Charles 1
HOEING, Frederick Waldbridge 4
HOEKENDIJK, Johannes Christiaan 6
HOELSCHER, Randolph Philip 5
HOELZEL, John P. 3
HOEN, August H
HOENSHEL, Eli J. 1
HOEPPEL, John Henry 6
HOERR, Normand Louis 4
HOERTER, Charles Richard 3
HOEY, Clyde Roark 3
HOEY, James J. 2
HOF, Samuel 1
HOFF, Charles Worthington 4
HOFF, Emanuel Buechley 1
HOFF, John Edward 4
HOFF, John Van Rensselaer 1
HOFF, Nelville Soule 1
HOFF, Olaf 1
HOFF, William Bainbridge 1
HOFFECKER, John H. 1
HOFFENSTEIN, Samuel Goodman 2
HOFFHERR, Frederic G. 3
HOFFLUND, John Leslie 4
HOFFMAN, Abram 2
HOFFMAN, Arnold 4
HOFFMAN, Arthur Gilman 2
HOFFMAN, Arthur Sullivant 6
HOFFMAN, Burton C. 3
HOFFMAN, Carl 4
HOFFMAN, Charles Fenno H
HOFFMAN, Charles Frederick 1
HOFFMAN, Charles W. 5
HOFFMAN, Christian Balzac 1
HOFFMAN, Clare E. 4
HOFFMAN, David 1
HOFFMAN, David Murray H
HOFFMAN, Dean Meck 5
HOFFMAN, Doretta Schlaphoff 6
HOFFMAN, Edward George 1
HOFFMAN, Edward Richard 3
HOFFMAN, Eugene Augustus 1
HOFFMAN, Frank Sargent 1
HOFFMAN, Fred William 4
HOFFMAN, Frederick John 5
HOFFMAN, Frederick Ludwig 2
HOFFMAN, George Matthias 1
HOFFMAN, Harold Giles 3
HOFFMAN, Harry Leslie 4
HOFFMAN, Heman Leslie 5
HOFFMAN, Henry William H
HOFFMAN, Herman S. 2
HOFFMAN, Horace Addison 1
HOFFMAN, Hugh French T. 3
HOFFMAN, James David 1
HOFFMAN, James Franklin 5
HOFFMAN, James I. 4
HOFFMAN, John C. 4
HOFFMAN, John Thompson H
HOFFMAN, John Washington 3
HOFFMAN, John Wesley 1
HOFFMAN, Joseph Gilbert 6
HOFFMAN, Josiah Ogden H
HOFFMAN, Leroy E. 5
HOFFMAN, Malvina 4
HOFFMAN, Mark 5
HOFFMAN, Michael H
HOFFMAN, Milton J. 4
HOFFMAN, Ogden H
HOFFMAN, Paul Gray 4
HOFFMAN, Ralph 1
HOFFMAN, Richard 1
HOFFMAN, Richard Curzon 1
HOFFMAN, Richard W. 6
HOFFMAN, Roy 5

HOFFMAN, Samuel David 3
HOFFMAN, W. D. 3
HOFFMAN, Wickham H
HOFFMAN, William George 3
HOFFMANN, Ernst 3
HOFFMANN, Francis Arnold 1
HOFFMANN, Ralph 1
HOFFSTOT, Frank N. 1
HOFFY, Alfred M. H
HOFFZIMMER, Ernest K(aspar) 5
HOFMAN, Heinrich Oscar 1
HOFMANN, Hans 4
HOFMANN, Herbert Andrew 5
HOFMANN, Hugo 5
HOFMANN, Josef 1
HOFMANN, Julius 1
HOFSTADTER, Richard 5
HOGAN, Aluysius Gonzaga Joseph 2
HOGAN, Bernard Francis 3
HOGAN, Dana 2
HOGAN, Daniel Wise 6
HOGAN, Denis Patrick 1
HOGAN, Edgar Poe 5
HOGAN, Edward A. Jr. 3
HOGAN, Frank J. 1
HOGAN, Frank J. 2
HOGAN, Frank Smithwick 6
HOGAN, George Archibald 5
HOGAN, Henry Michael 5
HOGAN, John H
HOGAN, John Henry 1
HOGAN, John Joseph 1
HOGAN, John Philip 4
HOGAN, John Vincent Lawiess 4
HOGAN, Louise E. Shimer 1
HOGAN, Michael J. 3
HOGAN, O. T. 5
HOGAN, William H
HOGAN, William Ransom 5
HOGATE, Enoch George 1
HOGATE, Kenneth Craven 2
HOGBEN, Lancelot 6
HOGE, Arthur Kenworthy 1
HOGE, James Doster 1
HOGE, James Fulton 5
HOGE, John H
HOGE, John H
HOGE, John Blair H
HOGE, Joseph Pendleton H
HOGE, Moses H
HOGE, Moses Drury H
HOGE, Peyton Harrison 4
HOGE, Vane Morgan 5
HOGE, William H
HOGE, William James H
HOGEBOOM, James H
HOGELAND, Albert 1
HOGELAND, Albert Harrison 1
HOGG, Astor 5
HOGG, George H
HOGG, Herschel M. 4
HOGG, James Stephen 1
HOGG, Samuel H
HOGG, William Clifford 1
HOGG, William Stetson 1
HOGGATT, Wilford Bacon 1
HOGGSON, William John 1
HOGLE, James A. 3
HOGNESS, Thorfin Rusten 6
HOGSETT, William Sloan 4
HOGUE, Addison 4
HOGUE, S. Fred 1
HOGUE, Walter Jenkins 1
HOGUE, Wilson Thomas 1
HOGUET, Robert Louis 3
HOGUN, James H
HOH, Paul Jacob 3
HOHENBERG, A. Elkan 1
HOHENTHAL, Emil Louis George 1
HOHF, Silas Matthew 5
HOHFELD, Edward 1
HOHFELD, Wesley Newcomb H
HOHFELD, Wesley Newcomb 4
HOHLFELD, Alexander Rudolf 2
HOHLFELD, Alexander Rudolf 3
HOHMAN, Leslie B. 5
HOIDALE, Einar 3
HOILES, Raymond Cyrus 5
HOISINGTON, Henry Richard H
HOIT, Henry Ford 5
HOITT, Charles William 4
HOKE, Elmer Rhodes 1
HOKE, Kremer J.

HOKE, Michael 2
HOKE, Robert Frederick 2
HOKE, Travis Henderson 3
HOKE, William Alexander 1
HOLABIRD, John Augur 2
HOLABIRD, Samuel 1
  Beckley
HOLADAY, Ross Edgar 1
HOLADAY, William P. 2
HOLAHAN, Maurice 1
  Fenelon
HOLAND, Hjalmar Rued 4
HOLAND, Hjalmar Rued 5
HOLBEN, Ralph Penrose 1
HOLBORN, Hajo 5
HOLBROOK, Alfred 1
HOLBROOK, Arthur 6
  Tenney
HOLBROOK, Donald 5
HOLBROOK, Dwight 4
HOLBROOK, Edward H
  Dexter
HOLBROOK, Elmer Allen 3
HOLBROOK, Evans 1
HOLBROOK, Florence 1
HOLBROOK, Frederick * 1
HOLBROOK, Henry Crosby 4
HOLBROOK, John 5
HOLBROOK, John Edwards H
HOLBROOK, John Swift 1
HOLBROOK, Josiah H
HOLBROOK, Lucius Roy 5
HOLBROOK, Martin 1
  Luther
HOLBROOK, Richard 1
  Thayer
HOLBROOK, Roland C. 3
HOLBROOK, Silas H
  Pinckney
HOLBROOK, Stewart Hall 4
HOLBROOK, Willard Ames 1
HOLCH, Arthur Everett 3
HOLCOMB, Amasa H
HOLCOMB, Horace Hale 1
HOLCOMB, Lynn Howe 2
HOLCOMB, Marcus 1
  Hensey
HOLCOMB, Oscar 5
  Raymond
HOLCOMB, Richard Roy 4
HOLCOMB, Silas 1
  Alexander
HOLCOMB, Thomas 4
HOLCOMBE, Amasa 5
  Maynard
HOLCOMBE, Armstead 1
  Richardson
HOLCOMBE, Chester 1
HOLCOMBE, George H
HOLCOMBE, Henry H
HOLCOMBE, James H
  Philemon
HOLCOMBE, John Lavallee 4
HOLCOMBE, John 1
  Marshall
HOLCOMBE, Oscar 5
  Fitzallen
HOLCOMBE, William 1
  Frederic
HOLCOMBE, William H
  Henry
HOLDAWAY, Charles 6
  William
HOLDEN, Albert James 1
HOLDEN, Alice M. 1
HOLDEN, Carl Frederick 3
HOLDEN, Charles Arthur 4
HOLDEN, Charles Revell 1
HOLDEN, Edgar 1
HOLDEN, Edward Henry 1
HOLDEN, Edward 1
  Singleton
HOLDEN, Edwin Chapin 2
HOLDEN, Frederick Clark 3
HOLDEN, George Parker 1
HOLDEN, George Walter 1
HOLDEN, Gerry Rounds 1
HOLDEN, Hale 1
HOLDEN, Hale 3
HOLDEN, Horace Moore 1
HOLDEN, James 1
HOLDEN, James Austin 2
HOLDEN, James Franklin 1
HOLDEN, James Stansbury 5
HOLDEN, John Burt 1
HOLDEN, Liberty Emery 1
HOLDEN, Louis Edward 1
HOLDEN, Louis Edward 1
HOLDEN, Louis Halsey 5
HOLDEN, Oliver 1
HOLDEN, Perry Greeley 4
HOLDEN, Roy Jay 1
HOLDEN, Thomas Steele 3
HOLDEN, Ward Andrews 1
HOLDEN, William Woods H

HOLDEN, Willis Sprague 6
HOLDER, Arthur Ernest 1
HOLDER, Charles Adams 3
HOLDER, Charles 1
  Frederick
HOLDER, Edward Perry 3
HOLDER, Francis Jerome 1
HOLDER, Ivan Wendell 6
HOLDER, Joseph Basset H
HOLDER, Oscar Curtis 4
HOLDERBY, Andrew 4
  Roberdeau
HOLDERBY, William 1
  Matthew
HOLDING, Archibald M. 1
HOLDING, Elisabeth 3
  Sanxay
HOLDING, Robert Powell 3
HOLDOM, Jesse 1
HOLDREGE, George Ward 1
HOLENSTEIN, Thomas 5
HOLGATE, Thomas 2
  Franklin
HOLIDAY, Eleanor 1
HOLIDAY, Herman Joe 4
HOLL, Carl Waldo 4
HOLL, Die Lewis 3
HOLLADAY, Alexander 1
  Quarles
HOLLADAY, Alexander H
  Richmond
HOLLADAY, Ben H
HOLLADAY, James 1
HOLLADAY, Waller 4
HOLLAMAN, Rich William 2
HOLLAND, Charles Hubert 6
HOLLAND, Clifford 1
  Milburn
HOLLAND, Cornelius H
HOLLAND, Edmund 1
  Milton
HOLLAND, Edward 1
  Everett
HOLLAND, Edwin Clifford H
HOLLAND, Elmer Joseph 5
HOLLAND, Elmer Leonard 4
  Jr.
HOLLAND, Ernest O. 3
HOLLAND, Frank P. 1
HOLLAND, Frederic May 1
HOLLAND, George 1
HOLLAND, Henry Finch 4
HOLLAND, James H
HOLLAND, James 1
  Buchanan
HOLLAND, James M. 1
HOLLAND, James William 1
HOLLAND, John Joseph 1
HOLLAND, John Philip H
HOLLAND, John Philip 1
HOLLAND, Joseph 1
  Jefferson
HOLLAND, Josiah Gilbert H
HOLLAND, Josiah Gilbert 6
HOLLAND, Laurier Fox- 3
  Strangways
HOLLAND, Leicester 3
  Bodine
HOLLAND, Louis Edward 4
HOLLAND, Madeline 5
  Oxford (Mrs. John N.
  McDonnell)
HOLLAND, Peter Olai 1
HOLLAND, Philip 5
HOLLAND, Robert Afton 1
HOLLAND, Robert Allen 1
HOLLAND, Rupert Sargent 3
HOLLAND, Rush LaMotte 2
HOLLAND, St. Clair Cecil 4
HOLLAND, Samuel Hyman 6
HOLLAND, Sidney George 4
HOLLAND, Spessard 5
  Lindsey
HOLLAND, Thomas Leroy 2
HOLLAND, Travis 4
HOLLAND, Ubert Cecil 3
HOLLAND, W. Bob 1
HOLLAND, William J. 1
HOLLAND, William 5
  Merideth
HOLLANDER, Franklin 4
HOLLANDER, Jacob H. 1
HOLLANDER, Sidney 5
HOLLANDS, Edmund 6
  Howard
HOLLEMAN, Joel H
HOLLEMAN, Willard Roy 5
HOLLENBACK, George H
  Matson
HOLLENBACK, John 1
  Welles
HOLLENBACK, Matthias H
HOLLENBECK, Don 3
HOLLERITH, Herman 1
HOLLERITH, Herman 2
HOLLERITH, Herman 4

HOLLEY, Alexander H
  Lyman
HOLLEY, Francis 1
HOLLEY, George Malvin 4
HOLLEY, Horace H
HOLLEY, Horace 4
HOLLEY, John Milton H
HOLLEY, John Milton 1
HOLLEY, Marietta 1
HOLLEY, Myron H
HOLLEY, William Welles H
HOLLICK, Arthur 1
HOLLIDAY, Carl 1
HOLLIDAY, Cyrus Kurtz 4
HOLLIDAY, Elias S. 1
HOLLIDAY, Houghton 5
HOLLIDAY, John 1
  Hampden
HOLLIDAY, Judy 4
HOLLIDAY, Robert Cortes 2
HOLLIDAY, Robert Paul 3
HOLLIDAY, Wallace 3
  Trevor
HOLLIDAY, William 4
  Harrison
HOLLIDAY, William H
  Helmus
HOLLIDAY, William 1
  Helmus
HOLLIDAY, William 4
  Helmus
HOLLING, Thomas Leslie 4
HOLLINGSHEAD, Stewart 4
HOLLINGSWORTH, Amor 3
HOLLINGSWORTH, David 4
  A.
HOLLINGSWORTH, Frank 4
HOLLINGSWORTH, 4
  William Franklin
HOLLINGTON, Richard 1
  Deming
HOLLINGWORTH, Harry 3
  Levi
HOLLINGWORTH, Leta S. 1
HOLLINS, George Nichols H
HOLLIS, Allen 3
HOLLIS, Ernest Victor 4
HOLLIS, Henry French 2
HOLLIS, Henry Leonard 1
HOLLIS, Ira Nelson 1
HOLLIS, W. Stanley 1
HOLLISTER, Buell 4
HOLLISTER, Clay Harvey 1
HOLLISTER, Fred H. 3
HOLLISTER, Gideon H
  Hiram
HOLLISTER, Granger A. 1
HOLLISTER, Horace 4
  Adelbert
HOLLISTER, Howard Clark 1
HOLLISTER, John 1
  Hamilcar
HOLLISTER, Joseph 3
HOLLISTER, Ned 1
HOLLISTER, Orlando 1
  Knapp
HOLLISTER, Richard 6
  Dennis Teall
HOLLISTER, William 1
  Henry Jr.
HOLLMANN, Harry 2
  Triebner
HOLLOMAN, Delmar 6
  Winston
HOLLOMON, James 1
  Arthur
HOLLOPETER, William 1
  Clarence
HOLLOWAY, David H
  Pierson
HOLLOWAY, Edward 1
  Stratton
HOLLOWAY, Harry Vance 4
HOLLOWAY, Jacob James 1
HOLLOWAY, John 4
HOLLOWAY, John Lindsay 4
HOLLOWAY, Joseph H
  Flavius
HOLLOWAY, Thomas 1
  Beaver
HOLLOWAY, William A. 4
HOLLOWAY, William 3
  Grace
HOLLOWAY, William 5
  James
HOLLOWAY, William 5
  Judson
HOLLOWAY, William 1
  Lawson
HOLLOWAY, William M. 4
HOLLOWAY, William 4
  Robeson
HOLLS, George Frederick 4
  William
HOLLUMS, Ellis Clyde 2
HOLLY, Charles Harden 4

HOLLY, Henry Hudson H
HOLLY, James Theodore 4
HOLLY, William H. 3
HOLLYDAY, Richard 4
  Carmichael
HOLLYER, Samuel 4
HOLM, Frits Vilhelm 1
HOLM, George Elmer 4
HOLM, Henry Jesse 5
HOLM, Theodor 1
HOLM, Victor S. 1
HOLMAN, Alfred 1
HOLMAN, Charles Thomas 4
HOLMAN, Eugene 4
HOLMAN, Frank 4
HOLMAN, Frank E. 4
HOLMAN, Frederick Van 5
  Voorhies
HOLMAN, Howard Francis 3
HOLMAN, Jesse Lynch 4
HOLMAN, Jud McCarty 5
HOLMAN, Louis Arthur 4
HOLMAN, Minard Lafever 1
HOLMAN, Rufus C. 4
HOLMAN, Russell Lowell 4
HOLMAN, William Henry 4
HOLMAN, William Kunkel 5
HOLMAN, William Steele 1
HOLMBERG, Adrian Otis 5
HOLMBERG, Allan 4
  Richard
HOLMBERG, George C. 1
HOLMBERG, Gustaf 1
  Fredrik
HOLME, John Francis 4
HOLME, Thomas H
HOLMES, Abiel H
HOLMES, Arthur 4
HOLMES, Bayard 1
HOLMES, Champneys Holt 3
HOLMES, Charles Elmer 4
HOLMES, Charles Horace H
HOLMES, Charles Shiveley 6
HOLMES, Christian R. 1
HOLMES, Clarence Leroy 1
HOLMES, David 1
HOLMES, David Eugene 4
HOLMES, Donald Safford 4
HOLMES, Dwight Oliver 5
  Wendell
HOLMES, Edward H
HOLMES, Edward Jackson 3
HOLMES, Edward Marion 1
  Jr.
HOLMES, Edward Thomas 5
HOLMES, Edwin Francis 4
HOLMES, Edwin Sanford 1
  Jr.
HOLMES, Elias Bellows 1
HOLMES, Ernest Shurtliff 4
HOLMES, Ezekiel 1
HOLMES, Frank G. 3
HOLMES, Frederick 4
HOLMES, Frederick Lionel 2
HOLMES, Frederick S. 4
HOLMES, Gabriel H
HOLMES, George Frederick H
HOLMES, George Kirby 4
HOLMES, George Robert 1
HOLMES, George Sanford 3
HOLMES, George William 4
HOLMES, Gerald Anderson 2
HOLMES, Gustavus S. 4
HOLMES, Guy Earl 2
HOLMES, Harry Nicholls 4
HOLMES, Henry Alfred 4
HOLMES, Henry Wyman 4
HOLMES, Howard Carleton 1
HOLMES, Isaac Edward H
HOLMES, Israel H
HOLMES, Jack Alroy 5
HOLMES, James Thomas 4
HOLMES, Jesse Herman 2
HOLMES, John 4
HOLMES, John * 4
HOLMES, John Haynes 4
HOLMES, John McClellan 1
HOLMES, John P. 4
HOLMES, John Simcox 5
HOLMES, Joseph Addison 4
HOLMES, Joseph Austin 1
HOLMES, Joses B. S. 5
HOLMES, Julius Cecil 4
HOLMES, Ludvig 1
HOLMES, Major Edward 4
HOLMES, Malcolm 3
  Haughton
HOLMES, Mary Caroline 4
HOLMES, Mary Elisabeth 1
HOLMES, Mary Emilie 1
HOLMES, Mary Jane 1
HOLMES, Merrill Jacob 5
HOLMES, Morris Grant 2
HOLMES, Nathaniel 1

HOLMES, Oliver Wendell H
HOLMES, Oliver Wendell 1
HOLMES, Pehr G. 3
HOLMES, Phillips 1
HOLMES, Ralph Clinton 3
HOLMES, Ralston Smith 4
HOLMES, Richard Sill 1
HOLMES, Robert 4
HOLMES, Robert Shailor 1
HOLMES, Rudolph Wieser 3
HOLMES, Samuel Foss 4
HOLMES, Samuel Jackson 5
HOLMES, Samuel Van 1
  Vranken
HOLMES, Sidney Tracy H
HOLMES, Theophilus H
  Hunter
HOLMES, Thomas James 3
HOLMES, Urban Tigner 5
HOLMES, Uriel 1
HOLMES, Walton H. 4
HOLMES, Wilbur Fisk 4
HOLMES, William Henry 1
HOLMES, William Henry 2
HOLMGREN, John R. 4
HOLMQUIST, Claire 5
  Walfred
HOLMSTROM, Andrew 5
  Birger
HOLMSTROM, Gus Edgar 5
HOLSAPPLE, Cortell Rose 4
HOLSCLAW, Charles H. 6
HOLSEY, Hopkins 1
HOLSEY, Lucius Henry 4
HOLSMAN, Henry K. 5
HOLST, Edvard H
HOLSTEIN, Henry Lincoln 4
HOLSTEIN, Otto 1
HOLT, Adoniram Judson 4
HOLT, Andrew 2
HOLT, Andrew Hall 3
HOLT, Arthur Erastus 1
HOLT, Byron Webber 1
HOLT, Charles Sumner 1
HOLT, Edwin Bissell 3
HOLT, Edwin Michael 4
HOLT, Erastus Eugene Sr. 1
HOLT, Erwin Allen 5
HOLT, Frank O. 4
HOLT, Fred Park 4
HOLT, George Chandler 1
HOLT, George Hubbard 1
HOLT, Guy 1
HOLT, Hamilton 3
HOLT, Hamilton Tatum 4
HOLT, Harold Edward 4
HOLT, Harry Howard Jr. 4
HOLT, Henry 1
HOLT, Henry Chandler 3
HOLT, Henry Winston 2
HOLT, Hines H
HOLT, Homer Adams 6
HOLT, Ivan Lee 4
HOLT, John H
HOLT, John Herrimon 4
HOLT, Joseph 1
HOLT, L. Emmett 1
HOLT, L. Emmett Jr. 6
HOLT, Lawrence 1
  Shackleford
HOLT, Lee Cone 3
HOLT, Lucius Hudson 3
HOLT, Marshall Keyser 5
  (Mrs. Leland Wallace
  Holt)
HOLT, Orren Thaddeus 4
HOLT, Orrin H
HOLT, Rackham 4
HOLT, Robert Harold 6
HOLT, Roland 1
HOLT, Rosa Belle 5
HOLT, Rush Dew 3
HOLT, Walter Vincent 4
HOLT, William Franklin 3
HOLT, William Henry 1
HOLT, William Joseph 3
HOLT, William Sylvester 1
HOLT, Winifred 2
HOLTEN, Samuel H
HOLTER, Norman B. 3
HOLTHUSEN, Henry 5
  Frank
HOLTMAN, Dudley Frank 4
HOLTMAN, Louis 1
HOLTON, Edwin Lee 3
HOLTON, Elizabeth Curran 5
  (Mrs. Winfred Byron
  Holton Jr.)
HOLTON, George Van 5
  Syckel
HOLTON, Henry Dwight 1
HOLTON, Holland 2
HOLTON, Jessie Moon 1
HOLTON, M. Adelaide 4
HOLTON, Winfred B. Jr. 3

HOLTZCLAW, Jack Gilbert 3
HOLTZMAN, John W. 4
HOLTZMANN, Jacob L. 4
HOLTZOFF, Alexander 5
HOLTZWORTH, Bertram 5
Arthur
HOLY, Thomas Celestine 6
HOLYOKE, Edward 1
HOLYOKE, Edward H
Augustus
HOLYOKE, Samuel H
HOLZAPPLE, Joseph 6
Randall
HOLZBERG, Jules Donald 5
HOLZER, Charles Elmer 5
HOLZHEIMER, William 2
Andrew
HOLZINGER, Karl John 3
HOLZKNECHT, Karl J. 3
HOLZMAN, Benjamin Grad 6
HOMAN, Fletcher 5
HOMAN, Paul Thomas 5
HOMANS, Amy Morris 4
HOMBERGER, Alfred 3
William
HOMBERGER, Ludwig 3
Maximillian
HOMER, Arthur Bartlett 5
HOMER, Francis Theodore 5
HOMER, John L. 4
HOMER, Louise Dilworth 2
Beatty
HOMER, Sidney 3
HOMER, Soloman Jones 5
HOMER, William J. 1
HOMER, William Oscar 6
HOMER, Winslow 1
HOMES, Henry Augustus H
HONAN, James Henry 1
HONAN, William Francis 1
HONDA, Masujiro 4
HONDORP, Peter 5
HONE, Philip H
HONEGGER, Arthur 4
HONEY, Robertson 1
HONEY, Samuel Robertson 1
HONEYCUTT, Francis 1
Webster
HONEYCUTT, Jesse 5
Vernon
HONEYMAN, Nan Wood 6
(Mrs. David T.
Honeyman)
HONEYWELL, Mark C. 4
HONEYWELL, Miss M. A. H
HONIG, George Honig 6
HONLINE, Moses Alfred 1
HONNEN, George 6
HONNOLD, William 3
Lincoln
HONORE, Paul 3
HOO, Victor Chi-Tsai 5
HOOBLER, Bert Raymond 2
HOOD, Arthur A. 4
HOOD, Charles Crook 1
HOOD, Charles Emerson 4
HOOD, E. Lyman 1
HOOD, Edwin Milton 1
HOOD, Frazer 2
HOOD, Frederic Clark 2
HOOD, George E. 3
HOOD, Horace 1
HOOD, J. Douglas 4
HOOD, James Walker 1
HOOD, John 1
HOOD, John Bell H
HOOD, Kenneth Ogilvie 6
HOOD, Oliver Roland 5
HOOD, Ozni Porter 1
HOOD, Raymond 1
Mathewson
HOOD, Solomon Porter 4
HOOD, Washington H
HOOD, William 1
HOOGEWERFF, John 1
Adrian
HOOK, Charles Ruffin Jr. 4
HOOK, Enos 1
HOOK, James William 3
HOOK, Walter Williams 1
HOOK, William Cather 1
HOOKER, Charles Edward 1
HOOKER, Donald Russell 2
HOOKER, Edward 1
HOOKER, Edward Beecher 1
HOOKER, Ellen Kelley 1
HOOKER, Elon Huntington 1
HOOKER, Forrestine 1
Cooper
HOOKER, Frank Arthur 1
HOOKER, George 1
Ellsworth
HOOKER, Harry Mix 4
HOOKER, Henry Stewart 2
HOOKER, Isabella Beecher 1
HOOKER, James Murray 5

HOOKER, John Daggett 1
HOOKER, John Jay 5
HOOKER, Joseph H
HOOKER, Margaret 5
Huntington
HOOKER, Philip H
HOOKER, Richard 4
HOOKER, Thomas H
HOOKER, Thomas 1
HOOKER, Warren Brewster 1
HOOKER, William H
HOOKER, William Brian 2
HOOKER, William P. 4
HOOKER, Worthington H
HOOKS, Charles H
HOOLEY, Arthur 5
HOOLEY, Edwin Strange 4
HOON, Clarence Earl 1
HOOPER, Ben W. 3
HOOPER, Bert Leslie 6
HOOPER, C. E. 3
HOOPER, Charles Edward 1
HOOPER, Everett 4
HOOPER, Frank Finley 3
HOOPER, Franklin Henry 1
HOOPER, Franklin William 1
HOOPER, Sir Federic 4
Collins
HOOPER, Jessie Annette 1
Jack
HOOPER, John William 3
HOOPER, Johnson Jones H
HOOPER, Joseph Lawrence 1
HOOPER, Louis Leverett 4
HOOPER, Lucy Hamilton H
HOOPER, Osman Castle 1
HOOPER, Philo O. 1
HOOPER, Robert P. 3
HOOPER, Samuel H
HOOPER, Shadrach K. 1
HOOPER, Stanford 3
Caldwell
HOOPER, William H
HOOPER, William Henry 4
HOOPER, William Leslie 1
HOOPER, William Thomas 4
HOOPES, Josiah 1
HOOPINGARNER, Dwight 3
Lowell
HOOPINGARNER, 3
Newman Leander
HOOPLE, Gordon Douglass 6
HOOSE, James Harmon 1
HOOTON, Caradine Ray 4
HOOTON, Earnest Albert 3
HOOTON, Mott 1
HOOVER, Arthur McCall 5
HOOVER, Bessie Ray 5
HOOVER, Blaine 3
HOOVER, Calvin Bryce 6
HOOVER, Charles Franklin 1
HOOVER, Charles Lewis 2
HOOVER, Charles Ruglas 2
HOOVER, Donald Douglas 5
HOOVER, Frank G. 3
HOOVER, George 3
Pendelton
HOOVER, Harvey Daniel 2
HOOVER, Herbert 4
HOOVER, Herbert Jr. 5
HOOVER, Herbert William 3
HOOVER, Hubert Don 5
HOOVER, J(ohn) Edgar 5
HOOVER, John Howard 5
HOOVER, Lou Henry 4
HOOVER, Ray 4
HOOVER, Samuel Earle 2
HOOVER, Simon Robert 1
HOOVER, Stuart 1
HOOVER, Theodore Jesse 3
HOOVER, William D. 2
HOOVER, William H. 3
HOPE, Chester Raines 4
HOPE, Clifford Ragsdale 5
HOPE, Eliza Milford Tatum 6
HOPE, Francis Moffat 1
HOPE, James H
HOPE, James Barron 1
HOPE, James Haskell 5
HOPE, James William 4
HOPE, John 1
HOPE, Minnie Gazelle 5
Welborn (Mrs. Tom
Hope)
HOPE, Richard 3
HOPE, Robert Hervey 6
HOPE, Walter Ewing 2
HOPEKIRK, Helen 3
HOPEWELL, John 1
HOPEWELL-SMITH, 1
Arthur
HOPF, Harry Arthur 2
HOPFENBECK, George M. 4
HOPKINS, Abner Crump 1
HOPKINS, Albert J. 1
HOPKINS, Alphonso Alva 1

HOPKINS, Altis Skiles 5
HOPKINS, Amos Lawrence 4
HOPKINS, Anderson Hoyt 5
HOPKINS, Andrew Delmar 4
HOPKINS, Andrew Winkle 6
HOPKINS, Archibald 1
HOPKINS, Arthur Francis H
HOPKINS, Arthur John 1
HOPKINS, Arthur 2
Melancthon
HOPKINS, B. Smith 4
HOPKINS, Benjamin H
Franklin
HOPKINS, Benjamin 3
Franklin
HOPKINS, Charlotte 1
Everett
HOPKINS, Clarence Victor 6
HOPKINS, Cyril George 1
HOPKINS, E. Washburn 1
HOPKINS, Edna Boies 1
HOPKINS, Edward H
HOPKINS, Edward H
Augustus
HOPKINS, Edward Jerome H
HOPKINS, Edwin Butcher 1
HOPKINS, Edwin Mortimer 2
HOPKINS, Erasmus Guy 1
HOPKINS, Erastus 4
HOPKINS, Ernest Martin 4
HOPKINS, Esek H
HOPKINS, Evan Henry 1
HOPKINS, Frank A. 4
HOPKINS, Franklin 1
HOPKINS, Franklin 4
Whetstone
HOPKINS, Fred Mead 3
HOPKINS, Frederick Eli 4
HOPKINS, George H
Washington
HOPKINS, Grant Sherman 4
HOPKINS, Harry L. 2
HOPKINS, Henry 1
HOPKINS, Herbert Muller 1
HOPKINS, Isaac Stiles 1
HOPKINS, James Campbell H
HOPKINS, James Frederick 1
HOPKINS, James Love 1
HOPKINS, James R. 5
HOPKINS, Jay Paul 5
HOPKINS, John Appleton 5
Haven
HOPKINS, John Burroughs H
HOPKINS, John Henry 1
HOPKINS, John Henry 2
HOPKINS, John Henry Jr. H
HOPKINS, John Jay 3
HOPKINS, Johns 1
HOPKINS, Joseph Gardner 3
HOPKINS, Juliet Ann Opie H
HOPKINS, Lemuel 1
HOPKINS, Lindsey 1
HOPKINS, Louis Bertram 1
HOPKINS, Louise Virginia 4
Martin
HOPKINS, Margaret 4
Briscoe
HOPKINS, Mark H
HOPKINS, Miriam 5
HOPKINS, Nanette 1
HOPKINS, Nevil Monroe 2
HOPKINS, Percy Don 1
HOPKINS, Richard J. 2
HOPKINS, Robert Emmet 1
HOPKINS, Robert Holbrook 5
HOPKINS, Robert Milton 3
HOPKINS, Samuel * 1
HOPKINS, Samuel 1
Augustus
HOPKINS, Samuel Miles H
HOPKINS, Samuel Miles 1
HOPKINS, Scott 1
HOPKINS, Selden G. 1
HOPKINS, Sherburne 1
Gillette
HOPKINS, Stanley Marshall 6
HOPKINS, Stephen H
HOPKINS, Stephen Tyng H
HOPKINS, Theodore Weld 4
HOPKINS, Thomas Cramer 3
HOPKINS, Thomas Snell 1
HOPKINS, Walter Lee 3
HOPKINS, William Hersey 1
HOPKINS, William John 1
HOPKINS, William Karl 6
HOPKINS, William 4
Rowland
HOPKINSON, Charles 4
HOPKINSON, Edward Jr. 1
HOPKINSON, Ernest 1
HOPKINSON, Francis H
HOPKINSON, Joseph 1
HOPKIRK, Howard William 4
HOPLEY, Elizabeth 1
Sheppard
HOPLEY, John Edward 1

HOPLEY, Russell James 2
HOPPE, Herman Henry 1
HOPPER, Bruce Campbell 6
HOPPER, David Claude 5
HOPPER, DeWolf 1
HOPPER, Edna Wallace 3
HOPPER, Edward 3
HOPPER, Frances Peters 5
(Mrs. Eugene D. Hopper)
HOPPER, Franklin 3
Ferguson
HOPPER, Hedda 4
HOPPER, Isaac Tatem H
HOPPER, James Marie 3
HOPPER, Rex Devern 4
HOPPER, Vincent Foster 6
HOPPES, John J. 4
HOPPIN, Augustus 1
HOPPIN, James Mason 1
HOPPIN, Joseph Clark 1
HOPPIN, William Warner 1
HOPPIN, William Warner 2
HOPPING, Andrew Daniel 3
HOPSON, George Bailey 1
HOPSON, William Fowler 1
HOPWOOD, Avery 1
HOPWOOD, Erie Clark 1
HOPWOOD, Herbert 4
Gladstone
HOPWOOD, Josephus 4
HOPWOOD, Robert 4
Freeman
HORACK, Frank Edward 3
HORACK, Frank Edward 3
Jr.
HORAN, Hubert Joseph Jr. 5
HORAN, Philip Edward 5
HORAN, Walter Franklin 4
HORBERG, Leland 3
HORD, Donal 4
HORDYK, Gerard 3
HORENSTEIN, Jascha 4
HORGAN, Daniel Stephen 6
HORINE, John 5
Winebrenner
HORKAN, George Anthony 4
Philip
HORKHEIMER, Arthur 6
Philip
HORLICK, Alexander 3
James
HORLICK, William 1
HORLICK, William Jr. 1
HORMEL, George Albert 2
HORMEL, Jay Catherwood 3
HORMELL, Orren Chalmer 6
HORMELL, William 1
Garfield
HORN, Aaron Charles 3
HORN, Carlton William 5
HORN, Charles Edward H
HORN, Charles J. 5
HORN, Clinton Morris 5
HORN, Edward Charles 6
HORN, Edward Traill 1
HORN, Frank Churchill 1
HORN, George Henry H
HORN, Henry H
HORN, Henry John 1
HORN, Henry John 2
HORN, John Louis 6
HORN, Nelson Paxson 3
HORN, Paul Whitfield 1
HORN, Raymond Edwin 4
HORN, Robert Chisolm 4
HORN, Roy de Saussure 6
HORN, Tiemann Newell 4
HORN, William C. 4
HORN, William Melchior 1
HORNADAY, Clifford Lee 6
HORNADAY, James Parks 1
HORNADAY, William 1
Temple
HORNADY, John Randolph 2
HORNBEAK, Samuel Lee 2
HORNBECK, Donald 4
Warner
HORNBECK, John Wesley 1
HORNBECK, John H
Westbrook
HORNBECK, Marquis D. 4
HORNBECK, Stanley K. 4
HORNBECK, Vivienne B. 5
(Mrs. Stanley K.
Hornbeck)
HORNBERGER, Theodore 6
HORNBLOW, Arthur 2
HORNBLOWER, Henry 1
HORNBLOWER, Joseph H
Coerten
HORNBLOWER, Joseph 1
Coerten
HORNBLOWER, Josiah H
HORNBLOWER, Ralph 5
HORNBLOWER, William 1
Butler

HORNBOSTEL, Henry 4
HORNBROOK, Henry 1
Hallam
HORNE, Charles Francis 2
HORNE, Edmund Campion 1
HORNE, Frank Alexander 1
HORNE, Frank S(mith) 6
HORNE, Frederick Joseph 3
HORNE, Henry Abbott 4
HORNE, Herman Harrell 2
HORNE, Joseph A. 3
HORNE, Josh L. 6
HORNE, Mary Tracy Earle 5
HORNE, Nellie Mathes 5
HORNE, Perley Leonard 1
HORNER, Bernard Justine 5
HORNER, Charles Francis 4
HORNER, Harlan Hoyt 6
HORNER, Henry 1
HORNER, James Richey 2
HORNER, John B. 1
HORNER, Junius Moore 1
HORNER, Leonard 2
Sherman
HORNER, Wesley Winans 3
HORNER, William H
Edmonds
HORNEY, Karen 3
HORNEY, Odus Creamer 3
HORNIBROOK, William 2
Harrison
HORNIBROOKE, Isabel 5
(Isabel Hornibrook)
HORNICK, Charles W. 1
HORNING, William Allen 4
HORNOR, Lynn Sedwick 1
HORNSBY, John Allen 1
HORNSBY, Rogers H
HORNSBY, Rogers 4
HORNUNG, Christian 4
HOROWITZ, Louis Jay 3
HOROWITZ, Saul Jr. 6
HORR, Alfred Reuel 3
HORR, George Edwin 1
HORR, Ralph A. 3
HORR, Roswell Gilbert H
HORRAX, Gilbert 3
HORRELL, George Robert 5
HORROCKS, James H
HORRWORTH, Charles A. 4
HORSBURGH, Robert 2
Homer
HORSEY, Outerbridge H
HORSFALL, Frank Lappin 5
Jr.
HORSFALL, I. Owen 2
HORSFALL, Robert Bruce 2
HORSFIELD, Thomas H
HORSFORD, Cornelia 3
HORSFORD, Eben Norton H
HORSFORD, Jerediah H
HORSKY, Edward 2
HORSLEY, John Shelton 2
HORSMANDEN, Daniel H
HORST, Emil Clemens 1
HORST, George Philip 1
HORST, John Joseph 2
HORST, Louis 4
HORST, Miles 5
HORSTMAN, Albert Adam 4
HORSTMANN, Ignatius 1
Frederick
HORSTMANN, William H. H
HORSWELL, Charles 4
HORTENSTINE, Raleigh 5
HORTON, Albert Howell 1
HORTON, Arthur 6
HORTON, Benjamin Jason 4
HORTON, (Charles) Marcus H
HORTON, Douglas 5
HORTON, Edward 2
Augustus
HORTON, Edward Everett 5
HORTON, Elmer Grant 2
HORTON, Frank Ogilvie 2
HORTON, George 2
HORTON, George Terry 2
HORTON, Henry Hollis 1
HORTON, Herbert L. 3
HORTON, Herman DeWitt 2
HORTON, Horace Babcock 3
HORTON, J(oseph) Warren 4
HORTON, Jesse M. 1
HORTON, Katharine Loren 1
Pratt
HORTON, Lydiard 2
Honeage
HORTON, McDavid 1
HORTON, Oliver Harvey 1
HORTON, Robert Elmer 2
HORTON, Samuel Dana 1
HORTON, Thomas Corwin 1
HORTON, Thomas H
Raymond
HORTON, Valentine Baxter H
HORTON, Walter Marshall 4

HORTON, Walter Shurts 4
HORTON, Wilkins P. 2
HORTON, William Edward 1
HORTON, William S. 4
HORVATH, Imre 3
HORVITZ, Aaron 5
HORWITZ, Phineas 1
Jonathan
HORWITZ, Solis 5
HORWOOD, Murray Philip 3
HOSACK, Alexander Eddy H
HOSACK, David H
HOSAFROS, Wayne Orville 6
HOSFORD, Charles
Franklin Jr.
HOSFORD, Harry Lindley 2
HOSFORD, Willard Deere 5
HOSFORD, William Fuller 3
HOSHOUR, Harvey Sheely 3
HOSHOUR, Samuel H
Klinefelter
HOSIC, James Fleming 4
HOSKIER, Herman C. 1
HOSKIN, Arthur Joseph 1
HOSKIN, Robert 4
HOSKINS, Fermin Lincoln 1
HOSKINS, Franklin Evans 1
HOSKINS, Fred 4
HOSKINS, George Gilbert 1
HOSKINS, Halford 4
Lancaster
HOSKINS, J. Preston 1
HOSKINS, James Dickcason 3
HOSKINS, James Preston 1
HOSKINS, John Deane 1
Charles
HOSKINS, John Hobart 3
HOSKINS, John K. 6
HOSKINS, John M. 4
HOSKINS, Leander Miller 1
HOSKINS, Roy Graham 6
HOSKINS, William 1
HOSKINS, William Horace 1
HOSMER, Charles 2
Bridgham
HOSMER, Frank Alvin 3
HOSMER, Frederick Lucian 1
HOSMER, George Stedman 1
HOSMER, Harriet Goodhue 1
HOSMER, Hezekiah Lord * H
HOSMER, James Kendall 1
HOSMER, Ralph Sheldon 1
HOSMER, Samuel Monroe 1
HOSMER, Titus 1
HOSMER, William Howe H
Cuyler
HOSS, Elijah Embree 1
HOSS, George Washington 1
HOSTER, Herman Albert 3
HOSTETLER, Erwin Case 5
HOSTETLER, Joseph C. 3
HOSTETLER, Lowell Coy 5
HOSTETLER, Theodore 2
Allen
HOSTETTER, Jacob 1
HOSTY, Thomas Edward 5
HOTCHENER, Henry 6
HOTCHENER, Marie 4
Russak
HOTCHKIN, Samuel Fitch 1
HOTCHKISS, Benjamin H
Berkeley
HOTCHKISS, Chauncey 1
Crafts
HOTCHKISS, Clarence 3
Roland
HOTCHKISS, George 3
Burton
HOTCHKISS, George W. 1
HOTCHKISS, Giles Waldo H
HOTCHKISS, Henry 1
Dedwitt
HOTCHKISS, Henry 4
Greene
HOTCHKISS, Henry Stuart 2
HOTCHKISS, Horace Leslie 1
HOTCHKISS, J. Elizabeth 5
HOTCHKISS, Julius 1
HOTCHKISS, Loyal Durand 4
HOTCHKISS, Lucius Wales 1
HOTCHKISS, Willard 3
Eugene
HOTCHKISS, William 3
Horace
HOTCHKISS, William Otis 3
HOTCHKISS, Willis R. 5
HOTELLING, Harold 4
HOTTENROTH, Adolph 5
Christian
HOTTES, Charles Frederick 5
HOTZ, Ferdinand Carl 4
HOTZ, H(enry) G(ustave) 5
HOTZ, Robert Schuttler 1
HOUCK, Irvin Elmer 5
HOUCK, Jacob Jr. H
HOUCK, Louis 1

HOUDE, Camillien 3
HOUDINI, Harry 3
HOUGH, Alfred Lacey 1
HOUGH, Charles Merrill 1
HOUGH, David H
HOUGH, Emerson 1
HOUGH, Franklin Benjamin H
HOUGH, George Anthony 5
HOUGH, George 1
Washington
HOUGH, Henry Hughes 2
HOUGH, Lynn Harold 6
HOUGH, Robert Lee Jr. 6
HOUGH, Romeyn Beck 1
HOUGH, Samuel Strickler 2
HOUGH, Theodore 1
HOUGH, Walter 1
HOUGH, Warwick 1
HOUGH, William Jervis H
HOUGH, Williston Samuel 1
HOUGHTELING, James 1
Lawrence
HOUGHTELING, James 4
Lawrence
HOUGHTON, Alanson 1
Bigelow
HOUGHTON, Albert Balch 5
HOUGHTON, Dorothy 5
Deemer (Mrs. Hiram Cole
Houghton)
HOUGHTON, Douglass 1
HOUGHTON, Edward 4
Lovell
HOUGHTON, Edward 3
Rittenhouse
HOUGHTON, Frederick 4
Boies
HOUGHTON, Frederick 1
Lowell
HOUGHTON, Frederick 5
Percival
HOUGHTON, George 1
Clarke
HOUGHTON, George H
Heindric
HOUGHTON, H. Seymour 4
HOUGHTON, Henry 1
Clarke
HOUGHTON, Henry Oscar H
HOUGHTON, Henry 6
Spencer
HOUGHTON, Herbert 4
Pierrepont
HOUGHTON, James 1
Warren
HOUGHTON, John Henry 1
HOUGHTON, Louise 5
Phillips
HOUGHTON, Louise 1
Seymour
HOUGHTON, Lucile C. 6
HOUGHTON, Sherman 4
Otis
HOUGHTON, Will H. 2
HOUGHTON, William 1
Addison
HOUGHTON, William 4
Morris
HOUK, Eliza Phillips 1
Thruston
HOUK, George Washington H
HOUK, Leonidas Campbell H
HOUKOM, John Asbjorn 3
HOULIHAN, D. F. 4
HOULTON, Ruth 6
HOURIGAN, John A. 4
HOURWICH, Isaac A. 1
HOUSE, A. G. 4
HOUSE, Boyce 4
HOUSE, Byron Orvil 5
HOUSE, Edward Howard 1
HOUSE, Edward John 6
HOUSE, Edward Mandell 1
HOUSE, Elwin Lincoln 1
HOUSE, Francis Edwin 1
HOUSE, Garry Campbell 5
HOUSE, Henry Alonzo 4
HOUSE, Homer Clyde 1
HOUSE, Homer Doliver 2
HOUSE, James Alford 1
HOUSE, James Arthur 5
HOUSE, Jay Elmer 1
HOUSE, John Forde 1
HOUSE, John Henry 1
HOUSE, Joseph Warren 1
HOUSE, Ralph Emerson 1
HOUSE, Robert Ernest 1
HOUSE, Roy Temple 4
HOUSE, Royal Earl 1
HOUSE, Samuel Reynolds H
HOUSEMAN, Julius H
HOUSER, Daniel M. 1
HOUSER, Frederick 2
Wilhelm
HOUSER, Gerald Fred 5
Tillman

HOUSER, Gilbert L. 3
HOUSER, Karl Musser 1
HOUSER, Shaler Charles 2
HOUSER, Theodore V. 4
HOUSER, Walter L. 4
HOUSMAN, Laurence 3
HOUSSAY, Bernardo 5
Alberto
HOUSTON, Bryan 6
HOUSTON, Charles Albert 3
HOUSTON, Charles 3
Hamilton
HOUSTON, Clarence 4
Preston
HOUSTON, David Franklin 1
HOUSTON, Edwin James 1
HOUSTON, Edwin Samuel 1
HOUSTON, Frances C. 1
HOUSTON, Francis A. 1
HOUSTON, George 2
Harrison
HOUSTON, George Smith 1
HOUSTON, Grant 3
HOUSTON, Harry 6
Rutherford
HOUSTON, Henry A. 3
HOUSTON, Henry Howard H
HOUSTON, Herbert 3
Sherman
HOUSTON, James Garfield 6
HOUSTON, John M. 6
HOUSTON, John Wallace H
HOUSTON, Margaret Bell 4
HOUSTON, Oscar R. 5
HOUSTON, Persis Daniel 3
HOUSTON, Robert Griffith 2
HOUSTON, Samuel H
HOUSTON, Samuel 3
Frederic
HOUSTON, Victor Steuart 5
Kaleoaloha
HOUSTON, William 3
Cannon
HOUSTON, William H
Churchill
HOUSTOUN, John H
HOUSTOUN, William H
HOUTS, Charles Alfred 1
HOUX, Frank L. 3
HOVANNES, John 5
HOVDE, Bryn J. 3
HOVELL, Albert Armand 3
HOVENDEN, Thomas H
HOVER, William Adgate 5
HOVERMAN, Russell Maas 6
HOVEY, Alvah 1
HOVEY, Alvin Peterson H
HOVEY, Chandler 4
HOVEY, Charles Edward H
HOVEY, Charles Mason H
HOVEY, Chester Ralph 5
HOVEY, Edmund Otis 1
HOVEY, George Rice 2
HOVEY, Henriette (Mrs. 5
Richard Hovey formerly
Mrs. Russell)
HOVEY, Horace Carter 1
HOVEY, Otis Ellis 2
HOVEY, Rexford William 5
HOVEY, Richard 1
HOVEY, William Simmons 3
HOVGAARD, William 2
HOVING, Johannes 5
HOVIS, William Forney 4
HOVLAND, Carl I. 4
HOW, Louis 2
HOWARD, A. Philo 6
HOWARD, A. T. 3
HOWARD, Ada Lydia 1
HOWARD, (Alan) Campbell 5
Palmer
HOWARD, Albert Andrew 1
HOWARD, Alfred Taylor 2
HOWARD, Alice Sturtevant 2
HOWARD, Alvin Hayward 5
HOWARD, Arthur 1
Ethelbert Day
HOWARD, Arthur Platt 1
HOWARD, Bailey Kneiriem 6
HOWARD, Ben Odell 5
HOWARD, Benjamin H
HOWARD, Benjamin Chew H
HOWARD, Blanche Willis 1
HOWARD, Bronson 1
HOWARD, Burt Estes 1
HOWARD, Burton James 1
HOWARD, Cecil de 3
Blaquiere
HOWARD, Charles Abner 6
HOWARD, Charles 4
Benjamin
HOWARD, Charles 2
Danforth
HOWARD, Charles Lowell 6
HOWARD, Charles 4
Pagelsen

HOWARD, Charles S. 3
HOWARD, Clara Eliza 1
HOWARD, Clarence Henry 1
HOWARD, Claud 5
HOWARD, Clifford 2
HOWARD, Clinton Norman 3
HOWARD, Clinton Wilbur 3
HOWARD, Dowell J. 3
HOWARD, Earl Dean 3
HOWARD, Eddy 4
HOWARD, Edgar 3
HOWARD, Edgar Billings 2
HOWARD, Edward D. 6
HOWARD, Edward Orson 3
HOWARD, Emma Pease 1
HOWARD, Eric 2
HOWARD, Ernest E. 3
HOWARD, Sir Esme 3
William
HOWARD, Everette B. 3
HOWARD, Ezra Lee 5
HOWARD, Francis W. 2
HOWARD, Frank Atherton 4
HOWARD, Frank Eugene 1
HOWARD, Fred Leslie 1
HOWARD, Frederic Hollis 5
HOWARD, George Bronson 1
HOWARD, George C. H
HOWARD, George Elliott 1
HOWARD, George H. 1
HOWARD, George H. 4
HOWARD, Graeme Keith 4
HOWARD, Guy Clemens 5
HOWARD, H. Clay 1
HOWARD, Harry Clay 1
HOWARD, Harvey James 3
HOWARD, Hector 4
Holdbrook
HOWARD, Henry H
HOWARD, Henry * 1
HOWARD, Henry 3
HOWARD, Herbert Burr 1
HOWARD, Jacob Merritt H
HOWARD, James E. 1
HOWARD, James Leland 6
HOWARD, James Quay 3
HOWARD, James Raley 3
HOWARD, John Don 6
HOWARD, John Eager H
HOWARD, John Galen 1
HOWARD, John Raymond 1
HOWARD, John Tasker 4
HOWARD, Joseph Jr. 1
HOWARD, Joseph Henry 1
HOWARD, Joseph Whitney 5
HOWARD, Julia Palmer 5
HOWARD, Kathleen 4
HOWARD, Lawrence 6
Augustus
HOWARD, Leland Ossian 3
HOWARD, Leslie 2
HOWARD, Louis Orrin 4
HOWARD, Lowry Samuel 2
HOWARD, Margaret 6
Douglas
HOWARD, Marion Edith 4
HOWARD, Mildred 6
Langford
HOWARD, Milford W. 4
HOWARD, Nathaniel 2
Lamson
HOWARD, Oliver Otis 1
HOWARD, Perry W. 3
HOWARD, Perry Wilbon 5
HOWARD, Philip Eugene 1
HOWARD, Ralph Hills 1
HOWARD, Robert 4
Mayburn
HOWARD, Rossiter 2
HOWARD, Roy Wilson 1
HOWARD, Seth Edwin 1
HOWARD, Sidney Coe 1
HOWARD, Thomas Benton 1
HOWARD, Tilgham H
Ashurst
HOWARD, Timothy 1
Edward
HOWARD, Velma Swanston 5
HOWARD, Volney Erskine H
HOWARD, Walter 1
HOWARD, Walter Eugene 1
HOWARD, Walter 2
Lafayette
HOWARD, Wendell 4
Stanton
HOWARD, Wesley O. 1
HOWARD, Wilbert Harvard 4
HOWARD, William H
Alanson
HOWARD, William Clyde 3
HOWARD, William Eager 5
Jr.
HOWARD, William Gibbs 2
HOWARD, William 1
Lauriston

HOWARD, William Lee 1
HOWARD, William 1
Marcellus
HOWARD, William Schley 5
HOWARD, William Travis 1
HOWARD, Willie 3
HOWARTH, Ellen 1
Clementine
HOWAT, William Frederick 1
HOWBERT, Irving 1
HOWDEN, Frederick 2
Bingham
HOWE, Albert Richards H
HOWE, Albion Parris H
HOWE, Andrew Jackson H
HOWE, Anna Belknap 1
HOWE, Archibald Murray 1
HOWE, Arthur 3
HOWE, Arthur Millidge 2
HOWE, Burton Alonzo 2
HOWE, Carl 2
HOWE, Carl Ellis 4
HOWE, Charles Sumner 1
HOWE, Church 1
HOWE, Clarence Decatur 4
HOWE, Daniel Wait 1
HOWE, Edgar F. 5
HOWE, Edgar Watson 1
HOWE, Edmund Grant 3
HOWE, Edward Gardner 1
HOWE, Edward Leavitt 3
HOWE, Elias 1
HOWE, Ernest 1
HOWE, Frank William 1
HOWE, Frederic Clemson 1
HOWE, Frederic William 3
HOWE, Frederic William Jr. 4
HOWE, Frederick Stanley 1
HOWE, Frederick Webster 1
HOWE, Gene Alexander 3
HOWE, George 1
HOWE, George 1
HOWE, George 3
HOWE, George 5
HOWE, George Augustus 4
HOWE, George Maxwell 5
HOWE, Harland Bradley 2
HOWE, Harley Earl 4
HOWE, Harold 5
HOWE, Harrison Estell 4
HOWE, Helen 6
HOWE, Henry 1
HOWE, Henry Marion 1
HOWE, Henry Saltonstall 1
HOWE, Henry V(an 6
Wagsten)
HOWE, Herbert Alonzo 1
HOWE, Herbert Crombie 1
HOWE, Herbert Marshall 1
HOWE, J. Olin 1
HOWE, James Blake 1
HOWE, James Lewis 3
HOWE, John Benedict 1
HOWE, John H. H
HOWE, John Ireland 1
HOWE, John Lynn 6
HOWE, John W. H
HOWE, Jonas Holland 1
HOWE, Julia Ward 1
HOWE, Lois Lilley 4
HOWE, Louis McHenry 1
HOWE, Lucien 1
HOWE, Malverd Abijah 4
HOWE, Mark Antony De 1
Wolfe
HOWE, Mark De Wolfe 4
HOWE, Mark-Anthony De H
Wolfe
HOWE, Marshall Avery 1
HOWE, Mary 4
HOWE, Percival S. Jr. 4
HOWE, Percival Spurr 4
HOWE, Percy Rogers 2
HOWE, Ralph S. 1
HOWE, Reginald Heber * 1
HOWE, Richard Flint 1
HOWE, Robert H
HOWE, Samuel 1
HOWE, Samuel Burnett 1
HOWE, Samuel Gridley 1
HOWE, Stanley H. 3
HOWE, Stewart Samuel 5
HOWE, Thomas Carr 1
HOWE, Thomas Marshall H
HOWE, Thomas Y. Jr. H
HOWE, Timothy Otis H
HOWE, Wallis Eastburn 1
HOWE, Walter 1
HOWE, Walter 2
HOWE, Walter Bruce 3
HOWE, Will David 2
HOWE, Willard B. 1
HOWE, William * H
HOWE, William Augustus 1
HOWE, William Francis 3
HOWE, William Henry 1

HOWE, William Wirt 1
HOWE, Wirt 1
HOWEL, Clayton James 6
HOWELL, A. Brazier 4
HOWELL, Alfred Corey 4
HOWELL, Arthur Holmes 1
HOWELL, Benjamin
 Franklin
HOWELL, Charles Cook 4
HOWELL, Charles Fish 2
HOWELL, Charles Robert 6
HOWELL, Clark 1
HOWELL, Clark 4
HOWELL, Corwin 6
HOWELL, Daniel Lane
HOWELL, Daniel William 2
HOWELL, David H
HOWELL, Edward H
HOWELL, Edward Vernon 2
HOWELL, Edwin Eugene
HOWELL, Edwin Hite 4
HOWELL, Elias
HOWELL, Evan P. 1
HOWELL, Francis Singleton 1
HOWELL, George 4
HOWELL, George Blaine 4
HOWELL, Herbert P. 2
HOWELL, Hilton Emory 5
HOWELL, J. Morton 1
HOWELL, James Albert Jr. 6
HOWELL, James Bruen 1
HOWELL, James Edward 1
HOWELL, Jeremiah Brown H
HOWELL, John Adams 1
HOWELL, John Adams 4
HOWELL, John Carnett 1
HOWELL, John White 1
HOWELL, Joseph H
HOWELL, Joseph A. 3
HOWELL, Julius Franklin 2
HOWELL, Mary Seymour 1
HOWELL, Max Don 4
HOWELL, Meta Pauline 5
HOWELL, Nathaniel H
 Woodhull
HOWELL, R. Beecher
HOWELL, Reese M. 4
HOWELL, Richard H
HOWELL, Robert Boyte H
 Crawford
HOWELL, Roger William 5
HOWELL, Walter Rufus 2
HOWELL, William Barberle 1
HOWELL, William Henry 2
HOWELL, Williamson S. Jr. 2
HOWELLS, John Mead 3
HOWELLS, Mildred 5
HOWELLS, William Dean 1
HOWER, Harry Sloan 2
HOWER, Milton Otis 1
HOWER, Paul Allen 4
HOWER, Ralph M. 6
HOWERTH, Ira Woods 1
HOWERTON, James
 Robert
HOWES, Benjamin Alfred 3
HOWES, Ernest Grant 3
HOWES, Ethel Dench 3
 Puffer
HOWES, Frank Stewart 6
HOWES, George Edwin 4
HOWES, Herbert Harold 1
HOWES, Royce B. 5
HOWES, William 4
 Washington
HOWEY, Benjamin Franklin H
HOWEY, Walter Crawford 3
HOWEY, William John 2
HOWIE, Robert George 3
HOWISON, George Holmes 1
HOWISON, Henry 1
 Lycurgus
HOWISON, Robert Reid 1
HOWKINS, Elizabeth 5
 Penrose
HOWLAND, Alfred 1
 Cornelius
HOWLAND, Arthur
 Charles
HOWLAND, Benjamin H
HOWLAND, Charles P. 1
HOWLAND, Charles 2
 Roscoe
HOWLAND, Emily 1
HOWLAND, Frances 4
 Louise
HOWLAND, Fred Arthur 3
HOWLAND, Frederick 1
 Hoppin
HOWLAND, Gardiner H
 Greene
HOWLAND, Gardiner 2
 Greene
HOWLAND, Garth A. 3
HOWLAND, Harold 4
HOWLAND, Henry Elias 1

HOWLAND, Henry 1
 Raymond
HOWLAND, Hewitt 2
 Hanson
HOWLAND, John 1
HOWLAND, Joseph Briggs 5
HOWLAND, Leroy Albert 6
HOWLAND, Louis 1
HOWLAND, Marguerite 6
 Elizabeth Smith (Mrs.
 Cecil M. Howland)
HOWLAND, Murray 3
 Shipley
HOWLAND, Paul 2
HOWLAND, Richard Smith 4
HOWLAND, Silas Wilder 1
HOWLAND, Thomas Smith 1
HOWLAND, William 2
HOWLAND, William Bailey 1
HOWLETT, Freeman 5
 S(mith)
HOWLETT, James David 1
HOWLETT, Walter Main 5
HOWRY, Richard H
HOWRY, Charles Bowen 1
HOWSE, Hilary Ewing 1
HOWSE, William Massy 6
 Godwin
HOWSON, Elmer Thomas 2
HOWSON, Roger 4
HOWZE, Henry Russell 5
HOWZE, Robert Lee 1
HOXIE, George Luke 5
HOXIE, Harold Jennings 5
HOXIE, Richard Leveridge 1
HOXIE, Robert Franklin 1
HOXIE, Solomon 1
HOXIE, Vinnie Ream 1
HOXTON, Archibald 5
 Robinson
HOXTON, Llewellyn 4
 Griffith
HOXTON, William Winslow 1
HOXWORTH, Stephen A. 4
HOY, Albert Harris 5
HOY, Carson 4
HOY, Patrick Henry 6
HOYER, Theodore 4
HOYLE, Eli DuBose 1
HOYME, Gjermund H
HOYNE, Archibald 4
 Lawrence
HOYNE, Thomas Maclay 1
HOYNE, Thomas Temple 2
HOYNES, William 1
HOYNS, Henry 2
HOYO, John Charles 3
HOYT, Albert Ellis 4
HOYT, Albert Harrison 4
HOYT, Alex Crawford 6
HOYT, Allen Grey 1
HOYT, Arthur Stephen 4
HOYT, Burnham 3
HOYT, Charles Albert 4
HOYT, Charles Hale 1
HOYT, Charles Kimball 4
HOYT, Charles Oliver 1
HOYT, Colgate 1
HOYT, Colgate 3
HOYT, Creig Simmons 3
HOYT, David Webster 1
HOYT, Deristhe Lavinta 5
HOYT, Edward C. 1
HOYT, Elizabeth Stone 6
HOYT, Elton II 4
HOYT, Francis Southack 1
HOYT, Franklin Chase 1
HOYT, Harold Wardwell 3
HOYT, Helen Brown 4
HOYT, Henry Augustus 4
HOYT, Henry Martyn H
HOYT, James Alfred 3
HOYT, James Humphrey 1
HOYT, James Phillips 1
HOYT, John Clayton 2
HOYT, John Philo 1
HOYT, John Sherman 3
HOYT, John Wesley 1
HOYT, Lucius Warner 1
HOYT, Minerva Hamilton 4
HOYT, Phillis Lucille 5
HOYT, Ralph H
HOYT, Ralph Wilson 4
HOYT, Richard Farnsworth 1
HOYT, Robert Stuart 5
HOYT, W. Henry 3
HOYT, Wayland 1
HOYT, Wilbur Franklin 1
HOYT, William Dana 2
HOYT, William Greeley 4
HRDLICKA, Ales 1
HROMADKA, Josef Luki 5
HSIA, David Yi-Yung 5
HSU, Mo 5
HUARD, Leo A(lbert) 5

HUBARD, Edmund Wilcox H
HUBARD, Robert Thruston 1
HUBARD, William James H
 Skinner
HUBBARD, Adolphus 1
 Skinner
HUBBARD, Alice 1
HUBBARD, Anita Day 1
HUBBARD, Asahel Wheeler H
HUBBARD, Bernard 4
 Rosecrans
HUBBARD, Carlisle Le 6
 Compte
HUBBARD, Charles J. 3
HUBBARD, Charles Wells 3
HUBBARD, Chester 1
 Dorman
HUBBARD, David H
HUBBARD, Demas Jr. H
HUBBARD, Elbert 1
HUBBARD, Elbert H
 Hamilton
HUBBARD, Elijah Kent 1
HUBBARD, Frances 5
 Virginia
HUBBARD, Frank Gaylord 1
HUBBARD, Frank 1
 McKinney
HUBBARD, Frank W. 2
HUBBARD, Frederick A. 3
HUBBARD, Gardiner H
 Greene
HUBBARD, George David 3
HUBBARD, George Henry 4
HUBBARD, George 4
 Whipple
HUBBARD, Giles Munro 3
HUBBARD, Gurdon H
 Saltonstall
HUBBARD, Harry H
HUBBARD, Havrah William 5
 Lines
HUBBARD, Henry H
HUBBARD, Henry H
 Griswold
HUBBARD, Henry 1
 Guernsey
HUBBARD, Henry Vincent 2
HUBBARD, Henry Wright 1
HUBBARD, Howard S. 4
HUBBARD, John * 1
HUBBARD, John 1
HUBBARD, John Charles 3
HUBBARD, John Henry 1
HUBBARD, John W. 2
HUBBARD, Jonathan Hatch H
HUBBARD, Joseph Stillman H
HUBBARD, Kin 1
HUBBARD, Leslie Elmer 4
HUBBARD, L(everett) 6
 Marsden
HUBBARD, Levi 1
HUBBARD, Lucius 1
 Frederick
HUBBARD, Lucius Lee 1
HUBBARD, Moses Gilbert 4
HUBBARD, Nathaniel 3
 Mead Jr.
HUBBARD, Oliver Payson 1
HUBBARD, Richard Bennet 1
HUBBARD, Richard 1
 Bennett
HUBBARD, Richard Dudley H
HUBBARD, Russell Sturgis 5
HUBBARD, S. Dana 1
HUBBARD, Samuel H
 Dickinson
HUBBARD, Samuel 1
 Fairfield
HUBBARD, Sara Anderson 1
HUBBARD, Theodora 1
 Kimball
HUBBARD, Thomas 4
HUBBARD, Thomas 1
 Hamlin
HUBBARD, Thomas Hill H
HUBBARD, Walter 1
 Comstock
HUBBARD, Walton 3
HUBBARD, William 1
HUBBARD, William H. 1
HUBBARD, William Henry 1
HUBBARD, William 1
 Pallister
HUBBARD, Wynant Davis 4
HUBBART, Henry Clyde 4
HUBBART, Ralph 3
HUBBELL, Alvin Allace 1
HUBBELL, Benjamin S. 4
HUBBELL, Burt G. 1
HUBBELL, Charles Bulkley 1
HUBBELL, Clarence W. 3
HUBBELL, Edwin Nelson 1
HUBBELL, Frederick 1
 Marion
HUBBELL, Frederick 3
 Windsor

HUBBELL, Grover Cooper 3
HUBBELL, Harry Mortimer 5
HUBBELL, Harvey 5
HUBBELL, Henry Salem 1
HUBBELL, Henry Salem 5
HUBBELL, Henry Wilson 1
HUBBELL, James Randolph H
HUBBELL, James Wakeman 2
HUBBELL, Jay Abel 1
HUBBELL, Raymond 1
HUBBELL, William Spring H
HUBBERT, James Monroe 3
HUBBLE, Edwin Powell 3
HUBBS, John Brewster 1
HUBBS, Rebecca 1
HUBENY, Maximilian John 2
HUBER, Carl Parker 1
HUBER, Charles Frederick 4
HUBER, Charles Henry 4
HUBER, Edward Godfrey 2
HUBER, G. Carl 1
HUBER, Harold 4
HUBER, Harvey Evert 3
HUBER, Henry Allen 4
HUBER, John Bessner 1
HUBER, John Greenleaf 4
HUBER, Max 3
HUBER, Miriam Blanton 3
HUBER, Phil 3
HUBER, Ray Allen 3
HUBER, Seba Cormany 2
HUBER, Walter Leroy 4
HUBERICH, Charles Henry 2
HUBERMAN, Leo 5
HUBERT, Benjamin 1
 Franklin
HUBERT, Conrad H
HUBERT, Conrad 4
HUBERT, Philip Aklis 1
HUBERT, Philip Gengembre 1
HUBERTH, Martin Francis 4
HUBERTY, Martin R. 4
HUBLER, Edward Lorenzo 4
HUBLEY, Edward Burd H
HUBLEY, George Wilbur 2
HUBNER, Charles William 1
HUBSCHMAN, Albert 3
HUCHINGSON, James 6
 Edwin
HUCKEL, Oliver 1
HUDD, Thomas Richard H
HUDDE, Andries H
HUDDLE, J. Klahr 3
HUDDLESON, I. Forest 4
HUDDLESTON, George 1
HUDDLESTON, George Jr. 5
HUDDLESTON, John 1
 Henry
HUDDY, George Henry Jr. 1
HUDDY, R(ichard) 6
 T(homas)
HUDGENS, Robert Smith 4
HUDGINS, Edward Wren 3
HUDGINS, Houlder 4
HUDGINS, Morgan Hughes 6
HUDNUT, Joseph 4
HUDNUT, William Herbert 4
HUDSON, Albert Blellock 2
HUDSON, Buell W. 4
HUDSON, Ceylon E. 6
HUDSON, Charles H
HUDSON, Claude Silbert 3
HUDSON, Daniel E. 4
HUDSON, Edward H
HUDSON, Erasmus Darwin H
HUDSON, Eric 1
HUDSON, Frederic H
HUDSON, Frederick 6
 Mitchell
HUDSON, George Elford 6
HUDSON, Grant Martin 3
HUDSON, Henry H
HUDSON, Henry Norman H
HUDSON, Hoyt Hopewell 2
HUDSON, James Fairchild 1
HUDSON, James Henry 2
HUDSON, Jay William 3
HUDSON, John Elbridge 1
HUDSON, John Rogers 4
HUDSON, Joseph Kennedy 1
HUDSON, Joseph Lowthian 1
HUDSON, Manley Ottmer 4
HUDSON, Millard Fillmore 4
HUDSON, Paul Bateman 5
HUDSON, Ralph 5
HUDSON, Richard 1
HUDSON, Richard 3
 Bradshaw
HUDSON, Richard Furman 4
HUDSON, Richard Furman 1
 Jr.
HUDSON, Robert Littleton 6
HUDSON, Samuel Eddy 4
HUDSON, Samuel Henry 4
HUDSON, Thomas Henry 4
HUDSON, Thomson Jay 1

HUDSON, Washington 4
 Elias
HUDSON, William 1
 Cadwalader
HUDSON, William Henry 4
HUDSON, William 4
 Mestrezat
HUDSON, William Smith H
HUDSON, Woodward 1
HUDSPETH, Andrew H. 5
HUDSPETH, Benoni 5
HUDSPETH, C. B. 5
HUDSPETH, Robert Hill 5
HUDSPETH, Robert S. 1
HUDTLOFF, Martin John 5
HUEBNER, Clarence R. 5
HUEBNER, Herbert 6
 Alloway
HUEBNER, Solomon 4
 Stephen
HUEBSCH, B. W. 4
HUETER, Hans Herbert 6
HUEY, Samuel Baird 1
HUFF, George A. 1
HUFF, George Franklin 1
HUFF, Joseph Bascomb 2
HUFF, Slaughter William 2
HUFF, William Bashford 4
HUFFARD, James Hudson 5
HUFFARD, Paul Phillippi 4
HUFFCUT, Ernest Wilson 1
HUFFMAN, Eugene Harvey 6
HUFFMAN, Laton Alton H
HUFFMAN, Laton Alton 4
HUFFMAN, Oscar 1
 Caperton
HUFNAGEL, Edward 2
 Henry
HUFNAGEL, Frederick 6
 Bernhard
HUFTY, Jacob H
HUG, George Willard 1
HUGE, Wilbert Erwin 1
HUGER, Alfred 1
HUGER, Benjamin * H
HUGER, Daniel H
HUGER, Daniel Eliott H
HUGER, Francis Kinloch H
HUGER, Isaac H
HUGER, John H
HUGER, William Harleston 1
HUGET, J. Percival 4
HUGGARD, Vincent P. 6
HUGGENVIK, Theodore 5
HUGGINS, Eli Lundy 1
HUGGINS, George 4
 Augustus
HUGGINS, Miller James H
HUGGINS, Miller James 1
HUGGINS, R. Paul 4
HUGGINS, Raleigh Russell 1
HUGGINS, Richard 5
 Emmett
HUGGINS, William Lloyd 1
HUGGINS, William Ogburn 1
HUGHAN, Jessie Wallace 4
HUGHES, Aaron Konkle 1
HUGHES, Adella Prentiss 4
HUGHES, Albert Raymond 4
HUGHES, Charles H
HUGHES, Charles Colfax 2
HUGHES, Charles Evans 2
HUGHES, Charles Evans Jr. 2
HUGHES, Charles Frank 3
HUGHES, Charles 1
 Frederick
HUGHES, Charles Hamilton 4
HUGHES, Charles Haynes 1
HUGHES, Charles James Jr. 1
HUGHES, Christopher H
HUGHES, Daphne 6
HUGHES, David Edward H
HUGHES, Donald James 4
HUGHES, Dudley Mays 2
HUGHES, Edward 1
 Smallwood
HUGHES, Edwin 4
HUGHES, Edwin Holt 2
HUGHES, Ellwood Clarke 1
HUGHES, Eugene Melvin 4
HUGHES, Everett S. 3
HUGHES, Francis Massie 4
HUGHES, Fred C. 1
HUGHES, George E. 4
HUGHES, George Wurtz H
HUGHES, Gerald 3
HUGHES, Harold L. 3
HUGHES, Hatcher 1
HUGHES, Hector James 1
HUGHES, Helen Sard 3
HUGHES, Henry H
HUGHES, Herman Yeary 1
HUGHES, Hermann James 3
HUGHES, Howard Robard 6
HUGHES, I. Lamont; 6
HUGHES, James H

* Indicates More Than One Such Name Listed

HUGHES, James Anthony 1
HUGHES, James Fredric 1
HUGHES, James H. 3
HUGHES, James Madison H
HUGHES, James Monroe 6
HUGHES, James P. 4
HUGHES, John Chambers 5
HUGHES, John H. 3
HUGHES, John Henry 5
HUGHES, John Joseph 4
HUGHES, John Newton 2
HUGHES, John T. 5
HUGHES, J(ohn) W(illiam) 6
HUGHES, Joseph E. 4
HUGHES, Langston 1
HUGHES, Levi Allen 1
HUGHES, Louis C. 1
HUGHES, Mack F. 6
HUGHES, Matt Simpson 5
HUGHES, Merritt Yerkes 5
HUGHES, Mildred E. 5
HUGHES, Oliver John 1
  Davis
HUGHES, Percy 3
HUGHES, Percy Meredith 1
HUGHES, Peter Davis 1
HUGHES, Phillip Samuel 1
HUGHES, Price H
HUGHES, Ray Osgood 3
HUGHES, Raymond 3
  Mollyneaux
HUGHES, Rees Hopkins 6
HUGHES, Reynold King 6
HUGHES, Richard Cecil 1
HUGHES, Robert Ball H
HUGHES, Robert Hugh 6
HUGHES, Robert M. Jr. 3
HUGHES, Robert Morton 1
HUGHES, Robert Patterson 1
HUGHES, Robert William 1
HUGHES, Rowland Roberts 3
HUGHES, Royal Delaney 1
HUGHES, Rupert 3
HUGHES, Russell Houston 5
HUGHES, Simon P. 1
HUGHES, Talmage Coates 4
HUGHES, Thomas Aloysius 4
HUGHES, Thomas Hurst 1
HUGHES, Thomas Patrick 1
HUGHES, Thomas Welburn 2
HUGHES, Wilburn Patrick 6
HUGHES, William 1
HUGHES, William Edgar 4
HUGHES, William F. 1
HUGHES, William Joseph 1
HUGHES, William Leonard 3
HUGHEY, Allen Harrison 6
HUGHITT, Marvin 1
HUGHITT, Marvin Jr. 2
HUGHSTON, Jonas Abbott H
HUGO, Albert Carl 3
HUGO, Trevanion William 4
HUGUELET, Guy 3
  Alexander
HUGUNIN, Daniel Jr. H
HUGUS, Wright 1
HUHLEIN, Charles 1
  Frederic
HUHN, John Ernest 6
HUHNER, Leon 3
HUHNER, Max 1
HUIDEKOPER, Arthur 1
  Clarke
HUIDEKOPER, Frederic H
HUIDEKOPER, Frederic 1
  Louis
HUIDEKOPER, Frederic 5
  Wolters
HUIDEKOPER, Harm Jan 1
HUIDEKOPER, Henry H
  Shippen
HUIDEKOPER, Reginald 2
  Shippen
HUIDEKOPER, Rush 1
  Shippen
HUIZENGA, Lee Sjoerds 2
HUIZINGA, Arnold van C. 3
  P.
HUIZINGA, Henry 2
HUKILL, Edwin Martin 4
HUKILL, Ralph LeRoy 5
HUKRIEDE, Theodore W. 6
HULBERT, Archer Butler 1
HULBERT, Calvin Butler 1
HULBERT, Edmund Daniel 1
HULBERT, Eri Baker 1
HULBERT, Geroge Murray 3
HULBERT, Henry Carlton 1
HULBERT, Henry 1
  Woodward
HULBERT, Homer B. 1
HULBERT, John Whitefield H
HULBERT, Milan Hulbert 1
HULBERT, William 1
  Davenport
HULBURD, Calvin Tilden H

HULBURD, Charles Henry 1
HULBURT, David Willey 1
HULBURT, Lorrain 2
  Sherman
HULBURT, Ray Garland 2
HULEN, John Augustus 3
HULEN, Rubey Mosley 5
HULETT, Edwin Lee 2
HULETT, George Augustus 3
HULICK, George 3
  Washington
HULICK, Peter Vaughn 5
HULING, Ray Greene 1
HULING, Sara Hawks 1
HULINGS, Garnet 1
HULINGS, Willis James 1
HULINGS, Willis James 4
HULL, Albert Wallace 4
HULL, Alexander 3
HULL, Charles Henry 1
HULL, Clark Leonard 3
HULL, Cordell 3
HULL, David Carlisle 1
HULL, David Denton 2
HULL, George Huntington 1
HULL, George Ross 3
HULL, Gordon Ferrie 1
HULL, Harry Edward 1
HULL, Isaac H
HULL, James Meriwether 6
HULL, (James) Roger 5
HULL, John H
HULL, John Adley 2
HULL, John Albert Tiffin 1
HULL, John Edwin 6
HULL, Josephine 3
HULL, Lawrence Cameron 4
HULL, Merlin 3
HULL, Morton Denison 1
HULL, Nathan P. 3
HULL, Robert Johnson 4
HULL, Robert William 5
HULL, Roger Benton 1
HULL, Theodore Young 1
HULL, Thomas Everett 4
HULL, William H
HULL, William Chase 6
HULL, William Edgar 2
HULL, William Isaac 1
HULLEY, Lincoln 1
HULLFISH, H. Gordon 4
HULLIHEN, Simon P. H
HULLIHEN, Walter 1
HULLINGER, Edwin Ware 5
HULME, Edward Maslin 5
HULME, Thomas Wilkins 1
HULME, William Henry 1
HULSE, George Egbert 4
HULSE, Hiram Richard 1
HULSHIZER, Stanford 5
HULST, Nelson Powell 1
HULSWIT, Charles Louis 6
HULSWIT, Frank Theodore 4
HULT, Adolf 1
HULT, Gottfried Emanuel 3
HULTEN, Charles M. 4
HULTEN, Herman H. 5
HULTMAN, Ivar Ninus 4
HULTZ, Fred Samuel 4
HULVEY, Otey Crawford 5
HUMASON, Harry Byrd 5
HUMASON, M. L. 5
HUMBER, Robert Lee 5
HUMBERT, Jean Joseph H
  Amable
HUMBERT, Russell J. 4
HUMBIRD, John Alexander 4
HUME, Alfred 4
HUME, Cyril 4
HUME, David 5
HUME, David Milford 6
HUME, Edgar Erskine 3
HUME, Edward Hicks 4
HUME, H. Harold 5
HUME, James Cleland 4
HUME, Leland 4
HUME, Nelson 3
HUME, Omer Forest 3
HUME, Robert Allen 1
HUME, Robert Ernest 2
HUME, Thomas 1
HUME, William H
HUME, William 2
HUMES, Augustine 3
  Leftwich
HUMES, Harold Louis 5
HUMES, Thomas William H
HUMMEL, Arthur William 6
HUMMEL, George F. 3
HUMMEL, George Henry 2
HUMMEL, R. A. 3
HUMMEL, William 3
  Grandville
HUMPHREY, Alexander 1
  Pope

HUMPHREY, Arthur 1
  Luther
HUMPHREY, Caroline 5
  Louise
HUMPHREY, Charles H
HUMPHREY, Charles 1
  Frederic
HUMPHREY, Charles 5
  Frederick Jr.
HUMPHREY, Doris 3
HUMPHREY, Edward 3
  Frank
HUMPHREY, Evan H. 5
HUMPHREY, George 2
  Colvin
HUMPHREY, George Duke 6
HUMPHREY, George 5
  Magoffin
HUMPHREY, George 5
  Thomas
HUMPHREY, Harry Baker 3
HUMPHREY, Harry Jasper 6
HUMPHREY, Helen F. 4
HUMPHREY, Heman H
HUMPHREY, Henry H. 2
HUMPHREY, Herman 1
  Leon
HUMPHREY, Herman Loin 1
HUMPHREY, J. Otis 1
HUMPHREY, James H
HUMPHREY, Lewis Craig 1
HUMPHREY, Lyman 1
  Underwood
HUMPHREY, Marie E. Ives 1
HUMPHREY, Nina S. 6
HUMPHREY, Reuben 1
HUMPHREY, Richard 1
  Lewis
HUMPHREY, Seth King 1
HUMPHREY, Walter R. 5
HUMPHREY, William 4
  Armine
HUMPHREY, William 4
  Brewster
HUMPHREY, William E. 1
HUMPHREY, William 3
  Francis
HUMPHREYS, Abram 4
  Stephanus
HUMPHREYS, Albert 5
  Edmund
HUMPHREYS, Albert 5
  Edmund
HUMPHREYS, Alexander 1
  Crombie
HUMPHREYS, Andrew H
  Atkinson
HUMPHREYS, Benjamin H
  Grubb
HUMPHREYS, Benjamin 1
  Grubb
HUMPHREYS, Charles H
HUMPHREYS, David H
HUMPHREYS, David 1
  Carlisle
HUMPHREYS, Frank 1
  Landon
HUMPHREYS, H. E. Jr. 4
HUMPHREYS, Harrie 2
  Moreland
HUMPHREYS, James H
HUMPHREYS, John J. H
HUMPHREYS, Joshua H
HUMPHREYS, Lester 1
  Warren
HUMPHREYS, Marie 1
  Champney
HUMPHREYS, Mary Gay 1
HUMPHREYS, Milton 1
  Wylie
HUMPHREYS, Parry H
  Wayne
HUMPHREYS, Richard 5
  F(ranklin)
HUMPHREYS, Robert 4
HUMPHREYS, Solon 1
HUMPHREYS, T(homas) 5
  Hadden
HUMPHREYS, Walter 5
HUMPHREYS, West H
  Hughes
HUMPHREYS, Willard 1
HUMPHREYS, William 2
  Jackson
HUMPHREYS, William 1
  Yerger
HUMPHRIES, (George) 5
  Rolfe
HUMPHRIES, John 1
  Edmund
HUMPHRISS, Charles H. 4
HUMPSTONE, Henry 3
  Judson
HUMSTONE, Walter 1
  Coutant
HUN, Henry 1

HUN, John Gale 2
HUND, H. E. H
HUNDLEY, Henry Rhodes 1
HUNDLEY, John Robinson 5
  Jr.
HUNDLEY, John Trible 4
  Thomas
HUNDLEY, Oscar R. 1
HUNEKE, William August 1
HUNEKER, James Gibbons 1
HUNGERFORD, Charles 5
  William
HUNGERFORD, Clark 4
HUNGERFORD, Edward 2
HUNGERFORD, Frank 1
  Louis
HUNGERFORD, John 1
  Newton
HUNGERFORD, John 1
  Pratt
HUNGERFORD, Orville H
HUNGERFORD, Samuel 3
  James
HUNKELER, Edward 5
  J(oseph)
HUNKER, John Jacob 1
HUNN, John 4
HUNNEMAN, William 3
  Cooper Jr.
HUNNER, Guy LeRoy 3
HUNNEWELL, Horatio H
  Hollis
HUNNEWELL, James H
HUNNEWELL, James 1
  Frothingham
HUNNEWELL, Walter 1
HUNNICUTT, Warren 5
  Towers
HUNSAKER, Walter 1
  Jerome
HUNSICKER, William 6
  Cosgrove Jr.
HUNT, Albert Clarence 3
HUNT, Albert Henry 4
HUNT, Alfred Ephraim H
HUNT, Andrew Murray 1
HUNT, Arthur Prince 1
HUNT, Benjamin Weeks 1
HUNT, Carleton 1
HUNT, Caroline Louisa 1
HUNT, Charles Wallace 1
HUNT, Charles Warren 1
HUNT, Charles Wesley 6
HUNT, Clara Whitehill 3
HUNT, Clyde Du Vernet 4
HUNT, D. F. 3
HUNT, Duane Garrison 4
HUNT, Edward Eyre 2
HUNT, Emory William 1
HUNT, Ernest Leroi 2
HUNT, Evert Merle 5
HUNT, Frank W. 1
HUNT, Frazier H
HUNT, Frederick Salisbury 2
HUNT, Frederick Vinton 5
HUNT, Freeman H
HUNT, Gaillard 1
HUNT, George Edwin 1
HUNT, George Wylie Paul 1
HUNT, Graham Putnam 3
HUNT, Haroldson Lafayette 6
HUNT, Harriet Larned 4
HUNT, Harriot Kezia H
HUNT, Harry Hampton 1
HUNT, Henry Jackson H
HUNT, Henry Thomas 6
HUNT, Henry Warren 1
HUNT, Hiram Paine 1
HUNT, Isaac H
HUNT, Isaac Hamilton 1
HUNT, James Bennett H
HUNT, James Gallaway 1
HUNT, James Ramsay 2
HUNT, James Stone 1
HUNT, James Winford 5
HUNT, Joe Byron 6
HUNT, John Thomas 4
HUNT, Jonathan H
HUNT, Leigh 3
HUNT, Leigh S. J. 1
HUNT, Lester Callaway 3
HUNT, Levi Clarence 1
HUNT, LeRoy Philip 4
HUNT, Livingston 2
HUNT, Mabel Leigh 5
HUNT, Marion Palmer 5
HUNT, Mary Hannah 1
HUNT, Myron 3
HUNT, Nathan H
HUNT, O(ra) E(lmer) 5
HUNT, Ormond Edson 4
HUNT, Ralph Hudson 3
HUNT, Ralph Leslie 6
HUNT, Ralph Waldo 5
  Emerson
HUNT, Reid 2

HUNT, Richard Carley 3
HUNT, Richard Howland H
HUNT, Richard Morris H
HUNT, Robert H
HUNT, Robert Woolston 1
HUNT, Roy Arthur 4
HUNT, Samuel H
HUNT, Samuel Furman 1
HUNT, Seth Bliss 2
HUNT, Sumner P. 1
HUNT, Theodore Gallard 1
HUNT, Theodore Whitefield 1
HUNT, Thomas Forsyth 1
HUNT, Thomas Sterry H
HUNT, Walter Reid 5
HUNT, Ward H
HUNT, Washington H
HUNT, Westley Marshall 3
HUNT, William Chamberlin 4
HUNT, William Gibbes H
HUNT, William Henry 2
HUNT, William Henry H
HUNT, William Morris H
HUNT, William Peter H
HUNT, William Prescott 1
HUNT, William Southworth 1
HUNT, Wilson Price H
HUNTER, Aaron Burtis 3
HUNTER, Adison I. 1
HUNTER, Alexander Stuart 1
HUNTER, Alfred M. 1
HUNTER, Andrew H
HUNTER, Andrew Jackson 4
HUNTER, Arthur 1
HUNTER, Charles Francis 6
HUNTER, Charles O. 5
HUNTER, Croil 5
HUNTER, Dard H
HUNTER, David H
HUNTER, Edward 1
HUNTER, Fred Heaton 5
HUNTER, Frederick 6
  Maurice
HUNTER, George Bowditch 4
HUNTER, George King 1
HUNTER, George Leland 1
HUNTER, George 2
  McPherson
HUNTER, George William 2
HUNTER, Guy 4
  Breckenridge
HUNTER, Hiram Tyram 2
HUNTER, Horace Talmage 4
HUNTER, Howard Louis 6
HUNTER, Howard Owen 4
HUNTER, Hubert Samuel 1
HUNTER, James Boyd 1
HUNTER, James Joseph 6
HUNTER, Jay Tyler 3
HUNTER, Jesse Coleman 2
HUNTER, Joel 3
HUNTER, John H
HUNTER, John 1
HUNTER, John F. 3
HUNTER, John Lathrop 1
HUNTER, Joseph Rufus 3
HUNTER, Kent A. 3
HUNTER, Louis James 1
HUNTER, Matthew Albert 4
HUNTER, Merlin Harold 2
HUNTER, Morton Craig H
HUNTER, Narsworthy 1
HUNTER, Oscar Benwood 3
HUNTER, Paull Stuart 5
HUNTER, R. M. 3
HUNTER, Richard 1
HUNTER, Richard Stockton 4
HUNTER, Robert H
HUNTER, Robert Mercer H
  Taliaferro
HUNTER, Rudolph Melville 1
HUNTER, Samuel John 2
HUNTER, Stephen 1
  Alexander
HUNTER, Thomas H
HUNTER, Thomas 1
HUNTER, Thomas 3
HUNTER, W. Godfrey 1
HUNTER, Walter David 1
HUNTER, Walter Samuel 5
HUNTER, Warren Clair 3
HUNTER, Wiles Robert 2
HUNTER, William * H
HUNTER, William 1
  Armstrong
HUNTER, William Boyd 5
HUNTER, William Forrest 1
HUNTER, William Forrest 1
HUNTER, William H. H
HUNTING, Fred Stanley 5
HUNTING, Gardner 4
HUNTING, George 1
  Coolidge
HUNTING, Walter Judson 5
HUNTINGTON, Abel H

HUNTINGTON, Adoniram 1
  Judson
HUNTINGTON, Albert 6
  Tracy
HUNTINGTON, Anna 6
  Hyatt (Mrs Archer M.
  Huntington)
HUNTINGTON, Archer 3
  Milton
HUNTINGTON, Arria 4
  Sargent
HUNTINGTON, Arthur 5
  Franklin
HUNTINGTON, Baldwin 3
  Gwynne
HUNTINGTON, Benjamin H
HUNTINGTON, Charles 4
  Clifford
HUNTINGTON, Charles 1
  Pratt
HUNTINGTON, Clarence 1
  William
HUNTINGTON, Collis
  Potter
HUNTINGTON, Daniel 1
HUNTINGTON, Daniel 3
  Trumbull
HUNTINGTON, David
  Lynde
HUNTINGTON, DeWitt 1
  Clinton
HUNTINGTON, Dorothy 5
  Phillips
HUNTINGTON, Ebenezer H
HUNTINGTON, Edward 3
  Vermilye
HUNTINGTON, Elisha H
HUNTINGTON, Ellsworth 2
HUNTINGTON, Emily 1
HUNTINGTON, Faye 4
HUNTINGTON, Ford 2
HUNTINGTON, Frances
  Carpenter (Mrs. William
  Chapin)
HUNTINGTON, Frank 1
HUNTINGTON, Frederic 1
  Dan
HUNTINGTON, George 1
HUNTINGTON, George 3
  Herbert
HUNTINGTON, George 1
  Sumner
HUNTINGTON, Harwood 1
HUNTINGTON, Henry 1
  Alonzo
HUNTINGTON, Henry 4
  Barrett
HUNTINGTON, Henry 1
  Edwards
HUNTINGTON, Jabez H
HUNTINGTON, Jabez H
  Williams
HUNTINGTON, James Otis 1
  Sargent
HUNTINGTON, Jedediah H
HUNTINGTON, Lloyd Lee 4
HUNTINGTON, Margaret 1
  Evans
HUNTINGTON, Oliver
  Whipple
HUNTINGTON, Richard 5
  Lee
HUNTINGTON, Robert 2
  Watkinson
HUNTINGTON, Samuel H
HUNTINGTON, Theodore 1
  Sollace
HUNTINGTON, Thomas 1
  Waterman
HUNTINGTON, Thomas 6
  Waterman
HUNTINGTON, Tuley 1
  Francis
HUNTINGTON, Warner 1
  Dare
HUNTINGTON, Whitney 4
  Clark
HUNTINGTON, William 3
  Chapin
HUNTINGTON, William 1
  Edwards
HUNTINGTON, William
  Reed
HUNTLEY, Charles R. 1
HUNTLEY, Chester Robert 6
  (Chet)
HUNTLEY, Elias DeWitt 1
HUNTLEY, Florence 1
HUNTLEY, Samantha 2
  Littlefield
HUNTLEY, Victoria Hutson 6
HUNTLEY, William Russell 6
HUNTON, Eppa 1
HUNTON, Eppa Jr. 1
HUNTON, William Lee 2

HUNTOON, Benjamin 1
  Bussey
HUNTOON, Gardner A. 5
HUNTOON, Louis 2
  Doremus
HUNTRESS, Carroll Benton 3
HUNTRESS, Frank G. 3
HUNTSMAN, Adam H
HUNTSMAN, Owen H
  Benjamin
HUNTSMAN, Robert F. R. 2
HUNZIKER, Otto Frederick 3
HUNZIKER, Richard 6
  Overton
HUPP, John Cox 4
HUPPER, Roscoe 4
  Henderson
HUPPERTZ, John William 6
HUPPUCH, Winfield A. 4
HURBAN, Vladimir S. 2
HURD, Albert Arthur 1
HURD, Archer Willis 3
HURD, Arthur William 1
HURD, Charles Edwin 1
HURD, Charles W.B. 5
HURD, Edward Melville 1
HURD, Edward Payson * 1
HURD, Eugene 1
HURD, Frank Hunt H
HURD, George Arthur 1
HURD, George Edward 5
HURD, Guilford Lansing 5
HURD, Harry Boyd 1
HURD, Harvey Bostwick 1
HURD, Henry Mills 1
HURD, John Codman H
HURD, Lee Maidment 2
HURD, Louis Guthrie 1
HURD, Nathaniel H
HURD, Richard Melancthon 1
HURD, William Daniel 1
HURDLE, James Ernest 5
HURDON, Elizabeth 4
HURFF, Lindley Scarlett 5
HURIE, Wiley Lin 5
HURLBERT, William Henry H
HURLBUT, Byron Satterlee 1
HURLBUT, Edwin Wilcox 1
HURLBUT, Jesse Lyman 1
HURLBUT, Stephen H
  Augustus
HURLBUT, William N. 3
HURLEY, Charles Francis 2
HURLEY, Edward Nash 1
HURLEY, Edward Timothy 4
HURLEY, George 3
HURLEY, James E. 1
HURLEY, James Franklin 1
HURLEY, John Patrick 2
HURLEY, John Richard 3
HURLEY, Joseph Patrick 4
HURLEY, Lawrence Francis 3
HURLEY, Leonard B. 4
HURLEY, Margaret Helene 4
HURLEY, Neil C. 2
HURLEY, Neil C. Jr. 4
HURLEY, Patrick Jay 1
HURLEY, Pearley B(liss) 1
HURLEY, Robert Augustine 5
HURLEY, Roy T. 5
HURLEY, Stephen Edward 1
HURLEY, William E. 3
HURLL, Estelle May 1
HUROK, Sol 6
HURRELL, Alfred 1
HURREY, Clarence Barzillai 5
HURSH, Ralph Kent 4
HURST, Albert S. 2
HURST, Carlton Bailey 2
HURST, Charles Warner 2
HURST, Clarence Thomas 2
HURST, Fannie 5
HURST, Harold Emerson 5
HURST, John 1
HURST, John Fletcher 1
HURST, Peter F(rederick) 5
HURST, William Henry 4
HURSTON, Zora Neale 3
HURT, Huber William 4
HURT, John Jeter 5
HURT, John Smith 4
HURT, Rollin 4
HURTH, Peter Joseph . 1
HURTY, John N. 1
HURTZ, Leonard E. 6
HURWITZ, Henry 4
HURWITZ, Wallie Abraham 3
HUSAIN, Zaklr 5
HUSBAND, George 3
  Rosewall
HUSBAND, Joseph 1
HUSBAND, Richard 1
  Wellington
HUSBAND, William Walter 2
HUSBANDS, Hermon H
HUSBANDS, Sam Henry 3

HUSE, Charles Phillips 3
HUSE, Charles Wells 6
HUSE, Harry Pinckney 2
HUSE, Raymond Howard 3
HUSE, William 3
HU-SHIH 4
HUSIK, Isaac 1
HUSING, Edward B. 4
HUSKINS, C. Leonard 2
HUSKINS, James Preston 3
HUSS, George Morehouse 2
HUSS, Henry Holden 1
HUSSAKOF, Louis 6
HUSSEIN, Taha 6
HUSSERL, Edmond H
HUSSERL, Edmond 1
HUSSEY, Charles Lincoln 1
HUSSEY, Curtis Grubb H
HUSSEY, John Brennan 4
HUSSEY, Obed H
HUSSEY, Raymond 3
HUSSEY, Roland Dennis 4
HUSSEY, Tacitus 4
HUSSEY, William Joseph 1
HUSSLEIN, Joseph 3
HUSSMAN, George 1
HUSSON, Chesley Hayward 5
HUSTED, James Delno 1
HUSTED, James William 1
HUSTED, James William 6
HUSTED, Ladley * 1
HUSTING, Berthold Juneau 2
HUSTING, Paul Oscar 1
HUSTIS, James H. 1
HUSTON, Abraham Francis 1
HUSTON, Charles H
HUSTON, Charles Andrews 1
HUSTON, Charles Lukens 3
HUSTON, Claudius Hart 4
HUSTON, Henry Augustus 5
HUSTON, Howard Riggins 3
HUSTON, Joseph Waldo 1
HUSTON, Luther Allison 6
HUSTON, Ralph Chase 5
HUSTON, Ralph Ernest 5
HUSTON, S(imeon) Arthur 5
HUSTON, Stewart 5
HUSTON, Thad 1
HUSTON, Walter 4
HUTCHENS, Frank 1
  Townsend
HUTCHEON, Robert James 1
HUTCHERSON, Dudley 4
  Robert
HUTCHESON, Allen 4
  Carrington Jr.
HUTCHESON, David 4
HUTCHESON, Grote 2
HUTCHESON, John Bell 1
HUTCHESON, John Redd 1
HUTCHESON, Joseph C. 5
  Jr.
HUTCHESON, Joseph 4
  Chappell
HUTCHESON, Martha 5
  Brookes
HUTCHESON, William 2
  Anderson
HUTCHESON, William L. 3
HUTCHINGS, Frank Day 1
HUTCHINGS, George 6
  Ernest
HUTCHINGS, John Richard 3
  Jr.
HUTCHINGS, Leslie 3
  Morton
HUTCHINGS, Leslie
  Morton
HUTCHINGS, Lester 3
HUTCHINGS, Richard 2
  Henry
HUTCHINS, Augustus 2
  Schell
HUTCHINS, Charles 4
  Clifford
HUTCHINS, Charles Henry 1
HUTCHINS, Charles Lewis 1
HUTCHINS, Charles Pelton 1
HUTCHINS, Charles 1
  Thomas
HUTCHINS, Edward 1
  Webster
HUTCHINS, Frank Avery 3
HUTCHINS, Frank Frazier 2
HUTCHINS, Harry Burns 1
HUTCHINS, James Calhoun 3
HUTCHINS, Jere 1
  Chamberlain
HUTCHINS, John H
HUTCHINS, John Corbin 1
HUTCHINS, Lee Wilson 3
HUTCHINS, Stilson 1
HUTCHINS, Thomas H
HUTCHINS, Waldo H
HUTCHINS, Wells Andrews H
HUTCHINS, Will 2

HUTCHINS, William J. 3
HUTCHINSON, Adoniram H
  Judson Joseph
HUTCHINSON, Anne H
  Vaughan
HUTCHINSON, Aubry 4
HUTCHINSON, B. Edwin 4
HUTCHINSON, Benjamin 1
  Peters
HUTCHINSON, Cary 1
  Talcott
HUTCHINSON, Charles 1
  Lawrence
HUTCHINSON, Edith 5
  Stotesbury
HUTCHINSON, Elijah 1
  Cubberley
HUTCHINSON, Ely 3
  Champion
HUTCHINSON, Emlen 4
HUTCHINSON, Forney 5
HUTCHINSON, Frederick 1
  Lane
HUTCHINSON, George 3
  Alexander
HUTCHINSON, J. 4
  Raymond B.
HUTCHINSON, James H
HUTCHINSON, John 1
  Corrin
HUTCHINSON, John 4
  Wallace
HUTCHINSON, John Irwin 1
HUTCHINSON, John 1
  Wallace
HUTCHINSON, Joseph 1
  Baldwin
HUTCHINSON, Knox 3
  Thomas
HUTCHINSON, Mark 5
  Eastwood
HUTCHINSON, Melvin 6
  Tyler
HUTCHINSON, Myron 3
  Wells Jr.
HUTCHINSON, Norman 1
HUTCHINSON, Paul 3
HUTCHINSON, Ray 6
  Coryton
HUTCHINSON, Robert 3
  Orland
HUTCHINSON, S. 1
  Pemberton
HUTCHINSON, Thomas H
HUTCHINSON, William K. 3
HUTCHINSON, William 2
  Spencer
HUTCHINSON, Woods 1
HUTCHISON, Benjamin 1
  Franklin
HUTCHISON, Frances 4
  Kinsley
HUTCHISON, Frederick 3
  William
HUTCHISON, George 2
  Wayland
HUTCHISON, Harvey 6
  Macleary
HUTCHISON, James 1
  Brewster
HUTCHISON, James Edgar 4
HUTCHISON, Martin Bell 1
HUTCHISON, Miller Reese 2
HUTCHISON, Ralph 4
  Cooper
HUTCHISON, Robert 1
  Alden
HUTCHISON, Stuart Nye 1
HUTCHISON, Stuart Nye 5
HUTCHISON, Thomas L. 4
HUTCHISON, William 1
  Easton
HUTCHMAN, J(ohnston) 5
  Harper
HUTSON, Charles 1
  Woodward
HUTSON, Frederick Leroy 3
HUTSON, John B. 4
HUTSON, Joshua Brown 4
HUTSON, Leander C. 5
HUTSON, Richard H
HUTT, Henry 2
HUTTER, Francis 4
HUTTIG, Charles Henry 5
HUTTON, Colin Osborne 5
HUTTON, Edward F. 4
HUTTON, Edward Hyatt 1
HUTTON, Frederick 1
  Remsen
HUTTON, Hugh McMillen 6
HUTTON, James Buchanan 1
HUTTON, James Morgan 1
HUTTON, John Edward 5
HUTTON, Josiah Lawson 4
HUTTON, Laurence 1
HUTTON, Leon 6
HUTTON, Levi W. 1

HUTTON, Mancius Holmes 1
HUTTON, Norman 1
HUTTON, Samuel Reed 4
HUTTON, William Edward 3
HUTTY, Alfred 3
HUTZLER, Albert David 4
HUXFORD, Walter Scott 3
HUXLEY, Aldous Leonard 4
HUXLEY, Henry Minor 3
HUXLEY, Sir Julian Sorell 5
HUXMAN, Walter A. 5
HUYCK, Edmund Niles 4
HUYKE, Juan Bernardo 6
HUYLER, John H
HUYSMANS, Camille 5
HYAM, Leslie Abraham 4
HYAMSON, Moses 2
HYATT, Alpheus 1
HYATT, Carl Britt 5
HYATT, Charles Eliot 1
HYATT, Edward 1
HYATT, Francis Marion 6
HYATT, Frank Kelso 3
HYATT, James Philip 6
HYATT, John Wesley 1
HYDE, Albert Alexander 1
HYDE, Ammi Bradford 1
HYDE, Arthur Knox 5
HYDE, Arthur M. 2
HYDE, Charles Cheney 3
HYDE, Charles Gilman 6
HYDE, Charles Leavitt 1
HYDE, Clarence Ludlam 1
HYDE, Clayton H. 4
HYDE, Cornelius Willet 4
  Gillam
HYDE, D. Clark 3
HYDE, Donald Frizell 4
HYDE, Edward * H
HYDE, Edward Pechin 6
HYDE, Edward Warden 1
HYDE, Edward Wyllys 1
HYDE, Edwin Francis 1
HYDE, Elizabeth A(dshead) 5
HYDE, George Merriam 1
HYDE, Grant Milnor 5
HYDE, Helen 1
HYDE, Henry Baldwin H
HYDE, Henry Morrow 5
HYDE, Howard Elmer 5
HYDE, Howard Kemper 5
HYDE, Howard Linton 5
HYDE, Ida Henrietta 3
HYDE, James Francis Clark 2
HYDE, James Hazen 3
HYDE, James Macdonald 4
HYDE, James Nevins 1
HYDE, Jeannette Acord 1
HYDE, Jesse Earl 1
HYDE, Joel Wilbur 1
HYDE, John 1
HYDE, John Bachman 1
HYDE, John McEwen 1
HYDE, John Sedgwick 1
HYDE, Joseph H
HYDE, Louis Kepler 4
HYDE, Mary Backus 5
HYDE, Mary Caroline 1
HYDE, Mary Kendall 1
HYDE, Miles Goodyear 4
HYDE, Nelson Collingwood 5
HYDE, Roscoe Raymond 2
HYDE, Walter Woodburn 6
HYDE, William Dewitt 1
HYDE, William Henry 2
HYDE, William Waldo 1
HYDE DE NEUVILLE, H
  Anne-Marguerite-
  Henriette
HYDRICK, Daniel Edward 1
HYER, David Burns Jr. 5
HYER, Frank Sidney 3
HYER, Julien Capers 6
HYER, Robert Stewart 1
HYLAN, John F. 1
HYLAN, John Perham 5
HYLAND, Francis E. 5
HYLAND, Philip David 3
HYLAND, William A. 4
HYLE, Michael William 4
HYLLESTED, August 4
  Frederick Ferdinand
HYLTON, John Dunbar 4
HYLTON, Joseph Roy 2
HYLTON-FOSTER, Harry 4
HYMAN, Albert Salisbury 5
HYMAN, Irving 4
HYMAN, John Adams H
HYMAN, Libbie Henrietta 5
HYMAN, Marion LaRoche 5
  Strobel (Mrs. John Patrick
  Hyman)
HYMAN, Stanley Edgar 5
HYMANS, Max 4
HYMON, Mary Watson 6

HYNDMAN, James Gilmore 1
HYNDS, John Arthur 2
HYNEMAN, John M. H
HYNES, John B. 5
HYNES, John William 3
HYNES, William J. 1
HYNICKA, Rudolph Kelker 1
HYNNINEN, P. J. 4
HYPES, Benjamin Murray 1
HYPES, Oran Faville 1
HYPES, Samuel L. 4
HYPES, William Findley 3
HYRE, Sarah Emma Cadwallader 5
HYRNE, Edmund Massingberd H
HYSLOP, James Augustus 3
HYSLOP, James Hervey 1
HYVERNAT, Henry 1
HYZER, Edward M. 1
HYZER, W. Edward 5

I

IARDELLA, Francisco H
IBANEZ DEL CAMPO, Carlos 4
IBAVIOSA, Alfred Cruz 6
IBERT, Jacques 4
IBSEN, Heman Lauritz 3
ICE, Harry Lawrence 4
ICHAILOVITCH, Lioubomir 5
ICKELHEIMER, Henry R. 4
ICKES, Harold L. 3
IDDINGS, Andrew Sheets 6
IDDINGS, Edward John 3
IDDINGS, Joseph Paxson 1
IDDINGS, Lewis Morris 1
IDE, Alba M. 1
IDE, Charles Edward 3
IDE, Fannie Ogden 1
IDE, George Edward 1
IDE, George Elmore 1
IDE, Henry Clay 1
IDE, John Jay 4
IDE, William B. H
IDELL, Albert Edward 3
IDEMA, Henry 3
IDESON, Julia Bedford 2
IDLEMAN, Finis Schuyler 1
IDLEMAN, Silas Ellsworth 1
IFFT, George Nicolas 2
IGLAUER, Samuel 2
IGLEHART, David Stewart 2
IGLEHART, Fanny Chambers Gooch 4
IGLEHART, Ferdinand Cowle 1
IGLESIAS, Santiago 1
IGOE, James Thomas 5
IGOE, Michael Lambert 4
IGOE, William L. 3
IHLDER, John 3
IHLE, Leo 3
IHLSENG, Axel Olaf 1
IHLSENG, Magnus Colbjorn 4
IHMSEN, Maximilian Frederick 1
IHRIE, Peter Jr. H
IHRIG, Harry Karl 4
IIAMS, Thomas Marion 4
IJAMS, Frank Burch 4
IJAMS, George Edwin 4
IKEDA, Hayato 4
ILAK, Abdul 3
ILES, George 4
ILES, Malvern Wells 4
ILES, Orlando Buff 1
ILGENFRITZ, Carl A. 4
ILGENFRITZ, E. K. 3
ILIFF, Thomas Corwin 1
ILL, Edward Joseph 2
ILLGES, John P. 3
ILLINGTON, Margaret 1
ILLINGWORTH, Sir Cyril Gordon 3
ILLOWAY, Henry 1
ILSLEY, Daniel H
ILSLEY, James Keeler 1
ILSLEY, James Lorimer 4
ILSLEY, Samuel Marshall 4
IMAHORN, Albert Peter 3
IMBERT, Antoine H
IMBODEN, John Daniel H
IMBRIE, James 6
IMES, Birney Sr. 2
IMLAY, Gilbert H
IMLAY, James Henderson H
IMLAY, Lorin Everett 1
IMMEL, Ray Keeslar 2
IMMELL, Ruth 6
IMPERATORI, Charles Johnstone 3
INCE, Charles R. 4
INCE, Thomas Harper 1
INCH, Richard 1
INCH, Robert Alexander 4
INCH, Sydney Richard 4
INFELD, Leopold 4
INGALLS, Charles Russell 1
INGALLS, Fay 3
INGALLS, George Hoadly 1
INGALLS, James Monroe 1
INGALLS, Jeremiah H
INGALLS, John James 1
INGALLS, Marilla Baker H
INGALLS, Melville Ezra 1
INGALLS, Robert Ingersoll 3
INGALLS, Roscoe Cunningham 5
INGALLS, Walter Renton 3
INGALS, E. Fletcher 1
INGALSBE, Grenville Mellen 1
INGE, Francis Harrison 3
INGE, Samuel Williams H
INGE, William 5
INGE, William Marshall H
INGE, Zebulon Montgomery Pike 3
INGERSOLL, A. C. Jr. 4
INGERSOLL, Charles Edward 1
INGERSOLL, Charles Henry 2
INGERSOLL, Charles Jared H
INGERSOLL, Colin Macrae 2
INGERSOLL, Ebon Clark H
INGERSOLL, Edward H
INGERSOLL, Edward Payson 1
INGERSOLL, Ernest 2
INGERSOLL, George Pratt 1
INGERSOLL, Henry Hulbert 1
INGERSOLL, Henry Wallace 2
INGERSOLL, Jared H
INGERSOLL, Joseph Reed H
INGERSOLL, Leonard Rose 3
INGERSOLL, Ralph Eugene 6
INGERSOLL, Ralph Isaacs H
INGERSOLL, Raymond Vail 1
INGERSOLL, Robert Green 1
INGERSOLL, Robert Hawley 1
INGERSOLL, Roy Claire 4
INGERSOLL, Royal Rodney 1
INGERSOLL, Simon H
INGERSOLL, Tyrrell Meyer 5
INGERSOLL, William Harrison 2
INGHAM, Charles Cromwell H
INGHAM, Charles Samuel 2
INGHAM, Charles T(attersall) 6
INGHAM, Harvey 2
INGHAM, John Albertson 2
INGHAM, Lucius Edwin 3
INGHAM, Samuel H
INGHAM, Samuel Delucenna H
INGHAM, William Armstrong 1
INGLE, David 6
INGLE, Edward 1
INGLE, James Addison 1
INGLE, Richard H
INGLE, William 4
INGLESON, Robert G. 4
INGLEY, Fred 3
INGLIS, Alexander James 1
INGLIS, Charles H
INGLIS, James 2
INGLIS, Richard 3
INGLIS, William Wallace 5
INGMANSON, William Leslie 4
INGRAHAM, Darius Holbrook 1
INGRAHAM, Duncan Nathaniel H
INGRAHAM, Edgar Shugert 5
INGRAHAM, Edward Duffield H
INGRAHAM, Franc Douglas 4
INGRAHAM, Frances Adelaide Leverich 1
INGRAHAM, George Landon 1
INGRAHAM, Henry A. 4
INGRAHAM, Henry Cruise Murphy 1
INGRAHAM, John Phillips Thurston 1
INGRAHAM, Joseph H
INGRAHAM, Joseph Holt H
INGRAHAM, Prentiss 1
INGRAHAM, William Moulton 3
INGRAM, Augustus Eugenio 4
INGRAM, Dwight 5
INGRAM, Edward Lovering 4
INGRAM, Eleanor Marie 1
INGRAM, Everett Jefferson 6
INGRAM, Frederick Fremont 1
INGRAM, Henry Atlee 4
INGRAM, Jonas Howard 3
INGRAM, Leon John 5
INGRAM, Orrin Henry 4
INGVOLDSTAD, Orlando 5
INGWERSEN, John Arthur 3
INLOW, Richard Morehead 3
INMAN, Arthur Charles 4
INMAN, Edward Hamilton 1
INMAN, George H
INMAN, Henry H
INMAN, Henry 1
INMAN, Henry Arthur 5
INMAN, John H
INMAN, John Hamilton H
INMAN, Samuel Guy 4
INMAN, Walker Patterson 3
INNES, Frederick Neil 1
INNES, George 3
INNES, Harry H
INNES, James H
INNES, Katherine 1
INNES, Thomas Christie 4
INNESS, George H
INNESS, George Jr. 1
INNIS, George Swan 4
INNIS, William Reynolds 1
INNOKENTII H
INONU, Ismet 6
INSKEEP, Annie Dolman 3
INSKIP, John Swanel H
INSLEY, William Henry 5
INSULL, Frederick William 1
INSULL, Martin John 5
INSULL, Samuel 1
INVERCHAPEL, Lord Archibald John Kerr Clark Kerr 3
INVERFORTH, Lord 3
INVILLIERS, Edward Vincent d 4
IOASAF H
IOOR, William H
IPATIEFF, Vladimir Nikolaevich 5
IPPEN, Arthur Thomas 6
IPSEN, Ernest Ludvig 3
IRBY, John Laurens Manning 1
IRBY, John St John 1
IRBY, Nolen Meaders 3
IREDELL, Francis Raymond 5
IREDELL, James * H
IRELAN, Singer B. 3
IRELAND, Alleyne 5
IRELAND, Charles Thomas Jr. 5
IRELAND, Clifford 1
IRELAND, John H
IRELAND, John 1
IRELAND, John 4
IRELAND, Joseph Norton H
IRELAND, Josias Alexander 4
IRELAND, Lloyd Owen 5
IRELAND, Mary E. 4
IRELAND, Merritte Weber 3
IRELAND, Oscar Brown 1
IRELAND, R. W. 5
IRELAND, Robert Livingston 1
IRELAND, Thomas Saxton 5
IRELAND, William 1
IRELAND, William Dunning 6
IRENE, Sister H
IRETON, Peter L. 3
IREY, Elmer Lincoln 2
IREYS, Charles Goodrich 2
IRION, Theophil William Henry 3
IRISH, Edwin M. 4
IRISH, Fred Abbott 3
IRISH, John Powell 1
IRISH, Rolland E. 4
IRLAND, George Allison 5
IRONQUILL 1
IRONS, Ernest Edward 3
IRONS, Henry Clay 4
IRONS, James Anderson 1
IRONSIDE, Henry Allan 3
IRVIN, Alexander H
IRVIN, Donald F. 3
IRVIN, James H
IRVIN, Leslie LeRoy 4
IRVIN, Rea 5
IRVIN, William Adolf 3
IRVIN, William W. H
IRVINE, Alexander Fitzgerald 1
IRVINE, Alonzo Blair 1
IRVINE, Benjamin Franklin 1
IRVINE, Clarence (Shortridge) 6
IRVINE, Fergus Albert 5
IRVINE, Frank 1
IRVINE, James H
IRVINE, James 4
IRVINE, Julia Josephine 1
IRVINE, Leigh Hadley 2
IRVINE, Robert Tate 1
IRVINE, William * H
IRVINE, William 1
IRVINE, William 4
IRVINE, William Bay 4
IRVINE, William Burriss 1
IRVINE, William Mann 1
IRVINE, Wilson Henry 1
IRVING, Frederick Carpenter 3
IRVING, George Henry Jr. 1
IRVING, George Milton 4
IRVING, Sir Henry Brodribb 1
IRVING, Isabel 2
IRVING, John Beaufain H
IRVING, John Duer 1
IRVING, John Treat 1
IRVING, Minna 1
IRVING, Paulus A. 4
IRVING, Peter H
IRVING, Pierre Munro H
IRVING, Roland Duer H
IRVING, Thomas Patrick 4
IRVING, Washington H
IRVING, William H
IRWIN, Agnes 1
IRWIN, Bernard John Dowling 1
IRWIN, Charles Walter 1
IRWIN, Clinton Fillmore 4
IRWIN, Edith Alice 6
IRWIN, Edward M. 1
IRWIN, Elisabeth Antoinette 2
IRWIN, Frederick Charles 5
IRWIN, George Le Roy 1
IRWIN, Harry N. 3
IRWIN, Harvey S. 4
IRWIN, Inez Haynes 5
IRWIN, James Ellis 6
IRWIN, Jared H
IRWIN, John 1
IRWIN, John Arthur 4
IRWIN, John Nichol 1
IRWIN, John Scull 1
IRWIN, Kilshaw McHenry 4
IRWIN, May 1
IRWIN, Noble Edward 1
IRWIN, Richard William 1
IRWIN, Robert Benjamin 3
IRWIN, Robert Forsythe Jr. 4
IRWIN, Robert Winfred 5
IRWIN, Solden H
IRWIN, Staford LeRoy 3
IRWIN, Thomas H
IRWIN, W. Francis 1
IRWIN, Wallace 3
IRWIN, Walter McMaster 5
IRWIN, Warren W. 4
IRWIN, William Andrew 4
IRWIN, William Glanton 2
IRWIN, William Henry 2
IRWIN, William Wallace H
ISAAC, Joseph Elias 6
ISAACS, Abram Samuel 1
ISAACS, Asher 4
ISAACS, Charles Applewhite 1
ISAACS, Edith J. R. 3
ISAACS, Hart 4
ISAACS, Hart 5
ISAACS, Henry G. H
ISAACS, John Dove 4
ISAACS, Lewis Montefiore 2
ISAACS, Moses Legis 5
ISAACS, Myer Samuel 1
ISAACS, Nathan 1
ISAACS, Raphael 4
ISAACS, Samuel Myer H
ISAACS, Stanley Myer 4
ISAACSON, Charles David 1
ISAAK, Nicholas 6
ISACKS, Jacob C. H
ISBELL, Egbert Raymond 5
ISBRANDTSEN, Hans J. 3
ISELIN, Adrian 1
ISELIN, Charles Oliver 1
ISELIN, Columbus O'Donnell 5
ISELIN, Columbus O'Donnell 1
ISELIN, Ernest 3
ISELIN, Oliver 4
ISELY, Frederick B. 2
ISENSTEAD, Joseph Herman 6
ISERMAN, Michael 5
ISHAM, Asa Brainerd 4
ISHAM, Frederic Stewart 1
ISHAM, Henry Porter 5
ISHAM, Howard Edwin 6
ISHAM, Mary Keyt 2
ISHAM, Norman Morrison 2
ISHAM, Ralph Heyward 3
ISHAM, Samuel 1
ISHERWOOD, Benjamin Franklin 1
ISLE, Walter Whitfield 3
ISMAY, Lord 4
ISOM, Edward Whitten 4
ISOM, Mary Frances 1
ISRAEL, Arthur Jr. 4
ISRAEL, Edward L. 1
ISRAEL, Harold Edward 4
ISRAEL, Rogers 1
ISRAELS, Carlos Lindner 5
ISSEKS, Samuel Shepp 3
ISSERMAN, Ferdinand Myron 5
ISTEL, Andre 4
ITTEL, George Alfred 4
ITTLESON, Henry 2
ITTLESON, Henry Jr. 6
ITTNER, Martin Hill 2
ITTNER, William Butts 1
IVANOWSKI, Sigismond de 5
IVEAGH, The Earl of 4
IVERSEN, Lorenz 4
IVERSEN, Lorenz 6
IVERSON, Alfred H
IVERSON, Samuel Gilbert 1
IVES, Augustus Wright 4
IVES, Brayton 1
IVES, Charles E. 3
IVES, Charles John 4
IVES, Charles Taylor 4
IVES, Chauncey Bradley H
IVES, Clarence Albert 5
IVES, Eli H
IVES, Frederic Eugene 1
IVES, Frederick Manley 3
IVES, George Burnham 1
IVES, Halsey Cooley 1
IVES, Herbert Eugene 3
IVES, Howard Chapin 2
IVES, Irving McNeil 4
IVES, James Edmund 2
IVES, James Merritt H
IVES, Joel Stone 1
IVES, John Hiett 5
IVES, John Winsor 3
IVES, Joseph Christmas H
IVES, Joseph Moss 1
IVES, Levi Silliman H
IVES, Percy 1
IVES, Ralph Burkett 1
IVES, Sarah Noble 5
IVES, Sumner Albert 2
IVES, Willard H
IVEY, Alphonso Lynn 2
IVEY, George Melvin 5
IVEY, Herbert Dee 4
IVEY, Joseph Benjamin 3
IVEY, Thomas Neal 1
IVIE, John Mark 6
IVIE, Joseph Henry 2
IVIE, William Noah 5
IVINS, Anthony W. 1
IVINS, Antoine Ridgway 5
IVINS, Benjamin Franklin Price 4
IVINS, James S. Y. 4
IVINS, Lester Sylvan 4
IVINS, William Mills 1
IVINSON, Edward 4
IVISON, David Brinkerhoff 1
IVY, Hardy H
IVY, Robert Henry 6
IYENAGA, Toyokichi 3
IZARD, George H
IZARD, Ralph H
IZARD, Thomas C. 4

J

JACCARD, Walter M. 5
JACCHIA, Agide 1
JACK, Frederick Lafayette 1
JACK, George Whitfield 1
JACK, James Robertson 3
JACK, John George 3
JACK, Summers Melville 4
JACK, Theodore Henley 4
JACK, William H
JACK, William Blake 2
JACKLIN, Edward G. 5
JACKLING, Daniel Cowan 3
JACKMAN, Charles Lyman 3
JACKMAN, Howard Hill 4
JACKMAN, Wilbur Samuel 1
JACKS, Allen 6
JACKS, Horace Leonard 4
JACKS, Leo Vincent 5
JACKSON, A. V. Williams 1
JACKSON, Abraham H
Reeves
JACKSON, Abraham 1
Willard
JACKSON, Al 6
JACKSON, Albert Atlee 1
JACKSON, Albert Mathews 1
JACKSON, Allan 4
JACKSON, Amos Henry 3
JACKSON, Amos Wade 5
JACKSON, Andrew H
JACKSON, Arnold S. 4
JACKSON, Arthur C. 3
JACKSON, Arthur Conard 4
JACKSON, Bennett Barron 4
JACKSON, Burris C. 4
JACKSON, Carl Newell 2
JACKSON, Carlton 6
JACKSON, Charles H
JACKSON, Charles 5
(Reginald)
JACKSON, Charles 4
Akerman
JACKSON, Charles Cabot 1
JACKSON, Charles Douglas 4
JACKSON, Charles H. 4
Spurgeon
JACKSON, Charles Loring 1
JACKSON, Charles Samuel 1
JACKSON, Charles Tenney 5
JACKSON, Charles Thomas H
JACKSON, Charles Warren 1
JACKSON, Chevalier 3
JACKSON, Chevalier L. 4
JACKSON, Claiborne Fox H
JACKSON, Clarence Martin 2
JACKSON, Clifford Linden 4
JACKSON, Daniel Dana 1
JACKSON, David H
JACKSON, David E. H
JACKSON, David Sherwood H
JACKSON, Dorothy Branch 1
JACKSON, Dugald Caleb 3
JACKSON, Dunham 2
JACKSON, E. Hilton 3
JACKSON, Ebenezer Jr. 1
JACKSON, Ed 3
JACKSON, Edward 2
JACKSON, Edward Brake 1
JACKSON, E(dward) 6
Franklin
JACKSON, Edward Payson 1
JACKSON, Elihu Emory 1
JACKSON, Elizabeth 6
Noland
JACKSON, Ernest Bryan 4
JACKSON, Francis H
JACKSON, Frank Dar 1
JACKSON, Frank Lee 5
JACKSON, Fred Schuyler 1
JACKSON, Frederic Ellis 2
JACKSON, Frederick John 1
Foakes
JACKSON, Frederick 3
Mitchell
JACKSON, Gabrielle Snow 4
JACKSON, George H
JACKSON, George 1
JACKSON, George Anson 1
JACKSON, George B. 4
JACKSON, George Edwards 1
JACKSON, George K. H
JACKSON, George Leroy 5
JACKSON, George Pullen 3
JACKSON, George 2
Somerville
JACKSON, George Thomas 1
JACKSON, George 2
Washington
JACKSON, Hall H
JACKSON, Helen Maria H
Fiske Hunt
JACKSON, Henry 1
JACKSON, Henry Ezekiel 1

JACKSON, Henry Hollister 3
JACKSON, Henry Melville 1
JACKSON, Henry Rootes H
JACKSON, Henry S. 1
JACKSON, Herbert Spencer 3
JACKSON, Herbert W. Jr. 4
JACKSON, Herbert Worth 4
JACKSON, Holland Taylor 4
JACKSON, Holmes Condict 1
JACKSON, Howard H
Campbell Sr.
JACKSON, Howell H
Edmunds
JACKSON, J. Hugh 4
JACKSON, Jabez North 1
JACKSON, Jabez Young H
JACKSON, James * H
JACKSON, James A. 4
JACKSON, James Arthur 3
JACKSON, James Caleb 1
JACKSON, James F. 1
JACKSON, James Frederick 1
JACKSON, James 2
Hathaway
JACKSON, James Kirkman 1
JACKSON, James Streshly H
JACKSON, Jesse Benjamin 1
JACKSON, John Adams H
JACKSON, John 1
Brinckerhoff
JACKSON, John Davies H
JACKSON, John Day 4
JACKSON, John Edward * 5
JACKSON, John Edwin 5
JACKSON, John George H
JACKSON, John Gillespie 4
JACKSON, John Gillespie 6
Jr.
JACKSON, John Henry 1
JACKSON, John J. 5
JACKSON, John Jay 1
JACKSON, John Long 2
JACKSON, Jonathan H
JACKSON, Joseph 2
JACKSON, Joseph Cooke 1
JACKSON, Joseph Henry 4
JACKSON, Joseph Henry 6
JACKSON, Joseph 5
Raymond
JACKSON, Joseph Webber 4
JACKSON, Josephine Agnes 2
JACKSON, Katharine 4
Johnson
JACKSON, Katherine Gauss 6
JACKSON, Lambert Lincoln 3
JACKSON, Leonora (Mrs. 6
William Duncan McKim)
JACKSON, Leroy Freeman 6
JACKSON, Lyman E. 6
JACKSON, Mahalia 5
JACKSON, Margaret Doyle 4
JACKSON, Margaret 4
Weymouth
JACKSON, Martha 5
JACKSON, Mary Anna 1
JACKSON, McStay 4
JACKSON, Mercy Ruggles H
Bisbe
JACKSON, Mortimer H
Melville
JACKSON, N. Baxter 6
JACKSON, Patrick Tracy H
JACKSON, Paul Rainey 5
JACKSON, Percival E. 5
JACKSON, Percy 4
JACKSON, Philip Ludwell 3
Donelson
JACKSON, Rachel H
JACKSON, Ralph LeRoy 3
JACKSON, Raymond 5
Thomas
JACKSON, Reginald Henry 4
JACKSON, Richard 1
Arbuthnot
JACKSON, Richard 5
Harrison
JACKSON, Richard Jr. H
JACKSON, Richard 6
Seymour
JACKSON, Richard Webber 3
JACKSON, Robert 1
JACKSON, Robert 3
Houghwout
JACKSON, Robert Manson 6
JACKSON, Robert Tracy 2
JACKSON, Roscoe 1
Bradbury
JACKSON, Russell H
JACKSON, Samuel H
JACKSON, Samuel Dillon 3
JACKSON, Samuel 1
Macauley
JACKSON, Samuel Morley 2
JACKSON, Samuel P. H
JACKSON, Schuyler Wood 4
JACKSON, Sheldon 1

JACKSON, Shirley 4
JACKSON, Theodore 4
Fredlinghuysen
JACKSON, Thomas Birdsall H
JACKSON, Thomas Broun 5
JACKSON, Thomas Herbert 4
JACKSON, Thomas H
Jonathan
JACKSON, Thomas Wright 5
JACKSON, V. T. 3
JACKSON, Virgil Thomas H
Sr.
JACKSON, Wilfrid J. 3
JACKSON, William * H
JACKSON, William 4
Alexander
JACKSON, William 1
Benjamin
JACKSON, William 5
H(arding)
JACKSON, William Henry 2
JACKSON, William Hicks 1
JACKSON, William H
Humphreys
JACKSON, William J. 2
JACKSON, William 1
Kenneth
JACKSON, William Neil 6
JACKSON, William Nichols 5
JACKSON, William Payne 1
JACKSON, William Purnell 1
JACKSON, William Terry H
JACKSON, William Trayton 1
JACKVONY, Louis V. 3
JACOB, Richard Taylor 1
JACOB, Robert Byron 5
JACOBBERGER, Francis 1
Benedict
JACOBI, Abraham 1
JACOBI, Frederick 3
JACOBI, Herbert P. 5
JACOBI, Mary Putnam 1
JACOBS, Arthur P. 6
JACOBS, Benjamin Franklin 1
JACOBS, Bernard 6
JACOBS, Carl Marlon 4
JACOBS, Charles M. 1
JACOBS, Charles Michael 4
JACOBS, Edwin Elmore 3
JACOBS, Elbridge Churchill 5
JACOBS, Fenton Stratton 4
JACOBS, Ferris Jr. H
JACOBS, Fred Clinton 4
JACOBS, Harold Duane 3
JACOBS, Henry Barton 1
JACOBS, Henry Eyster 1
JACOBS, Henry L. 4
JACOBS, Israel H
JACOBS, J. Arthur 4
JACOBS, Jay Wesley 5
JACOBS, John Hall 4
JACOBS, John Marshall 4
JACOBS, Joseph 1
JACOBS, Joseph Earle 5
JACOBS, Joshua W. 1
JACOBS, Melville 5
JACOBS, Michael H
JACOBS, Michael William 4
JACOBS, Michel 1
JACOBS, Myrl Lamont 3
JACOBS, Nathan Bernd 4
JACOBS, Nehemiah Pitman 4
Mann
JACOBS, Pattie Ruffner 1
JACOBS, Randall 4
JACOBS, Tevis 6
JACOBS, Thornwell 3
JACOBS, Walter Abraham 4
JACOBS, Walter Ballou 1
JACOBS, Whipple 3
JACOBS, William Plummer 2
JACOBS, William States 1
JACOBSEN, A. P. 6
JACOBSEN, Alfred 4
JACOBSEN, Bernhard 4
Martin
JACOBSEN, Carlyle 6
JACOBSEN, Einar A. 5
JACOBSEN, Elnar A. 5
JACOBSEN, Jerome 5
Vincent
JACOBSEN, Norman 6
JACOBSOHN, Simon 1
Eberhard
JACOBSON, Arthur 3
Clarence
JACOBSON, Belle Elizabeth 5
JACOBSON, Carl Alfred 5
JACOBSON, Carl Frederick 2
JACOBSON, Fritz 1
JACOBSON, Gabe 2
JACOBSON, John Christian H
JACOBSON, Morris 4
Lazarev

JACOBSON, Moses 5
Abraham
JACOBSON, Samuel 6
JACOBSSON, Per 4
JACOBSTEIN, Meyer 4
JACOBUS, David Schenck 1
JACOBUS, Melancthon 1
Williams
JACOBY, George W. 1
JACOBY, Harold 1
JACOBY, Henry Sylvester 3
JACOBY, J(ames) Ralph 6
JACOBY, Ludwig Sigmund 1
JACOBY, Raymond W. 4
JACOBY, William Lawall 1
JACOWAY, Henderson 5
Madison
JACQUES, Sidney Bennett 4
JACQUES, William White 1
JADWIN, Edgar 1
JAECKEL, Theodore 4
JAEGER, Alphons Otto 3
JAEGER, Gebhard 4
JAEGER, Werner Wilhelm 5
JAEGERS, Albert 1
JAEGERS, Augustine 5
JAEKEL, Frederic Blair 2
JAFFA, Myer Edward 1
JAFFE, David Lawrence 6
JAFFE, Louis Isaac 4
JAFFRAY, Clive Talbot 3
JAGEMANN, Hans Carl 1
Gunther von
JAGGAR, Thomas Augustus 1
JAGGAR, Thomas Augustus 3
JAGGARD, Edwin Ames 1
JAHN, Gunnar 5
JAHN, Walter J. 5
JAHNCKE, Ernest Lee 4
JAHNCKE, P. F. Sr. 4
JAHR, Torstein (Knutsson 5
Torstensen)
JAINSEN, Wilson Carl 6
JAKOSKY, John Jay 4
JALLADE, Louis Eugene 3
JAMERSON, G(eorge) H. 5
JAMES, Addison Davis 4
JAMES, Albert Calder 4
JAMES, Albert William 6
JAMES, Alexander 2
JAMES, Alfred Farragut 3
JAMES, Alice Archer 3
Sewall
JAMES, Amaziah Bailey H
JAMES, Aphie 5
JAMES, Arthur Curtiss 1
JAMES, Arthur Horace 5
JAMES, Bartlett Burleigh 3
JAMES, Ben 5
JAMES, Benjamin F. 4
JAMES, Bushrod 1
Washington
JAMES, Charles 1
JAMES, Charles Fenton 1
JAMES, Charles P. 1
JAMES, Charles Tillinghast H
JAMES, D. Bushrod 1
JAMES, D. Willis 1
JAMES, Darwin Rush * 1
JAMES, Donald Denny 5
JAMES, Edmund Janes 1
JAMES, Edward H
Christopher
JAMES, Edward David 5
JAMES, Edward Holton 4
JAMES, Edward 2
Washington
JAMES, Edwin H
JAMES, Edwin Leland 3
JAMES, Edwin Warley 5
JAMES, Eldon Revare 2
JAMES, Elias Olan 6
JAMES, Fleming 3
JAMES, Francis H
JAMES, Francis Bacon 1
JAMES, Frank Cyril 5
JAMES, Frank Lowber 1
JAMES, George 5
JAMES, George Francis 1
JAMES, George Oscar 1
JAMES, George Roosa 1
JAMES, George Wharton 1
JAMES, Harlean 6
JAMES, Henry * H
JAMES, Henry 1
JAMES, Henry 2
JAMES, Henry 4
JAMES, Herman Brooks 5
JAMES, James Alton 4
JAMES, James Charles 4
JAMES, Jesse Woodson H
JAMES, John Edwin 1
JAMES, Joseph Hidy 2
JAMES, Louis 1
JAMES, Marquis 3
JAMES, Mary E. 1

JAMES, May Hall (May 6
Winsor Hall)
JAMES, Minnie Kennedy 5
(Mrs. Wm. Carey James)
JAMES, Ollie M. 1
JAMES, Ollie Murray 5
JAMES, Philip (Frederick 6
Wright)
JAMES, Phillip 6
JAMES, Reese D. 4
JAMES, Samuel Catlett 4
JAMES, Samuel Humphreys 4
JAMES, Thomas H
JAMES, Thomas Chalkley H
JAMES, Thomas Lemuel 1
JAMES, Thomas Potts H
JAMES, W. Frank 4
JAMES, Walter Belknap 1
JAMES, Walter Gilbert 2
JAMES, Warren William 2
JAMES, William 1
JAMES, William 4
JAMES, William Carey 3
JAMES, William Hartford 1
JAMES, William John 1
JAMES, William Knowles 1
JAMES, William M. 3
JAMES, William P. 1
JAMES, William Roderick 2
JAMES, William Stubbs 5
JAMESON, Edwin Cornell 2
JAMESON, Henry 1
JAMESON, Horatio Gates 1
JAMESON, John H
JAMESON, John Alexander H
JAMESON, John Butler 5
JAMESON, John Franklin 1
JAMESON, P. Henry 4
JAMESON, Patrick Henry 4
JAMESON, Robert Willis 5
JAMESON, Russell Parsons 3
JAMIESON, Charles Clark 1
JAMIESON, Douglas James 6
JAMIESON, Edmund 1
Scudder
JAMIESON, Francis 4
Anthony
JAMIESON, Guy Arthur 4
JAMIESON, Robert Cary 4
JAMIESON, Thomas N. 4
JAMIESON, William D. 2
JAMIESON, William 4
Edward
JAMISON, Alpha Pierce 5
JAMISON, Atha Thomas 2
JAMISON, Cecilia Viets 4
JAMISON, Charles Laselle 4
JAMISON, David H
JAMISON, David Lee 2
JAMISON, Joseph Warren 4
JAMISON, Minnie Lou 4
JAMISON, Monroe 1
Franklin
JAMISON, Paul Bailey 5
JAMISON, Robert H. 4
JAMISON, Thomas Worth 4
Jr.
JAMISON, William 1
Arbuckle
JANAUSHEK, Francesca 1
JANE, Robert Stephen 3
JANES, George Milton 1
JANES, Henry Fisk H
JANES, John Valle 5
JANES, Lewis George 1
JANES, Lewis George 1
JANEWAY, Edward 1
Gamaliel
JANEWAY, Frank Latimer 4
JANEWAY, Phineas Allen 4
JANEWAY, Theodore 1
Caldwell
JANIS, Elsie 3
JANISSE, Denis R. 6
JANNEY, O. Edward 1
JANNEY, Russell 4
JANNEY, Samuel H
McPherson
JANNEY, Thomas B. 1
JANNOTTA, Alfred Vernon 5
JANSEN, Ernest George 4
JANSEN, Marie 1
JANSEN, Peter 4
JANSEN, Reinier H
JANSEN, William 4
JANSS, Peter W(illiam) 5
JANSSEN, E. C. 2
JANSSEN, Henry 2
JANSSEN, John 1
JANSSENS, Francis 1
JANSSON, Edward Fritiof 4
JANUARY, William Louis 1
JANVIER, Caesar A. 1
Rodney
JANVIER, Catharine Ann 1
JANVIER, Charles 4

---

* Indicates More Than One Such Name Listed

JANVIER, Margaret Thomson 1
JANVIER, Thomas Allibone 1
JANVRIN, Joseph Edward 1
JANZEN, Assar Gotrik 5
JANZEN, Danile H(ugo) 5
JAQUA, Albert Roscoe 3
JAQUA, Ernest James 5
JAQUES, Alfred 1
JAQUES, Bertha E. 2
JAQUES, Charles Everett 1
JAQUES, Francis Lee 5
JAQUES, Herbert 1
JAQUES, Willard W. 1
JAQUES, William Henry 1
JAQUESS, James Frazier H
JAQUESS, William Thomas 4
JAQUITH, Harold Clarence 2
JARBOE, Henry Lee 4
JARDINE, David H
JARDINE, James Tertius 3
JARDINE, John Earle 1
JARDINE, John Earle Jr. 5
JARDINE, William M. 3
JARECKY, Herman 4
JARMAN, Joseph Leonard 2
JARMAN, Lewis Wilson 3
JARMAN, Pete 3
JARMAN, Sanderford 3
JARNAGIN, Milton Preston 6
JARNAGIN, Spencer H
JARRATT, Devereaux H
JARRATT, Hill 5
JARRELL, Albert Polk 4
JARRELL, Albert Polk 5
JARRELL, Charles Crawford 5
JARRELL, Randall 4
JARRETT, Benjamin 2
JARRETT, Cora Hardy 5
JARRETT, Edwin Seton 1
JARRETT, Harry B. 6
JARRETT, William Ambrose 3
JARRETT, William Paul 1
JARRETT, William Paul 1
JARROLD, Ernest 4
JARVES, James Jackson 1
JARVIE, James Newbegin 1
JARVIS, Charles H. H
JARVIS, Chester Deacon 2
JARVIS, David Henry 1
JARVIS, De Forest Clinton 4
JARVIS, Deming H
JARVIS, Edward 1
JARVIS, George Tibbals 5
JARVIS, Harry Aydelotte H
JARVIS, John Wesley H
JARVIS, Leonard 1
JARVIS, Robert Edward Lee 5
JARVIS, Samuel M. 1
JARVIS, Thomas Jordan 1
JARVIS, Thomas Neilson 1
JARVIS, William H
JARVIS, William Chapman H
JASPER, William H
JASSPON, William Henry 3
JASTRAM, Edward Perkins 3
JASTROW, Joseph 2
JASTROW, Marcus 1
JASTROW, Morris Jr. 1
JASZI, Oscar 4
JAUNCEY, George Eric MacDonnell 1
JAUREGUI, Guillermo Patterson y 1
JAVIS, Abraham H
JAVITS, Benjamin Abraham 6
JAY, Clarence Hollingsworth 4
JAY, Sir James 4
JAY, John * H
JAY, John Clarkson 1
JAY, John Edwin 4
JAY, Lawrence Merton 1
JAY, Mary Rutherford 3
JAY, Milton 1
JAY, Nelson Dean 5
JAY, Peter Augustus H
JAY, Peter Augustus 2
JAY, Pierre 2
JAY, William * H
JAY, William 1
JAYCOX, Walter Husted 2
JAYNE, Anselm Helm 1
JAYNE, Benaiah Gustin 4
JAYNE, Caroline Furness 1
JAYNE, Henry LaBarre 1
JAYNE, Horace 1
JAYNE, Horace Howard Furness 6
JAYNE, Joseph Lee 1
JAYNE, Walter Addison 1
JAYNES, Allan Brown 1

JEAN, Sister Anne 5
JEAN, Sally Lucas 5
JEANMARD, Jules Benjamin 3
JEANS, Philip Charles 5
JECK, George G. 5
JEFFERIES, Emily Brown 1
JEFFERIS, Albert Webb 4
JEFFERIS, William W. 1
JEFFERS, Clyde G. 6
JEFFERS, Eliakim Tupper 1
JEFFERS, Henry William 3
JEFFERS, Katharine R. 3
JEFFERS, LeRoy 1
JEFFERS, Robinson 4
JEFFERS, William Hamilton 1
JEFFERS, William Martin 3
JEFFERS, William Nicholson H
JEFFERSON, Benjamin Lafayette 5
JEFFERSON, Bradley Carter 4
JEFFERSON, Charles Edward 1
JEFFERSON, Clarence Ernest 4
JEFFERSON, Cornelia Burke H
JEFFERSON, Floyd Wellman 5
JEFFERSON, Floyd Wellman 6
JEFFERSON, Floyd Wellman Jr. 6
JEFFERSON, John Percival 1
JEFFERSON, Joseph 1
JEFFERSON, Joseph * 1
JEFFERSON, Mark 4
JEFFERSON, Martha Wayles 1
JEFFERSON, Robert 4
JEFFERSON, Samuel Mitchell 1
JEFFERSON, Thomas H
JEFFERY, Edward Turner 1
JEFFERY, Elmore Berry 1
JEFFERY, Robert Emmett 1
JEFFERY, Rosa Griffith Vertner Johnson 1
JEFFERYS, Charles William 3
JEFFERYS, Edward Miller 2
JEFFERYS, William Hamilton 2
JEFFORDS, Elza H
JEFFORDS, Joe Sam 6
JEFFORDS, Lawrence Suggs 6
JEFFORDS, Olin Merrill 4
JEFFREY, Edward Charles 4
JEFFREY, Frank Rumer 2
JEFFREY, Robert Hutchins 6
JEFFREY, Walter Roland 5
JEFFRIES, Benjamin Joy 1
JEFFRIES, Edward J. 3
JEFFRIES, John H
JEFFRIES, Louis Eugene 1
JEFFRIES, Millard Dudley 1
JEFFRIES, Walter Sooy 3
JEFFRIES, Zay 6
JEFFRIS, Malcolm George 1
JEFFS, Charles Richardson 3
JEIDELS, Otto H
JELKE, Ferdinand Frazier 3
JELKE, John Faris 4
JELKS, James Thomas 4
JELKS, John Lemuel 1
JELKS, William Dorsey 1
JELLEMA, William Harry 6
Jr.
JELLIFF, Horatio F. H
JELLIFFE, Smith Ely 2
JELLINEK, Elvin M. 4
JELLINGHAUS, C. L. 3
JELLISON, Walter Fremont 4
JEMISON, David Vivian 4
JEMISON, Mary H
JEMISON, Robert Jr. 6
JEMISON, Robert Sr. 1
JENCKES, Joseph * H
JENCKES, Joseph Sherburne Jr. 5
JENCKES, Marcien 5
JENCKES, Thomas Allen H
JENCKES, Virginia Ellis 6
JENCKS, Millard Henry 2
JENIFER, Daniel * H
JENKINS, Albert Gallatin H
JENKINS, Alfred Alexander 3
Jr.
JENKINS, Arthur 1
JENKINS, Burris Jr. 4
JENKINS, Burris Atkins 2
JENKINS, C. Bissell 3
JENKINS, Charles Francis 1

JENKINS, Charles Francis 3
JENKINS, Charles Jones H
JENKINS, Charles Rush 5
JENKINS, Daniel Edwards 1
JENKINS, David Rhys 3
JENKINS, Douglas 6
JENKINS, E. Fellows 1
JENKINS, Edward Corbin 5
JENKINS, Edward Elmer 5
JENKINS, Edward Hopkins 1
JENKINS, Florence Foster 4
JENKINS, Frances 5
JENKINS, Francis A. 4
JENKINS, Frank Edwin 1
JENKINS, Frederick Warren 1
JENKINS, George Franklin 1
JENKINS, Harry Hibbs 6
JENKINS, Herbert F(ranklin) 1
JENKINS, Herbert Theodore 5
JENKINS, Hermon Dutilh 1
JENKINS, Herschel V. 4
JENKINS, Hilger Perry 5
JENKINS, Howard Malcolm 1
JENKINS, J. Caldwell 3
JENKINS, James Alexander 4
JENKINS, James Alexander 5
JENKINS, James Graham 1
JENKINS, John H
JENKINS, John J. 1
JENKINS, John Murray 3
JENKINS, John S. Jr. H
JENKINS, John Stilwell H
JENKINS, Joseph Harley 6
JENKINS, Joseph J. 4
JENKINS, Lemuel H
JENKINS, MacGregor 3
JENKINS, Micah H
JENKINS, Michael 1
JENKINS, Nathaniel H
JENKINS, Oliver Peebles 1
JENKINS, Paul Burrill 1
JENKINS, Perry Wilson 3
JENKINS, Ralph Carlton 2
JENKINS, Robert 1
JENKINS, Robert Edwin 1
JENKINS, Romilly James Heald 5
JENKINS, Stephen 1
JENKINS, Thomas 5
JENKINS, Thomas Albert 1
JENKINS, Thomas Atkinson 1
JENKINS, Thornton Alexander H
JENKINS, Timothy H
JENKINS, Vernon Henry 3
JENKINS, William Adrian 6
JENKINS, William Dunbar 1
JENKINS, Will(iam) F(itzgerald) 6
JENKINS, William J. 3
JENKINS, William Leroy 3
JENKINS, William M. 1
JENKINS, William Oscar 4
JENKINS, William Robert 5
JENKINSON, Isaac 1
JENKINSON, Richard C. 1
JENKS, Albert Ernest 4
JENKS, Almet H
JENKS, Almet Francis 4
JENKS, Arthur Byron 2
JENKS, Arthur Whipple 1
JENKS, Benjamin L. 4
JENKS, Clarence Wilfred 6
JENKS, Edward Watrous 1
JENKS, Edwin Hart 1
JENKS, George Augustus 1
JENKS, George Charles 1
JENKS, Henry Fitch 4
JENKS, James Lawrence 4
JENKS, Jeremiah Whipple 1
JENKS, John Edward 1
JENKS, John Story 2
JENKS, John Whipple Potter 1
JENKS, Joseph H
JENKS, Michael Hutchinson H
JENKS, Orrin Roe 3
JENKS, Phoebe A. 1
Pickering
JENKS, Stephen Moore 6
JENKS, Tudor 1
JENKS, William H
JENKS, William Jackson 3
JENNE, James Nathaniel 1
JENNESS, Benning Wentworth H
JENNESS, Leslie George 5
JENNESS, Lyndon Yates 4
JENNESS, Theodora Robinson 1
JENNEY, Charles Albert 4
JENNEY, Charles Francis 1

JENNEY, Chester Ezekiel 6
JENNEY, Ralph E. 2
JENNEY, William Le Baron 1
JENNEY, William Sherman 5
JENNINGS, Andrew 1
Jackson
JENNINGS, B. Brewster 5
JENNINGS, Charles Godwin 1
JENNINGS, David H
JENNINGS, David 3
JENNINGS, Dean Southern 5
JENNINGS, Edward Henry 1
JENNINGS, Edwin B. 4
JENNINGS, Elzy Dee 5
JENNINGS, Frank E. 5
JENNINGS, Frederic Beach 1
JENNINGS, Hennen 1
JENNINGS, Henry Burritt 1
JENNINGS, Henry C. 1
JENNINGS, Herbert Spencer 2
JENNINGS, Isaac Jr. 5
JENNINGS, Joe Leslie 5
JENNINGS, John H
JENNINGS, John Jr. 3
JENNINGS, John Edward 6
Jr.
JENNINGS, John Joseph 1
JENNINGS, Jonathan H
JENNINGS, Judson Toll 2
JENNINGS, Leslie Nelson 5
JENNINGS, Louis John H
JENNINGS, Maria Croft 1
JENNINGS, Martin Luther 1
JENNINGS, Newell 4
JENNINGS, O. E. 4
JENNINGS, Oliver Gould 1
JENNINGS, Percy Hall 6
JENNINGS, Richard William 1
JENNINGS, Robert William 4
JENNINGS, Roscoe G. 4
JENNINGS, Rudolph D. 3
JENNINGS, Samuel Clemens 1
JENNINGS, Sidney Johnston 1
JENNINGS, Stephen Richard 5
JENNINGS, W. Beatty 1
JENNINGS, Walter 1
JENNINGS, Walter Louis 2
JENNINGS, Wesley William 5
JENNINGS, William Sherman H
JENNNINGS, T. Albert 1
JENSEN, Ben Franklin 5
JENSEN, Christen 6
JENSEN, Christian Nephi 4
JENSEN, Elmer C. 3
JENSEN, Frank A. 2
JENSEN, Howard C. 5
JENSEN, Jens 3
JENSEN, Johannes V. 3
JENSEN, John Christian 3
JENSEN, Leslie 4
JENSEN, Ralph Adelbert 2
JENT, John William 1
JENTE, Richard 3
JENTZSCH, Richard Alvin 6
JEPPSON, George Nathaniel 4
JEPSEN, Glenn Lowell 6
JEPSON, Harry B. 3
JEPSON, Ivar Per 5
JEPSON, Samuel L. 1
JEPSON, William 1
JERGENS, Andrew 4
JERMAN, Mrs. Cornelia 5
Petty
JERMAIN, Louis Francis 1
JERMAN, Thomas Palmer 4
JERMANE, William 4
Wallace
JERNBERG, Reinert 2
August
JERNEGAN, Marcus 2
Wilson
JERNEGAN, Prescott Ford 4
JERNIGAN, Charlton C. 3
JEROLOMAN, John 4
JEROME, Brother 3
JEROME, Chauncey H
JEROME, Harry 1
JEROME, William Travers 1
JERSILD, Marvin A(mble) 5
JERTBERG, Gilbert H. 6
JERVEY, Harold Edward 4
JERVEY, Henry 2
JERVEY, Huger Wilkinson 2
JERVEY, James Postell 2
JERVEY, James Wilkinson 2
JERVIS, John Bloomfield H
JESSE, Richard Henry 2

JESSE, Richard Henry 3
JESSE, William H(erman) 5
JESSEN, Karl Detlev 1
JESSOPP, Dudley Frederick 4
JESSUP, Charles Augustus 4
JESSUP, Edgar B. 4
JESSUP, Everett Colgate 5
JESSUP, Henry Harris 1
JESSUP, Henry Wynans 1
JESSUP, Joseph John 3
JESSUP, Samuel 1
JESSUP, Walter Albert 2
JESTER, Beauford Halbert 2
JESTER, John Roberts 5
JESUP, Henry Griswold 1
JESUP, Morris Ketchum 1
JESUP, Thomas Sidney H
JETER, Frank Hamilton 3
JETER, Jeremiah Bell H
JETT, Ewell Kirk 4
JETT, Robert Carter 4
JETT, Thomas M. 4
JEWELL, Bert Mark 6
JEWELL, Edward Alden 2
JEWELL, Frederick Swartz 1
JEWELL, Harvey H
JEWELL, James Ralph 6
JEWELL, Jesse Dale 6
JEWELL, John Franklin 1
JEWELL, Louise Pond 1
JEWELL, Marshall H
JEWELL, Theodore Frelinghuysen 1
JEWELL, William Henry 3
JEWETT, Arthur Crawford 4
JEWETT, Charles 1
JEWETT, Charles Coffin H
JEWETT, David H
JEWETT, Edward Hurtt 1
JEWETT, Frances Gulick 1
JEWETT, Frank Baldwin 2
JEWETT, Frank Fanning 3
JEWETT, Frederick Stiles H
JEWETT, Freeborn Garrettson H
JEWETT, George Anson 1
JEWETT, George Franklin 3
JEWETT, George Frederick 3
JEWETT, Harry Mulford 1
JEWETT, Harvey C. 1
JEWETT, Harvey Chase Jr. 3
JEWETT, Hugh 6
JEWETT, Hugh Judge H
JEWETT, James Richard 2
JEWETT, John Howard 1
JEWETT, John Howard H
JEWETT, John Punchard H
JEWETT, Joshua Husband H
JEWETT, Luther H
JEWETT, Milo Parker 1
JEWETT, Nelson J. 3
JEWETT, Rutger Bleecker 1
JEWETT, Sarah Orne 1
JEWETT, Sophie H
JEWETT, Stephen Perham 4
JEWETT, Stephen Shannon 1
JEWETT, William H
JEWETT, William Cornell H
JEWETT, William Samuel Lyon H
JEWETT, William Smith H
JIGGITTS, Louis Meredith 2
JIMENEZ, Juan Ramon 3
JIMENEZ OREAMUNO, 2
Ricardo
JINNAH, Mahomed Ali 2
JLLEK, Lubor 6
JOANNES, Francis Y. 3
JOAREZ, Benito H
JOB, Frederick William 1
JOB, Herbert Keightley 4
JOB, Robert 4
JOB, Thomas 5
JOBES, Harry C. 5
JOBIN, Raoul 6
JOBLING, James Wesley 4
JOBST, Norbert Raymond 6
JOCELYN, Nathaniel H
JOCELYN, Simeon Smith H
JOCELYN, Stephen Perry 1
JOCHEM, Anita M. 4
JOCHEMS, William Dennis 4
JOEHR, Adolf 6
JOEKEL, Samuel Levinson 3
JOEL, George William Freeman 3
JOERG, W. L. G. 3
JOESTING, Henry Rochambeau 4
JOGUES, Isaac H
JOHANN, Carl
JOHANNES, Francis 4
JOHANNSEN, Oskar Augustus
JOHANSEN, George P. 4
JOHANSEN, John C. 2

JOHL, Edwin Phillips 4
JOHN XXIII, His Holiness 4
JOHN, Augustus E. 4
JOHN, Francis Sister Mary 5
JOHN, John Price Durbin 1
JOHN, Samuel Will 4
JOHN, Waldemar Alfred Paul 4
JOHN, William Mestrezat 4
JOHN, William Scott 3
JOHNES, Edward Rodolph 4
JOHNS, Carl Oscar 2
JOHNS, Charles A. 4
JOHNS, Choate Webster 4
JOHNS, Clarence D. 3
JOHNS, Clayton 1
JOHNS, Cyrus N. 5
JOHNS, Frank Stoddert 5
JOHNS, George Sibley 1
JOHNS, John H
JOHNS, Joshua Leroy 2
JOHNS, Kensey H
JOHNS, Kensey Jr. H
JOHNS, Roy William 4
JOHNS, William Hingston 2
JOHNSEN, Erik Kristian 1
JOHNSON, Aben 1
JOHNSON, Adam Rankin 4
JOHNSON, Adelaide McFadyen 4
JOHNSON, Adna Romulus 4
JOHNSON, Alba Boardman 1
JOHNSON, Albert 3
JOHNSON, Albert Henry 5
JOHNSON, Albert Mussey 2
JOHNSON, Albert Richard 4
JOHNSON, Albert Rittenhouse 3
JOHNSON, Albert Williams 3
JOHNSON, Albinus Alonzo 4
JOHNSON, Alden Porter 5
JOHNSON, Alex Carlton 1
JOHNSON, Alexander H
JOHNSON, Alexander Bryan H
JOHNSON, Alexander Smith H
JOHNSON, Alfred Le Roy 4
JOHNSON, Alfred Sidney 3
JOHNSON, Alice Frein 6
JOHNSON, Allan Chester 3
JOHNSON, Allen 1
JOHNSON, Alvin Saunders 5
JOHNSON, Amos Neill 6
JOHNSON, Andrew H
JOHNSON, Andrew Gustavus 1
JOHNSON, Andrew W. 4
JOHNSON, Anna 3
JOHNSON, Anton J. 6
JOHNSON, Arnold Milton 3
JOHNSON, Arthur Charles 3
JOHNSON, Arthur Monrad 2
JOHNSON, Arthur Newhall 1
JOHNSON, Ashley Sidney 1
JOHNSON, Axel Petrus 4
JOHNSON, Bascom 3
JOHNSON, Ben * H
JOHNSON, Benjamin Alvin 2
JOHNSON, Benjamin Franklin 1
JOHNSON, Benjamin Newhall 1
JOHNSON, Benjamin Pierce H
JOHNSON, Bernard Lyman 2
JOHNSON, Bolling Arthur 1
JOHNSON, Bradley Tyler 1
JOHNSON, Buford Jeanette 6
JOHNSON, Burt W. H
JOHNSON, Bushrod Rust H
JOHNSON, Byron H
JOHNSON, Byron Arthur 4
JOHNSON, Byron Bancroft 1
JOHNSON, Campbell Carrington 5
JOHNSON, Carl Edward 5
JOHNSON, Carl Gunnard 4
JOHNSON, Carl W. 3
JOHNSON, Cave H
JOHNSON, Chapman H
JOHNSON, Charles 5
JOHNSON, Charles Ellicott 5
JOHNSON, Charles Eugene 1
JOHNSON, Charles F Jr. 3
JOHNSON, Charles F. H. 1
JOHNSON, Charles Fletcher 4
JOHNSON, Charles Frederick 1
JOHNSON, Charles Henry 4
JOHNSON, Charles Nelson 3
JOHNSON, Charles Oscar 4
JOHNSON, Charles Philip 1
JOHNSON, Charles Price 5

JOHNSON, Charles Spurgeon 3
JOHNSON, Charles Sumner 4
JOHNSON, Charles Williamson 4
JOHNSON, Charles Willis 4
JOHNSON, Charles Willison 1
JOHNSON, Charles Willison 2
JOHNSON, Clarence Hazelton 6
JOHNSON, Clarence S. 3
JOHNSON, Clarke Howard 1
JOHNSON, Claude M. 4
JOHNSON, Clifton 1
JOHNSON, Clinton Charles 6
JOHNSON, Cone 6
JOHNSON, Constance Fuller Wheeler (Mrs. Burges Johnson) 6
JOHNSON, Crawford Toy 4
JOHNSON, Crawford Toy 5
JOHNSON, Crockett (David Johnson Leisk) 6
JOHNSON, Curtis Boyd 3
JOHNSON, David 1
JOHNSON, David Bancroft 1
JOHNSON, David Clayton 2
JOHNSON, Douglas Wilson 2
JOHNSON, Duncan Starr 1
JOHNSON, E. Fred 5
JOHNSON, Earl A. 4
JOHNSON, Earle Frederick 3
JOHNSON, Earle George 4
JOHNSON, Eastman 1
JOHNSON, Eben Samuel 1
JOHNSON, Edgar Augustus Jerome 5
JOHNSON, Edgar Hutchinson 2
JOHNSON, Edgar N(athaniel) 5
JOHNSON, Edith Christina 3
JOHNSON, Edward * H
JOHNSON, Edward Bryant 1
JOHNSON, Edward Gilpin 5
JOHNSON, Edward Payson 1
JOHNSON, Edward Roberts 4
JOHNSON, Edwin Carl 5
JOHNSON, Edwin Clifford 4
JOHNSON, Edwin Ferry H
JOHNSON, Edwin S. 1
JOHNSON, Effie 1
JOHNSON, Elbert Leland 2
JOHNSON, Eldridge Reeves 2
JOHNSON, Elias Finley 1
JOHNSON, Elias Henry 1
JOHNSON, Elijah H
JOHNSON, Elizabeth H
JOHNSON, Elizabeth Forrest 6
JOHNSON, Elizabeth Winthrop 4
JOHNSON, Ellen H
JOHNSON, Ellen Cheney H
JOHNSON, Ellis Adolph 6
JOHNSON, Elvera Crosby (Mrs. John Alex Johnson) 6
JOHNSON, Emil Fritiof 4
JOHNSON, Emory Richard 1
JOHNSON, Emsley Wright 3
JOHNSON, Ernest Amos 4
JOHNSON, Evan Malbone 1
JOHNSON, Francis H
JOHNSON, Francis Ellis 5
JOHNSON, Francis Howe 4
JOHNSON, Francis Kirk 4
JOHNSON, Francis Rarick 4
JOHNSON, Francis Raymond 1
JOHNSON, Frank Asbury 4
JOHNSON, Frank Fisk 5
JOHNSON, Frank Pearson 4
JOHNSON, Frank Seward 1
JOHNSON, Frank Tenney 4
JOHNSON, Franklin 1
JOHNSON, Franklin 2
JOHNSON, Franklin Paradise H
JOHNSON, Franklin Winslow 3
JOHNSON, Fred G. 5
JOHNSON, Fred Page 5
JOHNSON, Frederick 5
JOHNSON, Frederick Avery 5
JOHNSON, Frederick Ernest 5
JOHNSON, Frederick Foote 1
JOHNSON, Frederick Green 1
JOHNSON, Frederick William 3
JOHNSON, George 2
JOHNSON, George 1
JOHNSON, George C. 4

JOHNSON, George E. Q. 2
JOHNSON, George Ellsworth 1
JOHNSON, George Francis 2
JOHNSON, George H. 3
JOHNSON, George K. 1
JOHNSON, George W. 3
JOHNSON, George William 2
JOHNSON, Glover 6
JOHNSON, Gove Griffith 2
JOHNSON, Grace Allen 3
JOHNSON, Gustavus 4
JOHNSON, Guy H
JOHNSON, Hale 1
JOHNSON, Hallett 5
JOHNSON, Hansford Duncan 4
JOHNSON, Harold Bowtell 2
JOHNSON, Harry McCrindell 1
JOHNSON, Harry Miles 3
JOHNSON, Harvey Hull H
JOHNSON, Hayden 1
JOHNSON, Helen Kendrick 1
JOHNSON, Helgi 6
JOHNSON, Henry H
JOHNSON, Henry Clark 1
JOHNSON, Henry Herbert 1
JOHNSON, Henry Lincoln 1
JOHNSON, Henry Lowry Emilius 1
JOHNSON, Henry Mortimer 3
JOHNSON, Henry U. 4
JOHNSON, Henry Viley 1
JOHNSON, Herbert 2
JOHNSON, Herbert Fisk 1
JOHNSON, Herbert Morris 1
JOHNSON, Herbert Spencer 2
JOHNSON, Herman E. 5
JOHNSON, Herrick 1
JOHNSON, Herschel V. 4
JOHNSON, Herschel Vespasian H
JOHNSON, Hewlett 1
JOHNSON, Hiram Warren 4
JOHNSON, Homer Hosea 4
JOHNSON, Horace 2
JOHNSON, Howard 5
JOHNSON, Howard Albert 6
JOHNSON, Howard Cooper 3
JOHNSON, Hugh McCain 2
JOHNSON, Hugh S. 2
JOHNSON, Irving Peska 2
JOHNSON, Isaac Cureton 3
JOHNSON, J. Ford 4
JOHNSON, J. Lovell 1
JOHNSON, J. Sidney 5
JOHNSON, Jackson 1
JOHNSON, Jacob 3
JOHNSON, James * H
JOHNSON, James Augustus H
JOHNSON, James Buford 3
JOHNSON, James Clarence 4
JOHNSON, James Gibson 1
JOHNSON, James Granville 1
JOHNSON, James Hutchins H
JOHNSON, James Leeper 1
JOHNSON, James McIntosh 3
JOHNSON, James Weldon 1
JOHNSON, Jed Joseph 4
JOHNSON, Jefferson Deems Jr. 1
JOHNSON, Jeremiah Augustus 1
JOHNSON, Jeromus H
JOHNSON, Jesse 3
JOHNSON, John H
JOHNSON, Sir John H
JOHNSON, John A. 1
JOHNSON, John Albert 1
JOHNSON, John B. 1
JOHNSON, John Beauregard 6
JOHNSON, John Bockover Jr. 5
JOHNSON, John Butler 1
JOHNSON, John David 6
JOHNSON, John Davis 4
JOHNSON, John Edward 1
JOHNSON, John Edward 5
JOHNSON, John Gilmore 1
JOHNSON, John Graver 1
JOHNSON, John Lipscomb 1
JOHNSON, John Mitchell 4
JOHNSON, John Monroe 4
JOHNSON, John Samuel Adolphus 1
JOHNSON, John T. 4
JOHNSON, John Telemachus H
JOHNSON, John Theodore 4

JOHNSON, John William 1
JOHNSON, Jonathan H
JOHNSON, Jonathan Eastman 4
JOHNSON, Joseph * H
JOHNSON, Joseph French 1
JOHNSON, Joseph Horsfall 1
JOHNSON, Joseph Lowery 5
JOHNSON, Joseph Taber 1
JOHNSON, Joseph Travis 4
JOHNSON, Joseph Travis 4
JOHNSON, Jotham 4
JOHNSON, Julia Macfarlane 1
JOHNSON, Justin H
JOHNSON, Justin 4
JOHNSON, Kate Burr (Mrs. Clarence A. Johnson) 6
JOHNSON, Keen 5
JOHNSON, Kenneth D. 3
JOHNSON, Lambert Dunning 3
JOHNSON, Lee Payne 4
JOHNSON, Leighton Foster 3
JOHNSON, Leon H. 5
JOHNSON, Lester 6
JOHNSON, Lester Bicknell 5
JOHNSON, Levi 1
JOHNSON, Lewis Edgar 2
JOHNSON, Lewis Jerome 3
JOHNSON, Ligon 3
JOHNSON, Lilian Wyckoff 4
JOHNSON, Lincoln 3
JOHNSON, Lindsay Franklin 6
JOHNSON, Livingston 1
JOHNSON, Loren Bascom Tabor 2
JOHNSON, Lorenzo M. 1
JOHNSON, Louis Arthur 4
JOHNSON, Lucius E. 1
JOHNSON, Lucius Henry 1
JOHNSON, Luther Alexander 4
JOHNSON, Luther Appeles 1
JOHNSON, Lyndon Baines 5
JOHNSON, Magnus 3
JOHNSON, Malcolm 3
JOHNSON, Margaret 4
JOHNSON, Margaret Louise 6
JOHNSON, Marietta Louise 1
JOHNSON, Marion Alvin 4
JOHNSON, Marmaduke H
JOHNSON, Martin 1
JOHNSON, Martin Nelson 1
JOHNSON, Max Sherred 4
JOHNSON, Melvin Maynard 3
JOHNSON, Melvin Maynard Jr. 4
JOHNSON, Merle DeVore 1
JOHNSON, Milbank 2
JOHNSON, Mortimer Lawrence 1
JOHNSON, Nathaniel H
JOHNSON, Nels G. 3
JOHNSON, Nelson Trusler 3
JOHNSON, Noadiah H
JOHNSON, Oliver H
JOHNSON, Oliver Francis 1
JOHNSON, Osa Helen 3
JOHNSON, Oscar John 2
JOHNSON, Otis Coe 1
JOHNSON, Otis R. 3
JOHNSON, Owen 3
JOHNSON, Palmer O. 3
JOHNSON, Paul Burney 4
JOHNSON, Paul Emanuel 6
JOHNSON, Paul Luther 6
JOHNSON, Paul Rodgers 2
JOHNSON, Perley Brown 1
JOHNSON, Philander Chase 1
JOHNSON, Philip H
JOHNSON, Philip Gustav 2
JOHNSON, Ralph Blake 4
JOHNSON, Randall Edward 6
JOHNSON, Ray Prescott 4
JOHNSON, Reginald Davis 3
JOHNSON, Reverdy H
JOHNSON, Richard Ellis 6
JOHNSON, Richard H. 3
JOHNSON, Richard Harvey 1
JOHNSON, Richard Mentor H
JOHNSON, Richard Newhall 5
JOHNSON, Richard W. H
JOHNSON, Richard Zina 1
JOHNSON, Robert 4
JOHNSON, Robert Livingston 5
JOHNSON, Robert Livingston Jr. 1
JOHNSON, Robert Underwood H

JOHNSON, Robert V. 6
JOHNSON, Robert W. 4
JOHNSON, Robert Ward H
JOHNSON, Robert Wilkinson 1
JOHNSON, Robert Wood 5
JOHNSON, Robert Wood Jr. 5
JOHNSON, Roger Bruce Cash 3
JOHNSON, Rosamond 3
JOHNSON, Rossiter 1
JOHNSON, Roy Melisander 6
JOHNSON, Roy William 1
JOHNSON, Royal Cleaves 1
JOHNSON, S. Arthur 4
JOHNSON, Samuel * H
JOHNSON, Samuel William 1
JOHNSON, Silas 3
JOHNSON, Simeon Moses 1
JOHNSON, Stanley 2
JOHNSON, Stanley H. 1
JOHNSON, Sveinbjorn 1
JOHNSON, Sylvanus Elihu 1
JOHNSON, Talmage Casey 1
JOHNSON, Theodore 3
JOHNSON, Thomas 1
JOHNSON, Thomas Cary 1
JOHNSON, Thomas Humrickhouse 1
JOHNSON, Thomas Joseph Allan 1
JOHNSON, Thomas Moore 1
JOHNSON, Tillman Davis 1
JOHNSON, Tom Loftin 1
JOHNSON, Treat Baldwin 1
JOHNSON, Virgil Lamont 4
JOHNSON, Virginia Wales 1
JOHNSON, W. Ogden 4
JOHNSON, Waldo Porter H
JOHNSON, Wallace 1
JOHNSON, Wallace Clyde 1
JOHNSON, Walter H. 4
JOHNSON, Walter Lathrop 4
JOHNSON, Walter Nathan 3
JOHNSON, Walter Perry 1
JOHNSON, Walter Perry 4
JOHNSON, Walter Richard 6
JOHNSON, Wanda Mae 5
JOHNSON, Wayne 4
JOHNSON, Wendell A. L. 4
JOHNSON, William H
JOHNSON, Sir William H
JOHNSON, William Allen 1
JOHNSON, William Arthur 3
JOHNSON, William Bullein H
JOHNSON, William Burdett 3
JOHNSON, William C. 3
JOHNSON, William Christie H
JOHNSON, William Cost 5
JOHNSON, William Driscoll H
JOHNSON, William Eugene 2
JOHNSON, William F. 4
JOHNSON, William Franklin 4
JOHNSON, William Geary 4
JOHNSON, William Hallock 4
JOHNSON, William Hannibal 1
JOHNSON, William Harold 5
JOHNSON, William Henry 1
JOHNSON, William Houston 4
JOHNSON, William Howard 1
JOHNSON, William Martin 4
JOHNSON, William Mindred 1
JOHNSON, William Ransom H
JOHNSON, William Samuel H
JOHNSON, William Samuel 1
JOHNSON, William Templeton 3
JOHNSON, William Woolsey 3
JOHNSON, Willis Ernest 1
JOHNSON, Willis Fletcher 1
JOHNSON, Willis Grant 1
JOHNSON, Wingate M. 1
JOHNSTON, Adelia Antoinette Field 1
JOHNSTON, Albert Sidney H
JOHNSTON, Alexander H
JOHNSTON, Alva 3
JOHNSTON, Alvanley 1
JOHNSTON, Annie Fellows 1
JOHNSTON, Archibald 4
JOHNSTON, Augustus H
JOHNSTON, Charles 1
JOHNSTON, Charles 1
JOHNSTON, Charles H
JOHNSTON, Charles Clement

JOHNSTON, Charles Eugene 3
JOHNSTON, Charles G. 4
JOHNSTON, Charles Haven Ladd 2
JOHNSTON, Charles Hughes 1
JOHNSTON, Charles Worth 1
JOHNSTON, Christopher 1
JOHNSTON, Clarence Howard 1
JOHNSTON, Clarence Thomas 5
JOHNSTON, David Claypoole H
JOHNSTON, David E. 4
JOHNSTON, David Ira 3
JOHNSTON, Douglas T. 4
JOHNSTON, Elizabeth Bryant 1
JOHNSTON, Ella Bond 4
JOHNSTON, Eric A. 4
JOHNSTON, Forney 4
JOHNSTON, Frances Benjamin 3
JOHNSTON, Francis Wayland 4
JOHNSTON, Franklin Davis 5
JOHNSTON, Gabriel H
JOHNSTON, George Ben 1
JOHNSTON, George Doherty 1
JOHNSTON, Gordon 1
JOHNSTON, Gordon 3
JOHNSTON, Harold Whetstone 1
JOHNSTON, Harry Lang 2
JOHNSTON, Harry Raymond 6
JOHNSTON, Harvey Pollard 5
JOHNSTON, Henrietta 1
JOHNSTON, Henry Alan 3
JOHNSTON, Henry Donaldson 4
JOHNSTON, Henry Phelps 1
JOHNSTON, Herrick Lee 4
JOHNSTON, Howard Agnew 1
JOHNSTON, Hugh 1
JOHNSTON, Ivan Murray 4
JOHNSTON, J. Stoddard 1
JOHNSTON, James 4
JOHNSTON, James A. 1
JOHNSTON, James Martin 4
JOHNSTON, James Steptoe 1
JOHNSTON, John H
JOHNSTON, John 1
JOHNSTON, John 3
JOHNSTON, John Alexander 1
JOHNSTON, John Black 2
JOHNSTON, John Lawrence 3
JOHNSTON, John T. M. 1
JOHNSTON, John Taylor H
JOHNSTON, John Warfield H
JOHNSTON, Joseph Eggleston 1
JOHNSTON, Joseph Forney 1
JOHNSTON, Josiah Stoddard H
JOHNSTON, Julia Harriette 1
JOHNSTON, Kilbourne 5
JOHNSTON, L. S. 3
JOHNSTON, Lawrence Albert 1
JOHNSTON, Leon H. 4
JOHNSTON, Leslie Morgan 5
JOHNSTON, Lucy Browne 1
JOHNSTON, Marbury 1
JOHNSTON, Maria Isabella 5
JOHNSTON, Mary 1
JOHNSTON, Myrtle Alice Dean (Mrs. Carl Edward Johnston) 6
JOHNSTON, Nathan Robinson 4
JOHNSTON, Olin Dewitt 4
JOHNSTON, Oliver Martin 4
JOHNSTON, Oscar Goodbar 3
JOHNSTON, Percy Hampton 3
JOHNSTON, Peter H
JOHNSTON, Richard Hall 5
JOHNSTON, Richard Holland 3
JOHNSTON, Richard Malcolm H
JOHNSTON, Rienzi Melville 1
JOHNSTON, Robert Born 5
JOHNSTON, Robert Daniel 4

JOHNSTON, Robert Matteson 1
JOHNSTON, Robert Story 2
JOHNSTON, Rowland L. 1
JOHNSTON, Rufus Perry 1
JOHNSTON, Russell M. 4
JOHNSTON, Samuel H
JOHNSTON, Samuel 4
JOHNSTON, Samuel M. 5
JOHNSTON, Stanley 4
JOHNSTON, Stewart 1
JOHNSTON, Thomas H
JOHNSTON, Thomas Alexander 1
JOHNSTON, Thomas Murphy H
JOHNSTON, Thomas William 1
JOHNSTON, Victor A. 4
JOHNSTON, W. DAWSON 1
JOHNSTON, W. Dawson * 1
JOHNSTON, W. Fenton 4
JOHNSTON, W(illia)m Allen 5
JOHNSTON, Walter Vail 4
JOHNSTON, Wayne Andrew 4
JOHNSTON, William H
JOHNSTON, William 1
JOHNSTON, William Agnew 1
JOHNSTON, William Atkinson 1
JOHNSTON, William Drumm Jr. 5
JOHNSTON, William Greer 3
JOHNSTON, William Hugh 1
JOHNSTON, William Milton 1
JOHNSTON, William Pollock H
JOHNSTON, William Preston 1
JOHNSTON, William Waring 1
JOHNSTON, Wirt 1
JOHNSTON, Zachariah H
JOHNSTONE, Arthur Edward 5
JOHNSTONE, Bruce 5
JOHNSTONE, Edward Ransom 2
JOHNSTONE, Edward Robert 1
JOHNSTONE, Ernest Kinloch 2
JOHNSTONE, Henry Fraser 4
JOHNSTONE, Henry Webb 5
JOHNSTONE, Job H
JOHNSTONE, John Humphreys 4
JOHNSTONE, William Jackson 1
JOHONNOTT, Edwin Sheldon 1
JOINER, Otis William 6
JOLIET, Louis H
JOLINE, Adrian Hoffman 1
JOLIOT-CURIE, Frederic 3
JOLIOT-CURIE, Irene 3
JOLIVET, Andre 4
JOLLES, Otto Jolle Matthijs 5
JOLLIFFE, Charles Byron 5
JOLLIFFE, Norman H. 4
JOLLY, Austin Howell 4
JOLLY, Robert Garland 3
JOLSON, Al 3
JOME, Hiram L. 4
JONAH, Frank Gilbert 2
JONAS, August Frederick 1
JONAS, Benjamin Franklin 1
JONAS, Charles Andrew 4
JONAS, Edgar A. 4
JONAS, Franz 6
JONAS, Jack Henry 5
JONAS, Maryla 3
JONAS, Nathan S. 4
JONAS, Ralph 3
JONAS, Russell E. 5
JONES, Aaron 4
JONES, Abner 4
JONES, Ada 4
JONES, Adam Leroy 1
JONES, Albert Marshall 4
JONES, Albert Monmouth 4
JONES, Albert R. 5
JONES, Alexander H
JONES, Alexander Francis 4
JONES, Alfred 1
JONES, Alfred 4
JONES, Alfred B. 4
JONES, Alfred Miles 1
JONES, Allen 1
JONES, Allen Northey 3
JONES, Amanda Theodosia 1

JONES, Andrieus Aristieus 1
JONES, Anson H
JONES, Archibald A. 4
JONES, Arthur Gray 1
JONES, Arthur Julius 1
JONES, Arthur Woodruff 6
JONES, Augustine 1
JONES, Barton Mills 3
JONES, Bassett 3
JONES, Benjamin H
JONES, Benjamin Franklin * 1
JONES, Benjamin Franklin Jr. 1
JONES, Bob 4
JONES, Breckinridge 1
JONES, Brian 5
JONES, Bruce Carr 3
JONES, Buell Fay 2
JONES, Burr W. 1
JONES, Burton Rensselaer 1
JONES, C. Edward 1
JONES, C. Hampson 1
JONES, Calvin H
JONES, Carl H. 3
JONES, Carl Waring 3
JONES, Carlton Allen 1
JONES, Carter Helm 2
JONES, Catesby Ap Roger H
JONES, Charles Alfred 2
JONES, Charles Alvin 4
JONES, Charles Andrews 3
JONES, Charles Colcock 1
JONES, Charles Colcock III 5
JONES, Charles Davies 1
JONES, Charles F. 1
JONES, Charles Fremont 1
JONES, Charles Henry 1
JONES, Charles Hodge 6
JONES, Charles Paul 1
JONES, Charles Reading 2
JONES, Charles S. 5
JONES, Charles Sumner 1
JONES, Cheney Church 3
JONES, Chester Lloyd 1
JONES, Chester Morse 5
JONES, Claud Ashton 2
JONES, Clement Ross 1
JONES, Cliff C. 4
JONES, Clyde E. 3
JONES, Cyril Hamlen 1
JONES, Daniel Fiske 1
JONES, Daniel Jonathan 4
JONES, Daniel Terryll H
JONES, Daniel Webster 1
JONES, David H
JONES, David 6
JONES, David Dallas 3
JONES, David Hugh 4
JONES, David Percy 1
JONES, David Rumph H
JONES, Donald Forsha 4
JONES, Dwight Bangs 3
JONES, E. Lester 1
JONES, E(mmett) Milton 5
JONES, Earl J. 3
JONES, Edgar DeWitt 3
JONES, Edgar Laroy 1
JONES, Edith Kathleen 4
JONES, Edmund Adams 1
JONES, Edward Campbell 1
JONES, Edward David 3
JONES, Edward E. 2
JONES, Edward Franc 1
JONES, Edward Groves 1
JONES, Edward Perry 1
JONES, Edwin Frank 1
JONES, Edwin Lee 5
JONES, Edwin Leslie 6
JONES, Edwin Whiting 4
JONES, Eleanor Louise 5
JONES, Eli Stanley 5
JONES, Eliot 1
JONES, Elizabeth Dickson 4
JONES, Ella Virginia 4
JONES, Elmer Ellsworth 5
JONES, Elmer Ray 5
JONES, Elton B. 4
JONES, Evan J. 5
JONES, Evelyn Tubb 5
JONES, Everett Starr 4
JONES, F. Robertson 1
JONES, Fernando 1
JONES, Floyd William 1
JONES, Forrest Robert 4
JONES, Francis H
JONES, Francis Coates 1
JONES, Francis Ilah 3
JONES, Frank 1
JONES, Frank Cazenove 2
JONES, Frank Johnston 1
JONES, Frank Leonard 3
JONES, Frank Pierce 5
JONES, Franklin D. 1
JONES, Franklin Elmore 5
JONES, Frederic Marshall 2

JONES, Frederic Randolph 6
JONES, Frederick E. 6
JONES, Frederick Robertson 2
JONES, Gabriel H
JONES, Gaius J. 4
JONES, Gardner Maynard 1
JONES, George * H
JONES, George H. 1
JONES, George Heber 1
JONES, George Herbert 1
JONES, George James 4
JONES, George Lewis Jr. 5
JONES, George Salley 1
JONES, George Wallace H
JONES, George Washington H
JONES, George Washington 1
JONES, George William 1
JONES, Grinnell 2
JONES, Guernsey 1
JONES, H. Bolton 1
JONES, Harold Ellis 4
JONES, Harold Wellington 3
JONES, Harriot Hamblen 3
JONES, Harrison 1
JONES, Harry Burnell 5
JONES, Harry Clary 1
JONES, Harry Stewart 1
JONES, Harry Stuart Vedder 4
JONES, Harry Wild 1
JONES, Heber 1
JONES, Henrietta Ord 4
JONES, Henry Craig 4
JONES, Henry Lawrence 4
JONES, Henry N(eely) 6
JONES, Herbert Coffin 6
JONES, Herbert Vincent 2
JONES, Herschell V. 1
JONES, Hilary Pollard 1
JONES, Hilton Ira 3
JONES, Horace Conrad 1
JONES, Howard 4
JONES, Howard Palfrey 6
JONES, Hugh H
JONES, Hugh McK 1
JONES, I. Howland 5
JONES, Idwal 1
JONES, Ilion Tingnal 5
JONES, Isaac Dashiell 1
JONES, Isaac Thomas 1
JONES, Isham 1
JONES, J. Catron 1
JONES, J. Claude 1
JONES, J. Levering 1
JONES, J. Morris 4
JONES, J. S. William 2
JONES, J. Shirley 3
JONES, J. Sparhawk 1
JONES, J. William 1
JONES, Jacob H
JONES, James * H
JONES, James Archibald 4
JONES, James Chamberlayne 1
JONES, James Coulter 2
JONES, James Emlyn 1
JONES, James Hazlitt 5
JONES, James Kimbrough 1
JONES, James Marion Jr. 1
JONES, James Mills 1
JONES, James Sumner 1
JONES, James Taylor H
JONES, Jefferson 4
JONES, Jehu Glancy 1
JONES, Jenkin Lloyd 1
JONES, Jerome 1
JONES, Jesse Holman 3
JONES, Joe 1
JONES, Joel H
JONES, John H
JONES, John B. H
JONES, John Beauchamp H
JONES, John Carleton 1
JONES, John Edward 1
JONES, John George 3
JONES, John Logan 4
JONES, John Paul H
JONES, John Paul 1
JONES, John Percival 1
JONES, John Price 1
JONES, John Sills 1
JONES, John Taylor 4
JONES, John Wesley 4
JONES, John William 4
JONES, John Winston H
JONES, Jonathan 1
JONES, Joseph * H
JONES, Joseph Addison 2
JONES, Joseph Merrick 4
JONES, Joseph Russell 1
JONES, Joseph Seawell 1
JONES, Joseph Stevens H
JONES, Joshua H. 1
JONES, Kate Emery Sanborn 4

JONES, Lake 1
JONES, Laurence Clifton 6
JONES, Lawrence Clark 5
JONES, Lawrence Donald 4
JONES, Lawrence E. 4
JONES, Leonard Augustus 1
JONES, Lester Martin 3
JONES, Lewis Barrett 4
JONES, Lewis Henry * 1
JONES, Lewis Howel 5
JONES, Lewis Ralph 2
JONES, Lewis Webster 6
JONES, Livingston Erringer 2
JONES, Livingston French 1
JONES, Llewellyn 1
JONES, Lloyd E. 3
JONES, Louis R. 5
JONES, Louise Tayler 2
JONES, Loyd Ancile 3
JONES, Lynds 1
JONES, Mabel Cronise 1
JONES, Marcus Eugene 1
JONES, Marvin Fisher 3
JONES, Mary Harris H
JONES, Mary Harris 1
JONES, Matt Bushnell 1
JONES, Mattison Boyd 2
JONES, Melvin 4
JONES, Meredith Ashby 2
JONES, Millard Franklin 4
JONES, Minetry Leigh 1
JONES, Montfort 3
JONES, Morgan H
JONES, Morton Tebbs 4
JONES, Nard 5
JONES, Nathaniel H
JONES, Nellie Sawyer Kedzie 3
JONES, Nelson Edwards 1
JONES, Newell N. 5
JONES, Noble Wymberley H
JONES, Norman Edward 5
JONES, Norman L. 1
JONES, O. Garfield 3
JONES, Olin McKendree 4
JONES, Olive M. (Olivia Mary) 5
JONES, Ollie E. 6
JONES, Owen H
JONES, Paul 4
JONES, Paul 6
JONES, Paul Fouts 3
JONES, Peter Smith 5
JONES, Philip Harold 5
JONES, Philip Lovering 1
JONES, Philip Mills 1
JONES, Phineas 3
JONES, Quill 3
JONES, Ralph Beaumont 4
JONES, Ralph M. 2
JONES, Reginald Lamont 2
JONES, Richard 1
JONES, Richard Channing 1
JONES, Richard Hugh 6
JONES, Richard Lee 4
JONES, Richard Lloyd 4
JONES, Richard Mott 1
JONES, Richard Saxe 1
JONES, Richard Uriah 1
JONES, Richard Walter 1
JONES, Richard Watson 1
JONES, Robert Edmond 3
JONES, Robert Ellis 1
JONES, Robert Franklin 5
JONES, Robert Haydon 6
JONES, Robert Lee 1
JONES, Robert Looney 4
JONES, Robert Martin 6
JONES, Robert Otis 4
JONES, Robert Taylor 5
JONES, Robert Tyre Jr. (Bobby Jones) 5
JONES, Robert Vernon 5
JONES, Robinson Godfrey 1
JONES, Rodney Wilcox 6
JONES, Roland H
JONES, Roy Bergstresser 4
JONES, Roy Childs 4
JONES, Rufus Matthew 4
JONES, Samuel * H
JONES, Samuel Augustus 5
JONES, Samuel Fosdick 4
JONES, Samuel J. 1
JONES, Samuel Milton 1
JONES, Samuel Porter 1
JONES, Seaborn 1
JONES, Sebastian Chatham 1
JONES, Seth Benjamin 4
JONES, Seward William 4
JONES, Stephen Alfred 1
JONES, Sullivan W. 3
JONES, Sybil 1
JONES, T. Sambola H
JONES, Thomas H
JONES, Thomas Alfred 1

JONES, Thomas Ap Catesby H
JONES, Thomas Clive 2
JONES, Thomas Davies 1
JONES, Thomas Dow H
JONES, Thomas Elsa 6
JONES, Thomas Goode 1
JONES, Thomas Hoyt 2
JONES, Thomas Hudson 5
JONES, Thomas Jesse 2
JONES, Thomas Laurens H
JONES, Thomas P. H
JONES, Thomas Samuel Jr. 1
JONES, Victor Owen 5
JONES, Vincent Lloyd 4
JONES, Virginia Smith 1
JONES, W. A. Fleming 1
JONES, Mrs. W. J. (Mollie Roberts Jones) 5
JONES, W. Paul 3
JONES, Walk Claridge 4
JONES, Wallace Thaxter 2
JONES, Walter * H
JONES, Walter 1
JONES, Walter Burgwyn 4
JONES, Walter Clinton 2
JONES, Walter Clyde 1
JONES, Walter Parker 6
JONES, Warren Francis 5
JONES, Washington 1
JONES, Wesley Livsey 1
JONES, Wharton Stewart 1
JONES, Wiley Emmet 1
JONES, Wilie 4
JONES, Will Owen 1
JONES, William * H
JONES, William A. 4
JONES, William Albert 1
JONES, William Alexander 1
JONES, William Alfred 1
JONES, William Alton 4
JONES, William Ambrose 1
JONES, William Atkinson 1
JONES, William Carey * 1
JONES, William Jackson 6
JONES, William James 6
JONES, William James Jr. 1
JONES, William Larimer Jr. 3
JONES, William Otterbein 1
JONES, William Palmer H
JONES, William Patterson H
JONES, William Ralph 6
JONES, William Richard H
JONES, William Russell 5
JONES, William Theopilus H
JONES, Willie H
JONGERS, Alphonse 3
JONSON, Jep C. 4
JONSON, Libby Anne 6
JONSSON, Axel 3
JOPLIN, Janis 5
JOPP, Charles B. 5
JOPSON, John Howard 3
JORDAN, Arthur 1
JORDAN, Arthur Wheeler 6
JORDAN, Benjamin Everett 6
JORDAN, Charles Bernard 2
JORDAN, Charles Edward 6
JORDAN, Chester Bradley 1
JORDAN, Clarence Lorin 5
JORDAN, Conrad N. 1
JORDAN, David Francis 2
JORDAN, David Starr 1
JORDAN, Eben Dyer 1
JORDAN, Edward Benedict 3
JORDAN, Edward Stanlaw 3
JORDAN, Edwin Oakes 1
JORDAN, Elizabeth 2
JORDAN, Floyd 4
JORDAN, Francis Jr. 1
JORDAN, Frank Craig 1
JORDAN, Frank Morrill 5
JORDAN, Frederick Freas 1
JORDAN, G. Gunby 1
JORDAN, G. Ray 4
JORDAN, Harvey Bryant 4
JORDAN, Harvey Ernest 6
JORDAN, Harvey Herbert 5
JORDAN, Harvie 5
JORDAN, Henry Donaldson 6
JORDAN, Howard William 4
JORDAN, Isaac M. H
JORDAN, James Henry 1
JORDAN, John H. 4
JORDAN, John Woolf 4
JORDAN, Jules 1
JORDAN, Kate 1
JORDAN, Lyman Granville 1
JORDAN, Mahlon Kline 4
JORDAN, Marian 4
JORDAN, Mary Augusta 1
JORDAN, Ralph Curtis 4
JORDAN, Richard Henry 5
JORDAN, Riverda Harding 3
JORDAN, Samuel Martin 3
JORDAN, Sara Murray 3
JORDAN, Thomas H
JORDAN, Thomas Walden 1
JORDAN, Virgil 4
JORDAN, Weymouth Tyree 5
JORDAN, Whitman Howard 1
JORDAN, William Frederick 1
JORDAN, William George 1
JORDAN, William Mark 4
JORDEN, Edward Fletcher 1
JORGENSEN, Joseph H
JORGENSON, Ralph Enoch 6
JORGENSON, Theodore 6
JORN, Asger 6
JORPES, J. Erik 6
JOSAPHARE, Lionel 5
JOSEPH, Don Rosco 1
JOSEPH, Lawrence Edgar 3
JOSEPH, Lazarus 4
JOSEPHI, Isaac A. 5
JOSEPHSON, Aksel Gustav Salomon 2
JOSEPHSON, Clarence Egbert 5
JOSHI, Samuel Lucas 1
JOSLIN, Cedric Freeman 1
JOSLIN, Elliott Proctor 4
JOSLIN, Falcon 1
JOSLIN, Harold Vincent 1
JOSLIN, Theodore Goldsmith 2
JOSLIN, William Cary 1
JOSLYN, Marcellus Lindsey 4
JOSS, John 3
JOSSELYN, Benage S. 4
JOSSELYN, Charles 4
JOSSELYN, Freeman Marshall 1
JOSSELYN, John H
JOSSET, Raoul Jean 3
JOST, Henry Lee 3
JOST, Hudson 4
JOSTEN, Werner Eric 4
JOSTES, Frederick Augustus 3
JOUBERT DE LA MURAILLE, James Hector Marie Nicholas H
JOUETT, Edward Stockton 5
JOUETT, James Edward 1
JOUETT, John H
JOUETT, John Hamilton 5
JOUETT, Matthew Harris H
JOUHAUX, Leon 3
JOUIN, Louis 1
JOURARD, Sidney Marshall 6
JOURDAN, James H. 1
JOURNET, Marcel 1
JOUTEL, Henri H
JOUVENAL, Jacques H
JOWETT, John Henry 1
JOY, Agnes Elisabeth Winona Leclercq 4
JOY, Agnes Elisabeth Winona Leclercq H
JOY, Charles Frederick 4
JOY, Charles Turner 3
JOY, Henry Bourne 1
JOY, James Frederick H
JOY, James Richard 3
JOY, Richard Pickering 5
JOY, Thomas H
JOYCE, Adrian Dwight 3
JOYCE, Charles Herbert 4
JOYCE, Dwight P. 5
JOYCE, Isaac W. 1
JOYCE, J(ames) Wallace 5
JOYCE, James 3
JOYCE, John Alexander 1
JOYCE, John Michael 4
JOYCE, Kenyon Ashe 3
JOYCE, Matthew M. 3
JOYCE, Nedra Norton 6
JOYCE, Patrick H. 2
JOYCE, R. Edwin 3
JOYCE, Thomas Martin 2
JOYCE, Walter Eves 5
JOYCE, Walter Frank 5
JOYCE, William B. 4
JOYCE, William Henry 1
JOYES, John Warren 2
JOYNER, Fred Bunyan 4
JOYNER, James Yadkin 3
JOYNES, Edward Southey 1
JUBE, Albert Riordan 5
JUCH, Emma Antonia Joanna 1
JUCHHOFF, Frederick 3
JUDAH, Noble Brandon * 1
JUDAH, Samuel H
JUDAH, Samuel Benjamin Helbert H
JUDAH, Theodore Dehone H
JUDAY, Chancey 2
JUDD, Bertha Grimmell 2
JUDD, Charles Hubbard 2
JUDD, Climena Lyman 5
JUDD, Deane Brewster 5
JUDD, Edward Starr 1
JUDD, Gerrit Parmele H
JUDD, Gerrit Parmele IV 5
JUDD, James Robert 2
JUDD, John Waltus 4
JUDD, Lawrence McCully 5
JUDD, Norman Buel H
JUDD, Orange H
JUDD, Orrin Reynolds 3
JUDD, Sylvester H
JUDD, Zebulon 4
JUDGE, William John 5
JUDGE, William Quan H
JUDKINS, Charles Otis 1
JUDSON, Adoniram H
JUDSON, Adoniram Brown 1
JUDSON, Alexander Corbin 6
JUDSON, Andrew Thompson H
JUDSON, Ann Hasseltine H
JUDSON, Arthur 6
JUDSON, Charles Wingfield 5
JUDSON, Clara Ingram 4
JUDSON, Clay 4
JUDSON, Edward 1
JUDSON, Edward Zane Carroll H
JUDSON, Egbert Putnam H
JUDSON, Emily Chubbuck H
JUDSON, Fletcher Wesley 5
JUDSON, Frederick Newton 1
JUDSON, Harry Pratt 1
JUDSON, Sarah Hall Boardman H
JUDSON, Wilber 3
JUDSON, William Lees 1
JUDSON, William Pierson 1
JUDSON, William Voorhees 1
JUDY, Arthur Markley 4
JUDY, Clinton Kelly 6
JUENGLING, Frederick H
JUERGENS, Alfred 1
JUETTNER, Otto 1
JUHAN, Frank Alexander 4
JUHRING, John Christopher 1
JUIN, Alphonse Henri 4
JULDOON, Peter J. 1
JULIA, Sister H
JULIAN, George Washington H
JULIAN, George Washington 1
JULIAN, Isaac Hoover 1
JULIAN, John Herndon 4
JULIAN, Percy Lavon 6
JULIAN, William Alexander 2
JULIEN, Alexis Anastay 1
JULIEN, Juliette Marie 5
JULL, Morley Allan 3
JULLIARD, Augustus D. 1
JULLIARD, Frederic A. 1
JUMEL, Stephen H
JUMP, Herbert Atchinson 1
JUMP, William Ashby 2
JUMPER, Royal Thiesen 4
JUNEAU, Solomon Laurent H
JUNELL, John 3
JUNG, Carl Gustav 3
JUNG, Carl Gustav 4
JUNG, Franz August Richard 5
JUNGE, Carl Stephen 5
JUNGMAN, John George H
JUNKERMAN, Gustavus S. 1
JUNKERMANN, Charles Franklin 4
JUNKERSFELD, Peter 1
JUNKIN, Francis Thomas Anderson 1
JUNKIN, George H
JUNOD, Henri Pell 6
JURENEV, Serge B. 4
JURGATIS, John Paul 3
JURICA, Hilary Stanislaus 5
JUSSERAND, Jean Adrien Antoine Jules 1
JUST, Ernest Everett 1
JUST, Theodor Karl 4
JUSTICE, Edwin Judson 1
JUSTIN, Margaret M. 5
JUUL, Niels 1

K

KABLE, Harry G. 3
KABRICH, William Camillus 2
KADING, Charles August 3
KAEDING, Charles Deering 2
KAELBER, William G. 2
KAELIN, Charles Salis 1
KAEMMERLING, Gustav 1
KAEMPFFERT, Waldemar Bernhard 3
KAGAN, Henry Enoch 5
KAGEY, Charles L. 2
KAGY, Elbert Osborn 5
KAHANAMOKU, Duke Paoa 4
KAHANE, Benjamin Bertram 4
KAHIN, George 5
KAHLENBERG, Louis 1
KAHLER, Erich Gabriel 5
KAHLER, Frederick August 1
KAHLER, Harry Adams 3
KAHLER, Hugh MacNair 5
KAHLER, John Henry 1
KAHLKE, Charles Edwin 5
KAHN, Albert 2
KAHN, Ely Jacques 5
KAHN, Florence Prag 2
KAHN, Gilbert W(olff) 6
KAHN, Henry Kastor 4
KAHN, Herman 6
KAHN, Howard 3
KAHN, Julius 1
KAHN, Julius Bahr Jr. 5
KAHN, Lazard 1
KAHN, Louis I. 6
KAHN, Maurice Guthman 3
KAHN, Milton 6
KAHN, Otto Hermann 1
KAHN, Samuel 3
KAIN, George Hay 3
KAIN, John Joseph 1
KAINS, Archibald Chetwode 2
KAINS, Maurice Grenville 2
KAISER, Albert David 3
KAISER, Henry J. 4
KAISER, John Boynton 6
KAISER, Lewis 4
KAISER, Louis Anthony 5
KAIV, Johannes 4
KAL, Norman Coleman 5
KALANIANAOLE, J. KUHIO 1
KALB, Johann H
KALB, Lewis Powell 3
KALBFLEISCH, Martin H
KALBFUS, Edward Clifford 3
KALDENBERG, Frederick Robert 1
KALEKO, Mascha (Mrs. Chemjo Vinaver) 6
KALER, James Otis 1
KALES, Albert Martin 1
KALISCH, Isidor H
KALISCH, Samuel 1
KALISH, Max 2
KALISKI, Sidney Richard 6
KALKSTEIN, Mennasch 5
KALLAY DE NAGY KALLO, Miklos 4
KALLEN, Horace Meyer 6
KALLENBACH, Walter Dustin 2
KALLET, Arthur 5
KALLGREN, Carl Alfred 5
KALLIO, Elmer William 5
KALLMANN, Franz J. 4
KALLOCH, Parker Cromwell 3
KALMAN, Charles Oscar 1
KALMAN, Charles Oscar 3
KALMAN, Paul Jerome 1
KALMENSON, Benjamin 6
KALMUS, Herbert Thomas 4
KALTENBORN, Hans V. 4
KALVEN, Harry Jr. 6
KAMAIAKAN H
KAMBESTAD, Howard S. 3
KAMEHAMEHA I H
KAMEHAMEHA III H
KAMENSKY, Theodore 1
KAMIENSKI, Bogdan 6
KAMINSKI, Stephan 4
KAMMAN, William F. 4
KAMMER, Adolph Gottlieb 4
KAMMER, Alfred Charles 5
KAMMER, Edward Joseph 6
KAMMER, Herbert Anthony 4
KAMMERER, Frederic 1
KAMMERER, Percy Gamble 3
KAMMERER, Webb Louis 5
KAMMERT, Donald Milton 5
KAMMEYER, Julius Ernest 1
KAMPER, Louis 3
KAMPHUISEN, Pieter Wilhelmus 4
KANALEY, Byron Vincent 4
KANAVEL, Allen Buckner 1
KANBENSHUE, Paul 2
KANDEL, Isaac Leon 4
KANDER, Allen 5
KANDINSKY, Vasily 4
KANE, Elias Kent H
KANE, Elisha Kent H
KANE, Elisha Kent 1
KANE, Francis Fisher 3
KANE, Grenville 2
KANE, Howard Francis 2
KANE, James Johnson 1
KANE, John Kintzing H
KANE, Leo Aloysius 4
KANE, Matthew John 1
KANE, Nicholas Thomas H
KANE, Paul V. 3
KANE, Richmond Keith 6
KANE, Theodore Porter 2
KANE, Thomas Franklin 5
KANE, Thomas Leiper H
KANE, Thomas Leo 4
KANE, William Patterson 1
KANE, William T. 2
KANNER, Irving F. 6
KANNER, Samuel Jacob 5
KANOUSE, Theodore Dwight 4
KANSKI, Francis 5
KANTER, Aaron E. 5
KANTER, Arron E. 4
KANTER, Charles Andrew 3
KANTOR, Morris 6
KANTOROWICZ, Ernst H. 4
KANTZLER, George R. 3
KANZLER, Ernest Carlton 4
KAPELL, William 3
KAPENSTEIN, Ira 5
KAPLAN, Abraham David Hannath 6
KAPLAN, Benjamin 5
KAPLAN, Bernard Michael 1
KAPLAN, Ellezer 3
KAPLAN, Frank R. S. 3
KAPLAN, Harry 5
KAPLAN, Jacob Joseph 4
KAPLAN, Kivie 6
KAPLAN, Milton Lewis 5
KAPLAN, Mordecai Menahem 6
KAPLAN, Morris 4
KAPLAN, Samuel 5
KAPP, Friedrich H
KAPP, Jack 2
KAPPEL, Gertrude 5
KAPPEL, Samuel 3
KAPPER, Isaac M. 4
KARAPETOFF, Vladimir 2
KARAVONGSE, Phya Prabha 5
KARCH, Charles Adam 1
KARCHER, Walter Thompson 3
KAREL, John Connell 5
KARELITZ, George Boris 2
KARFIOL, Bernard 3
KARGER, Gustav J. 1
KARIG, Walter 3
KARKER, Maurice Harmon 3
KARL, Tom 4
KARLEN, Sven Bernhard 5
KARLOFF, Boris 5
KARN, Daniel Earl 5
KARN, Harry Wendell 5
KARNES, Joseph V. C. 1
KARNEY, Rex Lambert 4
KAROLIK, Maxim 4
KARPINSKI, Louis Charles 3
KARPOVICH, Michael 3
KARR, Edmund Joseph 5
KARR, Elizabeth 5
KARR, Frank 5
KARR, Robert McNary 6
KARRER, Enoch 2
KARRER, Paul 5
KARRER, Sebastian 6
KARRICK, David Brewer 4
KARSNER, Howard 5
KARSTEN, Gustaf E. 1
KARTAK, Franz August 3
KARTHEISER, Frank 6
KARWOSKI, Theodore F. 3
KASANIN, Jacob Sergi 2
KASAVUBU, Joseph 5
KASBERG, Karl Gary 5
KASE, Max 6
KASEBIER, Gertrude 1
KASNER, Edward 3
KASSABIAN, Mihran Krikor 1
KASSAY, Allan Attila 6
KASSEL, Charles 2
KASSLER, Edwin Stebbins 4
KASSLER, Kenneth Stone 4
KASSON, Frank H. 4
KASSON, John Adam 1
KAST, Ludwig 1

* Indicates More Than One Such Name Listed

KAST, Miller I. 2
KASTEN, Harry Edward 5
KASTEN, Walter 3
KASTEN, William Henry 4
KASTER, John P. 1
KASTLE, Joseph Hoeing 1
KASTNER, Erhart 6
KASTNER, Erich 6
KATCHEN, Julius 5
KATCHER, Archie 6
KATEK, Charles 5
KATHRENS, Richard 4
  Donland
KATO, Frederick 1
KATTE, Edwin Britton 1
KATTE, Walter 1
KATTERLE, Zeno Bernel 5
KATZ, Abner Roland 1
KATZ, Benjamin Samuel 5
KATZ, Frank J. 1
KATZ, Joseph 4
KATZ, Label Abraham 6
KATZ, Mark Jacob 1
KATZ, Michael H. 4
KATZENBACH, Edward 1
  Lawrence
KATZENBACH, Edward 6
  Lawrence Jr.
KATZENBACH, Frank S. 1
  Jr.
KATZENBERGER, William 5
  E.
KATZENELLENBOGEN, 4
  Adolf
KATZENTINE, A. Frank 3
KATZER, Frederic Xavier 1
KATZIN, Eugene M. 1
KATZ-SUCHY, Juliusz 5
KAUFFMAN, Benjamin 2
  Franklin
KAUFFMAN, Calvin Henry 1
KAUFFMAN, James Lee 5
KAUFFMAN, Lawrence A. 4
KAUFFMAN, Ruth Wright 3
KAUFFMAN, Treva Erdine 6
KAUFFMANN, Alfred Otto 1
KAUFFMANN, Rudolph 1
KAUFFMANN, Rudolph 3
  Max
KAUFFMANN, Samuel 1
  Hay
KAUFFMANN, Samuel 5
  Hay
KAUFMAN, Victor 5
KAUFMAN, Abraham 4
  Charles
KAUFMAN, David E. 1
KAUFMAN, David E. 5
KAUFMAN, David H
  Spangler
KAUFMAN, George S. 4
KAUFMAN, Herbert 2
KAUFMAN, Kenneth 2
  Carlyle
KAUFMAN, Louis 2
  Graveraet
KAUFMAN, Paul D. 3
KAUFMAN, Ralph Odell 3
KAUFMAN, Samuel H. 4
KAUFMANN, Christopher 4
  Alphonso
KAUFMANN, Ed 4
KAUFMANN, Edgar Jonas 3
KAUFMANN, Edmund I. 3
KAUFMANN, Gordon 3
  Bernie
KAUFMANN, John Heiden 5
KAUFMANN, Paul 4
KAUFMANN, Wilford E. 3
KAUL, John Lanzel 1
KAULBACK, Frank S. 3
KAUPER, Paul Gerhardt 6
KAUTZ, Albert 1
KAUTZ, August Valentine H
KAUTZ, John Arthur 1
KAUTZKY, Theodore 3
KAUVAR, C(harles) 5
  E(liezer) Hillel
KAVANAGH, Edward H
KAVANAGH, Francis 1
  Bernard
KAVANAGH, James 3
  Edward
KAVANAGH, Leslie J. 1
KAVANAGH, Marcus A. 1
KAVANAGH, Robert 3
  Vincent
KAVANAGH, Thomas 6
  Matthew
KAVANAUGH, John 5
  Michael
KAVANAUGH, William 1
  Harrison
KAVANAUGH, William 1
  Kerr

KAVANAUGH, Williams 1
  Marmaduke
KAVELER, Herman Henry 4
KAWABATA, Yasunari 5
KAWAKAMI, Jotaro 4
KAWAKAMI, K. K. 2
KAY, Edgar Boyd 1
KAY, George Frederick 2
KAY, (George) Marshall 6
KAY, Gertrude Alice 1
KAY, Joseph William 2
KAY, William Edward 1
KAYAN, Carl F(rederic) 5
KAYE, James Hamilton 1
  Barcroft
KAYE, John William 1
KAYE, Joseph 4
KAYE-SMITH, Sheila 3
KAYN, Hilde B. 3
KAYS, Donald Jackson 3
KAY-SCOTT, Cyril 6
  (Frederic Creighton)
KAZANJIAN, Varaztad 6
  Hovhannes
KAZANTZAKIS, Nikos 3
KAZANTZAKIS, Nikos 4
KEAGY, John Miller H
KEAGY, Walter R. 4
KEALING, Joseph B. 1
KEALY, Philip Joseph 2
KEAN, Charles H
KEAN, Charles Duell 4
KEAN, Edmund H
KEAN, Hamilton Fish 1
KEAN, Jefferson Randolph 3
KEAN, John H
KEAN, John 1
KEAN, Thomas H
KEANE, Doris 2
KEANE, James John 1
KEANE, John Joseph 1
KEANE, Lee 3
KEANE, Theodore John 3
KEANE, William Edward 3
KEARFUL, Francis Joseph 1
KEARL, Chase Delmar 6
KEARNEY, Andrew 4
  Thomas
KEARNEY, Belle 3
KEARNEY, Denis H
KEARNEY, Denis 4
KEARNEY, Drye H
KEARNEY, Edward Francis 1
KEARNEY, Edward James 1
KEARNEY, Erick Wilson 5
KEARNEY, Francis William 6
KEARNEY, George 1
  Fairchild
KEARNEY, Lawrence 4
  Francis
KEARNEY, Raymond 3
  Augustine
KEARNEY, Thomas Henry 3
KEARNS, Charles Cyrus 1
KEARNS, Gurney Harriss 4
KEARNS, John W. 3
KEARNS, Thomas 1
KEARNS, Thomas F. 4
KEARNS, William Michael 5
KEARNY, Francis H
KEARNY, Lawrence H
KEARNY, Philip H
KEARNY, Stephen Watts H
KEARNY, Warren 2
KEARSLEY, John H
KEASBEY, Edward Quinton 1
KEASBEY, George 1
  Macculloch
KEASBEY, Henry Miller 4
KEASBEY, Lindley Miller 4
KEATING, Anne C. 3
KEATING, Arthur 4
KEATING, Cecil A. 1
KEATING, Cletus 4
KEATING, Edward 4
KEATING, F(rancis) 5
  Raymond Jr.
KEATING, Frank Webster 1
KEATING, John 5
KEATING, John H. 4
KEATING, John Marie H
KEATING, John McLeod 1
KEATING, Kenneth B. 6
KEATING, Laurence 5
  Freeman
KEATING, William H
  Hypolitus
KEATON, Buster 4
KEATON, James R. 2
KEATOR, Alfred Decker 4
KEATOR, Frederic William 1
KEAYS, Hersilia A. 4
  Mitchell
KEBBON, Eric 4
KEBE, Kenneth Albert 4
KEBLER, Leonard 4

KEBLER, Lyman Frederic 3
KECK, Charles 3
KECK, Harry 4
KECK, Herbert Allen 6
KEDNEY, John Steinfort 1
KEDZIE, Frank Stewart 1
KEDZIE, Robert Clark 1
KEDZIE, William Roscoe 1
KEE, John 3
KEEBLE, Glendinning 2
KEEBLE, John Bell 1
KEEDICK, Lee 4
KEEDY, Charles Cochran 1
KEEDY, Edwin Roulette 6
KEEFE, Daniel C. 4
KEEFE, Daniel J. 1
KEEFE, David Andrew 5
KEEFE, Frank B. 3
KEEFE, John C. 4
KEEFE, John Hancock 5
KEEFE, John William 4
KEEFE, William J. 3
KEEFER, Chester Scott 4
KEEFER, Frank Royer 1
KEEFER, Joseph Isadore 1
KEEGAN, Gilbert Kearnie 4
KEEGAN, Harry Joseph 5
KEEGAN, Jane Claudia 6
KEEGAN, John Joseph 5
KEEHN, Clarence 1
  (Heckman)
KEEHN, Roy Dee 2
KEEL, Elmo W. 5
KEELER, Charles 1
KEELER, Ellen Coughlin 6
  (Mrs. Ralph Welles
  Keeler)
KEELER, Fred Lockwood 1
KEELER, Harriet Louise 1
KEELER, Harry Stephen 4
KEELER, James Edward 1
KEELER, John Everett 1
KEELER, Leonarde 2
KEELER, Ralph Olmstead H
KEELER, Ralph Welles 1
KEELER, Stephen Edwards 3
KEELEY, Edward S. 1
KEELEY, James 1
KEELEY, Leslie E. 1
KEELEY, Patrick C. H
KEELING, Hal Ray 1
KEELING, Walter Angus 2
KEELY, John Ernst Worrell H
KEELY, Robert Neff 1
KEEN, Edward Leggett 2
KEEN, Gregory Bernard 1
KEEN, James Velma 4
KEEN, Kennard Garton Jr. 1
KEEN, Morris Longstreth H
KEEN, Victor 3
KEEN, William Williams 1
KEENA, James Trafton 1
KEENA, Leo John 6
KEENA, Martin J. 4
KEENAN, Albert Joseph Jr. 5
KEENAN, Alexander 1
  Stanislaus
KEENAN, Frank 1
KEENAN, Geo M. 1
KEENAN, Henry Francis 4
KEENAN, James R. 3
KEENAN, Joseph Berry 3
KEENAN, Thomas 1
  Johnston
KEENE, Amor Frederick 1
KEENE, Arthur Samuel 1
KEENE, Carter Brewster 1
KEENE, Charles Herbert 6
KEENE, Edward Spencer 1
KEENE, Floyd Elwood 1
KEENE, James Robert 1
KEENE, Laura H
KEENE, Thomas Wallace H
KEENER, Gladys M. 4
KEENER, John Christian 1
KEENER, Walter Ney 1
KEENER, William Albert 1
KEENEY, Albert Lawrence 4
KEENEY, Francis B. 3
KEENEY, Frederick 1
  Thomas
KEENEY, Paul Aloysius 5
KEENEY, Mrs Ralph D. 3
KEENEY, Russell Watson 3
KEENEY, Willard F. 2
KEEP, Albert 1
KEEP, Charles Hallam 1
KEEP, Chauncey 1
KEEP, Henry H
KEEP, John Joseph 2
KEEP, Oliver Davis 1
KEEP, Robert Porter 1
KEEP, William John 1
KEESE, Richard H
KEESE, William Linn 1
KEESECKER, Raymond P. 4

KEESING, Felix Maxwell 4
KEESING, Frans Arnold 5
  George
KEESLING, Francis 4
  Valentine
KEETON, Robert Wood 3
KEEVIL, Charles Samuel 5
KEFAUVER, Clarence 5
  Eugene
KEFAUVER, Estes 4
KEFAUVER, Grayson 2
  Neikirk
KEFFER, Harry Joshua 1
KEFFER, Charles Albert 1
KEGEL, Arnold Henry 5
KEHL, John Elwin 5
KEHLENBECK, Alfred 5
  Paul
KEHOE, Arthur Henry 5
KEHOE, James N. 2
KEHOE, (James) Walter 4
KEHOE, Joseph W. 3
KEIDEL, George Charles 2
KEIFER, J. Warren 1
KEIGWIN, A. Edwin 3
KEILBERTH, Joseph 5
KEILEY, Benjamin J. 1
KEILLER, William 1
KEIM, Franklin David 3
KEIM, George de 1
  Benneville
KEIM, George May H
KEIM, William High H
KEIR, John Sibbit 4
KEIRN, Gideon Isaac 4
KEISER, Albert 4
KEISER, Edward Harrison 4
KEISER, George Camp 3
KEISER, Laurence Bollon 5
KEISTER, Abraham L. 1
KEITH, Adelphus Bartlett 1
KEITH, Allen Phelps 3
KEITH, Arthur 2
KEITH, Arthur Leslie 1
KEITH, Arthur Monroe 1
KEITH, Benjamin Franklin 1
KEITH, Charles Penrose 1
KEITH, Charles S. 2
KEITH, David 1
KEITH, David 2
KEITH, Dora Wheeler 1
KEITH, Elbridge G. 1
KEITH, George H
KEITH, George Eldon 1
KEITH, Harold Chessman 4
KEITH, James 1
KEITH, John Alexander 1
  Hull
KEITH, Lawrence Massillon H
KEITH, Marie Morrisey 4
KEITH, Minor Cooper 1
KEITH, Nathaniel S. 6
KEITH, Nathaniel Shepard 1
KEITH, Robert J. 6
KEITH, Sir William H
KEITH, William 1
KEITH, William Hammond 4
KEITHAHN, Edward 5
  Linnaeus
KEITT, George 5
  Wannamaker
KEITT, William Lawrence 6
KELBY, Charles Hendre 2
KELBY, James Edward 4
KELCE, L. Russell 5
KELCE, Merl C. 5
KELCEY, Guy 4
KELCEY, Herbert 1
KELEHER, William 5
  Aloysius
KELEHER, William L. 6
KELHAM, George William 1
KELIHER, John 4
KELIHER, John Austin 1
KELIHER, Sylvester 4
KELKER, James Joseph 6
  Arthur
KELKER, Rudolph 1
  Frederick Jr.
KELLAND, Clarence 1
  Budington
KELLAR, Chambers 3
KELLAR, Harry 1
KELLAR, Herbert Anthony 3
KELLAS, Eliza 1
KELLAWAY, Herbert John 2
KELLEHER, Daniel 1
KELLEHER, Louis Francis 4
KELLEHER, Michael T. 3
KELLEMS, Vivien 6
KELLEN, William Vail 1
KELLENBERGER, Hunter 4
KELLER, Adolph 5
KELLER, Albert Galloway 4
KELLER, Amelia R. (Mrs. 5
  Eugene Buehler)

KELLER, Arnold B. 4
KELLER, Arthur Ignatius 1
KELLER, Benjamin 1
  Franklin
KELLER, Carl Tilden 3
KELLER, Emil Ernest 4
KELLER, Frederick 4
KELLER, Gert 4
KELLER, Harry Frederick 1
KELLER, Helen Adams 5
KELLER, Henry 4
KELLER, Henry Jr. 3
KELLER, Henry Jr. 5
KELLER, Herbert Paist 6
KELLER, James Albert 2
KELLER, John William 1
KELLER, Kaufman Thuma 4
KELLER, Kent Ellsworth 3
KELLER, Lewis Henry 1
KELLER, Mathias 4
KELLER, May Lansfield 4
KELLER, Mollie V. Everett 5
  (Mrs. Charles C. Keller)
KELLER, Oliver James 4
KELLER, Oscar Edward 4
KELLER, Oscar H. 4
KELLER, Ralph Edward 4
KELLER, Walter 1
KELLER, Will E. 4
KELLER, William Huestis 2
KELLER, William Simpson 1
KELLERMAN, Karl 1
  Frederic
KELLERMAN, William 1
  Ashbrook
KELLERSBERGER, 4
  Eugene Roland
KELLETER, Paul Delmar 3
KELLEY, Albert Wesley 1
KELLEY, Alfred H
KELLEY, Alfred Kendall 1
KELLEY, Augustine 3
  Bernard
KELLEY, Bethel Bowles 6
KELLEY, Camille McGee 3
KELLEY, Clement Earl Jr. 5
KELLEY, Cornelius Francis 3
KELLEY, David Campbell 1
KELLEY, Edgar Stillman 2
KELLEY, Eugene Robert 1
KELLEY, Florence 1
KELLEY, Francis 1
  Alphonsus
KELLEY, Francis Clement 4
KELLEY, Frank Harrison 3
KELLEY, Hall Jackson H
KELLEY, Harold Hitchcock 4
KELLEY, Harrison 1
KELLEY, Hermon Alfred 1
KELLEY, Howard G. 1
KELLEY, J(ames) Herbert 5
  Jerrold
KELLEY, James Douglas 1
KELLEY, Jay George 1
KELLEY, Jerome Telfair 4
KELLEY, Jessie Stillman 4
KELLEY, Jessie Stillman 4
KELLEY, John S. 4
KELLEY, John William 1
KELLEY, Lilla Elizabeth 5
KELLEY, Louise 4
KELLEY, Nicholas 4
KELLEY, Oliver Hudson H
KELLEY, Oliver Hudson 4
KELLEY, Patrick Henry 1
KELLEY, Pearce Clement 5
KELLEY, Phelps 1
KELLEY, Robert Hamilton 4
KELLEY, Robert Michael 4
KELLEY, Robert Weeks 1
KELLEY, Samuel Walter 1
KELLEY, Selden Dee 4
KELLEY, Truman L. 4
KELLEY, Walter Pearson 4
KELLEY, William Andrew 1
  Gresham
KELLEY, William Darrah H
KELLEY, William Valentine 2
KELLEY, William 1
  Vallandigham
KELLICOTT, William 1
  Erskine
KELLNER, Elisabeth 1
  Willard Brooks
KELLNER, Max 1
KELLOGG, Abraham 2
  Lincoln
KELLOGG, Albert H
KELLOGG, Amos 1
  Markham
KELLOGG, Angel Ivey 6
  (Mrs. Karl Brittan
  Kellogg)
KELLOGG, Arthur Piper 1
KELLOGG, Arthur 5
  Remington

KELLOGG, Brainerd 5
KELLOGG, Charles H
KELLOGG, Charles Collins 1
KELLOGG, Charles 5
  Wetmore
KELLOGG, Clara Louise 1
KELLOGG, Daniel Fiske 1
KELLOGG, David 4
  Sherwood
KELLOGG, Edgar Romeyn 1
KELLOGG, Edward H
KELLOGG, Edward Brinley 4
KELLOGG, Edward Leland 2
KELLOGG, Elijah 1
KELLOGG, Elijah Chapman H
KELLOGG, Eva Mary H
  Crosby
KELLOGG, Francis William H
KELLOGG, Frank Billings 1
KELLOGG, Frederic Rogers 1
KELLOGG, Frederick 4
  Conway
KELLOGG, Frederick 1
  William
KELLOGG, George Dwight 3
KELLOGG, Gordon Hill 3
KELLOGG, Harold Field 4
KELLOGG, Henry 2
  Theodore
KELLOGG, Howard 6
KELLOGG, Howard Jr. 1
KELLOGG, James C. 1
KELLOGG, James G. 4
KELLOGG, James H. 5
KELLOGG, James 1
  Lawrence
KELLOGG, John Harvey 2
KELLOGG, John Morris 1
KELLOGG, John Prescott 1
KELLOGG, Joseph 1
  Augustus
KELLOGG, Laura Cornelius 5
  (Mrs. Orrin Joseph
  Kellogg)
KELLOGG, Louise Phelps 1
KELLOGG, Luther Laflin 1
KELLOGG, Martin 1
KELLOGG, Morris W. 3
KELLOGG, Olin Clay 2
KELLOGG, Oliver Dimon 1
KELLOGG, Orlando H
  Underwood
KELLOGG, Paul 5
KELLOGG, Peter Comstock 1
KELLOGG, Ralph Averill 4
KELLOGG, Robert James 3
KELLOGG, Samuel Henry H
KELLOGG, Scott D(ouglas) 1
KELLOGG, Spencer 1
KELLOGG, Stephen Wright 1
KELLOGG, Theodore H. 5
KELLOGG, Thomas Moore 1
KELLOGG, Vernon Lyman 1
KELLOGG, W. K. 6
KELLOGG, Walter Guest 3
KELLOGG, Warren 4
  Franklin
KELLOGG, Wilbur Ralph 3
KELLOGG, William H
KELLOGG, William Pitt 1
KELLOR, Frances 3
KELLS, Clarence Howard 1
KELLSTADT, Charles H. 6
KELLWAY, Cedric Vernon 4
KELLY, Alfred Hinsey 5
KELLY, Aloysius Oliver 1
  Joseph
KELLY, Bradley 5
KELLY, Charles E. 5
KELLY, David George 1
KELLY, Dennis Francis 4
KELLY, Edward A. 1
KELLY, Edward Joseph * 3
KELLY, Edward Wendell 6
  Jr.
KELLY, Eleanor 1
KELLY, Eric Philbrook 3
KELLY, Eugene H
KELLY, Eugene Hill 2
KELLY, Florence Finch 1
KELLY, Francis Martin 3
KELLY, Frank A. 2
KELLY, Frank V. 1
KELLY, Fred C. 3
KELLY, Frederick James 4
KELLY, Genevieve Ruth 5
KELLY, George 6
KELLY, George Alexander 4
KELLY, George Arthur 4
KELLY, George Henderson 1
KELLY, Sir Gerald 4
KELLY, Geroge B(radshaw) 5
KELLY, Guy Edward 1
KELLY, Harry Eugene 5
KELLY, Harry Francis 5
KELLY, Harry Joseph 4

KELLY, Harry McCormick 1
KELLY, Howard Atwood 2
KELLY, Howard Charles 3
KELLY, J. Redding 1
KELLY, James H
KELLY, James Edward 1
KELLY, James Kerr 1
KELLY, John H
KELLY, John C. 1
KELLY, John Clarence 6
KELLY, John Forrest 1
KELLY, John Grant 4
KELLY, John H. 1
KELLY, John William 5
KELLY, Joseph James 4
KELLY, Joseph Luther 1
KELLY, Judith 3
KELLY, Lawrence Vincent 6
KELLY, Lon Hamman 5
KELLY, Luther Sage H
KELLY, Luther Sage 4
KELLY, M. Clyde 1
KELLY, Mervin J. 5
KELLY, Michael D. 5
KELLY, Michael J. H
KELLY, Monroe 3
KELLY, Myra 2
KELLY, Orie R. 5
KELLY, Paul 3
KELLY, Percy R. 4
KELLY, Ralph 4
KELLY, Raymond 5
KELLY, Robert James 5
KELLY, Robert Lincoln 3
KELLY, Robert Morrow 5
KELLY, Stephen 4
KELLY, T(homas) Howard 1
KELLY, Walt 6
KELLY, William * H
KELLY, William 1
KELLY, William A. 4
KELLY, William Albert 4
KELLY, William Anthony 4
KELLY, William Arthur 4
KELLY, William F. 4
KELLY, William J. 3
KELLY, William Joseph 1
KELLY, William Louis 4
KELLY, William Powers 3
KELMAN, John 1
KELPIUS, Johann H
KELSEN, Hans 5
KELSER, David M. 6
KELSER, Raymond 3
  Alexander
KELSEY, Albert 3
KELSEY, Carl 5
KELSEY, Charles Boyd 1
KELSEY, Charles Edward 1
KELSEY, Clarence Hill 1
KELSEY, Francis Willey 1
KELSEY, Frederick 3
  Trowbridge
KELSEY, Frederick Wallace 1
KELSEY, Harlan Page 5
KELSEY, Harold 6
KELSEY, Henry Hopkins 1
KELSEY, Hugh Alexander 3
KELSEY, Joseph A. 1
KELSEY, Preston Telford 3
KELSEY, Rayner 1
  Wickersham
KELSEY, William Henry H
KELSO, James Anderson 3
KELSO, John Bolton 5
KELSO, John Russell 1
KELSO, Robert Wilson 6
KELTON, John H
  Cunningham
KELTON, Stanton Colt 3
KELTY, Paul Ray 2
KEM, James Preston 1
KEMBLE, Edward Windsor 1
KEMBLE, Frances Anne H
KEMBLE, Gouverneur 5
KEMERER, Benjamin 5
  Tibbits
KEMEYS, Edward 1
KEMLER, Walter James 4
KEMMERER, Edwin 2
  Walter
KEMMERER, John L. 2
KEMMERER, Walter Albert 3
KEMP, Agnes 1
KEMP, Alexander Nesbitt 3
KEMP, Bolivar Edwards 1
KEMP, (Clarence) Everett 1
KEMP, Ellwood Leitheiser 4
KEMP, Harold Augustus 5
KEMP, Harold Francis 3
KEMP, Harry Hibbard 4
KEMP, James H
KEMP, James Furman 1
KEMP, John 1
KEMP, Louis Wiltz 3
KEMP, Matthew Stanley 5

KEMP, Philip Claris 4
KEMP, Robert H. H
KEMP, Theodore 1
KEMP, W. Thomas 1
KEMP, William Webb 2
KEMP, Wyndham 1
KEMP, Zachariah Willis 1
KEMPER, Arthur Bernard 5
KEMPER, Charles 4
  Pendleton
KEMPER, General William 1
  Harrison
KEMPER, Graham Hawes 4
KEMPER, Jackson 1
KEMPER, James Lawson H
KEMPER, James Madison H
KEMPER, John Mason 5
KEMPER, Reuben H
KEMPER, William Mauzy 5
KEMPER, William 1
  Thornton
KEMPFF, Clarence S. 4
KEMPFF, Louis 1
KEMPNER, Aubrey John 5
KEMPNER, Isaac Herbert 5
KEMPNER, Isaac Herbert 5
  Jr.
KEMPSHALL, Thomas H
KEMPSTER, James Aquila 4
KEMPSTER, Walter 1
KEMPTON, Charles Walter 4
KEMSLEY, (James Gomer 5
  Berry)
KENAN, Thomas H
KENAN, William Rand Jr. 4
KENDAL, Mrs. 4
KENDAL, William Hunter 1
KENDALL, Amos H
KENDALL, Arthur Isaac 6
KENDALL, Calvin Noyes 1
KENDALL, Charles Harry 4
KENDALL, Charles 5
  Howard
KENDALL, Charles Pierce 5
KENDALL, Charles Shilling 5
KENDALL, Courts P. 5
KENDALL, Edward Calvin 5
KENDALL, Edward Hale 1
KENDALL, Elizabeth 3
  Kimball
KENDALL, Elva Roscoe 5
KENDALL, Ezra Fremont 1
KENDALL, George R. 5
KENDALL, George 5
  Valentine
KENDALL, George Wilkins H
KENDALL, Harry R. 5
KENDALL, Henry Hubbard 2
KENDALL, Henry Madison 4
KENDALL, Henry 3
  Plimpton
KENDALL, Henry 4
  Wiseman
KENDALL, James 5
KENDALL, John C. 3
KENDALL, John Chester 5
KENDALL, John Smith 5
KENDALL, John Wilkerson 6
KENDALL, Jonas H
KENDALL, Joseph Gowing H
KENDALL, Margaret 1
KENDALL, Margaret 4
KENDALL, Messmore 3
KENDALL, Myron A. 4
KENDALL, Nathan E. 1
KENDALL, Ralph Charles 4
KENDALL, Samuel Austin 1
KENDALL, Sergeant 4
KENDALL, Valerius 4
  Horatio
KENDALL, William 1
  Converse
KENDALL, William 1
  Mitchell
KENDALL, William 4
  Morgan
KENDELL, Robert Lothar 5
KENDIG, Bess Horton 6
  (Mrs. Andrew LeRoy
  Kendig)
KENDIG, Calvin Miles 3
KENDIG, H. Evert 3
KENDRICK, Asahel Clark 1
KENDRICK, Benjamin 2
  Burks
KENDRICK, Charles 5
KENDRICK, E. S. 4
KENDRICK, Eliza Hall 1
KENDRICK, Georgia 1
KENDRICK, John H
KENDRICK, John Benjamin 1
KENDRICK, John Mills 1
KENDRICK, John William 1
KENDRICK, Nathaniel 1
  Cooper
KENDRICK, Philip Eugene 6

KENDRICK, W. Freeland 3
KENDRICKS, Edward 3
  James
KENE, Joseph Alphonse 4
KENEALY, Ahmed John 4
KENEALY, Alexander C. 1
KENEALY, William James 6
KENEFICK, Daniel Joseph 2
KENERSON, Edward 6
  Hibbard
KENERSON, William 6
  Herbert
KENGLA, Hannah M. Egan 3
KENIN, Herman David 4
KENISTON, James 1
  Mortimer
KENISTON, (Ralph) 5
  Hayward
KENKEL, Frederick P. 3
KENLON, John 1
KENLY, John Reese 1
KENLY, Julie Woodbridge 2
  Terry
KENLY, Ritchie Graham 1
KENLY, William Lacy 1
KENNA, Edward Dudley 4
KENNA, Frank 2
KENNA, Howard James 6
KENNA, John Edward H
KENNA, Joseph Norris 3
KENNA, Roger 4
KENNAMER, Charles 3
  Brents
KENNAMER, Franklin 6
  Elmore
KENNAN, George 1
KENNARD, Frederic 1
  Hedge
KENNARD, Joseph Spencer 2
KENNARD, Samuel M. 1
KENNARD, William Jeffers 6
KENNEBECK, George 5
  Robert
KENNEDY, Albert Joseph 6
KENNEDY, Ambrose J. 3
KENNEDY, Andrew H
  Richardson
KENNEDY, Annie 3
KENNEDY, Anthony H
KENNEDY, Archibald H
KENNEDY, Arthur 3
  Garfield
KENNEDY, Charles A. 5
KENNEDY, Charles Rann 2
KENNEDY, Charles 1
  William
KENNEDY, Chase Wilmot 1
KENNEDY, Clarence 5
KENNEDY, Clarence 3
  Hamilton
KENNEDY, Clyde 5
  Raymond
KENNEDY, Crammond 1
KENNEDY, Daniel Joseph 1
KENNEDY, David Scott 1
KENNEDY, Elijah 1
  Robinson
KENNEDY, Elizabeth 6
  Smith
KENNEDY, Emma Baker 1
KENNEDY, F. Lowell 1
KENNEDY, Foster 3
KENNEDY, Francis Willard 1
KENNEDY, Frank J. 6
KENNEDY, Fred 5
  J(ohnston)
KENNEDY, Gall 1
KENNEDY, George A. 4
KENNEDY, Gilbert 5
  Falconer
KENNEDY, Henry L. 3
KENNEDY, Howard 1
  Samuel
KENNEDY, Howard 1
  Samuel
KENNEDY, James 1
KENNEDY, James Aloysius 6
  Charles
KENNEDY, James Arthur 1
KENNEDY, James Francis 6
  Jr.
KENNEDY, James Henry 1
KENNEDY, James Madison 1
KENNEDY, James Melvin 4
KENNEDY, John Bright 1
KENNEDY, John Bright 5
KENNEDY, John Doby H
KENNEDY, John Fitzgerald 4
KENNEDY, John 1
  Lauderdale
KENNEDY, John Louis 4
KENNEDY, John Pendleton H
KENNEDY, John Pendleton 5
KENNEDY, John Stewart 1
KENNEDY, John Thomas 3
KENNEDY, Joseph 1

KENNEDY, Joseph Camp H
  Griffith
KENNEDY, Joseph Patrick 5
KENNEDY, Joseph William 3
KENNEDY, Josiah Forrest 1
KENNEDY, Julian 1
KENNEDY, Lloyd Ellison 4
KENNEDY, Lorne Edward 4
KENNEDY, Margaret 4
KENNEDY, Margaret 1
KENNEDY, Martin J. 3
KENNEDY, Merton Grant 4
KENNEDY, Michael Joseph 2
KENNEDY, Miles 4
  Coverdale
KENNEDY, Moorhead 1
  Cowell
KENNEDY, Olin Wood 5
KENNEDY, Paca 1
KENNEDY, Philip 4
  Benjamin
KENNEDY, Ralph Dale 4
KENNEDY, Raymond 3
KENNEDY, Richard 3
  Oakley
KENNEDY, Robert Francis 5
KENNEDY, Robert 5
  MacMillan
KENNEDY, Robert Morris 2
KENNEDY, Robert 1
  Patterson
KENNEDY, Roger L. J. 4
KENNEDY, Ruby Jo 5
  Reeves
KENNEDY, Samuel Macaw 1
KENNEDY, Sara Beaumont 1
KENNEDY, Sidney 5
  Robinson
KENNEDY, Stanley 5
  Carmichael
KENNEDY, Sylvester 5
  Michael
KENNEDY, T. Blake 3
KENNEDY, Thomas 4
KENNEDY, Thomas F. 1
KENNEDY, W. McNeil 1
KENNEDY, Walker 1
KENNEDY, Willard John 2
KENNEDY, William H
KENNEDY, William 1
KENNEDY, William Henry 2
  Joseph
KENNEDY, William Parker 5
KENNEDY, William Pierce 5
KENNEDY, William Sloane 1
KENNEDY, Wray David 5
KENNELLY, Arthur Edwin 1
KENNELLY, Edward F. 4
KENNELLY, Martin H. 4
KENNER, Albert Walton 3
KENNER, Duncan Farrar 4
KENNER, Frank Terry 4
KENNERLEY, Mitchell 6
KENNERLY, John Hanger 1
KENNERLY, Thomas 4
  Martin
KENNERLY, Wesley Travis 2
KENNESON, Taddeus 1
  Davis
KENNETT, Luther Martin 1
KENNEY, Edward A. 1
KENNEY, James Francis 6
KENNEY, John Andrew 2
KENNEY, Richard Rolland 1
KENNEY, William Francis 1
KENNEY, William P. 1
KENNGOTT, George 4
  Frederick
KENNICOTT, Cass 5
  (Langdon)
KENNICOTT, Donald 4
KENNICOTT, Robert H
KENNISH, John 4
KENNON, Jack Ecclestone 4
KENNON, Lyman Walter 1
  Vere
KENNON, William Sr. H
KENNON, William Jr. H
KENNON, William Lee 3
KENNY, Albert Sewall 1
KENNY, Elizabeth 3
KENNY, John Edward 6
KENNY, John V. 6
KENNY, Michael 2
KENNY, Nicholas 6
  Napoleon
KENNY, Thomas James 5
KENNY, William John 1
KENRICK, Francis Patrick H
KENRICK, Peter Richard H
KENRICK, William 1
KENSETT, John Frederick H
KENT, Alexander 1
KENT, Arthur Atwater 2
KENT, Charles Artemas 1
KENT, Charles Foster 1

KIMBALL, Fiske 3
KIMBALL, G. Cook 1
KIMBALL, George Albert 1
KIMBALL, George Elbert 4
KIMBALL, George Henry 1
KIMBALL, George Selwyn 1
KIMBALL, George Turner 3
KIMBALL, Gilman H
KIMBALL, Gustavus Sylvester 1
KIMBALL, Hannah Parker 4
KIMBALL, Harriet McEwen 1
KIMBALL, Harry Swift 3
KIMBALL, Heber Chase H
KIMBALL, Henry Dox 1
KIMBALL, Herbert Harvey 5
KIMBALL, Jacob Jr. H
KIMBALL, James Henry 2
KIMBALL, James Putnam 1
KIMBALL, John C. 1
KIMBALL, John White 1
KIMBALL, Joseph C. 4
KIMBALL, Justin Ford 3
KIMBALL, Kate Fisher 1
KIMBALL, Katharine 2
KIMBALL, LeRoy Elwood 4
KIMBALL, Marie Goebel 3
KIMBALL, Nathan H
KIMBALL, Philip Horatio 2
KIMBALL, Ralph Horace 2
KIMBALL, Richard Burleigh H
KIMBALL, Robert Merriman 4
KIMBALL, Spofford Harris 4
KIMBALL, Stockton 3
KIMBALL, Sumner Increase 1
KIMBALL, Thomas Rogers 1
KIMBALL, Walter Gardner 3
KIMBALL, Willard 4
KIMBALL, William Coggin 1
KIMBALL, William Preston 4
KIMBALL, William Wallace 1
KIMBALL, William Wirt 1
KIMBELL, Kay 4
KIMBER, Arthur Clifford 4
KIMBER, Harry Goldring 4
KIMBERLY, Lewis Ashfield 1
KIMBLE, John Haines 1
KIMBLE, Joseph Chanslor 5
KIMBROUGH, Bradley Thomas 1
KIMBROUGH, Herbert 5
KIMBROUGH, Robert Alexander 5
KIMBROUGH, Robert Alexander Jr. 4
KIMBROUGH, Thomas Charles 2
KIMES, Russell A. 4
KIMM, Neal Edwin 4
KIMMEL, Gustav Bernard 1
KIMMEL, Husband Edward 5
KIMMEL, Lester Franklin 4
KIMMEL, William H
KIMMELSTIEL, Paul 5
KINARD, F. Marion 4
KINARD, James Pinckney 3
KINCAID, Charles Euston 1
KINCAID, Elbert Alvis 3
KINCAID, James Leslie 6
KINCAID, John H
KINCAID, Robert Lee 4
KINCAID, Trevor 5
KINCAID, William A. 1
KINCAID, William Wallace 2
KINCANNON, Andrew Armstrong 4
KINCER, Joseph Burton 5
KINCHELOE, David Hayes 3
KIND, John Louis 3
KINDEL, George John 1
KINDELBERGER, James Howard 4
KINDERMAN, Robert Henry 6
KINDIG, James William 4
KINDLE, Edward Martin 1
KINDLEBERGER, David 1
KINDLEBERGER, Jacob 3
KINDLER, Hans 2
KINDRED, John Joseph 1
KINEALY, John Henry 1
KINEON, George Goodhue 2
KING, Adam H
KING, Aden J(ackson) 5
KING, Albert Freeman Africanus 1
KING, Albion Roy 5
KING, Alexander 4
KING, Alexander Campbell 1
KING, Alfred Rufus 1
KING, Alvin Olin 3
KING, Andrew H
KING, Arno Warren 1
KING, Arthur Dale 3
KING, Arthur S. 3
KING, Austin Augustus H
KING, Basil 1
KING, Campbell 3
KING, Caroline Blanche 2
KING, Cecil 6
KING, Charles H
KING, Charles 1
KING, Charles Banks 5
KING, Charles Bird H
KING, Charles Burton 5
KING, Charles D. B. 4
KING, Charles Francis 1
KING, Charles Kelley 3
KING, Charles William H
KING, Clarence 1
KING, Clark W. 4
KING, Clifford William 2
KING, Clyde Lyndon 1
KING, Cora Smith 1
KING, Cyrus H
KING, D. J. 3
KING, D. Ward 4
KING, Dan H
KING, Daniel Putnam H
KING, David Bennett 4
KING, Dennis 5
KING, Dougall Macdougall 1
KING, Douglass Stone 6
KING, Edgar 5
KING, Edmund Burritt 1
KING, Edna Elvira Swanson (Mrs. Edgar J. King) 5
KING, Edward 1
KING, Edward Duncan 6
KING, Edward J. 1
KING, Edward Jasper 6
KING, Edward Lacy 4
KING, Edward Leonard 1
KING, Edward Postell Jr. 3
KING, Edward S. 1
KING, Edward Smith H
KING, Edwin Burruss 5
KING, Eldon Paul 4
KING, Elisha Alonzo 5
KING, Ernest Joseph 3
KING, Everett Edgar 5
KING, Fain White 5
KING, Francis Scott 1
KING, Frank Lamar 5
KING, Frank O. 5
KING, Franklin Hiram 1
KING, Frederick Allen 1
KING, George Anderson 1
KING, George B. 4
KING, George Gordon H
KING, Grace Elizabeth 1
KING, Hamilton 1
KING, Harold Davis 6
KING, Harold Joseph 4
KING, Harold William 4
KING, Harry Albert 6
KING, Harry Andrews 1
KING, Helen Dean 3
KING, Henry H
KING, Henry 1
KING, Henry Churchill 1
KING, Henry Lord Page 3
KING, Henry Melville 1
KING, Henry Stouffer 2
KING, Herbert Hiram 2
KING, Homer C. 4
KING, Horace Williams 3
KING, Horatio H
KING, Horatio Collins 1
KING, Howell Atwater 5
KING, Irving 5
KING, J. Cheston 4
KING, James A. 1
KING, James Aloysius 4
KING, James Gore H
KING, James H. 3
KING, James Harold 3
KING, James Joseph 1
KING, James Marcus 1
KING, James Moore 4
KING, James William 5
KING, James Wilson 4
KING, John * H
KING, John A. 1
KING, John Alsop H
KING, John Crookshanks H
KING, John Jefferson 1
KING, John Joseph 6
KING, John Lord 4
KING, John Pendleton H
KING, John Rigdon 1
KING, Jonas H
KING, Joseph Elijah 1
KING, Julie Rive 3
KING, LeRoy Albert 2
KING, Lida Shaw 1
KING, Lorenzo H. 2
KING, Louisa Yeomans (Mrs. Francis King) 5
KING, Margaret Isadora 6
KING, Martin Luther Jr. 4
KING, Mary Perry 5
KING, Maxwell Clark 5
KING, Melvin L. 2
KING, Merrill Jenks 4
KING, Morland 6
KING, Oscar A. 1
KING, Paul 2
KING, Paul Howard 2
KING, Preston H
KING, Putnam H
KING, Raymond Thomas 5
KING, Richard H
KING, Richard Hayne 2
KING, Robert Luther 5
KING, Roy Stevenson 3
KING, Rufus * H
KING, Rufus (Frederick) 6
KING, Rufus H. H
KING, Samuel H
KING, Samuel Archer H
KING, Samuel Archer 4
KING, Samuel Ward H
KING, Samuel Wilder 3
KING, Scott 6
KING, Stanley 3
KING, Stanton Henry 2
KING, Steve M. 3
KING, Stoddard 1
KING, Sylvan N. 4
KING, Theophilus 1
KING, Thomas Brown 4
KING, Thomas Butler H
KING, Thomas Luther 5
KING, Thomas Starr H
KING, Virginia Ann 4
KING, Wilburn Hill 1
KING, Wilford Isbell 4
KING, Will R. 1
KING, Willard Vinton 3
KING, William H
KING, William Albert 1
KING, William Bulluck 6
KING, William Fletcher 1
KING, William Frederick 1
KING, William Henry 2
KING, William Lyon Mackenzie 3
KING, William Perry 2
KING, William Peter 3
KING, William Reynolds 5
KING, William Robert 3
KING, William Rufus 4
KING, William Rufus Devane H
KING, William Wirt 3
KING, Willis L. 1
KING, Willis Percival 4
KINGDON, Frank 5
KINGERY, Hugh Macmaster 1
KINGMAN, A(lice) Salome (Mrs. Wyatt Kingman) 5
KINGMAN, Eugene 6
KINGMAN, Eugene A. 4
KINGMAN, Henry Selden 5
KINGMAN, John J. 2
KINGMAN, Lewis 1
KINGMAN, Matthew Henry 2
KINGMAN, Russell Barclay 3
KING OF WILLIAM, James H
KINGSBURY, Albert 2
KINGSBURY, Benjamin Freeman 2
KINGSBURY, Frederick John 1
KINGSBURY, Jerome 2
KINGSBURY, John H
KINGSBURY, John A. 3
KINGSBURY, Joseph Thomas 1
KINGSBURY, Kenneth Raleigh 1
KINGSBURY, Nathan Corning 1
KINGSBURY, Seldon Bingham 1
KINGSBURY, Susan Myra 2
KINGSBURY, William Wallace H
KINGSCOTT, Louis Clifton 4
KINGSFORD, Howard Nelson 2
KINGSFORD, Joan Elizabeth 5
KINGSFORD, Thomas H
KINGSLAND, Mrs. Burton 1
KINGSLEY, Bruce Gordon 5
KINGSLEY, Calvin H
KINGSLEY, Chester Ward 1
KINGSLEY, Clarence Darwin 1
KINGSLEY, Darwin Pearl 1
KINGSLEY, Elbridge 1
KINGSLEY, Florence Morse 1
KINGSLEY, Hiram Webster 5
KINGSLEY, Howard L. 2
KINGSLEY, J. Sterling 1
KINGSLEY, James Luce H
KINGSLEY, John H. 4
KINGSLEY, Norman William 1
KINGSLEY, Sherman Colver 4
KINGSLEY, Willey Lyon 1
KINGSLEY, William H. 2
KINGSLEY, William Morgan 2
KINGSMILL, Harold 2
KINGSMILL, Hugh 2
KINGSTON, George Frederick 3
KINKADE, Reynolds Robert 1
KINKAID, Mary Holland 2
KINKAID, Moses Pierce 1
KINKAID, Thomas Cassin 5
KINKAID, Thomas Wright 1
KINKEAD, Cleves 3
KINKEAD, Edgar Benton 1
KINKEAD, Elizabeth Shelby 5
KINKEAD, Eugene F. 4
KINKELDEY, Otto 4
KINKHEAD, John Henry 1
KINLEY, David 2
KINLEY, John James 6
KINLOCH, Cleland H
KINLOCH, Francis H
KINLOCH, Robert Alexander H
KINNAN, Alexander Phoenix Waldron 1
KINNAN, William Asahel 4
KINNANE, Charles Herman 3
KINNANE, John E. 1
KINNANE, Raphael Ignatius 6
KINNARD, George L. H
KINNARD, Leonard Hummel 5
KINNE, Edward DeWitt 1
KINNE, Helen 1
KINNE, La Vega G. 1
KINNEAR, James Wesley 1
KINNEAR, Wilson Sherman 1
KINNERSLEY, Ebenezer H
KINNETT, William Ennis 1
KINNEY, Abbot 1
KINNEY, Ansel McBryde 5
KINNEY, Antoinette Brown 2
KINNEY, Bruce 1
KINNEY, Charles Noyes 6
KINNEY, Clesson Selwyne 4
KINNEY, Coates 1
KINNEY, Edmund J. 6
KINNEY, Elizabeth Clementine Dodge Stedman H
KINNEY, Gilbert 3
KINNEY, Henry Walsworth 5
KINNEY, Laurence Forman 4
KINNEY, Lucien Blair 5
KINNEY, Margaret West 5
KINNEY, O. S. H
KINNEY, Thomas Tallmadge 1
KINNEY, Timothy 4
KINNEY, Troy 1
KINNEY, William Aloysius 6
KINNEY, William Burnet H
KINNEY, William Morton 4
KINNICUT, Lincoln Newton 1
KINNICUTT, Francis Parker 1
KINNICUTT, Leonard Parker 1
KINNOCH, P. A. 3
KINO, Eusebio Francisco H
KINSELL, Laurance Wilkie 5
KINSELLA, Thomas H
KINSELLA, Thomas James 5
KINSEY, Alfred Charles 3
KINSEY, Charles H
KINSEY, E. Lee 4
KINSEY, James H
KINSEY, John H
KINSEY, John De Cou 5
KINSEY, Oliver P. 4
KINSLER, James C. 5
KINSLEY, Albert Thomas 2
KINSLEY, Carl 5
KINSLEY, Martin H
KINSLEY, Philip 4
KINSLEY, William Wirt 1
KINSLOE, Charles Lambert 6
KINSMAN, David Nathaniel 1
KINSMAN, Delos Oscar 2
KINSMAN, Frederick Joseph 3
KINSMAN, J. Warren 4
KINSMAN, William A(bbot) 5
KINSOLVING, Arthur Barksdale 3
KINSOLVING, Arthur Barksdale Ii 4
KINSOLVING, George Herbert 1
KINSOLVING, Lucien Lee 1
KINSOLVING, Sally Bruce 4
KINSWORTHY, Edgar Burton 4
KINTER, William Lewis 1
KINTNER, Edwin G. 5
KINTNER, Robert Chester 6
KINTNER, Samuel Montgomery 1
KINTPUASH H
KINTZING, Pearce 1
KINTZINGER, John W. 2
KINYOUN, Joseph James 1
KINZER, J. Roland 3
KINZIE, John H
KIOKEMEISTER, Fred Ludwig 5
KIP, Abraham Lincoln 4
KIP, Frederic Ellsworth 4
KIP, Leonard 1
KIP, William Ingraham H
KIPLINGER, Willard Monroe 4
KIPP, Charles John 1
KIPP, George Washington 1
KIPP, Orin Lansing 3
KIPPAX, John R. 1
KIRBY, Absalom 1
KIRBY, C. Valentine 2
KIRBY, Daniel Bartholomew 3
KIRBY, Daniel Noyes 2
KIRBY, Edmund Burgis 1
KIRBY, Ephraim H
KIRBY, Frank E. 1
KIRBY, Fred Morgan 1
KIRBY, George Hughes 1
KIRBY, Harold 3
KIRBY, J. Hudson H
KIRBY, John Jr. 1
KIRBY, John Henry 1
KIRBY, Laverne Howe 6
KIRBY, R. Harper 1
KIRBY, Robert J. 2
KIRBY, Rollin 3
KIRBY, William Fosgate 1
KIRBY, William Gerard 5
KIRBY, William Maurice 4
KIRBYE, J. Edward 1
KIRBY-SMITH, Edmund H
KIRCHHOFF, Charles 1
KIRCHNER, Arthur Adolph 4
KIRCHNER, George H. 1
KIRCHNER, Henry Paul 3
KIRCHNER, Otto 1
KIRCHWEY, Freda 6
KIRCHWEY, George Washington 2
KIRCK, Charles Townsend 2
KIRK, Alan Goodrich 4
KIRK, Albert E. 6
KIRK, Arthur Dale 2
KIRK, Charles Albert 2
KIRK, Dolly Williams 5
KIRK, Edward Cameron 1
KIRK, Edward Norris H
KIRK, Ellen Olney 4
KIRK, Frank C. 4
KIRK, Harris C. 4
KIRK, Harris Elliott 3
KIRK, John Esben 6
KIRK, John Foster 1
KIRK, John Franklin 1
KIRK, John R. 1
KIRK, Lester King 5
KIRK, May 4
KIRK, Norman Thomas 4
KIRK, Ralph G. 6
KIRK, Raymond Eller 3
KIRK, Raymond V. 2
KIRK, Thomas Jefferson 4
KIRK, Waldorf Tilton 3
KIRK, William 4
KIRK, William Frederick 1
KIRK, William Talbot 6
KIRKBRIDE, Franklin Butler 3
KIRKBRIDE, Thomas Story H
KIRKBRIDE, Walter George 6
KIRKEBY, Arnold S. 4

* Indicates More Than One Such Name Listed

KIRKHAM, Harold Laurens 2
Dundas
KIRKHAM, John Henry 1
KIRKHAM, Stanton Davis 2
KIRKHAM, William Barri 5
KIRKLAND, Archie 1
Howard
KIRKLAND, Caroline H
Matilda Stansbury
KIRKLAND, Edward Chase 6
KIRKLAND, James 1
Hampton
KIRKLAND, James Robert 3
KIRKLAND, John H
Thornton
KIRKLAND, Joseph *
KIRKLAND, Samuel H
KIRKLAND, Weymouth 4
KIRKLAND, Winifred
Margaretta
KIRKLIN, Byrl Raymond 3
KIRKMAN, Marshall 1
Monroe
KIRKPATRICK, Andrew H
KIRKPATRICK, Andrew 1
KIRKPATRICK, Blaine 3
Evron
KIRKPATRICK, Carlos 3
Stevens
KIRKPATRICK, Clifford 5
KIRKPATRICK, Edwin 1
Asbury
KIRKPATRICK, Elbert W. 1
KIRKPATRICK, George 5
Holland
KIRKPATRICK, Ivone 4
Elliott
KIRKPATRICK, Leonard 4
Henry
KIRKPATRICK, Sanford 4
KIRKPATRICK, Sidney 5
Dale
KIRKPATRICK, Thomas Le 2
Roy
KIRKPATRICK, William H
KIRKPATRICK, William 4
Dawson
KIRKPATRICK, William 5
Huntington
KIRKPATRICK, William 1
James
KIRKPATRICK, William 1
Sebring
KIRKUS, William
KIRKWOOD, Arthur Carter 5
KIRKWOOD, Daniel H
KIRKWOOD, Irwin 1
KIRKWOOD, John Gamble 3
KIRKWOOD, Joseph 1
Edward
KIRKWOOD, Samuel H
Jordan
KIRKWOOD, William 4
Reeside
KIRN, George John 4
KIROACK, Howard 3
KIRSCH, John N. 4
KIRSCHBAUM, Arthur 3
KIRSHMAN, John Emmett 2
KIRSHNER, Charles Henry 2
KIRSTEIN, Arthur 1
KIRSTEIN, Louis Edward 2
KIRSTEIN, Max 5
KIRTLAND, Dorrance H
KIRTLAND, Fred Durrell 5
KIRTLAND, Jared Potter 1
KIRTLAND, John Copeland 3
KIRTLAND, Lucian Swift 4
KIRTLEY, James Samuel 3
KIRWAN, Albert Dennis 5
KIRWAN, Michael Joseph 5
KIRWIN, Thomas Joseph 3
KISELEV, Evgeny 4
Dmitrievich
KISER, Samuel Ellsworth 1
KISER, Samuel Ellsworth 2
KISSAM, Henry Snyder 1
KISSEL, John 1
KISSELL, Harry Seaman 4
KISTER, George Raphael 4
KISTLER, John Clinton 1
KISTLER, Raymon M. 4
KISTLER, Samuel Stephens 6
KITCHEL, Lloyd 3
KITCHEL, William Lloyd 1
KITCHELL, Aaron H
KITCHELL, Joseph Gray 2
KITCHEN, Bethuel H
KITCHEN, Joseph Ambrose 6
KITCHENS, Wade 4
Hampton
KITCHIN, Claude 1
KITCHIN, Thurman Delna 1
KITCHIN, William
Copeman
KITCHIN, William Walton 1

KITSON, Geoffrey Herbert 6
KITSON, Harry Dexter 3
KITSON, Henry Hudson 2
KITSON, Samuel James 1
KITSON, Theo Alice 1
Ruggles
KITTELL, Albert George 2
KITTELL, James Shepard 1
KITTELLE, Sumner Ely 3
Wetmore
KITTERA, John Wilkes H
KITTERA, Thomas H
KITTINGER, Harold D. 2
KITTLE, Charles Morgan 1
KITTREDGE, Abbott Eliot 1
KITTREDGE, Alfred Beard 1
KITTREDGE, Frank Alvah 3
KITTREDGE, George 1
Lyman
KITTREDGE, George H
Washington
KITTREDGE, George 2
Watson
KITTREDGE, Henry 1
Grattan
KITTREDGE, Josiah 1
Edwards
KITTREDGE, Mabel Hyde 3
KITTREDGE, Walter 1
KITTREDGE, Wheaton 3
KITTRELL, Norman Goree 1
KITTS, Joseph Arthur 2
KITTS, Willard Augustus 4
3rd
KITTSON, Norman Wolfred H
KIVEL, John 1
KIVETTE, Frederick 6
Norman
KIVLIN, Vincent Earl 5
KIXMILLER, Edgar Byron 6
KIXMILLER, William 2
KIZER, Benjamin Hamilton 6
KJELLGREN, Bengt R. F. 5
KJERSTAD, Conrad Lund 5
KLABER, Eugene Henry 5
KLABUNDE, Earl Horace 4
KLAEBER, Frederick 4
KLAERNER, Richard 4
Albert
KLAESTAD, Helge 4
KLAFFENBACH, Arthur 4
O.
KLAIN, Zora 3
KLAMMER, Aloysius A. 3
KLAPP, William Henry 1
KLAPPER, Paul 3
KLARE, Robert Edward 4
KLARMANN, Adolf D. 6
KLATH, Thormod Oscar 1
KLAUBER, Adolph 1
KLAUBER, Edward 3
KLAUBER, Laurence 5
Monroe
KLAUDER, Charles Zeller 1
KLAUS, Irving Goncer 5
KLAUSER, Karl 1
KLAUSMEYER, David 5
Michael
KLAW, Marc 1
KLAWANS, Arthur Herman 6
KLEBENOV, Louis H. 6
KLEBERG, Edward Robert 3
KLEBERG, Richard Miffin 5
KLEBERG, Robert Justus 6
Jr.
KLEBERG, Rudolph 1
KLEBS, Arnold Carl 2
KLECKI, Paul 6
KLECKNER, Martin Seler 1
KLEEGMAN, Sophia 5
Josephine *
KLEEMAN, Arthur S. 4
KLEENE, Gustav Adolph 2
KLEIN, Arthur George 4
KLEIN, Arthur Warner 6
KLEIN, Bruno Oscar 1
KLEIN, Charles 1
KLEIN, Eugene S. 5
KLEIN, Francis Joseph 5
KLEIN, Frederick B. 3
KLEIN, Frederick Charles 1
KLEIN, George H. 6
KLEIN, Gerald Brown 5
KLEIN, Harry Martin John 5
KLEIN, Harry Thomas 4
KLEIN, Henry Weber 5
KLEIN, Herman William 3
KLEIN, Hermann 1
KLEIN, Horace C. 4
KLEIN, Jacob 6
KLEIN, John Warren 3
KLEIN, Joseph Frederic 1
KLEIN, Joseph J(erome) 6
KLEIN, Julius 1
KLEIN, Manuel 4
KLEIN, Melanie 5

KLEIN, Sandor Sidney 5
KLEIN, Simon Robert 4
KLEIN, William Jr. 5
KLEIN, William M. 4
KLEINER, Hugo Gustav 5
KLEINER, Israel S. 4
KLEINPELL, William 3
Darwin
KLEINSCHMIDT, Edward 6
Ernst
KLEINSCHMIDT, Rudolph 2
August
KLEINSMID, Rufus 4
Bernard von
KLEISER, George William 3
KLEISER, Grenville 3
KLEISER, Lorentz 4
KLEIST, James Aloysius 3
KLEITZ, William L. 3
KLEMIN, Alexander 3
KLEMM, Louis Richard 1
KLEMME, Edward Julius 5
KLEMME, Randall Telford 6
KLEMME, Roland M. 3
KLEMPERER, Otto 5
KLENDSHOJ, Niels 6
Christian
KLENKE, William Walter 4
KLEPETKO, Frank 4
KLEPPER, Frank B. 3
KLEPPER, Max Francis 1
KLETZKI, Paul 5
KLIBANOW, William J. 5
KLIEFORTH, Ralph George 4
KLIEN, Arthur Jay 3
KLIEWER, John Walter 1
KLIKA, Ervin Robert 4
KLIMAS, John Edward 6
KLIMM, Lester E. 4
KLINCK, Arthur William 3
KLINCK, Leonard Silvanus 5
KLINE, Allan Blair 5
KLINE, Allen Marshall 6
KLINE, Ardolph L. 1
KLINE, Barton Leeorie 6
KLINE, C. Mahlon 4
KLINE, Charles H. 1
KLINE, Franz Josef 4
KLINE, George H
KLINE, George Milton 5
KLINE, George Washington 1
KLINE, I. Clinton 3
KLINE, Ira M. 6
KLINE, Jacob 1
KLINE, John Robert 3
KLINE, Marcus C. L. 1
KLINE, Marion Justus 4
KLINE, Paul Robert 5
KLINE, Quentin McKay 6
KLINE, Virgil Philip 1
KLINE, Walter Winter 6
KLINE, Whorten Albert 2
KLINE, William Fair 1
KLINE, William Jay 1
KLINEFELTER, Howard 4
Emanuel
KLING, Charles Fergus 6
KLINGAMAN, Orie Erb 4
KLINGBIEL, Ray I. 5
KLINGE, Ernest F. 3
KLINGENSMITH, John Jr. H
KLINGLER, Harry J. 4
KLINGMAN, William 6
(Washington)
KLIPPART, John Hancock H
KLIPSTEIN, Ernest Carl 1
KLIPSTEIN, Louis H
Frederick
KLOCK, Mabie Crouse 3
KLOEBER, Charles Edward 1
KLOEFFLER, Royce 6
Gerald
KLOPMAN, William 6
KLOPP, Edward Jonathan 1
KLOPP, Henry Irwin 2
KLOPSCH, Louis 1
KLOSS, Charles Luther 1
KLOSSNER, Howard Jacob 4
KLOTS, Allen Trafford 4
KLOTZ, Oskar H
KLOTZ, Robert 1
KLOTZBURGER, Edwin 4
Carl
KLUBERTANZ, George 5
Peter
KLUCKHOHN, Clyde Kay 4
Maben
KLUCKHOLN, Frank Louis 5
KLUCZYNSKI, John C. 6
KLUG, Norman R. 4
KLUGESCHEID, Richard 5
Charles
KLUGHERZ, John Anthony 3
KLUSS, Charles LaVerne 4
KLUTTZ, Theodore 1
Franklin

KLUTTZ, Whitehead 6
KLUYVER, Albert Jan 3
KLYCE, Scudder 1
KLYVER, Henry Peter 4
KNABE, Valentine Wilhelm H
Ludwig
KNABENSHUE, Paul 1
KNABENSHUE, Roy 3
KNABENSHUE, Samuel S. 1
KNAEBEL, Ernest 2
KNAPLUND, Paul 4
Alexander
KNAPP, A(rthur) Blair 5
KNAPP, Adeline 1
KNAPP, Andrew Stephen 4
KNAPP, Anthony Lausett H
KNAPP, Arnold Herman 3
KNAPP, Arthur May 2
KNAPP, Bliss 1
KNAPP, Bradford 1
KNAPP, Charles H
KNAPP, Charles 1
KNAPP, Charles Luman 1
KNAPP, Charles Welbourne 1
KNAPP, Chauncey Langdon H
KNAPP, Cleon Talboys 3
KNAPP, Francis Atherton 5
KNAPP, Frank Averill 1
KNAPP, Fred Church 2
KNAPP, George H
KNAPP, George Leonard 1
KNAPP, Grace Higley 5
KNAPP, Harold Everard 1
KNAPP, Harry Shepard 1
KNAPP, Henry Alonzo 1
KNAPP, Herman *
KNAPP, John Joseph 1
KNAPP, Joseph Palmer 3
KNAPP, Kemper K. 2
KNAPP, Lyman Enos 1
KNAPP, Martin Augustine 1
KNAPP, Philip Coombs 1
KNAPP, Robert Hampden 6
KNAPP, Robert Talbot 3
KNAPP, Samuel Lorenzo H
KNAPP, Seaman Asahel 1
KNAPP, Shepherd 2
KNAPP, Stanley Merrill 4
KNAPP, Thad Johnson 5
KNAPP, Thomas McCartan 4
KNAPP, Walter I(rving) 5
KNAPP, Willard A. 4
KNAPP, William Ireland 1
KNAPPEN, Loyal Edwin 1
KNAPPEN, Theodore 4
Macfarlane
KNAPPENBERGER, J. 4
William
KNAPPERTSBUSCH, Hans 4
KNATHS, (Otto) Karl 5
KNAUFFT, Ernest 4
KNAUSS, Harold Paul 4
KNAUTH, Arnold Whitman 4
KNAUTH, Oswald Whitman 4
KNEASS, George Bryan 5
KNEASS, Samuel H
Honeyman
KNEASS, Strickland 1
KNEASS, Strickland Landis 1
KNEASS, William 1
KNECHT, Andrew Wilson 6
KNECHT, Karl Kae 5
KNEEDLER, William L. 1
KNEELAND, Abner 1
KNEELAND, George H
Jackson
KNEELAND, Robert 5
Shepherd
KNEELAND, Samuel * H
KNEELAND, Stillman 1
Foster
KNEELAND, Yale Jr. 4
KNEIL, Robert Chipman 4
KNEIP, Herbert Joseph 3
KNEISEL, Franz 1
KNEISS, Gilbert Harold 4
KNEPPER, Edwin Garfield 4
KNEVELS, Gertrude 4
KNIBBS, Harry Herbert 1
KNICKERBOCKER, Fred 3
Hugh
KNICKERBOCKER, H
Harmen Jansen
KNICKERBOCKER, H
Herman
KNICKERBOCKER, 4
Hubert Renfro
KNICKERBOCKER, 4
William E.
KNICKERBOCKER, 5
William Skinkle
KNIFFIN, William Henry 4
KNIGHT, Adele Ferguson 4
KNIGHT, Albion 1
Williamson
KNIGHT, Alfred 6

KNIGHT, Arthur Merrill Jr. 6
KNIGHT, Augustus Smith 2
KNIGHT, Austin Melvin 1
KNIGHT, Charles 5
KNIGHT, Charles Landon 1
KNIGHT, Charles Mellen 2
KNIGHT, Charles Robert 5
KNIGHT, Clarence A. 1
KNIGHT, Edgar Wallace 3
KNIGHT, Edward Collings H
KNIGHT, Edward Henry H
KNIGHT, Edward Hooker 1
KNIGHT, Edward Wallace 1
KNIGHT, Erastus Cole 2
KNIGHT, Eric 2
KNIGHT, Eugene Herbert 5
KNIGHT, Felix Harrison 6
KNIGHT, Francis 3
McMaster
KNIGHT, Frank A. 3
KNIGHT, Frank Hyneman 5
KNIGHT, Frederic 2
Butterfield
KNIGHT, Frederic Harrison 1
KNIGHT, Frederick Irving 1
KNIGHT, George 1
Alexander
KNIGHT, George Laurence 5
KNIGHT, George Thomson 1
KNIGHT, George Wells 1
KNIGHT, Goodwin (Jess) 5
KNIGHT, Grant Cochran 3
KNIGHT, Harold Audas 3
KNIGHT, Harry Clifford 2
KNIGHT, Harry Edward 5
KNIGHT, Harry S. 3
KNIGHT, Henry Cogswell 1
KNIGHT, Henry Granger 2
KNIGHT, Howard Lawton 4
KNIGHT, Howard Roscoe 4
KNIGHT, James Ernest 5
KNIGHT, Jesse 1
KNIGHT, Jesse William 3
KNIGHT, John 1
KNIGHT, John George 1
David
KNIGHT, John Thornton 1
KNIGHT, Jonathan * 1
KNIGHT, Leona Kaiser 4
KNIGHT, Louis Aston 2
KNIGHT, Lucian Lamar 1
KNIGHT, Milton 5
KNIGHT, Montgomery 4
KNIGHT, Nehemiah H
KNIGHT, Nehemiah Rice H
KNIGHT, Nicholas 4
KNIGHT, Ora Willis 4
KNIGHT, Otis D. 4
KNIGHT, Peter Oliphant 2
KNIGHT, Ridgway 1
KNIGHT, Robert 1
KNIGHT, Robert Palmer 4
KNIGHT, Ryland 3
KNIGHT, Samuel 2
KNIGHT, Sarah Kemble H
KNIGHT, Stephen Albert 4
KNIGHT, Thomas Edmund 1
KNIGHT, Thomas Edmund 1
Jr.
KNIGHT, Walter David 3
KNIGHT, Webster 1
KNIGHT, Wilbur Clinton 1
KNIGHT, William Allen 1
KNIGHT, William D. 4
KNIGHT, William Henry 4
KNIPE, Alden Arthur 4
KNIPE, Emilie Benson 4
KNIPP, Charles Tobias 4
KNISKERN, Leslie Albert 4
KNISKERN, Philip Wheeler 4
KNISKERN, Warren B. 1
KNOBLOCH, Henry 4
F(rederick) J(acob)
KNODE, Oliver M. 4
KNODE, Ralph Howard 4
KNOLES, Tully Cleon 5
KNOLL, Hans G. 3
KNOLLENBERG, Bernhard 6
KNOLLYS, Edward George 4
William Tyrwhitt
KNOOP, Frederic Barnes 5
KNOPF, Adolph 5
KNOPF, Blanche 4
KNOPF, Blanche (Wolf) 5
KNOPF, Carl Sumner 2
KNOPF, Philip 1
KNOPF, S. Adolphus 2
KNOPF, William Cleveland 4
Jr.
KNOPP, Herbert William 4
Sr.
KNORR, Fred August 4
KNORR, Walter Herbert 6
KNORTZ, Karl 4
KNOTT, A. Leo 1
KNOTT, David H. 3

KNOTT, Emmet Kennard 4
KNOTT, James E. 4
KNOTT, James Proctor 1
KNOTT, John Francis 4
KNOTT, J(oseph) C(arlton) 6
KNOTT, Lester R. 4
KNOTT, Richard Wilson 4
KNOTT, Stuart R. 4
KNOTT, Thomas Albert 2
KNOTT, Van Buren 5
KNOTTS, Armanis F. 1
KNOTTS, Edward C. 1
KNOTTS, Howard Clayton 2
KNOTTS, Raymond 1
KNOUFF, Ralph Albert 4
KNOUS, William Lee 3
KNOWER, Henry McElderry 1
KNOWLAND, Joseph Russell 4
KNOWLAND, William Fife 6
KNOWLES, Archibald Campbell 5
KNOWLES, Daniel Clark 1
KNOWLES, Edward Gillett 5
KNOWLES, Edward Randall
KNOWLES, Edwin Blackwell 5
KNOWLES, Ellin J. 1
KNOWLES, Frederic Lawrence 1
KNOWLES, Frederick Milton 5
KNOWLES, Hiram 1
KNOWLES, Horace Greeley 1
KNOWLES, Lucius James H
KNOWLES, Melita 5
KNOWLES, Morris 1
KNOWLES, Nathaniel 5
KNOWLES, Robert Bell 3
KNOWLSON, James S. 3
KNOWLTON, Ansel Alphonse
KNOWLTON, Charles 1
KNOWLTON, Charles Osmond 4
KNOWLTON, Charles Osmond 5
KNOWLTON, Daniel Chauncey 5
KNOWLTON, Ebenezer H
KNOWLTON, Eliot A. 1
KNOWLTON, Frank Hall 4
KNOWLTON, Frank P(attengill) 5
KNOWLTON, George Willard 1
KNOWLTON, Helen Mary 1
KNOWLTON, Hosea Morrill
KNOWLTON, Marcus Perrin 1
KNOWLTON, P. Clarke 1
KNOWLTON, Philip Arnold 3
KNOWLTON, Robert Henry 4
KNOWLTON, Thomas H
KNOX, Adeline Trafton 3
KNOX, Mrs Charles B. 3
KNOX, Dudley Wright 4
KNOX, Mrs Frank 5
KNOX, George William 1
KNOX, Harry 1
KNOX, Henry 4
KNOX, James H
KNOX, James E. 3
KNOX, Jessie Juliet (Daily) 5
KNOX, John Barnett 1
KNOX, John Clark 4
KNOX, John Jay H
KNOX, Louis 2
KNOX, Martin Van Buren 1
KNOX, Mary Alice 1
KNOX, Philander Chase 1
KNOX, Raymond Collyer 5
KNOX, Robert White 5
KNOX, Rush Hightower 3
KNOX, Samuel H
KNOX, Samuel Lippincott Griswold
KNOX, Thomas Wallace H
KNOX, William Elliott 1
KNOX, William Franklin 1
KNOX, William Russell 6
KNOX, William Shadrach 4
KNOX, William White 1
KNUBEL, Frederick Hermann 2
KNUBEL, Frederick Ritscher 3
KNUDSEN, Charles William
KNUDSEN, Thorkild R. 4
KNUDSEN, Vern O. 6

KNUDSEN, William S. 2
KNUDSON, Albert Cornelius 3
KNUDSON, Bennett Olin 4
KNUDSON, James K. 4
KNUDSON, John Immanuel 3
KNUTSON, Harold 3
KNUTSON, Kent Siguart 5
KOBAK, Alfred Julian 6
KOBAK, Edgar 4
KOBBE, Gustav 1
KOBBE, William August 1
KOBELT, Karl 4
KOBER, Arthur 6
KOBER, George Martin 1
KOCH, Alfred 3
KOCH, Charles Rudolph Edward 1
KOCH, Edward William 2
KOCH, Elers 5
KOCH, Felix John 1
KOCH, Fred Chase 5
KOCH, Fred Conrad 5
KOCH, Frederick Henry 2
KOCH, George Price 5
KOCH, Henry G. H
KOCH, Julius Arnold 3
KOCH, Otto 3
KOCH, Theodore Wesley 5
KOCHAN, Edward John 5
KOCHER, A. Lawrence 5
KOCHERSPERGER, Hiram Miller 4
KOCHERTHAL, Josua von H
KOCHIN, Louis Mordecai 1
KOCHS, August 4
KOCIALKOWSKI, Leo 3
KOCKRITZ, Ewald 1
KOCOUREK, Albert 5
KOCSIS, Ann 6
KODALY, Zoltan 4
KOEBEL, Ralph Francis 4
KOEGEL, Otto Erwin 6
KOEHLER, Otto A. 5
KOEHLER, Robert 1
KOEHLER, Sylvester Rosa 1
KOEHLER, Wilhelm Reinhold Walter 3
KOEHRING, William J. 5
KOENIG, Adolph 1
KOENIG, Egmont Francis 6
KOENIG, George Augustus 1
KOENIG, Joseph Pierre 4
KOENIG, Louis F. 4
KOENIG, M(arshall) Glenn 6
KOENIG, Myron L(aw) 5
KOENIGSBERG, Moses 2
KOEPEL, Norbert Francis 4
KOERBLE, Charles Edward 6
KOERNER, Andrew 4
KOERNER, Gustave H
KOERNER, Theodor 3
KOERNER, Theodor 5
KOERNER, William 1
KOERNER, William Henry Dethlep 1
KOESTER, Frank 1
KOESTER, George Arthur 6
KOFFKA, Kurt 4
KOHL, Edwin Phillips 4
KOHLBECK, Valentine 1
KOHLER, Elmer Peter 1
KOHLER, Eric Louis 6
KOHLER, Fred 1
KOHLER, G. A. Edward 1
KOHLER, Herbert Calvin 3
KOHLER, Herbert Vollrath 5
KOHLER, Kaufmann 1
KOHLER, Max James 1
KOHLER, Ruth DeYoung 3
KOHLER, Walter Jodok 1
KOHLER, Wolfgang 4
KOHLER, Wolfgang 5
KOHLHEPP, Charles E. 1
KOHLMANN, Anthony H
KOHLMEIER, Albert L. 4
KOHLMER, Fred 5
KOHLSAAT, Christian Cecil
KOHLSAAT, Herman Henry 1
KOHLSTEDT, Donald Winston 5
KOHLSTEDT, Edward Delor 4
KOHN, August 1
KOHN, Gabriel 6
KOHN, Henry H. 2
KOHN, Jacob 5
KOHN, Louis A. 5
KOHN, Robert David 3
KOHNS, Lee 1
KOHNSTAMM, Frank R. 3
KOHUT, Alexander H
KOINER, C. Wellington 3

KOKATNUR, Vaman Ramachandra 3
KOKERITZ, K. A. Helge 4
KOKERNOT, Herbert Lee 5
KOKES, Richard Joseph 6
KOLAR, Victor 3
KOLB, Charles August 4
KOLB, Dielman H
KOLB, Ellsworth Leonardson 5
KOLB, James Monroe 6
KOLB, John Harrison 4
KOLB, Louis John 1
KOLBE, Parke Rexford 2
KOLE, Lessing Lawrence 5
KOLKER, Henry Joseph 2
KOLKEY, Eugene Louis 6
KOLLE, Frederick Strange 1
KOLLEN, Gerrit John 1
KOLLER, Carl 2
KOLLER, Paul Warren 1
KOLLOCK, Charles Wilson 1
KOLLOCK, Mary 4
KOLLOCK, Shepard H
KOLLWITZ, Kathe Schmidt 4
KOLMAN, Burton A. 5
KOLMER, John Albert 4
KOLOWICH, George J. 3
KOLSETH, J. Harold 5
KOMAREWSKY, Vasili Ilyich 3
KOMAROV, Vladimir 4
KOMMERS, William John 5
KOMORA, Paul O. 3
KOMP, William H. Wood 3
KOMROFF, Manuel 6
KONE, Edward Reeves 5
KONENKOV, Sergei Timopheevitch
KONIG, George 1
KONINGS, Anthony H
KONJOVIC, Petar 5
KONKLE, Burton Alva 2
KONOP, Thomas Frank 4
KONTA, Alexander 1
KONTA, Annie Lemp 5
KONTA, Geoffrey 2
KONTI, Isidore 1
KONTZ, Ernest Charles 2
KOON, Martin B. 1
KOONS, Charles Alfred 4
KOONS, Charles Alfred 6
KOONS, John Cornelius 1
KOONS, Tilghman Benjamin 4
KOONTZ, Arthur Burke 4
KOONTZ, Frederick Bowers 3
KOONTZ, James R. 4
KOONTZ, Louis Knott 2
KOOP, William H. 3
KOOPMAN, Augustus 1
KOOPMAN, Harry Lyman 1
KOOS, Leonard Vincent 6
KOPALD, Louis Joseph 1
KOPETZKY, Samuel Joseph 3
KOPF, Carl Heath 4
KOPLAR, Sam 4
KOPLIK, Henry 1
KOPMAN, Benjamin 4
KOPP, Arthur William 4
KOPP, Arthur William 5
KOPP, George A(dams) 5
KOPP, Otto 2
KOPP, William F. 1
KOPPER, Samuel Keene Claggett 3
KOPPERUD, Andrew 6
KOPPIUS, O. T. 4
KOPPLEMANN, Herman Paul 3
KORBEL, Mario 3
KORBLY, Charles Alexander 1
KORDA, Sir Alexander 3
KOREN, John 1
KOREN, Ulrik Vilhelm 1
KOREN, William Jr. 3
KORFF, Sergius Alexander 1
KORIN, Pavel Dmitrievich 5
KORN, Peter George 5
KORNEGAY, Wade Hampton
KORNER, Gustav Philipp H
KORNER, Jules Gilmer Jr. 4
KORNER, Theodor 5
KORNFELD, Albert 4
KORNFELD, Murray 5
KORNGOLD, Eric Wolfgang 4
KORNHAUSER, Sidney Isaac 3
KORSMEYER, Frederick August
KORSTIAN, Clarence Ferdinand 4

KORZYBSKI, Alfred Habdank 2
KOSA, Emil Jean Jr. 5
KOSANOVITCH, Sava N. 3
KOSCINSKI, Arthur A. 3
KOSCIUSZKO, Tadeusz Andrzej Bonawentura H
KOSER, Ralph B. 5
KOSER, Stewart Arment 5
KOSMAK, George William 3
KOSOLAPOFF, Gennady Michael 6
KOSSUTH, Lajos H
KOST, Frederick W. 1
KOST, John 1
KOSTALEK, John Anton 4
KOSTELLOW, Alexander Jusserand 3
KOSTER, Frederick Jacob 3
KOSTER, Willem 6
KOSTKA, William James 6
KOSTRZEWSKI, Jozef Wiadyslaw 6
KOSZALKA, Michael Francis 5
KOTANY, Ludwig 1
KOTH, Arthur William 4
KOUDELKA, Joseph Maria 1
KOUES, Helen 4
KOUNTZ, John S. 1
KOUNTZE, de Lancey 2
KOUNTZE, Augustus Frederick 1
KOUNTZE, Charles Thomas 5
KOUNTZE, Harold 4
KOUSSEVITZKY, Sergei 3
KOUTZEN, Boris 4
KOUWENHOVEN, William Bennett 6
KOVACH, George Stephen 4
KOVACS, Ernie 4
KOVACS, Richard 3
KOVARIK, Alois Francis 4
KOWAL, Chester * 4
KOWALSKI, Frank 6
KOWNATZKI, Hans 4
KOYL, Charles Herschel 1
KOYRE, Alexandre 5
KOZLOV, Frol Romanovich 4
KRACAUER, Siegfried 4
KRACKE, Frederick J. H. 3
KRACKE, Roy Rachford 3
KRAELING, Carl H. 4
KRAEMER, Casper John Jr. 3
KRAEMER, Henry 1
KRAETZER, Arthur Furman 1
KRAFFT, Carl R. 1
KRAFFT, Walter A. 3
KRAFFT, Walter E. 3
KRAFKA, Joseph Jr. 2
KRAFT, Edwin Arthur 4
KRAFT, James Lewis 3
KRAFT, John H. 5
KRAFT, Louis 6
KRAFVE, Richard Ernest 6
KRAL, Josef Jiri 4
KRAMER, A. Walter 5
KRAMER, Albert Ludlow 2
KRAMER, Andrew Anthony 5
KRAMER, Benjamin 6
KRAMER, Edwin Weed 2
KRAMER, Frederick Ferdinand 1
KRAMER, George Washington 1
KRAMER, Hans 3
KRAMER, Harold Morton 1
KRAMER, Herman Frederick 4
KRAMER, John F. 5
KRAMER, Raymond Charles 1
KRAMER, Rudolph Jesse 3
KRAMER, Samuel Edmond 4
KRAMER, Simon Gad 5
KRAMER, Simon Pendleton 4
KRAMER, Stephanie Shambaugh (Mrs. Ferd Kramer) 6
KRAMMES, Emma Ruess 3
KRANNERT, Herman C(harles) 5
KRANS, Horatio Sheafe 3
KRANS, Olaf H
KRANS, Olaf 4
KRANZ, Leon George 3
KRAPP, George Philip 1
KRASCHEL, Nelson George 4
KRASIK, Sidney 6
KRASS, Nathan 4
KRATHWOHL, William Charles 5
KRATT, Theodore 4

KRATZ, Alonzo Plumsted 5
KRATZ, Henry Elton 1
KRAUS, Adolf 1
KRAUS, Charles August 4
KRAUS, Edward Henry 5
KRAUS, John H
KRAUS, Milton 4
KRAUS, Rene Raoul 2
KRAUS, Walter Max 2
KRAUSE, Allen Kramer 1
KRAUSE, Carl Albert 1
KRAUSE, Chester T. 4
KRAUSE, Harry Theodore 5
KRAUSE, Louise B. 5
KRAUSE, Lyda Farrington 1
KRAUSE, Rudolph 4
KRAUSKOPF, Joseph 1
KRAUSS, Elmer Frederick 2
KRAUSS, William Christopher 1
KRAUSS-BOELTE, Maria 4
KRAUTBAUER, Franz Xaver H
KRAUTH, Charles Philip H
KRAUTH, Charles Porterfield H
KRAUTHOFF, Charles Rieseck 1
KRAUTHOFF, Louis Charles 1
KRAVCHENKO, Victor A. 4
KRAYBILL, Henry Reist 3
KREBS, Jacob H
KREBS, Stanley LeFevre 1
KREBS, Walter Winston 6
KREBS, William Samuel 3
KRECH, Alvin William 1
KRECKER, Frederick H(artzler) 6
KREEGER, Morris Harold 6
KREFELD, William John 4
KREGER, Clarence W. 4
KREGER, Edward Albert 3
KREGER, Henry Ludwig Flood 4
KREHBIEL, Christian H
KREHBIEL, Christian 4
KREHBIEL, Christian Emanuel 2
KREHBIEL, Edward 3
KREHBIEL, Henry Edward 1
KREIDER, Aaron Shenk 1
KREIDER, Charles Daniel 3
KREINHEDER, Oscar Carl 2
KREIS, Henry 4
KREISER, Edward Franklin 1
KREISINGER, Henry 2
KREISLER, Fritz 4
KREISMANN, Frederick Herman 5
KREJCI, Milo William 4
KREMER, Charles Edward 4
KREMER, Charles S. 4
KREMER, George H
KREMER, J. Bruce 1
KREMER, Walter Wall 4
KREMERS, Edward 1
KREMERS, J. H. 3
KREMPEL, John P. 1
KRESEL, Isidor Jacob 3
KRESGE, Sebastian S. 4
KRESS, Albert Leland 6
KRESS, C. Adam 3
KRESS, Claude Washington 1
KRESS, Daniel H. 4
KRESS, George Henry 1
KRESS, John Alexander 3
KRESS, Rush Harrison 4
KRESS, Samuel Henry 4
KRESS, Walter Jay 5
KRESSMAN, Mabel A. Gridley (Mrs. Frederick W. Kressman) 1
KRETSCHMER, Herman Louis 3
KRETZINGER, George Washington 1
KRETZMANN, M(artin) F(rederick) 6
KRETZMANN, Otto Paul 6
KREUDER, Ernst 6
KREUSCHER, Philip Heinrich 2
KREY, August Charles 4
KREYCHE, Robert Joseph 6
KREYMBORG, Alfred 4
KREZ, Konrad H
KRIBBEN, Earl 3
KRICK, Charles Shalter 2
KRICK, Edwin Vernon 3
KRIDL, Manfred 3
KRIEBEL, Oscar Schultz 1
KRIEBEL, William F. 3
KRIEBLE, Vernon Kriebel 4
KRIEG, Laurel Lee 6

KRIEGE, Otto Edward 5
KRIEGER, Knut Axel 6
KRIEHN, George 6
KRIENDLER, Maxwell Arnold 6
KRILL, Alex Eugene 5
KRIMMEL, John Lewis H
KRINER, Harry L(uther) 6
KRIPS, Henry Josef 6
KRISHNA, Menon Vengalil Krishman 6
KRISHNAN, Sir Kariamanikkam Srinivasa 4
KRISTOFFERSEN, Magnus K. 4
KRITZ, Karl 5
KRIZA, John 6
KROCK, Arthur 6
KROEBER, Alfred L. 4
KROECK, Louis Samuel 5
KROEGER, Adolph Ernst H
KROEGER, Ernest Richard 1
KROEGER, Frederick Charles 2
KROEH, Charles Frederick 2
KROEHLER, Peter Edward 4
KROEZE, Barend Herman 5
KROGER, Bernard Henry 2
KROHA, Jiri 6
KROHN, William Otterbein 1
KROL, Bastiaen Jansen H
KROLL, Jack 5
KROLL, Leon 6
KROMER, Leon Benjamin 4
KRON, Joseph 6
KRONBERG, Louis 4
KRONE, Max Thomas 5
KRONMILLER, John 4
KRONSHAGE, Theodore Jr. 5
KRONWALL, Konstantin 4
KROOS, Oscar August 5
KROOSS, Herman Edward 6
KROTEL, Gottlob Frederick 1
KROUT, Mary Hannah 1
KROYT, Boris 5
KRUCKMAN, Arnold 2
KRUEGER, Ernest Theodore
KRUEGER, John Frederick 1
KRUEGER, Otto 4
KRUEGER, Walter 4
KRUEGER, William Conrad 3
KRUELL, Gustav
KRUESI, Frank E. 2
KRUESI, John H
KRUESI, Paul John 4
KRUESI, Walter Edison 5
KRUETGEN, Ernest J. 2
KRUG, Henry Jr. 2
KRUG, Julius Albert 5
KRUGER, Frederick Konrad 3
KRUGER, Minna Nicola 6
KRUGER, Otto 6
KRULISH, Emil 6
KRUM, Chester Harding 1
KRUM, Howard Lewis 4
KRUMB, Henry 4
KRUMBEIN, Paul Otto 2
KRUMBHAAR, E. B. 4
KRUMREIG, Edward Ludwig 4
KRUMWIEDE, Charles 1
KRUPA, Gene 6
KRUPP, Alfried von Bohlen und Halbach 4
KRUPSHAW, David Loeb 4
KRUSE, E. T. 3
KRUSE, Frederick William 1
KRUSEN, Frank Hammond 6
KRUSEN, Ursula Leden 6
KRUSEN, Wilmer 2
KRUTCH, Joseph Wood 5
KRUTTSCHNITT, Ernest Benjamin
KRUTTSCHNITT, Julius 1
KRYL, Bohumir 5
KUBAT, Jerald Richard 5
KUBEL, Stephen Joseph 1
KUBELIK, Jan 1
KUBERT, Joseph Mandel 6
KUBIE, Lawrence S(chlesinger) 6
KUCERA, Louis Benedict 3
KUCZYNSKI, Robert Rene 4
KUDNER, Arthur Henry 2
KUEBLER, Clark George 4
KUEBLER, John R. 4
KUEHNE, Hugo Franz 4
KUEHNER, Quincy Adams 6
KUERSTEINER, Albert Frederick
KUESTER, Clarence Otto 2

KUETHER, Frederick William 5
KUFOID, Charles Atwood 2
KUH, Sydney 1
KUHL, Ernest Peter 6
KUHLMAN, Kathryn 6
KUHN, Adam H
KUHN, Arthur K. 3
KUHN, C. John 4
KUHN, Ferd William 3
KUHN, Franz Christian 1
KUHN, Harry Waldo 4
KUHN, Joseph Ernst 1
KUHN, Oliver Owen 1
KUHN, Walt 2
KUHN, William Frederick 1
KUHNS, Austin 4
KUHNS, Harold Samuel 4
KUHNS, Joseph Henry H
KUHNS, Luther Melanchthon 1
KUHNS, Oscar 1
KUHNS, William Rodney 5
KUICHLING, Emil 1
KUIPER, Gerard Peter 6
KUIST, Howard Tillman 4
KUIZENGA, John E. 3
KUJOTH, Jean Spealman 6
KULAS, Elroy John 3
KULDELL, Rudolph Charles 6
KULER, Fritz 5
KULIKOWSKI, Adam 4
KULIKOWSKI, Adam (Hyppolit) 4
KULJIAN, Harry A. 6
KULLMAN, Harold John Frederick 6
KULP, Clarence Arthur 4
KULP, Victor Henry 4
KUMLER, Henry H
KUMLER, John A. 4
KUMM, Einar Axel 3
KUMM, H. Karl William 4
KUMMEL, Henry Barnard 2
KUMMER, Frederic Arnold 2
KUMP, Herman Guy 4
KUNESH, Joseph Francis 4
KUNG, H. H. 4
KUNHARDT, Kingsley 3
KUNIANSKY, Max 4
KUNITZER, Robert 1
KUNIYOSHI, Yasuo 4
KUNKEL, A. William 5
KUNKEL, Beverly Waugh 5
KUNKEL, Frank Henry 3
KUNKEL, Jacob Michael H
KUNKEL, John Christian 3
KUNKEL, John Crain 5
KUNKEL, Louis Otto 4
KUNKEL, William Albert Jr. 2
KUNKLE, Bayard Dickenson 3
KUNO, Hisashi 5
KUNSMILLER, Adolph 6
KUNSTADTER, Albert 4
KUNSTADTER, Ralph Hess
KUNTZ, Albert 3
KUNTZ, Werner Hinrich 6
KUNWALD, Ernst 1
KUNZ, Adolf Henry 5
KUNZ, George Frederick 1
KUNZ, Jakob 1
KUNZ, Josef L(aurenz) 4
KUNZ, Stanley Henry 4
KUNZE, John Christopher H
KUNZE, Richard Ernest 1
KUNZE, William Frederick 5
KUNZEL, Fred 5
KUNZIG, Louis A. 3
KUNZMANN, Jacob Christoph
KUO, Ping Wen 5
KUPLIC, J. L. 5
KURCHATOV, Igor V. 5
KURLAND, Nancy Jamie (Mrs. Henry Hans-Heinz Schmidek) 6
KURN, James M. 2
KURRELMEYER, William 3
KURRIE, Harry Rushworth 1
KURT, Franklin Thomas 4
KURTH, Ernest Lynn 4
KURTH, Wilfred 3
KURTZ, Benjamin H
KURTZ, Benjamin Putnam 3
KURTZ, Charles Lindley 4
KURTZ, Charles M. 1
KURTZ, Daniel Webster 3
KURTZ, Ford 3
KURTZ, Jacob Banks 4
KURTZ, Louis Charles 5
KURTZ, Robert Merrill 1

KURTZ, Thomas Richardson 3
KURTZ, William Henry H
KURZ, Louis H
KURZ, Louis 4
KURZ, Louis Frederick 4
KURZ, Walter Charles 5
KURZMAN, Harold Phillip 5
KUSCHNER, Beatrice Barbara Katz (Mrs. Joseph P. Kuschner)
KUSHNER, Daniel Stephen 6
KUSKOV, Ivan Aleksandrovich H
KUSSY, Nathan 5
KUSTERMANN, Gustav 4
KUSWORM, Sidney Grover 5
KUTAK, Robert I. 3
KUTZ, Charles Willauer 1
KUTZ, George Fink 1
KUWATLY, Shukri Al 4
KUYKENDALL, Andrew Jackson H
KVALE, O. J. 1
KVALE, Walter Frederick 5
KYES, Preston 2
KYES, Roger M. 5
KYKER, Benjamin Franklin 4
KYLE, D. Braden 1
KYLE, Edwin Dewees 5
KYLE, Edwin Jackson 5
KYLE, Hugh Graham 1
KYLE, James Henderson 1
KYLE, John Johnson 1
KYLE, John Merrill 1
KYLE, John William 5
KYLE, Joseph 1
KYLE, Joseph Blair 4
KYLE, Laurence Harwood 5
KYLE, Melvin Grove 1
KYLE, Thomas Barton 4
KYLE, Willard Hugh 4
KYLE, William S. 1
KYLES, Lynwood Westinghouse 5
KYNE, Peter Bernard 3
KYNETT, Alpha Gilruth 1
KYNETT, Alpha Jefferson 5
KYNETT, Harold Havelock 6
KYRK, Hazel 6
KYSER, William D. 1
KYSTER, Olaf Helgesen Jr. 4

L

LA BACH, James Oscar 1
LABAREE, Benjamin 1
LABAREE, Mary Schauffler 3
LA BARGE, Joseph H
LABBE, Antoine G. 1
LABBERTON, John M. 3
LABEAUME, Louis 4
LABELLE, J. Edouard 3
LA BORDE, Maximilian H
LA BRANCHE, Alcee Louis H
LABRUM, J. Harry 5
LABUNSKI, Wiktor 6
LA BUY, Walter J. 4
LACASSE, Gustave 3
LA CAUZA, Frank Emilio 4
LA CAVA, Gregory 3
LACEY, Douglas Raymond 6
LACEY, Edward Samuel 1
LACEY, James D. 1
LACEY, John H
LACEY, John Fletcher 1
LACEY, John Wesley 1
LACEY, Raymond Henry 5
LACEY, Robert Alexander 6
LACHAISE, Gaston 1
LACHAISE, Gaston 4
LACHANCE, Leander Hansoom 5
LACHMAN, Arthur 5
LACHMAN, Harry 6
LACKAYE, Wilton 1
LACKEY, Henry Ellis 3
LACKEY, John Newton 2
LACKLAND, Frank Dorwin
LACLEDE, Pierre Ligueste H
LACOCK, Abner H
LACOMBE, Emile Henry 4
LACOSS, Louis 4
LA COSSITT, Henry 4
LACOUR-GAYET, Jacques 3
LA CROIX, Morris Felton 3
LACY, Arthur Jay 5
LACY, Ernest 1
LACY, George Carleton 2
LACY, James Horace 4
LACY, Paul B. 4
LACY, Thomas Norman 3
LACY, Walter Garner 4

LACY, William Henry 1
LACY, William Stokes 2
LADA-MOCARSKI, Valerian 5
LADD, Adoniram Judson 4
LADD, Alan Walbridge 4
LADD, Anna Coleman 1
LADD, Carl Edwin 2
LADD, Catherine H
LADD, Edwin Fremont 1
LADD, Eugene F. 1
LADD, George Edgar 1
LADD, George Tallman 2
LADD, George Trumbull 1
LADD, George Washington H
LADD, Herbert Warren 1
LADD, Horatio Oliver 1
LADD, Jesse A. 3
LADD, John W. 3
LADD, Joseph Brown H
LADD, Maynard 1
LADD, Niel Morrow 1
LADD, Sanford Burritt 1
LADD, Scott M. 1
LADD, William H
LADD, William Edwards 4
LADD, William Mead 1
LADD, William Palmer 1
LADD, William Sargeant 2
LADD, William Sargent H
LADD-FRANKLIN, Christine 1
LADDON, Isaac Machlin 6
LADDS, Herbert Preston 4
LADENBURG, Rudolf Walter 3
LADEW, Edward R. 1
LADNER, Albert H. 3
LADNER, Grover C. 3
LA DOW, George Augustus H
LA DU, Dwight B. 3
LADUE, Laurence Knight 3
LADUE, Pomeroy 5
LAEMMLE, Carl 1
LAESSLE, Albert 3
LAETSCH, Theodore (Carl Ferdinand) 5
LA FARGE, Bancel 1
LA FARGE, Christopher Grant 3
LA FARGE, Christopher 3
LA FARGE, John 1
LA FARGE, John 4
LA FARGE, Oliver 4
LAFAYETTE, Marquis de H
LAFEAN, Daniel Franklin 1
LA FETRA, Linnaeus Edword 1
LAFEVER, Minard H
LAFFAN, William M. 1
LAFFERTY, Abraham Walter 1
LAFFERTY, Abraham Walter 5
LAFFERTY, Alma V. 4
LAFFERTY, John James 1
LAFFERTY, William Thornton 1
LAFFITE, Jean H
LAFOLLETTE, Fola 5
LAFFOON, Ruby 1
LAFLECHE, Leo Richer 3
LA FLESCHE, Francis 1
LA FLESCHE, Susette H
LAFLIN, Addison Henry 1
LA FOLLETTE, Belle Case 1
LA FOLLETTE, Harvey Marion 1
LA FOLLETTE, Philip Fox 4
LA FOLLETTE, Robert Marion 1
LA FOLLETTE, Robert Marion Jr. 3
LA FOLLETTE, Robert Russell
LA FOLLETTE, William L. 1
LAFON, Thomy H
LA FONTAINE, Rachel Adelaide
LA FORGE, Laurence 3
LAFOUNT, Harold Arundel 3
LAFRENTZ, Ferdinand William
LA GARDE, Louis Anatole 1
LAGEN, Mary Huneker (Mrs.) 5
LAGER, Eric W. 6
LAGERCRANTZ, Herman Ludvig Fabian de
LAGERGREN, Carl Gustaf 1
LAGERKVIST, Par (Fabian) 6
LAGERQUIST, Walter Edwards
LA GORCE, John Oliver 5
LAGRANGE, Frank Crawford

LA GUARDIA, Fiorello H. 2
LAGUNA, Theodore de Leo de 1
LAHEE, Henry Charles 4
LAHEY, Edwin A. 5
LAHEY, Frank Howard 3
LAHM, Frank Purdy 4
LAHM, Frank Purdy 5
LAHM, Samuel H
LAHONTAN, baron de H
LAHR, Bert 6
LAHR, Raymond Merrill 6
LAI, Chia-Chiu 5
LAIDLAW, Alexander Hamilton 1
LAIDLAW, Alexander Hamilton Jr. 1
LAIDLAW, Harriet Barton 2
LAIDLAW, John Blake 6
LAIDLAW, Walter 1
LAIDLER, Harry Wellington 5
LAIDLEY, Roy Russell 1
LAING, Chester William 4
LAING, Gordon Jennings 2
LAING, John 2
LAING, John Albert 3
LAING, Samuel McPherson 2
LAIPPLY, Thomas Charles 5
LAIRD, Allison White 1
LAIRD, Edmund Cody 4
LAIRD, James H
LAIRD, John Baker 5
LAIRD, John Kenneth Jr. 1
LAIRD, Samuel 1
LAIRD, Warren Powers 2
LAIRD, William Ramsey III 6
LAIRY, Moses Barnett 1
LAIST, Theodore Frederick 1
LAISTNER, Max Ludwig Wolfram
LAIT, Jacquin L. 3
LAKANAL, Joseph H
LAKE, Charles H. 4
LAKE, Devereux 5
LAKE, Everett John 2
LAKE, Fred Wrightman 3
LAKE, George Burt 2
LAKE, Harry Beaston 3
LAKE, John 3
LAKE, Kirsopp 2
LAKE, Leonora Marie 4
LAKE, Mack Clayton 4
LAKE, Marshall E. 3
LAKE, Simon 2
LAKE, William Augustus H
LAKES, Arthur 4
LAKEY, Alice 1
LAKIN, Herbert Conrad 5
LAKIN, James Sansome 1
LA LANNE, Frank Dale 1
LALONE, Emerson Hugh 4
LALOR, Alice 1
LALUMIER, Edward Louis 6
LAMADE, Dietrick 1
LAMADE, George R.
LAMADE, Howard John 2
LAMAR, Andrew Jackson 1
LAMAR, Clarinda Pendleton
LAMAR, Gazaway Bugg H
LAMAR, Henry Graybill 1
LAMAR, James Sanford 4
LAMAR, John Basil 1
LAMAR, Joseph Rucker 1
LAMAR, Lucius Quintus Cincinnatus
LAMAR, Mirabeau Bonaparte H
LAMAR, William Harmong 1
LA MARR, Esther Bernice Randall 5
LAMB, Albert Richard 3
LAMB, Alfred William H
LAMB, Arthur Becket 3
LAMB, Charles Rollinson 2
LAMB, Daniel Smith 1
LAMB, Edwin Travis 1
LAMB, Ella Condie 1
LAMB, Frederick Stymetz 1
LAMB, Harold Albert 4
LAMB, Henry Whitney 1
LAMB, Hugh Louis 3
LAMB, Isaac Wixom 1
LAMB, James Gibson 1
LAMB, John 4
LAMB, John H
LAMB, John Edward 1
LAMB, Joseph F. 4
LAMB, Martha Joanna Reade Nash H
LAMB, Peter Oswald 1
LAMB, Richard Hubbert 1
LAMB, Robert Scott 3
LAMB, Roland O. 1
LAMB, William

LAMB, William Frederick 3
LAMBDIN, Alfred Cochran 1
LAMBDIN, James Reid H
LAMBDIN, Jerry Elmer 4
LAMBDIN, Milton Bennett 1
LAMBDIN, William 1
  Wallace
LAMBE, Sir Charles 4
  Edward
LAMBERSON, Ray 6
  Guernsey
LAMBERT, Adrian Van 5
  Sinderen
LAMBERT, Albert Bond 2
LAMBERT, Alexander 1
LAMBERT, Avery Eldorus 5
LAMBERT, Byron James 3
LAMBERT, Charles H
LAMBERT, Charles Irwin 3
LAMBERT, Fred Dayton 1
LAMBERT, Gerard Barnes 2
LAMBERT, Hubert Cottrell 6
LAMBERT, Jack Lincoln 4
LAMBERT, John H
LAMBERT, John 1
LAMBERT, John S. 3
LAMBERT, Louis A. 1
LAMBERT, Oscar Doane 4
LAMBERT, Robert 4
  Archibald
LAMBERT, Robert Eugene 5
LAMBERT, Samuel 2
  Waldron
LAMBERT, T. Arthur 4
LAMBERT, Tallmadge 4
  Augustine
LAMBERT, Walter Davis 6
LAMBERT, William 1
  Harrison
LAMBERT, W(illiam) 6
  V(incent)
LAMBERT, Wilton John 1
LAMBERTON, Benjamin 1
  Peffer
LAMBERTON, Chess 5
LAMBERTON, James 1
  McCormick
LAMBERTON, John A. 2
LAMBERTON, John Porter 1
LAMBERTON, Robert 1
  Eneas
LAMBERTON, William 1
  Alexander
LAMBERTSON, Genio 1
  Madison
LAMBERTSON, William 3
  Purnell
LAMBETH, William 1
  Alexander
LAMBETH, William Arnold 3
LAMBLE, John W. 5
LAMBRIGHT, Edwin Dart 3
LAMBRIX, Joseph H. 5
LAMBUTH, James William H
LAMBUTH, Walter Russell 1
LA MER, Victor Kuhn 4
LAMEY, Arthur Francis 4
LAMM, Henry 4
LAMM, Lynne M. 3
LAMME, Benjamin G. 1
LAMON, Ward Hill H
LAMONT, Daniel Scott 1
LAMONT, Forrest 4
LAMONT, Hammond 1
LAMONT, Peter T. 5
LAMONT, Robert Patterson 2
LAMONT, Thomas Stilwell 4
LAMONT, Thomas William 2
LA MONTE, John Life 3
LAMORISSE, Albert 6
LA MOTHE, John 1
  Dominique
LA MOTTE, Ellen Newbold 4
LAMOUNTAIN, John H
LA MOURE, Howard 5
  Alexander
LAMOUREUX, Silas 1
  Wright
LAMPE, Joseph Joachim 1
LAMPE, William Edmund 3
LAMPEN, Albert Eugene 4
LAMPERT, Floran 1
LAMPLAND, Carl Otto 4
LAMPMAN, Ben Hur 3
LAMPMAN, Lewis 1
LAMPORT, Harold 6
LAMPORT, William Henry H
LAMPRECHT, Sterling 4
  Power
LAMPREY, Louise 1
LAMPSON, Sir Curtis 4
  Miranda
LAMPTON, Thaddeus 1
  Booth
LAMPTON, Walter M. 4
LAMPTON, William James 1

LAMSON, Charles Henry 1
LAMSON, Charles Marion 1
LAMSON, Fred Mason 1
LAMSON, George Herbert 1
  Jr.
LAMSON, Guy Caleb 5
LAMSON, Julius Gustavus 2
LAMSON, Paul Dudley 4
LAMSON-SCRIBNER, 1
  Frank
LAMY, John Baptist H
LANAHAN, Francis H. Jr. 6
LANAHAN, Henry 4
LANAHAN, William 2
  Wallace
LANCASTER, Bruce 4
LANCASTER, Chester L. 3
LANCASTER, Columbia 1
LANCASTER, Dabney 6
  Stewart
LANCASTER, Ellsworth 3
  Gage
LANCASTER, Henry 3
  Carrington
LANCASTER, Hewes 1
LANCASTER, John 5
  Herrold
LANCASTER, John Lynch 4
LANCASTER, Richard 4
  Venable
LANCASTER, Walter B. 3
LAND, Aldred Dillingham 1
LAND, Charles Henry 1
LAND, Emory Scott 5
LAND, Fort Elmo 1
LAND, Frank Sherman 3
LAND, Frank Sherman 4
LAND, William Jesse Goad 2
LANDACRE, Francis Leroy 1
LANDACRE, Paul 4
  Hambleton
LANDAHL, Carl William 5
LANDAIS, Pierre H
LANDAU, Jacob 5
LANDAU, Lev Davidovich 5
LANDEGGER, Karl 6
  Francis
LANDER, Edward 1
LANDER, Frederick West H
LANDER, Jean Margaret 1
LANDER, Louisa 4
LANDERHOLM, Edwin 4
  Francis
LANDERS, George 1
  Foreman
LANDERS, George H
  Marcellus
LANDERS, Howe Stone 2
LANDERS, Joseph Samuel 4
LANDERS, Warren Prince 1
LANDERS, Wilbur Nelson 4
LANDES, Bertha Knight 2
LANDES, Henry 1
LANDES, Herbert Ellis 3
LANDES, William Grant 5
LANDFIELD, Jerome 3
LANDIS, Benson Young 4
LANDIS, Carney 4
LANDIS, Cary D. 1
LANDIS, Charles Beary 1
LANDIS, Charles Israel 1
LANDIS, Charles William 5
LANDIS, Frederick 1
LANDIS, Gerald Wayne 5
LANDIS, Harry DeWitt 4
LANDIS, Henry Robert 1
  Murray
LANDIS, James McCauley 4
LANDIS, Jessie Royce 5
LANDIS, John Howard 1
LANDIS, Josiah 1
  Pennabecker
LANDIS, Kenesaw 2
  Mountain
LANDIS, Kenesaw 2
  Mountain II
LANDIS, Mary Green (Mrs. 6
  Judson Taylor Landis)
LANDIS, Paul Nissley 5
LANDIS, Robert Kumler 4
LANDIS, William Weldon 2
LANDMAN, Isaac 2
LANDMAN, Jacob Henry 4
LANDMAN, Louis W. 3
LANDON, Charles 5
  Raeburne
LANDON, Hal D. 1
LANDON, Hugh 2
  McKennan
LANDON, Judson Stuart 1
LANDON, Melville De 1
  Lancey
LANDON, Thomas Durland 1
LANDON, Thompson 1
  Hoadley
LANDON, Warren Hall 1

LANDONE, Leon Elbert 4
LANDOWSKA, Wanda 3
LANDRETH, Burnet 1
LANDRETH, David 1
LANDRETH, Earl 5
LANDRETH, Olin Henry 1
LANDRETH, Symington 6
  Phillips
LANDRETH, William 4
  Barker
LANDRIGAN, Charles 4
  Raymond
LANDRITH, Ira 1
LANDRUM, John Morgan H
LANDRUM, Robert Dallas 2
LANDRUM, William 1
  Warren
LANDRY, Aubrey Edward 5
LANDRY, George A. 4
LANDRY, Joseph Aristide 2
LANDSBERG, Max 1
LANDSIEDEL, Harry 4
LANDSTEINER, Karl 2
LANDSTREET, Fairfax 1
  Stuart
LANDY, James H
LANE, Albert Grannis 1
LANE, Alfred Church 2
LANE, Sir Allen 5
LANE, Amos 1
LANE, Anna Eichberg King 4
LANE, Arthur Bliss 3
LANE, Charles Elmaar 5
LANE, Charles Homer 1
LANE, Charles Homer 2
LANE, Charles Stoddard 1
LANE, Chester T. 3
LANE, Clarence Guy 3
LANE, Clement Quirk 4
LANE, Edward Binney 1
LANE, Edward Hudson 6
LANE, Edward Wood 2
LANE, Elbert Clarence 3
LANE, Elinor Macartney 1
LANE, Everett Hale 5
LANE, Francis Ransom 4
LANE, Frank Hardy 5
LANE, Franklin Knight 1
LANE, Gardiner Martin 1
LANE, George Martin H
LANE, Gertrude Battles 2
LANE, Harry 1
LANE, Henry Higgins 6
LANE, Henry Marcus 1
LANE, Henry Smith H
LANE, Isaac 1
LANE, James Franklin 2
LANE, James H. 1
LANE, James Henry H
LANE, John 1
LANE, John Edward 1
LANE, Jonathan 1
LANE, Joseph H
LANE, La Fayette H
LANE, Laurence William 1
LANE, Levi 1
LANE, Loras T. 5
LANE, Merritt 1
LANE, Mills Bee 2
LANE, Otho Evans 4
LANE, Ralph H
LANE, Raymond A. 6
LANE, Robert Porter 3
LANE, Robert Ripley 5
LANE, Rose Wilder 5
LANE, Rufus Herman 2
LANE, Samuel Morse 5
LANE, Smith Edward 1
LANE, Stoddard 2
LANE, Thomas Alphonsus 6
LANE, Thomas Welsh 1
LANE, Tidence H
LANE, Victor Hugo 1
LANE, Wallace Rutherford 2
LANE, Walter Paye H
LANE, William Carr H
LANE, William Coolidge 1
LANE, William Preston Jr. 4
LANEY, Francis Baker 1
LANFORD, John Alexander 1
LANG, Arthur H. 5
LANG, Benjamin Johnson 1
LANG, C. Thompson 5
LANG, Charles B. 3
LANG, Charles H. Jr. 1
LANG, Charles Michael 1
  Angelo
LANG, Chester Henry 4
LANG, Donald Buzick 4
LANG, George 6
LANG, Henry Albert 4
LANG, Henry Roseman 1
LANG, Herbert (Otto 6
  Henry)
LANG, John Albert Jr. 6

LANG, Karl 5
LANG, Louis LaCourse 6
LANG, Merle Howie 5
LANG, Oscar Theodore 4
LANGDALE, John William 1
LANGDELL, Christopher 1
  Columbus
LANGDON, Andrew 1
LANGDON, Chauncey H
LANGDON, Courtney 1
LANGDON, Frank Warren 1
LANGDON, John H
LANGDON, Loomis Lyman 1
LANGDON, Russell 5
  (Creamer)
LANGDON, Samuel H
LANGDON, Stephen 1
  Herbert
LANGDON, William H
  Chauncy
LANGDON, William 2
  Chauncy
LANGDON, William Henry 1
LANGDON, Woodbury 1
LANGE, Alexis Frederick 1
LANGE, Dietrich 2
LANGE, Dorothea H
LANGE, Dorothea 4
LANGE, Frederick Edward 6
LANGE, Halvard Manthey 5
LANGE, Hans 4
LANGE, Louis 1
LANGE, Oscar Richard 4
LANGE, Ray Loomis 4
LANGENBECK, Karl 1
LANGENBERG, Harry Hill 3
LANGENWALTER, Jacob 5
  Hermann
LANGER, Charles 3
  Heinrichs
LANGER, William 3
LANGERFELDT, Theodore 1
  Otto
LANGERMAN, Joseph 3
LANGFELD, Herbert 3
  Sidney
LANGFELD, Millard 2
LANGFITT, J. Porter 4
LANGFITT, Joseph Alonzo 4
LANGFITT, William 1
  Campbell
LANGFORD, George W. 1
LANGFORD, Laura Carter 4
  Holloway
LANGFORD, Malcolm 4
  Sparhawk
LANGFORD, Nathaniel 1
  Pitt
LANGHAM, Jonathan 4
  Nicholas
LANGHORNE, George 4
  Tayloe
LANGHORNE, Marshall 2
LANGLEY, Ernest Felix 3
LANGLEY, James 5
  McLellan
LANGLEY, John Wesley 1
LANGLEY, John Williams 1
LANGLEY, Katherine 2
LANGLEY, Samuel 1
  Pierpont
LANGLEY, Samuel Sorrels 4
LANGLEY, William C. 4
LANGLEY, Wilson D(avis) 5
LANGLIE, Arthur Bernard 4
LANGLOIS, Ubald 3
LANGMADE, Stephen 4
  Wallace
LANGMUIR, Dean 2
LANGMUIR, Irving 3
LANGMUIR, Peter 4
  Bulkeley
LANGNER, Lawrence 4
LANGRETH, George 4
  Lillingston
LANGSDORF, Alexander 5
  Suss
LANGSDORF, William Bell 1
LANGSHAW, Walter 4
  Hamer
LANGSTON, John Mercer H
LANGSTROTH, Lorenzo H
  Lorraine
LANGTON, Clair Van 6
  Norman
LANGTON, Daniel Webster 1
LANGTON, James Ammon 2
LANGTRY, Albert Perkins 1
LANGTRY, Lillie 2
LANGTRY, Lillie 1
LANGWORTHY, Charles 1
  Ford
LANGWORTHY, Edward H
LANGWORTHY, Herman 3
  Moore

LANGWORTHY, James H
  Lyon
LANHAM, Fritz Garland 4
LANHAM, Henderson 3
  Lovelace
LANHAM, Samuel Willis 1
  Tucker
LANIEL, Joseph 6
LANIER, Alexander 2
  Cartwright
LANIER, Charles 1
LANIER, Clifford Anderson 1
LANIER, Edmond Raoul 6
  Henri
LANIER, George Huguley 2
LANIER, James Franklin H
  Doughty
LANIER, Powless William 3
LANIER, Raphael O'Hara 4
LANIER, Sidney 1
LANIGAN, George Thomas H
LANING, Harris 1
LANING, Jay Ford 3
LANING, Richard Henry 4
LANIUS, James Andrew 3
LANKERSHIM, James 4
  Boon
LANKES, Julius J. 4
LANKFORD, Menaicus 1
LANKFORD, William 5
  Chester
LANKFORD, Woodrow 6
  Wilson
LANMAN, Charles H
LANMAN, Charles 1
  Rockwell
LANMAN, James 1
LANMAN, Joseph 1
LANNEAU, John Francis 4
LANNING, Robert Lee 5
LANNING, William 1
  Mershon
LANNON, James Patrick 3
LANPHEAR, Emory 4
LANSDALE, Maria Hornor 5
LANSDELL, Rinaldo 3
  Addison
LANSDEN, Dick Latta 1
LANSDON, William 4
  Clarence
LANSIL, Walter Franklin 4
LANSING, Ambrose 3
LANSING, Eleanor Foster 5
  (Mrs. Robert Lansing)
LANSING, Frederick H
LANSING, Gerit Yates H
LANSING, Gulian 1
LANSING, John H
LANSING, John Belcher 5
LANSING, John Ernest 3
LANSING, Robert 1
LANSING, William 1
  Esselstyne
LANSINGH, Van 5
  Rensselaer
LANSTRUM, Oscar 1
  Monroe
LANTAFF, William C. 5
  (Bill)
LANTER, Fred Merrill 4
LANTZ, David Ernest 1
LANZA, Anthony Joseph 4
LANZA, Conrad Hammond 6
LANZA, Gaetano 1
LANZA, Mario 3
LANZA, Marquise Clara 4
LANZETTA, James J. 3
LAPHAM, Elbridge Gerry 1
LAPHAM, Increase Allen H
LAPHAM, J. H. 3
LAPHAM, John Raymond 4
LAPHAM, Oscar 1
LAPHAM, Roger Dearborn 4
LAPHAM, Samuel 5
LAPHAM, William Berry H
LA PIANA, George 5
LAPLACE, Ernest 1
LAPORTE, Alphonse A. 4
LAPORTE, Cloyd 6
LAPORTE, John H
LAPORTE, Otto 5
LAPORTE, Raymond 6
LA PORTE, William Ralph 3
LAPP, Claude Jerome 6
LAPP, John A. 4
LAPPIN, Warren Curtis 6
LA PRADE, Arthur 6
  Thornton
LAPRADE, Lloyd Stone 4
LAPRADE, William 6
  Thomas
LAPSLEY, Robert Alberti 1
LARABEE, Frank Sheridan 1
LARABEE, Lottie B(ertha) 4
LARAMIE, Jacques H
LARCO HERRERA, Rafael 5

LARCOM, Lucy H
LARD, Moses E. H
LARDNER, Henry Ackley 3
LARDNER, James Lawrence H
LARDNER, James Lawrence 5
LARDNER, John 3
LARDNER, John Joseph 2
LARDNER, Lena Bogardus 4
LARDNER, Ring W. 1
LARGE, George Elwyn 6
LARGE, John J. 1
LA RICHARDIE, Armand de H
LARIMER, Edgar Brown 5
LARIMER, Loyal Herbert 5
LARIMORE, Joseph William 5
LARIMORE, Louise Doddridge 2
LARIMORE, N. Greene 1
LARK-HOROVITZ, Karl 1
LARKIN, Adrian Hoffman 2
LARKIN, Edgar Lucien 1
LARKIN, Francis Marion 1
LARKIN, Fred Viall 3
LARKIN, John H
LARKIN, John Adrian 2
LARKIN, Joseph Maurice 1
LARKIN, Oliver Waterman 5
LARKIN, Rosemary Rita 6
LARKIN, Thomas B. 1
LARKIN, Thomas Oliver H
LARKIN, William Harrison 5
LARMON, Russell Raymond 5
LARNED, Augusta 4
LARNED, Charles William 1
LARNED, Ellen Douglas 4
LARNED, John Insley Blair 3
LARNED, Joseph Gay Eaton H
LARNED, Josephus Nelson 1
LARNED, Linda Hull 1
LARNED, Simon H
LARNED, Trowbridge 1
LARNED, Walter Cranston 1
LARNER, Edward Atkins 5
LARNER, John Bell 1
LARNER, Robert Martin 1
LA ROCHE, Rene H
LA ROCHELLE, Philippe de 5
LAROCQUE, Joseph 1
LAROE, Wilbur Jr. 3
LAROQUE, George Paul 3
LA ROQUE, O. K. 3
LARPENTEUR, Charles H
LARRABEE, C. R. 4
LARRABEE, Charles Hathaway H
LARRABEE, Edward Allan 1
LARRABEE, William 1
LARRABEE, William Clark H
LARRABEE, William Henry 1
LARRAZOLO, Octaviano Ambrosio 1
LARREMORE, Wilbur 1
LARRETA, Enrique 4
LARRICK, George P. 5
LARRIMORE, Francine 4
LARRINAGA, Tulio H
LARRINAGA, Tulio 4
LARSEN, Alfred 2
LARSEN, Christian 2
LARSEN, Ellouise Baker 4
LARSEN, Esper Signius Jr. 4
LARSEN, Finn Jacob 2
LARSEN, Hanna Astrup 2
LARSEN, Harold D. 4
LARSEN, Henning 5
LARSEN, Henry Louis 4
LARSEN, Jens Willard 6
LARSEN, Lauritz 1
LARSEN, Lewis A. 3
LARSEN, Lewis P. 3
LARSEN, Merwin John 4
LARSEN, Peter Laurentius 1
LARSEN, William 1
LARSEN, William Washington 1
LARSON, Agnes M(athilda) 5
LARSON, Algot J. E. 6
LARSON, Carl W. 3
LARSON, Christian Daa 5
LARSON, Cora Gunn 1
LARSON, Frank Oscar 6
LARSON, George Victor 3
LARSON, Gustus Ludwig 3
LARSON, John Augustus 4
LARSON, Lars Moore 3
LARSON, Laurence Marcellus 1
LARSON, Leonard W. 6
LARSON, O. T. 4

LARSON, Ralph Norman 6
LARSON, Randell 4
LARSON, Roy Frank 6
LARSON, Winford Porter 4
LARSSON, Gustaf 1
LA RUE, Carl Downey 3
LA RUE, Daniel Wolford 5
LA RUE, John W. 3
LA RUE, Mabel Guinnip 5
LA RUE, William Earl. 5
LA SALLE, sieur de H
LASATER, Ed Cunningham 1
LASBY, William Frederick 5
LASCARI, Salvatore 4
LASELLE, Mary Augusta 4
LA SERE, Emile H
LASH, Israel George 3
LASH, James Hamilton 3
LASHAR, Walter B. 3
LA SHELLE, Kirke 4
LASHER, George Starr 4
LASHER, George William 5
LASHLEY, K. S. 3
LASHLY, Arthur Valentine 3
LASHLY, Jacob Mark 4
LASKER, Albert Davis 3
LASKER, Bruno 4
LASKER, Loula Davis 4
LASKEY, John Ellsworth 2
LASKI, Harold Joseph 2
LASKOSKE, Aloysius William 5
LASKY, Jesse L. 3
LASKY, Wayne Edward 5
LA SPISA, Jake Anthony 5
LASSEN, Peter H
LASSER, Jacob Kay 3
LASSINGER, Larry Wayne 6
LASSITER, Francis Rives 1
LASSITER, Herbert Carlyle 3
LASSITER, Newton Hance 1
LASSITER, Robert 5
LASSITER, William 5
LASTINGER, John Williams 5
LATANE, James Allen 1
LATANE, John Holladay 1
LATCH, Edward Biddle 5
LATCHAW, David Austin 2
LATCHAW, John Roland Harris 3
LATHAM, Carl Ray 4
LATHAM, Charles Louis 5
LATHAM, Dana 6
LATHAM, Harold Strong 5
LATHAM, Louis Charles H
LATHAM, Milton Slocum H
LATHAM, Orval Ray 1
LATHAM, Rex Knight 1
LATHAM, Vida A. 4
LATHAN, Robert 1
LATHBURY, Albert Augustus 4
LATHBURY, Clarence 1
LATHBURY, Mary Artemisia 1
LATHE, Herbert William 1
LATHEM, Abraham Lance 3
LATHERS, Richard 1
LATHROP, Alanson P. 3
LATHROP, Austin Eugene 3
LATHROP, Bryan 1
LATHROP, Charles Newton 1
LATHROP, Francis 1
LATHROP, Gardiner 1
LATHROP, George Parsons H
LATHROP, Henry Burrowes 1
LATHROP, John 1
LATHROP, John 1
LATHROP, John Carroll 1
LATHROP, John Hiram H
LATHROP, John Howland 4
LATHROP, Julia Clifford 1
LATHROP, Palmer Jadwin 3
LATHROP, Rose Hawthorne H
LATHROP, Samuel 1
LATHROP, Walter W. 6
LATHROP, William Langson 1
LATIL, Alexandre H
LATIMER, Asbury Churchwell 1
LATIMER, Claiborne Green 4
LATIMER, Clyde Burney 3
LATIMER, Elizabeth Wormeley 1
LATIMER, Henry H
LATIMER, John Austin 6
LATIMER, Julian Lane 1
LATIMER, Margery Bodine 4
LATIMER, Samuel Lowry Jr. 6
LATIMER, Thomas Erwin 1
LATIMER, Thomas Sargent 1

LATIMER, Wendell Mitchell 3
LA TOUR, Le Blonde de H
LATOURETTE, Earl C. 3
LATOURETTE, Howard Fenton 3
LATROBE, Benjamin Henry * H
LATROBE, Charles Hazelhurst H
LATROBE, Fredinand Claiborne 1
LATROBE, John Hazelhurst Boneval H
LATSHAW, David Gardner 5
LATTA, Alexander Bonner H
LATTA, James P. 1
LATTA, Robert Edward 3
LATTA, Samuel Whitehill 4
LATTA, Thomas Albert 1
LATTIG, Herbert Elmer 3
LATTIMER, George W. 1
LATTIMORE, John Aaron Cicero 5
LATTIMORE, John Compere 1
LATTIMORE, Offa Shivers 1
LATTIMORE, Samuel Allan 1
LATTIMORE, William H
LATTIN, Leroy Emory 6
LATTMAN, Walter 4
LATTRE DE TASSIGNY, Jean Joseph Marie Gabriel de H
LATZER, John A. 3
LAU, Robert Frederick 2
LAUBACH, Charles 1
LAUBACH, Frank Charles 5
LAUBACH, Howard L. 5
LAUBENGAYER, Richard August 4
LAUBENGAYER, Robert J. 3
LAUBER, Joseph 2
LAUCHHEIMER, Charles Henry 1
LAUCK, William Jett 2
LAUD, Sam 4
LAUDER, Harry 4
LAUER, Conrad Newton 2
LAUER, Stewart Ellwood 4
LAUER, Walter Ernest 4
LAUFER, Berthold 1
LAUFER, Calvin Weiss 4
LAUGEL, Raymond William 4
LAUGHINGHOUSE, Charles O'Hagan 1
LAUGHLIN, Clara Elizabeth 1
LAUGHLIN, Frank C. 2
LAUGHLIN, Gail 3
LAUGHLIN, George Ashton 1
LAUGHLIN, George Mark 2
LAUGHLIN, George McCully Jr. 2
LAUGHLIN, Harry Hamilton 2
LAUGHLIN, Hugh C. 6
LAUGHLIN, Irwin 1
LAUGHLIN, James Laurence 1
LAUGHLIN, John Edward Jr. 5
LAUGHLIN, Julian 1
LAUGHLIN, Napoleon Bonaparte 4
LAUGHLIN, Samuel Ott Jr. 3
LAUGHLIN, Sceva Bright 2
LAUGHLIN, T. Cowden 5
LAUGHTON, Charles 4
LAUGHTON, George 1
LAUGHTON, Sarah Elizabeth 4
LAUNT, Francis Albemarle Delbretons 1
LAURANCE, John H
LAURENS, Henry H
LAURENS, John H
LAURENT, Robert 5
LAURENTI, Mario 1
LAURGAARD, Olaf 2
LAURIAT, Charles Emelius 1
LAURIE, James 4
LAURIE, James Woodin 5
LAURIE, Wilfrid Rhodes 6
LAURIE, William 1
LAURITSEN, Charles Christian 5
LAURITZEN, Ivar 6
LAURVIK, J(ohn) Nilsen 5
LAURYSSEN, Gaston 4
LAUT, Agnes C. 1
LAUTERBACH, Edward 1
LAUTERBACH, Jacob Zallel 2

LAUTERBACH, Richard E. 3
LAUTERPACHT, Hersch 4
LAUTMANN, Herbert Moses 5
LAUTZ, Henry B(itzel) 5
LAUX, August 1
LAVAKE, Rae Thornton 6
LAVAL, Jean M. 1
LAVALLE, John 5
LAVALLEE, Calixa 3
LAVEILLE, Joseph H
LAVELL, Cecil Fairfield 2
LAVELLE, Michael J. 1
LAVELY, Henry Alexander 4
LAVENDER, Harrison Morton 3
LA VERENDRYE, Pierre Gaultier de Varennes H
LAVERY, Urban A. 3
LAVES, Kurt 1
LAVIALLE, Peter Joseph 1
LAVIDGE, A. W. 4
LAVINDER, Claude Hervey 5
LAVIS, Fred 1
LAW, Andrew H
LAW, Arthur Ayer 1
LAW, Charles Blakeslee 1
LAW, Evander McIver 5
LAW, Francis Marion 5
LAW, Fred Hayes 2
LAW, Frederick Houk 3
LAW, George 5
LAW, Herbert Edward 5
LAW, James 1
LAW, James Richard 3
LAW, John H
LAW, John Adger 5
LAW, Jonathan H
LAW, Lyman 5
LAW, Richard H
LAW, Robert 1
LAW, Robert Adger 4
LAW, Russell 2
LAW, Sallie Chapman Gordon H
LAW, Thomas Hart 1
LAW, William Adger 1
LAWALL, Charles Elmer 5
LA WALL, Charles Herbert 1
LAWDER, Henry Miller 4
LAWES, Lewis E. 2
LAWLER, Frank H
LAWLER, Joab 1
LAWLER, John J. 2
LAWLER, Thomas Bonaventure 1
LAWLER, Thomas G. 1
LAWLESS, John T. 4
LAWLESS, Theodore Kenneth 5
LAWLOR, Daniel J. 4
LAWLOR, William F. 3
LAWLOR, William Patrick 4
LAWRANCE, Charles Lanier 3
LAWRANCE, Marion 1
LAWRANCE, William Irvin 1
LAWRENCE, Abbott H
LAWRENCE, Abraham Riker 1
LAWRENCE, Albert Lathrop 4
LAWRENCE, Amory Appleton 1
LAWRENCE, Amos H
LAWRENCE, Amos Adams H
LAWRENCE, Andrew Middleton 2
LAWRENCE, Armon Jay 4
LAWRENCE, Benjamin Franklin 1
LAWRENCE, Carl Gustavus 3
LAWRENCE, Charles Drummond 6
LAWRENCE, Charles Kennedy 1
LAWRENCE, Charles Solomon 1
LAWRENCE, Cornelius Van Wyck H
LAWRENCE, David 5
LAWRENCE, David Leo 4
LAWRENCE, E. George 1
LAWRENCE, Edwin Gordon 3
LAWRENCE, Edwin Winship 1
LAWRENCE, Effingham H
LAWRENCE, Egbert Charles 1
LAWRENCE, Ellis Fuller 2
LAWRENCE, Ernest Orlando 2
LAWRENCE, Florus Fremont 4

LAWRENCE, Frank Pell 3
LAWRENCE, George Andrew 6
LAWRENCE, George Newbold H
LAWRENCE, George Pelton 1
LAWRENCE, George Warren 1
LAWRENCE, Gertrude 3
LAWRENCE, Henry F. 4
LAWRENCE, Henry Wells 4
LAWRENCE, Howard C. 4
LAWRENCE, Isaac 1
LAWRENCE, James H
LAWRENCE, James Cooper 1
LAWRENCE, James Earnest 3
LAWRENCE, James Peyton Stuart 4
LAWRENCE, John Benjamin 6
LAWRENCE, John Marshall 6
LAWRENCE, John Silsbee 6
LAWRENCE, John Strachan 1
LAWRENCE, John Watson H
LAWRENCE, John William 5
LAWRENCE, Joseph 1
LAWRENCE, Joseph Stagg 3
LAWRENCE, Margaret 1
LAWRENCE, Newbold Trotter 5
LAWRENCE, Ralph Restieaux 5
LAWRENCE, Ray Ellsworth 6
LAWRENCE, Richard Smith H
LAWRENCE, Richard Wesley 2
LAWRENCE, Robert H. Jr. H
LAWRENCE, Robert H. Jr. 4
LAWRENCE, Robert Means 1
LAWRENCE, Samuel H
LAWRENCE, Samuel Crocker 1
LAWRENCE, Sidney H
LAWRENCE, Thomas 4
LAWRENCE, Victor H. 3
LAWRENCE, William * H
LAWRENCE, William * 1
LAWRENCE, William Appleton 1
LAWRENCE, William Beach 4
LAWRENCE, William Henry 3
LAWRENCE, William Hereford 1
LAWRENCE, William Howard 1
LAWRENCE, William Mangam 1
LAWRENCE, William Thomas H
LAWRENCE, William Van Duzer 1
LAWRENCE, William Witherle 3
LAWRIE, Lee 4
LAWRIE, Ritchie Jr. 1
LAWS, Annie 1
LAWS, Bolitha James 3
LAWS, Curtis Lee 2
LAWS, Elijah 1
LAWS, Frank Arthur 1
LAWS, George William 1
LAWS, George William 2
LAWS, Samuel Spahr 1
LAWSHE, Abraham Lincoln 1
LAWSON, Albert Gallatin 1
LAWSON, Albert Thomas 4
LAWSON, Alexander H
LAWSON, Alfred William 3
LAWSON, Andrew Cowper 3
LAWSON, Claude Sims 5
LAWSON, David A. 6
LAWSON, Douglas E. 4
LAWSON, Edward Burnett 4
LAWSON, Ernest 1
LAWSON, Evald Benjamin 1
LAWSON, George 1
LAWSON, George Benedict 3
LAWSON, Huron Willis 5
LAWSON, James H
LAWSON, James Gilchrist 2
LAWSON, James Joseph 4
LAWSON, John H
LAWSON, John Daniel H
LAWSON, John Davison 1
LAWSON, Joseph Albert 3
LAWSON, Joseph Warren 6
LAWSON, Laurin Leonard 3

LAWSON, Leonidas Merion H
LAWSON, Martin Emert 3
LAWSON, Paul Bowen 4
LAWSON, Publius Virgilius 1
LAWSON, Robert 3
LAWSON, Roberta 1
  Campbell
LAWSON, Thomas H
LAWSON, Thomas 1
  Goodwin
LAWSON, Thomas R. 3
LAWSON, Thomas William 1
LAWSON, Victor Fremont 1
LAWSON, W. Elsworth 4
LAWSON, Walter Carson 6
LAWSON, Warner 1
LAWSON, William C. 3
LAWTHER, Harry Preston 2
LAWTON, Alexander H
  Robert
LAWTON, Alexander 5
  Robert
LAWTON, Alexander 1
  Rudolf
LAWTON, Ezra Mills 1
LAWTON, Frederick 1
LAWTON, Frederick Joseph 6
LAWTON, Henry W. 1
LAWTON, Louis Bowen 1
LAWTON, Samuel Tilden 4
LAWTON, Shailer Upton 4
LAWTON, William 4
  Cranston
LAWTON, William Henry 1
LAWWILL, Stewart 5
LAWYER, George 4
LAWYER, Jay 4
LAWYER, Thomas 1
LAY, Alfred Morrison H
LAY, Benjamin 4
LAY, Charles Downing 3
LAY, Chester Frederic 6
LAY, Frank Morrill 3
LAY, George Washington H
LAY, George William 4
LAY, Henry Champlin H
LAY, John Louis 1
LAY, Julius Gareche 1
LAY, Robert Dwight 4
LAY, Wilfrid 5
LAYBOURNE, Lawrence 6
  Eugene
LAYCOCK, Charles Wilbur 1
LAYCOCK, Craven 4
LAYDEN, Elmer Francis 6
LAYLIN, Lewis Cass 4
LAYMAN, Waldo Arnold 1
LAYNE, J. Gregg 3
LAYNG, James D. 1
LAYTE, Ralph R. 4
LAYTON, Caleb Rodney 1
LAYTON, Frank Davis 3
LAYTON, Frederick 1
LAYTON, Joseph E. 4
LAYTON, Olivia Higgins 1
LAYTON, Walter Thomas 4
LAZAN, Benjamin J. 4
LAZAR, Benedict Joseph 1
LAZARO, Hipolito 6
LAZARO, Ladislas 1
LAZAROVICH-
HREBELIANOVICH,
  Princess
LAZAROW, Arnold 6
LAZARUS, Emma H
LAZARUS, Fred Jr. 6
LAZARUS, Reuben Avis 5
LAZARUS, Robert 5
LAZARUS, Simon 2
LAZEAR, Jesse H
LAZEAR, Jesse William 1
LAZELLE, Henry Martyn 1
LAZENBY, Albert 4
LAZENBY, William Rane 1
LAZO, Hector 4
LAZRUS, S. Ralph 3
LAZZARI, Carolina 2
  Antoinette
LEA, Clarence Frederick 4
LEA, Fanny Heaslip 3
LEA, Henry Charles 1
LEA, Homer 1
LEA, Isaac H
LEA, John McCormick 1
LEA, Luke 1
LEA, Luke 2
LEA, Mathew Carey 1
LEA, Mathew Carey 4
LEA, Preston 1
LEA, Pryor H
LEA, Robert Wentworth 3
LEACH, Abby 1
LEACH, Albert Ernest 1
LEACH, Arthur Burtis 1
LEACH, Charles Nelson 5
LEACH, Daniel Dyer H

LEACH, Dewitt Clinton 4
LEACH, Edmund C. 4
LEACH, Edward Giles 1
LEACH, Ellis 5
LEACH, Eugene Walter 1
LEACH, Frank Aleamon 4
LEACH, Frank Aleamon Jr. 5
LEACH, George E. 3
LEACH, Henry Goddard 4
LEACH, Howard Seavoy 1
LEACH, Hugh 5
LEACH, J. Granville 4
LEACH, James Madison H
LEACH, John Enfield 6
LEACH, John Sayles 1
LEACH, MacEdward 4
LEACH, Margaret 4
  Kernochan (Mrs. Ralph
  Pulitzer)
LEACH, Ralph Waldo 5
  Emerson
LEACH, Raymond 2
  Hotchkiss
LEACH, Shepherd H
LEACH, W(alter) Barton 5
LEACH, William Fillmore 5
LEACH, William Herman 4
LEACOCK, Arthur Gordner 2
LEACOCK, Stephen Butler 5
LEADBETTER, Caroline 1
  Pittock
LEADBETTER, Daniel H
  Parkhurst
LEADBETTER, Frederick 2
  William
LEADBETTER, Wyland F. 6
LEAHY, Edward L. 3
LEAHY, Frank 5
LEAHY, Lamar Richard 4
LEAHY, Paul 4
LEAHY, Timothy John 1
LEAHY, William Augustine 1
LEAHY, William D. 3
LEAHY, William Edward 3
LEAKE, Eugene W. 1
LEAKE, Frank 4
LEAKE, James Miller 6
LEAKE, James Payton 1
LEAKE, Joseph Bloomfield 1
LEAKE, Shelton Farrar H
LEAKE, Walter H
LEAKEY, Louis Seymour H
  Bazett
LEALE, Charles Augustus 4
LEALE, Medwin 1
LEAMAN, William Gilmore 6
  Jr.
LEAMING, Edmund 1
  Bennett
LEAMING, Jacob Spicer H
LEAMING, Jeremiah H
LEAMING, Thomas H
LEAMY, Frank Ashton 4
LEAMY, Frederick Walter 4
LEAMY, Hugh 1
LEAMY, James Patrick 4
LEANDER, Hugo Austin 5
LEAR, Ben 4
LEAR, Fred Roy 3
LEAR, Harry Bonnell 4
LEAR, Tobias H
LEARNARD, George 5
  Edward
LEARNARD, Henry Grant 1
LEARNED, Amasa 1
LEARNED, Arthur Garfield 3
LEARNED, Dwight 4
  Whitney
LEARNED, Ebenezer 1
LEARNED, Ellin Craven 1
LEARNED, Henry Barrett 1
LEARNED, Marion Dexter 1
LEARNED, Walter 1
LEARNED, William Law 1
LEARNED, William Setchel 2
LEARSI, Rufus 1
LEARY, Cornelius H
  Lawrence Ludlow
LEARY, Daniel Bell 2
LEARY, Francis Thomas 5
LEARY, Frederick 4
LEARY, Herbert Fairfax 3
LEARY, John Digney 6
LEARY, John Joseph Jr. 1
LEARY, Leo H. 4
LEARY, Lewis Gaston 1
LEARY, Montgomery Elihu 1
LEARY, Peter Jr. 1
LEARY, Richard Phillips 1
LEARY, Timothy 1
LEARY, William Henry 4
LEASE, Emory Bair 1
LEASE, Mary Elizabeth 1
  Mrs.
LEATHERS, Waller Smith 2

LEATHERS OF 4
  PURFLEET, Baron
LEATHERWOOD, Elmer 1
  O.
LEAVELL, Frank Hartwell 2
LEAVELL, James Berry 1
LEAVELL, James Reader 6
LEAVELL, Landrum Pinson 1
LEAVELL, Richard Marion 3
LEAVELL, Ullin Whitney 1
LEAVELL, William Hayne 1
LEAVELLE, Arnaud Bruce 3
LEAVELLE, Robert Bryan 5
LEAVENS, Robert French 6
LEAVENWORTH, Elias H
  Warner
LEAVENWORTH, Francis 1
  Preserved
LEAVENWORTH, Henry H
LEAVITT, Ashley Day 3
LEAVITT, Burke Fay 4
LEAVITT, Charles Welford 1
LEAVITT, Dudley 1
LEAVITT, Erasmus Darwin H
LEAVITT, Frank McDowell 1
LEAVITT, Halsey B. 4
LEAVITT, Humphrey Howe H
LEAVITT, John McDowell 1
LEAVITT, Joshua H
LEAVITT, Julius Adelbert 1
LEAVITT, Mary Greenleaf 1
  Clement
LEAVITT, Roger 3
LEAVITT, Scott 4
LEAVITT, Sheldon 1
LEAVY, Charles Henry 3
LEAYCRAFT, J. Edgar 1
LE BARON, John Francis 1
LE BARON, John Kittredge 1
LE BARON, William 3
LEBER, Charles Tudor 4
LEBHAR, Godfrey 1
  Montague
LE BLANC, Thomas John 2
LE BLOND, Charles Hubert 3
LE BLOND, Harold R. 5
LE BOEUF, Randall James 1
LE BOEUF, Randall James 6
  Jr.
LEBOLD, Foreman M. 3
LEBOUTILLIER, George 3
LE BRETON, Thomas 5
  Alberto
LE BRUN, Napoleon H
  Eugene Henry Charles
LEBRUN, Rico 4
LECHE, Paul 4
LECHE, Richard Webster 4
LECHER, Louis Arthur 2
LECHFORD, Thomas H
LECHNER, Carl Bernard 5
LECKIE, Adam Edward 1
  Lloyd
LECKIE, Katherine 1
LECKRONE, Walter 4
LECKWIJCK, William Peter 6
  Edward van
LECLAIR, Edward E(mile) 5
  Jr.
LECLAIR, Titus G. 5
LE CLEAR, Thomas H
LE CLERC, J. Arthur 4
LECOMPTE, Irville Charles 5
LECOMPTE, Joseph H
LECOMPTE, Karl Miles 5
LECONTE, John 1
LECONTE, John Lawrence H
LE CONTE, Joseph 1
LE CONTE, Joseph Nisbet 1
LE CONTE, Robert Grier 1
LE CORBUSIER, Charles- 5
  Edouard
LECOUNT, Edwin 1
  Raymond
LECUONA, Ernesto 4
LEDBETTER, Allison 4
  Woodville
LEDBETTER, Huddie 1
LEDBETTER, Walter A. 1
LEDDY, Bernard Joseph 5
LEDERER, Charles 1
LEDERER, Charles 3
LEDERER, Erwin Reginald 2
LEDERER, Francis Loeffler 5
LEDERER, George W. 1
LEDERER, John H
LEDERER, Norbert Lewis 3
LEDERER, Richard M. 1
LEDERLE, Ernst Joseph 1
LEDLIE, George 1
LEDNICKI, Waclaw 5
LEDNICKI, Waclaw 1
LEDOUX, Albert Reid 1
LEDOUX, John Walter 1
LEDOUX, Louis Vernon 2

LE DUC, William Gates 1
LEDVINA, Emmanuel B. 5
LEDWITH, William 1
  Laurence
LEDYARD, Erwin 1
LEDYARD, Henry 1
LEDYARD, Henry 1
  Brockholst
LEDYARD, John H
LEDYARD, Joshua Heard 5
LEDYARD, Lewis Cass 1
LEDYARD, Lewis Cass Jr. 1
LEDYARD, William 1
LEE, Agnes 1
LEE, Albert 2
LEE, Albert Lindley 1
LEE, Alexander Edmund 1
LEE, Alfred H
LEE, Alfred Emory 4
LEE, Algernon 3
LEE, Alice Louise 1
LEE, Alonzo Hester 6
LEE, Andrew Ericson 1
LEE, Ann H
LEE, Archie Laney 3
LEE, Arthur H
LEE, Arthur 4
LEE, Bee Virginia 1
LEE, Benjamin 1
LEE, Benjamin Fisler 1
LEE, Benjamin Franklin 1
LEE, Blair 2
LEE, Blewett 1
LEE, Bradner Wells 1
LEE, Burton James 1
LEE, Canada 3
LEE, Charles * H
LEE, Charles Alfred H
LEE, Charles Hamilton 1
LEE, David Aaron 6
LEE, David B. 5
LEE, David Russell 1
LEE, Delia Foreacre (Mrs. 5
  Blewett Lee)
LEE, E. Trumbull 1
LEE, Edgar Desmond 6
LEE, Edward Edson 2
LEE, Edward Hervey 1
LEE, Edward Thomas 2
LEE, Edwin Augustus 4
LEE, Edwin F. 2
LEE, Elisha 1
LEE, Eliza Buckminster H
LEE, Elmer 4
LEE, Elmo Pearce 2
LEE, Fitzhugh 1
LEE, Francis Bazley 1
LEE, Francis D. H
LEE, Francis Lightfoot H
LEE, Frank 1
LEE, Frank Augustus 4
LEE, Frank Hood 3
LEE, Frank Theodosius 2
LEE, Frederic Edward 1
LEE, Frederic Girard 1
LEE, Frederic Paddock 5
LEE, Frederic Schiller 1
LEE, Frederick Crosby 6
LEE, Gentry 4
LEE, George Bolling 2
LEE, George Cabot 1
LEE, George Washington 1
  Curtis
LEE, George Winthrop 2
LEE, Gerald Stanley 3
LEE, Gertrude Adams 3
LEE, Gordon 1
LEE, Gordon Canfield 5
LEE, Graham 3
LEE, Guy Carleton 1
LEE, Gypsy Rose (Rose 5
  Louise Hovick)
LEE, Halfdan 6
LEE, Hannah Sawyer 1
LEE, Harold B. 6
LEE, Harry 1
LEE, Harry Winfield 1
LEE, Henry * H
LEE, Henry 1
LEE, Henry Haworth 1
LEE, Henry Thomas 4
LEE, Hildegarde L. 1
LEE, Homer 1
LEE, Hugh Johnson 1
LEE, Ivy Ledbetter 1
LEE, James Beveridge 1
LEE, James Grafton 1
  Carleton
LEE, James J. 5
LEE, James Melvin 1
LEE, James P. 2
LEE, James Paris 1
LEE, James T. 1
LEE, James Wideman 1
LEE, Jason H
LEE, Jennette 3

LEE, Jennette 4
LEE, Jesse H
LEE, Jesse Matlock 1
LEE, John H
LEE, John Clarence 1
LEE, John Clifford Hodges 3
LEE, John Doyle 1
LEE, John Mallory 1
LEE, John Penn 4
LEE, John Stebbins 1
LEE, Jordan G. Jr. 3
LEE, Joseph 2
LEE, Joseph 4
LEE, Joseph Wilcox Jenkins 5
LEE, Joshua H
LEE, Joshua Bryan 4
LEE, Lansing B. 2
LEE, Laurence Frederick 4
LEE, Leslie Alexander 1
LEE, Luther H
LEE, Luther James Jr. 4
LEE, Manfred B. 5
LEE, Margaret 1
LEE, Mary C. Skeel 4
LEE, Mary Catherine 5
  (Jenkins)
LEE, Melicent Humason 2
LEE, Moses Lindley H
LEE, Muna 4
LEE, Oliver Justin 4
LEE, Oscar Grant 4
LEE, Otis 2
LEE, Paul Wayne 3
LEE, Peter Martinus 1
LEE, Porter Raymond 1
LEE, Ray Elmer 4
LEE, Raymond Eliot 3
LEE, Richard H
LEE, Richard Bland H
LEE, Richard Edwin 1
LEE, Richard Henry H
LEE, Robert C. 3
LEE, Robert Corwin 5
LEE, Robert E. 1
LEE, Robert Edward 4
LEE, Robert Edward 1
LEE, Robert H. 3
LEE, Roger Irving 4
LEE, Rose Hum 4
LEE, Samuel Henry 1
LEE, Samuel Hunt Jr. 6
LEE, Samuel Phillips H
LEE, Samuel Todd 3
LEE, Silas H
LEE, Stephen Dill 1
LEE, T. G. 1
LEE, Thomas * H
LEE, Thomas Bailey 2
LEE, Thomas Fitzhugh 5
LEE, Thomas George 1
LEE, Thomas Sim 1
LEE, Thomas Zanslaur 1
LEE, Umphrey 3
LEE, Voyd Frank 6
LEE, Wallace Howe 1
LEE, Wallace Rodgers 1
LEE, Walter Estell 6
LEE, Warren Isbell 3
LEE, Wesley T(erence) 5
LEE, William H
LEE, William 1
LEE, William C. 4
LEE, William Erwin 3
LEE, William Granville 1
LEE, William H. 1
LEE, William Henry H
  Fitzhugh
LEE, William L. 4
LEE, William Little H
LEE, William States 1
LEE, Willis Augustus Jr. 2
LEE, Willis Thomas 1
LEECH, Edward Towner 2
LEECH, Harper 3
LEECH, J. Russell 1
LEEDOM, Boyd Stewart 5
LEEDOM, John Peter H
LEEDS, Charles Tileston 3
LEEDS, Daniel H
LEEDS, John H
LEEDS, Jules C. 3
LEEDS, Morris Evans 3
LEEDS, Paul 1
LEEDS, Rudolph Gaar 4
LEEDS, Samuel Penniman 1
LEEDY, Charles Denoe 4
LEEDY, John W. 1
LEEK, John Halvor 5
LEEMAN, Paul James 1
LEEMING, Tom 1
LEERMAKERS, Peter 5
  Anthony
LEES, James Thomas 1
LEESER, Isaac H
LEESMAN, Elmer Martin 3

LEVERONI, Frank 2
LEVERSON, Montague R. 4
LEVESON GOWER, 3
  William Spencer
LEVETT, Benjamin Arthur 5
LEVETT, David Maurice 1
LEVEY, Charles Mack 1
LEVEY, Edgar Coleman 4
LEVEY, Martin 5
LEVI, Carlo 6
LEVI, Gerson Baruch 1
LEVI, Harry 5
LEVI, Julian Clarence 4
LEVI, Moritz 4
LEVIERO, Anthony Harry 3
LEVIN, Isaac 2
LEVIN, Joseph Jay 5
LEVIN, Jack 6
LEVIN, Leonard S. 5
LEVIN, Lewis Charles H
LEVIN, Theodore 5
LEVINE, Harry Harvey 4
LEVINE, Manuel 1
LEVINE, Marks 5
LEVINE, Maurice 5
LEVINE, Max 4
LEVINE, Morris 5
LEVINE, Samuel Albert 4
LEVINE, Victor Emanuel 4
LEVINGER, David 5
LEVINGER, Elma Ehrlich 3
LEVINGER, Lee Joseph 4
LEVINGS, Miriam Fairbank 5
  (Mrs. Nelson T. Levings)
LEVINS, Thomas C. H
LE VINSEN, Florenza 5
  d'Arona (Florence
  Roosevelt)
LEVINSON, Abraham 3
LEVINSON, David 6
LEVINSON, Norman 6
LEVINSON, Salmon Oliver 1
LEVINTHAL, Bernard 3
  Louis
LEVIS, J. Preston 6
LEVIS, William Edward 4
LEVISON, Jacob Bertha 2
LEVITAN, Solomon 1
LEVITAS, Arnold 5
LEVITAS, Samuel M. 4
LEVITSKY, Louis Moses 6
LEVITT, Albert 5
LEVITT, Robert Daniels 3
LEVITZKI, Mischa 1
LEVY, Adele Rosenwald 3
LEVY, Alexander Oscar 2
LEVY, Austin T. 3
LEVY, Clifton Harby 5
LEVY, David H
LEVY, Edgar M. 1
LEVY, Edward Dailey 4
LEVY, Ernest Coleman 1
LEVY, Felix Alexander 4
LEVY, Herbert 4
LEVY, Irving J. 3
LEVY, Isaac D(avid) 6
LEVY, J. Leonard 1
LEVY, Jefferson Monroe 1
LEVY, Leo S. 4
LEVY, Louis Edward 1
LEVY, Matthew Malltz 5
LEVY, Maurice Ambrose 1
LEVY, Max 1
LEVY, Nathan 6
LEVY, Newman 4
LEVY, Raphael 5
LEVY, Robert 2
LEVY, Robert J. 6
LEVY, Robert Louis 4
LEVY, Robert Michael 6
LEVY, Russell David 4
LEVY, Samuel D. 1
LEVY, Saul 4
LEVY, Uriah Phillips H
LEVY, William Mallory H
LE WALD, Leon Theodore 5
LEWELLING, Lorenzo D. 1
LEWERS, Robert 1
LEWI, Isidor 1
LEWIN, Charles J. 4
LEWIN, Kurt 2
LEWIN, Philip 4
LEWINE, Jerome 4
LEWING, Adele 4
LEWINTHAL, Isidore 1
LEWIS, Aaron Dennison 4
LEWIS, Abner H
LEWIS, Abram Herbert 1
LEWIS, Albert Buell 3
LEWIS, Alexander 1
LEWIS, Alfred Henry 4
LEWIS, Allen 1
LEWIS, Alma Dennie 4
LEWIS, Alvin Fayette 4
LEWIS, Andrew H
LEWIS, Arthur 5

LEWIS, Arthur R. Jr. 3
LEWIS, Austin Warren 6
LEWIS, B. Palmer 2
LEWIS, Barbour H
LEWIS, Bransford 3
LEWIS, Burdett Gibson 4
LEWIS, Burwell Boykin H
LEWIS, Calvin Leslie 1
LEWIS, Ceylon Harris 1
LEWIS, Charles Bertrand 4
LEWIS, Charles Clarke 4
LEWIS, Charles Levin 4
LEWIS, Charles Lundy 4
LEWIS, Charles Swearinger H
LEWIS, Charles Willard 5
LEWIS, Charlton Miner 1
LEWIS, Charlton Thomas 1
LEWIS, Clarence Irving 4
LEWIS, Clarke 1
LEWIS, Claude Isaac 1
LEWIS, Clive Staples 5
LEWIS, D(ominio) B(evan) 5
  Wyndham
LEWIS, Daniel 1
LEWIS, Daniel F. 4
LEWIS, Dave 5
LEWIS, David John 3
LEWIS, Dean 1
LEWIS, Diocesan H
LEWIS, Dixon Hall H
LEWIS, Ebenezer Ellesville 1
LEWIS, Edmund Harris 5
LEWIS, Edward Gardner 5
LEWIS, Edward Mann 1
LEWIS, Edward McElhiney 3
LEWIS, Edward Morgan 1
LEWIS, Edward Samuel 1
LEWIS, Edwin Herbert 1
LEWIS, Edwin James Jr. 1
LEWIS, Edwin Owen 6
LEWIS, Edwin Seelye 1
LEWIS, Elijah Banks 3
LEWIS, Elizabeth Foreman 4
LEWIS, Ellis H
LEWIS, Enoch 1
LEWIS, Ernest Irving 2
LEWIS, Ernest Sidney 1
LEWIS, Ernest William 1
LEWIS, Essington 4
LEWIS, Estelle Anna H
  Blanche Robinson
LEWIS, Eugene Howard 1
LEWIS, Eugene W. 3
LEWIS, Exum Percival 1
LEWIS, F. Park 1
LEWIS, Fielding H
LEWIS, Fletcher 3
LEWIS, Francis 1
LEWIS, Francis Albert 4
LEWIS, Frank Grant 2
LEWIS, Frank J. 4
LEWIS, Franklin Allan 5
LEWIS, Franklin Crocker 1
LEWIS, Franklin Fillmore 3
LEWIS, Fred 5
LEWIS, Fred B(radley) 6
LEWIS, Fred Ewing 2
LEWIS, Fred Justin 3
LEWIS, Frederic Thomas 4
LEWIS, Frederick Wheeler 4
LEWIS, Fulton Jr. 4
LEWIS, G. Griffin 1
LEWIS, George Albert 1
LEWIS, George Francis 4
LEWIS, George Morris 4
LEWIS, George William 2
LEWIS, Gilbert Newton 2
LEWIS, Grant Kirkland 1
LEWIS, H. Edgar 2
LEWIS, Harold C. 2
LEWIS, Harold M(acLean) 6
LEWIS, Harry Herbert 3
LEWIS, Henry H
LEWIS, Henry 1
LEWIS, Henry Carleton 5
LEWIS, Henry Harrison 4
LEWIS, Henry Steele 3
LEWIS, Henry Thomas 1
LEWIS, Herbert Lefkovitz 5
LEWIS, Herbert Wesley 4
LEWIS, Homer Pierce 4
LEWIS, Howard 1
LEWIS, Howard Augustus 4
LEWIS, Howard Bishop 5
LEWIS, Howard Corwin 4
LEWIS, Hugh Alban 4
LEWIS, Ida 1
LEWIS, Irving Jefferson 5
LEWIS, Irving Stanton 5
LEWIS, Isaac Newton 1
LEWIS, Ivy Foreman 4
LEWIS, J. Wilbur 1
LEWIS, James H
LEWIS, James Hamilton 4
LEWIS, James M. 1
LEWIS, James Malcolm 3

LEWIS, James Ogier 3
LEWIS, James Otto H
LEWIS, Jesse Willard 3
LEWIS, John Beavens 1
LEWIS, John F. Jr. 4
LEWIS, John Francis H
LEWIS, John Frederick 1
LEWIS, John Henry 3
LEWIS, John Kent 4
LEWIS, John L. 1
LEWIS, John L. 1
LEWIS, John Milligan 6
LEWIS, John Neher 5
LEWIS, John Philip 4
LEWIS, Joseph 5
LEWIS, Joseph Jr. H
LEWIS, Joseph H. 1
LEWIS J(oseph) Volney 5
LEWIS, Joseph William 1
LEWIS, Judd Mortimer 1
LEWIS, Kathryn 4
LEWIS, Kemp Plummer 3
LEWIS, L. Logan 4
LEWIS, Lafayette Arthur 4
LEWIS, Lawrence H
LEWIS, Lawrence 2
LEWIS, Lee Rich 2
LEWIS, Leicester Crosby 2
LEWIS, Leon Patteson 5
LEWIS, Lillian 1
LEWIS, Lloyd Downs 2
LEWIS, Lloyd Griffith 3
LEWIS, Loran Ludowick 1
LEWIS, Lowery Lamon 5
LEWIS, Lucy May 3
LEWIS, Lunsford Lomax 4
LEWIS, Mahlon Everett 4
LEWIS, Marion L. 3
LEWIS, Marvin Harrison 5
LEWIS, Mary Sybil 1
LEWIS, Mary Sybil 1
LEWIS, Mason Avery 4
LEWIS, Melvin S(owles) 5
LEWIS, Meriwether H
LEWIS, Merton Elmer 1
LEWIS, Merton Harry 5
LEWIS, Morgan 1
LEWIS, Morris James 1
LEWIS, Nancy Duke 5
LEWIS, Nelson Peter 1
LEWIS, Olin Bailey 4
LEWIS, Orlando Faulkland 1
LEWIS, Oscar 5
LEWIS, Paul A. 1
LEWIS, Reuben Alexander 2
  Jr.
LEWIS, Richard Henry 1
LEWIS, Richard Welborne 4
LEWIS, Robert 1
LEWIS, Robert E. 4
LEWIS, Samuel H
LEWIS, Sinclair 3
LEWIS, Spearman 1
LEWIS, Spencer Steen 3
LEWIS, Ted (Theodore 5
  Friedman)
LEWIS, Theodore Leonard 3
LEWIS, Thomas H
LEWIS, Thomas Hamilton 1
LEWIS, Virgil Anson 1
LEWIS, Vivian M. 2
LEWIS, Walker 1
LEWIS, Walter Oliver 4
LEWIS, Warren Harmon 4
LEWIS, Warren Kendall 6
LEWIS, Wilfred 1
LEWIS, William H
LEWIS, William Alexander 1
LEWIS, William Bennett 6
LEWIS, William Berkeley 1
LEWIS, William David H
LEWIS, William Dodge 4
LEWIS, William Draper 2
LEWIS, William Eugene 4
LEWIS, William Fisher 4
LEWIS, William Henry 4
LEWIS, William J. H
LEWIS, William Luther 3
LEWIS, William Mather 4
LEWIS, William Stanley 5
LEWIS, Sir Wilmet Harsant 2
LEWIS, Wilson Seeley 1
LEWIS, Winford Lee 4
LEWIS, Winslow H
LEWIS, Yancey 1
LEWISOHN, Adolph 1
LEWISOHN, Ludwig 5
LEWISOHN, Margaret S. 3
LEWISOHN, Sam A. 3
LEWMAN, Frank C. 4
LEWTON, Frederick Lewis 3
LEX, Charles E. 1
LEXOW, Clarence 1
LEY, Frederick Theodore 4
LEY, Harold Alexander 3
LEY, Willy 5
LEYDON, John Koebig 5

LEYENDECKER, Frank X. 1
LEYENDECKER, Joseph 3
  Christian
LEYMAN, Harry Stoll 5
LEYPOLDT, Frederick H
LEYS, James Farquharson 1
LEYS, Wayne Albert Risser 5
LEYSEN, Ralph J. 3
LEYSHON, Hal Irwin 4
L'HALLE, Constantin de 1
L'HEUREUX, Camille 4
L'HEUREUX, Herve Joseph 3
LHEVINNE, Josef 2
L'HOMMEDIEU, Ezra H
LHOTE, Andre 4
LI, Kuo-Ching 4
LIAUTAUD, Andre 3
LIBBEY, Edward 1
  Drummond
LIBBEY, Jonas Marsh 1
LIBBEY, Laura Jean 4
LIBBEY, William 1
LIBBY, Arthur Stephen 2
LIBBY, Charles Freeman 1
LIBBY, Edward Norton 1
LIBBY, Frederick Joseph 5
LIBBY, Melanchthon 1
  Fennessy
LIBBY, Orin Grant 3
LIBBY, Samuel Hammonds 5
LIBBY, Warren Edgar 3
LIBERMAN, Samuel 5
  Halpern
LIBERTE, Jean 4
LIBMAN, Emanuel 2
LICHITER, McIlyar 4
  Hamilton
LICHT, George Augustus 6
LICHTEN, Robert Lyon 6
LICHTENBERG, Bernard 2
LICHTENBERG, Leopold 1
LICHTENBERGER, Arthur 5
  Carl
LICHTENBERGER, James 3
  Pendleton
LICHTENSTEIN, Joy 5
LICHTENSTEIN, Walter 4
LICHTENTAG, Alexander 1
LICHTENWALTER, 5
  Franklin H.
LICHTY, John Alden 1
LICHTY, L(ester) (Clyde) 5
LICK, James H
LICK, Maxwell John 2
LIDBURY, Frank Austin 6
LIDDELL, Donald Macy 5
LIDDELL, Eva Louise 1
LIDDELL, Frank Austin 4
LIDDELL, Henry 4
LIDDELL, Howard Scott 4
LIDDELL, Mark Harvey 1
LIDDLE, Charles Allen 4
LIDDON, Benjamin Sullivan 1
LIE, Jonas 1
LIEB, Charles 3
LIEB, Charles Christian 3
LIEB, John William 1
LIEB, Joseph Patrick 6
LIEBEL, Michael Jr. 5
LIEBEL, Willard Koehler 4
LIEBER, B. Franklin 1
LIEBER, Eugene 4
LIEBER, Francis H
LIEBER, G. Norman 1
LIEBER, Hugh Gray 4
LIEBER, Richard 2
LIEBERMAN, Elias 5
LIEBERS, Otto Hugo 5
LIEBES, Mrs. Dorothy 5
  Wright
LIEBLING, Abbott Joseph 4
LIEBLING, Emil 1
LIEBLING, George 2
LIEBLING, Leonard 2
LIEBMAN, Joshua Loth 2
LIEBMAN, Julius 1
LIEBMANN, Philip 5
LIECTY, Austin N. 5
LIEDER, Frederick William 3
  Charles
LIEDER, Paul Robert 3
LIEFELD, Albert 1
LIEN, Arnold Johnson 4
LIEN, Elias Johnson 4
LIEN, Robert Cowles 6
LIENAU, Detlef H
LIES, Eugene Theodore 4
LIEURANCE, Thurlow 5
LIFE, Andrew Creamor 1
LIFE, Frank Mann 4
LIFSCHEY, Samuel 4
LIGGETT, Hunter 1
LIGGETT, Louis Kroh 2
LIGGETT, Walter William 1
LIGGINS, John 1

LIGHT, Charles Porterfield 3
LIGHT, Evelyn 3
LIGHT, Israel 6
LIGHT, Rudolph Alvin 5
LIGHTBURN, George 4
  William
LIGHTBURN, Joseph A. J. 1
LIGHTNER, Clarence 1
  Ashley
LIGHTNER, Ezra 5
  Wilberforce
LIGHTNER, Milton C. 5
LIGHTON, William Rheem 4
LIGON, Elvin Seth 6
LIGON, Elvin Seth Jr. 6
LIGON, Thomas Watkins H
LIHME, C. Bai 2
LIKLY, William F. 4
LILE, William Minor 1
LILES, Luther Brooks 1
LILIENTHAL, Howard 2
LILIENTHAL, Jesse 1
  Warren
LILIENTHAL, Joseph Leo 3
  Jr.
LILIENTHAL, Max H
LILIENTHAL, Samuel 3
LILIUOKALANI H
LILIUOKALANI 4
LILJENCRANTZ, Ottilie 1
  Adaline
LILJESTRAND, Goran 5
LILLARD, Benjamin 4
LILLARD, Walter Huston 4
LILLARD, Walter Huston 4
LILLEY, Charles Sumner 1
LILLEY, George 1
LILLEY, George Leavens 1
LILLEY, James E. 4
LILLEY, Robert 4
LILLIBRIDGE, William 1
  Otis
LILLICK, Ira S. 4
LILLIE, Abraham Bruyn 1
  Hasbrouck
LILLIE, Charles A. 4
LILLIE, Frank Rattray 2
LILLIE, Gordon William 2
LILLIE, Gordon William 2
LILLIE, Harold Irving 3
LILLIE, Howard Russell 4
LILLIE, Lucy Cecil 1
LILLIE, Ralph Stayner 3
LILLIE, Samuel Morris 1
LILLIS, Donald Chace 5
LILLIS, James F. 4
LILLIS, Thomas F. 1
LILLY, D. Clay 1
LILLY, Josiah Kirby 2
LILLY, Josiah Kirby 2
LILLY, Linus Augustine 2
LILLY, Richard C. 3
LILLY, Samuel H
LILLY, Thomas Jefferson 3
LILLY, William H
LIM, Pilar Hidalgo (Mrs. 6
  Vicente Lim)
LIMA, Manoel de Oliveira 1
LIMBACH, Russell 5
  Theodore
LIMBERT, Lee Middleton 4
LIMERICK, 2d earl H
LIMOGES, Joseph Eugene 6
LIMON, Jose Arcadio 5
LIN, Piao 5
LINCECUM, Gideon H
LINCOLN, Abraham 1
LINCOLN, Allen B. 1
LINCOLN, Arleigh Leon 4
LINCOLN, Asa Liggett 6
LINCOLN, Azariah Thomas 3
LINCOLN, Benjamin H
LINCOLN, Charles Clark 1
LINCOLN, Charles Monroe 3
LINCOLN, Charles Perez 1
LINCOLN, Charles 1
  Sherman
LINCOLN, Charles Zebina 4
LINCOLN, Daniel Waldo 5
LINCOLN, David Francis 1
LINCOLN, Edmond E. 3
LINCOLN, Enoch H
LINCOLN, Francis Church 5
LINCOLN, Gatewood 4
  Sanders
LINCOLN, George Arthur 6
LINCOLN, George Gould 6
LINCOLN, J. Freeman 4
LINCOLN, James Claiborne 1
LINCOLN, James Finney 4
LINCOLN, James Rush 1
LINCOLN, James Sullivan H
LINCOLN, Jeanie Gould 1
LINCOLN, John Cromwell 3
LINCOLN, John Larkin H
LINCOLN, Jonathan Thayer 2

* Indicates More Than One Such Name Listed

LINCOLN, Joseph Crosby 2
LINCOLN, Julius 3
LINCOLN, Leontine 1
LINCOLN, Leroy Alton 3
LINCOLN, Levi * H
LINCOLN, Mary Johnson 1
LINCOLN, Mary Todd H
LINCOLN, Murray 4
  Danforth
LINCOLN, Natalie Sumner 1
LINCOLN, Paul Martyn 2
LINCOLN, Robert Todd 1
LINCOLN, Rufus Pratt 1
LINCOLN, Solomon 1
LINCOLN, Sumner H. 1
LINCOLN, Waldo 1
LINCOLN, William Ensign 4
LINCOLN, William Henry 1
LINCOLN, William Slosson H
LIND, Ethel C. (Mrs. 5
  Walter C. Lind)
LIND, Jenny H
LIND, John 1
LIND, Samuel Colville 1
LINDABURY, Irvin L. 6
LINDABURY, Richard 1
  Vliet
LINDABURY, Richard 6
  Vliet
LINDAHL, Josua 1
LINDAHL, Oscar 3
  Nathanael
LINDBECK, John 5
  M(atthew) H(enry)
LINDBERG, Abram Frank 1
LINDBERG, Carl Otto 6
LINDBERG, Conrad Emil 1
LINDBERG, David Oscar 4
  Nathaniel
LINDBERG, Irving 3
  Augustus
LINDBERGH, Charles 1
  August
LINDBERGH, Charles 6
  Augustus
LINDBLAD, Bertil 4
LINDBLOOM, Pauline 6
  Funk
LINDE, Christian H
LINDEBERG, Harrie 3
  Thomas
LINDEGREN, Alina M. 3
LINDEMAN, Charles 5
  Bernard
LINDEMAN, Eduard 3
  Christian
LINDEMAN, Frank Jr. 4
LINDEMANN, Erich 6
LINDENKOHL, Adolph 1
LINDENTHAL, Gustav H
LINDER, Frederick M. 3
LINDER, Oliver Anderson 1
LINDERMAN, Frank Bird 3
LINDERMAN, Henry H
  Richard
LINDERMAN, Robert 1
  Packer
LINDERSTROM-LANG, 3
  Kaj
LINDGREN, Waldemar 1
LINDHEIMER, Ferdinand H
  Jacob
LINDLEY, Albert 4
LINDLEY, Curtis Holbrook 1
LINDLEY, Daniel H
LINDLEY, Erasmus 3
  Christopher
LINDLEY, Ernest Hiram 1
LINDLEY, Harlow 5
LINDLEY, Hervey 1
LINDLEY, Jacob H
LINDLEY, James Johnson 1
LINDLEY, John Franklin 6
LINDLEY, Paul Cameron 1
LINDLEY, Walter 1
LINDLEY, Walter C. 3
LINDNER, Clarence 3
  Richard
LINDNER, Robert M. 4
LINDQUIST, Francis O. 1
LINDQUIST, Robert John 3
LINDQUIST, Rudolph 2
  Daniel
LINDSAY, Alexander Jr. 1
LINDSAY, Anna Robertson 2
  Brown
LINDSAY, Arthur Hawes 2
LINDSAY, Arthur Oliver 1
LINDSAY, D. Moore 4
LINDSAY, F(rank) M(errill) 5
LINDSAY, George Henry 1
LINDSAY, George LeRoy 2
LINDSAY, George 1
  Washington
LINDSAY, Hal 4
LINDSAY, Henry Drennan 1

LINDSAY, Howard 4
LINDSAY, James Hubert 1
LINDSAY, John Douglas 1
LINDSAY, John 1
  Summerfield
LINDSAY, John Wesley 1
LINDSAY, Lynn Grout 5
LINDSAY, Marrill Kirk 4
LINDSAY, Maud McKnight 2
LINDSAY, Robert Burns 1
LINDSAY, The Rt. Hon. Sir 5
  Ronald
LINDSAY, Roy Wallace 4
LINDSAY, Samuel McCune 3
LINDSAY, Thomas Bond 1
LINDSAY, Thomas Corwin 1
LINDSAY, Vachel 1
LINDSAY, William 1
LINDSAY, William Sharp 1
LINDSEY, Benjamin Barr 2
LINDSEY, Daniel Weisiger 1
LINDSEY, Edward Allen 1
LINDSEY, Edward 2
  Sherman
LINDSEY, Harry W. Jr. 3
LINDSEY, Joseph Bridgeo 1
LINDSEY, Julian Robert 2
LINDSEY, Kenneth Lovell 1
LINDSEY, Louis 5
LINDSEY, Malcolm F. 6
LINDSEY, Stephen Decatur H
LINDSEY, Sterling Paul Jr. 3
LINDSEY, Therese Kayser 5
  (Mrs. S. A. Lindsey)
LINDSEY, Washington 1
LINDSEY, William 1
  Ellsworth
LINDSEY, William 1
LINDSEY, William Henry 1
LINDSLEY, Charles 1
  Augustus
LINDSLEY, Charles 4
  Frederick
LINDSLEY, Henry 1
  Dickinson
LINDSLEY, Herbert Kitchel 3
LINDSLEY, John Berrien H
LINDSLEY, Philip H
LINDSLEY, Smith M. 1
LINDSLEY, William Dell H
LINDSTROM, Carl E. 5
LINDSTROM, Ernest 2
  Walter
LINEBARGER, Charles 1
  Elijah
LINEBARGER, Paul Myron 4
  Anthony
LINEBARGER, Paul Myron 1
  Wentworth
LINEBAUGH, Daniel 1
  Haden
LINEBERGER, Walter 2
  Franklin
LINEHAN, John C. 1
LINEHAN, Neil J. 4
LINEN, James A. Jr. 3
LINES, Edwin Stevens 1
LINES, George 1
LINES, H. Wales 1
LINEWEAVER, Goodrich 1
  Wilson
LINFIELD, Adolphus 6
LINFIELD, Frances Eleanor 4
  Ross
LINFIELD, Frederick 3
  Bloomfield
LINFORD, James Henry 4
LINFORD, Leon Blood 3
LINFORTH, Ivan Mortimer 4
LING, Charles Joseph 5
LING, David W. 4
LING, Reese M. 4
LINGARD, James W. H
LINGELBACH, Anna Lane 4
LINGELBACH, William E. 4
LINGENFELTER, Mary 3
  Rebecca
LINGHAM, Fred J. 3
LINGLE, Bowman Church 1
LINGLE, David Judson 4
LINGLE, Elmore Yokum 6
LINGLE, Thomas Wilson 1
LINGLE, Walter Lee 3
LINGLEY, Charles 1
  Ramsdell
LINHART, Samuel Black 1
LINING, John H
LININGER, Frederick 6
  Fouse
LINK, Henry Charles 1
LINK, John Ephraim 4
LINK, Margaret C. Schott 6
  (Mrs. Joseph Link Jr.)
LINK, Samuel Albert 3
LINK, Theodore Carl 4
LINK, William W. 4
LINKLATER, Eric 6

LINN, Alonzo 1
LINN, Alvin Frank 1
LINN, Archibald Ladley 1
LINN, Henry W. 5
LINN, James H
LINN, James Weber 1
LINN, John 1
LINN, John Blair H
LINN, Lewis Fields H
LINN, Paul Hinkle 1
LINN, Robert A. 4
LINN, William Alexander 3
LINN, William Bomberger 3
LINNARD, Joseph 1
  Hamilton
LINNELL, William 4
  Shepherd
LINNEMAN, Herbert F. 5
LINNEN, Edward Bangs 1
LINNES, Lowell Claude 6
LINNEY, Frank Armfield 1
LINNEY, Robert Joseph 5
LINNIK, Iurii Vladimirovich 6
LINSCHEID, Adolph 3
LINSCOTT, Robert Newton 4
LINSLEY, Duncan 5
  Robertson
LINSON, Corwin Knapp 5
LINTHICUM, Charles 1
  Clarence
LINTHICUM, George 1
  Milton
LINTHICUM, John Charles 1
LINTHICUM, Richard 1
LINTNER, Joseph Albert 1
LINTON, Edwin 1
LINTON, Frank B. A. 2
LINTON, Morris Albert 4
LINTON, Ralph 3
LINTON, Robert 2
LINTON, William James H
LINTON, William Seelye 1
LINTOTT, Edward Barnard 3
LINVILLE, Clarence 6
  Philander
LINVILLE, Henry 2
  Richardson
LINZ, Paul Francis 6
LIONBERGER, Isaac H. 3
LIPCHITZ, Jacques 5
LIPMAN, Charles Bernard 2
LIPMAN, Clara 3
LIPMAN, Frederick 3
  Lockwood
LIPMAN, Jacob Goodale 1
LIPPARD, George H
LIPPHARD, William 5
  Benjamin
LIPPINCOTT, Charles 1
  Augustus
LIPPINCOTT, Craige 1
LIPPINCOTT, Ellis 6
  Ridgeway Jr.
LIPPINCOTT, Horace 4
  Mather
LIPPINCOTT, J. Bertram 1
LIPPINCOTT, James 1
LIPPINCOTT, James Starr H
LIPPINCOTT, Job H. 1
LIPPINCOTT, Joseph 2
  Barlow
LIPPINCOTT, Joshua H
  Ballinger
LIPPINCOTT, Martha 2
  Shepard
LIPPINCOTT, Richard H. 1
LIPPINCOTT, Sara Jane 1
LIPPINCOTT, William 1
  Adams
LIPPINCOTT, William 1
  Henry
LIPPITT, Charles Warren 1
LIPPITT, Charles Warren 5
LIPPITT, Francis James 1
LIPPITT, Henry 1
LIPPITT, Henry Frederick 1
LIPPITT, William Donald 1
LIPPMAN, Hyman Shalit 6
LIPPMAN, Leonard Bing 4
LIPPMANN, Julie Mathilde 3
LIPPMANN, Robert Korn 5
LIPPS, Oscar Hiram 4
LIPSCHULTZ, Samuel 4
LIPSCOMB, Abner Smith H
LIPSCOMB, Andrew H
  Adgate
LIPSCOMB, David 1
LIPSCOMB, Glenard P. 5
LIPSCOMB, William H. 3
LIPSEY, Plautus Iberus 2
LIPSEY, Plautus Iberus Jr. 5
LIPSITZ, Louis 1
LIPSKY, Louis 4
LIPSKY, Louis 5
LIPTON, Barbara 6

LIPTON, Sir Thomas 3
  Johnstone
LISA, Manuel H
LISCHER, Benno Edward 3
LISCUM, Emerson H. 1
LISLE, Arthur Beymer 2
LISLE, Marcus Claiborne H
LISLE, Robert Patton 1
LISMAN, Frederick J. 1
LISSER, Louis 1
LISSNER, Meyer 1
LIST, Ambrose Shaw 1
LIST, Carl F. 5
LIST, Emanuel 4
LIST, Georg Friedrich H
LIST, Kurt 5
LISTEMANN, Bernhard 1
LISTEMANN, Fritz 1
LISTER, Charles Baynard 3
LISTER, Ernest 1
LISTER, Walter Bartlett 4
LISTOE, Soren 4
LISTON, H. Sr. 3
LITCH, Ernest Wheeler 4
LITCHFIELD, Edward 5
  Harold
LITCHFIELD, Electus H
  Backus
LITCHFIELD, Electus 3
  Darwin
LITCHFIELD, Elisha H
LITCHFIELD, Grace Denio 2
LITCHFIELD, Lawrence 1
LITCHFIELD, Lawrence Jr. 4
LITCHFIELD, Mary 1
  Elizabeth
LITCHFIELD, Paul Weeks 3
LITCHFIELD, William 1
  Elias
LITCHMAN, Charles Henry 1
LITIN, Edward Mortimer 6
LITMAN, Simon 5
LITSEY, Edwin Carlile 5
LITSINGER, Edward 5
  Robert
LITT, Jacob 1
LITTAUER, Lucius Nathan 2
LITTEL, Emlyn T. H
LITTELL, Clair Francis 4
LITTELL, Clarence Guy 3
LITTELL, Eliakim 1
LITTELL, Frank Bowers 3
LITTELL, Isaac William 1
LITTELL, Philip 2
LITTELL, Robert 4
LITTELL, Samuel 4
  Harrington
LITTELL, Squier H
LITTELL, William 1
LITTEN, Frederic Nelson 3
LITTICK, Orville Beck 1
LITTIG, Lawrence William 1
LITTLE, Alden Howe 4
LITTLE, Archibald 4
  Alexander
LITTLE, Arthur 1
LITTLE, Arthur D. 5
LITTLE, Arthur Mitchell 1
LITTLE, Arthur W. 2
LITTLE, Arthur Wilde 1
LITTLE, Bascom 1
LITTLE, Charles 1
LITTLE, Charles Coffin H
LITTLE, Charles Eugene 4
LITTLE, Charles Joseph 1
LITTLE, Charles Newton 1
LITTLE, Chauncey B. 3
LITTLE, Clarence Belden 1
LITTLE, Clarence C(ook) 5
LITTLE, David M. 3
LITTLE, Edward Campbell 1
LITTLE, E(dward) 6
  H(erman)
LITTLE, Edward Preble H
LITTLE, Ernest 6
LITTLE, Frances 1
LITTLE, George H
LITTLE, George E. 6
LITTLE, George Obadiah 4
LITTLE, George Thomas 1
LITTLE, Gilbert Francis 4
LITTLE, Harry Britton 2
LITTLE, Henry G. 6
LITTLE, Herbert 1
  Satterthwaite
LITTLE, Homer Payson 4
LITTLE, J. Wesley 1
LITTLE, James Lovell 2
LITTLE, John Dozier 1
LITTLE, John Peter 6
LITTLE, John Sebastian 1
LITTLE, Joseph James 1
LITTLE, Kenneth Buxton 4
LITTLE, Louis McCarty 4
LITTLE, Lucius Freeman 2

LITTLE, Mitchell Stuart 5
LITTLE, Peter H
LITTLE, Philip 2
LITTLE, Richard Henry 1
LITTLE, Riley McMillan 1
LITTLE, Robbins 4
LITTLE, Robert Rice 2
LITTLE, Russell A. 1
LITTLE, S. George 6
LITTLE, Sidney Wahl 5
LITTLE, Tom 5
LITTLE, William Augustus 3
LITTLE, William Nelson II 1
LITTLE CROW V H
LITTLEDALE, Clara 3
  Savage
LITTLEFIELD, Charles 1
  Edgar
LITTLEFIELD, Charles 4
  William
LITTLEFIELD, Eben 1
  Northup
LITTLEFIELD, George 1
  Emery
LITTLEFIELD, George W. 4
LITTLEFIELD, Milton 1
  Smith
LITTLEFIELD, Nathan 1
  Whitman
LITTLEFIELD, Nathaniel H
  Swett
LITTLEFIELD, Walter 2
LITTLEHALES, George 1
  Washington
LITTLEJOHN, Abraham 1
  Newkirk
LITTLEJOHN, De Witt H
  Clinton
LITTLEJOHN, Elbridge 1
  Gerry
LITTLEJOHN, John Martin 4
LITTLEPAGE, Adam 4
  Brown
LITTLEPAGE, Lewis H
LITTLEPAGE, Thomas 2
  Price
LITTLETON, Arthur 6
LITTLETON, Benjamin H. 4
LITTLETON, Frank Leslie 1
LITTLETON, J. T. 4
LITTLETON, Jesse M. 1
LITTLETON, Jesse Talbot 1
LITTLETON, Martin Wiley 1
LITTLETON, William 1
  Graham
LITTLE TURTLE H
LITTLEWOOD, William 4
LITZENBERG, Homer 4
  Laurence
LITZENBERG, Jennings 2
  Crawford
LITZINGER, Marie 3
LIU, Shao-Chi 6
LIVELY, Charles Elson 5
LIVELY, Daniel O'Connell 1
LIVELY, Frank 2
LIVELY, Robert Alexander 6
LIVERIGHT, Horace 1
  Brisbin
LIVERMAN, Harry 4
LIVERMORE, Abiel Abbot H
LIVERMORE, Edward St H
  Loe
LIVERMORE, George H
LIVERMORE, George 4
  Robertson
LIVERMORE, Mary 1
  Ashton
LIVERMORE, Norman 5
  Banks
LIVERMORE, Russell B. 3
LIVERMORE, Samuel * H
LIVERMORE, Thomas 1
  Leonard
LIVERMORE, William 1
  Roscoe
LIVERNASH, Edward 4
  James
LIVERSIDGE, Horace 3
  Preston
LIVINGOOD, Charles 5
  Jacob
LIVINGSTON, Arthur 2
LIVINGSTON, Burton 1
  Edward
LIVINGSTON, Crawford 1
LIVINGSTON, Douglas 5
  Clermont
LIVINGSTON, Edward H
LIVINGSTON, George 3
LIVINGSTON, Goodhue 3
LIVINGSTON, Henry H
  Walter
LIVINGSTON, Homer J. 5
LIVINGSTON, James H

LIVINGSTON, James 1
Duane
LIVINGSTON, Jesse Elsmer 4
LIVINGSTON, John Henry H
LIVINGSTON, John H
William
LIVINGSTON, Leonidas 1
Felix
LIVINGSTON, Paul Yount 1
LIVINGSTON, Peter Van H
Brugh
LIVINGSTON, Philip H
LIVINGSTON, Philip 1
LIVINGSTON, Robert H
LIVINGSTON, Robert Irvin 4
LIVINGSTON, Robert Le H
Roy
LIVINGSTON, Robert R. * 4
LIVINGSTON, Robert 4
Teviot
LIVINGSTON, Sigmund 2
LIVINGSTON, Walter H
LIVINGSTON, William H
LIVINGSTON, William 1
Henry
LIVINGSTONE, Colin 2
Hamilton
LIVINGSTONE, John 1
Alexander
LIVINGSTONE, William 1
LIVINSTON, Henry H
Brockholst
LIZARS, Rawson Goodsir 5
LLEWELLYN, Fred Warde 6
LLEWELLYN, Frederick 5
Britton
LLEWELLYN, Joseph 1
Corson
LLEWELLYN, Karl 4
Nickerson
LLEWELLYN, Maxwell 6
Bowler
LLEWELLYN, Silas James 1
LLEWELLYN, William H. 3
H.
LLOYD, Alfred Henry 1
LLOYD, Alice Crocker 2
LLOYD, Arthur Selden 1
LLOYD, Bolivar Jones 3
LLOYD, Curtis Gates 1
LLOYD, David H
LLOYD, David Demarest 4
LLOYD, Demarest 1
LLOYD, E. Russell 1
LLOYD, Edmund Grindal 4
Rawson
LLOYD, Edward * H
LLOYD, Edward Lester 3
LLOYD, Edward Read 4
LLOYD, Edward VIII 2
LLOYD, Edward VIII 1
LLOYD, Ella Stryker Mapes 5
LLOYD, Francis Ernest 2
LLOYD, Frank S. 3
LLOYD, Frank T. 3
LLOYD, Frederic Ebenezer 1
John
LLOYD, Glen Alfred 6
LLOYD, Harold (Clayton) 5
LLOYD, Henry 1
LLOYD, Henry Demarest 1
LLOYD, Henry Demarest 5
LLOYD, Hinton 1
Summerfield
LLOYD, Horatio Gates 1
LLOYD, James * H
LLOYD, James Tighlman 2
LLOYD, John Uri 1
LLOYD, L(awrence) 5
Duncan
LLOYD, Marshall Burns 1
LLOYD, Morton Githens 1
LLOYD, Nelson McAllister 1
LLOYD, Ralph Bramel 3
LLOYD, Ralph Irving 1
LLOYD, Samuel 1
LLOYD, Samuel 1
LLOYD, Stacy Barcroft 1
LLOYD, Stewart Joseph 3
LLOYD, Thomas H
LLOYD, Walter Hamilton 3
Jr.
LLOYD, Wesley 1
LLOYD, William Allison 2
LLOYD, William Henry 1
LLOYD, Woodrow Stanley 5
LOAN, Benjamin Franklin H
LOAR, James Leazure 1
LOASBY, Arthur William 1
LOBDELL, Charles E. 1
LOBDELL, Effie L(eola) 5
LOBDELL, Harold E. 4
LOBECK, Armin Kohl 3
LOBECK, Charles O. 1
LOBENSTINE, Edwin 1
Carlyle

LOBER, Georg John 4
LOBERG, Harry John 4
LOBINGIER, Andrew 1
Stewart
LOBINGIER, Elizabeth 6
Miller
LOBO, Fernando 4
LOBRANO, Gustave S. 3
LOCHER, Casper William 1
LOCHER, Cyrus 1
LOCHMAN, John George H
LOCHNER, Louis Paul 6
LOCHNER, William 1
LOCHRIDGE, P. D. 1
LOCKE, Alain LeRoy 3
LOCKE, Alfred Hamilton 6
LOCKE, Bessie 3
LOCKE, Charles E. 2
LOCKE, Charles Edward 1
LOCKE, David Ross H
LOCKE, Edward 2
LOCKE, Edwin 1
LOCKE, Eugene Murphy 5
LOCKE, Eugene Perry 4
LOCKE, Francis H
LOCKE, Frank Lovering 1
LOCKE, Franklin Day 1
LOCKE, George Herbert 1
LOCKE, Harry Leslie 5
Franklin
LOCKE, James 1
LOCKE, James Dewitt 1
Clinton
LOCKE, James William 1
LOCKE, John * H
LOCKE, John Staples 1
LOCKE, M. Katherine 1
LOCKE, Matthew H
LOCKE, Richard Adams H
LOCKE, Robert Wynter 5
LOCKE, Robinson 1
LOCKE, Victor Murat Jr. 5
LOCKE, Walter 3
LOCKERBY, Frank 1
McCarthy
LOCKETT, Andrew M. 3
LOCKETT, James 4
LOCKEY, Joseph Byrne 3
LOCKEY, Mary Ishbel 1
LOCKHART, Arthur John 1
LOCKHART, Burton 3
Wellesley
LOCKHART, Caroline 5
LOCKHART, Charles 4
LOCKHART, Clinton 3
LOCKHART, Earl Granger 6
LOCKHART, Ernest Ray 5
LOCKHART, Frank P. 2
LOCKHART, Gene 2
LOCKHART, Henry Jr. 1
LOCKHART, James H
LOCKHART, James Henry 1
LOCKHART, Malcolm 1
Mabry
LOCKHART, Oliver Cary 6
LOCKHART, Walter 1
Samuel
LOCKHEED, Allan Haines 1
LOCKLEY, Fred 3
LOCKLEY, Lawrence 5
Campbell
LOCKMAN, DeWitt 3
McClellan
LOCKMAN, John Thomas 1
LOCKRIDGE, Frances 4
LOCKRIDGE, Ross 3
Franklin
LOCKRIDGE, Ross 2
Franklin Jr.
LOCKWOOD, Albert 1
LOCKWOOD, Alfred 5
Collins
LOCKWOOD, Belva Ann 1
Bennett
LOCKWOOD, Benjamin 1
Curtis
LOCKWOOD, Charles 4
Andrews Jr.
LOCKWOOD, Charles 3
Clapp
LOCKWOOD, Charles 1
Daniel
LOCKWOOD, Charles 3
Davenport
LOCKWOOD, Daniel 1
Newton
LOCKWOOD, Daniel 4
Wright
LOCKWOOD, Edward T. 4
Cummins
LOCKWOOD, Francis 1
Cummins
LOCKWOOD, George 1
Browning
LOCKWOOD, George Rae 4
LOCKWOOD, Harold J. 4
LOCKWOOD, Harold Paul 5

LOCKWOOD, Helen 5
Drusilla
LOCKWOOD, Henry 1
LOCKWOOD, Henry Hayes 1
LOCKWOOD, Henry 1
Roswell
LOCKWOOD, Homer 1
Nichols
LOCKWOOD, Ingersoll 4
LOCKWOOD, Ira Hiram 3
LOCKWOOD, James Booth H
LOCKWOOD, John 1
Alexander
LOCKWOOD, John Salem 3
LOCKWOOD, Laura Emma 4
LOCKWOOD, Luke Burnell 4
LOCKWOOD, Luke 3
Vincent
LOCKWOOD, Mary Smith 4
LOCKWOOD, Preston 1
LOCKWOOD, Ralph H
Ingersoll
LOCKWOOD, Richard John 4
LOCKWOOD, Samuel H
Drake
LOCKWOOD, Sara 4
Elizabeth Husted
LOCKWOOD, Stephen 5
Timothy
LOCKWOOD, Thomas B. 2
LOCKWOOD, Thomas 3
Dixon
LOCKWOOD, Wilton 1
LOCRAFT, Thomas Hall 4
LOCY, William Albert 1
LODGE, Edmund Anderson 6
LODGE, Gonzalez 1
LODGE, Henry Cabot 1
LODGE, John Christian 2
LODGE, John Ellerton 2
LODGE, Lee Davis 1
LODIAN, L. 4
LODOR, Richard 1
LOEB, Arthur Joseph 5
LOEB, Benjamin M. 4
LOEB, Carl M. 3
LOEB, G(erald) M(artin) 6
LOEB, Hanau Wolf 1
LOEB, Howard A. 3
LOEB, Isidor 3
LOEB, Jacob Moritz 2
LOEB, Jacques 1
LOEB, James 1
LOEB, Leo 1
LOEB, Louis 1
LOEB, Milton B. 5
LOEB, Morris 1
LOEB, Robert Frederick 6
LOEB, Sophie Irene 1
LOEB, William 1
LOEFFEL, William John 4
LOEFFLER, Carl August 5
LOEFFLER, Charles Martin 1
Tornov
LOEHWING, Walter 4
Ferdinand
LOESCH, Frank Joseph 2
LOESSER, Frank 6
LOETSCHER, Frederick 4
William
LOEVENHART, Arthur 1
Solomon
LOEW, Edward Victor 4
LOEW, Marcus 1
LOEWE, Dietrich Eduard 1
LOEWENBERG, Bert 6
James
LOEWENSTEIN, Karl 6
LOEWENTHAL, Isidor 1
LOEWI, Otto 4
LOEWY, Edwin 3
LOEWY, Erwin 5
LOFLAND, James Rush H
LOFT, George W. 4
LOFTIN, James Otis 3
LOFTIN, Scott Marion 3
LOFTING, Hugh 2
LOFTON, George Augustus 1
LOFTUS, Clarence James 5
LOFTUS, John Thomas 5
LOGAN, Albert J. 1
LOGAN, Archie Francis 5
LOGAN, Benjamin H
LOGAN, Charles Alexander 5
LOGAN, Cornelius H
Ambrose
LOGAN, Cornelius H
Ambrosius
LOGAN, Frank G. 1
LOGAN, George 1
LOGAN, Henry H
LOGAN, James * 1
LOGAN, James 1
LOGAN, James Addison Jr. 1
LOGAN, James Elmore 1
LOGAN, James Parmelee 1

LOGAN, Mrs. John A. 1
LOGAN, John Alexander H
LOGAN, John Alexander 1
Jr.
LOGAN, John Daniel 5
LOGAN, John Henry H
LOGAN, John Hubbard 1
LOGAN, Josephine 2
Hancock
LOGAN, Leavitt Curtis 1
LOGAN, Marvel Mills 1
LOGAN, Mercer Patton 1
LOGAN, Milburn Hill 4
LOGAN, Olive 1
LOGAN, Robert Fulton 3
LOGAN, Stephen Trigg 1
LOGAN, Thomas Dale 3
LOGAN, Thomas Francis 1
LOGAN, Thomas Moldrup H
LOGAN, Thomas Muldrup 1
LOGAN, W(illiam) Turner 1
LOGAN, Walter Seth 1
LOGAN, William H
LOGAN, William Hoffman 2
Gardiner
LOGAN, William Newton 2
LOGGINS, Vernon 1
LOGUE, J. Washington 1
LOGUE, John Terrell 2
LOGUEN, Jermain Wesley H
LOHMAN, Joseph D(ean) 5
LOHMANN, Carl Albert 3
LOHNES, Horace L. 3
LOHR, Lenox Riley 5
LOHRE, Nels J. 1
LOICHOT, Raymond 3
William
LOINES, Hilda 6
LOISEAU, John Elmer 4
LOKEY, Eugene 3
LOKKEN, Roscoe Leonard 6
LOKRANTZ, Sven 1
LOMAS, Alfred Jackson 3
LOMAX, Edward Lloyd 1
LOMAX, John Avery 2
LOMAX, John Tayloe H
LOMAX, Louis Emanuel 5
LOMAX, Lunsford Lindsay 1
LOMAX, Paul Sanford 6
LOMAX, Tennent 1
LOMBARD, Carole 1
LOMBARD, Frank Alanson 5
LOMBARD, Louis 4
LOMBARD, Warren 1
Plimpton
LOMBARDI, C. 1
LOMBARDI, Cornelius 3
Ennis
LOMBARDI, Vincent 1
Thomas
LOMEN, Gudbrand J. 1
LOMMEN, Christian Peter 1
LONARDI, Eduardo 3
LONDON, Alexander Troy 1
LONDON, Daniel Edwin 6
LONDON, Jack 1
LONDON, Meyer 1
LONERGAN, Augustine 1
LONERGAN, William 1
Ignatius
LONG, Albert Limerick 1
LONG, Alexander 1
LONG, Andrew Theodore 2
LONG, Armistead Lindsay H
LONG, Augustine J. 5
LONG, Augustine V. 3
LONG, Augustus White 3
LONG, Boaz Walton 4
LONG, Breckinridge 3
LONG, Charles D. 1
LONG, Charles Grant 2
LONG, Charles Ramsay 2
LONG, Chester I. 1
LONG, Crawford 1
Williamson
LONG, Cyril Norman Hugh 5
LONG, Daniel Albright 1
LONG, Earl Albert 5
LONG, Earl Kemp 4
LONG, Edward Harvey 4
LONG, Edward Henry 1
LONG, Edward Henry H
Carroll
LONG, Edward Vaughan 5
LONG, Eli 1
LONG, Ernest D. 5
LONG, Eugene Rufus 4
LONG, Frederick Able 4
LONG, George C. Jr. 3
LONG, George Edward 3
LONG, George Shannon 1
LONG, Haniel 1
LONG, Harriet Catherine 2
LONG, Henry Fletcher 1
LONG, Howard Hale 1
LONG, Huey Pierce 1

LONG, Hugh W. 4
LONG, James H
LONG, James Parker 5
LONG, John H
LONG, John D. 2
LONG, John Davis 1
LONG, John Dietrich 4
LONG, John G. 1
LONG, John Harper 1
LONG, John Luther 1
LONG, John Wesley 1
LONG, Joseph Harvey 3
LONG, Joseph Ragland 1
LONG, Le Roy 1
LONG, Lewis Marshall 3
LONG, LeRoy Downing 1
LONG, Lily Augusta 1
LONG, Lois 6
LONG, Luman Harrison 5
LONG, Mason 4
LONG, Maurice Alvin 1
LONG, Mitchell 3
LONG, Omera Floyd 2
LONG, Oren Ethelbirt 4
LONG, Orie William 3
LONG, Oscar Fitzalan 1
LONG, Percy Waldron 3
LONG, Perrin Hamilton 4
LONG, Pierse H
LONG, Ralph Herman 2
LONG, Ray 1
LONG, Robert Alexander 3
LONG, Robert Carey H
LONG, Robert Franklin 3
LONG, Rose McConnell 5
(Mrs. Huey P. Long)
LONG, Samuel Dismukes 4
LONG, Seely Frederick 1
LONG, Simon Cameron 1
LONG, Simon Peter 1
LONG, Stephen Harriman H
LONG, Theodore Kepner 2
LONG, Thomas George 6
LONG, Veldon Oscar 6
LONG, Walter 4
LONG, Walter E. 1
LONG, Wendell McLean 2
LONG, William Henry 1
LONG, William Joseph 3
LONG, William Lunsford 4
LONGACRE, Charles Smull 3
LONGACRE, James Barton H
LONGACRE, Lindsay 5
Bartholomew
LONGAN, Edward Everett 4
LONGAN, George Baker 1
LONGCOPE, Warfield 3
Theobald
LONGDEN, Aladine 1
Cummings
LONGDEN, Henry Boyer 2
LONGEST, Christopher 4
LONGEST, Christopher 5
Wadsworth
LONGFELLOW, A. 1
LONGFELLOW, Ernest H
Wadsworth
LONGFELLOW, Henry H
Wadsworth
LONGFELLOW, Samuel 1
LONGFELLOW, Stephen H
LONGFELLOW, Thomas 4
LONGFELLOW, William 1
Pitt Preble
LONGINO, Andrew 1
Houston
LONGINO, Olin Harrington 3
LONGLEY, Clifford Boles 3
LONGLEY, Edmund 1
Waters
LONGLEY, Francis 6
Fielding
LONGLEY, Harry Sherman 2
LONGLEY, W. H. 1
LONGLEY, William 6
Raymond
LONGMAID, Sydney 4
Esterbrook
LONGMAN, Evelyn 3
Beatrice
LONGNECKER, Edwin 1
LONGNECKER, Henry H
Clay
LONGSHORE, Hannah E. 1
LONGSTREET, Augustus H
Baldwin
LONGSTREET, Helen 4
Dortch
LONGSTREET, James 1
LONGSTREET, William H
LONGSTRETH, Charles 2
LONGSTRETH, Clyde 6
Marion
LONGSTRETH, Edward H
LONGSTRETH, Morris 4
LONGSWORTH, Walter Ira 4

LONGUA, Paul J. 6
LONGWELL, Chester Ray 6
LONGWELL, Daniel 5
LONGWELL, Oliver Henry 3
LONGWORTH, Nicholas H
LONGWORTH, Nicholas 1
LONGWORTH, Nicholas 4
  Murray
LONGWORTH, Raymond 6
  A.
LONGYEAR, Edmund 3
  Joseph
LONGYEAR, John Munro 1
LONGYEAR, John Wesley 6
LONGYEAR, Robert Davis 5
LONN, Ella 1
LONNQUIST, Carl Adolph 1
LONSDALE, John Gerdes 2
LONSDALE, John Tipton 4
LOOFBOUROW, John 3
  Robert
LOOKER, Thomas Henry 1
LOOMIS, Alfred F(ullerton) 5
LOOMIS, Alfred Lee 6
LOOMIS, Andrew Williams H
LOOMIS, Archibald Gilbert 1
LOOMIS, Arphaxed H
LOOMIS, Arthur Pope 4
LOOMIS, Benjamin 5
  Bloomfield
LOOMIS, C. Grant 4
LOOMIS, Charles Battell 1
LOOMIS, Charles Wheeler 3
LOOMIS, Chester 1
LOOMIS, Dwight 1
LOOMIS, Eben Jenks 1
LOOMIS, Edward Eugene 4
LOOMIS, Elmer Howard 1
LOOMIS, Francis Butler 2
LOOMIS, Francis Wheeler 6
LOOMIS, Frederic Brewster 1
LOOMIS, Frederic Morris 2
LOOMIS, Harold Francis 5
LOOMIS, Harvey 1
  Worthington
LOOMIS, Helen Augusta 5
LOOMIS, Henry M(eech) 3
LOOMIS, Henry P. 1
LOOMIS, James Lee 6
LOOMIS, John 5
LOOMIS, Kenneth Bradley 6
LOOMIS, Lafayette Charles 1
LOOMIS, Lee Pierson 4
LOOMIS, Leverett Mills 1
LOOMIS, Louise Ropes 3
LOOMIS, Madeleine 3
  Seymour
LOOMIS, Mahlon H
LOOMIS, Milton Early 6
LOOMIS, Nelson Henry 1
LOOMIS, Noel Miller 4
LOOMIS, Orland S. 2
LOOMIS, Robert H. 4
LOOMIS, Roger Sherman 4
LOOMIS, Ruth 3
LOOMIS, Samuel Lane 1
LOOMIS, Seymour Crane 1
LOOMIS, William 6
  Farnsworth
LOOMS, George 1
LOONEY, Marion A. 4
LOOP, Augustus Henry H
LOOP, Jennette Shepherd 1
LOOPER, Edward 3
  Anderson
LOOS, Charles Louis 4
LOOS, Isaac Althaus 1
LOOSE, Katharine Riegel 5
  ("Georg Schock")
LOPER, Don 5
LOPEZ, Aaron H
LOPEZ, Charles Albert 1
LOPEZ, Pumarejo Alfonso 5
LOPEZ-MATEOS, Adolfo 5
LOPP, William Thomas 1
LORAM, Charles 4
  Templeman
LORANCE, George Toel 6
LORAS, Jean Mathias H
  Pierre
LORBER, Herbert James 4
LORCH, Emil 5
LORD, Arthur 1
LORD, Asa Dearborn H
LORD, Augustus Mendon 4
LORD, Austin Willard 1
LORD, Bert 1
LORD, Charles Boyne 4
LORD, Charles King 4
LORD, Chester Bradford 1
LORD, Chester Sanders 1
LORD, Daniel 1
LORD, Daniel Aloysius 3
LORD, Daniel Miner 4
LORD, David Nevins H

LORD, Edward Thomas 5
  Sumner
LORD, Eleanor Louisa 4
LORD, Eleazar H
LORD, Everett William 4
LORD, Fred Townley 4
LORD, Frederic W. 3
LORD, Frederick Taylor 1
LORD, Frederick William H
LORD, George de Forest 2
LORD, Henry 1
LORD, Henry Curwen 1
LORD, Henry Gardner 4
LORD, Henry William H
LORD, Herbert Gardiner 1
LORD, Herbert Mayhew 1
LORD, Isabel Ely 1
LORD, J. Williams 1
LORD, James Brown 1
LORD, James Revell 6
LORD, John H
LORD, John 2
LORD, John Foley 5
LORD, John King 1
LORD, John Norton 4
LORD, John Prentiss 1
LORD, John W(hitaker) Jr. 1
LORD, Kenneth Prince 3
LORD, Lillos Montgomery 5
  (Mrs. John W. Lord Jr.)
LORD, Livingston G. 1
LORD, Louis Eleazer 3
LORD, Nathan 1
LORD, Nathaniel Wright 1
LORD, Otis Phillips 1
LORD, Pauline 3
LORD, Phillips H. 6
LORD, Rivington David 1
LORD, Robert Howard 3
LORD, Royal Bertram 5
LORD, Scott H
LORD, William Paine 1
LORD, William Sinclair 1
LORD, William Wilberforce 1
LORE, Charles Brown 1
LOREE, James Taber 5
LOREE, Leonor Fresnel 2
LORENZ, Daniel Edward 4
LORENZ, Henry William 5
  Frederick
LORENZ, Joseph 3
LORENZ, Julius 4
LORENZ, Keith 5
LORENZ, Max Otto 5
LORENZ, Richard 1
LORENZ, Rolland Carl 4
LORENZ, William 3
  Frederick
LORENZEN, Ernest Gustav 3
LORGE, Trving H
LORIGAN, William George 1
LORILLARD, Pierre H
LORILLARD, Pierre 1
LORIMER, George Claude 1
LORIMER, George Horace 1
LORIMER, William 1
LORIMER, Wright 1
LORIMIER, Pierre Louis H
LORING, Albert Carpenter 1
LORING, Augustus 1
  Peabody
LORING, Augustus 3
  Peabody Jr.
LORING, Charles 1
LORING, Charles Greely 1
LORING, Charles Harding 1
LORING, Edward Greely H
LORING, Ellis Gray 1
LORING, Emilie 3
LORING, Frederick H
  Wadsworth
LORING, George Bailey H
LORING, Homer 1
LORING, John Alden 2
LORING, Joshua * 1
LORING, Paule Stetson 5
LORING, Ralph Alden 3
LORING, Richard Tuttle 2
LORING, Victor Joseph 2
LORING, William Caleb 1
LORING, William Wing 1
LORNE, Marion 5
LORRE, Peter 4
LORTON, Eugene 2
LORWIN, Lewis L. 5
LORY, Charles Alfred 5
LOSE, George William 4
LOSEY, Frederick Douglas 1
LOSKIEL, George Henry H
LOSSING, Benson John H
LOSSING, Helen S. 4
LOTHIAN, Marquess of 1
LOTHROP, Amy 1
LOTHROP, Daniel 1
LOTHROP, Fannie Mack 5

LOTHROP, George Van H
  Ness
LOTHROP, Harriett 1
  Mulford
LOTHROP, Howard 1
  Augustus
LOTHROP, Marcus 1
  Thompson
LOTHROP, Samuel 4
  Kirkland
LOTHROP, Thornton 1
  Kirkland
LOTHROPP, John H
LOTKA, Alfred James 2
LOTSPEICH, Ethel Moore 4
LOTSPEICH, Roy Nicholas 3
LOTSPEICH, William 5
  Douglas
LOTT, Abraham Grant 1
LOTT, Charles H. 3
LOTT, Edson Schuyler 1
LOTTE, Edward F. L. 1
LOTTRIDGE, Silas A. 4
LOTZ, John 6
LOTZ, John R. 4
LOTZ, Oscar 1
LOUBAT, Joseph Florimund 4
  Duc de
LOUCHHEIM, Walter 5
  Clinton Jr.
LOUCKS, Charles Olney 4
LOUCKS, Elton Crocker 5
LOUCKS, Philip G. 4
LOUCKS, William Dewey 3
LOUD, Annie Frances 4
LOUD, Eugene Francis 1
LOUD, Frank Herbert 1
LOUD, George Alvin 1
LOUD, Henry Martin 4
LOUD, John Hermann 5
LOUDEN, Frederic Alic 4
LOUDEN, William 1
LOUDENSLAGER, Henry 1
  Clay
LOUDERBACK, George 3
  Davis
LOUDERBACK, Harold 1
LOUDERBACK, William 1
  Johnson
LOUDON, A. 3
LOUDON, Jonkheer John 4
LOUDON, Samuel H
LOUDOUN, 4th earl H
LOUGEE, Francis Eaton 6
LOUGEE, Willis Eugene 1
LOUGH, James Edwin 3
LOUGH, Samuel Alexander 4
LOUGH, William Henry 6
LOUGHAN, Mrs. Katherine 6
  O'Neil
LOUGHBOROUGH, James 2
  Fairfax
LOUGHEAD, Flora Haines 4
LOUGHEED, William 4
  Foster
LOUGHIN, Charles A. 4
LOUGHLIN, Gerald 2
  Francis
LOUGHLIN, John H
LOUGHRAN, John T. 3
LOUGHRIDGE, Robert 4
  Hills
LOUGHRIDGE, Robert H
  McGill
LOUGHRIDGE, William H
LOUIS, Andrew 5
LOUIS, John Jeffry 3
LOUIS, Max C. 4
LOUNSBERRY, Frank 1
  Burton
LOUNSBURY, Charles 3
  Edwin
LOUNSBURY, George 1
  Edward
LOUNSBURY, George 3
  Fenner
LOUNSBURY, James 6
  Breckinridge
LOUNSBURY, Phineas 1
  Chapman
LOUNSBURY, Ralph Reed 1
LOUNSBURY, Thomas 1
  Raynesford
LOURIE, Arthur 4
LOURIE, David A. 1
LOUTFI, Omar 4
LOUTHAN, Hattie Horner 5
LOUTHAN, Henry 3
  Thompson
LOUTHERBOURG, H
  Annibale Christian Henry
  de
LOUTTIT, Chauncey 3
  McKinley
LOUTTIT, George William 4

LOUTTIT, William Easton 5
  Jr.
LOUTZENHEISER, Joe L. 2
LOUW, Eric Hendrik 5
LOVATT, George Ignatius 5
LOVE, Albert Gallatin 5
LOVE, Albert Irving 5
LOVE, Alfred Henry 1
LOVE, Andrew Leo 4
LOVE, Charles Everts 3
LOVE, Cornelius Ruxton Jr. 5
LOVE, Don Lathrop 1
LOVE, Edgar Amos 6
LOVE, Edward Bainbridge 5
LOVE, Emanuel King H
LOVE, Frank Samuel 1
LOVE, Harry Houser 4
LOVE, J. Mack 1
LOVE, James H
LOVE, James Jay 4
LOVE, James Lee 5
LOVE, James Sanford Jr. 5
LOVE, James Spencer 4
LOVE, John H
LOVE, John W. 3
LOVE, Julian Price 5
LOVE, Peter Early H
LOVE, Robertus 1
LOVE, Smoloff Palace 1
LOVE, Stephen Hunter 1
LOVE, Thomas Bell 2
LOVE, Thomas Cutting H
LOVE, Thomas J. 3
LOVE, William Carter H
LOVE, William De Loss 1
LOVEJOY, Arthur Oncken 4
LOVEJOY, Asa Lawrence H
LOVEJOY, Clarence Earle 6
LOVEJOY, Elijah Parish 6
LOVEJOY, Esther Pohl 4
LOVEJOY, Francis Thomas 1
  Fletcher
LOVEJOY, Frank William 2
LOVEJOY, George Edwards 1
LOVEJOY, George Newell 4
LOVEJOY, Hatton 6
LOVEJOY, Jesse Robert 2
LOVEJOY, John Meston 5
LOVEJOY, Owen H
LOVEJOY, Owen Reed 4
LOVEJOY, Philip 4
LOVEJOY, Thomas E. 1
LOVELACE, Curtis M. 4
LOVELACE, Delos Wheeler 4
LOVELACE, Francis H
LOVELACE, William 4
  Randolph II
LOVELAND, Albert J. 4
LOVELAND, Edward 4
  Rutherford
LOVELAND, Francis 1
  William
LOVELAND, Gilbert 3
LOVELAND, Hansell 6
  William
LOVELAND, Seymour 4
  Austin Hamilton
LOVELAND, William H
LOVELL, Alfred Henry 4
LOVELL, Earl B. 4
LOVELL, Ernest James Jr. 6
LOVELL, George Blakeman 6
LOVELL, James H
LOVELL, John H
LOVELL, John Epy 1
LOVELL, John Harvey 1
LOVELL, Joseph H
LOVELL, Malcolm R. 6
LOVELL, Mansfield 1
LOVELL, Moses Richardson 2
LOVELL, Ralph L. 2
LOVELL, Walter Raleigh 5
LOVELY, John A. 1
LOVEMAN, Amy 5
LOVEMAN, Robert 1
LOVERIDGE, Blanche 1
  Grosbec
LOVERIDGE, Earl W. 3
LOVERING, Charles T. 4
LOVERING, Henry Bacon 1
LOVERING, Joseph 1
LOVERING, William C. 1
LOVET-LORSKI, Boris 4
LOVETT, Archibald Battle 2
LOVETT, Edgar Odell 3
LOVETT, John H
LOVETT, Robert H. 1
LOVETT, Robert Morss 1
LOVETT, Robert Scott 1
LOVETT, Robert 5
  Williamson
LOVETT, William Cuyler 5
LOVETTE, Joyce Metz 5
LOVETTE, Leland Pearson 4
LOVETTE, Leland Pearson 5
LOVETTE, Oscar Byrd 1

LOVEWELL, John H
LOVEWELL, Joseph Taplin 1
LOVEWELL, Samuel 4
  Harrison
LOVING, Starling 1
LOVINS, William Thomas 4
LOVITT, William Vernon 6
LOVRE, Harold O. 5
LOW, A. Augustus 4
LOW, Sir A. Maurice 1
LOW, Abiel Abbot H
LOW, Abraham Adolph 3
LOW, Albert Howard 1
LOW, Benjamin Robbins 1
  Curtis
LOW, Berthe Julienne 1
LOW, David 4
LOW, Ethelbert Ide 2
LOW, Francis Stuart 4
LOW, Frederick Ferdinand H
LOW, Frederick Rollins 1
LOW, Isaac H
LOW, Juliette Gordon H
LOW, Juliette Gordon 4
LOW, Marcus A. 1
LOW, Mrs. Marie Dickson 3
LOW, Mary Fairchild 2
LOW, Nicholas H
LOW, Seth 1
LOW, Will Hicok 1
LOW, William Gilman 1
LOWBER, James William 1
LOWDEN, Frank Orren 2
LOWDEN, Isabel 3
LOWDERMILK, Patricia 1
  Cannales
LOWDERMILK, Walter 6
  Clay
LOWE, Arthur Houghton 1
LOWE, Charles H
LOWE, Clarence George 4
LOWE, Clement Belton 4
LOWE, Clowney Oswald 6
LOWE, David Perley H
LOWE, Donald Vaughn 5
LOWE, Elias Avery 5
LOWE, Emily Lynch 4
LOWE, Ephraim Noble 1
LOWE, Frank E. 5
LOWE, George Hale 4
LOWE, Herman A. 4
LOWE, Joe 1
LOWE, John 1
LOWE, John Smith 3
LOWE, John William 2
LOWE, Louis Robert 5
LOWE, Louise 1
LOWE, Malcolm Branson 3
LOWE, Martha Perry 1
LOWE, Ralph Phillips H
LOWE, Richard Barrett 5
LOWE, Stanley 5
LOWE, Thaddeus S. C. 1
LOWE, Thomas Merritt 4
LOWE, Titus 3
LOWE, Walter Irenaeus 1
LOWE, William Baird 2
LOWE, William Herman 4
LOWE, William Webb 4
LOWELL, Abbott Lawrence 2
LOWELL, Amy H
LOWELL, Daniel Ozro 1
  Smith
LOWELL, Delmar Rial 1
LOWELL, Edward Jackson H
LOWELL, Francis Cabot H
LOWELL, Francis Cabot 1
LOWELL, Guy 1
LOWELL, James Arnold 1
LOWELL, James Harrison 2
LOWELL, James Russell H
LOWELL, Joan 4
LOWELL, John * H
LOWELL, John 1
LOWELL, Josephine Shaw 1
LOWELL, Joshua Adams H
LOWELL, Orson 3
LOWELL, Percival 1
LOWELL, Robert Traill H
  Spence
LOWELL, Sherman James 1
LOWEN, Charles Jules Jr. 3
LOWENBERG, Bettie 4
LOWENSTEIN, Henry Polk 5
LOWENSTEIN, Lloyd L. 4
LOWENSTEIN, Melvyn 5
  Gordon
LOWENSTEIN, Solomon 1
LOWENSTINE, Mandel 3
LOWER, Christian 4
LOWER, William Edgar 4
LOWEREE, F. Harold 1
LOWES, John Livingston 3
LOWETH, Charles 1
  Frederick
LOWIE, Robert Harry 3

LOWMAN, Arthur Ames 6
LOWMAN, Charles Le Roy 6
LOWMAN, Harmon 5
LOWMAN, Seymour 1
LOWMAN, Webster B. 1
LOWNDES, Arthur 1
LOWNDES, Charles Henry 5
 Tilghman
LOWNDES, Charles Lucien 4
 Baker
LOWNDES, Lloyd 1
LOWNDES, Mary Elizabeth 2
LOWNDES, Rawlins H
LOWNDES, Thomas 1
LOWNDES, William H
LOWNEY, Walter M. 1
LOWNSBERY, Charles 5
 Hatch
LOWREY, Bill G. 2
LOWREY, Frederick Jewett 4
LOWREY, Harvey H. 4
LOWREY, Lawson Gentry 3
LOWREY, Mark Perrin 4
LOWRIE, James Walter 4
LOWRIE, John Cameron 1
LOWRIE, Rebecca 6
 Lawrence
LOWRIE, Samuel 1
 Thompson
LOWRIE, Walter H
LOWRIE, Walter 5
LOWRIE, Will Leonard 2
LOWRY, D. R. 3
LOWRY, Edith Belle 2
LOWRY, Edith C. 5
LOWRY, Edward George 2
LOWRY, Fesington Carlyle 4
LOWRY, Frank Clifford 5
LOWRY, Frank J. 3
LOWRY, H(omer) H(iram) 5
LOWRY, Hiram Harrison 4
LOWRY, Horace 1
LOWRY, Howard Foster 4
LOWRY, Howard James 4
LOWRY, John 4
LOWRY, Joseph E. 4
LOWRY, Malcolm 4
LOWRY, Robert * 1
LOWRY, Thomas 4
LOWRY, Thomas Claude 2
LOWSLEY, Oswald 3
 Swinney
LOWSTUTER, William 3
 Jackson *
LOWTH, Frank James 5
LOWTHER, Granville 1
LOWTHER, Hugh Sears 3
LOWY, Alexander 1
LOY, Matthias 1
LOY, Sylvester K. 3
LOYALL, George H
LOYALL, George Robert 1
LOZIER, Clemence Sophia H
 Harned
LOZIER, Ralph Fulton 2
LOZNER, Joseph 6
LOZOWICK, Louis 6
LUBBOCK, Francis Richard 1
LUBECK, Henry 1
LUBEROFF, George 6
LUBIN, David 1
LUBIN, Simon Julius 1
LUBITSCH, Ernst 2
LUBKE, Carl Heinrich 5
LUBOMIRSKI, Prince 1
 Casimir
LUBSCHEZ, Ben Judah 6
LUBY, James 1
LUBY, Sylvester Daniel 4
LUCAS, Albert Hawley 5
LUCAS, Albert Pike 2
LUCAS, Anthony Francis 1
LUCAS, Arthur 4
LUCAS, Arthur Fletcher 2
LUCAS, Arthur Melville 2
LUCAS, Daniel Bedinger 1
LUCAS, Douglas P. 6
LUCAS, Edward H
LUCAS, Francis Ferdinand 4
LUCAS, Frederic Augustus 1
LUCAS, J. Lynn 6
LUCAS, James Clarence 6
 Merryman
LUCAS, James H. H
LUCAS, Jim Griffing 5
LUCAS, John Baptiste 1
 Charles
LUCAS, John Henry 1
LUCAS, John Porter 2
LUCAS, Johnathan 1
LUCAS, Jonathan H
LUCAS, Leo Sherman 4
LUCAS, Noah 4
LUCAS, Oliver G. 3
LUCAS, Robert 1
LUCAS, Robert H. 2

LUCAS, Scott Wike 4
LUCAS, Thomas John 4
LUCAS, William H
LUCAS, William Cardwell 3
LUCAS, William Palmer 4
LUCCHESI, Pascal Francis 6
LUCCOCK, Emory Wylie 1
LUCCOCK, George 1
 Naphtali
LUCCOCK, George 2
 Naphtall
LUCCOCK, Halford Edward 4
LUCCOCK, Naphtali 1
LUCE, Alice Hanson 1
LUCE, Cyrus Gray 1
LUCE, Edgar Augustine 3
LUCE, Harry James 4
LUCE, Henry Gardner 3
LUCE, Henry Robinson 4
LUCE, Robert 2
LUCE, Stephen Bleecker 1
LUCEY, Dennis Benedict 1
LUCEY, Patrick Joseph 4
LUCEY, Patrick Joseph 4
LUCEY, Thomas Elmore 5
LUCIER, Phillip Joseph 5
LUCKE, Balduin 3
LUCKE, Charles Edward 4
LUCKENBACH, Edgar 2
 Frederick
LUCKENBACH, Edgar 6
 Frederick Jr.
LUCKENBACH, John 3
 Lewis
LUCKENBILL, Daniel 1
 David
LUCKEY, David Franklin 5
LUCKEY, George 1
 Washington Andrew
LUCKEY, Henry Carl 3
LUCKEY, James S. 1
LUCKEY, Robert Burneston 6
LUCKHARDT, Arno 3
 Benedict
LUCKIESH, Matthew 4
LUCKING, Alfred 1
LUCKING, William Alfred 4
LUDDEN, Patrick Anthony 1
LUDDY, Michael G(abriel) 5
LUDELING, John Theodore H
LUDERS, Gustav Carl 1
LUDEWIG, Jos W. 3
LUDIN, Mohammed Kahir 1
 Crosby
LUDINGTON, Arthur 1
 Henry
LUDINGTON, Charles 1
 Henry
LUDINGTON, Marshall 1
 Independence
LUDLAM, Reuben 1
LUDLOW, Arthur Clyde 1
LUDLOW, Daniel H
LUDLOW, Edwin 1
LUDLOW, F. Milton 3
LUDLOW, Fitz Hugh H
LUDLOW, Gabriel George H
LUDLOW, George C. 1
LUDLOW, George Duncan H
LUDLOW, Henry Gilbert 1
LUDLOW, Henry Hunt 2
LUDLOW, Jacob Lott 1
LUDLOW, James Meeker 1
LUDLOW, James Minor 6
LUDLOW, Louis Leon 3
LUDLOW, Nicoll 1
LUDLOW, Noah Miller H
LUDLOW, Roger 1
LUDLOW, Theodore 4
 Russell
LUDLOW, Thomas William H
LUDLOW, William 1
LUDLOW, William Orr 3
LUDLUM, Clarence Allen 1
LUDLUM, Seymour DeWitt 3
LUDOVICI, Alice Emelie 1
LUDWELL, Philip 1
LUDWICK, Christopher H
LUDWIG, Charles H(eyler) 5
LUDWIG, Emil 4
LUDWIG, Sylvester 4
 Theodore
LUDY, Llewellyn V. 3
LUEBKE, Melvin William 6
LUECK, Martin Lawrence 4
LUECKE, John 3
LUECKE, Martin 1
LUEDDE, William Henry 3
LUEDEKING, Robert 1
LUEDER, Arthur Charles 3
LUEDKE, August J. 3
LUELLING, Henderson H
LUERS, John Henry H
LUETTE, Eleanor (Mrs. 5
 Paul Luette Jr.)
LUFF, Ralph Gordon 4
LUFKIN, Elgood Chauncey 1

LUFKIN, Garland 3
LUFKIN, Wilfred W. 1
LUFKIN, Willfred 3
 Weymouth Jr.
LUGG, Charles Henry 4
LUGG, Thomas Bransford 5
LUHAN, Mabel Dodge 4
LUHN, Hans Peter 4
LUHRING, Oscar Raymond 2
LUHRS, Henry Ernest 1
LUHRSEN, Julius G. 4
LUKA, Milo 3
LUKAS, Edwin Jay 6
LUKAS, Paul 3
LUKE, Arthur Fuller 1
LUKE, Edmon G. 5
LUKE, Thomas 2
LUKEMAN, Augustus 1
LUKEN, Martin Girard 5
LUKENS, Herman Tyson 2
LUKENS, Rebecca Webb H
 Pennock
LUKIN, Charles James 4
LUKS, George Benjamin 1
LULEK, Ralph Norbert 5
LULL, Cabot 5
LULL, Edward Phelps 1
LULL, Gerard Bramley 5
LULL, Henry Morris 2
LULL, Herbert Galen 1
LULL, Richard Swann 3
LUM, David Walker 1
LUM, Ralph Emerson 3
LUM, Ralph Emerson Jr. 6
LUMBROZO, Jacob 1
LUMLEY, Frederick Elmore 3
LUMMIS, Charles Fletcher 1
LUMMUS, Henry Tilton 4
LUMPKIN, Alva Moore 1
LUMPKIN, John Henry H
LUMPKIN, Joseph Henry 6
LUMPKIN, Joseph Henry 1
LUMPKIN, Samuel 1
LUMPKIN, Wilson H
LUMSDEN, Leslie Leon 2
LUMSDON, Christine 1
 Marie
LUNA, Solomon 1
LUNA, Tranquilino H
LUNA Y ARELLANO, H
 Tristan de
LUND, Charles Carroll 5
LUND, Chester Benford 4
LUND, Emil 1
LUND, Franze Edward 6
LUND, Fred Bates 4
LUND, Frederick Hansen 4
LUND, Lawrence Henry 3
LUND, Robert Leathan 3
LUNDAY, Charles G. 5
LUNDBECK, Gustaf Hilmer 2
LUNDBERG, Alfred J. 3
LUNDBERG, Charles J. 2
LUNDBERG, Clarence 1
 Harry
LUNDBERG, Frank A. 5
LUNDBORG, Florence 2
LUNDEBERG, Harry 3
LUNDEEN, Ernest 1
LUNDELL, Gustav Ernst 3
 Fredrick
LUNDERMAN, Charles 6
 Johnson Jr.
LUNDIE, Edwin Hugh 4
LUNDIE, John 1
LUNDIGAN, William 6
LUNDIN, Carl Axel Robert 1
LUNDIN, Frederick 1
LUND-QUIST, Carl E. 4
LUNDQUIST, Harold 3
 Leonard
LUNDSTRUM, Allan 5
 Winston
LUNDY, Ayres Derby 4
LUNDY, Benjamin H
LUNDY, Elmer Johnston 2
LUNDY, Frank Arthur 6
LUNDY, James Andrew 4
LUNDY, Wilson Thomas 4
LUNG, George Augustus 1
LUNGER, John B. 1
LUNGREN, Fernand 4
 Harvey
LUNING, Henry Herman 6
LUNKEN, Edmund H. 2
LUNKEN, Eshelby F. 3
LUNN, Arthur Constant 1
LUNN, George Richard 2
LUNSFORD, William 1
LUNT, George H
LUNT, Horace Gray 4
LUNT, Orrington 1
LUNT, William Edward 4
LUPTON, Charles Thomas 1
LUPTON, John Thomas 4
LUQUER, Lea McIlvaine 1

LUQUIENS, Frederick Bliss 1
LURCAT, Jean-Marie 4
LURIE, Harry Lawrence 6
LURIE, Louis Robert 5
LURIE, Ted R. 6
LURTON, Douglas 3
 Ellsworth
LURTON, Horace Harmon 1
LUSE, Claude Zeph 1
LUSH, Charles Keeler 4
LUSK, Clayton Riley 3
LUSK, Frank Stillman 1
LUSK, Georgia L. (Mrs.) 5
LUSK, Graham 1
LUSK, James Loring 1
LUSK, James W. 4
LUSK, Willard Clayton 1
LUSK, William Foster 5
LUSK, William Thompson H
LUST, Adeline Cohnfeld 1
LUSTIG, Alvin 3
LUSTMAN, Seymour 5
 Leonard
LUSTRAT, Joseph 1
LUTEN, Daniel Benjamin 2
LUTERBRIDGE, Eugene 1
 Harvey
LUTES, Delia Thompson 2
LUTHER, Edwin Cornelius 1
LUTHER, Flavel Sweeten 1
LUTHER, Hans 4
LUTHER, John Carlyle 5
LUTHER, Mark Lee 2
LUTHER, Seth H
LUTHER, Willard 4
 Blackinton
LUTHRINGER, George 3
 Francis
LUTHULI, Albert John 4
LUTHY, Fred 4
LUTKIN, Peter Christian 1
LUTTERBECK, Eugene 6
 Feistmann
LUTTRELL, John E. 5
LUTTRELL, John King H
LUTZ, Alma 6
LUTZ, Brenton Reid 4
LUTZ, Charles Abner 2
LUTZ, E. Russell 5
LUTZ, Edwin George 4
LUTZ, Frank Eugene 2
LUTZ, Frank J. 1
LUTZ, George Washington 4
LUTZ, Grace Livingston 2
LUTZ, Harley Leist 6
LUTZ, Parke Henry 2
LUTZ, Philip 2
LUTZ, Ralph Haswell 5
LUTZ, Samuel G. 3
LUTZ, William A. 4
LUXFORD, Ansel F(rank) 1
LUXFORD, G(eorge) 6
 A(lfred)
LUYTIES, Carl Johann 1
LUZ, Kadish 5
LYALL, James 1
LYALL, Toni Owen 5
LYBARGER, Donald Fisher 5
LYBARGER, Lee Francis 2
LYBRAND, Archibald 1
LYBRAND, Walter 6
 Archibald
LYBYER, Albert Howe 2
LYDECKER, Charles 1
 Edward
LYDECKER, F. A. 4
LYDECKER, Garit 1
 Abraham
LYDECKER, Garrett J. 1
LYDENBERG, Harry 3
 Miller
LYDENBERG, Harry 4
 Miller
LYDER, Jay W. 5
LYDICK, Jesse·Dean 2
LYDON, Eugene K. 4
LYDON, Richard Paul 2
LYDSTON, G. Frank 1
LYETH, J. M. Richardson 3
LYFORD, James Otis 1
LYFORD, Oliver Smith 1
LYFORD, Oliver Smith 3
LYFORD, Will Hartwell 1
LYKES, Joseph T. 4
LYLE, Aaron 1
LYLE, Benjamin Franklin H
LYLE, Clay 5
LYLE, Eugene P. Jr. 5
LYLE, Henry Hamilton 1
 Moore
LYLE, Hubert Samuel 1
LYLE, William Thomas 1
LYMAN, Albert Josiah 1
LYMAN, Alexander Steele 4
LYMAN, Amy Brown 4
LYMAN, Arthur Theodore 1

LYMAN, Benjamin Smith 1
LYMAN, Charles 1
LYMAN, Charles Baldwin 1
LYMAN, Charles 2
 Huntington
LYMAN, Charles 5
 Huntington III
LYMAN, Chester Smith H
LYMAN, Chester Wolcott 1
LYMAN, David Brainerd 1
LYMAN, David Russell 3
LYMAN, Edward Branch 5
LYMAN, Edward Brandon 6
LYMAN, Edward Dean 4
LYMAN, Elias 1
LYMAN, Elmer Adelbert 1
LYMAN, Eugene William 2
LYMAN, Evelyn May 6
LYMAN, Frank 4
LYMAN, Frank Hubbard 4
LYMAN, Frederick Wolcott 1
LYMAN, George Dunlap 3
LYMAN, George Richard 1
LYMAN, George Richards 1
LYMAN, Harry Webster 1
LYMAN, Hart 1
LYMAN, Henry Darius 1
LYMAN, Henry Munson 1
LYMAN, Homer Childs 1
LYMAN, James 1
LYMAN, Joseph H
LYMAN, Joseph 1
LYMAN, Joseph Bardwell H
LYMAN, Joseph Stebbins 1
LYMAN, Lauren Dwight 5
LYMAN, Mary Ely 6
LYMAN, Phineas H
LYMAN, Richard Roswell 1
LYMAN, Robert Hunt 1
LYMAN, Ronald Theodore 6
LYMAN, Rufus Ashley 3
LYMAN, Samuel H
LYMAN, Sarah E. 1
LYMAN, Theodore * H
LYMAN, Theodore 3
LYMAN, William H
LYMAN, William Denison 1
LYMER, Elmer E. 1
LYMER, William Barker 1
LYNCH, Anna 2
LYNCH, C. Arthur 4
LYNCH, Charles H
LYNCH, Charles 4
LYNCH, Charles F. 2
LYNCH, Charles Wesley 1
LYNCH, Clyde Alvin 3
LYNCH, Daniel Joseph 3
LYNCH, Edward James 2
LYNCH, Ella Frances 2
LYNCH, Florence 3
LYNCH, Frank Worthington 2
LYNCH, Frederick 1
LYNCH, Frederick Bicknell 1
LYNCH, Frederick J. 3
LYNCH, George Arthur 4
LYNCH, James Daniel 1
LYNCH, James Kennedy 1
LYNCH, James Mathew 1
LYNCH, James William 4
LYNCH, Jeremiah 1
LYNCH, Jerome Morley 3
LYNCH, John H
LYNCH, John A. 1
LYNCH, John David 1
LYNCH, John Fairfield 1
LYNCH, John Joseph 1
LYNCH, John Roy 1
LYNCH, Joseph Bertram 4
LYNCH, Joseph Patrick 3
LYNCH, Kenneth Merrill 6
LYNCH, Matthew 1
 Christoper
LYNCH, Patrick Neeson H
LYNCH, Raymond A. 5
LYNCH, Robert Newton 1
LYNCH, Thomas * H
LYNCH, Thomas Francis 5
LYNCH, Walter A. 3
LYNCH, Walton D. 4
LYNCH, Warren J. 1
LYNCH, Willard A. 5
LYNCH, William Francis 1
LYNCH, William Orlando 1
LYND, Robert Staughton 5
LYNDE, Benjamin H
LYNDE, Carleton John 5
LYNDE, Francis 1
LYNDE, Samuel Adams H
LYNDE, William Pitt 1
LYNDON, Lamar 4
LYNDS, Elam H
LYNE, James Garnett 4
LYNE, Wickliffe Campbell 1
LYNETT, Edward James 5
LYNETT, Edward James 5
LYNETT, Elizabeth Ruddy 6

LYNN, Charles J. 3
LYNN, David 4
LYNN, Harry Hudson 3
LYNN, Robert Henry 3
LYNN, Robert Marshall 1
LYNN, Thomas Edward 6
LYON, A. Maynard 1
LYON, Adrian 5
LYON, Alfred E. 4
LYON, Andrew Hutchinson 4
LYON, Anne Bozeman 4
LYON, Asa H
LYON, B. B. Vincent 6
LYON, Bertrand 6
LYON, Caleb H
LYON, Cecil Andrew 1
LYON, Charles Gershom 6
LYON, Clyde Laten 6
LYON, David Gordon 1
LYON, Dorsey Alfred 2
LYON, Edmund 1
LYON, Edmund Daniel 2
LYON, Edwin Bowman 4
LYON, Eldridge Merick 1
LYON, Elias Potter 1
LYON, Ernest 2
LYON, Ernest Neal 1
LYON, Francis Strother H
LYON, Frank 3
LYON, Frank Emory 2
LYON, Frederick Saxton 2
LYON, George Armstrong 1
LYON, George F. 1
LYON, George Harry 3
LYON, Gideon Allen 3
LYON, Hastings 3
LYON, Henry Ware 1
LYON, Herb 5
LYON, Homer LeGrand 4
LYON, J(ames) Adair 5
LYON, James H
LYON, James Alexander 3
LYON, John Denniston 1
LYON, John Stanley 4
LYON, Leonard Saxton 4
LYON, Leverett Samuel 4
LYON, LeRoy Springs 1
LYON, Lucius 6
LYON, Marcus Ward Jr. 2
LYON, Mary H
LYON, Matthew H
LYON, Milford Hall 5
LYON, Nathaniel H
LYON, Nelson Reed 5
LYON, Pritchett Alfred 4
LYON, Scott Cary 2
LYON, T. Lyttleton 1
LYON, Walter Jefferson 4
LYON, William Alexander 6
LYON, William Henry 1
LYON, William Penn 1
LYONS, Albert Brown 1
LYONS, Chalmers J. 1
LYONS, Champ 1
LYONS, Charles William 1
LYONS, Charlton Havard 5
LYONS, Coleburke 5
LYONS, Dennis Francis 4
LYONS, Gerald Edward 2
LYONS, James J. 1
LYONS, John Frederick 6
LYONS, John Sprole 2
LYONS, Joseph Henry 6
LYONS, Judson Whitlocke 1
LYONS, Julius J. 1
LYONS, Katharine 1
LYONS, Lucile Manning 1
LYONS, Peter H
LYONS, Robert Edward 2
LYONS, Samuel Ross 1
LYONS, Thomas Richard 1
LYONS, Timothy Augustine 1
LYSTER, Henry Francis Le H
Hunte
LYSTER, Theodore Charles 1
LYTE, E. Oram 1
LYTELL, Bert 3
LYTER, Jean Curtis 1
LYTLE, Almon Wheeler 4
LYTLE, J. Horace 4
LYTLE, Robert Todd H
LYTLE, William Haines H
LYTTLETON, Oliver 5
LYTTLETON, William 1
Henry
LYTTON, Bart 5

M

MAAG, William Frederick 5
Jr.
MAAS, Anthony J. 1
MAAS, Carlos J. 5
MAAS, Melvin Joseph 4
MAASKE, Roben J. 3

MAASS, Herbert Halsey 3
MAASS, Otto 4
MABBOTT, Thomas Ollive 5
MABEE, George W. 2
MABERY, Charles Frederic 5
MABEY, Charles R. 5
MABIE, Edward Charles 3
MABIE, Hamilton Wright 1
MABIE, Henry Clay 1
MABIE, Louise Kennedy 3
MABLEY, Jackie Moms 6
MABON, Thomas McCance 4
MABRY, Milton Harvey 4
MABURY, Margaret Ellis 1
MAC CALLUM, John 5
Bruce
MAC DONALD, William J. 5
MAC LEOD-THORP, L. E. 2
G.
MAC MULLAN, Ralph A. 5
MAC VEY, William Pitt 5
MAC ADAM, George 4
Hartley
MAC AFEE, John Blair 1
MACAGY, Douglas 6
Guernsey
MACALARNEY, Robert 2
Emmet
MACALESTER, Charles * H
MACALISTER, Sir Ian 3
MAC ALISTER, James 1
MACALLISTER, Archibald 4
Thomas Jr.
MAC ALPINE, Robert John 1
MACANALLY, James R. 5
MACARTHUR, Alfred 4
MAC ARTHUR, Archibald 1
MAC ARTHUR, Arthur * 1
MAC ARTHUR, Arthur 1
Frederic
MACARTHUR, Charles 3
MACARTHUR, Douglas 4
MACARTHUR, Harry 6
MAC ARTHUR, James 1
MACARTHUR, John R. 1
MACARTHUR, John R. 1
MACARTHUR, Robert 5
Helmer
MAC ARTHUR, Robert 1
Stuart
MACARTHUR, Ruth 6
Alberta Brown
MAC ARTHUR, Walter 4
MACARTNEY, Clarence 3
Edward Noble
MACARTNEY, John W. 5
MACARTNEY, Thomas 1
Benton Jr.
MACAULAY, Fannie 2
Caldwell
MACAULAY, Fannie 4
Caldwell
MACAULAY, Frederick 5
Robertson
MACAULAY, Malcolm 6
George
MACAULAY, Peter Stewart 4
MACAULEY, Alvan 3
MACAULEY, Charles 1
Raymond
MACAULEY, Charles 5
Raymond
MACAULEY, Edward 4
MACAULEY, Irving P. 4
MACBETH, Alexander 2
Barksdale
MACBETH, Florence 4
MACBETH, George 1
Alexander
MACBETH, George Duff 4
MACBETH, Henry 4
MACBRAYNE, Lewis E. 3
MACBRIDE, D. S. 3
MACBRIDE, Philip Douglas 4
MACBRIDE, Thomas 1
Huston
MACCALLA, Clifford 1
Sheron
MACCALLUM, John 2
Archibald
MACCALLUM, William 2
George
MAC CAMERON, Robert 1
MACCARTHY, Gerald 6
R(aleigh)
MACCARTY, William 1
Carpenter
MACCAUD, Francis 5
William
MACCAUGHEY, Vaughan 3
MAC CAULEY, Clay 1
MACCHESNEY, Chester 4
M.
MACCHESNEY, Clara 5
Taggart

MACCHESNEY, Nathan 3
William
MACCLINTOCK, Paul 5
MACCLINTOCK, Samuel 5
MAC CLINTOCK, William 1
Darnall
MACCLOSKEY, James 5
Edward Jr.
MACCOLL, Alexander 5
MAC COLL, James 1
Roberton
MAC COLL, William Bogle 1
MACCOLL, William 1
Hamilton
MAC CONNELL, Charles 1
Jenkins
MACCONNELL, John 3
Wilson
MAC CORD, Charles 1
William
MACCORKLE, Emmett 1
Wallace
MAC CORKLE, William 1
Alexander
MACCORMACK, Daniel 1
William
MACCORNACK, Walter 4
Roy
MACCORRY, P. J. 4
MAC COUN, Townsend 1
MACCOY, William Logan 2
MAC CRACKEN, Henry 1
Mitchell
MACCRACKEN, Henry 5
Noble
MACCRACKEN, John 2
Henry
MACCRACKEN, William 5
Patterson Jr.
MACCULLOUGH, Gleason 3
Harvey
MACCURDY, George 2
Grant
MACCUTCHEON, Aleck 3
MAC DANIEL, Frank 1
MACDANIEL, Robert D. 1
MAC DILL, David 1
MACDONALD, Alexander 1
MACDONALD, Alexander 2
Black
MACDONALD, Angus 3
Lewis
MACDONALD, Anna 1
Addams
MACDONALD, Archibald 1
Arnott
MAC DONALD, Arthur 1
MACDONALD, Arthur Jay 4
MACDONALD, Augustin 5
Sylvester
MACDONALD, Bernard 1
Callaghan
MACDONALD, Betty 3
MACDONALD, Byrnes 3
MACDONALD, Carlos 1
Frederick
MACDONALD, Charles 1
MACDONALD, Duncan 2
Black
MACDONALD, Edwina 6
LeVin
MACDONALD, George 4
MACDONALD, George 1
Alexander
MACDONALD, George 1
Everett
MACDONALD, George 2
Saxe
MACDONALD, Godfrey 4
MACDONALD, Gordon 1
MACDONALD, Henry 3
MACDONALD, Ian 5
(Gibbs)
MACDONALD, James 1
Allan
MACDONALD, James R. 4
MACDONALD, James H
Wilson Alexander
MACDONALD, James 1
Wilson Alexander
MACDONALD, Jeanette 4
MACDONALD, Jesse Juan 5
MACDONALD, John 2
Alexander
MACDONALD, John H. 4
MACDONALD, John 1
William
MACDONALD, Katherine 6
Cunningham (Mrs.George
Field MacDonald)
MACDONALD, Milton 4
Tenney
MACDONALD, Milton 6
Theodore
MACDONALD, Moses H

MACDONALD, Neil 1
Carnot
MACDONALD, Pirie 2
MACDONALD, Ranald H
MACDONALD, Robert 4
MACDONALD, Thomas 3
Harris
MAC DONALD, William 1
MACDONALD, William 4
Alexander
MACDONALD, William H. 1
MACDONALD, Willis 1
Goss
MACDONALD-WRIGHT, 6
Stanton
MACDONALL, Angus 1
MACDONNELL, James 6
Francis Carlin;
MACDONNELL, Ronald 6
Macalister
MACDONOUGH, Thomas H
MACDOUGAL, Daniel 3
Trembly
MACDOUGALD, Dan 3
MACDOUGALD, Mrs. 4
Alice Foote
MAC DOUGALL, Clinton 1
Dugald
MACDOUGALL, Edward 3
Archibald
MACDOUGALL, Frank 6
Henry
MACDOUGALL, Hamilton 2
Crawford
MACDOUGALL, Ranald 6
MAC DOUGALL, Robert 1
MACDOUGALL, William 2
Dugald
MACDOWELL, Charles 3
Henry
MACDOWELL, Mrs. 3
Edward
MACDOWELL, Edward 1
Alexander
MACDOWELL, Katherine H
Sherwood Bonner
MACDOWELL, Thain 4
Wendell
MACDUFFEE, Cyrus 4
Colton
MACDUFFIE, John 1
MACE, Daniel H
MACE, Frances Laughton 1
MACE, Frank William 4
MACE, Harold Loring 4
MACE, William Harrison 1
MACEACHERN, Malcolm 1
T.
MACEDO SOARES, Jose 5
Carlos
MAC ELREE, Wilmer W. 1
MAC ELROY, Andrew 4
Jackson
MACELROY, Andrew 5
Jackson
MACELWANE, Geraldine 6
Frances
MACELWANE, James B. 1
MACELWANE, John 5
Patrick
MACELWEE, Roy Samuel 1
MACENULTY, John 6
Forrest
MACEWEN, Ewen 2
Murchison
MACEWEN, Walter 2
MACFADDEN, Bernarr 3
MACFADYEN, Alexander 1
MACFARLAN, William 2
Charles
MACFARLAND, Charles 3
Stedman
MACFARLAND, Finlay 1
Leroy
MACFARLAND, Frank 3
Mace
MACFARLAND, Hays 6
MACFARLAND, Henry 1
Brown Floyd
MACFARLAND, Lanning 5
MACFARLAND, Robert 3
Alfred
MACFARLANE, Alexander 4
MACFARLANE, Catharine 5
MACFARLANE, Charles 5
William
MACFARLANE, David 3
Laing
MACFARLANE, Howard 5
Pettingill
MACFARLANE, James 6
MACFARLANE, John C. 3
MACFARLANE, John 1
Muirhead
MACFARLANE, Joseph 4
Arthur

MACFARLANE, Peter 3
MACFARLANE, Peter 1
Clark
MACFARLANE, Robert H
MACFARLANE, W. E. 2
MACFARLANE, William 6
MACFEELY, Robert 1
MAC GAHAN, Barbara 1
MACGAHAN, Januarius H
Aloysius
MAC GILLIVRAY, 1
Alexander Dyer
MACGILLIVRAY, William H
MACGILVARY, Norwood 2
MAC GILVARY, Paton 1
MACGINLEY, John 5
Bernard
MAC GINNISS, John 1
MACGLASHAN, David 1
Pollock
MAC GOWAN, Alice 4
MACGOWAN, David Bell 5
MACGOWAN, Gault 5
MAC GOWAN, Granville 1
MAC GOWAN, John Encil 1
MACGOWAN, John Koe 1
MACGOWAN, Kenneth 4
MAC GRATH, Harold 1
MACGREGOR, Charles 5
Peter
MACGREGOR, Clarence 3
MACGREGOR, David 3
Hutchison
MACGREGOR, David 5
Hutchison
MACGREGOR, Frank 5
Silver
MAC GREGOR, Henry 1
Frederick
MACGREGOR, Theodore 6
Douglas
MACHARG, John Brainerd 3
MACHARG, William 3
MACHEBEUF, Joseph H
Projectus
MACHEN, Arthur Webster 3
MACHEN, J. Gresham 3
MACHEN, Willis Benson H
MACHIR, James H
MACHLETT, Raymond R. 3
MACHMER, William 3
Lawson
MACHOLD, Earle John 4
MACHOLD, Henry 4
Edmund
MACHROWICZ, Thaddeus 5
M(ichael)
MACIEJEWSKI, Anton 3
Frank
MACINNES, Duncan 4
Arthur
MAC INNIS, John 1
Murdoch
MACINTOSH, Douglas 2
Clyde
MAC INTOSH, John 1
Alexander
MACINTYRE, Archibald 5
James
MACISAAC, Fred 1
MACIVER, Robert 5
Morrison
MACIVOR, John William 6
MACK, A. B. 1
MACK, Andrew 1
MACK, Augustus Frederick 4
Jr.
MACK, Carl Theodore 5
MACK, Connie 3
MACK, Edgar M. 2
MACK, Edward 3
MACK, Edwin S. 2
MACK, George Herbert 5
MACK, Henry Whitcomb 4
MACK, Howard 4
MACK, Isaac Foster 1
MACK, J(ames) S(tephen) 5
MACK, John E. 1
MACK, John Givan Davis 1
MACK, John M. 1
MACK, John Sephus 1
MACK, Julian Ellis 4
MACK, Julian William 2
MACK, Norman Edward 1
MACK, Pauline Beery 6
MACK, Richard Alfred 4
MACK, Russell Vernon 3
MACK, Warren Bryan 3
MACK, William 2
MACKALL, (Alexander) 5
Lawton
MACKALL, Leonard 1
Leopold
MACKALL, Louis 1
MACKALL, Paul 3

MACKAY, Clarence Hungerford 1
MACKAY, Constance D'Arcy 4
MACKAY, Donald Dundas 4
MACKAY, Donald Sage 1
MACKAY, Helen 4
MACKAY, Helen (Mrs. Archibald Mackay)
MACKAY, Henry Squarebriggs Jr. 3
MACKAY, James H
MACKAY, John Keiller 5
MACKAY, John William 1
MACKAY, Margaret 5
MACKAY, Robert 5
MACKAY, Roland Parks 4
MACKAY, William Andrew 1
MACKAY, William Eshorne 1
MACKAYE, Arthur Loring 4
MACKAYE, Benton 6
MACKAYE, Harold Steele 1
MACKAYE, James H
MACKAYE, James Morrison Steele
MACKAYE, Percy 3
MACKAY-SMITH, Alexander 1
MACKEACHIE, Douglas Cornell 2
MACKECHNIE, Hugh Neil 4
MACKEE, George Miller 3
MACKEEVER, John C. 3
MACKELLAR, Patrick H
MACKELLAR, Thomas H
MAC KELLAR, Thomas 4
MACKELLAR, William Henry Howard 2
MACKEN, Walter 4
MACKENZIE, A. Cameron 1
MACKENZIE, Alastair St. Clair 5
MACKENZIE, Alexander 1
MACKENZIE, Alexander Slidell H
MACKENZIE, Arthur 5
MACKENZIE, Arthur Stanley 4
MACKENZIE, Cameron 1
MACKENZIE, Donald 1
MACKENZIE, Donald 2
MACKENZIE, Donald Hector 3
MACKENZIE, Frederick William 1
MACKENZIE, George Henry H
MACKENZIE, J. Gazzam 5
MACKENZIE, James Cameron 1
MACKENZIE, Jean Kenyon 1
MACKENZIE, John Douglas 6
MACKENZIE, John Noland 1
MACKENZIE, Kenneth H
MACKENZIE, Kenneth Alexander J. 1
MACKENZIE, Kenneth Gerard 5
MACKENZIE, Morris Robinson Slidell 1
MACKENZIE, Murdo 1
MACKENZIE, Philip Edward 2
MACKENZIE, Ranald Slidell H
MACKENZIE, Robert 1
MACKENZIE, Robert Shelton H
MACKENZIE, Roderick Dempster 1
MACKENZIE, Tandy 4
MACKENZIE, Thomas Hanna 2
MACKENZIE, William H
MACKENZIE, William Adams 2
MACKENZIE, William Douglas 1
MACKENZIE, William Ross 3
MACKENZIE, William Roy 5
MACKEOWN, Samuel Stuart 3
MACKEY, Albert Gallatin H
MACKEY, Charles Osborn 4
MACKEY, Charles William 1
MACKEY, David Ray 6
MACKEY, Edmund William H McGregor
MACKEY, Harry A. 1
MACKEY, Joseph T. 4
MACKEY, Levi Augustus H
MACKEY, William Fleming 1
MACKIE, Alexander 4
MACKIE, David Ives 4

MACKIE, Ernest Lloyd 5
MACKIE, Joseph Bolton Cooper 2
MACKIE, Pauline Bradford 5 (Mrs. Herbert M. Hopkins)
MACKIE, Thomas Turlay 3
MACKIN, Joseph Hoover 5
MACKINNEY, Loren Carey 4
MACKINNON, Allan P. 1
MACKINNON, Eugene 3
MACKINNON, George V. 1
MACKINNON, Harold Alexander 5
MACKINNON, James Angus 3
MACKINNON, John C. 6
MACKINNON, Lee Warner 1
MACKINTOSH, Alexander 2
MACKINTOSH, George Lewis 1
MACKINTOSH, Harold Vincent 4
MACKINTOSH, Hugh 6
MACKINTOSH, Kenneth 5
MACKINTOSH, William Archibald 5
MACKLIN, James Edgar 4
MACKLIN, Justin Wilford 4
MACKLIN, W. A. Stewart 3
MACKNIGHT, Dodge 1
MACKUBIN, Florence 1
MACKY, Eric Spencer 3
MACLACHAN, David Cathcart 1
MACLACHLAN, Daniel A. 1
MACLACHLAN, James A. 4
MACLACHLAN, John Miller 4
MAC LACHLAN, Lachlan 1
MACLACHLAN, Margery Jean 4
MACLAFFERTY, James Henry 1
MACLANE, Gerald Robinson 5
MACLANE, M. Jean 4
MAC LANE, Mary 1
MACLANE, Mary 2
MAC LAREN, Archibald 1
MACLAREN, Malcolm 1
MACLAURIN, Richard Cockburn 1
MACLAURIN, William Rupert 3
MACLAY, Edgar Stanton 4
MACLAY, Isaac Walker 1
MACLAY, James 1
MACLAY, Otis Hardy 1
MACLAY, Robert Samuel 1
MACLAY, Samuel H
MACLAY, William * H
MACLAY, William Brown H
MACLAY, William Plunkett H
MACLAY, William Walter 3
MACLEAN, Alexander Tweedie 3
MACLEAN, Angus Dhu 1
MACLEAN, Annie Marion 1
MACLEAN, Arthur Winfield 2
MACLEAN, Basil Clarendon 4
MACLEAN, Charles Fraser 1
MACLEAN, Charles Thomas Agnew 1
MACLEAN, Clara Dargan 4
MACLEAN, Daniel 4
MACLEAN, George Edwin 1
MACLEAN, Henry Coit 4
MACLEAN, James Alexander 2
MACLEAN, John H
MACLEAN, John H
MACLEAN, John Norman 4
MACLEAN, Malcolm Shaw 6 Jr.
MACLEAN, Munroe Deacon 5
MACLEAN, Paul Robert 5
MACLEAN, Ray Butts 2
MACLEAN, Samuel Richter 4
MACLEAN, Stuart 5
MACLEAR, Anne Bush 1
MACLEARY, Bonnie 6
MACLEISH, Andrew 1
MACLEISH, Bruce 4
MACLEISH, John E. 5
MACLELLAN, Kenneth F. 1
MACLELLAN, Robert J. 3
MACLELLAN, Robert Llewellyn 1
MACLENNAN, Francis 1
MACLENNAN, Francis William 2

MACLENNAN, Frank Pitts 1
MACLENNAN, Simon Fraser 5
MACLEOD, Bruce Hamilton 4
MACLEOD, Colln Munro 5
MACLEOD, Donald Campbell 1
MACLEOD, Frederick Joseph 1
MACLEOD, Iain Norman 5
MACLEOD, John James Rickard 1
MACLEOD, Malcolm James 1
MACLEOD, Robert Brodie 5
MACLOSKIE, George 1
MACLURE, William H
MACMANUS, Seumas 4
MACMANUS, Seumas 5
MACMILLAN, Cargill 5
MACMILLAN, Conway 1
MACMILLAN, Cyrus 3
MACMILLAN, Donald Baxter 6
MACMILLAN, Sir Ernest Campbell 5
MACMILLAN, George Whitfield 5
MACMILLAN, Harvey Reginald 6
MACMILLAN, Hugh R. 3
MACMILLAN, Jason Leon 4
MACMILLAN, John Alwyn 3
MACMILLAN, John Hugh 4 Jr.
MACMILLAN, Kerr Duncan 1
MACMILLAN, Lucy Hayes 4
MACMILLAN, Richard F. 6
MAC MILLAN, Thomas C. 1
MACMILLAN, (William) Dougald III 6
MACMILLAN, William Duncan 2
MACMONNIES, Frederick 1
MACMULLEN, Wallace 2
MACMURRAY, James E. 2
MACMURRAY, John Van 4 Antwerp
MACNAIR, Florence Wheelock Ayscough 2
MACNAIR, Harley Farnsworth 2
MACNAIR, James Duncan 2
MACNAMARA, Arthur James 4
MACNAUGHTON, Edgar 5
MACNAUGHTON, Ernest 4 Boyd
MACNAUGHTON, James 2
MACNAUGHTON, Lewis 4 Winslow
MACNAUGHTON, Moray 4 Fraser
MACNEAL, Robert E. 4
MACNEAL, Ward J. 2
MACNEICE, Louis 4
MACNEIL, Carol Brooks 5
MACNEIL, Hermon Atkins 2
MACNEIL, Neil 5
MACNEIL, Sayre 4
MACNEIL, Virginia Allen 6 Bagby
MAC NEILL, Charles 1 Mather
MACNEILLE, Holbrook 6 Mann
MACNEILLE, Stephen 6 Mann
MACNEISH, Noel Stones 4
MACNEVEN, William H James
MACNICOL, Roy Vincent 5
MACNIDER, Hanford 2
MACNIDER, Hanford 5
MACNIDER, William de 3 Berniere
MACNULTY, William K. 4
MACOMB, Alexander H
MACOMB, Augustus 4 Canfield
MACOMB, David Betton 1
MACOMB, Montgomery 1 Meigs
MACOMBER, Alexander 3
MACOMBER, John R. 3
MACOMBER, William 1
MACON, Nathaniel H
MACON, Robert Bruce 1
MACPHAIL, Leland 6 Stanford (Larry)
MACPHAIL, William 4
MAC PHERSON, Earle 3 Steele

MACPHERSON, Leslie 6 Coombs Jr.
MACPHERSON, Walter 3 Henry
MACPHIE, Elmore I. 3
MAC PHIE, John Peter 4
MAC QUEARY, Thomas 1 Howard
MACQUEARY, Thomas 2 Howard
MACQUEEN, Donald 5 Bruce
MAC QUEEN, Peter 1
MACQUIGG, Charles 3 Ellison
MACRAE, Elliott Beach 4
MACRAE, Elmer 3 Livingston
MAC RAE, Floyd Willcox 4
MACRAE, George Wythe 4
MACRAE, Harry B. 3
MACRAE, Hugh 5
MAC RAE, James Cameron 1
MACRAE, John 3
MACRAE, William 1 Alexander
MACSHERRY, Charles 6 Whitman
MACSPARRAN, James H
MACTAVISH, William 5 Caruth
MACVANE, Edith 6
MACVANE, Silas Marcus 1
MACVEAGH, Charles 1
MACVEAGH, Ewen 5 Cameron
MACVEAGH, Franklin 1
MACVEAGH, Lincoln 5
MAC VEAGH, Wayne 1
MAC VICAR, John 4
MACVICAR, John George 2
MACVITTY, Karl de G. 3
MACWHORTER, H Alexander
MACY, Anne Mansfield 4 Sullivan
MACY, Arthur 1
MACY, C. Ward 4
MACY, Carleton 3
MACY, Edith Dewing 4
MACY, Edward Warren 3
MACY, George 3
MACY, Jesse 1
MACY, John 1
MACY, John B. H
MACY, Josiah H
MACY, Josiah Jr. 5
MACY, Nelson 3
MACY, Paul Griswold 4
MACY, V. Everit 1
MACY, Valentine E(verit) 5 Jr.
MACY, W. Kingsland 4
MADDEN, Edwin Charles 4
MADDEN, Eva Anne 4
MADDEN, James Loomis 5
MADDEN, John 3
MADDEN, John Fitz 2
MADDEN, John Griffith 4
MADDEN, John Joseph 4
MADDEN, John Thomas 2
MADDEN, Joseph Warren 5
MADDEN, Lillian Gertrude 6
MADDEN, M. Lester 4
MADDEN, Martin Barnaby 1
MADDEN, Mrs. Maude 4 Whitmore
MADDIN, Percy Downs 2
MADDOCK, Catharine 1 Young Glen
MADDOCK, Walter 4 Grierson
MADDOCK, William Eli 4
MADDON, John W. 3
MADDOX, Dwayne Depew 2
MADDOX, Fletcher 2
MADDOX, James Gray 6
MADDOX, John J. 2
MADDOX, Louis Wilson 4
MADDOX, Robert Charles 6
MADDOX, Robert Foster 5
MADDOX, Samuel T. 1
MADDOX, William Arthur 1
MADDOX, William Percy 5
MADDRY, Charles Edward 4
MADDUX, Jared 5
MADDUX, Parker Simmons 3
MADDY, Joseph Edgar 4
MADEIRA, Jean Browning 5
MADEIRA, Louis Childs 1
MADEIRA, Percy Child 2
MADELEVA, Sister Mary 4
MADERNA, Bruno 6
MADIGAN, LaVerne 4
MADILL, Grant Charles 2
MADISON, Charles C. 3

MADISON, Dorothea H Payne Todd
MADISON, Edmond H. 1
MADISON, Frank Dellno 2
MADISON, Harold Lester 3
MADISON, James * H
MADISON, Lucy Foster 1
MADSON, Norman Arthur 4
MAEDER, LeRoy M.A. 6
MAEGLI, Hallo 6
MAENNER, Theodore 3 Henry
MAES, Camillus Paul 1
MAES, Urban 6
MAESTRE, Sidney 4
MAESTRI, Robert S(idney) 6
MAETERLINCK, Maurice 2
MAFFITT, David 1
MAFFITTZ, John Newland H
MAGAN, Percy Tilson 2
MAGARY, Alvin Edwin 4
MAGAW, Charles Albert 5
MAGEE, Carlton Cole 2
MAGEE, Charles Lohr 5
MAGEE, Christopher 1 Lyman
MAGEE, Clare 5
MAGEE, J(unius) Ralph 5
MAGEE, James Carre 6
MAGEE, James Dysart 2
MAGEE, James M. 2
MAGEE, John H
MAGEE, John 4
MAGEE, John Benjamin 2
MAGEE, John Fackenthal 4
MAGEE, Rena Tucker 6
MAGEE, Walter Warren 1
MAGEE, Wayland Wells 6
MAGEE, William Addison 1
MAGEE, William Michael 4
MAGELLAN, Ferdinand H
MAGELSSEN, William 1 Christian
MAGER, Charles Augustus 3
MAGEVNEY, Eugene A. 4
MAGGARD, Edward Harris 5
MAGGS, Douglas Blount 4
MAGIE, David 5
MAGIE, William Francis 2
MAGIE, William Jay 1
MAGIL, Mary Ellen Ryan 5 (Mrs. Elias Magil)
MAGILL, Edmund Charles 1
MAGILL, Edward Hicks 1
MAGILL, Frank Stockton 3
MAGILL, George Paull 3
MAGILL, Hugh Stewart 3
MAGILL, James Phineas 6
MAGILL, Robert Edward 1
MAGILL, Roswell 4
MAGILL, Samuel Edward 1
MAGILL, William Seagrove 5
MAGILLIGAN, Donald 1 James
MAGIN, Francis W. 4
MAGINNES, Albert Bristol 4
MAGINNIS, Charles 5 Donagh
MAGINNIS, Martin 1
MAGINNIS, Samuel Abbot 1
MAGISTAD, Oscar Conrad 3
MAGLIN, William Henry 4
MAGNANI, Anna 6
MAGNER, F. J. 2
MAGNER, James Joseph 5
MAGNER, John F. 1
MAGNER, Thomas Francis 2
MAGNES, Judah Leon 2
MAGNIER, Anthony 3 Aloysius
MAGNUS, Joseph Emil 1
MAGNUSSON, Carl 1 Edward
MAGNUSSON, Magnus 5 Vignir
MAGNUSSON, Peter 4 Magnus
MAGOFFIN, Beriah H
MAGOFFIN, James Wiley H
MAGOFFIN, Ralph Van 2 Deman
MAGONE, Daniel 1
MAGONIGLE, Edith 5 Marion
MAGONIGLE, H. Van 1 Buren
MAGOON, Charles E. 1
MAGOON, Henry Sterling H
MAGOR, S. F. 3
MAGOUN, George Frederic H
MAGOUN, Henry A. 1
MAGOUN, Herbert William 3
MAGOUN, Jeanne 1 Bartholow (Mrs. Francis P.)
MAGOWAN, Sir John Hall 3

MAGRADY, Frederick W. 3
MAGRATH, Andrew H
  Gordon
MAGRATH, George 1
  Burgess
MAGRATH, William 3
MAGRAW, Lester Andrew 2
MAGRITTE, Rene 4
MAGRUDDER, Benjamin
  Drake
MAGRUDDER, David 1
  Lynn
MAGRUDER, Allan Bowie H
MAGRUDER, Bruce 3
MAGRUDER, Calvert 5
MAGRUDER, Frank 3
  Abbott
MAGRUDER, George 1
  Lloyd
MAGRUDER, John 3
MAGRUDER, John H
  Bankhead
MAGRUDER, John H. Jr. 4
MAGRUDER, Julia 1
MAGRUDER, Patrick H
MAGRUDER, Thomas 1
  Pickett
MAGRUDER, William 1
  Thomas
MAGSAYSAY, Ramon 3
MAGUIRE, Hamilton 5
  Ewing
MAGUIRE, James G. 4
MAGUIRE, Jeremiah De
  Smet
MAGUIRE, John Arthur 5
MAGUIRE, Matthew 4
MAGUIRE, Philip Francis 6
  Jr.
MAGUIRE, Raymer Francis 4
MAGUIRE, Russell 4
MAGUIRE, Walter N. 4
MAGUIRE, William G. 4
MAHAFFEY, Jesse Lynn 2
MAHAFFEY, John Quincy 4
MAHAFFIE, Charles 5
  Delahunt
MAHAN, Alfred Thayer 1
MAHAN, Asa 1
MAHAN, Bryan Francis 3
MAHAN, Dennis Hart 1
MAHAN, Dennis Hart 1
MAHAN, Edgar Clyde 2
MAHAN, George Addison 4
MAHAN, Lawrence Elmer 2
MAHAN, Milo 1
MAHAN, Patrick Joseph 1
MAHANA, George Shaw 4
MAHANEY, C. R. 6
MAHANY, Rowland 1
  Blennerhassett
MAHAR, Edward Albert 5
MAHENDRA, Bir Bikram 5
  Shah Deva
MAHER, Aldea 5
MAHER, Aly Pacha 4
MAHER, Chauncey Carter 5
MAHER, Dale Wilford 2
MAHER, George 1
  Washington
MAHER, James Denis 1
MAHER, James P. 1
MAHER, Stephen John 1
MAHESHWARI, 4
  Panchanan
MAHEU, Rene Gabriel 6
  Eugene
MAHIN, Edward Garfield 3
MAHIN, Frank Cadle 4
MAHIN, Frank Webster 1
MAHIN, John Lee 1
MAHL, William 1
MAHLE, Arthur Edwin 4
MAHLER, Ernst 4
MAHLER, Fritz 6
MAHLER, Gustav H
MAHLER, Gustav H
MAHON, Russell C. 3
MAHON, Stephen Keith 5
MAHON, Thaddeus Maclay 4
MAHON, Wilfred John 4
MAHON, William D. 2
MAHONE, William H
MAHONEY, Bernard 1
  Joseph
MAHONEY, Caroline 1
  Smith
MAHONEY, Charles H. 4
MAHONEY, Daniel Joseph 4
MAHONEY, Edward R. 1
MAHONEY, George 3
  William
MAHONEY, Jeremiah T. 5
MAHONEY, John C. 4
MAHONEY, John Dennis 5
MAHONEY, John Friend 3

MAHONEY, John Joseph 4
MAHONEY, Joseph 2
  Nathaniel
MAHONEY, Peter Paul H
MAHONEY, Walter Butler 3
MAHONEY, William Frank 1
MAHONEY, William J. 2
MAHONY, Emon Ossian 1
MAHONY, Michael Joseph 1
MAHONY, Thomas 5
  Harrison
MAHOOD, J. W. 4
MAHOOL, John Barry 1
MAHURAN, Stuart Ansala 3
MAHY, George Gordon 4
MAIDEN, Robert King 4
MAIER, Guy 2
MAIER, Walter Arthur * 2
MAILHOUSE, Max 2
MAILLER, William Henry 1
MAILLIARD, John Ward 3
  Jr.
MAILLY, William 1
MAIN, Archibald M. 4
MAIN, Arthur Elwin 1
MAIN, Charles Thomas 4
MAIN, Hanford 4
MAIN, Herschel 1
MAIN, Hubert Platt 1
MAIN, John Fleming 2
MAIN, John Hanson 1
  Thomas
MAIN, Marjorie 6
MAIN, William H
MAIN, William Holloway 1
MAINE, Mary Talulah 5
MAINS, George Preston 1
MAINS, Kathryn Pauline 1
MAINWARING, William 3
  Bernard
MAIR, William J. 4
MAIRS, Elwood Donald 5
MAIRS, Samuel 3
MAIRS, Thomas Isaiah 5
MAISCH, Henry Charles 1
  Christian
MAISCH, John Michael H
MAITLAND, George H. 4
MAITLAND, James Dreher 4
MAITLAND, Royal 2
  Lethington
MAJALI, Hazaa 4
MAJESKI, John F. 5
MAJOR, Alfred Job 4
MAJOR, Cedric A. 4
MAJOR, Charles 1
MAJOR, David R. 1
MAJOR, Duncan Kennedy 2
  Jr.
MAJOR, Elliott Woolfolk 2
MAJOR, J(ames) Earl 5
MAJOR, Samuel C. 1
MAJOR, William Warner 4
MAKEMIE, Francis H
MAKEPEACE, Charles D. 4
MAKEPEACE, Colin 4
  MacRae
MAKINSON, George 1
  Albert
MAKITA, Yolchiro 5
MAKUEN, G. Hudson 1
MALAKIS, Emile 3
MALAN, Clement Timothy 4
MALAN, Daniel Francois 3
MALAND, Talfourd Abbot 6
MALBONE, Edward H
  Greene
MALBONE, Francis 1
MALBURN, William 2
  Peabody
MALBY, George R. 1
MALCARNEY, Arthur 5
  Leno
MALCOLM, D. O. 3
MALCOLM, Daniel 1
MALCOLM, George Arthur 4
MALCOLM, Gilbert 1
MALCOLM, James Peller H
MALCOLM, Robert Bruce 6
MALCOLM, Roy 1
MALCOLM, Russell Laing 5
MALCOLM, William 2
  Lindsay
MALCOLM X 4
MALCOM, Howard H
MALCOMSON, Charles 1
  Tousley
MALCOMSON, James W. 1
MALDARELLI, Oronzio 4
MALIN, Patrick Murphy 4
MALINOVSKY, Rodion 4
  Yakovlevich
MALINOWSKI, Bronislaw 2
  Kasper
MALIPIERO, G. Francesco 6
MALISOFF, William Marias 2

MALITZ, Lester M. 4
MALKIEL, Leon Andrew 1
MALKO, Nicolai 4
MALL, Franklin Paine 1
MALLALIEU, Wilbur 2
  Vincent
MALLALIEU, Willard 1
  Francis
MALLARY, R. De Witt 1
MALLARY, Rollin Carolas H
MALLERY, Earl Dean 3
MALLERY, Garrick H
MALLERY, Otto Tod 3
MALLET, John William 1
MALLET-PREVOST, 2
  Severo
MALLETT, Daniel 4
  Trowbridge
MALLETT, Donald Roger 5
MALLETT, Reginald 4
MALLETT, Wilbert Grant 1
MALLINCKRODT, Edward 1
MALLINCKRODT, 6
  Laurence Edward
MALLINCKRODT, Pauline H
MALLINCKROOT, Edward 4
  Jr.
MALLISON, Richard 5
  Speight
MALLOCH, Douglas 1
MALLON, Alfred Edward 2
MALLON, Guy Ward 4
MALLON, Paul 3
MALLON, Winifred 3
MALLORY, C. C. 3
MALLORY, Clifford Day 1
MALLORY, Francis H
MALLORY, Frank Burr 2
MALLORY, Hugh 1
MALLORY, Hugh Shepherd 1
  Darby
MALLORY, Kathleen 6
  Moore
MALLORY, Meredith 1
MALLORY, Philip Rogers 6
MALLORY, Robert H
MALLORY, Rufus 4
MALLORY, Stephen H
  Russell
MALLORY, Stephen 1
  Russell
MALLORY, Tracy Burr 3
MALLOY, John Anthony 2
MALLY, Frederick William 4
MALM, Gustav Nathanael 1
MALONE, Booth M. 4
MALONE, Clarence M. 4
MALONE, Clifton J. 4
MALONE, Dana 1
MALONE, Dudley Field 3
MALONE, George Wilson 4
MALONE, J. Walter Jr. 1
MALONE, J. WALTER Jr. 4
MALONE, James C. 4
MALONE, James Thomas 4
MALONE, John Lee 6
MALONE, John Wesley 1
MALONE, Kemp 5
MALONE, Noel H. 4
MALONE, Paul Bernard 4
MALONE, Richard Harwell 1
MALONE, Rosser Lynn 4
MALONE, Thomas Henry 1
MALONE, Walter 1
MALONE, William Battle 1
MALONEY, Francis 2
MALONEY, John Philip 3
MALONEY, Joseph F. 4
MALONEY, Paul Herbert 5
MALONEY, Richard 6
  Clogher
MALONEY, Richard Lee 4
MALONEY, Robert S. 6
MALONEY, Walter H. 5
MALONEY, William J. M. 3
  A.
MALONY, Harry James 5
MALOTT, Clyde A. 3
MALSBARY, George Elmer 5
MALTBIE, Milo Roy 5
MALTBIE, William Henry 2
MALTBIE, William Mills 4
MALTBY, Margaret Eliza 4
MALTBY, Ralph B. 3
MALTER, Henry 1
MALTZ, George L. 4
MALTZAN, Adolf Georg 1
  Otto Freiherr Von
MALVERN, Viscount 5
MALZBERG, Benjamin 6
MAN, Alrick Hubbell 1
MAN, Ernest A. 1
MANAGAN, William 1
  Henry
MANAHAN, James 1
MANATT, J. Irving 1

MANCE, Grover Cleveland 3
MANCE, Robert Weston II 5
MANCHEE, Arthur 5
  Leavens
MANCHESTER, Arthur 2
  Livingston
MANCHESTER, Charles 1
  Howard
MANCHESTER, Earl 3
  Northup
MANCHESTER, Herbert A. 2
MANCUSO, Francis X. 5
MANDEL, Edwin Frank 4
MANDEL, John Aldred 1
MANDEL, Leon 6
MANDEL, Robert 5
MANDELBAUM, Samuel 2
MANDELL, George Snell 1
MANDERSON, Charles 1
  Frederick
MANDEVILLE, Giles 1
  Henry
MANDEVILLE, Hubert C. 2
MANDEVILLE, John 1
  Appleton
MANDEVILLE, William 3
  Hubert
MANES, Alfred 4
MANEY, George Alfred 2
MANEY, Richard 5
MANGAN, Thomas J. 2
MANGASARIAN, 4
  Mangasar Mugurditch
MANGEL, Sol 5
MANGELS, Hermann N. 4
MANGES, Morris 2
MANGIN, Joseph Francois H
MANGOLD, George 5
  Benjamin
MANGUM, Charles Staples 1
MANGUM, Josiah Thomas 5
MANGUM, Willie Person 4
MANGUM, Willis Lester 3
MANHART, Franklin 1
  Pierce
MANHOFF, Bill 6
MANICE, William DeForest 4
MANIERRE, Alfred Lee 3
MANIGAULT, Arthur H
  Middleton
MANIGAULT, Gabriel * H
MANIGAULT, Gabriel 1
  Edward
MANIGAULT, Peter H
MANIGAULT, Pierre H
MANIGAULT, R. S. 2
MANION, Edward J. 5
MANION, William Cecil 5
MANIS, Hubert Clyde 5
MANKIEWICZ, Herman J. 3
MANKINS, Elvin Orland 6
MANLEY, F. Nason 4
MANLEY, Frederick Willis 6
MANLEY, John H
MANLEY, John Ellis 3
MANLEY, Joseph Homan 1
MANLEY, Norman 5
  Washington
MANLEY, Thomas Henry 1
MANLY, Basil * H
MANLY, Basil 3
MANLY, Charles 1
MANLY, Charles Matthews 1
MANLY, Chesly 5
MANLY, George C. 1
MANLY, John Matthews 2
MANLY, Lewis Frederick 4
MANLY, Robert Emmet 3
MANLY, William Hester 1
MANN, Abijah Jr. H
MANN, Alan Newhall 4
MANN, Albert 1
MANN, Albert Clinton 2
MANN, Albert Russell 4
MANN, Albert Zachariah 1
MANN, Alden T. 1
MANN, Alexander 1
MANN, Ambrose Dudley 4
MANN, Anthony 4
MANN, Arthur 1
MANN, Arthur Robert 4
MANN, Arthur Teall 1
MANN, B. Pickman 1
MANN, Cameron 1
MANN, Charles August 2
MANN, Charles Holbrook 4
MANN, Charles Riborg 2
MANN, Charles William 1
MANN, Conrad Henry 3
MANN, Edward Ames 1
MANN, Edward Garnett 4
  Batson
MANN, Ellery Wilson 3
MANN, Erika (Mrs. Wystan 5
  Hugh Auden)
MANN, Frank Charles 4

MANN, Frank Hurt 3
MANN, Frank Irving 1
MANN, Fred Parker 5
MANN, Frederick Maynard 5
MANN, George Douglas 1
MANN, Gustav 4
MANN, Heinrich Ludwig 3
MANN, Henry 1
MANN, Henry 5
MANN, Horace 1
MANN, Horace Borchsenius 1
MANN, Horace L. 1
MANN, Isaac Thomas 1
MANN, James * H
MANN, James Robert 1
MANN, James Walter 1
MANN, Job H
MANN, Joel Keith H
MANN, John Joseph 6
MANN, Joseph F. 3
MANN, Klaus 3
MANN, Kristine 2
MANN, Lester Bradwell 3
MANN, Louis 1
MANN, Louis L. 4
MANN, Margaret 5
MANN, Mary Ridpath 4
MANN, Mary Tyler H
  Peabody
MANN, Matthew 1
  Derbyshire
MANN, Millicent E. 4
MANN, Nancy Murray 5
MANN, Newton 1
MANN, Parker 1
MANN, Paul Blakeslee 2
MANN, Rowena Morse 3
MANN, Seth 1
MANN, Stanley 3
MANN, Thomas 3
MANN, William Abram 1
MANN, William Alfred 5
MANN, William D'Alton 1
MANN, William Hodges 1
MANN, William Julius H
MANN, William M. 4
MANNER, Jane 2
MANNERS, J. Hartley 4
MANNES, David 3
MANNES, Leopold 6
  Damrosch
MANNEY, Charles Fonteyn 3
MANNEY, Henry Newman 1
MANNHEIM, Hermann 6
MANNHEIM, Jean 4
MANNING, Charles Henry 1
MANNING, Charles N. 2
MANNING, Clarence 5
  Augustus
MANNING, Daniel H
MANNING, Edward Betts 2
MANNING, Estelle 6
  Hempstead
MANNING, George 4
  Charles
MANNING, George H. 1
MANNING, Harry 6
MANNING, Henry Parker 2
MANNING, Isaac A. 4
MANNING, Isaac Hall 2
MANNING, James H
MANNING, James Hilton 1
MANNING, James Smith 1
MANNING, Jewel 6
  Evangeline Berger (Mrs.
  Harold E. Manning)
MANNING, John Charles 1
MANNING, John Joseph 4
MANNING, Joseph P. 2
MANNING, Joseph 5
  Thruston 3d
MANNING, Lucius Bass 2
MANNING, Marie 3
MANNING, Mary 1
  Margaretta Fryer
MANNING, Richard Irvine H
MANNING, Richard Irvine 1
MANNING, Robert H
MANNING, Thomas H
  Courtland
MANNING, Van H. 1
MANNING, Vannoy H
  Hartrog
MANNING, Walter 1
  Webster
MANNING, Warren Henry 1
MANNING, William Albert 5
MANNING, William Ray 1
MANNING, William T. 1
MANNING, William 2
  Thomas
MANNON, Floyd Ralph 4
MANNY, Frank Addison 5
MANSELL, O. S. 4
MANSER, Harry 4
MANSERGH, Robert 6

MANSFIELD, Archibald Romaine 1
MANSFIELD, Beatrice Cameron 4
MANSFIELD, Burton 1
MANSFIELD, Edward Deering H
MANSFIELD, Frederick William 3
MANSFIELD, George Rogers 5
MANSFIELD, Henry Buckingham 1
MANSFIELD, Howard 1
MANSFIELD, Ira Franklin 4
MANSFIELD, Jared H
MANSFIELD, Jayne 4
MANSFIELD, Joseph Jefferson 2
MANSFIELD, Joseph King Fenno H
MANSFIELD, Orlando Augustine 4
MANSFIELD, Richard H
MANSFIELD, Richard 1
MANSFIELD, Robert E. 1
MANSFIELD, Samuel Mather H
MANSFIELD, William Douglass 3
MANSHIP, Charles Phelps 2
MANSHIP, Paul 4
MANSKE, Walter Earl 6
MANSON, Daniel Edgar 2
MANSON, Frederic E. 4
MANSON, John Thomas 2
MANSON, Mahlon Dickerson H
MANSON, Marsden 1
MANSON, Otis Frederick H
MANSON, Ray H. 4
MANSON, Richard 3
MANSS, Harvey McKnight 3
MANSUR, Charles Harley H
MANSUR, Zophar M. 1
MANTELL, Robert Bruce 1
MANTER, Harold W(infred) 5
MANTEUFFEL, Tadeusz 6
MANTLE, Burns 2
MANTLE, Gladys Ann Doyle (Mrs. Arthur Claud-Mantle) 5
MANTLE, Lee 1
MANTON, Martin Thomas 2
MANTON, Walter Porter 1
MANTYNBAND, Louis M(artin) 5
MANTZ, H. J. 5
MANUCY, Dominic H
MANUEL, W(illiam) A(sbury) 5
MANUILSKY, Dmitry Zakharavish 3
MANVILLE, Edward Britton 2
MANVILLE, Hiram Edward 2
MANWARING, A. Homer II 3
MANWARING, Elizabeth Wheeler 2
MANWARING, Wilfred Hamilton 5
MANZANARES, Francisco Antonio 1
MAO TSE-TUNG 6
MAPES, Carl Edgar 1
MAPES, Carl Herbert 4
MAPES, Charles Victor 1
MAPES, Clarel Bowman 5
MAPES, James Jay 4
MAPES, Victor 5
MAPHIS, Charles Gilmore 1
MAPLES, Harold E. 2
MAPOTHER, Wible Lawrence
MAPOW, Abraham B. 6
MAPPA, Adam Gerard H
MARABLE, Fate 6
MARABLE, John Hartwell H
MARBLE, Annie Russell 1
MARBLE, Arthur H. 1
MARBLE, Charles Baldwin 1
MARBLE, Danforth H
MARBLE, Edgar M. 1
MARBLE, Fred Elmer 5
MARBLE, George Watson 1
MARBLE, John Hobart 1
MARBLE, John Putnam 1
MARBLE, Manton 1
MARBLE, Mitchell Stewart 4
MARBLE, Thomas Littlefield 3
MARBLE, William Allen 1
MARBURG, Edgar 1
MARBURG, Otto 3

MARBURG, Theodore 2
MARBURGER, Ralph E. 3
MARBURY, Elisabeth 1
MARBURY, William G. 5
MARBURY, William L. 1
MARBUT, Curtis Fletcher 1
MARBY, Giddings Edlon 6
MARC, Henri M. 4
MARCANTONIO, Vito 3
MARCEAU, Henri 4
MARCEL, Gabriel Honore 6
MARCH, Abraham W. 5
MARCH, Alden H
MARCH, Alden 2
MARCH, Anthony 6
MARCH, Charles Hoyt 2
MARCH, Daniel 1
MARCH, Francis Andrew 1
MARCH, Francis Andrew Jr. 1
MARCH, Fredric 5
MARCH, Hal 6
MARCH, H(erman) W(illiam) 6
MARCH, John Lewis 5
MARCH, Peyton Conway 4
MARCH, Thomas Stone 1
MARCHAND, Albert H
MARCHAND, David Gallatin
MARCHAND, John Bonnett H
MARCHANT, Edward Dalton H
MARCHANT, Henry H
MARCHANT, Trelawney E. 3
MARCHBANKS, Tom Earl 6
MARCHETTI, Andrew A. 5
MARCHEV, Alfred 2
MARCIAL-DORADO, Carolina
MARCIN, Max 6
MARCKWARDT, Albert Henry 6
MARCO, Herbert Francis 5
MARCO, Salvatore Michael 6
MARCONI, William Frederick 4
MARCOSSON, Isaac 4
MARCOSSON, Sol 1
MARCOTTE, Henry 3
MARCOU, John Belknap 4
MARCOU, Jules 1
MARCOUX, Vanni (Vanni-Marceux) 6
MARCUM, Thomas 4
MARCUS, Joseph Anthony 4
MARCUS, Louis 1
MARCUS, Louis William 1
MARCUS, Ralph 3
MARCUSE, Milton E. 2
MARCY, Daniel 1
MARCY, Erastus Edgerton 1
MARCY, George Edward 1
MARCY, Henry Orlando 1
MARCY, Oliver 1
MARCY, Randolph Barnes H
MARCY, William Learned H
MARDEN, Charles Carroll 1
MARDEN, George Augustus
MARDEN, Jesse Krekore 5
MARDEN, Orison Swett 1
MARDEN, Orison Swett 6
MARDEN, Oscar Avery 4
MARDEN, Philip Sanford 4
MARDEN, Robert Fiske 4
MARDIS, Samuel Wright H
MAREAN, Emma Endicott 1
MAREAN, Josiah Taylor 1
MAREAN, Willis Adams 1
MARECHAL, Ambrose 1
MAREK, Kurt W. (C.W. Ceram) 5
MARENO, Francisco Ildefonse H
MARES, Lumir Martin 5
MARESCA, Virginia Keller 6
MAREST, Pierre Gabriel H
MARETZEK, Max H
MARGET, Arthur William 4
MARGIL, Antonio H
MARGIOTTI, Charles Joseph 3
MARGOLD, Nathan Ross 2
MARGOLIS, Max Leopold 1
MARGOULIES, Vladimir de 4
MARGRAF, Gustav Bernhard 5
MARIENTHAL, George Edward 5
MARIETTA, Shelley Uriah 6
MARIGNY, Bernard H
MARIN, John 3
MARIN, Joseph 4

MARINDIN, Henri Louis Francois 1
MARINONI, Antonio 2
MARIO, Queena 3
MARION, Frances 6
MARION, Francis H
MARION, John Hardin 2
MARION, Robert H
MARITAIN, Jacques 5
MARIX, Adolph 1
MARJERISON, Howard Mitchell 3
MARK, Clarence 3
MARK, Clayton 1
MARK, Edgar H. 4
MARK, Edward Laurens 2
MARK, Kenneth Lamartine 5
MARK, Mary Louise 6
MARKBREIT, Leopold 1
MARKEE, Joseph Eldridge 5
MARKEL, Samuel A. 3
MARKELEY, Philip Swenk H
MARKELL, Charles 3
MARKELL, Charles Frederick 1
MARKELL, Henry H
MARKELL, Jacob H
MARKENS, Isaac H
MARKERT, Frederic Schaefer 3
MARKEY, Daniel Peter 4
MARKEY, John Clifton 5
MARKEY, Lawrence Morris 4
MARKHAM, Charles Henry 1
MARKHAM, Edward M. 3
MARKHAM, Edwin 1
MARKHAM, Edwin C. 4
MARKHAM, George C. 5
MARKHAM, George Dickson 2
MARKHAM, Henry Harrison 1
MARKHAM, Herbert Ira 4
MARKHAM, James Walter 5
MARKHAM, Jared Clark 3
MARKHAM, John Raymond 5
MARKHAM, Osmon Grant 2
MARKHAM, R. H. 3
MARKHAM, Reuel Finney 3
MARKHAM, Thomas F. 3
MARKHAM, Walter Tipton 5
MARKHAM, William H
MARKHAM, William Guy 4
MARKHAM, William Hugh 3
MARKIN, Morris 5
MARKINO, Yoshio 5
MARKLE, Alvan 1
MARKLE, John 1
MARKLEY, Alfred Collins 1
MARKLEY, Edward Anthony 3
MARKLEY, Joseph Lybrand 1
MARKLEY, Klare S(tephen) 6
MARKOE, Abraham H
MARKOE, Peter H
MARKOE, Thomas Masters 1
MARKS, Avery C. Jr. 1
MARKS, Bernard 1
MARKS, Bradley Cornelius 4
MARKS, Carl 4
MARKS, Edward Bennett 2
MARKS, Edwin I. 5
MARKS, Elias H
MARKS, Henry Kingdon 1
MARKS, Herbert S. 4
MARKS, J(ames) Christopher 5
MARKS, Jeanette 4
MARKS, Laurence Mandeville 3
MARKS, Leon John 5
MARKS, Lionel Simeon 3
MARKS, Marcus M. 1
MARKS, Mrs. L. S. 1
MARKS, Percy 3
MARKS, Sidney Jerome 5
MARKS, Solon 1
MARKS, Willard Leighton 2
MARKS, William H
MARKS, William Dennis 1
MARKS, Wirt Peebles Jr. 4
MARKWARD, Joseph Bradley 1
MARKWART, Arthur Hermann
MARKWOOD, Michael Edward 3
MARLAND, Ernest Whitworth 2
MARLAND, William C. 4
MARLATT, Abby Lillian 5
MARLATT, Charles Lester 3

MARLER, Herbert Meredith 1
MARLEY, James Preston 3
MARLIN, Harry Halpine 1
MARLING, Alfred Erskine 1
MARLING, James H. H
MARLING, John Leake H
MARLIO, Louis 6
MARLOR, Henry S. 4
MARLOW, Frank William 2
MARLOW, Thomas A. 1
MARLOWE, Julia 3
MARMADUKE, John Sappington H
MARMER, Harry Aaron 3
MARMER, Milton Jacob 5
MARMIER, Pierre Edouard 6
MARMION, Keith Robert 5
MARMION, Robert Augustine 1
MARMON, Howard C. 2
MARMON, Jeff Berry 1
MARMUR, Jacland 5
MARNELL, Robert Overton 1
MARON, Samuel Herbert 6
MARONEY, Frederick William 3
MAROT, Helen 1
MAROT, Mary Louise 5
MARQUAND, Allan 1
MARQUAND, Henry Gurdon 1
MARQUAND, John Phillips 4
MARQUARDT, Carl Eugene 5
MARQUARDT, Walter William 6
MARQUART, Edward John 3
MARQUAT, William Frederic 4
MARQUESS, William Hoge 1
MARQUETT, Turner Mastin H
MARQUETTE, Jacques H
MARQUIS, Albert Nelson 2
MARQUIS, David Calhoun 1
MARQUIS, Don 1
MARQUIS, Donald George 5
MARQUIS, George 4
MARQUIS, George Paull 1
MARQUIS, John Abner 1
MARQUIS, Robert Lincoln 1
MARQUIS, Rollin Ruthwin 1
MARQUIS, Samuel Simpson 1
MARQUIS, Vivienne 4
MARQUIS, William Stevenson 1
MARQUIS, William Vance 1
MARR, Alem 1
MARR, Carl 1
MARR, George Washington Lent H
MARRIAGE, E. Charles D. 5
MARRINER, Robie D. 3
MARRINER, Theodore 1
MARRIOTT, Abraham Robert 1
MARRIOTT, Arthur C. 3
MARRIOTT, Crittenden 4
MARRIOTT, Ross W. 3
MARRIOTT, W. Mckim 1
MARRON, Adrian Raphael 4
MARRONE, Joseph 4
MARRS, Starlin Marion Newberry 1
MARRS, Wyatt 4
MARSCH, Wolf Dieter 6
MARSCHALL, Nicola H
MARSCHALL, Nicola 1
MARSDEN, Raymond Robb 2
MARSDEN, Robert Samuel 4
MARSH, Arthur Merwin 2
MARSH, Ben R. 1
MARSH, Benjamin Clarke 5
MARSH, Benjamin F. 1
MARSH, C. Dwight 1
MARSH, Charles 4
MARSH, Charles Edward 4
MARSH, Cleta McGinn (Mrs. Myron G. Marsh) 6
MARSH, Edward Clark 1
MARSH, Egbert 1
MARSH, Ernest Sterling 6
MARSH, Francis Hedley 2
MARSH, Frank Burr 1
MARSH, Frank Earl Jr. 4
MARSH, Frank Edward 4
MARSH, Fred Dana 4
MARSH, George Havens 6
MARSH, George Perkins H
MARSH, George T. 2
MARSH, Gerald E(lmir) 6
MARSH, Herbert Eugene 2
MARSH, James H

MARSH, James A. 2
MARSH, James Prentiss 2
MARSH, John * H
MARSH, John Bigelow 4
MARSH, Joseph Franklin 3
MARSH, Joseph William 1
MARSH, Mae 4
MARSH, Myron Maurice 4
MARSH, Othniel Charles H
MARSH, Raymond E(ugene) 5
MARSH, Reginald 3
MARSH, Robert McCurdy 1
MARSH, Spencer Scott 2
MARSH, Susan Louise Cotton (Mrs. Eugene Marsh) 5
MARSH, Sylvester H
MARSH, Tamerlane Pliny 1
MARSH, Walter Randall 2
MARSH, William John 6
MARSHALL, Albert Brainerd 1
MARSHALL, Albert Edward 3
MARSHALL, Albert Ware 5
MARSHALL, Alexander Keith H
MARSHALL, Alfred H
MARSHALL, Alfred 1
MARSHALL, Alfred C. 2
MARSHALL, Arthur Lawrence 3
MARSHALL, Benjamin H
MARSHALL, Benjamin Howard 6
MARSHALL, Benjamin Tinkham 1
MARSHALL, Bernard Gay 4
MARSHALL, Caroline Louise 4
MARSHALL, Carrington Tanner 3
MARSHALL, Charles 1
MARSHALL, Charles Clinton 1
MARSHALL, Charles Donnell 1
MARSHALL, Charles Edward 1
MARSHALL, Charles Henry H
MARSHALL, Christopher H
MARSHALL, Clara 5
MARSHALL, Clarence James 1
MARSHALL, Daniel H
MARSHALL, E. Kennerly Jr. 4
MARSHALL, Edison 6
MARSHALL, Edward 1
MARSHALL, Edward Asaph 1
MARSHALL, Edward Chauncey 1
MARSHALL, Edwin Jessop 4
MARSHALL, Elder Watson 5
MARSHALL, Elton Lewis 5
MARSHALL, Francis Cutler 4
MARSHALL, Frank Anton 6
MARSHALL, Frank James 4
MARSHALL, Frederick Rupert 4
MARSHALL, George Anthony 3
MARSHALL, George Catlett 3
MARSHALL, Harold 1
MARSHALL, Harold Joseph 4
MARSHALL, Henry Rutgers 1
MARSHALL, Henry Wright 3
MARSHALL, Herbert 4
MARSHALL, Herbert Camp 5
MARSHALL, Howard Drake 5
MARSHALL, Humphrey * H
MARSHALL, James A. K. 3
MARSHALL, James Markham 1
MARSHALL, James Rush 1
MARSHALL, James Wilson H
MARSHALL, John H
MARSHALL, John * 1
MARSHALL, John Albert 2
MARSHALL, John Augustine 1
MARSHALL, John Daniel 4
MARSHALL, John Noble 3
MARSHALL, John Patten 1
MARSHALL, Lenore G. (Mrs. James Marshall)
MARSHALL, Leon Carroll 4
MARSHALL, Louis H

MARSHALL, Louis 1
MARSHALL, M. Lee 3
MARSHALL, Marguerite 4
  Mooers
MARSHALL, Marvin Gene 6
MARSHALL, Nira Lovering 4
MARSHALL, Peter 2
MARSHALL, Ray Gifford 2
MARSHALL, Raymond 4
  Willett
MARSHALL, Rembert 3
MARSHALL, Richard Coke 4
Jr.
MARSHALL, Richard 6
Jacquelin
MARSHALL, Robert 4
Bradford
MARSHALL, Robert 4
Edward
MARSHALL, Robert Eliot 1
MARSHALL, Rosamond 3
Van der Zee
MARSHALL, Ross Smiley 4
MARSHALL, Roujet De 1
Lisle
MARSHALL, Roy E. 4
MARSHALL, Roy E(dgar) 5
MARSHALL, Samuel Scott H
MARSHALL, Stewart M. 4
MARSHALL, Thomas H
MARSHALL, Thomas * 1
MARSHALL, Thomas H
Alexander
MARSHALL, Thomas 5
Alfred Jr.
MARSHALL, Thomas 5
Chalmers
MARSHALL, Thomas H
Francis
MARSHALL, Thomas 1
Frank
MARSHALL, Thomas 5
Franklin
MARSHALL, Thomas L. 4
MARSHALL, Thomas 1
Maitland
MARSHALL, Thomas Riley 1
MARSHALL, Thomas 3
Worth
MARSHALL, Tully Phillips 2
MARSHALL, Verne 4
MARSHALL, Wade 5
Hampton
MARSHALL, Waldo H. 1
MARSHALL, Walter P(eter) 5
MARSHALL, William A. 1
MARSHALL, William 1
Alexander
MARSHALL, William 4
Champe
MARSHALL, William 3
Gilbert
MARSHALL, William 4
Kennedy
MARSHALL, William 5
LeGrand
MARSHALL, William Louis 1
MARSHALL, William H
Rainey
MARSHALL, William 2
Stanley
MARSHALL, William 6
Worton
MARSHBURN, Joseph 6
Hancock
MARSHMAN, John Tryon 4
MARSHUTZ, Elmer 4
Glenville
MARSHUTZ, Joseph H. 3
MARSIGLIA, Gherlando H
MARSLAND, Cora 4
MARSTEN, Francis Edward 1
MARSTON, Anson 3
MARSTON, Edgar Lewis 1
MARSTON, George W. 1
MARSTON, George White 2
MARSTON, Gilman H
MARSTON, Percival 1
Freeman
MARSTON, Sylvanus 2
Boardman
MARSTON, William 2
Moulton
MART, Leon T. 4
MARTEL, Charles 2
MARTEL, Romeo Raoul 4
MARTELL, Eldred Roland 3
MARTENS, Frederick 1
Herman
MARTENS, Walter Frederic 5
MARTI-IBANEZ, Felix 5
MARTIN, A. C. H
MARTIN, Abe 1
MARTIN, Albert Thompson 4
MARTIN, Alexander H
MARTIN, Alfred Wilhelm 1

MARTIN, Alvah Howard 1
MARTIN, Andrew Bennett 4
MARTIN, Anne Henrietta 4
MARTIN, Artemas 1
MARTIN, Arthur T. 2
MARTIN, Asa Earl 4
MARTIN, Auguste Marie H
MARTIN, Barclay 1
MARTIN, Benjamin Ellis 1
MARTIN, Benjamin H
Franklin
MARTIN, Bradley 1
MARTIN, Bradley 4
MARTIN, Burton McMahan 1
MARTIN, Carey 1
MARTIN, Carl Neidhard 5
MARTIN, Celora M. 1
MARTIN, Chalmers 1
MARTIN, Charles Cyril 1
MARTIN, Charles Fletcher 3
MARTIN, Charles Henry 2
MARTIN, Charles Irving 4
MARTIN, Chester W. 4
MARTIN, Clarence 4
MARTIN, Clarence 2
Augustine
MARTIN, Clarence Eugene 3
MARTIN, Crawford Collins 5
MARTIN, Daniel J. 5
MARTIN, Daniel Strobel 1
MARTIN, David B. 1
MARTIN, David Grier 6
MARTIN, David Herron 4
MARTIN, Dempster 1
Disbrow
MARTIN, Douglas DeVeny 4
MARTIN, Earle 1
MARTIN, Earle D. 5
MARTIN, Eben Wever 1
MARTIN, Edgar 3
MARTIN, Edgar Stanley 1
MARTIN, Edward 1
MARTIN, Edward 4
MARTIN, Edward Hamilton 1
MARTIN, Edward H
Livingston
MARTIN, Edward Sandford 1
MARTIN, Edwin Manton 3
MARTIN, Edwin Moore 1
MARTIN, Elbert Sevier H
MARTIN, Ellis 1
MARTIN, Elsie Stark (Mrs. 6
William H. Martin)
MARTIN, Ernest Gale 1
MARTIN, Everett Dean 1
MARTIN, F. O. 3
MARTIN, Fernando Wood 1
MARTIN, Florence Arminta 5
DeLong (Minta Martin)
MARTIN, Floyd A. 3
MARTIN, Francois-Xavier H
MARTIN, Frank 3
MARTIN, Frank 6
MARTIN, Frank Joseph 1
MARTIN, Frank Lee 1
MARTIN, Franklin H. 1
MARTIN, Fred James 6
MARTIN, Frederick LeRoy 3
MARTIN, Frederick Roy 1
MARTIN, Frederick Stanley H
MARTIN, Frederick 1
Townsend
MARTIN, G. Forrest 1
MARTIN, George 1
MARTIN, George Abraham 2
MARTIN, George Brown 1
MARTIN, George Curtis 5
MARTIN, George E. 2
MARTIN, George Ellsworth 1
MARTIN, George Henry 1
MARTIN, George Madden 2
MARTIN, George Marshall 4
MARTIN, George R(ead) 6
MARTIN, George Riley 1
MARTIN, George 3
Washington
MARTIN, George Whitney 1
MARTIN, George William 4
MARTIN, Gertrude Shorb 1
MARTIN, Gertrude Shorb 5
MARTIN, Glenn L. 2
MARTIN, Gustav Julius 4
MARTIN, Guy H. 1
MARTIN, Harold 5
Montgomery
MARTIN, Harry Brownlow 1
MARTIN, Harry Leland 3
MARTIN, Helen 1
Reimensnyder
MARTIN, Henry Austin H
MARTIN, Henry Newell H
MARTIN, Herbert Spencer 1
MARTIN, Homer Dodge H
MARTIN, Hugh 5
MARTIN, Hugh Krepps 6
MARTIN, Isaac Jack 4

MARTIN, J. H. Thayer 3
MARTIN, James 1
MARTIN, James Green 4
MARTIN, James Lawrence 3
MARTIN, James Loren 1
MARTIN, James 3
MacDonald
MARTIN, James Royal 6
MARTIN, James Sankey 4
MARTIN, John 1
MARTIN, John 2
MARTIN, John 3
MARTIN, John Alexander H
MARTIN, John Andrew 1
MARTIN, John H
Blennerhasset
MARTIN, John C. 3
MARTIN, John Calvin 3
MARTIN, John Donelson 4
MARTIN, John Irwin 1
MARTIN, John James 1
MARTIN, John Preston H
MARTIN, John Wellborn 3
MARTIN, Joseph 2
MARTIN, Joseph I. 3
MARTIN, Joseph William 4
Jr.
MARTIN, Joshua Lanier 1
MARTIN, Josiah H
MARTIN, Julius Corpening 2
MARTIN, Kingsley 2
Leverich
MARTIN, Larkin Morris 1
MARTIN, Lawrence 6
MARTIN, Lawrence 5
Crawford
MARTIN, Leroy Albert 5
MARTIN, Lester 3
MARTIN, Lillien Jane 2
MARTIN, Louis Adolphe 1
Jr.
MARTIN, Luther H
MARTIN, Luther III 4
MARTIN, Mabel Wood 3
MARTIN, Martha Evans 1
MARTIN, Mellen 3
Chamberlain
MARTIN, Melvin Albert 1
MARTIN, Miles Macon 4
MARTIN, Milward Wyatt 6
MARTIN, Morgan Lewis H
MARTIN, Motte 3
MARTIN, Patrick Minor 1
MARTIN, Paul Alexander 4
MARTIN, Paul Curtis 1
MARTIN, Paul Leo 4
MARTIN, Paul Sidney 6
MARTIN, Percy Alvin 2
MARTIN, Ralph Andrew 5
MARTIN, Raymond George 6
MARTIN, Reginald Wesley 5
MARTIN, Renwick Harper 5
MARTIN, Riccardo 3
MARTIN, Robert Grant 1
MARTIN, Robert Hugh 1
MARTIN, Robert Nicols 1
MARTIN, Robert William 6
MARTIN, Roscoe Coleman 5
MARTIN, Royce George 5
MARTIN, Samuel Albert 1
MARTIN, Santford 3
MARTIN, Selden Osgood 2
MARTIN, Sylvester 1
Mitchell
MARTIN, T. T. 3
MARTIN, Thomas 1
Commerford
MARTIN, Thomas 3
Ellsworth
MARTIN, Thomas Joseph 5
MARTIN, Thomas Paul 4
MARTIN, Thomas 1
Powderly
MARTIN, Thomas Staples 1
MARTIN, Thomas Wesley 4
MARTIN, V. G. 3
MARTIN, Victoria Claffin 1
Woodhull
MARTIN, Wallace Harold 5
MARTIN, Walter 1
Bramblette
MARTIN, Walton 2
MARTIN, Warren Frederic 6
MARTIN, Whitmell Pugh 1
MARTIN, William 3
MARTIN, William 1
Alexander Parsons
MARTIN, William Dobbin 1
MARTIN, William Elejius 5
MARTIN, William Franklin 2
MARTIN, William 6
H(ennick)
MARTIN, William Hope 1
MARTIN, William Joseph 2
MARTIN, William Joseph 4
MARTIN, William Leslie 4

MARTIN, William Logan 3
MARTIN, William Logan 4
MARTIN, William 3
McChesney
MARTIN, William Oliver 6
MARTIN, William Thomas 4
MARTIN, William 3
Thompson
MARTIN, Winfred Robert 1
MARTINDALE, Earl 4
Henry
MARTINDALE, F. Carew 4
MARTINDALE, Henry H
Clinton
MARTINDALE, John 2
Henry
MARTINDALE, Thomas 1
MARTIN DU GARD, 3
Roger
MARTINE, James Edgar 1
MARTINEAU, Harriet 4
MARTINEAU, John Ellis 1
MARTINEAU, Roland Guy 6
MARTINEK, Frank V(ictor) 5
MARTINELLI, Giovanni 4
MARTINEZ, Felix 1
MARTINEZ, Xavier 2
MARTINI, Roland 4
MARTINO, Gaetano 4
MARTINON, Jean 6
MARTINOT, Sadie 4
MARTINS, Maria Alves 5
MARTINU, Bohuslav 3
MARTINY, Philip 1
MARTS, Arnaud Cartwright 5
MARTS, Carroll Hartman 4
MARTWICK, William 5
Lorimer
MARTY, Martin H
MARTYN, Carlos 1
MARTYN, Chauncey White 1
MARTYN, Sarah Towne H
Smith
MARTZ, Hyman Scher 5
MARTZ, Velorus 6
MARUSZEWSKI, Mariusz 6
MARVEL, Josiah 3
MARVELL, George Ralph 2
MARVIN, Charles Frederick 2
MARVIN, Cloyd Heck 5
MARVIN, Dudley H
MARVIN, Dwight 5
MARVIN, Dwight Edwards 1
MARVIN, Enoch Mather H
MARVIN, Frank Olin 1
MARVIN, Fred Richard 4
MARVIN, Frederic 1
Rowland
MARVIN, George 1
MARVIN, Henry Howard 3
MARVIN, James Arthur 4
MARVIN, Joseph Benson 1
MARVIN, Langdon Parker 3
MARVIN, Richard Pratt H
MARVIN, Thomas O. 1
MARVIN, Walter S(ands) 1
MARVIN, Walter Taylor 1
MARVIN, William Glenn 1
MARVIN, Winthrop Lippitt 1
MARWEDEL, Emma 1
Jacobina Christiana
MARX, Alexander 3
MARX, Charles David 1
MARX, Guido Hugo 1
MARX, Harry S. 2
MARX, Karl H
MARX, Oscar B. 1
MARX, Otto 4
MARX, Robert S. 1
MARX, Samuel Abraham 4
MARYE, George Thomas 1
MARZALL, John Adams 3
MARZO, Eduardo 1
MASARYK, Jan 2
MASCHKE, Maurice 1
MASCUCH, John Thomas 4
MASE, Stanley Wilson 4
MASEFIELD, John 4
MASENG, Sigurd 3
MASHBURN, (Arthur) 1
Gray
MASHBURN, Lloyd A. 4
MASLAND, John W(esley) 5
Jr.
MASLOW, Abraham Harold 5
MASON, A. Lawrence 4
MASON, Abraham John H
MASON, Alfred Bishop 1
MASON, Alfred De Witt 1
MASON, Alvin Hughlett 6
MASON, Amelia Gere 1
MASON, Armistead H
Thomson
MASON, Arthur Ellery 4
MASON, Augustus Lynch 1
MASON, Bernard Sterling 3

MASON, C. Avery 5
MASON, Caroline Atwater 1
MASON, Cassity E. 1
MASON, Charles H
MASON, Charles Frederick 4
MASON, Charles Harrison 4
MASON, Charles Noble 5
MASON, Claibourne Rice 1
MASON, Daniel Gregory 3
MASON, David Hastings 1
MASON, Edith (Barnes) 6
MASON, Edward 1
Tuckerman
MASON, Edward Wilson 2
MASON, Emily Virginia 1
MASON, Francis H
MASON, Frank Holcomb 1
MASON, Frank Stuart 1
MASON, George * H
MASON, George Allen 3
MASON, George Champlin H
MASON, George Dewitt 5
MASON, George Grant 3
MASON, G(eorge) Grant Jr. 5
MASON, George Jefferson 4
MASON, George W. 3
MASON, Guy 3
MASON, Harold Whitney 1
MASON, Harriet L. 4
MASON, Harry Howland 4
MASON, Henry H
MASON, Henry Freeman 1
MASON, Herbert Delavan 1
MASON, J. Alden 4
MASON, James Brown 1
MASON, James Monroe 5
MASON, James Murray 3
MASON, James Orley 1
MASON, James Tate 1
MASON, James Weir 1
MASON, Jeremiah H
MASON, Jesse Henry 2
MASON, John 1
MASON, John 1
MASON, John Calvin H
MASON, John Henry 1
MASON, John Mitchell 1
MASON, John Thomson 1
MASON, John William 1
MASON, John Young H
MASON, Jonathan H
MASON, Joseph Warren 1
Teets
MASON, Julian 3
Starkweather
MASON, L. Walter 1
MASON, Leslie Fenton 1
MASON, Lewis Duncan 1
MASON, Lowell H
MASON, Luther Whiting 1
MASON, Madison Charles 1
Butler
MASON, Mary Augusta 5
MASON, Mary Knight 4
Wood
MASON, Maud M. 3
MASON, Max 4
MASON, Michael L. 4
MASON, Miriam 6
Evangeline (Mrs. Miriam
Mason Swain)
MASON, (Mortimer) 5
Phillips
MASON, Moses Jr. H
MASON, Newton Eliphalet 2
MASON, Noah Morgan 5
MASON, Otis Tufton 1
MASON, Richard Barnes H
MASON, Roy Martell 5
MASON, Rufus Osgood 1
MASON, Samson H
MASON, Samuel 1
MASON, Silas Boxley 1
MASON, Silas Cheever 1
MASON, Stevens H
Thomson *
MASON, Thomson H
MASON, Victor Louis 1
MASON, Wallace Edward 2
MASON, Walt 1
MASON, Wilbur Nesbitt 1
MASON, William * H
MASON, William 1
MASON, William Clarke 3
MASON, William Ernest 1
MASON, William Madison 5
MASON, William Pitt 1
MASON, William Sanford H
MASON, William Smith 4
MASON, William Woodman 1
MASQUERAY, Emmanuel 1
Louis
MASQUERIER, Lewis H
MASSAGLIA, Joseph Jr. 5
MASSASSOIT H

MASSEE, Edward Kingsley 3
MASSEE, Jasper Cortenus 5
MASSEE, May 4
MASSEE, William Wellington 2
MASSEY, George Betton 1
MASSEY, George Valentine 1
MASSEY, John 4
MASSEY, Lucius Saunders 4
MASSEY, Luther M. 5
MASSEY, Mary Elizabeth 6
MASSEY, Richard W. 3
MASSEY, Vincent 4
MASSEY, Wilbur Fisk 1
MASSEY, William Alexander 1
MASSIE, David Meade 1
MASSIE, Eugene Carter 1
MASSIE, Robert Kinloch 1
MASSIE, Robert Kinloch Jr. 1
MASSINGALE, Sam Chapman 1
MASSLICH, Chester Bentley 1
MASSMANN, Frederick H. 5
MASSON, Henry James 6
MASSON, Robert Louis 5
MASSON, Thomas L. 1
MAST, Burdette Pond 4
MAST, Phineas Price H
MAST, Samuel Ottmar 2
MASTER, Arthur Matthew 6
MASTER, Henry Buck 1
MASTERS, Edgar Lee 2
MASTERS, Frank Meriro 2
MASTERS, Harris Kennedy 5
MASTERS, Howard Russell 4
MASTERS, John Volney 3
MASTERS, Josiah H
MASTERS, Keith 5
MASTERS, Victor Irvine 4
MASTERSON, John Joseph 4
MASTERSON, Kate 5
MASTERSON, Patrick J. 3
MASTERSON, William Barclay H
MASTERSON, William Barclay 4
MASTERSON, William Edward 5
MASTERSON, William Wesley 1
MASTICK, Seabury Cone 5
MASTIN, Claudius Henry H
MASTIN, William McDowell 1
MASTON, Robert H. 3
MASUR, Jack 5
MASURY, John Wesley H
MATAS, Rudolph 3
MATCHETT, Charles Horatio 1
MATCHETT, David Fleming 2
MATEER, Calvin Wilson 1
MATELIGER, Jan Ernst 1
MATHENY, Ezra Stacy 5
MATHER, Alonzo Clark 1
MATHER, Arthur 2
MATHER, Cotton H
MATHER, Elmer James 3
MATHER, Frank Jewett Jr. 3
MATHER, Fred 1
MATHER, Frederic Gregory 1
MATHER, Gordon Macdonald 3
MATHER, Increase H
MATHER, John Waterhouse 4
MATHER, Margaret 1
MATHER, Morgan Herbert
MATHER, Richard H
MATHER, Robert 1
MATHER, Rufus Graves 3
MATHER, S. Livingston 4
MATHER, Samuel H
MATHER, Samuel 1
MATHER, Samuel Holmes H
MATHER, Samuel Livingston H
MATHER, Stephen Tyng 1
MATHER, Thomas Ray 2
MATHER, William Allan 4
MATHER, William Gwinn 3
MATHER, William Tyler 1
MATHER, William Williams H
MATHERLY, Walter Jeffries
MATHERS, Frank C(urry) 5
MATHERS, Hugh Thompson 4
MATHES, James Monroe 3
MATHES, William C. 2
MATHESIUS, Walther Emil Ludwig 4
MATHESON, Alexander E. 1

MATHESON, George Wilson 3
MATHESON, James Pleasant 4
MATHESON, John F. 4
MATHESON, Kenneth Gordon 1
MATHESON, Martin 5
MATHESON, Robert 3
MATHESON, William John 1
MATHEWS, Albert 1
MATHEWS, Albert Prescott 3
MATHEWS, Alfred 1
MATHEWS, Alfred E. H
MATHEWS, Arthur Frank 1
MATHEWS, Basil Joseph 3
MATHEWS, Charles Thomson 1
MATHEWS, Clarence Wentworth 1
MATHEWS, Clifton 4
MATHEWS, Cornelius H
MATHEWS, David Oscar 6
MATHEWS, Delancey North 1
MATHEWS, Edward Bennett 1
MATHEWS, F. Schuyler 1
MATHEWS, Frances Aymar 2
MATHEWS, Frank A. Jr. 1
MATHEWS, Frank Stuart 1
MATHEWS, George 1
MATHEWS, George C. 4
MATHEWS, George Martin 1
MATHEWS, Henry Mason 1
MATHEWS, James H
MATHEWS, James Abram 1
MATHEWS, James Edward 1
MATHEWS, James Thomas 2
MATHEWS, Joanna Hooe 1
MATHEWS, John H
MATHEWS, John Alexander 1
MATHEWS, John Elie 3
MATHEWS, John Lathrop 1
MATHEWS, Joseph Howard 5
MATHEWS, Joseph McDowell 4
MATHEWS, S. Sherberne 1
MATHEWS, Samuel H
MATHEWS, Shailer 2
MATHEWS, Vincent H
MATHEWS, William 1
MATHEWS, William Burdette 2
MATHEWS, William Hooker 3
MATHEWS, William Rankin 5
MATHEWS, William Smith Babcock 1
MATHEWS, William T. H
MATHEWSON, Champion Herbert 6
MATHEWSON, Charles Frederick 1
MATHEWSON, Christopher H
MATHEWSON, Christopher 4
MATHEWSON, Edward Payson 5
MATHEWSON, Elisha H
MATHEWSON, Ozias Danforth 2
MATHEWSON, Stanley Bernard 2
MATHEY, Dean 5
MATHIAS, Henry Edwin 4
MATHIAS, Robert David 3
MATHIES, Wharton 5
MATHIESON, Samuel James 1
MATHIEU, Beltran 4
MATHIOT, Joshua H
MATHIS, Harry R. 4
MATHISON, Edward Thomson H
MATIGNON, John Kelly 6
MATIGNON, Francis Anthony H
MATILE, Leon Albert 1
MATISSE, Henri 3
MATISSE, Henri 4
MATLACK, James 1
MATLACK, Timothy H
MATRONE, Gennard 6
MATSCH, Franz 6
MATSON, Aaron 1
MATSON, Carlton Kingsbury 1
MATSON, Caroline Ruby 4
MATSON, Clarence Henry 2
MATSON, Courtland Cushing 1
MATSON, Donald Darrow 5

MATSON, Frederick Eugene 1
MATSON, George Charlton 1
MATSON, Henry 1
MATSON, Leroy E. 4
MATSON, Max M. 5
MATSON, Ralph Charles 2
MATSON, Robert H. 3
MATSON, Roderick Nathaniel 1
MATSON, Roy Lee 4
MATSON, Smith Corbin 1
MATSON, Theodore Malvin 3
MATSON, William 1
MATSUDAIRA, Tsuneo 2
MATTEI, Albert Chester 5
MATTERN, David Earl 3
MATTERSON, Clarence H. 4
MATTESON, Charles 1
MATTESON, Frank Willington 1
MATTESON, Herman Howard 3
MATTESON, Joel Aldrich H
MATTESON, Leonard Jerome 1
MATTESON, Orsamus Benajah H
MATTESON, Tompkins Harrison H
MATTESON, Victor Andre 1
MATTFELD, Marie 5
MATTHAEI, Frederick Carl 5
MATTHAI, William Henry 4
MATTHES, Francois Emile 2
MATTHES, Gerard Hendrik 3
MATTHEW, Allan Pomeroy 4
MATTHEW, Robert Hogg 6
MATTHEW, Robert John 6
MATTHEW, William Diller 1
MATTHEWMAN, Lisle de Vaux 1
MATTHEWS, Albert * 2
MATTHEWS, Armstrong R. 3
MATTHEWS, Arthur John 2
MATTHEWS, Brander 1
MATTHEWS, Burrows 1
MATTHEWS, Charles Herbert 4
MATTHEWS, Charles Samuel 5
MATTHEWS, Claude H
MATTHEWS, Edmund Orville 1
MATTHEWS, Ernest Crawford III 6
MATTHEWS, Eugene Alexander 5
MATTHEWS, Francis Patrick 3
MATTHEWS, Franklin 1
MATTHEWS, George Edward 1
MATTHEWS, Harlan Julius 3
MATTHEWS, H(arry) Alexander 6
MATTHEWS, Harry S. Jr. 3
MATTHEWS, Hugh 4
MATTHEWS, Isaac George 3
MATTHEWS, J. Merritt 1
MATTHEWS, John H
MATTHEWS, Mark Allison 1
MATTHEWS, Murrell O. 1
MATTHEWS, Nathan 1
MATTHEWS, Nelson Edwin 1
MATTHEWS, Orus Jones 4
MATTHEWS, Paul 3
MATTHEWS, Robert David 2
MATTHEWS, Robert Orville 2
MATTHEWS, Sir Ronald Wilfred 4
MATTHEWS, Stanley H
MATTHEWS, Stephen Johnson 5
MATTHEWS, Velma Dare 5
MATTHEWS, Walter Robert 6
MATTHEWS, Washington 1
MATTHEWS, William * H
MATTHEWS, William 6
MATTHEWS, William Albert 1
MATTHEWS, William Baynham 1
MATTHEWS, William Henry 2
MATTHEWS, William Henry 5
MATTHEWS, Zachariah Keodirelang 5
MATTHIAS, Edward Shiloh 3
MATTHIAS, John Marshall 5

MATTHIESSEN, Francis Otto 3
MATTHIESSEN, Ralph H. 6
MATTHISON, Edith Wynne 1
MATTIA, Virginius Dante 5
MATTICE, Burr 1
MATTIELLO, Joseph J. 2
MATTIMORE, John Clarke 6
MATTILL, Henry Albright 3
MATTINGLY, Barak Thomas 5
MATTINGLY, Frederick Browning 5
MATTINGLY, Garrett 4
MATTINGLY, Robert Edgar 4
MATTINGLY, William Francis 1
MATTIOLI, Lino 4
MATTISON, Donald Magnus 6
MATTISON, Fitch Champlin Edmonds 1
MATTISON, Hiram H
MATTISON, Richard Vanselous 1
MATTLIN, A. Homer 4
MATTOCKS, Charles Porter 1
MATTOCKS, John H
MATTOON, Arthur Martyn 1
MATTOON, Ebenezer H
MATTOON, Stephen H
MATTOX, William Earl 5
MATTSON, Bernard Gause 4
MATTSON, Hans 1
MATTSON, Karl Evald 4
MATTSON, Peter August 2
MATZ, Myron Harold 6
MATZ, Nicholas 1
MATZ, Philip Benjamin 1
MATZ, Rudolph 1
MATZEN, Herman N. 1
MATZENAUER, Margarete 4
MATZKE, Edwin Bernard 5
MATZKE, John Ernst 1
MAUBORGNE, Joseph Oswald 5
MAUCHLY, Sebastian Jacob 1
MAUCK, Joseph William 1
MAUCK, Wilfred Otto 6
MAUDE, Cyril Francis 3
MAUDE, William L. 4
MAUGH, Lawrence C(arnahan) 5
MAUGHAM, W. Somerset 4
MAUK, Charlotte E. 6
MAULDIN, Frank Gratin 1
MAULE, Frances 4
MAULE, Harry Edward 5
MAULE, Tallie Burton 6
MAUMUS, Achilles J. 4
MAURAN, John Lawrence 1
MAURER, Edward Rose 2
MAURER, Irving 2
MAURER, James Hudson 3
MAURER, James Hudson 5
MAURER, Oscar Edward 3
MAURER, Robert Adam 6
MAURER, William Allen 1
MAURIAC, Francois 5
MAURICE, Arthur Bartlett 1
MAURICE, James H
MAURILLO, Dominick 6
MAURITZSON, Jules Gote Ultimus 1
MAURO, Philip 3
MAUROIS, Andre 4
MAURY, Antonia Caetana de Paiva Pereira 3
MAURY, Carlotta Joaquina 1
MAURY, Dabney Herndon 1 *
MAURY, Francis Fontaine H
MAURY, John William 5
MAURY, Magruder Gordon 2
MAURY, Matthew Fontaine H
MAURY, Mytton 1
MAURY, Richard Brooke 1
MAURY, William Arden 1
MAUS, L. Mervin 1
MAUS, Marion Perry 1
MAUS, William Donald 4
MAUTHE, J. L. 4
MAUZé, Jean 6
MAUZE, Joseph Layton 4
MAVEETY, Patrick John 2
MAVER, William Jr. 1
MAVERICK, Maury 3
MAVERICK, Peter H
MAVERICK, Samuel H
MAWHINNEY, Robert James 3

MAXCY, Carroll Lewis 1
MAXCY, Charles Josiah 4
MAXCY, Gardiner Josiah 5
MAXCY, Jonathan 1
MAXCY, Kenneth Fuller 4
MAXCY, Virgil H
MAXEY, Edward Ernest 1
MAXEY, Edwin 5
MAXEY, George Wendell 2
MAXEY, Samuel Bell 1
MAXEY, Thomas S. 1
MAXFIELD, Ezra Kempton 1
MAXFIELD, Francis Norton 2
MAXIM, Hiram Percy 1
MAXIM, Hiram Stevens 1
MAXIM, Hudson 1
MAXIMILIAN H
MAXIMOS, Demetrios 3
MAXON, James Matthew 4
MAXON, Lou Russell 5
MAXON, William Densmore 1
MAXON, William Ralph 2
MAXSON, Ralph Nelson 2
MAXSON, Willis Edward 3
MAXWELL, Allison 2
MAXWELL, Archibald McIntyre 2
MAXWELL, Arthur Freeman 5
MAXWELL, Arthur Stanley 5
MAXWELL, Arthur Stanley 5
MAXWELL, Augustus Emmett 1
MAXWELL, Charles Augustus 4
MAXWELL, Charles Robert 1
MAXWELL, David Hervey H
MAXWELL, Elsa 4
MAXWELL, Evelyn Croom 3
MAXWELL, Francis Taylor 2
MAXWELL, Gavin 5
MAXWELL, George H
MAXWELL, George Clifford
MAXWELL, George Hebard 2
MAXWELL, George Holmes 1
MAXWELL, George Lawrence 2
MAXWELL, George Troup H
MAXWELL, Guy Everett 1
MAXWELL, Haymond 4
MAXWELL, Hugh 1
MAXWELL, James Angus 4
MAXWELL, James Hoyt 4
MAXWELL, John Mills 4
MAXWELL, John Milo 4
MAXWELL, John Patterson Bryan H
MAXWELL, John Rogers 1
MAXWELL, Joseph Raymond Nonnatus 5
MAXWELL, Lawrence 1
MAXWELL, Lee Wilder 2
MAXWELL, Leon Ryder 4
MAXWELL, Lewis H
MAXWELL, Lucien Bonaparte 1
MAXWELL, Margery 4
MAXWELL, Ralph Lester 3
MAXWELL, Russell Lamonte 5
MAXWELL, Samuel 1
MAXWELL, Samuel Steen 4
MAXWELL, Thomas H
MAXWELL, William * H
MAXWELL, William Allison Jr. 2
MAXWELL, William Cochrane 1
MAXWELL, William Donald 6
MAXWELL, William Henry 1
MAXWELL, William John 4
MAY, A. Wilfred 5
MAY, Alonzo Beryl 1
MAY, Andrew Jackson 3
MAY, Arthur James 5
MAY, Charles Henry 2
MAY, David 1
MAY, David William 1
MAY, Earl Chapin 4
MAY, Edna 1
MAY, Edward 1
MAY, Edward Harrison H
MAY, Edwin 1
MAY, Ernest H. 1
MAY, Geoffrey 4
MAY, George Oliver 4
MAY, George Storr 4
MAY, Henry 1
MAY, Herbert Arthur 4
MAY, Herbert Louis 4
MAY, Irving 1

MAY, Jacques Meyer 6
MAY, James Vance 2
MAY, Julia Harris 1
MAY, Luke S. 4
MAY, Max 1
MAY, Max Benjamin 1
MAY, Mortimer 6
MAY, Morton J. 5
MAY, Samuel Chester 3
MAY, Samuel Joseph H
MAY, Stella Burke 4
MAY, Thomas 1
MAY, Thomas 1
MAY, William Andrew 1
MAY, William Henry 5
MAY, William L. H
MAYALL, Samuel H
MAYBANK, Burnet Rhett 5
MAYBECK, Bernard Ralph 5
MAYBELL, Claude 5
MAYBURY, William Cotter 1
MAYER, Albert J. Jr. 4
MAYER, Alfred Marshall 3
MAYER, Andre 3
MAYER, Brantz H
MAYER, Charles Herbert 4
MAYER, Charles Holt 5
MAYER, Charles Raphael 4
MAYER, Constant 1
MAYER, Edgar 6
MAYER, Edward Everett 5
MAYER, Elias 2
MAYER, Emil 1
MAYER, Ernest De W(ael) 5
MAYER, Francis Blackwell H
MAYER, Gottfried Oscar 5
MAYER, Harry Hubert 5
MAYER, Henrik Martin 5
MAYER, Hy 3
MAYER, Isaac Henry 4
MAYER, John Ignatius 6
MAYER, Joseph 6
MAYER, Joseph Bell 3
MAYER, Julius M. 1
MAYER, Levy 1
MAYER, Lewis H
MAYER, Louis Burt 3
MAYER, Lucius W. 2
MAYER, Maria Goeppert 5
MAYER, Oscar F. 3
MAYER, Oscar Gottried 4
MAYER, Philip Frederick H
MAYER, Rene 5
MAYER, Richard 4
MAYER, Robert B. 6
MAYERS, Lawrence Seymour 3
MAYERS, Lewis 6
MAYES, Edward 1
MAYES, Joel Bryan H
MAYES, Robert Burns 1
MAYES, William Harding 4
MAYFIELD, Earle Bradford 4
MAYFIELD, Irving Hall 5
MAYFIELD, James Jefferson 1
MAYHAM, Ray Edwin 3
MAYHEW, Experience H
MAYHEW, George Noel 4
MAYHEW, Jonathan H
MAYHEW, Thomas * H
MAYLATH, Heinrich H
MAYNADIER, Gustavus Howard 4
MAYNARD, Charles Johnson 1
MAYNARD, Edward H
MAYNARD, Edwin Post 2
MAYNARD, Fred Augustus 4
MAYNARD, George Colton 1
MAYNARD, George William 1
MAYNARD, George Willoughby 1
MAYNARD, Harold Howard 3
MAYNARD, Harry Lee 4
MAYNARD, Horace H
MAYNARD, James 1
MAYNARD, John H
MAYNARD, John Albert 4
MAYNARD, John Blackwell 2
MAYNARD, John Walter 1
MAYNARD, John William 3
MAYNARD, La Salle Almeron 1
MAYNARD, Laurens 4
MAYNARD, Leonard Amby 5
MAYNARD, Lester 5
MAYNARD, Mila Tupper 4
MAYNARD, Poole 4
MAYNARD, Reuben Leslie 2
MAYNARD, Rezin Augustus 4

MAYNARD, Richard Field 4
MAYNARD, Robert Washburn 5
MAYNARD, Roger 5
MAYNARD, Samuel Taylor 1
MAYNARD, Theodore 3
MAYNARD, Walter 5
MAYNARD, Walter Effingham 1
MAYNARD, Washburn 1
MAYNARD, William Hale 1
MAYNE, Arthur Ferdinand 5
MAYNE, Dexter Dwight 4
MAYO, Amory Dwight 1
MAYO, Charles Horace 1
MAYO, Chester Garst 6
MAYO, Earl Williams 3
MAYO, Edmund Cooper 5
MAYO, Frank H
MAYO, Frederick Joseph 5
MAYO, George Elton 2
MAYO, Henry Thomas 1
MAYO, Katherine 1
MAYO, Nelson Slater 3
MAYO, Robert H
MAYO, Robert Murphy H
MAYO, Robert William Bainbridge 1
MAYO, Sarah Carter Edgarton 1
MAYO, William H
MAYO, William Benson 2
MAYO, William James 1
MAYO, William Kennon H
MAYO, William Kennon 1
MAYO, William Starbuck H
MAYOR, Alfred Goldsborough 1
MAYO-SMITH, Richmond 1
MAYRANT, William H
MAYS, Calhoun Allen 5
MAYS, Dannitte Hill 4
MAYS, David John 5
MAYS, Floyd Rosenbaum 3
MAYS, James H. 4
MAYS, Paul Kirtland 5
MAYS, Percy Joseph 6
MAYTAG, Fred II 4
MAYTAG, Frederick L. 5
MAYTAG, Lewis B. 4
MAZA, Jose 4
MAZE, Matthew T. 1
MAZER, Jacob 5
MAZER, Robert 2
MAZET, Robert H
MAZUREAU, Etienne H
MAZYCK, William Gaillard 2
MAZZANOVICH, Lawrence 4
MAZZEI, Philip H
MAZZILLI, Ranieri 6
MAZZUCHELLI, Samuel Charles H
M'BA, Leon 4
MCADAM, David 1
MCADAM, Dunlap Jamison 1
MCADAM, Edward Lippincott Jr. 5
MCADAM, George Harrison 1
MCADAMS, Clark 1
MCADAMS, John Pope 4
MCADAMS, Joseph Edward 6
MCADAMS, Thomas Branch 3
MCADIE, Alexander George 2
MCADOO, Henry Molseed 5
MCADOO, Mary Faith Floyd 5
MCADOO, William 1
MCADOO, William Gibbs 1
MCAFEE, Cleland Boyd 2
MCAFEE, John Armstrong H
MCAFEE, Joseph Ernest 2
MCAFEE, Lowell Mason 1
MCAFEE, Ralph Canfield 4
MCAFEE, Robert Breckinridge H
MCAFEE, Robert William 6
MCAFEE, William A(rchibald) 5
MCALEER, William 4
MCALESTER, Andrew Walker 1
MCALESTER, Andrew Walker Jr. 1
MCALEXANDER, Ulysses Grant 1
MCALISTER, Alexander Worth 3
MCALISTER, Heber Lowrey 3
MCALISTER, Hill 3
MCALISTER, John Barr 2

MCALISTER, Samuel Bertran 4
MCALISTER, William King 1
MCALL, Reginald Ley 3
MCALLESTER, Samuel Jackson 3
MCALLISTER, Addams Stratton 2
MCALLISTER, Alan H. 5
MCALLISTER, Archibald H
MCALLISTER, Charles Albert 1
MCALLISTER, Charles Eldridge 3
MCALLISTER, David 1
MCALLISTER, Elliott 5
MCALLISTER, Frank Winton 2
MCALLISTER, George Franklin 5
MCALLISTER, Hall H
MCALLISTER, Harry Lee 6
MCALLISTER, Henry 1
MCALLISTER, J(ames) Gray 5
MCALLISTER, Joseph Thompson 1
MCALLISTER, Matthew Hall H
MCALLISTER, Samuel Ward H
MCALLISTER, Sydney G. 4
MCALLISTER, Ward 1
MCALONEY, Thomas Simpson 1
MCALPIN, Benjamin Brandreth 1
MCALPIN, Edwin Augustus 1
MCALPINE, Charles Alonzo 2
MCALPINE, Kenneth 4
MCALPINE, William H. 3
MCALPINE, William Jarvis H
MCALVAY, Aaron Vance 1
MCANALLY, Arthur 5
MCANALLY, David Rice Monroe 1
MCANANY, Edwin Sebast H
MCANDLESS, Alva John 3
MCANDREW, James William 1
MCANDREW, William 1
MCANDREW, William Robert 5
MCANDREWS, James 2
MCANEENY, William Joseph 1
MCANENY, George 3
MCANNEY, B. O. 4
MCARDLE, Joseph A. 4
MCARDLE, Montrose Pallen 1
MCARDLE, Thomas Eugene 4
MCARTHUR, Charles Mortimer 6
MCARTHUR, Clifton Nesmith 1
MCARTHUR, Duncan H
MCARTHUR, John H
MCARTHUR, John 1
MCARTHUR, Lewis Linn 1
MCARTHUR, Lewis Linn Jr. 3
MCARTHUR, William Pope H
MCARTHUR, William Taylor 1
MCATEE, John Lind 1
MCAULEY, Thomas H
MCAULIFF, Cornelius 1
MCAULIFFE, Anthony C. 6
MCAULIFFE, Daniel J. 4
MCAULIFFE, Eugene 3
MCAULIFFE, John 4
MCAULIFFE, Joseph John 2
MCAULIFFE, Maurice Francis 2
MCAVITY, Malcolm 2
MCAVOY, Charles D. 1
MCAVOY, John Vincent 1
MC AVOY, Thomas D. 4
MCAVOY, Thomas Timothy 5
MCBAIN, Howard Lee 1
MCBAIN, James William 4
MCBAINE, James Patterson 4
MCBEAN, Atholl 6
MCBEAN, Thomas H
MCBEATH, James Mark 4
MCBEE, Earl Thurston 5
MCBEE, Mary Vardrine 4
MCBEE, Silas 1
MCBRAYER, Louis Burgin 1
MCBRIDE, Allan Clay 3
MCBRIDE, Andrew Jay 4
MCBRIDE, F. Scott 3

MCBRIDE, George McCutchen 5
MCBRIDE, George Wickliffe 1
MCBRIDE, Harold Herkimer 4
MCBRIDE, Harry Alexander 4
MCBRIDE, Henry 1
MCBRIDE, James Harvey 1
MCBRIDE, Karl R. Sr. 1
MCBRIDE, Malcolm Lee 2
MCBRIDE, Robert Edwin 2
MCBRIDE, Robert W. 1
MCBRIDE, Thomas Allen 1
MCBRIDE, Wilbert George 6
MCBRIDE, William Manley 3
MCBRIEN, Dean Depew 4
MCBRIEN, Jasper Leonidas 1
MCBROOM, Charles Emmett 4
MCBRYDE, Archibald 1
MCBRYDE, Charles Neil 5
MCBRYDE, James Bolton 1
MCBRYDE, John McLaren 1
MCBRYDE, Warren Horton 5
MCBURNEY, Charles 1
MCBURNEY, John White 4
MCBURNEY, Ralph 4
MCBURNEY, Robert Ross H
MCCABE, Charles B. 5
MCCABE, Charles Cardwell 1
MCCABE, Charles Martin 5
MCCABE, David Aloysius 5
MCCABE, Edward Raynsford Warner 5
MCCABE, Francis Xavier 1
MCCABE, Harriet Calista 1
MCCABE, James Dabney 4
MCCABE, John Collins H
MCCABE, Lida Rose 1
MCCABE, W. Gordon 1
MCCABE, William Hugh 4
MCCADDEN, John Edward 4
MCCAFFERTY, Don 5
MCCAFFERTY, Thomas Bowles 3
MCCAFFERY, Richard Stanislaus 2
MCCAFFREY, John H
MCCAGG, Ezra Butler 1
MCCAHAN, David 3
MCCAHEY, James B. 6
MCCAIG, William Dougal 5
MCCAIN, Charles Curtice 2
MCCAIN, Charles Simonton 3
MCCAIN, Dewey Marven 4
MCCAIN, George Nox 1
MCCAIN, Henry Pinckney 1
MCCAIN, James Ross 4
MCCAIN, John Sidney 2
MCCAIN, Paul Pressly 2
MCCAIN, Samuel Adams 4
MCCAIN, William Alexander 6
MCCAIN, William Dwight 6
MCCAIN, William Ross 6
MCCAINE, Alexander H
MCCALEB, Ella 1
MCCALEB, John Bell 1
MCCALEB, Theodore Howard 1
MCCALEB, Walter Flavius 5
MCCALL, Arthur G. 3
MCCALL, Edward Everett 1
MCCALL, Edward Rutledge H
MCCALL, Fred(erick) B(ays) 5
MCCALL, Harry 4
MCCALL, John A. 1
MCCALL, John Etheridge 1
MCCALL, John Opple 6
MCCALL, Milton Lawrence Samuel 4
MCCALL, Oswald Walter 3
MCCALL, Peter H
MCCALL, Samuel Walker 1
MCCALL, Thomas 2
MCCALL, Thomas Montgomery 4
MCCALLA, Albert 1
MCCALLA, Bowman Henry 1
MCCALLA, Elizabeth Hazard Sargent 4
MCCALLA, William Latta H
MCCALLAM, James Alexander 5
MCCALLEY, Henry 1
MCCALLIE, Robert Lewis 4
MCCALLIE, Samuel Washington 1
MCCALLIE, Spencer Jarnagin 2
MCCALLIE, Thomas Spencer 1
MCCALLUM, Angus 5

MCCALLUM, Daniel Craig H
MCCALLUM, Francis Marion 2
MCCAMANT, Wallace 4
MCCAMBRIDGE, William J. 4
MCCAMEY, Harold Emerson 4
MCCAMIC, Charles 3
MCCAMMON, George Edward 4
MCCAMMON, Joseph Kay 1
MCCAMMON, Milo Franklin 4
MCCAMPBELL, Charles Wilbur 4
MCCAMPBELL, Eugene Franklin 1
MCCAMPBELL, Leavelle 2
MCCANCE, Pressly Hodge 4
MCCANDLESS, Boyd Bowden 6
MCCANDLESS, Bruce 5
MCCANDLESS, Byron 6
MCCANDLESS, David Alexander 1
MCCANDLESS, James W. 4
MCCANDLESS, John Andrew 1
MCCANDLESS, Lincoln Loy 1
MCCANDLESS, Robert Buchanan 3
MCCANDLISH, Benjamin Vaughan 6
MCCANDLISS, Lester Chipman 2
MCCANN, Alfred W. 1
MCCANN, Charles Mallette 3
MCCANN, George 1
MCCANN, Harold Gilman 5
MCCANN, Harrison King 4
MCCANN, James J. 4
MCCANN, R. L. 5
MCCANN, Rebecca 1
MCCANN, Robert Caldwell 4
MCCANN, Thomas Addison 2
MCCANN, William Penn 1
MCCANN, William Sharp 6
MCCANNA, Henry Anthony 6
MCCANTS, E. Crayton 3
MCCARDELL, Claire 3
MCCARDELL, Lee Adrian 4
MCCARDELL, Roy Larcom 5
MCCARDLE, Carl Wesley 5
MCCAREY, (Thomas) Leo 5
MCCARL, John Raymond 1
MCCARN, Jeff 2
MCCARRAN, Patrick A. 3
MCCARRAN, Patrick H. 1
MCCARRENS, John S. 2
MCCARROLL, Henry Relton 5
MCCARROLL, James H
MCCARROLL, Russell Hudson 2
MCCARROLL, William 1
MCCARTAN, Edward 2
MCCARTEE, Divie Bethune H
MCCARTEN, John 6
MCCARTER, Henry 2
MCCARTER, James W. 1
MCCARTER, Margaret Hill 1
MCCARTER, Richard Farrell 1
MCCARTER, Robert Harris 1
MCCARTER, Thomas Nesbitt 1
MCCARTER, Thomas Nesbitt 3
MCCARTER, Thomas Nesbitt 4
MCCARTER, Thomas Nesbitt Jr. 1
MCCARTER, Uzal H. 1
MCCARTHY, Carlton 4
MCCARTHY, Charles 1
MCCARTHY, Charles Hallan 2
MCCARTHY, Charles James 1
MCCARTHY, Daniel Edward 1
MCCARTHY, Daniel J. 3
MCCARTHY, Denis Aloysius 1
MCCARTHY, Dennis H
MCCARTHY, Edward 4
MCCARTHY, Edward 5
MCCARTHY, Eugene 1
MCCARTHY, Eugene Ross 5
MCCARTHY, Frank Jeremiah 1

MCCARTHY, Henry Francis 4
MCCARTHY, J. A. 6
MCCARTHY, James Anthony Joseph 4
MCCARTHY, James E. 3
MCCARTHY, James Frederick 1
MCCARTHY, John E. 4
MCCARTHY, John Ralph 4
MCCARTHY, Joseph Edward 3
MCCARTHY, Joseph Francis 4
MCCARTHY, Joseph R. 3
MCCARTHY, Justin Howard 5
MCCARTHY, Kathryn O'loughlin 3
MCCARTHY, Kenneth Cecil 4
MCCARTHY, Leighton Goldie 3
MCCARTHY, Louise Roblee (Mrs. Eugene Ross McCarthy)
MCCARTHY, Michael Henry 1
MCCARTHY, P. H. 1
MCCARTHY, William Henry 5
MCCARTHY, Wilson 3
MCCARTNEY, Albert Joseph 4
MCCARTNEY, James Lincoln 5
MCCARTNEY, James S. 4
MCCARTNEY, Mary Elizabeth Maxwell H
MCCARTNEY, Washington H
MCCARTY, Andrew Zimmerman H
MCCARTY, C. Walter 4
MCCARTY, Charles Paschal 6
MCCARTY, Dan 3
MCCARTY, Dwight Gaylord 6
MCCARTY, E(dward) Prosper 5
MCCARTY, Franklin Bennett 6
MCCARTY, Johnathan H
MCCARTY, Milburn 4
MCCARTY, Orin Philip 1
MCCARTY, Richard H
MCCARTY, Richard Justin 3
MCCARTY, Sidney Louis 5
MCCARTY, Thomas J. 1
MCCARTY, William Mason H
MCCARTY, William Murdock 1
MCCARTY, William T. 5
MCCASH, Isaac Newton 5
MCCASKEY, Charles Irving 3
MCCASKEY, Hiram Dryer 1
MCCASKEY, John Piersol 3
MCCASKEY, William Spencer 1
MCCASKILL, James Lane 4
MCCASKILL, Oliver LeRoy 5
MCCASKILL, Virgil Everett 1
MCCASLAND, S(elby) Vernon 6
MCCASLIN, Frank Erwin 5
MCCASLIN, Robert Horace 3
MCCAUGHAN, Russell Craig 3
MCCAUGHAN, William John 1
MCCAULEY, Calvin Hudson 1
MCCAULEY, Charles Adam Hoke 4
MCCAULEY, Charles Stewart H
MCCAULEY, Clayton M. 3
MCCAULEY, David Vincent 2
MCCAULEY, Edward Yorke H
MCCAULEY, James Wayne 3
MCCAULEY, Jeremiah 1
MCCAULEY, Lena May 1
MCCAULEY, Mary Ludwig Hays H
MCCAULEY, William Fletcher 1
MCCAUSLEN, William Cochran H
MCCAUSTLAND, Elmer James 5
MCCAW, Henry 3
MCCAW, Walter Drew 1
MCCAWLEY, Alfred L. 4
MCCAWLEY, Charles Grymes

MCCAWLEY, Charles Laurie 1
MCCAY, Bruce Benjamin 4
MCCAY, Charles Francis H
MCCAY, Leroy Wiley 1
MCCLELLAN, Bryon Charles 2
MCCHESNEY, Calvin Stewart 1
MCCHESNEY, Dora Greenwell 1
MCCHESNEY, Elizabeth Studdiford 1
MCCHESNEY, May Louise (Logan) 5
MCCHESNEY, Wilbert Renwick 2
MCCHORD, Charles Caldwell 1
MCCLAIN, Dayton Ernest 5
MCCLAIN, Edward Lee 1
MCCLAIN, Emlin 1
MCCLAIN, John Wilcox 4
MCCLAIN, Joseph A. Jr. 5
MCCLAIN, Josiah 4
MCCLAMMY, Charles Washington H
MCCLANAHAN, Ellis Joshua 4
MCCLANAHAN, Harry Monroe 1
MCCLARAN, John Walter 3
MCCLARY, Nelson Alvin 5
MCCLASKEY, Henry Morrison Jr. 5
MCCLATCHY, Carlos Kelly 1
MCCLATCHY, Charles Kenny 1
MCCLATCHY, Valentine Stuart 1
MCCLAUGHRY, Robert Wilson 1
MCCLAVE, Charles Rowley 3
MCCLEAN, Harry J. 4
MCCLEAN, Moses H
MCCLEARY, James Thompson 1
MCCLEARY, Jesse Earl 6
MCCLEARY, Robert Altwig 5
MCCLEAVE, Robert 5
MCCLEERY, James H
MCCLELLAN, Abraham H
MCCLELLAN, Carswell H
MCCLELLAN, Elisabeth 1
MCCLELLAN, George H
MCCLELLAN, George Brinton H
MCCLELLAN, George Brinton 1
MCCLELLAN, Henry Brainerd H
MCCLELLAN, John H
MCCLELLAN, John Jasper 1
MCCLELLAN, Robert H
MCCLELLAN, Thomas Cowan 1
MCCLELLAN, Thomas Nicholas 1
MCCLELLAN, William 3
MCCLELLAND, Charles P. 2
MCCLELLAND, Charles Samuel 1
MCCLELLAND, George William 1
MCCLELLAND, Harold Mark 4
MCCLELLAND, Henry Thom 4
MCCLELLAND, James Farley 3
MCCLELLAND, James Henderson 1
MCCLELLAND, Robert H
MCCLELLAND, Ross St. John 5
MCCLELLAND, Silas Edward 3
MCCLELLAND, T. Calvin 1
MCCLELLAND, Thomas 1
MCCLELLAND, William H
MCCLELLAND, William 2
MCCLELLAND, William Craig 4
MCCLEMENT, John Hall 1
MCCLENACHAN, Blair H
MCCLENAGHAN, George Pinckney 4
MCCLENAHAN, David A. 4
MCCLENAHAN, Howard 1
MCCLENAHAN, Perry Eugene 5
MCCLENAHAN, Robert Stewart 5
MCCLENCH, William Wallace

MCCLENDON, James Wooten 6
MCCLENE, James H
MCCLENNEN, Edward Francis 2
MCCLENNY, George L. 2
MCCLERNAND, Edward John 1
MCCLERNAND, John A. H
MCCLINTIC, George Warwick 2
MCCLINTIC, Guthrie 4
MCCLINTIC, Howard H. 1
MCCLINTIC, James V. 2
MCCLINTIC, Robert Hofferd 5
MCCLINTOCK, Andrew Hamilton 1
MCCLINTOCK, Earl Irving 4
MCCLINTOCK, Emory 1
MCCLINTOCK, Euphemia E. 5
MCCLINTOCK, Franklin Trunkey 6
MCCLINTOCK, Gilbert Stuart 4
MCCLINTOCK, Harry Winfred 5
MCCLINTOCK, J. O. 1
MCCLINTOCK, James Harvey 1
MCCLINTOCK, John Calvin 1
MCCLINTOCK, John Calvin 5
MCCLINTOCK, Mary Law 1
MCCLINTOCK, Miller 3
MCCLINTOCK, Norman 1
MCCLINTOCK, Oliver 1
MCCLINTOCK, Walter 2
MCCLISH, Eli 1
MCCLOSKEY, Augustus 1
MCCLOSKEY, James Paul 2
MCCLOSKEY, John H
MCCLOSKEY, John Francis 3
MCCLOSKEY, Manus 5
MCCLOSKEY, Matthew H. 5
MCCLOSKEY, Robert Green 5
MCCLOSKEY, Thomas David 5
MCCLOSKEY, William George 1
MCCLOUD, Bentley Grimes 3
MCCLOUD, Charles A. 4
MCCLOUD, Earl 3
MCCLOW, Lloyd L. 4
MCCLOY, Charles Harold 3
MCCLUNG, Calvin Morgan 1
MCCLUNG, Clarence Erwin 2
MCCLUNG, George Harlan 3
MCCLUNG, Hugh Lawson 1
MCCLUNG, Lee 1
MCCLUNG, Reid Lage 4
MCCLUNG, Will Clinton 3
MCCLUNG, William H. 3
MCCLURE, Abbot 6
MCCLURE, Alexander Kelly 1
MCCLURE, Alexander Wilson H
MCCLURE, Alfred James Pollock 4
MCCLURE, Charles H
MCCLURE, Charles Freeman Williams 3
MCCLURE, Charles Wylie 4
MCCLURE, Daniel E. 1
MCCLURE, George H
MCCLURE, George Henry 4
MCCLURE, Grace Latimer Jones 6
MCCLURE, Harry Bell 6
MCCLURE, Howard (Orton) 5
MCCLURE, James Gore King 1
MCCLURE, James Gore King 1
MCCLURE, John Clarence 4
MCCLURE, Marjorie Barkley 1
MCCLURE, Martha 2
MCCLURE, Matthew Thompson Jr. 4
MCCLURE, Meade Lowrie 1
MCCLURE, Nathaniel Fish 2
MCCLURE, Norman Egbert 4
MCCLURE, Robert A. 3
MCCLURE, Robert Owen 4
MCCLURE, Roy Donaldson 3
MCCLURE, Russell Everett 6
MCCLURE, Samuel Grant 2
MCCLURE, Samuel Sidney 2

MCCLURE, W. Frank 3
MCCLURE, Walter Tennant 4
MCCLURE, William L. 3
MCCLURE, Worth 4
MCCLURG, Alexander Caldwell 1
MCCLURG, James H
MCCLURG, Joseph Washington H
MCCLURG, Walter 1
MCCLURKIN, John Knox 1
MCCLURKIN, Robert 3
MCCLURKIN, Robert J. G. 3
MCCLUSKEY, Edmund Roberts 4
MCCLUSKEY, Thomas Joseph 1
MCCOACH, David Jr. 3
MCCOBB, Paul (Winthrop) 5
MCCOLL, Jay Robert 1
MCCOLL, Robert Boyd 5
MCCOLLESTER, Lee Sullivan 4
MCCOLLESTER, Parker 1
MCCOLLESTER, Sullivan Holman 1
MCCOLLOCH, Frank Cleveland 5
MCCOLLOM, John Hildreth 1
MCCOLLOM, Vivian C. 4
MCCOLLUM, Earl 2
MCCOLLUM, Elmer Verner 4
MCCOMAS, Francis John 1
MCCOMAS, Henry Clay 5
MCCOMAS, Louis Emory 1
MCCOMAS, O. Parker 3
MCCOMAS, William H
MCCOMB, Arthur James 3
MCCOMB, Edgar 3
MCCOMB, Eleazer H
MCCOMB, John H
MCCOMB, Samuel 4
MCCOMB, William 4
MCCOMB, William Andrew 1
MCCOMB, William Randolph 1
MCCOMBS, Carl Esselstyn 5
MCCOMBS, Vernon Monroe 3
MCCOMBS, William Frank 1
MCCONACHIE, Harry Steele 4
MCCONACHIE, Lauros Grant 5
MCCONATHY, Osbourne 2
MCCONAUGHY, James 1
MCCONAUGHY, James Lukens 2
MCCONAUGHY, Robert 1
MCCONIHE, Malcolm Stuart 5
MCCONN, Charles Maxwell 3
MCCONNAUGHEY, George Carlton 4
MCCONNAUGHEY, Robert Kendall 4
MCCONNEL, John Ludlum H
MCCONNEL, Mervin Gilbert 3
MCCONNEL, Murray 4
MCCONNEL, Roger Harmon 4
MCCONNELL, Andrew M. 5
MCCONNELL, Charles Melvin 4
MCCONNELL, Felix Grundy H
MCCONNELL, Fernando Coello 1
MCCONNELL, Fowler Beery 4
MCCONNELL, Francis John 3
MCCONNELL, Franz 5
MCCONNELL, H. Hugh 3
MCCONNELL, H. S. 3
MCCONNELL, Henry 6
MCCONNELL, Herbert S(tevenson) 5
MCCONNELL, Ira Welch 1
MCCONNELL, James Eli 1
MCCONNELL, James Moore 1
MCCONNELL, John Griffith 6
MCCONNELL, John Preston 4
MCCONNELL, Joseph Moore 1
MCCONNELL, Lincoln 1

MCCONNELL, Luther Graham 4
MCCONNELL, Robert Darll 5
MCCONNELL, Robert Perche 5
MCCONNELL, Roy F. 4
MCCONNELL, Samuel David 1
MCCONNELL, Samuel Parsons 1
MCCONNELL, W. Joseph 3
MCCONNELL, Wallace Robert 4
MCCONNELL, William J. 1
MCCONNICO, Andrew Jackson 5
MCCONWAY, William 1
MCCOOK, Alexander McDowell 1
MCCOOK, Anson George 1
MCCOOK, Edward Moody 1
MCCOOK, Henry Christopher 1
MCCOOK, John James 1
MCCOOK, Willis Fisher 1
MCCORD, Alvin Carr 3
MCCORD, Andrew H
MCCORD, Andrew King 6
MCCORD, David James 1
MCCORD, George Herbert 1
MCCORD, James Nance 5
MCCORD, Joseph 2
MCCORD, Joseph Alexander 4
MCCORD, Leon 3
MCCORD, Louisa Susanna Cheves H
MCCORD, May Kennedy 6
MCCORD, Myron Hawley 1
MCCORD, Robert D. 4
MCCORD, William Clay 4
MCCORD, William H. 4
MCCORKLE, Graham K. 4
MCCORKLE, Joseph Walker H
MCCORKLE, Thomas Smith 3
MCCORMAC, Eugene Irving 2
MCCORMACK, Alfred 3
MCCORMACK, Arthur Thomas 2
MCCORMACK, Buren H. 5
MCCORMACK, Emmet J. 4
MCCORMACK, George Bryant 1
MCCORMACK, James 6
MCCORMACK, John 2
MCCORMACK, Joseph Nathaniel 1
MCCORMACK, M. Harriet Joyce (Mrs. John W. McCormack) 5
MCCORMACK, Thomas Joseph 1
MCCORMICK, Albert Edward 4
MCCORMICK, Albert M. D. 1
MCCORMICK, Alexander Agnew 1
MCCORMICK, Alexander Hugh 1
MCCORMICK, Andrew Phelps 1
MCCORMICK, Anne O'hare 3
MCCORMICK, Bradley Thomas 3
MCCORMICK, Charles Perry 5
MCCORMICK, Charles Tilford 4
MCCORMICK, Charles Wesley 1
MCCORMICK, Chauncey 3
MCCORMICK, Cyrus 5
MCCORMICK, Cyrus Hall H
MCCORMICK, Cyrus Hall 1
MCCORMICK, David 2
MCCORMICK, Donald 2
MCCORMICK, Edith Rockefeller 1
MCCORMICK, Edmund Burke 1
MCCORMICK, Edward James 6
MCCORMICK, Ernest O. 1
MCCORMICK, Fowler 5
MCCORMICK, Frederick 3
MCCORMICK, George Chalmers 5
MCCORMICK, George Wellesley 3

MCDOWELL, James Foster H
MCDOWELL, John H
MCDOWELL, John 1
MCDOWELL, John 3
MCDOWELL, John 6
MCDOWELL, John Anderson 3
MCDOWELL, John Sherman 1
MCDOWELL, Joseph H
MCDOWELL, Joseph Jefferson H
MCDOWELL, Louise Sherwood 4
MCDOWELL, Mary E. 1
MCDOWELL, Philetus H(arold) 5
MCDOWELL, Pierce Hubert 6
MCDOWELL, Rachel Kollock 2
MCDOWELL, Ralph Walker 1
MCDOWELL, Tremaine 3
MCDOWELL, William Fraser 1
MCDOWELL, William George 1
MCDOWELL, William Osborne 4
MCDUFFIE, Duncan 3
MCDUFFIE, George H
MCDUFFIE, John 3
MCDUFFIE, John Van H
MCDUFFIE, William C. 4
MCEACHERN, Daniel Victor 5
MCEACHERN, John Newton 3
MCEACHRON, Duncan Lendrum 1
MCEACHRON, Karl Boyer 3
MCELDOWNEY, Charles Roy 3
MCELDOWNEY, Henry C. 1
MCELDUFF, John Vincent 3
MCELFRESH, William Edward 2
MCELHANY, J. L. 3
MCELHINNEY, John H. 3
MCELMELL, Jackson 1
MCELRATH, Thomas H
MCELREATH, Walter 3
MCELROY, Benjamin Lincoln 3
MCELROY, Clarence Underwood 1
MCELROY, Frank D. 6
MCELROY, George Wightman 1
MCELROY, Henry F. 1
MCELROY, James W. 5
MCELROY, John H
MCELROY, John 1
MCELROY, Mary Arthur 1
MCELROY, Neil H. 5
MCELROY, Robert 3
MCELROY, William H. 1
MCELROY, William Thomas 4
MCELVEEN, William Thomas 1
MCELVENNY, Robert Talbot 4
MCELWAIN, Charles Church 5
MCELWAIN, Edwin 4
MCELWAIN, Frank Arthur 3
MCELWAIN, Henry Ely Jr. 4
MCELWAIN, J. Franklin 3
MCELWAIN, William Henry 5
MCENARY, Dale Robert 4
MCENERNEY, Garrett William 2
MCENERY, Samuel Douglas 1
MCENIRY, William Hugh Jr. 6
MCENTEE, Jervis H
MCENTEGART, Bryan J. 5
MCENTIRE, Richard Brooke 3
MCEVOY, James 1
MCEVOY, Joseph Patrick 3
MCEVOY, Reginald 6
MCEWAN, William Leonard 1
MCEWEN, James Henry 2
MCEWEN, Merrill Clyde 3
MCEWEN, Robert Ward 4
MCFADDEN, Effie Belle 5
MCFADDEN, George 1
MCFADDEN, George H. 1
MCFADDEN, James Augustine 3
MCFADDEN, John Francis 3
MCFADDEN, Joseph A. 6
MCFADDEN, Louis T. 1
MCFADDEN, Manus 3
MCFADDEN, Obadiah Benton H
MCFADDEN, S. Willis 4
MCFADDEN, William Hartman 3
MCFADEN, Frank Talbot 1
MCFADYEN, Bernice Musgrove 3
MCFALL, John Monteith 3
MCFALL, Merrill Borden 6
MCFARLAN, Duncan H
MCFARLAND, Archie J. 3
MCFARLAND, David Ford 3
MCFARLAND, Earl 5
MCFARLAND, Eugene James 3
MCFARLAND, Francis Patrick H
MCFARLAND, Gary 5
MCFARLAND, George Austin 1
MCFARLAND, Greyble Lewis Jr. 5
MCFARLAND, Jean Henderson 4
MCFARLAND, John Clemson 5
MCFARLAND, John Horace 2
MCFARLAND, John Thomas 1
MCFARLAND, Joseph 2
MCFARLAND, Kermit 5
MCFARLAND, Raymond 5
MCFARLAND, Robert White 1
MCFARLAND, Russell S(cott) 5
MCFARLAND, Samuel Gamble H
MCFARLAND, Silas Clark 1
MCFARLAND, Thomas Bard 1
MCFARLAND, Thomas C. 3
MCFARLAND, Walter Martin 1
MCFARLAND, Wilfred Myers 4
MCFARLANE, Arthur Emerson 2
MCFARLANE, Charles T. 5
MCFAUL, James Augustine 1
MCFAYDEN, Donald 5
MCFEE, Henry Lee 3
MCFEE, Inez N. 6
MCFEE, Lapsley Armstrong 1
MCFEE, William 4
MCFEELY, Richard Harding 4
MCFEELY, Wilbur Morris 6
MCFERRIN, John Berry H
MCFETRIDGE, William Lane 5
MCFIE, John Robert 1
MCGAFFEY, Ernest 4
MCGAFFIN, Alexander 1
MCGAFFIN, William 6
MCGAHAN, Paul James 5
MCGANN, Marion Eudora Hotchkiss (Mrs. James McGann) 5
MCGANNON, Matthew Charles 4
MCGARRAGHY, Joseph C. 6
MCGARRAH, Albert Franklin 4
MCGARRAH, Gates W. 1
MCGARRY, Edmund Daniels 6
MCGARRY, William James 1
MCGARRY, William Rutledge 5
MCGARVEY, John William 1
MCGARVEY, Robert Neill 3
MCGARVEY, William 1
MCGAUGH, Elmer Thomas 1
MCGAUGHEY, Edward Wilson H
MCGAUGHEY, William Ray 4
MCGAUGHY, James Ralph 3
MCGAURAN, John Baptist 5
MCGAVACK, Thomas Hodge 6
MCGAVICK, Alexander Joseph 2
MCGAVIN, Charles 5
MCGAVIN, Peter Murphy 6
MCGAVRAN, Edward G(rafton) 5
MCGAW, Alex James 5
MCGAW, George Keen 1
MCGEACHY, Archibald Alexander 1
MCGEE, Anita Newcomb 4
MCGEE, Clifford W. 3
MCGEE, Cushman 4
MCGEE, Frank 6
MCGEE, Homer Edgar 4
MCGEE, James Ellington 1
MCGEE, John Bernard 1
MCGEE, John Franklin 1
MCGEE, Milton H
MCGEE, Reginald Everett 6
MCGEE, Thomas D'Arcy H
MCGEE, W. J. 1
MCGEEHAN, William O. 1
MCGEEVER, John F. 5
MCGEHEE, Harvey 4
MCGEHEE, Harvey 5
MCGEHEE, Lucius Polk 1
MCGEHEE, Micijah C. Jr. 4
MCGEOCH, John Alexander 2
MCGEORGE, William Jr. 4
MCGETTIGAN, Margaret Mary 6
MCGHEE, James E. 4
MCGHEE, Paul Ansley 4
MCGIFFERT, Arthur Cushman 1
MCGIFFERT, James 2
MCGIFFERT, Julian Esselstyn 2
MCGIFFIN, Malcolm 1
MCGIFFIN, Philo Norton H
MCGIFFIN, William J. 3
MCGILL, Andrew Ryan 1
MCGILL, C. H. 4
MCGILL, David Frazier 1
MCGILL, George 4
MCGILL, J. Nota 1
MCGILL, James Henry 2
MCGILL, John H
MCGILL, John Dale 1
MCGILL, John Thomas 2
MCGILL, Ralph Emerson 5
MCGILL, Stephenson Waters 5
MCGILL, Thomas Julian 1
MCGILL, William L. 3
MCGILLICUDDY, Daniel John 1
MCGILLIVRAY, Alexander H
MCGILLYCUDDY, Valentine Trant O'Connell 4
MCGILVARY, Evander Bradley 3
MCGILVREY, John Edward 3
MCGINLEY, Anna Mathilda Agnes 4
MCGINLEY, Charles Calvin 4
MCGINLEY, Daniel Eugene 1
MCGINNESS, John Randolph 1
MCGINNIES, Joseph A. 2
MCGINNIS, Alan Ross 4
MCGINNIS, Edward Francis 6
MCGINNIS, Edwin 1
MCGINNIS, Felix Signoret 2
MCGINNIS, George 4
MCGINNIS, Patrick Benedict 5
MCGINNIS, William F. 1
MCGINNIS, William Hereford 1
MCGINTY, Francis Patrick 3
MCGINTY, George Banks 1
MCGIVERAN, Stanley J. 4
MCGIVNEY, Michael Joseph H
MCGLACHLIN, Edward Fenton 2
MCGLANNAN, Alexius 1
MCGLAUFLIN, William Henry 1
MCGLENNON, Cornelius A. 1
MCGLINN, John Alexander Jr. 6
MCGLOTHLIN, William Joseph 1
MCGLYNN, Edward 1
MCGLYNN, Frank 3
MCGLYNN, James Vincent 6
MCGOHEY, John F. X. 5
MCGOLDRICK, Thomas Aloysius 3
MCGOLRICK, James 1
MCGONAGLE, William Albert 1
MCGOODWIN, Henry Kerr 1
MCGOODWIN, Preston 6
MCGOORTY, John P. 3
MCGOVERN, Francis Edward 2
MCGOVERN, J. Raymond 6
MCGOVERN, John W. 6
MCGOVERN, James Lawrence 3
MCGOVERN, John 1
MCGOVERN, John Terence 4
MCGOVERN, Patrick Alphonsus 3
MCGOVERN, Philip Patrick 6
MCGOVERN, William Montgomery 4
MCGOVERN, William Robbins 4
MCGOVNEY, Dudley Odell 2
MCGOWAN, Arthur C. 3
MCGOWAN, Edwin W. 3
MCGOWAN, James Jr. 4
MCGOWAN, John 1
MCGOWAN, Lord 4
MCGOWAN, Samuel H
MCGOWAN, Samuel 1
MCGOWEN, James Greer 2
MCGOWN, Chester Stowe 5
MCGRADY, Edward Francis 4
MCGRADY, Thomas 1
MCGRANAHAN, James 1
MCGRANAHAN, Ralph Wilson 1
MCGRANAHAN, Raymond DePue 5
MCGRANERY, James Patrick 4
MCGRATH, Benjamin R. 1
MCGRATH, J. Howard 4
MCGRATH, James H
MCGRATH, John Joseph 3
MCGRATH, Joseph F. 3
MCGRATH, Justin 1
MCGRATH, Sister Mary 5
MCGRATH, Raymond Dyer 5
MCGRATH, William H. 3
MCGRAW, Curtis Whittlesey 3
MCGRAW, Donald C. 6
MCGRAW, Frank H. 6
MCGRAW, James H. 2
MCGRAW, James H. Jr. 5
MCGRAW, James J. 1
MCGRAW, John Harte 1
MCGRAW, John Joseph H
MCGRAW, John Joseph 4
MCGRAW, John Thomas 1
MCGRAW, Max 4
MCGRAW, Robert Bush 4
MCGRAW, Theodore Andrews 1
MCGREADY, James H
MCGREGOR, Alexander Grant 3
MCGREGOR, Douglas 4
MCGREGOR, George Wilbur 4
MCGREGOR, Gordon Roy 5
MCGREGOR, J. Harry 3
MCGREGOR, James Clyde 1
MCGREGOR, James Howard 3
MCGREGOR, Robert Gardner 2
MCGREGOR, Stuart Malcolm 4
MCGREGOR, Thomas 1
MCGREGOR, Thomas Burnett 4
MCGREGOR, Tracy W. 1
MCGREGOR, William Morrell 5
MCGREGORY, Joseph Frank 1
MCGREW, Clarence Alan 5
MCGREW, Dallas Dayton Lore 6
MCGREW, Donald Cargill 4
MCGREW, George Harrison 1
MCGREW, Henry Edwin 5
MCGREW, John Gilbert 5
MCGRIGOR, Sir Rhoderick 3
MCGROARTY, John Steven 2
MCGROARTY, Susan H
MCGUFFEY, William Holmes H
MCGUGIN, Dan E. 1
MCGUGIN, Harold 2
MCGUIGAN, F. H. 3
MCGUIGAN, Hugh 4
MCGUIGAN, Hugh (Alister) 5
MCGUIGAN, James Charles 6
MCGUIGAN, Joseph J. 5
MCGUINNESS, Eugene Joseph 3
MCGUIRE, Alice Brooks 6
MCGUIRE, Andrew Thomas 6
MCGUIRE, Bird Segle 4
MCGUIRE, Charles Bonaventure H
MCGUIRE, Edgar Robinson 1
MCGUIRE, George Alexander 1
MCGUIRE, Hunter Holmes 1
MCGUIRE, James Clark 1
MCGUIRE, James K. 3
MCGUIRE, John 4
MCGUIRE, John A. 2
MCGUIRE, Joseph Deakins 1
MCGUIRE, Joseph Hubert 2
MCGUIRE, Louis David 3
MCGUIRE, Martin Rawson Patrick 5
MCGUIRE, Michael Francis 3
MCGUIRE, Murray Mason 2
MCGUIRE, Ollie Roscoe 4
MCGUIRE, Stuart 2
MCGUIRE, Ulysses Melville 1
MCGUIRE, William Anthony 1
MCGUNNEGLE, George Kennedy 4
MCGURK, Joseph F. 4
MCHALE, Frank Martin 6
MCHALE, Kathryn 3
MCHANEY, Edgar La Fayette 2
MCHANEY, Powell B. 3
MCHARG, Henry K. 1
MCHARG, Ormsby 5
MCHATTIE, William Alexander 5
MCHATTON, Robert Lytle H
MCHENDRIE, Andrew Watson 5
MCHENRY, Carl Holbrook 4
MCHENRY, Donald Edward 5
MCHENRY, Edwin Harrison 4
MCHENRY, Henry Davis H
MCHENRY, James H
MCHENRY, John Geiser 1
MCHENRY, John Hardin H
MCHUGH, Daniel Joseph 4
MCHUGH, James F. (Jimmy) 5
MCHUGH, John 2
MCHUGH, Keith Stratton 6
MCHUGH, William Douglas 1
MCILHENNEY, Charles Morgan 1
MCILHENNEY, Francis Salisbury 1
MCILHENNEY, John D. 1
MCILHENNY, Edward Avery 2
MCILHENNY, John Avery 4
MCILHINEY, Parker Cairns 1
MCILROY, Malcolm Strong 3
MCILVAIN, Robert Wallace 3
MCILVAINE, Abraham Robinson H
MCILVAINE, Charles 1
MCILVAINE, Charles Pettit H
MCILVAINE, Harold Ralph Clair 4
MCILVAINE, James Hall 1
MCILVAINE, John Wilson 4
MCILVAINE, Joseph H
MCILVAINE, William H
MCILVAINE, William Brown 2
MCILWAIN, Charles Howard 6
MCILWAINE, Henry Read 1
MCILWAINE, Richard 4
MCILWAINE, William Baird 1
MCINALLY, William Keith 4
MCINDOE, Walter Duncan H
MCINERNEY, Francis Xavier 3
MCINERNEY, James Lawrence 5
MCINERNY, John Joseph 4
MCINERNY, Timothy A. 4
MCINNERNEY, Thomas H. 3
MCINNIS, Charles Ballard 5
MCINNIS, Edgar Wardwell 6
MCINTIRE, Albert Washington 1
MCINTIRE, Charles 1

* Indicates More Than One Such Name Listed

MCINTIRE, Clifford (Guy) 6
MCINTIRE, Paul Goodloe 3
MCINTIRE, Ross T. 3
MCINTIRE, Samuel H
MCINTIRE, Walter Oscar 5
MCINTIRE, Warren 1
  Wallace
MCINTOSH, Alexander 3
  Angus
MCINTOSH, Alexander 4
  Ennis
MCINTOSH, Arthur Tuttle 3
MCINTOSH, Benjamin 6
  Harrison
MCINTOSH, Burr William 2
MCINTOSH, Charles 5
  Herbert
MCINTOSH, Charles 3
  Kenneth
MCINTOSH, Donald 3
MCINTOSH, Henry Payne 1
MCINTOSH, Henry 4
  Thomas
MCINTOSH, James Henry 1
MCINTOSH, John Baillie 3
MCINTOSH, Joseph 3
  Wallace
MCINTOSH, Lachian H
MCINTOSH, Loy N. 6
MCINTOSH, Walter 2
  Kenneth
MCINTOSH, William 3
MCINTOSH, William M. 2
MCINTYRE, Alfred Robert 3
MCINTYRE, Augustine 3
MCINTYRE, Brouwer 4
  Davis
MCINTYRE, Frank 2
MCINTYRE, Frederick W. 4
MCINTYRE, Hugh Henry 1
MCINTYRE, John Francis 4
MCINTYRE, John T. 3
MCINTYRE, Marvin 2
  Hunter
MCINTYRE, Oscar Odd 1
MCINTYRE, Robert 1
MCINTYRE, Robson 5
  Duncan
MCINTYRE, Rufus H
MCINTYRE, William Davis 4
MCINTYRE, William H. 2
MCISAAC, Archibald 3
  MacDonald
MCIVER, Angus Vaughn 6
MCIVER, Charles Duncan 1
MCIVER, George Willcox 3
MCIVER, Henry 1
MCIVER, Joseph 1
MCIVER, Milo Kenneth 4
MCIVOR, Nicholas 1
  Williams
MCIVOR-TYNDALL, 1
  Alexander James
MCKAMY, David Knox 3
MCKAY, Ambrose Noble 1
MCKAY, Claude 2
MCKAY, Claude 5
MCKAY, David O. 5
MCKAY, Donald H
MCKAY, Donald Cope 3
MCKAY, Douglas 3
MCKAY, Frederick Sumner 3
MCKAY, James Iver 1
MCKAY, Kenneth Ivor 2
MCKAY, Llewelyn R. 6
MCKAY, Neal H. 3
MCKAY, Neil S. 4
MCKAY, Oscar Reed 2
MCKAY, Paul Leonard 5
MCKAY, Seth Shepard 5
MCKAY, Stanley Albert 4
MCKAY, Thomas Clayton 5
MCKAY, William M. 2
MCKAY, William O. 3
MCKEAG, Anna Jane 2
MCKEAN, Frank Chalmers 3
MCKEAN, Horace Grant 1
MCKEAN, Hugh Kiefer 4
MCKEAN, James Bedell H
MCKEAN, Joseph Borden H
MCKEAN, Josiah Slutts 3
MCKEAN, Samuel H
MCKEAN, Thomas H
MCKEAN, Thomas 1
MCKEAN, Thomas 3
MCKEAN, William Vincent 1
MCKEAN, William Wister H
MCKECHNIE, Neil 5
  Kenneth
MCKECHNIE, Robert 2
  Edward
MCKEE, Alexander 1
  Ellsworth
MCKEE, Andrew Irwin 4
MCKEE, Arthur G. 5
MCKEE, Captain William 6

MCKEE, David Harris 4
MCKEE, David Ritchie 1
MCKEE, Frederick 4
  Chadwick
MCKEE, George Colin H
MCKEE, Henry S. 3
MCKEE, Jesse Lynne 6
MCKEE, John H
MCKEE, John Dempster 4
MCKEE, Joseph V. 3
MCKEE, Oliver Jr. 2
MCKEE, Paul Boole 4
MCKEE, Paul Gordon 6
MCKEE, Ralph Harper 5
MCKEE, Rose 5
MCKEE, Ruth Karr 3
MCKEE, Samuel H
MCKEE, Sol Reid 5
MCKEE, William James 1
MCKEE, William Parker 1
MCKEEFRY, Peter 6
  Cardinal
MCKEEHAN, Charles 1
  Louis
MCKEEHAN, Hobart 1
  Deitrich
MCKEEHAN, Joseph 3
  Parker
MCKEEHAN, Louis 6
  Williams
MCKEEL, Ben S. 2
MCKEEN, Benjamin 2
MCKEEN, James 1
MCKEEN, Joseph H
MCKEEN, Stanley Stewart 4
MCKEEN, William Riley 5
MCKEEVER, Chauncey 1
MCKEEVER, Duncan Clark 4
MCKEEVER, Emmet G. 2
MCKEEVER, Francis 5
  Michael
MCKEEVER, Franklin 1
  Garrett
MCKEEVER, William Arch 1
MCKEIGHAN, William H
  Arthur
MCKEITH, David Jr. 4
MCKELDIN, Theodore 6
  Roosevelt
MCKELL, William E. 4
MCKELLAR, Kenneth 3
  Douglas
MCKELVEY, Graham 5
  Norton
MCKELVEY, John Jay 2
MCKELVEY, S. Willis 5
MCKELVIE, Samuel Roy 3
MCKELVY, Francis 3
  Graham
MCKELVY, J. D. 4
MCKELVY, William Rush 6
MCKELWAY, Alexander 1
  Jeffrey
MCKELWAY, St Clair 1
MCKENDREE, William H
MCKENDRICK, Edward 5
  John
MCKENDRY, John Joseph 4
MCKENNA, Charles 1
  Francis
MCKENNA, Edward 1
  William
MCKENNA, Joseph 1
MCKENNA, Brother Joseph 6
  G.
MCKENNA, Norbert 4
  Augustine
MCKENNA, Philip M. 5
MCKENNA, Roy Carnegie 3
MCKENNAN, Thomas
  McKean Thompson
MCKENNAN, Thomas 1
  McKean Thompson
MCKENNEY, A. Carlton 3
MCKENNEY, Frederic 2
  Duncan
MCKENNEY, James Hall 1
MCKENNEY, Robert Lee 2
MCKENNEY, Ruth 5
MCKENNEY, Thomas H
  Loraine
MCKENNY, Charles 1
MCKENNY, Francis Xavier 4
MCKENTY, Jacob Kerlin H
MCKENZIE, Alexander 1
MCKENZIE, Aline 2
MCKENZIE, Fayette Avery 3
MCKENZIE, George 1
MCKENZIE, Harry Carroll 4
MCKENZIE, James A. 1
MCKENZIE, John Charles 1
MCKENZIE, John 4
  Cummings
MCKENZIE, John Heyward 1
MCKENZIE, Kenneth 2
MCKENZIE, Lewis H

MCKENZIE, Robert Tait 1
MCKENZIE, Roderick 1
  Duncan
MCKENZIE, Vernon 4
MCKENZIE, William 5
  Dexter
MCKENZIE, William P. 1
MCKENZIE, William White 5
MCKEOGH, Arthur 1
MCKEON, John H
MCKEON, John J. 2
MCKEOWN, Tom D. 3
MCKERNAN, Maureen 5
  (Mrs. John Cooper Ross)
MCKERNON, Edward 2
MCKERR, George Joseph 4
MCKIBBEN, Frank Pape 1
MCKIBBEN, James A. 4
MCKIBBEN, Paul Stilwell 1
MCKIBBIN, Chambers 1
MCKIBBIN, George 4
  Baldwin
MCKIBBIN, John 4
MCKIBBIN, Joseph H
  Chambers
MCKIBBIN, William 1
MCKIM, Alexander H
MCKIM, Baltimore H
MCKIM, Charles Follen 1
MCKIM, Isaac H
MCKIM, James Miller H
MCKIM, John 1
MCKIM, Judson Jackson 2
MCKIM, Randolph Harrison 1
MCKIM, Robert James 6
MCKIM, William Duncan 1
MCKIMMON, Jane 5
  Simpson (Mrs. Charles
  McKimmon)
MCKINIRY, Richard F. 6
MCKINLAY, Arthur Patch 3
MCKINLAY, Chauncey 5
  Angus
MCKINLAY, Duncan E. 4
MCKINLAY, John 3
MCKINLEY, Abner 1
MCKINLEY, Albert 1
  Edward
MCKINLEY, Carlyle 1
MCKINLEY, Charles 5
  Ethelbert
MCKINLEY, Earl Baldwin 1
MCKINLEY, Ida Saxton 1
MCKINLEY, J. Charnley 3
MCKINLEY, James F. 1
MCKINLEY, James Wilfred 3
MCKINLEY, John H
MCKINLEY, Lloyd 4
MCKINLEY, William H
MCKINLEY, William 1
MCKINLEY, William 1
  Brown
MCKINLOCK, George 1
  Alexander
MCKINLY, John H
MCKINNEY, Alexander 1
  Harris
MCKINNEY, Annie 5
  (Valentine) Booth
MCKINNEY, Arthur 4
  Wesley
MCKINNEY, Buckner 1
  Abernathy
MCKINNEY, Colin Pierson 2
MCKINNEY, Corvell 6
MCKINNEY, David 1
MCKINNEY, Frank Cowen 3
MCKINNEY, Frank E. 6
MCKINNEY, Ida Scott 5
  Taylor
MCKINNEY, James 1
MCKINNEY, Kate 4
  Slaughter
MCKINNEY, Laurence 5
MCKINNEY, Luther 3
  Franklin
MCKINNEY, Madge M. 3
MCKINNEY, Philip 1
  Watkins
MCKINNEY, Robert C. 1
MCKINNEY, Theophilus 4
  Elisha
MCKINNEY, Thomas 1
  Emery
MCKINNEY, Walter H. 3
MCKINNEY, William Mark 3
MCKINNIE, James 4
  Renwick
MCKINNIS, George E. Sr. 1
MCKINNON, Neil John 6
MCKINSEY, Folger 1
MCKINSEY, J. C. C. 3
MCKINSEY, James O. 1
MCKINSTRY, Addis 1
  Emmett
MCKINSTRY, Alexander H

MCKINSTRY, Charles 4
  Hedges
MCKINSTRY, Elisha H
  Williams
MCKINSTRY, Grace E. 1
MCKINSTRY, Helen May 2
MCKISICK, Lewis 2
MCKISSICK, Anthony 1
  Foster
MCKISSICK, James Rion 5
MCKISSOCK, Thomas H
MCKISSON, Robert Erastus 4
MCKITTRICK, Roy 4
MCKITTRICK, Thomas 5
  Harrington
MCKITTRICK, William 1
  James
MCKNIGHT, Alexander G. 3
MCKNIGHT, Alexander 1
  Hearne
MCKNIGHT, Anna 2
  Caulfield
MCKNIGHT, Charles 1
MCKNIGHT, Douglas 6
MCKNIGHT, George 5
  Harley
MCKNIGHT, Harvey 1
  Washington
MCKNIGHT, Henry Turney 5
MCKNIGHT, James Rankin 3
MCKNIGHT, Robert 1
MCKNIGHT, Robert James 6
  George
MCKNIGHT, Roy Jerome 4
MCKNIGHT, William 6
  Hodges
MCKONE, Don Townsend 1
MCKOWEN, John Clay 6
MCKOWN, Edgar M. 5
MCKOWN, Harry Charles 4
MCKOWNE, Frank A. 2
MCKUSICK, Marshall Noah 3
MCLACHLAN, Archibald 4
  C.
MCLACHLAN, James 1
MCLACHLEN, Archibald 4
  Malcolm
MCLAGLEN, Victor 3
MCLAIN, Bobby Maurice 6
MCLAIN, Chester Alden 6
MCLAIN, Frank Alexander 4
MCLAIN, John Scudder 1
MCLAIN, John Speed 1
MCLAIN, Raymond S. 3
MCLALLEN, Walter Field 4
MCLANAHAN, Austin 2
MCLANAHAN, James H
  Xavier
MCLANE, A. V. 5
MCLANE, Allan H
MCLANE, Charles Keith 6
MCLANE, Charles Lourie 5
MCLANE, James Woods 1
MCLANE, John 1
MCLANE, John Roy 5
MCLANE, Louis H
MCLANE, Patrick 5
MCLANE, Robert Milligan 1
MCLANE, Ruby Roach 4
MCLANE, William Ward 1
MCLAREN, Donald 1
MCLAREN, Richard 6
  Wellington
MCLAREN, Walter Wallace 5
MCLAREN, William 1
  Edward
MCLAREN, William 5
  Gardner
MCLARTY, Norman 2
  Alexander
MCLAUGHLIN, Allan 1
  Joseph
MCLAUGHLIN, Andrew 1
  Cunningham
MCLAUGHLIN, Charles F. 6
MCLAUGHLIN, Charles 1
  V(incent)
MCLAUGHLIN, Chester 1
  Bentline
MCLAUGHLIN, Chester 3
  Bond
MCLAUGHLIN, Dean 1
  Benjamin
MCLAUGHLIN, Dorsey 2
  Elmer
MCLAUGHLIN, Edward 6
  Aloysius
MCLAUGHLIN, Edward H. 4
MCLAUGHLIN, Emma 5
  Moffat (Mrs. Alfred
  McLaughlin)
MCLAUGHLIN, George 1
  Asbury
MCLAUGHLIN, George 2
  Dunlap

MCLAUGHLIN, Harold 5
  Newell
MCLAUGHLIN, Henry 3
  Woods
MCLAUGHLIN, Hugh 1
MCLAUGHLIN, J. Frank 4
MCLAUGHLIN, James 1
MCLAUGHLIN, James 1
  Campbell
MCLAUGHLIN, James 4
  Matthew
MCLAUGHLIN, James W. 1
MCLAUGHLIN, Joseph 1
MCLAUGHLIN, Mary 1
  Louise
MCLAUGHLIN, Melvin 1
  Orlando
MCLAUGHLIN, Paul 5
MCLAUGHLIN, Robert 5
  Samuel
MCLAUGHLIN, Robert 1
  William
MCLAUGHLIN, Roland 1
  Rusk
MCLAUGHLIN, Stuart 5
  Watts
MCLAUGHLIN, Thomas 2
  H.
MCLAURIN, Anselm 1
  Joseph
MCLAURIN, John Lowndes 1
MCLAUTHLIN, Herbert 1
  Weston
MCLAWS, Lafayette H
MCLEAISH, Robert Burns 1
MCLEAN, A. Neil 4
MCLEAN, Alney H
MCLEAN, Andrew 1
MCLEAN, Angus 1
MCLEAN, Angus Wilton 1
MCLEAN, Archibald 1
MCLEAN, Arthur Edward 4
MCLEAN, David J. 6
MCLEAN, Donald 1
MCLEAN, Edward Beale 1
MCLEAN, Edward 5
  Cochrane
MCLEAN, Emily Nelson 1
  Ritchie
MCLEAN, Finis Ewing 1
MCLEAN, Franklin 5
  Chambers
MCLEAN, Fred 6
MCLEAN, George Payne 1
MCLEAN, Heber Hampton 5
MCLEAN, James Henry 1
MCLEAN, James Stanley 3
MCLEAN, John 1
MCLEAN, John Emery 4
MCLEAN, John Godfrey 6
MCLEAN, John Knox 1
MCLEAN, John M(ilton) 1
MCLEAN, John Roll 1
MCLEAN, Milton Robbins 3
MCLEAN, Ridley 1
MCLEAN, Robert Norris 4
MCLEAN, Samuel H
MCLEAN, Simon James 3
MCLEAN, Thomas 1
  Chalmers
MCLEAN, Wallace Donald 6
MCLEAN, Walter 1
MCLEAN, William H
MCLEAN, William L. 1
MCLEAN, William L. Jr. 3
MCLEAN, William Swan Jr. 1
MCLEARN, Frank Cecil 6
MCLEARY, James Harvey 1
MCLEES, Archibald H
MCLEISTER, Ira Ford 4
MCLELLAN, Archibald 1
MCLELLAN, Asahel 2
  Walker
MCLELLAN, Hugh Dean 6
MCLELLAN, Isaac 1
MCLELLAN, Thomas 5
  George
MCLEMORE, Albert 5
  Sydney
MCLEMORE, Jeff 1
MCLENDON, Lennox Polk 5
MCLENDON, Robert Burns 6
MCLENDON, Sol Brown 4
MCLENE, Jeremiah H
MCLENEGAN, Charles 1
  Edward
MCLENNAN, Donald 2
  Roderick
MCLENNAN, Grace Tytus 1
MCLENNAN, Peter Baillie 1
MCLEOD, Alexander H
MCLEOD, Clarence John 3
MCLEOD, Duncan Allen 6
MCLEOD, Frank Hilton 2
MCLEOD, Hugh H
MCLEOD, Malcolm 4

MCLEOD, Martin H
MCLEOD, Mary Louise 5
DeMarco
MCLEOD, Murdoch 3
MCLEOD, N. H. F. 5
MCLEOD, Nelson Wesley 4
MCLEOD, Scott 1
MCLEOD, Thomas Gordon 1
MCLEOD, Walter Herbert 4
MCLESKEY, Waymon B. 4
MCLESTER, James 3
Somerville
MCLESTER, Judson Cole 4
Jr.
MCLEVY, Jasper 4
MCLIN, Anna Eva 5
M'CLINTOCK, John H
MCLOUGHLIN, John H
MCLOUTH, Donald B. 3
MCLOUTH, Lawrence 1
Amos
MCLUCAS, Walter Scott 3
MCLURE, Charles 4
Derickson
MCMAHAN, Anna 1
Benneson
MCMAHAN, George 5
Thomas
MCMAHON, Alphonse 5
MCMAHON, Amos Philip 2
MCMAHON, Arthur 5
Laurence
MCMAHON, Bernard H
MCMAHON, Brien 3
MCMAHON, Henry George 5
MCMAHON, James 1
MCMAHON, John A. 1
MCMAHON, John Eugene 1
MCMAHON, John Joseph 1
MCMAHON, John Robert 3
MCMAHON, John Van H
Lear
MCMAHON, Joseph H. 1
MCMAHON, Lawrence H
Stephen
MCMAHON, Martin 1
Thomas
MCMAHON, Stephen John 3
MCMAHON, Thomas F. 2
MCMAHON, Thomas J. 3
MCMAIN, Eleanor Laura 2
MCMANAMAN, Edward 4
Peter
MCMANAMON, James 3
Emmett
MCMANAMY, Frank 2
MCMANES, James H
MCMANES, Kenmore 5
Mathew
MCMANIS, John Thomas 5
MCMANUS, Charles 2
Edward
MCMANUS, George 1
MCMANUS, George Henry 5
MCMANUS, Howard 6
Norbert Jr.
MCMANUS, John Joseph 4
MCMANUS, William H
MCMARTIN, Charles 3
MCMARTIN, William 5
Joseph
MCMASTER, Fitz Hugh 1
MCMASTER, Florence R. 6
MCMASTER, Guy H
Humphreys
MCMASTER, James H
Alphonsus
MCMASTER, John Bach 1
MCMASTER, John 1
Stevenson
MCMASTER, LeRoy 4
MCMASTER, Philip Duryee 5
MCMASTER, Ross 4
Huntington
MCMASTER, William 4
Henry
MCMASTER, William 5
Henry *
MCMATH, Francis Charles 1
MCMATH, Robert Edwin 5
MCMATH, Robert Emmett 4
MCMATH, Robert R. 4
MCMEANS, George Beale 4
MCMECHAN, Francis 1
Hoeffer
MCMEEN, Samuel 1
Groenendyke
MCMEIN, Neysa 2
MCMENAMIN, Hugh L. 2
MCMENAMY, Francis 1
Xavier
MCMENIMEN, William V. 4
MCMICHAEL, Clayton 1
MCMICHAEL, Morton H
MCMICHAEL, Thomas 1
Hanna

MCMILLAN, Alexander H
MCMILLAN, Alexander 4
MCMILLAN, Alfred E. 5
MCMILLAN, Charles 1
MCMILLAN, Claude 4
Richelieu
MCMILLAN, Daniel Hugh 4
MCMILLAN, Duncan J. 1
MCMILLAN, Edward John 4
MCMILLAN, Fred Orville 3
MCMILLAN, George 5
Scholefield
MCMILLAN, Homer 3
MCMILLAN, James 1
MCMILLAN, James Thayer 2
MCMILLAN, James 1
Winning
MCMILLAN, Neil 1
Alexander
MCMILLAN, Philip 1
Hamilton
MCMILLAN, Putnam Dana 4
Johnston
MCMILLAN, Robert 2
Johnston
MCMILLAN, Samuel 1
MCMILLAN, Samuel James H
Renwick
MCMILLAN, Thomas 1
Sanders
MCMILLAN, William H
Charles
MCMILLAN, William 1
Charles
MCMILLAN, William H. 1
MCMILLAN, William 5
Joshua
MCMILLAN, William Linn 1
MCMILLEN, Alonzo 1
Bertram
MCMILLEN, Dale Wilmore 5
MCMILLEN, Fred Ewing 4
MCMILLEN, James 3
Adelbert
MCMILLIN, Alvin Nugent 3
MCMILLIN, Benton 1
MCMILLIN, Emerson 1
MCMILLIN, Francis Briggs 1
Nelson
MCMILLIN, Frederick 1
MCMILLIN, John Milton 3
MCMILLIN, Lucille Foster 2
MCMILLIN, Stewart Earl 3
MCMINN, Joseph H
MCMORAN, George 6
Andrew
MCMORRAN, Henry 3
MCMORRIS, Charles H. 4
MCMORROW, Francis 4
Joseph
MCMORROW, Thomas 3
MCMULLAN, Harry 3
MCMULLAN, Oscar 4
MCMULLEN, Adam 5
MCMULLEN, Charles Bell 5
MCMULLEN, Chester 3
Bartow
MCMULLEN, Clements 3
MCMULLEN, Fayette H
MCMULLEN, Hugh 1
Aloysius
MCMULLEN, John H
MCMULLEN, John Joseph H
MCMULLEN, Lynn Banks 4
MCMULLEN, Richard 1
Cann
MCMURDY, Robert 2
MCMURRAY, Charles 1
Backman
MCMURRAY, DeWitt 4
MCMURRAY, Howard 4
Johnstone
MCMURRAY, James 5
Donald
MCMURRAY, James Henry 1
MCMURRAY, John 5
MCMURRAY, Orrin Kip 4
MCMURRAY, William 1
Josiah
MCMURRICH, J. Playfair 3
MCMURRICH, James H
Playfair
MCMURRICH, James 4
Playfair
MCMURRY, Charles 1
Alexander
MCMURRY, Frank Morton 4
MCMURRY, Lida Brown 4
MCMURRY, William 1
Fletcher
MCMURTRIE, Douglas 2
Crawford
MCMURTRIE, Uz 4
MCMURTRIE, William 1
Gilmer
MCMURTRY, James 3
MCMURTRY, John H
MCMURTRY, Lewis S. 1

MCMURTRY, William John 4
MCNAB, Alexander J. 3
MCNAB, Archibald Peter 1
MCNAB, Joe Hector 2
MCNABB, Samuel W. 1
MCNAGNY, Phil 5
McClellan
MCNAIR, Alexander H
MCNAIR, Frank 6
MCNAIR, Fred Walter 1
MCNAIR, Frederick 1
Vallette
MCNAIR, James Birtley 5
MCNAIR, John H
MCNAIR, John Babbitt 5
MCNAIR, Lesley James 2
MCNAIR, William Sharp 1
MCNALLY, Andrew 3
MCNALLY, Frederick 1
George
MCNALLY, George 6
Frederick
MCNALLY, James Clifford 4
MCNALLY, Joseph Thomas 5
MCNALLY, Paul Aloysius 3
MCNALLY, William 1
Duncan
MCNALLY, William J. 4
MCNAMARA, Harley 4
Vincent
MCNAMARA, John M. 4
MCNAMARA, Joseph 5
Augustine
MCNAMARA, Martin D. 4
MCNAMARA, Patrick 1
Vincent
MCNAMARA, Robert 4
Charles
MCNAMARA, Robert 5
Charles
MCNAMEE, C. Declian 4
MCNAMEE, Charles 4
Joseph
MCNAMEE, Graham 2
MCNAMEE, Luke 5
MCNAMEE, William John 2
Jr.
MCNARNEY, Josehh T. 5
MCNARY, Charles Linza 2
MCNARY, Henrietta 4
Williamson
MCNARY, James Graham 4
MCNARY, William S. 4
MCNAUGHER, John 2
MCNAUGHT, Francis 4
Hector
MCNAUGHT, James 4
MCNAUGHT, James B. 3
MCNAUGHTON, Andrew 4
George Latta
MCNAUGHTON, John 1
Hugh
MCNAUGHTON, John 4
Theodore
MCNAUGHTON, William 4
Francis
MCNAUGHTON, William 5
Francis
MCNEAL, Alice 4
MCNEAL, Donald Hamlin 4
MCNEAL, Edgar Holmes 3
MCNEAL, Joshua Vansant 1
MCNEAL, Thomas Allen 6
MCNEAL, William Horton 6
MCNEALY, Raymond 3
William
MCNEAR, George Plummer 2
Jr.
MCNEELY, Eugene 6
J(ohnson)
MCNEELY, Harry 5
G(regory)
MCNEELY, Robert 5
Whitehead
MCNEES, Sterling G. 3
MCNEIL, Edwin Colyer 4
MCNEIL, Elton Burbank 6
MCNEIL, Everett 1
MCNEIL, Hiram Colver 1
MCNEIL, Kenneth Gordon 5
MCNEIL, Sister Mary 5
Donald
MCNEIL, Robert Lincoln 1
MCNEILL, Archibald H
MCNEILL, Daniel H
MCNEILL, Edwin Ruthven 5
MCNEILL, George Edwin 1
MCNEILL, George 1
Rockwell
MCNEILL, Hector 1
MCNEILL, I. C. 4
MCNEILL, John Charles 1
MCNEILL, John Hanson 1
MCNEILL, John Thomas 6
MCNEILL, Neal Edward 1
MCNEILL, Robert Hayes 6

MCNEILL, Thomas W. 3
MCNEILL, William Gibbs H
MCNEIR, George 1
MCNEIR, William 4
MCNEIRNY, Francis H
MCNEW, John Thomas 2
Lamar
MCNICHOL, Paul John 5
MCNICHOLAS, John T. 3
MCNICHOLS, John Patrick 4
MCNIECE, Harold Francis 5
MCNIECE, Robert Gibson 1
MCNINCH, Frank R. 3
MCNULTA, John 1
MCNULTA, John 4
MCNULTY, C. H. 3
MCNULTY, Frank J. 5
MCNULTY, George Albert 4
MCNULTY, James 5
MCNULTY, John Laurence 3
MCNULTY, Robert 4
Wilkinson
MCNUTT, Alexander 1
MCNUTT, Anna Mary 5
MCNUTT, Paul Vories 4
MCNUTT, William Fletcher 4
MCNUTT, William Roy 6
MCPEAK, William Wallace 4
MCPHEE, Eugene Roderick 6
MCPHEE, Julian A. 4
MCPHEETERS, Chester 4
Amos
MCPHEETERS, William 4
Emmett
MCPHEETERS, William 1
Marcellus
MCPHERREN, Charles 5
Elmo
MCPHERRIN, John Weitz 6
MCPHERSON, Aimee 1
Semple
MCPHERSON, Aimee 2
Semple
MCPHERSON, Almee 4
Semple
MCPHERSON, Charles 2
MCPHERSON, Edward H
MCPHERSON, Harry 3
Wright
MCPHERSON, Hobart M. 3
MCPHERSON, Isaac V. 1
MCPHERSON, Isaac V. 4
MCPHERSON, James H
Birdseye
MCPHERSON, John 1
Bayard
MCPHERSON, John 1
Edward
MCPHERSON, John 3
Hanson Thomas
MCPHERSON, John H
Rhoderic
MCPHERSON, Logan 1
Grant
MCPHERSON, Ross 1
MCPHERSON, Samuel 3
Dace
MCPHERSON, Sherman 4
Tecumseh
MCPHERSON, Simon John 1
MCPHERSON, Smith 1
MCPHERSON, William 3
MCPHERSON, William 1
Lenhart
MCPIKE, Henry H. 1
MCQUADE, Vincent 5
Augustine
MCQUAID, Bernard John 1
MCQUAID, William 4
Ravenel
MCQUARRIE, Irvine 4
MCQUEEN, Elizabeth 6
Lippincott
MCQUEEN, Frederick Emil 4
MCQUEEN, Henry Clay 1
MCQUEEN, John H
MCQUEEN, L(oren) 5
A(ngus)
MCQUEEN, Stewart 1
MCQUIGG, John Rea 1
MCQUILKIN, Robert 3
Crawford
MCQUILLEN, John Hugh H
MCQUILLIN, Eugene 1
MCRAE, Austin Lee 1
MCRAE, Bruce 3
MCRAE, Duncan Kirkland H
MCRAE, George W. 3
MCRAE, James Henry 1
MCRAE, James Wilson 3
MCRAE, John Jones 1
MCRAE, Milton A. 1
MCRAE, Roderick 1
MCRAE, Thomas Chipman 1
MCRAE, William Allan Jr. 6

MCRCLOSKEY, George V. 1
A.
MCREYNOLDS, Frederick 5
Wilson
MCREYNOLDS, George 3
Edgar
MCREYNOLDS, James 2
Clark
MCREYNOLDS, John 2
Oliver
MCREYNOLDS, Peter 1
Wesley
MCREYNOLDS, Samuel 1
Davis
MCREYNOLDS, William 3
Henry
MCRILL, Albert Leroy 3
MCROBERTS, Harriet Pearl 2
Skinner
MCROBERTS, Samuel H
MCSHANE, Andrew James 1
MCSHERRY, James H
MCSHERRY, Richard H
MCSKIMMON, William 5
Bingham
MCSOLEY, Raymond 3
Joseph
MCSORLEY, Edward 4
MCSORLEY, Joseph 4
MCSPADDEN, Joseph 4
Walker
MCSPARRAN, John Aldus 5
MCSURELY, William 2
Harvey
MCSWAIN, John Jackson 1
MCSWEENEY, Henry 2
MCSWEENEY, John 5
MCSWEENEY, Miles 1
Benjamin
MCTAGUE, Charles Patrick 4
MCTAMMANY, John H
MCTAMMANY, John 4
MCTARNAHAN, William 3
Chamberlain
MCTYEIRE, Holland H
Nimmons
MCVAY, Charles Butler Jr. 2
MCVEA, Emilie Watts 5
MCVEAN, Charles H
MCVEIGH, John Newburn 3
MCVEY, Frank LeRond 3
MCVEY, William E. 1
MCVEY, William Estus 3
MCVICAR, Nelson 4
MCVICKAR, John H
MCVICKAR, William 1
Neilson
MCVICKER, James Hubert H
MCVINNEY, Russell J. 5
MCWADE, Robert Malachi 1
MCWANE, James Ransom 1
MCWHINNEY, Thomas 1
Martin
MCWHIRTER, Felix T. 1
MCWHIRTER, Luella 3
Frances Smith
MCWHIRTER, William 4
Allan
MCWHORTER, Ashton 1
Waugh
MCWHORTER, Ernest D. 2
MCWHORTER, Henry Clay 1
MCWILLIAM, John R. 4
MCWILLIAMS, Clarence 1
A.
MCWILLIAMS, John 5
Probasco
MCWILLIAMS, Roland 3
Fairbairn
MCWILLIAMS, Thomas 1
Samuel
MCWILLIE, Thomas 1
Anderson
MCWILLIE, William H
MEACHAM, James H
MEACHAM, W(illiam) 5
Banks
MEAD, Albert Davis 2
MEAD, Albert Edward 1
MEAD, Arthur Emett 4
MEAD, Arthur Raymond 6
MEAD, Charles Larew 1
MEAD, Charles Marsh 1
MEAD, Cowles H
MEAD, D. Irving 3
MEAD, Daniel Webster 2
MEAD, Edward Campbell 1
MEAD, Edward Sherwood 1
MEAD, Edwin Doak 1
MEAD, Elizabeth Storrs 1
MEAD, Elwood 1
MEAD, Frederick Sumner 1
MEAD, George Herbert 1
MEAD, George Houk 5
MEAD, George Jackson 2
MEAD, George Whitefield 2

MEAD, George Wilson 4
MEAD, Gilbert Wilcox 2
MEAD, Harry L. 4
MEAD, James M. 4
MEAD, John Abner 1
MEAD, Kate Campbell Hurd 1
MEAD, Larkin Goldsmith 1
MEAD, Leon 4
MEAD, Leonard Charles 1
MEAD, Lucia True Ames 1
MEAD, Nelson Prentiss 4
MEAD, Solomon Cristy 5
MEAD, Sterling V. 4
MEAD, Theodore Hoe 4
MEAD, Warren Judson 4
MEAD, William Edward 5
MEAD, William Henry 6
MEAD, William Rutherford 1
MEAD, William Whitman 1
MEADE, Edwin Ruthwen 1
MEADE, Eleanore Hussey 5
MEADE, Francis Louis 3
MEADE, Frank B. 2
MEADE, George
MEADE, George Edward 5
MEADE, George Gordon H
MEADE, George Peterkin 6
MEADE, James J. 3
MEADE, Janifer Dewitt 1
MEADE, Richard Kidder * H
MEADE, Richard Kidder 1
MEADE, Richard Worsam * H
MEADE, Richard Worsam 1
MEADE, Robert Douthat 6
MEADE, Robert Leamy 1
MEADE, William 1
MEADOR, Chastain Clark 1
MEADOWCROFT, William Henry 1
MEADOWS, Clarence Watson 4
MEADOWS, James Allen 5
MEAGHER, James Francis 1
MEAGHER, James Luke 1
MEAGHER, Raymond 3
MEAGHER, Thomas Francis H
MEAKIN, L. H. 1
MEALEY, Carroll Edward 4
MEANEY, Thomas Francis 5
MEANS, David MacGregor 1
MEANS, Earl A. 3
MEANS, Eldred Kurtz 3
MEANS, Emily Adams 5
MEANS, Frank Wilson 3
MEANS, Gaston Bullock 4
MEANS, George Hamilton 2
MEANS, Haston Bullock 4
MEANS, James Howard 4
MEANS, Philip Ainsworth 2
MEANS, Rice William 2
MEANS, Stewart
MEANS, Thomas Herbert 5
MEANWELL, Walter E. 3
MEANY, Edmond Stephen 1
MEANY, Edward P. 1
MEARA, Frank S. 1
MEARNS, Edgar A. H
MEARNS, Edgar Alexander 1
MEARNS, Hughes 4
MEARS, Brainerd 6
MEARS, David Otis 1
MEARS, Eliot Grinnell 2
MEARS, Frederick 1
MEARS, Helen Farnsworth 1
MEARS, J. EWING 4
MEARS, John William H
MEARS, Leverett 1
MEARS, Louise Wilhelmina 5
MEARS, Mary 5
MEASE, James H
MEASON, Isaac 1
MEBANE, Alexander H
MEBANE, B. Frank 4
MEBANE, Daniel 1
MEBANE, Harry Bartlett Jr. 5
MEBANE, Robert Sloan 1
MECH, Stephen John 5
MECHAU, Frank Jr. 2
MECHEM, Floyd Russell 1
MECHEM, Merritt Cramer 2
MECHEM, Philip 5
MECHERLE, George Jacob 3
MECHERLE, Raymond Perry
MECHLIN, Leila 2
MECKLIN, John Martin 5
MECKLIN, John Moffatt 3
MECOM, Benjamin
MEDALIE, George Zerdin 2
MEDARY, Milton Bennett 1
MEDARY, Samuel H
MEDBURY, Charles Sanderson 1

MEDEARIS, T(homas) W(hittier) 5
MEDFORD, William 5
MEDHURST, Sir Charles E. H. 3
MEDILL, Joseph H
MEDILL, William H
MEDLEY, Mat H
MEDSGER, Oliver Perry 5
MEE, William 1
MEECH, Ezra H
MEEHAN, M. Joseph 4
MEEHAN, Thomas 1
MEEHAN, Thomas A. 4
MEEK, Alexander Beaufort H
MEEK, Benjamin Franklin 1
MEEK, Charles Simpson 3
MEEK, Edward Roscoe 5
MEEK, Fielding Bradford H
MEEK, Howard Bagnall 5
MEEK, John Henry 1
MEEK, Joseph A(icinus) 5
MEEK, Joseph L. H
MEEK, Robert Abner 3
MEEK, Seth Eugene 1
MEEK, Sterner St Paul 5
MEEK, Theophile James 6
MEEK, Walter Joseph 6
MEEKER, Arthur 2
MEEKER, Arthur 5
MEEKER, Claude 1
MEEKER, Ezra 1
MEEKER, Frank Leroy 2
MEEKER, George Herbert 4
MEEKER, Jacob Edwin 1
MEEKER, James Rusling H
MEEKER, Jonathan Magie 1
MEEKER, Jotham H
MEEKER, Moses 1
MEEKER, Nathan Cook 1
MEEKER, Ralph Inman 6
MEEKER, Royal 3
MEEKINS, Isaac Melson 2
MEEKINS, Lynn Roby 1
MEEKISON, David 4
MEEKS, Benjamin Wiltshire 6
MEEKS, Carroll Louis Vanderslice
MEEKS, Clarence Gardner 3
MEEKS, Everett Victor 5
MEEKS, James A. 4
MEEM, Harry Grant 2
MEEMAN, Edward John 4
MEENES, Max 6
MEERSCHAERT, Theophile 1
MEES, Arthur 1
MEES, Carl Leo 1
MEES, Charles Edward Kenneth 4
MEES, Otto 3
MEES, Theophilus 1
MEESE, Alfred Hall 4
MEESE, William Henry 1
MEESER, Spenser Byron 4
MEESSEN, Hubert Joseph 4
MEFTAH, Davood Khan 5
MEGAN, Charles P. 2
MEGAPOLENSIS, Johannes H
MEGARGEE, Edwin 3
MEGARO, Gaudens 3
MEGGERS, William Frederick 4
MEGGINSON, William 5
MEGOWEN, Carl Robert 4
MEGRAN, Herbert Brown 3
MEGRAW, Herbert Ashton 3
MEGRUE, Roi Cooper 1
MEHAFFY, Tom Miller 2
MEHAN, John Dennis 4
MEHAN, Mona Catharine 4
MEHL, Robert Franklin 6
MEHLBERG, Josephine Janina Bednarski Spinner (Mrs. Henry Mehlberg)
MEHLER, John Sauter 4
MEHLIN, Theodore Grefe 5
MEHLING, Theodore John 4
MEHORNAY, Robert Lee 3
MEHREN, Edward J. 4
MEHTA, Gaganvihari L. 6
MEIDELL, Harold M. 1
MEIER, Fabian Allan 4
MEIER, Fred Campbell 1
MEIER, Julius L. 1
MEIER, Norman Charles 4
MEIER, Walter Frederick 4
MEIERE, M. Hildreth 4
MEIGGS, Henry H
MEIGHAN, Thomas 1
MEIGHEN, Arthur 3
MEIGHEN, John Felix Dryden
MEIGS, Arthur Ingersoll

MEIGS, Arthur Vincent 1
MEIGS, Charles Delucena H
MEIGS, Cornelia Lynde 6
MEIGS, Grace Lynde H
MEIGS, Henry H
MEIGS, James Aitken H
MEIGS, John 1
MEIGS, John Forsyth H
MEIGS, Josiah H
MEIGS, Merrill Church 4
MEIGS, Montgomery 1
MEIGS, Montgomery Cunningham H
MEIGS, Return Jonathan H
MEIGS, Return Jonathan Jr. *
MEIGS, Robert Van 5
MEIGS, William Montgomery 1
MEIKLE, George Stanley 3
MEIKLEJOHN, Alexander 4
MEIKLEJOHN, George De Rue 1
MEIKS, Lyman Thompson 3
MEILINK, John Girard 3
MEIN, John Gordon 5
MEIN, William Wallace 4
MEINE, Franklin Julius 5
MEINECKE, Emilio Pepe Michael 4
MEINEL, William John 4
MEINHOLD, H. E. 6
MEINHOLD, H. E. 6
MEINHOLTZ, Frederick E. 4
MEINRATH, Joseph 1
MEINS, Carroll Leach 3
MEINZER, Oscar Edward 2
MEISENHELDER, Edmund W.
MEISENHELTER, L. R. 6
MEISLE, Kathryn (Mrs. Calvin M. Franklin) 5
MEISS, Millard 6
MEISSNER, Edwin Benjamin 3
MEISSNER, K. W. 4
MEISTEN, John Nicholas 6
MEISTER, John William 6
MEITNER, Lise 5
MEJIA, Federico 4
MEKEEL, Haviland Scudder 4
MELANDER, A. L. 6
MELANDER, George Harold
MELBA, Mme Nellie 1
MELCHER, Carl A. 3
MELCHER, Columbus Rudolph 2
MELCHER, Frank Otis 1
MELCHER, Frederic Gershom 4
MELCHER, George 4
MELCHER, George B. 4
MELCHER, Joseph H
MELCHERS, Gari 1
MELCHERS, Leo Edward 6
MELCHETT, Julian Edward Alfred 6
MELCHIOR, Lauritz Lebrecht Hommel 5
MELCHOR, Oliver Hoffman 1
MELDEN, Charles Manly 1
MELDRIM, Peter W. 1
MELDRUM, Andrew Barclay 5
MELDRUM, A(ndrew) Mackenzie 5
MELDRUM, Herbert Alexander
MELDRUM, William Buell 3
MELEAR, James Melville 3
MELENCIO, Jose P. 3
MELENDY, Mary Ries 1
MELENEY, Clarence Edmund 1
MELENEY, Frank Lamont 4
MELHORN, Donald Franklin 6
MELHORN, Nathan R. 5
MELHUS, Irving E. 4
MELINE, Frank L. 2
MELINE, James Florant 4
MELIODON, Jules Andre 5
MELISH, John 4
MELISH, John Howard 5
MELISH, William Bromwell 4
MELIUS, L. Malcolm 4
MELL, Patrick H. H
MELL, Patrick Hues 1
MELLE, Rosine 4
MELLEN, Charles Sanger 1
MELLEN, Chase 1
MELLEN, George Frederick 1
MELLEN, Grenville H

MELLEN, Ida M. 6
MELLEN, Prentiss H
MELLER, Harry Bertine 3
MELLETT, Lowell 3
MELLETTE, Arthur Calvin H
MELLIN, Carl Johan 1
MELLINGER, Aubrey Hugo 4
MELLINGER, Samuel 4
MELLISH, David Batcheller H
MELLISH, Mary 3
MELLISS, David Ernest 1
MELLON, Andrew William 1
MELLON, James R. 1
MELLON, Richard Beatty 1
MELLON, Richard King 5
MELLON, Thomas 1
MELLON, Thomas Alexander H
MELLON, William Larimer 2
MELLOR, Charles Chauncey 1
MELLOR, Walter 4
MELLOTT, Arthur J. 3
MELLUISH, James George 5
MELONEY, Marie Mattingly 2
MELONEY, William Brown 1
MELONEY, William Brown 5
MELS, Edgar 1
MELSHEIMER, Friedrich Valentin H
MELTON, Charles Lewis 3
MELTON, James 4
MELTON, LeRoy 5
MELTON, Wightman Fletcher 2
MELTON, William D. 1
MELTON, William Walter 6
MELTZER, Charles Henry 1
MELTZER, Samuel James 1
MELVILLE, David H
MELVILLE, Frank Jr. 1
MELVILLE, George Wallace 1
MELVILLE, Henry 1
MELVILLE, Herman H
MELVILLE, K(enneth) I(van) 6
MELVILLE, Rose 2
MELVIN, Alonzo Dorus 1
MELVIN, Bradford Morse 4
MELVIN, Frank Worthington 4
MELVIN, Henry Alexander 1
MELVIN, Marion Edmund 3
MELVIN, Myron S. 4
MELVIN, Ridgely Prentiss 2
MEMBRE, Zenobius 1
MEMBRENO, Alberto 4
MEMINGER, James Wilbert 3
MEMMINGER, Allard 1
MEMMINGER, Christopher Gustavus H
MEMMINGER, Christopher Gustavus 1
MEMMINGER, Lucien 6
MENAGH, Louis Randolph Jr. 6
MENARD, Michel Branamour H
MENARD, Pierre H
MENARD, Rene H
MENCKEN, August 4
MENCKEN, Henry Louis 3
MENCKEN, Sara Powell Haardt 1
MENCONI, Ralph Joseph 6
MENDEL, Lafayette Benedict 1
MENDEL, Warner H(umphrey) 5
MENDELL, Clarence Whittlesey 5
MENDELL, Seth 1
MENDELSOHN, Charles Jastrow 1
MENDELSOHN, Erich H
MENDELSOHN, Erich 4
MENDELSOHN, Samuel 1
MENDELSSOHN, Louis 1
MENDENHALL, Charles Elwood 1
MENDENHALL, George Newton 6
MENDENHALL, Harlan George 1
MENDENHALL, Thomas Corwin 1
MENDENHALL, Walter Curran 3
MENDENHALL, William Orville 6
MENDERES, Adnan 4

MENDES, Frederick de Sola 1
MENDES, Henry Pereira 1
MENDES, Murilo Monteiro 6
MENDEZ, Joaquin 4
MENDLESON, Alan N. 3
MENEELY, A. Howard 4
MENEELY, Andrew H
MENEES, Thomas 1
MENEFEE, F(erdinand) N(orthrup)
MENEFEE, Richard Hickman H
MENENDEZ, Pedro de Aviles H
MENETREY, Joseph H
MENEWA H
MENGARINI, Gregory H
MENGE, Frederick 3
MENGEL, Levi Walter 1
MENGES, Franklin 3
MENGLE, Glenn A. 4
MENJOU, Adolphe Jean 4
MENKEN, Adah Isaacs H
MENKEN, Helen 4
MENKEN, S. Stanwood 3
MENNAN, William Gerhard 4
MENNER, Robert James 3
MENNINGER, William Claire 4
MENOCAL, Aniceto G. 1
MENOHER, Charles Thomas 1
MENOHER, Pearson 3
MENON, Maniketh Gopala 4
MENSEL, Ernst Edmund 4
MENSEL, Ernst Heinrich 2
MENTON, A(ndrew) Paul 5
MENTZ, George Francis Millen 3
MENTZER, William Cyrus 5
MENVILLE, Leon 3
MENVILLE, Raoul Louis 4
MENZIES, Alan Wilfrid Cranbrook 4
MENZIES, Alan Wilfrid Cranbrook 5
MENZIES, John Thomson 4
MENZIES, John William H
MENZIES, Percival Keith 6
MERAS, Albert Amedee 1
MERCER, Alfred Clifford 1
MERCER, Archibald 4
MERCER, Beverly Howard 6
MERCER, Charles Fenton H
MERCER, David Henry 1
MERCER, Eugene LeRoy 3
MERCER, Frederick Olin 4
MERCER, Henry Chapman 1
MERCER, Hugh H
MERCER, Hugh Victor 5
MERCER, James H
MERCER, Jesse H
MERCER, John Francis H
MERCER, Lauron W. 4
MERCER, Margaret H
MERCER, Samuel Alfred Browne 6
MERCER, Saul Erastus 4
MERCER, William Fairfield 1
MERCHANT, Frank Ivan 3
MERCIER, Armand Theodore 3
MERCIER, Charles Alfred 1
MERCK, George Wilhelm 3
MERCUR, Rodney Augustus 1
MERCUR, Ulysses H
MEREDITH, Albert Barrett 2
MEREDITH, Edna Elliott 6
MEREDITH, Edwin Thomas 1
MEREDITH, Edwin Thomas Jr. 4
MEREDITH, Ernest Sidney 6
MEREDITH, James Alva 1
MEREDITH, Joseph Carroll 1
MEREDITH, Samuel H
MEREDITH, Virginia Claypool 1
MEREDITH, William Henry 1
MEREDITH, William Morris H
MEREDITH, William Morton 4
MERGENTHALER, Ottmar H
MERGLER, Marie Josepha H
MERICA, Charles Oliver 1
MERICA, Paul Dyer 3
MERICKA, William John 5
MERIGOLD, Benjamin Shores 5
MERILH, Edmond L. 4

MERILLAT, Louis Adolph 6
MERINGTON, Marguerite 3
MERITT, Edgar Briant 5
MERIVALE, Philip 2
MERIWETHER, Colyer 1
MERIWETHER, David * H
MERIWETHER, Elizabeth 1
  Avery
MERIWETHER, James H
MERIWETHER, James A. H
MERIWETHER, Lee 4
MERKER, Harvey Milton 5
MERLEAU-PONTY, 4
  Maurice
MERLE-SMITH, Van 2
  Santvoord
MERLE-SMITH, Wilton 1
MERMEY, Maurice 6
MERNER, Garfield David 5
MEROLA, Gaetano 6
MERONEY, William Penn 1
MERORY, Joseph 5
MERRELL, Edgar Sanford 2
  Keen
MERRELL, George R. 4
MERRELL, Herman Stroup 6
MERRELL, Irvin Seward 3
MERRELL, John Hastings 5
MERRELL, John Porter 1
MERRELL, William Dayton 3
MERRIAM, Alexander Ross 1
MERRIAM, Augustus H
  Chapman
MERRIAM, Carroll 1
  Burnham
MERRIAM, Charles H
MERRIAM, Charles 3
  Edward
MERRIAM, Clinton Hart 1
MERRIAM, Edmund 1
  Franklin
MERRIAM, Frank Finley 3
MERRIAM, George Spring 1
MERRIAM, Henry Clay 1
MERRIAM, Henry M. 3
MERRIAM, John Campbell 2
MERRIAM, John Everett 4
MERRIAM, William Rush 1
MERRIAMN, Myra Hunt 1
  Kingman
MERRICK, Edward Steele 5
MERRICK, Edwin Thomas 1
MERRICK, Frank Anderson 2
MERRICK, Frederick H
MERRICK, George Edgar 2
MERRICK, George Peck 1
MERRICK, Harry Hopkins 5
MERRICK, Harry L. 1
MERRICK, J. Hartley 3
MERRICK, John Vaughan 1
MERRICK, Pliny H
MERRICK, Samuel H
  Vaughan
MERRICK, Walter 4
  Chapman
MERRICK, William H
  Duhurst
MERRICK, William H
  Matthew
MERRIFIELD, Fred 1
MERRIFIELD, Webster 1
MERRILL, Aaron Stanton 4
MERRILL, Abner Hopkins 1
MERRILL, Albert B. 3
MERRILL, Allyne 4
  Litchfield
MERRILL, Alma Lowell 4
MERRILL, Amos Newlove 5
MERRILL, Barzilee Winfred 3
MERRILL, Beardslee Bliss 4
MERRILL, Cassius Exum 4
MERRILL, Charles 4
  Clarkson
MERRILL, Charles Edward 3
MERRILL, Charles 3
  Washington
MERRILL, Charles White 1
MERRILL, Charles White 1
MERRILL, Cyrus Strong 1
MERRILL, Dana True 5
MERRILL, Daniel H
MERRILL, Edward Bagley 4
MERRILL, Edward Folsom 4
MERRILL, Edwin Godfrey 2
MERRILL, Edwin Katte 4
MERRILL, Elmer Drew 3
MERRILL, Elmer Truesdell 1
MERRILL, Francis 5
  Ellsworth
MERRILL, Frank D. 3
MERRILL, Frank Thayer 5
MERRILL, Frederick 5
  Augustus
MERRILL, Frederick James 1
  Hamilton
MERRILL, George Arthur 4

MERRILL, George Earnest 1
MERRILL, George 1
  Edmands
MERRILL, George Perkins 1
MERRILL, Henry 1
  Ferdinand
MERRILL, Hugh Davis 3
MERRILL, James Andrew 1
MERRILL, James Cushing 1
MERRILL, James Griswold 1
MERRILL, James Milford 1
MERRILL, John Buxton 3
MERRILL, John Fuller 2
  Appleton
MERRILL, John Lenord 2
MERRILL, John Lisgar 5
MERRILL, John Ogden 6
MERRILL, Joseph Francis 3
MERRILL, Joseph L. 5
MERRILL, Julia Wright 6
MERRILL, Leon Stephen 1
MERRILL, Louis Taylor 4
MERRILL, Lucius Herbert 1
MERRILL, Orsamus Cook H
MERRILL, Oscar Charles 3
MERRILL, Paul Willard 4
MERRILL, Payson 1
MERRILL, Richard Nye 6
MERRILL, Robert V. 3
MERRILL, Samuel H
MERRILL, Samuel * 1
MERRILL, Selah 1
MERRILL, Stephen Mason 1
MERRILL, Thais A. 6
MERRILL, Thomas Emery 2
MERRILL, William 4
  Augustus
MERRILL, William 1
  Bradford
MERRILL, William Emery H
MERRILL, William 1
  Fessenden *
MERRILL, William Henry 1
MERRILL, William J. 4
MERRILL, William Pierson 3
MERRIMAN, Daniel 1
MERRIMAN, Harry 3
  Morton
MERRIMAN, Helen 4
  Bigelow
MERRIMAN, Mansfield 1
MERRIMAN, Myra Hunt 1
  Kingman (Mrs. Josiah C.)
MERRIMAN, Roger 2
  Bigelow
MERRIMAN, San Lorenzo 3
MERRIMAN, Thaddeus 1
MERRIMAN, Truman H
  Adams
MERRIMON, Augustus H
  Summerfield
MERRITT, Abraham 2
MERRITT, Anna Lea 4
MERRITT, Arthur Hastings 5
MERRITT, Dixon Lanier 5
MERRITT, Edwin Atkins 5
MERRITT, Emma Laura 5
  Sutro (Mrs. George
  Washington Merritt)
MERRITT, Ernest George 2
MERRITT, Frank 1
MERRITT, Hulett Clinton 3
MERRITT, James White 6
MERRITT, Leonidas 1
MERRITT, LeRoy Charles 5
MERRITT, Matthew J. 2
MERRITT, Percival 1
MERRITT, Robert Clarence 1
MERRITT, Schuyler 3
MERRITT, Walter Gordon 5
MERRITT, Wesley 1
MERROW, Chester Earl 6
MERRY, Ann Brunton H
MERRY, John Fairfield 1
MERRY, Joseph James 5
MERRY, Robert Watson 6
MERRY, William Lawrence 1
MERRYFIELD, Mary 6
  Ainsworth
MERRYMAN, Andrew 1
  Curtis
MERRYWEATHER, 1
  George Edmund
MERSELES, Theodore 1
  Frelinghuysen
MERSEREAU, George 2
  Jefferson
MERSETH, Sidney Ingmar 5
MERSHON, Martin Luther 5
MERSHON, Ralph 3
  Davenport
MERSHON, William Butts 3
MERSON, Alexander 5
  J(ames)
MERTENS, George William 6

MERTINS, Gustave 5
  Frederick
MERTINS, Marshall Louis 5
MERTINS, (Marshall) Louis 6
MERTON, Holmes Whittier 2
MERTON, Thomas 5
MERTZ, Albert 1
MERVINE, William H
MERVIS, Meyer Bernard 5
MERWIN, Frederic Eaton 6
MERWIN, Henry Childs 1
MERWIN, Herbert Eugene 4
MERWIN, Loring Chase 5
MERWIN, Milton Hervey 4
MERWIN, Orange 1
MERWIN, Samuel 1
MERWIN, Samuel Edwin 1
MERWIN, Timothy Dwight 4
MERYMAN, Richard 5
  Sumner
MESEROLE, Clinton V. Jr. 5
MESEROLE, Clinton 3
  Vanderbilt
MESERVE, Charles Francis 1
MESERVE, Frederic Hill 4
MESERVE, Harry 1
  Chamberlain
MESERVE, John Bartlett 2
MESERVE, Nathaniel 4
MESICK, Jane Louise 4
MESICK, William S. 4
MESS, Otto 3
MESSENGER, J. Franklin 3
MESSENGER, North 1
  Overton
MESSENGER, Robert 4
  Pocock
MESSER, Alpha 1
MESSER, Asa H
MESSER, Edmund Clarence 1
MESSER, L. Wilbur 1
MESSER, Samuel 1
MESSER, William Stuart 4
MESSERSMITH, George S. 3
MESSERSMITH, George S. 4
MESSINA, Angelina Rose 5
MESSING, Abraham Joseph 5
MESSINGER, Charles 1
  Raymond
MESSINGER, Edwin John 4
MESSITER, Arthur Henry 1
MESSLER, Eugene 5
  Lawrence
MESSLER, Thomas H
  Doremus
MESSMER, Sebastian 1
  Gebhard
MESSNER, Julian 2
MESSNER, Kathryn G. 4
MESTA, Frank Albert 4
MESTA, L. W. 3
MESTA, Perle 5
MESTERN, H. Edward 5
MESTREZAT, Stephen 1
  Leslie
MESTROVIC, Ivan 4
METCALF, Arunah H
METCALF, Clarence 6
  Sheridan
METCALF, Clell Lee 2
METCALF, Edward Potter 4
METCALF, Frank Arthur 1
METCALF, George P. 3
METCALF, George Wallace 4
METCALF, Haven 2
METCALF, Henry Brewer 1
METCALF, Henry Harrison 1
METCALF, Irving Wight 1
METCALF, Jesse Houghton 2
METCALF, Joel Hastings 1
METCALF, John Calvin 2
METCALF, John Milton 4
  Putnam
METCALF, Leonard 1
METCALF, Lorettus Sutton 1
METCALF, Martin Kellogg 6
METCALF, Maynard Mayo 1
METCALF, Ralph 1
METCALF, Stephen Olney 3
METCALF, Theron H
METCALF, Victor Howard 1
METCALF, Wilder Stevens 1
METCALF, Willard Leroy 1
METCALF, William 1
METCALF, Zeno Payne 3
METCALFE, George 1
  Richmond
METCALFE, Henry 4
METCALFE, Henry H
  Bleecker
METCALFE, James Stetson 1
METCALFE, Richard Lee 3
METCALFE, Samuel Lytler H
METCALFE, Thomas 1
METCALFE, Tristram 1
  Walker

METEYARD, Thomas 1
  Buford
METTAUER, John Peter H
METTEN, John Farrell 5
METTEN, William F. 5
METTLER, John Wyckoff 3
METTLER, L. Harrison 4
METTS, John Van Bokkelen 5
METZ, Abraham Louis 4
METZ, Albert Frederick 4
METZ, Arthur Ray 4
METZ, Charles William 6
METZ, Christian H
METZ, Herman A. 1
METZDORF, Robert 6
  Frederick
METZENBAUM, Myron 2
  Firth
METZGAR, Charles Watson 4
METZGER, Delbert 5
  Everner
METZGER, Fraser 5
METZGER, Frederick Elder 3
METZGER, Herman Arthur 6
METZGER, Hutzel 3
METZGER, Irvin Dilling 2
METZGER, Ralph Alfred 5
METZLER, William Henry 4
METZMAN, Gustav 3
METZMAN, Gustav 4
MEUSER, Edwin Henry 2
MEY, Cornelius Jacobsen H
MEYER, Adolf 2
MEYER, Adolph 1
MEYER, Adolphus William 1
MEYER, Albert Gregory 4
MEYER, Alfred 3
MEYER, Alfred Henry 2
MEYER, Alfred Reuben 4
MEYER, Annie Nathan 3
MEYER, Arthur John 1
MEYER, Arthur Simon 3
MEYER, Arthur William 4
MEYER, B. G. 2
MEYER, Balthasar Henry 3
MEYER, Ben R. 3
MEYER, Charles F. 2
MEYER, Charles Garrison 4
MEYER, Charles Harrison 4
MEYER, Charles Zachary 5
MEYER, Christian 1
  Frederick Gottlieb
MEYER, Clarence Earle 4
MEYER, Edward Barnard 1
MEYER, Ely 5
MEYER, Estelle Reel (Mrs. 5
  Cort F. Meyer)
MEYER, Eugene 3
MEYER, Frank Straus 5
MEYER, Frederick H. 4
MEYER, Frederick Henry 4
MEYER, Fredrik 5
MEYER, George von 1
  Lengerke
MEYER, George A. 6
MEYER, George Homer 1
MEYER, George W. 4
MEYER, George William 3
MEYER, H. Kenneth 4
MEYER, Henry Coddington 3
  Jr.
MEYER, Henry Herman 3
MEYER, Herbert Alton 3
MEYER, Herbert Alton Jr. 5
MEYER, Herbert Willy 5
MEYER, Herman Henry 1
  Bernard
MEYER, Hugo Richard 4
MEYER, John Charles 6
MEYER, John Da Costa 6
MEYER, John Franklin 2
MEYER, John Jacob 5
MEYER, Joseph F. 1
MEYER, Julius Eduard H
MEYER, Julius Paul 2
MEYER, Karl Friedrich 5
MEYER, Karl Friedrich 6
MEYER, Lothar 5
MEYER, Lucy Rider 1
MEYER, Martin A. 1
MEYER, Max F(riedrich) 5
MEYER, Maximilian 3
  Courtland
MEYER, Paul D. 5
MEYER, Rudolph J. 1
MEYER, Schuyler Merritt 5
MEYER, Theodore 1
  Frederick
MEYER, Theodore Robert 6
MEYER, Wallace 5
MEYER, William Briggs 4
MEYER, Willy 1
MEYER, Wilson 5
MEYERCORD, George 1
  Rudolph

MEYERDING, Henry 5
  William
MEYERHOF, Otto 3
MEYERHOLZ, Charles 5
  Henry
MEYERS, Carl W. 3
MEYERS, Carlisle Paul 4
MEYERS, Erwin A. 4
MEYERS, George Julian 1
MEYERS, J. Edward 4
MEYERS, Joseph 3
MEYERS, Joseph Hugh 5
MEYERS, Robert C. V. 1
MEYERS, Sidney 5
  Stuyvesant
MEYERS, William John 1
MEYLAN, George Louis 3
MEYLAN, Paul Julien 4
MEYNE, Gerhardt 5
MEYNELL, Francis 6
MEYROWITZ, Emil B. 4
MEZES, Sidney Edward 1
MEZZROW, Mezz (Milton 5
  Mesirow)
MIANTONOMO H
MICH, Daniel D. 4
MICHAEL 3
MICHAEL, Arthur 1
MICHAEL, Arthur 2
MICHAEL, Elias 1
MICHAEL, Helen Abbott 1
MICHAEL, Jerome 3
MICHAEL, Max 5
MICHAEL, Moina Belle 4
MICHAEL, William Henry 1
MICHAELIDES, George 4
  Peter
MICHAELIS, George V. S. 5
MICHAELIS, Leonor 2
MICHAELIS, Richard C. 1
MICHAELIUS, Jonas H
MICHAELS, Charles 2
  Frederick
MICHAELS, Ernest Edwin 5
MICHAELS, Henry 3
MICHAELS, Hunter 4
MICHAELSON, M. Alfred 2
MICHAL, Aristotle D. 3
MICHALSON, Carl 4
MICHAUD, Gustave 1
MICHAUD, John Stephen 1
MICHAUD, Regis 1
MICHAUX, Andre H
MICHAUX, Francois Andre H
MICHEL, Charles E(ugene) 5
MICHEL, Ernest Adolph 2
MICHEL, Lincoln Mattheus 5
MICHEL, Richard Fraser 1
MICHEL, Virgil George H
MICHEL, Virgil George 4
MICHEL, William 4
MICHEL, William C. 5
MICHEL, William H
  Middleton
MICHELFELDER, 3
  Sylvester Clarence
MICHELS, Nicholas 5
  Aloysius
MICHELS, Walter Christian 6
MICHELSON, Albert 1
  Abraham
MICHELSON, Albert 1
  Heminway
MICHELSON, Albert 6
  Sidney
MICHELSON, Arnold 5
MICHELSON, Charles 2
MICHELSON, Henry 5
  E(rnest)
MICHELSON, Miriam 2
MICHELSON, Truman 1
MICHENER, Earl Cory 4
MICHENER, Ezra H
MICHENER, Louis 1
  Theodore
MICHI KINI KWA H
MICHIE, A. Hewson 3
MICHIE, H(enry) Stuart 5
MICHIE, James Newton 1
MICHIE, Peter Smith 1
MICHIE, Robert Edward 1
  Lee
MICHIE, Thomas Johnson 5
MICHINARD, Frank 4
MICHLER, Francis 3
MICHLER, Nathaniel H
MICKELSEN, Stanley R. 4
MICKELSON, George 4
  Theodore
MICKEY, Harold Chandler 5
MICKEY, John Hopwood 1
MICKLE, Joe J. 4
MICKLE, William English 1
MICOU, Richard Wilde 1

MIDDELSCHULTE, Wilhelm 2
MIDDLEBROOK, Louis Francis 1
MIDDLEBROOK, William Theophilus 6
MIDDLEBROOKS, Audy Jefferson 4
MIDDLEBUSH, Frederick Arnold 5
MIDDLESWARTH, Ner H
MIDDLETON, Arthur * H
MIDDLETON, Arthur D. H
MIDDLETON, Austin Ralph 3
MIDDLETON, Charles Gibson 3
MIDDLETON, Cornelius W. 4
MIDDLETON, George H
MIDDLETON, George 4
MIDDLETON, Henry 1
MIDDLETON, John Albert 6
MIDDLETON, John Izard H
MIDDLETON, Nathaniel Russell H
MIDDLETON, Peter 1
MIDDLETON, Stanley Grant 2
MIDDLETON, Thomas Cooke 4
MIDDLETON, William Shainline 6
MIDDLETON, William Vernon 4
MIDDOUR, Emory J. 3
MIDGLEY, Albert Leonard 6
MIDGLEY, John William 1
MIDGLEY, Thomas Jr. 2
MIEDEL, Robert Eugene 5
MIELATZ, Charles Frederick William 1
MIELZINER, Jo 6
MIELZINER, Leo 1
MIELZINER, Moses 1
MIERS, Earl Schenck 5
MIERS, Henry Virgil 1
MIERS, Robert Walter 1
MIERSCH, Paul Frederic Theodore 4
MIES VAN DER ROHE, Ludwig 5
MIESSNER, W(illiam) Otto 6
MIFFLIN, George Harrison 1
MIFFLIN, Lloyd 1
MIFFLIN, Thomas H
MIGATZ, Marshall 6
MIGEL, Julius A. 6
MIGHELS, Ella Sterling 1
MIGHELS, Ella Sterling 4
MIGHELS, Philip Verrill 1
MIGNONE, Albert Edmund 5
MIHALYFI, Erno 6
MIKELL, Henry Judah 2
MIKELL, William Ephraim 2
MIKESELL, Doyle 5
MIKESELL, Jerome Byron 5
MIKESELL, William Henry 5
MIKHALAPOV, George Sergei 5
MIKULES, T(homas) Leonard 6
MILAM, Arthur Yeager 3
MILAM, Carl Hastings 5
MILAS, Nicholas Althanasius 5
MILBANK, Albert Goodsell 3
MILBANK, Dunlevy 3
MILBANK, Jeremiah 5
MILBANK, Thomas Powell Fowler 6
MILBERT, Jacques Gerard H
MILBOURNE, Harvey Lee 4
MILBURN, Arthur W. 1
MILBURN, Edward Garland 5
MILBURN, George 1
MILBURN, George Roszelle 1
MILBURN, John George 1
MILBURN, William Henry 1
MILDEN, Alfred William 2
MILEN, Frederick Blumenthal 4
MILES, Basil 1
MILES, C. Edwin 1
MILES, Carlton Wright 3
MILES, Clarence Paul 1
MILES, Daniel Curtis 1
MILES, Dudley 3
MILES, Edson Russell 5
MILES, Ellen E. 4
MILES, Emma Bell 1
MILES, Evan 1
MILES, Frederick H
MILES, George Carpenter 6
MILES, Hooper Steele 4

MILES, Joshua Weldon 1
MILES, Louis Wardlaw 2
MILES, Lovick Pierce 3
MILES, Milton Edward 4
MILES, Nelson Appleton 1
MILES, Perry Lester 5
MILES, Robert Parker 1
MILES, Robert Whitfield 3
MILES, Vincent Morgan 2
MILES, Waldo Garland 6
MILES, Willard Wesbery 1
MILES, William Porcher 1
MILEY, Jess Wells 3
MILEY, John Henry 2
MILFORD, Morton Marshall 1
MILHAM, Willis Isbister 3
MILHAUD, Darius 6
MILHOLLAND, John Elmer 1
MILK, Arthur Leslie 4
MILKS, Howard Jay 3
MILLAR, Alexander Copeland 1
MILLAR, Edward Alexander 1
MILLAR, Preston Strong 2
MILLAR, Robert Cameron 5
MILLAR, Robert Wyness 3
MILLAR, Ronald 2
MILLAR, William Bell 1
MILLARD, Bailey 2
MILLARD, Charles Dunsmore 1
MILLARD, Charles Sterling 2
MILLARD, Clifford 4
MILLARD, Douglas 2
MILLARD, Earl 5
MILLARD, Everett Lee 1
MILLARD, Floyd Hays 3
MILLARD, Frank Ashley 4
MILLARD, Harrison 1
MILLARD, Joseph Hopkins 1
MILLARD, Paul Adsworth 2
MILLARD, Thomas Franklin Fairfax 1
MILLARD, Willard B(arrows) Jr. 5
MILLARD, William Barrett 4
MILLAY, Edna St Vincent 3
MILLAY, Kathleen Kalloch 2
MILLBERRY, Guy Stillman 5
MILLEDGE, John 1
MILLEDOLER, Philip H
MILLEN, John H
MILLENER, John A. 4
MILLER, A. Blanchard 1
MILLER, A. Blanchard 2
MILLER, A. K. 4
MILLER, Adolph Caspar 1
MILLER, Albert Edward 1
MILLER, Albert Fullerton 1
MILLER, Albert L. 3
MILLER, Alden Holmes 4
MILLER, Alexander Macomb 1
MILLER, Alfred Brashear 1
MILLER, Alfred Jacob H
MILLER, Alfred Parkin 1
MILLER, Alfred Stanley 1
MILLER, Alice Duer 2
MILLER, Amos Calvin 1
MILLER, Andrew 5
MILLER, Andrew Jackson Jr. 1
MILLER, Andrew James 4
MILLER, Andrew Joyce 1
MILLER, Anna Jenness 4
MILLER, Arthur 4
MILLER, Arthur Lewis 1
MILLER, Arthur McQuiston 1
MILLER, Arthur W. 5
MILLER, Augustus Samuel 1
MILLER, Austin Vicente 1
MILLER, Barse 5
MILLER, Benjamin Kurtz 1
MILLER, Benjamin LeRoy 2
MILLER, Benjamin M. 2
MILLER, Benjamin Orville 4
MILLER, Bert H. 2
MILLER, Bertha Everett Mahony 5
MILLER, Bina West 3
MILLER, Bloomfield Jackson 1
MILLER, Byron E. 1
MILLER, C. Jeff 1
MILLER, Carl A. 3
MILLER, Carl Wallace 4
MILLER, Carroll 2
MILLER, Charles 1
MILLER, Charles Addison 1
MILLER, Charles Armand 1
MILLER, Charles C. 1

MILLER, Charles Ervine 1
MILLER, Charles Franklin 5
MILLER, Charles Henry 1
MILLER, Charles Lewis 4
MILLER, Charles Mosher 6
MILLER, Charles R. 1
MILLER, Charles R. D. 4
MILLER, Charles Ransom 1
MILLER, Charles Russel 1
MILLER, Charles Wesley 1
MILLER, Charles Wilbur 3
MILLER, Charles William Emil 1
MILLER, Christian Otto Gerberding 3
MILLER, Cincinnatus Heine 1
MILLER, Clarence A. 3
MILLER, Clarence B. 1
MILLER, Clement Woodnutt 4
MILLER, Clyde Winwood 1
MILLER, Crosby Parke 1
MILLER, Daniel Fry H
MILLER, Daniel H. H
MILLER, Daniel Long 1
MILLER, Darius 1
MILLER, David Aaron 3
MILLER, David Lewis 5
MILLER, Dayton Clarence 1
MILLER, Dewitt 1
MILLER, Dick 5
MILLER, Dickinson Sergeant 4
MILLER, Don Clark 5
MILLER, Don Hugo 5
MILLER, Dudley Livingston 5
MILLER, E. P. Smith 1
MILLER, Edgar Calvin LeRoy 5
MILLER, Edgar Grim Jr. 3
MILLER, Edmund Howd 1
MILLER, Edmund Thornton 3
MILLER, Edmund W. 4
MILLER, Edward Alanson 4
MILLER, Edward Furber 1
MILLER, Edward Godfrey Jr. 5
MILLER, Edward Terhune 1
MILLER, Edward Tylor 4
MILLER, Edward Waite 1
MILLER, Edward Whitney 6
MILLER, Edwin Lee 2
MILLER, Edwin Lillie 1
MILLER, Edwin Morton 6
MILLER, Elihu Spencer H
MILLER, Elizabeth Smith 1
MILLER, Emerson R. 1
MILLER, Emily Huntington 1
MILLER, Emma Guffey 1
MILLER, Ephraim 1
MILLER, Ernest B. 3
MILLER, Ernest Henry 1
MILLER, Ernest Ivan 5
MILLER, Ethel Hull 4
MILLER, Eugene Harper 1
MILLER, E(ugene) K(earfott) 5
MILLER, Eugene Walter 1
MILLER, Ezra H
MILLER, Francis Garner 1
MILLER, Francis Trevelyn 1
MILLER, Frank A. 4
MILLER, Frank Augustus 1
MILLER, Frank Ebenezer 1
MILLER, Frank Harvey 1
MILLER, Frank Justus 1
MILLER, Frank William 4
MILLER, Franklin Thomas 1
MILLER, Fred J. 1
MILLER, Fred W. 2
MILLER, Frederic Howell 4
MILLER, Frederic K(epler) 1
MILLER, Frederic Magoun 1
MILLER, Frederick A. * 3
MILLER, Freeman Edwin 1
MILLER, Frieda Segelke 6
MILLER, G. F. 1
MILLER, Galen 5
MILLER, George 4
MILLER, George 1
MILLER, George Abram 1
MILLER, George Carter 1
MILLER, George E. 1
MILLER, George Frederick 4
MILLER, George Funston H
MILLER, George Henry 1
MILLER, George Henry 6
MILLER, George Lee 1
MILLER, George M. H
MILLER, George Macculloch 1
MILLER, George McAnelly 4
MILLER, George Morey 1
MILLER, George Noyes 1
MILLER, George Stewart 5

MILLER, Gerrit Smith 1
MILLER, Gerrit Smith Jr. 3
MILLER, Gilbert Heron 5
MILLER, Glenn 1
MILLER, Grace Moncrieff 1
MILLER, Gray 2
MILLER, Gustavus Hindman 1
MILLER, Harlan 5
MILLER, Harold C. 3
MILLER, Harriet Mann 1
MILLER, Harry Edward 1
MILLER, Harry (McKinley) 5
MILLER, Harry Irving 1
MILLER, Harvey H. 3
MILLER, Hazel Belle 6
MILLER, Helen Richards Guthrie 2
MILLER, Helen Topping 3
MILLER, Helen Topping 4
MILLER, Henry * 1
MILLER, Henry 4
MILLER, Henry B. 1
MILLER, Henry Russell 1
MILLER, Henry Watkins 1
MILLER, Herbert Adolphus 5
MILLER, Hilliard Eve 2
MILLER, Homer Virgil Milton H
MILLER, Horace Alden 1
MILLER, Howard Shultz 1
MILLER, Hugh 1
MILLER, Hugo Eugene 6
MILLER, Humphreys Henry Clay 1
MILLER, Irving Elgar 5
MILLER, Isaac Eugene 3
MILLER, J. Jay 1
MILLER, J. M. C. 4
MILLER, J. Martin 1
MILLER, J. Maxwell 1
MILLER, Jacob F. 1
MILLER, Jacob Welsh H
MILLER, Jacob William 1
MILLER, James 1
MILLER, James Alexander 2
MILLER, James Collins 1
MILLER, James Conelese 1
MILLER, James Decatur Jr. 5
MILLER, James Kenneth 1
MILLER, James Monroe 4
MILLER, James Russell 1
MILLER, Jesse H
MILLER, Jesse Isidor 2
MILLER, Joaquin 1
MILLER, John * H
MILLER, John 1
MILLER, John Anthony 5
MILLER, John Barnes 1
MILLER, John Bleecker 1
MILLER, John Briggs 1
MILLER, John Calvin 1
MILLER, John D. 2
MILLER, John Eschelman 1
MILLER, John Ford 1
MILLER, John Franklin 1
MILLER, John Franklin * 1
MILLER, John Gaines H
MILLER, John Henderson 1
MILLER, John Henry 1
MILLER, John King 6
MILLER, John Krepps 1
MILLER, John Maffit Jr. 1
MILLER, John Richardson 1
MILLER, John Rulon Jr. 1
MILLER, John S. 1
MILLER, John Stocker 1
MILLER, Jonathan Peckham H
MILLER, Joseph 1
MILLER, Joseph Dana 1
MILLER, Joseph Henry 3
MILLER, Joseph Hillis 3
MILLER, Joseph Leggett 1
MILLER, Joseph Nelson 1
MILLER, Joseph Torrence 1
MILLER, Josiah H
MILLER, Julian Creighton 5
MILLER, Julian Howell 4
MILLER, Julian Sidney 2
MILLER, Justin 5
MILLER, Kelly 2
MILLER, Kempster Blanchard 1
MILLER, Kenneth S. 6
MILLER, Kennth Hayes 5
MILLER, Knox Emerson 5
MILLER, Lawrence William 4
MILLER, Lee Graham 4
MILLER, Lee P. 1
MILLER, Leo Edward 3
MILLER, Leo L. 5
MILLER, Leslie Andrew 5
MILLER, Leslie Freeland 4
MILLER, Leslie William 1

MILLER, Leverett Saltonstall 1
MILLER, Lewis H
MILLER, Lewis Bennett 4
MILLER, Logan C. 3
MILLER, Loren 4
MILLER, Loren Barker 1
MILLER, Louise Klein 2
MILLER, Loye Holmes 5
MILLER, Lucius Hopkins 2
MILLER, Luther Deck 5
MILLER, M. V. 3
MILLER, Malcolm E. 4
MILLER, Marcus P. 1
MILLER, Marion Mills 1
MILLER, Mary Britton 6
MILLER, Mary Rogers 4
MILLER, Maude Murray 4
MILLER, Max 4
MILLER, Max 5
MILLER, Melville Winans 4
MILLER, Merrill 1
MILLER, Merritt Finley 5
MILLER, Michael A. 4
MILLER, Milton 1
MILLER, Milton A. 1
MILLER, Morris Smith 1
MILLER, Nathan H
MILLER, Nathan L. 3
MILLER, Nellie Burget 1
MILLER, Newton 4
MILLER, Olive Thorne 1
MILLER, Oscar Phineas 1
MILLER, Otto 3
MILLER, Park Hays 6
MILLER, Paul Duryea 3
MILLER, Paul E. 3
MILLER, Paul Gerard 3
MILLER, Perry 4
MILLER, Perry B. 1
MILLER, Pleasant Moorman H
MILLER, Pleasant Thomas 5
MILLER, R. Paul 4
MILLER, R. T. Jr. 3
MILLER, Ralph English 3
MILLER, Ransford Stevens 1
MILLER, Ray Haggard 6
MILLER, Ray T. 4
MILLER, Reed 1
MILLER, Richard E. 1
MILLER, Richard E. 1
MILLER, Richard Henry Thompson 1
MILLER, Richard 4
MILLER, Robert Frederick 1
MILLER, Robert Johnson 1
MILLER, Robert Netherland 4
MILLER, Robert Rowland 1
MILLER, Robert Talbott 1
MILLER, Robert Talbott Jr. 4
MILLER, Robert Walter 3
MILLER, Robert Warren 1
MILLER, Robert Watt 5
MILLER, Roger 1
MILLER, Roswell 1
MILLER, Rufus Wilder 1
MILLER, Russell 1
MILLER, Russell Benjamin 1
MILLER, Russell Cooper 1
MILLER, Russell King 1
MILLER, Rutger Bleecker H
MILLER, Samuel Charles 1
MILLER, Samuel Duncan 1
MILLER, Samuel Freeman H
MILLER, Samuel Haas 1
MILLER, Samuel Howard 1
MILLER, Samuel Warren 1
MILLER, Samuel William 1
MILLER, Seton Ingersoll 5
MILLER, Shackelford 1
MILLER, Sidney Lincoln 1
MILLER, Sidney Trowbridge 1
MILLER, Smith H
MILLER, Spencer Sr. 3
MILLER, Stephen Decatur H
MILLER, Stephen Ivan 5
MILLER, Sydney Robotham 2
MILLER, Theodore Joseph 6
MILLER, Thomas Condit 1
MILLER, Thomas Marshall 1
MILLER, Thomas Root 3
MILLER, Troup 3
MILLER, Vaughn 2
MILLER, W. Leslie 4
MILLER, Walter 2
MILLER, Walter 2
MILLER, Walter John 4
MILLER, Walter McNab 5
MILLER, Warner 1
MILLER, Warren Hastings 1
MILLER, Watson B. 4
MILLER, Webb 1

MILLER, Wilbur K. 6
MILLER, Wilhelm 5
MILLER, William H
MILLER, William 1
MILLER, William Davis 4
MILLER, William E. 3
MILLER, William Henry 1
MILLER, William Henry 1
Harrison
MILLER, William Jasper 4
MILLER, William Jennings 3
MILLER, William Morrison 4
MILLER, William 1
Niswonger
MILLER, William Rickarby H
MILLER, William Snow H
MILLER, William Starr H
MILLER, William Todd 4
MILLER, William Wilson H
MILLER, Willis Dance 5
MILLES, Carl Wilhelm Emil 3
MILLET, Clarence 3
MILLET, Francis Davis 1
MILLET, John Alfred 6
Parsons
MILLETT, Fred Benjamin 6
MILLETT, George Van 5
MILLETTE, John W. 2
MILLHAUSER, DeWitt 2
MILLIGAN, Alexander 1
Reed
MILLIGAN, Edward 1
MILLIGAN, Ezra McLeod 1
MILLIGAN, Harold V. 3
MILLIGAN, Jacob L. 3
MILLIGAN, John Jones H
MILLIGAN, Melvin Lee 4
MILLIGAN, Orlando 3
Howard
MILLIGAN, Robert Wiley 1
MILLIGAN, Samuel 1
MILLIGAN, William Edwin 1
MILLIKAN, Clark 4
Blanchard
MILLIKAN, George Lee 3
MILLIKAN, Max Franklin 5
MILLIKAN, Robert 3
Andrews
MILLIKEN, Arnold White 4
MILLIKEN, Carl Elias 4
MILLIKEN, Edwin C. 4
MILLIKEN, Gerrish H. 2
MILLIKEN, John David 4
MILLIKEN, Joseph K. 4
MILLIKEN, Joseph 1
Knowles
MILLIKEN, Seth Llewellyn H
MILLIKEN, Seth Mellen 1
MILLIKEN, William 6
Thomas
MILLIKIN, Benjamin L. 1
MILLIKIN, Eugene Donald 3
MILLIMAN, Elmer Edward 4
MILLIN, Sarah Gertrude 5
MILLING, Robert Edward 2
MILLING, Robert Edward 4
Jr.
MILLINGTON, Charles 1
Stephen
MILLINGTON, Ernest 3
John Oldknow
MILLION, John Wilson 1
MILLIS, Harry Alvin 2
MILLIS, Harry Lee 2
MILLIS, John 3
MILLIS, Wade 1
MILLIS, Walter 5
MILLIS, William Alfred 2
MILLMAN, Edward 4
MILLNER, Walker LeRoy 4
MILLOY, James S. 5
MILLS, Abbot Low 1
MILLS, Albert Leopold 1
MILLS, Alfred Elmer 1
MILLS, Anson 1
MILLS, Augustus K. III 3
MILLS, Benjamin H
MILLS, Benjamin Fay 1
MILLS, Blake David 3
MILLS, C. Wright 4
MILLS, Charles Burdick 4
MILLS, Charles Francis 1
MILLS, Charles Henry 4
MILLS, Charles Karsner 1
MILLS, Charles Smith 2
MILLS, Charles Wilson 2
MILLS, Charles Winfred 6
MILLS, Clark H
MILLS, Clyde Marvin 4
MILLS, Cyrus Taggart H
MILLS, Darius Ogden 1
MILLS, Dwight M. 5
MILLS, Earl Cuthbert 2
MILLS, Earle Watkins 6
MILLS, Edmund Mead 1

MILLS, Edward Kirkpatrick 4
Jr.
MILLS, Edwin Claude 3
MILLS, Elijah Hunt H
MILLS, Enos A. 1
MILLS, Frank Moody 4
MILLS, Frederick Cecil 4
MILLS, George Henry 6
MILLS, Harriet May 4
MILLS, Harriette Melissa 1
MILLS, Henry Edmund 4
MILLS, Herbert Elmer 3
MILLS, Herbert Hagerman 5
MILLS, Hillis 4
MILLS, Hiram Francis 1
MILLS, Isaac Newton 1
MILLS, J. Warner 1
MILLS, James Edward 2
MILLS, James Theodore 6
MILLS, Jesse T. 4
MILLS, Job Smith 1
MILLS, John 2
MILLS, John Sedwick 1
MILLS, Joseph John 4
MILLS, Lennox A(lgernon) 5
MILLS, Luther Laflin 1
MILLS, Matthew 5
MILLS, Ogden 1
MILLS, Ogden Livingston 1
MILLS, Robert * H
MILLS, Roger Quarles 1
MILLS, Samuel John H
MILLS, Samuel Myers 1
MILLS, Sebastian Bach 1
MILLS, Stephen Crosby 1
MILLS, Susan Lincoln 1
MILLS, Thomas Brooks 1
MILLS, Thornton Allen 1
MILLS, Thornton Anthony 1
MILLS, Weymer Jay 2
MILLS, William C. 1
MILLS, William Fitz 2
Randolph
MILLS, William Hayne 2
MILLS, William Howard 1
MILLS, William Joseph 1
MILLS, William McMaster 4
MILLS, William Merrill 4
MILLS, William O. 6
MILLS, William Webster 1
MILLSAPS, Reuben 1
Webster
MILLSON, John Singleton H
MILLSOP, Thomas E. 4
MILLSPAUGH, Arthur 3
Chester
MILLSPAUGH, Charles 1
Frederick
MILLSPAUGH, Frank 3
Crenshaw
MILLSPAUGH, Frank 1
Rosebrook
MILLSPAUGH, Jesse 1
Fonda
MILLSPAUGH, William 3
Hulse
MILLWARD, Russell 5
Hastings
MILLWARD, William H
MILMORE, Martin 1
MILNE, Alan Alexander 3
MILNE, Caleb Jones Jr. 1
MILNE, David 1
MILNE, Frances Margaret 5
(Tener)
MILNE, J. Scott 3
MILNE, James M. 1
MILNE, John 3
MILNE, William James 1
MILNER, Duncan 1
Chambers
MILNER, Henry Key 1
MILNER, John Turner H
MILNER, Moses Embree H
MILNER, Robert Teague 5
MILNER, Willis Justus Jr. 1
MILNES, William Jr. 1
MILNOR, George Sparks 3
MILNOR, James 1
MILNOR, William 1
MILOFSKY, Allan Henry 5
MILROY, Charles Martin 1
MILROY, Robert Arthur 6
MILROY, Robert Huston 1
MILROY, William Forsyth 2
MILROY, William 1
McCracken
MILTENBERGER, George 1
Warner
MILTNER, Charles 4
Christopher
MILTON, George Fort 1
MILTON, George Fort 3
MILTON, John 1
MILTON, John Brown 1
MILTON, William Hall 1

MILTON, William Hall 2
MILTON, William Hall 4
MILTON, William 4
Hammond
MILTOUN, Francis (Francis 5
Miltoun Mansfield)
MIMS, Edwin 3
MIMS, Livingston 1
MIMS, Stewart Lea 4
MINAHAN, Daniel Francis 5
MINAHAN, Victor Ivan 3
MINARD, Archibald 3
Ellsworth
MINARD, Duane Elmer 4
MINARY, Thomas Jay 1
MINCHIN, George H. 4
MINCHIN, Nina Mesirow 5
MINCKLER, Robert Lee 4
MINDSZENTY, H. E. 6
Cardinal Jozsef
MINEO, Sal 6
MINER, Ahiman Louis H
MINER, Alonzo Ames H
MINER, Asher 1
MINER, Carl Shelley 6
MINER, Charles H
MINER, Charles Wright 4
MINER, Edward Griffith 3
MINER, George Roberts 4
MINER, H. C. 3
MINER, Harlan Sherman 1
MINER, Jack 1
MINER, James A. 1
MINER, James Burt 2
MINER, Julius Howard 4
MINER, Luella 1
MINER, Myrtilla H
MINER, Phineas 1
MINER, Robert Bradford 5
MINER, Roy Waldo 3
MINER, William Harvey 1
MING, William Robert Jr. 6
MINGENBACK, Eugene 5
Carl
MINGOS, Howard L. 3
MINICH, Verne Elwood 3
MINICK, James William 3
MINIER, George 1
Washington
MINIFIE, William Charles 5
MINIGER, Clement Orville 2
MINIHAN, Jeremiah 6
Francis
MINITER, Edith (Dowe) 1
MINIUT, Peter H
MINKOWSKI, Rudolph Leo 6
B.
MINNAERT, Marcel Gilles 5
Jozef
MINNICH, Dwight Elmer 4
MINNICH, Harvey C. 3
MINNICK, John Harrison 5
MINNIGERODE, C. 3
Powell
MINNIGERODE, Lucy 4
MINNIGERODE, Meade 4
MINOR, Anne Rogers 2
MINOR, Benjamin Blake 1
MINOR, Benjamin Saunders 2
MINOR, Berkeley Jr. 4
MINOR, Charles Launcelot 1
MINOR, Clark Haynes 4
MINOR, Edward S. 1
MINOR, George Henry 4
MINOR, H. Dent 2
MINOR, John Barbee H
MINOR, Lucian H
MINOR, Milton Carlisle 6
MINOR, Raleigh Colston 1
MINOR, Robert 3
MINOR, Robert Crannell 1
MINOR, Thomas Chalmers 1
MINOR, Virginia Louisa H
MINOT, Charles Sedgwick 1
MINOT, George Evans 6
MINOT, George Richards 4
MINOT, George Richards 2
MINOT, John Clair 2
MINOT, Joseph Grafton 2
MINOT, William * 1
MINSCH, William J. 3
MINSHALL, Robert J. 3
MINSHALL, Thaddeus A. 4
MINTER, Mary Miles 4
MINTER, William Ramseur 4
MINTO, Walter H
MINTON, Henry Collin 1
MINTON, Maurice Meyer 4
MINTON, Melville 1
MINTON, Ollie Francis 6
MINTON, Sherman 4
MINTURN, James Francis 1
MINTURN, Robert Bowne H
MIRACLE, John Herbert 6
MIRANDA, Francisco de 1
MIRANDA, Heber Isaac 6

MIRICK, George Alonzo 4
MIRISCH, Harold Joseph 5
MIRKINE- 3
GUETZEVITCH, Boris
MIRO, Esteban Rodriguez H
MIRRIELEES, Edith 4
Ronald
MIRSKY, Alfred Ezra 6
MIRSKY, I. Arthur 6
MIRZA, Iskander 5
MIRZA, Youel Benjamin 2
MISBACH, Lorenz 3
MISER, Hugh Dinsmore 5
MISHIMA, Yukio (Kimitake 5
Hiraoka)
MISTRAL, Gabriela 3
MITCHAM, Orin 1
Burlingame
MITCHEL, Charles Burton H
MITCHEL, Edwin Kent 5
MITCHEL, Frederick 1
Augustus
MITCHEL, John Purroy 1
MITCHEL, Ormsby H
MacKnight
MITCHELL, Albert 3
MITCHELL, Albert Graeme 1
MITCHELL, Albert Roscoe 1
MITCHELL, Alexander 1
MITCHELL, Alfred 4
MITCHELL, Alfred Newton 5
MITCHELL, Allan Charles 4
Gray
MITCHELL, Anderson 1
MITCHELL, Arthur Evan 3
MITCHELL, Arthur W. 5
MITCHELL, Bruce 4
MITCHELL, C. Lionel 6
MITCHELL, Charles 1
Anderson
MITCHELL, Charles 1
Andrews
MITCHELL, Charles Bayard 2
MITCHELL, Charles Dennis 1
MITCHELL, Charles 1
Edward
MITCHELL, Charles Edwin 1
MITCHELL, Charles Elliott 1
MITCHELL, Charles F. H
MITCHELL, Charles 5
Franklin
MITCHELL, Charles Le 1
Moyne
MITCHELL, Charles Scott 5
MITCHELL, Charles 2
Tennant
MITCHELL, Clarence Blair 5
MITCHELL, Clifford 1
MITCHELL, Curtis 1
MITCHELL, David 1
MITCHELL, David Brydie H
MITCHELL, David Dawson H
MITCHELL, David Farrar 4
MITCHELL, David Ray 5
MITCHELL, Donald Grant 1
MITCHELL, Edmund 1
MITCHELL, Edward 1
Cushing
MITCHELL, Edward Page 1
MITCHELL, Edwin Knox 1
MITCHELL, Edwin Thomas 3
MITCHELL, Elisha 1
MITCHELL, Emory Forrest 5
MITCHELL, F. Edward 5
MITCHELL, G. P. 2
MITCHELL, George 4
Edward
MITCHELL, George 1
Franklin
MITCHELL, George 6
Frederick
MITCHELL, George T. 2
MITCHELL, George W. 4
MITCHELL, Guy Elliott 1
MITCHELL, Hal E. 2
MITCHELL, Harold E. 3
MITCHELL, Harry B. 3
MITCHELL, Harry Dawson 1
MISTRAL, Harry Luzerne 3
MITCHELL, Harry Walter 1
MITCHELL, Hazel Haynes 1
MITCHELL, Helen Codman 4
MITCHELL, Henry H
MITCHELL, Henry * 1
MITCHELL, Henry 3
Bedinger
MITCHELL, Henry Sewall 3
MITCHELL, Hinckley 1
Gilbert
MITCHELL, Homer 3
Rawlins
MITCHELL, Howard 2
MITCHELL, Howard 1
Walton

MITCHELL, Hugh Chester 3
MITCHELL, Hugh Gordon 5
MITCHELL, Humphrey 1
MITCHELL, Isaac H
MITCHELL, J. Murray 6
MITCHELL, James 1
MITCHELL, James Alfred 1
MITCHELL, James Coffield H
MITCHELL, James 4
Farnandis
MITCHELL, James George 4
MITCHELL, James Herbert 4
MITCHELL, James 2
McCormick
MITCHELL, James P. 4
MITCHELL, James S. 5
MITCHELL, James Tyndale 1
MITCHELL, John * H
MITCHELL, John 1
MITCHELL, John Ames 1
MITCHELL, John Blanton 5
MITCHELL, John Doyle 5
MITCHELL, John Fulton 3
Berrien
MITCHELL, John Gordon 6
MITCHELL, John H. 1
MITCHELL, John 6
Harrington
MITCHELL, John Inscho 1
MITCHELL, John J. 1
MITCHELL, John Joseph 1
MITCHELL, John Kearsley H
MITCHELL, John Kearsley 1
MITCHELL, John Lendrum 1
MITCHELL, John Marvin 5
MITCHELL, John 5
McKenney
MITCHELL, John Murray 1
MITCHELL, John Nicholas 4
MITCHELL, John R. 1
MITCHELL, John Raymond 1
MITCHELL, John William 1
MITCHELL, Jonathan H
MITCHELL, Julian 1
MITCHELL, Langdon 1
Elwyn
MITCHELL, Leander Perry 1
MITCHELL, Lebbeus 6
(Horatio)
MITCHELL, Leeds 1
MITCHELL, Lucy Myers H
Wright
MITCHELL, Lynn Boal 6
MITCHELL, Maggie 1
MITCHELL, Margaret 2
MITCHELL, Margaret 5
Johnes
MITCHELL, Maria H
MITCHELL, Martha 6
Elizabeth Beall Jennings
MITCHELL, Mason 1
MITCHELL, Nahum H
MITCHELL, Nathaniel H
MITCHELL, Nathaniel 4
McDonald
MITCHELL, O. W. H. 3
MITCHELL, Oscar 1
MITCHELL, Philip Henry 3
MITCHELL, R. Verne 1
MITCHELL, Ralph Clinton 1
Jr.
MITCHELL, Rexford 6
Samuel
MITCHELL, Richard Bland 4
MITCHELL, Richard 5
F(urlong)
MITCHELL, Robert H
MITCHELL, Robert 1
MITCHELL, Robert H
Byington
MITCHELL, Roland Burnell 6
MITCHELL, Roscoe Lee 5
MITCHELL, Ruth Comfort 3
MITCHELL, S. Weir 1
MITCHELL, Samuel Alfred 4
MITCHELL, Samuel Alfred 4
MITCHELL, Samuel 1
Augustus
MITCHELL, Samuel Chiles 3
MITCHELL, Samuel Phillips 4
MITCHELL, Samuel S. 1
MITCHELL, Samuel 1
Thomas
MITCHELL, Sidney 1
MITCHELL, Sidney 4
Alexander
MITCHELL, Sidney 2
Zollicoffer
MITCHELL, Steele 2
MITCHELL, Stephen 6
Arnold
MITCHELL, Stephen Mix H
MITCHELL, Stewart 3
MITCHELL, Sydney 1
Bancroft

MITCHELL, Sydney 3
Bancroft
MITCHELL, Sydney Knox 5
MITCHELL, Thomas 4
MITCHELL, Thomas A. 6
MITCHELL, Thomas Dache H
MITCHELL, Thomas 3
Edward
MITCHELL, Thomas 4
Edward
MITCHELL, Thomas H
Rothmaler
MITCHELL, Thompson 6
Hampton
MITCHELL, Viola 4
MITCHELL, Walter 1
MITCHELL, Walter Jenifer 3
MITCHELL, Walter Lee 5
MITCHELL, Walter Scott 5
MITCHELL, Wesley Clair 6
MITCHELL, Willard A. 2
MITCHELL, William * H
MITCHELL, William * 1
MITCHELL, William Carl 4
MITCHELL, William 3
DeWitt
MITCHELL, William 4
Edward
MITCHELL, William Henry 3
MITCHELL, William John 5
MITCHELL, William 4
Ledyard
MITCHELL, William 1
Samuel
MITCHELL, William 1
Whittier
MITCHELL, Wilmot 5
Brookings
MITCHILL, Samuel Latham H
MITCHILL, Theodore 4
Clarence
MITFORD, Nancy 6
MITKE, Charles A. 5
MITRE, Don Luis 3
MITROPOULOS, Dimitri 5
MITSCHER, Marc Andrew 4
MITTELMAN, Edward 4
MITTEN, Thomas Eugene 5
MITTON, George W. 2
MITTY, John Joseph 3
MIX, Arthur Jackson 3
MIX, Charles Louis 4
MIX, Edward Townsend H
MIX, Melville Walter 4
MIX, Tom 4
MIX, William Winter 4
MIXER, Albert Harrison 4
MIXTER, Charles Whitney 4
MIXTER, George 5
MIXTER, Samuel Jason 1
MIXTER, William Gilbert 1
MIZE, Robert Herbert 3
MIZE, Sidney Carr 4
MIZNER, Henry Rutgeras 1
MIZNER, Wilson 1
MOALE, Edward 4
MOBLEY, Ernest Cramer 6
MOBLEY, Lawrence 5
Eugene
MOBLEY, Mayor Dennis 6
MOBLEY, Radford E. 5
MOCK, Charles Adolphus 5
MOCK, Fred McKinley 4
MOCK, Harry Edgar 3
MOCKMORE, Charles 1
Arthur
MOCKRIDGE, John 5
Charles Hillier
MÓD, Aladár 6
MODARELLI, Alfred E. 3
MODDER, Montagu Frank 3
MODEL, Jean 5
MODELL, Clarion 5
MODERWELL, Charles 4
McClellan
MODJESKA, Helena 1
MODJESKI, Ralph 1
MODZELEWSKI, Zymunt 5
MOE, Alfred Kean 5
MOE, Henry Allen 6
MOEHLENPAH, Henry A. 2
MOEHLMAN, Arthur B. 3
MOEHLMAN, Conrad 6
Henry
MOEKLE, Herman 1
Liveright
MOELLER, Edith 6
MOELLER, Harold 5
Frederick
MOELLER, Henry 1
MOELLER, Louis 1
MOELLER, Philip 4
MOELLMANN, Albert 5
MOELLRING, George H. 1
MOELMANN, John 6
Matthew

MOEN, Reuben O. 4
MOENCH, Charles L. 1
MOENKHAUS, William J. 2
MOENKHAUS, William J. 5
MOERDYKE, Peter 1
MOERK, Frank Xavier 2
MOEUR, Benjamin Baker 1
MOFFAT, David Halliday 1
MOFFAT, David William 2
MOFFAT, Donald 3
MOFFAT, Douglas Maxwell H
MOFFAT, Frederick G. 1
MOFFAT, James Clement H
MOFFAT, James David 1
MOFFAT, James E. 3
MOFFAT, Jay Pierrepont 1
MOFFAT, John Little 1
MOFFATT, Fred Cushing 2
MOFFATT, James 2
MOFFATT, James Hugh 5
MOFFATT, James Strong 4
MOFFATT, Lucius Gaston 5
MOFFATT, Seth Crittenden H
MOFFET, John H
MOFFETT, Charles 3
Alexander
MOFFETT, Cleveland 1
MOFFETT, Donovan 4
Clifford
MOFFETT, Elwood Stewart 5
MOFFETT, George Monroe 3
MOFFETT, James Andrew 4
MOFFETT, James William 4
MOFFETT, Louis Burdelle 5
MOFFETT, Ross E. 6
MOFFETT, Samuel Austin 1
MOFFETT, Samuel 1
Erasmus
MOFFETT, Thomas Clinton 2
MOFFETT, William Adger 1
MOFFETT, William Walter 1
MOFFIT, Alexander 5
MOFFIT, S. P. 2
MOFFITT, Herbert Charles 5
MOFFITT, Hosea H
MOFFITT, James Kennedy 3
MOFFITT, Walter Volentine 5
MOFFLY, Charles K. 4
MOGENSEN, Walter 4
Alexander
MOHAMMED, V. 4
MOHLER, A. L. 1
MOHLER, Daniel Nathan 3
MOHLER, Henry Keller 3
MOHLER, Jacob Christian 3
MOHLER, John Frederick 1
MOHLER, John Robbins 5
MOHLER, Samuel Loomis 5
MOHN, Thorbjorn Nilson 1
MOHOLY-NAGY, Laszio 2
George
MOHR, Charles 1
MOHR, Charles Adam 5
MOHR, Charles Theodor 1
MOHR, Wesley George 6
MOHUN, Barry 1
MOINET, Edward Julien 3
MOIR, Henry 1
MOIR, John Troup 4
MOISE, Edwin Warren 4
MOISE, Harold A. 3
MOISE, Pennina 4
MOISEIWITSCH, Benno 4
MOISSEIFF, Leon Solomon 2
MOJICA, Jose 6
MOLDEHNKE, Edward 1
Frederick
MOLDENHAWER, Julius 2
Valdemar
MOLDENKE, Charles 1
Edward
MOLDENKE, Richard 1
MOLDVEEN- 5
GERONIMUS, Miriam
Esther
MOLE, Harvey E. 3
MOLEEN, George Arnold 5
MOLEY, Raymond 6
MOLINA, Edward Charles 4
Dixon
MOLINARE, Anthony 6
William
MOLINEUX, Edward Leslie 1
MOLINEUX, Marie Ada 5
MOLINEUX, Roland 4
Burnham
MOLITOR, David Albert 2
MOLITOR, Frederic Albert 1
MOLITOR, Hans 5
MOLLENHAUER, Emil 1
MOLLENHAUER, Henry 1
MOLLENKOPF, Jack 6
Kenneth Webster
MOLLER, Knud Ove 6
MOLLER, Mathias Peter 1
MOLLER, Mathias Peter Jr. 4

MOLLET, Guy 6
MOLLIN, Fernand E. 3
MOLLISON, Irvin Charles 4
MOLLISON, James 5
Alexander
MOLLOY, Sister Mary 3
Aloysius
MOLLOY, Thomas Marcus 2
MOLNAR, Ferenc 3
MOLNAR, Ferenc 4
MOLNAR, Julius Paul 2
MOLOHON, Albin 5
D(unlap)
MOLONEY, George Hale 4
MOLONEY, Herbert 4
William
MOLONEY, Thomas W. 4
MOLONEY, William Curry 5
MOLONY, Richard H
Sheppard
MOLONY, William Hayes 4
MOLTER, Harold 3
MOLYNEAUX, Joseph 1
West
MOLYNEUX, Robert H
MOMBERT, Jacob Isidor 1
MOMENT, John James 3
MOMMER, Peter Paul 4
MOMSEN, Charles B. 4
MOMSEN, Richard Paul 4
MONACHESI, Elio David 5
MONAELESSER, Adolph 1
MONAGHAN, Frank J. 2
MONAGHAN, J. F. 4
MONAGHAN, James 1
Charles
MONAGHAN, James 1
MONAGHAN, John James 1
MONAGHAN, Peter 2
Joseph
MONAHAN, Arthur 5
Coleman
MONAHAN, James Gideon 4
MONAHAN, Michael 1
MONAST, Louis 4
MONCHEUR, Baron 1
Ludovic
MONCKTON, Robert H
MONCKTON, Sir Walter H
Turner
MONCRIEF, John Wildman 1
MONCURE, Richard H
Cassius Lee
MONDELL, Frank Wheeler 1
MONDRIAN, Piet 4
MONELL, Ambrose 1
MONELL, Robert H
MONETTE, John Wesley H
MONEY, Hernando de Soto 1
MONFORT, Elias Riggs 1
MONFORT, Francis Cassatt 4
MONFORT, Joseph Glass 1
MONHELM, Leonard 5
Myers
MONIN, Louis Celestin 1
MONINO Y REDONDO, H
Jose
MONIS, Judah H
MONIZ, Egas 3
MONK, Wesley Elias 3
MONKS, George Howard 4
MONKS, John Austin Sands 1
MONKS, Leander John 1
MONKS, Lester Hawthorne 1
MONNET, Julian C. 4
MONNETT, Francis 3
Sylvester
MONNETT, Victor 5
MONNETTE, Mervin 1
Jeremiah
MONNETTE, Orra Eugene 1
MONOHAN, Edward 4
Sheehan III
MONOHAN, John M. 1
MONRO, Charles Bedell 5
MONRO, Hugh Reginald 3
MONRO, William Loftus 2
MONROE. Andrew Perrine 4
MONROE, Anne Shannon 2
MONROE, Arthur Eli 5
MONROE, Charles 4
MONROE, Charles Fraser 4
MONROE, Daniel L. 5
MONROE, Edwin Paul 4
MONROE, Frank Adair 1
MONROE, Harriet 1
MONROE, Harriet Earhart 1
MONROE, J. Blanc 4
MONROE, J. Raburn 4
MONROE, James * H
MONROE, Jay Randolph 5
MONROE, Lawrence 5
Alexander

MONROE, Marilyn 4
MONROE, Paul 2
MONROE, Pleasant Edgar 3
MONROE, Thomas 3
MONROE, Vaughn 6
MONROE, Will S. 1
MONROE, William Stanton 3
MONSARRAT, Nicholas 1
MONSEN, Frederick 1
Imman
MONSKY, Henry 2
MONSMAN, Gerald 5
MONSON, George S. 1
MONTAGUE, Abraham 4
MONTAGUE, Andrew 1
Jackson
MONTAGUE, Andrew 1
Philip
MONTAGUE, Dwight 1
Preston
MONTAGUE, Fairfax 5
Eubank
MONTAGUE, Gilbert 4
Holland
MONTAGUE, Helen 5
Weymouth
MONTAGUE, Henry James H
MONTAGUE, James 5
Edward Jr.
MONTAGUE, James 1
Jackson
MONTAGUE, James 2
Jackson
MONTAGUE, Joseph 6
Franklin
MONTAGUE, Richard 1
Ward
MONTAGUE, Robert 5
Latane
MONTAGUE, Robert H
Miller
MONTAGUE, Theodore 4
Giles
MONTAGUE, Wallace 3
Tenney
MONTAGUE, William 1
Lewis
MONTAGUE, William H
Pepperell
MONTANA, Bob 6
MONTAVON, William 5
Frederick
MONTEFIORE, Joshua H
MONTEITH, Walter 5
E(mbree)
MONTELEONE, Frank 3
Joseph
MONTENIER, Jules 4
Bernard
MONTE-SANO, Vincent 3
MONTES DE OCA, Luis 3
MONTEUX, Pierre 4
MONTEZ, Lola H
MONTEZUMA, Carlos 1
MONTEZUMA II H
MONTGOMERIE, John H
MONTGOMERY, A.E. 5
MONTGOMERY, Alfred E. 4
MONTGOMERY, Benjamin 5
F.
MONTGOMERY, Charles 2
Carroll
MONTGOMERY, Daniel 1
Jr.
MONTGOMERY, Douglass 4
William
MONTGOMERY, Edmund 1
Duncan
MONTGOMERY, Edna 5
Morley
MONTGOMERY, Edward 1
Emmet
MONTGOMERY, Edward 1
Gerrard
MONTGOMERY, Edward 1
Louis
MONTGOMERY, Emily P. 5
(Mrs. E. Geoffrey
Montgomery)
MONTGOMERY, Fletcher 2
H.
MONTGOMERY, Frank 1
Hugh
MONTGOMERY, George 1
MONTGOMERY, George 6
Granville
MONTGOMERY, George 3
Hugh Alexander
MONTGOMERY, George 3
Redington
MONTGOMERY, George H
Washington
MONTGOMERY, Guy 3

MONTGOMERY, Helen 1
Barrett
MONTGOMERY, Henry 3
Arthur
MONTGOMERY, J. Knox 1
MONTGOMERY, Jack 5
Percival
MONTGOMERY, James H
MONTGOMERY, James 5
Alan
MONTGOMERY, James 5
Eglinton
MONTGOMERY, James 5
Llewellyn
MONTGOMERY, James 3
Shera
MONTGOMERY, John H
MONTGOMERY, John H
Berrien
MONTGOMERY, John 3
Flournoy
MONTGOMERY, John 1
Gallagher
MONTGOMERY, John 1
Harold
MONTGOMERY, John 6
Rhea
MONTGOMERY, John 1
Rogerson
MONTGOMERY, Joseph H
Allen
MONTGOMERY, Mack 5
Allen
MONTGOMERY, Mary 1
Williams
MONTGOMERY, Morris 1
Carpenter
MONTGOMERY, Oscar 1
Hilton
MONTGOMERY, R. Ames 3
MONTGOMERY, Richard H
MONTGOMERY, Richard 3
D.
MONTGOMERY, Robert 3
MONTGOMERY, Robert 3
Hiester
MONTGOMERY, Robert 3
M.
MONTGOMERY, Robert 4
Nathaniel
MONTGOMERY, Roselle 1
Mercier
MONTGOMERY, S. A. 1
MONTGOMERY, Samuel 1
Thomas
MONTGOMERY, Thomas H
MONTGOMERY, Thomas 1
Harrison Jr.
MONTGOMERY, Thomas 1
Lynch
MONTGOMERY, Valda 3
Stewart
MONTGOMERY, Victor 1
MONTGOMERY, Whitney 1
Maxwell
MONTGOMERY, William H
*
MONTGOMERY, William 3
Coons
MONTGOMERY, William 1
Woodrow Jr.
MONTGOMERY OF 6
ALAMEIN, (Field
Marshall Bernard Law
Montgomery)
MONTHERLANT, Henry 5
de
MONTONNA, Ralph E. 3
MONTOYA, Atanasio 1
MONTOYA, Nestor 1
MONTRESOR, James H
Gabriel
MONTRESOR, John H
MONTROSS, Lynn 4
MONTZHEIMER, Arthur 5
MOOAR, George 1
MOOD, Francis Asbury H
MOOD, Orlando Clarendon 3
MOODIE, Campbell 5
MOODIE, Roy Lee 1
MOODY, Blair 3
MOODY, Dan 4
MOODY, Dwight Lyman H
MOODY, Ernest Addison 6
MOODY, Frank Sims 1
MOODY, Gideon Curtis 1
MOODY, H. W. 3
MOODY, Herbert Raymond 2
MOODY, James H
MOODY, Joseph Burnley 1
MOODY, Lewis Ferry 5
MOODY, Malcolm Adelbert 4
MOODY, Nelson Kingsland 5
MOODY, Paul H

MOODY, Paul Dwight 2
MOODY, Sidney Clarke 6
MOODY, Virginia Green 3
MOODY, Walter Dwight 1
MOODY, Walter Sherman 1
MOODY, William Henry 1
MOODY, William Lewis Jr. 1
MOODY, William Revell 1
MOODY, William Vaughn 1
MOODY, Winfield Scott 4
MOODY, Zenas Ferry 1
MOOG, Wilson Townsend 3
MOON, Carl 2
MOON, Don P. 2
MOON, Edwin G. 1
MOON, Franklin 1
MOON, Grace 2
MOON, Henry Dukso 6
MOON, John Austin 1
MOON, Parker Thomas 1
MOON, Reuben Osborne 1
MOON, Truman Jesse 3
MOON, Virgil Holland 6
MOONEY, Charles A. 1
MOONEY, Charles Patrick Joseph 1
MOONEY, Daniel Francis 1
MOONEY, Edmund L. 1
MOONEY, Edward Cardinal 3
MOONEY, Eugene Francis 5
MOONEY, Franklin D. 4
MOONEY, Guy 1
MOONEY, James 1
MOONEY, James David 3
MOONEY, James Elliott 5
MOONEY, James Garth 5
MOONEY, Joseph F. 1
MOONEY, Joseph W. 4
MOONEY, Robert Johnstone 1
MOONEY, Robert Lee 4
MOONEY, Urban Drening 1
MOONEY, William H
MOONEY, William C. 4
MOONEY, William M. 3
MOONLIGHT, Thomas 1
MOOR, Elizabeth I. 4
MOOR, Wyman Bradbury Seavy 1
MOORA, Robert L(orenzo) 5
MOORE, Addison Webster 1
MOORE, Albert Burton 4
MOORE, Albert Voorhis 3
MOORE, Albert Weston 4
MOORE, Alexander Pollock 1
MOORE, Alfred H
MOORE, Alfred Stibbs 1
MOORE, Alice Medora Rogers 1
MOORE, Allen II 2
MOORE, Allen Francis 5
MOORE, Andrew H
MOORE, Andrew Charles 4
MOORE, Anne Carroll 4
MOORE, Ansley Cunningham 5
MOORE, Arthur Harry 3
MOORE, Arthur James 6
MOORE, Aubertine Woodward 1
MOORE, Aubrey Shannon 3
MOORE, Austin Talley 1
MOORE, Bartholomew Figures H
MOORE, Ben Wheeler 3
MOORE, Benjamin H
MOORE, Bertha Pearl 1
MOORE, Blaine Free 1
MOORE, Bob 1
MOORE, Bryant Edward 1
MOORE, Burton Evans 1
MOORE, C. Ellis 1
MOORE, C. Ulysses 1
MOORE, Carl Allphin 6
MOORE, Carl Richard 1
MOORE, Carl Vernon 5
MOORE, Charles 2
MOORE, Charles Albert 1
MOORE, Charles Alexander 4
MOORE, Charles Arthur 1
MOORE, Charles Arthur 3
MOORE, Charles Brainard Taylor 1
MOORE, Charles Cadwell 1
MOORE, Charles Calvin 1
MOORE, Charles Forrest 4
MOORE, Charles Herbert 1
MOORE, Charles James 2
MOORE, Charles Leonard 1
MOORE, Charles Lothrop 5
MOORE, Clarence Bloomfield 1
MOORE, Clarence King 1
MOORE, Clarence Lemuel Elisha 1

MOORE, Clement Clarke H
MOORE, Clifford Herschel 1
MOORE, Clyde B. 6
MOORE, D. Mcfarlan 1
MOORE, Daniel Decatur 1
MOORE, David Hastings 1
MOORE, David Richard 3
MOORE, DeWitt Van Deusen 5
MOORE, Douglas Stuart 5
MOORE, Dunlop 1
MOORE, E. E. 4
MOORE, Edmond H. 1
MOORE, Edmund Joseph 4
MOORE, Edward Jr. 3
MOORE, Edward Bruce 1
MOORE, Edward Caldwell 2
MOORE, Edward Colman 1
MOORE, Edward H. 4
MOORE, Edward James 2
MOORE, Edward Jay 1
MOORE, Edward Mott 1
MOORE, Edward Roberts 3
MOORE, Edward Small 2
MOORE, Edward W. 1
MOORE, Edwin King 1
MOORE, Edwin Ward H
MOORE, Elbert Edmund 4
MOORE, Eliakim Hastings 1
MOORE, Ella Maude 1
MOORE, Elon Howard 3
MOORE, Ely 1
MOORE, Ernest Carroll 3
MOORE, Ernest Carroll Jr. 5
MOORE, Escum Lionel 6
MOORE, Ethelbert Allen 3
MOORE, Eva Perry 1
MOORE, Filmore 4
MOORE, Forris Jewett 1
MOORE, Francis 1
MOORE, Francis Cruger 4
MOORE, Frank A. 1
MOORE, Frank Gardner 4
MOORE, Frank Horace 5
MOORE, Frank Lincoln 1
MOORE, Frank R. 4
MOORE, Franklin Benjamin 1
MOORE, Fred Atkins 3
MOORE, Frederick 5
MOORE, Frederick Ferdinand 5
MOORE, Frederick Wightman 1
MOORE, G. Bedell 1
MOORE, Gabriel H
MOORE, George Andrew 2
MOORE, George Curtis 5
MOORE, George Edward 4
MOORE, George F. 2
MOORE, George Fleming H
MOORE, George Foot 1
MOORE, George Gail 5
MOORE, George Godfrey 1
MOORE, George Gordon 1
MOORE, George Henry H
MOORE, George Herbert 1
MOORE, George Thomas 1
MOORE, George Thomas 5
MOORE, Grace 2
MOORE, H. Humphrey 1
MOORE, Harold Emerson 6
MOORE, Harrie G. 1
MOORE, Harrison Bray 5
MOORE, Harry H. 3
MOORE, Harry Hascall 1
MOORE, Harry Tunis 5
MOORE, Harry William 5
MOORE, Helen 4
MOORE, Heman Allen H
MOORE, Henrietta Greer 1
MOORE, Sir Henry H
MOORE, Henry Dunning 1
MOORE, Henry Frank 2
MOORE, Henry Hoyt 4
MOORE, Henry Lynn 1
MOORE, Henry Trumbull 6
MOORE, Herbert McComb 1
MOORE, Hight C. 3
MOORE, Houston Burger 1
MOORE, Hoyt Augustus 3
MOORE, Hugh 4
MOORE, Hugh Benton 5
MOORE, Hugh Kelsea 5
MOORE, Irwin L. 5
MOORE, Isaac Sadler 5
MOORE, J. Howard 1
MOORE, J. Percey 4
MOORE, J. W. E. 5
MOORE, Jacob Bailey H
MOORE, James * 1
MOORE, James Edward 1
MOORE, James Gregory 5
MOORE, James Hobart 1
MOORE, James Miles 1
MOORE, James W. 1
MOORE, Jared Sparks 3

MOORE, Jere 2
MOORE, Jesse Hale H
MOORE, John * H
MOORE, John * 1
MOORE, John Bassett 2
MOORE, John Cecil 5
MOORE, John Chandler 2
MOORE, John Cunningham 4
MOORE, John D. 1
MOORE, John Ferguson 5
MOORE, John G. 4
MOORE, John Leverett 1
MOORE, John M. 1
MOORE, John Merrick 3
MOORE, John Milton 3
MOORE, John Monroe 5
MOORE, John Peabody 6
MOORE, John Small 5
MOORE, John Trotwood 1
MOORE, Mrs. John Trotwood 3
MOORE, John W. 1
MOORE, John Walker 3
MOORE, John Weeks H
MOORE, John White 1
MOORE, John William 2
MOORE, Joseph 1
MOORE, Joseph Arthur 1
MOORE, Joseph B. 1
MOORE, Joseph Earle 3
MOORE, Joseph Haines 2
MOORE, J(oseph) Hampton 5
MOORE, Joseph Waldron; 6
MOORE, Josiah John 4
MOORE, Josiah Staunton 3
MOORE, Julian H. 1
MOORE, Kenneth W. 5
MOORE, Laban Theodore H
MOORE, Lewis Baxter 4
MOORE, Lillian 4
MOORE, Lillian Russell 1
MOORE, Louis Herbert 1
MOORE, Lyle Stickley 3
MOORE, Lyman Sweet 3
MOORE, Marianne Craig 5
MOORE, Mark Egbert 5
MOORE, Mary 3
MOORE, Mary Norman 5
MOORE, Maurice H
MOORE, Maurice Malcolm 4
MOORE, Merrill 3
MOORE, Miles Conway 1
MOORE, Milton Harvey 5
MOORE, Mrs. N. Hudson 1
MOORE, Nathan Grier 2
MOORE, Nathaniel Drummond 1
MOORE, Nathaniel Fish H
MOORE, Orren Cheney 1
MOORE, Orval Floyd 3
MOORE, Oscar Fitzallen 1
MOORE, Paul 3
MOORE, Paul H. 4
MOORE, Paul J. 4
MOORE, Philip North 1
MOORE, Philip Wyatt 6
MOORE, Randle T. 5
MOORE, Ransom Asa 1
MOORE, Raymond Cecil 6
MOORE, Richard Bishop 1
MOORE, Richard Channing H
MOORE, Richard Curtis 4
MOORE, Robert H
MOORE, Robert 1
MOORE, Robert Allan 5
MOORE, Robert Foster 4
MOORE, Robert H(arris) 5
MOORE, Robert Lee 1
MOORE, Robert Lee 4
MOORE, Robert Lee 6
MOORE, Robert Martin 3
MOORE, Robert McDonald 4
MOORE, Robert Murray 4
MOORE, Robert S. 1
MOORE, Robert Thomas 3
MOORE, Robert Walton 1
MOORE, Robert Webber 4
MOORE, Roberts Cosby 5
MOORE, Roy 3
MOORE, Roy W. 5
MOORE, Rupert Eastmer 5
MOORE, Samuel H
MOORE, Samuel 1
MOORE, Samuel McDowell H
MOORE, Samuel Preston H
MOORE, Samuel Wallace H
MOORE, Sherwood 4
MOORE, Stephen 1
MOORE, Sydenham 1
MOORE, Thomas H
MOORE, Thomas Joseph 4
MOORE, Thomas Justin 3
MOORE, Thomas Love 1
MOORE, Thomas Morrell 1
MOORE, Thomas Overton H
MOORE, Thomas Verner 2

MOORE, Thomas Verner 5
MOORE, Thomas Waterman 5
MOORE, Veranus Alva 1
MOORE, Victor 4
MOORE, Victor F. 5
MOORE, Vida Frank 1
MOORE, Walter Bedford 1
MOORE, Walter William 1
MOORE, Walton Norwood 4
MOORE, Warren G. Sr. 4
MOORE, William * H
MOORE, William Charles 4
MOORE, William Emmet 1
MOORE, William Emmet 2
MOORE, William Eves 1
MOORE, William F. 1
MOORE, William Garrett 2
MOORE, William George 1
MOORE, William Henry 1
MOORE, William Sturtevant 1
MOORE, William Sutton 4
MOORE, William Thomas 4
MOORE, William Underhill 2
MOORE, Willis Luther 1
MOORE, Wilmer Lee 4
MOORE, Zephaniah Swift H
MOOREHEAD, Agnes Robertson 6
MOOREHEAD, Frederick Brown 2
MOOREHEAD, Singleton Peabody 6
MOOREHEAD, Warren King 1
MOOREHEAD, William Gallogly 1
MOORES, Charles Bruce Washington 1
MOORES, Charles 1
MOORES, J. Henry 1
MOORES, Merrill 1
MOORHEAD, Dudley Thomas 5
MOORHEAD, Frank Graham 3
MOORHEAD, Harley G. 2
MOORHEAD, James Kennedy H
MOORHEAD, Louis David 1
MOORHEAD, Louis David 3
MOORHEAD, Maxwell K. 1
MOORHEAD, Robert Lowry 5
MOORHEAD, William Singer 3
MOORHOUSE, Harold Roy 4
MOORMAN, Charles 1
MOORMAN, Henry DeHaven 6
MOORMAN, Robert Burrus Buckner 6
MOORMAN, Robert Wardlaw 6
MOOS, Charles J. 1
MOOSBRUGGER, Frederick 6
MOOSER, William H
MOOSMULLER, Oswald William H
MOOT, Adelbert 1
MOQUE, Alice Lee 1
MORA, F. Luis 1
MORA, Jose Antonio 6
MORA, Joseph Jacinto 2
MORAIS, Sabato H
MORALES, Sanchez 1
MORA MIRANDA, Marcial 5
MORAN, Alfred E. 6
MORAN, Annette 1
MORAN, Benjamin H
MORAN, Daniel Edward 1
MORAN, Daniel James 2
MORAN, Edward H
MORAN, Edward Carleton Jr. 1
MORAN, Eugene Francis 5
MORAN, Francis Thomas 1
MORAN, Fred T. 5
MORAN, James Thomas 1
MORAN, John Henry 3
MORAN, John Joseph 5
MORAN, Julia Porcelli 6
MORAN, Leon 1
MORAN, Percy 1
MORAN, Peter 1
MORAN, Richard Bartholomew 1
MORAN, Robert H
MORAN, Thomas 1
MORAN, Thomas 1
MORAN, Thomas 4
MORAN, Thomas A. 1

MORAN, Thomas Francis 1
MORAN, W(alter) H(arrison) 6
MORAN, William Edward Jr. 5
MORAN, William Joseph 4
MORANDI, Giorgio 4
MORAWETZ, Albert Richard 4
MORAWETZ, Victor 1
MORCOM, Clifford Bawden 3
MORDE, Theodore A. 3
MORDECAI, Alfred H
MORDECAI, Alfred 1
MORDECAI, Moses Cohen H
MORDECAI, Samuel Fox 1
MORDECAI, T. Moultrie 1
MORDEN, William J. 3
MORDVINOFF, Nicolas 6
MORE, Brookes 2
MORE, Charles Church 3
MORE, E. Anson 1
MORE, Herman 5
MORE, John Herron 5
MORE, Louis Trenchard 2
MORE, Nicholas H
MORE, Paul Elmer 1
MOREAU, Arthur Edmond 3
MOREAU DE SAINT MERY, Mederic-Louis-Elie H
MOREAU-LISLET, Louis Casimir Elisabeth H
MOREAUX, Amable Oli 2
MOREHEAD, Albert Hodges 4
MOREHEAD, Charles Allen 3
MOREHEAD, Charles Slaughter H
MOREHEAD, French Hugh 3
MOREHEAD, James Turner * 1
MOREHEAD, John Alfred 1
MOREHEAD, John Henry 2
MOREHEAD, John Lindsay 4
MOREHEAD, John Motley 1
MOREHEAD, John Motley 4
MOREHOUSE, Albert Kellogg 3
MOREHOUSE, Daniel Walter 1
MOREHOUSE, Frances Milton 2
MOREHOUSE, Frederic Cook 1
MOREHOUSE, George Pierson 4
MOREHOUSE, George Read 1
MOREHOUSE, Henry Lyman 1
MOREHOUSE, Juluis Stanley 4
MOREHOUSE, Linden Husted 1
MOREHOUSE, Linden Husted 4
MOREHOUSE, Lyman Foote 5
MOREHOUSE, P. Gad Bryan 5
MOREHOUSE, Ward 4
MOREHOUSE, William Russell 1
MOREL, Jean 6
MORELAND, Edward Leyburn 1
MORELAND, John Richard 2
MORELAND, William Hall 2
MORELAND, William Haywood 2
MORELL, George Webb H
MORELL, Parker 1
MORELL, Rosa Blanca Ortiz (Mrs. Ramon B. 6
MORELL, William Nelson 5
MORELOCK, George Leslie 6
MORELOCK, Horace Wilson 1
MORENCY, Paul Wilfrid 6
MORENO, Arthur Alphonse 3
MORENO, Jacob L. 6
MORENO-LACALLE, Julian 6
MORESCHI, Joseph V. 5
MORESI, Harry James Jr. 6
MOREY, Arthur Thornton 1
MOREY, Charles Rufus 1
MOREY, Charles William 4
MOREY, Chester S. 1
MOREY, Frank H
MOREY, Henry Martyn 3
MOREY, John William 3

MOREY, Lee B. 6
MOREY, Lloyd 4
MOREY, Samuel 4
MOREY, Sylvester Marvin 6
MOREY, Victor Pinkerton 3
MOREY, William Carey 1
MORFA, Raymond J. 3
MORFIT, Campbell H
MORFORD, Henry H
MORFORD, James Richard 4
MORGAN, Abel H
MORGAN, Alfred Powell 6
MORGAN, Angela 3
MORGAN, Ann Haven 4
MORGAN, Anna 1
MORGAN, Anne 1
MORGAN, Anne Eugenia Felicia 1
MORGAN, Appleton 1
MORGAN, Arthur Ernest 6
MORGAN, Bayard Quincy 4
MORGAN, Brooks Sanderson 5
MORGAN, Carey E. 1
MORGAN, Caroline Starr 5
MORGAN, Casey Bruce 1
MORGAN, Charles H
MORGAN, Charles 3
MORGAN, Charles Carroll 1
MORGAN, Charles Eldridge 2
MORGAN, Charles Henry 1
MORGAN, Charles Herbert 1
MORGAN, Charles Hill 1
MORGAN, Christopher H
MORGAN, Clifford Thomas 6
MORGAN, Clifford Veryl 3
MORGAN, Clinton Emory 3
MORGAN, Daniel H
MORGAN, Daniel Edgar 2
MORGAN, Daniel Nash 1
MORGAN, David E. 1
MORGAN, David Percy 6
MORGAN, DeWitt Schuyler 1
MORGAN, Dick Thompson 1
MORGAN, Edmund Morris Jr. 4
MORGAN, Edward Broadbent 1
MORGAN, Edward M. 1
MORGAN, Edwin Barber H
MORGAN, Edwin Denison H
MORGAN, Edwin Franklin Abell 4
MORGAN, Edwin Lee 4
MORGAN, Edwin Vernon 1
MORGAN, Elford C(hapman) 5
MORGAN, Eliot S. N. H
MORGAN, Ephraim Franklin 2
MORGAN, Ezra Leonidas 1
MORGAN, F. Coelies 1
MORGAN, Forrest 1
MORGAN, Francis Patterson 4
MORGAN, Frank 3
MORGAN, Frank Millett 4
MORGAN, Fred Bogardus 3
MORGAN, Fred Bruce Jr. 6
MORGAN, Frederic Lindley 5
MORGAN, G. Campbell 4
MORGAN, Geoffrey Francis 3
MORGAN, George 1
MORGAN, George 6
MORGAN, George Allen 5
MORGAN, George Hagar 4
MORGAN, George Horace 4
MORGAN, George O. 3
MORGAN, George Wagner 3
MORGAN, George Washbourne H
MORGAN, George Washington H
MORGAN, George Wilson 1
MORGAN, George Wilson 5
MORGAN, Harcourt Alexander 3
MORGAN, Harry Dale 3
MORGAN, Harry Hays 4
MORGAN, Henry A. 4
MORGAN, Henry William 1
MORGAN, Henry Williams Sr. 6
MORGAN, Herbert Rollo 4
MORGAN, Hugh Jackson 4
MORGAN, Ike 5
MORGAN, Isaac B. 5
MORGAN, Jacob L. 5
MORGAN, James H
MORGAN, James 3
MORGAN, James Bright 1
MORGAN, James Dada H

MORGAN, James Dudley 1
MORGAN, James Henry 1
MORGAN, James Norris 1
MORGAN, James W. 3
MORGAN, Jerome J. 4
MORGAN, Jesse Robert 6
MORGAN, John H
MORGAN, John Heath 5
MORGAN, John Hill 2
MORGAN, John Hunt H
MORGAN, John Jacob Brooke 2
MORGAN, John Jordan H
MORGAN, John Livingston Rutgers 1
MORGAN, John Paul 1
MORGAN, John Pierpont 1
MORGAN, John Pierpont 2
MORGAN, John Thoburn 5
MORGAN, John Tyler 1
MORGAN, Junius Spencer 3
MORGAN, Junius Spencer 4
MORGAN, Justin H
MORGAN, Justin Colfax 3
MORGAN, Lewis Henry 1
MORGAN, Lewis Lovering 5
MORGAN, Louis M. H
MORGAN, Sister M. Sylvia 4
MORGAN, Marshall Shapleigh 6
MORGAN, Matthew Somerville H
MORGAN, Maud 1
MORGAN, Michael Ryan 4
MORGAN, Minot Canfield 5
MORGAN, Monta B. Sr. 3
MORGAN, Morris Hicky 1
MORGAN, Octavius 1
MORGAN, Ora Sherman 4
MORGAN, Paul Beagary 3
MORGAN, Percy Tredegar 4
MORGAN, Peto Whittaker 4
MORGAN, Philip Hicky H
MORGAN, Philip M. 4
MORGAN, Ralph 4
MORGAN, Raymond A. 4
MORGAN, Robert Kenneth 4
MORGAN, Robert M. 3
MORGAN, Russell Van Dyke 3
MORGAN, Samuel Tate 4
MORGAN, Stephen 4
MORGAN, Stokeley Williams 4
MORGAN, Tali Esen 5
MORGAN, Theophilous John 5
MORGAN, Thomas H
MORGAN, Thomas Alfred 4
MORGAN, Thomas Francis Jr. 5
MORGAN, Thomas Hunt 2
MORGAN, Thomas J. 1
MORGAN, Thomas John 4
MORGAN, Thomas W. 1
MORGAN, Tom P. 4
MORGAN, Wallace 2
MORGAN, Walter Piety 3
MORGAN, Walter Sydney 3
MORGAN, William H
MORGAN, William 4
MORGAN, William Berry 4
MORGAN, William Conger 5
MORGAN, William Edgar 2d 4
MORGAN, William Fellowes 2
MORGAN, William Forbes 1
MORGAN, William Gerry 2
MORGAN, William Henry * 1
MORGAN, William M. 1
MORGAN, William McKendree H
MORGAN, William Sacheus 5
MORGAN, William Stephen H
MORGAN, William Thomas 2
MORGAN, William Yost 1
MORGENSTERN, Julian 6
MORGENSTIERNE, Wilhelm Thorleif Munthe 4
MORGENTHAU, Henry 4
MORGENTHAU, Henry Jr. 4
MORGULIS, Sergius 5
MORIARITY, Patrick Eugene H
MORIARTY, Charles Patrick 4
MORIARTY, Eugene 5
MORIARTY, William Daniel 1
MORIN, John M. 2
MORIN, Relman 4
MORINI, Erika 4
MORISON, George Abbot 4

MORISON, George Shattuck 1
MORISON, James Henderson Stuart 3
MORISON, Samuel Eliot 6
MORISSE, Richard Diehm 5
MORITZ, Adrianus Johannes Leonard 4
MORITZ, John A. 3
MORITZ, Richard Daniel 5
MORITZ, Robert Edouard 1
MORITZEN, Julius 3
MORK, P. Ralph 3
MORLAN, Webster Smith 1
MORLEY, Christopher 3
MORLEY, Clarence Joseph 5
MORLEY, Edward Williams 1
MORLEY, Frank 1
MORLEY, George Bidwell 1
MORLEY, John Henry 1
MORLEY, Margaret Warner 1
MORLEY, Sylvanus Griswold 2
MORLING, Edgar Alfred 1
MORMAN, James Bale 1
MORNINGSTAR, Thomas Wood 4
MORON, Alonzo Graseano 5
MORONEY, Carl J. 3
MORONEY, James McQueen 5
MOROSCO, Oliver 1
MOROSO, John Antonio 3
MORPHY, Paul Charles H
MORREL, William Griffin 6
MORRELL, Benjamin H
MORRELL, Daniel Johnson H
MORRELL, Edward De Veaux 4
MORRELL, Fred 6
MORRELL, Imogene Robinson 1
MORREY, Charles Bradfield 1
MORRILL, David Lawrence H
MORRILL, Albert Henry 4
MORRILL, Albro David 2
MORRILL, Anson Peaslee H
MORRILL, Charles Henry 1
MORRILL, Edmund N. 1
MORRILL, Henry Albert 4
MORRILL, John Adams 3
MORRILL, Justin H
MORRILL, Lot Myrick H
MORRILL, Mendon 4
MORRILL, Samuel Plummer H
MORRILL, Warren Pearl 2
MORRILL, William Kelso 5
MORRIS, Alice A. Parmelee 5
MORRIS, Alpheus Kaspar 4
MORRIS, Anthony * H
MORRIS, Arthur J. 6
MORRIS, Benjamin Wistar 1
MORRIS, Benjamin Wistar III 2
MORRIS, Bert Miller 6
MORRIS, Cadwalader H
MORRIS, Calvary H
MORRIS, Caspar H
MORRIS, Charles * 1
MORRIS, Charles * H
MORRIS, Charles Gould 4
MORRIS, Charles Harwood 5
MORRIS, Charles Shoemaker 3
MORRIS, Charles Wendel 5
MORRIS, Chester 5
MORRIS, Clara 1
MORRIS, Claude Frank 5
MORRIS, Clyde Tucker 5
MORRIS, Constance Lily 5
MORRIS, Daniel H
MORRIS, Dave Hennen 2
MORRIS, Dave Hennen Jr. 6
MORRIS, Don 5
MORRIS, Don Heath 6
MORRIS, Donald Florence 5
MORRIS, Douglas 1
MORRIS, Earl Halstead 3
MORRIS, Edgar Leslie 4
MORRIS, Edmund H
MORRIS, Edward 1
MORRIS, Edward Dafydd 1
MORRIS, Edward Joy H
MORRIS, Edward Parmelee 1
MORRIS, Edwin Bateman 5
MORRIS, Effingham Buckley 1
MORRIS, Elias Camp 1
MORRIS, Elisabeth Woodbridge (Mrs. Charles Gould Morris) 5
MORRIS, Elizabeth 1
MORRIS, Emory William 6
MORRIS, Ernest Melvin 3

MORRIS, Evangeline Hall 3
MORRIS, Felix James 1
MORRIS, Florance Ann 4
MORRIS, Frank Edward 4
MORRIS, Frank Hubbard 1
MORRIS, Frank R. 3
MORRIS, Frederick Kuhne 4
MORRIS, Frederick Wistar 5
MORRIS, George 2
MORRIS, George Davis 4
MORRIS, George Edward 1
MORRIS, George Ford 4
MORRIS, George Kenneth 1
MORRIS, George L. K. 6
MORRIS, George Maurice 5
MORRIS, George Perry 1
MORRIS, George Pope H
MORRIS, George Sylvester H
MORRIS, George Van Derveer 3
MORRIS, Gouverneur H
MORRIS, Gouverneur 3
MORRIS, Harold Cecil 4
MORRIS, Harrison Smith 2
MORRIS, Henry Crittenden 2
MORRIS, Homer Lawrence 4
MORRIS, Howard 1
MORRIS, Hugh Martin 4
MORRIS, Ira Nelson 1
MORRIS, Isaac Newton H
MORRIS, J. Cheston 1
MORRIS, Jack Sidney 6
MORRIS, James Charlton 4
MORRIS, James Cralk 2
MORRIS, James Ward 4
MORRIS, John 3
MORRIS, John Baptist 2
MORRIS, John Gottlieb H
MORRIS, Jonathan David 1
MORRIS, Joseph H
MORRIS, Joseph Chandler 5
MORRIS, Joseph E. 1
MORRIS, L. W. 3
MORRIS, Leland Burnette H
MORRIS, Lewis * H
MORRIS, Lewis Coleman H
MORRIS, Lewis Richard H
MORRIS, Lewis Spencer 2
MORRIS, Lloyd 3
MORRIS, Luzon Burritt H
MORRIS, Martin Ferdinand 1
MORRIS, Mathias H
MORRIS, Nelson 1
MORRIS, Newbold 1
MORRIS, Newbold H
MORRIS, Oscar Matison 2
MORRIS, Page 1
MORRIS, Pat G. 4
MORRIS, Percy Amos 5
MORRIS, Richard 1
MORRIS, Richard Lewis 4
MORRIS, Richard Valentine H
MORRIS, Robert * H
MORRIS, Robert Clark 1
MORRIS, Robert Eugene 5
MORRIS, Robert Hugh 1
MORRIS, Robert Hunter 4
MORRIS, Robert Nelson 5
MORRIS, Robert Seymour 5
MORRIS, Robert Tuttle 1
MORRIS, Roger H
MORRIS, Roger Sylvester 4
MORRIS, Roland Sletor H
MORRIS, Samuel Brooks 4
MORRIS, Samuel Henry 4
MORRIS, Samuel Leslie 1
MORRIS, Samuel Wells 1
MORRIS, Thomas * H
MORRIS, Thomas Armstrong H
MORRIS, Thomas John 1
MORRIS, Victor Pierpont 6
MORRIS, William 1
MORRIS, William Alfred 2
MORRIS, William Charles 1
MORRIS, William Henry Harrison 5
MORRIS, William Hicks 1
MORRIS, William Hopkins H
MORRIS, William Robert 4
MORRIS, William Shivers 1
MORRIS, William Sylvanus 4
MORRIS, William Thomas 2
MORRIS, William Torrey 4
MORRIS, William V. 1
MORRISON, A. Cressy 3
MORRISON, Albert Alexander 1
MORRISON, Alexander Francis 1
MORRISON, Cameron 4
MORRISON, Charles B. 4
MORRISON, Charles Clayton 4

MORRISON, Charles Munro 2
MORRISON, Charles Samuel 5
MORRISON, Charles Walthall 1
MORRISON, Clinton 1
MORRISON, deLesseps S. 4
MORRISON, Donald Harvard 3
MORRISON, Edward Lester 4
MORRISON, Edwin Rees 4
MORRISON, Frank 4
MORRISON, Frank Barron 3
MORRISON, Frederick Douglas 1
MORRISON, George Austin 1
MORRISON, George Washington H
MORRISON, Harry Steele 6
MORRISON, Harry Winford 5
MORRISON, Harvey Arch 6
MORRISON, Henry Clay 1
MORRISON, Henry Clay 2
MORRISON, Henry Clinton 3
MORRISON, Ivan 3
MORRISON, Jack Harold 5
MORRISON, James 6
MORRISON, James B(rown)
MORRISON, James Dalton 3
MORRISON, James Dow 1
MORRISON, James Frank 4
MORRISON, James Lowery Donaldson H
MORRISON, Jasper Newton 1
MORRISON, Jim 5
MORRISON, John Arch 4
MORRISON, John F. 4
MORRISON, John Irwin H
MORRISON, John Tracy 4
MORRISON, Joseph 4
MORRISON, Joseph L(ederman) 5
MORRISON, Joseph Peter 4
MORRISON, Levi 1
MORRISON, Lewis 1
MORRISON, Mary J. Whitney 1
MORRISON, Mrs. May Treat 4
MORRISON, Nathan Jackson 1
MORRISON, Ocie Butler Jr. 4
MORRISON, Phoebe 5
MORRISON, Ralph Waldo 2
MORRISON, Robert Hugh 5
MORRISON, Robert John 2
MORRISON, Robert Stewart 4
MORRISON, Roger Leroy 4
MORRISON, Sarah Elizabeth 5
MORRISON, Stanley 1
MORRISON, Theodore Nevin 1
MORRISON, Thomas Augustus 2
MORRISON, Wayland 3
MORRISON, Willard Langdon 4
MORRISON, William H
MORRISON, William Barrett 4
MORRISON, William Brown 1
MORRISON, William Ralls 4
MORRISON, William Shepherd 4
MORRISON, Zaidee 1
MORRISON, Zelma Reeves 4
MORRISS, Elizabeth Cleveland (Mrs. John) 1
MORRISSEY, Andrew 1
MORRISSEY, Andrew Marcus 1
MORRISSEY, Bernard Delbert 6
MORRISSEY, James Peter 5
MORRISSEY, John H
MORRISSEY, Michael A. 4
MORRISSEY, Patrick Henry 4
MORRON, John Reynolds 3
MORROW, Albert Sydney 4
MORROW, Cornelius Wortendyke
MORROW, Dwight Whitney 1
MORROW, Mrs. Dwight Whitney 5

MORROW, Edwin P. 1
MORROW, Frederick 3
  Keenan
MORROW, George Keenan 1
MORROW, George 1
  Washington
MORROW, Glenn R. 5
MORROW, Mrs. Honore 1
MORROW, Hubert T. 3
MORROW, Hugh 4
MORROW, James Binkley 1
MORROW, James E. 1
MORROW, Jay Johnson 1
MORROW, Jeremiah H
MORROW, John H
MORROW, John 1
MORROW, John D. A. 5
MORROW, Lester William 2
  Wallace
MORROW, Marco 5
MORROW, Prince Albert 1
MORROW, Theodore F. 4
MORROW, Thomas Robert 1
MORROW, Thomas 1
  Vaughan
MORROW, W. Carr 1
MORROW, W. K. 1
MORROW, Walter 2
  Alexander
MORROW, William 1
  Chambers
MORROW, William W. 1
MORROW, Winston 5
  Vaughan
MORROW, Wright Chalfant 5
MORSCH, Lucile M. 5
MORSCHAUSER, Joseph 2
MORSE, Albert Laverne 5
MORSE, Alexander Porter 1
MORSE, Alpheus H
MORSE, Anson Daniel 1
MORSE, Anson Ely 4
MORSE, Arthur David 5
MORSE, Arthur Henry 2
MORSE, Benjamin Clarke 1
MORSE, Charles Adelbert 1
MORSE, Charles Frederic 6
MORSE, Charles Henry 1
MORSE, Charles Hosmer 1
MORSE, Charles Hosmer 3
MORSE, Charles Wyman 1
MORSE, Charles Wyman 2
MORSE, Charles Wyman 4
MORSE, Clark T. 3
MORSE, David Sherman 4
MORSE, E. Rollins 4
MORSE, Edward Leland 4
  Clark
MORSE, Edward Lind 1
MORSE, Edward Peck 4
MORSE, Edward Sylvester 1
MORSE, Edwin Kirtland 2
MORSE, Edwin Wilson 1
MORSE, Elmer Addison 5
MORSE, Frank Lincoln 1
MORSE, Freeman Harlow H
MORSE, Fremont 1
MORSE, Glenn Tilley 3
MORSE, Godfrey 1
MORSE, Harmon Northrop 1
MORSE, Harold M. 1
MORSE, Harry Wheeler 1
MORSE, Henry Dutton H
MORSE, Horace Taylor 4
MORSE, Hosea Ballou 1
MORSE, Ira Herbert 5
MORSE, Irving Haskell 5
MORSE, Isaac Edward 1
MORSE, James Herbert 1
MORSE, Jedidiah H
MORSE, Jerome Edward 4
MORSE, John Lovett 1
MORSE, John Torrey Jr. 1
MORSE, Josiah 1
MORSE, Leon Jeremiah 3
MORSE, Leopold 1
MORSE, Lester Samuel 5
MORSE, Lucy Gibbons 1
MORSE, Margaret 5
  Fessenden
MORSE, Merrill Salisbury 4
MORSE, Oliver Andrew H
MORSE, Perley 2
MORSE, Richard Cary 1
MORSE, Richard Cary 1
MORSE, Robert Hosmer 4
MORSE, Robert Hosmer 6
  (Jr.)
MORSE, Robert McNeil 1
MORSE, Roy L. 1
MORSE, Samuel Finley H
  Breese
MORSE, Samuel Finley 5
  Brown
MORSE, Sidney 1
MORSE, Sidney Edwards H

MORSE, Waldo Grant 1
MORSE, Warner Jackson 1
MORSE, Wayne Lyman 6
MORSE, Wilbur Jr. 3
MORSE, Withrow 3
MORSELL, John Albert 6
MORSS, Charles Anthony 1
MORSS, Everett 1
MORSS, Samuel E. 1
MORSTEIN MARX, Fritz 5
MORT, Paul R. 4
MORTENSEN, Martin 5
MORTENSEN, Soren 6
  Hansen
MORTENSON, Ernest 5
  Dawson
MORTENSON, Peter Alvin 1
MORTEZA 4
MORTHLAND, David 6
  Vernon
MORTIMER, Alfred 4
  Garnett
MORTIMER, Frank 3
  Cogswell
MORTIMER, James Daniel 1
MORTIMER, Lee 4
MORTIMER, Mary H
MORTON, Alfred 6
  Hammond
MORTON, Asa Henry 4
MORTON, Charles H
MORTON, Charles 1
MORTON, Charles Adams 1
MORTON, Charles Gould 1
MORTON, Charles W. 4
MORTON, Conrad Vernon 5
MORTON, David 1
MORTON, Eliza Happy 1
MORTON, Ferdinand H
  Joseph La Menthe
MORTON, Ferdinand 4
  Joseph La Menthe
MORTON, Frank Roy 1
MORTON, Frederick 4
  William
MORTON, George * H
MORTON, George 1
  Carpenter
MORTON, George Edwin 1
MORTON, Henry 1
MORTON, Henry H. 1
MORTON, Howard 2
  McIlvain
MORTON, Ira Abbott 3
MORTON, Jack A. 5
MORTON, Jackson H
MORTON, James 1
  Ferdinand
MORTON, James Geary 4
MORTON, James Madison 1
  Jr.
MORTON, James Proctor 5
MORTON, James St Clair H
MORTON, Jennie Chinn 1
MORTON, Jeremiah H
MORTON, Jeremiah Rogers 1
MORTON, John 1
MORTON, John 4
MORTON, Joseph 2
MORTON, Joy 1
MORTON, Julius Sterling 1
MORTON, Levi Parsons 1
MORTON, Louis 6
MORTON, Marcus * H
MORTON, Nathaniel 1
MORTON, Oliver Hazard H
  Perry
MORTON, Oren Frederic 1
MORTON, Paul 1
MORTON, Perry William 4
MORTON, Richard Albert 3
  Dunlap
MORTON, Richard Lee 6
MORTON, Rosalie 5
  Slaughter
MORTON, Samuel George 1
MORTON, Samuel Walker 1
MORTON, Sarah H
  Wentworth Apthorpe
MORTON, Sterling 4
MORTON, Thomas 1
MORTON, Thomas George 4
MORTON, W. Brown 4
MORTON, William Henry 4
  Stephenson
MORTON, William Thomas H
  Green
MORWITZ, Edward H
MORWITZ, Samuel 6
  Mordecai
MORY, E. Lawrence 6
MOSBY, Charles Virgil 1
MOSBY, John Singleton 1
MOSCHCOWITZ, Alexis 1
  Victor
MOSCHCOWITZ, Paul 2

MOSCONA, Nicola 6
MOSCOSO de H
  ALVARADO, Luis de
MOSCOWITZ, Grover M. 2
MOSCRIP, William Smith H
MOSELEY, Ben Perley 4
  Poore
MOSELEY, Charles West 3
MOSELEY, Edward 1
  Augustus
MOSELEY, Edward 1
  Buckland
MOSELEY, Frederick S. Jr. 5
MOSELEY, George Van 4
  Horn
MOSELEY, Hal Walters 1
MOSELEY, John Ohleyer 3
MOSELEY, Jonathan H
  Ogden
MOSELEY, Lonzo B. 4
MOSELEY, Mercer Pamplin 1
MOSELEY, William Abbott H
MOSELY, Philip Edward 5
MOSENTHAL, Herman 3
MOSENTHAL, Joseph 1
MOSER, Alfred A. 5
MOSER, Charles Kroth 5
MOSER, Christopher Otto 1
MOSER, Clarence Patten 5
MOSER, Ellsworth 4
MOSER, Guy L. 4
MOSER, Henry S. 5
MOSER, Jefferson Franklin 1
MOSER, William 4
MOSES, Alfred Geiger 6
MOSES, Alfred Joseph 1
MOSES, Andrew 2
MOSES, Anna Mary 4
  Robertson
MOSES, Bernard 1
MOSES, C. A. 4
MOSES, Colter Hamilton 4
MOSES, Elbert Raymond 6
MOSES, Emile Phillips 6
MOSES, Frederick Taft 3
MOSES, George Higgins 2
MOSES, Harry Morgan 3
MOSES, Henry L. 4
MOSES, Horace Augustus 2
MOSES, John 1
MOSES, Montrose Jonas 1
MOSES, Siegfried 6
MOSES, Thomas 3
MOSES, Thomas Freeman 1
MOSES, Walter H. 6
MOSESSOHN, David N. 1
MOSESSOHN, Moses 1
  Dayyan
MOSESSOHN, Nehemiah 1
MOSHER, Aaron Alexander 3
  Roland
MOSHER, Clelia Duel 1
MOSHER, Eliza Marla 1
MOSHER, Esek Ray 2
MOSHER, George Clark 1
MOSHER, George Frank 1
MOSHER, Gouverneur 1
  Frank
MOSHER, Harris Peyton 3
MOSHER, Howard 1
  Townsend
MOSHER, Ira 4
MOSHER, Raymond Mylar 5
MOSHER, Robert Brent 1
MOSHER, Samuel Barlow 5
MOSHER, Thomas Bird 1
MOSHER, William Allison 5
MOSHER, William Eugene 2
MOSIER, Harold Gerard 5
MOSIER, Jeremiah George 1
MOSIER, Orval McKinley 4
MOSIMAN, Samuel K. 1
MOSKOWITZ, Belle Israels 1
MOSLER, Edwin H. 4
MOSLER, Henry 1
MOSS, Albert Bartlett 1
MOSS, Charles McCord 5
MOSS, Charles Melville 1
MOSS, Chase 6
MOSS, Emma Sadler 5
MOSS, Frank 1
MOSS, Frank J. 5
MOSS, Fred August 4
MOSS, Herbert James 3
MOSS, Hunter Holmes Jr. 1
MOSS, James Alfred 1
MOSS, John Calvin H
MOSS, Joseph 3
MOSS, Lemuel 1
MOSS, Leslie Bates 2
MOSS, Louis John 2
MOSS, Mary 1
MOSS, Maxmilian 4
MOSS, Ralph W. 4
MOSS, William Lorenzo 3
MOSS, William Washburn 2

MOSS, Woodson 1
MOSSADEGH, Mohammed 4
MOSSER, Charles Marcel 5
MOSSMAN, B. Paul 5
MOSSMAN, Frank E. 2
MOST, Johann Joseph H
MOST, Johann Joseph H
MOSTELLER, L. Karlton 5
MOTCHAN, Louis A. 6
MOTE, Carl Henry 2
MOTE, Donald Roosevelt 5
MOTEN, Bennie H
MOTEN, Roger Henwood 3
MOTHERWELL, Robert 2
  Burns II
MOTLEY, Emery Tyler 3
MOTLEY, John Lothrop 1
MOTLEY, Warren 5
MOTLEY, Willard Francis 4
MOTON, Robert Russa 1
MOTRY, Hubert Louis 3
MOTT, Charles Stewart 5
MOTT, Francis Edward 4
MOTT, Frank Luther 4
MOTT, George Scudder 1
MOTT, Gershom H
MOTT, Gordon Newell H
MOTT, James * H
MOTT, James Wheaton 2
MOTT, John Griffin 2
MOTT, John R. 3
MOTT, Jordan Lawrence 1
MOTT, Lewis Freeman 1
MOTT, Lucretia Coffin H
MOTT, Luther Wright 1
MOTT, Omer Hillman 2
MOTT, Richard H
MOTT, Rodney Loomer 5
MOTT, T. Bentley 3
MOTT, Valentine H
MOTT, Valentine 1
MOTT, William Elton 2
MOTTE, Isaac H
MOTTER, Orton B. 3
MOTTET, Henry 1
MOTTET, Jeanie Gallup 5
  (Mrs. Henry Mottet)
MOTTIER, David Myers 1
MOTZKIN, Theodore S. 5
MOUDY, Alfred L. 6
MOUDY, Walter Frank 5
MOUHTAR BEY, Ahmed 5
MOULD, Elmer Wallace 4
  King
MOULD, Jacob Wray H
MOULDS, George Henry 6
MOULTON, Arthur 4
  Wheelock
MOULTON, Charles Robert 2
MOULTON, Charles Wells 1
MOULTON, Charles 1
  William
MOULTON, Dudley 6
MOULTON, Earl L. 3
MOULTON, Edwin F. 1
MOULTON, Forest Ray 3
MOULTON, Frank Prescott 4
MOULTON, George 1
  Mayhew
MOULTON, Gertrude 6
  Evelyn
MOULTON, Harold Glen 4
MOULTON, Louise 1
  Chandler
MOULTON, Mace H
MOULTON, Mary 6
  Kennington
MOULTON, Richard Green 1
MOULTON, Robert Hurt 6
MOULTON, Sherman 1
  Roberts
MOULTON, Vern 3
MOULTON, Warren Joseph 2
MOULTON, William 4
  Horace
MOULTON, Willis Bryant 1
MOULTRIE, John H
MOULTRIE, William H
MOULTROP, Irving Edwin 4
MOUNGER, W. M. 3
MOUNT, Arnold John 2
MOUNT, Finley Pogue 1
MOUNT, George Haines 6
MOUNT, James Atwell 1
MOUNT, Oliver Erskine 1
MOUNT, Russell Theodore 6
MOUNT, Wallace 1
MOUNT, William Sidney H
MOUNTAIN, Harry 6
  Montgomery
MOUNTCASTLE, George 5
  Williams
MOUNTCASTLE, Robert 1
  Edward Lee
MOUNTIN, Joseph W. 3

MOURSUND, Andrew 5
  Fleming Jr.
MOURSUND, Walter 3
  Henrik
MOUSEL, Lloyd Harvey 4
MOUSER, Grant Earl Jr. 2
MOUTON, Alexander H
MOUZON, Edwin DuBose 1
MOUZON, James Carlisle 6
MOWAT, Magnus 5
MOWATT, Anna Cora H
  Ogden
MOWBRAY, Albert Henry 2
MOWBRAY, George H
  Mordey
MOWBRAY, H. Siddons 1
MOWBRAY-CLARKE, 3
  John
MOWER, Charles Drown 1
MOWER, Charles Drown 2
MOWER, Joseph Anthony H
MOWERY, William Byron 3
MOWRER, Frank Roger 5
MOWRER, Paul Scott 5
MOWRY, Daniel Jr. H
MOWRY, Harold 3
MOWRY, Ross Rutledge 3
MOWRY, William Augustus 1
MOXLEY, William J. 4
MOXOM, Philip Stafford 1
MOYER, Andrew Jackson 3
MOYER, Benton Leslie 4
MOYER, Burton Jones 5
MOYER, Charles H. 4
MOYER, David Gurstelle 5
MOYER, Gabriel Hocker 1
MOYER, Harold Nicholas 1
MOYER, Harvey Vernon 3
MOYER, James Ambrose 2
MOYER, Joseph Kearney 5
MOYER, William Henry 1
MOYLAN, Stephen H
MOYLE, Henry Dinwoodey 4
MOYLE, James Henry 2
MOYLE, Walter Gladstone 5
MOYNIHAN, James 4
  Humphrey
MOYNIHAN, P. H. 2
MOZEE, Phoebe Anne H
  Oakley
MOZEE, Phoebe Anne 4
  Oakley
MOZIER, Joseph H
MRAK, Ignatius 1
MUCKENFUSS, Anthony 1
  Moultrie
MUCKEY, Floyd Summer 1
MUCKLE, John Selser 1
MUCKLE, M. Richards 1
MUDD, Eugene J. 6
MUDD, Harvey Gilmer 1
MUDD, Harvey Seeley 3
MUDD, Mildred Esterbrook 3
MUDD, Seeley G. 4
MUDD, Seeley Wintersmith 1
MUDD, Stuart 6
MUDD, Sydney E. 1
MUDD, Sydney Emanuel 1
MUDD, William Swearingen 2
MUDGE, Alfred Eugene 2
MUDGE, Claire R. 4
MUDGE, Courtland Sawin 4
MUDGE, Edmund Webster 2
MUDGE, Enoch H
MUDGE, Henry U. 1
MUDGE, Isadore Gilbert 3
MUDGE, James 1
MUDGE, Lewis Seymour 1
MUDGE, Verne Donald 3
MUDGE, William Leroy 3
MUEHLBERGER, Clarence 4
  Weinert
MUEHLEISEN, Eugene 6
  Frederick
MUEHLING, John Adam 2
MUELLER, Adolph 2
MUELLER, Alfred 4
MUELLER, Arthur E. A. 4
MUELLER, Edward 3
MUELLER, Fred William 5
MUELLER, Hans 3
MUELLER, Hans 4
  Alexander
MUELLER, Hermann 1
MUELLER, John Henry 4
MUELLER, John Howard 3
MUELLER, John Victor 4
MUELLER, Karl Anton 5
MUELLER, Paul 4
MUELLER, Paul Albert 3
MUELLER, Paul Ferdinand 1
MUELLER, Paul John 4
MUELLER, Theodore 3
  Edward
MUELLER, Theodore 3
  Frederick

MUELLER, Theophil 4
  Herbert
MUELLER, Werner 4
MUENCH, Aloisius Joseph 4
MUENCH, Hugo Jr. 1
MUENCH, Hugo Jr. 5
MUENNICH, Ferenc 4
MUENSCHER, Walter C. 4
MUHAMMED, Elijah 6
  (Elijah Poole)
MUHLEMAN, George 5
  Washington
MUHLEMAN, Maurice 1
  Louis
MUHLENBERG, Francis H
  Swaine
MUHLENBERG, Frederick H
  Augustus Conrad
MUHLENBERG, Gotthilf H
  Henry Ernest
MUHLENBERG, Henry H
  Augustus
MUHLENBERG, Henry H
  Augustus Philip
MUHLENBERG, Henry H
  Melchior
MUHLENBERG, John H
  Peter Gabriel
MUHLENBERG, William H
  Augustus
MUHLFELD, George O. 2
MUHLMANN, Adolf 4
MUHSE, Albert Charles 4
MUILENBURG, James 6
MUIR, Andrew Forest 5
MUIR, Charles Henry 1
MUIR, Downie Davidson Jr. 1
MUIR, E. Stanton 4
MUIR, James 3
MUIR, James 4
MUIR, James Irvin 4
MUIR, Jere T. 5
MUIR, John * 1
MUIR, Joseph Johnstone 1
MUIR, Roy Cummings 6
MUIR, William 4
MUIRHEAD, James 1
  Fullarton
MUKERJI, Dhan Gopal 1
MULCAHY, Francis Patrick 6
MULDER, John 4
MULDOON, Hugh 3
  Cornelius
MULDOON, Peter J. 1
MULDOON, William H
MULDOON, William 4
MULEY SOLIMAN H
MULFINGER, George 1
  Abraham
MULFORD, Clarence 3
  Edward
MULFORD, Elisha H
MULFORD, John Willett 4
MULFORD, Prentice 4
MULFORD, Raymon 5
  Howard
MULFORD, Roland Jessup 5
MULFORD, Walter 5
MULHAUPT, Frederick J. 1
MULHAUSER, Frederick 6
  Ludwig
MULHERIN, William 2
  Anthony
MULHERON, Anne 2
  Morton
MULHOLLAND, Frank L. 2
MULHOLLAND, Henry 4
  Bearden
MULHOLLAND, John 5
MULHOLLAND, John 6
  Hugh
MULHOLLAND, William 1
MULKEY, Frederick 1
  William
MULL, George Fulmer 1
MULL, J. Harry 2
MULL, John Wesley 5
MULLALLY, Thornwell 2
MULLALY, Charles J. 1
MULLALY, John 1
MULLAN, Eugene Hagan 6
MULLAN, George Vincent 3
MULLAN, James 1
  McElwane
MULLAN, W. G. Read 4
MULLANEY, Eugene 6
  L(iguri)
MULLANEY, James 4
  Vincent
MULLANPHY, John 5
MULLANY, James Robert H
  Madison
MULLANY, John Francis 1
MULLANY, Patrick Francis H
MULLEN, Arthur Francis 1

MULLEN, James 4
MULLEN, James William 1
MULLEN, Joseph 6
MULLEN, Ruth Ackerman 5
  (Mrs. Frank A. Mullen)
MULLEN, Thomas Richard 3
MULLEN, Tobias 1
MULLEN, William E. 5
MULLENBACH, James 1
MULLENIX, Charles A. 3
MULLENIX, Rollin Clarke 2
MULLER, Adolf Lancken 5
MULLER, Amelia A. 3
MULLER, Carl 4
MULLER, Carl Christian 1
MULLER, Edouard 4
MULLER, George P. 2
MULLER, Henry Nicholas 6
  Jr.
MULLER, Herman Edwin 4
MULLER, Hermann Joseph 4
MULLER, James Arthur 2
MULLER, Jonas Norman 4
MULLER, Margarethe 3
MULLER, Nichols 4
MULLER, Siegfried 4
  Hermann
MULLER, Siemon William 5
MULLER, W. Max 1
MULLER, Walter J. 4
MULLER-URY, Adolfo 2
MULLETT, Mary B. 1
MULLGARDT, Louis 4
  Christian
MULLGARDT, William 6
  Oscar
MULLIGAN, Catharine 5
  A(rcher)
MULLIGAN, Charles J. 1
MULLIGAN, Charles Wise 5
MULLIGAN, David B. 3
MULLIGAN, James Hilary 1
MULLIGAN, Richard 1
  Thomas
MULLIGAN, William 6
  Joseph
MULLIKEN, Alfred Henry 1
MULLIKEN, Otis E. 5
MULLIKEN, Samuel 1
  Parsons
MULLIKIN, Sidney Albert 1
MULLIN, Francis Anthony 1
MULLIN, Joseph H
MULLIN, Sam S. 5
MULLIN, William Valentine 1
MULLINNIX, Henry 2
  Maston
MULLINS, D. Frank Jr. 6
MULLINS, Edgar Young 1
MULLINS, George Walker 3
MULLINS, Isla May 4
MULLINS, James H
MULLINS, Thomas C. 5
MULLOWNEY, John James 3
MULLOY, William 3
  Theodore
MULROONEY, Edward 5
  Pierce
MULRY, Joseph Aloysius 1
MULTER, Smith Lewis 1
MULVANE, David Winfield 1
MULVANIA, Maurice 6
MULVIHILL, Michael 1
  Joseph
MUMFORD, Charles 2
MUMFORD, Charles 1
  Carney
MUMFORD, Ethel Watts 1
MUMFORD, Frederick 3
  Blackmar
MUMFORD, George H
MUMFORD, George 2
  Saltonstall
MUMFORD, Gurdon H
  Saltonstall
MUMFORD, Herbert 1
  Windsor
MUMFORD, James 1
  Gregory
MUMFORD, John Kimberly 1
MUMFORD, Mary Eno 4
MUMFORD, Philip G. 3
MUMFORD, Samuel 1
  Cranage
MUMMA, Harlan L. 5
MUMMA, James Hebron 5
MUMMA, Morton Claire Jr. 5
MUMMA, Walter Mann 4
MUMMART, Clarence 3
  Allen
MUMPER, Norris 2
  McAllister
MUMPER, William Norris 4
MUNCE, Robert J(ohn) 6
MUNCH, Edvard 4
MUNCIE, Curtis Hamilton 4

MUNCIE, J. H. 3
MUNDE, Paul Fortunatus 1
MUNDELEIN, George 1
  William
MUNDEN, Kenneth White 6
MUNDHEIM, Samuel 1
MUNDIE, William Bryce 1
MUNDT, G. Henry 4
MUNDT, Karl Earl 6
MUNDT, Walter J. 5
MUNDY, Ethel Frances 4
MUNDY, Ezekiel Wilson 1
MUNDY, Johnson H
  Marchant
MUNDY, Talbot 1
MUNDY, William Nelson 2
MUNFORD, Mary Cooke 1
  Branch
MUNFORD, Robert H
MUNFORD, Walter F. 3
MUNFORD, William H
MUNGEN, William H
MUNGER, Claude Worrell 3
MUNGER, Dell H. 4
MUNGER, Harold Henry 5
MUNGER, Royal Freeman 4
MUNGER, Theodore 1
  Thornton
MUNGER, Thomas Charles 1
MUNGER, William Henry 1
MUNHALL, Leander 1
  Whitcomb
MUNIZ, Joao Carlos 4
MUNK, Joseph Amasa 1
MUNKITTRICK, Richard 1
  Kendall
MUNN, Charles Allen 1
MUNN, Charles Clark 1
MUNN, Hiram H. 4
MUNN, James Buell 4
MUNN, John Pixley 1
MUNN, Orson Desaix 1
MUNN, Orson Desaix 3
MUNN, Ralph 6
MUNN, William Phipps 1
MUNNIKHUYSEN, Walter 4
  Farnandis
MUNNS, Mrs. Margaret 3
  Cairns
MUNOZ GRANDES, 5
  Agustin
MUNOZ, Jorge 1
MUNRO, Annette Gardner 3
MUNRO, Dana Carleton 1
MUNRO, David Alexander 1
MUNRO, Donald 5
MUNRO, Emily Gardner 1
MUNRO, George H
MUNRO, H. G. 3
MUNRO, Henry H
MUNRO, James Alan 5
MUNRO, John Cummings 1
MUNRO, Leslie Knox 6
MUNRO, Robert Frater 5
MUNRO, Thomas 6
MUNRO, Walter J. 3
MUNRO, Walter Lee 1
MUNRO, Wilfred Harold 1
MUNRO, William Bennett 3
MUNROE, Charles 3
  Andrews
MUNROE, Charles Edward 1
MUNROE, Henry Smith 1
MUNROE, Hersey 1
MUNROE, James Phinney 1
MUNROE, John Alexander 5
MUNROE, Kirk 1
MUNROE, Robert Clifford 4
MUNROE, William Adams 1
MUNROE, William Robert 4
MUNSELL, Albert Henry 1
MUNSELL, Charles Edward 1
MUNSELL, Frank 4
MUNSELL, Harry B. 4
MUNSELL, Joel 1
MUNSELL, William Oliver 6
MUNSEY, Frank Andrew 1
MUNSN, John Maurice 3
MUNSON, C. La Rue 1
MUNSON, Edward Lyman 2
MUNSON, Edwin Sterling 5
MUNSON, Frank C. 1
MUNSON, Gorham B. 5
MUNSON, James Decker 1
MUNSON, James Eugene 1
MUNSON, John B. 4
MUNSON, John G. 3
MUNSON, John P. 1
MUNSON, Lewis S. Jr. 5
MUNSON, Loveland 1
MUNSON, Myron Andrews 1
MUNSON, Samuel Edgar 5
MUNSON, Samuel Lyman 1
MUNSON, Thomas Volney 1
MUNSON, Welton Marks 1

MUNSON, William 1
  Benjamin
MUNSTER, August W. 3
MUNSTERBERG, Hugo 1
MUNTER, Evelyn LaVon 6
  (Mrs. Robert Duane
  Munter)
MUNTER, Richard 6
  Strobach
MUNTZ, Earl Edward 4
MUNZ, Friedrich 1
MUNZ, Philip Alexander 6
MUNZIG, George 1
  Chickering
MURALT, Carl Leonard de 5
MURANE, Cornelius Daniel 4
MURAT, Achille Napoleon H
MURATORE, Lucien 3
MURCH, Chauncey 1
MURCH, James DeForest 6
MURCH, Maynard Hale 4
MURCH, Thompson Henry H
MURCH, Walter Tandy 4
MURCHIE, Alexander 3
MURCHIE, Harold Hale 1
MURCHIE, Robert Charles 2
MURCHISON, Carl 4
MURCHISON, Claudius 5
  Temple
MURCHISON, Clinton 5
  Williams
MURCHISON, Kenneth 1
  Mackenzie
MURDOCH, Frank H
  Hitchcock
MURDOCH, James Edward H
MURDOCH, James Vesey 6
MURDOCH, James Y. 4
MURDOCH, John 1
MURDOCH, John Gormley 1
MURDOCH, Thomas 1
MURDOCK, Charles Albert 1
MURDOCK, George John 2
MURDOCK, Harold 1
MURDOCK, Harris H. 3
MURDOCK, Henry Taylor 5
MURDOCK, James H
MURDOCK, John Robert 5
MURDOCK, John Samuel 2
MURDOCK, Joseph Ballard 1
MURDOCK, Kenneth 6
  Ballard
MURDOCK, Marcellus 5
  Marion
MURDOCK, Thomas 3
  Patrick
MURDOCK, Victor 1
MURFEE, Hopson Owen 3
MURFEE, James Thomas 1
MURFIN, James Orin 1
MURFIN, Orin Gould 3
MURFREE, Mary Noailles 1
MURFREE, Walter Lee 3
MURFREE, William Hardy 1
MURIE, Olaus Johan 4
MURKLAND, Charles 1
  Sumner
MURLIN, John Raymond 5
MURLIN, Lemuel Herbert 3
MURNANE, George 5
MURPH, Daniel Shuford 2
MURPHEY, Archibald De H
  Bow
MURPHEY, Charles H
MURPHEY, Robert Joseph 5
MURPHREE, Albert 1
  Alexander
MURPHREE, Eger V. 4
MURPHREE, Thomas 2
  Alexander
MURPHY, Albert S. 4
MURPHY, Alfred J. 1
MURPHY, Alice Harold 1
MURPHY, Arthur Alban 3
MURPHY, Arthur Edward 4
MURPHY, Arthur M. 1
MURPHY, Arthur Phillips 1
MURPHY, Carl 4
MURPHY, Charles F. 1
MURPHY, Charles Joseph 4
MURPHY, D. Hayes 1
MURPHY, Daniel D. 1
MURPHY, Daniel J. 3
MURPHY, Daniel Joseph 1
MURPHY, Dominic I. 1
MURPHY, Edgar Gardner 1
MURPHY, Edmond George 5
MURPHY, Edmund Albert 1
MURPHY, Edward Francis 4
MURPHY, Edward Jr. 1
MURPHY, Edward Thomas 3
MURPHY, Ernest 1
MURPHY, Eugene Edward 4
MURPHY, Eva Morley 1
MURPHY, Evert James 1
MURPHY, Francis 1

MURPHY, Francis Daniel 5
MURPHY, Francis P. 6
MURPHY, Francis Parnell 3
MURPHY, Francis S. 5
MURPHY, Frank 4
MURPHY, Frank Morrill 1
MURPHY, Franklin 1
MURPHY, Franklin William 1
MURPHY, Fred Towsley 2
MURPHY, Frederick E. 1
MURPHY, Frederick 3
  Vernon
MURPHY, George H. 4
MURPHY, Gerald 5
MURPHY, Grayson M. P. 1
MURPHY, Harry C. 4
MURPHY, Henry Constant 2
MURPHY, Henry Cruse H
MURPHY, Henry Killam 4
MURPHY, Herbert Francis 4
MURPHY, Hermann 4
  Dudley
MURPHY, Herschel 4
  Stratton
MURPHY, Howard Ansley 5
MURPHY, Isaac H
MURPHY, J. Edwin 2
MURPHY, J. Francis * 1
MURPHY, J. Harvey 1
MURPHY, James A. 3
MURPHY, James B. 3
MURPHY, James 1
  Cornelius *
MURPHY, James R. 4
MURPHY, James Shields 1
MURPHY, James William 3
MURPHY, Jeremiah Henry H
MURPHY, Jimmy 1
MURPHY, John * 1
MURPHY, John Benjamin * 1
MURPHY, John Donahoe 2
MURPHY, John H. 4
MURPHY, John Patrick 5
MURPHY, John T. 1
MURPHY, John Thomas 2
MURPHY, John Vernon 1
MURPHY, John W. H
MURPHY, John W. 4
MURPHY, Joseph Aloysius 1
  Charles
MURPHY, Joseph B. 3
MURPHY, Joseph Dudley 5
MURPHY, Joseph Nathaniel 4
MURPHY, Lambert 3
MURPHY, Laurence A. 4
MURPHY, Lawrence 5
  William
MURPHY, Loren Edgar 4
MURPHY, Mabel Ansley 5
MURPHY, Marvin 1
MURPHY, (Merle) Farmer 5
MURPHY, Michael Charles H
MURPHY, Michael Charles 4
MURPHY, Michael Thomas 1
MURPHY, Morgan 3
MURPHY, N. Barnard 3
MURPHY, Nathan Oakes 1
MURPHY, Nettie Seeley 4
MURPHY, Ray Dickinson 5
MURPHY, Richard Louis 1
MURPHY, Robert Cushman 5
MURPHY, Robert F. 2
MURPHY, Samuel Silenus 1
MURPHY, Samuel Wilson 4
MURPHY, Stanwood 5
MURPHY, Starr Jocelyn 1
MURPHY, Thomas 1
MURPHY, Thomas Dowler 1
MURPHY, Thomas Edward 4
MURPHY, Thomas Francis 4
MURPHY, Timothy Francis H
MURPHY, Vincent R. 6
MURPHY, W. Leo 1
MURPHY, Walter 2
MURPHY, Walter J. 5
MURPHY, Walter Patton 2
MURPHY, William Charles 2
  Jr.
MURPHY, William F. 2
MURPHY, William Gordon 3
MURPHY, William Larkin 1
MURPHY, William 1
  Mansuetus
MURPHY, William Robert 1
MURPHY, William Sumter H
MURPHY, William Walton 6
MURRAH, Alfred Paul 5
MURRAH, William Belton 1
MURRAY, A. N. 4
MURRAY, Alexander H
MURRAY, Alfred Lefurgy 4
MURRAY, Ambrose H
  Spencer
MURRAY, Arthur 1
MURRAY, Arthur T. 3
MURRAY, Augustus Taber 1

MURRAY, Benjamin 4
Franklin
MURRAY, Charles 5
MURRAY, Charles Bernard 1
MURRAY, Charles Burleigh 1
MURRAY, Charles H. 4
MURRAY, Charles 4
Theodore
MURRAY, David
MURRAY, David Ambrose 2
MURRAY, Dwight Harrison 6
MURRAY, Earle 3
MURRAY, Eugene 2
MURRAY, Frank Huron 6
MURRAY, George Dominic 3
MURRAY, George 2
Welwood
MURRAY, Gilbert 3
MURRAY, Grace Peckham 3
MURRAY, Howell Worth 4
MURRAY, James Edward 4
MURRAY, James Ormsbee H
MURRAY, James P. 5
MURRAY, James T. 5
MURRAY, Jennie Scudder 1
(Mrs. C. Edward Murray)
MURRAY, John * H
MURRAY, John Courtney 4
MURRAY, John Gardner 1
MURRAY, John Gregory 3
MURRAY, John Gwennap 2
MURRAY, John L. H
MURRAY, John O'Kane 1
MURRAY, John Scott 1
MURRAY, John Tucker 6
MURRAY, Johnston 6
MURRAY, Joseph 3
MURRAY, Joseph Wilson 3
MURRAY, Judith Sargent H
Stevens
MURRAY, Lawrence 5
N(ewbold)
MURRAY, Lawrence O. 1
MURRAY, Leo Tildon 5
MURRAY, Lindley H
MURRAY, Sister M.
Reparata
MURRAY, Maxwell 2
MURRAY, Nathaniel 3
Carleton
MURRAY, Nicholas H
MURRAY, O. Willard 5
MURRAY, Oscar G. 2
MURRAY, Owen Meredith 1
MURRAY, Peter 3
MURRAY, Philip 3
MURRAY, Reid Fred 3
MURRAY, Robert H
MURRAY, Robert 1
MURRAY, Robert B(laine) 1
Jr.
MURRAY, Robert Drake 1
MURRAY, Roy Irving 3
MURRAY, Samuel 1
MURRAY, Sidney Charles 1
MURRAY, Sidney Eugene 2
MURRAY, Thomas Jr. H
MURRAY, Thomas E. 4
MURRAY, Thomas 5
Hamilton
MURRAY, Thomas 4
Jefferson
MURRAY, Tom 5
MURRAY, Wallace 4
MURRAY, William 1
MURRAY, William D. 1
MURRAY, William Francis 1
MURRAY, William Henry 3
MURRAY, William Henry 1
Harrison
MURRAY, William Hilary 3
MURRAY, William Spencer 1
MURRAY, William Vans H
MURRAY-AARON, 4
Eugene
MURRAY-JACOBY, H. 1
MURRELL, John A. H
MURRIE, William F. R. 3
MURRIETA, Joaquin 1
MURRILL, William 3
Alphonso
MURROW, Edward R. 4
MURRY, John Middleton 3
MURTAGH, John Martin 6
MURTAUGH, Joseph Stuart 6
MURTFELDT, Edward 4
Warden
MUSCAT, Victor 6
MUSCHAMP, George 5
Morris
MUSCHENHEIM, 3
Frederick Augustus
MUSE, Vance 3
MUSE, William Foster 1
MUSE, William Sulivane 1
MUSE, William Taylor 5

MUSGRAVE, George 1
Clarke
MUSGRAVE, Harrison 1
MUSGRAVE, Walter 3
Emmett
MUSGRAVE, William 1
Everett
MUSICK, Charles Elvon 5
MUSICK, John Roy 5
MUSIN, Ovide 1
MUSMANNO, Michael 5
Angelo
MUSS-ARNOLT, William 4
MUSSELMAN, Clarence 2
Alfred
MUSSELMAN, Fren H
MUSSELMAN, J(ohn) 5
Rogers
MUSSELWHITE, Harry 3
Webster
MUSSER, George 1
Washington
MUSSER, John 2
MUSSER, John Herr 1
MUSSER, John Herr 1
MUSSER, Paul Howard 3
MUSSEY, Ellen Spencer 1
MUSSEY, Henry Raymond 2
MUSSEY, Reuben Dimond H
MUSSOLINI, Benito 4
MUSTAPHA II 1
MUSTARD, Harry Stoll 4
MUSTARD, Horace 4
Ransom
MUSTARD, Wilfred Pirt 1
MUSTON, Ronald C. G. 6
MUSULIN, Boris 6
MUSURILLO, Herbert 6
MUTCH, William James 2
MUTCHLER, William H
MUTER, Leslie Frederick 4
MUTESA, Edward 6
Frederick William
Walugembe Mutebi
Luwangula
MUTO, Anthony 4
MUYBRIDGE, Eadweard H
MUZIO, Claudia 1
MUZZALL, Ernest Linwood 4
MUZZARELLI, Antoine 1
MUZZEY, David Saville 4
MUZZY, H(enry) Earle 4
MYER, Albert James H
MYER, Albert Lee 1
MYER, Edmund John 4
MYER, Henry H
MYER, Isaac 1
MYER, Jesse Shire 1
MYER, John Walden 5
MYER, Joseph Charles 1
MYER, Sewall 1
MYER, Walter Evert 3
MYERBERG, Michael 6
MYERS, Abraham Charles 5
MYERS, Albert Cook 5
MYERS, Albert G. 6
MYERS, Alonzo Franklin 5
MYERS, Amos 1
MYERS, Barton 1
MYERS, Burton Dorr 1
MYERS, Charles Augustus 5
MYERS, Charles Franklin 1
MYERS, Clifford R. 1
MYERS, Clyde Hadley 2
MYERS, Cortland 4
MYERS, Curtis Clark 3
MYERS, David Albert 1
MYERS, David Jackson 5
Duke
MYERS, David Moffat 3
MYERS, Dean Wentworth 3
MYERS, Diller S. 1
MYERS, Edward Charles 6
MYERS, Edward DeLos 5
MYERS, Elizabeth (Fetter) 5
Lehman (Mrs. J. Upton
Myers)
MYERS, Francis John 3
MYERS, Frank Clayton 5
MYERS, Frank Kerchner 1
MYERS, Fred Edward Jr. 6
MYERS, Garry Cleveland 5
MYERS, George Boggan 6
MYERS, George Edmund 1
MYERS, George Hewitt 3
MYERS, George Sylvester 1
MYERS, George William 1
MYERS, Gustavus 1
MYERS, Harold B. 6
MYERS, Harry White 3
MYERS, Henry Alonzo 3
MYERS, Henry Guy 4
MYERS, Henry L. 2
MYERS, Howard 2
MYERS, Howard Barton 3
MYERS, Jack Allen 5

MYERS, James 4
MYERS, James Jefferson 1
MYERS, Jefferson 2
MYERS, Jerome 1
MYERS, John Dashiell 4
MYERS, John J. H
MYERS, John Llewellyn 5
MYERS, John Platt 4
MYERS, John Quincy 2
MYERS, John Sherman 5
MYERS, John Twiggs 5
MYERS, Johnston 1
MYERS, Joseph Simmons 3
MYERS, Lewis Edward 2
MYERS, Louis Robert 5
MYERS, Louis Wescott 5
MYERS, M. Lorton 4
MYERS, Minnie Walter 4
MYERS, Paul Noxon 5
MYERS, Philip Van Ness 1
MYERS, Quincy Alden 1
MYERS, Robert Holthy 4
MYERS, Sumner B. 5
MYERS, Theodore Walter 1
MYERS, Victor Caryl 5
MYERS, Walter Jr. 4
MYERS, Weldon Thomas 6
MYERS, Will Martin 4
MYERS, William Heyward 4
MYERS, William Kurtz 5
MYERS, William Shields 3
MYERS, William Starr 4
MYERSON, Abraham 2
MYGATT, Gerald 3
MYHRMAN, Othelia 1
MYLER, Joseph James 4
MYLER, Joseph Larkin 6
MYLES, Beverly Russell 3
MYLES, John H
MYLKS, Gordon Wright 6
MYNDERS, Alfred D. 5
MYNDERSE, Wilhelmus 1
MYRDDIN-EVANS, Sir 4
Guildhaume
MYRICK, Arthur Beckwith 5
MYRICK, Harry Pierce 5
MYRICK, Herbert 1
MYRICK, John Rencklin 1
MYRICK, Julian Southall 5
MYRICK, Shelby 4
MYRON, Paul 1

N

NABERS, Benjamin Duke H
NABERS, Jane Porter (Mrs. 6
Drayton Nabers)
NABESHIME, Isunatoshi 6
NABORS, Eugene Augustus 4
NABOURS, Robert 5
Kirkland
NABUCO, Joaquim 1
NACHT, Osias 6
NACHTRIEB, Henry 2
Francis
NACK, James M. H
NACY, Richard Robert H
NADAL, Charles Coleman 1
NADAL, Ehrman Syme 1
NADAL, Thomas William 3
NADEAU, Ira Alfred 4
NADLER, Carl S. 3
NADLER, Marcus 4
NAECKEL, Erwin George 3
NAEGELE, Charles 2
Frederick
NAFE, Cleon A. 4
NAFF, George Tipton 4
NAFFZIGER, Howard 4
Christian
NAFZIGER, Ralph LeRoy 4
NAFZIGER, Ralph Otto 6
NAGEL, Charles 1
NAGEL, Conrad 5
NAGEL, Conrad F. Jr. 3
NAGEL, Joseph Darwin 5
NAGEL, Stina (Mrs. Leon 5
Hill)
NAGER, Rudolf Felix 3
NAGLE, Charles Francis 1
NAGLE, Clarence Floyd 3
NAGLE, James C. 1
NAGLE, John Joseph 4
NAGLE, Patrick Sarsfield 1
NAGLE, Raymond Thomas 3
NAGLE, Urban 4
NAGLER, Floyd August 3
NAGLER, Forrest 3
NAGLEY, Frank Alvin 4
NAGY, Imre 4
NAHL, Charles Christian H
NAHL, Hugo Wilhelm H
Arthur
NAHM, Max Brunswick 3
NAIDEN, Earl L. 2

NAIL, James H. 1
NAIR, John Henry Jr. 5
NAIRN, Sir Michael 3
NAIRNE, Thomas H
NAISMITH, James 1
NALDER, Frank Fielding 1
NALLY, Edward Julian 3
NALLY, Francis Ignatius 6
NAMARA, Marguerite 6
NAMIER, Sir Lewis 4
Bernstein
NAMM, Benjamin Harrison 5
NAMMACK, Charles 1
Edward
NANCE, Albinus 1
NANCE, Ellwood Cecil 4
NANCE, Walter Buckner 4
NANCE, Willis Dean 5
NANCREDE, C. B. 1
Guerard de
NANCREDE, Paul Joseph H
Guerard de
NANGLE, John Joseph 4
NANKIVELL, Frank Arthur 5
NANZ, Robert Hamilton 5
NAON, Romulo S. 5
NAPHEN, Henry Francis 1
NAPIER, George Moultrie 1
NAPIER, J. Patton 6
NAPIER, Thomas Hewell 4
NAPIER, Walter Pharo 6
NAPOLI, Alexander J. 5
NAPTON, William Barclay H
NARAYANAN, Teralandur 4
Gopalacharya
NARDIN, Frances Louise 6
NARDIN, William 3
Thompson
NARRIN, Elgin Edwin 6
NARVAEZ, Panfilo H
NASH, Abner H
NASH, Albert C. H
NASH, Arthur 1
NASH, Bert Allen 2
NASH, C(arlton) Stewart 5
NASH, Charles Ellwood 1
NASH, Charles Sumner 2
NASH, Charles W. 2
NASH, Daniel H
NASH, Edgar Smiley 1
NASH, Edwin A. 1
NASH, Elliott E. 3
NASH, Ethel Miller Hughes 6
(Mrs. Arnold Samuel
Nash)
NASH, Francis H
NASH, Francis Philip 1
NASH, Frank C. 3
NASH, Frederick H
NASH, George Kilbon 1
NASH, George Williston 1
NASH, Harriet A. 1
NASH, Henry Sylvester 1
NASH, Herbert Charles 1
NASH, Isaac H(enry) 5
NASH, J. Newton 3
NASH, Jay Bryan 4
NASH, John Henry 1
NASH, Leonidas Lydwell 1
NASH, Louis Rogers 5
NASH, Luther Roberts 5
NASH, Lyman Junius 1
NASH, Ogden 5
NASH, Paul Cleveland 1
Bennett
NASH, Philip Curtis 2
NASH, Simeon H
NASH, Walter 5
NASH, William Alexander 5
NASH, William Holt 1
NASMYTH, George 1
NASON, Arthur Huntington 2
NASON, Elias H
NASON, Frank Lewis 1
NASON, Harry Baxter Jr. 5
NASON, Henry Bradford 1
NASON, Leonard Hastings 5
(Steamer)
NASON, Thomas H
Willoughby
NASSAU, Jason John 4
NASSAU, Robert Hamill 1
NASSER, Gamal Abdel 5
NAST, Albert Julius 2
NAST, Conde 1
NAST, Thomas H
NAST, Thomas 1
NAST, William H
NATE, Joseph Cookman 5
NATELSON, Morris 6
NATHAN, Alfred 1
NATHAN, Edgar Joshua 3
NATHAN, Edward Isaac 4
NATHAN, George Jean 3
NATHAN, J(acob) Philip 1

NATHAN, Maud 2
NATHANSON, Ira 3
Theodore
NATION, Carry Amelia H
Moore
NATION, Carry Amelia 4
Moore
NATIONS, Gilbert Owen 5
NATZLER, Gertrud Amon 6
(Mrs. Otto Natzler)
NAUDAIN, Arnold 1
NAUJOKS, Herbert Hugh 4
NAUMBURG, George 5
Washington
NAUMBURG, Walter 3
Wehle
NAUSS, Henry G. 5
NAVAGH, James Johnston 4
NAVARRO, Jose Antonio H
NAVE, Anna Eliza Semans 4
NAVE, Frederick Solomon 1
NAVE, Orville James 1
NAVIN, Robert B(ernard) 5
NAWN, Hugh 6
NAYLOR, Edmund Barry 5
NAYLOR, Addison Wood 4
NAYLOR, Charles H
NAYLOR, E. E. 1
NAYLOR, Emmett Hay 1
NAYLOR, James Ball 3
NAYLOR, John Calvin 4
NAYLOR, John Lewis 4
NAYLOR, Joseph Randolph 2
NAYLOR, William Keith 2
NAYLOR, Wilson Samuel 4
NAZIMOVA, Alla 2
NAZIMUDDIN, Al-Haj
Khwaja
NEAD, Benjamin Matthias 1
NEAGLE, John H
NEAGLE, Pickens 2
NEAL, Alva Otis 1
NEAL, David 1
NEAL, Ernest Eugene 5
NEAL, George Franklin 6
NEAL, George Ira 2
NEAL, Herbert Vincent 1
NEAL, James Arthur 1
NEAL, James Henry 1
NEAL, John H
NEAL, John Randolph 4
NEAL, John Randolph 3
NEAL, Joseph Clay H
NEAL, Josephine Bicknell 4
NEAL, Lawrence Talbott 1
NEAL, Mills Ferrell 5
NEAL, Paul Ardeen 3
NEAL, Phil Hudson 5
NEAL, Robert Wilson 1
NEAL, Thomas 1
NEAL, Will E. 3
NEAL, William Joseph 2
NEAL, William M. 4
NEAL, William Watt 5
NEAL, William Weaver 3
NEALE, John Ernest 6
NEALE, Laurance Irving 3
NEALE, Leonard H
NEALE, M. Gordon 4
NEALE, Raphael H
NEALE, Walter 1
NEAMAN, Pearson E.
NEARY, John Stuart 4
NEARY, William Herrmann 6
NEATH, Jasper Arthur 3
NEBEKER, Frank 5
Knowlton
NEBEL, Berthold 4
NECKERE, Leo Raymond H
De
NEDVED, Elizabeth 5
Kimball (Mrs. Rudolph
James Nedved)
NEE, Maurice Lyden
NEEDHAM, Charles Austin 1
NEEDHAM, Charles Willis 2
NEEDHAM, Claude Ervin 3
NEEDHAM, Daniel 1
NEEDHAM, Florian Berle 6
NEEDHAM, Henry Beach 1
NEEDHAM, James H
NEEDHAM, James Carson 2
NEEDHAM, Maurice
Henshaw
NEEDLES, Arthur Chase 4
NEEDLES, Enoch Ray 5
NEEF, Francis Joseph
Nicholas
NEEF, Frederick Emil 5
NEEL, William D. 1
NEELANDS, Thomas D. Jr. 5
NEELEY, George A. 1
NEELEY, John Lawton
NEELLEY, John Haven 4
NEELY, Charles Gracchus 1
NEELY, Henry Adams 1

NEELY, John Marshall III 5
NEELY, Matthew M. 3
NEELY, Thomas Benjamin 5
NEET, George W. 3
NEF, John Ulric 1
NEFF, Charles Thompson Jr.
NEFF, Elizabeth Hyer 5
NEFF, Elmer Hartshorn 2
NEFF, Frank Amandus 6
NEFF, Frank Chaffee 2
NEFF, Frank Howard 1
NEFF, George N. 1
NEFF, Grover Cleveland 5
NEFF, Harold Hopkins 5
NEFF, J. Louis 5
NEFF, Jay H. 4
NEFF, John Henry 1
NEFF, Joseph A. 5
NEFF, Joseph Seal 1
NEFF, Pat Morris 3
NEFF, Paul Joseph 3
NEFF, Silas S. 1
NEFF, Ward Andrew 3
NEFTEL, William B. 4
NEGLEY, Daniel H
NEGLEY, James Scott 1
NEGUS, Sidney Stevens 4
NEHER, Fred 1
NEHLIG, Victor 1
NEHRING, Millard J. 4
NEHRLING, Arno Herbert 6
NEHRLING, Henry 1
NEHRU, Jawaharlal 4
NEIDEG, William Jonathan 3
NEIDHARD, Charles H
NEIDLINGER, William Harold 1
NEIFERT, Ira Edward 3
NEIGHBORS, Robert Simpson H
NEIHARDT, John Gnelsenau 6
NEIL, Albert Bramlett 6
NEIL, Edward Wallace 1
NEIL, George M. 3
NEIL, Matt Marshall 1
NEILD, Edward Fairfax 3
NEILER, Samuel Graham 2
NEILL, Alexander Sutherland 6
NEILL, Charles Patrick 2
NEILL, Edward Duffield H
NEILL, James Maffett 4
NEILL, John H
NEILL, John Selby Martin 1
NEILL, Lelia Winslow Bray 5
(Mrs. Charles R. Neill)
NEILL, Paul 2
NEILL, Richard Renshaw 1
NEILL, Thomas Hewson H
NEILL, William H
NEILSON, Charles Hugh 3
NEILSON, Francis 4
NEILSON, Harry Rosengarten 2
NEILSON, Jason Andrew 5
NEILSON, John H
NEILSON, Lewis 4
NEILSON, Nellie 2
NEILSON, Nevin Paul 5
NEILSON, Raymond Perry Rodgers 4
NEILSON, Thomas Hall 4
NEILSON, Thomas Rundle 1
NEILSON, William Allan 2
NEILSON, William George 1
NEILSON, William LaCoste 3
NEISSER, Hans Philip 6
NEISWANGER, David 4
NEL, Louis Taylor 5
NELAN, Charles 1
NELL, Louis 4
NELL, Raymond Boyd 6
NELL, William Cooper H
NELLES, Percy W. 3
NELLIGAN, Howard Paul 3
NELMS, William Lewis 4
NELSON, Adolphus P. 1
NELSON, Alexander Lockhart H
NELSON, Alfred Brierley 3
NELSON, Alfred L. 4
NELSON, Arthur E. 3
NELSON, Benjamin F. 1
NELSON, Bertram Griffith 4
NELSON, Burton Edsal 5
NELSON, C. Ferdinand 3
NELSON, Carl K. 5
NELSON, Charles Alexander 1
NELSON, Charles Donald 4
NELSON, Charles Pembroke 5
NELSON, Clara Albertine 5
NELSON, Clarence 3

NELSON, Cleland Kinloch 1
NELSON, Daniel Thurber 1
NELSON, David H
NELSON, Donald Marr 3
NELSON, Dotson McGinnis 6
NELSON, Edgar Andrew 5
NELSON, Edward Beverly 4
NELSON, Edward William 1
NELSON, Elmer Martin 3
NELSON, Elnathan Kemper 1
NELSON, Erland Nels Peter 6
NELSON, Frank 4
NELSON, Frank Howard 1
NELSON, George Bliss 2
NELSON, George Francis 1
NELSON, George Herbert 4
NELSON, Godfrey Nicholas 3
NELSON, Harold Hayden 3
NELSON, Henry Addison 1
NELSON, Henry Loomis 1
NELSON, Herbert Undeen 3
NELSON, Homer Augustus H
NELSON, Hugh 1
NELSON, Irving Robert 6
NELSON, Jabez Curry 3
NELSON, James Boyd 3
NELSON, Jeremiah H
NELSON, John * 1
NELSON, John Edward 3
NELSON, John Evon 2
NELSON, John Mandt 5
NELSON, John Marbury Jr. 4
NELSON, Joseph David Jr. 4
NELSON, Joseph E. 4
NELSON, Julia Bullard 1
NELSON, Julius 1
NELSON, Knute 1
NELSON, Mack Barnabas 3
NELSON, Martin 5
NELSON, Martin Johan 4
NELSON, Nels Christian 4
NELSON, Nelson O. 4
NELSON, Ole C. 3
NELSON, Oliver Edward 6
NELSON, Orville Norman 4
NELSON, Oscar 1
NELSON, O(scar) A(lfred) (Ozzie) 6
NELSON, Perry Albert 5
NELSON, Peter Bering 4
NELSON, Ralph Thomas 5
NELSON, Rensselaer Russell 1
NELSON, Reuben 1
NELSON, Reuben Emmanuel H
NELSON, Richard Alfred 6
NELSON, Richard Arthur 4
NELSON, Richard Henry 1
NELSON, Richard J. 4
NELSON, Robert Franklin 4
NELSON, Robert Oliver 5
NELSON, Robert W. 1
NELSON, Robert William 5
NELSON, Roger 4
NELSON, Rufus Jerry 5
NELSON, Samuel H
NELSON, Samuel A. 1
NELSON, Sofus Bertelson 1
NELSON, Theodore 4
NELSON, Thomas * 1
NELSON, Thomas 4
NELSON, Thomas Amos Rogers H
NELSON, Thomas Kinloch 1
NELSON, Thomas Maduit H
NELSON, Thurlow C. 4
NELSON, Virginia Winslow 6
NELSON, Warren Otto 5
NELSON, William * H
NELSON, William * 1
NELSON, William 5
NELSON, William Hamilton 3
NELSON, William Lester 3
NELSON, William Rockhill 1
NELSON, Wolfred 5
NEMEROV, David 4
NEMEYER, S(idney) Lloyd 5
NEMMERS, Erwin Plein 2
NEPOMUK, Felix Constatin Alexander Johann H
NEPRASH, Jerry Alvin 3
NERAZ, John Claudius H
NERI, M. Philip 6
NERINCKX, Charles H
NERLOVE, Samuel Henry 5
NERUDA, Pablo 6
NES, Henry H
NESBIT, Charles Francis 1
NESBIT, Harrison 1
NESBIT, Otis Burgess 1
NESBIT, Valentine Jordan 5

NESBIT, Walter 6
NESBIT, Wilbur D. 1
NESBIT, William Marsiglia 1
NESBITT, Frank Watterson 2
NESBITT, John Maxwell H
NESBITT, Wilson H
NESLAGE, Oliver J. 3
NESLEN, C(harles) Clarence 6
NESLEN, Clarence Cannon 5
NESMITH, James Willis H
NESMITH, John H
NESS, Eliot 3
NESTOR, Agnes 2
NESTOS, Ragnvald Anderson 2
NETERER, Jeremiah 2
NETHERCUT, Edgar S. 5
NETHERSOLE, Olga 1
NETHERWOOD, Douglas Blakeshaw 2
NETTLETON, Alvred Bayard 1
NETTLETON, Asahel H
NETTLETON, Edwin S. H
NETTLETON, George Henry H
NETTLETON, Walter 1
NEUBERG, Carl Alexander 3
NEUBERG, Maurice Joseph 2
NEUBERGER, Richard Lewis
NEUBERGER, Richard Lewis 4
NEUBURGER, Rudolf 3
NEUENDORFF, Adolph Heinrich Anton Magnus H
NEUHAUS, Eugen 6
NEUHOFF, Charles Sidney 5
NEUMAN, Abraham C. 5
NEUMAN, Fred G. 3
NEUMANN, Arnold John Robert 2
NEUMANN, Edward Morsbach 5
NEUMANN, Ernest K. 3
NEUMANN, F. Wight 1
NEUMANN, Frank 4
NEUMANN, Henry 4
NEUMANN, John Nepomucene H
NEUMANN, Robert 6
NEUMANN, Sigmund 5
NEUMANN, William Louis 5
NEUMARK, Arthur Jay 4
NEUMARK, David 1
NEUMEYER, Albert 5
NEUMEYER, Carl Melvin H
NEUPERT, Carl Nicholas 5
NEUPERT, Edmund H
NEUTRA, Richard Joseph 5
NEUWIRTH, Isaac 5
NEVADA, Emma (Mrs. Raymond Palmer) 5
NEVE, Juergen Ludwig 2
NEVILLE, Donald Weston 5
NEVILLE, Edwin Lowe 2
NEVILLE, Glenn 4
NEVILLE, John H
NEVILLE, Joseph H
NEVILLE, Keith 3
NEVILLE, Paul Edwin 5
NEVILLE, Philip 6
NEVILLE, Robert 5
NEVILLE, Robert Henry 2
NEVILLE, Wendell Cushing 1
NEVILLE, William 1
NEVILS, W. Coleman 3
NEVIN, Alfred 1
NEVIN, Arthur Finley 2
NEVIN, Charles Merrick 6
NEVIN, Edwin Henry 1
NEVIN, Ethelbert 1
NEVIN, George Balch 1
NEVIN, Gordon Balch 1
NEVIN, James Banks 1
NEVIN, John Williamson H
NEVIN, Robert Jenkins 1
NEVIN, Robert Murphy 4
NEVIN, Robert Peebles 1
NEVIN, Robert Reasoner 3
NEVIN, Theodore Williamson 1
NEVIN, William Channing 4
NEVIN, William Latta 1
NEVINS, Allan 5
NEVINS, Bert 4
NEVINS, Ralph Griffith Jr. 6
NEVIUS, Henry M. 1
NEVIUS, John Livingston H
NEW, Anthony H
NEW, Catherine McLaen 5
NEW, Clarence Herbert 1
NEW, George Edward 4
NEW, Gordon Balgarnie 3

NEW, Harry Stewart 1
NEW, Jeptha Dudley H
NEW, John Chalfant 1
NEW, William Lafayette 6
NEWBERNE, Robert Edward Lee 1
NEWBERRY, Edgar A. 4
NEWBERRY, Farrar 5
NEWBERRY, John Josiah 3
NEWBERRY, John Stoughton H
NEWBERRY, John Strong 3
NEWBERRY, Mary Wheeler 3
NEWBERRY, Oliver H
NEWBERRY, Perry 1
NEWBERRY, Roger Wolcott 4
NEWBERRY, Truman Handy 3
NEWBERRY, Walter Cass 1
NEWBERRY, Walter Loomis H
NEWBERRY, William Belknap 4
NEWBILL, Willard Douglas 3
NEWBOLD, Fleming 2
NEWBOLD, Thomas H
NEWBOLD, W. Romaine 1
NEWBORG, Leonard David 5
NEWBRANCH, Harvey Ellsworth 3
NEWBROUGH, John Ballou H
NEWBURGER, Joseph 1
NEWBURGER, Joseph Emanuel 1
NEWBURGER, Morris 6
NEWBURN, Harry Kenneth 6
NEWBURY, Frank Davies 5
NEWBURY, Michael 5
NEWBURY, Mollie Netcher 3
NEWBY, Leonidas Perry 4
NEWBY, Nathan 3
NEWCOMB, Arthur Thurston 1
NEWCOMB, Charles Benjamin 1
NEWCOMB, Charles Leonard 1
NEWCOMB, Ezra Butler 1
NEWCOMB, Harry Turner 2
NEWCOMB, Harvey 1
NEWCOMB, Horatio Victor 1
NEWCOMB, James Edward 4
NEWCOMB, James Farmer 1
NEWCOMB, John Lloyd 3
NEWCOMB, Josephine Louise Le Monnier H
NEWCOMB, Josiah Turner 2
NEWCOMB, Kate Pelham 3
NEWCOMB, Katharine Hinchman 1
NEWCOMB, Simon 1
NEWCOMB, Wyllys Stetson 5
NEWCOMBE, Frederick Charles 1
NEWCOMER, Alphonso Gerald 1
NEWCOMER, Christian H
NEWCOMER, Henry Clay 4
NEWCOMER, Stanley J. 4
NEWCOMER, Waldo 1
NEWCOMET, Horace Edgar 2
NEWELL, Stanford 1
NEWELL, Charles Herbert 1
NEWELL, Cicero 1
NEWELL, Clarence DeRocha 5
NEWELL, Edward Jackson 4
NEWELL, Edward Theodore 1
NEWELL, Franklin Spilman 2
NEWELL, Frederick Haynes 1
NEWELL, George Edwards 1
NEWELL, George Glenn 1
NEWELL, George T. 6
NEWELL, Henry Clinton 1
NEWELL, Herman Wilson 3
NEWELL, Jake F. 2
NEWELL, James W. 5
NEWELL, Jessie Edna Whitehead 1
NEWELL, Joseph Shipley 3
NEWELL, Lyman Churchill 1
NEWELL, Peter 1
NEWELL, Quitman Underwood 1
NEWELL, Robert 1
NEWELL, Robert Brewer 2
NEWELL, Robert Henry 1
NEWELL, Robert Reid 4
NEWELL, Wilbur Charles 1

NEWELL, William Augustus 1
NEWELL, William Henry 1
NEWELL, William Reed 5
NEWELL, William Stark 1
NEWELL, William Wells 1
NEWELL, William Whiting 1
NEWELL, Wilmon 2
NEWENS, Adrian M. 5
NEWEY, Frederick John 2
NEWFANG, Oscar 2
NEWFIELD, Morris 2
NEWGARDEN, Paul W. 2
NEWHALL, Alfred Augustus 1
NEWHALL, Arthur Brock 3
NEWHALL, C. Stevenson 3
NEWHALL, Charles Francis 4
NEWHALL, Charles Francis 5
NEWHALL, Charles Stedman 4
NEWHALL, Charles Watson 2
NEWHALL, Henry Whiting 5
NEWHALL, J. Lincoln 3
NEWHALL, John Bailey 6
NEWHALL, Nancy 6
NEWHALL, Parker 4
NEWHALL, Richard Ager 6
NEWHALL, Thomas 2
NEWHARD, Peter 4
NEWHART, Horace 2
NEWHOUSE, Samuel 4
NEWHOUSE, Walter Harry 5
NEWKIRK, Clement Roy 4
NEWKIRK, Garrett 1
NEWKIRK, Matthew H
NEWKIRK, Newton 1
NEWKIRK, Samuel Drake 3
NEWLAND, Donald Elmer 6
NEWLANDS, Francis Griffith 1
NEWLEAN, John Walter 1
NEWLIN, Gurney Elwood 3
NEWLIN, Ora Allen 2
NEWLIN, Thomas 4
NEWLIN, William Jesse 3
NEWLON, Jesse H. 1
NEWMAN, Albert Broadus 3
NEWMAN, Albert Henry 1
NEWMAN, Alexander H
NEWMAN, Alfred 5
NEWMAN, Allen George 1
NEWMAN, Angelia French Thurston 1
NEWMAN, Barnett 4
NEWMAN, Barnett 5
NEWMAN, Bernard 5
NEWMAN, Bernard J. 1
NEWMAN, Carol Montgomery 1
NEWMAN, Charles Morehead 5
NEWMAN, Dora Lee 5
NEWMAN, E. M. 1
NEWMAN, Edgar Douglas 4
NEWMAN, Edwin A. 4
NEWMAN, Elliot Voss 6
NEWMAN, Ernest 3
NEWMAN, Erwin William 5
NEWMAN, Frances 1
NEWMAN, Helen Catherine 1
NEWMAN, Henry H
NEWMAN, Henry Parker 1
NEWMAN, Herman 5
NEWMAN, Horatio Hackett 3
NEWMAN, J. Kiefer Jr. 1
NEWMAN, Jacob 1
NEWMAN, Jacob Kiefer 2
NEWMAN, James Joseph 5
NEWMAN, James R. 4
NEWMAN, Jared Treman 1
NEWMAN, John Grant 1
NEWMAN, John Philip 1
NEWMAN, John Philip H
NEWMAN, John Urquhart 4
NEWMAN, Louis Israel 5
NEWMAN, Oliver Peck 5
NEWMAN, Robert 2
NEWMAN, Samuel Phillips H
NEWMAN, Stephen 1
NEWMAN, William H. 5
NEWMAN, William Truslow 1
NEWMAN, Willie Betty 4
NEWMARK, Harris 1
NEWMARK, Marco Ross 5
NEWMARK, Maurice Harris 1
NEWMARK, Nathan 6
NEWMYER, Alvin LeRoy 6
NEWMYER, Arthur Grover 3
NEWNAN, Daniel H

NEWPORT, Christopher H
NEWSAM, Albert H
NEWSHAM, Joseph Parkinson 3
NEWSOM, Curtis Bishop 3
NEWSOM, Edwin Earl 6
NEWSOM, Herschel D. 5
NEWSOM, John Flesher 1
NEWSOM, William Monypeny 1
NEWSOM, William Monypeny 2
NEWSOME, Albert Ray 3
NEWSON, Henry Byron 1
NEWTON, Alfred Edward 1
NEWTON, Arthur William 4
NEWTON, Byron R. 1
NEWTON, Charles Bertram 5
NEWTON, Charles Damon 1
NEWTON, Charles Howard 6
NEWTON, Clarence Lucian 3
NEWTON, Cleveland Alexander 2
NEWTON, Cosette Faust 6 (Mrs. Frank Hawley Newton)
NEWTON, Eben H
NEWTON, Edith 6
NEWTON, Elbridge Ward 4
NEWTON, Glenn D. 5
NEWTON, Henry Jotham H
NEWTON, Homer Curtis 3
NEWTON, Howard Chamberlian 4
NEWTON, Hubert Anson H
NEWTON, Isaac * H
NEWTON, Isaac Burkett 1
NEWTON, James Thornwell 1
NEWTON, John H
NEWTON, John Henry 2
NEWTON, John Orville 4
NEWTON, John Wharton 5
NEWTON, Joseph Fort 2
NEWTON, Maurice 5
NEWTON, McGuire 1
NEWTON, Oscar 1
NEWTON, R. Heber 1
NEWTON, Richard 1
NEWTON, Robert Safford H
NEWTON, Thomas * 1
NEWTON, Thomas H
NEWTON, Thomas Willoughby
NEWTON, Walter Hughes 1
NEWTON, Walter Russell 4
NEWTON, Watson J. 1
NEWTON, Willoughby Wilberforce 1
NEYLAN, John Francis 4
NEYLAND, Harry 3
NEYLAND, Robert Reese Jr. 4
NEYMANN, Clarence Adolph 3
NEZ COUPE H
NGO DINH DIEM 4
NIAS, Henry 3
NIBLACK, Albert Parker 1
NIBLACK, Silas Leslie H
NIBLACK, William Ellis H
NIBLEY, Charles Wilson 1
NIBLO, Urban 3
NIBLO, William 1
NICCOLLS, Samuel Jack 1
NICE, Harry 1
NICE, Margaret Morse 6 (Mrs. Leonard Blaine Nice)
NICELY, Harold Elliott 3
NICELY, James Mount 4
NICHOL, Edward Sterling 5
NICHOL, Francis David 4
NICHOL, Frederick William 3
NICHOLAS, Anna 1
NICHOLAS, Edwin August 3
NICHOLAS, George H
NICHOLAS, John H
NICHOLAS, John Spangler 4
NICHOLAS, Lindsley Vincent 6
NICHOLAS, Philip Norborne H
NICHOLAS, Richard Ulysses 3
NICHOLAS, Robert Carter H *
NICHOLAS, William Gardiner 1
NICHOLAS, William Oliver 5
NICHOLAS, Wilson Cary H
NICHOLL, Horace Wadham 1
NICHOLL, C. W. Delyon 1
NICHOLLS, Francis Tillon 1
NICHOLLS, George Heaton 5
NICHOLLS, John Calhoun 1
NICHOLLS, Rhoda Holmes 1

NICHOLLS, Richard H
NICHOLLS, Samuel Jones 1
NICHOLLS, Thomas David 5
NICHOLLS, William 3 Durrett
NICHOLS, Anne 4
NICHOLS, Arthur Burr 5
NICHOLS, Charles A. 1
NICHOLS, Charles Gerry 4
NICHOLS, Charles Henry 1
NICHOLS, Charles Lemuel 1
NICHOLS, Charles Walter 4
NICHOLS, Clarina Irene Howard 6
NICHOLS, Clark Asahel 5
NICHOLS, Edward Hall 1
NICHOLS, Edward Leamington 1
NICHOLS, Edward Tattnall 1
NICHOLS, Edward West 1
NICHOLS, Egbert Ray 3
NICHOLS, Ernest Fox 1
NICHOLS, Francis Henry 1
NICHOLS, Frank R. 1
NICHOLS, Frederick Day 5
NICHOLS, Frederick George 3
NICHOLS, George Elwood 4
NICHOLS, George Ward H
NICHOLS, Harry Peirce 4
NICHOLS, Henry Drew 4
NICHOLS, Henry Joseph 6
NICHOLS, Henry Sargent Prentiss 1
NICHOLS, Henry Windsor 4
NICHOLS, Herbert 1
NICHOLS, Herbert L. 4
NICHOLS, Hobart Jr. 4
NICHOLS, Ichabod H
NICHOLS, Isabel McIlhenny 2
NICHOLS, Jack John Conover 2
NICHOLS, James H
NICHOLS, James Robinson H
NICHOLS, James Walter 4
NICHOLS, Jesse Clyde 2
NICHOLS, John Benjamin 3
NICHOLS, John Francis 2
NICHOLS, John Grayson 2
NICHOLS, John Richard 1
NICHOLS, John Wesley 6
NICHOLS, Malcolm E. 4
NICHOLS, Mark Lovel 5
NICHOLS, Marvin Curtis 4
NICHOLS, Mary Sargeant Neal Gove H
NICHOLS, Matthias H. H
NICHOLS, Neil Ernest 3
NICHOLS, Othniel Foster 1
NICHOLS, Pierrepont Herrick 3
NICHOLS, Robert Hastings 3
NICHOLS, Roy Franklin 5
NICHOLS, Ruth Rowland 4
NICHOLS, Spencer Baird 3
NICHOLS, Spencer Van Bokkelen 2
NICHOLS, Thomas Flint 1
NICHOLS, Walter Edmond 5
NICHOLS, Walter Franklin 2
NICHOLS, Walter Hammond 1
NICHOLS, William Ford 1
NICHOLS, William Henry 1
NICHOLS, William LeRoy 3
NICHOLS, William Theophilus 1
NICHOLS, William Wallace 2
NICHOLSON, Alfred Osborn Pope H
NICHOLSON, Edward Everett 5
NICHOLSON, Eliza Jane Poitevent Holbrook H
NICHOLSON, Francis H
NICHOLSON, Frank Lee 3
NICHOLSON, Frank Walter 4
NICHOLSON, George Edward 1
NICHOLSON, George Mansel 5
NICHOLSON, George Robert Henderson 2
NICHOLSON, George T. 1
NICHOLSON, Hammond Burke 4
NICHOLSON, Harold George 5
NICHOLSON, Henry Hudson 1
NICHOLSON, Isaac Lea 1
NICHOLSON, J. Lee 4
NICHOLSON, James

NICHOLSON, James H Bartram
NICHOLSON, James 4 Bartram
NICHOLSON, James 5 Thomas
NICHOLSON, James 1 William
NICHOLSON, James H William Augustus
NICHOLSON, John * H
NICHOLSON, John 6 Frederick
NICHOLSON, John Page 1
NICHOLSON, John Reed 1
NICHOLSON, John 4 Rutherford
NICHOLSON, Joseph H Hopper
NICHOLSON, Leonard 3 Kimball
NICHOLSON, Meredith 2
NICHOLSON, Nollie Davis 6
NICHOLSON, Norman Edwin 5
NICHOLSON, Paul Coe 3
NICHOLSON, Ralph 5
NICHOLSON, Reginald Fairfax 1
NICHOLSON, Rex Lee 6
NICHOLSON, Robert 5 Harvey
NICHOLSON, Samuel H
NICHOLSON, Samuel D. 1
NICHOLSON, Samuel 1 Edgar
NICHOLSON, Samuel M. 1
NICHOLSON, Samuel 5 Thorne
NICHOLSON, Seth Barnes 4
NICHOLSON, Somerville 1
NICHOLSON, Soterios 3
NICHOLSON, Thomas 2
NICHOLSON, Timothy 4
NICHOLSON, Vincent DeWitt 2
NICHOLSON, Walter 4 Wicks
NICHOLSON, Watson 3
NICHOLSON, William Jones 1
NICHOLSON, William 6 McNeal
NICHOLSON, William 6 Ramsey Jr.
NICHOLSON, William Rufus 1
NICHOLSON, William H Thomas
NICKELS, John Augustine 1 Heard
NICKELS, Mervyn Millard 5 Stillman
NICKERSON, Frank 4 Robert
NICKERSON, Hiram 1 Robert
NICKERSON, Hoffman 4
NICKERSON, John 3
NICKERSON, Kingsbury S. 4
NICKEUS, Johnson 1
NICKLAS, Charles Aubrey 2
NICKS, F. William 5
NICODEMUS, Frank Courtney Jr. 3
NICOL, Alexander R. 4
NICOL, Charles Edgar 1
NICOL, Jacob 5
NICOLA, Lewis H
NICOLAI, Harry T. 3
NICOLASSEN, George Frederick 5
NICOLAY, Helen 3
NICOLAY, John George 1
NICOLET, Jean H
NICOLL, De Lancey 1
NICOLL, Henry H
NICOLL, James Craig 1
NICOLL, Matthias Jr. 1
NICOLLET, Joseph Nicolas H
NICOLLS, Matthias H
NICOLLS, Richard H
NICOLLS, William H
NICOLLS, William Jasper 1
NICUM, John 1
NIEBUHR, H. Richard 4
NIEBUHR, Reinhold 5
NIEDERMEYER, Frederick David 3
NIEDRINGHAUS, Frederick G. 1
NIEDRINGHAUS, George Hayward 2
NIEDRINGHAUS, George W. 1
NIEDRINGHAUS, Henry Frederick

NIEDRINGHAUS, J. P. 4 Erwin
NIEDRINGHAUS, Thomas 1 Key
NIEHAUS, Charles Henry 1
NIEHAUS, Fredrich 5 Wilhelm
NIELDS, John P. 2
NIELSEN, Alice 2
NIELSEN, Fred Kenelm 4
NIELSEN, Harald Herborg 5
NIELSEN, Johannes 5 Maagaard
NIEMAN, Lucius W. 1
NIEMANN, Carl 4
NIEMEYER, John Henry 1
NIERENSEE, John R. H
NIERMAN, John L. 3
NIES, James Buchanan 1
NIESET, Robert Thomas 4
NIESZ, Homer E. 1
NIETO Del RIO, Felix 3
NIEUWLAND, Julius Arthur 1
NIEZER, Charles M. 1
NIFONG, Frank Gosney 4
NIGGEMAN, Louis 6 William
NIGHTINGALE, Augustus 1 Frederick
NIGHTINGALE, William 4 Thomas
NIHART, Benjamin 3 Franklin
NIJINSKY, Vaslav 4
NIKANDER, John Kustaa 1
NIKOLSKY, Alexander A. 4
NILAN, John Joseph 1
NILES, Alfred Salem 1
NILES, Alva Joseph 2
NILES, Blair 3
NILES, Edward Hulbert 3
NILES, George McCallum 1
NILES, Henry Carpenter 3
NILES, Henry Clay 1
NILES, Henry Clay 6
NILES, Hezekiah H
NILES, Jason 1
NILES, John Milton H
NILES, Kossuth 1
NILES, Nathan Erie H
NILES, Nathaniel * H
NILES, Nathaniel 1
NILES, Philip Bradford 3
NILES, Samuel H
NILES, Walter Lindsay 2
NILES, William Harmon 1
NILES, William Henry 4
NILES, William White 1
NILES, William Woodruff 1
NILLES, Herbert George 4
NILSSON, Fritiof 6
NILSSON, Hjalmar 1
NILSSON, Victor 2
NIMITZ, Chester William 4
NIMKOFF, Meyer F. 1
NIMMONS, George Croll 2
NIMS, Eugene Dutton 3
NIMS, Harry Dwight 3
NINDE, Edward Summerfield 1
NINDE, William Xavier 1
NINNIS, Frederick Charles 6
NIPHER, Francis Eugene 1
NISBET, Charles William H
NISBET, Charles Richard 3
NISBET, Eugenius Aristides H
NISBET, James Douglas 1
NISBET, Robert Hogg 4
NISBET, Walter Olin Jr. 1
NISLEY, Harold A. 4
NISONGER, Herschel Ward 5
NISSEN, Harry Archibald 5
NISSEN, Hartvig 1
NISSEN, Henry W. 3
NISSEN, Ludwig 1
NITCHMANN, David H
NITZE, William Albert 3
NITZSCHE, Elsa Koenig 5
NITZSCHE, George E. 4
NIVEN, Archibald Campbell H
NIVEN, John Ballantine 3
NIVEN, William 1
NIVISON, Robert 6
NIX, James Thomas 5
NIXON, Brevard 1
NIXON, Charles Elston 4
NIXON, Eugene White 5
NIXON, George Felton 3
NIXON, George Stuart 1
NIXON, Howard Kenneth 4
NIXON, John * H
NIXON, John Thompson H
NIXON, Justin Wroe 1
NIXON, Lewis 1

NIXON, Oliver Woodson 1
NIXON, Pat Irland 4
NIXON, Paul 3
NIXON, Samuel F. 4
NIXON, Thomas Carlyle 5
NIXON, William C. 1
NIXON, William Penn 1
NIZA, Marcos de H
NKRUMAH, Kwame 5
NOA, Ernestine 5
NOAH, Mordecai Manuel H
NOAILLES, Louis Marie H
NOAKES, Edward Bruce 3
NOAKES, Frank LeRoy 5
NOBACK, Gustave J. 3
NOBILI, John H
NOBLE, Alfred 1
NOBLE, Annette Lucile 1
NOBLE, Charles 4
NOBLE, Charles C(asper) 5
NOBLE, Charles Franklin 1
NOBLE, Charles Henry 1
NOBLE, Charles P. 1
NOBLE, David Addison H
NOBLE, Edmund 1
NOBLE, Edward John 3
NOBLE, Eugene Allen 2
NOBLE, Frederick Alphonso 1
NOBLE, G. Kingsley 1
NOBLE, George Bernard 5
NOBLE, George Lawrence 4
NOBLE, Harold Joyce 3
NOBLE, Henry Smith 1
NOBLE, Howard Scott 4
NOBLE, James H
NOBLE, John 1
NOBLE, John 4
NOBLE, John Martin 1
NOBLE, John Willock 1
NOBLE, Marcus Cicero Stephens 2
NOBLE, Merrill Emmett 5
NOBLE, Nelle Sparks 6
NOBLE, Sir Percy Lockhart Harnam 3
NOBLE, Ralph Edward 5
NOBLE, Raymond Goodman 2
NOBLE, Robert Ernest 3
NOBLE, Robert Houston 1
NOBLE, Robert Peckham 5
NOBLE, Samuel H
NOBLE, Thomas Satterwhite H
NOBLE, Thomas Satterwhite 4
NOBLE, Thomas Tertius 3
NOBLE, Urbane Alexander 2
NOBLE, W. Clark 1
NOBLE, William Brown 1
NOBLE, William Henry H
NOBLE, William Lincoln 1
NOBLES, Milton 1
NOBLITT, Quintin G. 3
NOBS, Ernest 6
NOCE, Daniel 6
NOCK, Albert Jay 2
NOCK, Arthur Darby 4
NOE, Adolf Carl 1
NOE, James Thomas Cotton 4
NOE, Samuel VanArsdale 6
NOEGGERATH, Emil Oscar Jacob Bruno 1
NOEL, Cleo Allen Jr. 5
NOEL, Edmund Favor 1
NOEL, F. Regis 3
NOEL, James William 1
NOEL, Joseph Roberts 1
NOEL, Richard C. 3
NOELL, John William H
NOELL, Thomas Estes 2
NOELTE, Albert 3
NOEST, Jan Izaak 3
NOFER, Edward John 5
NOFFSINGER, Hugh Godwin
NOFFSINGER, John Samuel 4
NOGUCHI, Hideyo 1
NOLAN, Charles Paul 6
NOLAN, Dennis Edward 3
NOLAN, Edward James 3
NOLAN, James Bennett 4
NOLAN, Jeannette Covert 6 (Mrs. Val Nolan)
NOLAN, John Henry 3
NOLAN, John I. 3
NOLAN, John J. Jr. 1
NOLAN, Mae Ella 3
NOLAN, Philip H
NOLAN, Preston M. 1
NOLAN, Ralph Peter 6
NOLAN, Thomas 1
NOLAN, Val 6
NOLAN, William Ignatius 5

NOLAND, Edgar Smith 5
NOLAND, Iveson B. 6
NOLAND, Lloyd
NOLAND, Lowell E(van) 5
NOLAND, Stephen Croan 4
NOLAND, William 3
Churchill
NOLDE, Emil 4
NOLDE, O. Frederick 5
NOLEN, John 1
NOLEN, William Whiting 1
NOLI, Fan Stylian 4
NOLL, Arthur Howard 1
NOLL, Charles Franklin 3
NOLL, Edward Angus 3
August
NOLL, John Francis 3
NOLL, Raymond Rundell 6
NOLLEN, Gerard Scholte 4
NOLLEN, Henry Scholte 2
NOLLEN, John Scholte 3
NOLTE, Charles Beach 2
NOLTE, Fred Otto 4
NOLTE, Julius Mosher 4
NOLTE, Louis Gustavus 2
NOLTING, William 1
Greaner
NOMLAND, Ruben 3
NONES, Robert Hodgson 1
NOOE, Robert Sharpe 6
NOOE, Roger Theophilus 6
NOOJIN, Balpha Lonnie 3
NOON, Malik Firoz Khan 5
NOON, Paul A.T. 5
NOONAN, Edward J. 5
NOONAN, Edward T. 4
NOONAN, Greogory 4
Francis
NOONAN, Herbert C. 2
NOONAN, James Patrick H
NOONAN, James Patrick 4
NOONAN, John A. 4
NOONAN, Joseph Michael 3
NOONAN, Thomas Hazard 3
NOONAN, William T. 3
NORA, Joseph J. 5
NORBECK, Kermit George 3
NORBECK, Peter 3
NORBERG, Barbara Drew 6
Collins (Mrs. Nils Gunnar
Norberg)
NORBERG, Carl F. 5
NORBERG, Rudolph Carl 3
NORBLAD, Walter 4
NORBURY, Frank Parson 1
NORBY, Joseph Gerhard 4
NORCROSS, Bernard 6
Mallon
NORCROSS, Cleveland 2
NORCROSS, Frank Herbert 5
NORCROSS, George 1
NORCROSS, Grenville 1
Howland
NORCROSS, Orlando 1
Whitney
NORCROSS, Wilbur 1
Harrington
NORD, James Garesche 3
NORD, Walter Godfrey 5
NORDBERG, Bruno Victor 1
NORDBERG, Harry 1
Malcolm
NORDBY, Jorgen 3
NORDELL, Philip Augustus 1
NORDEN, Fred 5
Washington
NORDEN, N. Lindsay 5
NORDENHAUG, Josef 5
NORDFELDT, Bror Julius 3
Olsson
NORDHOFF, Charles 1
NORDHOFF, Charles 2
Bernard
NORDHOFF, Heinrich 5
NORDHOFF-JUNG, Sofie 1
Amalie
NORDICA, Lillian 1
NORDMARK, Godfrey 6
NORDSTROM, Lloyd 6
Walter
NORDSTROM, Sven Johan 3
NORELIUS, Eric 5
NORELL, Norman 5
NORFOLK, Duke of 6
NORGREN, Carl August 5
NORHEIMER, Isaac H
NORLIE, Olaf Morgan 4
NORLIN, George 2
NORMAN, Anne 5
NORMAN, Bradford Jr. 3
NORMAN, Carl Adolph 6
NORMAN, Edward A. 5
NORMAN, Fred 2
NORMAN, John H
NORMAN, Jonathan Van 3
Dyke

NORMAN, Mark Wilber 3
NORMAN, Montagu Collet 2
NORMAN, Robert Claude 1
NORMAN-WILCOX, 5
Gregor
NORMANDIN, Fortunal 4
Ernest
NORRELL, William F. 4
NORRIS, Benjamin White 4
NORRIS, Charles 1
NORRIS, Charles Camblos 5
NORRIS, Charles E. 1
NORRIS, Charles Gilman 2
NORRIS, Earle Bertram 5
NORRIS, Edgar Hughes 3
NORRIS, Edward H
NORRIS, Edwin Lee 1
NORRIS, Ernest Eden 1
NORRIS, Frank 1
NORRIS, Frank Callan 4
NORRIS, George H
Washington
NORRIS, George 3
Washington
NORRIS, George William * 1
NORRIS, Harry Waldo 2
NORRIS, Henry 1
NORRIS, Henry Hutchinson 1
NORRIS, Henry McCoy 1
NORRIS, Herbert T. 5
NORRIS, Homer Albert 1
NORRIS, Isaac * H
NORRIS, Isaac 4
NORRIS, James 3
NORRIS, James D. 4
NORRIS, James Flack 1
NORRIS, James Lawson 1
NORRIS, John Franklyn 3
NORRIS, Kathleen 4
NORRIS, Kenneth True 5
NORRIS, Lester J. Jr. 4
NORRIS, Mary Harriott 1
NORRIS, Moses Jr. H
NORRIS, Philip Ashton 2
NORRIS, Richard A. 6
NORRIS, Richard Cooper 2
NORRIS, Scott A. 4
NORRIS, True Livingston 1
NORRIS, Walter Blake 6
NORRIS, William 4
NORRIS, William 1
NORRIS, William Arthur Jr. 5
NORRIS, William Fisher 1
NORRIS, William Kibby 3
NORSWORTHY, Naomi 1
NORTH, Arthur A. 4
NORTH, Cecil Clare 4
NORTH, Charles Edward 4
NORTH, Charles H. 1
NORTH, Edward 1
NORTH, Elisha 1
NORTH, Emmett Pipkin 1
NORTH, Francis Reid 5
NORTH, Frank Joshua 1
NORTH, Frank Mason 1
NORTH, Harry B. 4
NORTH, Henry Emerson 4
NORTH, Isaac Franklin 4
NORTH, James Mortimer 3
NORTH, John Alden 5
NORTH, Ludlow Frey 4
NORTH, Orlando H
NORTH, Simeon * H
NORTH, Simon Newton 1
Dexter
NORTH, Solomon Taylor 4
NORTH, Sterling 6
NORTH, Walter Harper 3
NORTH, William 1
NORTHCOTE, Stafford 5
Mantle
NORTHCOTT, Elliott 2
NORTHCOTT, John A. Jr. 4
NORTHCOTT, William 1
Allen
NORTHCOTT, William 3
Newton
NORTHEN, Edwin Clyde 3
NORTHEN, William Ezra 1
NORTHEN, William 1
Jonathan
NORTHEND, Charles H
NORTHEND, Mary Harrod 1
NORTHEND, William 1
Dummer
NORTHINGTON, James 4
Montgomery
NORTHROP, Birdsey Grant H
NORTHROP, Cyrus 1
NORTHROP, David Ward 1
NORTHROP, Eugene 5
P(urdy)
NORTHROP, George 4
Norton
NORTHROP, Harry 1
Pinckney

NORTHROP, Henry 1
Davenport
NORTHROP, Herbert L. 1
NORTHROP, Lucius H
Bellinger
NORTHROP, Stephen 1
Abbott
NORTHRUP, Ansel Judd 1
NORTHRUP, Edwin Fitch 1
NORTHRUP, Elliott Judd 3
NORTHRUP, Frederic B. 4
NORTHRUP, George 1
Washington
NORTHRUP, William Perry 1
NORTHUP, Clark 4
Sutherland
NORTHUP, David 6
Wilmarth
NORTHUP, George Tyler 4
NORTHUP, John Eldridge 1
NORTHUP, William Guile 1
NORTON, Alice Peloubet 1
NORTON, Andrews H
NORTON, Arthur Brigham 1
NORTON, Arthur Henry 1
NORTON, A(rthur) Warren 5
NORTON, Charles Dyer 1
NORTON, Charles Eliot 1
NORTON, Charles 3
Hotchkiss
NORTON, Charles Ladd 1
NORTON, Charles Ledyard 1
NORTON, Charles Phelps 1
NORTON, Charles Stuart 1
NORTON, Daniel Field 3
NORTON, Daniel Sheldon H
NORTON, David Z. 1
NORTON, E. Hope 4
NORTON, Ebenezer Foote H
NORTON, Edith Eliza 1
Ames
NORTON, Edward Lee 4
NORTON, Edwin 1
NORTON, Edwin Clarence 2
NORTON, Eliot 1
NORTON, Eugene Levering 4
NORTON, Frederick Owen 1
NORTON, George Lowell 1
NORTON, George W. 1
NORTON, George 1
Washington
NORTON, Grace 1
NORTON, Grace Fallow 1
NORTON, Harold Percival 1
NORTON, Henry Kittredge 4
NORTON, Howard 1
Magruder
NORTON, J. Pease 3
NORTON, James 4
NORTON, James Albert 4
NORTON, Jesse Olds H
NORTON, John 1
NORTON, John Nathaniel 6
NORTON, John Nicholas 1
NORTON, John Pitkin H
NORTON, John Warner 1
NORTON, John William 6
Roy
NORTON, Laurence Harper 4
NORTON, Laurence J. 3
NORTON, Mary Teresa 3
NORTON, Miner Gibbs 4
NORTON, Nelson Ira 1
NORTON, Patrick Daniel 5
NORTON, Porter 1
NORTON, Ralph Hubbard 2
NORTON, Richard 1
NORTON, Robert Castle 4
NORTON, Roy 2
NORTON, Sidney Augustus 1
NORTON, Stephen Alison 1
NORTON, Thomas Herbert 2
NORTON, Wilbur H. 4
NORTON, William Bernard 1
NORTON, William Edward 1
NORTON, William Harmon 2
NORTON, William Warder 2
NORTONI, Albert Dexter 2
NORTONI, Albert Dexter 2
NORVAL, Theophilus 1
Lincoln
NORVELL, John H
NORVELL, Saunders 5
NORWICH, Viscount 3
NORWOOD, C. Augustus 1
NORWOOD, Charles 1
Joseph
NORWOOD, Edwin P. 1
NORWOOD, Elisabeth 6
Fessenden Gragg
NORWOOD, George 3
NORWOOD, John Nelson 4
NORWOOD, John Wilkins 2
NORWOOD, Maxwell C. 4
NORWOOD, Robert 1

NORWOOD, Thomas 1
Manson
NOSS, Theodore Bland 1
NOSTRAND, Peter Elbert 4
NOSWORTHY, Thomas 4
Arthur
NOTESTEIN, Jonas O. 1
NOTESTEIN, Wallace 5
NOTESTEIN, William Lee 1
NOTHSTEIN, Ira Oliver 5
NOTMAN, Arthur 4
NOTMAN, James Geoffrey 6
NOTMAN, John H
NOTNAGEL, Leland 3
Hascall
NOTOPOULOS, James A. 6
NOTT, Abraham H
NOTT, Charles Cooper 1
NOTT, Eliphalet 1
NOTT, Henry Junius H
NOTT, Josiah Clark H
NOTT, Otis Fessenden 1
NOTT, Samuel H
NOTT, Stanley Charles 3
NOTTER, Harley A. 3
NOTTINGHAM, Wayne B. 4
NOTTINGHAM, William 1
NOTZ, Frederick William 1
Augustus
NOTZ, William Frederick 2
NOURSE, Amos 1
NOURSE, Charles Joseph 6
NOURSE, Edward Everett 1
NOURSE, Edwin Griswold 5
NOURSE, Elizabeth 1
NOURSE, Henry Stedman 1
NOURSE, John Thomas Jr. 1
NOURSE, Joseph Pomeroy 1
NOVAK, Frank John Jr. 2
NOVAK, Ralph B(ernard) 5
NOVAK, Sonia 4
NOVARRO, Ramon (real 5
name Ramon Gil
Samaniego)
NOVELLO, Ivor 4
NOVER, Barnet 5
NOVOTNY, Antonin 5
NOVOTNY, Charles K. 4
NOVY, Frederick George 3
NOVY, Robert Lev 5
NOWELS, Trellyen Ernest 2
NOWLAN, George Clyde 4
NOWLIN, William Dudley 3
NOXON, Frank Wright 2
NOXON, Herbert Richards 5
NOYAN, Pierre-Jacques H
Payende
NOYES, Alexander Dana 2
NOYES, Alfred 3
NOYES, Arthur Amos 1
NOYES, Arthur P. 4
NOYES, C. Reinold 3
NOYES, Carleton 3
NOYES, Charles Floyd 4
NOYES, Charles Lothrop 1
NOYES, Charles Phelps 1
NOYES, Charles Rutherford 4
NOYES, Clara D. 1
NOYES, Crosby Stuart 1
NOYES, Daniel Rogers 1
NOYES, E. Louise 5
NOYES, Edward Allen 4
NOYES, Edward Follansbee H
NOYES, Edward 1
MacArthur
NOYES, Frank Brett 2
NOYES, Frank Eugene 1
NOYES, George Henry 1
NOYES, George Loftus 4
NOYES, George Rapail 1
NOYES, George Rapail H
NOYES, Guy Lincoln 1
NOYES, Harry Alfred 5
NOYES, Henry Drury 1
NOYES, Henry Erastus 1
NOYES, Irving George 4
NOYES, James Atkins 1
NOYES, Jansen 6
NOYES, John 1
NOYES, John Humphrey H
NOYES, John Rutherford 2
NOYES, Joseph Cobham 1
NOYES, La Verne W. 1
NOYES, Linwood Irving 4
NOYES, Marion Ingalls 5
NOYES, Morgan Phelps 5
NOYES, Newbold 2
NOYES, Pierrepont Burt 3
NOYES, Robert Gale 4
NOYES, Theodore Richards 1
NOYES, Theodore Williams 2
NOYES, Walter Chadwick 1
NOYES, William Albert 3
NOYES, William Curtis H
NUCKOLLS, Claiborne 6
George

NUCKOLLS, Stephen Friel H
NUELLE, Joseph Henry 4
NUELSEN, John Louis 2
NUESSLE, Francis E. 5
NUESSLE, William A. 3
NUFER, Albert F. 3
NUFFER, Joseph Henry 5
NUFFIELD, Viscount 4
NUGEN, Robert Hunter H
NUGENT, Daniel Cline 3
NUGENT, Frank Stanley 4
NUGENT, James Alexander 2
NUGENT, John F. 1
NUGENT, Paul Cook 1
NUGENT, Robert Logan 4
NUGENT, Thomas Joseph 3
NUGENT, Walter Henry 5
NUHN, Clifford Jeremiah 5
NUHN, John Alfred 1
NULSEN, Charles 3
Kilbourne
NULTON, Louis McCoy 1
NUNEMAKER, John 3
Horace
NUNEZ, Alvar Cabeza de H
Vaca
NUNLIST, Frank Joseph Jr. 6
NUNN, Clement Singleton 5
NUNN, Harold Francis 3
NUNN, Marshall 3
NUNN, Paul N. 1
NUNO, Jaime H
NUNO, Jaime 4
NUQUIST, Andrew 6
Edgerton
NURI AS-SAID 3
NURKSE, Ragnar 4
NURSE, Rebecca H
NUSE, Roy Cleveland 6
NUSSBAUM, Arthur 4
NUSSBAUM, Max 6
NUSSBAUM, Paul Joseph 1
NUTE, Alonzo H
NUTHEAD, William H
NUTT, Clifford Cameron 3
NUTT, Hubert Wilbur 5
NUTT, Joseph Randolph 2
NUTT, Robert Lee 2
NUTTALL, George Henry 1
Falkiner
NUTTALL, Leonard John 2
Jr.
NUTTALL, Thomas H
NUTTALL, Zelia 1
NUTTER, Donald Grant 4
NUTTER, Edmondson John 3
Masters
NUTTER, Edward Hoit 5
NUTTER, George Read 1
NUTTING, Charles 1
Cleveland
NUTTING, George Edward 4
NUTTING, Harold Judd 4
NUTTING, Herbert Chester 1
NUTTING, John Danforth 1
NUTTING, Margaret Ogden 5
NUTTING, Mary Adelaide 2
NUTTING, Mary Olivia 1
NUTTING, Newton Wright H
NUTTING, Perley Gilman 2
NUTTING, Wallace 1
NUTTLE, Harry (Hopkins) 5
NUTTMAN, Louis 1
Meredith
NUVEEN, John 2
NUVEEN, John 5
NUYTTENS, Pierre 3
NYBURG, Sidney Lauer 1
NYCE, Benjamin Markley 1
NYDEGGER, James 1
Archibald
NYDEN, John Augustus 1
NYE, Archibald 4
NYE, Edgar Hewitt 4
NYE, Edgar Wilson H
NYE, Frank E. 3
NYE, Frank Mellen 4
NYE, Gerald P. 5
NYE, Irene 4
NYE, James Warren 5
NYE, John Hooper 4
NYE, Reuben Lovell 4
NYE, Wallace George 4
NYE, Ward Higley 5
NYGAARD, Harlan 3
Kenneth
NYGAARD, Hjalmar C. 4
NYLANDER, Lennart 4
NYQUIST, Carl 3
NYQUIST, Edna Elvera 3
NYSTROM, Paul Henry 5
NYSTROM, Wendell 5
Clarence
NYSWANDER, Reuben 1
Edson Jr.

O

O'KELLY, James H
O'KELLY, Richard Mary 6
O'KELLY, Sean Thomas 4
OKEY, John Waterman H
OKIE, R. Brognard 2
OKKELBERG, Peter Olaus 6
OLANDER, Victor A. 2
O'LAUGHLIN, John Callan 2
OLAYA, Enrique 1
OLBRICH, Michael D. 1
OLCOTT, Ben Wilson 5
OLCOTT, Charles Sumner 1
OLCOTT, Chauncey 1
OLCOTT, Eben Erskine 1
OLCOTT, Frederic P. 1
OLCOTT, George N. 1
OLCOTT, Henry Steel 1
OLCOTT, Jacob Van Vechten 1
OLCOTT, Simeon H
OLCOTT, William James 4
OLCOTT, William Morrow Knox 1
OLCOTT, William Tyler 1
OLD, Francis Paxton 4
OLD, Howard Norman 3
OLD, William D. 4
OLDACRE, William Albert 6
OLDBERG, Arne 4
OLDBERG, Oscar 1
OLDEN, Charles Smith H
OLDER, Clifford 2
OLDER, Cora (Miranda) 5
OLDER, Fremont 1
OLDFATHER, William Abbott 2
OLDFIELD, William Allan 1
OLDHAM, G. Ashton 4
OLDHAM, John H
OLDHAM, Lemuel E. 5
OLDHAM, Robert Pollard 2
OLDHAM, William Fitzjames
OLDHAM, William K. 1
OLDHAM, Williamson Simpson H
OLDS, Edson Baldwin H
OLDS, Edwin Glenn 4
OLDS, George 4
OLDS, George Daniel 1
OLDS, Irving S. 4
OLDS, Leland 4
OLDS, Ransom Eli 3
OLDS, Robert 2
OLDS, Robert Edwin 1
OLDS, Walter 4
OLDSCHOOL, Oliver H
O'LEARY, Cornelius M. 1
O'LEARY, Daniel H
O'LEARY, Daniel 4
O'LEARY, Denis 4
O'LEARY, Edmund Bernard 4
O'LEARY, James A. 2
O'LEARY, James Lee 1
O'LEARY, John William 2
O'LEARY, Paul Arthur 1
O'LEARY, Thomas M. 2
O'LEARY, Wesley A. 1
O'LEARY, William Doris 1
OLEN, Walter A. 5
OLER, Wesley Marion 1
OLESHA, Yuri Karlovich 4
OLESON, John Prince 1
OLIN, Abram Baldwin H
OLIN, Arvin Solomon 1
OLIN, Franklin W. 3
OLIN, Gideon H
OLIN, Henry 1
OLIN, Hubert Leonard 4
OLIN, John Myers 1
OLIN, Richard M. 1
OLIN, Stephen H
OLIN, Stephen Henry 1
OLIN, Walter Herbert 1
OLIN, William Milo 1
OLINGER, Henri Cesar 4
OLINSKY, Ivan Gregorewitch
OLIPHANT, A. Dayton 4
OLIPHANT, Charles Lawrence 5
OLIPHANT, Ernest Henry Clark 1
OLIPHANT, Harold Duncan 5
OLIPHANT, Herman 1
OLITSKY, Peter Kosciusko 4
OLIVARES, Jose de 1
OLIVE, Edgar William 5
OLIVE, George Scott 4
OLIVE, John Ritter 6
OLIVER, Allen Laws 1
OLIVER, Andrew * H
OLIVER, Arthur L. 1
OLIVER, Augustus Kountze 3
OLIVER, Charles Augustus 1

OLIVER, Daniel Charles 1
OLIVER, Edna May 2
OLIVER, Edward Allen 1
OLIVER, Edwin Austin 1
OLIVER, Edwin Letts 3
OLIVER, Edwin Letts 4
OLIVER, Fitch Edward H
OLIVER, George Jeffries 6
OLIVER, George Sturges 4
OLIVER, George Tener 1
OLIVER, Grace Atkinson 1
OLIVER, Henry Kemble H
OLIVER, Henry Madison Jr. 5
OLIVER, Henry W. 1
OLIVER, James H
OLIVER, James Harrison 1
OLIVER, John Chadwick 4
OLIVER, John Rathbone 2
OLIVER, Joseph H
OLIVER, Joseph 4
OLIVER, Joseph Doty 1
OLIVER, L. Stauffer 4
OLIVER, Martha Capps 6
OLIVER, Paul Ambrose 1
OLIVER, Peter H
OLIVER, Robert Shaw 1
OLIVER, Thomas Edward 4
OLIVER, Webster J. 5
OLIVER, William Bacon 4
OLIVER, William Burns 6
OLIVER, William F(rederick) 5
OLIVER, William Morrison 4
OLIVETTI, Adriano 4
OLIVIER, Charles Pollard 6
OLIVIER, Stuart 4
OLLENHAUER, Erich 4
OLLESHEIMER, Henry 1
OLLMANN, Loyal Frank 4
OLMSTEAD, Albert Ten Eyck 2
OLMSTEAD, Frank Robert 3
OLMSTED, Charles Sanford 1
OLMSTED, Charles Tyler H
OLMSTED, Denison H
OLMSTED, E. Stanley 5
OLMSTED, Everett Ward 2
OLMSTED, Frederick Law 4
OLMSTED, Frederick Law 3
OLMSTED, George Welch 4
OLMSTED, Gideon H
OLMSTED, James Frederic 1
OLMSTED, James Greeley 3
OLMSTED, James Montrose Duncan 1
OLMSTED, John Bartow 4
OLMSTED, John Charles 1
OLMSTED, Marlin Edgar 1
OLMSTED, Millicent 1
OLMSTED, Victor Hugo 1
OLMSTED, William Beach 1
OLNEY, Albert J. 3
OLNEY, George W. 1
OLNEY, Jesse H
OLNEY, Louis Atwell 4
OLNEY, Peter Butler 1
OLNEY, Richard * 1
OLNEY, Warren 1
OLNEY, Warren Jr. 1
O'LOUGHLIN, John M(artin) 5
OLP, Ernest Everett 1
OLRICH, Ernest Louis 4
OLSEN, Clarence Edward 4
OLSEN, Herb 6
OLSEN, Herluf Vagn 4
OLSEN, Ingerval M. 4
OLSEN, John Charles 2
OLSEN, Julius 1
OLSEN, Leif Ericson 4
OLSEN, Nils Andreas 1
OLSEN, Thomas Siegfried 3
OLSEN, William Anderson 6
OLSON, Axel Ragnar 4
OLSON, Carl Walter 1
OLSON, Charles 5
OLSON, Culbert 1
OLSON, Edwin August 2
OLSON, Ernst William 3
OLSON, Floyd Bjerstjerne 2
OLSON, George Edgar 4
OLSON, Grant Franklin 4
OLSON, H. Edwin 4
OLSON, Harry 4
OLSON, Henry 4
OLSON, James Edward 5
OLSON, John Frederick 5
OLSON, Julius Emil 1
OLSON, Julius Johann 5
OLSON, Kenneth Eugene 4
OLSON, Norman O. 4
OLSON, Oscar Ludvig 3
OLSON, Oscar Thomas 4
OLSON, Oscar William 3
OLSON, Ralph J. 5

OLSON, Ralph O. 3
OLSON, Raymond 6
OLSON, Raymond Ferdinand 4
OLSON, Roy Howard 6
OLSSEN, William Whittingham 4
OLSSON, Alexander 3
OLSSON, Elis 3
OLSSON, Olof 1
OLSTON, Albert B. 4
OLT, George Russell 3
OLYPHANT, David Washington Cincinnatus H
OLYPHANT, John Kensett Jr. 6
OLYPHANT, Robert 1
OLYPHANT, Robert Morrison 1
O'MAHONEY, Joseph Christopher 4
O'MAHONEY, Joseph Michael 4
O'MAHONY, John H
O'MALLEY, Austin 1
O'MALLEY, Charles P. 5
O'MALLEY, Francis Joseph 6
O'MALLEY, Frank Ward 1
O'MALLEY, Henry 1
O'Malley, John Francis 1
O'MALLEY, Joseph Edward 6
O'MALLEY, Thomas F. 5
OMAN, Charles Malden 2
OMAN, Joseph Wallace 1
OMAR 1
O'MEALIA, E. Leo 4
O'MEARA, Mark 1
O'MEARA, Stephen 1
O'MELVENY, Henry William 1
OMWAKE, George L. 1
OMWAKE, Howard Rufus 2
OMWAKE, John 1
ONAHAN, William James 1
ONAN, David Warren 3
ONASSIS, Aristotle Socrates 6
ONATE, Juan de H
ONDERDONK, Adrian Holmes 5
ONDERDONK, Benjamin Tredwell H
ONDERDONK, Frank Scovill 1
ONDERDONK, Gilbert 4
ONDERDONK, Henry H
ONDERDONK, Henry Ustick H
ONDRAK, Ambrose Leo 4
O'NEAL, Charles Thomas 4
O'NEAL, Claude E(dgar) 5
O'NEAL, Edward Asbury III 3
O'NEAL, Edward Ashbury H
O'NEAL, Emmet 1
O'NEAL, Emmet 4
O'NEAL, Samuel Amos 1
O'NEAL, William Russell 2
O'NEALE, Margaret 1
O'NEALL, John Belton H
O'NEIL, Charles 1
O'NEIL, Frank R. 1
O'NEIL, George F. 5
O'NEIL, Hugh Roe 2
O'NEIL, James 1
O'NEIL, James Julian 4
O'NEIL, John Francis 1
O'NEIL, Joseph Henry 1
O'NEIL, Lew Drew 6
O'NEIL, Patrick Henry 1
O'NEIL, Ralph Thomas 1
O'NEIL, William Francis 4
O'NEILL, Albert T. 3
O'NEILL, Burke 4
O'NEILL, Charles 1
O'NEILL, Charles H
O'NEILL, Charles 2
O'NEILL, Charles Austin 1
O'NEILL, Edmond 1
O'NEILL, Edward Emerson 2
O'NEILL, Edward L. 2
O'NEILL, Eugene Gladstone 3
O'NEILL, Eugene M. 1
O'NEILL, Florence 4
O'NEILL, Frank J. 5
O'NEILL, Harry P. 3
O'NEILL, Hugh 1
O'NEILL, J. Henry 4
O'NEILL, J. Vincent 4
O'NEILL, James Albert 6
O'NEILL, James Lewis 1
O'NEILL, James Milton 5
O'NEILL, John H
O'NEILL, John Edward 4
O'NEILL, John J. 3

O'NEILL, Lewis Patrick 5
ONKEN, William Henry Jr. 5
OOMS, Casper W. 4
OOSTERMEYER, Jan 4
OOSTING, Henry J. 5
OPDYCKE, John Baker 3
OPDYCKE, Leonard Eckstein 1
OPDYKE, George H
OPDYKE, William Stryker 1
OPERTI, Albert 1
OPHEIM, Leonard Bertinius 5
OPHULS, William 1
OPIE, Eugene Lindsay 5
OPIE, Thomas 4
OPP, Julie 1
OPPELT, Wolfgang Walter 6
OPPENHEIM, Adolf Leo 6
OPPENHEIM, Amy Schwartz 1
OPPENHEIM, Ansel 1
OPPENHEIM, Edward Phillips 2
OPPENHEIM, James 1
OPPENHEIM, Nathan 1
OPPENHEIM, Samuel 1
OPPENHEIMER, Sir Ernest 3
OPPENHEIMER, Francis J. 6
OPPENHEIMER, Fritz Ernest 5
OPPENHEIMER, Robert 4
OPPER, Clarence Victor 4
OPPER, Frederick Burr 1
OPPICE, Harold Whinery 6
OPTIC, Oliver H
ORAHOOD, Harper M. 1
ORBISON, Thomas James 1
ORCHARD, John Ewing 4
ORCUTT, Calvin B. 1
ORCUTT, Hiram 1
ORCUTT, William Dana 3
ORCUTT, William Warren 2
ORD, Edward Otho Cresap H
ORD, George H
ORDAL, Ola Johannessen 1
ORDAL, Zakarias J. 3
ORDEAN, Albert Le Grand 1
ORDONEZ, Castor 1
ORDRONAUX, John 1
ORDWAY, Edward Warren 4
ORDWAY, J. G. 4
ORDWAY, John 1
ORDWAY, John Morse 1
ORDWAY, Samuel Hanson 1
ORDWAY, Samuel Hanson 5
ORDWAY, Thomas 5
ORE, Oystein 5
O'REAR, Edward Clay 5
O'REAR, John Davis 1
O'REGAN, Anthony H
O'REILLY, Alexander H
O'REILLY, Andrew John Goldsmith 2
O'REILLY, Bernard 1
O'REILLY, Bernard Patrick 1
O'REILLY, Charles J. 1
O'REILLY, Edward Synnott 6
O'REILLY, Gabriel 5
O'REILLY, Henry 1
O'REILLY, James 1
O'REILLY, James Thomas 4
O'REILLY, John Boyle 1
O'REILLY, Mary Boyle 1
O'REILLY, Peter J. 4
O'REILLY, Robert Maitland 1
O'REILLY, Thomas Charles 1
ORENDORFF, Alfred 1
ORLADY, George Boal 1
ORMAN, James Bradley 4
ORME, James Booth Lockwood 6
ORME, John Pinckney 1
ORMOND, Alexander Thomas 1
ORMOND, Jesse Marvin 4
ORMSBEE, Ebenezer Jolls 1
ORMSBEE, Thomas Hamilton 5
ORMSBY, Oliver Samuel 3
ORMSBY, Stephen 1
ORMSBY, Waterman Lilly H
ORMSTON, Mark D. 4
ORNDOFF, Benjamin Harry 5
ORNDORFF, William Ridgely 1
ORNDUFF, William Wilmer 1
ORNE, Caroline Frances 5
ORNE, John 1
ORNER, Irvin Melvin 4
ORNITZ, Samuel 3
O'ROURKE, Charles Edward 1

O'ROURKE, Fidelis (Arthur J.) 5
O'ROURKE, John Thomas 2
O'ROURKE, Lawrence James 4
O'ROURKE, Patrick Ira 2
O'ROURKE, William Thomas 3
OROZCO, Jose Clemente 4
ORR, Alexander Dalrymple H
ORR, Alexander Ector 1
ORR, Benjamin H
ORR, Carey 4
ORR, Charles 4
ORR, Charles Prentiss 1
ORR, Douglas William 5
ORR, Flora Gracia 3
ORR, George 1
ORR, Gustavus John H
ORR, H. Winnett 3
ORR, Hugh H
ORR, Isaac Henry 3
ORR, James Lawrence H
ORR, James Lawrence 1
ORR, James Washington 1
ORR, John Alvin 3
ORR, John Boyd (Lord Boyd of Brechin) 5
ORR, John William H
ORR, Joseph Kyle 1
ORR, Louis 4
ORR, Louis McDonald 4
ORR, Louis Thomas 5
ORR, Robert H
ORR, Robert Jr. H
ORR, Robert Hall 1
ORR, Robert McDaniel 6
ORR, Robert William 4
ORR, Robert Williamson 3
ORR, Thomas E. 4
ORR, Thomas Grover 3
ORR, Thomas L. 4
ORR, Walter Stuart 4
ORR, Warren Henry 4
ORR, William 1
ORR, William Anderson 3
ORRIS, S. Stanhope 1
ORROK, Douglas Hall 6
ORROK, George Alexander 2
ORRY-KELLY 4
ORT, Samuel Alfred 1
ORTEGA Y GASSET, Jose 3
ORTEGA Y GASSET, Jose 1
ORTEIG, Raymond 1
ORTH, Bertrand 1
ORTH, Charles J. 4
ORTH, Godlove Stein H
ORTH, John 1
ORTH, Lizette Emma 1
ORTH, O. Sidney 4
ORTH, Samuel Peter 1
ORTHWEIN, Charles F. H
ORTHWEIN, Percy James 3
ORTHWINE, Rudolf Adolf 5
ORTLOFF, Henry Stuart 4
ORTMANN, Arnold Edward 1
ORTON, Clayton Roberts 4
ORTON, Dwayne 5
ORTON, Edward 1
ORTON, Edward Jr. 1
ORTON, Harlow South 1
ORTON, Helen Fuller 4
ORTON, James H
ORTON, Samuel Torrey 1
ORTON, William H
ORTON, William Allen 1
ORTON, William Aylott 4
ORVILLE, Howard T. 4
ORVIS, Ellis Lewis 1
ORWELL, George 4
ORY, Edward Kid 5
O'RYAN, John F. 4
O'RYAN, William Francis 4
OSBON, Bradley Sillick 1
OSBORN, Abraham Coles 1
OSBORN, Albert Dunbar 5
OSBORN, Albert Sherman 2
OSBORN, Alexander Faickney 4
OSBORN, Alexander Perry 3
OSBORN, Charles H
OSBORN, Chase Salmon 2
OSBORN, Cyrus Richard 4
OSBORN, Edwin Faxon 1
OSBORN, Erastus William 4
OSBORN, Eugene Ernest 1
OSBORN, Fairfield 5
OSBORN, Frank Chittenden 1
OSBORN, Frederick Arthur 2
OSBORN, George Augustus 1
OSBORN, H. Fairfield 1
OSBORN, Henry Chisholm 1
OSBORN, Henry Leslie 1
OSBORN, Henry Stafford 1
OSBORN, Herbert 3

OSBORN, Hervey James 4
OSBORN, Laughton H
OSBORN, Loran David 3
OSBORN, Luther W. 1
OSBORN, Marvin Griffing 3
OSBORN, Merritt J. 3
OSBORN, Monroe 2
OSBORN, Norris Galpin 1
OSBORN, Selleck H
OSBORN, Sidney Preston 2
OSBORN, Stewart Patrick 4
OSBORN, Thomas Andrew H
OSBORN, Thomas Ogden 1
OSBORN, William Church 3
OSBORN, William H. 4
OSBORN, William Henry 4
OSBORNE, Antrim Edgar 1
OSBORNE, Arthur Dimon 1
OSBORNE, Charles Devens 4
OSBORNE, Duffield 1
OSBORNE, Earl Dorland 4
OSBORNE, Edward William 1
OSBORNE, Edwin Sylvanus 1
OSBORNE, Ernest G. 4
OSBORNE, Ernest Leslie 6
OSBORNE, Frank Wellman 6
OSBORNE, George Abbott 1
OSBORNE, Henry Zenas 1
OSBORNE, James Insley 3
OSBORNE, James Van Wyck 1
OSBORNE, John H
OSBORNE, John Ball 5
OSBORNE, John E. 4
OSBORNE, John Stuart 4
OSBORNE, Loyall Allen 2
OSBORNE, Margherita Osborn 6
OSBORNE, Milton Smith 5
OSBORNE, Oliver Thomas 4
OSBORNE, Reginald Stanley 5
OSBORNE, Thomas Burr H
OSBORNE, Thomas Burr 1
OSBORNE, Thomas Mott 1
OSBORNE, William Hamilton 2
OSBORNE, William McKinley 1
OSBORN-HANNAH, Jane 3
OSBOURN, Samuel Edmund 5
OSBOURNE, Alfred Slack 4
OSBOURNE, Lloyd 1
OSBURN, Worth James 3
OSCAR, Stephen A. 3
OSCEOLA H
OSENBAUGH, Charles Merril 1
OSEROFF, Abraham 4
OSGOOD, Alfred Townsend 3
OSGOOD, Charles Grosvenor 4
OSGOOD, Edwin Eugene 5
OSGOOD, Ellis Carlton 5
OSGOOD, Etta Haley 2
OSGOOD, Farley 1
OSGOOD, Frances Sargent Locke H
OSGOOD, Gayton Pickman H
OSGOOD, George Laurie 4
OSGOOD, Henry Brown 1
OSGOOD, Henry Osborne 4
OSGOOD, Herbert Levi 1
OSGOOD, Howard 1
OSGOOD, Irene 2
OSGOOD, Jacob H
OSGOOD, John Cleveland 1
OSGOOD, Phillips Endecott 3
OSGOOD, Robert Bayley 3
OSGOOD, Robert William 6
OSGOOD, Roy Clifton 3
OSGOOD, Samuel H
OSGOOD, Samuel Maurice 6
OSGOOD, Samuel Stillman 1
OSGOOD, Samuel Walter H
OSGOOD, Wilfred Hudson 2
OSGOOD, Willard Sumner 1
OSGOOD, William Fogg 2
O'SHAUGHNESSY, Edith Coues 1
O'SHAUGHNESSY, Elim 1
O'SHAUGHNESSY, Ignatius Aloysius 6
O'SHAUGHNESSY, John K. 3
O'SHAUGHNESSY, M. M. 1
O'SHAUNESSY, Nelson 1
O'SHAUNESSY, George Francis 1
O'SHEA, Benjamin 3
O'SHEA, John Augustine 3
O'SHEA, John J. 1
O'SHEA, Michael Vincent 1
O'SHEA, William James 3
O'SHEA, William Joseph 3

OSK, Roselle H. 3
OSKISON, John Milton 5
OSLAND, Birger 4
OSLER, William 1
OSMENA, Sergio 4
OSMOND, I. Thornton 1
OSMUN, A. Vincent 3
OSMUN, Russell A. 3
OSMUN, Thomas Embley 3
OSORIO, Oscar 5
OSORIO LIZARAZO, Jose Antonio 4
OSSERMAN, Kermit Edward 6
OSTENACO H
OSTENSO, Martha 4
OSTER, Henry Richard 2
OSTERBERG, Max 1
OSTERHAUS, Hugo 1
OSTERHAUS, Hugo Wilson 6
OSTERHAUS, Peter Joseph 1
OSTERHOLM, Martin John Vanleuven 1
OSTERHOUT, Winthrop 4
OSTERTAG, Blanche 5
OSTHAGEN, Clarence Hilmann 6
OSTHAUS, Carl Wilhelm Ferdinand 4
OSTHAUS, Edmund 1
OSTRAND, James Adolph 1
OSTRANDER, Dempster 1
OSTRANDER, Don Richard 5
OSTRANDER, Fannie Eliza 1
OSTRANDER, Isabel 1
OSTRANDER, John Edwin 1
OSTRANDER, Lee H. 6
OSTRANDER, Russell Cowles 1
OSTROLENK, Bernhard 2
OSTROM, Henry 1
OSTROM, Kurre Wilhelm 4
OSTROMISLENSKY, Iwan Iwanowich H
OSTROMISLENSKY, Iwan Iwanowich 4
OSTROWSKY, Abbo 6
O'SULLIVAN, Curtis D. 2
O'SULLIVAN, Frank 2
O'SULLIVAN, Jeremiah 1
O'SULLIVAN, John Louis H
O'SULLIVAN, Vincent 1
OSUNA, Juan Jose 3
OSWALD, Felix Leopold 1
OSWALD, John Clyde 5
OTERMEN, Antonio de H
OTERO, Miguel Antonio H
OTERO, Miguel Antonio 2
OTEY, Ernest Glenwood 4
OTEY, James Hervey H
OTEY, Peter Johnston 1
OTHMAN, Frederick C. 5
OTIS, Alphonse Elmer Spencer 4
OTIS, Arthur Sinton 4
OTIS, Ashton M. 6
OTIS, Bass H
OTIS, Charles 1
OTIS, Edward Osgood 1
OTIS, Elisha Graves H
OTIS, Elwell Stephen 1
OTIS, George Alexander H
OTIS, Harold 3
OTIS, Harrison Gray H
OTIS, Harrison Gray 1
OTIS, James H
OTIS, John 1
OTIS, Joseph Edward 3
OTIS, Joseph Edward 4
OTIS, Merrill E. 2
OTIS, Norton P. 1
OTIS, Philo Adams 1
OTIS, Samuel Allyne H
OTIS, Spencer 4
OTIS, William Augustus 1
OTIS, William Kelly 1
OTJEN, Theobald 1
OTJEN, William John 6
O'TOOLE, Donald Lawrence 4
O'TOOLE, William Joseph 1
OTSUKA, Raymond M. 5
OTT, Edward Amherst 4
OTT, Emil 4
OTT, George 1
OTT, Harvey Newton 1
OTT, Isaac 1
OTT, William Pinkerton 2
OTTAWAY, Elmer James 1
OTTE, Hugo Emil 2
OTTE, Louis Edward 3
OTTEMILLER, John H(enry) 5
OTTENDORFER, Anna Behr Uhl H

OTTENDORFER, Oswald 1
OTTER, John M. 4
OTTER, Thomas H
OTTERBEIN, H. C. 3
OTTERBEIN, Philip William H
OTTERBOURG, Edwin M. 4
OTTERSON, John Edward 4
OTTING, Bernard John 3
OTTING, Leonard Henry 3
OTTINGER, Albert 1
OTTINGER, Lawrence 3
OTTINGER, Simon 6
OTTLEY, John King 2
OTTLEY, Passie Fenton 4
OTTLEY, Roi 4
OTTMAN, Ford Cyrinde 1
OTTMANN, William 3
OTTO, Benjamin 2
OTTO, Bodo H
OTTO, Eberhard 6
OTTO, Henry J. 6
OTTO, John Conrad H
OTTO, Max Carl 5
OTTOERBOURG, Edwin M.
OTTOFY, Ladialaus Michael 2
OTTOFY, Louis 5
OTTS, John Martin Philip 1
OUCHTERLONEY, James Delgarens 4
OUCHTERLONY, John Arvid 1
OUDIN, Maurice Agnus 1
OUGHTERSON, Ashley W. 3
OUKRAINSKY, Serge (Léonide de Carva) 6
OULAHAN, Richard Victor 1
OURAY H
OURSLER, Fulton 3
OURSLER, Grace Perkins 3
OURY, Granville Henderson H
OUSDAL, Ashjorn Pedersen 6
OUSLEY, Clarence 2
OUTACITY H
OUTCAULT, Richard Felton 1
OUTERBRIDGE, Albert Albouy 1
OUTERBRIDGE, Alexander Ewing Jr.
OUTERBRIDGE, Eugene Harvey 1
OUTHWAITE, Joseph H. 1
OVENSHINE, Alexander Thompson 5
OVENSHINE, Samuel 1
OVERALL, John Wesley 1
OVERBECK, Reynolds Covel 5
OVERBY, Oscar Rudolph 4
OVERESCH, Harvey E. 5
OVERFIELD, Chauncey Percival 5
OVERFIELD, Peter D. 5
OVERHOLSER, Earle Long 2
OVERHOLSER, Edward 1
OVERHOLSER, Winfred 4
OVERMAN, Frederick H
OVERMAN, Lee Slater 1
OVERPECK, Areli Charles 6
OVERS, Walter Henry 1
OVERSTREET, Alan Burr 6
OVERSTREET, Harry Allen 5
OVERSTREET, James H
OVERSTREET, James Whetstone 4
OVERSTREET, Jesse 1
OVERSTREET, Lee-Carl 3
OVERTON, Daniel Hawkins 1
OVERTON, Eugene 6
OVERTON, Frank 3
OVERTON, Grant 1
OVERTON, Gwendolen 5
OVERTON, James Bertram 1
OVERTON, John H
OVERTON, John Holmes 2
OVERTON, Paul 6
OVERTON, Walter Hampden H
OVERTON, Watkins 3
OVERTON, Winston 3
OVIATT, Delmar Thomas 4
OVINGTON, Earle 1
OVINGTON, Irene Helen 1
OVINGTON, Mary White 4
OWEN, Allen Ferdinand 1
OWEN, Allison 4
OWEN, Arthur David Kemp 3
OWEN, Carl Maynard 1
OWEN, Charles Archibald 3
OWEN, Charles Sumner 2
OWEN, Clifford H. 6

OWEN, D. T. 2
OWEN, David Blair 4
OWEN, David Dale H
OWEN, David Edward 4
OWEN, David Edward 5
OWEN, Edward 1
OWEN, Emmett Marshall 1
OWEN, Fred K. 2
OWEN, George Hodges 6
OWEN, George Washington H
OWEN, Griffith H
OWEN, James H
OWEN, James 3
OWEN, John H
OWEN, John Paul 3
OWEN, John S. 1
OWEN, John Wilson 2
OWEN, Kenneth Marvin 4
OWEN, L. F. 3
OWEN, Mary Alicia 1
OWEN, Robert H
OWEN, Robert Dale H
OWEN, Robert Latham 2
OWEN, Russell 3
OWEN, Stephen Walker 5
OWEN, Stewart Douglas 5
OWEN, Thomas Henry 1
OWEN, Thomas McAdory 1
OWEN, Walter Cecil 1
OWEN, Walter Edwin 6
OWEN, Wesley M. 1
OWEN, William Baxter 1
OWEN, William Bishop 1
OWEN, William Frazer 1
OWEN, William Otway 1
OWEN, William Russell 1
OWENS, Frederick William 4
OWENS, George Welshman H
OWENS, Grover Thomas 3
OWENS, Hamilton 2
OWENS, James Francis 2
OWENS, John Edmond H
OWENS, John Edwin 1
OWENS, John Whitefield 5
OWENS, Leo Edward 6
OWENS, Madison Townsend 1
OWENS, Michael Joseph 1
OWENS, Ray L. 3
OWENS, Robert Bowie 1
OWENS, Thomas Leonard 2
OWENS, Walter D. 3
OWLETT, Gilbert Mason 3
OWRE, Alfred 1
OWSLEY, Alvin Mansfield 4
OWSLEY, Bryan Young H
OWSLEY, Charles Frederick 6
OWSLEY, Frank Lawrence 3
OWSLEY, William 1
OWST, Wilberfoss George 1
OXNAM, G. Bromley 4
OXNAM, Robert Fisher 6
OXNARD, Benjamin Alexander 1
OXNARD, Henry Thomas 1
OXNARD, Robert 1
OXNARD, Thomas 4
OXNER, George Dewey 4
OXTOBY, Frederic Breading 1
OXTOBY, Walter Ewing 1
OXTOBY, William Henry 1
OYEN, Henry 1
OYEN, Valborg Hansine (Mrs. Arnt J. Oyen) 5
OYSTER, James F. 1
OZBIRN, Mrs. E. Lee (Katie Freeman Ozbirn) 6
OZENFANT, Amedee-Jullen 4
OZLIN, Thomas William 2
OZMUN, Edward Henry 1

P

PAASIKIVI, Juho Kusti 5
PABST, Charles Frederick 5
PABST, Fred 3
PABST, Frederick 1
PACA, William H
PACE, Charles Nelson 4
PACE, Edward Aloysius 1
PACE, Frank 5
PACE, Homer St Clair 2
PACE, Jerome Grant 1
PACE, Julian Harrison 1
PACE, Leo L. 4
PACE, Mary Anna 1
PACE, Pearl Carter (Mrs. Stanley D. Pace) 5
PACE, Thomas A(ndrew) 5
PACENT, Louis Gerard 4
PACEY, William Cyril Desmond 6
PACH, Walter 3

PACHELBEL, Carl Theodorus H
PACHLER, William Joseph 5
PACHMANN, Vladimir de 1
PACHUCKI, Adolf Kasimer 6
PACK, Charles Lathrop 1
PACK, Frederick James 1
PACK, George Willis 4
PACK, Randolph Greene 3
PACK, Robert Francis 4
PACK, Robert Wallace 4
PACKARD, Alpheus Spring H
PACKARD, Alpheus Spring 1
PACKARD, Alton 1
PACKARD, Arthur Joseph 6
PACKARD, Arthur Worthington 3
PACKARD, Bertram E. 2
PACKARD, Burdett Aden 1
PACKARD, Charles Stuart Wood 1
PACKARD, Francis Randolph 3
PACKARD, Frank Edward 2
PACKARD, Frank Lucius 4
PACKARD, Frederick Adolphus H
PACKARD, George 2
PACKARD, George Arthur 5
PACKARD, George Byron 1
PACKARD, George Randolph 1
PACKARD, Horace 1
PACKARD, James Ward 1
PACKARD, Jasper 1
PACKARD, John Hooker 1
PACKARD, Joseph * 1
PACKARD, Laurence Bradford 1
PACKARD, Lewis Richard H
PACKARD, Ralph Gooding 4
PACKARD, Silas Sadler 1
PACKARD, Walter E. 4
PACKARD, William Alfred 1
PACKARD, Winthrop 2
PACKER, Asa H
PACKER, (Douglas) Frank (Hewson) 6
PACKER, Francis Herman 3
PACKER, Fred Little 3
PACKER, Herbert Leslie 5
PACKER, Horace Billings 3
PACKER, John Black H
PACKER, William Fisher H
PACKMAN, James Joseph 5
PADDLEFORD, Clementine Haskin 4
PADDOCK, Algernon Sidney H
PADDOCK, Benjamin Henry H
PADDOCK, Buckley B. 1
PADDOCK, Charles William 1
PADDOCK, George Arthur 4
PADDOCK, Hiram Lester 2
PADDOCK, John Adams H
PADDOCK, Lucius Carver 1
PADDOCK, Miner Hamlin 4
PADDOCK, R. B. 3
PADDOCK, Robert Lewis 1
PADDOCK, Wendell 3
PADDOCK, Willard Dryden 3
PADDOCK, Willard Dryden 2
PADELFORD, Frank William 1
PADELFORD, Frederick Morgan 2
PADELFORD, Silas Catching 5
PADEN, William Mitchel 4
PADEREWSKI, Ignace Jan 1
PADGETT, Dora Adele 6
PADGETT, Earl C. 2
PADGETT, Lemuel Phillips 1
PADGETT, Lemuel Phillips Jr. 4
PADILLA, Ezequiel 5
PADILLA, Juan de H
PADWAY, Joseph Arthur 2
PAEPCKE, Walter Paul 3
PAEPCKE, Walter Paul 4
PAETOW, Louis John 2
PAGAN, Bolivar 6
PAGAN, Oliver Elwood 6
PAGE, Alfred Rider 1
PAGE, Arthur Clinton 3
PAGE, Arthur Wilson 4
PAGE, Bertrand A. 1
PAGE, Calvin 1
PAGE, Carroll Smalley H
PAGE, Charles * 1
PAGE, Charles Grafton H
PAGE, Charles Randolph 6
PAGE, Curtis Hidden 2
PAGE, David Perkins H

PAGE, Earl Dexter 4
PAGE, Edward Day 1
PAGE, Elizabeth Fry 5
PAGE, Elwin Lawrence 5
PAGE, Frank Copeland 3
PAGE, Frederick Harlan 5
PAGE, George Bispham 2
PAGE, George T.
PAGE, Henry 1
PAGE, Herman 2
PAGE, Horace Francis H
PAGE, James 4
PAGE, James Morris 1
PAGE, James Rathwell 4
PAGE, John * H
PAGE, John Chatfield 3
PAGE, John Henry 1
PAGE, John Randolph 4
PAGE, Kirby 3
PAGE, Leigh 3
PAGE, Lewis Coues 5
PAGE, Logan Waller 4
PAGE, Mann * H
PAGE, Marie Danforth 1
PAGE, Nathaniel Clifford 4
PAGE, Ralph Walter 2
PAGE, Ralph Walter 5
PAGE, Richard Gregory 3
PAGE, Richard Lucian 5
PAGE, Robert H
PAGE, Robert G(uthrie) 4
PAGE, Robert M. 5
PAGE, Robert Newton 1
PAGE, Robert Powel Jr. 2
PAGE, Roger McKeene 2
PAGE, S. Davis 4
PAGE, Sherman H
PAGE, Thomas Jefferson 5
PAGE, Thomas Nelson 1
PAGE, Thomas Walker 1
PAGE, Walter Gilman 1
PAGE, Walter Hines 1
PAGE, William H
PAGE, William Herbert 3
PAGE, William Nelson 5
PAGE, William Tyler 2
PAGET, Lowell 4
PAGNOL, Marcel Paul 6
PAHLOW, Edwin William 2
PAHLOW, Gertrude Curtis 1
Brown
PAIGE, Calvin D. 1
PAIGE, Clifford E. 3
PAIGE, Del R. 4
PAIGE, Hildegard Brooks 4
PAIGE, Raymond North 4
PAIGE, Robert Myron 4
PAIGE, Sidney 6
PAIN, Philip H
PAINE, Albert Bigelow 1
PAINE, Albert Ware 1
PAINE, Bayard Henry 3
PAINE, Bryon 1
PAINE, Charles H
PAINE, Charles 1
PAINE, Charles Jackson 1
PAINE, Charles Leslie 5
PAINE, Clara Audrea (Mrs. 5
Clarence Summer Paine)
PAINE, Elijah H
PAINE, Ellery Burton 5
PAINE, Ephraim 1
PAINE, Francis Brinley 1
Hebard
PAINE, Francis Ward 1
PAINE, George Eustis 5
PAINE, George H. 3
PAINE, George Porter 6
PAINE, Gregory Lansing 1
PAINE, Halbert Eleazer 1
PAINE, Harlan Lloyd 5
PAINE, Harriet Eliza 1
PAINE, Henry Gallup 1
PAINE, Henry Warren H
PAINE, Horace Marshfield 1
PAINE, Howard Simmons 3
PAINE, Hugh E. 5
PAINE, James Lawrence 1
PAINE, John Alsop 1
PAINE, John Gregg 2
PAINE, John Knowles 1
PAINE, Karl 5
PAINE, Martyn H
PAINE, Nathaniel H
PAINE, Nathaniel Emmons 2
PAINE, Paul Mayo 3
PAINE, Ralph Delahaye 1
PAINE, Robert H
PAINE, Robert Findlay H
PAINE, Robert Treat * H
PAINE, Robert Treat 1
PAINE, Robert Treat 4
PAINE, Robert Treat II 2
PAINE, Roger W. 4
PAINE, Roland D. 5
PAINE, Rowlett 6

PAINE, Thomas H
PAINE, William Alfred 1
PAINE, William Wiseham H
PAINE, Willis Seaver 1
PAINTER, Carl Wesley 5
PAINTER, Charles Fairbank 1
PAINTER, Franklin 1
Verzelius Newton
PAINTER, Gamaliel H
PAINTER, George 4
Alexander Stephen
PAINTER, Henry 1
McMahan
PAINTER, Russell Floyd 5
PAINTER, Sidney 3
PAINTER, Theophilus 5
Shickel
PAINTER, William H
PAINTER, William 4
PAIST, Theresa Wilbur 6
PALACHE, Charles 3
PALACIOS, Alfredo L. 6
PALAMAR, Michael 5
PALEN, Frederick Pomeroy 1
PALEN, Rufus 5
PALEN, Rufus James 1
PALENCIA, Isabel de 6
PALEY, Samuel 4
PALFREY, John Gorham H
PALFREY, John Gorham 2
PALFREY, Sara Hammond 4
PALLEN, Conde Benoist 1
PALLETTE, Edward Choate 6
PALLETTE, Edward 2
Marshall
PALLISER, Charles 4
PALLISER, Melvin G. 1
PALLOTTI, Francis A. 4
PALM, Franklin Charles 6
PALMA, Tomas Estrada 1
PALMARO, Marcel A. 5
PALMA Y VELASQUEZ, 2
Rafael
PALMER, A. Emerson 1
PALMER, A. Mitchell 1
PALMER, A. Mitchell 1
PALMER, A. Mitchell 4
PALMER, Abraham John 1
PALMER, Agnes Lizzie 5
PALMER, Albert de Forest 1
PALMER, Albert Kenny 2
Craven
PALMER, Albert Marshman 1
PALMER, Albert Robert 2
PALMER, Albert 3
Wentworth
PALMER, Alden Claude 6
PALMER, Alice Freeman 1
PALMER, Alonzo Benjamin H
PALMER, Andrew Henry 2
PALMER, Anna Campbell 1
PALMER, Arthur 3
PALMER, Arthur Hubbell 1
PALMER, Arthur William 1
PALMER, Aulick 4
PALMER, Bartlett Joshua 4
PALMER, Bell Elliott (Mrs. 5
James Allerton Palmer)
PALMER, Benjamin 1
Morgan
PALMER, Beriah H
PALMER, Bertha Honore 1
PALMER, Bertha Rachel 3
PALMER, Bradley Webster 2
PALMER, Bruce Bartlett 6
PALMER, C. William 4
PALMER, Carleton H. 5
PALMER, Carroll 5
(Edwards)
PALMER, Charles Forrest 6
PALMER, Charles M. 2
PALMER, Charles Ray 1
PALMER, Charles Skeele 1
PALMER, Chase 4
PALMER, Chauncey D. 1
PALMER, Chesley Robert 5
PALMER, Claude Irwin 4
PALMER, Clyde Eber 3
PALMER, Cornelius 1
Solomon
PALMER, Daniel David H
PALMER, Daniel David 4
PALMER, David J. 3
PALMER, Dean 2
PALMER, Edgar 2
PALMER, Edward L. Jr. 3
PALMER, Edwin R. 4
PALMER, Elbridge 3
Woodman
PALMER, Elihu H
PALMER, E(phraim) 6
Laurence
PALMER, Erastus Dow 1
PALMER, Everett Walter 5
PALMER, Fanny Purdy 4

PALMER, Frances Flora H
Bond
PALMER, Francis Eber 5
PALMER, Francis Leseure 5
PALMER, Frank Herbert 1
PALMER, Frank Nelson 3
PALMER, Frank Wayland 1
PALMER, Fred Chester 5
PALMER, Frederic 1
PALMER, Frederic Jr. 4
PALMER, Frederick 1
PALMER, George Herbert 1
PALMER, George Louis 3
PALMER, George 4
Washington
PALMER, Gordon Davis 3
PALMER, Harold Gilbert 3
PALMER, Henrietta Lee 1
PALMER, Henry E. 1
PALMER, Henry L. 1
PALMER, Henry Robinson 4
PALMER, Henry Wilber 1
PALMER, Horatio 1
Richmond
PALMER, Howard 1
PALMER, Innis Newton H
PALMER, Irving Allston 1
PALMER, James Croxall H
PALMER, James Shedden 1
PALMER, Joel H
PALMER, John 1
PALMER, John McAuley 1
PALMER, John McAuley 3
PALMER, John William 1
PALMER, John Williamson 1
PALMER, Joseph 1
PALMER, Julius Auboineau 1
PALMER, Leigh Carlyle 3
PALMER, Leroy Sheldon 2
PALMER, Leslie Richard 1
PALMER, Loren 1
PALMER, Lynde 1
PALMER, Martin Franklin 4
PALMER, Nathaniel Brown H
PALMER, Pauline 1
PALMER, Philip Mason 3
PALMER, Potter 1
PALMER, Potter 2
PALMER, Mrs. Potter 1
PALMER, Ray H
PALMER, Ray 2
PALMER, Robert 1
PALMER, Samuel Sterling 1
PALMER, Silas H. 4
PALMER, Stanley Gustavus 6
PALMER, Stephen S. 1
PALMER, Stuart 4
PALMER, Theodore 3
Sherman
PALMER, Thomas Waverly 1
PALMER, Thomas Waverly 5
PALMER, Thomas 1
Witherell
PALMER, Truman Garrett 1
PALMER, Walter Launt 1
PALMER, Walter Walker 3
PALMER, Warren Sherman 4
PALMER, William Adams H
PALMER, William Beach 4
PALMER, William Henry H
PALMER, William Jackson 1
PALMER, William 1
Pendleton
PALMER, William Spencer 5
PALMER, Williston 6
Birkhimer
PALMERSTON, 3d H
viscount
PALMORE, William 1
Beverly
PALMQUIST, Elim Arthur 5
Eugene
PALOU, Francisco H
PALTSITS, Victor Hugo 3
PALUMBO, Leonard 6
PAM, Max 1
PAMMEL, Louis Hermann 1
PANARETOFF, Stephen 4
PANASSIE, Hughes Louis 6
Marle Henri
PANBOURNE, Oliver 1
PANCOAST, Henry 1
Khunrath
PANCOAST, Henry 1
Spackman
PANCOAST, Joseph H
PANCOAST, Russell Thorn 6
PANCOAST, Seth 1
PANCOAST, Thomas 1
Jessup
PANCOST, E. Ellsworth 3
PANDOLFI, Frank Louis 4
PANE-GASSER, John 4
PANETH, F. A. 6
PANGBORN, Earl Leroy 4

PANGBORN, Frederic 4
Werden
PANGBORN, Georgia 5
Wood
PANGBORN, Thomas 4
Wesley
PANICO, Giovanni 4
PANNELL, Faye 5
PANNELL, Henry Clifton 2
PANNELL, Charles Jackson 3
PANOFSKY, Erwin 4
PANSY 1
PANTON, William H
PANTSIOS, Athan 6
Anastason
PANUNZIO, Constantine 4
Maria
PANYUSHKIN, Alexander 6
S(emyenovich)
(nyoosh'kin)
PAPAGOS, Alexander 3
PAPANEK, Ernst 6
PAPANICOLAOU, George 4
Nicholas
PAPE, Eric 1
PAPE, William J. 4
PAPESH, Alexander 6
Anthony
PAPEZ, James Wenceslas 3
PAPI, Gennaro 1
PAPPENHEIMER, Alwin 3
M.
PAQUET, Anthony C. 4
PAQUETTE, Charles Alfred 5
PAQUIN, Albert Joseph Jr. 4
PAQUIN, Lawrence G. 4
PAQUIN, Paul 1
PAQUIN, Samuel Savil 1
PARADISE, Frank Ilsley 1
PARAMANANDA, Swami 4
PARCEL, John Ira 6
PARDEE, Ario H
PARDEE, Don Albert 1
PARDEE, George Cooper 1
PARDEE, Harold Ensign 5
Bennett
PARDEE, Israel Platt 1
PARDEE, James Thomas 2
PARDO, Felipe 4
PARDOW, William O'Brien 1
PARDRIDGE, William 6
Deweese
PARDUE, Louis A. 4
PARENT, Alphonse Marie 5
PARENTE, Pascal Prosper 4
PARET, J(ahial) Parmly 5
PARET, Thomas Dunkin 4
PARGELLIS, Stanley 4
PARHAM, Frederick 1
William
PARHAM, James A. 6
PARIS, Auguste Jean Jr. 3
PARIS, Charles Wesley 6
PARIS, W. Francklyn 3
PARISH, Elijah H
PARISH, John Carl 1
PARISH, Walter Alvis 3
PARISH, William Jackson 4
PARK, Charles Caldwell 1
PARK, Charles Edwards 1
PARK, Charles Francis 2
PARK, Edward Amasa 1
PARK, Edward Cahill 5
PARK, Edwards Albert * 4
PARK, Frank 4
PARK, Franklin Atwood 1
PARK, Guy Brasfield 2
PARK, Isabelle Springer 6
PARK, J. A. 3
PARK, J. Edgar 2
PARK, James H
PARK, John Alsey 5
PARK, Julian 4
PARK, Lawrence 1
PARK, Linton H
PARK, Marion Edwards 3
PARK, Maud Wood 3
PARK, Milton 1
PARK, Orville Augustus 2
PARK, Robert Emory 2
PARK, Robert Ezra 4
PARK, Roswell H
PARK, Royal Wheeler 1
PARK, Sam 1
PARK, Samuel Culver 4
PARK, Trenor William 1
PARK, William 4
PARK, William Hallock 1
PARK, William Lee 1
PARKE, Benjamin H
PARKE, Francis Neal 3
PARKE, Henry Walter 5
PARKE, John H

PARKE, John Grubb 1
PARKE, John Shepard 3
PARKE, William More 4
PARKER, A. Warner 4
PARKER, Addison Bennett 2
PARKER, Albert George Jr. 1
PARKER, Alexander Wilson 5
PARKER, Alexis du Pont 1
PARKER, Alton Brooks 1
PARKER, Amasa Junius H
PARKER, Amasa Junius 2
PARKER, Amory 4
PARKER, Andrew H
PARKER, Arthur Caswell 3
PARKER, Ben Hutchinson 5
PARKER, Benjamin 1
Franklin
PARKER, Charles A. 3
PARKER, Charles Barnsdall 4
PARKER, Charles H
Christopher
PARKER, Charles 5
Christopher
PARKER, Charles Edward * 1
PARKER, Charles Morton 1
PARKER, Charles Wolcott 2
PARKER, Chauncey David 5
PARKER, Chauncey 1
Goodrich
PARKER, Chauncey 3
Goodrich Jr.
PARKER, Cola Godden 4
PARKER, Cortlandt 1
PARKER, Cortlandt 3
PARKER, Daingerfield 1
PARKER, Daniel Francis 4
PARKER, DeWitt Henry 2
PARKER, Dorothy 4
Rothschild
PARKER, Edith Putnam 4
PARKER, Edmund 1
Southard
PARKER, Edward Burns 4
PARKER, Edward Cary 1
PARKER, Edward Frost 1
PARKER, Edward J. 4
PARKER, Edward Melville 1
PARKER, Edward Pickering 6
Jr.
PARKER, Edward Sanders 1
Jr.
PARKER, Edward Wheeler 4
PARKER, Edwin B. 1
PARKER, Edwin Pond 1
PARKER, Edwin Wallace 1
PARKER, Eila Moore 6
Johnson (Mrs. Barton
Wise Parker)
PARKER, Ely Samuel H
PARKER, Emmett Newton 5
PARKER, Evan James 4
PARKER, Fitzgerald Sale 1
PARKER, Fletcher Douglas 4
Alexander
PARKER, Foxhall H
Alexander
PARKER, Frances 5
PARKER, Francis Hubert 4
PARKER, Francis LeJau 5
PARKER, Francis Warner 1
PARKER, Francis Wayland 1
PARKER, Frank 1
PARKER, Frank Wilson 5
PARKER, Franklin Eddy 1
PARKER, Franklin Eddy Jr. 4
PARKER, Franklin Nutting 5
PARKER, Frederic Jr. 1
PARKER, Frederic Charles 1
Wesby
PARKER, Gabe Edward 6
PARKER, George Albert 1
PARKER, George Amos 1
PARKER, George B. 2
PARKER, George Frederick 1
PARKER, George Howard 4
PARKER, George Proctor 1
PARKER, George 3
Swinnerton
PARKER, Glenn Lane 2
PARKER, Grady P. 5
PARKER, H. E. 3
PARKER, H. Wayne 5
PARKER, Harry Lee 3
PARKER, Henry Griffith 3
PARKER, Henry Taylor 1
PARKER, Herbert 1
PARKER, Herschel Clifford 4
PARKER, Hilon Adelbert 1
PARKER, Homer Cling 2
PARKER, Horatio Newton 3
PARKER, Horatio William 1
PARKER, Hosea 1
Washington
PARKER, Isaac H
PARKER, Isaac Charles H
PARKER, J. Heber 3
PARKER, J. Roy 3
PARKER, James * H

PARKER, James 1
PARKER, James Cutler 1
Dunn
PARKER, James Edmund 2
PARKER, James Henry 1
PARKER, James I. 4
PARKER, James 1
Southworth
PARKER, James W. 3
PARKER, Jameson 5
PARKER, Jane Marsh 4
PARKER, Jo A. 5
PARKER, Joel * H
PARKER, John * H
PARKER, John 3
PARKER, John Adams 4
PARKER, John Bernard 3
PARKER, John Castiereagh 6
Jr.
PARKER, John D. 4
PARKER, John Gowans 3
PARKER, John Henry 2
PARKER, John Johnston 3
PARKER, John Mason H
PARKER, John Milliken 4
PARKER, Joseph Benson 1
PARKER, Josiah H
PARKER, Julia Evelina H
Smith
PARKER, Julius Frederick 4
PARKER, Junius 2
PARKER, Kenneth Colburn 4
PARKER, Laigh C. 3
PARKER, Lawton S. 3
PARKER, Leonard Fletcher 1
PARKER, Lewis Wardlwa 4
PARKER, Lottie Blair 1
PARKER, Lovell Hallet 4
PARKER, Marion W. 3
PARKER, Maude 3
PARKER, Maurice 6
PARKER, Millard Mayhew 4
PARKER, Moses Greeley 1
PARKER, Myron Melvin H
PARKER, Nahum H
PARKER, Peter H
PARKER, R. Wayne 1
PARKER, Ralph Robinson H
PARKER, Richard H
PARKER, Richard Elliot 1
PARKER, Richard Green H
PARKER, Robert 3
PARKER, Robert Hunt 4
PARKER, Robert Shumate 2
PARKER, Ross Isaac 6
PARKER, Samuel H
PARKER, Samuel Chester 1
PARKER, Samuel Wilson 1
PARKER, Severn Eyre H
PARKER, Stanley V. 5
PARKER, Theodore H
PARKER, Theodore Bissell 2
PARKER, Thomas H
PARKER, Thomas 4
Cleveland
PARKER, Torrance 2
PARKER, Valeria Hopkins 3
PARKER, Walter 5
Huntington
PARKER, Walter Robert 1
PARKER, Walter Winfield 3
PARKER, Wesby Reed 4
PARKER, Willard H
PARKER, Willard 4
PARKER, William Belmont 1
PARKER, William Edward 2
PARKER, William Gordon 5
PARKER, William H. 1
PARKER, William Harwar 4
PARKER, William Henry 3
PARKER, William M. 4
PARKER, William Riley 5
PARKER, William Stanley 5
PARKERSON, Jesse Jones 4
PARKES, Charles Herbert 5
PARKES, Henry Bamford 5
PARKES, William Ross 4
PARKHILL, Charles 4
Breckinridge
PARKHILL, James William 4
PARKHURST, C. Francis 1
PARKHURST, Charles 4
PARKHURST, Charles 1
Henry
PARKHURST, Frederic 5
Augustus
PARKHURST, Frederic 1
Hale
PARKHURST, Helen 6
PARKHURST, Helen Huss 3
PARKHURST, Howard 1
Elmore
PARKHURST, John 3
Adelbert
PARKHURST, John Foster 1
PARKHURST, John Gibson 1

PARKHURST, Lewis 2
PARKINS, Almon Ernest 1
PARKINSON, Burney 5
Lynch
PARKINSON, Daniel 1
Baldwin
PARKINSON, Donald 2
Berthold
PARKINSON, John Barber 1
PARKINSON, Robert 1
Henry
PARKINSON, Thomas I. 3
PARKINSON, William 4
Lynn
PARKINSON, William 5
Nimon
PARKMAN, Francis H
PARKMAN, Henry 1
PARKMAN, Henry 3
PARKS, Addison Karrick 2
PARKS, Charles Wellman 1
PARKS, Clifford C. 1
PARKS, E. Taylor 4
PARKS, Edd Winfield 5
PARKS, Edward Lamay 4
PARKS, Ethel R. 4
PARKS, Floyd Lavinius 3
PARKS, Frank Thomas 4
PARKS, Gorham H
PARKS, Henry Martin 4
PARKS, James Lewis * 1
PARKS, John Louis 5
PARKS, John Shields 5
PARKS, Leighton 1
PARKS, Marvin McTyeire 1
PARKS, Robert Lee 3
McAllister
PARKS, Rufus 1
PARKS, Samuel Conant 2
PARKS, Tilman Bacon 3
PARKS, Wilbur George 6
PARKS, William H
PARKS, Wythe Marchant 1
PARKYNS, George Isham 1
PARLANGE, Charles 1
PARLETTE, Ralph H
PARLEY, Peter H
PARLIN, Frank Edson 1
PARLIN, H. T. 1
PARLIN, William Henry 1
PARLOA, Maria 1
PARMELE, Harris Barnum 4
PARMELE, Mary Platt 1
PARMELEE, Cullen 3
Warner
PARMELEE, Henry Francis 1
PARMELEE, Howard Coon 3
PARMELEE, Julius Hall 4
PARMELEE, Lewis Dwight 3
PARMENTER, Bertice 2
Marvin
PARMENTER, Charles 1
Sylvester
PARMENTER, Charles 4
Winfield
PARMENTER, Christine 3
Whiting
PARMENTER, Frederick 6
James
PARMENTER, George 1
Freeman
PARMENTER, Roswell A. 4
PARMENTER, William H
PARMENTIER, Andrew H
PARMLEY, Joseph William 1
PARMLEY, Walter Camp 1
PARMLY, Eleazar H
PARNALL, Christopher 4
PARNELL, Harvey 1
PARPART, Arthur Kemble 4
PARR, Charles McKew 6
PARR, Harry L. 4
PARR, Jerome Henry 3
PARR, Joseph Greer 3
PARR, Samuel Wilson 1
PARR, William David 1
PARRAN, Thomas * 4
PARRETT, Arthur N. 1
PARRETT, William Fletcher H
PARRINGTON, Vernon 1
Louis
PARRIOTT, F. B. 3
PARRIOTT, James Deforis 2
PARRIS, Albion Keith 5
PARRIS, Alexander H
PARRIS, Samuel H
PARRIS, Virgil Delphini 4
PARRISH, Albert Garrett 1
PARRISH, Anne 1
PARRISH, Anne 4
PARRISH, Carl 4
PARRISH, Celestia 1
Susannah
PARRISH, Charles 1
PARRISH, Clara Weaver 1
PARRISH, Edward H

PARRISH, Isaac * H
PARRISH, John Bertrand 5
PARRISH, Joseph 1
PARRISH, Karl Calvin 1
PARRISH, Lucian Walton 1
PARRISH, Maxfield 4
PARRISH, Philip Hammon 3
PARRISH, Randall 1
PARRISH, Robert Lewis 1
PARRISH, Stephen 1
PARROTT, Alonzo Leslie 6
PARROTT, Claude Byron 5
PARROTT, Enoch H
Greenleafe
PARROTT, James Marion 1
PARROTT, John Fabyan 1
PARROTT, Marcus Junius 1
PARROTT, Percival John 3
PARROTT, Robert Parker 1
PARROTT, Thomas Marc 3
PARRY, Charles 1
Christopher
PARRY, Charles Thomas H
PARRY, David Maclean 1
PARRY, Emma Louise 1
PARRY, John Jay 3
PARRY, John Stubbs 1
PARRY, Sidney Loren 5
PARRY, Will H. 1
PARSELL, Charles Victor 1
PARSHALL, De Witt 3
PARSHALL, Howard 3
Madison
PARSON, Hubert 1
Templeton
PARSONS, Albert Richard 1
PARSONS, Albert Ross 1
PARSONS, Albert Stevens 1
PARSONS, Alice Beal 6
PARSONS, Alice Knight 4
PARSONS, Andrew 6
Clarkson
PARSONS, Archibald 3
Livingstone
PARSONS, Arthur Barrette 4
PARSONS, Arthur Hudson 3
Jr.
PARSONS, Azariah 1
Worthington
PARSONS, Charles H
PARSONS, Charles * 1
PARSONS, Charles 4
PARSONS, Charles B. 4
PARSONS, Charles Baldwin 1
PARSONS, Charles Francis 2
PARSONS, Charles Lathrop 3
PARSONS, C(hauncey) 6
Leland
PARSONS, Claude Van 1
PARSONS, Donald Johnson 5
PARSONS, Eben Burt 1
PARSONS, Edmund Byrd 4
PARSONS, Edward 4
Alexander
PARSONS, Edward Lambe 2
PARSONS, Edward Smith 2
PARSONS, Edward Young H
PARSONS, Elsie Clews 2
PARSONS, Emma Follin 5
(Mrs. Clifford W. Parsons)
PARSONS, Ernest William 5
PARSONS, Eugene 1
PARSONS, Fannie Griscom 1
PARSONS, Floyd William 1
PARSONS, Frances 4
Theodora
PARSONS, Francis 1
PARSONS, Frank 1
PARSONS, Frank Alvah 1
PARSONS, Frank Nesmith 1
PARSONS, Frederick 3
Williams
PARSONS, Geoffrey 3
PARSONS, Harry 1
deBerkeley
PARSONS, Mrs. Henry 1
PARSONS, Herbert 1
PARSONS, J. Lester 3
PARSONS, James Kelly 5
PARSONS, J(ames) Russell 5
PARSONS, James Russell 1
Jr.
PARSONS, John B. 4
PARSONS, John Calvin 5
PARSONS, John Edward 1
PARSONS, John Frederick 5
PARSONS, Lester Shields 4
PARSONS, Lewis Baldwin 1
PARSONS, Lewis Eliphalet H
PARSONS, Lewis Morgan 1
PARSONS, Llewellyn B. 4
PARSONS, Llewellyn 5
B(radley)
PARSONS, Louella O. 6
PARSONS, Marion Randall 6
PARSONS, Payn Bigelow 1

PARSONS, Philip Archibald 2
PARSONS, Ralph Monroe 5
PARSONS, Reginald 3
Hascall
PARSONS, Richard 1
PARSONS, Robert Stevens 1
PARSONS, Samuel 1
PARSONS, Samuel Holden H
PARSONS, Starr 1
PARSONS, Theophilus * H
PARSONS, Thomas Smith 1
PARSONS, Thomas William H
PARSONS, Usher 1
PARSONS, Wallace Emery 3
PARSONS, Wilfrid 3
PARSONS, Willard H. 5
PARSONS, William 1
PARSONS, William Barclay 1
PARSONS, William Barclay 5
PARSONS, William Edward 1
PARSONS, William Lewis 5
PARSONS, William Sterling 1
PARSONS, William Wood 1
PARSONS, Willis Edwards 4
PARTCH, Harry 6
PARTINGTON, Frederick 1
Eugene
PARTIPILO, Anthony 5
Victor
PARTLOW, Ira Judson 3
PARTLOW, William 5
Dempsey
PARTNER, Winnie Leroy 4
PARTON, Arthur 1
PARTON, Ernest 1
PARTON, Henry 1
Woodbridge
PARTON, James H
PARTON, Lemuel Frederick 2
PARTON, Sara Payson H
Willis
PARTRIDGE, Albert Gerry 3
PARTRIDGE, Alden 1
PARTRIDGE, Bellamy 4
PARTRIDGE, Charles 4
Patrick
PARTRIDGE, Donald 2
Barrows
PARTRIDGE, Edward 1
Lasell
PARTRIDGE, Everett 5
P(ercy)
PARTRIDGE, Frank 2
Charles
PARTRIDGE, George H
Everett
PARTRIDGE, George 3
Rudolph
PARTRIDGE, James H
Rudolph
PARTRIDGE, John Slater 1
PARTRIDGE, Richard 6
PARTRIDGE, Sidney Catlin 1
PARTRIDGE, William 1
Ordway
PARVIN, Theodore Sutton 1
PARVIN, Theophilus H
PAS, Ion 6
PASCALIS-OUVRIERE, 5
Felix
PASCALL, Thomas M. 6
PASCHAL, Franklin 2
Cressey
PASCHAL, George H
Washington
PASCHALL, John 3
PASCHALL, J(oshue) 6
E(rnest)
PASCO, Samuel 1
PASHKOVSKY, Theophilus 3
Nicholas
PASKO, Wesly Washington H
PASMA, Henry Kay 2
PASMORE, Henry Bickford 2
PASOLINI, Pier Paolo 6
PASQUIN, Anthony H
PASSANNATE, Charles H
PASSANO, Edward B. 2
PASSARELLI, Luigi 3
Alfonso
PASSAVANT, William H
Alfred
PASSMORE, Ellis Pusey 1
PASSMORE, Lincoln K. 1
PASTERNAK, Boris 4
Leonidovitch
PASTORIUS, Francis H
Daniel
PASVOLSKY, Leo 3
PATCH, Alexander 2
McCarrell Jr.
PATCH, Edith Marion 3
PATCH, Frank Wallace 1
PATCH, Helen Elizabeth 3
PATCH, Kate Whiting 1
PATCH, Nathaniel Jordan 1
Knight

PATCH, Ralph Reginald 3
PATCH, Sam H
PATCHEN, Kenneth 5
PATCHIN, Frank Glines 5
PATCHIN, Philip Halsey 3
PATCHIN, Robert Halsey 3
PATE, Maurice 4
PATE, Randolph McC 4
PATE, Walter Romny 5
PATEK, Stanislaw 4
PATENAUDE, Esioff Leon 5
PATENOTRE, Eleanor 5
Elverson
PATERSON, Albert Barnett 3
PATERSON, Donald 4
Gildersleeve
PATERSON, Isabel 4
PATERSON, James Venn 2
PATERSON, John H
PATERSON, Robert 4
Gildersleeve
PATERSON, Van 1
Rensselaer
PATERSON, William H
PATERSON, William Tait 5
PATIGIAN, Haig 3
PATILLO, Henry H
PATINO, Simon I. 2
PATMAN, Wright 6
PATMOS, Martin 6
PATON, James Morton 2
PATON, Lewis Bayles 1
PATON, Stewart 2
PATON, Thomas Bugard 1
PATON, William Agnew 1
PATON, William Kennell 3
PATRI, Angelo 4
PATRICK, David Lyall 5
PATRICK, Edwin Daviess 2
PATRICK, Fred Albert 1
PATRICK, George Edward 1
PATRICK, George Neill 6
PATRICK, George Thomas 2
White
PATRICK, Hugh Talbot 1
PATRICK, John Hayward 5
PATRICK, Joseph Cecil 5
PATRICK, Luther 3
PATRICK, Marsena H
Rudolph
PATRICK, Mary Mills 1
PATRICK, Mason Mathews 1
PATRICK, Ransom 5
Rathbone
PATRICK, Rembert Wallace 6
PATRICK, Robert F. 5
PATRICK, Robert Goodlett 1
PATRICK, Roy Leonard 5
PATRICK, Ted 4
PATT, John Francis 5
PATTANGALL, William 2
Robinson
PATTEE, Ernest Noble 2
PATTEE, Fred Lewis 3
PATTEE, William Sullivan 1
PATTEN, Amos Williams 1
PATTEN, Bradley Merrill 5
PATTEN, Charles Harreld 5
PATTEN, David 6
PATTEN, Everett Frank 4
PATTEN, George Yager 3
PATTEN, Gilbert 2
PATTEN, Helen Philbrook 4
PATTEN, Henry 3
PATTEN, James A. 1
PATTEN, James Horace 3
PATTEN, John 1
PATTEN, John A. 1
PATTEN, Simon Nelson 1
PATTEN, Thomas Gedney 1
PATTEN, William 1
PATTEN, Zeboim Charles 2
PATTERSON, A. L. 4
PATTERSON, Adoniram 1
Judson
PATTERSON, Alexander 2
Evans
PATTERSON, Alicia 4
PATTERSON, Alvah 1
Worrell
PATTERSON, Andrew 1
Henry
PATTERSON, Antoinette 1
De Courcey
PATTERSON, Archibald 4
Williams
PATTERSON, Austin 3
McDowell
PATTERSON, Burd 1
Shippen
PATTERSON, C. Stuart 1
PATTERSON, Caleb Perry 6
PATTERSON, Catherine 2
Norris
PATTERSON, Charles 1
Brodie

PATTERSON, Charles Edward 1
PATTERSON, Charles Howard 4
PATTERSON, Charles Loeser
PATTERSON, Charles Lord H
PATTERSON, Daniel Todd H
PATTERSON, David H. Jr. 5
PATTERSON, David Trotter H
PATTERSON, Edmund Booth 4
PATTERSON, Edward 1
PATTERSON, Edward White
PATTERSON, Edwin Wilhite 5
PATTERSON, Eleanor Medill 2
PATTERSON, Ernest Minor 5
PATTERSON, Ernest Odell 4
PATTERSON, Everett M.
PATTERSON, Flora Wambaugh
PATTERSON, Francis F. Jr. 1
PATTERSON, Frank Allen 2
PATTERSON, Frank Miner 1
PATTERSON, Frederick Beck 5
PATTERSON, Frederick William 4
PATTERSON, Gaylard Hawkins 1
PATTERSON, George Francis 5
PATTERSON, George Robert 1
PATTERSON, George Stuart 4
PATTERSON, George Washington H
PATTERSON, George Washington 1
PATTERSON, Gerard Francis 2
PATTERSON, Gilbert Brown 4
PATTERSON, Giles Jared 4
PATTERSON, Graham Creighton 5
PATTERSON, Grove Hiram 3
PATTERSON, Hannah Jane 6
PATTERSON, Harold C. 2
PATTERSON, Harry Jacob 2
PATTERSON, Harry Jacob 3
PATTERSON, Isaac Lee 1
PATTERSON, James 5
PATTERSON, James Albert 3
PATTERSON, James Kennedy 1
PATTERSON, James Lawson
PATTERSON, James O'Hanlon 1
PATTERSON, James Willis H
PATTERSON, Jane Lippitt
PATTERSON, John H
PATTERSON, John Fulton 1
PATTERSON, John Henry * 1
PATTERSON, John Letcher 1
PATTERSON, John Neville 5
PATTERSON, John Thomas 4
PATTERSON, Joseph McDowell
PATTERSON, Joseph Medill 2
PATTERSON, Joseph T. 5
PATTERSON, Lamar Gray 4
PATTERSON, Lemuel B. 1
PATTERSON, Lillian Beatrice 3
PATTERSON, Mrs. Lindsay 5 (Lucy Bramlette Patterson)
PATTERSON, Malcolm Rice 1
PATTERSON, Marion D. 2
PATTERSON, Mary King 6
PATTERSON, Morehead 4
PATTERSON, Morris H
PATTERSON, Otto 5
PATTERSON, Paul 3
PATTERSON, Paul Chenery 3
PATTERSON, Paul L. 3
PATTERSON, Ralph Morris 5
PATTERSON, Raymond Albert 1
PATTERSON, Richard Cunningham Jr. 4
PATTERSON, Robert * 1
PATTERSON, Robert Dempster 6

PATTERSON, Robert Foster 5
PATTERSON, Robert Franklin
PATTERSON, Robert Mayne 1
PATTERSON, Robert Porter 3
PATTERSON, Robert Urie 3
PATTERSON, Robert Wilson
PATTERSON, Roscoe Conkling 3
PATTERSON, Ross Vernet 1
PATTERSON, Rufus Lenoir II 2
PATTERSON, Samuel 4
PATTERSON, Samuel White 6
PATTERSON, Shirley Gale 1
PATTERSON, Thomas H
PATTERSON, Thomas 1
PATTERSON, Thomas Edward 4
PATTERSON, Thomas Harman H
PATTERSON, Thomas J. H
PATTERSON, Thomas Macdonald 1
PATTERSON, Virginia Sharpe
PATTERSON, Walter H
PATTERSON, Walter Kennedy 1
PATTERSON, William * H
PATTERSON, William Brown 1
PATTERSON, William Francis 4
PATTERSON, William Harvey 6
PATTERSON, William J. 3
PATTERSON, William Leslie 5
PATTERSON, William Morrison 6
PATTERSON, William R. 1
PATTERSON, Wright A. 3
PATTESON, S. Louise 4
PATTESON, Seargent Smith Prentiss 1
PATTI, Adelina
PATTIE, James Ohio H
PATTILLO, Nathan Allen 1
PATTISON, Everett Wilson 1
PATTISON, Granville Sharp H
PATTISON, Harold 1
PATTISON, Isaac Caldwell Jr. 4
PATTISON, James William 1
PATTISON, John 4
PATTISON, John M. 1
PATTISON, John R. 1
PATTISON, Martin 1
PATTISON, Robert Emory 1
PATTISON, Salem Griswold 4
PATTISON, Thomas H
PATTISON, Thomas Harwood
PATTISON, William J. 1
PATTON, Abigail Hutchinson H
PATTON, Albert F. 4
PATTON, Carl Safford 1
PATTON, Charles E. 4
PATTON, Cornelius Howard 1
PATTON, David Hubert 4
PATTON, Francis Landey 1
PATTON, Fred 3
PATTON, G. Farrar 1
PATTON, George Smith Jr. 2
PATTON, Haskell Riley 4
PATTON, Henry William 1
PATTON, Horace Bushnell 1
PATTON, Jacob Harris 1
PATTON, James McDowell 1
PATTON, James Welch 6
PATTON, John H
PATTON, John 1
PATTON, John Mercer H
PATTON, John Shelton 1
PATTON, Joseph McIntyre 1
PATTON, Katharine 2
PATTON, Leroy Thompson 3
PATTON, Nat 3
PATTON, Normand Smith 1
PATTON, Odis Knight 5
PATTON, Raymond Stanton 1
PATTON, Robert Howard 1
PATTON, Robert Williams 2
PATTON, Walter Melville 1
PATTON, Willard 1
PATTON, William H
PATTON, William Augustus 1

PATTON, William Macfarland 1
PATTON, William Weston H
PATTULLO, George 6
PATTY, Willard Walter 4
PATY, Raymond Ross 3
PAUGHER, Adrien de H
PAUKER, Ana 4
PAUL, A. J. Drexel 3
PAUL, Amasa Copp 1
PAUL, Arthur 6
PAUL, Charles Edward 5
PAUL, Charles Ferguson 4
PAUL, Charles Howard 1
PAUL, Charles Thomas 1
PAUL, Elliot Harold 3
PAUL, Gabriel H
PAUL, George Philip 6
PAUL, Harry Gilbert 2
PAUL, Henry Martyn 1
PAUL I H
PAUL, J. Gilman D'Arcy 5
PAUL, Jeremiah Jr. 1
PAUL, John * 1
PAUL, John 4
PAUL, John Benjamin 6
PAUL, John Harland 1
PAUL, John Haywood 5
PAUL, John R. 5
PAUL, John Rodman 5
PAUL, Joseph Edward 6
PAUL, Josephine Bay 4
PAUL, Joshua Hughes 1
PAUL, Maury Henry Biddle 2
PAUL, Nanette Baker 1
PAUL, Randolph Evernghim 3
PAUL, Ray Sherman 2
PAUL, Sarah Woodman 4
PAUL, Willard Augustus 4
PAUL, Willard Stewart 3
PAUL, William Brown 4
PAUL, William Edward 6
PAUL, William Glae 4
PAULDING, Charles Cook 5
PAULDING, Hiram H
PAULDING, James Kirke H
PAULDING, William Jr. H
PAULEN, Ben Sanford 4
PAULEN, Ben Sanford 4
PAULEY, Scott Samuel 5
PAULHAMUS, W. H. 1
PAULI, Hertha 5
PAULI, Wolfgang 4
PAULL, Lee Cunningham H
PAULLIN, Charles Oscar 2
PAULLIN, James Edgar 1
PAULSEN, Howard C. 4
PAULSON, Frederick Holroyd 4
PAULSON, Richard Hulet 4
PAULUS, Francis Petrus 1
PAULY, Karl Bone 4
PAUMGARTNER, Bernhard 5
PAUNACK, August Oscar 3
PAUR, Emil H
PAUST, Elnar Bernhardt 4
PAUSTOVSKY, Konstantin Georgievich 5
PAVLOSKA, Irene 4
PAVY, Octave H
PAWLING, Levi H
PAWLOWSKI, Bogumil 6
PAWLOWSKI, Felix Wladyslaw 3
PAWNEE BILL 1
PAX, Walter Thomas 1
PAXON, Frederic John 1
PAXSON, Edgar Samuel 1
PAXSON, Edward M. 1
PAXSON, Frederic Logan 2
PAXSON, Henry Douglas 6
PAXSON, W. A. 4
PAXTON, Alexander Gallatin 6
PAXTON, Edwin John 4
PAXTON, Edwin John 5
PAXTON, J. Hall 5
PAXTON, James Dunlop 1
PAXTON, John Gallatin 3
PAXTON, John Randolph 1
PAXTON, John Richard 5
PAXTON, Joseph Francis 1
PAXTON, Kenneth T. 5
PAXTON, Philip 1
PAXTON, Thomas B. 1
PAXTON, William Francis II 6
PAXTON, William McGregor 1
PAXTON, William Miller 1
PAXTON, William Percy 1
PAYEN DE NOYLAN, Gilles-Augustin H
PAYERAS, Mariano H

PAYNE, Anthony Monck-Mason 5
PAYNE, Bruce Ryburn 1
PAYNE, Byron Samuel 3
PAYNE, Charles Albert 4
PAYNE, Charles Edward 2
PAYNE, Charles Henry 1
PAYNE, Charles Rockwell 5
PAYNE, Christopher H. 4
PAYNE, Christy 1
PAYNE, Daniel Alexander H
PAYNE, E. George 3
PAYNE, Edward Waldron 1
PAYNE, Elisabeth Stancy 5
PAYNE, Eugene Beauharnais 4
PAYNE, F(anny) Ursula 5
PAYNE, Franklin Storey 5
PAYNE, Frederick Huff 2
PAYNE, George Frederick 1
PAYNE, George Henry 2
PAYNE, Henry B. 1
PAYNE, Henry C. 1
PAYNE, Jason 1
PAYNE, John A. 2
PAYNE, John Barton 1
PAYNE, John Bayly 4
PAYNE, John Carroll 4
PAYNE, John H. 5
PAYNE, John Howard 4
PAYNE, Kenneth Wilcox 4
PAYNE, Leon Mather 5
PAYNE, Leonidas Warren Jr. 6
PAYNE, Lewis Thornton Powell H
PAYNE, Montgomery Ashby 1
PAYNE, Oliver Hazard 1
PAYNE, Oliver Hiram 4
PAYNE, Philip 4
PAYNE, Robert Lee 1
PAYNE, Sereno Elisha 1
PAYNE, Will 3
PAYNE, William Harold 1
PAYNE, William Henry 1
PAYNE, William Kenneth 6
PAYNE, William Knapp 4
PAYNE, William Morton 1
PAYNE, William Wallace 1
PAYNE, William Winter 1
PAYNTER, Lemuel H
PAYNTER, Thomas H. 1
PAYSON, Edward 4
PAYSON, Edward Saxton 5
PAYSON, Eliot Robertson 2
PAYSON, Franklin Conant 1
PAYSON, George Shipman 1
PAYSON, Joan Whitney 6
PAYSON, Laurence G. 4
PAYSON, Seth 1
PAYSON, William Farquhar 1
PAYTON, Jacob Simpson 4
PAZ, Ezequiel P. 3
PEABODY, Andrew Preston H
PEABODY, Arthur 2
PEABODY, Augustus Stephen 1
PEABODY, Cecil Hobart 1
PEABODY, Charles 1
PEABODY, Charles Augustus * 1
PEABODY, Dean Jr. 3
PEABODY, Elizabeth Palmer H
PEABODY, Endicott 2
PEABODY, Ernest H. 4
PEABODY, Francis 1
PEABODY, Francis Greenwood 1
PEABODY, Francis Stuyvesant 1
PEABODY, Francis Weld 1
PEABODY, Frederick Forrest 1
PEABODY, Frederick William 1
PEABODY, George H
PEABODY, George Foster 1
PEABODY, George Harman 5
PEABODY, George Livingston 1
PEABODY, Harry Ernest 1
PEABODY, Helen Sophia 4
PEABODY, Henry Clay 1
PEABODY, Mrs. Henry Wayland 3
PEABODY, James Hamilton 1
PEABODY, Joseph H
PEABODY, Josephine Preston 1
PEABODY, Lucy Evelyn 4
PEABODY, Malcolm Endicott 6
PEABODY, Nathaniel H

PEABODY, Oliver William Bourn H
PEABODY, Robert Swain 1
PEABODY, Selim Hobart 1
PEABODY, Stuyvesant 2
PEABODY, William Bourn Oliver H
PEABODY, William Rodman 1
PEACE, Bony Hampton 4
PEACE, Roger Craft 5
PEACH, Robert English 5
PEACH, Robert Wesfly 1
PEACOCK, Dred 1
PEACOCK, Joseph Leishman 3
PEACOCK, M. A. 3
PEACOCK, Thomas Brower 1
PEACOCK, Virginia Tatnall 5
PEACOCK, Wesley Sr. 1
PEAIRS, Hervey B. 1
PEAK, J. Elmer 1
PEAK, John Lee 1
PEAKE, Alonzo William 3
PEAKE, Elmore Elliott 5
PEAKS, Archibald Garfield 1
PEALE, Albert Charles 1
PEALE, Anna Claypoole H
PEALE, Charles Clifford 3
PEALE, Charles Willson H
PEALE, Franklin H
PEALE, James H
PEALE, Mundy Ingalls 6
PEALE, Raphael H
PEALE, Rembrandt H
PEALE, Rembrandt 1
PEALE, Richard P. 6
PEALE, Sarah Miriam H
PEALE, Titian Ramsay H
PEARCE, Charles A. 4
PEARCE, Charles Edward 1
PEARCE, Charles Sidney 5
PEARCE, Charles Sprague H
PEARCE, Charles Sumner 4
PEARCE, Clinton Ellicott 4
PEARCE, Dutee Jerauld H
PEARCE, Eugene Hamer 1
PEARCE, Eva F. 5
PEARCE, Haywood Jefferson 1
PEARCE, J. Newton 1
PEARCE, James Alfred H
PEARCE, James Alfred 1
PEARCE, James William 6
PEARCE, John Elias 1
PEARCE, John Musser 3
PEARCE, Liston Houston 1
PEARCE, McLeod Milligan 3
PEARCE, Richard 4
PEARCE, Richard Mills Jr. 1
PEARCE, Stephen Austen H
PEARCE, Warren Frederick 4
PEARCE, Webster Houston 1
PEARCE, William 2
PEARCE, William Cliff 1
PEARCE, William Greene 3
PEARCY, Frank 6
PEARD, Frank Furnival 4
PEARE, Robert S. 3
PEARL, Joseph 6
PEARL, Mary Jeanette 5
PEARL, Raymond 1
PEARLSTONE, Hyman 4
PEARMAIN, Alice Whittemore Upton 4
PEARMAIN, Sumner Bass 4
PEARNE, Wesley Ulysses 1
PEARRE, George Alexander 1
PEARS, Sidney John 6
PEARSALL, Benjamin Simon 3
PEARSALL, Charles H. C. 3
PEARSALL, James Welch 4
PEARSALL, Robert Ellis 4
PEARSE, Arthur Sperry 4
PEARSE, Carroll Gardner 4
PEARSE, John Barnard 1
PEARSE, Langdon 3
PEARSON, Alfred John 1
PEARSON, Alfred L. 1
PEARSON, Andrew C. 1
PEARSON, Arthur Emmons 1
PEARSON, Charles William 1
PEARSON, Daniel Cecil 6
PEARSON, Drew (Andrew Russell) 5
PEARSON, Edmund Lester 1
PEARSON, Edward Jones H
PEARSON, Eliphalet 1
PEARSON, Frank Bail 4
PEARSON, Fred Stark 1
PEARSON, Gerald H(amilton) J(effrey) 5
PEARSON, Gustaf Adolph 2

PEARSON, Harry A.	6	PECK, George Record	1	PEET, William Wheelock
PEARSON, Henry Carr	5	PECK, George Washington	H	PEFFER, Harry Creighton
PEARSON, Henry Clemens	1	PECK, George Wesley	1	PEFFER, Henry Ira

PEARSON, Harry A. 6
PEARSON, Henry Carr 5
PEARSON, Henry Clemens 1
PEARSON, Henry Greenleaf
PEARSON, Herron Carney 3
PEARSON, Hesketh 4
PEARSON, James John 1
PEARSON, James Larkin 6
PEARSON, Jay Frederick Wesley 4
PEARSON, John James H
PEARSON, Joseph H
PEARSON, Joseph Thurman Jr. 3
PEARSON, Josephine Anderson 5
PEARSON, Leon Morris 4
PEARSON, Leonard 1
PEARSON, Lester Bowles 5
PEARSON, Lola Clark 3
PEARSON, Matthew Edgar 3
PEARSON, Norman Holmes 6
PEARSON, Oscar William 3
PEARSON, Paul Martin 1
PEARSON, Peter Henry 1
PEARSON, Ralph M. 3
PEARSON, Raymond Allen 1
PEARSON, Richard Metcalf 3
PEARSON, Richmond 1
PEARSON, Richmond Mumford H
PEARSON, Robert Logan 3
PEARSON, Samuel 4
PEARSON, Thomas 4
PEARSON, Thomas Gilbert 2
PEARSON, Walter Washington 4
PEARSON, William Alexander 3
PEARSON, William Lazarus 3
PEARSON, William Norman 1
PEARSONS, Daniel Kimball 1
PEARY, Josephine Diebitsch 3
PEARY, Robert Edwin 1
PEASE, Alan W. 3
PEASE, Alfred Humphreys H
PEASE, Arthur Stanley 4
PEASE, Calvin H
PEASE, Charles Giffin 1
PEASE, Charles Henry 1
PEASE, Elisha Marshall 1
PEASE, Ernest Mondell 1
PEASE, Francis Gladheim 1
PEASE, Frederick Henry 1
PEASE, Herbert Hoyt 6
PEASE, Joseph Ives H
PEASE, Kingsley Eugene 5
PEASE, Lucius Curtis (Lute Pease) 5
PEASE, Murray 4
PEASE, Robert Norton 4
PEASE, Rollin 6
PEASE, Theodore Calvin 2
PEASE, Zephaniah W. 1
PEASLEE, Amos Jenkins 5
PEASLEE, Charles Hazen H
PEASLEE, Edmund Randolph H
PEASLEE, Horace Whittier 3
PEASLEE, John Bradley 1
PEASLEE, Robert James 1
PEAT, Wilbur David 4
PEATE, John 1
PEATTIE, Donald Culross 4
PEATTIE, Elia Wilkinson 1
PEATTIE, Louise Redfield 4
PEATTIE, Robert 1
PEATTIE, Roderick 3
PEAVEY, Frank Hutchinson H
PEAVEY, Leroy Deering 3
PEAVY, George Wilcox 3
PEAY, Austin 1
PECH, James 1
PECHIN, Edmund Cash 1
PECK, Allen Steele 4
PECK, Annie Smith 1
PECK, Bayard Livingston 1
PECK, Cassius R. 6
PECK, Cecil Clay 6
PECK, Charles Horton 3
PECK, Charles Howard 1
PECK, Darius Edward 1
PECK, Edward Porter 1
PECK, Epaphroditus 1
PECK, Erasmus Darwin H
PECK, Ferdinand Wythe H
PECK, Frederick Burritt 1
PECK, Frederick Stanhope 2
PECK, George H
PECK, George Bacheler 1
PECK, George Clarke 1
PECK, George Lyman 1

PECK, George Record 1
PECK, George Washington H
PECK, George Wesley 1
PECK, George Wilbur 1
PECK, Harry Thurston 1
PECK, Harvey Whitefield 6
PECK, Henry Allen 1
PECK, Henry Austin 5
PECK, Herbert Massey 6
PECK, Hiram David 1
PECK, James Hawkins H
PECK, Jared Valentine 1
PECK, Jesse Truesdell H
PECK, John Hudson 1
PECK, John James H
PECK, John Mason H
PECK, John Sedgwick 5
PECK, John Weld 1
PECK, Lucius Benedict H
PECK, Luther Christopher H
PECK, Mark Barnet 1
PECK, Morton Eaton 5
PECK, Paul Frederick 1
PECK, Samuel Minturn 1
PECK, Staunton Bloodgood 5
PECK, Theodore Safford 1
PECK, Thomas Charles 4
PECK, Thomas Ephraim 1
PECK, Tracy 1
PECK, William Buckley 2
PECK, William Dandridge H
PECK, William Farley H
PECK, William Guy H
PECK, William Thane 4
PECK, Willys Ruggles 3
PECKHAM, Frank Edwin 1
PECKHAM, George Williams 1
PECKHAM, Howard Louis 5
PECKHAM, John J. 4
PECKHAM, Mary Chace H
PECKHAM, Orville 1
PECKHAM, Rufus Wheeler H
PECKHAM, Rufus Wheeler 1
PECKHAM, Stephen Farnum 1
PECKHAM, Wheeler Hazard 1
PECKHAM, William Clark 1
PECKHAM, William Gibbs 1
PECORA, Ferdinand 5
PECORA, William Thomas 4
PEDDER, James H
PEDDIE, Thomas Baldwin H
PEDDLE, John B. 1
PEDEN, Edward Andrew 1
PEDEN, Marie McKinney (Mrs. Ralph Hutchings Peden) 6
PEDERSEN, Niels Alvin 6
PEDERSEN, Victor Cox 3
PEDERSON, Lora Lee 4
PEDIGO, John Hardin 5
PEDRINI, Armando 1
PEEBLES, Alvin Roy 1
PEEBLES, Anna Davis 5
PEEBLES, Florence 5
PEEBLES, James Clinton 3
PEEBLES, James Martin 1
PEEBLES, John Bradbury 6
PEEBLES, Mary Louise 4
PEEK, Burton Francis 4
PEEK, Ernest Dichmann 1
PEEK, Frank William Jr. 1
PEEK, George Nelson 2
PEEK, Harmanus H
PEEK, Jesse Hope 4
PEEKE, George Hewson 1
PEEKE, Margaret Bloodgood 1
PEEL, William Lawson 1
PEELE, Robert 2
PEELE, Stanton Judkins 1
PEELE, William Walter 1
PEELER, Winston Snider 5
PEELLE, Stanton Canfield 2
PEEPLES, Thomas H. 4
PEERS, Benjamin Orrs H
PEERS, Robert Alway 6
PEERSON, Cleng H
PEERY, David Henry 4
PEERY, George Campbell 3
PEERY, John Carnahan 1
PEERY, Rufus Benton 1
PEERY, William Wallace 4
PEET, Albert W. 2
PEET, Charles Donald 4
PEET, Elizabeth 1
PEET, Harvey Prindle 1
PEET, Isaac Lewis H
PEET, Louis Harman 1
PEET, Lyman Plimpton 1
PEET, Max Minor 2
PEET, Roy William 5
PEET, Stephen Denison 1
PEET, William 1

PEET, William Wheelock 4
PEFFER, Harry Creighton 1
PEFFER, Henry Ira 3
PEFFER, Nathaniel 1
PEFFER, William Alfred 1
PEGLER, Westbrook James 5
PEGRAM, George Braxton 3
PEGRAM, George Herndon 1
PEGRAM, John 4
PEGRAM, John Combe 1
PEGRAM, Robert Baker III 5
PEGUES, Albert Shipp 4
PEGUES, Albert Shipp 5
PEGUES, Boykin Witherspoon 5
PEHRSONS, Ernest William 4
PEIK, Wesley Earnest 3
PEIRCE, Arthur Winslow 3
PEIRCE, Benjamin * H
PEIRCE, Benjamin Mills 5
PEIRCE, Benjamin Osgood 1
PEIRCE, Bradford Kinney H
PEIRCE, Charles Santiago Sanders 1
PEIRCE, Clarence Andrew 4
PEIRCE, Cyrus H
PEIRCE, Cyrus Newlin 1
PEIRCE, Frederic Marshall 6
PEIRCE, George James 3
PEIRCE, Harold 1
PEIRCE, Harry H. 3
PEIRCE, Henry Augustus 1
PEIRCE, Herbert Henry Davis 1
PEIRCE, James Mills 1
PEIRCE, Joseph H
PEIRCE, M. Fay 4
PEIRCE, Paul Skeels 3
PEIRCE, Silas 1
PEIRCE, Thomas May Jr. 6
PEIRCE, Thomas Mitchell 1
PEIRCE, Waldo 5
PEIRCE, William H
PEIRCE, William Foster 1
PEIRCE, William Henry 2
PEIRCE, William S. 1
PEIRSON, Alden 1
PEISER, Solomon 3
PEIXOTTO, Benjamin Franklin 1
PEIXOTTO, Ernest Clifford 1
PEIXOTTO, Jessica Blanche 1
PEIXOTTO, Sidney Salzado 1
PELENYI, John 6
PELHAM, Henry H
PELHAM, John H
PELHAM, John 1
PELHAM, Peter H
PELL, Edward Leigh 2
PELL, Ella Ferris 1
PELL, George Pierce 1
PELL, Herbert Claborne 4
PELL, James Albert 4
PELL, John L. E. 5
PELL, Philip H
PELL, Robert Paine 1
PELL, Stephen H. P. 3
PELL, William Henry Dannat 4
PELL, Williamson 2
PELL, Williamson Jr. 5
PELLETT, Frank Chapman 1
PELLEW, Charles Ernest 4
PELLEW, George H
PELLEW, Henry Edward 1
PELLEY, John Jeremiah 2
PELLEY, William Dudley 6
PELLICER, Anthony Dominic H
PELLY, Thomas Minor 6
PELOUBET, Francis Nathan 1
PELOUZE, William Nelson 2
PELTASON, Paul Evans 6
PELTER, Fred Paul 1
PELTIER, George Leo 6
PELTON, Guy Ray 4
PELTON, Roger Trowbridge 6
PELZ, Paul Johannes 1
PELZER, Louis 2
PEMBERTON, Brock 2
PEMBERTON, Henry 1
PEMBERTON, Israel 1
PEMBERTON, James H
PEMBERTON, John H
PEMBERTON, John deJarnette 4
PEMBERTON, John Clifford H
PEMBERTON, Ralph 2
PEMBERTON, William Young 1
PENALOSA BRICENO, Diego Dioniso de H

PENALVER Y CARDENAS, Luis Ignatius H
PENBERTHY, Grover Cleveland 3
PENCE, Arthur W. 3
PENCE, Edward Hart 1
PENCE, John Wesley 3
PENCE, Lafayette 1
PENCE, Thomas Jones 1
PENCE, William David 1
PENDELTON, Charles Sutphin 2
PENDER, Harold 3
PENDER, William Dorsey H
PENDERGAST, John Joseph 4
PENDEXTER, Hugh 1
PENDLETON, Albert Huntington 5
PENDLETON, Charles Rittenhouse 1
PENDLETON, Edmund H
PENDLETON, Edmund Henry H
PENDLETON, Edmund Monroe 1
PENDLETON, Edwin Conway 1
PENDLETON, Ellen Fitz 1
PENDLETON, Elliott Hunt 1
PENDLETON, Francis Key 1
PENDLETON, George Hunt 1
PENDLETON, James Madison H
PENDLETON, James Monroe H
PENDLETON, John B. H
PENDLETON, John Strother H
PENDLETON, Joseph Henry 1
PENDLETON, Louis 1
PENDLETON, Moses 3
PENDLETON, Nathanael Greene H
PENDLETON, Nathaniel Dandridge 1
PENDLETON, Robert L. 3
PENDLETON, Ruth Jane 6
PENDLETON, Thomas P. 3
PENDLETON, W. L. Marcy 4
PENDLETON, William Gibson 6
PENDLETON, William Kimbrough 1
PENDLETON, William Nelson 1
PENDLETON, William S. H
PENDRAY, Leatrice M. 5
PENFIELD, Clarence Miller 3
PENFIELD, Edward 1
PENFIELD, Frederic Courtland 1
PENFIELD, Jean Nelson 6
PENFIELD, Roderic Campbell 1
PENFIELD, Samuel Lewis 1
PENFIELD, Smith Newell 4
PENFIELD, Thornton B. 3
PENFIELD, Walter Scott 1
PENFIELD, William L. 1
PENGELLEY, Arthur Lorne 1
PENHALE, Clayton Archbold 3
PENHALLEGON, William Hitt 4
PENHALLOW, David Pearce 1
PENHALLOW, Dunlap Pearce 6
PENHALLOW, Samuel H
PENICK, Albert D. 4
PENICK, Charles Clifton 1
PENICK, Edwin Anderson 3
PENICK, Issac Newton 5
PENICK, John Newton 4
PENINGTON, Edward H
PENLAND, George Harvey 4
PENMAN, John Simpson 3
PENN, Albert Miller 4
PENN, Alexander Gordon H
PENN, Arthur A. 1
PENN, I. Garland 1
PENN, John * 1
PENN, John Cornelius 6
PENN, John Roby 3
PENN, Julius Augustus 1
PENN, Richard H
PENN, Thomas H
PENN, William H
PENNELL, Elizabeth 1

PENNELL, Joseph 1
PENNELL, Joseph Stanley 6
PENNELL, Ralph McT. 6
PENNELL, Walter Otis 5
PENNEWELL, Almer Mitchell 5
PENNEWILL, James 1
PENNEWILL, Simeon Selby 1
PENNEY, Charles George 1
PENNEY, James Cash 5
PENNEY, James Theophilus 4
PENNEY, John Stevens 4
PENNEY, Mark Embury 1
PENNEY, Minnie Freeman (Mrs. Edgar B. Penney) 5
PENNEY, Thomas 1
PENNIMAN, Ebenezer Jenckes H
PENNIMAN, James Hosmer 1
PENNIMAN, Josiah Harmar 1
PENNINGS, B. H. 3
PENNINGTON, Alexander Cumming McWhorter H
PENNINGTON, Alexander Cummings McWhorter 1
PENNINGTON, Edmund 1
PENNINGTON, Edward H
PENNINGTON, J. Rawson 1
PENNINGTON, James W. C. H
PENNINGTON, Leigh H. 1
PENNINGTON, Levi Talbott 5
PENNINGTON, Mary Engle 3
PENNINGTON, Samuel Hayes 1
PENNINGTON, William H
PENNINGTON, William Sandford H
PENNOCK, Alexander Mosley 1
PENNOCK, Gilbert Lee 6
PENNOVER, Charles Huntington 4
PENNOYER, Albert Sheldon 3
PENNOYER, Frederick William Jr. 5
PENNOYER, Paul Geddes 5
PENNOYER, Sylvester 1
PENNY, George Barlow 1
PENNY, Norman Frith 4
PENNYBACKER, Isaac Samuels 1
PENNYBACKER, Mrs. Percy V. 1
PENNYPACKER, Bevan Aubrey 3
PENNYPACKER, Elijah Funk H
PENNYPACKER, Galusha H
PENNYPACKER, Henry 1
PENNYPACKER, Isaac Rusling 1
PENNYPACKER, Samuel Whitaker 1
PENROSE, Boles 1
PENROSE, Charles 3
PENROSE, Charles Bingham H
PENROSE, Charles Bingham 1
PENROSE, Charles William 1
PENROSE, Clement Andariese 1
PENROSE, Clement Biddle 1
PENROSE, George Hoffman 4
PENROSE, Lionel Sharples 5
PENROSE, Richard Alexander Fullerton 1
PENROSE, Richard Alexander Fullerton Jr 1
PENROSE, Spencer 1
PENROSE, Stephen B. L. Jr. 3
PENROSE, Stephen Beasley Linnard 2
PENROSE, William Henry 1
PENTECOST, George Frederick 1
PENTON, John Augustus 1
PENZOLDT, Peter John 5
PEO, Ralph Frederick 4
PEO, Ralph Frederick 1
PEOPLES, Christian Joy 1
PEOPLES, James Alexander 5
PEOPLES, Richard Grier 5
PEOPLES, William Thaddeus 1
PEPLE, Edward Henry 1
PEPPARD, Murray Bisbee 6

PEPPER, Bailey B(reazeale) 5
PEPPER, Charles Hovey 3
PEPPER, Charles Melville 1
PEPPER, George Dana 1
Boardman
PEPPER, George Hubbard 1
PEPPER, George Seckel 1
PEPPER, George Wharton 4
PEPPER, Irvin St Clare 1
PEPPER, John Robertson 1
PEPPER, O. H. Perry 4
PEPPER, Stephen Coburn 5
PEPPER, William * H
PEPPER, William 2
PEPPER, William Mullin Jr. 6
PEPPERDAY, Thomas M. 3
PEPPERMAN, W(alter) 5
Leon
PEPPERRELL, Sir William H
PEPPLER, Charles H
PEQUIGNOT, Mary Boland 4
PERABO, Ernst 1
PERALTA, Pedro de 1
PERARD, Victor Semon 3
PERCHE, Napoleon Joseph H
PERCIVAL, Harold 4
Waldwin
PERCIVAL, Henry Robert 1
PERCIVAL, James Gates H
PERCIVAL, John 1
PERCIVAL, Olive May 4
Graves
PERCY, Atlee Lane 6
PERCY, Frederick Bosworth 1
PERCY, George 2
PERCY, James Fulton 2
PERCY, LeRoy 1
PERCY, Nelson Mortimer 3
PERCY, Walker 1
PERCY, William Alexander 1
PERDUE, Eugene Hartley 4
PEREA, Pedro 1
PEREIRA, I(rene) Rice 5
PERELLI, Achille H
PERES, Isreal Hyman 1
PEREZ DE VILLAGRA, H
Gaspar
PERGLER, Charles 3
PERHAM, Josiah H
PERHAM, Sidney 1
PERIGORD, Paul 3
PERIN, Charles Page 1
PERIN, Florence Hobart 5
PERIN, George Landor 1
PERINE, Edward Ten 1
Broeck
PERINI, Louis Robert Jr. 5
PERISHO, Elwood Chappell 1
PERITZ, Ismar John 3
PERKIN, Richard Scott 5
PERKINS, Agnes Frances 1
PERKINS, Albert 1
Thompson
PERKINS, Angle Villette 1
Warren
PERKINS, Bertram Lucius 5
PERKINS, Bishop H
PERKINS, Bishop Walden H
PERKINS, Carroll N. 3
PERKINS, Charles Albert 2
PERKINS, Charles Callahan H
PERKINS, Charles Edwin 5
PERKINS, Charles Elliott 1
PERKINS, Charles Elliott 2
PERKINS, Charles Enoch 1
PERKINS, Charles Harvey 4
PERKINS, Charles Plummer 1
PERKINS, Clarence 2
PERKINS, DeForest H. 1
PERKINS, Donald 6
PERKINS, Dwight Heald 1
PERKINS, E. Benson 4
PERKINS, Edmund Taylor 1
PERKINS, Edwin Ruthven 3
Jr.
PERKINS, Elias H
PERKINS, Elisha H
PERKINS, Elisha Henry 1
PERKINS, Elizabeth Ward 5
(Mrs. Charles Bruen
Perkins)
PERKINS, Emily Swan 1
PERKINS, Frances 4
PERKINS, Francis 5
Davenport
PERKINS, Frank Walley 1
PERKINS, Fred Bartlett 5
PERKINS, Frederic Beecher H
PERKINS, Frederic 2
Williams
PERKINS, Frederick 1
PERKINS, Frederick Orville 6
PERKINS, Frederick Powers 6
PERKINS, George Clement 1
PERKINS, George Douglas 1
PERKINS, George Hamilton H

PERKINS, George Henry 1
PERKINS, George 1
Walbridge
PERKINS, George 3
Walbridge
PERKINS, Harold E. 3
PERKINS, Henry Augustus 3
PERKINS, Henry Farnham 5
PERKINS, Herbert 1
Farrington
PERKINS, Jacob H
PERKINS, James Breck 1
PERKINS, James Handasyd H
PERKINS, James Handasyd 1
PERKINS, James McDaniel 4
PERKINS, Janet Russell 1
PERKINS, Jared H
PERKINS, John Jr. H
PERKINS, John Carroll 3
PERKINS, John Russell 1
PERKINS, Justin H
PERKINS, Lucy Ann 6
PERKINS, Lucy Fitch 1
PERKINS, Maurice 1
PERKINS, Maxwell Evarts 1
PERKINS, Milo Randolph 5
PERKINS, Nathaniel James 1
PERKINS, Ralph 4
PERKINS, Randolph 1
PERKINS, Reece Wilmer 1
PERKINS, Robert Patterson 1
PERKINS, Roger Griswold 1
PERKINS, S. Albert 3
PERKINS, Samuel Elliott 1
PERKINS, Thomas Clark 5
PERKINS, Thomas H
Handasyd
PERKINS, Thomas Jefferson 6
PERKINS, Thomas Lee 6
PERKINS, Thomas Nelson 1
PERKINS, Walter Eugene 5
PERKINS, Walton 1
PERKINS, William Allen 4
PERKINS, William Harvey 4
PERKINS, William Oscar 1
PERKINS, William R. 4
PERKINS, William 2
Robertson
PERKY, Kirtland Irving 1
PERLEA, Ionel 5
PERLEY, Ira H
PERLEY, Sidney 1
PERLITZ, Charles Albert Jr. 4
PERLMAN, David 6
PERLMAN, Jacob 5
PERLMAN, Nathan D. 3
PERLMAN, Philip B. 4
PERLMAN, Selig 3
PERLMANN, Gertrude 6
Erika
PERLMUTTER, Irving K. 5
PERLMUTTER, Oscar 6
William
PERLSTEIN, Meyer Aaron 5
PERLZWEIG, William A. 2
PERMAR, Robert 2
PERO, Giuseppe 4
PERON, Juan 6
PEROT, T. Morris Jr. 2
PEROT, Thomas Morris 1
PERRET, Auguste 3
PERRET, Frank Alvord 4
PERRIGO, James 3
PERRILL, Augustus H
Leonard
PERRIN, Bernadotte 1
PERRIN, Dwight Stanley 1
PERRIN, Fleming Allen 2
Clay
PERRIN, Frank L. 5
PERRIN, Halford Guy 6
PERRIN, Herbert Towle 4
PERRIN, John 1
PERRIN, John William 1
PERRIN, Lee J. 2
PERRIN, Marshall 1
PERRIN, Porter Gale 4
PERRIN, Raymond St 1
James
PERRIN, Willard Taylor 1
PERRINE, Charles Dillon 4
PERRINE, Enoch 1
PERRINE, Frederic Auten 1
Combs
PERRINE, Henry H
PERRINE, Henry Pratt 3
PERRINE, Irving 4
PERRINE, Van Dearing 3
PERROT, Nicholas H
PERRY, Aaron Fyfe H
PERRY, Albertus 1
PERRY, Alexander James 1
PERRY, Alfred Tyler 1
PERRY, Andre James 4
PERRY, Antoinette 1

PERRY, Antonio 2
PERRY, Arthur 1
PERRY, Arthur Cecil 4
PERRY, Arthur F. 2
PERRY, Arthur Latham 1
PERRY, Barbour 4
PERRY, Ben Edwin 5
PERRY, Benjamin Franklin H
PERRY, Bertrand James 4
PERRY, Bliss 3
PERRY, Carroll 1
PERRY, Charles 1
PERRY, Charles Milton 2
PERRY, Christopher H
Raymond
PERRY, Clarence Arthur 4
PERRY, Clay Lamont 5
PERRY, David 1
PERRY, David Brainerd 1
PERRY, Donald Putnam 4
PERRY, E. Wood 1
PERRY, Edward H
Aylesworth
PERRY, Edward Baxter 1
PERRY, Edward Delavan 1
PERRY, Eli H
PERRY, Ernest Bert 4
PERRY, Ernest James 2
PERRY, Everett Robbins 1
PERRY, George Dorn 1
PERRY, George Hough 2
PERRY, George Sessions 3
PERRY, Hector H. 5
PERRY, Henry Eldredge 2
PERRY, Hoyt Ogden 4
PERRY, Isaac Newton 1
PERRY, James Clifford 1
PERRY, James De Wolf 1
PERRY, James DeWolf 2
PERRY, John 5
PERRY, John Holliday 3
PERRY, John Hoyt 1
PERRY, John Jasiel H
PERRY, John Lester 3
PERRY, John Morris 2
PERRY, John Richard 1
PERRY, Joseph Franklin 1
PERRY, Kenneth 4
PERRY, Lawrence 3
PERRY, Lewis 4
PERRY, Lewis Ebenezer 4
PERRY, Lilla Cabot 1
PERRY, Louis Clausiel 1
PERRY, Lyman Spencer 6
PERRY, Marsden Jasiel 1
PERRY, Matthew Calbraith H
PERRY, Middleton Lee 5
PERRY, Nehemiah 1
PERRY, Nora H
PERRY, Oliver Hazard H
PERRY, Oscar Butler 2
PERRY, R. Ross 1
PERRY, Ralph Barton 5
PERRY, Richard Ross Jr. 5
PERRY, Roland Hinton 1
PERRY, Roy Vincelle 4
PERRY, Rufus Lewis 1
PERRY, Stella George Stern 3
PERRY, Stuart 1
PERRY, Stuart Hoffman 3
PERRY, Thomas 1
PERRY, Thomas Johns H
PERRY, Thomas Sergeant 1
PERRY, Wallace 1
PERRY, Walter Scott 1
PERRY, William * H
PERRY, William Flake 1
PERRY, William Graves 6
PERRY, William Hayes 4
PERRY, William L. 5
PERRY, William Stevens H
PERRYMAN, Francis 5
Spencer
PERRYMAN, Walter Lewis 4
Jr.
PERSE, Saint-John 6
PERSHING, Cyrus L. 1
PERSHING, Howell Terry 4
PERSHING, James 2
Hammond
PERSHING, John Joseph 2
PERSICO, E. Luigi H
PERSINGER, Louis 4
PERSKIE, Joseph B. 5
PERSON, Harlow Stafford 3
PERSON, Hiram Grant 4
PERSON, Hjalmar T. 6
PERSON, John Elmer 4
PERSON, John L. 5
PERSON, Robert S. 4
PERSON, Seymour Howe 3
PERSON, Thomas H
PERSONS, Augustus 1
Archilus
PERSONS, Frederick Torrel 2
PERSONS, Gordon 4

PERSONS, John Cecil 6
PERSONS, John Williams 5
PERSONS, Warren Milton 1
PERSONS, William Frank 3
PERTAIN, Charles Andree 6
PESCHAU, Ferdinand 1
William Elias
PESCHGES, John Hubert 2
PETEET, Walton 4
PETEGORSKY, David W. 3
PETER, Alfred Meredith 4
PETER, Arthur 2
PETER, George H
PETER, Hugh H
PETER, John Frederick 4
PETER, Luther Crouse 2
PETER, Marc 4
PETER, Marc 5
PETER, Philip Adam 4
PETER, Robert H
PETER, Sarah Worthington H
King
PETER, William Frederick 3
PETERKIN, Daniel 1
PETERKIN, George H
William
PETERKIN, Mrs. Julia 4
Mood
PETERKIN, William 2
Gardner
PETERMAN, Mynie 5
Gustav
PETERMANN, Albert E. 4
PETERS, Absalom H
PETERS, Albert Theodore 4
PETERS, Andrew James 1
PETERS, Charles Clinton 6
PETERS, Charles Rollo 4
PETERS, Christian Henry H
Frederick
PETERS, David Wilbur 3
PETERS, Edward Dyer 1
PETERS, Frederick Romer 4
PETERS, George Boddie 4
PETERS, George Henry 1
PETERS, Harry Alfred 6
PETERS, Heber Wallace 5
PETERS, J. A. 1
PETERS, James 5
PETERS, James Arthur 5
PETERS, James L. 3
PETERS, John Andrew 1
PETERS, John Andrew 4
PETERS, John Charles H
PETERS, John Dwight 4
PETERS, John Punnett 2
PETERS, John Punnett 3
PETERS, John Russell 1
PETERS, Le Roy Samuel 2
PETERS, Lewis Edwin 1
PETERS, Lulu Hunt 1
PETERS, Madison Clinton 1
PETERS, Marian Phelps * 4
PETERS, R. Earl 3
PETERS, Ralph 1
PETERS, Ralph Jr. 1
PETERS, Raymond Elmer 5
PETERS, Richard * H
PETERS, Russell Holt 6
PETERS, Samuel Andrew 1
PETERS, Samuel Ritter 1
PETERS, Thomas Pollock 1
PETERS, Thomas Willing 1
PETERS, Walter Harvest 3
PETERS, William Cumming H
PETERS, William E. 4
PETERS, William Henry 1
PETERS, William John 2
PETERSEN, Andrew N. 1
PETERSEN, Carl Edward 2
PETERSEN, Charles 4
PETERSEN, Harriet Lea 6
Murray (Mrs. Einer
Jalmer Petersen)
PETERSEN, Hjalmar 5
PETERSEN, Leroy A. 6
PETERSEN, Martin 3
PETERSEN, Martin 4
PETERSEN, Robert Warren 6
PETERSEN, Theodore 4
Scarborough
PETERSEN, William Earl 4
PETERSEN, William 3
Ferdinand
PETERSON, Albert 6
Edmund
PETERSON, Alfred 1
Emanuel
PETERSON, Alfred Walter 4
PETERSON, Arthur 1
PETERSON, Charles Jacobs H
PETERSON, Charles 5
Simeon
PETERSON, Donald Bolch 6
PETERSON, Elmer George 3

PETERSON, Elmer 5
Theodore
PETERSON, Frederick 1
PETERSON, Harry Claude 1
PETERSON, Henry H
PETERSON, Henry John 3
PETERSON, Herbert 2
PETERSON, J. Marvin 3
PETERSON, J. Whitney 5
PETERSON, James Earl Sr. 2
PETERSON, John B. 4
PETERSON, John Bertram 2
PETERSON, John Valdemar 5
PETERSON, Joseph H
PETERSON, Lawrence 1
Eugene
PETERSON, Lawrence John 3
PETERSON, May 3
PETERSON, Mell Andrew 5
PETERSON, Olof August 1
PETERSON, Peter 1
PETERSON, Reuben 1
PETERSON, Robert H
PETERSON, Virgil Lee 3
PETERSON, Virgilia 4
PETERSON, William H. 4
PETHICK, Harry H. 4
PETHICK-LAWRENCE,
Frederick William
PETIGRU, James Louis H
PETRI, Carl Johan 4
PETRIE, George 2
PETRIE, George 2
PETRIE, George Laurens 1
PETRIKIN, David H
PETRIKIN, William Lloyd 3
PETROFF, Strashimer 2
Alburtus
PETRUNKEVITCH, 4
Alexander
PETRY, Edward Jacob 1
PETTEE, Charles Holmes 3
PETTEE, George Daniel 4
PETTEE, James Horace 1
PETTEE, Lemuel Gardner 3
PETTEE, William Henry 1
PETTEE, William Jay 1
PETTEGREW, Jon Price 6
PETTEGREW, Marion 5
Edgar
PETTENGILL, George 3
PETTENGILL, Herman 1
Judson
PETTENGILL, Samuel 6
Barrett
PETTER, Rodolphe C. 2
PETTERSON, Leroy David 5
PETTET, Zellmer Roswell 5
PETTEYS, Alonzo 5
PETTIBONE, Augustus 1
Herman
PETTIBONE, Frank G. 4
PETTIBONE, George A. 4
PETTIBONE, Holman Dean 4
PETTIBONE, Wilson Boyd 4
PETTICORD, Paul Parker 6
PETTIGREW, Charles H
PETTIGREW, Ebenezer 1
PETTIGREW, George 1
Atwood
PETTIGREW, James H
Johnston
PETTIGREW, Richard 1
Franklin
PETTIJOHN, Charles Clyde 2
PETTIJOHN, John J. 1
PETTIJOHN, Julia Ivans 6
PETTINGELL, Frank 1
Hervey
PETTINGILL, William 3
LeRoy
PETTIS, Charles Emerson 5
PETTIS, Clifford Robert 1
PETTIS, Jerry Lyle 6
PETTIS, Spencer Darwin 4
PETTIT, Charles H
PETTIT, George Albert 1
Joseph
PETTIT, Harvey P. 4
PETTIT, Henry 1
PETTIT, John H
PETTIT, John Upfold H
PETTIT, Paul Bruce 6
PETTIT, Thomas McKean H
PETTITT, Byron Buck 1
PETTUS, Edmund Winston 1
PETTUS, Erle 4
PETTUS, James Thomas 3
PETTUS, Maia 3
PETTUS, Willaim Bacon 3
PETTUS, William Jerdone 5
PETTY, A. Ray 1
PETTY, Alonzo McAllister 1
PETTY, C. Wallace 1
PETTY, James William 4
PETTY, Orlando Henderson 1

PETTY, Orville Anderson 2
PETTY, William H
PETTYS, Anna C. 6
PETZOLDT, William A. 4
PEURIFOY, John E. 3
PEVSNER, Antoine 4
PEW, Arthur E. Jr. 4
PEW, J(ohn) Howard 5
PEW, James Edgar 2
PEW, John Brooks 4
PEW, John G. 3
PEW, Joseph Newton Jr. 4
PEW, Marien Edwin 1
PEXTON, George Ellsworth 1
PEYNADO, Francisco J. 4
PEYRAUD, Frank Charles 2
PEYSER, Ethan Allen 3
PEYSER, Julius I. 3
PEYSER, Theodore A. 4
PEYTON, Balie H
PEYTON, Bernard 6
PEYTON, Bernard 3
Robertson
PEYTON, Bertha Menzier 2
PEYTON, Charles Dewey 4
PEYTON, Ephraim 3
Goeffrey
PEYTON, Garland 5
PEYTON, Harlan Ide 3
PEYTON, John Howe 1
PEYTON, John Lewis 4
PEYTON, Joseph Hopkins H
PEYTON, Samuel Oldham H
PEZET, Frederico Alfonso 4
PFAFF, Franz 1
PFAFF, Orange Garrett 1
PFAFF, William 1
PFAHLER, George Edward 3
PFAHLER, William H. 4
PFANSTIEHL, Carl 2
PFATTEICHER, Ernst 2
Philip
PFEFFER, Delmont Kahler 6
PFEFFER, Edward Charles 3
PFEIFER, Joseph Lawrence 6
PFEIFFENBERGER, James 4
Mather
PFEIFFENSCHNEIDER, 4
Justus
PFEIFFER, Annie Merner 2
PFEIFFER, Carl H
PFEIFFER, Edward 4
PFEIFFER, Jacob 2
PFEIFFER, Oscar Joseph 4
PFEIFFER, Robert Henry 3
PFEIFFER, Timothy Newell 5
PFEIL, John Simon 5
PFEIL, Stephen 4
PFEILER, William Karl 5
PFINGST, Adolph O. 2
PFISTER, Jean Jacques 2
PFISTER, Joseph Clement 2
PFISTERER, Henry Albert 5
PFLAGER, Harry Miller 3
PFLAGER, Henry Barber 5
PFLUEGER, John 4
Seiberling
PFOHL, John Kenneth 4
PFORZHEIMER, Carl 3
Howard
PFOST, Gracie Bowers 6
PFOTENHAUER, Frederick 1
PFUND, A. Herman 2
PHAIR, John J(oseph) 5
PHALEN, Harold Romaine 1
PHALEN, James Matthew 3
PHALEN, Paul Stephens 1
PHANEUF, Louis Eusebe 5
PHARR, Hurieosco Austill 5
PHELAN, Andrew J. 6
PHELAN, Balfour 5
PHELAN, Edward Joseph 4
PHELAN, James * H
PHELAN, James Duval 1
PHELAN, James J. 1
PHELAN, James M. 6
PHELAN, John 3
PHELAN, Michael Francis 1
PHELAN, Richard 1
PHELAN, Sidney M. Jr. 3
PHELAN, Warren Waverly 1
PHELAN, William Rowe 6
PHELPS, Albert Charles 4
PHELPS, Almira Hart H
Lincoln
PHELPS, Andrew Henry 1
PHELPS, Anson Greene 1
PHELPS, Arthur Stevens 2
PHELPS, Ashton 1
PHELPS, Austin H
PHELPS, Charles 1
PHELPS, Charles Edward 1
PHELPS, Charles Edward 4
Davis
PHELPS, Charles Edward 1
Jr.

PHELPS, Charles Henry 1
PHELPS, Clarence Lucien 4
PHELPS, Darwin H
PHELPS, Delos Porter 1
PHELPS, Earle Bernard 3
PHELPS, Edward Bunnell 1
PHELPS, Edward John 1
PHELPS, Edward Shethar 1
PHELPS, Elisha H
PHELPS, Erskine Mason 1
PHELPS, Esmond 3
PHELPS, George Harrison 2
PHELPS, George Turner 1
PHELPS, Guy Fitch 1
PHELPS, Guy Merritt 2
PHELPS, Guy Rowland H
PHELPS, Harry 1
PHELPS, Helen Watson 2
PHELPS, Henry Willis 2
PHELPS, Isaac King 5
PHELPS, James H
PHELPS, James Ivey 5
PHELPS, J(ames) Manley 5
PHELPS, John Jay 2
PHELPS, John Noble 5
PHELPS, John Smith H
PHELPS, Lancelot 1
PHELPS, Lawrence 4
PHELPS, Marian 4
PHELPS, Oliver H
PHELPS, Ruth Shepard 4
PHELPS, Samuel Shethar 5
PHELPS, Shelton Joseph 4
PHELPS, Stephen 1
PHELPS, Thomas Stowell H
PHELPS, Thomas Stowell 1
Jr.
PHELPS, Timothy Guy 1
PHELPS, William Franklin 4
PHELPS, William Henry 1
PHELPS, William Lyon 2
PHELPS, William Wallace 1
PHELPS, William Walter 4
PHELPS, William H
Woodward
PHELPS-RIDER, Alice 6
PHEMISTER, Dallas B. 3
PHENIX, George Perley 1
PHIFER, Fred Wood 1
PHILBIN, Eugene A. 1
PHILBIN, Philip J. 5
PHILBRICK, Herbert Shaw 4
PHILBROOK, Warren 1
Coffin
PHILE, Philip H
PHILENIA H
PHILIP H
PHILIP, Andre 5
PHILIP, George 2
PHILIP, Hoffman 3
PHILIP, John Jay 6
PHILIP, John W. H
PHILIPP, Emanuel Lorenz 4
PHILIPP, Richard 3
PHILIPPE, Robert Rene 5
PHILIPPI, E. Martin 2
PHILIPS, Carlin 5
PHILIPS, George Morris 1
PHILIPS, Jesse Graves 4
PHILIPS, John F. 1
PHILIPS, Martin Wilson H
PHILIPS, William Pyle 3
PHILIPSE, Frederick H
PHILIPSON, David 2
PHILLER, George 1
PHILLIP, Hardie 6
PHILLIPPE, Gerald Lloyd 5
PHILLIPPI, Joseph Martin 1
PHILLIPPI, Stanley Isaac 5
PHILLIPS, Albanus 2
PHILLIPS, Albanus Jr. 5
PHILLIPS, Alexander 1
Hamilton
PHILLIPS, Alexander Lacy 1
PHILLIPS, Alexander Roy 5
PHILLIPS, Alexander Van 3
Cleve
PHILLIPS, Alfred Edward 1
PHILLIPS, Alfred Noroton 5
PHILLIPS, Andrew Wheeler 1
PHILLIPS, Arthur L. 1
PHILLIPS, Asa Emory 5
PHILLIPS, Barnet 1
PHILLIPS, Benjamin 5
Dwight
PHILLIPS, Bernard 6
PHILLIPS, Bert Geer 5
PHILLIPS, Cabell Beverly 6
Hatchett
PHILLIPS, Carl Chrisler 3
PHILLIPS, Carl L. 4
PHILLIPS, Catherine Coffin 2
PHILLIPS, Charles 1
PHILLIPS, Charles Gordon 4
PHILLIPS, Charles Henry 1
PHILLIPS, Charles L. 1

PHILLIPS, Charles Leonard 4
PHILLIPS, Chauncey Hatch 4
PHILLIPS, Coles 3
PHILLIPS, David Graham 1
PHILLIPS, Duane Seneca 1
PHILLIPS, Duncan 4
PHILLIPS, Edna M. 5
PHILLIPS, Edward Charles 5
PHILLIPS, Elliot Schuyler 4
PHILLIPS, Ellis Laurimore 4
PHILLIPS, Ethel Calvert 2
PHILLIPS, Everett Franklin 5
PHILLIPS, Francis Clifford 1
PHILLIPS, Frank 4
PHILLIPS, Frank McGinley 5
PHILLIPS, Frank Reith 5
PHILLIPS, George H
PHILLIPS, George Felter 4
PHILLIPS, George Wallace 6
PHILLIPS, Glenn Randall 5
PHILLIPS, Harmon 6
PHILLIPS, Harold Cooke 4
PHILLIPS, Harry Clinton 5
PHILLIPS, Harry 6
Hungerford Spooner Jr.
PHILLIPS, Harry Irving 4
PHILLIPS, Henry 3
PHILLIPS, Henry A. 3
PHILLIPS, Henry Albert 5
PHILLIPS, Henry Bayard 5
PHILLIPS, Henry Disbrow 1
PHILLIPS, Henry Lee 6
PHILLIPS, Henry Myer H
PHILLIPS, Henry Wallace 1
PHILLIPS, Herbert S. 4
PHILLIPS, Irna 5
PHILLIPS, James Andrew 2
PHILLIPS, James David 5
PHILLIPS, James Frederick 5
PHILLIPS, James Frederick 5
PHILLIPS, Jay Campbell 4
PHILLIPS, Jesse J. 1
PHILLIPS, Jesse Snyder 4
PHILLIPS, John * H
PHILLIPS, John 1
PHILLIPS, John Bakewell 1
PHILLIPS, John Burton 1
PHILLIPS, John C. 2
PHILLIPS, John Charles 1
PHILLIPS, John George 4
PHILLIPS, John Herbert 1
PHILLIPS, John Marshall 3
PHILLIPS, John McFarlane 1
PHILLIPS, John Sanburn 2
PHILLIPS, John Spinning 2
PHILLIPS, Kathryn Sisson 1
(Mrs. Ellis L. Phillips)
PHILLIPS, Lee Allen 1
PHILLIPS, Lee Eldas 2
PHILLIPS, Lena Madesin 4
PHILLIPS, Leon C. 3
PHILLIPS, Levi Benjamin 2
PHILLIPS, LeRoy 5
PHILLIPS, Llewellyn 4
PHILLIPS, Louis 3
PHILLIPS, Marie Tello 5
(Mrs. Charles J. Yaegle)
PHILLIPS, Maude Gillette 4
PHILLIPS, Merton Ogden 6
PHILLIPS, Michael James 4
PHILLIPS, Milton Eves 6
PHILLIPS, Morris 1
PHILLIPS, Nelson 4
PHILLIPS, Norman 4
Ethelbert
PHILLIPS, Paul Chrisler 3
PHILLIPS, Percival 1
PHILLIPS, Percy Wilson 5
PHILLIPS, Philip * H
PHILLIPS, Philip Lee 1
PHILLIPS, Ray Edmund 4
PHILLIPS, Richard Harvey 4
PHILLIPS, Richard Jones 5
PHILLIPS, Robert 2
PHILLIPS, Roger Sherman 5
PHILLIPS, Rowley Wilhelm 6
PHILLIPS, Samuel 4
PHILLIPS, Samuel Edgar 3
PHILLIPS, Stephen 5
Clarendon
PHILLIPS, T. D. 4
PHILLIPS, T. Redfield 5
PHILLIPS, Thomas Ashley 3
PHILLIPS, Thomas I. 5
PHILLIPS, Thomas Raphael 4
PHILLIPS, Thomas W. 1
PHILLIPS, Thomas 3
Wharton Jr.
PHILLIPS, Ulrich Bonnell 1
PHILLIPS, Waite 5
PHILLIPS, Wallace Banta 6
PHILLIPS, Walter Sargeant 6
PHILLIPS, Watson Lyman 2
PHILLIPS, Wendell H
PHILLIPS, Wendell 6

PHILLIPS, Wendell 1
Christopher
PHILLIPS, Willard H
PHILLIPS, William * H
PHILLIPS, William 4
PHILLIPS, William Addison H
PHILLIPS, William Battle 1
PHILLIPS, William Eric 6
PHILLIPS, William Fowke 4
Ravenel
PHILLIPS, William Irving 4
PHILLIPS, Ze Barney 2
Thorne
PHILLIPSON, Irving Joseph 3
PHILPOTTS, Eden 4
PHILP, John W. 1
PHILPOT, Gordon M. 4
PHILPOTT, Harvey Cloyd 5
Sr.
PHILPOTT, Peter Willey 1
PHILPUTT, Allan Bearden 1
PHILPUTT, James M. 1
PHILSON, Robert H
PHIN, John 1
PHINIZY, Bowdre 1
PHINIZY, Ferdinand 1
PHINIZY, Hamilton 1
PHIPPS, Don Holcomb 5
PHIPPS, Frank Huntington 3
PHIPPS, Henry 1
PHIPPS, John Shaffer 2
PHIPPS, Lawrence Cowle 3
PHIPPS, Michael Grace 5
PHIPS, Sir William 1
PHISTER, Elijah Conner H
PHISTER, Montgomery 4
PHLEGAR, Archer A. 1
PHOENIX, Charles E. 5
PHOENIX, Jonas Phillips 5
PHOENIX, Lloyd 1
PHOLIEN, Joseph 4
PHRANER, Wilson 4
PHYFE, Duncan H
PHYFE, William Henry 1
Pinkney
PHYSICK, Philip Syng H
PHYTHIAN, Robert Lees 1
PIAAT, Sarah Morgan 4
Bryan
PIAF, Edith 4
PIASECKI, Peter F. 5
PIASTRO, Mishel 5
PIATT, Donn 1
PIAZZA, Ferdinand 5
PIAZZONI, Gottardo 4
PIBUL SONGGRAM, 4
Luang
PICARD, Frank A. 4
PICARD, George Henry 1
PICARD, Ralph Alan 3
PICASSO, Pablo Ruiz 5
PICCARD, Jean Felix 4
PICCIRILLI, Attilio 2
PICCIRILLI, Furio 3
PICHEL, Irving 3
PICK, Albert 2
PICK, Bernhard 1
PICK, Lewis Andrew 3
PICKARD, Andrew Ezra 6
PICKARD, Florence 1
Willingham
PICKARD, Frederick 3
William
PICKARD, Greenleaf 3
Whittier
PICKARD, John 1
PICKARD, Josiah Little 1
PICKARD, Samuel Nelson 5
PICKARD, Samuel Thomas 1
PICKARD, Ward Wilson 4
PICKARD, William 3
Lowndes
PICKEL, Frank Welborn 1
PICKEL, Margaret Barnard 3
PICKELL, Frank Gerald 4
PICKELLS, Charles William 5
PICKEN, Lillian Hoxie 1
PICKENS, Andrew H
PICKENS, Andrew Calhoun 2
PICKENS, Francis 1
Wilkinson
PICKENS, Israel H
PICKENS, James Madison 5
PICKENS, Samuel O. 6
PICKENS, William 3
PICKENS, William 1
Augustus
PICKERELL, George Henry 4
PICKERING, Abner 4
PICKERING, Charles H
PICKERING, Edward 1
Charles
PICKERING, Ernest 6
PICKERING, John * H
PICKERING, Loring 3

PICKERING, Timothy H
PICKERING, William 1
Alfred
PICKERING, William 1
Henry
PICKET, Albert H
PICKETT, Albert James H
PICKETT, Bethel Stewart 6
PICKETT, Charles E. 1
PICKETT, Clarence Evan 4
PICKETT, Fermen Layton 4
PICKETT, George Edward H
PICKETT, Hugh Dale 5
PICKETT, James H
Chamberlayne
PICKETT, John Erasmus 3
PICKETT, La Salle Corbell 1
PICKETT, Thomas Edward 1
PICKETT, Warren Wheeler 3
PICKETT, William 1
Clendenin
PICKHARDT, William Paul 1
PICKING, Henry F. 1
PICKLE, George Wesley 4
PICKLESIMER, Hayes 5
PICKMAN, Benjamin Jr. H
PICKNELL, William Lamb H
PICKREL, William Gillespie 4
PICKRELL, Homer P. 5
PICOFF, Ronald Chester 6
PICOT, Louis Julien 1
PICQUET, Francois H
PICTON, Thomas H
PIDCOCK, Brian Morris 6
Henzell
PIDDOCK, Charles Albert 1
PIDGE, John Bartholomew 4
Gough
PIDGIN, Charles Felton 1
PIECK, Wilhelm 4
PIEPER, Emil G. 1
PIEPER, Ezra H. 3
PIEPER, Franz August Otto 1
PIEPER, John Jacob 1
PIEPER, William Charles 4
PIER, Arthur Stanwood 4
PIER, Garrett Chatfield 2
PIER, William Lauren 4
PIERCE, Alfred Mann 3
PIERCE, Anna Eloise 3
PIERCE, Arthur Henry 4
PIERCE, Arthur Sylvanus 4
PIERCE, Benjamin H
PIERCE, Bessie Louise 6
PIERCE, Byron Root 1
PIERCE, Carleton Custer 5
PIERCE, Charles Franklin 1
PIERCE, Charles Milton 5
PIERCE, Charles Sumner 3
PIERCE, Claude Connor 2
PIERCE, Clay Arthur 5
PIERCE, Clifford Davis 4
PIERCE, Daniel Thompson 5
PIERCE, Dante Melville 3
PIERCE, Earle Vaydor 6
PIERCE, Edward Allen 6
PIERCE, Edward J. 6
PIERCE, Edward Lillie H
PIERCE, Edward Lillie 1
PIERCE, Edward Peter 1
PIERCE, Francis Marshal 4
PIERCE, Frank 4
PIERCE, Frank Reynolds 3
PIERCE, Frank W. 4
PIERCE, Franklin H
PIERCE, Frederick Clifton 1
PIERCE, Frederick Ernest 4
PIERCE, Frederick Louis 1
PIERCE, George Edwin 3
PIERCE, George Foster 1
PIERCE, George Warren 4
PIERCE, George 3
Washington
PIERCE, George William 6
PIERCE, Gilbert Ashville 1
PIERCE, Grace Adele 1
PIERCE, H. Clay 1
PIERCE, Henry Hill 1
PIERCE, Henry Lillie H
PIERCE, Henry Niles 1
PIERCE, Jason Noble 2
PIERCE, John Davis 1
PIERCE, Joseph Hart 1
PIERCE, Josiah H. 1
PIERCE, Lawrence Blunt 4
PIERCE, Leonard A. 4
PIERCE, Lorne 4
PIERCE, Lyman L. 1
PIERCE, Marvin 5
PIERCE, Newton Barris 1
PIERCE, Norval Harvey 2
PIERCE, Oliver Willard 5
PIERCE, Palmer George 1
PIERCE, Ray Vaughn 4
PIERCE, Rice A. 4
PIERCE, Richard Donald 5

* Indicates More Than One Such Name Listed

PIERCE, Robert Fletcher Young 4
PIERCE, Robert L. 4
PIERCE, Roger 4
PIERCE, Shelly 3
PIERCE, Ulysses Grant Baker 2
PIERCE, Wallace Lincoln 1
PIERCE, Walter Marcus 3
PIERCE, Walworth 4
PIERCE, William H
PIERCE, William Kasson 4
PIERCE, William Leigh H
PIERCE, W(illis) Conway 6
PIERCE, Winslow Shelby 1
PIERI, Louis Arthur Raymond
PIERIOT, Lucille Georgette 6
PIERON, Henri 4
PIERPONT, Francis Harrison H
PIERPONT, Henry Edwards 5
PIERPONT, James 2
PIERPONT, James 1
PIERPONT, John H
PIERREPONT, Edwards H
PIERREPONT, Robert Low 1
PIERSEL, Alba Chambers
PIERSOL, George Arthur
PIERSOL, George Morris 4
PIERSON, Abraham * H
PIERSON, Arthur Tappan 1
PIERSON, Charles Ernest 4
PIERSON, Charles Wheeler 1
PIERSON, Coen Gallatin 5
PIERSON, Delavan Leonard 1
PIERSON, Hamilton Wilcox H
PIERSON, Isaac H
PIERSON, Isaac 1
PIERSON, Israel Coriell 1
PIERSON, J. Fred 1
PIERSON, Jeremiah Halsey H
PIERSON, Job 1
PIERSON, Lewis Eugene 3
PIERSON, Romaine 1
PIERSON, Silas Gilbert 2
PIERSON, William * 1
PIERZ, Franz H
PIETERS, Adrian John 1
PIETERS, Aleida Johanna 1
PIETRO, Cartaino di Sciarrine 1
PIETSCH, Karl 1
PIETSCH, Theodore Wells 1
PIEZ, Charles 1
PIFER, Drury Augustus 5
PIFFARD, Henry Granger 1
PIGEON, Richard H
PIGFORD, Clarence E. 2
PIGGOT, Charles Snowden 6
PIGGOT, James H
PIGGOT, Robert H
PIGMAN, George Wood 4
PIGOTT, James M. 5
PIGOTT, John Thomas 4
PIGOTT, Paul 4
PIGOTT, William Trigg 5
PIGUET, Leon A. 4
PIHLBLAD, Ernst Frederick 2
PIKE, Albert H
PIKE, Austin Franklin H
PIKE, Charles Burrall 2
PIKE, Clayton Warren 1
PIKE, Douglas Henry 6
PIKE, F. H. 3
PIKE, Frederick Augustus 4
PIKE, Granville Ross 4
PIKE, H. Harvey 6
PIKE, Harry Hale 5
PIKE, James H
PIKE, James Albert 5
PIKE, James Shepherd H
PIKE, Joseph Brown 4
PIKE, Nicolas H
PIKE, Percy M. 4
PIKE, Robert H
PIKE, Robert Gordon 1
PIKE, Sumner Tucker 6
PIKE, William John 1
PIKE, Zebulon Montgomery H
PILAT, Carl Francis 5
PILAT, Ignaz Anton 1
PILCHER, James Evelyn 1
PILCHER, James Taft 2
PILCHER, Joshua H
PILCHER, Lewis Frederick 1
PILCHER, Lewis Stephen 1
PILE, William Anderson H
PILES, Samuel Henry 1
PILGRIM, Charles Winfield 4
PILLARS, Charles Adrian 1
PILLEMER, Louis 3
PILLING, James Constantine
PILLOW, Gideon Johnson H

PILLSBURY, Albert Enoch 1
PILLSBURY, Alfred Fiske 3
PILLSBURY, Arthur Judson 1
PILLSBURY, Charles Alfred H
PILLSBURY, Charles Alfred 1
PILLSBURY, Charles Stinson 1
PILLSBURY, Edwin S. 4
PILLSBURY, Eleanor Bellows (Mrs. Philip Winston Pillsbury) 5
PILLSBURY, Evans Searle 4
PILLSBURY, George Bigelow 5
PILLSBURY, Harriette Brown 3
PILLSBURY, Harry N. 1
PILLSBURY, Henry Church 3
PILLSBURY, Horace Davis 1
PILLSBURY, John Elliott 1
PILLSBURY, John Henry 1
PILLSBURY, John Sargent 1
PILLSBURY, John Sargent 5
PILLSBURY, Parker H
PILLSBURY, Rosecrans W. 1
PILLSBURY, Walter Bowers 4
PILLSBURY, Walter Bowers 1
PILLSBURY, William Howard 3
PILMORE, Joseph H
PILSBRY, Henry Augustus 3
PILSBURY, Amos H
PILSBURY, Timothy H
PILSWORTH, Malcolm Nevil 4
PILZER, Maximilian 3
PIM, W. Paul 3
PINANSKI, Abraham Edward 2
PINANSKI, Samuel 5
PINCHBACK, Pinckney Benton Stewart 1
PINCHBECK, Raymond Bennett 3
PINCHOT, Amos Richard Eno 2
PINCHOT, Cornelia Bryce 4
PINCHOT, Gifford 2
PINCHOT, James W. H
PINCKARD, Harold Recenus 5
PINCKNEY, Charles H
PINCKNEY, Charles Cotesworth
PINCKNEY, Charles Cotesworth
PINCKNEY, Elizabeth Lucas 4
PINCKNEY, Francis Douglas 6
PINCKNEY, Henry Laurens H
PINCKNEY, John Adams 5
PINCKNEY, Josephine Lyons Scott 3
PINCKNEY, Merritt Willis 1
PINCKNEY, Thomas H
PINCUS, Gregory 4
PINDALL, James H
PINDALL, Xenophon Overton 1
PINDELL, Henry Means 4
PINE, David Andrew 5
PINE, Frank Woodworth 1
PINE, James 3
PINE, John B. 1
PINE, Robert Edge H
PINE, William Bliss 2
PINERO, Jesus T. 3
PINESS, George H
PINGREE, George Elmer 6
PINGREE, Hazen S. 1
PINGREE, Samuel Everett 1
PINK, Charlotte (Mrs. John M. Pink) 6
PINK, Louis Heaton 3
PINKERTON, Allan H
PINKERTON, Kathrene 4
PINKERTON, Lewis Letig H
PINKERTON, Lowell Call 3
PINKERTON, Roy David 6
PINKERTON, William Allan 1
PINKHAM, Lucile Deen 4
PINKHAM, Lucius Eugene 1
PINKHAM, Lydia Estes 4
PINKLEY, Roy H(enry) 6
PINKNEY, Edward Coote 1
PINKNEY, Ninian 1
PINKNEY, William H
PINNELL, Emmett Louis 5
PINNELL, LeRoy Kenneth 5
PINNEO, Dotha Stone 1
PINNER, Max H
PINNER, Max 2
PINNEY, E. Jay 4
PINNEY, George Miller Jr. 4

PINNEY, Harry Bowman 5
PINNEY, Norman H
PINSKI, David 5
PINSON, William Washington 1
PINTARD, John H
PINTARD, Lewis H
PINTEN, Joseph Gabriel 2
PINTNER, Rudolf 2
PINTO, Alva Sherman 4
PINTO, Isaac H
PINTO, Salvator 3
PINZA, Ezio 3
PIPER, Alexander Ross 3
PIPER, Arthur 4
PIPER, Charles Vancouver 1
PIPER, Edgar Bramwell 1
PIPER, Edwin Ford 1
PIPER, Fred LeRoy 4
PIPER, Horace L. 4
PIPER, James 4
PIPER, Margaret Rebecca 6
PIPER, Raymond F. 4
PIPER, William H
PIPER, William Thomas 5
PIPES, Louis A(lbert) 5
PIPES, Martin Luther 1
PIPKIN, Charles Wooten 1
PIPPENGER, Wayne Grise 6
PIPPETT, Roger 4
PIPPING, Hugo Edvard 6
PIQUENARD, Alfred H. 4
PIRANI, Eugenio di 4
PIRAZZINI, Agide 1
PIRCE, William Almy H
PIRE, Dominique Georges 5
PIRELLI, Alberto 3
PIRIE, Emma Elizabeth 3
PIRIE, Frederick W. 3
PIRIE, John Taylor 1
PIRIE, Samuel Carson H
PIRKEY, Everett Leighton 1
PIRKEY, Henry Warren Jr. 6
PIRQUET, Clemens Freiherr von
PIRSSON, James W. H
PIRSSON, Louis Valentine 1
PIRTLE, James Speed 1
PISAR, Charles Juneau 3
PISCATOR, Erwin 3
PISE, Charles Constantine H
PISER, Alfred Lionel 4
PISHTEY, Joseph Josephson 5
PITAVAL, John Baptist 1
PITCAIRN, Harold Frederick 4
PITCAIRN, John H
PITCAIRN, Norman Bruce 4
PITCAIRN, Raymond 4
PITCAIRN, Robert 1
PITCHER, Charles Sidney 5
PITCHER, Molly 1
PITCHER, Nathaniel 1
PITCHER, Zina 1
PITCHFORD, John H. 1
PITCHLYNN, Peter Perkins H
PITFIELD, Robert Lucas 6
PITKIN, Francis Alexander 5
PITKIN, Frederick Walker H
PITKIN, Timothy H
PITKIN, Walter Boughton 3
PITKIN, William * H
PITKIN, Wolcott H. 3
PITMAN, Benn 1
PITMAN, Frank Wesley 1
PITMAN, J. Asbury 3
PITMAN, James Hall 4
PITMAN, John 1
PITMAN, Norman Hinsdale 1
PITNER, Thomas Jefferson 1
PITNEY, John Oliver Halsted 1
PITNEY, Mahlon 1
PITNEY, Shelton 1
PITOU, Augustus 1
PITT, David Alexander 3
PITT, Louis Wetherbee 4
PITT, Robert Healy 1
PITT, William H
PITTENGER, Lemuel Arthur 3
PITTENGER, William 1
PITTENGER, William Alvin
PITTMAN, Alfred 2
PITTMAN, Charles Wesley H
PITTMAN, Ernest Wetmore 5
PITTMAN, Hannah Daviess 1
PITTMAN, Hobson 5
PITTMAN, Key 1
PITTMAN, Marvin 3
PITTMAN, Nathan Rowland 1
PITTMAN, Vail Montgomery 4

PITTMAN, William Buckner 1
PITTOCK, Henry Lewis 1
PITTS, Alexander Davidson 1
PITTS, Hiram Avery 1
PITTS, Llewellyn William 4
PITTS, Llewellyn William 5
PITTS, Mary Helen McCrea Weaver 5
PITZER, Alexander White 1
PIUS XII H
PIVER, Sara Elizabeth Early (Mrs. Sara Early Piver) 1
PIXLEY, Frank 1
PIXLEY, Henry David 4
PIZARRO, Francisco H
PIZITZ, Louis 2
PIZZETTI, Iidebrando 4
PLACE, Ira Adelbert 1
PLACE, Perley Oakland 2
PLACE, Roland Percy 4
PLACE, Wilard Fiske 4
PLACHY, Fred Joseph 5
PLACIDE, Alexander H
PLACIDE, Henry H
PLACK, William L. 2
PLAEHN, Erma Belle 6
PLAFKER, Nathan Victor 6
PLAGENS, Joseph Casimir 2
PLAISTED, Frederick William 1
PLAISTED, Harris Merrill H
PLAMENATZ, John Petrov 6
PLAMONDON, Alfred Daniel Jr. 4
PLANCK, Max Karl Ernst Ludwig 4
PLANJE, Christian William 6
PLANK, Kenneth Robert 6
PLANK, William Bertolette 4
PLANT, David H
PLANT, Henry Bradley 1
PLANT, Marion Borchers 5
PLANT, Morton F. 1
PLANT, Oscar Henry 1
PLANTS, Tobias Avery H
PLANTZ, Myra Goodwin 1
PLANTZ, Samuel 1
PLASCHKE, Paul Albert 4
PLASSMANN, Ernst H
PLASSMANN, Thomas 3
PLASTER, Jerry Glen 5
PLASTIRAS, Nicholas 4
PLATE, Walter 5
PLATER, George 1
PLATER, Thomas H
PLATH, Sylvia 4
PLATNER, John Winthrop 1
PLATNER, Samuel Ball 1
PLATOU, Ralph Victor 5
PLATT, Casper 4
PLATT, Charles 1
PLATT, Charles Adams 1
PLATT, Charles Alexander 4
PLATT, Edmund 1
PLATT, Eleanor 4
PLATT, Franklin 1
PLATT, Frederick Joseph 3
PLATT, Harvey P. 1
PLATT, Henry Clay 1
PLATT, Henry Russell 1
PLATT, Howard V. 4
PLATT, Isaac Hull 1
PLATT, James Henry Jr. H
PLATT, James Perry 1
PLATT, John 2
PLATT, John Osgood 1
PLATT, Jonas H
PLATT, Joseph Brereton 4
PLATT, Livingston 5
PLATT, Orville Hitchcock 1
PLATT, Robert Swanton 4
PLATT, Rutherford 6
PLATT, Samuel 1
PLATT, Thomas Collier 1
PLATT, William Popham 5
PLATT, Zephaniah H
PLATTEN, John Wesley 3
PLATZEK, M. Warley 1
PLATZMAN, Robert Leroy 6
PLAUT, Edward 2
PLAYER, William Oscar Jr. 3
PLAYTER, Harold 5
PLEADWELL, Frank Lester 3
PLEASANT, Ruffin Golson 1
PLEASANTS, Henry Jr. 4
PLEASANTS, J. Hall 3
PLEASANTS, James H
PLEASANTS, James Jay Jr. 3
PLEASANTS, John Hampden H
PLEASONTON, Alfred H
PLEASONTON, Augustus James H
PLEHN, Carl Copping 2
PLESSNER, Theodore 2

PLIMPTON, George Arthur 1
PLIMPTON, George Lincoln 3
PLIMPTON, Russell Arthur 6
PLOCK, Richard Henry 4
PLONK, Emma Laura 4
PLOWDEN, Eldridge Rodgers 6
PLOWHEAD, Ruth Gipson 6
PLOWMAN, George Taylor 1
PLUEMER, Adolph 4
PLUM, David Banks 2
PLUM, Harry Clarke 1
PLUM, Harry Grant 1
PLUMB, Albert Hale 1
PLUMB, Charles Sumner 1
PLUMB, Fayette Rumsey 4
PLUMB, Glenn Edward 1
PLUMB, Preston B. H
PLUMBE, George Edward 1
PLUMBE, John H
PLUME, Joseph Williams 1
PLUME, Stephen Kellogg 3
PLUMER, Arnold 1
PLUMER, George H
PLUMER, William 1
PLUMER, William Jr. H
PLUMER, William Swan 1
PLUMLEY, Charles Albert 4
PLUMLEY, Frank 1
PLUMMER, Charles Griffin 1
PLUMMER, Daniel Clarence 3
PLUMMER, Edward Clarence 1
PLUMMER, Edward Hinkley 1
PLUMMER, Frank Everett 4
PLUMMER, Franklin E. H
PLUMMER, Henry H
PLUMMER, James Kemp 3
PLUMMER, John Watrous 5
PLUMMER, Jonathan 1
PLUMMER, Mary Wright 1
PLUMMER, Ralph Walter 5
PLUMMER, Samuel C. 5
PLUMMER, Walter Percy 1
PLUMMER, William Alberto 1
PLUNKERT, William Joseph 6
PLUNKETT, Charles Peshall 1
PLUNKETT, Charles T. 1
PLUNKETT, Edward Milton 2
PLUNKETT, William Brown 1
PLYLER, Alva Washington 5
PLYLER, John Laney 4
PLYLER, Marion Timothy 5
PLYM, Francis John 1
PLYMIRE, Reginald Floyd 5
PLYMPTON, Eben 1
PLYMPTON, George Washington 1
PO-CHEDLEY, Donald Stephen 5
POAG, Thomas E. 6
POCAHONTAS H
POCKMAN, Philetus Theodore H
PODELL, David Louis 2
POE, Clarence 4
POE, Edgar Allan H
POE, Edgar Allan 4
POE, Elisabeth Ellicott 2
POE, Elizabeth Arnold H
POE, Floyd 5
POE, John Prentiss 1
POE, John William 1
POE, Orlando Metcalfe H
POE, Pascal Eugene Jr. 4
POEBEL, Arno 3
POEHLER, W(illiam) A(ugust) 5
POELS, Henry Andrew 4
POETKER, Albert H. 4
POFFENBARGER, George 4
POFFENBARGER, Livia Simpson 1
POGANY, Willi 3
POHLERS, Richard Camillo 3
POHLMAN, Augustus Grote 3
POHLMANN, Julius 1
POILLON, Howard Andrews 3
POILLON, William Clark 5
POINDEXTER, Claude Hendricks 6
POINDEXTER, George H
POINDEXTER, Joseph Boyd 3
POINDEXTER, Miles 1
POINSETT, Joel Roberts H
POINT, Nicholas H

POINT DU SABLE, Jean Baptiste H
POINTS, Arthur Jones 5
POLACCO, Giorgi 4
POLACHEK, Victor Henry 1
POLACK, William Gustave 3
POLAK, John Osborn 1
POLAKOV, Walter Nicholas 6
POLAND, Luke Potter H
POLAND, William Carey 1
POLANYI, Karl 4
POLASEK, Albin 4
POLDERVAART, Arie 5
POLE, Elizabeth H
POLE, John William 3
POLEMAN, Horace Irvin 4
POLERI, David Samuel 4
POLHAMUS, Jose Nelson 5
POLHEMUS, James H. 4
POLING, Daniel Alfred 5
POLING, Daniel V. 4
POLITELLA, Joseph 6
POLIVKA, Jaroslav Joseph 4
POLK, Albert Fawcett 5
POLK, Charles Peale H
POLK, Forrest Raymond 4
POLK, Frank Lyon 2
POLK, James G. 3
POLK, James Knox H
POLK, Leonidas H
POLK, Leonidas Lafayette H
POLK, Lucius Eugene H
POLK, Ralph Lane 1
POLK, Rufus King 1
POLK, Sarah Childress H
POLK, Thomas H
POLK, Trusten H
POLK, William H
POLK, William Hawkins H
POLK, William Mecklenburg H
POLLACK, Abou David 6
POLLACK, Ervin Harold 5
POLLACK, Louis 5
POLLAK, Egon 6
POLLAK, Gustav 1
POLLAK, Robert 5
POLLAK, Virginia Morris 4
POLLAK, Walter Hellprin 1
POLLAN, Arthur Adair 5
POLLARD, Arthur Gayton 1
POLLARD, Cash Blair 1
POLLARD, Charles Louis 2
POLLARD, Claude 1
POLLARD, Edward Alfred H
POLLARD, Edward Bagby 1
POLLARD, Ernest Mark 5
POLLARD, Harold Stanley 3
POLLARD, Harry Strange 4
POLLARD, Henry Douglas 2
POLLARD, Isaac 1
POLLARD, John Garland 1
POLLARD, John William Hobbs 5
POLLARD, Percival 1
POLLARD, Robert Nelson 6
POLLARD, Warren Randolph 4
POLLARD, William B. Sr. 3
POLLARD, William Jefferson 1
POLLEY, Samuel Cleland 2
POLLIA, Joseph P. 3
POLLITT, Levin Irving 5
POLLITZER, Anita 6
POLLITZER, Sigmund 1
POLLMAN, William 1
POLLOCK, Benjamin Reathe 4
POLLOCK, Channing 2
POLLOCK, Charles Andrew 1
POLLOCK, Clement Perry 6
POLLOCK, Edwin Taylor 2
POLLOCK, Horatio Milo 3
POLLOCK, Jackson H
POLLOCK, Jackson 4
POLLOCK, James H
POLLOCK, John C. 1
POLLOCK, Lewis John 4
POLLOCK, Oliver H
POLLOCK, Pinckney Daniel 1
POLLOCK, Simon Oscar 4
POLLOCK, Thomas Cithcart 2
POLLOCK, Walter Briesler 1
POLLOCK, Wayne 4
POLSKY, Bert Alfred 6
POLSLEY, Daniel Haymond H
POLTORATZKY, Marianna A. 5
POLYAK, Stephen 3
POLYZOIDES, Adamantios Theophilus 5

POMAREDE, Leon H
POMERAT, Charles Marc 4
POMERENE, Atlee 1
POMEROY, Allan H
POMEROY, Charles 4
POMEROY, Daniel Eleazer 4
POMEROY, Elizabeth Ella 4
POMEROY, Eltweed 1
POMEROY, Howard Edwin 6
POMEROY, John Larrabee 1
POMEROY, John Norton 1
POMEROY, John Norton 1
POMEROY, Marcus Mills 4
POMEROY, Ralph Brouwer 1
POMEROY, Samuel Clarke 1
POMEROY, Seth H
POMEROY, Theodore Medad H
POMPIDOU, Georges Jean Raymond 6
PONCE DE LEON, Juan H
PONCHER, Henry George 3
POND, Allen Bartlit 1
POND, Alonzo Smith 4
POND, Anson Phelps 4
POND, Ashley 1
POND, Bremer Whidden 3
POND, Charles Fremont 1
POND, Dana 4
POND, Enoch H
POND, Francis Jones 5
POND, Frederick Eugene 1
POND, George Edward 1
POND, George Gilbert 1
POND, Irving Kane 1
POND, James B. 4
POND, James Burton 1
POND, John Allan 5
POND, Peter H
POND, Philip 2
POND, Robert Andrew 5
POND, Samuel William 1
POND, Silvanus Billings H
POND, Theodore Hanford 1
POND, Wilf Pocklington 5
PONS, Lilly 6
PONT-AU-SABLE, Jean Baptiste
PONTIAC H
PONTIUS, Albert William 1
POOK, Samuel Hartt 1
POOL, David de Sola 5
POOL, Eugene Hillhouse 2
POOL, George Franklin 4
POOL, Joe 5
POOL, John 1
POOL, Judith Graham 6
POOL, Leonidas Moore H
POOL, Maria Louise H
POOL, Walter Freshwater 1
POOLE, Abram 4
POOLE, Cecil Percy 1
POOLE, Charles Augustus 4
POOLE, Charles Hubbard 1
POOLE, DeWitt Clinton 3
POOLE, Ernest 2
POOLE, Eugene Alonzo 1
POOLE, Fanny Huntington Runnells 2
POOLE, Fenn E. 3
POOLE, Fitch H
POOLE, Franklin Osborne 2
POOLE, Frederic 1
POOLE, Herman 4
POOLE, John 5
POOLE, Lynn D. 5
POOLE, Murray Edward 1
POOLE, Robert Franklin 3
POOLE, Rufus Gilbert 5
POOLE, Sidman Parmelee 3
POOLE, William Frederick H
POOLER, Charles Alfred H
POOLEY, Charles A. 1
POOLEY, Edward Murray 5
POOR, Agnes Blake 1
POOR, Charles Henry 4
POOR, Charles Lane 3
POOR, Charles Marshall 5
POOR, Daniel H
POOR, Enoch H
POOR, Frank A. 3
POOR, Fred Arthur 3
POOR, Henry Varnum III 5
POOR, Henry William 1
POOR, John H
POOR, John Alfred H
POOR, John Merrill 1
POOR, Ruel Whitcomb 5
POOR, Russell Spurgeon 5
POOR, Walter Everett 3
POOR, Wharton 6
POOR, William Bunker 6
POORE, Benjamin Andrew 1
POORE, Benjamin Perley H
POORE, Charles Graydon 5
POORE, Henry Rankin 1

POORMAN, Alfred Peter 3
POPE, Albert Augustus 1
POPE, Alexander 1
POPE, Alfred Atmore 1
POPE, Allan Melvill 4
POPE, Amy Elizabeth 1
POPE, Arthur 6
POPE, Arthur Upham 5
POPE, Bayard Foster 5
POPE, Carey Joseph 1
POPE, Clifford Hillhouse 6
POPE, Curran 1
POPE, Edward Waldron 4
POPE, Francis Horton 5
POPE, Franklin Leonard 4
POPE, Frederick 5
POPE, George 5
POPE, Gustavus Debrille 3
POPE, Harold Linder 6
POPE, Henry Francis 3
POPE, Herbert 3
POPE, James Worden 1
POPE, John * H
POPE, John Dudley 4
POPE, John Russell 1
POPE, Larry Jacob 6
POPE, Liston 6
POPE, Nathaniel H
POPE, Patrick Hamilton 1
POPE, Percival Clarence 1
POPE, Ralph Elton 1
POPE, Ralph Wainwright 1
POPE, Roy L(eon) 6
POPE, Walter Lyndon 5
POPE, William Hayes 1
POPE, Young John 1
POPEJOY, Thomas Lafayette 6
POPHAM, George H
POPMA, Gerritt Jacob 4
POPOFF, Stephen 1
POPOVIC, Vladimir 5
POPOV-VENIAMINOV, Joann H
POPPEN, Emmanuel Frederick 4
POPPENHEIM, Mary Barnett 1
POPPENHUSEN, Conrad Herman H
POPPER, William 4
PORCHER, Francis Peyre H
PORMORT, Philemon H
PORRAS, Belisario 1
PORRITT, Edward 1
PORRO, Thomas J. 4
PORTAL, Baron Wyndham Raymond H
PORTELA, Epifanio 4
PORTER, A. Kingsley 1
PORTER, A. W. Noel 4
PORTER, Albert 1
PORTER, Albert Gallatin H
PORTER, Alexander H
PORTER, Andrew H
PORTER, Arthur Le Moyne 5
PORTER, Augustus Seymour H
PORTER, Benjamin Curtis 1
PORTER, Bruce 5
PORTER, Charles Allen 1
PORTER, Charles Burnham 1
PORTER, Charles Howell 4
PORTER, Charles Scott 4
PORTER, Charles Vernon 5
PORTER, Charley Lyman 4
PORTER, Charlotte Williams 1
PORTER, Claude R. 2
PORTER, Cole 4
PORTER, Dana H
PORTER, David H
PORTER, David Dixon H
PORTER, David Dixon 2
PORTER, David Richard 6
PORTER, David Rittenhouse H
PORTER, Delia Lyman 1
PORTER, Dwight 1
PORTER, Earle S. 3
PORTER, Ebenezer H
PORTER, Edward Arthur Gribbon 1
PORTER, Eleanor Hodgman 1
PORTER, Ernest Warren 5
PORTER, Eugene Hoffman 1
PORTER, F. Addison 1
PORTER, Fairfield 6
PORTER, Fitz-John H
PORTER, Florence Collins 1
PORTER, Frank Chamberlin 2
PORTER, Frank M. 4
PORTER, Frank Monroe 5
PORTER, Fred Thomas 5
PORTER, Gene Stratton 1
PORTER, George French 1

PORTER, Gilbert Edwin 2
PORTER, Gilchrist H
PORTER, H. M. 1
PORTER, Harold Everett 1
PORTER, Henry Alford 2
PORTER, Henry Dwight 1
PORTER, Henry H. 1
PORTER, Henry (Harry) Alanson 5
PORTER, Henry Hobart 1
PORTER, Henry Kirke 1
PORTER, Holbrook Fitz-John 1
PORTER, Horace 1
PORTER, Hugh 4
PORTER, Hugh Omega 4
PORTER, Irvin Lourie 6
PORTER, James H
PORTER, James A. 5
PORTER, James Davis 1
PORTER, James Dunlop 5
PORTER, James Hyde 2
PORTER, James Madison H
PORTER, James Madison III
PORTER, James Pertice 3
PORTER, J(ames) Sherman 5
PORTER, James Temple 1
PORTER, James W. 3
PORTER, Jermain Gildersleeve 1
PORTER, Joe Frank 3
PORTER, John H
PORTER, John Addison H
PORTER, John Addison 1
PORTER, John Clinton 3
PORTER, John Henry 1
PORTER, John Jermain 6
PORTER, John Lincoln 1
PORTER, John Luke 1
PORTER, John Lupher 1
PORTER, John William 1
PORTER, Joseph Franklin 2
PORTER, Joseph Yates 1
PORTER, Kirk Harold 5
PORTER, L(ester) G(ilbert) 5
PORTER, Linn Boyd H
PORTER, Louis Hopkins 2
PORTER, Lucius Chapin 3
PORTER, Miles Fuller 1
PORTER, Newton Hazelton 2
PORTER, Noah H
PORTER, Paul Aldermandt 6
PORTER, Peter Buell H
PORTER, Phil 4
PORTER, Quincy 4
PORTER, Robert Langley 4
PORTER, Robert Percival 1
PORTER, Roland Guyer 3
PORTER, Rose H
PORTER, Royal A(rthur) 5
PORTER, Rufus H
PORTER, Russell Williams 2
PORTER, Samuel 1
PORTER, Sarah 1
PORTER, Seton 3
PORTER, Silas Wright 1
PORTER, Stephen Geyer 1
PORTER, Sydney 1
PORTER, Theodoric 1
PORTER, Thomas Conrad 1
PORTER, Timothy H. H
PORTER, Valentine Mott 1
PORTER, Washington Tullis 1
PORTER, Whitney Clair 5
PORTER, William Arnold 6
PORTER, William Curren 4
PORTER, William David 1
PORTER, William Gove 4
PORTER, William Henry * 1
PORTER, William Luther 4
PORTER, William N(ichols) 5
PORTER, William Townsend 1
PORTER, William Trotter H
PORTER, William Wagener 1
PORTER, William Wallace 3
PORTERFIELD, Allen Wilson 1
PORTERFIELD, Lewis Broughton 2
PORTERFIELD, Robert Huffard 5
PORTERIE, Gaston Louis 4
PORTEVIN, Albert Marcel Germain Rene 4
PORTIER, Michael H
PORTINARI, Candido 4
PORTMAN, Eric 5
PORTMANN, Ursus Victor 4
PORTNOFF, Alexander H
PORTOLA, Gaspar de H
PORTOR, Laura Spencer 4
PORY, John H
POSEGATE, Mabel 3
POSEY, Chester Alfred 5

POSEY, Leroy R. 6
POSEY, Thomas H
POSEY, William Campbell 1
POSNER, Edwin 5
POSNER, Harry 4
POSNER, Louis Samuel 5
POSNER, Stanley I. 4
POSSE, Rose (Baroness); also known as Rose Moore Strong. 5
POSSEL, René de 6
POST, Alice Thacher 2
POST, Chandler Rathfon 3
POST, Charles Addison 6
POST, Charles Johnson 3
POST, Charles William 1
POST, Chester Leroy 5
POST, Christian Frederick H
POST, Edwin 1
POST, Elwyn Donald 4
POST, Emily 1
POST, Frank Truman 1
POST, George Adams 1
POST, George Browne 1
POST, George Edward 1
POST, Herbert Wilson 4
POST, Hoyt Garrod 3
POST, Isaac H
POST, James D. 1
POST, James Howell 1
POST, James Otis 3
POST, Josephine Fowler 2
POST, Jotham Jr. H
POST, Kenneth 3
POST, Lawrence T. 3
POST, Levi Arnold 5
POST, Louis Freeland 1
POST, Marjorie Merriweather 6
POST, Martin Hayward 1
POST, Melville Davisson 1
POST, Philip Sidney H
POST, Regis Henri 2
POST, Roswell Olcott 4
POST, Truman Marcellus 1
POST, W. Merritt 1
POST, Waldron Kintzing 3
POST, Wilber E. 4
POST, Wiley 1
POST, William Stone 1
POST, Wright H
POSTL, Karl Anton H
POSTLE, Wilbur Everett 1
POSTLETHWAITE, Robert Hodgshon 4
POSTLETHWAITE, William Wallace 5
POSTNIKOV, Fedor Alexis (F. A. Post) 5
POSTON, Charles Pebrille H
POSTON, Elias McClellan 1
POSTON, Lawrence Sanford Jr. 6
POTEAT, Edwin McNeill 1
POTEAT, Edwin McNeill 3
POTEAT, Hubert McNeill 3
POTEAT, James Douglass 2
POTEAT, William Louis 1
POTHIER, Aram J. 1
POTOCKI, Jerzy 4
POTRATZ, Herbert August 6
POTT, Francis Lister Hawks 2
POTT, John H
POTT, William Sumner Appleton 4
POTTENGER, Francis Marion 4
POTTER, Albert Franklin 4
POTTER, Albert Knight 4
POTTER, Alfred Claghorn 1
POTTER, Alfred Knight 1
POTTER, Allen H
POTTER, Alonzo H
POTTER, Burton Willis 4
POTTER, Charles 5
POTTER, Charles Francis 4
POTTER, Charles Lewis 1
POTTER, Charles Nelson 1
POTTER, Chester Magee 6
POTTER, Clarkson 6
POTTER, Clarkson Nott 1
POTTER, Cora Urquhart 1
POTTER, David 5
POTTER, David Morris 5
POTTER, Delbert Maxwell 5
POTTER, Edward Clark 1
POTTER, Edward Eels 1
POTTER, Edwin Augustus 1
POTTER, Eliphalet Nott 1
POTTER, Elisha Reynolds * H
POTTER, Ellen Culver 3
POTTER, Emery Davis H
POTTER, Frank B(ell) 5
POTTER, Frank Maxson 2
POTTER, George Milton 5
POTTER, George W. 3

POTTER, Harry S. 5
POTTER, Henry Codman 1
POTTER, Henry Noel 5
POTTER, Henry Staples 1
POTTER, Homer Dexter 1
POTTER, Horatio H
POTTER, James H
POTTER, Mrs. James 1
Brown
POTTER, John Fox 1
POTTER, John Milton 4
POTTER, John Wesley 4
POTTER, Justin 1
POTTER, Louis 1
POTTER, Margaret Horton 1
POTTER, Marion E. 3
POTTER, Mark Winslow 2
POTTER, Mary Knight 1
POTTER, Mary Ross 5
POTTER, Nathaniel H
POTTER, Nathaniel 5
Bowditch
POTTER, Orlando Brunson H
POTTER, Orrin W. 1
POTTER, Paul Meredith 1
POTTER, Platt H
POTTER, Robert H
POTTER, Robert Brown H
POTTER, Rockwell Harmon 4
POTTER, Roderick 4
POTTER, Samuel John H
POTTER, Samuel Otway 4
Lewis
POTTER, Stephen 5
POTTER, Thomas Albert 2
POTTER, Thomas Paine 1
POTTER, Wilfrid Carne 2
POTTER, William H
POTTER, William Bancroft 1
POTTER, William Bleecker 1
POTTER, William Chapman 3
POTTER, William Henry 1
POTTER, William J. 4
POTTER, William James H
POTTER, William Parker 1
POTTER, William Plumer 1
POTTER, William W. 5
POTTER, William Warren 1
POTTER, William Wilson 1
POTTERTON, Thomas 1
Edward
POTTHAST, Edward Henry 1
POTTLE, Emory Bemsley H
POTTS, Alfred Fremont 1
POTTS, Benjamin Franklin H
POTTS, Charles Edwin 1
POTTS, Charles Sower 1
POTTS, David Jr. H
POTTS, James Henry 1
POTTS, James Henry 2
POTTS, Jonathan H
POTTS, Louis Moses 1
POTTS, Richard H
POTTS, Robert 1
POTTS, Robert Joseph 4
POTTS, Roy C. 6
POTTS, Templin Morris 1
POTTS, William 1
POTTS, Willis John 5
POTTS, Wylodine Gabbert 5
(Mrs. Thomas C. Potts)
POTZGER, John E. 3
POU, Edward William 1
POU, James Hinton 1
POUCH, William Henry 3
POUILLY, Jacques Nicholas H
Bussiere de
POUILLY, Joseph de H
POULENC, Francis 4
POULOS, Raleigh Anest 6
POULSON, Zachariah H
POULSSON, Anne Emilie 1
POUND, Arthur 4
POUND, Cuthbert Winfred 1
POUND, Earl Clifford 2
POUND, Ezra 5
POUND, G(rellet) C. 5
POUND, Jere M. 1
POUND, Jere M. 4
POUND, Louise 3
POUND, Roscoe 4
POUND, Thomas 4
POURTALES, Louis H
Francois de
POUSETTE-DART, 4
Nathaniel
POWDERLY, Terence 1
Vincent
POWDERMAKER, 5
Hortense
POWE, Thomas Erasmus 2
POWEL, Harford 3
POWEL, John Hare 1
POWELL H
POWELL, Aaron Macy 1

POWELL, Adam Clayton 5
Jr.
POWELL, Alden L. 3
POWELL, Alfred H. H
POWELL, Arthur Gray 3
POWELL, Arthur James 3
Emery
POWELL, Benjamin 4
Harrison
POWELL, Caroline Amelia 1
POWELL, Caroline Amelia 5
POWELL, Carroll A. 2
POWELL, Cecil Frank 5
POWELL, Charles Francis 1
POWELL, Charles L. 1
POWELL, Charles Stuart H
POWELL, Charles Underhill 3
POWELL, Cuthbert 1
POWELL, David 1
POWELL, Dawn 5
POWELL, Desmond Stevens 4
POWELL, Dick 5
POWELL, Doane 3
POWELL, Donald Adams 5
POWELL, E. Alxander 3
POWELL, E. Harrison 4
POWELL, Earl 4
POWELL, Edward 1
Alexander
POWELL, Edward Henry 4
POWELL, Edward Lindsay 1
POWELL, Edward Payson 1
POWELL, Edward Thomson 5
POWELL, Elmer Ellsworth 2
POWELL, Elmer Nathaniel 2
POWELL, Fred Wilbur 4
POWELL, Frederick 4
POWELL, G. Harold 1
POWELL, G. Thomas 4
POWELL, G. Thomas 5
POWELL, George May 1
POWELL, Hunter Holmes 1
POWELL, John 4
POWELL, John Benjamin 2
POWELL, John H. 1
POWELL, John Lee 4
POWELL, John Wesley 4
POWELL, Joseph Wright 3
POWELL, Joseph Yancey 1
POWELL, Junius L. 4
POWELL, Lazarus H
Whitehead
POWELL, Levin H
POWELL, Lucien Whiting 1
POWELL, Lula E. 3
POWELL, Lyman Pierson 2
POWELL, Lyman Theodore 6
Jr.
POWELL, Maud 1
POWELL, Nathan 5
POWELL, Noble Cilley 5
POWELL, Paul 5
POWELL, Paulus H
POWELL, Paulus Prince 4
POWELL, Rachel Hopper 4
POWELL, Ralph Lorin 6
POWELL, Ray E. 6
POWELL, Richard Holmes 2
POWELL, Richard Sterling 5
POWELL, Robert 1
POWELL, Samuel H
POWELL, Snelling 1
POWELL, Talcott Williams 1
POWELL, Thomas H
POWELL, Thomas 1
POWELL, Thomas Carr 2
POWELL, Thomas Edward 4
POWELL, Thomas Reed 4
POWELL, Warren Thomson 3
POWELL, Weldon 4
POWELL, William H
Bramwell
POWELL, William Byrd H
POWELL, William Dan 2
POWELL, William David 1
POWELL, William Frank 4
POWELL, William 1
Hamilton
POWELL, William Henry H
POWELL, William Henry 1
POWELL, William M. 4
POWELL, Wilson Marcy H
POWELL, Wilson Marcy 4
POWELSON, Abram James 6
POWELSON, Wilfrid Van H
Nest
POWER, Charles Gavan 5
POWER, Ethel B. 6
POWER, Frank W. 4
POWER, Frederick Belding 1
POWER, Frederick 1
Dunglison
POWER, Howard Anderson 3
POWER, James Edward 1
POWER, John H
POWER, John Joseph Jr. 5

POWER, Thomas Charles 1
POWER, Thomas S. 6
POWER, Tyrone 3
POWERS, Caleb 1
POWERS, Carol Hoyt 1
POWERS, Charles Andrew 1
POWERS, Daniel William H
POWERS, Delmar Thomas 2
POWERS, Edwin Booth 2
POWERS, Eugene Paul 5
POWERS, Franklin Brown 4
POWERS, Frederick Alton 1
POWERS, George 1
McClellan
POWERS, Gershom 1
POWERS, Grover Francis 5
POWERS, H. Henry 1
POWERS, Harry 4
Huntington
POWERS, Harry Joseph 1
POWERS, Harry Joseph 2
POWERS, Hiram 1
POWERS, Horatio Nelson 1
POWERS, Hugh Winfield 1
POWERS, James Knox 1
POWERS, James T. 1
POWERS, John Craig 3
POWERS, Joseph Harrell 5
POWERS, Joseph Neely 1
POWERS, Leland Todd 1
POWERS, Leon Walter 2
POWERS, Leonard Stewart 6
POWERS, Levi Moore 1
POWERS, LeGrand 4
POWERS, Llewellyn 1
POWERS, Luther Milton 1
POWERS, Orlando 1
Woodworth
POWERS, Pliny H. 4
POWERS, Ralph Averill 1
POWERS, Ridgely Ceylon 1
POWERS, Robert Davis Jr. 5
POWERS, Samuel Leland 1
POWERS, Samuel Ralph 5
POWERS, Sidney 1
POWERS, Sue McFall 6
POWERS, Thomas Jefferson 5
POWERS, Tom 3
POWERS, William Dudley 1
POWERS, William L. 1
POWERS, William 6
T(homas)
POWHATAN H
POWLEY, N. R. 3
POWLISON, Charles Ford 2
POWNALL, Mrs. H
POWNALL, Charles Alan 6
POWNALL, Thomas H
POWYS, John Cowper 4
POWYS, Llewelyn 2
POYDRAS, Julien de 1
Lallande
POYNTER, Charles William 3
McCorkle
POYNTER, Clara Martin 1
POYNTER, Henrietta 4
POYNTER, Juliet Jameson 6
POYNTER, Paul 3
POYNTER, William A. 1
POYNTON, John Albert 1
POYNTZ, James M. 1
POZNANSKI, Gustavus H
PRACHT, Charles Frederick 6
PRADO UGARTECHE, 4
Manuel
PRADT, Louis Augustus 1
PRAEGER, Otto 2
PRAHL, Augustus John 5
PRALL, Anning S. 1
PRALL, Charles Edward 1
PRALL, David Wight 1
PRALL, William 1
PRANG, Louis 1
PRANG, Mary Dana Hicks 1
PRANKARD, Harry Irving 1
II
PRASAD, Rajendra 4
PRATHER, Perry Franklin 4
PRATHER, Thomas J. 4
PRATT, Agnes Edwards 3
Rothery
PRATT, Arthur Peabody 5
PRATT, Auguste G. 1
PRATT, Bela Lyon 1
PRATT, Charles H
PRATT, Charles 3
PRATT, Charles C. 1
PRATT, Charles Dudley 5
PRATT, Charles Henry 1
PRATT, Charles Millard 1
PRATT, Charles Stebbins 5
PRATT, Charles Stuart 1
PRATT, Daniel * H
PRATT, Daniel 2
PRATT, Daniel Darwin H
PRATT, Don Forrester 2

PRATT, Dwight Mallory 1
PRATT, Edward Barton 4
PRATT, Edwin Hartley 1
PRATT, Ella Farman 1
PRATT, Enoch H
PRATT, Fletcher 3
PRATT, Florence Gibb 1
PRATT, Frank Randall 4
PRATT, Frederic Bayley 1
PRATT, Frederic Haven 3
PRATT, Frederick Sanford 5
PRATT, George Collins 1
PRATT, George Dupont 1
PRATT, George Dwight 1
PRATT, George K. 3
PRATT, Harcourt J. 4
PRATT, Harold Irving 1
PRATT, Harold Irving 6
PRATT, Harry Edward 4
PRATT, Harry Emerson 3
PRATT, Harry Hayt 1
PRATT, Harry Noyes 2
PRATT, Harry Rogers 3
PRATT, Henry Cheever H
PRATT, Henry Conger 4
PRATT, Henry Sherring 1
PRATT, Herbert Lee 2
PRATT, James Alfred 1
PRATT, James Bissett 2
PRATT, James Timothy 1
PRATT, John Francis 4
PRATT, John L. 6
PRATT, John Lowell 5
PRATT, John Teele 1
PRATT, Joseph Hersey 1
PRATT, Joseph Hyde 2
PRATT, Joseph M. 2
PRATT, Le Gage 1
PRATT, Lewellyn 1
PRATT, Lucy 5
PRATT, Matthew H
PRATT, Orson H
PRATT, Orville Clyde 3
PRATT, Parley Parker 1
PRATT, Pascal Paoli 1
PRATT, Richard Henry 1
PRATT, Richardson 1
PRATT, Ruth Sears Baker 3
PRATT, Samuel Wheeler 1
PRATT, Sedgwick 1
PRATT, Sereno S. 1
PRATT, Silas Gamaliel 1
PRATT, Steve 6
PRATT, Stewart Camden 3
PRATT, Thomas George 1
PRATT, Thomas Willis H
PRATT, Waldo Selden 1
PRATT, Wallace 1
PRATT, Walter Merriam 6
PRATT, William Veazie 3
PRATT, Zadock 1
PRATTE, Bernard H
PRAY, Charles Nelson 4
PRAY, Isaac Clark 1
PRAY, James Sturgis 1
PRAY, Theron Brown 1
PREBLE, Edward H
PREBLE, Edward A. 3
PREBLE, Fred Myron 1
PREBLE, George Henry H
PREBLE, Robert Bruce 2
PREBLE, William Pitt 1
PREBLE, William Pitt Jr. 1
PREETORIUS, Emil 1
PREGEANT, Victor Eugene 5
III
PRELLWITZ, Edith Mitchill 2
PRELLWITZ, Henry 1
PRENDERGAST, Albert 1
Collins
PRENDERGAST, Charles 2
Francis
PRENDERGAST, Edmond 1
Francis
PRENDERGAST, James M. 1
Brazil
PRENDERGAST, Maurice 1
PRENDERGAST, William 3
A.
PRENTICE, Bernon 2
Sheldon
PRENTICE, E. Parmalee 3
PRENTICE, George H
Dennison
PRENTICE, George Gordon 1
PRENTICE, James Stuart 5
PRENTICE, Samuel Oscar 1
PRENTICE, Sartell 1
PRENTICE, William Kelly 4
PRENTICE, William Packer 1
PRENTIS, Henning Webb 3
Jr.
PRENTIS, Robert Riddick 1
PRENTISS, Benjamin 1
Maybury
PRENTISS, Daniel Webster 1

PRENTISS, Elizabeth H
Payson
PRENTISS, Francis Fleury 1
PRENTISS, George Lewis 1
PRENTISS, Henry James 1
PRENTISS, John Holmes H
PRENTISS, John Wing 1
PRENTISS, Samuel 1
PRENTISS, Seargent Smith H
PRENTISS, Theodore 3
PRESBREY, Eugene W. 1
PRESBREY, Frank 1
PRESBY, Charlotte Sulley 5
PRESCOTT, Albert 1
Benjamin
PRESCOTT, Anson Ward 1
PRESCOTT, Arthur Taylor 5
PRESCOTT, Charles Henry 1
PRESCOTT, Daniel Alfred 5
PRESCOTT, Dorothy 1
PRESCOTT, Edward Purcell 5
PRESCOTT, Frank Clarke 1
PRESCOTT, Frederick 1
Clarke
PRESCOTT, George Bartlett H
PRESCOTT, Henry 2
Washington
PRESCOTT, John S. 3
PRESCOTT, Mary H
Newmarch
PRESCOTT, Oliver 1
PRESCOTT, Oliver 1
PRESCOTT, Samuel H
PRESCOTT, Samuel Cate 4
PRESCOTT, Stedman 5
PRESCOTT, William H
Hickling
PRESCOTT, William Ray 4
PRESS, Otto 6
PRESS, Samuel David 1
PRESSER, Theodore 1
PRESSEY, Henry Albert 1
PRESSLY, Frank Young 4
PRESSLY, Mason Wylie 4
PRESSMAN, Joel J. 4
PREST, William Morton 1
PRESTON, Adelaide B. 5
PRESTON, Andrew W. 1
PRESTON, Ann H
PRESTON, Arthur Murray 5
PRESTON, Austin Roe 1
PRESTON, Byron Webster 1
PRESTON, Cecil Anthony 1
PRESTON, Charles Miller 2
PRESTON, Douglas A. 1
PRESTON, Elwyn Greeley 3
PRESTON, Erasmus Darwin 1
PRESTON, Frances Folsom 2
PRESTON, Francis H
PRESTON, George H. 1
PRESTON, George Junkin 1
PRESTON, Guy Henry 3
PRESTON, Harold 1
PRESTON, Harriet Waters 1
PRESTON, Herbert R. 1
PRESTON, Howard Hall 4
PRESTON, Howard Payne 4
PRESTON, Howard Willis 1
PRESTON, Hulon 4
PRESTON, Jacob Alexander H
PRESTON, James Harry 1
PRESTON, John Fisher 5
PRESTON, John Smith 1
PRESTON, John White 5
PRESTON, Jonas 1
PRESTON, Jonathan H
PRESTON, Josephine 3
Corliss
PRESTON, Keith 1
PRESTON, Malcolm 5
Greenhough
PRESTON, Margaret Junkin H
PRESTON, Ord 3
PRESTON, Paul H
PRESTON, Robert J. 5
PRESTON, Robert Louis 6
PRESTON, Roger 3
PRESTON, Thomas Jex Jr. 4
PRESTON, Thomas L. 3
PRESTON, Thomas Ross 3
PRESTON, Thomas Scott 1
PRESTON, William H
PRESTON, William Ballard H
PRESTON, William H
Campbell
PRESTRIDGE, John 1
Newton
PRETTYMAN, Cornelius 2
William
PRETTYMAN, E(lijah) 5
Barrett
PRETTYMAN, Forrest 2
Johnston
PRETTYMAN, Virgil 5
PREUS, Jacob Aail Ottesen 4

PREUS, Ove J. H. 3
PREUSS, Arthur 1
PREUSS, Lawrence 3
PREVOST, Clifford Alfred 6
PREVOST, Eugene-Prosper H
PREVOST, Francois Marie H
PREWITT, Ethan C. 6
PREYER, Allan Talmage 4
PREYER, Carl Adolph 2
PREYER, William Yost 5
PRIBER, Christian H
PRIBRAM, Ernest August 1
PRICE, Abel Fitzwater 1
PRICE, Andrew 3
PRICE, Bertram John 2
PRICE, Bruce 1
PRICE, Burr 3
PRICE, Butler Delaplaine 1
PRICE, Carl Fowler 2
PRICE, Charles Browne 1
PRICE, Charles S. 4
PRICE, Charles Wilson 1
PRICE, Chester B. 4
PRICE, Christopher Herbert 6
PRICE, David James 3
PRICE, Edwin R. 4
PRICE, Eldridge Cowman 1
PRICE, Eli Kirk H
PRICE, Enoch Jones 2
PRICE, Francis 4
PRICE, Frank 1
PRICE, Frank J. 1
PRICE, Frank Wilson 6
PRICE, Franklin Haines 3
PRICE, George Clinton 4
PRICE, George Edmund 1
PRICE, George Hunter 1
PRICE, George McCready 4
PRICE, George Merriman 3
PRICE, George Moses 2
PRICE, Granville 6
PRICE, Hannibal 5
PRICE, Harrison Jackson 2
PRICE, Harvey Lee 3
PRICE, Henry Ferris 4
PRICE, Henry Vernon 6
PRICE, Hickman 1
PRICE, Hiram 1
PRICE, Hobert 4
PRICE, Homer Charles 3
PRICE, Howard Campbell 3
PRICE, Ira Maurice 1
PRICE, J. St. Clair 6
PRICE, Jacob Embury 1
PRICE, James Houston 4
PRICE, James Hubert 2
PRICE, James L. 1
PRICE, James Woods 3
PRICE, Jesse Dashiell 1
PRICE, John D. 3
PRICE, John G. 1
PRICE, John Roy 6
PRICE, Joseph Lindon 5
PRICE, Julian 2
PRICE, Lee 4
PRICE, Lucien 4
PRICE, Margaret (Mrs. Hickman Price Jr.) 5
PRICE, Margaret Wright 5
PRICE, Marshall Langton 1
PRICE, Miles Oscar 5
PRICE, Milo B. 1
PRICE, Ore Lee 5
PRICE, Orlo Josiah 2
PRICE, Oscar Jay 1
PRICE, Overton Westfeldt 1
PRICE, P. Frank 3
PRICE, R. Holleman 4
PRICE, Raymond B. 5
PRICE, Richard Nye 1
PRICE, Richard Rees 5
PRICE, Robert Beverly 4
PRICE, Robert Henderson 4
PRICE, Robert Martin 1
PRICE, Rodman McCamley H
PRICE, Sadie F. 1
PRICE, Samuel H
PRICE, Samuel D. 1
PRICE, Samuel Woodson H
PRICE, Samuel Woodson 4
PRICE, Silas Eber 1
PRICE, Stephen H
PRICE, Sterling H
PRICE, Theodore Hazeltine 1
PRICE, Thomas Lawson H
PRICE, Thomas Randolph 1
PRICE, Viola Millron (Mrs. Edmund Glen Price) 6
PRICE, Walter L. 4
PRICE, Walter Winston 2
PRICE, Warren Elbridge 4
PRICE, Warwick James 1
PRICE, William Cecil H
PRICE, William Cecil 4
PRICE, William Francis 6
PRICE, William Gray Jr. 5
PRICE, William Henry 4
PRICE, William Hundley Jr. 5
PRICE, William Jennings 3
PRICE, William Pierce 1
PRICE, William Raleigh 1
PRICE, William Sylvester 6
PRICE, William Thompson H
PRICE, William Thompson 1
PRICE, William Wightman 5
PRICHARD, Augustus Bedlow 4
PRICHARD, Frank Perley 1
PRICHARD, Harold Adye 2
PRICHARD, Lev H. 2
PRICHARD, Sarah Johnson 1
PRICHARD, Theodore Jan 6
PRICHARD, Vernon E. 2
PRICKETT, Alva LeRoy 6
PRICKETT, Joe Milroy 3
PRICKETT, William 4
PRICKITT, William Augustus 1
PRIDDY, Lawrence 2
PRIDE, Frederick W.R. 5
PRIDE, H(erbert) Hammond 6
PRIDE, Maynard Prince 6
PRIDGEON, Charles Hamilton 1
PRIDMORE, John Edmund Oldaker 1
PRIEST, Alan 5
PRIEST, George Madison 2
PRIEST, Henry Samuel 1
PRIEST, Ira Allen 4
PRIEST, Irwin G. 1
PRIEST, Ivy Baker 6
PRIEST, James Percy 3
PRIEST, Walter Scott 1
PRIEST, Wells Blodgett 3
PRIESTLEY, George Colin 1
PRIESTLEY, Herbert Ingram 2
PRIESTLEY, James H
PRIESTLEY, Joseph H
PRIME, Benjamin Youngs H
PRIME, Ebenezer Scudder 1
PRIME, Edward Dorr Griffin H
PRIME, Frederick 1
PRIME, Frederick Edward 1
PRIME, Nathaniel Scudder H
PRIME, Ralph Earl 1
PRIME, Samuel Irenaeus H
PRIME, Samuel Thornton Kemeys 1
PRIME, William Cowper 1
PRIMER, Sylvester 1
PRIME-STEVESON, Edward Irenaeus 4
PRIMROSE, John 3
PRIMS, James Edwin 5
PRINCE, Arthur Warren 3
PRINCE, Benjamin F. 1
PRINCE, Eugene Mitchell 4
PRINCE, Frank Moody 1
PRINCE, Frederick Henry 3
PRINCE, George Harrison 1
PRINCE, George W. 1
PRINCE, Helen Choate 4
PRINCE, John Dyneley 2
PRINCE, John Tilden 1
PRINCE, John W. 4
PRINCE, L. Bradford 1
PRINCE, Leon Cushing 1
PRINCE, Leon Nathaniel 5
PRINCE, Morton 1
PRINCE, Nathan Dyer 2
PRINCE, Oliver Hillhouse H
PRINCE, Sydney Rhodes 2
PRINCE, Thomas H
PRINCE, Walter Franklin 1
PRINCE, William * H
PRINCE, William Loftin 2
PRINCE, William Robert H
PRINDLE, Edwin Jay 2
PRINDLE, Elizur H. H
PRINDLE, Frances Weston Carruth 4
PRINDLE, Franklin Cogswell 1
PRING, Martin H
PRINGEY, Joseph Colburn 3
PRINGLE, Benjamin H
PRINGLE, Coleman Roberson 1
PRINGLE, Cyrus Guernsey 1
PRINGLE, Ernest Henry 3
PRINGLE, Henry Fowles 3
PRINGLE, Henry Nelson 2
PRINGLE, James Nelson 2
PRINGLE, Joel Roberts Poinsett 1
PRINGLE, John Julius H
PRINGLE, Kenneth Ralph 6
PRINGLE, Ralph 1
PRINGLE, Ralph W. 3
PRINGLE, Robert Smith 1
PRINGLE, William James 1
PRINGLE, William James 6
PRINGSHEIM, Neena Hamilton (Mrs.) 5
PRINOSCH, Francis J. 5
PRINTZ, Johan Bjornsson H
PRINZ, Hermann 3
PRINZMETAL, Isadore Harry 5
PRIOR, Harris King 6
PRIOR, Herbert M. 3
PRIOR, William Matthew H
PRISK, Charles Henry 1
PRISK, William Frederick 4
PRITCHARD, Arthur John 1
PRITCHARD, Arthur Thomas 1
PRITCHARD, Harry N. 5
PRITCHARD, Harry Otis 1
PRITCHARD, Jeter Connelly 1
PRITCHARD, John F. 4
PRITCHARD, John Wagner 1
PRITCHARD, Myron Thomas 1
PRITCHARD, Richard E. 4
PRITCHARD, Richard Edward 4
PRITCHARD, Samuel Reynolds 1
PRITCHARD, Stuart 1
PRITCHARD, William Hobbs 1
PRITCHETT, Carr Waller 1
PRITCHETT, Clifton Augustine 3
PRITCHETT, Henry Smith 1
PRITCHETT, Joseph Johnston 5
PRITCHETT, Lafayette Bow 4
PRITCHETT, Norton 4
PRITZKER, Donald Nicholas 5
PRIZER, Edward 1
PROBASCO, Henry 1
PROBASCO, Scott Livingston 4
PROBERT, Frank Holman 1
PROBERT, Lionel Charles 1
PROBST, Charles Oliver 1
PROBST, Marvin 5
PROBST, Nathan 5
PROCHNIK, Edgar Leo Gustav 4
PROCOPE, Hjalmar Johan Fredrik 3
PROCTER, Addison Gilbert 1
PROCTER, Arthur Wyman 4
PROCTER, William 3
PROCTER, William Cooper 1
PROCTOR, A. Phimister 3
PROCTOR, Bernard Emerson 3
PROCTOR, Carroll Leigh 5
PROCTOR, David 6
PROCTOR, Edna Dean 1
PROCTOR, Fletcher Dutton 1
PROCTOR, Frederick Cocke 1
PROCTOR, Henry Hugh 1
PROCTOR, James McPherson 3
PROCTOR, John Robert 1
PROCTOR, John Thomas 1
PROCTOR, Joseph H
PROCTOR, Lucien Brock H
PROCTOR, Mortimer Robinson 5
PROCTOR, Redfield 1
PROCTOR, Redfield 3
PROCTOR, Robert 5
PROCTOR, Thomas Redfield 1
PROCTOR, Thomas William 1
PROCTOR, William H
PROCTOR, William Martin 1
PROFFIT, George H. H
PROFFITT, Edward J. W. 4
PROFFITT, Henry Walton 5
PROFFITT, Maris Marion 6
PROHASKA, John Van 5
PROKOFIEFF, Serge 3
PROKOSCH, Eduard 1
PROPER, Datus DeWitt 4
PROPER, Datus Edwin 4
PROPPER DE CALLEJON, Don Eduardo 5
PROSCHOWSKI, Frantz James Edward 4
PROSKAUER, Joseph M. 5
PROSSER, Charles Allen 5
PROSSER, Charles Smith 1
PROSSER, Paul Pittman 1
PROSSER, Seward 2
PROSSWIMMER, Paul E. 6
PROTHERO, James Harrison 1
PROTHEROE, Daniel 1
PROTITCH, Dragoslav 6
PROTTENGEIER, Conrad Gettfried 2
PROUD, Robert H
PROUDFIT, David Law H
PROUT, Frank J. 4
PROUT, G. R. 3
PROUT, Henry Goslee 5
PROUT, William Christopher 1
PROUTY, Charles Azro 1
PROUTY, Charles Tyler 6
PROUTY, George Herbert 1
PROUTY, Olive Higgins 6
PROUTY, Solomon Francis 4
PROUTY, William Frederick 6
PROUTY, Winston Lewis 5
PROVENCE, Herbert Winston 5
PROVENCE, Samuel Moore 4
PROVINE, John William 2
PROVINE, Loring Harvey 6
PROVINE, Robert Calhoun 4
PROVINSE, John H. 4
PROVOOST, Samuel H
PROVOST, Etienne H
PROVOSTY, Olivier O. 1
PROWELL, George R. 1
PROWSE, Robert John 5
PRUDDEN, Russell Field 5
PRUDDEN, T. Mitchell 1
PRUDEN, Oscar L. 1
PRUD'HOMME, John Francis Eugene H
PRUGH, Byron Edgar Peart 1
PRUITT, Raymond S. 3
PRUNTY, Merle Charles 5
PRUSSING, Eugene Ernst 1
PRUTTON, Carl Frederick 5
PRUYN, H. Sewall 5
PRUYN, John Van Schaick Lansing H
PRUYN, Robert Clarence 4
PRUYN, Robert Hewson H
PRYOR, Arthur 2
PRYOR, Edward Bailey 1
PRYOR, Ike T. 1
PRYOR, James Chambers 2
PRYOR, Nathaniel H
PRYOR, Ralph H(untington) 5
PRYOR, Roger 6
PRYOR, Roger Atkinson 1
PRYOR, Samuel F. 1
PRYOR, Sara Agnes 1
PRYOR, Thomas Brady 3
PRYOR, William Rice 1
PUBLICKER, Harry 3
PUCHNER, Irving A. 5
PUCKETT, B. Earl 6
PUCKETT, Charles Alexander 5
PUCKETT, Erastus Paul 3
PUCKETT, Newbell Niles 4
PUCKETT, William Olin 5
PUCKETTE, Charles McDonald 3
PUCKNER, William August 1
PUDDEFOOT, William George 1
PUELICHER, Albert Siefert 4
PUELICHER, John Huegin 1
PUENTE, Giuseppe Del H
PUFFER, J. Adams 3
PUGET, Peter Richings H
PUGH, Arthur Benton 1
PUGH, Charles E. 1
PUGH, Ellis H
PUGH, Evan H
PUGH, George Bernard 1
PUGH, George Ellis H
PUGH, Griffith Thompson 5
PUGH, James Lawrence 1
PUGH, John H
PUGH, John Jones 2
PUGH, Robert Chalfant 1
PUGH, Samuel J. 4
PUGH, William Barrow 3
PUGH, William Leonard 5
PUGH, William Samuel 3
PUGMIRE, Ernest Ivison 3
PUGSLEY, Charles William 1
PUGSLEY, Chester DeWitt 6
PUGSLEY, Cornelius Amory 1
PUJO, Arsene Paulin 1
PULASKI, Casimir H
PULESTON, William Dilworth 6
PULIDO, Augusto F. 5
PULITZER, Albert 1
PULITZER, Joseph 1
PULITZER, Joseph 3
PULITZER, Ralph 1
PULITZER, Walter 1
PULLEN, Elisabeth 5
PULLEN, Herbert Armitage 1
PULLEN, Roscoe LeRoy 3
PULLEN, William Russell 6
PULLER, Edwin Seward 2
PULLEY, Frederick 5
PULLIAM, Eugene Collins 6
PULLIAM, Roscoe 2
PULLIAM, William Ellis 3
PULLING, Arthur Clement 4
PULLMAN, George Mortimer H
PULLMAN, James Minton 1
PULLMAN, John 5
PULLMAN, John Stephenson 2
PULLY, Bernard Shaw 5
PULSIFER, Harold Trowbridge 2
PULSIFER, Harry Bridgman 2
PULSIFER, Lawson Valentine 6
PULSIFER, Nathan Trowbridge 1
PULSIFER, William E. 1
PULTE, Joseph Hippolyt H
PULTZ, Leon M(erle) 5
PULVER, Arthur Wadworth 1
PULVERMACHER, Joseph 4
PUMPELLY, Josiah Collins 1
PUMPELLY, Raphael 1
PUNDERFORD, John Keeler 1
PUPIN, Michael Idvorsky 1
PUPPEL, I. Darin 6
PURCE, Charles Lee 1
PURCELL, Charles Henry 3
PURCELL, Francis Andrew 5
PURCELL, Ganson 4
PURCELL, George William 3
PURCELL, Henry 1
PURCELL, John Baptist H
PURCELL, Richard J. 3
PURCELL, Theodore Vincent 3
PURCELL, William 1
PURCELL, William E. 1
PURCELL, William Henry 2
PURDON, Alexander 5
PURDON, Charles de la Cherois 4
PURDUE, Albert Homer 1
PURDUE, John H
PURDUM, Smith White 2
PURDY, Corydon Tyler 2
PURDY, Edward A. 2
PURDY, George Flint 5
PURDY, Ken William 5
PURDY, Lawson 3
PURDY, Milton Dwight 1
PURDY, Richard Augustus 1
PURDY, Richard Townsend 5
PURDY, Ross Coffin 3
PURDY, Smith Meade H
PURDY, Thomas C. 4
PURDY, Victor William 4
PURDY, Warren Grafton 1
PURIN, Charles Maltador 5
PURINGTON, Florence 3
PURINGTON, George Colby 1
PURINTON, Daniel Boardman 1
PURINTON, Edward Earle 3
PURINTON, Herbert Ronelle 1
PURKISS, Albert C. 5
PURMORT, Charles Hiram 4
PURMORT, LaDoyt Gilman 4
PURNELL, Benjamin H
PURNELL, Benjamin 4
PURNELL, Frank 3
PURNELL, Fred Sampson 1
PURNELL, Maurice Eugene 6
PURNELL, Oscar M. 4
PURNELL, Thomas Richard 1
PURNELL, William C(hilds) 5
PURNELL, William Henry H
PURNELL, William Reynolds 3
PURPLE, Samuel Smith 1
PURRINGTON, William Archer 1
PURRY, Jean Pierre H
PURSH, Frederick H
PURUCKER, Gottfried de 2
PURVES, Clifford Burrough 4
PURVES, Dale Benson 4

* Indicates More Than One Such Name Listed

PURVES, Edmund Randolph 4
PURVES, George T. 1
PURVIANCE, David H
PURVIANCE, Samuel Anderson H
PURVIANCE, Samuel Dinsmore H
PURVIS, Charles B. 4
PURVIS, William Edmond 1
PURYEAR, Charles 3
PURYEAR, Richard Clausele
PURYEAR, Vernon John 6
PUSEY, Brown 3
PUSEY, Caleb H
PUSEY, Edwin Davis 5
PUSEY, William Allen 4
PUSHMAN, Hovsep 4
PUSHMATAHAW H
PUTERBAUGH, Jay G. 4
PUTERBAUGH, Leslie D. 1
PUTHUFF, Hanson Duvall 5
PUTMAN, Russell Lorain 6
PUTNAM, Albert William 3
PUTNAM, Alfred Porter 1
PUTNAM, Arthur 4
PUTNAM, Borden Roger 6
PUTNAM, Brenda 6
PUTNAM, Clarence Irwin 4
PUTNAM, Claude Adams 4
PUTNAM, Eben H
PUTNAM, Eben Fiske 3
Appleton
PUTNAM, Edward Kirby 1
PUTNAM, Edwin H
PUTNAM, Emily James 2
PUTNAM, Francis J. 1
PUTNAM, Frederic Ward 1
PUTNAM, George 3
PUTNAM, George 4
PUTNAM, George 1
Ellsworth
PUTNAM, George Haven 1
PUTNAM, George Jacob 4
PUTNAM, George Martin 3
PUTNAM, George Palmer H
PUTNAM, George Palmer 2
PUTNAM, George Rockwell 3
PUTNAM, Gideon 1
PUTNAM, H. St Clair 1
PUTNAM, Harrington 1
PUTNAM, Harvey H
PUTNAM, Helen Cordelia 1
PUTNAM, Herbert 3
PUTNAM, Israel H
PUTNAM, James Jackson 1
PUTNAM, James Osborne 1
PUTNAM, James William 1
PUTNAM, James Wright 1
PUTNAM, John Bishop 1
PUTNAM, John Pickering 1
PUTNAM, John Risley 2
PUTNAM, Mark Edson 4
PUTNAM, Nina Wilcox 4
PUTNAM, Rufus 1
PUTNAM, Russell Benjamin 3
PUTNAM, Ruth H
PUTNAM, Stephen Greeley 4
PUTNAM, Thomas Milton 4
PUTNAM, Warren Edward 1
PUTNAM, Warren Edward 2
PUTNAM, William 3
Hutchinson
PUTNAM, William Le 1
Baron
PUTNAM, William Lowell 1
PUTNAM, William Rowell 3
PUTNEY, Albert Hutchinson
PUTNEY, Elmore M. 3
PUZINAS, Paul Peter 5
PYE, William Satterlee 6
PYEATT, John Samuel 2
PYKE, W. E. 4
PYLE, Ernest Taylor 2
PYLE, Helen Mary 5
PYLE, Howard 1
PYLE, John Sherman 4
PYLE, Joseph Gilpin 1
PYLE, Katharine 1
PYLE, Robert 4
PYLE, Walter Lytle 1
PYLE, William H. 3
PYNCHON, John H
PYNCHON, Thomas 1
Ruggles
PYNCHON, William H
PYNE, Frederick Glover 4
PYNE, George Rovillo 1
PYNE, M. Taylor 1
PYNE, Percy Rivington II 1
PYNE, Percy Rivington II 1
PYRE, George John 5
PYRE, James Francis 1
Augustin

PYRKE, Berne Ashley 4
PYRON, Walter Braxton 3
PYRTLE, E. Ruth 5
PYUN, Yung-tai 5

Q

QASSIM, Abdul Karim 4
QUACKENBOS, John 1
Duncan
QUACKENBOSS, 4
Alexander
QUACKENBUSH, Larry 4
QUACKENBUSH, Stephen H
Platt
QUADE, Maurice Northrop 4
QUADE, Omar H. 4
QUAIFE, Milo Milton 3
QUAIL, Frank Adgate 5
QUAILE, George Emerson 5
QUAIN, Edwin Alphonsus 6
QUAIN, Eric P. 5
QUAINTANCE, Altus Lacy 5
QUALTROUGH, Edward 1
Francis
QUANAH H
QUANAH H
QUANTRELL, Ernest E. 4
QUANTRILL, William H
Clarke
QUARLES, Charles 1
QUARLES, Charles Bullen 5
QUARLES, Donald A. 3
QUARLES, Edwin Latham 5
QUARLES, James 3
QUARLES, James Addison 1
QUARLES, James Thomas 4
QUARLES, Joseph Very 1
QUARLES, Joseph Very III 2
QUARLES, Louis 5
QUARLES, Ralph P. 1
QUARLES, Tunstall H
QUARLES, William Charles H
QUARTER, William 1
QUARTLEY, Arthur H
QUASIMODO, Salvatore 5
QUATTROCCHI, Edmondo 4
QUAY, Arthur Hayes 1
QUAY, Matthew Stanley 1
QUAYLE, Henry Joseph 5
QUAYLE, John Francis 1
QUAYLE, John Harrison 2
QUAYLE, Oliver A. Jr. 3
QUAYLE, Osborne R. 3
QUAYLE, William Alfred 1
QUEALY, Patrick J. 1
QUEALY, Susan Jane 3
QUEEN, Walter H
QUEENY, Edgar Monsanto 5
QUEENY, John Francis 4
QUELCH, John 1
QUERBES, Andrew 1
QUEREAU, Edmund Chase 4
QUERY, Walter Graham 4
QUESADA, Manuel Castro 5
QUESNAY, Alexandre-Marie
QUESTA, Edward J. 4
QUEZON Y MOLINA, 2
Manuel Luis
QUIAT, Ira L(ouis) 5
QUICK, George W. 4
QUICK, Herbert 1
QUICK, Walter 4
QUICKERT, Marvin H. 6
QUIDOR, John H
QUIGG, James F. 4
QUIGG, Lemuel E. 1
QUIGGLE, Edmund 1
Blanchard
QUIGLEY, Harry Nelson 1
QUIGLEY, Jack Clement 6
QUIGLEY, James Cloyd 3
QUIGLEY, James Edward 1
QUIGLEY, John Paul 4
QUIGLEY, Martin Joseph 4
QUIGLEY, Samuel 3
QUIGLEY, Thomas M. 6
QUIGLEY, William 3
Middleton
QUILICI, George L. 1
QUILL, Michael J. 4
QUILLEN, I. James 4
QUILLEN, Robert 2
QUILLER-COUCH, Arthur 2
Thomas
QUILLIAN, Paul Whitfield 2
QUIMBY, Charles Elihu 1
QUIMBY, (Frank) Brooks 5
QUIMBY, Harriet 1
QUIMBY, Neal Frederic 4
QUIMBY, Phineas Parkhurst H
QUIN, Charles Kennon 1
QUIN, Clinton Simon 3
QUIN, Huston 1

QUIN, Percy Edwards 1
QUINAN, John Russell H
QUINBY, Frank Haviland 1
QUINBY, Henry Brewer 1
QUINBY, Isaac Ferdinand H
QUINBY, William Carter 5
QUINBY, William Emory H
QUINCEY, Josiah 1
QUINCY, Charles Frederick 1
QUINCY, Edmund H
QUINCY, Josiah H
QUINCY, Josiah 1
QUINCY, Josiah Phillips 1
QUINE, William E. 1
QUINLAN, George Austin 6
QUINLAN, John H
QUINLAN, Joseph A. 3
QUINLIVAN, Ray James 4
QUINN, Arthur Hobson 4
QUINN, Bernard G. 4
QUINN, Charles Henry 5
QUINN, Daniel Hellenist 1
QUINN, Daniel Joseph 1
QUINN, Edmond 1
QUINN, Edward James 6
QUINN, (Elisabeth) Vernon 6
QUINN, James Baird 1
QUINN, James H. 1
QUINN, James Leland 5
QUINN, John 1
QUINN, John Francis 5
QUINN, John Joseph 2
QUINN, Patrick Henry 3
QUINN, Ralph Hughes 1
QUINN, Robert Emmett 6
QUINN, Terence John 4
QUINN, Theodore Kinget 4
QUINN, Thomas Charles 4
QUINT, Wilder Dwight 1
QUINTARD, Charles Todd H
QUINTARD, Edward 1
QUINTARD, George 1
William
QUINTERO, Lamar Charles 1
QUINTON, Cornelia 1
Bentley Sage
QUINTON, Harold 5
QUINTON, John Henry 1
QUINTON, William 1
QUIRINO, Elpidio 3
QUIRK, Francis Joseph 6
QUIRK, James Robert 1
QUIRK, James Thomas 5
QUIRK, John F. 4
QUIRKE, Terence Thomas 2
QUISENBERRY, Anderson 1
Chenault
QUISENBERRY, Hiter 4
Nelson
QUISENBERRY, Russell A. 4
QUITMAN, John Anthony H
QUONIAM DE 1
SCHOMPRE, Guy Emile
Marie Joseph
QUYNN, Allen George 5

R

RAAB, Julius 4
RAAB, Wilhelm 5
RAABE, Arthur Edward 4
RAASCH, Richard Frederic 6
RABAUT, Louis Charles 4
RABB, Kate Milner 1
RABE, Robert Emanuel 6
RABEL, Ernst 5
RABENORT, William Louis 1
RABER, Oran Lee 1
RABIN, Michael 5
RABINOFF, Max 4
RABINOVITZ, Joseph 4
RABINOWITCH, Eugene 6
RABOCH, Wenzel Albert 2
RABOCH, Wenzel Albert 1
RABY, James Joseph 4
RACCA, Vittorio 1
RACE, John H. 3
RACHFORD, Benjamin 1
Knox
RACHMANINOFF, Sergei 2
RACHMIEL, Jean 5
RACKEMANN, Francis 4
Minot
RACKLEY, Frank Bailey 6
RACKLEY, John Ralph 5
RADBILL, Samuel 3
RADCLIFF, Jacob H
RADCLIFFE, Amos H. 3
RADCLIFFE, George L. 4
RADCLIFFE, Harry 1
Southwell
RADCLIFFE, Wallace 1
RADEMACHER, Hans 4
RADEMACHER, Joseph 1
RADER, Paul 1

RADER, Perry Scott 4
RADER, Robert Fort 4
RADER, William 1
RADFORD, Arthur William 6
RADFORD, Benjamin 1
Johnson
RADFORD, Cyrus S. 3
RADFORD, George Stanley 6
RADFORD, Robert 1
Somerville
RADFORD, William * H
RADFORD, William A. 4
RADFORD, William H. 4
RADHAKRISHNAM, 6
Sarvepalli
RADIN, Edward David 1
RADIN, Max 3
RADIN, Paul 3
RADINSKY, Ellis 3
RADISSON, Pierre Esprit H
RADNER, William 1
RADO, Sandor 5
RADO, Tibor 4
RADOSAVLJEVICH, Paul 3
Rankov
RADWAN, Edmund P. 4
RADZAT, Gilbert Francke 6
RAE, Bruce 4
RAE, Charles Whiteside 1
RAE, John H
RAE, John 4
RAE, William McLane 4
RAEGENER, Louis 1
Christian
RAEMAEKERS, Louis 3
RAEMER, Clifford M. 4
RAFF, Richard Davis 4
RAFFEINER, John Stephen H
RAFFERTY, James A. 3
RAFFERTY, William 1
Carroll
RAFFETY, W. Edward 1
RAFFMAN, Halsey Lester 6
RAFINESQUE, Constantine H
Samuel
RAFTERY, John Henry 4
RAFTERY, Oliver Tenry 1
RAGAN, Frank Xavier 6
RAGEN, Joseph Edward 5
RAGIR, Benjamin A. 3
RAGLAND, George 3
RAGLAND, Samuel Evan 1
RAGLAND, William T. 6
RAGO, Henry Anthony 5
RAGON, Heartsill 1
RAGOZIN, Zenaide 1
Alexeievna
RAGSDALE, Bartow Davis 2
RAGSDALE, Edward 4
Tillottson
RAGSDALE, J. Willard 1
RAGSDALE, James W. 4
RAGSDALE, Tallulah 3
RAGSDALE, Van Hubert 4
RAGUET, Condy H
RAHI, Michel 6
RAHMAN, Abdul 4
RAHMAN, Tunku Abdul 3
RAHMN, Elza Lothner 4
RAHN, Otto 4
RAHV, Philip 6
RAIBLE, John R. 2
RAIFORD, Lemuel Charles 4
RAIGUEL, George Earle 4
RAILEY, Fleming G. 4
RAILEY, Thomas Tarlton 3
RAIMONDI, Luigi 6
RAINE, James Watt 2
RAINE, William MacLeod 3
RAINER, Joseph 1
RAINES, George Neely 3
RAINES, John 1
RAINES, John Marlin 5
RAINEY, Anson 4
RAINEY, Henry Thomas 1
RAINEY, John W. 1
RAINEY, Joseph Hayne H
RAINEY, Lilius Bratton 5
RAINEY, Ma 4
RAINEY, Jean 4
RAINS, Claude 4
RAINS, Gabriel James H
RAINS, George Washington H
RAINS, Leon 1
RAINSFORD, William 1
Stephen
RAINWATER, Clarence 1
Elmer
RAIRDEN, Bradstreet 2
Stinson
RAISA, Rosa 4
RAITT, Effie Isabel 2
RAIZEN, Chales Sanford 4
RAJAGOPALACHARYA, 5
Chakravarti
RAK, Mary Kidder 3

RAKE, Geoffrey William 3
RAKE, John Frederick 6
RAKEMAN, Carl 6
RAKER, John Edward 1
RAKOTOMALALA, Louis 5
RALE, Sebastien H
RALEIGH, Henry Patrick 6
RALEIGH, Sir Walter H
RALEY, John Wesley 5
RALL, Edward Everett 5
RALL, Harris Franklin 4
RALLI, Elaine Pandia 5
RALLS, Arthur Williams 6
RALPH, James H
RALPH, Lester 2
RALPH, Stuart Harrison 3
RALSTON, Anderson 2
Wheeler
RALSTON, Burrell Otto 5
RALSTON, Byron Brown 5
RALSTON, Jackson Harvey 2
RALSTON, Hon. James 5
Layton K. C.
RALSTON, John Chester 1
RALSTON, Oliver Caldwell 4
RALSTON, Mrs. Samuel M. 3
RALSTON, Samuel Moffett 1
RALSTON, William H
Chapman
RALSTON, William 5
Chapman
RAMADIER, Paul 4
RAMAGE, Carroll Johnson 1
RAMAGE, James Savage 3
RAMAGE, John 1
RAMAKER, Albert John 2
RAMALEY, Francis 2
RAMAN, Chandrasekhara 6
Venkata
RAMANI, Radhakrishna 5
RAMBAUD, George Gibier 1
RAMBAUT, Mary Lucinda 1
Bonney
RAMBEAU, Morjorie 5
RAMEE, Joseph Jacques H
RAMEY, Frank Marion 4
RAMEY, Homer Alonzo 3
RAMIREZ, Pedro Pablo 4
RAMM, Charles Adolph 4
RAMMELKAMP, Charles 1
Henry
RAMMER, August J. 4
RAMSAY, Alexander H
RAMSAY, David H
RAMSAY, David Marshall 4
RAMSAY, Erskine 4
RAMSAY, Francis Munroe H
RAMSAY, George Douglas H
RAMSAY, Nathaniel H
RAMSAY, Robert Lee 6
RAMSAY, Robert Lincoln 5
RAMSAYE, Thomas Henry 4
RAMSAYE, Terry 3
RAMSBURG, C. J. 2
RAMSDELL, Charles 2
William
RAMSDELL, Edwin George 3
RAMSDELL, Lewis 5
Stephen
RAMSDELL, Washington 4
Irving
RAMSEN, Halsey Edmund 1
RAMSER, Charles Ernest 4
RAMSEUR, Stephen H
Dodson
RAMSEY, Alexander 1
RAMSEY, Alfred 4
RAMSEY, D. Hiden 5
RAMSEY, DeWitt Clinton 5
RAMSEY, George 2
RAMSEY, George Junkin 1
RAMSEY, George Samuel 2
RAMSEY, Horace Marion 2
RAMSEY, James B. 4
RAMSEY, James Basil 5
RAMSEY, James Gettys H
McGready
RAMSEY, John Patterson 4
RAMSEY, John Rathbone 1
RAMSEY, Jr. 1
RAMSEY, Leonidas Willing 1
RAMSEY, Marathon 4
Montrose
RAMSEY, Norman Foster 4
RAMSEY, Robert 5
RAMSEY, Rolla Roy 3
RAMSEY, William 1
RAMSEY, William F. 1
RAMSEY, William Sterrett 1
RAMSEY, Willis Hinksman 1
RAMSEYER, Christian 2
William
RAMSEYER, John Alvin 5
RAMSOWER, Harry 6
C(lifford)
RAMSPECK, Robert 5

RAMSTAD, N(iles) Oliver 5
RAMUS, Carl 5
RANCE, Sir Hubert Elvin 6
RANCK, Clayton 5
Haverstick
RANCK, Edward Carty 6
RANCK, George 1
Washington
RANCK, Henry Haverstick 2
RANCK, Samuel H. 3
RANCK, Than Vanneman 2
RAND, Addison Crittenden H
RAND, Arthur Henry Jr. 5
RAND, Benjamin 1
RAND, Charles Frederic 1
RAND, Christopher 5
RAND, Clayton Thomas 5
RAND, Edgar Eugene 3
RAND, Edward Augustus 1
RAND, Edward Kennard 2
RAND, Edward Lothrop 1
RAND, Edward Sprague H
RAND, Ellen Emmet 2
RAND, Frank Chambless 2
RAND, Frank Prentice 5
RAND, Frederick Henry 2
RAND, George Franklin 2
RAND, Gertrude 5
RAND, Henry Hale 4
RAND, Herbert Wilbur 4
RAND, James Henry 5
RAND, John Goffe H
RAND, John Langdon 2
RAND, John Prentice 1
RAND, Mary Frances 5
Abbott
RAND, Stephen 1
RAND, Theodore Dehon 1
RAND, William Jr. 1
RAND, William Blanchard 6
RAND, William Wilberforce 1
RANDALL, Albert Borland 2
RANDALL, Alexander H
RANDALL, Alexander 3
RANDALL, Alexander 1
Williams
RANDALL, Benjamin * H
RANDALL, Blanchard 2
RANDALL, Burton 1
Alexander
RANDALL, Charles Hiram 4
RANDALL, Clarence 4
Belden
RANDALL, Clyde 5
Nathaniel
RANDALL, Daniel Richard 1
RANDALL, David Anton 6
RANDALL, David Austin H
RANDALL, Edward 2
RANDALL, Edward Caleb 1
RANDALL, Edwin Jarvis 4
RANDALL, Edwin 1
Mortimer
RANDALL, Emilius Oviatt 1
RANDALL, Eugene Wilson 1
RANDALL, Frank Alfred 5
RANDALL, Frank Hall 4
RANDALL, Frank Lange 1
RANDALL, George 1
Archibald
RANDALL, George Morton 1
RANDALL, George William 6
RANDALL, Henry H
Stephens
RANDALL, J. G. 3
RANDALL, James Ryder 1
RANDALL, John Arthur 6
RANDALL, John 4
Hammond
RANDALL, John Herman 2
RANDALL, Lawrence 5
Merrill
RANDALL, Merle 2
RANDALL, Otis Everett 2
RANDALL, Paul King Jr. 5
RANDALL, R. C. 3
RANDALL, Robert Henry 4
RANDALL, Robert Richard H
RANDALL, Ruth Painter 4
RANDALL, Samuel H
RANDALL, Samuel Bond 1
RANDALL, Samuel Jackson H
RANDALL, Samuel Sidwell H
RANDALL, William 1
Harrison
RANDALL, William 4
Trafton
RANDALL, Wyatt William 1
RANDAU, Clem J. 3
RANDEGGER, Giuseppe 5
Aldo
RANDELL, Choice Boswell 4
RANDLE, C. Wilson 4
RANDLE, Thurman 5
RANDLES, Andrew J. 5
RANDOLPH, Alfred Magill 1

RANDOLPH, Bessie Carter 4
RANDOLPH, Beverley H
RANDOLPH, Carman Fitz 1
RANDOLPH, Edgar 6
Eugene
RANDOLPH, Edmund H
RANDOLPH, Edmund H
Jennings
RANDOLPH, Edward 1
RANDOLPH, Edward 1
Hughes
RANDOLPH, Epes 1
RANDOLPH, Francis Fitz 6
RANDOLPH, George F. 1
RANDOLPH, George H
Wythe
RANDOLPH, Harold 1
RANDOLPH, Harrison 3
Nicholas
RANDOLPH, Hollins 1
RANDOLPH, Isham 1
RANDOLPH, Jacob H
RANDOLPH, James Fitz H
RANDOLPH, John * H
RANDOLPH, Sir John H
RANDOLPH, John Cooper 4
Fitz
RANDOLPH, Joseph Fitz H
RANDOLPH, Joseph Fitz 1
RANDOLPH, Lee F. 6
RANDOLPH, Lewis Van 1
Syckle Fitz
RANDOLPH, Lingan 1
Strother
RANDOLPH, Peyton H
RANDOLPH, Robert Isham 3
RANDOLPH, Robert Lee 6
RANDOLPH, Sarah 1
Nicholas
RANDOLPH, Theodore H
Fitz
RANDOLPH, Thomas H
Jefferson
RANDOLPH, Thomas H
Mann
RANDOLPH, Tom 1
RANDOLPH, Wallace F. 1
RANDOLPH, William H
RANDOLPH, William 2
Mann
RANDOLPH, Woodruff 4
RANE, Frank William 1
RANEY, George Pettus 1
RANEY, McKendree 5
Llewellyn
RANEY, Richard Beverly 1
RANEY, William Eugene 4
Francis
RANGER, Henry Ward 1
RANGER, Richard H. 4
RANGER, Walter Eugene 1
RANK, Joseph Arthur 5
RANK, Otto 4
RANKIN, B. Kirk 4
RANKIN, Carroll Watson 3
RANKIN, Christopher H
RANKIN, David 1
RANKIN, Egbert Guernsey 4
RANKIN, Emmet Woollen 4
RANKIN, Fred Wharton 3
RANKIN, George Clark 1
RANKIN, Henry Bascom 1
RANKIN, Isaac Ogden 1
RANKIN, James Doig 2
RANKIN, Jeannette 1
RANKIN, Jeremiah Eames 1
RANKIN, John 1
RANKIN, John Chambers 1
RANKIN, John Elliott 3
RANKIN, John Hall 3
RANKIN, John Mercer 2
RANKIN, John Watkins 5
RANKIN, Joseph H
RANKIN, Milledge Theron 4
RANKIN, Rebecca 4
Browning
RANKIN, Thomas Ernest 3
RANKIN, Walter Mead 2
RANKIN, Watson Smith 6
RANKIN, Wellington 4
Duncan
RANKIN, William 1
Bradshaw
RANKIN, William Durham 2
RANKIN, William 4
Thomasson
RANNEY, Ambrose Arnold 1
RANNEY, Ambrose Loomis 1
RANNEY, George Alfred 2
RANNEY, Henry Clay 1
RANNEY, Henry Joseph 1
RANNEY, Leo 3
RANNEY, Rufus Percival 1
RANNEY, William Tylee H

RANNEY, Winthrop 3
Rodgers
RANNO, Frederick 4
Sebastian
RANOUS, Dora Knowlton 1
RANOW, George R. 3
RANSDELL, Daniel Moore 1
RANSDELL, Joseph 3
Eugene
RANSEEN, Mattis C. 1
RANSFORD, Charles Orrin 5
RANSIER, Alonzo Jacob H
RANSLEY, Harry C. 1
RANSOHOFF, Joseph 1
RANSOM, Brayton Howard 1
RANSOM, Caroline L. H
Ormes
RANSOM, Caroline L. 4
Ormes
RANSOM, Elmer 3
RANSOM, Frank Leslie 2
RANSOM, George 1
Brinkerhoff
RANSOM, John Crowe 6
RANSOM, Marion 4
RANSOM, Mathew 2
Whitaker
RANSOM, Rastus Seneca 1
RANSOM, Ronald 2
RANSOM, Thomas Edward H
Greenfield
RANSOM, William Lynn 3
RANSOME, Frederick 2
Leslie
RANSON, Arthur Jones 5
RANSON, Stephen Walter 2
RANTOUL, Augustus Neal 3
RANTOUL, Neal 3
RANTOUL, Robert * H
RANTOUL, Robert Samuel 1
RANTOUL, William 2
Gibbons
RANTZ, Lowell Addison 4
RANUM, Arthur 1
RAO, K. Kirshna 5
RAOUL, Gaston C. 4
RAPACKI, Adam 5
RAPEE, Erno 2
RAPEE, Leon Andre 5
RAPER, Charles L. 3
RAPER, Charles Lee 4
RAPER, John Robert 6
RAPHALL, Morris Jacob H
RAPIER, James Thomas H
RAPIER, Thomas Gwynn 5
RAPP, George 1
RAPP, Wilhelm 1
RAPP, William Jourdan 2
RAPPAPORT, Max Edward 4
RAPPAPORT, Percy 5
RAPPARD, William 3
Emmanuel
RAPPE, Louis Amadeus H
RAPPOLD, Marie 3
RAPPOLO, Joseph Leon 4
RAPPORT, David 5
RAPUANO, Michael 6
RAREY, John Solomon 1
RARICK, Clarence Edmund 2
RARIDEN, James H
RARIG, Frank M. R. 4
RASBACH, Oscar 6
RASCH, Albertina 4
RASCHEN, John Frederick 3
Louis
RASCHIG, Frank Elmer 1
RASCO, Richmond Austin 1
RASCOE, Burton 3
RASELY, Hiram Newton 3
RASH, Frank Dillman 4
RASHEVSKY, Nicolas 6
RASKOB, John J. 3
RASMUSEN, Bertil Mathias 4
RASMUSEN, Edward A. 2
RASMUSSEN, Albert 5
Terrill
RASMUSSEN, Frederik 1
RASMUSSEN, Marius Peter 5
RASMUSSEN, Otho Mills 3
RASOR, Samuel Eugene 3
RASSIEUR, Leo 1
RATCHFORD, Michael D. 4
RATCLIFF, John Moses 3
RATCLIFFE, John H
RATH, Howard Harbin 5
RATH, Ruben A. 3
RATH, W. John 3
RATHBONE, Albert 2
RATHBONE, Alfred Day 2
IV
RATHBONE, Henry Bailey 2
RATHBONE, Henry Riggs 1
RATHBONE, Jared 1
Lawrence
RATHBONE, John Finley 1

RATHBONE, Josephine 1
Adams
RATHBONE, Justus Henry H
RATHBONE, Philip St John 4
Basil
RATHBONE, St George 1
Henry
RATHBORNE, J. Cornelius 3
RATHBUN, Edward Harris 2
RATHBUN, Elmer Jeremiah 3
RATHBUN, George Oscar H
RATHBUN, H. H. 3
RATHBUN, John Campbell 6
RATHBUN, John Charles 3
RATHBUN, Mary Jane 4
RATHBUN, Richard 1
RATHER, Howard C. 3
RATHER, John Thomas Jr. 3
RATHJE, Frank C. 4
RATHMANN, Carl Gustav 3
RATHMANN, Walter 3
Lincoln
RATHOM, John Revelstoke 1
RATHVON, Nathaniel 5
Peter
RATHVON, William Roedel 1
RATLIFF, Alexander L. 4
RATNER, Bret 3
RATOFF, Gregory 4
RATSHESKY, Abraham C. 2
RATTELMAN, William 3
Adam
RATTIGAN, Charles F. 4
RATTNER, Herbert 4
RATZLAFF, Carl Johann 3
RAU, Albert George 2
RAU, Sir Benegal Rama 3
RAU, Charles H
RAU, Roscoe Russel 4
RAUB, Edward B. 3
RAUB, Kenneth Charles 4
RAUB, William Longstreth 4
RAUCH, Frederick H
Augustus
RAUCH, George W. 5
RAUCH, Harry Lee 3
RAUCH, John Henry H
RAUCH, Rudolph Stewart 5
RAUDENBUSH, David 5
Webb
RAUDENBUSH, George 3
King
RAUE, Charles Gottlieb H
RAUH, Bertha Floersheim 5
(Mrs. Enoch Rauh)
RAUL, Minnie Louise 3
RAULT, Joseph Matthew 4
RAUM, Green Berry 1
RAUSCH, Emil Henry 4
RAUSCHENBUSCH, 1
Augustus
RAUSCHENBUSCH, 1
Walter
RAUTENSTRAUCH, 3
Walter
RAVALLI, Antonio H
RAVDIN, Isidor Schwaner 5
RAVDIN, Robert Glenn 6
RAVEL, Vincent Marvin 5
RAVEN, Anton Adolph 1
RAVEN, John Howard 2
RAVENEL, Beatrice Witte 4
RAVENEL, Edmund H
RAVENEL, Harriott Harry 4
RAVENEL, Henry William H
RAVENEL, St Julien H
RAVENEL, Mazyck 2
Porcher
RAVENEL, William de 4
Chastignier
RAVENSCROFT, Edward 3
Hawks
RAVENSCROFT, John 1
Stark
RAVESON, Sherman 6
Harold
RAVLIN, Grace 3
RAVNDAL, Gabriel Bie 1
RAVOGLI, Augustus 2
RAWIDOWICZ, Simon 3
RAWL, Bernard Hazelius 1
RAWLE, Francis H
RAWLE, Francis 1
RAWLE, James 1
RAWLE, William H
RAWLE, William Henry H
RAWLEIGH, William 1
Thomas
RAWLES, Jacob Beekman 1
RAWLES, William A. 1
RAWLEY, Joseph Pearson 1
RAWLINGS, Eugene 1
Hubbard
RAWLINGS, Majorie 1
Kinnan
RAWLINGS, Norborne L. 5

RAWLINS, George 4
Herndon
RAWLINS, John Aaron H
RAWLINS, Joseph 1
Lafayette
RAWLINS, William Thomas 1
RAWLINSON, Frank 1
Joseph
RAWN, Arnold Edward 6
RAWN, Ira Griffith 1
RAWSON, Albert Leighton 1
RAWSON, Carl Wendell 5
RAWSON, Charles A. 1
RAWSON, Edward Kirk 1
RAWSON, Frederick 1
Holbrook
RAY, Anna Chapin 2
RAY, Arthur Benning 3
RAY, Charles Andrew 1
RAY, Charles Bennett H
RAY, Charles Henry H
RAY, Charles Wayne 1
RAY, David Heydorn 4
RAY, E. Lansing 3
RAY, Edward Chittenden 2
RAY, Franklin Arnold 1
RAY, Frederick Augustus Jr. 5
RAY, G. J. 4
RAY, George Washington 1
RAY, Guy W. 3
RAY, Herbert James 5
RAY, Isaac H
RAY, Jefferson Davis 3
RAY, John Arthur 6
RAY, John Edwin 1
RAY, John Henry 6
RAY, Joseph H
RAY, Joseph R. Sr. 4
RAY, Louise Crenshaw 3
RAY, Marle Beynon 5
RAY, Milton S. 2
RAY, Ossian H
RAY, P. Henry 1
RAY, P(erley) Orman 5
RAY, Philip Alexander 5
RAY, Randolph 4
RAY, S(ilvey) J(ackson) 5
RAY, T. Bronson * 1
RAY, William Henry H
RAY, William Wallace 6
RAYBOLD, Walter James 1
RAYBURN, Sam 4
RAYCORFT, Joseph 3
Edward
RAYMER, Albert Reesor 1
RAYMOND, Alexander 3
Gillespie
RAYMOND, Anan 6
RAYMOND, Andrew Van 1
Vranken
RAYMOND, Anna Almy 1
RAYMOND, Benjamin H
Wright
RAYMOND, Bradford Paul 1
RAYMOND, C. Rexford 3
RAYMOND, Charles Beebe 2
RAYMOND, Charles 1
Walker
RAYMOND, Clifford 3
Samuel
RAYMOND, Daniel H
RAYMOND, Donat 4
RAYMOND, Dora Neill 4
Mrs.
RAYMOND, Ernest 6
RAYMOND, Evelyn Hunt 1
RAYMOND, Fred Morton 2
RAYMOND, Frederick 5
Wingate
RAYMOND, George 1
Lansing
RAYMOND, Harry Howard 1
RAYMOND, Henry Ingle 4
RAYMOND, Henry Jarvis 1
RAYMOND, Henry Warren 1
RAYMOND, Howard 2
Monre
RAYMOND, Jerome Hall 1
RAYMOND, John Baldwin H
RAYMOND, John Howard H
RAYMOND, John T. H
RAYMOND, Jonathan 4
Stone
RAYMOND, Joseph 1
Howard
RAYMOND, Josephine 5
Hunt (Mrs. Jerome Hall
Raymond)
RAYMOND, Mary 3
Elizabeth
RAYMOND, Maud Mary 1
Wotring
RAYMOND, Miner H
RAYMOND, Nell C. 4
RAYMOND, Percy Edward 6
RAYMOND, Robert Fulton 1

REID, Kenneth Alexander 3
REID, Loudon Corsan 5
REID, Mont Rogers 2
REID, O. L. 5
REID, Ogden Mills 1
REID, Philip Joseph 1
REID, Richard 4
REID, Robert 1
REID, Robert Haley 5
REID, Robert Raymond H
REID, Samuel Chester H
REID, Silas Hinkle 3
REID, Sydney 4
REID, T. Roy 1
REID, Thomas Mayne H
REID, Thorburn 3
REID, W. Max 1
REID, Walter Williamson 3
REID, Whitelaw 1
REID, Will J. 3
REID, William 4
REID, William Alfred 5
REID, William Clifford 2
REID, William Duncan 2
REID, William James 1
REID, William James Jr. 1
REID, William R. 3
REID, William Shields 4
REID, William Thomas 4
REIDY, Daniel Joseph 1
REIDY, E. T. 6
REIDY, Peter J. 5
REIF, Edward C. 4
REIF, Herbert R. 5
REIFENSTEIN, Edward Conrad 6
REIFENSTEIN, Edward Conrad Jr. 6
REIFF, Cecil K. 3
REIFF, Evan Allard 4
REIFFEL, Charles 2
REIFSNIDER, Charles Shriver 3
REIFSNIDER, Lawrence Fairfax
REIGER, Siegfried Heinrich 5
REIGHARD, Jacob 1
REIK, Henry Ottridge 1
REIK, Theodor 5
REILAND, Karl 4
REILLEY, Mrs. J. Eugene 1
REILLY, Frank Joseph 4
REILLY, Frank Kennicott 1
REILLY, Henry Joseph 4
REILLY, James Aloysius 3
REILLY, James William 1
REILLY, John David 5
REILLY, John Liguori 2
REILLY, Joseph F. 6
REILLY, Joseph John 3
REILLY, Maurice T. 4
REILLY, Michael Kiernan 2
REILLY, Peter C. 1
REILLY, Thomas Daniel 6
REILLY, Thomas Lawrence 4
REILLY, Walter B. 4
REILLY, William John 5
REILLY, Wilson H
REILY, E. Mont 3
REILY, George W. 1
REILY, Luther H
REIMANN, Stanley P. 4
REIMER, Marie 5
REIMERS, Frederick W. 2
REIMERT, William Daniel 1
REIMOLD, Orlando Schairer 4
REINAGLE, Alexander H
REINDAHL, Knute 1
REINER, Fritz 4
REINER, Joseph 1
REINHARD, Adolph Earl 5
REINHARD, L. Andrew 4
REINHARDT, Ad 4
REINHARDT, Aurelia Henry 2
REINHARDT, Charles William 4
REINHARDT, Django 4
REINHARDT, Emil Fred 5
REINHARDT, Emma 6
REINHARDT, G(eorge) Frederick 5
REINHARDT, George Frederick 1
REINHARDT, Guenther 5
REINHARDT, Gustav Adolph 4
REINHARDT, James Melvin 6
REINHARDT, Max 1
REINHARDT, Ralph Homer 5
REINHART, Benjamin Franklin H

REINHART, Charles Stanley H
REINHART, Earl F. 3
REINHART, Joseph W. 1
REINHAUS, Stanley Marx 3
REINHEIMER, Bartel Hilen 2
REINHOLD, Eli Spayd 1
REINHOLD, James P. 4
REINHOLDT, Julius William 1
REINHOLDT, Julius William 4
REINICKE, Frederick George 5
REINKE, Edwin Eustace 2
REINKING, Otto August 4
REINSCH, Paul Samuel 4
REIRSEN, Johan Reinhart H
REIS, Arthur M. 2
REISER, Armand Edouard 5
REISER, Oliver Leslie 6
REISINGER, Curt H. 4
REISINGER, Harold Carusi 1
REISINGER, Hugo 4
REISMAN, Morton 5
REISNER, Christian Fichthorne 1
REISNER, Edward Hartman 2
REISNER, George Andrew 1
REISS, Jacob L. 3
REISSNER, Albert 5
REIST, Henry Gerber 2
REITER, Bernard L. 5
REITER, George Cook 1
REITH, Francis C. 4
REITZ, Walter R. 3
REITZEL, Albert Emmet 4
REITZEL, Marques E. 4
REITZEL, Robert H
RELFE, James Hugh H
RELIN, Bernard 6
RELLER, Charles J. 4
RELLSTAB, John 1
RELYEA, Charles M. 4
REMAK, Gustavus Jr. 2
REMANN, Frederick H
REMARQUE, Erich Maria 5
REMBAUGH, Bertha 3
REMBERT, Arthur Gaillard 4
REMBERT, George William Francis 6
REMENSNYDER, Junius Benjamin 1
REMENYI, Joseph 3
REMER, Charles Frederick 5
REMER, Helen 4
REMEY, Charles Mason 6
REMEY, George Collier 1
REMICK, Grace May 5
REMICK, J. Gould 4
REMICK, James Waldron 2
REMINGTON, Eliphalet 1
REMINGTON, Franklin 3
REMINGTON, Frederic 1
REMINGTON, Harold 4
REMINGTON, Harvey Foote 2
REMINGTON, Joseph Price 1
REMINGTON, Philo H
REMINGTON, Preston 3
REMINGTON, William Procter 4
REMLEY, Milton 1
REMMEL, Arthur Kizer 1
REMMEL, Ellen Cates 4
REMMEL, Harmon Liveright 1
REMMEL, Valentine 4
REMON, Cantera Alejandro 6
REMON CANTERA, Jose Antonio 3
REMOND, Charles Lenox H
REMONDINO, Peter Charles 1
REMSBURG, John Eleazer 1
REMSEN, Daniel Smith 1
REMSEN, Ira 1
REMSTER, Charles 1
REMY, Alfred 1
REMY, Charles Frederick 5
REMY, Henri 1
RENAUD, (Abel) Etienne Bernardeau 6
RENAUD, Ralph Edward 2
RENCHER, Abraham 1
REND, William Patrick H
RENDALL, John Ballard 1
RENDLEMAN, John Samuel 6
RENFRO, Harold Bell 6
RENFROW, William Cary 1
RENICK, Felix 1
RENIER, Joseph Emile 4
RENISON, Robert John 3

RENNAY, Léon 6
RENNEBOHM, Oscar 5
RENNELSON, Clara H. 4
RENNER, George Thomas Jr. 3
RENNER, Karl 3
RENNER, Otto 4
RENNERT, Hugo Albert 1
RENNIE, Joseph 2
RENNIE, Sylvester Wilding 5
RENNIE, Thomas A. C. 3
RENO, Claude Trexler 4
RENO, Conrad 1
RENO, Doris Smith (Mrs. Paul Halvor Reno) 5
RENO, Guy Benjamin 5
RENO, Itti Kinney 4
RENO, Jesse Lee H
RENO, Jesse Wilford 4
RENOUF, Edward 1
RENOUVIN, Pierre Eugene Georges 6
RENSHAW, Alfred Howard 1
RENSHAW, Raemer Rex 1
RENTSCHLER, Calvin Balthaser 6
RENTSCHLER, Frederick B. 3
RENTSCHLER, George Adam 5
RENTSCHLER, Gordon S. 2
RENTSCHLER, Harvey Clayton 2
RENWICK, Edward Sabine 1
RENWICK, Henry Brevoort H
RENWICK, James * 1
RENWICK, William Whetten 1
RENYX, Guy Worden 3
REPASS, Joseph Wharton 1
REPASS, William Carlyle 2
REPLOGLE, Jacob Leonard 2
REPPLIER, Agnes 3
REPPY, Alison 3
REPPY, Roy Valentine 2
REQUA, Earl Francis 5
REQUA, Mark Lawrence 1
REQUIER, Augustus Julian 1
RESE, Frederick H
RESNICK, Joseph Yale 5
RESOR, Stanley 4
RESSLER, Edwin DeVore 1
RESTARICK, Henry Bond 1
RETHERS, Harry Frederick 1
RETI-FORBES, Jean 6
RETTGER, Leo Frederick 3
RETTIG, H. Earl 5
REU, Johann Michael 2
REUBEN, Odell Richardson 5
REUBEN, Robert Ervin 4
REULING, George 1
REUTER, Edward Byron 5
REUTER, Irving Jacob 5
REUTER, Rudolph Ernst 5
REUTERDAHL, Arvid 1
REUTERDAHL, Henry 1
REUTHER, Walter Philip 5
REUTLINGER, Harry F. 4
REVEL, Bernard 1
REVELL, Alexander Hamilton 1
REVELL, Fleming H. Jr. 5
REVELL, Fleming Hewitt 1
REVELLE, Thomas P. 1
REVELS, Hiram Rhoades H
REVERE, Clinton T. 2
REVERE, Edward H. R. 3
REVERE, Joseph Warren H
REVERE, Paul H
REVERMAN, Theodore Henry 1
REVILL, Milton Kirtley 3
REVSON, Charles Haskell 6
REW, Irwin 3
REX, Charles Henry 6
REXDALE, Robert 1
REXFORD, Eben Eugene 1
REXFORD, Frank A. 1
REY, Anthony H
REYBOLD, Eugene 4
REYBURN, John Edgar 1
REYBURN, Laurens H. 4
REYBURN, Robert 4
REYBURN, Samuel Wallace 4
REYERSON, Lloyd Hilton 5
REYES, Alfonso 3
REYMERT, Martin 5
REYNAL, Eugene 5
REYNAL, Louis 5
REYNARD, Grant 5
REYNAUD, Paul 4
REYNDERS, John V. W. 2
REYNIERS, James A. 4
REYNOLDS, Alexander Welch H
REYNOLDS, Alfred 1

REYNOLDS, Allen Holbrook 1
REYNOLDS, Amesbury L. 4
REYNOLDS, Arthur 2
REYNOLDS, Bruce D. 3
REYNOLDS, Carl Vernon 5
REYNOLDS, Carroll Foster 6
REYNOLDS, Charles Alexander H
REYNOLDS, Charles Bingham 1
REYNOLDS, Charles Lee 5
REYNOLDS, Charles Ransom 5
REYNOLDS, Chester A. 3
REYNOLDS, Clarence 6
REYNOLDS, Conger 5
REYNOLDS, Cuyler Sharpe 4
REYNOLDS, Dudley 1
REYNOLDS, Edwin 4
REYNOLDS, Elmer Lewis 4
REYNOLDS, Elmer Robert 1
REYNOLDS, Ernest Shaw 4
REYNOLDS, Frank Bernard H
REYNOLDS, Frank James 3
REYNOLDS, Frank William 5
REYNOLDS, Frederick Jesse 4
REYNOLDS, George Delachaumette H
REYNOLDS, George Greenwood 1
REYNOLDS, George McClelland 1
REYNOLDS, George William 2
REYNOLDS, Gideon H
REYNOLDS, Grace Morrison 3
REYNOLDS, H. Walter 6
REYNOLDS, Henry James 2
REYNOLDS, Herbert Byron 5
REYNOLDS, Igantius Aloysius
REYNOLDS, Isham E. 2
REYNOLDS, Jackson Eli 5
REYNOLDS, James B. 4
REYNOLDS, James Bronson 1
REYNOLDS, James Burton 2
REYNOLDS, John * H
REYNOLDS, John Edwin 1
REYNOLDS, John Fulton H
REYNOLDS, John Gillilford 4
REYNOLDS, John Hazard H
REYNOLDS, John Henry 5
REYNOLDS, John Hughes 1
REYNOLDS, John Lacey Jr. 4
REYNOLDS, John Merriman 1
REYNOLDS, John Parker 1
REYNOLDS, John Whitcome 3
REYNOLDS, Joseph H
REYNOLDS, Joseph B. 1
REYNOLDS, Joseph Jones H
REYNOLDS, Joseph Jones 1
REYNOLDS, Joseph Smith 1
REYNOLDS, Lawrence 6
REYNOLDS, Milton 1
REYNOLDS, Myra 1
REYNOLDS, Myron Herbert 5
REYNOLDS, Oliver Charlick 6
REYNOLDS, Paul Revere 4
REYNOLDS, Powell Benton 1
REYNOLDS, Quentin 4
REYNOLDS, Richard J. 1
REYNOLDS, Richard Samuel 3
REYNOLDS, Robert J. 5
REYNOLDS, Robert Rice 4
REYNOLDS, Royal 6
REYNOLDS, Samuel Godfrey H
REYNOLDS, Samuel Guilford 4
REYNOLDS, Thomas Harvey 2
REYNOLDS, Victor George Fassett 6
REYNOLDS, Virginia Mrs. 1
REYNOLDS, Walter Ford 4
REYNOLDS, Wellington Jarard 4
REYNOLDS, Wiley Richard 2
REYNOLDS, William H
REYNOLDS, William Howard 1
REYNOLDS, William Neal 3

REZANOV, Nikolai Petrovich H
REZNIKOFF, Charles 6
RHAESA, William A. 5
RHEA, Hortense 1
RHEA, John H
RHEA, John S. 4
RHEA, William Edward 2
RHEA, William Francis 4
RHEAD, Louis John 3
RHEAUME, Louis 3
RHEE, Syngman 4
RHEEM, Richard Scoffield 5
RHEES, John Morgan H
RHEES, Rush 1
RHEES, William Jones 1
RHEINHARDT, Rudolph H. 4
RHEINSTROM, Henry 4
RHETT, Andrew Burnet 2
RHETT, Robert Barnwell H
RHETT, Robert Goodwyn 1
RHETTS, Charles Edward 5
RHIND, Alexander Colden H
RHIND, Charles 4
RHIND, J. Massey 1
RHINE, Abraham Benedict 1
RHINELANDER, Philip Mercer 1
RHINELANDER, T. J. Oakley 4
RHINOCK, Joseph Lafayette 1
RHOAD, Albert Oliver 4
RHOADES, Cornelia Harsen 1
RHOADES, Edward Henry Jr. 3
RHOADES, John Harsen 1
RHOADES, John Harsen 2
RHOADES, Lewis Addison 1
RHOADES, Lyman 4
RHOADES, Mabel Carter 5
RHOADES, Nelson Osgood 5
RHOADES, Ralph Omer 4
RHOADES, William Caldwell Plunkett 1
RHOADS, Charles James 3
RHOADS, Cornelius Packard 3
RHOADS, James H
RHOADS, Joseph J. 3
RHOADS, McHenry 2
RHOADS, Samuel H
RHOADS, Samuel Nicholson 5
RHODE, Clarence J. 3
RHODE, Paul Peter 2
RHODES, Bradford 1
RHODES, Charles Dudley 3
RHODES, Donald Gene 6
RHODES, Edward Everett 3
RHODES, Elisha Hunt 4
RHODES, Eugene Manlove 1
RHODES, Foster Twichell 5
RHODES, Frederic Harrison 1
RHODES, Frederick Leland 1
RHODES, George Pearson 4
RHODES, Harrison 1
RHODES, Henry Abraham 4
RHODES, James Ford 1
RHODES, Jeremiah 1
RHODES, John Bower 4
RHODES, John Franklin 2
RHODES, Marion Edward 1
RHODES, Mosheim 4
RHODES, Robert Clinton 2
RHODES, Rufus Napoleon 1
RHODES, Stephen Holbrook 1
RHODES, Willard E. 5
RHONE, Rosamond Dodson 4
RHYNE, Brice Wilson 5
RHYS, Noel Andrew 6
RIALE, Franklin Nelman 1
RIANO Y GAYANGOS, Don Juan 1
RIBAR, Ivan 5
RIBAUT, Jean H
RIBBLE, Frederick D. G. 5
RIBNER, Irving 5
RICARD, Jerome Sixtus 1
RICARDO, Harry Ralph 6
RICAUD, James Barroll H
RICCI, Ulysses Anthony 4
RICCIUS, Hermann Porter 4
RICCIUTO, Harry Adrian 6
RICE, Abigail Ruth Burton (Mrs. Carl V. Rice) 5
RICE, Albert E. 1
RICE, Albert White 1
RICE, Alexander Hamilton H
RICE, Alexander Hamilton 1
RICE, Alice Caldwell Hegan 1
RICE, Alonzo Leora 4

RICE, Arthur Henry 6
RICE, Arthur Louis 2
RICE, Arthur Wallace 1
RICE, Ben H. Jr. 4
RICE, Benjamin Franklin 1
RICE, Cale Young 2
RICE, Calvin Winsor 1
RICE, Charles H
RICE, Charles A. 5
RICE, Charles Allen H
Thorndike
RICE, Charles Atwood 6
RICE, Charles Edmund 1
RICE, Charles Francis 1
RICE, Charles M. 3
RICE, Claton Silas 5
RICE, Craig 3
RICE, Dan H
RICE, David H
RICE, Devereux Dunlap 2
RICE, Edmund H
RICE, Edmund 1
RICE, Edward Irving 1
RICE, Edward Loranus 3
RICE, Edward Young H
RICE, Edwin Wilbur 1
RICE, Edwin Wilbur Jr. 1
RICE, Elmer 4
RICE, Ernest 3
RICE, Eugene 4
RICE, F. Willis 1
RICE, Fenelon Bird H
RICE, Frank James 1
RICE, Franklin Pierce 1
RICE, Frederick Adolph 3
RICE, George Brackett 2
RICE, George Samuel 2
RICE, George Staples 1
RICE, Grantland 3
RICE, Greek Lent 3
RICE, Harmon Howard 5
RICE, Harry Lee 1
RICE, Heber Holbrook 3
RICE, Henry 1
RICE, Henry Izard Bacon 6
RICE, Henry Mower 1
RICE, Herbert Ambrose 1
RICE, Herbert Howard 1
RICE, Herbert Leigh 1
RICE, Herbert Wayland 1
RICE, Howard Crosby 4
RICE, Isaac Leopold 1
RICE, Jack Horton 4
RICE, James Edward 5
RICE, James Henry Jr. 1
RICE, John 5
RICE, John Andrew 1
RICE, John Andrew 5
RICE, John Birchard H
RICE, John Blake H
RICE, John Campbell 1
RICE, John Hodgen 1
RICE, John Holt H
RICE, John Hovey 1
RICE, John McConnell H
RICE, John Pierrepont 2
RICE, John Winter 5
RICE, Jonas Shearn 1
RICE, Joseph J. 1
RICE, Joseph Lee Jr. 6
RICE, Joseph Mayer 1
RICE, Kingsley Loring 4
RICE, Laban Lacy 5
RICE, Lewis Frederick 1
RICE, Lloyd Preston 3
RICE, Luther H
RICE, M. Wilfred 5
RICE, Maurice Smythe 4
RICE, Merton Stacher 2
RICE, Nathan Lewis 1
RICE, Paul Harper 3
RICE, Paul North 4
RICE, Philip Blair 3
RICE, Richard Ashley 1
RICE, Richard Austin 1
RICE, Richard Henry 1
RICE, Robert 5
RICE, Stephen Ewing 3
RICE, Stuart Arthur 5
RICE, Theron Hall 1
RICE, Theron Moses H
RICE, Thomas H
RICE, Thomas Dartmouth 1
RICE, Thomas Stevens 2
RICE, Thurman Brooks 3
RICE, Victor Moreau H
RICE, W. North 1
RICE, Wallace 1
RICE, Willard Martin 1
RICE, William 1
RICE, William Ball 1
RICE, William Gorham 1
RICE, William Marsh H
RICE, William Morton 1
Jackson
RICE, William Whitney H

RICH, Adelbert P. 1
RICH, Arnold Rice 5
RICH, Benjamin Leroy 6
RICH, Burdett Alberto 1
RICH, Carl W. 5
RICH, Charles H
RICH, Charles Alonzo 2
RICH, Edgar Judson 2
RICH, Ednah Anne 5
RICH, Edson Prosper 4
RICH, Edward P. 1
RICH, Edwin Gile 6
RICH, Elmer 4
RICH, Giles Willard 2
RICH, Isaac H
RICH, John A. 4
RICH, John Frederick 6
RICH, John Harrison 1
RICH, John Lyon 3
RICH, John T. 1
RICH, Obadiah H
RICH, Raymond Thomas 3
RICH, Richard H. 6
RICH, Sir Robert H
RICH, Robert Fleming 5
RICH, Ronald Emil 3
RICH, Samuel Heath 2
RICH, Thaddeus 5
RICH, Williston C. 3
RICHARD, Charles 1
RICHARD, Ernst D. 1
RICHARD, Gabriel H
RICHARD, Harold Charles 3
RICHARD, Irwin 6
RICHARD, James William 1
RICHARD, John H. H
RICHARD, Matthias 1
RICHARDS, Alfred Ernest 2
RICHARDS, Alfred Newton 4
RICHARDS, Alice 1
Haliburton
RICHARDS, Bernard 5
Gerson
RICHARDS, Charles 1
Brinckerhoff
RICHARDS, Charles 5
Gorman
RICHARDS, Charles 1
Herbert
RICHARDS, Charles 5
Lenmore
RICHARDS, Charles 5
Malone
RICHARDS, Charles Russ 1
RICHARDS, Charles Russell 1
RICHARDS, Charles Walter 1
RICHARDS, Cyril Fuller 3
RICHARDS, De Forest 1
RICHARDS, Dickinson W. 5
RICHARDS, Donald 3
RICHARDS, E. F. 4
RICHARDS, Eben 2
RICHARDS, Edgar 4
RICHARDS, Edward A. 3
RICHARDS, Ellen 1
Henrietta
RICHARDS, Emerson 4
Lewis
RICHARDS, Emily S. 1
Tanner
RICHARDS, Erwin Hart 1
RICHARDS, Eugene Lamb 1
RICHARDS, Eugene Scott 1
Thompson
RICHARDS, Frederick 1
RICHARDS, George * 1
RICHARDS, George 2
RICHARDS, George 3
Franklin
RICHARDS, George Gill 3
RICHARDS, George 3
Handyside
RICHARDS, George 5
Huntington
RICHARDS, George 3
Warren
RICHARDS, Harry Sanger 1
RICHARDS, Henry 1
Melchior Muhlenberg
RICHARDS, Herbert Maule 1
RICHARDS, Herbert 5
Montague
RICHARDS, Irving 4
Trefethen
RICHARDS, Jacob 1
RICHARDS, James Austin 6
RICHARDS, James L. 1
RICHARDS, Janet E. 2
Hosmer
RICHARDS, Jean Marie 5
RICHARDS, John * H
RICHARDS, John E. 1
RICHARDS, John Gardiner 1
RICHARDS, John Kelvey 1
RICHARDS, John Thomas 2
RICHARDS, Joseph H. 5

RICHARDS, Joseph Havens 1
Cowles
RICHARDS, Joseph William 1
RICHARDS, Laura 2
Elizabeth
RICHARDS, Lela Horn 5
(pseudonym Lee Neville)
RICHARDS, Lewis Loomis 1
RICHARDS, Louise 1
RICHARDS, Mark H
RICHARDS, Mary Anne 6
Mitchell
RICHARDS, Nathan 2
Charles
RICHARDS, Paul Stanley 5
RICHARDS, Paul William 3
RICHARDS, Preston 3
RICHARDS, Ralph H(are) 1
RICHARDS, Ralph Strother 2
RICHARDS, Ralph Webster 1
RICHARDS, Ray 3
RICHARDS, Rezin Howard 4
Hallowell
RICHARDS, Robert 2
Haven
RICHARDS, Robert Watt 4
RICHARDS, Roger G. 5
RICHARDS, Rosalind 5
(Miss)
RICHARDS, Samuel H. 3
RICHARDS, Stephen L. 3
RICHARDS, Stewart 6
Watson
RICHARDS, T. Addison 1
RICHARDS, Theodore 1
William
RICHARDS, Thomas Cole 1
RICHARDS, Mrs. Waldo 5
RICHARDS, William H
RICHARDS, William Alford 1
RICHARDS, William Henry 4
RICHARDS, William Joseph 4
RICHARDS, William 1
Rogers
RICHARDS, William Trost 1
RICHARDS, Zalmon H
RICHARDSON, Abby Sage 1
RICHARDSON, Albert H
Deane
RICHARDSON, Alexander 5
Henderson
RICHARDSON, Anna 1
Euretta
RICHARDSON, Anna 2
Steese
RICHARDSON, Basil 1
RICHARDSON, Charles 1
RICHARDSON, Charles 1
Francis
RICHARDSON, Charles 1
Freemont
RICHARDSON, Charles 1
Henry
RICHARDSON, Charles 6
Tiffany
RICHARDSON, Charles 1
Williamson
RICHARDSON, Clarence 3
H.
RICHARDSON, Clifford 1
RICHARDSON, David 4
Crockett
RICHARDSON, Donovan 4
MacNeely
RICHARDSON, Dorothy 3
RICHARDSON, Edmund H
RICHARDSON, Edward 3
Elliott
RICHARDSON, Edward 5
H(enderson)
RICHARDSON, Edward 2
Peirson
RICHARDSON, Edwin 3
Sanders
RICHARDSON, Ellen A. 1
Verne
RICHARDSON, Elliott 1
RICHARDSON, Ernest 1
Cushing
RICHARDSON, Ernest 2
Gladstone
RICHARDSON, Francis 1
Asbury
RICHARDSON, Francis 6
Harrie
RICHARDSON, Francis 1
Henry
RICHARDSON, Frank 1
Chase
RICHARDSON, Frank 6
Howard
RICHARDSON, Frederick 1
RICHARDSON, Frederick 5
Albert
RICHARDSON, Friend 2
William

RICHARDSON, George 3
Adams
RICHARDSON, George 5
Burr
RICHARDSON, George 1
Lynde
RICHARDSON, George 1
Tilton
RICHARDSON, Guy A. 4
RICHARDSON, H. George 5
RICHARDSON, Harry 1
Alden
RICHARDSON, Henry 1
Brown
RICHARDSON, Henry H
Hobson
RICHARDSON, Henry 5
Smith
RICHARDSON, Hester 1
Dorsey
RICHARDSON, Hilary 5
Goode
RICHARDSON, Holden 6
Chester
RICHARDSON, Hugh 5
RICHARDSON, Ira 3
RICHARDSON, Israel Bush H
RICHARDSON, James 1
Bailey
RICHARDSON, James 1
Daniel
RICHARDSON, James 4
Hugh
RICHARDSON, James 1
Julius
RICHARDSON, James 4
Montgomery
RICHARDSON, James Otto 6
RICHARDSON, James 2
Parmelee
RICHARDSON, John Peter H
RICHARDSON, John 5
S(anford)
RICHARDSON, John H
Smythe
RICHARDSON, Joseph * H
RICHARDSON, Katharine 1
Berry
RICHARDSON, Leon 4
Josiah
RICHARDSON, Lunsford 3
RICHARDSON, M. S. 5
RICHARDSON, Mark 5
E(dwin)
RICHARDSON, Mark 4
Wyman
RICHARDSON, Maurice 1
Howe
RICHARDSON, Norman 2
Egbert
RICHARDSON, Norval 1
RICHARDSON, Oliver 1
Huntington
RICHARDSON, Philip 2
RICHARDSON, Robert H
RICHARDSON, Robert 3
Charlwood Jr.
RICHARDSON, Robert 1
Kimball
RICHARDSON, Robert 1
Newton
RICHARDSON, Robert 5
Price
RICHARDSON, Robert 4
William
RICHARDSON, Roland 2
George Dwight
RICHARDSON, Roy 1
Mundy Davidson
RICHARDSON, Rufus 1
Byam
RICHARDSON, Russell 6
RICHARDSON, Seth 3
Whitley
RICHARDSON, Sid 3
Williams
RICHARDSON, Sid 1
Williams
RICHARDSON, Tobias 1
Gibson
RICHARDSON, W. 1
Symmes
RICHARDSON, Warfield 1
Creath
RICHARDSON, Wilds 1
Preston
RICHARDSON, Willard H
RICHARDSON, Willard 3
Samuel
RICHARDSON, William 1
Adams
RICHARDSON, William 1
Alexander
RICHARDSON, William 1
Cummings

RICHARDSON, William D. 1
RICHARDSON, William E. 1
RICHARDSON, William 1
Eddy
RICHARDSON, William 5
Edwin
RICHARDSON, William 1
Franklin
RICHARDSON, William 5
King
RICHARDSON, William 1
Lambert
RICHARDSON, William 5
Lloyd
RICHARDSON, William H
Merchant
RICHARDSON, William 4
Samuel
RICHART, Duncan Grant 3
RICHART, Frank Erwin 3
RICHBERG, Donald 4
Randall
RICHE, Charles Swift 1
RICHEL, George William 5
RICHESON, John Jacob 4
RICHESON, John Jacob 5
RICHEY, Albert Sutton 1
RICHEY, Frederick David 3
RICHEY, Lawrence 1
RICHEY, Thomas B. 2
RICHINGS, Peter H
RICHLING, Don Jose 5
RICHMAN, Arthur 2
RICHMAN, Frank Nelson 4
RICHMAN, Irving Berdine 1
RICHMOND, Adam 3
RICHMOND, Charles 1
Alexander
RICHMOND, Charles Blair 5
RICHMOND, Charles 1
Wallace
RICHMOND, Dean H
RICHMOND, Euphemia 1
Johnson
RICHMOND, Frederic 1
Courtis
RICHMOND, George 5
Chalmers
RICHMOND, Grace S. 3
RICHMOND, Harold Bours 5
RICHMOND, Hiram H
Lawton
RICHMOND, James Howell 2
RICHMOND, John Lambert H
RICHMOND, John Wilkes 1
RICHMOND, Jonathan H
RICHMOND, Kenneth 1
Calvin
RICHMOND, Mary Ellen 1
RICHTER, Conrad Michael 5
RICHTER, Emil Heinrich 5
RICHTER, Gisela Marie 5
Augusta
RICHTER, Henry Joseph 1
RICHTER, John Frederick 1
RICHTER, Julius 6
RICHTER, Paul E. 2
RICHTER, Richard Biddle 5
RICHTMYER, F. K. 1
RICKARD, Brent Neville 3
RICKARD, Edgar 1
RICKARD, George Lewis H
RICKARD, George Lewis 4
RICKARD, Richard Darke 1
RICKARD, Thomas Arthur 5
RICKARDS, George Collins 1
RICKARDS, James S. 2
RICKENBACKER, Edward 5
Vernon ("Eddie")
RICKER, George Alfred Joy 1
RICKER, Marilla M. 1
RICKER, N. Clifford 1
RICKERBY, Arthur 5
Burroughs
RICKERT, Edith 1
RICKERT, Thomas A. 1
RICKETSON, Daniel H
RICKETSON, Walton 1
RICKETTS, Claude Vernon 4
RICKETTS, James H
Brewerton
RICKETTS, Louis Davidson 1
RICKETTS, Palmer 1
Chamberlaine
RICKETTS, Pierre de 1
Peyster
RICKEY, Branch 4
RICKEY, James Walter 2
RICKS, Augustus J. 1
RICKS, James B. 1
RICKS, Jesse Jay 5
RICKS, William Benjamin 1
RICORD, Frederick William H
RICORD, Philippe H
RIDABOCK, Raymond 5
Budd

RIDDELL, Guy Crosby 4
RIDDELL, Herman Ellis 4
RIDDELL, John Leonard H
RIDDELL, Robert Gerald 3
RIDDELL, William Hugh 3
RIDDELL, William Renwick
RIDDER, Bernard Herman 6
RIDDER, Herman 1
RIDDER, Herman Henry 5
RIDDER, Joseph E. 4
RIDDER, Victor Frank 4
RIDDICK, Carl W. 5
RIDDICK, James Edward 1
RIDDICK, Thomas Kader 1
RIDDICK, Wallace Carl 2
RIDDICK, Walter Garrett 1
RIDDLE, Albert Gallatin 1
RIDDLE, George 1
RIDDLE, George Read H
RIDDLE, Haywood Yancey H
RIDDLE, James Marion Jr. 5
RIDDLE, John Wallace 2
RIDDLE, Lincoln Ware 1
RIDDLE, Matthew Brown 1
RIDDLE, Oscar 5
RIDDLE, Theodate Pope 2
RIDDLE, William 4
RIDDLEBERGER, Harrison H Holt
RIDEAL, Charles Frederick 4
RIDEAL, Eric Keightley 6
RIDEING, William Henry 1
RIDENOUR, Louis N. Jr. 3
RIDEOUT, Henry Milner 1
RIDER, Arthur William 4
RIDER, Charles R. 4
RIDER, Fremont 4
RIDER, Ira Edgar 4
RIDGAWAY, Henry H Baseom
RIDGE, Albert Alphonso 4
RIDGE, Major H
RIDGELEY, Charles H Goodwin
RIDGELEY, Daniel Bowly H
RIDGELEY, Henry Moore H
RIDGELEY, Nicholas H
RIDGELEY, Richard H
RIDGELY, Benjamin H. 1
RIDGELY, Henry 1
RIDGELY, Hilliard Samuel 5
RIDGELY, William Barret 1
RIDGES, Robert Paul 5
RIDGEWAY, George L. 5
RIDGLEY, Douglas Clay 3
RIDGWAY, Amos Caryl 4
RIDGWAY, Arthur H Osbourne
RIDGWAY, Erman Jesse 2
RIDGWAY, Grant 5
RIDGWAY, Howard 6 Eugene
RIDGWAY, Joseph H
RIDGWAY, Robert H
RIDGWAY, Robert * 1
RIDGWAY, Thomas H
RIDGWAY, William Hance 2
RIDINGS, Eugene Ware 4
RIDLEY, Clarence Self 5
RIDLON, John 1
RIDLON, Joseph Randall 6
RIDPATH, John Clark 1
RIDPATH, Robert Ferguson 3
RIDSDALE, Percival 3 Sheldon
RIEBEL, Frank A. 5
RIEBER, Charles Henry 1
RIEBER, Torkild 5
RIECHMANN, Donald 6 August
RIECKEN, William Emil 4
RIED, William Wharry 4
RIEDEL, Karl Heinrich 2
RIEFLER, Winfield William 6
RIEFSTAHL, Rudolf M. 6
RIEGEL, Benjamin D. 1
RIEGEL, Byron 5
RIEGEL, Catherine Thirza 6
RIEGER, Johann Georg 5 Joseph Anton
RIEGER, William Henry 4
RIEGGER, Wallingford 4
RIEHLE, Theodore Martin 2
RIEKE, Marcus Clarence 4
RIEL, Louis H
RIELY, John William 1
RIEMAN, Charles Ellet 5
RIEMENSCHNEIDER, 3 Albert
RIEMER, Guido Carl Leo 5
RIEPE, Carl Christoph 5
RIES, Elias Elkan 1
RIES, Heinrich 3
RIESENBERG, Felix 1
RIESENFELD, Hugo 5

RIESER, Leonard Moos 3
RIESMAN, David 1
RIESMAN, John Penrose 6
RIETHMULLER, Richard 1 Henri
RIETMULDER, James 5
RIETZ, Henry Lewis 2
RIEVE, Emil 5
RIFE, John Maynard 5
RIGBY, Edmund 4
RIGBY, William Cattron 2
RIGBY, William Otto 3
RIGBY, William Titus 4
RIGDON, Charles Loammi 5
RIGDON, Jonathan 1
RIGDON, Sidney H
RIGG, Ephraim 4
RIGG, George Burton 6
RIGGE, William Francis 1
RIGGINS, H. Mcleod 5
RIGGINS, Russell Myers 4
RIGGIO, Vincent 4
RIGGS, Alexander Brown 1
RIGGS, Alfred Longley 1
RIGGS, Arthur Stanley 6
RIGGS, Austen Fox 1
RIGGS, Charles Edward 4
RIGGS, Edward 1
RIGGS, Edward Gridley 4
RIGGS, Elias 1
RIGGS, Ernest Wilson 3
RIGGS, Francis Behn 4
RIGGS, George Washington H
RIGGS, Henry Earle 2
RIGGS, Henry Harrison 3
RIGGS, James Forsyth 4
RIGGS, James Gilbert 1
RIGGS, James Milton 1
RIGGS, James Stevenson 4
RIGGS, Jetur Rose 1
RIGGS, John Davis Seaton 1
RIGGS, John Mankey 1
RIGGS, Joseph A. 6
RIGGS, Kate Douglas 1 Wiggin
RIGGS, Lewis 1
RIGGS, Louis Warner 4
RIGGS, Norman Colman 2
RIGGS, Robert 1
RIGGS, Robert Baird 1
RIGGS, Stephen Return H
RIGGS, Theodore Foster 5
RIGGS, Theodore Scott 5
RIGGS, Thomas 2
RIGGS, Walter Merritt 1
RIGHTMIRE, George 3 Washington
RIGHTOR, Henry 1
RIGNALL, Raymond H. 4
RIGNEY, Hugh M. 5
RIGSBEE, Albert Vinson 5
RIHANI, Ameen 3
RIHBANY, Abraham Mitrie 2
RIHBANY, Abraham Mitrie 5
RIIS, Erling 5
RIIS, Jacob August 1
RIIS, Roger William 3
RIISAGER, Knudage 6
RIKER, Albert Burdsall 5
RIKER, Andrew Lawrence 1
RIKER, Carroll Livingston 1
RIKER, Franklin Wing 3
RIKER, Irving 5
RIKER, John L. 1
RIKER, Samuel 1
RIKER, Thad Weed 4
RILEA, Thomas Edward 3
RILEY, Benjamin Franklin 1
RILEY, Bennet H
RILEY, Bert Clair 4
RILEY, Bryan M. 4
RILEY, Cassius Marcellus 2
RILEY, Charles Valentine 1
RILEY, Earl 4
RILEY, Edward 1
RILEY, Franklin Lafayette 1
RILEY, George Washington 3
RILEY, Henry Alsop 5
RILEY, Henry Ware 1
RILEY, Herbert Douglas 5
RILEY, James 4
RILEY, James Breinig 1
RILEY, James Whitcomb 1
RILEY, John Alexander 4
RILEY, John B. 1
RILEY, John Jacob 4
RILEY, John Stewart 4
RILEY, Leonard William 2
RILEY, Lewis Adams 1
RILEY, Melville Fuller 1
RILEY, Phil Madison 1
RILEY, Philip Henry 4
RILEY, Thomas James 1
RILEY, Thomas Joseph 5
RILEY, Walter James 6
RILEY, William Bell 2

RILEY, William F. 3
RILEY, William G. 3
RILEY, Woodbridge 1
RILKE, Rainer Maria 4
RIMINGTON, Critchell 6
RIMINI, Giacomo 1
RIMMER, Caroline Hunt 4
RIMMER, Harry 3
RIMMER, John Wilfred 4
RIMMER, William H
RINAKER, Samuel Mayo 2
RINDISBACHER, Peter 4
RINEHART, George 4 Franklin
RINEHART, Henry R. 4
RINEHART, James Fleece 3
RINEHART, Mary Roberts 3
RINEHART, Roy James 3
RINEHART, Stanley 5 Marshall Jr.
RINEHART, William Henry H
RINER, John Alden 1
RINER, William A. 3
RINES, George Edwin 4
RINEY, Earl Alvin 3
RING, Blanche 1
RING, Floyd Orval 6
RING, Richard Warner 4
RING, Welding 1
RINGER, Paul Henry 3
RINGGOLD, Cadwalader H
RINGGOLD, Samuel 1
RINGLAND, Adam Weir 5
RINGLAND, Joseph Ford 3
RINGLE, Arthur Levi 4
RINGLEY, James Patrick 4
RINGLING, Charles 6
RINGLING, Charles 4
RINGLING, Henry E. 3
RINGLING, John 1
RINGLING, Robert Edward 2
RINGO, Helen 1
RINGO, Hugh Fay 2
RINGOLD, James 4
RINGSTAD, Edward Olson 5
RINGWALT, Ralph Curtis 1
RINKENBACH, William 4 Henry
RINKOFF, Barbara Jean 6
RINSLAND, Henry Daniel 5
RION, Hanna 1
RIORDAN, Daniel J. 1
RIORDAN, Leo (Thomas 6 Aloyslus)
RIORDAN, Patrick William 1
RIORDAN, Roger 1
RIORDAN, Timothy Allen 4
RIORDAN, William O. 3
RIORDON, Raymond 1
RIOS, Juan Antonio 2
RIPLEY, Alden Lassell 5
RIPLEY, Alfred Lawrence 2
RIPLEY, Charles Trescott 2
RIPLEY, Clements 3
RIPLEY, Edward Lafayette 3
RIPLEY, Edward Payson 1
RIPLEY, Eleazar Wheelock H
RIPLEY, Ezra 1
RIPLEY, Frederic Herbert 4
RIPLEY, George H
RIPLEY, Giles Emmett 2
RIPLEY, Hubert G. 2
RIPLEY, James Wheelock H
RIPLEY, James Wolfe H
RIPLEY, Joseph 1
RIPLEY, Joseph Pierce 6
RIPLEY, Katharine Ball 3
RIPLEY, Lauren William 4
RIPLEY, Lucy Fairfield 2 Perkins
RIPLEY, Mary Churchill 4
RIPLEY, Robert Harris 4
RIPLEY, Robert LeRoy 2
RIPLEY, Roswell Sabine 4
RIPLEY, Thomas C. H
RIPLEY, Thomas Emerson 4
RIPLEY, Wilber Franklin 6
RIPLEY, William Zebina 1
RIPPEL, Julius S. 3
RIPPERGER, Helmut 6 Lothar
RIPPEY, Edwin Floyd 4
RIPPEY, Harian Watson 3
RIPPIN, Jane Deeter 5
RIPPLE, Michael Joseph 1
RIPTON, Benjamin Henry 1
RISDON, Fulton 6
RISEMAN, Joseph Ephraim 6 Frank
RISER, William Henry Jr. 4
RISHELL, Charles Wesley 1
RISHELL, James Dyson 4
RISING, Henry 1
RISING, Johan Classon H
RISING, Willard Bradley 1
RISITINE, Frederick Pearce 4

RISK, Charles Francis 2
RISLEY, Edwin H. 4
RISLEY, Elijah H
RISLEY, Paul L(emuel) 5
RISLEY, Richard Voorhees 1
RISLEY, Samuel Doty 1
RISLEY, Theodore 4 Granville
RISNER, Henry Clay 2
RISSBERGER, Harold P. 6
RISSER, Hubert Elias 6
RISTAD, Ditlef G. 1
RISTER, Carl Coke 3
RISTINE, Frank Humphrey 3
RISTINE, George W. 1
RITCH, John Warren 4
RITCHEY, Charles James 4
RITCHEY, George Willis 4
RITCHEY, Thomas 4
RITCHIE, Adele 1
RITCHIE, Albert Cabell 1
RITCHIE, Alexander Hay H
RITCHIE, Andrew Jackson 1
RITCHIE, Arthur 1
RITCHIE, David H
RITCHIE, John H
RITCHIE, John 1
RITCHIE, John A. 6
RITCHIE, John Woodside 2
RITCHIE, Nelvia E. Webb 6
RITCHIE, Robert Welles 2
RITCHIE, Ryerson 1
RITCHIE, Thomas H
RITCHIE, William 3
RITER, Frank Miller 1
RITER, Franklin 4
RITER, Henry G. III 4
RITER, William Delamater 1
RITMAN, Louis 4
RITNER, Joseph H
RITSCHEL, Wilhelm 3
RITT, Joseph Fels 3
RITTENBERG, David 5
RITTENBERG, Henry H. 5
RITTENBERG, Louis 4
RITTENHOUSE, Daniel 2 Franklin
RITTENHOUSE, David 1
RITTENHOUSE, Elmer 1 Ellsworth
RITTENHOUSE, George 1 Brown
RITTENHOUSE, Jessie 2 Belle
RITTENHOUSE, Moses 1 Franklin
RITTENHOUSE, William 1
RITTER, Burwell Clarke H
RITTER, Claude Dowd 4
RITTER, Edward Frederick 1
RITTER, Frederic Louis H
RITTER, Halsted Lockwood 4
RITTER, Howard L(ester) 5
RITTER, John 4
RITTER, Joseph Elmer 4
RITTER, Louis E. 1
RITTER, Paul 1
RITTER, Thelma 5
RITTER, Verus Taggart 2
RITTER, William Emerson 2
RITTER, William Leonard 5
RITTERSPORN, Bernard 6 Andrew
RITTMAN, Walter Frank 3
RITTMASTER, Alexander 5 III
RITZ, Harold A. 2
RITZMAN, Ernest George 3
RIVAS, Damaso de 5
RIVENBURG, Romeyn 1 Henry
RIVERA CARBALLO, Julio 6 Adalberto
RIVERA, Diego 4
RIVERA, Jose Garibi 5
RIVERA, Luis Munoz 1
RIVERS, Eurith Dickinson 4
RIVERS, G. L. Buist 4
RIVERS, L. Mendel 5
RIVERS, Moultrie Rutledge 1
RIVERS, Thomas H
RIVERS, Thomas Milton 4
RIVERS, William Cannon 2
RIVERS, William Walter 4
RIVES, Alfred Landon 1
RIVES, Edwin Earle H
RIVES, Francis Everod H
RIVES, George Lockhart 1
RIVES, John Cook H
RIVES, Tom Christopher 4
RIVES, William Cabell H
RIVES, Zeno J. 1
RIVES-WHEELER, Hallie 1 Ermine
RIVINGTON, James H
RIVINUS, Francis Markoe 3

RIVITZ, Hiram S. 3
RIVKIN, William Robert 4
RIX, Carl Barnett 4
RIX, Charles Northrup 1
RIX, Frank Reader 1
RIXEY, George Foreman 6
RIXEY, John Franklin 1
RIXEY, Presley Marion 1
RIXFORD, Elizabeth M. 3 Leach
RIXFORD, Emmet 1
RIZER, Henry Clay 4
ROACH, Abby Meguire 5
ROACH, Alden G. 3
ROACH, David James 3
ROACH, John H
ROACH, John Millard 1
ROACH, Philip Francis 6
ROACH, Sidney C. 4
ROACH, Thomas Watson 1
ROADHOUSE, Chester 5 Linwood
ROADS, Charles 1
ROADSTRUM, Victor N. 4
ROANE, Archibald H
ROANE, John H
ROANE, John Jones H
ROANE, John Selden H
ROANE, Spencer H
ROANE, William Henry H
ROARK, Ruric Nevel 1
ROBB, Charles Henry 1
ROBB, Clair E. 4
ROBB, Eccles Donald 2
ROBB, Edward 4
ROBB, Elise de la Fontaine 5 (Mrs. Robert Cumming Robb)
ROBB, Eugene Spivey 5
ROBB, Hunter 1
ROBB, James 1
ROBB, James Hampden 1
ROBB, Max 6
ROBB, Richard Alexander 1
ROBB, Russell 1
ROBB, Russell 3
ROBB, Seymour 4
ROBB, Thomas Bruce 4
ROBB, Walter Johnson 6
ROBB, William Lispenard 1
ROBB, Willis Oscar 4
ROBBIE, Alexander 4 Cumming
ROBBINS, Alexander Henry 1
ROBBINS, Arthur Graham 4
ROBBINS, Asher H
ROBBINS, Benjamin H. 4
ROBBINS, Burnett W. 3
ROBBINS, Chandler H
ROBBINS, Charles Burton 1
ROBBINS, Charles F. 3
ROBBINS, Charles Leonidas 1
ROBBINS, Edmund Yard 2
ROBBINS, Edward 1 Denmore
ROBBINS, Edward Everett 1
ROBBINS, Edward Rutledge 5
ROBBINS, Edwin Clyde 2
ROBBINS, Francis LeBaron 1
ROBBINS, Franklin G. 5
ROBBINS, Frederick Wright 4
ROBBINS, Gaston A. 1
ROBBINS, George Ridgway 1
ROBBINS, George Robbins H
ROBBINS, Harry Clare 4
ROBBINS, Harry Pelham 2
ROBBINS, Harry Wolcott 2
ROBBINS, Hayes 1
ROBBINS, Henry Spencer 1
ROBBINS, Horace Wolcott 1
ROBBINS, Howard 3 Chandler
ROBBINS, Irvin 1
ROBBINS, Jim 4
ROBBINS, John H
ROBBINS, John Williams 1
ROBBINS, Joseph Chandler 4
ROBBINS, Joseph Chandler 5
ROBBINS, Laurence Ballard 4
ROBBINS, Leonard H. 2
ROBBINS, Mary Caroline 1
ROBBINS, Merton Covey 1
ROBBINS, Milton Herbert 5
ROBBINS, Milton Holley 5 Jr.
ROBBINS, Omer Ellsworth 6
ROBBINS, Reginald 3 Chauncey
ROBBINS, Richard 5 Whitfield
ROBBINS, Royal 1
ROBBINS, Samuel Dowse 5
ROBBINS, Thomas 1
ROBBINS, Thomas 5 Hinckley Jr.
ROBBINS, Walter 3

ROBINSON, John 6
Q(uentin)
ROBINSON, John S. 3
ROBINSON, John Sherman 3
ROBINSON, John Trumbull 1
ROBINSON, John W. 2
ROBINSON, Jonathan H
ROBINSON, Joseph 2
ROBINSON, Joseph E. 3
ROBINSON, Joseph Gibson 4
ROBINSON, Joseph Taylor 1
ROBINSON, Julia Almira 2
ROBINSON, Karl Frederic 4
ROBINSON, Lennox 3
ROBINSON, Leonard 2
George
ROBINSON, Leonidas 4
Dunlap
ROBINSON, Lewis Wood 1
ROBINSON, Louis Newton 3
ROBINSON, Lucien Moore 1
ROBINSON, Lucius 1
Franklin
ROBINSON, Lucius W. 1
ROBINSON, Lucius 1
Waterman
ROBINSON, Luther 3
Emerson
ROBINSON, Lydia 5
Gillingham
ROBINSON, Mabel Louise 4
ROBINSON, Mary 5
Dummett Nauman
ROBINSON, Mary Yandes 4
ROBINSON, Maurice 2
Henry
ROBINSON, Millard 2
Lyman
ROBINSON, Milton Stapp H
ROBINSON, Moncure H
ROBINSON, Moses 1
ROBINSON, Myron Wilber 6
ROBINSON, Noel 2
ROBINSON, Orin Pomeroy 3
Jr.
ROBINSON, Orville H
ROBINSON, P. Gervais 4
ROBINSON, Pat 4
ROBINSON, Remus Grant 5
ROBINSON, Richard 1
Hallett Meredith
ROBINSON, Richard Lee 1
ROBINSON, Robert 6
ROBINSON, Robert P. 1
ROBINSON, Rodney Potter 3
ROBINSON, Roscoe R. 2
ROBINSON, Rowland 1
Evans
ROBINSON, Samuel 2
ROBINSON, Samuel 1
Murray
ROBINSON, Sanford 2
ROBINSON, Sara Tappan 4
Doolittle
ROBINSON, Sidney W. 6
ROBINSON, Silas Arnold 1
ROBINSON, Solon H
ROBINSON, Solon 4
ROBINSON, Stephen 4
Bernard
ROBINSON, Stewart Mac 4
Master
ROBINSON, Stillman 1
Williams
ROBINSON, Stuart H
ROBINSON, Theodore H
ROBINSON, Theodore 1
Douglas
ROBINSON, Theodore 2
Winthrop
ROBINSON, Therese H
Albertine Louise von
Jakob
ROBINSON, Thomas Jr. H
ROBINSON, Thomas John 3
Bright
ROBINSON, Thomas 1
Linton
ROBINSON, Tracy 4
ROBINSON, Victor 2
ROBINSON, W. Courtland 1
ROBINSON, Waltour M. 4
ROBINSON, Wilfred Henry 3
ROBINSON, Wilfreid 5
ROBINSON, William * H
ROBINSON, William 4
ROBINSON, William 1
Alexander
ROBINSON, William 3
Alexander
ROBINSON, William 1
Callyhan
ROBINSON, William 4
Christopher
ROBINSON, William Dean 3

ROBINSON, William 1
Duffield
ROBINSON, William 5
Edward
ROBINSON, William H
Erigena
ROBINSON, William H. 5
ROBINSON, William Henry 1
ROBINSON, William Henry 3
ROBINSON, Wm Henry 3
ROBINSON, William J. 1
ROBINSON, William M. 4
ROBINSON, William 4
Morrison Jr.
ROBINSON, William S. 2
ROBINSON, William 1
Stevens
ROBINSON, William 3
Theodore
ROBINSON, William 1
Wallace Jr.
ROBINSON, Wirt 1
ROBISON, David Fullerton H
ROBISON, Henry Barton 3
ROBISON, Henry John 4
ROBISON, Samuel Shelburn 1
ROBISON, William Ferretti 2
ROBNETT, Ronald Herbert 3
ROBOT, Isidore H
ROBSION, John Marshall 1
ROBSON, Frank E. 2
ROBSON, James A. 1
ROBSON, Martin Cecil 5
ROBSON, May 2
ROBSON, May Waldron 1
ROBSON, Stuart 1
ROBUS, Hugo 4
ROBYN, Alfred George 1
ROBYN, Edward H
ROCAP, James E. 6
ROCHAMBEAU, comte de 1
ROCHE, Ambrose Francis 1
ROCHE, Arthur Somers 1
ROCHE, Frederick W. 5
ROCHE, James Jeffrey 1
ROCHE, John A. 1
ROCHE, John Joseph 4
ROCHE, John Pierre 3
ROCHE, Joseph T. 4
ROCHE, Martin 1
ROCHE, Michael Joseph 4
ROCHE, William James 1
ROCHESTER, Edward 2
Sudler
ROCHESTER, Nathaniel H
ROCHESTER, William H
Beatty
ROCHESTER, William 1
Beatty
ROCHLEN, Ava Michael 5
ROCK, George Frederick 2
ROCK, George Henry 2
ROCKEFELLER, John 1
Davison
ROCKEFELLER, John 4
Davison Jr.
ROCKEFELLER, Lewis 5
Kirby
ROCKEFELLER, Percy 1
Avery
ROCKEFELLER, William 1
ROCKEFELLER, William 1
Goodsell
ROCKEFELLER, Winthrop 5
ROCKEFELLER, Winthrop 6
ROCKENBACH, Samuel 1
Dickerson
ROCKETT, James Francis 2
ROCKEY, Alpha Eugene 1
ROCKEY, Howard 1
ROCKEY, Keller E. 5
ROCKHILL, William 1
ROCKHILL, William 1
Woodville
ROCKINGHAM, Charles H
Watson-Wentworth
ROCKNE, Knute Kenneth 1
Perkins
ROCKWELL, Alfred 1
ROCKWELL, Alphonso 1
David
ROCKWELL, Charles H. 1
ROCKWELL, Charles 1
Henry
ROCKWELL, David Ladd 5
ROCKWELL, Edward 2
Henry
ROCKWELL, Fletcher 5
Webster
ROCKWELL, Homer 1
ROCKWELL, John Arnold H
ROCKWELL, Joseph H. 1
ROCKWELL, Julius H
ROCKWELL, Julius Ensign 1
ROCKWELL, Kiffin Yates 1
ROCKWELL, Kiffin Yates 4

ROCKWELL, Maryelda 5
ROCKWELL, Robert Fay 3
ROCKWELL, Samuel 4
ROCKWELL, Walter F. 6
ROCKWELL, William 1
Hayden
ROCKWELL, William 3
Walker
ROCKWOOD, Charles 1
Greene
ROCKWOOD, Elbert 1
William
ROCKWOOD, Frank Ernest 1
ROCKWOOD, George 1
Gardner
ROCKWOOD, George I. 5
ROCKWOOD, Robert 3
Everett
RODALE, Jerome Irving 5
RODD, Thomas 4
RODDA, F. C. 4
RODDENBERY, Seaborn 1
Anderson
RODDEWIG, Clair M. 6
RODDEY, Philip Dale 4
RODDEY, William Joseph 4
RODDIS, Hamilton 3
RODDY, Gilbert Morgan 5
RODDY, Harry Justin 1
RODDY, Harry Justin 2
RODDY, James E. 4
RODDY, William Franklin 1
RODE, Alfred H
RODE, Ralph Becker 3
RODEBUSH, Worth Huff 4
RODEFER, Charles Mayger 4
RODEHEAVER, Homer 3
Alvan
RODELL, Marie Freid 6
RODEN, Carl Bismarck 3
RODEN, Henry Wisdom 1
RODENBAUGH, Henry 4
Nathan
RODENBECK, Adolph 3
Julius
RODENBERG, William A. 1
RODENBOUGH, 1
Theophilus Francis
RODER, Martin H
RODES, Robert Emmett H
RODEY, Bernard Shandon 1
RODEY, Pearce Coddington 3
RODGER, James George 4
RODGERS, Christopher 1
Raymond Perry
RODGERS, Cleveland 3
RODGERS, Cowan 1
RODGERS, David John 5
RODGERS, Frederick 1
RODGERS, George H
Washington *
RODGERS, Henry Darling 6
RODGERS, James Linn 1
RODGERS, John * H
RODGERS, John 1
RODGERS, John Augustus 1
RODGERS, John Gilmour 1
RODGERS, John Isaac 1
RODGERS, Philip R. 4
RODGERS, Raymond 5
RODGERS, Raymond Perry 1
RODGERS, Robert Lewis 4
RODGERS, Ted V. 4
RODGERS, Thomas Slidell 1
RODGERS, William 5
RODGERS, William 1
Blackstock
RODGERS, William 1
Cunningham
RODGERS, William 2
Ledyard
RODGERS, William S. S. 4
RODGERS, William 1
Thomas
RODKEY, Robert Gordon 4
RODMAN, Clarence James 5
RODMAN, Hugh 1
RODMAN, Isaac Peace 1
RODMAN, John Croom 1
RODMAN, John Stewart 3
RODMAN, T. Clifford 1
RODMAN, Thomas Jackson H
RODMAN, Walter Sheldon 2
RODMAN, Warren Anson 4
RODMAN, William 1
RODMAN, William Blount 2
RODMAN, William Louis 1
RODNEY, Caesar H
RODNEY, Caesar Augustus H
RODNEY, Daniel 1
RODNEY, George Brydges H
RODNEY, George Brydges 4
RODNEY, Richard 4
Seymour
RODNEY, Thomas H
RODRIGUEZ, Jose Ignacio 1

RODRIGUEZ-SERRA, 5
Manuel
RODRIQUEZ, Abelardo 4
RODZINSKI, Artur 3
ROE, Arthur 2
ROE, Azel Stevens H
ROE, Charles Francis 1
ROE, Clifford Griffith 1
ROE, Dudley George 6
ROE, Edward Drake Jr. 1
ROE, Edward Payson H
ROE, Francis Asbury 1
ROE, Frederick William 5
ROE, George 4
ROE, Gilbert Ernstein 1
ROE, Herman 4
ROE, James A. 4
ROE, John Orlando 1
ROE, Joseph Hyram 5
ROE, Joseph Wickham 4
ROE, Nora Ardella 4
ROE, Vingie Eve 3
ROE, William Edgar 1
ROEBER, Edward Charles 6
ROEBER, Eugene Franz 1
ROEBLING, Ferdinand W. 1
ROEBLING, Ferdinand 1
William Jr.
ROEBLING, John Augustus H
ROEBLING, Washington 1
Augustus
ROEBUCK, Arthur 6
Wentworth
ROEBUCK, John Ransom 4
ROEBUCK, John Ransom 5
ROEDDER, Edwin Carl 2
Lothar Clemens
ROEDER, Adolph 4
ROEDER, Bernard Franklin 5
ROEDER, Fred Vincent 5
ROEDER, Geraldine 4
Morgan
ROEHM, Alfred Isaac 2
ROEHR, Julius Edward 1
ROEHRIG, Frederic Louis 1
Otto
ROELKER, Charles Rafael 1
ROELKER, William Greene 3
ROELOFS, Howard 6
Dykema
ROEMER, Ferdinand H
ROEMER, Henry A. 5
ROEMER, John Lincoln 1
ROEMER, Joseph 3
ROEMERSHAUSER, Alvin 5
E(arl)
ROENNE, Torben Henning 6
ROERICH, Nicholas 2
Konstantin
ROESCH, Charles Edward 1
ROESCH, Karl Alexander 5
ROESCH, Walter Alfred 5
ROESSLER, John Edward 4
ROESSNER, Elmer 5
(Stirling)
ROETHKE, Theodore 4
ROETHKE, William A. C. 4
ROETHLISBERGER, Fritz 6
Jules
ROETTER, Paulus H
ROEVER, William Henry 3
ROGAN, Fred Leon 3
ROGAN, James S. 3
ROGAN, Ralph Frederic 3
ROGERS, Alfred Moore 4
ROGERS, Alfred Thomas 2
ROGERS, Allan Buttrick 4
ROGERS, Allen 1
ROGERS, Allen Hastings 1
ROGERS, Arthur 1
ROGERS, Arthur Amzi 6
ROGERS, Arthur Curtis 1
ROGERS, Arthur Kenyon 1
ROGERS, Arthur Small 4
ROGERS, Austin Flint 1
ROGERS, Austin Leonard 1
ROGERS, B. Talbot 5
ROGERS, Bernard 5
ROGERS, Bruce 3
ROGERS, Burton R(ay) 6
ROGERS, Cephas Brainerd 1
ROGERS, Charles H
ROGERS, Charles Butler 4
ROGERS, Charles Custis 1
ROGERS, Charles Darius 1
ROGERS, Charles Edwin 2
ROGERS, Charles Gardner 3
ROGERS, Charlotte 6
Boardman
ROGERS, Clara Kathleen 1
ROGERS, Daisy Fiske 5
ROGERS, David Banks 4
ROGERS, David Barss 4
ROGERS, David Camp 4
ROGERS, Donald Aquilla 5
ROGERS, Donald G. 3

ROGERS, Dwight L. 3
ROGERS, Edith Nourse 4
ROGERS, Edmund James 1
Armstrong
ROGERS, Edward H
ROGERS, Edward Sidney 2
ROGERS, Edward H
Standiford
ROGERS, Ernest Albert 5
ROGERS, Ernest Andrew 3
ROGERS, Ernest Elias 2
ROGERS, Eustace Barron 1
ROGERS, Fairman 1
ROGERS, Floyd Sterling Jr. 4
ROGERS, Francis 3
ROGERS, Frazier 3
ROGERS, Fred A. 3
ROGERS, Fred S. 2
ROGERS, Frederick Morris 5
ROGERS, Frederick 1
Titsworth
ROGERS, George Alfred 1
ROGERS, George Bartlett 4
ROGERS, George Blake 4
ROGERS, George F. 2
ROGERS, George McIntosh 3
ROGERS, George Vernor 1
ROGERS, Gordon B. 4
ROGERS, Haratio 1
ROGERS, Harriet Burbank H
ROGERS, Harriet Burbank 4
ROGERS, Harry Clayton 5
ROGERS, Harry H. 3
ROGERS, Harry Lovejoy 1
ROGERS, Harry Stanley 5
ROGERS, Henry Darwin H
ROGERS, Henry H. 1
ROGERS, Henry 4
Huddleston
ROGERS, Henry J. H
ROGERS, Henry Munroe 1
ROGERS, Henry Treat 1
ROGERS, Henry Wade 1
ROGERS, Herbert Wesley 1
ROGERS, Hopewell 2
Lindenberger
ROGERS, Howard J. 3
ROGERS, Howard Jason 1
ROGERS, Hubert E. 3
ROGERS, Isaiah H
ROGERS, J. Harris 1
ROGERS, J. Speed 3
ROGERS, James H
ROGERS, James Blythe H
ROGERS, James Frederick 4
ROGERS, James Gamble 2
ROGERS, James Grafton 5
ROGERS, James Harvey 1
ROGERS, James Hotchkiss 1
ROGERS, James Sterling 5
ROGERS, James Tracy 4
ROGERS, Jason 2
ROGERS, John * H
ROGERS, John * 1
ROGERS, John Edward 2
ROGERS, John Henry 1
ROGERS, John I. 1
ROGERS, John Jacob 1
ROGERS, John Rankin 1
ROGERS, John Raphael 1
ROGERS, John William 4
ROGERS, Joseph Egerton 1
ROGERS, Joseph Morgan 1
ROGERS, Julia Ellen 4
ROGERS, Lebbeus Harding 4
ROGERS, Lester Burton 5
ROGERS, Lester Cushing 5
ROGERS, Lore Alford 5
ROGERS, Louis William 4
ROGERS, Malcolm Joseph 5
ROGERS, Marvin Carson 5
ROGERS, Mary Cochrane 5
ROGERS, Max 4
ROGERS, May 4
ROGERS, McLain 3
ROGERS, Moses H
ROGERS, Oscar H. 1
ROGERS, Philip Fletcher 1
ROGERS, Pleas Blair 6
ROGERS, Randolph 1
ROGERS, Robert H
ROGERS, Robert Cameron 1
ROGERS, Robert Emmons 1
ROGERS, Robert Empie H
ROGERS, Robert Samuel 5
ROGERS, Robert William 1
ROGERS, Sampson Jr. 5
ROGERS, Samuel H. 5
ROGERS, Samuel Lyle 1
ROGERS, Sherman S. 1
ROGERS, Sion Hart H
ROGERS, Stephen H
ROGERS, Thomas H
ROGERS, Thomas Jones H
ROGERS, Thomas Wesley 6
ROGERS, Tyler Stewart 4

* Indicates More Than One Such Name Listed

ROGERS, Vance 4
ROGERS, Waldo Henry 4
ROGERS, Walter Alexander 2
ROGERS, Walter Stowell 4
ROGERS, Warren Lincoln 1
ROGERS, Weaver Henry 1
ROGERS, Will 1
ROGERS, Willard Benjamin 4
ROGERS, William Allen 1
ROGERS, William Arthur 1
ROGERS, William Augustus H
ROGERS, William Banks 1
ROGERS, William Barton H
ROGERS, William Boddie 1
ROGERS, William H
Crowninshield
ROGERS, William F. 4
ROGERS, William Harlow 4
ROGERS, William King 1
ROGERS, William Loveland 5
ROGERS, William 2
Nathaniel
ROGERS, William Oscar 4
ROGERS, William Pennock 1
ROGERS, William Perry 1
ROGERS, Wynne Grey 2
ROGERSON, Charles 1
Edward
ROGLIANO, Francis 6
Teobaldo
ROGOSIN, I. 5
ROHBACH, James 1
Alexander
ROHDE, Max Spencer 6
ROHDE, Ruth Bryan 3
ROHE, Charles Henry 1
ROHE, George Henry 1
ROHLFING, Charles 3
Carroll
ROHLFS, Anna Katharine 1
Green
ROHLFS, Charles 1
ROHLMAN, Henry P. 3
ROHN, Oscar 1
ROHNSTOCK, J. Henry 3
ROHR, Elizabeth 3
ROHR, Frederick Hilmer 1
ROHRBACH, John Francis 5
Deems
ROHRBACH, John J. 3
ROHRBOUGH, Edward G. 3
ROHRBOUGH, Ralph 4
Virgil
ROHRER, Albert Lawrence 3
ROHRER, Karl 1
ROHRLICH, Chester 6
ROHWER, Henry 1
ROIG, Antonio A. 3
ROIG, Harold Joseph 5
ROISMAN, Joseph 4
ROJANKOVSKY, Feodor S. 5
ROJAS, P. Ezequiel 1
ROJAS PINILLA, Gustavo 6
ROJTMAN, Marc B. 4
ROLAPP, Henry Hermann 1
ROLER, Edward Oscar 4
Fitzalan
ROLETTE, Jean Joseph H
ROLFE, Alfred Grosvenor 2
ROLFE, Charles Wesley 1
ROLFE, Daniel Thomas 5
ROLFE, George William 2
ROLFE, Henry Winchester 1
ROLFE, John H
ROLFE, John Carew 2
ROLFE, John Furman 1
ROLFE, Stanley Herbert 2
ROLFE, William James 1
ROLFING, R. C. 6
ROLFS, Fred Maas 5
ROLFS, Peter Henry 2
ROLLAND, Romaine 2
ROLLEFSON, Gerhard 1
Krohn
ROLLER, Charles S. Jr. 4
ROLLER, Robert Douglas 1
Jr.
ROLLER, Thomas J. 3
ROLLERT, Edward Dumas 5
ROLLINS, Alice Marland H
Wellington
ROLLINS, Carl Purington 4
ROLLINS, Charles E. Jr. 3
ROLLINS, Charles Leonard 4
ROLLINS, Clara Sherwood 5
(Mrs.)
ROLLINS, Edward Henry H
ROLLINS, Edward Warren 1
ROLLINS, Frank West 1
ROLLINS, George Sherman 1
ROLLINS, Hyder Edward 5
ROLLINS, James Sidney H
ROLLINS, James Wingate 1
ROLLINS, John Fox 4
ROLLINS, Montgomery 1
ROLLINS, Thornton 1

ROLLINS, Wallace Eugene 3
ROLLINS, Walter 1
Huntington
ROLLINSON, William H
ROLPH, James Jr. 1
ROLPH, John Gladwyn 3
ROLPH, Samuel Wyman 4
ROLSHOVEN, Julius 1
ROLT-WHEELER, Francis 4
William
ROLVAAG, Ole Edvart 1
ROLZ-BENNETT, Jose 5
ROMA, Caro 1
ROMAINS, Jules 5
ROMAN, Andre Bienvenu H
ROMAN, Frederick William 2
ROMAN, James Dixon 1
ROMAN, Victor M. Reyes 3
Y.
ROMANOWITZ, Harry 5
Alex
ROMANS, Bernard H
ROMANS, John Francis 6
ROMAYNE, Nicholas H
ROMBAUER, Roderick 4
Emile
ROMBERG, Sigmund 3
ROME, Charles A. 3
ROMEIKE, Henry 1
ROMER, Alfred Sherwood 6
ROMER, Arthur C. 4
ROMERA-NAVARRO, 4
Miguel
ROMFH, Edward Coleman 6
ROMIG, Edgar Franklin 4
ROMIG, John Samuel 1
ROMINGER, Carl Ludwig 4
ROMMEL, George 2
McCullough
ROMNES, H(aakon) 6
I(ngolf)
ROMODA, Joseph J. 4
ROMUALDEZ, Miguel 6
ROMUALDEZ, Norberto 5
RONAN, Daniel John 5
RONAN, James Joseph 4
RONAYNE, Maurice 1
RONDTHALER, Edward 1
RONDTHALER, Howard 3
Edward
RONGY, Abraham Jacob 2
RONNE, Torben 6
RONNEBECK, Arnold 2
RONNEBERG, Earl 5
Fridthjov
RONON, Gerald 4
ROOD, A. Edward 3
ROOD, Dorothy B. A. 4
ROOD, James Theron 1
ROOD, John 6
ROOD, Ogden Nicholas 1
ROOD, Paul William 3
ROOK, Charles Alexander 2
ROOK, Edward Francis 4
ROOK, Gustav S. 5
ROOKER, Frederick Zadok 1
ROOKS, Lowell W(ard) 4
ROOME, Kenneth Andrew 5
ROONEY, John J. 6
ROONEY, John Jerome 1
ROONEY, Marie Collins 2
ROOP, Hervin Ulysses 3
ROOP, James Clawson 3
ROORBACH, George Byron 1
ROOS, Charles Frederick 3
ROOS, Delmar Gerle 3
ROOS, Edwin G. 5
ROOS, Frank John Jr. 4
ROOS, Robert Achille 3
ROOS, Walter L. 5
ROOSA, Daniel Bennett St 1
John
ROOSEVELT, Anna 4
Eleanor
ROOSEVELT, Edith Kermit 2
Carow
ROOSEVELT, Franklin H
Delano
ROOSEVELT, Franklin 2
Delano
ROOSEVELT, Franklin 4
Delano
ROOSEVELT, George 4
Emlen
ROOSEVELT, George 1
Washington
ROOSEVELT, Henry 1
Latrobe
ROOSEVELT, Hilborne H
Lewis
ROOSEVELT, James I. H
ROOSEVELT, Kermit 2
ROOSEVELT, Nicholas J. H
ROOSEVELT, Philip James 2
ROOSEVELT, Robert 1
Barnwell

ROOSEVELT, S. 1
Montgomery
ROOSEVELT, Theodore H
ROOSEVELT, Theodore H
ROOSEVELT, Theodore 4
ROOSEVELT, Mrs 4
Theodore
ROOSEVELT, Theodore Jr. 2
ROOSEVELT, W. Emlen H
ROOT, Amos Ives 1
ROOT, Azariah Smith 1
ROOT, Chapman Jay 2
ROOT, Edward Clary 2
ROOT, Edward Tallmadge 2
ROOT, Edwin Alvin 4
ROOT, Edwin Park 1
ROOT, Elihu 1
ROOT, Elihu Jr. 4
ROOT, Elisha King H
ROOT, Erastus H
ROOT, Ernest Rob 5
ROOT, Frank Albert 1
ROOT, Frank Douglas 4
ROOT, Frederic Woodman 1
ROOT, Frederick Stanley 1
ROOT, George Frederick 1
ROOT, Howard Frank 4
ROOT, Jesse H
ROOT, Jesse L. 3
ROOT, John Wellborn H
ROOT, John Wellborn H
ROOT, Joseph Cullen 1
ROOT, Joseph Edward 1
ROOT, Joseph Mosley H
ROOT, Joseph Pomeroy H
ROOT, Louis Carroll 1
ROOT, Lyman C. 1
ROOT, Mary Pauline 4
ROOT, Milo Adelbert 1
ROOT, Oren 1
ROOT, Oren 2
ROOT, Robert Cromwell 4
ROOT, Robert Kilburn 3
ROOT, Walter Harold 3
ROOT, Walter Stanton 5
ROOT, William Campbell 5
ROOT, William Thomas 2
ROOT, William Webster 1
ROOT, Winfred Trexler 2
ROOTH, Ivar 5
ROOTS, Logan Herbert 2
ROOTS, Logan Holt H
ROPER, Alvin Whitehead 1
ROPER, Daniel Calhoun 2
ROPER, Denney Warren 4
ROPER, John Caswell 1
ROPER, John Wesley 5
ROPER, Lewis Murphree 1
ROPER, Robert Poore 4
ROPER, William Winston 2
ROPERS, Harold 1
ROPES, Charles Joseph 1
Hardy
ROPES, James Hardy 1
ROPES, John Codman 1
ROPES, Joseph H
ROPES, William Ladd 1
RORABACK, Alberto T. 1
RORABACK, J. Henry 1
RORABAUGH, Guy Oscar 4
RORER, David H
RORER, Gerald Francis 6
RORER, James Birch 5
RORER, Sarah Tyson 1
RORER, Virgil Eugene 2
RORICK, John C. 4
RORIMER, James J. 4
RORIMER, Louis 1
RORTY, James 6
RORTY, Malcolm Churchill 1
ROSA, Edward Bennett 1
ROSAMOND, William Irby 6
ROSANOFF, Martin Andre 3
ROSATI, Joseph H
ROSBAUD, Hans 4
ROSCH, Joseph 6
ROSE, Albert Chatellier 4
ROSE, Aquila 1
ROSE, Arnold M. 4
ROSE, Benjamin Morris 1
ROSE, Billy 5
ROSE, Carlton Raymond 5
ROSE, Charles Bedell 4
ROSE, Chauncey H
ROSE, D. Kenneth 4
ROSE, Dana 1
ROSE, David S. 4
ROSE, Don 6
ROSE, Donald Frank 4
ROSE, Dwight Chappell 5
ROSE, Edward H
ROSE, Edward Everley 1
ROSE, E(rnest) H(erbert) 5
ROSE, Ernestine Louise H
Silsmondi Potowski
ROSE, Flora 3

ROSE, Floyd 3
ROSE, Forrest Hobart 5
ROSE, Frank Bramwell 1
ROSE, Frank Watson 5
ROSE, George B. 2
ROSE, Guy 1
ROSE, Heloise Durant (Mrs. 5
C. H. M. Rose)
ROSE, Henry Howard 1
ROSE, Henry Martin 1
ROSE, Henry Reuben 1
ROSE, Herschel Hampton 2
ROSE, Hugh Edward 2
ROSE, John Carter 1
ROSE, John Kerr 6
ROSE, John Marshall 1
ROSE, Joseph Nelson 1
ROSE, Josiah Tryon 1
ROSE, Kurt Eugene 6
ROSE, Landon Cabell 1
ROSE, Lisle A. 3
ROSE, Marcus A. 4
ROSE, Martha Emily 1
Parmelee
ROSE, Mary D. Swartz 1
ROSE, Maurice 2
ROSE, Philip Sheridan 1
ROSE, Ray Clarke 5
ROSE, Robert Forest 4
ROSE, Robert Hugh 1
ROSE, Robert Lawson H
ROSE, Robert Selden 1
ROSE, Rufus Edwards 1
ROSE, S. Brandt 1
ROSE, Thomas Ellwood 1
ROSE, U. M. 1
ROSE, Wallace Dickinson 1
ROSE, Walter Malins 1
ROSE, Wickliffe 1
ROSE, William Brandon 2
ROSE, William Clayton 5
ROSE, William Ganson 3
ROSE, William Hazael 4
ROSEBAULT, Charles 2
Jerome
ROSEBUSH, Judson George 2
ROSECRANS, Egbert 1
ROSECRANS, Sylvester H
Horton
ROSECRANS, William H
Starke
ROSECRANS, William 5
Starke
ROSEKRANS, John 4
Newton
ROSEKRANS, Sarah H. 6
Didriksen (Mrs. Milton
Charles Rosekrans)
ROSELAND, Harry 3
ROSELIUS, Christian H
ROSEMAN, Alvin 6
ROSEN, Baron 1
ROSEN, Charles 3
ROSEN, Charles F. 4
ROSEN, Julius Jack 5
ROSEN, Max 3
ROSEN, Peter 3
ROSEN, Samuel 5
ROSEN, Victor Hugo 5
ROSENAU, Frederick J. 6
ROSENAU, Milton Joseph 2
ROSENBACH, Abraham S. 5
Wolf
ROSENBACH, Joseph 3
Bernhardt
ROSENBAUM, David 6
ROSENBAUM, Edward 4
Philip
ROSENBAUM, Lewis 3
Newman
ROSENBAUM, Otho Bane 5
ROSENBAUM, Samuel 5
Rawlins
ROSENBAUM, Solomon 1
Guedalia
ROSENBERG, Arthur 2
ROSENBERG, Henry H
ROSENBERG, Henry A. 3
ROSENBERG, Israel 5
ROSENBERG, James N. 2
ROSENBERG, S. L. Millard 1
ROSENBERG, Samuel 5
ROSENBERGER, Absalom 4
ROSENBERGER, Carl 2
ROSENBERGER, Gerald 4
E.
ROSENBERRY, Lois Carter 5
Kimball Mathews (Mrs.
Marvin Bristol
ROSENBERRY, M. Claude 5
ROSENBERRY, Marvin 3
Bristol
ROSENBLATT, Sol A(riah) 5
ROSENBLOOM, Benjamin 6
Louis

ROSENBLUETH, Arturo 5
Stearns
ROSENBLUM, Frank 5
ROSENBLUM, Herman 5
ROSENBLUM, Jacob 5
Joseph
ROSENBLUM, William 4
Franklin
ROSENDALE, Simon 1
Wolfe
ROSENFELD, Maurice 1
ROSENFELD, Paul 2
ROSENFELD, Sydney 1
ROSENFIELD, John 4
ROSENGARTEN, Adolph 2
George
ROSENGARTEN, Frederic 3
ROSENGARTEN, George 1
David
ROSENGARTEN, Joseph 4
George
ROSENGRANT, E. Judson 5
ROSENHEIM, Alfred Faist 2
ROSENHOLTZ, Joseph 4
Leon
ROSENKAMPFF, Arthur 3
H.
ROSENMAN, Samuel 5
Irving
ROSENMILLER, Joseph 4
Lewis
ROSENSOHN, Etta Lasker 4
ROSENSON, Alexander 5
Moses
ROSENSTEIN, David 4
ROSENSTENGEL, W. E. 3
ROSENSTERN, Iwan 6
ROSENSTIEL, Lewis S. 6
ROSENSTOCK, Arthur 6
ROSENSTOCK-HUESSY, 5
Eugen
ROSENTHAL, Albert 1
ROSENTHAL, Benjamin 1
ROSENTHAL, David S. 3
ROSENTHAL, Doris 1
ROSENTHAL, Herman 1
ROSENTHAL, Ida 5
ROSENTHAL, Jean 5
ROSENTHAL, Lessing 2
ROSENTHAL, Louis S. 2
ROSENTHAL, Max 1
ROSENTHAL, Moritz 1
ROSENTHAL, Morris 3
Sigmund
ROSENTHAL, Sam 6
ROSENTHAL, Sarah 5
G(ertrude)
ROSENTHAL, Toby E. 1
ROSENWALD, Julius 1
ROSER, Henry Harvoleau 4
ROSEWATER, Andrew 1
ROSEWATER, Charles 2
Colman
ROSEWATER, Edward 1
ROSEWATER, Stanley 3
Meinrath
ROSEWATER, Victor 1
ROSIER, Joseph 3
ROSIN, Harry 6
ROSING, Leonard August 1
ROSING, Vladimir 4
ROSLING, George 1
ROSS, Abel Hastings H
ROSS, Albert * 1
ROSS, Albert Randolph 3
ROSS, Alexander H
ROSS, Alexander Coffman 1
ROSS, Alfred Joseph 5
ROSS, Allan Charles 5
ROSS, Arthur Leonidas 4
ROSS, Arthur M(ax) 5
ROSS, Austin C. 3
ROSS, Bennett Battle 1
ROSS, Bernard Rogan H
ROSS, Betsy H
ROSS, Carmon 2
ROSS, Charles Ben 2
ROSS, Charles Griffith 3
ROSS, Clarence Frisbee 2
ROSS, Clarence Samuel 5
ROSS, Clay Campbell 2
ROSS, Clinton 1
ROSS, David H
ROSS, David 4
ROSS, David E. 2
ROSS, David Francis 6
ROSS, Denman Waldo 2
ROSS, Donald 4
ROSS, Earle D(udley) 5
ROSS, Edmund Gibson H
ROSS, Edmund Gibson 1
ROSS, Edward Alsworth 5
ROSS, Emory 5
ROSS, Erskine Mayo 1
ROSS, Frank Alexander 5
ROSS, Frank Elmore 4

ROSS, Frank James 4
ROSS, Frank MacKenzie 5
ROSS, Frederick Jeffery 3
ROSS, G. A. Johnston 1
ROSS, George H
ROSS, George H. 4
ROSS, Harold Ellis 6
ROSS, Harold Wallace 3
ROSS, Harry Seymour 2
ROSS, Henry Davis 2
ROSS, Henry Howard H
ROSS, Homer Lachlin 4
ROSS, J. Walker 1
ROSS, James H
ROSS, James Delmage 1
ROSS, James Lycurgus 4
ROSS, John * H
ROSS, John Alexander Jr. 6
ROSS, John Dawson 1
ROSS, John Elliot 2
ROSS, John Jacob 3
ROSS, John Mason 2
ROSS, John O. 4
ROSS, John Wesley 1
ROSS, John William 1
ROSS, John William * 4
ROSS, Jonathan 1
ROSS, Joseph 4
ROSS, Julian Lenhart 5
ROSS, Lawrence Sullivan H
ROSS, Leonard Fulton 1
ROSS, Leroy Williams 1
ROSS, Lester J. 3
ROSS, Letitia Roano Dowdell 3
ROSS, Lewis P. 1
ROSS, Lewis T. 3
ROSS, Lewis Winans H
ROSS, Luther Sherman 4
ROSS, Malcolm 4
ROSS, Martin H
ROSS, Michael 4
ROSS, Ogden 5
ROSS, Patrick Hore Warriner 1
ROSS, Perley Ason 1
ROSS, Peter V. 2
ROSS, Philip James 3
ROSS, Robert Edwin 1
ROSS, Samuel Louis 5
ROSS, Sarah Gridley 4
ROSS, Sobieski H
ROSS, Stoyte O. 6
ROSS, Thomas H
ROSS, Thomas Joseph 6
ROSS, Thomas Randolph H
ROSS, Walter L. 1
ROSS, Wilbert Davidson 2
ROSS, William Bradford 1
ROSS, William Horace 2
ROSS, William McAllister 1
ROSS, Worth Gwynn 1
ROSSBACH, Edgar Hilary 3
ROSSBY, Carl-Gustaf Arvid 3
ROSSDALE, Albert Berger 6
ROSSEAU, Lovell Harrison H
ROSSEAU, Percival Leonard 1
ROSSELL, John Settles 1
ROSSELL, William Trent 1
ROSSELLE, William Quay 5
ROSSEN, Ralph 6
ROSSEN, Robert 4
ROSSER, John Elijah 6
ROSSER, Luther Zeigler 1
ROSSER, Thomas Lafayette 1
ROSSETER, John Henry 5
ROSSETTER, George W. 3
ROSSETTI, Victor H. 4
ROSSEY, Chris C. 2
ROSSI, Angelo Joseph 2
ROSSI, Louis Mansfield 2
ROSSI, Luis Banchero 5
ROSSITER, Clinton 5
ROSSITER, Edward Van Wyck 1
ROSSITER, Ehrick Kensett 2
ROSSITER, Fred J. 4
ROSSITER, Frederick McGee 5
ROSSITER, Perceval Sherer 5
ROSSITER, Stealy Bales 1
ROSSITER, Thomas Prichard H
ROSSITER, William Sidney 1
ROSSLYN, John 4
ROSSMAN, George 4
ROSSMAN, Joseph 5
ROSSMAN, Samuel S. 5
ROSSO, Augusto 4
ROSTOCK, Frank Witte 4
ROSTOVTZEFF, Michael Ivanovich 3
ROSZEL, Brantz Mayer 1
ROTCH, A. Lawrence 1
ROTCH, Arthur H
ROTCH, Thomas Morgan 1
ROTCH, William H
ROTCH, William 1
ROTCHFORD, Hugh Babb 5
ROTH, Ben 3
ROTH, Feri 5
ROTH, Filibert 1
ROTH, Frederick George Richard 2
ROTH, George Byron 6
ROTH, Henry Warren 1
ROTH, John Ernest 4
ROTH, Paul Hoerlein 4
ROTH, Stephen John 6
ROTH, William P. 4
ROTHAFEL, Samuel Lionel H
ROTHAFEL, Samuel Lionel 4
ROTHBERG, Maurice 6
ROTHBERG, Sidney 5
ROTHE, Guillermo 6
ROTHENBERG, Milton 5
ROTHENBERG, Morris 3
ROTHENBURGER, William Frederic 5
ROTHERMEL, Amos Cornelius 2
ROTHERMEL, John Goodhart 1
ROTHERMEL, John H. 1
ROTHERMEL, Peter Frederick H
ROTHIER, Leon 5
ROTHKO, Mark 5
ROTHMAN, Stephen 4
ROTHROCK, Addison M(ay) 5
ROTHROCK, David Andrew 4
ROTHROCK, Edward Streicher 4
ROTHROCK, Joseph Trimble 1
ROTHSCHILD, Alonzo 1
ROTHSCHILD, Karl 5
ROTHSCHILD, Louis F. 3
ROTHSCHILD, Marcus A. 1
ROTHSCHILD, Maurice 2
ROTHSCHILD, Walter Nathan 4
ROTHSTEIN, Irma 5
ROTHWELL, Bernard Joseph 2
ROTHWELL, Gideon Frank H
ROTHWELL, Richard Pennefather 1
ROTHWELL, Will A. 1
ROTNEM, Ralph Arthur 5
ROTTGER, Curtis Hoopes 4
ROTZELL, Willett Enos 1
ROUAULT, Georges 3
ROUCOLLE, Adrienne (Miss) 5
ROUDEBUSH, Alfred Holt 2
ROUDEBUSH, Francis Wilshira 6
ROUILLER, Charles 6
ROULAND, Orlando 2
ROULHAC, Thomas Ruffin 4
ROULSTON, Marjorie Hillis 5
ROULSTONE, George H
ROUND, William Marshall Fitts 1
ROUNDS, Arthur Charles 1
ROUNDS, Leslie Raymond 4
ROUNDS, Ralph Stowell 2
ROUNSEVILLE, Robert Field 6
ROUNTREE, George 2
ROUQUETTE, Adrien Emmanuel H
ROUQUETTE, Francois Dominique H
ROURKE, Anthony J(ohn) J(oseph) 6
ROURKE, Constance Mayfield 1
ROURKE, Frank W. 4
ROUS, Peyton 5
ROUSE, Adelaide Louise 1
ROUSE, Arthur B. 5
ROUSE, Henry Clark 1
ROUSE, John Delos 4
ROUSE, John Gould 4
ROUSE, Louis Austin 6
ROUSH, Gar A. 3
ROUSH, Oliver Eugene 5
ROUSMANIERE, Edmund Swett 1
ROUSS, Charles Broadway 1
ROUSSE, Thomas Andrew 4
ROUSSEAU, Harry Harwood 1
ROUSSEAU, Theodore 6
ROUSSELOT, Louis M. 6
ROUSSEVE, Ferdinand Lucien 4
ROUTH, Eugene Coke 5
ROUTH, James (Edward) 6
ROUTLEY, Thomas Clarence 4
ROUTT, John Long 1
ROUTZAHN, Evart Grant 1
ROUTZOHN, Harry Nelson 3
ROUXEL, Gustave Augustin 1
ROVELSTAD, A(dolph) M(arius) 6
ROVENSKY, Joseph Charles 3
ROVENSTINE, E. A. 4
ROVER, Leo Aloysius 4
ROVERSI, Louis 1
ROW, Edgar Charles 6
ROW, Robert Keable 1
ROW, William Hamilton 4
ROWAN, Andrew Summers 2
ROWAN, Charles A. 1
ROWAN, Charles Joseph 2
ROWAN, Hugh Williamson 6
ROWAN, John H
ROWAN, Joseph 1
ROWAN, Richard Wilmer 4
ROWAN, Stephen Clegg H
ROWAN, Thomas Leslie 5
ROWAN, William A. 4
ROWBOTTOM, Harry E. 1
ROWCLIFF, Gilbert 4
ROWE, Albert Holmes 5
ROWE, Allan Winter 1
ROWE, Benjamin Ackley 1
ROWE, Clifford Paul 5
ROWE, Frederick William 2
ROWE, Gilbert Theodore 4
ROWE, Guy 5
ROWE, Hartley 4
ROWE, Henrietta Gould 1
ROWE, Henry Clarke 4
ROWE, Henry Kalloch 1
ROWE, Jesse Perry 5
ROWE, John Leroy 6
ROWE, Joseph Eugene 1
ROWE, L. Earle 1
ROWE, Leo S. 2
ROWE, Peter H
ROWE, Peter Trimble 2
ROWE, Robert G. 5
ROWE, Stuart Henry 5
ROWE, Theodore Spurling 6
ROWE, Walter Ellsworth 3
ROWE, William Stanhope 1
ROWELL, Chester Harvey 2
ROWELL, George Presbury 1
ROWELL, George Smith 4
ROWELL, Henry Thompson 6
ROWELL, Hugh Grant 4
ROWELL, James G. 3
ROWELL, John W. 1
ROWELL, Jonathan Harvey 1
ROWELL, Joseph Cummings 1
ROWELL, Ross Erastus 2
ROWELL, Wilbur Everett 2
ROWELL, Wilfrid Asa 3
ROWLAND, Adoniram Judson 1
ROWLAND, Arthur John 1
ROWLAND, Benjamin Jr. 5
ROWLAND, Charles H. 4
ROWLAND, Charles Leonard 1
ROWLAND, Clarence H. 5
ROWLAND, Dunbar 1
ROWLAND, Harry T. 3
ROWLAND, Henry Augustus 1
ROWLAND, Henry Cottrell 1
ROWLAND, James Marshall Hanna 3
ROWLAND, Joseph Medley 1
ROWLAND, Kate Mason 1
ROWLAND, Roger Whittaker 6
ROWLAND, Vernon Cecil 4
ROWLAND, William Samuel 1
ROWLANDS, William H
ROWLANDSON, Mary White H
ROWLEE, Willard Winfield 1
ROWLETT, Robert 1
ROWLEY, Francis Harold 3
ROWLEY, Frank S. 3
ROWLEY, George 4
ROWLEY, John 1
ROWLEY, William C. 4
ROWNTREE, Jennie 6
ROWSE, Samuel Worcester H
ROWSON, Susanna Haswell H
ROXAS, Manuel 2
ROY, Arthur Jay 2
ROY, Francis Albert 5
ROY, James Evans 6
ROY, Lillian Elizabeth 1
ROY, Percy Albert 2
ROY, Philip Seddon 4
ROY, Reuben Finnell 4
ROY, Sharat Kumar 4
ROY, Victor Leander Sr. 5
ROYAL, Forrest 2
ROYAL, George 1
ROYAL, Ralph 1
ROYALL, Anne Newport H
ROYALL, Kenneth Claiborne 5
ROYALL, Ralph 3
ROYALL, Tucker 1
ROYALL, William Bailey 1
ROYALTY, Paul 4
ROYCE, Alexander Burgess 4
ROYCE, Asa Marshfield 4
ROYCE, Donald 5
ROYCE, Frederick Page 1
ROYCE, George Monroe 1
ROYCE, Homer Elihu H
ROYCE, Josiah 1
ROYCE, Luman Herbert 1
ROYCE, Robert Russel 5
ROYCE, Sarah Eleanor Bayliss H
ROYE, Edward James H
ROYER, Arnold Lennel 5
ROYER, J. E. E. 3
ROYLE, Edwin Milton 2
ROYSE, Samuel Durham 2
ROYSTER, Hubert Ashley 5
ROYSTER, James Finch 1
ROYSTER, Lawrence Thomas 5
ROYSTER, Salibelle 6
ROZMAREK, Charles 6
RUARK, Robert Chester 4
RUBATTEL, Rodolphe 4
RUBEL, A. C. 4
RUBEN, Barney 3
RUBENDALL, Clarence 3
RUBENS, Harry 1
RUBENS, Horatio Seymour 1
RUBEY, Thomas Lewis 1
RUBEY, William Walden 6
RUBIN, J. Robert 3
RUBIN, Reuven 6
RUBIN, William Benjamin 5
RUBIN DE LA BORBOLLA, Daniel Fernando 5
RUBINKAM, Nathaniel Irwin 1
RUBINOVITZ, George 5
RUBINOW, Isaac Max 1
RUBINOWICZ, Wojciech 6
RUBINSTEIN, Beryl 3
RUBINSTEIN, Helena 4
RUBIO, Antonio 3
RUBIO, David 4
RUBLEE, George 3
RUBLEE, Horace H
RUBLEE, William Alvah 1
RUBSAMEN, Walter Howard 6
RUBY, Edward Ernest 5
RUBY, Harry 6
RUBY, Lionel 5
RUCH, Giles Murrel 2
RUCKER, Allen Willis 4
RUCKER, Atterson Walden 2
RUCKER, Casper Bell 2
RUCKER, D. H. H
RUCKER, Daniel Henry 1
RUCKER, Elbert Marion 1
RUCKER, Louis H. 1
RUCKER, Marvin Pierce 4
RUCKER, William Colby 1
RUCKER, William Waller 1
RUCKMAN, John Wilson 1
RUCKMICK, Christian Alban 4
RUCKSTULL, Fred Wellington 2
RUDD, Judson Archer 5
RUDD, Stephan A. 1
RUDD, Thomas Brown 3
RUDD, William Platt 1
RUDDER, James Earl 5
RUDDIMAN, Edsel Alexander 3
RUDDIMAN, Edsel Alexander 5
RUDDOCK, John Carroll 4
RUDDOCK, Malcolm Irving 4
RUDDY, Edward Michael 5
RUDDY, Howard Shaw 1
RUDE, Joe Christopher 6
RUDENBERG, Reinhold 4
RUDENKO, William Bernard 4
RUDER, William Ernst 4
RUDERMAN, James 6
RUDERSDORFF, Hermine H
RUDGE, William Edwin 1
RUDICK, Harry J. 4
RUDINGER, Ellen Eckstein (Mrs. George Rudinger) 5
RUDKIN, Frank H. 1
RUDKIN, Margaret Fogarty 4
RUDOLPH, Charles 4
RUDOLPH, Cuna H. 1
RUDOLPH, Herbert Blaine 3
RUDOLPH, Herman Louis 6
RUDOLPH, Irving 4
RUDOLPH, Jacob H. 3
RUDOLPH, Robert Livingston 1
RUE, Lars 4
RUE, Levi Lingo 1
RUE, Milton 5
RUE, Ralph H. 4
RUEBUSH, James Hott 3
RUEDEMANN, Albert Darwin 6
RUEDEMANN, Rudolf 3
RUEDIGER, Gustav F. 1
RUEDIGER, William Carl 2
RUEHE, Harrison August 3
RUETENIK, Herman Julius 4
RUFF, G. Elson 5
RUFF, Robert Hamric 2
RUFFIN, Edmund H
RUFFIN, Margaret Ellen Henry 5
RUFFIN, Sterling 2
RUFFIN, Thomas * H
RUFFINI, Elise Erna 5
RUFFNER, Charles Shumway 1
RUFFNER, Ernest Howard 4
RUFFNER, Henry H
RUFFNER, William Henry 1
RUFUS, Will Carl 2
RUGEN, Myrtle Louise 6
RUGER, Thomas Howard 1
RUGG, Arthur Prentice 1
RUGG, Charles Belcher 4
RUGG, Frederic Waldo 1
RUGG, Harold 4
RUGG, Henry Warren 1
RUGG, Herbert Dean 4
RUGG, Robert Billings 2
RUGGLES, Arthur Hiler 4
RUGGLES, Benjamin H
RUGGLES, Carl 5
RUGGLES, Charles 5
RUGGLES, Charles Herman H
RUGGLES, Clyde Orval 3
RUGGLES, Colden L'Hommedieu 1
RUGGLES, E. Wood 2
RUGGLES, George David 1
RUGGLES, Henry Joseph 1
RUGGLES, John H
RUGGLES, Nathaniel H
RUGGLES, Oliver W. 1
RUGGLES, Samuel Bulkley H
RUGGLES, Timothy H
RUGGLES, William Burroughs 4
RUGH, Charles Edward 4
RUHE, Percy Bott 4
RUHEMANN, Helmut 6
RUHL, Arthur Brown 5
RUHL, Christian H. 4
RUHL, James Brough 3
RUHL, Robert Waldo 4
RUHLENDER, Henry 4
RUHOFF, John Richard 6
RUHRAH, John 1
RUIZ, Cortines Adolfo 6
RUIZ, Jose Martinez 4
RUIZ GUINAZO, Enrique 4
RULAND, Lloyd Stanton 3
RULE, Arthur Richards 3
RULE, James Noble 1
RULE, William 1
RULON, Phillip Justin 5
RUMBLE, Douglas 6
RUMBOLD, Frank Meeker 4
RUMBOLD, Thomas Frazier 1
RUMELY, Edward A. 4
RUMELY, V. P. 4
RUMELY, William Nicholas 3
RUMFORD, Count H
RUML, Beardsley 3
RUMMEL, Joseph F. 4
RUMPF, Arthur Newell 5
RUMPLE, J. N. W. 1
RUMSEY, Benjamin H
RUMSEY, Charles Cary 1
RUMSEY, David H
RUMSEY, Dexter Phelps 4
RUMSEY, Edward H
RUMSEY, Israel Parsons 4
RUMSEY, James H

* Indicates More Than One Such Name Listed

RUMSEY, Mary Harriman 1
RUMSEY, William 1
RUNCIE, Constance Fauntleroy
RUNDALL, Charles O. 3
RUNDELL, Oliver Samuel 3
RUNDLE, George Mortimer 4
RUNDQUIST, George E. 5
RUNGE, Edith Amelie 5
RUNGIUS, Carl 3
RUNK, John H
RUNKLE, Benjamin Platt 1
RUNKLE, Delmer 1
RUNKLE, Erwin William 1
RUNKLE, Harry Godley 4
RUNKLE, Harry Maize 4
RUNKLE, John Daniel 1
RUNKLE, Lucia Isabella 4
RUNNELLS, Clive 1
RUNNELLS, John Sumner 1
RUNNELS, Orange Scott 1
RUNNELS, Richard Stitt 6
RUNNER, Harvey Evan 4
RUNNING, Theodore Rudolph 5
RUNYAN, Elmer Gardner 1
RUNYAN, William B. 3
RUNYON, Alfred Damon 2
RUNYON, John William 4
RUNYON, W. Parker 1
RUNYON, William Nelson 1
RUOFF, Henry Woldmar 1
RUOPP, Harold Washington 4
RUOTOLO, Onorio 4
RUPE, Dallas Gordon 5
RUPEL, I(saac) Walker 5
RUPERTUS, William Henry 2
RUPLEY, Arthur Ringwalt 4
RUPLEY, Joseph William 5
RUPP, Charles Jr. 5
RUPP, Israel Daniel H
RUPP, Lawrence Henry 4
RUPP, Otto Burton 4
RUPP, Werner Andrew 4
RUPP, William 1
RUPPEL, Louis 3
RUPPENTHAL, Jacob Christian 4
RUPPERT, George E. 2
RUPPERT, Jacob Jr. 1
RUPPERT, Max King 1
RUPPRECHT, Frederick Kelsey 3
RUSBY, Henry Hurd 1
RUSH, Benjamin H
RUSH, Benjamin 2
RUSH, Charles Andrew 4
RUSH, Franklin Smithwick 1
RUSH, Guy Mansfield 4
RUSH, Jacob H
RUSH, James H
RUSH, John Andrew 2
RUSH, Madelon Reine Francis (Mrs. Alan Sydney Rush) 6
RUSH, Olive 4
RUSH, Richard H
RUSH, Sylvester R. 1
RUSH, Thomas E. 1
RUSH, William H
RUSHING, James Andrew 5
RUSHMORE, David Barker 1
RUSHMORE, Edward 4
RUSHMORE, John Dikeman 4
RUSHMORE, Stephen 5
RUSHTON, Herbert J. 2
RUSHTON, Ray 1
RUSHTON, Richard Holt 1
RUSK, Henry Perly 5
RUSK, Jeremiah McLain H
RUSK, John 1
RUSK, Ralph Leslie 4
RUSK, Thomas Jefferson H
RUSKIN, Jerrold Harold 5
RUSLING, James Fowler 1
RUSS, Hugh McMaster 5
RUSS, John H
RUSS, John Denison 1
RUSS, John Megginson 5
RUSS, John T. 3
RUSSEL, Edgar 1
RUSSEL, George Howard 1
RUSSEL, Henry 1
RUSSEL, Walter S. 1
RUSSELL, Addison Peale 1
RUSSELL, Albert Hyatt 4
RUSSELL, Alexander 3
RUSSELL, Alexander Wilson 4
RUSSELL, Alfred 1
RUSSELL, Annie 1
RUSSELL, Arthur Joseph 4
RUSSELL, Arthur Perkins 2
RUSSELL, Benjamin * H

RUSSELL, Bertrand Earl Russell 5
RUSSELL, Bruce Alexander 4
RUSSELL, Charles 1
RUSSELL, Charles Addison 1
RUSSELL, Charles Augustus 4
RUSSELL, Charles Edward 1
RUSSELL, Charles Howland 1
RUSSELL, Charles Marion 1
RUSSELL, Charles Partridge 4
RUSSELL, Charles Taze 1
RUSSELL, Charles Tier 3
RUSSELL, Charles Wells 1
RUSSELL, Clinton Warden 4
RUSSELL, Daniel 2
RUSSELL, Daniel Lindsay 1
RUSSELL, David Abel H
RUSSELL, David Allen H
RUSSELL, Doris Aurelia 4
RUSSELL, Edmund A. 4
RUSSELL, Edward Hutson 5
RUSSELL, Edward Lafayette 1
RUSSELL, Elbert 3
RUSSELL, Elias Harlow 1
RUSSELL, Ernest John 3
RUSSELL, Faris M. 5
RUSSELL, Francis Thayer 1
RUSSELL, Francis Wayland 5
RUSSELL, Frank 1
RUSSELL, Frank F. 5
RUSSELL, Frank Marion 5
RUSSELL, Frederick Fuller 4
RUSSELL, George 1
RUSSELL, George Edmond 3
RUSSELL, George Harvey 5
RUSSELL, George Louis Jr. 1
RUSSELL, Gordon 1
RUSSELL, H(arry) Earle 5
RUSSELL, Harry Luman 5
RUSSELL, Harry Newton 5
RUSSELL, Helen Crocker 4
RUSSELL, Helen Gertrude 5
RUSSELL, Henry 2
RUSSELL, Henry Benajah 2
RUSSELL, Henry Dozier 5
RUSSELL, Henry Moore 1
RUSSELL, Henry Norris 3
RUSSELL, Herbert Edwin 1
RUSSELL, Herman 1
RUSSELL, Horace 1
RUSSELL, Horace 6
RUSSELL, Howard Hyde 1
RUSSELL, Irwin H
RUSSELL, Isaac Franklin 1
RUSSELL, Israel Cook 1
RUSSELL, J. Henry 1
RUSSELL, J. J. 3
RUSSELL, J. Stuart H
RUSSELL, James Earl 2
RUSSELL, James McPherson H
RUSSELL, James Solomon 1
RUSSELL, Jane Anne 4
RUSSELL, Jeremiah H
RUSSELL, John H
RUSSELL, John 3
RUSSELL, John Andrew 1
RUSSELL, John Edward 1
RUSSELL, John Henry 1
RUSSELL, John Henry 2
RUSSELL, Jonathan H
RUSSELL, Joseph * H
RUSSELL, Joseph Ballister 1
RUSSELL, Joseph Holt 4
RUSSELL, Joshua Edward Sherman 1
RUSSELL, Kenneth 6
RUSSELL, Lee Maurice 2
RUSSELL, Lillian 1
RUSSELL, Louis Arthur 1
RUSSELL, L(ulu) Case 5
RUSSELL, Manley Holland 5
RUSSELL, Martin J. 1
RUSSELL, Mother Mary Baptist H
RUSSELL, Melvin Gray Jr. 6
RUSSELL, Nelson Vance 3
RUSSELL, Norman Felt Shelton 3
RUSSELL, Osborne H
RUSSELL, Pastor 1
RUSSELL, Paul Snowden 2
RUSSELL, Richard Brevard 1
RUSSELL, Richard Brevard 5
RUSSELL, Richard Joel 5
RUSSELL, Robert 4
RUSSELL, Robert Lee 4
RUSSELL, Robert McWatty 1
RUSSELL, Robert Watrous 4
RUSSELL, Samuel Jr. 1
RUSSELL, Samuel Lyon H
RUSSELL, Scott 1
RUSSELL, Sol Smith 1
RUSSELL, Stanley Addison 3

RUSSELL, Talcott Huntington 1
RUSSELL, Thomas Halbert 1
RUSSELL, Thomas Herbert 4
RUSSELL, Thomas Wright 6
RUSSELL, Walter 1
RUSSELL, Walter C. 3
RUSSELL, Walter Earle 2
RUSSELL, Willard Lorane 2
RUSSELL, William * H
RUSSELL, William Eustus H
RUSSELL, William Fiero H
RUSSELL, William Fletcher 3
RUSSELL, William Henry H
RUSSELL, William Hepburn H
RUSSELL, William Hepburn 1
RUSSELL, William Logie 3
RUSSELL, William Logie 1
RUSSELL, William Loughlin 4
RUSSELL, William T. 1
RUSSELL, William 4
RUSSELL, William Worthington 1
RUSSUM, B. C. 3
RUSSUM, Sarah Elizabeth 5
RUSSWURM, John Brown 1
RUST, Adlai H. 6
RUST, Albert H
RUST, Charles Herbert 3
RUST, Henry Bedinger 1
RUST, John Daniel 3
RUST, Mack Donald 4
RUST, Walter L. 3
RUSTAD, Elmer Lewis 6
RUSTGARD, John 2
RUSTIN, Henry 4
RUSTON, John Edward 1
RUSTON, William Otis 1
RUSZNYAK, Istvan 6
RUTAN, Charles Hercules 1
RUTAN, Harold Duane 3
RUTGERS, Henry H
RUTH, Carl Douglas 1
RUTH, George Herman 2
RUTH, Henry Swartley 3
RUTH, John A. 5
RUTH, John P(illing) 5
RUTHERFORD, Albert Greig 1
RUTHERFORD, Alexander H. 3
RUTHERFORD, Charles Henry 6
RUTHERFORD, Clarendon 1
RUTHERFORD, George H. 4
RUTHERFORD, Margaret Lewis 1
RUTHERFORD, Mildred 1
RUTHERFORD, Robert H
RUTHERFORD, S. Morton 1
RUTHERFORD, Samuel 1
RUTHERFURD, John H
RUTHERFURD, John 4
RUTHERFURD, Lewis Morris H
RUTHRAUFF, John Mosheim 1
RUTHVEN, Alexander G(rant) 5
RUTLAND, James Richard 2
RUTLEDGE, Ann H
RUTLEDGE, Archibald (Hamilton) 6
RUTLEDGE, Benjamin Huger 4
RUTLEDGE, Carl P. 1
RUTLEDGE, Edward H
RUTLEDGE, George Perry 4
RUTLEDGE, John H
RUTLEDGE, John Jr. H
RUTLEDGE, Thomas G. 4
RUTLEDGE, Wiley Blount 2
RUTT, Christian Louis 1
RUTTENBER, Edward Manning 1
RUTTER, Frank Roy 1
RUTTER, Henley Chapman 1
RUTTER, Josiah Baldwin 3
RUTTER, Robert Lewis 4
RUUD, Martin Bronn 1
RUUTZ-REES, Caroline 3
RUYL, Beatrice Baxter 6
RUYLE, John Bryan 4
RUZICKA, Charles 3
RYALL, Daniel Bailey H
RYALS, Thomas Edward 5
RYAN, Abram Joseph H
RYAN, Archie Lowell 6
RYAN, Arthur 5
RYAN, Clement Daniel 1
RYAN, Clendenin J. 5
RYAN, Cornelius Edward 4
RYAN, Cornelius John 6
RYAN, Daniel Joseph 1
RYAN, Dennis 1
RYAN, Edward Francis H
RYAN, Edward George H

RYAN, Edward William 1
RYAN, Elmer James 3
RYAN, Evelyn Althea Murphy 3
RYAN, Francis Joseph 4
RYAN, Franklin Winton 3
RYAN, Frederick Behrens 3
RYAN, George Joseph 2
RYAN, Harris Joseph 1
RYAN, J. Harold 4
RYAN, James 1
RYAN, James 3
RYAN, James Augustine 3
RYAN, James Hugh 2
RYAN, James W. 4
RYAN, John Augustine 2
RYAN, John D. 1
RYAN, John J. Jr. 1
RYAN, John William 5
RYAN, Lewis Cook 1
RYAN, Marah Ellis 1
RYAN, Marah Ellis 1
RYAN, Martin Francis 1
RYAN, Michael J. 2
RYAN, Michael Sylvester 1
RYAN, O'Neill 1
RYAN, Patrick John 1
RYAN, Patrick John 1
RYAN, Patrick L. 1
RYAN, Raymond Richard 4
RYAN, Robert 1
RYAN, Stanley Martin 3
RYAN, Stephen Vincent H
RYAN, Thomas 1
RYAN, Thomas Curran 1
RYAN, Thomas Fortune 1
RYAN, Timothy Edward 1
RYAN, Vincent J. 3
RYAN, Will Carson 5
RYAN, William 1
RYAN, William Fitts 5
RYAN, William Henry 1
RYAN, William Patrick 1
RYAN, William Thomas 1
RYBNER, Martin Cornelius 1
RYBURN, Frank M. 4
RYCKMAN, Charles Silcott 4
RYCKMANS, Pierre 3
RYDBERG, Per Axel 1
RYDEN, George Herbert 1
RYDER, Albert Pinkham 1
RYDER, Arthur Hilton 1
RYDER, Arthur William 1
RYDER, Charles Jackson 1
RYDER, Charles Wolcott 5
RYDER, Chauncey Foster 2
RYDER, Frederick Milliachip 1
RYDER, George Hope 1
RYDER, Harry Osborne 1
RYDER, Oscar Baxter 5
RYDER, Robert Oliver 1
RYDER, Thomas Philander H
RYDER, William Henry 1
RYDSTROM, Arthur Gordon 6
RYERSON, Edward Larned 1
RYERSON, Edward Larned 5
RYERSON, Edwin Warner 1
RYERSON, Joseph Turner 3
RYERSON, Martin Antoine 1
RYERSON, William Newton 5
RYGEL, John 3
RYGG, Andrew Nilsen 3
RYGH, George Taylor 1
RYKEN, Theodore James H
RYKENS, Paul 5
RYLANCE, Joseph Hine 1
RYLAND, Edward 6
RYLAND, John Peter 1
RYLAND, Joseph R. 1
RYLAND, Robert 1
RYLAND, Robert Knight 4
RYLAND, William Semple 1
RYLEE, William Jackson 4
RYMAN, James H. T. 1
RYNEARSON, Edward 3
RYNNING, Ole H
RYON, Harrison 1
RYONS, Joseph Leslie 4
RYS, Carl Friedrich Wilheim 5
RYUS, Celeste Nellis 5

S

SAAL, Irving Randolph 6
SAALFIELD, Ada Louise (Ada Louise Sutton) 5
SAALFIELD, Albert George 1
SAAR, Louis Victor Franz 1
SAARINEN, Aline 5
Bernstein

SAARINEN, Eero 4
SAARINEN, Eliel 3
SABATH, Adolph J. 3
SABATINI, Rafael 2
SABEN, Mowry 3
SABIN, Alvah H
SABIN, Alvah Horton 1
SABIN, Charles Hamilton 1
SABIN, Dwight May 1
SABIN, Edwin Legrand 5
SABIN, Elbridge Hosmer 1
SABIN, Ellen Clara 2
SABIN, Florence Rena 3
SABIN, Frances Ellis 1
SABIN, Henry 1
SABIN, Joseph H
SABIN, Louis Carlton 1
SABIN, Wallace Arthur 1
SABINE, George Holland 4
SABINE, Lorenzo H
SABINE, Wallace Clement 1
SABINE, Wallace Clement 2
SABINE, William Tufnell 1
SACAGAWEA H
SACCO, Nicola 4
SACHS, Alexander 6
SACHS, Bernard 2
SACHS, Curt 3
SACHS, Ernest 3
SACHS, Howard Joseph 5
SACHS, James Henry 5
SACHS, Joseph 2
SACHS, Julius 1
SACHS, Morris Bernard 3
SACHS, Nelly 5
SACHS, Paul Joseph 4
SACHS, Teviah 1
SACHSE, Helena V. (Mrs. Sadtler)
SACHSE, Julius Friedrich 1
SACHSE, Richard 1
SACK, Alexander Naoum 1
SACK, Henri S(amuel) 5
SACK, Leo R. 3
SACKETT, Arthur Johnson 6
SACKETT, Carl Leroy 5
SACKETT, Earl L. 5
SACKETT, Frederic Moseley Jr. 1
SACKETT, Henry Woodward 1
SACKETT, Robert Lemuel 4
SACKETT, Samuel Jefferson 4
SACKETT, Sheldon F(red) 1
SACKETT, Walter George 6
SACKETT, William August H
SACKETT, William Edgar 1
SACKS, Emanuel 3
SACKVILLE, Lord H
SACKVILLE-WEST, Lionel H
SACKVILLE-WEST, Lionel 4
SACKVILLE-WEST, Victoria 4
SADACCA, Henri 5
SADD, Walter Allen 5
SADLAK, Antoni Nicholas 5
SADLEIR, Michael
SADLER, Everit Jay 3
SADLER, Frank Howard 4
SADLER, Herbert Charles 5
SADLER, Lena Kellogg 3
SADLER, McGruder Ellis 4
SADLER, Reinhold 1
SADLER, Sylvester Baker 1
SADLER, Thomas William H
SADLER, Wilbur Fisk 1
SADLIER, Denis H
SADOW, Leonard Bernard 6
SADOWSKI, George G. 4
SADTLER, John Phillip Benjamin H
SADTLER, Samuel Philip 1
SAENDERL, Simon H
SAENGER, Oscar 1
SAERCHINGER, Cesar (Victor Charles) 5
SAFANIE, Murray D. 4
SAFAY, Fred A. 3
SAFFIN, William 1
SAFFIN, William H
SAFFOLD, William Berney 2
SAFFORD, Agnes Mabel 1
SAFFORD, Harry Robinson 2
SAFFORD, James Merrill 1
SAFFORD, Mary Augusta 4
SAFFORD, Truman Henry 1
SAFFORD, William Edwin 1
SAGAZ, Angel 5
SAGE, Agnes Carolyn 4
SAGE, Bernard Janin 1
SAGE, Charles Gurdon 4
SAGE, Charles H(enry) 6
SAGE, Dean 2
SAGE, Eben Charles 1
SAGE, Ebenezer H
SAGE, Evan Taylor 1

* Indicates More Than One Such Name Listed

SCHARFF, Maurice Roos 5
SCHARL, Josef 3
SCHARNAGEL, Isabel 3
Mona
SCHARPS, Andrew 5
SCHATTSCHNEIDER, 5
Elmer Eric
SCHATZ, Carl F. 5
SCHATZ, Nathan Arthur 4
SCHAUB, Edward Leroy 3
SCHAUB, Frederick 1
SCHAUB, Howard Churchill 5
SCHAUB, Ira Obed 2
SCHAUB, Mother Jerome 2
SCHAUB, Robert C. 3
SCHAUFFLER, Adolph 1
Frederick
SCHAUFFLER, Edward 1
William
SCHAUFFLER, Goodrich 4
Capen
SCHAUFFLER, Henry Park 1
SCHAUFFLER, Rachel 5
Capen
SCHAUFFLER, Robert 4
Haven
SCHAUFFLER, William H
Gottlieb
SCHAUFFLER, William 1
Gray
SCHAUFUS, Charles 6
Patrick
SCHAYER, Milton M. 1
SCHEALER, Samuel 4
Raymond
SCHECHTER, Solomon 1
SCHEDLER, Carl Robert 4
SCHEDLER, Dean L. 5
SCHEELINE, Julia 6
Schoenfeld
SCHEER, Edward 2
Waldemar
SCHEETZ, Francis Harley 5
SCHEFF, Fritzl 3
SCHEFFAUER, Herman 1
George
SCHEFFEY, Lewis Cass 5
SCHEIBERLING, Edward 4
Nicholas
SCHEIBERLING, Edward 5
Nicholas
SCHEIBLE, Charles 1
Frederick
SCHEIDENHELM, 4
Frederick William
SCHEIN, Ernest 5
SCHEIN, Marcel 3
SCHELDRUP, Nicolay 1
Hilmar
SCHELE DE VERE, H
Maximilian
SCHELL, Augustus H
SCHELL, Edwin Allison 1
SCHELL, Frank Cresson 2
SCHELL, Herbert Hannan 6
SCHELL, Ralph Garfield 3
SCHELL, Richard 1
SCHELL, Samuel Duvall 6
SCHELL, William Elias 5
SCHELL, William Peter 6
SCHELLBERG, William 6
Henry
SCHELLING, Ernest Henry 1
SCHELLING, Felix 2
Emanuel
SCHEM, Alexander Jacob H
SCHEMAN, Louis 5
SCHENCK, Abraham Henry H
SCHENCK, Benjamin 1
Robinson
SCHENCK, Charles Meigs 5
SCHENCK, Edgar Craig 3
SCHENCK, Edwin Saxton 4
SCHENCK, Eunice Morgan 3
SCHENCK, Ferdinand H
Schureman
SCHENCK, Ferdinand 1
Schureman
SCHENCK, Hassil Eli 5
SCHENCK, Hollister V. 4
SCHENCK, Hubert Gregory 4
SCHENCK, James Findlay H
SCHENCK, Joseph M. 4
SCHENCK, Martin A. 3
SCHENCK, Michael 2
SCHENCK, Nicholas 5
SCHENCK, Paul F. 5
SCHENCK, Paul 5
Wadsworth
SCHENCK, Peter Lawrence 4
SCHENCK, Robert H
Cumming
SCHENCK, Robert 4
Cumming
SCHENCK, William Edward 1
SCHENK, Francis Joseph 5

SCHENK, Henry L. 5
SCHENUIT, Alfons William 4
SCHEPPEGRELL, William 4
SCHER, Phillip George 6
SCHERBAK, Boris 5
SCHERCHEN, Hermann 5
SCHERCK, Gordon 5
SCHERER, James Augustin 2
Brown
SCHERER, John Jacob Jr. 3
SCHERER, Melanchthon G. 1
G.
SCHERER, Paul Ehrman 5
SCHERER, Robert Pauli 5
SCHERER, Tilden 5
SCHERER, Walter H. 5
SCHERESCHEWSKY, John 5
Forby
SCHERESCHEWSKY, 1
Joseph Williams
SCHERESCHEWSKY, 1
Samuel Isaac Joseph
SCHERGER, George 1
Lawrence
SCHERMAN, Harry 5
SCHERMERHORN, H
Abraham Maus
SCHERMERHORN, Arthur 4
Frederic
SCHERMERHORN, 1
Frederick Augustus
SCHERMERHORN, James 2
SCHERMERHORN, Martin 4
Kellogg
SCHERMERHORN, 5
Richard Jr.
SCHERMERHORN, 2
William David
SCHERR, Harry 5
SCHERR, Harry Jr. 5
SCHERTZ, Helen Pitkin 5
SCHERZER, Albert H. 1
SCHEUCH, Frederick 5
Charles
SCHEUERMANN, Hugo E. 3
SCHEVE, Edward Benjamin 1
SCHEVILL, Ferdinand 2
SCHEVILL, Rudolph 2
SCHEVILL, William V. 4
SCHIAPARELLI, Elsa 6
SCHICK, Bela 5
SCHICK, Herman John 2
SCHICK, John Michael 1
SCHICK, Lawrence E. 5
SCHICK-GUTIERREZ, 4
Rene
SCHICKHAUS, Edward 5
SCHIEDT, Richard Conrad 1
Francis
SCHIEFFELEN, Ed 4
SCHIEFFELIN, Bradhurst 1
SCHIEFFELIN, Samuel 1
Bradhurst
SCHIEFFELIN, William Jay 5
SCHIERBERG, George 5
Bernard
SCHIEREN, Charles 1
Adolph
SCHIFF, Jacob Henry 1
SCHIFF, Leo F. 3
SCHIFF, Leonard Isaac 5
SCHIFF, Mortimer L. 1
SCHIFF, Robert William 5
SCHIFF, Sydney Kaufman 6
SCHIFFELER, Curt Conrad 5
SCHIFFER, Herbert 5
Michael
SCHIFFNER, Carl Edmund 3
SCHILDER, Paul Ferdinand 1
SCHILDKRAUT, Joseph 4
SCHILLER, Avery Reubens 6
SCHILLER, Max 3
SCHILLER, William Bacon 4
SCHILLING, George A. 4
SCHILLING, Gustav H
SCHILLING, Hugo Karl 1
SCHILLING, Joseph T. 5
SCHILLING, William Frank 5
SCHILLINGER, Arnold 4
Arthur
SCHIMPF, Henry William 4
SCHIMPFF, Charles Henry 6
SCHINDEL, John Randolph 1
SCHINDEL, S. John Bayard 1
SCHINDLER, Jacob John 1
SCHINDLER, Kurt 1
SCHINDLER, Raymond 3
Campbell
SCHINDLER, Rudolf 5
SCHINDLER, Solomon 1
SCHINE, J. Myer 5
SCHINNER, Augustin 1
Francis
SCHINZ, Albert 2
SCHIPA, Tito 4
SCHIRER, George 5

SCHIRM, Charles R. 4
SCHIRMER, Gustav H
SCHIRMER, Gustave 4
SCHIROKAUER, Arno C. 3
SCHJELDERUP, Harald 6
Krabbe
SCHLACKS, Charles Henry 1
SCHLADERMUNDT, 1
Herman T.
SCHLADERMUNDT, Peter 6
SCHLADITZ, E. 1
SCHLAEFER, Edward 4
George
SCHLAIKJER, Erich Maren 5
SCHLAIKJER, Erich Maren 6
SCHLAKE, William E. 1
SCHLANGER, Ben 5
SCHLAPP, Max Gustav 1
SCHLARMAN, Joseph H. 3
SCHLATTER, Michael H
SCHLEE, Stanley Curren 6
SCHLEGEL, H. Franklin 5
SCHLEICHER, Gustave 1
SCHLEIF, William 4
SCHLENZ, Harry Edward 5
SCHLERETH, C. Q. 4
SCHLESINGER, Armin 4
Ardery
SCHLESINGER, Arthur 4
Meier
SCHLESINGER, Benjamin H
SCHLESINGER, Benjamin 4
SCHLESINGER, Edward 6
Ralph
SCHLESINGER, Elmer 1
SCHLESINGER, Frank 2
SCHLESINGER, Hermann 4
I.
SCHLESINGER, Louis 1
SCHLESINGER, Louis 1
SCHLESSER, George 6
Ernest
SCHLEY, Evander Baker 3
SCHLEY, Grant Barney 1
SCHLEY, Julian Larcombe 4
SCHLEY, Kenneth Baker 4
SCHLEY, Reeve 4
SCHLEY, William H
SCHLEY, Winfield Scott 1
SCHLEYER, O. L. 3
SCHLIEDER, Frederick 5
(William)
SCHLIEMANN, Heinrich 1
SCHLING, Max 2
SCHLING, Max Jr. 5
SCHLOERB, Rolland 4
Walter
SCHLOSBERG, Harold 4
SCHLOSS, Oscar 3
Menderson
SCHLOSSBERG, Joseph 5
SCHLOTTERBECK, Julius 1
Otto
SCHLOTTERER, Ray C. 4
SCHLOTTMAN, Richard 3
Henry
SCHLUETER, Edward 5
Benjamin
SCHLUETER, Robert Ernst 3
SCHLUNDT, Herman 1
SCHLUTZ, Frederic William 2
SCHMAUK, Theodore 1
Emanuel
SCHMEDEMAN, Albert 2
George
SCHMEDTGEN, William 4
Herman
SCHMEISSER, Harry 5
Christian
SCHMERTZ, Robert J. 6
SCHMICK, Franklin Bush 6
SCHMICK, William 1
Frederick
SCHMIDLAPP, Carl Jacob 4
SCHMIDLAPP, Jacob 1
Godfrey
SCHMIDLIN, Theodor 6
SCHMIDT, Adolph D. Jr. 5
SCHMIDT, Alfred Francis 5
William
SCHMIDT, Arthur 5
Alexander
SCHMIDT, Austin G. 4
SCHMIDT, Carl Louis 2
August
SCHMIDT, Edward Charles 2
SCHMIDT, Edward William 4
SCHMIDT, Elmer Frederick 3
Edward
SCHMIDT, Emil G. 3
SCHMIDT, Erich Friedrich 3
SCHMIDT, Ernest R. 5
SCHMIDT, Erwin Rudolph 4
SCHMIDT, Francis Albert 2
SCHMIDT, Frank Henry 5

SCHMIDT, Frederick 4
Augustus
SCHMIDT, Friedrich Georg 2
Gottlob
SCHMIDT, George August 4
SCHMIDT, George Small 1
SCHMIDT, Harry 4
SCHMIDT, Herbert William 4
SCHMIDT, Joseph Martin 1
SCHMIDT, Karl P. 3
SCHMIDT, Louis Bernard 6
SCHMIDT, Louis Ernst 3
SCHMIDT, Nathaniel 1
SCHMIDT, Orvis Adrian 5
SCHMIDT, Otto L. 1
SCHMIDT, Paul Gerhard 3
SCHMIDT, Peter Paul 5
SCHMIDT, Petrus Johannes 3
SCHMIDT, Richard Ernst 3
SCHMIDT, Walter A. 6
SCHMIDT, Walter August 4
SCHMIDT, Walter Seton 3
SCHMIDT, William 1
SCHMIDT, William Jr. 3
SCHMIDT, William Richard 4
SCHMIDT-ISSERSTEDT, 6
Hans Paul Ernst
SCHMITT, Arthur J. 5
SCHMITT, Cooper Davis 5
SCHMITT, Gladys 5
SCHMITT, Oscar C. 3
SCHMITT, Roland G. 4
SCHMITT, Rupert P. 3
SCHMITZ, Carl Ludwig 4
SCHMITZ, Dietrich 5
SCHMITZ, Henry 4
SCHMITZ, Herbert Eugene 5
SCHMITZ, Joseph William 4
SCHMITZ, Leonard 6
Stockwell
SCHMITZ, Woodrow 6
Adolph
SCHMON, Arthur Albert 4
SCHMUCK, Elmer Nicholas 1
SCHMUCKER, Beale H
Melanchthon
SCHMUCKER, John 5
George
SCHMUCKER, Samuel 5
Christian
SCHMUCKER, Samuel D. 1
SCHMUCKER, Samuel H
Simon
SCHMUS, Elmer Ezra 3
SCHMUTZ, Charles Austin 6
SCHNABEL, Artur 5
SCHNABEL, Charles J. 1
SCHNABEL, Truman Gross 5
SCHNACKENBERG, 5
Elmer Jacob
SCHNADER, William 5
A(braham)
SCHNAKENBERG, Henry 5
SCHNAUFFER, Carl H
Heinrich
SCHNEBLY, John Thomas 6
SCHNECKER, Peter August 1
SCHNEDER, David 1
Bowman
SCHNEE, Verne H. 3
SCHNEEBELI, G. Adolph 3
SCHNEEBELI, G. Adolph 4
SCHNEIDER, Adolph 2
Benedict
SCHNEIDER, Albert 1
SCHNEIDER, Alma 6
Kittredge
SCHNEIDER, Benjamin H
SCHNEIDER, Carl E. 4
SCHNEIDER, Charles 1
Conrad
SCHNEIDER, Clement 5
Joseph
SCHNEIDER, Edward 4
Alexander
SCHNEIDER, Edward 3
Christian
SCHNEIDER, Erich 5
SCHNEIDER, Frederick 2
William
SCHNEIDER, George 5
SCHNEIDER, George J. 1
SCHNEIDER, Herman 1
SCHNEIDER, Joseph 1
SCHNEIDER, Oscar Albert 4
SCHNEIDER, Ralph 4
Edward
SCHNEIDER, Samuel 1
Hiram
SCHNEIDER, Stanley 6
Frederick
SCHNEIDER, Theodore H
SCHNEIDER, Walter 3
Arthur
SCHNEIDER, William B. 4

SCHNEIDER, Wilmar 6
Rufus
SCHNEIDERS, Alexander 5
A(loysius)
SCHNEIDEWIND, Richard 5
SCHNEIRLA, Theodore 5
Christian
SCHNELLER, Frederic 4
Andrew
SCHNELLER, George Otto H
SCHNERING, Otto 3
SCHNITZLER, John 1
William
SCHNUR, George Henry Jr. 1
SCHNURPEL, Hans Karl 6
SCHNURR, Martin K. 4
SCHNUTE, William Jacob 6
SCHOBECK, Arthur Ellwyn 4
SCHOCH, Eugene Paul 5
SCHOCKEN, Theodore 6
SCHODDE, George Henry 1
SCHODER, Ernest William 5
SCHOELLKOPF, Alfred 2
Hugo
SCHOELLKOPF, J. Fred IV 5
SCHOELLKOPF, Jacob F. 2
SCHOELLKOPF, Paul 2
Arthur
SCHOEMAKER, Daniel 3
Martin
SCHOEN, Charles T. 4
SCHOEN, Edward Jr. 6
SCHOEN, John Edmund 5
SCHOENBERG, Arnold 3
SCHOENE, William Jay 6
SCHOENECK, Edward 5
SCHOENEFELD, Henry 4
SCHOENEMANN, Oscar 6
Paul
SCHOENFELD, H. F. 3
Arthur
SCHOENFELD, Hermann 1
SCHOENFELD, William 3
Alfred
SCHOENSTEIN, Paul 6
SCHOEPF, W. Kesley 1
SCHOEPFLE, Chester S. 3
SCHOEPPEL, Andrew F. 4
SCHOEPPERLE, Victor 4
SCHOETZ, Max 1
SCHOFF, Hannah Kent 1
SCHOFF, Stephen Alonzo 1
SCHOFF, Wilfred Harvey 1
SCHOFIELD, Albert 5
George
SCHOFIELD, Charles 3
Edwin
SCHOFIELD, Frank 2
Herman
SCHOFIELD, Frank Lee 1
SCHOFIELD, Harvey A. 1
SCHOFIELD, Henry 1
SCHOFIELD, John 1
McAllister
SCHOFIELD, Mary Lyon 2
Cheney
SCHOFIELD, William 1
SCHOFIELD, William 1
Henry
SCHOITZ, Aksel 6
SCHOLER, Walter 5
SCHOLES, Charles Marcel 6
SCHOLES, Samuel Ray 6
SCHOLL, John William 3
SCHOLL, William M. 5
SCHOLLE, Hardinge 6
SCHOLTE, Hendrick Peter H
SCHOLTZ, Joseph D. 5
SCHOLZ, Emil Maurice 5
SCHOLZ, Karl William 4
Henry
SCHOLZ, Richard Frederick 1
SCHOMMER, John J. 4
SCHOMP, Albert L. 3
SCHONBERGER, 1
E(manuel) D(eo)
SCHONFELD, William A. 5
SCHONHARDT, Henri 3
SCHOOLCRAFT, Arthur 4
Allen
SCHOOLCRAFT, Henry H
Rowe
SCHOOLCRAFT, John H
Lawrence
SCHOOLER, Lewis 4
SCHOONHOVEN, Helen 3
Butterfield
SCHOONHOVEN, John 1
James
SCHOONMAKER, H
Cornelius Corneliusen
SCHOONMAKER, Edwin 1
Davies
SCHOONMAKER, Frederic 2
Palen

SCHOONMAKER, Nancy 4
M.
SCHOONOVER, Draper 3
Talman
SCHOONOVER, Frank 5
Earle
SCHOOTEN, Sarah 6
SCHOPF, Johann David H
SCHOPFLIN, Jack 4
Schilling
SCHORGER, Arlie William 4
SCHORLING, Raleigh 3
SCHORSCH, Alexander
Peter
SCHORTEMEIER, 4
Frederick Edward
SCHOTT, Charles Anthony 1
SCHOTT, Henry 1
SCHOTT, Lawrence 4
Frederick
SCHOTT, Max 3
SCHOULER, James 1
SCHOULER, John 1
SCHOULER, William H
SCHOUR, Isaac
SCHOYER, Alfred McGill 4
SCHRADE, Leo Franz 5
SCHRADER, Charles E. 5
SCHRADER, Frank Charles 2
SCHRADER, Franz 4
SCHRADER, Fred L. 4
SCHRADER, Frederick 2
Franklin
SCHRADER, George H. 5
SCHRADER, Robert Estes 6
SCHRADIECK, Henry 4
SCHRAKAMP, Josepha 5
SCHRAM, Jack Aron 4
SCHRAMM, E. Frank 4
SCHRANK, Raymond 6
Edward
SCHRATCHLEY, Francis 4
Arthur
SCHRECKENGAST, Isaac 1
Butler
SCHRECKER, Paul 4
SCHREIBER, Carl 3
Frederick
SCHREIBER, Manuel 6
SCHREIBER, Walter 3
SCHREINER, George Abel 5
SCHREINER, Oswald 5
SCHREMBS, Joseph 2
SCHRENK, Hermann von 3
SCHREYVOGEL, Charles 1
SCHRIBER, Louis 3
SCHRICKER, Henry 4
Frederick
SCHRIECK, Sister Louise H
Van der
SCHRIEVER, William 3
SCHRIVER, Edmund H
SCHRODER, William
Henry
SCHRÖDINGER, Erwin 4
SCHROEDER, Albert 4
William
SCHROEDER, Alwin 4
SCHROEDER, Bernard A. 4
SCHROEDER, Carl A. 4
SCHROEDER, Ernest
Charles
SCHROEDER, Frederick A. 1
SCHROEDER, George 6
William
SCHROEDER, Henry 6
Alfred
SCHROEDER, John 3
Charles
SCHROEDER, John H
Frederick
SCHROEDER, Joseph
Edwin
SCHROEDER, Paul Louis 4
SCHROEDER, Reginald 4
SCHROEDER, Rudolph 3
William
SCHROEDER, Seaton 1
SCHROEDER, Walter 4
SCHROEDER, Werner 1
William
SCHROEDER, William 1
Edward
SCHROFF, Joseph 4
SCHROPP, Rutledge Clifton 6
SCHRUNK, Terry Doyle 6
SCHUCHARDT, Rudolph
Frederick
SCHUCHARDT, William 3
Herbert
SCHUCHERT, Charles 2
SCHUCK, Arthur Aloys 3
SCHUCK, Arthur Frederick 5
SCHUELEIN, Hermann 5
SCHUERMAN, William 1
Henry

SCHUETTE, Conrad 1
Herman Louis
SCHUETTE, Curt Nicolaus 6
SCHUETTE, Walter Erwin 3
SCHUETTE, William 4
Herman
SCHUETZ, Leonard William 2
SCHUH, Henry Frederick 4
SCHUHMANN, George 1
William
SCHUIRMANN, Roscoe 5
Ernest
SCHULE, James Raymond 5
SCHULER, Anthony J. 2
SCHULER, Donald Vern 4
SCHULER, Hans 3
SCHULER, Loring Ashley 5
SCHULGEN, George
Francis
SCHULHOFF, Henry 5
Bernard
SCHULL, Herman Walter 5
SCHULLINGER, Rudolph 5
Nicholas
SCHULMAIER, A. Talmage 3
SCHULMAN, Jack Henry 4
SCHULMAN, Samuel 3
SCHULTE, David A. 2
SCHULTE, Herman von
Wechlinger
SCHULTE, William Henry 3
SCHULTHEISS, Carl Max 4
SCHULTZ, Alfred Paul 6
SCHULTZ, Alfred Reginald 4
SCHULTZ, Clifford Griffith 3
SCHULTZ, Clinton M. 4
SCHULTZ, Edward Waters 5
SCHULTZ, Ernst William 4
SCHULTZ, George F. 5
SCHULTZ, Henry 4
SCHULTZ, Henry 4
SCHULTZ, James Willard 2
SCHULTZ, John H. 6
SCHULTZ, John Richie 2
SCHULTZ, Louis 4
SCHULTZ, William Eben 4
SCHULTZE, Arthur 4
SCHULTZE, Augustus 1
SCHULTZE, Carl Emil 4
SCHULTZE, Leonard 3
SCHULZ, Carl Gustav 4
SCHULZ, Edward Hugh 3
SCHULZ, Leo 2
SCHULZE, Paul 3
SCHULZE, Paul Jr. 3
SCHUMACHER, Anton 5
Herbert
SCHUMACHER, Ferdinand 1
SCHUMACHER, Henry
Cyril
SCHUMACHER, Matthew 4
Aloysius
SCHUMACHER, Thomas
Milton
SCHUMAN, Robert 2
SCHUMANN, Edward
Armin
SCHUMANN, John Joseph 4
Jr.
SCHUMANN-HEINK, 1
Ernestine
SCHUMM, Herman Charles 3
SCHUMPETER, Joseph 2
Alois
SCHUNEMAN, Martin H
Gerretsen
SCHUNK, Arthur John 5
SCHUPP, Otto 4
SCHUPP, Robert William 1
SCHUREMAN, James H
SCHURICHT, Carl 4
SCHURMAN, George 1
Wellington
SCHURMAN, Jacob Gould 2
SCHURMAN, Jacob Gould 6
III
SCHURZ, Carl 1
SCHURZ, Carl Lincoln 4
SCHURZ, William Lytle 4
SCHUSSELE, Christian 4
SCHUSTER, George Lee 4
SCHUTT, Harold Smith 4
SCHUTTE, Louis Henry 3
SCHUTTLER, Peter H
SCHUTZE, Martin 3
SCHUTZER, Paul George 5
SCHUTZMAN, Julius 4
SCHUYLER, Aaron 1
SCHUYLER, Daniel J. 3
SCHUYLER, Eugene 4
SCHUYLER, George H
Washington
SCHUYLER, Hamilton 1
SCHUYLER, James Dix 1
SCHUYLER, Karl Cortlandt 1

SCHUYLER, Livingston 1
Rowe
SCHUYLER, Margurita H
SCHUYLER, Montgomery 1
SCHUYLER, Montgomery 3
SCHUYLER, Peter H
SCHUYLER, Philip H
Jeremiah
SCHUYLER, Philip John H
SCHUYLER, Philippa Duke 4
SCHUYLER, Walter 1
Scribner
SCHUYLER, William 1
SCHWAB, Charles M. 1
SCHWAB, Francis Xavier 2
SCHWAB, Gustav Henry 1
SCHWAB, Harvey A. 2
SCHWAB, John Christopher 1
SCHWAB, John George 2
SCHWAB, Martin Constan 2
SCHWAB, Paul Josiah 4
SCHWAB, Robert Sidney 5
SCHWAB, Roy Valentine 5
SCHWAB, Sidney Isaac 2
SCHWABACHER, Albert 4
E.
SCHWABACHER, James 3
Herbert
SCHWABE, George Blaine 3
SCHWABE, H. August 1
SCHWACKE, John Henry 2
SCHWAIN, Frank Robert 4
SCHWALM, Earl George 4
SCHWALM, Vernon 5
Franklin
SCHWAMB, Herbert H. 4
SCHWAMB, Peter 4
SCHWAMM, Harvey 3
SCHWAN, Theodore 1
SCHWARDT, Herbert 4
Henry
SCHWARTZ, A. Charles 4
SCHWARTZ, Andrew 2
Thomas
SCHWARTZ, B. Davis 5
SCHWARTZ, Charles 5
SCHWARTZ, Delmore 4
SCHWARTZ, Hans Jorgen 3
SCHWARTZ, Harwood 2
Muzzy
SCHWARTZ, Herbert J. 3
SCHWARTZ, Isaac Hillson 5
SCHWARTZ, Jack William 5
SCHWARTZ, John H
SCHWARTZ, Julia Augusta 5
SCHWARTZ, Karl 1
SCHWARTZ, Lew 5
SCHWARTZ, Louis 4
SCHWARTZ, Maurice 4
SCHWARTZ, Milton Henry 5
SCHWARTZ, Samuel D. 4
SCHWARTZ, Walter 5
Marshall Sr.
SCHWARTZ, William 5
Spencer
SCHWARZ, Berthold 5
Theodore Dominic
SCHWARZ, Edward R. 4
SCHWARZ, Frank Henry 3
SCHWARZ, Frederick 6
August Otto
SCHWARZ, George 1
Frederick
SCHWARZ, Guenter 6
SCHWARZ, Helen Geneva 4
Frederick
SCHWARZ, Henry 5
SCHWARZ, Otto Henry 3
SCHWARZ, William Tefft 4
SCHWARZBURGER, Carl 4
SCHWARZE, William 2
Nathaniel
SCHWARZENBACH, 5
Ernest Blackbrook
SCHWARZMANN, Herman H
J.
SCHWARZSCHILD, 3
William Harry
SCHWATKA, Frederick H
SCHWATT, Isaac Joachim 1
SCHWEBACH, James 1
SCHWEDTMAN, F. 3
Charles
SCHWEGLER, Raymond 3
Alfred
SCHWEIGARDT, Frederick 2
William
SCHWEIKERT, Harry 1
Christian
SCHWEINFURTH, Charles 1
Frederick
SCHWEINFURTH, Julius 1
Adolph
SCHWEINHAUT, Henry 5
Albert

SCHWEINITZ, Edmund H
Alexander
SCHWEINITZ, Emil 1
Alexander de
SCHWEINITZ, George 1
Edmund de
SCHWEITER, Leo Henry 5
SCHWEITZER, Albert 4
SCHWEITZER, Paul 1
SCHWEIZER, Albert 3
Charles
SCHWEIZER, J. Otto 1
SCHWELLENBACH, Edgar 3
Ward
SCHWELLENBACH, Lewis 2
Baxter
SCHWENGEL, Frank 6
Rudolph
SCHWENTKER, Francis 3
Frederic
SCHWEPPE, Charles 1
Hodgdon
SCHWERT, Pius Louis 3
SCHWERTNER, August 1
John
SCHWIDETZKY, Oscar O. 4
R.
SCHWIETERT, Arthur 4
Henry
SCHWINGEL, Vincent 1
John
SCHWINN, Frederick 5
Sievers
SCHWINN, Sidoine Jordon 4
SCHWITALLA, Alphonse 4
Mary
SCHWYZER, Arnold 2
SCIDMORE, Eliza 1
Ruhamah
SCIDMORE, George 1
Hawthorne
SCIPIO, Lynn A. 5
SCISM, Don 3
SCLATER, John Robert 3
Paterson
SCOFIELD, Carl Schurz 4
SCOFIELD, Cyrus Ingerson 1
SCOFIELD, Edward 1
SCOFIELD, Glenni William H
SCOFIELD, Louis A. 4
SCOFIELD, Perry Lee 6
SCOFIELD, Walter Keeler 1
SCOFIELD, William Bacon 1
SCOGGINS, Charles Elbert 3
SCOLLARD, Clinton 1
SCONCE, Harvey James 2
SCOON, Robert 5
SCOPES, John T. 5
SCORE, John Nelson 3
Russell
SCOTSON-CLARK, George 1
Frederick
SCOTT, Albert Lyon 2
SCOTT, Albert Woodburn 5
Jr.
SCOTT, Alexander 4
Armstrong
SCOTT, Alfred James Jr. 1
SCOTT, Alfred Witherspoon 6
SCOTT, Angelo Cyrus 2
SCOTT, Arthur Carroll 1
SCOTT, Arthur Curtis 5
SCOTT, Austin 1
SCOTT, Bruce 1
SCOTT, Buford 6
SCOTT, Carlyle MacRoberts 2
SCOTT, Carrie Emma 2
SCOTT, Charles H
SCOTT, Charles 1
SCOTT, Charles Felton 2
SCOTT, Charles Frederick 1
SCOTT, Charles Herrington 5
SCOTT, Charles L. 3
SCOTT, Charles Payson
Gurley
SCOTT, Charlotte Angas 1
SCOTT, Clyde F. 6
SCOTT, Colin Alexander 1
SCOTT, Cyril Meir 6
SCOTT, D. R. 3
SCOTT, David H
SCOTT, Donald 4
SCOTT, Donnell Everett 3
SCOTT, Dred H
SCOTT, Earl Francis 1
SCOTT, Eben Greenough 4
SCOTT, Edwin William 6
SCOTT, Ellen C. 1
SCOTT, Elmer 3
SCOTT, Elmon 4
SCOTT, Emily M. 4
SCOTT, Emmett Jay 4
SCOTT, Ernest 1
SCOTT, Ernest 6
SCOTT, Ernest Darius 5
SCOTT, Ernest Findlay 3

SCOTT, Eugene Crampton 5
SCOTT, Fitzhugh 3
SCOTT, Francis Markoe 1
SCOTT, Frank Augustus 2
SCOTT, Frank Hall 1
SCOTT, Frank Hamline 1
SCOTT, Frank Jesup 4
SCOTT, Fred Newton 1
SCOTT, Frederic William 1
SCOTT, Frederick Andrew 4
SCOTT, Frederick Hossack 3
SCOTT, Garfield 3
SCOTT, George 2
SCOTT, George Cromwell 2
SCOTT, George Eaton 1
SCOTT, George Gilmore 5
SCOTT, George Winfield 2
SCOTT, Gordon Hatler 5
SCOTT, Gustavus H
SCOTT, Guy Charles 1
SCOTT, Hamilton Gray 2
SCOTT, Harold Wilson 5
SCOTT, Harriet Maria 1
SCOTT, Harvey David H
SCOTT, Harvey W. 1
SCOTT, Henri 2
SCOTT, Henry Clay 6
SCOTT, Henry Dickerson 2
SCOTT, Henry Edwards 2
SCOTT, Henry Tiffany 1
SCOTT, Henry Wilson 5
SCOTT, Herbert 5
SCOTT, Hermon Hosmer 6
SCOTT, Hugh Briar 1
SCOTT, Hugh Lenox 1
SCOTT, Hugh McDonald 1
SCOTT, Irving Murray 1
SCOTT, Isaac MacBurney 2
SCOTT, Isaiah Benjamin 1
SCOTT, J. G. 2
SCOTT, Jack Garrett 2
SCOTT, James Brown 1
SCOTT, James Edward 5
SCOTT, James Hutchison 4
SCOTT, James Wilmot H
SCOTT, Jeannette 1
SCOTT, Job H
SCOTT, John * H
SCOTT, John 1
SCOTT, John Adams 3
SCOTT, John Addison 3
SCOTT, John Guier 4
SCOTT, John Hart 4
SCOTT, John Loughran 6
SCOTT, John Marcy 5
SCOTT, John Morin H
SCOTT, John Prindle 4
SCOTT, John R. K. 3
SCOTT, John Randolph H
SCOTT, John Reed 5
SCOTT, John William 1
SCOTT, Jonathan French 2
SCOTT, Joseph 3
SCOTT, Julia Green 1
SCOTT, Julian 1
SCOTT, Leroy 1
SCOTT, Leslie M. 4
SCOTT, Llewellyn Davis 6
SCOTT, Lon Allen 1
SCOTT, Louis Allen 6
SCOTT, Lucy Jameson 1
SCOTT, Martin J. 3
SCOTT, Mary Augusta 1
SCOTT, Miriam Finn 2
SCOTT, Nathan Bay 1
SCOTT, Norman 3
SCOTT, Norman H
SCOTT, Orange H
SCOTT, Oreon Earle 3
SCOTT, Paul Ryrie 4
SCOTT, Paul Whitten 3
SCOTT, Philip B. 4
SCOTT, Philip Drennen 2
SCOTT, Richard H. 1
SCOTT, Richard Hugh 2
SCOTT, Richard John Ernst 1
SCOTT, Robert 4
SCOTT, R(obert) D(ouglas) 6
SCOTT, Robert Kingston 1
SCOTT, Robert Lindsay 3
SCOTT, Robert Nicholson H
SCOTT, Roger Burdette 5
SCOTT, Roy Wesley 3
SCOTT, Russell B(urton) 5
SCOTT, S. Spencer 5
SCOTT, Samuel Parsons 1
SCOTT, Sutton Selwyn 1
SCOTT, Thomas H
SCOTT, Thomas Alexander H
SCOTT, Thomas Fielding 1
SCOTT, Thomas Morton 1
SCOTT, Tom 4
SCOTT, Tully H
SCOTT, Walter H
SCOTT, Walter 1

SCOTT, Walter Canfield 3
SCOTT, Walter Dill 3
SCOTT, Walter E. Jr. 3
SCOTT, Wendell G(arrison) 5
SCOTT, Wilfred Welday 1
SCOTT, Will 1
SCOTT, Willard 4
SCOTT, William 5
SCOTT, William 1
SCOTT, William Amasa 2
SCOTT, William Anderson 4
SCOTT, William Berryman 2
SCOTT, William Earl Dodge 4
SCOTT, William Edouard 4
SCOTT, William Forse 5
SCOTT, William Henry 1
SCOTT, William Kerr 3
SCOTT, William Lawrence 4
SCOTT, William R. 1
SCOTT, William Sherley 4
SCOTT, William Wilson 4
SCOTT, Willis Howard 4
SCOTT, Winfield H
SCOTT, Winfield Townley 5
SCOTT-HUNTER, George 5
SCOTTEN, Robert McGregor 5
SCOTTEN, Samuel Chatman 1
SCOTTI, Antonio 1
SCOULLER, James Brown 1
SCOULLER, John Crawford 1
SCOVEL, Sylvester 3
SCOVEL, Sylvester Fithian 1
SCOVELL, Melville Amasa 1
SCOVIL, Samuel 3
SCOVILLE, Annie Beecher 1
SCOVILLE, Harold Ralph 6
SCOVILLE, Jonathan H
SCOVILLE, Joseph Alfred 1
SCOVILLE, Robert 1
SCOVILLE, Samuel Jr. 3
SCOVILLE, Wilbur Lincoln 4
SCRANTON, Cassius A. 5
SCRANTON, George Whitefield H
SCRANTON, Marion Margery Warren 4
SCRANTON, Worthington 3
SCREWS, William Preston 5
SCREWS, William Wallace 1
SCRIBNER, Arthur Hawley 1
SCRIBNER, Charles H
SCRIBNER, Charles 1
SCRIBNER, Charles 3
SCRIBNER, Charles Ezra 3
SCRIBNER, Frank Jay 4
SCRIBNER, Frank Kimball 1
SCRIBNER, George Kline 4
SCRIBNER, Gilbert Hilton 1
SCRIBNER, Gilbert Hilton 4
SCRIBNER, Gilbert Hilton 5
SCRIBNER, Harvey 4
SCRIBNER, Mrs. Lucy Skidmore 1
SCRIPPS, Edward Wyllis 1
SCRIPPS, James Edmund 1
SCRIPPS, John Locke H
SCRIPPS, Robert Paine 1
SCRIPPS, William Edmund 3
SCRIPTURE, Edward Wheeler 4
SCRIPTURE, William Ellis 1
SCRIVEN, George Percival 4
SCROGGS, Joseph Whitefield 1
SCROGGS, William Oscar 3
SCRUGGS, Anderson M. 1
SCRUGGS, Loyd 5
SCRUGGS, William Lindsay 1
SCRUGGS, William Marvin 4
SCRUGHAM, James Graves 2
SCRUGHAM, William Warburton 2
SCRYMSER, James Alexander 1
SCUDDER, Charles Locke 2
SCUDDER, Doremus 1
SCUDDER, Edward Wallace 3
SCUDDER, Henry Joel H
SCUDDER, Horace Elisha 1
SCUDDER, Hubert B. 5
SCUDDER, Isaac Williamson H
SCUDDER, Janet 1
SCUDDER, John H
SCUDDER, John Anderson H
SCUDDER, John Milton H
SCUDDER, Moses Lewis 1
SCUDDER, Myron Tracy 1
SCUDDER, Nathaniel H
SCUDDER, Samuel Hubbard 1
SCUDDER, Townsend 3
SCUDDER, Tredwell H

SCUDDER, Vida Dutton 3
SCUDDER, Wallace McIlvaine 1
SCUDDER, Zeno H
SCULL, John H
SCULLEN, Anthony James 3
SCULLY, C. Alison 3
SCULLY, Cornelius Decatur 6
SCULLY, Hugh Day 5
SCULLY, James Wall 1
SCULLY, Thomas J. 1
SCULLY, William A. 5
SCULLY, William Augustine 1
SCUPHAM, George William 5
SCUPIN, Carl Albert 5
SCURRY, Richardson H
SEABERRY, Virgil Theodore 4
SEABROOK, C. F. 4
SEABROOK, William Buehler 2
SEABROOKE, Thomas Q. 1
SEABURY, Charles Ward 4
SEABURY, David 3
SEABURY, David 4
SEABURY, Francis William 2
SEABURY, George Tilley 1
SEABURY, Samuel * 1
SEABURY, Samuel 3
SEABURY, William Jones 1
SEABURY, William Marston 2
SEACHREST, Effie M. 1
SEACREST, Frederick Snively 5
SEACREST, Joseph Claggett 2
SEAGER, Allan 5
SEAGER, Charles Allen 2
SEAGER, Henry Rogers 1
SEAGER, Lawrence H. 1
SEAGLE, Oscar 2
SEAGO, Erwin 5
SEAGRAVE, Frank Evans 1
SEAGRAVE, Gordon Stiffer 4
SEAGRAVE, Louis H. 4
SEAGROVE, Gordon Kay 4
SEAL, John Frederick 4
SEALOCK, William Elmer 1
SEALS, Carl H. 3
SEALS, John H. 5
SEALSFIELD, Charles H
SEALY, Frank L. 1
SEAMAN, A(lbert) Owen 6
SEAMAN, Arthur Edmund 1
SEAMAN, Augusta Huiell 3
SEAMAN, Elizabeth Cochrane H
SEAMAN, Elizabeth Cochrane 4
SEAMAN, Eugene Cecil 3
SEAMAN, George Milton 1
SEAMAN, Gilbert Edmund 1
SEAMAN, Henry Bowman 1
SEAMAN, Henry John H
SEAMAN, Irving 6
SEAMAN, John Thompson 3
SEAMAN, Louis Livingston 1
SEAMAN, William Grant 4
SEAMAN, William Henry * 1
SEAMANS, Clarence Walker 1
SEARBY, Edmund Wilson 2
SEARCH, Preston Willis 1
SEARCH, Theodore Corson 1
SEARCY, Chesley Hunter 1
SEARCY, Mrs. Earle Benjamin 5
SEARCY, Hubert Floyd 5
SEARCY, James Thomas 4
SEARER, Jay Charles 1
SEARES, Frederick Hanley 6
SEARING, Hudson Roy 4
SEARING, John Alexander H
SEARING, Laura Catherine Redden 4
SEARLE, Alonzo T. 1
SEARLE, Arthur 1
SEARLE, Augustus Leach 3
SEARLE, Charles James 1
SEARLE, Charles Putnam 1
SEARLE, George Mary 1
SEARLE, Harriet Richardson (Mrs. William D. Searle) 5
SEARLE, James 1
SEARLE, John Preston 1
SEARLE, Robert Wyckoff 5
SEARLE, Robert Wycroff 4
SEARLES, Colbert 5
SEARLES, John Ennis 1
SEARLES, John William 1
SEARLES, William Henry 1
SEARLS, Carroll 5
SEARLS, David Thomas 5
SEARS, Barnas H

SEARS, Charles Brown 3
SEARS, Charles Hatch 2
SEARS, Clinton Brooks 1
SEARS, Edmund Hamilton H
SEARS, Edmund Hamilton 2
SEARS, Francis Philip 5
SEARS, Francis W(eston) 6
SEARS, Frank Irving 3
SEARS, Fred Coleman 4
SEARS, Frederic William 1
SEARS, Frederick W. 1
SEARS, George Gray 1
SEARS, George Wallace 6
SEARS, Herbert Mason 2
SEARS, Hess Thatcher 5
SEARS, Isaac H
SEARS, James Hamilton 1
SEARS, Jesse Brundage 5
SEARS, John Van Der Zee 4
SEARS, Joseph Hamblen 2
SEARS, Julian D(ucker) 5
SEARS, Kenneth Craddock 4
SEARS, Laurence 3
SEARS, Lester Merriam 4
SEARS, Lorenzo 1
SEARS, Nathan Pratt 2
SEARS, Nathaniel Clinton 1
SEARS, Philip Mason 6
SEARS, Philip S. 3
SEARS, Richard Warren 1
SEARS, Robert H
SEARS, Russell Adams 1
SEARS, Samuel Powers 1
SEARS, Sarah Choate 1
SEARS, Taber 1
SEARS, Walter Herbert 1
SEARS, Walter James 1
SEARS, Willard Thomas 1
SEARS, William Henry 1
SEARS, William Joseph 2
SEARS, Willis G. 5
SEARS, Zelda 1
SEARSON, James William 1
SEASHORE, August Theodore 1
SEASHORE, Carl Emil 4
SEASHORE, Robert Holmes 3
SEASTONE, Charles Victor 1
SEASTONE, Charles Victor 6
SEATON, Frederick Andrew 6
SEATON, John Lawrence 1
SEATON, John Lawrence 5
SEATON, Roy Andrew 5
SEATON, William Winston H
SEATTLE H
SEAVER, Ebenezer H
SEAVER, Edwin Pliny 1
SEAVER, Frank Roger 4
SEAVER, Fred Jay 5
SEAVER, Henry Latimer 5
SEAVER, Kenneth 5
SEAVERNS, Joel Herbert 4
SEAVEY, Clyde Leroy 2
SEAVEY, Warren Abner 4
SEAWELL, Aaron Ashley Flowers 3
SEAWELL, Emmet 1
SEAWELL, Herbert Floyd 5
SEAWELL, Molly Elliott 1
SEAY, Abraham Jefferson 1
SEAY, Edward Tucker 2
SEAY, Frank 1
SEAY, George James 1
SEAY, Harry Lauderdale 5
SEAY, William Albert 5
SEBALD, Weber William 4
SEBAST, Frederick Martin 3
SEBASTIAN, Benjamin 1
SEBASTIAN, Jerome D. 4
SEBASTIAN, John 1
SEBASTIAN, William King H
SEBELIUS, Sven Johan 3
SEBENIUS, John Uno 1
SEBREE, Edmund B. 4
SEBREE, Uriel 1
SEBRING, Harold Leon 5
SECCOMB, John H
SECHER, Samuel H
SECKENDORFF, Max Gebhard 1
SECKLER-HUDSON, Catheryn 4
SECONDARI, John Hermes 6
SECOR, John Alstyne 1
SECORD, Arthur Wellesley 3
SECORD, Frederick 4
SECRIST, Horace 2
SECUNDA, Sholom 6
SEDDON, James H
SEDDON, William Little 1
SEDER, Arthur Raymond 5
SEDGWICK, Allan E. 2
SEDGWICK, Anne Douglas 1
SEDGWICK, Arthur George 1

SEDGWICK, Catharine Maria H
SEDGWICK, Charles Baldwin H
SEDGWICK, Francis Minturn 5
SEDGWICK, Henry Dwight H
SEDGWICK, Henry Dwight 1
SEDGWICK, Henry Dwight 3
SEDGWICK, John H
SEDGWICK, Julius Parker 1
SEDGWICK, Paul J(oseph) 6
SEDGWICK, Robert 4
SEDGWICK, Samuel Hopkins 1
SEDGWICK, Theodore * H
SEDGWICK, Theodore 2d H
SEDGWICK, William Thompson 1
SEDITA, Frank Albert 6
SEDLANDER, Norman Robert 6
SEDLAR, Sasa 6
SEDLEY, Henry 1
SEDWICK, Ellery 1
SEE, Elliot M. 4
SEE, Harold Philip 6
SEE, Horace 1
SEE, Thomas Jefferson Jackson 1
SEEBIRT, Eli Fowler 3
SEEDS, Russel M. 1
SEEGAL, David 5
SEEGER, Alan 1
SEEGER, Charles Louis 2
SEEGER, Edwin W. 5
SEEGER, Eugene 1
SEEGER, Stanley Joseph 5
SEEGER, Walter G. 5
SEEGERS, John Conrad 1
SEEGMILLER, Wilhelmina 1
SEELBACH, Louis 5
SEELE, Keith C(edric) 5
SEELER, Albert Otto 6
SEELER, Edgar Viguers 1
SEELEY, Elias P. H
SEELEY, Frank Barrows 3
SEELEY, John Edward H
SEELEY, Levi 1
SEELEY, Walter James 5
SEELIG, M. G. 5
SEELOS, Francis X. 1
SEELVE, Laurens Hickok 4
SEELY, Fred Loring 2
SEELY, Henry Martyn 1
SEELY, Herman Gastrell 3
SEELY, Walter Hoff 1
SEELYE, Elizabeth Eggleston 3
SEELYE, Julius Hawley 1
SEELYE, L. Clark 1
SEELYE, Theodore Edward 4
SEEM, Ralph Berger 4
SEERLEY, Frank Newell 4
SEERLEY, Homer Horatio 4
SEES, John Vincent 1
SEESTED, August Frederick 1
SEEVER, William John 2
SEEVERS, Charles Hamilton 6
SEEVERS, William Henry H
SEFERIADES, George 5
SEFRIT, Frank Ira 5
SEGAL, Paul Moses 5
SEGAR, Joseph Eggleston H
SEGEL, David 5
SEGER, Charles Bronson 1
SEGER, George N. 1
SEGER, Gerhart Henry 4
SEGHERS, Charles Jean H
SEGNI, Antonio 5
SEGUIN, Edouard H
SEGUIN, Edward Constant H
SEIBEL, Frederick Otto 5
SEIBEL, George 3
SEIBELS, Edwin Granville 5
SEIBELS, George Goldthwaite 5
SEIBERLING, Charles Willard 2
SEIBERLING, Francis 1
SEIBERLING, Frank A. 5
SEIBERT, James Walter 4
SEIBERT, John F. 1
SEIBERT, Walter R. 4
SEIBERT, William Adam 1
SEIBOLD, Louis 1
SEIBOLD, Myron James 5
SEIDEL, Emil 2
SEIDEL, Harry George 6
SEIDEL, John George 4
SEIDEL, Toscha 1
SEIDEMANN, Henry Peter 3
SEIDENBUSH, Rupert 1
SEIDENSTICKER, Oswald H

SEIDERS, George Melville 1
SEIDL, Anton H
SEIDL, Frank J(oseph) Sr. 6
SEIDLITZ, Walter George 6
SEIDNER, Howard Mayo 5
SEIF, William Henry 1
SEIFERT, Mathias Joseph 1
SEIFRIZ, William 3
SEIGLE, John Sanders 5
SEIGNOBOSC, Francoise 4
SEIME, Reuben Ingmar 6
SEINSHEIMER, J. Fellman 3
SEIP, Theodore Lorenzo 1
SEISS, Joseph Augustus 1
SEITZ, Albert Blazier 4
SEITZ, Charles Edward 1
SEITZ, Don Carlos 1
SEITZ, Frank Noah 2
SEITZ, George Albert 2
SEITZ, Ira James 5
SEITZ, William Chapin 6
SEIVER, George Otto 4
SEIXAS, Gershom Mendes H
SEJOUR, Victor H
SEKERA, Zdenek 5
SEKERS, Nicholas Thomas 5
SELBY, Augustine Dawson 1
SELBY, Charles Baxter 1
SELBY, Clarence Davey 6
SELBY, Howard Williams 3
SELBY, Mark Webster 5
SELBY, Thomas Jefferson 1
SELBY, William H
SELDEN, Charles A(lbert) 1
SELDEN, Dudley H
SELDEN, George Baldwin 4
SELDEN, Lynde 5
SELDES, Gilbert (Vivian) 5
SELDOMRIDGE, Harry Hunter 4
SELECMAN, Charles Claude 3
SELEKMAN, Benjamin Morris 4
SELF, James C. 3
SELF, William King 6
SELFRIDGE, Harry Gordon 2
SELFRIDGE, Thomas Oliver * 1
SELIG, Lester North 4
SELIG, William Nicholas 2
SELIGER, Robert V. 3
SELIGMAN, Albert Joseph 1
SELIGMAN, Arthur 1
SELIGMAN, Ben B(aruch) 5
SELIGMAN, Edwin Robert Anderson 1
SELIGMAN, Henry 1
SELIGMAN, Isaac Newton 1
SELIGMAN, Jefferson 1
SELIGMAN, Jesse H
SELIGMAN, Joseph H
SELIGMAN, Selig Jacob 5
SELIGMANN, Kurt 4
SELIJNS, Henricus H
SELINGER, Jean Paul 1
SELKE, George Albert 5
SELKE, W(ilhelm) Erich (Christian) 5
SELL, Edward Herman Miller 1
SELL, Henry Blackman 6
SELL, Henry Thorne 1
SELL, Lewis L. 3
SELLAR, Robert F. 5
SELLARDS, Elias Howard 4
SELLARS, Roy Wood 6
SELLECK, Willard Chamberlain 2
SELLECK, William Alson 2
SELLEN, Arthur Godfrey 4
SELLEN, Coleman 1
SELLERS, Coleman Jr. 1
SELLERS, David Foote 2
SELLERS, Edwin Jaquett 1
SELLERS, Horace Wells 1
SELLERS, Isaiah H
SELLERS, James Clark 6
SELLERS, James Freeman 1
SELLERS, Kathryn 1
SELLERS, Matthew Bacon 1
SELLERS, Robert Daniel 4
SELLERS, Robert Henry 4
SELLERS, Sandford 1
SELLERS, Walton Preston 5
SELLERS, William 1
SELLERY, George Clarke 4
SELLEW, George Tucker 4
SELLEW, Walter Ashbel 1
SELLMAN, William Nelson 4
SELLS, Cato 5
SELLS, Elijah Watt 1
SELLSTEDT, Lars Gustaf 1
SELMER, Ernst Westerlund H
SELTZER, Charles Alden 1

SELTZER, Theodore 3
SELVAGE, Watson 5
SELVIDGE, Robert 2
Washington
SELVIG, Conrad George 3
SELWYN, Edgar 2
SELYE, Lewis H
SELZ, Lawrence 4
Hochstadter
SELZNICK, David Oliver 4
SEMAN, Philip Louis 3
SEMANS, Edwin Walker 5
SEMANS, Harry Merrick 5
SEMBACH, J. 6
SEMBOWER, Alta Brunt 4
SEMBOWER, Charles Jacob 5
SEMBRICH, Marcella 1
SEMELROTH, William 4
James
SEMLER, George Herbert 3
SEMMANN, Liborius 5
SEMMES, Alexander H
Jenkins
SEMMES, Benedict Joseph H
SEMMES, John Edward 4
SEMMES, Raphael H
SEMMES, Thomas Jenkins H
SEMNACHER, William M. 4
SEMPLE, Ellen Churchill 1
SEMPLE, Henry Churchill 1
SEMPLE, James H
SEMPLE, William Tunstall 4
SEMSCH, Otto Francis 5
SENAN, Jose Francisco de H
Paula
SENANAYAKE, Don 3
Stephen
SENANAYAKE, Dudley 5
Shelton
SENCENBAUGH, Charles 3
Wilber
SENEAR, Francis Eugene 3
SENEFF, Edward H. 1
SENER, James Beverley H
SENEY, George Ingraham H
SENEY, Henry William 4
SENEY, Joshua H
SENFT, Craig T. 6
SENGIER, Edgar 4
SENGSTACK, John 5
F(rederick)
SENIOR, Clair Marcil 4
SENIOR, Clarence 6
SENIOR, Harold Dickinson 1
SENIOR, John Lawson 4
SENIOR, Joseph Howe 5
SENIOR, Samuel Palmer 4
SENN, Nicholas 1
SENN, Thomas J. 2
SENNER, Joseph Henry 1
SENNET, George Burritt H
SENNETT, Mack 5
SENNETT, Mack 4
SENNING, John Peter 3
SENOUR, Charles H
SENSENBRENNER, Frank 3
Jacob
SENSENBRENNER, John 6
Stlip
SENSENEY, George Eyster 2
SENSENICH, Roscoe Lloyd 4
SENSENIG, David Martin 1
SENTELL, George 3
Washington
SENTELLE, Mark Edgar 3
SENTER, John Henry 1
SENTER, Leon B. 4
SENTER, Ralph Townsend 2
SENTER, William Tandy H
SENTNER, David 6
SENTNER, Richard 5
Faulkner
SEPPELT, Ian Howe 6
SEQUOYAH 4
SERAFIN, Tullio 4
SERAKOFF, Leonard 5
SERESS, Raoul 4
SERGEANT, Elizabeth 4
Shepley
SERGEANT, John * H
SERGEANT, Jonathan H
Dickinson
SERGEANT, Thomas H
SERGEL, Charles Hubbard 1
SERLES, Earl R. 3
SERLIN, Oscar 5
SERLING, Rod 6
SEROTTA, Elliott Cecil 6
SERPELL, Susan Watkins 1
SERRA, Junipero H
SERRELL, Edward 1
Wellmann
SERRIES, Mavis McGrew 6
SERRILL, William Jones 3
SERVEN, Abram Ralph 4
SERVICE, Robert William 4

SERVISS, Frederick 3
LeVerne
SERVISS, Garrett Putman 1
SERVOSS, Thomas Lowery H
SESKIS, I. J. 3
SESSINGHAUS, Gustavus H
SESSIONS, Charles H. 2
SESSIONS, Clarence 1
William
SESSIONS, Kenosha 5
SESSIONS, Walter Loomis H
SESSIONS, William Edwin 1
SESSUMS, Davis H
SESTINI, Benedict H
SETCHELL, William Albert 2
SETH, Julien Orem 4
SETON, Elizabeth Ann H
Bayley
SETON, Ernest Thompson 2
SETON, Grace Thompson 3
SETON, Julia 4
SETON, Robert 1
SETTERFIELD, Hugh E. 3
SETTI, Giulio H
SETTLE, Evan E. 1
SETTLE, George Thomas 4
SETTLE, Thomas * H
SETTLE, Warner Ellmore 4
SETZE, Julius Adolphus 3
SETZER, Richard Woodrow 5
SETZLER, Frank Maryl 6
SEUBERT, Edward George 4
SEVER, George Francis 4
SEVERANCE, Caroline 1
Maria Seymour
SEVERANCE, Cordenio 1
Arnold
SEVERANCE, Frank 1
Hayward
SEVERANCE, Henry 2
Ormal
SEVERANCE, John Long 1
SEVERANCE, Luther 4
SEVERANCE, Mark Sibley 4
SEVERENS, Henry 4
Franklin
SEVERN, Edmund 3
SEVERS, John Ward 4
SEVERSKY, Alexander P. 6
SEVERSON, Harold 6
Clifford
SEVERSON, Lewis Everett 4
SEVERY, Melvin Linwood 4
SEVEY, Robert 3
SEVIER, Ambrose Hundley H
SEVIER, Charles Edwin 3
SEVIER, Clara Driscoll 6
SEVIER, Henry Hulme 1
SEVIER, Henry Hulme 2
SEVIER, John H
SEVIER, Joseph Ramsey 5
SEVIER, Landers 3
SEVIER, Randolph 4
SEVIGNY, Albert 4
SEVITZKY, Fabien 4
SEWALL, Arthur H
SEWALL, Arthur Wollaston 1
SEWALL, Charles S. H
SEWALL, Edmund 4
Devereux
SEWALL, Frank 1
SEWALL, Harold Marsh 1
SEWALL, Harriet Winslow H
SEWALL, Henry 1
SEWALL, James Wingate 4
SEWALL, John Smith 3
SEWALL, Jonathan 1
SEWALL, Jonathan H
Mitchell
SEWALL, Lee Goodrich 5
SEWALL, May Wright 1
SEWALL, Rufus King H
SEWALL, Samuel * H
SEWALL, Stephen 1
SEWALL, Sydney 6
SEWARD, Allin Carey Jr. 5
SEWARD, Coy Avon 4
SEWARD, Frederick 1
William
SEWARD, George 1
Frederick
SEWARD, George Winn 6
SEWARD, Herbert Lee 4
SEWARD, James Lindsay H
SEWARD, John Perry 1
SEWARD, Samuel Swayze H
SEWARD, Samuel Swayze 1
Jr.
SEWARD, Theodore 1
Frelinghuysen
SEWARD, William H
SEWARD, William Henry 1
SEWARD, William Henry 1
SEWELL, Albert Henry 1
SEWELL, Amanda Brewster 1
SEWELL, Dan Roy 6

SEWELL, Jesse Parker 5
SEWELL, John Stephen 1
SEWELL, Oscar Marion 1
SEWELL, Robert van Vorst 1
SEWELL, Warren Pelmer 6
SEWELL, William Joyce 1
SEXSON, John Amherst 6
SEXTON, Anne Harvey 6
SEXTON, George Samuel 1
SEXTON, Harold Eustace 5
SEXTON, John Chase 1
SEXTON, John Moody 5
SEXTON, Lawrence Eugene 1
SEXTON, Leonidas 1
SEXTON, Lewis Albert 1
SEXTON, Pliny Titus 1
SEXTON, Sherman J. 3
SEXTON, Thomas 4
Lawrence
SEXTON, Thomas Scott 5
SEXTON, Walton Roswell 1
SEXTON, William Henry 4
SEXTON, William Thomas H
SEYBERT, Adam 1
SEYBERT, Henry 1
SEYBERT, John 1
SEYBOLT, Robert Francis 3
SEYFERT, Carl Keenan 4
SEYFFARTH, Gustavus 3
SEYFFERT, Leopold 3
SEYMORE, Truman 4
SEYMOUR, Alexander 3
Duncan Jr.
SEYMOUR, Arthur Bliss 1
SEYMOUR, Augustus 1
Theodore
SEYMOUR, Augustus 4
Theodore
SEYMOUR, Burge Miles 4
SEYMOUR, Charles 4
SEYMOUR, Charles Milne 3
SEYMOUR, David Lowrey H
SEYMOUR, Edward H
Woodruff
SEYMOUR, Flora Warren 1
SEYMOUR, Frederick 1
SEYMOUR, George Dudley 2
SEYMOUR, George 1
Franklin
SEYMOUR, George Steele 4
SEYMOUR, Gideon 5
SEYMOUR, Harold J. 5
SEYMOUR, Horatio * H
SEYMOUR, Horatio 1
Winslow
SEYMOUR, James Alward 2
SEYMOUR, John Sammis 1
SEYMOUR, Mary Harrison 3
SEYMOUR, Morris 1
Woodruff
SEYMOUR, Origen Storrs H
SEYMOUR, Ralph Fletcher 4
SEYMOUR, Robert Gillin 1
SEYMOUR, Samuel 1
SEYMOUR, Storrs Ozias 3
SEYMOUR, Thomas Day 1
SEYMOUR, Thomas Hart H
SEYMOUR, William 1
SEYMOUR, William 1
SEYMOUR, William 1
Wolcott
SEYMOUR, William 1
Wotkyns
SEYRIG, Henri Arnold 6
SHAAD, George Carl 4
SHABONEE H
SHACK, Ferdinand H
SHACKELFORD, Edward 2
Madison
SHACKELFORD, Francis 6
SHACKELFORD, James M. 1
SHACKELFORD, John 1
Williams
SHACKELFORD, Virginius 2
Randolph
SHACKFORD, John Walter 6
SHACKFORD, Martha Hale 5
SHACKLEFORD, Dorsey 4
W.
SHACKLEFORD, Robert 4
Wooten
SHACKLEFORD, Thomas 1
Mitchell
SHACKLEFORD, Thomas 5
Mitchell Jr.
SHACKLETON, Robert 1
SHADID, Michael Abraham 4
SHAFER, Don Cameron 6
SHAFER, George F. 2
SHAFER, George H. 2
SHAFER, Helen Almira 1
SHAFER, Jacob K. H
SHAFER, John Douglas 1
SHAFER, Morris Luther 6
SHAFER, Paul W. 3
SHAFER, Robert 3

SHAFER, Sara Andrew 1
SHAFFER, Bertram 6
SHAFFER, Charles Norman 4
SHAFFER, Cornelius 1
Thadeus
SHAFFER, Edward H. 2
SHAFFER, Elmer Ellsworth 6
Dale
SHAFFER, Floyd Elmer 4
SHAFFER, John Charles 2
SHAFFER, John Charles 5
SHAFFER, Joseph Crockett 3
SHAFFER, Lewis 1
SHAFFER, Newton 1
Melman
SHAFFER, Philip Anderson 4
SHAFFER, Ray Osborn 4
SHAFFER, Roy Lee 6
SHAFFER, William 4
Frederick
SHAFFNER, Henry Fries 2
SHAFFNER, Taliaferro H
Preston
SHAFROTH, John Franklin 1
SHAFROTH, John Franklin 4
SHAFTER, William Rufus 1
SHAFTESBURY, Archie D. 4
SHAHAN, Thomas Joseph 1
SHAHN, Ben 5
SHAIKEN, Joseph 6
SHAINMARK, Eliezer L. 6
SHAINWALD, Richard 3
Herman
SHAINWALD, Richard S. 3
SHAKESPEARE, William 1
Jr.
SHALER, Alexander 1
SHALER, Charles 1
SHALER, Clarence Addison 2
SHALER, Nathaniel 1
Southgate
SHALER, William H
SHALLBERG, Gustavus 3
Adolphus
SHALLCROSS, Cecil 2
Fleetwood
SHALLENBERGER, 1
Ashton C.
SHALLENBERGER, 3
Martin C.
SHALLENBERGER, 1
William Shadrach
SHALTER, Irwin Maurer 6
SHAMBAUGH, Benjamin 1
Franklin
SHAMBAUGH, Bertha M. 5
H. (Mrs. Benjamin F.
Shambaugh)
SHAMBAUGH, George 5
Elmer
SHAMBORA, William 6
E(dward)
SHAMBURGER, Carl 5
Shuford
SHAMEL, Archibald Dixon 6
SHAMROY, Leon 6
SHANAFELT, Thomas M. 4
SHANAHAN, David 1
Edward
SHANAHAN, Edmund 1
Thomas
SHANAHAN, Foss 4
SHANAHAN, John Daniel 4
SHANAHAN, John W. 1
SHANAHAN, T. J. 4
SHANANAN, Jeremiah H
Francis
SHAND, Robert Gordon 4
SHAND, James JAMES 3
SHANDS, Aurelius Rives 1
SHANDS, Courtney 5
SHANDS, Garvin Dugas 1
SHANE, George (Walker) 5
SHANE, Joseph Brooks 6
SHANK, Corwin Sheridan 2
SHANK, Donald J. 4
SHANK, Samuel Herbert 1
SHANKLAND, Edward 1
Clapp
SHANKLAND, Sherwood 2
Dodge
SHANKLIN, Arnold 4
SHANKLIN, George Sea H
SHANKLIN, John Gilbert 1
SHANKLIN, William 1
Arnold
SHANKS, David Carey 1
SHANKS, Henry Thomas 4
SHANKS, Lewis Piaget 1
SHANKS, Royal E. 4
SHANKS, William Franklin 1
Gore
SHANLEY, George Patrick 4
SHANLEY, James Andrew 4
SHANLEY, John 1

SHANNAHAN, John 1
Newton
SHANNON, Edgar Finley 1
SHANNON, Effie 5
SHANNON, Fred Albert 4
SHANNON, Frederick 5
Franklin
SHANNON, George Pope 4
SHANNON, J. J. 4
SHANNON, Joseph B. 2
SHANNON, Nellie 5
SHANNON, Richard Cutts 1
SHANNON, Robert 1
Thomas
SHANNON, Spencer Sweet 4
SHANNON, Thomas H
SHANNON, Thomas H
Bowles
SHANNON, Thomas 3
Vincent
SHANNON, Wilson H
SHANTZ, Homer LeRoy 4
SHAPIRO, Arthur 6
SHAPIRO, Harry 4
SHAPIRO, Joseph 4
SHAPIRO, Joseph M. 5
SHAPLEIGH, Alfred Lee 2
SHAPLEIGH, Bertram 2
SHAPLEIGH, Frank Henry 1
SHAPLEIGH, Waldron 1
SHAPLEY, Alan 6
SHAPLEY, Harlow 5
SHAPLEY, Rufus Edmonds 4
SHAPORIN, Yuri 4
SHARETT, Moshe 4
SHARKEY, Joseph Edward 5
SHARKEY, Thomas Clifford 6
SHARKEY, William Lewis H
SHARMAN, Jackson Roger 3
SHARON, William H
SHARP, Alexander 1
SHARP, Benjamin 1
SHARP, Carl J. 5
SHARP, Clarence Bryan 6
SHARP, Clayton Halsey 1
SHARP, Dallas Lore 1
SHARP, Daniel H
SHARP, Eckley Grant 4
SHARP, Edgar A. 2
SHARP, Edward Raymond 4
SHARP, Edwin Rees 1
SHARP, Frank Chapman 2
SHARP, George Clough 5
SHARP, George Gillies 4
SHARP, George Matthews 1
SHARP, George Winters 5
SHARP, Henry Staats 5
SHARP, Hugh Rodney 6
SHARP, Hunter 1
SHARP, James H. 6
SHARP, John H
SHARP, Mrs. John C. 1
SHARP, John Fletcher 1
SHARP, John H. 5
SHARP, Joseph C. 2
SHARP, Joseph Lessil 5
SHARP, Katharine Lucinda 1
SHARP, Marlay Albert 1
SHARP, Robert 1
SHARP, Robert Sherman 1
SHARP, Solomon P. 1
SHARP, Thomas Enoch 1
SHARP, Waldo Z. 1
SHARP, Walter Bedford 4
SHARP, William H
SHARP, William F. 4
SHARP, William Graves 1
SHARP, William Wilson 4
SHARPE. Alfred Clarence 1
SHARPE, Francis Robert 2
SHARPE, Henry Augustus 1
SHARPE, Henry Dexter 3
SHARPE, Henry Granville 4
SHARPE, Horatio 2
SHARPE, John C. 1
SHARPE, Merrell Quentin 4
SHARPE, Nelson 1
SHARPE, Peter H
SHARPE, Philip Burdette 4
SHARPE, William H
SHARPLES, James 1
SHARPLES, Philip M. 4
SHARPLES, Stephen 1
Paschall
SHARPLESS, Frederic Cope 5
SHARPLESS, Frederick F. 3
SHARPLESS, Isaac 1
SHARSWOOD, George H
SHARTS, Joseph William 5
SHASTID, Thomas Hall 4
SHASTRI, Lal Bahadur 4
SHATTUC, William B. 1
SHATTUCK, Aaron Draper 1
SHATTUCK, Arthur 4
SHATTUCK, Charles 1
Houston

SHATTUCK, Edward 4 Stevens	SHAW, Oliver H	SHEEDY, Joseph Edward 3	SHELFORD, Victor 5 E(rnest)	SHEPHERD, Patricia Drake 5 (Mrs. James Leftwich Shepherd III)

SHATTUCK, Edward 4
Stevens
SHATTUCK, Edwin Paul 4
SHATTUCK, Frederick 1
Cheever
SHATTUCK, George Brune 1
SHATTUCK, George 1
Burbank
SHATTUCK, George 5
Cheever
SHATTUCK, George H
Cheyne *
SHATTUCK, H. Morgan 4
SHATTUCK, Harriette Lucy 4
Robinson
SHATTUCK, Henry Lee 5
SHATTUCK, Howard 5
Francis
SHATTUCK, John Garrett 4
SHATTUCK, Lemuel H
SHATTUCK, Lemuel C. 1
SHATTUCK, Mayo Adams 3
SHATTUCK, Samuel 1
Walker
SHATTUCK, (Sidney) 6
Frank
SHATTUCK, William 3
SHATZER, Charles Gallatin 3
SHAUCK, John Allen 1
SHAUGHNESSY, Clark 5
Daniel
SHAUGHNESSY, Gerald 3
SHAUGHNESSY, Sir 1
Thomas George
SHAVER, Charles William 4
SHAVER, Clement 3
Lawrence
SHAVER, Dorothy
SHAVER, George Frederick 4
SHAVER, Jesse Milton 4
SHAVER, Robert Ezekiel 6
SHAW, Aaron H
SHAW, Albert 2
SHAW, Albert Duane 1
SHAW, Albert Sidney 6
Johnston
SHAW, Anna Howard 1
SHAW, Arch Wilkinson 4
SHAW, Avery Albert 2
SHAW, Charles Bunsen 4
SHAW, Charles Frederick 1
SHAW, Charles Gray 2
SHAW, Charles Green 6
SHAW, Clarence Reginald 3
SHAW, Dexter Nichols 6
SHAW, Earl 4
SHAW, Edgar Dwight 1
SHAW, Edward Richard 1
SHAW, Edwin Adams 3
SHAW, Edwin Coupland 2
SHAW, Elijah H
SHAW, Elwyn Riley 3
SHAW, Esmond 5
SHAW, Eugene 6
SHAW, Eugene Wesley 1
SHAW, Florence Sylvia 4
Berlowitz
SHAW, Frances Wills 1
SHAW, Frank L. 5
SHAW, Frederic Lonsdale 6
SHAW, Frederick Benjamin 5
SHAW, Frederick William 2
SHAW, G. Bernard 3
SHAW, Gardiner Howland 4
SHAW, George Bernard 6
SHAW, George Bullen H
SHAW, George Elmer 1
SHAW, George Hamlin 3
SHAW, Guy Loren 6
SHAW, Harriett McCreary 1
Jackson
SHAW, Henry * H
SHAW, Henry G(eorge) 6
SHAW, Henry Larned Keith 1
SHAW, Henry Marchmore
SHAW, Henry Wheeler H
SHAW, Hobart Doane 4
SHAW, Howard Burton
SHAW, Howard Van Doren 1
SHAW, J. W.
SHAW, James Byrnie 2
SHAW, James Edward 6
SHAW, John * H
SHAW, John Balcom 4
SHAW, John Jacob 6
SHAW, John Stewart 3
SHAW, John William 4
SHAW, Joseph Alden 1
SHAW, Joshua H
SHAW, Lemuel H
SHAW, Leo Nelson 5
SHAW, Leslie Mortier 1
SHAW, Lloyd 3
SHAW, Lucien 1
SHAW, Mary 1
SHAW, Nathaniel H

SHAW, Oliver H
SHAW, Oliver Abbott 2
SHAW, Patrick 6
SHAW, Phillips Bassett 4
SHAW, Quincy A. 4
SHAW, Quincy A. 5
SHAW, Ralph Martin 4
SHAW, Ralph Robert 5
SHAW, Reuben T. 5
SHAW, Richard 3
SHAW, Robert 5
SHAW, Robert 6
SHAW, Robert Alfred 2
SHAW, Robert Anderson 1
SHAW, Robert Gould H
SHAW, Robert Kendall 4
SHAW, Robert Sidey 3
SHAW, Roger 3
SHAW, Samuel * H
SHAW, Samuel Gormley 2
SHAW, Silas Frederick 6
SHAW, Sterling Price 5
SHAW, Sydney Dale 6
SHAW, Thomas H
SHAW, Thomas 3
SHAW, Thomas Mott 4
SHAW, Tristram 1
SHAW, Walter Adam 3
SHAW, Walter Carlyle 6
SHAW, Walter Keith 1
SHAW, William Bristol 2
SHAW, William Edward 4
SHAW, William Frederick 5
SHAW, William James 3
SHAW, William Smith H
SHAWHAN, Narcissa 5
Tayloe Maupin (Mrs.
Charles S.)
SHAWKEY, Morris Purdy 4
SHAWN, Edwin M. (Ted 5
Shawn)
SHAY, Frank 3
SHAYLER, Ernest Vincent 2
SHAYS, Daniel H
SHAZAR, Zalman 6
SHEA, Andrew Bernard 4
SHEA, Daniel William 1
SHEA, Edmund Burke 4
SHEA, Edward Lane 4
SHEA, James R. 3
SHEA, John Dawson H
Gilmary
SHEA, John J. 4
SHEA, John Joseph 5
SHEA, John Joseph 6
SHEA, Joseph Bernard 1
SHEA, Joseph Hooker 4
SHEA, Lewis Anthony 5
SHEA, William Joseph 4
SHEAFE, James H
SHEAFER, Arthur 1
Whitcomb
SHEAFFER, Craig Royer 4
SHEAFFER, Daniel Miller 4
SHEAFFER, Walter A. 2
SHEAN, Charles M. 1
SHEAR, Cornelius Lott 4
SHEAR, John Knox 3
SHEAR, Theodore Leslie 2
SHEARD, Titus 1
SHEARER, Andrew 1
SHEARER, Augustus Hunt 4
SHEARER, George Lewis 4
SHEARER, Henry 4
SHEARER, J. Harry 4
SHEARER, John Bunyan 1
SHEARER, John Louis 4
SHEARER, John Sanford 1
SHEARER, Maurice Edwin 6
SHEARER, Tom Ellas 4
SHEARER, Tom Ellas 5
SHEARIN, Hubert Gibson 1
SHEARMAN, Thomas 1
Gaskell
SHEARN, Clarence John 3
SHEATS, William Nicholas 1
SHEATSLEY, Clarence 4
Valentine
SHEATSLEY, Jacob 4
SHECUT, John Linnaeus H
Edward Whitridge
SHEDD, Clarence Prouty 6
SHEDD, Fred Fuller 1
SHEDD, George Clifford 4
SHEDD, J. Herbert 1
SHEDD, John Cutler 4
SHEDD, John Graves 1
SHEDD, Solon 2
SHEDD, Thomas Clark 3
SHEDD, William Alfred 4
SHEDD, William 1
Greenough Thayer
SHEDDEN, Lucian Love 1
SHEEAN, James B. 3
SHEEAN, James Vincent 6
SHEEDY, Dennis 1

SHEEDY, Joseph Edward 3
SHEEDY, Morgan M. 1
SHEEHAN, Daniel Michael 4
SHEEHAN, Donal 4
SHEEHAN, Donald Henry 6
SHEEHAN, J. Eastman 4
SHEEHAN, John Charles 1
SHEEHAN, Joseph 1
Raymond
SHEEHAN, Perley Poore 5
SHEEHAN, Robert Francis 2
Jr.
SHEEHAN, Robert John 4
SHEEHAN, Robert Wade 5
SHEEHAN, Timothy J. 4
SHEEHAN, William Francis 1
SHEEHAN, William Mark 4
SHEEHAN, Winfield R. 1
SHEEHY, Joe Warren 4
SHEEHY, Maurice 5
S(tephen)
SHEELER, Charles 4
SHEELY, William Clarence 5
SHEEN, Daniel Robinson 4
SHEEP, William L. 6
SHEERIN, Charles Wilford 2
SHEERIN, James 1
SHEETS, Frank Thomas 3
SHEETS, Harold F. 5
SHEETS, Millard Owen 4
SHEFFER, Daniel 6
SHEFFER, Henry Maurice 4
SHEFFEY, Daniel 4
SHEFFEY, Edward Fleming 1
SHEFFIELD, Alfred Dwight 4
SHEFFIELD, Devello Z. 1
SHEFFIELD, Frederick 5
SHEFFIELD, J. S. 4
SHEFFIELD, James 1
Rockwell
SHEFFIELD, Joseph Earl H
William Paine *
SHEIL, Bernard J(ames) 5
SHEIN, Harvey M. 6
SHEININ, John J(acobi) 5
SHELBURNE, James M. 3
SHELBURNE, Lord 1
SHELBY, David Davie 1
SHELBY, Evan 1
SHELBY, Gertrude 1
Singleton Mathews
SHELBY, Isaac H
SHELBY, John Todd 1
SHELBY, Joseph Orville H
SHELBY, Robert Evart 3
SHELBY, Thomas Hall 6
SHELBY, William Read 1
SHELDEN, Carlos Douglas 1
SHELDEN, Miriam 6
Aldridge
SHELDON, Addison Erwin 2
SHELDON, Arthur 1
Frederick
SHELDON, Caroline M. 1
SHELDON, Charles 1
SHELDON, Charles Mills 4
SHELDON, Charles 2
Monroe
SHELDON, Charles Stuart 1
SHELDON, David Newton H
SHELDON, Edward Austin H
SHELDON, Edward 2
Brewster
SHELDON, Edward Stevens 1
SHELDON, Edward Wright 1
SHELDON, Frederick 1
Beaumont
SHELDON, G. L. 5
SHELDON, George Lawson 3
SHELDON, George Preston 1
SHELDON, George Rumsey 1
SHELDON, George William 1
SHELDON, Grace Carew 1
SHELDON, Harold Horton 4
SHELDON, Henry Clay 1
SHELDON, Henry 2
Davidson
SHELDON, Henry Newton 1
SHELDON, John Lewis 3
SHELDON, John M. 4
SHELDON, Joseph 1
SHELDON, Lionel Allen 1
SHELDON, Ralph Edward 4
SHELDON, Rowland 1
Caldwell
SHELDON, Roy Horton 5
SHELDON, Samuel 1
SHELDON, Walter L. 1
SHELDON, William Evarts H
SHELDON, Wilmon Henry 5
SHELDON, Winthrop 4
Dudley
SHELEKHOV, Grigorii H
Ivanovich
SHELEY, Basil LeRoy 4

SHELFORD, Victor 5
E(rnest)
SHELLABARGER, Samuel H
SHELLABARGER, Samuel 3
SHELLEY, George Elgin 4
SHELLEY, Guy Morrell 6
SHELLEY, Harry Rowe 2
SHELLEY, Henry Charles 1
SHELLEY, Henry V. 3
SHELLEY, John Francis 6
SHELLEY, Oliver Hazard 2
Perry
SHELLEY, Tully 5
SHELMIRE, Horace Weeks 4
SHELTON, Charles Eldred 1
SHELTON, Don Odell 1
SHELTON, E. Kost 3
SHELTON, Frederick H
William
SHELTON, Jane de Forest 5
SHELTON, Louise 1
SHELTON, Orman Leroy 4
SHELTON, Samuel A. 4
SHELTON, Thomas Wall 1
SHELTON, Whitford 4
Huston
SHELTON, Willard 5
Ellington
SHELTON, William Arthur 5
SHELTON, William Henry 4
SHENEHON, Francis 1
Clinton
SHENEMAN, Hester Mary 5
Dickerson (Mrs. McKinley
Sheneman)
SHENK, Hirmna Herr 3
SHENK, John Wesley 3
SHENTON, Herbert 1
Newhard
SHEPARD, Andrew N. 1
SHEPARD, Bertram David 4
SHEPARD, C. Sidney 1
SHEPARD, Charles Biddle H
SHEPARD, Charles Edward 1
SHEPARD, Charles Henry 1
SHEPARD, Charles Upham H
SHEPARD, Earl Dorman 5
SHEPARD, Edward Martin 1
SHEPARD, Edward Morse 1
SHEPARD, Edwin M. 1
SHEPARD, Finley Johnson 2
SHEPARD, Frank Edward 4
SHEPARD, Frank Russell 3
SHEPARD, Fred Douglas 1
SHEPARD, Frederick Job 1
SHEPARD, George Wanzor 3
SHEPARD, Guy Conwell 1
SHEPARD, Harriett Elma 2
SHEPARD, Harvey Newton 1
SHEPARD, Helen Miller 1
SHEPARD, Horace B. 2
SHEPARD, Irwin 1
SHEPARD, James Edward 2
SHEPARD, James Henry 1
SHEPARD, John Jr. 1
SHEPARD, John Frederick 4
SHEPARD, Luther 1
Dimmick
SHEPARD, Odell 5
SHEPARD, Seth 1
SHEPARD, Stuart Gore 1
SHEPARD, Theodore F. 4
SHEPARD, Thomas H
SHEPARD, Walter James 1
SHEPARD, William H
SHEPARD, William Biddle H
SHEPARD, William Orville 1
SHEPARD, William Pierce 2
SHEPARD, Woolsey Adams 4
SHEPARDSON, Charles 6
Noah
SHEPARDSON, Francis 1
Wayland
SHEPARDSON, Frank 3
Lucius
SHEPARDSON, George 1
Defrees
SHEPARDSON, Ruth 2
Pearson Chandler
SHEPARDSON, Whitney 4
Hart
SHEPERD, James Edward 4
SHEPHERD, Alexander R. 1
SHEPHERD, Arthur 4
SHEPHERD, Charles 4
Reginald
SHEPHERD, Clifford John 1
SHEPHERD, Ernest Stanley 2
SHEPHERD, Fred N. 6
SHEPHERD, Grace M. 5
SHEPHERD, Harold 2
SHEPHERD, Henry Elliot 1
SHEPHERD, James 4
Leftwich
SHEPHERD, Mozelle 6
Miller

SHEPHERD, Patricia Drake 5
(Mrs. James Leftwich
Shepherd III)
SHEPHERD, Pearce 5
SHEPHERD, Russell E. 2
SHEPHERD, Theodosia 1
Burr
SHEPHERD, William 4
Chauncey
SHEPHERD, William Gunn 1
SHEPHERD, William R. 1
SHEPLER, Joseph McGuire 3
SHEPLER, Matthias 1
SHEPLEY, Ethan A.H. 6
SHEPLEY, Ether H
SHEPLEY, George Foster H
SHEPLEY, George Foster 1
SHEPLEY, George Leander 1
SHEPLEY, Henry 4
Richardson
SHEPPARD, Harry R. 5
SHEPPARD, Jack Murff 6
SHEPPARD, James Carroll 1
SHEPPARD, James J. 1
SHEPPARD, John Calhoun 1
SHEPPARD, John Levi 1
SHEPPARD, John 2
Rutherford
SHEPPARD, John 1
Shoemaker
SHEPPARD, Lawrence 5
Baker
SHEPPARD, Lucius Elmer 1
SHEPPARD, Morris 1
SHEPPARD, Robert 4
Dickinson
SHEPPARD, Samuel 2
Edward
SHEPPARD, Walter Wade 1
SHEPPARD, Warren 1
SHEPPARD, William 1
Bostwick
SHEPPARD, William Henry 4
SHEPPERD, Augustine H
Henry
SHEPPERD, John Henry 1
SHEPPERSON, Archibald 4
Bolling
SHEPPEY, Marshall 2
SHEPS, Mindel Cherniack 4
SHERBAKOFF, 1
Constantine Dmitriev
SHERBON, Florence Brown 2
SHERBURNE, Ernest C. 3
SHERBURNE, Harold 6
Hewitt
SHERBURNE, John Henry 4
SHERBURNE, John Samuel H
SHERBY, Daniel 5
SHERE, Lewis 3
SHEREDINE, Upton H
SHERER, Albert W. 6
SHERER, Dunham B. 4
SHERER, Rex W. 5
SHERER, William 4
SHERIDAN, Ann 4
SHERIDAN, Edward 6
Francis
SHERIDAN, George 1
Augustus
SHERIDAN, Harold James 4
SHERIDAN, John 4
Lawrence
SHERIDAN, Lawrence 5
Vinnedge
SHERIDAN, Leo J. 6
SHERIDAN, Michael 1
Vincent
SHERIDAN, Philip Henry H
SHERIDAN, Sarah M. 5
SHERIDAN, Thomas 4
Francis
SHERIDAN, Thomas 3
Harold
SHERIDAN, Wilbur 1
Fletcher
SHERIFF, Robert Cedric 6
SHERILL, George Raymond 4
SHERK, Kenneth Wayne 5
SHERLOCK, Charles 1
Reginald
SHERLOCK, Chesia C. 1
SHERMAN, Allan 6
SHERMAN, Althea Rosina 2
SHERMAN, Andrew 1
Magoun
SHERMAN, Buren 1
Robinson
SHERMAN, Carl 3
SHERMAN, Carl Benjamin 6
SHERMAN, Charles 1
Colebrook
SHERMAN, Charles 5
Lawrence

SHERMAN, Charles Lawton 3
SHERMAN, Charles Phineas 6
SHERMAN, Charles Pomeroy 2
SHERMAN, Christopher Elias 1
SHERMAN, Clifford Gould 4
SHERMAN, Clifton Lucien 2
SHERMAN, Edgar Jay 6
SHERMAN, Edward Augustine 1
SHERMAN, Elijah Bernis 1
SHERMAN, Ellen Burns 3
SHERMAN, Forrest Percival 3
SHERMAN, Frank 4
SHERMAN, Frank Asbury 1
SHERMAN, Frank Dempster 1
SHERMAN, Franklin 1
SHERMAN, Frederick C. 3
SHERMAN, Gordon Edward 1
SHERMAN, H. M. Jr. 4
SHERMAN, Harry Mitchell 1
SHERMAN, Henry Clapp 3
SHERMAN, Henry Stoddard 3
SHERMAN, Homer Henkel 2
SHERMAN, Hoyt 1
SHERMAN, James Morgan 3
SHERMAN, James Schoolcraft 1
SHERMAN, John H
SHERMAN, John 1
SHERMAN, John Dickinson 1
SHERMAN, John Francis 1
SHERMAN, John James 6
SHERMAN, John K(urtz) 5
SHERMAN, Judson W. H
SHERMAN, Lawrence William Jr. 5
SHERMAN, Lawrence Y. 1
SHERMAN, Lewis Frank 6
SHERMAN, Louis Ralph 3
SHERMAN, Lucius Adelno 1
SHERMAN, Mary Belle King 1
SHERMAN, Maurice Sinclair 2
SHERMAN, Merritt Masters 1
SHERMAN, Mildred P. 4
SHERMAN, Moses Hazeltine 1
SHERMAN, Philemon Tecumseh 4
SHERMAN, Philip Francis 6
SHERMAN, Ray Eugene 2
SHERMAN, Roger H
SHERMAN, Roger 3
SHERMAN, Socrates Norton H
SHERMAN, Stuart Pratt 1
SHERMAN, Thomas B. 5
SHERMAN, Thomas Ewing 4
SHERMAN, Thomas Townsend 1
SHERMAN, Thomas West H
SHERMAN, Wells Alvord 1
SHERMAN, William Arthur 3
SHERMAN, William Bowen 5
SHERMAN, William O'neill 1
SHERMAN, William Tecumseh H
SHERMAN, William Winslow 1
SHERO, Lucius Rogers 5
SHERO, William Francis 2
SHERPICK, Eugene Arthur 4
SHERRARD, Charles Cornell 1
SHERRARD, Glenwood John 3
SHERRARD, Thomas Herrick 1
SHERRERD, William D. H
SHERRIFF, Andrew Rothwell 1
SHERRILL, Alvan Foote 4
SHERRILL, Charles Hitchcock 1
SHERRILL, Clarence Osborne 5
SHERRILL, Edwin Stanton 4
SHERRILL, Eliakim 1
SHERRILL, Gibbs Wynkoop 3
SHERRILL, James Winn 3
SHERRILL, John Bascom 1
SHERRILL, Lewis Joseph 1
SHERRILL, Miles Osborne 1
SHERRILL, Miles Standish 4

SHERRILL, R. E. 3
SHERRILL, Ruth Erwin 4
SHERRILL, Samuel Wells 5
SHERRILL, Stephen H. 3
SHERRILL, William Lander 5
SHERRY, George Gregory 4
SHERWELL, G. Butler 4
SHERWELL, Guillermo Antonio 1
SHERWIN, Belle 3
SHERWIN, Carl Paxson 6
SHERWIN, Henry Alden 1
SHERWIN, John Collins 1
SHERWIN, Proctor Fenn 3
SHERWIN, Ralph Sidney 3
SHERWIN, Thomas H
SHERWIN, Thomas 1
SHERWOOD, Adiel H
SHERWOOD, Andrew 1
SHERWOOD, Arnold Cooper 5
SHERWOOD, Carl G. 1
SHERWOOD, Carlton Montgomery 5
SHERWOOD, Emily Lee 4
SHERWOOD, George Herbert 1
SHERWOOD, Granville Hudson 1
SHERWOOD, Henry H
SHERWOOD, Herbert Francis 1
SHERWOOD, Isaac R. 1
SHERWOOD, Katharine Margaret Brownlee 1
SHERWOOD, Margaret Pollock 3
SHERWOOD, Mary Elizabeth Wilson 1
SHERWOOD, Noble Pierce 4
SHERWOOD, Robert Emmet 3
SHERWOOD, Rosina Emmet 3
SHERWOOD, Samuel H
SHERWOOD, Samuel Burr 4
SHERWOOD, Sidney 1
SHERWOOD, Thomas Adiel 4
SHERWOOD, Thomas Kilgore 6
SHERWOOD, William 3
SHERWOOD, William Hall 5
SHERWOOD-DUNN, Berkeley 5
SHERZER, William Hittell 1
SHETTER, Stella Cross 1
SHEVELSON, S. Harris 3
SHEWHART, Walter Andrew 4
SHEWMAKE, Oscar Lane 4
SHEWMAN, Eben B. 2
SHIBER, Etta 4
SHIBLEY, Alice Smith Patterson 4
SHIDEHARA, Baron Kijuro 6
SHIDELER, W. H. 3
SHIDY, Leland Perry 1
SHIEL, George Knox H
SHIELD, Lansing P. 3
SHIELD, Lansing P. 4
SHIELDS, A. C. 2
SHIELDS, Benjamin Glover H
SHIELDS, Charles R. 1
SHIELDS, Charles Woodruff 1
SHIELDS, Ebenezer J. H
SHIELDS, Edmund Claude 2
SHIELDS, Edwin John 6
SHIELDS, Emily L. 4
SHIELDS, G. O. 3
SHIELDS, George Howell 1
SHIELDS, George Robert 2
SHIELDS, James * H
SHIELDS, John Franklin 2
SHIELDS, John Knight 1
SHIELDS, Paul Vincent 4
SHIELDS, Roy Franklin 4
SHIELDS, Thomas Edward 1
SHIELDS, Thomas Todhunter 3
SHIELDS, William S. 1
SHIELS, Albert 1
SHIELS, George Franklin 2
SHIELS, James 5
SHIENTAG, Bernard Lloyd 3
SHIER, Calrton S. 3
SHIGEMITSU, Mamoru 4
SHIKELLAMY, H
SHILLABER, Benjamin Penhallow 3
SHILLADY, John R. 5
SHILLING, Alexander 1
SHILLINGLAW, David Lee 6
SHILOAH, Reuven 5
SHIMEK, Bohumil 1

SHIMER, Hervey Woodburn 4
SHIMER, Porter William 1
SHIMP, Herbert Gilby 2
SHINE, Francis Eppes 4
SHINGLER, Don Gilmore 4
SHINKLE, Edward Marsh 4
SHINKMAN, Paul Alfred 6
SHINN, Asa H
SHINN, Charles Howard 1
SHINN, Everett 3
SHINN, Florence Scovel 4
SHINN, George Wolfe 1
SHINN, Henry Arthur 2
SHINN, John Calvin 6
SHINN, Milicent Washburn H
SHINN, William Norton H
SHIPHERD, H(enry) Robinson 6
SHIPHERD, John Jay H
SHIPHERD, Zebulon Rudd H
SHIPLE, George J. 3
SHIPLEE, Charles Raymond 4
SHIPLEY, Edward Ellis 1
SHIPLEY, Frederick William 2
SHIPLEY, George 2
SHIPLEY, Maynard 1
SHIPLEY, Richard Larkin 2
SHIPLEY, Samuel R. 1
SHIPLEY, Walter Penn 2
SHIPLEY, William Stewart 3
SHIPMAN, Arthur Leffingwell 1
SHIPMAN, Benjamin Jonson 4
SHIPMAN, Herbert 1
SHIPMAN, Louis Evan 1
SHIPMAN, Nathaniel 1
SHIPMAN, Samuel 1
SHIPMAN, William Rollin 1
SHIPP, Albert Micajah H
SHIPP, Barnard 4
SHIPP, Cameron 4
SHIPP, Frederic B. 1
SHIPP, Scott 1
SHIPP, Thomas Roerty 3
SHIPPEE, Lester Burrell 2
SHIPPEN, Edward * H
SHIPPEN, Edward 1
SHIPPEN, Eugene Rodman 3
SHIPPEN, Joseph 1
SHIPPEN, Rush Rhees 1
SHIPPEN, William * H
SHIPPEY, (Henry) Lee 5
SHIPSEY, Edward 1
SHIPSTEAD, Henrik 4
SHIPTON, A. W. 4
SHIPTON, Clifford Kenyon 6
SHIPTON, James Ancil 1
SHIR, Martin M. 6
SHIRAS, George III 2
SHIRAS, George Jr. 1
SHIRAS, Oliver Perry 1
SHIRER, John Wesley 6
SHIRLAW, Walter 1
SHIRLEY, Cassius Clay 4
SHIRLEY, Robert Kirby 3
SHIRLEY, William H
SHIVE, John W(esley) 5
SHIVELY, Benjamin Franklin 1
SHIVELY, Carlton Adamson 3
SHIVERICK, Asa 1
SHIVERS, R. Kevin 4
SHLENKER, Irvin Morris 5
SHOAFF, Fred B. 4
SHOALS, George 4
SHOBER, Francis E. 4
SHOBER, Francis Edwin H
SHOBER, John Bedford 1
SHOCK, Thomas Macy 4
SHOCK, William Henry 4
SHOCKLEY, Frank William 3
SHOCKLEY, M. Augustus Wroten 5
SHOEMAKER, Charles Chalmers 1
SHOEMAKER, Charles Frederick 1
SHOEMAKER, Daniel Naylor 5
SHOEMAKER, Harlan 2
SHOEMAKER, Henry Francis 1
SHOEMAKER, Henry Wharton 4
SHOEMAKER, John Vietch 1
SHOEMAKER, Joseph Addison 5
SHOEMAKER, Lazarus Denison H
SHOEMAKER, Michael Myers 1

SHOEMAKER, Rachel Hinkle 1
SHOEMAKER, Raymond L. 4
SHOEMAKER, Richard Heston 5
SHOEMAKER, Robert H
SHOEMAKER, Samuel Moor 4
SHOEMAKER, Waite Almon 1
SHOEMAKER, William Rawle 1
SHOENBERG, Sydney Melville 6
SHOFFSTALL, Arthur Scott 1
SHOFNER, Orman Eugene 6
SHOHAT, James Alexander 2
SHOHL, Walter Max 5
SHOLES, Christopher Latham H
SHOLLEY, Sidney Llewellyn 3
SHOLTZ, David 3
SHOMO, E. H. 5
SHONNARD, Christy Fox 6
SHONTS, Theodore Perry 4
SHONTZ, Vernon Lloyd 3
SHOOK, Alfred M. 1
SHOOK, Charles Francis 4
SHOOK, Edgar 5
SHOOK, Glenn Alfred 3
SHOONMAKER, Marius 1
SHOOP, Clarence Adelbert 4
SHOOP, Duke 3
SHOOP, John Daniel 1
SHOPE, Richard Edwin 4
SHOPE, Simeon P. 1
SHOR, Franc Marion Luther 6
SHOR, George Gershon 5
SHORE, Clarence Albert 1
SHORE, Maurice J. 4
SHORES, Robert James 6
SHOREY, Clyde Everett 4
SHOREY, Paul 1
SHORIKI, Matsutaro 5
SHORT, Albert H
SHORT, Charles H
SHORT, Charles Wilkins H
SHORT, Francis Burgette 1
SHORT, Frank Hamilton 1
SHORT, Joseph 3
SHORT, Joseph Hudson Jr. 4
SHORT, Josephine Helena 1
SHORT, Livingston Lyman 4
SHORT, Sidney Howe 1
SHORT, Wallace Mertin 5
SHORT, Walter Campbell 2
SHORT, William H
SHORT, William Harrison 1
SHORT, Zuber Nathaniel 5
SHORTALL, John G. 1
SHORTALL, Thomas Francis 4
SHORTER, Eli Sims H
SHORTER, John Gill H
SHORTLE, Abraham Given 1
SHORTLIDGE, Jonathan Chauncey 1
SHORTRIDGE, Charles M. 4
SHORTRIDGE, N. Parker 1
SHORTRIDGE, Samuel Morgan 3
SHORTRIDGE, Wilson Peter 6
SHORTS, Bruce Carman 4
SHORTS, Robert Perry 6
SHORTT, Elster Clayton 4
SHOSTAKOVICH, Dmitri 4
SHOTT, Hugh Ike 3
SHOTWELL, Abel V. 1
SHOTWELL, James Thomson 4
SHOUDY, Loyal Ambrose 4
SHOUDY, William Allen 6
SHOULDERS, Harrison H. 1
SHOUP, Arthur Glendinning 2
SHOUP, Earl Leon 1
SHOUP, Eldon Campbell 3
SHOUP, Francis Asbury H
SHOUP, George Laird 1
SHOUP, Guy V. 5
SHOUP, Merrill Edgar 4
SHOUP, Oliver Henry 1
SHOUP, Paul 2
SHOUSE, James D. 4
SHOUSE, Jouett 6
SHOVE, Eugene Percy 4
SHOW, Arley Barthlow 1
SHOWALTER, Anthony Johnson 1
SHOWALTER, Jackson Whipps 1

SHOWALTER, Joseph Baltzell 4
SHOWALTER, Noah David 1
SHOWALTER, William Joseph 1
SHOWER, George Theodore 1
SHOWER, Jacob H
SHOWERMAN, Grant 1
SHOWERS, J. Balmer 4
SHOWMAN, Harry Munson 2
SHRADY, George Frederick 1
SHRADY, Henry Merwin 1
SHREVE, Charles Everett 5
SHREVE, Earl Owen 6
SHREVE, Forrest 3
SHREVE, Henry Miller H
SHREVE, Milton William 1
SHREVE, Richmond Harold 2
SHREVE, Thomas Hopkins H
SHREVE, Wickliffe Winston 4
SHRINER, Charles Anthony 3
SHRINER, Herb 5
SHRIVER, Alfred H
SHRIVER, Alfred Jenkins 1
SHRIVER, George McLean 2
SHRIVER, John Shultz 1
SHRIVER, William Payne 3
SHRODER, William Jacob 5
SHROPSHIRE, Courtney William 4
SHROYER, Curtis Clinton 6
SHRUM, George Dixon 4
SHRYOCK, Burnett Henry Sr. 5
SHRYOCK, Gideon H
SHRYOCK, Henry William 1
SHRYOCK, Joseph Grundy 3
SHRYOCK, Richard Harrison 1
SHUBERT, Jacob J. 4
SHUBERT, Lee 3
SHUBRICK, John Templer H
SHUBRICK, William Branford H
SHUCK, Jehu Lewis 1
SHUEY, Edwin Longstreet 1
SHUEY, Lillian Hinman 4
SHUEY, William John 1
SHUFELDT, Robert Wilson H
SHUFELDT, Robert Wilson 1
SHUFF, John A. 5
SHUFORD, A. Alex Jr. 1
SHUFORD, Alonzo Craig 1
SHUFORD, Forrest Herman 4
SHUFORD, George A. 4
SHUGERMAN, Abe Louis 4
SHULER, Ellis W. 3
SHULER, Robert Pierce (Bob Shuler) 6
SHULL, A. Franklin 4
SHULL, Charles Albert 6
SHULL, Charles Graves 1
SHULL, Deloss Carlton 1
SHULL, Deloss P. 4
SHULL, Frank Leslie 1
SHULL, George Harrison 3
SHULL, James Marion 2
SHULL, Joseph H. 6
SHULLENBERGER, William Arthur 1
SHULMAN, Charles E. 5
SHULMAN, Harry 3
SHULTERS, Hoyt Volney 1
SHULTZ, William John 5
SHULZ, Adolph Robert 4
SHULZE, John Andrew H
SHUMAKER, E. Ellsworth 4
SHUMAKER, Edward Seitz 1
SHUMAKER, Ross W. 4
SHUMAN, Abraham 1
SHUMAN, Davis 4
SHUMAN, Edwin Llewellyn 1
SHUMAN, John Franklin 1
SHUMATE, Roger V. 3
SHUMATE, Wade Hampton 1
SHUMBERGER, John Calvin 4
SHUMWAY, Adelina Ritter 6
SHUMWAY, Daniel Bussier 1
SHUMWAY, Edgar Solomon 1
SHUMWAY, Edward D. 4
SHUMWAY, Sherman N. 3
SHUMWAY, Waldo 4
SHUMWAY, Walter Bradley 1
SHUNK, Francis Rawn H
SHUNK, Joseph Lorain 1
SHUNK, William Alexander 1
SHUNK, William Findlay 1
SHUPE, Henry Fox 1
SHUPING, Clarence Leroy 5
SHURCLIFF, Arthur Asahel 3
SHURLY, Burt Russell 5

SHURTER, Edwin DuBois 2
SHURTER, Robert LaFevre 6
SHURTLEFF, Charles Allerton
SHURTLEFF, Ernest Warburton 1
SHURTLEFF, Eugene 3
SHURTLEFF, Flavel 6
SHURTLEFF, Glen Kassimer 1
SHURTLEFF, Nathaniel Bradstreet H
SHURTLEFF, Roswell Morse 1
SHUSTER, W. Morgan 4
SHUTE, Abraham Lincoln 1
SHUTE, Daniel Kerfoot 1
SHUTE, Emmett R. 4
SHUTE, Henry Augustus 4
SHUTE, Nevil 3
SHUTE, Nevil 4
SHUTE, Samuel H
SHUTE, Samuel Moore 1
SHUTTER, Marion Daniel 1
SHUTTLEWORTH, V. Craven 4
SHUTTS, Frank Barker 1
SHVERNIK, Nikola (Mikhallvich) 5
SHY, George Milton 4
SIAS, Ernest J. 3
SIBELIUS, Jean Julius Christian
SIBERELL, Lloyd E. 5
SIBERT, William Luther 4
SIBLEY, Bolling 2
SIBLEY, Clyde Lawson 4
SIBLEY, Edwin Henry 4
SIBLEY, Frank J. 3
SIBLEY, Frederick Hubbard 1
SIBLEY, Frederick W. 1
SIBLEY, George Champlain H
SIBLEY, George H. 6
SIBLEY, Harper H
SIBLEY, Henry Hastings H
SIBLEY, Hiram H
SIBLEY, Hiram Luther 1
SIBLEY, John H
SIBLEY, John Langdon H
SIBLEY, Jonas 2
SIBLEY, Joseph Crocker 1
SIBLEY, Josiah 5
SIBLEY, Mark Hopkins H
SIBLEY, Robert 3
SIBLEY, Rufus Adams 4
SIBLEY, Samuel Hale 3
SIBLEY, Solomon H
SIBLEY, William Giddings 1
SICARD, Montgomery 1
SICELOFF, L(ewis) Parker 6
SICILIANOS, Demetrios Constantine 6
SICK, Emil George 4
SICKEL, William George 1
SICKELS, David Banks 1
SICKELS, Frederick Ellsworth H
SICKELS, Ivin 2
SICKELS, Nicholas H
SICKLES, Daniel Edgar 1
SIDAROUSS, Pasha 4
SIDBURY, James Buren 4
SIDDALL, Hugh Wagstaff 4
SIDDALL, John MacAlpine 1
SIDDONS, Frederick Lincoln 1
SIDELL, William Henry H
SIDERS, Walter Raleigh 1
SIDGREAVES, Sir Arthur F. 3
SIDI MUHAMMED H
SIDIS, Boris 1
SIDLEY, William Pratt 3
SIDLO, Thomas L. 3
SIDNEY, Margaret 1
SIDO, George Henry 3
SIDWELL, Thomas Watson 1
SIEBECKER, Robert George 1
SIEBEL, John Ewald 1
SIEBENTHAL, Claude Ellsworth
SIEBERT, Wilbur Henry 4
SIECK, Louis John 3
SIEDENBURG, Frederic 1
SIEDER, Otto F. 5
SIEFERT, Henry Otto Rudolf 1
SIEFF, Israel Moses 5
SIEFKIN, C. Gordon 4
SIEFKIN, Forest De Witt 4
SIEFKIN, George 4
SIEG, Lee Paul 4
SIEGEL, David Porter 3
SIEGEL, David Tevel 4
SIEGEL, Irwin 5

SIEGEL, Isaac 2
SIEGEL, Keeve Milton 6
SIEGEL, Lester 5
SIEGEL, Roy Richard 6
SIEGEL, William Ely 6
SIEGRIST, Mary 3
SIELAFF, Gustav Julius 4
SIEMON, Daniel William 4
SIEMONN, George 3
SIEMS, Allan Gleason 2
SIENI, Cyril 4
SIES, Raymond William 1
SIEVERS, Fred John 3
SIEVERS, Frederick William 4
SIEVERT, Leo Ellsworth 1
SIFTON, Harry Austin 4
SIFTON, Victor 4
SIGALL, Joseph de 3
SIGEL, Franz * 1
SIGERFOOS, Charles Peter 4
SIGERIST, Henry Ernest 4
SIGLER, Thomas Amon 3
SIGMAN, Jules Israel 6
SIGMUND, Frederick Lester 4
SIGMUND, Jay G. 1
SIGNER, Merton I. 3
SIGOURNEY, Lydia Howard Huntley H
SIGSBEE, Charles Dwight 1
SIHLER, Ernest Gottlieb 1
SIKES, Clarence S. 5
SIKES, Enoch Walter 1
SIKES, George Cushing 1
SIKES, William Wirt H
SIKORSKY, Igor I. 5
SILBERBERG, Mendel B. 4
SILBERMAN, Alfred M. 2
SILBERMAN, M. J. 4
SILBERSACK, Walter Frank 4
SILBERSTEIN, Ludwik 2
SILCOX, Ferdinand Augustus 1
SILCOX, John B. 4
SILER, Vinton Earnest 5
SILIN, Charles Intervale 6
SILKETT, Albert Frank 4
SILKNITTER, G. F. 3
SILL, Anna Peck H
SILL, Edward Rowland H
SILL, Frederick Herbert 3
SILL, John Mahelm Berry 1
SILL, Louise Morgan 4
SILL, Thomas Hale 4
SILLANPAA, Frans Emil 4
SILLEN, Lars Gunnar 5
SILLIMAN, Augustus Ely H
SILLIMAN, Benjamin H
SILLIMAN, Benjamin Jr. H
SILLIMAN, Charles Augustus 1
SILLIMAN, Harry Inness 5
SILLIMAN, Reuben Daniel 4
SILLOWAY, Thomas William 1
SILLS, Kenneth Charles Morton 3
SILLS, Milton 1
SILSBEE, Arthur Boardman 1
SILSBEE, Nathaniel H
SILSBY, Wilson 3
SILVA, William Posey 4
SILVER, Abba Hillel 4
SILVER, Arthur Elmer 3
SILVER, Ernest Leroy 3
SILVER, Francis Aloysius 6
SILVER, Gray 1
SILVER, H. Percy 4
SILVER, Jesse Forrest 5
SILVER, Maxwell 4
SILVER, Thomas H
SILVERA, Frank Alvin 5
SILVERCRUYS, Baron 4
SILVERCRUYS, Suzanne (Mrs. Edward Ford Stevenson) 6
SILVERMAN, Alexander 4
SILVERMAN, Archibald 4
SILVERMAN, David 3
SILVERMAN, Irving 3
SILVERMAN, Joseph 1
SILVERMAN, Leslie 5
SILVERMAN, Morris 5
SILVERMAN, Roland E. 6
SILVERMAN, Sime 1
SILVERMAN, Sime 4
SILVERS, Earl Reed 2
SILVESTER, Lindsay McDonald 4
SILVESTER, Peter H
SILVESTER, Peter Henry 4
SILVESTER, Richard William 4
SILVEUS, William Arents 5
SILZER, George S. 1

SIM, John Robert 1
SIMES, Lewis Mallalleu 6
SIMIC, Stanoje 5
SIMKHOVITCH, Mary Melinda Kingsbury 3
SIMKHOVITCH, Vladimir Gregorievitch 3
SIMKINS, Eldred H
SIMKINS, Henry Walter 1
SIMKINS, William Stewart 1
SIMLER, George Brenner 5
SIMLEY, Irvin T. 5
SIMMILL, Elvin Raymond 5
SIMMONDS, Albert Carleton Jr. 4
SIMMONDS, Frank William 5
SIMMONS, Daniel Augustus 5
SIMMONS, David Andrew 4
SIMMONS, Dayton Cooper 3
SIMMONS, Dwight Lane 5
SIMMONS, Edward 1
SIMMONS, Edward Alfred 1
SIMMONS, Edward Campbell 1
SIMMONS, Edward Henry Harriman 3
SIMMONS, Elizabeth Margret 2
SIMMONS, Ernest J. 5
SIMMONS, Franklin 1
SIMMONS, Furnifold McLendell 1
SIMMONS, Geo Finlay 3
SIMMONS, George Abel H
SIMMONS, George E(vans) 5
SIMMONS, George H. 1
SIMMONS, George Welch 1
SIMMONS, Grant G(ilbert) Sr. 6
SIMMONS, Henry Clay 1
SIMMONS, Henry Martyn 1
SIMMONS, J. Edward 1
SIMMONS, J. P. 4
SIMMONS, James Fowler H
SIMMONS, James Henry 5
SIMMONS, James Stevens 3
SIMMONS, James William 5
SIMMONS, John F. 4
SIMMONS, Leo Charles 3
SIMMONS, Lessie Southgate 1
SIMMONS, Robert Cantrell 4
SIMMONS, Thomas J. 3
SIMMONS, Thomas Jackson 2
SIMMONS, Thomas Jefferson H
SIMMONS, Virgil M. 3
SIMMONS, Wallace Delafield 4
SIMMONS, Warren Seabury 2
SIMMONS, Will 1
SIMMONS, William Marvin 1
SIMMS, Albert Gallatin 4
SIMMS, Jeptha Root H
SIMMS, John Field 3
SIMMS, Joseph 1
SIMMS, Lewis Wesley 3
SIMMS, Paris Marion 3
SIMMS, Ruth Hanna 2
SIMMS, S. Chapman 1
SIMMS, William Elliot H
SIMMS, William Gilmore H
SIMMS, William Philip 3
SIMON, Abram 1
SIMON, Andre Louis 5
SIMON, Charles Edmund 1
SIMON, Clarence Joseph 6
SIMON, Clarence Turkle 5
SIMON, Edward Paul 4
SIMON, Sir Francis 3
SIMON, Franklin 1
SIMON, Frederick M. 4
SIMON, Grant Miles 5
SIMON, Henry William 5
SIMON, Joseph 1
SIMON, Julian Edwin 4
SIMON, Leon Charles 3
SIMON, Louis A. 3
SIMON, Naif Louis 4
SIMON, Richard Leo 4
SIMON, Webster Godman 6
SIMON, William 3
SIMON, Yves R. 4
SIMOND, Louis H
SIMOND, Maynard Ewing 4
SIMONDS, Alvan Tracy 5
SIMONDS, Frank H. 1
SIMONDS, Frederic William 1
SIMONDS, George Sherwin 1
SIMONDS, Gifford 3
SIMONDS, Godfrey Baldwin 3
SIMONDS, James Persons 4
SIMONDS, Ossian Cole 1
SIMONDS, William H
SIMONDS, William Adams 4
SIMONDS, William Edgar 1
SIMONDS, William Edward 2
SIMONE, G. F. Edgardo 2
SIMONS, Algie Martin 3
SIMONS, Amory Coffin 5
SIMONS, Charles Casper 4
SIMONS, George Albert 3
SIMONS, Hans 5
SIMONS, Howard Perry 4
SIMONS, James 1
SIMONS, Kenneth W. 2
SIMONS, Manley Hale 6
SIMONS, May Wood 2
SIMONS, Minot 1
SIMONS, Samuel H
SIMONS, Sarah Emma 4
SIMONS, Wilford Collins 3
SIMONSON, Gustave 4
SIMONSON, Henry James Jr. 4
SIMONSON, Lee 3
SIMONSON, William A. 1
SIMONTON, Charles H. 1
SIMONTON, Ida Vera 1
SIMONTON, James H
SIMONTON, John Wiggins 1
SIMONTON, William H
SIMPICH, Frederick 2
SIMPKINS, George W. 4
SIMPSON, Albert B. 1
SIMPSON, Alex Jr. 1
SIMPSON, Alfred Dexter 3
SIMPSON, Charles Torrey 1
SIMPSON, Charles William 6
SIMPSON, Clarence 5
SIMPSON, Clarence L(orenzo) 4
SIMPSON, Clarence Oliver 6
SIMPSON, Cuthbert 5
SIMPSON, David Ferguson Aikman 1
SIMPSON, Edmund H
SIMPSON, Edward H
SIMPSON, Edward 1
SIMPSON, Floyd Robert 6
SIMPSON, Frances 4
SIMPSON, Frank Edward 2
SIMPSON, Frank Farrow 1
SIMPSON, Frank Leslie 5
SIMPSON, French 1
SIMPSON, Hartley 5
SIMPSON, Herbert Downs 5
SIMPSON, Herman 5
SIMPSON, Howard Edwin 1
SIMPSON, James 1
SIMPSON, James Jr. 3
SIMPSON, James Alexander 4
SIMPSON, James Clarke 2
SIMPSON, James Hervey H
SIMPSON, James Inglis 3
SIMPSON, Jerry 1
SIMPSON, Jesse L. 6
SIMPSON, John 1
SIMPSON, John A. 1
SIMPSON, John Childs 4
SIMPSON, John Dixon 4
SIMPSON, John Frederick 6
SIMPSON, John Nathan 2
SIMPSON, John R. 3
SIMPSON, John R. 6
SIMPSON, John William 6
SIMPSON, John Woodruff 1
SIMPSON, Joseph Warren 2
SIMPSON, Josephine Sarles 4
SIMPSON, Kemper 6
SIMPSON, Kenneth Farrand 1
SIMPSON, Kenneth Miller 4
SIMPSON, Kirke Larue 5
SIMPSON, Lola Jean 6
SIMPSON, Marcus De Lafayette 5
SIMPSON, Matthew H
SIMPSON, Michael Hodge H
SIMPSON, Richard Franklin H
SIMPSON, Richard Lee 5
SIMPSON, Richard Murray 3
SIMPSON, Richard Murray 4
SIMPSON, Robert 1
SIMPSON, Robert Edward 5
SIMPSON, Robert Tennent 1
SIMPSON, Samuel 3
SIMPSON, Sid 3
SIMPSON, Sidney Post 4
SIMPSON, Sloan 5
SIMPSON, Stephen H
SIMPSON, Sumner 3
SIMPSON, Sutherland 1
SIMPSON, Thomas McNider Jr. 4
SIMPSON, Virgil Earl 2

SIMPSON, William 4
SIMPSON, William Augustus
SIMPSON, William B. 2
SIMPSON, William Dunlap H
SIMPSON, William James 1
SIMPSON, William Kelly 1
SIMPSON, William Robert 6
SIMRALL, Josephine Price 2
SIMRELL, William Le Grand 1
SIMS, Alexander Dromgoole H
SIMS, Alva Ray 4
SIMS, Cecil 5
SIMS, Charles Abercrombie 2
SIMS, Charles N. H
SIMS, Charles N. 4
SIMS, Clifford Stanley 1
SIMS, Edwin W. 2
SIMS, Frederick Wilmer 4
SIMS, Harry Marion 4
SIMS, Henry Upson 4
SIMS, James Marion H
SIMS, John Francis 1
SIMS, Leonard Henly H
SIMS, Marian McCamy 4
SIMS, Newell LeRoy 4
SIMS, Richard Maury 1
SIMS, Thetus Wilrette 1
SIMS, W. Scott 1
SIMS, Walter Arthur 6
SIMS, William Sowden 1
SINCERBEAUX, Frank H. 5
SINCLAIR, Alexander Doull 4
SINCLAIR, Alexander Grant 1
SINCLAIR, Angus 1
SINCLAIR, Earle Westwood 2
SINCLAIR, Harold Augustus 4
SINCLAIR, Harry Ford 3
SINCLAIR, James Herbert 2
SINCLAIR, John Elbridge 1
SINCLAIR, John Franklin 3
SINCLAIR, John Stephens 5
SINCLAIR, Lee Wiley 1
SINCLAIR, Peter Thomas 5
SINCLAIR, Robert Soutter 1
SINCLAIR, W. R. 4
SINCLAIR, William 1
SINCLAIR, William Albert 4
SINDEBAND, Maurice Leonard 5
SINDELAR, Paul Joseph 6
SINEK, William J. 4
SINGER, Berthold 1
SINGER, Edgar Arthur Jr. 3
SINGER, Frederic 4
SINGER, Frederick George 5
SINGER, Harold Douglas 1
SINGER, Harold Ralph 2
SINGER, Henry B. 6
SINGER, Isaac Merrit H
SINGER, Isidore 1
SINGER, Israel Joshua 2
SINGER, Otto H
SINGER, Russell E. 6
SINGER, Willard Edison 5
SINGER, William H. Jr. 3
SINGERLY, William Miskey 1
SINGH, Raja Sir Maharaj 6
SINGLETARY, B. Henry 4
SINGLETON, Albert Olin 2
SINGLETON, Asa Leon 2
SINGLETON, Esther 1
SINGLETON, James Washington H
SINGLETON, Marvin Edward 1
SINGLETON, Otho Robards H
SINGLETON, Thomas Day 4
SINGLETON, William Daniel 5
SINGLEY, Albert Henry 6
SINGLEY, B. Lloyd 4
SINGMASTER, Elsie 3
SINGMASTER, James Arthur 4
SINGMASTER, John Alden 1
SINK, Charles Albert 5
SINK, Robert Frederick 4
SINKLER, John P. B. 3
SINKLER, Wharton 1
SINNICKSON, Thomas * H
SINNOTT, Alfred Arthur 3
SINNOTT, Arthur J. 2
SINNOTT, Edmund Ware 4
SINNOTT, Nicholas John 1
SINSEL, Rupert Alston 5
SINZ, Walter Alexander 4
SIODMAK, Robert 6
SIONS, Harry 6
SIOUSSAT, St George Leakin 4

SIPLE, Paul Allman	5			

SIPLE, Paul Allman 5
SIPPEL, Bettie Manroe 5
SIPPLE, Chester Ellsworth 4
SIPPLE, Leslie B. 6
SIPPY, Bertram Welton 1
SIPPY, John Johnson 1
SIQUEIROS, David Alfaro 6
SIQUELAND, Tryggve Albert 1
SIRES, Ronald Vernon 5
SIROIS, Edward D. 4
SIROKY, Villem 5
SIROVICH, William I. 1
SIRRINE, Joseph Emory 5
SISAM, Charles Herschel 3
SISAVANG VONG 3
SISCO, Frank Thayer 4
SISCO, Gordon A. 3
SISCOE, Frank Gotch 5
SISE, Lincoln Fleetford 2
SISE, Paul F. 3
SISLEY, Lyman A. 1
SISSON, Charles Newton 2
SISSON, Charles Peck 1
SISSON, Edgar Grant 2
SISSON, Edward Octavius 1
SISSON, Francis Hinckley 1
SISSON, Fred James 2
SISSON, Jean 5
SISSON, Septimus 1
SISSON, Thomas Upton 1
SISTO, Louis Stanley 5
SITES, Frank Crawford 4
SITGREAVES, Charles H
SITGREAVES, John H
SITGREAVES, Samuel H
SITJAR, Buenaventura H
SITTERLY, Charles Fremont 2
SITTING BULL H
SITWELL, Dame Edith H
SITWELL, (Sir) Osbert 5
SIVITER, Anna Pierpont 1
SIVITER, William Henry 1
SIVRIGHT, Cal 2
SIZER, Lawrence Bradford 5
SIZER, Nelson 4
SIZER, Theodore 4
SIZOO, Joseph Richard 5
SJOLANDER, John Peter 4
SJOQVIST, Erik 6
SKAGGS, William Henry 2
SKANIADARIIO H
SKAPSKI, Adam Stanislas 5
SKARIATINA, Irina 4
SKARSTEDT, Ernst Teofil 2
SKAUG, Arne 6
SKAUG, Julius 6
SKEEL, Adelaide 5
SKEEL, Franklin Deuel 1
SKEEL, Roland Edward 1
SKEELE, Walter Fisher 1
SKEELS, Wines Harris 5
SKEEN, John A. 1
SKELLEY, William Charles 3
SKELLEY, William Grove 1
SKELTON, Charles H
SKELTON, Henrietta 1
SKELTON, Leslie James 1
SKELTON, William B. 1
SKENANDOA H
SKENE, Alexander Johnston Chalmers 1
SKERPAN, Alfred Andrew 5
SKEVINGTON, Samuel John 2
SKEWES, James Henry 1
SKIDMORE, Charles H. 5
SKIDMORE, Hubert Standish 2
SKIDMORE, Lemuel 4
SKIDMORE, Louis 4
SKIDMORE, Louis 5
SKIFF, Frederick James Volney 1
SKIFTER, Hector Randolph 4
SKILES, Jonah William Durward 4
SKILES, William Vernon 2
SKILES, William Woodburn 1
SKILLERN, Ross Hall 1
SKILLIN, John H
SKILLIN, Simeon H
SKILLIN, Simeon Jr. H
SKILLING, David Miller 1
SKILLING, William Thompson 5
SKILLMAN, Thomas Julien 1
SKILTON, Charles Sanford 1
SKILTON, DeWitt Clinton 1
SKILTON, John Davis 3
SKINNER, Aaron Nichols 1
SKINNER, Alburn Edward 5
SKINNER, Avery Warner 1
SKINNER, Belle 1
SKINNER, Beverly Oden 5

SKINNER, Charles Drake 3
SKINNER, Charles Edward* 3
SKINNER, Charles H(enry) 6
SKINNER, Charles Montgomery 1
SKINNER, Charles Rufus 1
SKINNER, Charles Wilbur 2
SKINNER, Clarence Aurelius 5
SKINNER, Clarence Edward 4
SKINNER, Clarence Russell 2
SKINNER, Constance Lindsay 1
SKINNER, David A. 5
SKINNER, David William 6
SKINNER, Edward Holman 3
SKINNER, Eleanor Louise 3
SKINNER, Ernest Brown 1
SKINNER, Ernest M. 5
SKINNER, Eugene William 4
SKINNER, Frank Woodward 4
SKINNER, Halcyon H
SKINNER, Harold Stanfield 4
SKINNER, Harry 4
SKINNER, Henrietta Channing Dana 1
SKINNER, Henry 1
SKINNER, Howard K. 5
SKINNER, Hubert Marshall 1
SKINNER, James M. 3
SKINNER, James M(ortimer) Jr. 6
SKINNER, James W. 4
SKINNER, John Harrison 2
SKINNER, John Stuart H
SKINNER, Joseph Allen 2
SKINNER, Laurence Hervey 2
SKINNER, Lewis Bailey 5
SKINNER, Otis 1
SKINNER, Paul Butler 5
SKINNER, Richard H
SKINNER, Robert P. 4
SKINNER, Stella 1
SKINNER, Thomas Clagett 1
SKINNER, Thomas Harvey H
SKINNER, Thomson Joseph H
SKINNER, William 1
SKINNER, William 2
SKINNER, William Converse 1
SKINNER, William Woolford 5
SKIPPER, Glenn Blount 1
SKOG, Charles Arthur 4
SKOGH, Harriet Mathilda 4
SKOGMO, Philip Waldo 3
SKOOG, Andrew Leonard 4
SKOOG, Bertil O. 6
SKOOG, Karl Frederick 1
SKORNECK, Alan Bernard 4
SKOTTSBERG, Carl Johan F. 4
SKOURAS, George P. 4
SKOURAS, Spyros P. 5
SKUCE, Walter Charles 6
SKULNIK, Menasha 5
SLABAUGH, Harold Watson 5
SLACK, Charles Morse 5
SLACK, Charles William 2
SLACK, Leighton P. 1
SLACK, L(emuel) Ert(us) 5
SLACK, Munsey 4
SLADE, Albert Arthur 5
SLADE, Arthur Joseph 4
SLADE, Caleb Arnold 4
SLADE, Caroline McCormick 3
SLADE, Charles H
SLADE, Charles Blount 2
SLADE, Emma Maleen Hardy 4
SLADE, George Theron 1
SLADE, John C. 4
SLADE, Joseph Alfred H
SLADE, William 1
SLADE, William Adams 3
SLADEN, Fred Winchester 2
SLAFTER, Edmund Farwell 1
SLAGHT, William Ernest Andrew 1
SLAGLE, Dean 4
SLAGLE, Robert Lincoln 1
SLARROW, Malcolm G. 4
SLATE, Frederick 1
SLATE, William L. 4
SLATEN, Arthur Wakefield 2
SLATER, A. James 4
SLATER, Denniston Lyon 5
SLATER, Fred C. 4
SLATER, Harry George 1
SLATER, Hughes de Courcy 5

SLATER, John Fox H
SLATER, Samuel H
SLATER, William Albert 4
SLATER, William Kershaw 5
SLATER, Woodson Taylor 4
SLATON, John Marshall 3
SLATTERY, Charles Lewis 1
SLATTERY, Harry 2
SLATTERY, James M. 2
SLATTERY, John Lawrence 6
SLATTERY, John Theodore 1
SLATTERY, Margaret 2
SLATTON, Charles Stewart 3
SLAUGHT, Herbert Ellsworth 1
SLAUGHTER, Christopher C. 1
SLAUGHTER, Danely Philip 5
SLAUGHTER, Donald 3
SLAUGHTER, Harvey Leroy 4
SLAUGHTER, John Willis 1
SLAUGHTER, Moses Stephen 1
SLAUGHTER, Philip H
SLAUGHTER, Seth Warren 5
SLAVEN, Henry Bartholomew 1
SLAVENS, Thomas Horace 4
SLAVIN, Robert Joseph 4
SLAWSON, Chester Baker 4
SLAYDEN, James Luther 1
SLAYMAKER, Amos H
SLAYMAKER, Philip K. 3
SLAYTER, Games 4
SLECHTA, Mary Rose 6
SLEDD, Andrew 1
SLEDD, Benjamin 1
SLEDGE, William Whitfield 4
SLEE, John B. 2
SLEEPER, Albert E. 1
SLEEPER, Harold Reeve 4
SLEEPER, Henry Dike 2
SLEEPER, Jacob H
SLEETER, Richard L. 6
SLEICHER, John A. 1
SLEIGHT, Charles Lee 4
SLEMONS, Clyde C. 5
SLEMONS, Josiah Morris 2
SLEMP, Campbell 1
SLEMP, Campbell Bascom 2
SLENKER, Elmina Drake 1
SLENTZ, Samuel D. 3
SLEPIAN, Joseph 5
SLESER, James Clyde Jr. 2
SLEYSTER, Rock 2
SLEZAK, Leo 2
SLICER, Thomas Roberts 1
SLICHTER, Allen McKinnon 6
SLICHTER, Charles Sumner 2
SLICHTER, Sumner Huber 3
SLICHTER, Walter Irvine 5
SLICK, Thomas Baker 1
SLICK, Thomas Whitten 3
SLIDELL, John H
SLIFER, Hiram Joseph 1
SLIM, Mongi 5
SLIM, William 5
SLINGERLAND, John I. H
SLINGERLAND, Mark Vernon 1
SLINGLAND, George Kuett 6
SLINGLUFF, Jesse 3
SLINKER, Clay Dean 4
SLIPHER, Vesto Melvin 5
SLOAN, Alfred Pritchard Jr. 4
SLOAN, Andrew H
SLOAN, Andrew Scott H
SLOAN, Benjamin 4
SLOAN, Charles H. 2
SLOAN, Duncan Lindley 5
SLOAN, Edgar J. 2
SLOAN, Edwin P. 1
SLOAN, Fergus Martin 4
SLOAN, George A. 3
SLOAN, George Beale 4
SLOAN, Gordon McGregor 4
SLOAN, Harold Paul 4
SLOAN, Hubert John 6
SLOAN, James 1
SLOAN, James Forman 3
SLOAN, James Forman 4
SLOAN, John 3
SLOAN, Laurence Henry 2
SLOAN, LeRoy Hendrick 4
SLOAN, Marianna 1
SLOAN, Mary Herron 6
SLOAN, Matthew Scott 2
SLOAN, Richard E. 1
SLOAN, Robert James 5
SLOAN, Samuel * 1
SLOAN, Thomas Wylie 3

SLOAN, William Franklin 3
SLOANE, Alfred Baldwin 1
SLOANE, Charles Swift 1
SLOANE, John H
SLOANE, John 1
SLOANE, Jonathan H
SLOANE, Joseph Curtis 5
SLOANE, Rush Richard 5
SLOANE, T. O'Conor 1
SLOANE, Thomas Morrison 1
SLOANE, William 1
SLOANE, William A. 1
SLOANE, William Milligan 1
SLOANE, William (Milligan III) 6
SLOAT, John Drake 1
SLOBIN, Hermon Lester H
SLOBODKIN, Louis 6
SLOCTEMEYER, Hugo Ferdinand 1
SLOCUM, Arthur Gaylord 1
SLOCUM, Charles Elihu 1
SLOCUM, Clarence Alfred 3
SLOCUM, Clarence Rice 1
SLOCUM, Francis H
SLOCUM, Frederick 2
SLOCUM, George Warren 4
SLOCUM, Henry Warner H
SLOCUM, Herbert Jermain 1
SLOCUM, Joseph H
SLOCUM, Joshua 1
SLOCUM, Joshua 4
SLOCUM, Lorimer B. 1
SLOCUM, Richard William 3
SLOCUM, Samuel H
SLOCUM, Stephen Elmer 4
SLOCUM, Thomas Williams 1
SLOCUM, William Frederick 1
SLOCUMB, Jesse H
SLOMAN, Ernest Gaynor 3
SLONECKER, J. G. 4
SLONEKER, Howard L. 4
SLOPER, Andrew Jackson 1
SLOPER, Leslie Akers 4
SLOSS, James Withers H
SLOSS, Louis 1
SLOSS, Marcus Cauffman 4
SLOSSON, Annie Trumbull 1
SLOSSON, Edwin Emery 1
SLOSSON, Leonard Butler 4
SLOTKIN, Samuel 4
SLOTT, Mollie 6
SLOTTMAN, George Vincent 3
SLOVER, Samuel LeRoy 4
SLUSS, Homer Oscar 1
SLUSS, John William 4
SLUSSER, Charles Edward 4
SLUTER, George 1
SLUTZ, Frank D. 3
SLY, John Fairfield 4
SLY, William James 1
SLYE, Maud 3
SMADEL, Joseph Edwin 4
SMALL, Albion Woodbury 1
SMALL, Alex 4
SMALL, Alvan Edmond H
SMALL, Andrew Buchanan 1
SMALL, Benjamin Francis 5
SMALL, Charles C. 5
SMALL, Elden 1
SMALL, Ernest Gregor 2
SMALL, Francis Aloysius 4
SMALL, Frank Jr. 6
SMALL, Frederick Percival 3
SMALL, Harold Patten 2
SMALL, John Clay 5
SMALL, John D. 4
SMALL, John Humphrey 2
SMALL, John Kunkel 1
SMALL, Len 1
SMALL, Philip Lindsley 4
SMALL, Robert Scott 5
SMALL, Sam 1
SMALL, Sergine Anne (Mrs. Donald David Small) 6
SMALL, Sidney Aylmer 5
SMALL, Sydney French 6
SMALL, Vivian Blanche 2
SMALL, Willard Stanton 2
SMALL, W(illiam) A(rden) 6
SMALL, William Bradbury 1
SMALLENS, Alexander 5
SMALLEY, Bradley Barlow 1
SMALLEY, Eugene Virgil H
SMALLEY, Eugene Virgil 1
SMALLEY, Frank 1
SMALLEY, Frank Mather 5
SMALLEY, George Washburn 1
SMALLEY, Harrison Standish 1
SMALLEY, William Cameron 6

SMALLS, Robert H
SMALLS, Robert 4
SMALLSREED, George A. Sr. 4
SMALLWOOD, Della Graeme 5
SMALLWOOD, Robert Bartly 6
SMALLWOOD, William H
SMALLWOOD, William Martin 1
SMART, Charles 1
SMART, Charles Allen 4
SMART, David A. 3
SMART, Edmund Hodgson 2
SMART, Elizabeth Allen 4
SMART, Ephraim Knight H
SMART, Frank Leroy 1
SMART, George Thomas 1
SMART, Jackson Wyman 5
SMART, James D. 3
SMART, James Henry 1
SMART, John Stuart Jr. 5
SMART, Richard Addison 5
SMART, Walter Kay 6
SMATHERS, William H. 3
SMAY, Joseph Edgar 6
SMEALLIE, John Morris 2
SMEDLEY, Agnes 3
SMEDLEY, Graham B. 3
SMEDLEY, M(artin) Harvey 1
SMEDLEY, William Thomas 1
SMELO, Leon Samuel 6
SMELT, Dennis H
SMELTZ, George Washington 1
SMELTZER, Clarence Harry 5
SMELZER, Baxter Timothy 4
SMEMO, Johannes 4
SMERTENKO, Clara Millerd 5
SMET, Pierre-Jean de H
SMIBERT, John 6
SMIGEL, Erwin O. 6
SMILEY, Albert Keith 1
SMILEY, Charles Newton 1
SMILEY, Charles Wesley 5
SMILEY, Daniel 1
SMILEY, David Elmer 1
SMILEY, Dean Franklin 5
SMILEY, Elmer Ellsworth 1
SMILEY, Francis Edward 4
SMILEY, John Stanley 4
SMILEY, Lyda May 4
SMILEY, Sarah Frances 1
SMILEY, William Brownlee 1
SMILEY, William Henry 1
SMILEY, William Henry 2
SMILIE, John 4
SMILLIE, George Frederick Cumming 1
SMILLIE, George Henry 1
SMILLIE, Helen Sheldon Jacobs 1
SMILLIE, James H
SMILLIE, James David 1
SMILLIE, Thomas W. 4
SMILLIE, Wilson George 5
SMISER, James A. 1
SMISSMAN, Edward Ervin 6
SMITH, A. Alexander 1
SMITH, A. Donaldson 1
SMITH, A. Frank 4
SMITH, Abby Hadassah H
SMITH, Abiel Leonard 1
SMITH, Abraham E. 1
SMITH, Abraham Herr H
SMITH, Addison Romain 2
SMITH, Addison Taylor 3
SMITH, Adrian W. 1
SMITH, Albert * H
SMITH, Albert C. 5
SMITH, Albert Charles 5
SMITH, Albert Edward 4
SMITH, Albert Edwin 1
SMITH, Albert Holmes 1
SMITH, Albert William 1
SMITH, Albert William 1
SMITH, Albridge Clinton 1
SMITH, Alexander 1
SMITH, Alexander Coke 1
SMITH, Alexander Rogers 4
SMITH, Alexander Wyly 1
SMITH, Alfred Emanuel 2
SMITH, Alfred Franklin 5
SMITH, Alfred H. 1
SMITH, Alfred H. 4
SMITH, Alfred Theodore 1
SMITH, Alice Ravenel Huger 5
SMITH, Allard 1
SMITH, Allen 1
SMITH, Allen John 1

SMITH, Allen S. 4
SMITH, Alphonse J. 1
SMITH, Alson Jesse 5
SMITH, Alva J. 1
SMITH, Alvin Augustine 2
SMITH, Andrew Heermance 1
SMITH, Andrew Jackson H
SMITH, Andrew Thomas 1
SMITH, Anna Tolman 1
SMITH, Annie Morrill 4
SMITH, Archibald Cary 1
SMITH, Arthur H
SMITH, Arthur A. 5
SMITH, Arthur Cosslett 1
SMITH, Arthur George 1
SMITH, Arthur Henderson 1
SMITH, Arthur L. J. 2
SMITH, Arthur Mumford 5
SMITH, Arthur St Clair 2
SMITH, Asa Dodge H
SMITH, Ashbel H
SMITH, Augustus Wardlaw 1
SMITH, Azariah H
SMITH, B. Holly 1
SMITH, Barry Congar 3
SMITH, Barton 1
SMITH, Benjamin Eli 1
SMITH, Benjamin M. 3
SMITH, Benjamin Mosby H
SMITH, Bernard H
SMITH, Bessie H
SMITH, Bessie 4
SMITH, Betty 5
SMITH, Beverly Waugh Jr. 5
SMITH, Blaine Spray 3
SMITH, Bolton 1
SMITH, Boyd Milford 6
SMITH, Bradford 4
SMITH, Bridges 1
SMITH, Bruce 3
SMITH, Bruce D. 3
SMITH, Bryce Byram 4
SMITH, Buckingham H
SMITH, Burton 2
SMITH, Byron Caldwell H
SMITH, Byron Laflin 1
SMITH, C. Alphonso 1
SMITH, C. H. Erskine 6
SMITH, Caleb Blood H
SMITH, Cameron C. 1
SMITH, Carl T. 4
SMITH, Carroll Earll 4
SMITH, Cecil H. 4
SMITH, Cecil Michener 3
SMITH, Charles Axel 1
SMITH, Charles Bennett 1
SMITH, Charles Blood 1
SMITH, Charles Card 1
SMITH, Charles Carman 3
SMITH, Charles Copeland 6
SMITH, Charles Dennison 1
SMITH, Charles Edward 4
SMITH, Charles Edward 5
SMITH, Charles Emory 1
SMITH, Charles Ernest 1
SMITH, Charles Ferguson H
SMITH, Charles Foster 1
SMITH, Charles G. 4
SMITH, Charles George Percy (Lord Delacourt-Smith) 6
SMITH, Charles Grover 5
SMITH, Charles Henry * 1
SMITH, Charles Howard 3
SMITH, Charles J. 4
SMITH, Charles Jacob 4
SMITH, Charles Lavens 3
SMITH, Charles Lee 3
SMITH, Charles Lysle 5
SMITH, Charles Manley 1
SMITH, Charles Perley 2
SMITH, Charles Perrin H
SMITH, Charles Shaler H
SMITH, Charles Sidney 1
SMITH, Charles Spencer 1
SMITH, Charles Sprague 1
SMITH, Charles Stephenson 4
SMITH, Charles Stewart 1
SMITH, Charles Sumner 1
SMITH, Charles Theodore 1
SMITH, Charles Wenham 1
SMITH, Charles William 1
SMITH, Charles William 6
SMITH, Chauncey Wayland 1
SMITH, Chauncy H
SMITH, Chester Clinton 2
SMITH, Chester F. 4
SMITH, Clarence Beaman 5
SMITH, Clarence Edwin 4
SMITH, Clarence James 1
SMITH, Clay 1
SMITH, Clement Lawrence 1
SMITH, Clifford Pabody 2
SMITH, Clinton De Witt 1
SMITH, Clustor Quentin 4
SMITH, Clyde Harold 1
SMITH, Courtland 5
SMITH, Courtney Craig 5
SMITH, Cyril James 6
SMITH, D. Nevin 4
SMITH, Dan Morgan 2
SMITH, Daniel H
SMITH, Daniel Appleton White 1
SMITH, Daniel B. H
SMITH, Daniel Fletcher Jr. 5
SMITH, David 4
SMITH, David Eugene 2
SMITH, David H. H
SMITH, David Highbaugh 4
SMITH, David Morton 1
SMITH, David Stanley 2
SMITH, David Thomas 1
SMITH, David V. 6
SMITH, Dean Tyler 1
SMITH, Delavan 1
SMITH, Delazon H
SMITH, Delos Hamilton 4
SMITH, Delos Owen 6
SMITH, Dena (Mrs. Warren R. Smith) 5
SMITH, Dilman M. K. 5
SMITH, Donald Borden 3
SMITH, Donald Jenckes 4
SMITH, Dorman Henry 3
SMITH, Douglas Forrest 5
SMITH, Dudley Crofford 3
SMITH, E. C. E. 3
SMITH, E. Norman 3
SMITH, E. Otis 1
SMITH, E. Sumter 1
SMITH, Earl Baldwin 3
SMITH, Earl Baxter 6
SMITH, Earl Edward 4
SMITH, Earle Clement 4
SMITH, Ed Sinclair 4
SMITH, Edgar 1
SMITH, Edgar Bronson 1
SMITH, Edgar Fahs 1
SMITH, Edgar Moncena 3
SMITH, Edgar Wadsworth 4
SMITH, E(dmund) Howard 5
SMITH, Edmund Kirby H
SMITH, Edmund Kirby 1
SMITH, Edmund Munroe 4
SMITH, Edward B. 1
SMITH, Edward Curtis 1
SMITH, Edward Delafield H
SMITH, Edward Devereux 5
SMITH, Edward Everett 5
SMITH, Edward G. 3
SMITH, Edward Grandison 2
SMITH, Edward Hanson 4
SMITH, Edward Henry H
SMITH, Edward Laurence * 1
SMITH, Edward Lincoln 1
SMITH, Edward North 2
SMITH, Edward Parson 1
SMITH, Edward St. Clair 6
SMITH, Edward Warren 6
SMITH, Edward Willis 5
SMITH, Edwin 1
SMITH, Edwin Bert 6
SMITH, Edwin Bradbury 4
SMITH, Edwin Burritt 1
SMITH, Edwin E. 1
SMITH, Edwin Whittier 1
SMITH, Egbert Watson 2
SMITH, Elbert Luther Jr. 6
SMITH, Elbert Sidney 1
SMITH, Eli H
SMITH, Elias H
SMITH, Elias Anthon Cappelen 2
SMITH, Elihu Hubbard H
SMITH, Elizabeth Howell 4
SMITH, Elizabeth Oakes Prince H
SMITH, Ellen M. Cyr 1
SMITH, Elliott 2
SMITH, Ellison DuRant 2
SMITH, Ellison Griffith 1
SMITH, E(lmer) Boyd. 5
SMITH, Elmer Dennison 2
SMITH, Elmer William 3
SMITH, Elmo 5
SMITH, Elva Sophronia 5
SMITH, Erasmus Darwin H
SMITH, Erasmus Deshine H
SMITH, Erastus Gilbert 1
SMITH, Erminnie Adelle Platt H
SMITH, Ernest Ashton 1
SMITH, Ernest Charles 4
SMITH, Ernest Ellsworth 1
SMITH, Ernest Gray 2
SMITH, Erwin F. 1
SMITH, Erwin Fletcher 6
SMITH, Erwin Jesse 1
SMITH, Ethan Henry 1
SMITH, Ethan Henry 2
SMITH, Ethelbert Walton 3
SMITH, Eugene 1
SMITH, Eugene Allen 1
SMITH, Eugene Hanes 1
SMITH, Everett 4
SMITH, Everett William 4
SMITH, Ezekiel Ezra 3
SMITH, F. Berkeley 4
SMITH, F. Hopkinson 1
SMITH, F. Janney 5
SMITH, Ferdinand Conrad 3
SMITH, Ferris 3
SMITH, Fitz-Henry Jr. 5
SMITH, Forrest 4
SMITH, Frances Stanton 5
SMITH, Francis Alward 4
SMITH, Francis Asbury 1
SMITH, Francis Edward 6
SMITH, Francis Edwin 5
SMITH, Francis Henney H
SMITH, Francis Henry 1
SMITH, Francis Marion 1
SMITH, Francis Ormand Jonathan H
SMITH, Frank 1
SMITH, Frank Austin 2
SMITH, Frank Bulkeley 1
SMITH, Frank C. 5
SMITH, Frank Channing Jr. 3
SMITH, Frank Gerard 6
SMITH, Frank Grigsby 3
SMITH, Frank Leslie 3
SMITH, Frank Marshall 1
SMITH, Frank O. 1
SMITH, Frank Sullivan 1
SMITH, Frank Webster 2
SMITH, Frank Whitney 2
SMITH, Franklin G. 5
SMITH, Franklin Guest 1
SMITH, Franklin Orion 1
SMITH, Fred Andrew 5
SMITH, Fred B. 1
SMITH, Fred Emory 4
SMITH, Fred M. 2
SMITH, Frederic William 6
SMITH, Frederick Appleton 1
SMITH, Frederick Arthur 5
SMITH, Frederick Augustus 1
SMITH, Frederick C. 3
SMITH, Frederick H. 1
SMITH, Frederick Madison 2
SMITH, Frederick Miller 5
SMITH, G. WALLACE 3
SMITH, G. Williamson 1
SMITH, George H
SMITH, George Albert 1
SMITH, George Albert 3
SMITH, George Albert Jr. 5
SMITH, George Carson 1
SMITH, George C(line) 6
SMITH, George D. 4
SMITH, George Edson Philip 5
SMITH, George Frederick 6
SMITH, George Gilbert 4
SMITH, George Harris 2
SMITH, George Hathorn 3
SMITH, George Henry 1
SMITH, George Hunter 3
SMITH, George Jay 4
SMITH, George Joseph 4
SMITH, George L. 3
SMITH, George Luke H
SMITH, George M. 1
SMITH, George M. 4
SMITH, George Milton 3
SMITH, George Otis 2
SMITH, George P. F. 4
SMITH, George Rodney 4
SMITH, George Ross 4
SMITH, George Theodore 1
SMITH, George W. 1
SMITH, George Walter Vincent 1
SMITH, George Weissinger 1
SMITH, Gerald Birney 1
SMITH, Gerald Hewitt 3
SMITH, Gerrit H
SMITH, Gerrit 1
SMITH, Gertrude 1
SMITH, Gilbert Morgan 3
SMITH, Giles Alexander H
SMITH, Goldwin 1
SMITH, Gordon Arthur 2
SMITH, Grafton Adrian 5
SMITH, Green Clay H
SMITH, Gregory L. 1
SMITH, Gretchen Hart 6
SMITH, Griffin 3
SMITH, Gustavus Woodson H
SMITH, Guy Chester 6
SMITH, Guy Lincoln 5
SMITH, H. A. A. 1
SMITH, H. Allen 6
SMITH, H. Alexander 4
SMITH, H. Augustine 3
SMITH, H. Lester 3
SMITH, H. M. Jr. 1
SMITH, Hal Horace 2
SMITH, Hal Horace Jr. 5
SMITH, Hamilton H
SMITH, Hamilton Lamphere 1
SMITH, Hariette Knight 4
SMITH, Harlan Ingersoll 1
SMITH, Harmon 1
SMITH, Harold Babbitt 1
SMITH, Harold Dewey 2
SMITH, Harold Leonard 5
SMITH, Harold Stephen 5
SMITH, Harold Travis 3
SMITH, Harold Vincent 4
SMITH, Harold Wellington 3
SMITH, Harriet Lummis 2
SMITH, Harrison 5
SMITH, Harry de Forest 5
SMITH, Harry Alexander * 1
SMITH, Harry Bache 1
SMITH, Harry Eaton 1
SMITH, Harry James 1
SMITH, Harry Pearse 3
SMITH, Harry Worcester 2
SMITH, Haviland 5
SMITH, Hay Watson 1
SMITH, Helen Evertson 4
SMITH, Henry A. M. 1
SMITH, Henry Boynton H
SMITH, Henry Bradford 1
SMITH, Henry Cassorte 1
SMITH, Henry Cooper 4
SMITH, Henry Erskine 5
SMITH, Henry Gerrish 3
SMITH, H(enry) Gordon 6
SMITH, Henry Justin 1
SMITH, Henry Leavitt 1
SMITH, Henry Lee Jr. 5
SMITH, Henry Lester 4
SMITH, Henry Louis 3
SMITH, Henry Michelet 3
SMITH, Henry Monmouth 3
SMITH, Henry Preserved 1
SMITH, Henry Tomlinson 1
SMITH, Herbert Atwood 3
SMITH, Herbert Augustine 2
SMITH, Herbert Booth 4
SMITH, Herbert Edward 5
SMITH, Herbert Eugene 1
SMITH, Herbert Huntington 1
SMITH, Herbert Knox 1
SMITH, Herbert Wilson 5
SMITH, Herman Lyle 3
SMITH, Hezekiah H
SMITH, Hezekiah Bradley H
SMITH, Hiram H
SMITH, Hiram Moore 2
SMITH, Hiram Ypsilanti H
SMITH, Hoke 1
SMITH, Holland McTyeire 4
SMITH, Holmes 1
SMITH, Homer 1
SMITH, Homer William 4
SMITH, Horace H
SMITH, Horace Boardman H
SMITH, Horace Herbert 4
SMITH, Horatio Elwin 2
SMITH, Howard Anthony 4
SMITH, Howard Caswell 4
SMITH, Howard Dwight 3
SMITH, Howard Leland 6
SMITH, Howard Leslie 4
SMITH, Howard Remus 5
SMITH, Howard Wayne 3
SMITH, Hubert Winston 5
SMITH, Hugh Allison 5
SMITH, Hugh Carnes 2
SMITH, Hugh F. Jr. 2
SMITH, Hugh McCormick 1
SMITH, Huntington 4
SMITH, Hurlbut William 3
SMITH, Huron H. 1
SMITH, Ida B. Wise 3
SMITH, Ignatius 3
SMITH, Irving Gardner 4
SMITH, Isaac * H
SMITH, Isaac B. 2
SMITH, Isaac Townsend 4
SMITH, Isabel E. 1
SMITH, Isaiah Perley 4
SMITH, Israel H
SMITH, Israel A. 3
SMITH, J. Allen 1
SMITH, J. Burritt 1
SMITH, J. Frank 1
SMITH, J. M. Powis 1
SMITH, J. Paul 3
SMITH, J. Ritchie 1
SMITH, J. Waldo 1
SMITH, J. Warren 1
SMITH, J. Emil 5
SMITH, J. Neil 5
SMITH, Jacob Getlar 3
SMITH, Jacob Hurd 1
SMITH, James * H
SMITH, James Jr. 1
SMITH, James Allwood 1
SMITH, James Argyle 4
SMITH, James D. 3
SMITH, James Dickinson 1
SMITH, James Ellwood 1
SMITH, James Francis 1
SMITH, James Gerald 2
SMITH, James Henry Oliver 1
SMITH, James Irwin 4
SMITH, James Kellum 4
SMITH, James McCune H
SMITH, James McLain 1
SMITH, James Perrin 1
SMITH, James Porter 1
SMITH, James Power 4
SMITH, James Sheppard 1
SMITH, James Strudwick H
SMITH, James W. 3
SMITH, James Walter 2
SMITH, James Willison 2
SMITH, James Youngs H
SMITH, Jane Luella Dowd 4
SMITH, Jane Norman 3
SMITH, Jeanie Oliver Davidson 1
SMITH, Jedediah Kilburn H
SMITH, Jedediah Strong H
SMITH, Jeremiah H
SMITH, Jeremiah 1
SMITH, Jeremiah Jr. 1
SMITH, Jesse Merrick 1
SMITH, Jessie Willcox 1
SMITH, Jim Clifford 2
SMITH, Job Lewis H
SMITH, Joe Frazer 3
SMITH, Joe L. 4
SMITH, Joel Perry 6
SMITH, Joel West 1
SMITH, John * H
SMITH, John Addison Baxter 1
SMITH, John Ambler H
SMITH, John Armstrong H
SMITH, John Augustine H
SMITH, John Bernhardt 1
SMITH, John Blair H
SMITH, John Butler 1
SMITH, John Charles 4
SMITH, John Corson 1
SMITH, John Cotton * H
SMITH, John Day 1
SMITH, John Elijah 5
SMITH, John Eugene H
SMITH, John Frederick 3
SMITH, John Gregory H
SMITH, John Hammond 1
SMITH, John Henry Jr. 3
SMITH, John Hyatt H
SMITH, John Jay H
SMITH, John Joseph 5
SMITH, John Lawrence H
SMITH, John Lawrence 3
SMITH, John Lewis 3
SMITH, John M. C. 1
SMITH, John P. 2
SMITH, John Rowson H
SMITH, John Rubens H
SMITH, John Sloan 5
SMITH, John Speed H
SMITH, John T. H
SMITH, John Talbot 1
SMITH, John Thomas 2
SMITH, John Walter 1
SMITH, John Walter 5
SMITH, John Wesley 1
SMITH, Jonathan Bayard H
SMITH, Joseph * H
SMITH, Joseph * 1
SMITH, Joseph Adams 1
SMITH, Joseph Brodie 2
SMITH, Joseph Earl 5
SMITH, Joseph Fielding 1
SMITH, Joseph Fielding 4
SMITH, Joseph Fielding 5
SMITH, Joseph Francis 2
SMITH, Joseph Lindon 3
SMITH, Joseph Mather H
SMITH, Joseph Newton 3
SMITH, Joseph P. 4
SMITH, Joseph Rowe 1
SMITH, J(oseph) Russell 6
SMITH, Joseph Showalter H
SMITH, Joseph Thomas 4
SMITH, Josephine Wernicke 3
SMITH, Josiah H
SMITH, Josiah Renick 1
SMITH, Judson 1
SMITH, Jules Andre 6
SMITH, Julia Evelina H
SMITH, Julia Holmes 1
SMITH, Julius Clarence 5
SMITH, June C. 2
SMITH, Junius H
SMITH, Justin Harvey 1
SMITH, K. Wesley 4
SMITH, Kenneth Gladstone 2

* Indicates More Than One Such Name Listed

SMITH, Kirby Flower 1
SMITH, Langdon 1
SMITH, Laura Rountree 1
SMITH, Lawrence 1
SMITH, Lawrence Henry 3
SMITH, Lawrence Meredith 6
  Clemson
SMITH, Lawrence Weld 6
SMITH, Lee Thompson 4
SMITH, Lemuel Augustus 3
  Sr.
SMITH, Lemuel F. 3
SMITH, Leo R. 4
SMITH, Leon E. 4
SMITH, Leon Edgar 6
SMITH, Leon Perdue 4
SMITH, Leon Perdue 4
SMITH, Leona Jones (Mrs. 5
  Robert James Smith)
SMITH, Leonard Bacon 3
SMITH, Leonard Bacon 4
SMITH, Leonard Minuse 2
SMITH, Leonidas 1
  D'Entrecasteaux
SMITH, Levi Pease 5
SMITH, Lewis Elden 4
SMITH, Lewis Martin 3
SMITH, Lewis Wilbur 3
SMITH, Lewis Worthington 2
SMITH, Lillian 1
SMITH, Livingston 6
SMITH, Livingston Waddell 3
SMITH, Lloyd DeWitt 5
SMITH, Lloyd Gaston 3
SMITH, Lloyd Pearsall H
SMITH, Lloyd Raymond 2
SMITH, Lloyd Waddell 5
SMITH, Lloyd Weir 3
SMITH, Logan Pearsall 2
SMITH, Lothrop 3
SMITH, Louie Henrie 5
SMITH, Lowell H. 2
SMITH, Lura Eugenie 4
  Brown
SMITH, Luther Ely 3
SMITH, Luther Wesley 5
SMITH, Lybrand Palmer 2
SMITH, Lyman Cornelius 1
SMITH, Lyndon Ambrose 1
SMITH, Lynwood H. 3
SMITH, M. Ellwood 4
SMITH, Mabell Shippie 2
  Clarke
SMITH, Madison Roswell 4
SMITH, Marcus H
SMITH, Marcus Aurelius 1
SMITH, Margaret Bayard H
SMITH, Margaret Vowell 4
SMITH, Marion 2
SMITH, Marion Couthouy 1
SMITH, Marion Gertrude 3
SMITH, Marjorie C. 5
SMITH, Mark H
SMITH, Mark A. 2
SMITH, Martha Rose 5
  Kapantaes (Mrs. Robert
  Clifford Smith)
SMITH, Martin F. 3
SMITH, Martin Luther H
SMITH, Marvin Boren 3
SMITH, Mary Cynthia 6
SMITH, Mary Elizabeth 1
SMITH, Mary Prudence 1
  Wells
SMITH, Mason 4
SMITH, Matthew 3
SMITH, Matthew F. 1
SMITH, Matthew Hale H
SMITH, Matthew John 4
  Wilfred
SMITH, May Riley 1
SMITH, McGregor 5
SMITH, Melancton H
SMITH, Melvin 6
  Montgomery
SMITH, Meriwether 1
SMITH, Merle Negley 5
SMITH, Merriman 5
SMITH, Mildred Catharine 6
SMITH, Milton H. 1
SMITH, Milton Truman 1
SMITH, Minna Caroline 1
SMITH, Monroe William 6
SMITH, Mordon 6
SMITH, Morgan Lewis 1
SMITH, Moses 4
SMITH, Munroe 1
SMITH, Murray 1
SMITH, Myrtle Holm 3
SMITH, Nathan * 1
SMITH, Nathan Ryno H
SMITH, Nathaniel 1
SMITH, Nathaniel Waite 5
SMITH, Newman 1
SMITH, Nicholas 1
SMITH, Nicol Hamilton 5

SMITH, Nora Archibald 1
SMITH, Norman Kemp 5
SMITH, Norman Murray 5
SMITH, O. Warren 1
SMITH, Oberlin H
SMITH, O'Brien H
SMITH, Oliver H
SMITH, Oliver Hampton H
SMITH, Oramandal 3
SMITH, Orlando Jay 1
SMITH, Orma Jacob 2
SMITH, Ormond Gerald 1
SMITH, Orrin Harold 6
SMITH, Orson 1
SMITH, Otis David 1
SMITH, Otterbein Oscar 1
SMITH, Owen Lun West 4
SMITH, Paul Edward 5
SMITH, Paul Francis 4
SMITH, Paul Glen 6
SMITH, Paul Jordan 5
SMITH, Paul Kenneth 4
SMITH, Payson 4
SMITH, Percey Franklyn 1
SMITH, Percy William 4
SMITH, Perry H
SMITH, Perry Coke 6
SMITH, Perry Dunlap 4
SMITH, Persifor Frazer H
SMITH, Peter 4
SMITH, Peter P. 3
SMITH, Philip E. 5
SMITH, Philip Sidney 4
SMITH, Phillips Waller 4
SMITH, Preserved 4
SMITH, Quintius 4
  Cincinnatus
SMITH, R. Waverley 1
SMITH, Ralph Chester 4
SMITH, Ralph Eliot 5
SMITH, Ralph M. 3
SMITH, Ralph Tyler 5
SMITH, Ralph Winfield 5
SMITH, Randle Jasper 4
SMITH, Ray L. 3
SMITH, Raymond Abner 4
SMITH, Raymond 3
  Underwood
SMITH, Reed 2
SMITH, Reginald Heber 4
SMITH, Reuben Robert 5
SMITH, Rex 1
SMITH, Richard H
SMITH, Richard Hewlett 2
SMITH, Richard Paul 4
SMITH, Richard Penn H
SMITH, Richard R. 3
SMITH, Richard Root 1
SMITH, Richard Somers H
SMITH, Robert * H
SMITH, Robert A. C. 1
SMITH, Robert Armstrong 4
SMITH, Robert Aura 3
SMITH, R(obert) Blackwell 5
  Jr.
SMITH, Robert Brandon 2
SMITH, Robert Burns 1
SMITH, Robert Chester 4
SMITH, Robert Edwin 3
SMITH, Robert Edwin 1
SMITH, Robert Fitch 4
SMITH, Robert H. 4
SMITH, Robert Hardy 1
SMITH, Robert Hays 5
SMITH, Robert Keating 1
SMITH, Robert Lee 1
SMITH, Robert Metcalf 2
SMITH, Robert P. 4
SMITH, Robert Paterson 5
SMITH, Robert Seneca 1
SMITH, Robert Shufeldt 4
SMITH, Robert Sidney 5
SMITH, Robert Sidney 4
SMITH, Robert Sidney 5
SMITH, Robert William 6
SMITH, Robinson 2
SMITH, Rodney 1
SMITH, Roland Cotton 1
SMITH, Roland Kidder 1
SMITH, Roswell H
SMITH, Roy Campbell 1
SMITH, Roy Harmon 4
SMITH, Roy Leon 1
SMITH, Ruel Perley 1
SMITH, Rufus D. 3
SMITH, Russell H
SMITH, Ruth Ann Cook 5
SMITH, S. Archibald 3
SMITH, S. Calvin 1
SMITH, S. Jennie 1
SMITH, S. Stephenson 4
SMITH, Sadie Adams 5
SMITH, Samray 5
SMITH, Samuel * H
SMITH, Samuel 4
SMITH, Samuel A. H

SMITH, Samuel Axley H
SMITH, Samuel Edwin 1
SMITH, Samuel Francis 1
SMITH, Samuel George 1
SMITH, Samuel Harrison 1
SMITH, S(amuel) L(eonard) 5
SMITH, Samuel Stanhope H
SMITH, Samuel William 1
SMITH, Seba H
SMITH, Seth MacCuen 1
SMITH, Seymour Wemyss 1
SMITH, Sherman Everett 6
SMITH, Sherrill 3
SMITH, Shirley Wheeler 3
SMITH, Sidney 1
SMITH, Sidney 1
SMITH, Sidney Earle 3
SMITH, Sidney Irving 1
SMITH, Sidney Mason 1
SMITH, Sion Bass 3
SMITH, Soloman Franklin 1
SMITH, Solomon Albert 4
SMITH, Sophia 1
SMITH, Stephen 1
SMITH, Stevenson 3
SMITH, Stuart Robertson 1
SMITH, Susan T. 4
SMITH, Sydney 1
SMITH, Sylvester Clark 1
SMITH, T. Guilford 1
SMITH, T. V. 4
SMITH, Theobald 1
SMITH, Theodore Clarke 1
SMITH, Thomas * 4
SMITH, Thomas * 4
SMITH, Thomas Adams H
SMITH, Thomas Arthur 4
SMITH, Thomas Berry 1
SMITH, Thomas F. 1
SMITH, Thomas Franklin 1
SMITH, Thomas Jefferson 5
SMITH, Thomas Kilby 1
SMITH, Thomas Newill 5
SMITH, Thomas Octavius 1
SMITH, Thomas R. 2
SMITH, Thomas William 5
SMITH, (Thomas) Max 5
  Montgomery
SMITH, Thurber 3
SMITH, Truman 2
SMITH, Ulysses Simpson 2
SMITH, Uriah 1
SMITH, Vincent E. 5
SMITH, Vincent Weaver 4
SMITH, Vine Harold 5
SMITH, Vivian Thomas 3
SMITH, W. A. 3
SMITH, W. H. B. 4
SMITH, Wade Cothran 5
SMITH, Walt Allen 5
SMITH, Walter Bedell 4
SMITH, Walter Byron 2
SMITH, Walter Driscoll 1
SMITH, Walter George 1
SMITH, Walter Inglewood 1
SMITH, Walter Lloyd 1
SMITH, Walter McMynn 1
SMITH, Walter Robinson 1
SMITH, Walter Tenney 1
SMITH, Walter Tenney 1
SMITH, Walter Winfred 2
SMITH, Warren Du Pre 3
SMITH, Warren Lounsbury 5
SMITH, Warren Robert 3
SMITH, Wayne Carleton 1
SMITH, Wendell 5
SMITH, Weston 6
SMITH, Wilbert L. 1
SMITH, Wilbur Cleveland 3
SMITH, Wilbur Fisk 1
SMITH, Willard Adelbert 1
SMITH, William * H
SMITH, William 1
SMITH, William Alden 1
SMITH, William Alexander H
SMITH, William Alexander 1
SMITH, William Andrew 1
SMITH, William Anton 6
SMITH, William Austin 1
SMITH, William Benjamin 1
SMITH, William Clarke 1
SMITH, William Clarke 2
SMITH, William 2
  Cunningham
SMITH, William Eason 2
SMITH, William Edward 2
SMITH, William Ephraim H
SMITH, William Farrar 1
SMITH, William Francis 4
SMITH, William Griswold 2
SMITH, William Hall 4
SMITH, William Harrison 1
SMITH, William Hawley 1
SMITH, William Henry * H
SMITH, William Henry 1
SMITH, William Henry 4

SMITH, William Hinckle 2
SMITH, William Hopton 2
SMITH, William Jones 1
SMITH, William Loughton H
SMITH, William Mason 4
SMITH, William Nathan H
  Harrell
SMITH, William Oliver 4
SMITH, William Orlando 4
SMITH, William Owen 2
SMITH, William Owen 2
SMITH, William Robert 1
SMITH, William Roy 5
SMITH, William Russell 1
SMITH, William Ruthven 1
SMITH, William Skeldon 3
  Adamson
SMITH, William Sooy 1
SMITH, William Stephens 1
SMITH, William Stevenson 5
SMITH, William Strother 1
SMITH, William Thayer 1
SMITH, William Thomas 2
SMITH, William W. II 3
SMITH, William Walker 1
SMITH, William Walter 2
SMITH, William Ward 4
SMITH, William Waugh 1
SMITH, William Wilberforce 2
SMITH, Willis 3
SMITH, Willis Jr. 5
SMITH, Wilmot M. 1
SMITH, Wilson George 1
SMITH, Winchell 1
SMITH, Winford Henry 4
SMITH, Winthrop Hiram 4
SMITH, Worthington 1
SMITH, Worthington Curtis H
SMITH, Young Berryman 4
SMITH, Zachariah Frederick 1
SMITH, Zemro Augustus 1
SMITH, Zilpha Drew 1
SMITHEE, James Newton 1
SMITHER, Henry Carpenter 1
SMITHERS, Ernest Leonard 1
SMITHERS, Nathaniel H
  Barrett
SMITHERS, William West 2
SMITHEY, Louis Philippe 4
SMITHEY, Royall Bascom 1
SMITHEY, William Royall 5
SMITHIES, Frank 1
SMITH-PETERSEN, Marius 3
  Nygaard
SMITHSON, James H
SMITHSON, Noble 1
SMITHSON, William 1
  Walpole
SMITHWICK, John Harris 1
SMOCK, Harry Berdan 6
SMOCK, John Conover 1
SMOCK, P(eter) Monroe 5
SMOCK, Wendell Merritt 4
SMOHALLA H
SMOHALLA 4
SMOLEY, Constantine 3
  Kenneth
SMOOT, Charles Head 1
SMOOT, Reed 1
SMOOT, Thomas Arthur 1
SMULL, Jacob Barstow 4
SMULL, Thomas Jefferson 4
  Jr.
SMULSKI, John F. 1
SMUTNY, Rudolf 6
SMUTS, Jan Christiaan 3
SMYKAL, Richard 3
SMYSER, Martin L. 1
SMYSER, William Emory 1
SMYTH, Albert Henry 1
SMYTH, Alexander 1
SMYTH, Calvin Mason Jr. 4
SMYTH, Charles Henry Jr. 1
SMYTH, Clifford 1
SMYTH, Constantine Joseph 1
SMYTH, Egbert Coffin 1
SMYTH, Ellison Adger 1
SMYTH, Ellison Adger 2
SMYTH, Francis Scott 5
SMYTH, George H
  Washington
SMYTH, Henry Field 3
SMYTH, Henry Lloyd 2
SMYTH, Herbert 2
  Crommelin
SMYTH, Herbert Weir 1
SMYTH, James Adger 1
SMYTH, Julian Kennedy 1
SMYTH, Margarita 5
  Pumpelly
SMYTH, Newman 1
SMYTH, S. Gordon 3
SMYTH, Thomas 1
SMYTH, Timothy Clement 4
SMYTH, William * H
SMYTH, William Henry 1

SMYTH, Wilma Louise 5
SMYTH, Winfield Scott 1
SMYTHE, Augustine 1
  Thomas
SMYTHE, George Franklin 1
SMYTHE, George Winfred 5
SMYTHE, J. Henry Jr. 3
SMYTHE, Sidney Thomas 1
SMYTHE, William E. 1
SNAITH, William Theodore 6
SNAPE, John 2
SNAPP, Henry H
SNAPP, Howard Malcolm 4
SNARE, Frederick 3
SNARR, Frederic Earle 4
SNARR, Otto Welton 4
SNAVELY, Guy Everett 6
SNAVELY, John Robert 4
SNEAD, Thomas Lowndes H
SNEATH, E. Hershey 1
SNEATH, Mrs. Samuel B. 5
  (Laura S. Sneath)
SNEDDEN, David 5
SNEDECOR, George W. 6
SNEDECOR, James George 1
SNEDEKER, Caroline Dale 3
SNEDEKER, Charles 1
  Dippolt
SNEED, Albert Lee 4
SNEED, Frank Woolford 1
SNEED, John Louis Taylor 1
SNEED, William Henry H
SNEED, William Lent 2
SNELHAM, John Sydney 4
SNELL, Albert M. 3
SNELL, Bertrand H. 1
SNELL, Earl Wilcox 2
SNELL, George H
SNELL, Henry Bayley 2
SNELL, John Leslie 5
SNELL, Roy Judson 6
SNELLING Charles Mercer 1
SNELLING, Henry Hunt H
SNELLING, Josiah 1
SNELLING, Rodman Paul 1
SNELLING, Walter 1
  Otheman
SNELLING, William Joseph H
SNETHEN, Nicholas H
SNEVE, Haldor 1
SNEVILY, Henry Mansfield 3
SNIDER, Clyde Frank 5
SNIDER, Denton Jaques 1
SNIDER, Joseph Lyons 3
SNIDER, Luther Crocker 2
SNIDER, Samuel Prather 1
SNIFF, Littleton M. 1
SNIFFEN, Culver Channing 1
SNIVELY, Samuel Frisby 4
SNIVELY, William Andrew 1
SNOBERGER, Rantz 1
SNODDY, Elmer Ellsworth 1
SNODDY, Leland Bradley 3
SNODGRASS, Charles 4
  Edward
SNODGRASS, David E. 4
SNODGRASS, David La 1
  Fayette
SNODGRASS, George 1
  Merrill
SNODGRASS, John Fryall H
SNODGRASS, John Harold 2
SNODGRASS, Robert 1
SNODGRASS, Robert 5
  Evans
SNODGRASS, Robert 5
  Richard
SNODGRASS, Samuel 6
  Robert
SNOOK, Homer Clyde 3
SNOOK, John S. 5
SNOOK, John Wilson 5
SNOW, Albert Sydney 1
SNOW, Alpheus Henry 1
SNOW, Alva Edson 1
SNOW, Benjamin Warner 4
SNOW, Carmel 4
SNOW, Chalres Ernest 1
SNOW, Charles Armstrong 1
SNOW, Charles Henry 1
SNOW, Chauncey Depew 4
SNOW, Donald Francis 5
SNOW, Edgar Parks 5
SNOW, Elbert Clay 4
SNOW, Elbridge Gerry 1
SNOW, Eliza Roxey H
SNOW, Ernest Albert 1
SNOW, Francis 1
SNOW, Francis Huntington 1
SNOW, Franklin Augustus 2
SNOW, Frederic 4
SNOW, Henry Sanger 4
SNOW, J. Parker 4
SNOW, John Ben 5
SNOW, Leslie Perkins 1
SNOW, Leslie W. 3

SNOW, Lorenzo 1
SNOW, Louis Franklin 1
SNOW, Marshall Solomon 1
SNOW, Sydney Bruce 2
SNOW, Walter Bradlee 4
SNOW, Warren Howland 4
SNOW, William Benham 6
SNOW, William Dunham 1
SNOW, William Freeman 3
SNOW, William Josiah 1
SNOW, William W. H
SNOWDEN, A. Loudon 1
SNOWDEN, James Henry 1
SNOWDEN, James Ross H
SNOWDEN, Robert 1
Bogardus
SNOWDEN, R(obert) 5
Brinkley
SNOWDEN, Thomas 1
SNOWDEN, Yates 1
SNURE, John 1
SNYDER, A. Cecil 3
SNYDER, Adam Wilson 1
SNYDER, Addison Hogan 6
SNYDER, Alban Goshorn 5
SNYDER, Albert Whitcomb 1
SNYDER, Arthur 4
SNYDER, Baird III 2
SNYDER, Carl 2
SNYDER, Carl J. 3
SNYDER, Charles B. J. 4
SNYDER, Charles Edward 5
SNYDER, Charles McCoy 5
SNYDER, Charles Philip 4
SNYDER, Edgar Callender 1
SNYDER, Edward 1
SNYDER, Eldredge 4
SNYDER, Erwin Paul 6
SNYDER, Franklyn Bliss 3
SNYDER, Fred Beal 3
SNYDER, Frederic 5
Sylvester
SNYDER, George Gordon 6
SNYDER, Harry 1
SNYDER, Henry H
SNYDER, Henry George 3
SNYDER, Henry Nelson 1
SNYDER, Henry Steinman 1
SNYDER, Homer P. 4
SNYDER, Howard McC. 5
SNYDER, J. Ralph 3
SNYDER, Jefferson 1
SNYDER, John H
SNYDER, John Buell 2
SNYDER, John I. Jr. 4
SNYDER, John Otterbein 5
SNYDER, John Taylor 3
SNYDER, Jonathan Le 1
Moyne
SNYDER, Leroy Edwin 2
SNYDER, Meredith Pinxton 1
SNYDER, Monroe B. 1
SNYDER, Murray 5
SNYDER, Nicholas R. 4
SNYDER, Oliver P. H
SNYDER, Oscar John 2
SNYDER, Reginald Clare 1
SNYDER, Robert McClure 1
SNYDER, Simon H
SNYDER, Simon 1
SNYDER, Valentine P. 1
SNYDER, Virgil 2
SNYDER, William Edward 3
SNYDER, William 4
Lamartine
SNYDER, William P. Jr. 4
SNYDER, Zachariah 1
Xenophon
SOANS, Cyril Arthur 6
SOARES, Theodore Gerald 5
SOBEL, Bernard 4
SOBELOFF, Simon E. 6
SOBER, Herbert Alexander 6
SOBIESKI, John 4
SOBILOFF, Hyman Jordan 5
SOBOL, Louis 2
SOBOLEV, Arkady A. 4
SOBOLEWSKI, J. Friedrich H
Edvard
SOCKMAN, Ralph 5
Washington
SODDY, Frederick 3
SODT, William George 3
SOERGEL, E. W. 3
SOFFEL, Joseph August 6
SOGGE, Tillman M. 3
SOGLOW, Otto 6
SOHN, Joseph 1
SOHON, Frederick Wyatt 5
SOILAND, Albert 4
SOKOLOFF, Nikolai 4
SOKOLOFF, Ruth H. 4
Ottaway
SOKOLOW, Alexander 1
Theodore

SOKOLSKY, George 4
Ephraim
SOLBERG, Charles Orrin 2
SOLBERG, Thorvald 2
SOLBERT, Oscar Nathaniel 3
SOLER, Juan José é 6
SOLETHER, Pliny Louis 3
SOLEY, James Russell 1
SOLEY, Mayo Hallton 3
SOLF Y MURO, Alfredo 5
SOLGER, Reinhold Ernst H
Friedrich Karl
SOLHEIM, Arthur Oliver 4
SOLIDAY, David Shriver 5
SOLIDAY, Joseph Henry 2
SOLIS, Isaac Nathan 1
SOLIS-COREN, Solomon 2
SOLLENBERGER, Richard 6
Talbot
SOLLERS, Augustus H
Rhodes
SOLLITT, Sumner S. 4
SOLLMANN, Torald 4
Hermann
SOLLOTT, Ralph Preston 3
SOLLY, Samuel Edwin 1
SOLOMON, Edward Davis 4
SOLOMON, Louis H. 1
SOLOMON, Sidney L. 6
SOLON, Faustin Johnson 2
SOLON, Harry 5
SOLON, Leon Victor 3
SOLOW, Herbert 4
SOLTES, Mordecai 5
SOMERALL, James Bentley 6
SOMERDIKE, John Mason 1
SOMERS, Andrew L. 2
SOMERS, Joseph Patrick 6
SOMERS, Orlando Allen 1
SOMERS, Richard H. 6
SOMERVELL, Brehon 5
Burke
SOMERVILLE, Frederick 1
Howland
SOMERVILLE, Harry 4
Philip
SOMERVILLE, Henderson 1
Middleton
SOMERVILLE, James 1
Alexander
SOMERVILLE, James 2
Fownes
SOMERVILLE, Ormond 1
SOMERVILLE, Pearl Cliffe 1
SOMERVILLE, Randolph 3
SOMERVILLE, Thomas 4
Hugh
SOMERVILLE, William H
Clark
SOMES, Daniel Eton H
SOMMER, Alvin Henry 4
SOMMER, Charles G. 1
SOMMER, Daniel Philip 4
SOMMER, Ernst August 4
SOMMER, Frank Henry 3
SOMMER, Henry Getz 4
SOMMER, Luther Allen 2
SOMMER, Martin S. 5
SOMMER, Peter W. 1
SOMMER, Reuben E. 4
SOMMER, William H. 3
SOMMERICH, Otto 4
Charles
SOMMERS, Charles 5
Leissring
SOMMERS, Henry Cantine 4
SOMMERS, Martin 4
SOMMERS, Paul Bergen 3
SOMMERVILLE, Charles 1
William
SOMMERVILLE, Maxwell 1
SOMMERVILLE, Walter 6
Byers
SOMOZA, Anastasio 3
SOMOZA, Luis 4
SONDERN, Frederic Ewald 5
SONDLEY, F. A. 3
SONES, Warren Wesley 1
David
SONFIELD, Robert Leon 5
SONIAT, Leonce Martin 1
SONNABEND, Abraham 4
M.
SONNAKOLB, Franklin 4
Schuyler
SONNE, Fred Theodore 4
SONNECK, Oscar George 1
Theodore
SONNEDECKER, Thomas 4
Harry
SONNENBERG, Henry L. 5
SONNENSCHEIN, Hugo 3
SONNETT, John Francis 5
SONNEYSYN, H. O. 1
(Sonny)
SONNICHSEN, Albert 1

SONNICHSEN, Yngvar 1
SONNTAG, Marcus S. 1
SONNTAG, William Louis 1
SONSTEBY, John J. 1
SONTAG, Raymond James 5
SOONG, T.V. 1
SOOYSMITH, Charles 1
SOPER, Alexander Coburn 1
SOPER, Edmund Davison 4
SOPER, Erastus Burrows 1
SOPER, George Albert 2
SOPER, Henry Marlin 1
SOPER, Horace Wendell 5
SOPER, John Harris 1
SOPER, Morris Ames 4
SOPER, Pliny Leland 4
SOPHIAN, Lawrence Henry 3
SOPHOCLES, Evangelinus H
Apostolides
SOPHOULIS, Themistocles 5
SORDONI, Andrew John 5
Jr.
SORDONI, Andrew John 4
Sr.
SORENSEN, Charles E. 5
SORENSEN, John Hjelmhof 5
SORENSEN, Royal Wasson 4
SORENSON, Roy 5
SORG, Paul John 1
SORG, Theodore 3
SORIANO, Andres 4
SORIN, Edward Frederick H
SORLIE, Arthur Gustav 1
SOROKIN, Pitrim 4
Alexandrovitch
SORRELL, Lewis Carlyle 4
SORRELLS, John Harvey 2
SORSBY, William Brooks 1
SOSKIN, William 3
SOSMAN, Merrill C. 3
SOSMAN, Robert Browning 5
SOTHERAN, Alice 5
Hyneman
SOTHERAN, Charles 1
SOTHERN, Edward Askew H
SOTHERN, Edward Hugh 1
SOTTER, George William 3
SOTZIN, Heber Allen 3
SOUBY, A. Max 1
SOUCEK, Apollo 5
SOUCHON, Edmond 1
SOUDER, Edwin Mills 2
SOUERS, Loren Edmunds 4
SOUERS, Sidney William 5
SOUERS, Warren Earl 6
SOULE, Andrew MacNairn 1
SOULE, Asa Titus 4
SOULE, Caroline Gray 4
SOULE, Charles Carroll 1
SOULE, Edward Lee 5
SOULE, Elizabeth Sterling 4
SOULE, George 1
SOULE, Henri Remy 4
SOULE, Joshua 4
SOULE, Malcolm Herman 3
SOULE, Nathan 4
SOULE, Pierre H
SOULE, Robert Homer 3
SOULE, Winsor 3
SOULES, Mary E. (Mrs. 6
Powell J. Bing)
SOURDIS, Evarista 5
SOUSA, Carlos Martins 4
Pereira
SOUSA, John Philip 1
SOUSER, Kenneth 5
SOUTH, Jerry C. 1
SOUTH, John Glover 1
SOUTH, Lillian H. 6
SOUTHACK, Cyprian H
SOUTHALL, James Cocke H
SOUTHALL, James Powell 4
Cocke
SOUTHALL, Robert Goode 3
SOUTHAM, H. S. 3
SOUTHAM, J. D. 3
SOUTHARD, Elmer Ernest 1
SOUTHARD, George 1
Franklin
SOUTHARD, Harry Green 4
SOUTHARD, Henry 4
SOUTHARD, Isaac H
SOUTHARD, James 1
Harding
SOUTHARD, Louis Carver 1
SOUTHARD, Lucien 4
SOUTHARD, Samuel Lewis H
SOUTHER, Henry 1
SOUTHERD, Lucien H. 4
SOUTHERLAND, Clarence 6
Andrew
SOUTHERLAND, J. Julien 3
SOUTHERLAND, William 1
Henry Hudson
SOUTHERN, Allen Carriger 4

SOUTHERN, William Neil 3
Jr.
SOUTHGATE, George 2
Thompson
SOUTHGATE, Horatio 4
SOUTHGATE, James 1
Haywood
SOUTHGATE, Richard 2
SOUTHGATE, Thomas 1
Somerville
SOUTHGATE, William H
Wright
SOUTHWICK, Albert 4
Plympton
SOUTHWICK, George N. 1
SOUTHWICK, George 1
Rinaldo
SOUTHWICK, Henry 4
Lawrence
SOUTHWICK, John 5
Leonard
SOUTHWICK, Soloman H
SOUTHWORTH, Emma 1
Dorothy Eliza Nevitte
SOUTHWORTH, Franklin 2
Chester
SOUTHWORTH, George 4
Champlin Shepard
SOUTHWORTH, George 5
Clark
SOUTHWORTH, Melvin 4
Deane
SOUTHWORTH, Thomas 1
Shepard
SOWDON, Arthur John 1
Clark
SOWELL, Ashley B. 2
SOWELL, Ellis Mast 4
SOWELL, Ingram Cecil 2
SOWELL, Paul Dibrell 5
SOWER, Charles Gilbert Sr. 1
SOWER, Christopher * 1
SOWERBY, Leo 5
SOWERS, Don Conger 1
SOWERS, Joseph Cullen 5
SOYER, Moses 6
SPAAK, Paul Henri 5
SPAATZ, Carl 6
SPACHNER, John Victor 6
SPACKMAN, Cyril 4
Saunders
SPACKMAN, Harold 3
Burton
SPAETH, Adolph 1
SPAETH, Bernard Anton 4
SPAETH, J. Duncan 3
SPAETH, Otto Lucien 4
SPAETH, Reynold Albrecht 1
SPAETH, Sigmund 4
SPAFFORD, Edward Elwell 2
SPAFFORD, Frederick 1
Angier
SPAFFORD, George Catlin 2
SPAHR, Boyd Lee 5
SPAHR, Charles Barzillai 1
SPAHR, George W. 1
SPAHR, Herman Louis 3
SPAHR, Walter Earl 5
SPAID, Arthur Rusmiselle 4
Miller
SPAID, William Wesley 5
SPAID, William Winfield 1
SPAIGHT, Richard Dobbs H
SPAIGHT, Richard Dobbs H
Jr.
SPAIN, Charles Lyle 2
SPAIN, Charles R. 4
SPAIN, Gail Elliott 4
SPAIN, Will Cook 3
SPALDING, Albert 3
SPALDING, Albert 1
Goodwill
SPALDING, Alfred Baker 3
SPALDING, Alice 5
Huntington
SPALDING, Burleigh 1
Folsom
SPALDING, Catherine H
SPALDING, Charles 4
Hubbard
SPALDING, Eliza Hart H
SPALDING, Elizabeth Hill 4
SPALDING, Franklin 1
Spencer
SPALDING, Frederick 1
Putnam
SPALDING, George 4
SPALDING, George Burley 1
SPALDING, George R. 5
SPALDING, Henry Harmon H
SPALDING, Hughes 5
SPALDING, J. Walter 1
SPALDING, Jack Johnson 3
SPALDING, James Alfred 1
SPALDING, James Field 1
SPALDING, Jesse 1

SPALDING, John Franklin 1
SPALDING, John Lancaster 1
SPALDING, Keith 4
SPALDING, Keith 5
SPALDING, Lyman H
SPALDING, Martin John H
SPALDING, Phebe Estelle 1
SPALDING, Philip 1
Leffingwell
SPALDING, Rufus Paine H
SPALDING, Thomas H
SPALDING, Volney 1
Morgan
SPALDING, Walter 4
Raymond
SPALDING, William 1
Andrew
SPAMER, Richard 1
SPANG, Joseph Peter Jr. 5
SPANGENBERG, Augustus H
Gottlieb
SPANGLER, David H
SPANGLER, Harrison Earl 4
SPANGLER, Henry 4
Thomas
SPANGLER, Henry Wilson 1
SPANGLER, Jacob H
SPANGLER, James 5
Williams
SPANGLER, Timon John 1
SPANIER, Francis Joseph 4
SPANN, Otis 5
SPARBER, Jean Leah 6
Weinstein (Mrs. Howard
Sparber)
SPARGO, John 4
SPARGO, John Webster 3
SPARHAWK, Frances 4
Campbell
SPARKES, Boyden 3
SPARKMAN, Stephen M. 4
SPARKS, Arthur Watson 1
SPARKS, Charles I. 1
SPARKS, Chauncey 5
SPARKS, Edwin Erle 1
SPARKS, Frank Hugh 4
SPARKS, Frank Melville 3
SPARKS, George McIntosh 3
SPARKS, Jared H
SPARKS, John 1
SPARKS, Joseph 4
SPARKS, N(orman) 5
R(obert)
SPARKS, Sir T. Ashley 4
SPARKS, Thomas Ayres 1
SPARKS, Thomas J. 2
SPARKS, Will 1
SPARKS, Will Morris 2
SPARKS, William Henry H
SPARLING, Samuel Edwin 4
SPARROW, Carroll Mason 1
SPARROW, Ray F. 4
SPARROW, Stanwood 3
Willston
SPARROW, William H
SPARROW, William 1
Warburton Knox
SPATTA, George 5
SPAULDING, Edward 1
Gleason
SPAULDING, Elbridge H
Gerry
SPAULDING, Eugene 5
Ristine
SPAULDING, Forrest 4
Brisbin
SPAULDING, Francis Trow 3
SPAULDING, Frank 4
Ellsworth
SPAULDING, Frederic 6
Henry
SPAULDING, George 1
Lawson
SPAULDING, Helim G. 2
SPAULDING, Henry 1
George
SPAULDING, Huntley 1
Nowell
SPAULDING, John Cecil 3
SPAULDING, John Pearson 6
SPAULDING, Levi H
SPAULDING, Major 4
Franklin
SPAULDING, Nathan 1
Weston
SPAULDING, Oliver 1
Lyman
SPAULDING, Oliver 2
Lyman
SPAULDING, Rolland 2
Harty
SPAULDING, Sumner 3
SPAULDING, William 1
Stuart
SPAYD, Milferd Aaron 5
SPEAKMAN, Frank L. 1

SPEAKMAN, G. Dixon 3
SPEAKMAN, Harold 1
SPEAKS, John Charles 2
SPEAKS, Oley 2
SPEAR, Ray 6
SPEAR, Albert Moore 1
SPEAR, Arthur Prince 4
SPEAR, Charles H
SPEAR, Ellis 5
SPEAR, Ellwood Barker 5
SPEAR, John William 2
SPEAR, Lawrence York 3
SPEAR, Lewis Benson 5
SPEAR, Nathaniel 2
SPEAR, Samuel Thayer 1
SPEAR, William Thomas 1
SPEARE, Charles Frederic 4
SPEARE, Dorothy 4
SPEARE, Edward Ray 4
SPEARE, Frank Palmer 5
SPEARE, Morris Edmund 6
SPEARE, William Martin 5
SPEARING, J. Zach 1
SPEARING, Joseph Hall 4
SPEARL, George 1
SPEARMAN, Frank Hamilton 1
SPEARS, John Randolph 1
SPEARS, Lawrence Napoleon 6
SPEARS, Raymond Smiley 3
SPEARS, Samuel Tilden 1
SPEARS, William Oscar 1
SPEASE, Edward 3
SPECHT, Frederick William 6
SPECK, Frank Gouldsmith 2
SPECTHRIE, Samuel Waldo 6
SPECTOR, Benjamin 6
SPECTORSKY, Auguste C. 5
SPEED, Horace 1
SPEED, James H
SPEED, James Breckinridge 5
SPEED, John Gilmer 1
SPEED, Keats 3
SPEED, Kellogg 3
SPEED, Thomas H
SPEED, Thomas 1
SPEED, Virginia Perrin 5 (Mrs. W. S. Speed)
SPEED, William Shallcross 3
SPEER, Alfred Alten 1
SPEER, Emma Bailey 4
SPEER, Emory 1
SPEER, James Henry 4
SPEER, James Ramsey 2
SPEER, Peter Moore 1
SPEER, Robert Elliott 2
SPEER, Robert Kenneth 4
SPEER, Robert Milton H
SPEER, Robert Walter 1
SPEER, Thomas Jefferson H
SPEER, William 1
SPEER, William H. 3
SPEER, William McMurtrie 1
SPEERS, Chester Henry 4
SPEERS, James M. 4
SPEERS, Theodore Cuyler 4
SPEERS, William Ewing 4
SPEICHER, Eugene Edward 4
SPEIDEL, Edward 2
SPEIDEL, Merritt Charles 5
SPEIDEL, Thomas D. 3
SPEIGHT, Jesse H
SPEIR, Samuel Fleet H
SPEIS, August H
SPEISER, Ephraim Avigdor 4
SPEKKE, Arnolds 5
SPELFOGEL, Morris 5 Richard
SPELLACY, Edmund Frank 5
SPELLACY, Thomas Joseph 3
SPELLMAN, Francis 4 Cardinal
SPELLMEYER, Henry 1
SPENCE, Brent 4
SPENCE, Clara B. 1
SPENCE, Frederick 1
SPENCE, Homer Roberts 6
SPENCE, John Fletcher 1
SPENCE, John Lee 4
SPENCE, John Selby H
SPENCE, John Selby 1
SPENCE, Kenneth Monroe 3
SPENCE, Kenneth 4 Wartinbee
SPENCE, Thomas Ara H
SPENCE, Walter 4
SPENCE, William H. 1
SPENCE, William Kenneth 4
SPENCER, Alfred Jr. 1
SPENCER, Almon Edwin 4
SPENCER, Ambrose H
SPENCER, Anna Garlin 1
SPENCER, Arthur Coe 5
SPENCER, Bunyan 1
SPENCER, Byron 1

SPENCER, C. Luther 4
SPENCER, Charles Eldridge 3 Jr.
SPENCER, Claudius 1 Buchanan
SPENCER, Clayton C(reel) 6
SPENCER, Corwin H. 5
SPENCER, Edgar A. 1
SPENCER, Edward 2 Buckham Taylor
SPENCER, Elihu H
SPENCER, Elijah H
SPENCER, Evelene 4 Armstrong
SPENCER, Francis Marion 1
SPENCER, Frank E. 3
SPENCER, Frank Robert 3
SPENCER, George Albert 5
SPENCER, George Eliphaz H
SPENCER, George 1 Mazelton
SPENCER, Guilford Lawson 1
SPENCER, Guy Raymond 6
SPENCER, Harley Orton 6
SPENCER, Hazelton 2
SPENCER, Henry Russell 5
SPENCER, Herbert 4
SPENCER, Herbert Lincoln 3
SPENCER, Horatio Nelson 1
SPENCER, Howard Bonnell 6
SPENCER, Ichabod Smith H
SPENCER, Irene Keyes 6 (Mrs. Charles Truman Spencer)
SPENCER, J. Brookes 3
SPENCER, J. W. 1
SPENCER, James Bradley H
SPENCER, James Clark 1
SPENCER, James Harland 5
SPENCER, James Morton 4
SPENCER, Jesse Ames 1
SPENCER, John 3
SPENCER, John Canfield 3
SPENCER, John Mitchell 3
SPENCER, John R. 1
SPENCER, John Wesley 1
SPENCER, Joseph 1
SPENCER, Kenneth 2
SPENCER, Kenneth Aldred 3
SPENCER, Lee Bowen 4
SPENCER, Mrs. Lilian 3 White
SPENCER, Lorillard * 1
SPENCER, Lyle Manly 5
SPENCER, M(atthew) Lyle 5
SPENCER, Niles 3
SPENCER, Oliver Martin 4
SPENCER, Omar Corwin 6
SPENCER, Paul 1
SPENCER, Percy Craig 5
SPENCER, Percy LeBaron 5
SPENCER, Pitman Clemens H
SPENCER, Platt Rogers 1
SPENCER, Richard H
SPENCER, Richard 1
SPENCER, Robert 1
SPENCER, Robert Closson 5
SPENCER, Robert Lyle 2
SPENCER, Robert Nelson 5
SPENCER, Samuel 1
SPENCER, Samuel Riley 3
SPENCER, Sara Andrews 1
SPENCER, Selden Palmer 1
SPENCER, Theodore 2
SPENCER, Thomas 1
SPENCER, Vernon 5
SPENCER, Walker Brainerd 1
SPENCER, William Brinerd 6
SPENCER, William Homer 4
SPENCER, William L. 4
SPENCER, William Loring 5
SPENCER, William 1 Vaughan
SPENCER, Willing 5
SPENCER-NAIRN, Sir 4 Robert
SPENS, Conrad E. 1
SPENZER, John George 1
SPERANZA, Gino 1
SPERBER, Jacob 4
SPERLING, Melitta 6
SPERO, Sterling D. 6
SPERR, Frederick William 1
SPERRY, Charles Stilman 1
SPERRY, Earl Evelyn 1
SPERRY, Elmer Ambrose 1
SPERRY, Leavenworth 3 Porter
SPERRY, Lewis 4
SPERRY, Lyman Beecher 1
SPERRY, Marcy 1 Leavenworth
SPERRY, Nehemiah Day 1
SPERRY, Paul 6
SPERRY, Watson Robertson 1
SPERRY, Willard Gardner 4

SPERRY, Willard Learoyd 3
SPEWACK, Samuel 5
SPEYER, James 1
SPEYER, Leonora 3
SPEYERS, Arthur Bayard 1
SPEYERS, Anne Higginson 4
SPICER, Clarence Winfred 1
SPICER, Clinton Elbert 5
SPICER, Eleanor W. 6
SPICER, Henry Russell 5
SPICER, Robert Barclay 5
SPICER, William Ambrose 5
SPICER-SIMSON, Margaret 1
SPICER-SIMSON, Theodore 3
SPIEGEL, Edwin John 4
SPIEGEL, Frederick 1 Siegfried
SPIEGEL, Frederick 6 William
SPIEGEL, Modie Joseph 2
SPIEKER, Edward Henry 1
SPIEKER, George Frederick 1
SPIER, Leslie 4
SPIERING, Theodore 1
SPIES, Albert 1
SPIES, Tom Douglas 4
SPIESS, Carlos Augustus 4
SPIETH, Lawrence Caleb 4
SPIKE, Robert Warren 4
SPILLANE, Edward 4
SPILLANE, Richard 2
SPILLER, Harold Alfred 4
SPILLER, William Gibson 1
SPILLERS, Charles Lee 1
SPILLMAN, Ora Seldon 1
SPILLMAN, William Jasper 1 Washington
SPILMAN, Bernard 5
SPILMAN, Edward Guthrie 1
SPILMAN, Lewis Hopkins 1
SPILMAN, Robert Scott 3
SPILMAN, Robert Scott Jr. 5
SPILSBURY, Edmund 1 Gybbon
SPINDEN, Herbert Joseph 4
SPINDLER, Garold Ralph 4
SPINGARN, Arthur B. 5
SPINGARN, J. E. 1
SPINGOLD, Nathan Breiter 3
SPINING, George Lawrence 1
SPINK, Cyrus H
SPINK, J. G. Taylor 4
SPINK, Mary Angela 1
SPINK, Mary Angela 2
SPINK, Solomon Lewis H
SPINKA, Matthew 5
SPINKS, Lewis 2
SPINNER, Francis Elias H
SPINNEY, George Wilbur 4
SPINNEY, Louis Bevier 3
SPINNING, James M. 6
SPINOLA, Francis Barretto H
SPIRO, Charles 1
SPIRO, Solon 4
SPITZ, Armand 5 N(eustadter)
SPITZ, Leo 3
SPITZER, Ceilan Milo 5
SPITZKA, Edward Anthony 1
SPITZKA, Edward Charles 1
SPIVACK, Robert Gerald 5
SPIVAK, Charles David 1
SPIVEY, Ludd Myrl 4
SPIVEY, Thomas Sawyer 1
SPLINT, Sarah Field 2
SPOEHR, Herman Augustus 3
SPOFFORD, Ainsworth 1 Rand
SPOFFORD, Grace Harriet 6
SPOFFORD, Harriet 1 Prescott
SPOFFORD, W. E. 4
SPOHN, George Welda 2
SPONBERG, Harold 6 Eugene
SPONG, Harper W. 4
SPONSLER, Olenus Lee 3
SPOONER, Charles Horace 1
SPOONER, Edmund D. 4
SPOONER, Florence 1 Garrettson
SPOONER, Henry Joshua 1
SPOONER, John Colt 1
SPOONER, Lysander 1
SPOONER, Shearjashub H
SPOONTS, Morris Augustus 4
SPOOR, John Alden 1
SPORBORG, Constance A. 6
SPOTSWOOD, Alexander H
SPOTTED TAIL H
SPOTTS, William Bigler 3
SPOTTSWOOD, Stephen 6 Gill
SPRACHER, Dwight L. 5
SPRAGINS, Robert L. 4

SPRAGUE, Achsa W. H
SPRAGUE, Albert Arnold 1
SPRAGUE, Albert Arnold 2
SPRAGUE, Albert Tilden 5 Jr.
SPRAGUE, Augustus Brown 1 Reed
SPRAGUE, Austin Velorous 4 Milton
SPRAGUE, Benjamin 2 Oxnard
SPRAGUE, Carleton 1
SPRAGUE, Charles 6
SPRAGUE, Charles Arthur 5
SPRAGUE, Charles Ezra 1
SPRAGUE, Charles 1 Franklin
SPRAGUE, Charles James 1
SPRAGUE, Clifton Albert 3
SPRAGUE, Edward 6 Wharton
SPRAGUE, Ezra Kimball 2
SPRAGUE, Frank Headley 4
SPRAGUE, Frank Julian 1
SPRAGUE, Franklin M. 1
SPRAGUE, George Clare 4
SPRAGUE, Henry Harrison 1
SPRAGUE, Homer Baxter 1
SPRAGUE, Howard B. 5
SPRAGUE, Hugh Almeron 1
SPRAGUE, Jesse Rainsford 2
SPRAGUE, John Titcomb H
SPRAGUE, Julian King 4
SPRAGUE, Kate Chase H
SPRAGUE, Kenneth 4 Burdette
SPRAGUE, Kenneth 5 Burdette
SPRAGUE, Leslie Willis 1
SPRAGUE, Levi L. 1
SPRAGUE, Lucian C. 4
SPRAGUE, M. D. 1
SPRAGUE, Mary Aplin 1
SPRAGUE, Oliver Mitchell 3 Wentworth
SPRAGUE, Paul Epworth 6
SPRAGUE, Peleg * H
SPRAGUE, Robert James 1
SPRAGUE, Thomas Henry 1
SPRAGUE, Thomas 5 Lamison
SPRAGUE, William * H
SPRAGUE, William 1
SPRAGUE, William Buell H
SPRAGUE, William Cyrus 1
SPRAGUE, William Wallace 4
SPRAGUE-SMITH, Charles 1
SPRAGUE-SMITH, Isabelle 3 Dwight
SPRATLING, William 1
SPRATLING, William 4 Philip
SPRATT, Frederick 1
SPRATT, Nelson Tracy Jr. 6
SPRAY, Chalres Cranston 4
SPRAY, Ruth Hinshaw 1
SPRECKELS, Adolph 1 Bernard
SPRECKELS, Claus 1
SPRECKELS, John Diedrich 1
SPRECKELS, Rudolph 3
SPRENG, Samuel Peter 2
SPRENG, Theodore 4 Frederick Henry
SPRENGLING, Martin 3
SPRIGG, James Cresap 1
SPRIGG, John Thomas H
SPRIGG, Louis Rivers H
SPRIGG, Michael Cresap H
SPRIGG, Richard Jr. H
SPRIGG, Thomas H
SPRIGLE, Ray 3
SPRING, Alfred 1
SPRING, Gardiner H
SPRING, George E. 1
SPRING, Howard 4
SPRING, La Verne Ward 4
SPRING, Laurence 4 Ellsworth
SPRING, Leverett Wilson 1
SPRING, Samuel 1
SPRING, Samuel 6
SPRING, Samuel Newton 3
SPRINGER, Alfred 1
SPRINGER, Charles 1
SPRINGER, Durand 4 William
SPRINGER, Edward 4 Thomas
SPRINGER, Francis Edwin 1
SPRINGER, Frank 1
SPRINGER, Franklin 1 Wesley
SPRINGER, George Peter 5
SPRINGER, John Franklin 2

SPRINGER, John 5 McKendree
SPRINGER, John Wallace 4
SPRINGER, Raymond 2 Smiley
SPRINGER, Rebecca Ruter 1
SPRINGER, Reuben H Runyan
SPRINGER, Thomas Grant 5
SPRINGER, William 1 McKendree
SPRINGHORN, Carl 5
SPRINGMEYER, George 6
SPRING-RICE, Sir Cecil 1 Arthur
SPRINGS, Elliott White 3
SPRINGS, Holmes Buck 3
SPRINGS, Lena Jones 2
SPRINGS, Leroy 1
SPRINGWEILER, Erwin 5 Frederick
SPROGELL, Harry 6 E(dward)
SPRONG, Severn D. 2
SPROSS, Charles Gilbert 4
SPROSS, Charles Gilbert 4
SPROTT, Jarl S. 2
SPROUL, Elliott Wilford 1
SPROUL, Robert Gordon 6
SPROUL, William Cameron 1
SPROUL, William H. 1
SPROULE, Charles H. 1
SPROULE, William 1
SPROULL, Thomas H
SPROULL, William Oliver 1
SPROUSE, Claude Willard 3
SPROUT, Will Carleton 4
SPROWL, James Allen 4
SPROWLS, Joseph Barnett 5 Jr.
SPRUANCE, Benton M. 4
SPRUANCE, Presley H
SPRUANCE, Raymond 5 Ames
SPRUANCE, William Corbit 1
SPRUNT, Alexander 1
SPRUNT, Alexander Jr. 5
SPRY, William 1
SPURGEON, William 1 Porter
SPURGIN, William Fletcher 1
SPURR, Josiah Edward 2
SPURR, Josiah Edward 3
SPURR, William Alfred 6
SPURZHEIM, Johann H Kaspar
SPYKMAN, Nicholas John 2
SQUANTO H
SQUIBB, Edward Robinson 1
SQUIER, Carl B. 4
SQUIER, Ephraim George H
SQUIER, George Owen 1
SQUIER, John Bentley 2
SQUIER, Lee Welling 4
SQUIER, Miles Powell H
SQUIERS, Arnon Lyon 1
SQUIERS, Herbert 1 Goldsmith
SQUIRE, Amos Osborne 2
SQUIRE, Andrew 1
SQUIRE, Edward Jacob 1
SQUIRE, Frances 1
SQUIRE, Francis Hagar 1
SQUIRE, Watson Carvosso 1
SQUIRES, Charles William 2
SQUIRES, David Denton 6
SQUIRES, George Forbes 3
SQUIRES, Ralph Anthony 4
SQUIRES, Vernon Purinton 1
SQUIRES, Walter Albion 5
SQUIRES, William Henry 2 Tappey
STAACK, John George 6
STAAF, Oscar 3
STAAKE, William Heaton 2
STABLER, Herman 2
STABLER, Howard Douglas 4
STABLER, James Pleasants 4
STABLER, John Gates 1
STABLER, Jordan Herbert 1
STABLER, Laird Joseph 1
STABLETON, John Kay 4
STACE, Arthur William 2
STACE, Walter Terence 5
STACEY, Alfred Edwin 1
STACEY, Alfred Edwin Jr. 6
STACEY, Anna Lee 1
STACEY, John Franklin 1
STACEY, John Markell 6
STACK, Edmund John 5
STACK, Frederic William 5
STACK, J. W. 3
STACK, John 1
STACK, Joseph Michael 3
STACKHOUSE, Eli Thomas H

STACKHOUSE, Perry James 2
STACKHOUSE, Wesley Thomas 4
STACKPOLE, Albert Hummel 5
STACKPOLE, Edward J. 4
STACKPOLE, Edward James 1
STACKPOLE, Everett Schermerhorn 1
STACKPOLE, James Hall 4
STACKPOLE, Pierpont L. 4
STACY, Merrill E. 4
STACY, Thomas Hobbs 1
STACY, Walter Parker 3
STADDEN, Corry Montague 1
STADELMAN, William Francis 1
STADIE, William Christopher 3
STADLER, Charles A. 4
STADLER, Lewis John 4
STADLER, William Lewis 5
STADTFELD, Joseph 2
STAFFORD, Charles Lewis 1
STAFFORD, Clarence Eugene 6
STAFFORD, Cora Elder 4
STAFFORD, Dale Bernard 6
STAFFORD, Geoffrey Wardle 3
STAFFORD, John Aloysius 4
STAFFORD, John Richard 5
STAFFORD, Maurice L. 3
STAFFORD, Orin Fletcher 1
STAFFORD, Thomas Polhill 2
STAFFORD, Wendell Phillips 5
STAFFORD, William Bascom 4
STAFSETH, H(enrik) J(oakim) 5
STAGE, Charles Willard 2
STAGER, Anson H
STAGG, Amos Alonzo 4
STAGG, Charles H
STAGG, Charles Tracey 1
STAGG, John Weldon 1
STAHEL, Julius 1
STAHL, John Meloy 2
STAHL, Karl Friedrich 2
STAHL, William Harris 5
STAHLMAN, E. B. Jr. 6
STAHLMAN, Edward Bushrod 1
STAHLSCHMIDT, Arthur Edward 4
STAHR, Henry Irvin 4
STAHR, John Summers 1
STAINBACK, Ingram Macklin 4
STAIR, Charles Augustus 6
STAIR, Edward Douglas 5
STAKELY, Charles A. 5
STAKELY, Charles Averett 4
STALBERG, Jonah 3
STALDER, Jackson R. 5
STALDER, Walter 2
STALEY, A. Rollin 4
STALEY, Allen Conklin 4
STALEY, Augustus Eugene 1
STALEY, Augustus Eugene Jr. 6
STALEY, Cady 1
STALEY, John Richard 4
STALEY, John Wilson 4
STALEY, R. C. 4
STALIN, Joseph Vissarionovich 3
STALIN, Joseph Vissarionovich 4
STALKER, Arthur William 1
STALKER, John Nellis 6
STALL, Albert H. 6
STALL, Sylvanus 1
STALLARD, Carton Sherman 6
STALLINGS, Jesse F. 4
STALLINGS, Laurence 4
STALLO, John Bernhard 1
STALLWORTH, James Adams H
STALLWORTH, Nicholas Eugene 1
STALNAKER, Frank D. 1
STALNAKER, Luther Winfield 3
STAM, Colin Ferguson 4
STAM, Jacob 5
STAMBAUGH, Armstrong Alexander 4
STAMBAUGH, John 1
STAMM, Earle Williams 4
STAMM, Edward P. 4

STAMM, Frederick Keller 4
STAMM, John Samuel 3
STAMM, Vincil R. 5
STAMP, Adele H. 6
STAMPS, Thomas Dodson 4
STANARD, Edwin Obed 1
STANARD, Mary Newton 1
STANARD, William Glover 1
STANBERY, Henry H
STANBERY, William H
STANBRO, William Woodrow 6
STANBURY, Walter Albert 3
STANCHFIELD, John Barry 1
STANCLIFF, Evert Lee 3
STANCLIFT, Henry Clay 2
STANDEN, William Thomas 4
STANDER, Henricus Johannes 2
STANDEVEN, Herbert Leslie 2
STANDEVEN, James Wylie 5
STANDEVEN, James Wylie 6
STANDIFER, James H
STANDIFORD, Elisha David H
STANDISH, John Van Ness 1
STANDISH, Myles H
STANDISH, Myles 1
STANDISH, S. H. 3
STANDLEY, William Harrison 4
STANFIELD, J. Fisher 3
STANFIELD, Robert Nelson 2
STANFIELD, Theodore 5
STANFORD, Albert Clinton 3
STANFORD, Edward Valentine 4
STANFORD, Homer Reed 4
STANFORD, Jane Lathrop 1
STANFORD, John H
STANFORD, Leland H
STANFORD, Rawghlie Clement 4
STANFORD, Richard H
STANFORD, Wesley M. 4
STANGE, Charles Henry 1
STANGELAND, Charles Emil 1
STANGELAND, Katharina Marie (Mrs. Charles E. Stangeland) 5
STANGLAND, Benjamin F. 4
STANISLAUS, I(gnatius) V(alerius) Stanley 5
STANLAWS, Penrhyn 3
STANLEY, A. Owsley 2
STANLEY, Albert Augustus 1
STANLEY, Carleton Wellesley 5
STANLEY, Caroline Abbot 1
STANLEY, Cassius Miller 4
STANLEY, Clarance 5
STANLEY, David Sloane 1
STANLEY, Edmund 1
STANLEY, Edwin James 1
STANLEY, Edwin M(onroe) 5
STANLEY, Emory Day 4
STANLEY, Francis Edgar H
STANLEY, Francis Edgar 1
STANLEY, Frank Arthur 4
STANLEY, Frederic Bartlett 2
STANLEY, Frederick Jonte 4
STANLEY, Freelan O. 1
STANLEY, George James 4
STANLEY, Harold 4
STANLEY, Helen 4
STANLEY, Sir Henry Morton G. C. B. 1
STANLEY, Hiram Alonzo 4
STANLEY, Hugh Wright 3
STANLEY, James G. 2
STANLEY, John Joseph 1
STANLEY, John Mix H
STANLEY, Louise 3
STANLEY, Maurice 4
STANLEY, Osso Willis 4
STANLEY, Philip B. 4
STANLEY, Robert Crooks 3
STANLEY, Thomas Bahnson 4
STANLEY, W. E. 1
STANLEY, Wendell M(eredith) 5
STANLEY, William 1
STANLEY, William 2
STANLEY, William Eugene 4
STANLEY, William Henry 4
STANLEY-BROWN, Joseph 1
STANLEY-BROWN, Joseph 2
STANLY, Edward H
STANLY, John H

STANLY, Walter Lawrence 2
STANNARD, Albert Clinton 6
STANNARD, E. Tappan 2
STANNARD, Mrs. Margaret J. 4
STANSBURY, Ele 4
STANSBURY, Howard H
STANSBURY, Joseph H
STANSBURY, Karl E. 4
STANSBURY, Paul William 4
STANSELL, Robert Basil 5
STANTON, A. Glenn 5
STANTON, Benjamin H
STANTON, Charles Spelman 2
STANTON, Edwin McMasters H
STANTON, Elizabeth Cady 1
STANTON, Frank Lebby 1
STANTON, Frank M. 4
STANTON, Frank McMillan H
STANTON, Frederick Perry H
STANTON, Harry Leavenworth 1
STANTON, Henry Brewster H
STANTON, Henry Francis 3
STANTON, Henry Thompson 3
STANTON, Horace Coffin 1
STANTON, John 1
STANTON, John Gilman 1
STANTON, Jonathan Young 1
STANTON, Joseph Jr. H
STANTON, Lucy M. 1
STANTON, Oscar Fitzalan 1
STANTON, Philip Ackley 4
STANTON, Richard Henry H
STANTON, Robert 6
STANTON, Robert Brewster 1
STANTON, Stephen Berrien 5
STANTON, Thaddeus H. 1
STANTON, Theodore 1
STANTON, Thomas Elwood 6
STANTON, Timothy William 3
STANTON, William 1
STANWICK, John H
STANWOOD, Edward 1
STAPLES, Abram Penn 4
STAPLES, Abram Penn 3
STAPLES, Arthur Gray 1
STAPLES, Charles Henry 4
STAPLES, Charles Jason 4
STAPLES, Henry Franklin 1
STAPLES, John Norman 4
STAPLES, Percy A. 4
STAPLES, Philip Clayton 2
STAPLES, Seth Stitt 4
STAPLES, Thomas S. 3
STAPLES, Waller Redd H
STAPLES, William Read H
STAPLETON, Ammon 1
STAPLETON, Benjamin F. 3
STAPLETON, Luke D. 1
STAPLETON, William 4
STARBIRD, Alfred 3
STARBUCK, Edwin Diller 4
STARBUCK, Kathryn Helene 4
STARBUCK, Raymond Donald 4
STARCKE, Viggo 6
STAREK, Fred 5
STAREN, John Edgar 5
STARIHA, John 1
STARIN, John Henry 1
STARK, Abe 5
STARK, Albert Philander 4
STARK, Clarence Oscar 5
STARK, Dudley Scott 5
STARK, Edwin Jackson 4
STARK, Edwin M. 4
STARK, Francis Raymond 5
STARK, G. Harold 6
STARK, George W. 4
STARK, Harold Raynsford 4
STARK, Harry Rodgers 4
STARK, Henry Ignatius 2
STARK, Henry Jacob Lutcher 5
STARK, John H
STARK, Lloyd Crow 5
STARK, Louis 5
STARK, Orton K(irkwood) 5
STARK, Otto 1
STARK, Paul Clarence 6
STARK, Taylor 4
STARK, William Everett 4
STARK, William Ledyard 1
STARKEY, Harold Bellamy 6
STARKEY, Thomas Alfred 1

STARKLOFF, Max C(arl) 5
STARKS, William Henry Lord 4
STARKWEATHER, Chauncey Clark 1
STARKWEATHER, David H Austin
STARKWEATHER, George H Anson
STARKWEATHER, Henry H Howard
STARKWEATHER, John K. 5
STARKWEATHER, Louis Pomeroy 3
STARKWEATHER, William Edward Bloomfield 5
STARLING, William 1
STARNES, George Talmage 3
STARNES, Joe 5
STARR, Belle H
STARR, Cornelius V. 5
STARR, Eliza Allen 1
STARR, Frances (Grant) 6
STARR, Frederick 1
STARR, H. Danforth 6
STARR, Helen Knowlton 6
STARR, Henry Frank 5
STARR, Ida May Hill 4
STARR, Lee Anna 5
STARR, Louis 1
STARR, Louis Edward 4
STARR, M. Allen 1
STARR, Merritt 1
STARR, Nathan 3
STARR, Oliver 1
STARR, Paul Hart 6
STARR, Raymond Wesley 5
STARR, William G. 4
STARRETT, Helen Ekin 1
STARRETT, Henry Prince 1
STARRETT, Lewis Frederick 1
STARRETT, Milton Gerry 2
STARRETT, Paul 3
STARRETT, Theodore 1
STARRETT, Vincent (Charles Vincent Emerson) 6
STARRETT, William Aiken 1
STARRING, Frederick A. 1
STARRING, Mason Brayman 1
START, Charles Monroe 1
START, Edwin Augustus 1
START, Henry R. 1
STASON, E(dwin) Blythe 5
STASTNY, Olga Frances 3
STATE, Charles 1
STATHAS, Pericles Peter 5
STATHERS, Birk Smtih 2
STATLER, Alice Seidler (Mrs. Ellsworth Milton Statler) 5
STATLER, Ellsworth Milton 1
STATON, Adolphus 4
STATON, Harry 3
STATTER, Arthur Frederick 5
STATTON, Arthur Biggs 4
STAUB, Albert William 4
STAUB, Gordon James 3
STAUB, Walter Adolph 2
STAUBER, Leslie Alfred 5
STAUBLE, Wilbur Carl 5
STAUDINGER, Hermann 4
STAUFFACHER, Charles Henry 3
STAUFFACHER, Edward L. 4
STAUFFEN, Ernest Jr. 3
STAUFFER, Charles Albert 5
STAUFFER, Clinton Raymond 1
STAUFFER, David McNeely 1
STAUFFER, Donald Alfred 4
STAUFFER, Grant 2
STAUFFER, Herbert Milton 5
STAUFFER, Vernon 1
STAUGHTON, William H
STAUNTON, Sidney Augustus 1
STAUNTON, William H
STAUNTON, William Field 2
STAYTON, Edward M. 3
STAYTON, John William 1
STAYTON, Joseph Markham 1
STAYTON, Robert Weldon 4
STAYTON, William H. 2
STEACIE, Edgar William Richard 4
STEAD, Robert 2
STEAD, William Henry 3
STEADMAN, Alva Edgar 4

STEADMAN, Chester Chandler 6
STEADMAN, John Marcellus Jr. 2
STEADWELL, B. Samuel 2
STEAGALL, Henry Bascom 2
STEALEY, Orlando O. 1
STEALEY, Sydnor Lorenzo 5
STEARLEY, Ralph F. 5
STEARLY, Wilson Reiff 1
STEARNE, Allen Michener 3
STEARNES, Reaumur Coleman 2
STEARNS, Abel H
STEARNS, Albert Warren 2
STEARNS, Alfred Ernest 2
STEARNS, Arthur French 4
STEARNS, Asahel H
STEARNS, Carl Leo 5
STEARNS, Charles Cummings 1
STEARNS, Charles Falconer 2
STEARNS, Eben Sperry H
STEARNS, Edith Shaffer 4
STEARNS, Foster 3
STEARNS, Frank Preston 1
STEARNS, Frank Waterman 1
STEARNS, Frederic Pike 1
STEARNS, Frederick Sweet 6
STEARNS, Frederick William 1
STEARNS, George Luther H
STEARNS, Gustav 3
STEARNS, Harold Edmund 2
STEARNS, Henry Putnam 1
STEARNS, John Barker 6
STEARNS, John Newton 1
STEARNS, John William 4
STEARNS, Joyce Clennam 2
STEARNS, Junius Brutus H
STEARNS, Lutie Eugenia 4
STEARNS, Marshall Winslow 5
STEARNS, Neele Edward 4
STEARNS, Oliver 1
STEARNS, Osborne Putnam 4
STEARNS, Ozora Pierson H
STEARNS, Robert Edwards Carter 1
STEARNS, Sarah Burger 4
STEARNS, Shubal H
STEARNS, Theodore 3
STEARNS, Wallace Nelson 1
STEARNS, William Augustus H
STEARNS, William Guilford 1
STEARNS, William Marion 1
STEBBINS, Arthur D. 6
STEBBINS, Arthur D. 3
STEBBINS, Byron H. 4
STEBBINS, Edwin Allen 3
STEBBINS, Emma 1
STEBBINS, George Coles 2
STEBBINS, G(eorge) Waring 5
STEBBINS, Henry Endicott 6
STEBBINS, Henry George 4
STEBBINS, Henry Hamlin 3
STEBBINS, Homer Adolph 4
STEBBINS, Horatio H
STEBBINS, Joel 6
STEBBINS, John W. 4
STEBBINS, Kathleen B. 4
STEBBINS, Lucy Ward 6
STEBBINS, Rufus Phineas H
STEBLER, William John 4
STECHER, Henry William 1
STECHER, Robert Morgan 5
STECHOW, Wolfgang 6
STECHSCHULTE, Victor Cyril 3
STECIUK, Basil W. 6
STECK, Charles Calvin 5
STECK, Daniel Frederic 3
STECK, George 1
STECKEL, Abram Peters 3
STECKER, Robert Donald 4
STECKLER, Alfred 4
STEDDOM, Rice Price 5
STEDMAN, Charles Manly 1
STEDMAN, Edmund Clarence 1
STEDMAN, George Woolverton 3
STEDMAN, Giles Chester 4
STEDMAN, Henry Rust 1
STEDMAN, John Moore 2
STEDMAN, John Weiss 3
STEDMAN, Louise Adella 3
STEDMAN, Thomas Lathrop 1
STEDMAN, William H
STEED, J. Lyman 2
STEED, Robert Dennis 4

STEEDLY, Benjamin 1
Broadus
STEEDMAN, Charles H
STEEDMAN, Edwin 4
Harrison
STEEDMAN, James Blair H
STEEL, Alfred G. B. 2
STEEL, David 6
STEEL, George Alexander 1
STEEL, Rowe Summerville 1
STEEL, Westbrook 5
STEELE, Albert Wilbur 1
STEELE, Alfred N. 3
STEELE, Alice Garland 6
STEELE, Charles 1
STEELE, Daniel 1
STEELE, Daniel Atkinson 1
King
STEELE, David 1
STEELE, David McConnell 2
STEELE, Edgar Clarence 4
STEELE, Esther Baker 1
STEELE, Frank B. 5
STEELE, Frederic Dorr 2
STEELE, Frederick 1
STEELE, George W. H
STEELE, George 1
Washington
STEELE, Harry Lee 1
STEELE, Heath McClung 3
STEELE, Henry J. 1
STEELE, Henry Maynadier 1
STEELE, Hiram Roswell 1
STEELE, James Dallas 1
STEELE, James King 1
STEELE, Joel Dorman 1
STEELE, John H
STEELE, John 1
STEELE, John Benedict H
STEELE, John Dutton 5
STEELE, John Murray 5
STEELE, John Nelson 1
STEELE, John Nevett 5
STEELE, Joseph M. 5
STEELE, Leon Charles 1
STEELE, Leslie J. 1
STEELE, Robert Benson 5
STEELE, Robert Denham 5
STEELE, Robert Wilbur 1
STEELE, Robert Wilbur 5
STEELE, Rufus 1
STEELE, Sidney John 5
STEELE, Theodore Clement 1
STEELE, Thomas J. 1
STEELE, Thomas M. 2
STEELE, Thomas Sedgwick 1
STEELE, Walter Leak H
STEELE, Walter Simeon 3
STEELE, Wilbur Daniel 5
STEELE, Wilbur Fletcher 4
STEELE, William Gaston 1
STEELE, William La Barthe 2
STEELL, Willis 1
STEELL, Willis 2
STEEN, Fred E. 6
STEEN, Marguerite 6
STEENBERG, Richard 4
Wilbur
STEENBOCK, Harry 4
STEENDAM, Jacob H
STEENE, William 4
STEENERSON, Halvor 1
STEENROD, Lewis H
STEENROD, Norman Earl 5
STEENSTRA, Peter Henry 1
STEENWYCK, Cornelis H
STEEP, Thomas 2
STEERE, Joseph Beal 1
STEERE, Joseph Hall 1
STEERE, Kenneth David 4
STEERE, Lloyd Randol 4
STEERS, George H
STEERS, William Edward 6
STEESE, James Gordon 3
STEFAN, Karl 2
STEFANINI, Francois Ange 2
Antoine
STEFANSSON, Vilhjalmur 4
STEFFAN, Roger 3
STEFFENS, Cornelius M. 1
STEFFENS, Lincoln 1
STEFFENS, Theodore 3
Henry
STEFFENSEN, Vernal R. 1
STEFFIAN, Edwin 6
Theodore
STEGEMAN, Gebhard 2
STEGER, Christian Talbot 3
STEGER, Julius 3
STEGER, Peyton 1
STEHLE, Aurelius 2
STEICHEN, Edward 5
STEIDTMANN, Waldo E. 3
STEIGER, Ernst 1
STEIGER, George 2
STEIGERS, William Corbet 1

STEIGUER, Louis Rudolph 2
de
STEIL, William Nicholas 5
STEIN, Albert Harvey 5
STEIN, Edward Thomas 4
STEIN, Evaleen 1
STEIN, Fred W. Sr. 5
STEIN, Gertrude 2
STEIN, Hannah 6
STEIN, Harold 4
STEIN, I. Melville 4
STEIN, James Rauch 5
STEIN, John Philip 1
STEIN, Louis P. 3
STEIN, Robert 1
STEINBACH, Everett Mark 5
STEINBACH, Milton 5
STEINBECK, John Ernst 5
STEINBERG, Milton 3
STEINBERG, Samuel 4
Sidney
STEINBERGER, Franklin 6
Jennings
STEINBOCK, Max 6
STEINBRINK, Meier 4
STEINBRUGGE, Edward 6
Donald
STEINDEL, Bruno 5
STEINDLER, Arthur 3
STEINDORFF, Georg 3
STEINEM, Pauline 4
STEINER, Bernard 1
Christian
STEINER, Bernard Sigfried 6
STEINER, Celestin John 5
STEINER, Edward Alfred 5
STEINER, Jesse Frederick 6
STEINER, Leo K. 2
STEINER, Lewis Henry H
STEINER, Max 5
STEINER, Robert Eugene 3
STEINER, Walter Ralph 2
STEINER, William Howard 4
STEINER, Williams Kossuth 2
STEINERT, Alan 2
STEINERT, William Joseph 6
STEINETZ, Bernard G. 4
STEINFELD, Albert 5
STEINGRUBER-
WILDGANS, Ilona
STEINHARDT, Laurence 2
A.
STEINHART, Frank 1
STEINHART, Jesse H. 4
STEINHAUS, Arthur H. 5
STEINHAUS, Edward 5
A(rthur)
STEININGER, Fred H. 5
STEINITZ, William 1
STEINKRAUS, Herman W. 6
STEINLE, Roland Joseph 4
STEINLE, Roland Joseph 5
STEINMAN, Andrew 1
Jackson
STEINMAN, David Barnard 4
STEINMAN, James Hale 4
STEINMETZ, Charles 1
Proteus
STEINMETZ, Joseph 1
Allison
STEINMETZ, Maurice 5
STEINREICH, Kenneth 4
Pease
STEINSAPIR, Saul P. 5
STEINWAY, Charles 1
Herman
STEINWAY, Christian H
Friedrich Theodore
STEINWAY, Henry H
Engelhard
STEINWAY, Theodore E. 3
STEINWAY, William H
STEINWAY, William 4
Richard
STEINWEG, William Louis 4
STEIWER, Frederick 1
STEJNEGER, Leonhard 2
STELLA, Antonio 1
STELLA, Joseph 2
STELLE, Charles Clarkson 4
STELLE, John 4
STELLHORN, Frederick 1
William
STELLWAGEN, Edward 1
James
STELLWAGEN, Seitorde 2
Michael
STELTER, Benjamin F. 3
STELWAGON, Henry 1
Weightman
STELZLE, Charles 1
STEMBEL, Roger Nelson 1
STEMLER, Otto Adolph 1
STEMMLER, Theodore 6
Washington
STEMPEL, Guido Hermann 3

STEMPF, Victor Herman 2
STEMPLE, Frank 4
STENGEL, Alfred 1
STENGEL, (Charles Dillon) 6
Casey
STENGEL, Erwin 6
STENGEL, Frederick 5
William
STENGLE, Charles Irwin 3
STENTZ, John Clyde 6
STENZEL, Lula Vinette 5
STEPELTON, Norman 5
Allen
STEPHAN, Arthur 6
Theodore
STEPHAN, Frank Lawrence 3
STEPHAN, Frederick 5
Franklin
STEPHAN, George 2
STEPHEN, George 3
STEPHENS, A. E. S. 6
STEPHENS, Abraham P. H
STEPHENS, Albert Lee Sr. 4
STEPHENS, Alexander H
Hamilton
STEPHENS, Alice Barber 1
STEPHENS, Ambrose E. B. 1
STEPHENS, Ann Sophia H
Hughl
STEPHENS, Benjamin 5
STEPHENS, Charles Asbury 1
STEPHENS, Claude P. 4
STEPHENS, Clyde Harrison 4
STEPHENS, Dan Voorhees 1
STEPHENS, Daniel Mallory 4
STEPHENS, David Stubert 1
STEPHENS, Edwin Lewis 1
STEPHENS, Edwin William 1
STEPHENS, Ferris J. 5
STEPHENS, Frank 1
STEPHENS, Frank Fletcher 6
STEPHENS, George 1
STEPHENS, George Asbury 3
STEPHENS, George Ware 4
STEPHENS, Guy Frederic 4
STEPHENS, H. Morse 1
STEPHENS, Harley Clifford 5
STEPHENS, Harold 3
Montelle
STEPHENS, Harry T. 2
STEPHENS, Herbert Taylor 1
STEPHENS, Howard V. 3
STEPHENS, Hubert Durrett 2
STEPHENS, James 3
STEPHENS, James C(ollins) 4
STEPHENS, John Hall 4
STEPHENS, John Leonard 1
STEPHENS, John Lloyd H
STEPHENS, John Vant 2
STEPHENS, Kate 1
STEPHENS, Lawrence Vest 1
STEPHENS, Leroy 4
STEPHENS, Linton 4
STEPHENS, Louis L. 4
STEPHENS, Martin Bates 1
STEPHENS, Oren Melson 5
STEPHENS, Percy Rector 2
STEPHENS, Philander H
STEPHENS, Philip 5
B(lanton)
STEPHENS, Redmond 1
Davis
STEPHENS, Robert Allan 4
STEPHENS, Robert Neilson 1
STEPHENS, Roswell Powell 3
STEPHENS, Russell Stout 4
STEPHENS, Theodore 4
Pierson
STEPHENS, Uriah Smith H
STEPHENS, W(illiam) 5
Barclay
STEPHENS, Ward 1
STEPHENS, William 2
Dennison
STEPHENSON, Benjamin H
STEPHENSON, Benjamin H
Franklin
STEPHENSON, C. S. 4
STEPHENSON, Carl 3
STEPHENSON, Edward 1
Morris
STEPHENSON, Franklin 4
Bache
STEPHENSON, George 3
Malcolm
STEPHENSON, Gilbert 5
Thomas
STEPHENSON, Henry 5
Thew
STEPHENSON, Isaac 1
STEPHENSON, James H
STEPHENSON, James 2
STEPHENSON, James 3
Pomeroy
STEPHENSON, John H

STEPHENSON, Joseph 2
Maxwell
STEPHENSON, Nathaniel 1
Wright
STEPHENSON, Orlistus 4
Bell
STEPHENSON, Rome 2
Charles
STEPHENSON, S. Town 4
STEPHENSON, Sam 2
STEPHENSON, Wendell 5
Holmes
STEPHENSON, William H
STEPHENSON, William B. 3
Jr.
STEPHENSON, William 4
Benjamin
STEPHENSON, William 5
Lawrence
STEPHENSON, William 5
Prettyman
STEPHENSON, William 3
Worth
STEPPAT, Leo 5
STEPTOE, Philip Pendleton 2
STERETT, Andrew 1
STERETT, Samuel H
STERIGERE, John Benton 1
STERKI, Victor 1
STERLEY, William F. 4
STERLING, Ansel H
STERLING, Bruce F. 5
STERLING, Donald Justus 3
STERLING, Edward 1
Canfield
STERLING, Ernest Albert 6
STERLING, Frederick 5
Augustine
STERLING, George 1
Mathleson
STERLING, George 5
STERLING, Graham Lee 3
STERLING, Guy 1
STERLING, James H
STERLING, John A. 1
STERLING, John C. 4
STERLING, John Whalen H
STERLING, John William 1
STERLING, Micah H
STERLING, Ross Shaw 2
STERLING, Theodore 1
STERLING, Thomas 1
STERLING, W. T. 3
STERN, Adolph 6
STERN, Alfred Whital 4
STERN, Bernhard Joseph 3
STERN, Bill 5
STERN, Charles Frank 4
STERN, David Becker 4
STERN, Edgar Bloom 5
STERN, Edith Mendel 6
STERN, Elizabeth 3
STERN, Gladys Bertha 6
STERN, Henry Root 3
STERN, Horace 5
STERN, Isaac Farber 6
STERN, Jo Lane 1
STERN, Joseph Smith 5
STERN, Joseph William H
STERN, Joseph William 4
STERN, Julius David 5
STERN, Kurt Guenter 3
STERN, Lawrence Fish 2
STERN, Leo 6
STERN, Louis 1
STERN, Louis 5
STERN, Nathan 5
STERN, Oscar David 6
STERN, Sigmund 3
STERN, Simon Adler 1
STERN, William Bernhard 5
STERNBERG, Charles 2
Hazellus
STERNBERG, George 1
Miller
STERNBERG, Walter 3
STERNBERGER, Mrs. 5
Estelle Miller
STERNBURG, Herman von 1
Speck
STERNE, Albert Eugene 1
STERNE, Maurice 3
STERNE, Niel Paul 1
STERNE, Simon 1
STERNE, Theodore Eugene 5
STERNER, Albert 2
STERNHAGEN, John 3
Meler
STERNHELL, Charles Max 5
STERRETT, Frances 2
Roberta
STERRETT, Henry Hatch 6
Dent
STERRETT, James 1
Macbridge
STERRETT, James Ralston 1

STERRETT, John Robert 1
Sitlington
STETEFELDT, Carl August H
STETSON, Augusta E. 1
STETSON, Caleb Rochford 1
STETSON, Charles H
STETSON, Charles H
Augustus
STETSON, Charles Walter 1
STETSON, Eugene William 3
STETSON, Harlan True 3
STETSON, Henry Crosby 3
STETSON, Herbert Lee 4
STETSON, Isaiah Kidder 1
STETSON, John Batterson 1
STETSON, Lemuel H
STETSON, Paul Clifford 1
STETSON, Raymond 3
Herbert
STETSON, Thomas Drew 4
STETSON, William Wallace 1
STETSON, Willis Kimball 1
STETTEN, DeWitt 3
STETTINIUS, Edward R. 1
STETTINIUS, Edward R. 2
Jr.
STETTNER, Ludwig 4
Wilhelmin
STEUART, George Hume 1
STEUART, James Aloysius 1
STEUBEN, Friedrich H
Wilhelm Ludolf Gerhard
Augustin v
STEUER, Max David 1
STEUER, Max David 4
STEUERMANN, Edward 4
STEVENOT, Fred Gabriel 1
STEVENS, Aaron Fletcher H
STEVENS, Abel 1
STEVENS, Adie Allan 3
STEVENS, Albert Clark 1
STEVENS, Alden 5
STEVENS, Alexander H
Hodgdon
STEVENS, Alexander 5
Raymond
STEVENS, Alviso Burdett 1
STEVENS, Anna C. Mann 1
(Mrs. Frank Jay Stevens)
STEVENS, Arthur Albert 4
STEVENS, Ashton 4
STEVENS, Beatrice 2
STEVENS, Benjamin 1
Franklin
STEVENS, Bradford H
Newcomb
STEVENS, Charles A. 1
STEVENS, Charles Abbot H
STEVENS, Charles Brooks 3
STEVENS, Charles Ellis 1
STEVENS, Clement 1
Hoffman
STEVENS, Cyrus Lee 1
STEVENS, Daisy McLaurin 3
STEVENS, Daniel Gurden 1
STEVENS, David 5
STEVENS, Don Albert 5
STEVENS, Doris 4
STEVENS, Durham White 1
STEVENS, E. Ray 1
STEVENS, Eben Sutton 4
STEVENS, Edward Fletcher 2
STEVENS, Edward Francis 4
STEVENS, Edward 1
Lawrence
STEVENS, Edwin Augustus H
STEVENS, Edwin Augustus 1
STEVENS, Elbert Marcus 1
STEVENS, Elisha H
STEVENS, Ellen Yale 5
STEVENS, Elmer T. 5
STEVENS, Ernest James 5
STEVENS, Eugene Morgan 1
STEVENS, Evarts Chapman 3
STEVENS, Everett Duncan 5
STEVENS, Francis Bowden 5
STEVENS, Frank Jay 5
STEVENS, Frank Lincoln 1
STEVENS, Frank Walker 1
STEVENS, Frederic Bliss 2
STEVENS, Frederic Harper 6
STEVENS, Frederic William 1
STEVENS, Frederick 1
Charles
STEVENS, Frederick 1
Clement
STEVENS, Frederick Waeir 1
STEVENS, George 6
STEVENS, George Barker 1
STEVENS, George Thomas 1
STEVENS, George Walter 1
STEVENS, George 1
Washington
STEVENS, Gorham Phillips 4
STEVENS, Harry Clay 1
STEVENS, Hazard 1

STEVENS, Henry H
STEVENS, Henry Davis 4
STEVENS, Henry Leonidas 5 Jr.
STEVENS, Henry M. 3
STEVENS, Hestor Lockhart H
STEVENS, Hiram Fairchild 1
STEVENS, Hiram Sanford H
STEVENS, Horace Jared 1
STEVENS, Howard Eveleth 5
STEVENS, Inger 5
STEVENS, Isaac Ingalls H
STEVENS, Isaac Newton 1
STEVENS, J. Franklin 1
STEVENS, James H
STEVENS, James Floyd 5
STEVENS, James Franklin 1
STEVENS, James Stacy 1
STEVENS, James William 1
STEVENS, John * H
STEVENS, John Amos 1
STEVENS, John Austin H
STEVENS, John Austin 1
STEVENS, John Calvin 1
STEVENS, John F. 4
STEVENS, John Leavitt 1
STEVENS, John Loomis 4
STEVENS, John Milior 6
STEVENS, John Morgan 4
STEVENS, Lawrence M. 5
STEVENS, Leith 1
STEVENS, Leslie Clark 3
STEVENS, Lewis Miller 4
STEVENS, Lillian M. N. 1
STEVENS, Maltby 3
STEVENS, Milton J. 5
STEVENS, Nathaniel 2
STEVENS, Neil Everett 2
STEVENS, P. F. 1
STEVENS, Patricia 3
STEVENS, Ray Parker 4
STEVENS, Raymond 2 Bartlett
STEVENS, Raymond 1 William
STEVENS, Robert H Livingston
STEVENS, Robert Smith H
STEVENS, Robert Sproule 5
STEVENS, Rollin Howard 2
STEVENS, Roy George 2
STEVENS, Samuel Nowell 4
STEVENS, Sheppard 1
STEVENS, Solon Whithed 4
STEVENS, S(tanley) Smith 5
STEVENS, Sylvester K(irby) 6
STEVENS, Terrill D. 4
STEVENS, Thaddeus H
STEVENS, Thomas H Holdup *
STEVENS, Thomas Holdup 1 III
STEVENS, Thomas 2 McCorvey
STEVENS, Thomas Wood 1
STEVENS, Thomas Wood 2
STEVENS, Truman S. 3
STEVENS, Wallace 3
STEVENS, Walter Barlow 1
STEVENS, Walter E. 6
STEVENS, Walter Husted H
STEVENS, Walter Le Conte 1
STEVENS, Wayne Edson 3
STEVENS, Wayne 6 Mackenzie
STEVENS, William Arnold 1
STEVENS, William Bacon H
STEVENS, William 2 Bertrand
STEVENS, William 4 Burnham
STEVENS, William Chase 3
STEVENS, William Dodge 1
STEVENS, William 5 Harrison Spring
STEVENS, William Lester 5
STEVENS, William Oliver 3
STEVENSON, Adlai Ewing 1
STEVENSON, Adlai Ewing 4
STEVENSON, Alec Brock 5
STEVENSON, Alexander 2 Russell Jr.
STEVENSON, Andrew H
STEVENSON, Andrew 1
STEVENSON, Archibald 4 Ewing
STEVENSON, Archie Mac 4 Nicol
STEVENSON, Beulah 4
STEVENSON, Burton 1
STEVENSON, C. Albert 4
STEVENSON, Carter H Littlepage
STEVENSON, Charles 2 Hugh
STEVENSON, Coke Robert 6

STEVENSON, David Lloyd 6
STEVENSON, Edward 2 Irenaeus
STEVENSON, Edward 4 Irenaeus
STEVENSON, Edward 2 Luther
STEVENSON, Eldon Jr. 5
STEVENSON, Elliott 1 Grasette
STEVENSON, Elmo Nall 6
STEVENSON, Eugene 1
STEVENSON, Frank 1 Herbert
STEVENSON, Frederic 1 Augustus
STEVENSON, Frederick 2 Alfred
STEVENSON, Frederick 1 Boyd
STEVENSON, George 1
STEVENSON, George 6 Stanley
STEVENSON, Guy 4
STEVENSON, Holland 3 Newton
STEVENSON, Howard A. 3
STEVENSON, J. Ross 1
STEVENSON, James H
STEVENSON, James Henry 1
STEVENSON, James S. H
STEVENSON, John Alford 2
STEVENSON, John James 1
STEVENSON, John White 1
STEVENSON, Katharine 1 Adelia Lent
STEVENSON, Lewis Green 1
STEVENSON, Lionel 6
STEVENSON, Marcia 5 Jacobs
STEVENSON, Marion 5 Delimon
STEVENSON, Mark 1
STEVENSON, Markley 4
STEVENSON, Matilda 1 Coxe
STEVENSON, Paul Eve 1
STEVENSON, Richard 3 Corwine
STEVENSON, Richard 1 Taylor
STEVENSON, Robert 4 Montgomery
STEVENSON, Sara Yorke 1
STEVENSON, Sarah 1 Hackett
STEVENSON, Thomas 4 Patton
STEVENSON, W. C. 3
STEVENSON, Wade 5
STEVENSON, Walter 1 Anson
STEVENSON, Wilbert 4 Everett
STEVENSON, William 2 Francis
STEVENSON, William 3 Henry
STEVENSON, William Holmes
STEVENSON, William 1 Patton
STEVENSON, William Taylor
STEVICK, David William 1
STEWARD, Ira H
STEWARD, Joseph H
STEWARD, Julian H. 5
STEWARD, Lewis H
STEWARD, LeRoy T. 2
STEWARD, Thomas Gifford 1
STEWARDSON, Emlyn Lamar
STEWARDSON, John 4
STEWARDSON, Langdon 4 Cheves
STEWART, Adiel Fitzgerald 4
STEWART, Albert 4
STEWART, Alexander 1
STEWART, Alexander Mair 1
STEWART, Alexander P. 1
STEWART, Alexander H Turney
STEWART, Allison Vance 1
STEWART, Alpheus Lloyd 2
STEWART, Alphonso Chase 1
STEWART, Alvan H
STEWART, Andrew H
STEWART, Cecil Parker 2
STEWART, Charles *
STEWART, Charles Allan 5
STEWART, Charles D. 5
STEWART, Charles Leslie 6
STEWART, Charles 1 Seaforth

STEWART, Charles West 1
STEWART, Colin Campbell 2
STEWART, David H
STEWART, David 4
STEWART, David Denison 1
STEWART, De Lisle 3
STEWART, Donald 2 Farquharson
STEWART, Douglas 1
STEWART, Douglas Hunt 1
STEWART, Duncan 1
STEWART, Edwin 1
STEWART, Eliza Daniel 1
STEWART, Ella Seass 5
STEWART, Ethelbert 1
STEWART, Ford 5
STEWART, Francis Robert 5
STEWART, Francis Torrens 1
STEWART, Frank Mann 4
STEWART, Frank R. 4
STEWART, Fred 5
STEWART, Fred Carlton 2
STEWART, Frederick 1 William
STEWART, George 3
STEWART, George 5
STEWART, George Black 1
STEWART, George Craig 1
STEWART, George David 1
STEWART, George H. 1
STEWART, George James 3
STEWART, George Neil 1
STEWART, George Taylor 1
STEWART, George Walter 3
STEWART, Gideon Tabor 1
STEWART, Gilbert Henry 1
STEWART, Grace Bliss 5
STEWART, Graeme 1
STEWART, Harlon L. 4
STEWART, Harold Edison 5
STEWART, Humphrey John 1
STEWART, Isabel Maitland 4
STEWART, Ivey Withers 4
STEWART, J. D. 2
STEWART, Jacob Henry H
STEWART, James H
STEWART, James 3
STEWART, James Augustus H
STEWART, James Christian 2
STEWART, James Fleming 1
STEWART, James Garfield 3
STEWART, Jane Agnes 2
STEWART, John * H
STEWART, John 1
STEWART, John Aikman 1
STEWART, John Alexander 5
STEWART, John Appleton 1
STEWART, John David H
STEWART, John Hamilton 1
STEWART, John K. 4
STEWART, John Lammey 1
STEWART, John Leighton 1
STEWART, John Leslie 1
STEWART, John Minor 1
STEWART, John Quincy 5
STEWART, John Truesdale 1
STEWART, John Wolcott 1
STEWART, Joseph 1
STEWART, Joseph Spencer 1
STEWART, Joseph William 1 Alexander
STEWART, Judd 4
STEWART, Julius L. 4
STEWART, Lispenard 1
STEWART, Malcolm 5 Chilson
STEWART, Malcolm 1 Montrose
STEWART, Marshall 6 Bowyer
STEWART, Merch Bradt 1
STEWART, Morris Albion 4
STEWART, Nathaniel 1 Bacon
STEWART, Oline Johnson 5
STEWART, Oliver Wayne 1
STEWART, Oscar Milton 1
STEWART, Paul 3
STEWART, Paul Morton 1
STEWART, Paul Rich 6
STEWART, Paul William 3
STEWART, Percy Hamilton 3
STEWART, Philip Battell 1
STEWART, Philo Penfield H
STEWART, Randall 1
STEWART, Rex William 1
STEWART, Richard 1 Siegfried
STEWART, Robert H
STEWART, Robert Giffen 3
STEWART, Robert Laird 1
STEWART, Robert 1 Marcellus
STEWART, Robert Wright 3
STEWART, Rolland 6 Maclaren

STEWART, Ross 6
STEWART, Rowe 1
STEWART, Russ 6
STEWART, Russell C. 1
STEWART, Russell C. 2
STEWART, Samuel Vernon 1
STEWART, T. Mccants 4
STEWART, Thomas 1 Jamison
STEWART, Thomas Milton 2
STEWART, Tom 5
STEWART, Walter Allan 5
STEWART, Walter Leslie 6
STEWART, Walter W. 3
STEWART, Wilbur Filson 4
STEWART, William H
STEWART, William Alvah 3
STEWART, Sir William H Drummond
STEWART, William Finney 4 Bay
STEWART, William Henry 1
STEWART, William 2 Kilborne
STEWART, William Lyman 1
STEWART, William Lyman 4 Jr.
STEWART, William Morris 1
STEWART, William 1 Rhinelander
STEWART, William Shaw 1
STEYNE, Alan Nathaniel 2
STIBBS, John Henry 6
STIBITZ, George 2
STICKLE, John Wesley 5
STICKLES, Arndt Mathis 5
STICKLEY, Ezra Eugenius 3
STICKLEY, Gustav 4
STICKNEY, Albert 1
STICKNEY, Alpheus Beede 1
STICKNEY, Amos 1
STICKNEY, Herman 1 Osman
STICKNEY, Joseph L. 1
STICKNEY, Julia Noyes 4
STICKNEY, Louis R. 6
STICKNEY, Samuel Crosby 4
STICKNEY, William 1 Wallace
STIDGER, William Leroy 2
STIDLEY, Leonard Albert 3
STIEFFEL, Hermann H
STIEG, Max 5
STIEGEL, Henry William 1
STIEGLITZ, Alfred 2
STIEGLITZ, Julius 1
STIFLER, James Madison 1
STIFLER, James Madison 1
STIGLER, William G. 3
STIGNANI, Ebe 1
STILES, Charles Wardell 1
STILES, Edward H. 4
STILES, Ezra H
STILES, Fred Bailey 5
STILES, George K(ean) 5
STILES, Hinson 5
STILES, James Esmond 4
STILES, James F. Jr. 4
STILES, John Dodson 1
STILES, Meredith 1 Newcomb
STILES, Percy Goldthwait 1
STILES, Theodore Lamme 1
STILES, William Curtis 1
STILES, William Henry H
STILL, Alfred 5
STILL, Andrew Taylor 1
STILL, Clyfford 4
STILL, William 1
STILLE, Alfred 1
STILLE, Charles Janeway 1
STILLINGS, Charles Arthur 1
STILLINGS, Ephraim 1 Bailey
STILLMAN, Charles Clark 3
STILLMAN, James 1
STILLMAN, James 2 Alexander
STILLMAN, John Maxson 1
STILLMAN, Paul Roscoe 3
STILLMAN, Samuel H
STILLMAN, Stanley 1
STILLMAN, Thomas Bliss 1
STILLMAN, Walter N. 3
STILLMAN, William James 1
STILLMAN, William Olin 1
STILLWELL, Homer 1 Allison
STILLWELL, Leander 5
STILLWELL, Lewis Buckley 1
STILLWELL, Thomas Neel H
STILLWELL, William 1 Burney
STILSON, Oscar Reeves 5
STILWELL, Abner J. 4
STILWELL, Arthur Edward 1

STILWELL, Edmund 3 William
STILWELL, Herbert Fenton 1
STILWELL, Joseph W. 2
STILWELL, Silas Moore H
STILWELL, Wilber Moore H
STIMETS, Charles Calvin 4
STIMPSON, George 3 William
STIMPSON, Herbert Baird 1
STIMPSON, William 1
STIMPSON, William G. 1
STIMSON, Arthur Marston 5
STIMSON, Charles D. 1
STIMSON, Daniel 1 MacMartin
STIMSON, Frederic Jesup 2
STIMSON, Henry Albert 1
STIMSON, Henry Lewis 1
STIMSON, John Ward 1
STIMSON, Julia Catherine 2
STIMSON, Lewis Atterbury 1
STIMSON, Philip Moen 5
STIMSON, Rufus Whittaker 4
STIMSON, Thomas Douglas 1
STINCHFIELD, Frederick 2 Harold
STINCHFIELD, Roger 5 Adams
STINE, Charles Milton 3 Altland
STINE, John William Jr. 3
STINE, Milton Henry 1
STINE, Oscar Clemen 6
STINE, Wilbur Morris 1
STINESS, John Henry 1
STINESS, Walter Russell 1
STINSON, John Turner 5
STIRES, Ernest Milmore 3
STIRLEN, Eugene Dare 4
STIRLING, J. Bowman 5
STIRLING, John William 6
STIRLING, Matthew 6 Williams
STIRLING, Yates 1
STIRLING, Yates Jr. 2
STIRTON, Ruben Arthur 4
STITES, Fletcher Wilbur 1
STITES, John 1
STITES, Raymond Somers 6
STITH, William H
STITH, Wilmer Curtis 4
STITT, Edward Rhodes 1
STITT, Edward Walmsley 1
STITT, William Britton 1
STIVEN, Frederic Benjamin 2
STIVERS, Edwin Jacob 4
STIVERS, Kazia Armington 4
STIVERS, Moses Dunning H
STIX, Ernest William 3
STIX, Sylvan L. 5
STOAKS, Charles E. 4
STOBBS, George Russell 4
STOBO, Robert H
STOCK, Chester 3
STOCK, Frederick A. 2
STOCK, Harry T. 3
STOCK, Joseph Whiting H
STOCK, Leo Francis 6
STOCKARD, Charles 1 Rupert
STOCKARD, Henry Jerome 1
STOCKARD, Virginia Alice 1 Cottey
STOCKBARGER, Donald 3 C.
STOCKBERGER, Warner 2 W.
STOCKBRIDGE, Francis H Brown
STOCKBRIDGE, Frank 1 Parker
STOCKBRIDGE, Henry 1
STOCKBRIDGE, Henry H Smith
STOCKBRIDGE, Horace 1 Edward
STOCKDALE, Allen Arthur 5
STOCKDALE, Grant 4
STOCKDALE, Paris B. 4
STOCKDALE, Thomas H Ringland
STOCKDER, Archibald 4 Herbert
STOCKER, Harry Emilius 1
STOCKHAM, Alice Bunker 1
STOCKHAM, Edward 1 Villeroy
STOCKHAM, William 1 Henry
STOCKHAUSEN, William 6 Edward
STOCKING, Charles 5 Francis
STOCKING, Charles 3 Howard

STOCKING, George Ward 6
STOCKING, Jay Thomas 1
STOCKING, William Alonzo Jr. 1
STOCKMAN, Lowell 4
STOCKSLAGER, Charles O. 4
STOCKSTROM, Louis 2
STOCKTON, Charles G. 1
STOCKTON, Charles Herbert 1
STOCKTON, Edward A. Jr. 2
STOCKTON, Ernest 3
STOCKTON, Francis Richard 1
STOCKTON, Fred Everett 1
STOCKTON, George 1
STOCKTON, Howard 1
STOCKTON, J(ames) Roy 5
STOCKTON, John Potter H
STOCKTON, Joseph 1
STOCKTON, Joseph Denniston 4
STOCKTON, Kenneth E. 1
STOCKTON, Louise 5
STOCKTON, Philip H
STOCKTON, Richard * H
STOCKTON, Robert Field H
STOCKTON, Robert Henry 1
STOCKTON, Thomas Hewlings H
STOCKTON, William Tennent 1
STOCKWELL, Chester Twitchell 1
STOCKWELL, Eugene Lafayette 5
STOCKWELL, Frank Clifford 2
STOCKWELL, Frederick Emerson 1
STOCKWELL, Herbert Grant 4
STOCKWELL, John Nelson 1
STOCKWELL, John Wesley Jr. 5
STOCKWELL, Samuel B. H
STOCKWELL, Thomas Blanchard 1
STOCKWELL, Walter Lincoln 3
STODDARD, Alexander Jerry 4
STODDARD, Amos H
STODDARD, Anne (Mrs.) 6
STODDARD, A(rthur) E(lsworth) 5
STODDARD, Charles Augustus 1
STODDARD, Charles Coleman 5
STODDARD, Charles Warren 1
STODDARD, Cora Frances 4
STODDARD, David Tappan H
STODDARD, Ebenezer 1
STODDARD, Elizabeth Drew Barstow 1
STODDARD, Enoch Vine 1
STODDARD, Florence Jackson 5
STODDARD, Francis Hovey 1
STODDARD, Francis Russell 3
STODDARD, Harry G. 5
STODDARD, Henry Luther 2
STODDARD, Howard J. 5
STODDARD, James Alexander 5
STODDARD, John Fair H
STODDARD, John Lawson 1
STODDARD, John Tappan 1
STODDARD, Joshua C. H
STODDARD, Lothrop 3
STODDARD, Richard Henry 1
STODDARD, Robert Curtis 5
STODDARD, Sanford 1
STODDARD, Solomon H
STODDARD, Thomas A. 4
STODDARD, William Leavitt 3
STODDARD, William Osborn 1
STODDART, Charles William 5
STODDART, James Henry 1
STODDART, Joseph Marshall 1
STODDART, L(aurence) A. 5
STODDERT, Benjamin H
STODDERT, John Truman H
STOECKEL, Carl 1
STOECKEL, Gustave Jacob 1

STOECKEL, Robbins B. 4
STOEHR, Max W. 1
STOEK, Harry Harkness 1
STOEPLER, Ambrose M. 5
STOESSEL, Albert 2
STOETZER, Herman Goethe 1
STOEVER, Martin Luther H
STOEVER, William Caspar H
STOFFER, Bryan Sewall 4
STOHLMAN, Frederick Jr. 6
STOICA, Chivu 6
STOKDYK, Ellis Adolph 4
STOKE, John M. 4
STOKELY, Jehu Thomas 4
STOKELY, Samuel H
STOKELY, William Burnett Jr. 4
STOKES, Andrew Jackson 3
STOKES, Anson Phelps 1
STOKES, Anson Phelps 3
STOKES, Arthur Charles 1
STOKES, Charles Francis 1
STOKES, Charles Senseney 4
STOKES, Edward Casper 1
STOKES, Edward Lowber 4
STOKES, Francis Joseph 3
STOKES, Frank Wilbert 3
STOKES, Frederick Abbot 1
STOKES, Harold Phelps 5
STOKES, Henry Bolter 1
STOKES, Henry Newlin 5
STOKES, Henry Warrington 1
STOKES, Horace Winston Phelps 1
STOKES, Isaac Newton 2
STOKES, J. G. Phelps 3
STOKES, James William 1
STOKES, John Harrison Jr. 5
STOKES, John Patrick 1
STOKES, John Stogdell 2
STOKES, Joseph Jr. 6
STOKES, Milton Lonsdale 6
STOKES, Montfort H
STOKES, Richard Leroy 3
STOKES, Rose Pastor 1
STOKES, Thomas 6
STOKES, Thomas Lunsford Jr. 3
STOKES, William Brickly H
STOKES, William E. 6
STOKES, William Herman 1
STOLAND, Ole Olufson 3
STOLBERG, Benjamin 3
STOLEE, Michael J. 4
STOLL, Charles Augustus 1
STOLL, Harry 1
STOLL, Philip Henry 3
STOLL, Richard Charles 4
STOLLER, James Hough 1
STOLLER, Morton Joseph 4
STOLPER, Gustav 2
STOLTZ, Charles Edward 5
STOLTZ, Robert Bear 4
STOLZ, Benjamin 1
STOLZ, Joseph 1
STOLZ, Karl Ruf 3
STOLZ, Leon 5
STOMBERG, Andrew Adin 2
STONE, Abraham 4
STONE, Albert Jmes 3
STONE, Alfred 1
STONE, Alfred Holt 3
STONE, Alfred Parish 1
STONE, Allison 1
STONE, Amasa 1
STONE, Andrew Jackson 4
STONE, Arthur Fairbanks 2
STONE, Arthur John 1
STONE, Barton Warren H
STONE, Caleb H
STONE, Calvin Perry 3
STONE, Carlos Huntington 1
STONE, Charles Arthur 2
STONE, Charles Augustus 1
STONE, Charles Edwin 3
STONE, Charles Francis 1
STONE, Charles Frederic 1
STONE, Charles Holmes 4
STONE, Charles Newhall 4
STONE, Charles Pomeroy H
STONE, Charles Warren 1
STONE, Charles Waterman 1
STONE, Charles Wellington 1
STONE, Claudius Ulysses 3
STONE, Cliff Winfield 5
STONE, Clyde Ernest 2
STONE, David H
STONE, David Lamme 5
STONE, David Marvin H
STONE, Eben Francis H
STONE, Ebenezer Whittier H
STONE, Ellen Maria 1
STONE, Emanuel Olson 4
STONE, Emerson Law 3
STONE, Fred Andrew 3

STONE, Fred Denton 3
STONE, Frederick 1
STONE, Frederick E. 5
STONE, George Edward 5
STONE, George Frederick 1
STONE, George Hapgood 1
STONE, George Washington H
STONE, George Whitefield 1
STONE, H. Chase 5
STONE, Harlan Fiske 2
STONE, Harold 1
STONE, Harry Everette 5
STONE, Harry R. 4
STONE, H(enry) Charles 5
STONE, Henry Lane 1
STONE, Herbert Lawrence 1
STONE, Herbert Stuart 1
STONE, Horace Greeley 1
STONE, Horace M. 2
STONE, Horatio H
STONE, Hugh Lamar 4
STONE, Isaac Scott 4
STONE, Isabelle 5
STONE, Ivan McKinley 4
STONE, James Clifton 6
STONE, James Lauriston 5
STONE, James Samuel 1
STONE, James W. H
STONE, John Augustus 1
STONE, John Charles 1
STONE, John Francis 1
STONE, John Holden 1
STONE, John Marshall 1
STONE, J(ohn) McWilliams 5
STONE, John Paul 5
STONE, John Pittman 1
STONE, John Seely H
STONE, John Stone 1
STONE, John Theodore 1
STONE, John Wesley 1
STONE, Joseph Cecil 2
STONE, Joseph E. 5
STONE, Judson E. 3
STONE, Julius Frederick 4
STONE, Kenneth Franklin 5
STONE, Kimbrough 3
STONE, L. A. 2
STONE, Lauson 1
STONE, L(awrence) Joseph 6
STONE, Lee Alexander 6
STONE, Lewis 3
STONE, Livingston 1
STONE, Lucy 1
STONE, Malcolm Bowditch Barbour 1
STONE, Margaret Manson 4
STONE, Mason Sereno 4
STONE, Melville Elijah 1
STONE, Michael Jenifer H
STONE, N. I. 4
STONE, Nat 1
STONE, Ormond 1
STONE, Patrick Thomas 4
STONE, Philip Carlton 5
STONE, Raleigh Webster 5
STONE, Ralph 5
STONE, Ralph Walter 4
STONE, Robert Elwin 5
STONE, Robert Franklin 5
STONE, Robert Spencer 5
STONE, Royal Augustus 2
STONE, Rufus Barrett 1
STONE, Samuel H
STONE, Samuel M. 3
STONE, Theodore Thaddeus 3
STONE, Thomas H
STONE, Thomas Treadwell H
STONE, Ulysses Stevens 6
STONE, Walker 5
STONE, Walter King 3
STONE, Walter Robinson 1
STONE, Warren 1
STONE, Warren Sanford 1
STONE, Wilbur Fisk 1
STONE, Willard John 2
STONE, William * H
STONE, William Alexis H
STONE, William Alexis 1
STONE, William Joel 1
STONE, William Leete H
STONE, William Leete 1
STONE, William Oliver H
STONE, William S(ebastian) 5
STONE, Wilson S(tuart) 5
STONE, Winthrop Ellsworth 1
STONE, Witmer 1
STONEHOUSE, Ned Bernard 4
STONEMAN, Frank B. 1
STONEMAN, George H
STONER, Dayton 2
STONER, Frank E. 4
STONER, George Hiram 5

STONER, William David 4
STONER, Mrs. Winifred Sackville 1
STONG, Philip Duffield 3
STONIER, Harold 3
STONOROV, Oskar 5
STOOKEY, Byron 4
STOOKEY, Lyman Brumbaugh 1
STOOKEY, Stephen Wharton 3
STOOKSBURY, William Lafayette 4
STOOPS, John Dashiell 5
STOOTHOFF, Everett O. 5
STOPKA, Andrzej Wieslaw 6
STORCKMAN, Clem Franklin 4
STORER, Bellamy H
STORER, Bellamy 1
STORER, Clement 4
STORER, David Humphreys H
STORER, Francis Humphreys 1
STORER, George Butler 6
STORER, Horatio Robinson 1
STORER, John Humphreys 1
STORER, Maria Longworth 1
STORER, Norman Wilson 3
STORER, Robert Treat 4
STOREY, Moorfield 1
STOREY, Robert Gerald Jr. 4
STOREY, Thomas Andrew 2
STOREY, Walter Rendell 3
STOREY, Wilbur Fisk 1
STOREY, William Benson 1
STORING, James Alvin 4
STORK, Charles Wharton 6
STORKE, Arthur Ditchfield 2
STORKE, Thomas More 5
STORM, Hans Otto 2
STORM, Jack 6
STORM, John M. 2
STORM, Mildred Raum 5
(Mrs. Edward D. Storm)
STORMS, Albert Boynton 1
STORMZAND, Martin James 6
STORROW, James Jackson H
STORROW, James Jackson 1
STORRS, Caryl B. 1
STORRS, Harry Asahel 5
STORRS, Henry Randolph H
STORRS, John 1
STORRS, Leonard Kip 3
STORRS, Lewis Austin 2
STORRS, Lucius Seymour 1
STORRS, Richard Salter 1
STORRS, Richard Salter 1
STORRS, Robert Williamson 5
III
STORRS, William Lucius H
STORY, Douglas 5
STORY, Francis Quarles 4
STORY, George Henry 1
STORY, Isaac H
STORY, John Patten 1
STORY, Joseph H
STORY, Julian 1
STORY, Nelson Jr. 1
STORY, Russell McCulloch 2
STORY, Walter P. 5
STORY, Walter Scott 1
STORY, William Edward 1
STORY, William Wetmore H
STORZ, Todd 4
STOSE, George Willis 4
STOSKOPF, William Brewster 5
STOTESBURY, Edward Townsend 1
STOTESBURY, Louis William 2
STOTSENBURG, Evan Brown H
STOTT, Henry Gordon 1
STOTT, Roscoe Gilmore 5
STOTZ, Edward Jr. 4
STOUDT, John Baer 3
STOUFFER, Gordon A. 5
STOUFFER, Samuel Andrew 3
STOUFFER, Vernon Bigelow 6
STOUGH, Henry Wellington 1
STOUGHTON, Bradley 3
STOUGHTON, Charles William 2
STOUGHTON, Clarence Charles 6
STOUGHTON, Edwin Wallace H
STOUGHTON, William H

STOUGHTON, William Lewis H
STOUT, Aaron James 4
STOUT, Arlow Burdette 3
STOUT, Arthur Purdy 4
STOUT, Byron Gray H
STOUT, Charles Banks 5
STOUT, Charles Frederick Cloua 5
STOUT, Elmer William 4
STOUT, George Abeel 5
STOUT, George Clymer 5
STOUT, Henry Elbert 5
STOUT, Henry Rice 1
STOUT, Hiram Miller 5
STOUT, Howard A. 3
STOUT, Irving Wright 6
STOUT, James Coffin 1
STOUT, James Huff 1
STOUT, John Elbert 2
STOUT, Joseph Duerson 2
STOUT, Lansing H
STOUT, Lawrence Edward 5
STOUT, Oscar Van Pelt 1
STOUT, Ralph Emerson 1
STOUT, Rex Todhunter 6
STOUT, Selatie Edgar 5
STOUT, Tom 2
STOUT, Wesley Winans 5
STOUT, William Bushnell 3
STOVALL, Pleasant Alexander 1
STOVALL, Wallace Fisher 3
STOVALL, William Robert 4
STOVER, George Henry 1
STOVER, John Hubler H
STOVER, Jordan Homer III 6
STOVER, Martin Luther 1
STOVER, William Miller 4
STOW, Baron H
STOW, Charles Messer 3
STOW, Marcellus H. 4
STOW, Micollius Noel 4
STOW, Silas 1
STOWE, Ansel Roy Monroe 3
STOWE, Calvin Ellis H
STOWE, Charles Edward 1
STOWE, Frederick Arthur 1
STOWE, Harriet Elizabeth Beecher H
STOWE, Lyman Beecher 4
STOWE, Robert Lee 4
STOWELL, Calvin Llewellyn 1
STOWELL, Charles Frederick 1
STOWELL, Charles Henry 1
STOWELL, Ellery Cory 3
STOWELL, Frederick M. 1
STOWELL, Jay Samuel 4
STOWELL, Kenneth Kingsley 5
STOWELL, Leon Carl 6
STOWELL, Louise Maria Reed 4
STOWELL, Thomas Blanchard 1
STOWELL, William Henry Harrison 1
STOWER, John G. H
STRABEL, Thelma 3
STRACCIA, Frank Alexander 6
STRACHAN, Paul Ambrose 4
STRACHAN, Thomas Curr Jr. 4
STRACHAUER, Arthur C. 4
STRACHEY, John 4
STRACHEY, Lionel 1
STRACHEY, William H
STRADER, Bernard Earl 2
STRADER, Peter Wilson H
STRADLEY, Bland Lloyd 3
STRADLEY, Leighton Paxton 3
STRADLING, George Flowers 4
STRAEHLEY, Erwin Sr. 2
STRAFER, Harriette R. 5
STRAGNELL, Gregory 2
STRAHAN, Charles Morton 2
STRAHAN, Hazel Blair 4
STRAHAN, Kay Cleaver 1
STRAHM, Victor H. 3
STRAHORN, Robert Edmund 2
STRAIGHT, Herbert Randall 4
STRAIGHT, Willard Dickerman 1
STRAIN, Isaac G. H
STRAIT, Thomas Jefferson 1
STRAKE, George William 5
STRAKOSCH, Maurice H
STRALEM, Donald S. 6

642

STURGIS, Samuel Davis H
STURGIS, Samuel Davis 1
STURGIS, Samuel Davis Jr. 4
STURGIS, William
STURGIS, William Codman 2
STURGISS, George 1
Cookman
STURM, Ernest 1
STURM, Justin
STURTEVANT, Albert 3
Morey
STURTEVANT, Alfred 5
Henry
STURTEVANT, Benjamin H
Franklin
STURTEVANT, Carleton 4
William
STURTEVANT, Edgar 5
Howard
STURTEVANT, Edward H
Lewis
STURTEVANT, John 1
Loomis
STURTEVANT, Julian H
Monson
STURTEVANT, Sarah 2
Martha
STUTESMAN, James Flynn 1
STUTSMAN, Jesse O. 1
STUTZ, Harry C. 1
STUYVESANT, Petrus
STYER, Henry Delp 2
STYER, Wilhelm D. 6
STYGALL, James Henry 3
STYKA, Tade 3
SUAREZ-MUJICA, 4
Eduardo
SUBLETTE, William Lewis H
SUCKOW, Ruth 3
SUDDUTH, William Xavier
SUDJARWO, 5
Tjondronegoro
SUDLER, Arthur Emory 5
SUDLER, Mervin Tubman 5
SUDLOW, Elizabeth 3
Williams
SUDWORTH, George 1
Bishop
SUFFERN, Arthur Elliott 6
SUFFREN, Charles Carroll
SUGDEN, Walter S. 1
SUGG, Redding Stancil 3
SUGHRUE, Timothy 4
George
SUGRUE, Thomas 3
SUHR, Charles Louis 5
SUHR, Otto Ernst Heinrich
Hermann
SUHR, Robert Carl 6
SUHRIE, Ambrose L. 3
SUKARNO 5
SUKER, George Francis 1
SULERUD, Allen Christen 6
SULLAVAN, Margaret 1
SULLENS, Frederick 3
SULLIVAN, Alexander 4
SULLIVAN, Arthur George 2
SULLIVAN, Arthur George 3
SULLIVAN, Christopher D. 2
SULLIVAN, Corliss
Esmonde
SULLIVAN, Daniel Clifford 4
SULLIVAN, David 6
SULLIVAN, Dennis Francis 5
SULLIVAN, Donal Mark 5
SULLIVAN, Edward Dean 1
SULLIVAN, Edward 6
Vincent
SULLIVAN, Elizabeth 5
Higgins (Elizabeth
Higgins)
SULLIVAN, Eugene 4
Cornelius
SULLIVAN, Florence David 3
SULLIVAN, Francis John 1
SULLIVAN, Francis Loftus 3
SULLIVAN, Francis Paul 4
SULLIVAN, Francis
William
SULLIVAN, Frank (Francis 6
John Sullivan)
SULLIVAN, Gael 3
SULLIVAN, George H
SULLIVAN, George F. 2
SULLIVAN, George 3
Hammond
SULLIVAN, Harry Stack H
SULLIVAN, Harry Stack 4
SULLIVAN, Henry J. 4
SULLIVAN, Isaac Newton 1
SULLIVAN, James H
SULLIVAN, James 1
SULLIVAN, James Edward 1
SULLIVAN, James F. 1
SULLIVAN, James Mark 1
SULLIVAN, James William 4

SULLIVAN, Jeremiah 1
Francis
SULLIVAN, Jeremiah 5
Francis Jr.
SULLIVAN, Jeremiah J. 4
SULLIVAN, Jerry 2
Bartholomew
SULLIVAN, John H
SULLIVAN, John A. 4
SULLIVAN, John 3
Berchmans
SULLIVAN, John Francis 3
SULLIVAN, John J. 3
SULLIVAN, John L. H
SULLIVAN, John L. 4
SULLIVAN, John Lawrence 3
SULLIVAN, Lawrence 4
SULLIVAN, Leo Dennis 5
SULLIVAN, Louis Henry 4
SULLIVAN, Margaret 1
Frances
SULLIVAN, Margaret M. 4
SULLIVAN, Mark 1
SULLIVAN, Maurice J. * 4
SULLIVAN, Michael 1
Crowley
SULLIVAN, Michael Xavier 4
SULLIVAN, Oscar Matthias 3
SULLIVAN, Owen J. 3
SULLIVAN, Patrick 1
SULLIVAN, Patrick F. 1
SULLIVAN, Patrick J. 1
SULLIVAN, Patrick U. 2
SULLIVAN, Paul E. 5
SULLIVAN, Peter John H
SULLIVAN, Philip Leo 4
SULLIVAN, Raymond F. 5
SULLIVAN, Roger C. 1
SULLIVAN, Russell 6
SULLIVAN, Thomas Crook 1
SULLIVAN, Thomas Russell 1
SULLIVAN, Timothy D. 5
SULLIVAN, William H
SULLIVAN, William Cleary 1
SULLIVAN, William 1
Laurence
SULLIVAN, William 4
Lawrence
SULLIVAN, William Van 1
Amberg
SULLIVANT, William H
Starling
SULLOWAY, Alvah 1
Woodbury
SULLOWAY, Cyrus Adams 1
SULLY, Alfred H
SULLY, Alfred 1
SULLY, Daniel 1
SULLY, Daniel J. 1
SULLY, John Murchison 1
SULLY, Thomas H
SULTAN, Daniel Isom 2
SULZBACHER, Louis 1
SULZBERGER, Arthur 5
Hays
SULZBERGER, Cyrus L. 1
SULZBERGER, Mayer 1
SULZER, Albert Frederick 1
SULZER, Charles August 1
SULZER, Hans A. 3
SULZER, William 1
SUMICHRAST, Frederick 4
Caesar de
SUMMERALL, Charles 3
Pelot
SUMMERBELL, Carlyle 1
SUMMERBELL, Martyn 1
SUMMERBELL, Robert 4
Kerr
SUMMERFIELD, Arthur 5
E(llsworth)
SUMMERFIELD, Charles H
SUMMERFIELD, Lester D. 4
SUMMERFIELD, Solon E. 2
SUMMERFORD, DeAlva 5
Clinton
SUMMERLIN, George 2
Thomas
SUMMERS, Alex 1
SUMMERS, Andrew Rowan 5
Neander
SUMMERS, Cleon Aubrey 6
SUMMERS, Festus Paul 5
SUMMERS, George William H 4
SUMMERS, Henry Elijah 4
SUMMERS, James Colling 1
SUMMERS, John Edward * 1
SUMMERS, John William 1
SUMMERS, Leland Laflin 1
SUMMERS, Lewis Preston 3
SUMMERS, Lionel Morgan 6
SUMMERS, Maddin 1
SUMMERS, Thomas 1
Osmond
SUMMERS, Walter G. 1

SUMMERS, Walter Lee 4
SUMMERS, William Henry 3
SUMMERVILLE, Amelia 1
Shaw
SUMMEY, George 3
SUMNER, (Bertha) Cid 5
Ricketts
SUMNER, Caroline Louise 5
SUMNER, Charles H
SUMNER, Charles Allen 1
SUMNER, Charles Burt 4
SUMNER, Charles Ralsey 1
SUMNER, Clarence 3
SUMNER, Edward Alleyne 2
SUMNER, Edwin Vose H
SUMNER, Edwin Vose 1
SUMNER, Francis Bertody 2
SUMNER, Frederick Azel 1
SUMNER, G. Lynn 1
SUMNER, George Watson 1
SUMNER, Guilford Herman 1
SUMNER, Increase 1
SUMNER, James Batcheller 3
SUMNER, Jethro 1
SUMNER, John D. 3
SUMNER, John Osborne 1
SUMNER, John Saxton 5
SUMNER, Samuel Storrow 1
SUMNER, Walter Taylor 1
SUMNER, William Graham 1
SUMNERS, Chester Lamar 4
SUMNERS, Hatton W. 4
SUMPTER, William David 4
SUMTER, Thomas H
SUMTER, Thomas DeLage 1
SUNBERG, Carl Andrew 1
Lawrence
SUNDAY, William Ashley 1
SUNDBACK, G. 3
SUNDELIUS, Marie 1
SUNDERLAND, Edson 3
Read
SUNDERLAND, Edwin 4
Sherwood Stowell
SUNDERLAND, Eliza 1
Read
SUNDERLAND, Jabez 1
Thomas
SUNDERLAND, LeRoy H
SUNDERLAND, Wilfred 2
Wilt
SUNDERLIN, Charles 3
Algernon
SUNDFOR, Zalia Harbaugh 5
(Mrs. Guttorm Sundfor)
SUNDHEIM, Anders M. 2
SUNDHEIM, Trig 6
SUNDSTROM, Swan 1
Reuben
SUNDT, Edwin Einar 1
SUNDWALL, John 3
SUNNY, Bernard Edward 2
SUNSTROM, Mark A. 4
SUOZZO, John 6
SUPER, Charles William 1
SUPER, Ovando Byron 1
SUPLEE, Henry Harrison 1
SURAMARIT, Norodom 3
King of Cambodia
SURE, Barnett 4
SURETTE, Thomas 1
Whitney
SURFACE, Frank Macy 4
SURFACE, Harvey Adam 4
SURKAMP, Arthur 5
SURLES, Alexander Day 1
SURMANN, John Fred 5
SURRAN, Edna M. Walsh 5
SURRAT, Mary Eugenia H
Jenkins
SURRATT, John H. H
SUSANN, Jacqueline 6
SUSSMAN, Otto 1
SUTER, Charles Russell 1
SUTER, Francis L. 5
SUTER, Herbert Wallace Jr. 4
SUTER, John Wallace 1
SUTHERLAND, Abby Ann 6
SUTHERLAND, Allan 1
SUTHERLAND, Annie 2
SUTHERLAND, Arthur 5
Eugene
SUTHERLAND, Dan A. 3
SUTHERLAND, Earl 6
Wilbur Jr.
SUTHERLAND, Edward 1
Alexander
SUTHERLAND, Edwin 1
Hardin
SUTHERLAND, Evelyn 1
Greenleaf
SUTHERLAND, George * 2
SUTHERLAND, Gordon 3
Alexander
SUTHERLAND, Howard 1

SUTHERLAND, Howard 4
Vigne
SUTHERLAND, Joel H
Barlow
SUTHERLAND, John Bain 2
SUTHERLAND, John 1
Preston
SUTHERLAND, Joseph 5
Hooker
SUTHERLAND, Josiah H
SUTHERLAND, Richard K. 4
SUTHERLAND, Robert 6
Edward Lee
SUTHERLAND, Roderick 3
Dhu
SUTHERLAND, Thomas 1
Henry
SUTHERLAND, William A. 1
SUTHERLAND, William 1
James
SUTLIFF, Milo Joseph 4
SUTLIFF, Phebe 1
Temperance
SUTLIFF, Vincent E. 5
SUTPHEN, Duncan Dunbar 3
SUTPHEN, Henry 1
Randolph
SUTPHEN, William Gilbert 2
Van Tassel
SUTRO, Adolph Heinrich H
Joseph
SUTRO, Alfred 2
SUTRO, Florence Clinton 1
SUTRO, Oscar 1
SUTRO, Richard 1
SUTRO, Theodore 1
SUTTER, Harry Blair 4
SUTTER, John Augustus H
SUTTLE, Andrew Dillard 4
SUTTON, Charles Edward 6
SUTTON, Charles R(euel) 5
SUTTON, Charles Wood 1
SUTTON, Claude William 3
SUTTON, Dallas Gilchrist 4
SUTTON, David Nelson 5
SUTTON, Don C. 4
SUTTON, Donn 4
SUTTON, Frank 4
SUTTON, Frank Spencer 6
SUTTON, Frederick I. 5
SUTTON, John Brannen 2
SUTTON, Joseph Lee 5
SUTTON, Joseph Wilson 6
SUTTON, Lee Edwards Jr. 4
SUTTON, Louis Valvelle 5
SUTTON, Loyd Hall 2
SUTTON, Mary Wooster 5
Munson
SUTTON, Ransome 1
SUTTON, Rhoades 1
Stansbury
SUTTON, Richard 3
Lightburn
SUTTON, W. Henry 1
SUTTON, Wilbur Ervin 2
SUTTON, William 1
SUTTON, William Seneca 4
SUYDAM, Charles Crooke 4
SUYDAM, Henry 3
SUYDAM, John Howard 1
SUYDAM, Vernon Andrew 3
SUYKER, Hector 5
SUZUKI, Daisetsu Teitaro 1
SUZZALLO, Henry 1
SVANHOLM, Set 4
SVEDBERG, Theodor 5
SVEDELIUS, Nils Eberhard 4
SVENDSEN, (James) Kester 5
(Olaf)
SVERDRUP, Georg 1
SVERDRUP, George 1
SVERDRUP, Harald Ulrik 3
SVERDRUP, Leif John 6
SVIEN, Hendrik Julius 4
SVININ, Pavel Petrovitch H
SVOBODA, Ralph Edward 5
SWABEY, Marie Collins 4
SWACKER, Frank M. 3
SWADOS, Harvey 5
SWAIM, H. Nathan 4
SWAIM, Joseph Skinner 1
SWAIN, David Lowry H
SWAIN, George Fillmore 1
SWAIN, Henry Huntington 1
SWAIN, Henry Lawrence 1
SWAIN, James 1
SWAIN, James Ramsay 5
SWAIN, Joseph 1
SWAIN, Joseph Ward 5
SWAIN, Philip William 3
SWAIN, Robert Eckles 4
SWAINE, Robert Taylor 3
SWAINSON, William 1
SWALLOW, Alan 4
SWALLOW, George Clinton 1
SWALLOW, Silas C. 1

SWALM, Albert Winfield 1
SWALWELL, Joseph Arthur 5
SWAN, Clifford Melville 3
SWAN, Frank Herbert 3
SWAN, Gustaf Nilsson 1
SWAN, Henry Harrison 1
SWAN, James H
SWAN, James Edward 1
SWAN, John H
SWAN, John Mumford 3
SWAN, John Nesbit 1
SWAN, Joseph Edwards 4
Corson
SWAN, Joseph R. 4
SWAN, Joseph Rackwell 1
SWAN, Joseph Rockwell H
SWAN, Lowell Benjamin 1
SWAN, Nathalie Henderson 6
SWAN, Paul 5
SWAN, Samuel H
SWAN, Thomas Walter 4
SWAN, Timothy H
SWAN, Verne Sturges 5
SWANBERG, Harold 5
SWANDER, John I. 1
SWANEBECK, Clarence W. 5
SWANEY, William Bentley 2
SWANISH, Peter Theodore 5
SWANK, Fletcher B. 2
SWANK, James Moore 1
SWANLUND, Lester 1
Herman
SWANN, Edward 4
SWANN, Ralph Clay 4
SWANN, Thomas 4
SWANN, William Francis 4
Gray
SWANSEN, Sam T. 3
SWANSON, Albert E. 5
SWANSON, Albert Gustav 5
SWANSON, Charles 5
Edward
SWANSON, Clarence 5
Emanuel
SWANSON, Claude 1
Augustus
SWANSON, Edgar Walfred 5
SWANSON, John A. 2
SWANSON, Paul Gustaf 5
SWANSON, W. Clarke 4
SWANTEE, Paul Frederick 5
SWANTON, Gerald F. 3
SWANTON, John Reed 1
SWANTON, William T. 5
SWART, Joseph 4
SWART, Peter 1
SWART, Robert Emerson 2
SWART, Walter Goodwin 1
SWARTHOUT, Donald 4
Malcolm
SWARTHOUT, Elvin 1
SWARTHOUT, Gladys 5
SWARTHOUT, Max Van 1
Lewen
SWARTS, Gardner Taber 1
SWARTSBERG, Jerome F. 4
SWARTWOOD, Howard 1
Albright
SWARTWOUT, Egerton 2
SWARTWOUT, Mary 5
Cooke
SWARTWOUT, Richard 1
Henry
SWARTWOUT, Samuel H
SWARTZ, Charles Benjamin 3
SWARTZ, Charles Kephart 2
SWARTZ, Edward James 1
SWARTZ, Harry Raymond 2
SWARTZ, Herman Frank 5
SWARTZ, Jacob Hyams 6
SWARTZ, Joel 4
SWARTZ, Joshua W. 1
SWARTZ, Katherine H. 4
SWARTZ, Mifflin Wyatt 5
SWARTZ, Osman Ellis 5
SWARTZ, Peter Winferd 6
SWARTZ, Philip Allen 1
SWARTZ, Samuel Jackson 1
SWARTZ, Willis George 4
SWARTZBAUGH, William 1
Lamson
SWASEY, Albert Loring 3
SWASEY, Ambrose 1
SWATLAND, Donald 4
Clinton
SWAVELY, Eli 5
SWAYNE, Alfred Harris 1
SWAYNE, Charles 1
SWAYNE, Noah Haynes H
SWAYNE, Wager 1
SWAYZE, Francis Joseph 1
SWAYZE, George Banghart 1
Henry
SWEARINGEN, Embry L. 1
SWEARINGEN, Henry H

SWEARINGEN, Henry Chapman 1
SWEARINGEN, John Eldred 5
SWEARINGEN, Lloyd Edward 5
SWEARINGEN, Mack Buckley 5
SWEARINGEN, Van Cicero 5
SWEARINGEN, Victor Clarence 5
SWEATT, William R. 1
SWEENEY, Alvin Randolph 3
SWEENEY, Bo 1
SWEENEY, Edward C. 4
SWEENEY, George H
SWEENEY, George Clinton 5
SWEENEY, James G. 5
SWEENEY, James J. 5
SWEENEY, James P. 4
SWEENEY, John William 5
SWEENEY, Martin L. 5
SWEENEY, Mildred I. McNeal 5
SWEENEY, Orland Russell 3
SWEENEY, Thomas Bell Sr. 3
SWEENEY, Thomas William H
SWEENEY, Walter Campbell 4
SWEENEY, William Northcut H
SWEENEY, William R. 6
SWEENEY, Zachary Taylor 1
SWEENIE, Denis J. 1
SWEENY, Charles Amos 5
SWEENY, Peter Barr H
SWEENY, Peter Barr 4
SWEENY, William Montgomery 5
SWEET, Ada Celeste 3
SWEET, Ada Celeste 4
SWEET, Alexander Edwin 1
SWEET, Alfred Henry 3
SWEET, Carroll Fuller 3
SWEET, Cyrus Bardeen 4
SWEET, Edwin Forrest 1
SWEET, Ellingham Tracy 2
SWEET, Elnathan 1
SWEET, Frank Herbert 1
SWEET, Frederic E(lmore) 6
SWEET, George Sullivan 1
SWEET, Harold Edward 1
SWEET, John Edson 1
SWEET, John Henry Throop Jr. 3
SWEET, John Hyde 4
SWEET, Joshua Edwin 3
SWEET, Louis Dennison 1
SWEET, Louis Matthews 3
SWEET, Marion Atwood (Mrs. Hamilton Howard Sweet) 5
SWEET, Owen Jay 1
SWEET, Thaddeus C. 1
SWEET, Timothy Bailey 1
SWEET, William Ellery 2
SWEET, William Luther 4
SWEET, William Merrick 1
SWEET, William Warren 3
SWEETLAND, Cornelius Sowle 1
SWEETLAND, Leon Hiram 6
SWEETLAND, William Howard 1
SWEETS, David Matthis 1
SWEETS, Henry Hayes 3
SWEETSER, Arthur 1
SWEETSER, Charles H
SWEETSER, Delight 1
SWEETSER, Edwin Chapin 1
SWEETSER, John Anderson 2
SWEETSER, Kate Dickinson 1
SWEITZER, Caesar 5
SWEITZER, J. Mearl 6
SWEM, Lee Allan 3
SWENEY, Joseph Henry 1
SWENGEL, Uriah Frantz 1
SWENK, Myron Harmon 4
SWENSON, David Ferdinand 1
SWENSON, Eric P. 2
SWENSON, Laurits Selmer 2
SWENSON, Lowell Harvey 4
SWENSON, Merrill G. 4
SWENSON, Stanley 6
SWENSSON, Carl Aaron 1
SWEPSTON, John E. 4
SWERDFEGER, Elbert Byron 1
SWERTFAGER, Walter Milton 4

SWETLAND, Roger Williams 1
SWETT, Frank Tracy 5
SWETT, John 1
SWETT, Louis William 1
SWETT, Sophia Miriam 1
SWETT, Susan Hartley 1
SWEZEY, Goodwin Deloss 1
SWICK, J. Howard 6
SWIFT, Archie Dean 4
SWIFT, Benjamin H
SWIFT, Carl Brown 1
SWIFT, Charles Henry 2
SWIFT, Clarence Franklin 1
SWIFT, Douglas 2
SWIFT, Eben 1
SWIFT, Edgar James 1
SWIFT, Edward Foster 1
SWIFT, Edward Wellington 4
SWIFT, Elijah Kent 3
SWIFT, Ernest Fremont 5
SWIFT, Ernest John 1
SWIFT, Eugene Clinton 1
SWIFT, Fletcher Harper 2
SWIFT, George B. 4
SWIFT, George Wilkins 1
SWIFT, Gustavus Franklin 1
SWIFT, Gustavus Franklin 2
SWIFT, Harold Higgins 4
SWIFT, Harry Ladrew 3
SWIFT, Homer Fordyce 3
SWIFT, Innis Palmer 2
SWIFT, Ivan 2
SWIFT, James Carroll 1
SWIFT, James Marcus 1
SWIFT, Jireh Jr. 2
SWIFT, John Edward 6
SWIFT, John Franklin H
SWIFT, John Trumbull 1
SWIFT, Joseph Gardner H
SWIFT, Josiah Otis 1
SWIFT, Lewis 1
SWIFT, Lindsay 1
SWIFT, Louis Franklin 1
SWIFT, Lucian 3
SWIFT, Nathan Butler 1
SWIFT, Oscar William 1
SWIFT, Polemus Hamilton 1
SWIFT, Raymond W(alter) 6
SWIFT, Samuel 1
SWIFT, Willard Everett 2
SWIFT, William 1
SWIFT, William Henry H
SWIFT, Zephaniah H
SWIGART, Charles H. 1
SWIGART, Clyde Arthur 6
SWIGART, Edmund Kearsley 1
SWIGART, LaVern Lake 6
SWIGER, Wilbur Moore 1
SWIGGART, William Harris 4
SWIGGETT, Douglas Worthington 2
SWIGGETT, Douglas Worthington 3
SWIGGETT, Glen Levin 4
SWIM, Chester Lawrence 5
SWIM, Dudley 5
SWINBURNE, John H
SWINBURNE, William Thomas 1
SWINDALL, Charles 1
SWINDEREN, Jonkheer Reneke de Marees van 4
SWINDLER, Mary Hamilton 4
SWINEHART, Gerry 4
SWINERTON, Alfred B. 4
SWINEY, Daniel 1
SWINFORD, Mac 6
SWING, Albert Temple 1
SWING, David 1
SWING, Philip David 4
SWING, Raymond 5
SWINGLE, D. B. 2
SWINGLE, Frank Bell 5
SWINGLE, Walter T. 1
SWINGLE, William S. 6
SWINGLER, William S(herman) 5
SWINNERTON, James Guilford 6
SWINNEY, Edward Fletcher 1
SWINT, John J. 4
SWINT, Samuel H. 4
SWINTON, John 1
SWINTON, William H
SWIRBUL, Leon A. 4
SWIREN, Max 5
SWISHER, Benjamin Franklin 3
SWISHER, Charles Clinton 1
SWISSHELM, Jane Grey Cannon H
SWITZ, Theodore MacLean 5

SWITZER, George Washington 1
SWITZER, Mary Elizabeth 5
SWITZER, Maurice 1
SWITZER, Robert Mauck 4
SWOOPE, Jacob H
SWOOPE, William Irvin 1
SWOPE, Ammon 4
SWOPE, Charles Siegel 3
SWOPE, Gerard 3
SWOPE, Guy J. 5
SWOPE, Herbert Bayard 4
SWOPE, King 4
SWOPE, Samuel Franklin 1
SWORD, James Brade 1
SWORDS, Henry Cotheal 1
SYDENSTRICKER, Edgar 1
SYDENSTRICKER, Virgil Preston 4
SYDNESS, Joseph Truman 5
SYDNOR, Charles Sackett 3
SYDNOR, Giles Granville 2
SYKES, Charles Henry 1
SYKES, Edward 5
SYKES, Edward Turner 4
SYKES, Eugene Octave 2
SYKES, Frederick Henry 1
SYKES, George * 4
SYKES, Howard Calvin 4
SYKES, James H
SYKES, Jerome H. 1
SYKES, Mabel 1
SYKES, M'Cready 3
SYKES, Richard Eddy 2
SYKES, Wilfred 5
SYLE, Louis du Pont 1
SYLVA, Marguerita 3
SYLVESTER, Albert Lenthall 6
SYLVESTER, Allie Lewis 4
SYLVESTER, Emma 5
SYLVESTER, Evander Wallace 4
SYLVESTER, Frederick Oakes 1
SYLVESTER, Herbert Milton 4
SYLVESTER, James Joseph H
SYLVESTER, Robert 6
SYLVIS, William H. H
SYME, Conrad Hunt 2
SYME, John P. 5
SYMES, George Gifford 1
SYMES, J. Foster 3
SYMINGTON, Donald 2
SYMMERS, Douglas 3
SYMMES, Edwin Joseph 1
SYMMES, Frank Jameson 1
SYMMES, John Cleves H
SYMMES, Leslie Webb 6
SYMMONDS, Charles Jacobs 1
SYMONDS, Brandreth 1
SYMONDS, Frederick Martin 1
SYMONDS, Gardiner 5
SYMONDS, Joseph White 1
SYMONDS, Nathaniel Millberry 5
SYMONDS, Percival Mallon 4
SYMONDS, Walter Stout 3
SYMONS, Gardner 1
SYMONS, Noel S. 4
SYMONS, Thomas Baddeley 5
SYMONS, Thomas William 1
SYMS, Benjamin H
SYNG, Philip H
SYNNOTT, Joseph J. 1
SYNNOTT, Thomas Whitney 1
SYPHER, Josiah Rhinehart 1
SYPHERD, Wilbur Owen 5
SYVERTON, Jerome T. 4
SYVERTSEN, Rolf Christian 4
SZE, Sao-Ke Alfred 3
SZEKELY, Ernest 3
SZIGETI, Joseph 5
SZILARD, Leo 4
SZINNYEY, Stephen Ivor 2
SZOLD, Henrietta 2
SZUMOWSKA, Antoinette 1
SZYK, Arthur 4

T

TABB, John Banister 1
TABELL, Edmund Weber 4
TABER, David Fairman 3
TABER, Erroll James Livingstone 2

TABER, George Hathaway Jr. 3
TABER, Harry Persons 4
TABER, Henry 1
TABER, John 4
TABER, Louis John 4
TABER, Mary Jane Howland 4
TABER, Norman Stephen 3
TABER, Ralph Graham 4
TABER, Stephen H
TABER, Thomas 2d H
TABER, William Ira 1
TABOR, Carl Henry 3
TABOR, Edward A. 4
TABOR, Horace Austin Warner H
TABORS, Robert Gustav 4
TACK, Augustus Vincent 2
TACKETT, John Robert 4
TACKETT, William Clarence 3
TADD, J. Liberty 1
TAEUBER, Irene Barnes (Mrs. Conrad Taeuber) 6
TAEUSCH, Carl Frederick 4
TAFEL, Gustav 1
TAFF, Joseph Alexander 2
TAFFE, John H
TAFFINDER, Sherwoode Ayerst 4
TAFT, Alphonso H
TAFT, Charles Phelps 1
TAFT, David Gibson 4
TAFT, Elihu Barber 4
TAFT, George Wheaton 1
TAFT, Harry Deward 3
TAFT, Henry Waters 2
TAFT, Horace Dutton 3
TAFT, Hulbert 3
TAFT, Kendall B(enard) 5
TAFT, Kingsley A. 5
TAFT, Levi Rawson 4
TAFT, Lorado 1
TAFT, Lorado 4
TAFT, Robert 1
TAFT, Robert Alphonso 3
TAFT, Robert Burbidge 3
TAFT, Robert Wendell 1
TAFT, Royal Chapin 1
TAFT, Russell Smith 1
TAFT, William Howard 1
TAG, Casimir 1
TAGG, Francis Thomas 1
TAGGARD, Genevieve 2
TAGGART, Arthur Fay 3
TAGGART, David Alexander 5
TAGGART, David Arthur 1
TAGGART, Elmore Findlay 4
TAGGART, Eugene Francis 3
TAGGART, Frank Fulton 2
TAGGART, Joseph 1
TAGGART, Marion Ames 1
TAGGART, Ralph Enos 3
TAGGART, Rush 1
TAGGART, Samuel H
TAGGART, Thomas 1
TAGGART, Thomas Douglas 2
TAGGART, Walter Thomas 1
TAGLIABUE, Giuseppe H
TAGUE, Peter F. 1
TAINTER, Charles Sumner 1
TAINTOR, Henry Fox 1
TAINTOR, Jesse Fox 1
TAIT, Arthur Fitzwilliam 1
TAIT, Charles 4
TAIT, Frank Morrison 4
TAIT, George 3
TAIT, John Robinson 1
TAITT, Francis Marion 2
TAKACH, Basil 2
TAKAHIRA, Kogoro 4
TAKAMINE, Jokichi 1
TALBERT, Joseph Truitt 1
TALBERT, Samuel Stubbs 5
TALBERT, W. Jasper 1
TALBOT, Adolphus Robert 2
TALBOT, Arthur Newell 2
TALBOT, Edith Armstrong 5
TALBOT, Ellen Bliss 1
TALBOT, Ethelbert 1
TALBOT, Eugene Solomon 1
TALBOT, Francis Xavier 3
TALBOT, George Frederick 5
TALBOT, Guy Webster 3
TALBOT, Henry Paul 1
TALBOT, Howard 1
TALBOT, Isham H
TALBOT, Israel Tisdale 1
TALBOT, John H
TALBOT, John William 1
TALBOT, Marion 2
TALBOT, Mary White 3

TALBOT, M(urrell) W(illiams) 5
TALBOT, Silas H
TALBOT, Walter LeMar 2
TALBOT, Winifred Luella Winter (Mrs. John E. Talbot) 5
TALBOTT, Albert Gallatin H
TALBOTT, Everett Guy 2
TALBOTT, Harold E. 3
TALBOTT, Harold E. H
TALBOTT, Henry James 1
TALBOTT, J. Fred C. 1
TALBOTT, Nelson S. 3
TALBURT, Harold M. 4
TALCOTT, Andrew H
TALCOTT, Charles Andrew 1
TALCOTT, Edward N. Kirk 1
TALCOTT, James Frederick 2
TALCOTT, Joseph 1
TALIAFERRO, Benjamin H
TALIAFERRO, Harry Monroe 5
TALIAFERRO, Henry Beckwith 4
TALIAFERRO, James Piper 2
TALIAFERRO, John H
TALIAFERRO, Lawrence H
TALIAFERRO, Nicholas Lloyd 4
TALIAFERRO, Thomas Hardy 1
TALIAFERRO, Thomas Seddon Jr. 1
TALIAFERRO, William Booth H
TALIAFERRO, William Hay 6
TALL, Lida Lee 2
TALLANT, Hugh 3
TALLE, Henry O(scar) 2
TALLERDAY, Howard G. 2
TALLEY, Bascom 5
Destrehan Jr.
TALLEY, Dyer Findley 2
TALLEY, Lynn Porter 2
TALLEYRAND-PERIGORD, Charles Maurice de H
TALLIAFERO, Richard H
TALLICHET, Jules Henri 1
TALLMADGE, Benjamin H
TALLMADGE, Frederick Augustus H
TALLMADGE, Guy Kasten 4
TALLMADGE, James Jr. H
TALLMADGE, Nathaniel Pitcher H
TALLMADGE, Thomas Eddy 1
TALLMAN, Clay 5
TALLMAN, Peleg H
TALLY, Robert Emmet 1
TALLY, William F. 4
TALMADGE, Constance 6
TALMADGE, Eugene 2
TALMADGE, Norma 3
TALMAGE, James Edward 1
TALMAGE, John Van Nest H
TALMAGE, T. Dewitt 1
TALMAN, Charles Fitzhugh 1
TALMAN, E. Lee 4
TALON, Pierre H
TAMARKIN, Jacob David 2
TAMARON, Pedro H
TAMIRIS, Helen 4
TAMIROFF, Akim 5
TAMM, Igor 6
TAMM, Igor Y. 5
TAMMANY H
TAMMEN, Agnes Reid 2
TAMMEN, Harry Heye 1
TAMMEN, Harry Heye 4
TANAKA, Kotaro 6
TANEY, Roger Brooke H
TANG, K. Y. 4
TANGEMAN, Robert Stone 4
TANGEMAN, Walter W. 4
TANGLEY, Edwin Savory (Baron Tangley of Blackheath) 6
TANGUY, Yves 3
TANI, Masayuki 4
TANIZAKI, Junichiro 4
TANNAHILL, Samuel O. 1
TANNEBERGER, David H
TANNEHILL, Adamson H
TANNENBAUM, Samuel Aaron 2
TANNER, Adolphus Hitchcock H
TANNER, Benjamin H
TANNER, Benjamin Tucker 1
TANNER, Edwin Platt 1
TANNER, Eugene Simpson 5
TANNER, Fred Wilbur 3

TANNER, Frederick Chauncey 4
TANNER, George Clinton 4
TANNER, Harold Brooks 5
TANNER, Henry Ossawa 1
TANNER, Henry Schenck H
TANNER, Jacob 5
TANNER, James 1
TANNER, John Henry 1
TANNER, John Riley 1
TANNER, Kenneth Spencer 4
TANNER, Rollin Harvelle 5
TANNER, Sheldon C. 4
TANNER, Willard Brooks 4
TANNER, William Vaughn 3
TANNER, Zera Luther 1
TANNRATH, John Joseph 1
TANSEY, Patrick Henry 6
TANSIL, John Bell 3
TANSILL, Charles Callan 4
TANZER, Laurence Arnold 4
TAPLEY, Walter Moore Jr. 5
TAPLIN, Frank E. 1
TAPLINGER, Richard Jacques 5
TAPP, Ernest Marvin 6
TAPP, Jesse W. 2
TAPP, Sidney C. 5
TAPPAN, Arthur H
TAPPAN, Benjamin 5
TAPPAN, Benjamin 1
TAPPAN, David Stanton 4
TAPPAN, Eli Todd H
TAPPAN, Eva March 1
TAPPAN, Frank Girard 4
TAPPAN, Henry Philip H
TAPPAN, Lewis H
TAPPAN, Mason Weare H
TAPPAN, William Bingham H
TAPPEN, Frederick D. 1
TAPPEN, Paul W. 4
TAPPER, Bertha Feiring 1
TAPPER, Thomas 1
TAPPERT, Theodore Gerhardt 6
TAPPIN, John Lindsley 4
TAPSCOTT, Ralph Henry 4
TAQUINO, George James 3
TARACOUZIO, Timothy Andrew 3
TARBELL, Arthur Wilson 2
TARBELL, Edmund C. 1
TARBELL, Frank Bigelow 1
TARBELL, Gage E. 1
TARBELL, Horace Sumner 1
TARBELL, Ida Minerva 2
TARBELL, Joseph H
TARBELL, Martha 2
TARBELL, Thomas Freeman 3
TARBOUX, Joseph G. 3
TARBOX, Increase Niles H
TARBOX, John Kemble H
TARBUTTON, Ben James 4
TARCHER, Jack David 4
TARCHIANI, Alberto 3
TARKINGTON, Grayson Emery 1
TARKINGTON, John Stevenson 1
TARKINGTON, Newton Booth 2
TARLER, George Cornell 1
TARPEY, Michael Francis 1
TARR, Christian H
TARR, Frederick Courtney 3
TARR, Frederick Hamilton 2
TARR, Leslie Riley 5
TARR, Ralph Stockman 1
TARR, William Arthur 1
TARRANT, Warren Downes 1
TARRANT, William Theodore 5
TARSNEY, John C. 4
TARTAKOFF, Joseph 6
TARVER, Malcolm Connor 4
TARVER, William Allen 1
TASHLIN, Frank 5
TASKER, Cyril 3
TASKEY, Harry LeRoy 3
TASSIN, Algernon de Vivier 1
TASSIN, Wirt 1
TATE, Benjamin Ethan 4
TATE, Farish Carter 4
TATE, Fred N. 4
TATE, H. Theodore 3
TATE, H. Theodore 5
TATE, Hugh McCall 5
TATE, Jack Bernard 5
TATE, James Alexander 3
TATE, John Matthew Jr. 5
TATE, John Torrence 2
TATE, Magnus H
TATE, Robert 4
TATE, Sam 1

TATE, William Knox 1
TATGENHORST, Charles 4
TATHAM, William H
TATLOCK, Henry 2
TATLOCK, John 1
TATLOCK, John S. P. 2
TATMAN, Charles Taylor 2
TATNALL, Henry 1
TATOM, Absalom 1
TATSCH, J. Hugo 1
TATTNALL, Edward Fenwick H
TATTNALL, Josiah * H
TATUM, Arthur 4
TATUM, Arthur Lawrie 3
TATUM, Edward Lawrie 6
TAUB, Edward Allen 5
TAUB, Sam 2
TAUBE, Mortimer 4
TAUBENHAUS, Jacob Joseph 1
TAUBENHAUS, Leon Jair 6
TAUBER, Richard 2
TAUBMAN, George Primrose 2
TAUBMAN, Tom 4
TAUL, Micah H
TAULBEE, William Preston H
TAUSSIG, Albert Ernst 2
TAUSSIG, Charles William 2
TAUSSIG, Edward David 1
TAUSSIG, Francis Brewster 5
TAUSSIG, Frank William 1
TAUSSIG, Frederick Joseph 2
TAUSSIG, James Edward 2
TAUSSIG, Joseph Knefler 2
TAUSSIG, Rudolph Julius 1
TAUSSIG, William 1
TAVENNER, Clyde Howard H
TAVENNER, Clyde Howard 2
TAVENNER, Frank Stacy Jr. 4
TAVES, Brydon 2
TAWNEY, Guy Alan 2
TAWNEY, James A. 1
TAWRESEY, John Godwin 2
TAYLER, Benjamin Walter Rogers 1
TAYLER, Joseph Henry 3
TAYLER, Lewis H
TAYLER, Robert Walker 1
TAYLOR, Abner 4
TAYLOR, Alan Carey 6
TAYLOR, Albert Davis 3
TAYLOR, Albert Hoyt 4
TAYLOR, Albert Pierce 1
TAYLOR, Albert Reynolds 1
TAYLOR, Alexander Wilson H
TAYLOR, Alfred Alexander 1
TAYLOR, Alfred Simpson 2
TAYLOR, Alrutheus Ambush 3
TAYLOR, Alva Edwards 1
TAYLOR, Amos Elias 5
TAYLOR, Amos Leavitt 4
TAYLOR, Archer 6
TAYLOR, Archibald Wellington 3
TAYLOR, Arthur Nelson 1
TAYLOR, Asher Clayton 1
TAYLOR, Aubrey E. 2
TAYLOR, Barnard Cook 1
TAYLOR, Bayard H
TAYLOR, Benjamin Franklin H
TAYLOR, Benjamin Irving 1
TAYLOR, Bert Leston 1
TAYLOR, Burton Leo 6
TAYLOR, Caleb Newbold 4
TAYLOR, Carson Lee 4
TAYLOR, Charles Elisha 1
TAYLOR, Charles Fayette H
TAYLOR, Charles Fayette 1
TAYLOR, Charles Fremont 1
TAYLOR, Charles Gillies Jr. 3
TAYLOR, Charles Henry * 1
TAYLOR, Charles Jay 1
TAYLOR, Charles Keen 6
TAYLOR, Charles Lewis 1
TAYLOR, Charles Ralph 5
TAYLOR, Charles Vincent 2
TAYLOR, Charles William 2
TAYLOR, Charlotte De Bernier Scarbrough H
TAYLOR, Claude Ambrose 4
TAYLOR, Creed H
TAYLOR, Daniel Albert 6
TAYLOR, David Watson 1
TAYLOR, Deems 4
TAYLOR, Donald Stephen 5
TAYLOR, Donald Wayne 6
TAYLOR, E. Alexis 1
TAYLOR, E. Leland 2

TAYLOR, Earl Burt 2
TAYLOR, Edward 1
TAYLOR, Edward Ballinger 1
TAYLOR, Edward Livingston 1
TAYLOR, Edward R. 5
TAYLOR, Edward Randolph 1
TAYLOR, Edward Robeson 1
TAYLOR, Edward Thomas 1
TAYLOR, Edward Thompson H
TAYLOR, Edwin 3
TAYLOR, Edwy Lycurgus 2
TAYLOR, Emerson Gifford 5
TAYLOR, Emily (Heyward) Drayton 5
TAYLOR, Eugene Hartwell 4
TAYLOR, Ezra B. 1
TAYLOR, F. Carroll 3
TAYLOR, F. W. Howard 4
TAYLOR, F. Walter 1
TAYLOR, Floyd 1
TAYLOR, Francis Henry 3
TAYLOR, Francis Matthew Sill 1
TAYLOR, Frank 1
TAYLOR, Frank Bursley 4
TAYLOR, Frank Flagg 5
TAYLOR, Frank J. 5
TAYLOR, Frank L. 4
TAYLOR, Frank Mansfield 1
TAYLOR, Fred Manville 4
TAYLOR, Frederic William 2
TAYLOR, Frederic Eugene 1
TAYLOR, Frederick R. 3
TAYLOR, Frederick William 1
TAYLOR, Frederick Winslow 1
TAYLOR, G. Mosser 4
TAYLOR, Geoffrey Ingram 6
TAYLOR, George * H
TAYLOR, George Jr. 4
TAYLOR, George Boardman 1
TAYLOR, George Braxton 2
TAYLOR, George Chadbourne 4
TAYLOR, George Washington 1
TAYLOR, George William 5
TAYLOR, Graham 1
TAYLOR, Graham Romeyn 2
TAYLOR, H. Birchard 3
TAYLOR, H. Genet 1
TAYLOR, Hannis 1
TAYLOR, Harden Franklin 4
TAYLOR, Harris 1
TAYLOR, Harry 1
TAYLOR, Harry G. 1
TAYLOR, Harry Gordon 5
TAYLOR, Harry Leonard 3
TAYLOR, Henry A. Colt 1
TAYLOR, Henry Charles 6
TAYLOR, Henry Clay 1
TAYLOR, Henry Fitch 1
TAYLOR, Henry Kirby 1
TAYLOR, Henry Lewis 4
TAYLOR, Henry Ling 1
TAYLOR, Henry Longstreet 1
TAYLOR, Henry Osborn 1
TAYLOR, Herbert Addison 2
TAYLOR, Herbert Worthington 1
TAYLOR, Hillsman 4
TAYLOR, Horace A. 1
TAYLOR, Howard 1
TAYLOR, Howard Canning 2
TAYLOR, Howard Emerson 4
TAYLOR, Howard Floyd 4
TAYLOR, Howard Rice 3
TAYLOR, Hugh Stott 6
TAYLOR, Isaac Montrose 1
TAYLOR, Isaac Stockton 1
TAYLOR, J. Gurney 3
TAYLOR, J. Madison 1
TAYLOR, J. Will 1
TAYLOR, Jacob B. 4
TAYLOR, James Alfred 1
TAYLOR, James Anderson 1
TAYLOR, James Barnett H
TAYLOR, James Earl 1
TAYLOR, James H. 5
TAYLOR, James Henry 1
TAYLOR, James Henry 5
TAYLOR, James Knox 1
TAYLOR, James Loockerman 4
TAYLOR, James Milburn 5
TAYLOR, James Monroe 1
TAYLOR, James Morford 1
TAYLOR, James Sherwood 6
TAYLOR, James W. 1
TAYLOR, James Wickes H
TAYLOR, Jesse Reade 6

TAYLOR, John * H
TAYLOR, John Bellamy 4
TAYLOR, John Blyth 5
TAYLOR, John James H
TAYLOR, John Lampkin H
TAYLOR, John Louis 1
TAYLOR, John McNay 6
TAYLOR, John Metcalf 1
TAYLOR, John Phelps 1
TAYLOR, John Thomas 4
TAYLOR, John W. H
TAYLOR, John Yeatman 1
TAYLOR, Jonathan 1
TAYLOR, Joseph Fillmore 3
TAYLOR, Joseph Jackson 2
TAYLOR, Joseph Judson 1
TAYLOR, Joseph Richard 3
TAYLOR, Joseph Robert 5
TAYLOR, Joseph Russell 1
TAYLOR, Joseph S. 5
TAYLOR, Joseph Wright H
TAYLOR, Julian Daniel 1
TAYLOR, Katharine Haviland 1
TAYLOR, Laurette 2
TAYLOR, Lea Demarest 6
TAYLOR, Leland Russell 1
TAYLOR, Lewis Harvie 1
TAYLOR, Lillian E. 5
TAYLOR, Lily Ross 5
TAYLOR, Lloyd William 2
TAYLOR, Lodusky J. 4
TAYLOR, Louis Sherman 4
TAYLOR, Marian Young (Professionally Martha Deane) 6
TAYLOR, Marie Hansen 4
TAYLOR, Marion Sayle 1
TAYLOR, Maris 4
TAYLOR, Marshall William H
TAYLOR, Mary Imlay 1
TAYLOR, Maurice 3
TAYLOR, Merris 4
TAYLOR, Miles H
TAYLOR, Mills James 6
TAYLOR, Montgomery Meigs 3
TAYLOR, Moses H
TAYLOR, Moses 1
TAYLOR, Myron C. 3
TAYLOR, Nathaniel Green H
TAYLOR, Nathaniel William H
TAYLOR, Nelson H
TAYLOR, Nelson 1
TAYLOR, Norman 5
TAYLOR, Oliver Guy 3
TAYLOR, Ora Autumn 4
TAYLOR, Orville 1
TAYLOR, Oury Wilburn 3
TAYLOR, Paul Bennett 4
TAYLOR, R. Tunstall 1
TAYLOR, Ralph Wesley 6
TAYLOR, Raynor H
TAYLOR, Reese Hale 4
TAYLOR, Richard H
TAYLOR, Richard (Denison) 5
TAYLOR, Richard Cowling H
TAYLOR, Richard V. 1
TAYLOR, Robert 4
TAYLOR, Robert Fenwick 4
TAYLOR, Robert Howard 1
TAYLOR, Robert John 5
TAYLOR, Robert Lee 5
TAYLOR, Robert Longley 1
TAYLOR, Robert Love 1
TAYLOR, Robert Stewart 1
TAYLOR, Robert William 4
TAYLOR, S. Earl 5
TAYLOR, Samuel Alfred 1
TAYLOR, Samuel Harvey 1
TAYLOR, Samuel Mac 1
TAYLOR, Samuel Mitchell 1
TAYLOR, S(amuel) N(ewton) 5
TAYLOR, Thelma Marjorie Vogt (Mrs. Jean Landon Taylor) 6
TAYLOR, Thomas 2
TAYLOR, Thomas Hendricks 4
TAYLOR, Thomas Ivan 6
TAYLOR, Thomas Nicholls 3
TAYLOR, Thomas Ulvan 4
TAYLOR, Vernon F. 5
TAYLOR, Victor V. 2
TAYLOR, Vincent George 3
TAYLOR, Waller 1
TAYLOR, Walter Andrews 4
TAYLOR, Walter Herron 1
TAYLOR, Warner 2
TAYLOR, Wayne Chatfield 4
TAYLOR, Will Samuel 5
TAYLOR, William 1
TAYLOR, William 1

TAYLOR, William Albert 2
TAYLOR, William Alexander 1
TAYLOR, William Alton 2
TAYLOR, W(illiam) Bayard 6
TAYLOR, William C. 3
TAYLOR, William Dana 1
TAYLOR, William David Jr. 6
TAYLOR, William George Langworthy 1
TAYLOR, William H. 1
TAYLOR, William Henry 1
TAYLOR, William James 2
TAYLOR, William Johnson 1
TAYLOR, William Ladd 1
TAYLOR, William Mackergo H
TAYLOR, William Mode 1
TAYLOR, William Osgood 3
TAYLOR, William Penn H
TAYLOR, William Rivers 1
TAYLOR, William Rogers 1
TAYLOR, William Septimus 2
TAYLOR, William Sylvester 1
TAYLOR, William Vigneron H
TAYLOR, William Watts 1
TAYLOR, Willis Ratcliffe 2
TAYLOR, Zachary 1
TAZEWELL, Henry H
TAZEWELL, Littleton Waller H
TEACH, Edward H
TEACHENOR, Frank Randall 3
TEAD, Edward Sampson 1
TEAD, Ordway 6
TEAGARDEN, Florence M(abel) 6
TEAGARDEN, Jack Weldon Leo 4
TEAGLE, Walter Clark 4
TEAGUE, Charles C. 3
TEAGUE, Charles McKevett 6
TEAGUE, Walter Dorwin 4
TEAL, Joseph Nathan 1
TEALL, Edward Nelson 2
TEALL, Francis Augustus H
TEALL, Francis Horace 1
TEALL, Gardner 3
TEARSE, Harold Horton 5
TEASDALE, Kenneth 5
TEASDALE, Sara 1
TEASDALE, William Bernard 1
TEBBETTS, Charles Edwin 4
TECUMSEH H
TEDDER, Lord Arthur William 4
TEDESCHE, Leon G. 3
TEDROW, Harry B. 1
TEDYUSKUNG H
TEED, Ralph H. 3
TEEL, Forrest 3
TEEL, Warren Floyd 1
TEELE, Ray Palmer 1
TEELE, Ray Palmer 5
TEELE, Stanley Ferdinand 4
TEEPLE, John Edgar 1
TEESE, Frederick Halstead H
TEESING, H(ubert) P(aul) H(umphrey) 6
TEETER, Albert A. 3
TEETER, John Henry 4
TEETERS, Bert Alonzo 1
TEETERS, Negley King 5
TEETERS, Wilber John 5
TEETOR, Lothair 4
TEETS, Harley O. 3
TEE-VAN, John 4
TEEVAN, John Charles 2
TEFFT, Benjamin Franklin H
TEFFT, Lyman Beecher 1
TEFFT, Thomas A. H
TEFFT, William Wolcott 1
TEGARDEN, JB Hollis 3
TEGGART, Frederick John 2
TEGTMEYER, William Hahne 6
TEHON, Leo Roy 3
TEICH, Max Louis 4
TEICHMANN, William C. 4
TEIGAN, Henry George H
TEILHARD DE CHARDIN, Pierre H
TEILHARD DE CHARDIN, Pierre 4
TELFAIR, Edward H
TELFAIR, Thomas H
TELFORD, Robert Lee 1
TELLER, Henry Moore 1
TELLER, Hugh Harlow 5
TELLER, Isaac 1
TELLER, James Harvey 1
TELLER, John Du Bois 4
TELLER, Ludwig 4

THOMAS, John Lloyd 1
THOMAS, John Martin 3
THOMAS, John Montague 3
THOMAS, John Parnell 5
THOMAS, John Peyre Jr. 2
THOMAS, John Robert 1
THOMAS, John Rochester 1
THOMAS, John S. Ladd 3
THOMAS, John W. 2
THOMAS, John W. 3
THOMAS, John Wilson Jr. 1
THOMAS, Joseph H
THOMAS, Joseph Brown 3
THOMAS, Joseph Loren 5
THOMAS, Joseph Peter 2
THOMAS, Kirby 1
THOMAS, Lee Emmett 4
THOMAS, Lewis F. 3
THOMAS, Lewis Victor 4
THOMAS, Lorenzo H
THOMAS, Lot 1
THOMAS, Lucien Irving 3
THOMAS, M. Carey 1
THOMAS, M. Louise 2
THOMAS, Martin Henry 1
THOMAS, Mason Blanchard 1
THOMAS, Maurice J. 4
THOMAS, Nathaniel Seymour 1
THOMAS, Norman (Mattoon) 5
THOMAS, Paul Henwood 6
THOMAS, Paul Kirk Middlebrook 4
THOMAS, Percy Champion 5
THOMAS, Percy H. 3
THOMAS, Philemon H
THOMAS, Philip Evan H
THOMAS, Philip Francis H
THOMAS, P(urdom) C(lark) 5
THOMAS, Ralph Llewellyn 4
THOMAS, Ralph W. 1
THOMAS, Reuen 1
THOMAS, Richard H
THOMAS, Richard Curd Pope 1
THOMAS, Richard Henry 1
THOMAS, Robert Bailey H
THOMAS, Robert David 6
THOMAS, Robert Ellis 5
THOMAS, Robert McK. Jr. 1
THOMAS, Robert Young Jr. 1
THOMAS, Rolla L. 1
THOMAS, Rolland Jay 4
THOMAS, Roy Zachariah 6
THOMAS, Samuel 1
THOMAS, Samuel 3
THOMAS, Samuel Morgan 5
THOMAS, Seth H
THOMAS, Seth Edward Jr. 1
THOMAS, Stanley Judson 4
THOMAS, Stanley Powers Rowland 6
THOMAS, Stephen Seymour 3
THOMAS, T. Rowland 1
THOMAS, Thaddeus Peter 4
THOMAS, Theodore 1
THOMAS, Theodore Gaillard 1
THOMAS, Walter Horstmann 2
THOMAS, Warren H. 4
THOMAS, Washington Butcher 1
THOMAS, Wilbur Kelsey 3
THOMAS, William 1
THOMAS, William Aubrey 3
THOMAS, William David 1
THOMAS, William Davy 4
THOMAS, William Henry Griffith 1
THOMAS, William Holcombe 2
THOMAS, William Isaac 2
THOMAS, William Nathaniel 5
THOMAS, William Preston 4
THOMAS, William S. 1
THOMAS, William Sturgis 1
THOMAS, William Widgery 1
THOMASON, John William Jr. 2
THOMASON, Robert Ewing 6
THOMASON, Samuel Emory 2
THOMASSON, William Poindexter H
THOMEN, August A. 2
THOMES, William Henry H
THOMPKINS, Leonard Joseph 6
THOMPSON, Albert Clifton 1
THOMPSON, Albert F. 4

THOMPSON, Alexander Marshall 3
THOMPSON, Alfred Charles 4
THOMPSON, Alfred Clark 1
THOMPSON, Alfred Wordsworth H
THOMPSON, Almon Harris 1
THOMPSON, Amos Burt 4
THOMPSON, Arthur Scott 3
THOMPSON, Arthur Webster 1
THOMPSON, Augustus Charles 1
THOMPSON, Basil 1
THOMPSON, Beach 1
THOMPSON, Benjamin * H
THOMPSON, C. Seymour 3
THOMPSON, C. Woody 2
THOMPSON, Calvin Miles 2
THOMPSON, Carl Dean 2
THOMPSON, Carmi Alderman 2
THOMPSON, Cecil Vincent Raymond 3
THOMPSON, Cephas Giovanni H
THOMPSON, Charles Edwin 1
THOMPSON, Charles Fullington 3
THOMPSON, Charles H. 5
THOMPSON, Charles Impey 3
THOMPSON, Charles James 1
THOMPSON, Charles Lemuel 1
THOMPSON, Charles Manfred 4
THOMPSON, Charles Miner 2
THOMPSON, Charles Nebeker 3
THOMPSON, Charles Oliver H
THOMPSON, Charles Perkins H
THOMPSON, Charles Thaddeus 1
THOMPSON, Charles William 1
THOMPSON, Charles Willis 2
THOMPSON, Charles Winston 1
THOMPSON, Chester Charles 5
THOMPSON, Clara Elmer 3
THOMPSON, Clarence 2
THOMPSON, Clary 4
THOMPSON, Clem Oren 3
THOMPSON, Clifford Griffeth 4
THOMPSON, Cyrus 1
THOMPSON, Daniel Pierce H
THOMPSON, Daniel Varney 1
THOMPSON, David H
THOMPSON, David Alphaeus 1
THOMPSON, David Decamp 1
THOMPSON, David E. 2
THOMPSON, David Newton 4
THOMPSON, David P. 1
THOMPSON, Denman 4
THOMPSON, Dorothy 4
THOMPSON, Dwinel French 1
THOMPSON, E. E. 5
THOMPSON, Eben Francis 1
THOMPSON, Edward Archibald 3
THOMPSON, Edward Herbert 1
THOMPSON, Egbert H
THOMPSON, Elbert-Nevius Sebring 2
THOMPSON, Eliza Jane Trimble 3
THOMPSON, Elizabeth McArthur 3
THOMPSON, Ernest 2
THOMPSON, Ernest Othmer 4
THOMPSON, Erwin W. 4
THOMPSON, Fayette Lathrop 1
THOMPSON, Floyd E. 4
THOMPSON, Frank Abner 3
THOMPSON, Frank Dutton 1
THOMPSON, Frank E. 2

THOMPSON, Frank Forrester 1
THOMPSON, Frank M. 1
THOMPSON, Frank Victor 1
THOMPSON, Fred Lawrence 5
THOMPSON, Frederic Diodati Count 1
THOMPSON, Frederic Lincoln 1
THOMPSON, Frederick Gregg 5
THOMPSON, Frederick Henry 1
THOMPSON, Frederick Ingate 3
THOMPSON, George * 1
THOMPSON, George B. 4
THOMPSON, George David 4
THOMPSON, George Jarvis 4
THOMPSON, George Victor 5
THOMPSON, George Wallace 1
THOMPSON, George Western H
THOMPSON, George Williston 5
THOMPSON, Gilbert 1
THOMPSON, Gustave Whyte 2
THOMPSON, Guy A. 3
THOMPSON, Hal Charles 4
THOMPSON, Harry Arthur 1
THOMPSON, Harry LeRoy 3
THOMPSON, Heber Samuel 1
THOMPSON, Hedge H
THOMPSON, Helen Elizabeth 1
THOMPSON, Helen Mulford 6
THOMPSON, Henry Adams 1
THOMPSON, Henry Burling 1
THOMPSON, Henry Dallas 1
THOMPSON, Holland 1
THOMPSON, Hollis Ring 2
THOMPSON, Hugh Lindsay 2
THOMPSON, Hugh Miller 1
THOMPSON, Hugh Smith 1
THOMPSON, Huston 4
THOMPSON, Ira Francis 1
THOMPSON, J. Eric S. 6
THOMPSON, J. Milton 1
THOMPSON, Jacob H
THOMPSON, James Edwin 1
THOMPSON, James F. 3
THOMPSON, James Goodhart 6
THOMPSON, James Kidd 5
THOMPSON, James Livingston 4
THOMPSON, James Ralph 5
THOMPSON, James Stratton 1
THOMPSON, James Voorhees 3
THOMPSON, James Westfall 1
THOMPSON, Jean M. 5
THOMPSON, Jeremiah H
THOMPSON, Jerome B. H
THOMPSON, Joel H
THOMPSON, John * H
THOMPSON, John 2
THOMPSON, John 3
THOMPSON, John Bert 6
THOMPSON, John Burton 1
THOMPSON, John Cameron 1
THOMPSON, John Fairfield 5
THOMPSON, John Fawdrey Jr. 1
THOMPSON, John Gilbert 2
THOMPSON, John Graves 4
THOMPSON, John Kerwin 2
THOMPSON, John Q. 1
THOMPSON, John R. 8
THOMPSON, John Reuben H
THOMPSON, John Taliaferro 1
THOMPSON, John Winter 3
THOMPSON, Joseph Addison 1
THOMPSON, Joseph B. 1
THOMPSON, Joseph H. 5
THOMPSON, Joseph Osgood 3
THOMPSON, Joseph Parrish H
THOMPSON, Joseph S(exton) 5

THOMPSON, Joseph Whitaker 2
THOMPSON, Josiah Van Kirk 1
THOMPSON, Laforrest Holman 1
THOMPSON, Launt H
THOMPSON, Lawrance Roger 5
THOMPSON, Leslie Prince 4
THOMPSON, Lewis 1
THOMPSON, Lewis Eugene 5
THOMPSON, Lewis Ryers 3
THOMPSON, Llewellyn E. Jr. 5
THOMPSON, M. Gladys 6
THOMPSON, Marshall Putnam 5
THOMPSON, Martin E. H
THOMPSON, Maurice 1
THOMPSON, Maurice Wycliffe 3
THOMPSON, Melville Withington 1
THOMPSON, Merle Dow 5
THOMPSON, Mills 2
THOMPSON, Milo Milton 2
THOMPSON, Milton John 5
THOMPSON, Oscar 2
THOMPSON, Owen Pierce 4
THOMPSON, Paul 2
THOMPSON, Paul Jennings 4
THOMPSON, Percy Wallace 4
THOMPSON, Philip H
THOMPSON, Philip Rootes H
THOMPSON, Ralph Leroy 5
THOMPSON, Ralph Seymour 4
THOMPSON, Reuben Cyril Hill 3
THOMPSON, Richard Wigginton 1
THOMPSON, Robert Andrew 1
THOMPSON, Robert Augustine H
THOMPSON, Robert Bruce 5
THOMPSON, Robert Ellis 1
THOMPSON, Robert Elmo 2
THOMPSON, Robert Foster 5
THOMPSON, Robert Harvey 1
THOMPSON, Robert John 1
THOMPSON, Robert LeRoy 3
THOMPSON, Robert Long 4
THOMPSON, Robert Means 1
THOMPSON, Robert S. 5
THOMPSON, Roby Calvin 4
THOMPSON, Ronald Burdick 6
THOMPSON, Roy Leland 3
THOMPSON, Rupert Campbell Jr. 5
THOMPSON, Russell Irvin 3
THOMPSON, Sam H. 3
THOMPSON, Sam(uel) 5
THOMPSON, Samuel Evans 3
THOMPSON, Samuel Hunter 4
THOMPSON, Samuel Huston H
THOMPSON, Samuel Rankin 2
THOMPSON, Sanford Eleazer 1
THOMPSON, Slason 1
THOMPSON, Smith H
THOMPSON, Stith 6
THOMPSON, Theodore Strong 1
THOMPSON, Theos Jardin 5
THOMPSON, Thomas 4
THOMPSON, Thomas Barney 1
THOMPSON, Thomas Clarkson 2
THOMPSON, Thomas Edward 4
THOMPSON, Thomas Gordon 3
THOMPSON, Thomas Larkin 1
THOMPSON, Thomas Payne 4
THOMPSON, Thomas Weston 3
THOMPSON, Thor Arthur 1
THOMPSON, Vance 5
THOMPSON, W. Stuart 4
THOMPSON, W. Taliaferro H
THOMPSON, Waddy 1
THOMPSON, Waddy H
THOMPSON, Wallace 1
THOMPSON, Wiley H

THOMPSON, Will L. 1
THOMPSON, Will Scroggs 4
THOMPSON, Willard Chandler 3
THOMPSON, Willard Owen 3
THOMPSON, William * H
THOMPSON, William Barlum 4
THOMPSON, William Bess 1
THOMPSON, William Blaine Jr. 5
THOMPSON, William Boyce 1
THOMPSON, William Francis 4
THOMPSON, William Gilman 1
THOMPSON, William Goodrich 1
THOMPSON, William Hale 2
THOMPSON, William Henry 1
THOMPSON, William Herbert 1
THOMPSON, William Howard 1
THOMPSON, William Joseph 2
THOMPSON, William Leland 3
THOMPSON, William McLean 4
THOMPSON, William N. 6
THOMPSON, William Ormonde 2
THOMPSON, William Oxley 1
THOMPSON, William Tappan H
THOMPSON, William Thomas 3
THOMPSON, William Townsend 1
THOMPSON, William W. 5
THOMPSON, Zadock H
THOMS, Craig Sharpe 2
THOMS, Herbert 5
THOMS, William Edward 2
THOMS, William M. 4
THOMSEN, Mark Lawrence 1
THOMSEN, Rasmus 2
THOMSON, Alexander H
THOMSON, Alexander 1
THOMSON, Arthur Conover 2
THOMSON, Charles H
THOMSON, Charles Alexander 4
THOMSON, Charles Goff 1
THOMSON, Charles Marsh 2
THOMSON, David Sidney 3
THOMSON, Edgar Steiner 1
THOMSON, Edward H
THOMSON, Edward 1
THOMSON, Edward H. 4
THOMSON, Edward William 4
THOMSON, Elihu 1
THOMSON, Francis A. 3
THOMSON, Frank 1
THOMSON, Sir George Paget 6
THOMSON, Sir Godfrey Hilton 3
THOMSON, Henry Czar Merwin 1
THOMSON, James E. M. 4
THOMSON, James Lewis 1
THOMSON, James McIlhany 3
THOMSON, James Sutherland 5
THOMSON, James William 1
THOMSON, John H
THOMSON, John 1
THOMSON, John Cameron 4
THOMSON, John Edgar 1
THOMSON, John Renshaw H
THOMSON, Keith 4
THOMSON, Logan G. 2
THOMSON, Mark 1
THOMSON, Mortimer Neal 4
THOMSON, Osmund Rhoads Howard 2
THOMSON, Peter Gibson 1
THOMSON, Philip Livingston 5
THOMSON, Procter 6
THOMSON, Reginald Heber 3
THOMSON, Roy B. 3
THOMSON, Samuel H
THOMSON, Samuel Harrison 1

THOMSON, Samuel Harrison 6
THOMSON, T. Kennard 3
THOMSON, Thaddeus Austin 1
THOMSON, W. H. Seward 1
THOMSON, William H
THOMSON, William 1
THOMSON, William Archibald Jr. 6
THOMSON, William H. 2
THOMSON, William Hanna 1
THOMSON, William Judah 1
THOMSON, William McClure H
THOMSON, William Nobel 6
THORBORG, Kerstin 5
THORBURN, Grant H
THORBURN, Thomas Rankin 4
THOREAU, Henry David H
THOREK, Max 3
THOREZ, Maurice 4
THORFINN H
THORGRIMSON, Oliver Bernhard 5
THORINGTON, James 2
THORINGTON, William Sewell 1
THORKELSON, Halsten Joseph 5
THORKELSON, Jacob 5
THORN, Frank Manly 4
THORN, James 3
THORNAL, Benjamin Campbell 5
THORNBER, John James 5
THORNBURG, Charles Lewis 2
THORNBURG, Delmar Leon 6
THORNBURG, Zenas Charles 1
THORNBURGH, George 1
THORNBURGH, Jacob Montgomery H
THORNDIKE, Ashley Horace 1
THORNDIKE, Augustus 4
THORNDIKE, Edward Lee 2
THORNDIKE, Israel H
THORNDIKE, Lynn 4
THORNDIKE, Paul 1
THORNDIKE, Townsend William 1
THORNDIKE, Willis Hale 5
THORNE, Charles Embree 1
THORNE, Charles Hallett 2
THORNE, Charles Robert * H
THORNE, Chester 1
THORNE, Clifford 1
THORNE, Edwin 1
THORNE, Elisabeth Griffin 5
THORNE, Frederick Wisner 4
THORNE, James Reynolds 5
THORNE, Landon K. 4
THORNE, Lansing S. 4
THORNE, Oakleigh 2
THORNE, Robert Julius 3
THORNE, Samuel 1
THORNE, William 3
THORNE, William Henry 4
THORNE, William Van Schoonhoven 1
THORNHILL, Arthur H. 5
THORNLEY, Fant Hill 5
THORNTHWAITE, Charles Warren 4
THORNTON, Charles Stead 6
THORNTON, Dan 6
THORNTON, Edward Quin 2
THORNTON, Edwin William 3
THORNTON, Eric Laurence 6
THORNTON, Gustavus Brown 1
THORNTON, Hamilton 5
THORNTON, Harrison John 3
THORNTON, Sir Henry Worth 1
THORNTON, James Brown 1
THORNTON, Jessy Quinn H
THORNTON, John Randolph 1
THORNTON, John Wingate H
THORNTON, Leila Cameron Austell 1
THORNTON, Matthew H
THORNTON, Patrick M. 3
THORNTON, Robert Lee 4
THORNTON, T. Eugene 4
THORNTON, Walter Edwin 4
THORNTON, Walter Francis 4
THORNTON, William H
THORNTON, William D. 3
THORNTON, William Mynn 1
THORNTON, William Taylor 1
THORNTON, William Wheeler 1
THORNWELL, James Henley H
THORON, Benjamin Warder 6
THOROUGHMAN, James Chanslor 6
THORP, Charles Monroe 2
THORP, Clark Elwin 5
THORP, Frank 1
THORP, Frank Hall 4
THORP, George Gowen 4
THORP, Harry Walter 4
THORP, John H
THORP, Willard Brown 3
THORPE, Burton Lee 5
THORPE, Drew Maxwell 4
THORPE, Ervin Llewellyn 1
THORPE, Francis Newton 1
THORPE, George Cyrus 1
THORPE, James Francis H
THORPE, James Francis 4
THORPE, Merle 3
THORPE, Rose Hartwick 1
THORPE, Spencer Roane 4
THORPE, Thomas Bangs H
THORS, Olafur 4
THORS, Thor 4
THORSEN, David S. 5
THORSON, Gunnar Axel Wright 5
THORSON, Nelson Thor 3
THORSON, Thomas 1
THORSON, Truman C. 4
THORVALDSON, Gunnar S. 5
THORVALDSSON, Eric H
THRASHER, Allen Benton 1
THRASHER, Frederic Milton 4
THRASHER, John Sidney H
THRASHER, Max Bennett 1
THRASHER, Paul McNeel 2
THREADGILL, Frances Falwell (Mrs. John Threadgill) 5
THRELKELD, Clyde Hollis 4
THROCKMORTON, Archibald Hall 1
THROCKMORTON, Charlotte Edgerton Alvord ("Charles Eqerton") 5
THROCKMORTON, Cleon 4
THROCKMORTON, George Kenneth 3
THROCKMORTON, James Webb H
THROCKMORTON, Tom Bentley 4
THROGMORTON, William P. 1
THROOP, Enos Thompson H
THROOP, Frank Dwight 2
THROOP, George Reeves 2
THROOP, Montgomery Hunt H
THROPP, Joseph Earlston 5
THRUSTON, Buckner H
THRUSTON, Gates Phillips 1
THRUSTON, Lucy Meacham 4
THRUSTON, Rogers Clark Ballard 2
THULSTRUP, Thure de 1
THUM, Ernest Edgar 4
THUM, Patty Prather 1
THUM, William 4
THUMAN, J. Herman 4
THUMB, Gen Tom H
THURBER, Caroline 3
THURBER, Charles H
THURBER, Charles Herbert 1
THURBER, Edward Gerrish 1
THURBER, Francis Beatty 1
THURBER, George H
THURBER, Harry Raymond 4
THURBER, Howard Ford 1
THURBER, James Grover 4
THURMAN, Aaron 6
THURMAN, Allen Granberry H
THURMAN, Allen William 4
THURMAN, Hal C. 3
THURMAN, John Richardson H
THURMAN, Samuel R. 4
THURMON, Francis M. 4
THURMOND, Erasmus Khleber 5
THURMOND, John William 4
THURNAUER, Gustav 2
THURSBY, Emma Cecelia 2
THURSTON, Benjamin Babcock H
THURSTON, Charles Rawson 1
THURSTON, Edward Sampson 2
THURSTON, Elliott Ladd 6
THURSTON, Ernest Lawton 3
THURSTON, Henry Winfred 2
THURSTON, Howard 1
THURSTON, Ida Treadwell 1
THURSTON, John Foster 6
THURSTON, John Mellen 1
THURSTON, Lee Mohrmann 3
THURSTON, Lloyd 5
THURSTON, Lorrin Andrews 1
THURSTON, Robert Henry 1
THURSTON, Robert Lawton H
THURSTON, Samuel Royal H
THURSTON, Theodore Payne 1
THURSTON, Walter 6
THURSTON, William Ravenel 4
THURSTONE, Louis Leon 3
THWAITE, Charles Edward Jr. 4
THWAITES, Reuben Gold 1
THWING, Charles Burton 4
THWING, Charles Franklin 1
THWING, Edward Waite 4
THWING, Eugene 1
THYE, Edward John 5
TIBBALS, Charles Austin Jr. 2
TIBBALS, Seymour Selden 3
TIBBALS, William Huntington 4
TIBBATTS, John Wooleston H
TIBBETS, Addison S. 4
TIBBETT, Lawrence Mervil 4
TIBBETTS, Frederick Horace 1
TIBBITS, Charles Edward Dudley 1
TIBBITS, George H
TIBBLES, Thomas Henry 1
TIBOLT, Robert P. 5
TIBOR, Lee Anthony 4
TICE, Frederick 3
TICHBORNE, Josephine Caroline Sawyer 1
TICHENOR, Alfred Benton 5
TICHENOR, Austin Kent 5
TICHENOR, Isaac H
TICHENOR, Isaac Taylor H
TICKNOR, Caroline 1
TICKNOR, Elisha H
TICKNOR, Francis Orray H
TICKNOR, George H
TICKNOR, Howard Malcom 1
TICKNOR, William Davis H
TIDBALL, John Caldwell 1
TIDBALL, Thomas Allen 4
TIDEMANN, Karl 6
TIDWELL, Josiah Blake 2
TIEBOUT, Cornelius H
TIEBOUT, Harry Morgan 4
TIEDEMAN, Christopher Gustavus 1
TIEDEMANN, Tudor H. A. 3
TIEDJENS, Victor Alphons 6
TIEF, Francis Joseph 4
TIEKEN, Robert 6
TIEKEN, Theodore 1
TIEMANN, Daniel Fawcett 1
TIERNAN, Charles Bernard 1
TIERNEY, Harry Austin 4
TIERNEY, John M. 4
TIERNEY, John Thomas 2
TIERNEY, Leo Francis 5
TIERNEY, Michael 1
TIERNEY, Richard Henry 1
TIERNEY, William Laurence 3
TIERNON, John Luke 1
TIETJENS, Eunice 2
TIETJENS, Paul 5
TIETSORT, Franics Judson 5
TIFFANY, Alexander Ralston H
TIFFANY, Charles Comfort 1
TIFFANY, Charles Lewis 1
TIFFANY, Charles Lewis 2
TIFFANY, Flavel Benjamin 1
TIFFANY, Francis 1
TIFFANY, Francis Buchanan 3
TIFFANY, Hanford 4
TIFFANY, Herbert Thorndike 2
TIFFANY, J. Raymond 3
TIFFANY, Louis Comfort 1
TIFFANY, Louis McLane 1
TIFFANY, Nina Moore 3
TIFFANY, Orrin Edward 4
TIFFANY, Ross Kerr 1
TIFFANY, Walter Checkley 4
TIFFIN, Edward H
TIFFT, Henry Neville 1
TIFT, Nelson H
TIGERT, John James 1
TIGERT, John James 2
TIGERT, John James 4
TIGH, William Frederick 4
TIGHE, Ambrose 1
TIGHE, Laurence Gotzian 3
TIGHE, Lawrence Giblin 2
TIGHT, William George 1
TIHEN, John Henry 1
TILANDER, Artur Gunnar 6
TILDEN, Charles Joseph 3
TILDEN, Daniel Rose H
TILDEN, Douglas 1
TILDEN, Edward 1
TILDEN, Francis Calvin 4
TILDEN, George Thomas 1
TILDEN, John Henry 4
TILDEN, Joseph Mayo 1
TILDEN, Josephine Elizabeth 3
TILDEN, Louis Edward 5
TILDEN, Samuel Jones H
TILDEN, William Tatem H
TILDEN, William Tatem 1
TILDEN, William Tatem 4
TILDSLEY, John Lee 2
TILDY, Zoltan 4
TILESTON, Mary Wilder 1
TILESTON, Thomas H
TILESTON, Wilder 5
TILFORD, Frank 1
TILFORD, Henry Johnson 5
TILFORD, Joseph Green 1
TILGHMAN, Edward H
TILGHMAN, Matthew H
TILGHMAN, Richard Albert H
TILGHMAN, Tench H
TILGHMAN, William H
TILGHMAN, William Matthew H
TILGHMAN, William Matthew 4
TILLER, Theodore Hance 3
TILLERY, Lee 4
TILLES, Roy E. 4
TILLETT, Charles Walter 1
TILLETT, Charles Walter 3
TILLETT, Wilbur Fisk 1
TILLETT, William S. 6
TILLEY, Benjamin Franklin 1
TILLEY, Cecil Edgar 6
TILLEY, Morris Palmer 2
TILLICH, Paul Johannes 4
TILLINGHAST, Benjamin Franklin 1
TILLINGHAST, Benjamin Franklin 3
TILLINGHAST, Caleb Benjamin 1
TILLINGHAST, Charles Carpenter 4
TILLINGHAST, Harold Morton 3
TILLINGHAST, Joseph Leonard H
TILLINGHAST, Mary Elizabeth 1
TILLINGHAST, Pardon E. 1
TILLINGHAST, Thomas H
TILLMAN, Abram Martin 2
TILLMAN, Albert Gallatin III 6
TILLMAN, Benjamin Ryan 1
TILLMAN, George N. 1
TILLMAN, James Davidson 4
TILLMAN, John Newton 1
TILLMAN, John Plummer 1
TILLMAN, Lewis H
TILLMAN, Nathaniel Patrick 4
TILLMAN, Paul Edward 6
TILLMAN, Samuel Escue 2
TILLOTSON, Edwin Ward 4
TILLOTSON, Loyal Garis 4
TILLOTSON, Thomas H
TILLSON, George William 1
TILLSON, John Charles Fremont 1
TILLSON, John Charles Fremont 2
TILLY, David L. 2
TILNEY, Albert Arthur 1
TILNEY, Frederick 1
TILROE, William Edwin 1
TILSON, Ann Coe (Mrs. Donald Heath Tilson) 5
TILSON, John Quillin 3
TILSON, William Josiah 2
TILT, Charles Arthur 3
TILTON, Dwight 1
TILTON, Edward Lippincott 1
TILTON, Elizabeth (Mrs. William Tilton) 5
TILTON, Frederic Arthur 2
TILTON, George Henry 1
TILTON, Howard Winslow 1
TILTON, James H
TILTON, John Philip 3
TILTON, John Rollin H
TILTON, McLane Jr. 1
TILTON, Ralph 1
TILTON, Theodore 1
TILY, Herbert James 2
TILYOU, George Cornelius H
TILYOU, George Cornelius 4
TIMBERLAKE, Charles B. 1
TIMBERLAKE, Gideon 3
TIMBERLAKE, Henry H
TIMBERMAN, Andrew 2
TIMBLIN, Louis M. 3
TIMBY, Theodore Ruggles 1
TIMKEN, Henry H
TIMKEN, Henry 4
TIMKEN, Henry H. Jr. 4
TIMLIN, William Henry 1
TIMLOW, Elizabeth Weston 1
TIMM, Henry Christian H
TIMM, John A(rrend) 5
TIMME, Ernst G. 4
TIMME, Walter 3
TIMMERMAN, Arthur Henry 5
TIMMERMAN, George Bell 4
TIMMERMAN, George Bell 5
TIMMINS, Jules Robert 5
TIMMONS, Dever 4
TIMMONS, Edward J. Finley 4
TIMMONS, Wofford Colquitt 3
TIMON, John H
TIMOSHENKO, Stephen 5
TIMOTHY, Lewis H
TIMPY, Jack J. 3
TIMROD, Henry H
TIMS, John Chapel 1
TIMS, John Francis 5
TINCHER, J. N. 3
TINCKER, Mary Agnes 1
TINDALL, Glenn Means 5
TINGELSTAD, Oscar Adolf 3
TINGEY, Thomas H
TINGLE, John Bishop 3
TINGLE, Leonard 4
TINGLEY, Charles Love Scott 4
TINGLEY, Clyde 4
TINGLEY, Katherine 1
TINGLEY, Louisa Paine 3
TINGLEY, Richard Hoadley 1
TINKER, Chauncey Brewster 4
TINKER, Clarence L. 2
TINKER, Earl Warren 3
TINKER, Edward Larocque 5
TINKER, Edward Richmond 3
TINKER, Martin Buel 3
TINKHAM, Henry Crain 1
TINKHAM, Herbert Linwood 1
TINKHAM, Richard Parsons 5
TINKMAN, George Holden 3
TINLEY, Mathew Adrian 3
TINNEY, Frank 1
TINNON, Robert McCracken 1
TINNON, Thomas B. 6
TINSLEY, Gladney Jack 3
TINSLEY, John Francis 3
TINSLEY, Richard Parran 1
TINSMAN, Homer Ellsworth 2
TIPPET, Charles Frederick Basil 4
TIPPETS, Joseph Henderson 5
TIPPETTS, Charles Sanford 5
TIPPLE, Bertrand Martin 5
TIPPLE, Ezra Squier 1
TIPPY, William Bruce 6

* Indicates More Than One Such Name Listed

TIPPY, Worth Marion 4
TIPTON, Ernest Moss 3
TIPTON, John * H
TIPTON, Laurence B.
TIPTON, Royce Jay 4
TIPTON, Royce Jay 5
TIREY, Ralph Noble
TIRINDELLI, Pier Adolfo 4
TIRRELL, Charles Quincy
TIRRELL, Frank A. Jr. 3
TIRRELL, Henry Archelaus 5
TISCH, Alfred Francis 5
TISDALL, Fritz Gerald
TISDEL, Frederick Monroe 5
TISELIUS, Arne (Wilhelm 5
 Kaurin)
TISHER, Paul Winslow 6
TISINGER, Benjamin Louis 1
TISON, Alexander 1
TISQUANTUM H
TISSERANT, H. E. 5
 Cardinal Eugene
TITCHENER, Edward 1
 Bradford
TITCHENER, John 5
 Bradford
TITCOMB, Harvey Burgess 5
TITCOMB, John Wheelock 1
TITCOMB, Mary Lemist 1
TITCOMB, Miriam 6
TITCOMB, Virginia 5
 Chandler
TITHERINGTON, Richard 1
 Handfield
TITSWORTH, Alfred 1
 Alexander
TITSWORTH, Clarence E. 5
TITSWORTH, Grant 4
TITSWORTH, Judson 1
TITSWORTH, Paul 1
 Emerson
TITTERINGTON, Sophie 4
 Bronson
TITTLE, Elmer Anthony 5
TITTLE, Ernest Fremont 2
TITTLE, Walter 4
TITTMANN, Charles 4
 Trowbridge
TITTMANN, Otto Hilgard 1
TITUS, Andrew Phillips 5
TITUS, Bennett Eaton 1
TITUS, Edward Coddington 5
TITUS, Ellwood Valentine
TITUS, Louis 5
TITUS, Obadiah H
TITUS, Paul 3
TITUS, Paul 5
TITUS, Robert Cyrus 1
TIVNAN, Edward P. 1
TIYANOGA H
TJADER, Richard 1
TOASPERN, Otto 4
TOBENKIN, Elias 4
TOBEY, Charles William 3
TOBEY, Edward Silas H
TOBIAS, Channing Heggie 4
TOBIAS, Norman 6
TOBIN, Charles Milton 5
TOBIN, Daniel Aloysius 2
TOBIN, Daniel J. 3
TOBIN, Edmund Paul 4
TOBIN, George Timothy 4
TOBIN, James Edward 5
TOBIN, James F(rancis) 6
TOBIN, John Charles 3
TOBIN, Maurice Joseph 3
TOBIN, Ralph C. 2
TOBIN, Richard 3
 Montgomery
TOBIN, Robert Gibson 3
TOBIN, Robert James 5
TOBITT, Edith 3
TOBOLSKY, Arthur Victor 5
TOBY, Edward 2
TOCH, Ernst 4
TOCH, Maximilian 2
TOCQUEVILLE, Alexis
 Henri Maurice Clerel de
TOD, David H
TOD, George H
TOD, J. Kennedy 1
TOD, John H
TOD, John 3
TODARO, Vincent Settimo 6
TODD, Albert May 1
TODD, Albert W. 2
TODD, Ambrose Giddings 2
TODD, Arthur James 2
TODD, Casey 5
TODD, Chapman Coleman 1
TODD, Charles Burr 4
TODD, Charles Stewart H
TODD, Clare Chrisman 3
TODD, David 1
TODD, Earle Marion 1
TODD, Edward Howard 5

TODD, Eli H
TODD, Elmer Ely 4
TODD, Elmer Kenneth 5
TODD, Eugene A. 5
TODD, Fannie Burgess 5
 (Mrs. Harold Arthur
 Todd)
TODD, Forde Anderson 5
TODD, Frank Chisholm 1
TODD, George Carroll 2
TODD, George Davidson 4
TODD, George Walter
TODD, H. Stanley 4
TODD, Harold Arthur 4
TODD, Harry L.
TODD, Henry Alfred 1
TODD, Henry Davis 1
TODD, Hiram Charles 4
TODD, Hiram Eugene 2
TODD, James Edward 1
TODD, John H
TODD, John Blair Smith H
TODD, John Reynard 2
TODD, Joseph Clinton 5
TODD, Jouett Ross 4
TODD, Laurence 3
TODD, Lawrie H
TODD, Lemuel H
TODD, Luther Edward 1
TODD, M. Hampton 4
TODD, Mabel Loomis 1
TODD, Marion 4
TODD, Michael 3
TODD, Paul Harold 5
TODD, Percy R. 1
TODD, Robert Henry 4
TODD, Robert I. 1
TODD, Roscoe Johnson 6
TODD, Sereno Edwards H
TODD, T. Wingate 1
TODD, Thomas H
TODD, Thomas 3
TODD, Walter Edmond 5
 Clyde
TODD, Walter Ledyard 5
TODD, William Henry 1
TODD, William T. Jr. 3
TOEBBE, Augustus Marie H
TOFFENETTI, Dario Louis 4
TOFFTEEN, Olof Alfred 4
TOFTOY, Holger Nelson 4
TOGLIATTI, Palmiro 4
TOGNAZZINI, Roland 4
TOLAN, Edwin Kirkman 6
TOLAN, John Harvey 2
TOLAND, Clarence 5
 G(aines)
TOLAND, Edmund M. 2
TOLAND, Hugh Huger H
TOLANSKY, Samuel 4
TOLBERT, Benjamin Arthur 1
TOLBERT, Joseph W(arren) 5
TOLBERT, Raymond 4
 Augustine
TOLBERT, Ward Van der
 Hoof
TOLEDO-HERRARTE, 5
 Luis
TOLER, Fred W. 1
TOLFREE, James Edward 1
TOLIN, Ernest A. 4
TOLISCHUS, Otto David 4
TOLKIEN, John Ronald 6
 Reuel
TOLL, Henry Wolcott 6
TOLL, Roger Wolcott 1
TOLL, William Edward 4
TOLLEFSON, Martin 4
TOLLER, Ernst H
TOLLER, Ernst 4
TOLLES, Frederick Barnes 6
TOLLES, Marian Donahue 4
 (Mrs. N. Arnold Tolles)
TOLLES, Newman Arnold 4
TOLLES, Sheldon H
 Hitchcock
TOLLESON, William N. 1
TOLLETT, Raymond Lee 4
TOLLEY, Harold Sumner 3
TOLLEY, Howard Ross 3
TOLLMIEN, Walter Gustav 4
TOLMAN, Albert Harris 1
TOLMAN, Albert Walter 4
TOLMAN, Charles Prescott 4
TOLMAN, Cyrus Fisher Jr. 2
TOLMAN, Edgar Bronson 2
TOLMAN, Edward Chase 4
TOLMAN, Frank Leland 4
TOLMAN, Herbert Cushing 1
TOLMAN, Judson Allen 2
TOLMAN, Richard Chace 2
TOLMAN, Ruth S. 3
TOLMAN, Warren W. 1
TOLMAN, William Howe 1
TOLMIE, William Fraser H
TOLSON, Clyde Anderson 6

TOLSON, George Tolover 4
TOLSTOY, Count Alexei 4
 Nikolaevich
TOLTZ, Max 1
TOM, Howard 4
TOMAJAN, John S. 5
TOMBALBAYE, Francois 6
TOMBER, Max L. 5
TOME, Jacob 1
TOMEI, Peter Andrew 5
TOMKINS, Calvin H
TOMKINS, Floyd Williams 1
TOMKINS, Gordon Mayer 6
TOMLIN, Bradley Walker 3
TOMLIN, James Harvey 4
TOMLINS, William 4
 Lawrence
TOMLINSON, Allen U. 3
TOMLINSON, Arthur 1
 Hibbs
TOMLINSON, Charles C. 3
TOMLINSON, Charles 2
 Fawcett
TOMLINSON, Douglas 6
TOMLINSON, Edward 6
TOMLINSON, Everett 1
 Titsworth
TOMLINSON, George H
 Ashley
TOMLINSON, Gideon H
TOMLINSON, H. M. 3
TOMLINSON, Homer 5
 Aubrey
TOMLINSON, Roy Everett 5
TOMLINSON, Thomas Ash H
TOMLINSON, Vincent 1
 Eaton
TOMLINSON, William 5
 Gosnell
TOMOCHICHI H
TOMPERS, George Urban 1
TOMPERT, Russell Howard 1
TOMPKINS, Arnold 1
TOMPKINS, Arthur Sidney 1
TOMPKINS, Boylston 5
 Adams
TOMPKINS, Caleb 1
TOMPKINS, Charles Henry 1
TOMPKINS, Charles Hook H
TOMPKINS, Christopher H
TOMPKINS, Christopher 4
TOMPKINS, Cydnor Bailey H
TOMPKINS, Daniel A. 1
TOMPKINS, Daniel D. H
TOMPKINS, De Loss
 Monroe
TOMPKINS, Elizabeth 4
 Knight
TOMPKINS, Frank Hector 1
TOMPKINS, H. D. 3
TOMPKINS, Juliet Wilbor 5
TOMPKINS, Leslie Jay 3
TOMPKINS, Lucius 5
 Douglas
TOMPKINS, Nathaniel 1
TOMPKINS, Patrick H
 Watson
TOMPSON, Benjamin H
TOMS, Robert Morrell 3
TOMS, Zach 1
TONDORF, Francis 1
 Anthony
TONE, Franchot 5
TONE, Frank Jerome 2
TONER, Edward C. 1
TONER, James Vincent 3
TONER, Joseph Meredith H
TONG, Hollington K. 5
TONGUE, Thomas H. 1
TONKS, Oliver Samuel 3
TONNER, John Andrew 4
TONTY, Henry de H
TOOHEY, John Peter 2
TOOKER, Lewis Frank 1
TOOKER, Norman Brown 4
TOOKER, Sterling Twiss 4
TOOKEY, Clarence H(all) 5
TOOLE, Joseph Kemp 1
TOOLE, S. Westcott 5
TOOLIN, John Martin 5
TOOMBS, Henry Johnston 5
TOOMBS, Percy Walthall 5
TOOMBS, Robert Augustus H
TOOMEY, De Lally 1
 Prescott
TOOMEY, Floyd F(rancis) 6
TOON, Thomas Fentress 1
TOOPS, Herbert Anderson 6
TOOTELL, Robert Ballard 5
TOOTHAKER, Charles 3
 Robinson
TOOTLE, Milton Jr. 2
TOPAKYAN, Haigazoun 1
 Hohannes
TOPE, Homer W. 1
TOPLIFF, Samuel H

TOPLITZKY, Joe 1
TOPPAN, Charles H
TOPPAN, Robert Noxon 1
TOPPIN, Harry Pattinson 5
TOPPING, Daniel Reid 6
TOPPING, John Alexander 1
TORBERT, Alfred Thomas H
 Archimedes
TORBERT, John Bryant 1
TORBERT, William 5
 Sydenham
TORBETT, Joe Hall 3
TORCHIANA, Henry 1
 Albert van Coenen
TORCHIO, Philip 1
TORCHIO, Phillip Jr. 3
TOREK, Franz 2
TORGERSEN, Harold 4
TORGERSEN, Harold W. 4
TORIAN, Oscar Noel 5
TORKELSON, Martin 4
 Wilhelm
TORNEY, George Henry 1
TORNGREN, Ralf 4
TORO, Emilio del 4
TORRANCE, David 1
TORRANCE, Eli 1
TORRANCE, Francis J. 1
TORRANCE, Henry 5
TORRANCE, Stiles Albert 3
TORRE, Carlos de la 5
TORRENCE, George Paull 4
TORRENCE, Joseph H
 Thatcher
TORRENCE, Olivia 5
 Howard Dunbar
TORRENCE, Ridgely 3
TORRENS, D.T. 1
TORRENS, William Erskine 1
TORREY, Bradford 1
TORREY, Charles Cutler 5
TORREY, Charles Turner 6
TORREY, Clarence Ezra Jr. 6
TORREY, Elbridge 1
TORREY, Elliot Bouton 2
TORREY, George 1
 Burroughs
TORREY, Herbert Gray 1
TORREY, John H
TORREY, Joseph 1
 Hezekiah
TORREY, Marian Marsh 5
TORREY, Raymond 1
TORREYSON, Burr Walter 1
TORRISON, John William 4
TORRISON, Oscar M. 1
TORY, John Stewart Donald 4
TOSCANINI, Arturo 5
TOTH, William 4
TOTTEN, Charles Adiel 1
 Lewis
TOTTEN, George Muirson 1
TOTTEN, George Oakley 1
 Jr.
TOTTEN, Joe Byron 2
TOTTEN, Joseph Gilbert H
TOTTEN, Ralph James H
TOTTEN, Silas H
TOTTON, Frank Mortimer 4
TOTTY, S. V. 4
TOUCEY, Isaac H
TOULMIN, Harry H
TOULMIN, Harry Aubrey 4
 Jr.
TOULMIN, Harry 1
 Theophilus
TOULMIN, John Edwin 5
TOUMEY, James William 1
TOUPS, Roland Leon 5
TOUR, Reuben S. 3
TOUREL, Jennie 6
TOURET, Frank Hale 2
TOURGEE, Albion Winegar 1
TOURJEE, Eben H
TOURSCHER, Francis 1
 Edward
TOURTELLOT, George 2
 Platt
TOURTELLOTTE, Edward 1
 Everett
TOUSANT, Emma Sanborn 5
TOUSEY, Sinclair 1
TOUSEY, William George 1
TOUSSAINT
 L'OUVERTURE, Pierre
 Francois Dominique
TOUTON, Frank Charles 2
TOUVELLE, William E. 4
TOVEN, Joseph Richard 5
TOWAR, Albert Selah 4
TOWART, William G. 2
TOWER, Carl Vernon 5
TOWER, Charlemagne 1
TOWER, Edwin Briggs Hale 3
 Jr.

TOWER, George Edward 1
TOWER, George Warren Jr. 1
TOWER, James Eaton 2
TOWER, John H
TOWER, Olin Freeman 2
TOWER, Ralph Winfred 1
TOWER, Walter Sheldon 5
TOWER, William Lawrence 5
TOWERS, Albert Garey 5
TOWERS, John Alden 3
TOWERS, John Henry 3
TOWERS, Walter Kellogg 2
TOWL, Forrest Milton 2
TOWLE, Carroll S. 3
TOWLE, Charles Brother 3
TOWLE, Charlotte 4
TOWLE, George Makepeace H
TOWLE, J. Norman 3
TOWLE, Lawrence William 6
TOWLE, Norman Lincoln 4
TOWLER, John H
TOWLER, Thomas Willard 5
TOWN, David Edward 1
TOWN, Ithiel H
TOWNE, Arthur Whittlesey 3
TOWNE, Benjamin H
TOWNE, Charles Arnette 1
TOWNE, Charles Hanson 2
TOWNE, Charles Wayland 6
TOWNE, Edward Owings 4
TOWNE, Elizabeth 4
TOWNE, Ezra Thayer 3
TOWNE, George Lewis 1
TOWNE, Henry Robinson 1
TOWNE, John Henry 1
TOWNE, John Henry 2
TOWNE, Robert Duke 1
TOWNE, Salem B. 1
TOWNE, Walter James 1
TOWNE, William Elmer 5
TOWNER, Daniel Brink 1
TOWNER, Horace Mann 1
TOWNER, Neile Fassett 4
TOWNER, Rutherford 2
 Hamilton
TOWNER, Zealous Bates H
TOWNES, Edgar Eggleston 4
TOWNES, John Charles 1
TOWNLEY, Calvert 1
TOWNLEY, Sidney Dean 2
TOWNS, Charles B. 2
TOWNS, George H
 Washington Bonaparte
TOWNSEND, Amos 1
TOWNSEND, Charles H
 Elroy
TOWNSEND, Charles H
 Haskell
TOWNSEND, Charles 2
 Haskins
TOWNSEND, Charles 2
 Henry Tyler
TOWNSEND, Charles Orrin 1
TOWNSEND, Charles 1
 Wendell
TOWNSEND, Curtis 1
 McDonald
TOWNSEND, Dallas 4
 Selwyn
TOWNSEND, Edgar 1
 Jerome
TOWNSEND, Edward 1
 Davis
TOWNSEND, Edward 2
 Waterman
TOWNSEND, Edwin 1
 Franklin
TOWNSEND, Ernest 2
 Nathaniel
TOWNSEND, Francis 4
 Everett
TOWNSEND, Frederic 4
 Martin
TOWNSEND, Frederick 2
TOWNSEND, George H
 Alfred
TOWNSEND, George 2
 Washington
TOWNSEND, Harvey 2
 Gates
TOWNSEND, Henry C. 1
TOWNSEND, Horace 1
TOWNSEND, Hosea 1
TOWNSEND, James Bliss 1
TOWNSEND, James 1
 Mulford *
TOWNSEND, John G. Jr. 4
TOWNSEND, John Kirk H
TOWNSEND, John Wilson 4
TOWNSEND, Joseph 1
 Hendley
TOWNSEND, Julius Curtis 1
TOWNSEND, Lawrence 1
TOWNSEND, Luther Tracy 1
TOWNSEND, M. Clifford 3

TOWNSEND, Marion Ernest 1
TOWNSEND, Martin Ingham 1
TOWNSEND, Mary Ashley 1
TOWNSEND, Mary Evelyn 3
TOWNSEND, Mira Sharpless H
TOWNSEND, Oliver Henry 5
TOWNSEND, Oscar 5
TOWNSEND, Prescott Winson 4
TOWNSEND, Randolph W. 1
TOWNSEND, Robert H
TOWNSEND, Robert Donaldson 1
TOWNSEND, Smith DeLancey 2
TOWNSEND, Sylvester D. 2
TOWNSEND, Theodore Irving 1
TOWNSEND, Virginia Frances 4
TOWNSEND, Washington H
TOWNSEND, Wayne LaSalle 5
TOWNSEND, Willard Saxby 3
TOWNSEND, William H. 4
TOWNSEND, William Hay 1
TOWNSEND, William Kneeland 1
TOWNSEND, William Warren 1
TOWNSEND, Wilson 4
TOWNSEND, Wisner Robinson
TOWNSHEND, Charles H
TOWNSHEND, Norton Strange H
TOWNSHEND, Richard Wellington H
TOWNSLEY, Clarence Page 1
TOWNSLEY, Louis 5
TOWSE, J. Ranken 1
TOY, Crawford Howell 1
TOY, Harry Stanley 3
TOY, Walter Dallam 4
TOYNBEE, Arnold Joseph 6
TOZERE, Frederic 5
TOZIER, Josephine 4
TOZZER, Alfred Marston 4
TOZZER, Arthur Clarence 2
TRABERT, George Henry 1
TRABUE, Charles Clay 2
TRABUE, Edmund Francis 1
TRABUE, Isaac Hodgen 1
TRABUE, Marion Rex 5
TRACEWELL, Robert J. 1
TRACEY, Charles 1
TRACEY, James Frances 1
TRACHTMAN, Joseph 6
TRACY, Albert Haller H
TRACY, Andrew H
TRACY, Benjamin Franklin 1
TRACY, Charles Chapin 1
TRACY, Clarissa Tucker 4
TRACY, Daniel William 3
TRACY, Ernest B. 2
TRACY, Evarts 1
TRACY, Frank Basil 1
TRACY, Frank W. 1
TRACY, George Allison 5
TRACY, Henry Chester 3
TRACY, Henry Wells H
TRACY, Howard Van Sinderen 2
TRACY, James Grant 2
TRACY, James Madison 1
TRACY, John Clayton 3
TRACY, John Evarts 3
TRACY, Joseph H
TRACY, Joseph Powell 3
TRACY, Leo James 4
TRACY, Lyall 3
TRACY, Martha 4
TRACY, Merle Elliott 2
TRACY, Nathaniel H
TRACY, Phineas Lyman H
TRACY, Roger Sherman 1
TRACY, Roger Walker 4
TRACY, Russel Lord 2
TRACY, Samuel Mills 1
TRACY, Spencer 4
TRACY, Thomas Henry 4
TRACY, Uri H
TRACY, Uriah 1
TRACY, William W. 1
TRACY, (William) Lee 5
TRAEGER, Cornelius Horace 5
TRAEGER, William Isham 1
TRAER, Charles Solberg 2
TRAFFORD, Bernard Walton 1
TRAFTON, Gilbert Haven 2

TRAFTON, Mark 1
TRAFTON, William Henry 1
TRAIN, Arthur 2
TRAIN, Charles J. 1
TRAIN, Charles Russell H
TRAIN, Charles Russell 1
TRAIN, Elizabeth Phipps 4
TRAIN, Enoch 5
TRAIN, Ethel Kissam 1
TRAIN, George Francis 1
TRAIN, Harold Cecil 5
TRAIN, John Lambert 3
TRAINER, David Woolsey Jr. 1
TRAINER, Maurice Newlin 5
TRAISMAN, Alfred Stanley 6
TRAJETTA, Philip 2
TRALLE, Henry Edward 2
TRAMBURG, John William 4
TRAMMELL, Leander Newton 1
TRAMMELL, Niles 5
TRAMMELL, Park 1
TRAMMELL, Paul Barclay 4
TRANE, Reuben Nicholas 3
TRANER, Frederick W. 1
TRANER, Fredrick W. 5
TRANSEAU, Edgar Nelson 5
TRANT, James Buchanan 5
TRANTHAM, Henry 4
TRAP, William Martin 3
TRAPHAGEN, Frank Weiss 1
TRAPIER, Paul 4
TRAPNELL, Frederick Mackay 6
TRAPNELL, William Colston 6
TRAPNELL, William Holmes 6
TRAPP, Martin Edwin 3
TRASK, John Ellingwood Donnell 1
TRASK, John William 3
TRASK, Kate Nichols 1
TRASK, Spencer 4
TRASK, William Blake 1
TRATMAN, Edward Ernest Russell 5
TRATTNER, Ernest Robert 4
TRAUB, Peter Edward 3
TRAUBEL, Helen 5
TRAUBEL, Horace 1
TRAUDT, Bernard G. 5
TRAUGOTT, Albert Maser 4
TRAUTMAN, George M. 4
TRAUTMANN, William Emil 1
TRAUTWINE, John Cresson H
TRAUTWINE, John Cresson Jr. 1
TRAVEN, B. 5
TRAVER, John Gideon 2
TRAVERS, Edward Schofield 2
TRAVIS, Charles Mabbett 2
TRAVIS, Homer Lee 4
TRAVIS, Ira Dudley 5
TRAVIS, Judson Cooper 6
TRAVIS, Juluis Curtis 1
TRAVIS, Philip H. 2
TRAVIS, Robert Falligant 3
TRAVIS, Simeon Ezekiel 3
TRAVIS, Walter John 1
TRAVIS, Walter John 4
TRAVIS, Wesley Elgin 5
TRAVIS, William Barret 1
TRAWICK, Arcadius McSwain 5
TRAWICK, Henry 1
TRAWICK, Leonard M. 1
TRAYLOR, John H. 4
TRAYLOR, Melvin Alvah 1
TRAYLOR, Robert Lee 1
TRAYNOR, Philip Andrew 5
TRAYNOR, William Bernard 1
TRAYNOR, William James Henry 4
TRAYSER, Lewis W. 4
TREACY, John P. 4
TREADWAY, Allen Towner 2
TREADWAY, Charles Terry 1
TREADWAY, Walter Lewis 4
TREADWELL, Aaron Louis 2
TREADWELL, Daniel H
TREADWELL, Edward Francis 1
TREADWELL, George A. 5
TREADWELL, John 1
TREADWELL, Nancy Claar 5
TREANOR, Arthur Ryan 4
TREANOR, James Aloysius Jr. 4

TREANOR, John 1
TREANOR, Joseph Holland 4
TREANOR, Walter Emanuel 1
TREAT, Charles Gould 1
TREAT, Charles Henry 1
TREAT, Charles Payson 1
TREAT, Charles Watson 4
TREAT, George Winfield 3
TREAT, Jay Porter 4
TREAT, John Harvey 1
TREAT, Joseph Bradford 4
TREAT, Mary 1
TREAT, Payson Jackson 5
TREAT, Robert H
TREAT, Robert Byron 1
TREAT, Samuel 1
TREAT, Samuel Hubbel H
TRECKER, Joseph Leonard 2
TRECKER, Theodore 3
TREDER, Oscar F. R. 1
TREDTIN, Walter C. 6
TREDWAY, William Marshall H
TREDWELL, Daniel M. 1
TREDWELL, Thomas H
TREE, Herbert Beerbohm 1
TREE, Lambert 1
TREECE, Elbert Lee 4
TREES, Clyde C. 4
TREES, Harry A. 4
TREES, Joe Clifton 2
TREES, Merle Jay 5
TREFZGER, Emil Anton 4
TREGASKIS, Richard 6
TREGOE, James Harry 1
TRELEASE, Richard Mitchell 4
TRELEASE, Sam F. 3
TRELEASE, Sam Farlow 1
TRELEASE, William 2
TREMAIN, Albert Wright 5
TREMAIN, Eloise Ruthven 2
TREMAIN, George Lee 5
TREMAIN, Henry Edwin 1
TREMAIN, Lyman H
TREMAINE, Burton Gad 2
TREMAINE, Charles Milton 5
TREMAINE, Frederick Orlin 3
TREMAINE, Henry Barnes 1
TREMAN, Charles Edward 1
TREMAN, Robert Henry 1
TREMBLAY, Rene 4
TRENARY, James Marshall 4
TRENCH, William Washington 3
TRENCHARD, Edward C. H
TRENCHARD, Hugh Montague 3
TRENCHARD, Stephen Decatur H
TRENCHARD, Thomas Whitaker 1
TRENDLE, George Washington 5
TRENERY, Matthew John 5
TRENHOLM, George Alfred H
TRENHOLM, William Lee 1
TRENHOLME, Norman Maclaren 1
TRENT, Richard Henderson 1
TRENT, William H
TRENT, William Johnson 4
TRENT, William Peterfield 1
TRESCOT, William Henry H
TRESCOTT, Paul Henry 6
TRESIDDER, Donald Bertrand 2
TRESOLINI, Rocco John 5
TRESSLER, Irving Dart 2
TRESSLER, Jacob Cloyd 3
TRESSLER, Victor George Augustine 1
TRETTIEN, Augustus William 1
TREUDLEY, Frederick 4
TREVELLICK, Richard F. 1
TREVELYAN, George Macaulay 4
TREVER, Albert Augustus 1
TREVER, George Henry 1
TREVES, Norman 4
TREVISAN, Vittorio H
TREVOR, John Bond 3
TREVOR, Joseph Ellis 1
TREVORROW, Robert Johns 1
TREVOY, William Vivian 4
TREWIN, James Henry 1
TREXLER, Frank M. 3
TREXLER, Harry C. 1
TREXLER, Samuel Geiss 2
TREZVANT, James H

TRIBBLE, Lewis Herndon 4
TRIBBLE, Samuel Joel 1
TRIBUS, Louis Lincoln 1
TRICKETT, William 1
TRIEBEL, Frederick Ernst 4
TRIEBER, Jacob 1
TRIGG, Abram H
TRIGG, Ernest T. 3
TRIGG, John Johns H
TRIGGS, Flloyd Willding 1
TRIGGS, Oscar Lovell 1
TRILLEY, Joseph 1
TRILLING, Lionel 6
TRIM, Gordon Mariner 4
TRIMBLE, Allen 1
TRIMBLE, Carey Allen 1
TRIMBLE, David H
TRIMBLE, Ernest Greene 5
TRIMBLE, Harvey Marion 1
TRIMBLE, Isaac Ridgeway H
TRIMBLE, James W. 5
TRIMBLE, John H
TRIMBLE, Richard 1
TRIMBLE, Robert H
TRIMBLE, Robert Maurice 4
TRIMBLE, Selden Y. 4
TRIMBLE, South 2
TRIMBLE, South Jr. 6
TRIMBLE, William Allen 1
TRIMBLE, William Pitt 2
TRINE, Charles Clarke 4
TRINE, Ralph Waldo 5
TRINKLE, Elbert Lee 1
TRINKS, Willibald 5
TRIPLER, Charles E. 4
TRIPLETT, Arthur Fairfax 3
TRIPLETT, Elijah Henry 4
TRIPLETT, John Edwin 2
TRIPLETT, Norman 1
TRIPLETT, Philip H
TRIPP, Bartlett 1
TRIPP, Frank Elihu 1
TRIPP, Guy Eastman 1
TRIPP, Lena Elvina Flack 6
TRIPP, Louis H. 4
TRIPP, William Henry Jr. 5
TRIPPE, Andrew Cross 1
TRIPPE, James McConky 1
TRIPPE, John 4
TRIPPET, Oscar A. 1
TRISCOTT, Samuel Peter Rolt 1
TRISSAL, John Meredith 6
TRIST, Nicholas Philip H
TRITLE, John Stewart 2
TRIVELLI, Albert F. 4
TROBEC, James 1
TROCHE, Ernst Gunter 5
TROEGER, John Winthrop 1
TROLAND, Leonard Thompson 1
TROOP, J. G. Carter 1
TROOST, George Wilbur 3
TROOST, Gerard H
TROPER, Morris C. 4
TROTT, Benjamin H
TROTT, Clement Augustus 5
TROTT, Nicholas H
TROTT, Norman Liebman 4
TROTT, Stanley B. 3
TROTTER, Alfred Williams 1
TROTTER, Frank Butler 1
TROTTER, James Fisher 4
TROTTER, Melvin E. 1
TROTTER, Newbold Hough H
TROTTER, Spencer 1
TROTTI, Lamar 3
TROTTI, Samuel Wilds H
TROTTMAN, James Franklin 4
TROTZ, J. O. Emmanuel 1
TROUBETZKOY, Amelie Rives 2
TROUBETZKOY, Prince Pierre 1
TROUP, Alexander 1
TROUP, George Michael H
TROUP, Robert H
TROUT, Clement E. 4
TROUT, David McCamel 3
TROUT, Ethel Wendell 1
TROUT, Grace Wilbur 3
TROUT, Hugh Henry Sr. 2
TROUT, Michael Carver H
TROUYET, Carlos 5
TROW, John Fowler H
TROWBRIDGE, Alexander Buel 4
TROWBRIDGE, Alvah 1
TROWBRIDGE, Arthur Carleton 5
TROWBRIDGE, Augustus 1
TROWBRIDGE, Carl Hoyt 5
TROWBRIDGE, Charles Christopher 1
TROWBRIDGE, Edmund H

TROWBRIDGE, Edward Dwight 1
TROWBRIDGE, John 1
TROWBRIDGE, John Townsend 1
TROWBRIDGE, Mary Elizabeth Day 1
TROWBRIDGE, Perry Fox 1
TROWBRIDGE, Rowland Ebenezer H
TROWBRIDGE, S. Breck Parkman 1
TROWBRIDGE, Vaughan 5
TROWBRIDGE, William Pettit H
TROXELL, Edward Leffingwell 5
TROXELL, Millard Francis 4
TROXELL, Thomas Franklin 5
TROY, Alexander 1
TROY, George Francis 5
TROY, John Henry 3
TROY, John Weir 2
TROY, Peter Henry 4
TROY, Thomas Francis 4
TROYE, Edward H
TRUANT, Aldo Peter 6
TRUAX, Arthur Harold 4
TRUAX, Charles Henry 1
TRUAX, Charles Vilas 1
TRUAX, Chauncey Shaffer 1
TRUBY, Albert Ernest 5
TRUCCO, Manuel 5
TRUDE, Alfred Samuel 1
TRUDEAU, Edward Livingston 1
TRUDGIAN, Andrew B. 6
TRUE, Alfred Charles 1
TRUE, Allen Tupper 5
TRUE, Frederick William 1
TRUE, Gordon Haines 1
TRUE, Hiram L. 4
TRUE, John Preston 1
TRUE, Lilian (Sarah) Crawford 5
TRUE, Rodney Howard 1
TRUE, Theodore Edmond 1
TRUEBLOOD, Benjamin Franklin 1
TRUEBLOOD, Dennis Lee 4
TRUEBLOOD, Ralph Waldo 3
TRUEBLOOD, Robert Martin 6
TRUEBLOOD, Thomas Clarkson 3
TRUELL, Rohn 5
TRUELSEN, Henry 4
TRUEMAN, Walter Harley 5
TRUEMAN, William H. 5
TRUESDALE, Philemon E. 2
TRUESDALE, William Haynes 1
TRUESDELL, Hobart George 1
TRUESDELL, Karl 3
TRUETT, George W. 2
TRUETTE, Everett Ellsworth 1
TRUITT, James Steele 5
TRUITT, Max O'Rell 3
TRUITT, Ralph Purnell 4
TRUITT, Warren 1
TRUJILLO MOLINA, Rafael Leonidas 4
TRULLINGER, R. W. 3
TRULY, Jefferson 4
TRUMAN, Benjamin Cummings 1
TRUMAN, Harry S. 5
TRUMAN, James 1
TRUMAN, Ralph Emerson 4
TRUMBAUER, Frank 4
TRUMBAUER, Horace 1
TRUMBAUER, Horace 4
TRUMBO, Andrew 1
TRUMBO, Arthur Cook 3
TRUMBULL, Annie Eliot 2
TRUMBULL, Benjamin 1
TRUMBULL, Charles Gallaudet 1
TRUMBULL, Frank 1
TRUMBULL, Gurdon 1
TRUMBULL, Henry Clay 1
TRUMBULL, James Hammond H
TRUMBULL, John * H
TRUMBULL, John H. 4
TRUMBULL, Jonathan * H
TRUMBULL, Jonathan H
TRUMBULL, Joseph * H
TRUMBULL, Levi R. 1
TRUMBULL, Lyman H
TRUMP, Edward Needles 4
TRUMPLER, Robert Julius 3

VAN VLIET, Robert 2
  Campbell
VAN VOAST, James 1
VAN VOLKENBURG, Jack 4
  Lamont
VAN VOORHIS, Daniel 3
VAN VOORHIS, Henry 2
  Clay
VAN VOORHIS, John 1
VAN VOORHIS, Robert 4
  Henry
VAN VORHES, Nelson H
  Holmes
VAN VORHIS, Flavius 1
  Josephus
VAN VORST, Bessie 1
VAN VORST, Marie 1
VAN WAGENEN, 1
  Anthony
VAN WAGENEN, James 1
  Hubert
VAN WART, Walter Bright 5
VAN WATERS, Miriam 5
VAN WESEP, Alleda 4
VAN WESTRUM, Adriaan 1
  Schade
VAN WICKEL, Jesse 3
  Frederick
VAN WINKLE, Edgar 1
  Beach
VAN WINKLE, Isaac 2
  Homer
VAN WINKLE, Marshall 5
VAN WINKLE, Peter H
  Godwin
VAN WINKLE, Walling 1
  Wallenson
VAN WYCK, Augustus 1
VAN WYCK, Charles H
  Henry
VAN WYCK, Robert 1
  Anderson
VAN WYCK, William 3
VAN WYCK, William H
  William
VAN WYK, William P. 2
VAN ZANDT, Charles H
  Collins
VAN ZANDT, Clarence 1
  Duncan
VAN ZANDT, Clarence 1
  Elmer
VAN ZANDT, Khleber 1
  Miller
VAN ZANDT, Marie 1
VAN ZANDT, Richard 1
  Lipscomb
VANZETTI, Bartolomeo 4
VAN ZILE, Edward Sims 1
VAN ZILE, Philip Taylor 1
VARDAMAN, James 1
  Kimble
VARDELL, Charles 4
  Gildersleeve
VARDELL, Charles Graves 3
VARDEN, George 3
VARDILL, John H
VARE, William Scott 1
VARELA, Jacobo 5
VARELA Y MORALES, H
  Felix Francisco Jose Maria
  de la C
VARESE, Edgard 4
VARGAS, Getulio 3
VARIAN, Bertram Stetson 5
VARIAN, Charles Stetson 1
VARIAN, Donald Cord 5
VARIAN, George Edmund 1
VARIAN, Russell Harrison 3
VARICK, James H
VARICK, Richard H
VARIELL, Arthur Davis 1
VARLEY, John Philip 1
VARNEY, Charles Edward 4
VARNEY, William 4
  Frederick
VARNEY, William Henry 1
VARNEY, William Wesley 2
VARNUM, James M. 1
VARNUM, James Mitchell H
VARNUM, John H
VARNUM, Joseph Bradley H
VARNUM, William 1
  Harrison
VARSER, Lycurgus Rayner 4
VASCHE, Joseph Burton 4
VASEY, Frank Thomas 1
VASEY, George H
VASILIEFF, Nicholas 5
  Loanovich
VASILIEV, Alexander 5
  Alexandrovich
VASQUEZ, Francisco 4
  Leonte
VASS, Alonzo Frederick 4

VASSALIO, Edward 6
  Andrew
VASSALL, John H
VASSAR, Matthew H
VATTEMARE, Nicolas H
  Marie Alexandre
VAUCLAIN, Samuel 1
  Matthews
VAUDREUIL- H
  CAVAGNAL, Pierre de
  Rigaud
VAUGHAN, Alfred 1
  Jefferson
VAUGHAN, Arthur Winn 2
VAUGHAN, Benjamin H
VAUGHAN, Charles H
VAUGHAN, Charles Parker 1
VAUGHAN, Daniel 1
VAUGHAN, David Davies 5
VAUGHAN, Elmer E. 1
VAUGHAN, Floyd Lamar 3
VAUGHAN, George 2
VAUGHAN, George Tully 5
VAUGHAN, George 4
  William
VAUGHAN, Guy W. 4
VAUGHAN, Harold Stearns 5
VAUGHAN, Harry Briggs 1
  Jr.
VAUGHAN, Herbert 2
  Hunter
VAUGHAN, Horace Worth 1
VAUGHAN, John Colin 1
VAUGHAN, John Gaines 1
VAUGHAN, John George 2
VAUGHAN, John Henry 1
VAUGHAN, John Russell 3
VAUGHAN, John Samuel 1
VAUGHAN, John Walter 2
VAUGHAN, Lawrence J. 1
VAUGHAN, Richard Miner 3
VAUGHAN, T. Wayland 3
VAUGHAN, Victor 1
  Clarence
VAUGHAN, Warren Taylor 2
  Farries
VAUGHAN, Wayland 4
VAUGHAN, William 5
  Hutchinson
VAUGHAN, William Wirt H
VAUGHAN WILLIAMS, 3
  Ralph
VAUGHN, Earnest Van 5
  Court
VAUGHN, Francis Arthur 1
VAUGHN, Robert Gallaway 3
VAUGHN, Samuel Jesse 1
VAUGHN, William James 1
VAUGHT, Edgar Sullins 3
VAUX, Calvert 1
VAUX, George Jr. 1
VAUX, Richard H
VAUX, Roberts H
VAVRUSKA, Frank 6
VAWTER, Charles Erastus 1
VAWTER, John William 1
VAWTER, Keith 1
VAYHINGER, Monroe 1
VEACH, Robert Wells 5
VEAL, Frank Richard 4
VEASEY, Clarence 3
  Archibald
VEATCH, Arthur Clifford 1
VEATCH, Byron Elbert 1
VEATCH, Nathan Thomas 6
VEAZEY, I. PARKER 4
VEAZEY, Thomas Ward H
VEAZIE, George Augustus 1
VEBLEN, Andrew 1
  Anderson
VEBLEN, Oswald 4
VEBLEN, Thorstein B. 1
VECKI, Victor G. 1
VEDDER, Beverly Blair 3
VEDDER, Charles Stuart 1
VEDDER, Commodore 1
  Perry
VEDDER, Edward Bright 3
VEDDER, Elihu 1
VEDDER, Henry Clay 1
VEDITZ, Charles William 1
  Augustus
VEEDER, Albert Henry 1
VEEDER, Curtis Hussey 2
VEEDER, Henry 2
VEEDER, Major Albert 1
VEEDER, Van Vechten 2
VEENEMAN, William H. 1
VEITCH, Fletcher Pearre 2
VEKSLER, Vladimir I. 4
VELARDE, Hernan 1
VELAZQUEZ, Hector 4
VELTIN, Louise de Launay 1
VELVIN, Ellen 1
VENABLE, Abraham H
  Bedford

VENABLE, Abraham H
  Watkins
VENABLE, Charles Scott 1
VENABLE, Emerson 6
VENABLE, Francis Preston 1
VENABLE, Joseph Glass 1
VENABLE, Richard Morton 1
VENABLE, William Henry 1
VENABLE, William Mayo 3
VENABLE, William Webb 6
VENEMANN, H. Gerald 3
VENING MEINISZ, Felix 4
VENNEMA, Ame 1
VENNEMA, John 3
VENTH, Carl 1
VENTING, Albert 4
VENTRIS, Michael George 4
  Francis
VERBECK, Guido Fridolin 1
VERBECK, Guido Herman H
  Fridolin
VER BECK, Hanna 1
VERBECK, William 1
VER BECK, William Francis 1
VER BECK, William Francis 4
VERBEEK, Gustave 4
VERBEKE, Alexis O. 4
VERBRUGGHEN, Henri 1
VERDAGUER, Peter 1
VERDELIN, Henry 4
VERDI, William Francis 5
VEREEN, William Jerome 3
VERENDRYE, Sieur de la H
VERGENNES, comte de H
  Joseph
VERHAEGEN, Peter H
VERHAGEN, Aloysius 1
  Alphonsus
VERHOEFF, Frederick 5
  Herman
VERITY, George Matthew 2
VERKUYL, Gerrit 5
VERLENDEN, Jacob Serrill 6
VERMILION, Charles 1
  William
VERMILYA, Charles E. 5
VERMILYE, Mrs. Kate 1
  Jordan
VERMILYE, William 2
  Moorhead
VERMUELE, Cornelius 2
  Clarkson
VERNADSKY, George 6
VERNER, Samuel Phillips 5
VERNIER, Chester Garfield 2
VERNON, Ambrose White 5
VERNON, Clarence Clark 3
VERNON, James William 3
VERNON, Leroy Tudor 1
VERNON, Robert Orion 6
VERNON, Samuel 1
VERNON, Samuel Milton 1
VERNON, William H
VERNON, William 5
  Tecumseh
VERNOR, Richard Edward 3
VERONDA, Maurice 4
VEROT, Jean Marcel Pierre H
  Auguste
VERPLANCK, Daniel H
  Crommelin
VERPLANCK, Gulian 1
  Crommelin
VERRALL, Richard P. 1
VERRAZANO, Giovanni da H
VERREE, John Paul 1
VERRILL, Addison Emery 1
VERRILL, Alpheus Hyatt 3
VERRILL, Charles Henry 1
VERRILL, Elmer Russell 6
VERRILL, Harry Mighels 5
VERRILL, Robinson 3
VERSFELT, William H. 3
VERSON, David C. 5
VER STEEG, Karl 3
VERTES, Marcel 4
VERWOERD, Hendrik 4
  Frensch
VERY, Frank Washington 1
VERY, Jones H
VERY, Lydia Louisa Anna 1
VERY, Samuel Williams 1
VESEY, Denmark H
VESEY, William H
VESPUCCI, Amerigo H
VESSELLA, Oreste 5
VESSEY, Robert Scadden 4
VEST, George Graham 1
VEST, H. Grant 5
VEST, Samuel Alexander Jr. 1
VEST, Walter Edward 4
VESTAL, Albert Henry 1
VESTAL, Samuel Curtis 3
VESTIN, John 5
VESTINE, Ernest Harry 5
VESTLING, Axel Ebenezer 2

VETCH, Samuel H
VETH, Martin 5
VETHAKE, Henry H
VEYRA, Mrs. Jaime C. de 5
VEYRA, Jaime Carlos de 5
VEZIN, Charles 2
VIA, Lemuel R. 5
VIALL, Ethan 3
VIALL, Richmond Thomas 4
VIAUT, André Jules 6
  Armand
VIBBARD, Chauncey H
VIBBERT, William H. 1
VICHERT, John Frederick 2
VICK, James H
VICK, Robert Ellsworth 5
VICK, Walker Whiting 1
VICKERS, Alonzo Knox 1
VICKERS, Enoch Howard 5
VICKERS, George 1
VICKERS, George Morley 4
VICKERS, James Cator 5
VICKERY, Herman Frank 1
VICKERY, Howard Leroy 5
VICKREY, Charles Vernon 4
VICTOR, Alexander F. 4
VICTOR, Frances Fuller 4
VICTOR, John Harvey 3
VICTOR, Metta Victoria H
  Fuller
VICTOR, Orville James 1
VICTORY, John Patrick 4
VIDAL, Eugene Luther 5
VIDAL, Michel 1
VIDAVER, Sidney Joseph 5
VIDMER, George 5
VIEHOEVER, Arno 5
VIEL, Etienne Bernard 4
  Alexandre
VIELE, Aernout H
  Cornelissen
VIELE, Charles Delavan 1
VIELE, Egbert Ludovickus 1
VIELE, Egbert Ludovicus 1
VIELE, Herman 1
  Knickerbocker
VIERECK, George Sylvester 4
VIERECK, Louis C. 5
VIESSELMAN, Percival 2
  William
VIETH, Henry Alvin 5
VIETOR, George Frederick 1
VIETOR, Karl 3
VIETT, George Frederic 3
VIEWEG, Frederic 2
VIGNAUD, Henry 1
VIGNEC, Alfred J. 4
VIGNESS, Lauritz Andreas 2
VIGO, Joseph Maria H
  Francesco
VIGRAN, Nathan 5
VIGUERS, Richard 5
  Thomson
VIGUERS, Ruth Hill 5
VIJITAVONGS, Phya 5
VILAS, Charles Harrison 5
VILAS, George Byron 5
VILAS, William Freeman 1
VILATTE, Joseph Rene 4
VILBRANDT, Frank Carl 4
VILES, Blaine Spooner 2
VILES, Jonas 2
VILJOEN, Benjamin 4
  Johannis
VILLA, Francisco H
VILLA, Francisco 4
VILLAGRA, Gaspar Perez H
  de
VILLA-LOBOS, Heitor 3
VILLAMOR, Ignacio 1
VILLANI, Ralph A. 6
VILLARD, Henry H
VILLARD, Oswald Garrison 2
VILLA-REAL, Antonio 6
VILLAROEL, Gualberto 2
VILLEDA-MORALES, 5
  Ramon
VILLENEUVE, J. M. 2
  Rodrigue
VILLERE, Jacques Philippe H
VILLERS, Thomas Jefferson 1
VILLON, Jacques 4
VIMEUR, Jean Baptiste H
  Donatien de
VINAL, Harold 4
VINAL, William Gould 6
VINAVER, Chemjo 4
VINCENNES, sieur de * H
VINCENT, Bird J. 1
VINCENT, Boyd 1
VINCENT, Clarence 2
  Augustus
VINCENT, Clarence 1
  Cornelius
VINCENT, Clinton Dermott 3
VINCENT, Clive Belden 1

VINCENT, Earl W. 3
VINCENT, Edgar La Verne 4
VINCENT, Frank 1
VINCENT, George Edgar 1
VINCENT, Harold S(ellew) 1
VINCENT, Harry Aiken 1
VINCENT, Henry Bethuel 1
VINCENT, Jesse Gurney 4
VINCENT, John Carter 5
VINCENT, John Heyl 1
VINCENT, John Martin 1
VINCENT, Leon Henry 1
VINCENT, Marvin 1
  Richardson
VINCENT, Mary Ann H
  Farlow
VINCENT, Thomas 1
  MacCurdy
VINCENT, Walter B. 1
VINCENT, Wilber Ddwain 5
VINCENT, William David 1
VINCI, Henry 5
VINER, Jacob 5
VINES, Fred Daniel 4
VINES, John Finley 5
VINES, William Madison 5
VINING, Edward Payson 1
VINING, John H
VINJE, Aad John 1
VINSON, Albert Earl 5
VINSON, Arthur Ferle 4
VINSON, Frederic Moore 3
VINSON, Robert Ernest 2
VINSON, Taylor 1
VINSON, William Ashton 3
VINSONHALER, Frank 2
VINTON, Alexander H
  Hamilton
VINTON, Alexander 1
  Hamilton
VINTON, Arthur Dudley 1
VINTON, Francis H
VINTON, Francis Laurens H
VINTON, Frederic H
VINTON, Frederic Porter 1
VINTON, John Adams H
VINTON, Samuel Finley H
VINTON, Warren Jay 5
VIOLETTE, Ebal E. 6
VIOLETTE, Willis Gordon 4
VIPOND, Jonathan 3
VIPOND, Kenneth C(linton) 6
VIR DEN, Ray 3
VIRGIL, Almon Kincaid 4
VIRGIL, Antha Minerva 1
VIRGIN, Edward Harmon 5
VIRGIN, Herbert Whiting 5
VIRKUS, Frederick Adams 3
VIRTANEN, Artturi Ilmari 6
VIRTUE, Charles Franklin 5
VIRTUE, George Olien 1
VISCONTI, Luchino 5
VISHER, Stephen Sargent 4
VISHER, Stephen Sargent 5
VISHNIAC, Wolf Vladimir 6
VISSCHER, J. Paul 3
VISSCHER, William 1
  Lightfoot
VITALE, Ferruccio 1
VITETTL, Leonardo 6
VITS, George 1
VITT, Bruno Ceaser 4
VITTUM, Edmund March 1
VITTUM, Edmund March 2
VITTUM, Harriet E. 3
VIVIAN, Alfred 4
VIVIAN, Harold Acton 5
VIVIAN, John Charles 4
VIVIAN, John Frederick 3
VIVIAN, Thomas Jondrie 1
VIZCAINO, Sebastian H
VIZETELLY, Frank Horace 1
VOEGELI, Henry Edward 4
VOEGTLIN, Carl 6
VOEHRINGER, John 5
  Kasper Jr.
VOELKER, Paul Frederick 1
VOETTER, Thomas Wilson 5
VOGDES, Anthony Wayne 4
VOGEL, Augustus Hugo 3
VOGEL, Charles Pfister 4
VOGEL, Charles W. 3
VOGEL, Clayton Barney 4
VOGEL, Edwin Chester 6
VOGEL, Frank 1
VOGEL, Fred Jr. 1
VOGEL, Joseph Richard 5
VOGEL, Joshua Holmes 5
VOGEL, Leo E. 5
VOGEL, Robert Willis 5
VOGEL, Rudolph Emerson 5
VOGELBACK, William 3
  Edward
VOGELER, Rudolf 6
  Frederick

VOGELGESANG, Carl Theodore 1
VOGELGESANG, Shepard 5
VOGELSANG, Alexander Theodore 1
VOGELSTEIN, Hans Alfred 4
VOGELTANZ, Edward Louis 5
VOGLER, William L. 5
VOGT, Henry F. 6
VOGT, Paul Leroy 6
VOGT, V. Ogden 4
VOGT, William 5
VOIGT, Andrew George 1
VOIGT, Edward 1
VOIGT, Irma Elizabeth 3
VOISLAWSKY, Antonie Phineas
VOLD, George Bryan 4
VOLDENG, Mathew Nelson 1
VOLINI, Italo Frederick 3
VOLIVA, Wilbur Glenn 6
VOLK, Douglas 1
VOLK, Leonard Wells 4
VOLKER, William 2
VOLKERT, Edward Charles 1
VOLKOV, Vladislav N. 5
VOLLAND, Roscoe Henry 5
VOLLMER, August 3
VOLLMER, John Phillip 1
VOLLMER, Lula 3
VOLLMER, Philip 1
VOLLRATH, Edward 1
VOLPE, Arnold 1
VOLPE, Paul Anthony 5
VOLSTEAD, Andrew J. 2
VOLWILER, Albert Tangeman 3
VOLZ, Edward J. 6
VON BEKESY, Georg 5
VON BERTALANFFY, Ludwig 5
VON BONNEWITZ, Orlando R. 5
VON BRENTANO, Heinrich 4
VON CHOLTITZ, Dietrich 4
VONDER, HAAR Edward P. 6
VON DER HEYDE, Matthew Jennings 6
VON DER LAURITZ, Robert Eberhard Schmidt H
VONDERLEHR, Raymond Aloysius 5
VON DEWALL, Hans Werner 6
VON EGLOFFSTEIN, Frederick W. H
VON ELM, Henry C. 5
VON ENDE, Carl Leopold 1
VON ENGELKEN, Friedrich Johannes Hugo 6
VON ENGELN, Oskar Deitrich 6
VON EULER-CHELPIN, Hans 4
VON FABER DU FAUR, Curt 4
VON FERSEN, Count H
VON FIELITZ, Alexander 4
VON FREMD, Charles Spencer 4
VON GOTTSCHALCK, Oscar Hunt
VON GRAVE-JONAS, Elsa (Baroness) 5
VON GRUNEBAUM, Gustave E(dmund) 5
VON GUTTENBERG, Karl Theodore 5
VON HOFFMANN, Bernard 2
VON HOLST, Hermann Eduard 1
VON HUTTEN, Baroness Bettina 3
VON KAHLER, Erich Gabriel 5
VON KARMAN, Theodore 4
VON KELER, Theodore M. R. 1
VON KLEINWAECHTER, Ludwig Paul Viktor 5
VON KLENZE, Camillo 2
VON KOCHERTHAL, Josua H
VON LACKUM, John Peter 4
VON LAUE, Max 4
VON MACH, Edmund 1
VON MINDEN, William John 5
VON MISES, Ludwig Edler 6
VON MISES, Richard 3

VON MOSCHZISKER, Robert 1
VON NEUMANN, John 3
VONNOH, Bessie Potter 1
VONNOH, Robert 3
VON PAGENHARDT, Maximilian Hugo 1
VON PHUL, Anna Maria H
VON PHUL, William 2
VON PRITTWITZ UND GAFFRON, Friedrich Wilhelm 3
VON RUCK, Karl 1
VON SALLMANN, Ludwig 6
VON SALTZA, Charles Frederick 1
VON SCHIERBRAND, Wolf 4
VON SCHLIEDER, Albert 5
VON SCHON, Hans August Evald Conrad 4
VON SCHRENK, Hermann 3
VON SCHWEINITZ, Lewis David H
VON STEUBEN, Friedrich Wilhelm Ludolf Gerhard August H
VON STIEGEL, Baron H
VON STROHEIM, Erich 4
VON STRUVE, Henry Clay 1
VON TEMPSKI, Armine 2
VON TRESCKOW, Egmont Charles 5
VON TUNGELN, George Henry 4
VON WALTHER, Eckert 4
VON WENING, Anthony 5
VON WICHT, John 5
VON WELLER, Harry Walter 5
VOORHEES, Boynton Stephen 6
VOORHEES, Clark Greenwood 1
VOORHEES, Daniel Wolsey H
VOORHEES, Edward Burnett 1
VOORHEES, Foster MacGowan 1
VOORHEES, Henry Beiln 4
VOORHEES, James D. 5
VOORHEES, John Howard 2
VOORHEES, Louis Augustus 1
VOORHEES, Melvin 6
VOORHEES, Oscar McMurtrie 2
VOORHEES, Philip Falkerson H
VOORHEES, Samuel Stockton 1
VOORHEES, Stephen Francis 4
VOORHEES, Stephen Hegeman 1
VOORHEES, Theodore 1
VOORHEES, Tracy S. 6
VOORHEES, Willard Penfield 1
VOORHIES, Frank Corey 1
VOORHIES, Paul Warren 3
VOORHIS, Charles Brown 1
VOORHIS, Charles Henry H
VOORHIS, Warren Rollin 3
VOORSANGER, Jacob 1
VOPICKA, Charles J. 1
VORBERG, Martin Philip 6
VORENBERG, Felix 4
VORHAUER, John Cook 4
VORHIES, Charles Taylor 5
VORIS, John Ralph 4
VOROSHILOV, Mazshal Kliment Yefremovich 5
VORSE, Albert White 1
VORSE, Mary Heaton 4
VORWALD, Arthur John 6
VORYS, Arthur Isaiah 1
VORYS, John Martin 5
VORYS, Webb Isaiah 5
VOS, Bert John 2
VOS, Geerhardus 1
VOSBURGH, George Bedell 1
VOSBURGH, William Wallace 4
VOSE, Edward Neville 1
VOSE, James Wilson 6
VOSE, Robert Churchill 6
VOSE, Roger H
VOSE, William Preston 1
VOSHELL, Allen Fiske 4
VOSS, Carl August 2
VOSS, Ernst Karl Johann Heinrich 1
VOSS, Fred James 4

VOTAW, Albert Hiatt 1
VOTAW, Clyde Weber 4
VOTAW, Heber Herbert 4
VOTER, Perley Conant 3
VOTEY, Edwin Scott 1
VOTEY, Josiah William 1
VOTIPKA, Thelma 5
VOUGHT, Chance Milton H
VOUGHT, Chance Milton 4
VOX, Herman H(arold) 5
VREDENBURGH, William Henry 4
VREELAND, Albert Lincoln 6
VREELAND, Edward Butterfield 1
VREELAND, Hamilton Jr. 5
VREELAND, Herbert Harold 2
VREELAND, T. Reed 4
VREELAND, Walter J. 1
VREELAND, Williamson Updike 2
VROOM, Garret Dorset Wall 1
VROOM, Peter Dumont 4
VROOM, Peter Dumont 1
VROOM, Robert Allyn 4
VROOMAN, Carl 4
VROOMAN, Clare Martin 2
VROOMAN, John Wright 1
VUILLEUMIER, Ernest Albert 3
VULTEE, Howard Fleming 5
VURSELL, Charles W. 6
VU-VAN-MAU 4
VYSHINSKY, Andrei Yanuarievich 3

W

WABASHA H
WACH, Joachim 3
WACHENFELD, William A. 5
WACHENHEIMER, J. 1
WACHSMUTH, Charles H
WACHTER, Frank C. 1
WACK, Henry Wellington 3
WACK, Otis 1
WACKER, Charles Henry 1
WACKERNAGEL, William 1
WACKERNISTER, William 6
WACKMAN, Kenneth B. 6
WADDEL, James H
WADDEL, Louise Forsslund 1
WADDEL, Moses H
WADDELL, Alfred Moore 1
WADDELL, Charles Carey 1
WADDELL, Charles Edward 2
WADDELL, Charles Wilkin 5
WADDELL, Hugh 1
WADDELL, James Iredell H
WADDELL, John Alexander Low 1
WADDELL, John Newton H
WADDELL, Joseph Addison 1
WADDILL, Edmund Jr. 1
WADDINGTON, Conrad Hal 6
WADDINGTON, Ralph Henry 5
WADE, Benjamin Franklin H
WADE, Cyrus U. 4
WADE, Edward H
WADE, Festus John 1
WADE, Frank Bertram 3
WADE, Frank Edward 1
WADE, George Garretson 3
WADE, Harry Vincent 6
WADE, Herbert Treadwell 3
WADE, James Francis 4
WADE, James Franklin 1
WADE, Jason Lloyd 5
WADE, Jeptha Homer H
WADE, John Donald 4
WADE, John E. 5
WADE, Joseph Sanford 4
WADE, Lester A. 1
WADE, Martin Joseph 1
WADE, Mary Hazelton 4
WADE, Mary L. Hill 4
WADE, William Ligon 5
WADHAMS, Albion Varette 1
WADHAMS, Edgar Philip H
WADHAMS, Frederick Eugene 1
WADHAMS, Robert Pelton 1
WADHAMS, William Henderson 5
WADLEIGH, Bainbridge H
WADLEIGH, Francis Rawle 4

WADLEIGH, George Henry 1
WADLIN, Horace Greeley 1
WADSTED, Otto 6
WADSWORTH, Alfred Powell 3
WADSWORTH, Alice Hay 6
WADSWORTH, Arthur Littleford 5
WADSWORTH, Augustus Baldwin 3
WADSWORTH, Charles Jr. 1
WADSWORTH, Charles Curtiss 1
WADSWORTH, Craig Wharton 4
WADSWORTH, Craig Wharton 1
WADSWORTH, Daniel H
WADSWORTH, Eliot 3
WADSWORTH, Frank Lawton Olcott 1
WADSWORTH, George 3
WADSWORTH, Guy Woodbridge 1
WADSWORTH, Harrison Lowell 1
WADSWORTH, Hiram Warren 1
WADSWORTH, James * H
WADSWORTH, James Wolcott 1
WADSWORTH, James Wolcott 4
WADSWORTH, Jeremiah H
WADSWORTH, Marshman Edward 1
WADSWORTH, Oliver Fairfield 1
WADSWORTH, Peleg H
WADSWORTH, William H
WADSWORTH, William Austin 1
WADSWORTH, William Henry H
WADY, Clifton Sanford 3
WAESCHE, Russell Randolph 2
WAFFLE, Albert Edward 1
WAGENAAR, Bernard 5
WAGENER, Anthony Pelzer 5
WAGENER, David Douglas H
WAGENHEIM, Michael Benjamin 1
WAGER, Alan Turner 4
WAGER, Charles Henry 1
WAGER, Ralph Edmond 6
WAGGAMAN, George Augustus H
WAGGENER, Balie Payton 1
WAGGENER, Leslie Peyton 3
WAGGENER, William 2
WAGGONER, Alvin 1
WAGGONER, David E. 2
WAGNALLS, Adam Willis 1
WAGNER, Arthur Lockwood 1
WAGNER, Charles Gray 1
WAGNER, Charles L. 3
WAGNER, Charles Philip 4
WAGNER, Daniel 1
WAGNER, Frank Caspar 1
WAGNER, Frederick Runyon 1
WAGNER, George 4
WAGNER, H. Hughes 6
WAGNER, Harr 1
WAGNER, Henry Franklin 2
WAGNER, Henry Raup 3
WAGNER, Herbert Appleton 2
WAGNER, Herman Alexander 4
WAGNER, Hugh Kiernan 1
WAGNER, James Elvin 5
WAGNER, John Henry H
WAGNER, John Henry 4
WAGNER, Jonathan Howard 5
WAGNER, Kenneth Hall 4
WAGNER, Kip Lowell 6
WAGNER, Louis 1
WAGNER, Martin 5
WAGNER, Myron Leroy 6
WAGNER, Oscar 5
WAGNER, Peter Joseph H
WAGNER, Rob 2
WAGNER, Robert Ferdinand 3
WAGNER, Russell Halderman 3
WAGNER, Samuel 1
WAGNER, Samuel Tobias 1
WAGNER, Steward 4

WAGNER, Webster H
WAGNER, Wieland 4
WAGNER, William H
WAGNER, Wilmer Gouger 4
WAGONER, Philip Dakin 4
WAGONER, Winfred Ethestal 2
WAGSTAFF, Alfred 1
WAGSTAFF, Henry McGilbert 5
WAGSTAFF, Robert McAlpine 6
WAHL, George Moritz 1
WAHL, Lutz 1
WAHL, William Henry 1
WAHLSTROM, Matthias 4
WAHRHAFTIG, Felix Solomon 5
WAID, Dan Everett 4
WAID, George S. 4
WAIDNER, Charles William 1
WAILES, Benjamin Leonard Covington H
WAILES, Edward Thompson 5
WAILES, George Handy 4
WAILES, George Handy 5
WAILLY, Jacques Warnier de 6
WAINDLE, Roger F(rancis) 5
WAINWRIGHT, Dallas Bache 4
WAINWRIGHT, Guy Alwyn 3
WAINWRIGHT, John 4
WAINWRIGHT, Jonathan Mayhew H
WAINWRIGHT, Jonathan Mayhew 2
WAINWRIGHT, Jonathan Mayhew 3
WAINWRIGHT, Marie 1
WAINWRIGHT, Richard 1
WAINWRIGHT, Richard 1
WAINWRIGHT, Samuel Hayman 3
WAIT, Charles Edmund 1
WAIT, Henry Heileman 1
WAIT, Horatio Loomis 1
WAIT, John Cassan 1
WAIT, Lucien Augustus 1
WAIT, Robert T. P. H
WAIT, Samuel H
WAIT, William H
WAIT, William B. 1
WAIT, William Cushing 1
WAIT, William Henry 1
WAITE, Alice Vinton 2
WAITE, Byron Sylvester 1
WAITE, Catharine Van Valkenburg 4
WAITE, Charles Burlingame 1
WAITE, Clark Francis 3
WAITE, Davis Hanson 1
WAITE, Edward Foote 3
WAITE, Frederick Clayton 3
WAITE, George Thomas 1
WAITE, Harvey Rice 5
WAITE, Henry Matson 2
WAITE, Henry Randall 1
WAITE, Herbert Harold 1
WAITE, J. Herbert 3
WAITE, John David 4
WAITE, John Leman 1
WAITE, Merton Benway 2
WAITE, Morison Remich 4
WAITE, Morrison Remick H
WAITE, Sumner 3
WAITE, Warren C. 3
WAITS, Edward McShane 2
WAITT, Ernest Linden 5
WAKASUGI, Sueyuki 6
WAKE, Charles Staniland 1
WAKEFIELD, Arthur Paul 2
WAKEFIELD, Cyrus H
WAKEFIELD, Edmund Burritt 1
WAKEFIELD, Ernest Alonzo 4
WAKEFIELD, Eva Ingersoll 5
WAKEFIELD, Henriette (Mrs. Greek Evans) 6
WAKEFIELD, Lyman E. 2
WAKEFIELD, Milton C. 4
WAKEFIELD, Paul M. 5
WAKEFIELD, Ralph Bruchman 6
WAKEFIELD, Ray 1
WAKEFIELD, Ray Cecil 4
WAKEFIELD, Sherman Day 3
WAKEHURST, Lord (John deVere Loder) 5
WAKELAND, Charles Richard 4

WAKELEE, Edmund Waring 2
WAKELEY, Arthur Cooper 1
WAKELEY, Joseph Burton H
WAKELEY, Thompson Morris 5
WAKEMAN, Abram
WAKEMAN, Antoinette van Hoesen 4
WAKEMAN, Earl Seeley 6
WAKEMAN, Keith 1
WAKEMAN, Seth 1
WAKEMAN, Seth 5
WAKEMAN, Thaddeus Burr 1
WAKEMAN, Wilbur Fisk 1
WAKSMEN, Selman Abraham 6
WALBRIDGE, Cyrus Packard 1
WALBRIDGE, David Safford H
WALBRIDGE, Earle F. 4
WALBRIDGE, George Hicks 1
WALBRIDGE, Henry Sanford H
WALBRIDGE, Hiram H
WALBRIDGE, Nelson Lee 5
WALCOT, Charles Melton H
WALCOTT, Charles Doolittle 1
WALCOTT, Chester Howe 2
WALCOTT, Earle Ashley 1
WALCOTT, Frederic Collin 3
WALCOTT, Gregory Dexter 3
WALCOTT, Gregory Dexter 4
WALCOTT, Harry Mills 2
WALCOTT, Henry Pickering 1
WALCOTT, Robert 3
WALCUTT, Charles C. Jr. 1
WALCUTT, William H
WALD, Abraham 3
WALD, Gustavus Henry 1
WALD, Jerry 4
WALD, Lillian D. 1
WALDECK, Carl Gustav 1
WALDECK, Herman 3
WALDEN, Austin Thomas 4
WALDEN, Freeman 1
WALDEN, Hiram H
WALDEN, John Morgan 1
WALDEN, Lionel 1
WALDEN, Madison Miner H
WALDEN, Percy Talbot 2
WALDEN, Treadwell 1
WALDEN, Walter 5
WALDER, Ernest George 2
WALDERNE, Richard H
WALDO, Charles Gilbert 4
WALDO, Clarence Abiathar 1
WALDO, David H
WALDO, Dwight Bryant 1
WALDO, Frank 1
WALDO, Fullerton Leonard 5
WALDO, George C. 3
WALDO, George E. 2
WALDO, Leonard 1
WALDO, Lillian McLean 5
WALDO, Loren Pinckney H
WALDO, Rhinelander 1
WALDO, Richard H. 2
WALDO, Samuel H
WALDO, Samuel Lovett H
WALDO, Samuel Putnam H
WALDO, Selden Fennell 3
WALDO, William Earl 4
WALDON, Sidney Dunn 2
WALDORF, Ernest Lynn 2
WALDORF, Wilella Louise 2
WALDOW, William F. 1
WALDRIP, Marion Nelson 5
WALDROM, Alfred M. 4
WALDRON, Arthur Maxson 3
WALDRON, Clare Bailey 2
WALDRON, Henry H
WALDRON, James Albert 1
WALDRON, Jeremy Richard 3
WALDRON, John J. 5
WALDRON, John William 1
WALDRON, Webb 2
WALDRON, William Henry 2
WALDROP, R. Walter 2
WALDSEEMULLER, Martin H
WALDSTEIN, Louis 1
WALDSTEIN, Martin E. 4
WALES, George C. 1
WALES, George Edward 5
WALES, George Russell 1
WALES, Henry 3
WALES, James Albert H
WALES, James Albert 5

WALES, John H
WALES, Julia Grace 6
WALES, Leonard Eugene H
WALES, Philip Skinner 1
WALES, Royal Linfield 6
WALES, Salem Howe 1
WALES, Wellington H
WALET, Eugene Henry Jr. 5
WALGREEN, Charles Rudolph 1
WALK, Charles Edmonds 1
WALK, George Everett 4
WALK, James Wilson 1
WALKE, Frank Hicks 1
WALKE, Henry H
WALKE, Willoughby 1
WALKER, Aaron Thibaud (T-Bone) 6
WALKER, Abbie Phillips 2
WALKER, Albert Henry 1
WALKER, Albert Perry 1
WALKER, Aldace F. 1
WALKER, Alexander H
WALKER, Alexander Edward 4
WALKER, Alexander Stewart H
WALKER, Alexander 3
WALKER, Alfred 2
WALKER, Alice Johnstone 5
WALKER, Amasa H
WALKER, Annie Kendrick 5
WALKER, Arthur Lucian 3
WALKER, Arthur Tappan 2
WALKER, Asa H
WALKER, Benjamin H
WALKER, Bradford Hastings 2
WALKER, Bryant 1
WALKER, Buz M. 2
WALKER, C. Howard 1
WALKER, C. Irvine 4
WALKER, Chapman Johnston 6
WALKER, Charles Abbot 1
WALKER, Charles Bertram 5
WALKER, Charles Christopher Brainerd
WALKER, Charles Clement 5
WALKER, Charles Jabez 1
WALKER, Charles Manning 4
WALKER, Charles Rumford 6
WALKER, Charles Swan 1
WALKER, Charles Thomas 4
WALKER, Charles Wellington 5
WALKER, Charlotte Abell 4
WALKER, Clifford Mitchell 5
WALKER, Cornelius 1
WALKER, Curtis Howe 4
WALKER, Danton MacIntyre 4
WALKER, Darrell E. 6
WALKER, David * H
WALKER, David Harold 4
WALKER, David Shelby Beaconsfield 1
WALKER, Dow Vernon 4
WALKER, Dugald Stewart 4
WALKER, Edward Dwight H
WALKER, Edwin 1
WALKER, Edwin Robert 1
WALKER, Edwin Ruthven 6
WALKER, Elisha 3
WALKER, Emory Judson 1
WALKER, Faye 1
WALKER, Felix 1
WALKER, Francis H
WALKER, Francis 2
WALKER, Francis Amasa H
WALKER, Francis John Harwell 6
WALKER, Frank Banghart 1
WALKER, Frank Buckley 4
WALKER, Frank Comerford 3
WALKER, Frank Ray 2
WALKER, Frank Robinson 4
WALKER, Fred Allan 2
WALKER, Fred Livingood 5
WALKER, Frederick 4
WALKER, Ferdinand 1
WALKER, Graham H
WALKER, Freeman H
WALKER, Gayle Courtney 1
WALKER, George H
WALKER, George 1
WALKER, George Abram H
WALKER, George Henry 5
WALKER, George Leon 1
WALKER, George Levi H
WALKER, George Richard 4
WALKER, George Rowland 4
WALKER, George Winfield 2
WALKER, Gilbert Carlton H
WALKER, Guy Morrison 1
WALKER, Harry 5

WALKER, Harry Bruce 3
WALKER, Harry Leslie 5
WALKER, Harry Wilson 1
WALKER, Harvey 4
WALKER, Henry Clay Jr. 4
WALKER, Henry Hammersley 1
WALKER, Henry Lee 4
WALKER, Henry Oliver 1
WALKER, Henry Yonge 3
WALKER, Herbert William 4
WALKER, Hobart Alexander 5
WALKER, Horatio 1
WALKER, Hugh Kelso 2
WALKER, Irving Miller 5
WALKER, Irwin Nolan 6
WALKER, Isaac Pigeon H
WALKER, Ivan N. 1
WALKER, Jacob Garrett 1
WALKER, James * H
WALKER, James Alexander 1
WALKER, James Barr 1
WALKER, James Baynes 1
WALKER, James Everett 2
WALKER, James Herbert 2
WALKER, James J. 4
WALKER, James Peter H
WALKER, James V. 4
WALKER, James Wilson Grimes 3
WALKER, Jay P. 4
WALKER, John H
WALKER, John Baldwin 1
WALKER, John Brisben 1
WALKER, John Earl 1
WALKER, John Franklin 6
WALKER, John Grimes H
WALKER, John Leonard 5
WALKER, John Moore 3
WALKER, J(ohn) Randall 5
WALKER, John Williams H
WALKER, John Yates Gholson 1
WALKER, Jonathan Hoge H
WALKER, Joseph 2
WALKER, Joseph Albert 4
WALKER, J(oseph) Frederic 5
WALKER, Joseph Henry 1
WALKER, Joseph Reddeford H
WALKER, Kenneth N. 3
WALKER, Kenzie Wallace 3
WALKER, Lapsley Greene 1
WALKER, Leroy Pope 1
WALKER, Lewis 3d 5
WALKER, Lewis B. 4
WALKER, Lewis Carter 2
WALKER, Louis Carlisle 4
WALKER, Mary H
WALKER, Mary Adelaide 2
WALKER, Mary E. 1
WALKER, Meriwether Lewis 4
WALKER, Myron Hamilton 1
WALKER, Nat Gaillard 3
WALKER, Nathan Wilson 1
WALKER, Nellie Verne 5
WALKER, Nelson Macy 1
WALKER, Newton Farmer 1
WALKER, Norman McFarlane 1
WALKER, Paul Atlee 4
WALKER, Percy H
WALKER, Perley F. 1
WALKER, Pinkney Houston H
WALKER, Platt Dickinson 1
WALKER, Ralph Curry 1
WALKER, Ralph Thomas 5
WALKER, Ramsay M. 2
WALKER, Reuben Eugene 1
WALKER, Reuben Lindsay H
WALKER, Richard Wilde 1
WALKER, Robert 3
WALKER, Robert Barney 2
WALKER, Robert Coleman 3
WALKER, Robert E. 3
WALKER, Robert Franklin 1
WALKER, Robert James H
WALKER, Robert John H
WALKER, Robert Sparks H
WALKER, Roberts 1
WALKER, Roger A. P. 3
WALKER, Rollin Hough 2
WALKER, Ross H. 5
WALKER, Ruth Irene 6
WALKER, Ryan 1
WALKER, Samuel J. 4
WALKER, Scott Wells 4
WALKER, Sears Cook H
WALKER, Stanley 4
WALKER, Stanton 5
WALKER, Stewart McCulloch 4
WALKER, Stuart 1
WALKER, Stuart Wilson 1

WALKER, Theodore C. 4
WALKER, Theodore Penfield 3
WALKER, Thomas H
WALKER, Thomas Barlow 1
WALKER, Thomas Joseph 2
WALKER, Timothy * H
WALKER, Tom P. 4
WALKER, Walter 3
WALKER, Walter 4
WALKER, Walton Harris 3
WALKER, William H
WALKER, William Adams H
WALKER, William Alexander 6
WALKER, William David 1
WALKER, William G(eorge) 4
WALKER, William Henry 1
WALKER, William Henry Talbot H
WALKER, William Hultz 1
WALKER, William Johnson H
WALKER, William Kemble 1
WALKER, William May 6
WALKER, William S. 3
WALKER, Willis J. 2
WALKER, Williston 1
WALKINSHAW, Robert Boyd 4
WALKLEY, Raymond Lowery 1
WALKOWITZ, Abraham 4
WALL, Albert Chandler 2
WALL, Alexander James 2
WALL, Edward Clarence 1
WALL, Edward Everett 2
WALL, Edward John 1
WALL, Francis Lowry 4
WALL, Frank Jerome 2
WALL, Garret Dorset H
WALL, Garrett Buckner 1
WALL, George Willard *
WALL, Harry Rutherford 6
WALL, Hubert Stanley 5
WALL, James Walter H
WALL, Stuart S. 4
WALL, William H
WALL, William Guy H
WALL, William Guy 1
WALLACE, Addison Alexander 3
WALLACE, Alexander Gilfillan 1
WALLACE, Alexander Stuart H
WALLACE, Austin Edward 1
WALLACE, Benjamin Bruce 2
WALLACE, Bruce Hinds 1
WALLACE, Charles Frederick 4
WALLACE, Charles Hodge 2
WALLACE, Charles William 1
WALLACE, Charlton 2
WALLACE, Daniel H
WALLACE, Daniel Alden 3
WALLACE, David H
WALLACE, David A. 5
WALLACE, David Duncan 1
WALLACE, David M. 5
WALLACE, Dillon H
WALLACE, Donald H. 3
WALLACE, Edwin Sherman 1
WALLACE, Elizabeth 3
WALLACE, George Barclay 2
WALLACE, George Macdonald 3
WALLACE, George Selden 6
WALLACE, Grant 1
WALLACE, Harold Ayer 3
WALLACE, Harry Brookings 1
WALLACE, Henry 1
WALLACE, Henry Agard 4
WALLACE, Henry Cantwell 1
WALLACE, Horace Binney H
WALLACE, Howard T. 4
WALLACE, Hugh Campbell 1
WALLACE, Hugh D. 3
WALLACE, Ira 4
WALLACE, J. Sherman 1
WALLACE, James 1
WALLACE, James M. H
WALLACE, John Findlay 1
WALLACE, John J. 2
WALLACE, John William H
WALLACE, John Winfield H
WALLACE, Jonathan Hasson 1
WALLACE, Joseph 1
WALLACE, Karl Richards 6
WALLACE, Lawrence Wilkerson 6
WALLACE, Lewis 1

WALLACE, Lurleen Burns 5
WALLACE, Margaret Adair 5
WALLACE, Mary Kent 6
WALLACE, Nathaniel Dick H
WALLACE, Oates Charles Symonds 2
WALLACE, R. James 4
WALLACE, Robert Charles 3
WALLACE, Robert Dwight 4
WALLACE, Robert Minor 3
WALLACE, Robert Moore 1
WALLACE, Rothvin 1
WALLACE, Rush Richard 1
WALLACE, S(amuel) Mayner 4
WALLACE, Schuyler Crawford 5
WALLACE, Sebon Rains 6
WALLACE, Stuart Allen 4
WALLACE, Susan Elston 1
WALLACE, Thomas F. 5
WALLACE, Thomas Ross 3
WALLACE, Tom 4
WALLACE, William Jr. 1
WALLACE, William Alexander Anderson H
WALLACE, William Andrew 5
WALLACE, William Charles
WALLACE, William Henry 1
WALLACE, William Henry 3
WALLACE, William Henson
WALLACE, William James 1
WALLACE, William McLean
WALLACE, William Miller 4
WALLACE, William Robert 4
WALLACE, William Ross 1
WALLACK, Henry John H
WALLACK, James William *
WALLACK, John Johnstone Lester H
WALLAU, Herman L. 5
WALLEN, Saul 5
WALLEN, Theodore Clifford 1
WALLENBERG, Axel Fingal 5
WALLENBERG, Marc Jr. 5
WALLENIUS, Carl Gideon 2
WALLENSTEIN, Merrill Bernard 5
WALLER, Allen George 4
WALLER, Cecile Howell 3
WALLER, Claude 1
WALLER, Curtis L. 3
WALLER, David Jewett Jr. 1
WALLER, Edwin James 6
WALLER, Elwyn 1
WALLER, Emma H
WALLER, Frank 1
WALLER, George Platt 4
WALLER, Gilbert Johnson 4
WALLER, Helen Hiett 4
WALLER, Henry 1
WALLER, John Lightfoot H
WALLER, John Robert 4
WALLER, Lewis 1
WALLER, Littleton W. T. 4
WALLER, Littleton Waller Tazewell 1
WALLER, Mary Ella 1
WALLER, Osmar Lysander 1
WALLER, Peter August 1
WALLER, Rose 1
WALLER, Thomas 1
WALLER, Thomas McDonald 1
WALLER, Willard Walter 2
WALLER, Wilmer Joyce 5
WALLERSTEIN, Edward 5
WALLEY, Samuel Hurd H
WALLGREN, Monrad C. 4
WALLICHS, Glenn Everett 5
WALLIHAN, Allen Grant 1
WALLIN, Alfred 1
WALLIN, J(ohn) E(dward) Wallace 4
WALLIN, Samuel 4
WALLIN, Van Arthur 2
WALLIN, William John 4
WALLING, Anna Strunsky 4
WALLING, Ansel Tracy H
WALLING, Emory A. 1
WALLING, William English 1
WALLING, William Henry 5
WALLING, Willoughby George 1
WALLINGFORD, John Duvall 1
WALLINGTON, Nellie Urner 4
WALLIS, Everett Stanley 4

WALLIS, Frederick Alfred 3
WALLIS, George Edward 5
WALLIS, Jenny 1
WALLIS, Philip 4
WALLIS, Severn Teackle H
WALLIS, William Fisher 5
WALLS, David Crawford 3
WALLS, Frank Xavier 5
WALLS, William Jacob 6
WALLS, William L. 1
WALMSLEY, Walter Newbold Jr. 5
WALN, Nicholas H
WALN, Nora 4
WALN, Robert * H
WALRATH, Florence Dahl 3
WALRATH, John Henry 4
WALSH, Allan B. 5
WALSH, Arthur 2
WALSH, Basil Sylvester 2
WALSH, Benjamin Dann H
WALSH, Blanche 1
WALSH, Catherine Shellew 2
WALSH, Charles Clinton 2
WALSH, Correa Moylan 3
WALSH, Cyril Ambrose 6
WALSH, David Ignatius 2
WALSH, Edmund 1
WALSH, Edward Anthony 6
WALSH, Edward J. 2
WALSH, Emmet M. 4
WALSH, Frank P. 1
WALSH, Sister Frances Marie 5
WALSH, Frederick Harper 4
WALSH, George Ethelbert 1
WALSH, Gerald Groveland 4
WALSH, Gerald Powers 4
WALSH, Henry Collins 1
WALSH, James A. 4
WALSH, James Anthony 1
WALSH, James Joseph 2
WALSH, James Lawrence 3
WALSH, John 2
WALSH, John Edward 1
WALSH, John Gaynor 3
WALSH, John Henry 1
WALSH, John Klaerr 4
WALSH, Joseph 2
WALSH, J(oseph) Hartt 1
WALSH, Joseph Leonard 6
WALSH, Joseph Patrick 5
WALSH, Julius Sylvester 1
WALSH, Lawrence Aloysius 5
WALSH, Louis Sebastian 4
WALSH, Matthew James 4
WALSH, Michael H
WALSH, Philip F. 4
WALSH, Raycroft 3
WALSH, Raymond Arnold 1
WALSH, Raymond James 4
WALSH, Richard John 4
WALSH, Robert 1
WALSH, Robert Douglas 1
WALSH, Roy Edward 5
WALSH, Theodore Edwin 5
WALSH, Thomas 1
WALSH, Thomas F. 1
WALSH, Thomas James 1
WALSH, Thomas Joseph 3
WALSH, Thomas W. H
WALSH, Thomas Yates 1
WALSH, William H
WALSH, William 6
Concannon
WALSH, William Edwin 4
WALSH, William Francis 2
WALSH, William Henry 1
WALSH, William Thomas 1
WALSON, Charles Moore 3
WALSTER, Harlow Leslie 4
WALSTON, Charles 1
WALSTON, Vernon C. 4
WALTER, A. Henry 4
WALTER, Albert G. H
WALTER, Alfred 1
WALTER, Allan Wylie 4
WALTER, Bruno 3
WALTER, Ellery 1
WALTER, Elliot Vincent 5
WALTER, Eugene 1
WALTER, Francis Eugene 4
WALTER, Frank J. 4
WALTER, Frank Keller 2
WALTER, George William 1
WALTER, Herbert Eugene 2
WALTER, Howard Arnold 1
WALTER, Luther Mason 2
WALTER, M. E. 2
WALTER, Paul Alfred 6
Francis Jr.
WALTER, Raymond F. 1
WALTER, Robert 1
WALTER, Thomas H
WALTER, Thomas Ustick H
WALTER, William Emley 5

WALTER, William Henry H
WALTERS, Alexander 1
WALTERS, Anderson Howel
WALTERS, Basil L. 6
WALTERS, Carl 3
WALTERS, Charles S. 1
WALTERS, Francis Marion 3 Jr.
WALTERS, Frank Alexander 4
WALTERS, George Washington 3
WALTERS, Gus 2
WALTERS, Henry 1
WALTERS, Henry C. 1
WALTERS, Herbert Sanford 6
WALTERS, Jack Edward 4
WALTERS, Leon L. 3
WALTERS, Orville Selkirk 6
WALTERS, R. G. 3
WALTERS, Raymond 5
WALTERS, Rolland J. D. 2
WALTERS, Theodore Augustus 1
WALTERS, William H. 5
WALTERS, William Thompson H
WALTHALL, Edward Cary H
WALTHER, Carl Ferdinand H
Wilhelm
WALTHER, Henry Wellman Emile 2
WALTMAN, Harry Franklin 3
WALTMAN, William DeWitt 3
WALTON, Albert Douglass 3
WALTON, Alfred Grant 5
WALTON, Arthur Calvin 5
WALTON, Arthur Keith 5
WALTON, Charles Edgar 1
WALTON, Charles M(ilton) 5 Jr.
WALTON, Charles Spittall 6 Jr.
WALTON, Clifford Stevens 1
WALTON, Duane Edward 6
WALTON, Eleanor Going 5
WALTON, Eliakim Persons H
WALTON, Frank Richmond 3
WALTON, George H
WALTON, George 1 Augustus
WALTON, George Lincoln 1
WALTON, Howard Charles 4
WALTON, Howard Charles 5
WALTON, James Henry 2
WALTON, John Fawcett Jr. 6
WALTON, Lee Barker 1
WALTON, Lester Aglar 1
WALTON, Lucius Leedom 1
WALTON, Mason Augustus 1
WALTON, Matthew H
WALTON, Norman Burdett 2
WALTON, Norton Hall 5
WALTON, Sydney Grant 4
WALTON, Thomas Cameron 1
WALTON, Thomas Otto 4
WALTON, William 1
WALTON, William Bell 1
WALTON, William Randolph 3
WALTZ, Arthur David 6
WALTZ, Elizabeth Cherry 1
WALTZ, Millard Fillmore 4
WALWORTH, Clarence Alphonsus 1
WALWORTH, Ellen Hardin 1
WALWORTH, Jeanette Ritchie Hadermann 4
WALWORTH, Mansfield H
Tracy
WALWORTH, Reuben H
Hyde
WALZ, John Albrecht 3
WALZ, William Emanuel 4
WALZER, Elmer C. 6
WAMBAUGH, Eugene 1
WAMBAUGH, Sarah 3
WAMPLER, Cloud 6
WANAMAKER, Allison 2
Temple
WANAMAKER, John 1
WANAMAKER, Rodman 1
WANAMAKER, Thomas B. 1
WANDELL, Samuel Henry 2
WANDLESS, Edgar Griffin 5
WANDS, Ernest Henry 2
WANGCHUK, Maharaja 5
Jigme Dorji
WANGENHEIM, Julius 2
WANGER, Irving Price 4
WANGLER, Theodore 6
Joseph

WANK, Roland Anthony 5
WANKOWICZ, Melchior 6
WANLASS, Ralph Page 5
WANN, Frank B. 5
WANN, Louis 3
WANNAMAKER, John 2
Skottowe
WANNAMAKER, Olin 5
Dantzler
WANNAMAKER, William 5
Hane
WANSTROM, Ruth Cecilia 6
WANTLAND, Wayne 5
W(arde)
WANTON, Joseph H
WANTY, George Proctor 1
WANTZ, Ray 4
WANVIG, Chester Odin 3
WANZER, H. Stanley 4
WAPLES, Rufus 1
WAPPAT, Blanche King 1
Smith
WARBASSE, James Peter 5
WARBEKE, John Martyn 3
WARBOURG, Eugene H
WARBURG, Felix M. 1
WARBURG, Frederick 6
Marcus
WARBURG, Gerald Felix 5
WARBURG, James Paul 5
WARBURG, Otto Heinrich 5
WARBURG, Paul Moritz 1
WARBURTON, Barclay 3
Harding
WARBURTON, Clyde 6
Williams
WARBURTON, Stanton 3
WARD, Aaron H
WARD, Aaron 1
WARD, Aaron Montgomery H
WARD, Aaron Montgomery 4
WARD, Albert Norman 1
WARD, Alger Luman 5
WARD, Anna Lydia 1
WARD, Arch 5
WARD, Archibald Robinson 5
WARD, Artemas 1
WARD, Artemas Jr. H
WARD, Artemus H
WARD, Arthur Sprague 5
WARD, Cabot 1
WARD, Catharine Weed 1
Barnes
WARD, Charles Allen 3
WARD, Charles Augustus 5
WARD, Charles Bonnell 6
WARD, Charles Carroll 3
WARD, Charles Howell 2
WARD, Charles Sumner 1
WARD, Christopher 2
Longstreth
WARD, Clarence Richard 5
WARD, Clifford 4
WARD, Cyrenus Osborne H
WARD, David 1
WARD, David J. 4
WARD, Delancey Walton 4
WARD, Duren J. H. 4
WARD, E. G. 1
WARD, Edgar Melville 1
WARD, Edward Joshua 2
WARD, Elijah H
WARD, Elizabeth Stuart 1
Phelps
WARD, Evans 4
WARD, Fannie 1
WARD, Florence Elizabeth 3
WARD, Florence Jeanette 1
Baier
WARD, Florence 1
Nightingale Ferguson
WARD, Frank Edwin 3
WARD, Frank Gibson 1
WARD, Frank Trenwith Jr. 6
WARD, Franklin Wilmer 1
WARD, Frederick King 1
WARD, Frederick H
Townsend
WARD, Freeman 2
WARD, Genevieve 1
WARD, George Clinton 3
WARD, George Ehinger 5
WARD, George Gray 1
WARD, George Gray 1
WARD, George Morgan 1
WARD, Gilbert Oakley 5
WARD, Gordon Bert 6
WARD, Grant Eben 5
WARD, Hallett Sydney 5
WARD, Hamilton 1
WARD, Harry Edwin 1
WARD, Harry Frederick 4
WARD, Henry Augustus 1
WARD, Henry Baldwin 2
WARD, Henry Clay 1
WARD, Henry Dana H

WARD, Henry Galbraith 1
WARD, Henry Heber 5
WARD, Henry Levi 2
WARD, Henry Tibbels 1
WARD, Henry Winfield 4
WARD, Henshaw 1
WARD, Herbert Dickinson 1
WARD, Herbert Shaeffer 4
WARD, Herbert William 1
WARD, Holcombe 6
WARD, J. H. 3
WARD, Jacob C. H
WARD, James Edward H
WARD, James Harmon 1
WARD, James Warner H
WARD, James William 1
WARD, John Chamberlain 1
WARD, John Chamberlain 2
WARD, John Elliott 1
WARD, John Harris 6
WARD, John Henry Hobart 1
WARD, John Quincy 1
Adams
WARD, John Wesley 1
WARD, John William 2
George
WARD, Jonathan H
WARD, Joseph H
WARD, Joshua 5
WARD, Julia Elizabeth 1
WARD, Kenneth William 5
WARD, Leo L. 3
WARD, Leslie Dodd 1
WARD, Lester Frank H
WARD, Lester Frank 1
WARD, Lester Frank 4
WARD, Lydia Avery 1
Coonley
WARD, Lyman 2
WARD, Marcus Lawrence H
WARD, Marcus Llewellyn 4
WARD, Matthias 1
WARD, May Alden 1
WARD, Milan Lester 5
WARD, Montgomery 1
WARD, Nancy H
WARD, Nathaniel H
WARD, Orlando 5
WARD, Ossian Peay 5
WARD, Peirce Colton 5
WARD, Perley Erik 1
WARD, Ralph Ansel 5
WARD, Reginald Henshaw 1
WARD, Richard H
WARD, Richard Halsted 1
WARD, Robert De Courcy 1
WARD, Robert Stafford 6
WARD, Robert W. 5
WARD, Robert William 3
WARD, Samuel * H
WARD, Samuel 4
WARD, Samuel Bladwin 1
WARD, Samuel Ringgold H
WARD, Seth 1
WARD, Stevenson E. 3
WARD, Susan Hayes 4
WARD, Thomas * H
WARD, Thomas 1
WARD, Thomas Bayless 4
WARD, Thomas Johnson 4
WARD, Thomas Wren 3
WARD, Wilbert 3
WARD, Wilbur 1
WARD, Willard Parker 1
WARD, William H
WARD, William Allen 4
WARD, William Breining 1
WARD, William Edgar 5
WARD, William Evans 5
WARD, William G. 4
WARD, William Hayes 1
WARD, William Hilles 4
WARD, William I. 3
WARD, William Rankin 1
WARD, William Thomas 4
WARDALL, Ruth Aimee 1
WARDALL, William Jed 5
WARDE, Frederick 1
WARDE, Mary Francis H
Xavier
WARDELL, Justus S. 2
WARDELL, Morris L. 3
WARDEN, David Bailie H
WARDEN, James 6
WARDEN, Oliver Sherman 3
WARDEN, Robert Bruce 4
WARDENBURG, F. A. 4
WARDER, George 1
Woodward
WARDER, John Aston 1
WARDER, John Haines 1
WARDER, Robert Bowne 1
WARDER, Walter 4
WARDLAW, Joseph 2
Coachman
WARDLAW, Patterson 2

WARDLE, Robert Jr. 5
WARDLEY, Russell George 1
WARDMAN, Ervin 1
WARDROP, Robert 1
WARDWELL, Allen 3
WARDWELL, Daniel H
WARDWELL, Frank 5
Carlton
WARDWELL, Harold 4
Fletcher
WARDWELL, Sheldon 4
Eaton
WARDWELL, William 1
Thomas
WARE, Allison 6
WARE, Arthur 1
WARE, Ashur H
WARE, Edmund Asa H
WARE, Edward Twichell 1
WARE, Eugene F. 1
WARE, Franklin Backus 2
WARE, Harriet 4
WARE, Harry Hudnall Jr. 5
WARE, Helen 4
WARE, Henry H
WARE, Henry Jr. H
WARE, Horace Everett 4
WARE, John 5
WARE, John Fothergill H
Waterhouse
WARE, Lewis Sharpe 1
WARE, Mary S. 3
WARE, Nathaniel A. H
WARE, Nicholas H
WARE, Norman Joseph 2
WARE, Paul 5
WARE, Sedley Lynch 3
WARE, Walter Ellsworth 4
WARE, William 1
WARE, William Robert 1
WAREHAM, Harry F. 2
WAREHAM, John 6
Hamilton Dee
WAREING, Ernest Clyde 4
WARFIELD, Augustus 4
Bennett
WARFIELD, Benjamin 1
Breckinridge
WARFIELD, C. Dorsey 2
WARFIELD, Catherine Ann H
Ware
WARFIELD, David 3
WARFIELD, Edwin 1
WARFIELD, Ethelbert 6
WARFIELD, Ethelbert 1
Dudley
WARFIELD, George Alfred 1
WARFIELD, Harry Ridgely 5
Jr.
WARFIELD, Henry Mactier 4
WARFIELD, Henry Ridgely H
WARFIELD, R. Emory 1
WARFIELD, Ridgeley 1
Brown
WARFIELD, S. Davies 1
WARFIELD, William 2
WARHEIT, Isarel Albert 5
WARING, Clarence Henry 3
WARING, George Edwin 1
WARING, J. Waties 3
WARING, James Howard 1
WARING, James Johnston 3
WARING, Malvina Sarah 1
WARING, Roane 3
WARING, Thomas Richard 6
WARK, George H. 1
WARK, Homer Ethan 5
WARLICK, Hulon Otis Jr. 4
WARMAN, Cy 1
WARMAN, Edward B. 2
WARMAN, Philip Creveling 1
WARMOTH, Henry Clay 1
WARNACH, Paul Victor 6
WARNE, Francis Wesley 2
WARNE, Frank Julian 2
WARNER, Adoniram 1
Judson
WARNER, Albert 4
WARNER, Albert Lyman 4
WARNER, Alton G. 4
WARNER, Amos Griswold 1
WARNER, Anna Bartlett 1
WARNER, Anne 1
WARNER, Beverley Ellison 1
WARNER, Bradford 6
Newman
WARNER, Brainard Henry 1
WARNER, Charles 1
WARNER, C(harles) 5
A(lbert)
WARNER, Charles Dudley 1
WARNER, Charles 1
Mortimer
WARNER, David Ashley 4
WARNER, DeVer Howard 1
WARNER, Donald Ticknor 1

WARNER, Edward 3
WARNER, Ellsworth 2
  Colonel
WARNER, Eltinge Fowler 4
WARNER, Ernest Noble 1
WARNER, Everett Longley 4
WARNER, Ezra Joseph * 1
WARNER, Frank 2
WARNER, Franklin 6
  Humphrey
WARNER, Fred Maltby 1
WARNER, Gertrude Bass 3
WARNER, Glenn Scobey 3
WARNER, Hannah 1
WARNER, Harold 2
WARNER, Harry Jackson 3
WARNER, Harry Morris 3
WARNER, Harry O. 3
WARNER, Henry Byron 3
WARNER, Henry Edward 2
WARNER, Hiram H
WARNER, Horace Emory 4
WARNER, Horace Everett 1
WARNER, Ira David 4
WARNER, J. Foster 1
WARNER, Jack F. 6
WARNER, James H
  Cartwright
WARNER, James Edward 6
WARNER, John DeWitt 1
WARNER, John F. 4
WARNER, Jonathan 4
WARNER, Jonathan H
  Trumbull
WARNER, Joseph Bangs 1
WARNER, Joseph Everett 3
WARNER, Langdon 3
WARNER, Lucien Calvin 1
WARNER, Lucien 3
  Thompson
WARNER, Milo Joseph 4
WARNER, Milton Jones 3
WARNER, Olin Levi H
WARNER, Paul McC 4
WARNER, Rawleigh 5
WARNER, Richard 3
  Ambrose
WARNER, Robert 6
  Foreman
WARNER, Robert 4
  Wilberforce
WARNER, Samuel Larkin H
WARNER, Seth H
WARNER, Southard Parker 1
WARNER, Susan Bogert H
WARNER, Thor 3
WARNER, Vespasian 1
WARNER, W. Lloyd 6
WARNER, Willard 1
WARNER, William H
WARNER, William Bishop 2
WARNER, William Everett 5
WARNER, Worcester Reed H
WARNICK, Spencer 5
  K(ellogg)
WARNOCK, Arthur Ray 3
WARNOCK, Ernest Henry 6
WARNOCK, William 4
  Robert
WARNOW, Mark 2
WARNSHUIS, Abbe 3
  Livingston
WARRELL, James H
WARREN, Althea 3
WARREN, Arthur 1
WARREN, Arthur Fiske 5
WARREN, Avra Milvin 3
WARREN, Benjamin S. 1
WARREN, Bentley Wirt 2
WARREN, Casper Carl 6
WARREN, Charles 1
WARREN, Charles Beecher 1
WARREN, Charles Elliott 2
WARREN, Charles Howard 1
WARREN, Charles Hyde 3
WARREN, Constance 5
WARREN, Cornelia 5
WARREN, Cornelius 1
WARREN, Cyrus Moors H
WARREN, Earl 6
WARREN, Edward Allen H
WARREN, Edward Henry 2
WARREN, Edward K. 1
WARREN, Edward Leroy 1
WARREN, Edward Royal 2
WARREN, Edwin Walpole 1
WARREN, Fiske 1
WARREN, Francis Emory 1
WARREN, Frank Edward 1
WARREN, Frank Furniss 4
WARREN, Frank Lincoln 5
WARREN, Fred D. 3
WARREN, Frederick 2
  Andrew
WARREN, Frederick 2
  Emroy

WARREN, Frederick 1
  Morris
WARREN, Fuller 6
WARREN, George Earle 6
WARREN, George 1
  Frederick
WARREN, George 1
  Washington
WARREN, George William 1
WARREN, Gouverneur H
  Kemble
WARREN, Harold 1
  Broadfield
WARREN, Harry Marsh 1
WARREN, Henry Clarke H
WARREN, Henry Ellis 3
WARREN, Henry Kimball 4
WARREN, Henry Pitt 1
WARREN, Henry White 1
WARREN, Herbert 1
  Langford
WARREN, Howard Crosby 1
WARREN, Irene 5
WARREN, Israel Perkins H
WARREN, J. Collins 1
WARREN, James H
WARREN, James Carey 3
WARREN, James E. 3
WARREN, James Goold 4
WARREN, James Thomas 2
WARREN, John H
WARREN, John Collins 1
WARREN, John Davock 6
WARREN, Joseph H
WARREN, Joseph 2
WARREN, Joseph Mabbett 1
WARREN, Joseph H
  Weatherhead
WARREN, Josiah H
WARREN, Julius Ernest 4
WARREN, Leonard 3
WARREN, Lillie Eginton 4
WARREN, Lott H
WARREN, Maude Lavinia 1
WARREN, Mercy Otis H
WARREN, Minton 1
WARREN, Minton 2
  Machado
WARREN, Percy Holmes 4
WARREN, Sir Peter H
WARREN, Richard Henry 1
WARREN, Robert B. 2
WARREN, Russell H
WARREN, Samuel Dennis 1
WARREN, Samuel Edward 1
WARREN, Samuel Prowse 1
WARREN, Speed 5
WARREN, Stanley Perkins 4
WARREN, Thomas Davis 5
WARREN, Whitney 2
WARREN, Willard Clinton 1
WARREN, William * H
WARREN, William C. 1
WARREN, William Fairfield 1
WARREN, William Homer 4
WARREN, William 3
  Marshall
WARREN, William 2
  Robinson
WARREN, William Tilman 4
WARREN, William Wirt H
WARREN, Winslow 1
WARRICK, Dupuy Goza 4
WARRINER, Edward 1
  Augustus
WARRINER, Eugene 1
  Clarente
WARRINER, Lewis 1
  Legrand
WARRINER, Reuel Edward 5
WARRINER, Reuel Edward 6
WARRINER, Samuel 2
  Dexter
WARRING, Charles Bartlett 1
WARRINGTON, Albert 1
  Powell
WARRINGTON, George 1
  Howard
WARRINGTON, John W. 1
WARRINGTON, Lewis H
WARSHAW, Jacob 2
WARSHAWSKY, Abel 4
  George
WARTENBERG, Robert 3
WARTHEN, William 6
  Horace Franklin
WARTHIN, Aldred Scott 1
WARTON, Frank Riggs 3
WARVELLE, George 1
  William
WARWICK, C. Laurence 3
WARWICK, Charles 1
  Franklin
WARWICK, Edward 6
WARWICK, Herbert 5
  Sherwood Jr.

WARWICK, John George H
WARWICK, Walter Winter 1
WARWICK, William 1
  Edmund
WASCHER, Howard 4
  George
WASEY, L. 4
WASH, Carlyle Hilton 2
WASHABAUGH, Jacob 1
  Edgar
WASHAKIE H
WASHBURN, Albert Henry 1
WASHBURN, Alfred 5
  Hamlin
WASHBURN, Benjamin 4
  Martin
WASHBURN, Cadwallader 4
WASHBURN, Cadwallader 1
  Colden
WASHBURN, Charles H
  Ames
WASHBURN, Charles 1
  Grenfill
WASHBURN, Claude 1
  Carlos
WASHBURN, Edward Abiel H
WASHBURN, Edward 5
  Roger
WASHBURN, Edward 1
  Wight
WASHBURN, Emory 1
WASHBURN, F. S. 4
WASHBURN, Francis 1
WASHBURN, Frank 1
  Sherman
WASHBURN, Frederic 2
  Augustus
WASHBURN, Frederic 2
  Baldwin
WASHBURN, Frederic 1
  Leonard
WASHBURN, George 1
WASHBURN, George 4
  Frederic
WASHBURN, George 1
  Hamlin
WASHBURN, Henry 4
  Bradford
WASHBURN, Henry Dana H
WASHBURN, Henry 1
  Stevenson
WASHBURN, Homer 4
  Charles
WASHBURN, Ichabod H
WASHBURN, Israel H
WASHBURN, Ives 2
WASHBURN, Jed L. 1
WASHBURN, John 1
WASHBURN, John Henry 1
WASHBURN, John Hosea 1
WASHBURN, Louis Cope 1
WASHBURN, Margaret 1
  Floy
WASHBURN, Peter H
  Thacher
WASHBURN, Reginald 3
WASHBURN, Robert 2
WASHBURN, Stanley 3
WASHBURN, Victor Duke 4
WASHBURN, Watson 6
WASHBURN, William H
  Barrett
WASHBURN, William 1
  Drew
WASHBURN, William Ives 1
WASHBURN, William 1
  Sherman
WASHBURN, William 1
  Tucker
WASHBURNE, Elihu H
  Benjamin
WASHBURNE, George 2
  Adrian
WASHBURNE, Heluiz 5
  Chandler (Mrs. Carleton
  W. Washburne)
WASHINGER, William 1
  Henry
WASHINGTON, Booker 1
  Taliaferro
WASHINGTON, Bushrod H
WASHINGTON, George H
WASHINGTON, George 1
  Corbin
WASHINGTON, George 5
  Thomas
WASHINGTON, Henry 1
  Stephens
WASHINGTON, Horace 4
  Lee
WASHINGTON, John 1
  Macrae
WASHINGTON, Lawrence 1
WASHINGTON, Martha H
  Dandridge Custis
WASHINGTON, Thomas 3

WASHINGTON, W. Lanier 1
WASHINGTON, William H
  Henry
WASINGER, Gordon 5
  Bernard
WASKEY, Frank Hinman 4
WASKEY, Frank Hinman 5
WASLEY, Ruth Ellen 5
WASON, Charles William 1
WASON, Edward H. 1
WASON, Leonard Chase 1
WASON, Robert Alexander 3
WASON, Robert R. 3
WASON, William J. Jr. 3
WASSAM, Clarence 3
  Wyckliffe
WASSERMAN, Earl Reeves 5
WASSERMANN, Friedrich 5
WASSERVOGEL, Isidor 4
WASSON, Alfred 4
  Washington
WASSON, Alonzo 6
WASSON, George Savary 3
WASSON, Theron 5
WASSON, Thomas 2
  Campbell
WASSON, William Walter 5
WASTE, William Harrison 1
WATCHORN, Robert 1
WATERBURY, Frank C. 1
WATERBURY, Frederick 4
WATERBURY, Henry S. 3
WATERBURY, John Isaac 1
WATERFALL, Harry 2
  William
WATERFALL, Wallace 6
WATERHOUSE, Alfred 4
  James
WATERHOUSE, Benjamin H
WATERHOUSE, Frank 1
WATERHOUSE, George 3
  Booker
WATERHOUSE, George 5
  Shadford
WATERHOUSE, John 2
WATERHOUSE, Joseph 4
  Raymond
WATERHOUSE, Richard 1
  Green
WATERHOUSE, Sylvester H
WATERLOO, Stanley 1
WATERMAN, Alan Tower 4
WATERMAN, Arba Nelson 1
WATERMAN, Charles 1
  Dana
WATERMAN, Charles M. 1
WATERMAN, Charles 1
  Winfield
WATERMAN, Charles 4
  Winfield
WATERMAN, Earle Lytton 3
WATERMAN, Frank Allan 5
WATERMAN, Herbert 2
WATERMAN, Julian Seesel 2
WATERMAN, Leroy 5
WATERMAN, Lewis 1
  Anthony
WATERMAN, Lewis Edson H
WATERMAN, Lucius 1
WATERMAN, Marcus 4
WATERMAN, Nixon 1
WATERMAN, Robert H. H
WATERMAN, Sigismund 4
WATERMAN, Thomas H
  Whitney
WATERMAN, Warren 3
WATERMAN, Willoughby 4
  Cyrus
WATERMULDER, Louis F. 6
WATERS, Campbell Easter 5
WATERS, Clara Erskine 1
  Clement
WATERS, Daniel H
WATERS, Dudley E. 1
WATERS, Eugene A. 3
WATERS, Francis E. 1
WATERS, Henry Jackson 1
WATERS, James Stephen 4
WATERS, John H. 1
WATERS, Lewis William 2
WATERS, Moses H. 4
WATERS, N. Mcgee 1
WATERS, Robert 1
WATERS, Russell Judson 1
WATERS, Samuel M. 3
WATERS, Thomas Franklin 1
WATERS, Vincent S. 6
WATERS, William Everett 1
WATERS, William Laurence 3
WATERS, William Otis 1
WATERS, William P. 1
WATERSON, Karl William 1
WATHEN, John Roach 1
WATIE, Stand H
WATIES, James Rives 4

WATKEYS, Charles W. 5
WATKIN, William Ward 3
WATKINS, Aaron Sherman 1
WATKINS, Albert 1
WATKINS, Albert Galiton H
WATKINS, Alexander 1
  Farrar
WATKINS, Arthur Charles 3
WATKINS, Arthur V. 6
WATKINS, Charles D. 4
WATKINS, Charles L. 4
WATKINS, Charles W. 1
WATKINS, Dale Baxter 5
WATKINS, David Ogden 1
WATKINS, Dwight Everett 4
WATKINS, Edgar 2
WATKINS, Elton Sr. 3
WATKINS, Everett C. 3
WATKINS, Ferre C. 4
WATKINS, Frank Thomas 3
WATKINS, Franklin 5
  Chenault
WATKINS, Frederick 5
  Mundell
WATKINS, G. Robert 5
WATKINS, George H
  Claiborne
WATKINS, Harry Evans 4
WATKINS, Henry Hitt 5
WATKINS, Henry Vaughan 2
WATKINS, Jabez Bunting 1
WATKINS, James (Keir) 5
WATKINS, J(ames) Stephen 5
WATKINS, John Elfreth 1
WATKINS, John Elfreth 1
WATKINS, John Thomas 1
WATKINS, Joseph Conrad 5
WATKINS, Mark Hanna 6
WATKINS, Raymond 2
  Edward
WATKINS, Robert Henry 4
WATKINS, Thomas 6
  Franklin
WATKINS, Thomas H. 4
WATKINS, Thomas James 1
WATKINS, Vernon Phillips 5
WATKINS, Walter Kendall 4
WATKINS, William Turner 4
WATKINS, William 1
  Woodbury
WATLING, John Wright 3
WATMOUGH, James 1
  Horatio
WATMOUGH, John H
  Goddard
WATNER, Abraham 4
WATRES, Louis Arthur 1
WATROUS, Charles Leach 1
WATROUS, Elizabeth 1
  Snowden Nichols
WATROUS, George Ansel 1
WATROUS, George Dutton 1
WATROUS, Harry Willson 1
WATROUS, Richard 3
  Benedict
WATSON, Adolphus 2
  Eugene
WATSON, Albert 3
WATSON, Alfred Augustin 1
WATSON, Alonzo Richard 4
WATSON, Amelia 1
  Montague
WATSON, Andrew 1
WATSON, Archibald 3
  Robinson
WATSON, Arthur Clinton 6
WATSON, Arthur Kittredge 6
WATSON, Benjamin Frank 1
WATSON, Benjamin Philip 6
WATSON, Bruce Mervellon 2
WATSON, Burl Stevens 6
WATSON, Byron S. 2
WATSON, Charles G. 5
WATSON, Charles Henry 1
WATSON, Charles Roger 1
WATSON, Clarence 1
  Wayland
WATSON, Cooper H
  Kinderdine
WATSON, David Emmett 1
WATSON, David Kemper 4
WATSON, David Robert 5
WATSON, David Thompson 1
WATSON, Drake 3
WATSON, Dudley Crafts 5
WATSON, Earnest Charles 5
WATSON, Ebbie Julian 1
WATSON, Edith Sarah 3
WATSON, Edward Hann 6
WATSON, Edward Minor 1
WATSON, Edward Minor 2
WATSON, Edward Willard 1
WATSON, Edwin Martin 2
WATSON, Elizabeth Lowe 4
WATSON, Elkanah H
WATSON, Emile Emdon 1

* Indicates More Than One Such Name Listed

WATSON, Emory Olin 1
WATSON, Ernest W(illiam) 5
WATSON, Eugene Payne 1
WATSON, Eugene Winslow 1
WATSON, F. B. 3
WATSON, Floyd Rowe 5
WATSON, Frank Dekker 3
WATSON, Frank Rushmore 5
WATSON, G. Clarke 4
WATSON, George D. 1
WATSON, George Henry 3
WATSON, H. Sumner 1
WATSON, Harry Legare 3
WATSON, Henry Chapman 1
WATSON, Henry Clay H
WATSON, Henry Cood 1
WATSON, Henry David 1
WATSON, Henry Winfield 1
WATSON, Hugh Hammond 2
WATSON, Irving Allison 1
WATSON, James H
WATSON, James 1
WATSON, James Craig H
WATSON, James D. 1
WATSON, James E. 2
WATSON, James 6
  Fraughtman
WATSON, James Gray 3
WATSON, James Madison 1
WATSON, James Sibley 3
WATSON, James Webster 3
WATSON, John B. 3
WATSON, John Brown 1
WATSON, John Crittenden 1
WATSON, John Fanning 1
WATSON, John Franklin 5
WATSON, John H. Jr. 4
WATSON, John Henry 1
WATSON, John Jay 1
WATSON, John Jordan 1
  Crittenden
WATSON, John Thomas 3
WATSON, John William H
  Clark
WATSON, Joseph Franklin 1
WATSON, Kenneth Nicoll 1
WATSON, Leroy Hugh 6
WATSON, Lewis Findlay H
WATSON, Mark Skinner 1
WATSON, Paul Barron 2
WATSON, Ralph Hopkins 1
WATSON, Robert 1
WATSON, Robert 1
WATSON, Robert Walker 2
WATSON, Russell 5
  Ellsworth
WATSON, Samuel Newell 2
WATSON, Sereno H
WATSON, Thomas 1
  Augustus
WATSON, Thomas E. 1
WATSON, Thomas John 3
WATSON, Thomas Leonard 1
WATSON, Walter Allen 1
WATSON, Willard Oliphint 5
WATSON, William 1
WATSON, William Franklin 3
WATSON, William Gorrell 4
WATSON, William Henry 1
WATSON, William Richard 1
WATSON-WATT, Sir 6
  Robert (Alexander)
WATT, Barbara Hall 5
WATT, Ben H. 4
WATT, David Alexander 1
WATT, Homer Andrew 2
WATT, James Robert 1
WATT, Richard Morgan 1
WATT, Robert J. 2
WATT, Robert McDowell 4
WATT, Rolla Vernon 1
WATTERS, Henry Eugene 1
WATTERS, Philip 1
  Melancthon
WATTERS, Rev. Philip 5
  Sidney
WATTERS, Thomas 1
WATTERS, William Henry 3
WATTERSON, Harvey 1
  Magee
WATTERSON, Henry 1
WATTERSON, Joseph 6
WATTERSTON, George H
WATTIE, James 6
WATTIS, Edmund Orson 1
WATTLES, Gurdon Wallace 1
WATTLES, Willard Austin 3
WATTS, Alan Wilson 6
WATTS, Albert Edward 5
WATTS, Arthur S. 5
WATTS, Arthur Thomas 1
WATTS, Charles Henry 3
WATTS, Edward Seabrook 1
WATTS, Ethelbert 1
WATTS, Frank Overton 2
WATTS, Frederick H

WATTS, George 1
  Washington
WATTS, H. Bascom 3
WATTS, Harry Dorsey 3
WATTS, Harvey Maitland 4
WATTS, Herbert Charles 5
WATTS, John H
WATTS, John Clarence 5
WATTS, John Sebrie H
WATTS, Joseph Thomas 3
WATTS, Legh Richmond 1
WATTS, Lyle Ford 4
WATTS, Mary Stanbery 4
WATTS, May Petrea 6
  Theilgaard
WATTS, Ralph L. 2
WATTS, Richard Cannon 1
WATTS, Ridley 1
WATTS, Ridley 1
WATTS, Roderick John 3
WATTS, Stanley Saul 5
WATTS, Thomas Hill H
WATTS, Thomas Joseph 3
WATTS, William Carleton 1
WATTS, William Lord 4
WAUCHOPE, George 2
  Armstrong
WAUGH, Alfred S. H
WAUGH, Beverly H
WAUGH, Coulton 6
WAUGH, Evelyn Arthur St 4
  John
WAUGH, Frank Albert 1
WAUGH, Frederick Judd 1
WAUGH, Ida 1
WAUGH, John McMaster 4
WAUGH, Karl Tinsley 5
WAUGH, Samuel Bell H
WAUGH, Samuel Clark 5
WAUGH, Sidney 1
WAUGH, William Francis 1
WAUGH, William 5
  Hammond
WAUGH, William Jasper 1
WAUL, Thomas Neville 1
WAVELL, Archibald 3
  Percival
WAVERLEY, Viscount 3
WAXMAN, Franz 4
WAXMAN, Percy 2
WAY, Cassius 2
WAY, George Brevitt 4
WAY, Gordon L. 6
WAY, John 1
WAY, Joseph Howell 1
WAY, Luther B. 2
WAY, Royal Brunson 1
WAY, Sylvester Bedell 2
WAY, Warren Wade 2
WAY, William 5
WAYBURN, Ned 2
WAYLAND, Francis H
WAYLAND, Francis 1
WAYLAND, Julius 1
  Augustus
WAYLAND-SMITH, 4
  Robert
WAYMACK, William 4
  Wesley
WAYMAN, Alexander H
  Walker
WAYMAN, Dorothy C. 6
WAYMAN, Harry Clifford 6
WAYMOUTH, George H
WAYNE, Anthony H
WAYNE, Arthur Trezevant 4
WAYNE, Charles Stokes 4
WAYNE, Isaac H
WAYNE, James Moore H
WAYNE, Joseph Jr. 2
WAYSON, James Thomas 6
WEAD, Charles Kasson 1
WEAD, (Mary) Eunice 6
WEADOCK, Bernard 2
  Francis
WEADOCK, Edward E. 4
WEADOCK, John C. 3
WEADOCK, Thomas Addis 1
  Emmet
WEAGANT, Roy Alexander 2
WEAGLY, Mrs. Roy C. F. 3
WEAKLEY, Charles Enright 5
WEAKLEY, Robert 1
WEAKLEY, Samuel Davies 1
WEAR, D. Walker 4
WEAR, Frank Lucian 5
WEAR, Joseph W. 1
WEAR, Samuel McConnell 6
WEARE, Meshech H
WEARING, Thomas 4
WEART, Douglas Lafayette 6
WEATHERBY, Charles 2
  Alfred
WEATHERBY, LeRoy 2
  Samuel

WEATHERED, Roy Bishop 6
WEATHERFORD, William H
WEATHERFORD, Willis 5
  Duke
WEATHERHEAD, Albert 4
  J. Jr.
WEATHERLY, James 4
  Meriwether
WEATHERLY, Ulysses 1
  Grant
WEATHERLY, W(illiam) 5
  H.
WEATHERRED, Preston 5
  Alonzo
WEATHERWAX, Hazelett 5
  Paul
WEAVER, Aaron Ward 1
WEAVER, Andrew Thomas 4
WEAVER, Archibald Jerard H
WEAVER, Arthur J. 2
WEAVER, Bennett 5
WEAVER, Charles 4
  Blanchard
WEAVER, Charles Clinton 1
WEAVER, Charles Parsons 4
WEAVER, Clarence Eugene 1
WEAVER, Claude 3
WEAVER, Edward 1
  Ebenezer
WEAVER, Erasmus Morgan 1
WEAVER, Fred(erick) 5
  H(enry)
WEAVER, George Calvin 1
WEAVER, George Howitt 2
WEAVER, Gilbert Grimes 5
WEAVER, Harry Otis 1
WEAVER, Harry Sands 1
WEAVER, Henry Grady 5
WEAVER, James B. 1
WEAVER, James Bellamy 1
WEAVER, James Harvey 5
WEAVER, John 1
WEAVER, John Van Alstyn 1
WEAVER, Jonathan 1
WEAVER, Joseph B. 1
WEAVER, Junius Vaden 6
WEAVER, Martha Collins 4
WEAVER, Myron 4
  McDonald
WEAVER, Paul John 2
WEAVER, Philip H
WEAVER, Philip Johnson 5
WEAVER, Philip Tennant 6
WEAVER, Powell 2
WEAVER, R.C. 5
WEAVER, R(alph) H(older) 2
WEAVER, Rudolph 2
WEAVER, Rufus B. 1
WEAVER, Rufus 4
  Washington
WEAVER, Samuel Pool 4
WEAVER, Silas Matteson 1
WEAVER, Walter L. 1
WEAVER, Walter Reed 2
WEAVER, William Dixon 1
WEAVER, Zebulon 2
WEBB, Alexander Stewart 1
WEBB, Alexander Stewart 2
WEBB, Atticus 5
WEBB, Carl N. 3
WEBB, Charles Aurelius 2
WEBB, Charles Henry 1
WEBB, Charles M. 5
WEBB, Charles Wallace 2
WEBB, Clifton 4
WEBB, Sir Clifton 4
WEBB, Daniel H
WEBB, Daniel Clary 3
WEBB, Del E. 6
WEBB, Earle W. 2
WEBB, Edward Fleming 1
WEBB, Edwin Douglas 1
WEBB, Edwin Yates 3
WEBB, Ernest Clay 5
WEBB, Frank Elbridge 2
WEBB, Frank Rush 1
WEBB, George H. 1
WEBB, George James H
WEBB, George Thomas 4
WEBB, Gerald Bertram 2
WEBB, Hanor A. 4
WEBB, Henry Walter 1
WEBB, J. Burkitt 1
WEBB, James Avery 3
WEBB, James Duncan 4
WEBB, James Henry 1
WEBB, James Ruffin 6
WEBB, James Watson H
WEBB, John Maurice 1
WEBB, Joseph James 4
WEBB, Kenneth Seymour 4
WEBB, Nathan 1
WEBB, Richard L. 4
WEBB, Robert Alexander 1
WEBB, Robert H. 3

WEBB, Robert Thomas 1
WEBB, Robert Williams 2
WEBB, Stuart Weston 5
WEBB, Thomas H
WEBB, T(homes) Dwight 5
WEBB, Thomas Smith H
WEBB, Thompson 6
WEBB, Ulys Robert 3
WEBB, Ulysses Sigel 2
WEBB, Vanderbilt 3
WEBB, Vivian Howell (Mrs. 5
  Thompson Webb)
WEBB, Walter Loring 1
WEBB, Walter Prescott 4
WEBB, Willard Isaac Jr. 5
WEBB, William Alexander 1
WEBB, William Alfred 2
WEBB, William Henry 1
WEBB, William Robert 1
WEBB, William Seward 1
WEBB, William Snyder 4
WEBB, William Walter 1
WEBBER, Amos Richard 2
WEBBER, Charles Wilkins H
WEBBER, George Harris 1
WEBBER, Henry William 1
WEBBER, Herbert John 2
WEBBER, James Benson Jr. 3
WEBBER, Le Roy 1
WEBBER, Oscar 4
WEBBER, Richard Hudson 4
WEBBER, Samuel H
WEBBER, Samuel Gilbert 1
WEBBINK, Paul 5
WEBER, Adna Ferrin 5
WEBER, Albert 1
WEBER, Albert J. 4
WEBER, Alfred 3
WEBER, Arthur William 4
WEBER, Carl Jefferson 4
WEBER, Edouard 5
WEBER, Frederick Clarence 6
WEBER, Frederick 3
  Theodore
WEBER, Gustav C. E. 4
WEBER, Gustave Frederick 6
WEBER, Gustavus 2
  Adolphus
WEBER, Harry M. 3
WEBER, Henri Carleton 4
WEBER, Henry Adam 4
WEBER, Herman Carl 1
WEBER, Jessie Palmer 1
WEBER, Joe Nicholas 4
WEBER, John 1
WEBER, John B. 1
WEBER, John Langdon 1
WEBER, Joseph M. 2
WEBER, Lois 1
WEBER, Max 1
WEBER, Max 1
WEBER, Paul 3
WEBER, Randolph Henry 4
WEBER, Samuel Edwin 5
WEBER, William A. 6
WEBER, William Lander 1
WEBERN, Anton 4
WEBNER, Frank Erastus 4
WEBSTER, Arthur Gordon 1
WEBSTER, Benjamin 1
  Francis
WEBSTER, Bruce Peck 6
WEBSTER, Clyde Irvin 5
WEBSTER, Cornelius 2
  Crosby
WEBSTER, Daniel H
WEBSTER, David 1
WEBSTER, Edward Harlan 1
WEBSTER, Edward Jerome 4
WEBSTER, Edwin Hanson H
WEBSTER, Edwin Harrison 5
WEBSTER, Edwin Sibley 3
WEBSTER, Edwin Sibley Jr. 3
WEBSTER, Eugene Carroll 1
WEBSTER, Francis Marion 1
WEBSTER, Frank Daniel 1
WEBSTER, Frank G. 2
WEBSTER, Frederic Smith 4
WEBSTER, George Sidney 1
WEBSTER, George Smedley 1
WEBSTER, George Van 1
  O'Linda
WEBSTER, George 5
  Washington
WEBSTER, Harold E. 4
WEBSTER, Harold Tucker 3
WEBSTER, Harrie 1
WEBSTER, Helen 1
  Livermore
WEBSTER, Henry Kitchell 1
WEBSTER, Hutton 3
WEBSTER, Hutton Jr. 1
WEBSTER, J. Stanley 4
WEBSTER, James R. 3
WEBSTER, Jean 1

WEBSTER, Jerome Pierce 6
WEBSTER, John Clarence 2
WEBSTER, John Hunter 1
WEBSTER, John Lee 1
WEBSTER, John White H
WEBSTER, Joseph Dana H
WEBSTER, Leslie Tillotson 2
WEBSTER, Lorin 1
WEBSTER, Margaret 5
WEBSTER, Marjorie Fraser 4
WEBSTER, Nathan 1
  Burnham
WEBSTER, Noah H
WEBSTER, Paul Kimball 3
WEBSTER, Pelatiah 1
WEBSTER, Ralph Waldo 1
WEBSTER, Reginald H. 4
WEBSTER, Robert Morris 4
WEBSTER, Sidney 1
WEBSTER, Taylor H
WEBSTER, Warren 1
WEBSTER, William 5
WEBSTER, William 5
  Clarence
WEBSTER, William 4
  Franklin
WEBSTER, William Grant 1
WEBSTER, William Reuben 2
WECHSLER, Isreal Spanier 4
WECKLER, Herman L. 5
WECTER, Dixon 3
WEDDELL, Alexander 1
  Wilbourne
WEDDELL, Donald J. 3
WEDDERBURN, Joseph 2
  Henry Maclagan
WEDDERSPOON, William 1
  Rhind
WEDDINGTON, Frank 4
  Ruel
WEDEL, Paul John 5
WEDEL, Theodore Otto 5
WEDEMEYER, William 1
  Walter
WEE, Mons O. 1
WEED, Alonzo Rogers 1
WEED, Charles Frederick 1
WEED, Clarence Moores 2
WEED, Clive 1
WEED, Clyde E. 6
WEED, Edwin Gardner 1
WEED, Frank Watkins 1
WEED, George Ludington 1
WEED, Hugh Hourston 3
  Craigie
WEED, J. Spencer 5
WEED, Jefferson 1
WEED, Lewis Hill 3
WEED, LeRoy Jefferson 4
WEED, Samuel Richards 1
WEED, Smith Mead 1
WEED, Theodore Linus 5
WEED, Thurlow 1
WEED, Walter Harvey 2
WEEDEN, William Babcock 1
WEEDON, Leslie 1
  Washington
WEEKLEY, William Marion 1
WEEKS, Alanson 2
WEEKS, Andrew Jackson 1
WEEKS, Arland Deyett 1
WEEKS, Bartow Sumter 1
WEEKS, Benjamin D. 2
WEEKS, Carl 4
WEEKS, Charles Peter 1
WEEKS, David Fairchild 1
WEEKS, Edgar 1
WEEKS, Edwin Lord 1
WEEKS, Edwin Ruthven 1
WEEKS, Francis Darling 4
WEEKS, Frank Bentley 1
WEEKS, George H. 1
WEEKS, Grenville Mellen 1
WEEKS, H. Hobart 3
WEEKS, Harry Curtis 5
WEEKS, John A. 1
WEEKS, John Eliakim 2
WEEKS, John Elmer 2
WEEKS, John L. 3
WEEKS, John Wingate H
WEEKS, John Wingate 1
WEEKS, Joseph H
WEEKS, Joseph Dame H
WEEKS, Mary Harmon 1
WEEKS, Ralph Emerson 3
WEEKS, Raymond 1
WEEKS, Robert Kelley H
WEEKS, Rufus Wells 1
WEEKS, Sinclair 5
WEEKS, Stephen 1
  Beauregard
WEEKS, Stephen Holmes 1
WEEKS, Walter Scott 2
WEEKS, William Raymond 4

WEEMS, Capell Lain 4
WEEMS, John Crompton H
WEEMS, Julius Buel 1
WEEMS, Mason Locke H
WEEMS, Wharton Ewell 4
WEER, John Henry 2
WEESE, A. O. 3
WEET, Herbert Seeley 5
WEFALD, Knud 1
WEGEMANN, Carroll 6
Harvey
WEGENER, Theodore H. 4
WEGER, George Stephen 1
WEGG, David Spencer 1
WEGLEIN, David Emrich 5
WEGMANN, Edward 1
WEHE, Frank Rumrill 4
WEHLE, Louis Brandeis 3
WEHLER, Charles Emanuel 1
WEHLING, Louis Albert 6
WEHMEYER, Lewis 5
E(dgar)
WEHRHAN, Nelson W. 6
WEHRLE, Vincent 1
WEHRLE, William Otto 3
Joseph
WEHRMANN, Henry 5
WEHRWEIN, George 2
Simon
WEIBLE, Rillmond 5
Fernando
WEIBY, Maxwell Oliver 4
WEICHEL, Alvin F. 4
WEICHER, John 5
WEICHSEL, Christian 5
C(arl)
WEICKER, Theodore 1
WEICKER, Theodore 5
WEIDENMANN, Jacob H
WEIDIG, Adolf 5
WEIDLER, Albert Greer 3
WEIDLER, Deleth Eber 4
WEIDLER, Victor Otterbein 3
WEIDMAN, Charles 6
WEIDMAN, Frederick 3
Deforest
WEIDMAN, Samuel 2
WEIDNER, Carl A. 1
WEIDNER, Revere Franklin 1
WEIGEL, Albert Charles 4
WEIGEL, Eugene John 6
WEIGEL, George Kibler 1
WEIGEL, William 1
WEIGHTMAN, Richard 1
Coxe
WEIGHTMAN, Richard H
Hanson
WEIGLE, Luther Allen 6
WEIK, Jesse William 3
WEIKEL, Anna Hamlin 5
WEIKEL, Charles Henry 5
Harrison
WEIL, A. Leo 1
WEIL, Adolph Leopold 3
WEIL, Ann Yezner 5
WEIL, Carl 1
WEIL, Frank L. 3
WEIL, Fred Alban 1
WEIL, Irving 5
WEIL, Lee Herman 5
WEIL, Louis A. 3
WEIL, Oscar 4
WEIL, Richard Jr. 3
WEIL, Robert T. Jr. 6
WEILAND, Christian 1
Frederick van Leeuwen
WEILER, Royal William 1
WEILL, Kurt 3
WEILL, Milton 6
WEIMAN, Rita 4
WEIMER, Albert Barnes 1
WEIMER, Bernal Robinson 3
WEIMER, Claud F. 3
WEINBERG, Benjamin 5
Franklin
WEINBERG, Bernard 5
WEINBERG, Robert 6
Charles
WEINBERG, Sidney James 5
WEINBERG, Tobias 5
WEINBERGER, Jacob 6
WEINER, Joseph Lee 6
WEINERMAN, Edwin 5
Richard
WEINERT, Albert 2
WEINGARTEN, Joe 4
WEINGARTEN, Lawrence 6
A.
WEINHANDL, Ferdinand 6
WEINIG, Arthur John 4
WEINMAN, Adolph 3
Alexander
WEINMANN, Joseph Peter 4
WEINREICH, Uriel 5

WEINSTEIN, Alexander 2
WEINSTEIN, Jacob Joseph 6
WEINSTEIN, Joe 4
WEINSTOCK, Harris 5
WEINSTOCK, Herbert 5
WEINTAL, Edward 5
WEINTRAUB, Abraham 6
Allen
WEINZIRL, Adolph 4
WEIR, Ernest Tener 3
WEIR, F. Roney 1
WEIR, Hugh C. 1
WEIR, Irene 2
WEIR, J. Alden 1
WEIR, James Jr. 1
WEIR, John Ferguson 1
WEIR, John M. 2
WEIR, Levi Candee 1
WEIR, Paul 5
WEIR, Robert Fulton H
WEIR, Robert Walter H
WEIR, Samuel 2
WEIR, W. Victor 6
WEIR, William Clarence 1
WEIR, William Figley 3
WEIS, Mrs. Charles William 4
Jr.
WEISBERG, Harold Charles 5
WEISBERGER, David 4
WEISE, Arthur James 4
WEISENBURG, Theodore 1
WEISENBURGER, Walter 2
Bertheau
WEISER, Emilius James 1
WEISER, Harry Boyer 4
WEISER, Johann Conrad H
WEISER, Walter R. 1
WEISGERBER, William 3
Edwin
WEISIGER, Kendall 6
WEISL, Edwin Louis 5
WEISMAN, Russell 2
WEISMANN, Walter W. 5
WEISS, Adolph A. 5
WEISS, Albert Paul 1
WEISS, Anton Charles 1
WEISS, George 5
WEISS, John H
WEISS, John Morris 4
WEISS, Lewis Allen 3
WEISS, Louis Stix 3
WEISS, Richard Alexander 6
WEISS, Samuel 3
WEISS, Samuel 6
WEISS, Seymour 5
WEISS, William 3
WEISS, William Casper 1
WEISS, William Erhard 2
WEISSE, Charles H. 1
WEISSE, Faneuil Dunkin 1
WEISSERT, Augustus 4
Gordon
WEITZ, Rudolph Wilson 6
WEITZEL, George Thomas 1
WEITZEL, Godfrey H
WEITZMAN, Ellis 5
WEIZMANN, Chaim 4
WEIZMANN, Chalm 3
WELBORN, Curtis R. 5
WELBORN, Ira Clinton 5
WELBORN, Jesse Floyd 5
WELBY, Amelia Ball H
Coppuck
WELCH, Adonijah Strong H
WELCH, Anthony 4
Cummings
WELCH, Archibald Ashley 1
WELCH, Ashbel H
WELCH, Charles Edgar 4
WELCH, Charles Whitefield 2
WELCH, Dale Dennis 6
WELCH, Deshler 4
WELCH, Douglas 5
WELCH, Edward Sohier 2
WELCH, Frank H
WELCH, George Martin 4
WELCH, Herbert 5
WELCH, Howard A. 3
WELCH, J. Leo 4
WELCH, John 1
WELCH, John Collins 4
WELCH, John Edgar 1
WELCH, John R. 4
WELCH, Joseph N. 4
WELCH, Livingston 6
WELCH, Norman A. 4
WELCH, Paul M. 5
WELCH, Paul R. 3
WELCH, Philip Henry H
WELCH, Richard J. 1
WELCH, Roy Dickinson 4
WELCH, Samuel Wallace 1
WELCH, Stewart Henry 5
WELCH, Thomas Anthony 4
WELCH, Vincent S. 1
WELCH, W. S. 3

WELCH, William Addams 2
WELCH, William Henry * 1
WELCH, William McNair 5
WELCH, William Wickham 4
WELD, Alfred Winsor 4
WELD, C. Minot 4
WELD, Francis Minot 2
WELD, Frank Augustine 4
WELD, J. Linzee 3
WELD, Laenas Gifford 1
WELD, LeRoy Dougherty 6
WELD, Stephen Minot 1
WELD, Theodore Dwight H
WELD, Thomas H
WELD, William Ernest 3
WELD, William Ernest 4
WELDIN, John Chilcote H
WELDON, Charles Dater 1
WELDON, James Brewer 6
WELDON, Lawrence 1
WELDON, R. Laurence 5
WELFLE, Frederick Edgar 5
WELFORD, Walter 5
WELKE, Edward Arthur 3
WELKER, Herman 5
WELKER, Philip Albert 1
WELKER, William Henry 3
WELLBORN, Marshall H
Johnson
WELLBORN, Maximilian 4
Bethune
WELLBORN, Olin 1
WELLBORN, Olin III 1
WELLDON, Samuel A. 4
WELLER, Carl Vernon 3
WELLER, Charles Frederick 4
WELLER, Charles Heald 1
WELLER, Frank I. 3
WELLER, Fred Warren 4
WELLER, George Emery 1
WELLER, John B. H
WELLER, LeRoy 5
WELLER, Michael Ignatius 1
WELLER, Ovington E. 2
WELLER, Reginald Heber 1
WELLER, Royal H. 1
WELLER, Stuart 1
WELLES, Charles F. H
WELLES, Donald Phelps 6
WELLES, Edgar Thaddeus 1
WELLES, Edward Kenneth 5
WELLES, George Denison 1
WELLES, Gideon H
WELLES, Henry Hunter Jr. 2
WELLES, Kenneth Brakeley 3
WELLES, Noah 1
WELLES, Roger 1
WELLES, Sumner 4
WELLESZ, Egon Joseph 6
WELLFORD, Edwin 3
Taliaferro
WELLHOUSE, Frederick 1
WELLING, James Clarke H
WELLING, John C. 4
WELLING, Milton Holmes 5
WELLING, Richard 2
WELLINGTON, Arthur H
Mellen
WELLINGTON, C. G. 3
WELLINGTON, Charles 1
WELLINGTON, Charles 3
Oliver
WELLINGTON, George 1
Brainerd
WELLINGTON, George 1
Louis
WELLINGTON, Herbert 4
Galbraith
WELLINGTON, Richard 6
WELLINGTON, William H. 1
Churchill
WELLIVER, Judson 2
WELLIVER, Lester Allen 6
WELLMAN, Arthur 2
Holbrook
WELLMAN, Beth Lucy 3
WELLMAN, Charles Aaron 5
WELLMAN, Creighton 5
WELLMAN, Francis L. 2
WELLMAN, Guy 1
WELLMAN, Hiller Crowell 3
WELLMAN, Holley 6
Garfield
WELLMAN, Mabel 5
Thacher
WELLMAN, Paul Iselin 4
WELLMAN, Samuel 1
Thomas
WELLMAN, Sargent 4
Holbrook
WELLMAN, Walter 1
WELLMAN, William 6
Augustus
WELLONS, William Brock H
WELLS, Addison E. 1
WELLS, Agnes Ermina 1

WELLS, Alfred H
WELLS, Almond Brown 1
WELLS, Amos Russel 1
WELLS, Arthur George 1
WELLS, Arthur Register 3
WELLS, Benjamin Willis 1
WELLS, Brooks Hughes 1
WELLS, Bulkeley 1
WELLS, Calvin 1
WELLS, Carolyn 2
WELLS, Carveth 3
WELLS, Catherine Boott 4
WELLS, Channing 5
McGregory
WELLS, Charles Edwin 1
WELLS, Charles J(oseph) 6
WELLS, Charles Luke 1
WELLS, Charles Raymond 4
WELLS, Chester 2
WELLS, Daniel Halsey 1
WELLS, David Ames H
WELLS, David Collin 1
WELLS, David Dwight 1
WELLS, Donald A. 5
WELLS, Ebenezer Tracy 1
WELLS, Edgar Herbert 1
WELLS, Edgar Huidekoper 1
WELLS, Edward D. 1
WELLS, Edward Hubbard 1
WELLS, Edward L. 4
WELLS, Edward P. 1
WELLS, Erastus H
WELLS, Everett F. 5
WELLS, Frank Oren 1
WELLS, Frederic De Witt 1
WELLS, Frederic Lyman 4
WELLS, Frederick Brown 3
WELLS, George Burnham 1
WELLS, George Fitch 1
WELLS, George Harlan 6
WELLS, George Miller 3
WELLS, George Washington 1
WELLS, Harry Edward 2
WELLS, Harry Gideon 2
WELLS, Harry Lumm 6
WELLS, Heber Manning 1
WELLS, Henry H
WELLS, Henry Parkhurst 1
WELLS, Herbert George 2
WELLS, Herbert Johnson 1
WELLS, Hermon J. 2
WELLS, Horace H
WELLS, Horace Lemuel 1
WELLS, Ira Kent 1
WELLS, J. Brent 4
WELLS, James Earl 4
WELLS, James Madison H
WELLS, James Simpson 1
Chester
WELLS, Joel Cheney * 3
WELLS, Joel Reaves 5
WELLS, John * H
WELLS, John Barnes 1
WELLS, John Daniel 1
WELLS, John Edwin 2
WELLS, John Mason 5
WELLS, John Miller 2
WELLS, John Sullivan H
WELLS, John Walter 1
WELLS, Kenneth Robert 3
WELLS, Lemuel Henry 1
WELLS, Linton 6
WELLS, Marguerite Jo Van 1
Dalsem (Mrs. Thaddeus
R. Wells)
WELLS, Marguerite Milton 4
WELLS, Mary Evelyn 6
WELLS, Newell Woolsey 4
WELLS, Newton Alonzo 1
WELLS, Orlando William 1
WELLS, Oscar 3
WELLS, Philip Patterson 1
WELLS, Ralph Gent 6
WELLS, Ralph Olney 2
WELLS, Richard Harris 2
WELLS, Robert William H
WELLS, Roger Clark 2
WELLS, Rolla 2
WELLS, Samuel Calvin 1
WELLS, Samuel Roberts H
WELLS, Stuart Wilder 5
WELLS, Theodore D(onald) 2
WELLS, Thomas Bucklin 2
WELLS, Thomas Tileston 2
WELLS, Walter Farrington 3
WELLS, Webster 1
WELLS, William Calvin 2
WELLS, William Charles 1
WELLS, William Charles 1
WELLS, William Edwin 1
WELLS, William Harvey 1
WELLS, William Hill H
WELLS, William Hughes 1
WELLS, William Vincent 4
WELLS, William Widney 5
WELLSTOOD, William 1

WELSH, Ashton Leroy 4
WELSH, Charles 1
WELSH, George A. 6
WELSH, George A. 5
WELSH, George Wilson 6
WELSH, Herbert 1
WELSH, John H
WELSH, John Rushing III 6
WELSH, Judson Perry 4
WELSH, Lilian 1
WELSH, Robert James 5
WELSH, Robert Kaye 2
WELSH, Vernon M. 5
WELSHIMER, Helen 3
Louise
WELSHIMER, Pearl H. 3
WELTE, Carl Michael 3
WELTMER, (Cyrus) Ernest 6
WELTMER, Sidney Abram 1
WELTY, Benjamin Franklin 5
WEMPLE, William Lester 5
WEMPLE, William Yates 1
WEMYSS, Francis Courtney H
WEMYSS, William Hatch 5
WENCHEL, John Philip 4
WENCKEBACH, Carla 1
WENDE, Ernest 1
WENDEL, Hugo Christian 2
Martin
WENDELL, Arthur Rindge 3
WENDELL, Barrett 1
WENDELL, Edith 1
Greenough
WENDELL, George 1
Vincent
WENDELL, James Isaac 3
WENDELL, Oliver Clinton 1
WENDEROTH, Oscar 5
WENDLING, George 1
Reuben
WENDOVER, Peter H
Hercules
WENDT, Edwin Frederick 3
WENDT, Gerald (Louis) 6
WENDT, Henry W. 4
WENDT, Julia Bracken 2
WENDT, William 2
WENDTE, Charles William 1
WENE, Elmer H. 5
WENGER, Joseph Numa 5
WENGER, Oliver Clarence 3
WENGERT, Egbert 4
Semmann
WENIGER, Willibald 3
WENKE, Adolph E. 4
WENLEY, Archibald 5
Gibson
WENLEY, Robert Mark 1
WENNAGEL, Leonard 6
Alvin
WENNER, Frank 3
WENNER, George Unangst 1
WENNER, Howard 5
Theodore
WENNER, William Ervin 2
WENNING, T. H. 4
WENNINGER, Francis 1
Joseph
WENRICH, Calvin 5
Naftzinger
WENSLEY, Robert Lytle 4
WENTE, Carl Frederick 5
WENTE, Edward 5
Christopher
WENTWORTH, Benning H
WENTWORTH, Catherine 2
Denkman
WENTWORTH, Cecile De 1
WENTWORTH, Edward 3
Norris
WENTWORTH, Franklin 3
Harcourt
WENTWORTH, Fred 2
Wesley
WENTWORTH, George 1
Albert
WENTWORTH, John * H
WENTWORTH, John H
WENTWORTH, John Jr. H
WENTWORTH, Marion 5
Craig
WENTWORTH, Paul H
WENTWORTH, Tappan 1
WENTWORTH, Walter 5
Allerton
WENTWORTH, William H
Pitt
WENTZ, Daniel Bertsch Jr. 1
WENTZ, George Elmore 4
WENTZ, Louis Haines 2
WENTZ, Peter Leland 6
WENZEL, Caroline 3
WENZEL, Thomas Philip 6
WENZELL, Albert Beck 1
WENZELL, Henry Burleigh 4

WENZLAFF, Gustav Gottlieb 4
WEPPNER, Oliver A. 4
WERBE, Thomas Chandler Sr. 3
WERDEN, Reed H
WERDEN, Robert M. 5
WERDER, Xavier Oswald 4
WERFEL, Franz 2
WERKMAN, Chester Hamlin 4
WERLE, Edward C. 4
WERLEIN, Elizabeth Thomas 2
WERMUTH, Burt 6
WERNAER, Robert Maximilian 5
WERNER, Adolph 1
WERNER, Edwin H. 6
WERNER, Heinz 1
WERNER, Henry Paul 3
WERNER, Henry Paul 4
WERNER, Joseph Gustave 6
WERNER, Max 1
WERNER, Oscar Emil Wade 3
WERNER, Victor Davis 5
WERNER, William E. 1
WERNER, William 1
WERNTZ, William Welling 4
WERNWAG, Lewis H
WERRENRATH, Reinald 1
WERT, James Edwin 4
WERTENBAKER, Charles Christian 3
WERTENBAKER, Charles Poindexter 1
WERTENBAKER, Thomas Jefferson 4
WERTH, Alexander 5
WERTHEIM, Maurice 3
WERTMAN, Floyd Rollan 2
WERTMAN, Kenneth Franklin 4
WERTMULLER, Adolph Ulrich H
WERTS, George Theodore 1
WERTZ, Edwin Slusser 2
WERTZ, George M. 1
WESBROOK, Frank Fairchild 1
WESCOAT, L. S. 5
WESCOTT, Cassius Douglas 2
WESCOTT, James Barney 3
WESCOTT, John Wesley 1
WESCOTT, Orville De Witt 5
WESEEN, Maurice Harley 1
WESLEY, Charles Sumner 4
WESLEY, Clarence Newton 5
WESSELHOEFT, Conrad 1
WESSELHOEFT, Lily Foster 1
WESSELHOFT, Walter 4
WESSELINK, John 5
WESSELLS, Henry Walton Jr. 1
WESSLINK, Gerritt William 4
WESSON, Charles Macon 3
WESSON, Daniel Baird 1
WESSON, David 1
WESSON, Miley Barton 6
WEST, Allen Brown 1
WEST, Andrew Fleming 2
WEST, Anson 1
WEST, Archa Kelly 1
WEST, Arthur 1
WEST, Arthur Benjamin 5
WEST, Ben 6
WEST, Benjamin * H
WEST, Caleb Walton 1
WEST, Charles 5
WEST, Charles Cameron 3
WEST, Charles Edwin 1
WEST, Charles H. 1
WEST, Christopher 6
WEST, Clifford Hardy 1
WEST, DuVal 3
WEST, E. Lovette 2
WEST, Edward Augustus 3
WEST, Egbert Watson 2
WEST, Elizabeth Howard 2
WEST, Erdman 4
WEST, Ernest Holley 5
WEST, Francis H
WEST, George H
WEST, George Henry 1
WEST, George N. 1
WEST, George V. 6
WEST, Hamilton Atchison 1
WEST, Helen Hunt 4
WEST, Henry Litchfield 1
WEST, Henry Sergeant H
WEST, Henry Skinner 1
WEST, Herbert Faulkner 6
WEST, Howard H(iram) 5
WEST, James Edward 2

WEST, James Harcourt 4
WEST, James Hartwell 4
WEST, James Samuel 5
WEST, Jesse Felix 1
WEST, John Chester 4
WEST, Joseph H
WEST, Judson S. 3
WEST, Junius Edgar 2
WEST, Kenyon 4
WEST, Levon 5
WEST, Mary Brodie Crump 4
WEST, Max 1
WEST, Millard F. 1
WEST, Milton H. 2
WEST, Nathanael H
WEST, Nathanael 4
WEST, Olin 3
WEST, Oswald 5
WEST, Paul 1
WEST, Paul Brown 4
WEST, Preston C. 5
WEST, Raymond M. 1
WEST, Robert Rout 4
WEST, Roy Owen 3
WEST, Samuel H
WEST, Samuel H. 1
WEST, Samuel Wallens 5
WEST, Thomas H
WEST, Thomas Dyson 1
WEST, Thomas Franklin 1
WEST, Thomas Hector 6
WEST, Thomas Henry 1
WEST, Thomas Henry 4
WEST, Thomas Henry Jr. 1
WEST, Victor J. 1
WEST, William Edward H
WEST, William Henry 1
WEST, William Stanley 1
WEST, Willis Mason 1
WESTBROOK, Arthur E. 4
WESTBROOK, Elroy Herman 1
WESTBROOK, John H
WESTBROOK, Lawrence 4
WESTBROOK, Theodoric Romeyn 1
WESTCOTT, Allan Ferguson 3
WESTCOTT, Charles Drake 5
WESTCOTT, Edward Noyes H
WESTCOTT, Frank Nash 1
WESTCOTT, Harry R. 6
WESTCOTT, James Diament Jr. 1
WESTCOTT, John Howell 2
WESTCOTT, Richard Nutter 6
WESTCOTT, Thompson H
WESTCOTT, Thompson Seiser 3
WESTENGARD, Jens Iverson 1
WESTENHAVER, David C. 1
WESTERFIELD, Ray Bert 4
WESTERFIELD, Samuel Zaza Jr. 5
WESTERGAARD, Harald Malcolm 3
WESTERLO, Rensselaer H
WESTERMAN, Harry James 2
WESTERMANN, William Linn 3
WESTERMEYER, H(arry) E(dward) 6
WESTERN, Forrest 5
WESTERN, Lucille 4
WESTERVELT, Emery Emmanuel 4
WESTERVELT, Esther Julia Manning 6
WESTERVELT, Jacob Aaron H
WESTERVELT, Marvin Zabriskie 1
WESTERVELT, William Irving 1
WESTERVELT, William Young 2
WESTFALL, Alfred R. 4
WESTFALL, Byron Lee 5
WESTFALL, Katherine Storey 1
WESTFALL, Othel D. 4
WESTFALL, W. D. A. 3
WESTFELDT, George G(ustaf) 2
WESTGATE, John Minton 1
WESTGATE, Lewis Gardner 2
WESTHAFER, William Rader 1
WESTHUES, Henry J. 5
WESTINGHOUSE, George 1
WESTINGHOUSE, Henry Herman 1

WESTINGHOUSE, Marguerite Erskine Walker 1
WESTLAKE, Emory H. 4
WESTLAKE, J. Willis 1
WESTLEY, George Hembert 1
WESTMORE, George Bud 6
WESTON, Charles Sidney 4
WESTON, Charles Valentine 1
WESTON, Edmund Brownell 1
WESTON, Edward 1
WESTON, Edward 3
WESTON, Edward F. 6
WESTON, Edward Payson Stewart 1
WESTON, Elizabeth 4
WESTON, Eugene Jr. 5
WESTON, Francis Hopkins 4
WESTON, Frank Morey 5
WESTON, George 1
WESTON, Harold 5
WESTON, Harry Elisha 1
WESTON, Henry Griggs 1
WESTON, James Augustus 1
WESTON, James Francis 3
WESTON, John Burns 1
WESTON, John Francis 1
WESTON, Karl Ephraim 1
WESTON, Nathan Austin 1
WESTON, Robert Spurr 2
WESTON, S. Burns 1
WESTON, Sidney Adams 5
WESTON, Stephen Francis 1
WESTON, Theodore 1
WESTON, Thomas H
WESTON, William H
WESTON, William 5
WESTOVER, Myron F. 1
WESTOVER, Oscar 1
WESTOVER, Russell Channing 1
WESTOVER, Wendell 4
WESTWOOD, Horace 3
WESTWOOD, Richard W. 4
WETHERALD, Charles E. 5
WETHERBEE, Frank Irving 5
WETHERBEE, George 4
WETHERED, John H
WETHERELL, Elizabeth 1
WETHERILL, Charles Mayer H
WETHERILL, Horace Greeley 4
WETHERILL, Samuel * H
WETJEN, Albert Richard 2
WETMORE, Claude Hazeltine 4
WETMORE, Edmund 1
WETMORE, Edward Ditmars 2
WETMORE, Elizabeth Bisland 1
WETMORE, Frank O. 1
WETMORE, George Peabody 1
WETMORE, James Alphonso 1
WETMORE, Maude A. K. 4
WETMORE, Monroe Nichols 1
WETTACH, Robert Hasley 4
WETTEN, Albert Hayes 3
WETTEN, Emil C. 2
WETTERAU, Oliver George 6
WETTERAU, Theodore Carl Jr. 1
WETTLING, Louis Eugene 1
WETZEL, Harry H. 4
WETZEL, John Wesley 2
WETZEL, Lewis H
WETZLER, Joseph 1
WEXLER, Harry 4
WEXLER, Jacob 6
WEXLER, Solomon 1
WEYANDT, Carl Stanley 4
WEYBURN, Lyon 3
WEYER, Edward Moffat 2
WEYERHAEUSER, Charles Augustus 1
WEYERHAEUSER, Frederick 1
WEYERHAEUSER, Frederick Edward 1
WEYERHAEUSER, John Philip 1
WEYERHAEUSER, John Philip Jr. 1
WEYERHAEUSER, Rudolph Michael 1
WEYGANDT, Carl Victor 4
WEYGANDT, Cornelius 3
WEYHE, Erhard 6
WEYL, Charles 5

WEYL, Hermann 3
WEYL, Max 1
WEYL, Walter Edward 1
WEYL, Woldemar Anatol 6
WEYLER, George Lester 5
WEYMOUTH, Aubrey 1
WEYMOUTH, Clarence Raymond 2
WEYMOUTH, Frank Elwin 1
WEYMOUTH, George Warren 1
WEYMOUTH, Thomas Rote 3
WEYRAUCH, Martin Henry 3
WEYSSE, Arthur Wisswald 5
WHALEN, Grover A. 4
WHALEN, John 1
WHALEN, Robert E. 3
WHALEY, A. R. 1
WHALEY, George P. 2
WHALEY, James V. 4
WHALEY, Kellian Van Rensalear 1
WHALEY, Percival Huntington 4
WHALEY, Richard Smith 3
WHALING, Horace Morland Jr. 6
WHALING, Thornton 4
WHALLEY, Edward H
WHALLON, Edward Payson 1
WHALLON, Reuben H
WHALLON, Walter Lowrie 6
WHAM, Benjamin 5
WHAPLES, Meigs H. 1
WHAREY, James Blanton 1
WHARTON, Anne Hollingsworth 1
WHARTON, Arthur Orlando 5
WHARTON, Carol Forbes 3
WHARTON, Charles Henry H
WHARTON, Charles S. 5
WHARTON, Edith 1
WHARTON, Francis H
WHARTON, Henry Marvin 1
WHARTON, Henry Redwood 1
WHARTON, James E. 4
WHARTON, James Pearce 4
WHARTON, Jesse 1
WHARTON, Joseph 1
WHARTON, Lang 2
WHARTON, Morton Bryan 1
WHARTON, Richard H
WHARTON, Robert 1
WHARTON, Samuel H
WHARTON, Theodore Finley 2
WHARTON, Thomas 1
WHARTON, Thomas Isaac 1
WHARTON, Thomas Kelah H
WHARTON, Turner Ashby 1
WHARTON, Vernon Lane 4
WHARTON, William Fisher 1
WHARTON, William H. H
WHARTON, William P. 6
WHATCOAT, Richard H
WHATMOUGH, Joshua 4
WHEAT, Alfred Adams 1
WHEAT, Carl Irving 4
WHEAT, George Seay 1
WHEAT, Harry G(rove) 6
WHEAT, Renville 5
WHEAT, William Howard 1
WHEATLAND, Marcus Fitzherbert 1
WHEATLEY, Phillis 1
WHEATLEY, Richard 4
WHEATLEY, William H
WHEATLEY, William Alonzo 5
WHEATON, Frank 1
WHEATON, Henry H
WHEATON, Horace 1
WHEATON, Laban H
WHEATON, Loyd 1
WHEATON, Nathaniel Sheldon 1
WHEDON, Daniel Denison H
WHEDON, John Fielding 5
WHEELAN, Fairfax Henry 4
WHEELAN, James Nicholas 1
WHEELER, Albert Gallatin 1
WHEELER, Albert Harry 5
WHEELER, Alvin Sawyer 1
WHEELER, Andrew Carpenter 1
WHEELER, Arthur Dana 1
WHEELER, Arthur Leslie 1
WHEELER, Arthur Martin 1
WHEELER, Benjamin Ide 1
WHEELER, Burr 4

WHEELER, Burton Kendall 6
WHEELER, C. Gilbert 1
WHEELER, Candace Thurber 1
WHEELER, Candace Thurber 2
WHEELER, Charles Barker 1
WHEELER, Charles Brewster 2
WHEELER, Charles Francis 1
WHEELER, Charles Gardner 3
WHEELER, Charles Kennedy 4
WHEELER, Charles (Reginald) 6
WHEELER, Charles Stetson 1
WHEELER, Daniel Davis 1
WHEELER, Daniel Edwin 6
WHEELER, David Hilton 1
WHEELER, Earle Gilmore 6
WHEELER, Ebenezer Smith 1
WHEELER, Edward Jewitt 1
WHEELER, Edward Warren 4
WHEELER, Esther Willard 3
WHEELER, Everett Pepperrell 1
WHEELER, Ezra H
WHEELER, Franklin Carroll 4
WHEELER, Frederick Freeman 1
WHEELER, Frederick Seymour 1
WHEELER, George Bourne 2
WHEELER, George Carpenter 1
WHEELER, George Montague 4
WHEELER, George Wakeman 1
WHEELER, Grattan Henry H
WHEELER, Harold Francis 3
WHEELER, Harris Ansel 4
WHEELER, Harrison H. H
WHEELER, Harry A. 3
WHEELER, Henry 1
WHEELER, Henry Lord 1
WHEELER, Henry Nathan 1
WHEELER, Herbert Locke 1
WHEELER, Hiram C. 4
WHEELER, Hiram Nicholas 1
WHEELER, Homer Jay 1
WHEELER, Homer Webster 1
WHEELER, Howard Duryce 3
WHEELER, Howard V. 3
WHEELER, Hoyt Henry 1
WHEELER, James Cooper 1
WHEELER, James Everett 1
WHEELER, James Rignall 1
WHEELER, Janet 1
WHEELER, Jean Huleatt (Mrs. Joseph Coolidge Wheeler) 5
WHEELER, Jerome Byron 1
WHEELER, John Brooks 1
WHEELER, John DeBerry 5
WHEELER, John Egbert 2
WHEELER, John Hill H
WHEELER, John Martin 1
WHEELER, John Neville 6
WHEELER, John Samuel 1
WHEELER, John Taylor 3
WHEELER, John Wilson 1
WHEELER, Joseph 1
WHEELER, Joseph C. 5
WHEELER, Joseph Trank 1
WHEELER, Leslie Allen 5
WHEELER, Loren E. 1
WHEELER, Marianna 4
WHEELER, Mary Curtis 5
WHEELER, Mary Sparkes 1
WHEELER, Maxwell Stevenson 3
WHEELER, Nathaniel H
WHEELER, Nelson P. 4
WHEELER, Olin Dunbar 4
WHEELER, Post 6
WHEELER, Raymond Albert 1
WHEELER, Raymond Holder 4
WHEELER, Richard Smith 5
WHEELER, Rollo Clark 4
WHEELER, Royall Tyler 1
WHEELER, Ruth 2
WHEELER, Schuyler Skaats 1
WHEELER, Scott 1
WHEELER, Stephen Morse 4
WHEELER, Walter Heber Jr. 6
WHEELER, Walton M. Jr. 1
WHEELER, Wayne Bidwell 1
WHEELER, William Adolphus H

WHEELER, William Alman H
WHEELER, William Archie 5
WHEELER, William 1
   Morton
WHEELER, William 4
   Reginald
WHEELER, William Riley 1
WHEELER, William Webb 1
WHEELER, Wilmot Fitch 4
WHEELOCK, Charles 4
   Delorma
WHEELOCK, Edward 1
WHEELOCK, Edwin 4
   Dwight
WHEELOCK, Eleazar 1
WHEELOCK, Harry Bergen 1
WHEELOCK, Irene 1
   Grosvenor
WHEELOCK, John H
WHEELOCK, Joseph Albert 1
WHEELOCK, Lucy 2
WHEELOCK, Ward 3
WHEELOCK, William 1
   Almy
WHEELOCK, William 2
   Hawxhurst
WHEELWRIGHT, Edmund 1
   March
WHEELWRIGHT, John H
WHEELWRIGHT, John 1
   Tyler
WHEELWRIGHT, Mary 6
   Cabot
WHEELWRIGHT, Philip 5
   Ellis
WHEELWRIGHT, Robert 4
WHEELWRIGHT, Thomas 1
   Stewart
WHEELWRIGHT, William H
WHEELWRIGHT, William 1
   Dana
WHELAN, Charles A. 2
WHELAN, Charles Elbert 1
WHELAN, Edward J. 5
WHELAN, James H
WHELAN, Ralph 2
WHELAN, Richard Vincent H
WHELAND, Edward F. 3
WHELAND, Zenas Windsor 3
WHELCHEL, B. Frank 3
WHELCHEL, Clarence 6
   Anthony
WHELCHEL, John Esten 6
WHELEN, Townsend 1
WHELESS, Joseph 5
WHELPLEY, Benjamin 4
   Lincoln
WHELPLEY, Henry Milton 1
WHELPLEY, James 4
   Davenport
WHELPLEY, Medley 5
   Gordon Brittain
WHELPTON, Pascal Kidder 4
WHERRETT, Harry Scott 2
WHERRY, Arthur Cornelius 2
WHERRY, Elwood Morris 1
WHERRY, Frank Gilbert 6
WHERRY, John 1
WHERRY, Kenneth S. 3
WHERRY, William 1
   Buchanan
WHERRY, William Mackey 1
WHERRY, William Mackey 4
   Jr.
WHETSTONE, Walter 1
WHETZEL, Herbert Hice 2
WHICHER, George Frisbie 3
WHICHER, George Meason 1
WHIDDEN, Bruce 6
WHIDDEN, Ray Allen 6
WHIFFEN, Mrs. Thomas H
WHIFFEN, Mrs. Thomas 1
WHIGHAM, Henry James 3
WHILEY, Charles Whipple 1
WHINERY, Samuel 1
WHIPPLE, Abraham H
WHIPPLE, Allen Oldfather 4
WHIPPLE, Amiel Weeks H
WHIPPLE, Charles Henry 1
WHIPPLE, Charles John 3
WHIPPLE, Edwin Percy 1
WHIPPLE, George 1
   Chandler
WHIPPLE, George Hoyt 6
WHIPPLE, Guy Montrose 4
WHIPPLE, Harvey 3
WHIPPLE, Henry Benjamin 1
WHIPPLE, Howard Gregory 6
WHIPPLE, Jay Northam 6
WHIPPLE, Leonidas 1
   Rutledge
WHIPPLE, Lucius Albert 3
WHIPPLE, Oliver Mayhew 1
WHIPPLE, Ralph W. 3
WHIPPLE, Sherman Leland 1
WHIPPLE, Squire H

WHIPPLE, Thomas Jr. H
WHIPPLE, Wayne 2
WHIPPLE, William H
WHIPPLE, William Denison 1
WHIPPLE, William G. 5
WHISENAND, James 4
   Franklin
WHISTLER, George H
   Washington
WHISTLER, James Abbott 1
   McNeill
WHISTLER, Joseph Nelson 1
   Garland
WHISTON, Frank Michael 5
WHITACRE, Frank Edward 5
WHITACRE, Horace J. 2
WHITACRE, John J. 4
WHITAKER, Albert Conser 5
WHITAKER, Alexander H
WHITAKER, Alma 3
WHITAKER, Benjamin 6
   Palmer
WHITAKER, Charles Harris 1
WHITAKER, Clem 4
WHITAKER, Daniel H
   Kimball
WHITAKER, Douglas 6
WHITAKER, Edward 1
   Gascoigne
WHITAKER, Edwards 4
WHITAKER, Elbert 6
   Coleman
WHITAKER, Epher 1
WHITAKER, Frank M. 1
WHITAKER, George 1
WHITAKER, Harriet 5
   Catherine Reed (Mrs.
   Charles Richard Whitaker)
WHITAKER, Harriet Reed 4
WHITAKER, Herbert 1
   Coleman
WHITAKER, Herman 1
WHITAKER, Hervey 1
   Williams
WHITAKER, John Albert 3
WHITAKER, John 2
   Thompson
WHITAKER, Lewis Alfred 6
WHITAKER, Martin D. 4
WHITAKER, Mary 4
   Scrimzeour
WHITAKER, Milton C. 4
WHITAKER, Nathaniel 1
WHITAKER, Nelson L. 3
WHITAKER, Nicholas 1
   Tillinghast
WHITAKER, Orvil R(obert) 5
WHITAKER, Ozi William 1
WHITAKER, Robert 2
WHITAKER, Samuel Estill 4
WHITAKER, U. A. 6
WHITAKER, Walter 1
   Claiborne
WHITAKER, William Force 1
WHITALL, Samuel Rucker 1
WHITBECK, R. H. 1
WHITCHER, Frances H
   Miriam Berry
WHITCHER, Frank Weston 1
WHITCHER, Mary H
WHITCHURCH, Irl 5
   Goldwin
WHITCOMB, David 6
WHITCOMB, David 6
   Twining
WHITCOMB, G. Henry 1
WHITCOMB, Ida Prentice 1
WHITCOMB, James 1
WHITCOMB, Merrick 4
WHITCOMB, Selden 1
   Lincoln
WHITCOMB, William 2
   Arthur
WHITE, Aaron Pancoast 2
WHITE, Albert Beebe 1
WHITE, Albert Blakeslee 1
WHITE, Albert Easton 4
WHITE, Albert Smith 1
WHITE, Alexander H
WHITE, Mrs. Alexander B. 5
   (Rassie Hoskins)
WHITE, Alexander M. 1
WHITE, Alfred Holmes 3
WHITE, Alfred Ludlow 3
WHITE, Alfred Tredway 1
WHITE, Allison H
WHITE, Alma 3
WHITE, Alvan Newton 2
WHITE, Andrew H
WHITE, Andrew Dickson 1
WHITE, Andrew John Jr. 1
WHITE, Arthur Cleveland 4
WHITE, Arthur Fairchild 1
WHITE, Aubrey Lee 3
WHITE, Austin John 2
WHITE, Bartow H

WHITE, Benjamin H
WHITE, Benjamin Franklin 4
WHITE, Bessie Bruce 5
WHITE, Bouck 5
WHITE, Campbell Patrick H
WHITE, Canvass H
WHITE, Caroline Earle 1
WHITE, Charles Abiathar 1
WHITE, Charles Alexander 6
WHITE, Charles Daniel 3
WHITE, Charles Edgar 4
WHITE, Charles Elmer Jr. 1
WHITE, Charles Harrison 2
WHITE, Charles Henry 1
WHITE, Charles Henry 3
WHITE, Charles Ignatius H
WHITE, Charles James 4
WHITE, Charles Joyce 3
WHITE, Charles Lincoln 1
WHITE, Charles Stanley 5
WHITE, Charles Thomas 3
WHITE, Clarence Cameron 4
WHITE, Clarence H. 2
WHITE, Clarence Hudson 1
WHITE, Compton Ignatius 3
WHITE, Courtland Yardley 1
   Jr.
WHITE, David H
WHITE, David 1
WHITE, David Stuart 2
WHITE, Dudley Allen 3
WHITE, Edmund Valentine 3
WHITE, Edward Albert 2
WHITE, Edward Brickell 1
WHITE, Edward Douglass H
WHITE, Edward Douglass 1
WHITE, Edward Franklin 1
WHITE, Edward Higgins II 4
WHITE, Edward Joseph 1
WHITE, E(dward) Laurence 5
WHITE, Edward Lucas 1
WHITE, Edwin 1
WHITE, Edwin 3
WHITE, Edwin Augustine 1
WHITE, Egbert 6
WHITE, Elijah B. 1
WHITE, Eliza Orne 2
WHITE, Ellen Gould H
   Harmon
WHITE, Ellen Gould 4
   Harmon
WHITE, Emerson Elbridge 1
WHITE, Emma Eaton (Mrs. 5
   Edward Franklin White)
WHITE, Erskine Norman 1
WHITE EYES H
WHITE, Florence Donnell 3
WHITE, Frances Hodges 4
WHITE, Francis H
WHITE, Francis 1
WHITE, Francis Johnstone 5
WHITE, Francis Samuel 1
WHITE, Francis W. 3
WHITE, Frank * 1
WHITE, Frank Edson 1
WHITE, Frank Marshall 4
WHITE, Frank Newhall 1
WHITE, Frank Russell 1
WHITE, Frank Shelley 1
WHITE, Frank Thomas 6
   Matthews
WHITE, Frederick W. 1
WHITE, Gaylord Starin 1
WHITE, George H
WHITE, George 3
WHITE, George Ared 2
WHITE, George Avery 3
WHITE, George Edward 2
WHITE, George Frederic 1
WHITE, George Leonard H
WHITE, George Loring 5
WHITE, George Starr 4
WHITE, George W. H
WHITE, George Washington 1
WHITE, George Whitney 1
WHITE, Georgia Laura 3
WHITE, Gilbert 1
WHITE, Greenough 1
WHITE, H. Lee 5
WHITE, Harold Tredway 4
WHITE, Harry 3
WHITE, Harry Dexter H
WHITE, Harry Dexter 2
WHITE, Harry Dexter 4
WHITE, Hays B. 1
WHITE, Helen Constance 4
WHITE, Henry * 1
WHITE, Henry 1
WHITE, Henry Adelbert 3
WHITE, Henry Alexander 1
WHITE, Henry Clay * 1
WHITE, Henry Dale 5
WHITE, Henry Ford 4
WHITE, Henry Middleton 3
WHITE, Henry Seely 2
WHITE, Herbert Humphrey 1

WHITE, Herbert Judson 2
WHITE, Hervey 4
WHITE, Horace 1
WHITE, Horace 2
WHITE, Horace Greeley 4
WHITE, Horace Henry 2
WHITE, Horatio Stevens 1
WHITE, Howard Ganson 4
WHITE, Howard Judson 1
WHITE, Hugh H
WHITE, Hugh 1
WHITE, Hugh Lawson H
WHITE, Hugh Lawson 1
WHITE, Ike D. 5
WHITE, Isaac Deforest 4
WHITE, Israel C. 1
WHITE, J. Campbell 1
WHITE, J. Du Pratt 1
WHITE, J. Harrison 4
WHITE, J. Warren 4
WHITE, Jacob Lee 2
WHITE, James * H
WHITE, James A. 2
WHITE, James Andrew 4
WHITE, James Bain H
WHITE, James Barlow 4
WHITE, James Charles 5
WHITE, James Clarke 1
WHITE, James Dempsey 4
WHITE, James Gilbert 2
WHITE, James Halley 5
WHITE, James McLaren 1
WHITE, James Terry 1
WHITE, James Watson 2
WHITE, James William 1
WHITE, Jay 1
WHITE, Jesse Hayes 5
WHITE, Joan Fulton 6
WHITE, John * H
WHITE, John Baker 4
WHITE, John Barber 1
WHITE, (John) Beaver 5
WHITE, John Blake H
WHITE, John Blake 1
WHITE, John Campbell 4
WHITE, John Chanler 3
WHITE, John DeHaven 1
WHITE, John Ellington 1
WHITE, John Griswold 1
WHITE, John Hazen 1
WHITE, John P. 1
WHITE, John Phillip 5
WHITE, John Roberts 4
WHITE, John Stuart 1
WHITE, John Turner 2
WHITE, John W. 4
WHITE, John Williams 1
WHITE, John Z. 1
WHITE, Joseph Augustus 4
WHITE, Joseph Hill 1
WHITE, Joseph Livingston H
WHITE, Joseph M. 1
WHITE, Joseph H
   Worthington
WHITE, Josh 5
WHITE, Joshua Warren 3
WHITE, Kathleen Merell 6
WHITE, Kemble 1
WHITE, Lawrence Grant 1
WHITE, Lazarus 3
WHITE, Lee A. 5
WHITE, Leonard H
WHITE, Leonard Dupee 3
WHITE, Leslie Alvin 4
WHITE, Lewis Charles 6
WHITE, Llewellyn Brooke 4
WHITE, Lucien 6
WHITE, Luke Matthews 3
WHITE, Lynn Townsend 6
WHITE, Lynne Loraine 4
WHITE, Marcus 1
WHITE, Marian Ainsworth 5
WHITE, Matthew Jr. 1
WHITE, Michael Alfred 1
   Edwin
WHITE, Nehemiah 1
WHITE, Nelia Gardner 3
WHITE, Newman Ivey 2
WHITE, Octavius Augustus 1
WHITE, Paul Dudley 6
WHITE, Paul W. 3
WHITE, Pearl H
WHITE, Pearl 4
WHITE, Percival 5
WHITE, Peter 1
WHITE, Philip (Rodney) 5
WHITE, Phillips H
WHITE, Phineas H
WHITE, Ray Bridwell 2
WHITE, Richard Grant H
WHITE, Robe Carl 3
WHITE, Robert 4
WHITE, Robert Vose 4
WHITE, Rodney Douglas 4
WHITE, Rollin Henry 4

WHITE, Roy Barton 4
WHITE, Rufus Austin 1
WHITE, S. Etelka 6
WHITE, S. Marx 4
WHITE, Sallie Joy 1
WHITE, Samuel H
WHITE, Samuel Stockton H
WHITE, Sebastian Harrison 2
WHITE, Stanford 1
WHITE, Stanley 1
WHITE, Stephen Mallory 1
WHITE, Stephen Van Culen 1
WHITE, Stewart Edward 2
WHITE, Terence Hanbury 4
WHITE, Thomas Dresser 4
WHITE, Thomas Holden 3
WHITE, Thomas Justin 2
WHITE, Thomas Raeburn 1
WHITE, Thomas Willis H
WHITE, Trentwell Mason 3
WHITE, Trueman Clark 1
WHITE, Trumbull 1
WHITE, Trumbull 2
WHITE, W. Wilson 4
WHITE, Wallace Humphrey 1
   Jr.
WHITE, Walter 3
WHITE, Walter C. 1
WHITE, Walter Louis 4
WHITE, Walter Porter 2
WHITE, Walter W(illiam) 5
WHITE, Weldon Bailey 4
WHITE, Wendelyn Florence 6
   Wheeler
WHITE, Wilbert Webster 2
WHITE, Wilbur Wallace 3
WHITE, William H
WHITE, William 4
WHITE, William Alanson 1
WHITE, William Alfred 5
WHITE, William Allen 2
WHITE, William Chapman 3
WHITE, William Charles 2
WHITE, William Crawford 4
WHITE, William E. 1
WHITE, William Henry 1
WHITE, William Henry Jr. 6
WHITE, William Lawrence 4
WHITE, William L(indsay) 5
WHITE, William Lindsay 6
WHITE, William Mathews 1
WHITE, William Monroe 2
WHITE, William Nathaniel H
WHITE, William Parker 2
WHITE, William Pierrepont 1
WHITE, William Prescott 2
WHITE, William Wallace 1
WHITE, William Wurts 5
WHITE, Wilson Henry 6
   Stout
WHITE, Windsor T. 1
WHITEAKER, Robert O. 3
WHITEBROOK, Lloyd 4
   George
WHITEFIELD, Edwin H
WHITEFIELD, George H
   Hayes
WHITEFORD, Gilbert 2
   Hayes
WHITEFORD, Roger J. 4
WHITEFORD, William 5
   Kepler
WHITEHAIR, Charles 1
   Wesley
WHITEHEAD, Alfred 2
   North
WHITEHEAD, Asa Carter 6
WHITEHEAD, Cabell 1
WHITEHEAD, Charles 1
   Nelson
WHITEHEAD, Cortlandt 1
WHITEHEAD, Donald 3
   Strehle
WHITEHEAD, Edwin 1
   Kirby
WHITEHEAD, Ennis 4
   Clement
WHITEHEAD, Harold 6
WHITEHEAD, Henry C. 5
WHITEHEAD, James 1
   Thomas
WHITEHEAD, John 3
WHITEHEAD, John 3
   Boswell
WHITEHEAD, John Meek 1
WHITEHEAD, Joseph 4
WHITEHEAD, Ralph 1
   Radcliffe
WHITEHEAD, Richard 1
   Henry
WHITEHEAD, Robert 1
   Frederick
WHITEHEAD, T(homas) 1
   North
WHITEHEAD, Wilbur H
   Cherrier

WHITEHEAD, Wilbur Cherrier 4
WHITEHEAD, William Adee H
WHITEHILL, Clarence 1
WHITEHILL, Howard Joseph 4
WHITEHILL, James H
WHITEHILL, John H
WHITEHILL, Robert H
WHITEHORNE, Earl
WHITEHOUSE, Brooks 5
WHITEHOUSE, F. Cope 1
WHITEHOUSE, Florence Brooks 5
WHITEHOUSE, Henry Remsen 4
WHITEHOUSE, Horace 3
WHITEHOUSE, James Horton
WHITEHOUSE, John Osborne H
WHITEHOUSE, Robert Treat 5
WHITEHOUSE, Sheldon 4
WHITEHOUSE, Vira Boarman (Mrs. Norman de R. Whitehouse) 5
WHITEHOUSE, William Fitz Hugh 1
WHITEHOUSE, William Penn 1
WHITEHURST, Camelia 1
WHITEHURST, John Leyburn 4
WHITEIS, William Robert 5
WHITELAW, John Bertram 5
WHITELEY, Emily Stone 1
WHITELEY, Isabel Nixon 5
WHITELEY, James Gustavus 5
WHITELEY, Richard Henry H
WHITELEY, William Gustavus H
WHITELOCK, George 1
WHITELOCK, Louis Clarkson 1
WHITELOCK, Louise Clarkson 4
WHITELOCK, William Wallace
WHITEMAN, Paul 4
WHITEMAN, Samuel Dickey 5
WHITENER, Paul A. W. 3
WHITENTON, William Maynard 1
WHITER, Edward Tait 4
WHITESELL, William M. 4
WHITESIDE, Arthur Dare 4
WHITESIDE, Frank Reed 1
WHITESIDE, George Morris II 4
WHITESIDE, George Walter 4
WHITESIDE, Horace Eugene 3
WHITESIDE, James Leonard 1
WHITESIDE, Jenkin H
WHITESIDE, John H
WHITESIDE, Walker H
WHITFIELD, Albert Hall 4
WHITFIELD, Henry H
WHITFIELD, Henry Lewis 1
WHITFIELD, J. Edward 1
WHITFIELD, James 1
WHITFIELD, James Bryan 2
WHITFIELD, John Wilkins H
WHITFIELD, Robert Parr 1
WHITFORD, Alfred E(dward) 5
WHITFORD, Edward Everett 3
WHITFORD, Greeley Webster 1
WHITFORD, Oscar F. 1
WHITFORD, Robert Naylor 3
WHITFORD, William Calvin
WHITFORD, William Clarke 1
WHITHORNE, Emerson 3
WHITIN, Ernest Stagg 2
WHITING, Almon Clark 6
WHITING, Arthur 1
WHITING, Borden Durfee 1
WHITING, Charles Goodrich
WHITING, Charles Sumner 1
WHITING, Edward Clark 6
WHITING, Edward Elwell 3
WHITING, Fred 5
WHITING, Fred T. 5
WHITING, Frederic Allen 5
WHITING, George Elbrige 1

WHITING, Gertrude 3
WHITING, Harry Hayes 1
WHITING, Henry H
WHITING, Henry Hyer 1
WHITING, John Talman 1
WHITING, Justin Rice 1
WHITING, Justin Rice 4
WHITING, Lawrence Harley 6
WHITING, Lilian 2
WHITING, Mary Gray 2
WHITING, Percy Hollister 6
WHITING, Richard Henry H
WHITING, Robert Rudd 1
WHITING, Samuel H
WHITING, Sarah Frances 1
WHITING, Walter Rogers 5
WHITING, William H
WHITING, William 1
WHITING, William Alonzo 3
WHITING, William Fairfield 1
WHITING, William Henry 1
WHITING, William Henry Jr. 2
WHITING, William Henry Chase H
WHITLEY, Cora Call 1
WHITLEY, James Lucius 5
WHITLEY, Johnson DeCosta 5
WHITLEY, Mary Theodora 4
WHITLEY, Samuel Henry 2
WHITLOCK, Brand 1
WHITLOCK, Douglas 6
WHITLOCK, Eliza Kemble 1
WHITLOCK, Elliott Howland 5
WHITLOCK, Herbert Percy 2
WHITLOCK, Paul Cameron 6
WHITLOCK, William Francis 1
WHITMAN, Alfred 3
WHITMAN, Armitage Freeman
WHITMAN, Arthur Dudley 4
WHITMAN, Benaiah Longley 1
WHITMAN, Charles Huntington 1
WHITMAN, Charles Otis 1
WHITMAN, Charles Seymour 2
WHITMAN, Edmund Allen 5
WHITMAN, Edward A. 2
WHITMAN, Eugene Winfield 4
WHITMAN, Ezekiel H
WHITMAN, Ezra Bailey 4
WHITMAN, Frank Perkins 1
WHITMAN, Frank S. 1
WHITMAN, Hendricks Hallett 3
WHITMAN, Henry Harold 4
WHITMAN, Howard 6
WHITMAN, John Lorin 1
WHITMAN, John Munro 1
WHITMAN, Lemuel H
WHITMAN, LeRoy 5
WHITMAN, Malcolm Douglass 1
WHITMAN, Marcus H
WHITMAN, Narcissa Prentiss H
WHITMAN, Ralph 2
WHITMAN, Roger B. 2
WHITMAN, Roswell Hartson 4
WHITMAN, Royal 2
WHITMAN, Russell 2
WHITMAN, Russell Ripley 1
WHITMAN, Sarah Helen Power H
WHITMAN, Stephen F(rench) 6
WHITMAN, Walter 1
WHITMAN, Walter Gordon 6
WHITMAN, William 1
WHITMAN, William Edward Seaver
WHITMAN, William R. 6
WHITMARSH, Francis Leggett 5
WHITMARSH, Henry Allen 1
WHITMARSH, Hubert Phelps 4
WHITMARSH, Theodore Francis
WHITMER, David H
WHITMER, Robert Forster 4
WHITMORE, Annie Goodell
WHITMORE, Carl 3
WHITMORE, Elias H
WHITMORE, Eugene R(andolph) 5

WHITMORE, Frank Clifford 2
WHITMORE, George Washington H
WHITMORE, William Henry 1
WHITMYER, Edward Charles
WHITNALL, Harold Orville 2
WHITNER, Daniel Jay 4
WHITNEY, Adeline Dutton Train 1
WHITNEY, Alexander Fell 2
WHITNEY, Alfred Rutgers 2
WHITNEY, Allen Banks 5
WHITNEY, Allen Sisson 3
WHITNEY, Anne 1
WHITNEY, Asa * H
WHITNEY, Carl Everett 1
WHITNEY, Carrie Westlake 5
WHITNEY, Caspar 2
WHITNEY, Charles Smith 3
WHITNEY, Courtney 5
WHITNEY, David Day 6
WHITNEY, David Rice 1
WHITNEY, Edward Baldwin 1
WHITNEY, Edwin Morse 3
WHITNEY, Eli H
WHITNEY, Eli 1
WHITNEY, Emily Henrietta 4
WHITNEY, Frank I. 5
WHITNEY, George 1
WHITNEY, Gertrude Capen 1
WHITNEY, Gertrude Vanderbilt 2
WHITNEY, Guilford Harrison 5
WHITNEY, Gwin Allison 1
WHITNEY, Harry 1
WHITNEY, Harry Edward 1
WHITNEY, Harry Payne 1
WHITNEY, Henry Clay 4
WHITNEY, Henry Howard 2
WHITNEY, Henry Melville 1
WHITNEY, Henry Mitchell 1
WHITNEY, Herbert Baker 4
WHITNEY, James Amaziah 1
WHITNEY, James Lyman 1
WHITNEY, Jason F(ranklin) 6
WHITNEY, John Dunning 4
WHITNEY, Joseph Lafeton 2
WHITNEY, Josiah Dwight H
WHITNEY, Leon Fradley 6
WHITNEY, Loren Harper 1
WHITNEY, Marian Parker 2
WHITNEY, Mary Watson 1
WHITNEY, Milton 1
WHITNEY, Myron W. 1
WHITNEY, Nathaniel Ruggles 4
WHITNEY, Nelson Oliver 1
WHITNEY, Paul Clinton 5
WHITNEY, Payne 1
WHITNEY, Richard 6
WHITNEY, Robert Bacon 1
WHITNEY, Samuel Brenton 1
WHITNEY, Thomas Richard H
WHITNEY, Wheelock 3
WHITNEY, William Channing 2
WHITNEY, William Collins 1
WHITNEY, William Dwight H
WHITNEY, William Fiske 1
WHITNEY, William Locke 1
WHITNEY, Willis Rodney 1
WHITON, Herman Frasch 4
WHITON, James Morris 1
WHITRIDGE, Frederick Wallingford 1
WHITRIDGE, Morris 1
WHITSETT, William Thornton 1
WHITSIDE, Samuel Marmaduke 1
WHITSITT, William Heth 1
WHITSON, Andrew Robeson 5
WHITSON, Edward 1
WHITSON, John Harvey 1
WHITT, Hugh 1
WHITTAKER, Charles E(vans) 6
WHITTAKER, Edmund Boyd 3
WHITTAKER, James 4
WHITTAKER, James Thomas 1
WHITTAKER, Miller F. 3
WHITTED, Elmer Ellsworth 4
WHITTEKER, John Edwin 1
WHITTELSEY, Abigail Goodrich H
WHITTEMORE, Amos H

WHITTEMORE, Arthur Easterbrook 5
WHITTEMORE, Benjamin Franklin H
WHITTEMORE, Charles Otto 4
WHITTEMORE, Clark McKinley 3
WHITTEMORE, Don Juan 1
WHITTEMORE, Edward Loder 1
WHITTEMORE, Eugene Beede 4
WHITTEMORE, Harris 1
WHITTEMORE, Henry 4
WHITTEMORE, Herbert Lucius 3
WHITTEMORE, James Madison 1
WHITTEMORE, John Weed 4
WHITTEMORE, Laurence Frederick 4
WHITTEMORE, Luther Denny 4
WHITTEMORE, Thomas H
WHITTEMORE, Thomas 3
WHITTEMORE, William John 3
WHITTEMORE, Wyman 3
WHITTEN, John Charles 4
WHITTEN, Robert 1
WHITTHORNE, Washington Curran H
WHITTIER, Charles Comfort 5
WHITTIER, Charles Franklin 1
WHITTIER, Clarke Butler 2
WHITTIER, John Greenleaf H
WHITTIER, William Frank 1
WHITTINGHAM, William Rollinson H
WHITTINGHILL, Dexter Gooch 5
WHITTINGTON, William Madison 4
WHITTLE, Francis McNeece 1
WHITTLE, Stafford Gorman 1
WHITTLES, Thomas Davis 1
WHITTLESEY, Derwent 3
WHITTLESEY, Eliphalet H
WHITTLESEY, Elisha H
WHITTLESEY, Frederick 1
WHITTLESEY, Henry De Witt Sr. 4
WHITTLESEY, Thomas Tucker 1
WHITTLESEY, William Augustus H
WHITTON, Charlotte 6
WHITTREDGE, Worthington 1
WHITTY, Dame May 2
WHITTY, James Howard 1
WHITWELL, Frederick Silsbee 1
WHITWORTH, George Gillatt 1
WHITWORTH, Pegram 5
WHOLBERG, Gerald Walter 6
WHORF, John 3
WHORF, Richard 4
WHORTON, John Lacy 1
WHYBURN, Gordon Thomas 5
WHYBURN, William Marvin 5
WHYTE, Carl Barzellous 4
WHYTE, Frederick William Carrick 3
WHYTE, James Primrose 1
WHYTE, Jessel Stuart 3
WHYTE, John 3
WHYTE, Malcolm K. 1
WHYTE, William Pinckney 1
WIBORG, Frank Bestow 1
WICHER, Edward Arthur 3
WICK, Charles J. 4
WICK, James L. 4
WICK, Samuel 5
WICK, William Watson H
WICKARD, Claude Raymond 4
WICKENDEN, Arthur Consaul 4
WICKENDEN, William Elgin 2
WICKER, Cassius Milton 1
WICKER, George Ray 1
WICKER, John Jordan 3
WICKERSHAM, Cornelius Wendell

WICKERSHAM, Cornelius Wendell Jr. 4
WICKERSHAM, Edward Dean 4
WICKERSHAM, George Woodward 1
WICKERSHAM, James 1
WICKERSHAM, James Pyle H
WICKES, Eliphalet H
WICKES, Forsyth H
WICKES, Harvey Randall 6
WICKES, Lambert H
WICKES, Stephen H
WICKES, Thomas H. 1
WICKETT, Frederick Henry 1
WICKHAM, Henry Frederick
WICKHAM, Henry Taylor 3
WICKHAM, John H
WICKHEM, John Dunne 2
WICKLIFFE, Charles Anderson H
WICKLIFFE, Robert C. 1
WICKLIFFE, Robert Charles
WICKLOW, Norman Louis 6
WICKMAN, Carl Eric 3
WICKS, Frank Scott Corey 3
WICKS, Robert Russell 4
WICKSER, Philip John 2
WICKSON, Edward James 1
WICKWARE, Francis Graham 1
WICKWIRE, Theodore Harry Jr. 6
WICOFF, John Van Buren 3
WIDDEMER, Mabel Cleland 4
WIDEMAN, Francis James 3
WIDENER, George D. 5
WIDENER, Joseph E. 2
WIDENER, Joseph Early H
WIDENER, Joseph Early 4
WIDENER, Peter A. Brown 1
WIDGERY, William
WIDMANN, Bernard Pierre 5
WIDTMANN, Arthur Albert 6
WIDTSOE, John Andreas 4
WIDTSOE, Leah Dunford 5
WIEAND, Albert Cassel 5
WIEBOLDT, Elmer F. 5
WIEBOLDT, Raymond Carl 5
WIEBOLDT, Werner A. 6
WIECHMANN, Ferdinand Gerhard 1
WIECK, Fred Dernburg 6
WIECZOREK, Max 3
WIEDMANN, Francis Edward 6
WIEGAND, Charles Dudley 5
WIEGAND, Ernest Herman 6
WIEGAND, Gustave Adolph
WIEGAND, Karl McKay 2
WIEGMAN, Fred Conrad 3
WIEHE, Theodore Charles 5
WIELAND, Arthur J. 3
WIELAND, G. R. 3
WIELAND, Heinrich Otto 3
WIELBOLDT, William A. 5
WIEMAN, Elton Ewart 5
WIEMAN, Henry Nelson 6
WIENER, Leo 1
WIENER, Meyer 5
WIENER, Norbert 4
WIENER, Paul Lester 4
WIENS, Henry Warkentin 5
WIER, Jeanne Elizabeth 3
WIER, John 5
WIER, Robert Withrow 5
WIER, Roy W. 4
WIERS, Edgar Swan 1
WIESE, Otis L. 5
WIESENBERGER, Arthur 5
WIESS, Harry Carothers 2
WIEST, Edward 6
WIEST, Howard 2
WIESTLING, Helen Merwin 6
WIGFALL, Louis Tresevant H
WIGGAM, Albert Edward 2
WIGGANS, Cleo Claude 5
WIGGER, Winand Michael 1
WIGGERS, Carl John 4
WIGGIN, Albert Henry 3
WIGGIN, Frank H. 1
WIGGIN, Frederick Alonzo 1
WIGGIN, Frederick Holme 1
WIGGIN, Frederick Holme 4
WIGGIN, Kate Douglas 1
WIGGIN, Twing Brooks 4
WIGGINS, Benjamin Lawton 1
WIGGINS, Carleton 1

WIGGINS, Charles II 2
WIGGINS, Frank 1
WIGGINS, Guy 4
WIGGINS, Horace Leland 1
WIGGINS, Sterling Pitts 2
WIGGINS, William D. 3
WIGGINTON, George Peter 1
WIGGINTON, Peter Dinwiddie H
WIGGINTON, Thomas Albert 4
WIGGLESWORTH, Edward * H
WIGGLESWORTH, Edward 2
WIGGLESWORTH, George 1
WIGGLESWORTH, Michael H
WIGGLESWORTH, Richard Bowditch 4
WIGHT, Charles Albert 5
WIGHT, E. Van Dyke 3
WIGHT, Francis Asa 2
WIGHT, Frank Clinton 1
WIGHT, John Fitch 5
WIGHT, John Green 1
WIGHT, Orlando Williams H
WIGHT, Pearl 4
WIGHT, Peter Bonnett 4
WIGHT, Thomas 1
WIGHT, William Drewin 2
WIGHT, William Ward 1
WIGMORE, John Henry 2
WIGNELL, Thomas H
WIHT, Thomas 3
WIKOFF, Frank J. 4
WIKOFF, Henry H
WILBAR, Charles Luther Jr. 5
WILBER, David 1
WILBER, David Forrest 1
WILBER, Edward Bacon 3
WILBER, Francis Allen 4
WILBER, George M. 1
WILBER, Herbert Wray 4
WILBOR, William Chambers 4
WILBOUR, Isaac H
WILBUR, Charles Edgar 1
WILBUR, Charles Toppan 1
WILBUR, Cressy Livingston 1
WILBUR, Curtis Dwight 3
WILBUR, Elisha Packer 1
WILBUR, Henry W. 1
WILBUR, Hervey H
WILBUR, Hervey Backus 1
WILBUR, James Benjamin 1
WILBUR, John 1
WILBUR, John Milnor 5
WILBUR, Ray Lyman 2
WILBUR, Rollin Henry 1
WILBUR, Samuel H
WILBUR, Sibyl 2
WILBUR, William Allen 2
WILBY, Arthur Clyde 1
WILBY, Ernest 3
WILBY, Francis Bowditch 4
WILCOX, Alexander Martin 1
WILCOX, Ansley 1
WILCOX, Armour David 1
WILCOX, Cadmus Marcellus H
WILCOX, Carl C(lifford) 6
WILCOX, Charles Bowser 1
WILCOX, Clair 5
WILCOX, Clarence E. 3
WILCOX, Clarence Rothwell 1
WILCOX, Delos Franklin 1
WILCOX, DeWitt Gilbert 5
WILCOX, Edward Byers 5
WILCOX, Edwin Mead 1
WILCOX, Elgin Roscoe 6
WILCOX, Elias Bunn 5
WILCOX, Ella Wheeler 1
WILCOX, Elmer Almy 1
WILCOX, Frank Langdon 4
WILCOX, Frederick Bernon 4
WILCOX, George Horace 1
WILCOX, George Milo 5
WILCOX, Grafton Stiles 6
WILCOX, Henry Buckley 1
WILCOX, Herbert Budington 1
WILCOX, J. Mark 3
WILCOX, Jeduthun H
WILCOX, Jerome K. 4
WILCOX, John A. H
WILCOX, John C. 2
WILCOX, John Walter Jr. 2
WILCOX, Leonard 1
WILCOX, LeRoy T. 4
WILCOX, Lucius Merle 4
WILCOX, Marrion 1
WILCOX, Nelson James 2
WILCOX, Perley S. 3

WILCOX, Reynold Webb 1
WILCOX, Robert William 1
WILCOX, Roy C. 6
WILCOX, Roy Porter 2
WILCOX, Sheldon E. 4
WILCOX, Sidney Freeman 1
WILCOX, Stephen H
WILCOX, Timothy Erastus 1
WILCOX, Walter Dwight 3
WILCOX, Wayne Ayres 6
WILCOX, William Craig 1
WILCOX, William Walter 2
WILCZYNSKI, Ernest Julius 1
WILD, Fred 4
WILD, Harrison Major 4
WILD, Henry Daniel 4
WILD, John Caspar H
WILD, John Daniel 5
WILD, Laura Hulda 5
WILD, Norman Russell 6
WILDE, Arthur Herbert 4
WILDE, George Francis Faxon 1
WILDE, Norman 1
WILDE, Percival 3
WILDE, Richard Henry H
WILDENSTEIN, Lazare Georges 4
WILDENTHAL, Bryan 1
WILDER, Abel Carter H
WILDER, Alexander 1
WILDER, Amos Parker 1
WILDER, Arthur Ashford 1
WILDER, Burt Green 1
WILDER, Charles Wesley 5
WILDER, Charlotte Frances 1
WILDER, Daniel Webster 1
WILDER, George Warren 1
WILDER, Gerald Gardner 2
WILDER, Gerrit Parmile 1
WILDER, Harris Hawthorne 1
WILDER, Herbert Augustus 1
WILDER, Herbert Merrill 1
WILDER, Inez Whipple 1
WILDER, John Emery 1
WILDER, John Thomas 2
WILDER, Laura Ingalls 3
WILDER, Laurence Russell 1
WILDER, Mrs. Louise Beebe 1
WILDER, Marshall Pinckney H
WILDER, Marshall Pinckney 1
WILDER, Ralph Everett 1
WILDER, Robert Ingersoll 6
WILDER, Robert Parmelee 1
WILDER, Russell Morse 3
WILDER, Salmon Willoughby 1
WILDER, Sampson Uryling Stoddard H
WILDER, T. Edward 1
WILDER, Thornton Niven 6
WILDER, Wilbur Elliott 3
WILDER, William Hamlin 1
WILDER, William Henry * 1
WILDERMUTH, Joe Henry 6
WILDERMUTH, Ora Leonard 4
WILDES, Frank 1
WILDMAN, Clyde Everett 3
WILDMAN, Edwin 1
WILDMAN, Marian Warner 5
(Mrs. Jesse A. Fenner)
WILDMAN, Murray Shipley 1
WILDMAN, Zalmon H
WILDNER, Harry Charles 4
WILDRICK, Isaac H
WILDS, George James Jr. 3
WILDS, William Naylor 3
WILDT, Rupert 6
WILE, Frank Sloan 6
WILE, Frederic William 1
WILE, Frederic William Jr. 4
WILE, Ira Solomon 2
WILE, Udo Julius 4
WILE, William Conrad 1
WILES, Charles Peter 2
WILES, Irving Ramsay 1
WILES, John Henry 1
WILES, Kimball 5
WILES, Lemuel Maynard 1
WILEY, Alexander 4
WILEY, Andrew J. 1
WILEY, Ariosto Appling H
WILEY, Calvin Henderson H
WILEY, David 1
WILEY, Edwin H
WILEY, Ephraim Emerson H
WILEY, Franklin Baldwin 1
WILEY, H(enry) Orton 5
WILEY, Harvey Washington 1
WILEY, Henry Ariosto 2

WILEY, Herbert V. 3
WILEY, Hugh 5
WILEY, Isaac William H
WILEY, James Sullivan H
WILEY, John Alexander 1
WILEY, John Cooper 4
WILEY, Louis 1
WILEY, Robert Hopkins 3
WILEY, Samuel Ernest 5
WILEY, Walter H. 1
WILEY, William Foust 2
WILEY, William Halsted 1
WILEY, William Ogden 3
WILFLEY, Lebbeus Redman 1
WILFLEY, Xenophon Pierce 1
WILFORD, Loran Frederick 5
WILGRESS, L. Dana 5
WILGUS, Horace La Fayette 1
WILGUS, Sidney Dean 1
WILGUS, William John 2
WILHELM, Donald 2
WILHELM, Richard Herman 5
WILHELM, Stephen Roger 4
WILHELMINA, Helena Pauline Maria 1
WILHELMJ, Charles Martel 4
WILHELMSEN, Karl John 4
WILHOIT, Eugene Lovell 1
WILKE, Otto John 5
WILKER, Arthur V. 3
WILKERSON, Albert Wadsworth 1
WILKERSON, James Herbert 2
WILKERSON, Marcus Manley 1
WILKERSON, William Wesley Jr. 4
WILKES, Charles H
WILKES, Charles S. 6
WILKES, Eliza Tupper 4
WILKES, George H
WILKES, Jack Stauffer 5
WILKES, James Claiborne Sr. 1
WILKES, John 3
WILKES, John Summerfield 1
WILKESON, Frank 4
WILKESON, Samuel H
WILKIE, Franc Bangs H
WILKIE, Harold McLean 3
WILKIE, John Elbert 1
WILKIN, Jacob W. H
WILKIN, James Whitney H
WILKIN, Samuel Jones H
WILKINS, Beriah 1
WILKINS, Ernest Hatch 3
WILKINS, Frank Lemoyne 1
WILKINS, Harold Tom 4
WILKINS, Horace M. 3
WILKINS, J. Ernest 3
WILKINS, John A. 3
WILKINS, Lawrence Augustus 1
WILKINS, Lawson 4
WILKINS, Milan William 1
WILKINS, Raymond Sanger 5
WILKINS, Ross H
WILKINS, Thomas Russell 1
WILKINS, Thomas Russell 2
WILKINS, Vaughan 3
WILKINS, Walter 1
WILKINS, William H
WILKINS, William Glyde 1
WILKINS, William James 3
WILKINSON, Albert 6
WILKINSON, Alfred Edmund 1
WILKINSON, Alfred Ernest 1
WILKINSON, Andrew 1
WILKINSON, Cecil J. 4
WILKINSON, Charles Fore Jr. 1
WILKINSON, David H
WILKINSON, Elizabeth Hays 6
WILKINSON, Ford L. Jr. 3
WILKINSON, George Lawrence 3
WILKINSON, Horace Simpson 1
WILKINSON, Howard Sargent 2
WILKINSON, Ignatius Martin 3
WILKINSON, James H
WILKINSON, James Cuthbert 6
WILKINSON, Jasper Newton 4

WILKINSON, Jemima H
WILKINSON, Jeremiah H
WILKINSON, John H
WILKINSON, John 6
WILKINSON, Joseph A. 4
WILKINSON, Joseph Biddle 4
WILKINSON, Joseph Green 1
WILKINSON, Marguerite Ogden Bigelow 1
WILKINSON, Melville Le Vaunt 1
WILKINSON, Morton Smith H
WILKINSON, Robert Johnson 3
WILKINSON, Robert Shaw 1
WILKINSON, Theodore S. 2
WILKINSON, Warring 1
WILKINSON, William Albert 5
WILKINSON, William Cleaver 1
WILKINSON, William Cook 1
WILKINSON, William Donald 5
WILKINSON, William John 3
WILKS, Samuel Stanley 4
WILL, Allen Sinclair 1
WILL, Arthur A. 2
WILL, Arthur Percival 3
WILL, Louis 1
WILL, Thomas St. CLAIR 4
WILL, Thomas Elmer 1
WILLARD, Archibald M. H
WILLARD, Archibald M. 1
WILLARD, Arthur Cutts 1
WILLARD, Arthur Lee 1
WILLARD, Ashton Rollins 1
WILLARD, Charles Andrew 1
WILLARD, Charles J(ulius) 6
WILLARD, Charles Wesley H
WILLARD, Chester Ezra 1
WILLARD, Daniel 2
WILLARD, Daniel Everett 4
WILLARD, DeForest 1
WILLARD, DeForest P. 3
WILLARD, Edward Lawrence 6
WILLARD, Edward Smith 1
WILLARD, Eleanor Withey 4
WILLARD, Emma Hart 1
WILLARD, Ernest Russell 4
WILLARD, Frances Elizabeth Caroline H
WILLARD, Frank H. 3
WILLARD, Frank Henry 4
WILLARD, Frederic Wilson 2
WILLARD, Henry Augustus 1
WILLARD, Hobart Hurd 6
WILLARD, Horace Mann 1
WILLARD, Ira Farnum 4
WILLARD, James Field 1
WILLARD, John 1
WILLARD, John Artemas 1
WILLARD, Joseh Edward 1
WILLARD, Joseph * H
WILLARD, Joseph Augustus 4
WILLARD, Josiah Flynt 1
WILLARD, Julius Terrass 3
WILLARD, Leigh 1
WILLARD, Lillian Winifred 5
WILLARD, Monroe Livingstone 4
WILLARD, Roy H(obson) 5
WILLARD, Samuel * H
WILLARD, Sidney H
WILLARD, Simon * H
WILLARD, Solomon H
WILLARD, Sylvester David H
WILLARD, Theodore A. 2
WILLARD, Thomas Rigney 1
WILLARD, William A(lbert) 5
WILLARD, William Charles 1
WILLAUER, Whiting 4
WILLCOX, Cornelis de Witt 1
WILLCOX, David 1
WILLCOX, James M. 1
WILLCOX, Julius Abner 1
WILLCOX, Louise Collier 1
WILLCOX, Mary Alice 3
WILLCOX, Orlando Bolivar 1
WILLCOX, Walter Francis 4
WILLCOX, Walter Francis 6
WILLCOX, Walter Ross 2
WILLCOX, Westmore 5
WILLCOX, William G. 1
WILLCOX, William Henry 1
WILLCOX, William Russell H
WILLEBRANDT, Mabel Walker 4

WILLEN, Pearl Larner 5
(Mrs. Joseph Willen)
WILLET, Anne Lee 2
WILLETS, David Gifford 5
WILLETS, Gilson 5
WILLETT, George F. 5
WILLETT, Herbert Lockwood 2
WILLETT, Howard Levansellaer Sr. 4
WILLETT, Marinus 4
WILLETT, Oscar Louis 2
WILLETT, William Jr. 5
WILLETTS, Ernest Ward 6
WILLETTS, Herbert 5
WILLETTS, William Prentice 4
WILLEVER, John Calvin 1
WILLEY, Calvin H
WILLEY, Charles Herbert 1
WILLEY, D. Allen 1
WILLEY, Earle D. 5
WILLEY, Henry 1
WILLEY, John Heston 2
WILLEY, Malcolm Macdonald 6
WILLEY, Norman Bushnell 4
WILLEY, Norman LeRoy 4
WILLEY, Samuel Hopkins 1
WILLFORD, Albert Clinton 3
WILLGING, Eugene P. 4
WILLGING, Joseph C. 3
WILLHITE, Frank Vanatta 2
WILLI, Albert B(ond) 5
WILLIAM III H
WILLIAM, Maurice 4
WILLIAMS, A. J. 3
WILLIAMS, Abraham Pease 1
WILLIAMS, Alan Meredith 6
WILLIAMS, Albert Frank 3
WILLIAMS, Albert Nathaniel 4
WILLIAMS, Albert Rhys 5
WILLIAMS, Alexander Elliot 3
WILLIAMS, Alexander Scott 4
WILLIAMS, Alford Joseph Jr. 3
WILLIAMS, Alfred Brockenbrough 1
WILLIAMS, Alfred Hector 6
WILLIAMS, Alfred Hicks 5
WILLIAMS, Alfred Mason 1
WILLIAMS, Alfred Melvin 5
WILLIAMS, Alpheus 5
WILLIAMS, Alpheus Starkey H
WILLIAMS, Anna Bolles 4
WILLIAMS, Anna Wessels 4
WILLIAMS, Archibald Hunter Arrington H
WILLIAMS, Arthur 1
WILLIAMS, Arthur B. 1
WILLIAMS, Arthur Llewellyn 1
WILLIAMS, Ashton Hilliard 4
WILLIAMS, Aubrey Willis 4
WILLIAMS, B. Y. 3
WILLIAMS, Barney 1
WILLIAMS, Beatty Bricker 6
WILLIAMS, Ben Ames 3
WILLIAMS, Ben J. 3
WILLIAMS, Benjamin 1
WILLIAMS, Benjamin Harrison 6
WILLIAMS, Berkeley 3
WILLIAMS, Bert 1
WILLIAMS, Bert C. 3
WILLIAMS, Blanche Colton 2
WILLIAMS, Bradford 1
WILLIAMS, C. Arthur 3
WILLIAMS, Carl 3
WILLIAMS, Carlos Grant 2
WILLIAMS, Catharine Read H
WILLIAMS, Cecil Brown 1
WILLIAMS, Channing Moore 1
WILLIAMS, Charles Bray 3
WILLIAMS, Charles Burgess 2
WILLIAMS, Charles David 1
WILLIAMS, Charles Finn 1
WILLIAMS, Charles Grandison H
WILLIAMS, Charles Hamilton 6
WILLIAMS, Charles Ira 6
WILLIAMS, Charles Luther 1
WILLIAMS, Charles Mallory 3
WILLIAMS, Charles McCay 3
WILLIAMS, Charles Page 3
WILLIAMS, Charles Parker 3

WILLINGHAM, Edward 5
Bacon
WILLINGHAM, Henry J. 2
WILLINGHAM, Robert 1
Josiah
WILLINGHAM, William A. 2
WILLINGS, George Carke 3
WILLIS, Albert Shelby H
WILLIS, Alfred 4
WILLIS, Bailey 2
WILLIS, Benjamin H
Albertson
WILLIS, Charles Francis 5
WILLIS, Clodius Harris 4
WILLIS, Edwin Caldwell 3
WILLIS, Edwin Edward 5
WILLIS, Francis H
WILLIS, Frank Bartlette 1
WILLIS, George Francis 1
WILLIS, H. Parker 1
WILLIS, Harold Buckley 4
WILLIS, Henry 4
WILLIS, Herman Allen 5
WILLIS, Horace Harold 5
WILLIS, Jack Macy 4
WILLIS, Nathaniel H
WILLIS, Nathaniel Parker H
WILLIS, Olympia Brown 1
WILLIS, Park Weed 5
WILLIS, Paul 1
WILLIS, Raymond Eugene 3
WILLIS, Simeon S. 4
WILLIS, William H
WILLIS, William Darrell 6
WILLISON, George 5
F(indlay)
WILLISTON, Arthur 5
Lyman
WILLISTON, Edward 1
Bancroft
WILLISTON, Samuel H
WILLISTON, Samuel 4
WILLISTON, Samuel 1
Wendell
WILLISTON, Seth H
WILLITS, Albert Bower H
WILLITS, Edwin H
WILLITS, George Sidney 1
WILLITS, Oliver Gaston 5
WILLIUS, Frederick Arthur 4
WILLKIE, E. E. 3
WILLKIE, Herman 3
Frederick
WILLKIE, Philip Herman 6
WILLKIE, Wendell Lewis 2
WILLMAN, Leon Kurtz 5
WILLMARTH, James 1
Willard
WILLMERING, Henry 4
WILLNUS, Harry G. 5
WILLOUGHBY, Barrett 3
WILLOUGHBY, Benjamin 1
Milton
WILLOUGHBY, Charles A. 5
WILLOUGHBY, Charles 2
Clark
WILLOUGHBY, Charles 3
Grant
WILLOUGHBY, Edwin 3
Eliott
WILLOUGHBY, Harold 4
Rideout
WILLOUGHBY, Hugh 4
Laussaf
WILLOUGHBY, John 1
Edmund
WILLOUGHBY, Julius 2
Edgar
WILLOUGHBY, Westel Jr. H
WILLOUGHBY, Westel 2
Woodbury
WILLOUGHBY, William 4
Charles
WILLOUGHBY, William 4
Franklin
WILLOUGHBY, Woodbury 4
WILLS, Albert Potter 1
WILLS, Bob 6
WILLS, Charles Tomlinson 1
WILLS, David 4
WILLS, David Crawford 1
WILLS, F. Reed 4
WILLS, George Stockton 3
WILLS, Royal Barry 4
WILLS, William Henry 2
WILLSON, Augustus 1
Everett
WILLSON, Charles Albert 1
WILLSON, David Burt H
WILLSON, Forceythe H
WILLSON, Frederick 1
Newton
WILLSON, George 4
Hayward
WILLSON, James McCrorry 6
WILLSON, James William 1

WILLSON, John Owens 1
WILLSON, Lester Sebastian 1
WILLSON, Marcius 1
WILLSON, Robert Newton 1
WILLSON, Robert Wheeler 1
WILLSON, Russell 2
WILLSON, Sidney Louis 2
WILLYS, John North 1
WILM, Emil Carl 1
WILM, Grace Gridley (Mrs. 5
Emil Carl Wilm)
WILMARTH, Lemuel 1
Everett
WILMER, Cary 3
Breckinridge
WILMER, Frank J. 2
WILMER, James Jones H
WILMER, Joseph Pere Bell H
WILMER, Richard Hooker H
WILMER, Richard Hooker 6
WILMER, William Holland H
WILMER, William Holland 1
WILMERDING, Lucius 1
Kellogg
WILMETH, Frank Lincoln 1
WILMETH, James Lillard 3
WILMORE, Augustus 1
Cleland
WILMORE, John Jenkins 2
WILMOT, David H
WILMOT, Frank Moore 1
WILMOT, George 1
Washington
WILMOT, Nellie Maroa 4
WILMOT, R. J. 3
WILMS, John Henry 1
WILNER, Robert Franklin 3
WILSHIRE, Gaylord 1
WILSHIRE, Joseph 3
WILSHIRE, William H
Wallace
WILSON, Adair 4
WILSON, Albert Dwight 3
WILSON, Albert Frederick 4
WILSON, Alexander * H
WILSON, Alexander 3
WILSON, Alexander 2
Massey
WILSON, Mrs. Alfred 5
Gaston (Matilda Raush
Wilson)
WILSON, Allen Benjamin H
WILSON, Alonzo Edes 2
WILSON, Alpheus Waters 1
WILSON, Andrew 3
WILSON, Andrew Gordon 4
WILSON, Andrew Wilkins 1
Jr.
WILSON, Arthur Orville H
WILSON, Arthur Riehl 3
WILSON, Augusta Jane 1
Evans
WILSON, Benjamin 3
WILSON, Benjamin Lee 4
WILSON, Bert 5
WILSON, Bird H
WILSON, Burwell L. 3
WILSON, Byron Henry 1
WILSON, Cairine Reay M. 4
WILSON, Calvin Dill 1
WILSON, Carey 4
WILSON, Carroll Atwood 2
WILSON, Carroll Louis 2
WILSON, Carroll Louis 3
WILSON, Charles H
WILSON, Charles 4
WILSON, Charles A. 5
WILSON, Charles Alfred 1
WILSON, Charles Branch 1
WILSON, Charles Bundy 1
WILSON, Charles Edward 5
WILSON, Charles Erwin 4
WILSON, Charles Gustavas 4
WILSON, Charles Henry 3
WILSON, Charles Henry 6
WILSON, Charles Irving 3
WILSON, Charles Scoon 1
WILSON, Charles Stuart 6
WILSON, Clarence Hall 5
WILSON, Clarence Rich 1
WILSON, Clarence True 4
WILSON, Clifford Brittin 2
WILSON, Daniel Munro 4
WILSON, David Cooper 1
WILSON, David Gilbert Jr. 1
WILSON, David Mathias 1
WILSON, David Roger 2
WILSON, David Wright 1
WILSON, Dunning Steele 1
WILSON, E. Graham 4
WILSON, Earl B. 6
WILSON, Edgar 1
WILSON, Edgar Bright 3
WILSON, Edgar Campbell H
WILSON, Edmund 1
WILSON, Edmund 5

WILSON, Edmund Beecher 1
WILSON, Edward Arthur 5
WILSON, Edward Clarkson 2
WILSON, Edward Harlan 5
WILSON, Edward Latimer 5
WILSON, Edward 1
Livingston
WILSON, Edward Preble 4
WILSON, Edward Stansbury 1
WILSON, Edward Taylor 5
WILSON, Edward William 5
WILSON, Edwin Bidwell 4
WILSON, Edwin Carleton 5
WILSON, Edwin Mood 5
WILSON, Edwin Walter 1
WILSON, Ella Calista 4
WILSON, Ellen Axson 1
WILSON, Ephraim King * H
WILSON, Erasmus 1
WILSON, Ernest Dana 3
WILSON, Ernest Henry 1
WILSON, Ernest Theodore 6
WILSON, Eugene Benjamin 1
WILSON, Eugene Edward 6
WILSON, Eugene H
McLanahan
WILSON, Eugene Smith 1
WILSON, Felix Zollicoffer 4
WILSON, Fletcher Aloysius 1
WILSON, Floyd Baker 4
WILSON, Floyd M. 1
WILSON, Francis 1
WILSON, Francis Cushman 1
WILSON, Francis Mairs 2
Huntington
WILSON, Francis Murray 3
WILSON, Francis Servis 1
WILSON, Frank Elmer 2
WILSON, Frank John 5
WILSON, Frank N. 3
WILSON, Frank Robert 6
WILSON, Franklin 1
Augustus
WILSON, G. Lloyd 3
WILSON, George * 1
WILSON, George Allison 4
WILSON, George Arthur 4
WILSON, George Arthur 5
WILSON, George Barry 2
WILSON, George Francis 1
WILSON, George Grafton 3
WILSON, George Henry 1
WILSON, George Henry 4
WILSON, George P(ickett) 5
WILSON, George Smith 1
WILSON, George W. * 2
WILSON, George West 1
WILSON, Gilbert 4
WILSON, Gill Robb 4
WILSON, Grafton Lee 5
WILSON, Grenville Dean H
WILSON, Grove 3
WILSON, Guy Mitchell 4
WILSON, H. Augustus 3
WILSON, Halsey William 3
WILSON, Harley Peyton 4
WILSON, Harold Albert 4
WILSON, Harold Edward 4
WILSON, Harold J. 6
WILSON, Harold Kirby 3
WILSON, Harry Bruce 4
WILSON, Harry Langford 1
WILSON, Harry Leon 2
WILSON, Harry Robert 5
WILSON, Henry * H
WILSON, Henry Braid 3
WILSON, Henry H. 4
WILSON, Henry Harrison 1
WILSON, Henry Lane 1
WILSON, Henry Van Peters 1
WILSON, Henyr Parke H
Custis
WILSON, Herbert Couper 1
WILSON, Herbert Michael 1
WILSON, Hiram Roy 5
WILSON, Howard E. 4
WILSON, Howard Stebbins 3
WILSON, Hugh Robert 2
WILSON, I. H. 1
WILSON, Ida Lewis 1
WILSON, Irving Livingstone 2
WILSON, Isaac H
WILSON, J. C. 4
WILSON, J. Christy 6
WILSON, J. Frank 5
WILSON, Jackson Stitt 1
WILSON, James * H
WILSON, James * 1
WILSON, James A. 1
WILSON, James Cornelius 2
WILSON, James 1
Cunningham
WILSON, James Falconer H
WILSON, James Grant 1
WILSON, James Harrison 1

WILSON, James Jefferson H
WILSON, James Knox H
WILSON, James Ormond 1
WILSON, James Walter 5
WILSON, James Wilbur 5
WILSON, Jesse Everett 2
WILSON, Joel 4
WILSON, John * H
WILSON, John 1
WILSON, John Arthur 2
WILSON, John David 5
WILSON, John Fleming 1
WILSON, John Franklin 4
WILSON, John Fry 1
WILSON, John G. 3
WILSON, John Gordon 2
WILSON, John Haden 5
WILSON, John Henry 3
WILSON, John L. 1
WILSON, John Leighton H
WILSON, John Madison 5
WILSON, John McCalmont 1
WILSON, John McMillan 4
WILSON, John Moulder 1
WILSON, John P. 2
WILSON, John P. 3
WILSON, John Reid 2
WILSON, John Thomas 1
WILSON, John Timothy 1
WILSON, Joseph 5
C(hamberlain)
WILSON, Joseph 1
Chamberlain
WILSON, Joseph G. 3
WILSON, Joseph Gardner H
WILSON, Joseph Miller 1
WILSON, Joseph R. 2
WILSON, Joseph Robert 3
WILSON, Joseph Rogers 1
WILSON, Joshua Lacy 1
WILSON, Julian Alexander 5
WILSON, Julian DuBois 3
WILSON, Julian Morris 1
WILSON, L. B. 3
WILSON, Lawrence Glass 3
WILSON, Leonard 5
WILSON, Leonard Seltzer 1
WILSON, Leroy A. 5
WILSON, Lester MacLean 1
WILSON, Lewis Albert 5
WILSON, Lewis Gilbert 4
WILSON, Lloyd Tilghman 1
WILSON, Lorenzo Arthur 1
WILSON, Louis Blanchard 1
WILSON, Louis N. 1
WILSON, Louis Round 5
WILSON, Lucius Edward 2
WILSON, Lucy Langdon 1
Williams
WILSON, Luther Barton 1
WILSON, Lyle Campbell 4
WILSON, Lyman Perl 3
WILSON, Mardon Dewees 4
WILSON, Margaret Barclay 1
WILSON, Margaret 2
Woodrow
WILSON, Mary Elizabeth 3
WILSON, Matthew 1
WILSON, Maurice Emery 1
WILSON, Milburn Lincoln 4
WILSON, Millard Thomas 4
WILSON, Mira Bigelow 3
WILSON, Morris Watson 1
WILSON, Mortimer 1
WILSON, Moses Fleming 1
WILSON, Murray Alderson 5
WILSON, Myron Henry Jr. 4
WILSON, Nathan H
WILSON, Nathaniel 1
WILSON, Orlando Winfield 5
WILSON, Orme 4
WILSON, Otis Guy 5
WILSON, Paul Oran 1
WILSON, Percy 1
WILSON, Peter H
WILSON, Philip Duncan 5
WILSON, Philip Sheridan 1
WILSON, Philip St Julien 1
WILSON, Philip Whitwell 1
WILSON, Respess S. 3
WILSON, Richard Henry 4
(Richard Fisguill)
WILSON, Richard Hulbert 4
WILSON, Riley Joseph 2
WILSON, Robert H
WILSON, Robert 2
WILSON, Robert Burns 1
WILSON, Robert Cade 2
WILSON, Robert Christian 6
WILSON, Robert Dick 1
WILSON, Robert Edward 1
Lee
WILSON, Robert Erastus 4
WILSON, Robert Forrest 2

WILSON, Robert Lee 3
WILSON, Robert North 5
WILSON, Robert Perry 5
WILSON, Robert Wilbar 6
WILSON, Roy William 5
WILSON, Rufus Rockwell 2
WILSON, Rufus Rockwell 1
WILSON, Russell 2
WILSON, Russell H. 1
WILSON, Ruth 6
Danenhower (Mrs. Albert
Frederick Wilson)
WILSON, S. Davis 1
WILSON, Samuel H
WILSON, Samuel Bailey 3
WILSON, Samuel Graham 1
WILSON, Samuel Knox 3
WILSON, Samuel Mackay 2
WILSON, Samuel 1
Mountford
WILSON, Samuel Ramsay H
WILSON, Samuel Thomas H
WILSON, Samuel Tyndale 4
WILSON, Scott 1
WILSON, Sol 1
WILSON, Stanley Calef 4
WILSON, Stanley Kidder 6
WILSON, Stanyarne 1
WILSON, Stephen 4
WILSON, Stephen Fowler 1
WILSON, T. B. 3
WILSON, Theodore H
Delavan
WILSON, Thomas * H
WILSON, Thomas * 1
WILSON, Thomas A. 4
WILSON, Thomas Bayne 4
WILSON, Thomas Edward 3
WILSON, Thomas Henry 4
WILSON, Thomas James 5
WILSON, Thomas Murray 4
WILSON, Thomas R(ichard) 1
WILSON, Thomas Webber 2
WILSON, Thomas William 2
WILSON, Val Haining 4
WILSON, Vincent Edward 6
WILSON, Walter K. 3
WILSON, Walter Lewis 6
WILSON, Walter Sibbald 4
WILSON, Warren Hugh 1
WILSON, Webster Hill 6
WILSON, Wilbur M. 3
WILSON, Wilford Murry 4
WILSON, Willard 1
WILSON, William * H
WILSON, William 1
WILSON, William B. 1
WILSON, William Bauchop 1
WILSON, William Earl 1
WILSON, William Edward 4
WILSON, William Edward 5
WILSON, William Hasell 1
WILSON, William Henry 1
WILSON, William 5
Huntington
WILSON, William James 5
WILSON, William Joseph 6
WILSON, William Lyne 3
WILSON, William Oliver 3
WILSON, William Otis 1
WILSON, William Powell 1
WILSON, William Ralph 6
WILSON, William Riley 5
WILSON, William Robert 1
Anthony
WILSON, William Warfield 1
WILSON, Willian Lyne 2
WILSON, Wlmo C. 4
WILSON, Woodrow 1
WILSON, Woodrow 1
WILSON, Mrs. Woodrow 1
WILSTACH, Frank Jenners 1
WILSTACH, Paul 3
WILT, Napier 1
WILTBANK, William White 1
WILTSE, Sara Eliza 1
WILTSEE, William Pharo 1
WILTSIE, Charles Hastings 1
WILTZ, Louis Alfred 1
WILWERDING, Walter 4
Joseph
WIMAN, Charles Deere 3
WIMAN, Erastus 1
WIMAR, Carl 1
WIMBERLY, Charles 1
Franklin
WIMBERLY, Lowry 3
Charles
WIMMER, Boniface H
WIMSATT, William Kurtz 6
WINANS, Charles Sumner H
WINANS, Edwin Baruch H
WINANS, Edwin Baruch 2
WINANS, Henry Morgan 4

* Indicates More Than One Such Name Listed

WINANS, James Albert 5
WINANS, James January H
WINANS, James Merritt H
WINANS, Ross H
WINANS, Samuel Ross H
WINANS, Thomas DeKay H
WINANS, Wilfred Hughes 6
WINANS, William H
WINANT, John Gilbert 2
WINBIGLER, Charles 1
  Fremont
WINBORNE, John Wallace 5
WINBOURN, Robert 1
  Emmet
WINBURN, Hardy Lathan 1
WINCH, Horace Carlton 5
WINCHELL, Alexander H
WINCHELL, Alexander 3
  Newton
WINCHELL, Benjamin La 2
  Fon
WINCHELL, Horace 1
  Vaughn
WINCHELL, John H. 5
WINCHELL, Newton 1
  Horace
WINCHELL, Samuel 4
  Robertson
WINCHELL, Walter 5
WINCHESTER, Benjamin 3
  Severance
WINCHESTER, Caleb 1
  Thomas
WINCHESTER, Charles 1
  Wesley
WINCHESTER, Elhanan H
WINCHESTER, James H
WINCHESTER, James Price 2
WINCHESTER, James 1
  Ridout
WINCHESTER, Millard E. 4
WINCHESTER, Oliver 1
  Fisher
WINCHESTER, William 2
  Eugene
WIND, Edgar 5
WINDELS, Paul 4
WINDELS, Paul 5
WINDER, Adam Heber 1
WINDER, G. Norman 4
WINDER, John Henry H
WINDER, Levin H
WINDER, William Henry H
WINDES, Thomas G. 1
WINDET, Victor 1
WINDGASSEN, Wolfgang 6
  Friedrich Hermann
WINDHOLZ, Louis H. 2
WINDINGSTAD, Ole 5
WINDMULLER, Louis 1
WINDOM, William H
WINDRIM, James Hamilton 1
WINDRIM, John Torrey H
WINDRIM, John Torrey 4
WINDSOR, H. R. H. 5
WINDSOR, Henry Haven H
WINDSOR, Henry Haven 4
  Jr.
WINDSOR, James H(arvey) 5
  II
WINDSOR, Phineas 5
  Lawrence
WINDSOR, Wilbur 3
  Cunningham
WINDSOR, William 1
  Augustus
WINE, William E. 3
WINEBRENNER, John H
WINEMAN, Henry 6
WINEMAN, Mode H
WINES, Enoch Cobb H
WINES, Frederick Howard 1
WINFIELD, Arthur M. 1
WINFIELD, Charles Henry H
WINFIELD, George 2
  Freeman
WINFIELD, James 1
  Macfarlane
WINFIELD, James 4
  Macfarlane
WINFREY, Elisha William 1
WING, Asa Shove 1
WING, Austin Eli H
WING, Charles Benjamin 2
WING, Charles Hallet 1
WING, Daniel Gould 1
WING, Francis Joseph 1
WING, Frank (Francis 5
  Marion)
WING, Henry Hiram 1
WING, John Durham 3
WING, Leonard Fred 4
WING, Mrs. Lucy Madeira 4
WING, Orion N. 1
WING, Russell Merritt 3
WING, Wilson Gordon 2

WING, Wilson Munford 5
WINGATE, Charles Edgar 2
  Lewis
WINGATE, Charles 1
  Frederick
WINGATE, George Wood 1
WINGATE, Joseph H
  Ferdinand
WINGATE, Paine H
WINGATE, Uranus Owen 1
  Brackett
WINGE, Ojvind 4
WINGER, Albert E. 5
WINGER, Maurice Homer 3
WINGER, Otho 2
WINGERT, Emmert 5
  Laurson
WINGET, Arthur Knox 5
WINGET, Benjamin 4
WINGFIELD, Edward H
  Maria
WINGFIELD, George 4
WINGFIELD, Marshall 4
WINGO, Otis Theodore 1
WINKELMAN, Nathaniel 3
  William
WINKELMANN, Christian 2
  H.
WINKENWERDER, Hugo 6
  August
WINKING, Cyril H. 5
WINKLER, Edwin H
  Theodore
WINKLER, Ernest William 4
WINKLER, John K. 3
WINKLER, Max 1
WINKWORTH, Edwin 3
  David
WINLOCK, Herbert Eustis 4
WINLOCK, Joseph H
WINLOW, Clara Vostrovsky 5
  (Mrs. Albert E. Winlow)
WINN, Charles V. 2
WINN, Frank Long 1
WINN, James Herbert 4
WINN, Jane Frances 1
WINN, John F. 4
WINN, John Sheridan 1
WINN, Milton 4
WINN, Richard H
WINN, Robert Hiner 2
WINN, Thomas Clay 4
WINN, William Alma 5
WINNEMUCCA, Sarah H
WINNER, Clifford 4
WINNER, Percy 6
WINNER, Septimus 1
WINNETT, Percy G(len) 6
WINSBOROUGH, Hallie 1
  Paxson
WINSER, Beatrice 2
WINSER, Henry Jacob H
WINSEY, A(lexander) Reid 5
WINSHIP, Albert Edward 1
WINSHIP, Blanton 2
WINSHIP, Laurence Leathe 6
WINSHIP, Walter Edwin 5
WINSLOW, Alfred 1
  Augustus
WINSLOW, Arthur 1
WINSLOW, Arthur 3
  Ellsworth
WINSLOW, Benjamin 4
  Emanuel
WINSLOW, Cameron 1
  McRae
WINSLOW, Carleton 2
  Monroe
WINSLOW, Carroll Dana 1
WINSLOW, Catherine Mary 1
WINSLOW, Charles-Edward 3
  Amory
WINSLOW, E. Eveleth 1
WINSLOW, Edward * 1
WINSLOW, Edward Delbert 1
WINSLOW, Erving 1
WINSLOW, Francis Asbury 1
WINSLOW, Frederic I. 1
WINSLOW, George 1
  Frederick
WINSLOW, Guy Monroe 3
WINSLOW, Helen Maria 4
WINSLOW, Herbert H
WINSLOW, Hubbard H
WINSLOW, John H
WINSLOW, John Ancrum H
WINSLOW, John Bradley 1
WINSLOW, John Flack H
WINSLOW, John Randolph 4
WINSLOW, Josiah H
WINSLOW, Kate Reignolds 1
WINSLOW, Leon Loyal 4
WINSLOW, Miron 1
WINSLOW, Randolph 4
WINSLOW, Rex (Shelton) 5
WINSLOW, Robert Lane Jr. 5

WINSLOW, Samuel 4
  Ellsworth
WINSLOW, Sidney Wilmot 1
WINSLOW, Sidney Wilmot 4
  Jr.
WINSLOW, Thacher 3
WINSLOW, Thyra Samter 4
WINSLOW, Warren H
WINSLOW, William Copley 1
WINSOR, Frank Edward 1
WINSOR, Frederick 1
WINSOR, James Davis Jr. 3
WINSOR, Justin H
WINSOR, Mulford 3
WINSOR, Paul 4
WINSOR, Robert 1
WINSTEIN, S(aul) 5
WINSTON, Annie Steger 1
WINSTON, Charles Henry 4
WINSTON, Francis Donnell 2
WINSTON, Frederick 1
  Hampden
WINSTON, Frederick 1
  Seymour
WINSTON, Garrard 3
WINSTON, George Taylor 4
WINSTON, Gilmer 2
WINSTON, Isaac 1
WINSTON, John Anthony H
WINSTON, John Clark 1
WINSTON, Joseph H
WINSTON, Patrick Henry 6
WINSTON, Robert Watson 2
WINSTON, Sanford Richard 5
WINT, Theodore Jonathan 1
WINTER, Alice Ames 2
WINTER, Alice Beach 2
WINTER, Andrew 3
WINTER, Charles Allan 2
WINTER, Charles Edwin 2
WINTER, Elisha I. H
WINTER, Elizabeth 1
  Campbell
WINTER, Emil 1
WINTER, Ezra Augustus 2
WINTER, Ferdinand 1
WINTER, Francis Anderson 1
WINTER, George 1
WINTER, George Ben 1
  Wade
WINTER, Herman 3
WINTER, Irvah Lester 1
WINTER, John Garrett 3
WINTER, Nevin Otto 1
WINTER, Thomas Daniel 1
WINTER, Thomas Gerald 1
WINTER, William 1
WINTER, William D. 3
WINTERBOTHAM, Joseph 3
WINTERBURN, Florence 5
  (May) Hull
WINTERBURN, George 1
  William
WINTERHALTER, Albert 1
  Gustavus
WINTERNITZ, Milton 3
  Charles
WINTERS, Allen Charles 6
WINTERS, Harry 5
  S(underland)
WINTERS, Robert (Henry) 5
WINTERS, Yvor 4
WINTERSTEINER, Oskar 5
  Paul
WINTHER, Oscar Osburn 5
WINTHROP, Beekman 1
WINTHROP, Bronson 2
WINTHROP, Henry Rogers 3
WINTHROP, James H
WINTHROP, John * H
  Charles
WINTHROP, Robert H
  Charles
WINTHROP, Theodore H
WINTNER, Aurel 4
WINTON, Alexander 1
WINTON, Andrew Lincoln 1
WINTON, George Beverly 1
WINZLER, Richard John 5
WIRE, G. E. 1
WIREBAUGH, Evelyn 5
  Burbank (Mrs. Harold W.
  Wirebaugh)
WIRJOPRANOTO, 4
  Sukardjo
WIRKA, Herman Wenzel 6
WIRT, Loyal Lincoln 5
WIRT, William Albert 1
WIRTH, Fremont Philip 4
WIRTH, Louis 3
WIRTH, Russell D. L. 5
WIRTH, William Joseph 4
WIRTHLIN, Joseph L. 4
WIRTSCHAFTER, Zolton 5
  Tillson

WIRTZ, Alvin J. 3
WIRZ, Henry H
WISCOTT, William Joseph 5
WISE, Aaron H
WISE, Arthur Chamberlin 3
WISE, Boyd Ashby 5
WISE, Byrd Douglas 5
WISE, Claude Merton 4
WISE, Daniel H
WISE, Edmond E. 1
WISE, Edward 1
WISE, Harold A. 3
WISE, Harold Edward H
WISE, Henry Alexander H
WISE, Henry Augustus H
WISE, Henry Morris 4
WISE, Isaac Mayer H
WISE, James 1
WISE, James Walter 1
WISE, Jennings Cropper 6
WISE, John * H
WISE, John Sergeant 1
WISE, Jonah Bondi 3
WISE, Leo Henry 1
WISE, Louise Waterman 2
WISE, Marion Johnson 1
WISE, Otto Irving 1
WISE, Peter Manuel 1
WISE, Russell Vincent 5
WISE, Stephen Samuel 2
WISE, Thomas Alfred 1
WISE, William Clinton 1
WISE, William Frederic 3
WISEMAN, Bruce Kenneth 3
WISEMAN, Joseph 6
  R(osenfeld)
WISEMAN, Sir William 4
WISH, Harvey 5
WISHARD, John G. 1
WISHARD, Luther 2
  Deloraine
WISHARD, Samuel Ellis 1
WISHARD, William Niles 1
WISHARD, William Niles 6
  Jr.
WISHART, Alfred Wesley 1
WISHART, Charles 3
  Frederick
WISHART, John Elliott 1
WISHART, William C. 4
WISHON, A. Emory 1
WISHON, Albert Graves 1
WISLIZENUS, Frederick H
  Adolph
WISLOCKI, George Bernays 3
WISMER, Harry 6
WISNER, Frank George 1
WISNER, George Monroe 1
WISNER, George Y. 1
WISNER, Henry H
WISNER, Oscar Francis 2
WISSER, John Philip 1
WISSLER, Clark 2
WISSLER, Jacques 1
WIST, Benjamin Othello 3
WISTAR, Caspar * H
WISTAR, Isaac Jones 1
WISTER, Annis Lee 1
WISTER, Owen 1
WISTER, Sally H
WISTRAND, Karl Knutsson 6
WISWALL, Frank Lawrence 5
WISWALL, Richard H. 3
WISWELL, Andrew Peters 1
WISWELL, George Nelson 4
WITEBSKY, Ernest 5
WITHAM, Ernest C. 3
WITHAM, Henry Bryan 6
WITHERBEE, Frank 1
  Spencer
WITHERELL, James H
WITHEROW, William 3
  Porter
WITHERS, Frederick Clarke H
WITHERS, Garrett Lee 3
WITHERS, Harry Clay 3
WITHERS, John Thomas 4
WITHERS, John William 4
WITHERS, Robert Edwin 3
WITHERS, Robert Enoch 1
WITHERS, William 1
  Alphonso
WITHERSPOON, Archibald 3
  William
WITHERSPOON, Herbert H
WITHERSPOON, John H
WITHERSPOON, John A. 1
WITHERSPOON, Robert H
WITHERSPOON, Samuel 1
  Andrew
WITHERSPOON, Thomas 3
  Casey
WITHERSPOON, William 5
  Wallace
WITHERSTINE, 1
  Christopher Sumner

WITHEY, Henry Franklin 6
WITHEY, Morton Owen 4
WITHINGTON, Charles 1
  Francis
WITHINGTON, David 1
  Little
WITHINGTON, Irving Platt 4
WITHINGTON, Leonard 1
WITHINGTON, Robert 3
WITHINGTON, Winthrop 3
WITHROW, Gardner 4
  Robert
WITHROW, James Renwick 6
WITHROW, John Lindsay 1
WITHYCOMBE, James 1
WITMER, Charles B. 1
WITMER, David Julius 6
WITMER, Francis Potts 5
WITMER, Lightner 5
WITMER, R(obert) 5
  B(onner)
WITSCHEY, Robert E. 4
WITSCHI, Emil 5
WITSELL, Edward Fuller 4
WITSELL, William Postell 4
WITT, Edgar E. 6
WITT, John Henry H
WITT, Joshua Chitwood 5
WITT, Max Siegfried 1
WITTE, Edwin Emil 4
WITTE, Fred(erick) 5
  C(hristopher)
WITTE, Max Ernest 1
WITTE, William Henry H
WITTEN, Harold Bryan 5
WITTENMYER, Edmund 1
WITTER, Dean 5
WITTER, Jean Carter 5
WITTGENSTEIN, Ludwig 4
  Josef Johann
WITTHAUS, Rudolph 1
  August
WITTICH, Fred William 4
WITTIG, Gustav Frederick 3
WITTKE, Carl Frederick 5
WITTKOWER, Rudolf 5
WITTMER, John L. 3
WITTNER, Fred 5
WITTWER, Eldon E. 4
WITTY, Paul Andrew 4
WITTY, William Henry 5
WITWER, Harry Charles 1
WITZEMANN, Edgar John 2
WIXSON, Franklin 4
WIXSON, Helen Marsh 1
WOBBER, Herman 4
WODEHOUSE, Pelham 6
  Grenville
WOEHLKE, Walter Victor 3
WOELFKIN, Cornelius 1
WOELFLE, Arthur W. 1
WOELK, Norma Marie 6
WOELPER, Benjamin 1
  Franklin Jr.
WOERMANN, John 2
  William
WOERNER, William F. 1
WOERTENDYKE, James 5
  H.
WOFFORD, Kate Vixon 3
WOFFORD, William Tatum H
WOGAN, John B. 3
WOGLOM, William Henry 4
WOHL, David Philip 3
WOHLENBERG, Ernest T. 4
  F.
WOHLENBERG, Walter 3
  Jacob
WOHLLEBEN, William 4
  Joseph
WOHLSEN, Ralph J. 5
WOJDYLA, Henry Edward 5
WOLBACH, Edwin J. 3
WOLBACH, Simeon Burt 3
WOLBARST, Abraham Leo 5
WOLCOTT, Daniel Fooks 6
WOLCOTT, Edward Oliver 1
WOLCOTT, Frank Bliss 4
WOLCOTT, Henry Merrill 6
WOLCOTT, Henry Roger 1
WOLCOTT, Jesse Paine 5
WOLCOTT, John Dorsey 2
WOLCOTT, Josiah Oliver 1
WOLCOTT, L. W. 3
WOLCOTT, Oliver H
WOLCOTT, Robert Henry 1
WOLCOTT, Roger H
WOLCOTT, Roger 5
WOLCOTT, Roger Henry 2
WOLCOTT, Samuel 4
  Huntington
WOLD, Peter Irving 2
WOLD, Theodore 2
WOLDMAN, Albert 5
  Alexander

WOLF, Adolph Grant 2
WOLF, Arnold Veryl 6
WOLF, August Stephen 5
WOLF, Charles George 5
Lewis
WOLF, Edmund Jacob 1
WOLF, Emma 4
WOLF, Frank 2
WOLF, George H
WOLF, George W. 4
WOLF, H. Carl 3
WOLF, H. D. 4
WOLF, Henry 1
WOLF, Henry John 6
WOLF, Henry Milton 1
WOLF, Irwin Damasius 3
WOLF, Isaac Jr. 4
WOLF, Joseph 3
WOLF, Leonard George 5
WOLF, Luther Benaiah 1
WOLF, Orrin E. 4
WOLF, Paul Alexander 3
WOLF, Rennold 1
WOLF, Robert Bunsen 3
WOLF, Simon 1
WOLF, William A. 4
WOLF, William Penn H
WOLFE, Albert Benedict 1
WOLFE, Arthur Lester 1
WOLFE, Catharine Lorillard H
WOLFE, Clayton A. 3
WOLFE, Edgar Thurston 5
WOLFE, Harry Deane 6
WOLFE, Harry Kirke 1
WOLFE, Harry Preston 2
WOLFE, J. Theodore 4
WOLFE, James H
WOLFE, James Edward 5
WOLFE, James H. 3
WOLFE, James Jacob 1
WOLFE, John David H
WOLFE, John Marcus 6
WOLFE, Kenneth B. 5
WOLFE, Lawrence 3
WOLFE, Manson Horatio 4
WOLFE, Paul Austin 4
WOLFE, Richard Russell 5
WOLFE, Robert Frederick 1
WOLFE, S. Herbert 1
WOLFE, Simeon Kalfius 1
WOLFE, Theodore 1
Frelinghuysen
WOLFE, Thomas Clayton 1
WOLFE, Thomas Kennerly 5
WOLFE, William Henry 6
WOLFEL, Paul Ludwig 4
WOLFENBARGER, 4
Andrew G.
WOLFENDEN, James 2
WOLFER, John A. 3
WOLFERMAN, Fred 5
WOLFERS, Arnold Oscar 5
WOLFF, Frank Alfred 5
WOLFF, George Dering H
WOLFF, Harold G. 4
WOLFF, John Eliot 1
WOLFF, William Almon 1
WOLFIT, Donald 4
WOLFIT, Donald 5
WOLFKILL, Guy Fontelle 6
WOLFMAN, Augustus 6
WOLFORD, Frank Lane H
WOLFORD, Leo Thorp 5
WOLFROM, Melville 5
L(awrence)
WOLFSKILL, William H
WOLFSOHN, Joel David 4
WOLFSON, Erwin Service 4
WOLFSON, Harry Austryn 6
WOLFSON, Howard 5
E(dward)
WOLFSON, Kurt 4
WOLFSTEIN, David I. 2
WOLL, Fritz Wilhelm 1
WOLL, Matthew 3
WOLLE, John Frederick 1
WOLLENHAUPT, H
Hermann Adolf
WOLLENWEBER, Ludwig H
August
WOLMAN, Leo 4
WOLPE, Stefan 5
WOLSEY, Louis 5
WOLTERS, Larry (Lorenz 5
Gerhard)
WOLTERSDORF, Arthur 2
Fred
WOLTMAN, Frederick 5
Enos
WOLTMAN, Henry 5
WOLVERTON, Charles A. 5
WOLVERTON, Charles 1
Edwin
WOLVERTON, John 5
Marshall
WOLVIN, Augustus B. 1

WOMACK, Ennis Bryan 6
WOMACK, Joseph Pitts 5
WOMACK, Nathan 5
Anthony
WOMBLE, John Philip Jr. 3
WOMELDORPH, Stuart 4
Early
WOMER, Parley Paul 3
WONDERLEY, Anthony 6
Wayne
WONNACOTT, Norman 6
WONSON, Roy Warren 2
WOOD, Abiel H
WOOD, Abraham H
WOOD, Alexander C. 4
WOOD, Alexander Thomas 4
WOOD, Alice Holabird 1
WOOD, Amos Eastman H
WOOD, Andrew Hollister 5
WOOD, Ann Van Cleef 6
WOOD, Arthur B. 3
WOOD, Arthur D. 3
WOOD, Arthur Evans 6
WOOD, Arthur Julius 1
WOOD, Asa Butler 2
WOOD, Austin Voorhees 6
WOOD, Barry 5
WOOD, Benjamin H
WOOD, Benjamin 4
WOOD, Benson H
WOOD, Bernard Augustine 4
WOOD, Bradford Ripley H
WOOD, Carl Bruce 4
WOOD, Carroll David 1
WOOD, Casey Albert 1
WOOD, Chandler Mason 1
WOOD, Charles 2
WOOD, Charles Erskine 2
Scott
WOOD, Charles Milton 1
WOOD, Charles P. 5
WOOD, Charles Seely 1
WOOD, Clark Verner 4
WOOD, Clement 3
WOOD, Clinton Tyler 4
WOOD, Corydon L. 1
WOOD, David Duffie 1
WOOD, David Muir 3
WOOD, De Volson H
WOOD, Edgar Liberty 3
WOOD, Edith Elmer 2
WOOD, Edmund Palmer 5
WOOD, Edward Edgar 1
WOOD, Edward Jenner 1
WOOD, Edward Stickney 1
WOOD, Edwin Ellsworth 1
WOOD, Edwin Orin 1
WOOD, Eric Fisher 4
WOOD, Ernest Edward 5
WOOD, Eugene 1
WOOD, Fernando H
WOOD, Floyd Bernard 4
WOOD, Frances Gilchrist 2
WOOD, Francis Asbury 2
WOOD, Francis Carter 3
WOOD, Frank Hoyt 1
WOOD, Frederic Taylor 3
WOOD, Frederick Hill 2
WOOD, Frederick William 2
WOOD, George * H
WOOD, George 1
WOOD, George Arthur 1
WOOD, George Bacon H
WOOD, George Henry 2
WOOD, George McLane 1
WOOD, George Willard 1
WOOD, Grant 1
WOOD, Guy Bussey 3
WOOD, Harold E. 4
WOOD, Harry Parker 1
WOOD, Hart 3
WOOD, Henry * 1
WOOD, Henry 2
WOOD, Henry A. Wise 1
WOOD, Henry Clay 1
WOOD, Horatio C. 1
WOOD, Horatio Charles 1
WOOD, Horatio Charles Jr. 3
WOOD, Horatio D. 1
WOOD, Howland 1
WOOD, Hudson A. 4
WOOD, Ira Wells 1
WOOD, Irving Francis 1
WOOD, Isaac Lemuel 4
WOOD, Isabel Warwick 5
WOOD, James H
WOOD, James 1
WOOD, James Anderson 2
WOOD, James Craven 2
WOOD, James Frederick H
WOOD, James J. 1
WOOD, James Madison 3
WOOD, James Perry 1
WOOD, James R. 1
WOOD, James Rushmore 1
WOOD, Jethro H

WOOD, John * H
WOOD, John Anderson 1
WOOD, John C(lark) 5
WOOD, John Enos 4
WOOD, John Hepler 1
WOOD, John Jacob H
WOOD, John M. H
WOOD, J(ohn) Perry 4
WOOD, John Quinby 4
WOOD, John S. 4
WOOD, John Scott 3
WOOD, John Seymour 1
WOOD, John Stephens 5
WOOD, John Travers 5
WOOD, John Walter 3
WOOD, John Wilson 2
WOOD, Joseph * H
WOOD, Joseph 1
WOOD, Kenneth Foster 4
WOOD, Laurence Irven 6
WOOD, Ledger 5
WOOD, Leonard 4
WOOD, Leonard Earle 6
WOOD, Lewis 4
WOOD, Lloyd Fuller 4
WOOD, Loren Newton 4
WOOD, Lydia Collins 4
WOOD, Marshall William 4
WOOD, Mary I. 3
WOOD, Matthew Laurence 5
WOOD, Meredith 6
WOOD, Montraville 1
WOOD, Moses Lindley 4
WOOD, Myron Ray 1
WOOD, Nathan Eusebius 1
WOOD, Nathan Robinson 1
WOOD, Oliver Ellsworth 1
WOOD, Palmer Gaylord 1
WOOD, Paul Meyer 4
WOOD, Paul Spencer 4
WOOD, Pierpont Jonathan 3
Edwards
WOOD, Ralph 3
WOOD, Reuben 3
WOOD, Reuben Terrell 3
WOOD, Richard 1
WOOD, Richard D. H
WOOD, Robert E. 5
WOOD, Robert Williams 3
WOOD, Samuel H
WOOD, Samuel Grosvenor 2
WOOD, Samuel Newitt H
WOOD, Sarah Sayward H
Barrell Keating
WOOD, Silas 1
WOOD, Spencer Shepard 1
WOOD, Stella Louise 3
WOOD, Sterling Alexander 4
WOOD, Stuart 1
WOOD, Theodore Thomas 4
WOOD, Thomas H
WOOD, Thomas Denison 3
WOOD, Thomas Edward 6
WOOD, Thomas John 1
WOOD, Thomas John 6
WOOD, Thomas Waterman 1
WOOD, Waddy Butler 2
WOOD, Walter 1
WOOD, Walter 1
WOOD, Walter Aaron 5
WOOD, Walter Abbott H
WOOD, Will Christopher 1
WOOD, William H
WOOD, William Allen 4
WOOD, William Barry Jr. 5
WOOD, William Burke H
WOOD, William Carleton 6
WOOD, William Elliott 3
WOOD, William H. S. 1
WOOD, William Hamilton 3
WOOD, William Madison 1
WOOD, William Robert 1
WOOD, William Roscoe 2
WOOD, William Thomas 2
WOOD, Willis Delano 5
WOOD, Word Harris 3
WOOD-ALLEN, Mary 1
WOODARD, Charles 5
Augustus
WOODARD, Frederick 1
Augustus
WOODARD, G. C. 1
WOODARD, James Edward 2
WOODBERRY, George 1
Edward
WOODBERRY, Miriam L. 5
WOODBERRY, Rosa 1
WOODBERRY, D. Hoyt 6
WOODBINE, George 3
Edward
WOODBRIDGE, Charles 4
Kingsley
WOODBRIDGE, Dudley 5
Warner
WOODBRIDGE, Dwight 5
Edwards

WOODBRIDGE, Frederick H
Enoch
WOODBRIDGE, Frederick 6
James
WOODBRIDGE, Frederick 1
James Eugene
WOODBRIDGE, Homer 3
Edwards
WOODBRIDGE, John H
WOODBRIDGE, John 5
Arven
WOODBRIDGE, Samuel 1
Homer
WOODBRIDGE, Samuel 1
Merrill
WOODBRIDGE, William H
WOODBRIDGE, William H
Channing
WOODBURN, Ethelbert 4
Cooke
WOODBURN, James Albert 2
WOODBURN, William 6
WOODBURNE, Angus 1
Stewart
WOODBURY, Charles 1
Herbert
WOODBURY, Charles J. 4
WOODBURY, Charles 1
Jeptha Hill
WOODBURY, Daniel H
Phineas
WOODBURY, Ellen 1
Carolina de Quincy
WOODBURY, Frank Porter 4
WOODBURY, Gordon 1
WOODBURY, Helen 1
Sumner
WOODBURY, Ida Sumner 1
Vose
WOODBURY, Isaac Baker H
WOODBURY, Levi H
WOODBURY, Malcolm 1
Sumner
WOODBURY, Marcia 1
Oakes
WOODBURY, Mildred 6
Fairchild
WOODBURY, Robert 5
Morse
WOODBURY, Urban 1
Andrain
WOODBURY, Walter E. 4
WOODCOCK, Amos 4
Walter Wright
WOODCOCK, Charles 1
Edward
WOODCOCK, David 1
WOODDY, Claiborne 1
Alphonso
WOODFORD, Arthur 4
Burnham
WOODFORD, Frank B. 4
WOODFORD, M. Dewitt 1
WOODFORD, Stewart 1
Lyndon
WOODFORD, William 1
WOODHEAD, Harry 4
WOODHEAD, William 4
WOODHOUSE, Arthur 4
Sutherland Pigott
WOODHOUSE, Charles 4
Williamson
WOODHOUSE, James H
WOODHOUSE, Samuel W. H
WOODHULL, Alfred 1
Alexander
WOODHULL, Daniel Ellis 5
WOODHULL, John Francis 1
WOODHULL, Maxwell Van 1
Zandt
WOODHULL, Nathaniel H
WOODHULL, Victoria H
Claflin
WOODHULL, Victoria 4
Claflin
WOODHULL, Zula Maud 5
WOODIN, William 1
Hartman
WOODING, Hugh Olliviere 6
Beresford
WOODLEY, Oscar Israel 1
WOODLOCK, Thomas 4
Francis
WOODMAN, Abby 4
Johnson
WOODMAN, Albert 1
Stanton
WOODMAN, Alpheus 5
Grant
WOODMAN, Clarence 1
Eugene
WOODMAN, Durand 1
WOODMAN, Frederic 3
Thomas
WOODMAN, J. Edmund 1
WOODMAN, John H

WOODMAN, Lawrence 5
Ewalt
WOODMAN, Raymond 2
Huntington
WOODRING, Harry Hines 4
WOODROW, H. R. 1
WOODROW, James 1
WOODROW, Jay W. 3
WOODROW, Nancy Mann 1
Waddel
WOODROW, Samuel 2
Hetherington
WOODRUFF, Anne Helena 4
WOODRUFF, Carle 1
Augustus
WOODRUFF, Caroline 2
Salome
WOODRUFF, Charles 1
Albert
WOODRUFF, Charles 1
Edward
WOODRUFF, Clinton 2
Rogers
WOODRUFF, Edwin 5
Blanchard
WOODRUFF, Edwin 1
Hamlin
WOODRUFF, Elmer Grant 3
WOODRUFF, Ernest 4
WOODRUFF, Francis Eben 4
WOODRUFF, Frank 4
Edward
WOODRUFF, Frederick 3
William
WOODRUFF, George 2
Catlin
WOODRUFF, George H
Hobart
WOODRUFF, George 2
Washington
WOODRUFF, George 1
Hobart
WOODRUFF, Harvey T. 1
WOODRUFF, Helen S. 1
WOODRUFF, Henry 1
Mygatt
WOODRUFF, Isaac Ogden 6
WOODRUFF, James Albert 5
WOODRUFF, John 6
WOODRUFF, John T. 2
WOODRUFF, Joseph 1
Talmage Battis
WOODRUFF, Julia Louisa 1
Matilda
WOODRUFF, Lorande Loss 2
WOODRUFF, Marston 6
True
WOODRUFF, Nathan H. 4
WOODRUFF, Olive 4
WOODRUFF, Robert 4
Eastman
WOODRUFF, Rollin 1
Simmons
WOODRUFF, Roy Orchard 3
WOODRUFF, Theodore H
Tuttle
WOODRUFF, Thomas 1
Adams
WOODRUFF, Thomas M. 4
WOODRUFF, Timothy 1
Lester
WOODRUFF, Wilford H
WOODRUFF, William H
Edward
WOODRUFF, William 5
Wight
WOODRUM, Clifton 3
Alexander
WOODS, Alan Churchill 4
WOODS, Albert Fred 2
WOODS, Alfred W. 3
WOODS, Alice (Miss) 5
WOODS, Alva 1
WOODS, Andrew Henry 5
WOODS, Arthur 2
WOODS, Baldwin Munger 3
WOODS, Bertha Gerneaux 3
WOODS, Bill Milton 6
WOODS, Charles Albert 1
WOODS, Charles Carroll 1
WOODS, Charles Dayton 1
WOODS, Charles Robert 1
WOODS, Cyrus E. 1
WOODS, David Walker Jr. 4
WOODS, Edgar Hall 3
WOODS, Edgar Lyons 4
WOODS, Edward Augustus 1
WOODS, Francis Marion 4
WOODS, Frank Henry 4
WOODS, Frank P. 4
WOODS, Frederick Adams 1
WOODS, Frederick 3
Shenstone
WOODS, George Benjamin 3
WOODS, George Herbert 6
WOODS, Granville Cecil 6
WOODS, Harry Irwin 5

* Indicates More Than One Such Name Listed   669

WRIGHT, Donald S. 3
WRIGHT, Donald Thomas 4
WRIGHT, Dudley Hugh 6
  Aloysius
WRIGHT, Edmond Fleming 6
WRIGHT, Edward Bingham 1
WRIGHT, Edward Everett 1
WRIGHT, Edward Pulteney 4
WRIGHT, Edward R. 3
WRIGHT, Edward Richard 1
WRIGHT, Edwin Ruthvin H
  Vincent
WRIGHT, Eliphalet Nott 4
WRIGHT, Elizabeth 5
  Washburne (Mrs.
  Hamilton Wright)
WRIGHT, Elizur H
WRIGHT, Ernest Hunter 5
WRIGHT, Ernest Linwood 6
WRIGHT, Fielding Lewis 3
WRIGHT, Frances 1
WRIGHT, Francis Marion 1
WRIGHT, Frank Ayres 2
WRIGHT, Frank C. 2
WRIGHT, Frank James 3
WRIGHT, Frank Lee 2
WRIGHT, Frank Lloyd 3
WRIGHT, Frederick Eugene 1
WRIGHT, George Bohan 1
WRIGHT, George E. 1
WRIGHT, G(eorge) Ernest 6
WRIGHT, George Francis 4
WRIGHT, George Francis 5
WRIGHT, George Frederick H
WRIGHT, George Frederick 1
WRIGHT, George Grover H
WRIGHT, George Hand 4
WRIGHT, George Mann 6
WRIGHT, George Murray 4
WRIGHT, George 5
  Washington
WRIGHT, George William 4
WRIGHT, Gilbert G. 1
WRIGHT, Graham 3
WRIGHT, Grant 4
WRIGHT, Hamilton 1
WRIGHT, Hamilton Mercer 3
WRIGHT, Harold Abbott 4
WRIGHT, Harold Bell 2
WRIGHT, Harry Noble 5
WRIGHT, Helen R. 5
WRIGHT, Helen Smith 5
WRIGHT, Hendrick Bradley H
WRIGHT, Henry Burt 1
WRIGHT, Henry Clarke 1
WRIGHT, Henry Collier 1
WRIGHT, Henry Harry H
WRIGHT, Henry John 1
WRIGHT, Henry Parks 1
WRIGHT, Henry Wilkes 5
WRIGHT, Herbert E. 2
WRIGHT, Herbert E. 2
WRIGHT, Herbert Perry 2
WRIGHT, Horace Caldwell 4
WRIGHT, Horace Melville 3
WRIGHT, Horatio H
  Governeur
WRIGHT, Irene Aloha 5
WRIGHT, Isaac Miles 2
WRIGHT, J. Butler 1
WRIGHT, J. Montgomery 1
WRIGHT, James Elwin 6
WRIGHT, James Franklin 4
WRIGHT, James Frederick 6
WRIGHT, James Harris 2
WRIGHT, James Homer 1
WRIGHT, James Lendrew H
WRIGHT, James Lloyd 3
WRIGHT, Jessie 5
WRIGHT, Joanna Maynard 4
  Shaw
WRIGHT, John 1
WRIGHT, John Bittinger 1
WRIGHT, John Calvin 5
WRIGHT, John Crafts H
WRIGHT, John Henry 1
WRIGHT, John Kirtland 5
WRIGHT, John Lloyd 5
WRIGHT, John Pilling 2
WRIGHT, John Stephen 1
WRIGHT, John Vines 1
WRIGHT, John Wells 1
WRIGHT, John Westley 1
WRIGHT, John Westley 2
WRIGHT, John Womack 3
WRIGHT, Jonathan Jasper H
WRIGHT, Joseph H
WRIGHT, Joseph Albert 4
WRIGHT, Joseph Alexander 5
WRIGHT, Joseph Jefferson H
  Burr
WRIGHT, Joseph Purdon 1
WRIGHT, Julia MacNair 1
WRIGHT, Julian May 4
WRIGHT, Leroy A. 2
WRIGHT, Louis Clinton 6

WRIGHT, Louis Tompkins 3
WRIGHT, Louise Sophie 4
  Wigfall
WRIGHT, Loyd 6
WRIGHT, Luke E. 1
WRIGHT, Luther Lamphear 1
WRIGHT, Mabel Osgood 1
WRIGHT, Marcellus Eugene 4
WRIGHT, Marcus Joseph 1
WRIGHT, Marie Robinson 1
WRIGHT, Mary Clabaugh 5
  (Mrs. Arthur F. Wright)
WRIGHT, Mary Tappan 1
WRIGHT, Maurice Lauchlin 1
WRIGHT, Merle St Croix 1
WRIGHT, Milton 1
WRIGHT, Milton H
WRIGHT, Moorhead 2
WRIGHT, Muriel Hazel 6
WRIGHT, Myron Benjamin H
WRIGHT, Nathaniel Curwin 1
WRIGHT, Norris N. 3
WRIGHT, Ora Campbell 6
WRIGHT, Orville 2
WRIGHT, Patience Lovell H
WRIGHT, Paul 4
WRIGHT, Peter Clark 2
WRIGHT, Purd B. 4
WRIGHT, Quincy 5
WRIGHT, Richard 4
WRIGHT, Richard Robert 4
WRIGHT, Richard Robert 4
  Jr.
WRIGHT, Richardson Little 4
WRIGHT, Robert H
WRIGHT, Robert 4
WRIGHT, Robert Charlton 2
WRIGHT, Robert Clinton 1
WRIGHT, Robert Herring 1
WRIGHT, Robert William H
WRIGHT, Ross Pier 4
WRIGHT, Roydon Vincent 2
WRIGHT, Rufus 1
WRIGHT, Samuel Gardiner H
  Mrs.
WRIGHT, Selden Stuart 4
WRIGHT, Silas Jr. H
WRIGHT, Stanley Willard 5
WRIGHT, Stephen Mott 1
WRIGHT, Sydney 5
  Longstreth
WRIGHT, Theodore 4
WRIGHT, Theodore Francis 1
WRIGHT, Theodore Lyman 1
WRIGHT, Theodore Paul 5
WRIGHT, Thew 5
WRIGHT, Thomas Roane 4
  Barnes
WRIGHT, Turbutt 2
WRIGHT, Walter Henry 3
WRIGHT, Walter King 1
WRIGHT, Walter 2
  Livingston Jr.
WRIGHT, Warren 3
WRIGHT, Wilbur 1
WRIGHT, Wilbur Seaman 1
WRIGHT, Wilfred L. 2
WRIGHT, Willard 1
WRIGHT, William 1
  Huntington
WRIGHT, William H
WRIGHT, William Bleecker 4
WRIGHT, William Bull H
WRIGHT, William Burnet 1
WRIGHT, William Carter 1
WRIGHT, William 4
  Frederick
WRIGHT, William 3
  Hammond
WRIGHT, William Janes 1
WRIGHT, William Kelley 5
WRIGHT, William Mason 2
WRIGHT, William Ryer 1
WRIGHT, William Thomas 3
  Jr.
WRIGHT, William Wood 5
WRIGHT, Wirt 6
WRIGHTSMAN, Charles 3
  John
WRIGHTSON, George D. 4
WRIGLEY, Thomas 4
WRIGLEY, William Jr. 1
WRINCH, Dorothy 6
WRISLEY, George A. 4
WROBLEWSKI, Wladyslaw 4
WROCK, Arthur Henry 4
WRONG, H. Hume 3
WROTH, Edward Pinkney 1
WU, Chao-Chu 1
WU TING-FANG H
WUERPEL, Edmund Henry 5
WULLING, Frederick John 2
WULSIN, Frederick Roelker 4
WULSIN, Lucien 1
WULSIN, Lucien 5
WUNDER, Charles 4
  Newman

WUNDER, Clarence 1
  Edmond
WUNDERLICH, Fritz 4
WUNDHEILER, Alexander 3
  Wundt
WUNSCH, Ernest Conrad 1
WUORINEN, John H. 5
WURDEMANN, Audrey 4
  May
WURDEMANN, Harry 1
  Vanderbilt
WURLITZER, Farny R. 5
WURLITZER, Rudolph H. 2
WURMAN, Harry P. 4
WURSTER, William Wilson 6
WURTS, Alexander Jay 1
WURTS, John H
WURTS, John 4
WURTS, John Halsey 1
WURTSMITH, Paul Bernard 2
WURTTEMBERG, H
  Friedrich Paul Wilhelm
WURZ, John Francis 4
WURZBACH, Harry 1
  McLeary
WURZBURG, Francis Lewis 3
WYANT, Adam Martin 1
WYANT, Alexander Helwig H
WYANT, Paul Byron 3
WYATT, Bernard Langdon 4
WYATT, Edith Franklin 3
WYATT, Sir Francis H
WYATT, J. B. Noel 1
WYATT, Landon R. 5
WYATT, Lee B. 3
WYATT, Robert H. 6
WYATT-BROWN, Hunter 3
WYCHE, Charles Cecil 4
WYCHE, Richard Thomas 1
WYCKOFF, Albert Clarke 5
WYCKOFF, Ambrose 4
  Barkley
WYCKOFF, Arcalous 1
  Welling
WYCKOFF, Cecelia G. 4
WYCKOFF, Cecelia G. 5
WYCKOFF, Charles 1
  Truman
WYCKOFF, John 1
WYCKOFF, Richard 5
  DeMille
WYCKOFF, Walter 1
  Augustus
WYER, James Ingersoll 3
WYER, Malcolm Glenn 4
WYER, Samuel S. 3
WYETH, John H
WYETH, John Allan 1
WYETH, Nathan C. 4
WYETH, Nathaniel Jarvis H
WYETH, Newell Convers 2
WYKA, Kazimierz 6
WYKOFF, Leward 4
  Cornelius
WYLEGALLA, Victor 4
  Bernard
WYLES, Tom Russell 3
WYLIE, Andrew H
WYLIE, Andrew 1
WYLIE, David Gourley 1
WYLIE, Douglas M. 4
WYLIE, Dwight 1
  Witherspoon
WYLIE, Edna Edwards 1
WYLIE, Elinor Hoyt 1
WYLIE, Herbert George 4
WYLIE, Ida Alexa Ross 6
WYLIE, James Renwick Jr. 6
WYLIE, Laura Johnson 1
WYLIE, Max 6
WYLIE, Philip Gordon 5
WYLIE, Richard Cameron 1
WYLIE, Robert H
WYLIE, Robert Bradford 4
WYLIE, Robert H. 4
WYLIE, Samuel Brown H
WYLIE, Samuel Joseph 6
WYLIE, Walker Gill 1
WYLLIE, Irvin Gordon 5
WYLLIE, John Cook 5
WYLLIE, Robert (Edward) 1
  Evan
WYLLYS, George 1
WYMAN, Alfred Lee 3
WYMAN, Bruce 1
WYMAN, Charles Alfred 5
WYMAN, Eugene Lester 5
WYMAN, Frank Theodore 4
WYMAN, Hal C. 1
WYMAN, Henry Augustus 1
WYMAN, Herbert Gardner 4
WYMAN, Jefferies 1
WYMAN, Levi Parker 1
WYMAN, Lillie Buffum 1
  Chace
WYMAN, Morrill H

WYMAN, Phillips 3
WYMAN, Robert Harris H
WYMAN, Seth H
WYMAN, Walter 1
WYMAN, Walter Forestus 1
WYMAN, Walter Scott 2
WYMAN, Willard Gordon 5
WYMAN, William D. 1
WYMAN, William Frizzell 4
WYMAN, William Stokes 1
WYNEGAR, Howard 3
  LaVerne
WYNKOOP, Asa 2
WYNKOOP, Bernard 1
  Martell
WYNKOOP, Henry H
WYNN, Ed 4
WYNN, James Oscar 6
WYNN, William Joseph 4
WYNN, William Thomas 3
WYNNE, Cyril 4
WYNNE, Madeline Yale 1
WYNNE, Robert John 1
WYNNE, Shirley Wilmott 2
WYNNE, Thomas Neil 3
WYNNS, Thomas H
WYNTER, Bryan Herbert 6
WYTHE, George H
WYUM, Obed Alonzo 5
WYVELL, Manton M. 1

X

XANTUS, Janos H
XCERON, Jean 4

Y

YACKER, Julius S. 6
YADEN, James Garfield 6
YAGER, Arthur 4
YAGER, Joseph Arthur 4
YAGER, Louis 1
YAGER, Vincent 3
YAGLOU, Constantin 4
  Prodromos
YALE, Caroline Ardelia 1
YALE, Elihu H
YALE, Leroy Milton 1
YALE, Linus H
YANCEY, Bartlett H
YANCEY, Edward 2
  Burbridge
YANCEY, George Richard 6
YANCEY, James 1
YANCEY, Joel 1
YANCEY, Richard Hunter 1
YANCEY, William Lowndes H
YANDELL, David Wendel 1
YANDELL, Enid 1
YANDELL, Lunsford Pitts H
YANES, Francisco Javier 1
YANGCO, Teodore R. 4
YANKWICH, Leon Rene 4
YANNEY, Benjamin 3
  Franklin
YANT, William Parks 4
YANTIS, George Franklin 2
YARBOROUGH, Warren 1
  Furman
YARBROUGH, William 6
  Thomas (Tom)
YARD, Robert Sterling 2
YARDLEY, Farnham 3
YARDLEY, Herbert O. 4
YARGER, Henry Lee 1
YARMOLINSKY, 6
  Avrahm(Abraham)
YARNALL, Alexander 1
  Coxe
YARNALL, D. Robert 4
YARNALL, Stanley Rhoads 4
YARNALL, Harry Ervin 2
YARNELL, Ray 4
YARNELLE, Edward Ralph 6
YARROW, Harry Crecy 1
YARROW, Philip 3
YARYAN, Homer T. 4
YATES, Abraham H
YATES, Arthur Gould 1
YATES, Arthur Wolcott 1
YATES, Charles Colt 1
YATES, Cullen 2
YATES, Eugene Adams 6
YATES, Gilbert E. 5
YATES, Henry A. 4
YATES, Henry Whitefield 1
YATES, Herbert John 4
YATES, John Barentse 1
YATES, John Lawrence 1
YATES, John Van Ness H
YATES, Julian Emmet 5
YATES, Katherine Merritte 4
YATES, Kyle Monroe 6
YATES, Lorenzo Gordin 1

YATES, Matthew Tyson H
YATES, Paul Clifford 4
YATES, Peter Waldron H
YATES, Raymond Francis 4
YATES, Richard H
YATES, Richard 1
YATES, Robert 4
YATES, Robert Carl 4
YATES, Stephen 5
YATES, Ted 4
YATMAN, Marion Fay 3
YAW, Ellen Beach 2
YAWKEY, Cyrus Carpenter 1
YEAGER, Albert Franklin 4
YEAGER, Howard Austin 4
YEAGER, Joseph H
YEAMAN, George Helm 1
YEAMAN, Malcolm 1
YEAMANS, Sir John 1
YEAPLE, Whitney S. K. 4
YEARDLEY, Sir George 1
YEARDON, Richard H
YEASTING, William Henry 5
YEATER, Charles Emmett 4
YEATES, Jasper H
YEATES, Jesse Johnson 1
YEATES, William Smith 1
YEATMAN, James E. 1
YEATMAN, Pope 3
YEATMAN, Richard 1
  Thompson
YEATON, Arthur Charles 3
YECHTON, Barbara 1
YEISER, John O. 1
YEISER, John Otho III 6
YEISLEY, George Conrad 1
YELL, Archibald H
YELLIN, Samuel 1
YELLOWLEY, Edward C. 5
YENDES, Lucy A. 1
YENS, Karl 2
YEOMANS, Charles 3
YEOMANS, Earl Raymond 5
YEOMANS, Frank Clark 5
YEOMANS, George Dallas 1
YEOMANS, Henry Aaron 5
YEOMANS, James D. 1
YEOMANS, John William H
YEOMANS, Robert 4
  DeWitte
YEPSEN, Lloyd Nicoll 3
YERBY, William James 3
YERGER, William H
YERGIN, Howard Vernon 3
YERKES, Charles Tyson 1
YERKES, John Watson 1
YERKES, Leonard A. 4
YERKES, Robert Mearns 4
YERKES, Royden Keith 4
YERUSHALMY, Jacob 6
YESKO, Elmer George 4
YEUELL, Gladstone Horace 4
YEWELL, George Henry 1
YI, Ha-yun 6
YLVISAKER, Ivar Daniel 1
YLVISAKER, Lauritz S. 4
YNTEMA, Hessell Edward 4
YOAKUM, Benjamin F. 1
YOAKUM, Clarence Stone 2
YOAKUM, Henderson H
YOCHUM, H(arold) 6
  L(eland)
YOCUM, A. Duncan 1
YOCUM, Seth Hartman H
YOCUM, Wilbur Fisk 4
YODER, Albert Henry 2
YODER, Anne Elizabeth 6
YODER, David Carl 4
YODER, Jocelyn Paul 6
YODER, Lloyd Edward 4
YODER, Robert Anderson 1
YODER, Robert McAyeal 4
YODER, Worth Nicholas 4
YOHN, Frederick Coffay 1
YOKOYAMA, Taiwan 3
YON, Pietro A. 2
YONGE, Julien C(handler) 6
YONGE, Philip Keyes 1
YOOK, Young-Soo 6
YORAN, George Francis 4
YORE, Clem 1
YORE, Amos Chesley 3
YORK, Edward Howard Jr. 5
YORK, Edward Palmer 1
YORK, Francis Lodowick 3
YORK, Frank 4
YORK, Harlan Harvey 4
YORK, Harry Clinton 5
YORK, Miles Frederick 6
YORK, Robert 4
YORK, Samuel Albert 4
YORKE, George Marshall 1
YORKE, Peter Christopher 1
YORKE, Thomas Jones H
YOSHIDA, Shigeru 4
YOSHIDA, Tomizo 6

YOST, Bartley Francis 5
YOST, Casper Salathiel 1
YOST, Fielding Harris 2
YOST, Gaylord 3
YOST, Jacob 4
YOST, Jacob Senewell H
YOST, Joseph Warren 4
YOST, Lenna Lowe 6
YOST, Mary 3
YOU, Dominique H
YOUMANS, Edward H
Livingston
YOUMANS, Frank A. 1
YOUMANS, William Jay H
YOUNG, Aaron H
YOUNG, Abram Van Eps 1
YOUNG, Agatha (Mrs. 6
George Benham Young)
YOUNG, Alexander H
YOUNG, Alfred H
YOUNG, Allyn Abbott 1
YOUNG, Ammi Burnham H
YOUNG, Andrew Harvey 1
YOUNG, Archer Everett 5
YOUNG, Art 4
YOUNG, Arthur Howland 4
YOUNG, Arthur J. 4
YOUNG, Augustus 4
YOUNG, Benjamin 4
YOUNG, Benjamin E. 3
YOUNG, Benjamin Loring 4
YOUNG, Bennett 1
Henderson
YOUNG, Bert Edward 2
YOUNG, Bicknell 1
YOUNG, Brigham H
YOUNG, Bryan Rust 4
YOUNG, C. Griffith 4
YOUNG, C. Jac 1
YOUNG, Charles Augustus 1
YOUNG, Charles 3
Duncanson
YOUNG, Charles Henry 1
YOUNG, Charles Luther 4
YOUNG, Charles Sommers 5
YOUNG, Charles Van 5
Patten
YOUNG, Chic 6
YOUNG, Chic (Murat 5
Bernard Young)
YOUNG, Claiborne Addison 5
YOUNG, Clara Kimball 4
YOUNG, Clarence Hoffman 5
YOUNG, Clarence Marshall 5
YOUNG, Clark 1
Montgomery
YOUNG, Clement Calhoun 2
YOUNG, Courtland H. 1
YOUNG, D. Philip 6
YOUNG, David H
YOUNG, Denton True 1
YOUNG, Denton True 4
YOUNG, Dwight Edwin 4
YOUNG, Ebenezer H
YOUNG, Edward Joseph 5
YOUNG, Edward M. 1
YOUNG, Edward T. 4
YOUNG, Elizabeth Guion 5
(Bab Sears)
YOUNG, Ella Flagg 1
YOUNG, Ernest Charles 5
YOUNG, Evan E. 1
YOUNG, Ewing H
YOUNG, Francis Brett 3
YOUNG, Frank Herman 4
YOUNG, Frank Mobley Jr. 4
YOUNG, Franklin Knowles 1
YOUNG, Frederic George 1
YOUNG, George 3
YOUNG, George Jr. 3
YOUNG, George A. 4
YOUNG, George Brigham 1
YOUNG, George Bright 1
YOUNG, George Brooks 1
YOUNG, George Gilray 3
YOUNG, George Henry 5
YOUNG, George Husband 4
YOUNG, George Joseph 5
YOUNG, George Morley 1
YOUNG, George Rude 4
YOUNG, George Ulysses 4
YOUNG, George 1
Washington
YOUNG, Gilbert Amos 2
YOUNG, Gladwin E(llis) 6
YOUNG, Gordon 3
YOUNG, Gordon Elmo 5
YOUNG, H. Olin 4
YOUNG, Helen Louise 2
YOUNG, Henry Lane 4
YOUNG, Herbert A. 4
YOUNG, Horace Autrey 6
YOUNG, Horace Gedney 4
YOUNG, Howard Isaac 4
YOUNG, Howard Sloan 6
YOUNG, Hugh Hampton 2

YOUNG, J. Addison 4
YOUNG, J. H. 2
YOUNG, Jacob William 2
Albert
YOUNG, James 4
YOUNG, James Carleton 1
YOUNG, James Henry 1
YOUNG, James Kelly 1
YOUNG, James Nicholas 3
YOUNG, James Rankin 1
YOUNG, James Scott 1
YOUNG, James Thomas 5
YOUNG, James Webb 5
YOUNG, Jeremiah Simeon 1
YOUNG, Jesse Bowman 1
YOUNG, John H
YOUNG, John Clarke H
YOUNG, John Edwin 1
YOUNG, John Philip 1
YOUNG, John Richardson H
YOUNG, John Russell H
YOUNG, John Russell 4
YOUNG, John Wesley 1
YOUNG, Joseph Hardie 3
YOUNG, Josue Maria 1
YOUNG, Julia Evelyn 4
YOUNG, Karl 4
YOUNG, Kenneth Todd 5
YOUNG, Kimball 6
YOUNG, Lafayette 1
YOUNG, Lafayette Jr. 1
YOUNG, Laurence W. 5
YOUNG, Leon Decatur 2
YOUNG, Leonard 5
YOUNG, Leonard Augustus 4
YOUNG, Lester Willis 5
YOUNG, Levi Edgar 5
YOUNG, Lewis Emanuel 1
YOUNG, Lucien 1
YOUNG, Mahonri 3
YOUNG, Margaret Rankin 2
YOUNG, Mary Vance 2
YOUNG, Morrison Waite 1
YOUNG, Newton Clarence 1
YOUNG, Odus Graham 1
YOUNG, Otto 1
YOUNG, Owen D. 4
YOUNG, Percy S. 3
YOUNG, Philip 3
YOUNG, Philip Endicott 3
YOUNG, Pierce Manning H
Butler
YOUNG, Plummer Bernard 4
YOUNG, Richard 5
YOUNG, Richard Hale 5
YOUNG, Richard H
Montgomery
YOUNG, Richard 1
Whitehead
YOUNG, Rida Johnson 1
YOUNG, Robert Anderson 1
YOUNG, Robert Nicholas 4
YOUNG, Robert Ralph 3
YOUNG, Robert Thompson 5
YOUNG, Robert Winthrop 4
YOUNG, Rodney Stuart 6
YOUNG, Roland 3
YOUNG, Rose 1
YOUNG, Roy Archibald 4
YOUNG, Roy Odo 3
YOUNG, S. Edward 1
YOUNG, Sam Martin 1
YOUNG, Samuel Baldwin 1
Marks
YOUNG, Samuel Hall 2
YOUNG, Sanborn 5
YOUNG, Smith Gresham 4
YOUNG, Stanley (Preston) 6
YOUNG, Stark 4
YOUNG, Stewart Woodford 1
YOUNG, Thomas H
YOUNG, Thomas Crane 1
YOUNG, Thomas Gorsuch 3
YOUNG, Thomas Kay 3
YOUNG, Thomas Lowry H
YOUNG, Thomas Shields 1
YOUNG, Thomas White 4
YOUNG, Truman Post 2
YOUNG, Udell Charles 4
YOUNG, Victor 3
YOUNG, Wallace Jesse 1
YOUNG, Walter Jorgensen 1
YOUNG, Walter Stevens 2
YOUNG, Whitney Moore 5
Jr.
YOUNG, William 1
YOUNG, William A. 4
YOUNG, William Brooks 4
YOUNG, William Foster 1
YOUNG, William 5
Lesquereux
YOUNG, William Lindsay 3
YOUNG, William Singleton H
YOUNG, William Wesley 4
YOUNGBERG, Gilbert 5
A(lbin)

YOUNGBLOOD, Bonney 6
YOUNGDAHL, Benjamin 5
Emanuel
YOUNGDAHL, Oscar 2
Ferdinand
YOUNGDAHL, Reuben 5
Kenneth Nathaniel
YOUNGER, Jesse Arthur 4
YOUNGER, John 2
YOUNGER, John Elliott 3
YOUNGER, Thomas H
Coleman
YOUNGER, Thomas 4
Coleman
YOUNGERT, Sven Gustaf 1
YOUNGGREEN, Charles 2
Clark
YOUNG-HUNTER, John 3
YOUNGKEN, Heber 4
Wilkinson
YOUNGMAN, Frank 5
Nourse
YOUNGQUIST, G. Arron 3
YOUNGS, John H
YOUNGS, J(ohn) W(illiam) 5
T(heodore)
YOUNGS, Merle L. 4
YOUNGS, William J. 1
YOUNGSON, William 5
Wallace
YOUNT, Barton Kyle 2
YOUNT, George H
Concepcion
YOUNT, Miles Frank 1
YOUNT, Norman Fleming 5
YOUTZ, Herbert Alden 4
YOUTZ, Lewis Addison 3
YOUTZ, Philip Newell 5
YOWELL, Everett Irving 3
YSAYE, Eugene 1
YUDAIN, Theodore 5
YUDKIN, Arthur M. 3
YUGOV, Anton 4
YUI, O. K. 4
YULEE, David Levy 1
YUNCKER, Truman George 4
YUNG, Julius Rudolph 6
YUNG, Wing 1
YUNGBLUTH, Bernard 3
Joseph
YURKA, Blanche 6
YUST, Walter 5
YUST, William Frederick 2
YUSUF KARAMANLI 1
YUTZY, Henry Clay 4
YUTZY, Thomas Daniel 4

Z

ZABEL, Morton Dauwen 4
ZABINSKI, Jan Franciszek 6
ZABRISKIE, Andrew 1
Christian
ZABRISKIE, Edwin G. 3
ZABRISKIE, George 1
ZABRISKIE, George Albert 3
ZABRISKIE, Robert 5
Lansing
ZACH, Leon 4
ZACH, Max Wilhelm 1
ZACHARIAS, Ellis Mark 4
ZACHER, Clarence Henry 6
ZACHER, Louis Edmund 2
ZACHOS, John Celivergas H
ZADEIKIS, Povilas 3
ZADKINE, Ossip 4
ZAENGLEIN, Paul Carl 5
ZAHARIAS, Babe H
Didrikson
ZAHARIAS, Mildred 4
Didrikson
ZAHEDI, Fazlollah 4
ZAHM, Albert Francis 3
ZAHM, John Augustine 1
ZAHN, Edward James Jr. 4
ZAHNISER, Arthur 1
DeFrance
ZAHNISER, Charles Reed 5
ZAHNISER, Howard 4
ZAHORSKY, John 4
ZAIN, Rebyl (Mrs. George 6
K. Zain)
ZAKRZEWSKA, Marie H
Elizabeth
ZALDIVAR, Rafael 1
ZALESKI, Alexander 6
ZALINSKI, Edmund Louis 1
Gray
ZALINSKI, Moses Gray 1
ZALVIDEA, Jose Maria de H
ZAMORANO, Austin Juan H
Vincente
ZAND, Stephen Joseph 4
ZANDER, Arnold Scheuer 6
ZANDER, Henry George 1

ZANE, Abraham Vanhoy 1
ZANE, Charles S. 4
ZANE, Ebenezer H
ZANE, John Maxcy 1
ZANETTI, Joaquin Enrique 6
ZANGERIE, John A. 5
ZANTZINGER, Clarence 3
Clark
ZAPFFE, Frederick Carl 3
ZAPOTOCKY, Antonin 4
ZAPP, Carroll Francis 5
ZARING, Clarence Arthur 4
ZARING, E. Robb 4
ZAROUBIN, Georgi N. 3
ZARTMANN, Parley 5
Emmett
ZAUGG, Walter Albert 4
ZAVITZ, Edwin Cornell 4
ZAWADZKI, Aleksander 5
ZDANOWICZ, Casimir 1
Douglass
ZECH, Frederick Jr. 1
ZECHMEISTER, Laszlo 5
Karoly Erno
ZECKWER, Richard 1
ZEDER, Fred Morrell 3
ZEDLER, John 1
ZEHNDER, Charles Henry 1
ZEHNER, J. Alexander 4
ZEHRING, Blanche 1
ZEHRUNG, Winfield Scott 4
ZEIDLER, Carl Frederick 2
ZEIGEN, Frederic 2
ZEIGLER, Lee Woodward 3
ZEILIN, Jacob H
ZEISBERGER, David H
ZEISLER, Fannie 1
Bloomfield
ZEISLER, Joseph 1
ZEISLER, Sigmund 1
ZEIT, F. Robert 1
Aenishaenslin
ZEITLER, Emerson Walter 5
ZEITLIN, Jacob 2
ZELENY, Anthony 2
ZELENY, Charles 1
ZELENY, John 3
ZELIE, John Sheridan 2
ZELLER, George Anthony 1
ZELLER, Harry A. 6
ZELLER, Joseph William 4
ZELLER, Julius Christian 1
ZELLER, Walter George 5
ZELLER, Walter Philip 3
ZELLERBACH, Isadore 2
ZELLERBACH, James 4
David
ZEMLINSKY, Alexander 1
Von
ZEMURRAY, Samuel 4
ZENDER, Austin R. 5
ZENGER, John Peter H
ZENNER, Philip McKnight 4
ZENOR, William T. 4
ZENOS, Andrew C. 1
ZENTMAYER, Joseph H
ZENTMAYER, William 5
ZERAN, Franklin Royalton 6
ZERBAN, Frederick 3
William
ZERBE, Alvin Sylvester 4
ZERBE, Farran 2
ZERBE, James Slough 1
ZERBE, Karl 5
ZERBEY, Joseph Henry 4
ZEREGA DIZEREGA, 1
Louis Augustus
ZERNIKE, Frits 4
ZETTERSTRAND, Ernst 1
Adrian
ZETTLER, Emil Robert 2
ZEUCH, Herman J. 1
ZEUNER, Charles H
ZHDANOV, Andrei 3
Alexandrovich
ZHUKOV, Georgi 6
Konstantnovich
ZIEGEMEIER, Henry 1
Joseph
ZIEGENFUSS, Samuel 1
Addison
ZIEGENHEIN, William J. 4
ZIEGET, Julius 1
ZIEGFELD, Florenz * 1
ZIEGLER, Charles Edward 5
ZIEGLER, David H
ZIEGLER, Edward 2
ZIEGLER, Edwin Allen 4
ZIEGLER, Karl 6
ZIEGLER, Lloyd Hiram 3
ZIEGLER, Maxine Evelyn 5
Hogue (Mrs. James R.
Ziegler)
ZIEGLER, S. Lewis 2
ZIEGLER, William 1
ZIEGLER, William Jr. 3

ZIEGLER, William Jr. 4
ZIEGLER, Winfred Hamlin 5
ZIELKE, George Robert 6
ZIER, Merlin William 5
ZIESING, August 2
ZIESING, Richard Jr. 4
ZIETLOW, John L. W. 4
ZIFF, William Bernard 3
ZIGROSSER, Carl 6
ZIGLER, David Howard 1
ZIGLER, John Darrel 4
ZIHLMAN, Frederick N. 1
ZILBOORG, Gregory 3
ZIMAND, Savel 4
ZIMBALIST, Mary Louise 5
Curtis
ZIMM, Bruno Louis 2
ZIMMER, Bernard Nicolas 5
ZIMMER, H. Ward 3
ZIMMER, Henry Wenzell 4
ZIMMER, John Todd 3
ZIMMER, Verne A. 2
ZIMMER, William Homer 5
ZIMMERER, Charles John 4
ZIMMERLEY, Howard 2
Henry
ZIMMERMAN, Charles 1
Ballard
ZIMMERMAN, Charles 5
Fishburn
ZIMMERMAN, Edward 4
Americus
ZIMMERMAN, Edward 6
August
ZIMMERMAN, Eugene 1
ZIMMERMAN, Fred R. 3
ZIMMERMAN, Harvey J. 5
ZIMMERMAN, Henry 1
Martin
ZIMMERMAN, Herbert 4
John
ZIMMERMAN, Hyman 5
Harold
ZIMMERMAN, James 2
Fulton
ZIMMERMAN, Jeremiah 1
ZIMMERMAN, Leander M. 5
ZIMMERMAN, Louis 2
Seymour
ZIMMERMAN, M(ax) 6
M(andell)
ZIMMERMAN, Orville 3
ZIMMERMAN, Percy 3
White
ZIMMERMAN, Rufus 3
Eicher
ZIMMERMAN, Thomas C. 1
ZIMMERMAN, William 4
ZIMMERMAN, William 5
Carbys
ZIMMERMANN, Erich 3
Walter
ZIMMERMANN, Herbert 3
George
ZIMMERMANN, Herbert 4
P.
ZIMMERMANN, John 2
Edward
ZIMMERN, Sir Alfred 3
ZINK, Harold 4
ZINKE, E. Gustav 1
ZINN, Aaron Stanton 1
ZINN, Alpha Alexander 1
ZINN, Charles James 5
ZINN, George A. 2
ZINN, James Alexander 5
ZINNECKER, Wesley 3
Daniel
ZINSSER, August 2
ZINSSER, Hans 1
ZINSSER, Rudolph 2
ZINZENDORF, Nicholaus H
Ludwig
ZIONCHECK, Marion A. 1
ZIRATO, Bruno 5
ZIRKLE, Conway 5
ZIROLI, Nicola Victor 4
ZISKIN, Daniel E. 3
ZITO, Frank J. 3
ZIWET, Alexander 1
ZNANIECKI, Florian 4
Witold
ZOBEL, Alfred Jacob 3
ZOBEL, Harold 6
ZOELLER, Henry Adolph 5
ZOELLNER, Joseph Sr. 4
ZOERNER, Carl Bernard 4
ZOFFMAN, George F. 1
ZOGBAUM, Rufus 1
Fairchild
ZOLLARS, Ely Vaughan 1
ZOLLICOFFER, Felix Kirk H
ZOLLINGER, Gulielma 1
ZOLNAY, George Julian 2
ZON, Raphael 3
ZONDERVAN, B. D. 4

ZOOK, George Frederick 3
ZOPPI, Vittorio 4
ZORACH, William 4
ZORBACH, William Werner 6
ZORBAUGH, Charles Louis 2
ZORBAUGH, Harvey 4
  Warren
ZORLU, Fatin Rustu 4
ZORN, Edwin George 3
ZORN, Paul Manthey 5
ZOSHCHENKO, Mikhail 4
  Mikhailovich
ZOVICKIAN, Anthony 5
ZUBLY, John Joachim H
ZUCKER, Paul 5
ZUCKERBROD, Morris 6
ZUCKERMAN, Harry 6
ZUCKERMAN, Paul Stuart 4
ZUEBLIN, Charles 1
ZUGGER, Aloysius Henry 5
ZUKER, William Berdette 4
ZUKOR, Adolph 6
ZULAUF, Romeo Maxwell 3
ZULAUF, Romeo Maxwell 4
ZUNDEL, John H
ZUNTS, James Edwin 4
ZUPPKE, Robert Carl 3
ZUR BURG, Frederick 6
  William
ZURCHER, Arnold John 6
ZURCHER, George 1
ZURLINDEN, Frank J. 2
ZURN, Melvin Ackerman 5
ZWEIFEL, Henry 5
ZWEIG, Ben 6
ZWEIG, Stefan 2
ZWICKY, Fritz 6